MOTOR

IMPORTED CAR REPAIR MANUAL

18th Edition, Volume 2

First Printing

John R. Lypen, SAE
Editorial Director

Marian A. Maasshoff, SAE
Executive Managing Editor

EDITORIAL DEVELOPMENT

Senior Editor
Warren Schildknecht, SAE

Associate Editor
Daniel Reynolds

Quality Assurance Editor
Richard G. Glover, SAE

Assistant Special Projects Editor
Ron Lathrop

For Information On
MOTOR Products
Call
1-800-4A-MOTOR

Authorized Publisher Representative

EDITORIAL PRODUCTION

Production Manager
Richard C. Grunz

Production Assistants
Lynda Slater
Michele L. Hawley

PRODUCT SUPPORT

Product Support Specialist
Richard F. Cahoon

BOOK PRODUCTION

Director of Technology
Robert Jaramillo

Information Systems Manager
Kirk D. Lashbrook

Production Manager
Tracy Flynn

Production Group
Catherine Cardon
Elizabeth Matteini
Sergio Mautone
Kristen Parsons
Elizabeth A. Summers

Published by
MOTOR
A Division of Hearst Business Publishing, Inc.
5600 Crooks Road, Troy, MI 48098
Printed in the U.S.A.

ISBN 0-87851-887-8

Frank A. Bennack, Jr.
President

Gilbert C. Maurer
Executive Vice President

Richard P. Malloch
Vice President/General Manager Hearst Books/Business Publishing Group

Nelson J. Maione
Vice President & Resident Controller

George R. Hearst, Jr.
Chairman

Victor F. Ganzi
Senior Vice President

William K. Baker
Vice President/General Manager Hearst Business Publishing, Inc.

Kevin F. Carr
Vice President/General Manager Motor Publications

Richard B. Laimbeer
Publisher Motor Books

[redacted]

VEHICLE IDENTIFICATION

INDEX

	Page No.	Fig. No.
Mitsubishi	0-1	1
Nissan Passenger Cars	0-2	2
Nissan Light Duty Trucks	0-2	3
Porsche	0-3	4
Saab	0-3	4
Subraru	0-4	6
Suzuki	0-4	7
1993-95 Toyota Passenger Cars	0-5	8
1996 Toyota Passenger Cars	0-5	9
1993-95 Toyota Light Duty Trucks	0-6	10
1996 Toyota Light Duty Trucks	0-6	11
Volkswagen	0-7	12
Volvo	0-7	13

1st POSITION
COUNTRY OF ORIGIN
J = Japan
K = Korea
4 = U.S.A.
6 = Australia

2nd POSITION
MANUFACTURER
A = Mitsubishi
M = Mitsubishi
M = Hyundai (Precis)
P = Hyundai (Precis)

3rd POSITION
VEHICLE TYPE
H = Passenger Car
M = Passenger Car
3 = Passenger Car
4 = MPV
7 = Truck

4th POSITION - CARS
EXCEPT PRECIS
RESTRAINT SYSTEM
A = Driver & Pass Air Bag
B = Active Seat Belt (91-92)
B = Driver Air Bag (1993)
C = Passive Seat Belt
D = Active Seat Belt
E = Driver Air Bag
X = Driver Air Bag
PRECIS
DRIVE LINE TYPE
U = Right Hand Drive
V = Left Hand Drive

4th POSITION - TRUCKS/MPV
GVWR & BRAKE SYSTEM
HYDRAULIC
F = 4001 - 5000 lbs.
G = 5001 - 6000 lbs.
L = 4001 - 5000 lbs.
M = 5001 - 6000 lbs.

5th POSITION
EXCEPT PRECIS
VEHICLE LINE
A = Mirage
B = Expo LRV (FWD)
C = Diamante
C = Expo LRV (AWD)
D = 3000GT (FWD)
D = Expo (FWD)
D = Precis 3DR HB
E = 3000GT (AWD)
E = Expo (AWD)
F = Eclipse (FWD)
G = Eclipse (AWD)
H = Galant (FWD) 1993
J = Montero
J = Galant (1994-96)
K = Montero
K = Eclipse (FWD) (95-96)
L = Truck (RWD)
L = Eclipse (AWD)
L = Eclipse GSX (95-96)
M = Truck (4WD)

5th POSITION (Cont'd)
M = 3000GT (FWD)
N = 3000GT (AWD) VR4
P = Diamante
R = Galant (FWD)
EXCEPT PRECIS
VEHICLE LINE
R = Montero
S = Eclipse (FWD)
S = Truck (RWD)
T = Eclipse (AWD)
T = Truck (4WD)
U = Mirage
V = Expo LRV (FWD)
V = 3000GT Conv. (FWD)
W = Expo LRV (AWD)
W = 3000GT Conv. (AWD)
X = Galant (AWD)
X = Eclipse Conv.
Y = Expo (FWD)
Z = Expo (AWD)
PRECIS
BODY TYPE
A = 5 Door Sedan
D = 3 Door Sedan
F = 4 Door Sedan

6th POSITION
EXCEPT PRECIS
SERIES
1 = Economy/Base
2 = Low
3 = Medium
4 = High
5 = Premium
5 = Sports
6 = Special
6 = Premium
7 = Ultimate
8 = Sports
8 = Special
PRECIS
BODY STYLE & VERSION
1 = Standard
2 = Deluxe (GL)
3 = Super Deluxe (GLS)

7th POSITION - CARS
EXCEPT PRECIS
BODY STYLE
0 = 4 Door Wagon
1 = 2 Door Sedan
4 = 3 Door Hatchback
5 = 2 Door Convertible
6 = 4 Door Sedan
7 = 4 Door Hardtop (Pillared)
9 = 5 Door Wagon
PRECIS
RESTRAINT SYSTEM
1 = Active
1 = Passive (1994)
2 = Passive

7th POSITION - TRUCKS/MPV
BODY STYLE
1 = 5 Door Wagon
1 = Pickup - Short
2 = Pickup - Long

7th POSITION (Cont'd)
3 = 3 Door Metal Top
3 = Pickup - Extended Cab
4 = Pickup - Standard Cab
5 = Pickup - Extended Cab
9 = Pickup - Long Cab

8th POSITION
ENGINE CODE
A = 1.5L SOHC, MPI
A = 1.5L SOHC, MFI
B = 3.0L DOHC, MPI
B = 1.8L SOHC, MFI
C = 3.0L DOHC, Turbo
C = 1.8L SOHC, MFI
D = 1.8L SOHC, MPI
D = 2.0L SOHC, MFI
E = 2.6L
E = 2.0L DOHC, MFI
F = 2.0L DOHC, Turbo
G = 2.4L SOHC, MFI
H = 3.0L SOHC, MFI
J = 1468cc (Precis)
J = 3.0L DOHC, MFI
J = 1.5L MPI
K = 3.0L DOHC, Turbo
L = 2.4L DOHC, MFI
M = 3.5L
N = 2.5l SOHC, MPI
R = 2.0L DOHC, MPI
S = 3.0L SOHC, MPI
T = 1.8L SOHC, MPI
U = 2.0L DOHC, Turbo
V = 2.0L SOHC, MPI
W = 2.4L SOHC, MPI
Y = 1.6L DOHC, MPI
Y = 2.0L DOHC, MFI

9th POSITION
CHECK DIGIT

10th POSITION
MODEL YEAR
M = 1991
N = 1992
P = 1993
R = 1994
S = 1995
T = 1996

11th POSITION
ASSEMBLY PLANT
B = Bromont (Precis Only)
E = DSM (Diamond Star)
J = Nagoya-3
P = Nagoya
T = Tonsley Park
U = Mizushima
U = Ulsan (Precis only)
Y = Nagoya-1
Z = Okazaki

12th THRU 17th POSITION
PRODUCTION SEQUENCE NUMBER

MT1139300190000X

Fig. 1 Mitsubishi

...DE, 2.4L-4cyl.

...MA

C = VQ30DE, 3.0L-V6
E = VE30DE, 3.0L-V6
H = VG30I, 3.0L-V6

SENTRA/NX COUPE

E = GA16DE, 1.6L-4cyl.
G = SR20DE, 2.0L-4cyl.

STANZA

F = KA24E, 2.4L-4cyl.

200SX

A = GA16DE, 1.6L-4cyl.
B = SR20DE, 2.0L-4cyl.

240SX

A = KA24DE, 2.4L-4cyl.
H = KA24E, 2.4L-4cyl.
M = KA24DE, 2.4L-4cyl.

300ZX

C = VG30DETT, 3.0L-V6 (twin turbo)
R = VG30DE, 3.0L-V6

5th & 6th POSITION
MODEL & SERIES

A2 = Maxima (A32)
B3 = Sentra / NX Coupe (B13)
B4 = Sentra / 200SX (B14)
J0 = Maxima (J30)
S3 = 240SX (S13)
S4 = 240SX (S14)
U2 = Stanza (U12)
U3 = Altima (U13)
Z2 = 300ZX (Z32)

7th POSITION
BODY TYPE CODE

1 = 4 Door Sedan
2 = 2 Door Sedan
2 = 2 Door Coupe (200SX)
4 = Coupe (240SX, Sentra/NX Coupe)
4 = 2 Seater (300ZX)
5 = 4 Door Sedan
6 = Coupe, T-Bar Roof (Sentra/NX Coupe)
6 = Fastback & Convertible (240SX)
6 = 2+2 Seater (300ZX)
7 = Convertible (1993-95)

8th POSITION
RESTRAINT SYSTEM

A = Passive 3 Point (Mechanical)
B = Passive 2 Point (Motorized)
B = Air Bag
C = Air Bag & Passive Belt
D = Driver & Pass Air Bag
F = Air Bag & Passive Belt
H = Air Bag & Passive Belt
J = Passive 2 Point (Motorized) 4WD
P = Passive 2 Point (Motorized) 2WD
S = Active Belt

9th POSITION
CHECK DIGIT

10th POSITION
MODEL YEAR

M = 1991
N = 1992
P = 1993
R = 1994
S = 1995
T = 1996

11th POSITION
ASSEMBLY PLANT

C = Smyrna, Tennessee
T = Oppama
U = Zama
W = Kyushu
X = Nissha-Hiratsuka

12th Thru 17th POSITION
PRODUCTION SEQUENCE NUMBER

NS1139300145000X

Fig. 2 Nissan Passenger Cars

1st POSITION
NATION OF ORIGIN

J = Japan
1 = U.S.A.
4 = U.S.A.

2nd POSITION
MANUFACTURER

N = Nissan

3rd POSITION
VEHICLE TYPE

2 = MPV, U.S.A.
4 = Cargo, U.S.A.
6 = Commercial, Japan
6 = Truck, U.S.A.
8 = MPV, Japan

4th POSITION - EXC QUEST
ENGINE TYPE

PICK-UP

H = VG30E, 3.0L V6
S = KA24E, 2.4L 4cyl.

PATHFINDER

H = VG30i, 3.0L V6

4th POSITION - QUEST
G.V.W.R. & BRAKE SYSTEM ASSIGNED BY CLASS

5th & 6th POSITION
MODEL & SERIES

D1 = Truck (D21)
D1 = Pathfinder (WD21)
N1 = Quest MPV(V40)
N4 = Quest Cargo (V40)

7th POSITION
BODY TYPE CODE

1 = Standard Wheelbase (Truck)
1 = MPV (Quest)
2 = Long Wheelbase (Truck)
4 = Cargo (Quest)
4 = 2 Door Pathfinder
6 = King Cab (Truck)
6 = 2 Door Pathfinder
7 = 4 Door Pathfinder
8 = 4 Door Pathfinder

8th POSITION - EXC QUEST
MISCELLANEOUS INFORMATION

H = Heavy Duty
S = 2 Wheel Drive
Y = 4 Wheel Drive

8th POSITION - QUEST
ENGINE TYPE

W = VG30E

9th POSITION
CHECK DIGIT

10th POSITION
MODEL YEAR

M = 1991
N = 1992
P = 1993
R = 1994
S = 1995
T = 1996

11th POSITION
ASSEMBLY PLANT

C = Smyrna, Tennessee
D = Avon Lake, Ohio
W = Kyushyu
X = Nissha-Hiratsuka

12th Thru 17th POSITION
PRODUCTION SEQUENCE NUMBER

NS1139300146000X

Fig. 3 Nissan Light Duty Trucks

1st Thru 3rd POSITION
MANUFACTURER
WPO = Porsche, West Germany

4th POSITION
SERIES
A = 911 & 924S Coupe
A = 911 Carrera, 2 & 4WD Coupe
A = 911 RS America
A = 911 Turbo
A = 928 S4 Coupe
A = 928 GTS
A = 944, 944S & 944 Turbo Coupe
A = 968 Coupe
B = 911 Carrera, 2 & 4WD Targa
C = 911 Carrera, 2 & 4WD Cabriolet
C = 911 Carrera Speedster
C = 911 America Roadster
C = 911 Carrerra, 2 door Convertible (1996)
C = 944 S2 Cabriolet
C = 968 Cabriolet
D = 911 Carrera, 2 Door Targa (1996)
E = 911 Targa & Cabriolet
E = 911 Turbo Targa & Cabriolet
J = 928 S4 Coupe
J = 911 Turbo Coupe

5th POSITION
ENGINE TYPE
1983
A = 928S Model-4664cc, 234hp-8 Cyl
A = 911SC Model-2994cc, 172hp-6 Cyl
A = 944 Model-2479cc, 4 Cyl
1984-86
A = 944 Model-2479cc, 4 Cyl
A = 944 Model-3164cc, 6 Cyl Turbo
B = 911 Model-3164cc, 6 Cyl
B = 928 Model-4664cc, 8 Cyl
1987
A = 911-3164cc, 6 Cyl-300hp, Turbo
A = 944 Model-2479cc, 4 Cyl-190/220hp
B = 911-3164cc, 6 Cyl-217hp
B = 944 & 924 Model-2479cc, 4 Cyl-150hp
1988-95
A = Varies w/Models - 968, 928, 911
B = Varies w/Models - 911 Carrera 2 & 4
B = Varies w/Models - RS America & Speedster
C = 911 Turbo
1996
A = 3.6L 6 Cyl, 282hp
C = 3.6L 6 Cyl Turbo, 400hp

6th POSITION
RESTRAINT SYSTEM
0 = Active
2 = Passive
9 = Passive

7th & 8th POSITION
MODEL LINE
91 = 911, 924 & 928
92 = 924, 924S, 928, & 928S
92 = 928 GTS
93 = 911 Turbo
94 = 944, 944S & 944 Turbo
95 = 944 Turbo
96 = 968, 911 Carrera 2 & 4WD
96 = 911 RS America & America Roadster
96 = 911 Turbo
99 = 911 Carrera

9th POSITION
CHECK DIGIT

10th POSITION
MODEL YEAR
D = 1983
E = 1984
F = 1985
G = 1986
H = 1987
J = 1988
K = 1989
L = 1990
M = 1991
N = 1992
P = 1993
R = 1994
S = 1995
T = 1996

11th POSITION
ASSEMBLY PLANT
N = Neckarsulm
S = Stuttgart

12th Thru 17th POSITION
PRODUCTION SEQUENCE NUMBER

PR1139300008000X

Fig. 4 Porsche

1st Thru 3rd POSITION
MANUFACTURER CODE
YK1 = Saab of Finland
YS3 = Saab of Sweden

4th POSITION
PRODUCTION LINE CODE
A = 900
C = 9000
D = 900 (94-96)

5th POSITION, 1983-86
SERIES CODE
B = Base Series
C = S Series
D = Turbo Series
E = S Series (4 Door)
G = Base Series
H = S Series
M = Base Series
S = S Series (3 Door)
T = Turbo Series

5TH POSITION, 1987-96
SERIES/RESTRAINT
D = S, CD/CS w/Dual Air Bags
F = SE, CDE/CSE w/Dual Air Bags
H = Aero w/Dual Air Bags
J = Base/Passive
K = Base, S/Driver Air Bag
L = Turbo/Driver Air Bag
M = Non Turbo/Dual Air Bag
N = Turbo/Dual Air Bag
R = Base/Active
S = S/Active
T = Turbo/Active

6th POSITION
BODY TYPE
2 = 2 Door Notchback
3 = 3 Door Hatchback (900)
4 = 4 Door Sedan
5 = 5 Door Hatchback (900)
6 = 5 Door Hatchback (9000 CS)
7 = Convertible (900)

7th POSITION, 1983
ENGINE CODE
3 = 2.0L Fuel Injection
4 = 2.0L Turbo

7th POSITION, 1984-96
TRANSMISSION TYPE
5 = 5 Speed Manual
6 = 3 Speed Automatic (900)
8 = 4 Speed Automatic (9000)

8th POSITION, 1983
RESTRAINT SYSTEM
A = Air Bag
P = Passive Belt
S = Active Belt

8th POSITION, 1984-96
ENGINE CODE
B = 2.3L Fuel Inj., 16 Valve
D = 2.0L Fuel Inj., 16 Valve
E = 2.1L Fuel Inj., 16 Valve
J = 2.0L Fuel Inj., 8 Valve
L = 2.0L Turbo, 16 Valve
M = 2.3L Turbo, 16 Valve
N = 2.0L Turbo, Intercooled
R = 2.3L Turbo, Intercooled
S = 2.0L Turbo
T = 2.0L Turbo, Intercooled
U = 2.3L Turbo
V = 2.5L Fuel Inj., V6
W = 3.0L Fuel Inj., V6

9th POSITION
CHECK DIGIT

10th POSITION
MODEL YEAR
D = 1983
E = 1984
F = 1985
G = 1986
H = 1987
J = 1988
K = 1989
L = 1990
M = 1991
N = 1992
P = 1993
R = 1994
S = 1995
T = 1996

11th POSITION
ASSEMBLY PLANT
1 = Trollhatten, Sweden
2 = Trollhatten, Sweden
3 = Arlov, Sweden
4 = Malmo, Sweden
5 = Malmo, Sweden
6 = Nystad, Finland
7 = Nystad, Finland
8 = Nystad, Finland
9 = Trollhattan, Sweden

12th Thru 17th POSITION
PRODUCTION SEQUENCE NUMBER

SA1139300022000X

Fig. 5 Saab

1st POSITION
NATION OF ORIGIN
J = Japan
4 = USA

2nd POSITION
MANUFACTURER
F = Fuji Heavy Industries LTD.
S = Subaru-Isuzu Automotive

3rd POSITION
VEHICLE TYPE
1 = Passenger Vehicle
2 = Multipurpose Vehicle (MPV)
3 = Passenger Vehicle
4 = Multipurpose Vehicle (MPV)
7 = Truck

4th POSITION
LINE TYPE
A = Fuji Subaru, L Line (82-89)
A = Loyal & XT Line (90-94)
B = Legacy Line (90-96)
C = SVX Line
G = Impreza Line
K = Justy Line

5th POSITION
BODY TYPE
A = Justy 3 Door
B = 4 Door Sedan (82-84)
C = 4 Door Sedan (85-92)
C = Impreza & Legacy 4D
D = Justy 5 Door
D = Legacy Sedan
F = Hatchback (82-89)
F = Legacy Touring Wagon
F = Impreza Station Wagon
G = 3 Door Coupe
J = Legacy Station Wagon
K = Touring Wagon (1989)
K = Loyale Touring Wagon
K = Legacy Station Wagon
M = Station Wagon (82-84)
M = Impreza Coupe
N = Station Wagon (85-89)
N = Loyale Station Wagon
T = Brat (82-85)
U = Brat (86-87)
W = Hardtop (82-84)
X = XT & XT6
X = SVX

6th POSITION
ENGINE TYPE
1 = 1300cc
1 = 1800cc FWD (95-96)
2 = 1600cc
2 = 1800cc
2 = 2200cc AWD (95-96)
3 = 1600cc 4WD
3 = 2200cc FWD (95-96)
3 = 3300cc
4 = 1800cc
4 = 2200cc AWD (95-96)
5 = 1800cc 4WD
6 = 2200cc & 2200cc 4WD
6 = 2500cc AWD (95-96)
7 = 1800cc 4WD L Line & 1200cc J Line
8 = 2700cc L Line & 1200cc 4WD J Line
9 = 2700cc 4WD L Line (w/Air Susp.)

7th POSITION
MODEL INFORMATION
1 = Standard, Non Turbo RS, L
1 = Impreza Base
2 = DL, RS, Legacy Base & Loyale
2 = Impreza L & L+ M.T.
3 = GL, RS Justy, Legacy L & L+
4 = GL 10, XT6, Legacy LS, SVX
4 = Impreza L+ AT & LS
5 = GL 10 Turbo, GL F4WD 3D
5 = Legacy LS & LS-L, SVX
5 = Impreza LS, LSI, LX
6 = RX Turbo, Loyale Turbo
6 = Legacy LSI
7 = GL Turbo, Loyale Turbo
7 = Legacy GT
7 = Legacy Turbo
8 = Legacy Outback, Impreza Outback
9 = Legacy Postal vehicle

8th POSITION
WEIGHT CLASS/RESTRAINT
PASSENGER CAR
1 = Active Restraint
2 = Passive Restraint
3 = Air Bag
5 = Active w/Dual Air Bags
TRUCK
A = Under 3000lb. GVW / Active
B = 3001 - 4000lb. GVW / Passive
1 = Under 3000lb. GVW / Active
2 = 3001 - 4000lb. GVW / Passive
MPV
A = Under 3000lb. GVW
B = 3001 - 4000lb. GVW
C = 4001 - 5000lb. GVW

9th POSITION
CHECK DIGIT

10th POSITION
MODEL YEAR
C = 1982
D = 1983
E = 1984
F = 1985
G = 1986
H = 1987
J = 1988
K = 1989
L = 1990
M = 1991
N = 1992
P = 1993
R = 1994
S = 1995
T = 1996

11th POSITION
ASSY PLANT/TRANSMISSION
GUNMA
A = Manual 4 Speed
B = Manual 5 Speed
C = Automatic 3 Speed, ECTV, 4EAT
D = Manual 5 Speed (4WD)
E = 4 Speed Dual Range
F = Automatic 3 Speed & ECTV (4WD)
G = Manual 5 Speed Full Time (4WD)
H = Elect Auto 4 Sp Full Time (4WD)
J = Dual Range-5MT Full Time (4WD)
K = Electronic Automatic 4 Speed
LAFAYETTE
1 = Manual 5 Speed
2 = Automatic 3 Speed, ECTV, 4EAT
3 = Manual 5 Speed (4WD)
5 = Automatic 3 Speed & ECTV (4WD)
6 = Manual 5 Speed Full Time (4WD)
7 = Elect Auto 4 Sp Full Time (4WD)
9 = Electronic Automatic 4 Speed

12th THRU 17th POSITION
PRODUCTION SEQUENCE NUMBER

SB1139300046000X

Fig. 6 Subaru

1st POSITION
NATION OF ORIGIN
J = Japan
2 = Canada

2nd POSITION
MANUFACTURER
S = Suzuki

3rd POSITION
VEHICLE TYPE
2 = Passenger Car
3 = Multipurpose Vehicle (MPV)
4 = Truck W/2 Seats When Factory Delivers

4th POSITION
VEHICLE LINE
A = Swift
G = Esteem
J = Samurai
L = X-90
T = Sidekick

5th POSITION - PASSENGER CARS
SERIES & RESTRAINT SYSTEM
A = 2 Door Hatchback, Active
A = 2WD, Active (1995)
B = 4 Door Hatchback, Active
B = 2WD, Active w/Air Bags (95-96)
C = 2 Door Hatchback, Passive
D = 4 Door Hatchback, Passive
E = 4 Door Notchback, Passive
H = 4 Door Notchback, Active

5th POSITION - TRUCKS/MPV
SERIES
A = X-90, 2 Door (2WD)
A = Sidekick, 2 Door (4WD)
B = X-90, 2 Door (4WD)
C = Sidekick, 2 Door (2WD)
C = Samurai, (4WD)
D = Sidekick, 4 Door (4WD)
D = Samurai, (2WD)
E = Sidekick, 4 Door (2WD)

6th POSITION
ENGINE CODE
0 = 1.6L, 4 Cylinder
1 = 1.0L, 3 Cylinder (Swift)
1 = 1.6L, 4 Cylinder

6th POSITION (Cont'd)
2 = 1.3L, 4 Cylinder (Swift)
2 = 1.8l, 4 Cylinder (Sidekick Sport)
3 = 1.3L, 4 Cylinder
4 = 1.0L, 3 Cylinder (Swift)
5 = 1.3L, 4 Cylinder

7th POSITION
DESIGN SEQUENCE
1 = Original Design
2 = Original Design
3 = Original Design
4 = Swift GTI
5 = Swift GA

8th POSITION
BODY TYPE
C = Canvas Top
H = 3 Door Hatchback
S = Sedan
S = T-Bar Top
T = Truck
V = Hardtop (Van)
W = Wagon

9th POSITION
CHECK DIGIT

10th POSITION
MODEL YEAR
G = 1986
H = 1987
J = 1988
K = 1989
L = 1990
M = 1991
N = 1992
P = 1993
R = 1994
S = 1995
T = 1996

11th POSITION
ASSEMBLY PLANT
4 = Iwata
5 = Kosai
6 = CAMI

12th Thru 17th POSITION
PRODUCTION SEQUENCE NUMBER

SK1139300054000X

Fig. 7 Suzuki

1st POSITION
NATION OF ORIGIN
- J = Japan
- T = U.S.A.
- 1 = U.S.A.
- 2 = Canada

2nd POSITION
MANUFACTURER
- T = Toyota
- N = New United Mfg., Inc.

3rd POSITION
VEHICLE TYPE
- X = Passenger Car, U.S.A.
- 2 = Passenger Car

4th POSITION
ENGINE CODE
- AVALON
  - G = 1MZ-FE
- CAMRY
  - G = 1MZ-FE (94-95)
  - S = 3S-FE (90-91)
  - S = 5S-FE (92-95)
  - V = 2VZ-FE (90-91)
  - V = 3VZ-FE (92-93)
- CELICA
  - A = 4A-FE, 7A-FE
  - S = 3S-GTE, 5S-FE
- COROLLA
  - A = 4A-FE, 4A-GE
  - A = 7A-FE
- CRESSIDA
  - M = 7M-GE
- MR2
  - S = 3S-GTE, 5S-FE
- PASEO
  - E = 5E-FE
- SUPRA
  - J = 2JZ-GE, 2JZ-GTE
  - M = 7M-GE, 7M-GTE
- TERCEL
  - E = 3E, 3E-E
  - E = 5E-FE

5th POSITION
VEHICLE LINE
- A = Supra
- B = Avalon
- E = Corolla
- K = Camry
- L = Tercel
- L = Paseo
- T = Celica
- V = Camry
- W = MR2
- X = Cressida

6th POSITION
MODEL CODE
- AVALON
  - 1 = MCX10
- CAMRY
  - 1 = SXV10, VCV10
  - 1 = MCV10
  - 2 = SV21, SV25, VZV21
- CELICA
  - 8 = AT180, ST184, ST185
  - 0 = AT200, ST204

6th POSITION (Cont'd)
MODEL CODE
- COROLLA
  - 9 = AE92, AE95
  - 0 = AE101, AE102
- CRESSIDA
  - 8 = MX83
- MR2
  - 2 = SW20, SW21
- PASEO
  - 4 = EL44
- SUPRA
  - 7 = MA70
  - 8 = JZA80
- TERCEL
  - 3 = EL31
  - 4 = EL42
  - 5 = EL53

7th POSITION
SERIES / GRADE
- AVALON
  - 0 = XL
  - 1 = XLS
- CAMRY
  - 1 = DLX
  - 1 = DX
  - 2 = LE
  - 3 = XLE
  - 4 = Standard
  - 4 = SE
- CELICA
  - 0 = ST
  - 5 = GT-S
  - 6 = ST
  - 7 = GT
  - 8 = Turbo All-Trac
- COROLLA
  - 0 = LE
  - 1 = Standard
  - 4 = DLX
  - 4 = Std/DX
  - 6 = SR5
  - 7 = LE
  - 7 = DX
  - 8 = GT-S
  - 9 = DX/LE
- CRESSIDA
  - 3 = GLX
- MR2
  - 1 = Base
  - 2 = Base
- PASEO
  - 5 = Base
- SUPRA
  - 0 = GT
  - 1 = GT
  - 2 = GT
- TERCEL
  - 1 = Standard
  - 2 = DLX
  - 3 = Standard (1990)
  - 3 = DX (91-95)
  - 4 = DLX (1990)
  - 4 = LE (91-95)
  - 5 = Standard
  - 6 = Base (1990)
  - 6 = Standard (91-94)
  - 6 = DX (1995)

8th POSITION
BODY TYPE
- AVALON
  - E = 4 Door Sedan
- CAMRY
  - C = 2 Door Coupe
  - E = 4 Door Sedan
  - F = 4 Door Sedan
  - J = 4 Door Sedan
  - W = 5 Door Wagon
- CELICA
  - F = Coupe
  - K = Convertible
  - N = Liftback
  - P = Liftback
- COROLLA
  - A = 4 Door Sedan
  - B = 4 Door Sedan
  - E = 4 Door Sedan
  - J = 2 Door Coupe
  - K = 5 Door Wagon
  - M = Station Wagon
  - R = 4 Door Sedan
  - V = 5 Door Wagon
  - W = 5 Door Wagon
- CRESSIDA
  - E = 4 Door Sedan
- MR2
  - M = 2 Door Coupe
  - N = 2 Door Coupe w/T-Bar Roof
- PASEO
  - F = 2 Door Coupe
  - U = 2 Door Coupe
- SUPRA
  - J = Liftback w/Sport Roof
  - L = Liftback
  - M = Liftback
  - N = Sport Roof
- TERCEL
  - A = 4 Door Sedan
  - B = 2 Door Sedan
  - D = 2 Door Sedan
  - E = 4 Door Sedan
  - F = 2 Door Sedan
  - M = 3 Door Sedan & EZ
  - S = 2 Door Sedan
  - T = 4 Door Sedan

9th POSITION
CHECK DIGIT

10th POSITION
MODEL YEAR
- L = 1990
- M = 1991
- N = 1992
- P = 1993
- R = 1994
- S = 1995

11th POSITION
ASSEMBLY PLANT

12th Thru 17th POSITION
PRODUCTION SEQUENCE NUMBER

TY1139300283000X

Fig. 8 1993–95 Toyota Passenger Cars

1st POSITION
NATION OF ORIGIN
- J = Japan
- T = U.S.A.

2nd POSITION
MANUFACTURER
- T = Toyota

3rd POSITION
VEHICLE TYPE
- 2 = Passenger Vehicle
- 5 = Incomplete Vehicle

4th POSITION
BODY / DRIVE TYPE
- A = 2 Door Sedan 2WD
- B = 4 Door Sedan 2WD
- C = 2 Door Coupe 2WD
- D = 3 Door Liftback 2WD
- E = 4 Door Wagon 2WD
- F = 2 Door Convertible 2WD

5th POSITION
ENGINE CODE
- A = 4A-FE
- B = 7A-FE
- C = 5E-FE
- D = 2JZ-GE
- E = 2JZ-GTE
- F = 1MZ-FE
- G = 5S-FE
- L = 2TZ-FE

6th POSITION
SERIES CODE
- 1 = 10, 111 SERIES
- 2 = 20, 110 SERIES
- 3 = 30, 130 SERIES
- 4 = 40, 140 SERIES

7th POSITION
RESTRAINT / GRADE
- 1 = Manual Belt
- 2 = Manual Belt w/ Air Bag

8th POSITION
CARLINE
- A = Supra
- B = Avalon
- E = Corolla
- H = Paseo
- K = Camry
- L = Tercel
- T = Celica

9th POSITION
CHECK DIGIT

10th POSITION
MODEL YEAR
- T = 1996

11th POSITION
ASSEMBLY PLANT

12th Thru 17th POSITION
PRODUCTION SEQUENCE NUMBER

TY1139600284000X

Fig. 9 1996 Toyota Passenger Cars

1st POSITION
NATION OF ORIGIN
J = Japan
T = U.S.A.

2nd POSITION
MANUFACTURER
T = Toyota

3rd POSITION
VEHICLE TYPE
3 = MPV
4 = Truck
5 = Incomplete Vehicle

4th POSITION
ENGINE CODE
LAND CRUISER
F = 3F-E, 1FZ-FE
PICK-UP & 4 RUNNER
R = 22R, 22R-E
V = 3VZ-E
PREVIA
A = 2TZ-FE, 2TZ-FZE
T-100
U = 3RZ-FE
V = 3VZ-E, 5VZ-FE

5th POSITION
VEHICLE LINE
C = Previa
D = T-100
J = Land Cruiser
N = Pick-Up & 4 Runner

6th POSITION
MODEL CODE
LAND CRUISER
6 = FJ62
8 = FJ80, FZJ80
PICK-UP
0 = RN101, RN106
0 = VZN100, VZN105
1 = RN110, VZN110
8 = RN80, RN85, VZN85
9 = RN90, VZN90, VZN95
PREVIA
1 = TCR10
2 = TCR20
T-100
1 = VCK10, VCK11, RCK10
2 = VCK20, VCK21
4 RUNNER
2 = RN120, RN121, VZN120
3 = RN130, RN131
3 = VZN130, VZN131

7th POSITION
SERIES / GRADE
LAND CRUISER
0 = GX
1 = VX
2 = GX
PICK-UP
1 = Standard, DLX
1 = SR5, SR5V6
2 = DLX, SR5, Standard
3 = DLX, SR5, SR5V6
4 = Standard

SERIES / GRADE
PREVIA
1 = DLX
2 = LE
3 = DLX
4 = LE
T-100
0 = Standard, SR5
1 = Standard, DLX
1 = SR5
2 = DLX, SR5
4 RUNNER
5 = SR5, SR5V6
6 = SR5, SR5V6
7 = SR5
9 = SR5V6

8th POSITION
BODY TYPE
LAND CRUISER
G = Wagon
W = Wagon
PICK-UP, RN80
A = Short Wheel Base
D = Short Wheel Base
R = Short Wheel Base
P = Short Wheel Base
PICK-UP, RN85
D = Long Wheel Base
P = Long Wheel Base
S = Long Wheel Base
PICK-UP, RN90
D = Extra Long
P = Extra Long
PICK-UP, RN101
P = Short Wheel Base
S = Short Wheel Base
PICK-UP, RN106
P = Long Wheel Base
PICK-UP, RN110
P = Extra Long
S = Extra Long
PICK-UP, VZN85
D = Long Wheel Base
N = 1 Ton (1990)
N = Long Wheel Base (91-92)
R = Long Wheel Base
T = Dual Rear Wheel (1990)
T = Long Wheel Base (91-92)

8th POSITION (Cont'd)
PICK-UP, VZN90
D = Extra Long
G = Extra Long
PICK-UP, VZN95
T = Dual Rear Wheel (1990)
T = Super Long (91-93)
PICK-UP, VZN100
D = Short Wheel Base
G = Short Wheel Base
PICK-UP, VZN105
D = Long Wheel Base
PICK-UP, VZN110
D = Extra Long
G = Extra Long
PREVIA
R = Wagon
S = Wagon
T-100, RCK10
D = Regular Cab 1/2 Ton

BODY TYPE
T-100, VCK10
A = Regular Cab 1/2 Ton
B = Regular Cab 1 Ton
C = Regular Cab 1 Ton
T-100, VCK11
E = Reg. Or Extra Cab 1/2 Ton
F = Reg. Or Extra Cab 1/2 Ton
G = Regular Cab 1 Ton
H = Regular Cab 1/2 Ton
T-100, VCK20
A = Regular Cab 1/2 Ton
C = Regular Cab 1/2 Ton
T-100, VCK21
E = Reg. Or Extra Cab 1/2 Ton
F = Reg. Or Extra Cab 1/2 Ton
4 RUNNER
H = 2 or 4 Door Van
J = 2 Door Wagon
S = 2 or 4 Door Van
V = 4 Door Wagon
W = 4 Door Wagon

9th POSITION
CHECK DIGIT

10th POSITION
MODEL YEAR
L = 1990
M = 1991
N = 1992
P = 1993
R = 1994
S = 1995

11th POSITION
ASSEMBLY PLANT

12th Thru 17th POSITION
PRODUCTION SEQUENCE NUMBER

TY1139300285000X

Fig. 10 1993–95 Toyota Light Duty Trucks

1st POSITION
NATION OF ORIGIN
J = Japan
T = U.S.A.

2nd POSITION
MANUFACTURER
T = Toyota

3rd POSITION
VEHICLE TYPE
3 = MPV
4 = Truck
5 = Incomplete Vehicle
6 = Bus

4th POSITION
BODY / DRIVE TYPE
G = 3 Door Wagon 2WD
H = 4 Door Wagon (ALL TRAC) 4WD
J = STD Cab 1/2 Ton 2WD
K = STD Cab 1/2 Ton 4WD
L = STD Cab 1 Ton 2WD
M = STD Cab 1 Ton 4WD
N = STD Cab, Short Wheel Base, 2WD
P = STD Cab, Short Wheel Base, 4WD
T = EXT Cab 1/2 Ton 2WD
U = EXT Cab 1/2 Ton 4WD
V = EXT Cab, Extra Long WB, 2WD
W = EXT Cab, Extra Long WB, 4WD

5th POSITION
ENGINE CODE
J = 1FZ-FE
K = 2TZ-FZE
L = 2TZ-FE
M = 3RZ-FE
N = 5VZ-FE

6th POSITION
SERIES CODE
1 = 10, 111 SERIES
2 = 20, 110 SERIES
3 = 30, 130 SERIES
4 = 40, 140 SERIES

7th POSITION
RESTRAINT SYSTEM / GRADE
1 = STD
2 = DLX
3 = LE
4 = SR 5
5 = VX
6 = SR 5 V6

8th POSITION
CARLINE
M = Previa
D = T100
J = Land Cruiser
N = Tacoma Pickup
R = 4 Runner
V = RAV 4

9th POSITION
CHECK DIGIT

10th POSITION
MODEL YEAR
T = 1996

11th POSITION
ASSEMBLY PLANT

12th Thru 17th POSITION
PRODUCTION SEQUENCE NUMBER

TY1139600286000X

Fig. 11 1996 Toyota Light Duty Trucks

1st Thru 3rd POSITION
MANUFACTURERS CODE
WVW = Europe, Passenger Car
WV1 = Europe, Truck
WV2 = Europe, MPV
WV3 = Europe, Incomplete Vehicle
3VW = Mexico, Passenger Car
9BW = Brazil, Passenger Car

4th POSITION
BODY TYPE
A = Cabriolet Base
B = Fox Economy, 2 Door (91)
B = Fox Base, 2 Door (92-93)
B = Golf GL, 2 Door
B = Cabriolet Classic
B = Cabrio, 2 Door (95-96)
B = Golf Sport, 2 Door (1995)
C = Cabriolet Custom (91)
C = Cabriolet Base (92)
C = Passat GLS, 4 Door (1995)
D = Cabriolet Carat
D = Corrado Sport/G60
D = Golf GTI-8V, 2 Door
D = GTI VR6, 2 Door (1994)
D = Passat GLS, Wagon (1995)
E = Cabriolet Etienne Aigner
E = Corrado SLC
E = Passat GLX, 4 Door (95-96)
E = Eurovan, Panel Van (1995)
F = Golf GL, 4 Door
F = Passat GL, 4 Door (91-93)
F = Passat CL (92)
F = Passat GLX, Wagon (95-96)
G = Fox GL, 4 Door
G = Passat GL Wagon, 4 Door
G = Passat GLS, 4 Door
H = Golf GTI-16V, 2 Door
H = Passat GLS / Wagon
H = Eurovan CL
H = Eurovan GL, 3 Door (94-95)
H = GTI VR6, 2 Door (95-96)
J = Golf City, 4 Door (1995)
J = Passat GLS Wagon
J = Passat GLX
J = Eurovan GL, 4 Door (1995)
K = Golf, 4 Door (1995)
K = Eurovan GL
K = Eurovan GLS, 3 Door (94-95)
L = Eurovan GLS, 4 Door (1995)
L = Golf Celebration Ed., 4 Door
M = Jetta Custom, 2 Door (91)
M = Eurovan MV Camper
M = Eurovan Multivan (1995)
N = Passat GLX Wagon
P = Jetta 4 Door (1995)
R = Jetta Custom, 4 Door (91)
R = Jetta GL (92-96)
S = Jetta Carat (92)
S = Jetta GLS (93-96)
T = Jetta GLI-16V (91-92)
T = Jetta GLX (93-96)
T = Vanagon Multi-Van (91)
V = Jetta City, 4 Door (1995)
W = Jetta Celebration Ed., 4 Door
Y = Vanagon Bus (91)
Z = Vanagon Camper (91)

5th POSITION
ENGINE CODE
CABRIO
B = 1984cc 115hp 4 Cyl
C = 1984cc 115hp 4 Cyl

CABRIOLET
B = 1780cc 94hp 4 Cyl, Fed
C = 1780cc 94hp 4 Cyl, Calif

CORRADO
B = 1780cc 158hp 4 Cyl, Fed
C = 1780cc 158hp 4 Cyl, Calif
D = 2792cc 178hp 6 Cyl, Calif
E = 2792cc 178hp 6 Cyl, Fed
F = 2792cc 178hp 6 Cyl

EUROVAN
C = 2461cc 109hp 5 Cyl, Fed
D = 2461cc 109hp 5 Cyl, Calif
D = 2461cc 109hp 5 Cyl (1994)
E = 2461cc 109hp 5 Cyl (1995)

FOX
A = 1780cc 81hp 4 Cyl, Fed
B = 1780cc 81hp 4 Cyl, Calif

GTI
A = 1984cc 115hp 4 Cyl, Fed
F = 1896cc 90hp 4 Cyl, Diesel
G = 1896cc 90hp 4 Cyl, Diesel
S = 2792cc 172hp 6 Cyl

GOLF
A = 1780cc 100hp 4 Cyl, Fed
A = 1984cc 115hp 4 Cyl, Fed
B = 1780cc 105hp 4 Cyl, Fed
B = 1984cc 115hp 4 Cyl, Calif
C = 1984cc 115hp 4 Cyl
D = 2771cc 172hp 6 Cyl, Fed
D = 2792cc 172hp 6 Cyl, Fed
E = 1984cc 134hp 4 Cyl, Fed
E = 2771cc 172hp 6 Cyl, Calif
F = 1896cc 90hp 4 Cyl, Diesel
G = 1896cc 90hp 4 Cyl, Diesel
H = 1896cc 90hp 4 Cyl, Diesel
J = 1984cc 134hp 4 Cyl, Calif
K = 1780cc 100hp 4 Cyl, Calif
L = 1984cc 115hp 4 Cyl, Fed
R = 1984cc 115hp 4 Cyl, Calif

JETTA
A = 1780cc 100hp 4 Cyl, Fed
A = 1984cc 115hp 4 Cyl, Fed
B = 1780cc 105hp 4 Cyl, Fed
B = 1984cc 115hp 4 Cyl, Calif
C = 1984cc 115hp 4 Cyl
D = 2771cc 172hp 6 Cyl, Fed
D = 2792cc 172hp 6 Cyl, Fed
E = 1984cc 134hp 4 Cyl, Calif
E = 2771cc 172hp 6 Cyl, Calif
F = 1588cc 59hp 4 Cyl, Fed
F = 1896cc 90 hp 4 Cyl, Diesel
G = 1896cc 90 hp 4 Cyl, Diesel
G = 1588cc 52hp 4 Cyl, Fed
H = 1896cc 90hp 4 Cyl, Diesel
J = 1984cc 134hp 4 Cyl, Fed
K = 1780cc 100hp 4 Cyl, Calif
L = 1984cc 115hp 4 Cyl, Fed
M = 2792cc 172hp 6 Cyl, Fed
R = 1984cc 115hp 4 Cyl, Calif
S = 2792cc 172hp 6 Cyl, Calif
S = 2792cc 172hp 6 Cyl (1994)

5th POSITION (Cont'd)
PASSAT
B = 1984cc 134hp 4 Cyl, Fed
C = 1984cc 134hp 4 Cyl, Calif
D = 2792cc 172hp 6 Cyl, Fed
E = 2792cc 172hp 6 Cyl,
E = 2771cc 172hp 6 Cyl
F = 2792cc 172hp 6 Cyl
G = 1896cc 90hp 4 Cyl, Diesel

VANAGON
B = 2109cc 90hp 4 Cyl

6th POSITION
RESTRAINT SYSTEM
0 = Active
2 = Passive W/Manual Lap
4 = ELRA W/Manual Lap
5 = Driver Air Bag
8 = Driver & Pass Air Bag

7th & 8th POSITION
MODEL LINE
1E = Cabrio
1G = Golf/Jetta
1H = Golf III, GTI VR6
1H = Jetta III
15 = Cabriolet
25 = Vanagon
3A = Passat
30 = Fox
31 = Passat
50 = Corrado
70 = Eurovan

9th POSITION
CHECK DIGIT

10th POSITION
MODEL YEAR
M = 1991
N = 1992
P = 1993
R = 1994
S = 1995
T = 1996

11th POSITION
ASSEMBLY PLANT
A = Ingolstadt
E = Emden
G = Graz
H = Hanover
K = Osnabrueck
M = Mexico
N = Necharsulm
P = Brazil
W = Wolfsburg

12th Thru 17th POSITION
PRODUCTION SEQUENCE NUMBER

VW1139300035000X

Fig. 12 Volkswagen

1st Thru 3rd POSITION
MANUFACTURER CODE
YV1 = Volvo

4th POSITION
SERIES
A = 240 Series
B = 260 Series
D = 700 Series (83-85)
F = 740 Series
G = 760 Series
H = 780 Series
J = 940 Series
K = 940SE/960 Series
L = 850 Series

5th POSITION, 1980-91
RESTRAINT SYSTEM
A = 3 Point Seat Belt & Air Bag
X = 3 Point Seat Belt

5th POSITION, 1992-96
BODY TYPE / RESTRAINT SYSTEM
S = 4 Door, Driver Air Bag (92-93)
S = 4 Door, Dual Air Bags (93-95)
W = 5 Door, Driver Air Bag (92-93)
W = 5 Door, Dual Air Bags (93-95)

6th & 7th POSITION
ENGINE CODE
41 = B21A
45 = B21F Non-MPG
47 = B21FT
48 = B21F LH
49 = B21F MPG
55 = B5254F, B5254S
57 = B5234FT, B5234T
58 = B5234T5
69 = B28F, 280F
76 = D24T
77 = D24
82 = B230F
83 = B230FD
84 = B23E
86 = B230FT w/EGR Pulsair
87 = B230FT, B23FT
88 = B230F, B23F
89 = B234F
93 = B6254S
95 = B6304F
96 = B63042S

8th POSITION, 1980-91
BODY TYPE
2 = 2 Door
4 = 4 Door
5 = 5 Door Wagon

8th POSITION, 1992-96
EMISSIONS CODE
0 = 49 State w/o EGR, Bosch (92-94)
0 = 50 State w/o EGR (1995)
1 = 50 State w/EGR, Bosch
3 = 49 State w/o EGR, Bendix (92-93)
3 = 49 State w/o EGR, Siemons (1994)
3 = 50 State w/EGR (1995)

9th POSITION
CHECK DIGIT

10th POSITION
MODEL YEAR
A = 1980
B = 1981
C = 1982
D = 1983
E = 1984
F = 1985
G = 1986
H = 1987
J = 1988
K = 1989
L = 1990
M = 1991
N = 1992
P = 1993
R = 1994
S = 1995
T = 1996

11th POSITION
ASSEMBLY PLANT
A = Uddevalla, Sweden
0 = Kalmar, Sweden
1 = Torslanda, Sweden
1 = Gothenburg, Sweden
2 = Ghent, Belgium
2 = Volvo Europe
3 = Halifax, Canada

12th Thru 17th POSITION
PRODUCTION SEQUENCE NUMBER

VV1139300032000X

Fig. 13 Volvo

AIR BAG SYSTEM PRECAUTIONS

INDEX

	Page No.
Mitsubishi	0-8
Arming	0-8
Disarming	0-8
Nissan	0-8
Arming	0-8
Disarming	0-8
Porsche	0-8
Arming	0-8
Disarming	0-8
Saab	0-8
Arming	0-8
Disarming	0-8
Subaru	0-8
Arming	0-8
Disarming	0-8
Suzuki	0-8
Arming	0-8
Disarming	0-8
Toyota	0-9
Arming	0-9
Disarming	0-9
Volkswagen	0-9
Arming	0-9
Disarming	0-9
Volvo	0-9
Arming	0-9
Disarming	0-9

MITSUBISHI

DISARMING

1. Turn ignition switch to Lock position.
2. Disconnect and isolate battery ground cable.
3. **Wait at least 60 seconds after disconnection before performing repair procedures.** The SRS is designed to retain enough deployment voltage for a short time even after battery has been disconnected.

ARMING

1. Ensure no one is inside vehicle.
2. Connect battery ground cable and start engine.
3. Ensure SRS warning lamp lights for approximately seven seconds, then goes off and remains off for at least 45 seconds.
4. If lamp operates as described, SRS is functioning properly.
5. If lamp does not operate as described, an SRS malfunction is indicated. Diagnose and repair as necessary.

NISSAN

DISARMING

1. Turn ignition switch to off position, then disconnect battery cables.
2. **Wait a minimum of ten minutes for air bag system to discharge. System will retain power for approximately ten minutes after disconnection. It is possible for air bag to deploy during this time.**
3. Remove steering wheel lower lid, then disconnect air bag module electrical connector.

ARMING

1. With battery cables disconnected, connect air bag module connector.
2. Ensure no one is inside vehicle, then connect battery cables.
3. Turn ignition switch to On position and observe SRS warning lamp.
4. SRS lamp should light for approximately seven seconds, then go off. This indicates SRS is functioning properly.
5. If SRS warning lamp does not function as described, an SRS malfunction is indicated. Diagnose and repair as necessary.

PORSCHE

DISARMING

1. Turn ignition switch to off position.
2. Disconnect and isolate battery ground cable.
3. **Wait at least 20 minutes before beginning diagnosis or repairs. This is necessary to allow air bag back-up power supply to discharge.**

ARMING

1. Turn ignition switch to off position.
2. Connect battery ground cable.
3. Turn ignition switch to On position and note air bag warning lamp operation.
4. **On 928, 968 and 1993–94 911 models,** lamp should light for approximately 2½ seconds, then go off.
5. **On 1995–96 911 models,** lamp should light for approximately four seconds, then go off.
6. **On all models,** if lamp fails to light or remains illuminated, an air bag system malfunction is indicated. Diagnose and repair as necessary.

SAAB

DISARMING

1. Disconnect battery ground cable.
2. Prior to performing any service or diagnostic procedure, wait at least 20 minutes for back up power supply to deplete.

ARMING

1. Connect battery ground cable. **Ensure no one is inside vehicle when connecting battery ground cable.**
2. Turn ignition switch to On position and note SRS warning lamp operation. The SRS warning lamp should light for approximately six seconds, then go off. If lamp remains illuminated or fails to light, an SRS malfunction is indicated. Diagnose and repair as necessary.

SUBARU

DISARMING

1. Place ignition switch in off position.
2. Disconnect battery ground cable, then the positive cable.
3. **Wait 20 seconds before beginning repair procedures.**

ARMING

1. Ensure no one is inside vehicle.
2. With ignition switch in off position, connect battery positive cable, then the ground cable.
3. Wait at least 20 seconds, then turn ignition switch to On position and note air bag warning lamp operation. Lamp should light for approximately eight seconds, then go off. If lamp remains illuminated or fails to light, an air bag system malfunction is indicated. Diagnose and repair as necessary.

SUZUKI

DISARMING

1. Place front wheels in straight ahead position.
2. Turn ignition switch to Lock position and remove key, then disconnect battery ground cable.
3. Remove Air Bag-IG fuse from air bag fuse panel, **Fig. 1.** Air bag fuse box is located under lefthand side of instrument panel near junction/fuse panel.
4. Remove lefthand upper steering column cap, then unlock and disconnect driver's air bag module yellow connector.
5. Open glove compartment while pushing stopper from left and righthand sides, then remove compartment.
6. Disconnect passenger's air bag yellow connector.

ARMING

1. Turn ignition switch to Lock position and remove key.
2. Connect passenger's and driver's air bag yellow connectors. **Ensure connector lock levers lock securely.**
3. Install glove compartment and steering column upper lefthand cap, then install Air Bag-IG fuse.
4. Ensure no one is inside vehicle, then connect battery ground cable.
5. Turn ignition switch to On position and note air bag lamp operation.
6. If air bag lamp does not flash seven times, then go off, an SRS malfunction is indicated. Diagnose and repair as necessary.

TOYOTA

DISARMING

1. Note radio station settings before disconnecting battery, as all vehicle memory will be lost.
2. Turn ignition switch to Lock position, then disconnect battery ground cable.
3. **Wait at least 90 seconds after disconnection before proceeding with any service procedures.** Supplemental Restraint System (SRS) incorporates a back-up energy source that can maintain sufficient deployment voltage for up to 90 seconds after ignition switch has been placed in off position and battery disconnected.
4. **Never use an auxiliary power source during this procedure.**

ARMING

1. Ensure ignition switch is in Lock position and no one is inside vehicle.
2. Connect battery ground cable.
3. **Wait at least ten seconds before turning ignition switch from Lock position.**
4. Place ignition switch in Accessory or On position and ensure SRS lamp lights, then goes off after approximately six seconds.
5. If SRS warning lamp does not go off after six seconds, an SRS malfunction is stored in system memory. Diagnose and repair as necessary.
6. Reset radio stations and clock.

VOLKSWAGEN

DISARMING

Do not use the computer memory saver tool on air bag equipped models. Using this tool will keep the system charged and may cause unexpected air bag unit activation. Obtain the radio security code prior to disconnecting the battery ground cable. After service has been completed and the cable connected, use this code to activate the radio.

1. Disconnect battery ground cable.
2. **Wait 20 minutes to allow air bag/ Supplemental Restraint System (SRS) capacitor to discharge prior to performing any service procedures.**

ARMING

1. **Ensure no one is in vehicle, then connect battery ground cable.**
2. Turn ignition switch to On position and note air bag warning lamp operation. Lamp should light for three to eight seconds, then go off. If lamp fails to light or remains lit after eight seconds, an SRS malfunction is indicated. Diagnose and repair as necessary.

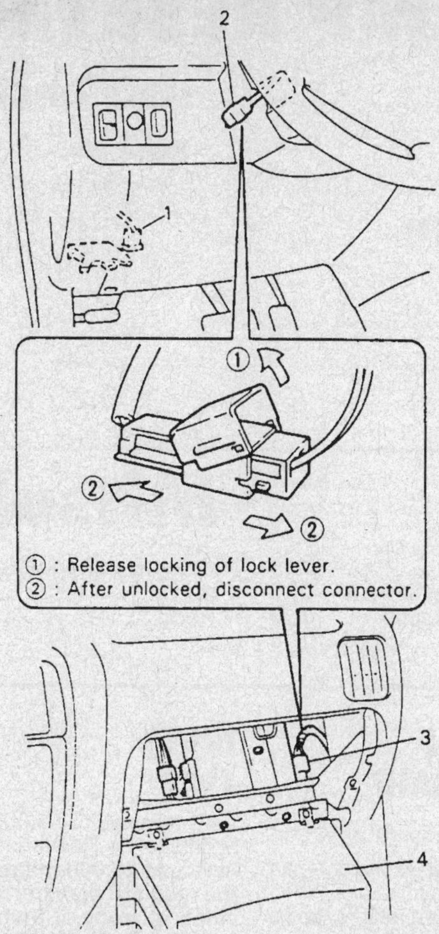

2
1
① : Release locking of lock lever.
② : After unlocked, disconnect connector.
3
4

1. Air bag fuse box
2. Yellow connector of driver air bag (inflator) module
3. Yellow connectors of passenger air bag (inflator) module
4. Glove box

MT1138500001000X

Fig. 1 Air bag system fuse & panel. Suzuki

VOLVO

DISARMING

On models equipped with a microprocessor radio, always turn the radio off before disconnecting or connecting the battery ground cable to prevent radio damage.

To disarm air bag/Supplemental Restraint System (SRS), turn the ignition switch to the off position, then disconnect the battery ground cable. Wait at least ten seconds after disconnection to perform any service procedures. The SRS is designed to retain deployment voltage for a short time even after the battery ground cable has been disconnected. Performing service before the minimum ten second wait may cause unexpected deployment and possible injury.

ARMING

To arm the SRS, turn the ignition switch to the off position, then connect the battery ground cable. Wait at least ten seconds, then turn the ignition switch to the On position. The SRS warning lamp should light for approximately ten seconds, then go off. If the lamp does not light or remains lit after the ten second interval, an SRS malfunction is indicated. Diagnose and repair as necessary.

SERVICE REMINDER & WARNING LAMP RESET PROCEDURES

TABLE OF CONTENTS

	Page No.		Page No.
MITSUBISHI	0-10	STERLING	0-22
NISSAN/DATSUN	0-12	SUBARU	0-22
PEUGEOT	0-18	SUZUKI	0-24
PORSCHE	0-19	TOYOTA	0-25
RENAULT	0-20	VOLKSWAGEN	0-31
SAAB	0-21	VOLVO	0-32

Mitsubishi

Air Bag Warning Lamp 0-10
Anti-Lock Brake Warning Lamp .. 0-10
Maintenance Reminder Lamp 0-10
Montero & Truck 0-10
Maintenance Required Lamp 0-10
Montero 0-10
Truck 0-10
Van & Wagon 0-10
Malfunction Indicator Lamp (MIL) 0-10

MALFUNCTION INDICATOR LAMP (MIL)

The MIL will illuminate to indicate an emission control item malfunction. When the malfunctioning system returns to its normal state, the MIL will go out.

Immediately after the ignition switch is placed in the On position, the MIL will light for five seconds to indicate proper operation.

MAINTENANCE REMINDER LAMP

MONTERO & TRUCK

An EGR warning lamp on the dash will illuminate at 50,000 miles to alert the driver to have the EGR system inspected and serviced.

Following inspection and maintenance, reset mileage sensor. Reset switch is located on the back of instrument panel either to the left of or below speedometer cable junction, **Fig. 1.** Slide switch to the opposite position to reset sensor lamp.

MAINTENANCE REQUIRED LAMP

VAN & WAGON

At 50,000, 80,000 and 100,000 miles the Maintenance Required lamp will be illuminated. **After performing the required service, reset switch located at rear of instrument cluster to turn lamp off, Fig. 2. At 120,000 miles, the bulb should be removed from the Maintenance Required lamp.**

TRUCK

1988

At mileage of 50,000 and 100,000 the Maintenance Required lamp will be illuminated. **At 50,000 miles, after performing the required service, reset the switch located at front of instrument cluster to turn lamp off, Fig. 3. At 100,000 miles, the bulb should be removed from the Maintenance Required lamp.**

1989-95

At mileage of 50,000, 80,000 and 100,000 the Maintenance Required lamp will be illuminated. **At 50,000, 80,000 and 100,000 miles, after performing the required service, reset switch located at front of instrument cluster to turn lamp off, Fig. 3. At mileage above 120,000 miles, the bulb should be removed from the Maintenance Required lamp.**

MONTERO

1988

At mileage of 50,000 and 100,000 the Maintenance Required lamp will be illuminated. **At 50,000 miles, after performing the required service, reset switch located at rear of instrument cluster to turn lamp off, Fig. 4. At 100,000 miles, the bulb should be removed from the Maintenance Required lamp.**

1989-95

At mileage of 50,000, 80,000 and 100,000 the Maintenance Required lamp will be illuminated. **After performing the required service, reset switch located at rear of instrument cluster to turn lamp off, Figs. 4 through 6. At mileage above 120,000 miles on 1989 models, 150,000 miles on 1990–91 models or 100,000 miles on 1992–95 models, the bulb should be removed from the Maintenance Required lamp.**

ANTI-LOCK BRAKE WARNING LAMP

The Anti-Lock warning lamp is used to warn of a system malfunction. It will be lit during engine start-up, but should go out when the self-diagnostic system determines that the system is functioning properly. If the lamp remains lit, a malfunction in the anti-lock brake system is indicated. **Following diagnosis and repair of the system, the lamp may be turned off using a Multi-Use Tester (MUT) diagnostic scan tool. Follow tool manufacturer's instructions.**

AIR BAG WARNING LAMP

The diagnosis unit monitors the Supplemental Restraint System (SRS) and stores data concerning any faults detected in the system. When the ignition key is in the On or Start positions, the lamp should illuminate for approximately seven seconds, then turn off. This indicates the system is operating properly.

If the air bag warning lamp does not illuminate as described, stays on for longer than seven seconds or illuminates during vehicle operation, a system malfunction is indicated. **To reset the lamp, it is necessary to use a Multi-Use Tester (MUT) diagnostic scan tool. Follow tool manufacturer's instructions.**

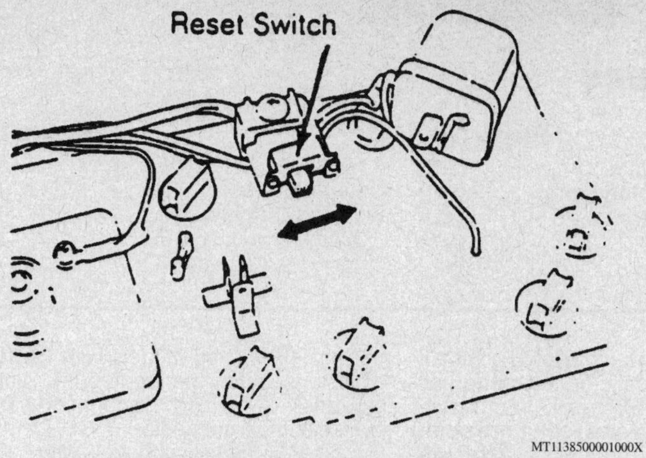
Reset Switch
MT1138500001000X
Fig. 1 EGR/Maintenance reminder lamp reset. 1985-86 Montero

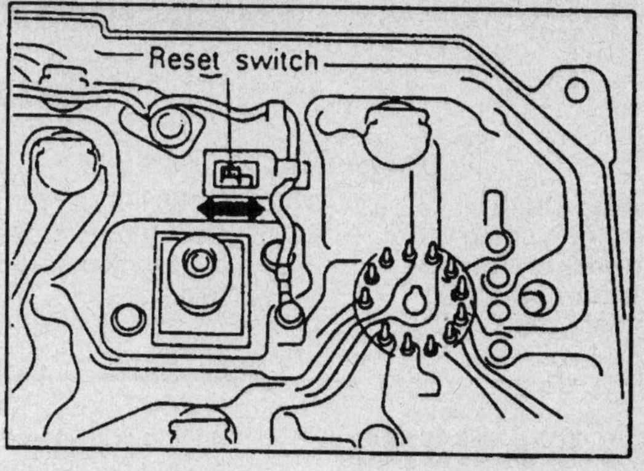
Reset switch
MT1138500002000X
Fig. 2 Maintenance Required lamp reset. Van & Wagon

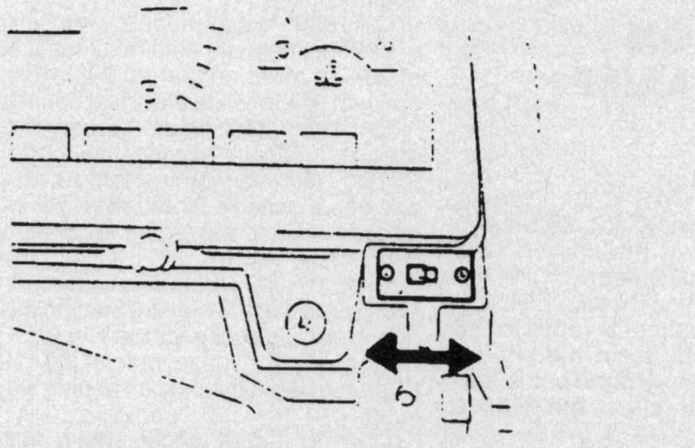
MT1139000003000X
Fig. 3 EGR/Maintenance Required lamp reset. Truck

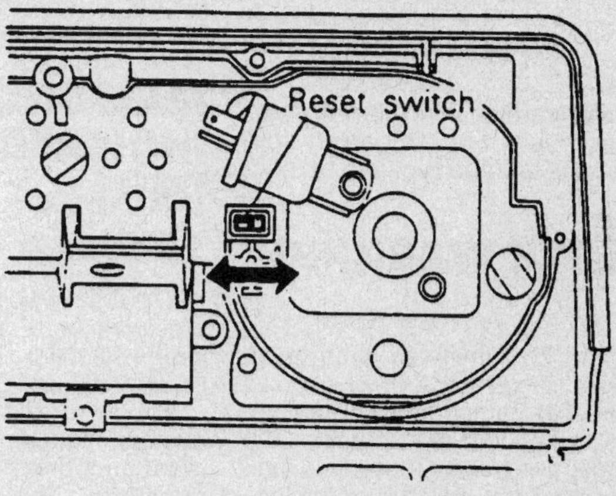
Reset switch
MT1138800004000X
Fig. 4 EGR/Maintenance Required lamp reset. 1988–91 Montero

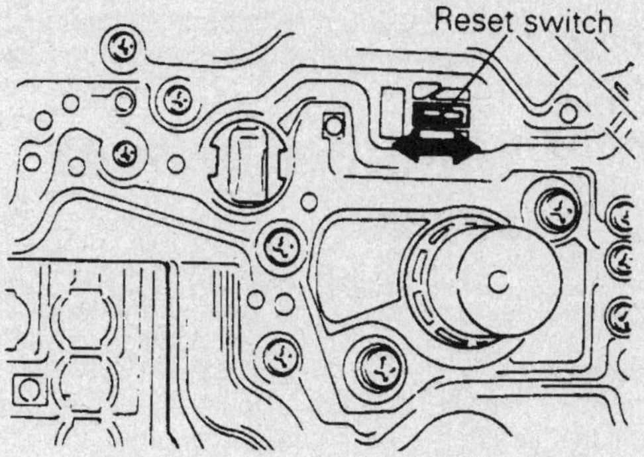
Reset switch
MT1139200005000X
Fig. 5 EGR/Maintenance Required lamp reset. 1992–93 Montero

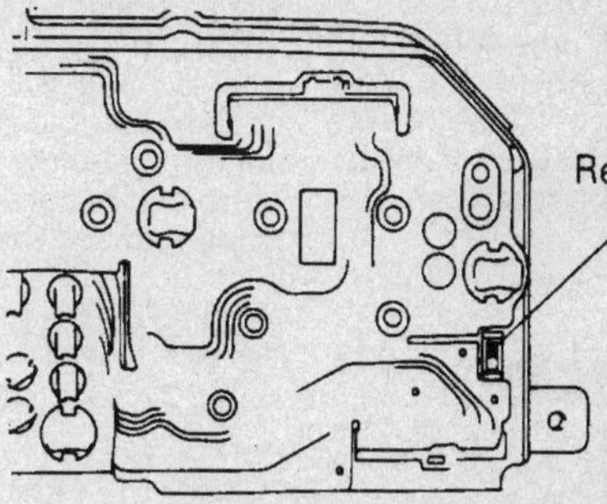
Reset switch
MT1139400006000X
Fig. 6 EGR/Maintenance Required lamp reset. 1994–95 Montero

Nissan/Datsun

INDEX

	Page No.
Air Bag Warning Lamp	0-12
Anti-Lock Warning Lamp	0-12
Automatic Transmission Oil Temperature Warning Lamp	0-12
"Check Engine" Lamp	0-12
1988–92	0-12
Coolant Level Warning Lamp	0-12
Malfunction Indicator Lamp (MIL)	0-12
1993–96	0-12
Oxygen Sensor	0-12
Warning Display	0-12
300ZX	0-12

AIR BAG WARNING LAMP

When the ignition key is placed in the On or Start positions, the air bag warning lamp will illuminate for approximately seven seconds, then turn off. This lamp cycle indicates the air bag system is functioning properly.

If the air bag warning lamp does not perform as described, the air bag system should be inspected and repaired as necessary.

ANTI-LOCK WARNING LAMP

This lamp will be illuminated when the ignition switch is placed in the On position as a bulb check. If the lamp remains illuminated or lights during vehicle operation, an anti-lock brake system malfunction is indicated. When the lamp is illuminated, place the ignition switch in the off position, then restart the engine. If the lamp still remains lit, the anti-lock brake system should be serviced. The basic brake system will remain functional, but without the assistance of anti-lock features. **After servicing the anti-lock brake system, the lamp will reset automatically when the ignition switch has been cycled to the off position and the vehicle has been driven at a speed exceeding 19 mph.**

AUTOMATIC TRANSMISSION OIL TEMPERATURE WARNING LAMP

This lamp will be illuminated when the automatic transmission fluid temperature is excessive. **When the transmission fluid has returned to its normal temperature, the lamp will reset automatically.**

"CHECK ENGINE" LAMP

1988–92

The "Check Engine" lamp will be illuminated when the ignition switch is in the On position with engine not running. When the engine is started, the lamp should go out. If it does not, a diagnostic trouble code has been stored by the electronic control system. **After diagnosis and repair are complete, place the ignition switch in the off position, then clear stored diagnostic trouble codes by disconnecting battery ground cable momentarily.**

MALFUNCTION INDICATOR LAMP (MIL)

1993–96

The MIL will illuminate to indicate the presence of a system malfunction. The lamp will blink simultaneously with the ECM's red Light Emitting Diode (LED).

Following diagnosis and repair of all system malfunctions, reset the MIL by disconnecting battery ground cable momentarily. This will clear the ECM's memory.

COOLANT LEVEL WARNING LAMP

This lamp will be illuminated when the coolant level in the cooling system reservoir drops below the "MIN" level mark. **The lamp will reset when the coolant level is raised above the "MIN" mark.**

OXYGEN SENSOR

Refer to Figs. **Figs. 1 through 26** when performing the following procedures.

After the vehicle has been operated for 30,000 or 50,000 miles, depending on model, the oxygen sensor warning lamp located on the instrument panel will illuminate, indicating that the oxygen sensor should be checked.

On 1980–85 models except 1985 Pickup, after the appropriate service has been performed, disconnect warning lamp electrical connector to prevent the light from illuminating again.

On 1986–89 models except Pickup and Stanza Wagon, reset the warning lamp hold relay. After the third interval, at 90,000 miles, disconnect warning lamp electrical connector to prevent the light from illuminating again.

On 1985 Pickup models with California emissions, after the appropriate service has been performed, disconnect warning lamp electrical connector.

On 1985–86 Pickup models with Federal emissions, disconnect the yellow wiring harness connector at 50,000 miles and the yellow/black wiring harness connector at 100,000 miles.

On 1986 Pickup models with California emissions, depress hold relay reset button at 30,000 miles and, at 90,000 miles, disconnect yellow white electrical connector.

On 1986–87 Stanza Wagon models, after appropriate service has been performed, remove warning lamp hold relay and use a suitable tool to reset. At 90,000 miles, disconnect warning lamp electrical connector.

On 1987 300ZX models with an analog instrument cluster, after inspecting the oxygen sensor, disconnect the electrical connector for the mileage interval indicated in **Fig. 11,** to reset the oxygen sensor warning lamp.

On 1987 300ZX models with a digital instrument cluster, after inspecting the oxygen sensor, depress and hold relay button to reset the oxygen sensor warning lamp at 30,000 and 60,000 mile intervals, **Fig. 27.** At the 90,000 mile interval, disconnect the warning lamp electrical connector, **Fig. 11.**

WARNING DISPLAY

300ZX

This system monitors engine coolant level, washer fluid level and exterior lamp operation. When the ignition switch is placed in the On position, the "WASH" and "WATER" lamps should illuminate and, if systems are satisfactory, the "OK" lamp should also illuminate. Operation of the headlamps, stop lamps and tail lamps will not be checked until the system has been activated by depressing the brake pedal or placing the light switch in the On position. If a problem is detected in one of the monitored systems, the red warning display indicator lamp will be illuminated. Depressing the warning display check button will indicate which system is in need of attention. **After the indicated system has been serviced, the warning display will reset automatically.**

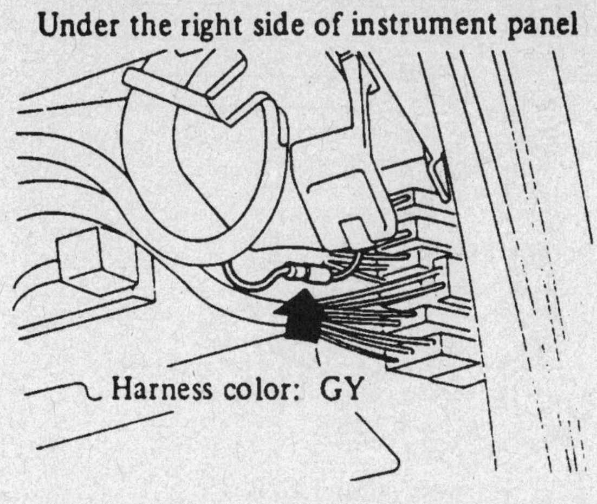
Under the right side of instrument panel
Harness color: GY

NS1138000001000X

Fig. 1 Oxygen sensor warning lamp electrical connector location. 1980–81 810

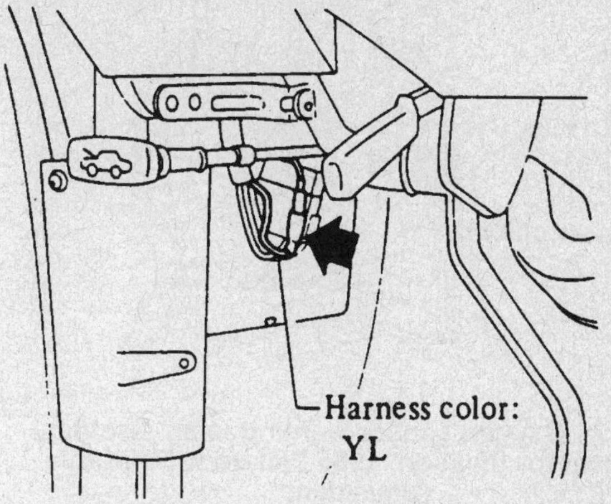
Harness color:
YL

NS1138000002000X

Fig. 2 Oxygen sensor warning lamp electrical connector location. 1981–83 200SX

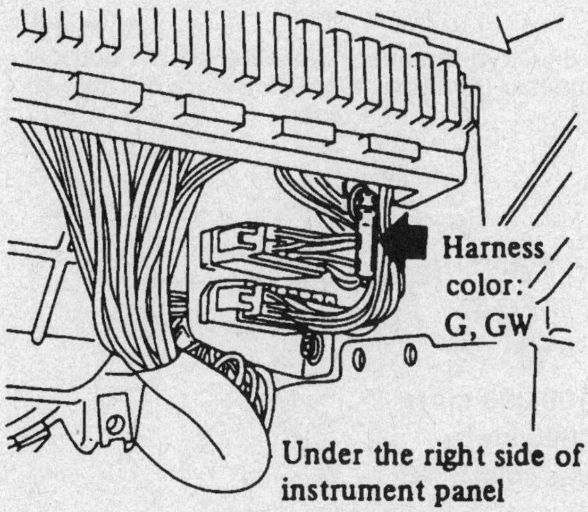
Harness
color:
G, GW
Under the right side of
instrument panel

NS1138100003000X

Fig. 3 Oxygen sensor warning lamp electrical connector location. 1980–83 280ZX

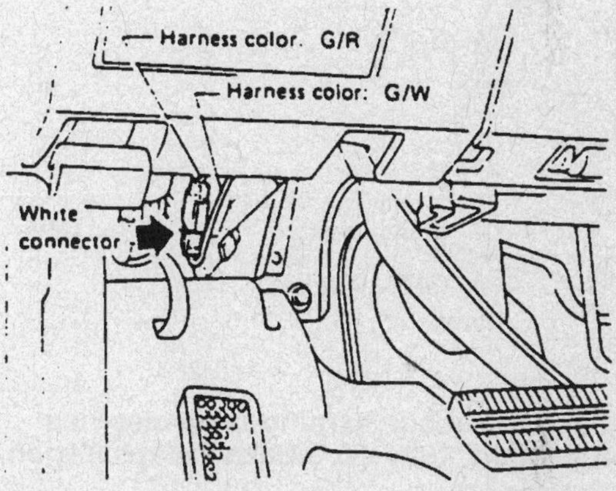
Harness color. G/R
Harness color: G/W
White
connector

NS1138200004000X

Fig. 4 Oxygen sensor warning lamp electrical connector location. 1982–83 Sentra & 1982–84 Pulsar

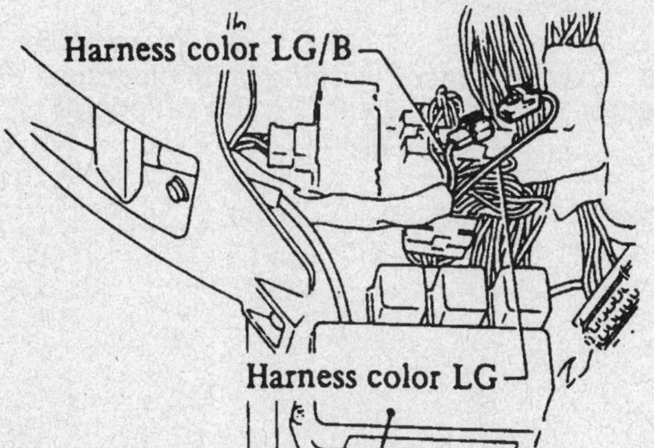
Harness color LG/B
Harness color LG
Fuse box

NS1138300005000X

Fig. 5 Oxygen sensor warning lamp electrical connector location. 1983–87 Maxima

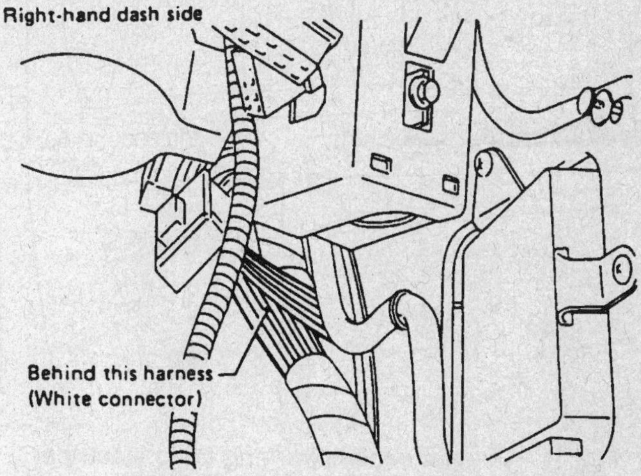
Right-hand dash side
Behind this harness
(White connector)

NS1138400006000X

Fig. 6 Oxygen sensor warning lamp electrical connector location. 1984 200SX

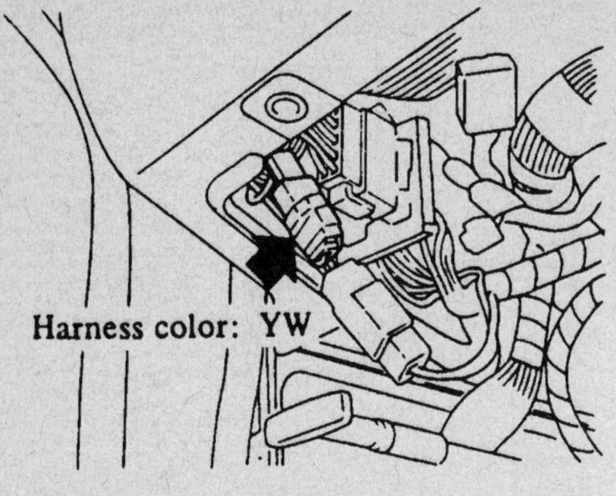
Harness color: YW

NS1138500007000X

Fig. 7 Oxygen sensor warning lamp electrical connector location. 1985 Pickup w/California emissions

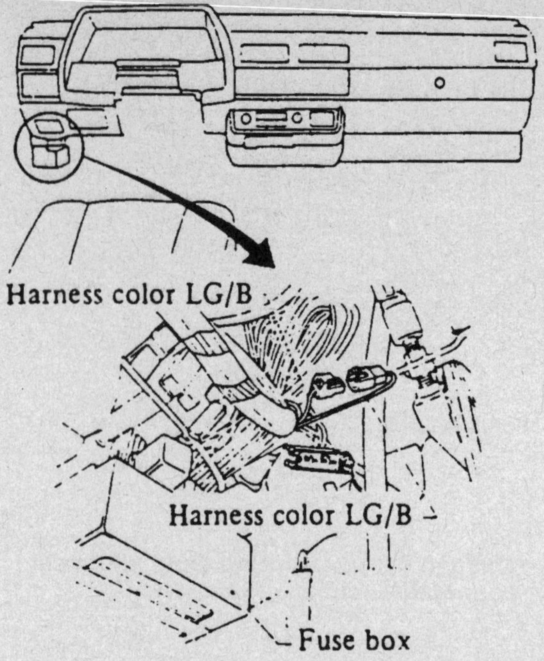
Harness color LG/B
Harness color LG/B
Fuse box

NS1138400008000X

Fig. 8 Oxygen sensor warning lamp electrical connector location. 1984–86 Sentra & 1985–86 Pulsar

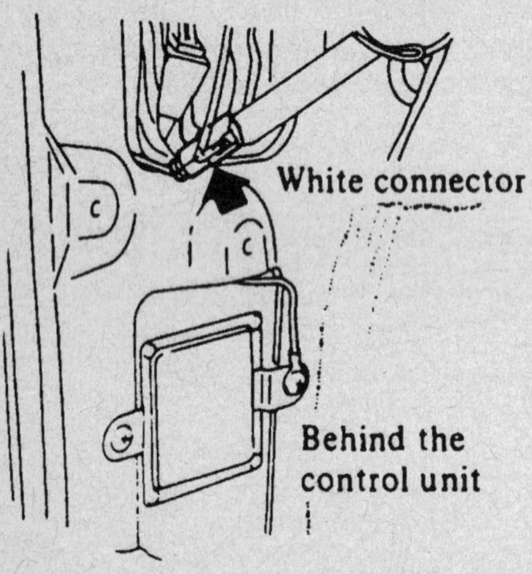
White connector
Behind the
control unit

NS1138400009000X

Fig. 9 Oxygen sensor warning lamp electrical connector location. 1984–86 Stanza except Wagon

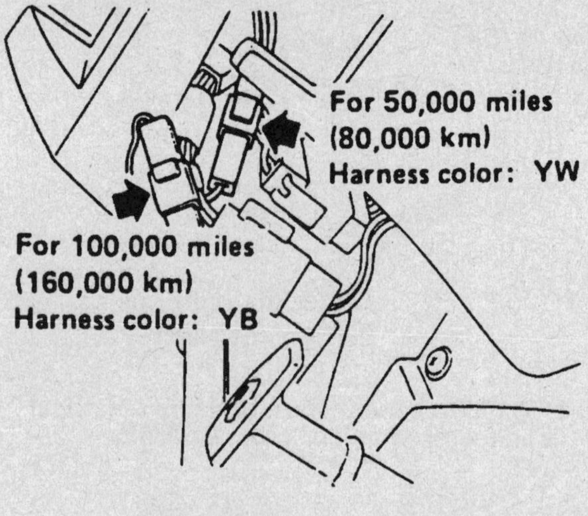
For 50,000 miles
(80,000 km)
Harness color: YW
For 100,000 miles
(160,000 km)
Harness color: YB

NS1138500010000X

Fig. 10 Oxygen sensor warning lamp electrical connector location. 1985–86 Pickup w/Federal emissions

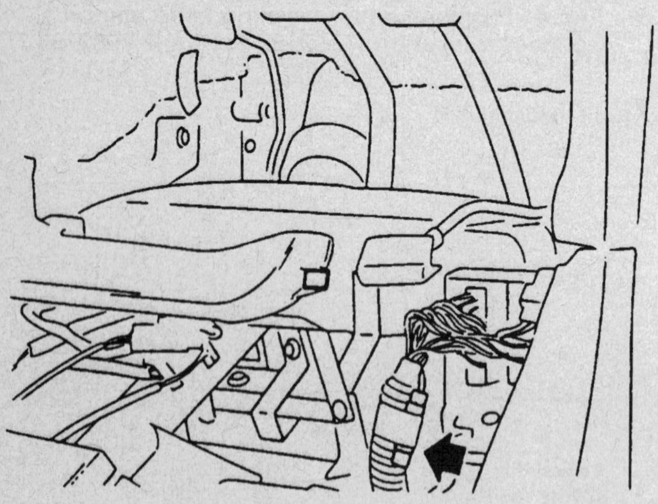

NS1138400011000X

Fig. 11 Oxygen sensor warning lamp electrical connector location. 1984–87 300ZX

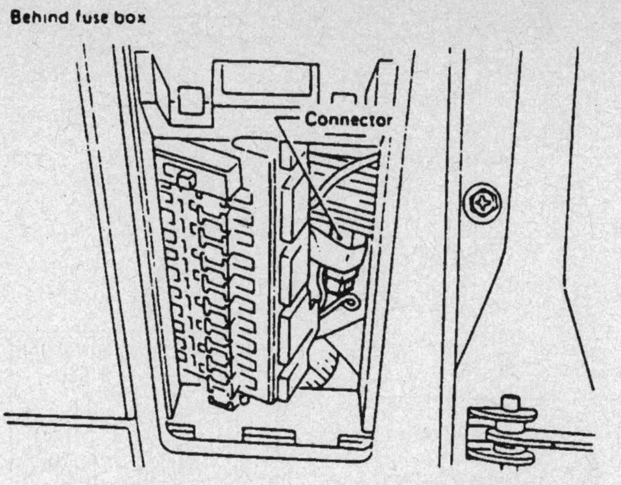
Behind fuse box
Connector

NS1138500012000X

Fig. 12 Oxygen sensor warning lamp electrical connector location. 1985–87 200SX

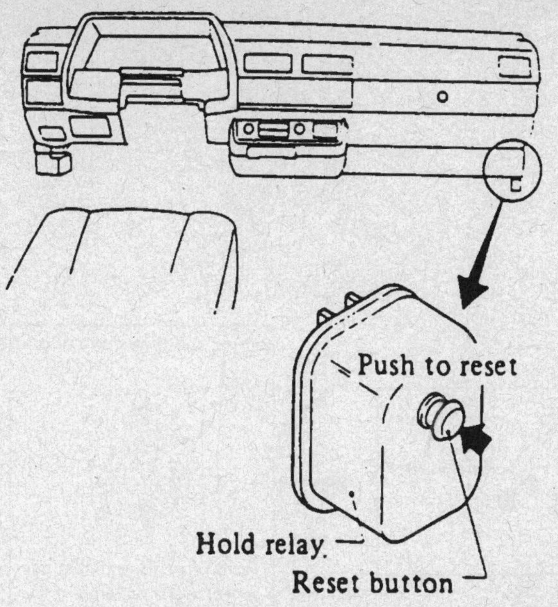
Push to reset
Hold relay
Reset button

NS1138600013000X

Fig. 13 Oxygen sensor warning lamp hold relay location. 1986 Pulsar & 1986–89 Sentra

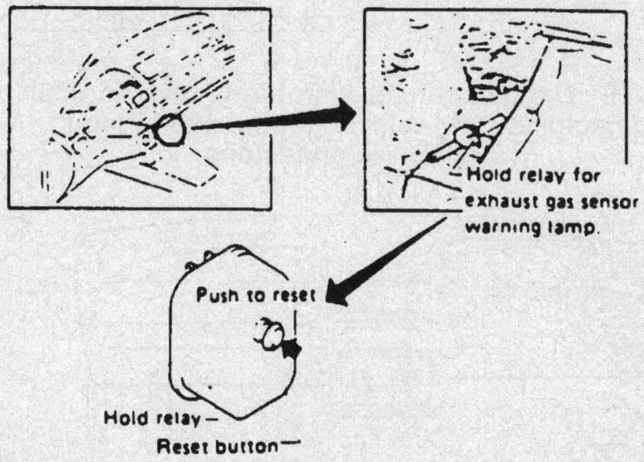
Hold relay for
exhaust gas sensor
warning lamp.
Push to reset
Hold relay
Reset button

NS1138600014000X

Fig. 14 Oxygen sensor warning lamp hold relay location. 1986–87 200SX

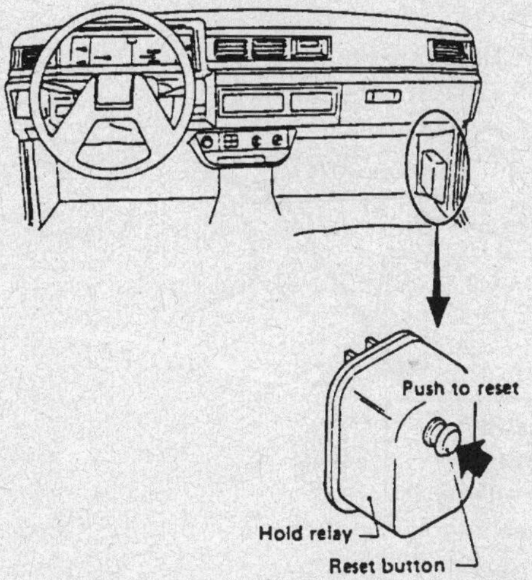
Push to reset
Hold relay
Reset button

NS1138600015000X

Fig. 15 Oxygen sensor warning lamp hold relay location. 1986 Stanza except Wagon

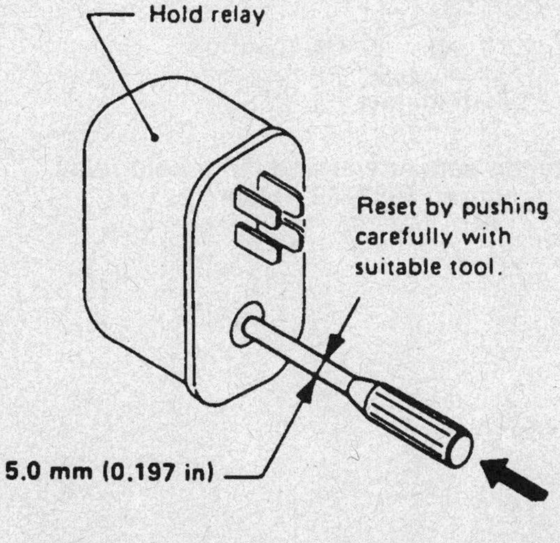
Hold relay
Reset by pushing
carefully with
suitable tool.
5.0 mm (0.197 in)

NS1138600016000X

Fig. 16 Oxygen sensor warning lamp hold relay location. 1986 Maxima

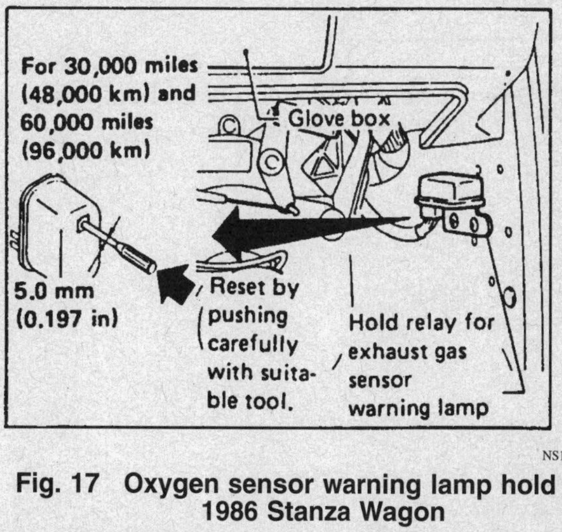
For 30,000 miles
(48,000 km) and
60,000 miles
(96,000 km)
Glove box
5.0 mm
(0.197 in)
Reset by
pushing
carefully
with suita-
ble tool.
Hold relay for
exhaust gas
sensor
warning lamp

NS1138600017000X

Fig. 17 Oxygen sensor warning lamp hold relay. 1986 Stanza Wagon

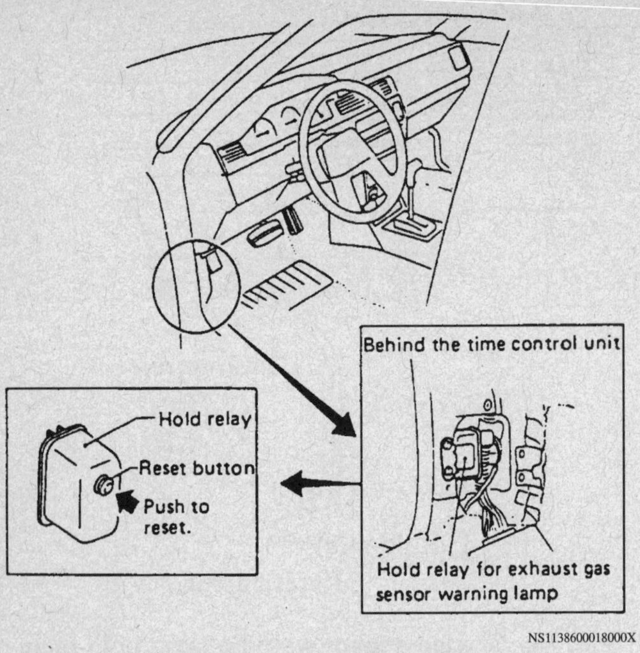
Behind the time control unit
Hold relay
Reset button
Push to reset.
Hold relay for exhaust gas sensor warning lamp
NS1138600018000X

Fig. 18 Oxygen sensor warning lamp hold relay location. 1987 Maxima

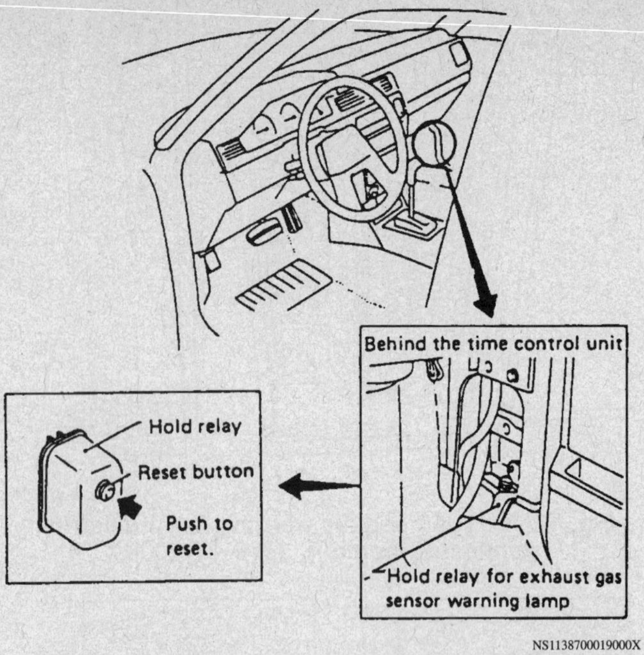
Behind the time control unit
Hold relay
Reset button
Push to reset.
Hold relay for exhaust gas sensor warning lamp
NS1138700019000X

Fig. 19 Oxygen sensor warning lamp electrical connector & hold relay location. 1986 Pickup w/California emissions

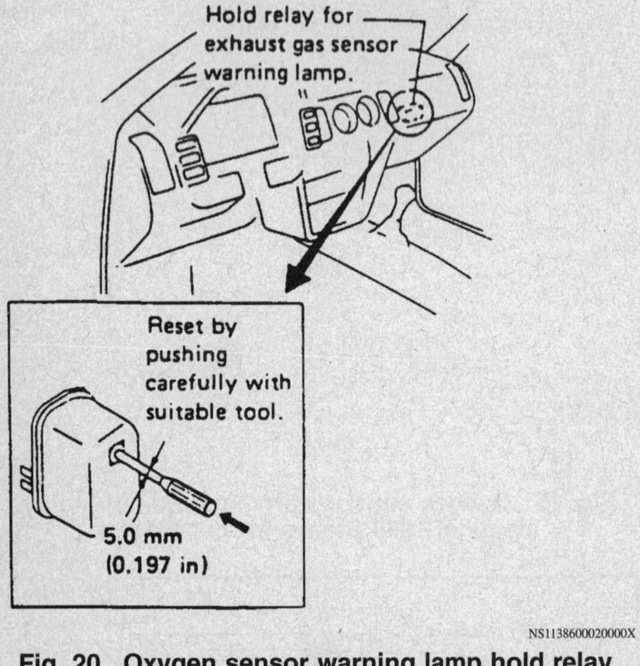
Hold relay for exhaust gas sensor warning lamp.
Reset by pushing carefully with suitable tool.
5.0 mm (0.197 in)
NS1138600020000X

Fig. 20 Oxygen sensor warning lamp hold relay location. 1986 300ZX

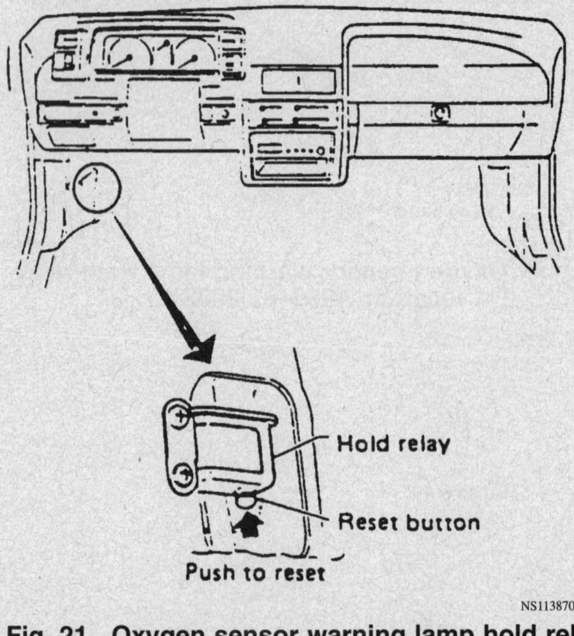
Hold relay
Reset button
Push to reset
NS1138700021000X

Fig. 21 Oxygen sensor warning lamp hold relay location. 1987–89 Pulsar

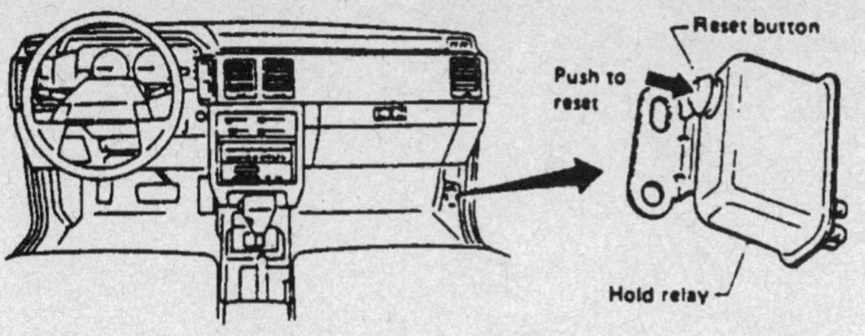
Reset button
Push to reset
Hold relay

NS1138700022000X

Fig. 22 Oxygen sensor warning lamp electrical connector location. 1987 Stanza except Wagon

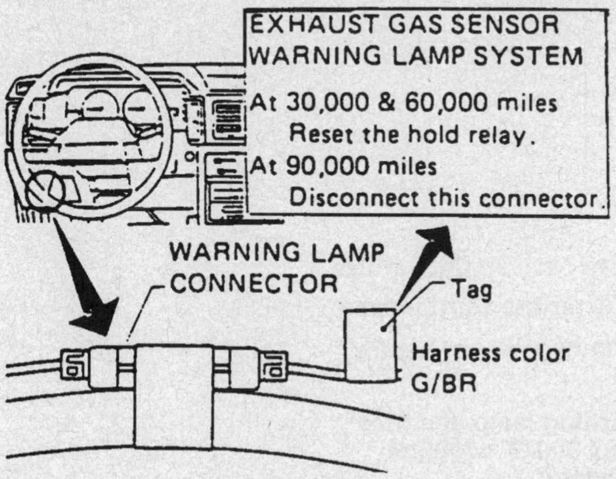
EXHAUST GAS SENSOR
WARNING LAMP SYSTEM
At 30,000 & 60,000 miles
Reset the hold relay.
At 90,000 miles
Disconnect this connector.
WARNING LAMP
CONNECTOR
Tag
Harness color
G/BR

NS1138700024000X

Fig. 24 Oxygen sensor warning lamp electrical connector location. 1987 Pulsar

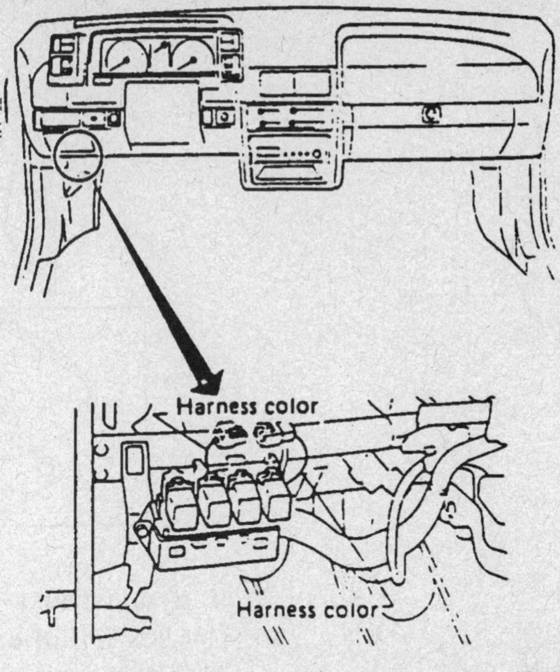
Harness color
Harness color

NS1138700023000X

Fig. 23 Oxygen sensor warning lamp hold relay location. 1987 Stanza except Wagon

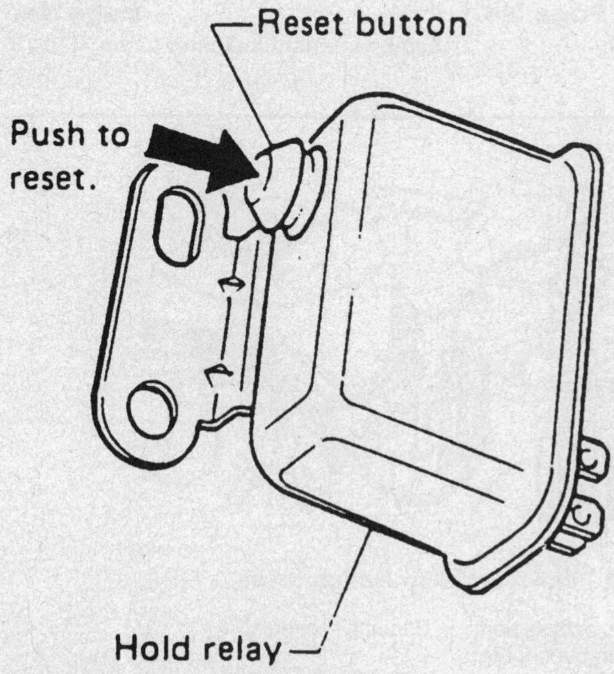
Reset button
Push to
reset.
Hold relay

NS1138700025000X

Fig. 25 Oxygen sensor warning lamp hold relay. 1987 Stanza Wagon

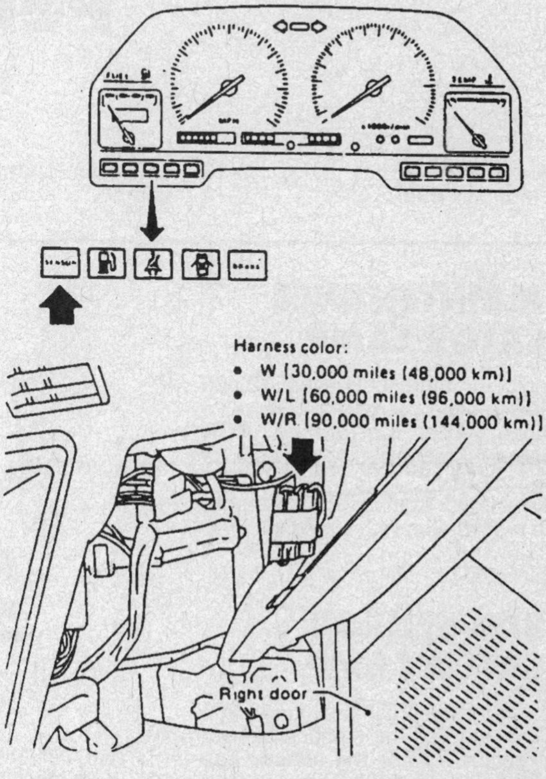
Harness color:
• W (30,000 miles (48,000 km))
• W/L (60,000 miles (96,000 km))
• W/R (90,000 miles (144,000 km))
Right door

NS1138700026000X

Fig. 26 Oxygen sensor warning lamp electrical connectors location. 1987 300ZX w/analog instrument cluster

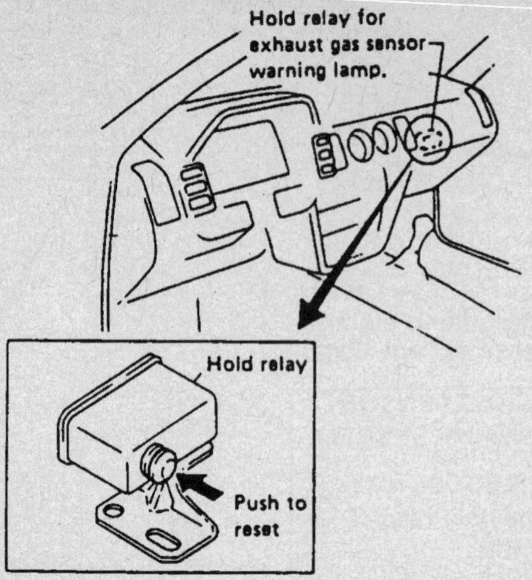
Hold relay for
exhaust gas sensor
warning lamp.
Hold relay
Push to
reset

If sensor should be checked at 90,000 miles (144,000 km) of operation (After the third inspection), disconnect warning lamp harness connector.

NS1138700027000X

Fig. 27 Oxygen sensor warning lamp electrical connectors location. 1987 300ZX w/digital instrument cluster

Peugeot

INDEX

Page No.		Page No.		Page No.	
"Check Engine" Lamp	0-19	**EGR Maintenance Indicator Lamp**	0-18	**Lambda Sensor Indicator Lamp**	0-18
Bosch Motronic Fuel System	0-19				

EGR MAINTENANCE INDICATOR LAMP

This indicator lamp lights every 12,500 miles to indicate the interval for EGR valve maintenance. **After performing EGR maintenance, the lamp may be reset as follows:**

1. Remove cover from reset access port.
2. Push reset button with pin punch, **Fig. 1.**
3. Install cover.

LAMBDA SENSOR INDICATOR LAMP

This indicator lamp lights every 30,000 miles to indicate that the Lambda Sensor must be replaced. **After the sensor has been replaced, reset the lamp as follows:**

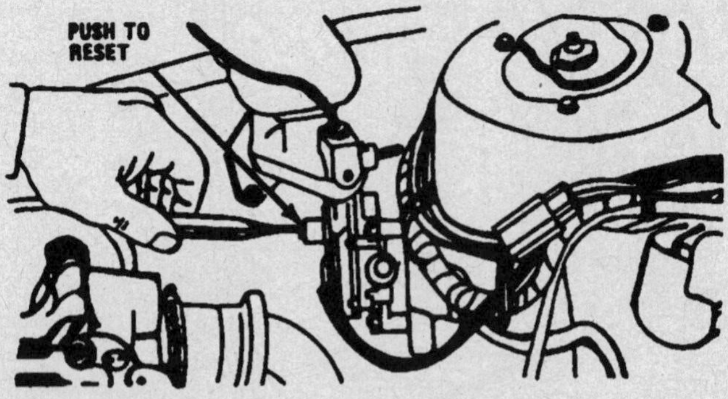
PUSH TO
RESET

PE1139000001000X

Fig. 1 Indicator lamp switch reset

1. Remove cover from reset access port.
2. Push reset button with pin punch, **Fig. 1.**
3. Install cover.

"CHECK ENGINE" LAMP

BOSCH MOTRONIC FUEL SYSTEM

The "Check Engine" lamp will be illuminated when the ignition switch is in the On position with the engine not running. When the engine is started, the lamp should go out. If the lamp remains lit, a diagnostic trouble code has been stored by the Electronic Control Unit (ECU). **After diagnosis and repair are complete, retrieve all diagnostic trouble codes until Diagnostic Trouble Code 11 is displayed. Depress the jumper harness switch for more than ten seconds to clear ECU memory and reset the "Check Engine" lamp.**

Porsche

INDEX

	Page No.
"Check Engine" Lamp	0-19
DME & LH-Jetronic Fuel Systems	0-19
EGR Indicator Lamp	0-19
924 & 944 Turbo	0-19
Oxygen Sensor Lamp	0-19
911	0-19
924 & 944	0-19
928	0-19

EGR INDICATOR LAMP

924 & 944 TURBO

After completing EGR system service, reset lamp by pushing in pin on elapsed mileage odometer. The elapsed mileage odometer is located behind the instrument cluster.

OXYGEN SENSOR LAMP

924 & 944

On 924 models, an OXS lamp will light at 30,000 mile intervals as a reminder to replace the oxygen sensor. **The 944 models do not use a warning lamp. On these models, however, it is recommended that the oxygen sensor be replaced every 60,000 miles.**

On 924 models, after replacing oxygen sensor and with vehicle still raised, locate mileage counter on left engine mount, then use a thick wire or thin metal rod to push in reset button. Ensure to push button in all the way to stop and that OXS lamp goes out.

911

An OXS lamp will light at 30,000 mile intervals as a reminder to replace the oxygen sensor. **After replacing the oxygen sensor, disconnect battery ground cable and remove speedometer. The mileage counter will be visible through speedometer mounting hole. Use a thick piece of wire or a thin rod to press white reset button on counter. Push button all the way in against stop.** Ensure warning lamp goes off.

928

The 928S (with LH Jetronic system) does not use a warning lamp. On these models, however, it is recommended that the oxygen sensor be replaced every 60,000 miles. On 928 and 928S (with CIS system) models, after replacing the oxygen sensor, reset the mileage counter which is located to the right of the passenger seat floor. Remove counter cover retaining screw and cover. Press reset button all the way in to against stop. Ensure warning lamp goes off.

"CHECK ENGINE" LAMP

DME & LH-JETRONIC FUEL SYSTEMS

The "Check Engine" lamp will be illuminated when the ignition switch is in the On position with engine not running. When the engine is started, the lamp should go out. If the lamp remains lit, a diagnostic trouble code has been stored by the Electronic Control Unit (ECU). **After diagnosis and repair are complete, place ignition switch in On position without starting engine, then depress accelerator pedal fully for more than 11 seconds. ECU memory should be cleared and the "Check Engine" lamp should be reset.**

Renault

INDEX

	Page No.
EGR Maintenance Indicator......	0-20
Oxygen Sensor Indicator	0-20

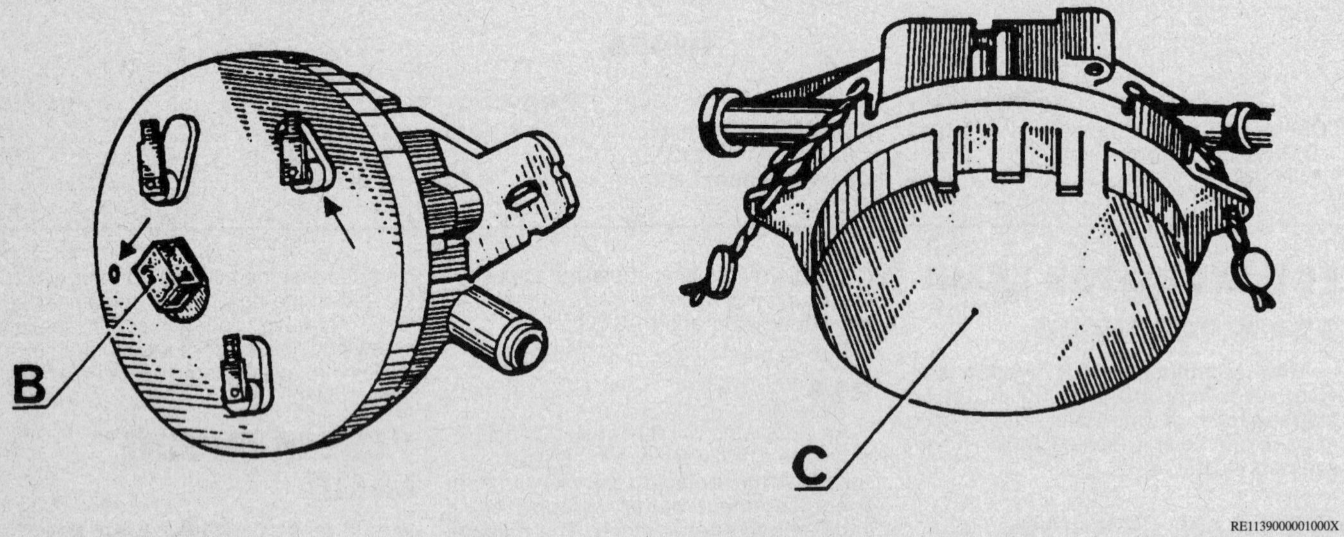
B
C
RE1139000001000X

Fig. 1 Resetting emission maintenance reminder lamps

EGR MAINTENANCE INDICATOR

On some models, an EGR maintenance indicator is placed in the speedometer cable between the transmission and the speedometer. This indicator is also attached to the air filter bracket and activates a warning lamp on the instrument panel at 25,000 mile intervals.

After the proper maintenance has been performed, the indicator lamp should be reset. To reset the indicator, follow the procedure as outlined below:

1. Using a suitable tool, cut seal plug wires from indicator cover, **Fig. 1,** then remove cover by disengaging clips.
2. Turn button (B) one quarter turn in direction of arrow and towards the "O" mark on indicator.
3. Replace cover and secure using wire.

OXYGEN SENSOR INDICATOR

On some vehicles equipped with an oxygen sensor, a maintenance indicator is placed in the speedometer cable between the transmission and the speedometer. The indicator, usually attached to the air filter bracket, closes an electrical contact and activates a warning lamp on the instrument panel, alerting the driver to replace the sensor. The maintenance indicator will activate at approximately 30,000 mile intervals.

After the proper maintenance has been performed, the indicator lamp should be reset. To reset the indicator, follow the procedure as outlined below:

1. Using a suitable tool, cut seal plug wires from indicator cover, **Fig. 1,** then remove cover by disengaging clips.
2. Turn button (B) one quarter turn in direction of arrow and toward "O" mark on indicator.
3. Replace cover and secure using wire.

Saab

INDEX

	Page No.
"Check Engine" Lamp	0-21
Oxygen Sensor Maintenance Reminder Lamp	0-21

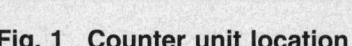

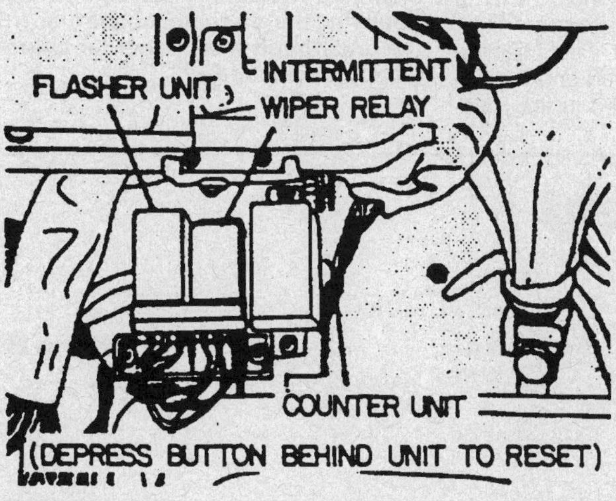
FLASHER UNIT
INTERMITTENT WIPER RELAY
COUNTER UNIT
(DEPRESS BUTTON BEHIND UNIT TO RESET)
SA1139000001000X

Fig. 1 Counter unit location

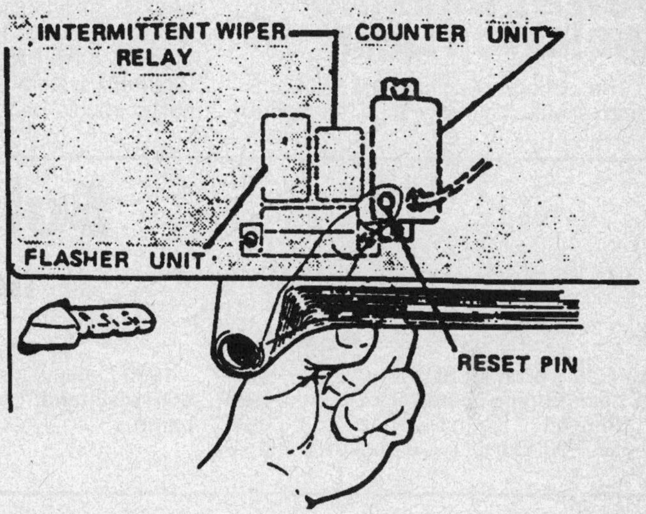
INTERMITTENT WIPER RELAY
COUNTER UNIT
FLASHER UNIT
RESET PIN
SA1139000002000X

Fig. 2 Resetting counter unit

"CHECK ENGINE" LAMP

The "Check Engine" lamp illuminates to indicate an electronic system malfunction and can also be used to display diagnostic trouble codes. **Following diagnosis and repair of a malfunction, the lamp will no longer illuminate if the system is operating properly.**

OXYGEN SENSOR MAINTENANCE REMINDER LAMP

The oxygen sensor warning lamp, marked EXH, is located on the instrument panel and will illuminate, at 15,000 mile intervals for 1980 models and 30,000 mile intervals for later models, as a service reminder. **After the appropriate service has been performed, reset counter unit as shown in Figs. 1 and 2,** using the following procedure:

1. Remove padding from under instrument panel.
2. Remove counter unit cover retaining screws, then the cover.
3. Depress counter unit reset pin. Depressing reset pin will turn the EXH warning lamp off and reset the counter to zero.
4. Install counter unit cover, then install and tighten retaining screws.
5. Install padding under instrument panel.

Sterling

INDEX

Page No.
"Check Engine"/PGM-FI Warning Indicator Lamp 0-22

"CHECK ENGINE"/ PGM-FI WARNING INDICATOR LAMP

The Check Engine/PGM-FI warning lamp should be illuminated for approximately two seconds after the ignition switch is placed in the On position as a bulb check. After approximately two seconds, the lamp should go out. If the lamp remains lit, a problem in the Programmed Fuel Injection (PGM-FI) system is indicated and a diagnostic trouble code is stored in the Electronic Control Unit (ECU) memory. **After diagnosis and repair are complete, the PGM-FI ECU memory can be cleared by removing the alternator sense fuse from the underhood relay panel for approximately ten seconds.**

Subaru

INDEX

Page No.
Air Bag Warning Lamp 0-24
"Check Engine" Lamp 0-23
1985–86 0-23
1987–96 Except 1990 Legacy .. 0-23
1990 Legacy 0-23
EGR Maintenance Reminder Lamp 0-24
Malfunction Indicator Lamp (MIL) 0-24
Impreza 0-24

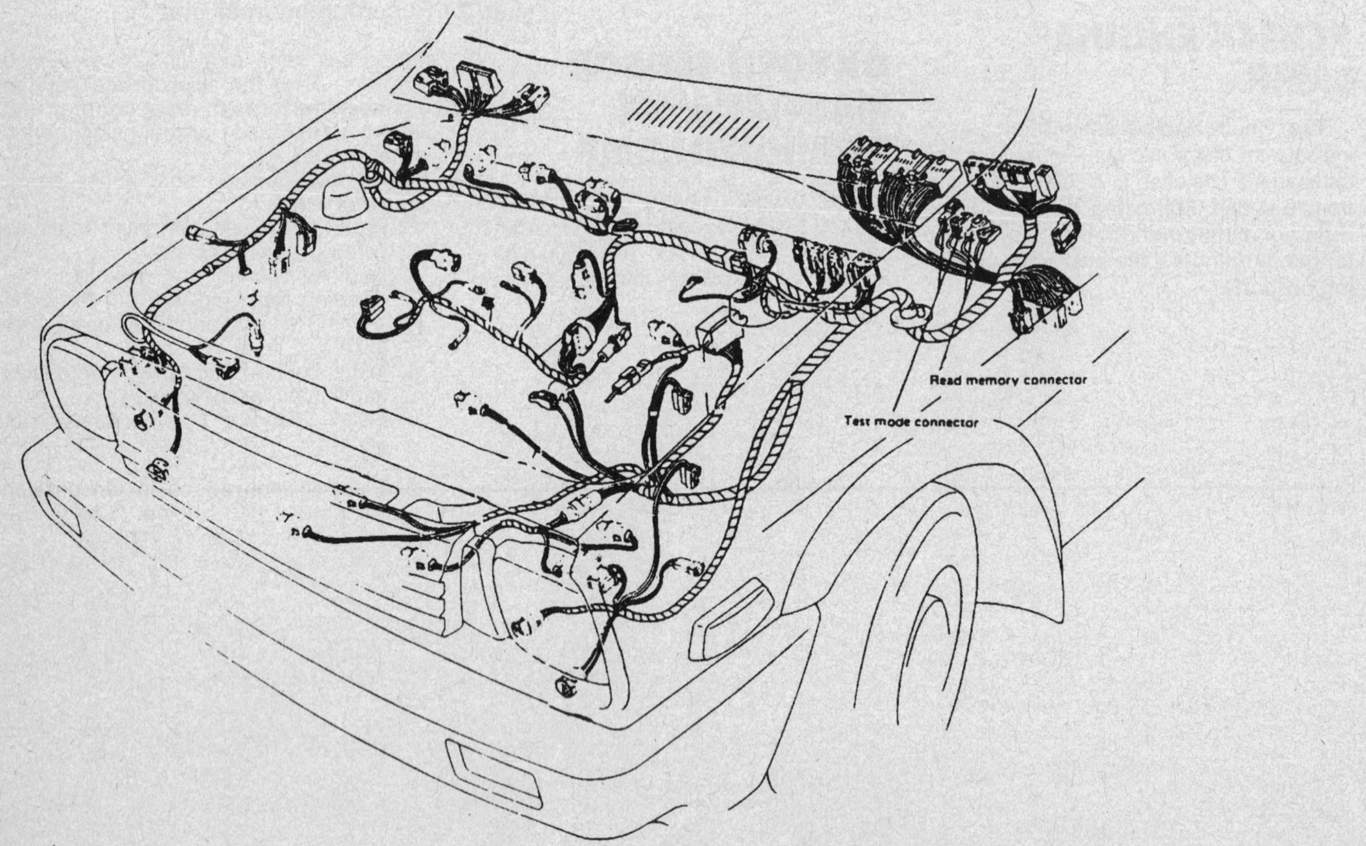
Read memory connector
Test mode connector
SB1139100036000X

Fig. 1 Read & test connector locations. Justy

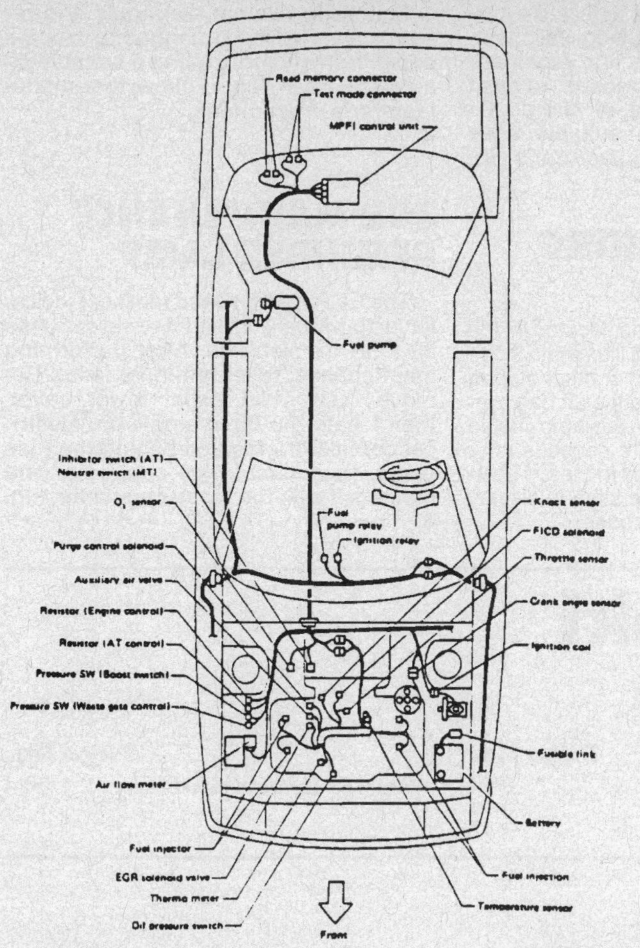
Read memory connector
Test mode connector
MPFI control unit
Fuel pump
Inhibitor switch (AT)
Neutral switch (MT)
O2 sensor
Fuel pump relay
Ignition relay
Purge control solenoid
Auxiliary air valve
Resistor (Engine control)
Resistor (AT control)
Pressure SW (Boost switch)
Pressure SW (Waste gate control)
Air flow meter
Knock sensor
FICD solenoid
Throttle sensor
Crank angle sensor
Ignition coil
Fusible link
Battery
Fuel injector
EGR solenoid valve
Thermo meter
Oil pressure switch
Fuel injection
Temperature sensor
Front

SB1139100037000X

Fig. 2 Read & test connector locations. XT

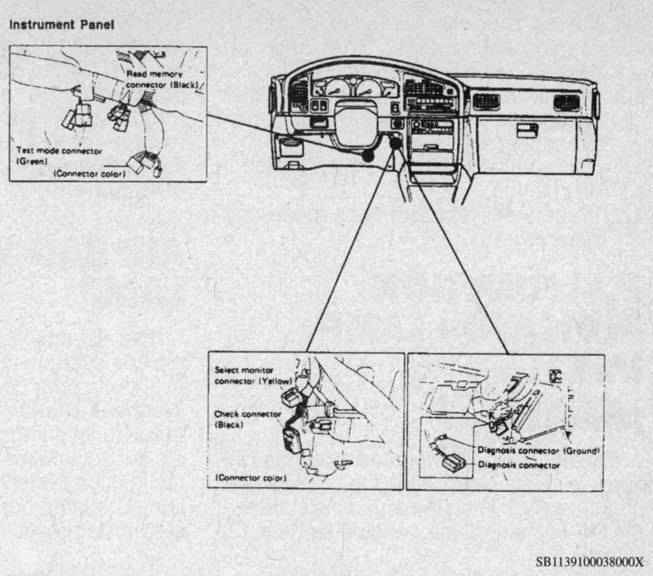
Instrument Panel
Read memory connector (Black)
Test mode connector (Green)
(Connector color)
Select monitor connector (Yellow)
Check connector (Black)
(Connector color)
Diagnosis connector (Ground)
Diagnosis connector

SB1139100038000X

Fig. 3 Read & test connector locations. Except Justy & XT

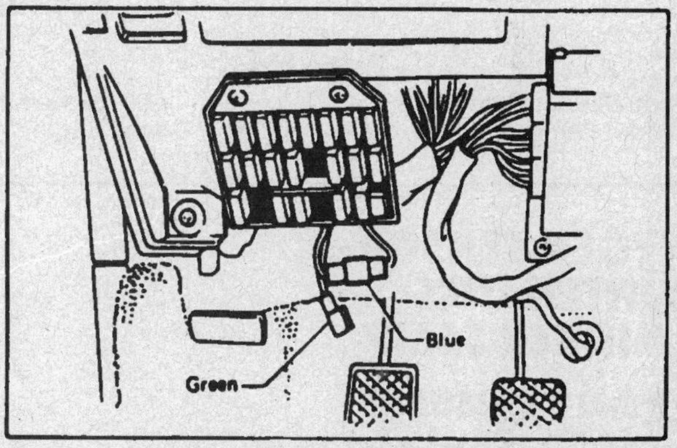
Blue
Green

SB1139000001000X

Fig. 4 EGR maintenance lamp reset

"CHECK ENGINE" LAMP

1985-86

The "Check Engine" lamp will illuminate when the ignition switch is in the On position. The lamp should go out shortly after the engine has been started. If it does not, the self-diagnostic system has detected a problem and stored a diagnostic trouble code. **After diagnosis and repair are complete, the self-diagnostic system memory will automatically be cleared of any stored diagnostic trouble codes.**

1987-96 EXCEPT 1990 LEGACY

The "Check Engine" lamp will be illuminated when the ignition switch is placed in the On position. When the engine is started, the lamp should go out. If it remains lit after engine start-up, the self-diagnostic system has detected a problem and stored a diagnostic trouble code. **After diagnosis and repair are complete, the self-diagnostic system memory can be cleared as follows:**

1. Start engine and run until normal operating temperature is reached.
2. Place ignition switch in off position, then connect test mode and read memory connectors, **Figs. 1 through 3.**
3. Place ignition switch in On position without starting engine. "Check Engine" lamp should be illuminated.
4. Depress accelerator pedal completely, then return to half throttle and hold for two seconds.
5. Release accelerator pedal and start engine.
6. Drive vehicle at a speed above 5 mph for approximately one minute.
7. Allow engine to reach operating temperature at an engine speed above 1500 RPM. "Check Engine" lamp should blink.
8. Place ignition switch in off position, then disconnect test mode and read memory connectors.

1990 LEGACY

The "Check Engine" lamp will be illuminated when the ignition switch is placed in the On position. When the engine is started, the lamp should go out. If it remains lit after engine start-up, the self-diagnostic system has detected a problem and stored a diagnostic trouble code. **After diagnosis and repair are complete, the self-diagnostic system memory can be cleared as follows:**

1. Start engine and allow to reach operating temperature.
2. Place ignition switch in off position, then connect test mode and read memory connectors, **Fig. 3.**
3. Place ignition switch in On position without starting engine. "Check Engine" lamp should be illuminated.
4. Depress accelerator pedal completely, then return to half throttle and hold for two seconds.
5. Release accelerator pedal and start engine.
6. If "Check Engine" lamp remains lit, proceed as follows:
   a. Confirm diagnostic trouble code.
   b. Perform sequential checks of diagnostic trouble codes.
7. If lamp goes out, drive at a speed exceeding 7 mph for at least one minute.
8. **On models equipped with manual transaxle,** perform a fourth speed shift.

9. **On all models,** warm up engine by running above 2000 RPM, then observe "Check Engine" lamp.
10. If lamp does not blink, check again for diagnostic trouble codes, then repeat preceding step.
11. If lamp blinks, place ignition switch in off position.
12. Disconnect test and read mode connectors.

MALFUNCTION INDICATOR LAMP (MIL)

IMPREZA

The MIL will be illuminated when the ignition switch is placed in the On position, and should go out when the engine is started. If the MIL remains lit after engine start-up, the self-diagnostic system has detected a malfunction and has stored a diagnostic trouble code. **After diagnosis and repair are complete, the self-diagnostic system memory can be cleared of diagnostic trouble codes using a suitable scan tool. Follow tool manufacturer's instructions.**

AIR BAG WARNING LAMP

The air bag warning lamp, located inside the combination meter, will illuminate in the event of a poor connection or other air bag system malfunction. When the air bag system is functioning properly, the lamp should go out approximately eight seconds after the ignition switch is placed in the On position. The lamp can also be used to display stored diagnostic trouble codes.

Following system diagnosis and repair, clear air bag diagnostic trouble codes from memory using a suitable diagnostic scan tool. Follow tool manufacturer's instructions.

EGR MAINTENANCE REMINDER LAMP

The EGR maintenance reminder indicator lamp will be illuminated to indicate time for EGR maintenance. **After performing maintenance, reset reminder lamp. Remove instrument panel lower cover, then locate the three single pin electrical connectors located behind the fuse panel. Disconnect blue connector and connect it with the green connector, Fig. 4.**

Suzuki

INDEX

	Page No.
Oxygen Sensor Maintenance Reminder Lamp	0-24
1986–87 Samurai	0-24
"Check Engine" Light	0-24
1988–91 Samurai & Sidekick	0-24

OXYGEN SENSOR MAINTENANCE REMINDER LAMP

1986–87 SAMURAI

A sensor lamp is located on the instrument panel to indicate proper operation of the oxygen sensor feedback circuit. Every 60,000 miles of vehicle operation, the lamp will begin to flash. **When the lamp begins to flash, the feedback circuit should be checked and the lamp reset using the following procedure:**

1. Ensure ignition switch is in the off position, then remove fuse panel cover and move cancel switch to On position, **Fig. 1.**
2. Turn ignition switch to On position and observe Sensor lamp. If lamp does not light (without flashing), inspect for defective bulb or open feed circuit and repair as necessary.
3. After lamp lights, start engine and allow to reach normal operating temperature.
4. Operate engine at 1500–2000 RPM while observing lamp.
5. If lamp flashed, system is operating properly. If lamp does not flash, a problem in the Computer Engine Control System is indicated and diagnosis and system testing is required.
6. After proper system operation has been verified, place cancel switch in off position to reset automatic indicator system.

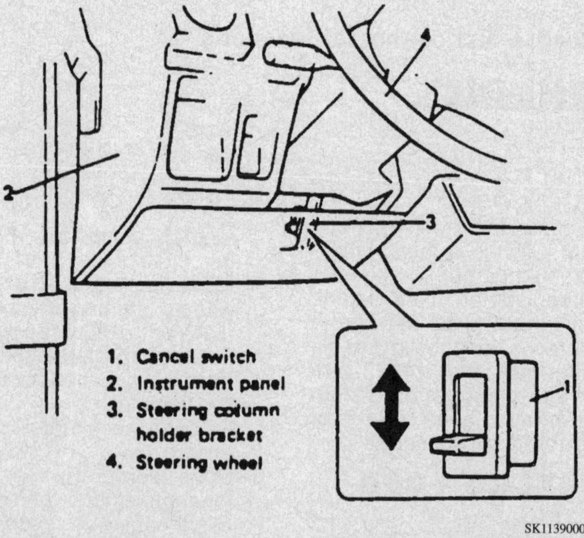

1. Cancel switch
2. Instrument panel
3. Steering column holder bracket
4. Steering wheel
1
2
3
4
SK1139000001000X

Fig. 1 Oxygen sensor indicator lamp cancel switch

"CHECK ENGINE" LIGHT

1988–91 SAMURAI & SIDEKICK

The "Check Engine" light will flash or illuminate at 50,000, 80,000 and 100,000 miles to indicate emission maintenance is required. After performing the required maintenance the light may be reset by moving cancel switch to opposite position. Cancel switch is located under instrument panel to the left of the steering column.

Toyota

INDEX

	Page No.
Air Bag System Warning Lamp	0-30
Except RAV4	0-30
RAV4	0-30
Anti-Lock Brake System Warning Lamp	0-25
Avalon & Camry	0-25
Celica & Paseo	0-25
Cressida	0-25
Land Cruiser & Tacoma	0-25
MR2	0-27
Pickup & 4Runner	0-26
Previa	0-26
RAV4	0-26
Supra	0-25
T100	0-27
Automatic Transmission Oil Temperature Warning Lamp	0-27
Automatic Transmission Overdrive Lamp	0-27
Engine Oil Reminder Lamp	0-31
Previa	0-31
Low Coolant Level Lamp	0-29
Low Oil Level Warning Lamp	0-29
Malfunction Indicator Lamp (MIL)	0-28
Camry, Celica, Paseo & Supra	0-28
Corolla & Tercel	0-28
Cressida & Van	0-28
Land Cruiser, Pickup, Previa, Tacoma, T100 & 4Runner	0-29
MR2	0-29
RAV4	0-29
Oxygen Sensor Maintenance Reminder Lamp	0-29
4 Cylinder Engine	0-29
Timing Belt Maintenance Indicator Lamp	0-30
Pickup	0-30

ANTI-LOCK BRAKE SYSTEM WARNING LAMP

The anti-lock warning lamp is used to warn of a system malfunction. The lamp will be lit during engine start-up, but should go out when the self-diagnostic system verifies proper anti-lock operation. If the lamp remains lit, a malfunction in the anti-lock brake system is indicated. **After system diagnosis and repair are complete, the lamp can be reset using the following procedures.**

AVALON & CAMRY

1990-91

1. Place ignition switch in On position.
2. Disconnect check connector, **Fig. 1.**
3. Depress brake pedal completely at least eight times within three seconds, then ensure warning lamp diagnostic trouble code display indicates normal condition, **Fig. 2.**
4. Connect check connector.
5. Anti-lock warning lamp should not be illuminated. If it is, repeat reset procedure, ensuring all requirements are met.

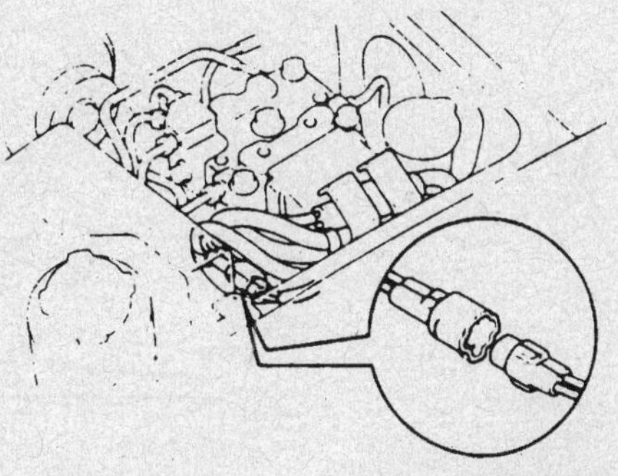

TY1139000213000X

Fig. 1 Check connector location. 1990–91 Camry

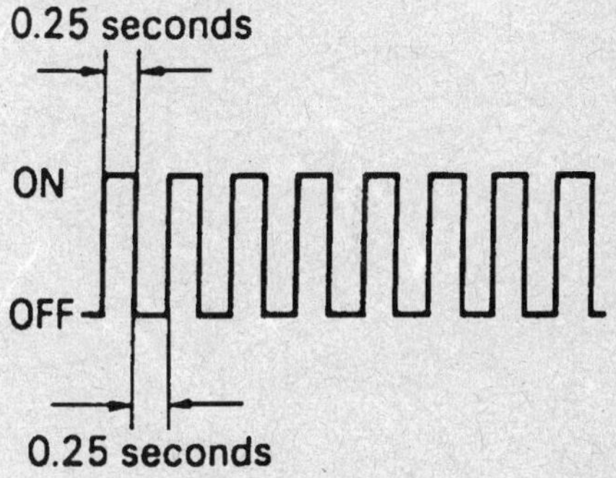
0.25 seconds
ON
OFF
0.25 seconds

TY1139100214000X

Fig. 2 Normal indication

1992-96

1. Place ignition switch in On position.
2. Connect jumper tool No. 09843-18020, or equivalent, to terminals T_C and E1 of diagnostic connector link, **Figs. 3 and 4.** Vehicle must be stopped at this time.
3. Clear diagnostic trouble codes from ECU by fully depressing brake pedal at least eight times within three seconds.
4. Ensure warning lamp diagnostic trouble code display indicates a normal condition, **Fig. 2.**
5. Remove check connectors, then ensure ABS warning lamp goes out.

CELICA & PASEO

1987-89

1. Place ignition switch in On position.
2. **On FWD models,** remove control relay bracket attaching bolt, **Fig. 5.**
3. **On all models,** disconnect check connector, **Figs. 5 and 6.**
4. Cycle brake pedal at least eight times within three seconds, then ensure warning lamp diagnostic trouble code display indicates a normal condition, **Fig. 2.**
5. Connect check connector.
6. Anti-lock warning lamp should not be illuminated.
7. **On FWD models,** install control relay attaching bolt.

1990-96

1. Place ignition switch in On position.
2. Connect jumper tool No. 09843-18020, or equivalent, to terminals T_C and E1 of diagnostic connector link, **Figs. 7 and 8.** Vehicle must be stopped at this time.
3. Clear ECU diagnostic trouble codes by fully depressing brake pedal at least eight times within three seconds.
4. Ensure warning lamp diagnostic trouble code display indicates a normal condition.
5. Remove jumper tool and ensure ABS warning lamp goes out.

CRESSIDA

1. Place ignition switch in On position.
2. Connect a suitable jumper wire between terminals T_C and E1 of diagnostic connector link, **Fig. 9.**
3. Fully depress brake pedal at lease eight times within three seconds, then ensure warning lamp diagnostic trouble code display indicates a normal condition, **Fig. 2.**
4. Disconnect jumper wire from diagnostic connector link.
5. Anti-lock warning lamp should not be illuminated.

LAND CRUISER & TACOMA

1. Place ignition switch in On position.
2. Connect jumper tool No. 09843-18020, or equivalent, to terminals T_C and E1 of diagnostic connector link, **Fig. 8.** Vehicle must be stopped at this time.
3. Clear diagnostic trouble codes from ECU by fully depressing brake pedal at least eight times within three seconds.
4. Ensure warning lamp diagnostic trouble code display indicates a normal condition.
5. Remove jumper tool, then ensure ABS warning lamp goes out.

SUPRA

1988-92

1. Place ignition switch in On position.
2. Disconnect actuator check connector, **Fig. 10.**

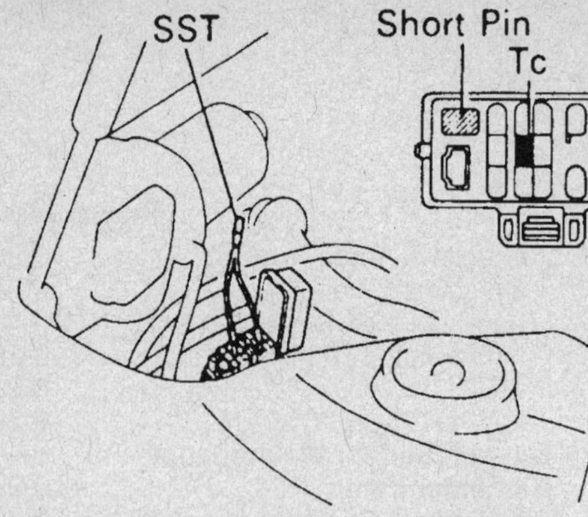
SST
Short Pin
Tc
E_1

TY1139200215000X

Fig. 3 Check connector location & terminal identification. 1992–96 Camry

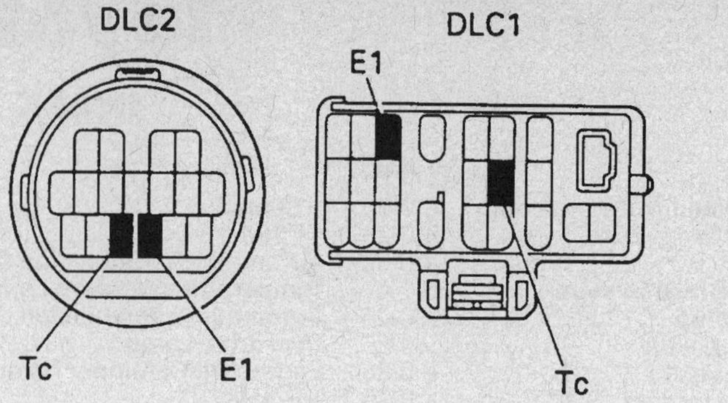
DLC2
DLC1
E1
Tc
E1
Tc

TY1139500262000X

Fig. 4 Check connector terminal identification. Avalon

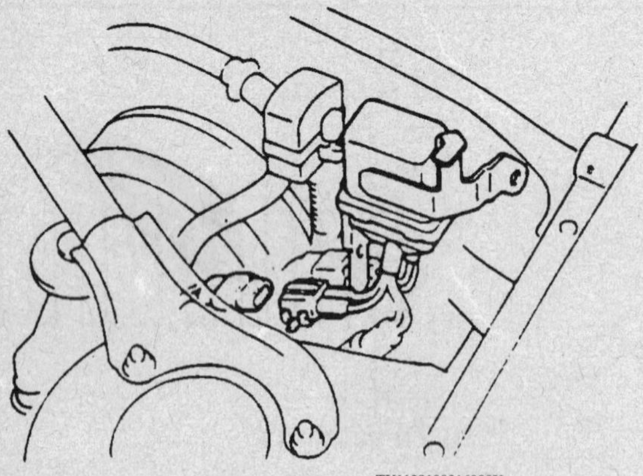

TY1139100216000X

Fig. 5 Check connector location. 1987–89 Celica FWD

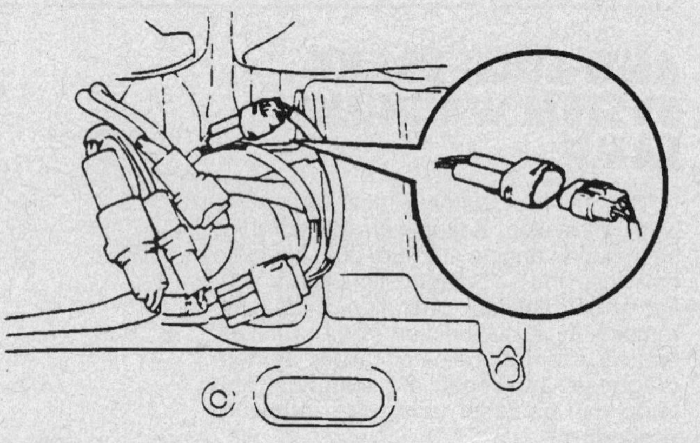

TY1139100217000X

Fig. 6 Check connector location. 1987–89 Celica AWD

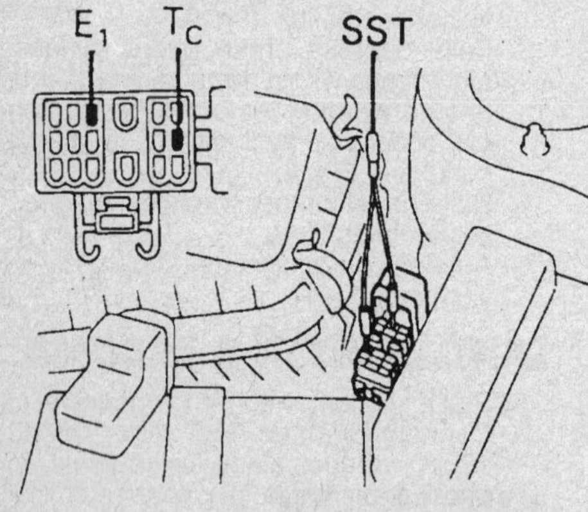
E_1
T_C
SST

TY1139000218000X

Fig. 7 Check connector location & terminal identification. 1990–93 Celica

3. Fully depress brake pedal at least eight times within three seconds, then ensure warning lamp diagnostic trouble code display indicates a normal condition, **Fig. 2.**
4. Connect actuator check connector.
5. Anti-lock warning lamp should not be illuminated. If it is, repeat reset procedure, ensuring all requirements are met.

1993–96

1. Using a suitable jumper, connect DLC1 or DLC2 terminals T_C and E1, **Fig. 11.**
2. Fully depress brake pedal at least eight times within three seconds, then ensure warning lamp diagnostic trouble code display indicates a normal condition.
3. Remove jumper, then connect short pin to DLC1.

PICKUP & 4RUNNER

1. Place ignition switch in On position.
2. Disconnect service connector, **Fig. 12.** Ensure vehicle is not moving.
3. Connect a suitable jumper wire between terminals T_C and E_1 of check connector, **Figs. 13 and 14.**
4. Fully depress brake pedal at least eight times within three seconds, then ensure warning lamp diagnostic trouble code display indicates a normal condition, **Fig. 2.**
5. Connect service connector and remove jumper wire. Ensure warning lamp goes out.

RAV4

1. Using jumper tool No. 09843-18020, or equivalent, connect Data Link Connector (DLC1) terminals T_C and E1, **Fig. 8.**
2. Disconnect short pin from DLC1, then place ignition switch in On position.
3. **On AWD models,** fully depress brake pedal at least eight times within three seconds.
4. **On FWD models,** fully depress brake pedal at least eight times within five seconds.
5. **On all models,** ensure warning lamp diagnostic trouble code display indicates a normal condition.
6. Remove jumper tool and connect short pin to DLC1.

PREVIA

1. Place ignition switch in On position.
2. Disconnect service connector, **Fig. 15.**
3. Connect jumper wire tool No. 09843-18020, or equivalent, to check connector terminals T_C and E_1, **Fig. 16.** Ensure vehicle is not moving.
4. Clear ECU diagnostic trouble codes by fully depressing brake pedal at least eight times within three seconds.
5. Ensure warning lamp diagnostic trouble code display indicates a normal condition, then connect service connector.

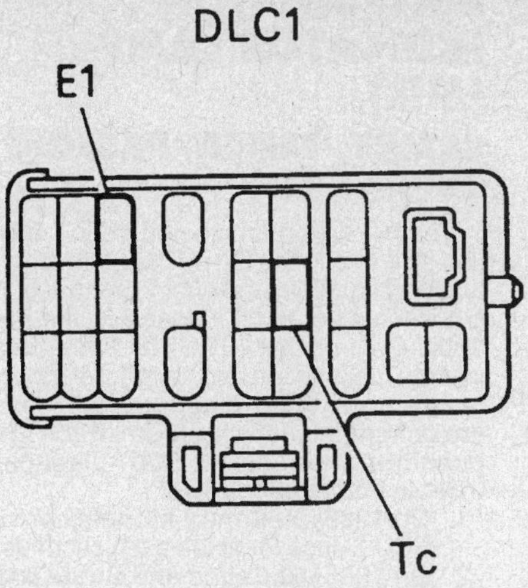
DLC1
E1
Tc

TY1139500263000X

Fig. 8 Check connector terminal identification. RAV4 & 1994–96 Celica, Land Cruiser & Tacoma

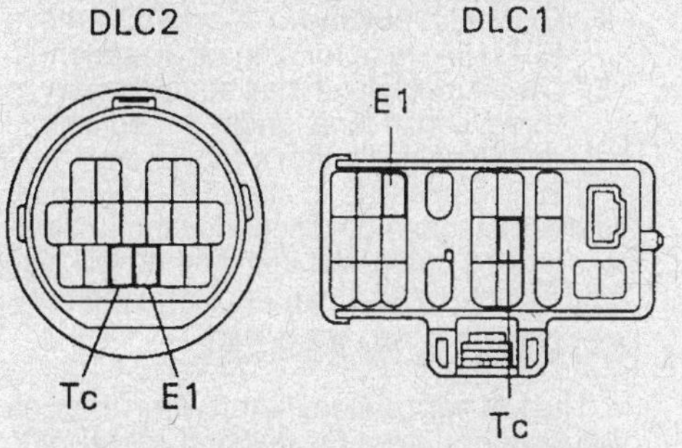
DLC2
DLC1
E1
Tc
E1
Tc

TY1139300221000X

Fig. 11 Check connector terminal identification. 1993–96 Supra

6. Remove jumper wire tool and ensure ABS warning lamp goes out.

MR2

1. Place ignition switch in On position.
2. Connect jumper wire tool No. 09843-18020, or equivalent, to check connector terminals T_C and E1, **Fig. 17.** Ensure vehicle is not moving.
3. Clear ECU diagnostic trouble codes by fully depressing brake pedal at least eight times within three seconds.
4. Ensure warning lamp diagnostic trouble code display indicates a normal condition, then remove jumper tool.
5. Ensure ABS warning lamp goes out.

T100

1. Place ignition switch in On position.
2. Connect jumper tool No. 09843-18020, or equivalent, to diagnostic connector link terminals T_C and E_1, **Fig. 18.** Ensure vehicle is not moving.
3. Clear ECU diagnostic trouble codes by fully depressing brake pedal at least eight times within three seconds.

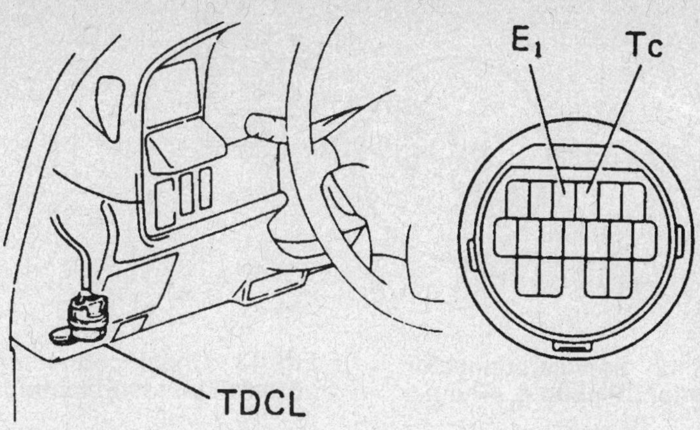
E1
Tc
TDCL

TY1139100219000X

Fig. 9 Check connector location. Cressida

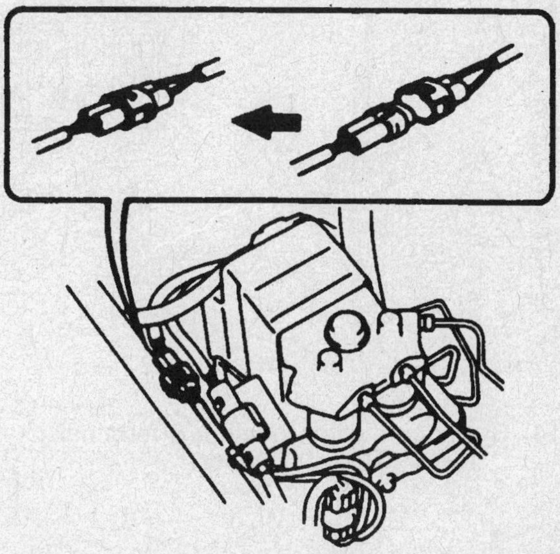

TY1138800220000X

Fig. 10 Check connector location. 1988–92 Supra

4. Ensure warning lamp diagnostic trouble code display indicates a normal condition.
5. Remove jumper tool and ensure ABS warning lamp goes out.

AUTOMATIC TRANSMISSION OVERDRIVE LAMP

The "OD off" lamp will be illuminated when the ignition switch is in the On position and the Overdrive (OD) switch is in the off position. When the OD switch is placed in the On position, the "OD off" lamp should go out. If the lamp flashes when the switch is placed in the On position, a malfunction has been detected by the electronic control system. **After diagnosis and repair are complete, place the ignition switch in the off position, then clear ECU of diagnostic trouble codes as follows:**

1. **On Celica, MR2, Pickup, Previa, T100 and 4Runner models,** remove EFI fuse (15A) for at least ten seconds.
2. **On Cressida models,** remove EFI fuse (20A) for at least ten seconds.
3. **On Supra models,** remove DOME fuse for at least ten seconds.
4. **On all models,** it may be necessary to remove fuse for a longer period of time in cold weather conditions.

AUTOMATIC TRANSMISSION OIL TEMPERATURE WARNING LAMP

This lamp will be illuminated when automatic transmission or transfer case fluid temperature exceeds 302°F. If the lamp lights, allow vehicle to operate at idle speed until fluid temperature falls below 248°F;

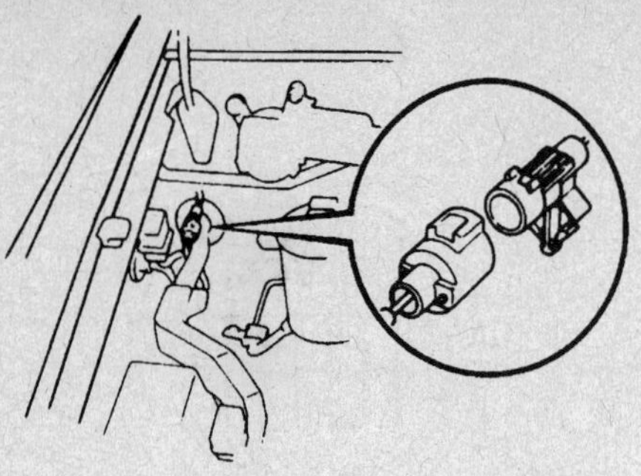

TY1139100222000X

Fig. 12 Service connector location. Pickup & 4Runner

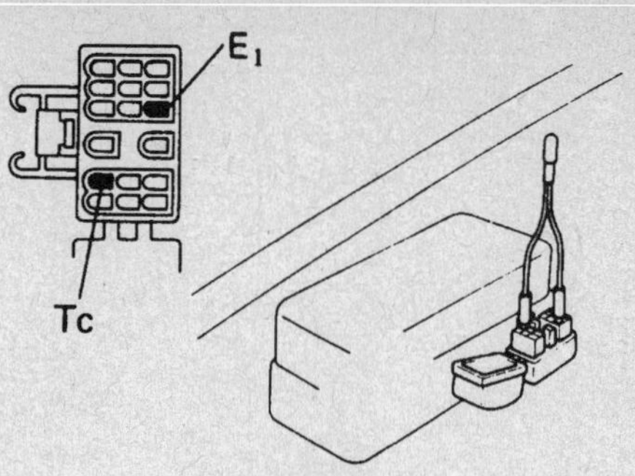
E1
Tc

TY1139100223000X

Fig. 13 Check connector location & terminal identification. Pickup

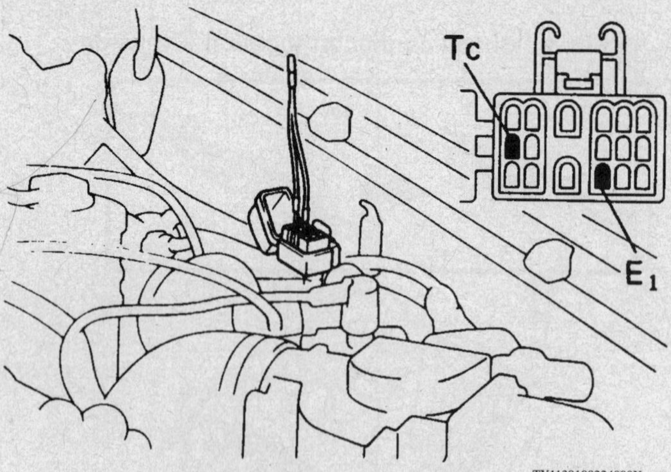
Tc
E1

TY1139100224000X

Fig. 14 Check connector location & terminal identification. 4Runner

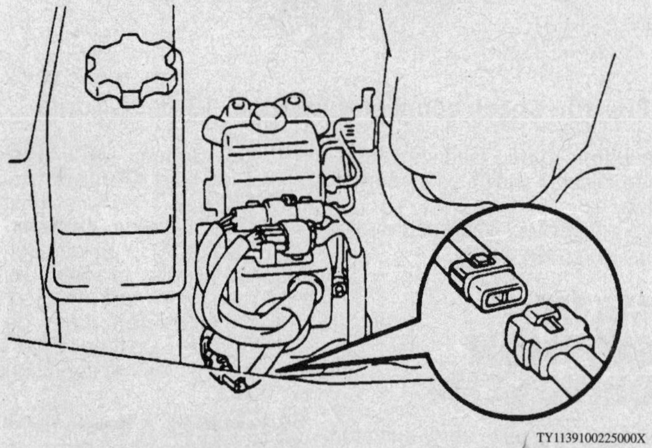

TY1139100225000X

Fig. 15 Service connector location. Previa

the lamp should go out. If it remains lit, the transmission or transfer case may require service.

When transmission or transfer case fluid has returned to its normal temperature, the lamp will reset automatically.

MALFUNCTION INDICATOR LAMP (MIL)

CAMRY, CELICA, PASEO & SUPRA

The MIL will be illuminated when the ignition switch is in the On position with engine not running. When the engine is started, the MIL should go out. If it does not, the Electronic Control Unit (ECU) has detected a system malfunction and stored a diagnostic trouble code. **After diagnosis and repair are complete, place ignition switch in off position, then clear ECU diagnostic trouble codes as follows:**

1. **On 1985–86 Camry models,** remove ECU-B fuse for at least ten seconds.
2. **On 1985–86 Celica and Supra models,** remove STOP fuse for at least ten seconds.
3. **On 1987–89 models and 1990–96 models except Supra,** remove EFI fuse for at least ten seconds.
4. **On 1990–96 Supra models,** remove EFI (15A) fuse for at least 30 seconds.
5. **On all models,** it may be necessary to remove fuse for a longer period of time during cold weather conditions.

It is also possible to clear ECU diagnostic trouble codes by disconnecting the battery ground cable, but this method will also erase clock, radio and radio alarm memory.

COROLLA & TERCEL

The MIL will be illuminated when the ignition switch is in the On position with engine not running. When the engine has been started, the MIL should go out. If it does not, the Electronic Control Unit (ECU) has detected a system malfunction and stored a diagnostic trouble code. **After diagnosis and repair are complete, place ignition switch in off position, then clear ECU diagnostic trouble codes as follows:**

1. **On all models except 1990–96 Tercel,** remove STOP (15A) fuse, **Fig. 19,** for at least ten seconds.
2. **On 1990–96 Tercel models,** remove EFI (15A) fuse for at least ten seconds.
3. **On all models,** it may be necessary to remove fuse for a longer period of time during cold weather conditions.

It is also possible to clear ECU diagnostic trouble codes by disconnecting the battery ground cable, but this method will also erase clock, radio and radio alarm memory.

CRESSIDA & VAN

The MIL will be illuminated when the ignition switch is in the On position with engine not running. When the engine has been started, the MIL should go out. If it remains lit, a diagnostic trouble code has been stored by the Electronic Control Unit

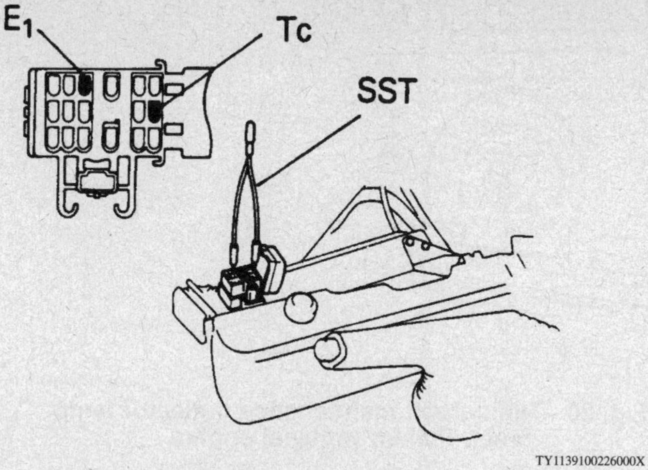
E1
Tc
SST
TY1139100226000X

Fig. 16 Check connector location & terminal identification. Previa

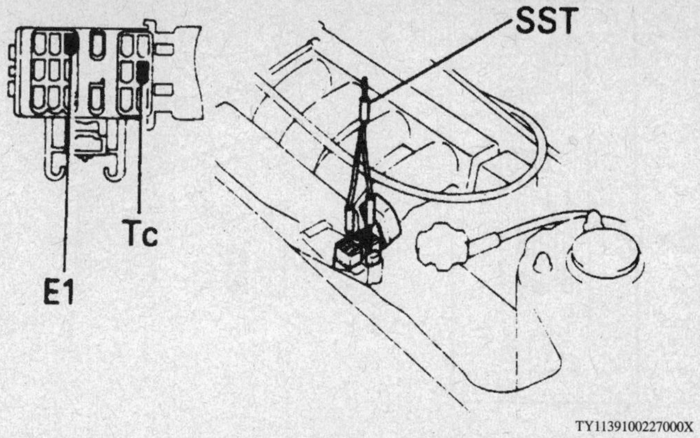
SST
Tc
E1
TY1139100227000X

Fig. 17 Check connector location & terminal identification. MR2

(ECU). **After diagnosis and repair are complete, place ignition switch in off position, then clear diagnostic trouble codes from the ECU by removing the EFI (20A) fuse from the passenger compartment fuse panel for at least ten seconds. It may be necessary to remove the fuse for a longer period of time during cold weather conditions.** It is also possible to clear ECU diagnostic trouble codes by disconnecting the battery ground cable, but this method will also erase clock and radio memory.

LAND CRUISER, PICKUP, PREVIA, TACOMA, T100 & 4RUNNER

The MIL will be illuminated when the ignition switch is in the On position with engine not running. When the engine has been started, the lamp should go out. If it remains lit, a diagnostic trouble code has been stored by the Electronic Control Unit (ECU). **After diagnosis and repair are complete, place the ignition switch in the off position, then clear ECU diagnostic trouble codes as follows:**

1. **On models equipped with carbureted engine,** remove HAZ-HORN fuse from engine compartment relay panel.
2. **On models equipped with fuel injected engine,** remove EFI (15A) fuse from passenger compartment fuse panel.
3. **On all models,** the fuse must be removed for at least 30 seconds, possibly longer during cold weather conditions.

Diagnostic trouble codes can also be erased by disconnecting the battery ground cable, but this method will also erase clock and radio memory.

RAV4

The MIL should light when the ignition switch is placed in the On position without starting the engine. When the engine is started, the lamp should go out. If it remains lit, a malfunction has been detected by the diagnostic system and has logged a diagnostic trouble code. If the malfunction does

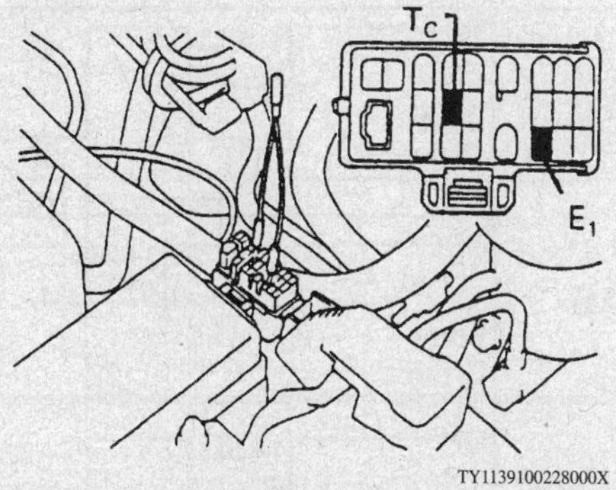
Tc
E1
TY1139100228000X

Fig. 18 Check connector location & terminal identification. T100

not occur again within three trips, the lamp will go out but a diagnostic trouble code will remain stored. **The lamp will reset automatically when diagnosis and repair are complete and diagnostic trouble codes have been cleared using one of the following procedures:**

1. Connect a suitable OBD II scan tool to instrument panel data link connector, then use tool to erase stored diagnostic trouble codes. Follow tool manufacturer's instructions.
2. Disconnect battery ground cable or EFI fuse. **Disconnecting ground cable will also erase clock and radio memory.**

MR2

The MIL will be illuminated when the ignition switch is in the On position with engine not running. When the engine has been started, the lamp should go out. If it remains lit, a diagnostic trouble code has been stored by the Electronic Control Unit (ECU). **After diagnosis and repair are complete, place ignition switch in off position, then remove the AM-2 fuse from the engine compartment relay panel on pre-1991 models or the EFI (15A) fuse on 1991–95 models.** The fuse must be removed for at least ten seconds, possibly longer during cold weather conditions. The lower the ambient temperature, the longer the fuse will have to be removed. Another method to erase stored diagnostic trouble codes is to disconnect the battery ground cable, but this method will also erase other memory, including clock and radio.

LOW COOLANT LEVEL LAMP

This lamp will be illuminated when the coolant level in the radiator drops below a pre-determined point. **To reset the lamp, bring the coolant to the proper level. Be sure to inspect the cooling system for leaks that may have precipitated the low coolant level condition.**

LOW OIL LEVEL WARNING LAMP

This lamp lights to indicate that the engine oil level is below a specified level. The lamp will be illuminated during engine startup. If oil level is sufficient, the lamp will go out during engine operation. **The lamp will reset automatically when the oil level is corrected.**

OXYGEN SENSOR MAINTENANCE REMINDER LAMP

4 CYLINDER ENGINE

This lamp illuminates at 30,000 mile intervals. After performing the required service, reset lamp cancel switch. On Corolla models equipped with 3T-C engine and Celica and Corona models, the cancel switch is clipped to lefthand kick panel. On Corolla models equipped with 3A-C engine and Cressida and Tercel models, the cancel switch is located under instrument panel on the lower lefthand side. On 1980 Supra models, the cancel switch is located under the instrument panel to the left of the steering column. On 1981 Supra models, the cancel switch is clipped to the lefthand kick panel.

On 1980 models, use tool No. 09810-25010, or equivalent, to remove switch

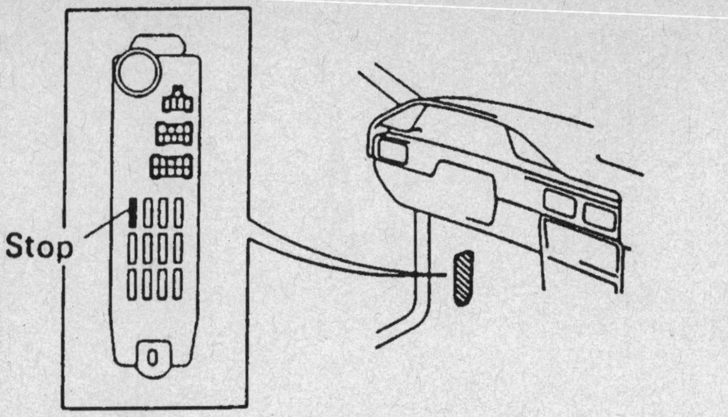
Stop

TY1139100229000X

Fig. 19 STOP fuse location. Corolla & Tercel

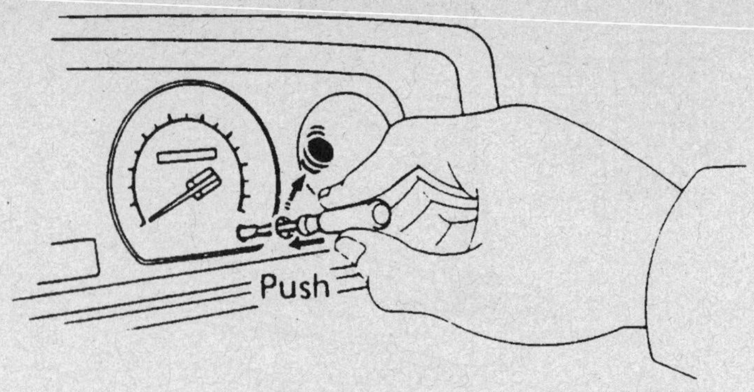
Push

TY1139100230000X

Fig. 20 Timing belt maintenance indicator lamp reset. Pickup w/diesel engine

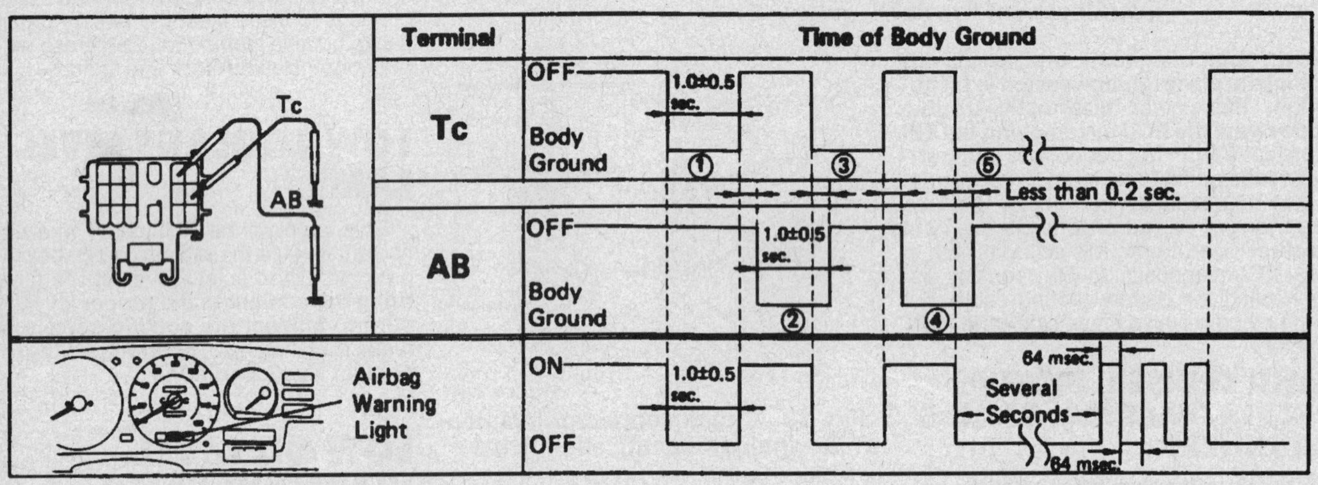
Tc
AB
Terminal
Time of Body Ground
OFF
Body Ground
1.0±0.5 sec.
Less than 0.2 sec.
Airbag Warning Light
ON
64 msec.
Several Seconds

TY1139100231000X

Fig. 21 Air bag warning lamp connector terminals

cover, then move switch lever to opposite position. On 1981 models, open the switch cover; then, using a screwdriver and working through the cover opening, move the switch lever to the opposite position.

TIMING BELT MAINTENANCE INDICATOR LAMP

PICKUP

Diesel Engine

After the timing belt has been replaced, the maintenance indicator lamp may be reset as follows:

1. Remove grommet from speedometer lens.
2. Insert a screwdriver into grommet hole and depress reset switch, **Fig. 20.**
3. Install grommet on speedometer lens.

AIR BAG SYSTEM WARNING LAMP

EXCEPT RAV4

The air bag system warning lamp is used to warn of a system malfunction. The lamp will light during engine start-up, but should go out when the self-diagnostic system determines that no malfunctions are present. If the lamp remains lit, a malfunction in the air bag system is indicated. **The air bag system must be diagnosed and repaired, then the following procedures can be used to reset the warning lamp.**

1. If Diagnostic Trouble Code 41 is not indicated, proceed as follows:
   a. Ensure ignition switch is in off position.
   b. Disconnect battery ground cable or remove ECU-B fuse for at least ten seconds.
   c. Connect battery ground cable or install ECU-B fuse. **Ensure ignition switch is in Lock position, or diagnostic system damage may occur.**
2. If Diagnostic Trouble Code 41 is indicated, proceed as follows:
   a. Connect service wires to check connector terminals T_C and AB.
   b. Place ignition switch in Accessory or On positions and wait approximately six seconds.
   c. Apply body ground to terminals T_C and AB alternately, twice in .5–1.5 second intervals beginning with terminal T_C, **Fig. 21.** When alternating ground applications, release one terminal from ground while applying it to other terminal.
   d. After a few seconds, the air bag lamp will blink in a 64 millisecond cycle, indicating cancellation is complete.

RAV4

The air bag or SRS warning lamp is intended to warn the driver of an air bag system malfunction. It is activated by the air bag sensor assembly. If the system is functioning properly, the lamp should light when the ignition switch is placed in the Accessory or On positions and should remain lit for approximately six seconds. If the lamp does not go out after this time or flashes, a malfunction has been detected and a diagnostic trouble code has been stored. **When diagnosis and repair are complete, placing the ignition switch in the off position will clear diagnostic trouble codes. This, in turn, will reset the warning lamp.**

ENGINE OIL REMINDER LAMP

PREVIA

At the specified engine oil change interval of 6,000 miles, an Oil Change reminder lamp on the instrument panel will be illuminated. After changing the engine oil and filter the lamp must be reset. To rest lamp, remove cover from instrument cluster, **Fig. 22,** then insert a small screwdriver or equivalent into plug opening to depress reset button.

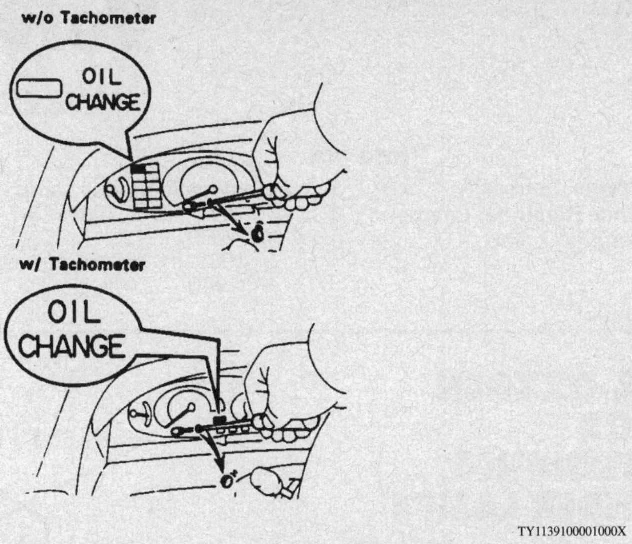
w/o Tachometer
OIL CHANGE
w/ Tachometer
OIL CHANGE
TY1139100001000X

Fig. 22 Engine oil service reminder lamp reset. Previa

Volkswagen

INDEX

Page No.		Page No.		Page No.	
EGR Warning Lamp	0-31	Emission Control System (ESC) Lamp	0-31	Service Reminder Indicator Lamp	0-31
		Oxygen Sensor Warning Lamp	0-31		

EGR WARNING LAMP

After performing the required service, turn off warning lamp, by pushing in reset button. On Jetta, GTI, Rabbit, Cabriolet, Golf and Scirocco models, remove instrument panel cover plate and insert a piece of wire, with a hooked end, through opening at top left corner of speedometer and pull left counter release arm. On Vanagon models, push in on raised area of reset module, which is located in line with speedometer cable.

Service Performed	Displays To Reset
7500 Mile/6 Month	OEL
15,000 Mile/12 Month	OEL, IN 01
22,500 Mile/18 Months	OEL
30,000 Mile/24 Months	OEL, IN 01, IN 02
37,500 Mile/30 Months	OEL
45,000 Mile/36 Months	OEL, IN 01
52,500 Mile/42 Months	OEL
60,000 Mile/48 Months	OEL, IN 01, IN 02

Fig. 1 SRI display reset

EMISSION CONTROL SYSTEM (ESC) LAMP

This lamp should be illuminated when the ignition switch is placed in the On position. After engine is started the lamp should go off, unless a problem has been detected by the emission control system self-diagnostic computer. **After diagnosis and repair, the lamp will automatically reset when stored diagnostic trouble codes are cleared from the system memory.**

OXYGEN SENSOR WARNING LAMP

After performing the required service, turn off warning lamp by pushing in reset button. On Fox, Jetta, GTI, Rabbit, Cabriolet, Golf and Scirocco models, remove instrument panel cover plate and insert a piece of wire, with a hooked end, through opening at top left corner of speedometer and pull right counter release arm. On Vanagon models, push in on raised area of reset module, located in line with speedometer cable.

SERVICE REMINDER INDICATOR LAMP

On all 1993–96 Cabrio, Golf, GTI, and Jetta models, the Service Reminder Indicator (SRI) alerts the driver when a vehicle service is needed. The system uses a hard permanent-type memory which will not erase if the battery is disconnected.

This reminder appears in the odometer display window. When the ignition is turned On, the following displays will appear for about three seconds: IN 00, no service required; OEL, 7500 miles/6 month engine oil change; IN 01, 15,000 miles/12 month maintenance and inspection; IN 02, 30,000 miles/24 month maintenance and inspection.

After required procedures are completed, reset the SRI displays to those shown **Fig. 1.**

Volvo

INDEX

	Page No.
EGR & Oxygen Sensor Maintenance Reminder Lamps	0-32
"Check Engine" Lamp	0-32
Service Indicator Lamp	0-32
1987 760 & 1987–90 740 & 780	0-32
1988–91 760 & 1991–96 740 & 940	0-32
1989–92 240	0-32
1992–96 850	0-32

EGR & OXYGEN SENSOR MAINTENANCE REMINDER LAMPS

After completing required service, turn EGR and oxygen sensor maintenance reminder lamps off. Remove the counter unit cover retaining screw, then the cover, **Fig. 1,** which is an in line unit of the speedometer cable. Press the reset button on the counter unit, until warning lamp goes off.

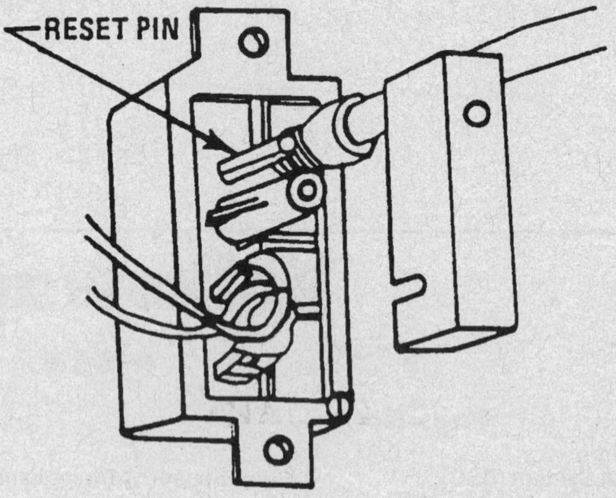
RESET PIN
VV1139000001000X

Fig. 1 Maintenance reminder mileage counter

"CHECK ENGINE" LAMP

This lamp should be illuminated when the ignition switch is placed in the On position. After the engine has been started, the lamp should go out. If it remains lit, a problem has been detected by the engine's self-diagnostic system. **After diagnosis and repair are complete and any stored diagnostic trouble codes are cleared, the lamp will reset automatically.**

SERVICE INDICATOR LAMP

1989–92 240

At the specified engine oil change interval of 5,000 miles, an oil change interval reminder lamp on the instrument panel will be illuminated for two minutes following each engine start. After changing engine oil and filter the lamp must be reset. To reset counter, press upward on lever located at the rear of the instrument cluster, **Fig. 2.**

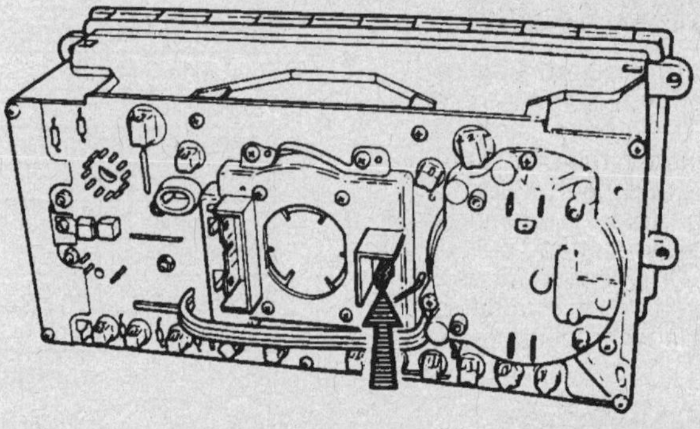
VV1138900002000X

Fig. 2 Service indicator lamp reset. 1989–92 240

1987 760 & 1987–90 740 & 780

At the specified engine oil change interval of 5,000 miles, an oil change interval reminder lamp on the instrument panel will be illuminated for two minutes following each engine start. After changing the engine oil and filter, the lamp must be reset. To reset lamp, depress reset knob located at the rear of the instrument cluster, **Fig. 3.**

1988–91 760 & 1991–96 740 & 940

At the specified engine oil change interval of 5,000 miles an oil change interval reminder lamp on the instrument panel will be illuminated for two minutes following each engine start. After changing the engine oil and filter, the lamp must be reset. To reset lamp, remove rubber grommet from the front of the instrument cluster, left of the odometer, **Fig. 4,** then insert a small screwdriver or equivalent into grommet opening to depress the reset button.

1992–96 850

The service reminder lamp will illuminate for approximately 2 minutes, after the vehicle has been started, at intervals of 12 month, 9,300 miles or 750 driving hours. After completing the required service, the lamp may be reset as follows:

1. Place ignition switch in the On position.
2. Select position 7 on diagnostic output unit A, **Fig. 5.**
3. Briefly depress button four times. System is now in diagnostic test mode 4.
4. When LED emits steady glow, enter code 151 as follows:
   a. While LED is glowing, depress button one time, then wait until LED emits a steady glow.
   b. While LED is glowing, depress button five times, then wait until LED emits a steady glow.
   c. While LED is glowing, depress button one time.
   d. Confirmation of code being received will be indicated by rapid flashes of the LED.

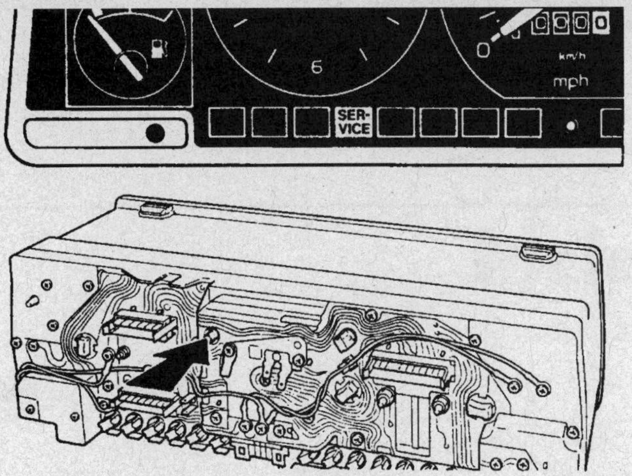
6
0
km/h
mph
SER-
VICE

VV1138900003000X

Fig. 3 Service indicator lamp reset. 1987 760 & 1987–90 740 & 780

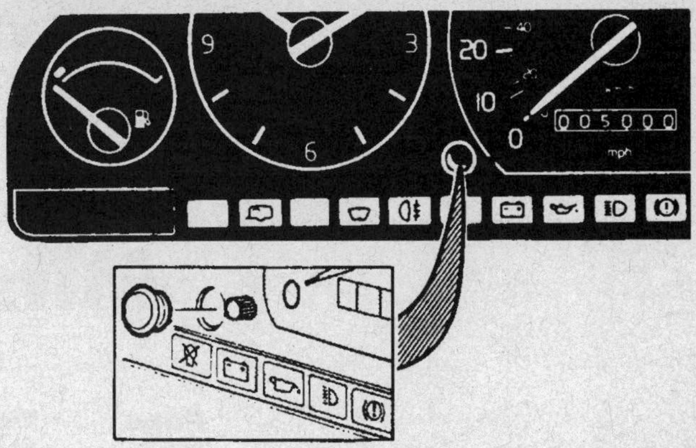
9
3
6
20
10
0
005000
mph

VV1138800004000X

Fig. 4 Service indicator lamp reset. 1988–91 760 & 1991 740

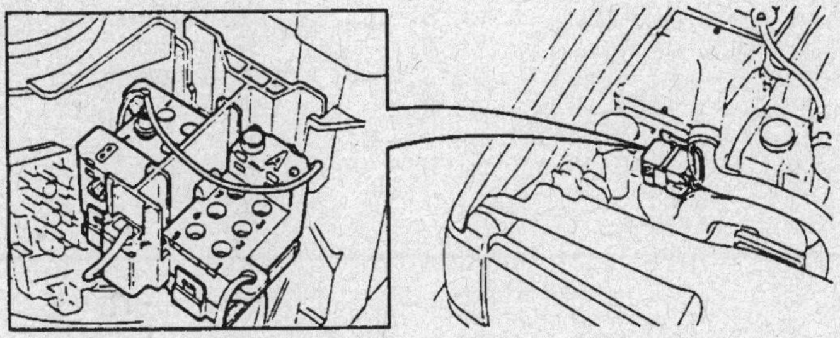

VV1139200005000X

Fig. 5 Diagnostic output unit A. 1992–96 850

VEHICLE LIFT POINTS

INDEX

	Page No.
Mitsubishi	0-34
Nissan	0-45
Porsche	0-51
Saab	0-52
Subaru	0-53
Suzuki	0-56
Toyota	0-59
Volkswagen	0-68

Mitsubishi

INDEX

	Page No.	Fig. No.
Diamante		
Floor Jack	0-35	2
Hoist	0-34	1
Expo	0-35	3
Mirage	0-36	4
Precis		
Floor Jack	0-36	5
Hoist	0-37	6
Truck		
Floor Jack	0-39	8
Hoist	0-38	7
1993-94 Eclipse	0-40	9
1995-96 Eclipse		
Floor Jack	0-41	10
Hoist	0-42	11
1993 Galant	0-42	12
1994-96 Galant		
Floor Jack	0-43	14
Hoist	0-43	13
1996 Galant		
Floor Jack	0-43	15
1993-94 Montero	0-43	16
1995-96 Montero		
Floor Jack	0-44	17
Hoist	0-44	18
3000GT	0-44	19

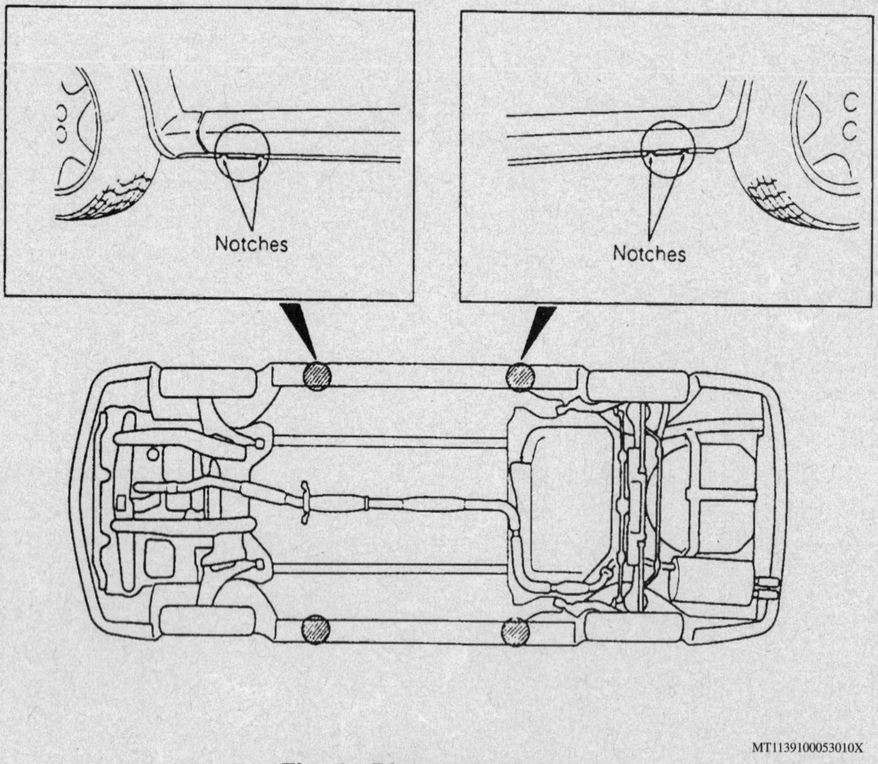

Notches
Notches
MT1139100053010X

Fig. 1 Diamante. Hoist

FLOOR JACK

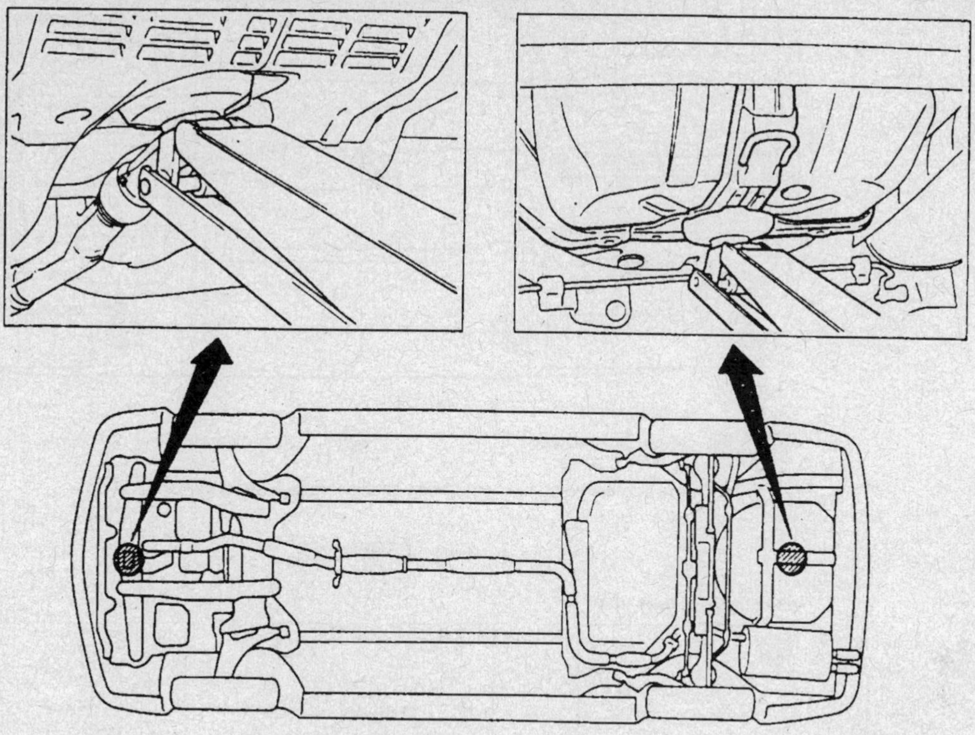

MT1139100053020X

Fig. 2 Diamante. Floor Jack

<FWD>

<AWD>

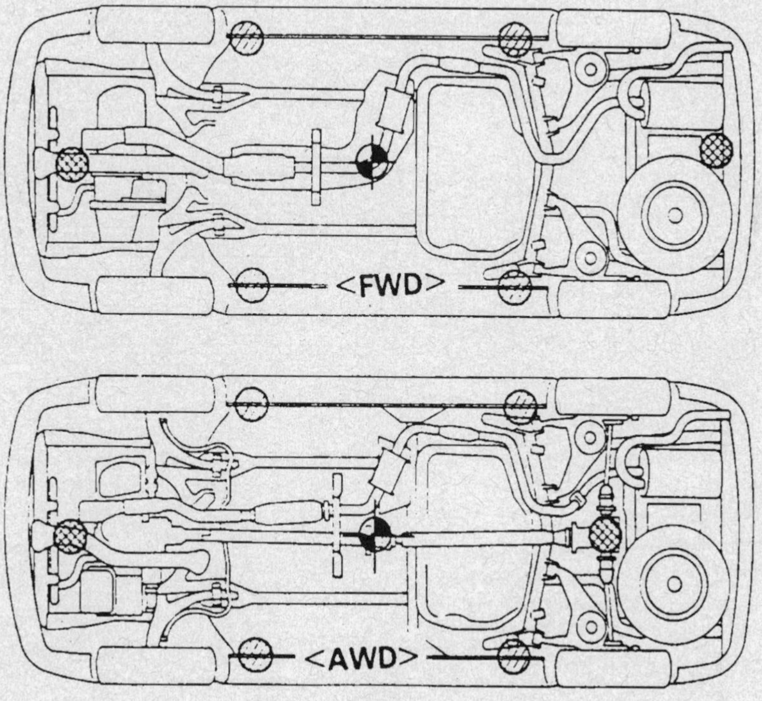

<FWD>
<AWD>

Floor jack locations

Approximate center of gravity

Frame contact hoist, twin post hoist or scissores jack (energency) locations

MT1139100055000X

Fig. 3 Expo

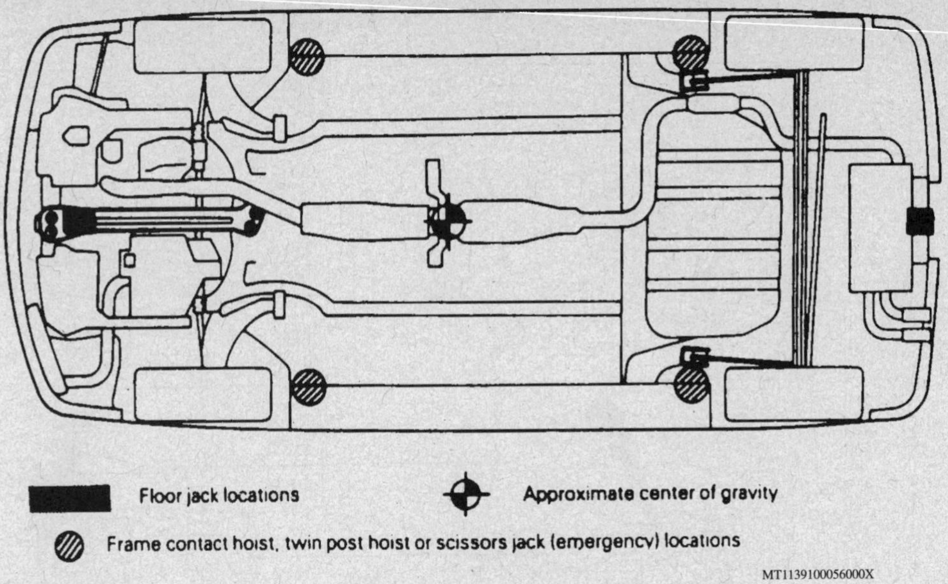
Floor jack locations
Approximate center of gravity
Frame contact hoist, twin post hoist or scissors jack (emergency) locations

MT1139100056000X

Fig. 4 Mirage

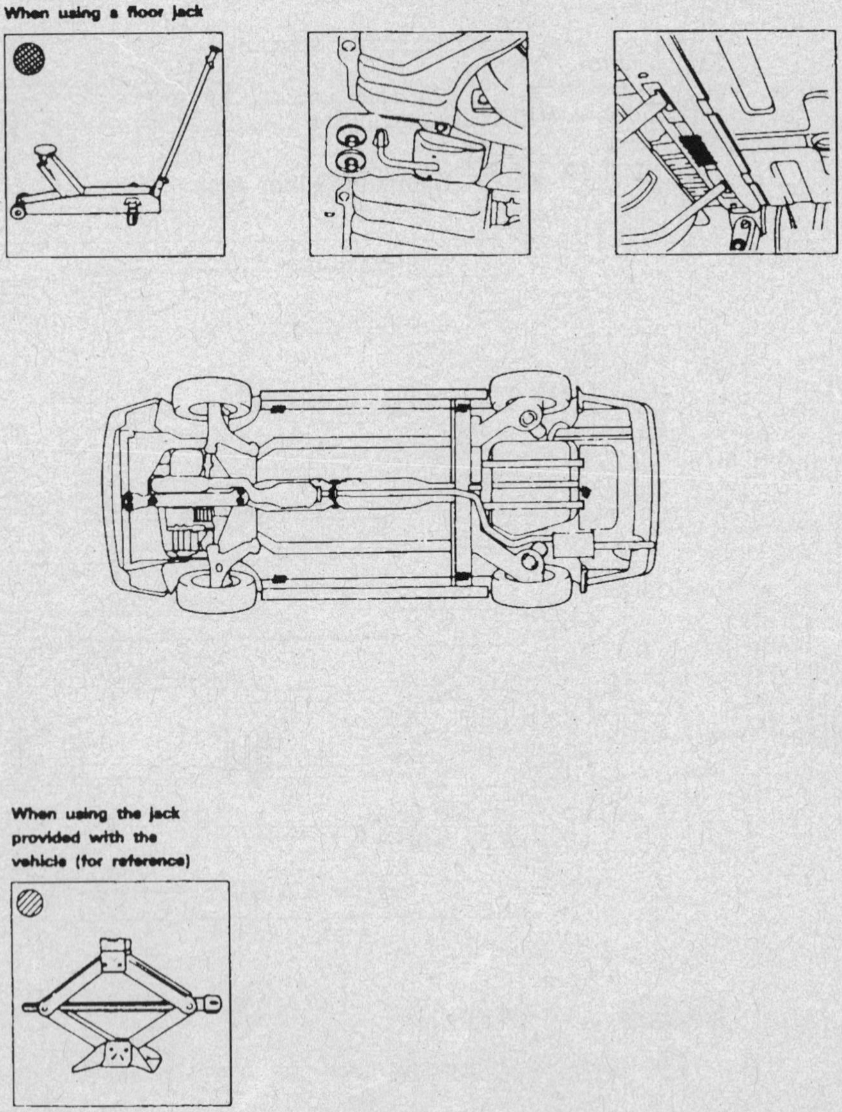
When using a floor jack
When using the jack provided with the vehicle (for reference)

MT1139100058000X

Fig. 5 Precis. Floor Jack

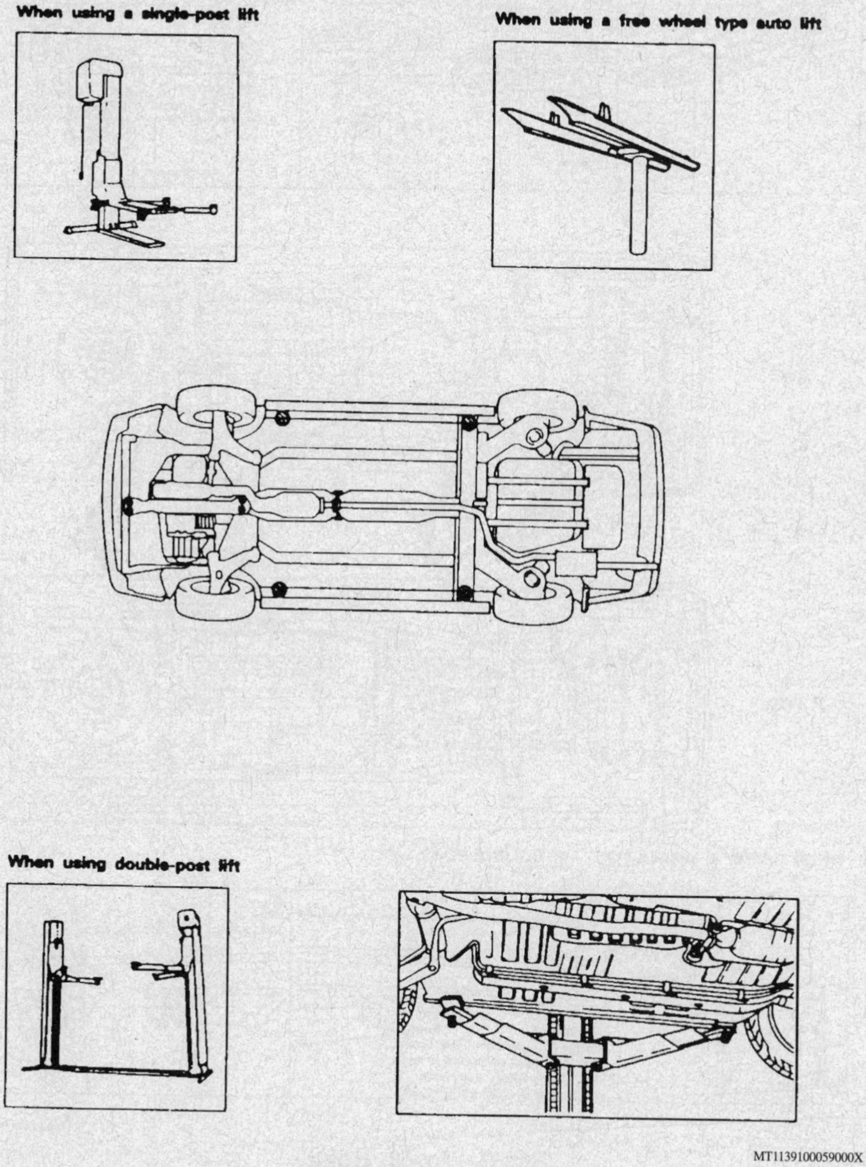
When using a single-post lift
When using a free wheel type auto lift
When using double-post lift
MT1139100059000X

Fig. 6 Precis. Hoist

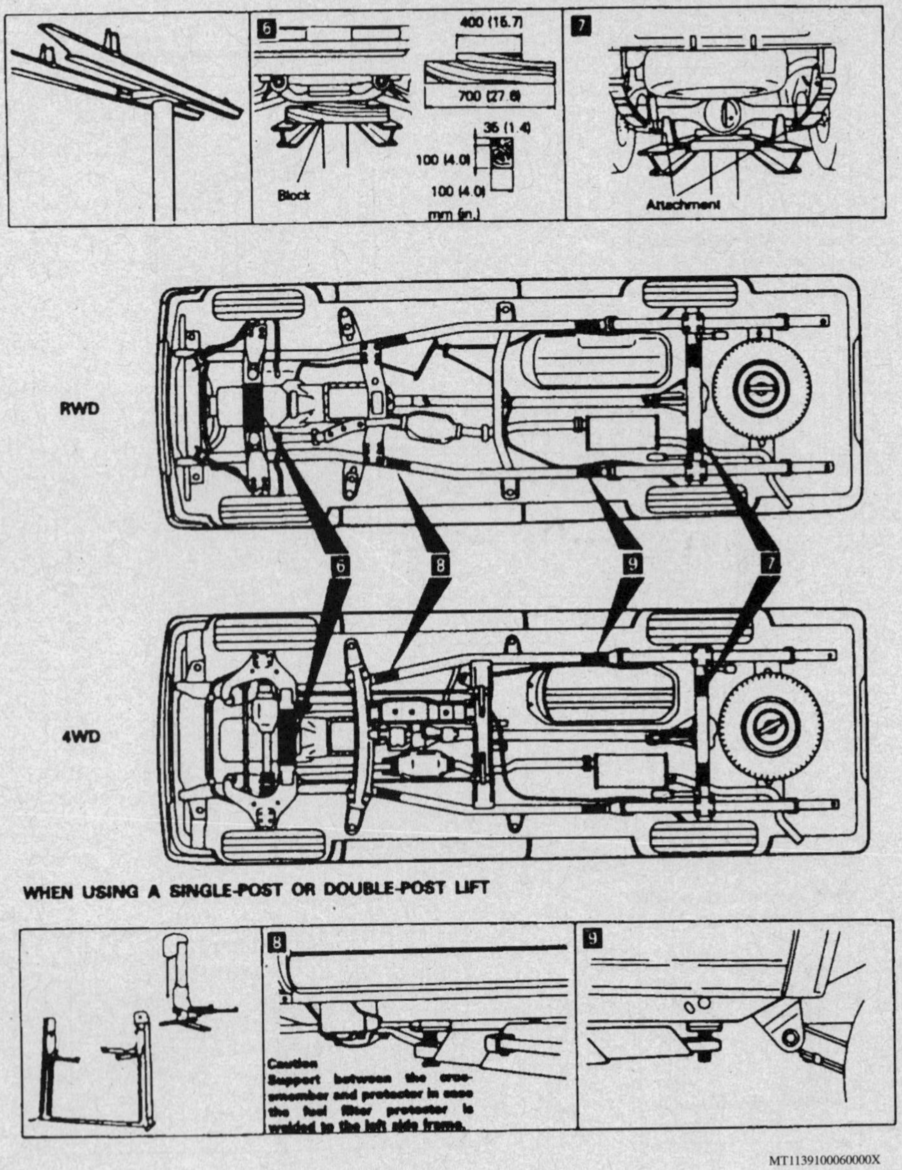
6
400 (15.7)
700 (27.6)
35 (1.4)
100 (4.0)
100 (4.0)
mm (in.)
Block
7
Attachment
RWD
4WD
6
8
9
7
WHEN USING A SINGLE-POST OR DOUBLE-POST LIFT
8
Caution
Support between the crossmember and protector in case the fuel filter protector is welded to the left side frame.
9
MT1139100060000X

Fig. 7 Truck. Hoist

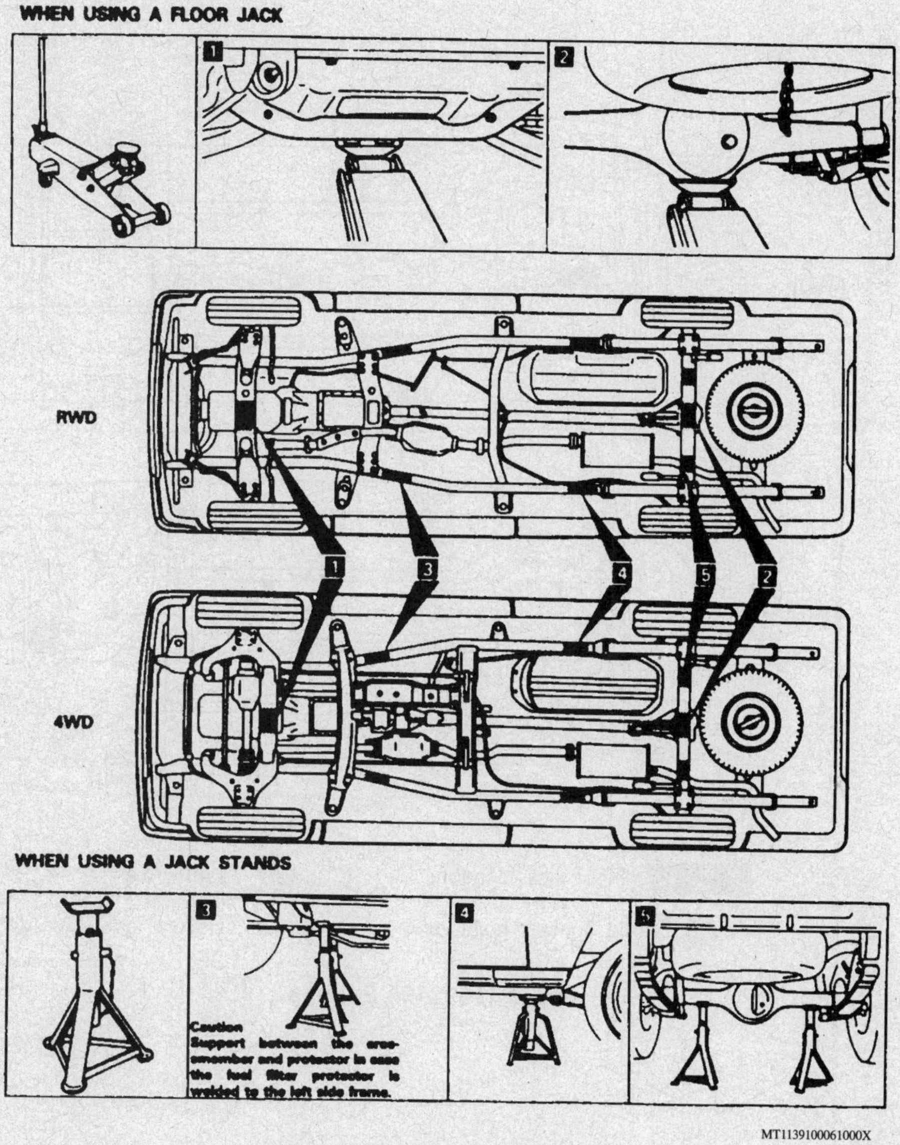
WHEN USING A FLOOR JACK
1
2
RWD
1
3
4
5
2
4WD
WHEN USING A JACK STANDS
3
Caution
Support between the cross-member and protector in case the fuel filter protector is welded to the left side frame.
4
5
MT1139100061000X

Fig. 8 Truck. Floor Jack

<2WD>

<4WD>

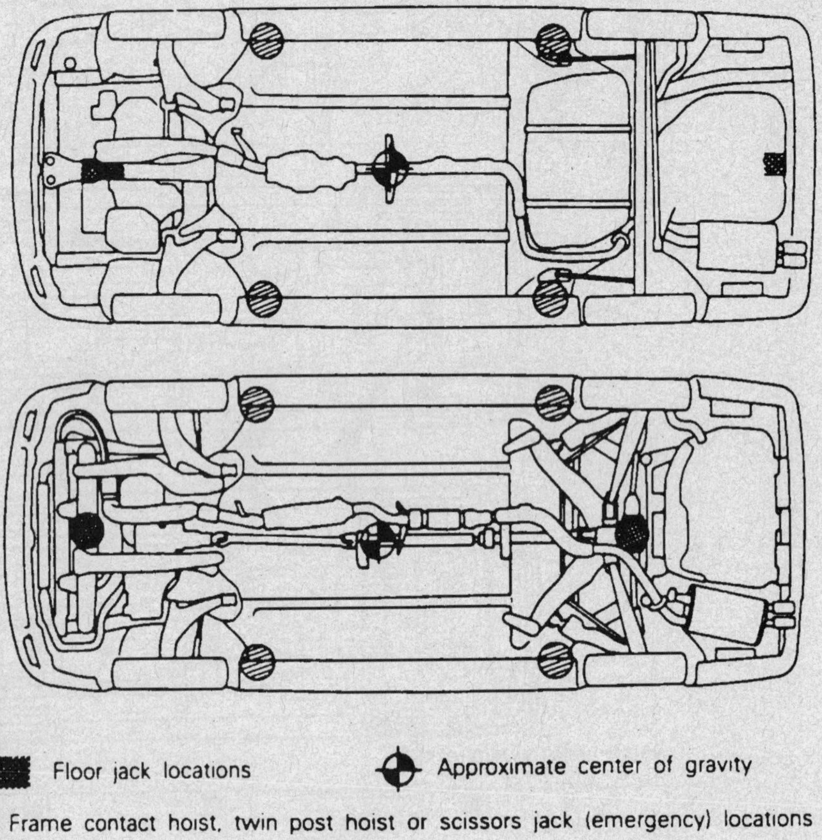
Floor jack locations
Approximate center of gravity
Frame contact hoist, twin post hoist or scissors jack (emergency) locations
MT1139100054000X

Fig. 9 1993–94 Eclipse

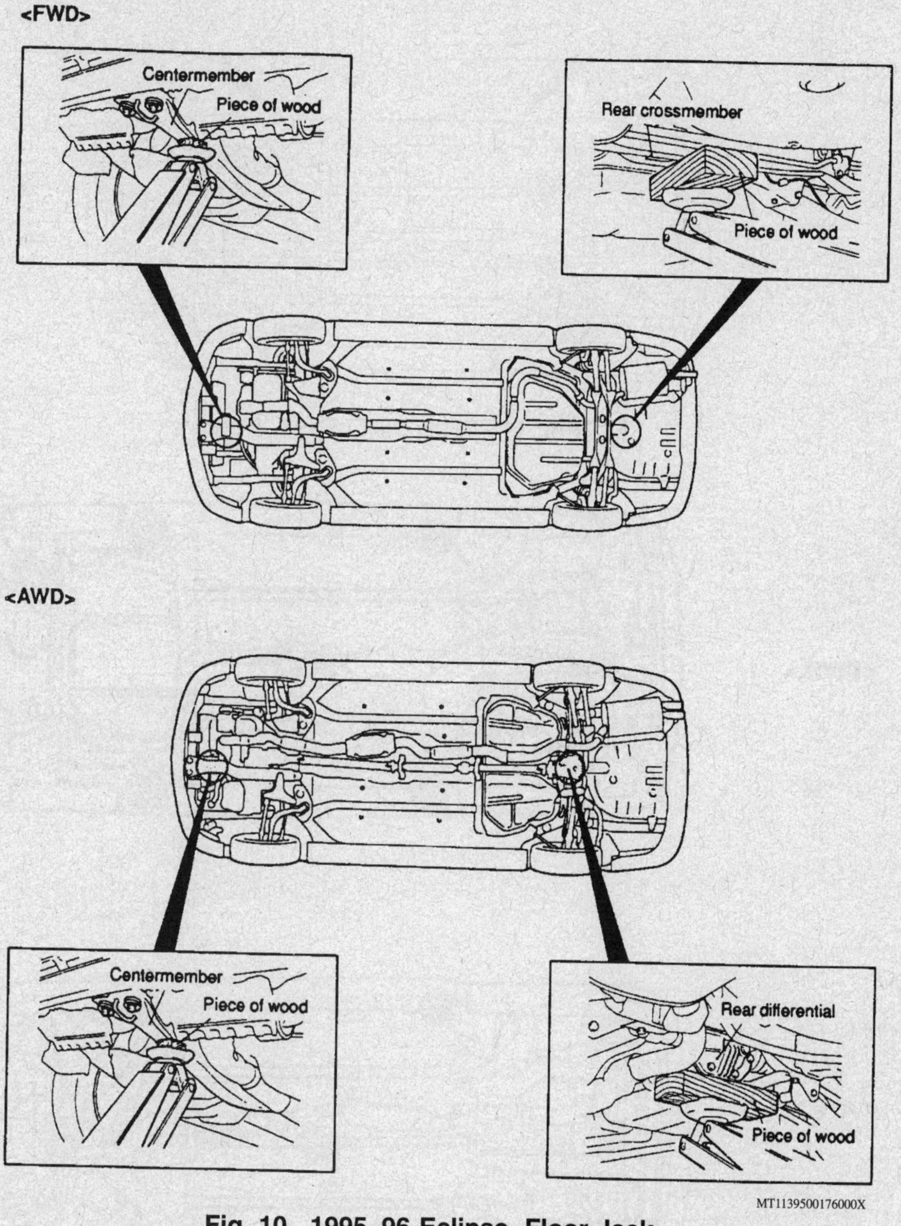
<FWD>
Centermember
Piece of wood
Rear crossmember
Piece of wood
<AWD>
Centermember
Piece of wood
Rear differential
Piece of wood
MT1139500176000X

Fig. 10 1995–96 Eclipse. Floor Jack

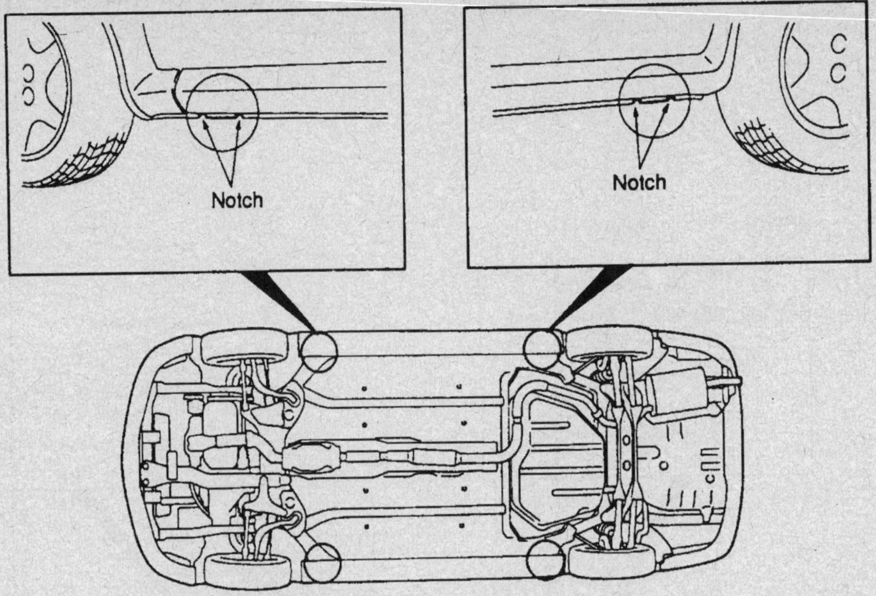
Notch
Notch

MT1139500177000X

Fig. 11 1995–96 Eclipse. Hoist

<FWD>

<AWD>

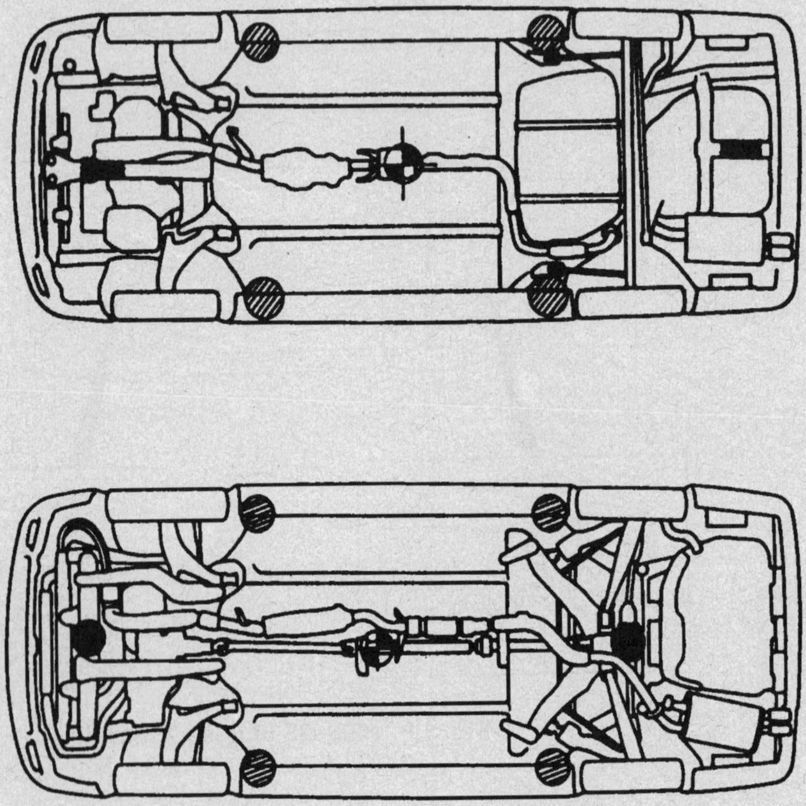

Floor jack locations

Approximate center of gravity

Frame contact hoist, twin post hoist or scissors jack (emergency) locations

MT1139100052000X

Fig. 12 1993 Galant

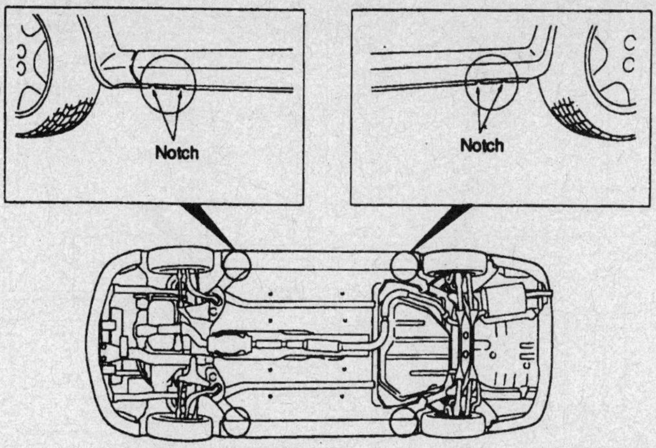
Notch
Notch

MT1139400193000X

Fig. 13 1994–96 Galant. Hoist

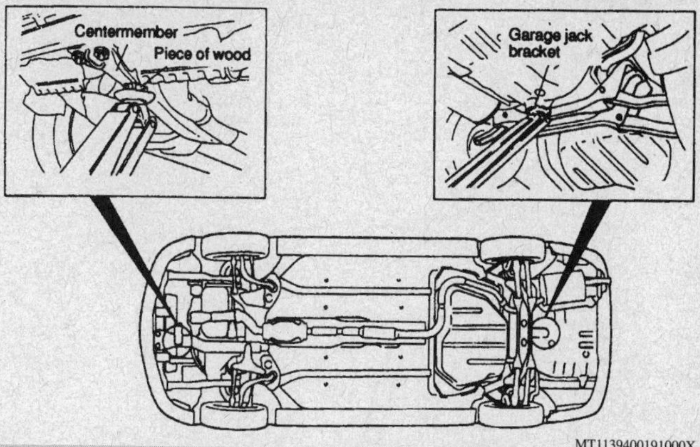
Centermember
Piece of wood
Garage jack bracket

MT1139400191000X

Fig. 14 1994–96 Galant. Floor Jack

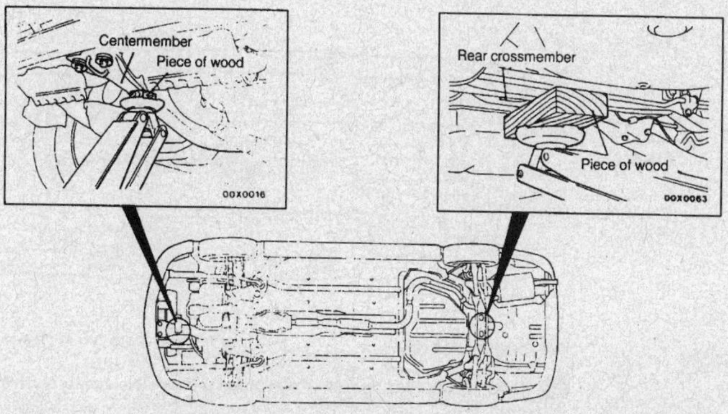
Centermember
Piece of wood
00X0016
Rear crossmember
Piece of wood
00X0063

MT1139600192000X

Fig. 15 1996 Galant. Floor Jack

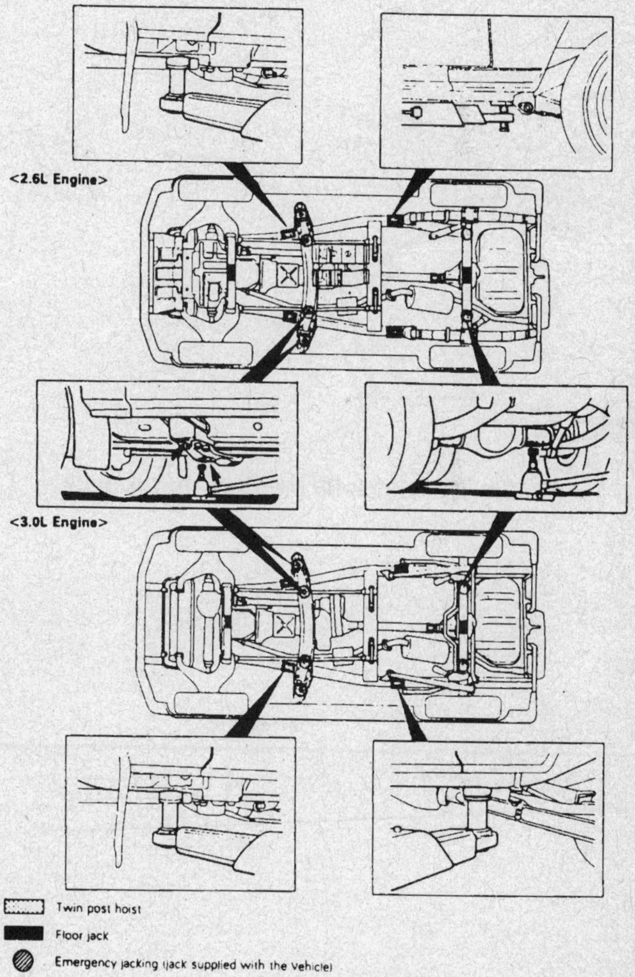
<2.6L Engine>
<3.0L Engine>
Twin post hoist
Floor jack
Emergency jacking (jack supplied with the vehicle)

MT1139100057000X

Fig. 16 1993–94 Montero

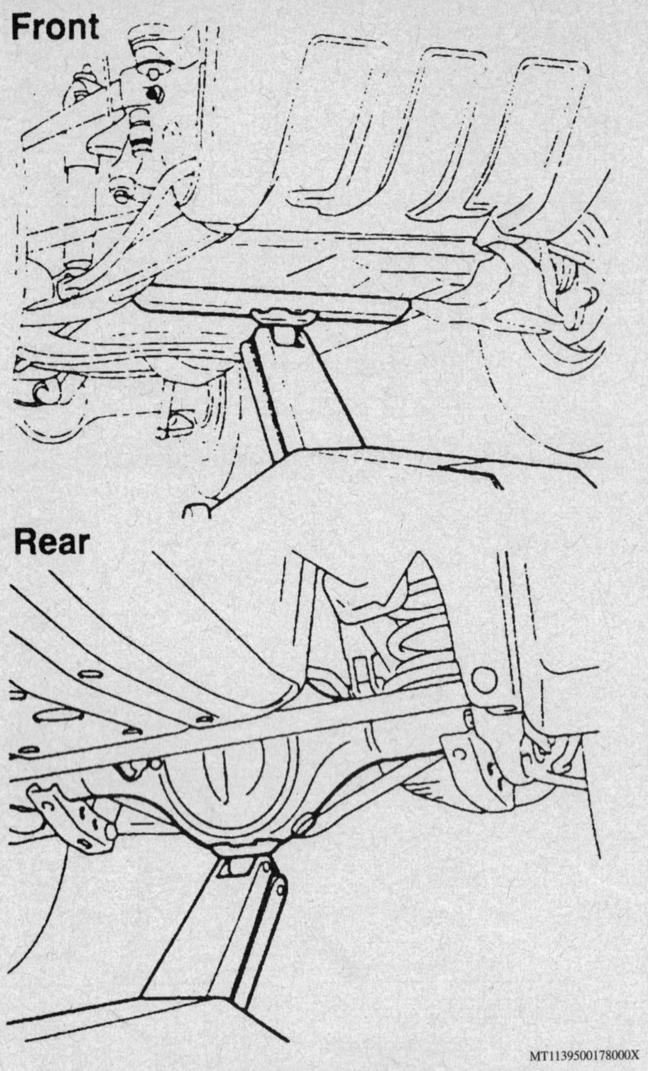
Front
Rear
MT1139500178000X

Fig. 17 1995–96 Montero. Floor Jack

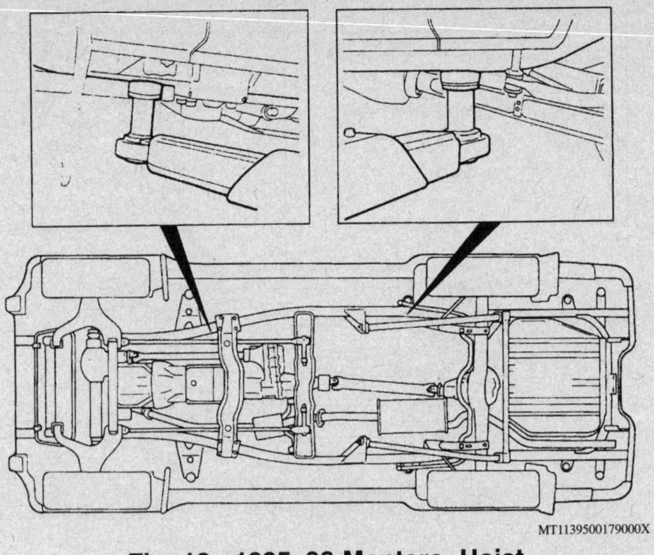
MT1139500179000X

Fig. 18 1995–96 Montero. Hoist

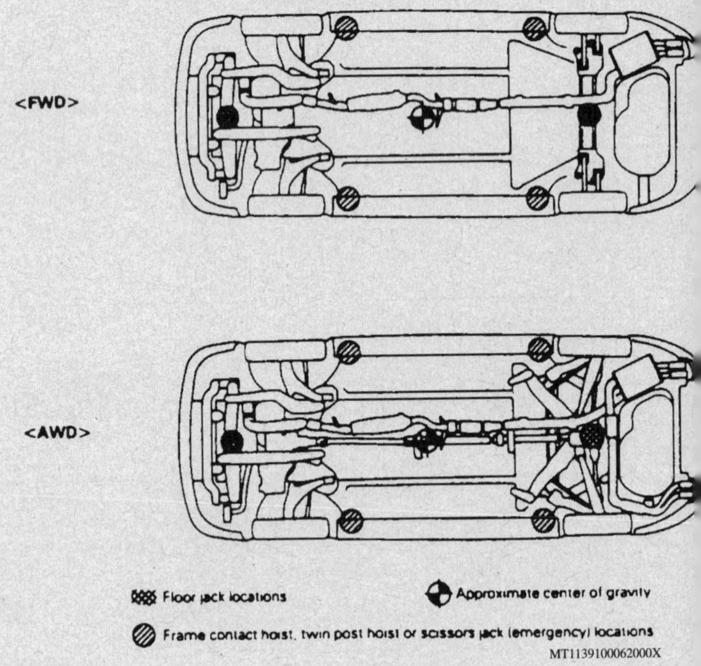
<FWD>
<AWD>
Floor jack locations
Approximate center of gravity
Frame contact hoist, twin post hoist or scissors jack (emergency) locations
MT1139100062000X

Fig. 19 3000GT

VEHICLE LIFT POINTS
Nissan

INDEX

	Page No.	Fig. No.
Altima		
Floor Jack	0-45	1
Hoist	0-46	2
Maxima		
Hoist	0-46	3
1993–95		
Floor Jack	0-46	4
1996		
Floor Jack	0-46	5
NX1600 & NX2000		
Floor Jack	0-47	6
NX1600, NX2000. Sentra, 200SX & 1993–94 240SX		
Hoist	0-47	7
Pathfinder & Pickup		
1993–95		
Hoist	0-47	9
Floor Jack	0-48	12
Pathfinder		
1996		
Hoist	0-48	10
Floor Jack	0-48	13
Pickup		
1996		
Hoist	0-48	11
Quest	0-47	8
Sentra & 200SX		
Floor Jack	0-49	14
240SX		
1993–94		
Floor Jack	0-49	16
1995–96		
Hoist	0-49	15
Floor Jack	0-49	17
300ZX		
Hoist	0-50	18
Floor Jack	0-50	19

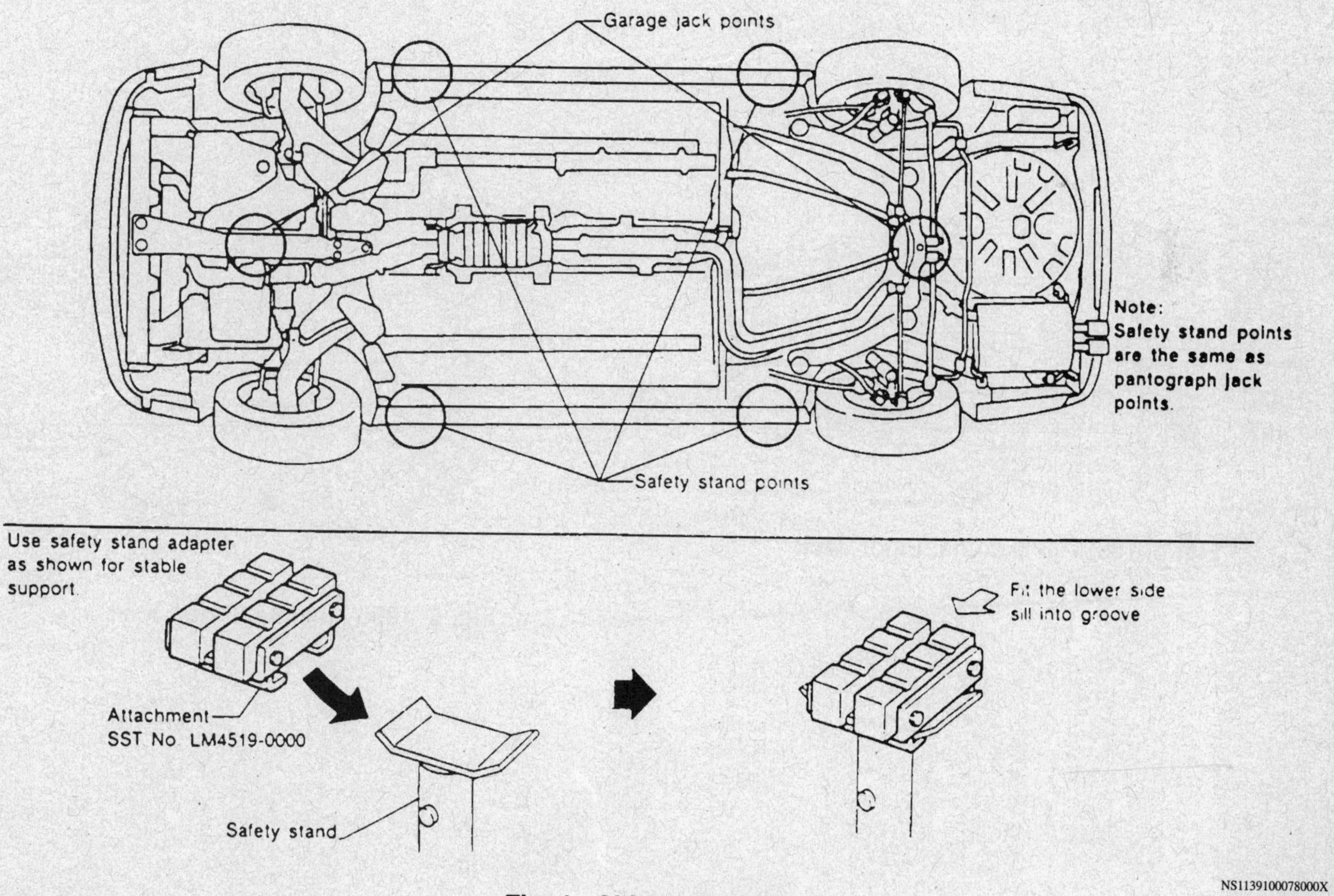

Garage jack points
Note: Safety stand points are the same as pantograph jack points.
Safety stand points
Use safety stand adapter as shown for stable support.
Fit the lower side sill into groove
Attachment SST No. LM4519-0000
Safety stand
NS1139100078000X

Fig. 1 Altima. Floor Jack

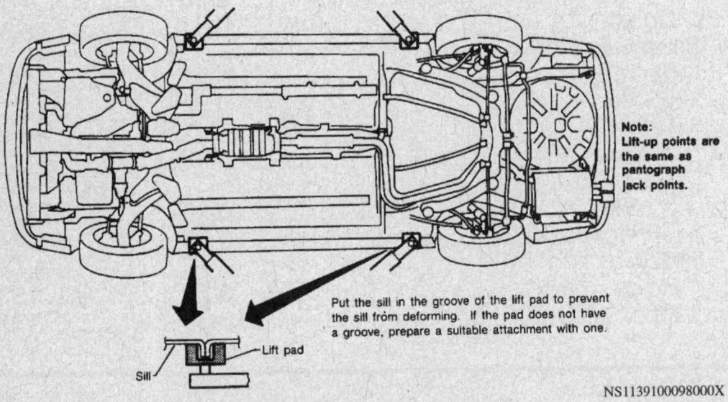
Note:
Lift-up points are the same as pantograph jack points.
Put the sill in the groove of the lift pad to prevent the sill from deforming. If the pad does not have a groove, prepare a suitable attachment with one.
Lift pad
Sill
NS1139100098000X

Fig. 2 Altima. Hoist

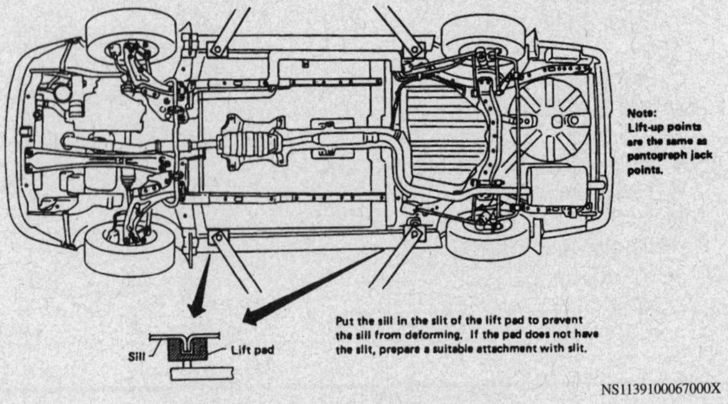
Note:
Lift-up points are the same as pantograph jack points.
Put the sill in the slit of the lift pad to prevent the sill from deforming. If the pad does not have the slit, prepare a suitable attachment with slit.
Sill
Lift pad
NS1139100067000X

Fig. 3 Maxima. Hoist

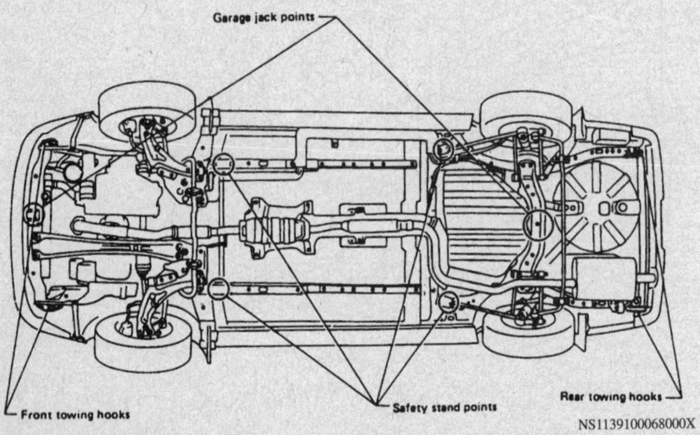
Garage jack points
Front towing hooks
Safety stand points
Rear towing hooks
NS1139100068000X

Fig. 4 1993–95 Maxima. Floor Jack

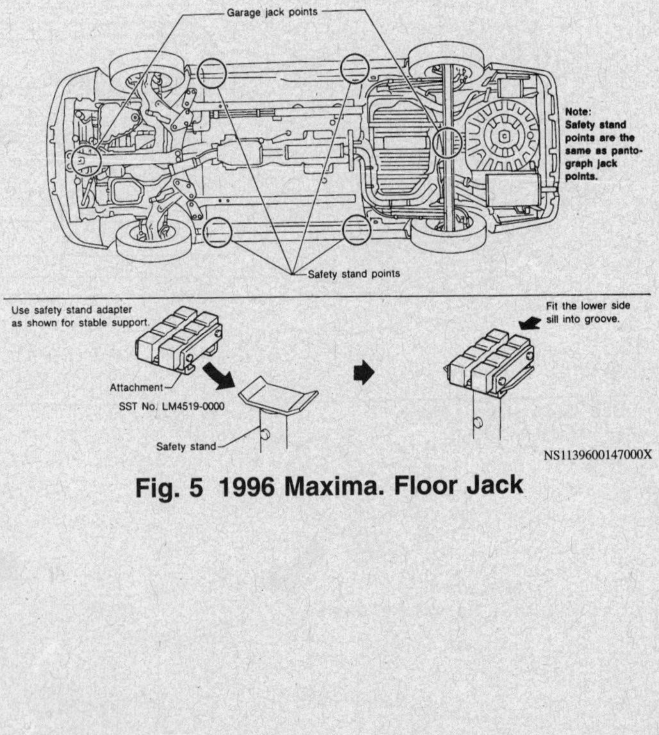
Garage jack points
Note:
Safety stand points are the same as pantograph jack points.
Safety stand points
Use safety stand adapter as shown for stable support.
Fit the lower side sill into groove.
Attachment
SST No. LM4519-0000
Safety stand
NS1139600147000X

Fig. 5 1996 Maxima. Floor Jack

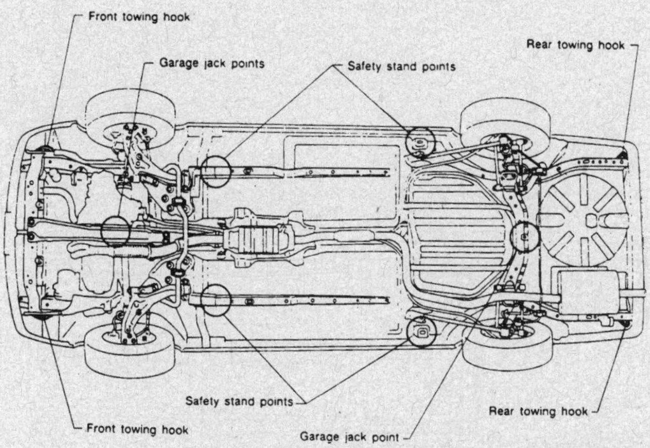
Front towing hook
Garage jack points
Safety stand points
Rear towing hook
Safety stand points
Rear towing hook
Front towing hook
Garage jack point
NS1139100073000X

Fig. 6 NX1600 & NX2000. Floor Jack

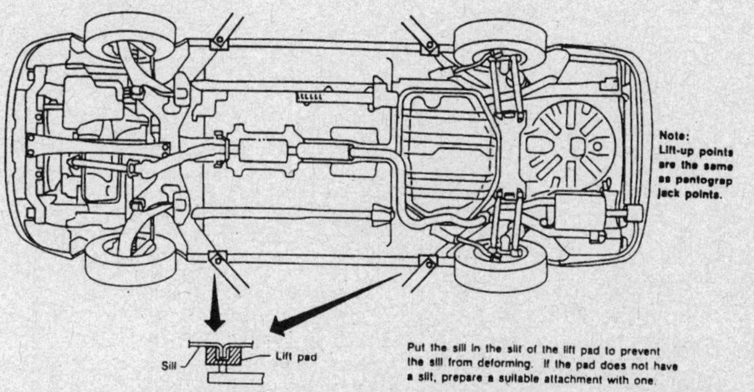
Note:
Lift-up points are the same as pentograp jack points.
Sill
Lift pad
Put the sill in the slit of the lift pad to prevent the sill from deforming. If the pad does not have a slit, prepare a suitable attachment with one.
NS1139100071000X

Fig. 7 NX1600, NX2000, Sentra, 200SX & 1993–94 240SX. Hoist

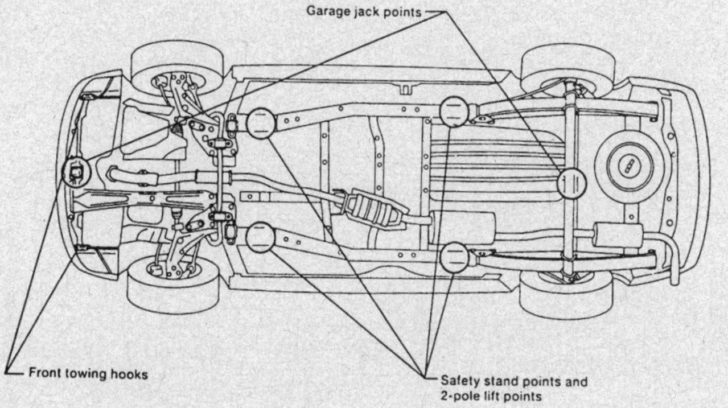
Garage jack points
Front towing hooks
Safety stand points and 2-pole lift points
NS1139100077000X

Fig. 8 Quest

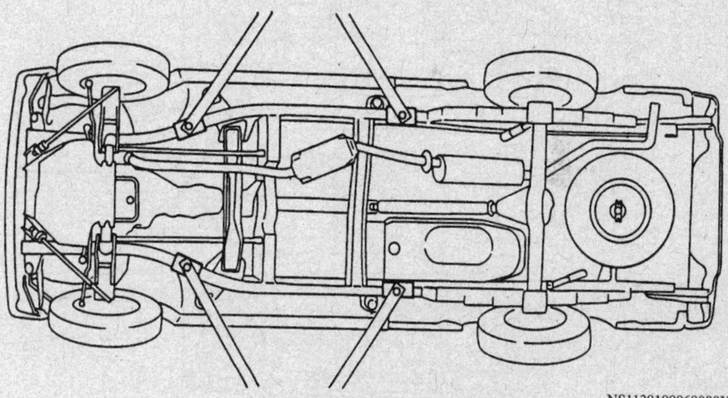
NS1139100069000X

Fig. 9 1993-95 Pathfinder & Pickup. Hoist

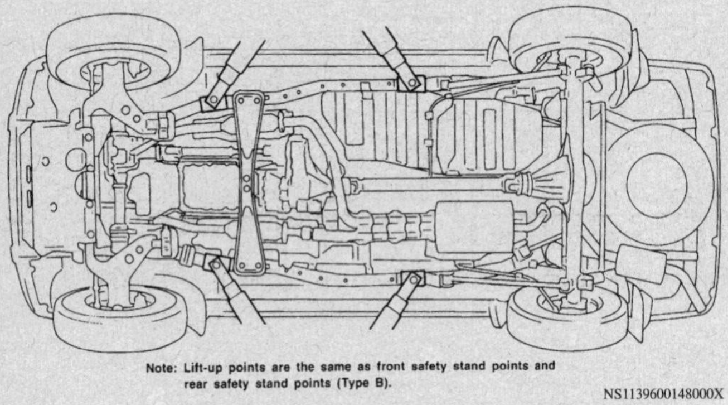
Note: Lift-up points are the same as front safety stand points and rear safety stand points (Type B).
NS1139600148000X

Fig. 10 1996 Pathfinder. Hoist

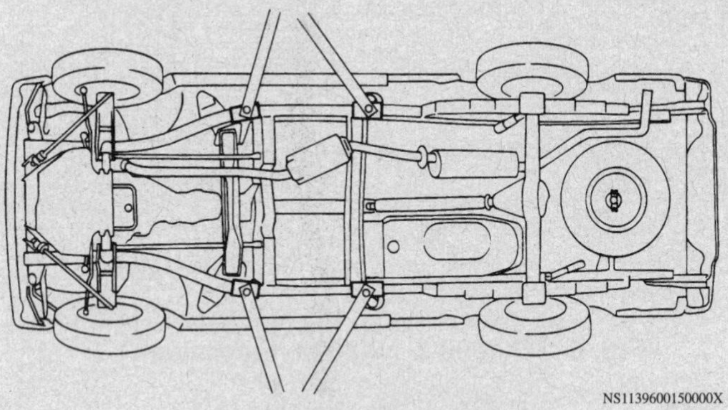
NS1139600150000X

Fig. 11 1996 Pickup. Hoist

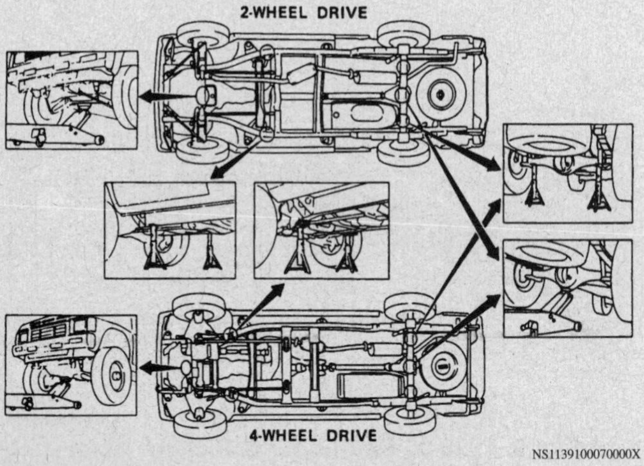
2-WHEEL DRIVE
4-WHEEL DRIVE
NS1139100070000X

Fig. 12 Pickup & 1993–95 Pathfinder. Floor Jack

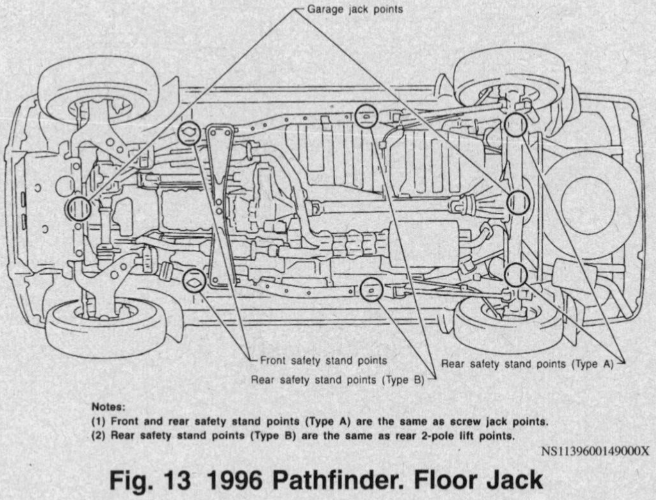
Garage jack points
Front safety stand points
Rear safety stand points (Type B)
Rear safety stand points (Type A)
Notes:
(1) Front and rear safety stand points (Type A) are the same as screw jack points.
(2) Rear safety stand points (Type B) are the same as rear 2-pole lift points.
NS1139600149000X

Fig. 13 1996 Pathfinder. Floor Jack

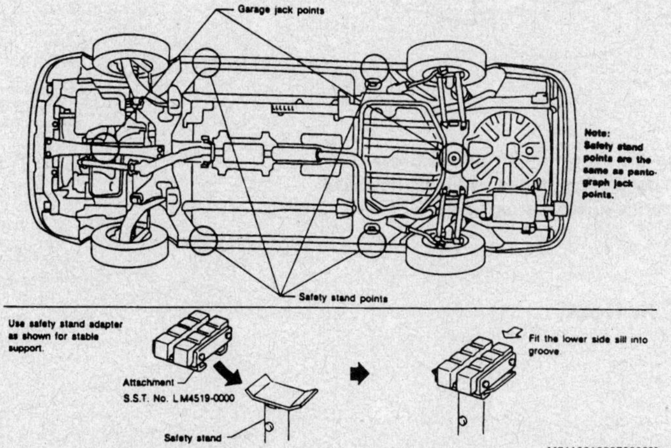
Garage jack points
Note:
Safety stand points are the same as pantograph jack points.
Safety stand points
Use safety stand adapter as shown for stable support.
Attachment
S.S.T. No. LM4519-0000
Safety stand
Fit the lower side sill into groove

NS1139100072000X

Fig. 14 Sentra & 240SX. Floor Jack

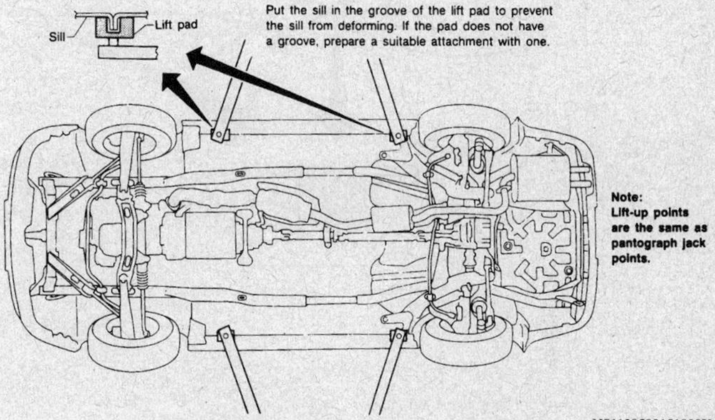
Sill
Lift pad
Put the sill in the groove of the lift pad to prevent the sill from deforming. If the pad does not have a groove, prepare a suitable attachment with one.
Note:
Lift-up points are the same as pantograph jack points.

NS1139500151000X

Fig. 15 1995–96 240SX. Hoist

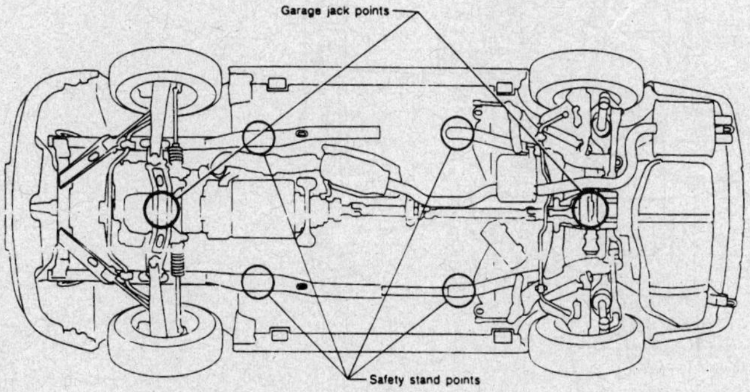
Garage jack points
Safety stand points

NS1139100074000X

Fig. 16 1993–94 240SX. Floor Jack

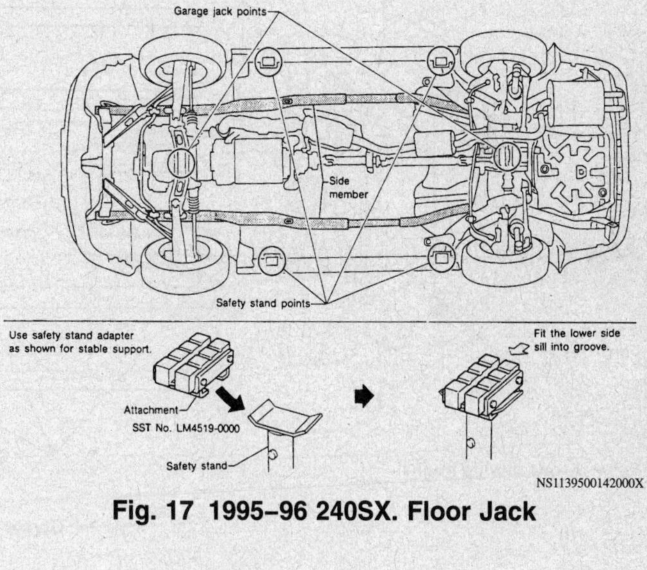
Garage jack points
Side member
Safety stand points
Use safety stand adapter as shown for stable support.
Attachment
SST No. LM4519-0000
Safety stand
Fit the lower side sill into groove.

NS1139500142000X

Fig. 17 1995–96 240SX. Floor Jack

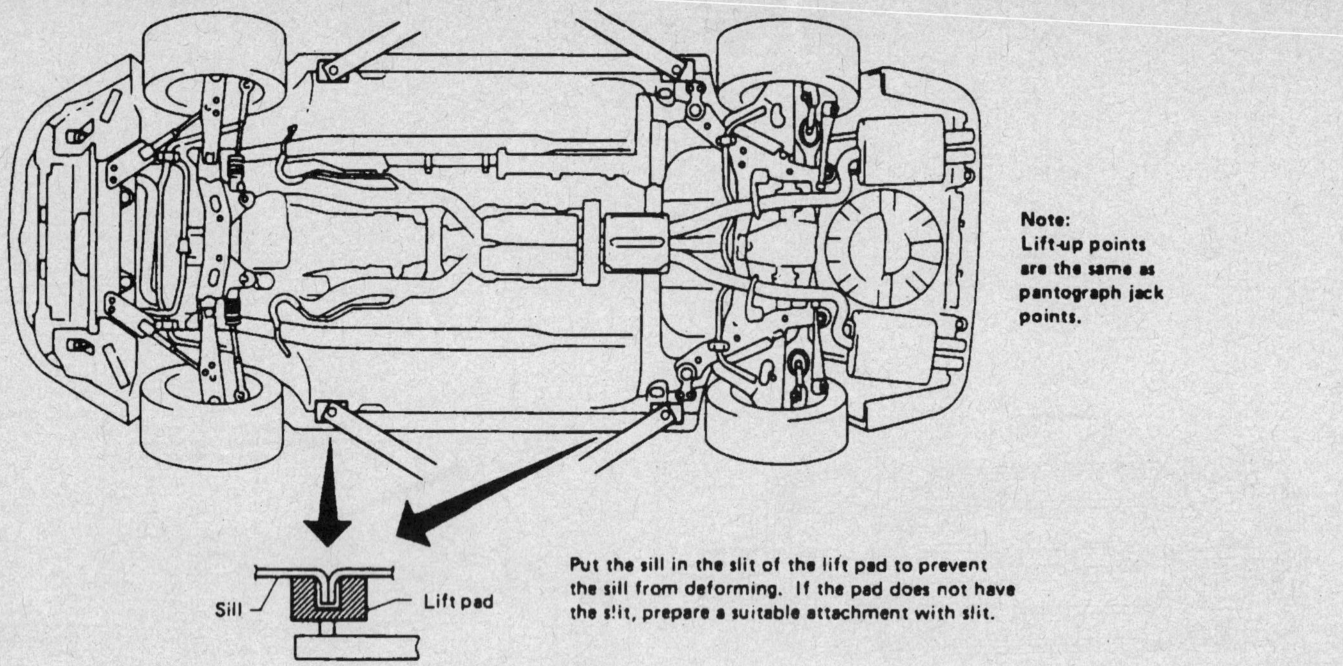
Note:
Lift-up points are the same as pantograph jack points.
Sill
Lift pad
Put the sill in the slit of the lift pad to prevent the sill from deforming. If the pad does not have the slit, prepare a suitable attachment with slit.

NS1139100075000X

Fig. 18 300ZX. Hoist

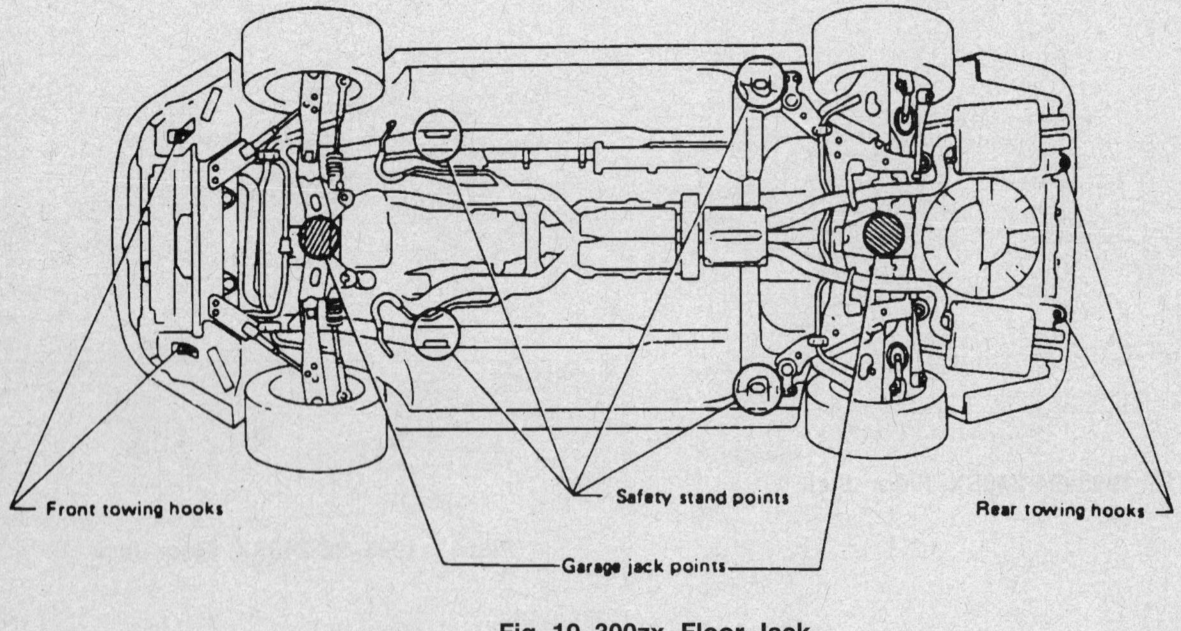
Front towing hooks
Safety stand points
Rear towing hooks
Garage jack points

NS1139100076000X

Fig. 19 300zx. Floor Jack

VEHICLE LIFT POINTS
Porsche

INDEX

	Page No.	Fig. No.		Page No.	Fig. No.
911 Carrera	0-51	1			

The vehicle may only be raised at the jacking points illustrated. When driving the vehicle onto a lifting platform, make sure that there is sufficient clearance between the platform and the vehicle.

Front **Rear**

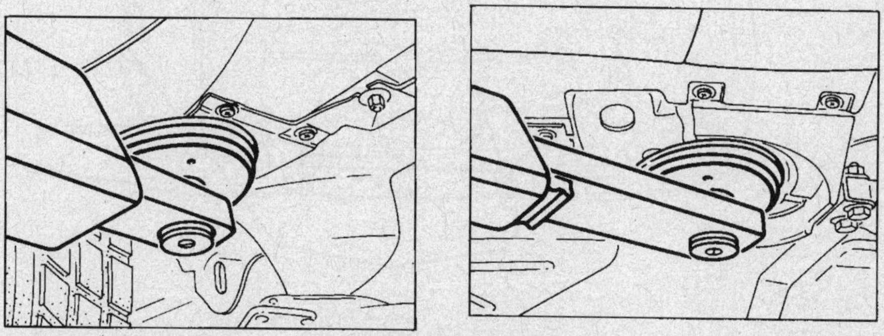

PR1139400009000X

Fig. 1 911 Carrera

VEHICLE LIFT POINTS
Saab

INDEX

	Page No.	Fig. No.		Page No.	Fig. No.
900	0-52	1	9000	0-52	2

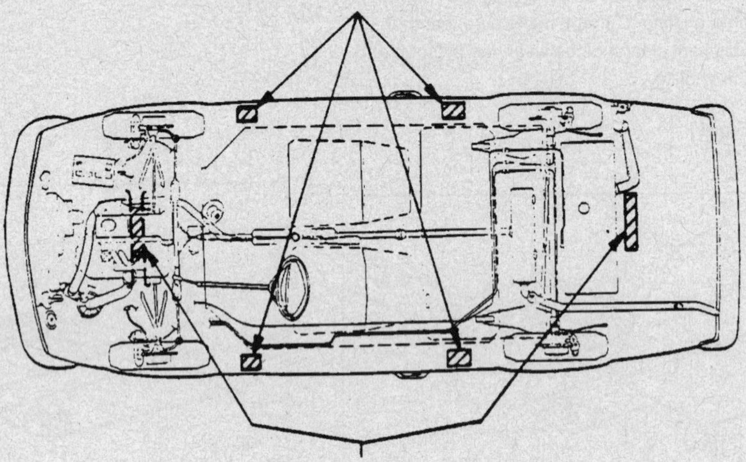

Lift Points for Car Hoist and Jack Stands
(wheel change jack head reinforcements)
Floor Jack Lift Points
(floorpan reinforcement crossmembers)
SA1139100009000X

Fig. 1 900

A Front jack attachments and application points for hoist

B and C Alternate front application points for hoist

D Rear jack attachments and appliction points for hoist

E Front application point for floor jack

F Rear application point for floor jack

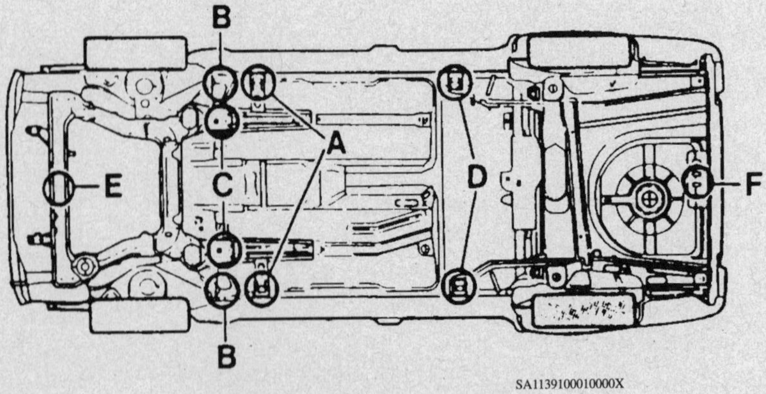

B
A
E
C
D
F
B
SA1139100010000X

Fig. 2 9000

VEHICLE LIFT POINTS
Subaru

INDEX

	Page No.	Fig. No.
Justy	0-53	1
Impreza		
Floor Jack	0-55	5
Hoist	0-55	6
Loyale	0-53	2
Legacy	0-54	3
SVX	0-54	4

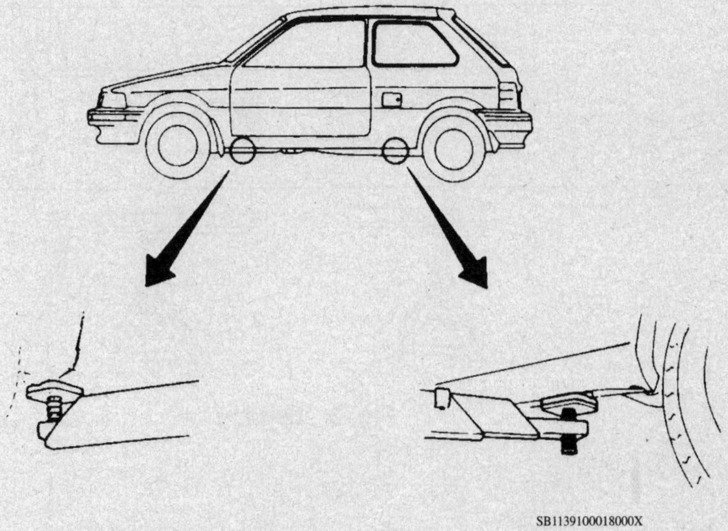

SB1139100018000X

Fig. 1 Justy

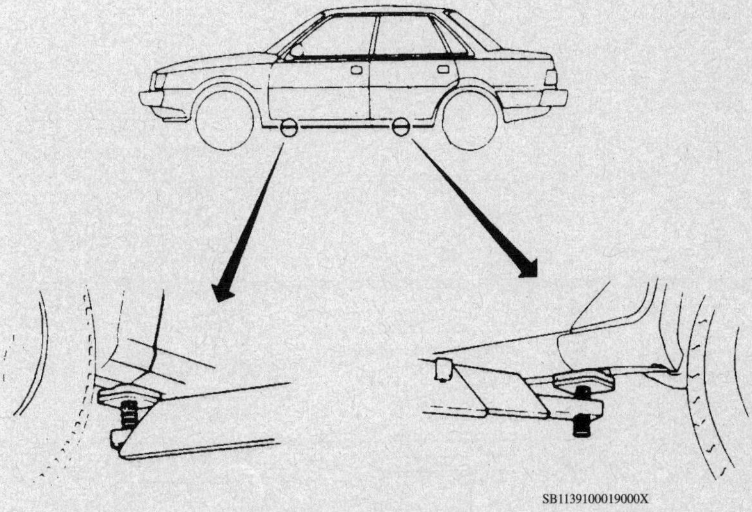

SB1139100019000X

Fig. 2 Loyale

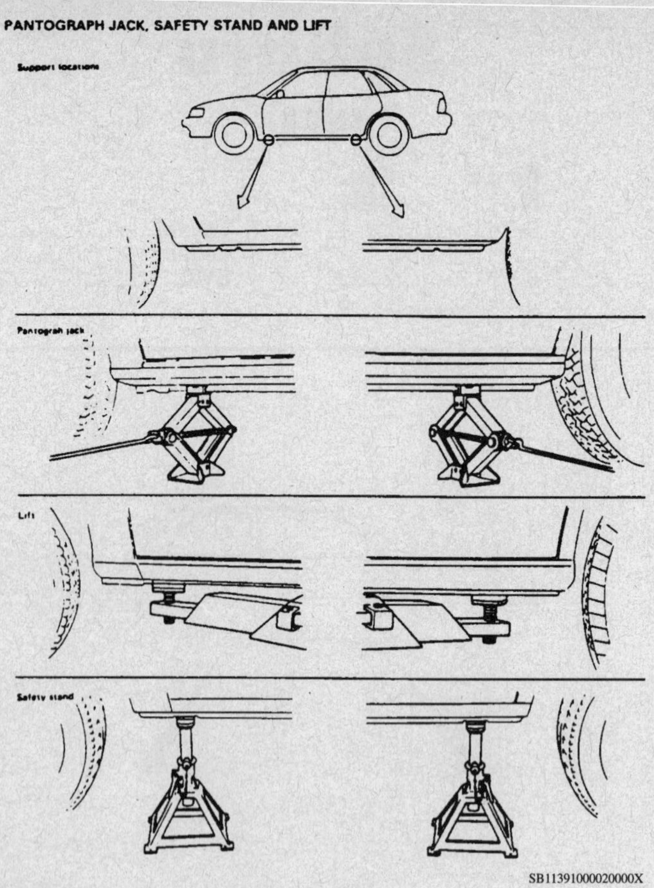
PANTOGRAPH JACK, SAFETY STAND AND LIFT
Support locations
Pantograph jack
Lift
Safety stand
SB11391000020000X

Fig. 3 Legacy

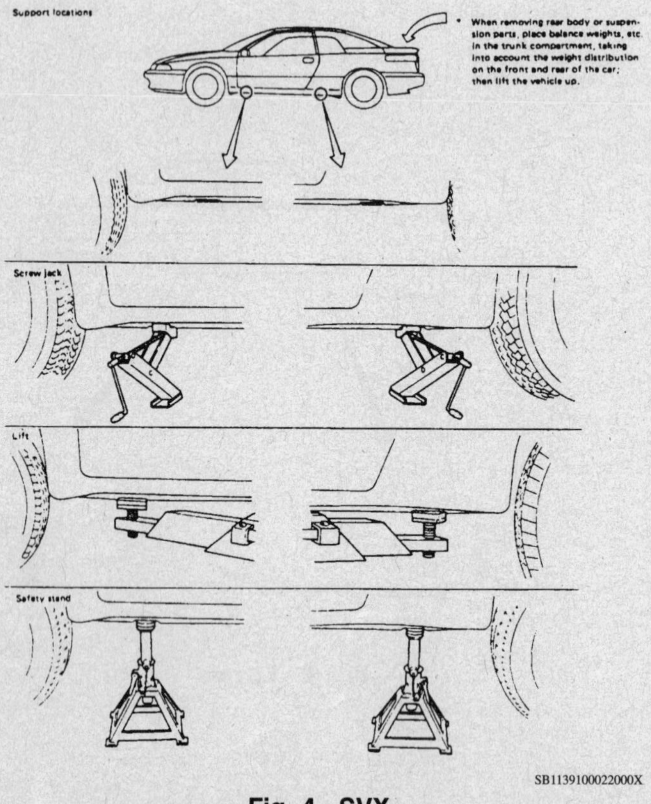
Support locations
When removing rear body or suspension parts, place balance weights, etc. in the trunk compartment, taking into account the weight distribution on the front and rear of the car; then lift the vehicle up.
Screw jack
Lift
Safety stand
SB1139100022000X

Fig. 4 SVX

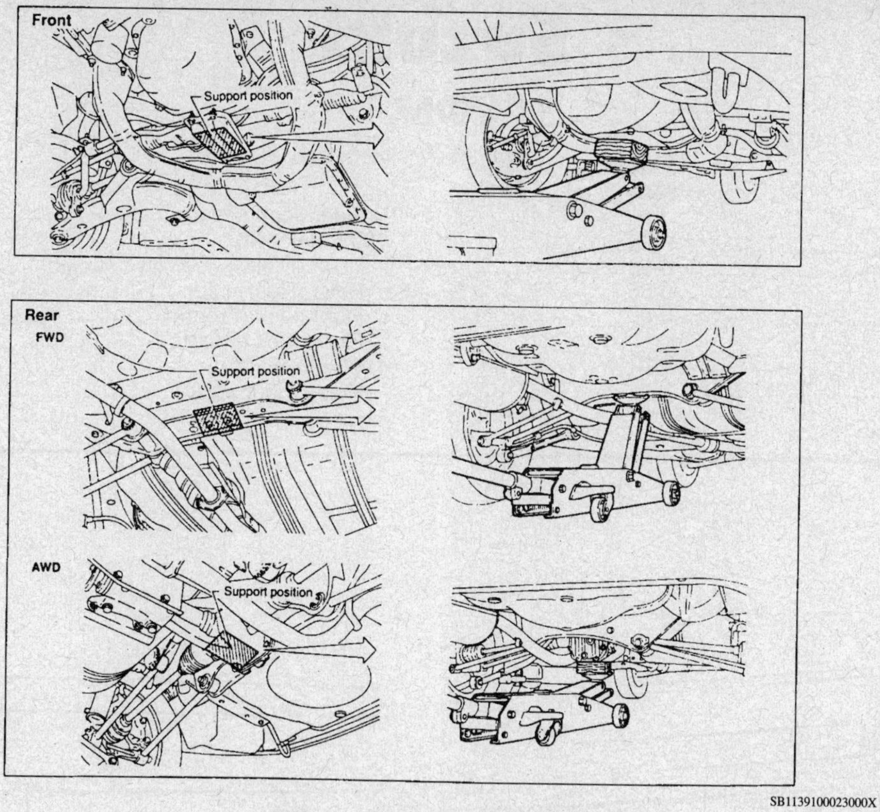
Front
Support position
Rear
FWD
Support position
AWD
Support position
SB1139100023000X

Fig. 5 Impreza. Floor Jack

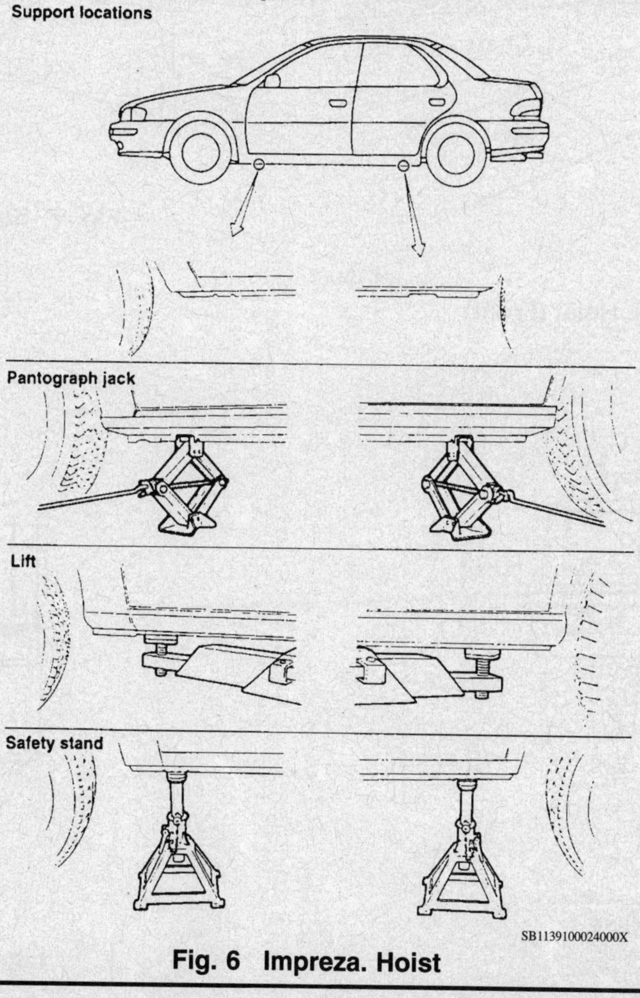
Support locations
Pantograph jack
Lift
Safety stand
SB1139100024000X

Fig. 6 Impreza. Hoist

VEHICLE LIFT POINTS
Suzuki

INDEX

	Page No.	Fig. No.
Samurai		
Hoist (Front)	0-56	1
Hoist (Rear)	0-56	2
Floor Jack (Front)	0-56	3
Floor Jack (Rear)	0-56	4
Sidekick		
Hoist (Front)	0-57	5
Hoist (Rear)	0-57	6
Floor Jack (Front)	0-57	7
Floor Jack (Rear)	0-57	8
1993–94 Swift		
Hoist (Front)	0-57	9
Hoist (Rear)	0-57	10
Floor Jack (Front)	0-58	11
Floor Jack (Rear)	0-58	12
1995–96 Swift		
Hoist. Floor Jack	0-58	13

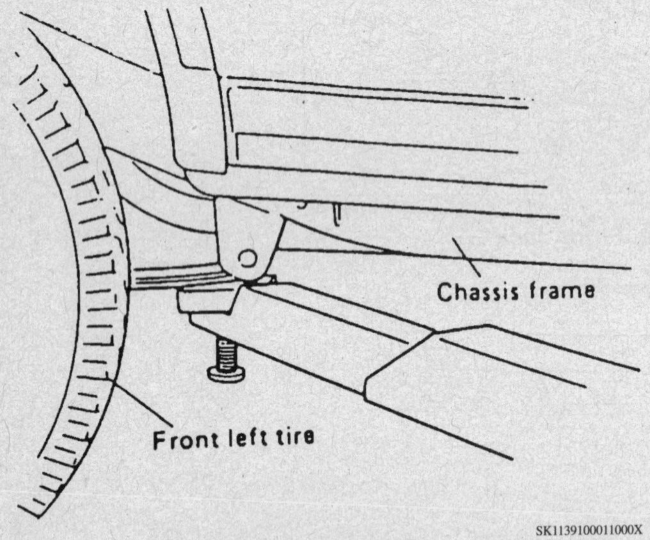

Chassis frame
Front left tire
SK1139100011000X

Fig. 1 Samurai. Hoist (Front)

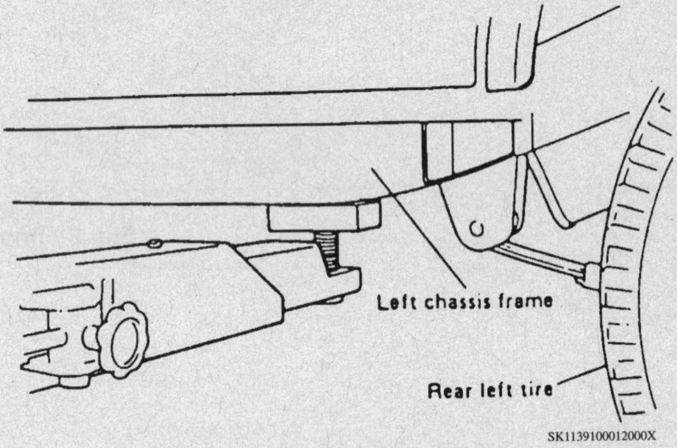

Left chassis frame
Rear left tire
SK1139100012000X

Fig. 2 Samurai. Hoist (Rear)

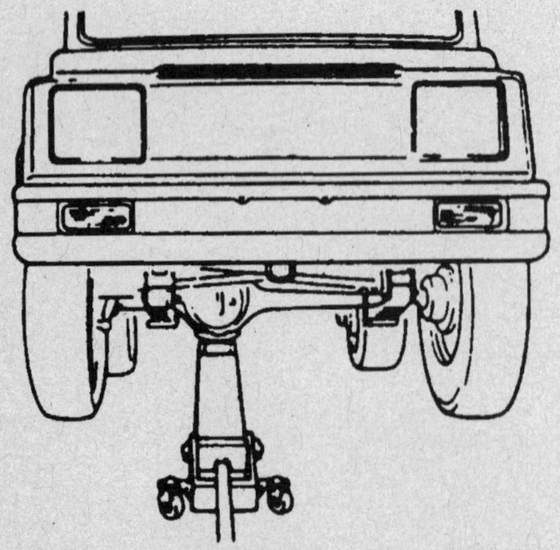

SK1139100013000X

Fig. 3 Samurai. Floor Jack (Front)

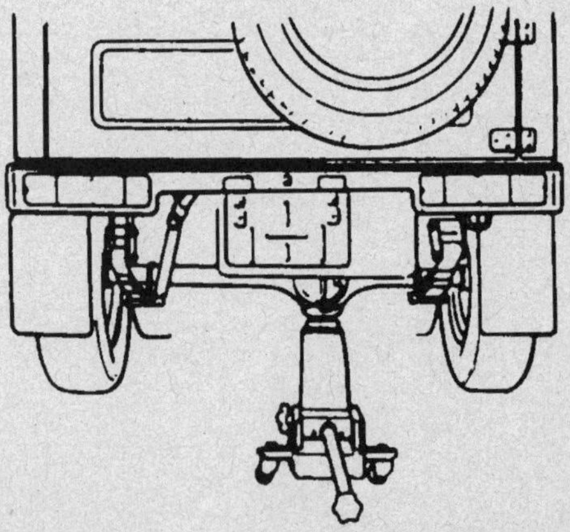

SK1139100014000X

Fig. 4 Samurai. Floor Jack (Rear)

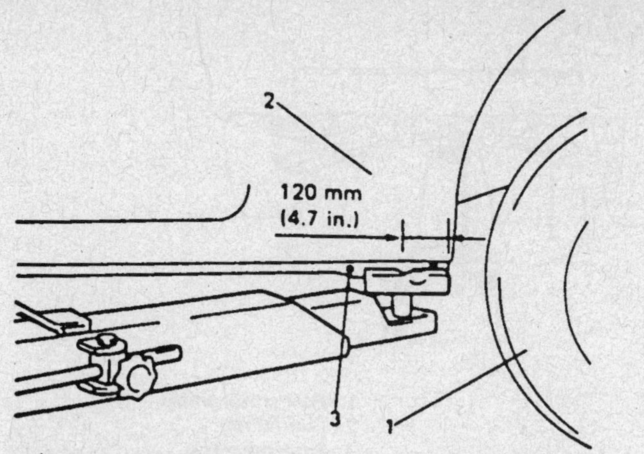
2
120 mm
(4.7 in.)
3
1

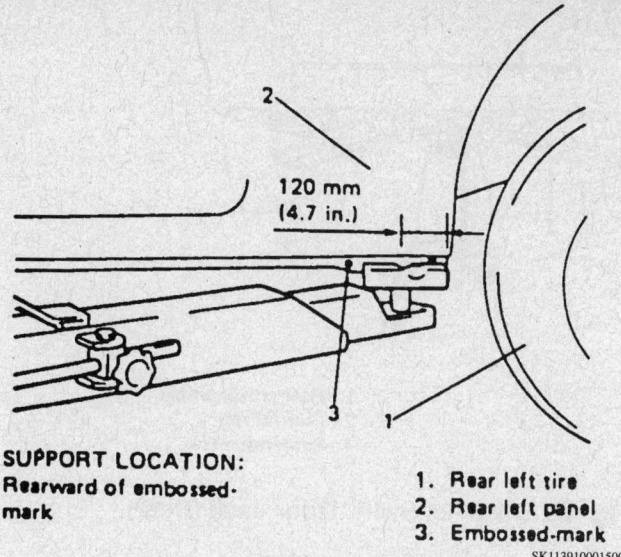

SUPPORT LOCATION:
Rearward of embossed-mark

1. Rear left tire
2. Rear left panel
3. Embossed-mark

SK1139100015000X

Fig. 5 Sidekick. Hoist (Front)

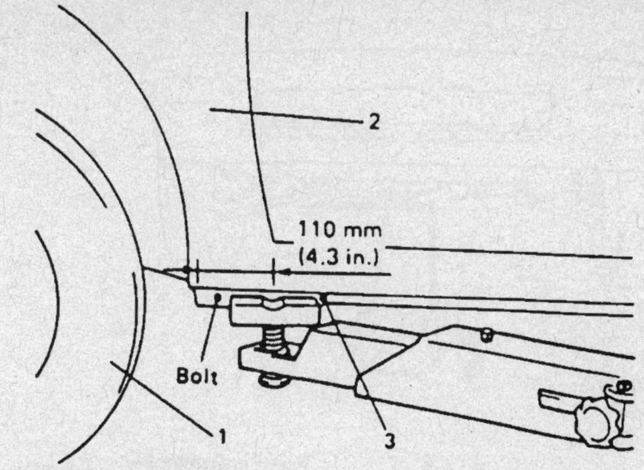
2
110 mm
(4.3 in.)
Bolt
1
3

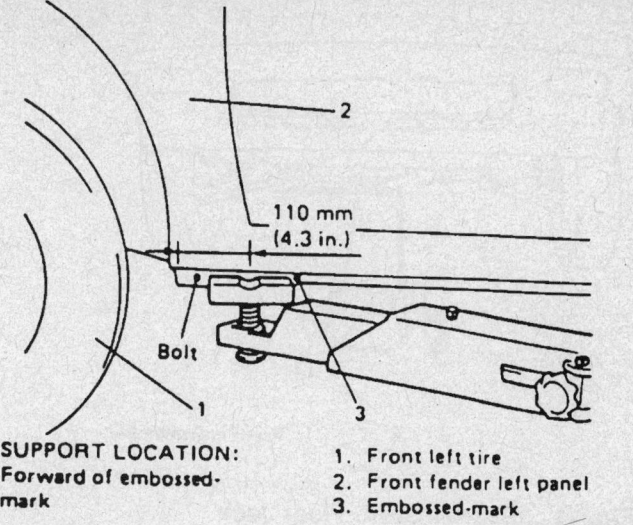

SUPPORT LOCATION:
Forward of embossed-mark

1. Front left tire
2. Front fender left panel
3. Embossed-mark

SK1139100016000X

Fig. 6 Sidekick. Hoist (Rear)

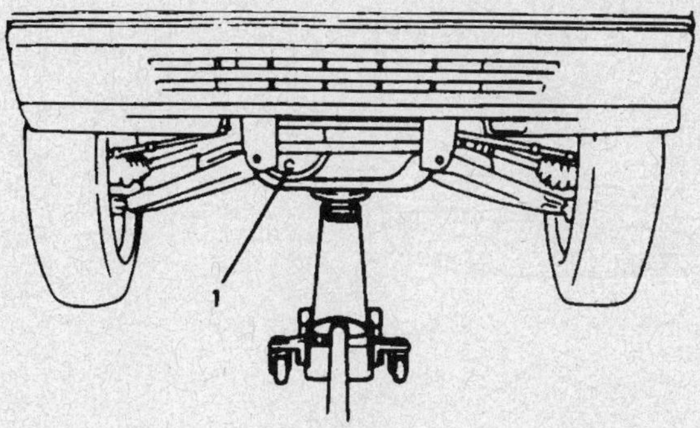
1

1. Front differential housing

SK1139100017000X

Fig. 7 Sidekick. Floor Jack (Front)

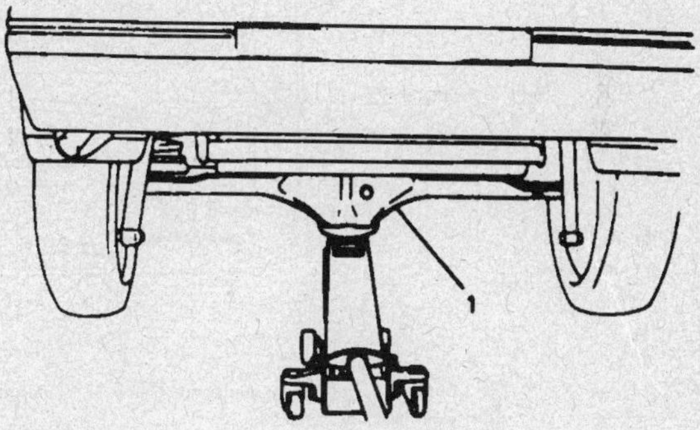
1

1. Rear axle

SK1139100018000X

Fig. 8 Sidekick. Floor Jack (Rear)

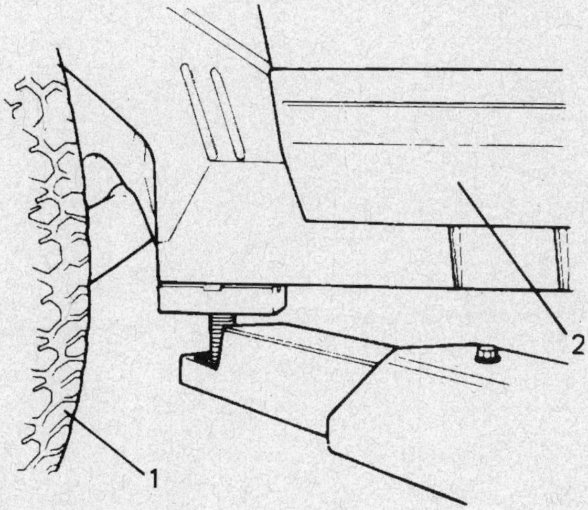
2
1

1. Front left tire
2. Front fender left panel

SK1139100019000X

Fig. 9 1993–94 Swift. Hoist (Front)

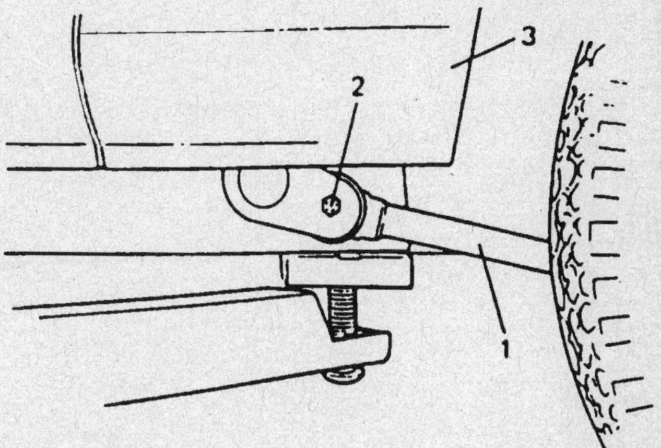
3
2
1

1. Trailing rod
2. Trailing rod bolt
3. Rear panel

SK1139100020000X

Fig. 10 1993–94 Swift. Hoist (Rear)

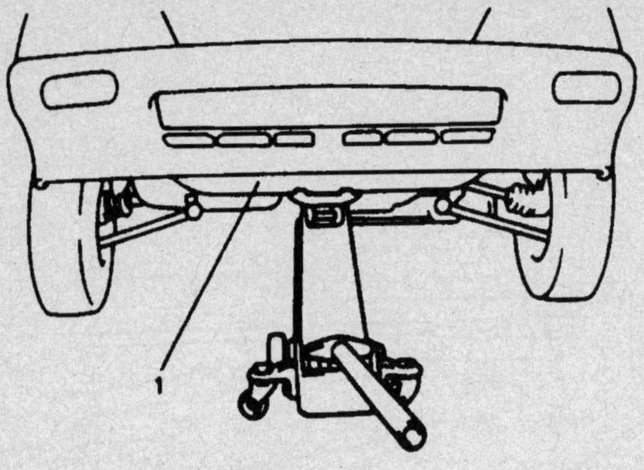
1
1. Front crossmember
SK1139100021000X

Fig. 11 1993–94 Swift. Floor Jack (Front)

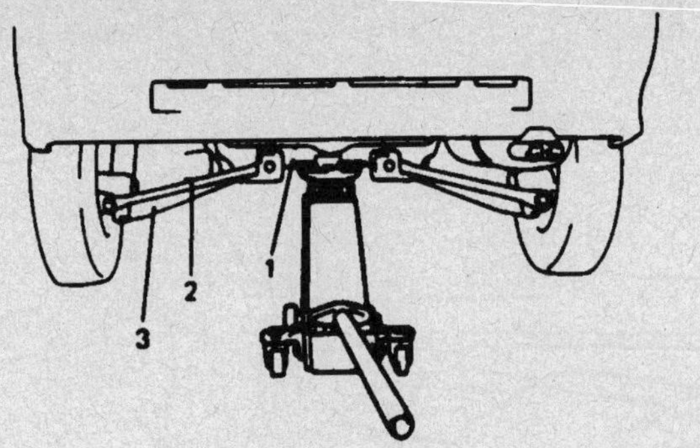
1
2
3
1. Rear crossmember
2. Control rod
3. Suspension arm
SK1139100022000X

Fig. 12 1993–94 Swift. Floor Jack (Rear)

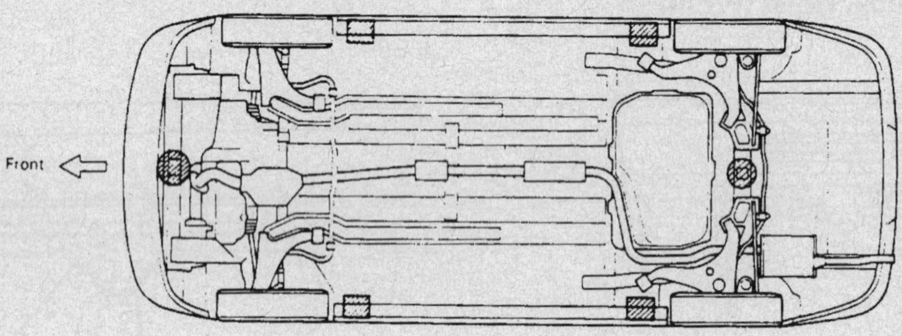
Front
: Support position for frame contact hoist and safety stand
: Floor jack position
SK1139500053000X

Fig. 13 1995–96 Swift

VEHICLE LIFT POINTS
Toyota

INDEX

	Page No.	Fig. No.
Avalon	0-59	1
Camry		
1993–95	0-60	2
1996	0-61	3
Celica	0-61	4
Corolla	0-62	5
Land Cruiser		
1993-94	0-62	6
1995–96	0-61	3
MR2	0-63	8
Paseo	0-64	9
Pickup & T100	0-64	10
Previa	0-65	11
RAV4	0-65	12
Supra	0-66	13
Tacoma	0-66	14
Tercel	0-67	15
4Runner		
1993–95	0-67	16
1996	0-67	17

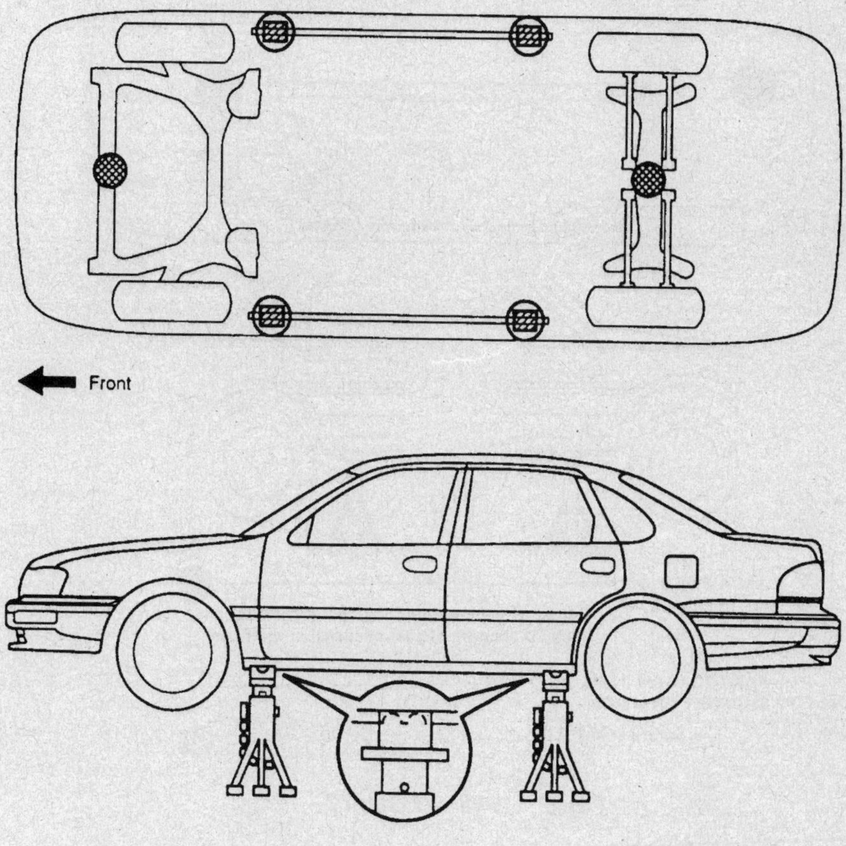

Front

JACK POSITION

Front .... Front crossmember
Rear .... Rear axle beam

CAUTION: Before jacking-up the rear and front, make sure the car is not carrying any extra weight.

PANTOGRAPH JACK POSITION

SUPPORT POSITION

Safety stand and swing arm type lift ....

TY1139500254000X

Fig. 1 Avalon

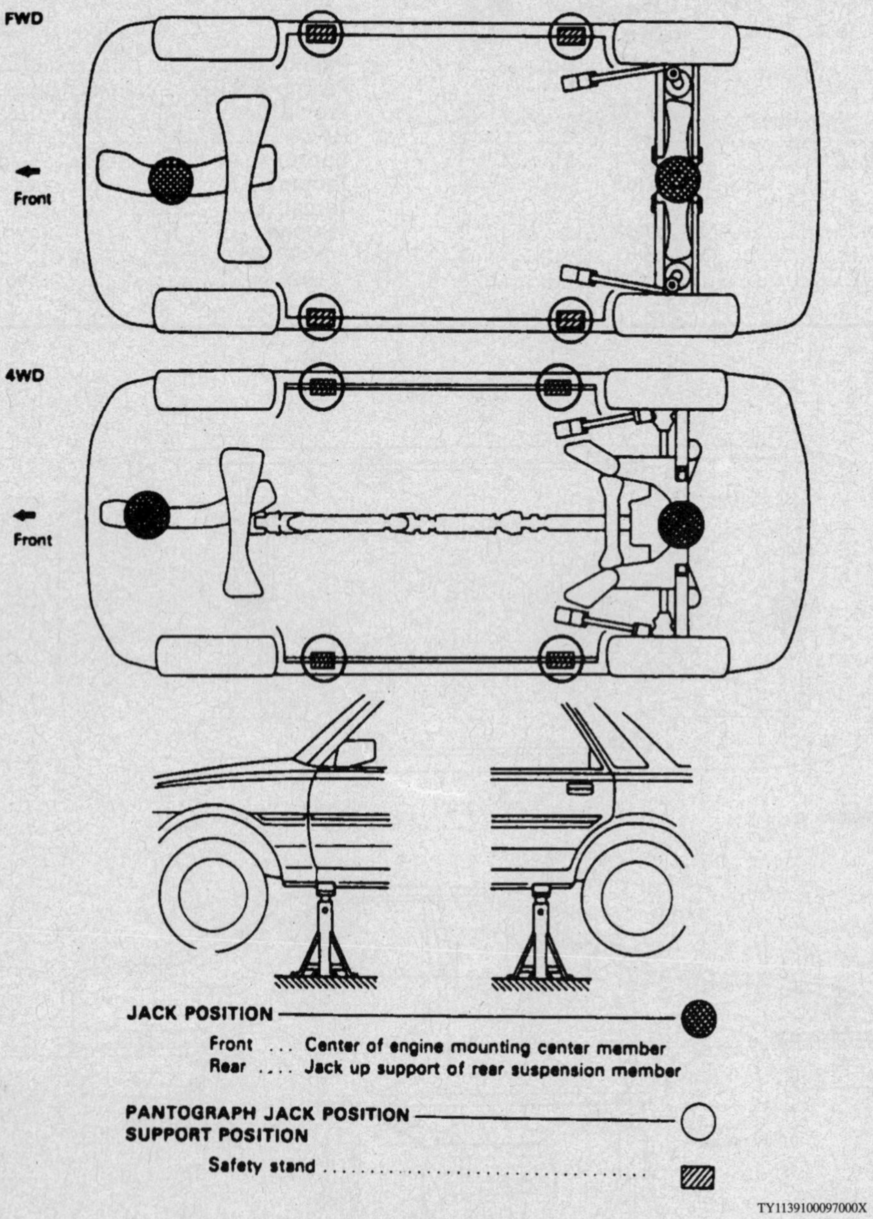
FWD
Front
4WD
Front
JACK POSITION
Front ... Center of engine mounting center member
Rear .... Jack up support of rear suspension member
PANTOGRAPH JACK POSITION
SUPPORT POSITION
Safety stand ....
TY1139100097000X

Fig. 2 1993–95 Camry

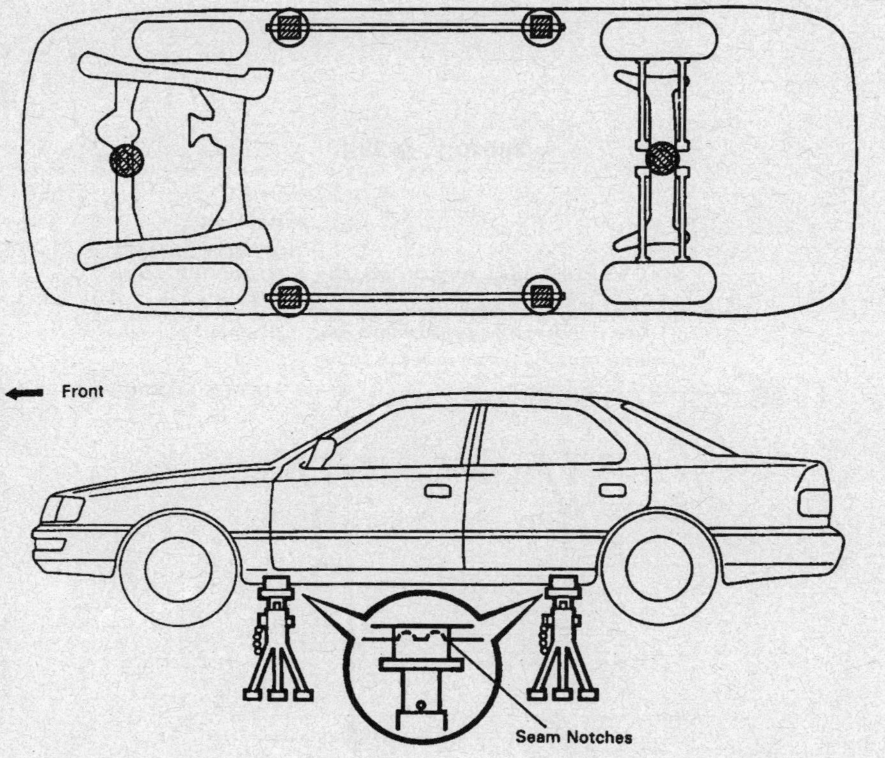

Front
Seam Notches

JACK POSITION
- Front .... Front crossmember
- Rear .... Rear axle beam

CAUTION: Before jacking-up the rear and front, make sure the car is not carrying any extra weight.

PANTOGRAPH JACK POSITION

SUPPORT POSITION
- Safety stand and swing arm type lift ....

TY1139600287000X

Fig. 3 1996 Camry

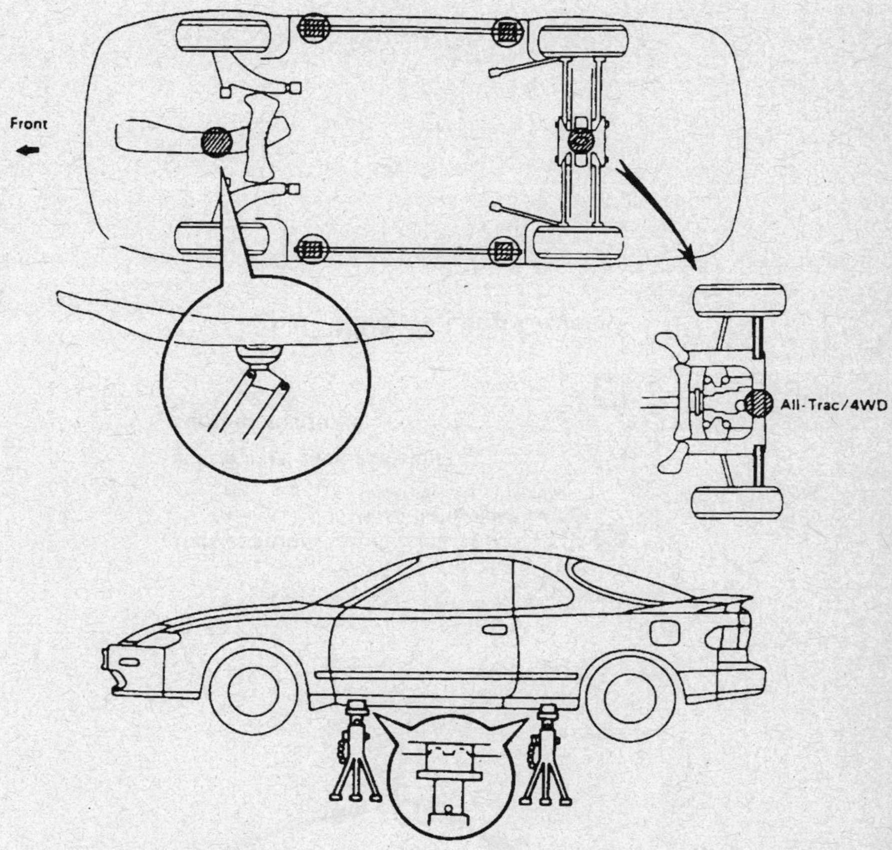

Front
All-Trac/4WD

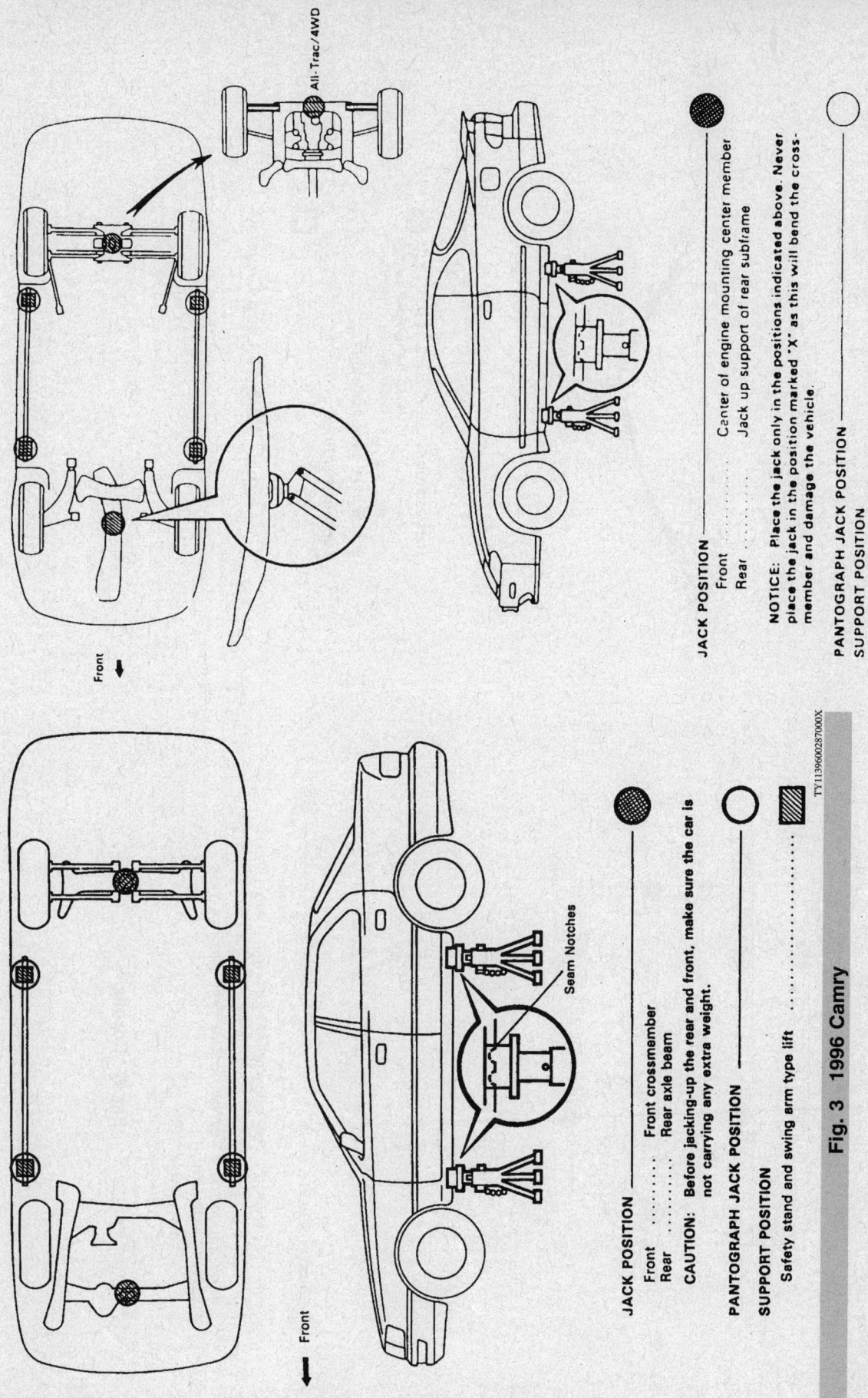

JACK POSITION
- Front .... Center of engine mounting center member
- Rear .... Jack up support of rear subframe

NOTICE: Place the jack only in the positions indicated above. Never place the jack in the position marked "X" as this will bend the cross-member and damage the vehicle.

PANTOGRAPH JACK POSITION

SUPPORT POSITION
- Safety stand and swing arm type lift

TY1139100098000X

Fig. 4 Celica

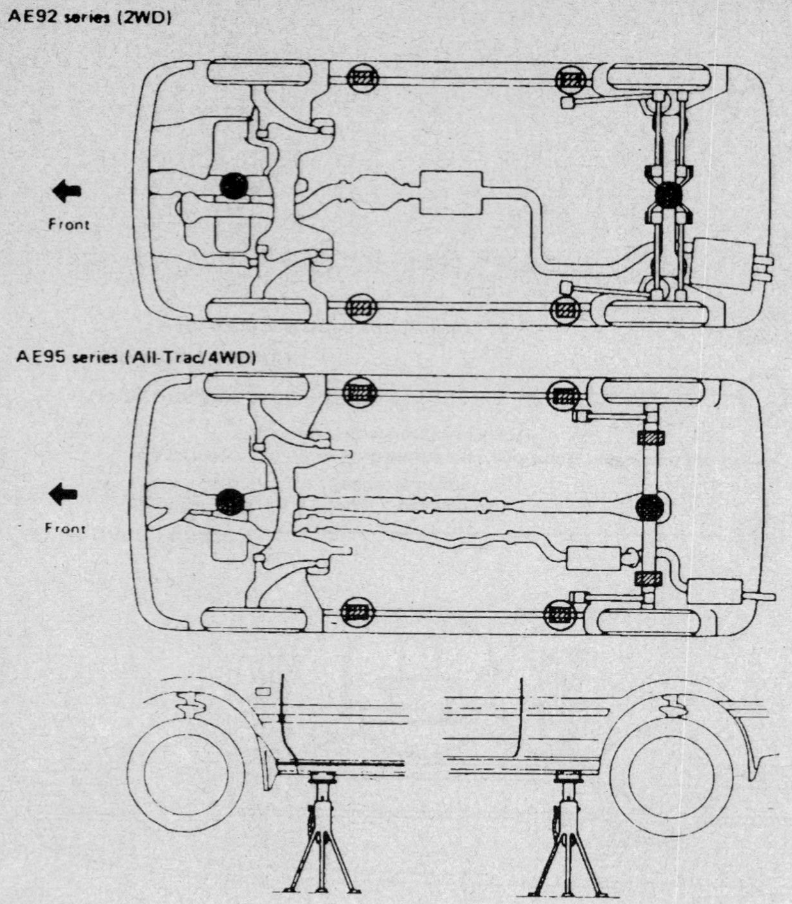
AE92 series (2WD)
Front
AE95 series (All-Trac/4WD)
Front

JACK POSITION

Front .... Center of engine mounting center member

Rear .... Rear subframe (AE92 series)
Jack up support of rear axle housing (AE95 series)

PANTOGRAPH JACK AND SWING ARM TYPE LIFT POSITION

SUPPORT POSITION

Safety stand

TY1139100099000X

Fig. 5 Corolla

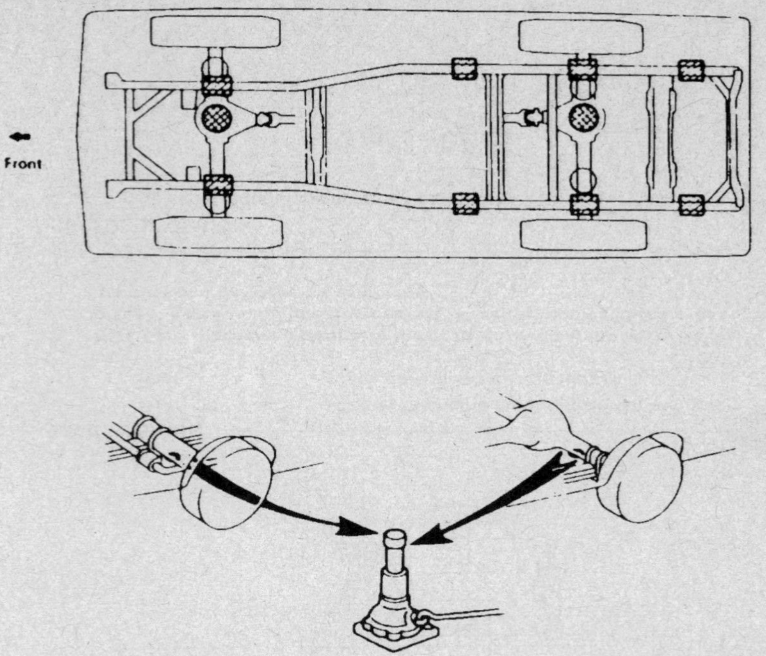
Front

JACK POSITION

Front Under the front differential

Rear Under the rear differential

SCREW TYPE JACK POSITION

SUPPORT POSITION

Safety stand

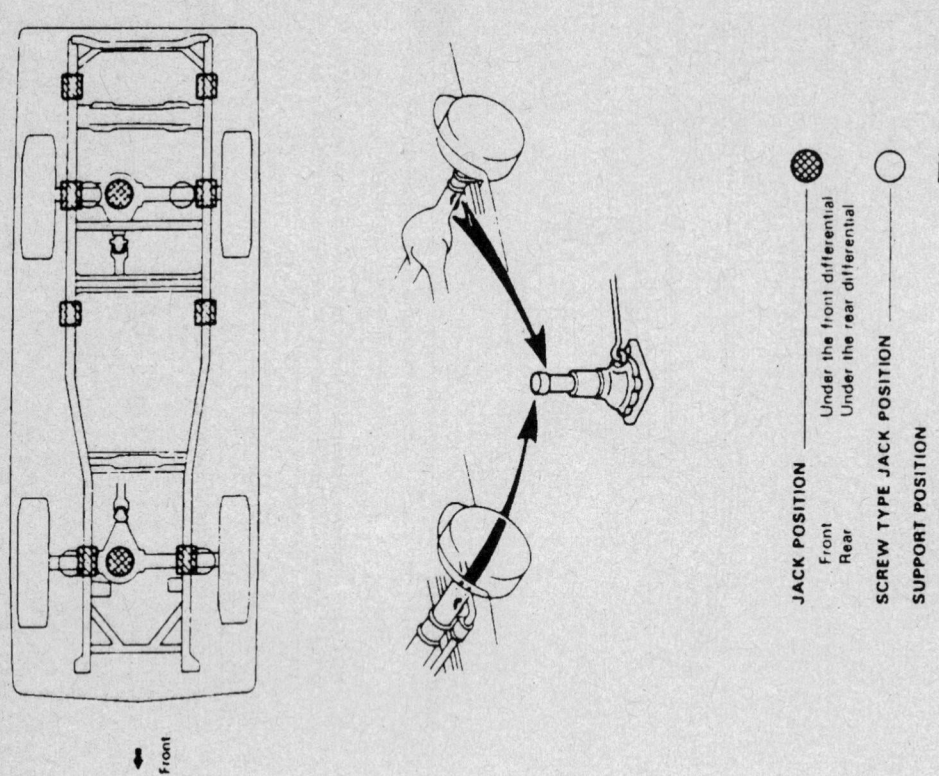

TY1139100109000X

Fig. 6 1993–94 Land Cruiser

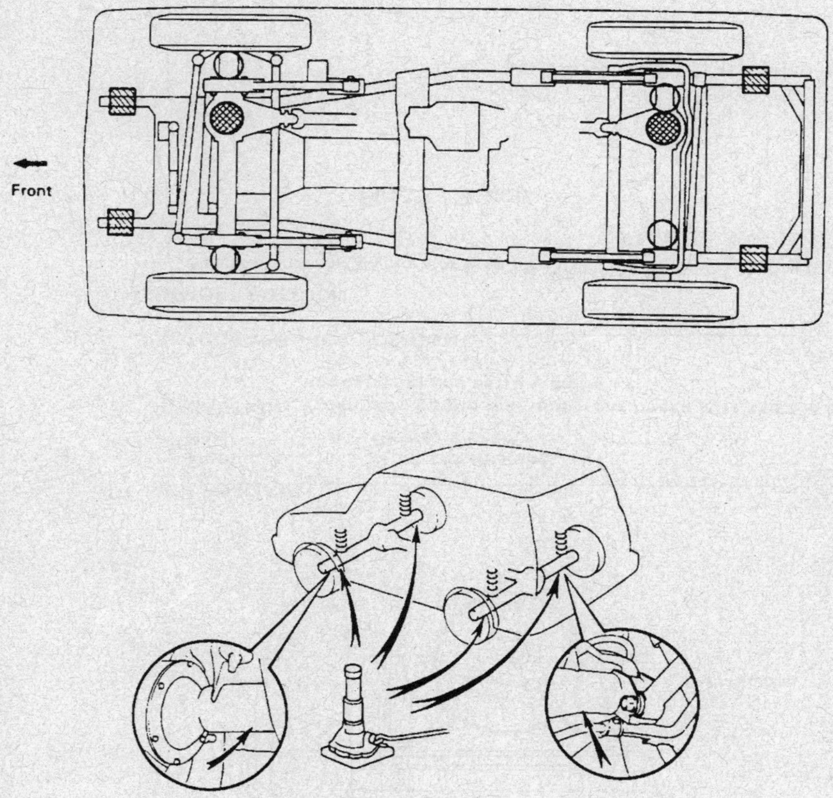
Front

JACK POSITION
- Front .... Under the front differential
- Rear .... Under the rear differential

SCREW TYPE JACK POSITION

SUPPORT POSITION
- Safety stand ....

TY1139500255000X

Fig. 7 1995–96 Land Cruiser

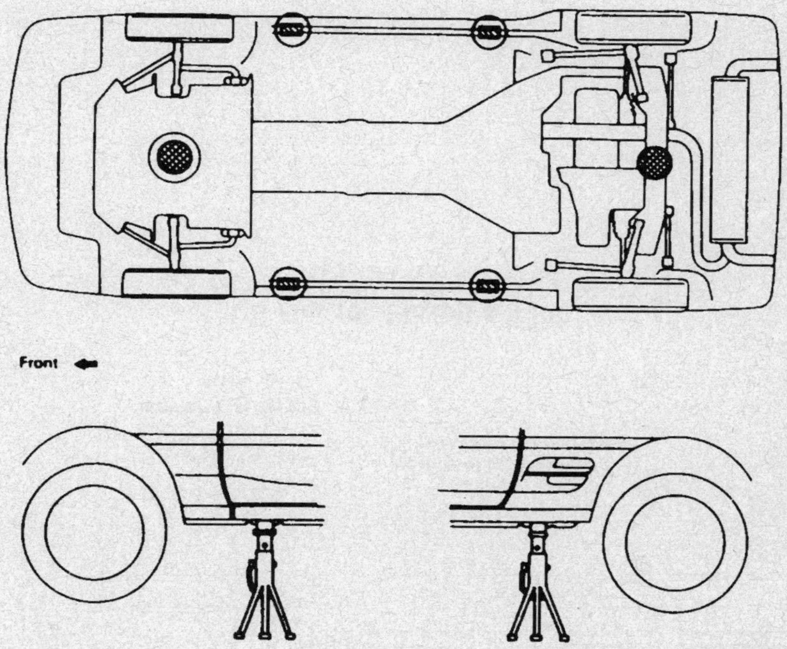
Front

JACK POSITION
- Front .... Jack up support of front under cover center
- Rear ..... Rear suspension crossmember

PANTOGRAPH JACK POSITION

SUPPORT POSITION
- Safety stand ....

TY1139100101000X

Fig. 8 MR2

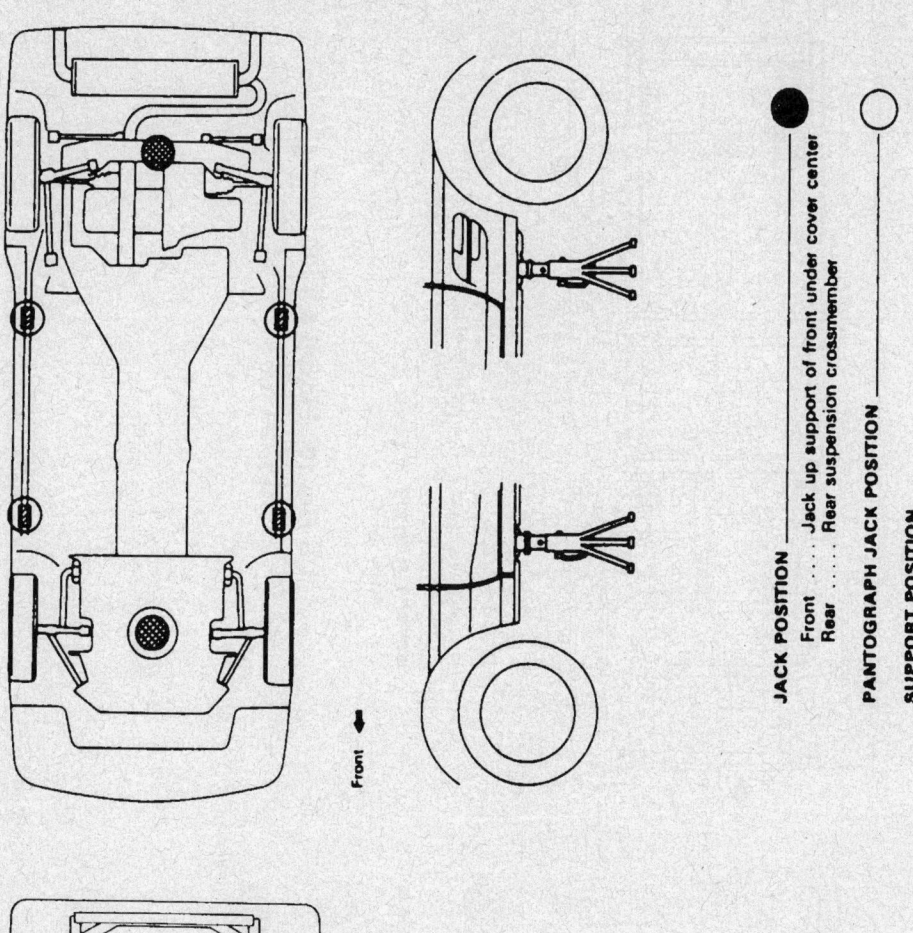

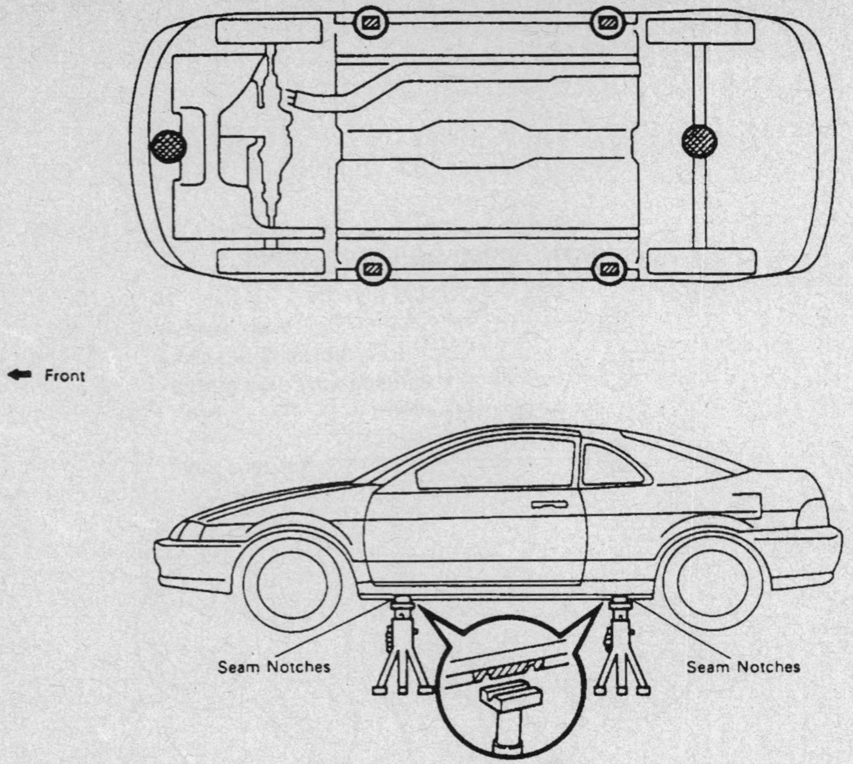
Front
Seam Notches
Seam Notches

JACK POSITION

Front .... Front crossmember
Rear .... Rear axle beam

CAUTION: When jack-up the rear and front, make sure the car is not carrying any extra weight.

PANTOGRAPH JACK POSITION

SUPPORT POSITION

Safety stand and swing arm type lift ....

TY1139100108000X

Fig. 9 Paseo

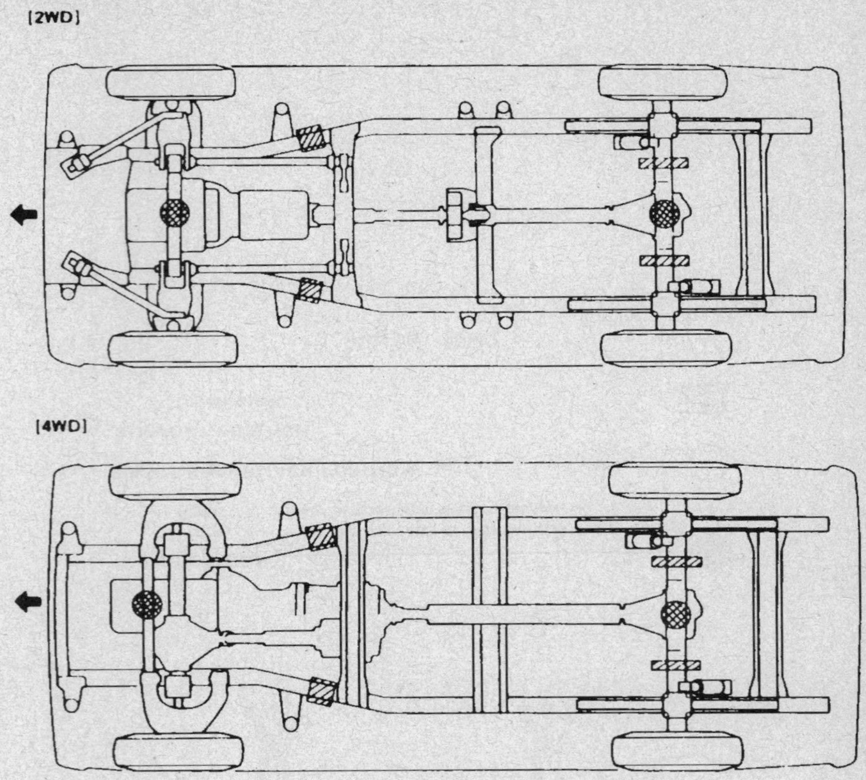
[2WD]
[4WD]

JACK POSITION

Front .... Center of crossmember
Rear .... Under the rear differential

SUPPORT POSITION

Safety stand ....

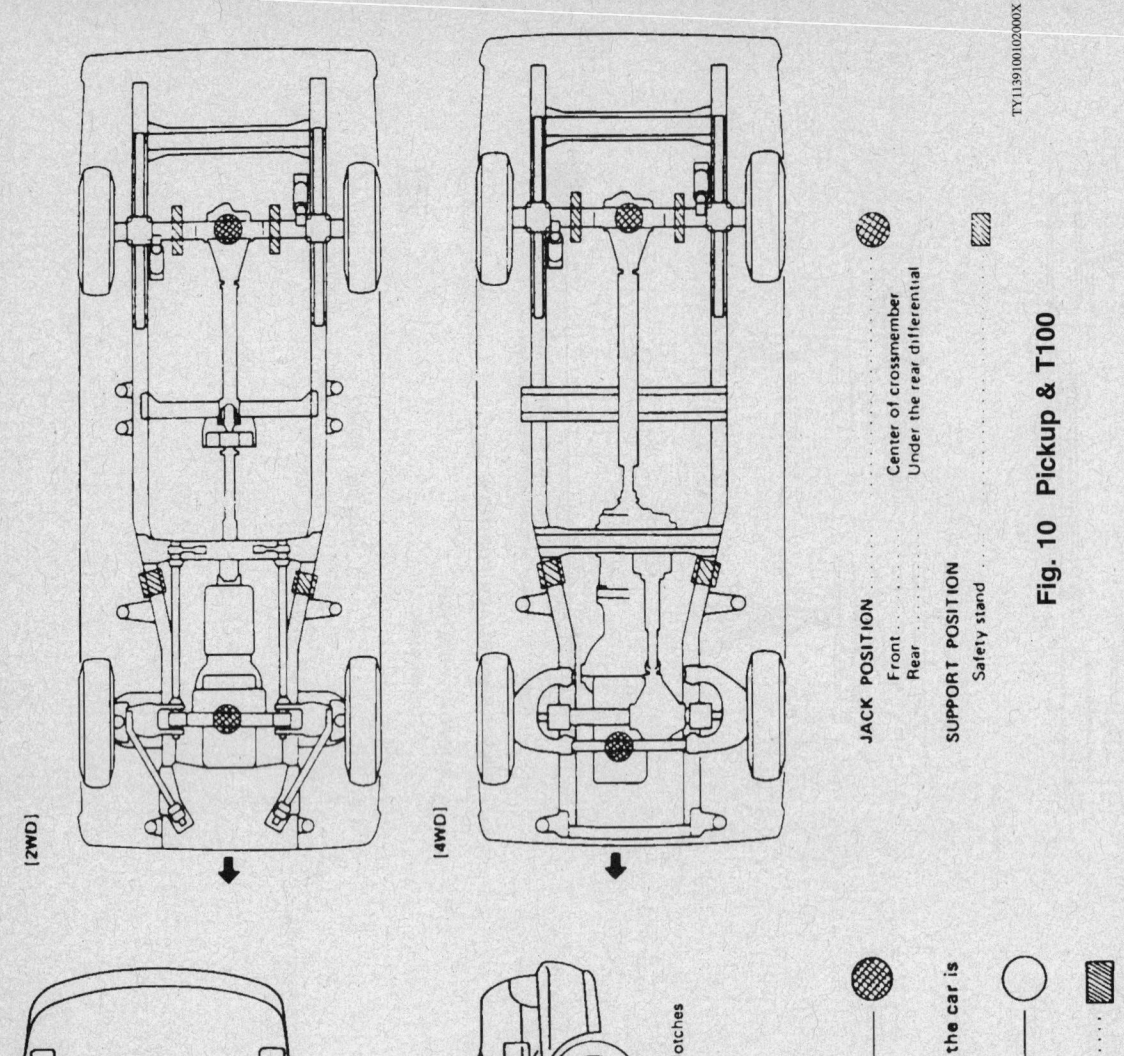

TY1139100102000X

Fig. 10 Pickup & T100

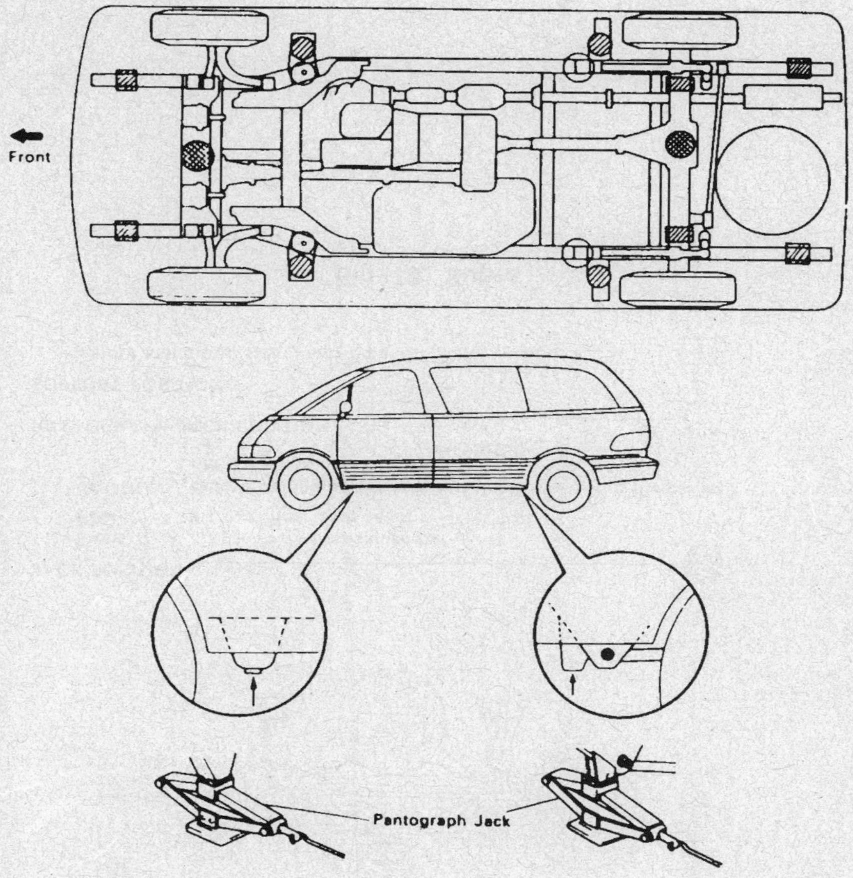
Front
Pantograph Jack

JACK POSITION ———— (hatched circle)

Front .... Center of front suspension crossmember
Rear .... Center of rear axle housing

PANTOGRAPH JACK POSITION ———— (open circle)
SUPPORT POSITION

Safety stand .... (hatched box)

SWING ARM TYPE LIFT POSITION ———— (dark circle)

TY1139300106000X

Fig. 11 Previa

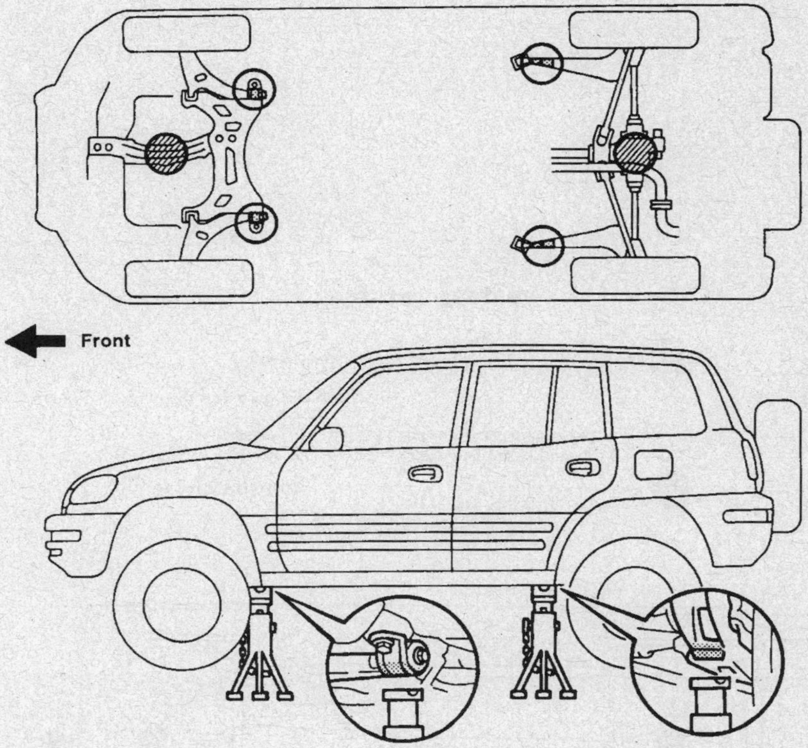
Front

JACK POSITION ———— (hatched circle)

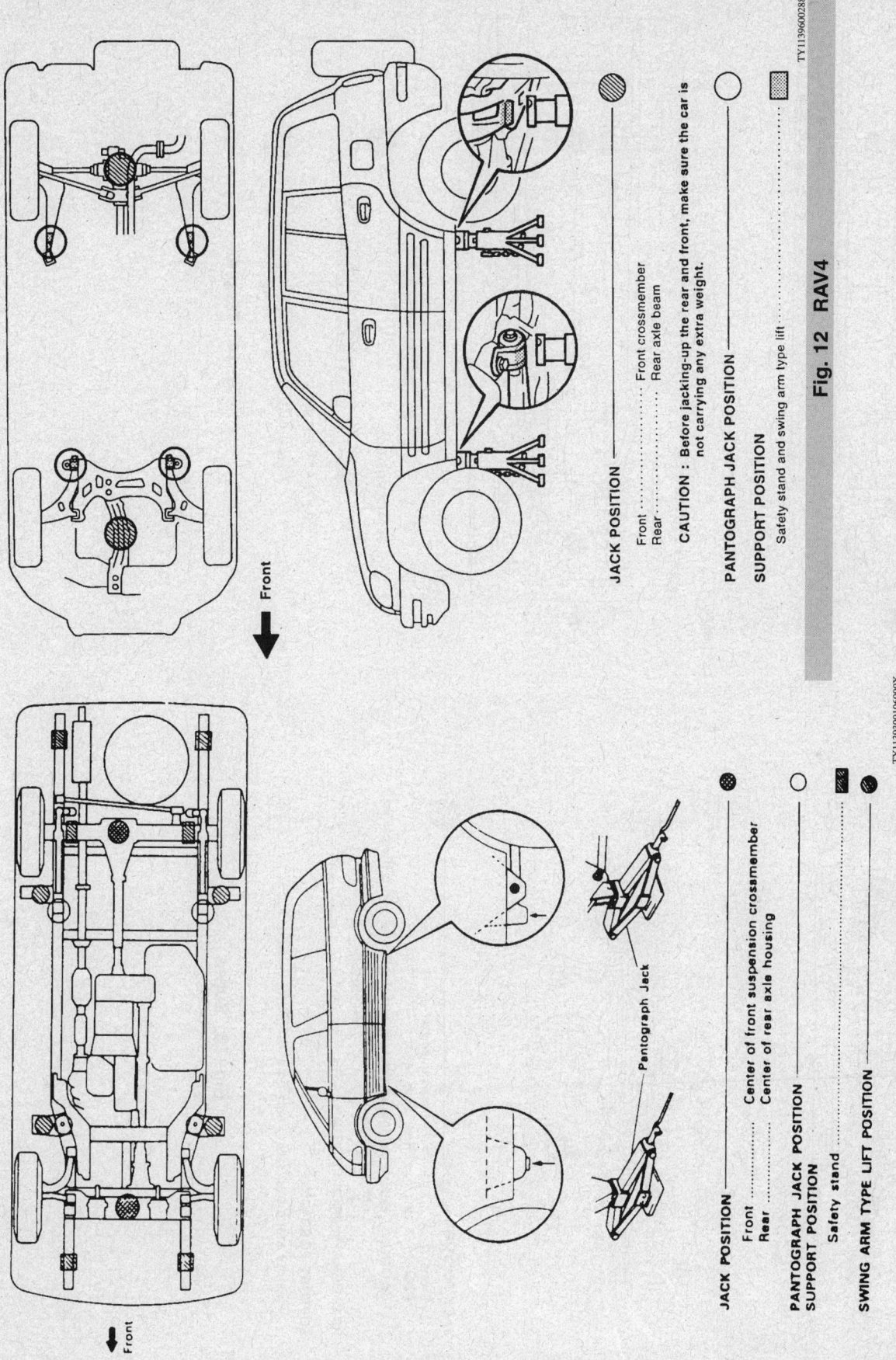

Front .... Front crossmember
Rear .... Rear axle beam

CAUTION : Before jacking-up the rear and front, make sure the car is not carrying any extra weight.

PANTOGRAPH JACK POSITION ———— (open circle)

SUPPORT POSITION

Safety stand and swing arm type lift .... (shaded box)

TY1139600288000X

Fig. 12 RAV4

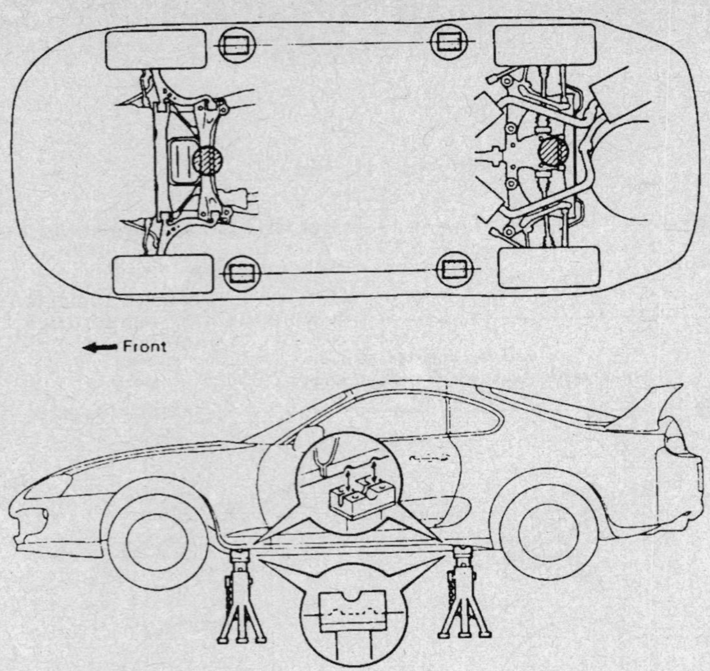
Front

JACK POSITION

Front .... Front crossmember
Rear .... Rear axle beam

CAUTION: Before jacking-up the rear and front, make sure the car is not carrying any extra weight.

PANTOGRAPH JACK POSITION

SUPPORT POSITION

Safety stand and swing arm type lift ....

TY1139300104000X

Fig. 13 Supra

[2WD]

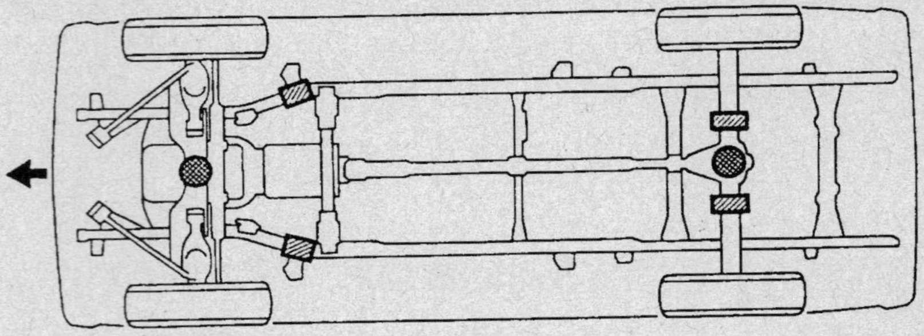

[4WD]

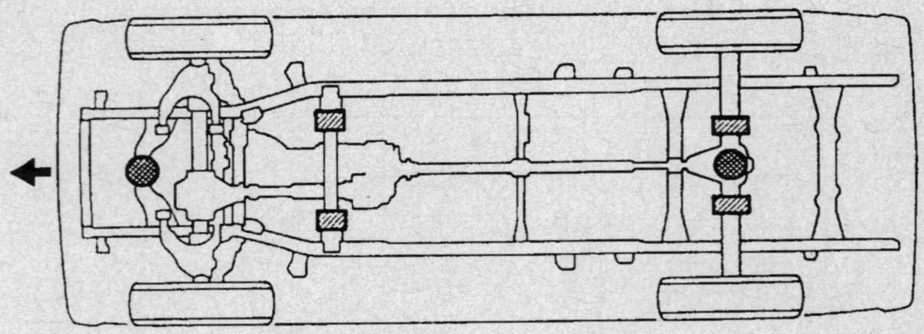

JACK POSITION . . . .

Front . . . . Center of crossmember
Rear . . . . Under the rear differential

SUPPORT POSITION

Safety stand . . . .

TY1139500256000X

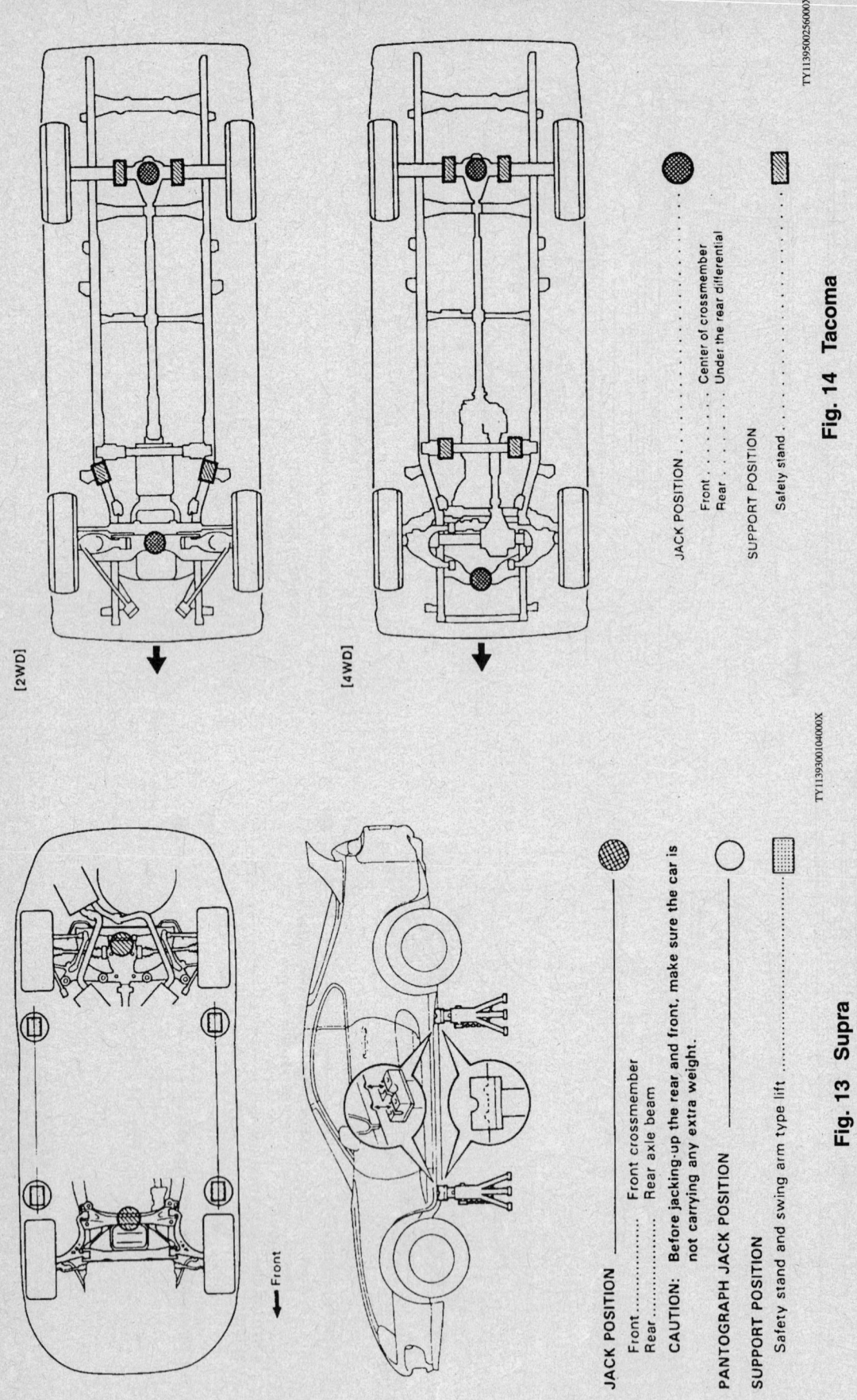

Fig. 14 Tacoma

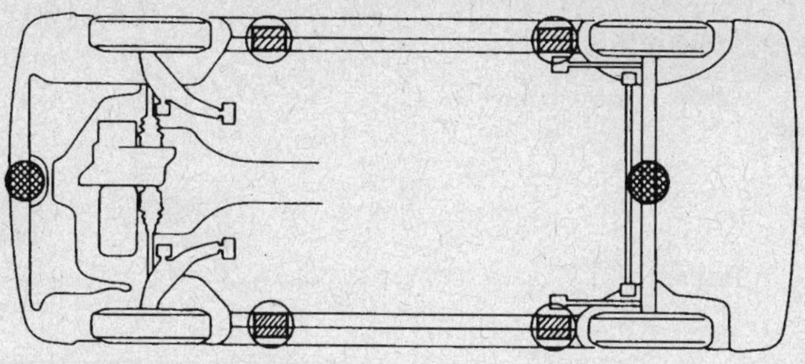
Front

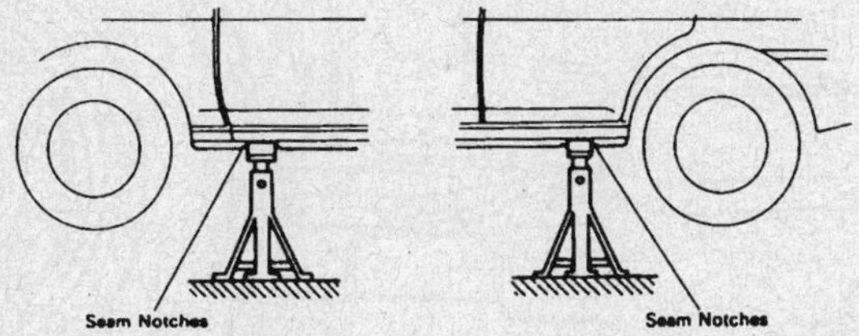
Seam Notches
Seam Notches

JACK POSITION (●)

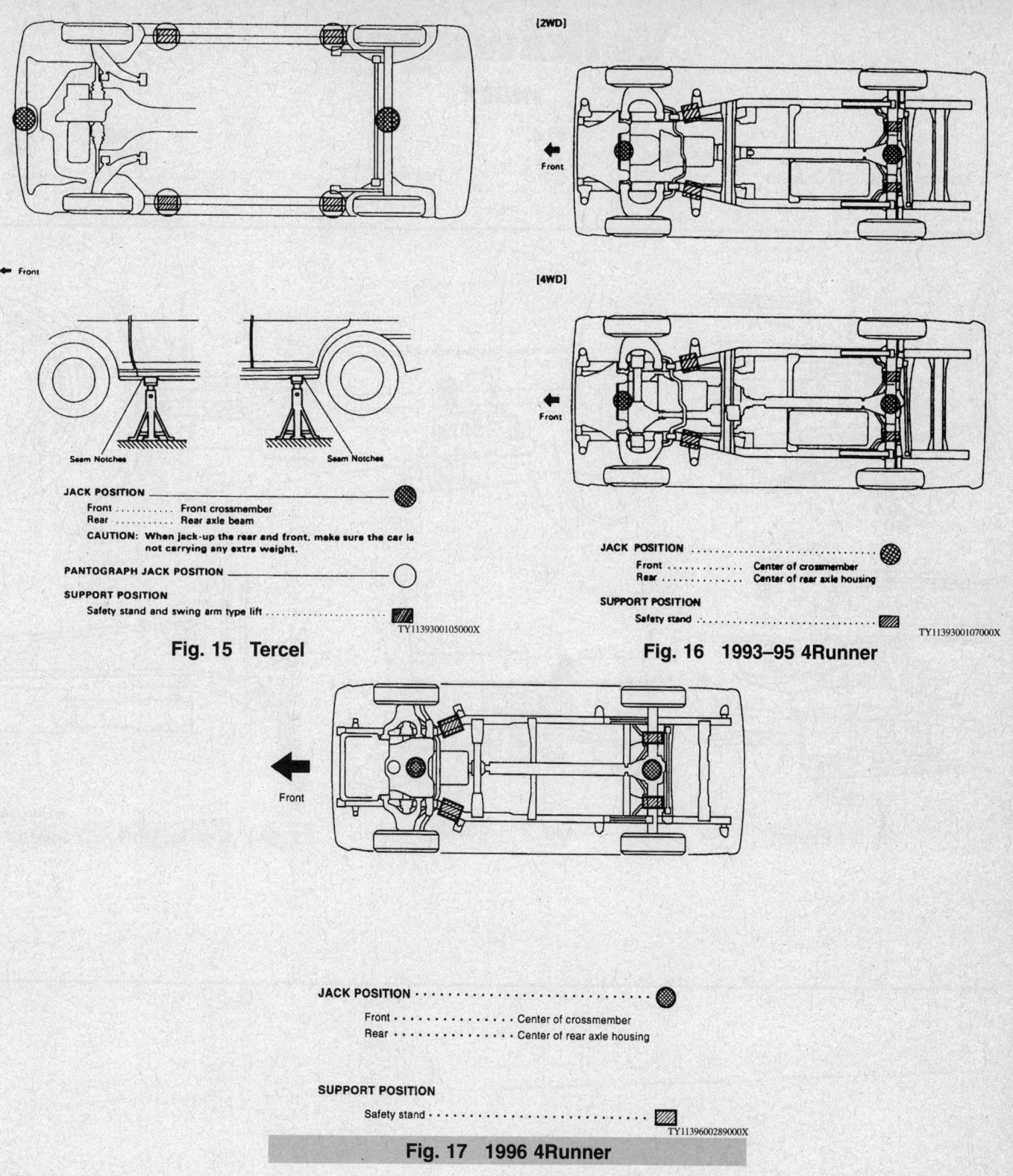

Front .... Front crossmember
Rear .... Rear axle beam

CAUTION: When jack-up the rear and front, make sure the car is not carrying any extra weight.

PANTOGRAPH JACK POSITION (○)

SUPPORT POSITION

Safety stand and swing arm type lift .... (▨)

TY1139300105000X

Fig. 15 Tercel

[2WD]

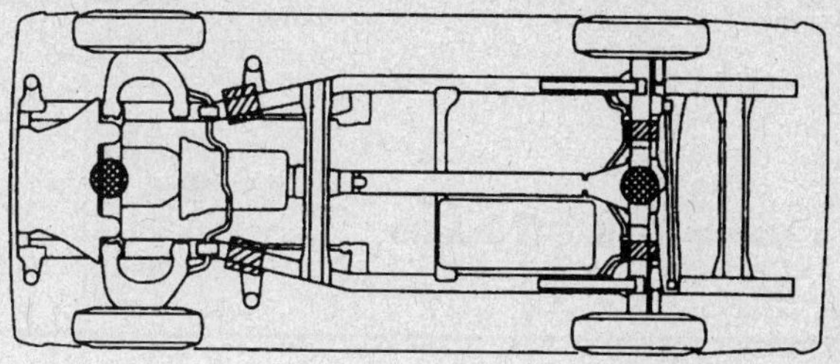
Front

[4WD]

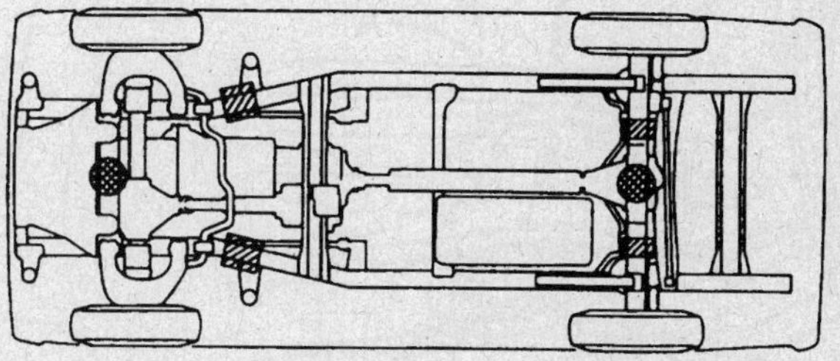
Front

JACK POSITION .... (●)

Front .... Center of crossmember
Rear .... Center of rear axle housing

SUPPORT POSITION

Safety stand .... (▨)

TY1139300107000X

Fig. 16 1993–95 4Runner

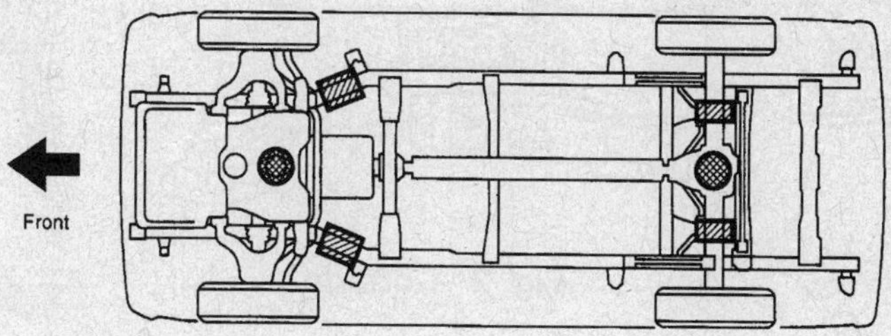
Front

JACK POSITION .... (●)

Front .... Center of crossmember
Rear .... Center of rear axle housing

SUPPORT POSITION

Safety stand .... (▨)

TY1139600289000X

Fig. 17 1996 4Runner

VEHICLE LIFT POINTS
Volkswagen

INDEX

	Page No.	Fig. No.
Cabrio, Golf, GTI & Jetta	0-68	3
Corrado	0-68	2
Passat	0-68	1

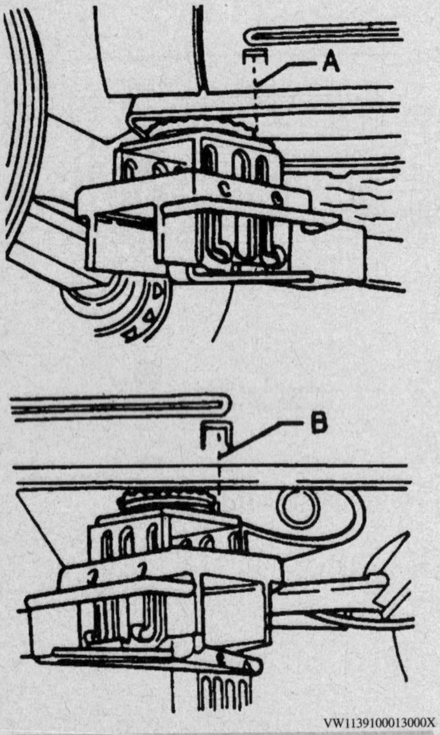

A
B
VW1139100013000X

Fig. 1 Passat

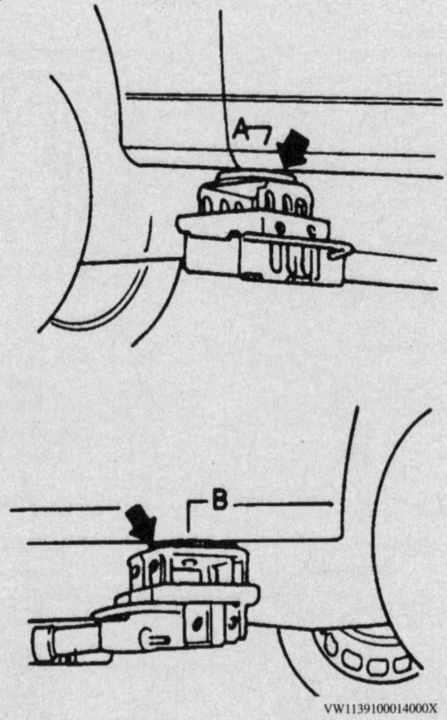

A
B
VW1139100014000X

Fig. 2 Corrado

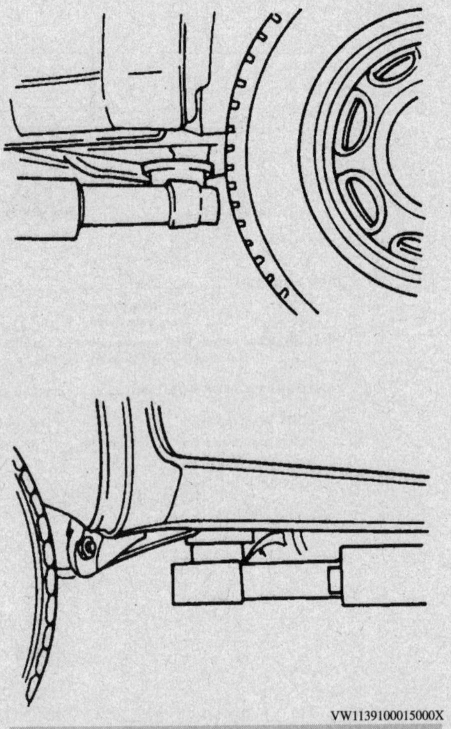

VW1139100015000X

Fig. 3 Cabrio, Golf, GTI & Jetta

VEHICLE MAINTENANCE SCHEDULES

TABLE OF CONTENTS

	Page No.
MITSUBISHI	0-69
NISSAN	0-89
PORSCHE	0-98
SAAB	0-101
SUBARU	0-104
SUZUKI	0-108
TOYOTA	0-113
VOLKSWAGEN	0-133
VOLVO	0-135

Mitsubishi

INDEX

	Page No.	Fig. No.
Diamante		
1993	0-69	1
1994	0-70	2
1995–96	0-71	3
Eclipse		
1993–94	0-71	4
1995	0-72	5
1996	0-72	6
Expo		
1993	0-73	7
1994	0-73	8
1995	0-74	9
1996	0-74	10
Galant		
1993	0-75	11
1994	0-75	12
1995	0-76	13
1996	0-77	14
Mirage		
1993	0-77	15
1994–96	0-78	16
Montero		
1993–94	0-79	17
1995	0-80	18
1996	0-82	19
Pickup		
1993–94	0-84	20
1995	0-85	21
1996	0-86	22
Precis		
3000GT		
1993–94	0-87	24
1995–96	0-88	25

No	Emission Control System Maintenance	Service Intervals	Kilometers in Thousands	24	48	72	80	96
			Mileage in Thousands	15	30	45	50	60
1	Check Fuel System (Tank, Pipe Line and Connections and Fuel Filler Cap) for Leaks Every 5 Years		or				X	
2	Check Fuel Hoses for Leaks or Damage Every 2 Years		or		X			X
3	Replace Air Cleaner Element		at		X			X
4	Replace Spark Plugs	with SOHC engine	at		X			X
		with DOHC engine	at					X
No	General Maintenance	Service Intervals	Kilometers in Thousands	24	48	72	80	96
			Mileage in Thousands	15	30	45	50	60
5	Timing Belt	Replace	at					X
6	Drive Belt (for Alternator)	Inspect for Tension	at		X			X
7	Engine Oil	Change Every Year	or	Every 12,000 km (7,500 miles)				
8	Engine Oil Filter	Replace Every Year	or	X	X	X		X
9	Automatic Transaxle Fluid	Inspect Fluid Level Every Year	or	X	X	X		X
		Change Fluid	at		X			X
10	Engine Coolant	Replace Every 2 Years	or		X			X
11	Disc Brake Pads	Inspect for Wear Every Year	or	X	X	X		X
12	Brake Hoses	Check for Deterioration or Leaks Every Year	or	X	X	X		X
13	Ball Joint and Steering Linkage Seals	Inspect for Grease Leaks and Damage Every 2 Years	or		X			X
14	Drive Shaft Boots	Inspect for Grease Leaks and Damage Every Year	or	X	X	X		X
15	S.R.S.* airbag system	Inspect at 10 years						
16	Exhaust System (Connection Portion of Muffler, Pipings and Converter Heat Shields)	Check and Service as Required Every 2 Years	or		X			X

NOTE
* Supplemental Restraint System

MT1139200169000X

Fig. 1 Diamante. 1993

No.	Emission control system maintenance	Service to be performed	Kilometers in thousands	24	48	72	96	120	144	168
			Mileage in thousands	15	30	45	60	75	90	105
1	Fuel system (Tank, pipe line and connection, and fuel tank filler tube cap)*	Check for leaks Every 5 years	or				×			
2	Fuel hoses	Check condition Every 2 years	or		×		×		×	
3	Air cleaner element	Replace	at		×		×		×	
4	Evaporative emission control system (except evaporative emission canister)*	Check for leaks and clogging Every 5 years	or				×			
5	Spark plugs	Replace	at		×		×		×	
6	Ignition cables*	Replace Every 5 years	or				×			
7	Distributor cap and rotor*	Check Every 5 years	or				×			

*: For California only

GENERAL MAINTENANCE SERVICE FOR PROPER VEHICLE PERFORMANCE

No	General maintenance	Service to be performed	Kilometers in thousands	24	48	72	96	120	144	168
			Mileage in thousands	15	30	45	60	75	90	105
8	Timing belt	Replace	at				×*1			
9	Drive belt (for generator)	Check condition	at		×		×		×	
10	Engine oil	Change Every year	or	Every 12,000 km (7,500 miles)						
11	Engine oil filter	Replace Every year	or	×	×	×	×	×	×	×
12	Automatic transmission fluid	Inspect fluid level Every year	or	×	×	×	×	×	×	×
		Change fluid	at		×		×		×	
13	Engine coolant	Change Every 2 years	or		×		×		×	
14	Disc brake pads	Inspect for wear Every year	or	×	×	×	×	×	×	×
15	Brake hoses	Check for deterioration or leaks Every year	or	×	×	×	×	×	×	×
16	Ball joint and steering linkage seals	Inspect for grease leaks and damage Every 2 years	or		×		×		×	
17	Drive shaft boots	Inspect for grease leaks and damage Every year	or	×	×	×	×	×	×	×
18	S.R.S.*2 air bag system	Inspect system		At 10 years						
19	Exhaust system (Connection portion of muffler, pipings and converter heat shields)	Check and service as required Every 2 years	*, or		×		×		×	

NOTE
*: For California, this maintenance is recommended but not required
*2: Supplemental Restraint System

MT1139400170000X

Fig. 2 Diamante. 1994

No.	Emission control system maintenance	Service to be performed		Kilometers in thousands	24	48	72	96	120	144	168
				Mileage in thousands	15	30	45	60	75	90	105
1	Fuel system (Tank, pipe line and connection, and fuel tank filler tube cap)	Check for leaks Every 5 years		or				×			
2	Fuel hoses	Check condition Every 2 years		or		×		×		×	
3	Air cleaner element	Replace		at		×		×		×	
4	Evaporative emission control system (except evaporative emission canister)	Check for leaks and clogging Every 5 years		or				×			
5	Spark plugs	Replace	except platinum plugs			×		×		×	
			platinum plugs only					×			
6	Ignition cables	Replace Every 5 years		or				×			
7	Distributor cap and rotor	Check Every 5 years		or				×			

No.	General maintenance	Service to be performed	Kilometers in thousands	24	48	72	96	120	144	168
			Mileage in thousands	15	30	45	60	75	90	105
8	Timing belt	Replace	at				×*1		At 160,000 km*2 (100,000 miles)	
9	Drive belt (for generator, water pump, power steering pump)	Check condition	at		×		×		×	
10	Engine oil	Change Every year	or	Every 12,000 km (7,500 miles)						
11	Engine oil filter	Replace Every year*3	or	×	×	×	×	×	×	×
12	Automatic transmission fluid	Inspect fluid level Every year	or	×	×	×	×	×	×	×
		Change fluid	at		×		×		×	
13	Engine coolant	Change Every 2 years	or		×		×		×	
14	Disc brake pads	Inspect for wear Every year	or	×	×	×	×	×	×	×
15	Brake hoses	Check for deterioration or leaks Every year	or	×	×	×	×	×	×	×
16	Ball joint and steering linkage seals	Inspect for grease leaks and damage Every 2 years	or		×		×		×	
17	Drive shaft boots	Inspect for grease leaks and damage Every year	or	×	×	×	×	×	×	×
18	SRS*4 air bag system	Inspect system		At 10 years						
19	Exhaust system (Connection portion of muffler, pipings and converter heat shields)	Check and service as required Every 2 years	or		×		×		×	

NOTE
*1: For California, this maintenance is recommended but not required.
*2: Not required if belt was previously changed.
*3: If the mileage is less than 12,000 km (7,500 miles) each year, the oil filter should be replaced at every oil change.
*4: Supplemental Restraint System

MT1139500199000X

Fig. 3 Diamante. 1995–96

No.	Emission Control System Maintenance	Service Intervals	Kilometers in Thousands	24	48	72	80	96
			Mileage in Thousands	15	30	45	50	60
1	Check Fuel System (Tank, Line and Connections and Fuel Filler Cap) for Leaks Every 5 Years		or				X	
2	Check Fuel Hoses Every 2 Years for leaks or damage		or		X			X
3	Replace Air Cleaner Element		at		X			X
4	Replace Spark Plugs		at		X			X

No.	General Maintenance		Service Intervals	Kilometers in Thousands	24	48	72	80	96
				Mileage in Thousands	15	30	45	50	60
5	Timing Belt (Including the Balancer Belt)		Replace	at					X
6	Drive Belt (for Water Pump and Alternator)		Inspect for tension	at		X			X
7	Engine Oil	Non-Turbo	Change Every Year	or	Every 12,000 km (7,500 miles)				
		Turbo	Change Every 6 Months		Every 8,000 km (5,000 miles)				
8	Engine Oil Filter	Non-Turbo	Change Every Year	or	X	X	X		X
		Turbo	Change Every Year		Every 16,000 km (10,000 miles)				
9	Manual Transaxle Oil		Inspect Oil Level	at		X			X
10	Automatic Transaxle Fluid		Inspect Fluid Level Every Year	or	X	X	X		X
			Change Fluid	at		X			X
11	Engine Coolant		Replace Every 2 Years	or		X			X
12	Disc Brake Pads		Inspect for Wear Every Year	or	X	X	X		X
13	Brake Hoses		Check for Deterioration or Leaks Every Year	or	X	X	X		X
14	Ball Joint and Steering Linkage Seals		Inspect for Grease Leaks and Damage Every 2 Years	or		X			X
15	Drive Shaft Boots		Inspect for Grease Leaks and Damage Every Year	or	X	X	X		X
16	Rear Axle <AWD>	With LSD	Change Oil			X			X
		Without LSD	Inspect Oil Level			X			X
17	Exhaust System (Connection Portion of Muffler, Pipings and Converter Heat Shields)		Check and Service as Required Every 2 Years	or		X			X

NOTE
LSD: Limited-slip differential

MT1139100166000X

Fig. 4 Eclipse. 1993–94

No.	Emission control system maintenance	Service to be performed		Kilometers in thousands	24	48	72	96	120	144	168
				Mileage in thousands	15	30	45	60	75	90	105
1	Fuel system (Tank, pipe line and connection, and fuel tank filler tube cap)	Check for leaks Every 5 years	or					×			
2	Fuel hoses	Check condition Every 2 years	or			×		×		×	
3	Air cleaner element	Replace	at			×		×		×	
4	Evaporative emission control system (except evaporative emission canister)	Check for leaks and clogging Every 5 years	or					×			
5	Spark plugs	Replace	at			×		×		×	
6	Ignition cables	Replace Every 5 years	or					×			

No.	General maintenance		Service to be performed		Kilometers in thousands	24	48	72	96	120	144	168
					Mileage in thousands	15	30	45	60	75	90	105
7	Timing belts		Replace	at					×*1		160,000 km*2 (100,000 miles)	
8	Drive belt (for generator, water pump, power steering pump)		Check condition	at			×		×		×	
9	Engine oil	Non-turbo	Change Every 6 months	or		Every 12,000 km (7,500 miles)						
			Change Every year	or								
		Turbo	Change Every 6 months	or		Every 8,000 km (5,000 miles)						
10	Engine oil filter	Non-turbo	Replace Every Year*3	or		×	×	×	×	×	×	×
		Turbo	Replace Every Year	or		Every 16,000 km (10,000 miles)						
11	Manual transaxle oil (including transfer)		Inspect oil level	at			×		×		×	
12	Automatic transaxle fluid		Inspect fluid level Every year	or		×	×	×	×	×	×	×
			Change fluid*4	at			×		×		×	
13	Engine coolant		Change Every 2 years	or			×		×		×	
14	Disc brake pads		Inspect for wear Every year	or		×	×	×	×	×	×	×
15	Rear drum brake linings and rear wheel cylinders (except vehicles with disc brakes for all wheels)		Inspect for wear and leaks Every 2 years	or			×		×		×	
16	Brake hoses		Check for deterioration or leaks Every year	or		×	×	×	×	×	×	×
17	Ball joint and steering linkage seals		Inspect for grease leaks and damage Every 2 years	or			×		×		×	
18	Drive shaft boots		Inspect for grease leaks and damage Every year	or		×	×	×	×	×	×	×
19	Rear axle oil		Inspect oil level	at			×		×		×	
20	SRS*5 system		Inspect system			At 10 years						
21	Exhaust system (connection portion of muffler, pipings and converter heat shields)		Check and service as required Every 2 years	or			×		×		×	

NOTES
*1: For California, this maintenance is recommended but not required
*2: Not required if belt was previously changed.
*3: If the mileage is less than 12,000 km (7,500 miles) each year, the oil filter should be replaced at every oil change.
*4: Vehicles with turbocharger
*5: Supplemental Restraint system

MT1139500186000X

Fig. 5 Eclipse. 1995

No.	Emission control system maintenance		Service to be performed	Kilometers in thousands	24	48	72	96	120	144	168
				Mileage in thousands	15	30	45	60	75	90	105
1	Fuel system (Tank, pipe line and connection, and fuel tank filler tube cap)		Check for leaks Every 5 years or					×			
2	Fuel hoses		Check condition Every 2 years or			×		×		×	
3	Air cleaner element		Replace at			×		×		×	
4	Evaporative emission control system (except evaporative emission canister)		Check for leaks and clogging Every 5 years or					×			
5	Spark plugs		Replace at			×		×		×	
6	Ignition cables		Replace Every 5 years or					×			
7	Timing belts		Replace at					×*1		160,000 km*2 (100,000 miles)	
8	Drive belt (for generator, water pump, power steering pump)		Check condition at			×		×		×	
9	Engine oil	Non-turbo	Change Every 6 months or		Every 12,000 km (7,500 miles)						
		Turbo			Every 8,000 km (5,000 miles)						
10	Engine oil filter	Non-turbo	Replace Every Year*3 or		×	×	×	×	×	×	×
		Turbo	Replace Every Year or		Every 16,000 km (10,000 miles)						
11	Manual transaxle oil		Check oil level at			×		×		×	
12	Automatic transaxle fluid		Check fluid level Every year or		×	×	×	×	×	×	×
			Change fluid*4 at			×		×		×	
13	Transfer oil		Check oil level at			×		×		×	
14	Engine coolant		Change Every 2 years or			×		×		×	
15	Disc brake pads		Check for wear Every year or		×	×	×	×	×	×	×
16	Rear drum brake linings and rear wheel cylinders (vehicles without disc brakes for all wheels)		Check for wear and leaks Every 2 years or			×		×		×	
17	Brake hoses		Check for deterioration or leaks Every year or		×	×	×	×	×	×	×
18	Ball joint and steering linkage seals		Check for grease leaks and damage Every 2 years or			×		×		×	
19	Drive shaft boots		Check for grease leaks and damage Every year or		×	×	×	×	×	×	×
20	Rear axle oil		Check oil level at			×		×		×	
21	SRS*5 system		Check system		At 10 years						
22	Exhaust system (connection portion of muffler, pipings and converter heat shields)		Check and service as required Every 2 years or			×		×		×	

NOTES
*1: For California, this maintenance is recommended but not required
*2: Not required if belt was previously changed.
*3: If the mileage is less than 12,000 km (7,500 miles) each year, the oil filter should be replaced at every oil change.
*4: Vehicles with turbocharger
*5: Supplemental Restraint system

MT1139600187000X

Fig. 6 Eclipse. 1996

No.	Emission Control System Maintenance	Service Intervals		Kilometers in Thousands	24	48	72	80	96
				Mileage in Thousands	15	30	45	50	60
1	Check Valve Clearance and Adjust as required (1.8 Liter Engine)			at	X	X	X		X
2	Check Fuel System (Tank, Lines, Connections and Fuel Filter Cap) for Leaks Every 5 Years			or				X	
3	Check Fuel Hoses for Leaks or Damage Every 2 Years			or		X			X
4	Replace Air Cleaner Element			at		X			X
5	Replace Spark Plugs			at		X			X

GENERAL MAINTENANCE SERVICE FOR PROPER VEHICLE PERFORMANCE

No.	General maintenance		Service Intervals	Kilometers in Thousands	24	48	72	80	96
				Mileage in Thousands	15	30	45	50	60
6	Timing Belt		Replace	at					X
7	Drive Belt	For Water Pump and Alternator (2.4 Liter Engine) / For Alternator (1.8 Liter Engine)	Check for damage	at		X			X
8	Engine Oil		Change every year	or	Every 12,000 km (7,500 miles)				
9	Engine Oil Filter		Change every year	or	X	X	X		X
10	Manual Transaxle Oil		Inspect oil level	at		X			X
11	Automatic Transaxle Fluid		Inspect fluid level every year	or	X	X	X		X
			Change fluid	at		X			X
12	Engine Coolant		Replace every 2 years	or		X			X
13	Disc Brake Pads		Inspect for wear every year	or	X	X	X		X
14	Rear Drum Brake Linings and Rear Wheel Cylinders		Inspect for wear and leaks every 2 years	or		X			X
15	Brake Hoses		Check for deterioration or leaks every year	or	X	X	X		X
16	Ball Joint and Steering Linkage Seals		Inspect for grease leaks and damage every 2 years	or		X			X
17	Drive Shaft Boots		Inspect for grease leaks and damage every year	or	X	X	X		X
18	Rear Axle (AWD)	Cars with L.S.D.*	Change oil	at		X			X
		Cars without L.S.D.*	Inspect oil level	at		X			X
19	Exhaust System (Connection Portion of Muffler, Pipings and Converter Heat Shields)		Check and service as required every 2 years	or		X			X

*L.S.D.: Limited-Slip Differential

MT1139200167000X

Fig. 7 Expo. 1993

No.	Emission control system maintenance	Service to be performed	Kilometers in thousands	24	48	72	96	120	144	168
			Mileage in thousands	15	30	45	60	75	90	105
1	Valve clearances (1.8L engine models)	Check and adjust as required	at	X	X	X	X	X	X	X
2	Fuel system (Tank, pipe line and connection, and fuel tank filler tube cap)	Check for leaks Every 5 years	or				X			
3	Fuel hoses	Check condition Every 2 years	or		X		X		X	
4	Air cleaner element	Replace	at		X		X		X	
5	Evaporative emission control system (except evaporative emission canister)	Check for leaks and clogging Every 5 years	or				X			
6	Spark plugs	Replace	at		X		X		X	
7	Ignition cables	Replace Every 5 years	or				X			
8	Distributor cap and rotor	Check Every 5 years	or				X			

GENERAL MAINTENANCE SERVICE FOR PROPER VEHICLE PERFORMANCE

No.	General maintenance		Service to be performed	Kilometers in thousands	24	48	72	96	120	144	168
				Mileage in thousands	15	30	45	60	75	90	105
9	Timing Belts		Replace	at				X*3			
10	Drive Belt	for Water Pump and generator (2.4L engine) / for generator (1.8L engine)	Check condition	at		X		X		X	
11	Engine Oil		Change Every year	or	Every 12,000 km (7,500 miles)						
12	Engine Oil Filter		Replace Every Year	or	X	X	X	X	X	X	X
13	Manual Transaxle Oil		Inspect oil level	at		X		X		X	
14	Automatic Transaxle Fluid		Inspect fluid level Every year	or	X	X	X	X	X	X	X
			Change fluid	at		X		X		X	
15	Engine coolant		Change Every 2 years	or		X		X		X	
16	Disc Brake Pads		Inspect for wear Every year	or	X	X	X	X	X	X	X
17	Rear Drum Brake Linings and Rear Wheel Cylinders		Inspect for wear and leaks Every 2 years	or		X		X		X	
18	Brake Huses		Check for deterioration or leaks Every year	or	X	X	X	X	X	X	X
19	Ball Joint and Steering Linkage Seals		Inspect for grease leaks and damage Every 2 years	or		X		X		X	
20	Drive Shaft Boots		Inspect for grease leaks and damage Every year	or	X	X	X	X	X	X	X
21	Rear Axle (All-wheel drive cars)	cars with L.S.D.*1	Change oil	at		X		X		X	
		cars without L.S.D.*1	Inspect oil level	at		X		X		X	
22	Exhaust System (Connection Portion of Muffler, Pipings and Converter Heat Shields)		Check and service as required Every 2 years	or		X		X		X	
23	SRS*2 air bag		Inspection system	at	10 years						

*1 L.S.D.: Limited Slip Differential
*2 SRS: Supplemental Restraint System
*3. For California, this maintenance is recommended but not required.

MT1139400168000X

Fig. 8 Expo. 1994

No.	Emission control system maintenance	Service to be performed	Kilometers in thousands / Mileage in thousands	24 / 15	48 / 30	72 / 45	96 / 60	120 / 75	144 / 90	168 / 105
1	Valve clearances (1.8L Engine)	Check and adjust as required at		×	×	×	×	×	×	×
2	Fuel system (Tank, pipe line and connection, and fuel tank filler tube cap)	Check for leaks Every 5 years or					×			
3	Fuel hoses	Check condition Every 2 years or			×		×		×	
4	Air cleaner element	Replace at			×		×		×	
5	Evaporative emission control system (except evaporative emission canister)	Check for leaks and clogging Every 5 years or					×			
6	Spark plugs	Replace at			×		×		×	
7	Ignition cables	Replace Every 5 years or					×			
8	Distributor cap and rotor	Check Every 5 years or					×			

No.	General maintenance	Service to be performed	Kilometers in thousands / Mileage in thousands	24 / 15	48 / 30	72 / 45	96 / 60	120 / 75	144 / 90	168 / 105
9	Timing Belts	Replace at					×*1		160,000 km*2 (100,000 miles)	
10	Drive Belt (for generator, water pump power steering pump)	Check condition at			×		×		×	
11	Engine Oil	Change Every year or		Every 12,000 km (7,500 miles)						
12	Engine Oil Filter	Replace Every Year or		×	×	×	×	×	×	×
13	Manual Transaxle Oil (Including transfer)	Inspect oil level at			×		×		×	
14	Automatic Transaxle Fluid	Inspect fluid level Every year or		×	×	×	×	×	×	×
		Change fluid at			×		×		×	
15	Engine coolant	Change Every 2 years or			×		×		×	
16	Disc Brake Pads	Inspect for wear Every year or		×	×	×	×	×	×	×
17	Rear Drum Brake Linings and Rear Wheel Cylinders (Vehicles with rear drum brakes)	Inspect for wear and leaks Every 2 years or			×		×		×	
18	Brake Hoses	Check for deterioration or leaks Every year or		×	×	×	×	×	×	×
19	Ball Joint and Steering Linkage Seals	Inspect for grease leaks and damage Every 2 years or			×		×		×	
20	Drive Shaft Boots	Inspect for grease leaks and damage Every year or		×	×	×	×	×	×	×
21	Rear Axle Oil	Inspect oil level at			×		×		×	
22	SRS*3 air bag	Inspection system at		10 years						
23	Exhaust System (Connection Portion of Muffler, Pipings and Converter Heat Shields)	Check and service as required Every 2 years or			×		×		×	

*1 For California, this maintenance is recommended but not required.
*2 Not required if belt was previously changed.
*3 SRS: Supplemental Restraint System

MT1139500187000X

Fig. 9 Expo. 1995

No.	Emission control system maintenance	Service to be performed	Kilometers in thousands / Mileage in thousands	24 / 15	48 / 30	72 / 45	96 / 60	120 / 75	144 / 90	168 / 105
1	Valve clearances (1.8L Engine)	Check and adjust as required at		×	×	×	×	×	×	×
2	Fuel system (Tank, pipe line and connection, and fuel tank filler tube cap)	Check for leaks Every 5 years or					×			
3	Fuel hoses	Check condition Every 2 years or			×		×		×	
4	Air cleaner element	Replace at			×		×		×	
5	Evaporative emission control system (except evaporative emission canister)	Check for leaks and clogging Every 5 years or					×			
6	Spark plugs	Replace at			×		×		×	
7	Ignition cables	Replace Every 5 years or					×			
8	Distributor cap and rotor	Check Every 5 years or					×			

No.	General maintenance	Service to be performed	Kilometers in thousands / Mileage in thousands	24 / 15	48 / 30	72 / 45	96 / 60	120 / 75	144 / 90	168 / 105
9	Timing belts	Replace at					×*1		160,000 km*2 (100,000 miles)	
10	Drive belt (for generator, water pump, power steering pump)	Check condition at			×		×		×	
11	Engine oil	Change Every year or		Every 12,000 km (7,500 miles)						
12	Engine oil filter	Replace Every Year or		×	×	×	×	×	×	×
13	Manual transaxle oil	Check oil level at			×		×		×	
14	Automatic transaxle fluid	Check fluid level Every year or		×	×	×	×	×	×	×
		Change fluid at			×		×		×	
15	Transfer oil	Check oil level			×		×		×	
16	Engine coolant	Change Every 2 years or			×		×		×	
17	Disc brake pads	Inspect for wear Every year or		×	×	×	×	×	×	×
18	Rear drum brake linings and rear wheel cylinders	Inspect for wear and leaks Every 2 years or			×		×		×	
19	Brake hoses	Check for deterioration or leaks Every year or		×	×	×	×	×	×	×
20	Ball Joint and steering linkage seals	Inspect for grease leaks and damage Every 2 years or			×		×		×	
21	Drive shaft boots	Inspect for grease leaks and damage Every year or		×	×	×	×	×	×	×
22	Rear axle oil	Check oil level at			×		×		×	
23	SRS*3 air bag	Inspection system at		10 years						
24	Exhaust system (connection portion of muffler, pipings and converter heat shields)	Check and service as required Every 2 years or			×		×		×	

*1 For California, this maintenance is recommended but not required.
*2 Not required if belt was previously changed.
*3 SRS: Supplemental Restraint System

MT1139600198000X

Fig. 10 Expo. 1996

No.	Emission Control System Maintenance	Service Intervals	Kilometers in Thousands / Mileage in Thousands	24 / 15	48 / 30	72 / 45	80 / 50	96 / 60
1	Check Fuel System (Tank, Line and Connections and Fuel Filler Cap) for Leaks Every 5 Years		or				X	
2	Check Fuel Hoses Every 2 Years for leaks or damage		or		X			X
3	Replace Air Cleaner Element		at		X			X
4	Replace Spark Plugs		at		X			X

GENERAL MAINTENANCE SERVICE FOR PROPER VEHICLE PERFORMANCE

No.	General Maintenance		Service Intervals	Kilometers in Thousands / Mileage in Thousands	24 / 15	48 / 30	72 / 45	80 / 50	96 / 60
5	Timing Belt (Including the Balancer Belt)		Replace	at					X
6	Drive Belt (for Water Pump and Alternator)		Inspect for tension	at		X			X
7	Engine Oil	Non-Turbo	Change Every Year	or	Every 12,000 km (7,500 miles)				
		Turbo	Change Every 6 Months	or	Every 8,000 km (5,000 miles)				
8	Engine Oil Filter	Non-Turbo	Change Every Year	or	X	X	X		X
		Turbo	Change Every Year	or	Every 16,000 km (10,000 miles)				
9	Manual Transaxle Oil		Inspect Oil Level	at		X			X
10	Automatic Transaxle Fluid		Inspect Fluid Level Every Year	or	X	X	X		X
			Change Fluid	at		X			X
11	Engine Coolant		Replace Every 2 Years	or		X			X
12	Disc Brake Pads		Inspect for Wear Every Year	or	X	X	X		X
13	Drum Brake Linings and Rear Wheel Cylinders		Inspect for Wear and Leaks Every 2 Years	or		X			X
14	Brake Hoses		Check for Deterioration or Leaks Every Year	or	X	X	X		X
15	Ball Joint and Steering Linkage Seals		Inspect for Grease Leaks and Damage Every 2 Years	or		X			X
16	Drive Shaft Boots		Inspect for Grease Leaks and Damage Every Year	or	X	X	X		X
17	Rear Axle <AWD>		Change Oil	at		X			X
18	Exhaust System (Connection Portion of Muffler, Pipings and Converter Heat Shields)		Check and Service as Required Every 2 Years	or		X			X

MT1139100162000X

Fig. 11 Galant. 1993

No.	Emission control system maintenance	Service to be performed	Kilometers in thousands / Mileage in thousands	24 / 15	48 / 30	72 / 45	96 / 60	120 / 75	144 / 90	168 / 105
1	Fuel system (Tank, pipe line and connection, and fuel tank filler tube cap)	Check for leaks Every 5 years	or				×			
2	Fuel hoses	Check condition Every 2 years	or		×		×		×	
3	Air cleaner element	Replace	at		×		×		×	
4	Evaporative emission control system (except evaporative emission canister)	Check for leaks and clogging Every 5 years	or				×			
5	Spark plugs	Replace	at		×		×		×	
6	Ignition cables	Replace Every 5 years	or				×			
7	Distributor cap and rotor	Check Every 5 years	or				×			

GENERAL MAINTENANCE SERVICE FOR PROPER VEHICLE PERFORMANCE

No.	General maintenance	Service to be performed	Kilometers in thousands / Mileage in thousands	24 / 15	48 / 30	72 / 45	96 / 60	120 / 75	144 / 90	168 / 105
8	Timing belts	Replace	at				×			
9	Drive belt (for water pump and generator)	Check condition	at		×		×		×	
10	Engine oil	Change Every year	or	Every 12,000 km (7,500 miles)						
11	Engine oil filter	Replace Every Year	or	×	×	×	×	×	×	×
12	Manual transaxle oil	Inspect oil level	at		×		×		×	
13	Automatic transaxle fluid	Inspect fluid level Every year	or	×	×	×	×	×	×	×
		Change fluid	at		×		×		×	
14	Engine coolant	Change Every 2 years	or		×		×		×	
15	Disc brake pads	Inspect for wear Every year	or	×	×	×	×	×	×	×
16	Rear drum brake linings and rear wheel cylinders	Inspect for wear and leaks Every 2 years	or		×		×		×	
17	Brake hoses	Check for deterioration or leaks Every year	or	×	×	×	×	×	×	×
18	Ball joint and steering linkage seals	Inspect for grease leaks and damage Every 2 years	or		×		×		×	
19	Drive shaft boots	Inspect for grease leaks and damage Every year	or	×	×	×	×	×	×	×
20	S.R.S.* air bag system	Inspect system		At 10 years						
21	Exhaust system (connection portion of muffler, pipings and converter heat shields)	Check and service as required Every 2 years	or		×		×		×	

* Supplemental Restraint System

MT1139400163000X

Fig. 12 Galant. 1994

No.	Emission control system maintenance	Service to be performed	Kilometers in thousands	24	48	72	96	120	144	168
			Mileage in thousands	15	30	45	60	75	90	105
1	Fuel system (Tank, pipe line and connection, and fuel tank filler tube cap)	Check for leaks Every 5 years or					×			
2	Fuel hoses	Check condition Every 2 years or			×		×		×	
3	Air cleaner element	Replace at			×		×		×	
4	Evaporative emission control system (except evaporative emission canister)	Check for leaks and clogging Every 5 years or					×			
5	Spark plugs	Replace at			×		×		×	
6	Ignition cables	Replace Every 5 years or					×			
7	Distributor cap and rotor	Check Every 5 years or					×			

MT1139500183010X

Fig. 13 Galant (Part 1 of 3). 1995

No.	General maintenance	Service to be performed	Kilometers in thousands	24	48	72	96	120	144	160	168
			Mileage in thousands	15	30	45	60	75	90	100	105
8	Timing belts	Replace at					×*1			×*2	
9	Drive belt (for water pump and generator)	Check condition at			×		×		×		
10	Engine oil	Change Every year or		Every 12,000 km (7,500 miles)							
11	Engine oil filter	Replace Every Year or*3		×	×	×	×	×	×	×	×
12	Manual transaxle oil	Inspect oil level at			×		×		×		
13	Automatic transaxle fluid	Inspect fluid level Every year or		×	×	×	×	×	×	×	×
		Change fluid at			×		×		×		
14	Engine coolant	Change Every 2 years or			×		×		×		
15	Disc brake pads	Inspect for wear Every year or		×	×	×	×	×	×	×	×
16	Rear drum brake linings and rear wheel cylinders	Inspect for wear and leaks Every 2 years or			×		×		×		
17	Brake hoses	Check for deterioration or leaks Every year or		×	×	×	×	×	×	×	×
18	Ball joint and steering linkage seals	Inspect for grease leaks and damage Every 2 years or			×		×		×		
19	Drive shaft boots	Inspect for grease leaks and damage Every year or		×	×	×	×	×	×	×	×
20	S.R.S.*4 air bag system	Inspect system		At 10 years							
21	Exhaust system (connection portion of muffler, pipings and converter heat shields)	Check and service as required Every 2 years or			×		×		×		

NOTE
*1: For California, this maintenance is recommended but not required.
*2: Not erquired if belt was previously changed.
*3: If the mileage is less than 12,000 km (7,500 miles) each year, the oil filter should be replaced at oil change.
*4: Supplemental Restraint System

MT1139500183020X

Fig. 13 Galant (Part 2 of 3). 1995

No.	Maintenance item	Service to be performed	Kilometers in thousands	24	48	72	96	120	144	168
			Mileage in Thousands	15	30	45	60	75	90	105
22	Engine oil	Change Every 3 months or		Every 4,800 km (3,000 miles)						
23	Engine oil filter	Replace Every 6 months or		Every 9,600 km (6,000 miles)						
24	Air cleaner element	Replace		×	×	×	×	×	×	×
25	Spark plugs	Replace		×	×	×	×	×	×	×
26	Manual transaxle oil	Change oil at			×		×		×	
27	Disc brake pads	Inspect for wear and leaks Every 6 months or		Every 9,600 km (6,000 miles)						
28	Rear drum brake linings and rear wheel cylinders	Inspect for wear and leaks Every year or		×	×	×	×	×	×	×

MT1139500183030X

Fig. 13 Galant (Part 3 of 3). 1995

No.	Emission control system maintenance	Service to be performed	Kilometers in thousands	24	48	72	96	120	144	168
			Mileage in thousands	15	30	45	60	75	90	105
1	Fuel system (Tank, pipe line and connection, and fuel tank filler tube cap)	Check for leaks Every 5 years or					×			
2	Fuel hoses	Check condition Every 2 years or			×		×		×	
3	Air cleaner element	Replace at			×		×		×	
4	Evaporative emission control system (except evaporative emission canister)	Check for leaks and clogging Every 5 years or					×			
5	Spark plugs	Replace at			×		×		×	
6	Ignition cables	Replace Every 5 years or					×			
7	Distributor cap and rotor	Check Every 5 years or					×			
8	Timing belts	Replace at					×*1		160,000Km*2 (100,000 miles)	
9	Drive belt (for generator, water pump, power steering pump)	Check condition at			×		×		×	
10	Engine oil	Change Every year or		Every 12,000 km (7,500 miles)						
11	Engine oil filter	Replace Every Year or*3		×	×	×	×	×	×	×
12	Manual transaxle oil	Check oil level at			×		×		×	
13	Automatic transaxle fluid	Check fluid level Every year or		×	×	×	×	×	×	×
		Change fluid at			×		×		×	
14	Engine coolant	Change Every 2 years or			×		×		×	
15	Disc brake pads	Inspect for wear Every year or		×	×	×	×	×	×	×
16	Rear drum brake linings and rear wheel cylinders	Inspect for wear and leaks Every 2 years or			×		×		×	
17	Brake hoses	Check for deterioration or leaks Every year or		×	×	×	×	×	×	×
18	Ball joint and steering linkage seals	Inspect for grease leaks and damage Every 2 years or			×		×		×	
19	Drive shaft boots	Inspect for grease leaks and damage Every year or		×	×	×	×	×	×	×
20	SRS *4 air bag system	Inspect system		At 10 years						
21	Exhaust system (connection portion of muffler, pipings and converter heat shields)	Check and service as required Every 2 years or			×		×		×	

NOTE
*1: For California, this maintenance is recommended but not required.
*2: Not erquired if belt was previously changed.
*3: If the mileage is less than 12,000 km (7,500 miles) each year, the oil filtter should be replaced at oil change.
*4: Supplemental Restraint System

MT1139600195000X

Fig. 14 Galant. 1996

No.	Emission Control System Maintenance	Service Intervals	Kilometers in Thousands	24	48	72	80	96
			Mileage in Thousands	15	30	45	50	60
1	Check Valve Clearance and Adjust as Required (4G15 only)		at	X	X	X		X
2	Check Fuel System (Tank, Line, Connections and Fuel Filler Cap) for Leaks Every 5 Years		or				X	
3	Check Fuel Hoses for Leaks or Damage Every 2 Years		or		X			X
4	Replace Air Cleaner Element		at		X			X
5	Replace Spark Plugs		at		X			X
No.	General Maintenance	Service Intervals	Kilometers in Thousands	24	48	72	80	96
			Mileage in Thousands	15	30	45	50	60
6	Timing Belt	Replace	at					X
7	Drive Belt (for Water Pump and Alternator)	Inspect for Tension	at		X			X
8	Engine Oil	Change Every Year	or	Every 12,000 km (7,500 miles)				
9	Engine Oil Filter	Change Every Year	or	X	X	X		X
10	Manual Transmission Oil	Inspect Oil Level	at		X			X
11	Automatic Transmission Fluid	Inspect Fluid Level Every Year	or	X	X	X		X
		Change Fluid	at		X			X
12	Engine Coolant	Replace Every 2 Years	or		X			X
13	Disc Brake Pads	Inspect for Wear Every Year	or	X	X	X		X
14	Drum Brake Linings and Rear Wheel Cylinders	Inspect for Wear and Leaks Every 2 Years	or		X			X
15	Brake Hoses	Check for Deterioration or Leaks Every Year	or	X	X	X		X
16	Ball Joint and Steering Linkage Seals	Inspect for Grease Leaks and Damage Every 2 Years	or		X			X
17	Drive Shaft Boots	Inspect for Grease Leaks and Damage Every Year	or	X	X	X		X
18	Exhaust System (Connection Portion of Muffler, Pipings and Converter Heat Shields)	Check and Service as Required Every 2 Years	or		X			X

MT1139100160000X

Fig. 15 Mirage. 1993

No.	Emission control system maintenance	Service to be performed	Kilometers in thousands / Mileage in thousands	24 / 15	48 / 30	72 / 45	96 / 60	120 / 75	144 / 90	168 / 105
1	Valve clearances	Check and adjust as required at		×	×	×	×	×	×	×
2	Fuel system (tank, pipe line and connection, and fuel tank filler tube cap)	Check for leaks Every 5 years or					×			
3	Fuel hoses	Check condition Every 2 years or			×		×		×	
4	Air cleaner element	Replace at			×		×		×	
5	Evaporative emission control system (except evaporative emission canister)*	Check for leaks and clogging Every 5 years or					×			
6	Spark plugs	Replace at			×		×		×	
7	Ignition cables*	Replace Every 5 years or					×			
8	Distributor cap and rotor*	Check Every 5 years or					×			

*: For California only <Up to 1993 models>

MT1139500182010X

Fig. 16 Mirage (Part 1 of 2). 1994–96

No.	General maintenance	Service to be performed	Kilometers in thousands / Mileage in thousands	24 / 15	48 / 30	72 / 45	96 / 60	120 / 75	144 / 90	160 / 100	168 / 105
9	Timing belt	Replace at					×[*2]			×[*3]	
10	Drive belt: for water pump and generator (1.5L Engine); for generator (1.8L Engine)	Check condition at			×		×		×		
11	Engine oil	Change Every year or		Every 12,000 km (7,500 miles)							
12	Engine oil filter	Replace Every year or[*4]		×	×	×	×	×	×	×	×
13	Manual transmission oil	Inspect oil level at			×		×		×		
14	Automatic transmission fluid	Inspect fluid level Every year or		×	×	×	×	×	×	×	×
		Change fluid at			×		×		×		
15	Engine coolant	Change Every 2 years or			×		×		×		
16	Disc brake pads	Inspect for wear Every year or		×	×	×	×	×	×	×	×
17	Rear drum brake linings and rear wheel cylinders (except vehicles with disc brakes for all wheels)	Inspect for wear and leaks Every 2 years or			×		×		×		
18	Brake hoses	Check for deterioration or leaks Every year or		×	×	×	×	×	×	×	×
19	Ball joint and steering linkage seals	Inspect for grease leaks and damage Every 2 years or			×		×		×		
20	Drive shaft boots	Inspect for grease leaks and damage Every year or		×	×	×	×	×	×	×	×
*1 21	SRS air bag	Inspect System		At 10 years							
22	Exhaust system (Connection portion of muffler, pipings and converter heat shields)	Check and service as required Every 2 years or			×		×		×		

NOTE <1994 models>
(1) SRS: Supplementally Restraint System
(2) *1: <From 1994 models>
(3) *2: For California, this maintenance is recommended but not required.
(4) *3: Not required if belt was previously changed. <1995 models>
(5) *4: If the mileage is less than 12,000 km (7,500 miles) each year, the oil filter should be replaced at every oil change. <1995 models>

MT1139500182020X

Fig. 16 Mirage (Part 2 of 2). 1994–96

No.	Emission control system maintenance	Service to be performed	Kilometers in thousands	24	48	72	96	120	144	168
			Mileage in thousands	15	30	45	60	75	90	105
1	Fuel system (tank, pipe line and connection, and fuel tank filler tube cap)*	Check for leaks Every 5 years or					×			
2	Fuel hoses	Check condition Every 2 years or			×		×		×	
3	Air cleaner element	Replace at			×		×		×	
4	Evaporative emission control system (except evaporative emission canister)*	Check for leaks and clogging Every 5 years or					×			
5	Sparks plugs	Replace	except platinum plugs		×		×		×	
			platinum plugs only				×			
6	Ignition cables*	Replace Every 5 years or					×			

NOTE
*: Except for Federal

No.	General maintenance		Service to be performed	Kilometers in thousands	24	48	72	96	120	144	168
				Mileage in thousands	15	30	45	60	75	90	105
7	Timing belt		Replace at					×*			
8	Drive belt (for Generator)		Check condition at			×		×		×	
9	Engine oil	Non-Turbo	Change Every year or		Every 12,000 km (7,500 miles)						
		Turbo	Change Every 6 months or		Every 8,000 km (5,000 miles)						
10	Engine oil filter	Non-Turbo	Replace Every year or		×	×	×	×	×	×	×
		Turbo	Replace Every year or		Every 16,000 km (10,000 miles)						
11	Manual transmission (incl. transfer) oil		Inspect oil level at			×		×		×	
12	Automatic transmission fluid		Inspect fluid level Every year or		×	×	×	×	×	×	×
			Change fluid at			×		×		×	
13	Engine coolant		Change Every 2 years or			×		×		×	
14	Disc brake pads		Inspect for wear Every year or		×	×	×	×	×	×	×

NOTE
*: For California, this maintenance is recommended but not required.

MT1139500184010X

Fig. 17 Montero (Part 1 of 2). 1993–94

No.	General maintenance	Service to be performed	Kilometers in thousands	24	48	72	96	120	144	168
			Mileage in thousands	15	30	45	60	75	90	105
15	Brake hoses	Check for deterioration or leaks Every year or		×	×	×	×	×	×	×
16	Ball joint and steering linkage seals	Inspect for grease leaks and damage Every 2 years or			×		×		×	
17	Drive shaft boots	Inspect for grease leaks and damage Every year or		×	×	×	×	×	×	×
18	Rear axle oil <AWD>	Change oil			×		×		×	
19	SRS airbag	Inspect system		At 10 years						
20	Exhaust system (connection portion of muffler, pipings and converter heat shields)	Check and service as required Every 2 years or			×		×		×	

MT1139500184020X

Fig. 17 Montero (Part 2 of 2). 1993–94

No.	Emission Control System Maintenance	Service Intervals	Kilometers in Thousands	24	48	72	96	120	144	160	168	192
			Mileage in Thousands	15	30	45	60	75	90	100	105	120
1	Fuel System (Tank, Pipe Line and Connection, and Fuel Tank Filler Tube Cap)	Check for Leaks Every 5 Years or					X					X
2	Fuel Hoses	Check Condition Every 2 Years or			X		X		X			X
3	Air Cleaner Element	Replace at			X		X		X			X
4	Positive Crankcase Ventilation System (PCV system)*	Clean at		Every 160,000 km (100,000 miles)								
5	Evaporative Emission Control System* (Except for Evaporative Emission Canister)	Check for Leaks and Clogging Every 5 Years or					X					X
6	Evaporative Emission Canister*	Replace at		Every 160,000 km (100,000 miles)								
7	Spark Plugs	Replace	Except Platinum Plugs at		X		X		X			X
			Platinum Plugs Only at				X					X
8	Ignition Cables*	Replace Every 5 Years or					X					X
9	EGR System* (Except 6G72 MFI Engine)	EGR Valve	Replace at	Every 160,000 km (100,000 miles)								
10	Distributor Cap and Rotor (6G72-12 VALVE Engine)	Check Every 5 Years or					X					X

NOTE
*: Except for California

MT1139500185010X

Fig. 18 Montero (Part 1 of 2). 1995

No.	General Maintenance	Service Intervals	Kilometers in Thousands	24	48	72	96	120	144	160	168	192
			Mileage in Thousands	15	30	45	60	75	90	100	105	120
11	Timing Belt	Replace at					X*3			X*4		X*3
12	Drive Belt (for Generator, Water Pump, Power Steering Pump)	Check Condition at			X		X		X			X
13	Engine Oil	Change Oil Every 12 Months or		Every 12,000 km (7,500 miles)								
14	Engine Oil Filter	Replace Every 12 Months or*5		X	X	X	X	X	X		X	X
15	Manual Transmission and Transfer Oil	Check Oil Level at			X		X		X			X
16	Automatic Transmission Fluid	Check Fluid Level Every 12 Months or		X	X	X	X	X	X		X	X
17	Automatic Transmission and Transfer Fluid	Change Fluid at			X		X		X			X
18	Engine Coolant	Change Coolant Every 2 Years or			X		X		X			X
19	Disc Brake Pads	Inspect for Wear Every 12 Months or		X	X	X	X	X	X		X	X
20	Brake Hoses	Check for Deterioration or Leaks Every 12 Months or		X	X	X	X	X	X		X	X
21	Ball Joint and Steering Linkage Seals	Inspect for Grease Leaks and Damage Every 2 Years or			X		X		X			X
22	Drive Shaft Boots	Inspect for Grease Leaks and Damage Every 12 Months or		X	X	X	X	X	X		X	X
23	Ball Joints With Grease Fitting	Lubricate with Grease Every 2 Years or			X		X		X		X	X
24	Front Axle and Rear Axle — With LSD*1	Change Oil at			X		X		X		X	X
	Front Axle and Rear Axle — Without LSD*1	Inspect Oil Level at			X		X		X		X	X
25	Propeller Shaft Joints	Lubricate with Grease Every 2 Years or			X		X		X		X	X
26	Exhaust System Connection Portion of Muffler, Piping and Converter Heat Shields	Check and Service as Required Every 2 Years or			X		X		X		X	X
27	SRS*2 air bag	Inspect the SRS System at		10 years								

NOTE
*1: LSD: Limited-slip differential
*2: SRS: Supplemental Restraint System
*3: For California, this maintenance is recommended but not required
*4: Not required if belt was previously changed
*5: If the mileage is less than 12,000 km (7,500 miles) each year, the oil filter should be replaced at every oil change

MT1139500185020X

Fig. 18 Montero (Part 2 of 2). 1995

No.	Emission Control System Maintenance	Service Intervals										
			Kilometers in Thousands	24	48	72	96	120	144	160	168	192
			Mileage in Thousands	15	30	45	60	75	90	100	105	120
1	Fuel System (Tank, Pipe Line and Connection, and Fuel Tank Filler Tube Cap)	Check for Leaks Every 5 Years or					X					X
2	Fuel Hoses	Check Condition Every 2 Years or			X		X		X			X
3	Air Cleaner Element	Replace at			X		X		X			X
4	Evaporative Emission Control System* (Except for Canister)	Check for Leaks and Clogging Every 5 Years or					X					X
5	Spark Plugs	Replace	Except Platinum Plugs at		X		X		X			X
			Platinum Plugs Only at				X					X
6	Ignition Cables	Replace Every 5 Years or					X					X
7	Distributor Cap and Rotor (3.0L-12 VALVE Engine)	Check Every 5 Years or					X					X

MT1139600196010X

Fig. 19 Montero (Part 1 of 2). 1996

No.	General Maintenance	Service Intervals	Kilometers in Thousands	24	48	72	96	120	144	160	168	192
			Mileage in Thousands	15	30	45	60	75	90	100	105	120
8	Timing Belt	Replace at					X*3			X*4		X*3
9	Drive Belt (for Generator, Water Pump, Power Steering Pump)	Check Condition at			X		X		X			X
10	Engine Oil	Change Oil Every 12 Months or		Every 12,000 km (7,500 miles)								
11	Engine Oil Filter	Replace Every 12 Months or*5		X	X	X	X	X	X		X	X
12	Manual Transmission oil	Check Oil Level at			X		X		X			X
13	Automatic Transmission Fluid	Check Fluid Level Every 12 Months or		X	X	X	X	X	X		X	X
14	Automatic Transmission Fluid	Change Fluid at			X		X		X			X
15	Transfer oil	Check oil level			X		X		X			X
16	Engine Coolant	Change Coolant Every 2 Years or			X		X		X			X
17	Disc Brake Pads	Inspect for Wear Every 12 Months or		X	X	X	X	X	X		X	X
18	Brake Hoses	Check for Deterioration or Leaks Every 12 Months or		X	X	X	X	X	X		X	X
19	Ball Joint and Steering Linkage Seals	Inspect for Grease Leaks and Damage Every 2 Years or			X		X		X			X
20	Drive Shaft Boots	Inspect for Grease Leaks and Damage Every 12 Months or		X	X	X	X	X	X		X	X
21	Ball Joints With Grease Fitting	Lubricate with Grease Every 2 Years or			X		X		X		X	X
22	Front Axle and Rear Axle — With LSD*1	Change Oil at			X		X		X		X	X
	Front Axle and Rear Axle — Without LSD*1	Inspect Oil Level at			X		X		X		X	X
23	Propeller Shaft Joints	Lubricate with Grease Every 2 Years or			X		X		X		X	X
24	Exhaust System Connection Portion of Muffler, Piping and Converter Heat Shields	Check and Service as Required Every 2 Years or			X		X		X		X	X
25	SRS*2 air bag	Inspect the SRS System at		10 years								

NOTE
*1: LSD: Limited-slip differential
*2: SRS: Supplemental Restraint System
*3: For California, this maintenance is recommended but not required
*4: Not required if belt was previously changed
*5: If the mileage is less than 12,000 km (7,500 miles) each year, the oil filter should be replaced at every oil change

MT1139600196020X

Fig. 19 Montero (Part 2 of 2). 1996

No	Emission Control System Maintenance	Service Intervals	Kilometers in Thousands	24	48	72	80	96	120	128	144	160	168	192
			Mileage in Thousands	15	30	45	50	60	75	80	90	100	105	120
1	Check Fuel System (Tank, Pipe Line Connection, and Fuel Filler Cap) for Leaks Every 5 Years	or					×					×		
2	Replace Vacuum Hoses, Crankcase Ventilation Hoses and Water Hoses Every 5 Years	or						×						×
3	Check Fuel Hoses Every 2 Years	or			×			×			×			×
4	Replace Air Cleaner Element	at			×			×			×			×
5	Clean Crankcase Emission Control System (PCV Valve)*	at								×				
6	Check Evaporative Emission Control System (except Canister) for Leaks and Clogging* Every 5 Years	or						×						×
7	Replace Canister*	at										×		
8	Replace Spark Plugs	at			×			×			×			×
9	Replace Ignition Cables* Every 5 Years	or						×						×
10	Replace EGR System (EGR valve) <2.4L Engine>*	at					×					×		
11	Replace Oxygen Sensor*	at								×				
12	Check Distributor Cap and Rotor Every 5 Years	or						×						×
13	Check Intake Temperature Control System* Every 5 Years	or						×						×

MT1139100158010X

Fig. 20 Pickup (Part 1 of 2). 1993–94

No	General Maintenance		Service Interval		Kilometers in Thousands	12	24	36	48	60	72	84	96
					Mileage in Thousands	7.5	15	22.5	30	37.5	45	52.5	60
14	Timing Belt		Replace	at									×
15	Drive belt (For Water Pump, Alternator)		Check	at					×				×
16	Engine Oil		Change Every Year	or		×	×	×	×	×	×	×	×
17	Engine Oil Filter		Change Every Year	or			×		×		×		×
18	Manual Transmission (include Transfer) Oil		Check Oil Level	at					×				×
19	Automatic Transmission Fluid		Check Fluid Level Every Year	or			×		×		×		×
20	Automatic Transmission and Transfer Fluid*1		Change Fluid	or					×				×
21	Engine Coolant		Change Every 2 Years	or					×				×
22	Disc Brake Pads		Inspect for Wear Every Year	or			×		×		×		×
23	Drum Brake Linings and Wheel Cylinders		Inspect for Wear and Leaks Every 2 years	or					×				×
24	Brake Hoses		Check for Deterioration or Leaks Every Year	or			×		×		×		×
25	Ball Joint and Steering Linkage Seals		Inspect for Grease Leaks and Damage Every 2 Years	or					×				×
26	Drive Shaft Boots		Inspect for Grease Leaks and Damage Every Year	or			×		×		×		×
27	Ball Joints with Grease Fitting		Lubricate Grease Every Year	or			×		×		×		×
28	Front Axle and Rear Axle	With LSD*2	Change Oil	at					×				×
		Without LSD*2	Inspect Oil Level	at					×				×
29	Propeller Shaft Joint		Lubricate Grease Every 2 Years	or					×				×
30	Exhaust System (Connection Portion of Muffler, Pipings and Converter Heat Shields)		Check and Service as Required Every 2 Years	or					×				×

NOTE
*1 In case of RWD, change fluid when severe usage conditions only.
*2 LSD – Limited slip differential

MT1139100158020X

Fig. 20 Pickup (Part 2 of 2). 1993–94

No.	Emission Control System Maintenance	Service Intervals		Kilometers in Thousands	24	48	72	96	120	144	160	168	192
				Mileage in Thousands	15	30	45	60	75	90	100	105	120
1	Fuel System (Tank, Pipe Line and Connection and Fuel Tank Filler Tube Cap)	Check for Leaks	Every 5 Years	or				x					x
2	Fuel Hoses	Check	Every 2 years	or		x		x		x			x
3	Air Cleaner Element	Replace		at		x		x		x			x
4	Positive Crankcase Ventilation System* (PCV System)	Clean		at							x		
5	Evaporative Emission Control System (except Evaporative Emission Canister)	Check for Leaks and Clogging	Every 5 Years	or				x					x
6	Evaporative Emission Canister*	Replace		at							x		
7	Spark Plugs	Replace		at		x		x		x			x
8	Ignition Cables	Replace	Every 5 Years	or				x					x
9	EGR System (EGR valve) <2.4L Engine>*	Replace		at							x		
11	Distributor Cap and Rotor	Check	Every 5 Years	or				x					x

NOTE
* For Federal only

MT1139500181010X

Fig. 21 Pickup (Part 1 of 2). 1995

No.	General Maintenance		Service Interval		Kilometers in Thousands	24	48	72	96	120	144	160	168	192
					Mileage in Thousands	15	30	45	60	75	90	100	105	120
12	Timing Belt		Replace		at				x*1			x*2		x*1
13	Drive belt		Check		at		x		x		x			x
14	Engine Oil		Change	Every Year	or	Every 12,000 km (7,500 Miles)								
15	Engine Oil Filter		Change	Every Year*3	or	x	x	x	x	x	x		x	x
16	Manual Transmission (include Transfer) Oil		Check Oil Level		at		x		x		x			x
17	Automatic Transmission Fluid		Check Fluid Level	Every Year	or	x	x	x	x	x	x		x	x
19	Engine Coolant		Change	Every 2 Years	or		x		x		x			x
20	Disc Brake Pads		Inspect for Wear	Every Year	or	x	x	x	x	x	x		x	x
21	Drum Brake Linings and Wheel Cylinders		Inspect for Wear and Leaks	Every 2 years	or		x		x		x			x
22	Brake Hoses		Check for Deterioration or Leaks	Every Year	or	x	x	x	x	x	x		x	x
23	Ball Joint and Steering Linkage Seals		Inspect for Grease Leaks and Damage	Every 2 Years	or		x		x		x			x
24	Drive Shaft Boots		Inspect for Grease Leaks and Damage	Every Year	or	x	x	x	x	x	x		x	x
25	Ball Joints with Grease Fitting		Lubricate Grease	Every 2 Years	or		x		x		x			x
26	Front Axle and Rear Axle	With LSD*4	Change Oil		at		x		x		x			x
		Without LSD*4	Inspect Oil Level		at		x		x		x			x
27	Propeller Shaft Joint		Lubricate Grease	Every 2 Years	or		x		x		x			x
28	Exhaust System (Connection Portion of Muffler, Pipings and Converter Heat Shields)		Check and Service as Required	Every 2 Years	or		x		x		x			x

NOTE
*1: For California, this maintenance is recommended but not required
*2: Not required if belt was previously changed
*3: If the mileage is less than 12,000 km (7,500 miles) each year, the oil filter should be replaced at every oil change.
*4: LSD – Limited slip differential

MT1139500181020X

Fig. 21 Pickup (Part 2 of 2). 1995

No.	Emission Control System Maintenance	Service Intervals		Kilometers in Thousands / Mileage in Thousands	24 / 15	48 / 30	72 / 45	96 / 60	120 / 75	144 / 90	160 / 100	168 / 105	192 / 120
1	Fuel System (Tank, Pipe Line and Connection, and Fuel Tank Filler Tube Cap)	Check for Leaks	Every 5 Years	or				×					×
2	Fuel Hoses	Check	Every 2 years	or		×		×		×			×
3	Air Cleaner Element	Replace		at		×		×		×			×
5	Evaporative Emission Control System (except Evaporative Emission Canister)	Check for Leaks and Clogging	Every 5 Years	or				×					×
7	Spark Plugs	Replace		at		×		×		×			×
8	Ignition Cables	Replace	Every 5 Years	or				×					×
11	Distributor Cap and Rotor	Check	Every 5 Years	or				×					×

MT1139600194010X

Fig. 22 Pickup (Part 1 of 2). 1996

No.	General Maintenance		Service Interval		Kilometers in Thousands / Mileage in Thousands	24 / 15	48 / 30	72 / 45	96 / 60	120 / 75	144 / 90	160 / 100	168 / 105	192 / 120
12	Timing Belt		Replace		at				×*1			×*2		×*1
13	Drive belt		Check		at		×		×		×			×
14	Engine Oil		Change	Every Year	or	Every 12,000 km (7,500 Miles)								
15	Engine Oil Filter		Change	Every Year*3	or	×	×	×	×	×	×		×	×
16	Manual Transmission Oil		Check Oil Level		at		×		×		×			×
17	Automatic Transmission Fluid		Check Fluid Level	Every Year	or	×	×	×	×	×	×		×	×
19	Engine Coolant		Change	Every 2 Years	or		×		×		×			×
20	Disc Brake Pads		Inspect for Wear	Every Year	or	×	×	×	×	×	×		×	×
21	Drum Brake Linings and Wheel Cylinders		Inspect for Wear and Leaks	Every 2 years	or		×		×		×			×
22	Brake Hoses		Check for Deterioration or Leaks	Every Year	or	×	×	×	×	×	×		×	×
23	Ball Joint and Steering Linkage Seals		Inspect for Grease Leaks and Damage	Every 2 Years	or		×		×		×			×
24	Drive Shaft Boots		Inspect for Grease Leaks and Damage	Every Year	or	×	×	×	×	×	×		×	×
25	Ball Joints with Grease Fitting		Lubricate Grease	Every 2 Years	or		×		×		×			×
26	Front Axle and Rear Axle	With LSD*4	Change Oil		at		×		×		×			×
		Without LSD*4	Inspect Oil Level		at		×		×		×			×
27	Propeller Shaft Joint		Lubricate Grease	Every 2 Years	or		×		×		×			×
28	Exhaust System (Connection Portion of Muffler, Pipings and Converter Heat Shields)		Check and Service as Required	Every 2 Years	or		×		×		×			×

NOTE
*1: For California, this maintenance is recommended but not required.
*2: Not required if belt was previously changed.
*3: If the mileage is less than 12,000 km (7,500 miles) each year, the oil filter should be replaced at every oil change.
*4: LSD – Limited slip differential

MT1139600194020X

Fig. 22 Pickup (Part 2 of 2). 1996

R : REPLACE
I : INSPECT, AFTER INSPECTION, CLEAN, ADJUST, REPAIR OR REPLACE IF NECESSARY

NO	DESCRIPTION	MILES X 1000 / KILOMETERS X 1000	7.5 / 12	15 / 24	22.5 / 36	30 / 48	37.5 / 60	45 / 72	52.5 / 84	60 / 96
	EMISSION CONTROL ITEMS									
1	ENGINE OIL AND FILTER*		R	R	R	R	R	R	R	R
2	VALVE CLEARANCE			I		I		I		I
3	FUEL FILTER								R	
4	FUEL LINES AND CONNECTIONS								I	
5	VACUUM, CRANKCASE VENTILATION HOSES								I	
6	FUEL HOSE, VAPOR HOSE & FUEL FILLER CAP								I	
7	AIR CLEANER FILTER					R				R
8	SPARK PLUGS					R				R

*Replace oil and filter at mileage interval or 6 months whichever occurs first.

MT1139100159010X

Fig. 23 Precis (Part 1 of 2)

NO	DESCRIPTION	MILES X 1000	7.5	15	22.5	30	37.5	45	52.5	60
		KILOMETERS X 1000	12	24	36	48	60	72	84	96
	GENERAL ITEMS									
1	DRIVE BELT (WATER PUMP AND ALTERNATOR)					I				I
2	ENGINE COOLANT*					R				R
3	TIMING BELT									R
4	MANUAL TRANSAXLE OIL					I				I
5	AUTO TRANSAXLE OIL			I		R		I		R
6	BRAKE FLUID*					R				R
7	BRAKE HOSES, LINES			I		I		I		I
8	REAR BRAKE DRUMS/LININGS/PARKING BRAKE					I				I
9	BRAKE PADS, CALIPERS, ROTORS			I		I		I		I
10	EXHAUST PIPE CONNECTIONS, MUFFLER & SUSPENSION BOLTS					I				I
11	STEERING GEAR RACK, LINKAGE & BOOTS					I				I
12	WHEEL BEARING GREASE					I				I
13	DRIVESHAFTS & BOOTS			I		I		I		I

*Change coolant and fluid at mileage interval or at 2 years whichever occurs first.

MT1139100159020X

Fig. 23 Precis (Part 2 of 2)

No.	General Maintenance		Service Intervals	Kilometers in Thousands	24	48	72	80	96
				Mileage in Thousands	15	30	45	50	60
5	Timing Belt		Replace	at					X
6	Drive Belt (for Alternator)		Inspect for Tension	at		X			X
7	Engine Oil	Non-Turbo	Change Every Year	or	Every 12,000 km (7,500 miles)				
		Turbo	Change Every 6 Months		Every 8,000 km (5,000 miles)				
8	Engine Oil Filter	Non-Turbo	Change Every Year	or	X	X	X		X
		Turbo	Change Every Year		Every 16,000 km (10,000 miles)				
9	Manual Transaxle Oil		Inspect Oil Level	at		X			X
10	Automatic Transaxle Fluid		Inspect Fluid Level Every Year	or	X	X	X		X
			Change Fluid	at		X			X
11	Engine Coolant		Replace Every 2 Years	or		X			X
12	Disc Brake Pads		Inspect for Wear Every Year	or	X	X	X		X
13	Brake Hoses		Check for Deterioration or Leaks Every Year	or	X	X	X		X
14	Ball Joint and Steering Linkage Seals		Inspect for Grease Leaks and Damage Every 2 Years	or		X			X
15	Drive Shaft Boots		Inspect for Grease Leaks and Damage Every Year	or	X	X	X		X
16	Rear Axle <AWD>	With LSD	Change Oil			X			X
		Without LSD	Inspect Oil Level			X			X
17	Exhaust System (Connection Portion of Muffler, Pipings and Converter Heat Shields)		Check and Service as Required Every 2 Years	or		X			X

MT1139100157000X

Fig. 24 3000GT. 1993–94

No.	Emission control system maintenance	Service to be performed		Kilometers in thousands	24	48	72	96	120	144	168
				Mileage in thousands	15	30	45	60	75	90	105
1	Fuel system (tank, pipe line and connection, and fuel tank filler tube cap)[*1]	Check for leaks Every 5 years or						×			
2	Fuel hoses	Check condition Every 2 years or				×		×		×	
3	Air cleaner element	Replace at				×		×		×	
4	Evaporative emission control system (except evaporative emission canister)[*1]	Check for leaks and clogging Every 5 years or						×			
5	Sparks plugs	Replace	except platinum plugs			×		×		×	
			platinum plugs only					×			
6	Ignition cables[*1]	Replace Every 5 years or						×			

NOTE
*1: Except for Federal

No.	General maintenance		Service to be performed	Kilometers in thousands	24	48	72	96	120	144	168
				Mileage in thousands	15	30	45	60	75	90	105
7	Timing belt		Replace at					×[*1]			At 160,000 km[*2] (100,000 miles)
8	Drive belt (for Generator, Water pump, Power steering pump)		Check condition at			×		×		×	
9	Engine oil	Non-Turbo	Change Every year or		Every 12,000 km (7,500 miles)						
		Turbo	Change Every 6 months or		Every 8,000 km (5,000 miles)						
10	Engine oil filter	Non-Turbo	Replace Every year[*3] or		×	×	×	×	×	×	×
		Turbo	Replace Every year or		Every 16,000 km (10,000 miles)						
11	Manual transmission (incl. transfer) oil		Inspect oil level at			×		×		×	
12	Automatic transmission fluid		Inspect fluid level Every year or		×	×	×	×	×	×	×
			Change fluid at			×		×		×	

NOTE
*1: For California, this maintenance is recommended but not required.
*2: Not required if belt was previously changed.
*3: If the mileage is less than 12,000 km (7,500 miles) each year, the oil filter should be replaced at every oil change.

MT1139500180010X

Fig. 25 3000GT (Part 1 of 2). 1995–96

No.	General maintenance	Service to be performed	Kilometers in thousands	24	48	72	96	120	144	168
			Mileage in thousands	15	30	45	60	75	90	105
13	Engine coolant	Change Every 2 years or			×		×		×	
14	Disc brake pads	Inspect for wear Every year or		×	×	×	×	×	×	×
15	Brake hoses	Check for deterioration or leaks Every year or		×	×	×	×	×	×	×
16	Ball joint and steering linkage seals	Inspect for grease leaks and damage Every 2 years or			×		×		×	
17	Drive shaft boots	Inspect for grease leaks and damage Every year or		×	×	×	×	×	×	×
18	Rear axle oil <AWD>	Inspect oil level			×		×		×	
19	SRS airbag	Inspect system		At 10 years						
20	Exhaust system (connection portion of muffler, pipings and converter heat shields)	Check and service as required Every 2 years or			×		×		×	

MT1139500180020X

Fig. 25 3000GT (Part 2 of 2). 1995–96

VEHICLE MAINTENANCE SCHEDULES

Nissan

INDEX

	Page No.	Fig. No.
Altima		
1993–95	0-89	1
1996	0-90	2
Maxima		
1993–94	0-90	3
1995	0-91	4
1996	0-91	5
NX1600, NX2000 & 1993–95 Sentra & 200SX		
All	0-92	6
Pathfinder & Pickup		
1993–95	0-92	7
Pathfinder		
1996	0-93	8
Pickup		
1996	0-93	9
Quest		
1993–95	0-94	10
1996	0-94	11
Sentra & 200SX		
1996	0-95	12
240SX		
1993–95	0-95	13
1996	0-96	14
300ZX		
1993–95	0-96	15
1996	0-97	17

Abbreviations: R = Replace. I = Inspect. Correct or replace if necessary.

[ ]: At the mileage intervals only

MAINTENANCE OPERATION		MAINTENANCE INTERVAL															
Perform at number of miles, kilometers or months, whichever comes first.	Miles x 1,000 (km x 1,000) Months	3.75 (6) 3	7.5 (12) 6	11.25 (18) 9	15 (24) 12	18.75 (30) 15	22.5 (36) 18	26.25 (42) 21	30 (48) 24	33.75 (54) 27	37.5 (60) 30	41.25 (66) 33	45 (72) 36	48.75 (78) 39	52.5 (84) 42	56.25 (90) 45	60 (96) 48
Emission control system maintenance																	
Drive belts	See NOTE (1)																I*
Air cleaner filter	See NOTE (2)								[R]								[R]
Vapor lines									I*								I*
Fuel lines									I*								I*
Fuel filter	See NOTE (3)*																
Engine coolant	See NOTE (4)																R*
Engine oil		R	R	R	R	R	R	R	R	R	R	R	R	R	R	R	R
Engine oil filter (Use Nissan PREMIUM type or equivalent)		R	R	R	R	R	R	R	R	R	R	R	R	R	R	R	R
Spark plugs									[R]								[R]
Intake & exhaust valve clearance	See NOTE (5)*																
Chassis and body maintenance																	
Brake lines & cables					I				I				I				I
Brake pads, discs, drums & linings			I		I		I		I		I		I		I		I
Manual & automatic transaxle oil	See NOTE (6)				I				I				I				I
Steering gear & linkage, axle & suspension parts			I		I		I		I		I		I		I		I
Steering linkage ball joints & front suspension ball joints			I		I		I		I		I		I		I		I
Exhaust system			I		I		I		I		I		I		I		I
Drive shaft boots			I		I		I		I		I		I		I		I
Air bag system	See NOTE (7)																

NOTE: (1) After 60,000 miles (96,000 km) or 48 months, inspect every 15,000 miles (24,000 km) or 12 months.
(2) If operating mainly in dusty conditions, more frequent maintenance may be required.
(3) If vehicle is operated under extremely adverse weather conditions or in areas where ambient temperatures are either extremely low or extremely high, the filters might become clogged. In such an event, replace them immediately.
(4) After 60,000 miles (96,000 km) or 48 months, replace every 30,000 miles (48,000 km) or 24 months.
(5) If valve noise increases, inspect valve clearance.
(6) If towing a trailer, using a camper or a car-top carrier, or driving on rough or muddy roads, change (not just inspect) oil at every 30,000 miles (48,000 km) or 24 months.
(7) Inspect the air bag system 10 years after the date of manufacture as noted on the F.M.V.S.S. certification label.
(8) Maintenance items and intervals with "*" are recommended by NISSAN for reliable vehicle operation. The owner need not perform such maintenance in order to maintain the emission warranty or manufacturer recall liability. Other maintenance items and intervals are required.

NS1139100136000X

Fig. 1 Altima. 1993–95

Abbreviations: R = Replace. I = Inspect. Correct or replace if necessary. [ ]: At the mileage intervals only

MAINTENANCE OPERATION Perform at number of miles, kilometers or months, whichever comes first.	Miles x 1,000 (km x 1,000) Months	7.5 (12) 6	15 (24) 12	22.5 (36) 18	30 (48) 24	37.5 (60) 30	45 (72) 36	52.5 (84) 42	60 (96) 48
Emission control system maintenance									
Drive belts	See NOTE (1)								I*
Air cleaner filter					[R]				[R]
Vapor lines					I*				I*
Fuel lines					I*				I*
Fuel filter	See NOTE (2)*								
Engine coolant	See NOTE (3)								R*
Engine oil		R	R	R	R	R	R	R	R
Engine oil filter (Use Nissan PREMIUM type or equivalent)		R	R	R	R	R	R	R	R
Spark plugs					[R]				[R]
Intake & exhaust valve clearance	See NOTE (4)*								
Chassis and body maintenance									
Brake lines & cables			I		I		I		I
Brake pads, discs, drums & linings			I		I		I		I
Manual & automatic transaxle oil			I		I		I		I
Steering gear linkage, axle & suspension parts					I				I
Exhaust system					I				I
Drive shaft boots			I		I		I		I
Air bag system	See NOTE (5)								

NOTE: (1) After 60,000 miles (96,000 km) or 48 months, inspect every 15,000 miles (24,000 km) or 12 months.
(2) If vehicle is operated under extremely adverse weather conditions or in areas where ambient temperatures are either extremely low or extremely high, the filters might become clogged. In such an event, replace them immediately.
(3) After 60,000 miles (96,000 km) or 48 months, replace every 30,000 miles (48,000 km) or 24 months.
(4) If valve noise increases, inspect valve clearance.
(5) Inspect the air bag system 10 years after the date of manufacture noted on the FMVSS certification label.
*** Maintenance items and intervals with "*" are recommended by NISSAN for reliable vehicle operation. The owner need not perform such maintenance in order to maintain the emission warranty or manufacturer recall liability. Other maintenance items and intervals are required.**

NS1139600152000X

Fig. 2 Altima. 1996

Abbreviations: R = Replace I = Inspect. Correct or replace if necessary [ ]: At the mileage intervals only

MAINTENANCE OPERATION Perform at number of miles, kilometers or months, whichever comes first.	Miles x 1,000 (km x 1,000) Months	3.75 (6) 3	7.5 (12) 6	11.25 (18) 9	15 (24) 12	18.75 (30) 15	22.5 (36) 18	26.25 (42) 21	30 (48) 24	33.75 (54) 27	37.5 (60) 30	41.25 (66) 33	45 (72) 36	48.75 (78) 39	52.5 (84) 42	56.25 (90) 45	60 (96) 48
Emission control system maintenance																	
Drive belts	See NOTE (1)																I*
Air cleaner filter	See NOTE (2)								[R]								[R]
Vapor lines									I*								I*
Fuel lines									I*								I*
Fuel filter	See NOTE (3)*																
Engine coolant									R*								R*
Engine oil		R	R	R	R	R	R	R	R	R	R	R	R	R	R	R	R
Engine oil filter (Use Nissan PREMIUM type or equivalent.)		R	R	R	R	R	R	R	R	R	R	R	R	R	R	R	R
Spark plugs									[R]								[R]
Chassis and body maintenance																	
Brake lines & cables					I				I				I				I
Brake pads, discs, drums & linings			I		I		I		I		I		I		I		I
Manual & automatic transaxle oil (Transfer & differential gear oil 4WD)	See NOTE (4)				I				I				I				I
Steering gear & linkage, axle & suspension parts			I		I		I		I		I		I		I		I
Steering linkage ball joints & front suspension ball joints			I		I		I		I		I		I		I		I
Exhaust system			I		I		I		I		I		I		I		I
Drive shaft boots, (Propeller shaft 4WD)			I		I		I		I		I		I		I		I

NOTE: (1) After 60,000 miles (96,000 km) or 48 months, inspect every 15,000 miles (24,000 km) or 12 months.
(2) If operating mainly in dusty conditions, more frequent maintenance may be required.
(3) If vehicle is operated under extremely adverse weather conditions or in areas where ambient temperatures are either extremely low or extremely high, the filters might become clogged. In such an event, replace them immediately.
(4) If towing a trailer, using a camper or a car-top carrier, or driving on rough or muddy roads, change (not just inspect) oil at every 30,000 miles (48,000 km) or 24 months.
(5) Maintenance items and intervals with "*" are recommended by NISSAN for reliable vehicle operation. The owner need not perform such maintenance in order to maintain the emission warranty or manufacturer recall liability. Other maintenance itmes and intervals are required.

NS1139100133000X

Fig. 3 Maxima. 1993–94

Abbreviations: R = Replace. I = Inspect. Correct or replace if necessary.

[ ]: At the mileage intervals only

MAINTENANCE OPERATION		MAINTENANCE INTERVAL							
Perform at number of miles, kilometers or months, whichever comes first.	Miles x 1,000	7.5	15	22.5	30	37.5	45	52.5	60
	(km x 1,000)	(12)	(24)	(36)	(48)	(60)	(72)	(84)	(96)
	Months	6	12	18	24	30	36	42	48
Emission control system maintenance									
Drive belts	See NOTE (1)								I*
Air cleaner filter					[R]				[R]
Vapor lines					I*				I*
Fuel lines					I*				I*
Fuel filter	See NOTE (2)*								
Engine coolant	See NOTE (3)								R*
Engine oil		R	R	R	R	R	R	R	R
Engine oil filter (Use part No. 15208-31U00 or equivalent.)			R		R		R		R
Spark plugs (Use PLATINUM-TIPPED type)									[R]
Intake & exhaust valve clearance	See NOTE (4)								
Chassis and body maintenance									
Brake lines & cables			I		I		I		I
Brake pads & discs			I		I		I		I
Manual & automatic transaxle oil			I		I		I		I
Steering gear linkage, axle & suspension parts					I				I
Exhaust system					I				I
Drive shaft boots			I		I		I		I
Air bag system	See NOTE (5)								

NOTE: (1) After 60,000 miles (96,000 km) or 48 months, inspect every 15,000 miles (24,000 km) or 12 months.
(2) If vehicle is operated under extremely adverse weather conditions or in areas where ambient temperatures are either extremely low or extremely high, the filters might become clogged. In such an event, replace them immediately.
(3) After 60,000 miles (96,000 km) or 48 months, replace every 30,000 miles (48,000 km) or 24 months.
(4) If valve noise increases, inspect valve clearance.
(5) Inspect the air bag system 10 years after the date of manufacture as noted on the F.M.V.S.S. certification label.
(6) Maintenance items and intervals with "*" are recommended by NISSAN for reliable vehicle operation. The owner need not perform such maintenance in order to maintain the emission warranty or manufacturer recall liability. Other maintenance items and intervals are required.

NS1139500144000X

Fig. 4 Maxima. 1995

Abbreviations: R = Replace. I = Inspect. Correct or replace if necessary.

[ ]: At the mileage intervals only

MAINTENANCE OPERATION		MAINTENANCE INTERVAL							
Perform at number of miles, kilometers or months, whichever comes first.	Miles x 1,000	7.5	15	22.5	30	37.5	45	52.5	60
	(km x 1,000)	(12)	(24)	(36)	(48)	(60)	(72)	(84)	(96)
	Months	6	12	18	24	30	36	42	48
Emission control system maintenance									
Drive belts	See NOTE (1)								I*
Air cleaner filter					[R]				[R]
Vapor lines					I*				I*
Fuel lines					I*				I*
Fuel filter	See NOTE (2)*								
Engine coolant	See NOTE (3)								R*
Engine oil		R	R	R	R	R	R	R	R
Engine oil filter (Use part No. 15208-31U00 or equivalent.)		R	R	R	R	R	R	R	R
Spark plugs (Use PLATINUM-TIPPED type)									[R]
Intake & exhaust valve clearance	See NOTE (4)								
Chassis and body maintenance									
Brake lines & cables			I		I		I		I
Brake pads & discs			I		I		I		I
Manual & automatic transaxle oil			I		I		I		I
Steering gear linkage, axle & suspension parts					I				I
Exhaust system					I				I
Drive shaft boots			I		I		I		I
Air bag system	See NOTE (5)								

NOTE: (1) After 60,000 miles (96,000 km) or 48 months, inspect every 15,000 miles (24,000 km) or 12 months.
(2) If vehicle is operated under extremely adverse weather conditions or in areas where ambient temperatures are either extremely low or extremely high, the filters might become clogged. In such an event, replace them immediately.
(3) After 60,000 miles (96,000 km) or 48 months, replace every 30,000 miles (48,000 km) or 24 months.
(4) If valve noise increases, inspect valve clearance.
(5) Inspect the air bag system 10 years after the date of manufacture noted on the FMVSS certification label.
★ Maintenance items and intervals with "*" are recommended by NISSAN/INFINITI for reliable vehicle operation. The owner need not perform such maintenance in order to maintain the emission warranty or manufacturer recall liability. Other maintenance items and intervals are required.

NS1139600153000X

Fig. 5 Maxima. 1996

Abbreviations: R = Replace. I = Inspect. Correct or replace if necessary.

[ ]: At the mileage intervals only

MAINTENANCE OPERATION — Perform at number of miles, kilometers or months, whichever comes first.		3.75	7.5	11.25	15	18.75	22.5	26.25	30	33.75	37.5	41.25	45	48.75	52.5	56.25	60	SR series	GA series
	(km x 1,000)	(6)	(12)	(18)	(24)	(30)	(36)	(42)	(48)	(54)	(60)	(66)	(72)	(78)	(84)	(90)	(96)		
	Months	3	6	9	12	15	18	21	24	27	30	33	36	39	42	45	48		
Emission control system maintenance																			
Drive belts	See NOTE (1).																I*		
Air cleaner filter	See NOTE (2)								[R]								[R]		
Vapor lines									I*								I*		
Fuel lines									I*								I*		
Fuel filter	See NOTE (3)*.																		
Engine coolant	See NOTE (4).																R*		
Engine oil		R	R	R	R	R	R	R	R	R	R	R	R	R	R	R	R		
Engine oil filter (Use Nissan PREMIUM type or equivalent for GA16DE engine.)		R	R	R	R	R	R	R	R	R	R	R	R	R	R	R	R		
Spark plugs — GA16DE engine									[R]								[R]		
Spark plugs — SR20DE engine (Use PLATINUM-TIPPED type.) See NOTE (5)																	[R]		
Idle rpm (GA16DE engine)									I*								I*		
Intake & exhaust valve clearance (GA16DE engine)	See NOTE (6)*.																		
Chassis and body maintenance																			
Brake lines & cables					I				I				I				I		
Brake pads, discs, drums & linings			I		I		I		I		I		I		I		I		
Manual & automatic transaxle oil	See NOTE (7).				I				I				I				I		
Steering gear & linkage, axle & suspension parts			I		I		I		I		I		I		I		I		
Steering linkage ball joints & front suspension ball joints			I		I		I		I		I		I		I		I		
Exhaust system			I		I		I		I		I		I		I		I		
Drive shaft boots			I		I		I		I		I		I		I		I		
Air bag system (Coupe models)	See NOTE (8).																		

NOTE: (1) After 60,000 miles (96,000 km) or 48 months, inspect every 15,000 miles (24,000 km) or 12 months.
(2) If operating mainly in dusty conditions, more frequent maintenance may be required.
(3) If vehicle is operated under extremely adverse weather conditions or in areas where ambient temperatures are either extremely low or extremely high, the filters might become clogged. In such an event, replace them immediately.
(4) After 60,000 miles (96,000 km) or 48 months, replace every 30,000 miles (48,000 km) or 24 months.
(5) Original equipment platinum-tipped plugs should be replaced at 60,000 miles (96,000 km). Conventional spark plugs can be used but should be replaced at 30,000 mile (48,000 km) intervals.
(6) If valve noise increases, inspect valve clearance.
(7) If towing a trailer, using a camper or a car-top carrier, or driving on rough or muddy roads, change (not just inspect) oil at every 30,000 miles (48,000 km) or 24 months.
(8) Inspect the air bag system 10 years after the date of manufacture as noted on the F.M.V.S.S. certification label.
(9) Maintenance items and intervals with "*" are recommended by NISSAN for reliable vehicle operation. The owner need not perform such maintenance in order to maintain the emission warranty or manufacturer recall liability. Other maintenance items and intervals are required.

NS1139100135000X

Fig. 6 NX1600, NX2000 & 1993–95 Sentra & 200SX

Abbreviations: R = Replace I = Inspect. Correct or replace if necessary.

[ ]: At the mileage intervals only

MAINTENANCE OPERATION — Perform at number of miles, kilometers or months, whichever comes first.	Miles x 1,000	3.75	7.5	11.25	15	18.75	22.5	26.25	30	33.75	37.5	41.25	45	48.75	52.5	56.25	60
	(km x 1,000)	(6)	(12)	(18)	(24)	(30)	(36)	(42)	(48)	(54)	(60)	(66)	(72)	(78)	(84)	(90)	(96)
	Months	3	6	9	12	15	18	21	24	27	30	33	36	39	42	45	48
Emission control system maintenance																	
Drive belts									I*								:
Air cleaner filter	See NOTE (1)								[R]								[R]
Positive crankcase ventilation (P.C.V.) filter (KA24E engine only)	See NOTE (3)								[R]								[R]
Pulsed secondary air injection valve filter (KA24E engine only)	See NOTE (2)																
Vapor lines									I*								I*
Fuel lines									I*								I*
Fuel filter	See NOTE (3)*																
Engine coolant	See NOTE (4)																R*
Engine oil		R	R	R	R	R	R	R	R	R	R	R	R	R	R	R	R
Engine oil filter (Use Nissan PREMIUM type or equivalent)		R	R	R	R	R	R	R	R	R	R	R	R	R	R	R	R
Spark plugs									[R]								[R]
Timing belt (VG30E engine only)																	[R]
Chassis and body maintenance																	
Brake lines & cables					I				I				I				I
Brake pads, discs, drums & linings			I		I		I		I		I		I		I		I
Manual and automatic transmission, transfer & differential gear oil (exc. L.S.D.)	See NOTE (5)				I				I				I				I
Limited-slip differential (L.S.D.) gear oil	See NOTE (5)				I				R				I				R
Steering gear (box) & linkage, (steering damper 4x4), axle & suspension parts			I		I		I		I		I		I		I		I
Drive shaft boots & propeller shaft (4x4)			I		I		I		I		I		I		I		I
Steering linkage ball joints & front suspension ball joints			I		I		I		I		I		I		I		I
Front wheel bearing grease (4x2)									I								I
Front wheel bearing grease & free-running hub grease (4x4)	See NOTE (6)				I				R				I				R
Exhaust system			I		I		I		I		I		I		I		I

NOTE: (1) If operating mainly in dusty conditions, more frequent maintenance may be required.
(2) If operating mainly in dusty conditions, replace every 30,000 miles (48,000 km).
(3) If vehicle is operated under extremely adverse weather conditions or in areas where ambient temperatures are either extremely low or extremely high, the filters might become clogged. In such an event, replace them immediately.
(4) After 60,000 miles (96,000 km) or 48 months, replace every 30,000 miles (48,000 km) or 24 months.
(5) If towing a trailer, using a camper or a car-top carrier, or driving on rough or muddy roads, change (not just inspect) oil at every 30,000 miles (48,000 km) or 24 months except for L.S.D. Change L.S.D. gear oil every 15,000 miles (24,000 km) or 12 months.
(6) If operating frequently in water, replace grease every 3,750 miles (6,000 km) or 3 months.
(7) Maintenance items and intervals with "*" are recommended by NISSAN for reliable vehicle operation. The owner need not perform such maintenance in order to maintain the emission warranty or manufacturer recall liability. Other maintenance items and intervals are required.

NS1139100134000X

Fig. 7 Pathfinder & Pickup. 1993–95

Abbreviations: R = Replace I = Inspect. Correct or replace if necessary. L = Lubricate [ ]: At the mileage intervals only

MAINTENANCE OPERATION		MAINTENANCE INTERVAL							
Perform at number of miles, kilometers or months, whichever comes first.	Miles x 1,000	7.5	15	22.5	30	37.5	45	52.5	60
	(km x 1,000)	(12)	(24)	(36)	(48)	(60)	(72)	(84)	(96)
	Months	6	12	18	24	30	36	42	48
Emission control system maintenance									
Drive belts					I*				I*
Air cleaner filter					[R]				[R]
Vapor lines					I*				I*
Fuel lines					I*				I*
Fuel filter	See NOTE (1)*								
Engine coolant	See NOTE (2)								R*
Engine oil		R	R	R	R	R	R	R	R
Engine oil filter (Use Part No. 15208 31U00 or equivalent)		R	R	R	R	R	R	R	R
Spark plugs					[R]				[R]
Timing belt		Replace every 105,000 miles (168,000 km)							
Chassis and body maintenance									
Brake lines & cables			I		I		I		I
Brake pads, discs, drums & linings			I		I		I		I
Manual and automatic transmission, transfer & differential gear oil (exc. LSD)			I		I		I		I
Limited-slip differential (LSD) gear oil			I		R		I		R
Steering gear, linkage & transfer gear, axle & suspension parts					I				I
Drive shaft boots & propeller shaft (4x4)			I		I		I		I
Propeller shaft	See NOTE (3)		L		L		L		L
Steering linkage ball joints & front suspension ball joints									I
Front wheel bearing grease (4x2)					I				I
Front wheel bearing grease (4x4)			I		R		I		R
Exhaust system					I				I
Air bag system	See NOTE (4)								

NOTE: (1) If vehicle is operated under extremely adverse weather conditions or in areas where ambient temperatures are either extremely low or extremely high, the filters might become clogged. In such an event, replace them immediately.
(2) After 60,000 miles (96,000 km) or 48 months, replace every 30,000 miles (48,000 km) or 24 months.
(3) The propeller shaft should be re-greased daily if it is immersed in water.
(4) Inspect the air bag system 10 years after the date of manufacture noted on the FMVSS certification label.
★ Maintenance items and intervals with "*" are recommended by NISSAN for reliable vehicle operation. The owner need not perform such maintenance in order to maintain the emission warranty or manufacturer recall liability. Other maintenance items and intervals are required.

NS1139600154000X

Fig. 8 Pathfinder. 1996

Abbreviations: R = Replace I = Inspect. Correct or replace if necessary. [ ]: At the mileage intervals only

MAINTENANCE OPERATION		MAINTENANCE INTERVAL							
Perform at number of miles, kilometers or months, whichever comes first.	Miles x 1,000	7.5	15	22.5	30	37.5	45	52.5	60
	(km x 1,000)	(12)	(24)	(36)	(48)	(60)	(72)	(84)	(96)
	Months	6	12	18	24	30	36	42	48
Emission control system maintenance									
Drive belts					I*				I*
Air cleaner filter					[R]				[R]
Positive crankcase ventilation (PCV) filter	See NOTE (1)				[R]				[R]
Vapor lines					I*				I*
Fuel lines					I*				I*
Fuel filter	See NOTE (1)*								
Engine coolant	See NOTE (2)								R*
Engine oil		R	R	R	R	R	R	R	R
Engine oil filter		R	R	R	R	R	R	R	R
Spark plugs					[R]				[R]
Chassis and body maintenance									
Brake lines & cables			I		I		I		I
Brake pads, discs, drums & linings			I		I		I		I
Manual and automatic transmission, transfer fluid & differential gear oil (exc. LSD)			I		I		I		I
Limited-slip differential (LSD) gear oil			I		R		I		R
Steering gear (box) & linkage, (steering damper 4x4), axle & suspension parts					I				I
Drive shaft boots & propeller shaft (4x4)			I		I		I		I
Steering linkage ball joints & front suspension ball joints									I
Front wheel bearing grease (4x2)					I				I
Front wheel bearing grease & free-running hub grease (4x4)			I		R		I		R
Exhaust system					I				I
Air bag system	See NOTE (3)								

NOTE: (1) If vehicle is operated under extremely adverse weather conditions or in areas where ambient temperatures are either extremely low or extremely high, the filters might become clogged. In such an event, replace them immediately.
(2) After 60,000 miles (96,000 km) or 48 months, replace every 30,000 miles (48,000 km) or 24 months.
(3) Inspect the air bag system 10 years after the date of manufacture noted on the FMVSS certification label.
★ Maintenance items and intervals with "*" are recommended by NISSAN for reliable vehicle operation. The owner need not perform such maintenance in order to maintain the emission warranty or manufacturer recall liability. Other maintenance items and intervals are required.

NS1139600155000X

Fig. 9 Pickup. 1996

Abbreviations: R = Replace I = Inspect. Correct or replace if necessary. [ ]: At the mileage intervals only

MAINTENANCE OPERATION		MAINTENANCE INTERVAL															
Perform at number of miles, kilometers or months, whichever comes first.	Miles × 1,000	3.75	7.5	11.25	15	18.75	22.5	26.25	30	33.75	37.5	41.25	45	48.75	52.5	56.25	60
	(km × 1,000)	(6)	(12)	(18)	(24)	(30)	(36)	(42)	(48)	(54)	(60)	(66)	(72)	(78)	(84)	(90)	(96)
	Months	3	6	9	12	15	18	21	24	27	30	33	36	39	42	45	48
Emission control system maintenance																	
Drive belts	See NOTE (1)																I*
Air cleaner filter	See NOTE (2)								[R]								[R]
Vapor lines									I*								I*
Fuel lines									I*								I*
Fuel filter	See NOTE (3)*																
Engine coolant	Replace every 30,000 miles (48,000 km) or 36 months*																
Engine oil		R	R	R	R	R	R	R	R	R	R	R	R	R	R	R	R
Engine oil filter (Use Nissan PREMIUM type or equivalent.)		R	R	R	R	R	R	R	R	R	R	R	R	R	R	R	R
Spark plugs									[R]								[R]
Timing belt	Replace every 105,000 miles (168,000 km)																
Chassis and body maintenance																	
Brake lines & cables					I				I				I				I
Brake pads, discs, drums & linings			I		I		I		I		I		I		I		I
Automatic transaxle oil	See NOTE (4)				I				I				I				I
Steering gear & linkage, axle & suspension parts			I		I		I		I		I		I		I		I
Steering linkage ball joints & front suspension ball joints			I		I		I		I		I		I		I		I
Exhaust system			I		I		I		I		I		I		I		I
Drive shaft boots			I		I		I		I		I		I		I		I
Supplemental air bag system	See NOTE (5)																

NOTE: (1) After 60,000 miles (96,000 km) or 48 months, inspect every 15,000 miles (24,000 km) or 12 months.
(2) If operating mainly in dusty conditions, more frequent maintenance may be required.
(3) If vehicle is operated under extremely adverse weather conditions or in areas where ambient temperatures are either extremely low or extremely high, the filters might become clogged. In such an event, replace them immediately.
(4) If towing a trailer, using a camper or a car-top carrier, or driving on rough or muddy roads, change (not just inspect) oil at every 30,000 miles (48,000 km) or 24 months.
(5) Inspect the supplemental air bag system 10 years after the date of manufacture as noted on the F.M.V.S.S. certification label.
(*) Maintenance items and intervals with "*" are recommended by NISSAN for reliable vehicle operation. The owner need not perform such maintenance in order to maintain the emission warranty or manufacturer recall liability. Other maintenance items and intervals are required.

NS1139100139000X

Fig. 10 Quest. 1993–95

Abbreviations: R = Replace I =Inspect. Correct or replace if necessary. [ ]: At the mileage intervals only

MAINTENANCE OPERATION		MAINTENANCE INTERVAL							
Perform at number of miles, kilometers or months, whichever comes first.	Miles × 1,000	7.5	15	22.5	30	37.5	45	52.5	60
	(km × 1,000)	(12)	(24)	(36)	(48)	(60)	(72)	(84)	(96)
	Months	6	12	18	24	30	36	42	48
Emission control system maintenance									
Drive belts	See NOTE (1)								I*
Air cleaner filter					[R]				[R]
Vapor lines					I*				I*
Fuel lines					I*				I*
Fuel filter	See NOTE (2)*								
Engine coolant	Replace every 30,000 miles (48,000 km) or 36 months*								
Engine oil		R	R	R	R	R	R	R	R
Engine oil filter (Use Nissan PREMIUM type or equivalent.)		R	R	R	R	R	R	R	R
Spark plugs					[R]				[R]
Timing belt	Replace every 105,000 miles (168,000 km)								
Chassis and body maintenance									
Brake lines & cables			I		I		I		I
Brake pads, discs, drums & linings			I		I		I		I
Automatic transaxle oil			I		I		I		I
Steering gear linkage, axle & suspension parts					I				I
Exhaust system					I				I
Drive shaft boots			I		I		I		I
Air bag system	See NOTE (3)								

NOTE: (1) After 60,000 miles (96,000 km) or 48 months, inspect every 15,000 miles (24,000 km) or 12 months.
(2) If vehicle is operated under extremely adverse weather conditions or in areas where ambient temperatures are either extremely low or extremely high, the filters might become clogged. In such an event, replace them immediately.
(3) Inspect the air bag system 10 years after the date of manufacture noted on the FMVSS certification label.
(*) Maintenance items and intervals with "*" are recommended by NISSAN for reliable vehicle operation. The owner need not perform such maintenance in order to maintain the emission warranty or manufacturer recall liability. Other maintenance items and intervals are required.

NS1139600156000X

Fig. 11 Quest. 1996

Abbreviations: R = Replace. I = Inspect. Correct or replace if necessary. [ ]: At the mileage intervals only

MAINTENANCE OPERATION		MAINTENANCE INTERVAL									
Perform at number of miles, kilometers or months, whichever comes first.	Miles x 1,000	7.5	15	22.5	30	37.5	45	52.5	60		
	(km x 1,000)	(12)	(24)	(36)	(48)	(60)	(72)	(84)	(96)		
	Months	6	12	18	24	30	36	42	48		
Emission control system maintenance											
Drive belts	See NOTE (1).								I*		
Air cleaner filter					[R]				[R]		
Vapor lines					I*				I*		
Fuel lines					I*				I*		
Fuel filter	See NOTE (2)*.										
Engine coolant	See NOTE (3).								R*		
Engine oil		R	R	R	R	R	R	R	R		
Engine oil filter (Use Part No. 15208-H8903 for GA16DE engine and 15208-65F00 for SR20DE engine.)		R	R	R	R	R	R	R	R		
Spark plugs GA16DE engine					[R]				[R]	—	
Spark plugs SR20DE engine (Use PLATINUM-TIPPED type.) See NOTE (4).									[R]		—
Idle rpm (GA16DE engine)					I*				I*	—	
Intake & exhaust valve clearance (GA16DE engine)	See NOTE (5)*.									—	
Chassis and body maintenance											
Brake lines & cables			I		I		I		I		
Brake pads, discs, drums & linings			I		I		I		I		
Manual & automatic transmission oil			I		I		I		I		
Steering gear linkage, axle & suspension parts					I				I		
Exhaust system					I				I		
Drive shaft boots			I		I		I		I		
Air bag system	See NOTE (6).										

NOTE: (1) After 60,000 miles (96,000 km) or 48 months, inspect every 15,000 miles (24,000 km) or 12 months.
(2) If vehicle is operated under extremely adverse weather conditions or in areas where ambient temperatures are either extremely low or extremely high, the filters might become clogged. In such an event, replace them immediately.
(3) After 60,000 miles (96,000 km) or 48 months, replace every 30,000 miles (48,000 km) or 24 months.
(4) Original equipment platinum-tipped plugs should be replaced at 60,000 miles (96,000 km). Conventional spark plugs can be used but should be replaced at 30,000 mile (48,000 km) intervals.
(5) If valve noise increases, inspect valve clearance.
(6) Inspect the air bag system 10 years after the date of manufacture noted on the FMVSS certification label.
* Maintenance items and intervals with "*" are recommended by NISSAN for reliable vehicle operation. The owner need not perform such maintenance in order to maintain the emission warranty or manufacturer recall liability. Other maintenance items and intervals are required.

NS1139600157000X

Fig. 12 Sentra & 200SX. 1996

Abbreviations: R = Replace I = Inspect. Correct or replace if necessary. [ ]: At the mileage intervals only

MAINTENANCE OPERATION		MAINTENANCE INTERVAL															
Perform at number of miles, kilometers or months, whichever comes first.	Miles x 1,000	3.75	7.5	11.25	15	18.75	22.5	26.25	30	33.75	37.5	41.25	45	48.75	52.5	56.25	60
	(km x 1,000)	(6)	(12)	(18)	(24)	(30)	(36)	(42)	(48)	(54)	(60)	(66)	(72)	(78)	(84)	(90)	(96)
	Months	3	6	9	12	15	18	21	24	27	30	33	36	39	42	45	48
Emission control system maintenance																	
Drive belts	See NOTE (1)																I*
Air cleaner filter	See NOTE (2)								[R]								[R]
Vapor lines									I*								I*
Fuel lines									I*								I*
Fuel filter	See NOTE (3)*																
Engine coolant	See NOTE (4)																R*
Engine oil		R	R	R	R	R	R	R	R	R	R	R	R	R	R	R	R
Engine oil filter (Use Nissan PREMIUM type or equivalent.)		R	R	R	R	R	R	R	R	R	R	R	R	R	R	R	R
Spark plugs									[R]								[R]
Intake & exhaust valve clearances	See NOTE (5)*																
Chassis and body maintenance																	
Brake lines & cables					I				I				I				I
Brake pads & discs			I		I		I		I		I		I		I		I
Manual and automatic transmission oil, & differential gear oil	See NOTE (6)				I				I				I				I
Steering gear & linkage, axle & suspension parts			I		I		I		I		I		I		I		I
Steering linkage ball joints & front suspension ball joints			I		I		I		I		I		I		I		I
SUPER HICAS linkage			I		I		I		I		I		I		I		I
Exhaust system			I		I		I		I		I		I		I		I

NOTE: (1) After 60,000 miles (96,000 km) or 48 months, inspect every 15,000 miles (24,000 km) or 12 months.
(2) If operating mainly in dusty conditions, more frequent maintenance may be required.
(3) If vehicle is operated under extremely adverse weather conditions or in areas where ambient temperatures are either extremely low or extremely high, the filters might become clogged. In such an event, replace them immediately.
(4) After 60,000 miles (96,000 km) or 48 months, replace every 30,000 miles (48,000 km) or 24 months.
(5) If valve noise increases, inspect valve clearances.
(6) If towing a trailer, using a camper or a car-top carrier, or driving on rough or muddy roads, change (not just inspect) oil at every 30,000 miles (48,000 km) or 24 months.
(7) Maintenance items and intervals with "*" are recommended by NISSAN for reliable vehicle operation. The owner need not perform such maintenance in order to maintain the emission warranty or manufacturer recall liability. Other maintenance items and intervals are required.

NS1139100137000X

Fig. 13 240SX. 1993–95

Abbreviations: R = Replace I = Inspect. Correct or replace if necessary. [ ]: At the mileage intervals only

MAINTENANCE OPERATION		MAINTENANCE INTERVAL							
Perform at number of miles, kilometers or months, whichever comes first.	Miles x 1,000	7.5	15	22.5	30	37.5	45	52.5	60
	(km x 1,000)	(12)	(24)	(36)	(48)	(60)	(72)	(84)	(96)
	Months	6	12	18	24	30	36	42	48
Emission control system maintenance									
Drive belts	See NOTE (1)								I*
Air cleaner filter					[R]				[R]
Vapor lines					I*				I*
Fuel lines					I*				I*
Fuel filter	See NOTE (2)*								
Engine coolant	See NOTE (3)								R*
Engine oil		R	R	R	R	R	R	R	R
Engine oil filter (Use Nissan PREMIUM type or equivalent.)		R	R	R	R	R	R	R	R
Spark plugs (Use PLATINUM-TIPPED type)									[R]
Intake & exhaust valve clearances	See NOTE (4)*								
Chassis and body maintenance									
Brake lines & cables			I		I		I		I
Brake pads & discs			I		I		I		I
Manual and automatic transmission oil, & differential gear oil			I		I		I		I
Steering gear linkage, axle & suspension parts					I				I
Exhaust system					I				I
Air bag system	See NOTE (5)								

NOTE: (1) After 60,000 miles (96,000 km) or 48 months, inspect every 15,000 miles (24,000 km) or 12 months.
(2) If vehicle is operated under extremely adverse weather conditions or in areas where ambient temperatures are either extremely low or extremely high, the filters might become clogged. In such an event, replace them immediately.
(3) After 60,000 miles (96,000 km) or 48 months, replace every 30,000 miles (48,000 km) or 24 months.
(4) If valve noise increases, inspect valve clearances.
(5) Inspect the air bag system 10 years after the date of manufacture noted on the FMVSS certification label.
★ Maintenance items and intervals with "*" are recommended by NISSAN for reliable vehicle operation. The owner need not perform such maintenance in order to maintain the emission warranty or manufacturer recall liability. Other maintenance items and intervals are required.

NS1139600158000X

Fig. 14 240SX. 1996

Abbreviations: R = Replace I = Inspect. Correct or replace if necessary. [ ]: At the mileage intervals only

MAINTENANCE OPERATION		MAINTENANCE INTERVAL																
Perform at number of miles, kilometers or months, whichever comes first.	Miles x 1,000	3.00	3.75	7.5	11.25	15	18.75	22.5	26.25	30	33.75	37.5	41.25	45	48.75	52.5	56.25	60
	(km x 1,000)	(5)	(6)	(12)	(18)	(24)	(30)	(36)	(42)	(48)	(54)	(60)	(66)	(72)	(78)	(84)	(90)	(96)
	Months	3	3	6	9	12	15	18	21	24	27	30	33	36	39	42	45	48
EMISSION CONTROL SYSTEM MAINTENANCE																		
Drive belts	See NOTE (1).																	I*
Air cleaner filter	See NOTE (2).									[R]								[R]
Vapor lines										I*								I*
Fuel lines										I*								I*
Fuel filter	See NOTE (3).*																	
Engine coolant	See NOTE (4).																	R*
Engine oil			R	R	R	R	R	R	R	R	R	R	R	R	R	R	R	R
Engine oil filter (Use part No. 15208-60U00 or equivalent.)			R	R	R	R	R	R	R	R	R	R	R	R	R	R	R	R
Spark plugs (PLATINUM-TIPPED type)																		[R]
Timing belt	See NOTE (5).																	
CHASSIS AND BODY MAINTENANCE																		
Brake lines & cables						I				I				I				I
Brake pads & discs				I		I		I		I		I		I		I		I
Manual & automatic transmission oil, & differential gear oil	See NOTE (6).					I				I				I				I
Steering gear & linkage, axle & suspension parts				I		I		I		I		I		I		I		I
Steering linkage ball joints & front suspension ball joints				I		I		I		I		I		I		I		I
Exhaust system				I		I		I		I		I		I		I		I
Air bag system	See NOTE (7).																	

NOTE: (1) After 60,000 miles (96,000 km) or 48 months, inspect every 15,000 miles (24,000 km) or 12 months.
(2) If operating mainly in dusty conditions, more frequent maintenance may be required.
(3) If vehicle is operated under extremely adverse weather conditions or in areas where ambient temperatures are either extremely low or extremely high, the filters might become clogged. In such an event, replace them immediately.
(4) After 60,000 miles (96,000 km) or 48 months, replace every 30,000 miles (48,000 km) or 24 months.
(5) Replace every 105,000 miles (168,000 km).
(6) If towing a trailer, using a camper or a car-top carrier, or driving on rough or muddy roads, change (not just inspect) oil at every 30,000 miles (48,000 km) or 24 months.
(7) Inspect the air bag system 10 years after the date of manufacture as noted on the F.M.V.S.S. certification label.
(8) Maintenance items and intervals with " * " are recommended by NISSAN for reliable vehicle operation. The owner need not perform such maintenance in order to maintain the emission warranty or manufacturer recall liability. Other maintenance items and intervals are required.

NS1139100138000X

Fig. 15 300ZX. 1993–95

Abbreviations: R = Replace I = Inspect. Correct or replace if necessary. [ ]: At the mileage intervals only

MAINTENANCE OPERATION		MAINTENANCE INTERVAL								
Perform at number of miles, kilometers or months, whichever comes first.	Miles x 1,000	5.0	7.5	15	22.5	30	37.5	45	52.5	60
	(km x 1,000)	(8)	(12)	(24)	(36)	(48)	(60)	(72)	(84)	(96)
	Months	6	6	12	18	24	30	36	42	48
EMISSION CONTROL SYSTEM MAINTENANCE										
Drive belts	See NOTE (1).									I*
Air cleaner filter						[R]				[R]
Vapor lines						I*				I*
Fuel lines						I*				I*
Fuel filter	See NOTE (2)*.									
Engine coolant	See NOTE (3).									R*
Engine oil			R	R	R	R	R	R	R	R
	Turbocharger model	R	Then replace every 5,000 miles (8,000 km) or 6 months.							
Engine oil filter (Use part No. 15208-60U00 or equivalent.)			R	R	R	R	R	R	R	R
	Turbocharger model	R	Then replace every second oil change.							
Spark plugs (PLATINUM-TIPPED type)										[R]
Timing belt	See NOTE (4).									[R]
CHASSIS AND BODY MAINTENANCE										
Brake lines & cables				I		I		I		I
Brake pads & discs				I		I		I		I
Manual & automatic transmission oil, & differential gear oil				I		I		I		I
Steering gear & linkage, axle & suspension parts						I				I
SUPER HICAS linkage (Turbocharger model)						I				I
Exhaust system				I		I		I		I
Air bag system	See NOTE (5).									

NOTE: (1) After 60,000 miles (96,000 km) or 48 months, inspect every 15,000 miles (24,000 km) or 12 months.
(2) If vehicle is operated under extremely adverse weather conditions or in areas where ambient temperatures are either extremely low or extremely high, the filters might become clogged. In such an event, replace them immediately.
(3) After 60,000 miles (96,000 km) or 48 months, replace every 30,000 miles (48,000 km) or 24 months.
(4) Replace every 105,000 miles (168,000 km) on non-turbocharged models. On turbocharged models, replace every 60,000 miles (96,000 km).
(5) Inspect the air bag system 10 years after the date of manufacture noted on the FMVSS certification label.
* Maintenance items and intervals with " * " are recommended by NISSAN for reliable vehicle operation. The owner need not perform such maintenance in order to maintain the emission warranty or manufacturer recall liability. Other maintenance items and intervals are required.

NS1139600159000X

Fig. 16 300ZX. 1996

VEHICLE MAINTENANCE SCHEDULES

Porsche

INDEX

	Page No.	Fig. No.
911 Carrera		
Except 1994-96	0-98	1
1994-96	0-100	2

☐ **Maintenance 3,000 to 4,000 km/2,000 to 2,500 mls**
(working position 03 01 00 ..)

The terms "inspect" and "check" include all associated work such as adjustments readjustments corrections and replenishment They do not include the repair replacement or overhaul of components or assemblies The maintenance points stated above are valid for all vehicle types of the model line in question

Type ⇒	968	911 Turbo	911	928
Tires: Check condition and pressure (928 with system tester)	●	●	●	●
Front axle Check toe adjustment				●
Diagnosis system Read out fault memory	●	●	●	●
V-belt and Polyno belt: Check tension		●		●
Toothed belt for camshafts Check tension				●
Toothed belt for balance shafts Check tension	●			
Visual inspection for leaks Oils and fluids	●	●	●	●
Coolant: Check level	●			●
Windshield washer, headlight washer Check fluid level in winter months top up with anti-freeze as necessary	●	●	●	●
Check operation of lighting system	●	●	●	●
Exhaust system Visual inspection for leaks and damage	●	●	●	●
Test idle speed		●		
Perform system adaptation on vehicles without catalytic converter Test CO content			●	●
Convertible top Check operation	●	●	●	
Test drive:				
Foot brake and handbrake, clutch automatic speed control, steering, heating air conditioning and instruments Check operation	●	●	●	●
Visual inspection for leaks Oils and fluids	●	●	●	●

PR1139100006020X

Fig. 1 Except 1994–96 911 Carrera (Part 1 of 5). 1993–94

☐ **Maintenance every 20,000 km/12,000 mls**
(working position 03 20 00..)

The terms "inspect" and "check" include all associated work such as adjustments readjustments corrections and replenishment They do not include the repair replacement or overhaul of components or assemblies The maintenance points stated above are valid for all vehicle types of the model line in question

Type ⇒	968	911 Turbo	911	928
Diagnosis system Read out fault memory	●	●	●	●
Change engine oil and oil filter	●	●	●	●
Check valve clearance		●	●	
V belt or Polyrib belt Check condition and tension	●	●	●	●
Toothed belt for camshafts Check condition and tension				●
Toothed belt for power steering Check condition		●	●	
Toothed belt tensioner Check oil level				●
Change spark plugs (only on vehicles without catalytic converter)	●	●	●	●
Check boost pressure safety switch		●		
Visual inspection for leaks Oils and fluids	●	●	●	●
Coolant hoses: Check condition Radiator Visual inspection for external fouling Coolant Check level and anti-freeze content	●			●
Air filter Replace filter element				●
Crankcase ventilation Check tightness of hose connections		●	●	●
Fuel system Visual inspection for damage, correct position and tightness of connections	●	●	●	●
Intake air system Check hoses lines and connections for tightness	●	●	●	●
Handbrake Check free travel of handbrake lever	●	●	●	●
Brake system Visual inspection of brake pads and disks for wear	●	●	●	●
Brake hoses and lines Visual inspection for damage, correct position and corrosion, check brake fluid level For 928 Visual inspection of components for Tire Pressure Monitoring System	●	●	●	●
Clutch Check play or final position of clutch pedal	●	●	●	●
Throttle valve actuation Check for ease of movement and full throttle position	●	●	●	●
Resonance flap Check operation			●	●
Steering gear: Visual check of bellows for damage Track rod links Check play and dust caps	●	●	●	●
Power steering Check fluid level	●	●	●	●
Axle joints Visual inspection of dust caps for damage Screw connections of suspension adjustment system Check for tightness front and rear	●	●	●	●
Front wheel bearings Check play	●			●
Manual transmission/axle drives Check oil level	●	●	●	●
Automatic transmission Check fluid level	●		●	●
Drive shafts Visual inspection of sleeves for leaks and damage	●	●	●	●
Exhaust system Visual inspection for leaks and damage, check attachment	●	●	●	●
Tires: Check condition and pressure (928 with system tester)	●	●	●	●
Door hinges: Lubricate		●	●	
Check door, lid locks and safety hooks on front lid for tightness and operation	●	●	●	●
Hinges for rear lid Lubricate				●
Safety belts: Check operation and condition	●	●	●	●

PR1139100006010X

Fig. 1 911 Carrera (Part 2 of 5). Except 1994–96

Maintenance every 20,000 km/12,000 mls

Type ⇒	968	911 Turbo	911	928
Seals for doors, compartment lids and roof: remove abraded rubber. Apply suitable lubricant	●	●	●	●
Check operation of vehicle lighting All headlights: Check setting Horn: Check operation	●	●	●	●
Pop-up headlights: Lubricate linkages	●			●
Windshield washer, headlight washer: Check fluid levels and nozzle settings; in the winter months top up with anti-freeze as necessary	●	●	●	●
All other electrical equipment as well as indicator and warning lights: Check operation	●	●	●	●
Ignition circuit 1 and 2: Check operation			●	
Additional:				
☐ **every 40,000 km/24,000 mls**				
Automatic transmission: Change fluid, clean ATF strainer or change filter	●		●	●
Replace fuel filter	●	●	●	●
Air filter: Replace filter element	●	●	●	
Auxiliary air pump: Replace filter element		●		●
Toothed belt for balance shafts: Check condition and tension	●			
Toothed belt for camshafts: Check condition	●			
Replace spark plugs (only in vehicles with catalytic converter)	●	●	●	●
☐ **every 80,000 km/48,000 mls**				
Manual transmission/axle drives: Change oil	●	●	●	●
Automatic transmission: Change oil in axle drive	●		●	●
Toothed belt for camshafts: Replace (Check tension of balance shaft belt after 3 000-4 000 km/2 000-2 500 mls if replaced)	●			
☐ **every 100,000 km/60,000 mls**				
Replace toothed belt for camshafts (check tension after 3 000-4 000 km/2 000-2 500 mls)				●
☐ **Yearly – after the first 2 years**				
Fill Status Report for Long life guarantee	●	●	●	●
☐ **every 2 years**				
Change brake fluid	●	●	●	●
Change coolant	●			●
☐ **after 4, 8 and 10 years, thereafter every 2 years**				
Check airbag system	●	●	●	●
Test drive:				
Foot brake and handbrake, clutch, automatic speed control, steering, heating, air conditioning and instruments: Check operation	●	●	●	●
Visual inspection for leaks: Oils and fluids	●	●	●	●

PR1139100006030X

Fig. 1 911 Carrera (Part 3 of 5). Except 1994–96

☐ Recommended Yearly Maintenance

Vehicles with a low yearly mileage between two required service intervals (working position 03 50 00...)

The terms "inspect" and "check" include all associated work such as adjustments, readjustments, corrections and replenishment. They do not include the repair, replacement or overhaul of components or assemblies. The maintenance points stated above are valid for all vehicle types of the model line in question.

Type ⇒	968	911 Turbo	911	928
Visual inspection for leaks: Oils and fluids	●	●	●	●
Diagnosis system: Read out fault memory	●	●	●	●
Handbrake: Check free travel of handbrake lever	●	●	●	●
Brake system: Visual inspection of brake pads and disks for wear	●	●	●	●
Check brake fluid level	●	●	●	●
Steering gear: Visual inspection of bellows for damage Track rod joints: Check play and dust caps	●	●	●	●
Axle joints: Visual inspection of dust caps for damage	●	●	●	●
Drive shafts: Visual inspection of cup seals for leaks and damage	●	●	●	●
Exhaust system: Visual inspection for leaks and damage, check attachment	●	●	●	●
Tires: Check condition and pressure (928 with system tester)	●	●	●	●
Seals for doors, compartment lids and roof: remove abraded rubber. Apply suitable lubricant	●	●	●	●
Check operation of lighting system	●	●	●	●
Windshield washer, headlight washer: Check fluid level and nozzle settings; in the winter months top up with anti-freeze as necessary	●	●	●	●
Battery: Check electrolyte level and density	●	●	●	●
All other electrical equipment as well as indicator and warning lights: Check operation	●	●	●	●
Fill Status Report for Long life guarantee (after the first 2 years)	●	●	●	●
Test drive:				
Foot brake and handbrake, clutch, automatic speed control, steering, heating, air conditioning and instruments: Check operation	●	●	●	●
Visual inspection for leaks: Oils and fluids	●	●	●	●

PR1139100006040X

Fig. 1 911 Carrera (Part 4 of 5). Except 1994–96

Additional service every 60 000 miles / 96 000 km	968	911 Turbo	911	928
Camshafts' drive belt: replacement required	●			
Camshafts' drive belt: replace. Check tension after 2 000 - 2 500 miles/3 200 - 4 000 km and document in space provided				●
Manual transmission and axle drives: change oil	●	●	●	●
Automatic transmission: change oil in differential	●		●	●

Service every 2 years	968	911 Turbo	911	928
Cooling system: change coolant	●			●

Service every 3 years	968	911 Turbo	911	928
Brake system: change brake fluid (only use Original Porsche Brake Fluid)	●	●	●	●

Service after 4, 8, 10 and then every 2 years	968	911 Turbo	911	928
Air bag supplemental restraint system scheduled maintenance	●	●	●	●

PR1139100006050X

Fig. 1 911 Carrera (Part 5 of 5). Except 1994–96

Service every 20,000 km
Diagnosis system: read out fault memory
Change engine oil
Air cleaner: replace filter element
Particle filter: replace filter element
V-belt or Polyrib belt: check condition and tension
Replace spart plugs (only on vehicles without catalytic converter)
Visual check for leaks: oils and fluids
Crankcase ventilation: check tightness of hose connections
Fuel system: visual inspection for damage, routing and tight fit of line and hose connections
Intake air system: check hoses, lines and connections for tight fit
Parking brake: check free travel of parking brake lever
Brake system: visual check of brake pads and brake discs for wear
Brake hoses and pipes: visual check for damage, routing and corrosion
Clutch: check free travel and pedal end position
Throttle actutator: check for smooth operation and full-load position
Check operation of resonance flap
Steering gear: visual check of rubber bellows for damage. Tie rod joints: check play and condition of dust caps
Power steering: check fluid level
Ball joints: visual inspection of dust caps for damage. Check bolt connections of front and rear suspension alignment for tight fit
Transmission / final drives: check oil levels
Automatic transmission: check ATF fluid level
Drive shafts: visual inspection of bellows for leaks and damage
Exhaust system: visual inspection for leaks and damage, check fitting
Tires: check condition and tire pressure
Door hinges: lubricate with oil
Check door and hinge locks and safety hook of front hood for tightness and operation
Seat belts: check operation and condition
Seals of doors, hoods and roof: remove rubber abrasions. Apply suitable lubricant.
Check operation of vehicle lighting. All headlights: check adjustment. Signal horn: check operation
Windshield washer system, headlight cleaning system: Check fluid level and nozzle adjustment, check antifreeze content in winter season
All other electrical systems, monitor lamps and warning lamps: check operation
Ignition circuits 1 and 2: check operation
Test drive: Brake pedal and parking brake, clutch, automatic speed control, steering, heater, air conditioning and instruments: check operation
Visual inspection for leaks: oils and fluids

PR1139400010010X

Fig. 2 911 Carrera (Part 1 of 2). 1994–96

Additional service every 40,000 km
Automatic transmission: change ATF and ATF filter
Toothed belt for power steering: check condition
Replace spark plugs (only for vehicles with catalytic converter)
Replace both engine oil filters
Additional service every 80,000 km
Replace fuel filter
Manual transmission / final drives: change oil
Automatic transmission: change oil in final drive
Yearly service – starting after the first 2 years
File Status Report for Long-life warranty
Service every 3 years
Change brake fluid (use only genuine Porsche brake fluid)
Service every 4, 8, 10 years and then every 2 years
Check airbag system
Recommended annual service
Visual inspection for leaks: oils, fluids
Diagnosis system: read out fault memory
Parking brake: check free travel of parking brake lever
Brake system: visual check of brake pads and brake discs for wear
Check brake fluid level
Steering gear: visual inspection of bellows for damage Tie rod joints: check play and condition of dust caps
Ball joints: visual inspection of dust caps for damage
Drive shafts: visual inspection of bellows for leaks and damage
Exhaust system: visual inspection for leaks and damage, check fitting,
Tires: check condition and tire pressure
Seals of doors, hoods and roof: remove rubber abrasions. Apply suitable lubricant.
Check operation of vehicle lighting.
Windshield washer system, headlight cleaning system: Check fluid level and nozzle adjustment, check antifreeze content in winter season.
Battery: Check electrolyte level and electrolyte density
All other electrical systems and monitor lamps and warning lamps: check operation
File Status Report for Long-life warranty (first report after 2 years)
Test drive: Brake pedal and parking brake, clutch, automatic speed control, steering, heater, air conditioning and instruments: check operation
Visual inspection for leaks: oils and fluids

PR1139400010020X

Fig. 2 911 Carrera (Part 2 of 2). 1994–96

VEHICLE MAINTENANCE SCHEDULES

Saab

INDEX

	Page No.	Fig. No.
900	0-101	1
9000	0-102	2

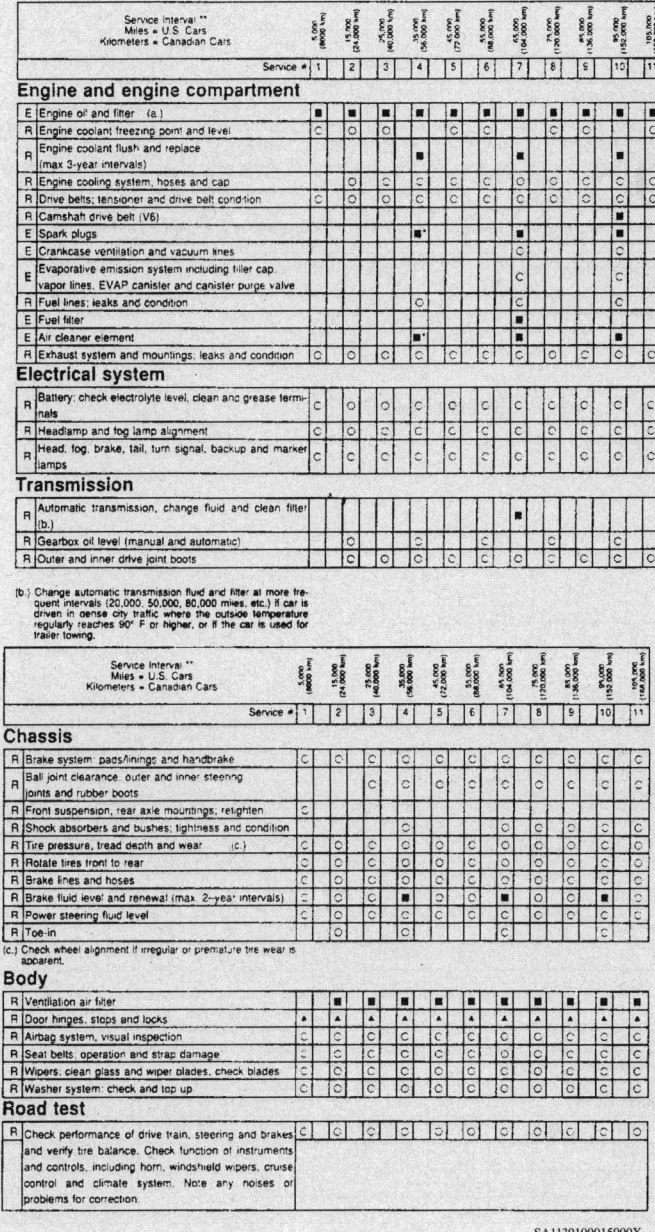

	Service Interval ** Miles = U.S. Cars Kilometers = Canadian Cars	5,000 (8000 km)	15,000 (24,000 km)	25,000 (40,000 km)	35,000 (56,000 km)	45,000 (72,000 km)	55,000 (88,000 km)	65,000 (104,000 km)	75,000 (120,000 km)	85,000 (136,000 km)	95,000 (152,000 km)	105,000 (168,000 km)
	Service #	1	2	3	4	5	6	7	8	9	10	11

Engine and engine compartment

		1	2	3	4	5	6	7	8	9	10	11
E	Engine oil and filter (a.)	■	■	■	■	■	■	■	■	■	■	■
R	Engine coolant freezing point and level	○	○	○		○	○		○	○		○
R	Engine coolant flush and replace (max 3-year intervals)				■			■			■	
R	Engine cooling system, hoses and cap		○	○	○	○	○	○	○	○	○	○
R	Drive belts; tensioner and drive belt condition	○	○	○	○	○	○	○	○	○	○	○
R	Camshaft drive belt (V6)										■	
E	Spark plugs				■*			■			■	
E	Crankcase ventilation and vacuum lines							○			○	
E	Evaporative emission system including filler cap, vapor lines, EVAP canister and canister purge valve							○			○	
R	Fuel lines; leaks and condition				○			○			○	
E	Fuel filter							■				
E	Air cleaner element				■*			■			■	
R	Exhaust system and mountings; leaks and condition	○	○	○	○	○	○	○	○	○	○	○

Electrical system

		1	2	3	4	5	6	7	8	9	10	11
R	Battery; check electrolyte level, clean and grease terminals	○	○	○	○	○	○	○	○	○	○	○
R	Headlamp and fog lamp alignment	○	○	○	○	○	○	○	○	○	○	○
R	Head, fog, brake, tail, turn signal, backup and marker lamps	○	○	○	○	○	○	○	○	○	○	○

Transmission

		1	2	3	4	5	6	7	8	9	10	11
R	Automatic transmission, change fluid and clean filter (b.)							■				
R	Gearbox oil level (manual and automatic)		○		○		○		○		○	
R	Outer and inner drive joint boots		○	○	○	○	○	○	○	○	○	○

(b.) Change automatic transmission fluid and filter at more frequent intervals (20,000, 50,000, 80,000 miles, etc.) if car is driven in dense city traffic where the outside temperature regularly reaches 90° F or higher, or if the car is used for trailer towing.

	Service Interval ** Miles = U.S. Cars Kilometers = Canadian Cars	5,000 (8000 km)	15,000 (24,000 km)	25,000 (40,000 km)	35,000 (56,000 km)	45,000 (72,000 km)	55,000 (88,000 km)	65,000 (104,000 km)	75,000 (120,000 km)	85,000 (136,000 km)	95,000 (152,000 km)	105,000 (168,000 km)
	Service #	1	2	3	4	5	6	7	8	9	10	11

Chassis

		1	2	3	4	5	6	7	8	9	10	11
R	Brake system: pads/linings and handbrake	○	○	○	○	○	○	○	○	○	○	○
R	Ball joint clearance, outer and inner steering joints and rubber boots			○	○	○	○	○	○	○	○	○
R	Front suspension, rear axle mountings; retighten	○										
R	Shock absorbers and bushes; tightness and condition				○			○	○	○	○	○
R	Tire pressure, tread depth and wear (c.)	○	○	○	○	○	○	○	○	○	○	○
R	Rotate tires front to rear	○	○	○	○	○	○	○	○	○	○	○
R	Brake lines and hoses	○	○	○	○	○	○	○	○	○	○	○
R	Brake fluid level and renewal (max. 2–year intervals)	○	○	○	■	○	○	■	○	○	■	○
R	Power steering fluid level	○	○	○	○	○	○	○	○	○	○	○
R	Toe-in		○		○			○			○	

(c.) Check wheel alignment if irregular or premature tire wear is apparent.

Body

		1	2	3	4	5	6	7	8	9	10	11
R	Ventilation air filter		■	■	■	■	■	■	■	■	■	■
R	Door hinges, stops and locks	▲	▲	▲	▲	▲	▲	▲	▲	▲	▲	▲
R	Airbag system, visual inspection	○	○	○	○	○	○	○	○	○	○	○
R	Seat belts: operation and strap damage	○	○	○	○	○	○	○	○	○	○	○
R	Wipers: clean glass and wiper blades, check blades	○	○	○	○	○	○	○	○	○	○	○
R	Washer system: check and top up	○	○	○	○	○	○	○	○	○	○	○

Road test

		1	2	3	4	5	6	7	8	9	10	11
R	Check performance of drive train, steering and brakes and verify tire balance. Check function of instruments and controls, including horn, windshield wipers, cruise control and climate system. Note any noises or problems for correction.	○	○	○	○	○	○	○	○	○	○	○

SA1139100015000X

Fig. 1 900

Service Interval** Miles = U.S. Cars Kilometers = Canadian Cars		5,000 (8,000 km)	15,000 (24,000 km)	25,000 (40,000 km)	35,000 (56,000 km)	45,000 (72,000 km)	55,000 (88,000 km)	65,000 (104,000 km)	75,000 (120,000 km)	85,000 (136,000 km)	95,000 (152,000 km)	105,000 (168,000 km)
	Service #	1	2	3	4	5	6	7	8	9	10	11
Engine and engine compartment												
E	Engine oil and filter (a.)	■	■	■	■	■	■	■	■	■	■	■
R	Coolant freezing point and level	○	○	○		○	○		○	○		○
R	Coolant flush and replace (max. 3-year intervals)				■			■			■	
R	Cooling system, hoses and cap	○			○			○			○	
R	Drive belt tensioner function and belt condition)	○	○	○	○	○	○	■	○	○	○	○
E	Spark plugs				■*			■			■	
E	Crankcase ventilation and vacuum lines							○			○	
E	Evaporative control system including filler cap, vapor lines, canister and purge							○			○	
R	Fuel lines; leaks and condition				○			○			○	
E	Fuel filter							■				
E	Air cleaner element				■*			■			■	
R	Exhaust system and mountings; leaks and condition	○	○	○	○	○	○	○	○	○	○	○
R	Calibration, idle speed (Traction Control System) (b.)	○										

* For vehicles certified for sale and registered in California, these are the minimum required Emission Control System maintenance steps. Saab urges that all recommended maintenance procedures be performed according to this program.

(a.) Engine oil and filter should be changed at least once a year. Intermediate oil and filter changes (halfway between indicated intervals) suggested for cars primarily used for driving in dense city traffic or for repeated short trip operation without sufficient engine warm up.

(b.) TCS calibration must be performed by an authorized Saab dealer.

****Service Intervals:** Repeat service procedures for Service #2 at 115,000/135,000/145,000 etc.; Service #7 at 125,000; Service #4 at 155/185,000

Application/type of service (col. 1)
E = emission service
R = regular maintenance

Service Procedure
○ = check - top up, adjust or replace if necessary
■ = replace
▲ = lubricate

SA1139100016010X

Fig. 2 9000 (Part 1 of 3)

Service Interval Miles = U.S. Cars Kilometers = Canadian Cars		5,000 (8,000 km)	15,000 (24,000 km)	25,000 (40,000 km)	35,000 (56,000 km)	45,000 (72,000 km)	55,000 (88,000 km)	65,000 (104,000 km)	75,000 (120,000 km)	85,000 (136,000 km)	95,000 (152,000 km)	105,000 (168,000 km)
	Service #	1	2	3	4	5	6	7	8	9	10	11
Electrical system												
R	Battery; check electrolyte level, clean and grease terminals	○	○	○	○	○	○	○	○	○	○	○
R	Headlamp and fog lamp alignment				○			○			○	
R	Head, fog, brake, tail, turn signal, backup and marker lamps	○	○	○	○	○	○	○	○	○	○	○
Transmission												
R	Automatic transmission fluid and filter change (c.)	■			■			■			■	
R	Gearbox oil level (manual and automatic)	○	○	○	○	○	○	○	○	○	○	○
R	Outer and inner drive joint boots	○	○	○	○	○	○	○	○	○	○	○
Chassis												
R	Hand brake function	○			○			○			○	
R	Hand brake cable adjustment	○										
R	Ball joint clearance, outer and inner steering joints and rubber boots				○			○			○	
R	Front suspension, rear axle mountings; retighten	○										
R	Shock absorbers and bushes; tightness and condition				○			○			○	
R	Tire pressure tread depth and wear (d.)	○	○	○	○	○	○	○	○	○	○	○
R	Rotate tires, front to rear	○	○	○	○	○	○	○	○	○	○	○
R	Brake pads and discs; wear and condition	○	○	○	○	○	○	○	○	○	○	○

(c.) Change automatic transmission fluid and filter at more frequent intervals (20,000, 50,000, 80,000 miles, etc.) If car is driven in dense city traffic where the outside temperature regularly reaches 90° F or higher, or if car is used in a mountainous/high altitude area or for trailer towing.

(d.) Check wheel alignment if irregular or premature tire wear is apparent.

SA1139100016020X

Fig. 2 9000 (Part 2 of 3)

	Service Interval Miles = U.S. Cars Kilometers = Canadian Cars	5,000 (8,000 km)	15,000 (24,000 km)	25,000 (40,000 km)	35,000 (56,000 km)	45,000 (72,000 km)	55,000 (88,000 km)	65,000 (104,000 km)	75,000 (120,000 km)	85,000 (136,000 km)	95,000 (152,000 km)	105,000 (168,000 km)
	Service #	1	2	3	4	5	6	7	8	9	10	11
Chassis (continued)												
R	Brake lines and hoses	○	○	○	○	○	○	○	○	○	○	○
R	Brake fluid level and renewal (max. 2-year intervals)	○	○	○	■	○	○	■	○	○	■	○
R	Power steering fluid level	○	○	○	○	○	○	○	○	○	○	○
R	Toe-in				○			○			○	
Body												
R	Ventilation air filter				■			■			■	
R	Door hinges, stops and locks				▲			▲			▲	
R	Airbag system (check after 10 years)											
Road Test												
R	Check performance of drive train, steering and brakes and verify tire balance. Check function of instruments and controls, including horn, windshield wipers, cruise control and climate system. Note any noises or problems for correction.	○	○	○	○	○	○	○	○	○	○	○

SA1139100016030X

Fig. 2 9000 (Part 3 of 3)

VEHICLE MAINTENANCE SCHEDULES

Subaru

INDEX

	Page No.	Fig. No.
Impreza	0-104	1
Justy	0-105	2
Legacy & Loyale	0-106	3
SVX	0-107	4

Continue periodic maintenance beyond 96,000 km (60,000 miles) or 60 months by returning to the first column of the maintenance schedule and adding 96,000 km (60,000 miles) or 60 months to the column headings.

Symbols used:
R: Replace
I: Inspect, and then adjust, correct or replace if necessary.
P: Perform
(I) or (P): Recommended service for safe vehicle operation
*: This maintenance operation is required for all states except California. However, we do recommend that this operation be performed on California vehicles as well.

MAINTENANCE ITEM		MAINTENANCE INTERVAL (Number of months or km (miles), whichever occurs first)										REMARKS
		Months	3	7.5	15	22.5	30	37.5	45	52.5	60	
		x 1,000 km	4.8	12	24	36	48	60	72	84	96	
		x 1,000 miles	3	7.5	15	22.5	30	37.5	45	52.5	60	
1	Drive belt(s) [Except camshaft] (Inspect drive belt tension)						I				R	
2	Camshaft drive belt						I*				R	
3	Engine oil		R	R	R	R	R	R	R	R	R	See NOTE 1)
4	Engine oil filter		R	R	R	R	R	R	R	R	R	
5	Replace engine coolant and inspect cooling system, hoses and connections						P				P	
6	Replace fuel filter and inspect fuel system hoses and connections						(P)				P	See NOTE 2), 6) & 7)
7	Air cleaner						R				R	
8	Spark plug						R				R	
9	Transmission/Differential (Front & Rear) Lubricants (Gear oil)						I					See NOTE 3)
10	Automatic transmission fluid						I					See NOTE 4)
11	Brake fluid						R				R	See NOTE 5)
12	Disc brake pad and disc, Front and rear axle boots and axle shaft joints				I		I		I		I	See NOTE 6)
13	Brake linings and drums (Parking brake)						I				I	See NOTE 6)
14	Inspect brake line and check operation of parking and service brake system				P		P		P		P	See NOTE 6)
15	Clutch and hill-holder system				I		I		I		I	
16	Steering and suspension				I		I		I		I	See NOTE 6)
17	Front and rear wheel bearing lubricant										(I)	
18	Supplemental restraint system		Inspect every 10 years									

SB1139100044010X

Fig. 1 Impreza (Part 1 of 2)

NOTE:

1) **When the vehicle is used under severe driving conditions such as those mentioned below*, the engine oil should be changed more often.**
2) **When the vehicle is used in extremely cold or hot weather areas, contamination of the filter may occur and filter replacement should be performed more often.**
3) **When the vehicle is frequently operated under severe conditions, replacement should be performed every 48,000 km (30,000 miles).**
4) **When the vehicle is frequently operated under severe conditions, replacement should be performed every 24,000 km (15,000 miles).**
5) **When the vehicle is used in high humidity areas or in mountainous areas, change the brake fluid every 24,000 km (15,000 miles) or 15 months, whichever occurs first.**
6) **When the vehicle is used under severe driving conditions such as those mentioned below*, inspection should be performed every 12,000 km (7,500 miles) or 7.5 months, whichever occurs first.**
7) **This inspection is not required to maintain emission warranty eligibility and it does not affect the manufacturer's obligations under EPA's in-use compliance program.**

* Examples of severe driving conditions:
(1) Repeated short distance driving. (Items 3, 12 and 13 only)
(2) Driving on rough and/or muddy roads. (Items 12, 13 and 16 only)
(3) Driving in dusty conditions.
(4) Driving in extremely cold weather. (Items 3 and 16 only)
(5) Driving in areas where roads salts or other corrosive materials are used. (Items 6, 12, 13, 14 and 16 only)
(6) Living in coastal areas. (Items 6, 12, 13, 14 and 16 only)

SB1139100044020X

Fig. 1 Impreza (Part 2 of 2)

Continue periodic maintenance beyond 96,000 km (60,000 miles) or 60 months by returning to the first column of the maintenance schedule and adding 96,000 km (60,000 miles) or 60 months to the column headings.

Symbols used
- R : Replace
- I : Inspect, and then adjust, correct or replace if necessary
- P : Perform
- (I) or (P) : Recommended service for safe vehicle operation

	MAINTENANCE ITEM	MAINTENANCE INTERVAL [Number of months or km (miles), whichever occurs first]										REMARKS
		Months	3	7.5	15	22.5	30	37.5	45	52.5	60	
		x 1,000 km	4.8	12	24	36	48	60	72	84	96	
		x 1,000 miles	3	7.5	15	22.5	30	37.5	45	52.5	60	
1	Drive belt(s) [Except camshaft]						I				R	
2	Camshaft drive belt										R	
3	Engine oil and oil filter		R	R	R	R	R	R	R	R	R	See NOTE 1)
4	Replace engine coolant and inspect cooling system, hose and connections						P				P	
5	Replace fuel filter and inspect fuel system, line and connections						(P)				P	See NOTE 2), 6) & 7)
6	Air filter elements (Air filter, PCV air filter*)						R				R	*: On carburetor engine only
7	Spark plugs						R				R	
8	Intake and exhaust valve clearance				I		I		I		I	
9	Transmission/Differential (Front & Rear) lubricants (Gear oil)				I		I		I		I	See NOTE 3)
10	ECVT fluid						R				R	See NOTE 4)
11	ECVT system (Accelerator pedal switch, selector switch and carbon brush)						I				I	
12	Brake fluid						R				R	See NOTE 5)
13	Disc brake pad and disc/Front and rear axle boots and axle shaft joint portions				I		I		I		I	See NOTE 6)
14	Brake linings and drums						I				I	See NOTE 6)
15	Inspect brake line and check operation of parking and service brake system				P		P		P		P	See NOTE 6)
16	Clutch pedal operation				I		I		I		I	
17	Steering and suspension system				I		I		I		I	See NOTE 6)
18	Front and rear wheel bearings lubricant										(I)	

NOTES:

1. When the vehicle is used under severe driving conditions such as those mentioned below**, the engine oil should be changed more often.
2. When the vehicle is used in extremely cold or hot weather areas, contamination of the filter may occur and filter replacement should be performed more often.
3. When the vehicle is frequently operated under severe driving conditions, replacement should be performed every 48,000 km (30,000 miles).
4. When the vehicle is frequently operated under severe driving conditions, such as mountain driving replacement should be performed every 24,000 km (15,000 miles).
5. When the vehicle is used in high humidity areas or in mountainous areas, change the brake fluid every 24,000 km (15,000 miles) or 15 months, whichever occurs first.
6. When the vehicle is used under severe driving conditions such as those mentioned below**, inspection should be performed every 12,000 km (7,500 miles) or 7.5 months, whichever occurs first.
7. This inspection is not required to maintain emission warranty eligibility and it does not affect the manufactuer's obligations under EPA's in-use compliance program.

** Examples of severe driving conditions:
- (1) Repeated short distance driving. (Items 3, 13 and 14 only)
- (2) Driving on rough and/or muddy roads. (Ktems 13, 14 and 17 only)
- (3) Driving in dusty conditions.
- (4) Driving in extremely cold weather. (Items 3 and 17 only)
- (5) Driving in areas where roads salts or other corrosive materials are used. (Item 5, 13, 14, 15 and 17 only)
- (6) Living in coastal areas. (Items 5, 13, 14, 15 and 17 only)

SB1139100040000X

Fig. 2 Justy

Continue periodic maintenance beyond 96,000 km (60,000 miles) or 60 months by returning to the first column of the maintenance schedule and adding 96,000 km (60,000 miles) or 60 months to the column headings.

Symbols used:
R: Replace
I: Inspect, and then adjust, correct or replace if necessary.
P: Perform
(I) or (P): Recommended service for safe vehicle operation
*: This maintenance operation is required for all states except California. However, we do recommend that this operation be performed on California vehicles as well.

	MAINTENANCE ITEM	MAINTENANCE INTERVAL (Number of months or km (miles), whichever occurs first)										REMARKS
		Months	3	7.5	15	22.5	30	37.5	45	52.5	60	
		x1,000 km	4.8	12	24	36	48	60	72	84	96	
		x1,000 miles	3	7.5	15	22.5	30	37.5	45	52.5	60	
1	Drive belt(s) [Except camshaft] (Inspect drive belt tension)						I				R	
2	Camshaft drive belt						I*				R	
3	Engine oil		R	R	R	R	R	R	R	R	R	See NOTE 1)
4	Engine oil filter		R	R	R	R	R	R	R	R	R	
5	Replace engine coolant and inspect cooling system, hoses and connections						P				P	
6	Replace fuel filter and inspect fuel system hoses and connections						(P)				P	See NOTE 2), 6) & 7)
7	Air filter elements						R				R	
8	Spark plug						R				R	
9	Transmission/Differential (Front & Rear) Lubricants (Gear oil)						I					See NOTE 3)
10	Automatic transmission fluid						I					See NOTE 4)
11	Brake fluid						R				R	See NOTE 5)
12	Disc brake pad and disc, Front and rear axle boots and axle shaft joints				I		I		I		I	See NOTE 6)
13	Brake linings and drums (Parking brake)						I				I	See NOTE 6)
14	Inspect brake line and check operation of parking and service brake system				P		P		P		P	See NOTE 6)
15	Clutch and hill-holder system				I		I		I		I	
16	Steering and suspension				I		I		I		I	See NOTE 6)
17	Front and rear wheel bearing lubricant										(I)	
18	Supplemental Restraint System		Inspect every 10 years									

1) When the vehicle is used under severe driving conditions such as those mentioned below**, the engine oil should be changed more often.
2) When the vehicle is used in extremely cold or hot weather areas, contamination of the filter may occur and filter replacement should be performed more often.
3) When the vehicle is frequently operated under severe conditions, replacement should be performed every 48,000 km (30,000 miles).
4) When the vehicle is frequently operated under severe conditions, replacement should be performed every 24,000 km (15,000 miles).
5) When the vehicle is used in high humidity areas or in mountainous areas, change the brake fluid every 24,000 km (15,000 miles) or 15 months, whichever occurs first.
6) When the vehicle is used under severe driving conditions such as those mentioned below*, inspection should be performed every 12,000 km (7,500 miles) or 7.5 months, whichever occurs first.

SB1139100041000X

Fig. 3 Legacy & Loyale

Continue periodic maintenance beyond 96,000 km (60,000 miles) or 60 months by returning to the first column of the maintenance schedule and adding 96,000 km (60,000 miles) or 60 months to the column headings.

Symbols used:
R: Replace
I: Inspect, and then adjust, correct or replace if necessary.
P: Perform
(I) or (P): Recommended service for safe vehicle operation
*: This maintenance operation is required for all states except California.
However, we do recommend that this operation be performed on California vehicles as well.

	MAINTENANCE ITEM	MAINTENANCE INTERVAL (Number of months or km (miles), whichever occurs first)									REMARKS
	Months	3	7.5	15	22.5	30	37.5	45	52.5	60	
	x1,000 km	4.8	12	24	36	48	60	72	84	96	
	x1,000 miles	3	7.5	15	22.5	30	37.5	45	52.5	60	
1	Drive belt(s) [Except camshaft] (Inspect drive belt tension)					I				R	
2	Timing belt (Camshaft drive belt)					I*				R	
3	Engine oil	R	R	R	R	R	R	R	R	R	See NOTE 1)
4	Engine oil filter	R	R	R	R	R	R	R	R	R	
5	Replace engine coolant and inspect cooling system, hoses and connections					P				P	
6	Replace fuel filter and inspect fuel system hoses and connections					(P)				P	See NOTE 2), 6) & 7)
7	Air filter elements					R				R	
8	Spark plug									R	
9	Differential (Front & Rear) Lubricants (Gear oil)					I					See NOTE 3)
10	Automatic transmission fluid					I					See NOTE 4)
11	Brake fluid					R				R	See NOTE 5)
12	Disc brake pad and disc, Front and rear axle boots and axle shaft joints			I		I		I		I	See NOTE 6)
13	Brake linings and drums (Parking brake)					I				I	See NOTE 6)
14	Inspect brake line and check operation of parking and service brake system			P		P		P		P	See NOTE 6)
15	Steering and suspension			I		I		I		I	See NOTE 6)
16	Front and rear wheel bearing lubricant									(I)	
17	Supplemental restraint system	Inspect every 10 years.									

1) When the vehicle is used under severe driving conditions such as those mentioned below**, the engine oil should be changed more often.
2) When the vehicle is used in extremely cold or hot weather areas, contamination of the filter may occur and filter replacement should be performed more often.
3) When the vehicle is frequently operated under severe conditions, replacement should be performed every 48,000 km (30,000 miles).
4) When the vehicle is frequently operated under severe conditions, replacement should be performed every 24,000 km (15,000 miles).
5) When the vehicle is used in high humidity areas or in mountainous areas, change the brake fluid every 24,000 km (15,000 miles) or 15 months, whichever occurs first.
6) When the vehicle is used under severe driving conditions such as those mentioned below**, inspection should be performed every 12,000 km (7,500 miles) or 7.5 months, whichever occurs first.

SB1139100043000X

Fig. 4 SVX

VEHICLE MAINTENANCE SCHEDULES

Suzuki

INDEX

	Page No.	Fig. No.
Samurai		
All	0-108	1
Sidekick		
1993–95	0-109	2
1996	0-111	3
1996 w/California Emissions	0-111	3
1996 w/Federal Emissions	0-110	3
Swift		
All	0-112	4

Interval: This interval should be judged by odometer reading or months, whichever comes first.	miles (x 1,000)	7.5	15	22.5	30	37.5	45	52.5	60	67.5	75	82.5	90	97.5	105	112.5	120
	km (x 1,000)	12	24	36	48	60	72	84	96	108	120	132	144	156	168	180	192
	months	6	12	18	24	30	36	42	48	54	60	66	72	78	84	90	96
ENGINE & EMISSION CONTROL																	
1. Fan (Water pump) drive belt		–	–	–	I	–	–	–	R	–	–	–	I	–	–	–	R
2. Camshaft timing belt		–	–	–	–	–	–	–	I	–	–	–	I	–	–	–	I
3. Valve lash (clearance)		–	I	–	I	–	I	–	I	–	I	–	I	–	I	–	I
4. Engine oil and oil filter		R	R	R	R	R	R	R	R	R	R	R	R	R	R	R	R
5. Cooling system hoses and connections		–	–	–	**I	–	–	–	I	–	–	–	I	–	–	–	I
6. Engine coolant		–	–	–	**R	–	–	–	R	–	–	–	R	–	–	–	R
7. Exhaust pipes and mountings		–	–	–	**I	–	–	–	I&(R)	–	–	–	I	–	–	–	I&(R)
8. PCV valve		Replace at 50,000 miles (80,000 km) and 100,000 miles (160,000 km)															
9. Oxygen sensor		Replace at 80,000 miles (128,000 km)															
10. Catalytic converter		Inspect at 100,000 miles (160,000 km)															
11. Charcoal canister		Replace at 100,000 miles (160,000 km)															
12. Emission-related hoses & tubes		–	–	–	–	–	–	–	I	–	–	–	–	–	–	–	I
13. EGR system		Inspect at 50,000 miles (80,000 km) and 100,000 miles (160,000 km)															
14. ECM & associated sensors		Inspect at 100,000 miles (160,000 km)															
15. Wiring harness and connections		–	–	–*	–	–	–	–	I	–	–	–	–	–	–	–	I
16. Spark plugs		–	–	–	R	–	–	–	R	–	–	–	R	–	–	–	R
17. Distributor cap and rotor		–	–	–	–	–	–	–	I	–	–	–	–	–	–	–	I
18. Ignition wiring		–	–	–	–	–	–	–	R	–	–	–	–	–	–	–	R
19. Ignition timing		–	–	–	–	–	–	–	I	–	–	–	–	–	–	–	I
20. Distributor advance		–	–	–	–	–	–	–	I	–	–	–	–	–	–	–	I

NOTES:
"R": Replace or change
"I" : Inspect and correct or replace if necessary
"T": Tighten to the specified torque
"L": Lubricate

- *Item 7 (R) is applicable to the exhaust mounting rubber only.*
- *(For U.S.A. specification vehicle) Item 5 **I, Item 6 **R and Item 7 **I are recommended maintenance items.*

SK1139100048010X

Fig. 1 Samurai (Part 1 of 2)

Interval: This interval should be judged by odometer reading or months, whichever comes first.	miles (x 1,000)	7.5	15	22.5	30	37.5	45	52.5	60	67.5	75	82.5	90	97.5	105	112.5	120
	km (x 1,000)	12	24	36	48	60	72	84	96	108	120	132	144	156	168	180	192
	months	6	12	18	24	30	36	42	48	54	60	66	72	78	84	90	96
21. Fuel tank cap		–	–	–	**I	–	–	–	R	–	–	–	I	–	–	–	R
22. Air cleaner filter element		–	–	–	R	–	–	–	R	–	–	–	R	–	–	–	R
23. Thermostatically controlled air cleaner system		–	–	–	I	–	–	–	I	–	–	–	I	–	–	–	I
24. Choke system		–	–	–	I&L	–	–	–	I&L	–	–	–	I&L	–	–	–	I&L
25. Fuel filter		–	–	–	**R	–	–	–	R	–	–	–	R	–	–	–	R
26. Fuel lines and connections		–	–	–	**I	–	–	–	R	–	–	–	I	–	–	–	R
*27. Idle speed		–	I	–	I	–	I	–	I	–	I	–	I	–	I	–	I
28. Idle mixture		–	–	–	–	–	–	–	I	–	–	–	–	–	–	–	I
29. Carburetor		Inspect at 100,000 miles (160,000 km)															
CHASSIS AND BODY																	
30. Clutch		–	I	–	I	–	I	–	I	–	I	–	I	–	I	–	I
31. Brake discs and pads (front) Brake drums and shoes (rear)		–	I	–	I	–	I	–	I	–	I	–	I	–	I	–	I
32. Brake hoses and pipes		–	I	–	I	–	I	–	I	–	I	–	I	–	I	–	I
33. Brake fluid		–	I	–	I	–	I	–	R	–	I	–	I	–	I	–	R
34. Brake pedal		–	I	–	I	–	I	–	I	–	I	–	I	–	I	–	I
35. Brake lever and cable		–	I	–	I	–	I	–	I	–	I	–	I	–	I	–	I
36. Tires		I	I	I	I	I	I	I	I	I	I	I	I	I	I	I	I
37. Wheel discs and free wheeling hubs (if equipped)		I	I	I	I	I	I	I	I	I	I	I	I	I	I	I	I
38. Steering knuckle oil seals		–	–	R	–	–	R	–	–	R	–	–	R	–	–	R	–
39. Wheel bearings		–	I	–	*I	–	I	–	*I	–	I	–	*I	–	I	–	*I
40. Shock absorbers		I	I	–	I	–	I	–	I	–	I	–	I	–	I	–	I
41. Propeller shafts		–	I&L	–	I&L	–	I&L	–	I&L	–	I&L	–	I&L	–	I&L	–	I&L
42. Transmission, transfer and differential oil		R	I	I	R	I	I	I	R	I	I	I	R	I	I	I	R
43. Leaf springs		–	–	–	I	–	–	–	I	–	–	–	I	–	–	–	I
44. Bolts and nuts		T	T	–	T	–	T	–	T	–	T	–	T	–	T	–	T
45. Steering system		I	I	I	I	I	I	I	I	I	I	I	I	I	I	I	I
46. Door hinges		L	L	L	L	L	L	L	L	L	L	L	L	L	L	L	L

NOTES:

"R": Replace or change

"I" : Inspect and correct or replace if necessary

"T": Tighten to the specified torque

"L": Lubricate

- *(For U.S.A. specification vehicle) Item 21 **I, Item 25 **R and Item 26 **I are recommended maintenance items.*
- *Item 26 R is applicable to the fuel hose and clamp only.*
- *Item *27 is recommended maintenance item.*
- *Item 39 *I is applicable to not only rattled wear but also their grease.*

SK1139100048020X

Fig. 1 Samurai (Part 2 of 2)

Interval: This interval should be judged by odometer reading or months, whichever comes first.	miles (x 1,000)	7.5	15	22.5	30	37.5	45	52.5	60	67.5	75	82.5	90	97.5	105	112.5	120
	km (x 1,000)	12.5	25	37.5	50	62.5	75	87.5	100	112.5	125	137.5	150	162.5	175	187.5	200
	months	7.5	15	22.5	30	37.5	45	52.5	60	67.5	75	82.5	90	97.5	105	112.5	120
ENGINE & EMISSION CONTROL																	
1. Fan (Water pump) drive belt		–	–	–	I	–	–	–	R	–	–	–	I	–	–	–	R
2. Camshaft timing belt		–	–	–	–	–	–	–	I	–	–	–	I	–	–	–	I
3. Valve lash (clearance)		–	I	–	I	–	I	–	I	–	I	–	I	–	I	–	I
4. Engine oil and oil filter		R	R	R	R	R	R	R	R	R	R	R	R	R	R	R	R
5. Cooling system hoses and connections		–	–	–	**I	–	–	–	I	–	–	–	I	–	–	–	I
6. Engine coolant		–	–	–	**R	–	–	–	R	–	–	–	R	–	–	–	R
7. Exhaust pipes and mountings		–	–	–	**I	–	–	–	I&(R)	–	–	–	I	–	–	–	I&(R)
8. PCV valve		Replace at 50,000 miles (83,000 km) and 100,000 miles (166,000 km)															
9. Oxygen sensor		Replace at 80,000 miles (133,000 km)															
10. Catalytic converter		Inspect at 100,000 miles (166,000 km)															
11. Charcoal canister		Replace at 100,000 miles (166,000 km)															
12. Emission-related hoses & tubes		–	–	–	–	–	–	–	I	–	–	–	–	–	–	–	I
*13. EGR system		Inspect at 50,000 miles (83,000 km) and 100,000 miles (166,000 km)															
14. ECM & associated sensors		Inspect at 100,000 miles (166,000 km)															
15. Wiring harness and connections		–	–	–	–	–	–	–	I	–	–	–	–	–	–	–	I
IGNITION SYSTEM																	
16. Spark plugs		–	–	–	R	–	–	–	R	–	–	–	R	–	–	–	R
17. Distributor cap and rotor		–	–	–	–	–	–	–	I	–	–	–	–	–	–	–	I
18. Ignition wiring		–	–	–	–	–	–	–	R	–	–	–	–	–	–	–	R
19. Ignition timing		–	–	–	–	–	–	–	I	–	–	–	–	–	–	–	I
20.		BLANK															
FUEL																	
21. Fuel tank cap		–	–	–	**I	–	–	–	R	–	–	–	I	–	–	–	R
22. Air cleaner filter element		–	–	–	R	–	–	–	R	–	–	–	R	–	–	–	R
23. Fuel filter		–	–	–	**R	–	–	–	R	–	–	–	R	–	–	–	R
24. Fuel lines and connections		–	–	–	**I	–	–	–	I	–	–	–	I	–	–	–	I
*25. Idle speed		–	I	–	I	–	I	–	I	–	I	–	I	–	I	–	I
26. Fuel injector		Inspect at 100,000 miles (166,000 km)															

SK1139100049010X

Fig. 2 Sidekick (Part 1 of 2). 1993–95

NOTES:
"R": Replace or change
"I" : Inspect and correct or replace if necessary
*• Item 5 **I, Item 6 **R and Item 7 **I are recommended mintenance items.*
• Item 7 (R) is applicable to exhaust mounting rubber only.
*• Item 21 **I, Item 23 **R and Item 24 **I are recommended maintenance items.*
*• Item *25 is recommended maintenance item.*

Interval: This interval should be judged by odometer reading or months, whichever comes first.																		
		miles (x 1,000)	7.5	15	22.5	30	37.5	45	52.5	60	67.5	75	82.5	90	97.5	105	112.5	120
		km (x 1,000)	12.5	25	37.5	50	62.5	75	87.5	100	112.5	125	137.5	150	162.5	175	187.5	200
		months	7.5	15	22.5	30	37.5	45	52.5	60	67.5	75	82.5	90	97.5	105	112.5	120
CHASSIS AND BODY																		
1. Clutch (For manual transmission)			–	I	–	I	–	I	–	I	–	I	–	I	–	I	–	I
2. Brake discs and pads (front) Brake drums and shoes (rear)			–	I	–	I	–	I	–	I	–	I	–	I	–	I	–	I
3. Brake hoses and pipes			–	I	–	I	–	I	–	I	–	I	–	I	–	I	–	I
4. Brake fluid			–	I	–	I	–	I	–	R	–	I	–	I	–	I	–	R
5. Brake pedal			–	I	–	I	–	I	–	I	–	I	–	I	–	I	–	I
6. Brake lever and cable			–	I	–	I	–	I	–	I	–	I	–	I	–	I	–	I
7. Tires			I	I	I	I	I	I	I	I	I	I	I	I	I	I	I	I
8. Wheel discs and free wheeling hubs (if equipped)			I	I	I	I	I	I	I	I	I	I	I	I	I	I	I	I
9. Wheel bearings			–	I	–	*I	–	I	–	*I	–	I	–	*I	–	I	–	*I
10. Suspension system			I	I	–	I	–	I	–	I	–	I	–	I	–	I	–	I
11. Propeller shafts			–	I	–	I	–	I	–	I	–	I	–	I	–	I	–	I
12. Transmission oil (Manual)			R	I	I	R	I	I	I	R	I	I	I	R	I	I	I	R
13. Automatic transmission	Fluid level		I	I	I	I	I	I	I	I	I	I	I	I	I	I	I	I
	Fluid change		Replace every 100,000 miles (166,000 km)															
	Fluid hose		–	–	–	–	–	R	–	–	–	–	–	R	–	–	–	–
14. Transfer and differential oil			R	I	I	R	I	I	I	R	I	I	I	R	I	I	I	R
15. Steering system			I	I	I	I	I	I	I	I	I	I	I	I	I	I	I	I
16. Power steering system (if equipped)			I	I	I	I	I	I	I	I	I	I	I	I	I	I	I	I
17. Door hinges			L	L	L	L	L	L	L	L	L	L	L	L	L	L	L	L

NOTES:
"R": Replace or change
"I" : Inspect and correct or replace if necessary
"L": Lubricate
*• Item 9 *I is applicable to not only rattled wear but also their grease.*

SK1139100049020X

Fig. 2 Sidekick (Part 2 of 2). 1993–95

Interval: This interval should be judged by odometer reading or months, whichever comes first.																	
	miles (x 1,000)	7.5	15	22.5	30	37.5	45	52.5	60	67.5	75	82.5	90	97.5	105	112.5	120
	km (x 1,000)	12.5	25	37.5	50	62.5	75	87.5	100	112.5	125	137.5	150	162.5	175	187.5	200
	months	7.5	15	22.5	30	37.5	45	52.5	60	67.5	75	82.5	90	97.5	105	112.5	120
ENGINE & EMISSION CONTROL																	
1. Drive belt		–	–	–	I	–	–	–	R	–	–	–	I	–	–	–	R
2. Camshaft timing belt		–	–	–	–	–	–	–	* *R	–	–	–	I	–	–	–	R
3. Valve lash (clearance)		–	I	–	I	–	I	–	I	–	I	–	I	–	I	–	I
4. Engine oil and oil filter		R	R	R	R	R	R	R	R	R	R	R	R	R	R	R	R
5. Cooling system hoses and connections		–	–	–	* *I	–	–	–	I	–	–	–	I	–	–	–	I
6. Engine coolant		–	–	–	* *R	–	–	–	R	–	–	–	R	–	–	–	R
7. Exhaust pipes and mountings		–	–	–	* *I	–	–	–	I&(R)	–	–	–	I	–	–	–	I&(R)
8. PCV valve		Replace at 50,000 miles (83,000 km) and 100,000 miles (166,000 km)															
9.		BLANK															
10. Three way catalytic converter		Inspect at 100,000 miles (166,000 km)															
11. EVAP canister		Replace at 100,000 miles (166,000 km)															
12. Emission-related hoses & tubes		–	–	–	–	–	–	–	I	–	–	–	–	–	–	–	I
13.		BLANK															
14.		BLANK															
15. Wiring harness and connections		–	–	–	–	–	–	–	I	–	–	–	–	–	–	–	I
IGNITION SYSTEM																	
16. Spark plugs		–	–	–	R	–	–	–	R	–	–	–	R	–	–	–	R
17. Distrubutor cap and rotor		–	–	–	–	–	–	–	I	–	–	–	–	–	–	–	I
18. Ignition wiring		–	–	–	–	–	–	–	R	–	–	–	–	–	–	–	R
19. Ignition timing		–	–	–	–	–	–	–	* *I	–	–	–	–	–	–	–	* *I
20.		BLANK															
FUEL																	
21. Fuel tank cap		–	–	–	* *I	–	–	–	R	–	–	–	I	–	–	–	R
22. Air cleaner filter element		–	–	–	R	–	–	–	R	–	–	–	R	–	–	–	R
23. Fuel filter		–	–	–	* *R	–	–	–	R	–	–	–	R	–	–	–	R
24. Fuel lines and connections		–	–	–	* *I	–	–	–	I	–	–	–	I	–	–	–	I
25. Idle speed		–	* *I	–	* *I	–	* *I	–	* *I	–	* *I	–	* *I	–	* *I	–	* *I
26. Fuel injector		Inspect at 100,000 miles (166,000 km)															

SK113960005501AX

Fig. 3 Sidekick (Part 1 of 2). 1996 w/Federal Emission

Interval: This interval should be judged by odometer reading or months, whichever comes first.																	
	miles (x 1,000)	7.5	15	22.5	30	37.5	45	52.5	60	67.5	75	82.5	90	97.5	105	112.5	120
	km (x 1,000)	12.5	25	37.5	50	62.5	75	87.5	100	112.5	125	137.5	150	162.5	175	187.5	200
	months	7.5	15	22.5	30	37.5	45	52.5	60	67.5	75	82.5	90	97.5	105	112.5	120
ENGINE & EMISSION CONTROL																	
1. Drive belt		–	–	–	I	–	–	–	* *R	–	–	–	I	–	–	–	R
2. Camshaft timing belt		–	–	–	–	–	–	–	* *R	–	–	–	* *I	–	–	–	R
3. Valve lash (clearance)		–	I	–	I	–	I	–	I	–	I	–	I	–	I	–	I
4. Engine oil and oil filter		R	R	R	R	R	R	R	R	R	R	R	R	R	R	R	R
5. Cooling system hoses and connections		–	–	–	* *I	–	–	–	I	–	–	–	I	–	–	–	I
6. Engine coolant		–	–	–	* *R	–	–	–	R	–	–	–	R	–	–	–	R
7. Exhaust pipes and mountings		–	–	–	* *I	–	–	–	*I*&(R)	–	–	–	I	–	–	–	I&(R)
8. PCV valve		Replace at 50,000 miles (83,000 km) and 100,000 miles (166,000 km)															
9.		BLANK															
10. Three way catalytic converter		Inspect at 100,000 miles (166,000 km)															
11. EVAP canister		Replace at 100,000 miles (166,000 km)															
12. Emission-related hoses & tubes		–	–	–	–	–	–	–	* *I	–	–	–	–	–	–	–	I
13.		BLANK															
14.		BLANK															
15. Wiring harness and connections		–	–	–	–	–	–	–	* *I	–	–	–	–	–	–	–	I
IGNITION SYSTEM																	
16. Spark plugs		–	–	–	R	–	–	–	R	–	–	–	R	–	–	–	R
17. Distributor cap and rotor		–	–	–	–	–	–	–	* *I	–	–	–	–	–	–	–	I
18. Ignition wiring		–	–	–	–	–	–	–	R	–	–	–	–	–	–	–	R
19. Ignition timing		–	–	–	–	–	–	–	* *I	–	–	–	–	–	–	–	* *I
20.		BLANK															
FUEL																	
21. Fuel tank cap		–	–	–	* *I	–	–	–	* *R	–	–	–	* *I	–	–	–	R
22. Air cleaner filter element		–	–	–	R	–	–	–	R	–	–	–	R	–	–	–	R
23. Fuel filter		–	–	–	* *R	–	–	–	* *R	–	–	–	* *R	–	–	–	R
24. Fuel lines and connections		–	–	–	* *I	–	–	–	* *I	–	–	–	* *I	–	–	–	I
25. Idle speed		–	–	–	* *I	–	–	–	* *I	–	–	–	* *I	–	–	–	* *I
26. Fuel injector		Inspect at 100,000 miles (166,000 km)															

NOTE:
- *The maintenance services with ** are recommended maintenance items.*
- *Item 7 (R) is applicable to the exhaust mounting rubber only.*
- *"R": Replace or change*
- *"I": Inspect and correct or replace if necessary*

NOTE:
For Maintenance Schedule of CHASSIS / BODY, refer to p. 0B-3.

SK113960005501BX

Fig. 3 Sidekick (Part 1 of 2). 1996 w/California Emissions

NOTES:
"R": Replace or change
"I": Inspect and correct or replace if necessary
- *The maintenance services with * * (asterisks) are recommended maintenance items.*
- *Item 7 (R) is applicable to exhaust mounting rubber only.*

Interval: This interval should be judged by odometer reading or months, whichever comes first.																	
	miles (x 1,000)	7.5	15	22.5	30	37.5	45	52.5	60	67.5	75	82.5	90	97.5	105	112.5	120
	km (x 1,000)	12.5	25	37.5	50	62.5	75	87.5	100	112.5	125	137.5	150	162.5	175	187.5	200
	months	7.5	15	22.5	30	37.5	45	52.5	60	67.5	75	82.5	90	97.5	105	112.5	120
CHASSIS AND BODY																	
1. Clutch (For manual transmission)		–	I	–	I	–	I	–	I	–	I	–	I	–	I	–	I
2. Brake discs and pads (front) Brake drums and shoes (rear)		–	I	–	I	–	I	–	I	–	I	–	I	–	I	–	I
3. Brake hoses and pipes		–	I	–	I	–	I	–	I	–	I	–	I	–	I	–	I
4. Brake fluid		–	I	–	I	–	I	–	R	–	I	–	I	–	I	–	R
5. Brake pedal		–	I	–	I	–	I	–	I	–	I	–	I	–	I	–	I
6. Brake lever and cable		–	I	–	I	–	I	–	I	–	I	–	I	–	I	–	I
7. Tires		I	I	I	I	I	I	I	I	I	I	I	I	I	I	I	I
8. Wheel discs and free wheeling hubs (if equipped)		I	I	I	I	I	I	I	I	I	I	I	I	I	I	I	I
9. Wheel bearings		–	I	–	*I	–	I	–	*I	–	I	–	*I	–	I	–	*I
10. Suspension system		I	I	–	I	–	I	–	I	–	I	–	I	–	I	–	I
11. Propeller shafts		–	I	–	I	–	I	–	I	–	I	–	I	–	I	–	I
12. Transmission oil (Manual)		I	I	I	R	I	I	I	R	I	I	I	R	I	I	I	R
13. Automatic transmission	Fluid level	I	I	I	I	I	I	I	I	I	I	I	I	I	I	I	I
	Fluid change	Replace every 100,000 miles (166,000 km) ... 4 A/T No replacement required ... 3 A/T															
	Fluid hose	–	–	–	–	–	R	–	–	–	–	–	R	–	–	–	–
14. Transfer and differential oil		I	I	I	R	I	I	I	R	I	I	I	R	I	I	I	R
15. Steering system		I	I	I	I	I	I	I	I	I	I	I	I	I	I	I	I
16. Power steering system (if equipped)		I	I	I	I	I	I	I	I	I	I	I	I	I	I	I	I
17. Door hinges		L	L	L	L	L	L	L	L	L	L	L	L	L	L	L	L

NOTES:
"R": Replace or change
"I": Inspect and correct or replace if necessary
"L": Lubricate
- *Item 9 *I : Inspect for rattled wear and proper lubrication.*

SK1139600055020X

Fig. 3 Sidekick (Part 2 of 2). 1996

Interval: This interval should be judged by odometer reading or months, whichever comes first.		This table includes services as scheduled up to 120,000 miles (200,000 km) mileage. Beyond 120,000 miles (200,000 km), carry out the same services at the same intervals respectively.															
	miles (x 1,000)	7.5	15	22.5	30	37.5	45	52.5	60	67.5	75	82.5	90	97.5	105	112.5	120
	km (x 1,000)	12.5	25	37.5	50	62.5	75	87.5	100	112.5	125	137.5	150	162.5	175	187.5	200
	months	7.5	15	22.5	30	37.5	45	52.5	60	67.5	75	82.5	90	97.5	105	112.5	120
1. ENGINE																	
1-1. Water pump belt (tension, damage)		–	–	–	I	–	–	–	I	–	–	–	I	–	–	–	I
1-1'. Camshaft timing belt		–	–	–	–	–	–	–	*R	–	–	–	I	–	–	–	R
1-2. Valve lash (clearance) (except GT)		–	I	–	I	–	I	–	I	–	I	–	I	–	I	–	I
1-3. Engine oil and oil filter	except GT	R	R	R	R	R	R	R	R	R	R	R	R	R	R	R	R
	GT	Replace every 5,000 miles (8,000 km) or 12 months															
1-4. Cooling system hoses and connections (leakage, damage)		–	*I	–	*I	–	*I	–	I	–	I	–	I	–	I	–	I
1-5. Engine coolant		–	–	–	R	–	–	–	R	–	–	–	R	–	–	–	R
1-6. Exhaust system		–	–	–	I	–	–	–	I	–	–	–	I	–	–	–	I
1-7. Wiring harness and connections		–	–	–	–	–	–	–	I	–	–	–	–	–	–	–	I
2. IGNITION SYSTEM																	
2-1. Spark plugs		–	–	–	R	–	–	–	R	–	–	–	R	–	–	–	R
2-2. Ignition wiring		–	–	–	–	–	–	–	R	–	–	–	–	–	–	–	R
3. FUEL SYSTEM																	
3-1. Air cleaner filter element	Paved-road	–	–	–	R	–	–	–	R	–	–	–	R	–	–	–	R
3-2. Fuel tank, cap & lines		–	*I	–	*I	–	*I	–	I	–	I	–	I	–	I	–	I
3-3. Fuel filter		–	–	–	R	–	–	–	R	–	–	–	R	–	–	–	R
4. BRAKE																	
4-1. Brake discs and pads (thickness, wear, damage) Brake drums and shoes (wear, damage)		I	–	I	–	I	–	I	–	I	–	I	–	I	–	I	–
4-2. Brake hoses and pipes (leakage, damage, clamp)		I	–	I	–	I	–	I	–	I	–	I	–	I	–	I	–
4-3. Brake fluid			I	–	I	–	I	–	R	–	I	–	I	–	I	–	R
4-4. Brake lever and cable (damage, stroke, operation)		I	–	I	–	I	–	I	–	I	–	I	–	I	–	I	–
4-5. Brake pedal		–	I	–	I	–	I	–	I	–	I	–	I	–	I	–	I
5. CHASSIS AND BODY																	
5-1. Clutch (For manual transmission) pedal free travel		I	I	I	I	I	I	I	I	I	I	I	I	I	I	I	I
5-2. Tires/wheel discs (wear, damage, rotation)		I	I	I	I	I	I	I	I	I	I	I	I	I	I	I	I
5-3. Drive axle boots (breakage, damage)		I	I	I	I	I	I	I	I	I	I	I	I	I	I	I	I
5-4. Suspension system (tightness, damage, rattle, breakage)		I	I	I	I	I	I	I	I	I	I	I	I	I	I	I	I
5-5. Steering system (tightness, damage, breakage, rattle)		I	I	I	I	I	I	I	I	I	I	I	I	I	I	I	I
5-6. Manual transmission oil (leakage, level)		I	I	I	R	I	I	I	R	I	I	I	R	I	I	I	R
5-7. Automatic transmission	Fluid level	I	I	I	I	I	I	I	I	I	I	I	I	I	I	I	I
	Fluid change	Replace every 100,000 miles (160,000 km)															
	Fluid hose	–	–	–	–	–	R	–	–	–	–	–	R	–	–	–	–
5-8. Door hinges & Gear shift control lever shaft		I	I	I	I	I	I	I	I	I	I	I	I	I	I	I	I
5-9. Power steering system		I	I	I	I	I	I	I	I	I	I	I	I	I	I	I	I

NOTES:

"R": Replace or change

"I" : Inspect and correct or replace if necessary

- *The maintenance services with * (asterisk) are recommended maintenance items. (After 120,000 miles (200,000 km), they are not recommended maintenance items.)*

SK1139100050010X

Fig. 4 Swift (Part 1 of 2)

Interval: This interval should be judged by odometer reading or months, whichever comes first.		This table includes services as scheduled up to 120,000 miles (200,000 km) mileage. Beyond 120,000 miles (200,000 km), carry out the same services at the same intervals respectively.															
	miles (x 1,000)	7.5	15	22.5	30	37.5	45	52.5	60	67.5	75	82.5	90	97.5	105	112.5	120
	km (x 1,000)	12.5	25	37.5	50	62.5	75	87.5	100	112.5	125	137.5	150	162.5	175	187.5	200
	months	7.5	15	22.5	30	37.5	45	52.5	60	67.5	75	82.5	90	97.5	105	112.5	120
1. ENGINE																	
1-1. Water pump belt (tension, damage)		–	–	–	I	–	–	–	I	–	–	–	I	–	–	–	I
1-1'. Camshaft timing belt		–	–	–	–	–	–	–	*R	–	–	–	*I	–	–	–	R
1-2. Valve lash (clearance) (except GT)		–	I	–	I	–	I	–	I	–	I	–	I	–	I	–	I
1-3. Engine oil and oil filter	except GT	R	R	R	R	R	R	R	R	R	R	R	R	R	R	R	R
	GT	Replace every 5,000 miles (8,000 km) or 12 months															
1-4. Cooling system hoses and connections (leakage, damage)		–	*I	–	*I	–	*I	–	I	–	I	–	I	–	I	–	I
1-5. Engine coolant		–	–	–	R	–	–	–	R	–	–	–	R	–	–	–	R
1-6. Exhaust system		–	–	–	*I	–	–	–	*I	–	–	–	*I	–	–	–	I
1-7. Wiring harness and connections		–	–	–	–	–	–	–	*I	–	–	–	–	–	–	–	I
2. IGNITION SYSTEM																	
2-1. Spark plugs		–	–	–	R	–	–	–	R	–	–	–	R	–	–	–	R
2-2. Ignition wiring		–	–	–	–	–	–	–	R	–	–	–	–	–	–	–	R
3. FUEL SYSTEM																	
3-1. Air cleaner filter element	Paved-road	–	–	–	R	–	–	–	R	–	–	–	R	–	–	–	R
3-2. Fuel tank, cap & lines		–	*I	–	*I	–	*I	–	*I	–	*I	–	*I	–	I	–	I
3-3. Fuel filter		–	–	–	*R	–	–	–	*R	–	–	–	*R	–	–	–	R

NOTES:

"R": Replace or change

"I" : Inspect and correct or replace if necessary

- *The maintenance services with * (asterisk) are recommended maintenance items. (After 120,000 miles (200,000 km), they are not recommended maintenance items.)*

SK1139100050020X

Fig. 4 Swift (Part 2 of 2)

VEHICLE MAINTENANCE SCHEDULES

Toyota

INDEX

	Page No.	Fig. No.
Avalon		
1995	0-113	1
Celica		
1993	0-114	2
1994–95	0-115	3
Camry		
1993	0-116	4
1994–95	0-116	5
Corolla		
1993–95	0-117	6
Land Cruiser		
1993–94	0-118	7
1995	0-118	8
MR2		
1993–95	0-119	9
Previa		
1993–95	0-120	10
Pickup		
All	0-121	11
Supra		
1993–95	0-122	12
Tacoma		
1995	0-123	13
Tercel		
1993–95	0-124	14
T100		
1993–95	0-125	15
4Runner		
1993	0-126	16
1994–95	0-127	17
Paseo		
1993–95	0-128	18
Except Land Cruiser, Pickup, Previa, RAV4 & 4Runner		
1996	0-129	19
Land Cruiser, Pickup, Previa, RAV4 & 4Runner		
1996	0-131	20

Maintenance operation: A = Check and adjust if necessary.
R = Replace, change or lubricate.
I = Inspect and correct or replace if necessary.

System	Service interval (Use odometer reading or months, whichever comes first) / Maintenance items	Maintenance services beyond 96,000 km (60,000 miles) should continue to be performed at the same intervals shown for each maintenance schedule.									
		x 1,000 km	12	24	36	48	60	72	84	96	Months
		x 1,000 miles	7.5	15	22.5	30	37.5	45	52.5	60	
ENGINE	Valve clearance									A	A: Every 72 months
	Drive belt		I: First period 96,000 km (60,000 miles) or 72 months. I: After that every 12,000 km (7,500 miles) or 12 months.								
	Engine oil and oil filter★		R	R	R	R	R	R	R	R	R: Every 12 months
	Engine coolant		R: First period 72,000 km (45,000 miles) or 36 months. R: After that every 48,000 km (30,000 miles) or 24 months.								
	Exhaust pipes and mountings					I				I	I: Every 36 months
FUEL	Air filter★					R				R	R: Every 36 months
	Fuel lines and connections (1)					I				I	I: Every 36 months
	Fuel tank cap gasket									R	R: Every 72 months
IGNITION	Spark plugs (Platinum tipped type)★*									R	R: Every 72 months
EVAP	Charcoal canister (2)									I	I: Every 72 months
BRAKES	Brake linings and drums (3)			I		I		I		I	I: Every 24 months
	Brake pads and discs (Front and rear)			I		I		I		I	I: Every 24 months
	Brake line pipes and hoses			I		I		I		I	I: Every 24 months
CHASSIS	Steering linkage			I		I		I		I	I: Every 24 months
	SRS airbag		I: First period 10 years. I: After that every 2 years.								
	Ball joints and dust covers			I		I		I		I	I: Every 24 months
	Drive shaft boots			I		I		I		I	I: Every 24 months
	Automatic transmission and differential oil (4)			I		I		I		I	I: Every 24 months
	Steering gear housing oil (5)			I		I		I		I	I: Every 24 months
	Bolts and nuts on chassis and body (6)			I		I		I		I	I: Every 24 months

TY1139500259010X

Fig. 1 Avalon (Part 1 of 2). 1995

★ or ∗ marks indicates maintenance which is part of the warranty conditions for the Emission Control Systems. The warranty period is in accordance with the owner's guide or the warranty booklet.

★: For vehicles sold in California and Massachusetts only

∗ : For vehicles sold outside California and Massachusetts

(1) Includes inspection of fuel tank band and vapor vent system.
(2) Non–maintenance item except for California and Massachusetts.
(3) Also applicable to drum lining for parking brake.
(4) Check for leakage.
(5) Check for oil leaks from steering gear housing.
(6) The applicable parts are listed below.

- Front and rear suspension member to cross body
- Strut bar bracket to body
- Bolts for seat installation

TY1139500259020X

Fig. 1 Avalon (Part 2 of 2). 1995

CONDITIONS: Conditions other than those listed for SCHEDULE A.

System	Service interval (Odometer reading or months, whichever comes first) / Maintenance items		7.5	15	22.5	30	37.5	45	52.5	60	Months
			Maintenance service beyond 60,000 miles (96,000 km) should continue to be performed at the same intervals shown for each maintenance schedule.								
		Miles x 1,000	7.5	15	22.5	30	37.5	45	52.5	60	Months
		km x 1,000	12	24	36	48	60	72	84	96	
ENGINE	Valve clearance									A	A: Every 72 months
	Drive belt		I: First period, 60,000 miles (96,000 km) or 72 months. I. After that every 7,500 miles (12,000 km) or 12 months.								
	Engine oil*	3S-GTE engine	R Every 5,000 miles (8,000 km) or 6 months*								
		Others	R	R	R	R	R	R	R	R	R: Every 12 months
	Engine oil filter*	3S-GTE engine	R Every 10,000 miles (16,000 km) or 12 months								
		Others	R	R	R	R	R	R	R	R	R: Every 12 months
	Engine coolant		R. First period, 45,000 miles (72,000 km) or 36 months R. After that every 30,000 miles (48,000 km) or 24 months.								
	Exhaust pipes and mountings					I				I	I. Every 36 months
FUEL	Idle speed	4A-FE engine	A Adjust at first 7,500 miles (12,000 km) or 12 months, and at 15,000 miles (24,000 km) or 24 months. Then adjust every 15 000 miles (24,000 km) or 24 months.								
	Air filter*					R				R	R: Every 36 months
	Fuel lines and connections (1)					I				I	I: Every 36 months
	Fuel tank cap gasket									R	R. Every 72 months
IGNITION	Speak plugs	4A-FE engine**				R				R	R: Every 36 months
		Others								R	R: Every 72 months
EVAP	Charcoal canister									I	I. Every 72 months
BRAKES	Brake linings and drums (2)			I		I		I		I	I. Every 24 months
	Brake pads and discs (Front and rear)			I		I		I		I	I: Every 24 months
	Brake line pipes and hoses			I		I		I		I	I: Every 24 months
CHASSIS	Steering linkage			I		I		I		I	I: Every 24 months
	SRS airbag		I: First period, 10 years I. After that every 2 years.								
	Drive shaft boots			I		I		I		I	I. Every 24 months
	Ball joints and dust covers			I		I		I		I	I: Every 24 months
	Manual transaxle, automatic transaxle and differential (3)			I		I		I		I	I: Every 24 months
	Steering gear housing oil (4)			I		I		I		I	I: Every 24 months
	Bolts and nuts on chassis and body (5)			I		I		I		I	I: Every 24 months

* and * marks indicate maintenance which is part of the warranty conditions for the Emission Control System. The warranty period is in accordance with the owner's guide or the warranty booklet.

(*: California specification vehicles *: Other specification vehicles)

(1) Includes inspection of fuel tank band and vapor vent system.
(2) Also applicable to lining drum for parking brake.
(3) Check for leakage.
(4) Check for oil leaks from steering gear housing.
(5) The applicable parts are listed below.

- Front and rear suspension member to cross body
- Strut bar bracket to body bolt
- Bolts for seat installation

TY1139100233000X

Fig. 2 Celica. 1993

System	Service interval (Use odometer reading or months, whichever comes first) / Maintenance items	Maintenance services beyond 96,000 km (60,000 miles) should continue to be performed at the same intervals shown for each maintenance schedule																	
		× 1,000 km	6	12	18	24	30	36	42	48	54	60	66	72	78	84	90	96	Months
		× 1,000 miles	3.75	7.5	11.25	15	18.75	22.5	26.25	30	33.75	37.5	41.25	45	48.75	52.5	56.25	60	
ENGINE	Timing belt (1)																	R	-
	Valve clearance																	A	A: Every 72 months
	Drive belt	I: First period 96,000 km (60,000 miles) or 72 months I: After that every 12,000 km (7,500 miles) or 12 months																	
	Engine oil and oil filter★		R	R	R	R	R	R	R	R	R	R	R	R	R	R	R	R	R: Every 6 months
	Engine coolant	R: First period 72,000 km (45,000 miles) or 36 months R: After that every 48,000 km (30,000 miles) or 24 months																	
	Exhaust pipes and mountings					I				I				I				I	I: Every 24 months
FUEL	Air filter (2)★		I	I	I	I	I	I	I	R	I	I	I	I	I	I	I	R	I: Every 6 months R: Every 36 months
	Fuel lines and connections (3)									I								I	I: Every 36 months
	Fuel tank cap gasket																	R	R: Every 72 months
IGNITION	Spark plugs ★◆									R								R	R: Every 36 months
EVAP	Charcoal canister (4)																	I	I: Every 72 months
BRAKES	Brake linings and drums (5)			I		I		I		I		I		I		I		I	I: Every 12 months
	Brake pads and discs			I		I		I		I		I		I		I		I	I: Every 12 months
	Brake line pipes and hoses					I				I				I				I	I: Every 24 months
CHASSIS	Steering linkage			I		I		I		I		I		I		I		I	I: Every 12 months
	SRS airbag	I: First period 10 years. I: After that every 2 years																	
	Ball joints and dust covers			I		I		I		I		I		I		I		I	I: Every 12 months
	Drive shaft boots			I		I		I		I		I		I		I		I	I: Every 12 months
	Manual transaxle, automatic transaxle and differential					R				R				R				R	R: Every 24 months
	Steering gear housing oil (6)					I				I				I				I	I: Every 24 months
	Bolts and nuts on chassis and body (7)			I		I		I		I		I		I		I		I	I: Every 12 months

TY1139400234010X

Fig. 3 Celica (Part 1 of 2). 1994–95

★ and ◆ marks indicates maintenance which is part of the warranty conditions for the Emission Control Systems.

★: California and New York specification vehicles
◆: Other specification vehicles

(1) Applicable to vehicles operated under conditions of extensive idling and/or low speed driving for long distances such as police, taxi or door-to-door delivery use.
(2) Applicable when operating mainly on dusty roads.
(3) Includes inspection of fuel tank band and vapor vent system.
(4) Non-maintenance item except for California and New York.
(5) Also applicable to drum lining for parking brake.

(6) Check for oil leaks from steering gear housing.
(7) Applicable only when operating mainly on rough, muddy roads. The applicable parts are listed below.
- Front and rear suspension member to cross body.
- Bolts for seat installation.

TY1139400234020X

Fig. 3 Celica (Part 2 of 2). 1994–95

CONDITIONS: Conditions other than those listed for SCHEDULE A

System	Service interval (Odometer reading or months, whichever comes first)	Maintenance service beyond 60,000 miles (96,000 km) should continue to be performed at the same intervals shown for each maintenance schedule.								
		Miles x 1,000	7.5	15	22.5	30	37.5	45	52.5	60	Months
	Maintenance items	km x 1,000	12	24	36	48	60	72	84	96	
ENGINE	Valve clearance									A	A: Every 72 months
	Drive belts	I: First period, 60,000 miles (96,000 km) or 72 months I: After that every 7,500 miles (12,000 km) or 12 months									
	Engine oil and oil filter*		R	R	R	R	R	R	R	R	R: Every 12 months
	Engine coolant	R: First period, 45,000 miles (72 000 km) or 36 months R: After that every 30,000 miles (48,000 km) or 24 months									
	Exhaust pipes and mountings					I				I	I: Every 36 months
FUEL	Air filter*					R				R	R: Every 36 months
	Fuel lines and connections(1)					I				I	I: Every 36 months
	Fuel tank cap gasket									R	R: Every 72 months
IGNITION	Spark plugs (Platinum tipped type)									R	R: Every 72 months
EVAP	Charcoal canister									I	I: Every 72 months
BRAKES	Brake linings and drums(2)			I		I		I		I	I: Every 24 months
	Brake pads and discs (Front and rear)			I		I		I		I	I: Every 24 months
	Brake line pipes and hoses			I		I		I		I	I: Every 24 months
CHASSIS	Steering linkage			I		I		I		I	I: Every 24 months
	SRS airbag	I: First period, 10 years I: After that every 2 years									
	Drive shaft boots			I		I		I		I	I: Every 24 months
	Ball joints and dust covers			I		I		I		I	I: Every 24 months
	Manual transaxle, automatic transaxle and differential(3)			I		I		I		I	I: Every 24 months
	Steering gear housing oil(4)			I		I		I		I	I: Every 24 months
	Bolts and nuts on chassis and body(5)			I		I		I		I	I: Every 24 months

* Mark indicates maintenance which is part of the warranty conditions for the Emission Control System. The warranty period is in accordance with the owner's guide or the warranty booklet. (*: California specification vehicles)

(1) Includes inspection of fuel tank band and vapor vent system.

(2) Also applicable to lining drum for parking brake.

(3) Check for leakage.

(4) Check for oil leaks from steering gear housing.

(5) The applicable parts are listed below.

- Front and rear suspension member to cross body
- Strut bar bracket to body bolt
- Bolts for sheet installation

TY1139100235000X

Fig. 4 Camry. 1993

System	Service interval (Use odometer reading or months, whichever comes first)	Maintenance services beyond 96 000 km (60,000 miles) should continue to be performed at the same intervals shown for each maintenance schedule																
		x 1,000 km	6	12	18	24	30	36	42	48	54	60	66	72	78	84	90	96	Months
	Maintenance items	x 1,000 miles	3.75	7.5	11.25	15	18.75	22.5	26.25	30	33.75	37.5	41.25	45	48.75	52.5	56.25	60	
ENGINE	Timing belt (1)																	R	-
	Valve clearance																	A	A: Every 72 months
	Drive belts	I: First period 96,000 km (60,000 miles) or 72 months. I: After that every 12 000 km (7,500 miles) or 12 months																	
	Engine oil and oil filter*		R	R	R	R	R	R	R	R	R	R	R	R	R	R	R	R	R: Every 6 months
	Engine coolant	R: First period 72 000 km (45,000 miles) or 36 months. R: After that every 48 000 km (30,000 miles) or 24 months																	
	Exhaust pipes and mountings					I				I				I				I	I: Every 24 months
FUEL	Air filter (2)*		I	I	I	I	I	I	I	R	I	I	I	I	I	I	I	R	I: Every 6 months R: Every 36 months
	Fuel lines and connections (3)									I								I	I: Every 36 months
	Fuel tank cap gasket																	R	R: Every 72 months
IGNITION	Spark plugs (Platinum tipped type)																	R	R: Every 72 months
EVAP	Charcoal canister (4)																	I	I: Every 72 months
BRAKES	Brake linings and drums (5)			I		I		I		I		I		I		I		I	I: Every 12 months
	Brake pads and discs (Front and rear)			I		I		I		I		I		I		I		I	I: Every 12 months
	Brake line pipes and hoses					I				I				I				I	I: Every 24 months

TY1139400236010X

Fig. 5 Camry (Part 1 of 2). 1994–95

System	Service interval (Use odometer reading or months, whichever comes first) / Maintenance items		Maintenance services beyond 96,000 km (60,000 miles) should continue to be performed at the same intervals shown for each maintenance schedule.																Months
		x 1,000 km	6	12	18	24	30	36	42	48	54	60	66	72	78	84	90	96	
		x 1,000 miles	3.75	7.5	11.25	15	18.75	22.5	26.25	30	33.75	37.5	41.25	45	48.75	52.5	56.25	60	
CHASSIS	Steering linkage			I		I		I		I		I		I		I		I	I: Every 12 months
	SRS airbag		I: First period 10 years. I: After that every 2 years																
	Drive shaft boots			I		I		I		I		I		I		I		I	I: Every 12 months
	Ball joints and dust covers			I		I		I		I		I		I		I		I	I: Every 12 months
	Manual transaxle, automatic transaxle and differential (5)					R				R				R				R	R: Every 24 months
	Steering gear housing oil (7)					I				I				I				I	I: Every 24 months
	Bolts and nuts on chassis and body (8)			I		I		I		I		I		I		I		I	I: Every 12 months

★ marks indicates maintenance which is part of the warranty conditions for the Emission Control Systems.

★: California and New York specification vehicles

(1) Applicable to vehicles operated under conditions of extensive idling and/or low speed driving for long distances such as police, taxi or door-to-door delivery use.
(2) Applicable when operating mainly on dusty roads.
(3) Includes inspection of fuel tank band and vapor vent system.
(4) Non-maintenance item except for California and New York.
(5) Also applicable to drum lining for parking brake.

(6) Check for leakage.
(7) Check for oil leaks from steering gear housing.
(8) Applicable only when operating mainly on rough, muddy roads. The applicable parts are listed below. For other usage conditions, refer to SCHEDULE B.
- Front and rear suspension member to cross body.
- Strut bar bracket to body bolts.
- Bolts for seat installation.

TY1139400236020X

Fig. 5 Camry (Part 2 of 2). 1994–95

CONDITIONS: Conditions other than those listed for SCHEDULE A.

System	Service interval (Odometer reading or months, whichever comes first) / Maintenance items		Maintenance service beyond 96,000 km (60,000 miles) should continue to be performed at the same intervals shown for each maintenance schedule.								Months
		km × 1,000	12	24	36	48	60	72	84	96	
		Miles × 1,000	7.5	15	22.5	30	37.5	45	52.5	60	
ENGINE	Valve clearance									A	A: Every 72 months
	Drive belts		I: First period, 96,000 km (60,000 miles) or 72 months. I: After that every 12,000 km (7,500 miles) or 12 months								
	Engine oil and oil filter*		R	R	R	R	R	R	R	R	R: Every 12 months
	Engine coolant		R: First period, 72,000 km (45,000 miles) or 36 months. R: After that every 48,000 km (30,000 miles) or 24 months								
	Exhaust pipes and mountings					I				I	I: Every 36 months
FUEL	Air filter*					R				R	R: Every 36 months
	Fuel lines and connections (1)					I				I	I: Every 36 months
	Fuel tank cap gasket									R	R: Every 72 months
IGNITION	Spark plugs					R				R	R: Every 36 months
EVAP	Charcoal canister									I	I: Every 72 months
BRAKES	Brake linings and drums (2)			I		I		I		I	I: Every 24 months
	Brake pads and discs			I		I		I		I	I: Every 24 months
	Brake line pipes and hoses			I		I		I		I	I: Every 24 months
CHASSIS	Steering linkage			I		I		I		I	I: Every 24 months
	SRS airbag		I: First period, 10 years. I: After that every 2 years.								
	Drive shaft boots			I		I		I		I	I: Every 24 months
	Ball joints and dust covers			I		I		I		I	I: Every 24 months
	Manual transaxle, automatic transaxle and differential (3)			I		I		I		I	I: Every 24 months
	Steering gear housing oil (4)			I		I		I		I	I: Every 24 months
	Bolts and nuts on chassis and body (5)			I		I		I		I	I: Every 24 months

* and * marks indicate maintenance which is part of the warranty conditions for the Emission Control System. The warranty period is in accordance with the owner's guide or the warranty booklet. (*: California specification vehicles *: Other specification vehicles)
(1) Includes inspection of fuel tank band and vapor vent system.
(2) Also applicable to lining drum for parking brake.
(3) Check for leakage.
(4) Check for oil leaks from steering gear housing.
(5) The applicable parts are listed below.
- Front and rear suspension member to cross body
- Strut bar bracket to body bolt
- Bolts for seat installation

TY1139100237000X

Fig. 6 Corolla. 1993-95

Conditions: Conditions other than those listed for SCHEDULE A.

Maintenance operations: A = Check and adjust if necessary.
R = Replace, change or lubricate.
I = Inspect and correct or replace if necessary

System	Service interval (Odometer reading or months, whichever comes first) / Maintenance items	km x 1 000	12	24	36	48	60	72	84	96	Months
		Miles x 1 000	7.5	15	22.5	30	37.5	45	52.5	60	
	Maintenance service beyond 96,000 km (60,000 miles) should be performed at the same intervals shown in each maintenance schedule.										
ENGINE	Valve clearance*									A	A: Every 72 months
	Drive belts(1)					I				I	I: 36 months, 72 months
	Engine oil and oil filter*		R	R	R	R	R	R	R	R	R: Every 12 months
	Engine coolant(2)							R			R: 36 months
	Exhaust pipes and mountings					I				I	I: Every 36 months
FUEL	Air Filter*					R				R	R: Every 36 months
	Fuel lines and connections(3)					I				I	I: Every 36 months
	Fuel tank cap gasket									R	R: Every 72 months
IGNITION	Spark plugs**					R				R	R: Every 36 months
EVAP	Charcoal canister	California only								I	I: Every 72 months
EXHAUST	Heated oxygen sensors	Except california	R: 128,000 km (80,000 miles) only								
BRAKES	Brake linings and drums(4)			I		I		I		I	I: Every 24 months
	Brake pads discs (Front and rear)			I		I		I		I	I: Every 24 months
	Brake line pipes and hoses			I		I		I		I	I: Every 24 months
CHASSIS	Steering linkage			I		I		I		I	I: Every 24 months
	Ball joints and dust covers			I		I		I		I	I: Every 24 months
	Front wheel bearing and thrust bush grease					R				R	R: Every 36 months
	Steering knuckle and chassis grease(5)			R		R		R		R	R: Every 24 months
	Propeller shaft grease(5)			R		R		R		R	R: Every 24 months
	Automatic transmission			I		I		I		I	I: Every 24 months
	Transfer, differential and steering gear box oil(6)			I		I		I		I	I: Every 24 months
	Bolt and nuts on chassis and body(7)			I		I		I		I	I: Every 24 months

Maintenance service indicated by a star (★) or asterisk (*) are required under the terms of the Emission Control Systems Warranty (ECSW). See Owner's Guide or Warranty Booklet for complete warranty information.

★ For vehicle sold in California * For vehicle sold outside California

HINT:

(1) After 96,000 km (60,000 miles) or 72 months, inspect every 12,000 km (7,500 miles) or 12 months
(2) After 72,000 km (45,000 miles) or 36 months, replace every 48,000 km (30,000 miles) or 24 months
(3) Includes inspection of fuel tank band vapor vent system
(4) Also applicable to lining drum for parking brake
(5) If the propeller shaft has been immersed in water, it should be re-greased within a day
(6) Inspect the steering gear box for oil leakage only
(7) The applicable parts are listed below
• Bolts for sheet installation

TY1139100239000X

Fig. 7 Land Cruiser. 1993–94

Maintenance operation: A = Check and adjust if necessary.
R = Replace, change or lubricate.
I = Inspect and correct or replace if necessary.

System	Service interval (Odometer reading or months, whichever comes first) / Maintenance items	x 1,000 km	6	12	18	24	30	36	42	48	54	60	66	72	78	84	90	96	Months
		x 1,000 miles	3.75	7.5	11.25	15	18.75	22.5	26.25	30	33.75	37.5	41.25	45	48.75	52.5	56.25	60	
	Maintenance services beyond 96,000 km (60,000 miles) should continue to be performed at the same intervals shown in each maintenance schedule.																		
ENGINE	Valve clearance																	A	A: Every 72 months
	Drive belts (1)									I								I	I: 36 months, 72 months
	Engine oil and oil filter ★		R	R	R	R	R	R	R	R	R	R	R	R	R	R	R	R	R: Every 6 months
	Engine coolant (2)													R					R: 36 months
	Exhaust pipes and mountings					I				I				I				I	I: Every 24 months
FUEL	Air Filter ★ (3)		I	I	I	I	I	I	I	R	I	I	I	I	I	I	I	R	I: Every 6 months R: Every 36 months
	Fuel lines and connections (4)									I								I	I: Every 36 months
	Fuel tank cap gasket																	R	R: Every 72 months
IGNITION	Spark plugs ★ ◆									R								R	R: Every 36 months
EVAP	Charcoal canister (5)																	I	I: Every 72 months
BRAKES	Brake linings and drums			I		I		I		I		I		I		I		I	I: Every 12 months
	Brake pads and discs (Front and rear)			I		I		I		I		I		I		I		I	I: Every 12 months
	Brake line pipes and hoses					I				I				I				I	I: Every 24 months
CHASSIS	Steering linkage			I		I		I		I		I		I		I		I	I: Every 12 months
	SRS airbag		I: First period, 10 years. I. After that every 2 years.																
	Ball joints and dust covers			I		I		I		I		I		I		I		I	I: Every 12 months
	Automatic transmission					R				R				R				R	R: Every 24 months
	Transfer and differential					R				R				R				R	R: Every 24 months
	Steering gear box oil (6)					I				I				I				I	I: Every 24 months
	Front wheel bearing and thrust bush grease									R								R	R: Every 36 months
	Steering knuckle and chassis grease (7)			R		R		R		R		R		R		R		R	R: Every 12 months
	Propeller shaft grease (7)			R		R		R		R		R		R		R		R	R: Every 12 months
	Bolts and nuts on chassis and body (8)			I		I		I		I		I		I		I		I	I: Every 12 months

TY1139500260010X

Fig. 8 Land Cruiser (Part 1 of 2). 1995

Maintenance services indicated by ★ or ◆ are required under the terms of the Emission Control Systems Warranty. See Owner's Guide or Warranty Booklet for complete warranty information.

★: For vehicles sold in California and Massachusetts

◆: For vehicles sold outside California and Massachusetts

(1) After 96,000 km (60,000 miles) or 72 months, inspect every 12,000 km (7,500 miles) or 12 months.

(2) After 72,000 km (45,000 miles) or 36 months, replace every 48,000 km (30,000 miles) or 24 months.

(3) Applicable when operating mainly on dusty roads.

(4) Includes inspection of fuel tank band vapor vent system.

(5) For vehicles sold in California and Massachusetts.

(6) Inspect the steering gear box for oil leakage only.

(7) If the propeller shaft has been immersed in water, it should be re−greased within a day.

(8) Applicable only when operating mainlv on rough, muddy roads. The applicable parts are listed below.

- Bolts for seat installation.

TY1139500260020X

Fig. 8 Land Cruiser (Part 2 of 2). 1995

System	Service interval (Use odometer reading or months, whichever comes first) / Maintenance items	Maintenance services beyond 96,000 km (60,000 miles) should continue to be performed at the same intervals shown for each maintenance schedule																Months
	x 1,000 km	6	12	18	24	30	36	42	48	54	60	66	72	78	84	90	96	
	x 1,000 miles	3.75	7.5	11.25	15	18.75	22.5	26.25	30	33.75	37.5	41.25	45	48.75	52.5	56.25	60	
ENGINE	Timing belt (1)																R	-
	Valve clearance																A	A Every 72 months
	Drive belt	I First period 96 000 km (60 000 miles) or 72 months I After that every 12 000 km (7 500 miles) or 12 months																
	Engine oil*	R Every 4,000 km (2 500 miles) or 3 months																
	Engine oil filter*	R Every 8,000 km (5,000 miles) or 5 months																
	Engine coolant	R First period 72,000 km (45,000 miles) or 36 months R After that every 48,000 km (30,000 miles) or 24 months																
	Exhaust pipes and mountings				I				I				I				I	I: Every 24 months
FUEL	Air filter (2)★	I	I	I	I	I	I	I	R	I	I	I	I	I	I	I	R	I Every 6 months R: Every 36 months
	Fuel lines and connections (3)								I								I	I: Every 36 months
	Fuel tank cap gasket																R	R Every 72 months
IGNITION	Spark plugs (Platinum tipped type)																R	R Every 72 months
EVAP	Charcoal canister																I	I: Every 72 months
BRAKES	Brake pads and discs (Front and rear)		I		I		I		I		I		I		I		I	I Every 12 months
	Brake line pipes and hoses				I				I				I				I	I Every 24 months
CHASSIS	Steering linkage		I		I		I		I		I		I		I		I	I: Every 12 months
	SRS airbag	I First period 10 years I After that every 2 years																
	Ball joints and dust covers		I		I		I		I		I		I		I		I	I Every 12 months
	Drive shaft boots		I		I		I		I		I		I		I		I	I: Every 12 months
	Manual transaxle				R				R				R				R	R Every 24 months
	Steering gear housing oil (4)				I				I				I				I	I: Every 24 months
	Bolts and nuts on chassis and body (5)		I		I		I		I		I		I		I		I	I: Every 12 months

TY1139100240010X

Fig. 9 MR2 (Part 1 of 2). 1993–95

★ mark indicates maintenance which is part of the warranty conditions for the Emission Control Systems. The warranty period is in accordance with the owner's guide or the warranty booklet. (★: California and New York specification vehicles)

(1) Applicable to vehicles operated under conditions of extensive idling and/or low speed driving for long distances such as police, taxi or door—to—door delivery use.
(2) Applicable when operating mainly on dusty roads.If not apply SCHEDULE B.
(3) Includes inspection of fuel tank band and vapor vent system.
(4) Check for oil leaks from steering gear housing.
(5) Applicable only when operating mainly on rough, muddy roads. The applicable parts are listed below. For other usage conditions, refer to SCHEDULE B.
- Front and rear suspension member to cross body.
- Strut bar bracket to body bots.
- Bolts for seat installation.

TY1139100240020X

Fig. 9 MR2 (Part 2 of 2). 1993–95

Maintenance operation: A = Check and adjust if necessary;
R = Replace, change or lubricate;
I = Inspect and correct or replace if necessary

CONDITION

- Towing a trailer, using a camper or car top carrier.
- Repeat short trips less than 5 miles (8 km) and outside temperatures remain below freezing.
- Extensive idling and/or low speed driving for a long distance such as police, taxi or door-to-door delivery use.
- Operating on dusty, rough, muddy or salt spread roads.

System	Service interval (Odometer reading or months, whichever comes first) / Maintenance items		Maintenance services beyond 60,000 miles (96,000 km) should be performed at the same intervals shown in each maintenance schedule.																
			Miles x 1,000	3.75	7.5	11.25	15	18.75	22.5	26.25	30	33.75	37.5	41.25	45	48.75	52.5	56.25	60	Months
			km x 1,000	6	12	18	24	30	36	42	48	54	60	66	72	78	84	90	96	
ENGINE	Valve clearance																		A	A: Every 72 months
	Drive belts			I: First period 60,000 miles (96,000 km) or 72 months I: After that every 7,500 miles (12,000 km) or 12 months																
	Engine oil and oil filter★			R	R	R	R	R	R	R	R	R	R	R	R	R	R	R	R	R: Every 6 months
	Engine coolant			R: First period 45,000 miles (72,000 km) or 36 months R: After that every 30,000 miles (48,000 km) or 24 months																
	Exhaust pipes and mountings						I				I				I				I	I: Every 24 months
FUEL	Air filter★ (1)			I	I	I	I	I	I	I	R	I	I	I	I	I	I	I	R	I: Every 6 months R: Every 36 months
	Fuel lines and connections (2)										I								I	I: Every 36 months
	Fuel tank cap gasket																		R	R: Every 72 months
IGNITION	Spark plugs*																		R	R: Every 72 months
EVAP	Charcoal canister	California only																	I	I: Every 72 months
EXHAUST	Oxygen sensors	Fed. and Canada only		R: 80,000 miles (129,000 km) only																
BRAKES	Brake linings and drums (3)				I		I		I		I		I		I		I		I	I: Every 12 months
	Brake pads and discs				I		I		I		I		I		I		I		I	I: Every 12 months
	Brake line pipes and hoses						I				I				I				I	I: Every 24 months

TY1139100241010X

Fig. 10 Previa (Part 1 of 2). 1993–95

System	Service interval (Odometer reading or months, whichever comes first) / Maintenance items		Maintenance services beyond 60,000 miles (96,000 km) should be performed at the same intervals shown in each maintenance schedule.																
		Miles x 1,000	3.75	7.5	11.25	15	18.75	22.5	26.25	30	33.75	37.5	41.25	45	48.75	52.5	56.25	60	Months
		km x 1,000	6	12	18	24	30	36	42	48	54	60	66	72	78	84	90	96	
CHASSIS	Steering linkage			I		I		I		I		I		I		I		I	I: Every 12 months
	SRS airbag		I: First Period 10 years. I: After that every 2 years																
	Ball joint and dust covers			I		I		I		I		I		I		I		I	I: Every 12 months
	Drive shaft boots	4WD		I		I		I		I		I		I		I		I	I: Every 12 months
	Automatic transmission, manual transmission, transfer (4WD) and differential oil					R				R				R				R	R: Every 24 months
	Steering gear housing oil (4)					I				I				I				I	I: Every 24 months
	Propeller shaft grease (5)	4WD		R		R		R		R		R		R		R		R	R: Every 12 months
	Bolts and nuts on chassis and body (6)			I		I		I		I		I		I		I		I	I: Every 12 months

* or * mark indicates maintenance which is part of the warranty conditions for the engine control system. The warranty period is in accordance with the owner's guide or the warranty booklet.

* : California specification vehicles.

* : Vehicles other than California specification vehicle.

HINT:

(1) Applicable when operating mainly on dusty roads.

(2) Includes inspection of vapor vent system.

(3) Also applicable to lining drum for parking brake.

(4) Check for oil leaks from steering gear box.

(5) If the propeller shaft has been immersed in water, it should be re-greased daily.

(6) Applicable only when operating mainly on rough, muddy roads. The applicable parts are listed below.

- Bolts for seat installation.

TY1139100241020X

Fig. 10 Previa (Part 2 of 2). 1993-95

Maintenance operation: A = Check and adjust if necessary;
R = Replace, change or lubricate;
I = Inspect and correct or replace if necessary

CONDITIONS:

- Towing a trailer, using a camper or car top carrier.
- Repeated short trips less than 5 miles (8 km) and outside temperature remains below freezing.
- Extensive idling and/or low speed driving for long distances such as police, taxi or door-to-door delivery use.
- Operating on dusty, rough, muddy or salt spread roads.

System	Service interval (Odometer reading or months, whichever comes first) / Maintenance items		Maintenance services beyond 60,000 miles (96,000 km) should be continue to performed at the same intervals shown in each maintenance schedule.																
		Miles x 1,000	3.75	7.5	11.25	15	18.75	22.5	26.25	30	33.75	37.5	41.25	45	48.75	52.5	56.25	60	Months
		km x 1,000	6	12	18	24	30	36	42	48	54	60	66	72	78	84	90	96	
ENGINE	Timing belt (1)	3VZ-E engine																R	–
	Valve clearance*	22R-E engine								A								A	A: Every 36 months
	Valve clearance	3VZ-E engine																A	A: Every 72 months
	Drive belts		I: First period. 30,000 miles (48,000 km) or 36 months, second period, 60,000 miles (96,000 km) or 72 months I: After that, every 7,500 miles (12,000 km) or 12 months																
	Engine oil and oil filter*		R	R	R	R	R	R	R	R	R	R	R	R	R	R	R	R	R: Every 6 months
	Engine coolant		R: First period 45,000 miles (72,000 km) or 36 months R: After that every 30,000 miles (48,000 km) or 24 months																
	Exhaust pipes and mounting					I				I				I				I	I: Every 24 months
FUEL	Idle speed		A: First period. 7,500 miles (12,000 km) or 12 months, second period, 15,000 miles (24,000 km) or 24 months A: After that, every 15,000 miles (24,000 km) or 24 months																
	Air filter* (2)		I	I	I	I	I	I	I	R	I	I	I	I	I	I	I	R	I: Every 6 months R: Every 36 months
	Fuel lines and connection (3)									I								I	I: Every 36 months
	Fuel tank cap gasket																	R	R: Every 72 months
IGNITION	Spark plugs* *									R								R	R: Every 36 months
EVAP	Charcoal canister	Calif. only																I	I: Every 72 months
EXHAUST	Oxygen sensor	Fed. and Canada only	R: 80,000 miles (129,000 km) only																
BRAKES	Brake linings and drums			I		I		I		I		I		I		I		I	I: Every 12 months
	Brake pads and discs			I		I		I		I		I		I		I		I	I: Every 12 months
	Brake line pipes and hoses					I				I				I				I	I: Every 24 months

TY1139100242010X

Fig. 11 Pickup (Part 1 of 2)

System	Service interval (Odometer reading or months, whichever comes first) / Maintenance items		Maintenance services beyond 60,000 miles (96,000 km) should continue to be performed at the same intervals shown in each maintenance schedule.																Months
		Miles × 1,000	3.75	7.5	11.25	15	18.75	22.5	26.25	30	33.75	37.5	41.25	45	48.75	52.5	56.25	60	
		km × 1,000	6	12	18	24	30	36	42	48	54	60	66	72	78	84	90	96	
CHASSIS	Steering linkage			I		I		I		I		I		I		I		I	I: Every 12 months
	Ball joints and dust covers			I		I		I		I		I		I		I		I	I: Every 12 months
	Drive shaft boots	4WD		I		I		I		I		I		I		I		I	I: Every 12 months
	Automatic transmission, manual transmission, transfer (4WD) and differential					R				R				R				R	R: Every 24 months
	Steering gear housing oil (4)					I				I				I				I	I: Every 24 months
	Front wheel bearing and thrust bush grease (4WD)	2WD								R								R	R: Every 48 months
		4WD								R								R	R: Every 36 months
	Propeller shaft grease (5)	4WD		R		R		R		R		R		R		R		R	R: Every 12 months
	Bolts and nuts on chassis and body (6)			I		I		I		I		I		I		I		I	I: Every 12 months

* or * mark indicates maintenance which is part of the warranty conditions for the Emission Control System. The warranty period is in accordance with the owner's guide or the warranty booklet.

* : California specification vehicles.

* : Vehicles other than California specification vehicles.

HINT:

(1) Applicable to vehicles operated under conditions of extensive idling and / or low speed driving for long distances such as police, taxi or door-to-door delivery use.

(2) Applicable when operating mainly on dusty roads.

(3) Includes inspection of vapor vent system.

(4) Check for oil leaks from steering gear box.

(5) If the propeller shaft has been immersed in water, it should be re-greased daily.

(6) Applicable only when operating mainly on rough, muddy roads. The applicable parts are listed below.

- Front and rear suspension member to cross body.
- Bolts for sheet installation.

TY1139100242020X

Fig. 11 Pickup (Part 2 of 2)

System	Service interval (Use odometer reading or months, whichever comes first) / Maintenance items		Maintenance services beyond 96,000 km (60,000 miles) should continue to be performed at the same intervals shown for each maintenance schedule.																	Months
		× 1,000 km	1.6	6	12	18	24	30	36	42	48	54	60	66	72	78	84	90	96	
		× 1,000 miles	1	3.75	7.5	11.25	15	18.75	22.5	26.25	30	33.75	37.5	41.25	45	48.75	52.5	56.25	60	
ENGINE	Timing belt (1)																		R	–
	Valve clearance																		A	A: Every 72 months
	Drive belt		I: First period 96,000 km (60,000 miles) or 72 months I: After that every 12,000 km (7,500 miles) or 12 months																	
	Engine oil	2JZ-GE engine	R	R	R	R	R	R	R	R	R	R	R	R	R	R	R	R	R	R: Every 6 months
		2JZ-GTE engine	R: Every 2,500 miles (4,000 km) or 3 months																	
	Engine oil filter	2JZ-GE engine	R	R	R	R	R	R	R	R	R	R	R	R	R	R	R	R	R	R: Every 6 months
		2JZ-GTE engine	R: Every 5,000 miles (8,000 km) or 6 months																	
	Engine coolant		R: First period 72,000 km (45,000 miles) or 36 months R: After that every 48,000 km (30,000 miles) or 24 months.																	
	Exhaust pipes and mountings						I				I				I				I	I: Every 24 months
FUEL	Air filter (2)*			I	I	I	I	I	I	I	R	I	I	I	I	I	I	I	R	I: Every 6 months R: Every 36 months
	Fuel lines and connections (3)										I								I	I: Every 36 months
	Fuel tank cap gasket																		R	R: Every 72 months
IGNITION	Spark plugs (Platinum tipped type)																		R	R: Every 72 months
EVAP	Charcoal canister	New York and California only																	I	I: Every 72 months
BRAKES	Brake linings and drums (4)				I		I		I		I		I		I		I		I	I: Every 12 months
	Brake pads and discs (Front and rear)				I		I		I		I		I		I		I		I	I: Every 12 months
	Brake line pipes and hoses						I				I				I				I	I: Every 24 months
CHASSIS	Steering linkage				I		I		I		I		I		I		I		I	I: Every 12 months
	SRS airbag		I: First period 10 years I: After that every 2 years.																	
	Ball joints and dust covers				I		I		I		I		I		I		I		I	I: Every 12 months
	Automatic transmission, manual transmission and differential oil						R				R				R				R	R: Every 24 months
	Steering gear housing oil (5)						I				I				I				I	I: Every 24 months
	Bolts and nuts on chassis and body (6)				I		I		I		I		I		I		I		I	I: Every 12 months

TY1139300244010X

Fig. 12 Supra (Part 1 of 2). 1993–95

★ mark indicates maintenance which is part of the warranty conditions for the Emission Control Systems. The warranty period is in accordance with the owner's guide or the warranty booklet. (★: California and New York specification vehicles)

(1) Applicacable to vehicles operated under conditions of extensive idling and/or low speed driving for long distances such as police, taxi or door—to—door delivery use.
(2) Applicable when operating mainly on dusty roads.
(3) Includes inspection of fuel tank band and vaper vent system.
(4) Also applicable to drum lining for parking brake.

(5) Check for oil leaks from steering gear housing.
(6) Applicable only when operating mainly on rough, muddy roads. The applicable parts are listed below.
- Front and rear suspension member to cross body.
- Bolts for sheat installation.

TY1139300244020X

Fig. 12 Supra (Part 2 of 2). 1993–95

Maintenance operation: A = Check and adjust if necessary.
R = Replace, change or lubricate.
I = Inspect and correct or replace if necessary.

System	Service interval (Use odometer reading or months, whichever comes first) / Maintenance items		Maintenance services beyond 96,000 km (60,000 miles) should continue to be performed at the same intervals shown in each maintenance schedule.								Months
		km x 1,000	12	24	36	48	60	72	84	96	
		Miles x 1,000	7.5	15	22.5	30	37.5	45	52.5	60	
ENGINE	Valve clearance									A	A: Every 72 months
	Drive belts		I: First period 96,000 km (60,000 miles) or 72 months I: After that, every 12,000 km (7,500 miles) or 12 months								
	Engine oil and oil filter*		R	R	R	R	R	R	R	R	R: Every 12 months
	Engine coolant		R: First period 72,000 km (45,000 miles) or 36 months R: After that, every 48,000 km (30,000 miles) or 24 months								
	Exhaust pipes and mountings					I				I	I: Every 36 months
FUEL	Air filter*					R				R	R: Every 36 months
	Fuel lines and connections (1)					I				I	I: Every 36 months
	Fuel tank cap gasket									R	R: Every 72 months
IGNITION	Spark plugs*◆					R				R	R: Every 36 months
EVAP	Charcoal canister (2)									I	I: Every 72 months
EXHAUST	Heated oxygen sensor ◆		R: 129,000 km (80,000 miles) only								
BRAKES	Brake linings and drums			I		I		I		I	I: Every 24 months
	Brake pads and discs			I		I		I		I	I: Every 24 months
	Brake line pipes and hoses			I		I		I		I	I: Every 24 months
CHASSIS	Steering linkage			I		I		I		I	I: Every 24 months
	SRS airbag		I: First period 10 years. I. After that every 2 years.								
	Ball joints and dust covers			I		I		I		I	I: Every 24 months
	Drive shaft boots	4WD		I		I		I		I	I: Every 24 months
	Automatic transmission, manual transmission, transfer (4WD) and differential (3)			I		I		I		I	I: Every 24 months
	Steering gear housing oil (4)			I		I		I		I	I: Every 24 months
	Front wheel bearing and thrust bush grease (4WD)	2WD				R				R	R: Every 48 months
		4WD				R				R	R: Every 36 months
	Propeller shaft grease (5)	4WD		R		R		R		R	R: Every 24 months
	Bolts and nuts on chassis and body (6)			I		I		I		I	I: Every 24 months

TY1139500261010X

Fig. 13 Tacoma (Part 1 of 2). 1995

★ or ◆ mark indicates maintenance which is part of the warranty conditions for the Emission Control Systems. The warranty period is in accordance with the owner's guide or the warranty booklet.

★: For vehicles sold in california and Massachusetts.
◆: For vehicles sold outside california and Massachusetts.

(1) Includes inspection of fuel tank band and vapor vent system.
(2) Non−maintenance item except for California and Massachusetts.
(3) Check for oil level.
(4) Check for oil leaks from steering gear box.
(5) If the propeller shaft has been immersed in water, it should be re−greased daily.
(6) The applicable parts are listed below.
- Front and rear suspension member to cross body.
- Strut bar bracket to body.
- Leaf spring U−bolt.
- Bolts for seat installation.

TY1139500261020X

Fig. 13 Tacoma (Part 2 of 2). 1995

CONDITIONS:

Maintenance operation: A = Check and adjust if necessary;
R = Replace, changer or lubricate;
I = Inspect and correct to replace if necessary

- Towing a trailer, using a camper or car top carrier.
- Repeated short trips of less than 8 km (5 miles) and outside temperature remains below freezing.
- Extensive idling and/or low speed driving for long distances such as police, taxi or door-to-door delivery use.
- Operating on dusty, rough, muddy or salt spread roads.

System	Service interval (Odometer reading or months, whichever comes first) / Maintenance items	Maintenance services beyond 96,000 km (60,000 miles) should continue to be performed as the same intervals shown in each maintenance schedule.																
		km x 1,000	6	12	18	24	30	36	42	48	54	60	66	72	78	84	90	96	Months
		Miles x 1,000	3.75	7.5	11.25	15	18.75	22.5	26.25	30	33.75	37.5	41.25	45	48.75	52.5	56.25	60	
ENGINE	Timing belt (1)																	R	–
	Valve clearance★									A								A	A: Every 36 months
	Drive belts	I: First period, 96,000 km (60,000 miles) or 72 months I: After that, every 12,000 km (7,500 miles) or 12 months																	
	Engine oil and oil filter★		R	R	R	R	R	R	R	R	R	R	R	R	R	R	R	R	R: Every 6 months
	Engine coolant	R: First period, 72,000 km (45,000 miles) or 36 months R: After that, every 48,000 km (30,000 miles) or 24 months																	
	Exhaust pipes and mountings					I				I				I				I	I: Every 24 months
FUEL	Idle speed	A: First period, 12,000 km (7,500 miles) or 12 months, and 24,000 km (15,000 miles) or 24 months A: After that, every 24,000 km (15,000 miles) or 24 months																	
	Air filter★ (2)		I	I	I	I	I	I	I	R	I	I	I	I	I	I	I	R	I: Every 6 months R: Every 36 months
	Fuel lines and connections (3)									I								I	I: Every 36 months
	Fuel tank cap gasket																	R	R: Every 72 months
IGNITION	Spark plugs★•									R								R	R: Every 36 months
EVAP	Charcoal canister																	I	I: Every 72 months

TY1139100245010X

Fig. 14 Tercel (Part 1 of 2). 1993-95

System	Service interval (Odometer reading or months, whichever comes first) / Maintenance items	6	12	18	24	30	36	42	48	54	60	66	72	78	84	90	96	Months
		Maintenance services beyond 96,000 km (60,000 miles) should continue to be performed as the same intervals shown in each maintenance schedule.																
	km x 1,000	6	12	18	24	30	36	42	48	54	60	66	72	78	84	90	96	Months
	Miles x 1,000	3.75	7.5	11.25	15	18.75	22.5	26.25	30	33.75	37.5	41.25	45	48.75	52.5	56.25	60	
BRAKES	Brake linings and drums		I		I		I		I		I		I		I		I	I: Every 12 months
	Brake pads and discs		I		I		I		I		I		I		I		I	I: Every 12 months
	Brake line pipes and hoses				I				I				I				I	I: Every 24 months
CHASSIS	Steering linkage		I		I		I		I		I		I		I		I	I: Every 12 months
	SRS airbag	I: First period, 10 years. I: After that every 2 years.																
	Ball joints and dust covers		I		I		I		I		I		I		I		I	I: Every 12 months
	Drive shaft boots		I		I		I		I		I		I		I		I	I: Every 12 months
	Automatic transmission, manual transmission and differential oil				R				R				R				R	R: Every 24 months
	Steering gear housing oil (4)				I				I				I				I	I: Every 24 months
	Rear wheel bearing								R									R: Every 48 months
	Bolts on body (5)		I		I		I		I		I		I		I		I	I: Every 12 months

★ or • mark indicates maintenance which is part of the Emission Control System. The warranty period is in accordance with the owner's guide or the warranty booklet.

★: California specification vehicles.

•: Vehicles other than California specification vehicles.

NOTE:

(1) Applicable to vehicle operated under conditions of extensive idling and/or low speed driving for long distances such as police, taxi or door-to-door delivery use.

(2) Applicable when operating mainly on dusty roads.

(3) Includes inspection of vapor vent system.

(4) Check for oil leaks from steering gear box.

(5) Applicable only when operating mainly on rough, muddy roads. The applicable parts are listed below.

- Bolts for sheet installation.

TY1139100245020X

Fig. 14 Tercel (Part 2 of 2). 1993–95

System	Service interval (Use odometer reading or months, whichever comes first) / Maintenance items		6	12	18	24	30	36	42	48	54	60	66	72	78	84	90	96	Months
			Maintenance services beyond 96,000 km (60,000 miles) should continue to be performed at the same intervals shown in each maintenance schedule.																
		km x 1,000	6	12	18	24	30	36	42	48	54	60	66	72	78	84	90	96	Months
		Miles x 1,000	3.75	7.5	11.25	15	18.75	22.5	26.25	30	33.75	37.5	41.25	45	48.75	52.5	56.25	60	
ENGINE	Timing belt (1)																	R	–
	Valve clearance																	A	A: Every 72 months
	Drive belts		I: First period. 48,000 km (30,000 miles) or 36 months, second period, 96,000 km (60,000 miles) or 72 months I: After that, every 12,000 km (7,500 miles) or 12 months																
	Engine oil and oil filter*		R	R	R	R	R	R	R	R	R	R	R	R	R	R	R	R	R: Every 6 months
	Engine coolant		R: First period 72,000 km (45,000 miles) or 36 months R: After that every 48,000 km (30,000 miles) or 24 months																
	Exhaust pipes and mounting					I				I				I				I	I: Every 24 months
FUEL	Idle speed		A: First period. 12,000 km (7,500 miles) or 12 months, second period, 24,000 km (15,000 miles) or 24 months A: After that, every 24,000 km (15,000 miles) or 24 months																
	Air filter* (2)		I	I	I	I	I	I	I	R	I	I	I	I	I	I	I	R	I: Every 6 months R: Every 36 months
	Fuel lines and connection (3)									I								I	I: Every 36 months
	Fuel tank cap gasket																	R	R: Every 72 months
IGNITION	Spark plugs* •									R								R	R: Every 36 months
EVAP	Charcoal canister (4)																	I	I: Every 72 months
EXHAUST	Heated oxygen sensor	Ex. Calif. and N.Y.	R: 129,000 km (80,000 miles) only																
BRAKES	Brake linings and drums			I		I		I		I		I		I		I		I	I: Every 12 months
	Brake pads and discs			I		I		I		I		I		I		I		I	I: Every 12 months
	Brake line pipes and hoses					I				I				I				I	I: Every 24 months
CHASSIS	Steering linkage			I		I		I		I		I		I		I		I	I: Every 12 months
	SRS airbag		I: First Period 10 years. I: After that every 2 years.																
	Ball joints and dust covers			I		I		I		I		I		I		I		I	I: Every 12 months
	Drive shaft boots	4WD		I		I		I		I		I		I		I		I	I: Every 12 months
	Automatic transmission, manual transmission, transfer (4WD) and differential					R				R				R				R	R: Every 24 months
	Steering gear housing oil (5)					I				I				I				I	I: Every 24 months
	Front wheel bearing and thrust bush grease (4WD)	2WD								R								R	R: Every 48 months
		4WD								R								R	R: Every 36 months
	Propeller shaft grease (6)	4WD		R		R		R		R		R		R		R		R	R: Every 12 months
	Bolts and nuts on chassis and body (7)			I		I		I		I		I		I		I		I	I: Every 12 months

TY1139100246010X

Fig. 15 T100 (Part 1 of 2). 1993–95

★ or ◆ mark indicates maintenance which is part of the warranty conditions for the Emission Control Systems. The warranty period is in accordance with the owner's guide or the warranty booklet.

★: California and New York specification vehicles

◆: Vehicles other than California and New York specification vehicles

(1) Applicacable to vehicles operated under conditions of extensive idling and/or low speed driving for long distances such as police, taxi or door−to−door delivery use.
(2) Applicable when operating mainly on dusty roads
(3) Includes inspection of fuel tank band and vaper vent system.
(4) Non−maintenance item except for California and New York.
(5) Check for oil leaks from steering gear box.
(6) If the propeller shaft has been immersed in water, it should be re−greased daily.
(7) Applicable only when operating mainly on rough, muddy roads. The applicable parts are listed below.
- Front and rear suspension member to cross body.
- Strut bar bracket to body.
- Leaf spring U−bolt.
- Bolts for sheat installation.

TY1139100246020X

Fig. 15 T100 (Part 2 of 2). 1993–95

System	Service interval (Use odometer reading or months, whichever comes first) / Maintenance items		Maintenance services beyond 60,000 miles (96,000 km) should continue to be performed at the same intervals shown in each maintenance schedule.								
		Miles × 1,000	7.5	15	22.5	30	37.5	45	52.5	60	Months
		km × 1,000	12	24	36	48	60	72	84	96	
ENGINE	Valve clearance*	22R-E engine				A				A	A: Every 36 months
	Valve clearance	3VZ-E engine								A	A: Every 72 months
	Drive belts		I: First period. 30,000 miles (48,000 km) or 36 months, second period, 60,000 miles (96,000 km) or 72 months I: After that, every 7,500 miles (12,000 km) or 12 months								
	Engine oil and oil filter*		R	R	R	R	R	R	R	R	R: Every 12 months
	Engine coolant		R: First period. 45,000 miles (72,000 km) or 36 months R: After that, every 30,000 miles (48,000 km) or 24 months								
	Exhaust pipes and mountings					I				I	I: Every 36 months
FUEL	Idle speed		A: First period. 7,500 miles (12,000 km) or 12 months, second period, 15,000 miles (24,000 km) or 24 months A: After that, every 15,000 miles (24,000 km) or 24 months								
	Air filter*					R				R	R: Every 36 months
	Fuel lines and connections (1)					I				I	I: Every 36 months
	Fuel tank cap gasket									R	R: Every 72 months
IGNITION	Spark plugs**					R				R	R: Every 36 months
EVAP	Charcoal canister	Calif. only								I	I: Every 72 months
EXHAUST	Oxygen sensor	Fed. and Canada only	R: 80,000 miles (129,000 km) only								
BRAKES	Brake lining and drums			I		I		I		I	I: Every 24 months
	Brake pads and discs			I		I		I		I	I: Every 24 months
	Brake line pipes and hoses			I		I		I		I	I: Every 24 months

TY1139100247010X

Fig. 16 4Runner (Part 1 of 2). 1993

System	Service interval (Use odometer reading or months, whichever comes first) / Maintenance items		Maintenance services beyond 60,000 miles (96,000 km) should continue to be performed at the same intervals shown in each maintenance schedule.								
		Miles × 1,000	7.5	15	22.5	30	37.5	45	52.5	60	Months
		km × 1,000	12	24	36	48	60	72	84	96	
CHASSIS	Steering linkage			I		I		I		I	I: Every 24 months
	Ball joints and dust covers			I		I		I		I	I: Every 24 months
	Drive shaft boots	4WD		I		I		I		I	I: Every 24 months
	Automatic transmission, manual transmission, transfer (4WD) and differential (2)			I		I		I		I	I: Every 24 months
	Steering gear housing oil (3)			I		I		I		I	I: Every 24 months
	Front wheel bearing and thrust bush grease (4WD)	2WD				R				R	R: Every 48 months
		4WD				R				R	R: Every 36 months
	Propeller shaft grease (4)	4WD		R		R		R		R	R: Every 24 months
	Bolts and nuts on chassis and body (5)			I		I		I		I	I: Every 24 months

* or * mark indicates maintenance which is part of the warranty conditions for the Emission Control System. The warranty period is in accordance with the owner's guide or the warranty booklet.

* : California specification vehicles.

* : Vehicles other than California specification vehicles.

HINT:

(1) Includes inspection of vapor vent system.

(2) Check for oil level.

(3) Check for oil leaks from steering gear box.

(4) If the propeller shaft has been immersed in water, it should be re-greased daily.

(5) The applicable parts are listed below.

- Front and rear suspension member to cross body.
- Bolts for sheet installation.

TY1139100247020X

Fig. 16 4Runner (Part 2 of 2). 1993

System	Service interval (Use odometer reading or months, whichever comes first) / Maintenance items		Maintenance services beyond 96,000 km (60,000 miles) should continue to be performed at the same intervals shown in each maintenance schedule.																
		km x 1,000	6	12	18	24	30	36	42	48	54	60	66	72	78	84	90	96	Months
		Miles x 1,000	3.75	7.5	11.25	15	18.75	22.5	26.25	30	33.75	37.5	41.25	45	48.75	52.5	56.25	60	
ENGINE	Timing belt (1)	3VZ-E engine																R	–
	Valve clearance*	22R-E engine								A								A	A: Every 36 months
	Valve clearance	3VZ-E engine																A	A: Every 72 months
	Drive belts		I: First period. 48,000 km (30,000 miles) or 36 months, second period, 96,000 km (60,000 miles) or 72 months I: After that, every 12,000 km (7,500 miles) or 12 months																
	Engine oil and oil filter*		R	R	R	R	R	R	R	R	R	R	R	R	R	R	R	R	R: Every 6 months
	Engine coolant		R: First period 72,000 km (45,000 miles) or 36 months R: After that every 48,000 km (30,000 miles) or 24 months																
	Exhaust pipes and mounting					I				I				I				I	I: Every 24 months
FUEL	Idle speed		A: First period. 12,000 km (7,500 miles) or 12 months, second period, 24,000 km (15,000 miles) or 24 months A: After that, every 48,000 km (30,000 miles) or 24 months																
	Air filter* (2)		I	I	I	I	I	I	I	R	I	I	I	I	I	I	I	R	I: Every 6 months R: Every 36 months
	Fuel lines and connection (3)									I								I	I: Every 36 months
	Fuel tank cap gasket																	R	R: Every 72 months
IGNITION	Spark plugs* *									R								R	R: Every 36 months
EVAP	Charcoal canister	Calif. and N.Y. only																I	I: Every 72 months
EXHAUST	Heated oxygen sensor	Ex. Calif. and N.Y.	R: 129,000 km (80,000 miles) only																
BRAKES	Brake linings and drums			I		I		I		I		I		I		I		I	I: Every 12 months
	Brake pads and discs			I		I		I		I		I		I		I		I	I: Every 12 months
	Brake line pipes and hoses					I				I				I				I	I: Every 24 months
CHASSIS	Steering linkage			I		I		I		I		I		I		I		I	I: Every 12 months
	Ball joints and dust covers			I		I		I		I		I		I		I		I	I: Every 12 months
	Drive shaft boots	4WD		I		I		I		I		I		I		I		I	I: Every 12 months
	Automatic transmission, manual transmission, transfer (4WD) and differential					R				R				R				R	R: Every 24 months
	Steering gear housing oil (4)					I				I				I				I	I: Every 24 months
	Front wheel bearing and thrust bush grease (4WD)	2WD								R								R	R: Every 48 months
		4WD								R								R	R: Every 36 months
	Propeller shaft grease (5)	4WD		R		R		R		R		R		R		R		R	R: Every 12 months
	Bolts and nuts on chassis and body (6)			I		I		I		I		I		I		I		I	I: Every 12 months

TY1139400248010X

Fig. 17 4Runner (Part 1 of 2). 1994–95

★ or ◆ mark indicates maintenance which is part of the warranty conditions for the Emission Control Systems. The warranty period is in accordance with the owner's guide or the warranty booklet.

★: California and New York specification vehicles

◆: Vehicles other than California and New York specification vehicles

(1) Applicacable to vehicles operated under conditions of extensive idling and/or low speed driving for long distances such as police, taxi or door–to–door delivery use.
(2) Applicable when operating mainly on dusty roads
(3) Includes inspection of fuel tank band and vaper vent system.
(4) Check for oil leaks from steering gear box.
(5) If the propeller shaft has been immersed in water, it should be re–greased daily.
(6) Applicable only when operating mainly on rough, muddy roads. The applicable parts are listed below.

- Front and rear suspension member to cross body.
- Bolts for sheet installation.

TY1139400248020X

Fig. 17 4Runner (Part 2 of 2). 1994–95

System	Service interval (Use odometer reading or months, whichever comes first) / Maintenance items		Maintenance services beyond 96,000 km (60,000 miles) should continue to be performed at the same intervals shown for each maintenance schedule.																
		x 1,000 km	6	12	18	24	30	36	42	48	54	60	66	72	78	84	90	96	Months
		x 1,000 miles	3.75	7.5	11.25	15	18.75	22.5	26.25	30	33.75	37.5	41.25	45	48.75	52.5	56.25	60	
ENGINE	Timing belt (1)																	R	–
	Valve clearance																	A	A Every 72 months
	Drive belt		I First period 96,000 km (60,000 miles) or 72 months. I: After that every 12,000 km (7 500 miles) or 12 months																
	Engine oil and oil filter★		R	R	R	R	R	R	R	R	R	R	R	R	R	R	R	R	R Every 6 months
	Engine coolant		R First period 72,000 km (45,000 miles) or 36 months. R After that every 48,000 km (30,000 miles) or 24 months																
	Exhaust pipes and mountings					I				I				I				I	I: Every 24 months
FUEL	Idle speed		A First period 12,000 km (7,500 miles) or 12 months, second period 24,000 km (15,000 miles) or 24 months. A After that every 24,000 km (15,000 miles) or 24 months																
	Air filter (2)★		I	I	I	I	I	I	I	R	I	I	I	I	I	I	I	R	I: Every 6 months R. Every 36 months
	Fuel lines and connections (3)									I								I	I: Every 36 months
	Fuel tank cap gasket																	R	R: Every 72 months
IGNITION	Spark plugs★ ◆									R								R	R. Every 36 months
EVAP	Charcoal canister																	I	I: Every 72 months
BRAKES	Brake linings and drums (4)			I		I		I		I		I		I		I		I	I. Every 12 months
	Brake pads and discs			I		I		I		I		I		I		I		I	I: Every 12 months
	Brake line pipes and hoses					I				I				I				I	I: Every 24 months
CHASSIS	Steering linkage			I		I		I		I		I		I		I		I	I: Every 12 months
	SRS airbag		I: First period 10 years. I: After that every 2 years.																
	Drive shaft boots			I		I		I		I		I		I		I		I	I Every 12 months
	Ball joints and dust covers			I		I		I		I		I		I		I		I	I: Every 12 months
	Transaxle oil					R				R				R				R	R: Every 24 months
	Steering gear housing oil (5)					I				I				I				I	I: Every 24 months
	Rear wheel bearing									R								I	I. Every 48 months
	Bolts on body (6)			I		I		I		I		I		I		I		I	I. Every 12 months

TY1139100249010X

Fig. 18 Paseo (Part 1 of 2). 1993–95

★ and * marks indicates maintenance which is part of the warranty conditions for the Emission Control Systems. The warranty period is in accordance with the owner's guide or the warranty booklet.

★: California and New York specification vehicles

*: Other specification vehicles

(1) Applicacable to vehicles operated under conditions of extensive idling and/or low speed driving for long distances such as police, taxi or door—to—door delivery use.

(2) Applicable when operating mainly on dusty roads.

(3) Includes inspection of fuel tank band and vaper vent system.

(4) Also applicable to drum lining for parking brake.

(5) Check for oil leaks from steering gear housing.

(6) Applicable only when operating mainly on rough, muddy roads. The applicable parts are listed below.

- Bolts for seat installation.

TY1139100249020X

Fig. 18 Paseo (Part 2 of 2). 1993–95

Maintenance Required	Mileage (Thousands)/Months							
	7.5/6	15/12	22.5/18	30/24	37.5/30	45/36	52.5/42	60/48
Rotate Tires	X	X	X	X	X	X	X	X
Replace Engine Oil & Filter	X	X	X	X	X	X	X	X
Replace Engine Air Filter	—	—	—	X	—	—	—	X
Inspect SRS Air Bag	⑥	⑥	⑥	⑥	⑥	⑥	⑥	⑥
Inspect Exhaust System	—	X	—	X	—	X	—	X
Inspect Brake System	—	X	—	X	—	X	—	X
Inspect Steering Linkages	—	X	—	X	—	X	—	X
Inspect Rack & Pinion For Leakage	—	X	—	X	—	X	—	X
Inspect Ball Joints & Dust Covers	—	X	—	X	—	X	—	X
Inspect Driveshaft Boots & Re-Torque Flange Bolts	—	X	—	X	—	X	—	X
Inspect A/T & Differential Oil	—	X	—	X	—	X	—	X
Inspect Limited Slip Differential Oil①	—	X	—	—	—	X	—	—
Replace Limited Slip Differential Oil①	—	—	—	X	—	—	—	X
Replace Non-Platinum Spark Plugs②	—	—	—	X	—	—	—	X
Replace Platinum Spark Plugs	—	—	—	—	—	—	—	X
Replace Engine Coolant	—	—	—	X	—	—	—	X
Repack Rear Wheel Bearings③	—	—	—	X	—	—	—	X
Inspect Fuel Lines & Connections, Fuel Tank Vapor Vent System Hoses & Fuel Tank Band	—	—	—	X	—	—	—	X
Inspect Fuel Tank Cap Gasket	—	—	—	X	—	—	—	X
Inspect Valve Adjustment④	—	—	—	—	—	—	—	X
Inspect Drive Belts	—	—	—	—	—	—	—	X
Inspect Charcoal Canister⑤	—	—	—	—	—	—	—	X

① — Supra.
② — Celica w/7AFE engine, Corolla, Paseo & Tercel.
③ — Paseo & Tercel.
④ — Audible inspection.
⑤ — Non-maintenance item except in California, Massachusetts & New York.
⑥ — Inspect every ten years.

Fig. 19 Except Land Cruiser, Pickup, Previa, RAV4 & 4Runner (Part 1 of 2). 1996

Maintenance Required	Mileage (Thousands)/Months							
	67.5/54	75/60	82.5/66	90/72	97.5/78	105/84	112.5/90	120/96
Rotate Tires	X	X	X	X	X	X	X	X
Replace Engine Oil & Filter	X	X	X	X	X	X	X	X
Replace Engine Air Filter	—	—	—	X	—	—	—	X
Inspect SRS Air Bag	①	①	①	①	①	①	①	①
Inspect Drive Belts	—	X	—	X	—	X	—	X
Inspect Exhaust System	—	X	—	X	—	X	—	X
Inspect Brake System	—	X	—	X	—	X	—	X
Inspect Steering Linkages	—	X	—	X	—	X	—	X
Inspect Rack & Pinion For Leakage	—	X	—	X	—	X	—	X
Inspect Ball Joints & Dust Covers	—	X	—	X	—	X	—	X
Inspect Driveshaft Boots & Re-Torque Flange Bolts	—	X	—	X	—	X	—	X
Inspect A/T & Differential Oil	—	X	—	X	—	X	—	X
Inspect Limited Slip Differential Oil②	—	X	—	—	—	X	—	—
Replace Limited Slip Differential Oil②	—	—	—	X	—	—	—	X
Replace Non-Platinum Spark Plugs③	—	—	—	X	—	—	—	X
Replace Platinum Spark Plugs	—	—	—	—	—	—	—	X
Repack Rear Wheel Bearings④	—	—	—	X	—	—	—	X
Inspect Fuel Lines & Connections, Fuel Tank Vapor Vent System Hoses & Fuel Tank Band	—	—	—	X	—	—	—	X
Inspect Tank Cap Gasket	—	—	—	X	—	—	—	X
Inspect Charcoal Canister⑤	—	—	—	—	—	—	—	X
Inspect Valve Adjustment⑥	—	—	—	—	—	—	—	X

① — Inspect every ten years.
② — Supra.
③ — Celica w/7AFE engine, Corolla, Paseo & Tercel.
④ — Paseo & Tercel.
⑤ — Non-maintenance item except in California, Massachusetts & New York.
⑥ — Audible inspection.

Fig. 19 Except Land Cruiser, Pickup, Previa, RAV4 & 4Runner (Part 2 of 2). 1996

Maintenance Required	Mileage (Thousands)/Months							
	7.5/6	15/12	22.5/18	30/24	37.5/30	45/36	52.5/42	60/48
Rotate Tires	X	X	X	X	X	X	X	X
Replace Engine Oil & Filter	X	X	X	X	X	X	X	X
Inspect SRS Air Bag	①	①	①	①	①	①	①	①
Lubricate Steering Knuckle②	—	X	—	X	—	X	—	X
Lubricate Propeller Shaft & Re-Torque Bolts③	—	X	—	X	—	X	—	X
Inspect Exhaust System	—	X	—	X	—	X	—	X
Inspect Brake System	—	X	—	X	—	X	—	X
Inspect Steering Linkages	—	X	—	X	—	X	—	X
Inspect Steering Gearbox For Leakage	—	X	—	X	—	X	—	X
Inspect Ball Joints & Dust Covers	—	X	—	X	—	X	—	X
Inspect Driveshaft Boots & Re-Torque Flange Bolts④⑤	—	X	—	X	—	X	—	X
Inspect Limited Slip Differential Oil⑤	—	X	—	—	—	X	—	—
Replace Limited Slip Differential Oil⑤	—	—	—	X	—	—	—	X
Inspect A/T, Transfer & Differential Oil	—	X	—	X	—	X	—	X
Lubricate Driveshaft Bushing⑥	—	—	—	X	—	—	—	X
Replace Engine Air Filter	—	—	—	X	—	—	—	X
Replace Non-Platinum Spark Plugs⑦	—	—	—	X	—	—	—	X
Replace Platinum Spark Plugs	—	—	—	—	—	—	—	X
Replace Engine Coolant	—	—	—	X	—	—	—	X
Repack Front Wheel Bearings⑦	—	—	—	X	—	—	—	X
Inspect Non-Ribbed Drive Belts	—	—	—	X	—	—	—	X
Inspect All Drive Belts	—	—	—	—	—	—	—	X
Inspect Fuel Lines & Connections, Fuel Tank Vapor Vent System Hoses & Fuel Tank Band	—	—	—	X	—	—	—	X
Inspect Fuel Cap Gasket	—	—	—	X	—	—	—	X
Inspect Supercharger Gear Oil⑧	—	—	—	X	—	—	—	X
Inspect Valve Adjustment⑨	—	—	—	—	—	—	—	X
Inspect Charcoal Canister⑩	—	—	—	—	—	—	—	X

① — Inspect every ten years.
② — Land Cruiser.
③ — Except RAV4.
④ — 4WD models except Land Cruiser.
⑤ — RAV4.
⑥ — 4WD models except Previa.
⑦ — Except Previa & RAV4.
⑧ — Previa.
⑨ — Audible inspection.
⑩ — Non-maintenance item except in California, Massachusetts & New York.

Fig. 20 RAV4, Land Cruiser, Pickup, Previa & 4Runner (Part 1 of 2). 1996

Maintenance Required	Mileage (Thousands)/Months							
	67.5/54	75/60	82.5/66	90/72	97.5/78	105/82	112.5/88	120/96
Rotate Tires	X	X	X	X	X	X	X	X
Replace Engine Oil & Filter	X	X	X	X	X	X	X	X
Inspect SRS Air Bag	①	①	①	①	①	①	①	①
Lubricate Steering Knuckle②	—	X	—	X	—	X	—	X
Lubricate Propeller Shaft & Re-Torque Bolts③	—	X	—	X	—	X	—	X
Inspect Exhaust System	—	X	—	X	—	X	—	X
Inspect Brake System	—	X	—	X	—	X	—	X
Inspect Steering Linkages	—	X	—	X	—	X	—	X
Inspect Steering Gearbox For Leakage	—	X	—	X	—	X	—	X
Inspect Ball Joints & Dust Covers	—	X	—	X	—	X	—	X
Inspect Driveshaft Boots & Re-Torque Flange Bolts④⑤	—	X	—	X	—	X	—	X
Inspect Limited Slip Differential Oil⑤	—	X	—	—	—	X	—	—
Replace Limited Slip Differential Oil⑤	—	—	—	X	—	—	—	X
Inspect A/T, Transfer & Differential Oil	—	X	—	X	—	X	—	X
Lubricate Driveshaft Bushing⑥	—	—	—	X	—	—	—	X
Replace Engine Air Filter	—	—	—	X	—	—	—	X
Replace Non-Platinum Spark Plugs⑦	—	—	—	X	—	—	—	X
Replace Platinum Spark Plugs	—	—	—	—	—	—	—	X
Replace Engine Coolant	—	—	—	X	—	—	—	X
Repack Front Wheel Bearings⑦	—	—	—	X	—	—	—	X
Inspect Non-Ribbed Drive Belts	—	—	—	X	—	—	—	X
Inspect All Drive Belts	—	—	—	—	—	—	—	X
Inspect Fuel Lines & Connections, Fuel Tank Vapor Vent System Hoses & Fuel Tank Band	—	—	—	X	—	—	—	X
Inspect Fuel Cap Gasket	—	—	—	X	—	—	—	X
Inspect Supercharger Gear Oil⑧	—	—	—	X	—	—	—	X
Inspect Valve Adjustment⑨	—	—	—	—	—	—	—	X
Inspect Charcoal Canister⑩	—	—	—	—	—	—	—	X

① — Inspect every ten years.
② — Land Cruiser.
③ — Except RAV4.
④ — 4WD models except Land Cruiser.
⑤ — RAV4.
⑥ — 4WD models except Previa.
⑦ — Except Previa & RAV4.
⑧ — Previa.
⑨ — Audible inspection.
⑩ — Non-maintenance item except in California, Massachusetts & New York.

Fig. 20 RAV4, Land Cruiser, Pickup, Previa & 4Runner (Part 2 of 2). 1996

VEHICLE MAINTENANCE SCHEDULES

Volkswagen

INDEX

	Page No.	Fig. No.
All	0-133	1

Maintenance Required	Model									
	Fox	Golf/ GTI	Golf III	Jetta/ GLI	Jetta III	Jetta Diesel	Cab- riolet	Co- rrado	Passat	Euro Van
7500 MILE INTERVALS										
Change Engine Oil	X	X	X	X	X	X	X	X	X	X
Replace Engine Oil Filter①	X	X	X	X	X	—	X	X	X	X
Inspect Auto Shift Lock Operation②	—	X	X	X	X	—	X	X	X	X
Inspect Clutch Adjustment	X	—	—	—	—	—	X	—	—	—
Inspect Brake Pads⑥	—	—	—	—	—	—	—	—	—	X
Rotate Tires③	—	—	—	—	—	—	—	X	X	—
15,000 & 45,000 MILES										
Change Engine Oil & Filter	X	X	X	X	X	X	X	X	X	X
Inspect Battery Electrolyte Level	X	X	X	X	X	—	X	X	X	X
Inspect Coolant Level	X	X	X	X	X	X	X	X	X	X
Clean Snow Screen⑦	—	—	—	—	—	—	—	X	—	—
Inspect Timing Belt Tension & Condition	—	—	—	—	—	—	—	—	X	—
Inspect Auto Shift Lock Operation②	—	X	X	X	X	—	X	X	X	X
Inspect Manual Trans. For Leaks	X	X	X	X	X	X	X	X	X	X
Inspect Clutch Adjustment & Wear	X	—	—	—	—	—	X	—	—	—
Inspect All Tire Pressures	X	X	X	X	X	X	X	X	X	X
Inspect Brake System For Leakage, Damage, Low Fluid Level & Pad Wear⑥	X	X	X	X	X	X	X	X	X	X
Inspect Driveshaft Boots	X	X	X	X	X	X	X	X	X	X
Inspect Auto Seat Belt Operation	—	—	—	—	—	—	—	X	X	—
Inspect OBD System w/VAG 1551 Scan Tool	X	X	X	X	—	X	X	X	X	—
Drain Water Separator	—	—	—	—	—	X	—	—	—	—
Inspect Electrical Systems	X	X	X	X	—	X	X	X	X	—
Inspect Engine Idle Speed⑤	X	X	X	X	X	X	X	X	X	X
Inspect Auto. Trans. Fluid④	—	X	X	X	X	—	X	X	X	X
Inspect Power Steering Fluid Level	—	X	X	X	X	X	X	X	X	X
Inspect Exhaust System	X	X	X	X	X	X	X	X	X	X

Fig. 1 Vehicle Maintenance Schedule (Part 1 of 2)

Maintenance Required	Model									
	Fox	Golf/ GTI	Golf III	Jetta/ GLI	Jetta III	Jetta Diesel	Cab-riolet	Co-rrado	Passat	Euro Van
30,000 & 60,000 MILES										
Change Engine Oil & Filter	X	X	X	X	X	X	X	X	X	X
Inspect Battery Electrolyte Level	X	X	X	X	X	X	X	X	X	X
Inspect Coolant Level	X	X	X	X	X	X	X	X	X	X
Replace Air Filter	X	X	X	X	X	X	X	X	X	X
Clean Snow Screen⑦	—	—	—	—	—	—	—	X	—	—
Inspect Passenger Compartment Dust & Pollen Filter	—	X	X	X	X	—	—	—	—	—
Inspect V-Belt Tension & Condition	—	—	—	—	—	—	—	X	—	X
Inspect Ribbed V-Belt Condition	—	—	—	—	—	X	—	X	X	X
Inspect Toothed Belt Tension & Condition	—	—	—	—	—	X	—	—	—	—
Inspect Timing Belt Tension⑧	—	—	—	—	—	—	—	—	X	—
Replace Timing Belt⑧⑨	—	—	—	—	—	—	—	—	X	—
Replace Spark Plugs	X	X	X	X	X	—	X	X	X	X
Replace Oxygen Sensor⑨	X	—	—	—	—	—	—	—	—	—
Drain Water Separator	—	—	—	—	—	X	—	—	—	—
Inspect Clutch Adjustment & Condition	X	—	—	—	—	—	X	—	—	—
Inspect Auto Shift Lock Operation②	—	X	X	X	X	—	X	X	X	X
Inspect Manual Trans. For Leaks	X	X	X	X	X	X	X	X	X	X
Inspect Front Axle Ball Joint Dust Seals & Tie Rod Ends	X	X	X	X	X	X	X	X	X	X
Clean & Lubricate Sliding Roof Guide Rails w/Silicone Spray	—	X	X	X	X	X	—	—	—	—
Inspect Auto Seat Belt Operation	—	—	—	—	—	—	—	X	X	—
Inspect Tire Condition & Pressures	X	X	X	X	X	X	X	X	X	X
Inspect Brake System For Leakage, Damage, Low Fluid Level & Pad Wear⑥	X	X	X	X	X	X	X	X	X	X
Inspect Driveshaft Boots	X	X	X	X	X	X	X	X	X	X
Inspect OBD System w/VAG 1551 Scan Tool	X	X	X	X	—	X	X	X	X	—
Inspect Electrical Systems	X	X	X	X	—	X	X	X	X	—
Inspect Engine Idle Speed⑤	X	X	X	X	X	X	X	X	X	X
Inspect Auto. Trans. Fluid④	—	X	X	X	X	—	X	X	X	X
Inspect Power Steering Fluid Level	—	X	X	X	X	X	X	X	X	X
Inspect Exhaust System	X	X	X	X	X	X	X	X	X	X

① — Replace first @ 7500 & 15,000 miles, then @ 15,000 mile intervals.
② — Including park/neutral position switch.
③ — Rotate first @ 7500 miles, then @ 12,000 mile intervals.
④ — Under severe conditions, such as extreme high temperatures, continuous mountain driving, towing or frequent stop & go traffic, change fluid every 30,000 miles.
⑤ — Except California models.
⑥ — Replace brake fluid every two years, regardless of mileage.
⑦ — VR6 engine.
⑧ — 16V engine.
⑨ — At 60,000 miles.

Fig. 2 Vehicle Maintenance Schedule (Part 2 of 2)

VEHICLE MAINTENANCE SCHEDULES

Volvo

INDEX

	Page No.	Fig. No.
B230F Non-Turbocharged Engine	0-135	1
B230F Turbocharged Engine	0-135	2
B234F Engine	0-136	3
240 Chassis	0-136	4
700 Series Chassis	0-136	5
850	0-136	6
940	0-137	7
960	0-138	8

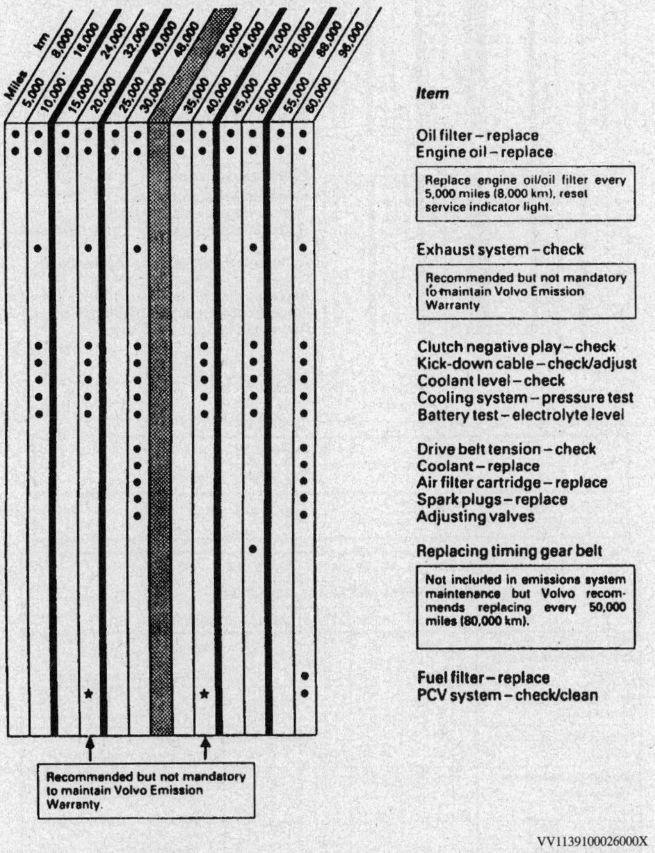

Miles km
5,000 8,000
10,000 16,000
15,000 24,000
20,000 32,000
25,000 40,000
30,000 48,000
35,000 56,000
40,000 64,000
45,000 72,000
50,000 80,000
55,000 88,000
60,000 96,000
Item
Oil filter – replace
Engine oil – replace
Replace engine oil/oil filter every 5,000 miles (8,000 km), reset service indicator light.
Exhaust system – check
Recommended but not mandatory to maintain Volvo Emission Warranty
Clutch negative play – check
Kick-down cable – check/adjust
Coolant level – check
Cooling system – pressure test
Battery test – electrolyte level
Drive belt tension – check
Coolant – replace
Air filter cartridge – replace
Spark plugs – replace
Adjusting valves
Replacing timing gear belt
Not included in emissions system maintenance but Volvo recommends replacing every 50,000 miles (80,000 km).
Fuel filter – replace
PCV system – check/clean
Recommended but not mandatory to maintain Volvo Emission Warranty.
VV1139100026000X

Fig. 1 B230F Non-Turbocharged Engine. 1993–94

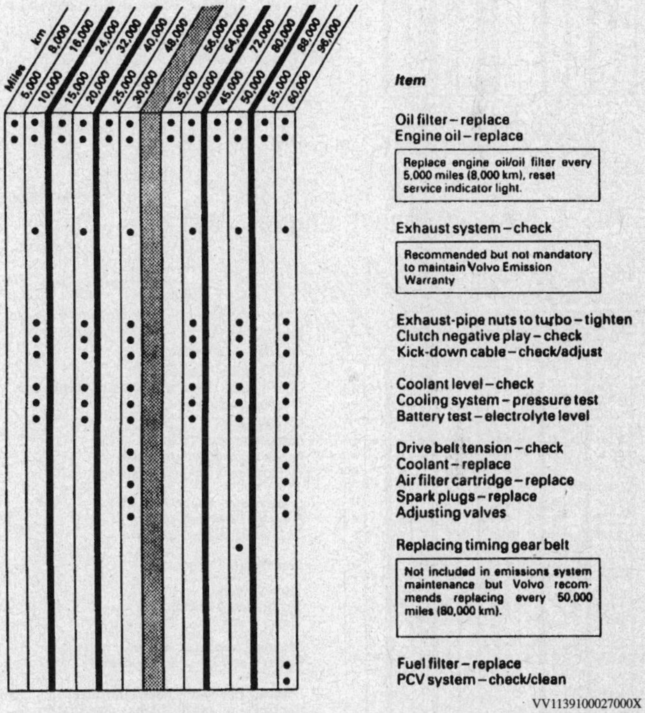

Miles km
5,000 8,000
10,000 16,000
15,000 24,000
20,000 32,000
25,000 40,000
30,000 48,000
35,000 56,000
40,000 64,000
45,000 72,000
50,000 80,000
55,000 88,000
60,000 96,000
Item
Oil filter – replace
Engine oil – replace
Replace engine oil/oil filter every 5,000 miles (8,000 km), reset service indicator light.
Exhaust system – check
Recommended but not mandatory to maintain Volvo Emission Warranty
Exhaust-pipe nuts to turbo – tighten
Clutch negative play – check
Kick-down cable – check/adjust
Coolant level – check
Cooling system – pressure test
Battery test – electrolyte level
Drive belt tension – check
Coolant – replace
Air filter cartridge – replace
Spark plugs – replace
Adjusting valves
Replacing timing gear belt
Not included in emissions system maintenance but Volvo recommends replacing every 50,000 miles (80,000 km).
Fuel filter – replace
PCV system – check/clean
VV1139100027000X

Fig. 2 B230F Turbocharged Engine. 1993–94

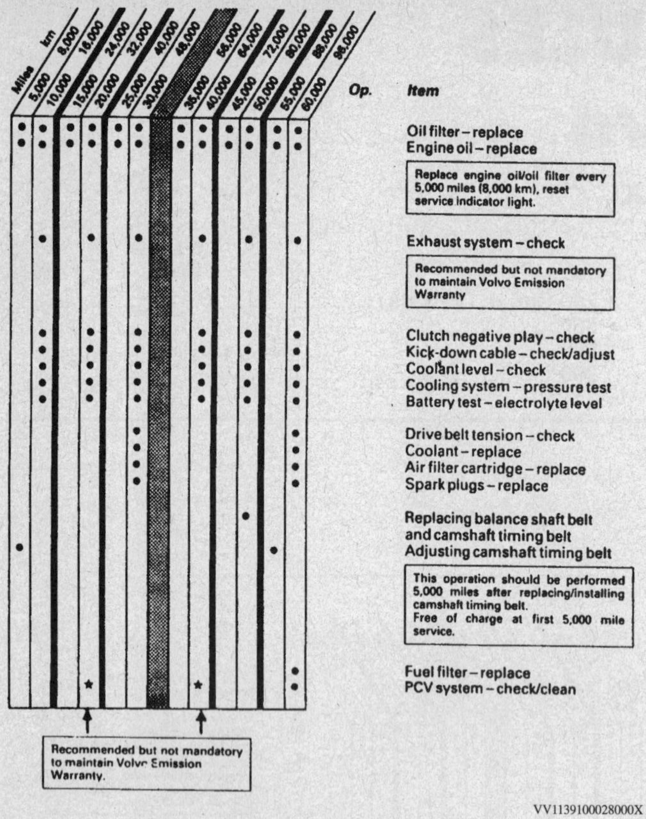
Miles km
5,000 8,000
10,000 16,000
15,000 24,000
20,000 32,000
25,000 40,000
30,000 48,000
35,000 56,000
40,000 64,000
45,000 72,000
50,000 80,000
55,000 88,000
60,000 96,000
Op.
Item
Oil filter – replace
Engine oil – replace
Replace engine oil/oil filter every 5,000 miles (8,000 km), reset service indicator light.
Exhaust system – check
Recommended but not mandatory to maintain Volvo Emission Warranty
Clutch negative play – check
Kick-down cable – check/adjust
Coolant level – check
Cooling system – pressure test
Battery test – electrolyte level
Drive belt tension – check
Coolant – replace
Air filter cartridge – replace
Spark plugs – replace
Replacing balance shaft belt and camshaft timing belt
Adjusting camshaft timing belt
This operation should be performed 5,000 miles after replacing/installing camshaft timing belt. Free of charge at first 5,000 mile service.
Fuel filter – replace
PCV system – check/clean
Recommended but not mandatory to maintain Volvo Emission Warranty.
VV1139100028000X

Fig. 3 B234F Engine. 1993–94

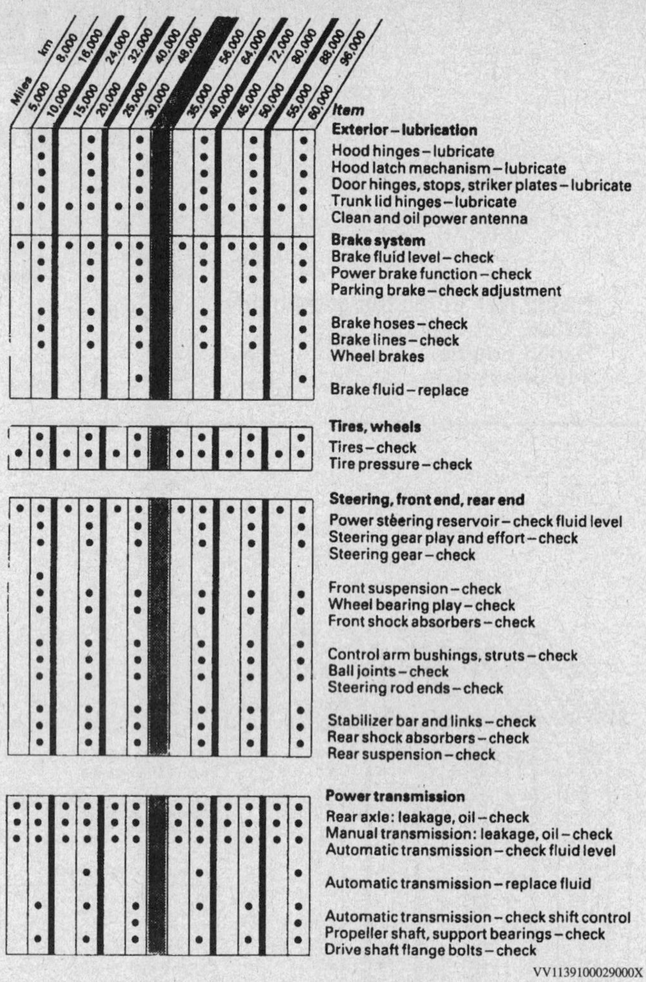
Miles km
5,000 8,000
10,000 16,000
15,000 24,000
20,000 32,000
25,000 40,000
30,000 48,000
35,000 56,000
40,000 64,000
45,000 72,000
50,000 80,000
55,000 88,000
60,000 96,000
Item
Exterior – lubrication
Hood hinges – lubricate
Hood latch mechanism – lubricate
Door hinges, stops, striker plates – lubricate
Trunk lid hinges – lubricate
Clean and oil power antenna
Brake system
Brake fluid level – check
Power brake function – check
Parking brake – check adjustment
Brake hoses – check
Brake lines – check
Wheel brakes
Brake fluid – replace
Tires, wheels
Tires – check
Tire pressure – check
Steering, front end, rear end
Power steering reservoir – check fluid level
Steering gear play and effort – check
Steering gear – check
Front suspension – check
Wheel bearing play – check
Front shock absorbers – check
Control arm bushings, struts – check
Ball joints – check
Steering rod ends – check
Stabilizer bar and links – check
Rear shock absorbers – check
Rear suspension – check
Power transmission
Rear axle: leakage, oil – check
Manual transmission: leakage, oil – check
Automatic transmission – check fluid level
Automatic transmission – replace fluid
Automatic transmission – check shift control
Propeller shaft, support bearings – check
Drive shaft flange bolts – check
VV1139100029000X

Fig. 4 240 Chassis

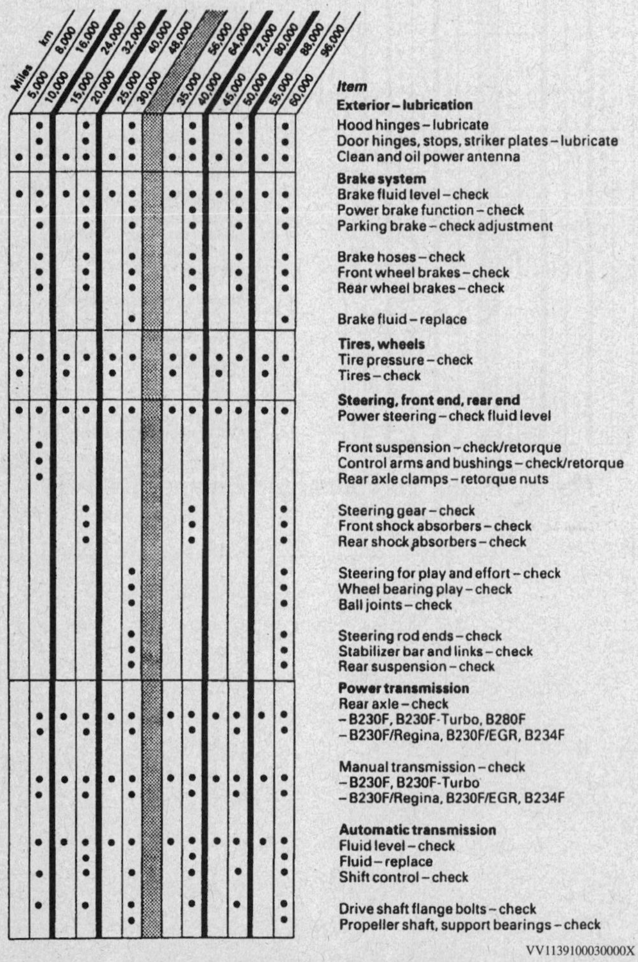
Miles km
5,000 8,000
10,000 16,000
15,000 24,000
20,000 32,000
25,000 40,000
30,000 48,000
35,000 56,000
40,000 64,000
45,000 72,000
50,000 80,000
55,000 88,000
60,000 96,000
Item
Exterior – lubrication
Hood hinges – lubricate
Door hinges, stops, striker plates – lubricate
Clean and oil power antenna
Brake system
Brake fluid level – check
Power brake function – check
Parking brake – check adjustment
Brake hoses – check
Front wheel brakes – check
Rear wheel brakes – check
Brake fluid – replace
Tires, wheels
Tire pressure – check
Tires – check
Steering, front end, rear end
Power steering – check fluid level
Front suspension – check/retorque
Control arms and bushings – check/retorque
Rear axle clamps – retorque nuts
Steering gear – check
Front shock absorbers – check
Rear shock absorbers – check
Steering for play and effort – check
Wheel bearing play – check
Ball joints – check
Steering rod ends – check
Stabilizer bar and links – check
Rear suspension – check
Power transmission
Rear axle – check
– B230F, B230F-Turbo, B280F
– B230F/Regina, B230F/EGR, B234F
Manual transmission – check
– B230F, B230F-Turbo
– B230F/Regina, B230F/EGR, B234F
Automatic transmission
Fluid level – check
Fluid – replace
Shift control – check
Drive shaft flange bolts – check
Propeller shaft, support bearings – check
VV1139100030000X

Fig. 5 700 Series Chassis

	miles 5,000	
	km 8,000	Comments
B5234T (Turbo): retorque exhaust pipe attachment to turbo	X	

miles x 1000	10	20	30	40	50	60	70	80	90	100	
km x 1000	16	32	48	64	80	96	112	128	144	160	
Months	12	24	36	48	60	72	84	96	108	120	Comments
Shift control, automatic transmission – check	X	X	X	X	X	X	X	X	X	X	Check when driving into shop.
Parking brake – check/adjust	X	X	X	X	X	X	X	X	X	X	Check when driving into shop.
Exterior lighting, controls – check	X	X	X	X	X	X	X	X	X	X	Check when driving into shop.
Windshield/headlamp wiper/washer – check/adjust	X	X	X	X	X	X	X	X	X	X	
PCV – inspect flame guard, clean nipple and hoses						X				X	No flame guard on Turbo engines.
Engine/transmission – check for leaks	X	X	X	X	X	X	X	X	X	X	From above.
Lift vehicle to permit inspection from below											
Engine/transmission – check for leaks	X	X	X	X	X	X	X	X	X	X	From below. In case of leakage, check fluid level in transmission.
Drain engine oil replace oil filter	X	X	X	X	X	X	X	X	X	X	
IMPORTANT! Turbo engine: Oil and oil filter to be replaced every 5,000 miles = 8,000 km.											
Drive shaft joints – check for wear/play						X	X	X	X	X	
– check boots	X	X	X	X	X	X	X	X	X	X	

VV1139300033010X

Fig. 6 850 (Part 1 of 3)

miles x 1000	10	20	30	40	50	60	70	80	90	100	
km x 1000	16	32	48	64	80	96	112	128	144	160	
Months	12	24	36	48	60	72	84	96	108	120	Comments
Tires – check – rotate	X	X	X	X	X	X	X	X	X	X	Check for damage and wear. Recommend every service.
Brake pads – check	X	X	X	X	X	X	X	X	X	X	Minimum lining thickness, front 0.12"= 3 mm, rear 0.08"= 2 mm. Check brake disc thickness when replacing brake pads.
Brake hoses – check for damage/leaks						X	X	X	X	X	
Brake/fuel lines – check for damage/leaks						X	X	X	X	X	
Fuel filter – replace										X	
Exhaust system – check condition/leaks/ suspension						X	X	X	X	X	
Lift front end so wheels and suspension hang free											
Steering/front suspension – check						X	X	X	X	X	Includes checking front shock absorbers.
Rear suspension – check for wear						X	X	X	X	X	Includes checking rear shock absorbers
Lower vehicle to ground											
Air cleaner cartridge – replace			X			X			X		
Spark plugs – replace			X			X			X		
Fill engine oil	X	X	X	X	X	X	X	X	X	X	
Turbo engine: Oil and oil filter to be replaced every 5,000 miles = 8,000 km.											
Fluid levels – check/adjust	X	X	X	X	X	X	X	X	X	X	Check levels of coolant, brake fluid, power steering fluid, washer fluid.
Battery – fluid level and clamping	X	X	X	X	X	X	X	X	X	X	

VV1139300033020X

Fig. 6 850 (Part 2 of 3)

miles x 1000	10	20	30	40	50	60	70	80	90	100	
km x 1000	16	32	48	64	80	96	112	128	144	160	
Months	12	24	36	48	60	72	84	96	108	120	Comments
Timing belt – replace							X				Recommended for proper function of the emission control system.
Auxiliary drive belt – replace						X					
EGR system – clean										X	
Doors, engine hood – lubricate hinges, latches, sliding parts	X	X	X	X	X	X	X	X	X	X	Also lubricate door stops, striker plates and locks.
Power antenna – clean											Recommend every service.
Brake fluid – replace											Recommend two year interval. If car is driven in mountainous areas or moist climate, recommend one year interval.
Reset service reminder indicator	X	X	X	X	X	X	X	X	X	X	Turbo: every 5,000 miles.

VV1139300033030X

Fig. 6 850 (Part 3 of 3)

miles x 1000	10	20	30	40	50	60	70	80	90	100	
km x 1000	16	32	48	64	80	96	112	128	144	160	
Months	12	24	36	48	60	72	84	96	108	120	Comments
Shift control, automatic transmission – check/adjust	X	X	X	X	X	X	X	X	X	X	Check when driving into shop.
Parking brake – check/adjust	X	X	X	X	X	X	X	X	X	X	Check when driving into shop.
Exterior lighting, controls – check	X	X	X	X	X	X	X	X	X	X	Check when driving into shop.
Windshield wiper/washer – check/adjust	X	X	X	X	X	X	X	X	X	X	
Kick-down cable – check/adjust		X		X		X		X		X	
PCV – inspect flame guard, clean nipple and hoses						X				X	No flame guard on Turbo engines.
Engine – check for leaks	X	X	X	X	X	X	X	X	X	X	From above.
Lift vehicle to permit inspection from below.											
Engine/transmission – check for leaks	X	X	X	X	X	X	X	X	X	X	From below. In case of leakage, check fluid level in transmission.
Drain engine oil replace oil filter	X	X	X	X	X	X	X	X	X	X	
IMPORTANT! **Turbo models:** Oil and oil filter to be replaced every 5,000 miles = 8,000 km.											
Automatic transmission fluid – drain				X				X			
– check/adjust level	X	X	X	X	X	X	X	X	X	X	
Tires – check – rotate	X	X	X	X	X	X	X	X	X	X	Check for damage and wear. Recommend every service.
Brake pads – check	X	X	X	X	X	X	X	X	X	X	Minimum lining thickness, front 0.12"= 3 mm, rear 0.08"= 2 mm. Check brake disc thickness when replacing brake pads.
Brake hoses – check for damage/leaks				X	X	X	X	X	X	X	
Brake/fuel lines – check for damage/leaks				X	X	X	X	X	X	X	

VV1139300034010X

Fig. 7 940 (Part 1 of 3)

miles x 1000	10	20	30	40	50	60	70	80	90	100	
km x 1000	16	32	48	64	80	96	112	128	144	160	
Months	12	24	36	48	60	72	84	96	108	120	Comments
Fuel filter – replace										X	
Rear axle – check for leaks	X	X	X	X	X	X	X	X	X	X	Check level in case of leakage.
Exhaust system – check				X	X	X	X	X	X	X	Check condition, leaks and suspension.
Lift front end so wheels and suspension hang free											
Steering/front suspension – retorque	X										Includes checking front shock absorbers.
– check for wear				X	X	X	X	X	X	X	
Propeller shaft, support bearings, u-joints – check for wear				X	X	X	X	X	X	X	
Rear suspension – retorque	X										Includes checking rear shock absorbers.
– check for wear				X	X	X	X	X	X	X	
Lower vehicle to ground											
Air cleaner cartridge – replace			X			X			X		
Spark plugs – replace			X			X			X		
Valve clearance, B230FD, B230F-Turbo (EGR) – check/adjust			X			X			X		
Fill engine oil	X	X	X	X	X	X	X	X	X	X	
Automatic transmission fluid – fill				X				X			
Fluid levels – check/adjust	X	X	X	X	X	X	X	X	X	X	Check levels of coolant, brake fluid, power steering fluid, washer fluid.
Battery – check fluid level and clamping	X	X	X	X	X	X	X	X	X	X	

VV1139300034020X

Fig. 7 940 (Part 2 of 3)

miles x 1000	10	20	30	40	50	60	70	80	90	100	
km x 1000	16	32	48	64	80	96	112	128	144	160	
Months	12	24	36	48	60	72	84	96	108	120	Comments
Auxiliary drive belt – check/adjust tension			X			X			X		
Timing belt – replace										X	Readjustment 10,000 miles after replacement.
– readjust	X										
EGR system – clean										X	
Doors, engine hood – lubricate hinges, latches, sliding parts	X	X	X	X	X	X	X	X	X	X	Also lubricate door stops, striker plates and locks.
Power antenna – clean											Recommend every service.
Brake fluid – replace											Recommend two year interval. If car is driven in mountainous areas or moist climate, recommend one year interval.
Reset service reminder indicator	X	X	X	X	X	X	X	X	X	X	Turbo: every 5,000 miles.

VV1139300034030X

Fig. 7 940 (Part 3 of 3)

miles x 1000	10	20	30	40	50	60	70	80	90	100	
km x 1000	16	32	48	64	80	96	112	128	144	160	
Months	12	24	36	48	60	72	84	96	108	120	Comments
Shift control, automatic transmission – check	X	X	X	X	X	X	X	X	X	X	Check when driving into shop.
Parking brake – check/adjust	X	X	X	X	X	X	X	X	X	X	Check when driving into shop.
Exterior lighting, controls – check	X	X	X	X	X	X	X	X	X	X	Check when driving into shop.
Windshield wiper/washer – check/adjust	X	X	X	X	X	X	X	X	X	X	
PCV – inspect flame guard, clean nipple and hoses						X				X	
Engine – check for leaks	X	X	X	X	X	X	X	X	X	X	From above.
Lift vehicle to permit inspection from below.											
Engine/transmission – check for leaks	X	X	X	X	X	X	X	X	X	X	From below. In case of leakage, check fluid level in transmission.
Drain engine oil replace oil filter	X	X	X	X	X	X	X	X	X	X	
Tires – check – rotate	X	X	X	X	X	X	X	X	X	X	Check for damage and wear. Recommend every service.
Brake pads – check	X	X	X	X	X	X	X	X	X	X	Minimum lining thickness, front 0.12"= 3 mm, rear 0.08"= 2 mm. Check brake disc thickness when replacing brake pads.
Brake hoses – check for damage/leaks				X	X	X	X	X	X	X	
Brake/fuel lines – check for damage/leaks				X	X	X	X	X	X	X	
Fuel filter – replace										X	

VV1139300035010X

Fig. 8 960 (Part 1 of 3)

miles x 1000	10	20	30	40	50	60	70	80	90	100	
km x 1000	16	32	48	64	80	96	112	128	144	160	
Months	12	24	36	48	60	72	84	96	108	120	Comments
Rear axle – check for leaks	X	X	X	X	X	X	X	X	X	X	Check level in case of leakage.
Exhaust system – check				X	X	X	X	X	X	X	Check condition, leaks and suspension.
Lift front end so wheels and suspension hang free											
Steering/front suspension – check for wear				X	X	X	X	X	X	X	Includes checking front shock absorbers.
Propeller shaft, support bearings, u-joints – check for wear				X	X	X	X	X	X	X	
Rear suspension – check for wear				X	X	X	X	X	X	X	Includes checking rear shock absorbers.
Lower vehicle to ground											
Air cleaner cartridge – replace			X			X			X		
Spark plugs – replace			X			X			X		
Fill engine oil	X	X	X	X	X	X	X	X	X	X	
Fluid levels – check/adjust	X	X	X	X	X	X	X	X	X	X	Check levels of coolant, brake fluid, power steering fluid, washer fluid.
Battery – check fluid level and clamping	X	X	X	X	X	X	X	X	X	X	
Auxiliary drive belt – replace						X					

VV1139300035020X

Fig. 8 960 (Part 2 of 3)

miles x 1000	10	20	30	40	50	60	70	80	90	100	
km x 1000	16	32	48	64	80	96	112	128	144	160	
Months	12	24	36	48	60	72	84	96	108	120	Comments
Timing belt – replace							X				Recommended for proper function of emission control system.
EGR system – clean										X	
Doors, engine hood – lubricate hinges, latches, sliding parts	X	X	X	X	X	X	X	X	X	X	Also lubricate door stops, striker plates and locks.
Power antenna – clean											Recommend every service.
Brake fluid – replace											Recommend two year interval. If car is driven in mountainous areas or moist climate, recommend one year interval.
Reset service reminder indicator	X	X	X	X	X	X	X	X	X	X	

VV1139300035030X

Fig. 8 960 (Part 3 of 3)

ELECTRICAL SYMBOL & WIRE COLOR CODE IDENTIFICATION

TABLE OF CONTENTS

	Page No.
ELECTRICAL SYMBOL IDENTIFICATION	0-139
WIRE COLOR CODE IDENTIFICATION	0-144

Electrical Symbol Identification

INDEX

	Page No.	Fig. No.
Mitsubishi	0-139	1
Nissan	0-140	2
Porsche	0-140	3
Saab	0-141	4
Subaru	0-141	5
Suzuki	0-142	6
Toyota	0-142	7
Volkswagen	0-143	8
Volvo	0-144	9

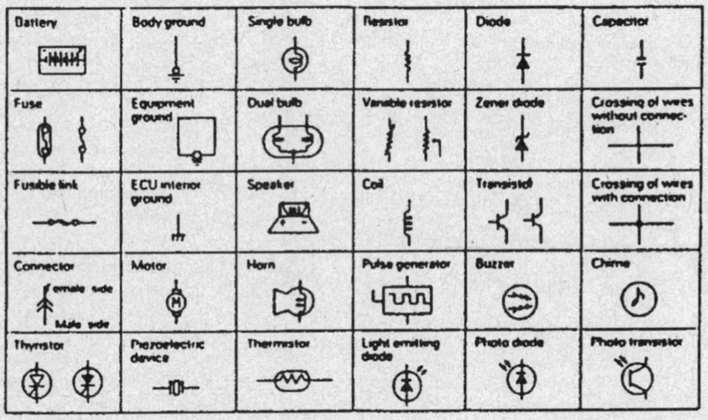

Battery
Body ground
Single bulb
Resistor
Diode
Capacitor
Fuse
Equipment ground
Dual bulb
Variable resistor
Zener diode
Crossing of wires without connection
Fusible link
ECU interior ground
Speaker
Coil
Transistor
Crossing of wires with connection
Connector
Female side
Male side
Motor
Horn
Pulse generator
Buzzer
Chime
Thyristor
Piezoelectric device
Thermistor
Light emitting diode
Photo diode
Photo transistor
MT1139100171000X

Fig. 1 Mitsubishi

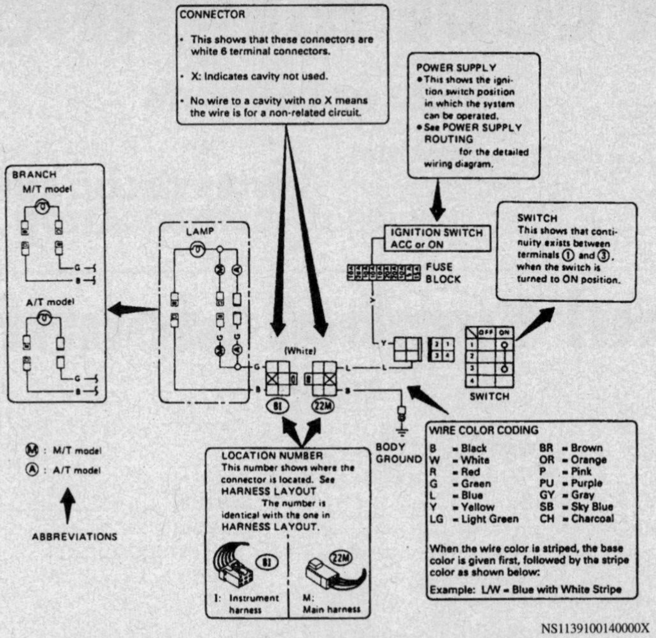

CONNECTOR
• This shows that these connectors are white 6 terminal connectors.
• X: Indicates cavity not used.
• No wire to a cavity with no X means the wire is for a non-related circuit.
POWER SUPPLY
• This shows the ignition switch position in which the system can be operated.
• See POWER SUPPLY ROUTING for the detailed wiring diagram.
BRANCH
M/T model
A/T model
LAMP
IGNITION SWITCH
ACC or ON
FUSE BLOCK
SWITCH
This shows that continuity exists between terminals ① and ③, when the switch is turned to ON position.
(White)
OFF
ON
SWITCH
81
22M
BODY GROUND
Ⓜ : M/T model
Ⓐ : A/T model
ABBREVIATIONS
LOCATION NUMBER
This number shows where the connector is located. See HARNESS LAYOUT
The number is identical with the one in HARNESS LAYOUT.
I: Instrument harness
M: Main harness
WIRE COLOR CODING
B = Black
W = White
R = Red
G = Green
L = Blue
Y = Yellow
LG = Light Green
BR = Brown
OR = Orange
P = Pink
PU = Purple
GY = Gray
SB = Sky Blue
CH = Charcoal
When the wire color is striped, the base color is given first, followed by the stripe color as shown below:
Example: L/W = Blue with White Stripe
NS1139100140000X

Fig. 2 Nissan

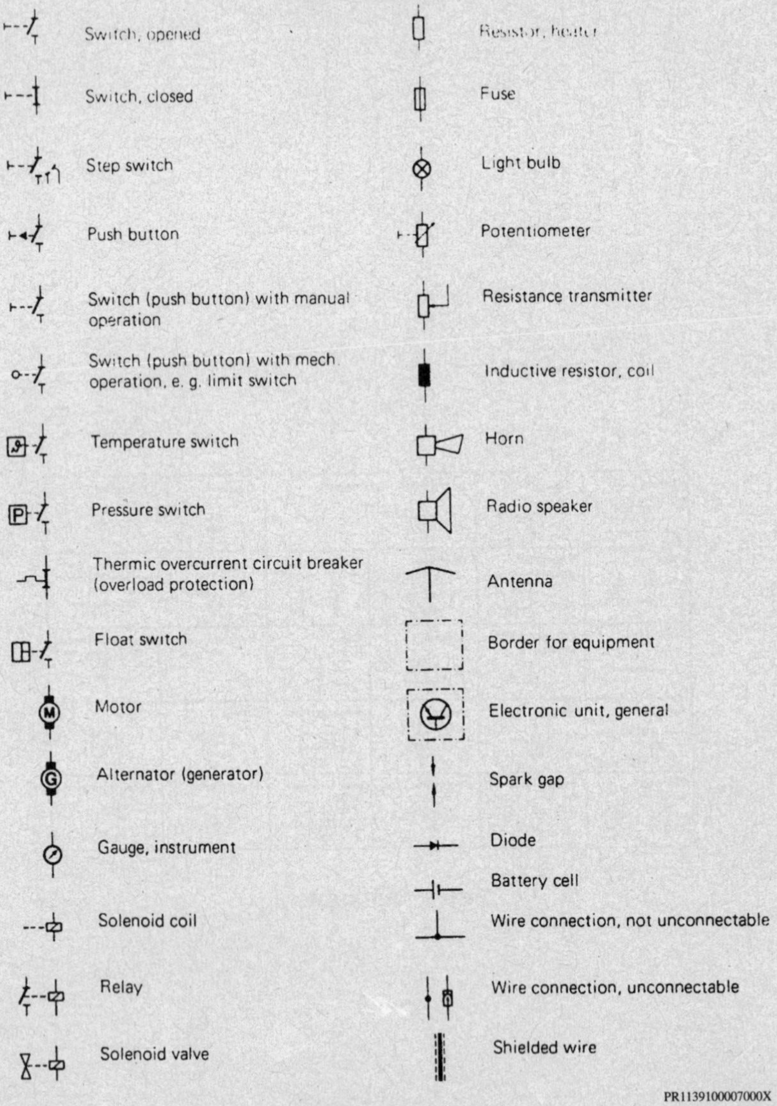

Switch, opened
Switch, closed
Step switch
Push button
Switch (push button) with manual operation
Switch (push button) with mech operation, e. g. limit switch
Temperature switch
Pressure switch
Thermic overcurrent circuit breaker (overload protection)
Float switch
Motor
Alternator (generator)
Gauge, instrument
Solenoid coil
Relay
Solenoid valve
Resistor, heater
Fuse
Light bulb
Potentiometer
Resistance transmitter
Inductive resistor, coil
Horn
Radio speaker
Antenna
Border for equipment
Electronic unit, general
Spark gap
Diode
Battery cell
Wire connection, not unconnectable
Wire connection, unconnectable
Shielded wire
PR1139100007000X

Fig. 3 Porsche

Fuses

In the wiring diagrams, every subsystem is generally shown from the relevant fuse in the electrical distribution box, up to the relevant component(s) and on to the grounding point or direct chassis connection.

The power supply to each fuse is shown separately in the section headed "Power supply systems", which also covers the car's electrical distribution box, ignition switch, etc.

Example:

When the power supply to a fuse comes from the +30 terminal, the supply from the battery to the respective fuse can be seen in the section entitled "+30 power supply".

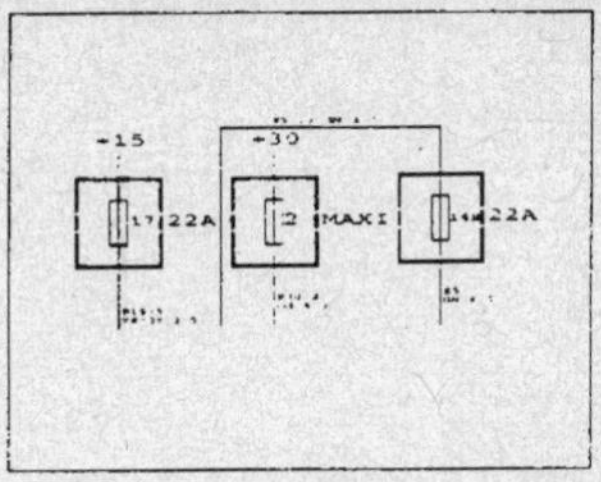

+15
+30
22A
MAXI
22A

Grounding points

Most of the car's grounding points have a component number consisting of a letter and a number, e.g. G2 or G29. The location of the grounding points on the car is given in the section of the manual entitled "Grounding points".

Switches, relays and components

Unless otherwise indicated, switches and relays are drawn in unenergized and unactivated state.
When the frame round the component is drawn with an unbroken line, the whole component is shown.
When the frame round the component is drawn with a broken line, only part of the component is shown.

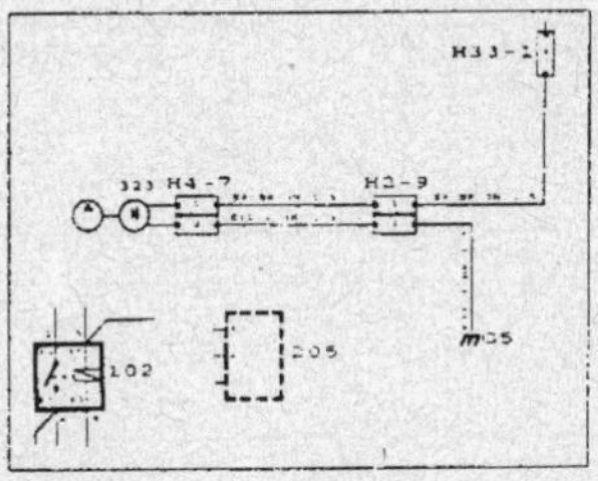

H33-1
H4-7
H2-9
102
205

Crimped connections

To reduce the number of connectors, the car's wiring contains several crimped connections. The symbol for these connections on the wiring diagrams is shown in the adjacent diagram.

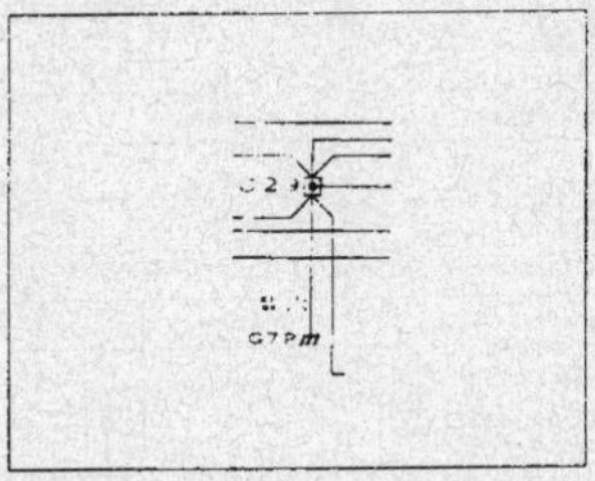

SA1139100017000X

Fig. 4 Saab

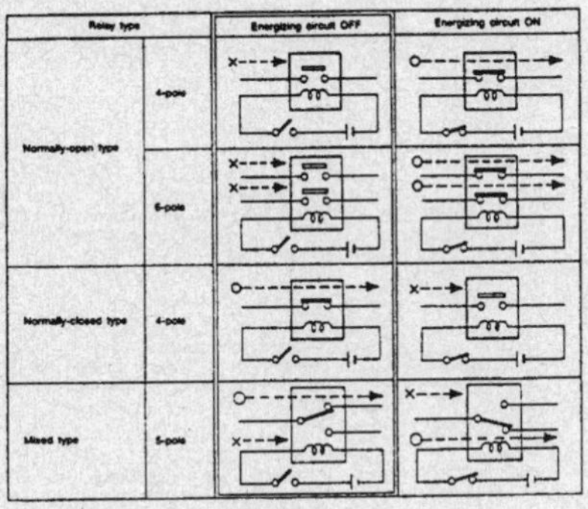

Relay type
Energizing circuit OFF
Energizing circuit ON
Normally-open type
4-pole
5-pole
Normally-closed type
4-pole
Mixed type
5-pole

The first character of each connector number refers to the area or system of the vehicle, as indicated in table below.

Symbol	Wiring harness and Cord
F	Front wiring harness LH & RH
B	Bulkhead wiring harness
E	Engine wiring harness, Engine module wiring harness
T	Transmission cord
D	Door cord LH & RH, Rear door adapter cord LH & RH
I	Instrument panel wiring harness
R	Rear wiring harness, Rear defogger cord Room light cord, Fuel tank cord, Sunroof cord, Rear gate cord, Rear gate lock adapter cord
P	Power window main harness

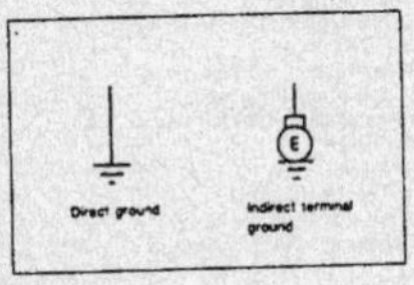

Direct ground
Indirect terminal ground

The ground points shown in the wiring diagr
the following:
(GB) Body ground
(GE) Engine ground
(GR) Radio ground
(GD) Rear defogger ground
All wiring harnesses are provided with a g
which should be securely connected.

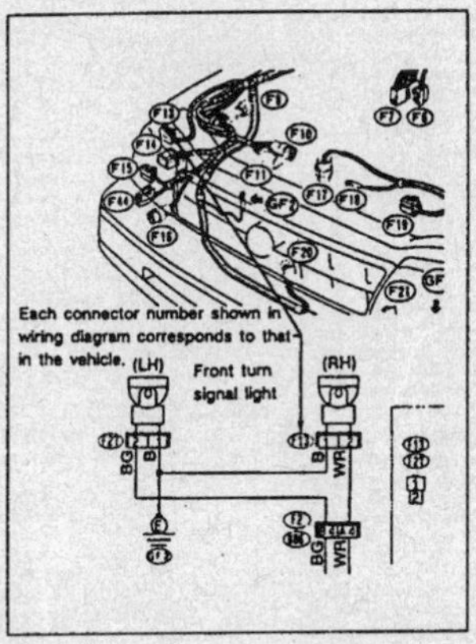

Each connector number shown in wiring diagram corresponds to that in the vehicle.
(LH)
(RH)
Front turn signal light
BG
B
WR

SB1139100045000X

Fig. 5 Subaru

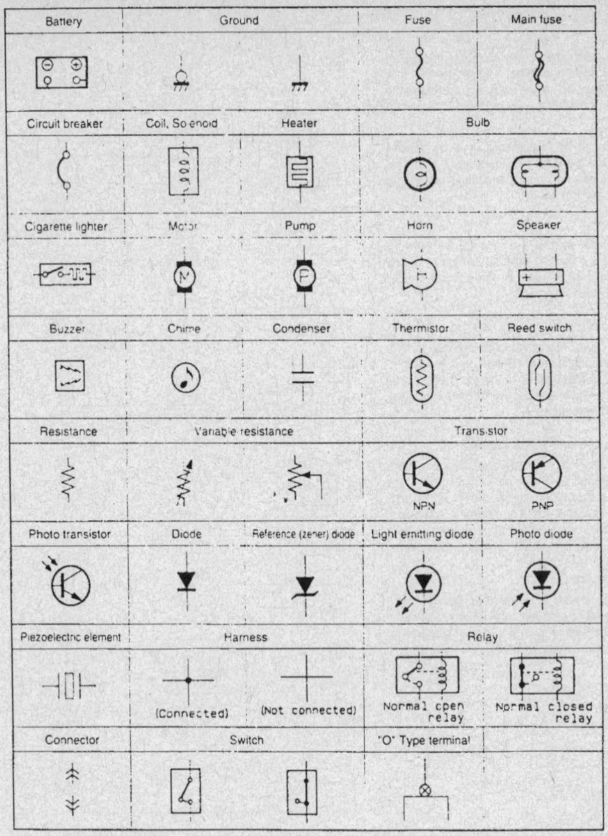

Battery
Ground
Fuse
Main fuse
Circuit breaker
Coil, Solenoid
Heater
Bulb
Cigarette lighter
Motor
Pump
Horn
Speaker
Buzzer
Chime
Condenser
Thermistor
Reed switch
Resistance
Variable resistance
Transistor
NPN
PNP
Photo transistor
Diode
Reference (zener) diode
Light emitting diode
Photo diode
Piezoelectric element
Harness
(Connected)
(Not connected)
Relay
Normal open relay
Normal closed relay
Connector
Switch
"O" Type terminal

SK1139100051000X

Fig. 6 Suzuki

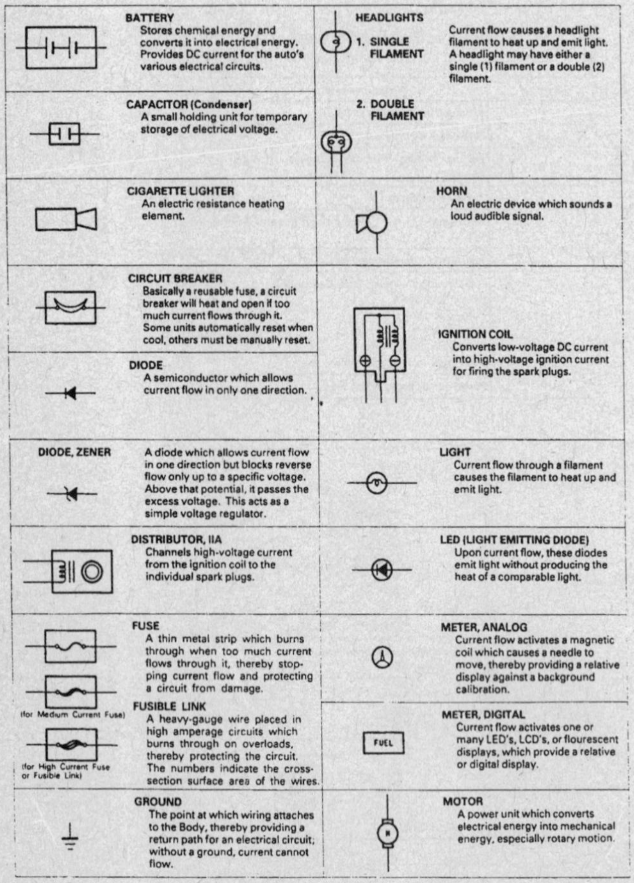

BATTERY
Stores chemical energy and converts it into electrical energy. Provides DC current for the auto's various electrical circuits.
HEADLIGHTS
1. SINGLE FILAMENT
2. DOUBLE FILAMENT
Current flow causes a headlight filament to heat up and emit light. A headlight may have either a single (1) filament or a double (2) filament.
CAPACITOR (Condenser)
A small holding unit for temporary storage of electrical voltage.
CIGARETTE LIGHTER
An electric resistance heating element.
HORN
An electric device which sounds a loud audible signal.
CIRCUIT BREAKER
Basically a reusable fuse, a circuit breaker will heat and open if too much current flows through it. Some units automatically reset when cool, others must be manually reset.
IGNITION COIL
Converts low-voltage DC current into high-voltage ignition current for firing the spark plugs.
DIODE
A semiconductor which allows current flow in only one direction.
DIODE, ZENER
A diode which allows current flow in one direction but blocks reverse flow only up to a specific voltage. Above that potential, it passes the excess voltage. This acts as a simple voltage regulator.
LIGHT
Current flow through a filament causes the filament to heat up and emit light.
DISTRIBUTOR, IIA
Channels high-voltage current from the ignition coil to the individual spark plugs.
LED (LIGHT EMITTING DIODE)
Upon current flow, these diodes emit light without producing the heat of a comparable light.
FUSE
A thin metal strip which burns through when too much current flows through it, thereby stopping current flow and protecting a circuit from damage.
(for Medium Current Fuse)
FUSIBLE LINK
A heavy-gauge wire placed in high amperage circuits which burns through on overloads, thereby protecting the circuit. The numbers indicate the cross-section surface area of the wires.
(for High Current Fuse or Fusible Link)
METER, ANALOG
Current flow activates a magnetic coil which causes a needle to move, thereby providing a relative display against a background calibration.
METER, DIGITAL
Current flow activates one or many LED's, LCD's, or flourescent displays, which provide a relative or digital display.
FUEL
GROUND
The point at which wiring attaches to the Body, thereby providing a return path for an electrical circuit; without a ground, current cannot flow.
MOTOR
A power unit which converts electrical energy into mechanical energy, especially rotary motion.

TY1139100250010X

Fig. 7 Toyota (Part 1 of 2)

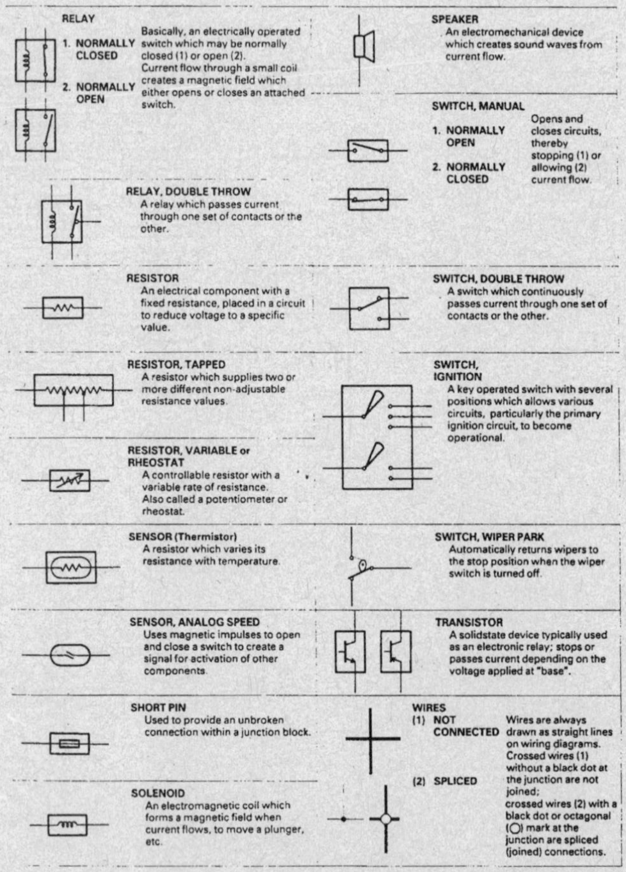

RELAY
1. NORMALLY CLOSED
2. NORMALLY OPEN
Basically, an electrically operated switch which may be normally closed (1) or open (2). Current flow through a small coil creates a magnetic field which either opens or closes an attached switch.
SPEAKER
An electromechanical device which creates sound waves from current flow.
SWITCH, MANUAL
1. NORMALLY OPEN
2. NORMALLY CLOSED
Opens and closes circuits, thereby stopping (1) or allowing (2) current flow.
RELAY, DOUBLE THROW
A relay which passes current through one set of contacts or the other.
RESISTOR
An electrical component with a fixed resistance, placed in a circuit to reduce voltage to a specific value.
SWITCH, DOUBLE THROW
A switch which continuously passes current through one set of contacts or the other.
RESISTOR, TAPPED
A resistor which supplies two or more different non-adjustable resistance values.
SWITCH, IGNITION
A key operated switch with several positions which allows various circuits, particularly the primary ignition circuit, to become operational.
RESISTOR, VARIABLE or RHEOSTAT
A controllable resistor with a variable rate of resistance. Also called a potentiometer or rheostat.
SENSOR (Thermistor)
A resistor which varies its resistance with temperature.
SWITCH, WIPER PARK
Automatically returns wipers to the stop position when the wiper switch is turned off.
SENSOR, ANALOG SPEED
Uses magnetic impulses to open and close a switch to create a signal for activation of other components.
TRANSISTOR
A solidstate device typically used as an electronic relay; stops or passes current depending on the voltage applied at "base".
SHORT PIN
Used to provide an unbroken connection within a junction block.
WIRES
(1) NOT CONNECTED
(2) SPLICED
Wires are always drawn as straight lines on wiring diagrams. Crossed wires (1) without a black dot at the junction are not joined; crossed wires (2) with a black dot or octagonal (○) mark at the junction are spliced (joined) connections.
SOLENOID
An electromagnetic coil which forms a magnetic field when current flows, to move a plunger, etc.

TY1139100250020X

Fig. 7 Toyota (Part 2 of 2)

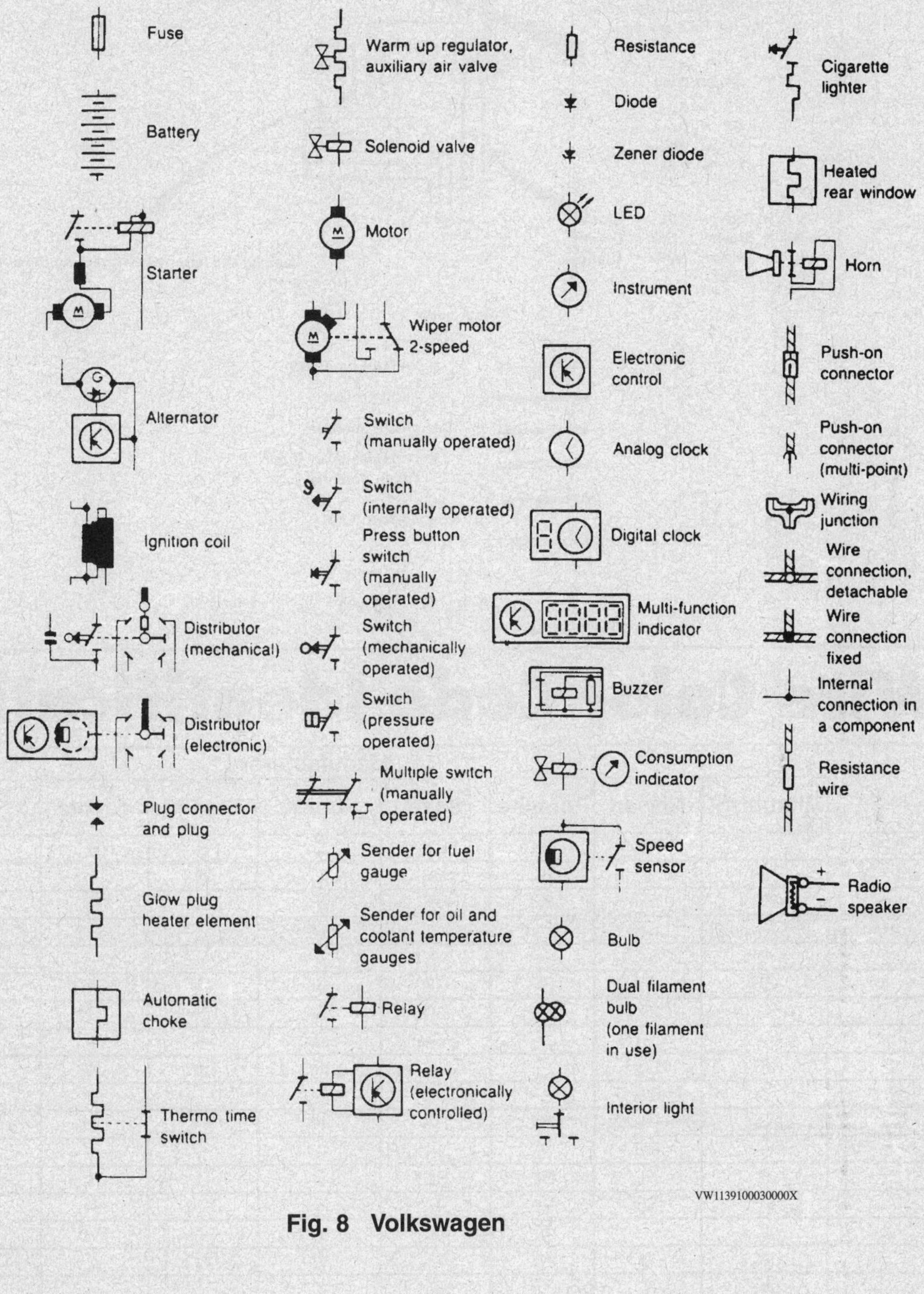
Fuse
Battery
Starter
Alternator
Ignition coil
Distributor (mechanical)
Distributor (electronic)
Plug connector and plug
Glow plug heater element
Automatic choke
Thermo time switch
Warm up regulator, auxiliary air valve
Solenoid valve
Motor
Wiper motor 2-speed
Switch (manually operated)
Switch (internally operated)
Press button switch (manually operated)
Switch (mechanically operated)
Switch (pressure operated)
Multiple switch (manually operated)
Sender for fuel gauge
Sender for oil and coolant temperature gauges
Relay
Relay (electronically controlled)
Resistance
Diode
Zener diode
LED
Instrument
Electronic control
Analog clock
Digital clock
Multi-function indicator
Buzzer
Consumption indicator
Speed sensor
Bulb
Dual filament bulb (one filament in use)
Interior light
Cigarette lighter
Heated rear window
Horn
Push-on connector
Push-on connector (multi-point)
Wiring junction
Wire connection, detachable
Wire connection fixed
Internal connection in a component
Resistance wire
Radio speaker
VW1139100030000X

Fig. 8 Volkswagen

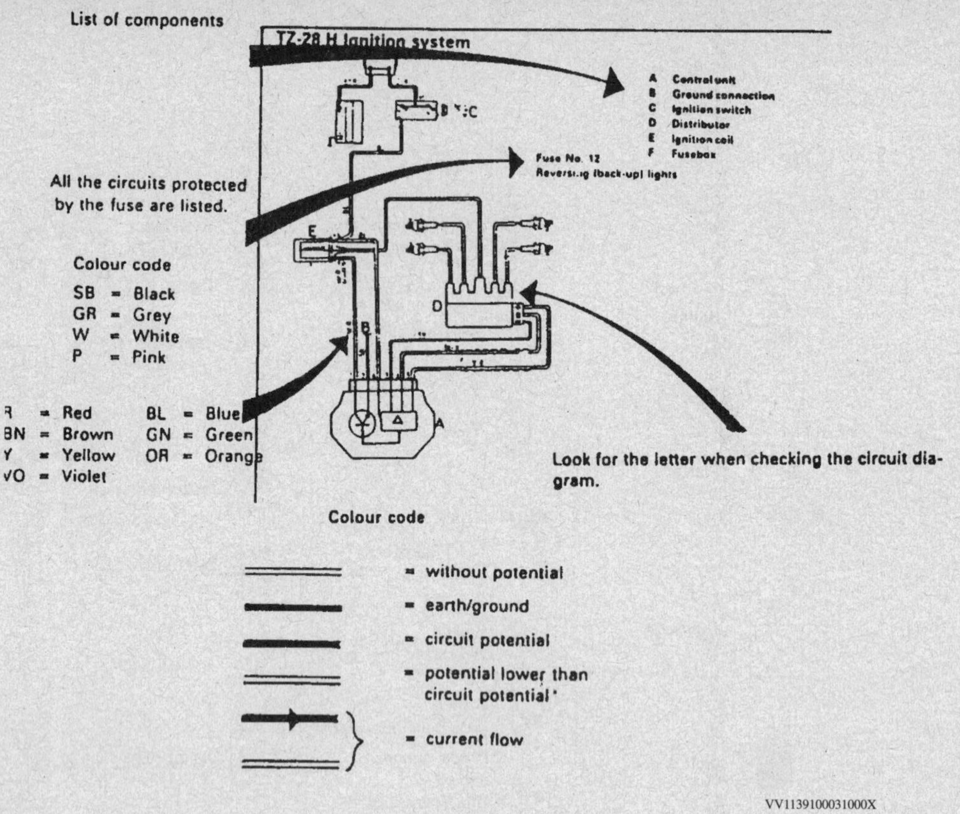
List of components
TZ-28 H Ignition system
A Control unit
B Ground connection
C Ignition switch
D Distributor
E Ignition coil
F Fusebox
Fuse No. 12
All the circuits protected by the fuse are listed.
Colour code
SB = Black
GR = Grey
W = White
P = Pink
R = Red
BN = Brown
Y = Yellow
VO = Violet
BL = Blue
GN = Green
OR = Orange
Look for the letter when checking the circuit diagram.
Colour code
= without potential
= earth/ground
= circuit potential
= potential lower than circuit potential
= current flow
VV1139100031000X

Fig. 9 Volvo

Wire Color Code Identification

Color	Manufacturer								
	Mitsubishi	Nissan	Porsche	Saab	Subaru	Suzuki	Toyota	Volks-wagen	Volvo
Black	B	B	BK	SV	B	B	B	BK	SB
Blue	L	L	BL	BL	L	Bl	L	BL	BL
Brown	BR	BR	BR	BR	Br	Br	BR	BR	BN
Charcoal	—	CH	—	—	—	—	—	—	—
Clear	—	—	—	—	—	—	—	CV	—
Gray	GR	GY	GR	GR	Gr	—	GR	GY	GR
Green	G	G	GN	GN	G	G	G	G	GN
Light Blue	—	—	—	—	Lb	—	—	—	—
Light Green	LG	LG	—	—	Lg	Lg	LG	LTG	—
Orange	O	OR	—	OG	Or	—	O	OR	OR
Pink	P	P	—	RA	P	—	P	—	P
Purple	—	PU	—	—	—	—	—	—	—
Red	R	R	RE	RD	R	R	R	R	R
Sky Blue	SB	SB	—	—	—	—	—	—	—
Violet	V	—	VI	VL	—	V	V	V	VO
White	W	W	WT	VT	W	W	W	W	W
Yellow	Y	Y	YE	GL	Y	Y	Y	Y	Y

Page No.

MITSUBISHI:

VEHICLE SERVICE:

Diamante 23-1

Eclipse & 3000GT 24-1

Expo 25-1

Galant 26-1

Mirage & Precis 27-1

Montero & Pickups 28-1

UNIT REPAIR 29-1

GENERAL INFORMATION

Manual Information Locator, Inside Rear Cover

Vehicle Identification 0-1

Air Bag System Precautions. 0-8

Service Reminder & Warning Lamp Reset Procedures 0-10

Vehicle Lift Points 0-34

Vehicle Maintenance Schedules. 0-69

Electrical Symbol & Wire Color Code Identification 0-139

Page No.

MITSUBISHI:

VEHICLE SERVICE:

Diamante 23-1

Eclipse & 3000GT 24-1

Expo 25-1

Galant 26-1

Mirage & Precis 27-1

Montero & Pickups 28-1

UNIT REPAIR 29-1

GENERAL INFORMATION

Manual Information Locator, Inside Rear Cover

Vehicle Identification 0-1

Air Bag System Precautions 0-8

Service Reminder & Warning Lamp Reset Procedures 0-10

Vehicle Lift Points 0-34

Vehicle Maintenance Schedules 0-69

Electrical Symbol & Wire Color Code Identification 0-139

MITSUBISHI DIAMANTE

INDEX OF SERVICE OPERATIONS

	Page No.
AIR BAG SYSTEM PRECAUTIONS	0-8
AUTOMATIC TRANSMISSIONS/ TRANSAXLES	29-1
BRAKES	
Anti-Lock Brakes	29-1
Disc Brakes	29-1
Drum Brakes	29-1
Hydraulic Brake Units	29-1
Power Brake Units	29-1
ELECTRICAL	
Air Bags	29-1
Air Conditioning	29-1
Alternators	29-1
Alternator, Replace	23-4
Blower Motor, Replace	23-6
Coil Pack, Replace	23-5
Cooling Fans	29-1
Cruise Control	29-1
Dash Gauges	29-1
Dash Panels	29-1
Distributor, Replace	23-4
Evaporator Core, Replace	23-6
Fuel Pump Relay Location	23-4
Fuse Panel & Flasher Location	23-4
Heater Core, Replace	23-6
Ignition Lock, Replace	23-5
Ignition Switch, Replace	23-5
Instrument Cluster, Replace	23-5
Multi-Function Switch, Replace	23-5
Neutral Safety Switch, Replace	23-5
Passive Restraints	29-1
Precautions	23-4
Radio, Replace	23-5
Relay Center Location	23-4
Speed Controls	29-1
Starter Motors	29-1
Starter, Replace	23-4
Steering Columns	29-1
Steering Wheel, Replace	23-5
Wiper Motor, Replace	23-6
Wiper Switch, Replace	23-6
Wiper Systems	29-1
ELECTRICAL SYMBOL IDENTIFICATION	0-139
FRONT SUSPENSION & STEERING	
Ball Joint, Replace	23-32
Control Arm, Replace	23-33
Manual Steering Gears	29-1
Power Steering	29-1
Power Steering Gear, Replace	23-33
Power Steering Pump, Replace	23-33
Precautions	23-31
Rear Power Cylinder, Replace	23-35
Rear Power Cylinder Control Valve, Replace	23-35
Stabilizer Bar, Replace	23-33
Strut, Replace	23-32
Tightening Specifications	23-38
Wheel Bearing, Adjust	23-31
Wheel Hub & Steering Knuckle, Replace	23-31
FRONT WHEEL DRIVE AXLES	29-1
REAR AXLE & SUSPENSION	
Coil Spring, Replace	23-27
Control Arm, Replace	23-27
Hub & Bearing, Replace	23-26
Rear Suspension, Replace	23-26
Shock Absorber, Replace	23-26
Stabilizer Bar, Replace	23-28
Tightening Specifications	23-30
Trailing Arm, Replace	23-28
SERVICE REMINDER & WARNING LAMP RESET PROCEDURES	0-10
SPECIFICATIONS	
Fluid Capacities & Cooling System Data	23-3
Front Wheel Alignment Specifications	23-3
General Engine Specifications	23-2
Lubricant Data	23-3
Rear Wheel Alignment Specifications	23-3
Tune Up Specifications	23-2
VEHICLE IDENTIFICATION	0-1
VEHICLE LIFT POINTS	0-34
VEHICLE MAINTENANCE SCHEDULES	0-69
WHEEL ALIGNMENT	
Front Wheel Alignment	23-39
Preliminary Inspection	23-39
Rear Wheel Alignment	23-39
Vehicle Ride Height	23-39
Wheel Alignment Specifications	23-3
WIRE COLOR CODE IDENTIFICATION	0-144
3.0L ENGINE	
Belt Tension Data	23-18
Camshaft, Replace	23-16
Compression Pressure	23-8
Cooling System Bleed	23-18
Crankshaft Seal, Replace	23-17
Cylinder Head, Replace	23-9
Engine Rebuilding Specifications	29-1
Engine, Replace	23-8
Engine Mount, Replace	23-8
Exhaust Manifold, Replace	23-9
Fuel Filter, Replace	23-19
Fuel Pump, Replace	23-19
Intake Manifold, Replace	23-8
Oil Pan, Replace	23-18
Oil Pump, Replace	23-18
Piston & Rod Assembly	23-17
Precautions	23-8
Radiator, Replace	23-18
Rocker Arms	23-10
Technical Service Bulletins	23-19
Thermostat, Replace	23-18
Tightening Specifications	23-24
Timing Belt, Replace	23-12
Valve Adjustment	23-10
Valve Arrangement	23-10
Valve Clearance Specifications	23-10
Water Pump, Replace	23-18

Specifications

GENERAL ENGINE SPECIFICATIONS

Year	Engine	Fuel System	Bore & Stroke	Compression Ratio	Maximum Net H.P. @ RPM	Maximum Torque, Ft. Lbs. @ RPM
1993–96	3.0L SOHC	MPI	3.587 X 2.992	10.0	175 @ 5500	185 @ 3000
	3.0L DOHC	MPI	3.587 X 2.992	10.0	202 @ 6000	201 @ 3500

TUNE UP SPECIFICATIONS

Year	Engine	Spark Plug Gap, Inch	Ignition Timing			Idle Speed, RPM		Fuel Pump Pressure, psi	Valve Lash	
			Firing Order	Timing, °BTDC	Timing Mark Location	Curb	Fast		Intake	Exhaust
1993–96	3.0L SOHC	.041	③	5④	Pulley	700N	①	47.6②	⑦	⑦
	3.0L DOHC	.051	③	5⑤	⑥	700N	①	47.6②	⑦	⑦

BTDC — Before Top Dead Center.

N — Neutral.

① — Controlled by idle speed control servo.

② — With fuel pressure regulator vacuum hose disconnected & plugged.

③ — Cylinder numbering from front of engine to rear: right bank, 1, 3, 5; left bank, 2, 4, 6. Firing order: 1–2–3–4–5–6. On SOHC engines, refer to Fig. A. On DOHC engines, refer to Fig. B.

④ — With jumper wire connected between ignition timing adjustment connector & ground. Refer to Fig. C.

⑤ — Electronically controlled.

⑥ — Equipped w/crankshaft position sensor.

⑦ — Hydraulic valve lifters, no adjustment required.

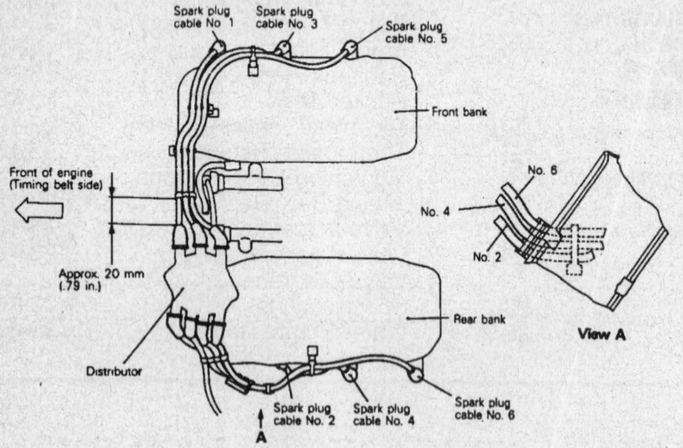
Spark plug cable No. 1
Spark plug cable No. 3
Spark plug cable No. 5
Front bank
Front of engine (Timing belt side)
No. 6
No. 4
No. 2
Approx. 20 mm (.79 in.)
Rear bank
View A
Distributor
Spark plug cable No. 2
Spark plug cable No. 4
Spark plug cable No. 6
A

MT1138800016000X

Fig. A

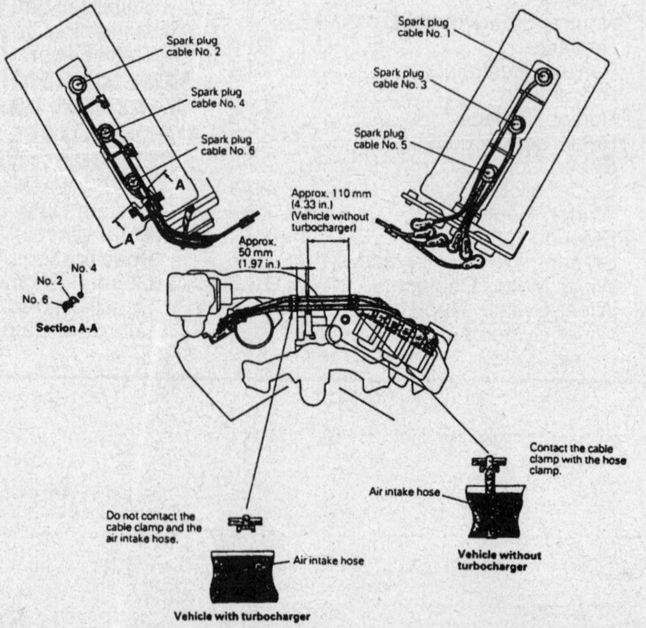
Spark plug cable No. 2
Spark plug cable No. 4
Spark plug cable No. 6
Spark plug cable No. 1
Spark plug cable No. 3
Spark plug cable No. 5
A
A
Approx. 110 mm (4.33 in.) (Vehicle without turbocharger)
Approx. 50 mm (1.97 in.)
No. 4
No. 2
No. 6
Section A-A
Contact the cable clamp with the hose clamp.
Air intake hose
Do not contact the cable clamp and the air intake hose.
Air intake hose
Vehicle without turbocharger
Vehicle with turbocharger

MT1138800014000X

Fig. B

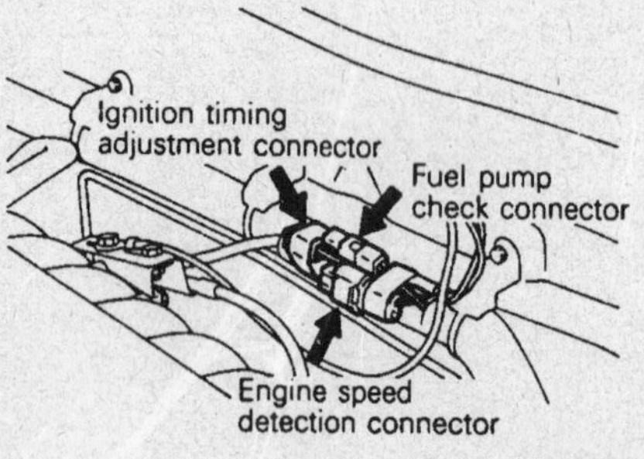
Ignition timing adjustment connector
Fuel pump check connector
Engine speed detection connector

MT1138800019000X

Fig. C

FRONT WHEEL ALIGNMENT SPECIFICATIONS

Year	Model	Caster Angle, Deg.		Camber Angle, Deg.		Toe, Inch①	Ball Joint Inspection⑤
		Limits	Desired	Limits	Desired		
1993	Diamante②	+2¼ to +3¼	+2 ¾	−½ to +½	0	−.12 to +.12	86.8–191.0④
	Diamante③	+1½ to +2½	+2	−⅙ to +⅚	+⅓	−.03 to +.12	86.8–191.0④
1994–96	Diamante	+2¼ to +3¼	+2 ¾	−½ to +½	0	−.12 to +.12	86.8–191.0④

① — Toe-in (+); toe-out (-).
② — Less active electronic control suspension.
③ — With active electronic control suspension.
④ — Breakaway torque measurement using special service tool No. MB990326, or equivalent.
⑤ — Inch lbs.

REAR WHEEL ALIGNMENT SPECIFICATIONS

Year	Model	Camber Angle, Deg.		Toe, Inch①	Ball Joint Inspection, Inch Lbs.
		Limits	Desired		
1993–96	Sedan	−½ to +½	0	②	17.36–78.11③
	Wagon	−¼ to +¼	0	−.012 to +.012	17.36–78.11③

① — Toe-in (+); toe-out (-).
② — Models less 4 wheel steering, −.12 to +.12 inch. Models w/4 wheel steering, −.08 to +.12 inch.
③ — Breakaway torque measurement using special service tool No. MB990326, or equivalent.

FLUID CAPACITIES & COOLING SYSTEM DATA

Year	Model/Engine	Coolant Capacity, Qts.	Radiator Cap Relief Pressure, Lbs.	Thermo. Opening Temp., Deg. F	Fuel Tank, Gals.	Engine Oil Refill, Qts. ①	Trans. Fluid, Qts. ②
1993–94	Sedan SOHC	8.50	13	190	19.0	4.5	7.9
	Sedan DOHC	8.50	13	180	19.0	4.5	7.9
	Wagon	10.04	13	190	19.0	4.7	7.9
1995–96	Sedan SOHC	8.50	13	190	19.0	4.5	7.9
	Sedan DOHC	8.50	13	180	19.0	4.5	7.9
	Wagon	10.04	13	190	18.7	4.7	7.9

① — Includes filter.

② — Approximate; make final check with dipstick.

LUBRICANT DATA

Year	Lubricant Type		
	Automatic Transaxle	Power Steering	Brake System
1993–96	Diamond ATF SP	Dexron II/IIE/III	DOT 3 or DOT 4

Electrical

NOTE: On Air Bag Equipped Models, Refer To "Air Bag System Precautions" Located In Front Of This Manual For System Disarming and Arming Procedures.

INDEX

	Page No.
Air Bags	29-1
Air Conditioning	29-1
Alternators	29-1
Alternator, Replace	23-4
DOHC	23-4
SOHC	23-4
Blower Motor, Replace	23-6
Coil Pack, Replace	23-5
3.0L DOHC Engine	23-5
Cooling Fans	29-1
Cruise Control	29-1
Dash Gauges	29-1
Dash Panels	29-1
Distributor, Replace	23-4
SOHC	23-4
Evaporator Core, Replace	23-6
Fuel Pump Relay Location	23-4
Fuse Panel & Flasher Location	23-4
Heater Core, Replace	23-6
Ignition Lock, Replace	23-5
Ignition Switch, Replace	23-5
Instrument Cluster, Replace	23-5
Multi-Function Switch, Replace	23-5
Neutral Safety Switch, Replace	23-5
Passive Restraints	29-1
Precautions	23-4
Air Bag Systems	23-4
Radio, Replace	23-5
Relay Center Location	23-4
Speed Controls	29-1
Starter Motors	29-1
Starter, Replace	23-4
Steering Columns	29-1
Steering Wheel, Replace	23-5
Wiper Motor, Replace	23-6
Wiper Switch, Replace	23-6
Wiper Systems	29-1

PRECAUTIONS

AIR BAG SYSTEMS

Refer to "Air Bag System Precautions" in front of this manual for system disarming and arming procedures.

FUSE PANEL & FLASHER LOCATION

Engine compartment fuse panel is located on righthand front corner of engine compartment, near battery. Multi-purpose fuse block is located behind lefthand side of instrument panel, left of steering column. Hazard and turn signal flasher unit is mounted on multi-purpose fuse block under lefthand side of instrument panel.

FUEL PUMP RELAY LOCATION

The fuel pump relay, also known as the multi-port fuel injection relay, is located on the blower motor assembly housing, **Fig. 1.**

RELAY CENTER LOCATION

Main relay center is located on righthand front side of engine compartment, near battery. An auxiliary relay cluster is located above righthand front wheel housing.

STARTER

REPLACE

1. Place gear selector lever in Neutral position.
2. Raise and support vehicle.
3. Drain transaxle oil and remove side undercover.

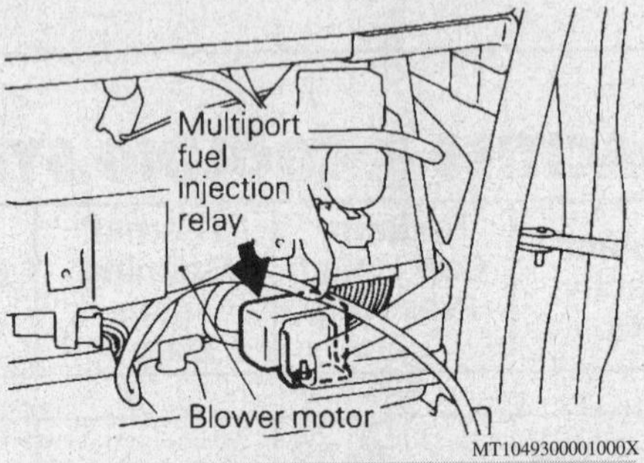

Multiport fuel injection relay
Blower motor
MT1049300001000X

Fig. 1 Fuel pump relay location. Diamante

4. Remove air cleaner cover and air intake hose.
5. Remove electronically controlled suspension compressor assembly leaving hoses attached. Secure to body using suitable wire.
6. Disconnect transaxle control and speedometer cables.
7. Disconnect oil cooler lines.
8. Disconnect Park/Neutral position and kickdown servo switches.
9. Disconnect pulse generator and oil temperature sensor.
10. Raise transaxle to release pressure on transaxle mount bracket using suitable jack stand then disconnect transaxle mount.
11. Remove 4 wheel steering (4WS) pump heat shield and pump assembly, leaving hoses attached. Secure pump to body using suitable wire.
12. Disconnect front height sensor rod.
13. Loosen tie rod end nut then disconnect tie rod from knuckle using steering linkage puller tool No. MB991113-01, or equivalent. **Ensure tie cord of tool is tied off correctly.**
14. With transaxle properly supported, remove righthand crossmember.
15. Remove starter electrical connections, then starter assembly.
16. Reverse procedure to install.

ALTERNATOR

REPLACE

SOHC

1. Remove intake air hose, then alternator drive belt.
2. Remove roll stopper stay, then EGR temperature sensor connection.
3. Remove EGR pipe, then air intake plenum stay.
4. Remove alternator mounting nut and bolt, then alternator from transaxle side through bottom of air intake plenum.
5. Reverse procedure to install.

DOHC

1. Remove headlamp washer pump tank, then condenser fan assembly.
2. Drain coolant into a suitable container.
3. Remove radiator upper hose, then alternator drive belt.
4. Disconnect and remove alternator and alternator bracket assembly.
5. Remove alternator bracket, then alternator.
6. Reverse procedure to install, setting alternator in place prior to mounting alternator bracket.

DISTRIBUTOR

REPLACE

SOHC

1. Disconnect coil and spark plug wires. **Mark position for installation reference.**

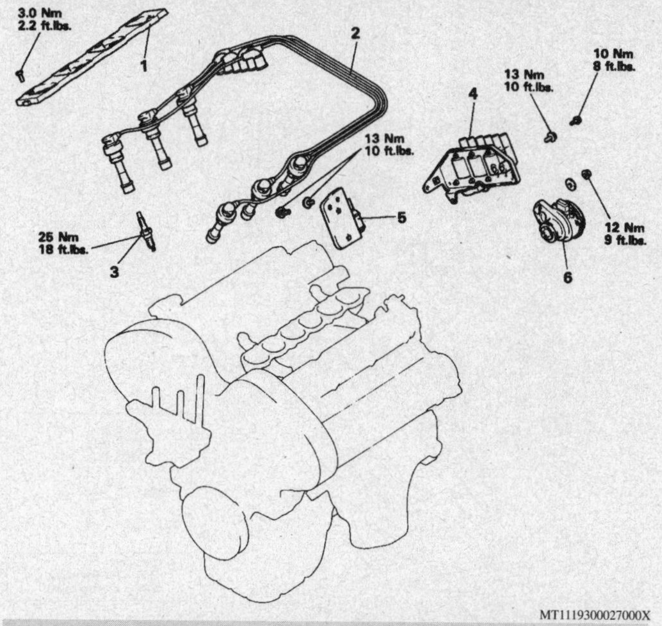
3.0 Nm
2.2 ft.lbs.
2
1
10 Nm
8 ft.lbs.
13 Nm
10 ft.lbs.
4
13 Nm
10 ft.lbs.
5
25 Nm
18 ft.lbs.
3
12 Nm
9 ft.lbs.
6
MT1119300027000X

Fig. 2 Coil pack replacement.

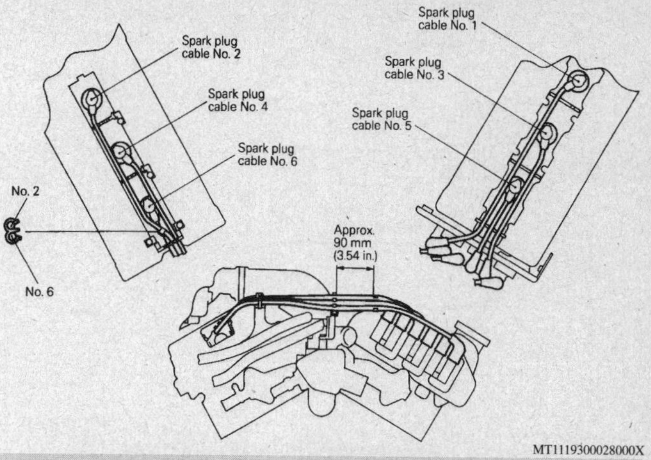
Spark plug cable No. 1
Spark plug cable No. 2
Spark plug cable No. 3
Spark plug cable No. 4
Spark plug cable No. 5
Spark plug cable No. 6
No. 2
No. 6
Approx. 90 mm (3.54 in.)
MT1119300028000X

Fig. 3 Coil pack spark plug wire routing.

2. Rotate engine to position No. 1 cylinder at top dead center (TDC) on compression stroke.
3. Mark position of distributor rotor on distributor housing and distributor housing on intake manifold for correct installation.
4. Remove distributor mounting nut and distributor from engine.
5. Reverse procedure to install, aligning marks made during disassembly.

COIL PACK, REPLACE

3.0L DOHC ENGINE

1. Disconnect battery ground cable.
2. Remove center cover.
3. Remove spark plug wires.
4. Remove coil pack, refer to **Figs. 2 through 4,** for removal and installation purposes.
5. Reverse procedure to install.

IGNITION LOCK

REPLACE

1. Remove steering wheel as outlined under "Steering Wheel, Replace."
2. Remove upper and lower steering column covers.
3. Remove column switch as outlined under "Column Switch, Replace."
4. Remove key interlock cover and cable.
5. Remove slide lever, **Fig. 5.**
6. Remove steering lock by cutting special bolts using a suitable hacksaw, **Fig. 6.**
7. Reverse procedure to install, noting the following:
   a. Temporarily install steering column lock using new special bolts and ensure proper operation.
   b. Tighten special bolts until heads twist off.

IGNITION SWITCH

REPLACE

1. Remove steering wheel as outlined under "Steering Wheel, Replace."
2. Remove upper and lower steering column covers.
3. Remove knee protector.
4. Remove column switch as outlined under "Column Switch, Replace."
5. Remove ignition key illumination ring.
6. Insert ignition key into ignition lock cylinder and turn to Acc position.
7. Press lock cylinder lockpin down, **Fig. 7,** and remove lock cylinder.
8. Remove key reminder switch segment.
9. Disconnect and remove ignition switch assembly.
10. Reverse procedure to install.

NEUTRAL SAFETY SWITCH

REPLACE

1. Place selector lever in Neutral position.
2. Place manual control lever in Neutral position, then remove control lever retainer and lever.
3. Disconnect electrical harness, then remove switch retaining bolts and switch assembly.
4. Reverse procedure to install, then adjust as follows:
   a. With manual control lever in Neutral position, rotate switch body until hole in end of manual control lever and hole in flange of inhibitor switch are aligned, **Fig. 8.**
   b. Hold switch body in position, then **torque** retaining bolts to 7–8 ft. lbs.
   c. Lightly pull transaxle control cable and tighten adjusting nut.
   d. Ensure selector lever is in Neutral position.
   e. Check for proper operation.

MULTI-FUNCTION SWITCH

REPLACE

1. Remove steering wheel as outlined under "Steering Wheel, Replace."
2. Remove upper and lower steering column covers.
3. Remove knee protector.
4. Remove lefthand column switch (illumination switch).
5. Remove righthand column switch (wiper switch).
6. Reverse procedure to install.

STEERING WHEEL

REPLACE

1. Position front wheels in straight ahead position.
2. Remove air bag module as outlined under "Passive Restraint Systems " section.
3. Remove steering wheel using suitable steering wheel puller.
4. Reverse procedure to install.

INSTRUMENT CLUSTER

REPLACE

1. Remove cluster bezel.
2. Remove cluster retaining screws.
3. Disconnect speedometer cable at transaxle end.
4. Pull cluster rearward slightly and disconnect electrical connectors and speedometer cable.
5. Release speedometer adapter by turning adapter left or right then remove adapter.
6. Reverse procedure to install.

RADIO

REPLACE

1. Remove radio trim panel.
2. Remove floor console as outlined under "Dash Panel Service."

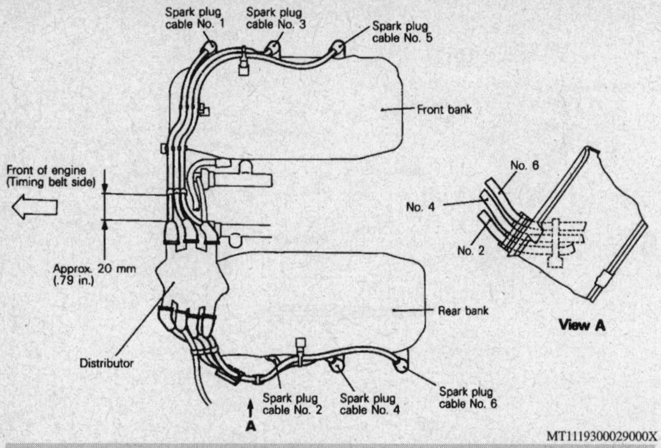
Spark plug cable No. 1
Spark plug cable No. 3
Spark plug cable No. 5
Front bank
Front of engine (Timing belt side)
No. 6
No. 4
No. 2
Approx. 20 mm (.79 in.)
Rear bank
View A
Distributor
Spark plug cable No. 2
Spark plug cable No. 4
Spark plug cable No. 6
A
MT1119300029000X

Fig. 4 Engine spark plug routing.

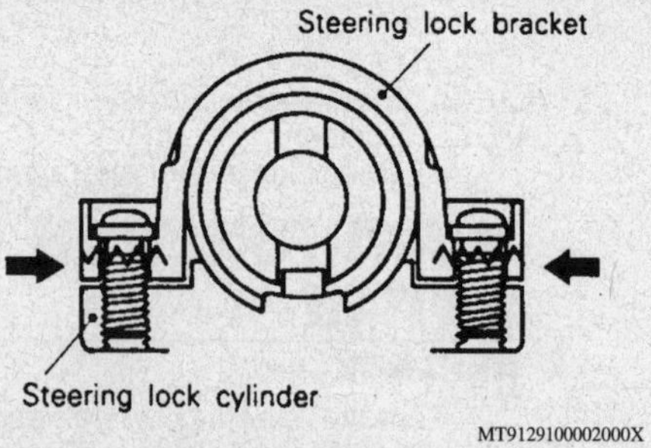
Steering lock bracket
Steering lock cylinder
MT9129100002000X

Fig. 6 Steering lock removal

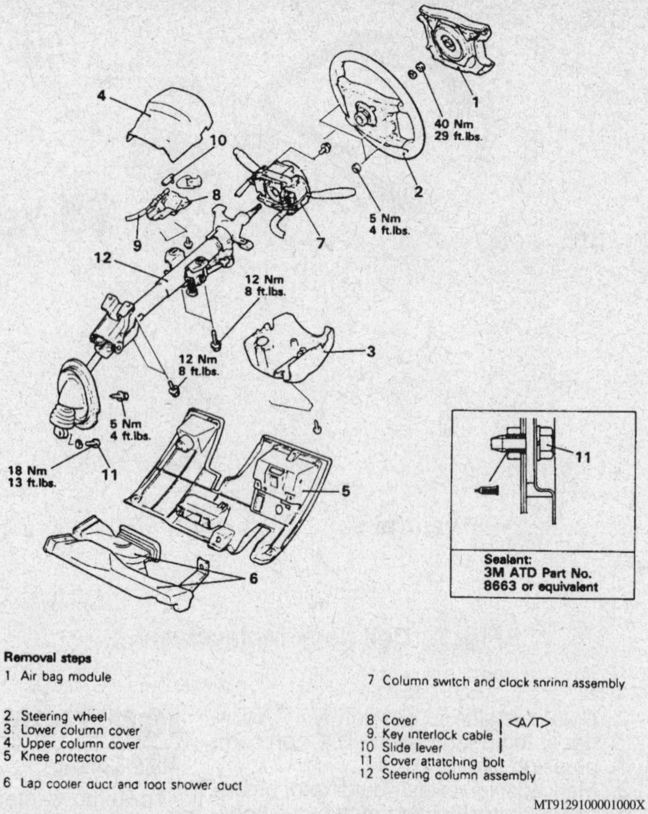
40 Nm
29 ft.lbs.
5 Nm
4 ft.lbs.
12 Nm
8 ft.lbs.
12 Nm
8 ft.lbs.
5 Nm
4 ft.lbs.
18 Nm
13 ft.lbs.
Sealant:
3M ATD Part No.
8663 or equivalent
Removal steps
1 Air bag module
2. Steering wheel
3. Lower column cover
4 Upper column cover
5 Knee protector
6 Lap cooler duct and foot shower duct
7 Column switch and clock spring assembly
8 Cover
9. Key interlock cable
10 Slide lever
<A/T>
11 Cover attaching bolt
12 Steering column assembly
MT9129100001000X

Fig. 5 Exploded view of steering column assembly

3. Remove radio, cassette player and/or CD player with bracket attached.
4. Remove bracket from radio, cassette player and/or CD player.
5. Reverse procedure to install.

WIPER MOTOR

REPLACE

1. Disconnect battery ground cable.
2. Remove wiper arms and blades.
3. Remove air inlet grille.
4. Loosen wiper motor bolts, then remove wiper motor assembly and disconnect linkage.
5. Reverse procedure to install.

WIPER SWITCH

REPLACE

Refer to "Multi-Function Switch, Replace" for wiper switch replacement procedure.

BLOWER MOTOR

REPLACE

1. Remove glove compartment and glove compartment outer case.
2. Remove passenger side lower cover.
3. Remove passenger foot shower duct.
4. Disconnect and remove blower motor assembly.
5. Reverse procedure to install.

HEATER CORE

REPLACE

1. Drain cooling system into a suitable container.
2. Remove instrument panel as outlined under "Dash Panel Service" section.
3. Replace heater unit in numbered sequence shown in **Fig. 9.**
4. Reverse procedure to install.

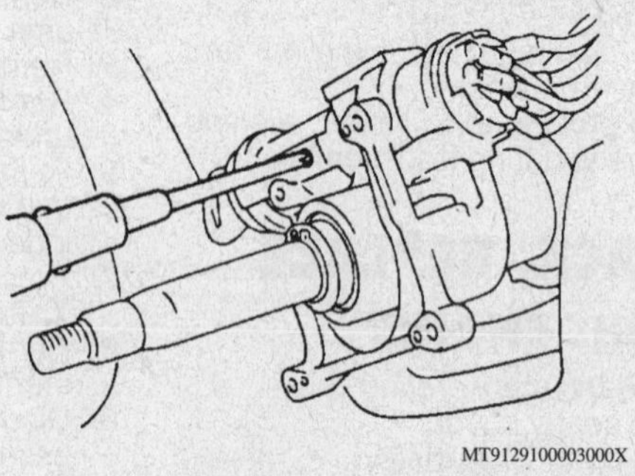
MT9129100003000X

Fig. 7 Ignition lock cylinder removal

EVAPORATOR CORE

REPLACE

1. Using approved refrigerant collection device and following manufacturer's instructions, discharge cooling system.
2. Remove glove compartment and glove compartment outer case.
3. Remove evaporator case assembly in numbered sequence shown in **Fig. 10.**
4. Disassemble evaporator case assembly in numbered sequence shown in **Fig. 11.**
5. Reverse procedure to install.

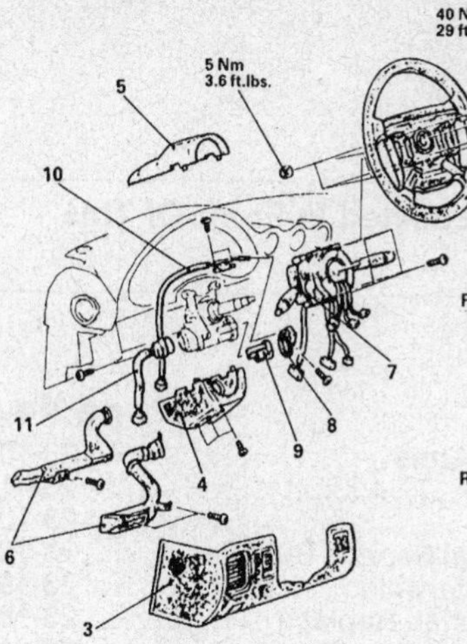
40 Nm
29 ft.lbs.
5 Nm
3.6 ft.lbs.

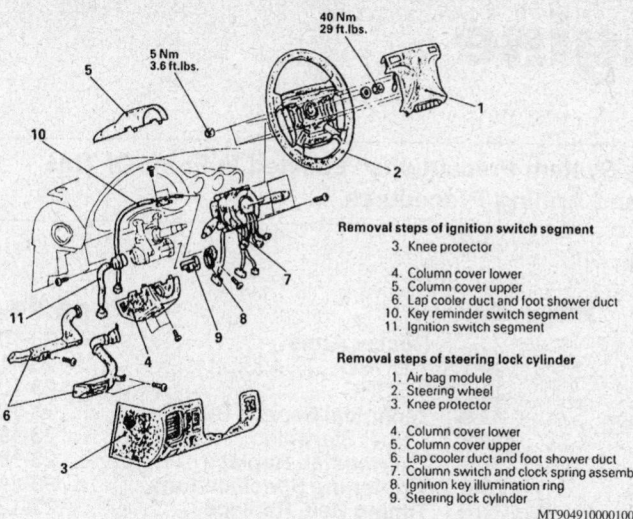

Removal steps of ignition switch segment

3. Knee protector
4. Column cover lower
5. Column cover upper
6. Lap cooler duct and foot shower duct
10. Key reminder switch segment
11. Ignition switch segment

Removal steps of steering lock cylinder

1. Air bag module
2. Steering wheel
3. Knee protector
4. Column cover lower
5. Column cover upper
6. Lap cooler duct and foot shower duct
7. Column switch and clock spring assembly
8. Ignition key illumination ring
9. Steering lock cylinder

MT9049100001000X

Fig. 8 Neutral start switch alignment

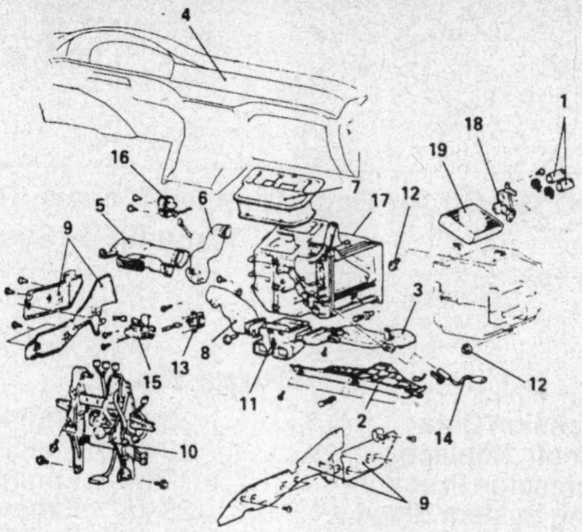

Removal steps

1. Connection of heater hoses
2. Passenger side under cover
3. Foot shower duct (right side)
4. Instrument panel
5. Foot shower nozzle
6. Lap cooler duct A
7. Center duct assembly
8. Foot shower duct (left side)
9. Front and rear center reinforcement
10. Center stay assembly
11. Distribution duct assembly
12. Installation of coolant unit
13. Power transistor
14. Engine coolant temperature sensor
15. Air mix damper motor assembly
16. Outlet selector damper motor assembly
17. Heater unit
18. Plate
19. Heater core

MT7029100069000X

Fig. 9 Heater unit replacement

Removal steps

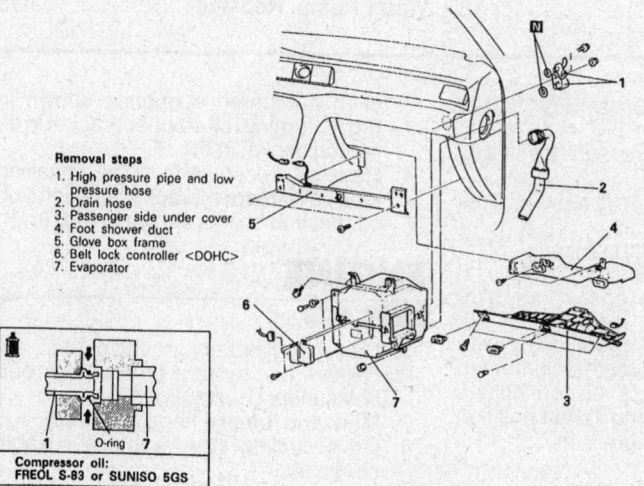

1. High pressure pipe and low pressure hose
2. Drain hose
3. Passenger side under cover
4. Foot shower duct
5. Glove box frame
6. Belt lock controller <DOHC>
7. Evaporator

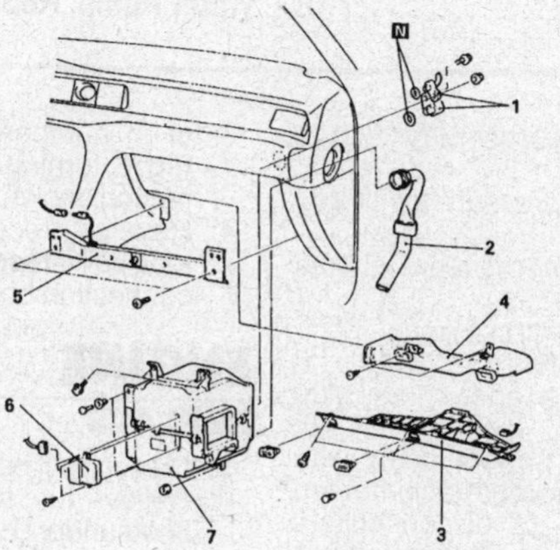

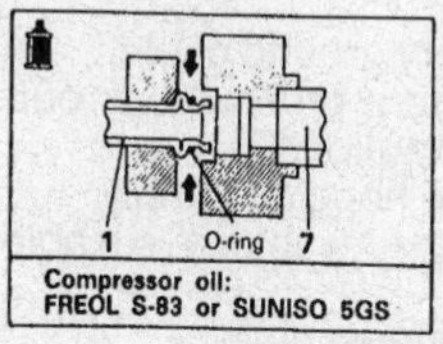
O-ring
Compressor oil:
FREOL S-83 or SUNISO 5GS

MT7029100070000X

Fig. 10 Evaporator unit replacement

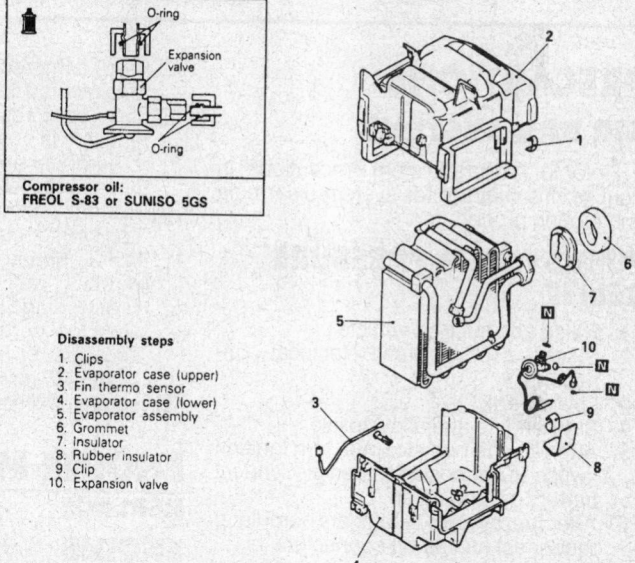

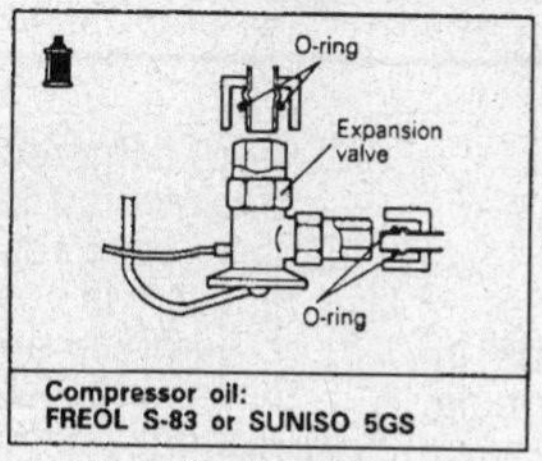
O-ring
Expansion valve
O-ring
Compressor oil:
FREOL S-83 or SUNISO 5GS

Disassembly steps

1. Clips
2. Evaporator case (upper)
3. Fin thermo sensor
4. Evaporator case (lower)
5. Evaporator assembly
6. Grommet
7. Insulator
8. Rubber insulator
9. Clip
10. Expansion valve

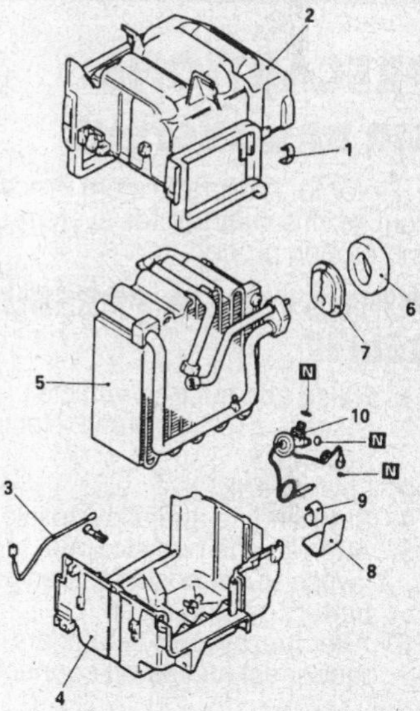

MT7029100071000X

Fig. 11 Exploded view of evaporator unit

3.0L Engine

NOTE: On Air Bag Equipped Models, Refer To "Air Bag System Precautions" Located In Front Of This Manual For System Disarming and Arming Procedures.

INDEX

	Page No.
Belt Tension Data	23-18
Camshaft, Replace	23-16
Compression Pressure	23-8
Cooling System Bleed	23-18
Crankshaft Seal, Replace	23-17
Front	23-17
Rear	23-17
Cylinder Head, Replace	23-9
DOHC	23-9
SOHC	23-9
Engine Mount, Replace	23-8
Engine Roll Stopper & Damper	23-8
Engine	23-8
Transaxle	23-8
Engine Rebuilding Specifications	29-1
Engine, Replace	23-8
Exhaust Manifold, Replace	23-9
Fuel Filter, Replace	23-19
Fuel Pump, Replace	23-19
Intake Manifold, Replace	23-8
Oil Pan, Replace	23-18
Oil Pump, Replace	23-18
Piston & Rod Assembly	23-17
Precautions	23-8
Air Bag Systems	23-8
Fuel System Pressure Relief	23-8
Radiator, Replace	23-18
Rocker Arms	23-10
DOHC	23-11
SOHC	23-10
Technical Service Bulletins	23-19
Fuel Starvation	23-19
Thermostat, Replace	23-18
Tightening Specifications	23-24
Timing Belt, Replace	23-12
DOHC	23-15
SOHC	23-14
Valve Adjustment	23-10
Valve Arrangement	23-10
Valve Clearance Specifications	23-10
Water Pump, Replace	23-18

PRECAUTIONS

AIR BAG SYSTEMS

Refer to "Air Bag System Precautions" in front of this manual for system disarming and arming procedures.

FUEL SYSTEM PRESSURE RELIEF

1. Raise and support vehicle.
2. Disconnect fuel pump electrical connector.
3. Lower vehicle.
4. Start engine and allow to idle.
5. After engine has stopped, turn ignition switch to Off position, then disconnect battery ground cable.
6. After fuel system repairs are complete, reconnect fuel pump connector.

COMPRESSION PRESSURE

Ensure engine oil, starter motor and battery are in satisfactory condition. When checking compression, engine coolant should be at normal operating temperature, spark plugs should be removed and throttle valve should be wide open. Perform engine compression pressure test as follows:

1. Ensure lights, electric cooling fan and accessories are OFF.
2. Disconnect distributor or crankshaft position sensor, **Fig. 1.**
3. Install compression gauge in spark plug holes.
4. With throttle valve fully open, crank engine at 250–400 RPM and record compression pressure.
5. Standard compression pressure for SOHC engines is 196 psi.
6. Standard compression pressure for DOHC engines is 185 psi.
7. Limit compression pressure for SOHC engines is 149 psi.
8. Limit compression pressure for DOHC engines is 139 psi.
9. Difference between cylinders should not exceed 14 psi.
10. Connect distributor or crankshaft position sensor connector.
11. Install spark plugs and spark plug wires.
12. Erase diagnostic trouble code with scan tool or reconnect battery after ten seconds or more of disconnection. Code will set when crankshaft position sensor is disconnected.

ENGINE MOUNT

REPLACE

ENGINE

1. Disconnect battery ground cable.
2. Using suitable floor jack, raise engine to release weight off mounts.
3. Replace engine mounts in numbered sequence shown in **Fig. 2,** installing mounting stopper in direction shown, **Fig. 3.**

TRANSAXLE

1. Disconnect battery ground cable.
2. Using suitable floor jack, raise transaxle to release weight off mounts.
3. Replace transaxle mounts in numbered sequence shown in **Fig. 4,** installing mounting stopper in direction shown, **Fig. 5.**

ENGINE ROLL STOPPER & DAMPER

1. Disconnect battery ground cable.
2. Using suitable floor jack raise transaxle to release weight off mounts.
3. Replace engine roll stopper and damper in numbered sequence shown in **Fig. 6,** turning roll stopper bracket in direction shown in **Fig. 7.**
4. Reverse procedure to install, installing rear roll stopper bracket and engine connection bolt as shown in **Fig. 8.**

ENGINE

REPLACE

1. Disconnect battery ground cable.
2. Relieve fuel system pressure as outlined under "Precautions."
3. Mark and remove hood assembly.
4. Drain cooling system into a suitable container.
5. Remove front exhaust pipe.
6. Remove transaxle assembly as outlined under "Automatic Transaxle" section.
7. Remove radiator assembly.
8. Remove engine assembly from vehicle in numbered sequence shown in **Figs. 9 and 10,** noting the following:
   a. Remove power steering pump and air conditioner compressor and position aside, leaving hoses attached.
   b. Disconnect alternator wiring from engine compartment relay block.
   c. Support engine assembly using a suitable engine lifting device, then remove engine mounting bolts.
   d. After ensuring all hoses and electrical connections are disconnected, raise engine out of engine compartment.
9. Reverse procedure to install, installing engine mount bracket stopper as shown in **Fig. 3.**

INTAKE MANIFOLD

REPLACE

1. Disconnect battery ground cable.

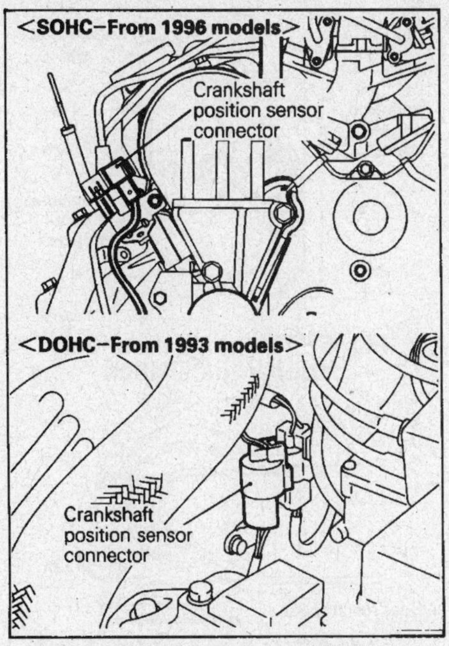
<SOHC–From 1996 models>
Crankshaft position sensor connector
<DOHC–From 1993 models>
Crankshaft position sensor connector
MT1119300030000X

Fig. 1 Distributor & crankshaft position sensor connector locations.

2. Release fuel system pressure as outlined under "Precautions."
3. Replace air plenum and intake manifold in numbered sequence shown in **Figs. 11 and 12,** noting the following:
   a. Install throttle body gasket as shown in **Fig. 13.**
   b. Rotate engine to position No. 1 cylinder at top dead center.
   c. **On DOHC engines,** line up match marks on crank angle sensor, then install into engine.
   d. **On SOHC engines,** align distributor housing and gear mating marks, then install distributor into engine keeping mounting stud located in center of adjusting slot in distributor.
   e. **On all engines,** lubricate fuel pressure regulator and fuel injector O-rings with clean engine oil for easy installation.
   f. Install injector into delivery pipe installing clip as shown, **Fig. 14.**

EXHAUST MANIFOLD

REPLACE

1. Disconnect battery ground cable.
2. Release fuel system pressure as outlined under "Precautions."
3. Replace exhaust manifold in numbered sequence shown in **Figs. 15 through 18,** noting the following:
   a. **On DOHC engines,** remove air conditioner compressor and position aside, leaving hoses attached.
   b. **On all engines,** disconnect front exhaust pipe.

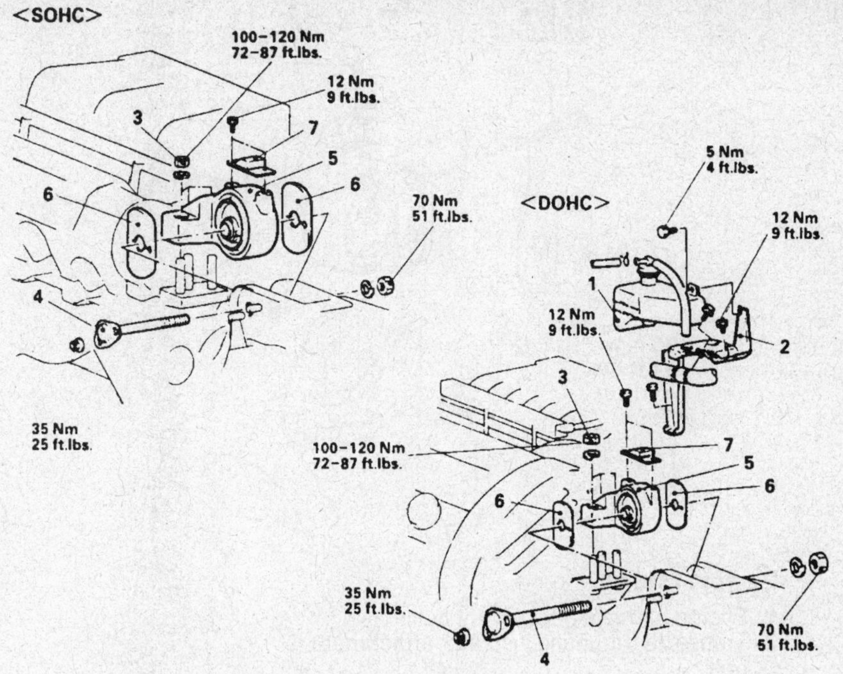
<SOHC>
100–120 Nm
72–87 ft.lbs.
12 Nm
9 ft.lbs.
70 Nm
51 ft.lbs.
35 Nm
25 ft.lbs.
<DOHC>
5 Nm
4 ft.lbs.
12 Nm
9 ft.lbs.
12 Nm
9 ft.lbs.
100–120 Nm
72–87 ft.lbs.
35 Nm
25 ft.lbs.
70 Nm
51 ft.lbs.

Removal steps

1 Reserve tank <Vehicles with ABS>
2 Reserve tank bracket <Vehicles with ABS>
3 Engine mount bracket mounting nuts
4 Engine mount bracket and body connection bolt
5 Engine mount bracket
6 Mounting stopper
7 Dynamic damper

MT1069100001000X

Fig. 2 Engine mount replacement

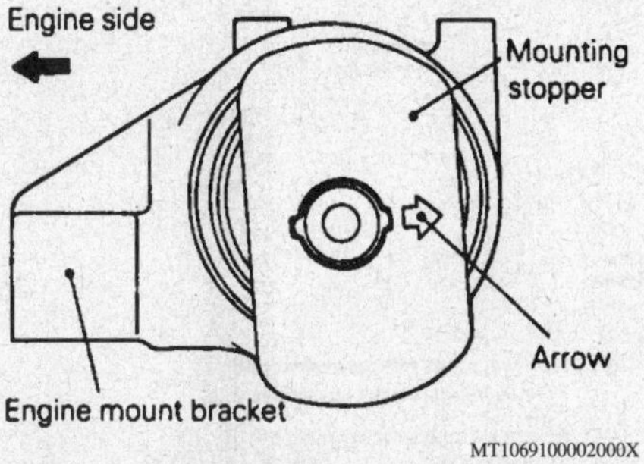
Engine side
Mounting stopper
Arrow
Engine mount bracket
MT1069100002000X

Fig. 3 Engine mounting stopper installation

CYLINDER HEAD

REPLACE

SOHC

1. Disconnect battery ground cable.
2. Relieve fuel system pressure as outlined under "Precautions."
3. Drain engine coolant into an approved container.
4. Remove exhaust manifold as outlined under "Exhaust Manifold, Replace."
5. Remove air plenum and intake manifold as outlined under "Air Plenum & Intake Manifold, Replace."
6. Remove timing belt as outlined under "Timing Belt, Replace."
7. Remove cylinder head in numbered sequence shown in **Fig. 19** using socket tool No. MD998051-01, or equivalent.
8. Reverse procedure to install, noting the following:
   a. Lay cylinder head gasket on block with identification mark at front top, **Fig. 20.**
   b. Using special socket tool, tighten cylinder head bolts to specifications in two or three steps, **Fig. 21.** Install cylinder head bolt washers as shown.

DOHC

1. Remove timing belt as outlined under "Timing Belt, Replace."
2. Remove camshafts as outlined under "Camshaft & Rocker Arm Service."
3. Remove exhaust manifolds as outlined under "Exhaust Manifold, Replace."
4. Drain engine coolant into an approved container.
5. Remove cylinder head in numbered sequence shown in **Fig. 22,** using cylinder head bolt wrench tool No. MD998051-01, or equivalent, to remove cylinder head bolts.
6. Using a suitable straightedge and feeler gauge, measure flatness of cylinder head and ensure head flatness is 0.0012 inch or less. If specification is

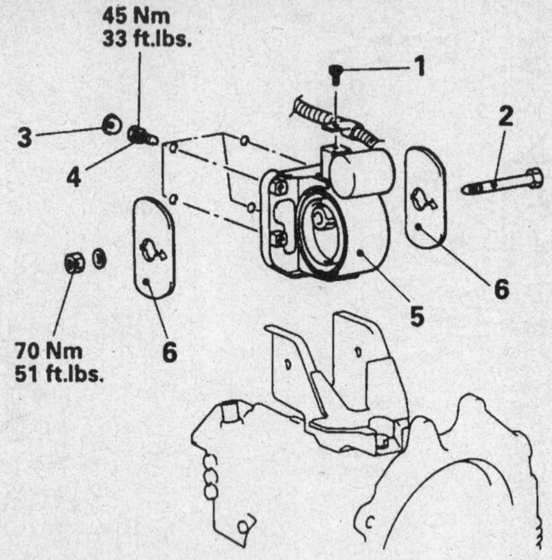
45 Nm
33 ft.lbs.
1
2
3
4
5
6
6
70 Nm
51 ft.lbs.

Removal steps

1. Engine harness attachment bolt
2. Transaxle mounting insulator attachment bolt
3. Cap
4. Transaxle mounting attachment bolt
5. Transaxle mounting bracket
6. Transaxle mounting stopper

MT1069100003000X

Fig. 4 Transaxle mount replacement

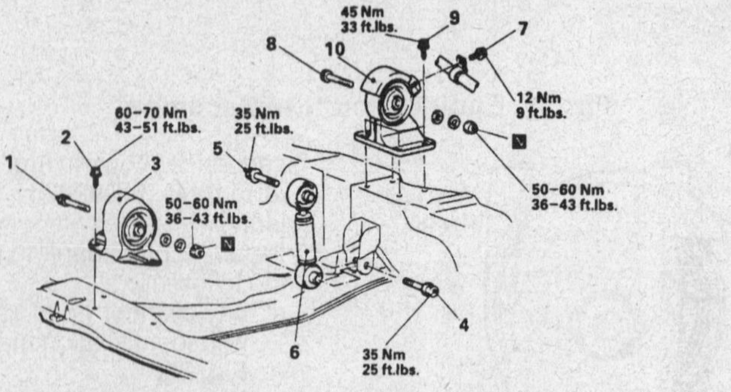
45 Nm
33 ft.lbs.
9
7
8
10
12 Nm
9 ft.lbs.
60–70 Nm
43–51 ft.lbs.
35 Nm
25 ft.lbs.
2
1
3
5
50–60 Nm
36–43 ft.lbs.
50–60 Nm
36–43 ft.lbs.
4
6
35 Nm
25 ft.lbs.

Removal steps for front roll stopper

1. Front roll stopper attachment bolt (engine side)
2. Front roll stopper attachment bolt (No.1 crossmember side)
3. Front roll stopper

Removal steps for engine damper

4. Engine damper lower attachment bolt
5. Engine damper upper attachment bolt
6. Engine damper

Removal steps for rear roll stopper

7. Hose installation bolt <Vehicles with 4WS>
8. Rear roll stopper attachment bolt (engine side)
9. Rear roll stopper attachment bolt (crossmember side)
10. Rear roll stopper

MT1069100005000X

Fig. 6 Engine roll stopper & engine damper replacement

exceeded, grind head no more than 0.008 inch.

7. Reverse numbered sequence shown in **Fig. 22** to install cylinder head, noting the following:
   a. Lay cylinder head gasket on block with identification mark at front top, **Fig. 20.**
   b. Using cylinder head bolt wrench tool, tighten cylinder head bolts to specifications in two to three stages in sequence shown, **Fig. 21.**
   c. Tighten rocker cover bolts in sequence shown in **Fig. 23.** Install black colored bolts on engine front bank and green colored bolts on

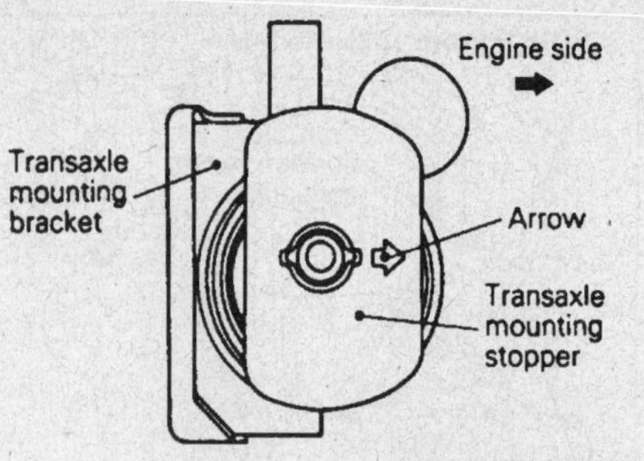
Engine side
Transaxle mounting bracket
Arrow
Transaxle mounting stopper

MT1069100004000X

Fig. 5 Transaxle mounting stopper installation

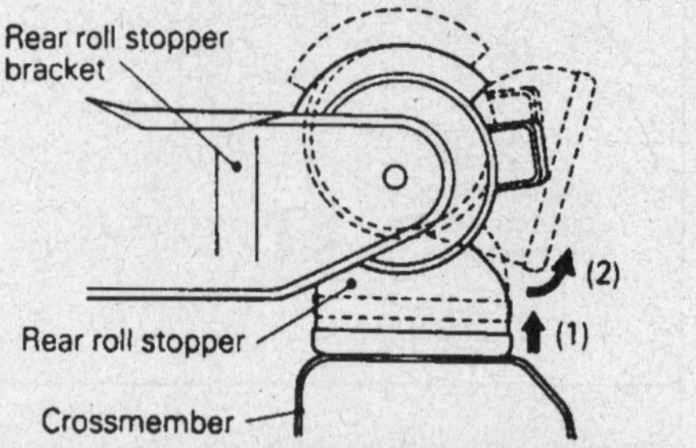
Rear roll stopper bracket
(2)
(1)
Rear roll stopper
Crossmember

MT1069100006000X

Fig. 7 Rotating roll stopper bracket

rear bank. Bolt No. 5 is longer than other bolts used.

VALVE ARRANGEMENT

Intake valves are on inside of cylinder head and exhaust valves are on outside of cylinder head.

VALVE CLEARANCE SPECIFICATIONS

Stem-To-Guide Clearance, Inch①	
Intake	Exhaust
SOHC ENGINE	
.0012–.0024	.0020–.0035
DOHC ENGINE	
.0008–.0020	.0020–.0035

① — Not adjustable.

VALVE ADJUSTMENT

Automatic lash adjusters are used; therefore no adjustment is necessary.

ROCKER ARMS

SOHC

1. Disconnect battery ground cable.
2. Release fuel system pressure as outlined under "Precautions."

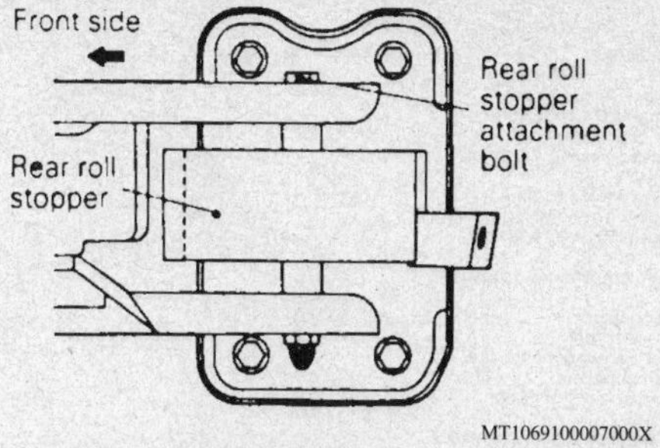
Front side
Rear roll stopper attachment bolt
Rear roll stopper
MT1069100007000X

Fig. 8 Roll stopper bracket bolt installation

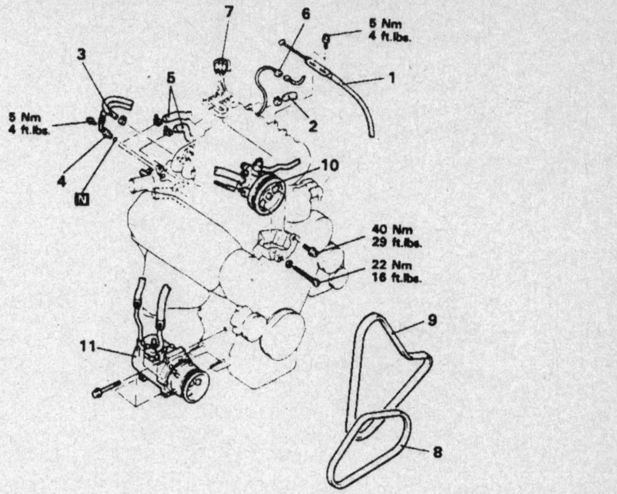
5 Nm
4 ft.lbs.
40 Nm
29 ft.lbs.
22 Nm
16 ft.lbs.

Removal steps

1. Accelerator cable connection
2. Brake booster vacuum hose connection
3. Fuel return hose connection
4. Fuel high pressure hose connection
5. Heater hose connection
6. EGR temperature sensor connector <Vehicles for California>
7. Vacuum hose connector

• Adjustment Drive Belt Tension

8. Drive belt (air conditioner)
9. Drive belt (alternator and power steering)
10. Power steering oil pump
11. Air conditioner compressor

MT1069100008010X

Fig. 9 Engine assembly removal (Part 1 of 2). SOHC engine

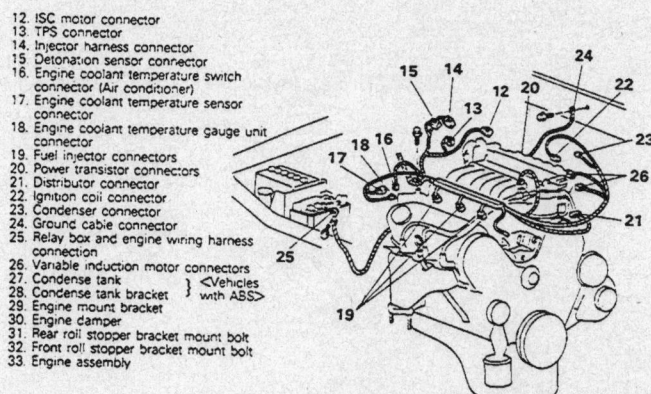

12. ISC motor connector
13. TPS connector
14. Injector harness connector
15. Detonation sensor connector
16. Engine coolant temperature switch connector (Air conditioner)
17. Engine coolant temperature sensor connector
18. Engine coolant temperature gauge unit connector
19. Fuel injector connectors
20. Power transistor connectors
21. Distributor connector
22. Ignition coil connector
23. Condenser connector
24. Ground cable connector
25. Relay box and engine wiring harness connection
26. Variable induction motor connectors
27. Condense tank } <Vehicles with ABS>
28. Condense tank bracket }
29. Engine mount bracket
30. Engine damper
31. Rear roll stopper bracket mount bolt
32. Front roll stopper bracket mount bolt
33. Engine assembly

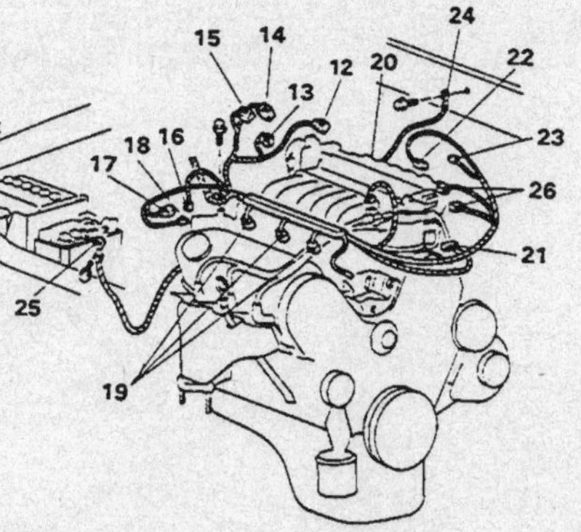

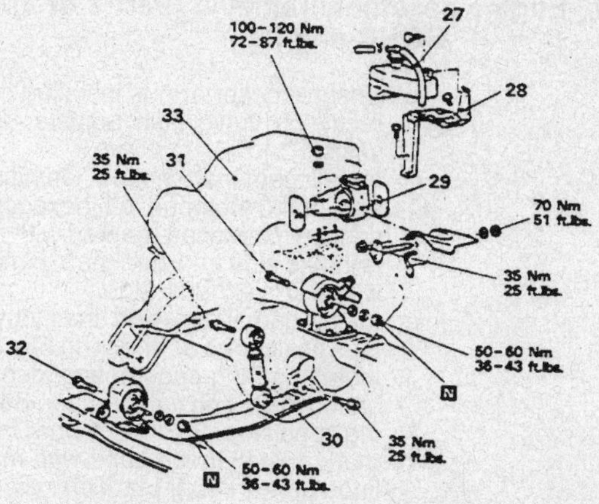
100–120 Nm
72–87 ft.lbs.
35 Nm
25 ft.lbs.
70 Nm
51 ft.lbs.
35 Nm
25 ft.lbs.
50–60 Nm
36–43 ft.lbs.
35 Nm
25 ft.lbs.
50–60 Nm
36–43 ft.lbs.
MT1069100008020X

Fig. 9 Engine assembly removal (Part 2 of 2). SOHC engine

3. Remove timing belt as outlined under "Timing Belt, Replace."
4. Remove camshaft sprocket bolt using end yoke holder tool No. MB990767 and MD998719, or equivalents.
5. Attach lash adjuster retainer tool No. MD998443-01, or equivalent, before removing rocker assembly.
6. Remove camshaft and rocker arms in numbered sequence shown in **Fig. 24**, noting the following:
   a. Immerse lash adjuster in clean diesel fuel. Using small wire, move plunger up and down four to five times while pushing down lightly on check ball to bleed out air. Install lash adjuster into cylinder head.
   b. Apply sealant at four places shown in **Fig. 25.** Ensure sealant does not contact cam journal surface.
   c. Install rocker arms, shafts and bearing caps so mark on bearing cap faces same direction as arrow mark on cylinder head, **Fig. 26.**
   d. Install camshaft oil seal as outlined under "Camshaft Oil Seal, Replace."
   e. Install a 0.020 inch spacer onto circular packing driver tool No. MD998714-01, or equivalent, then install circular packing.

DOHC

1. Disconnect battery ground cable.
2. Release fuel system pressure as outlined under "Precautions."
3. Remove timing belt as outlined under "Timing Belt, Replace."
4. Remove camshaft oil seal as outlined under "Camshaft Oil Seal, Replace."
5. Replace rocker arm and camshaft in numbered sequence shown in **Fig. 27,** noting the following:

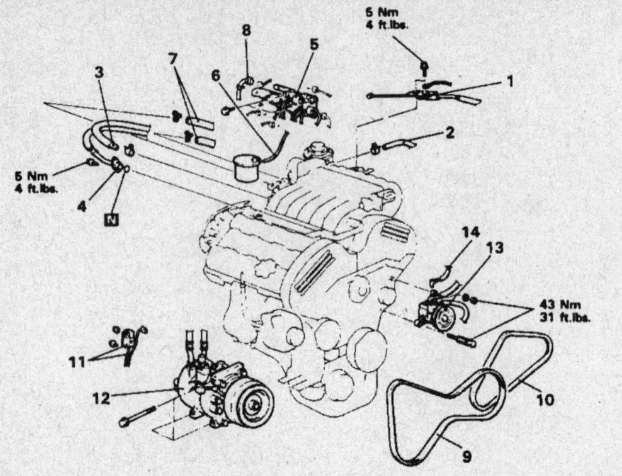
5 Nm
4 ft.lbs.
5 Nm
4 ft.lbs.
43 Nm
31 ft.lbs.

Removal steps

1. Accelerator cable connection
2. Brake booster vacuum hose connection
3. Fuel return hose connection
4. Fuel high pressure hose connection
5. Solenoid valve assembly
6. Vapor hose connection
7. Heater hose connection
8. EGR temperature sensor connector <Vehicles for California>
9. Drive belt (Generator and air conditioning)
10. Drive belt (Power steering)
11. Generator harness connection
12. Air conditioning compressor
13. Power steering oil pump
14. Oil pressure switch connection (Power steering)

MT1069100009010X

Fig. 10 Engine assembly removal (Part 1 of 2). DOHC engine

15. APS connector
16. ISC motor connector
17. TPS connector
18. Oil pressure switch connector
19. Fuel injector harness connector
20. Knock sensor connector
21. Crankshaft position sensor connector <1992 models>
22. Air conditioning engine coolant temperature switch connector
23. Engine coolant temperature sensor connector
24. Engine coolant temperature gauge unit connector
25. Ignition coil connector
26. Condenser connection
27. Ignition power transistor connector
28. Fuel injectors connector
29. Variable induction control motor connectors

29-1. Camshaft position sensor connector <From 1993 models>
29-2. Crankshaft position sensor connector <From 1993 models>

30. Condense tank } <Vehicles with ABS>
31. Condense tank bracket } <Vehicles with ABS>
32. Engine mounting bracket
33. Engine damper
34. Rear roll stopper bracket and engine connection bolt
35. Front roll stopper bracket and engine connection bolt
36. Engine assembly

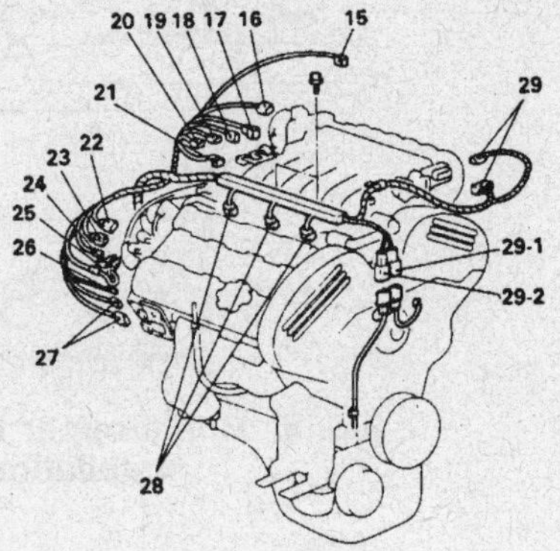

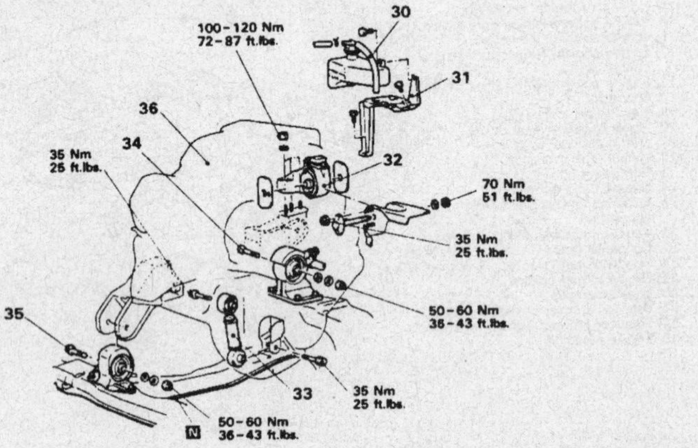
100-120 Nm
72-87 ft.lbs.
35 Nm
25 ft.lbs.
70 Nm
51 ft.lbs.
35 Nm
25 ft.lbs.
50-60 Nm
36-43 ft.lbs.
35 Nm
25 ft.lbs.
50-60 Nm
36-43 ft.lbs.

MT1069100009020X

Fig. 10 Engine assembly removal (Part 2 of 2). DOHC engine

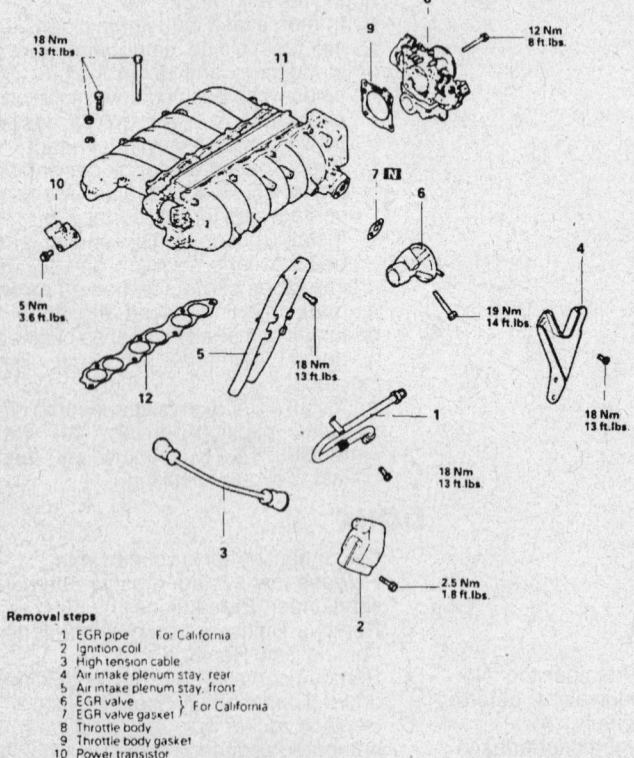

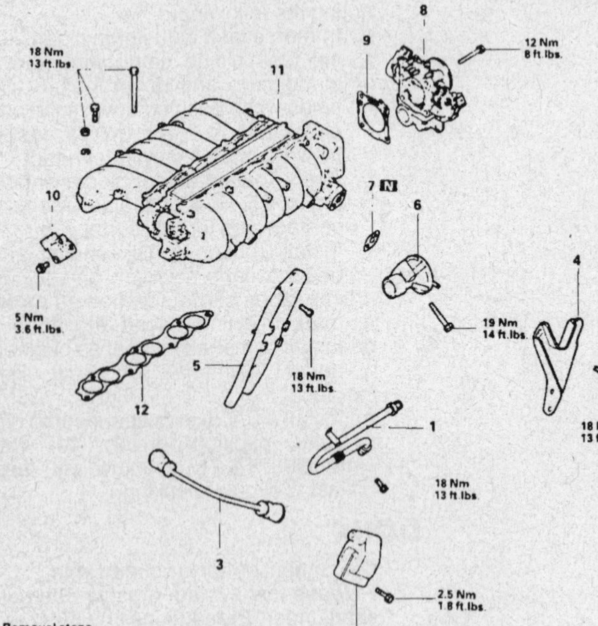
18 Nm
13 ft.lbs
12 Nm
8 ft.lbs.
5 Nm
3.6 ft.lbs.
19 Nm
14 ft.lbs.
18 Nm
13 ft.lbs.
18 Nm
13 ft.lbs.
18 Nm
13 ft.lbs.
2.5 Nm
1.8 ft.lbs.

Removal steps

1. EGR pipe — For California
2. Ignition coil
3. High tension cable
4. Air intake plenum stay, rear
5. Air intake plenum stay, front
6. EGR valve } For California
7. EGR valve gasket } For California
8. Throttle body
9. Throttle body gasket
10. Power transistor
11. Air intake plenum
12. Air intake plenum gasket

MT1059100001010X

Fig. 11 Intake manifold replacement (Part 1 of 3). SOHC engine

a. Immerse lash adjuster in clean diesel fuel. Using small wire, move plunger up and down four to five times while pushing down lightly on check ball to bleed out air. Install lash adjuster into cylinder head.
b. Turn crankshaft to bring No. 1 cylinder to TDC.
c. Ensure rocker arm is installed correctly on valve lash adjuster and valve.
d. Install camshaft noting identification mark stamped on hexagonal section. Camshaft marked with a V is intake side and camshaft marked with a D is exhaust side.
e. Install camshafts with their dowel pins positioned as shown in **Fig. 28.**
f. Install bearing caps noting identification mark and cap number. Bearing caps Nos. 2, 3 and 4 bear front mark. Install these caps with mark lined up with front mark on cylinder head. Caps marked with a "I" are for intake side and caps marked with an " E" are exhaust side.
g. Tighten bearing cap bolts gradually in two or three steps and finally tighten to specification.
h. Using circular packing installer tool No. MD998762, or equivalent, install circular packing.

TIMING BELT

REPLACE

With the timing belt removed, avoid turning the camshaft or crankshaft. If movement is required, exercise extreme caution to avoid valve damage caused by piston contact.

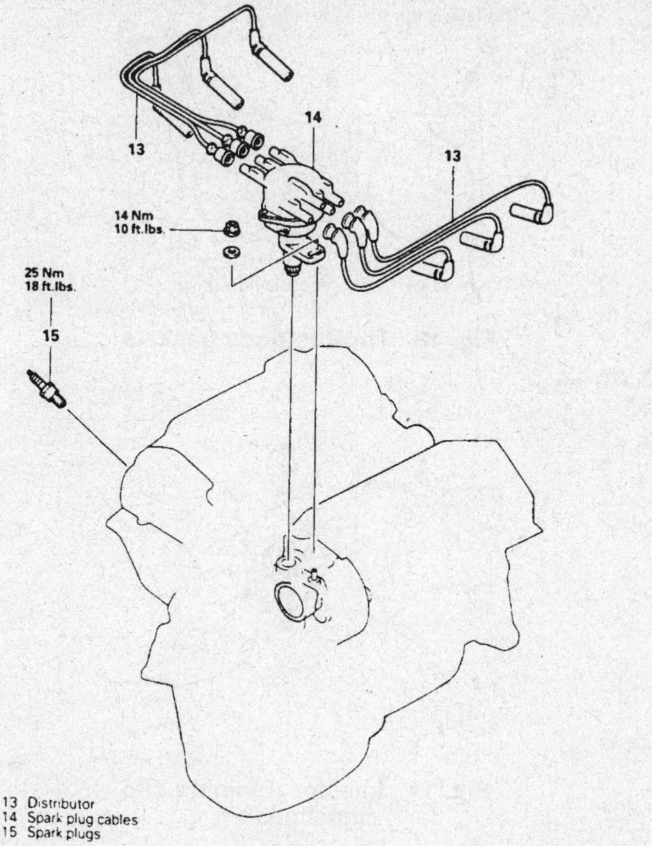
14 Nm
10 ft.lbs.
25 Nm
18 ft.lbs.
13 Distributor
14 Spark plug cables
15 Spark plugs
MT1059100001020X

Fig. 11 Intake manifold replacement (Part 2 of 3). SOHC engine

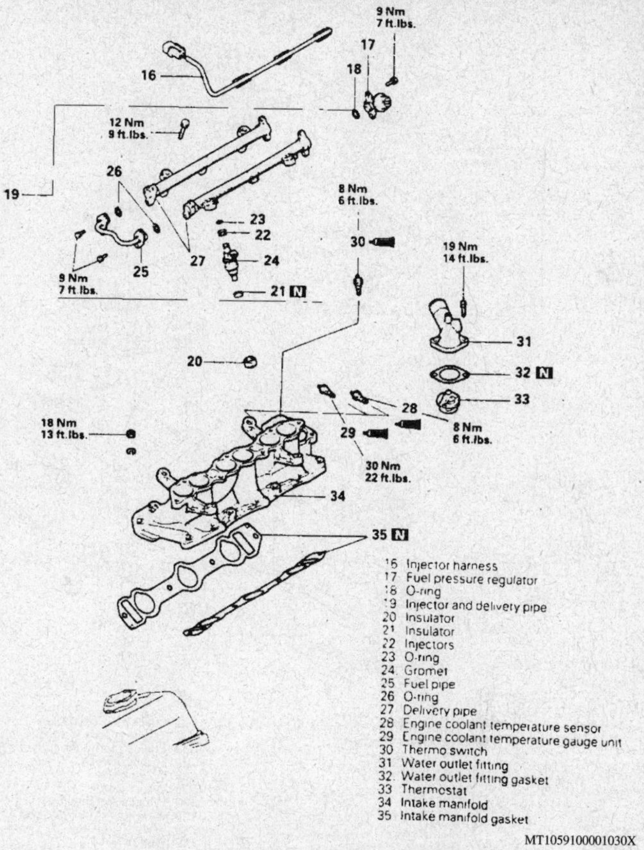
9 Nm
7 ft.lbs.
12 Nm
9 ft.lbs.
8 Nm
6 ft.lbs.
19 Nm
14 ft.lbs.
18 Nm
13 ft.lbs.
30 Nm
22 ft.lbs.
16 Injector harness
17 Fuel pressure regulator
18 O-ring
19 Injector and delivery pipe
20 Insulator
21 Insulator
22 Injectors
23 O-ring
24 Gromet
25 Fuel pipe
26 O-ring
27 Delivery pipe
28 Engine coolant temperature sensor
29 Engine coolant temperature gauge unit
30 Thermo switch
31 Water outlet fitting
32 Water outlet fitting gasket
33 Thermostat
34 Intake manifold
35 Intake manifold gasket
MT1059100001030X

Fig. 11 Intake manifold replacement (Part 3 of 3). SOHC engine

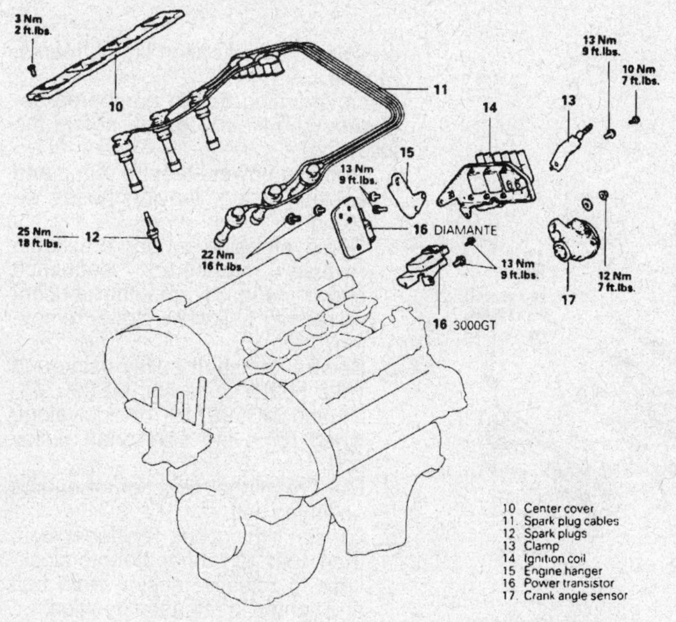
3 Nm
2 ft.lbs.
13 Nm
9 ft.lbs.
10 Nm
7 ft.lbs.
25 Nm
18 ft.lbs.
22 Nm
16 ft.lbs.
12 Nm
7 ft.lbs.
16 DIAMANTE
16 3000GT
10 Center cover
11 Spark plug cables
12 Spark plugs
13 Clamp
14 Ignition coil
15 Engine hanger
16 Power transistor
17 Crank angle sensor
MT1059100002010X

Fig. 12 Intake manifold replacement (Part 1 of 3). DOHC engine

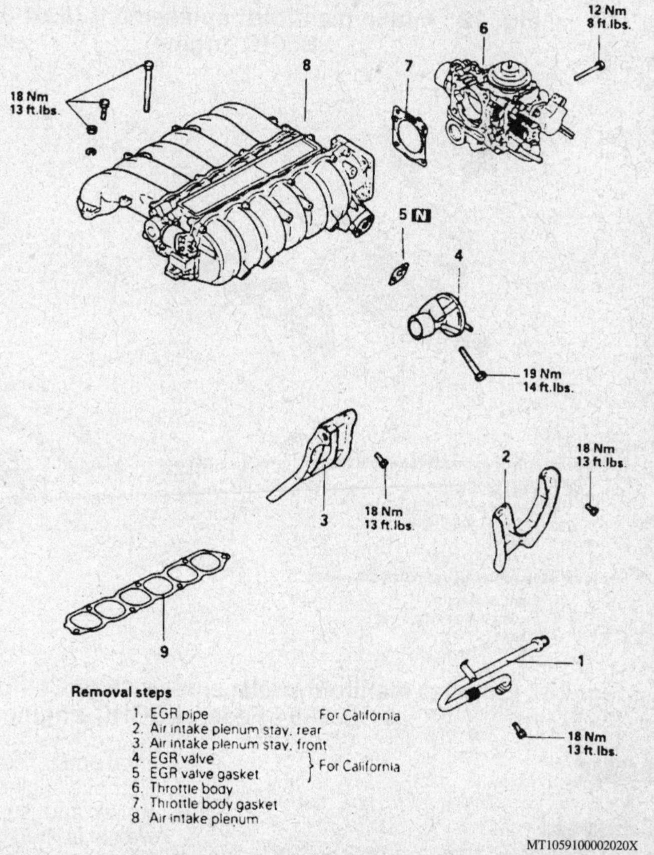
12 Nm
8 ft.lbs.
18 Nm
13 ft.lbs.
19 Nm
14 ft.lbs.
Removal steps
1. EGR pipe — For California
2. Air intake plenum stay, rear
3. Air intake plenum stay, front
4. EGR valve
5. EGR valve gasket — For California
6. Throttle body
7. Throttle body gasket
8. Air intake plenum
MT1059100002020X

Fig. 12 Intake manifold replacement (Part 2 of 3). DOHC engine

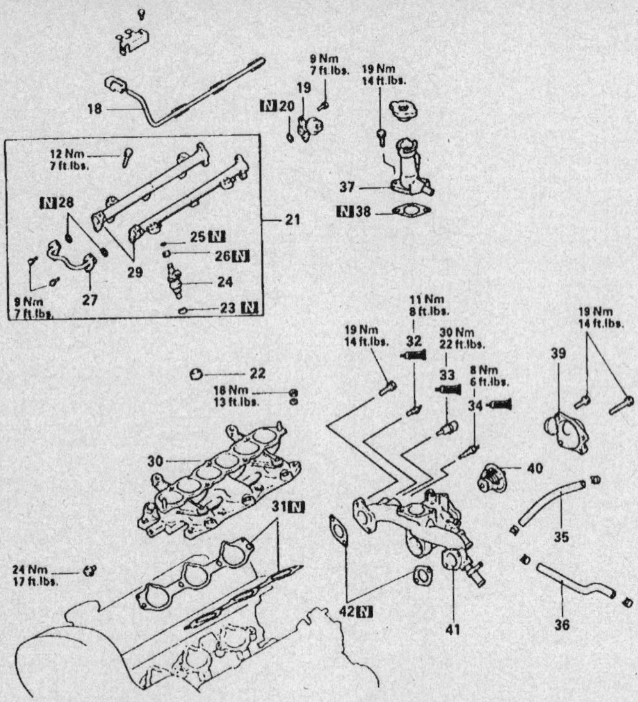

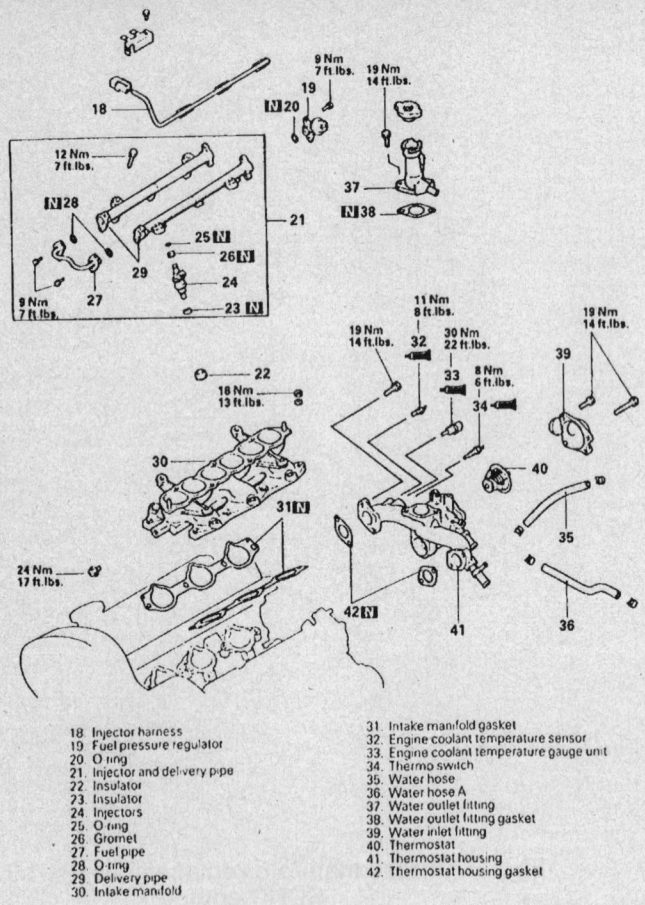

18. Injector harness
19. Fuel pressure regulator
20. O-ring
21. Injector and delivery pipe
22. Insulator
23. Insulator
24. Injectors
25. O-ring
26. Gromet
27. Fuel pipe
28. O-ring
29. Delivery pipe
30. Intake manifold
31. Intake manifold gasket
32. Engine coolant temperature sensor
33. Engine coolant temperature gauge unit
34. Thermo switch
35. Water hose
36. Water hose A
37. Water outlet fitting
38. Water outlet fitting gasket
39. Water inlet fitting
40. Thermostat
41. Thermostat housing
42. Thermostat housing gasket

MT1059100002030X

Fig. 12 Intake manifold replacement (Part 3 of 3). DOHC engine

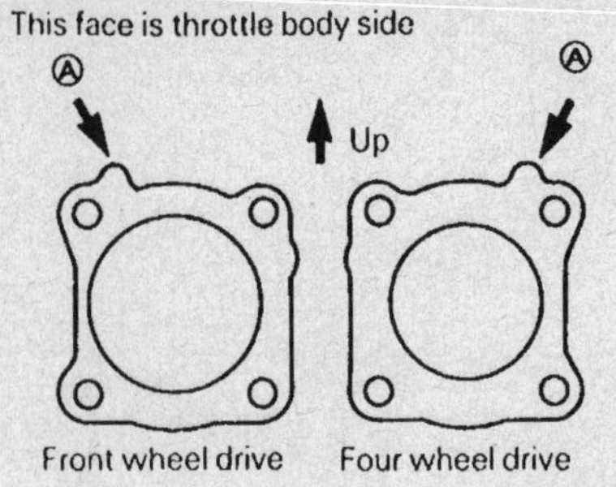
This face is throttle body side
Up
Front wheel drive
Four wheel drive

MT1069100318000X

Fig. 13 Throttle body gaskets

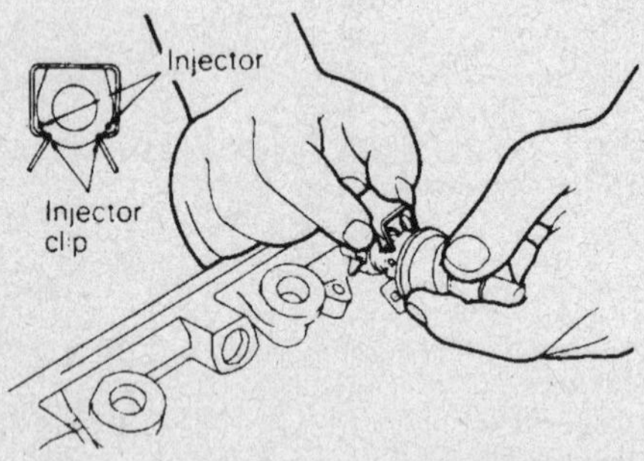
Injector
Injector clip

MT1069100319000X

Fig. 14 Injector retaining clip installation

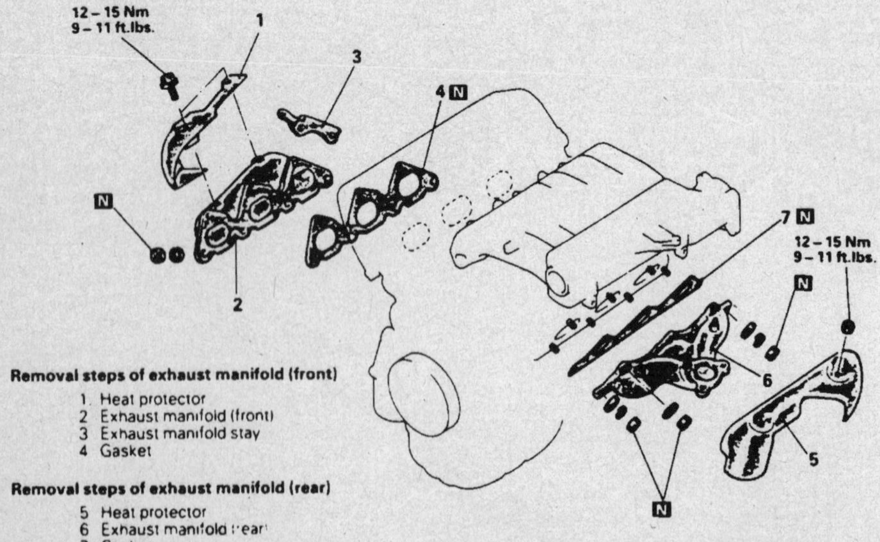
12 – 15 Nm
9 – 11 ft.lbs.
Removal steps of exhaust manifold (front)
1 Heat protector
2 Exhaust manifold (front)
3 Exhaust manifold stay
4 Gasket
Removal steps of exhaust manifold (rear)
5 Heat protector
6 Exhaust manifold (rear)
7 Gasket

MT1079100005000X

Fig. 15 Exhaust manifold replacement. 1993 California SOHC engine & 1993–94 Federal SOHC engine

SOHC

Removal

1. Disconnect battery ground cable.
2. Release fuel system pressure as outlined under "Precautions."
3. Remove engine lower cover.
4. Raise and support engine ensuring weight is lifted off mounts.
5. Rotate engine to position No. 1 cylinder at top dead center (TDC) on compression stroke to align timing marks, **Fig. 29.**
6. Remove timing belt in numbered sequence shown in **Fig. 30,** noting the following:
   a. Remove power steering pump and position aside, leaving hoses attached.
   b. Remove engine support bracket in reverse numbered sequence shown in **Fig. 31,** spraying lubricant on reamer bolt while slowly removing.
   c. Secure camshaft pulley using end yoke holder tools No. MB990767-01 and MD998719, or equivalent, when removing crankshaft pulley bolt.
   d. Mark rotational direction of engine on timing belt.
   e. Loosen timing belt tensioner bolt, then turn tensioner counterclockwise to release tension from belt and tighten in released position.

Installation

Reverse numbered sequence shown in **Fig. 30** to install, noting the following:

1. Align timing marks, **Fig. 29.**
2. Install timing belt as follows, keeping belt tight between each sprocket:
   a. Install timing belt on crankshaft sprocket.

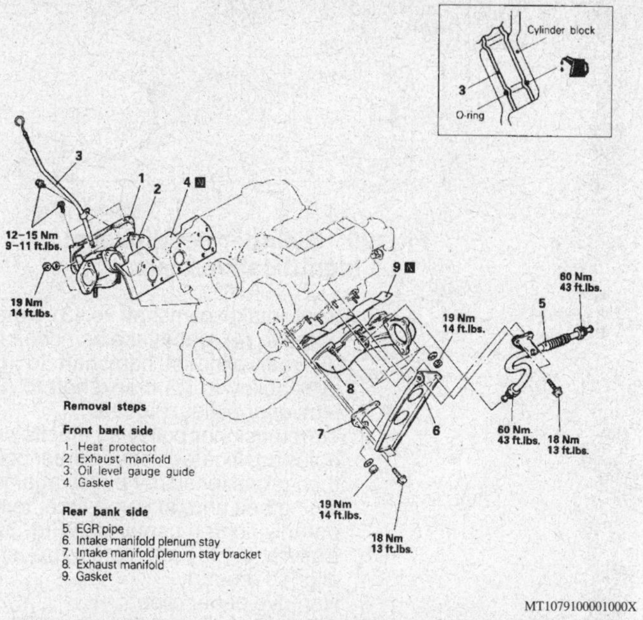
Cylinder block
O-ring
12–15 Nm
9–11 ft.lbs.
19 Nm
14 ft.lbs.
60 Nm
43 ft.lbs.
18 Nm
13 ft.lbs.
Removal steps
Front bank side
1. Heat protector
2. Exhaust manifold
3. Oil level gauge guide
4. Gasket
Rear bank side
5. EGR pipe
6. Intake manifold plenum stay
7. Intake manifold plenum stay bracket
8. Exhaust manifold
9. Gasket
MT1079100001000X

Fig. 16 Exhaust manifold replacement. 1994–96 California SOHC engine & 1995–96 Federal SOHC engine

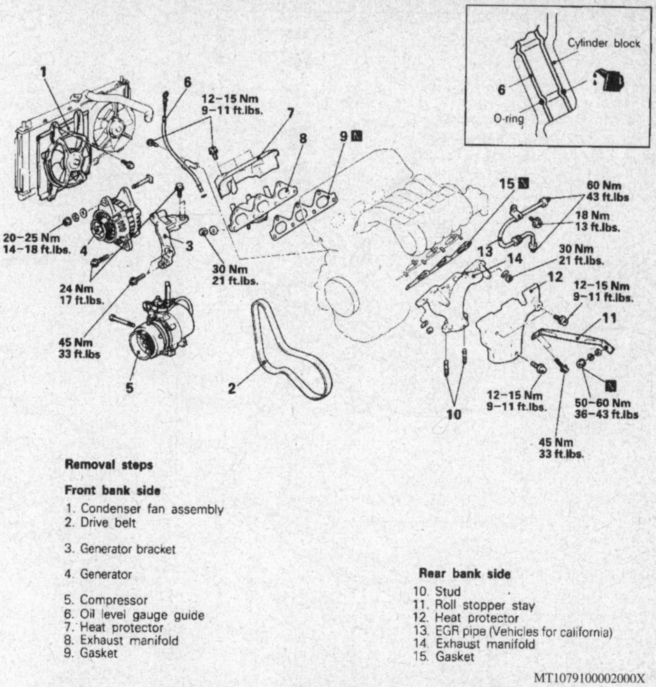
Cylinder block
O-ring
12–15 Nm
9–11 ft.lbs.
20–25 Nm
14–18 ft.lbs.
24 Nm
17 ft.lbs.
30 Nm
21 ft.lbs.
45 Nm
33 ft.lbs
60 Nm
43 ft.lbs
18 Nm
13 ft.lbs.
50–60 Nm
36–43 ft.lbs
Removal steps
Front bank side
1. Condenser fan assembly
2. Drive belt
3. Generator bracket
4. Generator
5. Compressor
6. Oil level gauge guide
7. Heat protector
8. Exhaust manifold
9. Gasket
Rear bank side
10. Stud
11. Roll stopper stay
12. Heat protector
13. EGR pipe (Vehicles for california)
14. Exhaust manifold
15. Gasket
MT1079100002000X

Fig. 17 Exhaust manifold replacement. 1993 California DOHC engine & 1993–94 Federal DOHC engine

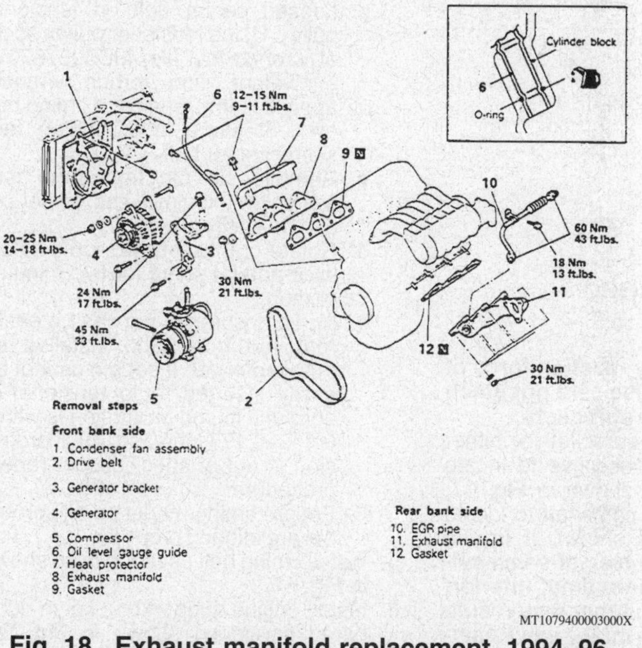
Cylinder block
O-ring
12–15 Nm
9–11 ft.lbs.
20–25 Nm
14–18 ft.lbs.
24 Nm
17 ft.lbs.
30 Nm
21 ft.lbs.
45 Nm
33 ft.lbs.
60 Nm
43 ft.lbs.
18 Nm
13 ft.lbs.
Removal steps
Front bank side
1. Condenser fan assembly
2. Drive belt
3. Generator bracket
4. Generator
5. Compressor
6. Oil level gauge guide
7. Heat protector
8. Exhaust manifold
9. Gasket
Rear bank side
10. EGR pipe
11. Exhaust manifold
12. Gasket
MT1079400003000X

Fig. 18 Exhaust manifold replacement. 1994–96 California DOHC engine & 1995–96 Federal DOHC engine

   b. Route belt over lefthand camshaft sprocket.
   c. Route belt onto water pump sprocket.
   d. Route belt over righthand camshaft sprocket.
   e. Route belt over tensioner pulley.
3. Adjust timing belt as follows:
   a. Install crankshaft flange.
   b. Loosen tensioner retainer bolt and allow tensioner spring tension to tighten timing belt.
   c. Turn crankshaft smoothly two turns clockwise.
   d. Realign timing marks. **Do not turn crankshaft counterclockwise as damage to valve components or pistons may occur.**
   e. Tighten tensioner retainer bolts.
   f. Measure timing belt tension using a suitable belt tension gauge. Belt tension should be 44.1–66.1 lbs.
4. Install timing belt cover bolts as shown in **Fig. 32.**
5. Tighten crankshaft pulley using end yoke holder tools No. MD990767-01 and MD998719, or equivalents.
6. Install engine support bracket in numbered sequence shown in **Fig. 31.** Note bolt size when installing.
7. Install engine mount bracket stopper as shown in **Fig. 3.**

DOHC

Removal

1. Disconnect battery ground cable.
2. Release fuel system pressure as outlined under "Precautions."
3. Remove engine undercover.
4. Remove alternator as outlined under "Alternator, Replace" in "Electrical."
5. Raise and support engine ensuring weight is lifted off mounts.
6. Rotate engine to position No. 1 cylinder at top dead center on compression stroke to align (TDC) timing marks, **Fig. 33.**
7. Remove timing belt in numbered sequence shown in **Fig. 34,** noting the following:
   a. Secure camshaft pulley using end yoke holder tools No. MB990767-01 and MD998719, or equivalents, then remove crankshaft pulley bolt.
   b. Remove engine support bracket in reverse numbered sequence shown in **Fig. 31,** spraying lubricant on reamer bolt while slowly removing.
   c. Mark rotational direction of engine on timing belt.
   d. Loosen timing belt tensioner pulley center bolt, then remove timing belt.

Installation

Reverse numbered sequence shown in **Fig. 34** to install, noting the following:

1. Align timing marks, **Fig. 33.**

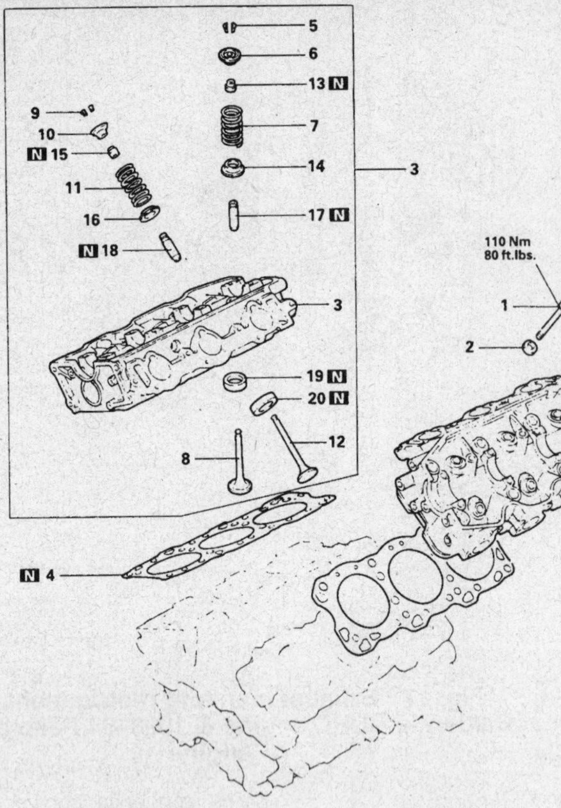
5
6
13 N
9
10
N 15
7
14
3
11
16
17 N
N 18
110 Nm
80 ft.lbs.
1
2
19 N
20 N
12
8
N 4

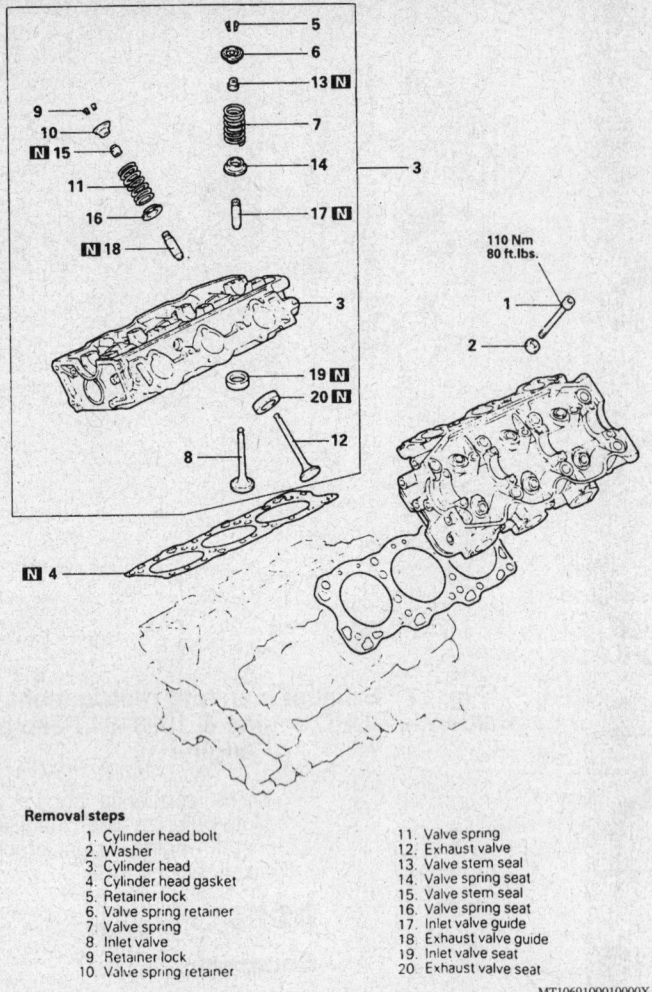

Removal steps

1. Cylinder head bolt
2. Washer
3. Cylinder head
4. Cylinder head gasket
5. Retainer lock
6. Valve spring retainer
7. Valve spring
8. Inlet valve
9. Retainer lock
10. Valve spring retainer
11. Valve spring
12. Exhaust valve
13. Valve stem seal
14. Valve spring seat
15. Valve stem seal
16. Valve spring seat
17. Inlet valve guide
18. Exhaust valve guide
19. Inlet valve seat
20. Exhaust valve seat

MT1069100010000X

Fig. 19 Cylinder head & valve replacement. SOHC engine

2. Install auto tensioner as follows:
   a. Clamp auto tensioner level and clamp in a soft jawed vise, **Fig. 35.**
   b. Close vise slowly until set hole in rod (A) is aligned with hole in cylinder (B).
   c. Insert a 0.055 inch diameter wire into set holes.
   d. Unclamp tensioner and install onto engine.
3. With timing marks aligned, install timing belt as follows keeping belt tight between each sprocket:
   a. Shift timing mark on crankshaft sprocket by three teeth to lower position on No. 1 cylinder slightly from TDC position on compression stroke. **Turning camshaft sprocket with piston in No. 1 cylinder at TDC may cause valves to interfere with piston.**
   b. Ensure timing marks on camshaft sprockets for intake and exhaust valves are not within range A in **Fig. 36.** If timing mark is within range A, turn camshaft sprocket to move timing mark to area closest to range A. **In range A, cam lobe on camshaft lifts valve through rocker arm and camshaft sprocket is apt to rotate by reaction force of valve spring. Use care not pinch finger between sprockets.**
   c. Turn camshaft sprocket for either intake or exhaust valve to locate timing mark as shown in **Fig. 37,** then turn other camshaft to locate timing mark as shown. **If intake and exhaust valves of same cylinder lift at same time, interference with each other may result. Therefore, turn intake valve camshaft sprocket and exhaust valve camshaft alternately.**
   d. Turn camshaft sprocket clockwise to align timing marks. If camshaft sprocket has been turned excessively, turn it counterclockwise to align timing marks.
   e. Align timing mark of crankshaft sprocket. **Shift timing mark of crankshaft sprocket one tooth in counterclockwise direction to aid in belt installation.**
   f. Using spring loaded paper clips, secure camshaft sprockets with suitable box end wrenches, then install timing belt in following order, ensuring not to allow belt to slack: (1) Front exhaust camshaft to (2)

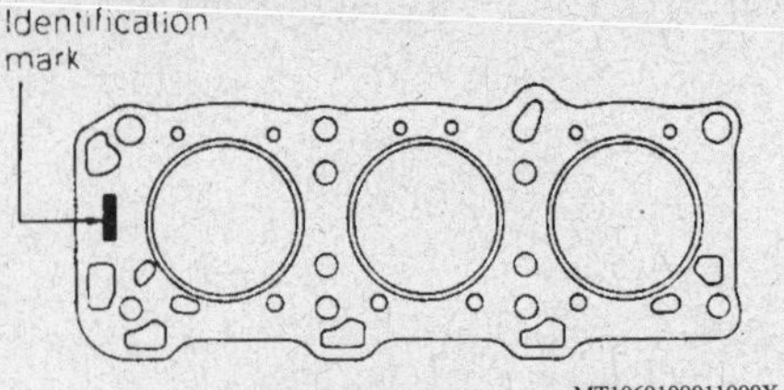
Identification
mark

MT1069100011000X

Fig. 20 Cylinder head gasket identification mark

front intake camshaft to (3) water pump to (4) rear intake camshaft to (5) rear exhaust camshaft to (6) idler pulley to (7) crankshaft to (8) tensioner pulley, **Fig. 38.**
   g. Turn tensioner pulley so that its pin holes are located above center bolt, then press tensioner pulley against timing belt and, at same time, temporarily tighten center bolt **Fig. 39.**
   h. Ensure all timing marks are still aligned properly.
   i. Remove paper clips.
4. Adjust timing belt as follows:
   a. Rotate crankshaft ¼ turn counterclockwise, then rotate crankshaft clockwise until timing marks are aligned.
   b. Loosen center bolt on tensioner pulley. Using tensioner pulley socket wrench tool No. MD998767, or equivalent, and torque wrench, apply 7 ft. lbs. tension to timing belt and, at same time, tighten tensioner center bolt.
   c. Remove set pin from auto tensioner. At this time, ensure set pin can be easily removed.
   d. Rotate crankshaft two turns clockwise and let stand for five minutes or more.
   e. Again ensure set pin can be easily removed from, and installed to, auto tensioner. If set pin cannot be easily inserted, auto tensioner is normal if its rod protrusion is within 0.149–0.177 inch, **Fig. 40.** If protrusion is out of specification, repeat procedure.
   f. Ensure timing marks on all sprockets are aligned properly.
5. Install timing belt cover bolts as shown in **Fig. 41.**
6. Install engine support bracket in numbered sequence shown in **Fig. 31.** Note bolt size when installing.
7. Tighten crankshaft pulley using end yoke holder tools No. MD990767-01 and MD998719, or equivalents.
8. Install engine mount bracket stopper as shown in **Fig. 3.**

CAMSHAFT

REPLACE

1. Disconnect battery ground cable.
2. Release fuel system pressure as outlined under "Precautions."
3. Remove timing belt as outlined under "Timing Belt, Replace."
4. **On SOHC engines,** remove camshaft

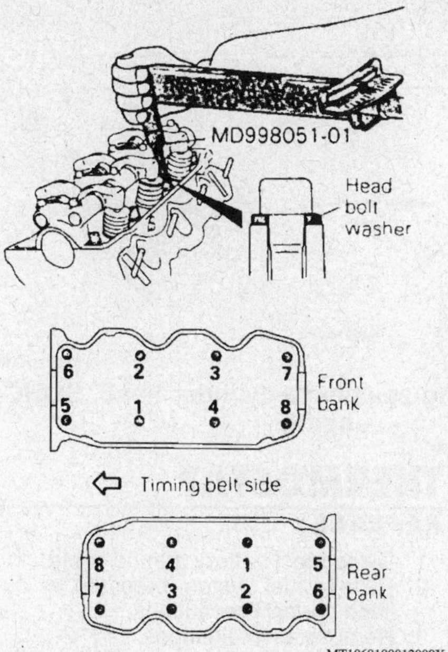
MD998051-01
Head bolt washer
6 2 3 7
5 1 4 8
Front bank
Timing belt side
8 4 1 5
7 3 2 6
Rear bank

MT1069100012000X

Fig. 21 Cylinder head bolt tightening sequence

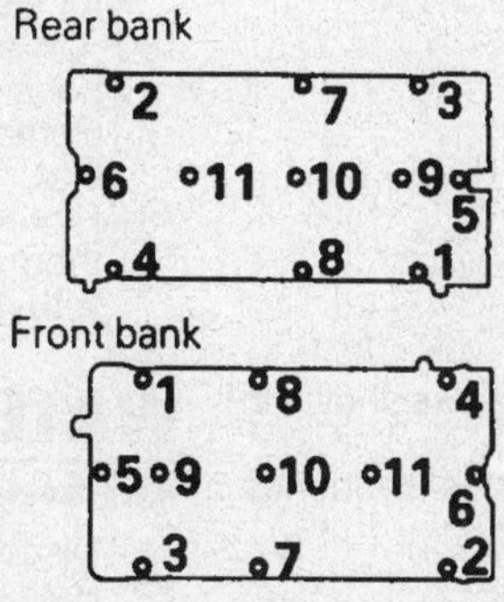
Rear bank
2 7 3
6 11 10 9 5
4 8 1
Front bank
1 8 4
5 9 10 11 6
3 7 2

MT1069100014000X

Fig. 23 Valve cover bolt tightening sequence

sprocket bolt using end yoke holder tool No. MB990767 and MD998719, or equivalents.

5. **On DOHC engines,** remove rocker covers. Remove camshaft sprocket bolts by securing camshaft with a suitable wrench as shown, **Fig. 42.**
6. **On all models,** cut out a portion in camshaft oil seal lip, **Fig. 43.**
7. Cover tip of a suitable screwdriver with a clean soft cloth and pry out seal at cut out portion of seal. **Use care not to damage camshaft or cylinder head.**
8. Lift camshaft from engine.
9. Reverse procedure to install, noting the following:
   a. Install oil seals using seal installation tool, No. MD998713-01, or equivalent, on SOHC engines or tool No. MD998761, or equivalent, on DOHC engines.
   b. **On DOHC engines,** tighten rocker cover bolts in sequence shown in **Fig. 23.** Install black colored bolts on engine front bank and green colored bolts on rear bank. Bolt No. 5 is longer than other bolts used.

PISTON & ROD ASSEMBLY

1. Disconnect battery ground cable.
2. Release fuel system pressure as outlined under "Precautions."
3. Drain engine coolant into an approved container.
4. Remove engine assembly as outlined under "Engine, Replace."
5. Remove timing belt as outlined under "Timing Belt, Replace."
6. Remove exhaust manifolds as outlined under "Exhaust Manifold, Replace."
7. Remove air plenum and intake manifold as outlined under "Air Plenum & Intake Manifold, Replace."
8. Remove cylinder head as outlined under "Cylinder Head, Replace."
9. Remove engine oil pan.
10. Replace piston and connecting rod in numbered sequence shown in **Fig. 44.**
11. Reverse procedure to install.

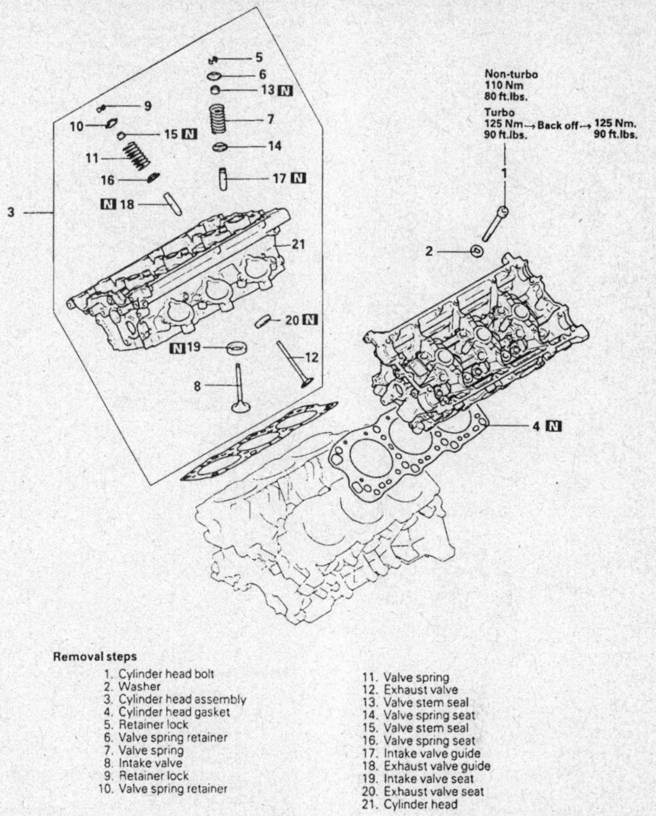
Non-turbo
110 Nm
80 ft.lbs.
Turbo
125 Nm → Back off → 125 Nm.
90 ft.lbs. 90 ft.lbs.
Removal steps
1. Cylinder head bolt
2. Washer
3. Cylinder head assembly
4. Cylinder head gasket
5. Retainer lock
6. Valve spring retainer
7. Valve spring
8. Intake valve
9. Retainer lock
10. Valve spring retainer
11. Valve spring
12. Exhaust valve
13. Valve stem seal
14. Valve spring seat
15. Valve stem seal
16. Valve spring seat
17. Intake valve guide
18. Exhaust valve guide
19. Intake valve seat
20. Exhaust valve seat
21. Cylinder head

MT1069100013000X

Fig. 22 Cylinder head & valve replacement. DOHC engine

CRANKSHAFT SEAL

REPLACE

FRONT

1. Disconnect battery ground cable.
2. Release fuel system pressure as outlined under "Precautions."
3. Remove timing belt as outlined under "Timing Belt, Replace."
4. Remove crankshaft sprocket.
5. Cut out a portion in camshaft oil seal lip, **Fig. 43.**
6. Cover tip of a suitable screwdriver with a clean soft cloth and pry out seal at cut out portion of seal. **Use care not to damage camshaft or cylinder head.**
7. Reverse procedure to install, using seal installer tool No. MD998717, or equivalent, to install oil seal.

REAR

1. Disconnect battery ground cable.
2. Release fuel system pressure as outlined under "Precautions."
3. Remove transaxle as outlined under "Automatic Transaxle" section.
4. Secure crankshaft using end yoke holder tool No. MD998719, or equivalent, on SOHC engines or No. MD998754, or equivalent, on DOHC engines.
5. Remove adapter and driveplates.

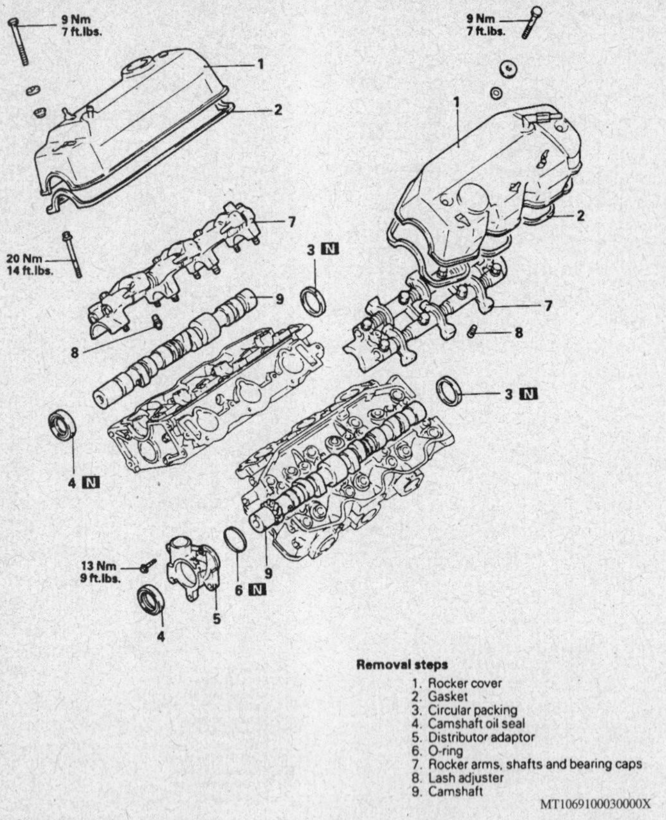
9 Nm
7 ft.lbs.
9 Nm
7 ft.lbs.
20 Nm
14 ft.lbs.
13 Nm
9 ft.lbs.
Removal steps
1. Rocker cover
2. Gasket
3. Circular packing
4. Camshaft oil seal
5. Distributor adaptor
6. O-ring
7. Rocker arms, shafts and bearing caps
8. Lash adjuster
9. Camshaft
MT1069100030000X

Fig. 24 Camshaft & rocker arm replacement. SOHC engine

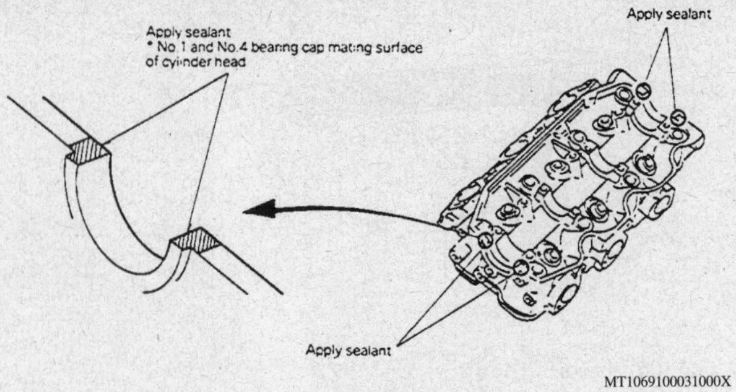
Apply sealant
* No.1 and No.4 bearing cap mating surface of cylinder head
Apply sealant
Apply sealant
MT1069100031000X

Fig. 25 Applying sealant to cylinder head. SOHC engine

6. Cut out a portion in camshaft oil seal lip, **Fig. 43.**
7. Cover tip of a suitable screwdriver with a clean soft cloth and pry out seal at cut out portion of seal. **Use care not to damage camshaft or cylinder head.**
8. Reverse procedure to install, using seal installer tool No. MD998718-01, or equivalent, to install rear main oil seal.

OIL PAN

REPLACE

1. Disconnect battery ground cable.
2. Release fuel system pressure as outlined under "Precautions."
3. Remove engine assembly as outlined under "Engine, Replace."
4. Remove timing belt as outlined under "Timing Belt, Replace."
5. Remove front exhaust pipe.
6. Drain engine oil into a suitable container.
7. Remove engine undercover.
8. Remove oil pan in numbered sequence shown in **Fig. 45.**
9. Reverse procedure to install, noting the following:
   a. Check oil pump components for cracks and wear.
   b. Install rotor on oil pump and ensure clearance is 0.0039–0.0071 inch for body clearance and 0.0016–0.0037 inch for side clearance, **Fig. 46.**
   c. Ensure oil cooler valve moves smoothly.
   d. Apply sealant to oil pan as shown in **Fig. 47.**
   e. Tighten oil pan bolts in sequence shown in **Fig. 48.**

OIL PUMP

REPLACE

Refer to "Oil Pan, Replace" for oil pump replacement procedure.

BELT TENSION DATA

Belt	Deflection At 22 Lbs. New, Inch	Deflection At 22 Lbs. Used, Inch
SOHC ENGINE		
Alternator/Power Steering	.157–.197	.236–.315
A/C	.256–.275	.275–.335
DOHC ENGINE		
Alt. & A/C	.138–.157	.157–.196
Power Steering	.300–.350	.410–.490

COOLING SYSTEM BLEED

These engines do not require a specified bleed procedure. After filling cooling system, run engine to operating temperature with radiator/pressure cap off. Air will then be automatically bled through cap opening.

THERMOSTAT

REPLACE

1. Disconnect battery ground cable.
2. Relieve fuel system pressure as outlined under "Precautions."
3. Remove air intake hose.
4. **On SOHC engines,** disconnect radiator upper hose.
5. **On DOHC engines,** disconnect radiator lower hose.
6. **On all engines,** remove water outlet housing.
7. Remove housing gasket and thermostat.
8. Reverse procedure to install. Position thermostat with jiggle valve lined up with mark on housing, **Fig. 49.**

WATER PUMP

REPLACE

1. Disconnect battery ground cable.
2. Release fuel system pressure as outlined under "Precautions."
3. Remove timing belt as outlined under "Timing Belt, Replace."
4. Drain engine coolant into a suitable container.
5. Replace engine water pump in numbered sequence shown in **Figs. 50 and 51,** noting the following during installation:
   a. Coat inlet pipe O-ring with water to ease installation.
   b. **On DOHC engines,** install water pump bolts as shown, **Fig. 52.**

RADIATOR

REPLACE

1. Drain engine coolant, then remove drain plug and radiator cap.
2. Remove overflow hose and reserve tank, then the upper and lower radiator hoses.
3. Disconnect ATF cooler hoses from radiator, then plug and cover hoses and nipples.
4. Disconnect condenser and radiator fan motor connections, then remove upper insulator and radiator.
5. Remove condenser fan motor assembly.
6. **On 1993 models,** remove thermo sensor connector.

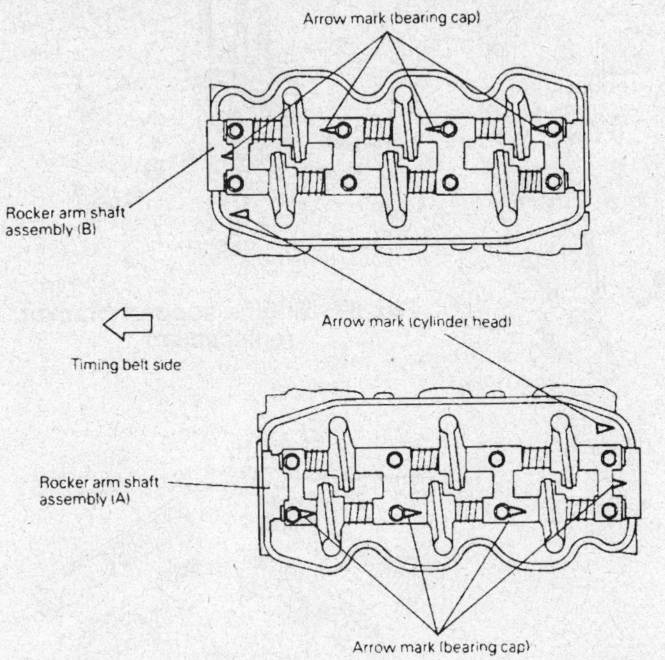
Arrow mark (bearing cap)
Rocker arm shaft assembly (B)
Arrow mark (cylinder head)
Timing belt side
Rocker arm shaft assembly (A)
Arrow mark (bearing cap)

MT1069100032000X

Fig. 26 Camshaft bearing caps installation. SOHC engine

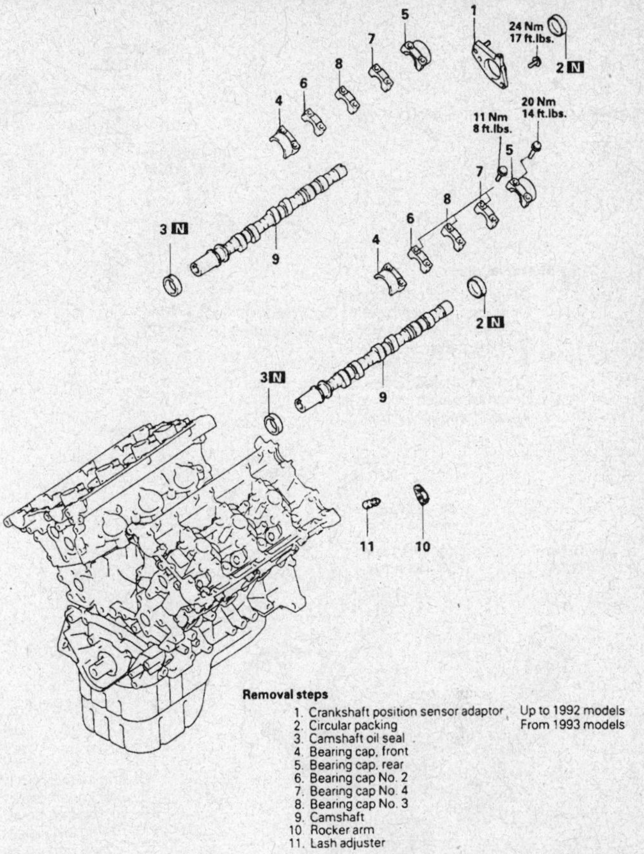
24 Nm
17 ft.lbs.
20 Nm
14 ft.lbs.
11 Nm
8 ft.lbs.
Removal steps
1. Crankshaft position sensor adaptor
2. Circular packing
3. Camshaft oil seal
4. Bearing cap, front
5. Bearing cap, rear
6. Bearing cap No. 2
7. Bearing cap No. 4
8. Bearing cap No. 3
9. Camshaft
10. Rocker arm
11. Lash adjuster
Up to 1992 models
From 1993 models

MT1069100033000X

Fig. 27 Camshaft & rocker arms replacement. DOHC engine

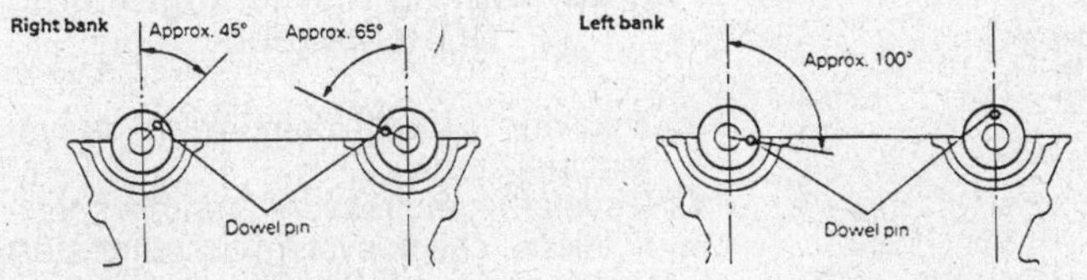
Right bank
Approx. 45°
Approx. 65°
Left bank
Approx. 100°
Dowel pin
Dowel pin

MT1069100034000X

Fig. 28 Camshaft dowel alignment. DOHC engine

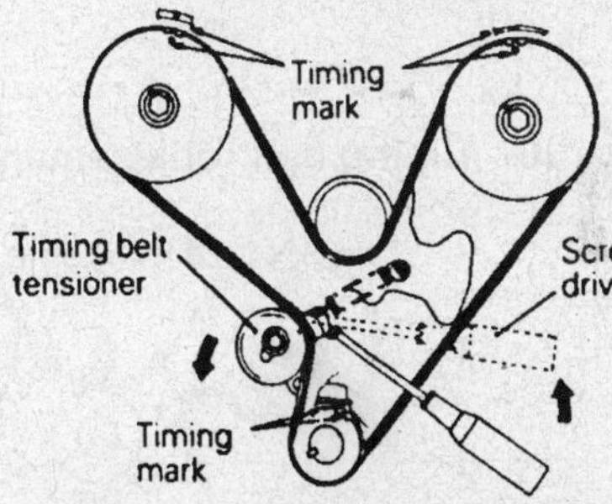
Timing mark
Timing belt tensioner
Screw-driver
Timing mark

MT1069100015000X

Fig. 29 Timing marks alignment. SOHC engine

7. **On all models,** remove radiator fan motor assembly.
8. **On 1993 models,** remove condenser and radiator fan thermo sensors.
9. **On all models,** remove lower insulator and fan, then resistor, fan motor and shroud.
10. Reverse procedure to install.

FUEL PUMP

REPLACE

Prior To Performing Any Service Operations Listed In This Section, Consult "Technical Service Bulletins" Section For Related Information.

1. Disconnect battery ground cable.
2. Relieve fuel system pressure as outlined under "Precautions."
3. Drain fuel into an approved container.
4. Remove fuel pump in numbered sequence shown in **Fig. 53,** noting the following:
   a. Remove rear wheel steering cylinder attachment bolts and lower cylinder to provide working space.
   b. Remove center exhaust pipe and suspend to frame using wire.
5. Reverse procedure to install.

FUEL FILTER

REPLACE

Prior To Performing Any Service Operations Listed In This Section, Consult "Technical Service Bulletins" Section For Related Information.

1. Disconnect battery ground cable.
2. Relieve fuel system pressure as outlined under "Precautions."
3. Drain fuel into an approved container.
4. Remove air intake hose.
5. Holding fuel filter with spanner, remove high pressure fuel hose and eye bolt. **Fuel pipe line has some residual pressure, cover with a rag to prevent spraying.**
6. Loosen flare nut to release connection with fuel main pipe, then remove fuel filter, **Fig. 54.**
7. Reverse procedure to install, **Fig. 55.**

TECHNICAL SERVICE BULLETINS

FUEL STARVATION

Fuel starvation can occur when in-tank fuel filter is clogged, typically by contaminated fuel.

To correct problem, proceed as follows:

1. Activate fuel pump with scan tool, then measure pump's supply voltage.
2. If voltage is less than 8 volts, inspect and repair fuel pump wiring harness.

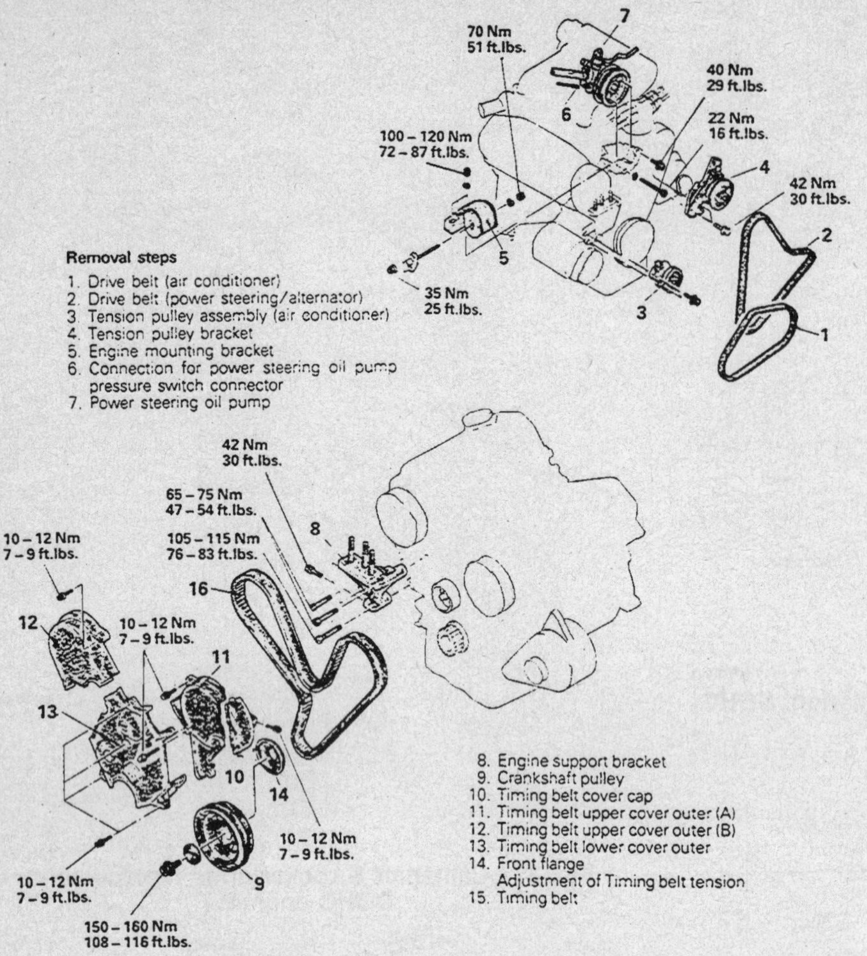
70 Nm
51 ft.lbs.
40 Nm
29 ft.lbs.
22 Nm
16 ft.lbs.
100 – 120 Nm
72 – 87 ft.lbs.
42 Nm
30 ft.lbs.
35 Nm
25 ft.lbs.
Removal steps
1. Drive belt (air conditioner)
2. Drive belt (power steering/alternator)
3. Tension pulley assembly (air conditioner)
4. Tension pulley bracket
5. Engine mounting bracket
6. Connection for power steering oil pump pressure switch connector
7. Power steering oil pump
42 Nm
30 ft.lbs.
65 – 75 Nm
47 – 54 ft.lbs.
10 – 12 Nm
7 – 9 ft.lbs.
105 – 115 Nm
76 – 83 ft.lbs.
10 – 12 Nm
7 – 9 ft.lbs.
10 – 12 Nm
7 – 9 ft.lbs.
10 – 12 Nm
7 – 9 ft.lbs.
150 – 160 Nm
108 – 116 ft.lbs.
8. Engine support bracket
9. Crankshaft pulley
10. Timing belt cover cap
11. Timing belt upper cover outer (A)
12. Timing belt upper cover outer (B)
13. Timing belt lower cover outer
14. Front flange
Adjustment of Timing belt tension
15. Timing belt
MT1069100016000X

Fig. 30 Timing belt replacement. SOHC engine

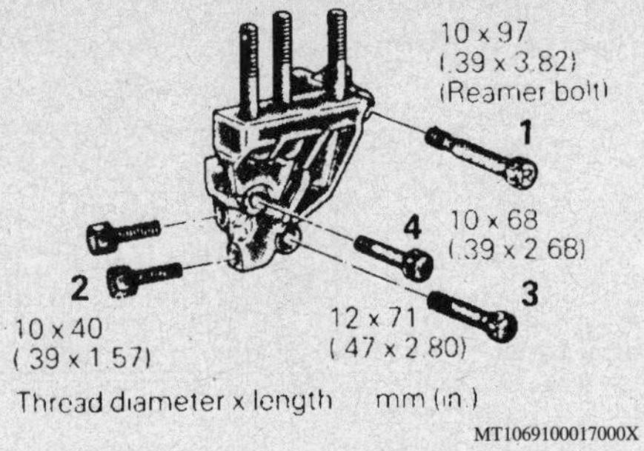
10 x 97
(.39 x 3.82)
(Reamer bolt)
10 x 68
(.39 x 2.68)
10 x 40
(.39 x 1.57)
12 x 71
(.47 x 2.80)
Thread diameter x length mm (in.)
MT1069100017000X

Fig. 31 Engine support bracket replacement

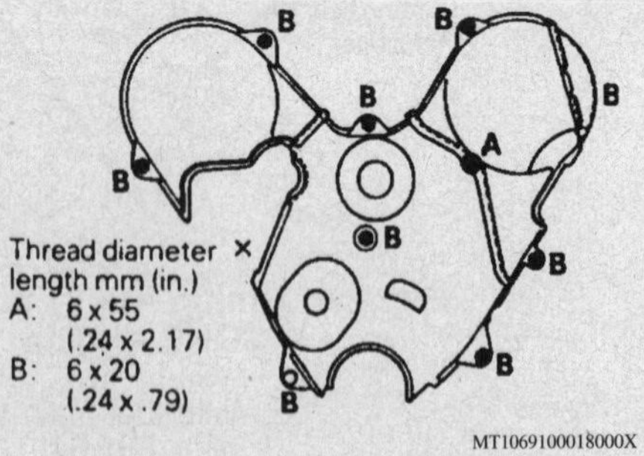
Thread diameter x
length mm (in.)
A: 6 x 55
(.24 x 2.17)
B: 6 x 20
(.24 x .79)
MT1069100018000X

Fig. 32 Timing belt cover bolt location. SOHC engine

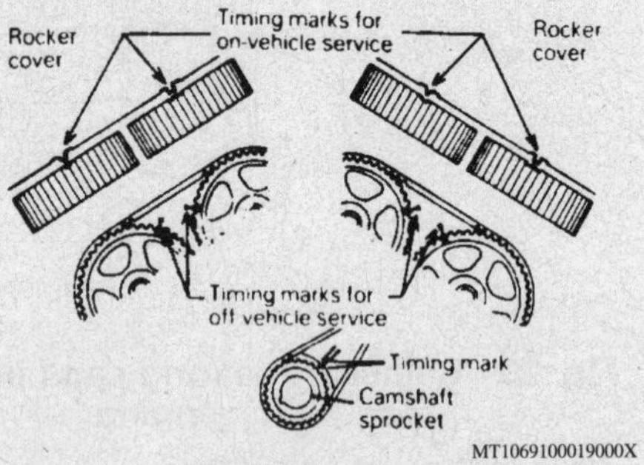
Rocker cover
Timing marks for on-vehicle service
Rocker cover
Timing marks for off vehicle service
Timing mark
Camshaft sprocket
MT1069100019000X

Fig. 33 Timing marks alignment. DOHC engine

3. If voltage is 8 volts or more, check system fuel pressure.
4. If system fuel pressure is within specifications, check system for other starvation problems. Specification is 38 psi at curb idle with fuel pressure regulator vacuum hose attached and 47–50 psi with hose disconnected.
5. If fuel system pressure is not within specifications, remove fuel pump as outlined under "Fuel Pump, Replace" and check filter.
6. If filter is clean, replace fuel pump. If filter is clogged, proceed as follows:
   a. Carefully dislodge pump motor from bracket. On some models it may be necessary to remove lower bracket clamp to dislodge motor.
   b. Remove rubber pump vibration dampener, then retaining clip (or nut) and filter.
   c. Replace filter.
   d. **If filter is severely clogged, clean inside of fuel tank.**

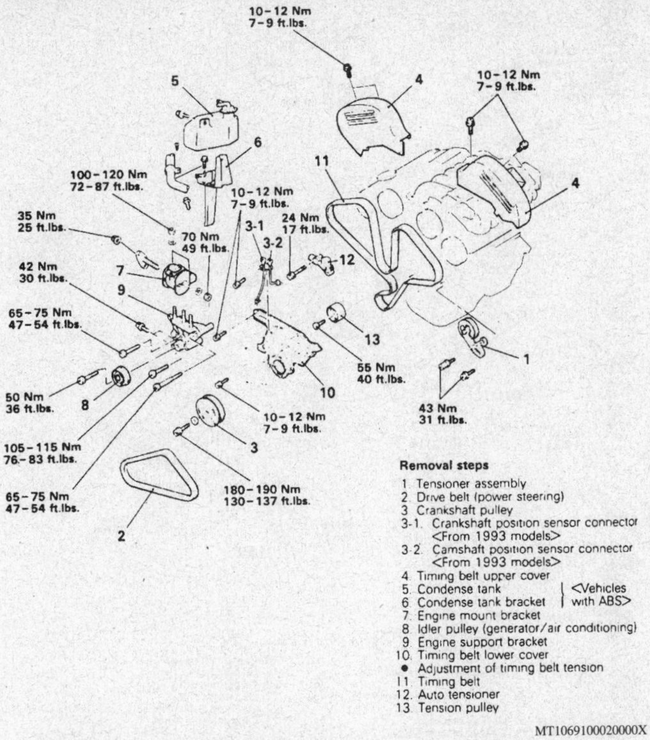

10-12 Nm
7-9 ft.lbs.
100-120 Nm
72-87 ft.lbs.
35 Nm
25 ft.lbs.
42 Nm
30 ft.lbs.
65-75 Nm
47-54 ft.lbs.
50 Nm
36 ft.lbs.
105-115 Nm
76-83 ft.lbs.
70 Nm
49 ft.lbs.
24 Nm
17 ft.lbs.
55 Nm
40 ft.lbs.
43 Nm
31 ft.lbs.
180-190 Nm
130-137 ft.lbs.
Removal steps
1. Tensioner assembly
2. Drive belt (power steering)
3. Crankshaft pulley
3-1. Crankshaft position sensor connector <From 1993 models>
3-2. Camshaft position sensor connector <From 1993 models>
4. Timing belt upper cover
5. Condense tank
6. Condense tank bracket
<Vehicles with ABS>
7. Engine mount bracket
8. Idler pulley (generator/air conditioning)
9. Engine support bracket
10. Timing belt lower cover
• Adjustment of timing belt tension
11. Timing belt
12. Auto tensioner
13. Tension pulley
MT1069100020000X

Fig. 34 Timing belt replacement. DOHC engine

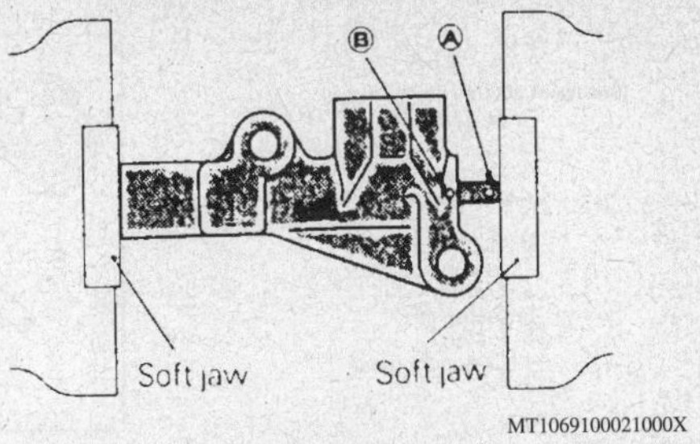

Ⓑ
Ⓐ
Soft jaw
Soft jaw
MT1069100021000X

Fig. 35 Auto tensioner set holes. DOHC engine

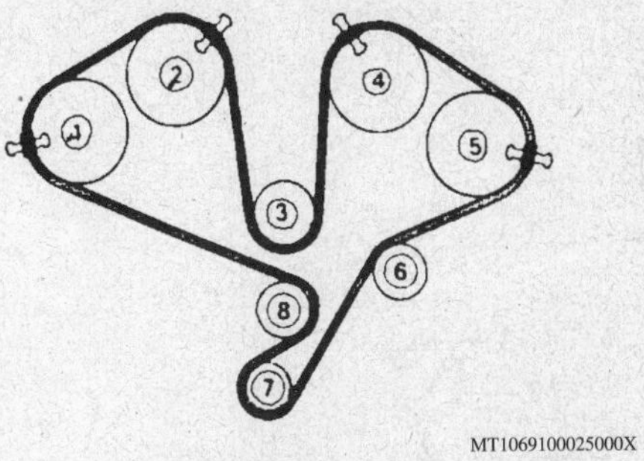

MT1069100025000X

Fig. 38 Timing belt installation. DOHC engine

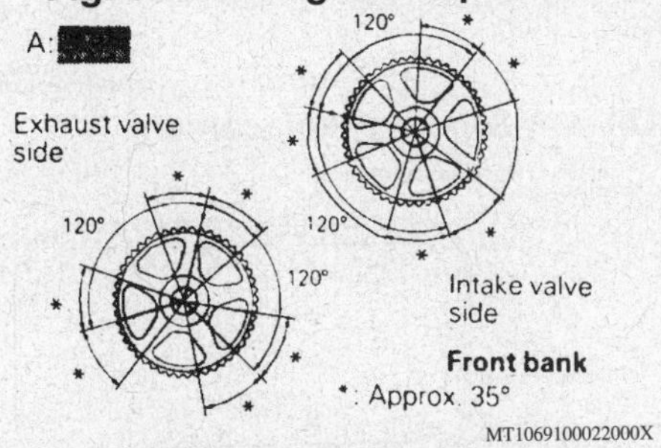

A: [redacted]
120°
Exhaust valve side
Intake valve side
Front bank
*: Approx. 35°
MT1069100022000X

Fig. 36 Camshaft alignment positions. DOHC engine

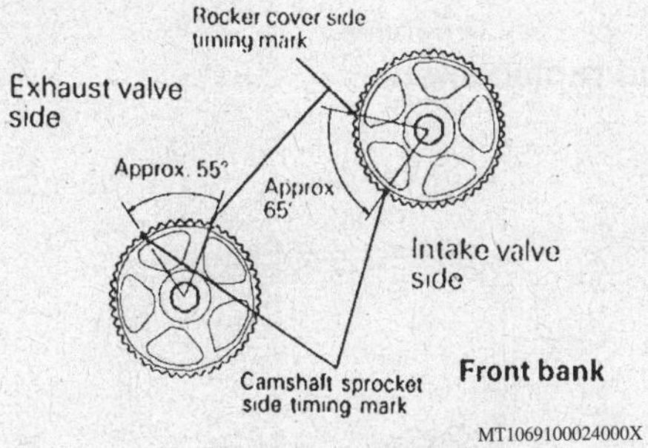

Rocker cover side timing mark
Exhaust valve side
Approx. 55°
Approx. 65°
Intake valve side
Camshaft sprocket side timing mark
Front bank
MT1069100024000X

Fig. 37 Timing mark alignment. DOHC engine

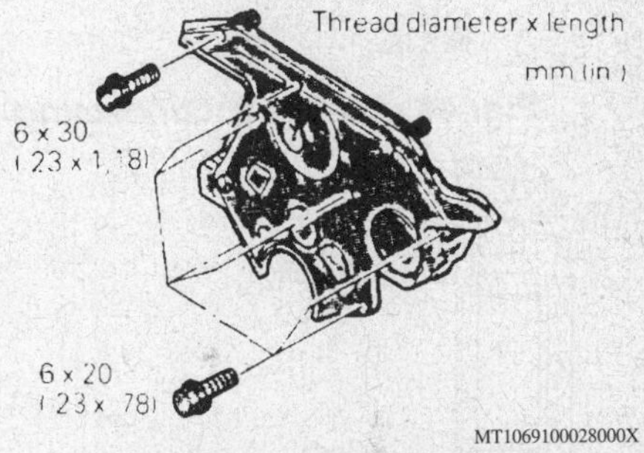

Thread diameter x length
mm (in.)
6 x 30
(.23 x 1.18)
6 x 20
(.23 x .78)
MT1069100028000X

Fig. 41 Timing belt lower cover bolt location. DOHC engine

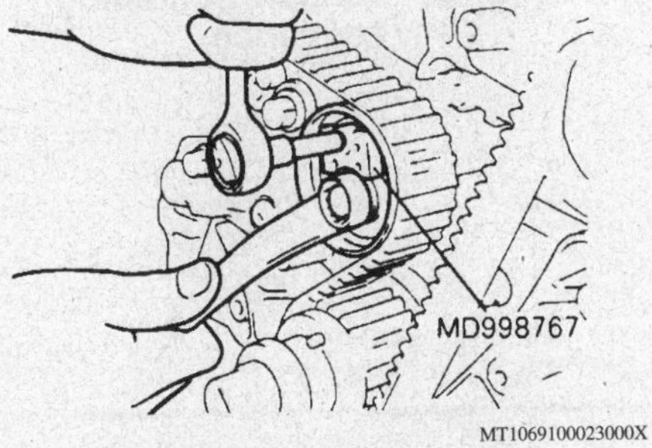

MD998767
MT1069100023000X

Fig. 39 Tensioner pulley adjustment. DOHC engine

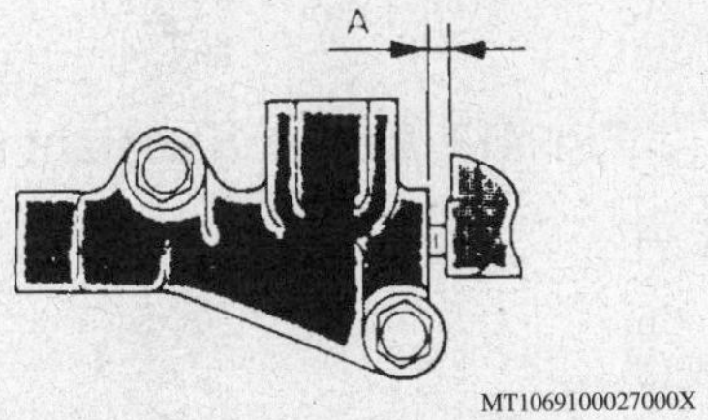

A
MT1069100027000X

Fig. 40 Auto tensioner rod protrusion. DOHC engine

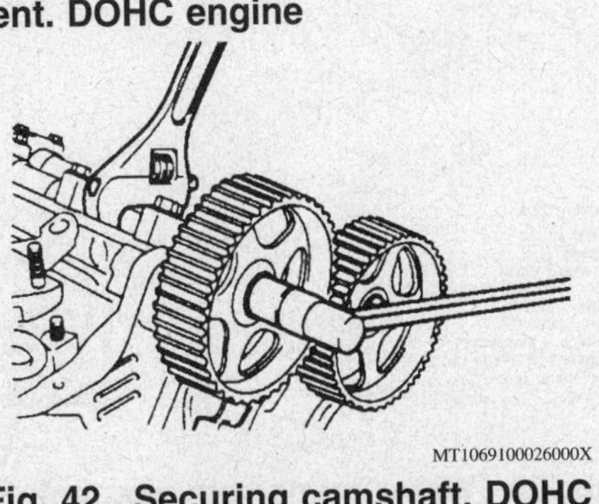

MT1069100026000X

Fig. 42 Securing camshaft. DOHC engine

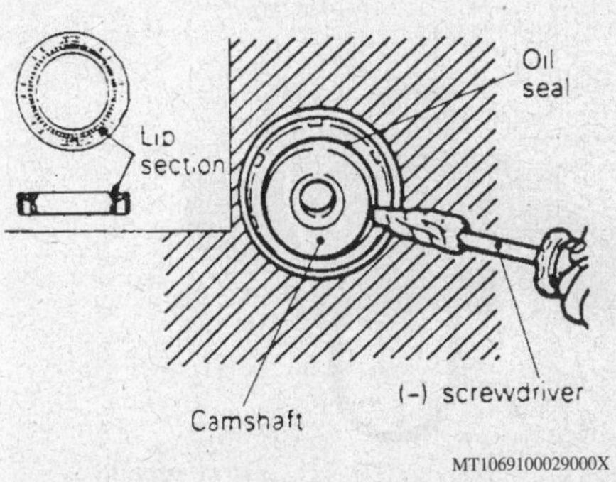

Oil seal
Lip section
Camshaft
(-) screwdriver
MT1069100029000X

Fig. 43 Oil seal removal

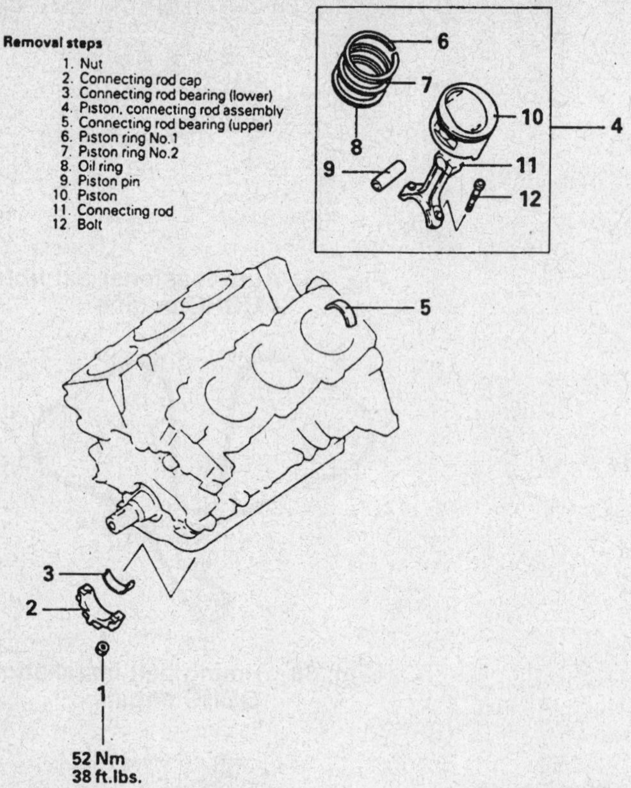

52 Nm
38 ft.lbs.

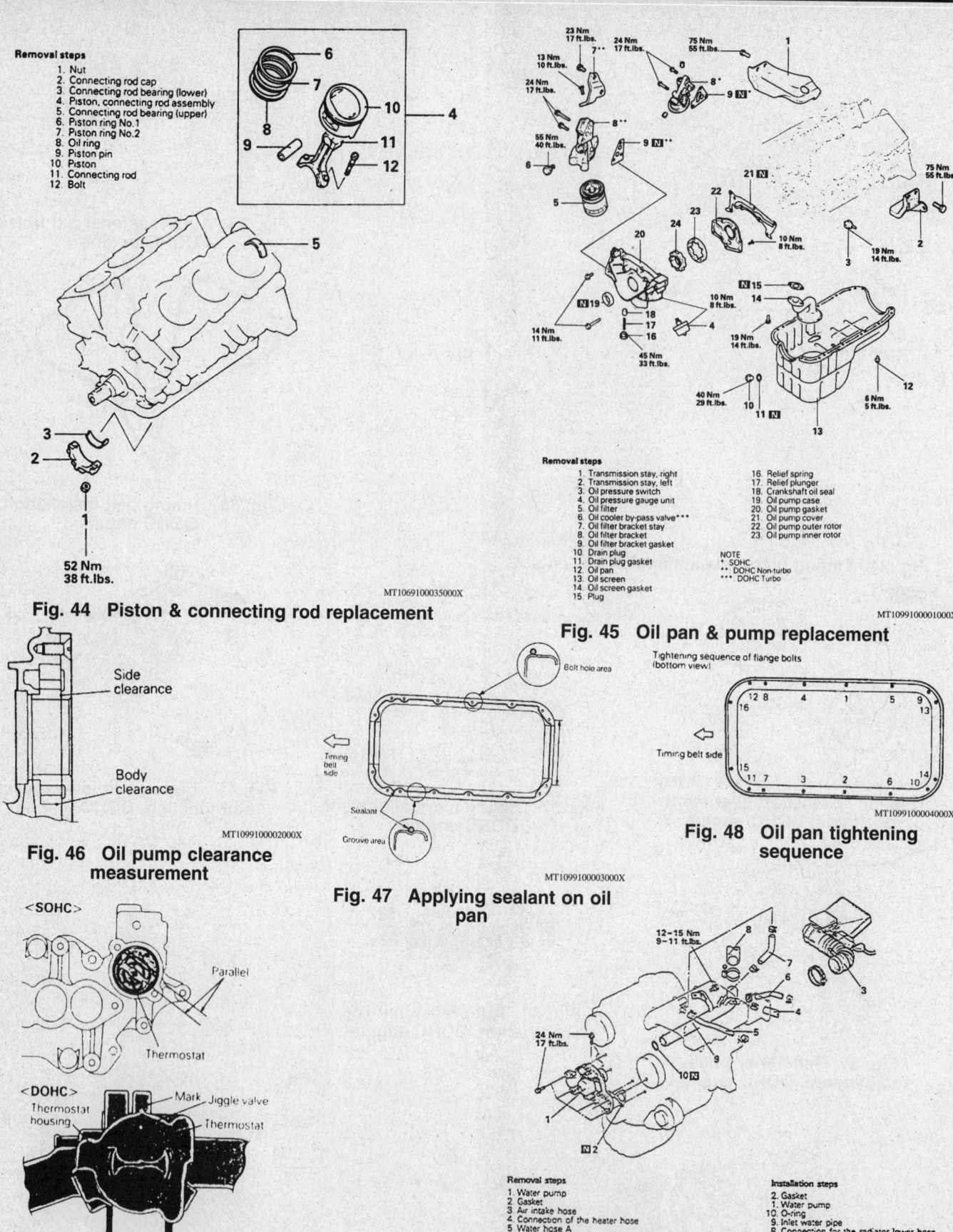

Removal steps
1. Nut
2. Connecting rod cap
3. Connecting rod bearing (lower)
4. Piston, connecting rod assembly
5. Connecting rod bearing (upper)
6. Piston ring No.1
7. Piston ring No.2
8. Oil ring
9. Piston pin
10. Piston
11. Connecting rod
12. Bolt

MT1069100035000X

Fig. 44 Piston & connecting rod replacement

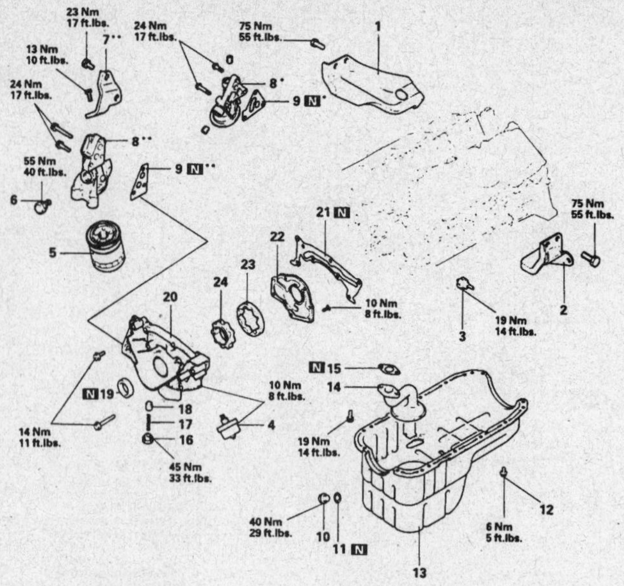

Removal steps
1. Transmission stay, right
2. Transmission stay, left
3. Oil pressure switch
4. Oil pressure gauge unit
5. Oil filter
6. Oil cooler by-pass valve***
7. Oil filter bracket stay
8. Oil filter bracket
9. Oil filter bracket gasket
10. Drain plug
11. Drain plug gasket
12. Oil pan
13. Oil screen
14. Oil screen gasket
15. Plug
16. Relief spring
17. Relief plunger
18. Crankshaft oil seal
19. Oil pump case
20. Oil pump gasket
21. Oil pump cover
22. Oil pump outer rotor
23. Oil pump inner rotor

NOTE
* : SOHC
** : DOHC Non-turbo
*** : DOHC Turbo

MT1099100001000X

Fig. 45 Oil pan & pump replacement

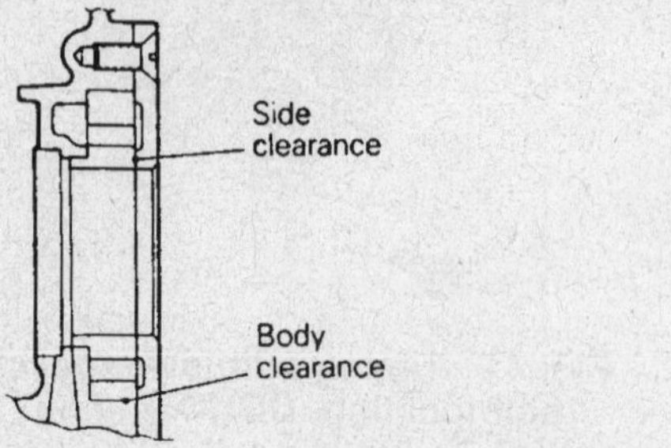

Side
clearance
Body
clearance

MT1099100002000X

Fig. 46 Oil pump clearance measurement

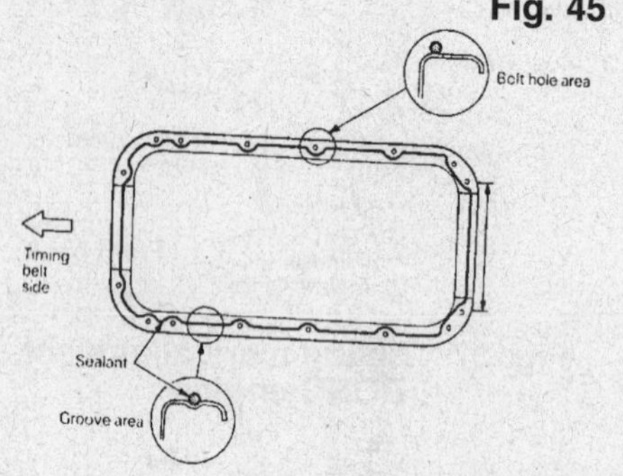

Bolt hole area
Timing
belt
side
Sealant
Groove area

MT1099100003000X

Fig. 47 Applying sealant on oil pan

Tightening sequence of flange bolts
(bottom view)

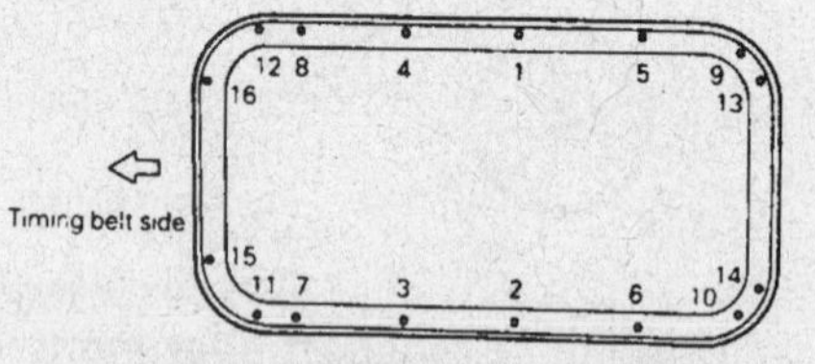

Timing belt side

MT1099100004000X

Fig. 48 Oil pan tightening sequence

<SOHC>

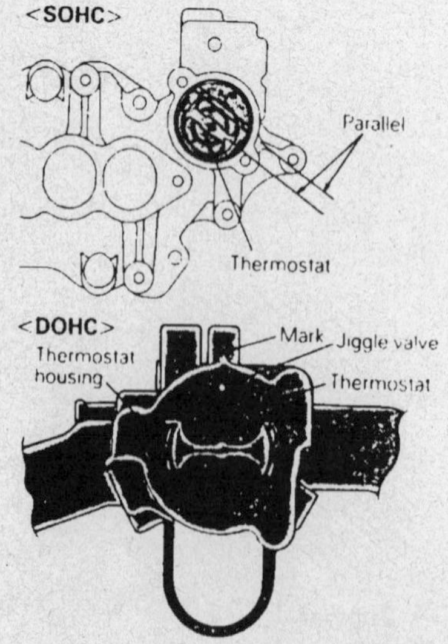

Parallel
Thermostat
<DOHC>
Mark
Jiggle valve
Thermostat
housing
Thermostat

MT1089100001000X

Fig. 49 Thermostat installation

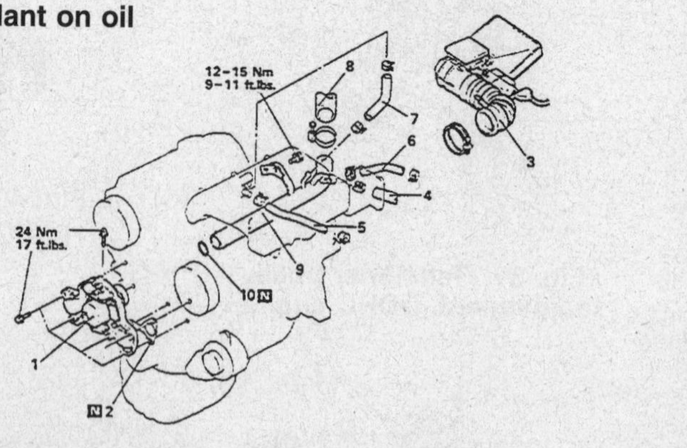

12-15 Nm
9-11 ft.lbs.
24 Nm
17 ft.lbs.

Removal steps
1. Water pump
2. Gasket
3. Air intake hose
4. Connection of the heater hose
5. Water hose A
6. Water hose B
7. By-pass water hose
8. Connection of the radiator lower hose
9. Inlet water pipe
10. O-ring

Installation steps
2. Gasket
1. Water pump
10. O-ring
9. Inlet water pipe
8. Connection for the radiator lower hose
7. By-pass water hose
6. Water hose B
5. Water hose A
4. Connection for the heater hose
3. Air intake hose

MT1089100002000X

Fig. 50 Water pump replacement. SOHC engine

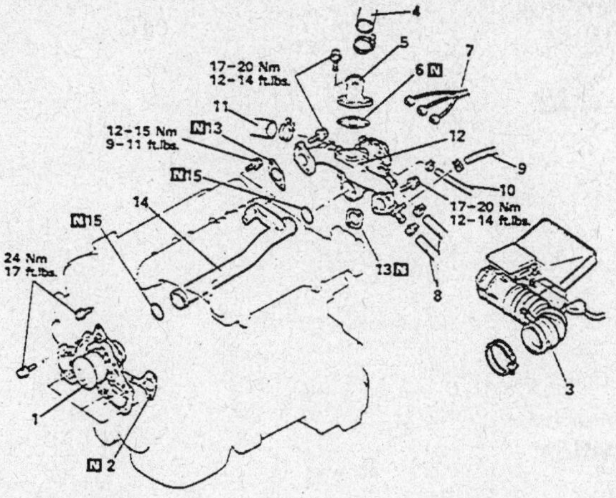
17-20 Nm
12-14 ft.lbs.
12-15 Nm
9-11 ft.lbs.
24 Nm
17 ft.lbs.
17-20 Nm
12-14 ft.lbs.

Removal steps

1. Water pump
2. Gasket
3. Air intake hose
4. Connection of radiator upper hose
5. Water outlet fitting
6. Gasket
7. Connection of harness
8. Connection of heater hose
9. Connection of water hose A
10. Connection of water hose
11. Connection of radiator lower hose
12. Thermostat housing
13. Gasket
14. Inlet water pipe
15. O-ring

Installation steps

2 Gasket
1. Water pump
15 O-ring
14. Inlet water pipe
13 Gasket
12 Thermostat housing
11. Connection of radiator lower hose
10 Connection of water hose
9 Connection of water hose A
8 Connection of heater hose
7. Connection of harness
6 Gasket
5 Water outlet fitting
4 Connection of radiator upper hose
3. Air intake hose

MT1089100003000X

Fig. 51 Water pump replacement. DOHC engine

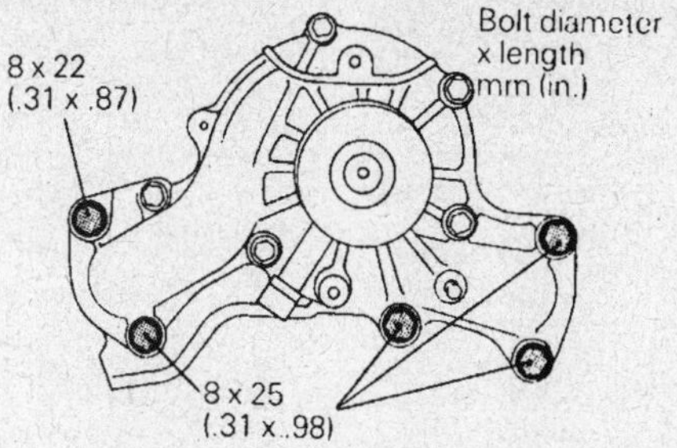
8 x 22
(.31 x .87)
Bolt diameter
x length
mm (in.)
8 x 25
(.31 x .98)

MT1089100004000X

Fig. 52 Water pump bolt locations. DOHC engine

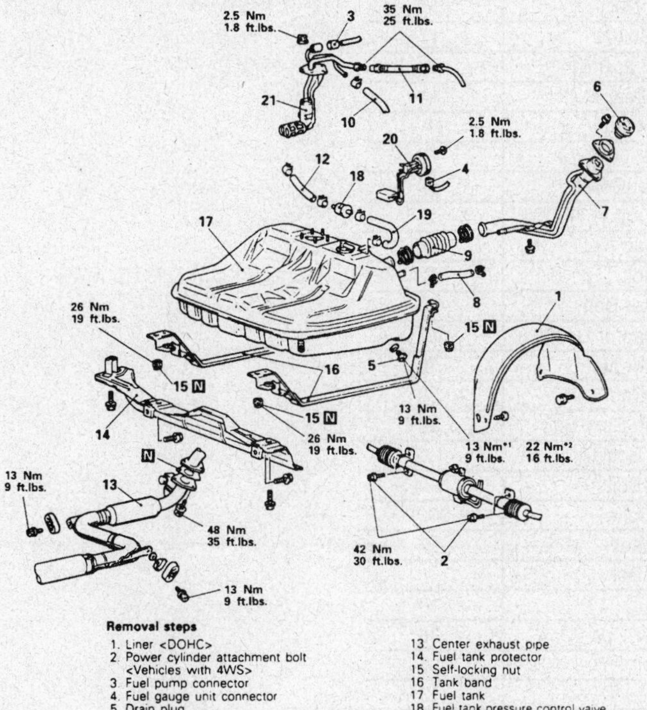
2.5 Nm
1.8 ft.lbs.
35 Nm
25 ft.lbs.
2.5 Nm
1.8 ft.lbs.
26 Nm
19 ft.lbs.
13 Nm
9 ft.lbs.
26 Nm
19 ft.lbs.
13 Nm*1
9 ft.lbs.
22 Nm*2
16 ft.lbs.
13 Nm
9 ft.lbs.
48 Nm
35 ft.lbs.
42 Nm
30 ft.lbs.
13 Nm
9 ft.lbs.

Removal steps

1. Liner <DOHC>
2. Power cylinder attachment bolt <Vehicles with 4WS>
3. Fuel pump connector
4. Fuel gauge unit connector
5. Drain plug
6. Fuel tank filler tube cap
7. Fuel tank filler tube
8. Vapor hose
9. Filler hose
10. Return hose
11. Fuel high-pressure hose
12. Vapor hose
13. Center exhaust pipe
14. Fuel tank protector
15. Self-locking nut
16. Tank band
17. Fuel tank
18. Fuel tank pressure control vaive
19. Vapor hose
20. Fuel gauge unit
21. Fuel pump unit

MT1029100001000X

Fig. 53 Fuel tank & pump replacement

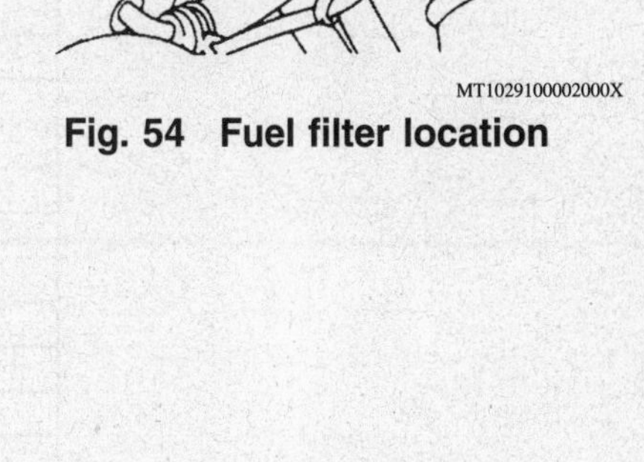
Fuel filter

MT1029100002000X

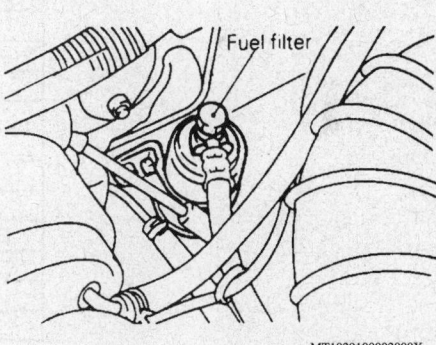

Fig. 54 Fuel filter location

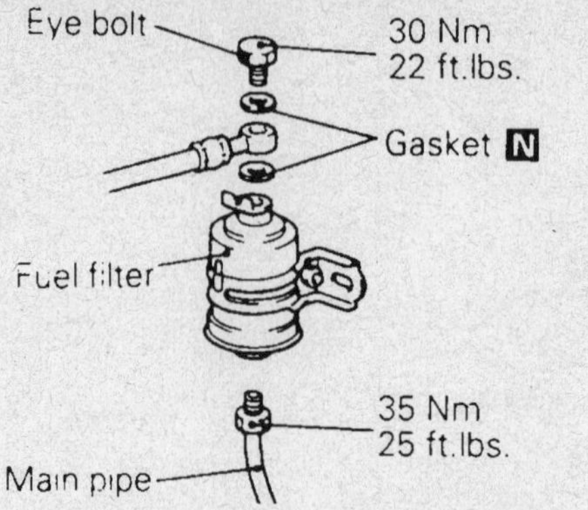
Eye bolt
30 Nm
22 ft.lbs.
Gasket N
Fuel filter
35 Nm
25 ft.lbs.
Main pipe
MT1029100003000X

Fig. 55 Fuel filter installation

TIGHTENING SPECIFICATIONS

Year	Component	Torque/Ft. Lbs.
1993–96	Air Intake Plenum Bolt & Nut	13
	Air Intake Plenum Stay Bolt	13
	Alternator	17
	Alternator Brace Bolt	10
	Alternator Bracket Bolt	17
	Alternator Bracket Side Bolt	7
	Alternator Pivot Nut	17
	Auto Tensioner Bolt②	17
	Bearing Caps Bolts No. 2, 3 & 4②	8
	Bearing Caps, Front & Rear Bolts②	14
	Bellhousing Cover Bolt	7
	Bracket Bolt	17
	Camshaft Sprocket Bolt	65
	Center Cover Bolt	2
	Connecting Rod Cap Nut	⑧
	Cooling Fan Bolt	8
	Cooling Fan Bracket Bolt	30
	Crank Angle Sensor Adapter Bolt②	17
	Crank Angle Sensor Nut	9
	Crankshaft Bearing Cap Bolt	⑦
	Crankshaft Bearing Cap Stay Bolt	35
	Crankshaft Pulley Bolt①	112
	Crankshaft Pulley Bolt②	134
	Cylinder Head Bolts	80⑨
	Detonation Sensor	17
	Distributor Adapter Bolts①	9
	Distributor Nut	10
	Drive Belt Tensioner Nut①	36
	Driveplate Bolt	54
	EGR Pipe	13
	EGR Pipe Clamp Bolts	13
	EGR Pipe Flare Nuts	43
	EGR Valve Bolt	14
	Engine Coolant Temperature Gauge Unit	8
	Engine Coolant Temperature Sensor	22
	Engine Support Bracket①	43③
	Engine Support Bracket①	80④

Continued

TIGHTENING SPECIFICATIONS—Continued

Year	Component	Torque/Ft. Lbs.
1993–96	Engine Support Bracket②	51③
	Engine Support Bracket②	80④
	Exhaust Manifold Heat Protector	10
	Exhaust Manifold Nut①	14
	Exhaust Manifold Nut②	21
	Exhaust Manifold Stay Bolt	44
	Exhaust Manifold Tightening Side Nut	9
	Fan Pulley Bolt	8
	Flywheel Bolt	54
	Fuel Pipe①	7
	Fuel Pressure Regulator Bolt	7
	Heat Pipe Bolt①	9
	Idler Pulley Bolt①	36
	Idler Pulley Bolt②	40
	Idler Pulley Bracket Bolt②	30
	Ignition Coil Bolt①	2
	Ignition Coil Bolt②	7③
	Ignition Coil Bolt②	9④
	Injector & Delivery Pipe Bolt	9
	Intake Manifold Front Side Nut	17
	Intake Manifold Nut	13
	Oil Filler①	7
	Oil Filter Bracket Stay	⑤
	Oil Filter Bracket	⑥
	Oil Pan Bolt	4
	Oil Pan Drain Plug	29
	Oil Pressure Switch①	7
	Oil Pressure Switch②	14
	Oil Pump Cane Bolt	10
	Oil Pump Cover Bolt	7
	Oil Screen Bolt	14
	Oil Seal Case Bolt	8
	Oil Level Gauge Assembly Bolt	10
	Power Transistor Bolt①	3.6
	Power Transistor Bolt②	16
	Rear Plate Bolt	8
	Rocker Arms, Shaft & Bearing Cap Bolts①	14
	Rocker Cover Bolt①	7
	Rocker Cover Bolt②	2
	Roll Stopper Bracket	30③
	Roll Stopper Bracket	54④
	Spark Plug	18
	Tensioner Arm Bolt②	30
	Tensioner Bracket Bolt①	30
	Tensioner Bracket Bolt②	17
	Tensioner Bracket Stay Bolt	17
	Tensioner Lock Bolt①	19
	Tensioner Pulley Nut②	35
	Tensioner Pulley Nut	36
	Thermo Switch	6
	Thermostat Housing Bolt	14
	Throttle Body Bolt	9
	Timing Belt Rear Cover Center Bolt②	17
	Transmission Stay	54

Continued

TIGHTENING SPECIFICATIONS—Continued

Year	Component	Torque/Ft. Lbs.
1993–96	Water Inlet Fitting Bolt	14
	Water Inlet Pipe Bolt	10
	Water Outlet Fitting Bolt	14
	Water Pump Bolt	17

① — SOHC engines.
② — DOHC engines.
③ — 10mm bolts.
④ — 12mm bolts.
⑤ — 8mm bolts, 9 ft. lbs.; 10mm bolts, 17 ft. lbs.
⑥ — Bolts marked '4', 17 ft. lbs.; bolts marked '7', 10 ft. lbs.
⑦ — Bolts marked '9', 58 ft. lbs.; bolts marked '10', 69 ft. lbs.
⑧ — 25 ft. lbs. plus an additional 1/4 turn.
⑨ — Tighten in three steps in sequence, refer to "Cylinder Head, Replace" for procedure.

Rear Axle & Suspension

INDEX

	Page No.
Coil Spring, Replace	23-27
Control Arm, Replace	23-27
Hub & Bearing, Replace	23-26
Rear Suspension, Replace	23-26
Shock Absorber, Replace	23-26
Stabilizer Bar, Replace	23-28
Tightening Specifications	23-30
Trailing Arm, Replace	23-28

HUB & BEARING

REPLACE

1. Disconnect battery ground cable.
2. Raise and support vehicle, then remove rear tire and wheel assembly.
3. Remove rear axle hub in numbered sequence shown in **Fig. 1,** noting the following:
   a. When removing rear speed sensor, use care not to strike pole piece against teeth of rotor or other components.
   b. Remove brake caliper leaving brake hose attached, then support to frame using suitable wire. **Do not allow caliper to hang by hose.**
   c. Care must be taken not to scratch or damage teeth of speed sensor rotor. Rotor must never be dropped.
4. Reverse procedure to install, noting the following:
   a. After tightening flange nut, crimp nut at concave portion of spindle.
   b. Install rear speed sensor and insert a 0.008–0.028 inch feeler gauge between speed sensor pole piece and rotor's toothed surface and tighten.

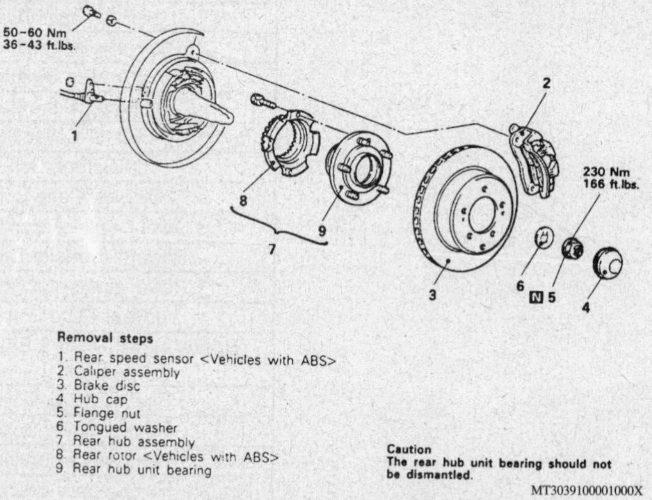

50-60 Nm
36-43 ft.lbs.
230 Nm
166 ft.lbs.
1
2
3
4
5
6
7
8
9
Removal steps
1. Rear speed sensor <Vehicles with ABS>
2. Caliper assembly
3. Brake disc
4. Hub cap
5. Flange nut
6. Tongued washer
7. Rear hub assembly
8. Rear rotor <Vehicles with ABS>
9. Rear hub unit bearing
Caution
The rear hub unit bearing should not be dismantled.
MT3039100001000X

Fig. 1 Rear axle hub replacement

REAR SUSPENSION

REPLACE

1. Disconnect battery ground cable.
2. Raise and support vehicle, then remove rear tire and wheel assembly.
3. **On sedan models,** remove trunk side trim panel.
4. **On all models,** support rear suspension using suitable jack stands.
5. Remove rear suspension in numbered sequence as shown in, **Figs. 2 through 4,** noting the following:
   a. Remove parking brake cable end.
   b. Prior to removing crossmember mounting nuts, support rear suspension using suitable jack stands.
   c. Remove crossmember mounting nuts and lower rear suspension out of vehicle.
6. Reverse procedure to install, noting the following on wagon models:
   a. Temporarily tighten lateral rod, upper control arms, shock absorbers and axle assembly attaching bolts.
   b. Install upper control arms ensuring attaching bolts are installed in proper direction, and tighten to specifications.
   c. Install rear springs with small end on top, ensuring step in pad aligns with end of spring.

SHOCK ABSORBER

REPLACE

1. Disconnect battery ground cable.
2. Raise and support vehicle, then remove rear tire and wheel assembly.

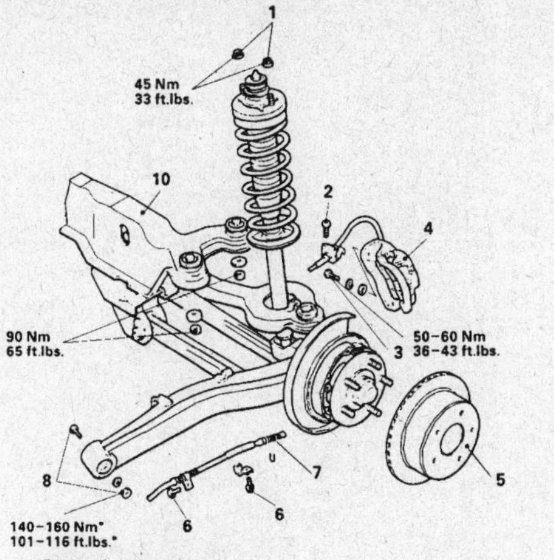
45 Nm
33 ft.lbs.
90 Nm
65 ft.lbs.
50-60 Nm
36-43 ft.lbs.
140-160 Nm*
101-116 ft.lbs.*

Removal steps

1. Shock absorber upper mounting nuts
2. Bolt
3. Brake caliper mounting bolts
4. Brake caliper assembly
5. Brake disk
6. Bolt
7. Parking brake cable end
8. Trailing arm mounting bolt and nut
9. Crossmember mounting nuts
10. Reat suspension assembly

* Indicates parts which should first be temporarily tightened, then fully tightened with the vehicle on the ground with no load (kerb weight).

MT2039100001000X

Fig. 2 Rear suspension assembly replacement. Sedan less 4WS

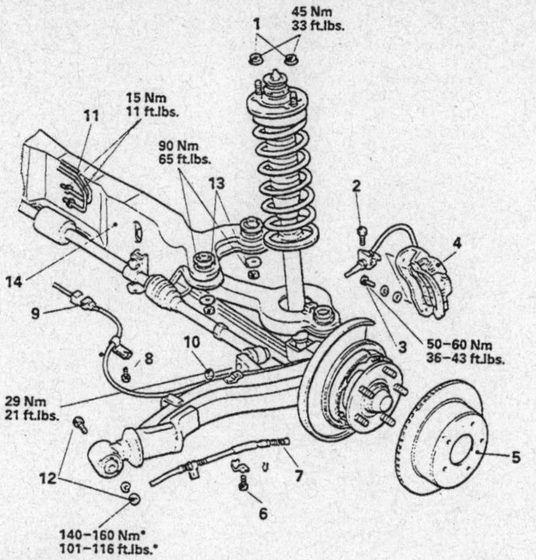
45 Nm
33 ft.lbs.
15 Nm
11 ft.lbs.
90 Nm
65 ft.lbs.
50-60 Nm
36-43 ft.lbs.
29 Nm
21 ft.lbs.
140-160 Nm*
101-116 ft.lbs.*

Removal steps

1. Shock absorber upper mounting nuts
2. Bolt
3. Brake caliper mounting bolts
4. Brake caliper assembly
5. Brake disk
6. Bolt
7. Parking brake cable end
8. Bolt (Vehicles equipped with ABS)
9. Connector
10. Power cylinder tie-rod connection nut
11. Power cylinder and pipe connection
12. Trailing arm mounting bolt and nut
13. Crossmember mounting nut
14. Rear suspension assembly

* Indicates part which should first be temporarily tightened, then fully tightened with the vehicle on the ground with no load (kerb weight).

MT2039100002000X

Fig. 3 Rear suspension assembly replacement. Sedan w/4WS

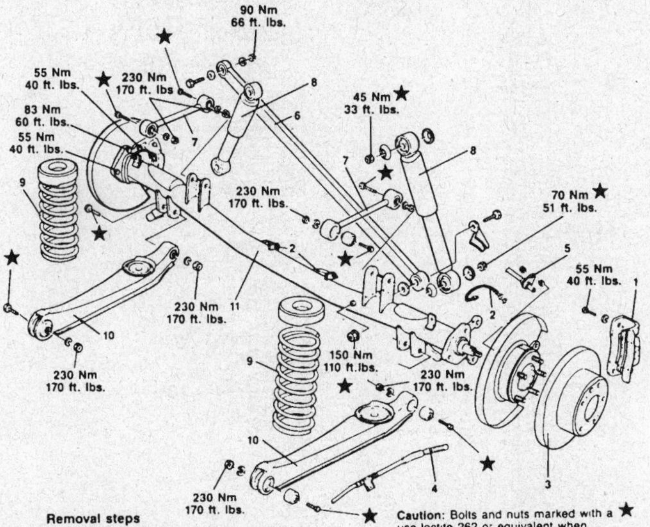
90 Nm
66 ft. lbs.
55 Nm
40 ft. lbs.
230 Nm
170 ft. lbs
83 Nm
60 ft. lbs.
55 Nm
40 ft. lbs.
45 Nm
33 ft. lbs.
230 Nm
170 ft. lbs.
70 Nm
51 ft. lbs.
55 Nm
40 ft. lbs.
230 Nm
170 ft. lbs.
150 Nm
110 ft.lbs.
230 Nm
170 ft. lbs.
230 Nm
170 ft. lbs.
230 Nm
170 ft. lbs.

Removal steps

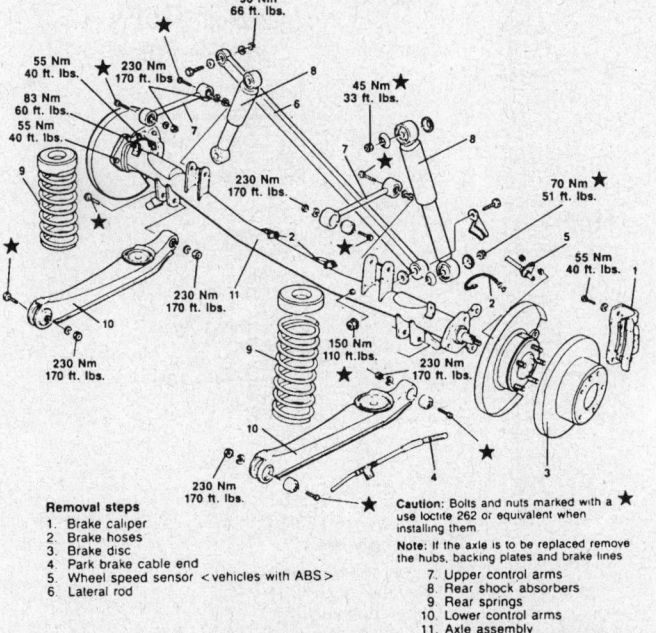

1. Brake caliper
2. Brake hoses
3. Brake disc
4. Park brake cable end
5. Wheel speed sensor <vehicles with ABS>
6. Lateral rod
7. Upper control arms
8. Rear shock absorbers
9. Rear springs
10. Lower control arms
11. Axle assembly

Caution: Bolts and nuts marked with a ★ use loctite 262 or equivalent when installing them.

Note: If the axle is to be replaced remove the hubs, backing plates and brake lines

MT2039100003000X

Fig. 4 Rear suspension assembly replacement. Wagon

3. Remove trunk side trim panel.
4. Remove shock absorber in numbered sequence shown in **Fig. 5** for models less active electronic controlled suspension (ECS), or **Fig. 6** for models with (ECS).
5. Reverse procedure to install. On models with active-electronic controlled suspension note the following:
   a. Apply a coat of rubber grease to O-ring on shock air tube connection, **Fig. 7.**
   b. Insert air tube until resistance is felt, then push tube in to paint mark on tube.
   c. After connecting air tube, to prevent double folding of diaphragm, with vehicle still raised and supported, press vehicle height switch (High) for two seconds or longer to select Extra High mode so air will be supplied to air springs.

COIL SPRING

REPLACE

1. Disconnect battery ground cable.
2. Raise and support vehicle, then remove rear tire and wheel assembly.
3. Remove shock absorber as outlined under "Shock Absorber, Replace."
4. Compress coil spring using coil spring compression tools No. MB991237 & MB991239, or equivalent.
5. Separate coil spring from other shock absorber components in numbered sequence shown in **Fig. 8** for models less active electronic controlled suspension (ECS) or **Fig. 9** for models with (ECS).
6. Reverse procedure to install, noting the following:
   a. Align edge of coil spring as shown in **Fig. 10.**
   b. Position upper bracket as shown in **Fig. 11,** then tighten nuts and bolts to specifications.
   c. **On models less (ECS),** apply a coat of rubber grease to air inlet joint O-ring then install it in joint then onto shock absorber.

CONTROL ARM

REPLACE

1. Disconnect battery ground cable.
2. Raise and support vehicle, then remove rear tire and wheel assembly.
3. Remove shock absorber as outlined under "Shock Absorber, Replace."
4. Remove assist link, lower and upper arm in numbered sequence shown in **Fig. 12,** noting the following:
   a. Remove ball joints using steering linkage puller tool No. MB991113, or equivalent.
   b. Loosen, but do not remove, crossmember mounting nuts to lower crossmember.
5. Reverse procedure to install.

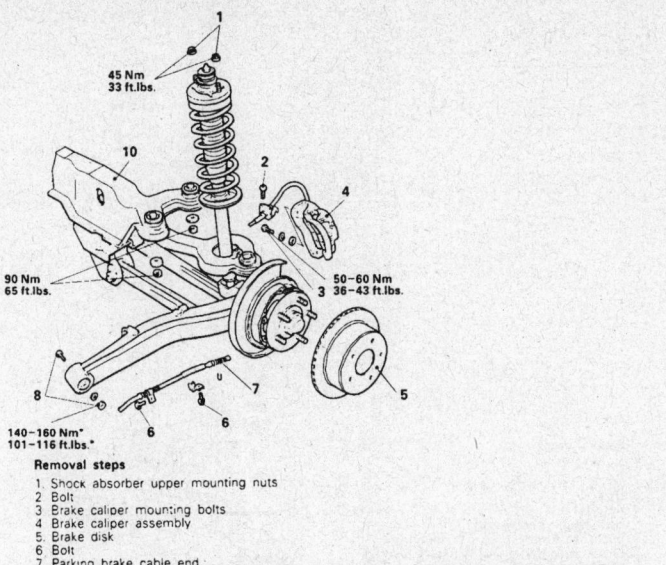

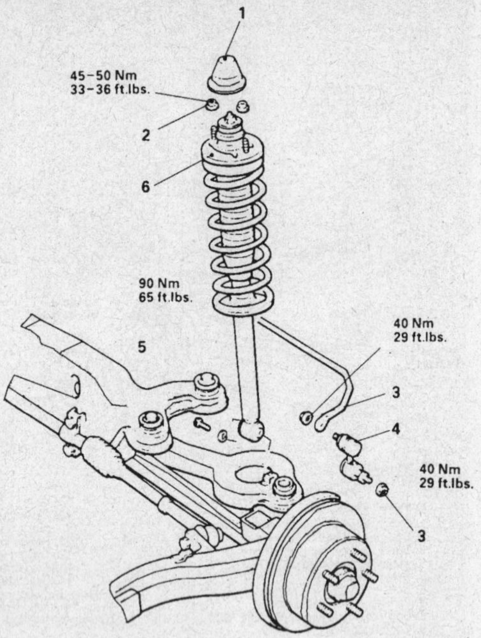
1
45-50 Nm
33-36 ft.lbs.
2
6
90 Nm
65 ft.lbs.
5
40 Nm
29 ft.lbs.
3
4
40 Nm
29 ft.lbs.
3
Removal steps
1. Cap
2. Shock absorber upper mounting nuts
3. Stabilizer link mounting nuts
4. Stabilizer link
5. Shock absorber mounting bolt
6. Shock absorber assembly
MT2039100004000X

Fig. 5 Shock absorber replacement. Models less active ECS

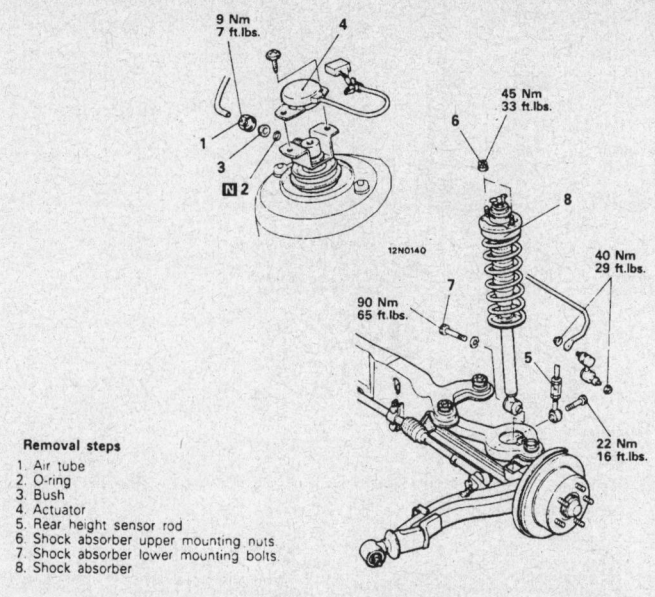

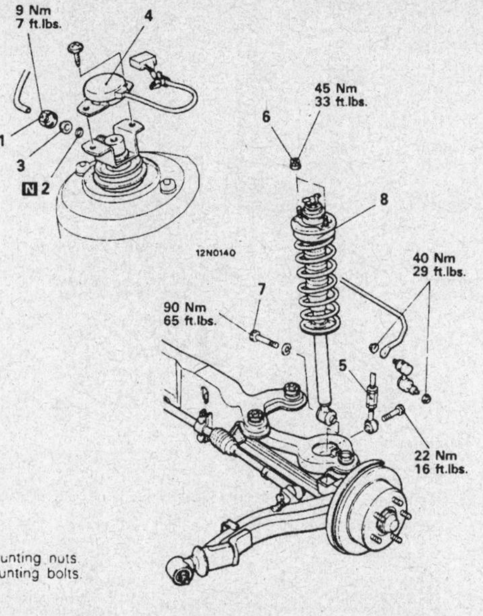
9 Nm
7 ft.lbs.
4
1
3
N 2
45 Nm
33 ft.lbs.
6
8
12N0140
40 Nm
29 ft.lbs.
90 Nm
65 ft.lbs.
7
5
22 Nm
16 ft.lbs.
Removal steps
1. Air tube
2. O-ring
3. Bush
4. Actuator
5. Rear height sensor rod
6. Shock absorber upper mounting nuts
7. Shock absorber lower mounting bolts.
8. Shock absorber
MT2039100005000X

Fig. 6 Shock absorber replacement. Models w/active ECS

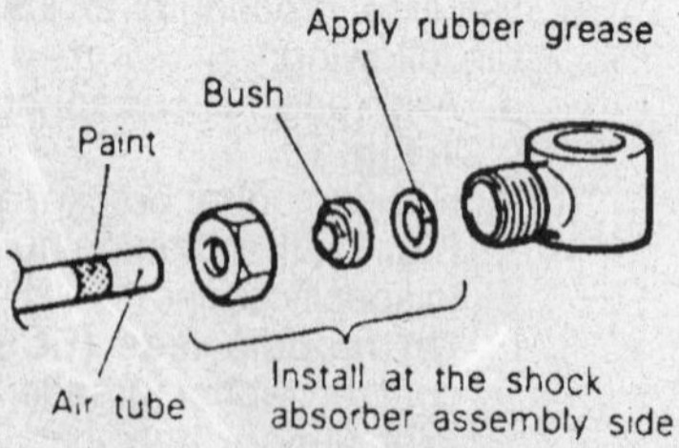
Apply rubber grease
Bush
Paint
Air tube
Install at the shock absorber assembly side
MT2039100006000X

Fig. 7 Air tube connection. Models w/Active ECS

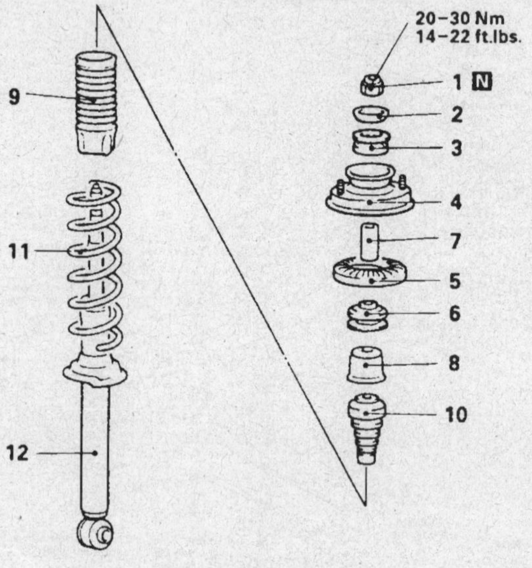
20-30 Nm
14-22 ft.lbs.
1 N
2
3
4
7
5
6
8
10
9
11
12
Disassembly steps
1. Piston rod tightening nut
2. Washer
3. Upper bushing (A)
4. Bracket assembly
5. Upper spring pad
6. Upper bushing (B)
7. Collar
8. Cup assembly
9. Dust cover
10. Bump rubber
11. Coil spring
12. Shock absorber
MT2039100007000X

Fig. 8 Exploded view of rear shock absorber assembly. Models less active ECS

TRAILING ARM

REPLACE

1. Disconnect battery ground cable.
2. Raise and support vehicle, then remove rear tire and wheel assembly.
3. Remove trailing arm in numbered sequence shown in **Fig. 13,** removing ball joints using steering linkage puller tool No. MB991113, or equivalent.
4. Reverse procedure to install.

STABILIZER BAR

REPLACE

1. Disconnect battery ground cable.
2. Raise and support vehicle, then remove rear tire and wheel assembly.
3. Remove stabilizer bar assembly in numbered sequence shown in **Fig. 14.**
4. Reverse procedure to install.

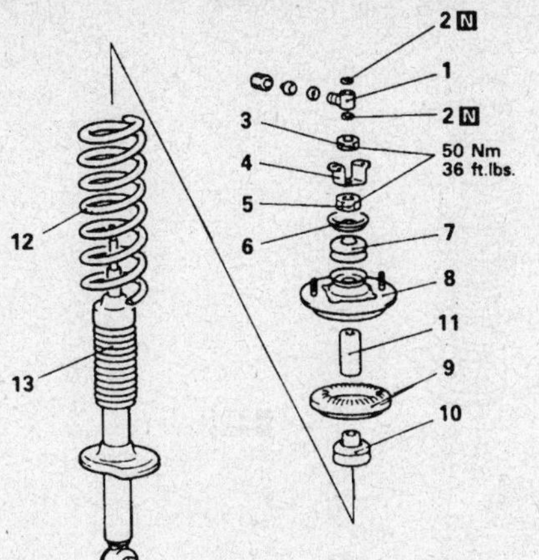

2 N
1
2 N
3
4
50 Nm
36 ft.lbs.
5
6
7
8
11
9
10
12
13

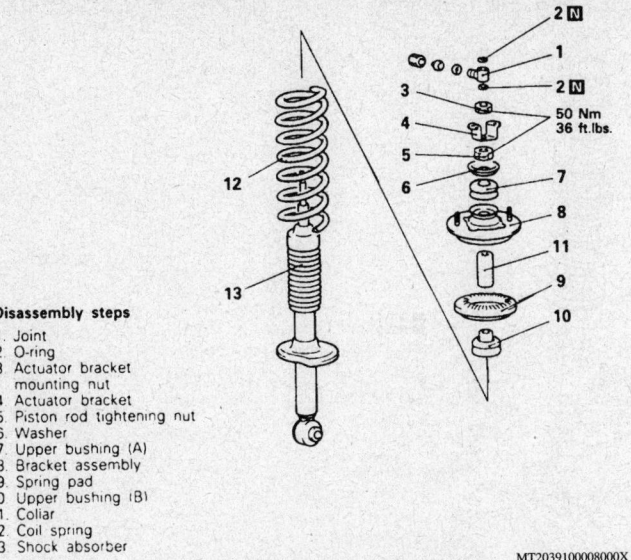

Disassembly steps

1. Joint
2. O-ring
3. Actuator bracket mounting nut
4. Actuator bracket
5. Piston rod tightening nut
6. Washer
7. Upper bushing (A)
8. Bracket assembly
9. Spring pad
10. Upper bushing (B)
11. Collar
12. Coil spring
13. Shock absorber

MT2039100008000X

Fig. 9 Exploded view of rear shock absorber assembly. Models w/active ECS

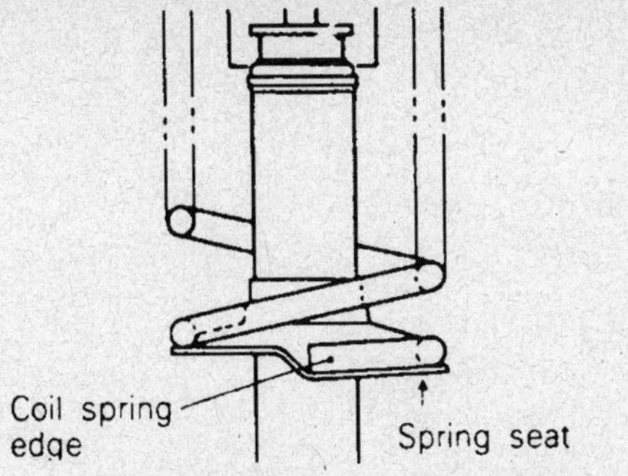

Coil spring
edge
Spring seat

MT2039100009000X

Fig. 10 Coil spring installation

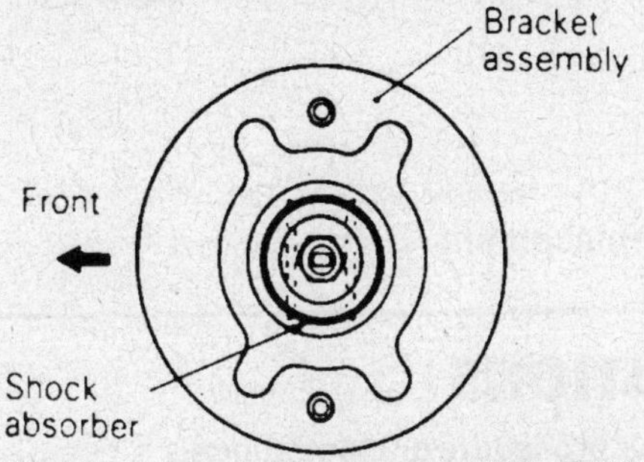

Bracket
assembly
Front
Shock
absorber

MT2039100010000X

Fig. 11 Upper bracket installation

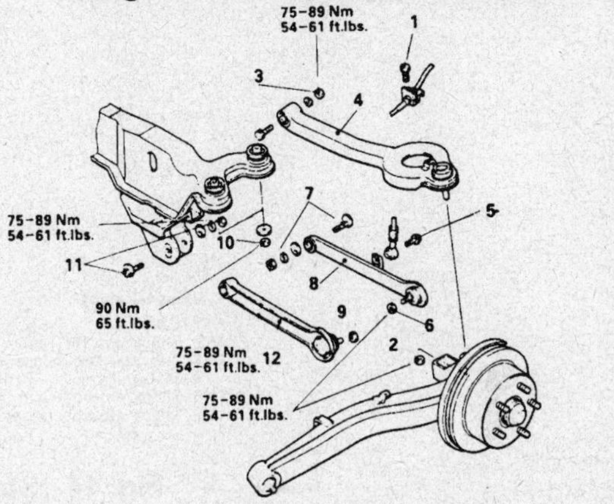

75-89 Nm
54-61 ft.lbs.
1
3
4
75-89 Nm
54-61 ft.lbs.
7
5
10
11
8
90 Nm
65 ft.lbs.
9
6
75-89 Nm
54-61 ft.lbs.
12
2
75-89 Nm
54-61 ft.lbs.

Upper arm removal steps

Removal of shock absorber

1. Brake line clamp bolt
2. Self lock nut
3. Upper arm mounting bolt and nut
4. Upper arm

Lower arm removal steps

5. ECS height sensor rod <Vehicle equipped with ECS>
6. Self lock nut
7. Lower arm mounting bolt and nut
8. Lower arm

Assist link removal steps

9. Self lock nut
10. Crossmember mounting nuts
11. Assist link mounting bolt and nut
12. Assist link

MT2039100011000X

Fig. 12 Assist link, lower & upper arm replacement

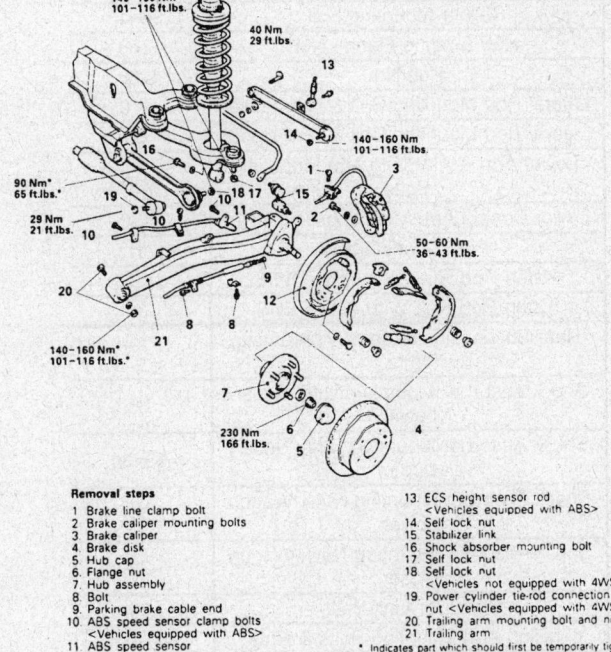

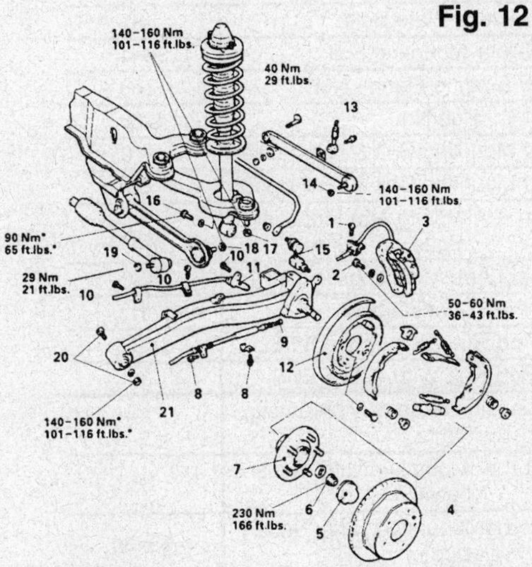

140-160 Nm
101-116 ft.lbs.
40 Nm
29 ft.lbs.
13
14
140-160 Nm
101-116 ft.lbs.
16
1
3
90 Nm*
65 ft.lbs.*
19
10
18
17
15
11
2
29 Nm
21 ft.lbs.
10
50-60 Nm
36-43 ft.lbs.
20
9
12
8
8
21
140-160 Nm*
101-116 ft.lbs.*
7
230 Nm
166 ft.lbs.
6
5
4

Removal steps

1. Brake line clamp bolt
2. Brake caliper mounting bolts
3. Brake caliper
4. Brake disk
5. Hub cap
6. Flange nut
7. Hub assembly
8. Bolt
9. Parking brake cable end
10. ABS speed sensor clamp bolts <Vehicles equipped with ABS>
11. ABS speed sensor <Vehicles equipped with ABS>
12. Backing plate
13. ECS height sensor rod <Vehicles equipped with ABS>
14. Self lock nut
15. Stabilizer link
16. Shock absorber mounting bolt
17. Self lock nut
18. Self lock nut <Vehicles not equipped with 4WS>
19. Power cylinder tie-rod connection nut <Vehicles equipped with 4WS>
20. Trailing arm mounting bolt and nut
21. Trailing arm

* Indicates part which should first be temporarily tightened, then fully tightened with the vehicle on the ground with no load (kerb weight)

MT2039100013000X

Fig. 13 Trailing arm replacement

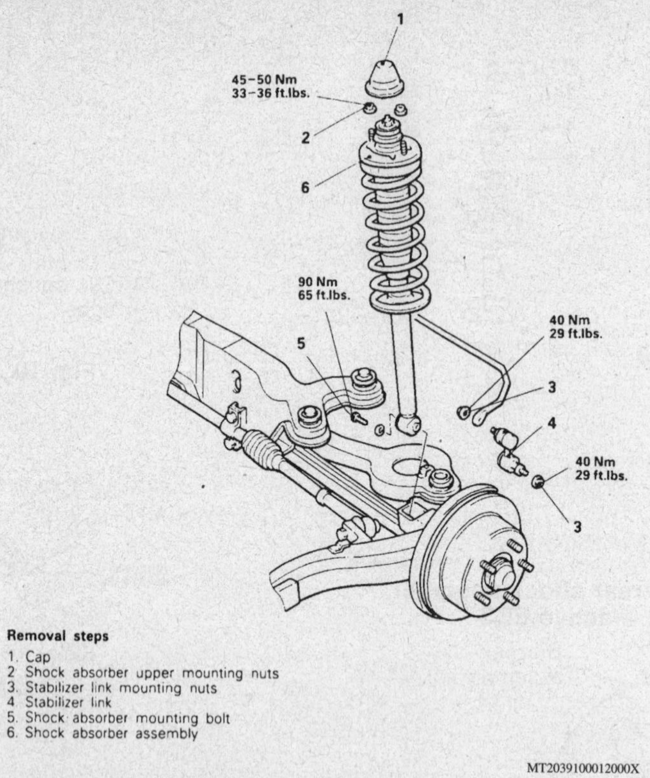
1
45–50 Nm
33–36 ft.lbs.
2
6
90 Nm
65 ft.lbs.
5
40 Nm
29 ft.lbs.
3
4
40 Nm
29 ft.lbs.
3
Removal steps
1. Cap
2. Shock absorber upper mounting nuts
3. Stabilizer link mounting nuts
4. Stabilizer link
5. Shock absorber mounting bolt
6. Shock absorber assembly
MT2039100012000X

Fig. 14 Stabilizer bar assembly replacement

TIGHTENING SPECIFICATIONS

For tightening specifications, refer to individual repair procedure or illustrations.

Year	Component	Torque/Ft. Lbs
1993–96	Air Tube Nuts	7
	Axle Nut	166
	Backing Plate Bolts	40
	Caliper Mounting Bolt	36–43
	Hub Bearing Flange Nut	166
	Hub Nut	166
	Lateral Rod Mounting Bolt & Nut, Lower	110
	Lateral Rod Mounting Bolt & Nut, Upper	66
	Lower Arm & Assisting Arm Mounting Bolts	54–61
	Lower Control Arm Mounting Bolt & Nut	170
	Pipe Connections	11
	Piston Rod Nut, Less Active ECS	14–33
	Piston Rod Nut, With Active ECS	36
	Rear Suspension Assembly Mounting Nuts	65
	Shock Absorber Mounting Nuts, Sedan Lower	65
	Shock Absorber Mounting Nuts, Sedan Upper	33–36
	Shock Absorber Mounting Nuts, Wagon Lower	51
	Shock Absorber Mounting Nuts, Wagon Upper	33
	Stabilizer Link Bolts	29
	Trailing Arm Mounting Bolts & Nuts	101–116
	Upper Arm Mounting Bolts & Nuts	54–61

Front Suspension & Steering

NOTE: On Air Bag Equipped Models, Refer To "Air Bag System Precautions" Located In Front Of This Manual For System Disarming & Arming Procedures.

INDEX

	Page No.
Ball Joint, Replace	23-32
Control Arm, Replace	23-33
Manual Steering Gears	29-1
Power Steering	29-1
Power Steering Gear, Replace	23-33
Power Steering Pump, Replace	23-33
Front	23-33
Rear	23-33
Precautions	23-31
Air Bag Systems	23-31
Rear Power Cylinder, Replace	23-35
Rear Power Cylinder Control Valve, Replace	23-35
Stabilizer Bar, Replace	23-33
Strut, Replace	23-32
Less Active Electronic Control Suspension (ECS)	23-32
With Active Electronic Control Suspension (ECS)	23-32
Tightening Specifications	23-38
Wheel Bearing, Adjust	23-31
Wheel Hub & Steering Knuckle, Replace	23-31

PRECAUTIONS

AIR BAG SYSTEMS

Refer to "Air Bag System Precautions" in front of this manual for system disarming and arming procedures.

WHEEL BEARING

ADJUST

Bearing preload is preset to specified value by design and cannot be adjusted.

WHEEL HUB & STEERING KNUCKLE

REPLACE

1. Replace hub, knuckle and bearing in numbered sequence shown in **Figs. 1 and 2,** noting the following:
   a. Use care when handling pole piece at tip of speed sensor and toothed edge of rotor, if equipped.
   b. Apply brake pressure, then remove driveshaft nut. **Do not apply vehicle weight to wheel bearing while loosening driveshaft nut.**
   c. Disconnect ball joint and tie rod end using steering linkage puller tool No. MB990635-01, or equivalent. **Loosen but do not remove ball joint and tie rod end nuts until knuckle is ready to be removed.**
   d. Using axle puller tool No. MB990241-01, or equivalent, press driveshaft from front hub.
   e. Install height sensor rod assembly, if equipped, install so that dimensions of rod are as shown in **Fig. 3.**
   f. Ensure driveshaft nut and washer are installed in direction shown in **Fig. 4.**
   g. Temporarily install speed sensor to knuckle, if equipped, then insert a suitable thickness gauge between sensor pole piece and rotor toothed surface, **Fig. 5,** and tighten speed sensor at a position where clearance is 0.012–0.035 inch. **If clearance cannot be obtained, check for improper installation of rotor.**
   h. Remove hub, or hub and rotor, by attaching front hub remover/installer tool No. MB990998-01 and knuckle arm bridge tool No. MB991355, or equivalents to knuckle and hub. Secure knuckle in vise, then tighten nut of front hub remover/installer to remove hub, or hub and rotor from knuckle.
   i. Remove wheel bearing inner race from front hub using side bearing puller tool No. MB990810-01, or equivalent. First, crush oil seal in two places to allow tabs of side bearing puller clearance to get under inner race.
   j. Drive wheel bearing out using knuckle arm bridge tool No. MB991355, remover/installer disc tool No. MB990932-01 and handle tool No. MB990938-01, or equivalents.
   k. Fill wheel bearing with multi-purpose grease and apply a thin coating to knuckle and bearing contact surfaces, then press in wheel bearing using rear suspension bushing base tool No. MB990890-01 and rear suspension arbor tool No. MB990883-01, or equivalents.
   l. Drive oil seal into knuckle using lower arm bushing arbor tool No. MB990947 and oil seal installer tool No. MB990955-01, or equivalents. Apply multi-purpose grease to lip of oil seal and surfaces of oil seal which contact front hub.
   m. Use front hub remover/installer tool No. MB990998-01, or equivalent, to mount hub or hub and rotor onto

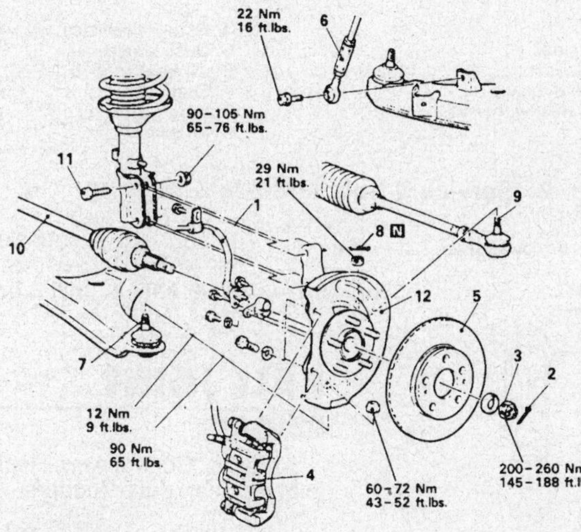

22 Nm
16 ft.lbs.
6
90–105 Nm
65–76 ft.lbs.
11
29 Nm
21 ft.lbs.
1
9
8 N
10
12
5
3
2
7
12 Nm
9 ft.lbs.
90 Nm
65 ft.lbs.
4
60–72 Nm
43–52 ft.lbs.
200–260 Nm
145–188 ft.lbs.

Removal steps
1. Front speed sensor <Vehicles with ABS>
2. Cotter pin
3. Drive shaft nut
4. Caliper assembly
5. Brake disc
6. Front height sensor <Vehicles with ACTIVE-ECS>
7. Connection for lower arm ball join
8. Cotter pin
9. Connection for tie rod end
10. Drive shaft
11. Front strut mounting bolt
12. Hub and knuckle

MT2049100001000X

Fig. 1 Hub, knuckle & bearing replacement

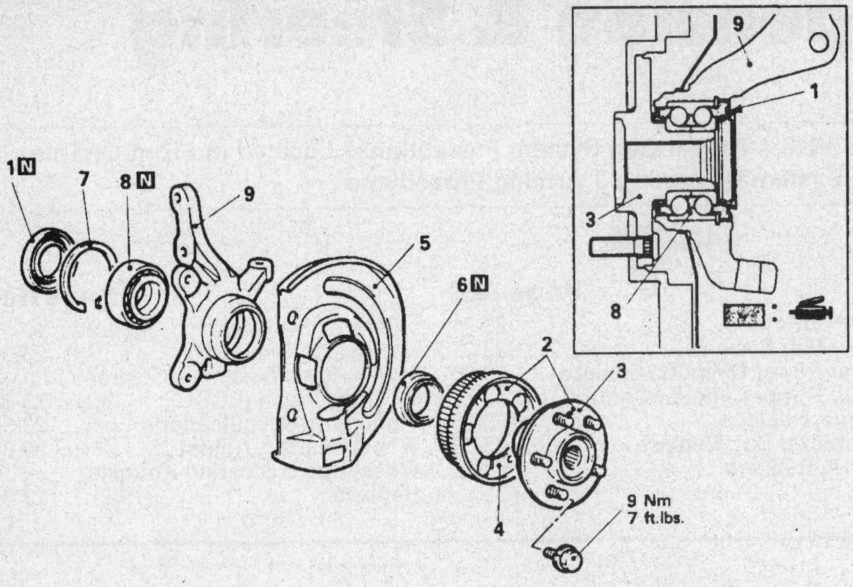
9 Nm
7 ft.lbs.

Disassembly steps

1. Oil seal (drive shaft side)
- Adjustment of wheel bearing starting torque
- Adjustment of hub end play
2. Hub and rotor <Vehicles with ABS>
3. Hub
4. Rotor <Vehicles with ABS>
5. Dust shield
6. Oil seal (hub side)
7. Snap ring
8. Wheel bearing
9. Knuckle

MT2049100002000X

Fig. 2 Servicing hub, knuckle & bearing

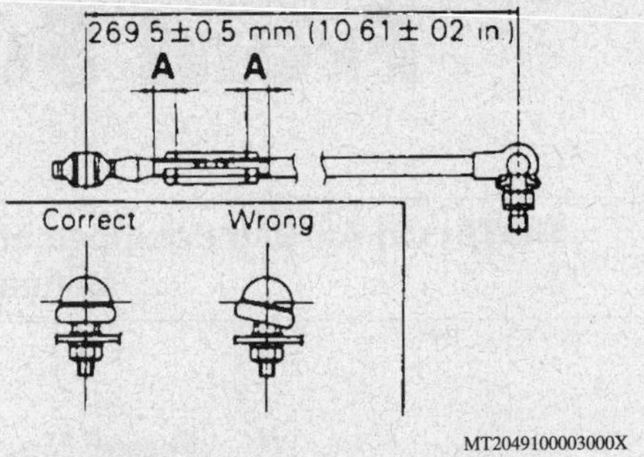
269 5±0 5 mm (10 61± 02 in)
A A
Correct
Wrong

MT2049100003000X

Fig. 3 Front height sensor installation. Models w/active ECS

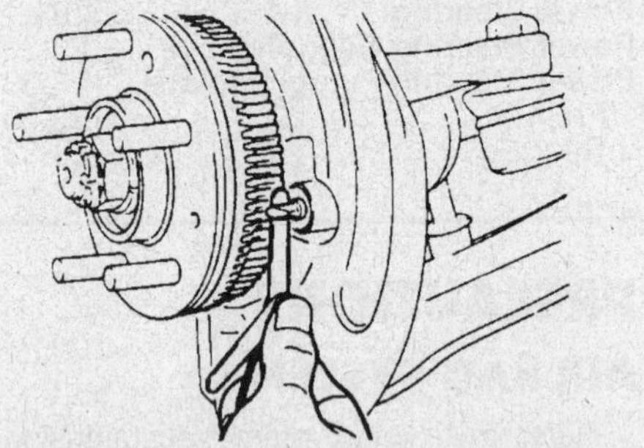

MT2049100005000X

Fig. 5 Speed sensor pole piece clearance check. Models w/ABS

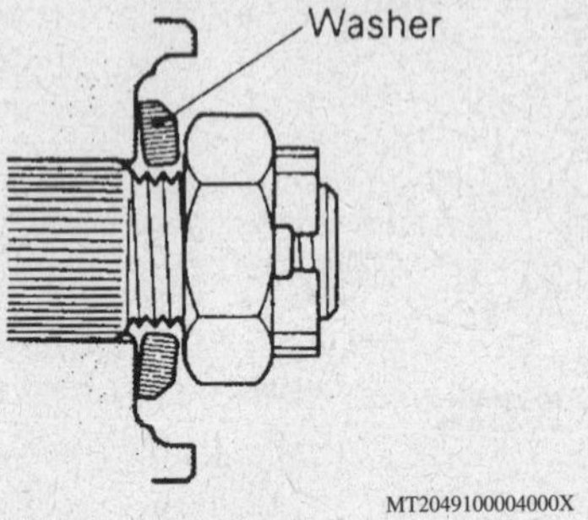
Washer

MT2049100004000X

Fig. 4 Driveshaft nut & washer installation

knuckle. Tighten nut of hub remover/installer to specifications while rotating hub to seat bearing. Leave hub remover/installer in place while taking measurements described in Steps n and o.

n. Measure wheel bearing starting torque using hub remover/installer and a suitable inch pound torque wrench. Starting torque must be 16 inch lbs. or less and bearing must not feel rough when rotated.
o. Measure hub endplay using hub remover/installer and a suitable dial indicator. Endplay must be within .002 inch. If starting torque and endplay are not within limits specified, bearing, hub and/or knuckle may have been incorrectly installed. Repeat disassembly and assembly procedures.
p. Apply multi-purpose grease to lip and install driveshaft side oil seal into knuckle using rear suspension bushing base tool No. MB990890-01 and rear suspension arbor tool No. MB990883-01, or equivalents. Drive seal in until it contacts snap ring.

BALL JOINT

REPLACE

Refer to "Control Arm, Replace" for ball joint replacement procedure.

STRUT

REPLACE

LESS ACTIVE ELECTRONIC CONTROL SUSPENSION (ECS)

1. Remove, install, disassemble and assemble strut assembly in numbered sequence shown in **Figs. 6 and 7,** noting the following:
   a. Hold spring upper seat using spring seat holder tool No. MB991176, or equivalent, then loosen but do not remove self-locking nut.
   b. Using spring compressor body and arm set tools No. MB991237 and MB991238, or equivalents, compress coil spring and remove self-locking nut.
   c. Line up holes in strut assembly spring lower seat with hole in spring upper seat. **This is more easily accomplished using a piece of pipe 10 mm x 300 mm.**
   d. Correctly align both ends of coil spring with grooves in spring seat.
   e. Apply multi-purpose grease to bearing portion of strut insulator. **Do not allow grease to adhere to insulator's rubber portion.**

WITH ACTIVE ELECTRONIC CONTROL SUSPENSION (ECS)

1. Remove, install, disassemble and assemble strut assembly in numbered sequence shown in **Figs. 8 and 9,** noting the following:
   a. Coat O-ring with rubber grease, then install O-ring, bush and flare nut to strut assembly as shown in **Fig. 10,** then slide air tube in up to painted portion. **O-ring may be damaged if installed at air tube side when connection is made. Air leak may occur if air tube connection is not complete and secure.**
   b. After connecting air tube, press vehicle height switch (High) for two seconds or longer to select Extra High mode. Air will be supplied to air springs, in order to prevent double folding of diaphragm while still in lifted condition.
   c. Hold spring upper seat using spring seat holder tool No. MB991176, or equivalent, then loosen but do not remove self-locking nut.
   d. Using spring compressor body and arm set tools No. MB991237 and MB991238, or equivalents, compress coil spring and remove self-locking nut.
   e. Install spring upper seat to piston rod, aligning notched part of piston rod and hole in spring seat.
   f. Align bead of spring upper seat and facing direction of knuckle bracket.

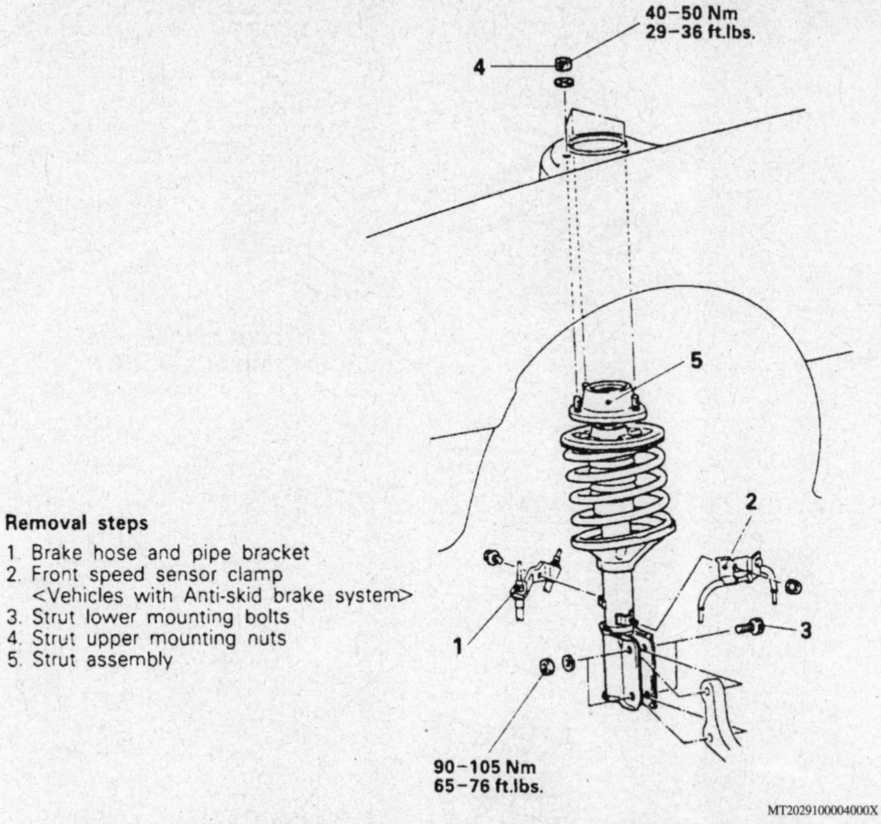
40–50 Nm
29–36 ft.lbs.
4
5
2
1
3
90–105 Nm
65–76 ft.lbs.
Removal steps
1. Brake hose and pipe bracket
2. Front speed sensor clamp
<Vehicles with Anti-skid brake system>
3. Strut lower mounting bolts
4. Strut upper mounting nuts
5. Strut assembly
MT2029100004000X

Fig. 6 Strut assembly replacement. Models less active ECS

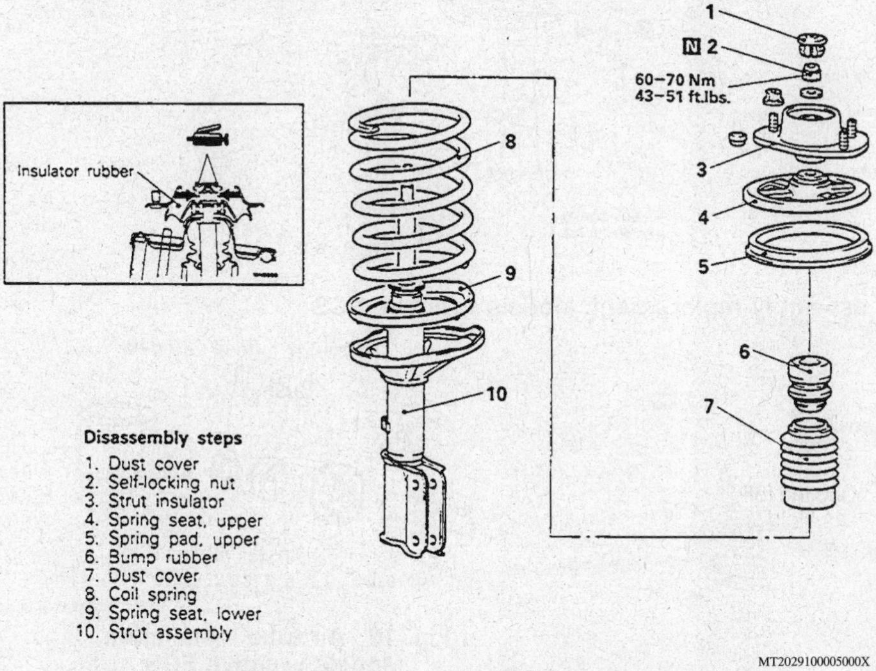
Insulator rubber
1
N 2
60–70 Nm
43–51 ft.lbs.
3
4
5
6
7
8
9
10
Disassembly steps
1. Dust cover
2. Self-locking nut
3. Strut insulator
4. Spring seat, upper
5. Spring pad, upper
6. Bump rubber
7. Dust cover
8. Coil spring
9. Spring seat, lower
10. Strut assembly
MT2029100005000X

Fig. 7 Servicing strut assembly. Models less active ECS

g. Apply multi-purpose grease to insulator bearing channel. **Do not allow grease to adhere to insulator's rubber portion.**

CONTROL ARM

REPLACE

1. Replace lower control arm and ball joint in numbered sequence shown in **Figs. 11 and 12,** noting the following:
   a. Remove ball joint using ball joint remover tool No. MB991113, or equivalent. **Loosen but do not remove ball joint nut until lower control arm is ready to be removed.**
   b. Place lower arm bushing bracket so that its mounting surface tilts 5–7° with respect to bottom surface of lower arm, then install self-locking nut, **Fig. 13.**

STABILIZER BAR

REPLACE

Replace stabilizer bar in numbered sequence shown in **Fig. 14.**

POWER STEERING GEAR

REPLACE

1. Replace power steering gearbox in numbered sequence shown in **Fig. 15,** noting the following:
   a. Disconnect tie rod ends using steering linkage puller tool No. MB991113-01, or equivalent.
   b. Disconnect lines as necessary from control valve, remove control valve from gearbox, then secure to crossmember with wire.
   c. Move rack completely to right, remove gearbox from crossmember, then tilt gearbox downward and remove to left. **Pull out carefully and slowly to avoid damaging boots.**
   d. When installing mounting rubber, align projection of mounting rubber with indentation in crossmember.

POWER STEERING PUMP

REPLACE

FRONT

1. Replace power steering pump in numbered sequence shown in **Figs. 16 and 17,** noting the following:
   a. **On SOHC engine,** raise connector of oil pressure hose upright and lift upward, then align concave portion of pump cover with fuel pipe and remove pump.
   b. **On all engines,** connect pressure hose so that slit part contacts oil pumps guide bracket.

REAR

1. Replace rear power steering pump in

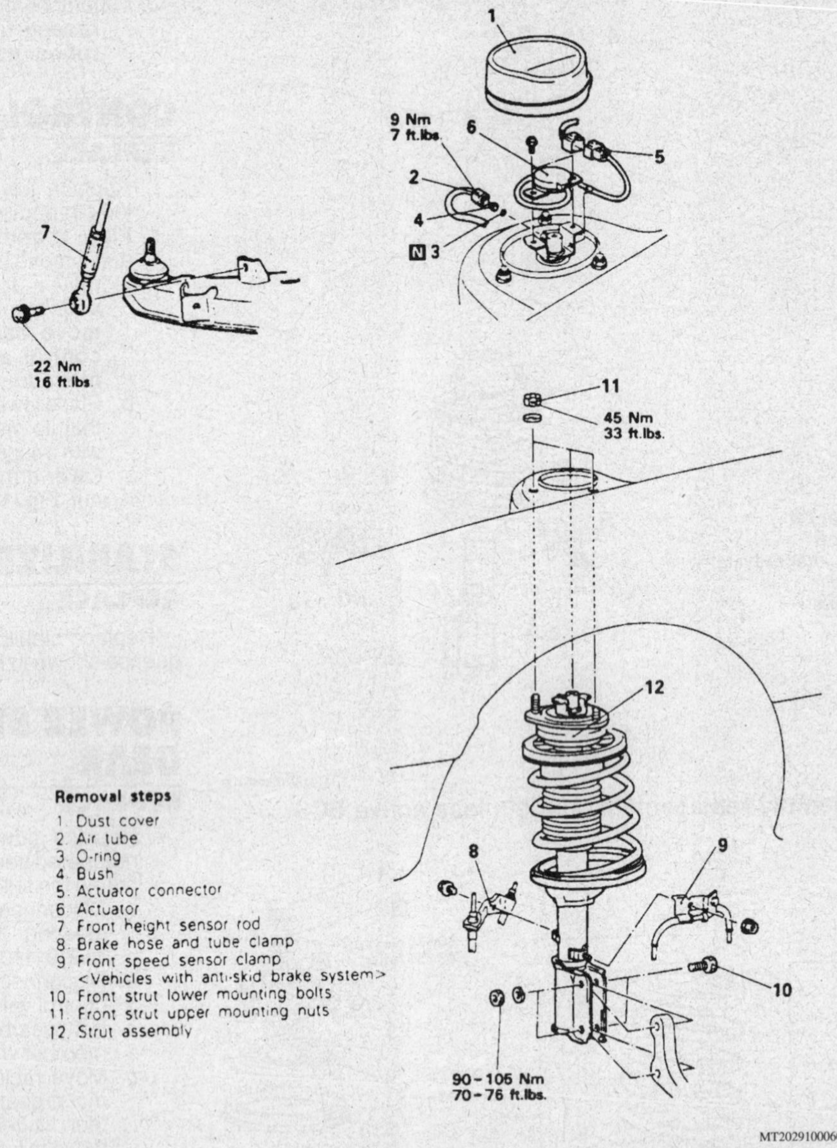
1
9 Nm
7 ft.lbs.
6
5
2
4
N 3
7
22 Nm
16 ft.lbs.
11
45 Nm
33 ft.lbs.
12
Removal steps
1. Dust cover
2. Air tube
3. O-ring
4. Bush
5. Actuator connector
6. Actuator
7. Front height sensor rod
8. Brake hose and tube clamp
9. Front speed sensor clamp
<Vehicles with anti-skid brake system>
10. Front strut lower mounting bolts
11. Front strut upper mounting nuts
12. Strut assembly
8
9
10
90-105 Nm
70-76 ft.lbs.
MT202910006000X

Fig. 8 Strut assembly replacement. Models w/Active ECS

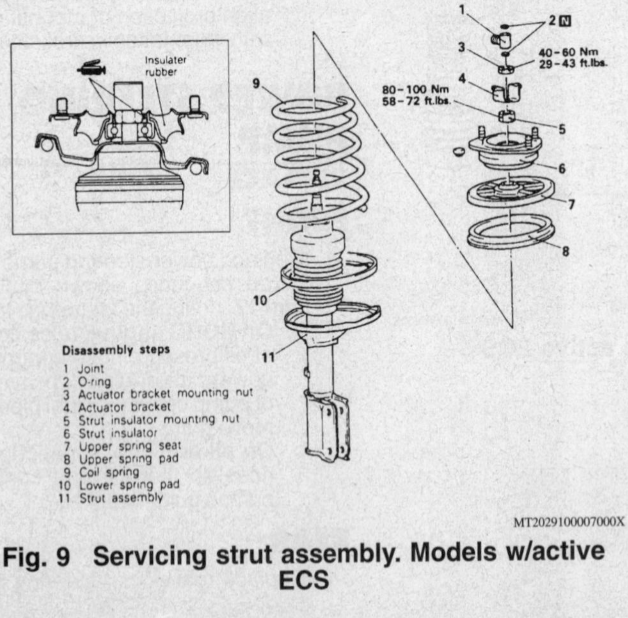
Insulater rubber
1
2 N
3
40-60 Nm
29-43 ft.lbs.
4
80-100 Nm
58-72 ft.lbs.
5
6
7
8
9
10
11
Disassembly steps
1 Joint
2 O-ring
3 Actuator bracket mounting nut
4 Actuator bracket
5 Strut insulator mounting nut
6 Strut insulator
7 Upper spring seat
8 Upper spring pad
9 Coil spring
10 Lower spring pad
11 Strut assembly
MT2029100007000X

Fig. 9 Servicing strut assembly. Models w/active ECS

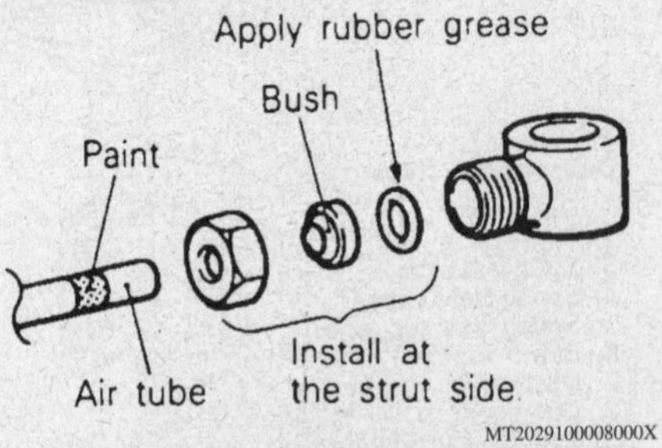
Apply rubber grease
Bush
Paint
Air tube
Install at the strut side
MT2029100008000X

Fig. 10 Air tube installation. Models w/active ECS

numbered sequence shown in **Fig. 18**, noting the following:

a. **On models with 4 wheel steering,** bleed 4 wheel steering (4WS) system as outlined under "Four Wheel Steering (4WS)."

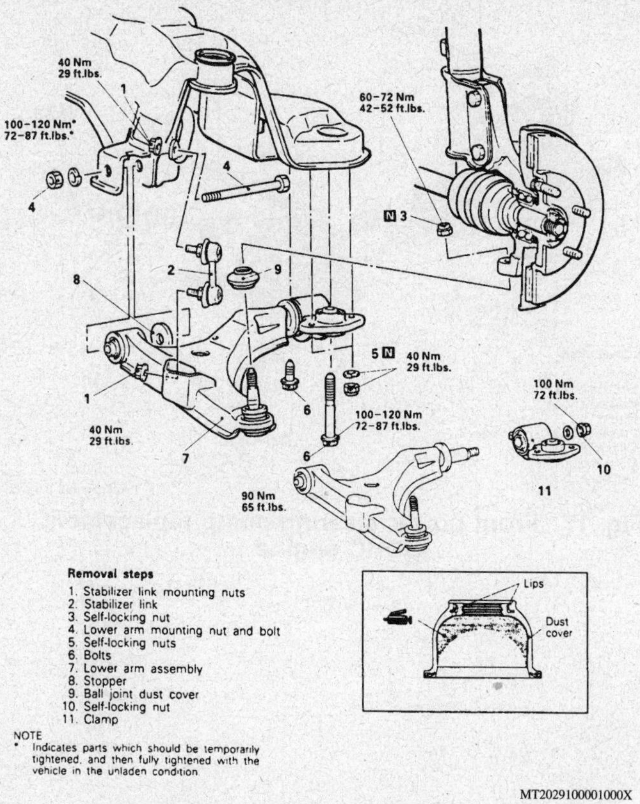
40 Nm
29 ft.lbs.
100–120 Nm*
72–87 ft.lbs.*
60–72 Nm
42–52 ft.lbs.
40 Nm
29 ft.lbs.
100 Nm
72 ft.lbs.
100–120 Nm
72–87 ft.lbs.
40 Nm
29 ft.lbs.
90 Nm
65 ft.lbs.
Removal steps
1. Stabilizer link mounting nuts
2. Stabilizer link
3. Self-locking nut
4. Lower arm mounting nut and bolt
5. Self-locking nuts
6. Bolts
7. Lower arm assembly
8. Stopper
9. Ball joint dust cover
10. Self-locking nut
11. Clamp
Lips
Dust cover
NOTE
* Indicates parts which should be temporarily tightened, and then fully tightened with the vehicle in the unladen condition
MT2029100001000X

Fig. 11 Lower control arm & ball joint replacement. Models less active ECS

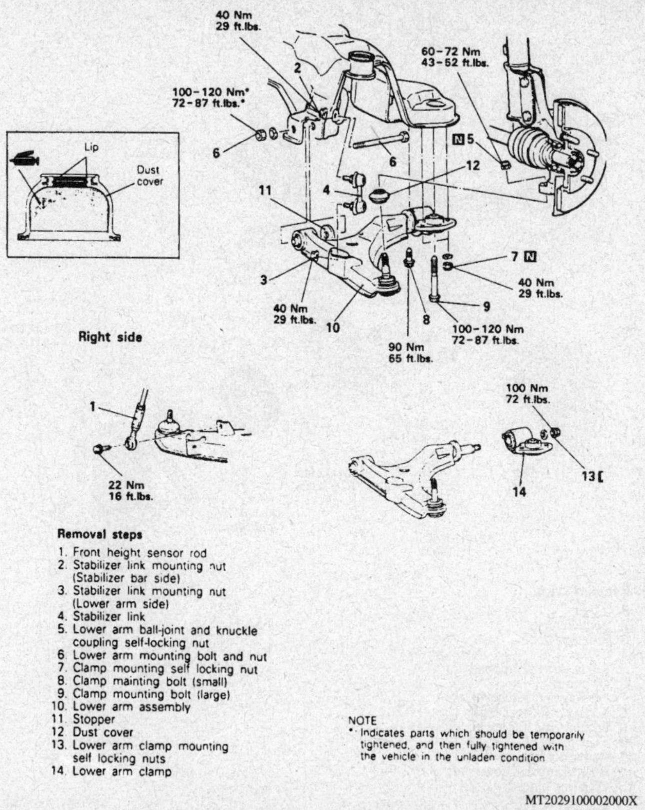
40 Nm
29 ft.lbs.
60–72 Nm
43–52 ft.lbs.
100–120 Nm*
72–87 ft.lbs.*
Lip
Dust cover
40 Nm
29 ft.lbs.
40 Nm
29 ft.lbs.
100–120 Nm
72–87 ft.lbs.
90 Nm
65 ft.lbs.
Right side
100 Nm
72 ft.lbs.
22 Nm
16 ft.lbs.
Removal steps
1. Front height sensor rod
2. Stabilizer link mounting nut (Stabilizer bar side)
3. Stabilizer link mounting nut (Lower arm side)
4. Stabilizer link
5. Lower arm ball-joint and knuckle coupling self-locking nut
6. Lower arm mounting bolt and nut
7. Clamp mounting self locking nut
8. Clamp mainting bolt (small)
9. Clamp mounting bolt (large)
10. Lower arm assembly
11. Stopper
12. Dust cover
13. Lower arm clamp mounting self locking nuts
14. Lower arm clamp
NOTE
*: Indicates parts which should be temporarily tightened, and then fully tightened with the vehicle in the unladen condition
MT2029100002000X

Fig. 12 Lower control arm & ball joint replacement. Models w/active ECS

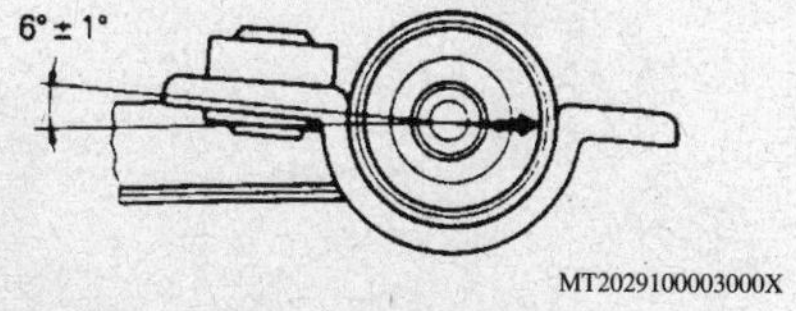
6° ± 1°
MT2029100003000X

Fig. 13 Lower arm clamp nut installation

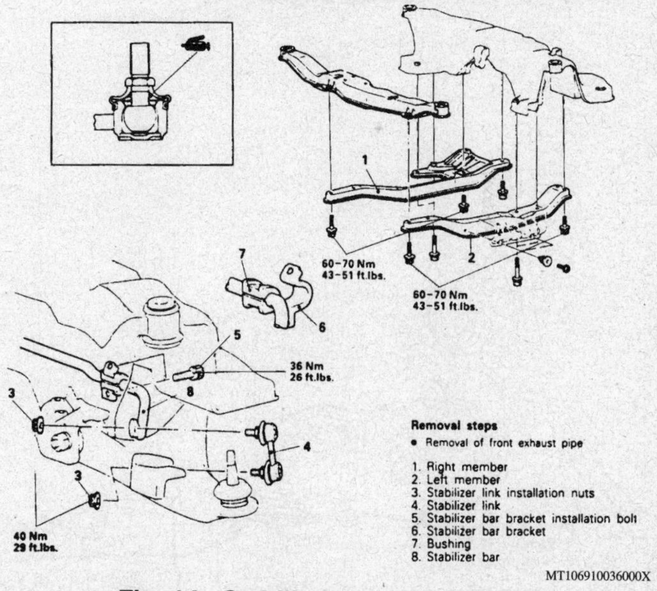
60–70 Nm
43–51 ft.lbs.
60–70 Nm
43–51 ft.lbs.
36 Nm
26 ft.lbs.
40 Nm
29 ft.lbs.
Removal steps
• Removal of front exhaust pipe
1. Right member
2. Left member
3. Stabilizer link installation nuts
4. Stabilizer link
5. Stabilizer bar bracket installation bolt
6. Stabilizer bar bracket
7. Bushing
8. Stabilizer bar
MT106910036000X

Fig. 14 Stabilizer bar replacement

REAR POWER CYLINDER

REPLACE

1. Replace power cylinder in numbered sequence shown in **Fig. 19,** noting the following during installation:
   a. Secure power cylinder to cross-member, then move cylinder piston rod through full stroke to determine neutral position.
   b. Align tie rod ends and installation holes at trailing arms.
   c. If tie rod ends and installation holes do not align, disconnect boot clips, then loosen tie rod end securing nut and adjust length so that difference between lengths of left and right tie rods is less than 0.039 inch. **Threads of tie rod ends may be used as a guide.**
   d. **On models with 4 wheel steering,** bleed four wheel steering (4WS) system as outlined under "Four Wheel Steering (4WS)."

REAR POWER CYLINDER CONTROL VALVE

REPLACE

1. Replace rear power cylinder control valve in numbered sequence shown in **Fig. 20,** noting the following:
   a. Remove left member first, then control valve.
   b. When installing control valve, hand tighten mounting bolts, connect pressure pipe, then tighten mounting bolts to specifications.
   c. **On models equipped with 4 wheel steering,** bleed Four Wheel Steering (4WS) System as outlined under "Four Wheel Steering (4WS)" section.

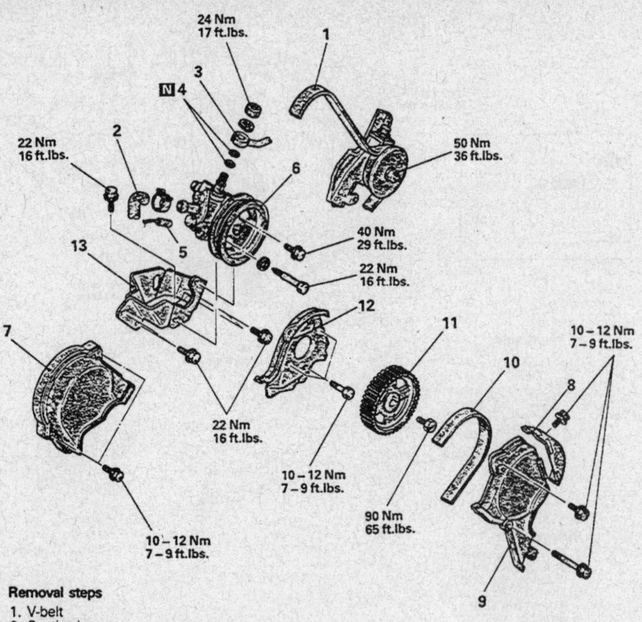
24 Nm
17 ft.lbs.
1
3
N 4
2
22 Nm
16 ft.lbs.
50 Nm
36 ft.lbs.
6
5
40 Nm
29 ft.lbs.
13
22 Nm
16 ft.lbs.
12
7
11
10 – 12 Nm
7 – 9 ft.lbs.
10
8
22 Nm
16 ft.lbs.
10 – 12 Nm
7 – 9 ft.lbs.
90 Nm
65 ft.lbs.
10 – 12 Nm
7 – 9 ft.lbs.
9

Removal steps
1. V-belt
2. Suction hose
3. Pressure hose
4. O-ring
5. Pressure switch connector
6. Oil pump
7. Front timing belt cover, right
8. Timing belt cover cap
9. Front timing belt cover, left
10. Timing belt
11. Camshaft sprocket
12. Rear timing belt cover, left
13. Oil pump bracket

MT1069100037000X

Fig. 16 Front power steering pump replacement. SOHC engine

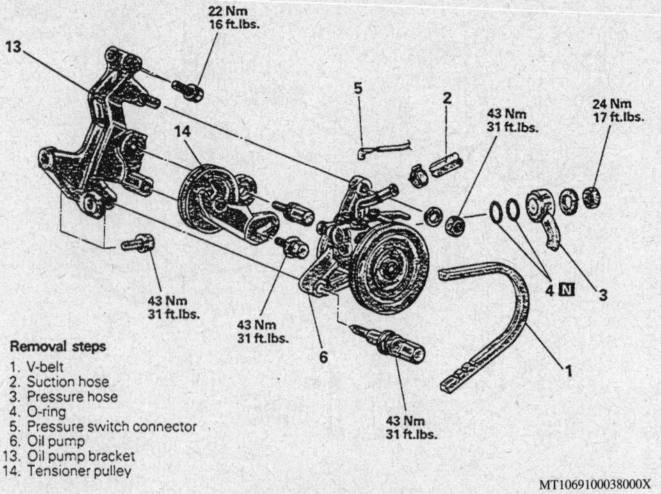
22 Nm
16 ft.lbs.
13
5
2
43 Nm
31 ft.lbs.
24 Nm
17 ft.lbs.
14
4 N
3
43 Nm
31 ft.lbs.
43 Nm
31 ft.lbs.
6
1
43 Nm
31 ft.lbs.

Removal steps
1. V-belt
2. Suction hose
3. Pressure hose
4. O-ring
5. Pressure switch connector
6. Oil pump
13. Oil pump bracket
14. Tensioner pulley

MT1069100038000X

Fig. 17 Front power steering pump replacement. DOHC engine

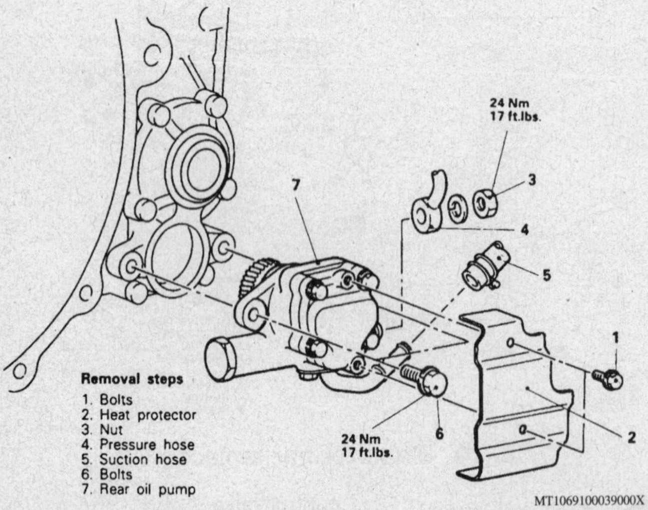
24 Nm
17 ft.lbs.
3
7
4
5
1
24 Nm
17 ft.lbs.
6
2

Removal steps
1. Bolts
2. Heat protector
3. Nut
4. Pressure hose
5. Suction hose
6. Bolts
7. Rear oil pump

MT1069100039000X

Fig. 18 Rear power steering pump replacement

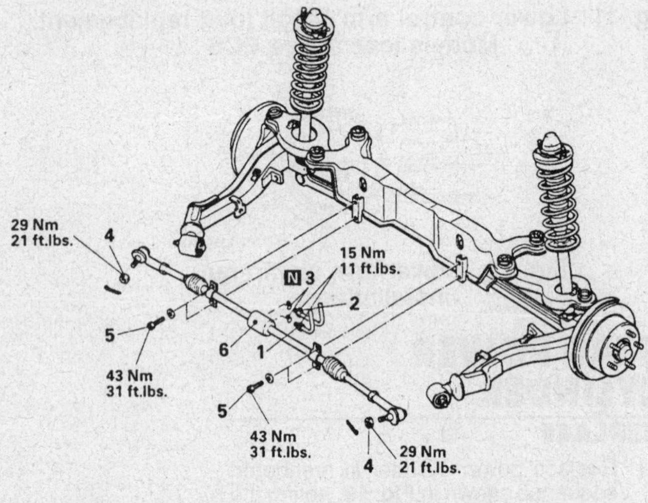
29 Nm
21 ft.lbs.
4
15 Nm
11 ft.lbs.
N 3
2
5
6
1
43 Nm
31 ft.lbs.
5
43 Nm
31 ft.lbs.
4
29 Nm
21 ft.lbs.

Removal steps
1. Pressure pipe RR
2. Pressure pipe RL
3. O-ring
4. Tie-rod end nuts
5. Bolts
6. Power cylinder

MT106910040000X

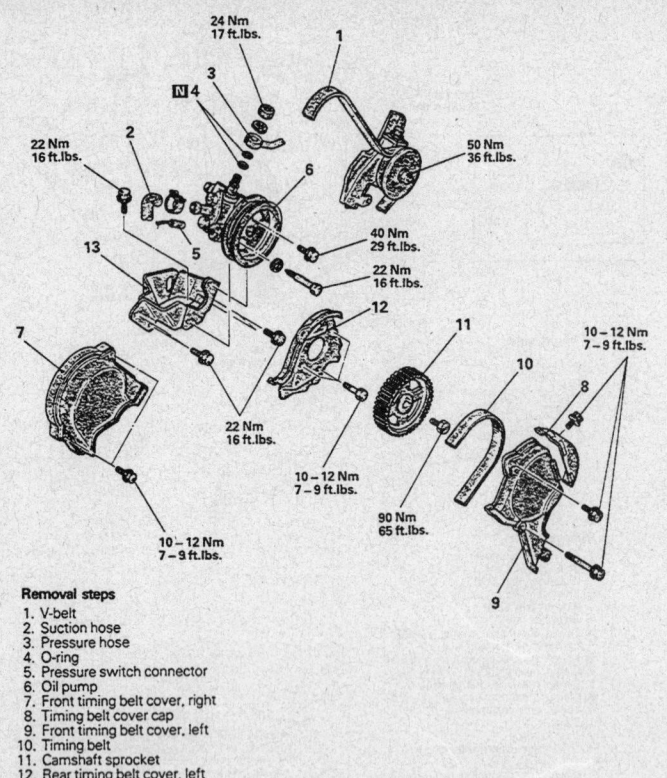

Fig. 19 Rear power cylinder (steering gear) replacement

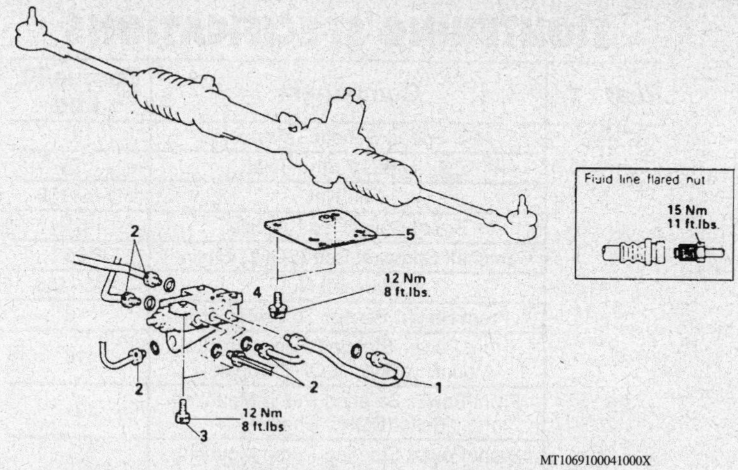
Fluid line flared nut
15 Nm
11 ft.lbs.
2
5
12 Nm
8 ft.lbs.
4
2
1
2
12 Nm
8 ft.lbs
3
MT1069100041000X

Fig. 20 Rear cylinder control valve replacement

TIGHTENING SPECIFICATIONS

Year	Component	Torque/Ft. Lbs
1993–96	ABS Speed Sensor To Knuckle	9
	Air Line To Strut Joint	7
	Axle Nut	145–188
	Brake Caliper To Knuckle	65
	Camshaft Sprocket Bolt (SOHC Engine)	65
	Driveshaft Nut	145–188
	Front Height Sensor To Lower Arm	16
	Front Power Steering Pump Bracket Mounting Bolts (DOHC Engine)	16
	Front Power Steering Pump Mounting Bolts (DOHC Engine)	31
	Front Power Steering Pump Mounting Bolts (SOHC Engine)	16
	Front Power Steering Pump Pressure Hose To Pump	17
	Hub Nut	145–188
	Hub To ABS Rotor	7
	Knuckle To Ball Joint	43–52
	Knuckle To Strut Assembly	65–76
	Knuckle To Tie Rod Assembly	21
	Lower Arm Clamp To Lower Arm	72
	Lower Arm To Crossmember Bolt	72–87
	Lower Arm To Crossmember Self Locking Nuts	29
	Lower Arm To Crossmember Through Bolt & Nut	72–87①
	Power Cylinder Control Valve To Mounting Plate	8
	Power Cylinder Lines	11
	Power Cylinder To Crossmember②	31
	Power Cylinder To Trailing Arm②	21
	Power Steering Control Valve Mounting Plate To Valve Bracket	8
	Power Steering Control Valve To Mounting Plate	8
	Power Steering Gearbox Coupling Bolt	13
	Power Steering Gearbox To Crossmember	51
	Power Steering Lines	11
	Rear Power Steering Pump Mounting Bolts②	17
	Rear Power Steering Pump Pressure Hose To Pump②	17
	Right & Left Member Bolts	43–51
	Stabilizer Bar Bracket	26
	Stabilizer Link Mounting Nut	29
	Strut To Strut Tower	29–36
	Strut Assembly Self Locking Nut, Less ECS	43–51
	Strut Actuator Bracket Mounting Nut, w/ECS	29–43
	Strut Insulator Mounting Nut, w/ECS	58–72
	Timing Cover Mounting Bolts (SOHC Engine)	7–9
	Wheel Lug Nuts	65–79

① — Must be tightened while vehicle is unladen.

② — 4 wheel steering system (4WS).

Wheel Alignment

INDEX

	Page No.
Front Wheel Alignment	23-39
Camber	23-39
Caster	23-39
Toe-In	23-39
Preliminary Inspection	23-39
Rear Wheel Alignment	23-39
Camber	23-39
Toe-In	23-39
Vehicle Ride Height	23-39
Wheel Alignment Specifications	23-3

PRELIMINARY INSPECTION

1. Ensure tires are inflated to correct pressure, then check for uneven wear.
2. Check front wheel bearings, suspension arm and ball joints for damage. Replace components as necessary, to eliminate improper alignment due to faulty components.
3. Check steering gear for damage and adjust as necessary.
4. Check shocks for damage and replace as necessary.
5. Rock vehicle backward and forward and bounce it upward and downward to settle vehicle prior to alignment.
6. Ensure vehicle is unloaded and on a suitable alignment rack according to manufacturer's instructions. **When measuring equipment is attached directly to outer end of driveshaft and front wheels are on turntables, apply brake to prevent improper vehicle movement.**

FRONT WHEEL ALIGNMENT

CAMBER

Camber is preset during production and is not adjustable. If camber is out of specification, replace bent or damaged components.

CASTER

Caster has been preset during production and is not adjustable.

TOE-IN

1. Adjust toe-in by loosening clips and turning left and right tie rod turnbuckles equally in opposite directions, **Fig. 1.**
2. To increase toe-out, turn left turnbuckle toward front of vehicle and right turnbuckle toward rear of vehicle. To increase toe-in, turn turnbuckles in other direction.
3. Amount of toe-in adjustment is 0.24 inch for each half turn of left and right tie rods.

REAR WHEEL ALIGNMENT

CAMBER

1. Turn lower arm mounting bolt to adjust rear camber, **Fig. 2.**

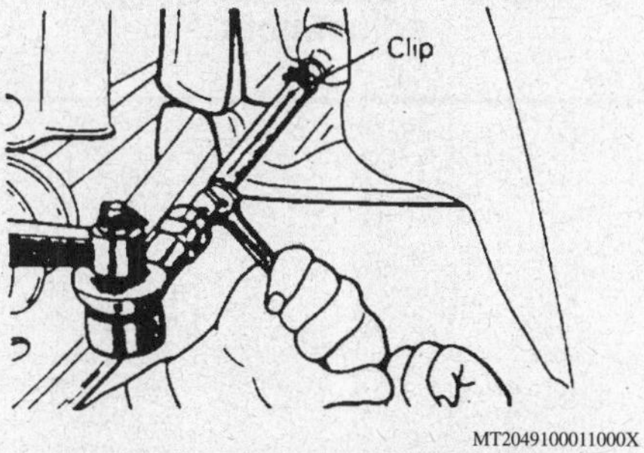
Clip
MT2049100011000X

Fig. 1 Front toe-in adjustment

<Vehicles not equipped with 4WS>

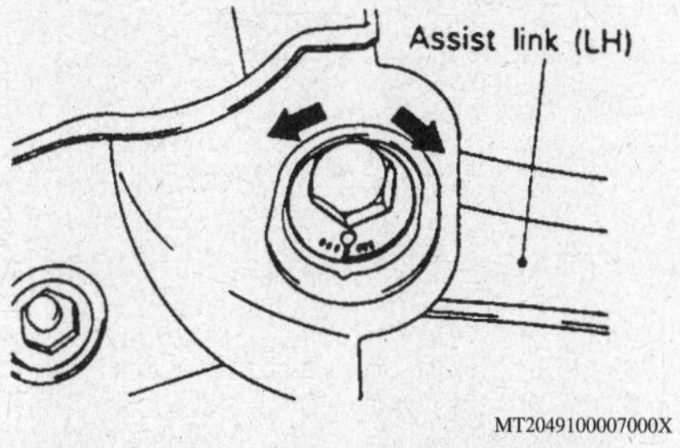
Assist link (LH)
MT2049100007000X

Fig. 3 Rear toe-in adjustment. 2WS

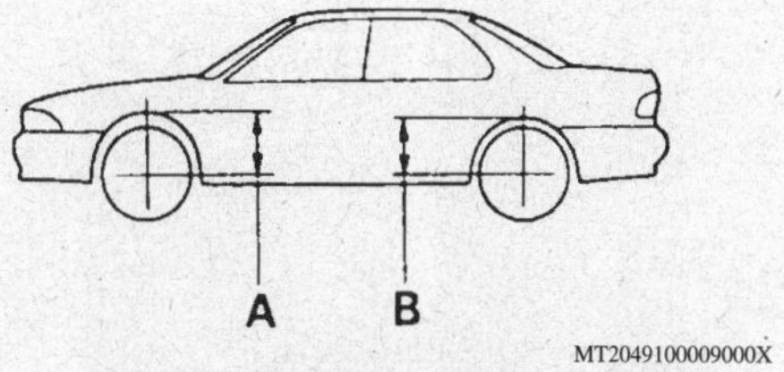
A
B
MT2049100009000X

Fig. 5 Vehicle ride height measurements

2. **On models with 2 wheel steering,** loosen assist link mounting bolt prior to camber adjustment.
3. **On models with 4 wheel steering,** disconnect power cylinder tie rod end from knuckle prior to adjustment.
4. **On all models,** difference between both wheels should not exceed ½°.

TOE-IN

2 Wheel Steering

Adjust rear toe-in by turning assist link mounting bolt an equal amount on both sides, **Fig. 3.**

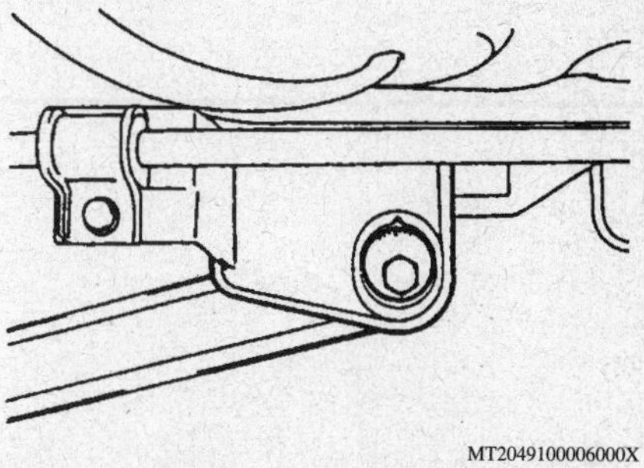
MT2049100006000X

Fig. 2 Rear camber adjustment

<Vehicles equipped with 4WS>

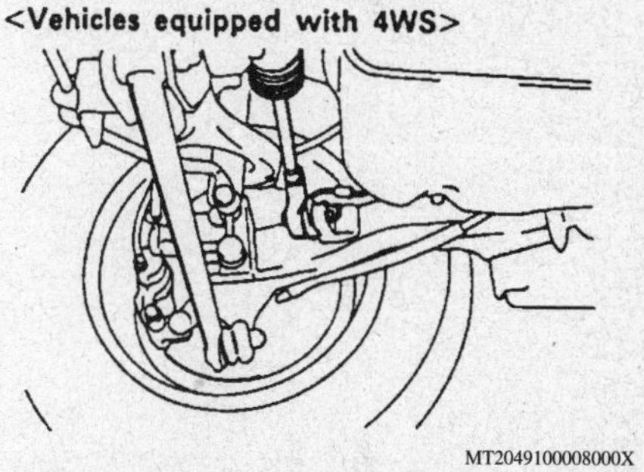
MT2049100008000X

Fig. 4 Rear toe-in adjustment. 4WS

4 Wheel Steering

Adjust rear toe-in by turning power cylinder tie rod screw an equal amount on both sides, **Fig. 4.**

VEHICLE RIDE HEIGHT

Vehicle ride height must be checked with vehicle stopped and engine at idle.

1. Park unloaded vehicle on a flat surface, then start engine.
2. Measure distance between wheel arch and center of axle for right front and left rear wheels, **Fig. 5.** Standard values are as follows:
   a. Distance at front wheel (dimension "A") should be 15.4–15.8 inches.
   b. Distance at rear wheel (dimension "B") should be 14.3–14.6 inches.
3. If vehicle height is not within specified range, loosen front and rear height sensor turnbuckles and rotate rods, **Fig. 6.** One turn of nut will raise front of vehicle approximately .24 inch or rear of vehicle approximately .12 inch.
4. Recheck both front and rear height dimensions after adjustment, even if only one was altered.

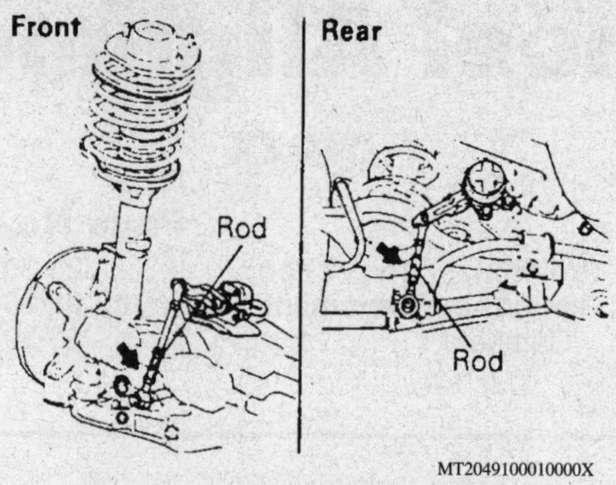
Front
Rear
Rod
Rod
MT2049100010000X

Fig. 6 Vehicle ride height adjustment

MITSUBISHI ECLIPSE & 3000GT

INDEX OF SERVICE OPERATIONS

Page No.

AIR BAG SYSTEM PRECAUTIONS 0-8
AUTOMATIC TRANSMISSIONS/ TRANSAXLES 29-1
BRAKES
Anti-Lock Brakes 29-1
Disc Brakes 29-1
Drum Brakes
Hydraulic Brake Systems 29-1
Power Brake Units 29-1
CLUTCH & MANUAL TRANSAXLES
Adjustments 24-68
Clutch, Replace 24-69
Hydraulic System Service 24-69
Precautions 24-68
Shift Cable, Replace 24-70
Technical Service Bulletins 24-72
Tightening Specifications 24-78
Transaxle, Replace 24-70
ELECTRICAL
Air Bags 29-1
Air Conditioning 29-1
Alternators 29-1
Blower Motor, Replace 24-13
Coil Pack, Replace 24-7
Combination Switch, Replace . 24-8
Cooling Fans 29-1
Cruise Control 29-1
Dash Gauges 29-1
Dash Panels 29-1
Dimmer Switch, Replace 24-10
Distributor, Replace 24-7
Evaporator Core, Replace 24-14
Fuel Pump Relay Location 24-5
Fuse Panel & Flasher Location 24-5
Headlamp Switch, Replace ... 24-8
Heater Core, Replace 24-14
Ignition Lock, Replace 24-7
Ignition Switch, Replace 24-8
Instrument Cluster, Replace ... 24-10
Neutral Safety Switch, Replace 24-8
Passive Restraints 29-1
Precautions 24-5
Radio, Replace 24-11
Relay Center Location 24-5
Speed Controls 29-1
Starter, Replace 24-5
Starter Motors 29-1
Steering Columns 29-1
Steering Wheel, Replace 24-10
Wiper Motor, Replace 24-11
Wiper Switch, Replace 24-13
Wiper Systems 29-1
ELECTRICAL SYMBOL IDENTIFICATION 0-144
FRONT SUSPENSION & STEERING
Ball Joint, Replace 24-96
Control Arm, Replace 24-98
Hub & Bearing Service 24-96
Manual Steering Gears 29-1
Manual Steering Gear, Replace 24-99
Power Steering 29-1
Power Steering Gear, Replace 24-99
Power Steering Pump, Replace 24-99
Precautions 24-94
Rear Power Cylinder, Replace 24-100
Rear Power Cylinder Control Valve, Replace 24-100
Stabilizer Bar, Replace 24-98
Strut, Replace 24-97
Strut Service 24-97
Tightening Specifications 24-106
Wheel Bearing, Adjust 24-94
Wheel Hub & Steering Knuckle, Replace 24-94
FRONT WHEEL DRIVE AXLES 29-1
REAR AXLE & SUSPENSION
Coil Spring, Replace 24-82
Control Arm, Replace 24-83
Differential Carrier, Replace ... 24-79
Hub & Bearing, Replace 24-80
Lateral Rod, Replace 24-91
Propeller Shaft, Replace 24-79
Rear Suspension, Replace 24-81
Shock Absorber, Replace 24-82
Stabilizer Bar, Replace 24-84
Tightening Specifications 24-91
Torsion Bar, Replace 24-91
Trailing Arm, Replace 24-83
Wheel Bearing, Adjust 24-80
SERVICE REMINDER & WARNING LAMP RESET PROCEDURES 0-10
SPECIFICATIONS
Fluid Capacities & Cooling System Data 24-4
Front Wheel Alignment Specifications 24-3
General Engine Specifications 24-2
Lubricant Data 24-4
Rear Wheel Alignment Specifications 24-3
Tune Up Specifications 24-2
TRANSFER CASE
Transfer Case, Replace 24-94
VEHICLE IDENTIFICATINS . 0-1
VEHICLE LIFT POINTS 0-34
VEHICLE MAINTENANCE SCHEDULES 0-69
WHEEL ALIGNMENT
Front Wheel Alignment 24-109
Preliminary Inspection 24-109
Rear Wheel Alignment 24-109
Vehicle Ride Height 24-109
Wheel Alignment Specifications 24-3
WIRE COLOR CODE IDENTIFICATION 0-144
1.8L & 2.0L ENGINES
Belt Tension Data 24-30
Camshaft, Replace 24-27
Compression Pressure 24-18
Cooling System Bleed 24-30
Crankshaft, Replace 24-22
Cylinder Head, Replace 24-20
Engine Mount, Replace 24-18
Engine Rebuilding Specifications 29-1
Engine, Replace 24-19
Exhaust Manifold, Replace 24-20
Front Cover, Replace 24-23
Fuel Filter, Replace 24-33
Fuel Pump, Replace 24-32
Intake Manifold, Replace 24-19
Main & Rod Bearings 24-29
Oil Pan, Replace 24-29
Oil Pump, Replace 24-29
Piston & Rod Assembly 24-29
Precautions 24-18
Radiator, Replace 24-31
Rocker Arms, Replace 24-22
Silent Shaft, Replace 24-29
Thermostat, Replace 24-30
Tightening Specifications 24-47
Timing Belt, Replace 24-23
Turbocharger, Replace 24-33
Valve Adjustment 24-22
Valve Arrangement 24-22
Valve Clearance Specifications 24-22
Valve Lifters 24-22
Water Pump, Replace 24-31
2.4L ENGINE
Engine Rebuilding Specifications 29-1
Engine, Replace 24-50
Tightening Specifications 24-51
3.0L ENGINE
Belt Tension Data 24-58
Camshaft, Replace 24-57
Compression Pressure 24-53
Cooling System Bleed 24-58
Cylinder Head, Replace 24-55
Engine Mount, Replace 24-53
Engine Rebuilding Specifications 29-1
Engine, Replace 24-54
Exhaust Manifold, Replace 24-55
Fuel Filter, Replace 24-60
Fuel Pump, Replace 24-58
Intake Manifold, Replace 24-54
Oil Cooler, Replace 24-58
Oil Pan, Replace 24-58
Oil Pump, Replace 24-58
Oil Pump Service 24-58
Piston & Rod Assembly 24-57
Precautions 24-53
Radiator, Replace 24-58
Thermostat, Replace 24-58
Tightening Specifications 24-67
Timing Belt, Replace 24-56
Turbocharger, Replace 24-60
Valve Adjustment 24-56
Valve Clearance Specifications 24-56
Valve Cover, Replace 24-
Water Pump, Replace .

Specifications

GENERAL ENGINE SPECIFICATIONS

Year	Engine Liter	Fuel System	Bore & Stroke	Compression Ratio	Maximum Net H.P. @ RPM	Maximum Torque, Ft. Lbs. @ RPM	Normal Oil Pressure, psi
1993	1.8L	Fuel Inj.	3.17 X 3.39	9.0	92 @ 5500	105 @ 3500	11.4②
	2.0L	Fuel Inj.	3.35 X 3.46	9.0	135 @ 5000	125 @ 3000	11.4②
	2.0L①	Fuel Inj.	3.35 X 3.46	7.8	190 @ 5000	203 @ 3000	11.4②
	3.0L	Fuel Inj.	3.59 X 2.99	10.0	222 @ 6000	201 @ 4500	11.4②
	3.0L①	Fuel Inj.	3.59 X 2.99	8.0	300 @ 6000	307 @ 2500	11.4②
1994	1.8L	Fuel Inj.	3.17 X 3.39	9.0	92 @ 5000	105 @ 3500	11.4②
	2.0L	Fuel Inj.	3.35 X 3.46	9.0	135 @ 6000	125 @ 3000	11.4②
	2.0L①	Fuel Inj.	3.35 X 3.46	7.8	195 @ 6000	203 @ 3000	11.4②
	3.0L	Fuel Inj.	3.59 X 2.99	10.0	222 @ 6000	205 @ 4500	11.4②
	3.0L①	Fuel Inj.	3.59 X 2.99	8.0	320 @ 6000	315 @ 2500	11.4②
1995	2.0L	Fuel Inj.	3.45 X 3.27	9.6	140 @ 6000	130 @ 4800	4.0③
	2.0L①	Fuel Inj.	3.35 X 3.46	8.5	210 @ 6000	214 @ 3000	11.4②
	3.0L	Fuel Inj.	3.59 X 2.99	10.0	222 @ 6000	205 @ 4500	11.4②
	3.0L①	Fuel Inj.	3.59 X 2.99	8.0	320 @ 6000	315 @ 2500	11.4②
1996	2.0L	Fuel Inj.	3.45 X 3.27	9.6	140 @ 6000	130 @ 4800	11.4①
	2.0L①	Fuel Inj.	3.35 X 3.46	8.5	210 @ 6000	214 @ 3000	11.4①
	2.4L	Fuel Inj.	3.41 X 3.94	9.5	141 @ 5500	148 @ 3000	11.4①
	3.0L	Fuel Inj.	3.59 X 2.99	10.0	218 @ 6000	205 @ 4500	11.4①
	3.0L①	Fuel Inj.	3.59 X 2.99	8.0	320 @ 6000	315 @ 2500	11.4①

① — Turbocharged engine.
② — At idle speed w/oil temperature between 167 to 194°F.
③ — At idle speed.

TUNE UP SPECIFICATIONS

Year	Engine Liter	Spark Plug Gap, Inch	Ignition Timing			Idle Speed, RPM				Fuel Pump Pressure, psi	Valve Lash
						Curb②		Fast			
			Firing Order	Timing, °BTDC	Timing Mark Location	Man. Trans.	Auto. Trans.	Man. Trans.	Auto. Trans.		
1993–94	1.8L	.041	1-3-4-2	5③	Pulley	700	700N	④	④	50	⑪
	2.0L	.041	1-3-4-2	5③	Pulley	750	750N	④	④	50	⑪
	2.0L⑤	.029	1-3-4-2	5③	Pulley	750	750N	④	④	⑥	⑪
	3.0L	.041	1-2-3-4-5-6	5①	⑦	700	700N	④	④	38	⑪
1995	2.0L	.050	⑧	12①	⑦	700	700N	④	④	48	⑪
	2.0L⑤	.030	⑧	5⑨	⑦	750	750N	④	④	42-45⑩	⑪
	3.0L	.041	1-2-3-4-5-6	5①	⑦	700	700N	④	④	38	⑪
1996	2.0L	.500	1-3-4-2	①	⑦	800	800N	④	④	47-50	⑪
	2.0L⑤	.300	1-3-4-2	5⑨	⑦	750	750N	④	④	33	⑪
	2.4L	.400	1-3-4-2	5⑨	⑦	750	750N	④	④	38	⑪
	3.0L	.410	1-2-3-4-5-6	5①	⑦	700	700N	④	④	38	⑪
	3.0L⑤	.410	1-2-3-4-5-6	5①	⑦	700	700N	④	④	34	⑪

BTDC — Before Top Dead Center.
N — Neutral.
① — Electronically controlled.
② — When adjusting idle speed, set parking brake & chock drive wheels.
③ — With jumper wire connected between ignition timing adjustment connector and ground. Refer to Fig. A.
④ — Controlled by idle speed control servo.
⑤ — Turbocharged engine.
⑥ — Models w/manual transaxle, 37 psi; models w/automatic transaxle, 43.5 psi.
⑦ — Equipped w/crankshaft position sensor.
⑧ — Cylinder numbering from front of engine to rear, 1, 2, 3, 4; firing order, 1–3–4–2.
⑨ — With jumper wire connected between ignition timing adjustment connector & ground. Refer to Fig. B.
⑩ — Pressure regulator vacuum hose disconnected at curb idle.
⑪ — Equipped w/hydraulic lash adjusters.

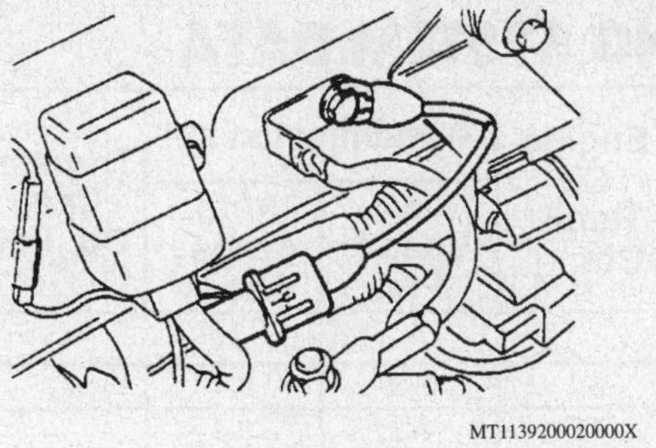
MT1139200020000X

Fig. A

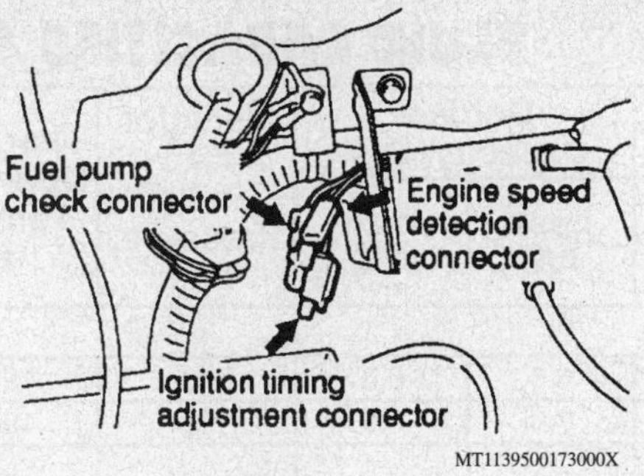
Fuel pump
check connector
Engine speed
detection
connector
Ignition timing
adjustment connector
MT1139500173000X

Fig. B

FRONT WHEEL ALIGNMENT SPECIFICATIONS

Year	Model	Caster Angle, Deg.		Camber Angle, Deg.		Toe, Inch①	Ball Joint Wear
		Limits	Desired	Limits	Desired		
1993–94	Eclipse FWD 1.8L	+1 5/6 to +2 5/6	+2 1/3	–4/15 to +11/15	+7/30	–.12 to +.12	⑥
	Eclipse FWD 2.0L	+1 9/10 to +2 9/10	+2 2/5	–5/12 to +7/12	+1/12	–.12 to +.12	⑥
	Eclipse AWD	+1 4/5 to +2 4/5	+2 3/10	–1/3 to +2/3	+1/6	–.12 to +.12	⑥
	3000GT	+3 5/12 to +4 5/12	+3 11/12	–1/2 to +1/2	0	–.12 to +.12	⑤
1995-96	Eclipse②	+3 1/6 to +6 1/6	+4 2/3	-7/12 to +5/12	-1/12	–.12 to +.12	④
	Eclipse③	+3 1/6 to +6 1/6	+4 2/3	-5/6 to +1/6	-1/3	–.12 to +.12	④
	3000GT	+3 5/12 to +4 5/12	+3 11/12	–1/2 to +1/2	0	–.12 to +.12	⑤

AWD — All Wheel Drive.
FWD — Front Wheel Drive.
① — Toe-in (+); toe-out (-).
② — With 14 inch wheels.
③ — With 16 inch wheels.

④ — Lateral lower arm ball joint breakaway torque, 9–30 ft. lbs.; stabilizer link ball joint breakaway torque, 4–13 inch lbs.
⑤ — Lateral lower arm ball joint breakaway torque, 86–191 inch lbs.; stabilizer link ball joint breakaway torque, 15–28 inch lbs.
⑥ — Lateral lower arm ball joint breakaway torque, 26–87 inch lbs.; stabilizer link ball joint breakaway torque, 15–28 inch lbs.

REAR WHEEL ALIGNMENT SPECIFICATIONS

Year	Model	Camber Angle, Deg.		Toe, Inch①
		Limits	Desired	
1993	Eclipse FWD	–1 1/4 to –1/4	–3/4	–.12 to +.12
	Eclipse AWD	–2 1/20 to –1 1/20	–1 11/20	+.02 to +.26
	3000GT FWD	–1/2 to +1/2	0	②
	3000GT AWD	–1/3 to +2/3	1/6	②
1994	Eclipse FWD	–1 1/4 to –1/4	–3/4	–.12 to +.12
	Eclipse AWD	–2 1/20 to –1 1/20	–1 11/20	+.02 to +.26
	3000GT FWD	–1/2 to +1/2	0	-.08 to +.10
	3000GT AWD	–1/3 to +2/3	1/6	-.08 to +.10
1995–96	Eclipse AWD③	-1 5/6 to -5/6	-1 1/3	0 to +.24
	Eclipse AWD④	-2 1/6 to -1 1/6	-1 2/3	0 to +.24
	Eclipse FWD⑤	-1 5/6 to -5/6	-1 1/3	0 to +.24
	Eclipse FWD⑥	-2 1/6 to -1 1/6	-1 2/3	0 to +.24
	3000GT FWD	–1/2 to +1/2	0	-.08 to +.10
	3000GT AWD	–1/3 to +2/3	1/6	-.08 to +.10

AWD — All Wheel Drive.
FWD — Front Wheel Drive.
① — Toe-in (+); toe-out (-).
② — Less Electronic Control Suspension, –.08 to +.10; w/Electronic Control Suspension, –.10 to +.12.
③ — Manual transaxle.
④ — Automatic transaxle.
⑤ — With 14 inch wheels.
⑥ — With 16 inch wheels

FLUID CAPACITIES & COOLING SYSTEM DATA

Model & Engine	Coolant Capacity, Qts. Less A/C	Coolant Capacity, Qts. With A/C	Radiator Cap Relief Pressure, Lbs.	Thermo. Opening Temp., °F	Fuel Tank, Gals.	Engine Oil Refill, Qts. ①	Transmission Oil 5 Speed, Pts.	Transmission Oil Auto. Trans., Qts.②	Transfer Case Oil, Pts.	Rear Drive Axle Oil, Pts.
1993										
Eclipse 1.8L	6.6	6.6	13	190	15.9	4.1	3.8	6.4	—	—
Eclipse 2.0L	7.6	7.6	13	190	15.9	4.6	3.8	6.4	—	—
Eclipse FWD 2.0L Turbo	7.6	7.6	13	190	15.9	4.8	4.8	7.4	—	—
Eclipse AWD 2.0L Turbo	7.6	7.6	13	190	15.9	4.8	4.8	7.4	1.26	1.48
3000GT 3.0L	8.5	8.5	13	170	19.8	4.5	4.2	7.9	—	—
3000GT 3.0L Turbo	8.5	8.5	13	170	19.8	4.9	5.0	7.9	1.58	2.40
1994										
Eclipse 1.8L	6.6	6.6	13	190	15.9	4.1	3.8	6.4	—	—
Eclipse 2.0L	7.6	7.6	13	190	15.9	4.6	3.8	6.4	—	—
Eclipse FWD 2.0L Turbo	7.6	7.6	13	190	15.9	4.8	4.8	7.4	—	—
Eclipse AWD 2.0L Turbo	7.6	7.6	13	190	15.9	4.8	4.8	7.4	1.26	1.48
3000GT 3.0L	8.5	8.5	13	170	19.8	4.5	4.8	7.9	—	—
3000GT 3.0L Turbo	8.5	8.5	13	170	19.8	4.9	5.0	7.9	③	2.40
1995–96										
Eclipse 2.0L Non-Turbo	7.4	7.4	13	195	16	4.5	4.2	9.1	—	—
Eclipse 2.0L FWD Turbo	7.4	7.4	13	180	16	4.5	4.2	7.1	—	—
Eclipse 2.0L AWD Turbo	7.4	7.4	13	180	16	4.5	4.6	7.1	1.06	1.80
3000GT 3.0L	8.5	8.5	13	170	19.8	4.5	4.8	7.9	—	—
3000GT 3.0L Turbo	8.5	8.5	13	170	19.8	4.9	5.0	7.9	③	2.40

AWD — All Wheel Drive.
DOHC — Dual Overhead Cam.
SOHC — Single Overhead Cam.
FWD — Front Wheel Drive.
① — Includes filter.
② — Approximate; make final check with dipstick.
③ — 5 MT, 1.58 pts.; 6 MT, 1.64 pts.

LUBRICANT DATA

Year	Lubricant Type: Transmission Manual	Transmission Automatic	Transfer Case	Rear Axle	Power Steering	Brake System
ECLIPSE						
1993–94	75w/90 GL-4/5	Dia ATF SP	75w/90 GL-4/5	GL-5	Dexron II/IIE/III	DOT 3
1995–96①	③	Dia ATF SP	—	—	Dexron II/IIE/III	DOT 3 or 4
1995–96②	75w/90 GL-4	Dia ATF SP	75w/90 GL-4	GL-5	Dexron II/IIE/III	DOT 3 or 4
3000GT						
1993–96	75w/90 GL-4/5	Dia ATF SP	75w/90 GL-4/5	GL-5	Dexron II/IIE/III	DOT 3

① — With non-turbocharged engine.

② — With turbocharged engine.

③ — Texaco MTX fluid FM or equivalent.

Electrical

NOTE: On Air Bag Equipped Models, Refer To "Air Bag System Precautions" Located In The Front Of This Manual For System Disarming & Arming Procedures.

INDEX

	Page No.
Air Bags	29-1
Air Conditioning	29-1
Alternators	29-1
Blower Motor, Replace	24-13
Eclipse	24-13
3000GT	24-13
Coil Pack, Replace	24-7
Eclipse	24-7
3000GT	24-7
Combination Switch, Replace	24-8
Eclipse	24-8
3000GT	24-9
Cooling Fans	29-1
Cruise Control	29-1
Dash Gauges	29-1
Dash Panels	29-1
Dimmer Switch, Replace	24-10
Distributor, Replace	24-7
1.8L Engine	24-7
Evaporator Core, Replace	24-14
Eclipse	24-14
3000GT	24-15
Fuel Pump Relay Location	24-5
Eclipse	24-5
3000GT	24-5
Fuse Panel & Flasher Location	24-5
Eclipse	24-5
3000GT	24-5
Headlamp Switch, Replace	24-8
Heater Core, Replace	24-14
Eclipse	24-14
3000GT	24-14
Ignition Lock, Replace	24-7
Eclipse	24-7
3000GT	24-7
Ignition Switch, Replace	24-8
Instrument Cluster, Replace	24-10
Eclipse	24-10
3000GT	24-10
Neutral Safety Switch, Replace	24-8
Passive Restraints	29-1
Precautions	24-5
Air Bag Systems	24-5
Radio, Replace	24-11
Eclipse	24-11
3000GT	24-11
Relay Center Location	24-5
Eclipse	24-5
3000GT	24-5
Speed Controls	29-1
Starter, Replace	24-5
Eclipse	24-5
3000GT	24-6
Starter Motors	29-1
Steering Columns	29-1
Steering Wheel, Replace	24-10
Eclipse	24-10
3000GT	24-10
Wiper Motor, Replace	24-11
Eclipse	24-11
3000GT	24-12
Wiper Switch, Replace	24-13
Wiper Systems	29-1

PRECAUTIONS

AIR BAG SYSTEMS

Refer to "Air Bag System Precautions" in the front of this manual for system disarming and arming procedures.

FUSE PANEL & FLASHER LOCATION

ECLIPSE

1993-94

The fuse panel is located under the lefthand side of the instrument panel. There are fuses located in a relay box on the right inner fender in the engine compartment. The A/C dedicated fuses are located in the engine compartment, behind the right front strut tower. The turn signal and hazard flasher unit is located under the lefthand side of the instrument panel, near the fuse panel.

1995-96

The multi-purpose fuse panel and dedicated fuse panel are located under the driver's side instrument panel.

The hazard and turn signal flasher are located behind the center console.

On non-turbo models, the dedicated fuse panel/power distribution block is located in the front lefthand side of the engine compartment.

On turbo models, the dedicated fuse panel/power distribution block is located in the righthand side of the engine compartment.

3000GT

The fuse panel is located under the lefthand side of the instrument panel. There are fuses located in the relay box on the right and left fender inner fender in the engine compartment. The turn signal and hazard flasher unit is located under the lefthand side of the instrument panel, near the lower kick panel.

FUEL PUMP RELAY LOCATION

ECLIPSE

1993-94

The fuel pump relay is located behind the center instrument panel.

1995-96

On non-turbo models, the fuel pump relay is located in the lefthand rear corner of the engine compartment.

On turbo models, the fuel pump relay is located behind center instrument panel.

3000GT

The fuel pump relay is located in the righthand side of the engine compartment, near the relay box.

RELAY CENTER LOCATION

ECLIPSE

1993-94

The main relay centers are located on the center righthand side and rear lefthand side of the engine compartment.

1995-96

On non-turbo models, the main relay centers are located on the front lefthand side and rear lefthand side of the engine compartment.

On turbo models, the main relay centers are located on the center righthand side of the engine compartment.

3000GT

The main relay centers are located on the center righthand side and lefthand rear corner of the engine compartment.

STARTER

REPLACE

ECLIPSE

1993-94

1. Disconnect battery cables, then remove battery sheet and battery tray.
2. Disconnect connection on transaxle side of speedometer cable.

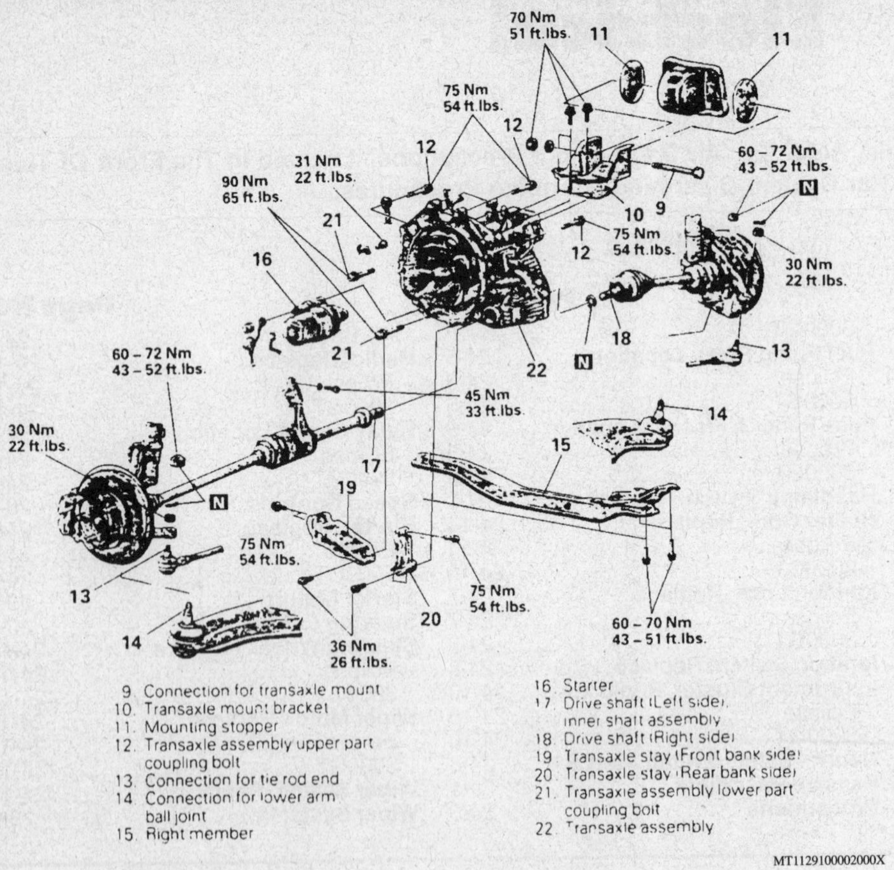

70 Nm
51 ft.lbs.
75 Nm
54 ft.lbs.
31 Nm
22 ft.lbs.
90 Nm
65 ft.lbs.
60 – 72 Nm
43 – 52 ft.lbs.
75 Nm
54 ft.lbs.
30 Nm
22 ft.lbs.
60 – 72 Nm
43 – 52 ft.lbs.
45 Nm
33 ft.lbs.
30 Nm
22 ft.lbs.
75 Nm
54 ft.lbs.
75 Nm
54 ft.lbs.
60 – 70 Nm
43 – 51 ft.lbs.
36 Nm
26 ft.lbs.
9. Connection for transaxle mount
10. Transaxle mount bracket
11. Mounting stopper
12. Transaxle assembly upper part coupling bolt
13. Connection for tie rod end
14. Connection for lower arm ball joint
15. Right member
16. Starter
17. Drive shaft (Left side), inner shaft assembly
18. Drive shaft (Right side)
19. Transaxle stay (Front bank side)
20. Transaxle stay (Rear bank side)
21. Transaxle assembly lower part coupling bolt
22. Transaxle assembly
MT1129100002000X

Fig. 1 Starter replacement. 3000GT FWD w/manual transaxle

3. **On models with 1.8L engine,** remove intake manifold stay.
4. **On all models,** disconnect starter wiring harness connection.
5. Remove starter mounting bolts, then the starter.
6. Reverse procedure to install.

1995–96

1. Disconnect battery ground cable, then raise and support vehicle.
2. **On non-turbo models with manual transmission,**remove aspirator assembly.
3. **On turbo models,** remove air hose.
4. **On all models,** remove starter terminal and connector.
5. Remove starter.
6. Reverse procedure to install.

3000GT

MANUAL TRANSAXLE

FWD Models

1. Raise and support vehicle.
2. Drain transmission fluid into appropriate container.
3. Remove engine lower cover.
4. Remove battery and battery tray, then the washer tank.
5. Remove air cleaner cover and air intake hose.
6. Remove clutch release cylinder and oil line bracket without disconnecting oil coupling, then secure to body using suitable wire.
7. Disconnect transaxle control and speedometer cables.
8. Raise transaxle with suitable jack to release pressure on transaxle mount bracket, then disconnect transaxle mount.
9. Remove transaxle mounting stopper, **Fig. 1.**
10. Loosen tie rod end nut then disconnect tie rod from knuckle using steering linkage puller tool No. MB991113-01, or equivalent. **Ensure tie cord of tool is tied off correctly.**
11. Repeat step 10 on lower ball joint.
12. With transaxle properly supported, remove righthand crossmember.
13. Remove starter electrical connections, then the starter assembly.
14. Reverse procedure to install, noting the following:
    a. Install mounting stopper as shown, **Fig. 2.**
    b. **Torque** starter bolts to 65 ft. lbs.
    c. **Torque** righthand crossmember bolts to 43–51 ft. lbs.
    d. **Torque** lower ball joint nut to 43–52 ft. lbs. and tie rod end nut to 22 ft. lbs.
    e. **Torque** transaxle mount bracket bolts to 51 ft. lbs.
    f. **Torque** clutch tube bracket bolts to 13 ft. lbs.

AWD Models

1. Raise and support vehicle.
2. Drain transaxle oil into appropriate

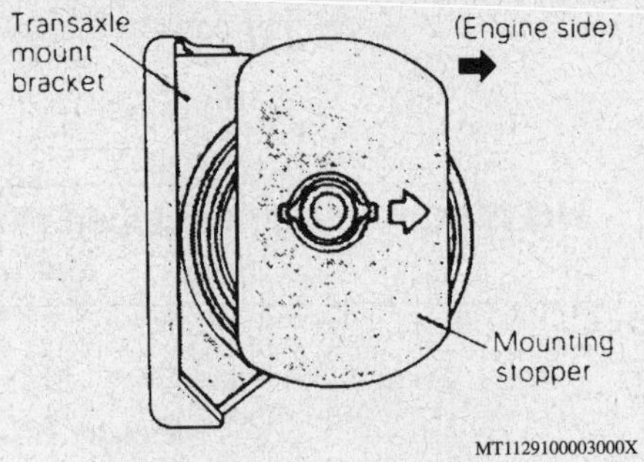

Transaxle mount bracket
(Engine side)
Mounting stopper
MT1129100003000X

Fig. 2 Mounting stopper installation. 3000GT

container and remove engine lower cover.
3. Disconnect front exhaust pipe and support from frame.
4. Remove rear propeller shaft and support aside. **Suspend propeller shaft so it is not sharply bent.**
5. Remove transfer assembly mounting bolts, then the transfer assembly.
6. Remove air cleaner hoses, air cleaner, air intake hose and vacuum pipe.
7. Remove battery and battery tray, then the washer tank.
8. Disconnect transaxle control cable.
9. Remove clutch release cylinder and oil line bracket without disconnecting oil coupling, then secure to body using suitable wire.
10. Raise transaxle to release pressure on transaxle mount bracket using suitable jack stand then disconnect transaxle mount.
11. Remove transaxle mounting stopper, **Fig. 3.**
12. Loosen tie rod end nut, then disconnect tie rod from knuckle using steering linkage puller tool No. MB991113-01, or equivalent. **Ensure tie cord of tool is tied off correctly.**
13. Repeat step 12 on lower ball joint.
14. With transaxle properly supported, remove righthand crossmember.
15. Remove starter electrical connections, then the starter assembly.
16. Reverse procedure to install, noting the following:
    a. Install mounting stopper as shown, **Fig. 2.**
    b. **Torque** starter bolts to 65 ft. lbs.
    c. **Torque** righthand crossmember bolts to 43–51 ft. lbs.
    d. **Torque** lower ball joint nut to 43–52 ft. lbs. and tie rod end nut to 36 ft. lbs.
    e. **Torque** transaxle mount bracket bolts to 51 ft. lbs.
    f. **Torque** clutch tube bracket bolts to 13 ft. lbs.
    g. **Torque** transfer assembly mounting bolts to 61–65 ft. lbs.

AUTOMATIC TRANSAXLE

1. Place gear selector lever into Neutral position.
2. Raise and support vehicle.
3. Drain transaxle oil into appropriate container and remove front and side lower covers.
4. Remove battery and battery tray, then

the washer tank.
5. Remove air cleaner cover and air intake hose.
6. Disconnect transaxle control and speedometer cables.
7. Disconnect oil cooler lines.
8. Disconnect Park/Neutral position and kickdown servo switches.
9. Disconnect pulse generator and oil temperature sensor.
10. Raise transaxle to release pressure on transaxle mount bracket using suitable jack stand, then disconnect transaxle mount.
11. Loosen tie rod end nut then disconnect tie rod from knuckle using steering linkage puller tool No. MB991113-01, or equivalent. **Ensure tie cord of tool is tied off correctly.**
12. Repeat step 11 on lower ball joint.
13. With transaxle properly supported, remove righthand crossmember, **Fig. 4.**
14. Remove starter electrical connections, then the starter assembly.
15. Reverse procedure to install, noting the following:
    a. **Torque** starter bolts to 22 ft. lbs.
    b. **Torque** righthand crossmember bolts to 43–51 ft. lbs.
    c. **Torque** lower ball joint nut to 43–52 ft. lbs. and tie rod end nut to 22 ft. lbs.
    d. **Torque** transaxle mount bracket bolts to 51 ft. lbs.

DISTRIBUTOR

REPLACE

1.8L ENGINE

1. Disconnect battery ground cable.
2. Mark and remove spark plug cables.
3. Mark location of distributor rotor on distributor body.
4. Mark location of distributor body on cylinder head.
5. Remove distributor hold-down nut, then the distributor.
6. Reverse procedure to install, noting the following:
    a. Align marks made during removal to install.
    b. If crankshaft or camshaft was moved while distributor was removed, turn crankshaft so that No. 1 cylinder is at top dead center (TDC).
    c. Align distributor housing and gear mating marks, **Fig. 5.**
    d. Install distributor on engine while aligning fine groove of distributor installation flange with center of distributor installation stud.
    e. **Torque** hold-down nut to 7–9 ft. lbs.

COIL PACK

REPLACE

ECLIPSE

1. **On all 1993–94 models and 1995–96 turbo models,** remove center cover.
2. **On all models,** disconnect spark plug cables from ignition coil. **Label cables for installation reference.**

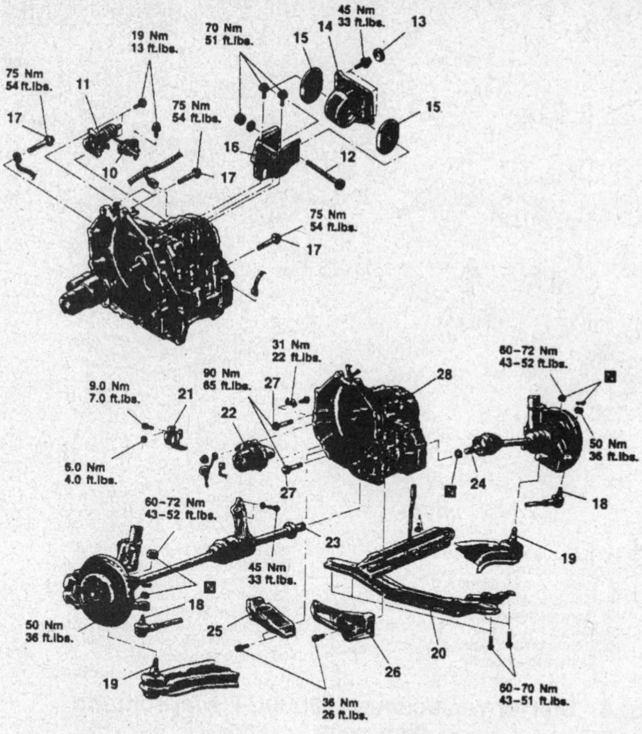
45 Nm
33 ft.lbs.
13
14
19 Nm
13 ft.lbs.
70 Nm
51 ft.lbs.
15
75 Nm
54 ft.lbs.
11
75 Nm
54 ft.lbs.
17
15
16
12
10
17
75 Nm
54 ft.lbs.
17
31 Nm
22 ft.lbs.
90 Nm
65 ft.lbs.
27
28
60-72 Nm
43-52 ft.lbs.
9.0 Nm
7.0 ft.lbs.
21
22
50 Nm
36 ft.lbs.
6.0 Nm
4.0 ft.lbs.
27
24
18
60-72 Nm
43-52 ft.lbs.
23
45 Nm
33 ft.lbs.
19
18
50 Nm
36 ft.lbs.
25
20
26
19
36 Nm
26 ft.lbs.
60-70 Nm
43-51 ft.lbs.

10. Clutch tube bracket connection
11. Clutch release cylinder connection
12. Transaxle mount connection
13. Plug
14. Transaxle mount bracket (Body side)
15. Mounting stopper
16. Transaxle mount bracket (Transaxle side)
17. Transaxle assembly lower part coupling bolt
18. Tie rod end connection
19. Lower arm ball joint connection
20. Right member
21. Starter cover
22. Starter
23. Drive shaft (Left side), Inner shaft assembly
24. Drive shaft (Right side)
25. Transaxle stay connection (Front bank side)
26. Transaxle stay connection (Rear bank side)
27. Transaxle assembly lower part coupling bolt
28. Transaxle assembly

MT1129500034000X

Fig. 3 Starter replacement. 3000GT AWD w/manual transaxle

3. Remove coil pack mounting screws, then the coil pack.
4. Reverse procedure to install.

3000GT

1. Disconnect spark plug cables from ignition coil. **Label cables for installation reference.**
2. Remove coil pack mounting screws, then the coil pack.
3. Reverse procedure to install.

IGNITION LOCK

REPLACE

ECLIPSE

1. Remove steering wheel as outlined under "Steering Wheel Replace."
2. Remove instrument panel lower cover.
3. Remove plug, then remove hood lock release handle, **Figs. 6 and 7.**
4. Remove upper and lower column covers.
5. **On air bag equipped models,** remove clock spring.
6. **On 1995–96 models,** remove column switch.
7. **On all models,** remove ignition key illumination light.
8. Insert key in ignition lock cylinder and turn to Acc position.
9. Using a Phillips tip screwdriver, or equivalent, push lockpin of ignition lock cylinder inward, then pull ignition lock cylinder out, **Fig. 8.**
10. **On 1993–94 models,** remove lap cooler, foot shower duct, cable band, key interlock cable and slide lever.
11. **On 1995–96 models,** remove key reminder switch segment and key hole illumination lamp if equipped.
12. **On all models,** remove ignition switch segment.
13. Reverse procedure to install, noting the following:
    a. **On 1993–94 models,** with ignition key removed, install slide lever to ignition lock cylinder, then connect key interlock cable to slide lever as shown, **Fig. 9.**
    b. Apply a light coat of multi-purpose grease to areas shown, then ensure proper operation of key interlock system.

3000GT

1. Remove ignition switch or lock cylinder in numbered sequence as shown, **Fig. 10,** noting the following:
    a. Remove steering wheel as outlined under "Steering Wheel, Replace."
    b. To remove clockspring connector

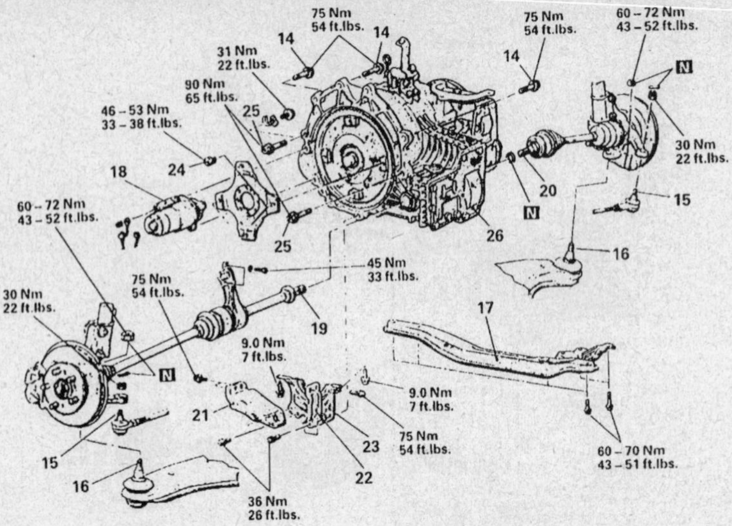
75 Nm
54 ft.lbs.
31 Nm
22 ft.lbs.
90 Nm
65 ft.lbs.
46 – 53 Nm
33 – 38 ft.lbs.
60 – 72 Nm
43 – 52 ft.lbs.
30 Nm
22 ft.lbs.
45 Nm
33 ft.lbs.
9.0 Nm
7 ft.lbs.
36 Nm
26 ft.lbs.
60 – 70 Nm
43 – 51 ft.lbs.
N

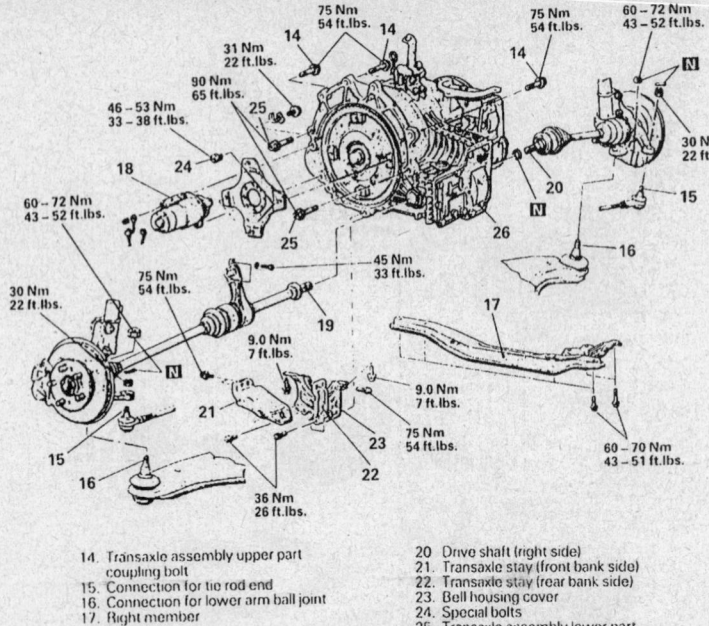

14. Transaxle assembly upper part coupling bolt
15. Connection for tie rod end
16. Connection for lower arm ball joint
17. Right member
18. Starter
19. Drive shaft (left side), Inner shaft assembly
20. Drive shaft (right side)
21. Transaxle stay (front bank side)
22. Transaxle stay (rear bank side)
23. Bell housing cover
24. Special bolts
25. Transaxle assembly lower part coupling bolt
26. Transaxle assembly

MT1129100005000X

Fig. 4 Starter replacement. 3000GT w/automatic transaxle

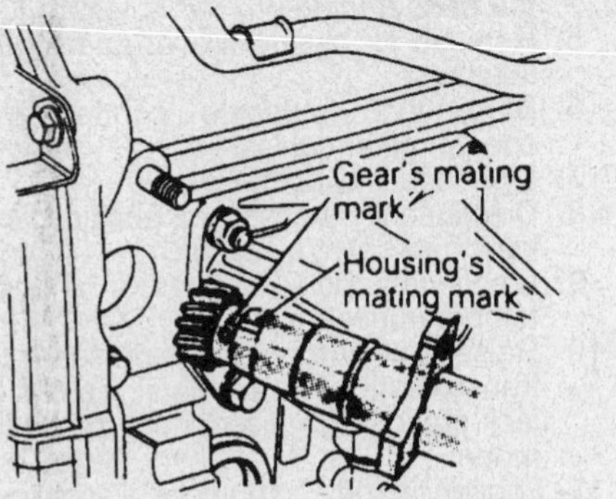
Gear's mating mark
Housing's mating mark

MT1119100001000X

Fig. 5 Distributor mating marks. 1.8L engine

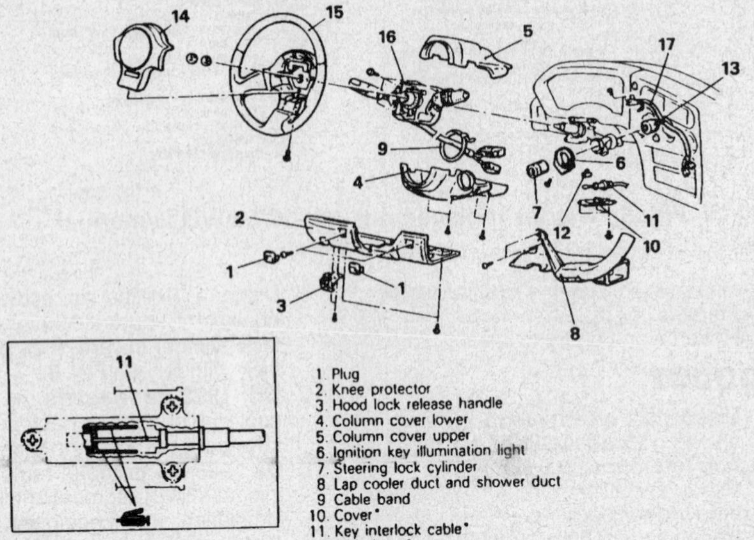

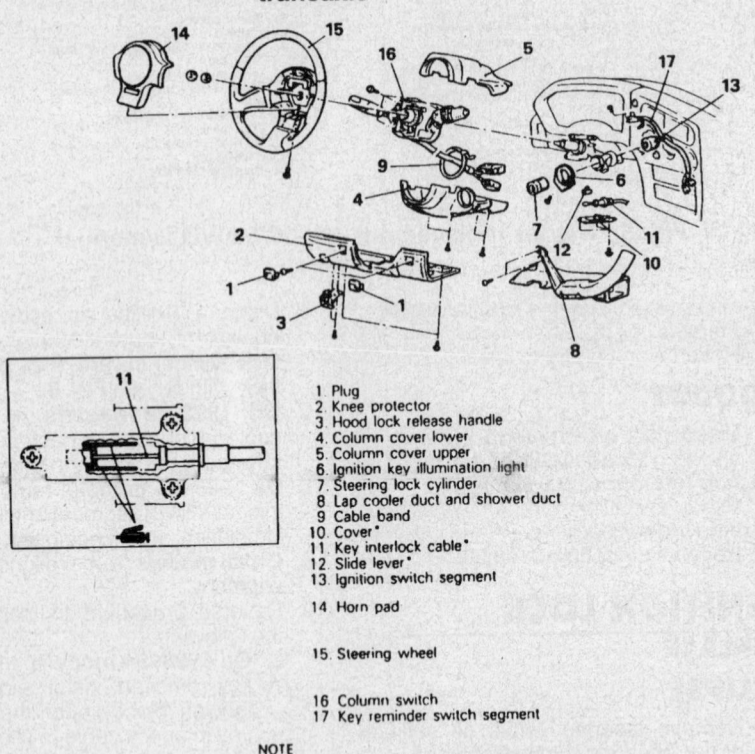

1. Plug
2. Knee protector
3. Hood lock release handle
4. Column cover lower
5. Column cover upper
6. Ignition key illumination light
7. Steering lock cylinder
8. Lap cooler duct and shower duct
9. Cable band
10. Cover*
11. Key interlock cable*
12. Slide lever*
13. Ignition switch segment
14. Horn pad
15. Steering wheel
16. Column switch
17. Key reminder switch segment

NOTE
* indicates vehicles with A/T safety-lock system

MT9129100006000X

Fig. 6 Ignition switch replacement. 1993–94 Eclipse

from air bag module, force lock outward and pry it with a suitable screwdriver as shown, **Fig. 11.** Ensure no excessive force is applied when connector is removed. **The removed air bag module should be stored in a clean, dry, flat place with pad cover facing up.**

c. Remove upper and lower steering column cover screws and covers, ensuring not to break cover grippers, **Fig. 12.**
d. Insert ignition key into ignition lock cylinder and turn to Acc position.
e. Press down lockpin using a suitable Phillips head screwdriver to remove lock cylinder, **Fig. 13.**

2. Reverse numbered sequence as shown, **Fig. 10**to assemble, noting the following:
   a. Line up "Neutral" mark of clockspring with mating mark to center clockspring. **If clockspring is not centered, problems such as intermediate failure of steering wheel to turn or broken ribbon cable in clockspring could occur. As a result, they might hinder proper operation of SRS, resulting in serious injury.**

IGNITION SWITCH

REPLACE

Refer to "Ignition Lock, Replace" for ignition switch replacement procedures.

NEUTRAL SAFETY SWITCH

REPLACE

1. Place selector lever in Neutral position.
2. Place manual control lever in Neutral position, then remove control lever retainer and lever.
3. Disconnect electrical harness, then remove switch retaining bolts and switch assembly.
4. Reverse procedure to install, then adjust as follows:
   a. With manual control lever in Neutral position, rotate switch body until wide end of control lever overlaps switch body flange.
   b. Hold switch body in position, then **torque** retaining bolts to 7–9 ft. lbs.

HEADLAMP SWITCH

REPLACE

Refer to "Combination Switch, Replace" for headlamp switch replacement procedure.

COMBINATION SWITCH

REPLACE

ECLIPSE

1993–94

1. Disconnect battery ground cable.

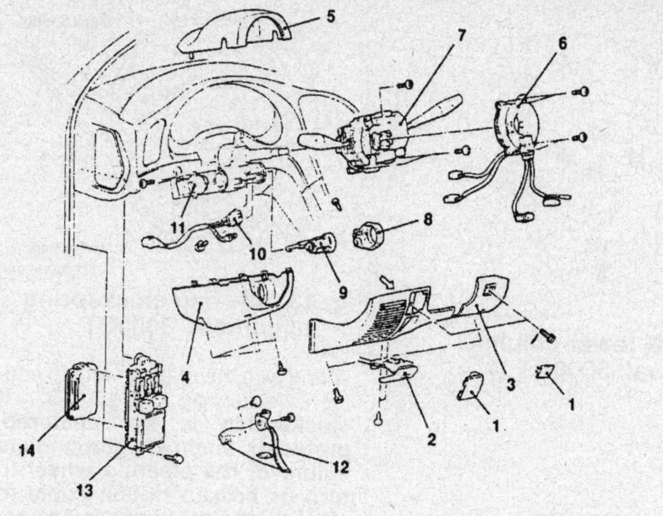
1
2
3
4
5
6
7
8
9
10
11
12
13
14

1. Plug
2. Hood lock release handle
3. Instrument under cover
4. Column cover lower
5. Column cover upper
6. Clock spring
7. Column switch
8. Ignition key illumination ring or ring cover
9. Steering lock cylinder
10. Key reminder switch segment or key hole illumination light
11. Ignition switch segment
12. Cowl side trim (LH)
13. Junction block
14. ETACS-ECU

MT9129500009000X

Fig. 7 Ignition switch replacement. 1995–96 Eclipse

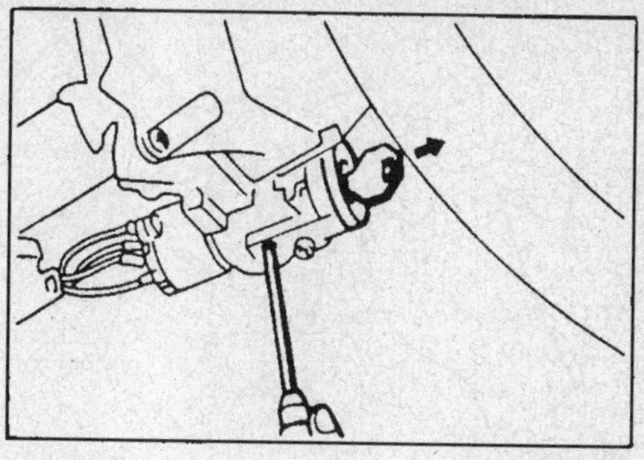

MT9129100004000X

Fig. 8 Lock cylinder removal. Eclipse

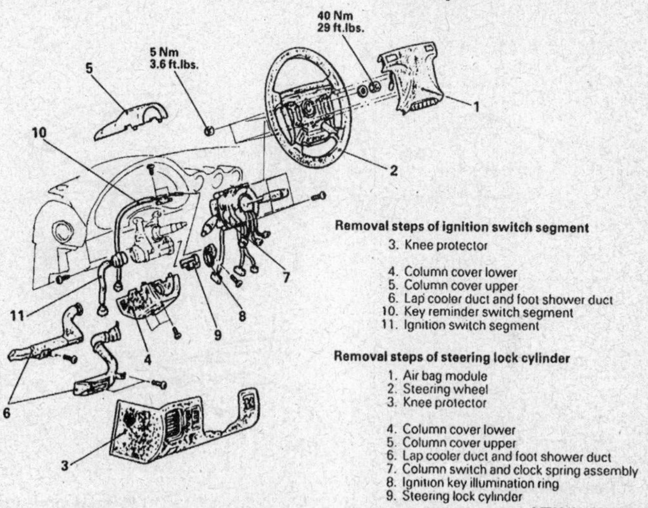
40 Nm
29 ft.lbs.
5 Nm
3.6 ft.lbs.
1
2
3
4
5
6
7
8
9
10
11
Removal steps of ignition switch segment
3. Knee protector
4. Column cover lower
5. Column cover upper
6. Lap cooler duct and foot shower duct
10. Key reminder switch segment
11. Ignition switch segment
Removal steps of steering lock cylinder
1. Air bag module
2. Steering wheel
3. Knee protector
4. Column cover lower
5. Column cover upper
6. Lap cooler duct and foot shower duct
7. Column switch and clock spring assembly
8. Ignition key illumination ring
9. Steering lock cylinder

MT9049100001000X

Fig. 10 Ignition switch replacement. 3000GT

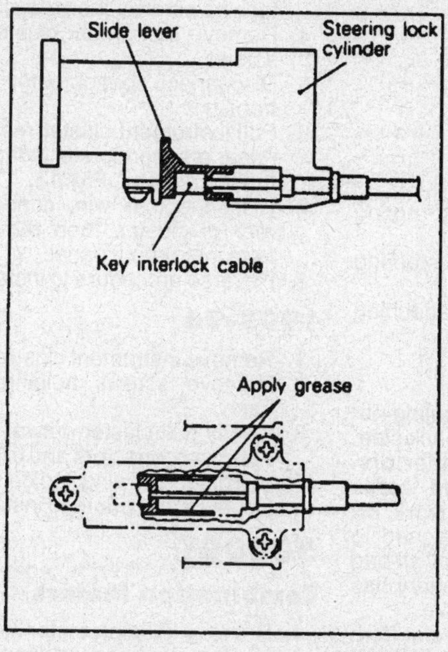
Slide lever
Steering lock cylinder
Key interlock cable
Apply grease

MT9129100005000X

Fig. 9 Slide lever installation. 1993–94 Eclipse

2. Remove steering wheel as outlined under "Steering Wheel, Replace."
3. Remove knee protector and hood lock handle, **Fig. 14.**
4. Remove upper and lower steering column covers.
5. Remove lap cooler and foot shower duct.
6. Remove cable band.
7. Disconnect column switch electrical connections and remove column switch.
8. Reverse procedure to install.

1995–96

1. Remove air bag module as outlined under "Air Bag System."
2. Remove steering wheel as outlined under "Steering Wheel, Replace."
3. Remove column switch in numbered sequence, **Fig. 15.**
4. Reverse procedure to install.

3000GT

1. Remove steering wheel as outlined under "Steering Wheel, Replace."
2. Remove knee protector as follows:
   a. Remove hood lock handle.
   b. Remove rheostat and switch garnish.
   c. Remove knee protector screws and knee protector, **Fig. 16.**
3. Remove upper and lower steering column cover screws, then remove covers ensuring not to break cover grippers, **Fig. 12.**
4. Remove lap cooler and foot shower duct.
5. Remove right and left column switches.

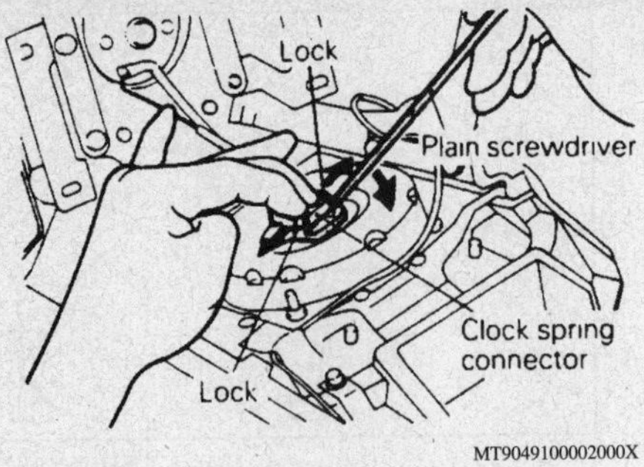

Lock
Plain screwdriver
Clock spring
connector
Lock
MT9049100002000X

Fig. 11 Air bag clockspring connector removal. 3000GT

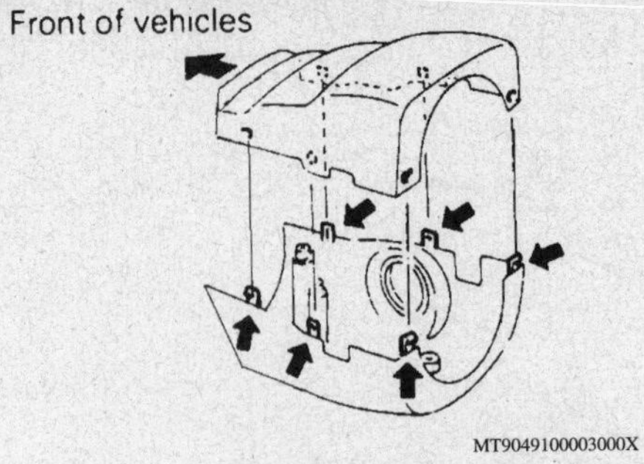

Front of vehicles
MT9049100003000X

Fig. 12 Upper & lower column cover removal. 3000GT

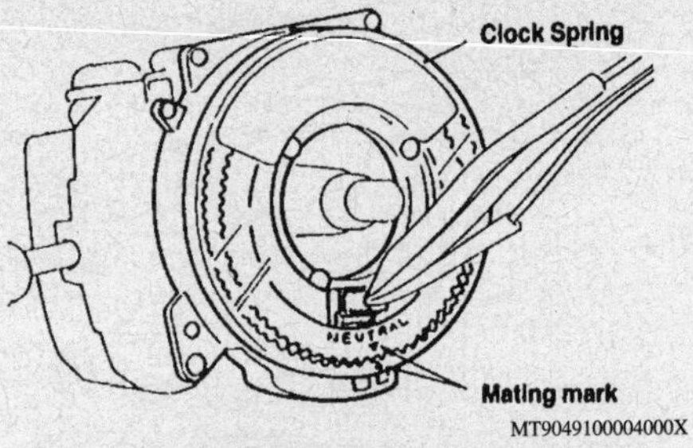

Clock Spring
Mating mark
MT9049100004000X

Fig. 13 Air bag clockspring alignment. 3000GT

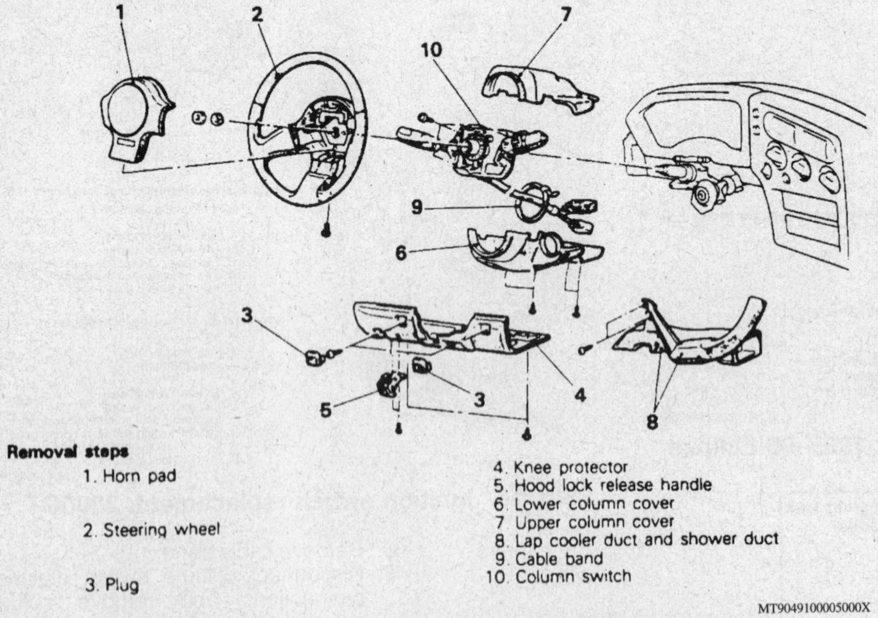

Removal steps
1. Horn pad
2. Steering wheel
3. Plug
4. Knee protector
5. Hood lock release handle
6. Lower column cover
7. Upper column cover
8. Lap cooler duct and shower duct
9. Cable band
10. Column switch
MT9049100005000X

Fig. 14 Column switch replacement. 1993–94 Eclipse

6. Reverse procedure to install.

DIMMER SWITCH

REPLACE

Refer to "Combination Switch, Replace" for dimmer switch replacement procedure.

STEERING WHEEL

REPLACE

ECLIPSE

1. Disconnect battery ground cable.
2. **On models with air bag,** remove air bag mounting nut from back side, then disconnect electrical connection.
3. **On models less air bag,** remove horn pad attaching screws and pad.
4. Remove steering wheel attaching nut.
5. Scribe mating marks on steering shaft and steering wheel for installation reference.
6. Using a suitable steering wheel puller, remove steering wheel. **Do not hammer on steering wheel to remove. Damage to collapsible mechanism may occur.**
7. Reverse procedure to install, noting the following:
   a. Align mating marks on steering shaft and steering wheel.
   b. **Torque** steering wheel attaching nut to 25–36 ft. lbs.

3000GT

1. Remove air bag module mounting nut using a socket wrench from back side. **Wait at least one minute after disconnecting battery ground cable before doing any further work on vehicle.** SRS system is designed to retain enough voltage to deploy air bag for a short time even after battery has been disconnected.
2. To remove clockspring connector from air bag module, force lock outward and pry it with a suitable screwdriver as shown, **Fig. 11.** Ensure no undue force is applied when connector is removed. **The removed air bag module should be stored in a clean, dry, flat place with pad cover facing up.**
3. Remove steering wheel using suitable puller.
4. Reverse procedure to install, noting the following:
   a. Line up the "Neutral" mark of clockspring with the mating mark to center clockspring, **Fig. 13. If clockspring is not centered, problems such as intermediate failure of the steering wheel to turn or broken ribbon cable in clockspring could occur. As a result, they might hinder proper operation of SRS, resulting in serious injury.**

INSTRUMENT CLUSTER

REPLACE

ECLIPSE

1993–94

1. Disconnect battery ground cable.
2. Remove cover from instrument cluster panel, **Fig. 17.**
3. Remove cluster panel assembly attaching screws, then the cluster panel.
4. Remove instrument cluster attaching screws.
5. Disconnect speedometer cable from transaxle.
6. Pull instrument cluster rearward, then release speedometer adapter lock by turning adapter, **Fig. 18.**
7. Disconnect all wire connectors from rear of cluster, then remove cluster from instrument panel.
8. Reverse procedure to install.

1995–96

1. Remove instrument cluster bezel.
2. Remove screws holding cluster to dash.
3. Gently pull cluster outward enough to remove connectors and clips from rear of cluster, allowing it to be removed.
4. Reverse procedure to install.

3000GT

Combination Meters

1. Remove knee protector as follows:
   a. Remove hood lock handle.
   b. Remove rheostat and switch garnish.
   c. Remove knee protector screws and knee protector.
2. Remove upper and lower steering column cover screws then remove covers ensuring not to break cover grippers, **Fig. 12.**
3. Remove metal bezel, **Fig. 19.**
4. Remove combination meter attaching screws.

5. **On models with mechanical speedometer,** disconnect speedometer cable at transaxle end of cable.
6. **On all models,** pull combination meter slightly toward vehicle interior, release wiring harness and speedometer adapter (if equipped) by turning to left or right.
7. Reverse procedure to install.

Combination Gauges

1. Remove instrument panel as outlined under "Instrument Panel, Replace" in "Dash Panel Service."
2. Remove air distribution duct.
3. Disconnect combination gauge electrical connections.
4. Remove combination gauge attaching screws, then the combination gauges.
5. Reverse procedure to install.

RADIO

REPLACE

ECLIPSE

1993–94

Remove radio in numbered sequence, **Fig. 20,** noting the following:

1. Use plastic trim tool to pry lower part of radio panel out of console.
2. Remove side cover of console box, then the amplifier.
3. Reverse procedure to install.

1995–96

1. Use plastic trim tool to pry lower part of radio panel out of console.
2. Remove floor console assembly.
3. Remove radio bracket.
4. Gently pull outward on radio assembly enough to remove connectors from rear of unit.
5. Reverse procedure to install.

3000GT

1. Disconnect battery ground cable.
2. Remove air bag module, clockspring and radio remote control switch.
3. Pry off radio panel using a suitable tool, then remove panel from floor console.
4. Remove radio bracket attaching screws, then disconnect antenna and radio electrical connector.
5. Remove radio from floor console.
6. Reverse procedure to install.

WIPER MOTOR

REPLACE

ECLIPSE

1993–94

Front

Remove front windshield wiper motor and transmission in numbered sequence, **Fig. 21,** noting the following:

1. Mark position of wiper arms before removal.
2. When mounting wiper arms check identification marks. "Dr" indicates driver side, "As" indicates passenger side.

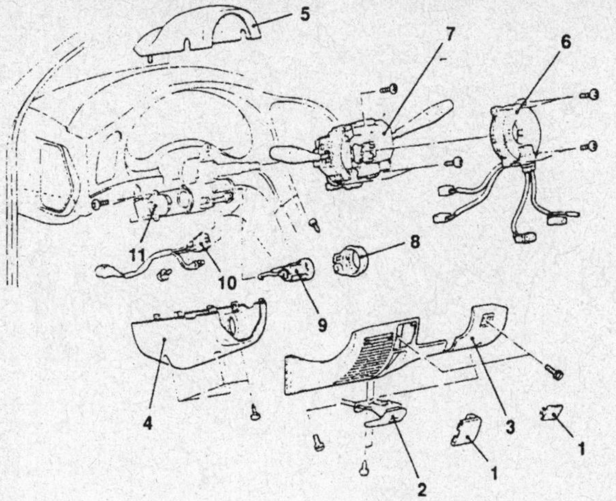
5
7
6
8
11
10
9
4
3
1
1
2

Steering lock cylinder removal steps
- Steering wheel

1. Plug
2. Hood lock release handle
3. Instrument under cover
4. Column cover lower
5. Column cover upper
6. Clock spring
7. Column switch
8. Ignition key illumination ring or ring cover
9. Steering lock cylinder

Key reminder switch segment or key hole illumination light removal steps

4. Column cover lower
5. Column cover upper
10. Key reminder switch segment or key hole illumination light

Ignition switch segment removal steps

4. Column cover lower
5. Column cover upper
11. Ignition switch segment

CR9049500067000X

Fig. 15 Combination switch removal. 1995–96 Eclipse

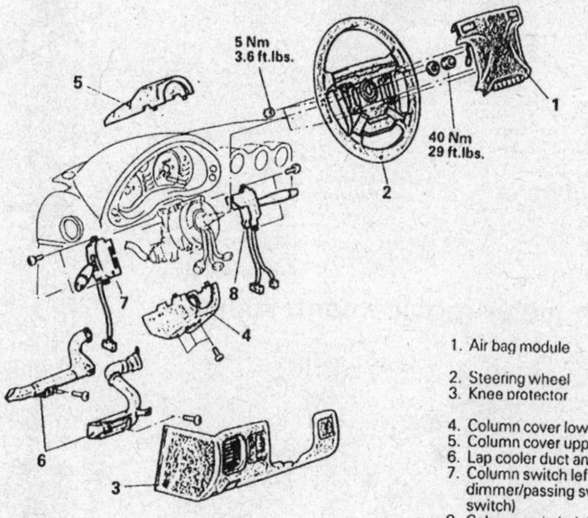
5 Nm
3.6 ft.lbs.
5
1
40 Nm
29 ft.lbs.
2
7
8
4
6
3

1. Air bag module
2. Steering wheel
3. Knee protector
4. Column cover lower
5. Column cover upper
6. Lap cooler duct and foot shower duct
7. Column switch left (For lighting switch, dimmer/passing switch and turn signal switch)
8. Column switch right (For wiper and washer switch)

MT9049100006000X

Fig. 16 Column switch replacement. 3000GT

3. Install wiper arm to pivot shaft so when in stop position wiper blades will be one inch from deck garnish.
4. Reverse procedure to install.

Rear

Remove rear windshield wiper motor and transmission in numbered sequence, **Fig. 22,** noting the following:

1. Using plastic trim tool, remove clip mounting areas on back of liftgate, then remove trim.
2. Install grommet with arrow positioned up.
3. Install wiper arm to pivot shaft so that blade will stop one inch from end liftgate glass.
4. Reverse procedure to install.

1995–96

Front

Remove front windshield wiper motor and transmission in numbered sequence, **Fig. 23,** noting the following:

1. Mark position of wiper arms before removal.
2. Reverse procedure to install.

Rear

Remove rear windshield wiper motor

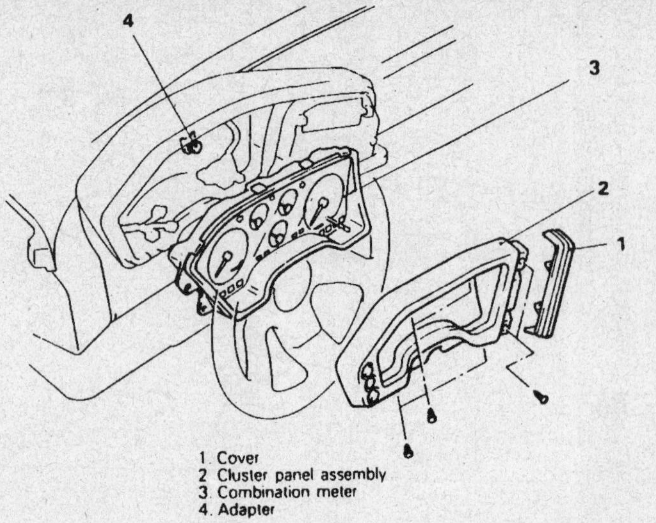
4
3
2
1
1. Cover
2. Cluster panel assembly
3. Combination meter
4. Adapter

MT9099100001000X

Fig. 17 Instrument cluster replacement. Eclipse

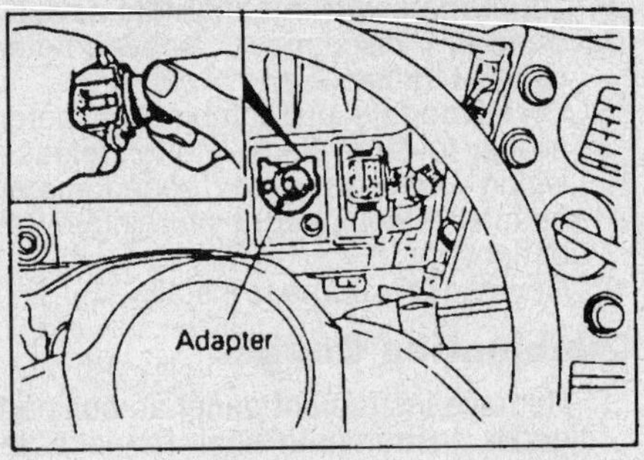
Adapter

MT9099100002000X

Fig. 18 Speedometer adapter lock removal. Eclipse

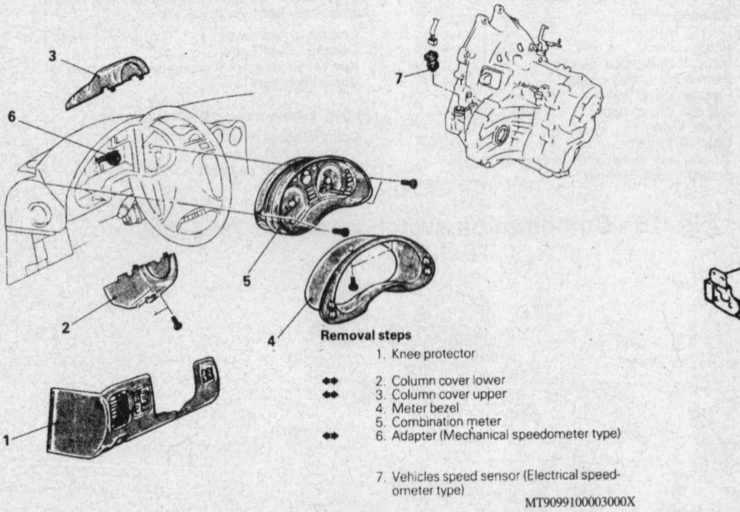
3
6
7
5
2
4
1
Removal steps
1. Knee protector
2. Column cover lower
3. Column cover upper
4. Meter bezel
5. Combination meter
6. Adapter (Mechanical speedometer type)
7. Vehicles speed sensor (Electrical speedometer type)

MT9099100003000X

Fig. 19 Combination meter replacement. 3000GT

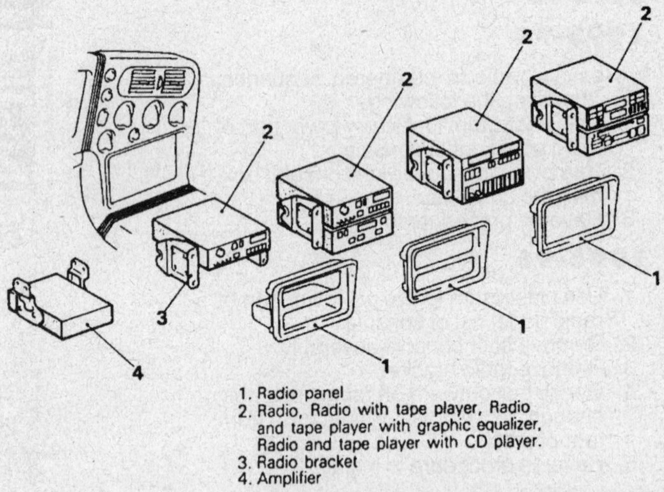
2
2
2
2
1
1
1
3
4
1. Radio panel
2. Radio, Radio with tape player, Radio and tape player with graphic equalizer, Radio and tape player with CD player.
3. Radio bracket
4. Amplifier

CR9039100001000X

Fig. 20 Radio replacement. 1993–94 Eclipse

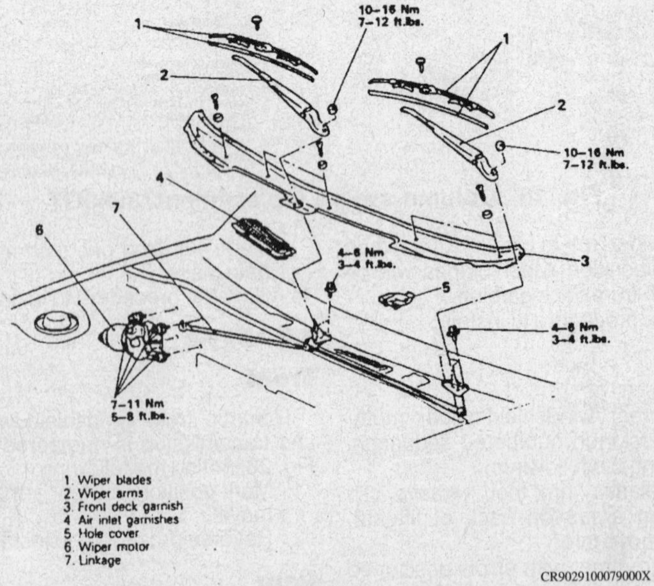
10–16 Nm
7–12 ft.lbs.
1
2
1
2
10–16 Nm
7–12 ft.lbs.
4
7
6
4–6 Nm
3–4 ft.lbs.
3
5
4–6 Nm
3–4 ft.lbs.
7–11 Nm
5–8 ft.lbs.
1. Wiper blades
2. Wiper arms
3. Front deck garnish
4. Air inlet garnishes
5. Hole cover
6. Wiper motor
7. Linkage

CR9029100079000X

Fig. 21 Front wiper motor replacement. 1993–94 Eclipse

and transmission in numbered sequence, **Fig. 24,** noting the following:

1. Mark position of wiper arm before removal.
2. Reverse procedure to install.

3000GT

FRONT

1. Disconnect battery ground cable.
2. Remove wiper arm attaching bolt, then remove wiper arm.
3. Unsnap hole cover assembly, **Fig. 25.**
4. Disconnect wiper motor electrical connector.
5. Remove wiper motor attaching bolts, then remove wiper motor.
6. Reverse procedure to install. **Torque** wiper motor attaching bolts to 7 ft. lbs. **Torque** wiper arm attaching nuts to 9.4 ft. lbs.

REAR

1. Disconnect battery ground cable.
2. Remove wiper arm and wiper blade, **Fig. 26.**

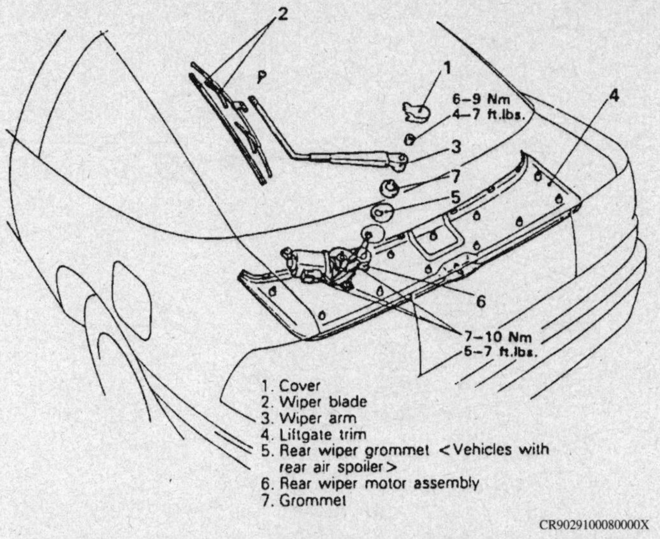
2
P
1
6–9 Nm
4–7 ft.lbs.
4
3
7
5
6
7–10 Nm
5–7 ft.lbs.
1. Cover
2. Wiper blade
3. Wiper arm
4. Liftgate trim
5. Rear wiper grommet <Vehicles with rear air spoiler>
6. Rear wiper motor assembly
7. Grommet
CR9029100080000X

Fig. 22 Rear wiper motor replacement. 1993–94 Eclipse

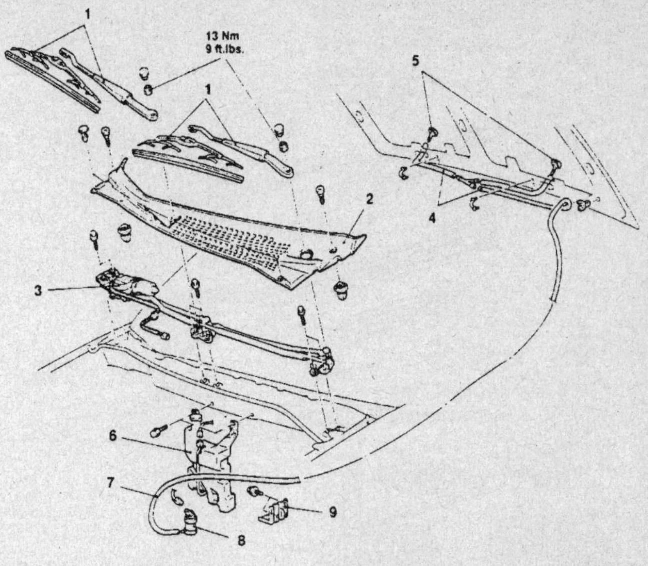
1
13 Nm
9 ft.lbs.
5
1
2
4
3
6
7
9
8

Motor and link assembly removal steps
1. Wiper arm and blade assembly
2. Front deck garnish
3. Motor and link assembly

Washer nozzle removal steps
4. Washer hose connection
5. Washer nozzle

Washer tank removal steps
6. Windshield washer tank
7. Washer hose
8. Washer motor
9. Washer tank bracket

CR9029500132000X

Fig. 23 Front wiper motor replacement. 1995–96 Eclipse

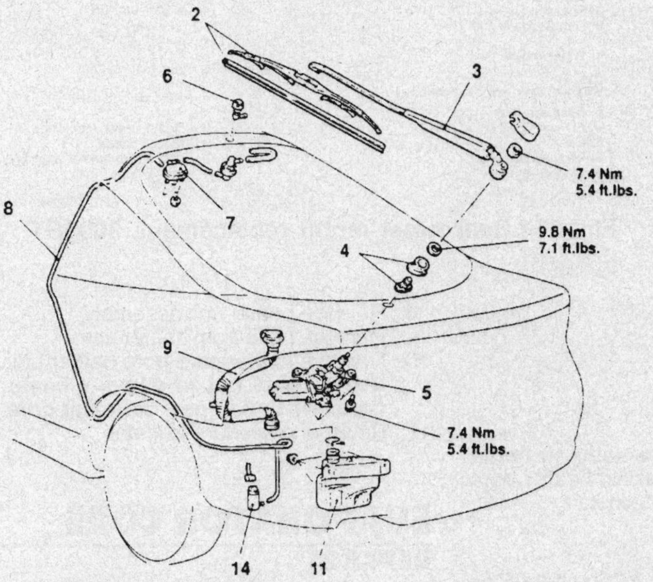
2
6
3
7.4 Nm
5.4 ft.lbs.
8
7
9.8 Nm
7.1 ft.lbs.
4
9
5
7.4 Nm
5.4 ft.lbs.
14
11

Rear wiper motor removal steps
2. Wiper blade
3. Wiper arm
4. Spacer assembly
- Liftgate lower trim

5. Rear wiper motor

Rear washer tank and hose removal steps
- Quarter upper trim (LH)
- Quarter lower trim (LH)
- Rear end trim
- Rear side trim
- Liftgate upper trim

6. Washer nozzle
7. Joint assembly
8. Tube assembly
9. Hose assembly
11. Rear washer tank
14. Rear washer motor

CR9029500133000X

Fig. 24 Rear wiper motor replacement. 1995–96 Eclipse

3. Remove wiper arm spacer, then the hatch trim.
4. Remove rear wiper motor bracket mounting nuts, then remove rear wiper motor assembly from hatch.
5. Reverse procedure to install.

WIPER SWITCH

REPLACE

Refer to "Combination Switch, Replace" procedure.

BLOWER MOTOR

REPLACE

ECLIPSE

1993–94

Remove blower motor in numbered sequence, **Fig. 27,** noting the following:
1. Clean blower case before installation.
2. Replace packing if cracked.
3. Reverse procedure to install.

1995–96

Remove blower motor in numbered sequence, **Fig. 28,** noting the following:
1. Clean blower case before installation.
2. Reverse procedure to install.

3000GT

1. Remove instrument panel lower cover.

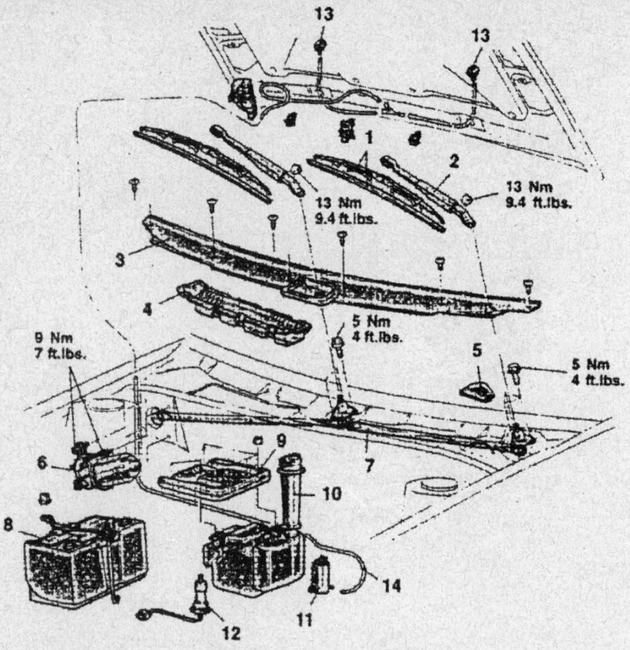
13
13
1
2
13 Nm
9.4 ft.lbs.
13 Nm
9.4 ft.lbs.
3
4
5 Nm
4 ft.lbs.
9 Nm
7 ft.lbs.
5
5 Nm
4 ft.lbs.
6
9
7
10
8
14
12
11

Linkage removal steps

1. Wiper blade
2. Wiper arm
3. Front deck garnish
4. Air inlet garnish (RH)
5. Hole cover
6. Wiper motor
7. Linkage

Wiper motor removal steps

1. Wiper blade
2. Wiper arm
5. Hole cover
6. Wiper motor

CR9029200081000X

Fig. 25 Front wiper motor replacement. 3000GT

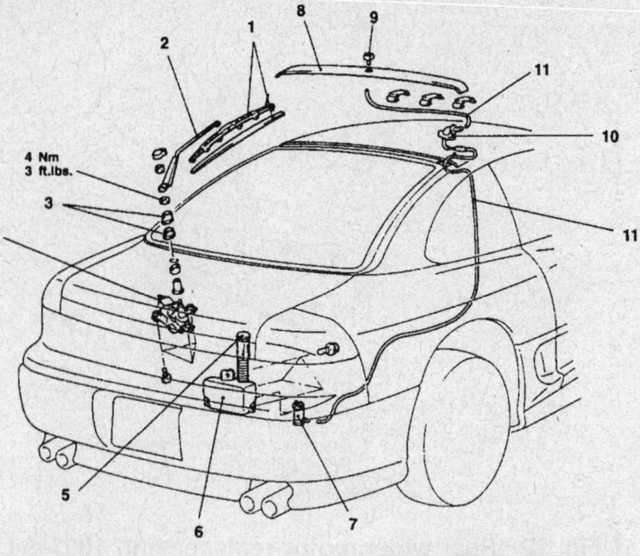
8
9
1
2
11
10
4 Nm
3 ft.lbs.
3
4
11
5
6
7

Wiper motor removal steps

1. Wiper blade
2. Wiper arm
3. Spacer
- Liftgate lower trim

4. Wiper motor

Washer tank removal steps

- Rear end trim

5. Cap
6. Washer tank
7. Washer motor

Washer tube removal steps

- Front pillar trim (RH)
- Quarter trim (RH)
- Quarter upper trim (RH)
- Rear roof rail trim
- Rear side trim (RH)

8. Liftgate upper moulding
9. Washer nozzle
10. Tube and grommet assembly
11. Washer tube

MT9029500051000X

Fig. 26 Rear wiper motor replacement. 3000GT

2. Remove blower motor attaching bolts, then the blower motor.
3. Reverse procedure to install.

HEATER CORE

REPLACE

ECLIPSE

1993-94

1. Disconnect battery ground cable.
2. Drain coolant into a suitable container.
3. Remove floor console and instrument panel as outlined under "Dash Panel Service."
4. Remove center reinforcement, **Fig. 29.**
5. Remove righthand foot shower, distribution and center ducts.
6. **On models with A/C,** remove evaporator assembly as outlined under "Evaporator Core, Replace."
7. **On all models,** to prevent bolts from falling into blower assembly, set air selection damper to outside air induction position.
8. Remove heater unit assembly.
9. Remove plate from heater unit, **Fig. 30.**
10. Remove heater core from heater unit. **Use caution not to damage heater core fins or pad part of heater core.**
11. Reverse procedure to install.

1995-96

Remove heater unit in numbered sequence, **Fig. 31,** noting the following:

1. Drain engine coolant.
2. Remove instrument panel as outlined in "Dash Panel Service."
3. Reverse procedure to install. Refill engine coolant.

3000GT

1. Drain coolant into a suitable container and disconnect heater hoses.
2. Remove center console and instrument panel as outlined under "Instrument Panel, Replace" in "Dash Panel Service."
3. Remove center reinforcement, **Fig. 32.**
4. Remove lower cover, foot shower, distribution and lap cooler ducts.
5. **On models with A/C,** remove evaporator assembly as outlined under "Evaporator Core, Replace."
6. **On all models,** remove center duct.
7. To prevent bolts from falling into blower assembly, set air selection damper to outside air induction position.
8. Remove heater unit assembly.
9. Remove plate from heater unit.
10. Remove heater core from heater unit. **Use caution not to damage heater core fins or pad part of heater core.**
11. Reverse procedure to install.

EVAPORATOR CORE

REPLACE

ECLIPSE

1993-94

Remove evaporator unit in numbered sequence, **Fig. 33,** noting the following:

1. Properly discharge refrigerant from A/C system as outlined under "Air Conditioning."
2. Remove floor console as shown in **Fig. 34.**
3. Remove instrument panel as outlined in "Dash Panel Service."
4. To prevent bolts from falling into blower assembly, set air selection damper to outside air introduction.
5. Remove evaporator core from case, **Fig. 35,** noting the following:
   a. Remove case clips using a flat blade screw driver covered with shop towel to prevent damage to case.
   b. Remove expansion valve by using two wrenches, one inlet side, one outlet side.
6. Pull evaporator core from evaporator

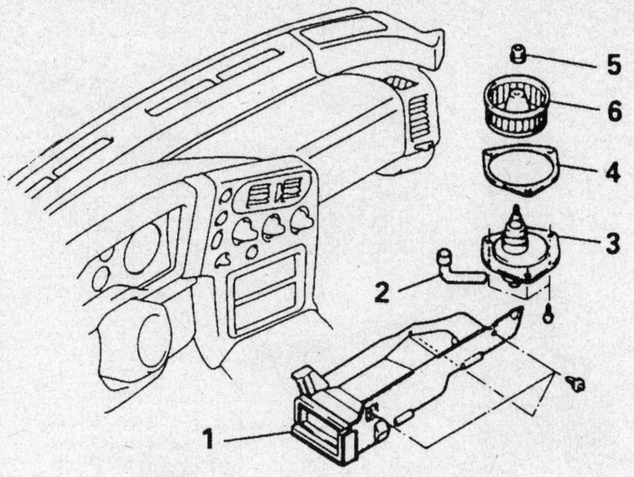

5
6
4
3
2
1

1. Shower duct R.H. <if so equipped>
2. Hose
3. Blower motor assembly
4. Packing
5. Fan installation nut
6. Fan

CR7029100047000X

Fig. 27 Blower motor replacement. 1993–94 Eclipse

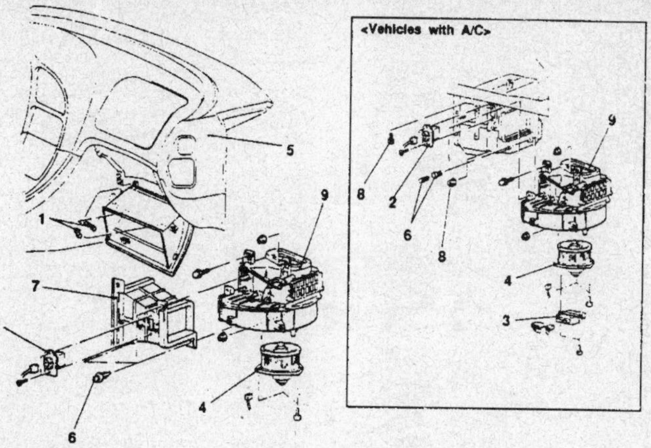

<Vehicles with A/C>

Resistor removal steps
1. Stopper
2. Resistor

Blower fan and motor removal steps
3. Automatic compressor ECM <Vehicles with A/C>
4. Blower fan and motor

Blower unit removal steps
5. Instrument panel
6. Clip
7. Joint duct <Vehicles without A/C>
8. Evaporator installation bolts and nut <Vehicles with A/C>
9. Blower unit assembly

CR7029500230000X

Fig. 28 Blower motor replacement. 1995–96 Eclipse

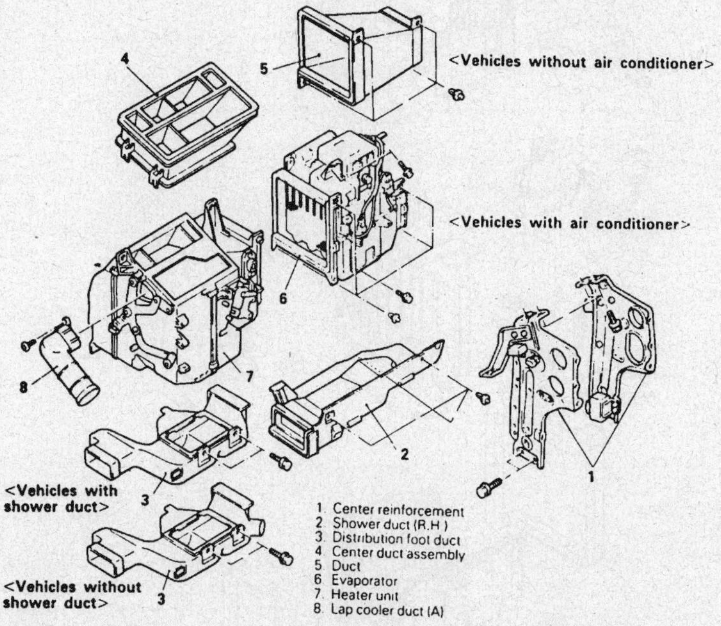

<Vehicles without air conditioner>
<Vehicles with air conditioner>
<Vehicles with shower duct>
<Vehicles without shower duct>
1. Center reinforcement
2. Shower duct (R.H.)
3. Distribution foot duct
4. Center duct assembly
5. Duct
6. Evaporator
7. Heater unit
8. Lap cooler duct (A)

MT7029100072000X

Fig. 29 Exploded view of heater unit. 1993–94 Eclipse

Plate

MT7029100073000X

Fig. 30 Heater core plate removal. 1993–94 Eclipse

case. **Do not damage fin or pad part of evaporator core.**

7. Reverse procedure to install, ensuring to properly recharge A/C system as outlined under "Air Conditioning."

1995-96

Remove evaporator unit in numbered sequence, **Figs. 36 and 37,** noting the following:

1. Properly discharge refrigerant from A/C system as outlined in "Air Conditioning."
2. Plug refrigerant lines to prevent air from mixing when disconnecting them.
3. **On non-turbo models,** refill evaporator with 1.35 fl. oz. ND-OIL 8 compressor oil, or equivalent, before replacing evaporator.
4. **On turbo models,** refill evaporator with 2.03 fl. oz. SUN PAG 56 compressor oil, or equivalent, before replacing evaporator.
5. Reverse procedure to install, properly recharge A/C system as outlined in "Air Conditioning."

3000GT

1. Disconnect battery ground cable, then discharge refrigerant into an approved recovery device as outlined in "Air Conditioning."
2. Disconnect suction hose and liquid pipe from evaporator.
3. Remove glove compartment stoppers, then the glove compartment, **Fig. 38.**
4. Remove lower frame, then the right-hand foot shower duct, if applicable.
5. Disconnect body wiring harness and A/C wiring harness connectors.
6. Remove A/C control unit.
7. Remove drain hose, then the evaporator.
8. Remove evaporator core from case as shown, **Fig. 39.**
9. Reverse procedure to install.

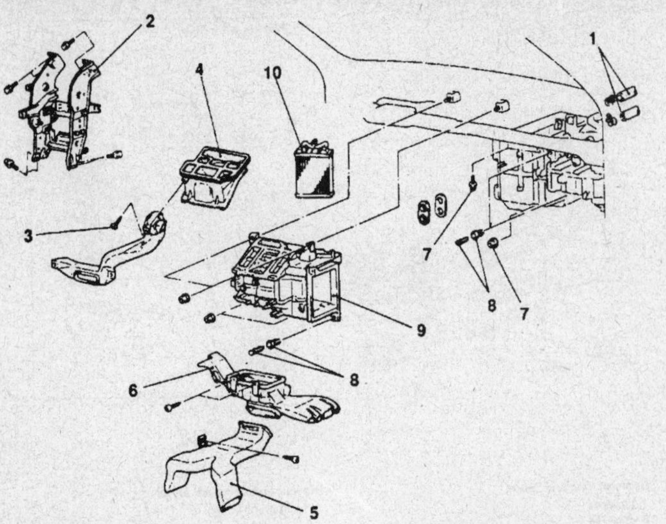

Removal steps

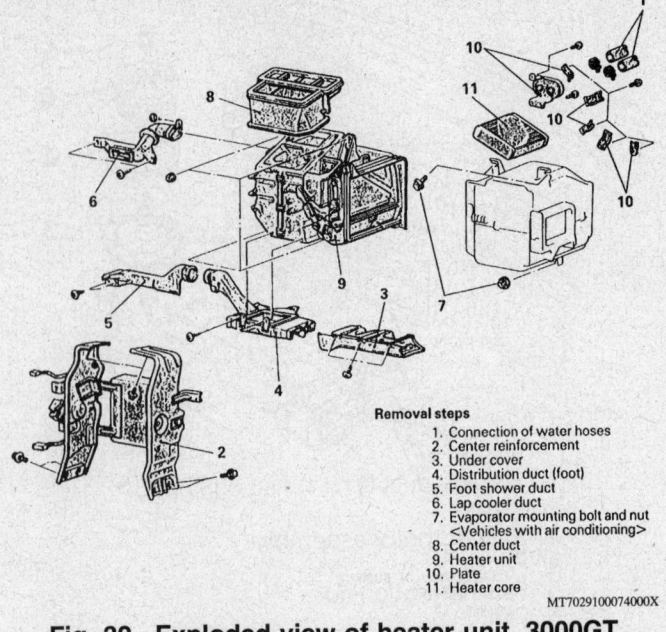

- Instrument panel

1. Heater hose connection
2. Center stay
3. Lap cooler duct installation screw
4. Center duct
5. Semi rear heater duct
6. Foot distribution duct
7. Evaporator installation bolt and nut <Vehicles with A/C>
8. Clip
9. Heater unit
10. Heater core

CR7029500231000X

Fig. 31 Exploded view of heater unit. 1995–96 Eclipse

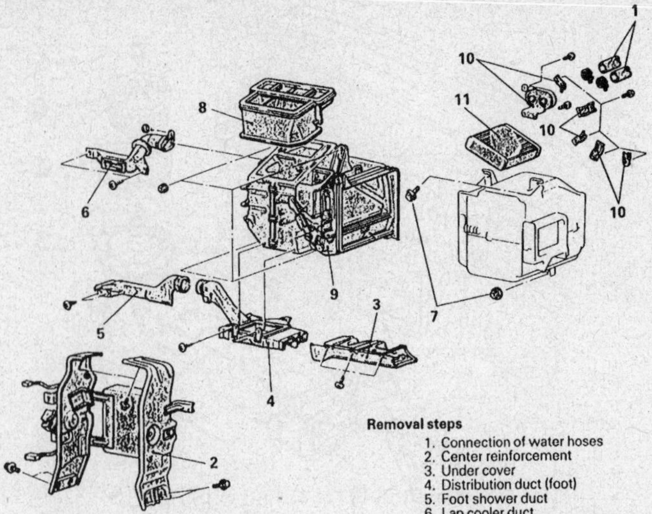

Removal steps

1. Connection of water hoses
2. Center reinforcement
3. Under cover
4. Distribution duct (foot)
5. Foot shower duct
6. Lap cooler duct
7. Evaporator mounting bolt and nut <Vehicles with air conditioning>
8. Center duct
9. Heater unit
10. Plate
11. Heater core

MT7029100074000X

Fig. 32 Exploded view of heater unit. 3000GT

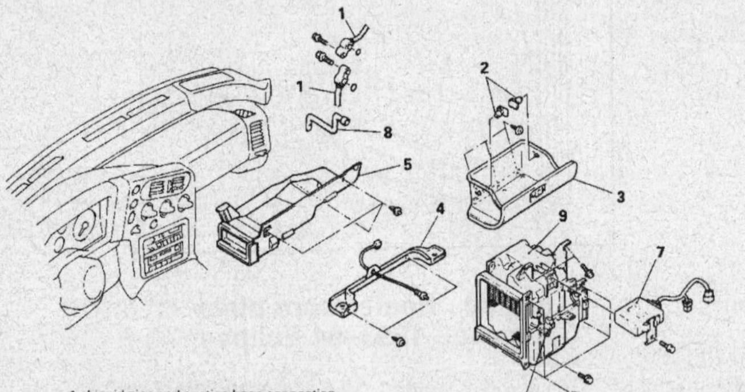

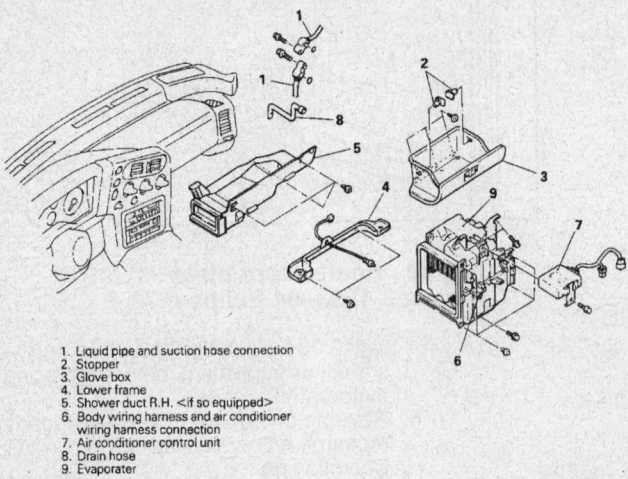

1. Liquid pipe and suction hose connection
2. Stopper
3. Glove box
4. Lower frame
5. Shower duct R.H. <if so equipped>
6. Body wiring harness and air conditioner wiring harness connection
7. Air conditioner control unit
8. Drain hose
9. Evaporater

CR7029100051000X

Fig. 33 Evaporator replacement. 1993–94 Eclipse

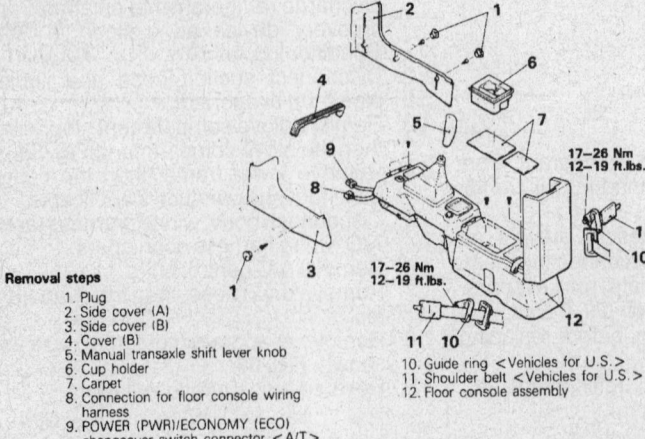

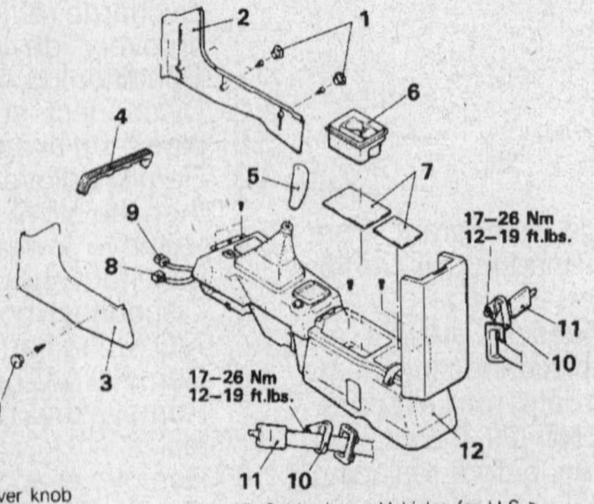
17–26 Nm
12–19 ft.lbs.
17–26 Nm
12–19 ft.lbs.

Removal steps

1. Plug
2. Side cover (A)
3. Side cover (B)
4. Cover (B)
5. Manual transaxle shift lever knob
6. Cup holder
7. Carpet
8. Connection for floor console wiring harness
9. POWER (PWR)/ECONOMY (ECO) changeover switch connector <A/T>
10. Guide ring <Vehicles for U.S.>
11. Shoulder belt <Vehicles for U.S.>
12. Floor console assembly

CR7029100049000X

Fig. 34 Floor console removal. 1993–94 Eclipse

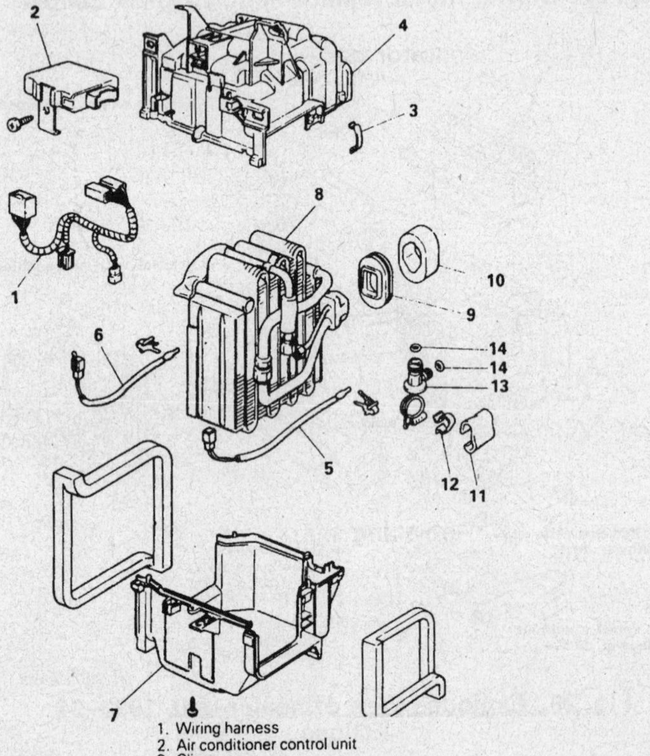

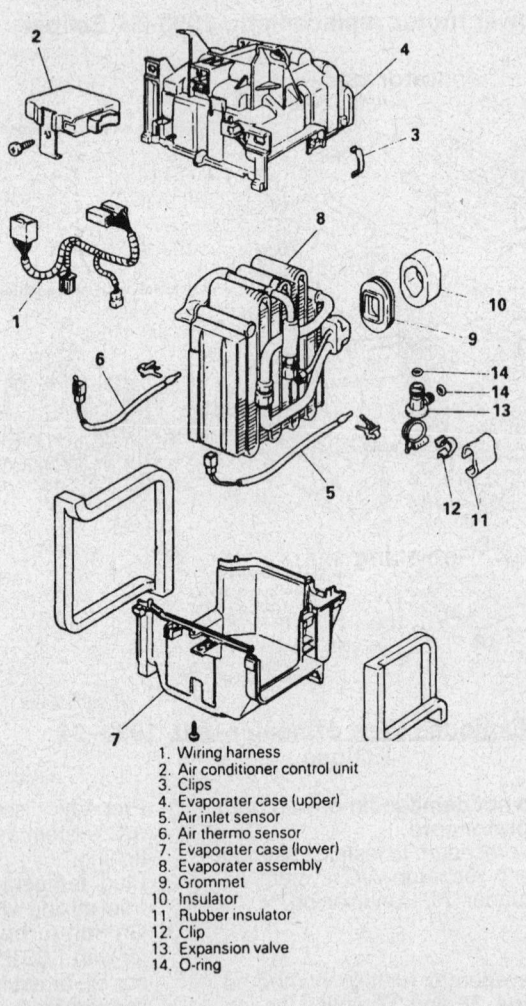

1. Wiring harness
2. Air conditioner control unit
3. Clips
4. Evaporator case (upper)
5. Air inlet sensor
6. Air thermo sensor
7. Evaporator case (lower)
8. Evaporater assembly
9. Grommet
10. Insulator
11. Rubber insulator
12. Clip
13. Expansion valve
14. O-ring

CR7029100052000X

Fig. 35 Exploded view of evaporator unit. 1993–94 Eclipse

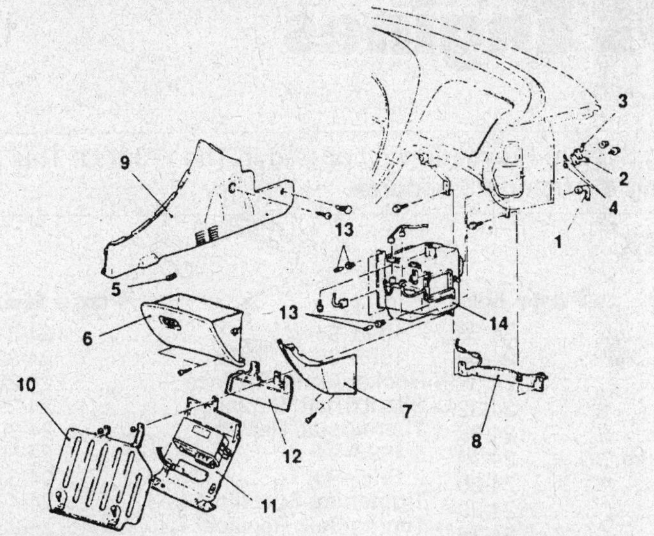

Removal steps

1. Drain hose
2. Suction pipe <Non-turbo> or suction hose <Turbo> connection
3. Liquid pipe connection
4. O-ring
5. Stopper
6. Glove box
7. Corner panel
8. Glove box under frame
9. Console side cover <RH>
10. Control unit cover
11. ABS-ECU bracket
12. Harness protector <Turbo>
13. Clip
14. Evaporator

CR7029500232000X

Fig. 36 Evaporator replacement. 1995–96 Eclipse

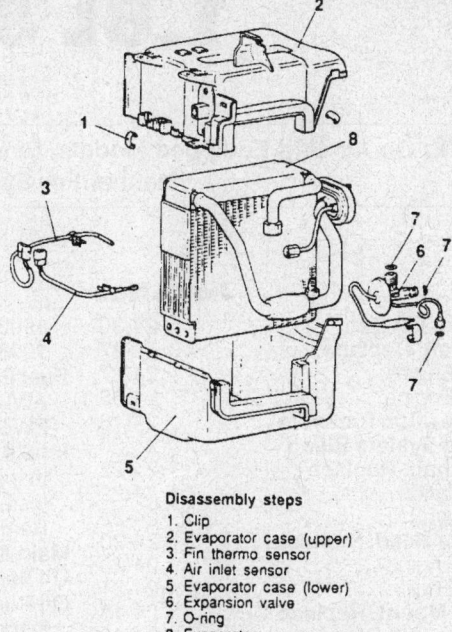

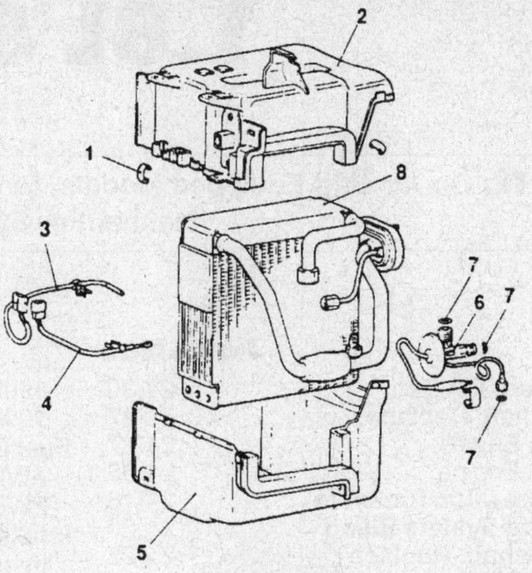

Disassembly steps

1. Clip
2. Evaporator case (upper)
3. Fin thermo sensor
4. Air inlet sensor
5. Evaporator case (lower)
6. Expansion valve
7. O-ring
8. Evaporator

Fig. 37 Exploded view of evaporator unit. 1995–96 Eclipse

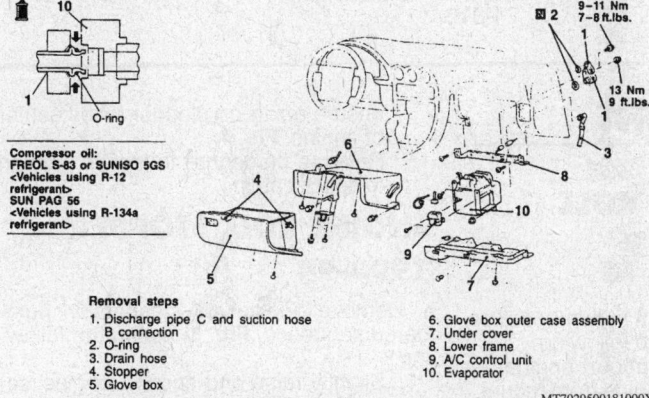

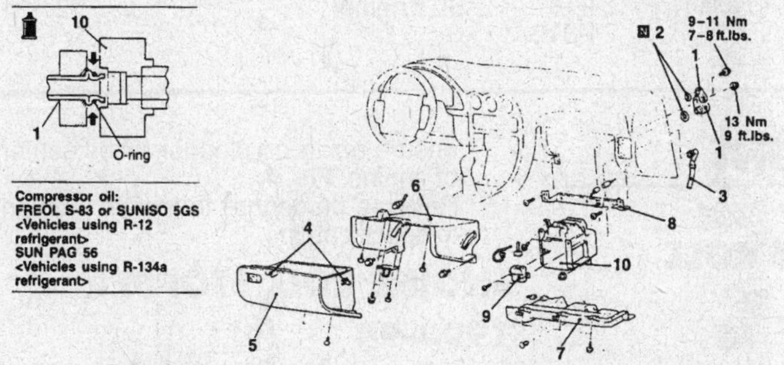
O-ring
Compressor oil:
FREOL S-83 or SUNISO 5GS
<Vehicles using R-12 refrigerant>
SUN PAG 56
<Vehicles using R-134a refrigerant>
9–11 Nm
7–8 ft.lbs.
13 Nm
9 ft.lbs.

Removal steps

1. Discharge pipe C and suction hose B connection
2. O-ring
3. Drain hose
4. Stopper
5. Glove box
6. Glove box outer case assembly
7. Under cover
8. Lower frame
9. A/C control unit
10. Evaporator

MT7029500181000X

Fig. 38 Replacing evaporator core. 3000GT

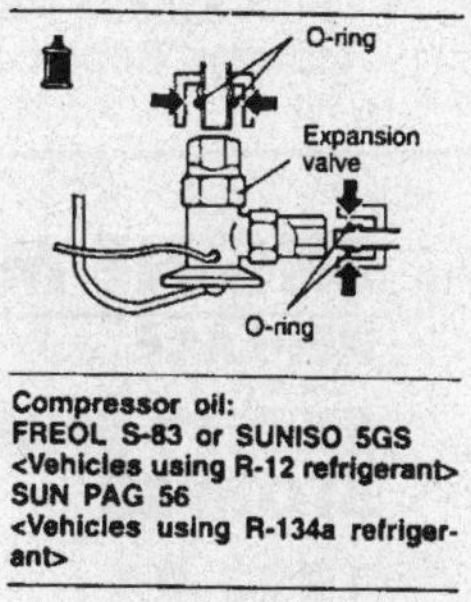
O-ring
Expansion valve
O-ring
Compressor oil:
FREOL S-83 or SUNISO 5GS
<Vehicles using R-12 refrigerant>
SUN PAG 56
<Vehicles using R-134a refrigerant>

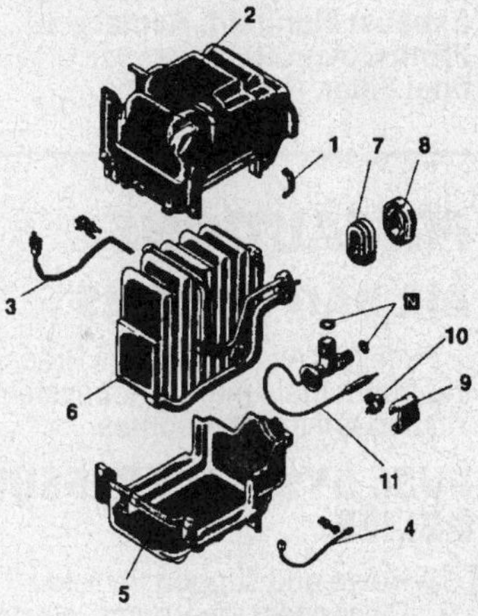

Disassembly steps

1. Clips
2. Evaporater case (upper)
3. Fin thermo sensor
4. Air inlet sensor <Vehicles with manual air conditioning>
5. Evaporator case (lower)
6. Evaporator assembly
7. Grommet
8. Insulator
9. Rubber insulator
10. Clip
11. Expansion valve

MT7029500182000X

Fig. 39 Exploded view of evaporator unit. 3000GT

1.8L & 2.0L Engines

NOTE: On Air Bag Equipped Models, Refer To "Air Bag System Precautions" Located In The Front Of This Manual For System Disarming & Arming Procedures.

INDEX

	Page No.
Belt Tension Data	24-30
Camshaft, Replace	24-27
1.8L Engine	24-27
2.0L Engine	24-28
Compression Pressure	24-18
Cooling System Bleed	24-30
Crankshaft, Replace	24-22
Installation	24-22
Removal	24-22
Cylinder Head, Replace	24-20
1.8L Engine	24-20
2.0L Engine	24-21
Engine Mount, Replace	24-18
Engine Roll Stopper	24-18
Except Engine Roll Stopper	24-18
Engine Rebuilding Specifications	28-1
Engine, Replace	24-19
Exhaust Manifold, Replace	24-20
Front Cover, Replace	24-23
Fuel Filter, Replace	24-33
1993–94	24-33
1995–96	24-33
Fuel Pump, Replace	24-32
AWD Models	24-32
FWD Models	24-32
Intake Manifold, Replace	24-19
Inspection	24-20
Installation	24-20
Removal	24-19
Main & Rod Bearings	24-29
Oil Pan, Replace	24-29
Oil Pump, Replace	24-29
Inspection	24-29
Installation	24-29
Removal	24-29
Piston & Rod Assembly	24-29
Precautions	24-18
Air Bag Systems	24-18
Fuel System Pressure Relief	24-18
Radiator, Replace	24-31
1993–94	24-31
1995–96	24-32
Rocker Arms, Replace	24-22
Silent Shaft, Replace	24-29
Thermostat, Replace	24-30
1993–94	24-30
1995–96	24-31
Tightening Specifications	24-47
Timing Belt, Replace	24-23
1.8L Engine	24-23
2.0L Engine	24-24
Turbocharger, Replace	24-33
Valve Adjustment	24-22
Valve Arrangement	24-22
Valve Clearance Specifications	24-22
Valve Lifters	24-22
Inspection	24-22
Water Pump, Replace	24-31
1.8L Engine	24-31
2.0L Engine	24-31

PRECAUTIONS

AIR BAG SYSTEMS

Refer to "Air Bag System Precautions" in the front of this manual for system disarming and arming procedures.

FUEL SYSTEM PRESSURE RELIEF

1. Raise and support vehicle.
2. Disconnect fuel pump electrical connector. **Failure to relieve fuel system pressure prior to disconnecting fuel system components may cause fire or personal injury.**
3. Lower vehicle.
4. Start and run engine until it stops. Allow engine to deplete fuel supply, then turn ignition off.
5. Disconnect battery ground cable.
6. Crank engine two or three times to release remaining fuel pressure.
7. After fuel system repairs are completed, reconnect fuel pump electrical connector.

COMPRESSION PRESSURE

Refer to **Fig. 1** for compression pressure data.

ENGINE MOUNT

REPLACE

EXCEPT ENGINE ROLL STOPPER

1993-94

Remove engine mount in numbered sequence, **Fig. 2,** noting the following:

1. Slightly raise and support engine, removing weight of engine from mount.
2. **On 1.8L engines,** bracket (2) is not used.
3. **On all engines,** inspect insulators for damage or cracks and replace as necessary.
4. Check brackets and replace if deformed or damaged.
5. When installing mounting stoppers, ensure arrow on stopper faces center of engine.
6. Reverse procedure to install.

1995-96

Remove engine mount in numbered sequence, **Fig. 3,** noting the following:

1. Slightly raise and support engine, removing weight of engine from mount.
2. Inspect insulators for damage or cracks and replace as necessary.
3. Check brackets and replace if deformed or damaged.
4. When installing mounting stoppers, ensure arrow on stopper faces center of engine, **Fig. 4.**
5. Reverse procedure to install. Tighten to specifications.

ENGINE ROLL STOPPER

1993-94

Remove engine roll stoppers in numbered sequence, **Fig. 5,** noting the following:

1. Slightly raise and support engine, removing weight of engine from mount.
2. Inspect insulators for damage or cracks and replace as necessary.
3. Inspect brackets and replace if deformed or damaged.
4. Discard and replace front roll stopper bracket installation nuts. When installing new nuts, first snug nuts to bolts, then lower engine and tighten to specifications once weight of engine is applied to mount.
5. When installing rear roll stopper bracket on models with automatic transmission, ensure distance between center hole and lower edge of bracket is as shown in **Fig. 6.**
6. Install front roll stopper bracket with hole positioned as shown in **Fig. 7.**
7. When installing front roll stopper bracket, ensure distance between center hole of insulator and lower edge of bracket is as shown, **Fig. 8.**

Year	Engine Liter	Compression Pressure, psi①	Minimum Pressure, psi	Max. Variation Between Cylinders, psi
1993–94	1.8L	185	131	14
	2.0L②	192	145	14
	2.0L③	164	121	14
1995–96	2.0L②	170–225	100	④
	2.0L③	178	133	14

①— At 250–400 psi.
②— Models less turbo.
③— Models w/turbo.
④— 25 max. variation between cylinders.

Fig. 1 Compression pressure data. Eclipse

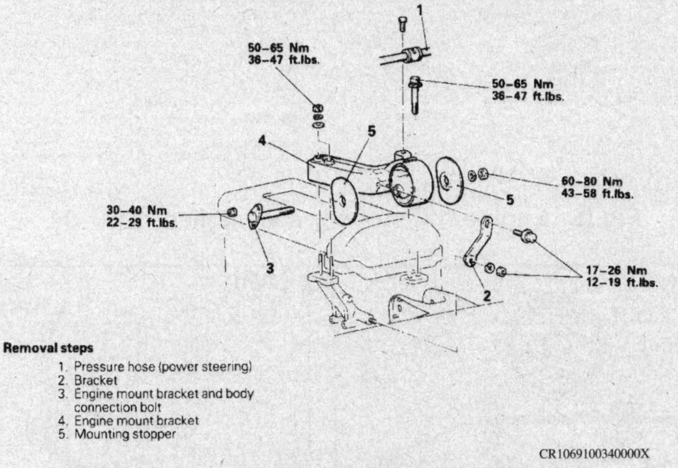
50-65 Nm
36-47 ft.lbs.
50-65 Nm
36-47 ft.lbs.
60-80 Nm
43-58 ft.lbs.
30-40 Nm
22-29 ft.lbs.
17-26 Nm
12-19 ft.lbs.
Removal steps
1. Pressure hose (power steering)
2. Bracket
3. Engine mount bracket and body connection bolt
4. Engine mount bracket
5. Mounting stopper
CR1069100340000X

Fig. 2 Engine mount assembly. 1993–94

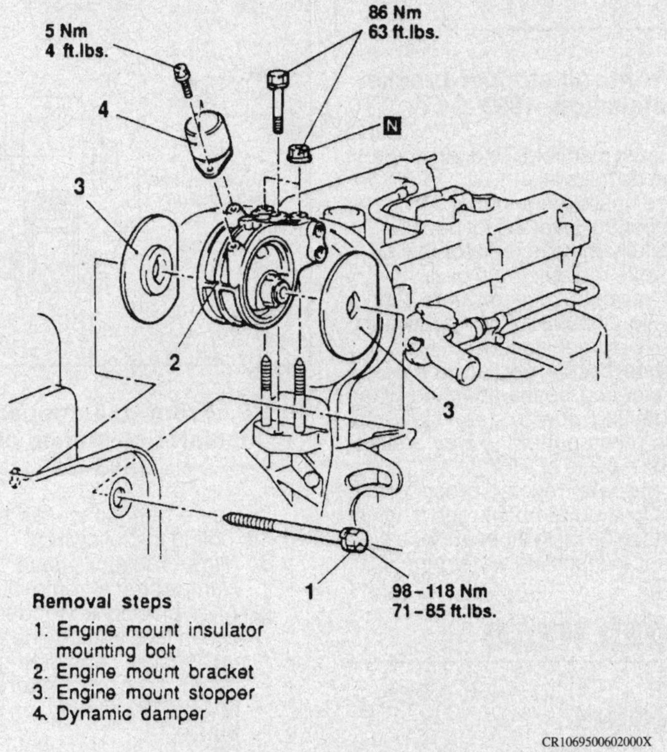
5 Nm
4 ft.lbs.
86 Nm
63 ft.lbs.
N
98-118 Nm
71-85 ft.lbs.
Removal steps
1. Engine mount insulator mounting bolt
2. Engine mount bracket
3. Engine mount stopper
4. Dynamic damper
CR1069500602000X

Fig. 3 Engine mount assembly. 1995–96

8. Reverse procedure to install.

1995–96

Remove engine roll stoppers in numbered sequence, **Fig. 9,** noting the following:

1. Slightly raise and support engine, removing weight of engine from mount.
2. Inspect insulators for damage or cracks and replace as necessary.
3. Inspect brackets and replace if deformed or damaged.
4. Inspect front roll stopper bracket assembly. If the dimension shown in **Fig. 10** is not 1.57–1.81 inches when the weight of the engine is on the body, replace the front roll stopper assembly.
5. When installing mounting stoppers, ensure arrow on stopper faces center of engine, **Fig. 4.**
6. Reverse procedure to install. Tighten to specifications.

ENGINE

REPLACE

1. Release fuel system pressure as outlined under "Precautions."
2. Disconnect battery ground cable.
3. Scribe reference marks between hood and hood hinges, then remove hood.
4. Drain cooling system as follows:
   a. Place temperature control lever in Hot position.
   b. Carefully remove radiator cap, then the radiator drain plug.
5. Remove transaxle assembly. On models with automatic transaxle, refer to procedure outlined under "Transaxle, Replace" in "Automatic Transaxle." On models with manual transaxle, refer to procedure outlined under "Transaxle, Replace" in "Clutch & Manual Transaxle."
6. Remove radiator as outlined under "Radiator Replace."
7. Remove engine components in numbered sequence as shown in **Fig. 11** on models with 1.8L engine and **Fig. 12** on models with 2.0L engine, noting the following:
   a. Remove power steering pump from bracket with hoses attached, then secure pump aside with a piece of wire.
   b. Remove A/C compressor from bracket with hoses attached, then compressor pump aside with a piece of wire.
   c. Using a suitable engine hoist, slightly raise engine, then remove engine mount bracket.
   d. Ensure all cables, connectors and hoses are disconnected, then remove engine from engine compartment.
8. Reverse procedure to install.

INTAKE MANIFOLD

REPLACE

REMOVAL

Remove intake manifold in numbered sequence, **Figs. 13 and 14,** noting the following:

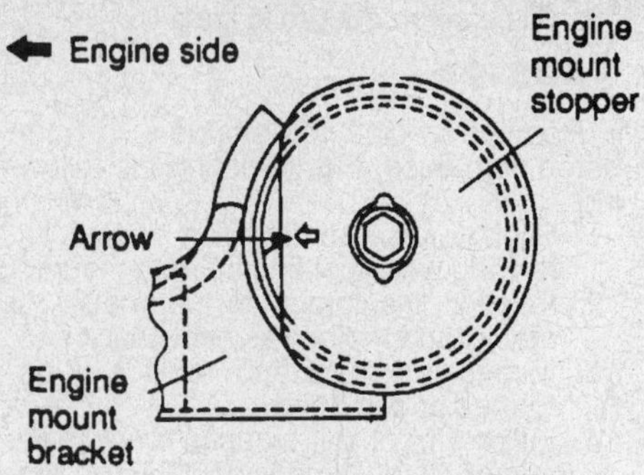
Engine side
Engine mount stopper
Arrow
Engine mount bracket

CR1069500603000X

Fig. 4 Engine mount stopper installation. 1995–96

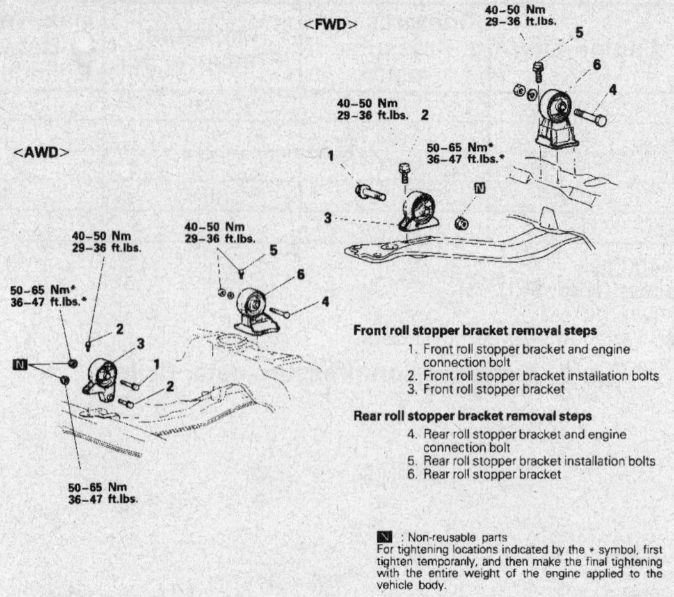
<FWD>
40-50 Nm
29-36 ft.lbs.
5
6
4
40-50 Nm
29-36 ft.lbs. 2
50-65 Nm*
36-47 ft.lbs.*
1
3
<AWD>
40-50 Nm
29-36 ft.lbs.
40-50 Nm
29-36 ft.lbs.
5
6
4
50-65 Nm*
36-47 ft.lbs.*
2
3
1
2
50-65 Nm
36-47 ft.lbs.
Front roll stopper bracket removal steps
1. Front roll stopper bracket and engine connection bolt
2. Front roll stopper bracket installation bolts
3. Front roll stopper bracket
Rear roll stopper bracket removal steps
4. Rear roll stopper bracket and engine connection bolt
5. Rear roll stopper bracket installation bolts
6. Rear roll stopper bracket
: Non-reusable parts
For tightening locations indicated by the * symbol, first tighten temporarily, and then make the final tightening with the entire weight of the engine applied to the vehicle body.

CR1069100341000X

Fig. 5 Engine roll stopper assemblies. 1993–94

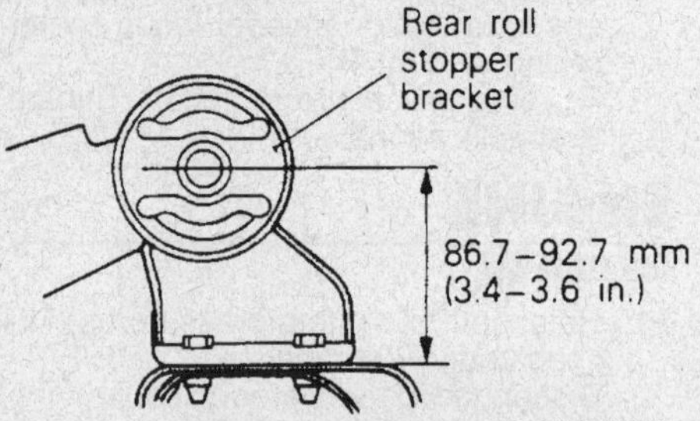
Rear roll stopper bracket
86.7–92.7 mm
(3.4–3.6 in.)

CR1069100342000X

Fig. 6 Rear roll stopper bracket clearance. 1993–94

1. Drain coolant as follows:
   a. Place instrument panel temperature control lever in Hot position.
   b. Carefully remove radiator cap.
   c. Remove radiator drain plug.
2. **On 1.8L engines,** when removing upper radiator hose, mark hose clamp in relation to hose for assembly reference.
3. **On all engines,** before disconnecting high pressure fuel line, release fuel pressure as outlined under "Precautions."
4. Remove delivery pipe, fuel injector and regulator as an assembly.

INSPECTION

Inspect intake manifold and air intake plenum (if equipped) as follows:

1. Check for damage, cracks or defects.
2. Ensure coolant and jet air passages are clear.
3. Check installation surfaces with a straightedge. Replace if deflection exceeds .012 inch.

INSTALLATION

Reverse removal procedure to install. On 2.0L engines, when installing throttle body, refer to bolt length chart, **Fig. 15.**

EXHAUST MANIFOLD

REPLACE

Remove exhaust manifold in numbered sequence, referring to **Fig. 16** on 1.8L engines, **Fig. 17** on non-turbocharged 2.0L engines and **Fig. 18** on turbocharged 2.0L engines, noting the following:

1. **On 2.0L turbocharged engine,** drain engine oil and coolant prior to removing exhaust manifold. To drain coolant, proceed as follows:
   a. Place instrument panel temperature control lever in Hot position.
   b. Carefully remove radiator cap.
   c. Remove radiator drain plug.
2. **On all models,** use oxygen sensor socket No. MD998703, or equivalent, to remove oxygen sensor.
3. **On 2.0L turbocharged engine,** leave power steering hoses attached when disconnecting power steering pump. Position pump out of the way and secure with a piece of wire.
4. **On all models,** reverse procedure to install. On 2.0L turbocharged engine, apply machine oil to inner surface pipe flare prior to installing water pipe (18), **Fig. 18.**

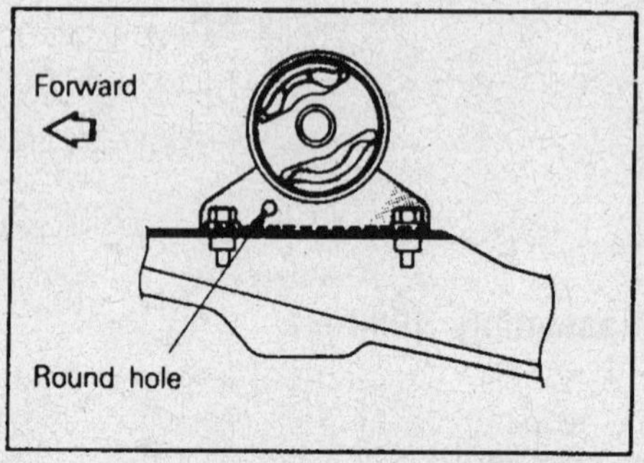
Forward
Round hole

CR1069100343000X

Fig. 7 Front roll stopper bracket installation. 1993–94

CYLINDER HEAD

REPLACE

1.8L ENGINE

1. Release fuel system pressure as outlined under "Precautions."
2. Drain cooling system into an appropriate container.
3. Remove cylinder head and gasket in numbered sequence as shown, **Fig. 19,** noting the following:
   a. Mark radiator hose and hose clamps prior to removal.
   b. After placing a wooden block between jack and engine oil pan, jack up vehicle and remove engine mount bracket. **Ensure pressure is applied evenly on engine oil pan.**
   c. Prior to removing timing belt, turn crankshaft clockwise and align timing marks, **Fig. 20.**
   d. Mark direction of rotation on timing belt if belt is to be reused.

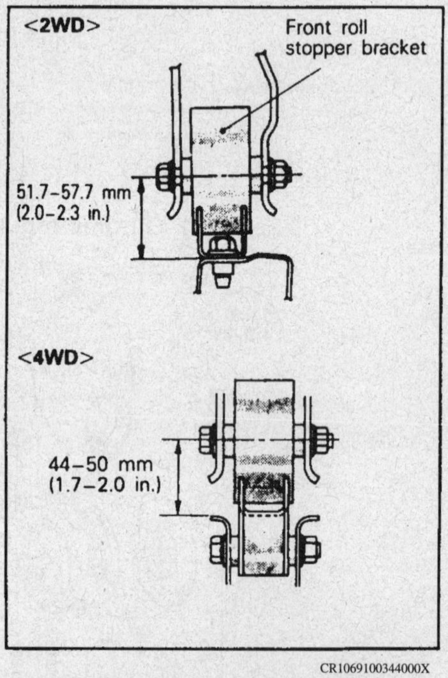
<2WD>
Front roll stopper bracket
51.7-57.7 mm
(2.0-2.3 in.)
<4WD>
44–50 mm
(1.7–2.0 in.)

CR1069100344000X

Fig. 8 Front roll stopper bracket insulator clearance check. 1993–94

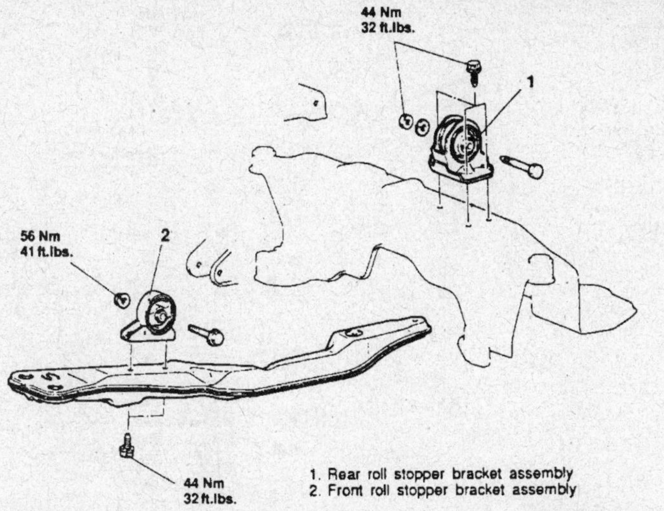
44 Nm
32 ft.lbs.
1
56 Nm
41 ft.lbs.
2
44 Nm
32 ft.lbs.
1. Rear roll stopper bracket assembly
2. Front roll stopper bracket assembly
CR1069500604000X

Fig. 9 Engine roll stopper assemblies. 1995–96

e. Remove camshaft sprocket with timing belt attached and secure timing belt in lower cover, ensuring pressure is kept on crankshaft pulley.
f. Using socket tool No. MD998360, or equivalent, remove cylinder head bolts in sequence as shown, **Fig. 21.**

4. Reverse procedure to install, noting the following:
   a. Clean both cylinder head and cylinder block gasket surfaces.
   b. Install gasket with identification mark toward cylinder head, **Fig. 22.**
   c. Using sequence shown in **Fig. 23, torque** cylinder head bolts in two or three steps to 51–54 ft. lbs.
   d. Install intake and exhaust manifolds and gaskets. Tighten bolts to specifications.

2.0L ENGINE

1995–96 Turbo

1. Release fuel system pressure as outlined under "Precautions."
2. Remove cylinder head in numbered sequence as shown, **Fig. 24.**
3. Disconnect battery ground cable, then drain cooling system into an appropriate container.
4. Prior to removing upper radiator hose, mark hose clamp in relation to hose for installation reference.
5. When disconnecting high pressure fuel hose, cover fuel pipe line with a shop towel. Some residual fuel pressure may be present.
6. Remove timing belt as outlined under "Timing Belt, Replace."
7. Using wrench tool No. MD998051, or equivalent, remove cylinder head attaching bolts in sequence as shown, **Fig. 21.** Loosen head bolts evenly, in two or three steps to prevent cylinder head warpage. When removing cylinder head use care not to disturb camshaft sprockets. After removing cylinder head, clean gasket surfaces on head and block.
8. Remove intake and exhaust manifolds.
9. Reverse procedure to install, noting the following:
   a. Tighten exhaust manifold nuts and intake manifold bolts to specifications.
   b. Clean both cylinder head and cylinder block gasket surfaces, then install gasket with identification mark toward cylinder head, **Fig. 22.**
   c. Using sequence shown in **Fig. 23, torque** cylinder head bolts in five steps: first, to 58 ft. lbs.; second, fully loosen all bolts; third, to 15 ft. lbs.; fourth, tighten each bolt an additional 90°; then finally, tighten each bolt an additional 90°. **Ensure head bolt washers are correctly installed.**
   d. Ensure camshaft and crankshaft timing marks are correctly aligned.
   e. Tighten auto tensioner bolt and timing cover bolts to specifications.
   f. Tighten tensioner pulley bolt and crankshaft pulley bolts to specifications.
   g. Tighten water pump pulley bolts and top engine mount bolt to specifications.
   h. Tighten top engine mount bracket bolts and intake manifold support bolts to specifications.
   i. Tighten engine center cover and rocker cover bolts to specifications.
   j. When installing rocker cover, apply 3M sealant No. 8660, or equivalent, to semicircular packing.
   k. When installing high pressure fuel line, apply a small amount of gasoline to hose union. **Use caution not to damage O-ring.**
   l. **Torque** fuel return hose fitting bolts to 3–4 ft. lbs.

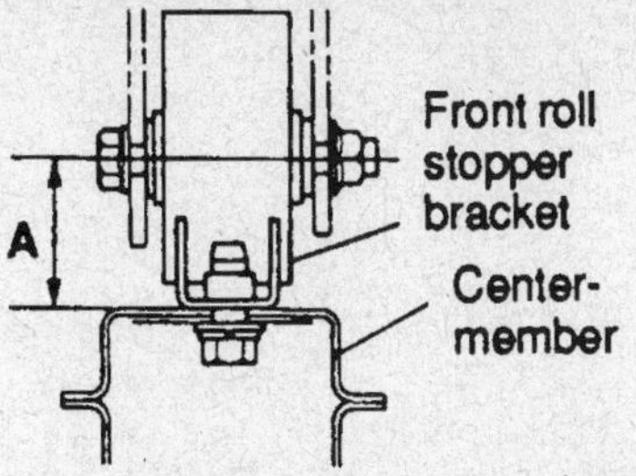
Front roll
stopper
bracket
A
Center-
member
CR1069500605000X

Fig. 10 Front roll stopper clearance. 1995–96

1995–96 Non-Turbo

1. Disconnect battery ground cable.
2. Relieve fuel system pressure as outlined under "Precautions."
3. Drain engine coolant, then drain crankcase.
4. Disconnect electrical connectors from A/C compressor clutch, power steering pump switch, oxygen sensor, engine coolant temperature switch and sensor, MAP sensor and intake air temperature sensor.
5. Disconnect accelerator cable.
6. Disconnect TPS, IAC motor and injector harness electrical connectors.
7. Disconnect ignition coil, camshaft position sensor and EGR solenoid electrical connectors.
8. Disconnect heater hose, upper radiator hose, overflow tube and water hose connection. **Mark relationship between radiator hose and clamp for installation reference.**
9. Disconnect fuel high pressure and return hoses.
10. Disconnect purge air hose.
11. Disconnect power brake booster vacuum hose connection.
12. Remove intake manifold stay.
13. Remove intake and exhaust camshafts as outlined under "Camshaft, Replace."
14. Disconnect exhaust pipe from exhaust manifold.
15. Remove cylinder head attaching bolts, then remove cylinder head and gasket. After cylinder head removal, remove intake and exhaust manifold as necessary.
16. Reverse procedure to install, noting the following:
    a. Prior to installation, inspect cylinder head bolts for stretching by placing a straightedge against bolt threads. If all threads do not contact straightedge, replace bolt.
    b. Clean bolt threads and lubricate with clean engine oil.
    c. Using sequence shown in **Fig. 25, torque** cylinder head bolts in four steps: first, **torque** bolts 1 through 6 to 24 ft. lbs., then bolts 7 through 10 to 20 ft. lbs.; second, **torque** bolts 1 through 6 to 48 ft. lbs., then bolts 7 through 10 to 20 ft. lbs.; third, **torque** bolts 1 through 6 to 48 ft. lbs., then bolts 7 through 10 to 20 ft.

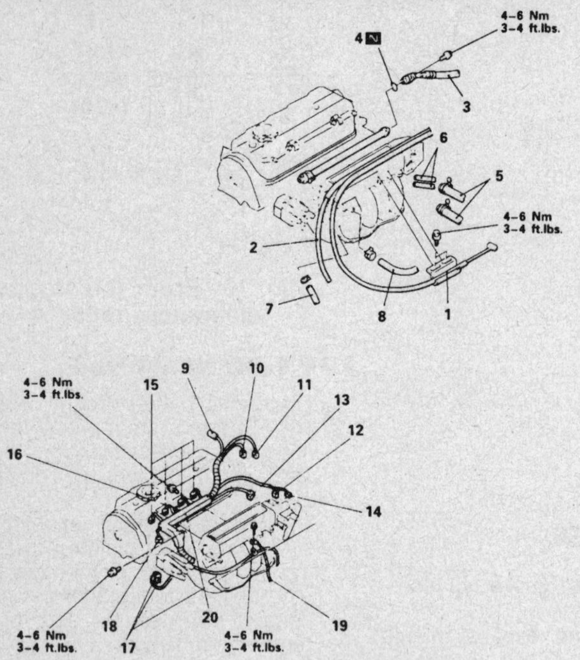
4-6 Nm
3-4 ft.lbs.
4-6 Nm
3-4 ft.lbs.
4-6 Nm
3-4 ft.lbs.
4-6 Nm
3-4 ft.lbs.
4-6 Nm
3-4 ft.lbs.

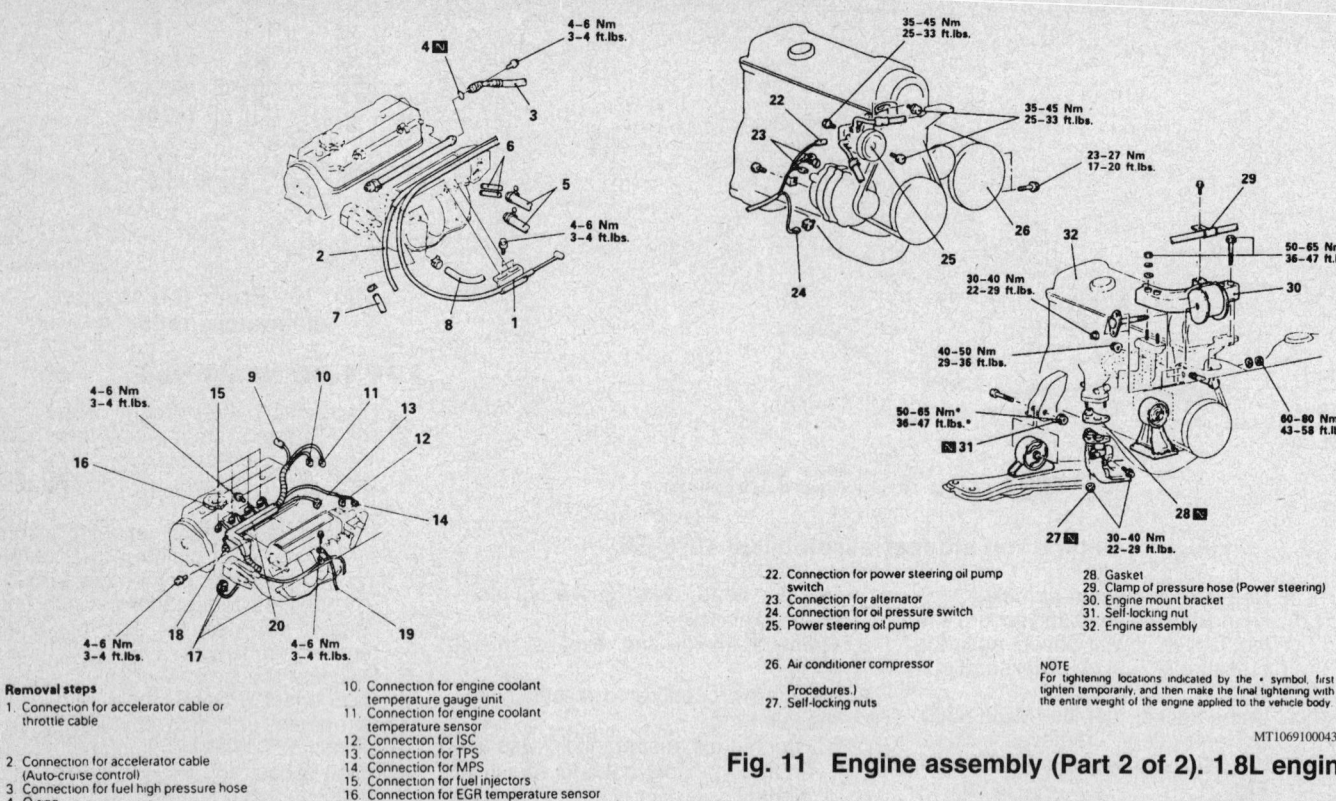

Removal steps

1. Connection for accelerator cable or throttle cable
2. Connection for accelerator cable (Auto-cruise control)
3. Connection for fuel high pressure hose
4. O-ring
5. Connection for heater hoses
6. Connection for vacuum hoses
7. Connection for fuel return hose
8. Connection for brake booster vacuum hose
9. Connection for oxygen sensor
10. Connection for engine coolant temperature gauge unit
11. Connection for engine coolant temperature sensor
12. Connection for ISC
13. Connection for TPS
14. Connection for MPS
15. Connection for fuel injectors
16. Connection for EGR temperature sensor
17. Connection for distributor
18. Connection for CRC filter
19. Connection for ground cable
20. Control wiring harness

MT1069100043010X

Fig. 11 Engine assembly (Part 1 of 2). 1.8L engine

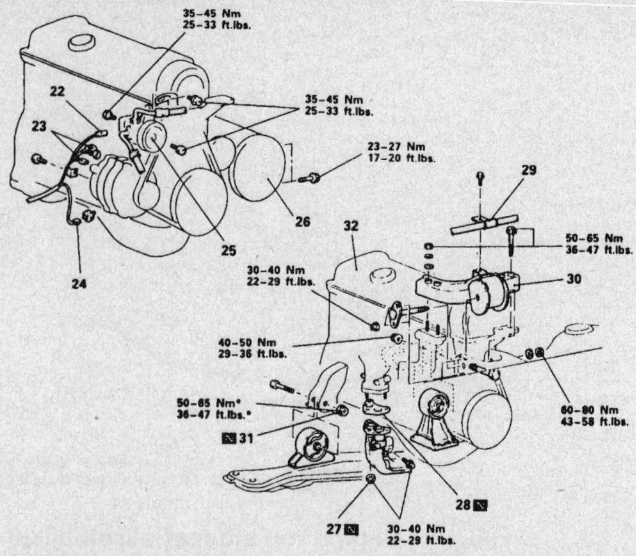
35-45 Nm
25-33 ft.lbs.
35-45 Nm
25-33 ft.lbs.
23-27 Nm
17-20 ft.lbs.
50-65 Nm
36-47 ft.lbs.
30-40 Nm
22-29 ft.lbs.
40-50 Nm
29-36 ft.lbs.
50-65 Nm*
36-47 ft.lbs.*
60-80 Nm
43-58 ft.lbs.
30-40 Nm
22-29 ft.lbs.

22. Connection for power steering oil pump switch
23. Connection for alternator
24. Connection for oil pressure switch
25. Power steering oil pump
26. Air conditioner compressor Procedures.)
27. Self-locking nuts
28. Gasket
29. Clamp of pressure hose (Power steering)
30. Engine mount bracket
31. Self-locking nut
32. Engine assembly

NOTE
For tightening locations indicated by the • symbol, first tighten temporarily, and then make the final tightening with the entire weight of the engine applied to the vehicle body.

MT1069100043020X

Fig. 11 Engine assembly (Part 2 of 2). 1.8L engine

lbs.; then finally, tighten all bolts an additional ¼ turn (90°).

d. When installing radiator hoses, align marks on clamps and respective hoses.

CRANKSHAFT

REPLACE

REMOVAL

Refer to **Fig. 26**when removing crankshaft and main bearings.

INSTALLATION

Refer to **Fig. 26**when installing crankshaft and main bearings, noting the following:

1. **On 2.0L engines, torque** main bearing caps to 47–51 ft. lbs.
2. **On all models,** install main upper bearing on cylinder block and lower bearing on main bearing caps.
3. Install crankshaft and apply engine oil to journals.
4. Caps should be installed with arrows facing forward and in proper number order, **Fig. 27.**
5. Tighten main bearing cap bolts to specification and check to ensure crankshaft rotates freely and has proper endplay.
6. Using crankshaft rear oil seal installer tool No. MD998011, or equivalent, install seal in case.
7. Install oil separator into case with 0.16 inch diameter oil hole in lowest position.
8. Install new oil seal case gasket and oil seal case assembly.
9. Install rear plate to cylinder block.
10. **On models with manual transaxle,** install flywheel and tighten bolts to specification, then check clutch mounting surface for runout.
11. **On models with automatic transaxle,** install adapter plates and driveplate, then tighten bolts to specifications.

VALVE ARRANGEMENT

Intake valves are on the righthand side of the engine and the exhaust valves are on the lefthand side of the engine.

VALVE LIFTERS

INSPECTION

If an abnormal noise is heard from the lash adjusters, check as follows:

1. Operate engine to normal operating temperature.
2. While installed to cylinder head, press part of rocker arm that contacts lash adjuster.
3. If, when pressed, rocker arm is very hard to be depressed, adjuster is operating correctly.
4. If, when pressed, rocker arm is very easily depressed replace lash adjuster.
5. If there is a spongy feeling when pressed, air is mixed in with engine oil. The cause is insufficient amount of engine oil or damage to oil screen and/or gasket.
6. After finding and correcting cause, warm engine and drive at low speed for a short time. Then, after stopping engine and waiting a few minutes, drive again at low speed. Repeat this step to bleed air out of oil system.

VALVE CLEARANCE SPECIFICATIONS

Engine Liter	Clearance	
	Intake	Exhaust
1.8L	.0012-.0024	.0020-.0035
2.0L①	.0008–.0020	.0020–.0035
2.0L②	.0019–.0026	.0029–.0037

① — With turbo.
② — Less turbo.

VALVE ADJUSTMENT

These engines use hydraulic auto-lash adjusters. No adjustments are required.

ROCKER ARMS

REPLACE

Refer to “Camshaft, Replace” for rocker arm replacement procedure.

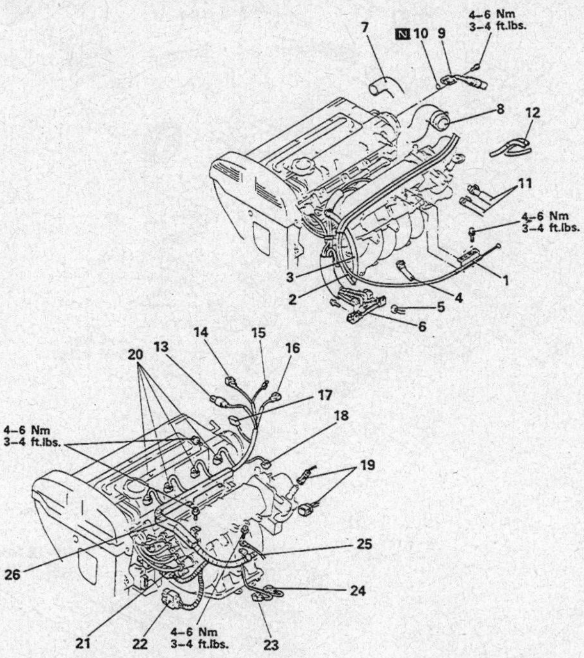
4-6 Nm
3-4 ft.lbs.
7
10
9
8
12
11
4-6 Nm
3-4 ft.lbs.
1
2
3
4
5
6
14
15
16
13
20
17
18
4-6 Nm
3-4 ft.lbs.
19
25
26
24
21
22
4-6 Nm
3-4 ft.lbs.
23

Removal steps

1. Connection for accelerator cable or throttle cable
2. Connection for accelerator cable (Auto-cruise control)
3. Connection for fuel return hose
4. Connection for brake booster vacuum hose
5. Connection for solenoid valve (Turbo)
6. Solenoid valve bracket (Turbo)
7. Connection for air hose A (Turbo)
8. Connection for air hose C (Turbo)
9. Connection for fuel high pressure hose
10. O-ring
11. Connection for heater hoses
12. Connection for vacuum hoses
13. Connection for oxygen sensor
14. Connection for engine coolant temperature sensor
15. Connection for engine coolant temperature gauge unit
16. Connection for air conditioning engine coolant temperature switch
17. Connection for crankshaft position sensor
18. Connection for TPS
19. Connection for ISC and closed throttle position switch
20. Connection for fuel injectors
21. Connection for ignition coil
22. Connection for ignition power transistor
23. Connection for knock sensor (Turbo)
24. Connection for EGR temperature sensor (California vehicles only)
25. Connection for ground cable
26. Control wiring harness

MT1069100044010X

Fig. 12 Engine assembly (Part 1 of 2). 2.0L engine

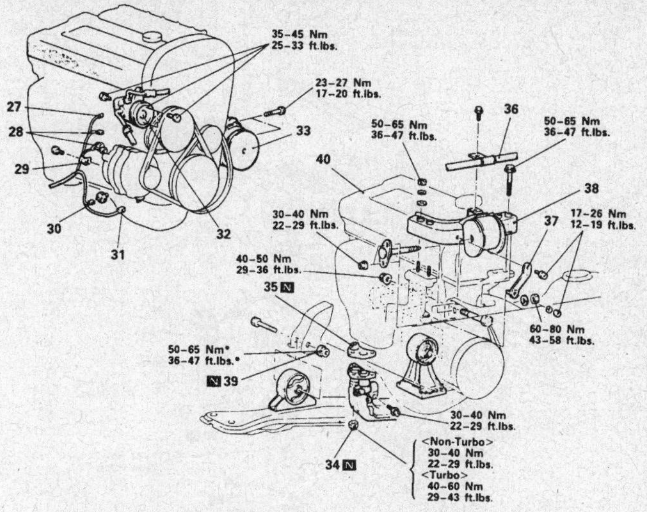
35-45 Nm
25-33 ft.lbs.
23-27 Nm
17-20 ft.lbs.
27
28
29
30
31
32
33
36
50-65 Nm
36-47 ft.lbs.
50-65 Nm
36-47 ft.lbs.
40
38
30-40 Nm
22-29 ft.lbs.
37
17-26 Nm
12-19 ft.lbs.
40-50 Nm
29-36 ft.lbs.
35
60-80 Nm
43-58 ft.lbs.
50-65 Nm*
36-47 ft.lbs.*
39
30-40 Nm
22-29 ft.lbs.
34
<Non-Turbo>
30-40 Nm
22-29 ft.lbs.
<Turbo>
40-60 Nm
29-43 ft.lbs.

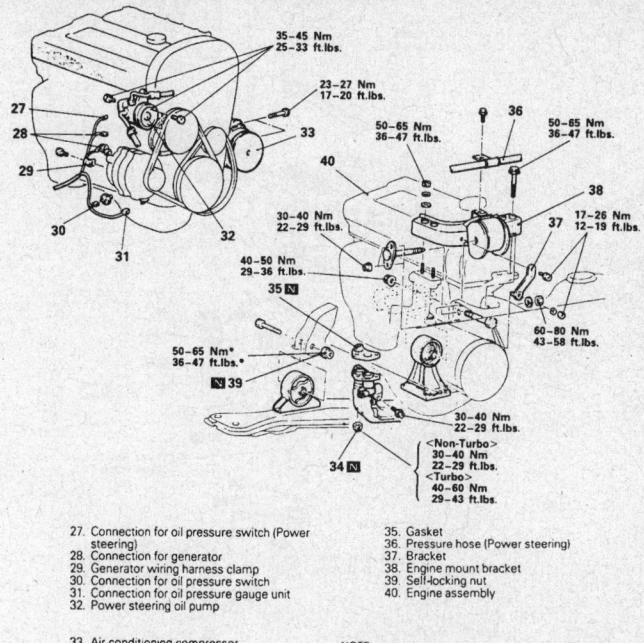

27. Connection for oil pressure switch (Power steering)
28. Connection for generator
29. Generator wiring harness clamp
30. Connection for oil pressure switch
31. Connection for oil pressure gauge unit
32. Power steering oil pump
33. Air conditioning compressor
34. Self-locking nuts
35. Gasket
36. Pressure hose (Power steering)
37. Bracket
38. Engine mount bracket
39. Self-locking nut
40. Engine assembly

NOTE
For tightening locations indicated by the • symbol, first tighten temporarily, and then make the final tightening with the entire weight of the engine applied to the vehicle body.

MT1069100044020X

Fig. 12 Engine assembly (Part 2 of 2). 2.0L engine

FRONT COVER

REPLACE

Refer to "Oil Pump, Replace" for front cover replacement procedure.

TIMING BELT

REPLACE

With the timing belt removed, avoid turning the camshaft or crankshaft. If movement is required, exercise extreme caution to avoid valve damage caused by piston contact.

1.8L ENGINE

REMOVAL

1. Release fuel system pressure as outlined under "Precautions."
2. Disconnect battery ground cable, then remove hood and lower cover.
3. Remove timing belt in numbered sequence as shown, **Fig. 28,** noting the following:
   a. Jack up vehicle after placing a wooden block between jack and engine oil pan and remove engine mount bracket. **Ensure pressure is applied equally on engine oil pan.**
   b. Prior to removing timing belt, turn crankshaft clockwise and align timing marks, **Fig. 20.**
   c. Mark direction of rotation on timing belt if belt is to be reused.
   d. Loosen timing belt tensioner bolt, then move tensioner toward water pump and tighten temporarily. Remove timing belt.
   e. Remove plug in side of cylinder block and insert a Phillips screwdriver to block silent shaft.
   f. Remove oil pump sprocket nut and sprocket.
   g. Mark direction of rotation on timing belt "B"if belt is to be reused.

INSTALLATION

Reverse numbered sequence to assemble, as shown in **Fig. 28,** noting the following:

1. Install crankshaft sprocket "B" as shown, **Fig. 29.**
2. Apply a thin coat of engine oil to outer circumference of right silent shaft sprocket spacer, then install spacer with chamfered end facing oil seal.
3. Align crankshaft sprocket "B" timing mark and silent shaft sprocket timing marks.
4. Install timing belt "B" over crankshaft and silent shaft sprockets. Ensure there is no slack in belt.
5. Adjust timing belt "B" as follows:
   a. Temporarily position timing belt "B" tensioner so that center of tensioner pulley is to left and above center of installation bolt, then temporarily install tensioner pulley so that flange is toward front of engine, **Fig. 30.**
   b. While holding timing belt "B" tensioner up, apply pressure on timing belt ensuring tension side of belt is taut, then tighten tensioner pulley bolt, **Fig. 31.**
   c. Depress belt with finger ensuring deflection is 0.20–0.28 inch. Adjust, if necessary.
6. Install flange as shown, **Fig. 32.**
7. Install tensioner spring, tensioner spacer and timing belt tensioner.
8. Place upper end of tensioner spring against water pump body.
9. Move tensioner fully toward water and temporarily secure.
10. Install timing belt as follows:
    a. Align timing marks on camshaft, oil pump and crankshaft sprockets, **Fig. 33.**
    b. When aligning timing marks on oil pump sprocket, remove plug from side of cylinder block and insert a Phillips head screwdriver with a shaft diameter of 0.31 inch into hole. Ensure screwdriver can be inserted 2.36 inches, if not, turn sprocket one rotation and align timing mark to ensure screwdriver can be installed 2.36 inches. Do not remove screwdriver until timing belt is completely installed.
    c. Install, in order, timing belt onto crankshaft sprocket, oil pump sprocket and camshaft sprocket

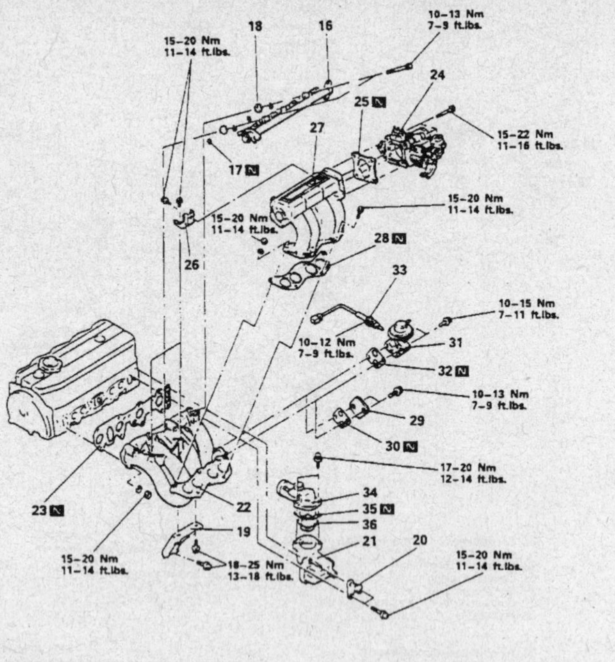
15–20 Nm
11–14 ft.lbs.
10–13 Nm
7–9 ft.lbs.
15–22 Nm
11–16 ft.lbs.
15–20 Nm
11–14 ft.lbs.
10–15 Nm
7–11 ft.lbs.
10–12 Nm
7–9 ft.lbs.
17–20 Nm
12–14 ft.lbs.
18–25 Nm
13–18 ft.lbs.

Removal steps

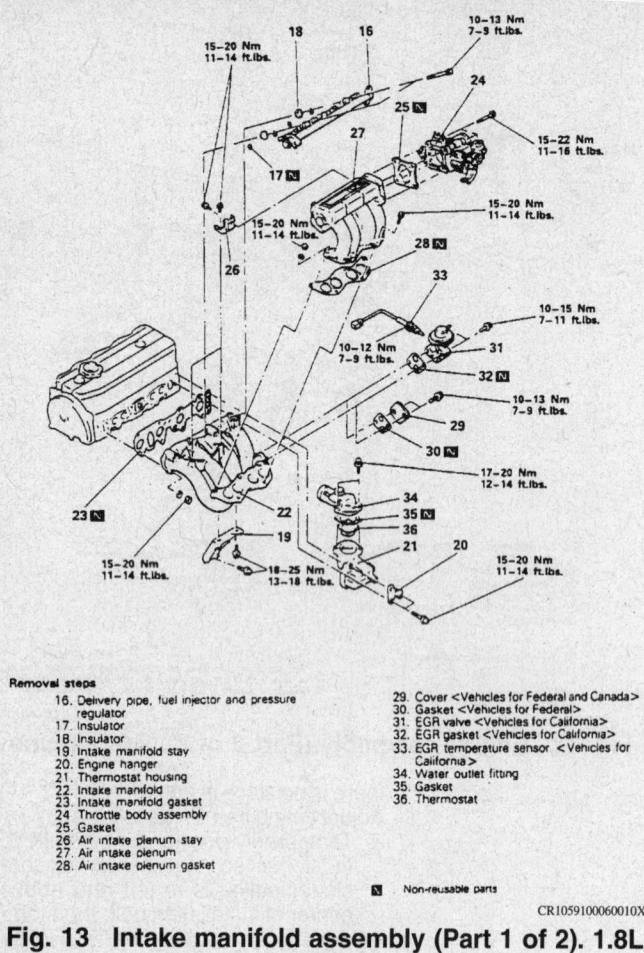

16. Delivery pipe, fuel injector and pressure regulator
17. Insulator
18. Insulator
19. Intake manifold stay
20. Engine hanger
21. Thermostat housing
22. Intake manifold
23. Intake manifold gasket
24. Throttle body assembly
25. Gasket
26. Air intake plenum stay
27. Air intake plenum
28. Air intake plenum gasket
29. Cover <Vehicles for Federal and Canada>
30. Gasket <Vehicles for Federal>
31. EGR valve <Vehicles for California>
32. EGR gasket <Vehicles for California>
33. EGR temperature sensor <Vehicles for California>
34. Water outlet fitting
35. Gasket
36. Thermostat

N Non-reusable parts

CR1059100060010X

Fig. 13 Intake manifold assembly (Part 1 of 2). 1.8L engine

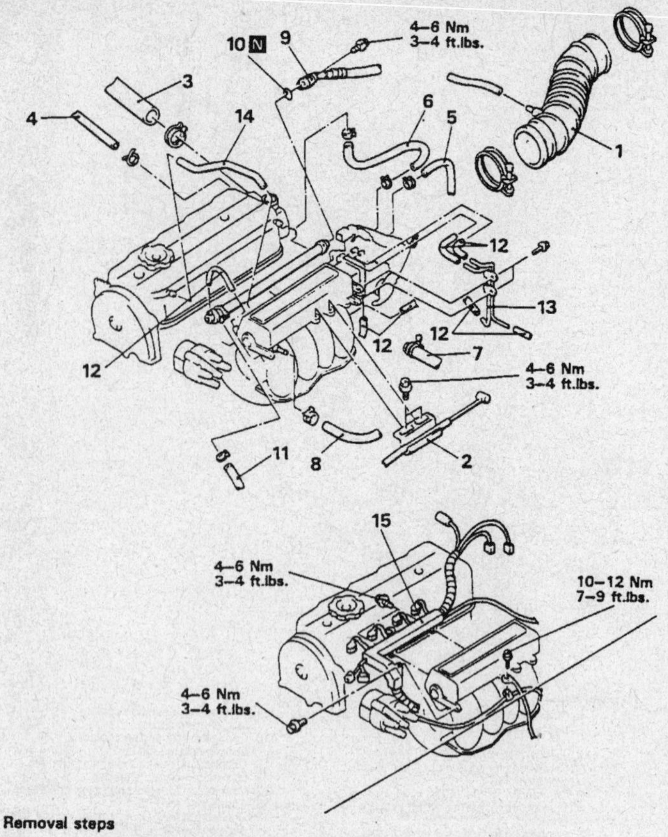
4–6 Nm
3–4 ft.lbs.
10–12 Nm
7–9 ft.lbs.

Removal steps

1. Air intake hose
2. Connection for accelerator cable
3. Connection for radiator upper hose
4. Connection for overflow tube
5. Connection for water by-pass hose
6. Water hose
7. Connection for heater hose
8. Connection for brake booster vacuum hose
9. Connection for fuel high pressure hose
10. O-ring
11. Connection for fuel return hose
12. Connection for vacuum hoses
13. Vacuum pipe
14. PCV hose
15. Connection for control harness

N : Non-reusable parts

CR1059100060020X

Fig. 13 Intake manifold assembly (Part 2 of 2). 1.8L engine

while keeping tension side of belt tight.

11. Adjust timing belt as follows:
    a. Loosen tensioner mounting nut and allow tensioner spring to push tensioner against belt.
    b. Ensure each sprocket is aligned with each timing mark.
    c. Turn crankshaft clockwise by two teeth of camshaft sprocket. **As this step is to apply proper amount of tension on timing belt, be sure not to rotate crankshaft counterclockwise or place pressure on belt to check amount of tension.**
    d. Apply pressure on tensioner in direction of arrow, ensuring no portion of timing belt raises out of position marked "A," **Fig. 34.**
    e. Tighten tensioner bolt, then tensioner spacer.
    f. Ensure clearance between outside of timing belt and cover is 0.40 inch with pinching belt and cover at a point between camshaft and oil pump sprockets.
12. Install upper and lower timing belt cover bolts as shown, **Fig. 35.**

2.0L ENGINE

EXCEPT 1995–96 NON-TURBO

Removal

1. Release fuel system pressure as outlined under "Precautions."
2. Remove lower cover and disconnect battery ground cable.
3. Remove clamp securing power steering pressure hose and air conditioner high pressure hose to body.
4. Using a wood block and a jack, place wood block on engine oil pan and raise engine enough to relieve tension on top engine mount, then remove mount and bracket.
5. Remove engine drive belts. **Prior to removing water pump drive belt, loosen water pump pulley bolts.**
6. Remove tensioner pulley and bracket.
7. Remove crankshaft pulley and water pump pulley.
8. Remove upper and lower timing covers.
9. Disconnect PCV and breather hoses, then remove center cover, spark plug wires, rocker cover, gasket and semicircular packing.
10. Rotate crankshaft clockwise to bring No. 1 cylinder to top dead center (TDC) compression stroke. **Rotate crankshaft only in clockwise direction.** No. 1 cylinder is at TDC of compression stroke when timing marks on camshaft sprockets are aligned with upper surface of cylinder head and dowel pins on camshaft sprockets are facing up as shown, **Fig. 36.**
11. Remove auto tensioner, **Fig. 37.**
12. Remove timing belt. If timing belt is to be reused, mark timing belt indicating direction of rotation.
13. Remove tensioner pulley and arm, then the idler pulley.
14. Using a wrench, hold camshaft at hexagonal portion (between Nos. 2 and 3 journals) and remove camshaft sprocket bolt, then the camshaft sprockets. **Locking camshaft sprocket with a tool may damage sprocket.**
15. Remove plug on left side of cylinder block. Retaining left silent shaft, use a suitable screwdriver to remove oil

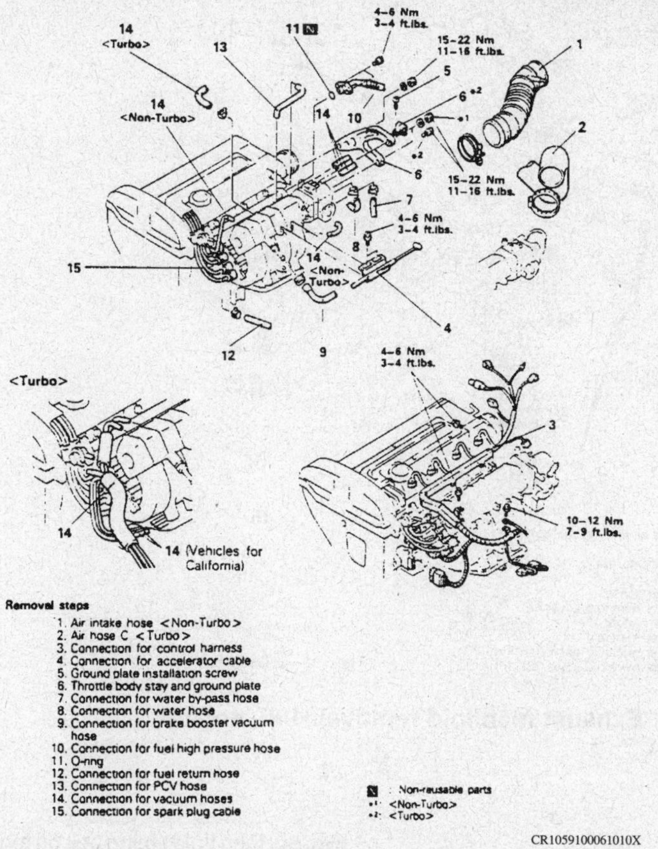
14 <Turbo>
14 <Non-Turbo>
4-6 Nm
3-4 ft.lbs.
15-22 Nm
11-16 ft.lbs.
<Turbo>
14 (Vehicles for California)
10-12 Nm
7-9 ft.lbs.
Removal steps
1. Air intake hose <Non-Turbo>
2. Air hose C <Turbo>
3. Connection for control harness
4. Connection for accelerator cable
5. Ground plate installation screw
6. Throttle body stay and ground plate
7. Connection for water by-pass hose
8. Connection for water hose
9. Connection for brake booster vacuum hose
10. Connection for fuel high pressure hose
11. O-ring
12. Connection for fuel return hose
13. Connection for PCV hose
14. Connection for vacuum hoses
15. Connection for spark plug cable
: Non-reusable parts
*1: <Non-Turbo>
*2: <Turbo>
CR1059100061010X

Fig. 14 Intake manifold assembly (Part 1 of 2). 2.0L engine

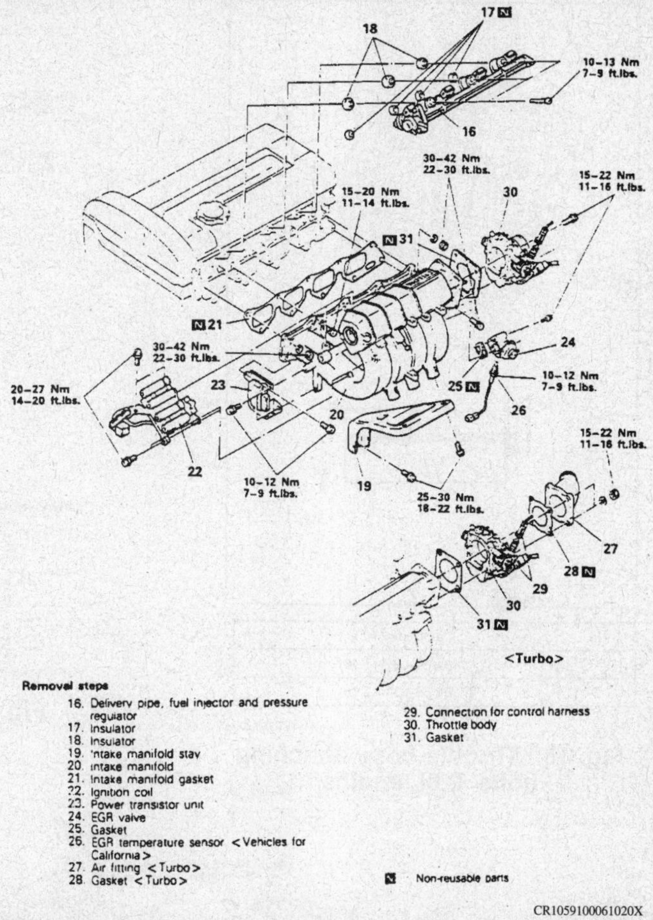
10-13 Nm
7-9 ft.lbs.
30-42 Nm
22-30 ft.lbs.
15-20 Nm
11-14 ft.lbs.
15-22 Nm
11-16 ft.lbs.
20-27 Nm
14-20 ft.lbs.
10-12 Nm
7-9 ft.lbs.
25-30 Nm
18-22 ft.lbs.
<Turbo>
Removal steps
16. Delivery pipe, fuel injector and pressure regulator
17. Insulator
18. Insulator
19. Intake manifold stay
20. Intake manifold
21. Intake manifold gasket
22. Ignition coil
23. Power transistor unit
24. EGR valve
25. Gasket
26. EGR temperature sensor <Vehicles for California>
27. Air fitting <Turbo>
28. Gasket <Turbo>
29. Connection for control harness
30. Throttle body
31. Gasket
Non-reusable parts
CR1059100061020X

Fig. 14 Intake manifold assembly (Part 2 of 2). 2.0L engine

pump sprocket retaining nut and sprocket.

16. Remove crankshaft sprocket bolt, special washer, sprocket and flange.
17. Remove tensioner "B," then mark normal direction of rotation on timing belt "B" and remove belt.
18. Remove silent shaft sprocket and spacer, then crankshaft sprocket "B" and timing belt lower covers.

Installation

1. Install rear timing belt covers.
2. Install crankshaft sprocket "B" as shown, **Fig. 38.**
3. Install silent shaft sprocket spacer and sprocket. Install spacer as follows:
   a. Apply a thin coat of engine oil to outer circumference of spacer.
   b. Install spacer with chamfered end facing oil seal as shown, **Fig. 39,** then tighten silent shaft bolt to specification.
4. Align timing marks of silent shaft sprocket and crankshaft sprocket "B," **Fig. 40,** then install timing belt "B" over both sprockets and ensure belt has no slack.
5. Adjust timing belt "B" tension as follows:
   a. Temporarily install timing belt "B" tensioner ensuring center of tensioner pulley is to left and above center of installation bolt, then attach tensioner pulley ensuring flange is toward front of engine, **Fig. 41.**
   b. Hold timing belt "B" tensioner up in direction shown by arrow, **Fig. 42,** then place pressure on timing belt ensuring tension side of belt is taut.
   c. Tighten tensioner "B" bolt to specification. **When tightening bolt, do not allow tensioner pulley shaft to rotate.**
   d. To check belt tension, depress belt at point (A), **Fig. 43.** Belt deflection should be 0.20–0.28 inch (5–7 mm). If not, adjust belt tension.
6. Install crankshaft sprocket flange, sprocket and special washer. Tighten crankshaft sprocket bolt to specification. **Ensure flange and sprocket are correctly installed as shown, Fig. 44.**
7. Insert a Phillips screwdriver with a shaft diameter of 0.31 inch (8 mm) through plug hole on left side of cylinder head to retain left silent shaft, **Fig. 45,** then install oil pump sprocket and tighten attaching nut to specification.
8. Install camshaft sprockets. Using a wrench, hold camshaft at hexagonal portion (between Nos. 2 and 3 journals) and tighten attaching bolt to specification. **Locking camshaft sprocket with a tool may damage sprocket.**
9. Install auto tensioner, then if tensioner rod is fully extended, proceed as follows:
   a. Position auto tensioner level in a soft jawed vise. If plug at bottom of tensioner protrudes, apply a plain washer to prevent plug from direct contact with vise.
   b. Using a suitable vise, slowly push tensioner rod in until set hole (A) is aligned with hole (B) in tensioner cylinder, **Fig. 46.**
   c. Insert a wire 0.055 inch (1.4 mm) in diameter into set holes, then remove auto tensioner from vise.
   d. Install auto tensioner, tighten attaching bolt to specification. **Leave wire installed in auto tensioner.**
10. Install tensioner pulley onto tensioner arm, then position hole in pulley shaft to left of center bolt. Tighten center bolt finger tight.
11. Rotate camshaft sprockets ensuring dowel pins are located on top, then align timing marks facing each other with top surface of cylinder head, **Fig. 47.** When exhaust camshaft is released, it will rotate one tooth in counterclockwise direction. **The camshaft sprockets are interchangeable and have two sets of timing marks. When sprocket is mounted on exhaust camshaft, use timing mark on right with dowel pin hole on top. For intake sprocket, use mark on left**

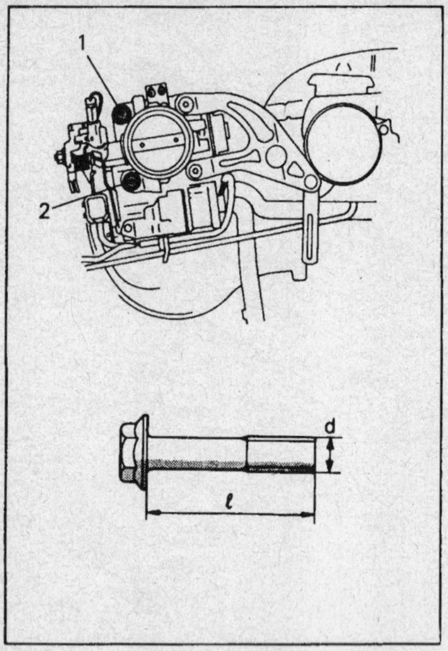
1
2
d
ℓ

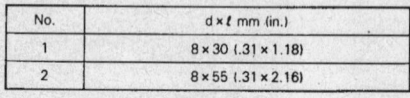

No.	d × ℓ mm (in.)
1	8 × 30 (.31 × 1.18)
2	8 × 55 (.31 × 2.16)

CR1059100062000X

Fig. 15 Throttle body attaching bolts. 2.0L engine

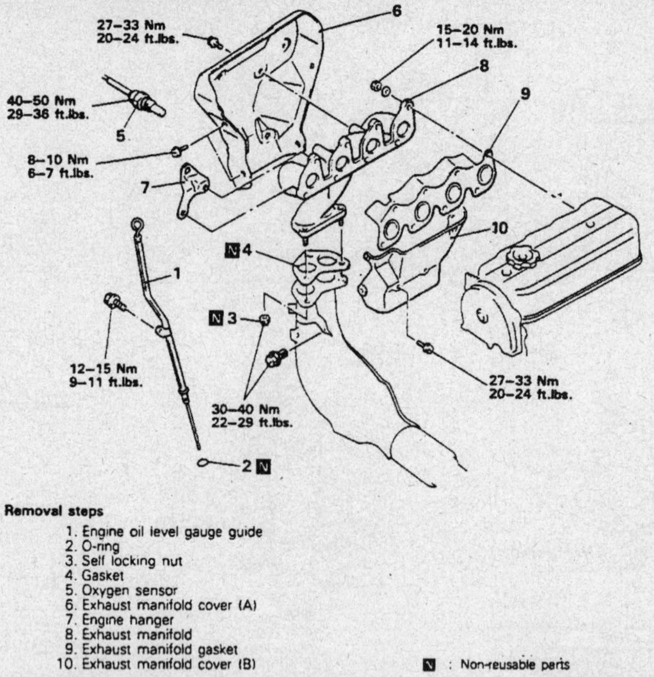
27–33 Nm
20–24 ft.lbs.
40–50 Nm
29–36 ft.lbs.
8–10 Nm
6–7 ft.lbs.
15–20 Nm
11–14 ft.lbs.
12–15 Nm
9–11 ft.lbs.
30–40 Nm
22–29 ft.lbs.
27–33 Nm
20–24 ft.lbs.
Removal steps
1. Engine oil level gauge guide
2. O-ring
3. Self locking nut
4. Gasket
5. Oxygen sensor
6. Exhaust manifold cover (A)
7. Engine hanger
8. Exhaust manifold
9. Exhaust manifold gasket
10. Exhaust manifold cover (B)
N : Non-reusable parts

CR1079100006000X

Fig. 16 Exhaust manifold removal. 1.8L engine

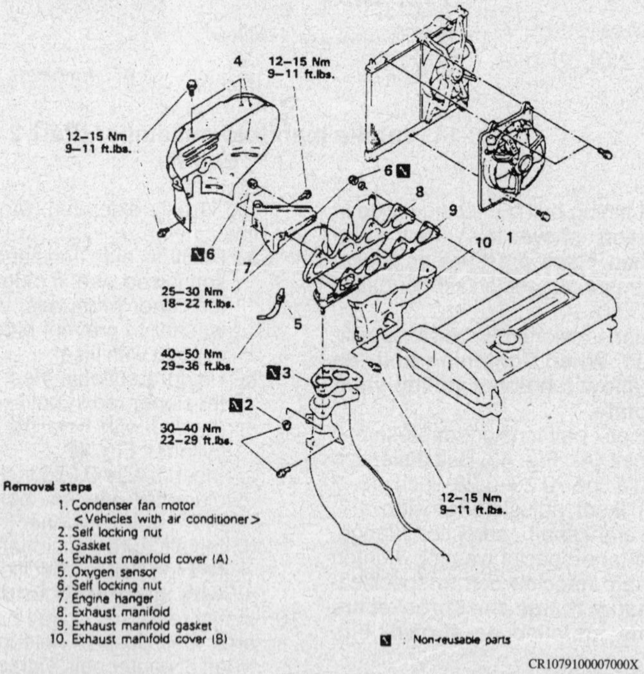
12–15 Nm
9–11 ft.lbs.
12–15 Nm
9–11 ft.lbs.
25–30 Nm
18–22 ft.lbs.
40–50 Nm
29–36 ft.lbs.
30–40 Nm
22–29 ft.lbs.
12–15 Nm
9–11 ft.lbs.
Removal steps
1. Condenser fan motor
<Vehicles with air conditioner>
2. Self locking nut
3. Gasket
4. Exhaust manifold cover (A)
5. Oxygen sensor
6. Self locking nut
7. Engine hanger
8. Exhaust manifold
9. Exhaust manifold gasket
10. Exhaust manifold cover (B)
N : Non-reusable parts

CR1079100007000X

Fig. 17 Exhaust manifold removal. 2.0L non-turbo engine

with dowel pin hole on top, Fig. 48.

12. Align crankshaft and oil pump sprocket timing marks as shown, **Fig. 49.**
13. With oil pump sprocket timing marks aligned, remove plug from lefthand side of cylinder block and insert a screwdriver with a shaft diameter of 0.3 inch. If screwdriver can be inserted 2.4 inches or more, alignment is correct, if not, rotate oil pump sprocket one revolution and realign timing marks. Ensure screwdriver can be inserted 2.4 inches or more properly positioning silent shaft and oil pump sprocket. Leave screwdriver inserted in hole until after timing belt has been installed.
14. Install timing belt as follows:
    a. Install timing belt around tensioner pulley and crankshaft sprocket, **Fig. 50,** then hold timing belt on tensioner pulley with your left hand.
    b. Pulling timing belt with your right-hand, install belt around oil pump sprocket.
    c. Install timing belt around idler pulley, then around intake camshaft sprocket.
    d. Rotate exhaust camshaft sprocket one tooth clockwise to align timing mark with cylinder head top surface; then, pulling belt with both hands, install around exhaust camshaft sprocket.
    e. Gently raise tensioner pulley in direction shown by arrow in **Fig. 50** so belt does not sag, then temporarily tighten center bolt.
15. Adjust timing belt tension as follows:
    a. Rotate crankshaft ¼ turn counterclockwise, then rotate clockwise to move No. 1 cylinder to top dead center.
    b. Loosen tensioner pulley center bolt, then using wrench tool No. MD998752, or equivalent, and a torque wrench, apply a **torque** of 1.88–2.03 ft. lbs., **Fig. 51.** If vehicle body interferes with torque wrench, use a jack to slightly raise engine.
    c. Holding tensioner pulley with wrench tool, tighten tensioner pulley center bolt to specification.
    d. Screw setscrew tool No. MD998738, or equivalent, into left engine support bracket until end of tool makes contact with tensioner arm, **Fig. 52.** Turn tool enough to relieve tension on auto tensioner rod, then remove set wire previously installed in auto tensioner.

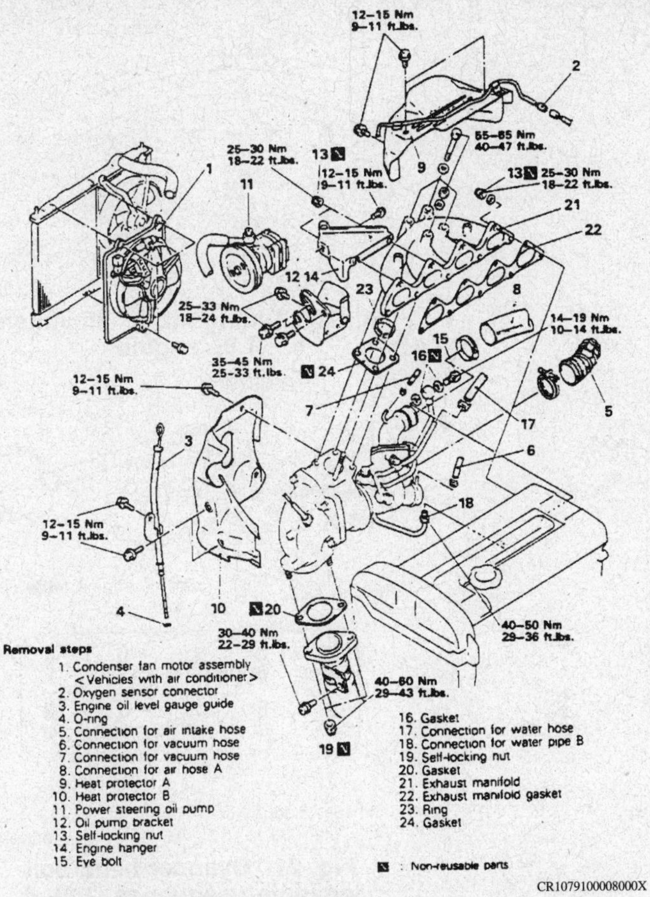
Removal steps
1. Condenser fan motor assembly <Vehicles with air conditioner>
2. Oxygen sensor connector
3. Engine oil level gauge guide
4. O-ring
5. Connection for air intake hose
6. Connection for vacuum hose
7. Connection for vacuum hose
8. Connection for air hose A
9. Heat protector A
10. Heat protector B
11. Power steering oil pump
12. Oil pump bracket
13. Self-locking nut
14. Engine hanger
15. Eye bolt
16. Gasket
17. Connection for water hose
18. Connection for water pipe B
19. Self-locking nut
20. Gasket
21. Exhaust manifold
22. Exhaust manifold gasket
23. Ring
24. Gasket
: Non-reusable parts
CR1079100008000X

Fig. 18 Exhaust manifold removal. 2.0L turbo engine

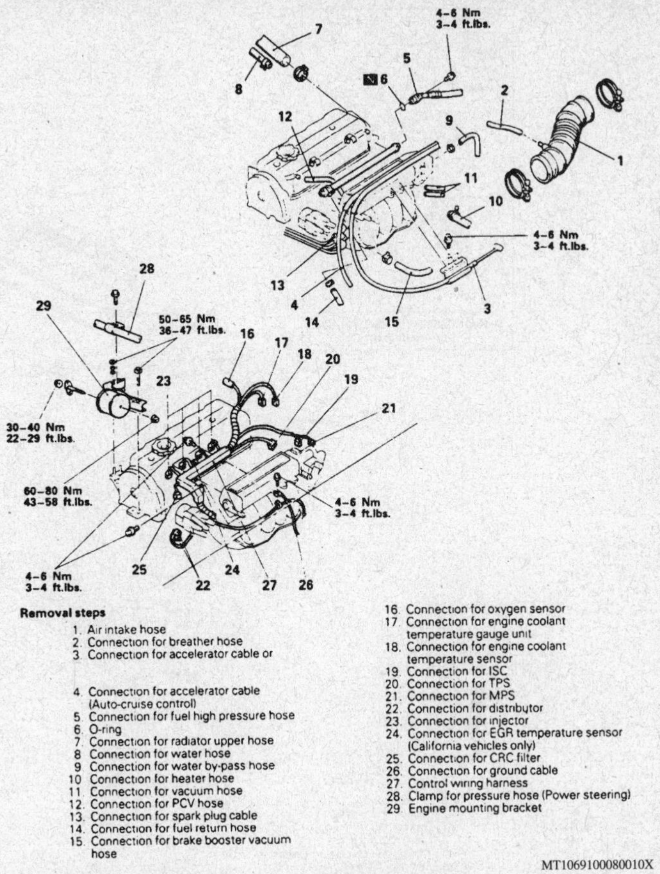
Removal steps
1. Air intake hose
2. Connection for breather hose
3. Connection for accelerator cable or
4. Connection for accelerator cable (Auto-cruise control)
5. Connection for fuel high pressure hose
6. O-ring
7. Connection for radiator upper hose
8. Connection for water hose
9. Connection for water by-pass hose
10. Connection for heater hose
11. Connection for vacuum hose
12. Connection for PCV hose
13. Connection for spark plug cable
14. Connection for fuel return hose
15. Connection for brake booster vacuum hose
16. Connection for oxygen sensor
17. Connection for engine coolant temperature gauge unit
18. Connection for engine coolant temperature sensor
19. Connection for ISC
20. Connection for TPS
21. Connection for MPS
22. Connection for distributor
23. Connection for injector
24. Connection for EGR temperature sensor (California vehicles only)
25. Connection for CRC filter
26. Connection for ground cable
27. Control wiring harness
28. Clamp for pressure hose (Power steering)
29. Engine mounting bracket
MT1069100080010X

Fig. 19 Cylinder head removal (Part 1 of 2). 1.8L engine

e. Remove setscrew tool.
f. Rotate crankshaft clockwise two complete turns, then let sit for 15 minutes.
g. Measure clearance (A) between tensioner arm and auto tensioner body, **Fig. 53.** If clearance is not 0.15–0.18 inch (3.8–4.5 mm), repeat steps a through g until clearance is correct.
h. If clearance (A) cannot be measured with engine in vehicle, screw in setscrew tool No. MD998738, or equivalent, until end of tool makes contact with tensioner arm.
i. Starting in this position, count number of turns of tool required to bring tensioner arm in contact with auto tensioner body. Ensure contact is made within 2.5–3 turns.
j. Install rubber plug into timing belt rear cover.

16. Reverse procedure to install remaining components. When installing rocker cover, apply 3M sealant No. 8660, or equivalent, to semicircular packing.

1995-96 NON-TURBO

Removal

Remove timing belt in numbered sequence as shown in **Fig. 54,** noting the following:

1. Remove crankshaft pulley as shown in **Fig. 55.**
2. Remove power steering pump from the bracket with hose attached and secure out of the way.
3. Place a suitable jack and wood block beneath engine and slightly raise engine to remove engine mount bracket.
4. Align timing marks on camshaft intake and exhaust sprockets before loosening belt tensioner to remove timing belt, **Fig. 56.** Ensure camshaft and crankshaft are not rotated after belt is removed.
5. When belt tensioner is removed, it is necessary to compress the plunger into the tensioner body:
   a. Place tensioner in a suitable vise and slowly compress the plunger, **Fig. 57.**
   b. Index the tensioner in the vise the same way it is installed on the engine to ensure proper pin orientation when installed on engine.
   c. When plunger is compressed into tensioner body, install a pin through the body and plunger to retain plunger in place until tensioner is installed.

Installation

Reverse removal procedure to install noting:

1. Set the crankshaft sprocket to TDC by aligning the sprocket with the arrow on the oil pump housing, **Fig. 58.**
2. Using a suitable wrench, move crankshaft to ½ notch before TDC.
3. Set the camshaft timing marks by aligning the notches on sprockets, **Fig. 56.**
4. Install timing belt, starting at crankshaft, around water pump sprocket, idler pulley, camshaft pulleys and tensioner pulley, **Fig. 59.**
5. Move crankshaft sprocket to TDC to take up belt slack.
6. Install belt tensioner to engine block but do not tighten fasteners.
7. Using a suitable torque wrench on the tensioner pulley, **torque** to 28 ft. lbs.
8. With torque being applied to the tensioner pulley, **Fig. 60** move the tensioner up against the tensioner pulley bracket and **torque** fasteners to 23 ft. lbs.
9. Pull the tensioner plunger pin. Pretension is correct when pin can be easily removed or installed.
10. Rotate crankshaft two revolutions and check alignment of timing marks. If not correct, repeat procedure.

CAMSHAFT

REPLACE

1.8L ENGINE

1. Release fuel system pressure as outlined under "Precautions."
2. Disconnect battery ground cable.

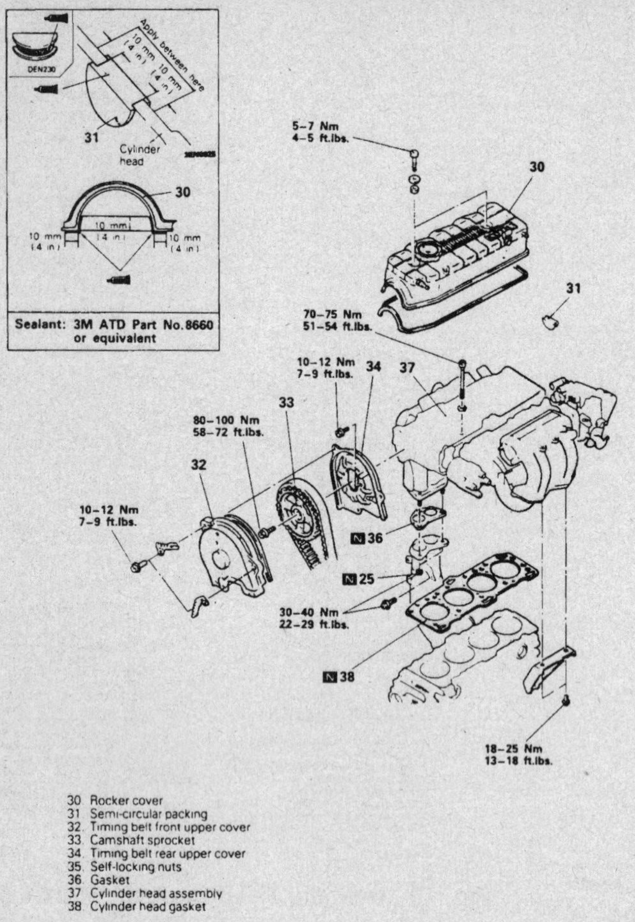
Apply between here
10 mm (.4 in.)
DEN230
31
Cylinder head
30
10 mm (.4 in.)
Sealant: 3M ATD Part No.8660 or equivalent
5–7 Nm
4–5 ft.lbs.
70–75 Nm
51–54 ft.lbs.
10–12 Nm
7–9 ft.lbs.
80–100 Nm
58–72 ft.lbs.
30–40 Nm
22–29 ft.lbs.
18–25 Nm
13–18 ft.lbs.
30 Rocker cover
31 Semi-circular packing
32 Timing belt front upper cover
33 Camshaft sprocket
34 Timing belt rear upper cover
35 Self-locking nuts
36 Gasket
37 Cylinder head assembly
38 Cylinder head gasket
MT1069100080020X

Fig. 19 Cylinder head removal (Part 2 of 2). 1.8L engine

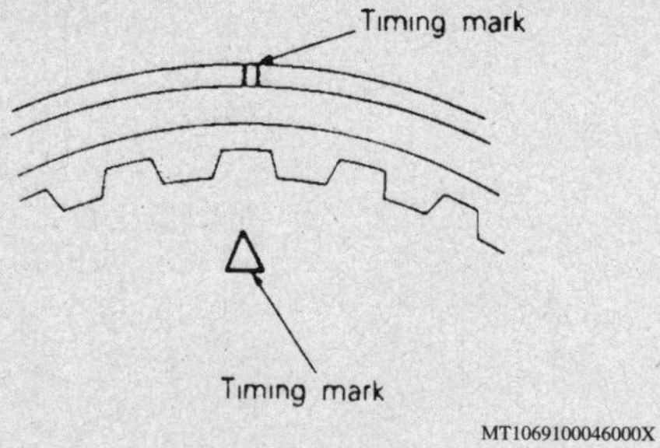
Timing mark
Timing mark
MT1069100046000X

Fig. 20 Timing marks alignment. 1.8L engine

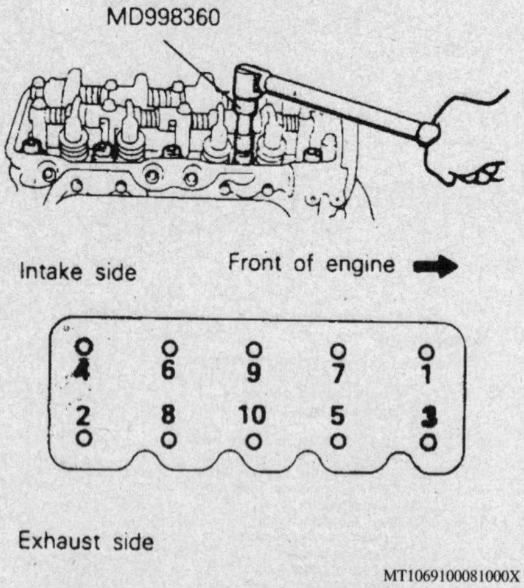
MD998360
Intake side
Front of engine
4
6
9
7
1
2
8
10
5
3
Exhaust side
MT1069100081000X

Fig. 21 Cylinder head bolt loosening sequence. 1.8L & 1995–96 2.0L turbo engines

3. Remove breather hose and PCV hose from rocker cover.
4. Remove oil filler cap attaching bolt, then the oil filler cap assembly, **Fig. 61.** Remove rocker cover, then the gasket.
5. Rotate crankshaft in normal direction of rotation until No. 1 cylinder is at top dead center and camshaft and crankshaft timing marks are aligned.
6. Place a chalk mark between timing belt and camshaft sprocket, then after removing camshaft sprocket bolt, separate sprocket from camshaft leaving belt in place on sprocket. Secure sprocket and belt on lower timing cover ensuring sprocket does not disengage from belt and fall. **Do not rotate crankshaft after sprocket is removed from camshaft.**
7. Prior to removal of rocker arm and rocker shaft assembly, install auto-lash adjuster holder tool No. MD998443, or equivalent, to ensure auto-lash adjuster is not allowed to fall.
8. Remove semicircular packing, then the oil seal.
9. Remove rocker arm and shaft assembly, then the auto-lash adjuster.
10. Remove camshaft.
11. Reverse procedure to install, noting the following:
    a. Insert rocker arm shafts into holes in front bearing cap and temporarily install bolts to hold shafts into place. When rocker arm shafts are inserted, ensure shaft front end cuts are facing up as shown, **Fig. 62.**
    b. Install bearing cap Nos. 2, 3 and 4. Caps can be identified by front mark, cap number and rocker cover attaching bolt hole, **Fig. 63.**
    c. Install wave washers as shown, **Fig. 64.**
    d. Use suitable gasket sealant for valve cover installation.

2.0L ENGINE

EXCEPT 1995–96 NON-TURBO

Removal

1. Release fuel system pressure as outlined under "Precautions."
2. Disconnect battery ground cable, then the accelerator cable from throttle body.
3. Remove timing belt as outlined under "Timing Belt, Replace."
4. Using a suitable screwdriver, remove camshaft oil seals, **Fig. 65. Use caution not to damage front camshaft bearing caps or camshafts.**
5. Loosen camshaft bearing cap bolts in two or three steps, then remove bolts and bearing caps, **If bearing caps are difficult to remove, use a plastic hammer to lightly tap rear part of camshaft, then remove bearing caps.**
6. Remove intake and exhaust camshafts.
7. Remove rocker arms.

Installation

1. Install rocker arms.
2. Apply engine oil to journals and lobes of camshafts, then install camshafts on cylinder head. **Ensure camshafts are correctly installed. Intake camshaft has a slit on rear end for driving crankshaft angle sensor. Also ensure dowel pins on sprocket ends are positioned on top.**
3. Install camshaft bearing caps. Bearing caps 2 through 5 are of identical shape. Check identification marks on bearing caps to determine correct location, **Fig. 66, and ensure rocker arms are correctly mounted on lash adjusters and valve stem ends.**
4. Tighten camshaft bearing caps in sequence as shown, **Fig. 67,** in two or three stages by torquing progressively. Tighten to specification in final sequence.
5. Install guide tool No. MD998307-01, or equivalent, on camshaft, then apply oil to camshaft oil seal and insert oil seal along guide tool until it contacts cylinder head. Using installer tool No. MD998306-01, or equivalent, press oil

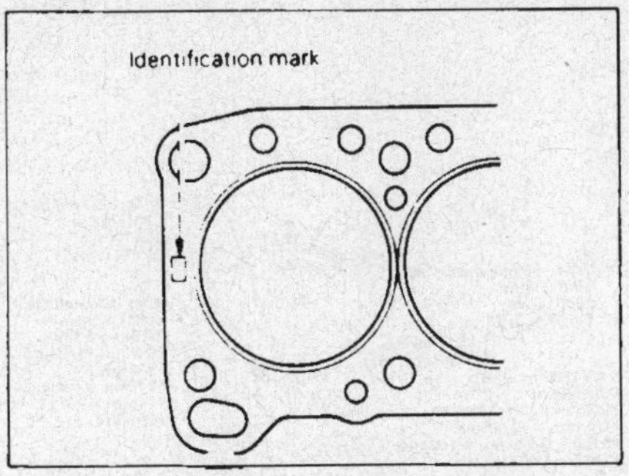
Identification mark

MT1069100082000X

Fig. 22 Cylinder head gasket identification mark. 1.8L & 1995–96 2.0L turbo engines

seal into cylinder head, then remove tools.

6. Install camshaft sprockets and tighten attaching bolts to specifications.
7. Install crankshaft angle sensor as follows:
   a. Position dowel pin on intake camshaft on top.
   b. Align punch mark on crankshaft angle sensor housing with notch in plate as shown, **Fig. 68.**
   c. Install crankshaft angle sensor on cylinder head. Tighten attaching nut to specifications. **Ensure crankshaft angle sensor does not turn when tightening attaching nut.**
8. Reverse remaining procedure to complete installation, noting the following:
   a. Ensure camshaft and crankshaft timing marks are correctly aligned.
   b. Tighten auto tensioner bolt, timing cover bolts and tensioner pulley bolt to specifications.
   c. Tighten crankshaft pulley bolts and water pump pulley bolts to specifications.
   d. Tighten engine center cover and rocker cover bolts to specifications.
   e. When installing rocker cover, apply 3M sealant No. 8660, or equivalent, to semicircular packing.
   f. Check and adjust ignition timing to specifications.

1995-96 NON-TURBO

Removal

Remove camshaft in numbered sequence, **Fig. 69,** noting the following:

1. Use camshaft sprocket holder and adapter tools No. C-4687 and C-4687–1, or equivalents, to ensure camshaft sprockets do not turn during removal.
2. Mark and identify intake camshaft and exhaust camshaft before removal as they are not interchangeable.
3. Loosen camshaft bearing cap attaching bolts in sequence shown in **Fig. 70,** one camshaft at a time.
4. Remove camshaft oil seals using suitable screwdriver to pry seal out.

Installation

1. Install new camshaft oil seals using special oil seal seating tools No. MB991554 and MB998713, or equivalents, **Fig. 71.**
2. Install camshaft bearing cap attaching bolts in sequence shown in **Fig. 70,** one camshaft at a time. Tighten to specifications.
3. Use camshaft sprocket holder and adapter tools No. C-4687 and C-4687–1, or equivalents, to ensure camshaft sprockets do not turn during installation.
4. Install cylinder head cover assembly to head and tighten in sequence shown in **Fig. 72. Torque** in three steps: first to 3.3 ft. lbs., then to 6.6 ft. lbs., finally to 8.9 ft. lbs.

SILENT SHAFT

REPLACE

Refer to "Oil Pump, Replace" for silent shaft replacement procedure.

PISTON & ROD ASSEMBLY

Refer to **Fig. 73** when removing piston and rod assembly. Keep all components, such as connecting rod caps and bearings, in proper order for installation. Position each piston ring gap as far apart as possible and ensure each piston and rod are installed in the same cylinder bore as removed. Ensure connecting rod caps and bearings are placed on proper connecting rods, then tighten bolts to specification.

Pistons and rings are available in standard sizes and oversizes of 0.010, 0.020, 0.030 and 0.039 inch. Measure piston as shown, **Fig. 74.** Oversize pins are not available.

MAIN & ROD BEARINGS

Refer to "Crankshaft, Replace" for main bearing replacement.

OIL PAN

REPLACE

1. Remove oil pan mounting bolts, then tap oil pan remover tool between cylinder block and oil pan.
2. Remove oil pan by placing a brass bar at corner of oil pan remover tool, then tap with a hammer. **Do not use a screwdriver, chisel or similar tool when removing oil pan.**
3. Check oil pan and screen for damage, cracks or clogging and replace as necessary.
4. Using a wire brush, scrape clean all gasket surfaces of cylinder block and oil pan ensuring all loose material is removed.
5. Ensuring gasket surfaces are free of oil and dirt, apply sealant, No. MD970389, or equivalent, around gasket surface of oil pan. Sealant should be applied in a continuous bead approximately 0.16 inch in diameter.
6. Assemble oil pan to cylinder block within 15 minutes after applying sealant. **After installing oil pan, wait at least 30 minutes before starting engine.**

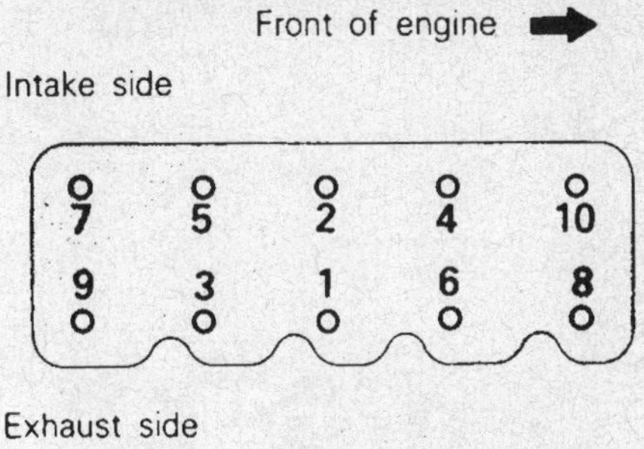
Front of engine
Intake side
7
5
2
4
10
9
3
1
6
8
Exhaust side

MT1069100083000X

Fig. 23 Cylinder head bolt tightening sequence. 1.8L & 1995–96 2.0L turbo engines

OIL PUMP

REPLACE

REMOVAL

Refer to **Figs. 75 through 78** when removing silent shaft, oil pump and front case, noting the following:

1. Position a suitable screwdriver between oil pan and cylinder block and slide along groove to remove.
2. Keep silent shaft in position by inserting a screwdriver through plug hole in left side of cylinder block, **Fig. 77.** Remove oil pump driven gear flange bolt.
3. If front case is sticking to cylinder, insert a suitable screwdriver into slot and pry up, **Fig. 78. Never attempt to pry at any other positions where flange is thinner. Avoid impacting front of case for removal.**
4. Using removal tool No. MD998282-01, or equivalent, remove front and rear bearings from cylinder block.

INSPECTION

1. Ensure silent shaft oil holes are not clogged and journal is inspected for seizure, damage or contact with bearing. If so, replace bearing or front case assembly.
2. Measure silent shaft clearance. If clearance is excessive due to wear, replace silent shaft bearing, silent shaft or front case assembly. Clearance should be as follows:
   a. Right: front, 0.0008–0.0024 inch; rear, 0.0020–0.0036 inch.
   b. Left: front, 0.0008–0.0021 inch; rear, 0.0020–0.0036 inch.
3. Ensure oil pump side clearance of each gear is as follows:
   a. Drive gear: 0.0031–0.0055 inch.
   b. Driven gear: 0.0024–0.0047 inch.

INSTALLATION

1. Install silent shaft in cylinder block.
2. Install oil pump drive and driven gears in front case, ensuring gear timing marks are aligned, **Fig. 79.**
3. Using small end of oil seal guide tool No. MD998375-01, or equivalent, for

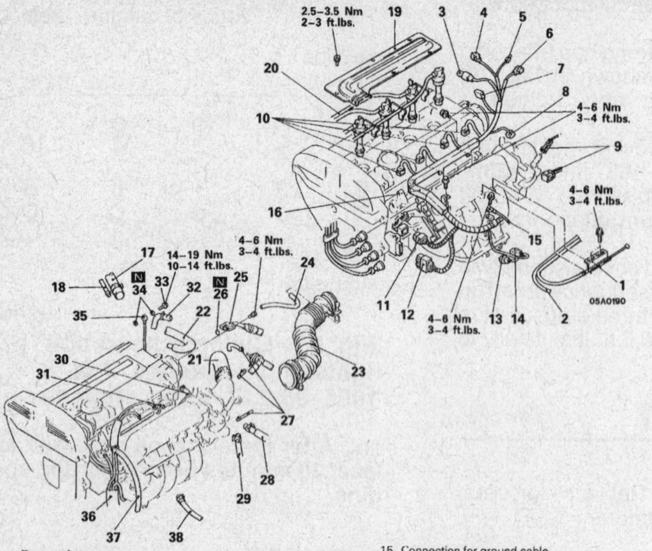
2.5–3.5 Nm
2–3 ft.lbs.
4–6 Nm
3–4 ft.lbs.
4–6 Nm
3–4 ft.lbs.
4–6 Nm
3–4 ft.lbs.
14–19 Nm
10–14 ft.lbs.
4–6 Nm
3–4 ft.lbs.
05A0190

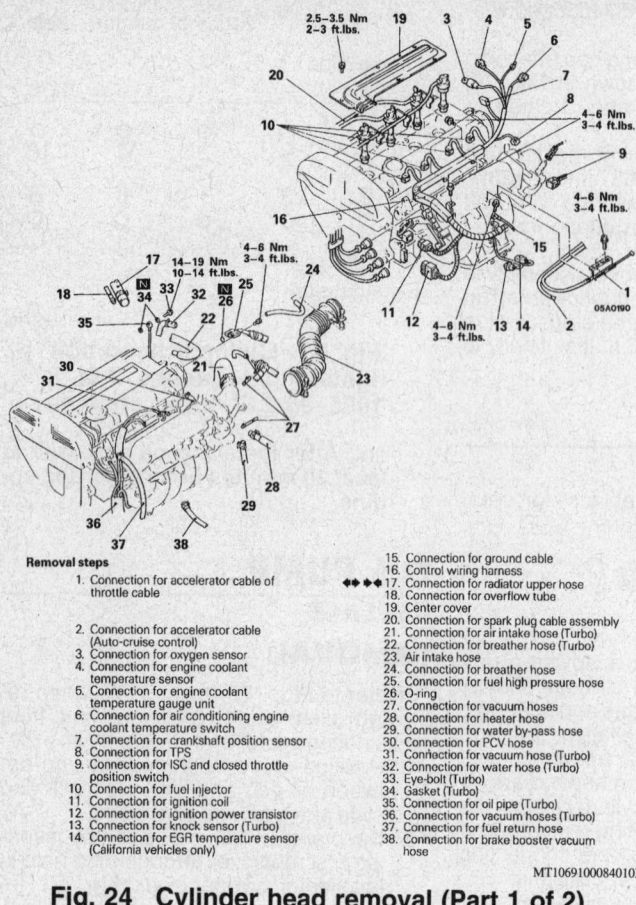

Removal steps

1. Connection for accelerator cable of throttle cable
2. Connection for accelerator cable (Auto-cruise control)
3. Connection for oxygen sensor
4. Connection for engine coolant temperature sensor
5. Connection for engine coolant temperature gauge unit
6. Connection for air conditioning engine coolant temperature switch
7. Connection for crankshaft position sensor
8. Connection for TPS
9. Connection for ISC and closed throttle position switch
10. Connection for fuel injector
11. Connection for ignition coil
12. Connection for ignition power transistor
13. Connection for knock sensor (Turbo)
14. Connection for EGR temperature sensor (California vehicles only)
15. Connection for ground cable
16. Control wiring harness
17. ◆◆ ◆◆ Connection for radiator upper hose
18. Connection for overflow tube
19. Center cover
20. Connection for spark plug cable assembly
21. Connection for air intake hose (Turbo)
22. Connection for breather hose (Turbo)
23. Air intake hose
24. Connection for breather hose
25. Connection for fuel high pressure hose
26. O-ring
27. Connection for vacuum hoses
28. Connection for heater hose
29. Connection for water by-pass hose
30. Connection for PCV hose
31. Connection for vacuum hose (Turbo)
32. Connection for water hose (Turbo)
33. Eye-bolt (Turbo)
34. Gasket (Turbo)
35. Connection for oil pipe (Turbo)
36. Connection for vacuum hoses (Turbo)
37. Connection for fuel return hose
38. Connection for brake booster vacuum hose

MT1069100084010X

Fig. 24 Cylinder head removal (Part 1 of 2). 1995–96 turbo

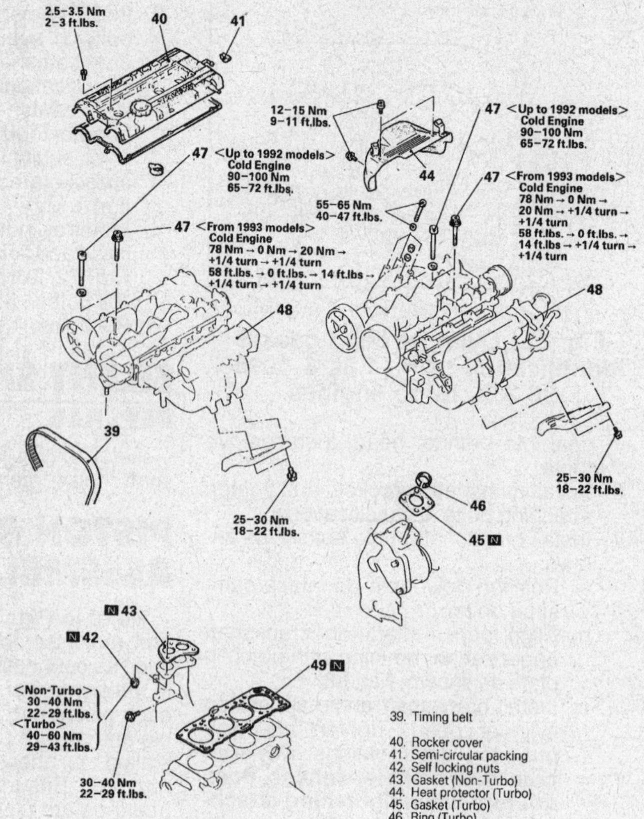
2.5–3.5 Nm
2–3 ft.lbs.
12–15 Nm
9–11 ft.lbs.
<Up to 1992 models>
Cold Engine
90–100 Nm
65–72 ft.lbs.
<From 1993 models>
Cold Engine
55–65 Nm
40–47 ft.lbs.
25–30 Nm
18–22 ft.lbs.
<Non-Turbo>
30–40 Nm
22–29 ft.lbs.
<Turbo>
40–60 Nm
29–43 ft.lbs.
30–40 Nm
22–29 ft.lbs.

39. Timing belt
40. Rocker cover
41. Semi-circular packing
42. Self locking nuts
43. Gasket (Non-Turbo)
44. Heat protector (Turbo)
45. Gasket (Turbo)
46. Ring (Turbo)
47. Cylinder head bolt
48. Cylinder head assembly
49. Cylinder head gasket

MT1069100084020X

Fig. 24 Cylinder head removal (Part 2 of 2). 1995–96 turbo

2.0L engines or No. MD998304, or equivalent, for 1.8L engines, install crankshaft front oil seal, **Figs. 80 and 81. If crankshaft front oil seal is already mounted to front case, use oil seal guide for protection of oil seal.**

4. Install front case.
5. Insert a screwdriver through plug hole in left side of cylinder block to keep shaft in position, **Fig. 45,** then tighten bolt to specification.
6. Install oil filter bracket assembly and gasket, then tighten front case bolts and oil filter bracket bolts to specification.
7. Install plug cap.
8. Install oil screen and gasket, then clean gasket surfaces of cylinder block and oil pan.
9. Install oil pan gasket, if equipped, using a small amount of suitable gasket sealant. If no gasket is used, apply a 0.16 inch (4 mm) wide bead of suitable sealant to entire circumference of oil pan flange.
10. Install oil pan and tighten bolts to specification. Note difference in bolt length as shown, **Fig. 82.**

BELT TENSION DATA

Refer to **Fig. 83**for belt tension data.

COOLING SYSTEM BLEED

These engines do not require a specified bleed procedure. After filling cooling system, run engine to operating temperature with radiator/pressure cap off. Air will then be automatically bled through the cap opening.

THERMOSTAT

REPLACE

1993–94

Removal

Do not remove pressure cap while engine is hot or under pressure.

1. Drain coolant to below level of thermostat housing.
2. Remove radiator upper hose from engine.
3. Remove two retaining bolts, water outlet fitting, gasket and thermostat.
4. Clean mating surfaces.

Installation

1. Reverse removal procedures to install.
2. Install thermostat so that the flange seats in recess of intake manifold and thermostat case, **Fig. 84.**
3. Install retaining bolts. **Torque** to 12–14 ft. lbs.
4. Ensure drain is closed, then refill coolant. Replace cap, then start engine until warm. Check for leaks, then recheck coolant and fill if necessary.

1995–96

Do not remove pressure cap while engine is hot or under pressure.

Remove thermostat in numbered sequence, **Fig. 85,** noting the following:

1. Drain coolant to below level of thermostat housing.
2. Mark and note the position of the hose clamps before removal.
3. Clean mating surfaces.
4. Reverse procedure to install, noting the following:
   a. Install retaining bolts and tighten to specification
   b. Align hose clamps in position as marked.
   c. Ensure drain is closed, then refill coolant. Replace cap, then start engine until warm. Check for leaks,

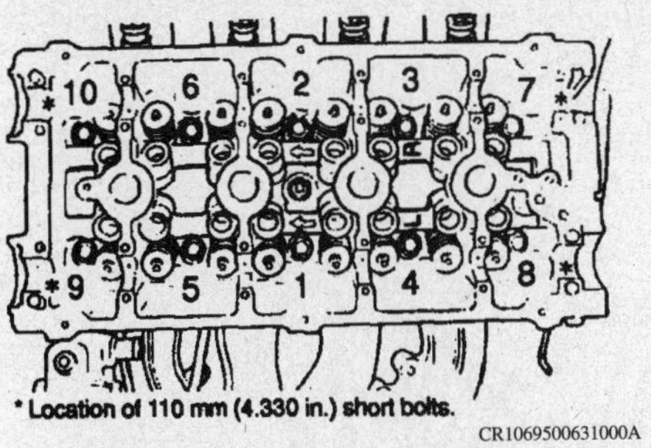
10
6
2
3
7
9
5
1
4
8
* Location of 110 mm (4.330 in.) short bolts.
CR1069500631000A

Fig. 25 Cylinder head bolt tightening sequence. 1995–96 non-turbo

then recheck coolant and fill if necessary.

WATER PUMP

REPLACE

1.8L ENGINE

REMOVAL

Remove water pump in numbered sequence, **Fig. 86,** noting the following:

1. Remove lower engine compartment cover.
2. Drain engine coolant as follows:
   a. Place instrument panel temperature control lever in Hot position.
   b. Carefully remove radiator cap.
   c. Remove radiator drain plug.
3. To remove engine mount bracket, slightly raise and support engine, removing weight of engine from mount.
4. Before removing water pump drive belt, loosen water pump pulley installation bolt.
5. Remove rocker cover, timing belt covers, timing belt and timing belt B as outlined under "Timing Belt, Replace."

INSTALLATION

Reverse removal procedure to install, noting the following:

1. Coat the O-ring (26) with water to ease installation.
2. Refer to bolt length chart, **Fig. 87,** when installing water pump attaching bolts.

2.0L ENGINE

1993–94

Removal

Remove water pump in numbered sequence, **Fig. 88,** noting the following:

1. Remove lower engine compartment cover.
2. Drain engine coolant as follows:
   a. Place instrument panel temperature control lever in Hot position.
   b. Carefully remove radiator cap.
   c. Remove radiator drain plug.
3. To remove engine mount bracket, slightly raise and support engine, removing weight of engine from mount.
4. Remove automatic tensioner, timing belt and timing belt B as outlined under "Timing Belt, Replace."

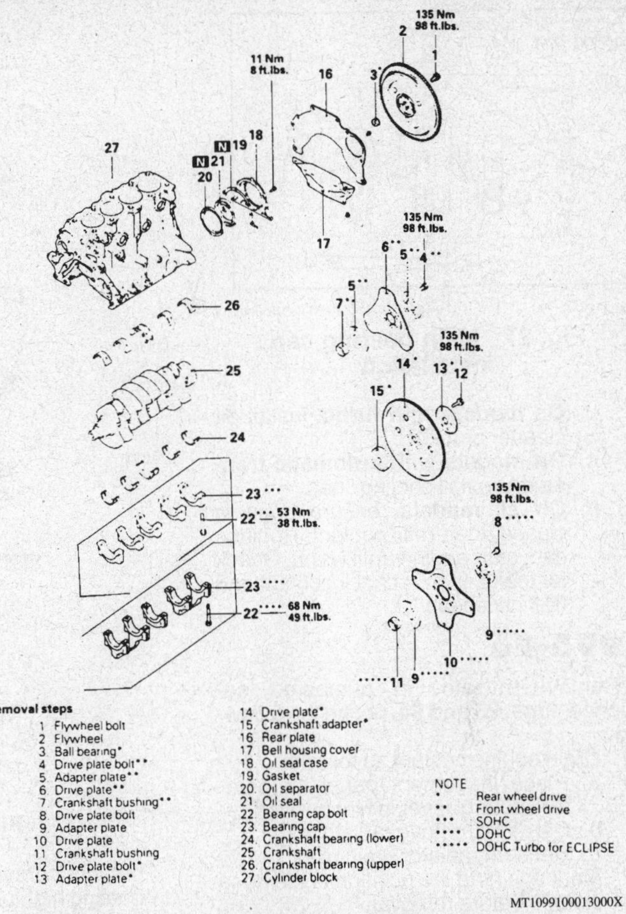
Removal steps
1 Flywheel bolt
2 Flywheel
3 Ball bearing*
4 Drive plate bolt**
5 Adapter plate**
6 Drive plate**
7 Crankshaft bushing**
8 Drive plate bolt
9 Adapter plate
10 Drive plate
11 Crankshaft bushing
12 Drive plate bolt*
13 Adapter plate*
14. Drive plate*
15. Crankshaft adapter*
16. Rear plate
17. Bell housing cover
18. Oil seal case
19. Gasket
20. Oil separator
21. Oil seal
22. Bearing cap bolt
23. Bearing cap
24. Crankshaft bearing (lower)
25 Crankshaft
26. Crankshaft bearing (upper)
27. Cylinder block
NOTE
* Rear wheel drive
** Front wheel drive
*** SOHC
**** DOHC
***** DOHC Turbo for ECLIPSE
MT1099100013000X

Fig. 26 Exploded view of cylinder block & crankshaft assembly

Installation

Reverse removal procedure to install, noting the following:

1. Coat the O-ring (26) with water to ease installation.
2. Refer to bolt length chart, **Fig. 89,** when installing water pump attaching bolts.

1995–96

Non-Turbo

Remove water pump in numbered sequence, **Fig. 90,** noting the following:

1. Drain engine coolant as follows:
   a. Place instrument panel temperature control lever in Hot position.
   b. Carefully remove radiator cap.
   c. Remove radiator drain plug.
2. Remove timing belt rear cover as outlined under "Timing Belt, Replace."
3. Reverse procedure to install. Coat O-ring with water or coolant to ease installation.

Turbo

Remove water pump in numbered sequence, **Fig. 91,** noting the following:

1. Drain engine coolant as follows:
   a. Place instrument panel temperature control lever in Hot position.
   b. Carefully remove radiator cap.
   c. Remove radiator drain plug.
2. Remove timing belt rear cover as outlined under "Timing Belt, Replace."
3. Reverse procedure to install, noting the following:
   a. Coat O-ring with water or coolant to ease installation.
   b. Refer to bolt inset, **Fig. 91,** when installing water pump attaching bolts.

RADIATOR

REPLACE

1993–94

Remove radiator in numbered sequence, **Fig. 92,** noting the following:

1. Drain engine coolant as follows:
   a. Place instrument panel temperature control lever in Hot position.
   b. Carefully remove radiator cap.
   c. Remove radiator drain plug.
2. Mark and note the position of the hose clamps before removal.
3. **On models with turbo,** remove air cleaner bracket.
4. **On models with automatic transaxle,** plug or cover nipples and hoses for cooling lines to ensure dust, dirt or other contaminants do not enter lines.
5. **On all models,** reverse procedure to install, noting the following
   a. Align hose clamps in position as marked.

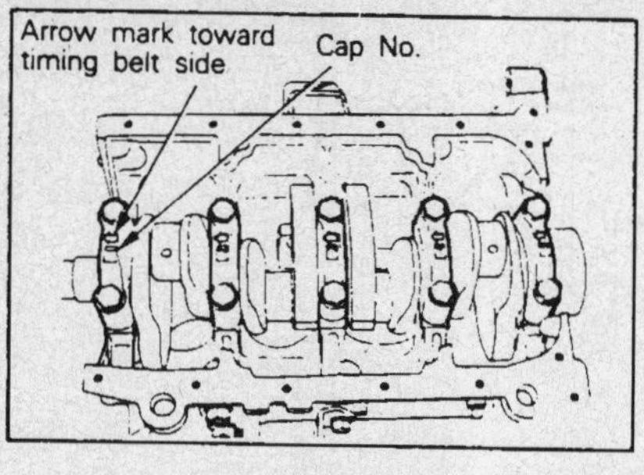
Arrow mark toward timing belt side
Cap No.
MT1099100014000X

Fig. 27 Main bearing cap installation

b. **On models with turbo,** install air cleaner bracket
c. **On models with automatic transaxle,** install cooling lines.
d. **On all models,** ensure drain is closed, then refill coolant. Replace cap, start engine until warm. Check for leaks, then recheck coolant and fill if necessary.

1995-96

Remove radiator in numbered sequence, **Figs. 93 and 94,** noting the following:

1. Drain engine coolant as follows:
   a. Place instrument panel temperature control lever in Hot position.
   b. Carefully remove radiator cap.
   c. Remove radiator drain plug.
2. Mark and note the position of the hose clamps before removal.
3. **On models with turbo,** remove air cleaner bracket.
4. **On models with automatic transaxle,** plug or cover nipples and hoses for cooling lines to ensure dust, dirt or other contaminants do not enter lines.
5. **On all models,** reverse procedure to install, noting the following:
   a. Align hose clamps in position as marked.
   b. **On models with turbo,** install air cleaner bracket
   c. **On models with automatic transaxle,** install cooling lines.
   d. **On all models,** ensure drain is closed, then refill coolant. Replace cap, start engine until warm. Check for leaks, then recheck coolant and fill if necessary.

FUEL PUMP

REPLACE

FWD MODELS

1993-94

Removal

Remove fuel pump in numbered sequence, **Fig. 95,** noting the following:

1. Relieve fuel system pressure as outlined under "Precautions."
2. Remove fuel from fuel tank into a suitable container.
3. Cover fuel line connection with rags to prevent spraying of fuel when disconnecting high pressure fuel line.
4. Loosen the two self-locking nuts (3) to the end of the stud bolt.
5. After disconnecting the lateral rod and body (5), lower the lateral rod and suspend from axle beam using a piece of wire.

Installation

Reverse removal procedure to install, noting the following:

1. Install overfill limiter in the direction as shown, **Fig. 96.**
2. When installing fuel gauge unit, align the two positioning projections as shown, **Fig. 97.** Ensure bend in float assembly is pointed to left during installation.
3. When installing fuel pump, O-ring and attaching bolt, proceed as follows:
   a. Align three positioning projections of packing with holes in fuel pump.
   b. Install lowest holding bolt first, ensuring O-ring is not pinched.
4. Tighten self-locking nuts until rear end of tank band contacts body.

1995-96

Removal

Remove fuel pump in numbered sequence, **Fig. 98.**

1. Relieve fuel pressure as outlined under "Precautions."
2. Remove fuel from fuel tank into a suitable container.
3. When disconnecting high pressure fuel line, cover fuel line connection with rags to prevent spraying of fuel.
4. Remove rear seat cushion and floor plate for access to fuel pump.
5. Disconnect hoses and connectors to remove fuel pump

Installation

Reverse removal procedure to install, noting the following:

1. Align packing position projections with holes in fuel pump assembly.
2. Ensure fuel pump assembly and hoses are not leaking.
3. Before installing hole cover plate, apply suitable sealant to rear floor pan.

AWD MODELS

1993-94

Removal

1. Relieve fuel pressure as outlined under "Precautions."
2. Remove fuel pump in numbered sequence, **Fig. 99.** When disconnecting high pressure fuel line, cover fuel line connection with rags to prevent spraying of fuel.

Installation

Reverse removal procedure to install, noting the following:

1. When installing fuel pump and fuel gauge unit assembly, align three positioning projections of packing with

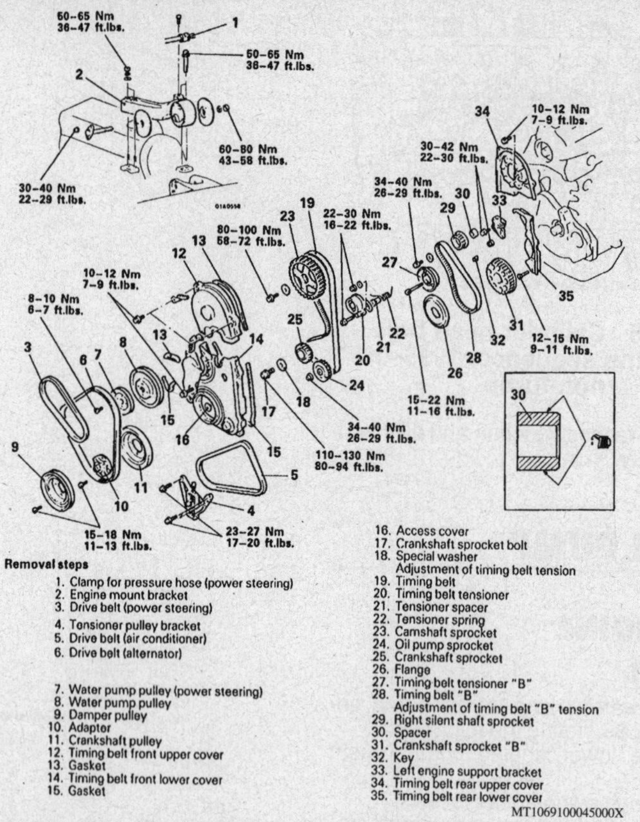
50-65 Nm
36-47 ft.lbs.
50-65 Nm
36-47 ft.lbs.
60-80 Nm
43-58 ft.lbs.
30-40 Nm
22-29 ft.lbs.
80-100 Nm
58-72 ft.lbs.
22-30 Nm
16-22 ft.lbs.
10-12 Nm
7-9 ft.lbs.
8-10 Nm
6-7 ft.lbs.
10-12 Nm
7-9 ft.lbs.
30-42 Nm
22-30 ft.lbs.
34-40 Nm
26-29 ft.lbs.
12-15 Nm
9-11 ft.lbs.
15-22 Nm
11-16 ft.lbs.
34-40 Nm
26-29 ft.lbs.
110-130 Nm
80-94 ft.lbs.
15-18 Nm
11-13 ft.lbs.
23-27 Nm
17-20 ft.lbs.
Removal steps
1. Clamp for pressure hose (power steering)
2. Engine mount bracket
3. Drive belt (power steering)
4. Tensioner pulley bracket
5. Drive belt (air conditioner)
6. Drive belt (alternator)
7. Water pump pulley (power steering)
8. Water pump pulley
9. Damper pulley
10. Adaptor
11. Crankshaft pulley
12. Timing belt front upper cover
13. Gasket
14. Timing belt front lower cover
15. Gasket
16. Access cover
17. Crankshaft sprocket bolt
18. Special washer
Adjustment of timing belt tension
19. Timing belt
20. Timing belt tensioner
21. Tensioner spacer
22. Tensioner spring
23. Camshaft sprocket
24. Oil pump sprocket
25. Crankshaft sprocket
26. Flange
27. Timing belt tensioner "B"
28. Timing belt "B"
Adjustment of timing belt "B" tension
29. Right silent shaft sprocket
30. Spacer
31. Crankshaft sprocket "B"
32. Key
33. Left engine support bracket
34. Timing belt rear upper cover
35. Timing belt rear lower cover
MT1069100045000X

Fig. 28 Timing belt replacement. 1.8L engine

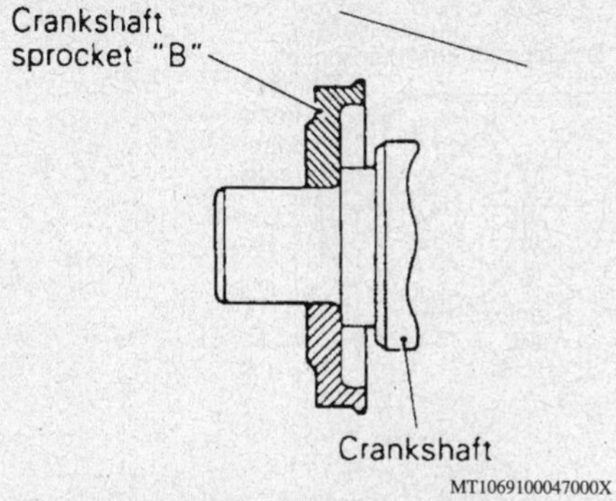
Crankshaft sprocket "B"
Crankshaft
MT1069100047000X

Fig. 29 Crankshaft sprocket "B" installation. 1.8L engine

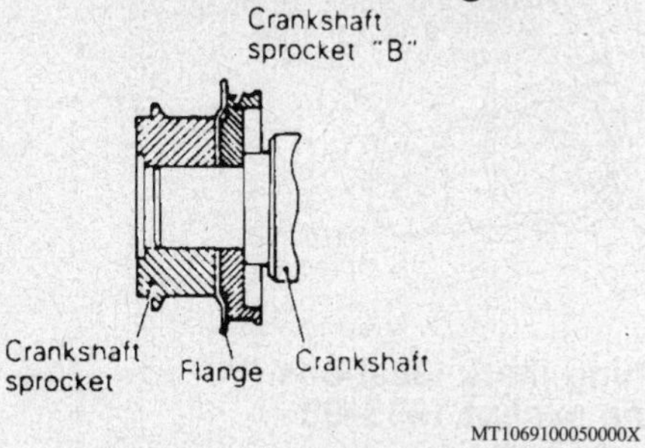
Crankshaft sprocket "B"
Crankshaft sprocket
Flange
Crankshaft
MT1069100050000X

Fig. 32 Crankshaft flange installation. 1.8L engine

holes in pump and gauge assembly.

2. Before installing hole cover plate, apply suitable sealant to rear floor pan.

1995-96

Removal

Relieve fuel pressure as outlined under "Precautions."

Remove fuel pump in numbered sequence, **Fig. 100.**

1. Remove fuel from fuel tank into a suitable container.
2. When disconnecting high pressure fuel line, cover fuel line connection with rags to prevent spraying of fuel.
3. Remove rear seat cushion and floor plate for access to fuel pump.
4. Disconnect hoses and connectors to remove fuel pump

Installation

Reverse removal procedure to install, noting the following:

1. Ensure packing seal is not damaged or deformed.
2. Apply soapy water to fuel tank threads, then install fuel pump and cap.
3. Using special cap tightening tool No. MB991480, or equivalent, **Fig. 101, torque** cap to 36 ft. lbs.
4. Ensure fuel pump assembly and hoses are not leaking.

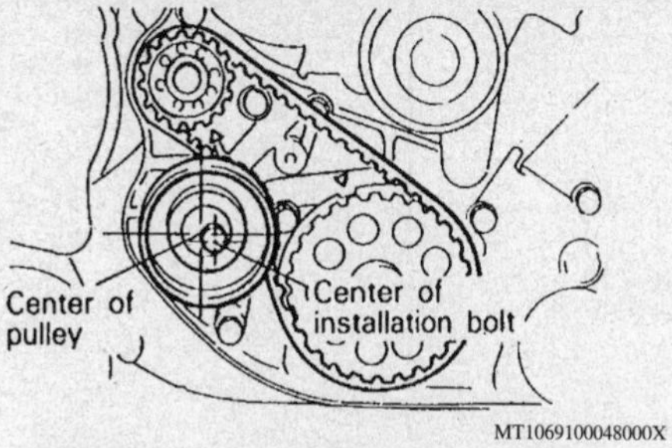
Center of pulley
Center of installation bolt
MT1069100048000X

Fig. 30 Silent shaft tensioner pulley installation. 1.8L engine

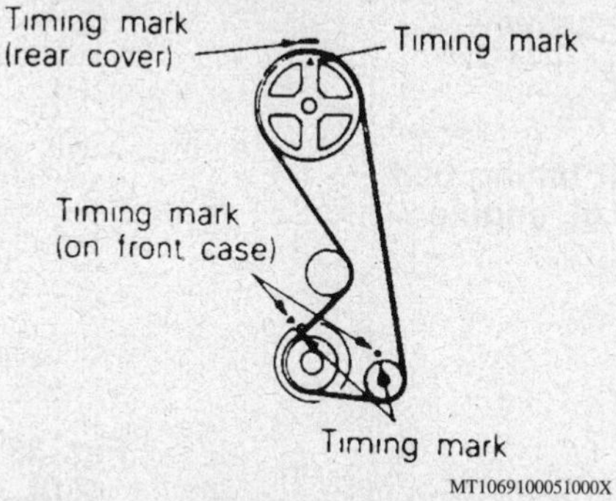
Timing mark (rear cover)
Timing mark
Timing mark (on front case)
Timing mark
MT1069100051000X

Fig. 33 Timing marks alignment. 1.8L engine

FUEL FILTER

REPLACE

1993-94

When replacing fuel filter, refer to **Fig. 102**for removal and installation procedure.

Relieve fuel pressure as outlined under "Precautions."

1995-96

When replacing fuel filter, refer to **Fig. 103** for removal and installation procedure.

1. Relieve fuel pressure as outlined under "Precautions."
2. Remove battery and air intake hose to access fuel filter.
3. Reverse procedure to install.

TURBOCHARGER

REPLACE

1. Remove turbocharger components in order as shown, **Fig. 104.**
2. Disconnect battery ground cable, then drain cooling system as follows:
   a. Place temperature control lever in Hot position.
   b. Carefully remove radiator cap.
   c. Remove radiator drain plug.
3. Drain engine oil into appropriate container.

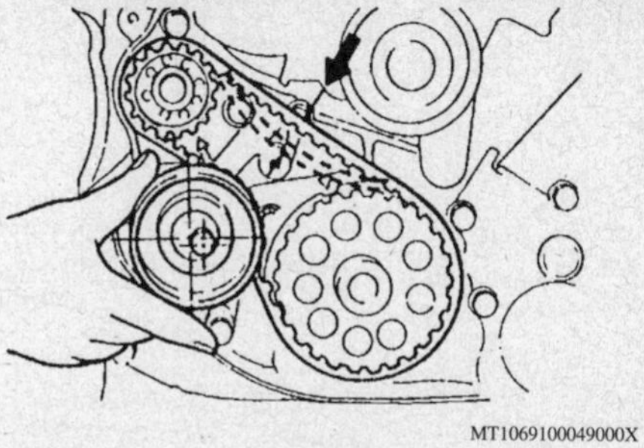
MT1069100049000X

Fig. 31 Timing belt "B" tension adjustment. 1.8L engine

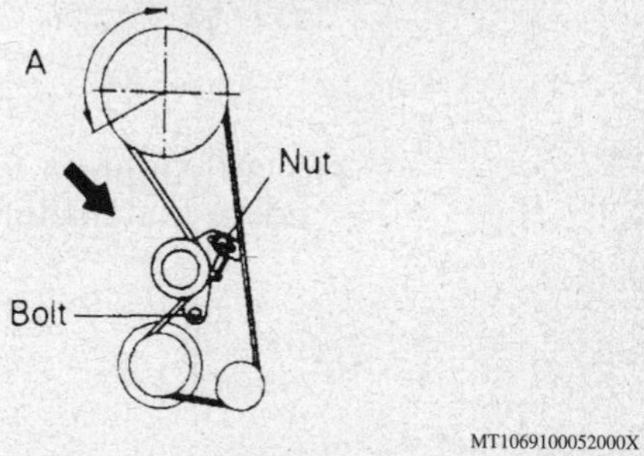
A
Nut
Bolt
MT1069100052000X

Fig. 34 Timing belt installation. 1.8L engine

4. Disconnect oxygen sensor electrical connector, then using oxygen sensor wrench tool No. MD998748, or equivalent, and an offset box-end wrench, remove oxygen sensor.
5. Remove power steering pump from bracket with hoses attached, then secure pump aside with a piece of wire.
6. Remove turbocharger assembly with exhaust fitting, water pipes A and B and oil pipe attached.
7. **After disconnecting oil pipe, ensure foreign material does not enter oil passage hole of turbocharger.**
8. Reverse procedure to install, noting the following:
   a. Prior to installing turbocharger assembly, pour a small quantity of clean engine oil into oil supply pipe fitting hole in turbocharger.
   b. Clean alignment surfaces of turbocharger as shown, **Fig. 105. Use caution not to allow gasket or other foreign material to enter oil passage hole.**
   c. Use new gaskets, locknuts and O-rings.
   d. Install oxygen sensor using oxygen sensor wrench tool No. MD998748, or equivalent, and an offset box-end wrench, then connect oxygen sensor electrical connector.

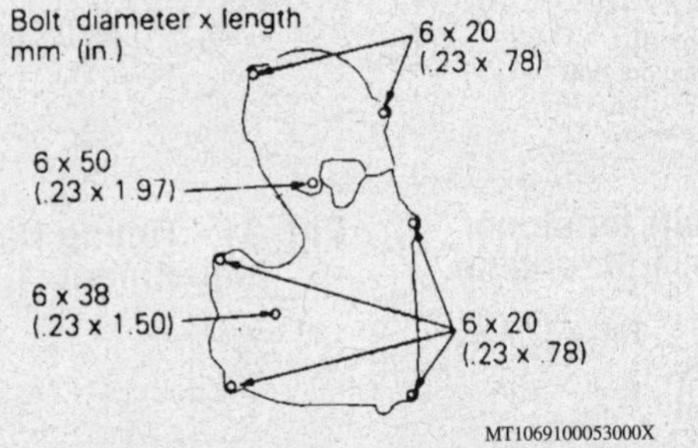
Bolt diameter x length
mm (in.)
6 x 20
(.23 x .78)
6 x 50
(.23 x 1.97)
6 x 38
(.23 x 1.50)
6 x 20
(.23 x .78)
MT1069100053000X

Fig. 35 Upper & lower timing belt cover installation. 1.8L engine

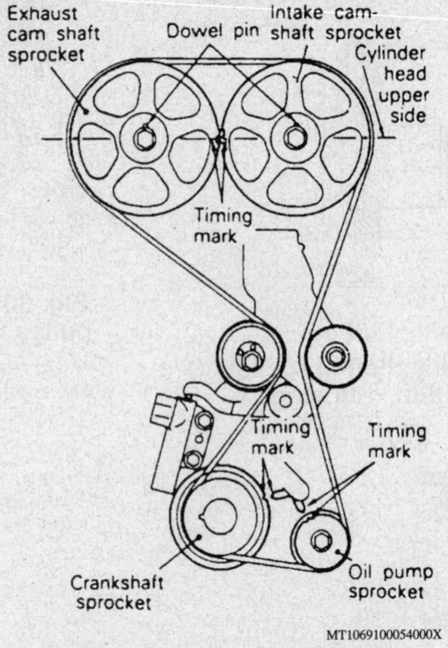
Exhaust
cam shaft
sprocket
Dowel pin
Intake cam-
shaft sprocket
Cylinder
head
upper
side
Timing
mark
Timing
mark
Timing
mark
Crankshaft
sprocket
Oil pump
sprocket
MT1069100054000X

Fig. 36 Timing mark locations. 2.0L engine except 1995–96 non-turbo

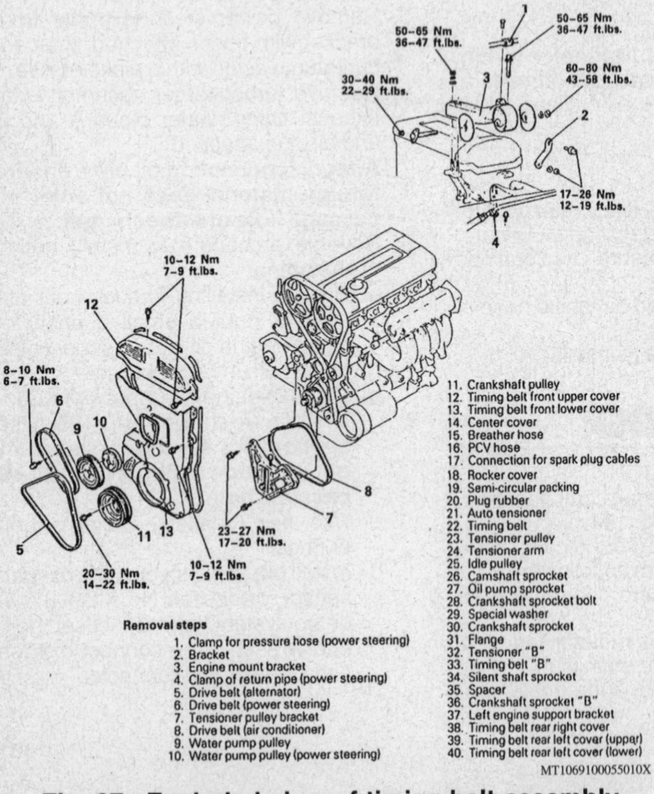
50–65 Nm
36–47 ft.lbs.
50–65 Nm
36–47 ft.lbs.
30–40 Nm
22–29 ft.lbs.
60–80 Nm
43–58 ft.lbs.
17–26 Nm
12–19 ft.lbs.
10–12 Nm
7–9 ft.lbs.
8–10 Nm
6–7 ft.lbs.
23–27 Nm
17–20 ft.lbs.
10–12 Nm
7–9 ft.lbs.
20–30 Nm
14–22 ft.lbs.
11. Crankshaft pulley
12. Timing belt front upper cover
13. Timing belt front lower cover
14. Center cover
15. Breather hose
16. PCV hose
17. Connection for spark plug cables
18. Rocker cover
19. Semi-circular packing
20. Plug rubber
21. Auto tensioner
22. Timing belt
23. Tensioner pulley
24. Tensioner arm
25. Idle pulley
26. Camshaft sprocket
27. Oil pump sprocket
28. Crankshaft sprocket bolt
29. Special washer
30. Crankshaft sprocket
31. Flange
32. Tensioner "B"
33. Timing belt "B"
34. Silent shaft sprocket
35. Spacer
36. Crankshaft sprocket "B"
37. Left engine support bracket
38. Timing belt rear right cover
39. Timing belt rear left cover (upper)
40. Timing belt rear left cover (lower)
Removal steps
1. Clamp for pressure hose (power steering)
2. Bracket
3. Engine mount bracket
4. Clamp of return pipe (power steering)
5. Drive belt (alternator)
6. Drive belt (power steering)
7. Tensioner pulley bracket
8. Drive belt (air conditioner)
9. Water pump pulley
10. Water pump pulley (power steering)
MT1069100055010X

Fig. 37 Exploded view of timing belt assembly (Part 1 of 2). 2.0L engine except 1995–96 non-turbo

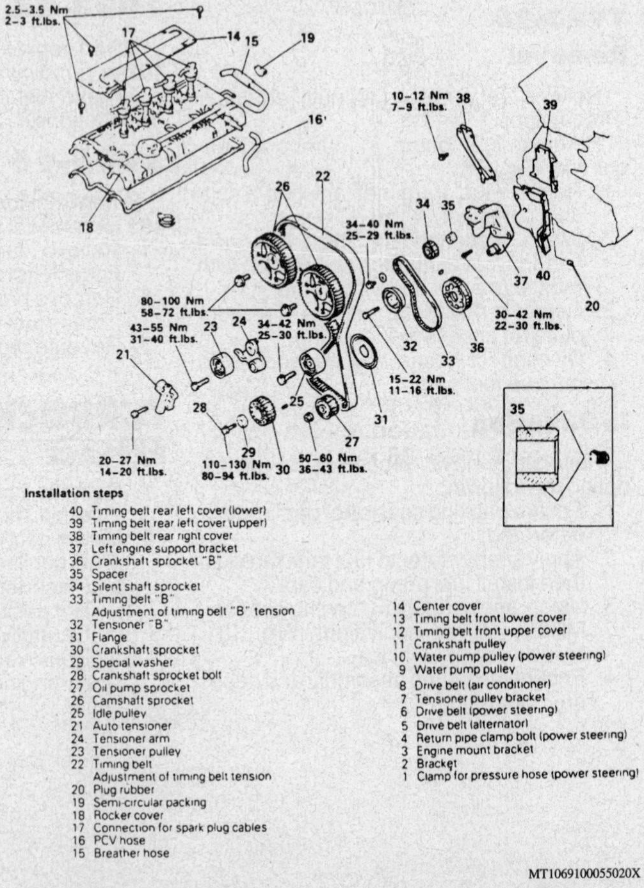
2.5–3.5 Nm
2–3 ft.lbs.
10–12 Nm
7–9 ft.lbs.
34–40 Nm
25–29 ft.lbs.
80–100 Nm
58–72 ft.lbs.
43–55 Nm
31–40 ft.lbs.
34–42 Nm
25–30 ft.lbs.
30–42 Nm
22–30 ft.lbs.
15–22 Nm
11–16 ft.lbs.
20–27 Nm
14–20 ft.lbs.
110–130 Nm
80–94 ft.lbs.
50–60 Nm
36–43 ft.lbs.
Installation steps
40 Timing belt rear left cover (lower)
39 Timing belt rear left cover (upper)
38 Timing belt rear right cover
37 Left engine support bracket
36 Crankshaft sprocket "B"
35 Spacer
34 Silent shaft sprocket
33 Timing belt "B"
Adjustment of timing belt "B" tension
32 Tensioner "B"
31 Flange
30 Crankshaft sprocket
29 Special washer
28 Crankshaft sprocket bolt
27 Oil pump sprocket
26 Camshaft sprocket
25 Idle pulley
21 Auto tensioner
24 Tensioner arm
23 Tensioner pulley
22 Timing belt
Adjustment of timing belt tension
20 Plug rubber
19 Semi-circular packing
18 Rocker cover
17 Connection for spark plug cables
16 PCV hose
15 Breather hose
14 Center cover
13 Timing belt front lower cover
12 Timing belt front upper cover
11 Crankshaft pulley
10 Water pump pulley (power steering)
9 Water pump pulley
8 Drive belt (air conditioner)
7 Tensioner pulley bracket
6 Drive belt (power steering)
5 Drive belt (alternator)
4 Return pipe clamp bolt (power steering)
3 Engine mount bracket
2 Bracket
1 Clamp for pressure hose (power steering)
MT1069100055020X

Fig. 37 Exploded view of timing belt assembly (Part 2 of 2). 2.0L engine except 1995–96 non-turbo

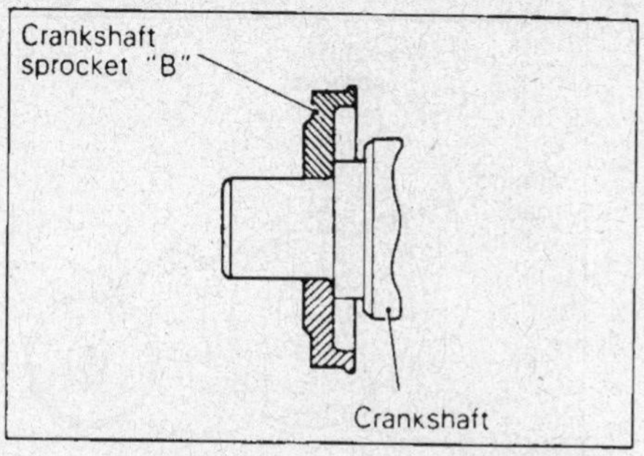
Crankshaft
sprocket "B"
Crankshaft
MT1069100056000X

Fig. 38 Crankshaft sprocket "B" installation. 2.0L engine except 1995–96 non-turbo

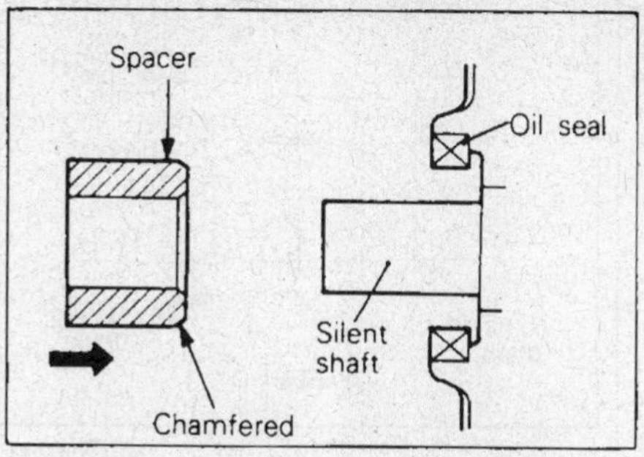
Spacer
Oil seal
Silent
shaft
Chamfered
MT1069100057000X

Fig. 39 Silent shaft sprocket spacer installation. 2.0L engine except 1995–96 non-turbo

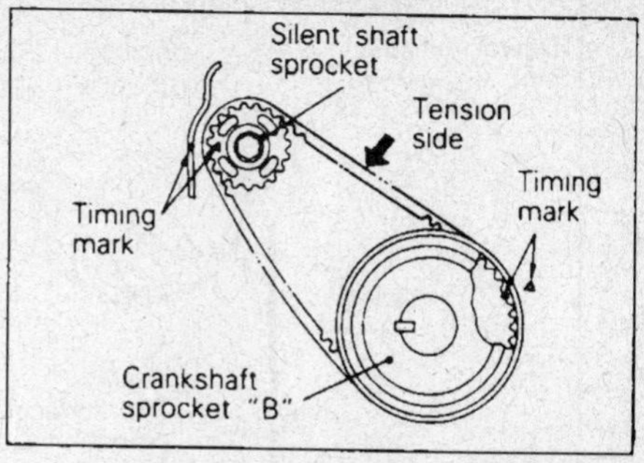
Silent shaft
sprocket
Tension
side
Timing
mark
Timing
mark
Crankshaft
sprocket "B"
MT1069100058000X

Fig. 40 Timing belt "B" installation. 2.0L engine except 1995–96 non-turbo

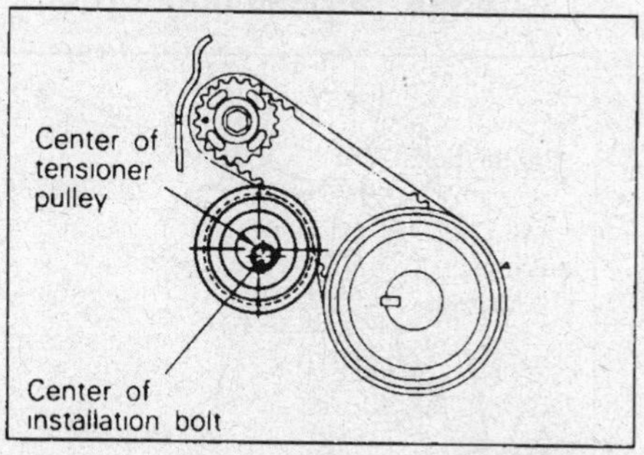
Center of
tensioner
pulley
Center of
installation bolt
MT1069100059000X

Fig. 41 Timing belt "B" tensioner pulley installation. 2.0L engine except 1995–96 non-turbo

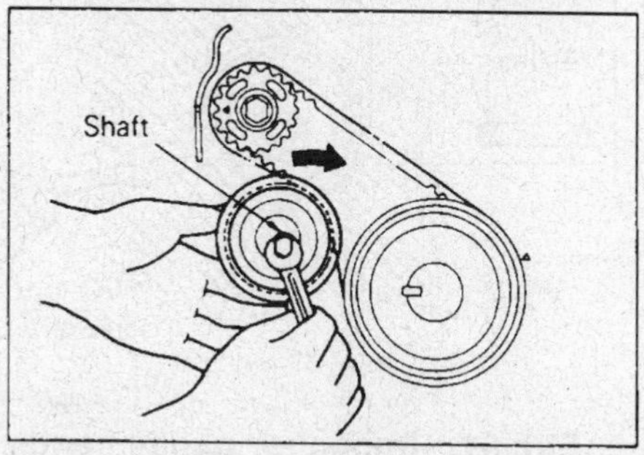
Shaft
MT1069100060000X

Fig. 42 Timing belt "B" tension adjustment. 2.0L engine except 1995–96 non-turbo

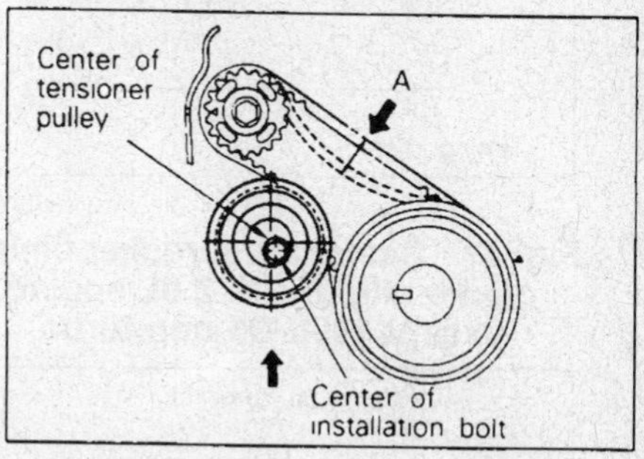
Center of
tensioner
pulley
A
Center of
installation bolt
MT1069100061000X

Fig. 43 Timing belt "B" tension check. 2.0L engine except 1995–96 non-turbo

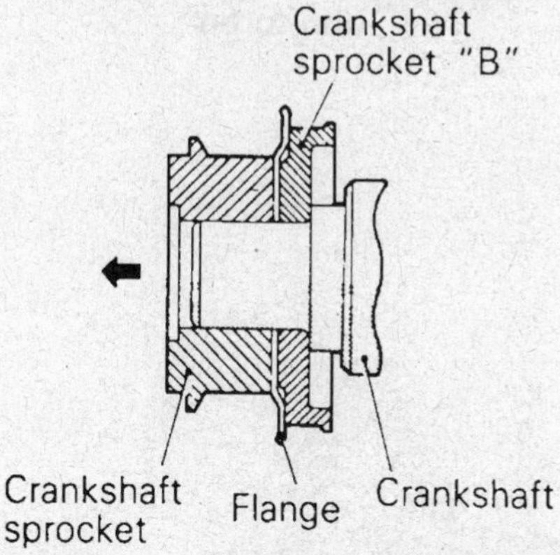
Crankshaft
sprocket "B"
Crankshaft
sprocket
Flange
Crankshaft
MT1069100062000X

Fig. 44 Crankshaft "B" sprocket & flange installation. 2.0L engine except 1995–96 non-turbo

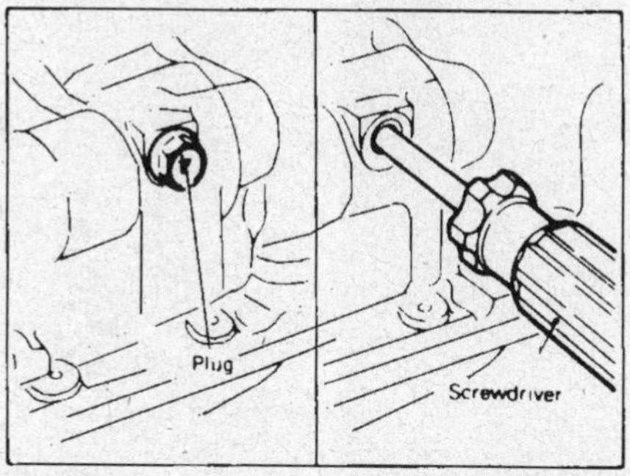
Plug
Screwdriver
MT1069100063000X

Fig. 45 Securing silent shaft. 2.0L engine except 1995–96 non-turbo

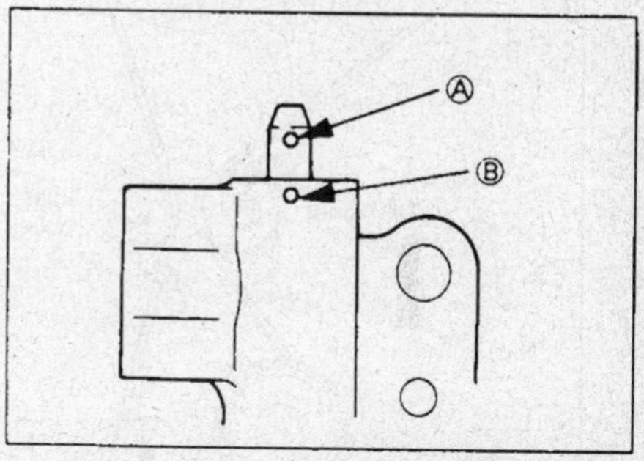
Ⓐ
Ⓑ
MT1069100064000X

Fig. 46 Tensioner rod alignment. 2.0L engine except 1995–96 non-turbo

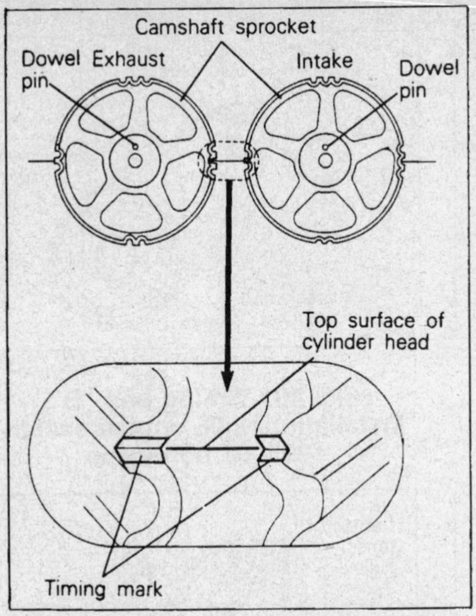
Camshaft sprocket
Dowel pin
Exhaust
Intake
Dowel pin
Top surface of cylinder head
Timing mark

MT1069100065000X

Fig. 47 Camshaft sprocket timing marks alignment. 2.0L engine except 1995–96 non-turbo

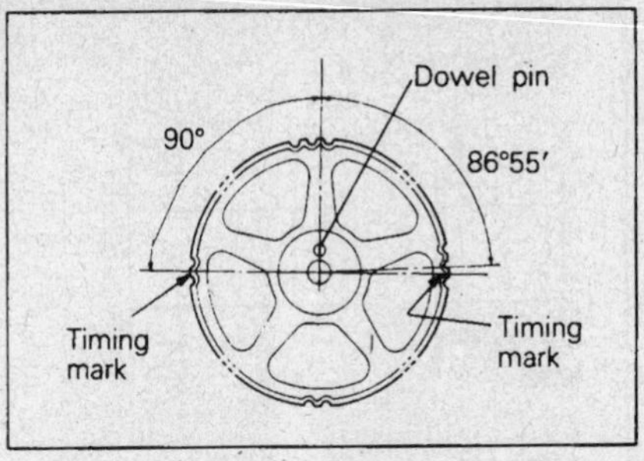
Dowel pin
90°
86°55′
Timing mark
Timing mark

MT1069100066000X

Fig. 48 Camshaft sprocket installation. 2.0L engine except 1995–96 non-turbo

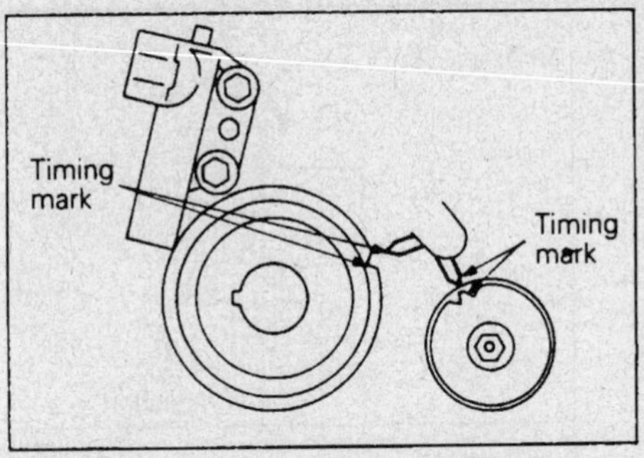
Timing mark
Timing mark

MT1069100067000X

Fig. 49 Crankshaft & oil pump sprockets installation. 2.0L engine except 1995–96 non-turbo

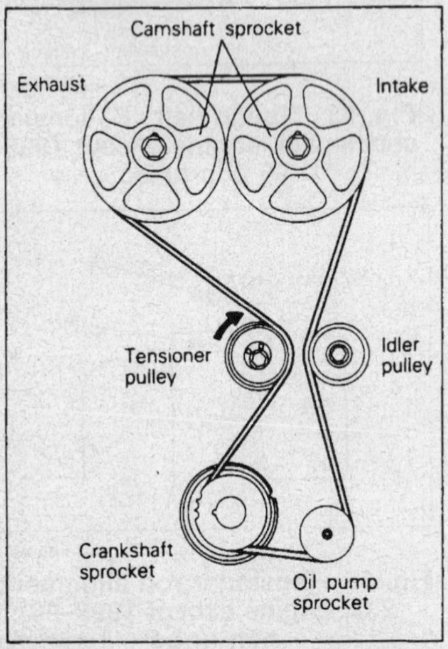
Camshaft sprocket
Exhaust
Intake
Tensioner pulley
Idler pulley
Crankshaft sprocket
Oil pump sprocket

MT1069100068000X

Fig. 50 Timing belt installation. 2.0L engine except 1995–96 non-turbo

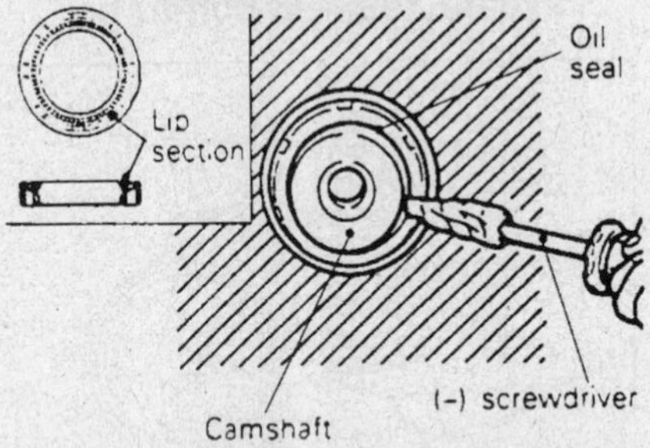
Oil seal
Lip section
Camshaft
(-) screwdriver

MT1069100029000X

Fig. 51 Tensioner pulley center bolt. 2.0L engine except 1995–96 non-turbo

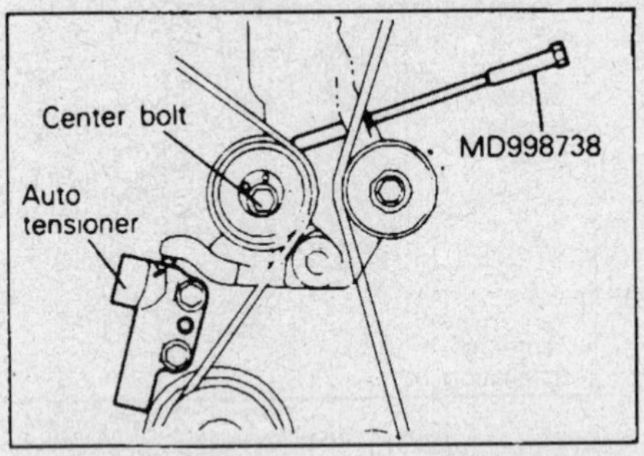
Center bolt
MD998738
Auto tensioner

MT1069100070000X

Fig. 52 Setscrew tool installation. 2.0L engine except 1995–96 non-turbo

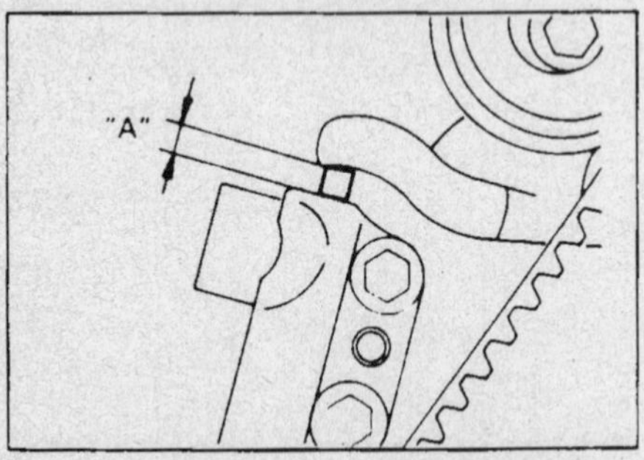
"A"

MT1069100071000X

Fig. 53 Tensioner arm clearance inspection. 2.0L engine except 1995–96 non-turbo

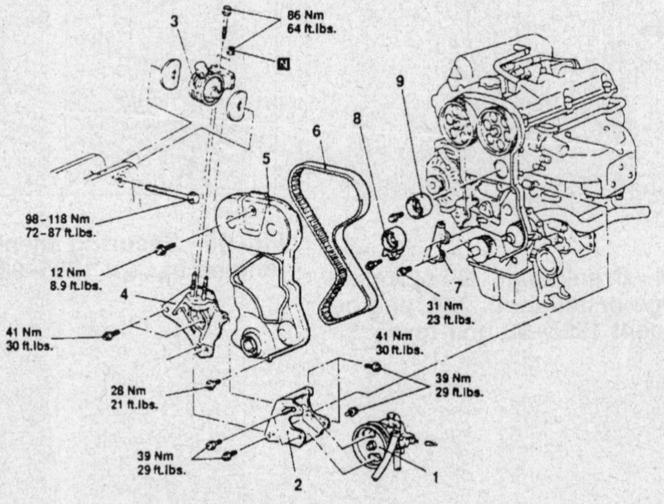
86 Nm
64 ft.lbs.
98 - 118 Nm
72 - 87 ft.lbs.
12 Nm
8.9 ft.lbs.
41 Nm
30 ft.lbs.
31 Nm
23 ft.lbs.
41 Nm
30 ft.lbs.
28 Nm
21 ft.lbs.
39 Nm
29 ft.lbs.
39 Nm
29 ft.lbs.

Removal steps

1. Power steering pump connection
2. Power steering pump bracket
3. Engine mount bracket assembly
4. Engine mount bracket
5. Front timing belt cover
6. Timing belt
7. Timing belt tensioner
8. Tensioner pulley
9. Idle pulley

CR1069500607000X

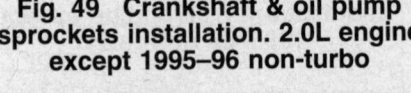

Fig. 54 Timing belt assembly. 1995–96 2.0L non-turbo engine

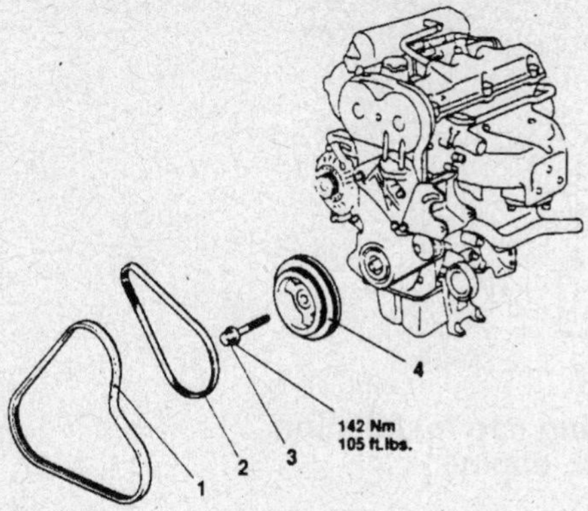
142 Nm
105 ft.lbs.
1
2
3
4

Removal steps
1. Drive belt (Power steering and A/C)
2. Drive belt (Generator)
3. Crankshaft bolt
4. Crankshaft pulley

CR1069500608000X

Fig. 55 Crankshaft pulley removal. 1995–96 2.0L non-turbo engine

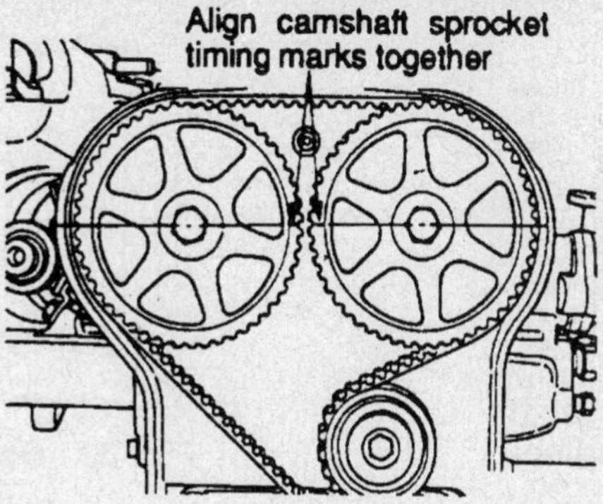
Align camshaft sprocket
timing marks together

CR1069500609000X

Fig. 56 Camshaft sprocket timing alignment. 1995–96 2.0L non-turbo engine

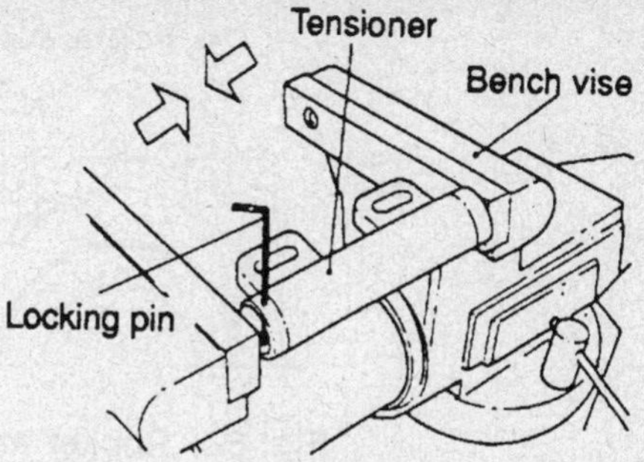
Tensioner
Bench vise
Locking pin

CR1069500610000X

Fig. 57 Timing belt tensioner compression. 1995–96 2.0L non-turbo engine

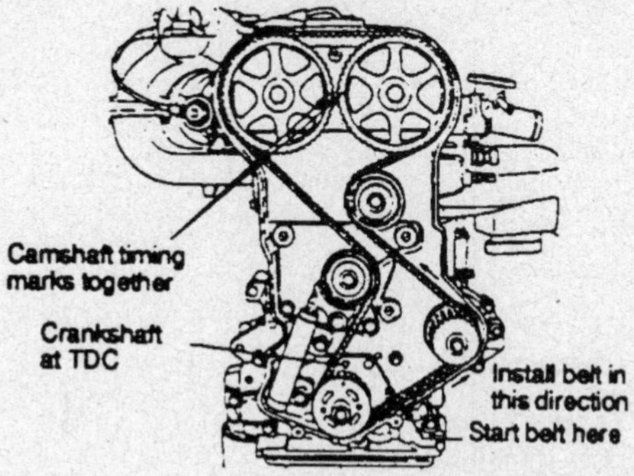
Camshaft timing
marks together
Crankshaft
at TDC
Install belt in
this direction
Start belt here

CR1069500612000X

Fig. 59 Timing belt installation. 1995-96 2.0L non-turbo engine

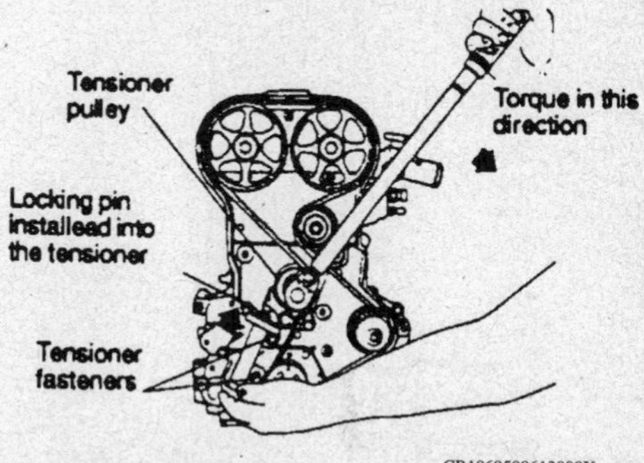
Tensioner
pulley
Torque in this
direction
Locking pin
installed into
the tensioner
Tensioner
fasteners

CR1069500613000X

Fig. 60 Timing belt adjustment. 1995–96 2.0L non-turbo engine

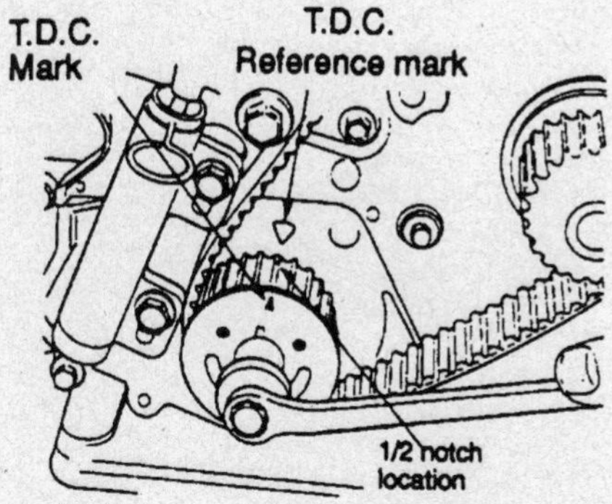
T.D.C.
Mark
T.D.C.
Reference mark
1/2 notch
location

CR1069500611000X

Fig. 58 Crankshaft sprocket alignment. 1995–96 2.0L non-turbo engine

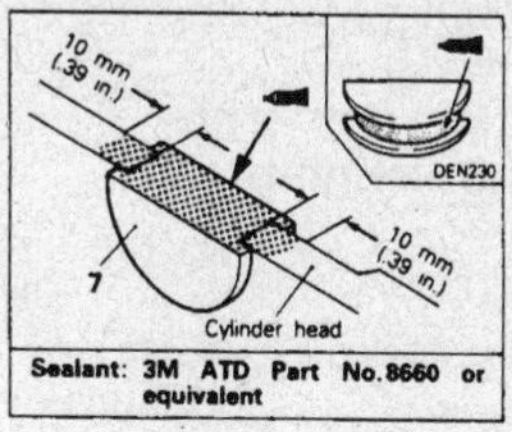
10 mm
(.39 in.)
10 mm
(.39 in.)
7
Cylinder head
DEN230
Sealant: 3M ATD Part No.8660 or
equivalent

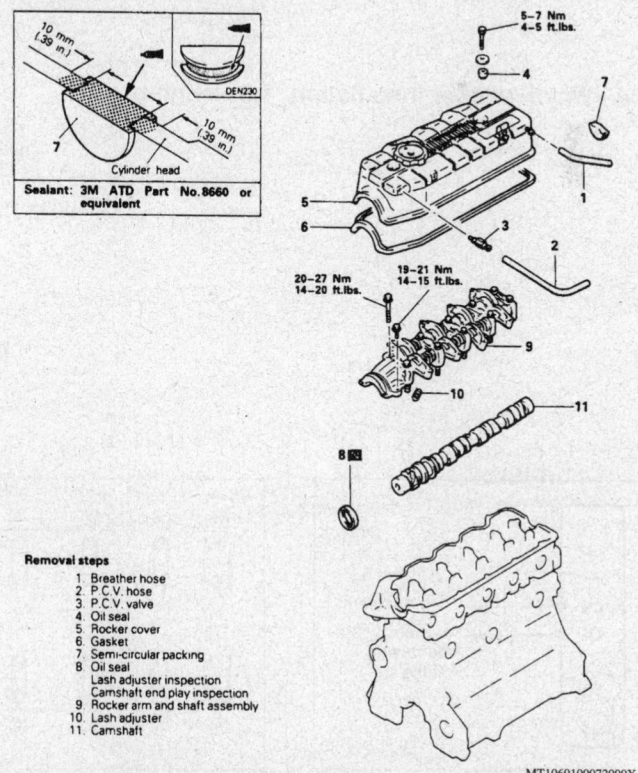

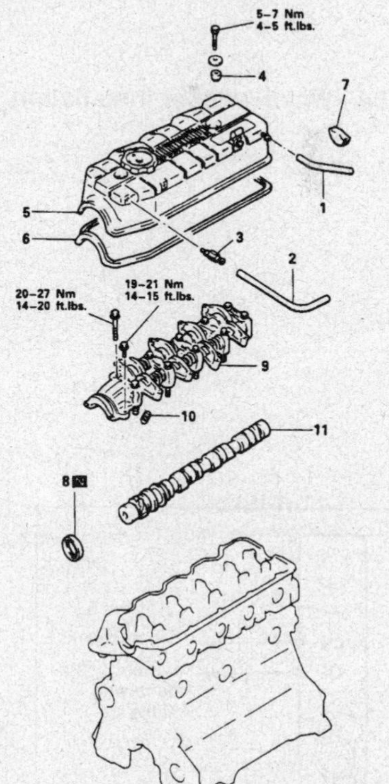
5–7 Nm
4–5 ft.lbs.
4
7
5
1
6
3
2
20–27 Nm
14–20 ft.lbs.
19–21 Nm
14–15 ft.lbs.
9
10
11
8

Removal steps
1. Breather hose
2. P.C.V. hose
3. P.C.V. valve
4. Oil seal
5. Rocker cover
6. Gasket
7. Semi-circular packing
8. Oil seal
   Lash adjuster inspection
   Camshaft end play inspection
9. Rocker arm and shaft assembly
10. Lash adjuster
11. Camshaft

MT1069100072000X

Fig. 61 Exploded view of camshaft, rocker arm & rocker shaft assemblies. 1.8L engine

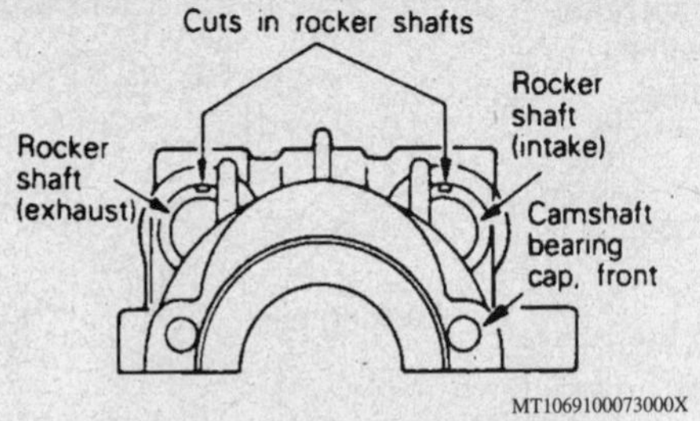
Cuts in rocker shafts
Rocker shaft (intake)
Rocker shaft (exhaust)
Camshaft bearing cap, front
MT1069100073000X

Fig. 62 Rocker arm shaft installation. 1.8L engine

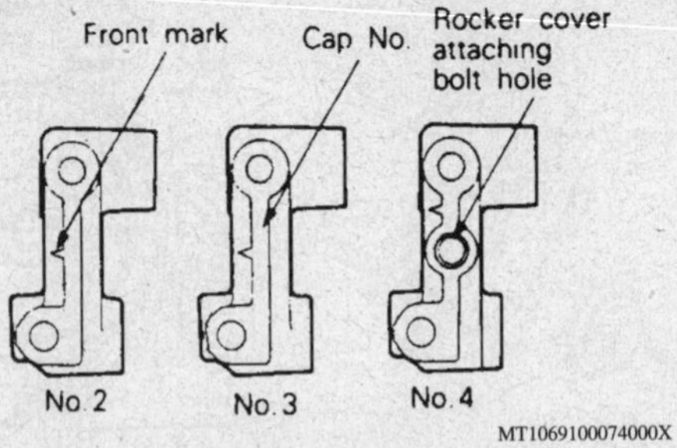
Front mark
Cap No.
Rocker cover attaching bolt hole
No. 2
No. 3
No. 4
MT1069100074000X

Fig. 63 Bearing cap installation. 1.8L engine

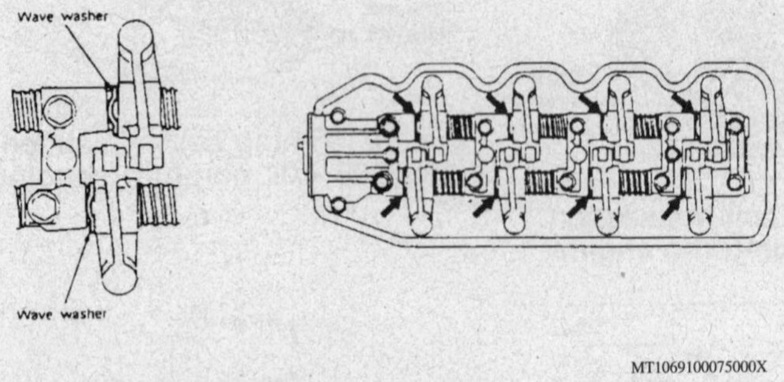
Wave washer
Wave washer
MT1069100075000X

Fig. 64 Wave washer installation. 1.8L engine

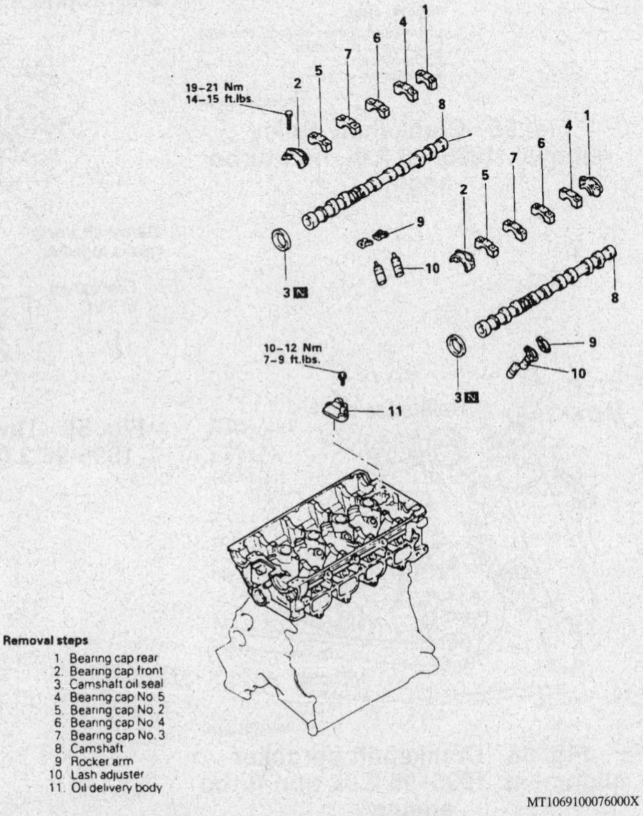
19–21 Nm
14–15 ft.lbs.
10–12 Nm
7–9 ft.lbs.
Removal steps
1. Bearing cap rear
2. Bearing cap front
3. Camshaft oil seal
4. Bearing cap No. 5
5. Bearing cap No. 2
6. Bearing cap No. 4
7. Bearing cap No. 3
8. Camshaft
9. Rocker arm
10. Lash adjuster
11. Oil delivery body
MT1069100076000X

Fig. 65 Exploded view of camshaft, rocker arm & rocker arm shaft. 2.0L engine except 1995–96 non-turbo

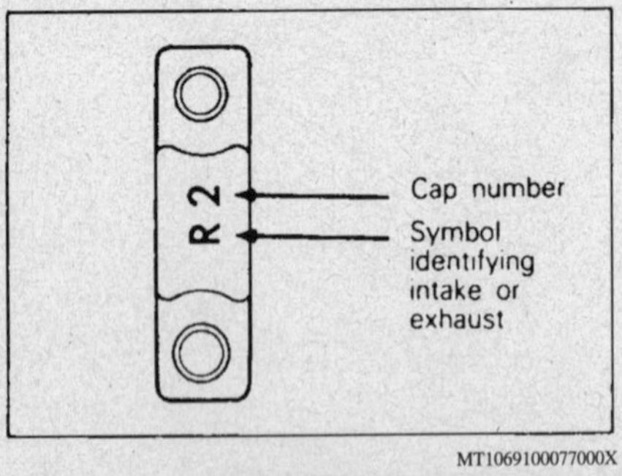
R 2
Cap number
Symbol identifying intake or exhaust
MT1069100077000X

Fig. 66 Camshaft bearing cap identification marks. 2.0L engine except 1995–96 non-turbo

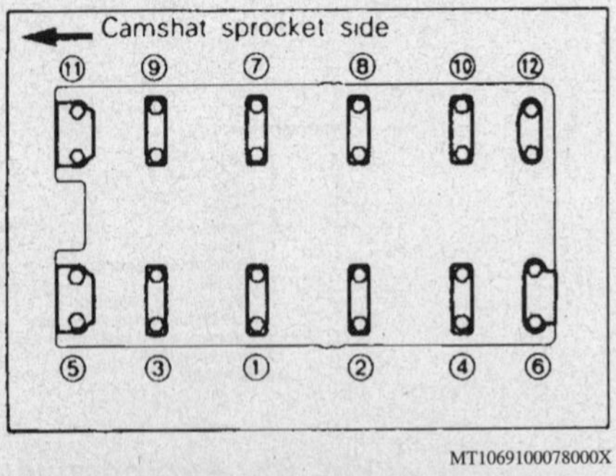
Camshat sprocket side
⑪ ⑨ ⑦ ⑧ ⑩ ⑫
⑤ ③ ① ② ④ ⑥
MT1069100078000X

Fig. 67 Camshaft bearing cap bolt tightening sequence. 2.0L engine except 1995–96 non-turbo

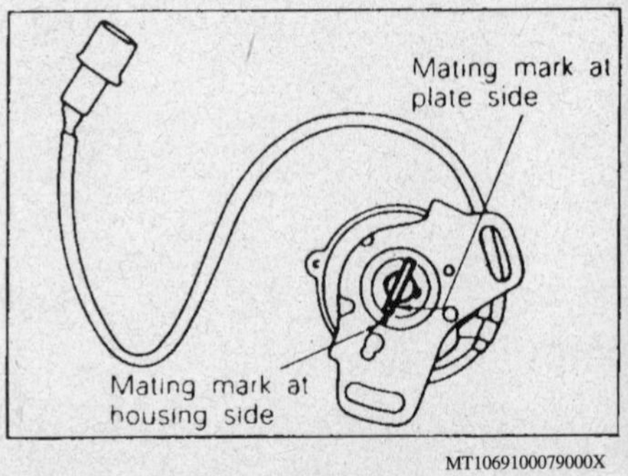
Mating mark at plate side
Mating mark at housing side
MT1069100079000X

Fig. 68 Crankshaft angle sensor mating marks alignment. 2.0L engine except 1995–96 non-turbo

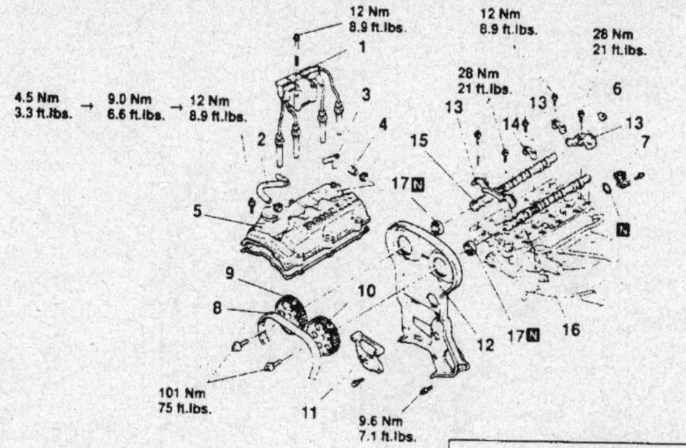
12 Nm
8.9 ft.lbs.
12 Nm
8.9 ft.lbs.
28 Nm
21 ft.lbs.
28 Nm
21 ft.lbs.
4.5 Nm
3.3 ft.lbs.
9.0 Nm
6.6 ft.lbs.
12 Nm
8.9 ft.lbs.
101 Nm
75 ft.lbs.
9.6 Nm
7.1 ft.lbs.

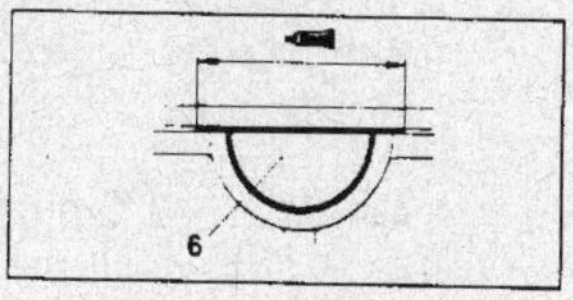

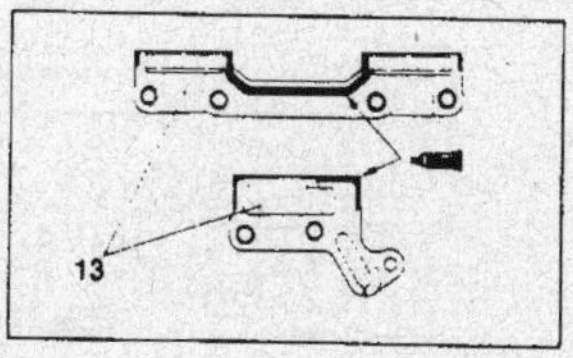

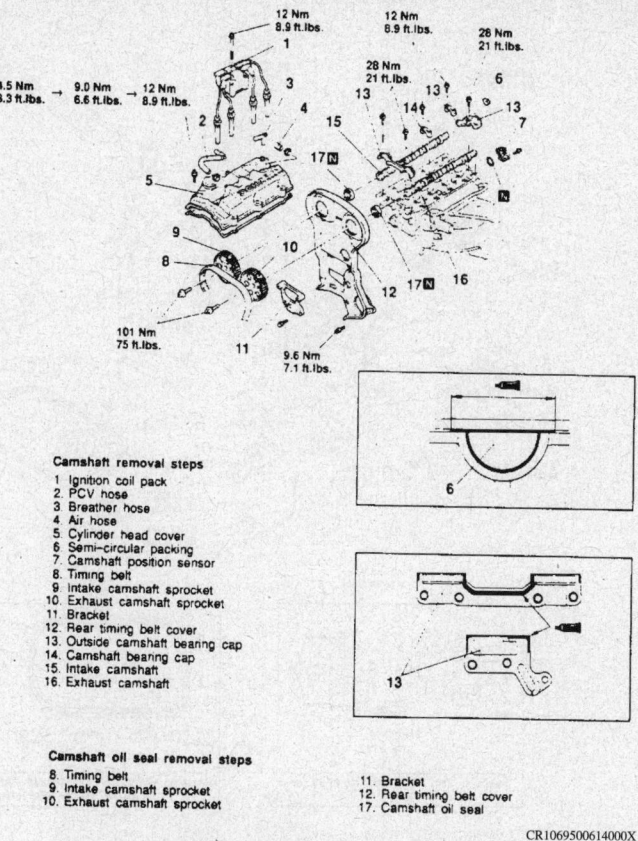

Camshaft removal steps

1. Ignition coil pack
2. PCV hose
3. Breather hose
4. Air hose
5. Cylinder head cover
6. Semi-circular packing
7. Camshaft position sensor
8. Timing belt
9. Intake camshaft sprocket
10. Exhaust camshaft sprocket
11. Bracket
12. Rear timing belt cover
13. Outside camshaft bearing cap
14. Camshaft bearing cap
15. Intake camshaft
16. Exhaust camshaft

Camshaft oil seal removal steps

8. Timing belt
9. Intake camshaft sprocket
10. Exhaust camshaft sprocket
11. Bracket
12. Rear timing belt cover
17. Camshaft oil seal

CR1069500614000X

Fig. 69 Camshaft assembly. 1995–96 2.0L non-turbo engine

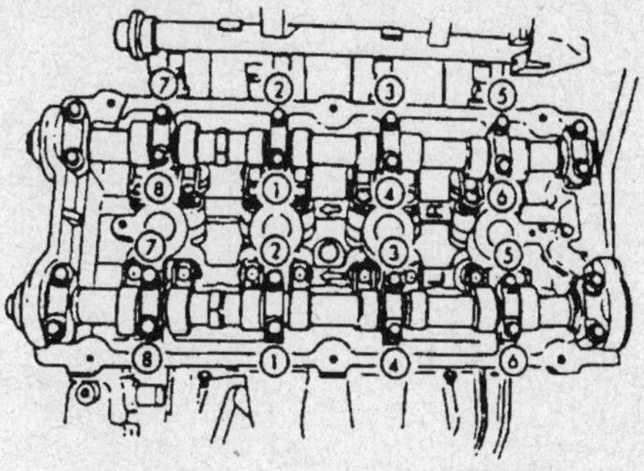

CR1069500615000X

Fig. 70 Camshaft bearing caps. 1995–96 2.0L non-turbo engine

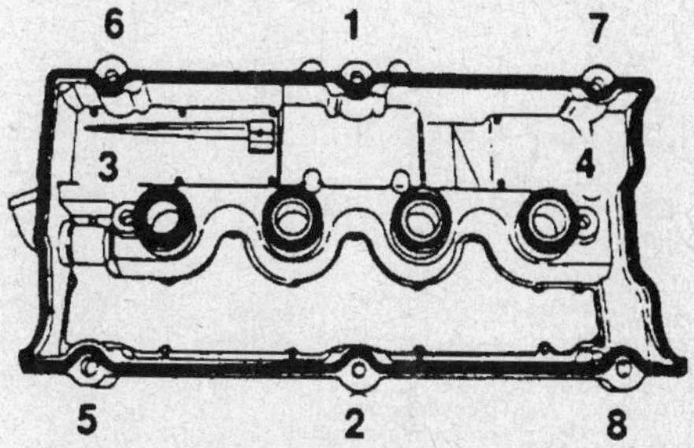
6
1
7
3
4
5
2
8

CR1069500616000X

Fig. 72 Cylinder head cover installation. 1995–96 2.0L non-turbo engine

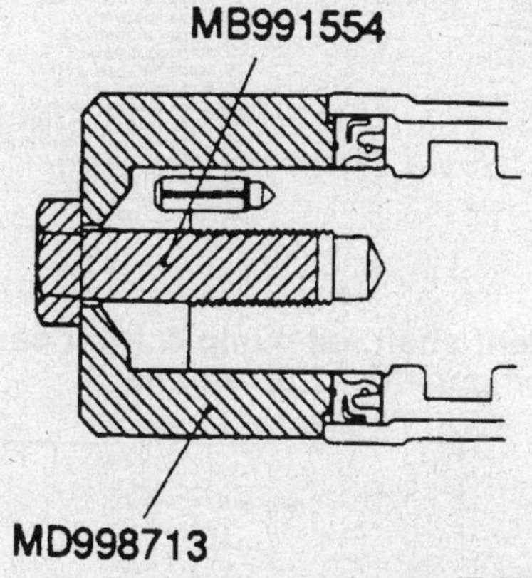
MB991554
MD998713

CR1069500617000X

Fig. 71 Camshaft oil seal installation. 1995–96 2.0L non-turbo engine

Tightening torque Nm (ft-lbs)

(1) Nut (8)
(2) Bearing cap (4)
(3) Bearing (4)
(4) Piston and connecting rod assembly (4)
- (1) Bearing (4)
- (2) Piston pin (4)
- (4)-(3) Connecting rod (4)
- (4) Bolt (8)
- (5) No. 1 piston ring (4)
- (6) No. 2 piston ring (4)
- (7) Oil ring (4)
- (8) Piston (4)

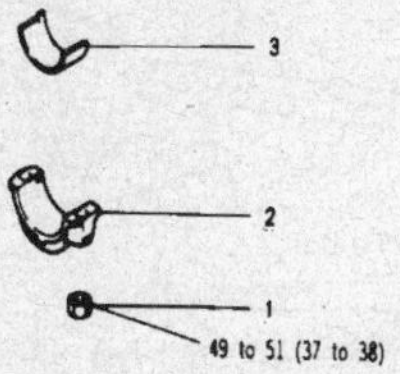
3
2
1
49 to 51 (37 to 38)

MT1069100087000X

Fig. 73 Piston & rod disassembly

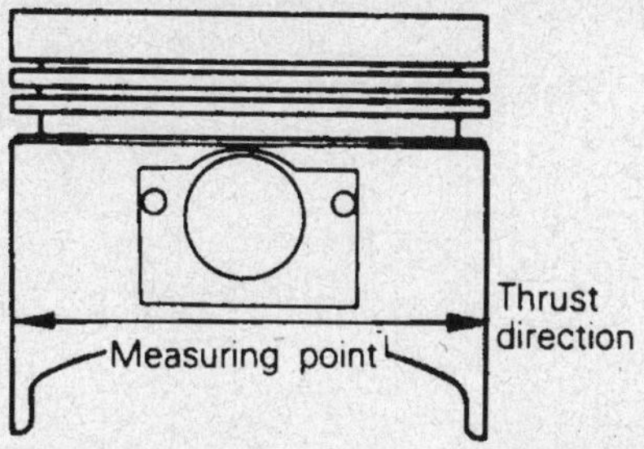
Thrust direction
Measuring point

MT1069100088000X

Fig. 74 Piston measurements

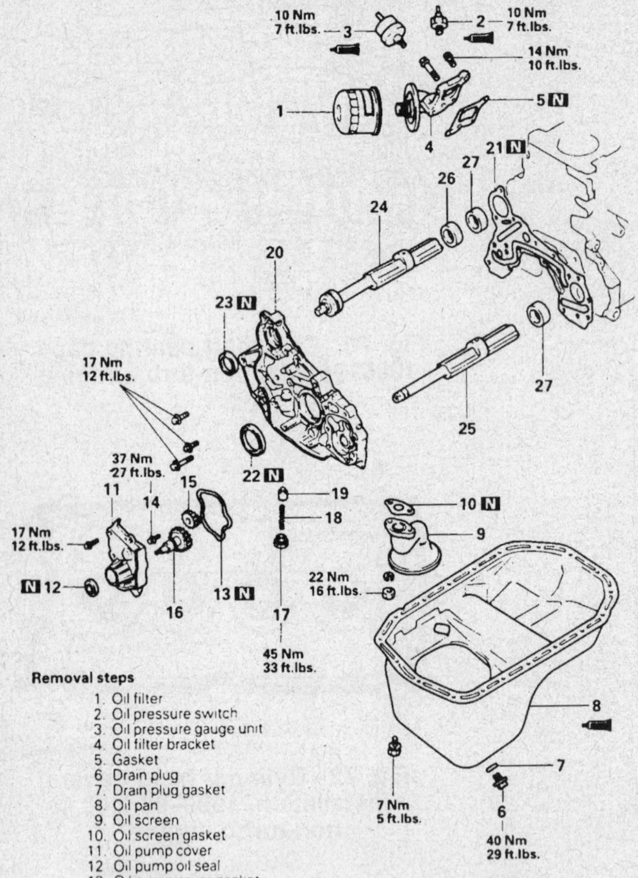
10 Nm
7 ft.lbs.
10 Nm
7 ft.lbs.
14 Nm
10 ft.lbs.
17 Nm
12 ft.lbs.
37 Nm
27 ft.lbs.
17 Nm
12 ft.lbs.
22 Nm
16 ft.lbs.
45 Nm
33 ft.lbs.
7 Nm
5 ft.lbs.
40 Nm
29 ft.lbs.

Removal steps

1. Oil filter
2. Oil pressure switch
3. Oil pressure gauge unit
4. Oil filter bracket
5. Gasket
6. Drain plug
7. Drain plug gasket
8. Oil pan
9. Oil screen
10. Oil screen gasket
11. Oil pump cover
12. Oil pump oil seal
13. Oil pump cover gasket
14. Flange bolt
15. Oil pump driven gear
16. Oil pump drive gear
17. Plug
18. Relief spring
19. Relief plunger
20. Front case
21. Front case gasket
22. Silent shaft oil seal
23. Crankshaft oil seal
24. Silent shaft, right
25. Silent shaft, left
26. Silent shaft front bearing
27. Silent shaft rear bearing

MT1099100005000X

Fig. 75 Silent shaft, oil pump & front case components. 1.8L engine

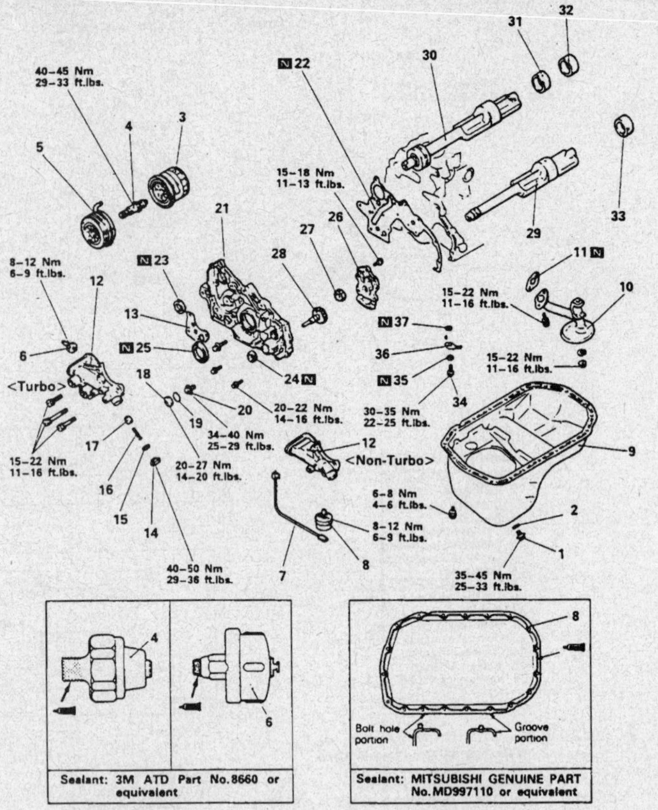
40–45 Nm
29–33 ft.lbs.
15–18 Nm
11–13 ft.lbs.
8–12 Nm
6–9 ft.lbs.
<Turbo>
15–22 Nm
11–16 ft.lbs.
20–22 Nm
14–16 ft.lbs.
34–40 Nm
25–29 ft.lbs.
20–27 Nm
14–20 ft.lbs.
40–50 Nm
29–36 ft.lbs.
<Non-Turbo>
30–35 Nm
22–25 ft.lbs.
15–22 Nm
11–16 ft.lbs.
6–8 Nm
4–6 ft.lbs.
8–12 Nm
6–9 ft.lbs.
35–45 Nm
25–33 ft.lbs.
Bolt hole portion
Groove portion
Sealant: 3M ATD Part No.8660 or equivalent
Sealant: MITSUBISHI GENUINE PART No.MD997110 or equivalent

Disassembly steps

1. Drain plug
2. Gasket
3. Oil filter
4. Oil cooler bolt (Turbo)
5. Oil cooler (Turbo)
6. Oil pressure switch
7. Harness assembly
8. Oil pressure gauge unit
9. Oil pan
10. Oil screen
11. Gasket
12. Oil filter bracket
13. Gasket
14. Relief plug
15. Gasket
16. Relief spring
17. Relief plunger
18. Plug cap
19. O-ring
20. Driven gear bolt
21. Front case
22. Gasket
23. Oil seal
24. Silent shaft oil seal
25. Crankshaft front oil seal
26. Oil pump cover
27. Oil pump driven gear
28. Oil pump drive gear
29. Left silent shaft
30. Right silent shaft
31. Silent shaft front bearings
32. Right silent shaft rear bearing
33. Left silent shaft rear bearing
34. Check valve (Turbo)
35. Gasket (Turbo)
36. Oil jet (Turbo)
37. Gasket (Turbo)

MT1099100006000X

Fig. 76 Silent shaft, oil pump & front case components. 2.0L engine

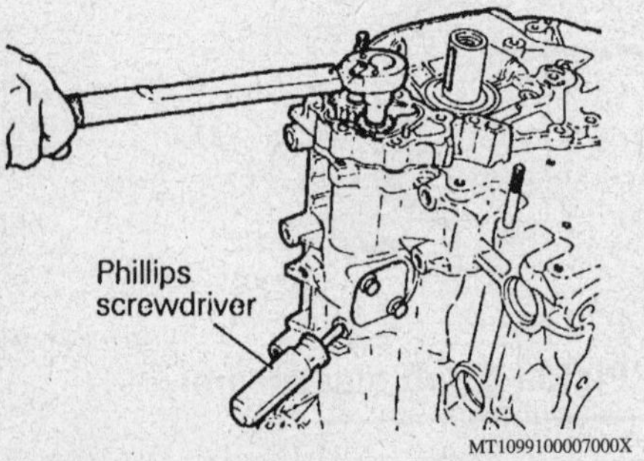
Phillips screwdriver

MT1099100007000X

Fig. 77 Flange bolt removal

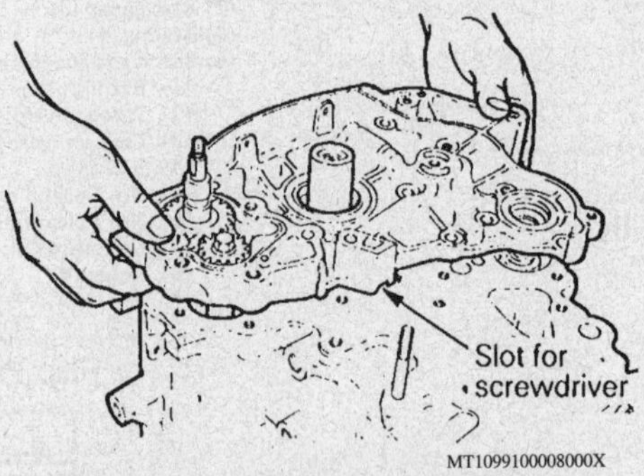
Slot for screwdriver

MT1099100008000X

Fig. 78 Front case removal

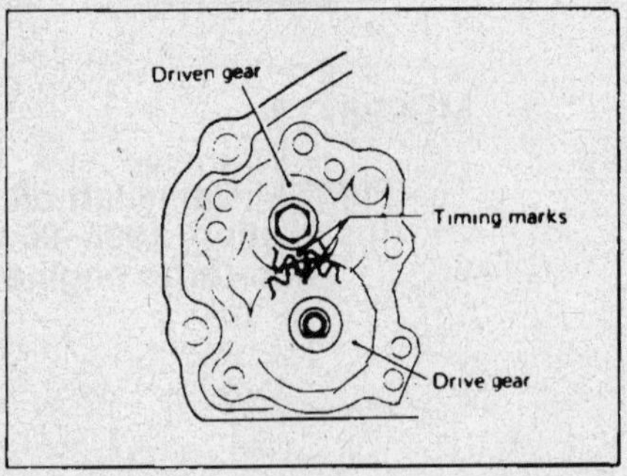
Driven gear
Timing marks
Drive gear

MT1099100009000X

Fig. 79 Oil pump gear timing marks

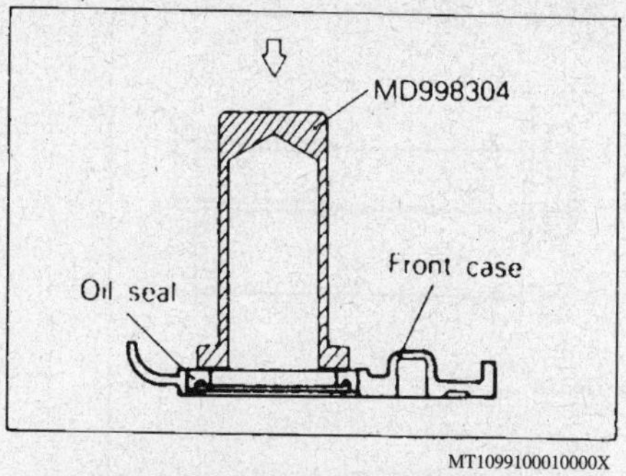
MD998304
Oil seal
Front case
MT1099100010000X

Fig. 80 Crankshaft front oil seal installation. 1.8L engine

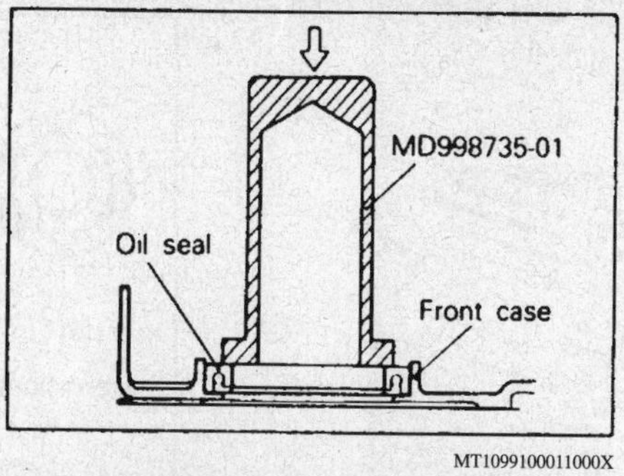
MD998735-01
Oil seal
Front case
MT1099100011000X

Fig. 81 Crankshaft front oil seal installation. 2.0L engine

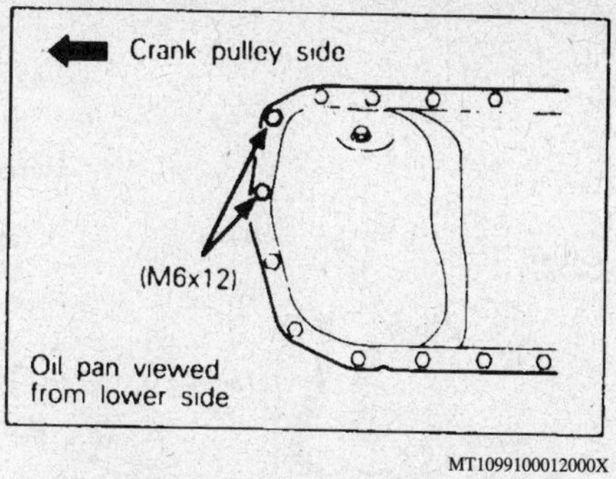
Crank pulley side
(M6x12)
Oil pan viewed from lower side
MT1099100012000X

Fig. 82 Oil pan bolt location

Year	Engine	Belt	New, Lbs.	Used, Lbs.
1993–94	All	A/C	104–126	71–88
		Alt.	110–154	88
1995–96	Non-Turbo	A/C	137–159	93–115
		Alt.	110–160	90–110
		Power Steering	137–159	93–115
1995–96	Turbo	A/C	86–99	57–75
		Alt.	110–154	88
		Power Steering	110–154	77–99

Fig. 83 Belt tension data

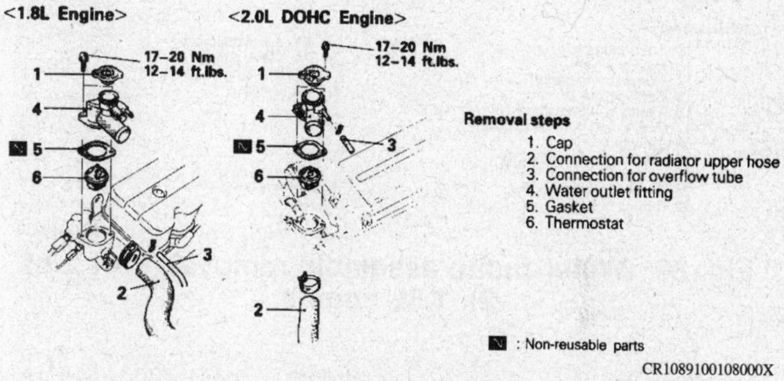
<1.8L Engine>
<2.0L DOHC Engine>
17–20 Nm
12–14 ft.lbs.
Removal steps
1. Cap
2. Connection for radiator upper hose
3. Connection for overflow tube
4. Water outlet fitting
5. Gasket
6. Thermostat
: Non-reusable parts
CR1089100108000X

Fig. 84 Thermostat replacement. 1993–94

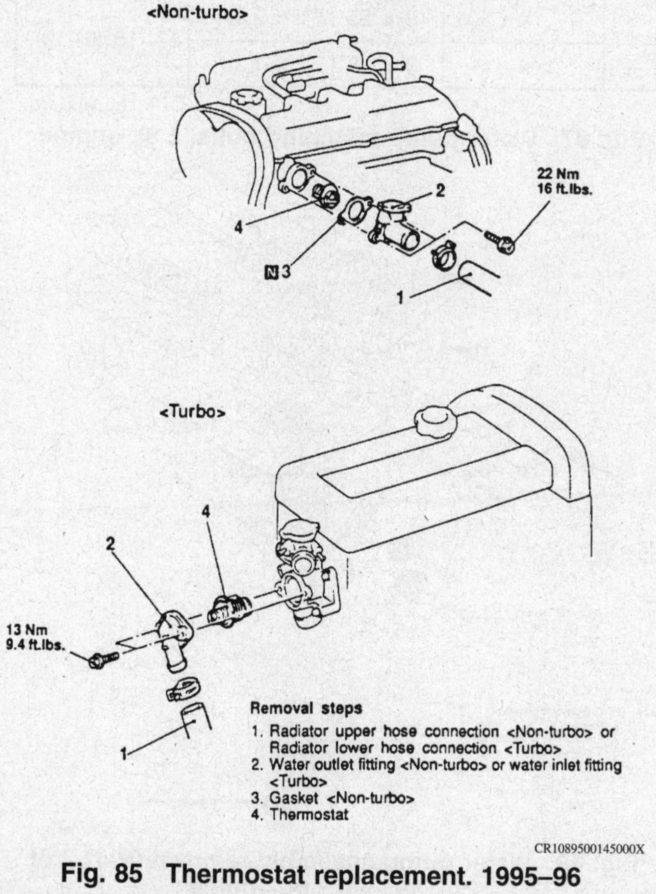
<Non-turbo>
22 Nm
16 ft.lbs.
<Turbo>
13 Nm
9.4 ft.lbs.
Removal steps
1. Radiator upper hose connection <Non-turbo> or Radiator lower hose connection <Turbo>
2. Water outlet fitting <Non-turbo> or water inlet fitting <Turbo>
3. Gasket <Non-turbo>
4. Thermostat
CR1089500145000X

Fig. 85 Thermostat replacement. 1995–96

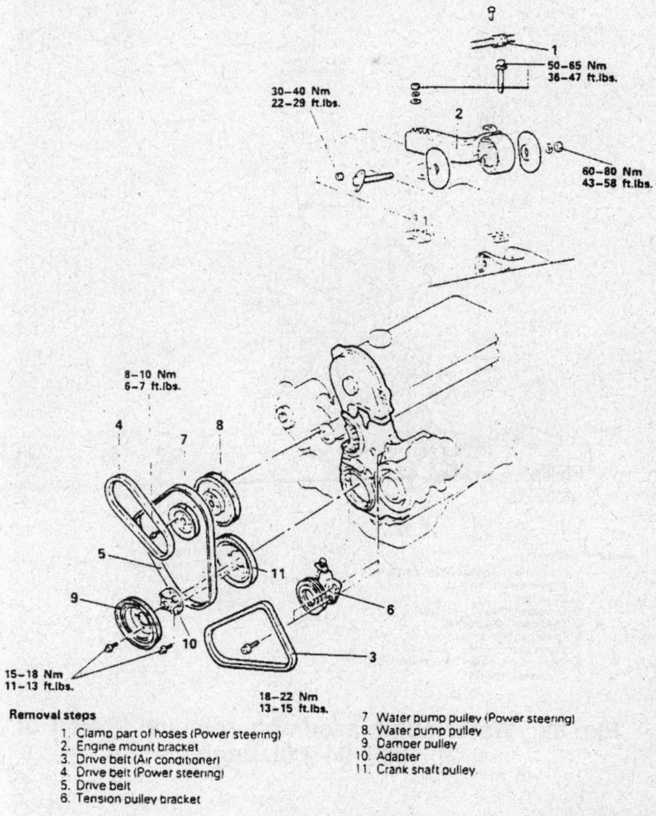
50–65 Nm
36–47 ft.lbs.
30–40 Nm
22–29 ft.lbs.
60–80 Nm
43–58 ft.lbs.
8–10 Nm
6–7 ft.lbs.
15–18 Nm
11–13 ft.lbs.
18–22 Nm
13–15 ft.lbs.
Removal steps
1. Clamp part of hoses (Power steering)
2. Engine mount bracket
3. Drive belt (Air conditioner)
4. Drive belt (Power steering)
5. Drive belt
6. Tension pulley bracket
7. Water pump pulley (Power steering)
8. Water pump pulley
9. Damper pulley
10. Adapter
11. Crank shaft pulley
CR1089100109010X

Fig. 86 Water pump assembly removal (Part 1 of 2). 1.8L engine

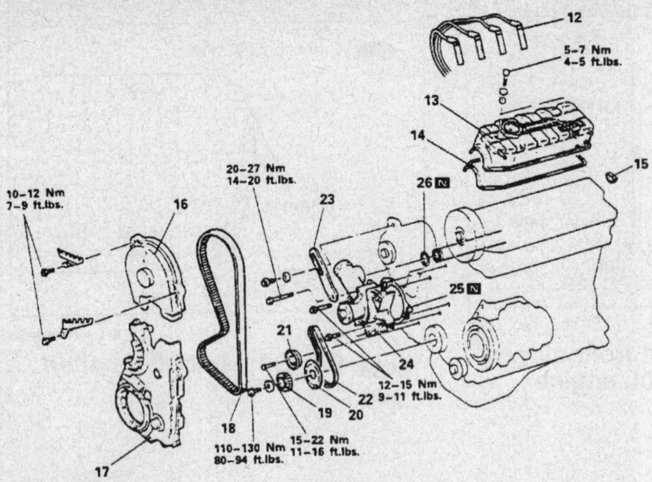

Removal steps

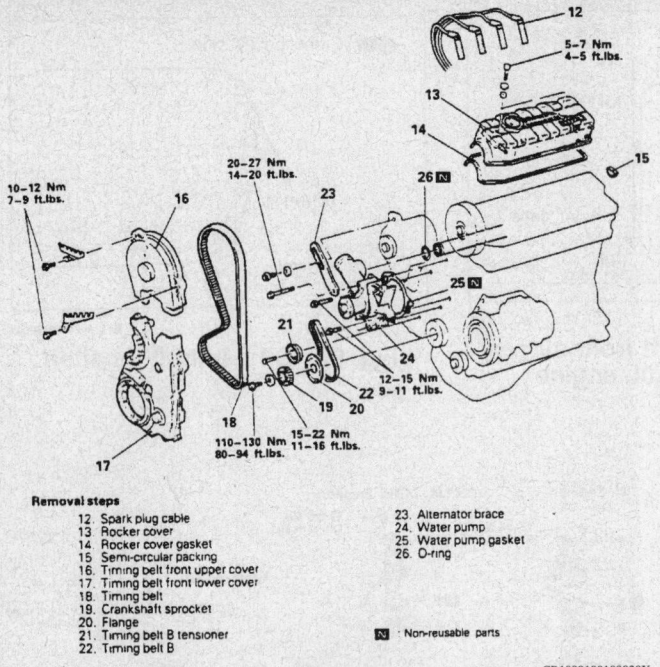

12. Spark plug cable
13. Rocker cover
14. Rocker cover gasket
15. Semi-circular packing
16. Timing belt front upper cover
17. Timing belt front lower cover
18. Timing belt
19. Crankshaft sprocket
20. Flange
21. Timing belt B tensioner
22. Timing belt B
23. Alternator brace
24. Water pump
25. Water pump gasket
26. O-ring

N : Non-reusable parts

CR1089100109020X

Fig. 86 Water pump assembly removal (Part 2 of 2). 1.8L engine

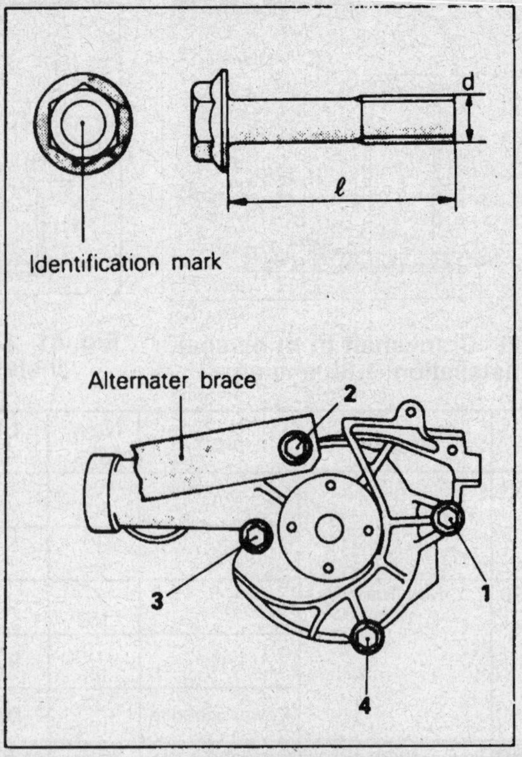

No.	Identification mark	Bolt diameter (d) x length (ℓ) mm (in.)	Torque Nm (ft.lbs.)
1	4	8 x 28 (.31 x 1.1)	12–15 (9–10)
2	7	8 x 70 (.31 x 2.76)	20–27 (15–19)
3	4	8 x 55 (.31 x 2.17)	12–15 (9–10)
4	4	8 x 28 (.31 x 1.1)	

CR1089100110000X

Fig. 87 Water pump attaching bolts. 1.8L engine

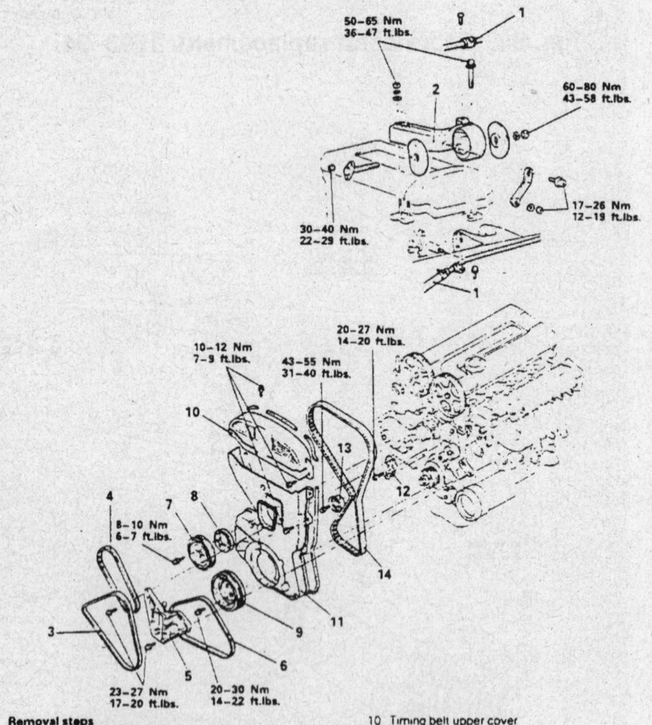

Removal steps

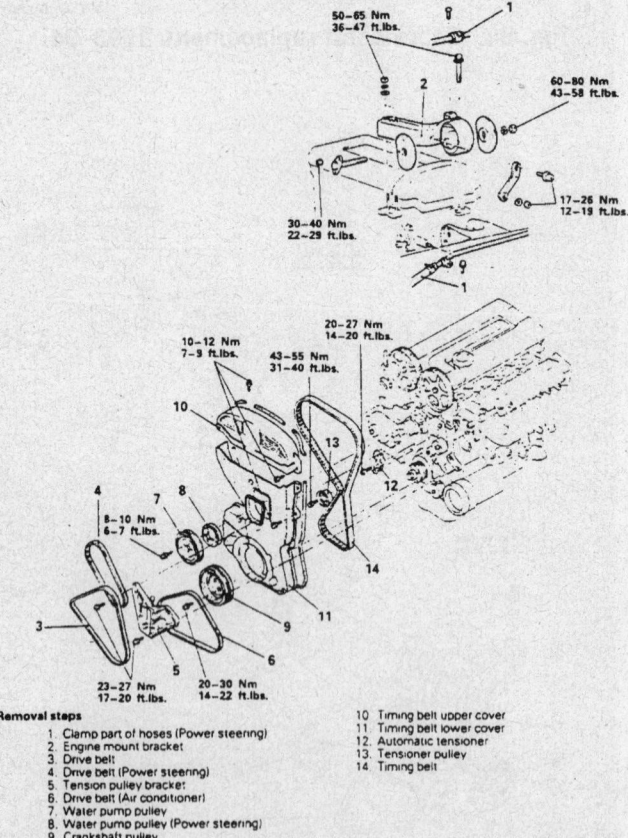

1. Clamp part of hoses (Power steering)
2. Engine mount bracket
3. Drive belt
4. Drive belt (Power steering)
5. Tension pulley bracket
6. Drive belt (Air conditioner)
7. Water pump pulley
8. Water pump pulley (Power steering)
9. Crankshaft pulley
10. Timing belt upper cover
11. Timing belt lower cover
12. Automatic tensioner
13. Tensioner pulley
14. Timing belt

CR1089100111010X

Fig. 88 Water pump assembly removal (Part 1 of 2). 1993–94 2.0L engine

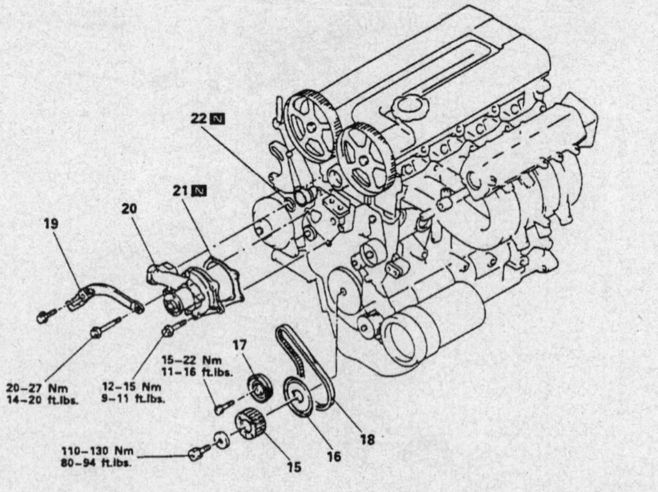

15. Crankshaft sprocket
16. Flange
17. Timing belt B tensioner
18. Timing belt B
19. Alternator brace
20. Water pump
21. Water pump gasket
22. O-ring

N : Non-reusable parts

CR1089100111020X

Fig. 88 Water pump assembly removal (Part 2 of 2). 1993–94 2.0L engine

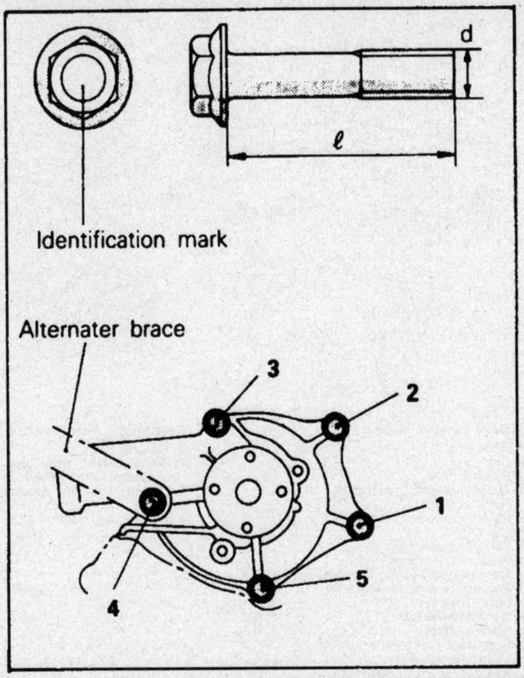
d
ℓ
Identification mark
Alternater brace
3
2
1
5
4

No.	Identification mark	Bolt diameter (d) x length (ℓ) mm (in.)	Torque Nm (ft.lbs.)
1	4	8 x 14 (.31 x .55)	12–15 (9–10)
2	4	8 x 22 (.31 x .87)	
3	4	8 x 30 (.31 x 1.18)	
4	7	8 x 65 (.31 x 2.56)	20–27 (15–19)
5	4	8 x 28 (.31 x 1.10)	12–15 (9–10)

CR1089100112000X

Fig. 89 Water pump attaching bolts. 1993–94 2.0L engine

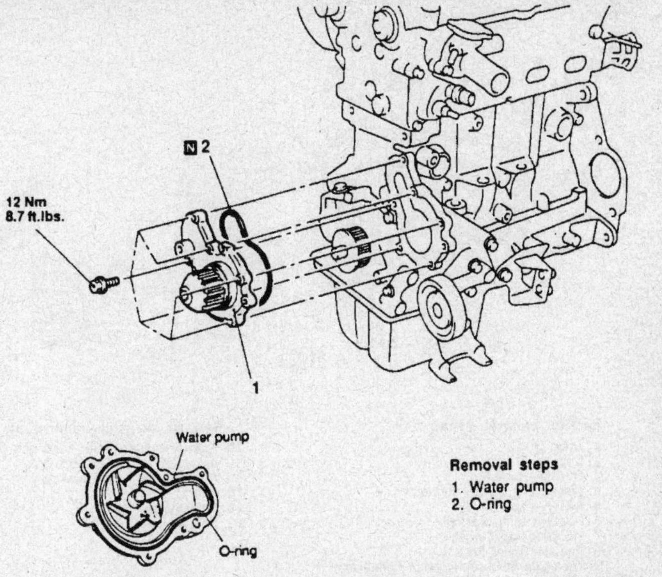
12 Nm
8.7 ft.lbs.
N 2
1
Water pump
O-ring
Removal steps
1. Water pump
2. O-ring

CR1089500146000X

Fig. 90 Water pump assembly removal. 1995–96 non-turbo

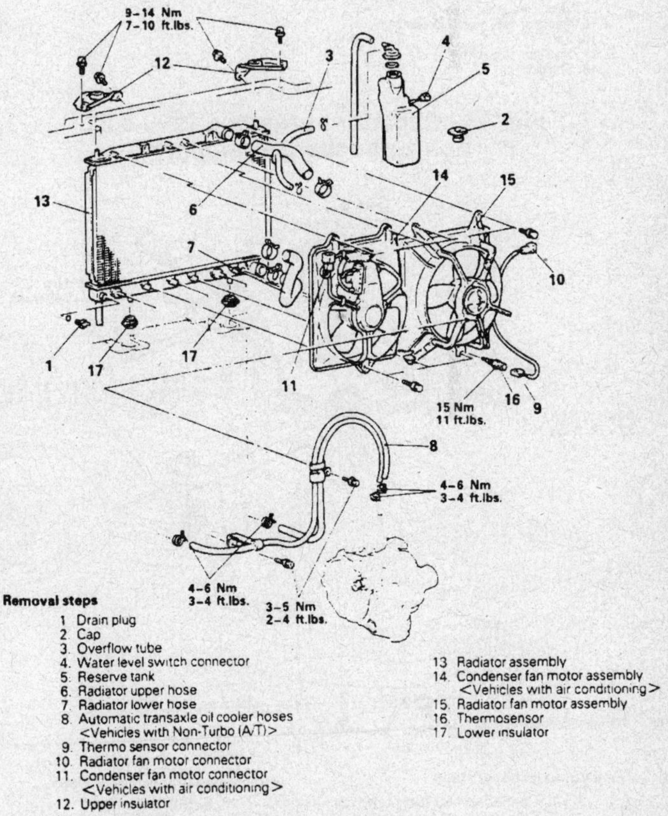
9–14 Nm
7–10 ft.lbs.
12
3
4
5
2
13
6
14
15
7
10
1
17
17
11
15 Nm
11 ft.lbs.
16
9
8
4–6 Nm
3–4 ft.lbs.
4–6 Nm
3–4 ft.lbs.
3–5 Nm
2–4 ft.lbs.
Removal steps
1. Drain plug
2. Cap
3. Overflow tube
4. Water level switch connector
5. Reserve tank
6. Radiator upper hose
7. Radiator lower hose
8. Automatic transaxle oil cooler hoses <Vehicles with Non-Turbo (A/T)>
9. Thermo sensor connector
10. Radiator fan motor connector
11. Condenser fan motor connector <Vehicles with air conditioning>
12. Upper insulator
13. Radiator assembly
14. Condenser fan motor assembly <Vehicles with air conditioning>
15. Radiator fan motor assembly
16. Thermosensor
17. Lower insulator

CR1089400148000X

Fig. 92 Radiator assembly. 1993–94

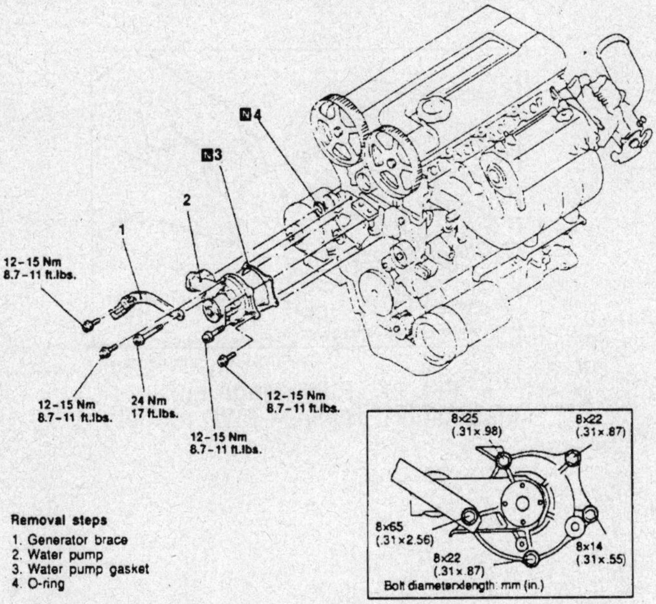
N 4
N 3
2
1
12–15 Nm
8.7–11 ft.lbs.
12–15 Nm
8.7–11 ft.lbs.
24 Nm
17 ft.lbs.
12–15 Nm
8.7–11 ft.lbs.
12–15 Nm
8.7–11 ft.lbs.
Removal steps
1. Generator brace
2. Water pump
3. Water pump gasket
4. O-ring
8x25 (.31x.98)
8x22 (.31x.87)
8x65 (.31x2.56)
8x14 (.31x.55)
8x22 (.31x.87)
Bolt diameterxlength: mm (in.)

CR1089500147000X

Fig. 91 Water pump assembly removal. 1995–96 turbo

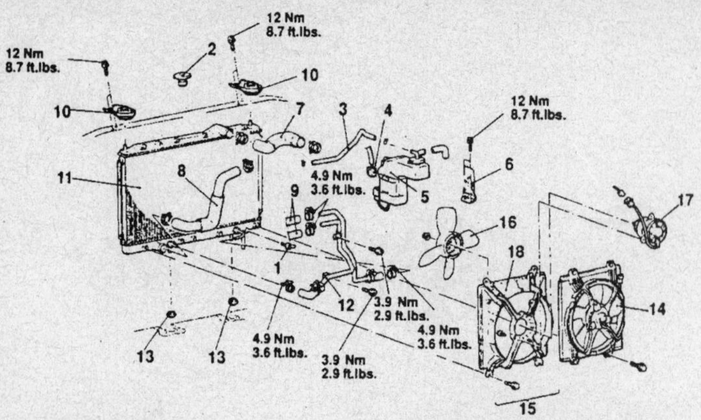
12 Nm
8.7 ft.lbs.
4.9 Nm
3.6 ft.lbs.
3.9 Nm
2.9 ft.lbs.

Radiator removal steps

1. Drain plug
2. Cap
3. Overflow tube
4. Water level switch connector
5. Reserve tank
6. Reserve tank bracket
7. Radiator upper hose
8. Radiator lower hose
9. Transaxle fluid cooler hose connection <Vehicles with A/T>
10. Upper insulator
11. Radiator assembly
12. Transaxle fluid cooler hose and pipe assembly <Vehicles with A/T>
13. Lower insulator
14. Condenser fan motor assembly <Vehicles with A/C>
15. Radiator fan motor assembly
16. Fan
17. Radiator fan motor
18. Shroud

Radiator fan motor removal steps

12. Transaxle fluid cooler hose and pipe assembly <Vehicles with A/T>
15. Radiator fan motor assembly
16. Fan
17. Radiator fan motor
18. Shroud

CR1089500149000X

Fig. 93 Radiator assembly. 1996 2.0L non-turbocharged engine

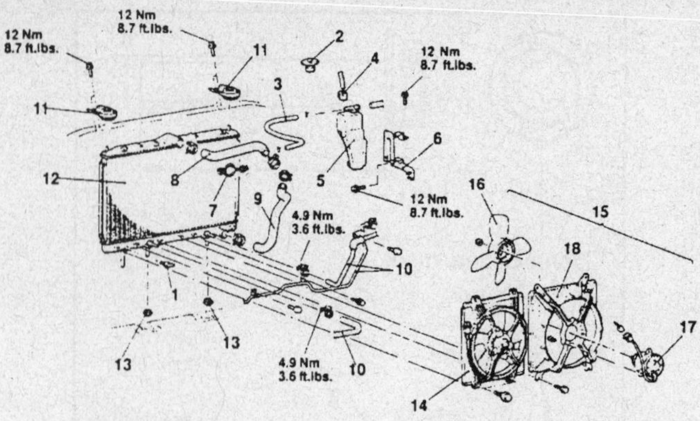
12 Nm
8.7 ft.lbs.
4.9 Nm
3.6 ft.lbs.

Radiator removal steps

1. Drain plug
2. Cap
3. Overflow tube
4. Water level switch connector
5. Reserve tank
6. Reserve tank bracket
7. Clip
8. Radiator upper hose
9. Radiator lower hose
10. Transaxle fluid cooler hose and pipe assembly <Vehicles with A/T>
11. Upper insulator
12. Radiator assembly
13. Lower insulator
14. Condenser fan motor assembly <Vehicles with A/C>
15. Radiator fan motor assembly
16. Fan
17. Radiator fan motor
18. Shroud

Radiator fan motor removal steps

5. Reserve tank
10. Transaxle fluid cooler hose and pipe assembly <Vehicles with A/T>
15. Radiator fan motor assembly
16. Fan
17. Radiator fan motor
18. Shroud

CR1089500150000X

Fig. 94 Radiator assembly. 1996 2.0L turbocharged engine

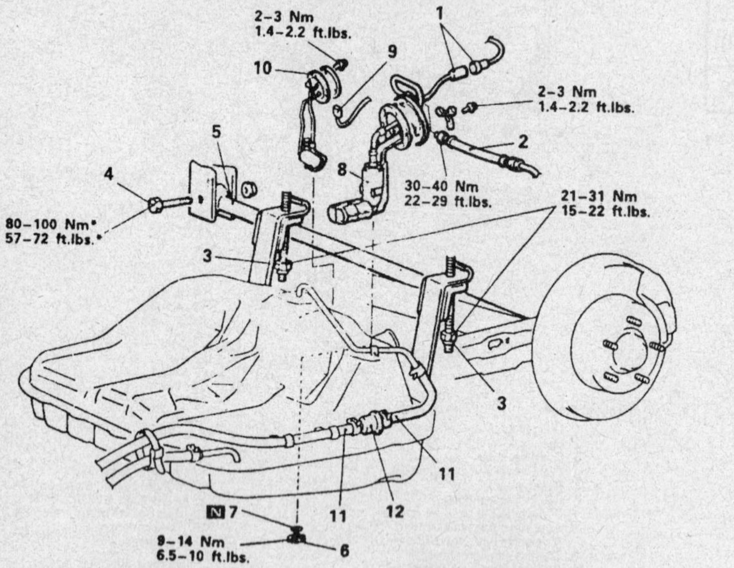
2–3 Nm
1.4–2.2 ft.lbs.
30–40 Nm
22–29 ft.lbs.
21–31 Nm
15–22 ft.lbs.
80–100 Nm*
57–72 ft.lbs.*
9–14 Nm
6.5–10 ft.lbs.

Fuel pump removal steps

1. Connection for fuel pump connector
2. High pressure fuel hose
3. Self locking nut
4. Lateral rod attaching bolt
5. Lateral rod and body connection
6. Bolt
7. O-ring
8. Electric fuel pump

Fuel gauge unit removal steps

3. Self locking nut
4. Lateral rod attaching bolt
5. Lateral rod and body connection
9. Connection for fuel gauge unit connector
10. Fuel gauge unit

Overfill limiter removal steps

11. Connection for vapor hose
12. Overfill limiter (Two-way valve)

CR1029102520000X

Fig. 95 Fuel pump assembly removal. 1993–94 FWD models

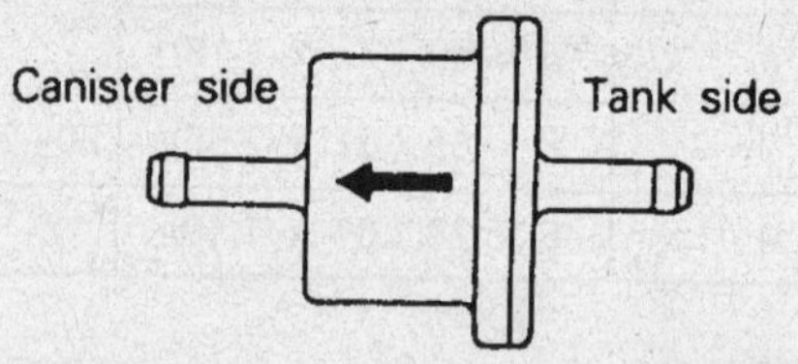
Canister side
Tank side

CR1029102521000X

Fig. 96 Fuel tank overfill limiter. 1993–94 FWD models

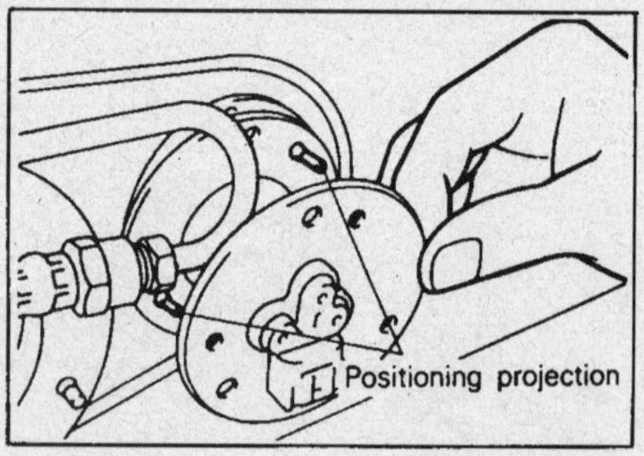
Positioning projection

CR1029102522000X

Fig. 97 Fuel gauge unit installation. 1993–94 FWD models

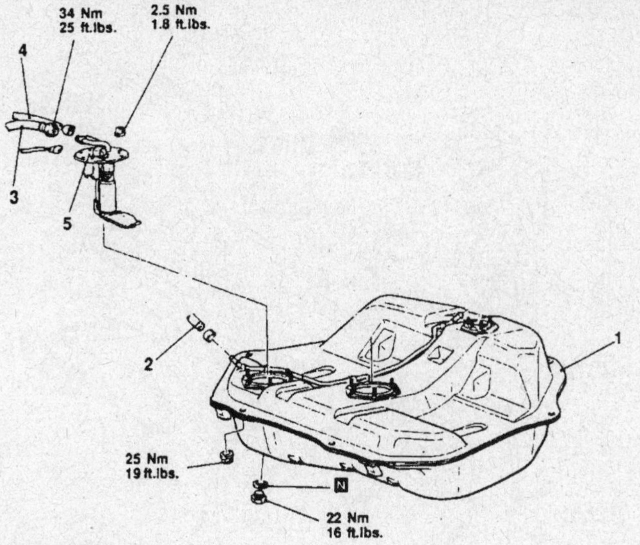
34 Nm
25 ft.lbs.
2.5 Nm
1.8 ft.lbs.
25 Nm
19 ft.lbs.
22 Nm
16 ft.lbs.
N

Removal steps

1. Fuel tank
2. Vapor hose
3. High-pressure fuel hose
4. Return hose
5. Fuel pump assembly

CR1029503772000X

Fig. 98 Fuel pump assembly removal. 1995–96 FWD models

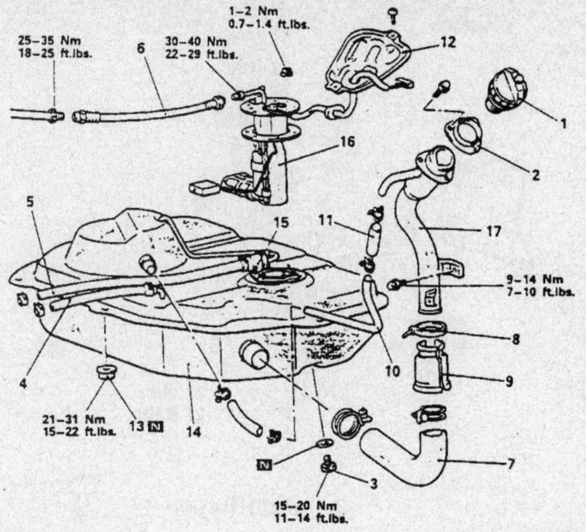
1–2 Nm
0.7–1.4 ft.lbs.
25–35 Nm
18–25 ft.lbs.
30–40 Nm
22–29 ft.lbs.
9–14 Nm
7–10 ft.lbs.
21–31 Nm
15–22 ft.lbs.
15–20 Nm
11–14 ft.lbs.

Removal steps

1. Fuel tank cap
2. Packing
3. Drain plug
4. Return hose
5. Vapor hose
6. High pressure fuel hose
7. Fuel filler hose
8. Cable band
9. Protector
10. Vapor pipe
11. Vapor hose
12. Hole cover
13. Self-locking nut
14. Fuel tank
15. Overfill limiter (Two-way valve)
16. Fuel pump and fuel gauge unit assembly
17. Fuel filler neck

N : Non-reusable parts

CR1029102523000X

Fig. 99 Fuel pump assembly removal. 1993–94 AWD models

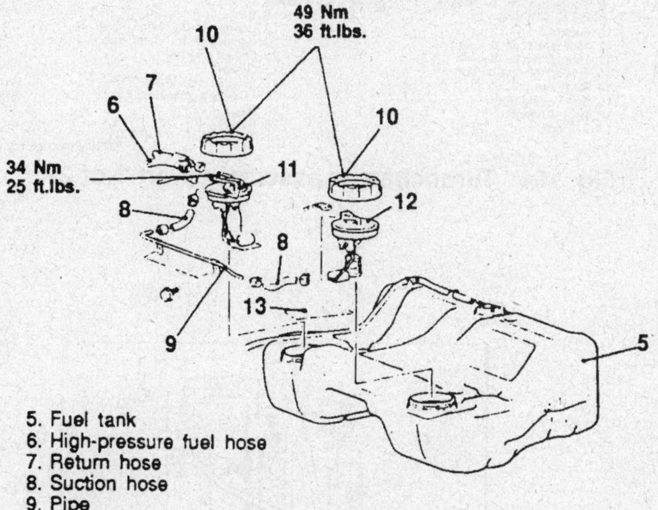
49 Nm
36 ft.lbs.
34 Nm
25 ft.lbs.

5. Fuel tank
6. High-pressure fuel hose
7. Return hose
8. Suction hose
9. Pipe
10. Cap
11. Fuel gauge unit and pump assembly
12. Fuel gauge unit and pipe assembly

CR1029503773000X

Fig. 100 Fuel pump assembly removal. 1995–96 AWD models

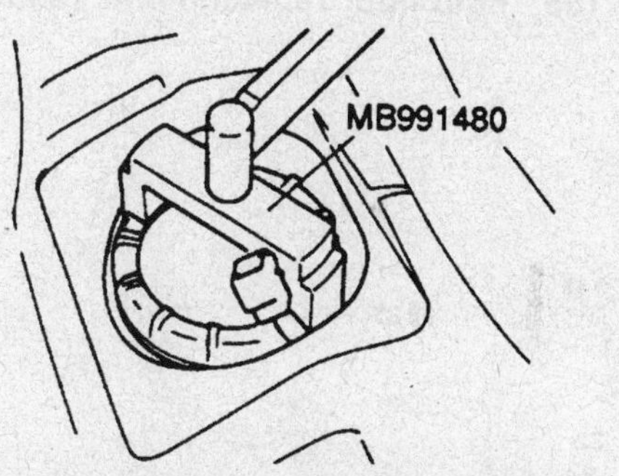
MB991480

CR1029503774000X

Fig. 101 Fuel pump cap installation. 1995–96 AWD models

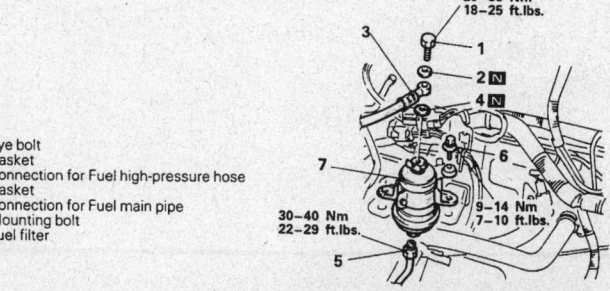

1. Eye bolt
2. Gasket
3. Connection for Fuel high-pressure hose
4. Gasket
5. Connection for Fuel main pipe
6. Mounting bolt
7. Fuel filter

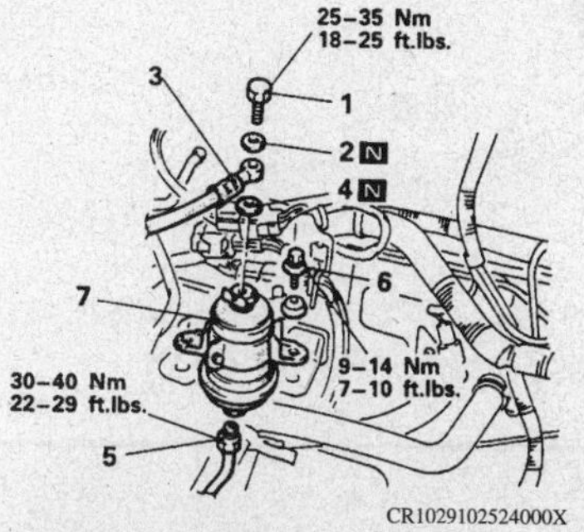
25–35 Nm
18–25 ft.lbs.
30–40 Nm
22–29 ft.lbs.
9–14 Nm
7–10 ft.lbs.

CR1029102524000X

Fig. 102 Fuel filter replacement. 1993–94

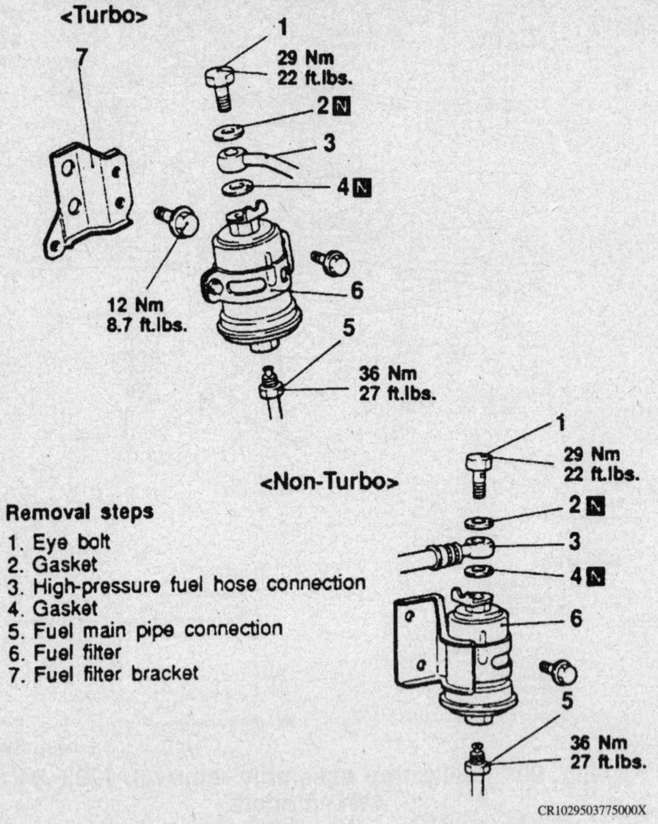
<Turbo>
29 Nm
22 ft.lbs.
12 Nm
8.7 ft.lbs.
36 Nm
27 ft.lbs.
<Non-Turbo>
29 Nm
22 ft.lbs.
36 Nm
27 ft.lbs.
Removal steps
1. Eye bolt
2. Gasket
3. High-pressure fuel hose connection
4. Gasket
5. Fuel main pipe connection
6. Fuel filter
7. Fuel filter bracket
CR1029503775000X

Fig. 103 Fuel filter replacement. 1995–96

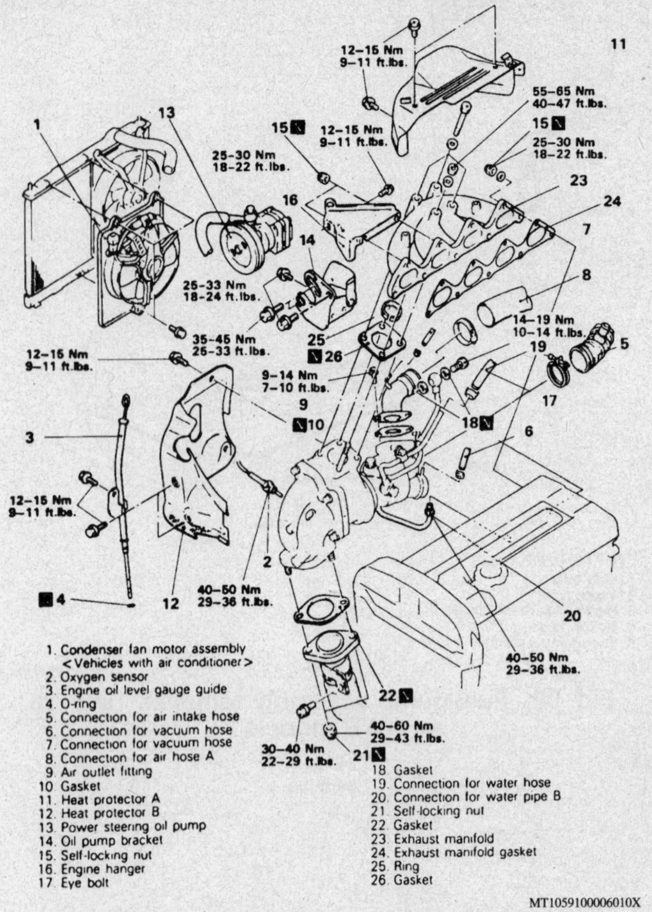
12–15 Nm
9–11 ft.lbs.
55–65 Nm
40–47 ft.lbs.
25–30 Nm
18–22 ft.lbs.
25–33 Nm
18–24 ft.lbs.
35–45 Nm
26–33 ft.lbs.
9–14 Nm
7–10 ft.lbs.
14–19 Nm
10–14 ft.lbs.
40–50 Nm
29–36 ft.lbs.
40–60 Nm
29–43 ft.lbs.
30–40 Nm
22–29 ft.lbs.
1. Condenser fan motor assembly
<Vehicles with air conditioner>
2. Oxygen sensor
3. Engine oil level gauge guide
4. O-ring
5. Connection for air intake hose
6. Connection for vacuum hose
7. Connection for vacuum hose
8. Connection for air hose A
9. Air outlet fitting
10. Gasket
11. Heat protector A
12. Heat protector B
13. Power steering oil pump
14. Oil pump bracket
15. Self-locking nut
16. Engine hanger
17. Eye bolt
18. Gasket
19. Connection for water hose
20. Connection for water pipe B
21. Self-locking nut
22. Gasket
23. Exhaust manifold
24. Exhaust manifold gasket
25. Ring
26. Gasket
MT1059100006010X

Fig. 104 Turbocharger assembly (Part 1 of 2)

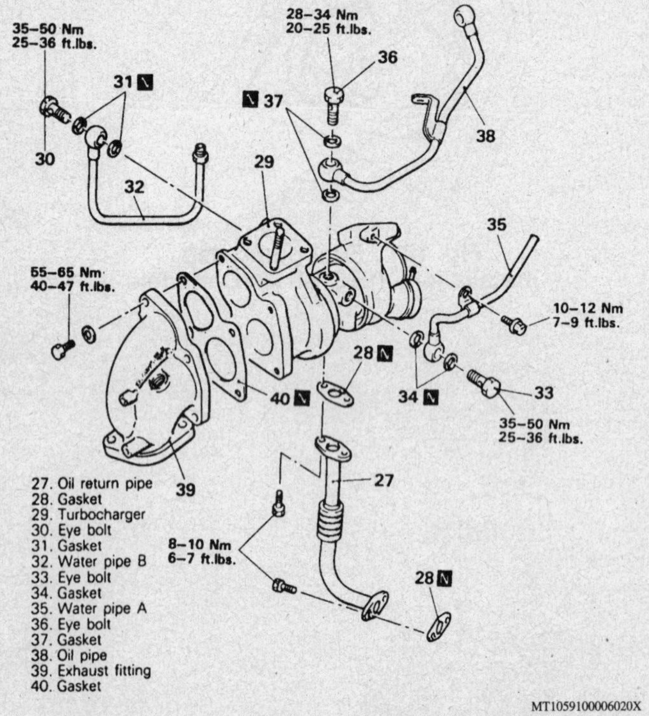
35–50 Nm
25–36 ft.lbs.
28–34 Nm
20–25 ft.lbs.
55–65 Nm
40–47 ft.lbs.
10–12 Nm
7–9 ft.lbs.
35–50 Nm
25–36 ft.lbs.
8–10 Nm
6–7 ft.lbs.
27. Oil return pipe
28. Gasket
29. Turbocharger
30. Eye bolt
31. Gasket
32. Water pipe B
33. Eye bolt
34. Gasket
35. Water pipe A
36. Eye bolt
37. Gasket
38. Oil pipe
39. Exhaust fitting
40. Gasket
MT1059100006020X

Fig. 104 Turbocharger assembly (Part 2 of 2)

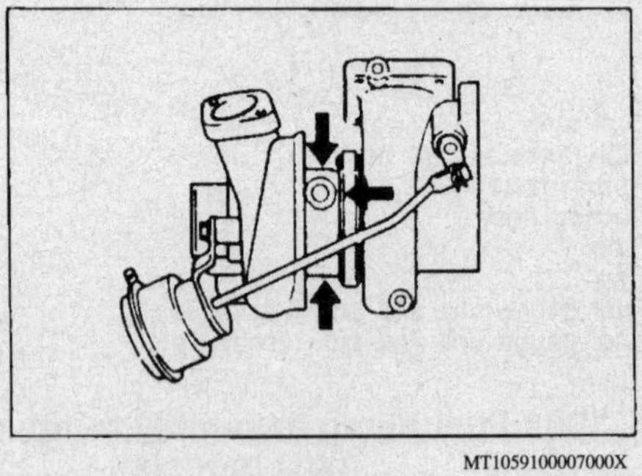
MT1059100007000X

Fig. 105 Turbocharger alignment surfaces

TIGHTENING SPECIFICATIONS

Year	Component	Torque/Ft. Lbs.
1993–94	A/C Compressor Bracket	17–20
	Air Cleaner Resonator	7–9
	Air Cleaner	6–7
	Auto Tensioner	14–20
	Camshaft Bearing Cap Bolt (Long)①	14–15
	Camshaft Bearing Cap Bolt (Short)①	14–20
	Camshaft Sprocket	58–72
	Center Cover⑪	2–3
	Centermember Bolt⑪	58–72
	Connecting Rod Bearing Cap①	24–25
	Crankshaft Bearing Cap①	37–39
	Crankshaft Pulley	②
	Crankshaft Sprocket	80–94
	Cylinder Head Bolts	③
	Distributor①	7–9
	Driveplate	94–101
	EGR Valve	⑤
	Electric Fuel Pump (Bolt)	6.5–10
	Electric Fuel Pump (Screws)	1.4–2.2
	Engine Coolant Temperature Sensor⑪	15–29
	Engine Cooler Pipe⑪	29–33
	Engine Mount Bracket Nut	36–47
	Engine Mount Bracket	36–51
	Engine Mount Insulator Nut (Large)	43–58
	Engine Mount Insulator Nut (Small)	22–29
	Engine Oil Cooler Mounting Nut⑪	6–9
	Engine Oil Hose Mounting Nut⑪	2–4
	Exhaust Manifold To Engine	18–22
	Exhaust Manifold To Turbocharger (Turbo)⑪	40–47
	Exhaust Pipe Clamp Bolt	22–29
	Exhaust Pipe Support Bracket	22–30
	Exhaust Pipe To Hanger	7–11
	Exhaust Pipe To Manifold (Non-Turbo)	22–29
	Exhaust Pipe To Manifold (Turbo)⑪	29–43
	Eye Bolt (Engine Oil Cooler Side)⑪	22–25
	Eye Bolt (Oil Filter Bracket Side)⑪	29–33
	Flywheel	94–101
	Front Case	14–16
	Front Roll Stopper Bracket To Body	40–54
	Front Roll Stopper Bracket To Centermember	29–36
	Front Roll Stopper Insulator Nut	36–47
	Fuel Gauge Unit	1.4–2.2
	Fuel Tank Self-Locking Nut	57–72
	Heat Shield⑪	9–11
	Intake Manifold Stay Bolt	⑥
	Intake Manifold To Engine (M8)	11–14
	Intake Manifold To Engine (M10)	22–30
	Intercooler Air Bypass Valve⑪	11–16
	Intercooler Air Pipe B⑪	9–11
	Intercooler⑪	9–11
	Left Engine Support Bracket	22–30
	Oil Filter Bracket	11–16

Continued

TIGHTENING SPECIFICATIONS—Continued

Year	Component	Torque/Ft. Lbs.
1993–94	Oil Level Gauge Mounting Bolt	9–11
	Oil Pan (Bolts)	4–6
	Oil Pan (Nuts)	3.5–5
	Oil Pan Drain Plug	25–33
	Oil Pipe-to-Engine (Turbo)⑪	10–14
	Oil Pressure Gauge Unit	6–9
	Oil Pressure Switch	6–9
	Oil Pump Cover	29–36
	Oil Pump Driven Gear	25–29
	Oil Pump Sprocket	⑦
	Oil Return Pipe-to-Oil Pan (Turbo)⑪	6–7
	Oil Screen	11–16
	Oxygen Sensor⑪	29–36
	Power Steering Bracket	25–33
	Radiator Upper Insulator	7–10
	Relief Plug	11–13
	Rocker Cover	2–3
	Silent Shaft Sprocket	⑧
	Tensioner Pulley Bracket	17–20
	Thermo Valve①	14–28
	Thermo Sensor To Radiator	2–3
	Throttle Body	⑨
	Throttle Position Sensor	1.1–1.8
	Timing Belt B Tensioner Bolt	11–16
	Timing Belt Front Cover	7–9
	Timing Belt Idle Pulley	25–30
	Timing Belt Rear Cover	7–9
	Timing Belt Tensioner Pulley	⑩
	Transaxle Mount Insulator Nut	43–58
	Transaxle Mount To Body	29–36
	Wastegate Actuator⑪	7–9
	Water Outlet⑪	12–14
	Water Pipe To Engine⑪	10–14
	Water Pipe To Turbocharger⑪	25–36
	Water Pump Bolt (4T)	9–11
	Water Pump Bolt (7T)	14–20
	Water Pump Pulley	6–7
1995–96	A/C Compressor Bracket	17–20
	Air Cleaner	6–7
	Auto Tensioner (Non-Turbo)	23
	Auto Tensioner (Turbo)	17
	Camshaft Bearing Cap Bolt (Non-Turbo)	⑫
	Camshaft Bearing Cap Bolt (Turbo)	14–15
	Camshaft Sprocket (Non-Turbo)	75
	Camshaft Sprocket (Turbo)	65
	Center Cover (Turbo)	2.2
	Connecting Rod Bearing Caps (Turbo)	16
	Connecting Rod Bearing Caps (Non-Turbo)	④
	Crankshaft Bearing Caps (Non-Turbo)	⑭
	Crankshaft Bearing Cap (Turbo)	⑬
	Crankshaft Pulley (Non-Turbo)	105
	Crankshaft Pulley (Turbo)	18
	Crankshaft Sprocket (Turbo)	80–94
	Cylinder Head Bolt (Non-Turbo)	③
	Cylinder Head Bolt (Turbo)	③

Continued

TIGHTENING SPECIFICATIONS—Continued

Year	Component	Torque/Ft. Lbs.
1995–96	EGR Valve	16
	Electric Fuel Pump (Bolt)	1.8
	Engine Coolant Temperature Sensor	5
	Engine Oil Cooler Mounting Bolt (Turbo)	29–33
	Exhaust Manifold To Engine (Non-Turbo)	17
	Exhaust Manifold To Engine (Turbo)	22
	Exhaust Manifold To Turbocharger (Turbo)	44–47
	Exhaust Pipe Clamp Bolt	9.4
	Exhaust Pipe To Hanger	9.4
	Exhaust Pipe To Manifold (Non-Turbo)	33
	Exhaust Pipe To Manifold (Turbo)	33–36
	Flywheel	94–101
	Fuel Gauge Unit (FWD)	1.8
	Fuel Gauge Unit (AWD)	36
	Heat Shield To Exhaust Manifold (Turbo)	9–11
	Intake Manifold To Engine (Non-Turbo)	17
	Intake Manifold To Engine (Turbo)	14
	Oil Filter Bracket (Turbo)	11–16
	Oil Pan (Non-Turbo)	8.9
	Oil Pan (Turbo)	5.1
	Oil Pan Drain Plug (Non-Turbo)	25
	Oil Pan Drain Plug (Turbo)	29
	Oil Pressure Gauge Unit (Turbo)	7
	Oil Pressure Switch (Turbo)	7
	Oil Pump Cover (Non-Turbo)	17
	Oil Pump Cover (Turbo)	9–12
	Oil Pump Driven Gear (Turbo)	7
	Oil Return Pipe To Oil Pan (Turbo)	6.5
	Oil Screen (Non-Turbo)	21
	Oil Screen (Turbo)	14
	Oxygen Sensor	22
	Tensioner Pulley Bracket (Turbo)	17–20
	Throttle Body	11–16
	Timing Belt Tensioner Bolt (Turbo)	17–20
	Timing Belt B Tensioner (Turbo)	14
	Timing Belt Front Cover, Top (Non-Turbo)	8.9
	Timing Belt Front Cover, Bottom (Non-Turbo)	21
	Timing Belt Front Cover (Turbo)	7.2–8.7
	Timing Belt Tensioner Pulley (Non-Turbo)	30
	Water Pump (Non-Turbo)	8.7
	Water Pump (Turbo)	8.7–11

① — 1.8L engine.
② — 1.8L engine, 11–13 ft. lbs.; 2.0L engine, 14–22 ft. lbs.
③ — Refer to "Cylinder Head Replace."
④ — 20 ft. lbs., then tighten an additional 90°.
⑤ — 1.8L engine, 7–11 ft. lbs.; 2.0L engine, 11–16 ft. lbs.
⑥ — 1.8L engine, 13–18 ft. lbs.; 2.0L engine, 18–22 ft. lbs.
⑦ — 1.8L engine, 26–29 ft. lbs.; 2.0L engine, 36–43 ft. lbs.
⑧ — 1.8L engine, 25–29 ft. lbs.; 2.0L engine, 31–35 ft. lbs.
⑨ — 1.8L engine, 7–9 ft. lbs.; 2.0L engine, 11–16 ft. lbs.
⑩ — 1.8L engine, 16–22 ft. lbs.; 2.0L engine, 31–40 ft. lbs.
⑪ — 2.0L engine.
⑫ — Main camshaft bearing caps, 21 ft. lbs.; small camshaft bearing caps, 8.9 ft. lbs.
⑬ — 18 ft. lbs., then tighten an additional 90–100°.
⑭ — Inner crankshaft bearing caps, 55 ft. lbs.; outer crankshaft bearing caps, 20 ft. lbs.

2.4L Engine

NOTE: For Procedures Not Found In This Section, Refer To The Galant Engine Section In The Mitsubishi Chapter.

NOTE: On Air Bag Equipped Models, Refer To "Air Bag System Precautions" Located In The Front Of This Manual For System Disarming & Arming Procedures.

INDEX

	Page No.
Engine Rebuilding Specifications	29-1
Engine, Replace	24-50
Tightening Specifications	24-51

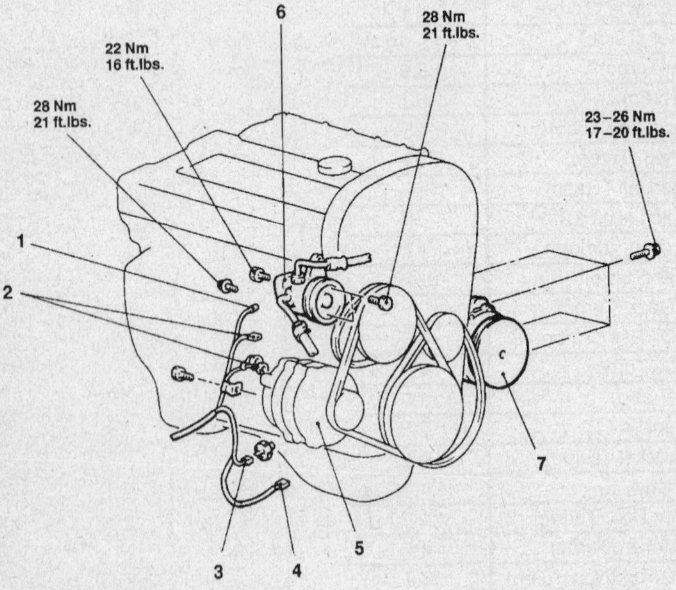

22 Nm
16 ft.lbs.
28 Nm
21 ft.lbs.
28 Nm
21 ft.lbs.
23–26 Nm
17–20 ft.lbs.

Removal steps
1. Power steering pressure switch connector
2. Generator connectors
3. Oil pressure switch connector
4. Oil pressure gauge unit connector
5. Generator
6. Power steering pump connection
7. A/C compressor connection

MT1069600342010X

Fig. 1 Engine assembly (Part 1 of 3). 2.4L engine

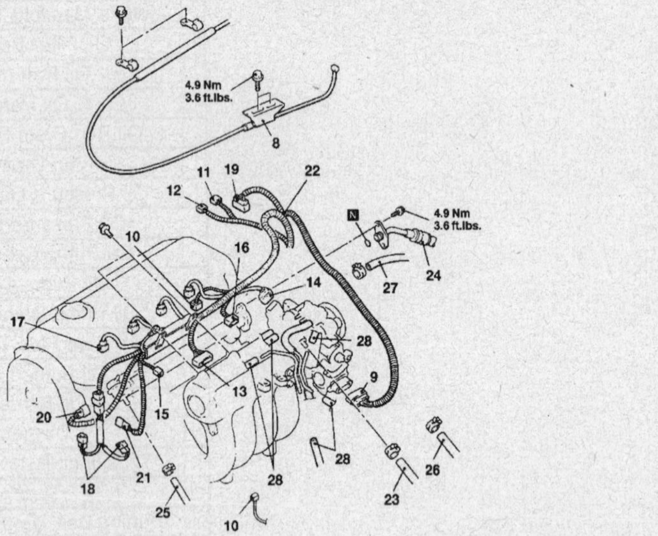

4.9 Nm
3.6 ft.lbs.
4.9 Nm
3.6 ft.lbs.

8. Accelerator cable connection
9. Idle air control motor connector
10. Heated oxygen sensor connector
11. Engine coolant temperature gauge unit connector
12. Engine coolant temperature sensor connector
13. Ignition power transistor connector
14. Throttle position sensor connector
15. Capacitor connector
16. Manifold differential pressure sensor connector
17. Injector connectors
18. Ignition coil connector
19. Camshaft position sensor connector
20. Crankshaft position sensor connector
21. Air conditioning compressor connector
22. Control wiring harness
23. Brake booster vacuum hose connection
24. High-pressure fuel hose connection
25. Fuel return hose connection
26. Water hose A connection
27. Water hose B connection
28. Vacuum hoses connection

MT1069600342020X

Fig. 1 Engine assembly (Part 2 of 3). 2.4L engine

ENGINE

REPLACE

1. Relieve fuel system pressure as outlined under "Precautions," then scribe and remove hood.
2. Drain engine coolant into a suitable container, then remove transaxle as outlined under "Transaxle, Replace" in "Clutch & Manual Transaxle" or "Automatic Transaxle."
3. Remove radiator as outlined under "Radiator, Replace," then the engine lower cover.
4. Remove engine assembly in numbered sequence shown in **Fig. 1,** noting the following:
   a. When removing power steering pump and A/C compressor, leave hoses attached and support aside.
   b. Ensure engine is supported when transaxle is removed. A block of wood placed between oil pan and a floor jack will suffice until a suitable engine lifting device can be installed.
5. Reverse procedure to install. Tighten all engine mounting bolts and nuts to specifications.

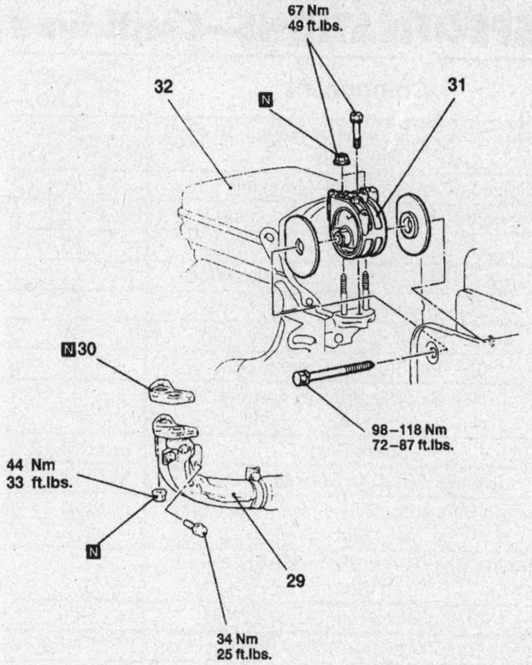
67 Nm
49 ft.lbs.
32
31
N
N 30
98–118 Nm
72–87 ft.lbs.
44 Nm
33 ft.lbs.
N
29
34 Nm
25 ft.lbs.

29. Front exhaust pipe connection
30. Gasket
31. Engine mount bracket assembly
32. Engine assembly

MT1069600342030X

Fig. 1 Engine assembly (Part 3 of 3). 2.4L engine

TIGHTENING SPECIFICATIONS

Year	Component	Torque/ Ft. Lbs.
1996	Accelerator Cable Bracket	3.6
	Air Intake Hose Clamp	3
	Alternator Adjustment Bolt	10
	Alternator Bracket Pivot Bolt	17
	Bellhousing Cover Bolts	7
	Camshaft Position Sensor Bolt	9
	Center Member Attaching Bolts (Front)	64
	Center Member Attaching Bolts (Rear)	50–56
	Crankshaft Pulley Bolts	18
	Dynamic Damper Mounting Bolts	4
	Engine Hanger To Exhaust Manifold Nuts	18–21
	Engine Mount Bracket Through Bolt	85
	Engine Mount Bracket To Engine Bolt & Nut	49
	Exhaust Manifold Mounting Nuts	20-22
	Front Exhaust Pipe Bracket Bolts	25
	Front Exhaust Pipe To Exhaust Manifold Nuts	33
	Front Roll Stopper Bracket Bolts	32
	Front Roll Stopper Bracket Through Bolt Nut	41
	Heat Protector	10

Continued

TIGHTENING SPECIFICATIONS—Continued

Year	Component	Torque/ Ft. Lbs.
1996	High Pressure Fuel Hose Flange To Fuel Rail Bolts	3.6
	Ignition Coil Assembly Mounting Bolt	7
	Ignition Power Transistor Mounting Bolt	3.6
	Oil Dipstick Tube Guide Bolt	43
	Power Steering Pump Mounting Bolt	21
	Power Steering Pump Pivot Bolt	16
	Power Steering Pump Pulley Bolts	21
	Rear Roll Stopper Bracket Bolts	32
	Rear Roll Stopper Bracket Through Bolt Nut	32
	Spark Plugs	18
	Timing Belt Auto Tensioner Bolt	17
	Timing Belt Auto Tensioner Pulley Center Bolt	35
	Timing Belt "B" Tensioner Pulley Center Bolt	14
	Timing Belt Front Cover Bolts	②
	Timing Belt Tensioner Pulley Bracket Bolts	17–19
	Transaxle Mount Bracket Bolt	51
	Transaxle Mount Bolt	①
	Water Inlet Pipe Bracket	10
	Water Pump Pulley Bolts	8

① — 6 mm diameter bolts, 8 ft. lbs.; 8 mm diameter bolts, 20 ft. lbs.; 10 mm diameter bolt, 36 ft. lbs.

② — M6 flange bolt, 8 ft. lbs.; M6 washer bolt, 7 ft. lbs.; M8 bolt, 10 ft. lbs.

3.0L Engine

NOTE: On Air Bag Equipped Models, Refer To "Air Bag System Precautions" Located In The Front Of This Manual For System Disarming & Arming Procedures.

INDEX

	Page No.
Belt Tension Data	24-58
Camshaft, Replace	24-57
Compression Pressure	24-53
Cooling System Bleed	24-58
Cylinder Head, Replace	24-55
Engine Mount, Replace	24-53
Engine Mounts	24-53
Engine Roll Stopper	24-53
Transaxle Mounts	24-53
Engine Rebuilding Specifications	29-1
Engine, Replace	24-54
Exhaust Manifold, Replace	24-55
Fuel Filter, Replace	24-60
Fuel Pump, Replace	24-58
Intake Manifold, Replace	24-54
Air Intake Manifold	24-55
Air Intake Plenum	24-54
Oil Cooler, Replace	24-58
Oil Pan, Replace	24-58
Oil Pump, Replace	24-58
Oil Pump Service	24-58
Piston & Rod Assembly	24-57
Precautions	24-53
Air Bag Systems	24-53
Fuel System Pressure Relief	24-53
Radiator, Replace	24-58
Thermostat, Replace	24-58
Tightening Specifications	24-67
Timing Belt, Replace	24-56
Turbocharger, Replace	24-60
Valve Adjustment	24-56
Valve Clearance Specifications	24-56
Valve Cover, Replace	24-56
Water Pump, Replace	24-58

PRECAUTIONS

AIR BAG SYSTEMS

Refer to "Air Bag System Precautions" in the front of this manual for system disarming and arming procedures.

FUEL SYSTEM PRESSURE RELIEF

Before any fuel system service can be performed, the fuel pressure in the fuel system must be released to prevent personal injury or damage to the vehicle.

1. Remove fuel gauge cover in luggage compartment.
2. Disconnect fuel pump harness connector.
3. Start engine and allow to idle.
4. When engine stops idling, turn ignition switch to Off position.
5. After fuel system repairs are complete, connect fuel pump harness connector.
6. Apply body sealant No. 8509, or equivalent, to fuel gauge cover, then install cover.

COMPRESSION PRESSURE

Refer to **Fig. 1** for compression pressure data.

Engine	Standard, psi @ RPM	Minimum, psi @ RPM	Maximum Variation Between Cylinders, psi
SOHC	171 @ 250-400	127 @ 250-400	14
DOHC①	185 @ 250-400	139 @ 250-400	14
DOHC②	156 @ 250-400	115 @ 250-400	14

① — Non-turbocharged. ② — Turbocharged.

Fig. 1 Compression pressure data. 3000GT

ENGINE MOUNT

REPLACE

ENGINE MOUNTS

1. Raise and support engine to remove weight off mounts using suitable engine jack.
2. Replace engine mounts in numbered sequence as shown, **Fig. 2,** moving cruise control actuator out of the way.
3. Ensure arrow mark on mounting stopper is pointing away from engine when installing engine mounting bracket, **Fig. 3.**

TRANSAXLE MOUNTS

1. Using suitable transmission jack, raise and support transaxle to remove weight off mounts.
2. Remove air cleaner assembly.
3. Replace transaxle mounts in numbered sequence as shown, **Fig. 4.**
4. Ensure arrow mark on mounting stopper is pointing toward engine when attaching transaxle mounting bracket, **Fig. 5.**

ENGINE ROLL STOPPER

1. **On turbocharged models,** remove condenser, then condenser cooling fan assembly and left catalytic converter.
2. **On all models,** replace engine front and rear roll stopper brackets in numbered sequence as shown, **Fig. 6.** Slightly raise rear roll stopper bracket, then twist rear roll stopper bracket up and lift upward to remove, **Fig. 7.**
3. When installing rear roll stopper bracket, install bracket and bracket to engine bolt as shown, **Fig. 8.**

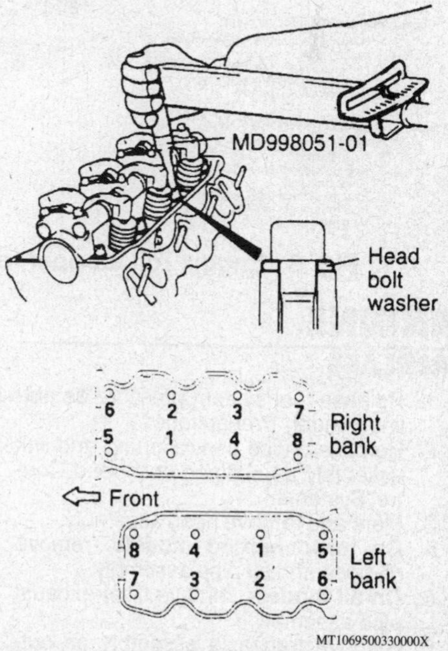

MD998051-01
Head
bolt
washer
6
2
3
7
5
1
4
8
Right bank
Front
8
4
1
5
7
3
2
6
Left bank
MT1069500330000X

Fig. 2 Engine mount replacement

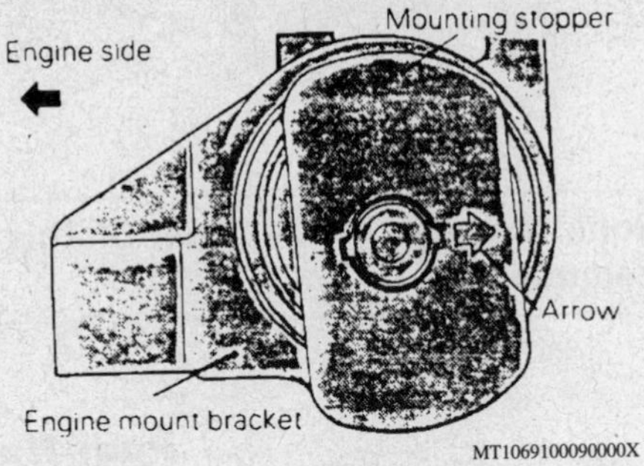

Engine side
Mounting stopper
Arrow
Engine mount bracket
MT1069100090000X

Fig. 3 Engine mounting stopper installation

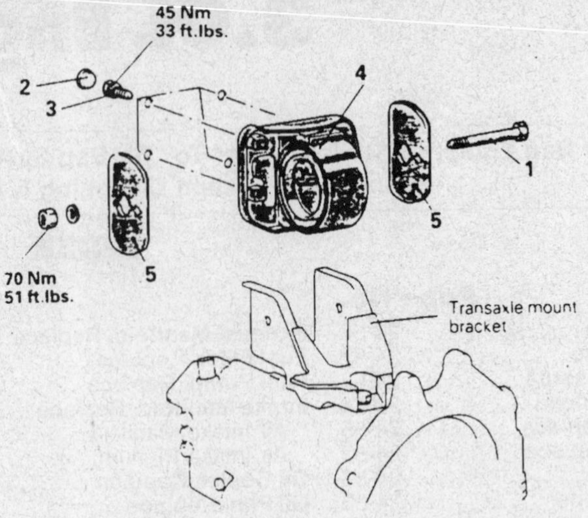

45 Nm
33 ft.lbs.
2
3
4
1
5
70 Nm
51 ft.lbs.
5
Transaxle mount bracket

Removal steps

1. Transaxle mount bracket and transaxle connection bolt
2. Cap
3. Transaxle mount bracket installation bolt
4. Transaxle mount bracket
5. Mounting stopper

MT1069100092000X

Fig. 4 Transaxle mount replacement

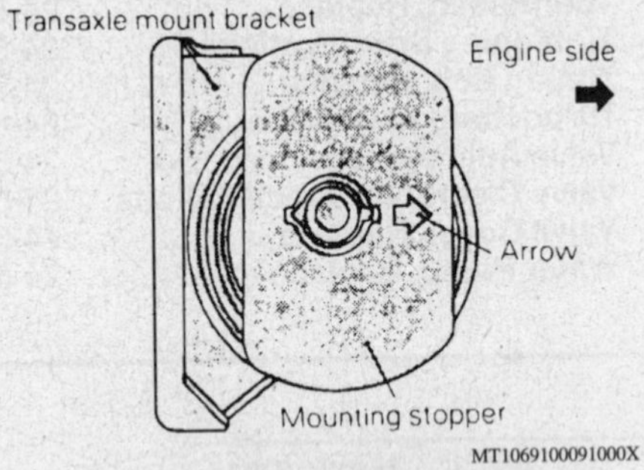

Transaxle mount bracket
Engine side
Arrow
Mounting stopper
MT1069100091000X

Fig. 5 Transaxle mounting stopper installation

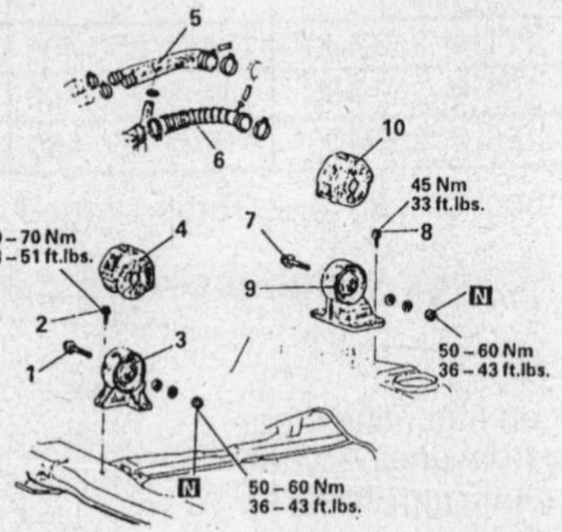

5
6
10
45 Nm
33 ft.lbs.
60 - 70 Nm
43 - 51 ft.lbs.
4
7
8
9
2
3
1
50 - 60 Nm
36 - 43 ft.lbs.
50 - 60 Nm
36 - 43 ft.lbs.

Front stopper bracket removal steps

1. Front roll stopper bracket and engine connection bolt
2. Front roll stopper bracket installation bolt
3. Front roll stopper bracket
4. Heat protector <Turbo>

Rear roll stopper bracket removal steps

5. Air hose A <Turbo>
6. Air intake hose C <Turbo>
7. Rear roll stopper bracket and engine connection bolt
8. Rear roll stopper bracket installation bolt
9. Rear roll stopper bracket
10. Heat protector <Turbo>

MT1069100093000X

Fig. 6 Engine roll stopper replacement

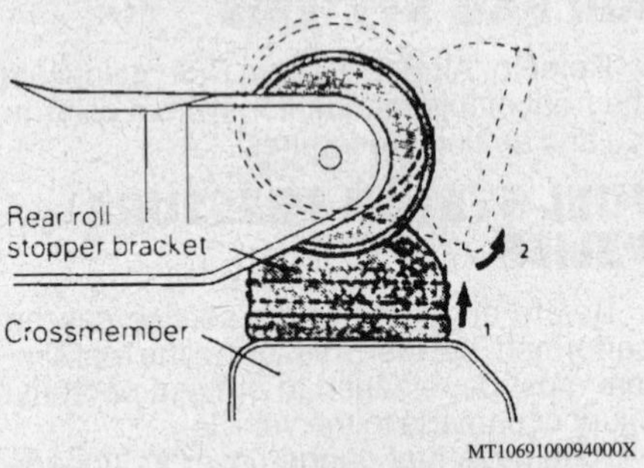

Rear roll stopper bracket
Crossmember
2
1
MT1069100094000X

Fig. 7 Rear roll stopper removal

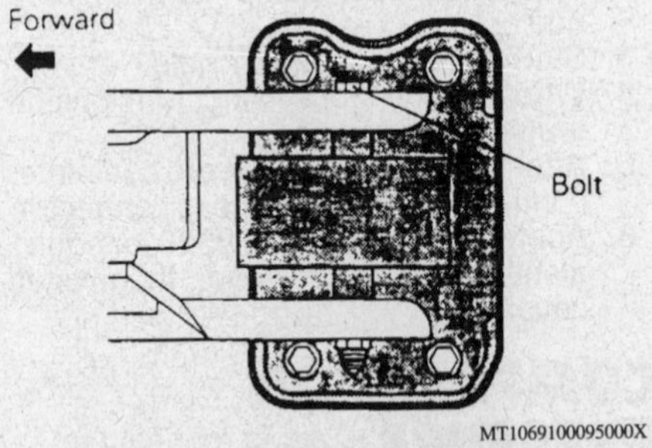

Forward
Bolt
MT1069100095000X

Fig. 8 Rear roll stopper installation

ENGINE

REPLACE

1. Release fuel system pressure as outlined under "Precautions."
2. Remove cruise control pump and link assembly as outlined in "Speed Control Systems."
3. Mark and remove hood assembly.
4. **On turbocharged models,** remove air hose and air pipe assembly.
5. **On all models,** remove front exhaust pipe assembly.
6. Remove transaxle assembly as outlined under "Transaxle, Replace" in "Clutch & Manual Transaxle"or "Automatic Transaxle."
7. Remove radiator assembly.
8. Remove engine assembly in numbered sequence as shown, **Fig. 9,** noting the following:
   a. Disconnect air conditioner compressor and power steering oil pump leaving hoses connected.
   b. Using suitable engine lifting device, raise and support engine to remove weight off mounts, then remove engine mount bracket as outlined under "Engine Mount, Replace."
   c. Ensuring cables, hoses and wire harness connectors are removed, raise engine assembly upward out of engine compartment.
9. Reverse procedure to install, **Fig. 9,** noting the following:
   a. Ensure all cables hoses and wire harness connectors are in correct position before completing engine installation.
   b. Ensure arrow mark on stopper is in direction shown, **Fig. 3,** when attaching engine mounting bracket.

INTAKE MANIFOLD

REPLACE

AIR INTAKE PLENUM

1. Release fuel system pressure as outlined under "Precautions."
2. Replace air intake plenum in numbered sequence shown, **Figs. 10 and**

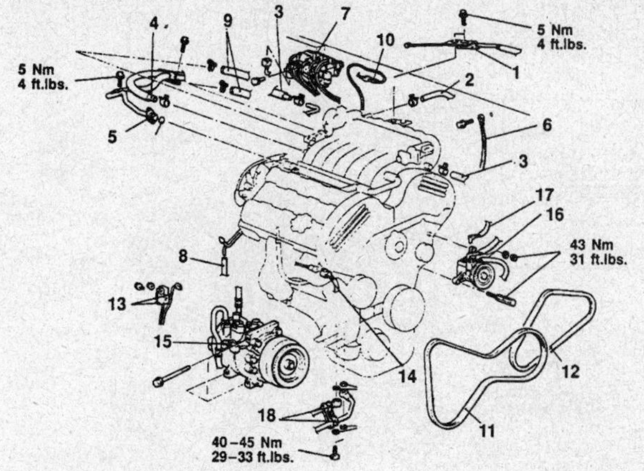
5 Nm
4 ft.lbs.
5 Nm
4 ft.lbs.
43 Nm
31 ft.lbs.
40–45 Nm
29–33 ft.lbs.

Removal steps

1. Accelerator cable connection
2. Brake booster vacuum hose connection
3. Booster vacuum hose connection <Turbo>
4. Fuel return hose connection
5. Fuel high pressure hose connection
6. Ground cable connection
7. Solenoid valve assembly
8. Vapor hose connection
9. Heater hose connection
10. EGR temperature sensor connector <Vehicles for California>
11. Drive belt (Generator and air conditioning)
12. Drive belt (Power steering)
13. Generator harness connection
14. Heated oxygen sensor connector <Turbo>
15. Air conditioning compressor
16. Power steering oil pump
17. Oil pressure switch connector (Power steering)
18. Oil cooler pipes connection <Turbo>

MT1069500332010X

Fig. 9 Engine assembly replacement (Part 1 of 2)

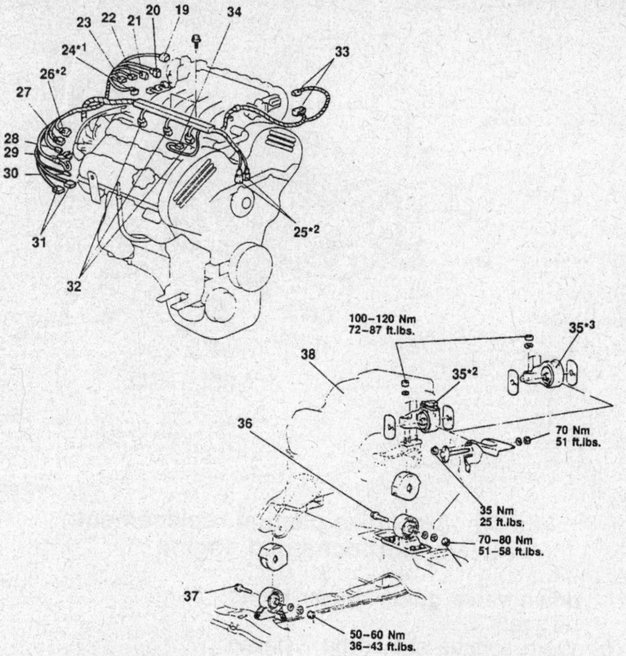
100–120 Nm
72–87 ft.lbs.
70 Nm
51 ft.lbs.
35 Nm
25 ft.lbs.
70–80 Nm
51–58 ft.lbs.
50–60 Nm
36–43 ft.lbs.

19. Idle air control motor connector
20. TPS connector
21. Oil pressure switch and oil pressure gauge unit connector
22. Fuel injector harness connector
23. Knock sensor connector
24. Crankshaft position sensor connector*1
25. Crankshaft position sensor and camshaft position sensor connector*2
26. Engine coolant temperature switch connector (Air conditioning)*2
27. Engine coolant temperature sensor connector
28. Engine coolant temperature gauge unit connector
29. Condenser connector
30. Ignition coil connector
31. Ignition power transistor connector
32. Fuel injector connector
33. Variable induction motor connector <Non-Turbo>
34. Heated oxygen sensor connector <Turbo>
35. Engine mounting bracket
36. Rear roll stopper bracket and engine connection bolt
37. Front roll stopper bracket and engine connection bolt
38. Engine assembly

NOTE
*1 1992 model
*2 1993 model
*3 1994 model

MT1069500332020X

Fig. 9 Engine assembly replacement (Part 2 of 2)

11, leaving hoses attached to throttle body when removing plenum.

3. When installing throttle body, ensure gasket protrusion is toward top.

AIR INTAKE MANIFOLD

1. Release fuel system pressure as outlined under “Precautions.”
2. Drain engine coolant into an appropriate container.
3. Remove air intake plenum as outlined previously.
4. Replace intake manifold in numbered sequence shown, **Fig. 12.**
5. Install gaskets with protrusions in position shown, **Fig. 13.**
6. **On turbocharged models,** tighten intake manifold mounting nuts using the following procedure:
   a. **Torque** nuts in front bank to 2.2–3.6 ft. lbs.
   b. **Torque** nuts in rear bank to 9–11 ft. lbs.
   c. **Torque** nuts in front bank to 9–11 ft. lbs.
   d. Repeat steps b and c one more time.
7. **On all models,** apply lubricant sparingly to intake manifold mounting nuts.

EXHAUST MANIFOLD

REPLACE

1. **On turbocharged models,** remove turbocharger assembly as outlined under “Turbocharger, Replace.”
2. **On non-turbocharged models,** remove front exhaust pipe and condenser fan motor assembly.
3. **On all models,** replace exhaust manifold in numbered sequence as shown, **Figs. 14 and 15.**
4. **On turbocharged models,** install rear exhaust manifold nuts in the following order:
   a. **Torque** nuts marked A to 22 ft. lbs., **Fig. 16.**
   b. **Torque** nuts marked B to 34–38 ft. lbs.
   c. Back off nuts marked B until a **torque** of 7 ft. lbs. is reached.
   d. **Torque** nuts marked B to 21–22 ft. lbs.
   e. Install cone disc spring with grooved side facing up, then the nut, cone disc spring and washer in direction shown.
5. **On turbocharged models,** with the exhaust manifold stay resting on exhaust manifold, fit it along manifold over studs.
6. **On turbocharged models,** install front exhaust manifold nuts in the following order:
   a. **Torque** nuts marked C to 22 ft. lbs., **Fig. 17.**
   b. Temporarily install turbocharger assembly.
   c. **Torque** nut marked D to 22 ft, lbs.
   d. **Torque** nuts marked E and F to 34–38 ft. lbs.
   e. Back off nuts marked E and F until a **torque**of 7 ft. lbs. is reached.
   f. **Torque** nuts marked E and F to 21–22 ft. lbs.
   g. Install cone disc spring with grooved side facing up, then the nut, cone disc spring and washer in direction shown.

CYLINDER HEAD

REPLACE

1. Remove timing belt as outlined under “Timing Belt, Replace.”
2. Remove camshafts as outlined under “Camshaft Replace.”
3. Remove exhaust manifolds as outlined under “Exhaust Manifold, Replace.”
4. Remove cylinder head and valves in numbered sequence as shown, **Fig. 18,** noting the following:
   a. Using cylinder head bolt wrench tool No. MD998051-01, or equivalent, remove cylinder head bolts.
   b. Using suitable valve spring compressor tool, remove valve spring retaining locks.
5. Using a suitable straightedge and feeler gauge, measure flatness of cylinder head ensuring head flatness is 0.0012 inch or less. If specification is greater, grind head no more than 0.008 inch.
6. Reverse procedure to install, **Fig. 18,** noting the following:
   a. Install spring seat, then the valve stem oil seal using valve stem oil seal installer tool No. MD998763, or equivalent. **Incorrect installation of seal without using oil seal installer tool will result in poor sealing and cause oil leakage**

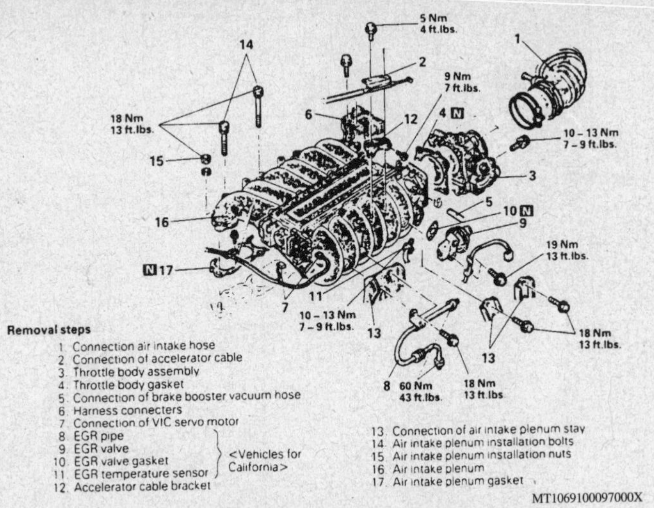

5 Nm
4 ft.lbs.
9 Nm
7 ft.lbs.
18 Nm
13 ft.lbs.
10 – 13 Nm
7 – 9 ft.lbs.
19 Nm
13 ft.lbs.
60 Nm
43 ft.lbs.
Removal steps
1. Connection air intake hose
2. Connection of accelerator cable
3. Throttle body assembly
4. Throttle body gasket
5. Connection of brake booster vacuum hose
6. Harness connecters
7. Connection of VIC servo motor
8. EGR pipe
9. EGR valve
10. EGR valve gasket
11. EGR temperature sensor
12. Accelerator cable bracket
<Vehicles for California>
13. Connection of air intake plenum stay
14. Air intake plenum installation bolts
15. Air intake plenum installation nuts
16. Air intake plenum
17. Air intake plenum gasket
MT1069100097000X

Fig. 10 Air intake plenum replacement. Non-turbocharged engine

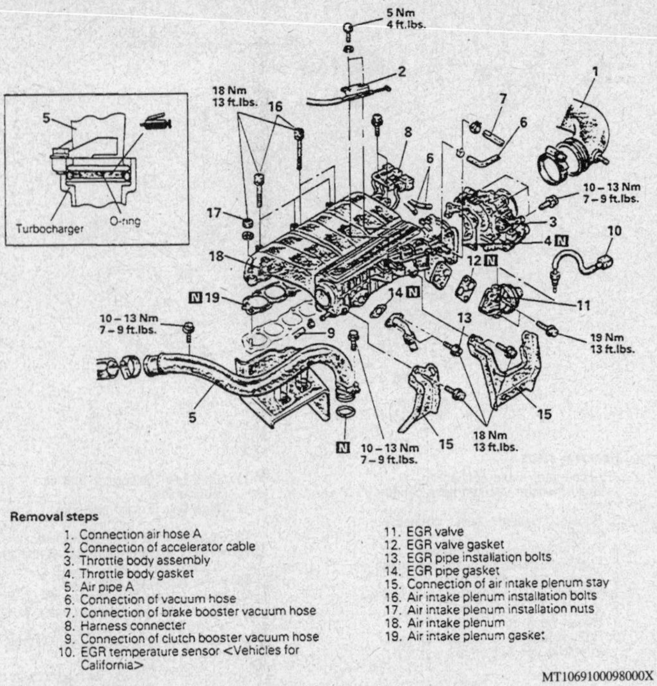

Turbocharger
O-ring
5 Nm
4 ft.lbs.
18 Nm
13 ft.lbs.
10 – 13 Nm
7 – 9 ft.lbs.
19 Nm
13 ft.lbs.
Removal steps
1. Connection air hose A
2. Connection of accelerator cable
3. Throttle body assembly
4. Throttle body gasket
5. Air pipe A
6. Connection of vacuum hose
7. Connection of brake booster vacuum hose
8. Harness connecter
9. Connection of clutch booster vacuum hose
10. EGR temperature sensor <Vehicles for California>
11. EGR valve
12. EGR valve gasket
13. EGR pipe installation bolts
14. EGR pipe gasket
15. Connection of air intake plenum stay
16. Air intake plenum installation bolts
17. Air intake plenum installation nuts
18. Air intake plenum
19. Air intake plenum gasket
MT1069100098000X

Fig. 11 Air intake plenum replacement. Turbocharged engine

down valve guide. Never reuse oil seals.

b. Valve springs should be installed with enamel coated side toward valve spring retainer.
c. Using suitable valve spring compression tool, install valve spring retainers.
d. Ensure correct head gasket is used on engine. Cylinder head gaskets marked with a 2DN are for non-turbocharged engines and cylinder head gaskets marked with a 2DT are for turbocharged engines.
e. Using sequence shown in **Fig. 19, torque** cylinder head bolts in two or three steps to 80 ft. lbs.
f. **On turbo models,** loosen head bolts, then repeat step e.

VALVE COVER

REPLACE

1. Remove timing belt as outlined under "Timing Belt, Replace."
2. Remove intake manifold as outlined under "Intake Manifold, Replace."
3. Replace camshaft oil seals in numbered sequence as shown, **Fig. 20,** noting the following:
   a. Using a suitable wrench on hexagonal part of camshaft, loosen camshaft sprocket bolt.
   b. Cut out a portion in camshaft oil seal lip, **Fig. 21.**
   c. Cover tip of a suitable screwdriver with a clean soft cloth and pry out seal at cut out portion of seal. **Use care not to damage camshaft or cylinder head.**
4. Reverse procedure to install, **Fig. 20,** noting the following:
   a. Apply small amount of engine oil to seal lip.
   b. Using camshaft oil seal installer tool No. MD998761, or equivalent, insert oil seal.
   c. Using a suitable wrench on hexagonal part of camshaft, tighten camshaft sprocket pulley bolt to specifications.
   d. Tighten valve cover bolts in order as shown, **Fig. 22. No. 5 bolt (0.79 inch) in rear bank differs from other bolts in length. Remaining bolts in rear bank are 0.39 inch long. Bolts are color coded for installation, front bank bolts are black and rear bank bolts are green. When rocker cover gasket has been replaced, tighten bolts in this order and then torque** bolts 1 through 6 to 2.9 ft. lbs.

VALVE CLEARANCE SPECIFICATIONS

Valve Clearance	
Intake	**Exhaust**
.0008–.0020	.0020–.0035

VALVE ADJUSTMENT

Because automatic lash adjusters are used, no adjustment is necessary.

TIMING BELT

REPLACE

The timing belt should be replaced every 60,000 miles.

1. **On models less active aero system,** remove lefthand lower cover.
2. **On models with active aero system,** remove front lower cover in numbered sequence as shown, **Fig. 23.** Install air dam link assembly in the operative condition for ease of front lower cover panel.
3. **On all models,** remove cruise control pump and link assembly as outlined in "Speed Control Systems."
4. Remove alternator assembly.
5. Using suitable engine lifting device, raise and support engine to remove weight off engine mounts.
6. Remove timing belt in numbered sequence as shown, **Fig. 24,** noting the following:
   a. Using crankshaft pulley holder and end yoke holder tools, No. MD998754 and MB990767-01, or equivalents, remove crankshaft pulley.
   b. Remove engine support bracket in numbered sequence as shown, **Fig. 25.** While spraying lubricant, slowly remove reamer bolt.
   c. Remove timing belt as outlined in steps d through f.
   d. Align timing marks, **Fig. 26.**
   e. Mark rotational direction on back side of timing.
   f. Loosen center bolt on tensioner pulley, then remove timing belt. **Coolant or oil on timing belt shortens belt life drastically, removed timing belt, sprocket and tensioner must be free from oil and coolant.**
7. Install auto tensioner as follows:
   a. Secure auto tensioner in a soft jaw vise in a level position, **Fig. 27.**
   b. Push in rod slowly with vise until set hole (A) is aligned with pin hole (B).
   c. Insert a 0.055 inch thick wire into set and pin holes.
   d. Remove auto tensioner from vise and install on engine.
8. Align timing marks on camshaft or crankshaft sprocket.
9. Install crankshaft pulley. Shift timing mark on crankshaft sprocket by three

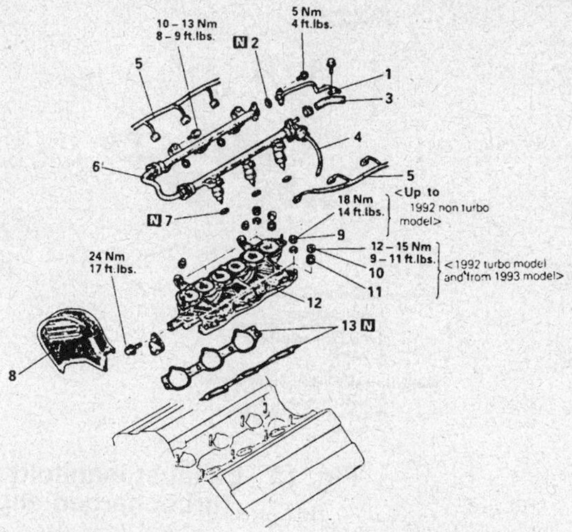
10 – 13 Nm
8 – 9 ft.lbs.
5 Nm
4 ft.lbs.
18 Nm
14 ft.lbs.
<Up to
1992 non turbo
model>
12 – 15 Nm
9 – 11 ft.lbs.
<1992 turbo model
and from 1993 model>
24 Nm
17 ft.lbs.

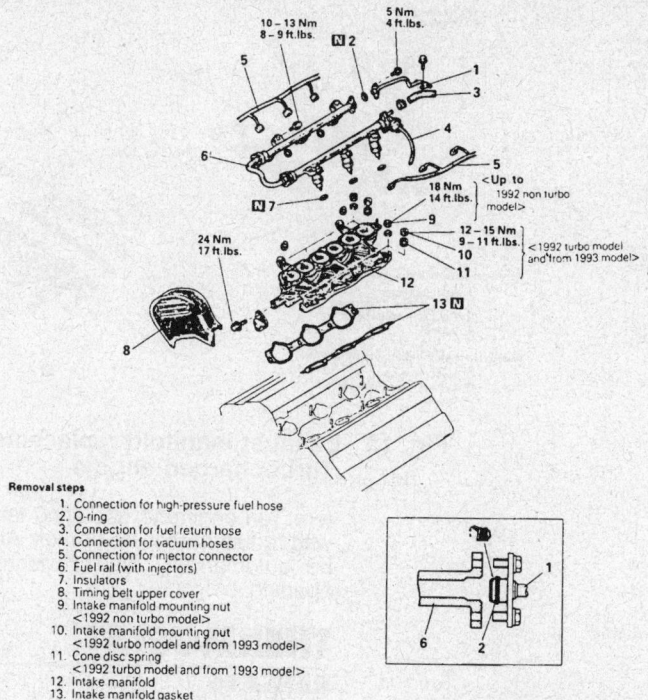

Removal steps
1. Connection for high-pressure fuel hose
2. O-ring
3. Connection for fuel return hose
4. Connection for vacuum hoses
5. Connection for injector connector
6. Fuel rail (with injectors)
7. Insulators
8. Timing belt upper cover
9. Intake manifold mounting nut
<1992 non turbo model>
10. Intake manifold mounting nut
<1992 turbo model and from 1993 model>
11. Cone disc spring
<1992 turbo model and from 1993 model>
12. Intake manifold
13. Intake manifold gasket

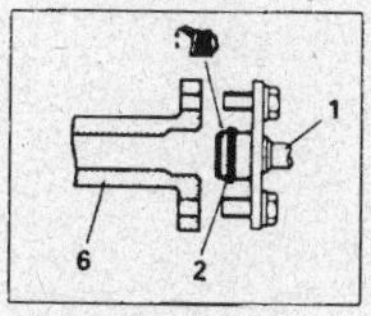

MT1059100008000X

Fig. 12 Intake manifold replacement

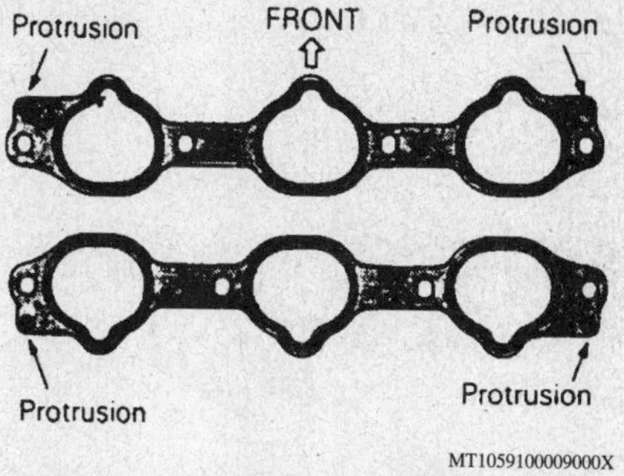
Protrusion
FRONT
Protrusion
Protrusion
Protrusion

MT1059100009000X

Fig. 13 Intake manifold gasket installation

teeth to lower the position on the No. 1 cylinder slightly from the TDC position on compression stroke. **Turning camshaft sprocket with piston in No. 1 cylinder at TDC may cause valves to interfere with piston.**

10. Ensure timing marks on camshaft sprockets for intake and exhaust valves are not within range A in **Fig. 28.** If timing mark is within range A, turn camshaft sprocket to move timing mark to area closest to range A. **In range A, cam lobe on camshaft lifts valve through rocker arm and camshaft sprocket is apt to rotate by reaction force of valve spring. Use care not to have finger pinched between sprockets.**
11. Turn camshaft sprocket for either intake or exhaust valve to locate timing mark as shown, **Fig. 29,** then turn other camshaft to locate timing mark as shown. **If intake and exhaust valves of same cylinder lift at the same time, interference with each other may result. Therefore, turn intake valve camshaft sprocket and exhaust valve camshaft alternately.**
12. Turn camshaft sprocket clockwise to align timing marks. If camshaft sprocket has been turned excessively, turn it counterclockwise to align timing marks.
13. Align timing mark of crankshaft sprocket. **Shift timing mark of crankshaft sprocket one tooth in counterclockwise direction to aid in belt installation.**
14. Using spring loaded paper clips, secure camshaft sprockets with suitable box end wrenches, then install timing belt in the following order: (1) Front exhaust camshaft to (2) front intake camshaft to (3) water pump to (4) rear intake camshaft to (5) rear exhaust camshaft to (6) idler pulley to (7) crankshaft to (8) tensioner pulley, **Fig. 30.** Do not allow belt to slacken.
15. Turn tensioner pulley ensuring pin holes are located above center bolt, then press tensioner pulley against timing belt and, at the same time, temporarily tighten center bolt, **Fig. 31.**
16. Ensure all timing marks are still aligned properly.
17. Remove loaded paper clips.
18. Adjust timing belt as follows:
    a. Rotate crankshaft ¼ turning counterclockwise, then rotate clockwise until timing marks are aligned.
    b. Loosen center bolt on tensioner pulley. Using tensioner pulley socket wrench tool No. MD998767, or equivalent, and torque wrench, apply a **torque** of 7 ft. lbs. to timing belt and tighten tensioner center bolt simultaneously.
    c. Remove set pin from auto tensioner, ensuring set pin cam be easily removed.
    d. Rotate crankshaft two turns clockwise and let stand for five minutes or more.
    e. Ensure set pin can be easily removed from, and installed to, the auto tensioner. If set pin cannot be easily inserted, the auto tensioner is normal if its rod protrusion is within 0.149–0.177 inch, **Fig. 32.** If protrusion is out of specification, repeat procedure.
    f. Ensure timing marks on all sprockets are aligned properly.
19. Reverse procedure to install as shown, **Fig. 24,** noting the following:
    a. Install lower timing cover bolts as shown, **Fig. 33.**
    b. Install engine support bracket bolts as shown, **Fig. 34.** While installing reamer bolt, tighten slowly while spraying lubricant on reamer area.
    c. Install crankshaft pulley using removal tools.

CAMSHAFT

REPLACE

1. Remove valve covers as outlined under "Valve Cover, Replace."
2. Replace rocker arm and camshaft in numbered sequence as shown, **Fig. 35,** noting the following:
    a. Immerse lash adjuster in clean diesel fuel. Using small wire, move plunger up and down four to five times while pushing down lightly on the check ball to bleed out air. Install lash adjuster into cylinder head.
    b. Turn crankshaft to bring No. 1 cylinder to TDC.
    c. Ensure rocker arm is installed correctly on valve lash adjuster and valve.
    d. Install camshaft noting identification mark stamped on hexagonal section. Camshaft marked with a V is the intake side and camshaft marked with a C is exhaust side.
    e. Install camshafts with their dowel pins positioned as shown, **Fig. 36.**
    f. Install bearing caps noting identification mark and cap number. Bearing caps Nos. 2, 3 and 4 bear the front mark. Install these caps with mark lined up with front mark on cylinder head. Caps marked with an I are for intake side and caps marked with an E are exhaust side, **Fig. 37.**
    g. Tighten bearing cap bolts gradually in two or three steps, then tighten to specifications.
    h. Using semicircular packing installer tool No. MD998762, or equivalent, install semicircular packing.

PISTON & ROD ASSEMBLY

When installing piston and rod assemblies, ensure front marks are pointed toward front of engine (timing belt side), **Fig. 38.**

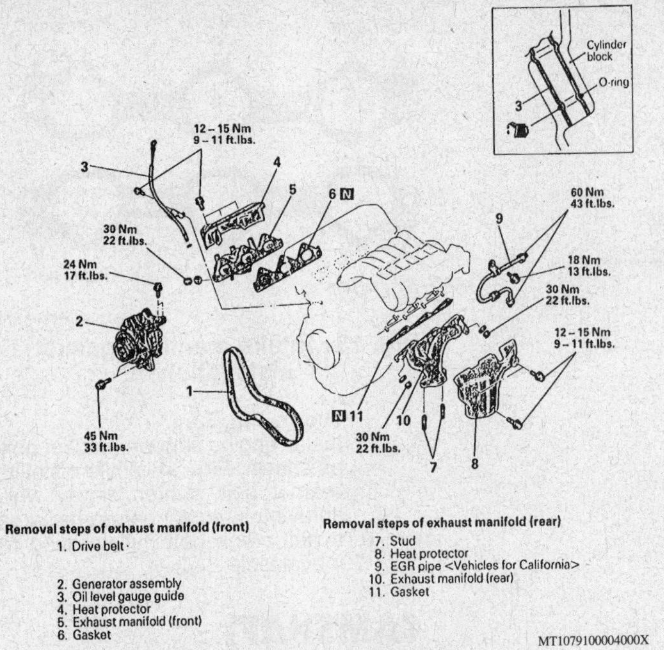
Cylinder block
O-ring
12 – 15 Nm
9 – 11 ft.lbs.
30 Nm
22 ft.lbs.
24 Nm
17 ft.lbs.
45 Nm
33 ft.lbs.
60 Nm
43 ft.lbs.
18 Nm
13 ft.lbs.
30 Nm
22 ft.lbs.
12 – 15 Nm
9 – 11 ft.lbs.
30 Nm
22 ft.lbs.
Removal steps of exhaust manifold (front)
1. Drive belt
2. Generator assembly
3. Oil level gauge guide
4. Heat protector
5. Exhaust manifold (front)
6. Gasket
Removal steps of exhaust manifold (rear)
7. Stud
8. Heat protector
9. EGR pipe <Vehicles for California>
10. Exhaust manifold (rear)
11. Gasket
MT1079100004000X

Fig. 14 Exhaust manifold replacement. Non-turbocharged engine

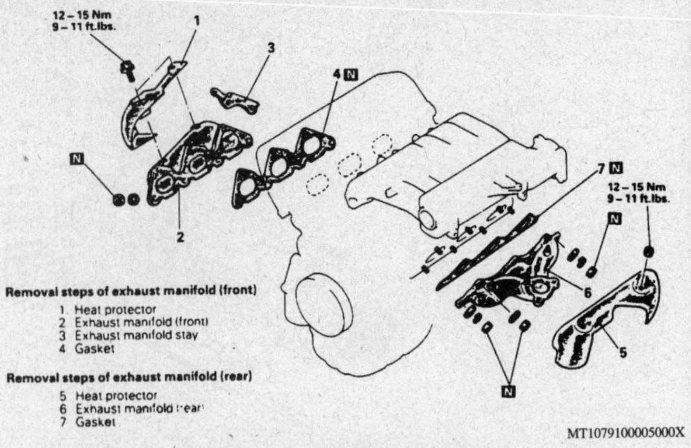
12 – 15 Nm
9 – 11 ft.lbs.
12 – 15 Nm
9 – 11 ft.lbs.
Removal steps of exhaust manifold (front)
1. Heat protector
2. Exhaust manifold (front)
3. Exhaust manifold stay
4. Gasket
Removal steps of exhaust manifold (rear)
5. Heat protector
6. Exhaust manifold (rear)
7. Gasket
MT1079100005000X

Fig. 15 Exhaust manifold replacement. Turbocharged engine

OIL PAN

REPLACE

1. Drain engine oil into an appropriate container.
2. **On models with active aero system,** remove front lower cover in numbered sequence as shown, **Fig. 23,** then install air dam link assembly in operative condition for ease of front lower cover panel installation.
3. **On all models,** remove engine lower cover.
4. Remove front exhaust pipe.
5. Remove transfer assembly as outlined under "Transfer Case, Replace" in "Clutch & Manual Transaxle" or "Automatic Transaxle."
6. Replace oil pan and screen in numbered sequence as shown, **Fig. 39.**
7. Reverse procedure to install, noting the following:
   a. Apply a 0.16 inch diameter bead of sealant around oil pan flange.
   b. Tighten oil pan bolts in sequence as shown, **Fig. 40.**

OIL PUMP

REPLACE

1. Remove engine assembly as outlined under "Engine, Replace."
2. Remove timing belt as outlined under "Timing Belt, Replace."
3. Remove oil pan and pump assembly in numbered sequence as shown, **Fig. 41.**
4. Reverse procedure to install, **Fig. 41,** noting the following:
   a. Install front oil seal using oil seal installer tool No. MD998717, or equivalent.
   b. Apply a 0.16 inch diameter bead of sealant around oil pan flange.
   c. Tighten oil pan bolts in sequence as shown, **Fig. 40.**

OIL PUMP SERVICE

1. Inspect oil pump by assembling rotor on oil pump. Ensure a 0.0039–0.0071 inch body and 0.0016–0.0037 inch side clearance, **Fig. 42.**
2. **On turbocharged models,** ensure oil cooler bypass valve moves smoothly and dimension marked L is 1.358 inches long under normal temperature and humidity and 1.57 inches long after being dipped into oil with a temperature of 212°F.

OIL COOLER

REPLACE

1. Drain engine oil into an appropriate container.
2. Remove front splash shield, then the oil cooler engine oil feed hose.
3. Remove oil cooler engine oil return hose, then the oil cooler engine oil return tube.
4. Remove engine oil cooler.
5. Reverse procedure to install.

BELT TENSION DATA

Adjust belts by applying 22 lbs. of force to belt midway between pulleys as shown, **Fig. 43,** ensuring deflection is as specified in **Fig. 44.**

COOLING SYSTEM BLEED

These engines do not require a specified bleed procedure. After filling cooling system, run engine to operating temperature with radiator/pressure cap off. Air will then be automatically bled through the cap opening.

THERMOSTAT

REPLACE

1. Drain coolant into an appropriate container.
2. Remove thermostat in numbered sequence as shown, **Fig. 45.**
3. Reverse procedure to install, noting the following:
   a. Install thermostat with jiggle valve lined up with mark on thermostat housing, **Fig. 46.**
   b. Align air intake hose "A" notches with marks on air intake hoses "B and C." Insert hoses into air intake hose "A" until bottomed out, **Fig. 47.**

WATER PUMP

REPLACE

1. Drain engine coolant into an appropriate container.
2. Remove power transistor and ignition coil assembly.
3. Remove timing belt as outlined under "Timing Belt, Replace."
4. Remove water pump.
5. Reverse procedure to install, **Fig. 48,** noting the following:
   a. Install water pump bolts in correct location as shown, **Fig. 49.**
   b. Replace inlet water pipe O-ring at both ends and apply water to O-ring to help installation. **Do not allow engine oil or other contaminates to adhere to O-ring.**

RADIATOR

REPLACE

Refer to **Fig. 50,**when replacing radiator.

FUEL PUMP

REPLACE

1. Drain fuel from fuel tank into an appropriate container.

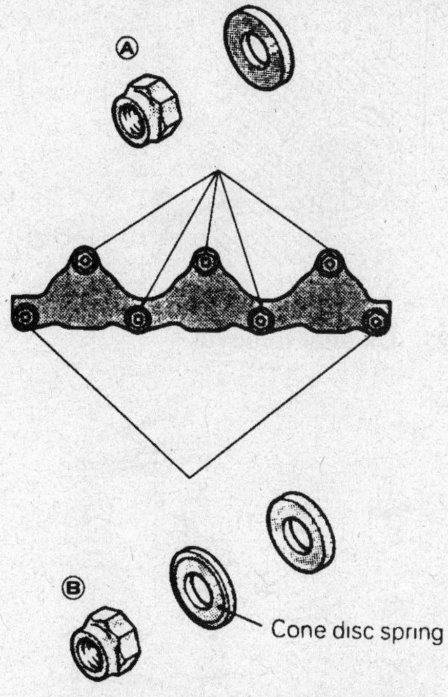
A
B
Cone disc spring

MT1079100006000X

Fig. 16 Rear exhaust manifold nut installation. Turbocharged engine

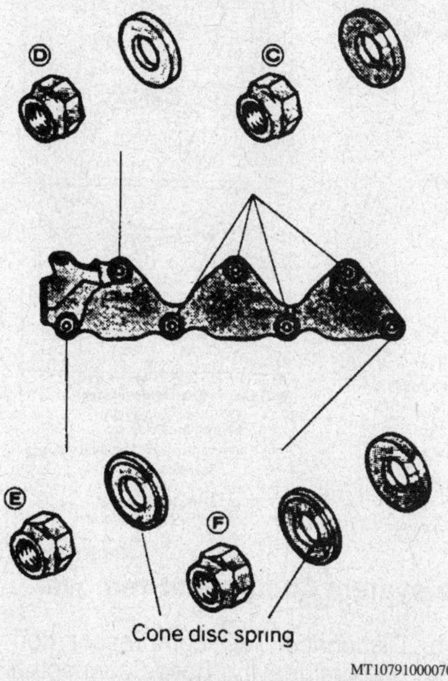
D
C
E
F
Cone disc spring

MT1079100007000X

Fig. 17 Front exhaust manifold nut installation. Turbocharged engine

2. Release fuel system pressure as outlined under "Precautions."
3. Remove fuel pump in numbered sequence as shown, **Fig. 51,** noting the following:
   a. Cover body side high pressure fuel hose connection with a shop towel to prevent splash of fuel that could be caused by residual pressure in fuel line.
   b. Hold pump side nut while disconnecting pump side of high pressure fuel hose.

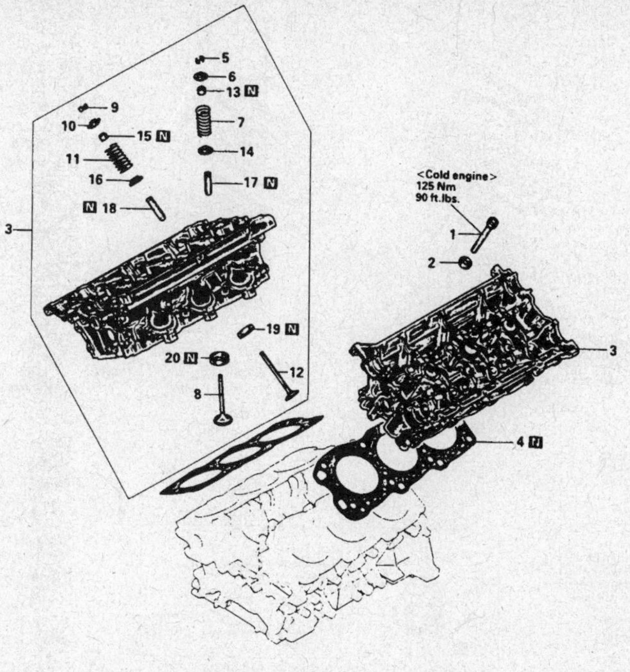
<Cold engine>
125 Nm
90 ft.lbs.

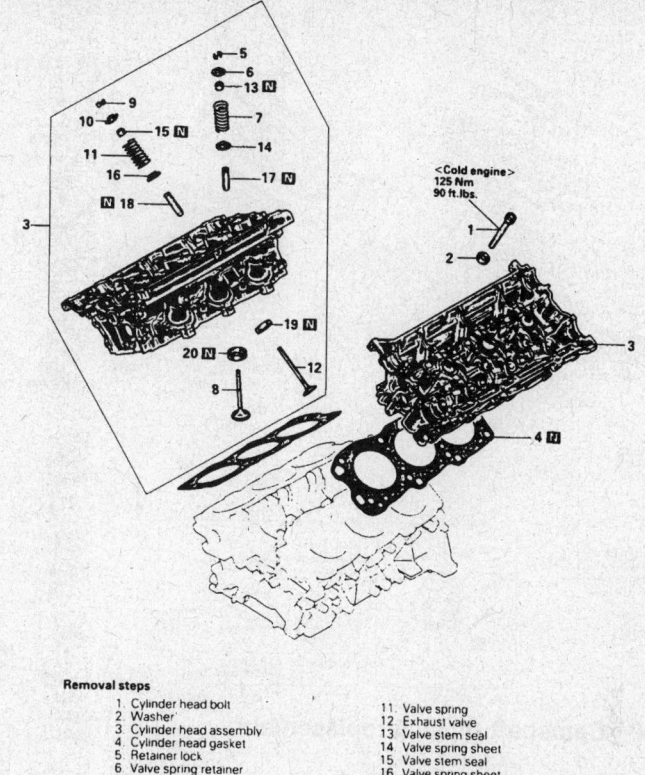

Removal steps

1. Cylinder head bolt
2. Washer
3. Cylinder head assembly
4. Cylinder head gasket
5. Retainer lock
6. Valve spring retainer
7. Valve spring
8. Intake valve
9. Retainer lock
10. Valve spring retainer
11. Valve spring
12. Exhaust valve
13. Valve stem seal
14. Valve spring sheet
15. Valve stem seal
16. Valve spring sheet
17. Intake valve guide
18. Exhaust valve guide
19. Intake valve sheet
20. Exhaust valve sheet

MT1099100032000X

Fig. 18 Cylinder head & valve replacement

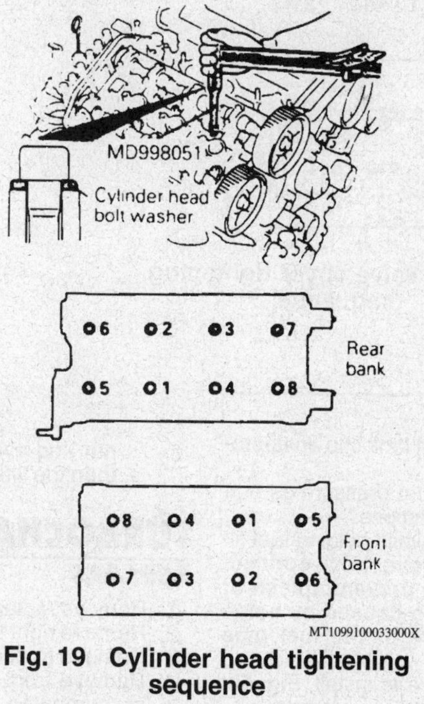
MD998051
Cylinder head bolt washer
Rear bank
Front bank

MT1099100033000X

Fig. 19 Cylinder head tightening sequence

4. Reverse procedure to install, noting the following:
   a. Align three projections of packing with holes in fuel pump and gauge assembly.
   b. Install overfill limiter valve as shown, **Fig. 52.**
   c. Apply body sealant to fuel gauge cover.
5. Reverse procedure to install.

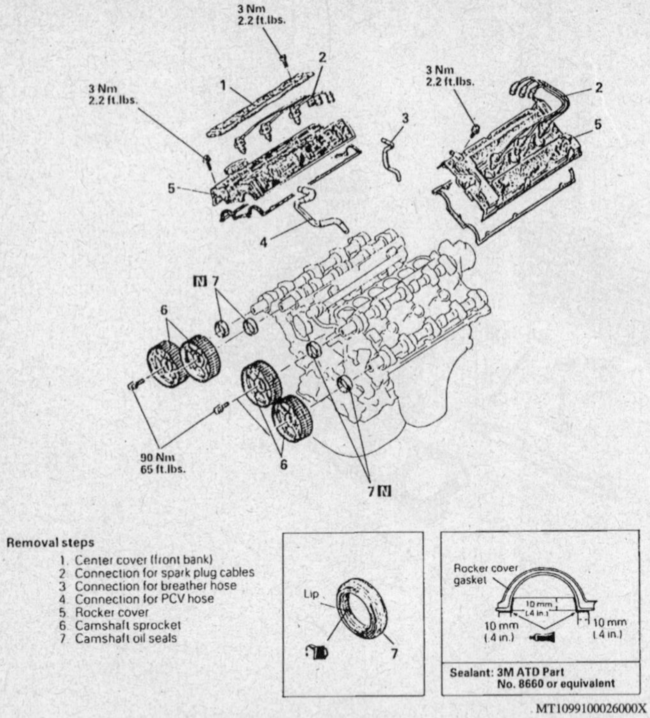
3 Nm
2.2 ft.lbs.
3 Nm
2.2 ft.lbs.
3 Nm
2.2 ft.lbs.
90 Nm
65 ft.lbs.
Removal steps
1. Center cover (front bank)
2. Connection for spark plug cables
3. Connection for breather hose
4. Connection for PCV hose
5. Rocker cover
6. Camshaft sprocket
7. Camshaft oil seals
Lip
Rocker cover gasket
10 mm (.4 in.)
10 mm (.4 in.)
10 mm (.4 in.)
Sealant: 3M ATD Part No. 8660 or equivalent
MT1099100026000X

Fig. 20 Camshaft oil seal replacement

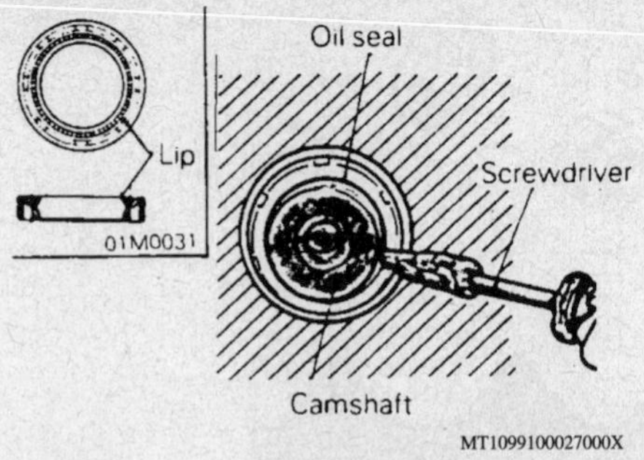
Oil seal
Lip
01M0031
Screwdriver
Camshaft
MT1099100027000X

Fig. 21 Oil seal removal

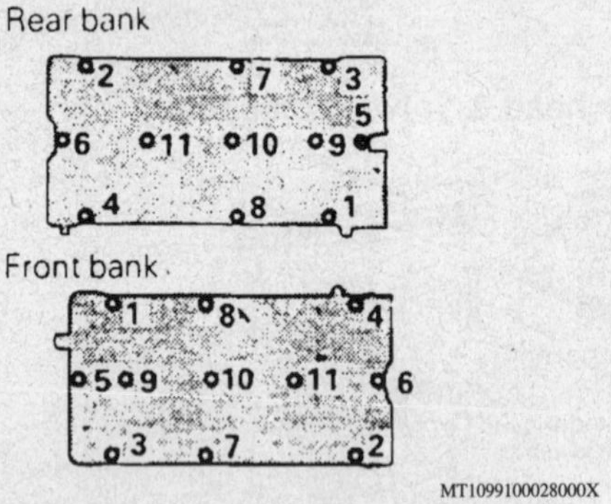
Rear bank
Front bank
MT1099100028000X

Fig. 22 Valve cover tightening sequence

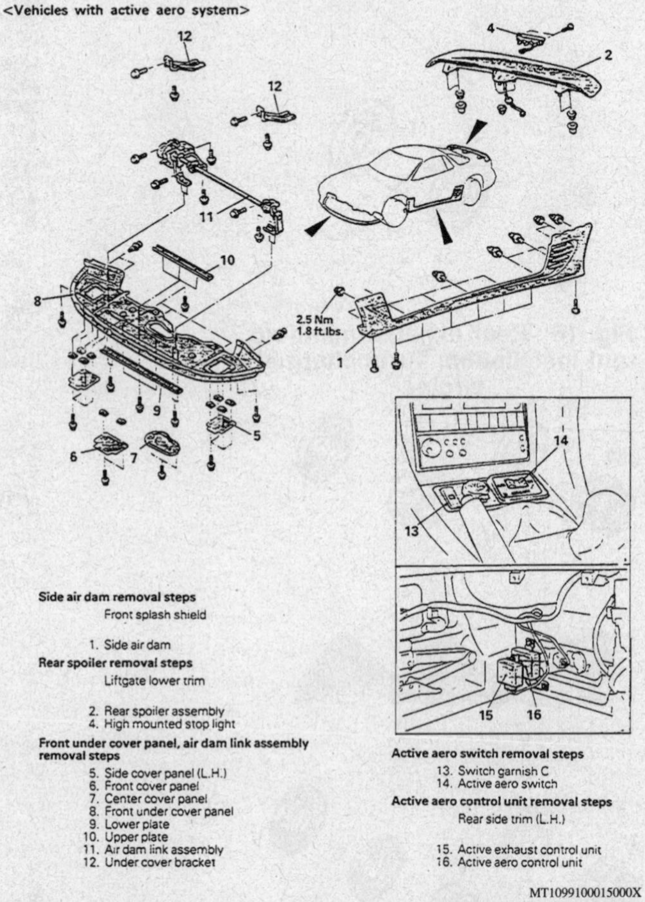
<Vehicles with active aero system>
2.5 Nm
1.8 ft.lbs.
Side air dam removal steps
Front splash shield
1. Side air dam
Rear spoiler removal steps
Liftgate lower trim
2. Rear spoiler assembly
4. High mounted stop light
Front under cover panel, air dam link assembly removal steps
5. Side cover panel (L.H.)
6. Front cover panel
7. Center cover panel
8. Front under cover panel
9. Lower plate
10. Upper plate
11. Air dam link assembly
12. Under cover bracket
Active aero switch removal steps
13. Switch garnish C
14. Active aero switch
Active aero control unit removal steps
Rear side trim (L.H.)
15. Active exhaust control unit
16. Active aero control unit
MT1099100015000X

Fig. 23 Active aero system component removal

FUEL FILTER

REPLACE

1. Drain fuel from fuel tank into an appropriate container.
2. Release fuel system pressure as outlined under "Precautions."
3. Remove eye bolt while holding fuel filter nut securely. **Cover hose connection with rags to prevent splash of fuel that could be caused by some residual pressure in the fuel pipe line.**
4. Reverse procedure to install, **Fig. 53,** noting the following:
   a. Insert main pipe at connector part of the high pressure fuel pipe, **Fig. 54,** then manually screw in main pipe flare nut.
   b. Holding fuel filter nut, tighten flare nut and eye bolt to specifications, then the filter to the bracket.

TURBOCHARGER

REPLACE

1. Remove radiator assembly.
2. Remove right transaxle stay.
3. Remove front exhaust pipe.
4. Remove front turbocharger assembly in numbered sequence as shown, **Figs. 55 and 56,** noting the following:
   a. Disconnect oxygen sensor connector, then remove oxygen sensor using oxygen sensor wrench tool No. MD998770, or equivalent.
   b. Disconnect A/C compressor connectors, leaving hoses connected.
5. Reverse numbered sequence as shown, **Figs. 55 and 56.**
6. Install front turbocharger, noting the following:
   a. Clean alignment surfaces as shown, **Fig. 57,** then apply clean engine oil through oil pipe hole.
   b. Install oxygen sensor using oxygen sensor tool.
   c. Align marks indicated by arrows and insert securely into stepped portion of pipe or until seated, **Figs. 58 through 62.**

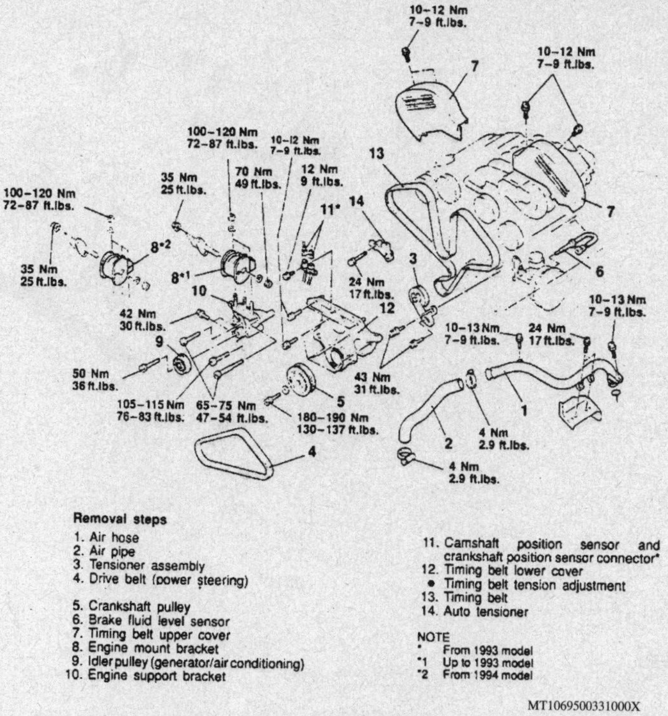
10-12 Nm
7-9 ft.lbs.
10-12 Nm
7-9 ft.lbs.
100-120 Nm
72-87 ft.lbs.
10-12 Nm
7-9 ft.lbs.
35 Nm
25 ft.lbs.
70 Nm
49 ft.lbs.
12 Nm
9 ft.lbs.
100-120 Nm
72-87 ft.lbs.
35 Nm
25 ft.lbs.
42 Nm
30 ft.lbs.
24 Nm
17 ft.lbs.
10-13 Nm
7-9 ft.lbs.
10-13 Nm
7-9 ft.lbs.
24 Nm
17 ft.lbs.
50 Nm
36 ft.lbs.
43 Nm
31 ft.lbs.
105-115 Nm
76-83 ft.lbs.
65-75 Nm
47-54 ft.lbs.
180-190 Nm
130-137 ft.lbs.
4 Nm
2.9 ft.lbs.
4 Nm
2.9 ft.lbs.
Removal steps
1. Air hose
2. Air pipe
3. Tensioner assembly
4. Drive belt (power steering)
5. Crankshaft pulley
6. Brake fluid level sensor
7. Timing belt upper cover
8. Engine mount bracket
9. Idler pulley (generator/air conditioning)
10. Engine support bracket
11. Camshaft position sensor and crankshaft position sensor connector*
12. Timing belt lower cover
• Timing belt tension adjustment
13. Timing belt
14. Auto tensioner
NOTE
* From 1993 model
*1 Up to 1993 model
*2 From 1994 model
MT1069500331000X

Fig. 24 Timing belt replacement

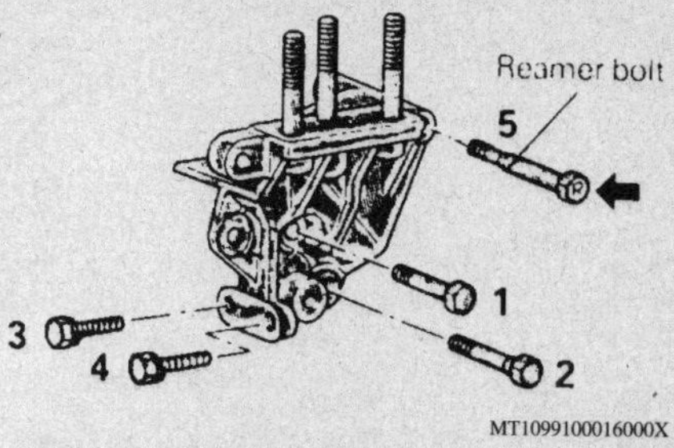
Reamer bolt
5
1
2
3
4
MT1099100016000X

Fig. 25 Engine support bracket removal

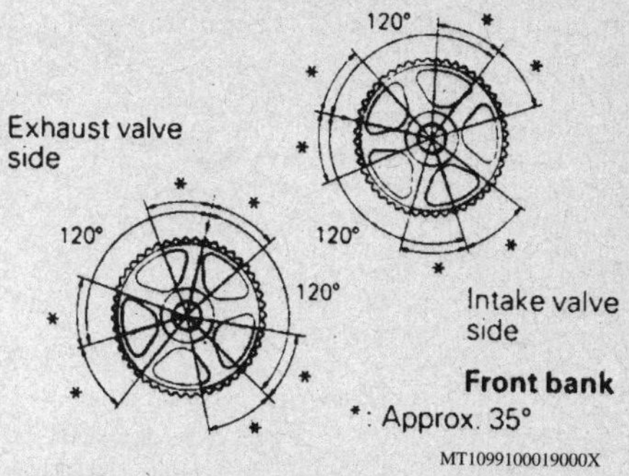
120°
Exhaust valve side
120°
120°
120°
Intake valve side
Front bank
*: Approx. 35°
MT1099100019000X

Fig. 28 Intake & exhaust alignment

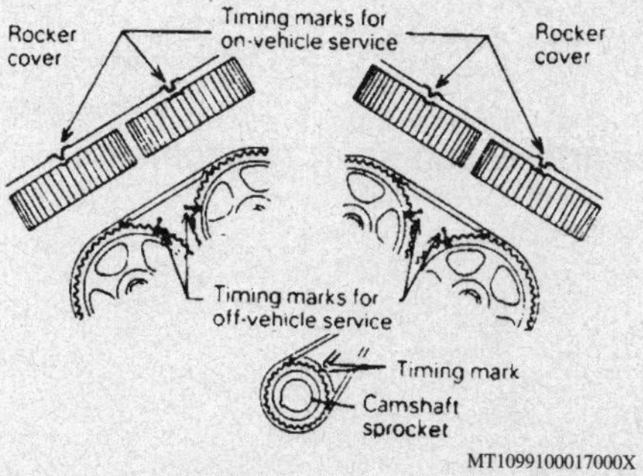
Rocker cover
Timing marks for on-vehicle service
Rocker cover
Timing marks for off-vehicle service
Timing mark
Camshaft sprocket
MT1099100017000X

Fig. 26 Timing mark alignment

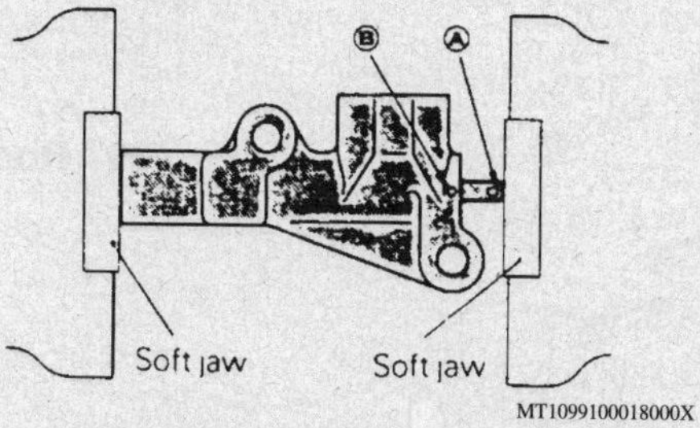
B
A
Soft jaw
Soft jaw
MT1099100018000X

Fig. 27 Timing belt auto tensioner adjustment

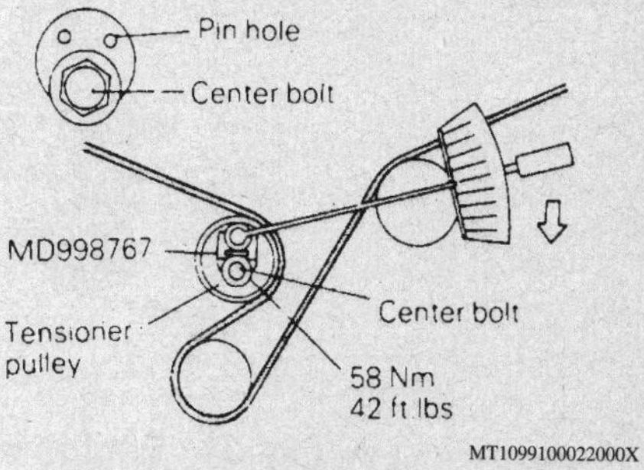
Pin hole
Center bolt
MD998767
Center bolt
Tensioner pulley
58 Nm
42 ft lbs
MT1099100022000X

Fig. 31 Timing belt tension adjustment

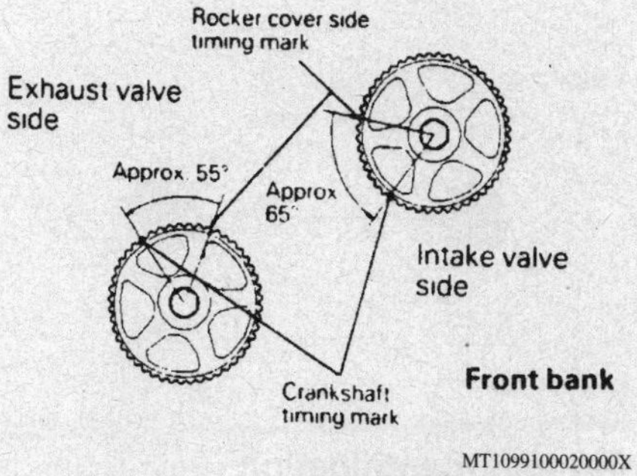
Rocker cover side timing mark
Exhaust valve side
Approx. 55°
Approx 65°
Intake valve side
Crankshaft timing mark
Front bank
MT1099100020000X

Fig. 29 Intake & exhaust camshaft alignment

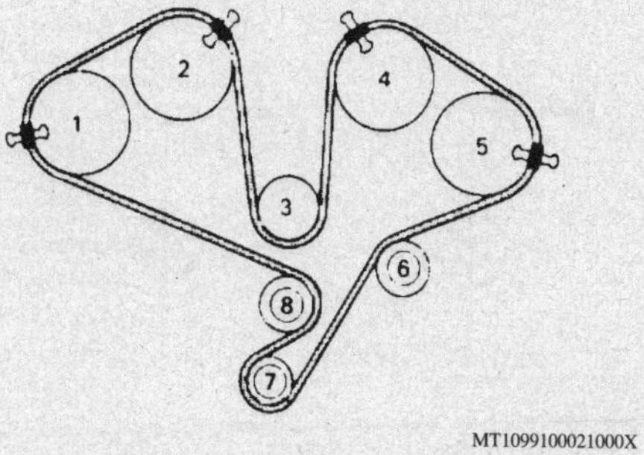
1
2
3
4
5
6
7
8
MT1099100021000X

Fig. 30 Timing belt installation

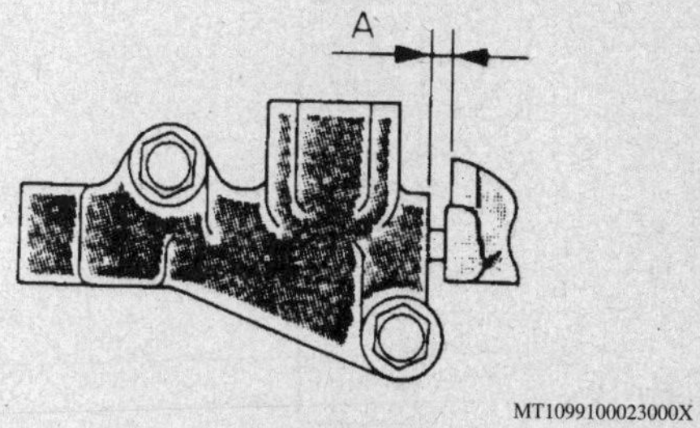
A
MT1099100023000X

Fig. 32 Auto adjuster rod protrusion

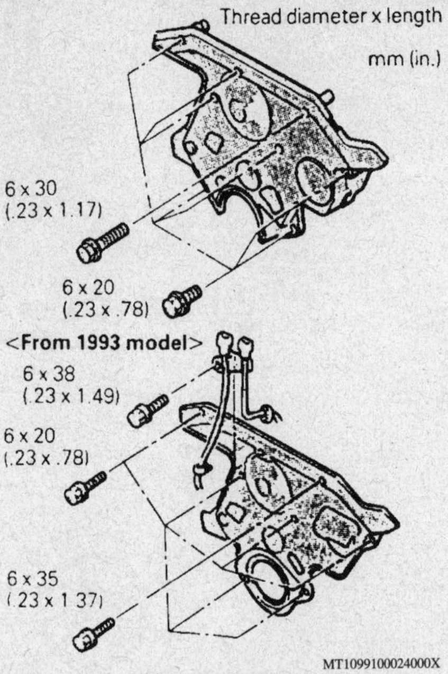
Thread diameter x length
mm (in.)
6 x 30
(.23 x 1.17)
6 x 20
(.23 x .78)
<From 1993 model>
6 x 38
(.23 x 1.49)
6 x 20
(.23 x .78)
6 x 35
(.23 x 1.37)
MT1099100024000X

Fig. 33 Lower timing belt cover installation

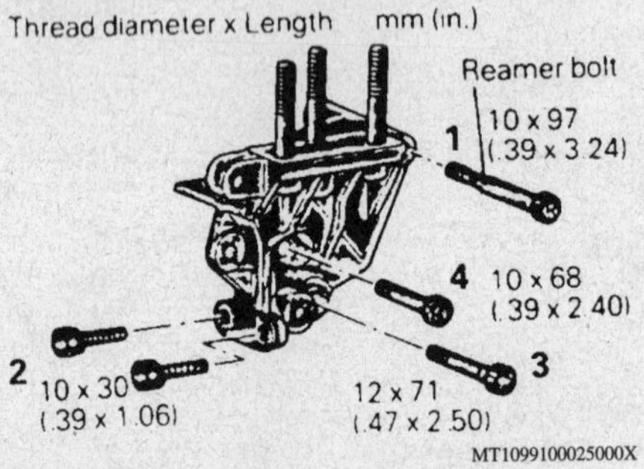
Thread diameter x Length mm (in.)
Reamer bolt
1
10 x 97
(.39 x 3.24)
4
10 x 68
(.39 x 2.40)
2
10 x 30
(.39 x 1.06)
3
12 x 71
(.47 x 2.50)
MT1099100025000X

Fig. 34 Engine support bracket installation

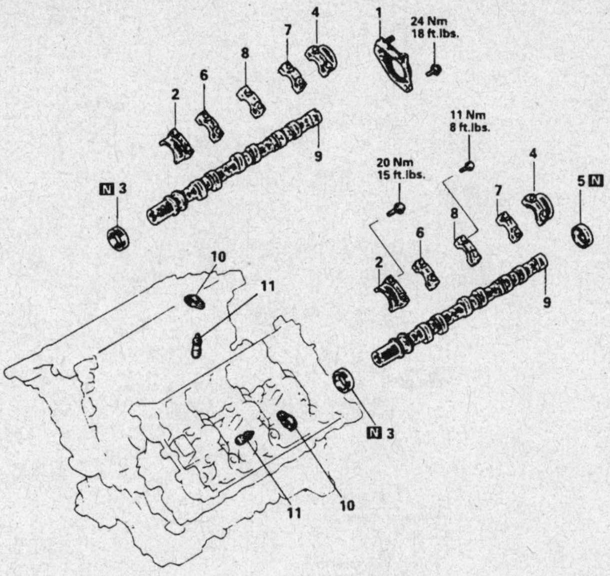
24 Nm
18 ft.lbs.
11 Nm
8 ft.lbs.
20 Nm
15 ft.lbs.

Removal steps

1. Crank angle sensor adaptor
2. Bearing cap front
3. Oil seal
4. Bearing cap rear
5. Circular packing
6. Bearing cap No. 2
7. Bearing cap No. 4
8. Bearing cap No. 3
9. Camshaft
10. Rocker arm
11. Lash adjuster

Installation steps

11. Lash adjuster
10. Rocker arm
9. Camshaft
8. Bearing cap No. 3
7. Bearing cap No. 4
6. Bearing cap No. 2
4. Bearing cap rear
2. Bearing cap front
5. Circular packing
3. Oil seal
1. Crank angle sensor adaptor

MT1099100029000X

Fig. 35 Rocker arm & camshaft replacement

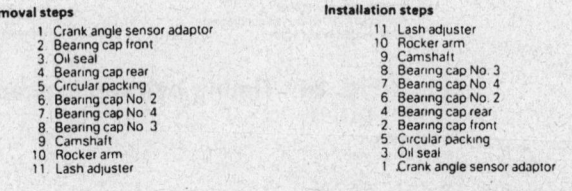

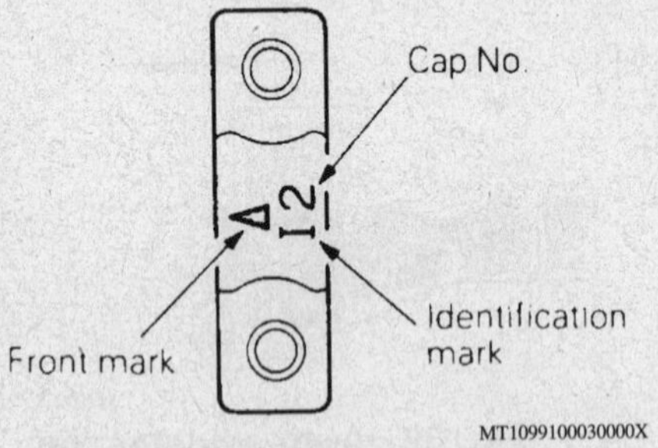
Cap No.
I2
Front mark
Identification mark
MT1099100030000X

Fig. 36 Camshaft installation

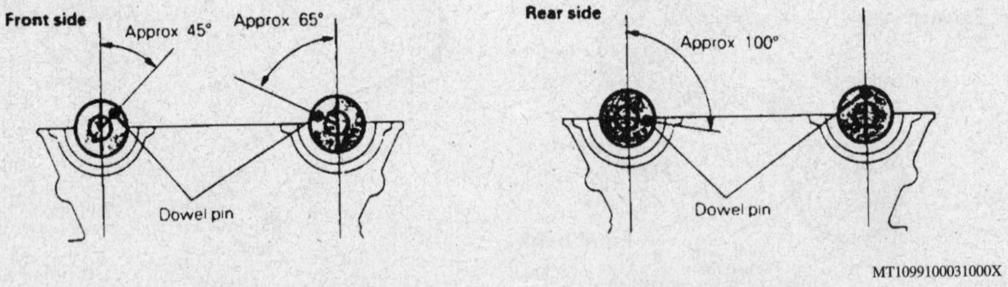
Front side
Approx 45°
Approx 65°
Dowel pin
Rear side
Approx 100°
Dowel pin
MT1099100031000X

Fig. 37 Camshaft bearing cap identification

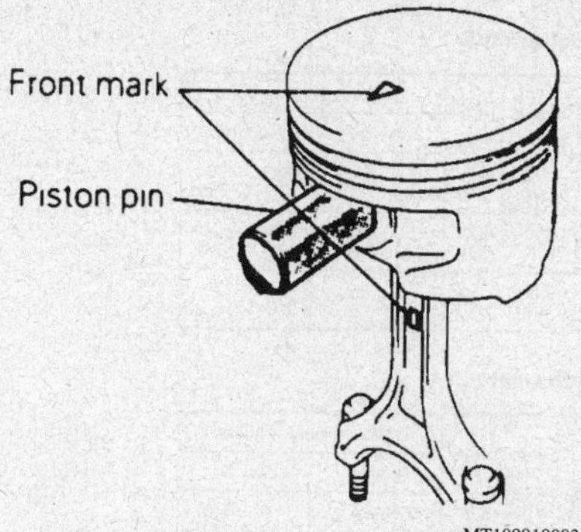
Front mark
Piston pin

MT1099100034000X

Fig. 38 Piston front marks

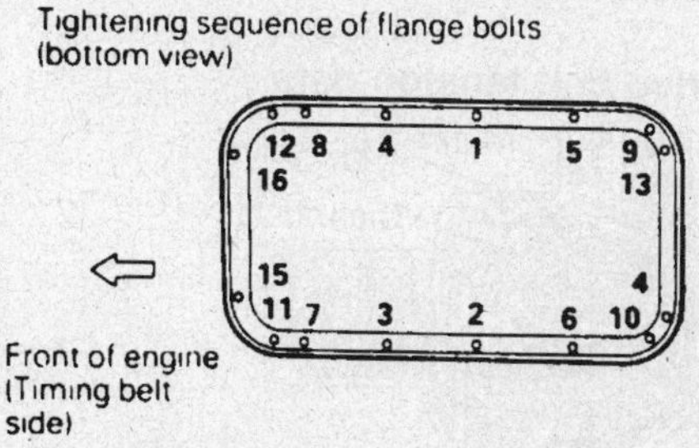
Tightening sequence of flange bolts
(bottom view)
12 8 4 1 5 9
16 13
15 4
11 7 3 2 6 10
Front of engine
(Timing belt
side)

MT1099100036000X

Fig. 40 Oil pan tightening sequence

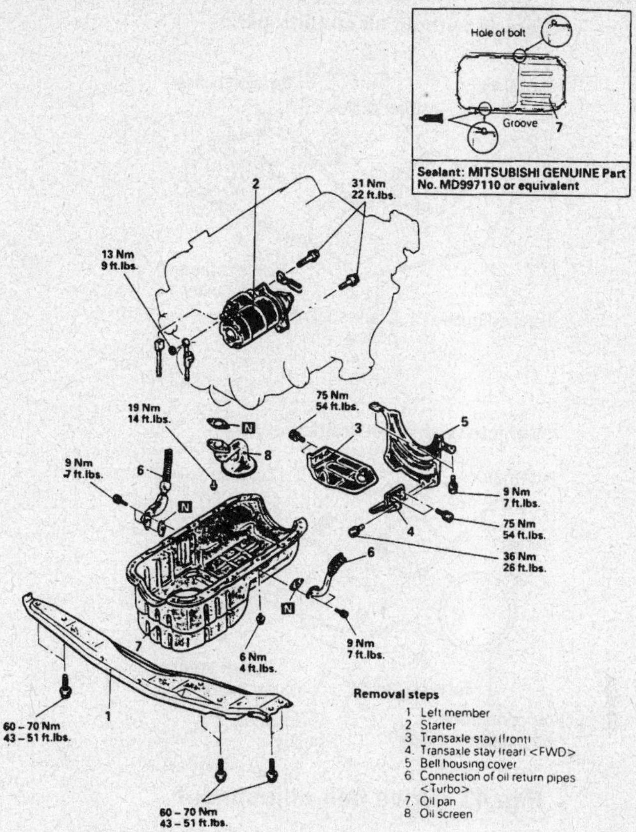
Hole of bolt
Groove
7
Sealant: MITSUBISHI GENUINE Part No. MD997110 or equivalent
31 Nm
22 ft.lbs.
13 Nm
9 ft.lbs.
19 Nm
14 ft.lbs.
75 Nm
54 ft.lbs.
9 Nm
7 ft.lbs.
36 Nm
26 ft.lbs.
6 Nm
4 ft.lbs.
60 – 70 Nm
43 – 51 ft.lbs.
Removal steps
1. Left member
2. Starter
3. Transaxle stay (front)
4. Transaxle stay (rear) <FWD>
5. Bell housing cover
6. Connection of oil return pipes <Turbo>
7. Oil pan
8. Oil screen

MT1099100035000X

Fig. 39 Oil pan & screen replacement

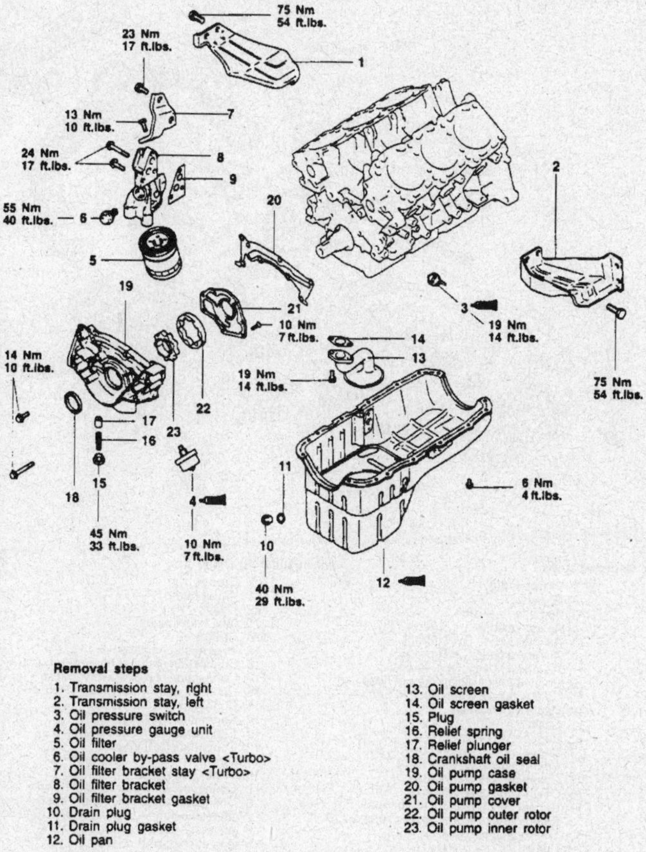
75 Nm
54 ft.lbs.
23 Nm
17 ft.lbs.
13 Nm
10 ft.lbs.
24 Nm
17 ft.lbs.
55 Nm
40 ft.lbs.
10 Nm
7 ft.lbs.
19 Nm
14 ft.lbs.
14 Nm
10 ft.lbs.
6 Nm
4 ft.lbs.
45 Nm
33 ft.lbs.
40 Nm
29 ft.lbs.
Removal steps
1. Transmission stay, right
2. Transmission stay, left
3. Oil pressure switch
4. Oil pressure gauge unit
5. Oil filter
6. Oil cooler by-pass valve <Turbo>
7. Oil filter bracket stay <Turbo>
8. Oil filter bracket
9. Oil filter bracket gasket
10. Drain plug
11. Drain plug gasket
12. Oil pan
13. Oil screen
14. Oil screen gasket
15. Plug
16. Relief spring
17. Relief plunger
18. Crankshaft oil seal
19. Oil pump case
20. Oil pump gasket
21. Oil pump cover
22. Oil pump outer rotor
23. Oil pump inner rotor

MT1099500060000X

Fig. 41 Oil pan & pump replacement

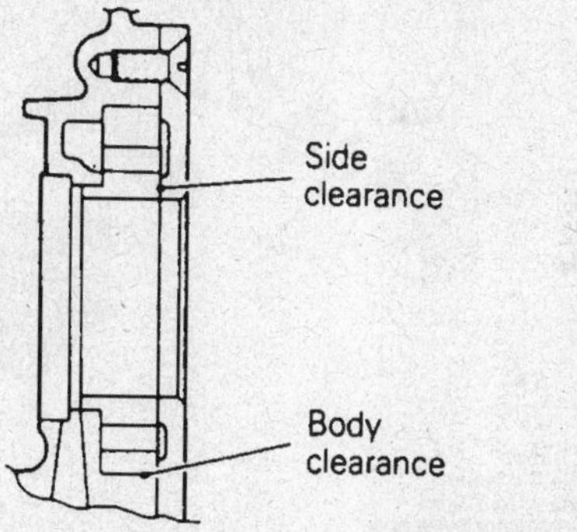
Side
clearance
Body
clearance

MT1099100038000X

Fig. 42 Oil pump inspection

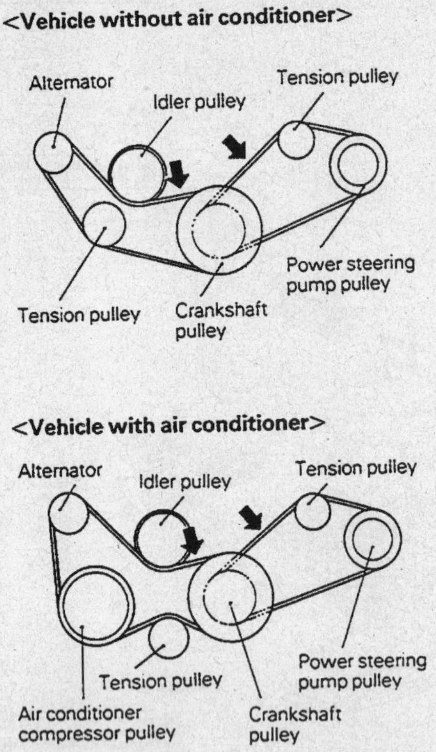
<Vehicle without air conditioner>
Alternator
Idler pulley
Tension pulley
Power steering pump pulley
Tension pulley
Crankshaft pulley
<Vehicle with air conditioner>
Alternator
Idler pulley
Tension pulley
Power steering pump pulley
Tension pulley
Air conditioner compressor pulley
Crankshaft pulley

MT1069100101000X

Fig. 43 Drive belt adjustment

<Vehicle without air conditioner>

Items		Check value	Adjustment value	
			New belt	Used belt
For alter-nator	Deflection mm (in.)	4.0 - 5.5 (.157 - .216)	3.5 - 4.0 (.138 - .157)	4.0 - 5.0 (.157 - .197)
	Tension N lbs.	350 - 600 (77 - 132)	650 - 850 (143 - 187)	450 - 600 (99 - 132)
For P/S pump	Deflection mm (in.)	9.0 11.0 (.354 - .433)	←	←

<Vehicle with air conditioner>

Items		Check value	Adjustment value	
			New belt	Used belt
For alter nator and A C compressor	Deflection mm (in.)	4.0 5.5 (.157 - .216)	3.5 - 4.0 (.138 - .157)	4.0 5.0 (.157 .197)
For P S pump	Deflection mm (in.)	9.0 - 11.0 (.354 - .433)	←	←

MT1069100100000X

Fig. 44 Drive belt tension data

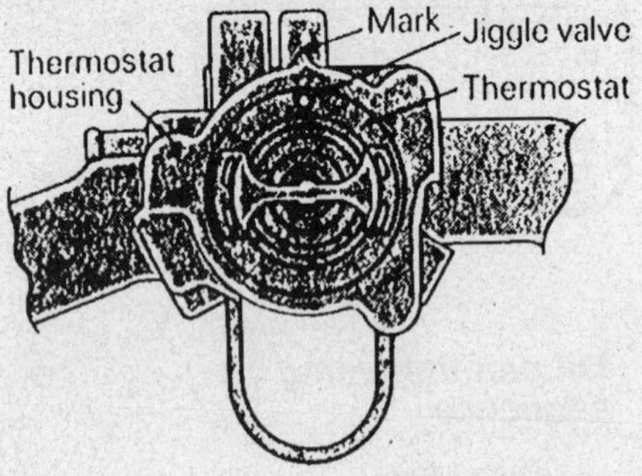
Mark
Jiggle valve
Thermostat housing
Thermostat

MT1089100010000X

Fig. 46 Thermostat installation

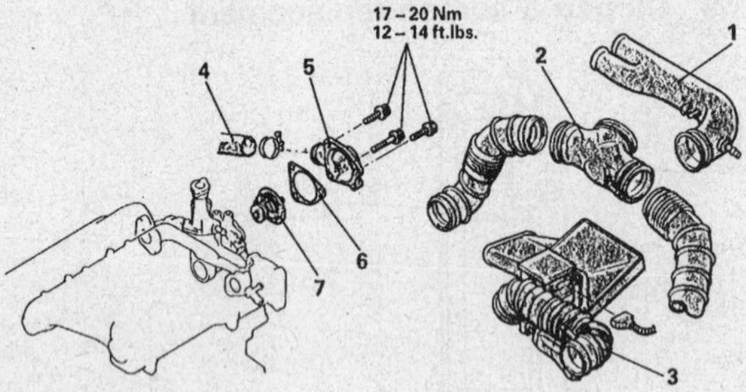
17 – 20 Nm
12 – 14 ft.lbs.
1
2
3
4
5
6
7

Removal steps

1. Air hose A <Turbo>
2. Air intake hose A <Turbo>
3. Air intake hose <Non-Turbo>
4. Connection of radiator lower hose
5. Water inlet fitting
6. Gasket
7. Thermostat

MT1089100009000X

Fig. 45 Thermostat replacement

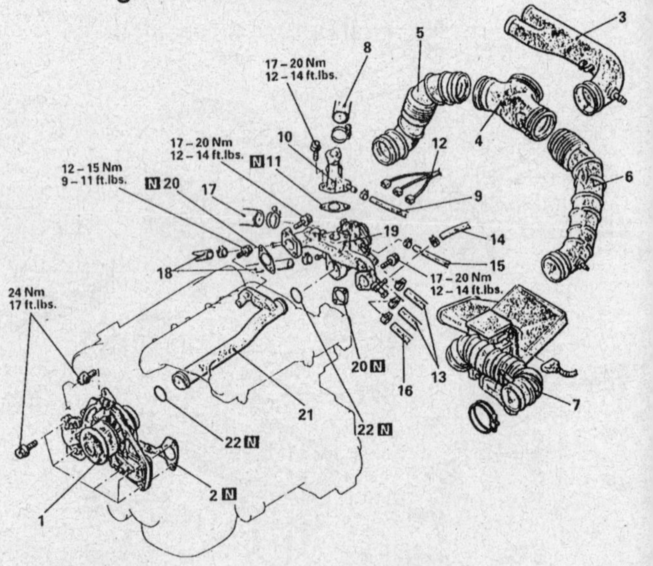
17 – 20 Nm
12 – 14 ft.lbs.
17 – 20 Nm
12 – 14 ft.lbs.
12 – 15 Nm
9 – 11 ft.lbs.
17 – 20 Nm
12 – 14 ft.lbs.
24 Nm
17 ft.lbs.

Removal steps

1. Water pump
2. Gasket
3. Air hose A <Turbo>
4. Air intake hose A <Turbo>
5. Air intake hose B <Turbo>
6. Air intake hose C <Turbo>
7. Air intake hose <Non-Turbo>
8. Connection of radiator upper hose
9. Connection of water hose <Turbo>
10. Water outlet fitting
11. Gasket
12. Connection of harness
13. Connection of heater hose
14. Connection of water hose A
15. Connection of water hose
16. Connection of water hose <Turbo>
17. Connection of radiator lower hose
18. Connection of water hose <Turbo>
19. Thermostat housing
20. Gasket
21. Inlet water pipe
22. O-ring

Installation steps

2. Gasket
1. Water pump
22. O-ring
21. Inlet water pipe
20. Gasket
19. Thermostat housing
18. Connection of water hose <Turbo>
17. Connection of radiator lower hose
16. Connection of water hose <Turbo>
15. Connection of water hose
14. Connection of water hose A
13. Connection of heater hose
12. Connection of harness
11. Gasket
10. Water outlet fitting
9. Connection of water hose <Turbo>
8. Connection of radiator upper hose
7. Air intake hose <Non-Turbo>
6. Air intake hose C <Turbo>
5. Air intake hose B <Turbo>
4. Air intake hose A <Turbo>
3. Air hose A <Turbo>

MT1089100012000X

Fig. 48 Water pump installation

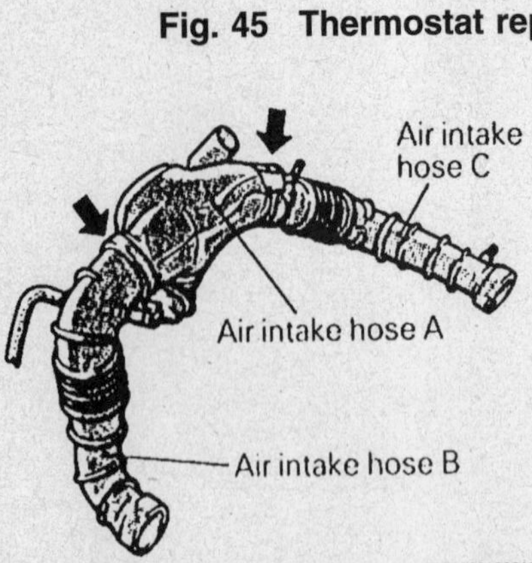
Air intake hose C
Air intake hose A
Air intake hose B

MT1089100011000X

Fig. 47 Air intake hose "A" installation

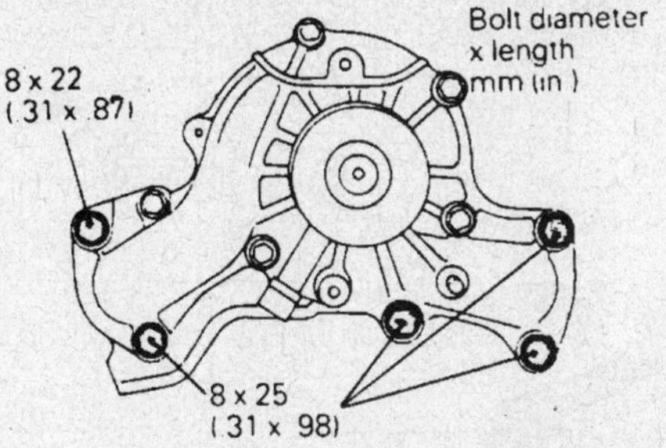
Bolt diameter
x length
mm (in.)
8 x 22
(.31 x .87)
8 x 25
(.31 x .98)

MT1089100013000X

Fig. 49 Water pump replacement

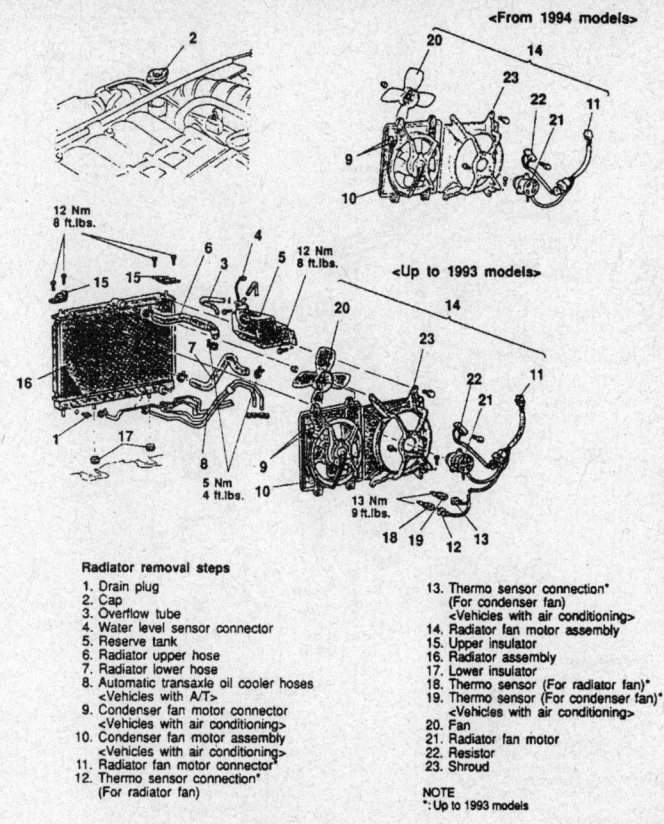

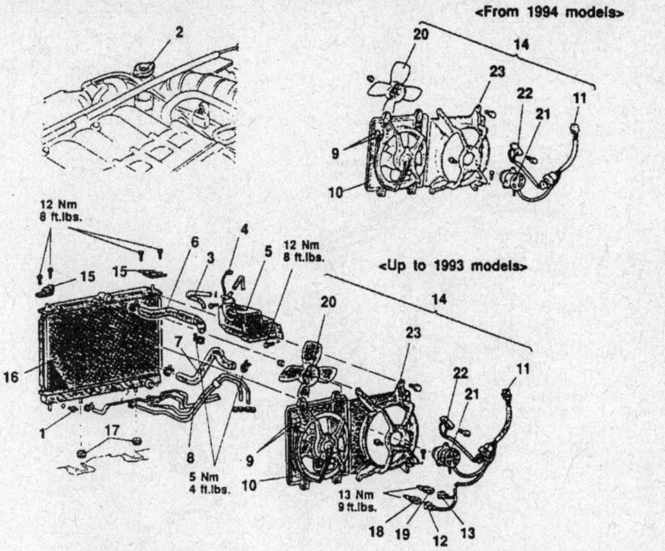
<From 1994 models>
<Up to 1993 models>
12 Nm
8 ft.lbs.
12 Nm
8 ft.lbs.
5 Nm
4 ft.lbs.
13 Nm
9 ft.lbs.

Radiator removal steps

1. Drain plug
2. Cap
3. Overflow tube
4. Water level sensor connector
5. Reserve tank
6. Radiator upper hose
7. Radiator lower hose
8. Automatic transaxle oil cooler hoses <Vehicles with A/T>
9. Condenser fan motor connector <Vehicles with air conditioning>
10. Condenser fan motor assembly <Vehicles with air conditioning>
11. Radiator fan motor connector*
12. Thermo sensor connection* (For radiator fan)
13. Thermo sensor connection* (For condenser fan) <Vehicles with air conditioning>
14. Radiator fan motor assembly
15. Upper insulator
16. Radiator assembly
17. Lower insulator
18. Thermo sensor (For radiator fan)*
19. Thermo sensor (For condenser fan)* <Vehicles with air conditioning>
20. Fan
21. Radiator fan motor
22. Resistor
23. Shroud

NOTE
*: Up to 1993 models

MT1089500079000X

Fig. 50 Radiator Replacement

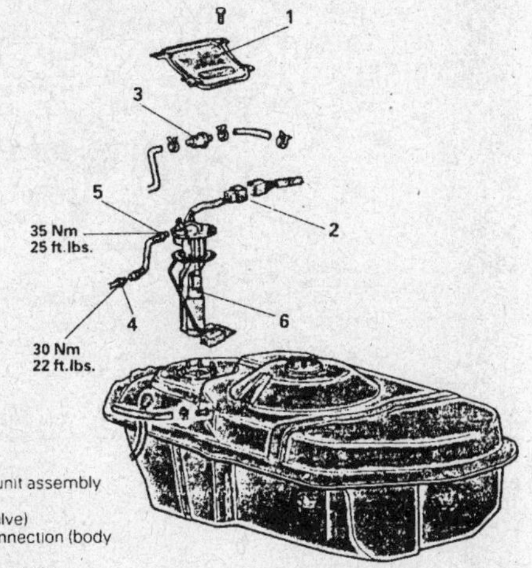
35 Nm
25 ft.lbs.
30 Nm
22 ft.lbs.

Removal steps

1. Fuel gauge cover
2. Fuel pump and fuel gauge unit assembly connector
3. Overfill limiter (Two-way valve)
4. High pressure fuel hose connection (body side)
5. High pressure fuel hose connection (fuel pump side)
6. Fuel pump and fuel gauge unit assembly

MT1029100006000X

Fig. 51 Fuel pump replacement

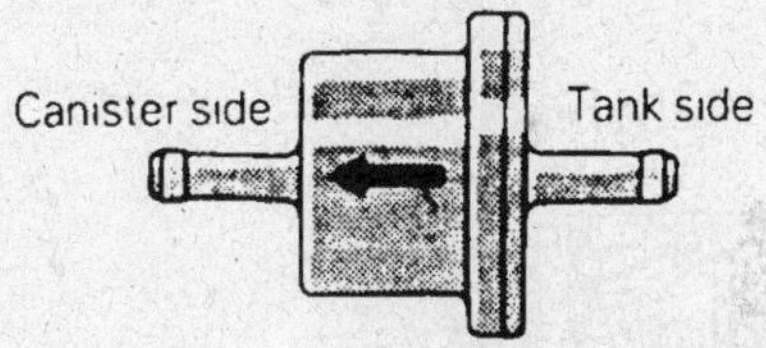
Canister side
Tank side

MT1029100007000X

Fig. 52 Overfill limiter valve installation

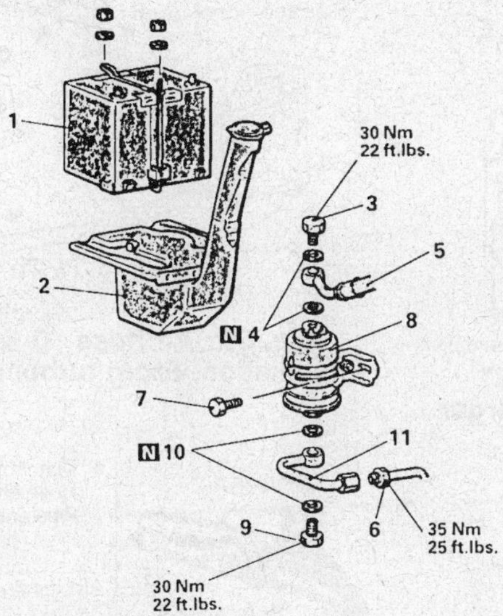
30 Nm
22 ft.lbs.
35 Nm
25 ft.lbs.
30 Nm
22 ft.lbs.

Removal steps

1. Battery
2. Battery tray with washer tank assembly
3. Eye bolt
4. Gasket
5. High pressure fuel hose
6. Connection of fuel main pipe
7. Mounting bolt
8. Fuel filter
9. Eye bolt
10. Gasket
11. High pressure fuel pipe

MT1029100008000X

Fig. 53 Fuel filter removal

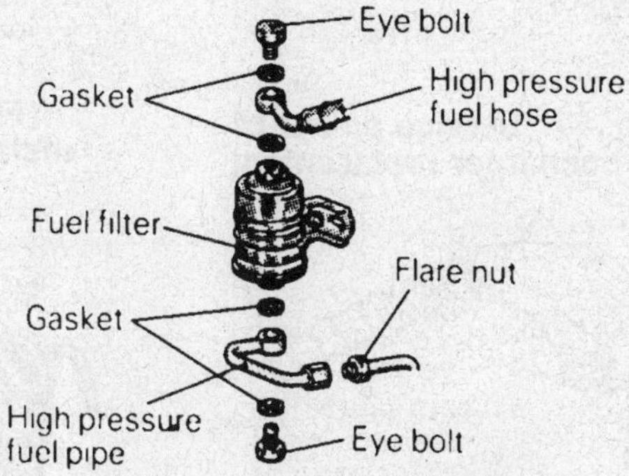
Eye bolt
Gasket
High pressure
fuel hose
Fuel filter
Flare nut
Gasket
High pressure
fuel pipe
Eye bolt

MT1029100009000X

Fig. 54 Fuel filter installation

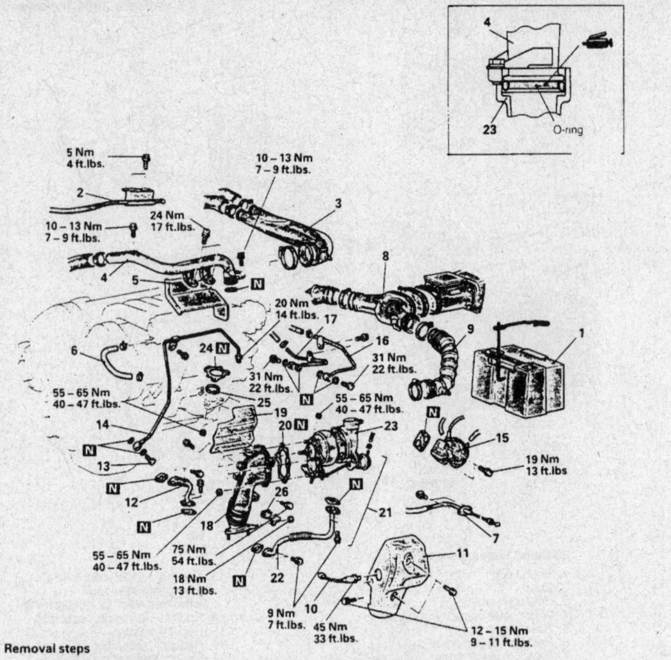
O-ring
5 Nm
4 ft.lbs.
10 – 13 Nm
7 – 9 ft.lbs.
24 Nm
17 ft.lbs.
20 Nm
14 ft.lbs.
31 Nm
22 ft.lbs.
55 – 65 Nm
40 – 47 ft.lbs.
19 Nm
13 ft.lbs.
75 Nm
54 ft.lbs.
18 Nm
13 ft.lbs.
9 Nm
7 ft.lbs.
45 Nm
33 ft.lbs.
12 – 15 Nm
9 – 11 ft.lbs.

Removal steps

1. Battery
2. Connection of accelerator cable (engine side)
3. Air hose A
4. Air pipe A
5. Heat protector F
6. Clutch booster vacuum hose
7. Connection of accelerator cable (pedal side)
8. Air intake hose A
9. Air intake hose C
10. Oxygen sensor
11. Heat protector D
12. EGR pipe
13. Eye bolt
14. Oil pipe
15. EGR valve
16. Water pipe A
17. Water pipe B
18. Exhaust fitting
19. Heat protector E
20. Gasket
21. Turbocharger & return pipe assembly
22. Oil return pipe
23. Turbocharger assembly
24. Gasket
25. Ring
26. Exhaust fitting stay

MT1059100040000X

Fig. 55 Front turbocharger replacement

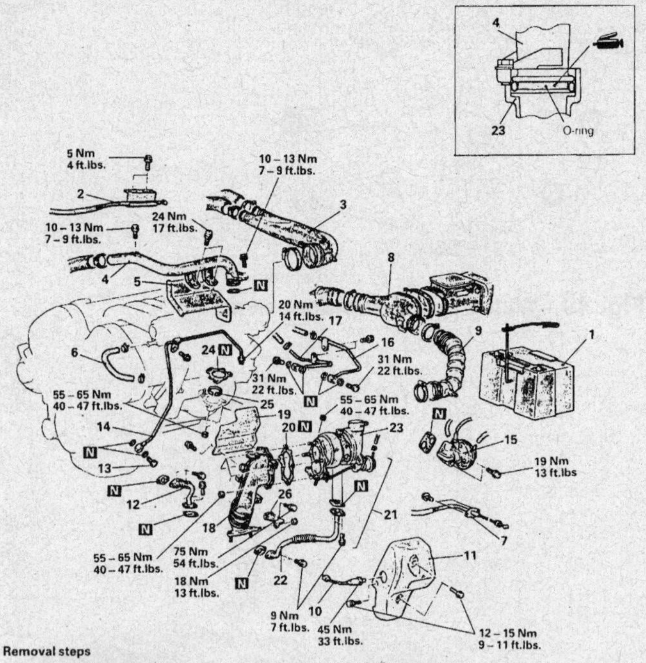
O-ring
5 Nm
4 ft.lbs.
10 – 13 Nm
7 – 9 ft.lbs.
24 Nm
17 ft.lbs.
20 Nm
14 ft.lbs.
31 Nm
22 ft.lbs.
55 – 65 Nm
40 – 47 ft.lbs.
19 Nm
13 ft.lbs.
75 Nm
54 ft.lbs.
18 Nm
13 ft.lbs.
9 Nm
7 ft.lbs.
45 Nm
33 ft.lbs.
12 – 15 Nm
9 – 11 ft.lbs.

Removal steps

1. Battery
2. Connection of accelerator cable (engine side)
3. Air hose A
4. Air pipe A
5. Heat protector F
6. Clutch booster vacuum hose
7. Connection of accelerator cable (pedal side)
8. Air intake hose A
9. Air intake hose C
10. Oxygen sensor
11. Heat protector D
12. EGR pipe
13. Eye bolt
14. Oil pipe
15. EGR valve
16. Water pipe A
17. Water pipe B
18. Exhaust fitting
19. Heat protector E
20. Gasket
21. Turbocharger & return pipe assembly
22. Oil return pipe
23. Turbocharger assembly
24. Gasket
25. Ring
26. Exhaust fitting stay

MT1059100041000X

Fig. 56 Rear turbocharger replacement

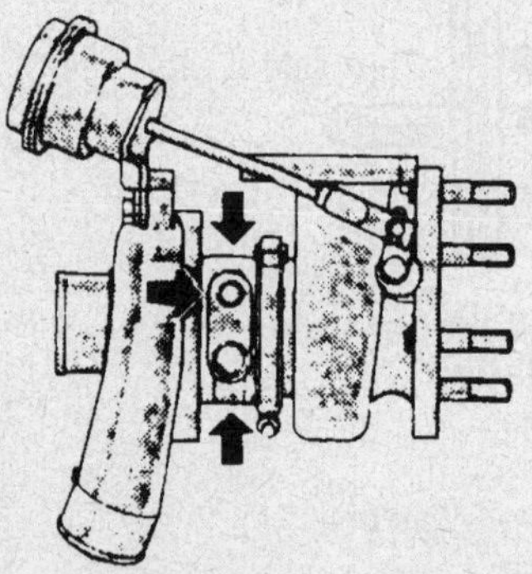

MT1059100010000X

Fig. 57 Service points of turbocharger replacement

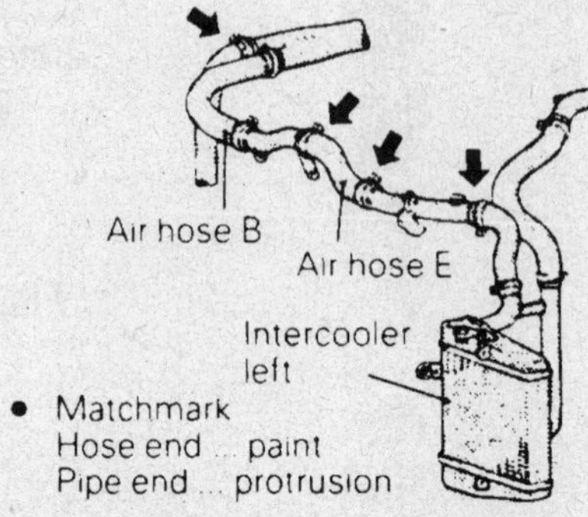
Air hose B
Air hose E
Intercooler left
• Matchmark
Hose end ... paint
Pipe end ... protrusion

MT1059100011000X

Fig. 58 Air hose "E & B" installation. Front turbocharger

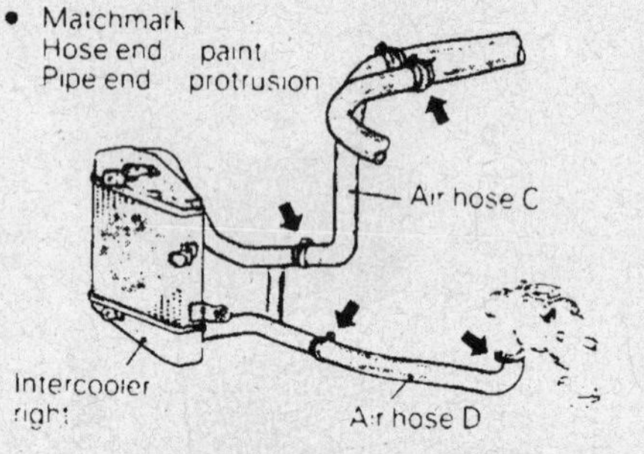
• Matchmark
Hose end paint
Pipe end protrusion
Air hose C
Intercooler right
Air hose D

MT1059100012000X

Fig. 59 Air hose "D & C" installation. Front turbocharger

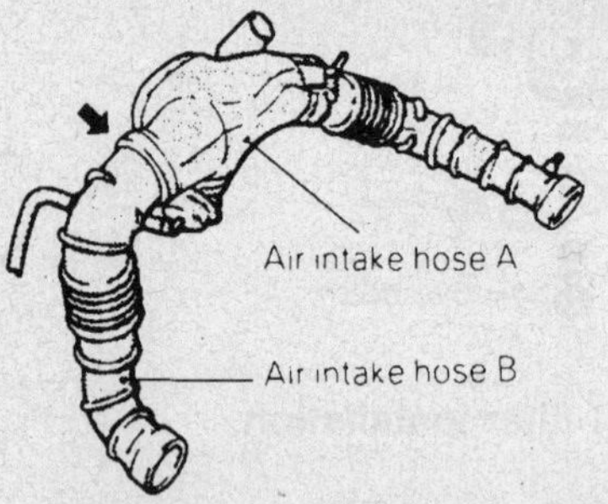
Air intake hose A
Air intake hose B

MT1059100013000X

Fig. 60 Air intake hose "B" installation. Front turbocharger

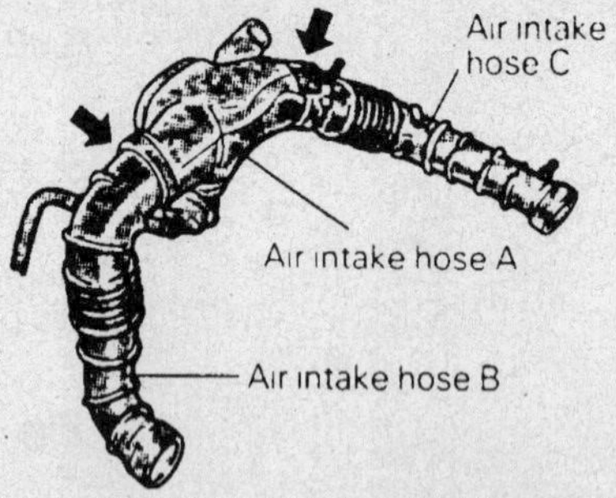
Air intake hose C
Air intake hose A
Air intake hose B

MT1059100014000X

Fig. 61 Air intake hose "A & C" installation. Rear turbocharger

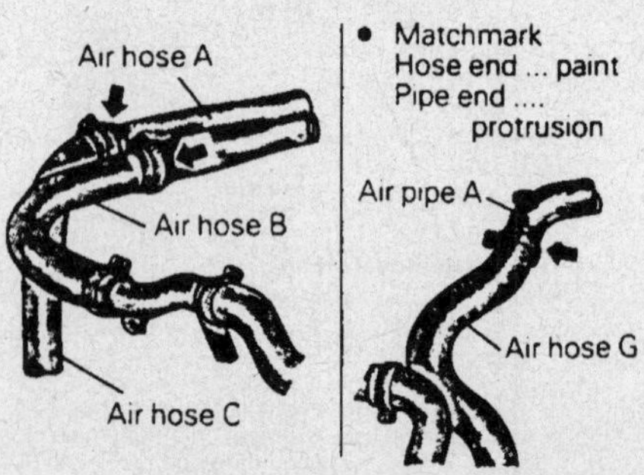
Air hose A
Air hose B
Air hose C
• Matchmark
Hose end ... paint
Pipe end .... protrusion
Air pipe A
Air hose G

MT1059100015000X

Fig. 62 Air pipe & hose "A" installation. Rear turbocharger

TIGHTENING SPECIFICATIONS

For rear axle and suspension tightening specifications, refer to individual repair or replacement procedure and illustrations.

Year	Component	Torque/ Ft. Lbs.
1993–96	Air Intake Plenum Bolt & Nut	13
	Air Intake Plenum Stay Bolt	13
	Alternator Brace Bolt	10
	Alternator Bracket Bolt	17
	Alternator Bracket Side Bolt	7
	Alternator Pivot Nut	17
	Alternator	17
	Auto Tensioner Bolt	17
	Bearing Caps Bolts No. 2, 3 & 4	8
	Bearing Caps, Front & Rear	14
	Bellhousing Cover Bolt	7
	Bracket Bolts	17
	Camshaft Sprocket Bolt	65
	Center Cover Bolt	2
	Connecting Rod Cap Nut	38
	Cooling Fan Bolt	8
	Cooling Fan Bracket Bolt	30
	Crank Angle Sensor Adapter Bolt	17
	Crank Angle Sensor Nut	9
	Crankshaft Bearing Cap Bolt	①
	Crankshaft Pulley Bolt	138
	Cylinder Head Bolts	⑦
	Detonation Sensor	17
	EGR Pipe	13
	EGR Valve	14
	Engine Coolant Temperature Gauge Unit	8
	Engine Coolant Temperature Sensor	22
	Engine Support Bracket	②
	Exhaust Manifold Heat Protector	10
	Exhaust Manifold Nut	21
	Exhaust Manifold Stay Bolt	44
	Exhaust Manifold Tightening Side Nut	9
	Fan Pulley Bolt	8
	Flywheel Bolt	54
	Fuel Pressure Regulator Bolt	7
	Idler Pulley Bolt	40
	Idler Pulley Bracket Bolt	30
	Ignition Coil Bolt	③
	Injector & Delivery Pipe Bolt	9
	Intake Manifold Front Side Nut	17
	Intake Manifold Nut	13
	Oil Filter Bracket Stay	④
	Oil Filter Bracket	⑤
	Oil Pan Bolt	4
	Oil Pan Drain Plug	29
	Oil Pressure Switch	14
	Oil Pump Case Bolt	10
	Oil Pump Cover Bolt	10
	Oil Screen Bolt	14
	Oil Seal Case Bolt	8
	Oil Level Gauge Assembly Bolt	10
	Power Transistor Bolt	16
	Rear Plate Bolt	8
	Rocker Cover Bolt	2
	Roll Stopper Bracket	⑥

Continued

Year	Component	Torque/ Ft. Lbs.
1993–96	Spark Plug	18
	Tensioner Arm Bolt	30
	Tensioner Bracket Bolt	17
	Tensioner Bracket Stay Bolt	17
	Tensioner Pulley Nut	35
	Thermo Switch	6
	Thermostat Housing Bolt	14
	Throttle Body Bolt	9
	Timing Belt Rear Cover Center Bolt	17
	Transmission Stay	54
	Water Inlet Fitting Bolt	14
	Water Inlet Pipe Bolt	10
	Water Outlet Fitting Pipe Bolt	14
	Water Pump Bolt	17

① — Bolts marked No. 9, 58 ft. lbs. ; bolts marked No. 10, 69 ft. lbs.
② — 10 mm bolts, 51 ft. lbs.; 12 mm bolts, 80 ft. lbs.
③ — 10 mm bolts, 7 ft. lbs.; 12 mm bolts, 9 ft. lbs.
④ — 8 mm bolts, 9 ft. lbs.; 10 mm bolts, 17 ft. lbs.
⑤ — Bolts marked No. 4, 17 ft. lbs. ; bolts marked No. 7, 10 ft. lbs.
⑥ — 10 mm bolts, 36–43 ft. lbs.; 12 mm bolts, 51–58 ft. lbs.
⑦ — Refer to "Cylinder Head, Replace."

Clutch & Manual Transaxle

NOTE: On Air Bag Equipped Models, Refer To "Air Bag System Precautions" Located In The Front Of This Manual For System Disarming & Arming Procedures.

INDEX

	Page No.
Adjustments	24-68
Clutch Booster Pushrod & Piston Clearance	24-69
Clutch Pedal	24-68
Clutch, Replace	24-69
Hydraulic System Service	24-69
Clutch Booster Inspection	24-69
Clutch Control Components, Replace	24-69
Clutch Master Cylinder Service	24-69
Precautions	24-68
Air Bag Systems	24-68
Shift Cable, Replace	24-70
Technical Service Bulletins	24-72
Manual Transaxle Gear Oil Specification	24-72
Tightening Specifications	24-78
Transaxle, Replace	24-70
Eclipse	24-70
3000GT	24-71

PRECAUTIONS

AIR BAG SYSTEMS

Refer to "Air Bag System Precautions" in the front of this manual for system disarming and arming procedures.

ADJUSTMENTS

CLUTCH PEDAL

Eclipse

1. Measure clutch pedal height "A" and clutch pedal clevis pin play "B," **Fig. 1.**
2. Clutch pedal height "A" should be 6.9–7.1 inches.
3. Clevis pin play "B" should be 0.04–0.12 inch.
4. If either "A" or "B"are not within specification, adjust as follows:
   a. **On models less cruise control,** turn and adjust bolt ensuring pedal height is correct, then secure by tightening locknut, **Fig. 2.**
   b. **On models with cruise control,** disconnect clutch switch connector and turn the switch for standard clutch pedal height, then lock with the locknut.
   c. **On all models,** turn pushrod, **Fig. 3,** to adjust clutch pedal clevis pin play to proper value, then secure pushrod with locknut. **When adjusting clutch pedal clevis pin play, ensure pushrod is not pushed toward the master cylinder.**
5. Upon completing adjustments above, ensure clutch pedal freeplay (C) is 0.2–0.5 inch.
6. **On 1993–94 models,** ensure distance (D) between clutch pedal pad and firewall, when clutch pedal is disengaged, **Fig. 4,** is 2.2 inches or more.
7. **On 1995–96 models,** ensure distance (D) between clutch pedal pad and firewall, when clutch pedal is disengaged, **Fig. 4,** is 2.76 inches or more.
8. **On all models,** if clutch pedal freeplay (C) and distance (D) are not within specification, check for air in hydraulic system or a defective clutch or master cylinder assembly.

3000GT

1. Measure clutch pedal height as

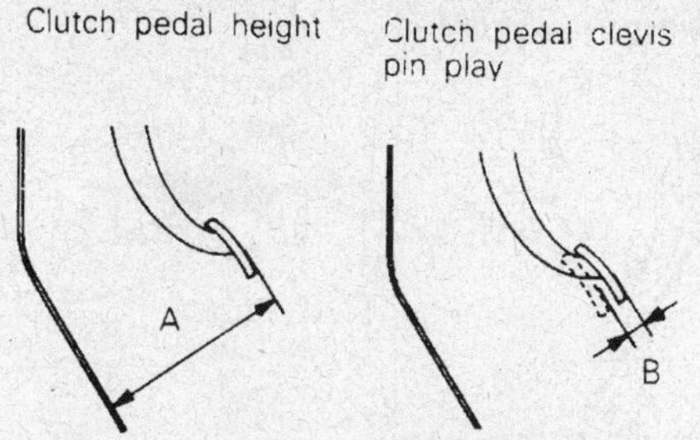
Clutch pedal height
Clutch pedal clevis pin play
A
B
MT5049100001000X

Fig. 1 Clutch pedal height & clevis pin play. Eclipse

shown, **Fig. 5.**

2. **On FWD models,** clutch pedal height should be 6.97–7.17 inches.
3. **On AWD models,** clutch pedal height should be 7.20–7.40 inches.
4. If clutch pedal height is not as specified, adjust as follows:
   a. **On models less cruise control,** turn and adjust bolt to obtain correct pedal height.
   b. **On models with cruise control,** disconnect clutch switch and turn switch to obtain correct pedal height.
5. Measure clutch pedal stroke, **Fig. 6.** If pedal stroke is not 6.29 inches or more, turn pushrod to obtain correct stroke.
6. Release pedal gradually from its full stroke position to measure amount of return made by pedal until interlock switch makes as operating sound, **Fig. 7.**
7. If amount of pedal return is not 0.394–0.591 inch, adjust by loosening locknut and turning interlock switch.
8. **On AWD models,** measure pedal play by depressing pedal two or three times to eliminate booster negative pressure with engine off, then push pedal with finger to measure play, **Fig. 8.**
9. **On all models,** measure clearance at point where clutch disengages, **Fig. 9.** On AWD models, engine must be idling.
10. Bleed hydraulic system or check master cylinder, release cylinder and hoses if clutch pedal play and clearance are not as follows:
    a. **On FWD models,** total play should be .24–.51 inch.
    b. **On AWD models,** total play should be .49–.79 inch.
    c. **On all models,** clearance from floorboard to clutch pedal pad with pedal depressed should be 2.2 inches or more.

CLUTCH BOOSTER PUSHROD & PISTON CLEARANCE

1. Measure dimension (B) between master cylinder and face and piston, **Fig. 10.** Measure with square placed on master cylinder end face then subtract thickness of square equaling (B).
2. Obtain dimension (C) between clutch booster mounting surface and master cylinder end face, **Fig. 11.**

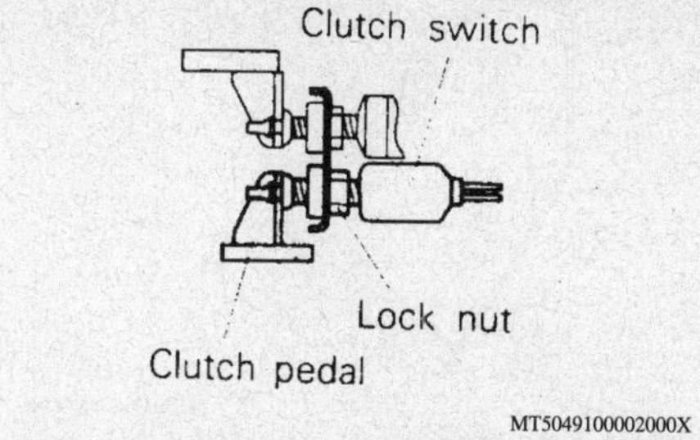
Clutch switch
Lock nut
Clutch pedal
MT5049100002000X

Fig. 2 Locknut location. Eclipse

3. Measure dimension (D) between master cylinder mounting surface on clutch booster and the pushrod end, **Fig. 12.** Measure with square placed on clutch booster, then subtract thickness of square equaling (D).
4. Using measured values obtained in steps 1 through 3, obtain clearance for dimension (A), **Fig. 13,** between clutch booster pushrod and piston using following formula: (A (A = B - C - D)).
5. If clearance is not within 0.0082–0.0181 inch, adjust by changing pushrod length by turning adjustable end of pushrod. **When clutch booster negative pressure of 9.7 psi is applied, the clearance (A) becomes 0.0039–0.0118 inch.**

HYDRAULIC SYSTEM SERVICE

CLUTCH BOOSTER INSPECTION

1. Run engine for one minute or more, then turn engine off.
2. Step on clutch pedal several times with normal pressure.
3. If pedal depressed fully the first time but gradually becomes higher when depressed several times, the booster is operating correctly.
4. If pedal height remains unchanged, booster is faulty.
5. With engine off, step on clutch pedal several times with same foot pressure, then step on clutch pedal and start engine.
6. If pedal moves downward slightly, booster is in good condition. If there is no change in pedal height, booster is faulty.
7. With engine idling, step on clutch pedal and turn engine off.
8. If pedal height does not change, booster is operating correctly. If pedal height rises, booster is faulty.
9. If one or more of the above tests fail, ensure condition of valve and vacuum hose and if necessary, replace booster.

CLUTCH CONTROL COMPONENTS, REPLACE

1. Remove air cleaner assembly.
2. Drain clutch system fluid into an appropriate container.
3. Remove clutch control components in numbered sequence as shown, **Figs. 14 through 17,** noting the following:

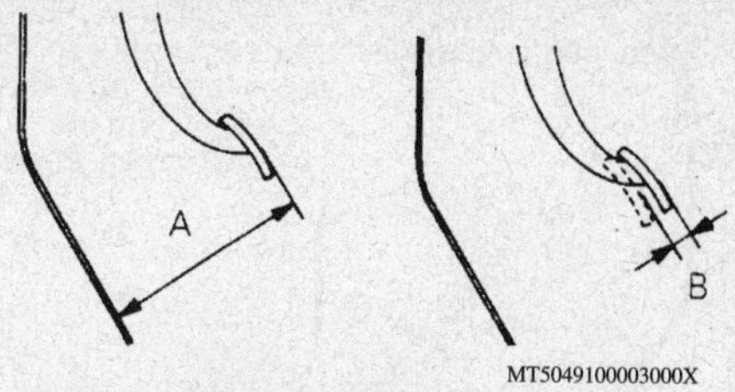
A
B
MT5049100003000X

Fig. 3 Clutch pedal clevis pin play. Eclipse

   a. Disconnect clutch hose from tube by securing nut on clutch hose, then loosen flare nut on clutch tube. Remove clip from clutch hose to remove clutch hose from bracket.
   b. **On 3000GT AWD,** use a flat type box wrench to remove clutch release cylinder bolts.
4. Reverse procedure to install. Temporarily tighten flare nut by hand, then tighten to specifications and ensure clutch hose does not become twisted.
5. **On 3000GT AWD,** adjust clearance between clutch booster pushrod and piston as outlined under "Clutch Booster Pushrod & Piston Clearance Adjust."

CLUTCH MASTER CYLINDER SERVICE

1. **On Eclipse,** remove piston stop ring, **Figs. 18** and **19.**
2. **On 3000GT,** remove piston stop ring (FWD) or the snap ring (AWD) while depressing the piston, **Fig. 20.**
3. **On all models,** remove piston assembly. **Do not damage master cylinder body or piston assembly. Do not disassemble piston assembly.**
4. Inspect inside cylinder body and piston for rust or scars and the piston cup for wear or deformation, replace as necessary.
5. Inspect clutch tube connection part for clogging.
6. Reverse procedure to assemble, tightening reservoir band.

CLUTCH

REPLACE

1. Remove transaxle as outlined under "Manual Transaxle, Replace."
2. Insert clutch disc guide tool No. MD998126, or equivalent, into center hole to prevent dropping of clutch disc, then diagonally loosen bolts that hold clutch cover assembly to remove clutch cover assembly. **Do not clean clutch disc or release bearing with cleaning solvent.**
3. Remove snap ring and clevis pin, then the release cylinder assembly, if equipped.
4. Remove return clip, then the release bearing.
5. Remove spring pins from clutch release fork and shaft using a suitable punch.
6. Install release shaft and packing, then the return spring and release fork.

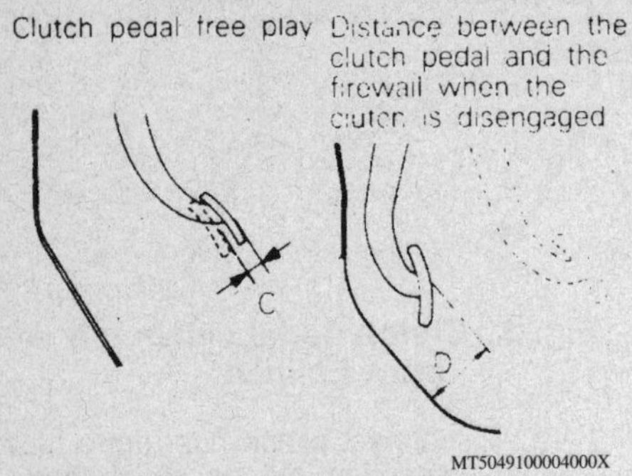
Clutch pedal free play
Distance between the clutch pedal and the firewall when the clutch is disengaged
C
D
MT5049100004000X

Fig. 4 Clutch pedal freeplay & distance to firewall. Eclipse

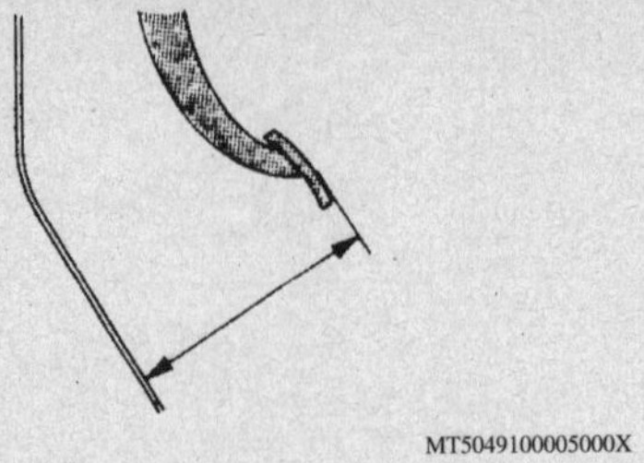
MT5049100005000X

Fig. 5 Clutch pedal height inspection. 3000GT

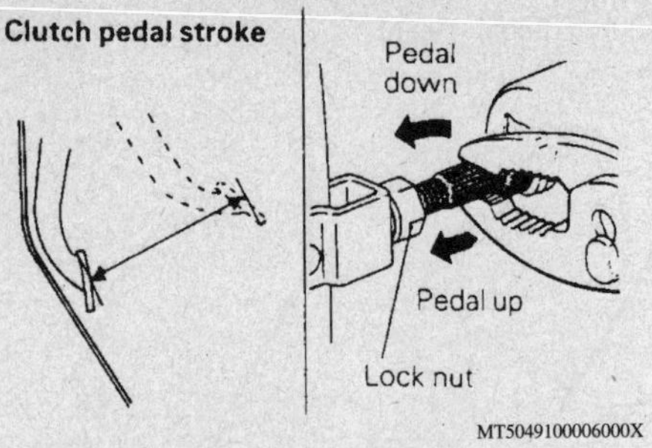
Clutch pedal stroke
Pedal down
Pedal up
Lock nut
MT5049100006000X

Fig. 6 Clutch pedal stroke inspection. 3000GT

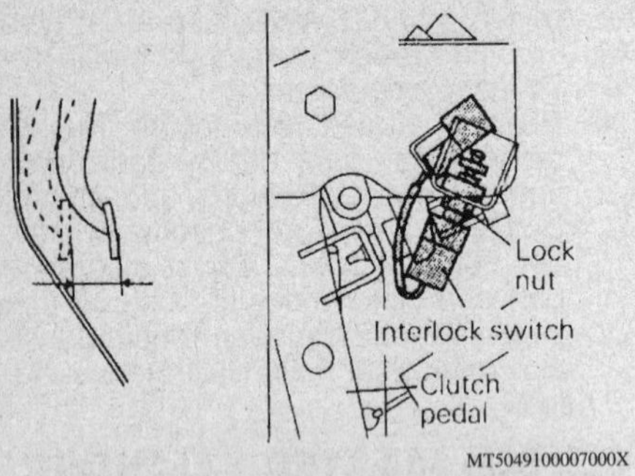
Lock nut
Interlock switch
Clutch pedal
MT5049100007000X

Fig. 7 Clutch pedal interlock operation inspection. 3000GT

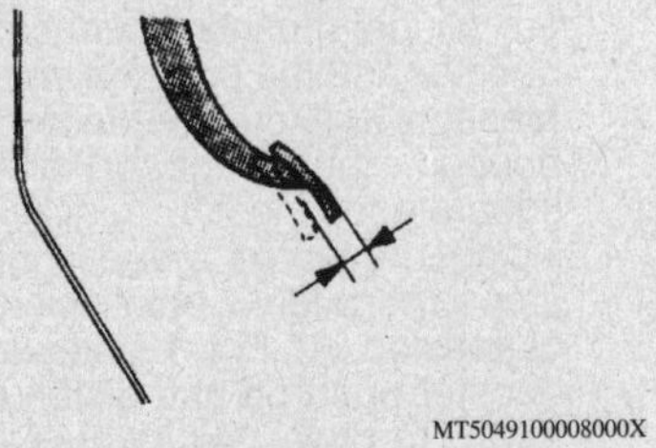
MT5049100008000X

Fig. 8 Clutch pedal freeplay check. 3000GT AWD

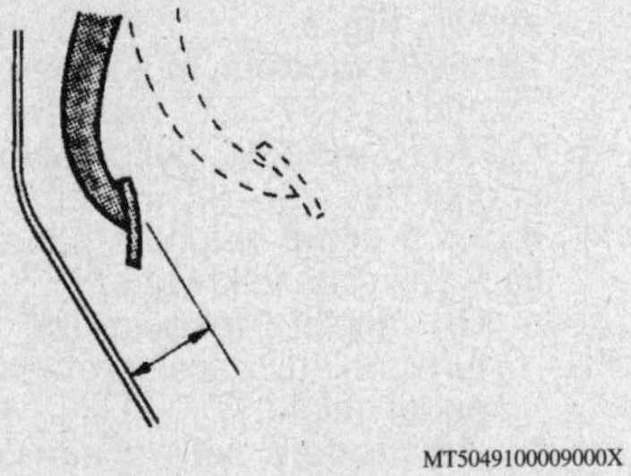
MT5049100009000X

Fig. 9 Clutch disengagement check. 3000GT

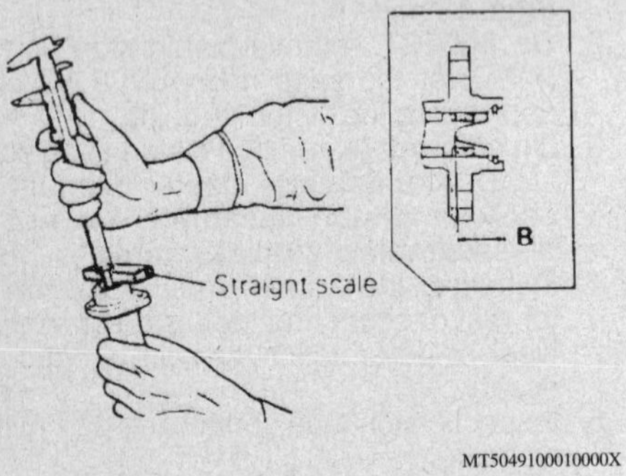
B
Straight scale
MT5049100010000X

Fig. 10 Pushrod clearance measurement (B). 3000GT AWD

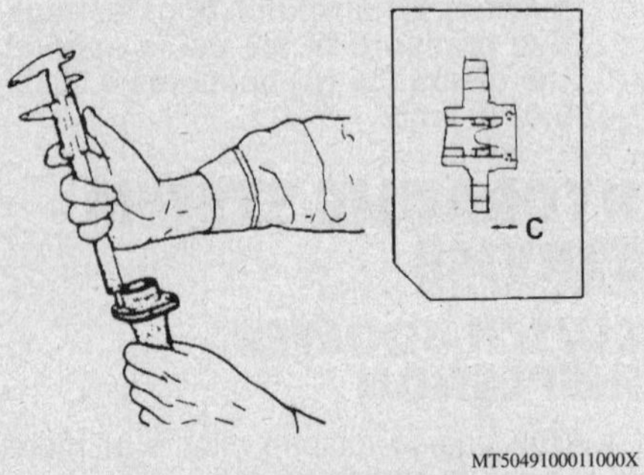
C
MT5049100011000X

Fig. 11 Pushrod clearance measurement (C). 3000GT AWD

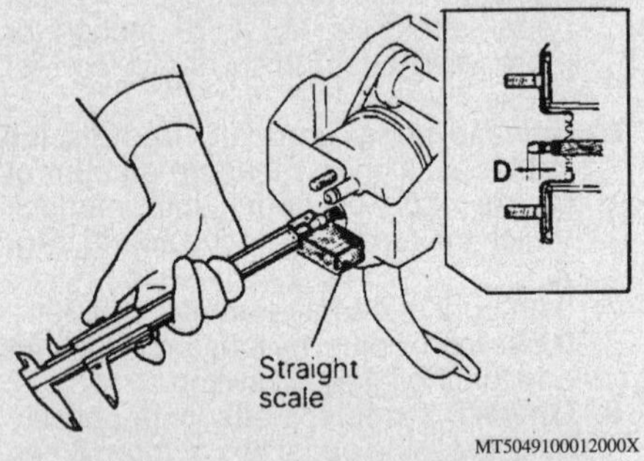
D
Straight scale
MT5049100012000X

Fig. 12 Pushrod clearance measurement (D). 3000GT AWD

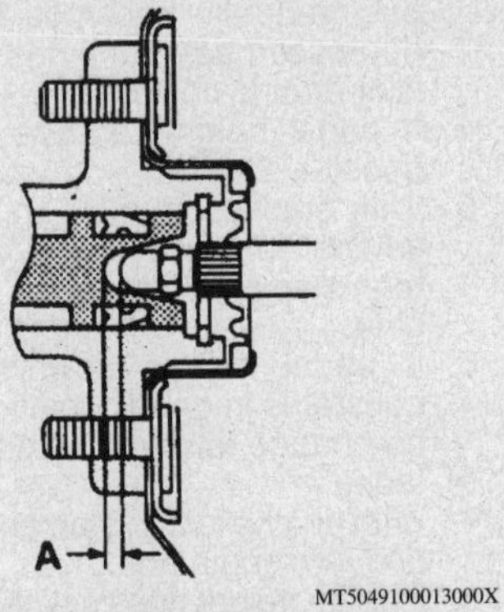
A
MT5049100013000X

Fig. 13 Pushrod clearance measurement (A). 3000GT AWD

7. Align lockpin holes of shift arm and control shaft, then drive in two new spring pins.
8. When installing spring pins, ensure spring pin slot direction is at right angles to center line of control shaft.
9. Remove grease from clutch facing by wiping with clean cloth.
10. Apply small amount of grease to clutch disc spline and input shaft spline.
11. Using clutch installer tool No. MD998126, or equivalent, install clutch disc and clutch cover assembly to flywheel. When installing clutch disc, ensure surface with manufacturer's stamped mark is on pressure plate side.

SHIFT CABLE

REPLACE

Replace transaxle shift cables in numbered sequences shown in **Figs. 21 through 23,** noting the following when installing:

1. Install shift lever assembly bushings with the side marked UP facing upward.
2. Install select cable as follows:
   a. Install select cable on the transaxle end.
   b. Place transaxle in Neutral position.
   c. Place gear selector in Neutral position.
   d. Adjust length of select cable then install cable onto gear selector assembly as shown, **Fig. 24.**
3. Install shift cable as follows:
   a. Install shift cable on the transaxle end.
   b. Keeping select lever on transaxle in the Neutral position, move shift lever on transaxle into 4th gear as shown, **Fig. 25.**
   c. Position gear selector lever into the 4th gear position, **Fig. 26,** and adjust length of shift cable and install cable onto the gear selector lever as shown.
4. Ensure transaxle controls function properly.

TRANSAXLE

REPLACE

ECLIPSE

1993–94

1. Disconnect battery cables, then remove battery.

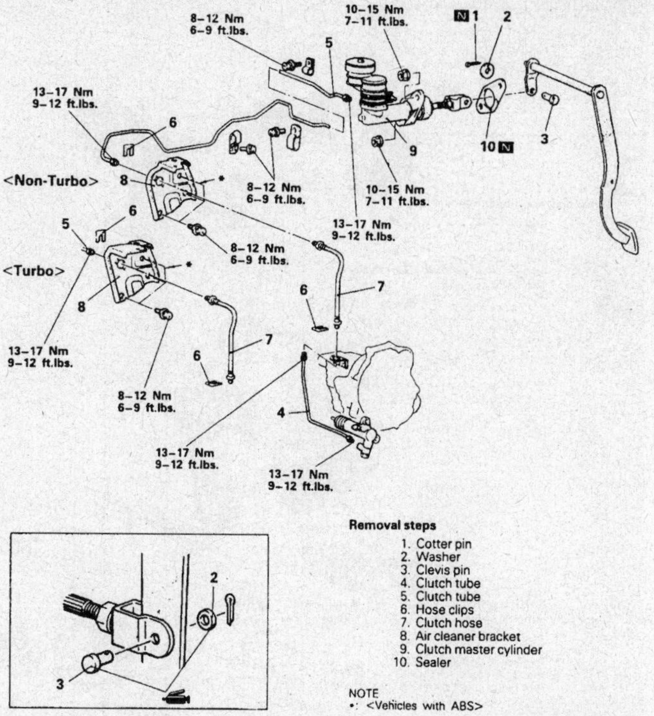
8–12 Nm
6–9 ft.lbs.
10–15 Nm
7–11 ft.lbs.
13–17 Nm
9–12 ft.lbs.
<Non-Turbo>
<Turbo>
Removal steps
1. Cotter pin
2. Washer
3. Clevis pin
4. Clutch tube
5. Clutch tube
6. Hose clips
7. Clutch hose
8. Air cleaner bracket
9. Clutch master cylinder
10. Sealer
NOTE
•: <Vehicles with ABS>
MT5049100014000X

Fig. 14 Clutch control component replacement. 1993–94 Eclipse

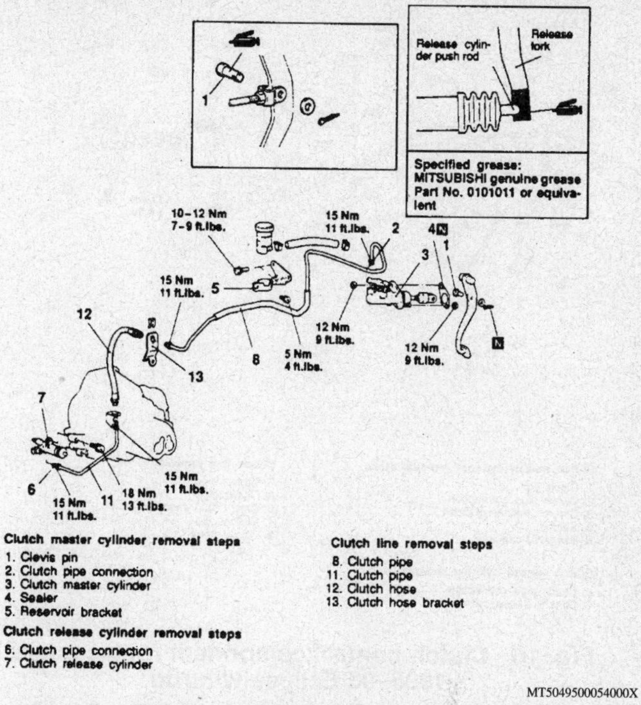
Release cylinder push rod
Release fork
Specified grease:
MITSUBISHI genuine grease Part No. 0101011 or equivalent
10–12 Nm
7–9 ft.lbs.
15 Nm
11 ft.lbs.
12 Nm
9 ft.lbs.
5 Nm
4 ft.lbs.
18 Nm
13 ft.lbs.
Clutch master cylinder removal steps
1. Clevis pin
2. Clutch pipe connection
3. Clutch master cylinder
4. Sealer
5. Reservoir bracket
Clutch release cylinder removal steps
6. Clutch pipe connection
7. Clutch release cylinder
Clutch line removal steps
8. Clutch pipe
11. Clutch pipe
12. Clutch hose
13. Clutch hose bracket
MT5049500054000X

Fig. 15 Clutch control component replacement. 1995–96 Eclipse less turbo

2. Drain transmission fluid into a suitable container.
3. Remove air cleaner hoses and air cleaner assembly.
4. Remove transaxle in numbered sequence shown in **Figs. 27 and 28,** noting the following:
   a. Remove clutch release cylinder bolt and oil line bracket and secure to body side without disconnecting the oil line.
   b. Loosen ball joint stud nut, then break ball joint loose from steering knuckle using a suitable tool.
   c. Loosen tie rod end stud nut, then disconnect tie rod end from steering knuckle using a suitable tool.
   d. **On FWD models,** remove driveshaft by placing a suitable pry bar between the transaxle and the driveshaft. **To avoid damaging oil seal, do not insert screwdrivers more than necessary.**
   e. **On AWD models,** remove right-hand driveshaft by placing a suitable pry bar between the transaxle and the driveshaft. **To avoid damaging oil seal, do not insert screwdrivers more than necessary.**
   f. Secure driveshaft to body, keeping as far away as possible from transaxle case.
   g. **On all models,** support transaxle assembly suing a suitable jack then move transaxle to the right and slowly lower transaxle from vehicle.
5. Reverse numbered sequence shown in **Figs. 27 and 28** to install transaxle, noting the following:
   a. Install driveshaft with the inboard joint of the driveshaft is straight relative to the transaxle.
   b. Align serrations and securely insert driveshaft into transaxle.
   c. Ensure starter ground cable connections.
   d. Fill transaxle with fluid, install battery and air cleaner. Check for proper operation of transaxle.

1995–96

1. Drain transaxle oil into a suitable container, then remove battery and engine undercover.
2. **On AWD models,** remove transfer assembly as outlined in "Transfer Cases."
3. Remove transaxle in numbered sequences shown, **Figs. 29 and 30,** noting the following:
   a. When removing transaxle mounting bracket nuts, use a suitable garage jack to raise transaxle assembly slightly. **Do not allow transaxle to tilt.**
   b. Support engine using support tool No. MZ203827, or equivalent.
   c. Use separator tool No. MB991113, or equivalent, to free tie rod end, lateral lower arm and compression lower arm.
   d. Use a suitable pry bar to separate driveshaft from transaxle case.
   e. Insert plug tool No. MB991460, or equivalent, into transaxle case to prevent entry of foreign matter.
   f. Support driveshaft to prevent joints from flexing excessively.
   g. When removing clutch release cylinder, it is not necessary to disconnect hydraulic line; simply support cylinder aside.
4. Reverse procedure to install, noting the following:
   a. Do not allow serrated portion of driveshaft to damage oil seal.
   b. **On AWD models,** ensure driveshaft washer is installed with convex side facing outward, then use a torque wrench and holding tool No. MB990767, or equivalent, to **torque** driveshaft nut to 145–188 ft. lbs.

3000GT

1. Drain transaxle fluid into an appropriate container.
2. **On models with an active aero system,** remove active front venturi skirt in numbered sequence as shown, **Fig. 31.**
3. **On AWD models,** remove transfer assembly as outlined under "Transfer Case, Replace."
4. **On all models,** remove front exhaust pipe.
5. Remove front lower cover.
6. Remove transaxle in numbered sequence as shown, **Figs. 32 and 33,** noting the following:
   a. Remove clutch release cylinder and clutch oil line bracket bolts, then secure to body using suitable wire without disconnecting oil line coupling.
   b. Raise transaxle assembly using suitable transmission stand to release weight off mounts, then remove transaxle mount insulator bolt.
   c. Loosen, but do not remove, tie rod ends using ball joint puller tool No. MB991113-01, or equivalent.
   d. Loosen, but do not remove, lower arm ball joint using ball joint tool.

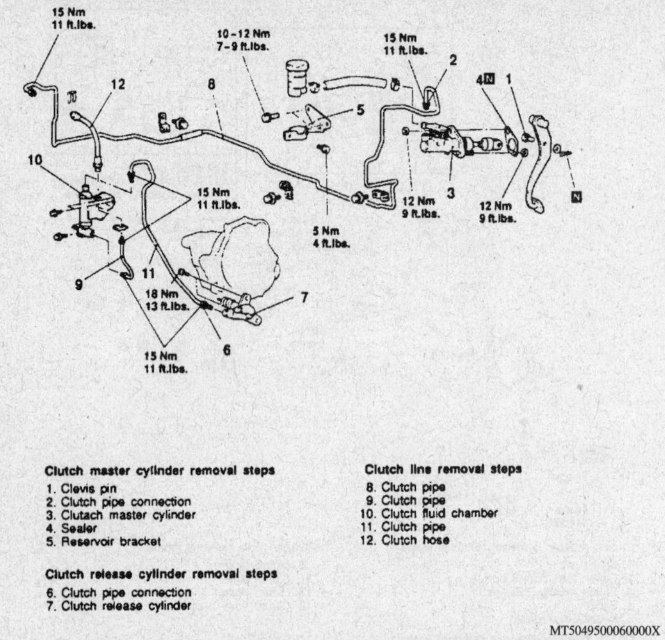
Clutch master cylinder removal steps
1. Clevis pin
2. Clutch pipe connection
3. Clutach master cylinder
4. Sealer
5. Reservoir bracket
Clutch line removal steps
8. Clutch pipe
9. Clutch pipe
10. Clutch fluid chamber
11. Clutch pipe
12. Clutch hose
Clutch release cylinder removal steps
6. Clutch pipe connection
7. Clutch release cylinder
MT5049500060000X

Fig. 16 Clutch control component replacement. 1995–96 Eclipse w/turbo

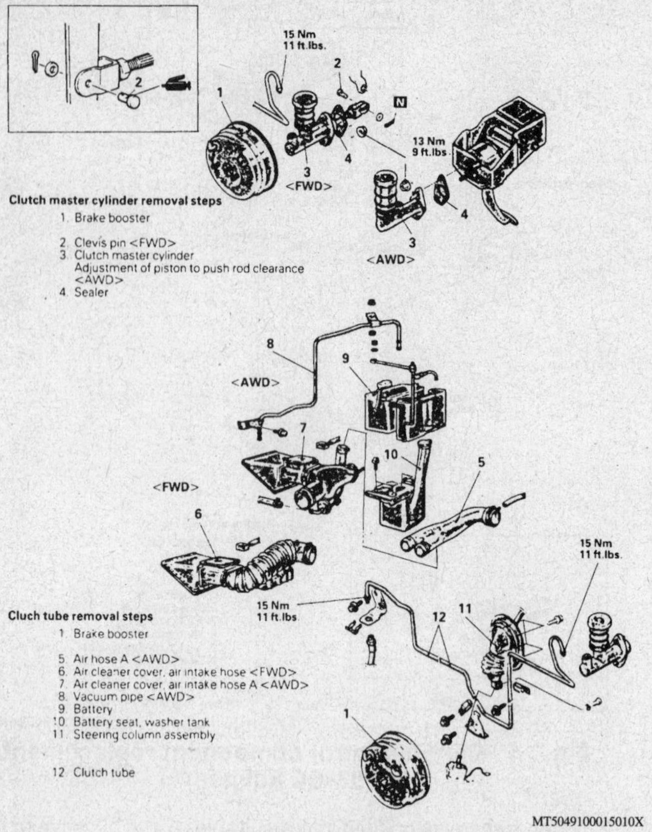
Clutch master cylinder removal steps
1. Brake booster
2. Clevis pin <FWD>
3. Clutch master cylinder
Adjustment of piston to push rod clearance <AWD>
4. Sealer
Cluch tube removal steps
1. Brake booster
5. Air hose A <AWD>
6. Air cleaner cover, air intake hose <FWD>
7. Air cleaner cover, air intake hose A <AWD>
8. Vacuum pipe <AWD>
9. Battery
10. Battery seat, washer tank
11. Steering column assembly
12. Clutch tube
MT5049100015010X

Fig. 17 Clutch control component replacement (Part 1 of 2). 3000GT

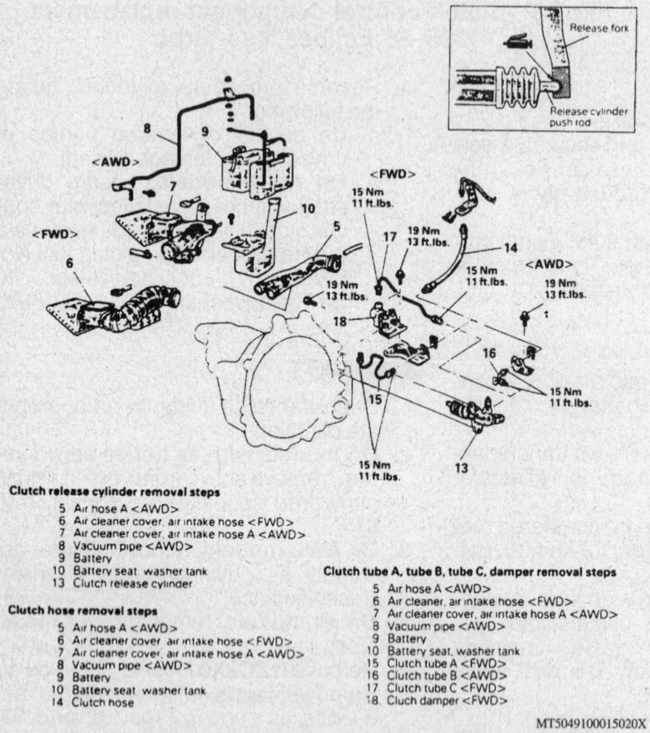
Release fork
Release cylinder push rod
Clutch release cylinder removal steps
5 Air hose A <AWD>
6 Air cleaner cover, air intake hose <FWD>
7 Air cleaner cover, air intake hose A <AWD>
8 Vacuum pipe <AWD>
9 Battery
10 Battery seat, washer tank
13 Clutch release cylinder
Clutch hose removal steps
5 Air hose A <AWD>
6 Air cleaner cover, air intake hose <FWD>
7 Air cleaner cover, air intake hose A <AWD>
8 Vacuum pipe <AWD>
9 Battery
10 Battery seat, washer tank
14 Clutch hose
Clutch tube A, tube B, tube C, damper removal steps
5 Air hose A <AWD>
6 Air cleaner, air intake hose <FWD>
7 Air cleaner cover, air intake hose A <AWD>
8 Vacuum pipe <AWD>
9 Battery
10 Battery seat, washer tank
15 Clutch tube A <FWD>
16 Clutch tube B <AWD>
17 Clutch tube C <FWD>
18. Cluch damper <FWD>
MT5049100015020X

Fig. 17 Clutch control component replacement (Part 2 of 2). 3000GT

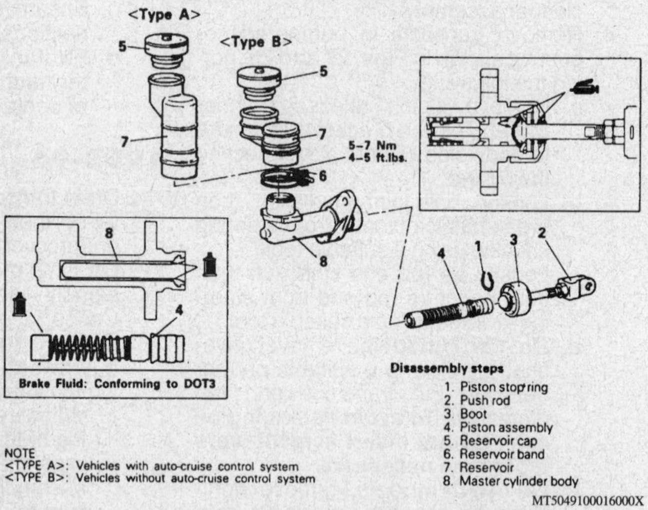
<Type A>
<Type B>
5–7 Nm
4–5 ft.lbs.
Brake Fluid: Conforming to DOT3
NOTE
<TYPE A>: Vehicles with auto-cruise control system
<TYPE B>: Vehicles without auto-cruise control system
Disassembly steps
1. Piston stop ring
2. Push rod
3. Boot
4. Piston assembly
5. Reservoir cap
6. Reservoir band
7. Reservoir
8. Master cylinder body
MT5049100016000X

Fig. 18 Clutch master cylinder. 1993–94 Eclipse

e. Remove lefthand driveshaft bearing bracket bolts, then insert pry bar between bearing bracket and cylinder block, **Fig. 34.**

f. Remove lefthand driveshaft and inner shaft assembly from transaxle. **Remove driveshaft and inner shaft as an assembly together with hub, knuckle and other parts.**

g. Suspend removed lefthand driveshaft and inner shaft assembly with suitable wire to prevent shaft from sharply bending or turning at each joint.

h. To remove righthand driveshaft from transaxle assembly, apply pry bar to protrusion, **Fig. 35.** Remove driveshaft as an assembly together with hub, knuckle and other parts.

i. Suspend removed lefthand driveshaft assembly with suitable wire to prevent shaft from sharply bending or turning at each joint.

j. Support transaxle assembly with a suitable transaxle stand, then remove transaxle assembly lower part coupling and lower transaxle assembly.

7. Reverse procedure to install, **Fig. 36.**

TECHNICAL SERVICE BULLETINS

MANUAL TRANSAXLE GEAR OIL SPECIFICATION

Manual transaxles in these vehicles require API GL-4 gear oil. Use of other API

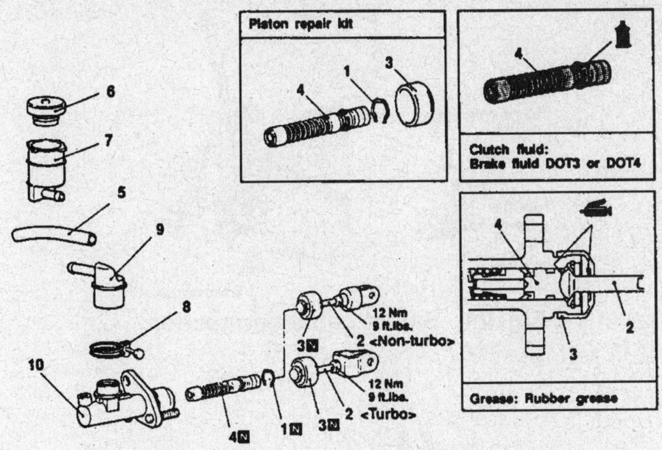
Piston repair kit
Clutch fluid:
Brake fluid DOT3 or DOT4
Grease: Rubber grease
12 Nm
9 ft.lbs.
2 <Non-turbo>
12 Nm
9 ft.lbs.
2 <Turbo>

Disassembly steps

1. Piston stopper ring
2. Push rod assembly
3. Boot
4. Piston assembly
5. Reservoir hose
6. Reservoir cap
7. Reservoir tank
8. Reservoir band
9. Nipple
10. Clutch master cylinder body

MT5049500062000X

Fig. 19 Clutch master cylinder. 1995–96 Eclipse

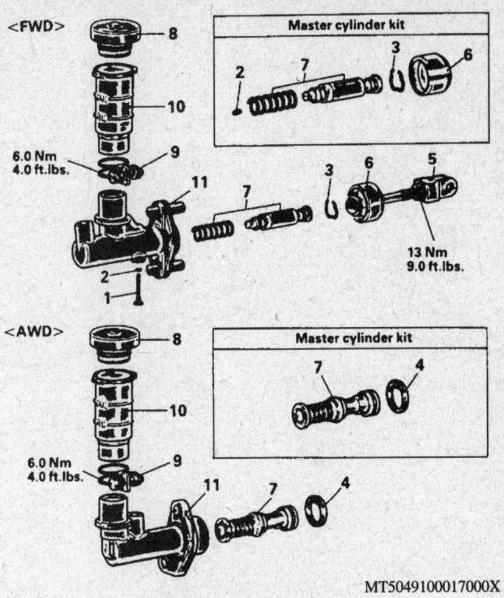
<FWD>
<AWD>
Master cylinder kit
6.0 Nm
4.0 ft.lbs.
13 Nm
9.0 ft.lbs.
Brake fluid:
Conforming to DOT3 or DOT4

Disassembly steps

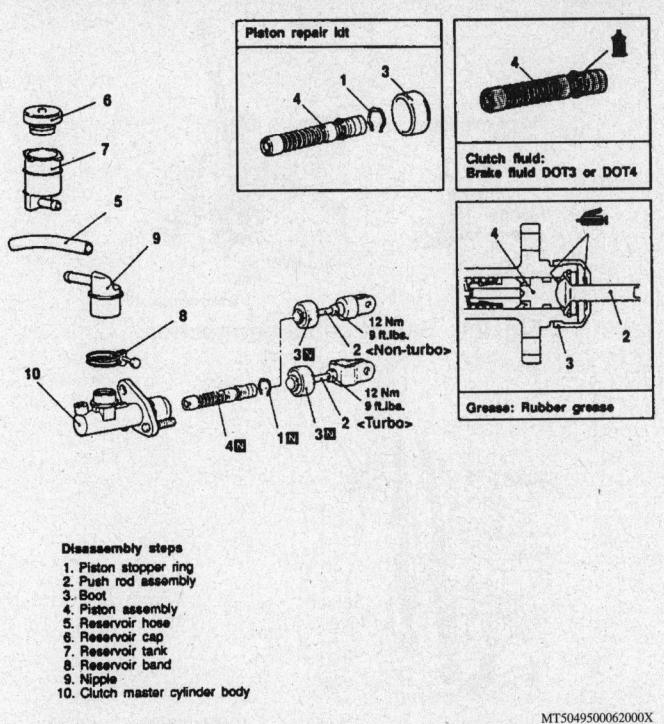

1. Piston stop bolt <FWD>
2. Gasket <FWD>
3. Piston stop ring <FWD>
4. Snap ring <AWD>
5. Push rod <FWD>
6. Boot <FWD>
7. Piston assembly
8. Reservoir cap
9. Reservoir band
10. Reservoir
11. Master cylinder body

MT5049100017000X

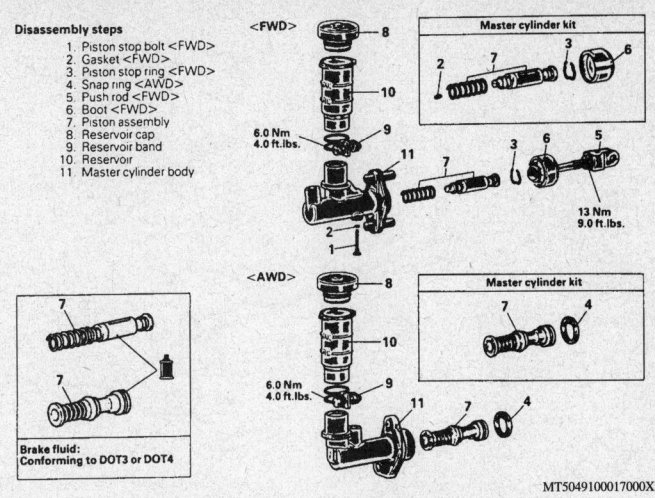

Fig. 20 Clutch master cylinder. 3000GT

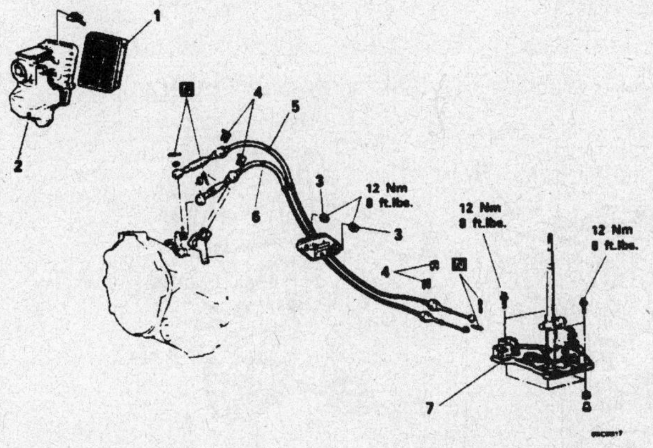
12 Nm
8 ft.lbs.

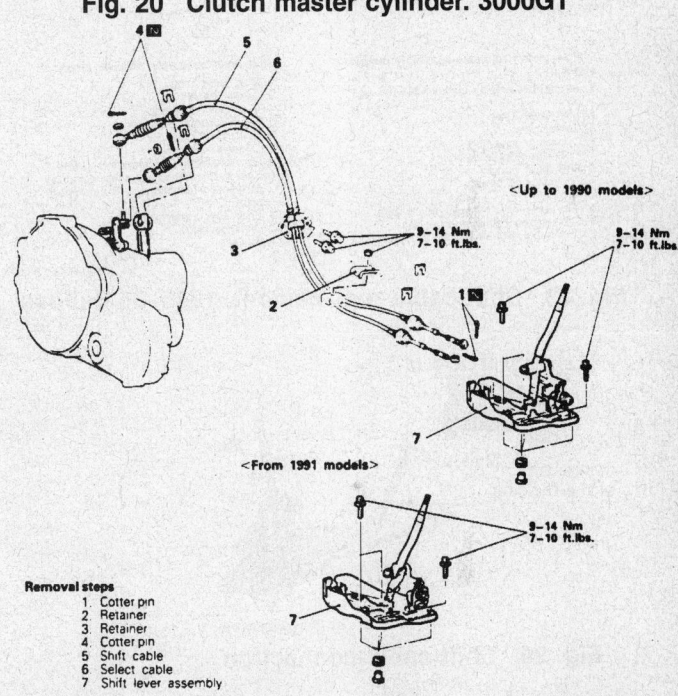

Removal steps of the transaxle control cable assembly

1. Air cleaner element
2. Air cleaner cover
3. Nut
4. Clip
5. Shift cable
6. Select cable

Removal of the shift lever assembly

7. Shift lever assembly

MT5038900125000X

Fig. 21 Shift cable replacement. 3000GT

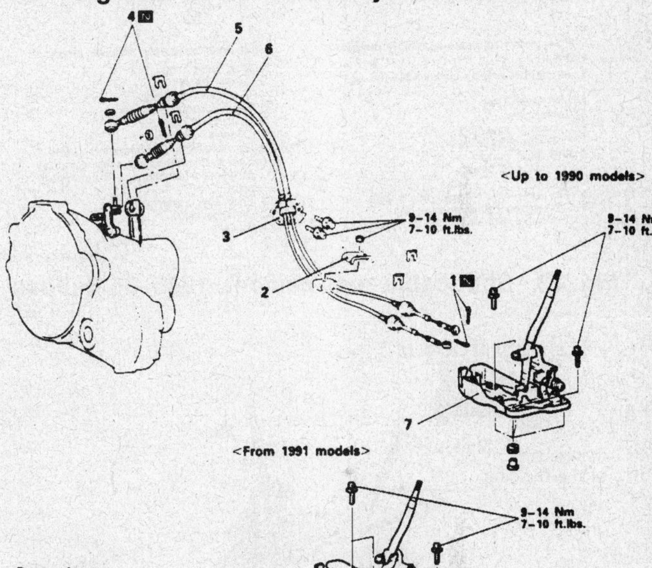
<Up to 1990 models>
<From 1991 models>
9–14 Nm
7–10 ft.lbs.

Removal steps

1. Cotter pin
2. Retainer
3. Retainer
4. Cotter pin
5. Shift cable
6. Select cable
7. Shift lever assembly

MT5038900126000X

Fig. 22 Shift cable replacement. 1993–94 Eclipse

gear oils, such as GL-5, may affect shift effort and result in internal transaxle damage due to chemical reactions with copper synchronizer rings. Mitsubishi Diamond Gear Lube No. A991ZC2X01 (SAE 75W–85W GL-4) or equivalent is recommended.

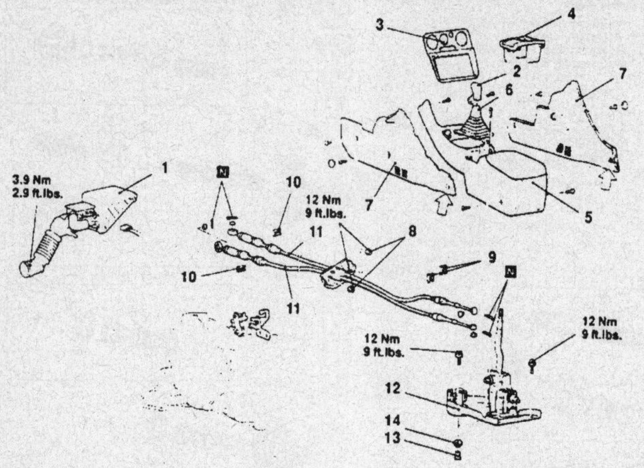
3.9 Nm
2.9 ft.lbs.
12 Nm
9 ft.lbs.
12 Nm
9 ft.lbs.
12 Nm
9 ft.lbs.

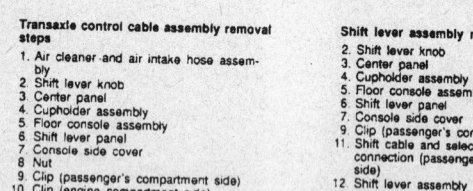

NOTE
⇦ : Resin clip position

Transaxle control cable assembly removal steps

1. Air cleaner and air intake hose assembly
2. Shift lever knob
3. Center panel
4. Cupholder assembly
5. Floor console assembly
6. Shift lever panel
7. Console side cover
8. Nut
9. Clip (passenger's compartment side)
10. Clip (engine compartment side)
11. Shift cable and select cable assembly

Shift lever assembly removal steps

2. Shift lever knob
3. Center panel
4. Cupholder assembly
5. Floor console assembly
6. Shift lever panel
7. Console side cover
9. Clip (passenger's compartment side
11. Shift cable and select cable assembly connection (passenger's compartment side)
12. Shift lever assembly
13. Distance piece
14. Bushing

MT5039500128000X

Fig. 23 Shift cable replacement. 1995–96 Eclipse

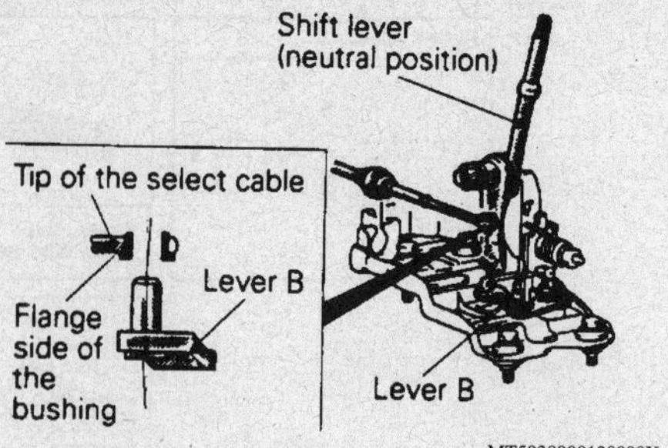
Shift lever
(neutral position)
Tip of the select cable
Lever B
Flange side of the bushing
Lever B

MT5038900128000X

Fig. 24 Select cable connection

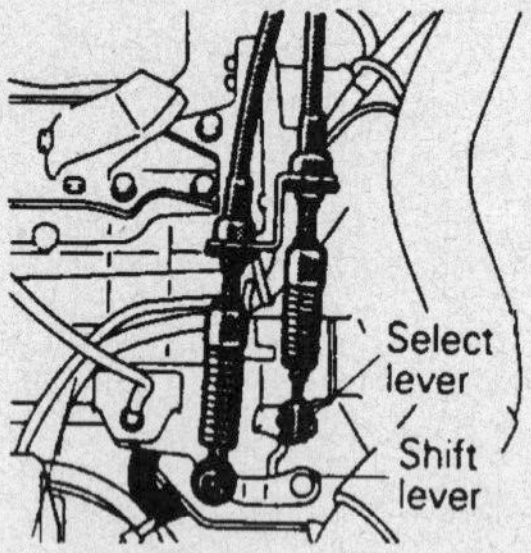
Select lever
Shift lever

MT5038900129000X

Fig. 25 Transaxle control position

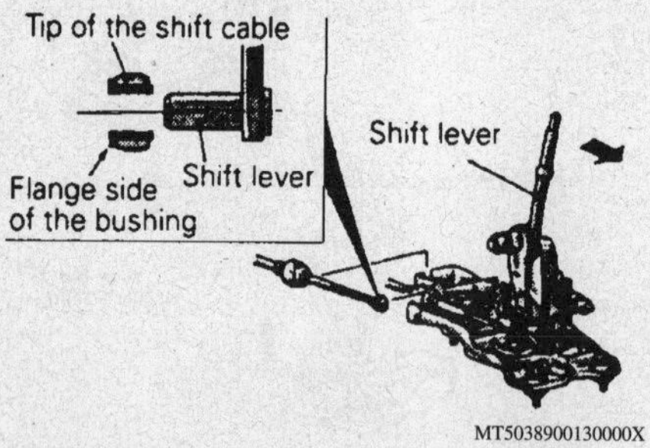
Tip of the shift cable
Shift lever
Flange side of the bushing
Shift lever

MT5038900130000X

Fig. 26 Shift cable connection

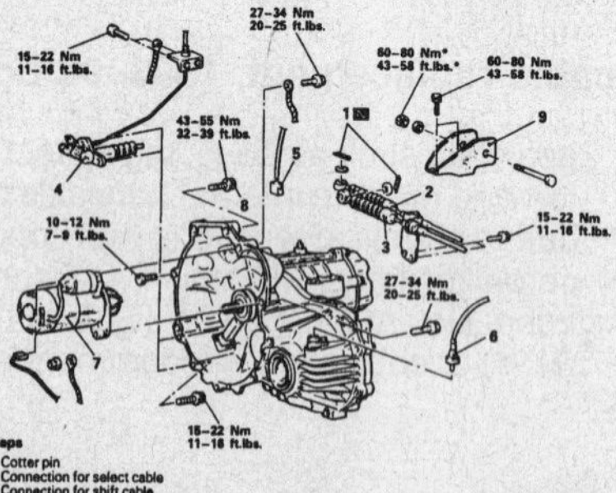
15–22 Nm
11–16 ft.lbs.
27–34 Nm
20–25 ft.lbs.
60–80 Nm*
43–58 ft.lbs.*
60–80 Nm
43–58 ft.lbs.
43–55 Nm
32–39 ft.lbs.
10–12 Nm
7–9 ft.lbs.
15–22 Nm
11–16 ft.lbs.
27–34 Nm
20–25 ft.lbs.
15–22 Nm
11–16 ft.lbs.

Removal steps

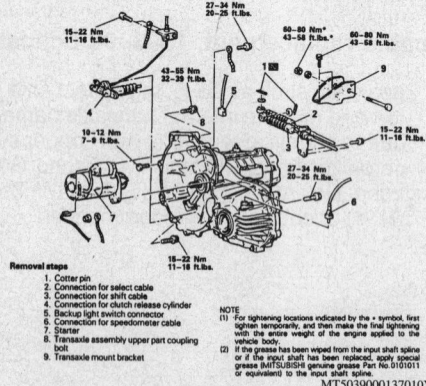

1. Cotter pin
2. Connection for select cable
3. Connection for shift cable
4. Connection for clutch release cylinder
5. Backup light switch connector
6. Connection for speedometer cable
7. Starter
8. Transaxle assembly upper part coupling bolt
9. Transaxle mount bracket

NOTE
(1) For tightening locations indicated by the * symbol, first tighten temporarily, and then make the final tightening with the entire weight of the engine applied to the vehicle body.
(2) If the grease has been wiped from the input shaft spline or if the input shaft has been replaced, apply special grease (MITSUBISHI genuine grease Part No.0101011 or equivalent) to the input shaft spline.

MT5039000137010X

Fig. 27 Transaxle replacement (Part 1 of 2). 1993–94 Eclipse FWD

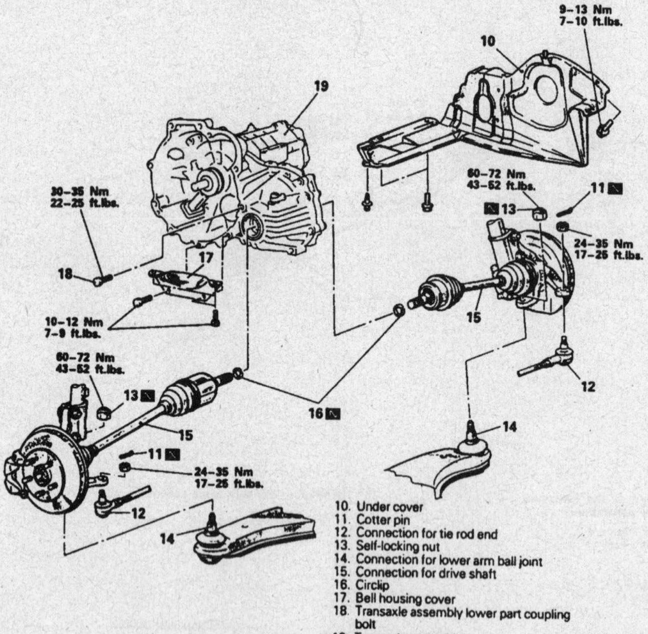
9–13 Nm
7–10 ft.lbs.
30–35 Nm
22–25 ft.lbs.
60–72 Nm
43–52 ft.lbs.
24–35 Nm
17–25 ft.lbs.
10–12 Nm
7–9 ft.lbs.
60–72 Nm
43–52 ft.lbs.
24–35 Nm
17–25 ft.lbs.

10. Under cover
11. Cotter pin
12. Connection for tie rod end
13. Self-locking nut
14. Connection for lower arm ball joint
15. Connection for drive shaft
16. Circlip
17. Bell housing cover
18. Transaxle assembly lower part coupling bolt
19. Transaxle assembly

MT5039000137020X

Fig. 27 Transaxle replacement (Part 2 of 2). 1993–94 Eclipse FWD

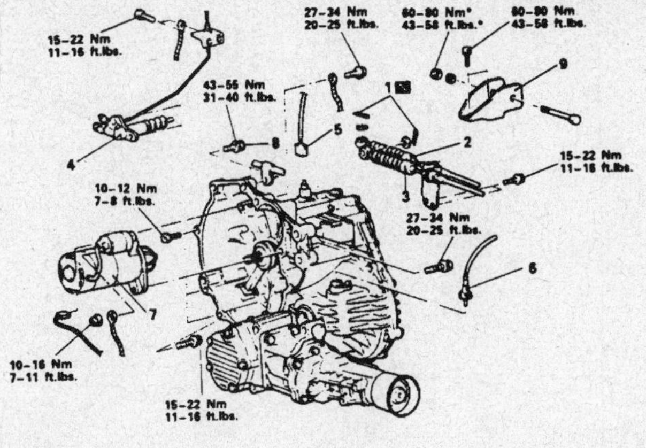
15-22 Nm
11-16 ft.lbs.
27-34 Nm
20-25 ft.lbs.
60-80 Nm*
43-58 ft.lbs.*
60-80 Nm
43-58 ft.lbs.
43-55 Nm
31-40 ft.lbs.
15-22 Nm
11-16 ft.lbs.
10-12 Nm
7-8 ft.lbs.
27-34 Nm
20-25 ft.lbs.
10-16 Nm
7-11 ft.lbs.
15-22 Nm
11-16 ft.lbs.

Removal steps

1. Cotter pin
2. Connection for select cable
3. Connection for shift cable
4. Connection for clutch release cylinder
5. Backup light switch connector
6. Connection for speedometer cable
7. Starter
8. Transaxle assembly upper part coupling bolt
9. Transaxle mount bracket

NOTE
(1) For tightening locations indicated by the * symbol, first tighten temporarily, and then make the final tightening with the entire weight of the engine applied to the vehicle body.
(2) If the grease has been wiped from the input shaft and center shaft splines or if the input shaft and center shaft have been replaced, apply special grease (MITSUBISHI genuine grease Part No. 0101011) or equivalent) to the input shaft and center shaft splines

MT5039000138010X

Fig. 28 Transaxle replacement (Part 1 of 2). 1993–94 Eclipse AWD

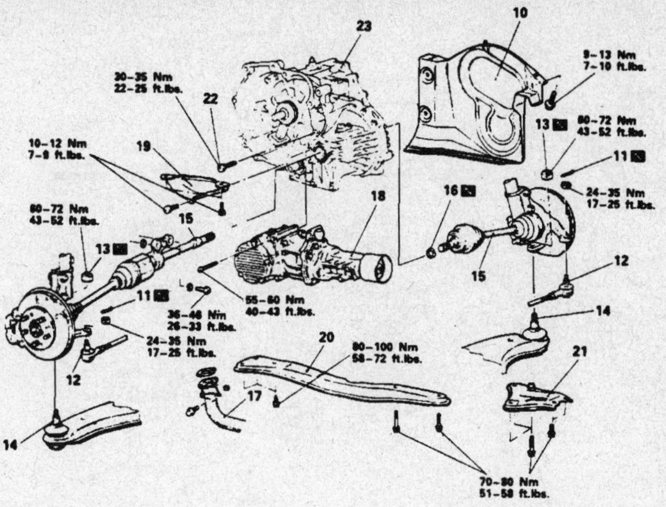
30-35 Nm
22-25 ft.lbs.
9-13 Nm
7-10 ft.lbs.
60-72 Nm
43-52 ft.lbs.
10-12 Nm
7-9 ft.lbs.
60-72 Nm
43-52 ft.lbs.
24-35 Nm
17-25 ft.lbs.
55-60 Nm
40-43 ft.lbs.
36-46 Nm
26-33 ft.lbs.
24-35 Nm
17-25 ft.lbs.
80-100 Nm
58-72 ft.lbs.
70-80 Nm
51-58 ft.lbs.

10. Under cover
11. Cotter pin
12. Connection for tie rod end
13. Self-locking nut
14. Connection for lower arm ball joint
15. Connection for drive shaft
16. Circlip
17. Front exhaust pipe
18. Transfer assembly
19. Bell housing cover
20. Right member
21. Gusset
22. Transaxle assembly lower part coupling bolt
23. Transaxle assembly

MT5039000138020X

Fig. 28 Transaxle replacement (Part 2 of 2). 1993–94 Eclipse AWD

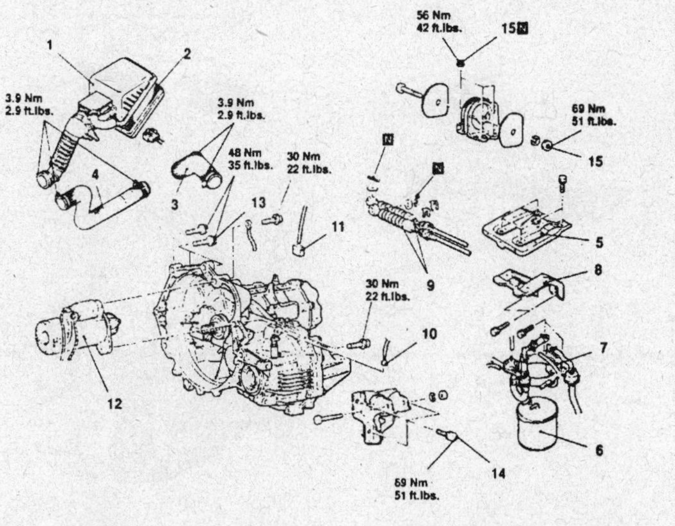
56 Nm
42 ft.lbs.
3.9 Nm
2.9 ft.lbs.
3.9 Nm
2.9 ft.lbs.
69 Nm
51 ft.lbs.
48 Nm
35 ft.lbs.
30 Nm
22 ft.lbs.
30 Nm
22 ft.lbs.
69 Nm
51 ft.lbs.

Removal steps

1. Air cleaner cover and air intake hose assembly
2. Air cleaner element
3. Air hose C
4. Air hose A
5. Battery tray
6. Evaporative emission canister
7. Evaporative emission canister holder
8. Battery tray stay
9. Shift cable and select cable connection
10. Backup light switch connector
11. Vehicle speed sensor connector
12. Starter motor
13. Transaxle assembly mounting bolts
14. Rear roll stopper bracket mounting bolts
15. Transaxle mounting bracket mounting nuts
• Supporting engine assembly

MT5039500130010X

Fig. 29 Transaxle replacement (Part 1 of 2). 1995–96 Eclipse FWD

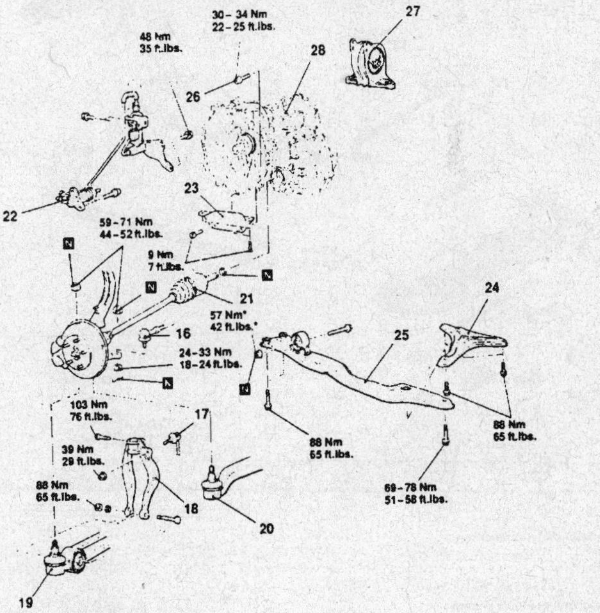
48 Nm
35 ft.lbs.
30-34 Nm
22-25 ft.lbs.
59-71 Nm
44-52 ft.lbs.
9 Nm
7 ft.lbs.
57 Nm*
42 ft.lbs.*
24-33 Nm
18-24 ft.lbs.
103 Nm
76 ft.lbs.
39 Nm
29 ft.lbs.
88 Nm
65 ft.lbs.
88 Nm
65 ft.lbs.
88 Nm
65 ft.lbs.
69-78 Nm
51-58 ft.lbs.

Lifting up of the vehicle

16. Tie rod end connection
17. Stabilizer link connection
18. Damper fork
19. Lateral lower arm connection
20. Compression lower arm connection
21. Drive shaft connection
22. Clutch release cylinder connection
23. Bell housing cover
24. Stay (R.H.)
25. Center member assembly
26. Transaxle assembly mounting bolt
27. Transaxle mounting
28. Transaxle assembly

Caution
*: Indicates parts which should be temporarily tightened, and then fully tightened with the vehicle on the ground in the unladen condition.

MT5039500130020X

Fig. 29 Transaxle replacement (Part 2 of 2). 1995–96 Eclipse FWD

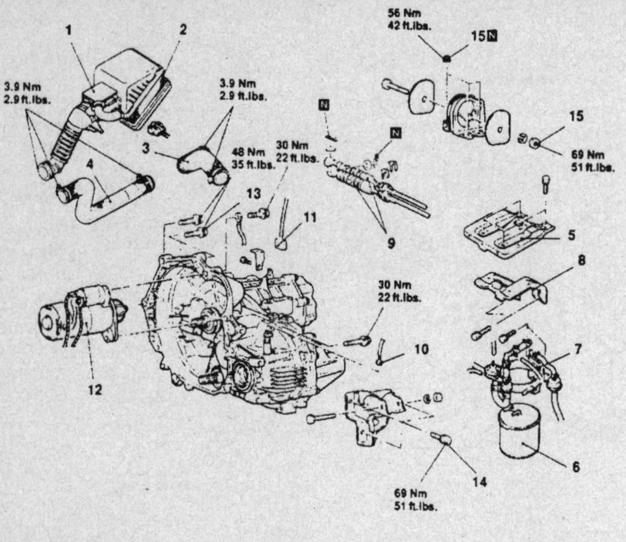
56 Nm
42 ft.lbs.
3.9 Nm
2.9 ft.lbs.
48 Nm
35 ft.lbs.
30 Nm
22 ft.lbs.
69 Nm
51 ft.lbs.

Removal steps

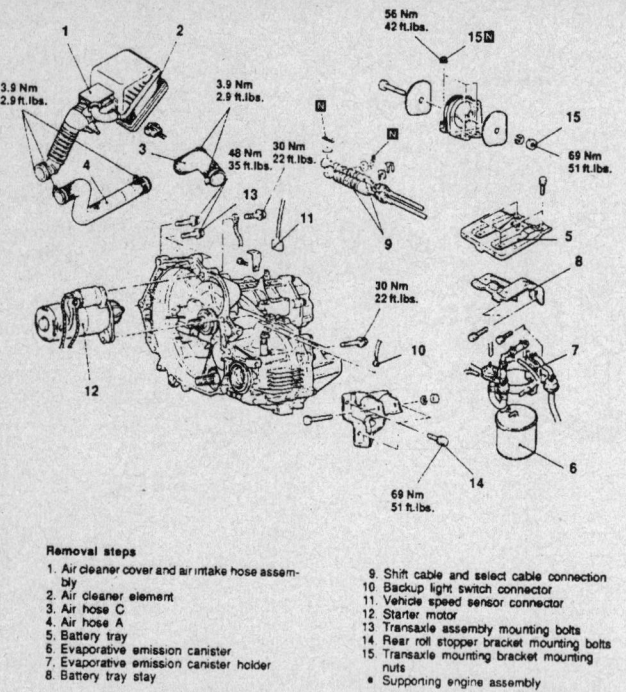

1. Air cleaner cover and air intake hose assembly
2. Air cleaner element
3. Air hose C
4. Air hose A
5. Battery tray
6. Evaporative emission canister
7. Evaporative emission canister holder
8. Battery tray stay
9. Shift cable and select cable connection
10. Backup light switch connector
11. Vehicle speed sensor connector
12. Starter motor
13. Transaxle assembly mounting bolts
14. Rear roll stopper bracket mounting bolts
15. Transaxle mounting bracket mounting nuts

• Supporting engine assembly

MT5039500131010X

Fig. 30 Transaxle replacement (Part 1 of 2). 1995–96 Eclipse AWD

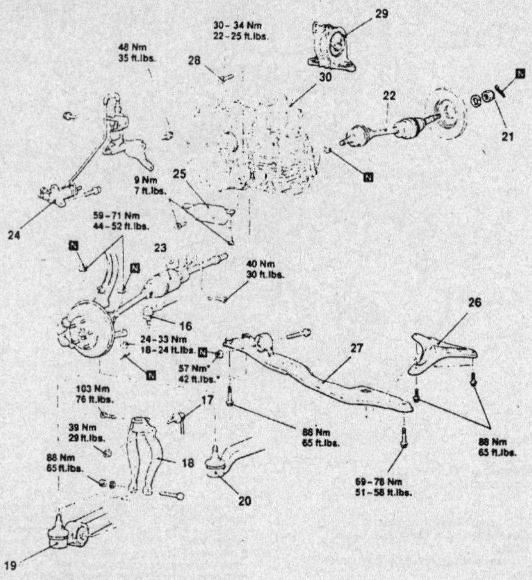
30 - 34 Nm
22 - 25 ft.lbs.
48 Nm
35 ft.lbs.
9 Nm
7 ft.lbs.
59 - 71 Nm
44 - 52 ft.lbs.
40 Nm
30 ft.lbs.
24 - 33 Nm
18 - 24 ft.lbs.
57 Nm*
42 ft.lbs.*
103 Nm
76 ft.lbs.
39 Nm
29 ft.lbs.
88 Nm
65 ft.lbs.
69 - 78 Nm
51 - 58 ft.lbs.

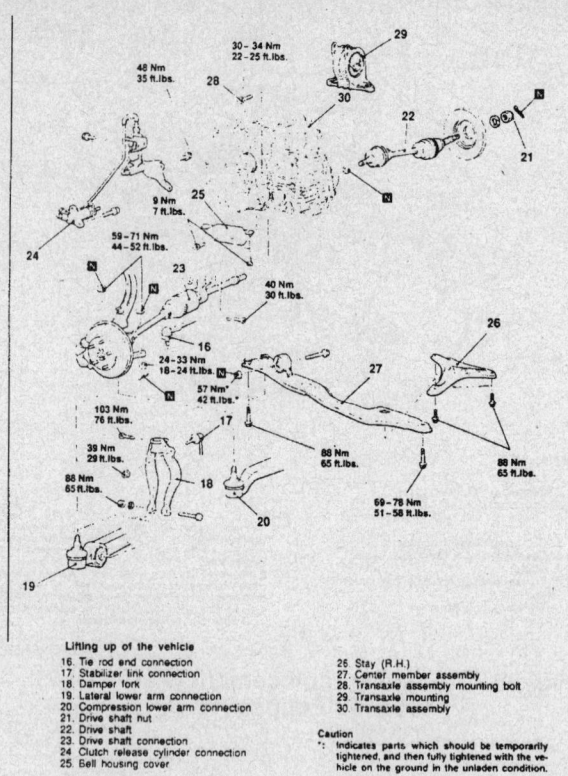

Lifting up of the vehicle

16. Tie rod end connection
17. Stabilizer link connection
18. Damper fork
19. Lateral lower arm connection
20. Compression lower arm connection
21. Drive shaft nut
22. Drive shaft
23. Drive shaft connection
24. Clutch release cylinder connection
25. Bell housing cover
26. Stay (R.H.)
27. Center member assembly
28. Transaxle assembly mounting bolt
29. Transaxle mounting
30. Transaxle assembly

Caution

*: Indicates parts which should be temporarily tightened, and then fully tightened with the vehicle on the ground in the unladen condition.

MT5039500131020X

Fig. 30 Transaxle replacement (Part 2 of 2). 1995–96 Eclipse AWD

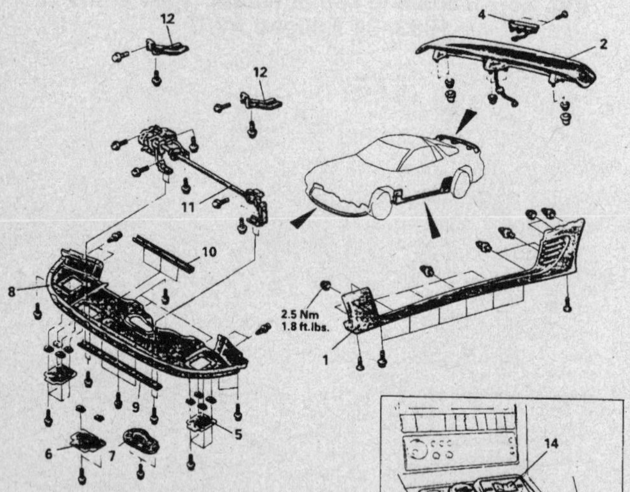
2.5 Nm
1.8 ft.lbs.

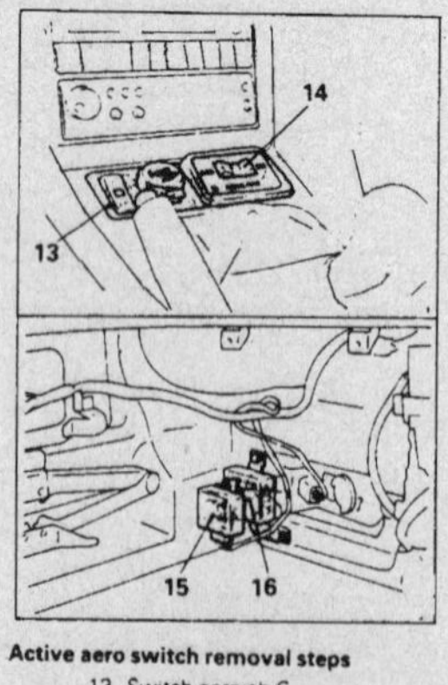

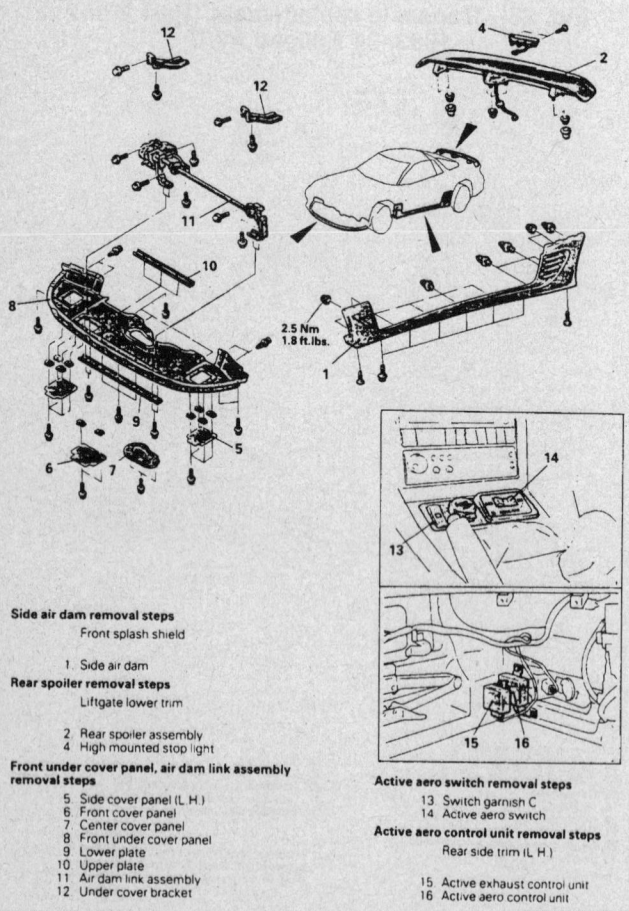

Side air dam removal steps

Front splash shield

1. Side air dam

Rear spoiler removal steps

Liftgate lower trim

2. Rear spoiler assembly
4. High mounted stop light

Front under cover panel, air dam link assembly removal steps

5. Side cover panel (L.H.)
6. Front cover panel
7. Center cover panel
8. Front under cover panel
9. Lower plate
10. Upper plate
11. Air dam link assembly
12. Under cover bracket

Active aero switch removal steps

13. Switch garnish C
14. Active aero switch

Active aero control unit removal steps

Rear side trim (L.H.)

15. Active exhaust control unit
16. Active aero control unit

MT5039100097000X

Fig. 31 Active aero component replacement. 3000GT

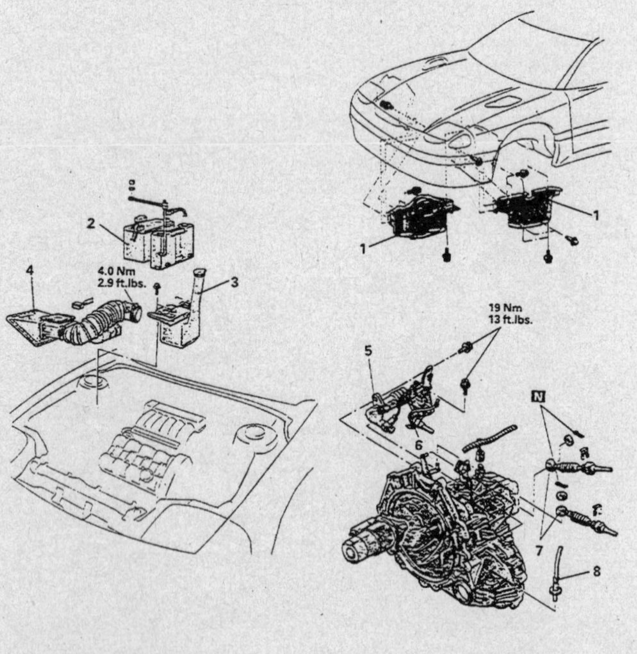
4.0 Nm
2.9 ft.lbs.
19 Nm
13 ft.lbs.

Removal steps

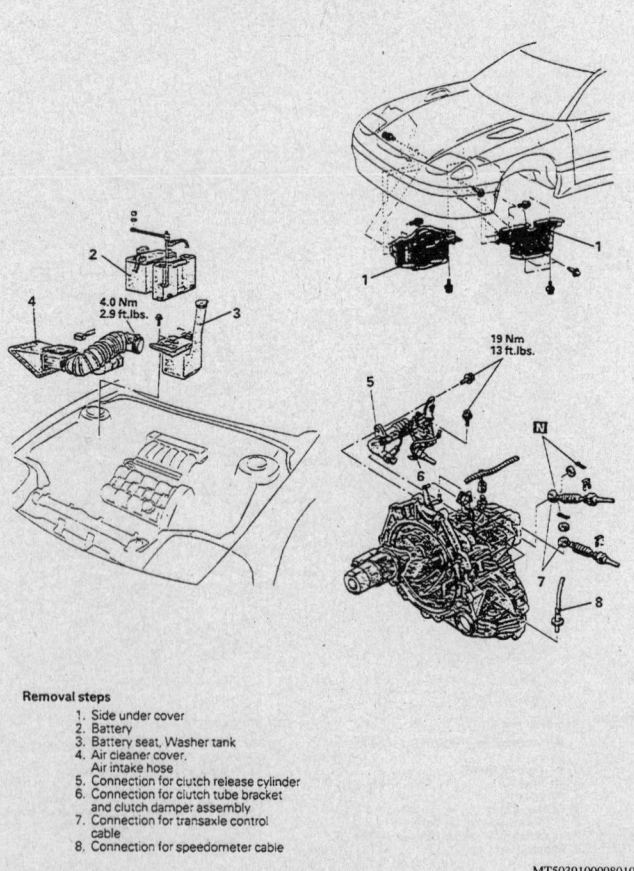

1. Side under cover
2. Battery
3. Battery seat, Washer tank
4. Air cleaner cover, Air intake hose
5. Connection for clutch release cylinder
6. Connection for clutch tube bracket and clutch damper assembly
7. Connection for transaxle control cable
8. Connection for speedometer cable

MT5039100098010X

Fig. 32 Transaxle assembly replacement (Part 1 of 2). 3000GT FWD

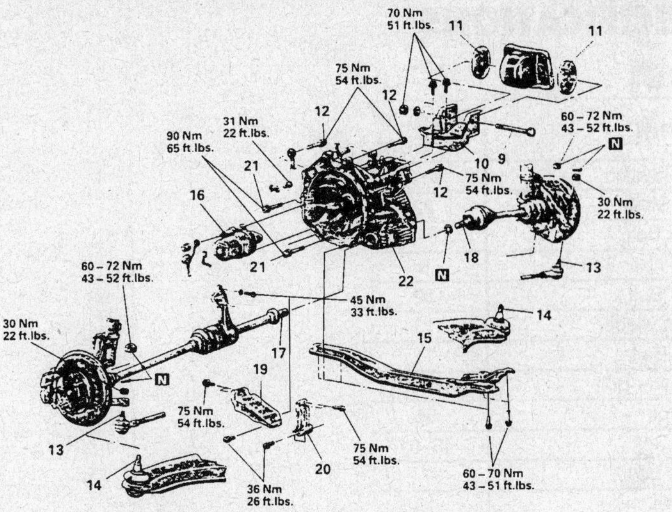
70 Nm
51 ft.lbs.
75 Nm
54 ft.lbs.
31 Nm
22 ft.lbs.
90 Nm
65 ft.lbs.
60 – 72 Nm
43 – 52 ft.lbs.
75 Nm
54 ft.lbs.
30 Nm
22 ft.lbs.
60 – 72 Nm
43 – 52 ft.lbs.
45 Nm
33 ft.lbs.
30 Nm
22 ft.lbs.
75 Nm
54 ft.lbs.
75 Nm
54 ft.lbs.
36 Nm
26 ft.lbs.
60 – 70 Nm
43 – 51 ft.lbs.

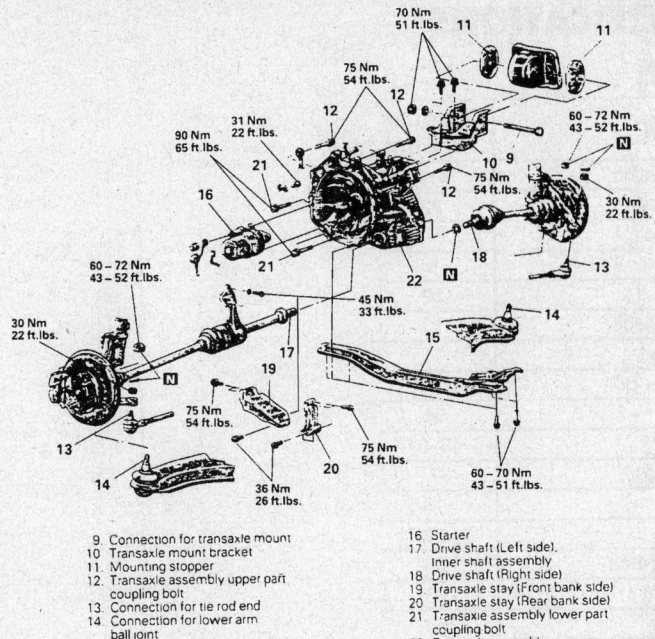

9. Connection for transaxle mount
10. Transaxle mount bracket
11. Mounting stopper
12. Transaxle assembly upper part coupling bolt
13. Connection for tie rod end
14. Connection for lower arm ball joint
15. Right member
16. Starter
17. Drive shaft (Left side), Inner shaft assembly
18. Drive shaft (Right side)
19. Transaxle stay (Front bank side)
20. Transaxle stay (Rear bank side)
21. Transaxle assembly lower part coupling bolt
22. Transaxle assembly

MT5039100098020X

Fig. 32 Transaxle assembly replacement (Part 2 of 2). 3000GT FWD

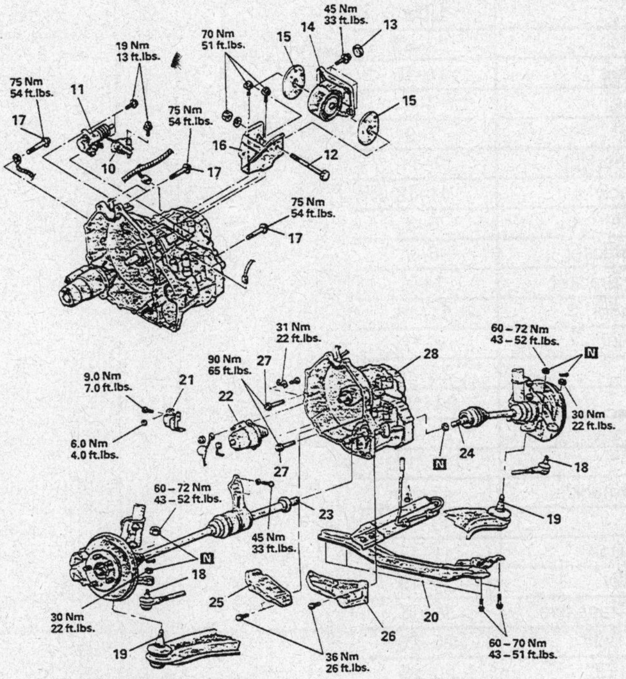
45 Nm
33 ft.lbs.
19 Nm
13 ft.lbs.
70 Nm
51 ft.lbs.
75 Nm
54 ft.lbs.
75 Nm
54 ft.lbs.
75 Nm
54 ft.lbs.
31 Nm
22 ft.lbs.
60 – 72 Nm
43 – 52 ft.lbs.
90 Nm
65 ft.lbs.
9.0 Nm
7.0 ft.lbs.
30 Nm
22 ft.lbs.
6.0 Nm
4.0 ft.lbs.
60 – 72 Nm
43 – 52 ft.lbs.
45 Nm
33 ft.lbs.
30 Nm
22 ft.lbs.
36 Nm
26 ft.lbs.
60 – 70 Nm
43 – 51 ft.lbs.

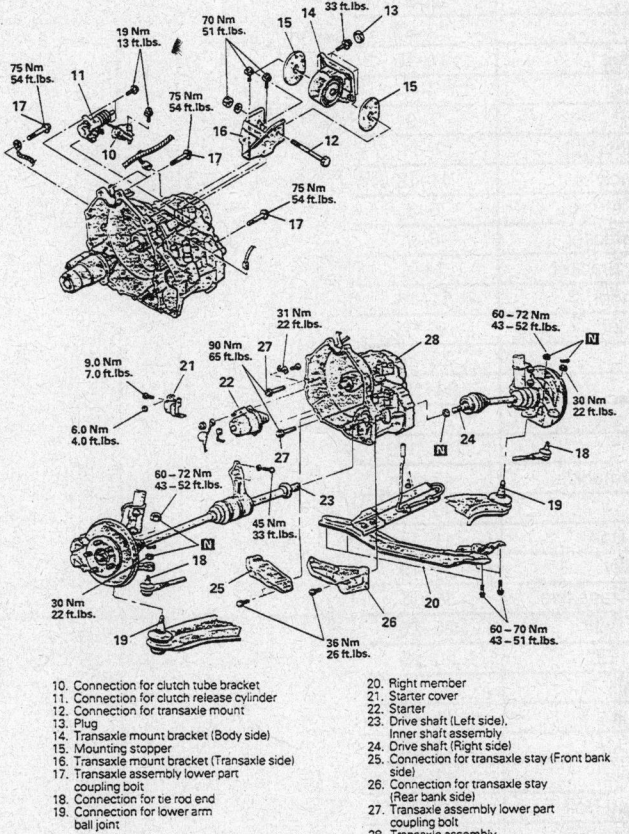

10. Connection for clutch tube bracket
11. Connection for clutch release cylinder
12. Connection for transaxle mount
13. Plug
14. Transaxle mount bracket (Body side)
15. Mounting stopper
16. Transaxle mount bracket (Transaxle side)
17. Transaxle assembly lower part coupling bolt
18. Connection for tie rod end
19. Connection for lower arm ball joint
20. Right member
21. Starter cover
22. Starter
23. Drive shaft (Left side), Inner shaft assembly
24. Drive shaft (Right side)
25. Connection for transaxle stay (Front bank side)
26. Connection for transaxle stay (Rear bank side)
27. Transaxle assembly lower part coupling bolt
28. Transaxle assembly

MT5039100099020X

Fig. 33 Transaxle assembly replacement (Part 2 of 2). 3000GT AWD

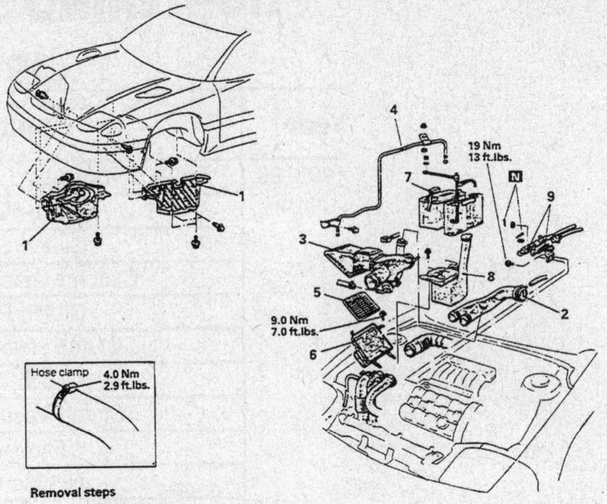
19 Nm
13 ft.lbs.
9.0 Nm
7.0 ft.lbs.
Hose clamp
4.0 Nm
2.9 ft.lbs.

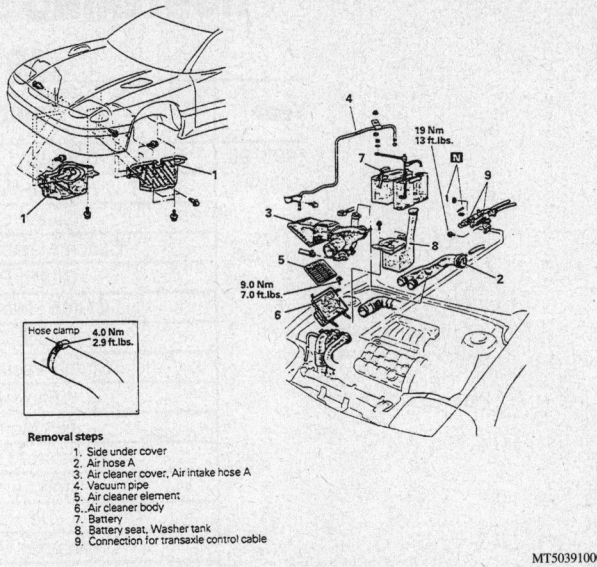

Removal steps

1. Side under cover
2. Air hose A
3. Air cleaner cover, Air intake hose A
4. Vacuum pipe
5. Air cleaner element
6. Air cleaner body
7. Battery
8. Battery seat, Washer tank
9. Connection for transaxle control cable

MT5039100099010X

Fig. 33 Transaxle assembly replacement (Part 1 of 2). 3000GT AWD

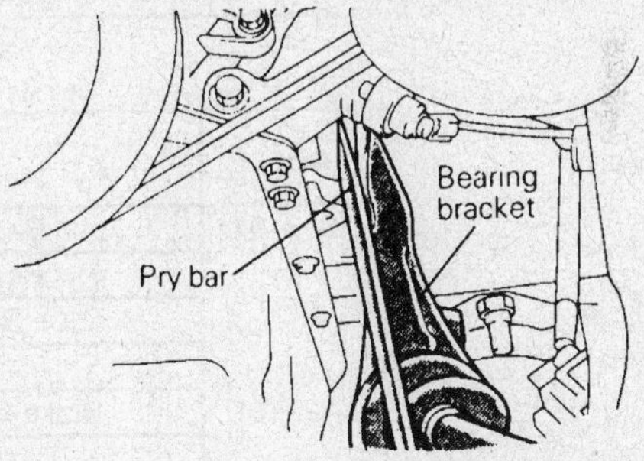
Bearing
bracket
Pry bar

MT5039100100000X

Fig. 34 Lefthand driveshaft removal. 3000GT

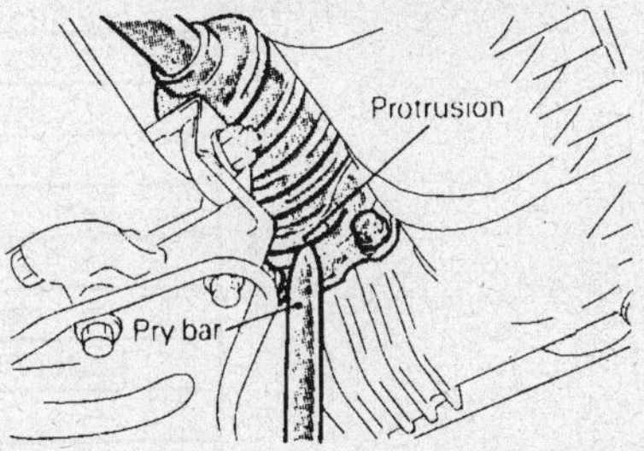
Protrusion
Pry bar

MT5039100101000X

Fig. 35 Righthand driveshaft removal. 3000GT

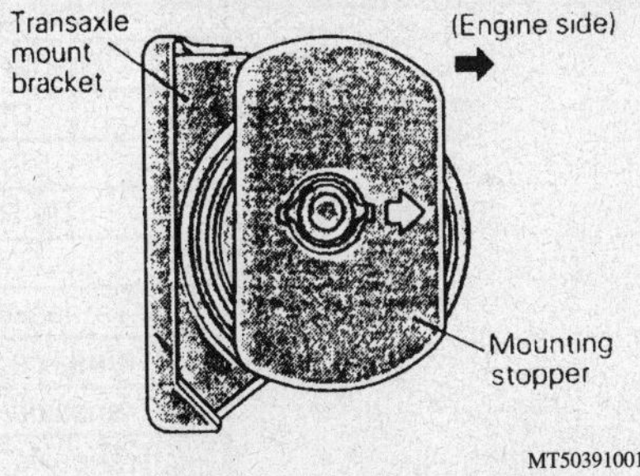
Transaxle
mount
bracket
(Engine side)
Mounting
stopper

MT5039100102000X

Fig. 36 Mounting stopper installation. 3000GT

TIGHTENING SPECIFICATIONS

3000GT

Year	Component	Torque/ Ft. Lbs.
1993–96	Back-Up Lamp Switch	14–22
	Brake Pedal Shaft	22
	Clutch Cover Bolt	11–15
	Clutch Master Cylinder Bolt	9
	Clutch Pedal Bolt	22
	Clutch Release Cylinder	13
	Clutch Tube Bolt	11
	Clutch Vacuum Line Bolt	11–13
	Flywheel Bolt	55
	RH Member Bolt	43–51
	Starter Cover Bolt	7
	Stop Lamp Switch	10
	Tie Rod End	22
	Transaxle Coupling Bolt	65
	Transaxle Mount	33
	Transaxle Stay	54
	Transfer Case To Transaxle	64

ECLIPSE

Year	Component	Torque/Ft. Lbs.
1993–94	Back-up Lamp Switch	22–25
	Bearing Retainer Bolt	11–15
	Bellhousing Cover	7–9
	Bleeder Plug	7–9
	Brake Booster Installation Nut	7–11
	Clutch Cover Assembly	11–16
	Clutch Pedal Bracket	6–9
	Clutch Pedal Support Bracket	6–9
	Clutch Pedal To Support Bracket	14–8
	Clutch Release Cylinder	11–16
	Clutch Tube Flare Nut	9–12
	Drain Plug	22–25
	Flywheel Bolts	94–191
	Fulcrum	25–30
	Input Shaft Locknut	102–115
	Lower Arm Ball Joint To Knuckle	43–52
	Poppet Plug	43–52
	Rear Housing Cover Bolt	11–15
	Restrict Ball Assembly	11–15
	Shift And Select Cable To Transaxle	11–16
	Speedometer Sleeve Bolt	20–25
	Starter Motor Mounting Bolt	20–25
	Stop Lamp Switch	7–11
	Stopper Bracket Bolt	11–15
	Tie Rod End To Knuckle	17–25
	Transaxle Bracket	43–58
	Transaxle Case Tightening Bolt	26–30
	Transaxle Mounting Bolt (.47 inch)	32–39
	Transaxle Mounting Bolt (.40 inch)	22–25
	Transaxle Mounting Bolt (.31 inch)	7–9
	Transfer Assembly Mounting Bolt	40–43
	Back-up Lamp Switch	22
	Bearing Retainer Bolt	14

Continued

Year	Component	Torque/Ft. Lbs.
1995–96	Clutch Cover Assembly	11–16
	Clutch Pedal Bracket	6–9
	Clutch Pedal Support Bracket	6–9
	Clutch Pedal To Support Bracket	14–18
	Clutch Release Cylinder	11–16
	Compression Lower Arm	44–52
	Flywheel Bolts	55
	Lower Arm Ball Joint To Knuckle	44–52
	Poppet Plug	27
	Rear Housing Cover Bolt	14
	Rear Roll Stopper Bracket	51
	Restrict Ball Assembly	24
	Shift And Select Cable To Transaxle	11–16
	Speedometer Sleeve Bolt	3
	Starter Motor Mounting Bolt	40
	Stop Lamp Switch	24
	Tie Rod End To Knuckle	18–24
	Transaxle Case Tightening Bolt	29
	Transaxle Mounting Bolt	35
	Transfer Assembly Mounting Bolt	40–44

Rear Axle & Suspension

INDEX

Page No.

Coil Spring, Replace 24-82
Control Arm, Replace 24-83
1995–96 Eclipse 24-83
3000GT & 1993–94 Eclipse
AWD Models 24-83
3000GT FWD Models........... 24-83
Differential Carrier, Replace 24-79
1995–96 Eclipse 24-79
3000GT & 1993–94 Eclipse..... 24-79
Hub & Bearing, Replace 24-80
AWD Models 24-80
FWD Models.................... 24-80
Lateral Rod, Replace............. 24-91
Eclipse 24-91
Propeller Shaft, Replace 24-79
Rear Suspension, Replace....... 24-81
Eclipse 24-81
3000GT 24-82
Shock Absorber, Replace........ 24-84
Stabilizer Bar, Replace.......... 24-83
1995–96 Eclipse 24-91
3000GT & 1993–94 Eclipse
AWD Models 24-84
3000GT FWD Models........... 24-84
Tightening Specifications 24-92
Eclipse 24-93
3000GT 24-92
Torsion Bar, Replace............ 24-92
Eclipse 24-91
Trailing Arm, Replace 24-83
1995–96 Eclipse 24-83
3000GT & 1993–94 Eclipse
AWD Models 24-83
3000GT FWD Models........... 24-83
Wheel Bearing, Adjust 24-80
AWD Models 24-80
FWD Models.................... 24-80

DIFFERENTIAL CARRIER

REPLACE

3000GT & 1993-94 ECLIPSE

1. Drain differential fluid into an appropriate container.
2. Remove center exhaust pipe.
3. Remove driveshaft as outlined under "Driveshaft, Replace" in "All Wheel Drive."
4. Remove propeller shaft.
5. Remove differential carrier in numbered sequence as shown, **Figs. 1 and 2,** noting the following:
   a. **On 3000GT,** hold bottom of differential carrier and remove rear wheel oil pump through mounting hole, then the differential carrier.
6. **On all models,** reverse procedure to install.

1995-96 ECLIPSE

1. Drain differential fluid, then drain brake fluid into an appropriate container.
2. Remove differential carrier in numbered sequence as shown, **Fig. 3,** noting the following:
   a. Scribe marks on differential companion flange and flange yoke for installation reference, then separate differential carrier and propeller shaft. Suspend propeller shaft from vehicle body with wire ensuring there are no sharp bends in shaft assembly.
   b. Push lower part of knuckle to outside of vehicle, then separate driveshaft from differential carrier. Suspend driveshaft from vehicle body with wire so as not to damage driveshaft joint.
   c. Removal differential carrier, then cover openings to prevent entry of foreign objects.
3. Reverse procedure to install.

PROPELLER SHAFT

REPLACE

1. Remove spacers, **Fig. 4.** Number of spacers differs on each vehicle. Note number of spacers and use for reference during installation.
2. Remove propeller shaft. Make mating marks on differential companion flange and flange yoke for reference during installation.
3. Insert piece of cloth or rag into boot opening, then remove propeller shaft in a straight and level manner ensuring boot is not damaged through pinching.
4. **Do not lower rear end of vehicle as the oil will flow out of the transfer case and be cautious to avoid damage to the oil seal lip of the transfer case.**
5. **Use special tool provided as a cover**

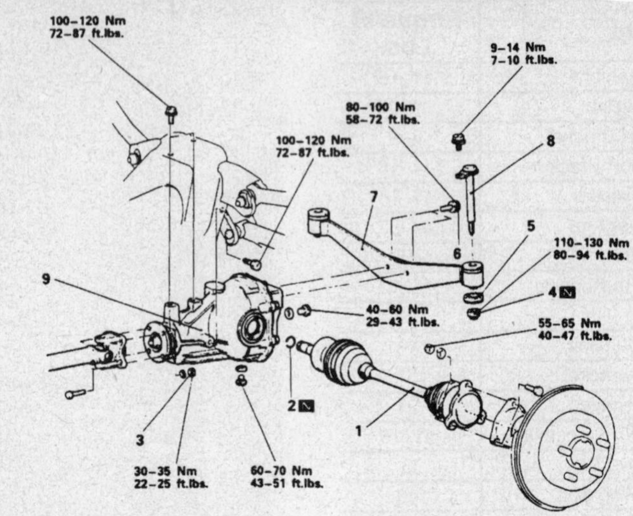
100-120 Nm
72-87 ft.lbs.
9-14 Nm
7-10 ft.lbs.
80-100 Nm
58-72 ft.lbs.
100-120 Nm
72-87 ft.lbs.
110-130 Nm
80-94 ft.lbs.
40-60 Nm
29-43 ft.lbs.
55-65 Nm
40-47 ft.lbs.
30-35 Nm
22-25 ft.lbs.
60-70 Nm
43-51 ft.lbs.

Removal steps

1. Drive shaft
2. Circlip
3. Propeller shaft connection
4. Differential support member installation nut
5. Stopper (lower)
6. Differential support member installation bolt
7. Differential support member
8. Differential support member installation bolt
9. Differential carrier

MT3019100001000X

Fig. 1 Differential carrier replacement. 1993–94 Eclipse AWD

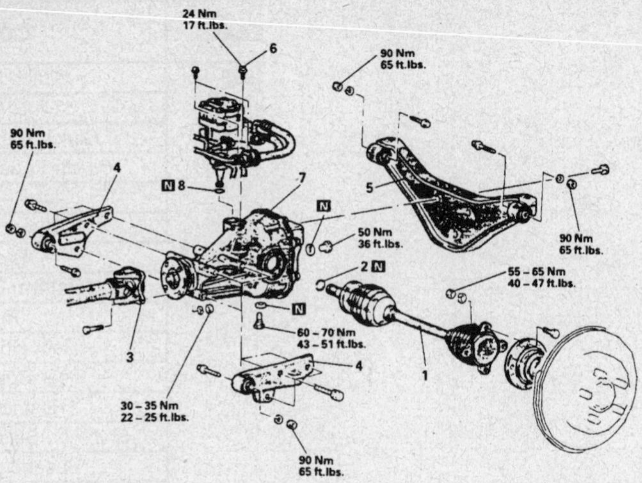
24 Nm
17 ft.lbs.
90 Nm
65 ft.lbs.
90 Nm
65 ft.lbs.
50 Nm
36 ft.lbs.
90 Nm
65 ft.lbs.
55-65 Nm
40-47 ft.lbs.
60-70 Nm
43-51 ft.lbs.
30-35 Nm
22-25 ft.lbs.
90 Nm
65 ft.lbs.

Removal steps

1. Drive shaft
2. Circlip
3. Propeller shaft connection
4. Differential support assembly
5. Differential support member assembly
6. Rear wheel oil pump installation bolt
7. Differential carrier
8. O-ring

MT3019100002000X

Fig. 2 Differential carrier replacement. 3000GT AWD

to prevent the entry of foreign materials into the transfer case.

6. Inspect sleeve yoke, center yoke, flange yoke and propeller shaft yokes for wear damage or cracks and replace as necessary.
7. Using a suitable dial indicator, measure propeller shaft runout. Runout for the front, center and rear propeller shafts should be 0.024 inch (0.6 mm).
8. Set V-blocks as much as possible to the end of the shaft, then measure the deflection at the center of the shaft.
9. Inspect universal joints for smooth operation in all directions, then the center bearing for smooth movement and mounting rubber for damage or deterioration and replace as necessary.
10. Reverse procedure to install, noting the following:
    a. Install spacers and insulators as shown, **Fig. 5.**
    b. When installing center bearing, assemble the same spacers as removed from the bearing or new spacers of equal thickness.

HUB & BEARING

REPLACE

FWD MODELS

Replace rear axle hub assembly in numbered sequence as shown, **Figs. 6 through 8,** noting the following:

1. **Care must be used when handling the pole piece at tip of ABS speed sensor and toothed edge of rotor so as not to damage them or striking against other components.**
2. Remove caliper assembly and support to frame using suitable wire.
3. **Care must be taken not to scratch or scar ABS rotor's tooth surface and not to drop it. If rotor's toothed surface is chipped or is deformed, the ABS brake system might not operate accurately.**

AWD MODELS

1. Remove rear axle hub in numbered sequence as shown, **Figs. 5, 9, and 10** noting the following:
    a. **Care must be used when handling the pole piece at the tip of the ABS speed sensor and toothed edge of rotor ensuring not to damage them or strike against other components.**
    b. Remove caliper assembly and support to frame using suitable wire.
    c. Using end yoke holder tool No. MB990767-01, or equivalent, secure axle hub and remove companion flange self-locking nut.
    d. Using axle puller and slide hammer tools, No. MB990211-01 and MB990241-01, or equivalents, remove rear axle hub.
    e. Press off ABS rotor from axle hub.
    f. Press off outer bearing and dust shield from axle hub.
    g. Using seal remover tool No. MB990938-01 and MB990928-01, or equivalents, remove axle hub seal and inner bearing from axle housing.
2. Reverse procedure to install, noting the following:
    a. Install inner bearing using bearing installer tool Nos. MB990931-01 and MB990938-01, or equivalents.
    b. Install oil seal using oil seal installer tool No. MB990931-01, or equivalent. Apply multi-purpose grease to lip of oil seal.
    c. Install dust shields using ball joint dust cover installer tool No. MB990799-01, or equivalent.
    d. Install outer bearing after applying multi-purpose grease to bearing surfaces.
    e. Install ABS rotor with groove in surface pointing toward axle shaft flange.

WHEEL BEARING

ADJUST

FWD MODELS

1. Raise and support vehicle.
2. Remove caliper assembly and support to frame using suitable wire.
3. Turn hub several times to seat bearings.
4. Using a suitable spring scale, measure rotary starting torque.
5. Loosen or tighten hub nut to obtain a starting torque of 9 inch lbs. or less. Replace rear hub bearing if necessary.

AWD MODELS

1. Raise and support vehicle.
2. Remove driveshaft from companion flange.
3. Remove caliper assembly and support to frame using suitable wire.

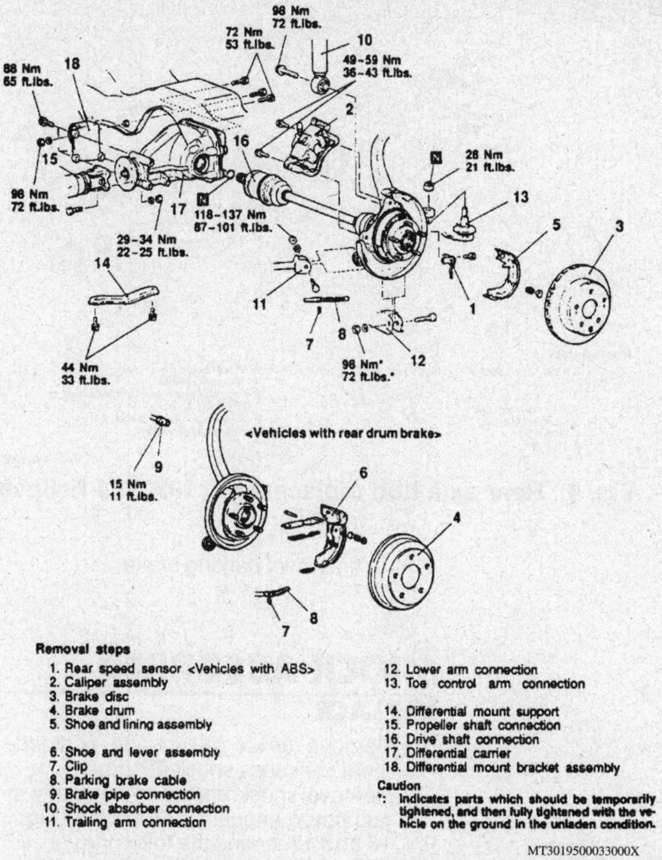
98 Nm
72 ft.lbs.
72 Nm
53 ft.lbs.
49–59 Nm
36–43 ft.lbs.
88 Nm
65 ft.lbs.
98 Nm
72 ft.lbs.
28 Nm
21 ft.lbs.
118–137 Nm
87–101 ft.lbs.
29–34 Nm
22–25 ft.lbs.
44 Nm
33 ft.lbs.
98 Nm*
72 ft.lbs.*
15 Nm
11 ft.lbs.
<Vehicles with rear drum brake>
Removal steps
1. Rear speed sensor <Vehicles with ABS>
2. Caliper assembly
3. Brake disc
4. Brake drum
5. Shoe and lining assembly
6. Shoe and lever assembly
7. Clip
8. Parking brake cable
9. Brake pipe connection
10. Shock absorber connection
11. Trailing arm connection
12. Lower arm connection
13. Toe control arm connection
14. Differential mount support
15. Propeller shaft connection
16. Drive shaft connection
17. Differential carrier
18. Differential mount bracket assembly
Caution
*: Indicates parts which should be temporarily tightened, and then fully tightened with the vehicle on the ground in the unladen condition.
MT3019500033000X

Fig. 3 Differential carrier replacement. 1995–96 Eclipse AWD

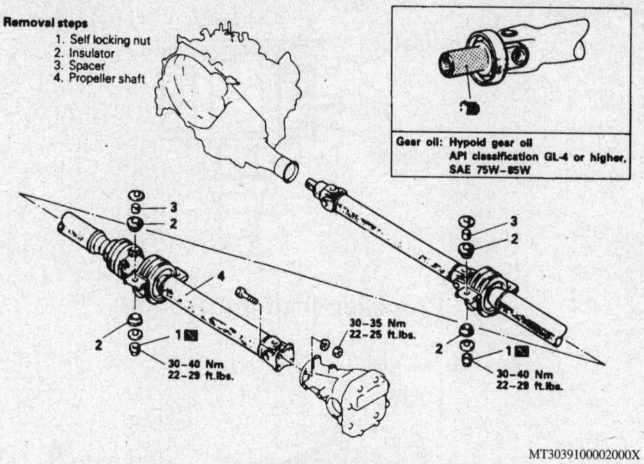
Removal steps
1. Self locking nut
2. Insulator
3. Spacer
4. Propeller shaft
Gear oil: Hypoid gear oil
API classification GL-4 or higher,
SAE 75W–85W
30–35 Nm
22–25 ft.lbs.
30–40 Nm
22–29 ft.lbs.
30–40 Nm
22–29 ft.lbs.
MT3039100002000X

Fig. 4 Propeller shaft removal

4. Turn hub several times to seat bearings.
5. Using a suitable spring scale, measure rotary starting torque.
6. If starting torque is not 6 inch lbs. or less, ensure torque of axle hub companion flange nut is correct. If flange torque is correct, replace axle hub bearing.

REAR SUSPENSION

REPLACE

ECLIPSE

1993–94

FWD Models

1. Raise and support vehicle, then remove rear wheels.
2. Disconnect parking brake cable from rear brake assembly and from the torsion axle and arm assembly, **Fig. 11.**
3. Remove brake hose bracket from torsion axle and arm assembly.
4. Remove rear brake assembly and secure out of way.
5. Support torsion axle and arm assembly with a jack.
6. Remove lateral rod from body. Refer to "Lateral Rod, Replace" procedure.
7. Remove torsion axle and arm assembly from body, then disconnect top of shock absorber.
8. Lower jack, then remove rear suspension assembly from body.
9. Reverse procedure to install.

AWD Models

1. Raise and support vehicle, then remove rear wheels.
2. Remove upper shock absorber attaching nuts, then the brake hose bracket from torsion axle and arm assembly.
3. Disconnect parking brake cable from caliper, then remove rear brake caliper assembly and secure out of way **Fig. 12.**
4. Remove center exhaust pipe and gaskets.
5. Remove propeller shaft installation nuts and bolts. Place mating marks on differential shaft and propeller shaft flange yoke, to be used for installation reference.
6. Support differential case with a suitable jack.
7. Remove self-locking nut from differential support member, then the support member.
8. Remove crossmember bracket attaching nuts and bolts, then the bracket.
9. Remove parking brake cable, then disconnect rear speed sensor electrical connector, if applicable.
10. Lower jack, then remove rear suspension assembly from body. **Ensure propeller shaft does not bend excessively and joint does not receive any shock.**
11. Reverse procedure to install, noting the following:
    a. Install propeller shaft to the differential carrier, ensuring mating marks are aligned.
    b. Install parking brake cable, then connect a parking brake cable end to parking brake lever. Pry up the parking brake lever, then install other cable end at this time.

1995–96

1. Remove service lid trim from interior of vehicle, then raise and support vehicle.
2. Remove rear crossmember under cover panel, then remove center exhaust pipe.
3. **On models with AWD,** remove propeller shaft assembly, **Fig. 13. Scribe marks on differential companion flange and flange yoke for installation reference, then separate differential carrier and propeller shaft. Suspend propeller shaft from vehicle body with wire ensuring there are no sharp bends in shaft assembly.**
4. **On all models,** remove brake caliper and brake assembly.
5. Remove parking brake cable.
6. **On models with drum brakes,** remove brake hose connection.
7. **On all models,** remove upper arm bracket, then shock absorber cap and mounting nuts.
8. **On models with ABS,** remove speed sensor electrical connection.
9. **On all models,** remove trailing arm grommet and mounting bolt.
10. **On models with AWD,** support differential case with suitable jack stand, then remove crossmember mounting nuts.
11. **On models with FWD,** support crossmember with suitable jack stand, then remove crossmember mounting nuts.
12. **On all models,** reverse procedure to install, noting the following:
    a. Bleed brake system as outlined under "Hydraulic Brake Systems" in "Unit Repair."
    b. Inspect rear wheel alignment as outlined under "Wheel Alignment."

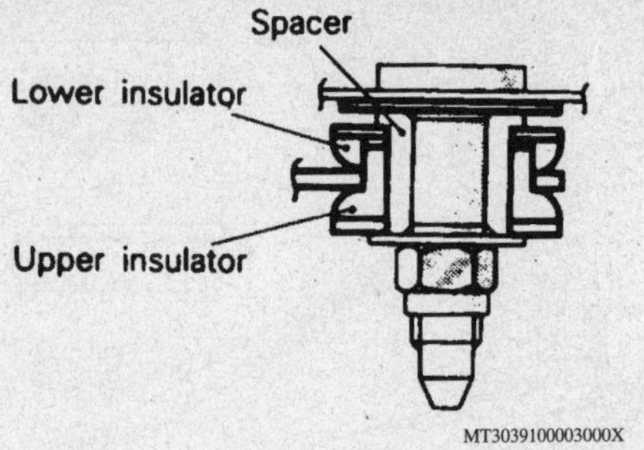
Spacer
Lower insulator
Upper insulator
MT3039100003000X

Fig. 5 Propeller shaft installation

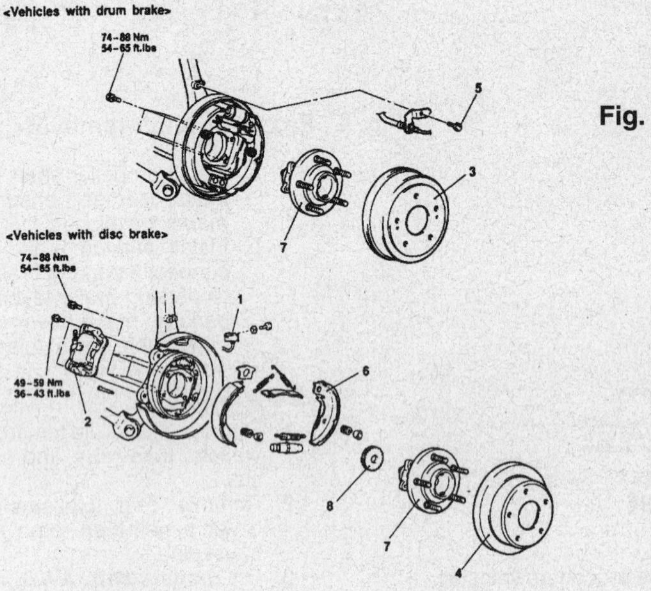
<Vehicles with drum brake>
74–88 Nm
54–65 ft.lbs
<Vehicles with disc brake>
74–88 Nm
54–65 ft.lbs
49–59 Nm
36–43 ft.lbs

Removal steps
1. Rear speed sensor <Vehicles with ABS>
2. Caliper assembly
3. Brake drum
4. Brake disc
5. Clip mounting bolt
6. Shoe and lining assembly
7. Rear hub assembly
8. Rotor<Vehicles with ABS>

Caution
The rear hub assembly should not be disassembled.

MT2049500054000X

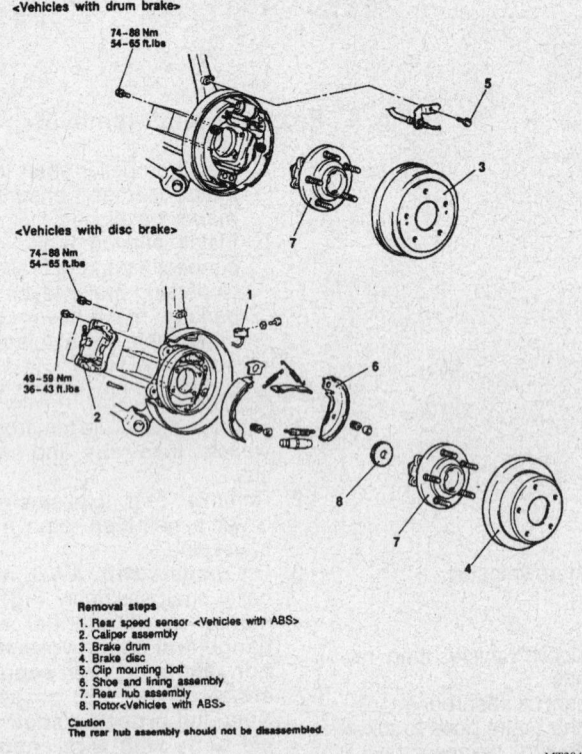

Fig. 7 Rear axle hub replacement. 1995–96 Eclipse FWD

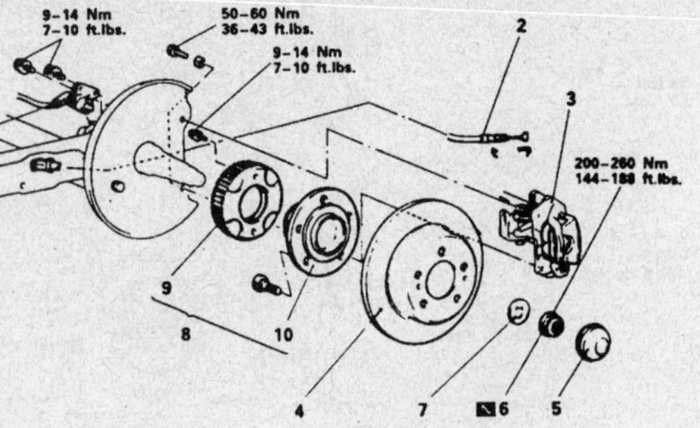
9–14 Nm
7–10 ft.lbs.
50–60 Nm
36–43 ft.lbs.
9–14 Nm
7–10 ft.lbs.
200–260 Nm
144–188 ft.lbs.

Removal steps
1. Rear speed sensor <Vehicles with A B S>
2. Parking brake cable
3. Caliper assembly
4. Brake disc
5. Hub cap
6. Wheel bearing nut
7. Tongued washer
8. Rear hub assembly <Vehicles with A B S>
9. Rear rotor <Vehicles with A B S>
10. Rear hub bearing unit

MT2049100012000X

Fig. 6 Rear axle hub replacement. 1993–94 Eclipse FWD

3000GT

FWD MODELS

1. Raise and support vehicle, then remove rear wheels.
2. Remove shock absorber trim cover from inside luggage compartment.
3. Remove exhaust muffler assembly.
4. Remove rear suspension assembly in numbered sequence as shown, **Fig. 14,** supporting crossmember with transmission jack, then remove crossmember mounting nut and rear suspension assembly.
5. Reverse procedure to install, noting the following:
   a. Install exhaust muffler.
   b. Verify rear wheel alignment.
   c. Verify parking brake operation.
   d. Install shock absorber trim cover in luggage compartment.

AWD MODELS

1. Remove shock absorber cover from luggage compartment.
2. Remove center exhaust pipe and main muffler.
3. Remove rear suspension in numbered sequence as shown, **Fig. 15,** noting the following:
   a. Before removing crossmember bracket, support differential case with a suitable transmission jack.
   b. Remove crossmember mounting nuts and bolts.
   c. Lower rear suspension using two assistants to help support suspension on transmission stand. **Rear suspension is very heavy and damage or personal injury could occur if rear suspension is not supported correctly.**
4. Reverse procedure to install, noting the following:
   a. Bleed power steering system as outlined under "Bleeding System" in "Power Steering Service."
   b. Verify rear wheel alignment and operation of parking brake.

SHOCK ABSORBER

REPLACE

1. Remove cover in luggage compartment to access shock absorber.
2. Remove shock absorber assembly in numbered sequence as shown, **Figs. 16 and 17,** noting the following:
   a. Raise and support rear suspension before removing shock absorber.
   b. Remove shock absorber upper and lower mounting bolts, then the shock absorber assembly.
3. Disassemble shock absorber assembly in numbered sequence as shown, **Figs. 18 and 19,** noting the following:
   a. Before removing piston rod nut, compress coil spring using suitable coil spring compression tool.
   b. While holding piston rod, remove piston rod nut.
4. Reverse procedure to install, noting the following:
   a. Using a suitable coil spring, compress and insert coil spring on shock absorber.
   b. Align edge of coil spring to position as shown, **Fig. 20.**
   c. Fit dust cover over dust cup as shown, **Fig. 21.**
   d. Position upper bracket as shown, then tighten piston nut to specifications.
   e. Install coil spring ensuring lower edge fits into spring seat groove and upper edge fits into spring pad groove, then remove compression tool, **Figs. 22 through 24.**

COIL SPRING

REPLACE

Remove and disassemble shock absorber assembly as outlined under "Shock Absorber, Replace."

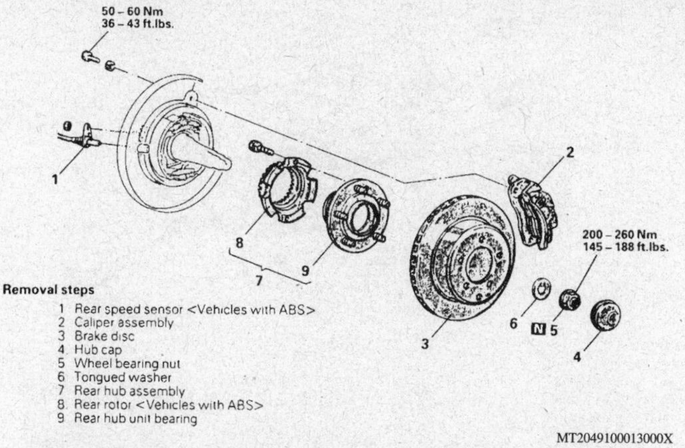
50 – 60 Nm
36 – 43 ft.lbs.
200 – 260 Nm
145 – 188 ft.lbs.
Removal steps
1 Rear speed sensor <Vehicles with ABS>
2 Caliper assembly
3 Brake disc
4 Hub cap
5 Wheel bearing nut
6 Tongued washer
7 Rear hub assembly
8 Rear rotor <Vehicles with ABS>
9 Rear hub unit bearing
MT2049100013000X

Fig. 8 Rear axle hub replacement. 3000GT FWD

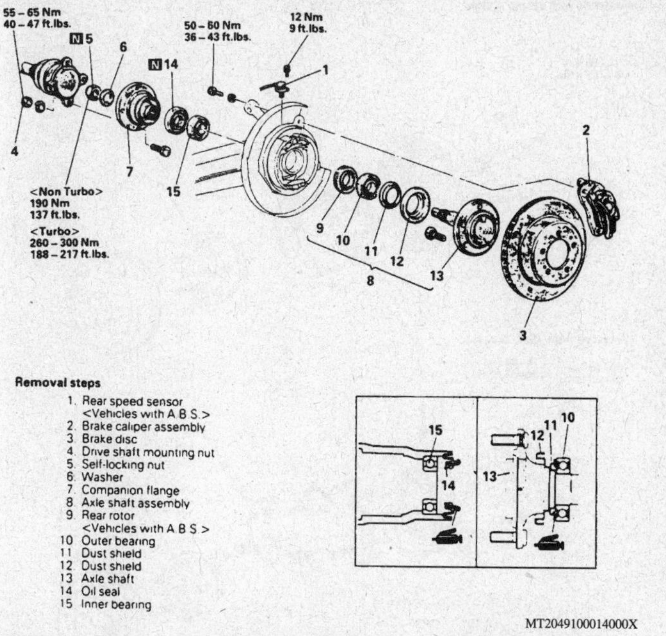
55 – 65 Nm
40 – 47 ft.lbs.
50 – 60 Nm
36 – 43 ft.lbs.
12 Nm
9 ft.lbs.
<Non Turbo>
190 Nm
137 ft.lbs.
<Turbo>
260 – 300 Nm
188 – 217 ft.lbs.
Removal steps
1. Rear speed sensor <Vehicles with A B S.>
2. Brake caliper assembly
3. Brake disc
4. Drive shaft mounting nut
5. Self-locking nut
6. Washer
7. Companion flange
8. Axle shaft assembly
9. Rear rotor <Vehicles with A B S >
10. Outer bearing
11. Dust shield
12. Dust shield
13. Axle shaft
14. Oil seal
15. Inner bearing
MT2049100014000X

Fig. 9 Rear axle hub replacement. 3000GT AWD & 1993–94 Eclipse AWD

CONTROL ARM

REPLACE

3000GT & 1993-94 ECLIPSE AWD MODELS

Remove upper and lower control arms in numbered sequence as shown, **Figs. 25 and 26,** then using ball joint remover tool No. MB991113-01, or equivalent, disconnect upper and lower arm ball joint from knuckle. **Loosen, but do not remove ball joint nut.**

3000GT FWD MODELS

1. Remove shock absorber assembly as outlined under "Shock Absorber, Replace."
2. Remove upper and lower control arms and assist link in numbered sequence as shown, **Fig. 27,** noting the following:
   a. Using ball joint remover tool No. MB991113-01, or equivalent, remove ball joints from the knuckle. **Loosen but do not remove ball joint nut.**

1995-96 ECLIPSE

Upper

1. Remove upper arm and connecting bolt, **Fig. 28.**
2. Remove upper arm assembly mounting bolts, then upper arm assembly.
3. Remove upper arm bracket.
4. Reverse procedure to install, noting the following:
   a. Install the upper arm bracket so that dimension "A" is 1.46 ± 0.08 inch, **Fig. 29.**
   b. Install the upper arm bracket so that dimension "B" is 8.40 inch, **Fig. 30.**
   c. Install the upper arm bracket so that dimension "C" is 10.6 inch.

Lower

1. **On models with aero parts,** remove lower arm cover.
2. **On all models,** remove stabilizer link, **Fig. 31.**
3. **On models with ABS,** remove speed sensor clamp bolts.
4. **On all models,** remove lower arm assembly and knuckle connecting bolt.
5. Remove lower arm assembly mounting bolt, then lower arm assembly.
6. Loosen toe control arm joint and knuckle connection using steering linkage puller tool No. MB991113 or equivalent. **Tie cord from tool to vehicle, then loosen but do not remove nut, Fig. 32.**
7. Scribe installation reference marks on toe control arm assembly mounting bolt, **Fig. 33,** then remove bolt and toe control arm assembly.
8. Reverse procedure to install.

TRAILING ARM

REPLACE

3000GT FWD MODELS

1. Remove trailing arm in numbered sequence as shown, **Fig. 34,** noting the following:
   a. Using ball joint remover tool No. MB991113-01, or equivalent, remove knuckle from lower arm, upper arm and assist link.
   b. **Do not remove nut from ball joint. Suspend special tool with a rope to prevent it from dropping.**
2. Reverse procedure to install, noting the following:
   a. Install stabilizer link as describer under "Stabilizer Bar, Replace."
   b. Verify wheel alignment and operation of parking brake.

3000GT & 1993-94 ECLIPSE AWD MODELS

1. Remove trailing arm in numbered sequence as shown, **Figs. 35 and 36,** noting the following:
   a. Using end yoke holder tool No. MB990767-01, or equivalent, secure rear axle shaft then remove self-locking nut.
   b. Using axle puller and slide hammer tools, No. MB990211-01 and MB990241-01, or equivalents, remove rear axle hub.
   c. Using ball joint remover tool No. MB991113-01, or equivalent, loosen and disconnect ball joint from knuckle. **Loosen, but do not remove ball joint nut.**
2. Replace connecting rod as follows:
   a. Remove trailing arm bushing.
   b. Remove connecting rod nut and bolt.
   c. Install rod remover and installer tool No. MB9911254, or equivalent, as shown in **Fig. 37.**
   d. Apply lubricant to sliding points (A). Install bolt (B) in trailing arm.
   e. Using a suitable wrench, turn screw (C) to remove connecting rod.
   f. Installation of special tool should be performed with screw shaft and guide shaft center lines oriented as shown, **Fig. 38.**
   g. Apply soapy water to rubber portion of connecting rod, then reverse procedure to install connecting rod.
3. Reverse procedure to install.

1995-96 ECLIPSE

1. Remove knuckle and trailing arm assembly connecting bolt, **Fig. 39.**
2. Remove trailing arm assembly grommet, mounting bolt and stopper.
3. Remove trailing arm assembly.
4. Reverse procedure to install.

STABILIZER BAR

REPLACE

3000GT FWD MODELS

Replace stabilizer bar in numbered sequence as shown, **Fig. 40,** noting the following:

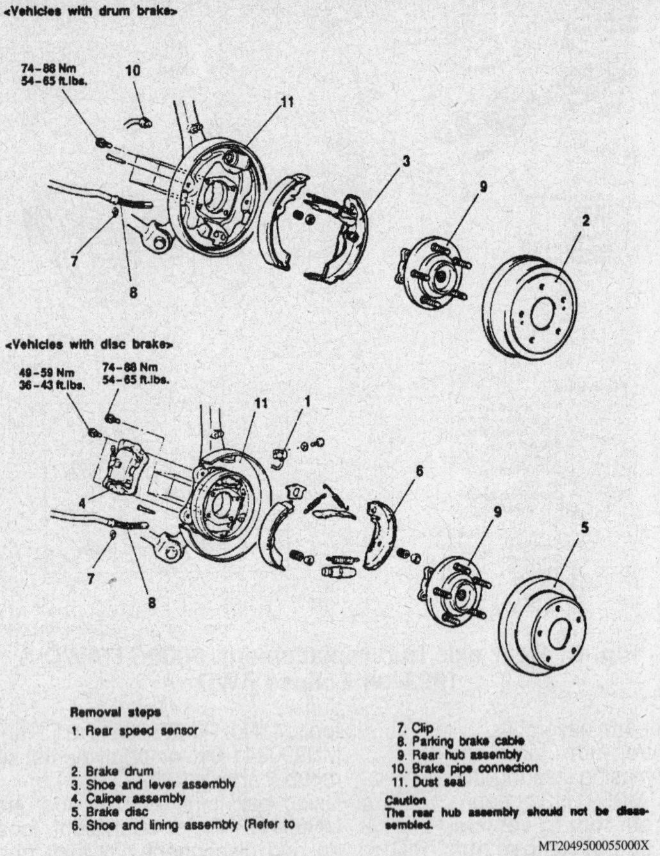
<Vehicles with drum brake>
74–88 Nm
54–65 ft.lbs.
<Vehicles with disc brake>
49–59 Nm
36–43 ft.lbs.
74–88 Nm
54–65 ft.lbs.
Removal steps
1. Rear speed sensor
2. Brake drum
3. Shoe and lever assembly
4. Caliper assembly
5. Brake disc
6. Shoe and lining assembly (Refer to
7. Clip
8. Parking brake cable
9. Rear hub assembly
10. Brake pipe connection
11. Dust seal
Caution
The rear hub assembly should not be disassembled.
MT2049500055000X

Fig. 10 Rear axle hub replacement. 1995–96 Eclipse/AWD

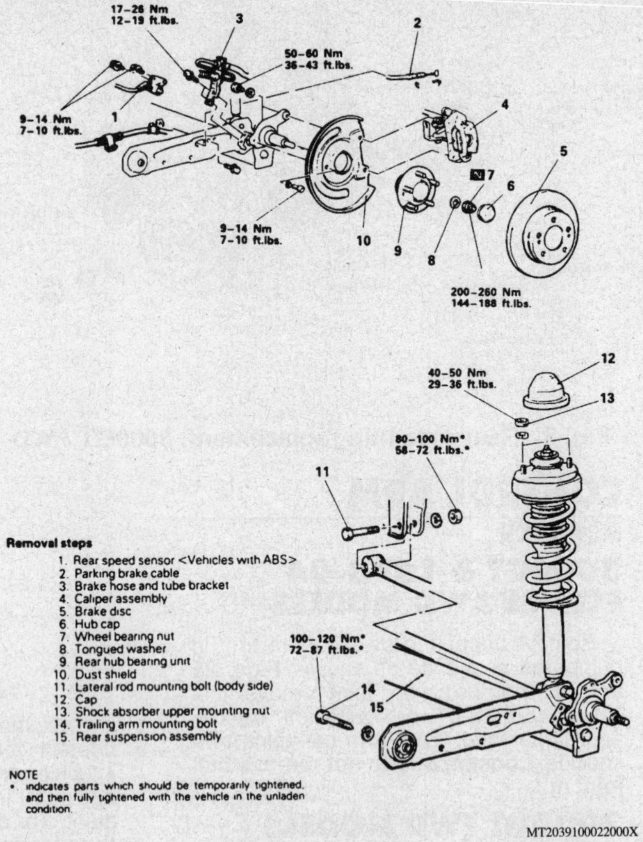
17–26 Nm
12–19 ft.lbs.
50–60 Nm
36–43 ft.lbs.
9–14 Nm
7–10 ft.lbs.
9–14 Nm
7–10 ft.lbs.
200–260 Nm
144–188 ft.lbs.
40–50 Nm
29–36 ft.lbs.
80–100 Nm*
58–72 ft.lbs.*
100–120 Nm*
72–87 ft.lbs.*
Removal steps
1. Rear speed sensor <Vehicles with ABS>
2. Parking brake cable
3. Brake hose and tube bracket
4. Caliper assembly
5. Brake disc
6. Hub cap
7. Wheel bearing nut
8. Tongued washer
9. Rear hub bearing unit
10. Dust shield
11. Lateral rod mounting bolt (body side)
12. Cap
13. Shock absorber upper mounting nut
14. Trailing arm mounting bolt
15. Rear suspension assembly
NOTE
• indicates parts which should be temporarily tightened, and then fully tightened with the vehicle in the unladen condition.
MT2039100022000X

Fig. 11 Rear suspension assembly. Eclipse FWD

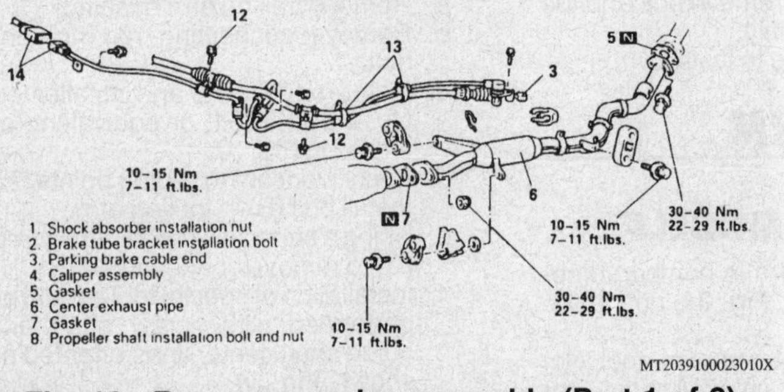
10–15 Nm
7–11 ft.lbs.
30–40 Nm
22–29 ft.lbs
10–15 Nm
7–11 ft.lbs.
30–40 Nm
22–29 ft.lbs.
10–15 Nm
7–11 ft.lbs.
1. Shock absorber installation nut
2. Brake tube bracket installation bolt
3. Parking brake cable end
4. Caliper assembly
5. Gasket
6. Center exhaust pipe
7. Gasket
8. Propeller shaft installation bolt and nut
MT2039100023010X

Fig. 12 Rear suspension assembly (Part 1 of 2). Eclipse AWD

1. Hold stabilizer link ball studs with wrench and install self-locking nuts (A), **Fig. 41.**
2. Holding stabilizer bar link with wrench, tighten self-locking nut "B" ensuring protrusion of stabilizer link is 0.197–0.276 inch.
3. Align left frame bushing with stabilizer bar marking end and temporarily tighten stabilizer bar bracket, **Fig. 42.**
4. Mount right stabilizer bar bracket and temporarily tighten.
5. Temporarily install both ends of stabilizer bar onto links and tighten stabilizer bar bracket bolts.

3000GT & 1993–94 ECLIPSE AWD MODELS

1. Remove rear suspension in numbered sequence as shown, **Figs. 43 and 44,** noting the following:
   a. Support rear suspension with a suitable transmission jack.
   b. Remove crossmember bracket nut and bracket.
   c. Lower transmission jack to obtain a gap between rear suspension and body.
   d. Remove stabilizer bar.
2. Check stabilizer link ball joint stud starting torque as follows:
   a. Move stabilizer link ball joint stud from side to side several times.
   b. Install two nuts on ball joint and measure ball joint starting torque, **Fig. 45.**
   c. If starting **torque** is not 15–28 lbs.,

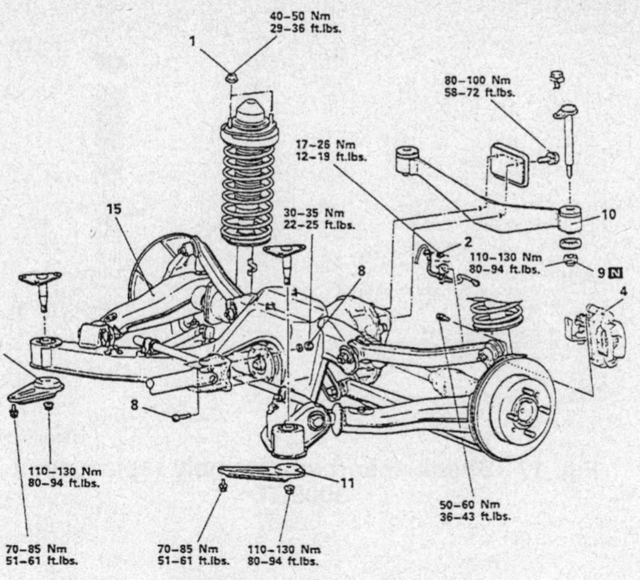

40–50 Nm
29–36 ft.lbs.
80–100 Nm
58–72 ft.lbs.
17–26 Nm
12–19 ft.lbs.
30–35 Nm
22–25 ft.lbs.
110–130 Nm
80–94 ft.lbs.
110–130 Nm
80–94 ft.lbs.
50–60 Nm
36–43 ft.lbs.
70–85 Nm
51–61 ft.lbs.
70–85 Nm
51–61 ft.lbs.
110–130 Nm
80–94 ft.lbs.

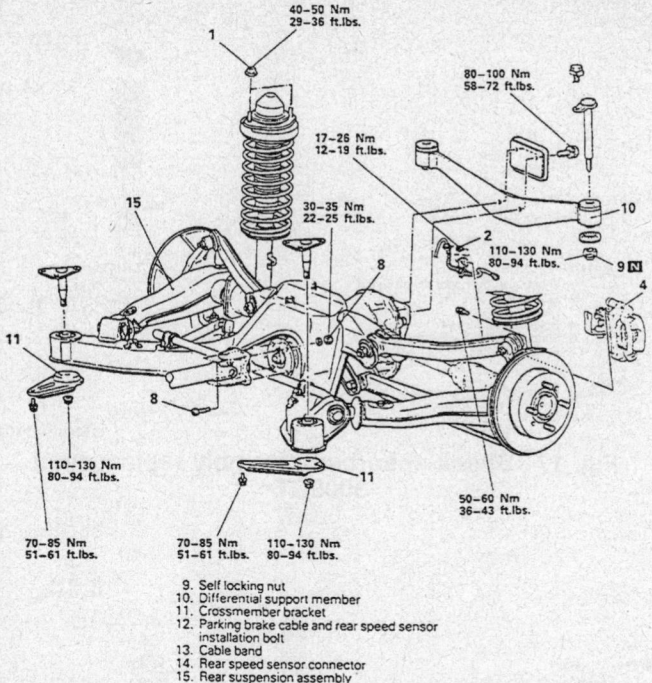

9. Self locking nut
10. Differential support member
11. Crossmember bracket
12. Parking brake cable and rear speed sensor installation bolt
13. Cable band
14. Rear speed sensor connector
15. Rear suspension assembly

MT2039100023020X

Fig. 12 Rear suspension assembly (Part 2 of 2). Eclipse AWD

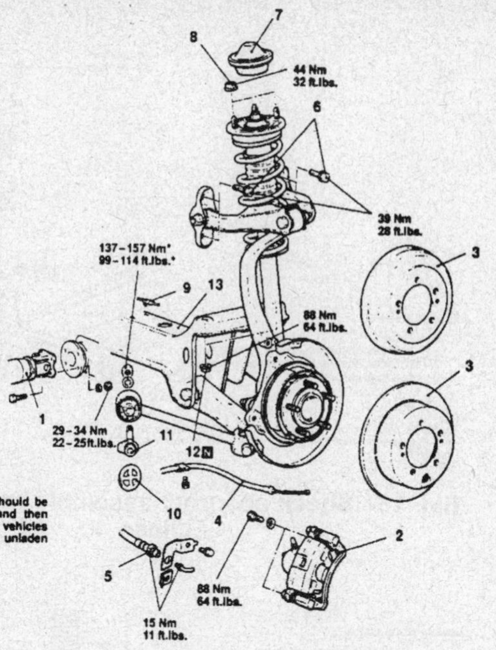

44 Nm
32 ft.lbs.
39 Nm
28 ft.lbs.
137–157 Nm*
99–114 ft.lbs.*
88 Nm
64 ft.lbs.
29–34 Nm
22–25ft.lbs.
88 Nm
64 ft.lbs.
15 Nm
11 ft.lbs.

Caution
: **Indicates parts which should be temporarily tightened, and then fully tightened with the vehicles on the ground in the unladen condition.**

Removal steps

1. Propeller shaft connection <AWD>
2. Brake caliper assembly <Vehicles with disc brakes>
3. Brake disc <Vehicles with disc brakes> or brake drum <Vehicles with drum brakes>
4. Parking brake cable end (Refer to GROUP 36-Parking Brake Cable)
5. Brake hose connection <Vehicles with drum brakes>
6. Upper arm bracket mounting bolts
7. Cap
8. Shock absorber mounting nuts
9. Rear wheel-speed sensor connector <Vehicles with ABS>
10. Grommet
11. Trailing arm mounting bolt
12. Crossmember mounting self-locking nuts
13. Rear suspension assembly

MT2039500094000X

Fig. 13 Rear suspension assembly. 1995–96 Eclipse

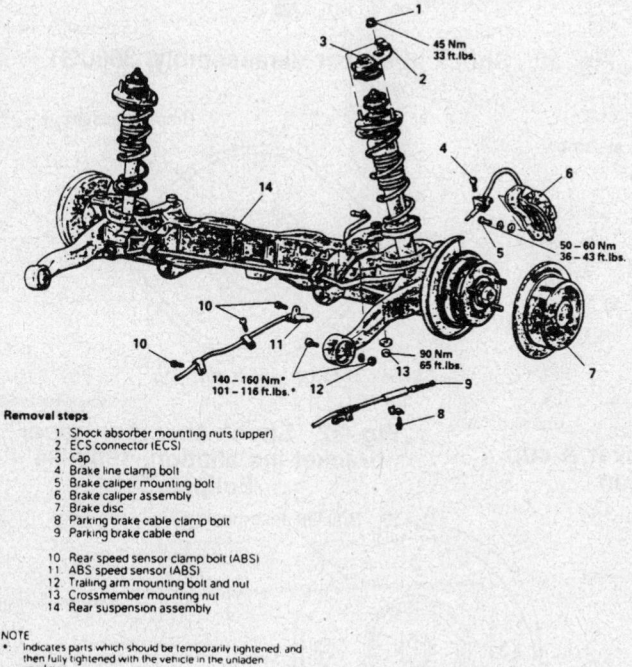

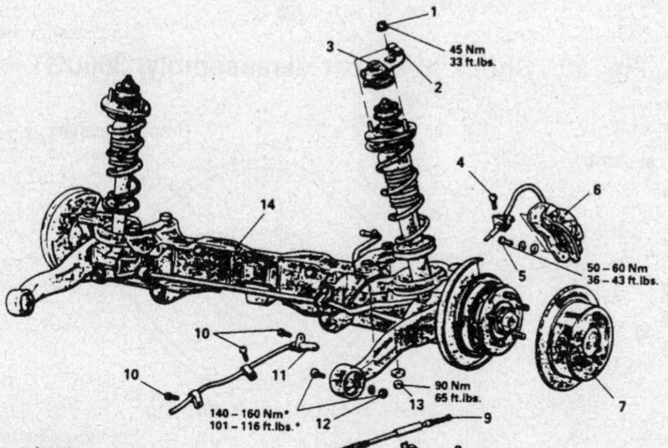

45 Nm
33 ft.lbs.
50–60 Nm
36–43 ft.lbs.
90 Nm
65 ft.lbs.
140–160 Nm*
101–116 ft.lbs.*

Removal steps

1. Shock absorber mounting nuts (upper)
2. ECS connector (ECS)
3. Cap
4. Brake line clamp bolt
5. Brake caliper mounting bolt
6. Brake caliper assembly
7. Brake disc
8. Parking brake cable clamp bolt
9. Parking brake cable end
10. Rear speed sensor clamp bolt (ABS)
11. ABS speed sensor (ABS)
12. Trailing arm mounting bolt and nut
13. Crossmember mounting nut
14. Rear suspension assembly

NOTE
*: Indicates parts which should be temporarily tightened, and then fully tightened with the vehicle in the unladen condition

MT2039100024000X

Fig. 14 Rear suspension assembly replacement. 3000GT FWD

Removal steps

1. Shock absorber mounting nuts (upper)*
2. ECS connector <ECS>*
3. Cap*
4. Brake tube to brake hose connection*
5. Brake caliper*
6. Brake disc*
7. Parking brake cable end*

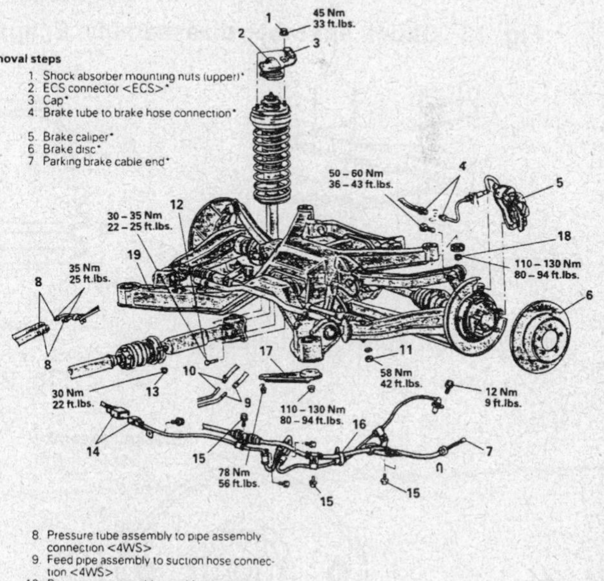

45 Nm
33 ft.lbs.
50–60 Nm
36–43 ft.lbs.
30–35 Nm
22–25 ft.lbs.
35 Nm
25 ft.lbs.
110–130 Nm
80–94 ft.lbs.
58 Nm
42 ft.lbs.
12 Nm
9 ft.lbs.
30 Nm
22 ft.lbs.
110–130 Nm
80–94 ft.lbs.
78 Nm
56 ft.lbs.

8. Pressure tube assembly to pipe assembly connection <4WS>
9. Feed pipe assembly to suction hose connection <4WS>
10. Return pipe assembly to rubber hose connection <4WS>
11. Power cylinder tie rod coupling nut <4WS>*
12. Differential carrier to propeller shaft coupling bolt and nut
13. Center bearing mounting nut
14. Harness connector connection <ABS>*
15. Parking brake cable and ABS sensor fixing bolt <ABS>*
16. Cable band*
17. Crossmember bracket*
18. Crossmember mounting nut (on differential side)*
19. Rear suspension assembly

NOTE
Parts marked with * are symmetrical

MT2039100025000X

Fig. 15 Rear suspension assembly replacement. 3000GT AWD

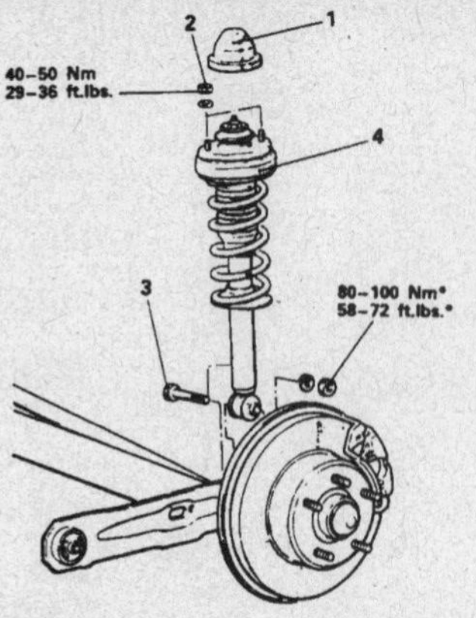
40-50 Nm
29-36 ft.lbs.
80-100 Nm*
58-72 ft.lbs.*
1
2
3
4

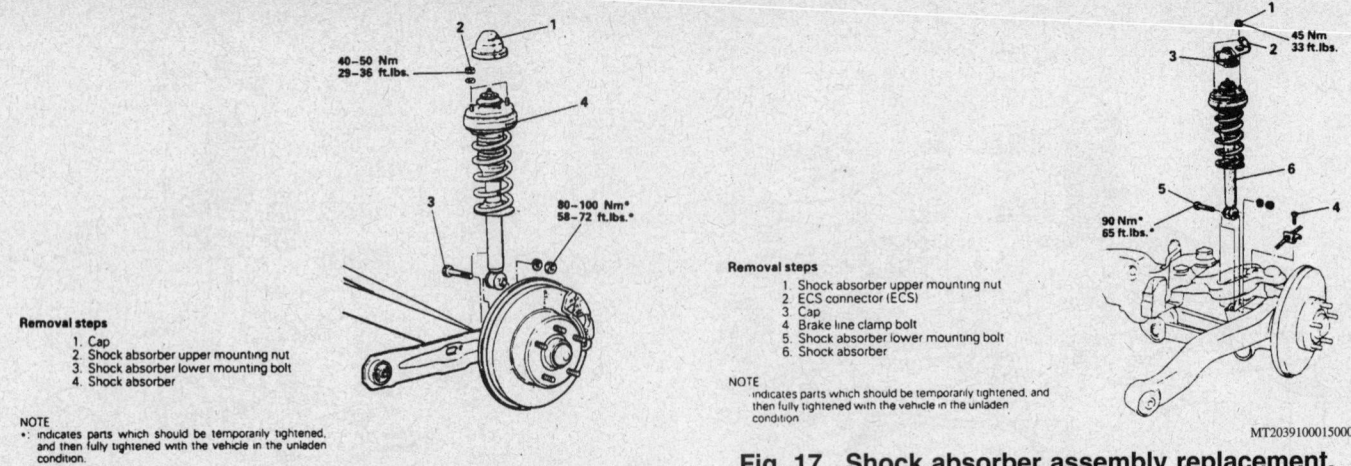

Removal steps
1. Cap
2. Shock absorber upper mounting nut
3. Shock absorber lower mounting bolt
4. Shock absorber

NOTE
*: indicates parts which should be temporarily tightened, and then fully tightened with the vehicle in the unladen condition.

MT2039100014000X

Fig. 16 Shock absorber assembly replacement. Eclipse

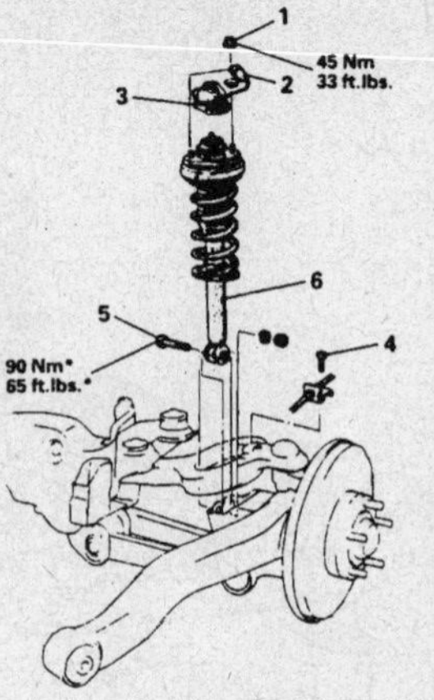
45 Nm
33 ft.lbs.
90 Nm*
65 ft.lbs.*
1
2
3
4
5
6

Removal steps
1. Shock absorber upper mounting nut
2. ECS connector (ECS)
3. Cap
4. Brake line clamp bolt
5. Shock absorber lower mounting bolt
6. Shock absorber

NOTE
*: indicates parts which should be temporarily tightened, and then fully tightened with the vehicle in the unladen condition

MT2039100015000X

Fig. 17 Shock absorber assembly replacement. 3000GT

Disassembly steps
1. Piston rod tightening nut
2. Washer
3. Upper bushing (A)
4. Bracket assembly
5. Upper spring pad
6. Upper bushing (B)
7. Collar
8. Cup assembly
9. Dust cover
10. Bump rubber
11. Coil spring
12. Shock absorber

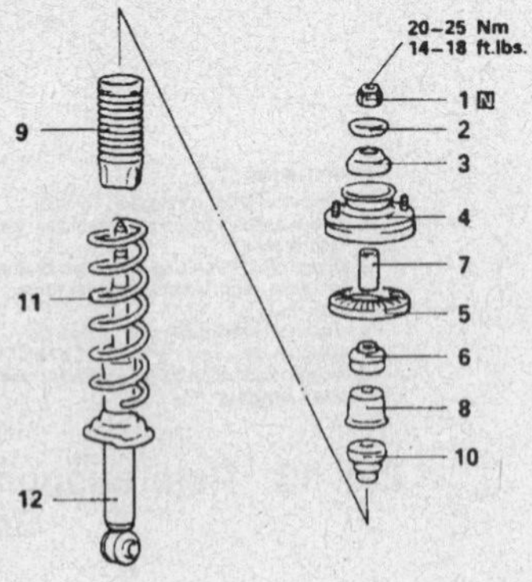
20-25 Nm
14-18 ft.lbs.
1 N
2
3
4
5
6
7
8
9
10
11
12

MT2039100016000X

Fig. 18 Shock absorber disassembly. Eclipse

Disassembly steps
1. Piston rod tightening nut
2. Washer
3. Upper bushing (A)
4. Bracket assembly
5. Upper spring pad
6. Upper bushing (B)
7. Collar
8. Cup assembly
9. Dust cover
10. Bump rubber
11. Coil spring
12. Shock absorber

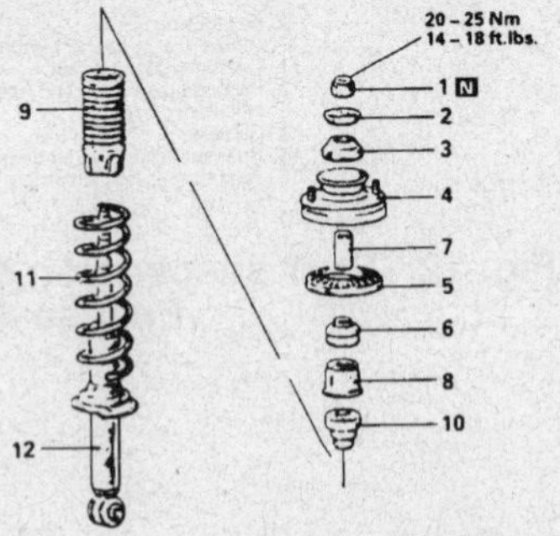
20-25 Nm
14-18 ft.lbs.
1 N
2
3
4
5
6
7
8
9
10
11
12

MT2039100017000X

Fig. 19 Shock absorber disassembly. 3000GT

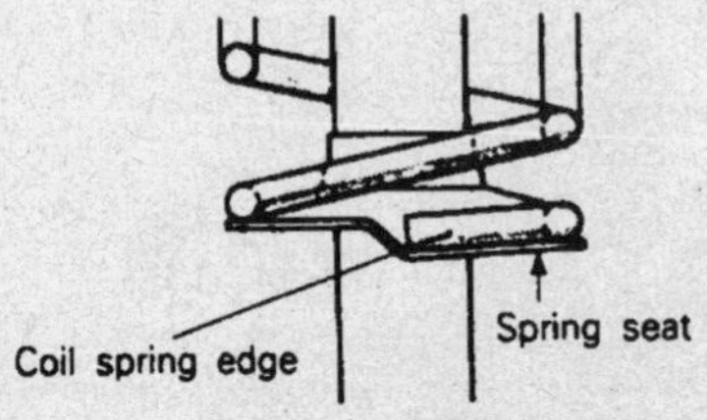
Coil spring edge
Spring seat

MT2039100018000X

Fig. 20 Coil spring installation

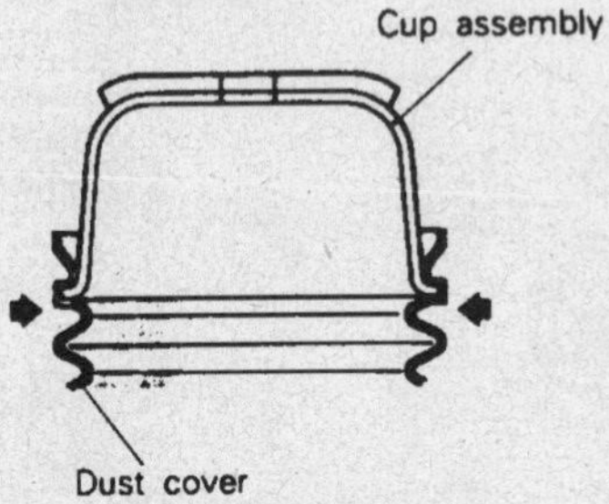
Cup assembly
Dust cover

MT2039100019000X

Fig. 21 Dust cover & cup installation

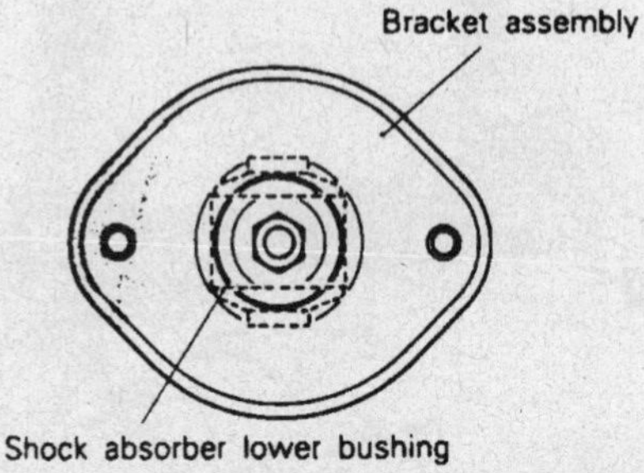
Bracket assembly
Shock absorber lower bushing

MT2039100020000X

Fig. 22 Shock absorber upper bracket installation. 1993–94 Eclipse

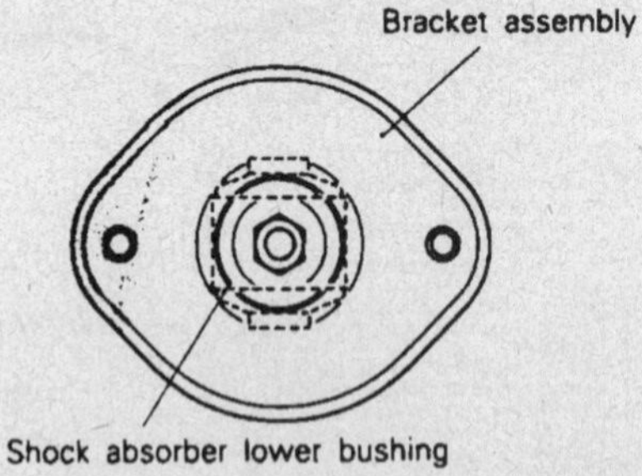
Bracket assembly
Shock absorber lower bushing

MT2039100020000X

Fig. 23 Shock absorber upper bracket installation. 1995–96 Eclipse

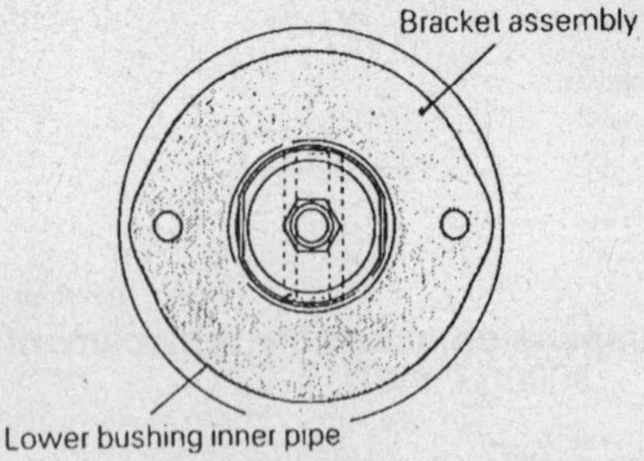
Bracket assembly
Lower bushing inner pipe

MT2039100021000X

Fig. 24 Shock absorber upper bracket installation. 3000GT

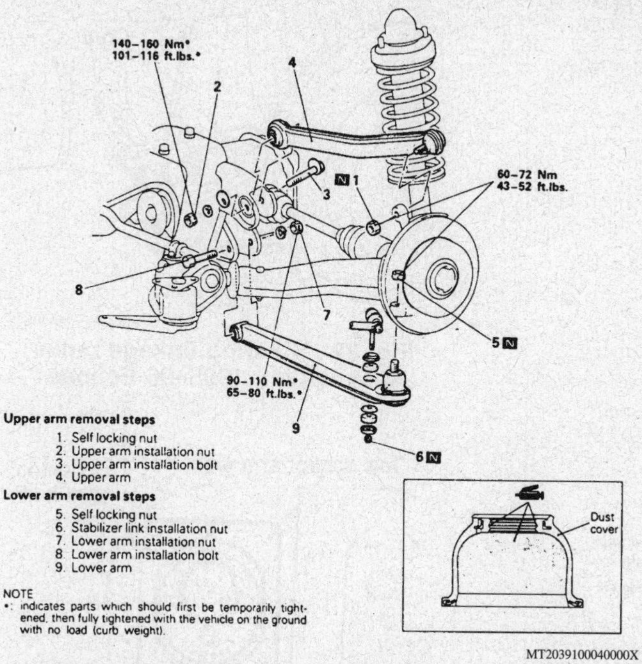
140–160 Nm*
101–116 ft.lbs.*
60–72 Nm
43–52 ft.lbs.
90–110 Nm*
65–80 ft.lbs.*
Upper arm removal steps
1. Self locking nut
2. Upper arm installation nut
3. Upper arm installation bolt
4. Upper arm
Lower arm removal steps
5. Self locking nut
6. Stabilizer link installation nut
7. Lower arm installation nut
8. Lower arm installation bolt
9. Lower arm
NOTE
*: indicates parts which should first be temporarily tightened, then fully tightened with the vehicle on the ground with no load (curb weight).
Dust cover
MT2039100040000X

Fig. 25 Upper & lower control arm replacement. 1993-94 Eclipse AWD

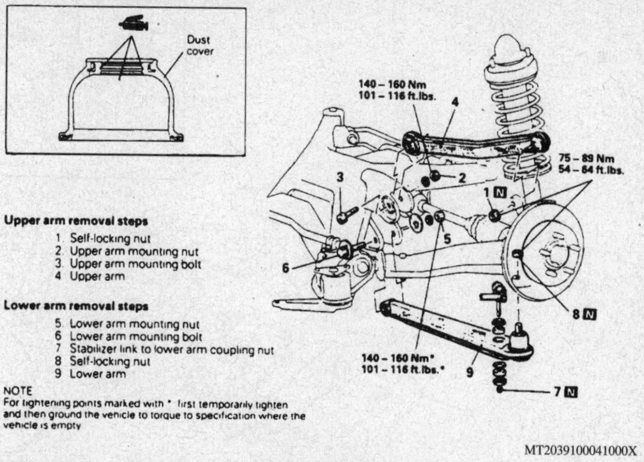
Dust cover
140–160 Nm
101–116 ft.lbs.
75–89 Nm
54–64 ft.lbs.
140–160 Nm*
101–116 ft.lbs.*
Upper arm removal steps
1. Self-locking nut
2. Upper arm mounting nut
3. Upper arm mounting bolt
4. Upper arm
Lower arm removal steps
5. Lower arm mounting nut
6. Lower arm mounting bolt
7. Stabilizer link to lower arm coupling nut
8. Self-locking nut
9. Lower arm
NOTE
For tightening points marked with * first temporarily tighten and then ground the vehicle to torque to specification where the vehicle is empty
MT2039100041000X

Fig. 26 Upper & lower control arm replacement. 3000GT AWD

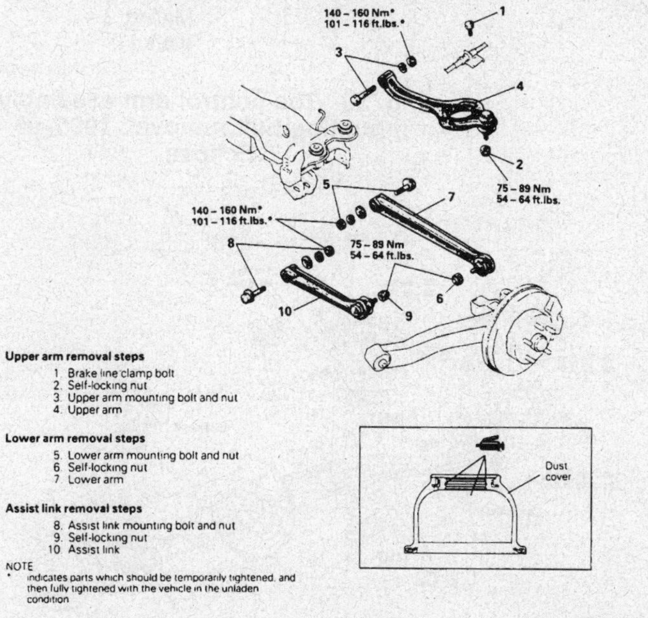
140–160 Nm*
101–116 ft.lbs.*
75–89 Nm
54–64 ft.lbs.
140–160 Nm*
101–116 ft.lbs.*
75–89 Nm
54–64 ft.lbs.
Upper arm removal steps
1. Brake line clamp bolt
2. Self-locking nut
3. Upper arm mounting bolt and nut
4. Upper arm
Lower arm removal steps
5. Lower arm mounting bolt and nut
6. Self-locking nut
7. Lower arm
Assist link removal steps
8. Assist link mounting bolt and nut
9. Self-locking nut
10. Assist link
NOTE
* indicates parts which should be temporarily tightened, and then fully tightened with the vehicle in the unladen condition
Dust cover
MT2039100042000X

Fig. 27 Upper & lower control arm & assist link replacement. 3000GT FWD

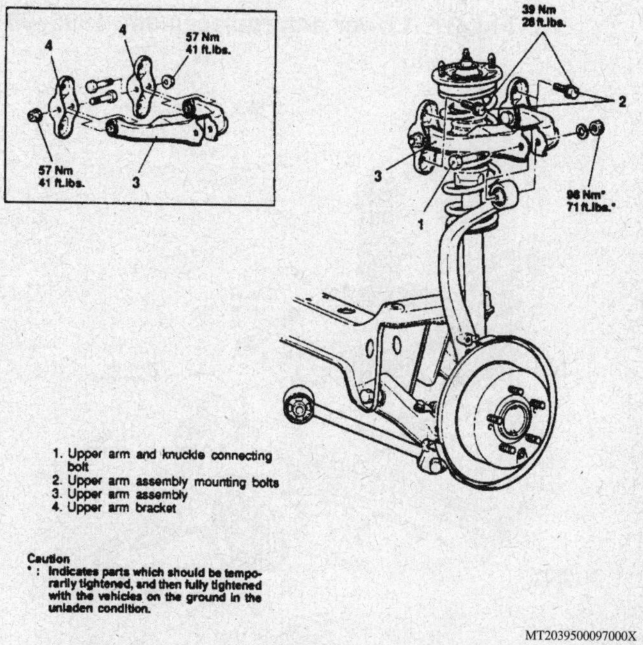
57 Nm
41 ft.lbs.
57 Nm
41 ft.lbs.
39 Nm
28 ft.lbs.
98 Nm*
71 ft.lbs.*
1. Upper arm and knuckle connecting bolt
2. Upper arm assembly mounting bolts
3. Upper arm assembly
4. Upper arm bracket
Caution
*: Indicates parts which should be temporarily tightened, and then fully tightened with the vehicles on the ground in the unladen condition.
MT2039500097000X

Fig. 28 Upper arm assembly. 1995–96 Eclipse

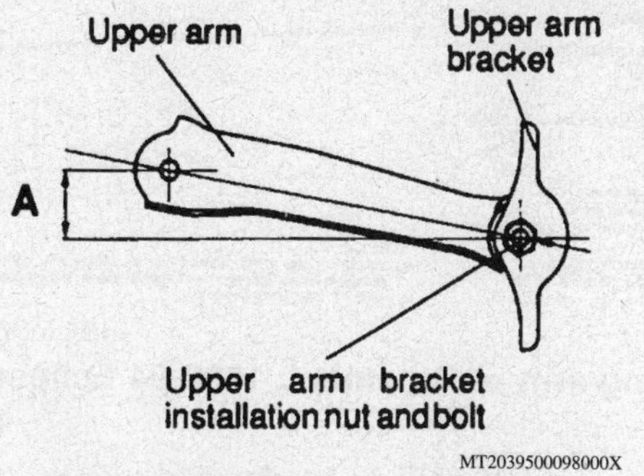
Upper arm
Upper arm bracket
A
Upper arm bracket installation nut and bolt
MT2039500098000X

Fig. 29 Upper arm bracket dimension A. 1995–96 Eclipse

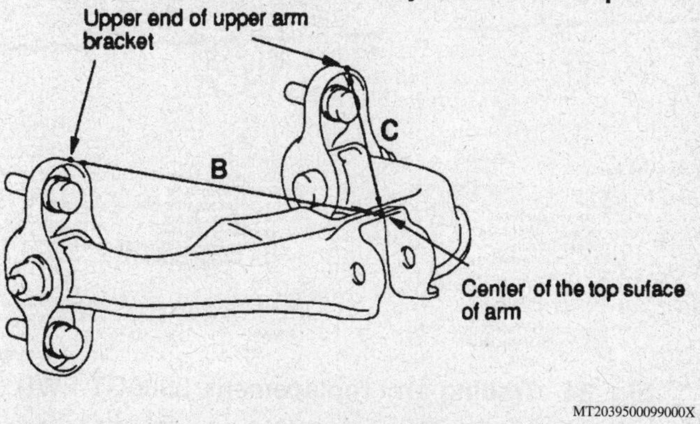
Upper end of upper arm bracket
B
C
Center of the top suface of arm
MT2039500099000X

Fig. 30 Upper arm bracket dimensions B & C. 1995–96 Eclipse

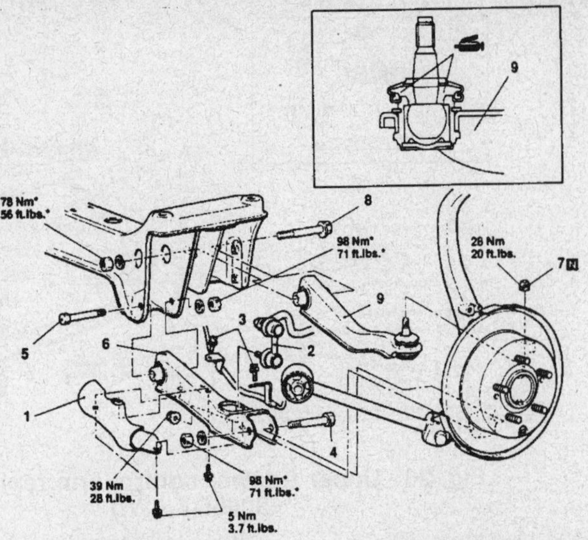
69–78 Nm*
50–56 ft.lbs.*
98 Nm*
71 ft.lbs.*
28 Nm
20 ft.lbs.
39 Nm
28 ft.lbs.
98 Nm*
71 ft.lbs.*
5 Nm
3.7 ft.lbs.

Lower arm assembly removal steps

1. Lower arm cover <Vehicles with aero parts>
2. Stabilizer link
3. ABS wheel-speed sensor clamp bolts <Vehicles with ABS>
4. Lower arm assembly and knuckle connecting bolt
5. Lower arm assembly mounting bolt
6. Lower arm assembly

Toe control arm assembly removal steps

7. Toe control arm ball joint and knuckle connection
8. Toe control arm assembly mounting bolt
9. Toe control arm assembly

Caution
* : Indicates parts which should be temporarily tightened, and then fully tightened with the vehicles on the ground in the unladen condition.

MT2039500100000X

Fig. 31 Lower arm replacement. 1995–96 Eclipse

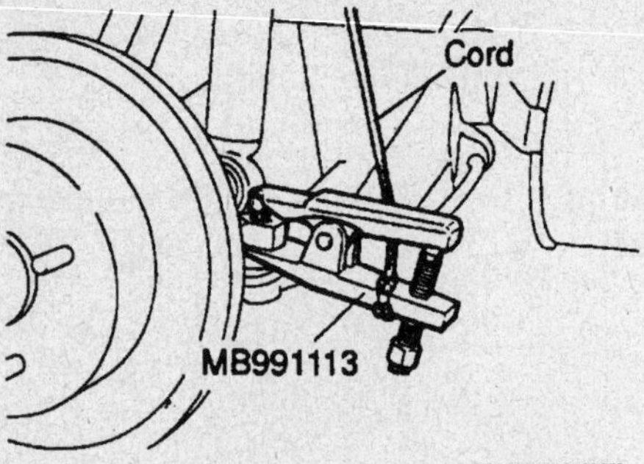
Cord
MB991113

MT2039500101000X

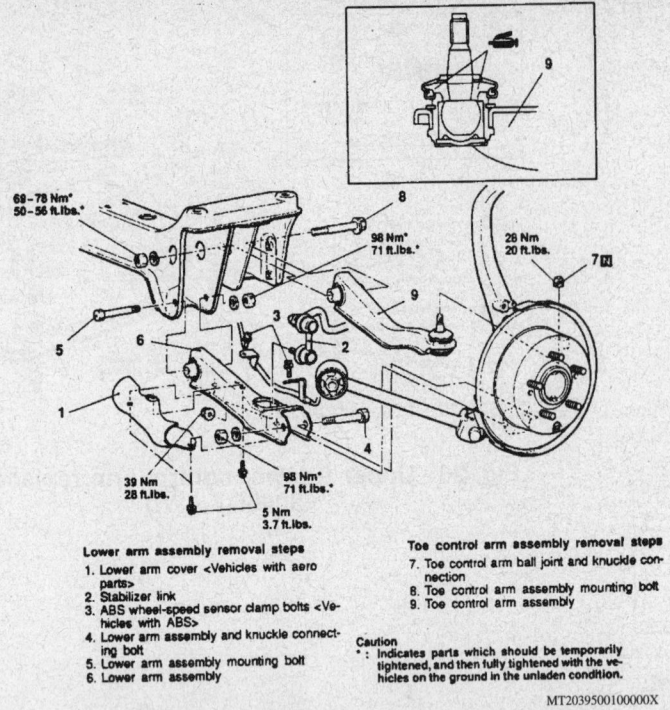

Fig. 32 Steering linkage puller installation. 1995–96 Eclipse

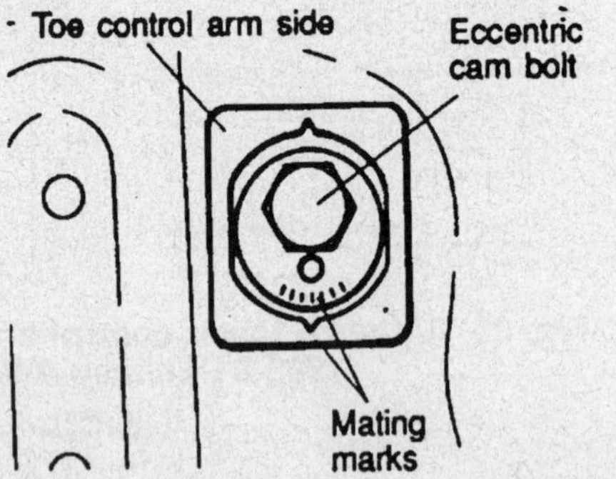
Toe control arm side
Eccentric cam bolt
Mating marks

MT2039500102000X

Fig. 33 Toe control arm assembly mounting bolt removal. 1995–96 Eclipse

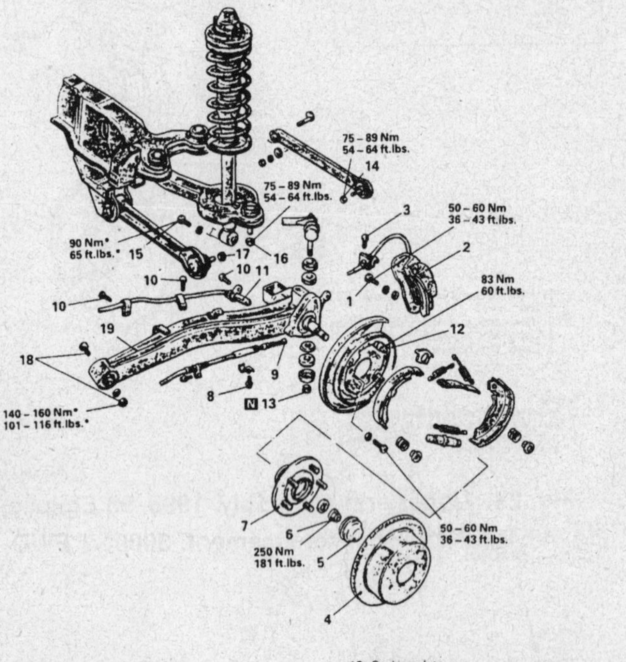
75–89 Nm
54–64 ft.lbs.
75–89 Nm
54–64 ft.lbs.
50–60 Nm
36–43 ft.lbs.
90 Nm*
65 ft.lbs.*
83 Nm
60 ft.lbs.
140–160 Nm*
101–116 ft.lbs.*
250 Nm
181 ft.lbs.
50–60 Nm
36–43 ft.lbs.

Removal steps

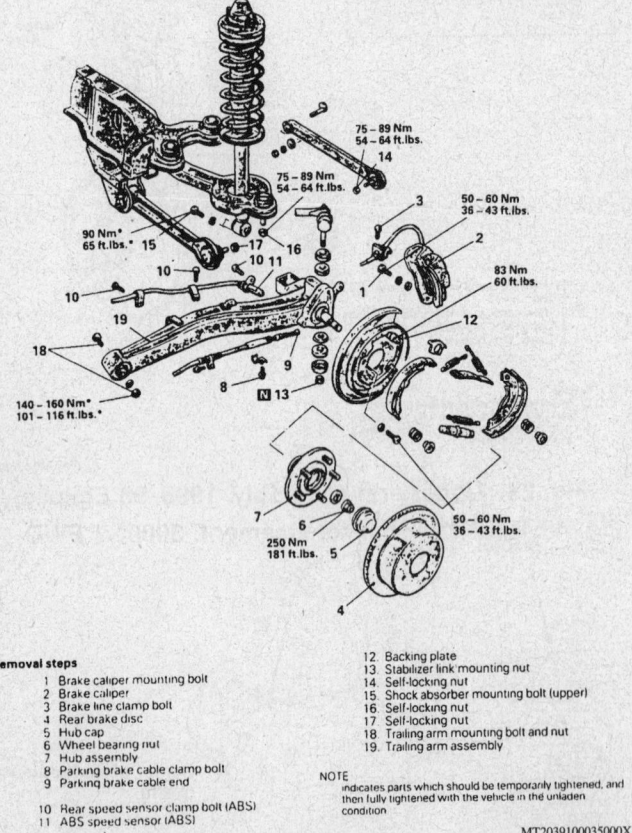

1. Brake caliper mounting bolt
2. Brake caliper
3. Brake line clamp bolt
4. Rear brake disc
5. Hub cap
6. Wheel bearing nut
7. Hub assembly
8. Parking brake cable clamp bolt
9. Parking brake cable end
10. Rear speed sensor clamp bolt (ABS)
11. ABS speed sensor (ABS)
12. Backing plate
13. Stabilizer link mounting nut
14. Self-locking nut
15. Shock absorber mounting bolt (upper)
16. Self-locking nut
17. Self-locking nut
18. Trailing arm mounting bolt and nut
19. Trailing arm assembly

NOTE
* indicates parts which should be temporarily tightened, and then fully tightened with the vehicle in the unladen condition

MT2039100035000X

Fig. 34 Trailing arm replacement. 3000GT FWD

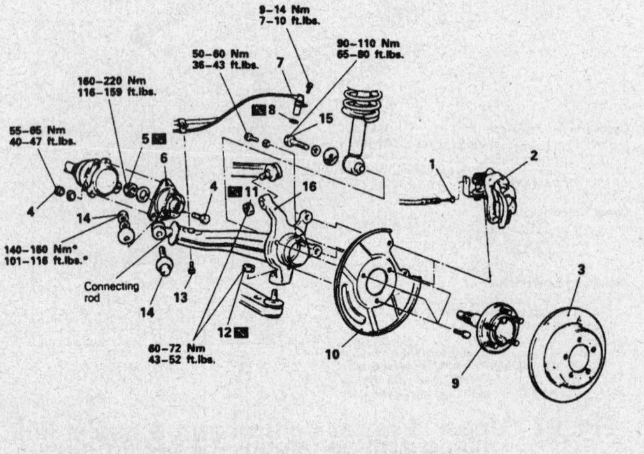
9–14 Nm
7–10 ft.lbs.
90–110 Nm
65–80 ft.lbs.
50–60 Nm
36–43 ft.lbs.
160–220 Nm
116–159 ft.lbs.
55–65 Nm
40–47 ft.lbs.
140–160 Nm*
101–116 ft.lbs.*
Connecting rod
60–72 Nm
43–52 ft.lbs.

Removal steps

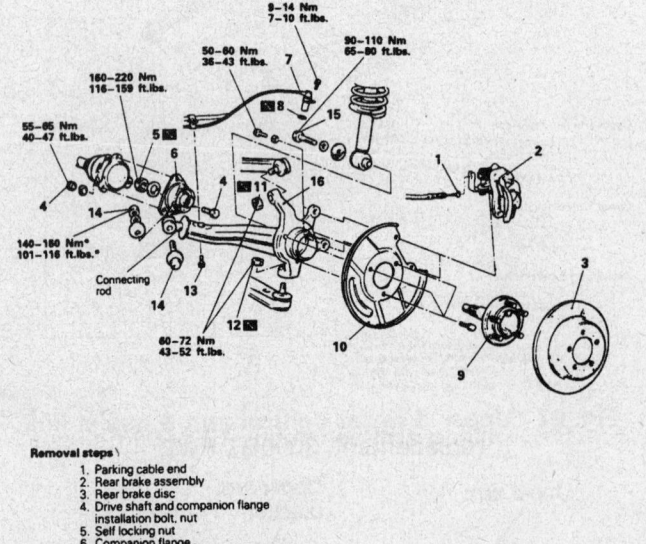

1. Parking cable end
2. Rear brake assembly
3. Rear brake disc
4. Drive shaft and companion flange installation bolt, nut
5. Self locking nut
6. Companion flange
7. Rear speed sensor <Vehicles with ABS>
8. O-ring
9. Rear axle shaft
10. Dust shield
11. Self locking nut (upper arm)
12. Self locking nut (lower arm)
13. Parking brake cable and rear speed sensor installation bolt
14. Trailing arm installation bolt, nut
15. Rear shock absorber installation bolt
16. Trailing arm

NOTE
*: indicates parts which should first be temporarily tightened, then fully tightened with the vehicle on the ground with no load (curb weight).

MT2039100036000X

Fig. 35 Trailing arm replacement. 1993-94 Eclipse AWD

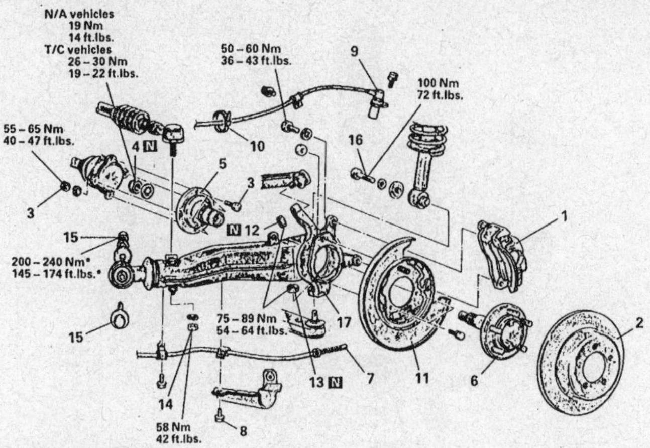
N/A vehicles
19 Nm
14 ft.lbs.
T/C vehicles
26 – 30 Nm
19 – 22 ft.lbs.
50 – 60 Nm
36 – 43 ft.lbs.
100 Nm
72 ft.lbs.
55 – 65 Nm
40 – 47 ft.lbs.
200 – 240 Nm*
145 – 174 ft.lbs.*
75 – 89 Nm
54 – 64 ft.lbs.
58 Nm
42 ft.lbs.

Removal steps

1. Rear brake caliper assembly
2. Rear brake disc
3. Drive shaft to companion flange mounting bolt and nut
4. Self-locking nut
5. Companion flange
6. Rear axle shaft
7. Parking brake cable end
8. Parking brake cable clamp bolt
9. Rear speed sensor (ABS)
10. Rear speed sensor cable and parking brake cable bands (ABS)
11. Dust shield
12. Self-locking nut (upper arm)
13. Self-locking nut (lower arm)
14. Tie rod end mounting nut
15. Trailing arm mounting bolt and nut
16. Rear shock absorber mounting bolt
17. Trailing arm

NOTE
For tightening points marked with *, first temporarily tighten and then ground the vehicle to torque to specification where the vehicle is empty

MT2039100037000X

Fig. 36 Trailing arm replacement. 3000GT AWD

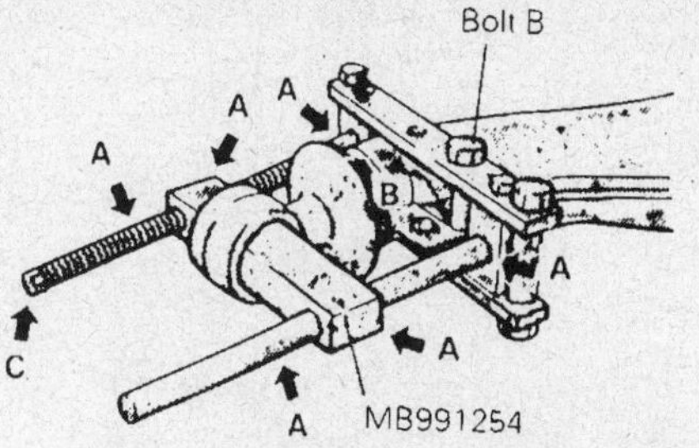
Bolt B
A
B
C
MB991254

MT2039100038000X

Fig. 37 Trailing arm connecting rod replacement

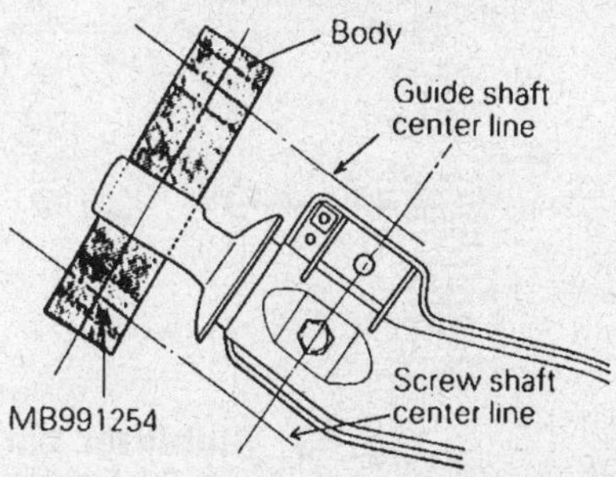
Body
Guide shaft center line
MB991254
Screw shaft center line

MT2039100039000X

Fig. 38 Trailing arm connecting rod installation

Removal steps

1. Knuckle and trailing arm assembly connecting bolt
2. Grommet
3. Trailing arm assembly mounting bolt
4. Stopper
5. Trailing arm assembly

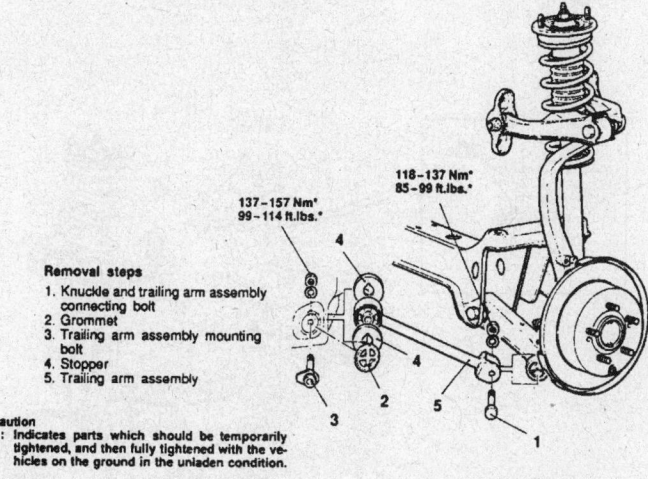

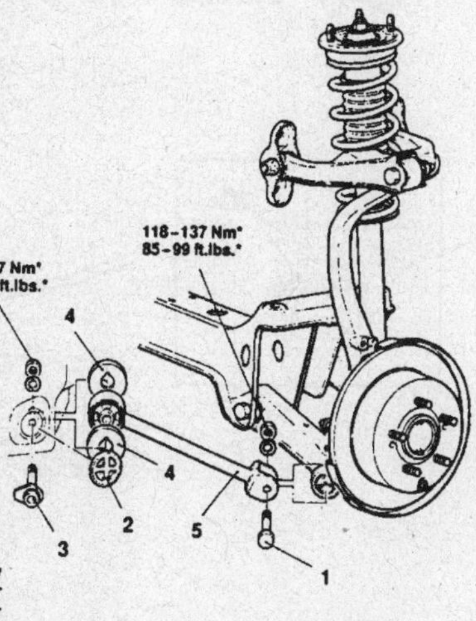
118 – 137 Nm*
85 – 99 ft.lbs.*
137 – 157 Nm*
99 – 114 ft.lbs.*

Caution
* : Indicates parts which should be temporarily tightened, and then fully tightened with the vehicles on the ground in the unladen condition.

MT2039500103000X

Fig. 39 Trailing arm assembly. 1995–96 Eclipse

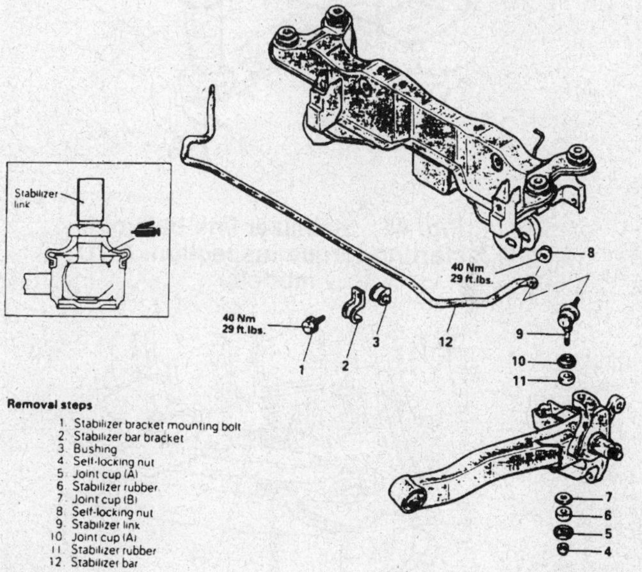
Stabilizer link
40 Nm
29 ft.lbs.
40 Nm
29 ft.lbs.

Removal steps

1. Stabilizer bracket mounting bolt
2. Stabilizer bar bracket
3. Bushing
4. Self-locking nut
5. Joint cup (A)
6. Stabilizer rubber
7. Joint cup (B)
8. Self-locking nut
9. Stabilizer link
10. Joint cup (A)
11. Stabilizer rubber
12. Stabilizer bar

MT2039100026000X

Fig. 40 Stabilizer bar replacement. 3000GT FWD

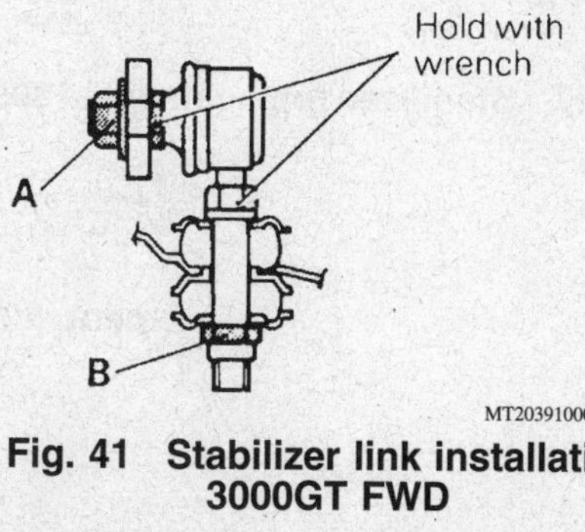
Hold with wrench
A
B

MT2039100027000X

Fig. 41 Stabilizer link installation. 3000GT FWD

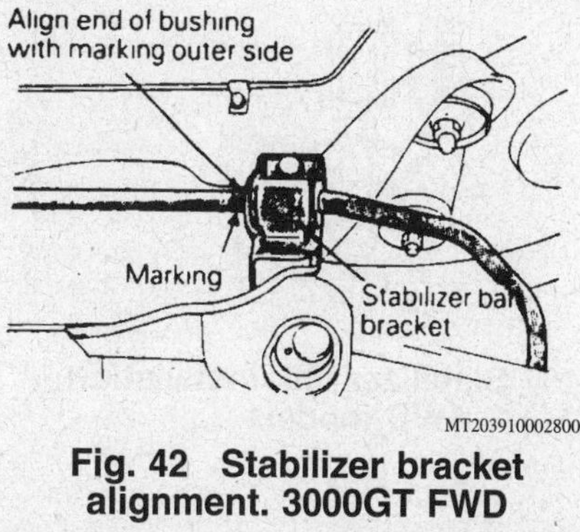
Align end of bushing with marking outer side
Marking
Stabilizer bar bracket

MT2039100028000X

Fig. 42 Stabilizer bracket alignment. 3000GT FWD

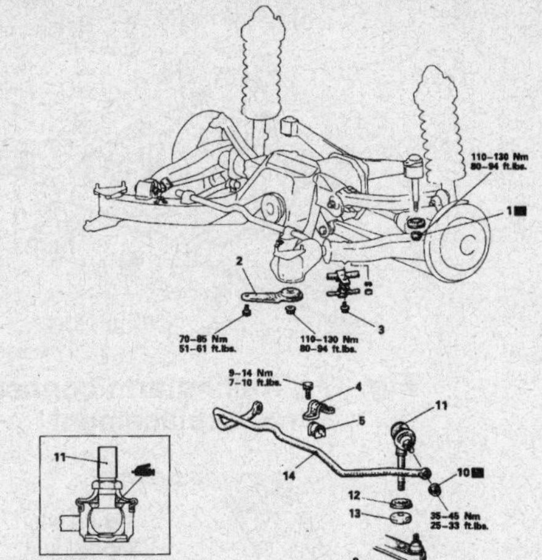
110–130 Nm
80–94 ft.lbs.
70–85 Nm
51–61 ft.lbs.
110–130 Nm
80–94 ft.lbs.
9–14 Nm
7–10 ft.lbs.
35–45 Nm
25–33 ft.lbs.

Removal steps

1. Self locking nut
2. Crossmember bracket
3. Parking brake cable and rear speed sensor installation bolt
4. Stabilizer bracket
5. Bushing
6. Self locking nut
7. Joint cup (A)
8. Stabilizer rubber
9. Joint cup (B)
10. Self locking nut
11. Stabilizer link
12. Joint cup (A)
13. Stabilizer rubber
14. Stabilizer bar

MT2039100029000X

Fig. 43 Stabilizer bar replacement. 1993-94 Eclipse AWD

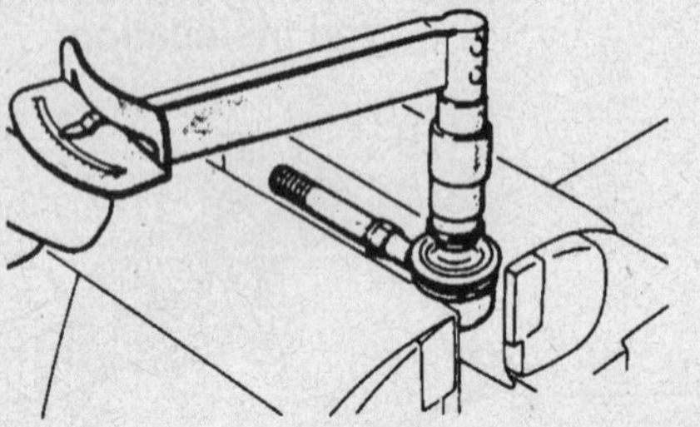

MT2039100031000X

Fig. 45 Stabilizer link ball joint starting torque inspection. AWD models

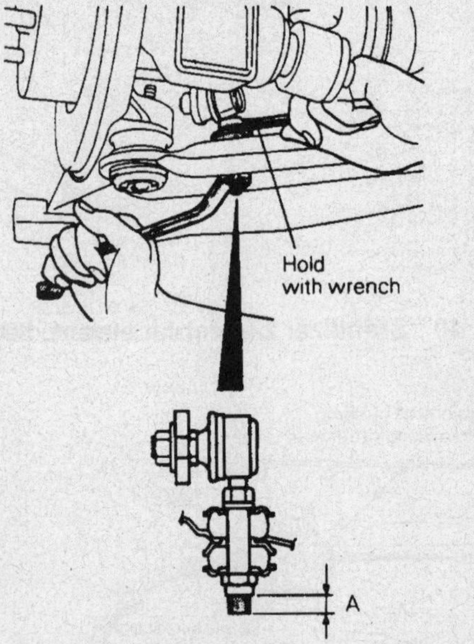
Hold
with wrench
A

MT2039100032000X

Fig. 46 Stabilizer link installation. AWD models

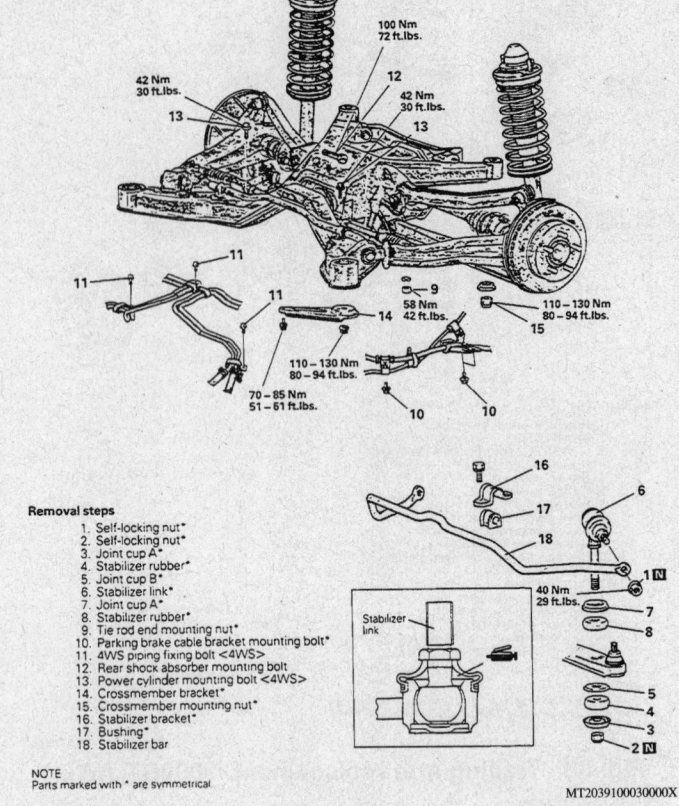

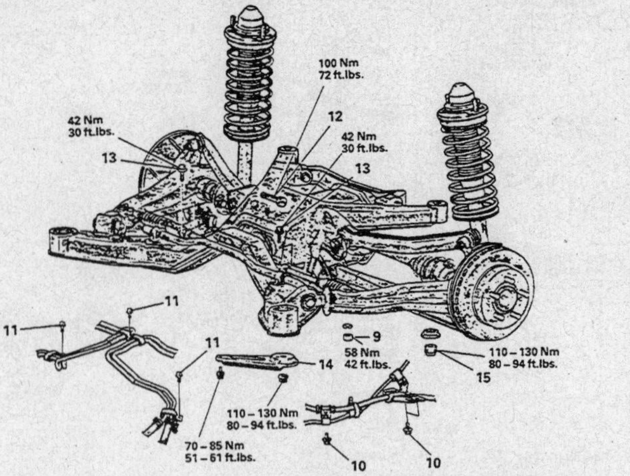
100 Nm
72 ft.lbs.
42 Nm
30 ft.lbs.
42 Nm
30 ft.lbs.
58 Nm
42 ft.lbs.
110 – 130 Nm
80 – 94 ft.lbs.
110 – 130 Nm
80 – 94 ft.lbs.
70 – 85 Nm
51 – 61 ft.lbs.

Removal steps

1. Self-locking nut*
2. Self-locking nut*
3. Joint cup A*
4. Stabilizer rubber*
5. Joint cup B*
6. Stabilizer link*
7. Joint cup A*
8. Stabilizer rubber*
9. Tie rod end mounting nut*
10. Parking brake cable bracket mounting bolt*
11. 4WS piping fixing bolt <4WS>
12. Rear shock absorber mounting bolt
13. Power cylinder mounting bolt <4WS>
14. Crossmember bracket*
15. Crossmember mounting nut*
16. Stabilizer bracket*
17. Bushing*
18. Stabilizer bar

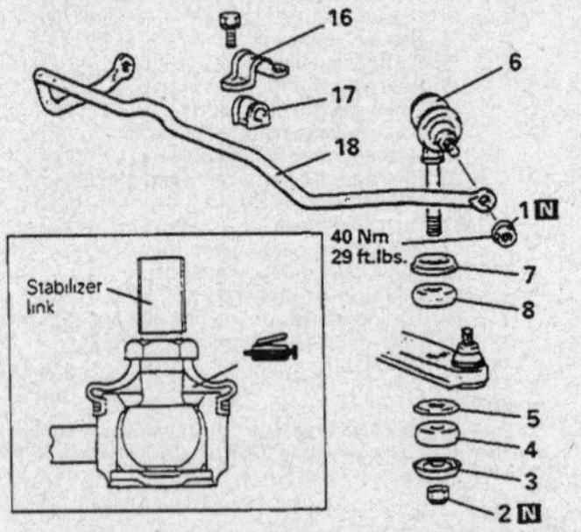
40 Nm
29 ft.lbs.
Stabilizer
link

NOTE
Parts marked with * are symmetrical

MT2039100030000X

Fig. 44 Stabilizer bar replacement. 3000GT AWD

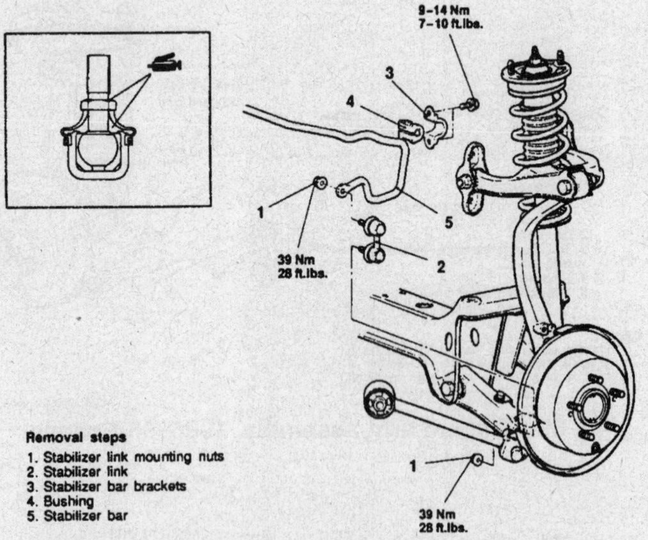
9–14 Nm
7–10 ft.lbs.
39 Nm
28 ft.lbs.
39 Nm
28 ft.lbs.

Removal steps

1. Stabilizer link mounting nuts
2. Stabilizer link
3. Stabilizer bar brackets
4. Bushing
5. Stabilizer bar

MT2039500095000X

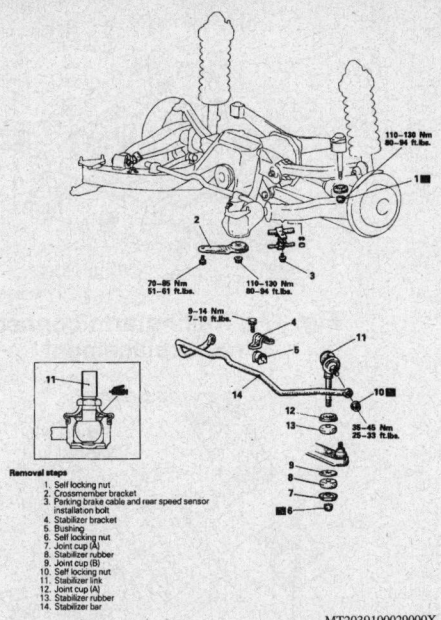

Fig. 47 Stabilizer replacement. 1995-96 Eclipse

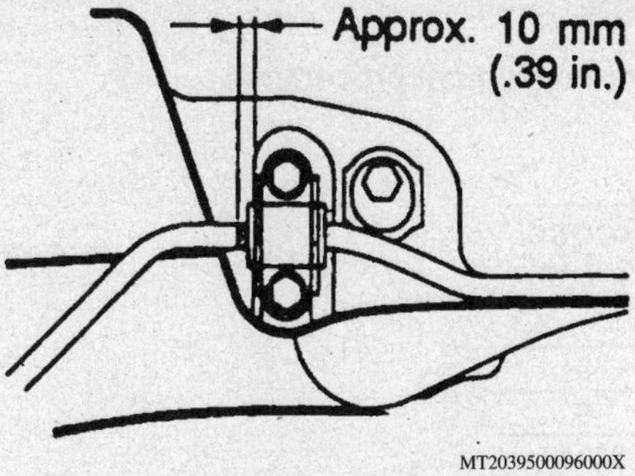
Approx. 10 mm
(.39 in.)
MT2039500096000X

Fig. 48 Stabilizer bar bushing installation. 1995-96 Eclipse

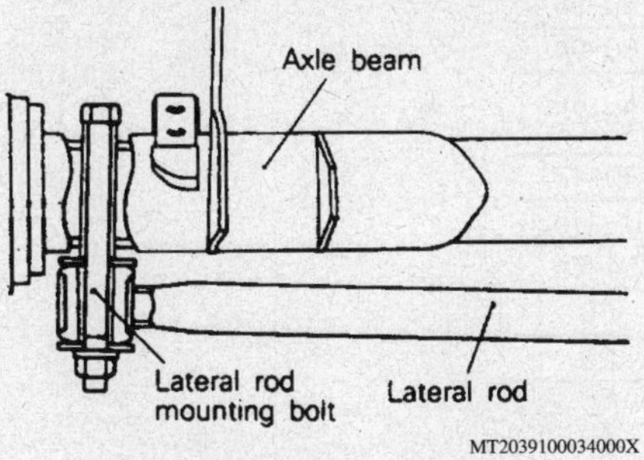
Axle beam
Lateral rod mounting bolt
Lateral rod
MT2039100034000X

Fig. 50 Lateral rod bolt installation. Eclipse FWD

replace stabilizer link.

3. Reverse procedure to install, noting the following:
   a. Hold stabilizer link with wrench and tighten locknut so that protrusion is 0.354–0.433 inch on Eclipse and 0.197–0.276 inch on 3000GT, **Fig. 46.**

1995-96 ECLIPSE

1. **On models with aero parts,** remove lower arm cover.
2. **On all models,** remove stabilizer link mounting nuts, then stabilizer link, **Fig. 47.**
3. Remove stabilizer bar brackets, bushing and stabilizer bar.
4. Inspect bushings for wear and deterioration, then inspect stabilizer bar for deterioration or damage.
5. Inspect stabilizer link ball joint dust cover for cracks. If dust cover is defective replace as follows:
   a. Remove clip ring and dust cover.
   b. Apply multi-purpose grease to the lip and inside of dust cover.
   c. Using vinyl tape, tape stabilizer link on protruding end, then install dust cover to stabilizer link.
   d. Secure dust cover by the clip ring.

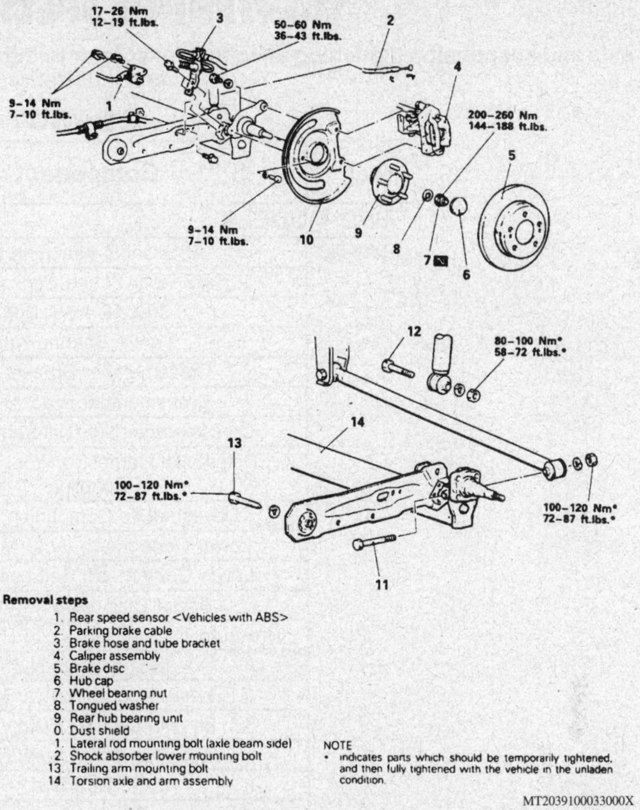
17-26 Nm
12-19 ft.lbs.
50-60 Nm
36-43 ft.lbs.
9-14 Nm
7-10 ft.lbs.
200-260 Nm
144-188 ft.lbs.
9-14 Nm
7-10 ft.lbs.
80-100 Nm*
58-72 ft.lbs.*
100-120 Nm*
72-87 ft.lbs.*
100-120 Nm*
72-87 ft.lbs.*
Removal steps
1. Rear speed sensor <Vehicles with ABS>
2. Parking brake cable
3. Brake hose and tube bracket
4. Caliper assembly
5. Brake disc
6. Hub cap
7. Wheel bearing nut
8. Tongued washer
9. Rear hub bearing unit
0. Dust shield
1. Lateral rod mounting bolt (axle beam side)
2. Shock absorber lower mounting bolt
13. Trailing arm mounting bolt
14. Torsion axle and arm assembly
NOTE
• indicates parts which should be temporarily tightened, and then fully tightened with the vehicle in the unladen condition.
MT2039100033000X

Fig. 49 Torsion axle & arm assembly replacement. Eclipse FWD

6. Inspect all bolts for condition and straitness.
7. Reverse procedure to install, noting the following:
   a. Install stabilizer bar so ID mark is at the left, then install bushing as shown in **Fig. 48.**

TORSION BAR

REPLACE

ECLIPSE

1. Remove torsion axle and arm assembly in numbered sequence as shown, **Fig. 49,** noting the following:
   a. Remove caliper assembly and support to frame using suitable wire.
   b. Remove rear hub as outlined under "Rear Axle Hub, Replace."
   c. Raise and support torsion axle and arm assembly.
   d. Remove shock absorber and trailing arm mounting bolts.
   e. Lower torsion axle and arm assembly slowly, then remove from vehicle.
2. Reverse procedure to install, then install lateral rod mounting bolt to axle beam as shown, **Fig. 50.**

LATERAL ROD

REPLACE

ECLIPSE

FWD Models

1. Raise and support vehicle, then remove rear wheels.
2. Remove lateral rod attaching nuts and bolts, then the lateral rod.
3. Reverse procedure to install, tightening lateral rod attaching nuts and bolts to specifications.

TIGHTENING SPECIFICATIONS

For rear axle and suspension tightening specifications, refer to individual repair or replacement procedures and illustrations.

3000GT

Year	Component	Torque/ Ft. Lbs.
AWD MODELS		
1993–96	ABS Cable Attaching Bolt	9
	ABS Rear Speed Sensor Bolt	9
	Brake Caliper Bolt	36–43
	Center Bearing Nut	22
	Crossmember Bracket Bolt	51–61
	Crossmember Bracket Nut	80–94
	Crossmember Nut (Differential Side)	80–94
	Differential Carrier To Propeller Shaft Coupling	22–25
	Driveshaft To Companion Flange	40–47
	Lower Control Arm Inner Nut & Bolt	101–116①
	Lower Control Arm Self-Locking Nut	54–64
	Power Cylinder Bolt (4WS)	30
	Pressure Tube Assembly To Pump (4WS)	25
	Self-Locking Nut	②
	Shock Absorber Lower Mount	72
	Shock Absorber Piston Rod	14–18
	Shock Absorber Upper Mount	33
	Tie Rod End	42
	Trailing Arm	145–174①
	Upper Control Arm Inner Nut & Bolt	101–116①
	Upper Control Arm Self-Locking Nut	54–64
	Wheel Lug Nuts	87–101
FWD MODELS		
1993–96	Assist Arm Self-Locking Nut	54–64
	Brake Caliper	36–43
	Crossmember Nut	65
	Lower Control Arm Self-Locking Nut	54–64
	Shock Absorber Lower Mount	65①
	Shock Absorber Piston Rod Nut	14–18
	Shock Absorber Upper Mount	33
	Stabilizer Bar Bolt	29
	Stabilizer Bar Self-Locking Nut	29
	Trailing Arm Nut & Bolt	101–116①
	Upper Control Arm Self-Locking Nut	54–64
	Wheel Bearing Nut	145–188
	Wheel Lug Nuts	87–101

① — Tighten temporarily, then tighten to specifications once vehicle is unladen.
② — Non-turbo, 137 ft. lbs.; turbo, 188–217 ft. lbs.

ECLIPSE

Year	Component	Torque/ Ft. Lbs.
1993–94	Brake Tube Bracket To Rear Shock Absorber	12–19
	Center Exhaust Pipe To Front Exhaust Pipe Installation Nut	22–29
	Center Exhaust Pipe To Main Muffler Installation Bolt	29–36
	Companion Flange To Driveshaft	40–47
	Companion Flange To Rear Axle Shaft	116–159
	Crossmember Bracket To Body	51–61
	Crossmember Bracket To Crossmember	80–94
	Differential Carrier To Differential Support Member	58–72
1993–94	Differential Carrier To Propeller Shaft	22–25
	Differential Support Member To Body	80–94
	Hanger Installation Bolt	7–11
	Hook Installation Bolt	7–11
	Lateral Rod Mounting Nut (Body Side)	58–72
	Lateral Rod Mounting Nut (Axle Beam Side)	72–87
	Lower Arm To Knuckle	43–52
	Lower Arm To Crossmember	65–80
	Piston Rod Nut	14–18
	Rear Brake Assembly Installation Bolt	36–43
	Rear Speed Sensor Installation Bolt	7–10
	Shock Absorber Upper Mounting Nut	29–36
	Shock Absorber Lower Mounting Nut	58–72
	Stabilizer Link To Stabilizer Bar	25–33
	Trailing Arm Mounting Bolt	72–87
	Trailing Arm To Crossmember	101–116
	Upper Arm To Crossmember	101–116
	Upper Arm To Knuckle	43–52
	Wheel Bearing Nut	144–188
	Wheel Lug Nuts	87–101
1995–96	Axle Nut	145–188
	Crossmember Self-Locking	64
	Differential Carrier To Differential Support Member	72
	Driveshaft Nut	145–188
	Hub Nut	145–188
	Lower Arm Assembly Mounting	71
	Lower Arm To Knuckle	71
	Piston Rod Nut	16
	Propeller Shaft To Differential	22–25
	Rear Brake Assembly Installation Bolt	64
	Shock Absorber Upper Mounting Nut	32
	Shock Absorber Lower Mounting Nut	71
	Stabilizer Bar Bracket	7–10
	Stabilizer Link Mounting	28
	Stabilizer Link To Stabilizer Bar	28
	Toe Control Arm Assembly Mounting	50–56
	Toe Control Arm Ball Joint to Knuckle	20
	Trailing Arm Mounting Bolt	99–114
	Trailing Arm To Knuckle	85–99
	Upper Arm Assembly	71
	Upper Arm Bracket	41
	Upper Arm Mounting	28
	Wheel Lug Nuts	65–80

Transfer Case

INDEX

Page No.
Transfer Case, Replace... 24-94

TRANSFER CASE

REPLACE

1. Disconnect battery ground cable.
2. Disconnect front exhaust pipe from engine.
3. Remove transfer case attaching bolts, then move transfer case to the left and lower front of transfer case.
4. Remove transfer case from propeller shaft, noting the following:
   a. Use caution not to damage transfer case oil seal lip.
   b. Suspend propeller shaft to prevent bending.
   c. Cover transfer case opening using plug tool No. MB991193, or equivalent, to prevent oil leakage and entry of foreign material.
5. Reverse procedure to install, tightening transfer case to transaxle attaching bolts to specifications.

Front Suspension & Steering

NOTE: On Air Bag Equipped Models, Refer To "Air Bag System Precautions" Located In The Front Of This Manual For System Disarming & Arming Procedures.

INDEX

	Page No.
Ball Joint, Replace	24-96
Control Arm, Replace	24-98
Lower	24-98
Hub & Bearing Service	24-96
Eclipse	24-96
Manual Steering Gears	29-1
Manual Steering Gear, Replace	24-99
Eclipse	24-99
Power Steering	29-1
Power Steering Gear, Replace	24-99
Eclipse	24-99
3000GT	24-99
Power Steering Pump, Replace	24-99
Eclipse	24-99
3000GT	24-99
Precautions	24-94
Air Bag Systems	24-94
Rear Power Cylinder, Replace	24-100
Rear Power Cylinder Control Valve, Replace	24-100
Stabilizer Bar, Replace	24-98
Eclipse	24-98
3000GT	24-98
Strut, Replace	24-97
Eclipse	24-97
3000GT	24-97
Strut Service	24-97
Eclipse	24-97
Tightening Specifications	24-106
Wheel Bearing, Adjust	24-94
Wheel Hub & Steering Knuckle, Replace	24-94
Eclipse	24-94
3000GT	24-95

PRECAUTIONS

AIR BAG SYSTEMS

Refer to "Air Bag System Precautions" in the front of this manual for system disarming and arming procedures.

WHEEL BEARING

ADJUST

1. Inspect play of bearings while vehicle is jacked up and resting on floor jack.
2. Remove hub cap, then release parking brake.
3. Remove caliper assembly and brake disc, then measure bearing endplay.
4. Placing dial gauge against hub surface, move hub in axial direction and check for endplay.
5. Endplay should be 0.004 inch or less; if greater, the locknut should be tightened to specification and endplay measured again.
6. Replace rear hub bearing unit if an adjustment cannot be made to within limit.

WHEEL HUB & STEERING KNUCKLE

REPLACE

ECLIPSE

1993-94

Removal

Remove knuckle and hub assembly in numbered sequence, **Fig. 1,** noting the following:

1. Loosen driveshaft nut with vehicle on floor and brakes applied.
2. Remove speed sensor mounting bolts, then the sensor. **Use care not to damage pole piece at tip of speed sensor and the toothed edge of the rotor.**
3. Remove and suspend caliper assembly using a piece of wire.
4. Insert pry bar between transaxle case and driveshaft, **Fig. 2,** then pry driveshaft from transaxle. **Do not pull on driveshaft.**

Installation

Reverse removal procedure to install, noting the following:

1. Install washer and wheel bearing nut in direction shown, **Fig. 3.**
2. After installing wheel, lower vehicle to ground, then final tighten wheel bearing nut.
3. If cotter pin holes do not match, tighten to specification.

1995-96

Removal

Remove knuckle and hub assembly in numbered sequence, **Fig. 4,** noting the following:

1. Loosen driveshaft nut with vehicle on floor and brakes applied.
2. Loosen, but do not remove, tie rod end nut.
3. Remove and suspend caliper assembly out of the way using a piece of wire.
4. Shift the knuckle to the outside in order to maintain the clearance between the front hub assembly mounting bolts and

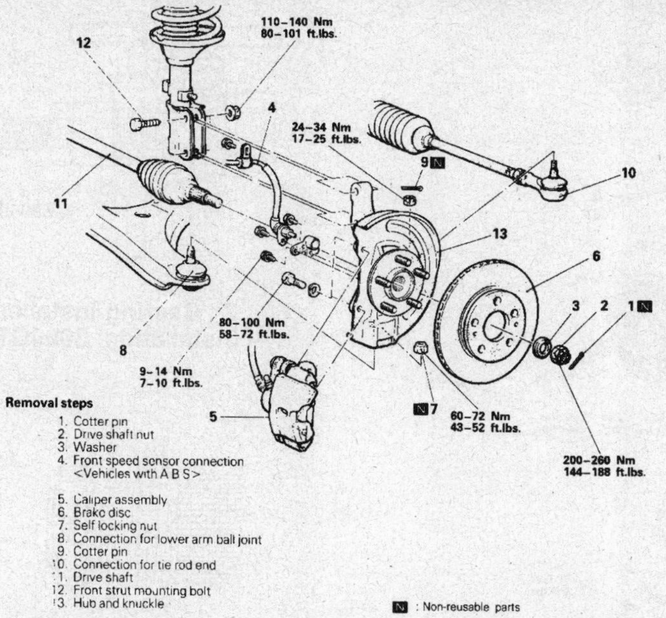
110–140 Nm
80–101 ft.lbs.
12
4
24–34 Nm
17–25 ft.lbs.
9 N
10
11
13
6
3
2
1 N
80–100 Nm
58–72 ft.lbs.
8
9–14 Nm
7–10 ft.lbs.
Removal steps
1. Cotter pin
2. Drive shaft nut
3. Washer
4. Front speed sensor connection
<Vehicles with A B S>
5. Caliper assembly
6. Brake disc
7. Self locking nut
8. Connection for lower arm ball joint
9. Cotter pin
10. Connection for tie rod end
11. Drive shaft
12. Front strut mounting bolt
13. Hub and knuckle
5
N 7
60–72 Nm
43–52 ft.lbs.
200–260 Nm
144–188 ft.lbs.
N : Non-reusable parts
CR3039100318000X

Fig. 1 Hub & knuckle assembly removal. 1993–94 Eclipse

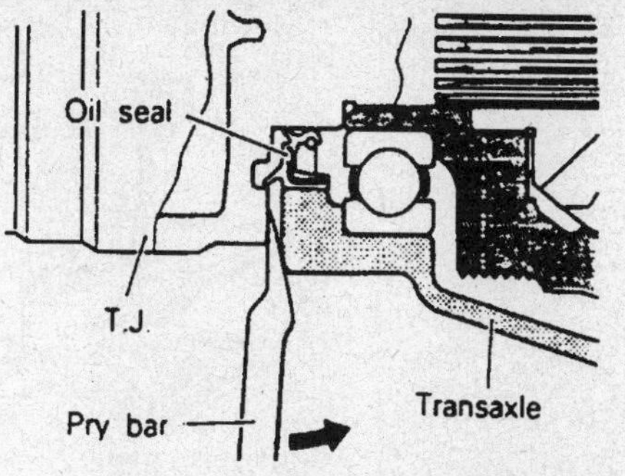
Oil seal
T.J.
Pry bar
Transaxle
CR3039100319000X

Fig. 2 Driveshaft removal. 1993–94 Eclipse

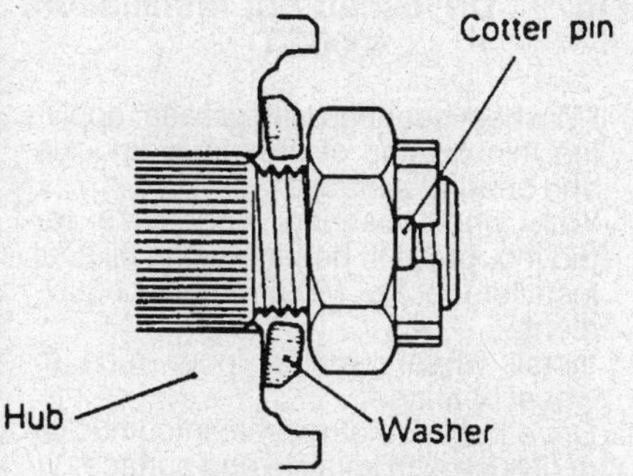
Cotter pin
Hub
Washer
CR3039100321000X

Fig. 3 Washer installation. 1993–94 Eclipse

the driveshaft. **Do not damage the ball joint boot.**

5. **On models with ABS,** ensure to not damage rotor.

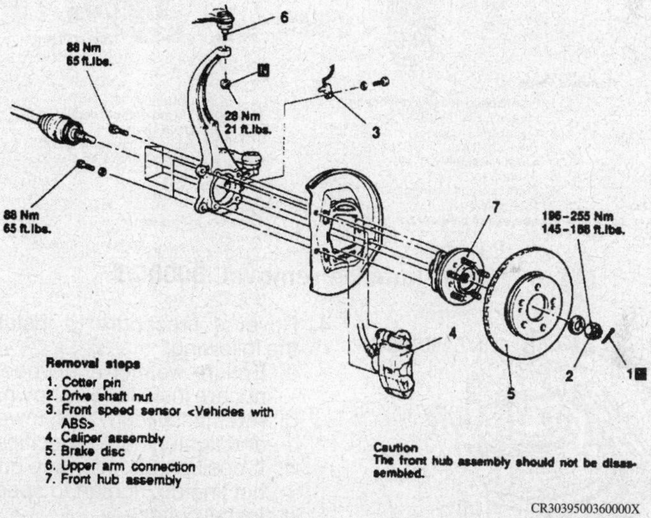
6
88 Nm
65 ft.lbs.
28 Nm
21 ft.lbs.
3
88 Nm
65 ft.lbs.
7
196–255 Nm
145–188 ft.lbs.
4
5
2
1
Removal steps
1. Cotter pin
2. Drive shaft nut
3. Front speed sensor <Vehicles with ABS>
4. Caliper assembly
5. Brake disc
6. Upper arm connection
7. Front hub assembly
Caution
The front hub assembly should not be disassembled.
CR3039500360000X

Fig. 4 Hub & knuckle assembly removal. 1995–96 Eclipse

Installation

Reverse removal procedure to install, noting the following:

1. Ensure to install driveshaft washer as shown, **Fig. 5.**
2. After installing wheel, lower vehicle to ground, then final tighten driveshaft nut.
3. If cotter pin holes do not match, tighten to specification.

3000GT

1. Raise and support vehicle.
2. Remove hub and knuckle in numbered sequence as shown, **Fig. 6,** noting the following:
   a. Remove front speed sensor bracket to knuckle mounting bolt, then the speed sensor. **Use care when handling the pole piece at the tip of the speed sensor and toothed surface of the ABS rotor so as not to strike or damage them.**

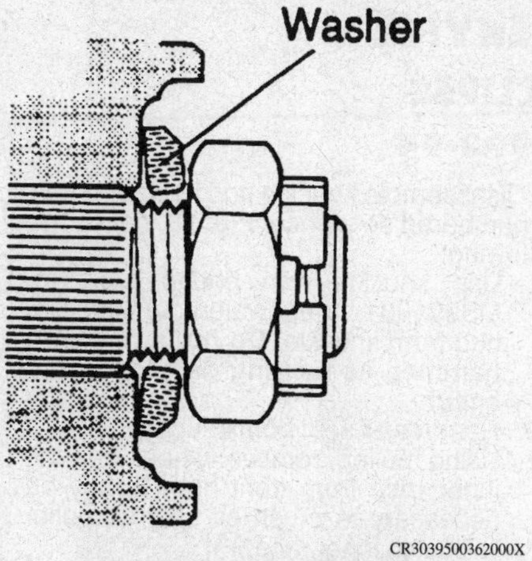
Washer
CR3039500362000X

Fig. 5 Driveshaft washer installation. 1995–96 Eclipse

   b. Loosen driveshaft nut while vehicle is on floor with brakes applied. **Do not apply full vehicle load on wheel bearing when loosening.**
   c. Remove caliper assembly mount bolts and suspend from frame using suitable wire without disconnecting the brake hose.
   d. Disconnect lower ball joint using ball joint remover tool No. MB990635-01, or equivalent. **Loosen, but do not remove ball joint nut.**
   e. Disconnect tie rod end using ball joint remover tool. **Loosen, but do not remove tie rod end locknut.**
   f. Remove driveshaft using axle puller tool No. MB990241-01, or equivalent.
   g. **On AWD models with anti-lock brakes,** use care not to damage

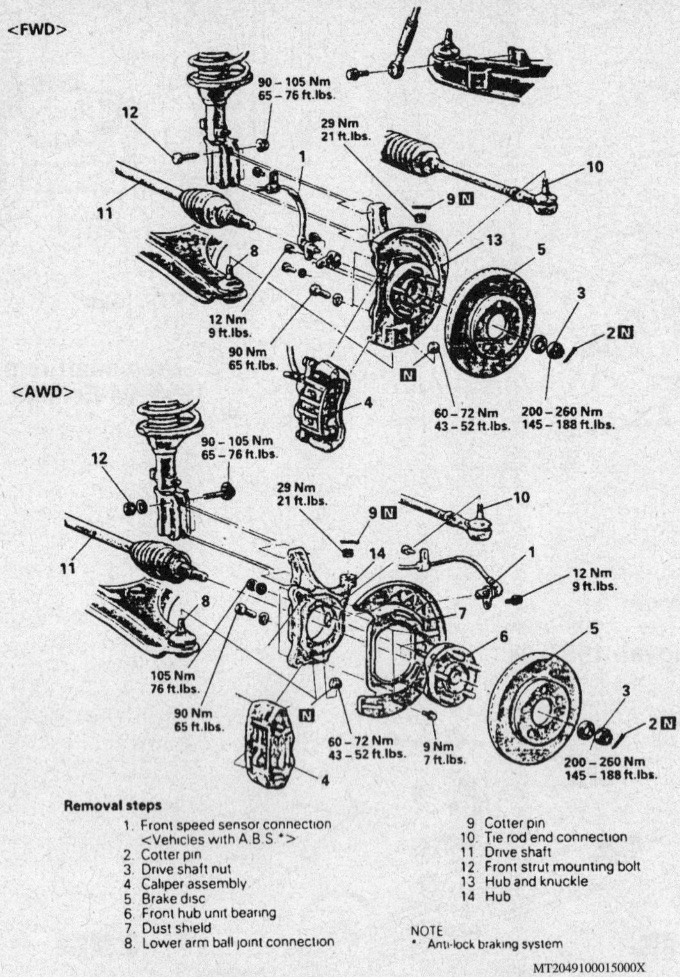

<FWD>
90 - 105 Nm
65 - 76 ft.lbs.
29 Nm
21 ft.lbs.
12 Nm
9 ft.lbs.
90 Nm
65 ft.lbs.
60 - 72 Nm
43 - 52 ft.lbs.
200 - 260 Nm
145 - 188 ft.lbs.
<AWD>
90 - 105 Nm
65 - 76 ft.lbs.
29 Nm
21 ft.lbs.
12 Nm
9 ft.lbs.
105 Nm
76 ft.lbs.
90 Nm
65 ft.lbs.
60 - 72 Nm
43 - 52 ft.lbs.
9 Nm
7 ft.lbs.
200 - 260 Nm
145 - 188 ft.lbs.
Removal steps
1. Front speed sensor connection <Vehicles with A.B.S.*>
2. Cotter pin
3. Drive shaft nut
4. Caliper assembly
5. Brake disc
6. Front hub unit bearing
7. Dust shield
8. Lower arm ball joint connection
9. Cotter pin
10. Tie rod end connection
11. Drive shaft
12. Front strut mounting bolt
13. Hub and knuckle
14. Hub
NOTE
*: Anti-lock braking system
MT2049100015000X

Fig. 6 Hub & knuckle removal. 3000GT

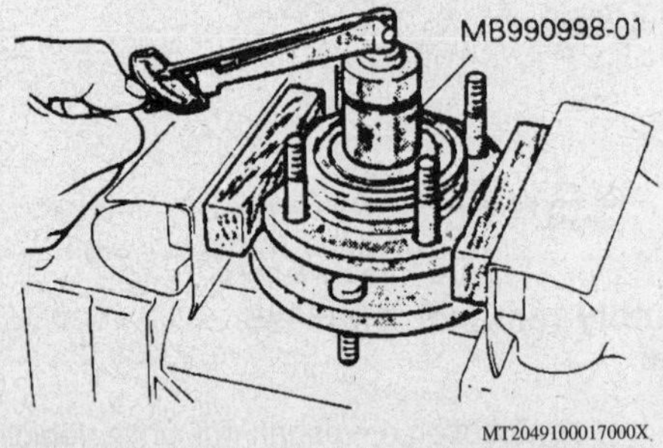

MB990998-01
MT2049100017000X

Fig. 8 Hub torque measurement. 3000GT

ABS rotor installed to the outer driveshaft outer race when removing hub.

3. **On all models,** measure front hub unit bearing rotation starting torque as follows:
   a. Install front hub remover and installer tool No. MB990998-01, or equivalent, on the front hub unit bearing, **Fig. 7.**
   b. While holding tool bolt, tighten to specification.
   c. Turn hub to seat bearing in grease.
   d. Measure rotation starting **torque** and ensure it is 16 inch lbs. or less, **Fig. 8.**
4. Reverse procedure to install, noting the following:
   a. Ensure washer and wheel bearing nut are installed as shown, **Fig. 9.**
   b. After installing wheel, lower vehicle and tighten nut to specifications.
   c. If position of cotter key holes does not line up, tighten to specification.
   d. Install cotter key.

HUB & BEARING SERVICE

ECLIPSE

1993–94

Disassemble knuckle and hub assembly in numbered sequence, **Fig. 10,** noting the following:

1. Use knuckle arm bridge tool No. MB991001, or equivalent, to separate hub from knuckle. **Do not strike with hammer, as bearing damage could occur.**
2. Remove oil seal from knuckle.
3. Using puller, remove wheel bearing inner race from front hub. It may be necessary to crush oil seal so puller will catch inner race.
4. Remove snap ring from knuckle.
5. Remove bearings from knuckle.

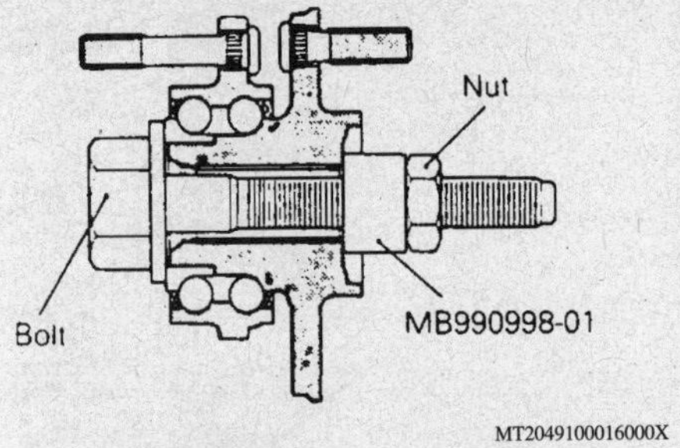

Nut
Bolt
MB990998-01
MT2049100016000X

Fig. 7 Bearing installer tool installation. 3000GT

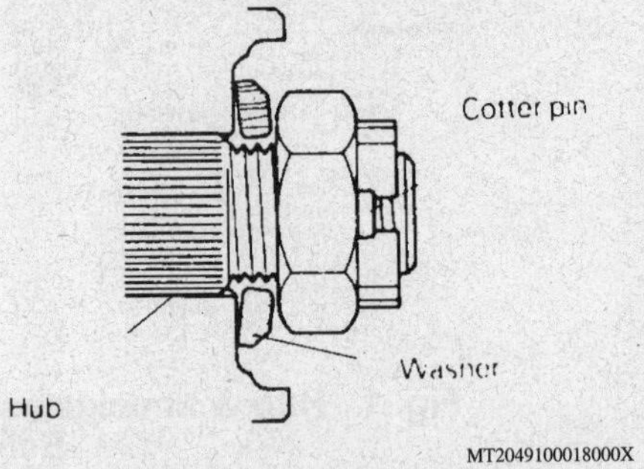

Cotter pin
Washer
Hub
MT2049100018000X

Fig. 9 Driveshaft nut installation. 3000GT

6. Fill wheel bearings with grease, applying thin coating of grease to knuckle and bearing surfaces.
7. With wheel bearing inner race removed, press in bearing using oil seal installer tool No. MB990985, or equivalent.
8. Install wheel bearing inner race to wheel bearing.
9. Drive hub side of oil seal into knuckle until flush with knuckle end surface.
10. Mount hub assembly to knuckle and tighten to specifications.
11. Rotate hub assembly to seat bearing.
12. Measure wheel bearing starting torque; **torque** should be 16 inch lbs.
13. Measure endplay of hub; Endplay should be .008 inch.
14. If starting torque and hub endplay are not within specification, it is possible that assembly has not been installed correctly. Repeat disassembly and assembly procedure.

1995–96

The front hub assembly should not be disassembled. If required by damage or wear, it should be replaced.

Disassemble knuckle assembly in numbered sequence, **Fig. 11,** noting the following:

1. Loosen, but do not remove, tie rod end nut.
2. Loosen, but do not remove, compression lower arm nut.
3. Loosen, but do not remove, lateral lower arm nut.

BALL JOINT

REPLACE

Refer to "Control Arm, Replace" for ball joint replacement procedure.

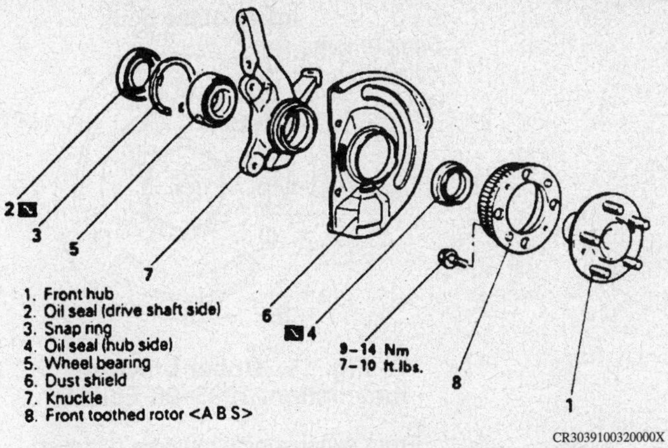
1. Front hub
2. Oil seal (drive shaft side)
3. Snap ring
4. Oil seal (hub side)
5. Wheel bearing
6. Dust shield
7. Knuckle
8. Front toothed rotor <A B S>
9–14 Nm
7–10 ft.lbs.
CR3039100320000X

Fig. 10 Hub & knuckle disassembly. 1993–94 Eclipse

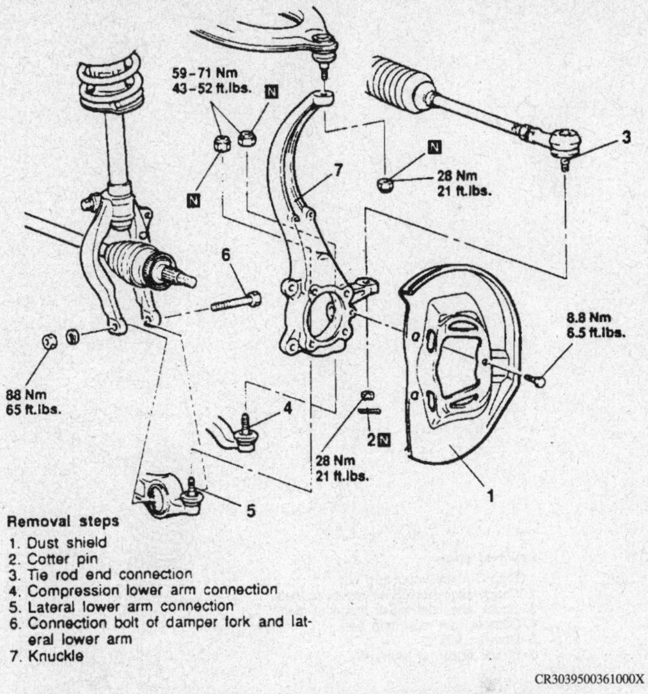
59–71 Nm
43–52 ft.lbs.
28 Nm
21 ft.lbs.
8.8 Nm
6.5 ft.lbs.
88 Nm
65 ft.lbs.
28 Nm
21 ft.lbs.
Removal steps
1. Dust shield
2. Cotter pin
3. Tie rod end connection
4. Compression lower arm connection
5. Lateral lower arm connection
6. Connection bolt of damper fork and lateral lower arm
7. Knuckle
CR3039500361000X

Fig. 11 Knuckle assembly. 1995–96 Eclipse

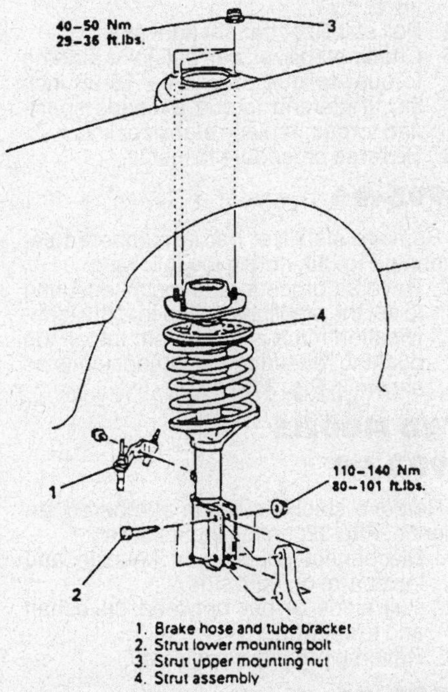
40–50 Nm
29–36 ft.lbs.
110–140 Nm
80–101 ft.lbs.
1. Brake hose and tube bracket
2. Strut lower mounting bolt
3. Strut upper mounting nut
4. Strut assembly
CR2029100057000X

Fig. 12 Strut assembly removal. 1993–94 Eclipse

STRUT

REPLACE

ECLIPSE

1993-94

Removal

Remove strut assembly in numbered sequence, **Fig. 12,** noting the following:

1. Do not pry brake hose and line away from strut.

Installation

Reverse removal procedure to install, noting the following:

1. Install strut assembly insulator as shown, **Fig. 13.**

1995-96

Removal

Remove strut assembly in numbered sequence, **Fig. 14.**

Installation

Reverse removal procedure to install, noting the following:

1. Ensure spring is properly seated in upper and lower spring seat when installing.
2. Install strut upper bracket as shown in **Fig. 15,** then tighten strut rod nut to specifications.

3000GT

1. Replace strut assembly in numbered sequence as shown, **Fig. 16.**
2. If necessary, disassemble strut assembly in numbered sequence as shown, **Fig. 17,** noting the following:
   a. Secure upper seat using spring seat holder tool No. MB991176, or equivalent, then loosen strut self-locking nut. **Loosen, but do not remove self-locking nut until the next step is performed.**
   b. Compress coil spring using a suitable coil spring compression tool, then remove self-locking nut.
3. Reverse procedure to assemble and install, noting the following:
   a. Assemble spring upper seat on piston rod of strut aligning notch in rod with notch in seat.
   b. Install coil spring while aligning four holes in upper seat with four holes in lower seat using a 0.3 inch diameter by 11.8 inch long rod, **Fig. 18.**
   c. With coil spring still compressed, secure upper seat and finger-tighten the self-locking nut.

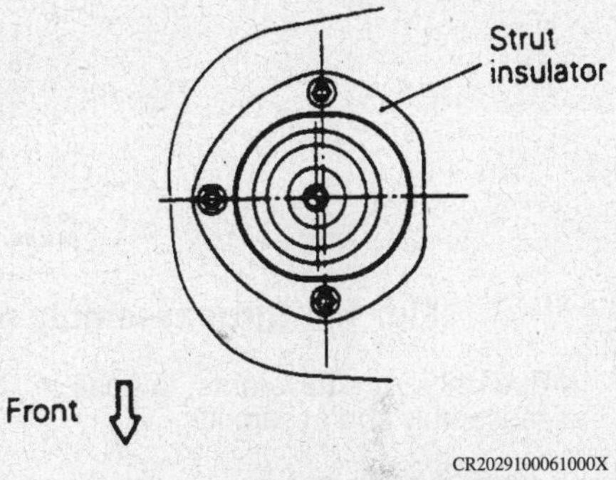
Strut insulator
Front
CR2029100061000X

Fig. 13 Insulator position. 1993–94 Eclipse

   d. Align both ends of the coil spring with grooves in spring seat, then slowly loosen compression tool.
   e. Using seat holder tool, **torque** strut rod self-locking nut to 56 ft. lbs.

STRUT SERVICE

ECLIPSE

1993-94

Disassemble strut in numbered sequence, **Fig. 19,** noting the following:

1. Compress coil spring, **Fig. 20,** then remove locknut.
2. Join dust cover and bump rubber, **Fig. 21.**
3. Line up holes in spring upper and lower seats.

1995-96

Disassemble strut in numbered sequence, **Fig. 22,** noting the following:

1. Compress spring using spring compression tools No. MB991237 and

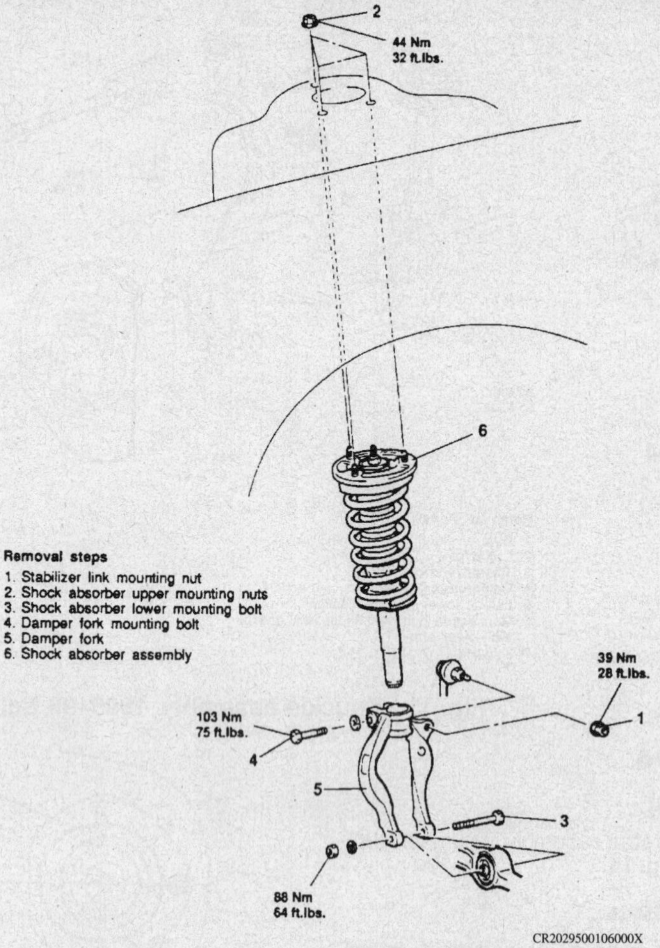
2
44 Nm
32 ft.lbs.
6
Removal steps
1. Stabilizer link mounting nut
2. Shock absorber upper mounting nuts
3. Shock absorber lower mounting bolt
4. Damper fork mounting bolt
5. Damper fork
6. Shock absorber assembly
39 Nm
28 ft.lbs.
1
103 Nm
75 ft.lbs.
4
5
3
88 Nm
64 ft.lbs.
CR2029500106000X

Fig. 14 Strut assembly removal. 1995–96 Eclipse

MB991239, or equivalents, to ease in disassembly and assembly.

CONTROL ARM

REPLACE

LOWER

ECLIPSE

1993-94

Remove lower control arm in numbered sequence, **Figs. 23 and 24,** noting the following:

1. Check ball joint starting torque. Torque should be 26–87 inch lbs. If reading exceeds specified amount, replace lower arm assembly.
2. Reverse procedure to install.

1995-96

Remove compression and lateral lower control arms in numbered sequence, **Fig. 25,** noting the following:

1. Loosen but do not remove compression lower arm ball joint.
2. Check compression lower arm ball joint breakaway torque. Torque should be 4–13 inch lbs. If reading exceeds specified amount, replace lower arm assembly.
3. Loosen but do not remove knuckle/lateral lower arm ball joint.
4. Check lateral lower arm ball joint breakaway torque. Torque should be 9–30 inch lbs. If reading exceeds specified amount, replace lower arm assembly.

3000GT

1. Replace lower control arm and ball joint in numbered sequence as shown, **Fig. 26,** noting the following:
   a. Remove ball joint using ball joint remover tool No. MB991113-01, or equivalent. **Loosen, but do not remove ball joint nut until lower control arm is ready to be removed.**
   b. Position lower arm bushing bracket with mounting surface tilting 5–7° with respect to bottom surface of lower arm, then install self-locking nut, **Fig. 27.**

STABILIZER BAR

REPLACE

ECLIPSE

FWD MODELS

1993-94

Remove stabilizer bar in numbered sequence, **Figs. 28 and 29,** noting the following:

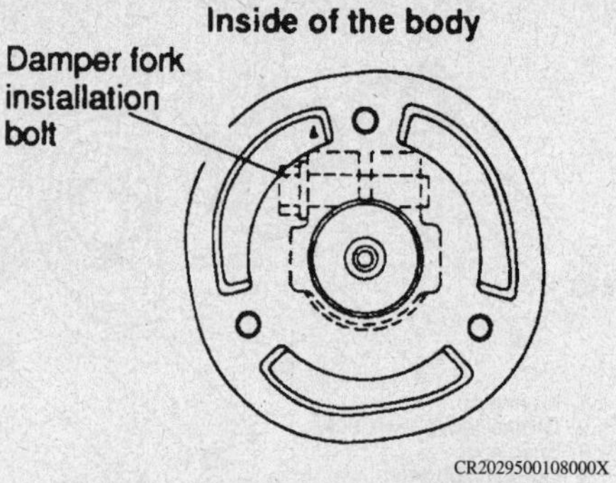
Inside of the body
Damper fork
installation
bolt
CR2029500108000X

Fig. 15 Upper bracket installation. 1995–96 Eclipse

1. Front exhaust pipe must be removed.
2. Pull both ends of stabilizer bar to rear of driveshaft.
3. Move right side of bar until it clears lower arm.
4. Pull stabilizer bar out right side.
5. Check stabilizer bar ball joint starting torque; **torque** should be 15-28 inch lbs. If starting torque exceeds specified torque, replace stabilizer link.
6. Reverse procedure to install.

1995-96

Remove stabilizer bar in numbered sequence, **Fig. 30,** noting the following:

1. Reverse procedure to install ensuring to set the stabilizer bar so that the identification mark is at the left. Install the bushing, ensuring the dimension is as shown in **Fig. 31.**

AWD MODELS

1993-94

Remove stabilizer bar in numbered sequence, **Fig. 32,** noting the following:

1. Disconnect coupling of knuckle and lower arm on right side.
2. Pull sides of bar between driveshaft and lower arm.
3. Reverse procedure to install.

1995-96

1. Remove stabilizer bar in numbered sequence, **Fig. 30.**
2. Reverse procedure to install. Ensure stabilizer bar is set so identification mark is at the left. Install bushing, ensuring the dimension is as shown in **Fig. 31.**

3000GT

1. Remove front exhaust pipe, then the front lower cover.
2. Remove right and left members in numbered sequence as shown, **Fig. 33.**
3. Replace stabilizer bar in numbered sequence shown, **Fig. 34.**
4. Reverse procedure to install, noting the following:
   a. Align left stabilizer bar bushing with marking on bar and temporarily tighten stabilizer bar bracket, **Fig. 35.**
   b. Mount stabilizer bar right bracket and temporarily tighten.
   c. Temporarily install both ends of the

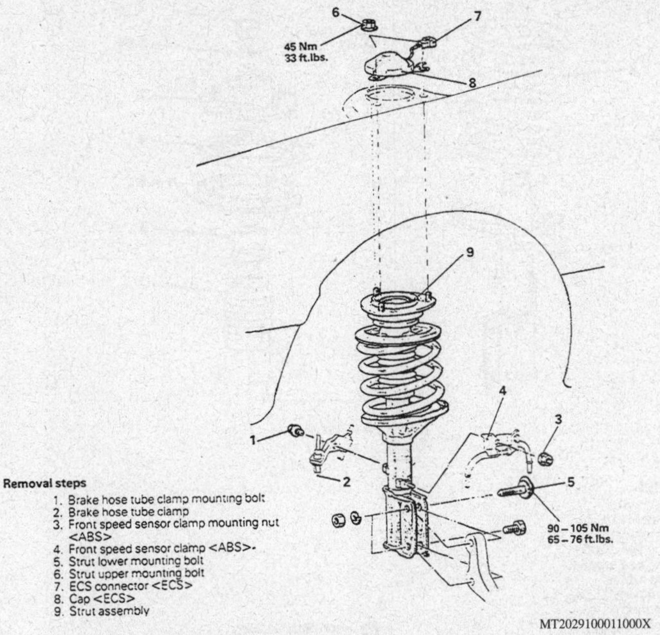
45 Nm
33 ft.lbs.
90–105 Nm
65–76 ft.lbs.
Removal steps
1. Brake hose tube clamp mounting bolt
2. Brake hose tube clamp
3. Front speed sensor clamp mounting nut <ABS>
4. Front speed sensor clamp <ABS>
5. Strut lower mounting bolt
6. Strut upper mounting bolt
7. ECS connector <ECS>
8. Cap <ECS>
9. Strut assembly
MT2029100011000X

Fig. 16 Strut assembly replacement. 3000GT

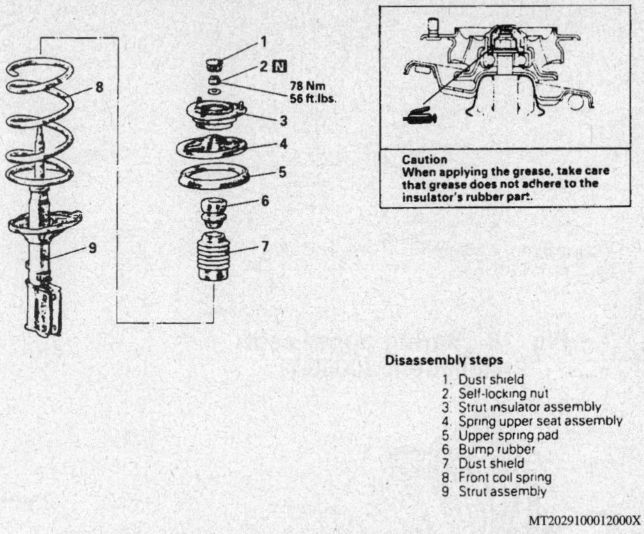
78 Nm
56 ft.lbs.
Caution
When applying the grease, take care that grease does not adhere to the insulator's rubber part.
Disassembly steps
1. Dust shield
2. Self-locking nut
3. Strut insulator assembly
4. Spring upper seat assembly
5. Upper spring pad
6. Bump rubber
7. Dust shield
8. Front coil spring
9. Strut assembly
MT2029100012000X

Fig. 17 Strut assembly removal. 3000GT

stabilizer bar on the links, then tighten stabilizer bar mounting brackets bolts.

d. Bleed power steering system and align front suspension. Refer to "Bleeding System" as outlined under "Power Steering Service."

POWER STEERING GEAR

REPLACE

ECLIPSE

Remove rack & pinion in numbered sequence, **Fig.36,** noting the following:

1. Turn rack completely to right, the disconnect gearbox from crossmember.
2. While tilting gearbox downward, remove from left side.
3. Reverse procedure to install.

3000GT

1. Drain power steering system fluid into an appropriate container.
2. Remove front exhaust pipe, then the transfer assembly.
3. Remove power steering gear in numbered sequence as shown, **Fig. 37,** noting the following:
   a. Disconnect tie rod end using ball joint remover tool No. MB991113-01, or equivalent.
   b. When removing steering gear, move gear completely to right and then remove gear from crossmember.
   c. Tilt steering gear downward and remove from left side.
4. Ensure total pinion **torque** while rotating pinion gear at a rate of one rotation every four to six seconds is 5–11 inch lbs.
5. Reverse procedure to install, noting the following:
   a. Keep projection of mounting rubber as shown, **Fig. 38.**
   b. Bleed power steering system as outlined under "Bleeding System" in "Power Steering Service."

POWER STEERING PUMP

REPLACE

ECLIPSE

1993–94

Remove steering pump in numbered sequence, **Fig. 39,** noting the following:

1. Remove reservoir cap and disconnect return hose to drain fluid.
2. Raise and support vehicle.
3. Disconnect high tension cable, then turn crank engine to drain fluid from gearbox.
4. Cover alternator (located under oil pump) if any hoses are removed.
5. Reverse procedure to install. When connecting pressure hose, ensure slit contacts oil pump guide bracket.

1995–96

Remove steering pump in numbered sequence, **Figs. 40 and 41,** noting the following:

1. Remove reservoir cap and disconnect return hose to drain fluid.
2. Raise and support vehicle.
3. Cover alternator (located under oil pump) if any hoses are removed
4. Reverse procedure to install, ensuring to install oil pump in a position towards the front of the bracket, and adjust the belt tension using the air conditioning tension pulley.

3000GT

Front

1. Drain power steering fluid into an appropriate container.
2. Replace power steering pump in numbered sequence as shown, **Fig. 42,** noting the following:
   a. Connect pressure hose ensuring slit part contacts the oil pump guide bracket, **Fig. 43.**
   b. Bleed power steering system as outlined under "Bleeding System" in "Power Steering Service."

Rear

1. Drain power steering fluid into an appropriate container.
2. Remove main muffler assembly.
3. Remove rear power steering pump in numbered sequence as shown, **Fig. 44,** noting the following:
   a. Support differential case using a suitable transmission jack, then remove crossmember bracket and crossmember mounting nuts on differential side.
   b. Slightly lower crossmember assembly.
4. Reverse procedure to install, noting the following:
   a. Bleed power steering system as outlined under "Bleeding System" in "Power Steering Service."
   b. Bleed the four wheel steering (4WS) system as outlined under "Bleeding System" in "Power Steering Service."

MANUAL STEERING GEAR

REPLACE

ECLIPSE

1. Raise and support front of vehicle, then remove wheel and tire assembly.
2. Remove shaft assembly and gearbox attaching bolt.

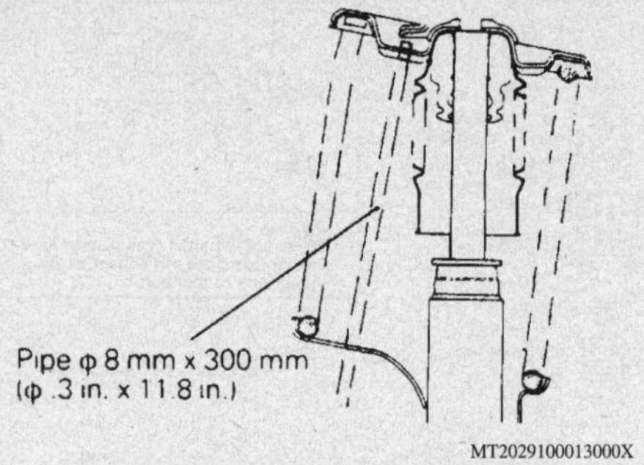
Pipe φ 8 mm x 300 mm
(φ .3 in. x 11.8 in.)
MT2029100013000X

Fig. 18 Spring upper seat installation. 3000GT

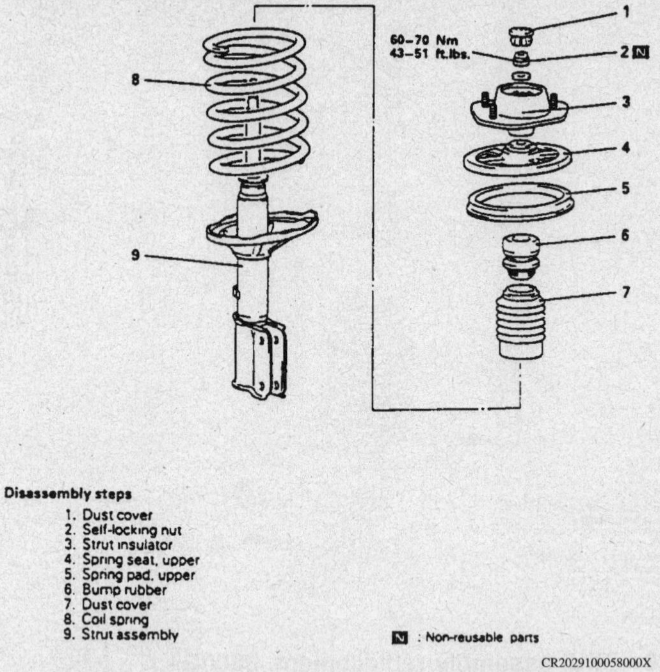
60–70 Nm
43–51 ft.lbs.
1
2 N
3
4
5
6
7
8
9
Disassembly steps
1. Dust cover
2. Self-locking nut
3. Strut insulator
4. Spring seat, upper
5. Spring pad, upper
6. Bump rubber
7. Dust cover
8. Coil spring
9. Strut assembly
N : Non-reusable parts
CR2029100058000X

Fig. 19 Strut disassemble. 1993–94 Eclipse

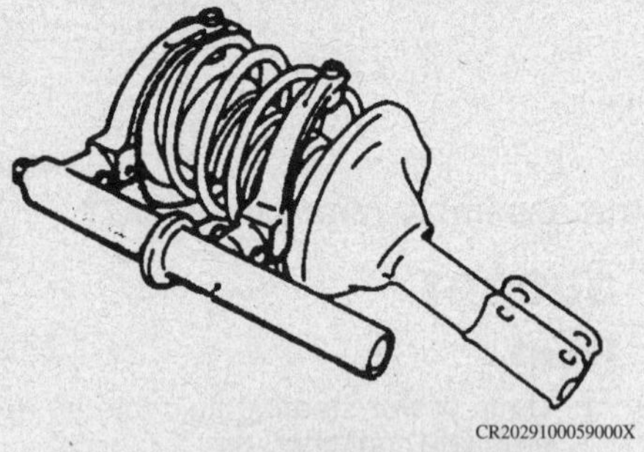
CR2029100059000X

Fig. 20 Spring compression. 1993–94 Eclipse

3. Remove tie rod end ball joint from knuckle using a suitable ball joint puller.
4. Remove dust cover band.
5. Remove gear housing clamp attaching bolts, then the gear housing clamps.
6. Remove gear housing mounting rubber, then the steering gear assembly.
7. Reverse procedure to install.

REAR POWER CYLINDER

REPLACE

1. Raise and support vehicle.
2. Clean steering system piping using suitable steam cleaner or equivalent.
3. Drain steering system fluid into an appropriate container.
4. Remove main muffler assembly.
5. Remove rear power cylinder in numbered sequence as shown, **Fig. 45**, noting the following:
   a. Before removing crossmember self-locking nut, support differential case with a suitable transmission jack, then remove self-locking nut.
   b. Secure power cylinder on tie rod side with a suitable spanner wrench and remove power cylinder mounting nut.
6. Inspect tie rod swing torque as follows:
   a. Swing tie rod ten times, hard.
   b. Point tie rod end down, then attach a suitable spring scale as shown and measure swing torque, **Fig. 46.**
   c. If swing **torque** is more than 26 inch lbs., replace tie rod.
   d. If swing **torque** is less than 4 inch lbs., the ball joint may be reused as long as it operates smoothly and is not loose.
7. Inspect power cylinder slide resistance as follows:
   a. Place piston in Neutral position.
   b. Wrap wire around tie rod end, then measure slide resistance using a suitable spring scale, **Fig. 47.**
   c. If slide resistance is more than 15 lbs., replace power cylinder.
   d. If resistance is less than 15 lbs., the power cylinder may be reused as long as it slides smoothly and is not loose.
8. Reverse procedure to install, noting the following:
   a. Secure power cylinder to crossmember.
   b. Move power cylinder piston rod over its full stroke to determine its Neutral position.
   c. Align tie rod ends and installation holes at trailing arm.
   d. When tie rod ends and installation holes on the trailing arm do not meet, loosen tie rod end securing nut, then adjust length. **The dust cover fastener clip should be removed for this step.**
   e. The difference between lengths of left and right tie rods should be less than 0.039 inch. **The threads of the tie rod ends may be used as a guide for this step.**
   f. Bleed four wheel steering (4WS) system as outlined under "Bleeding System" in "Power Steering System."

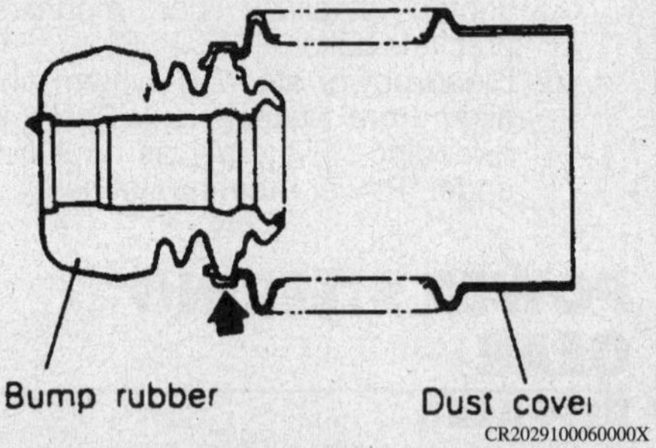
Bump rubber
Dust covei
CR2029100060000X

Fig. 21 Dust cover installation. 1993–94 Eclipse

REAR POWER CYLINDER CONTROL VALVE

REPLACE

1. Raise and support vehicle.
2. Clean steering system piping using suitable steam cleaner or equivalent.
3. Drain steering system fluid into an appropriate container.
4. Remove the rear suspension assembly as outlined under "Rear Suspension, Replace" in "Rear Axle & Suspension."
5. Replace control valve and related components in numbered sequence as shown, **Fig. 48.**
6. Reverse procedure to install, bleeding four wheel steering (4WS) system as outlined under "Bleeding System" in "Power Steering System."

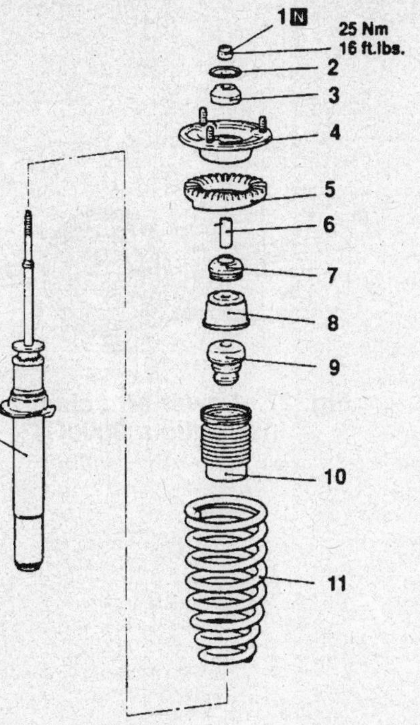

1
25 Nm
16 ft.lbs.
2
3
4
5
6
7
8
9
10
11
12

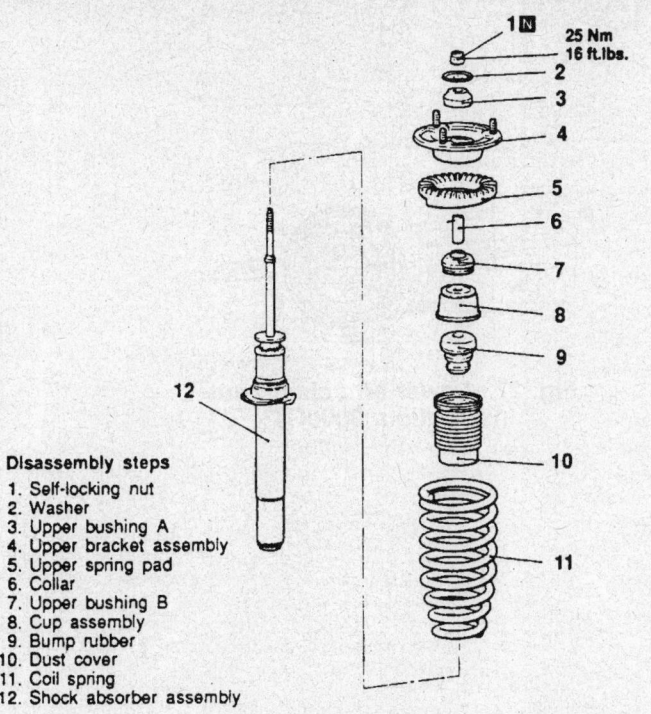

Disassembly steps

1. Self-locking nut
2. Washer
3. Upper bushing A
4. Upper bracket assembly
5. Upper spring pad
6. Collar
7. Upper bushing B
8. Cup assembly
9. Bump rubber
10. Dust cover
11. Coil spring
12. Shock absorber assembly

CR2029500107000X

Fig. 22 Strut disassembly. 1995–96 Eclipse

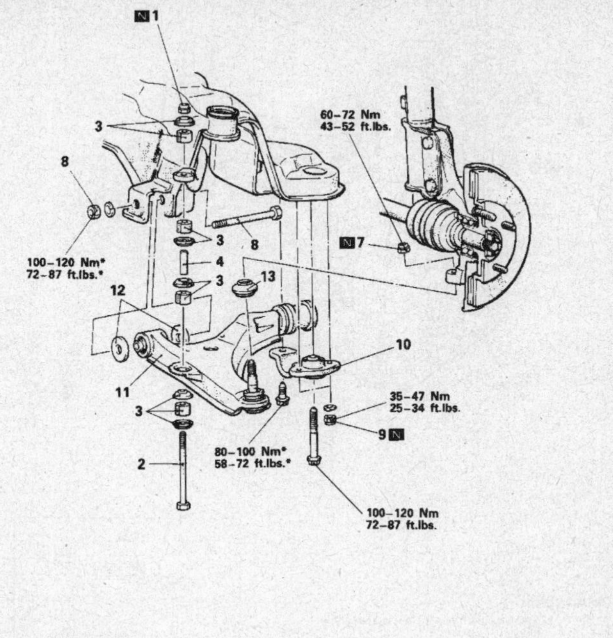

60–72 Nm
43–52 ft.lbs.
100–120 Nm*
72–87 ft.lbs.*
35–47 Nm
25–34 ft.lbs.
80–100 Nm*
58–72 ft.lbs.*
100–120 Nm
72–87 ft.lbs.

Removal step

1. Stabilizer bar mounting nut
2. Stabilizer bar mounting bolt
3. Joint cups and bushing
4. Collar
7. Self-locking nut
8. Lower arm mounting nut and bolt
9. Self-locking nut
10. Clamp
11. Lower arm
12. Stopper
13. Ball joint dust cover

N : Non-reusable parts
* : Indicates parts which should be temporarily tightened, and then fully tightened with the vehicle in the unladen condition.

CR2029100065000X

Fig. 23 Lower control arm removal. 1993–94 Eclipse w/rubber bushing stabilizer

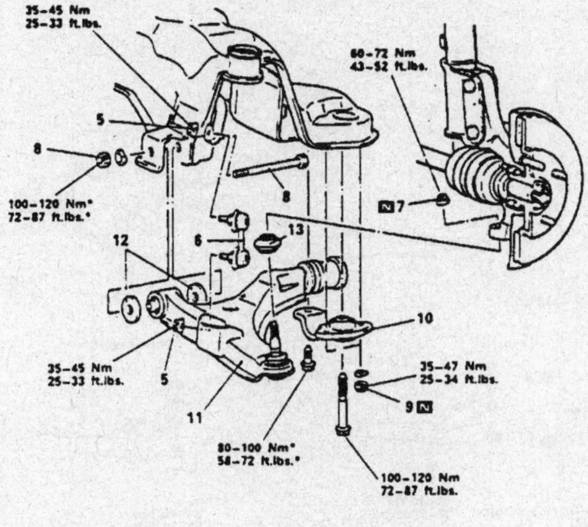

35–45 Nm
25–33 ft.lbs.
60–72 Nm
43–52 ft.lbs.
100–120 Nm*
72–87 ft.lbs.*
35–45 Nm
25–33 ft.lbs.
35–47 Nm
25–34 ft.lbs.
80–100 Nm*
58–72 ft.lbs.*
100–120 Nm
72–87 ft.lbs.

Removal step

5. Stabilizer link mounting nut
6. Stabilizer link
7. Self-locking nut
8. Lower arm mounting nut and bolt
9. Self-locking nut
10. Clamp
11. Lower arm
12. Stopper
13. Ball joint dust cover

N : Non-reusable parts
* : Indicates parts which should be temporarily tightened, and then fully tightened with the vehicle in the unladen condition.

CR2029100066000X

Fig. 24 Lower control arm removal. 1993–94 Eclipse w/pillow-ball stabilizer

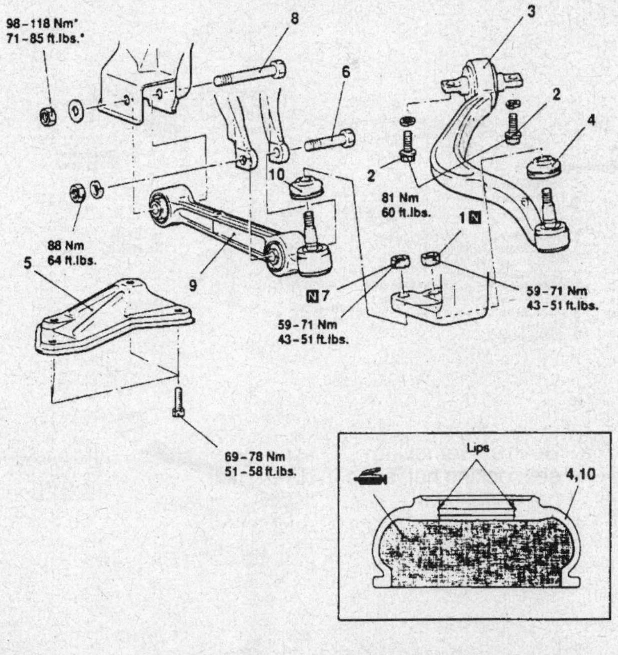

98–118 Nm*
71–85 ft.lbs.*
81 Nm
60 ft.lbs.
88 Nm
64 ft.lbs.
59–71 Nm
43–51 ft.lbs.
59–71 Nm
43–51 ft.lbs.
69–78 Nm
51–58 ft.lbs.
Lips
4,10

Compression lower arm assembly removal steps

1. Compression lower arm ball joint and knuckle connection
2. Compression lower arm mounting bolts
3. Compression lower arm assembly
4. Dust cover

Lateral lower arm assembly removal steps

5. Stay
6. Shock absorber lower mounting bolt
7. Lateral lower arm ball joint and knuckle connection
8. Lateral lower arm mounting bolt
9. Lateral lower arm assembly
10. Dust cover

Caution
*: **Indicates parts which should be temporarily tightened, and then fully tightened with the vehicle on the ground in the unladen condition.**

CR2029500109000X

Fig. 25 Compression & lateral lower arm assemblies. 1995–96 Eclipse

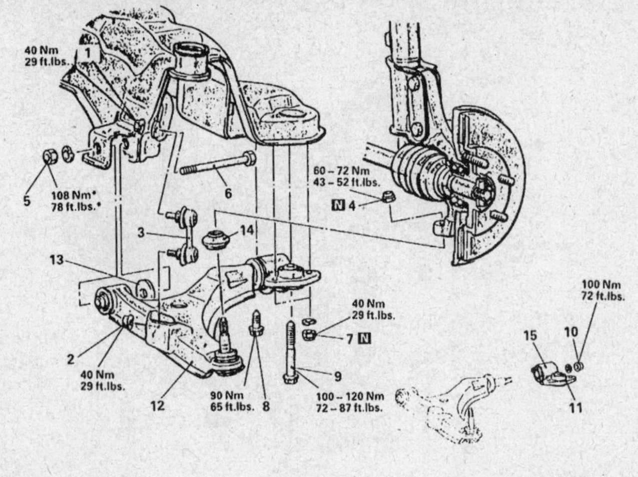
40 Nm
29 ft.lbs.
108 Nm*
78 ft.lbs.*
60 – 72 Nm
43 – 52 ft.lbs.
40 Nm
29 ft.lbs.
100 Nm
72 ft.lbs.
40 Nm
29 ft.lbs.
90 Nm
65 ft.lbs.
100 – 120 Nm
72 – 87 ft.lbs.

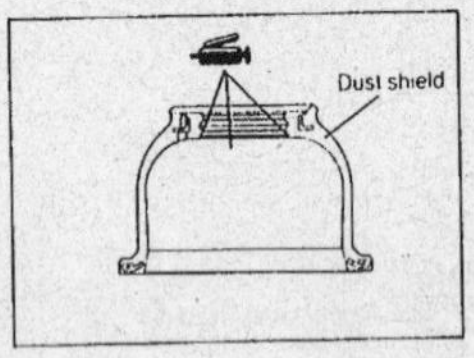
Dust shield

Removal steps
1. Stabilizer link mounting nut (stabilizer bar side)
2. Stabilizer link mounting nut (lower arm side)
3. Stabilizer link
4. Self-locking nut connecting lower arm ball joint to knuckle
5. Lower arm mounting nut
6. Lower arm mounting bolt
7. Clamp mounting self-locking nut
8. Clamp mounting bolt (small)
9. Clamp mounting bolt (large)
10. Lower arm clamp mounting self-locking nut
11. Lower arm mounting clamp
12. Lower arm
13. Stopper
14. Dust shield
15. Rod bushing

NOTE
For tightening points marked with *, first temporarily tighten them, then ground the vehicle and torque to specification where the vehicle is empty.

MT2029100009000X

Fig. 26 Lower control arm & ball joint replacement. 3000GT

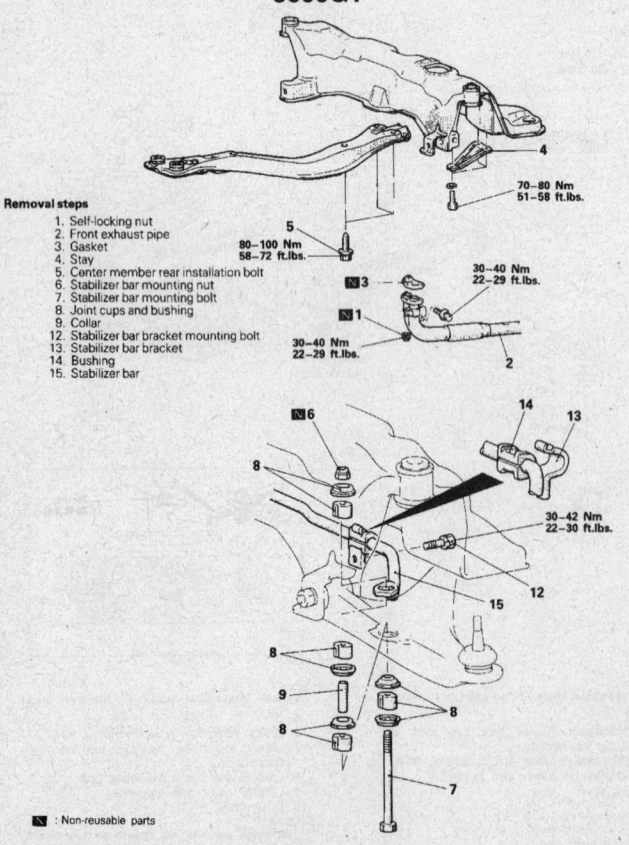

6° ± 1°

MT2029100010000X

Fig. 27 Lower arm clamp nut installation. 3000GT

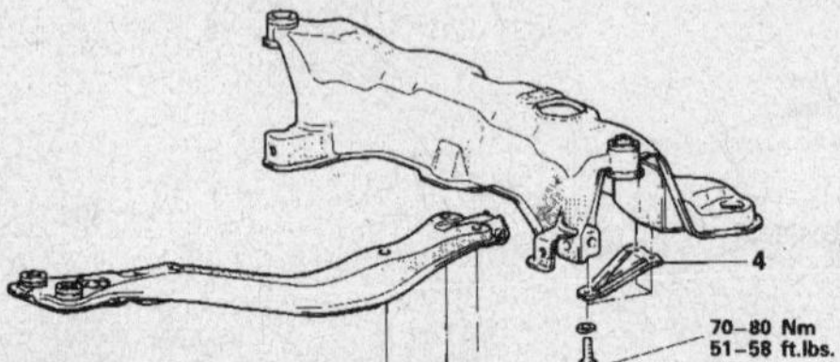
70–80 Nm
51–58 ft.lbs.
80–100 Nm
58–72 ft.lbs.

30–40 Nm
22–29 ft.lbs.
30–40 Nm
22–29 ft.lbs.

Removal steps
1. Self-locking nut
2. Front exhaust pipe
3. Gasket
4. Stay
5. Center member rear installation bolt
6. Stabilizer bar mounting nut
7. Stabilizer bar mounting bolt
8. Joint cups and bushing
9. Collar
12. Stabilizer bar bracket mounting bolt
13. Stabilizer bar bracket
14. Bushing
15. Stabilizer bar

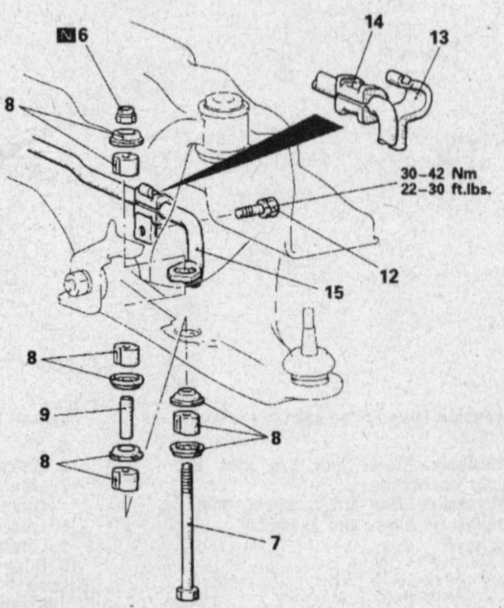
30–42 Nm
22–30 ft.lbs.

N : Non-reusable parts

CR2029100062000X

Fig. 28 Stabilizer bar removal. 1993–94 FWD w/rubber bushing stabilizer

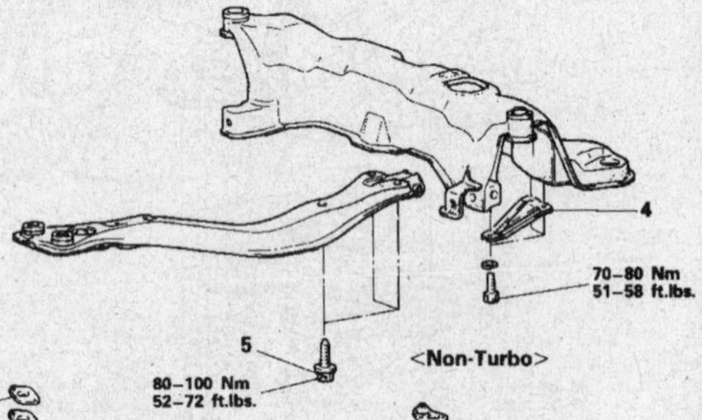
70–80 Nm
51–58 ft.lbs.
80–100 Nm
52–72 ft.lbs.

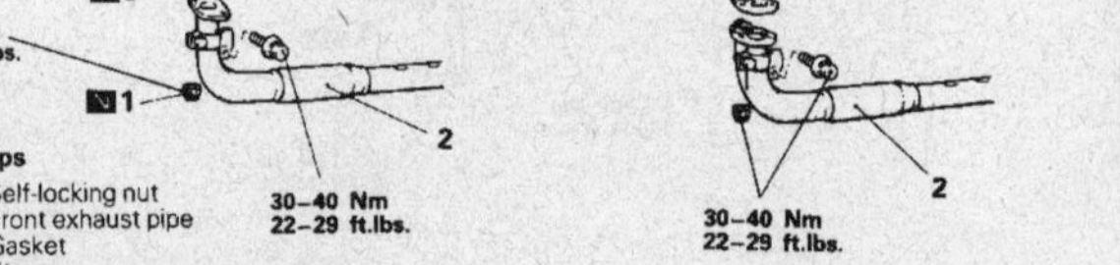
<Turbo>
<Non-Turbo>
40–60 Nm
29–43 ft.lbs.
30–40 Nm
22–29 ft.lbs.
30–40 Nm
22–29 ft.lbs.

Removal steps
1. Self-locking nut
2. Front exhaust pipe
3. Gasket
4. Stay
5. Center member rear installation bolt
10. Stabilizer link mounting nut
11. Stabilizer link
12. Stabilizer bar bracket mounting bolt
13. Stabilizer bar bracket
14. Bushing
15. Stabilizer bar

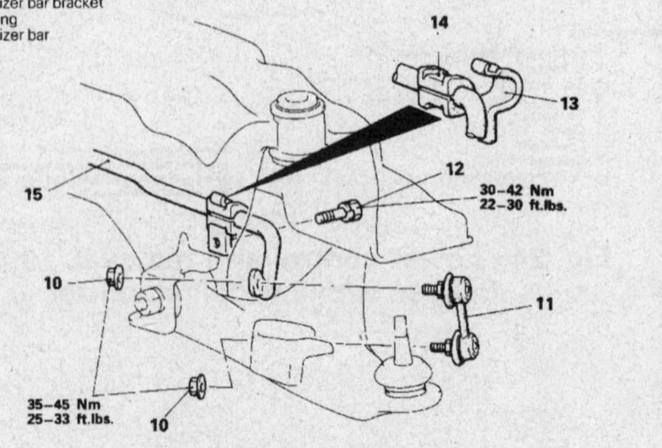
30–42 Nm
22–30 ft.lbs.
35–45 Nm
25–33 ft.lbs.

N : Non-reusable parts

CR2029100063000X

Fig. 29 Stabilizer bar removal. 1993–94 FWD w/pillow-ball stabilizer

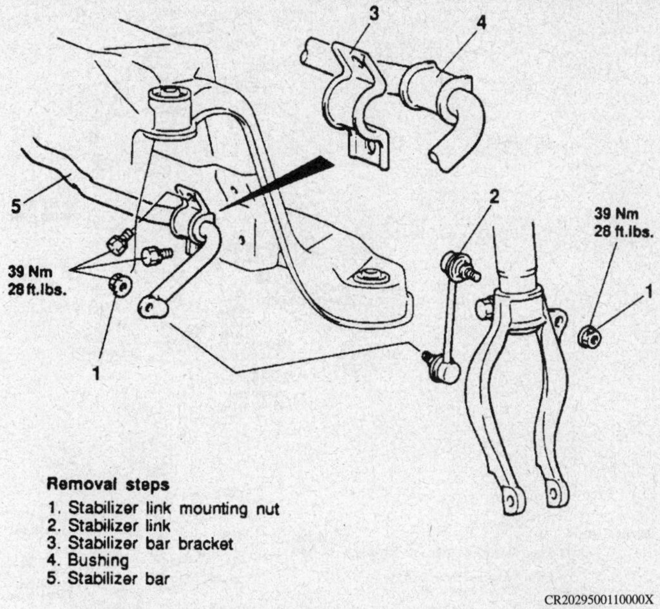
3
4
5
2
39 Nm
28 ft.lbs.
39 Nm
28 ft.lbs.
1
1
Removal steps
1. Stabilizer link mounting nut
2. Stabilizer link
3. Stabilizer bar bracket
4. Bushing
5. Stabilizer bar
CR2029500110000X

Fig. 30 Stabilizer bar removal. 1995–96 FWD

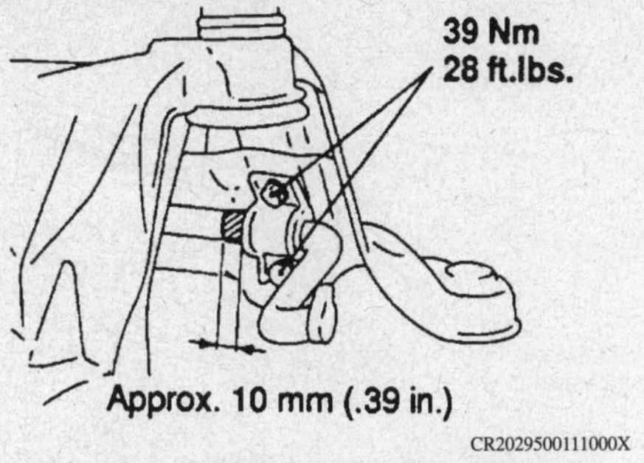
39 Nm
28 ft.lbs.
Approx. 10 mm (.39 in.)
CR2029500111000X

Fig. 31 Stabilizer bar bushing alignment. 1995–96 FWD

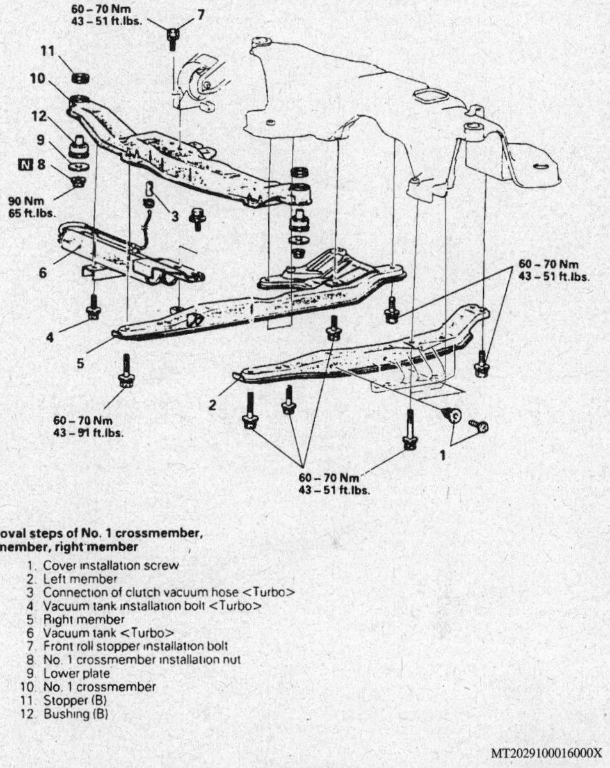
60 – 70 Nm
43 – 51 ft.lbs.
7
11
10
12
9
N 8
90 Nm
65 ft.lbs.
3
6
60 – 70 Nm
43 – 51 ft.lbs.
4
5
2
60 – 70 Nm
43 – 51 ft.lbs.
1
60 – 70 Nm
43 – 51 ft.lbs.
Removal steps of No. 1 crossmember, left member, right member
1. Cover installation screw
2. Left member
3. Connection of clutch vacuum hose <Turbo>
4. Vacuum tank installation bolt <Turbo>
5. Right member
6. Vacuum tank <Turbo>
7. Front roll stopper installation bolt
8. No. 1 crossmember installation nut
9. Lower plate
10. No. 1 crossmember
11. Stopper (B)
12. Bushing (B)
MT2029100016000X

Fig. 33 Right & left member replacement. 3000GT

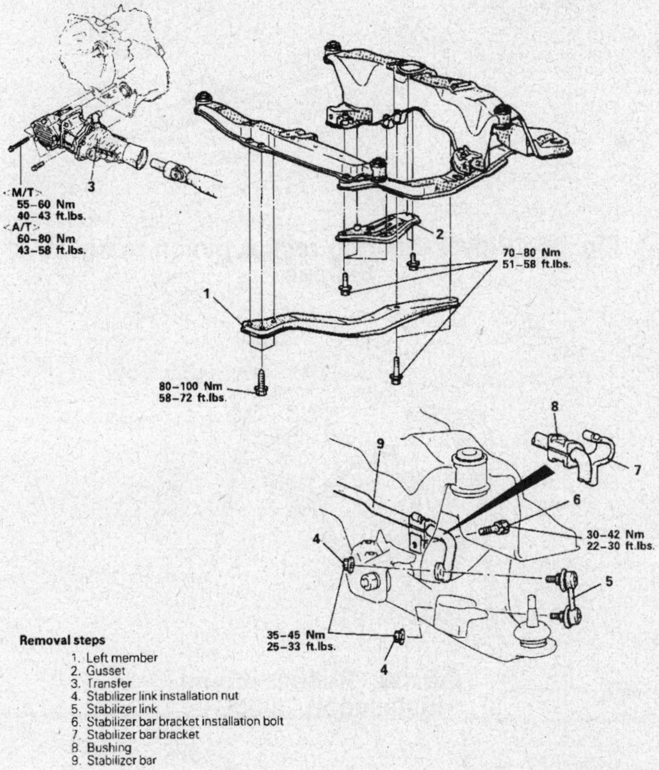
<M/T>
55–60 Nm
40–43 ft.lbs.
<A/T>
60–80 Nm
43–58 ft.lbs.
3
2
70–80 Nm
51–58 ft.lbs.
1
80–100 Nm
58–72 ft.lbs.
8
9
7
6
30–42 Nm
22–30 ft.lbs.
4
5
35–45 Nm
25–33 ft.lbs.
4
Removal steps
1. Left member
2. Gusset
3. Transfer
4. Stabilizer link installation nut
5. Stabilizer link
6. Stabilizer bar bracket installation bolt
7. Stabilizer bar bracket
8. Bushing
9. Stabilizer bar
CR2029100064000X

Fig. 32 Stabilizer bar removal. 1993–94 AWD models

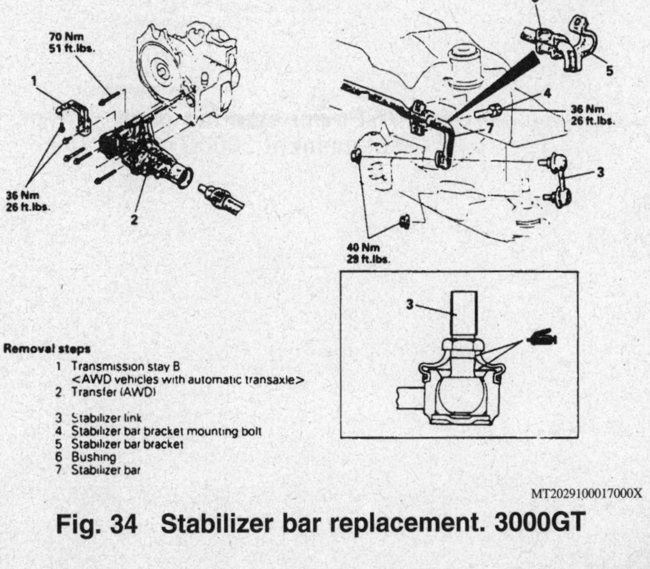
70 Nm
51 ft.lbs.
1
36 Nm
26 ft.lbs.
2
6
5
4
36 Nm
26 ft.lbs.
7
3
40 Nm
29 ft.lbs.
3
Removal steps
1 Transmission stay B
<AWD vehicles with automatic transaxle>
2 Transfer (AWD)
3 Stabilizer link
4 Stabilizer bar bracket mounting bolt
5 Stabilizer bar bracket
6 Bushing
7 Stabilizer bar
MT2029100017000X

Fig. 34 Stabilizer bar replacement. 3000GT

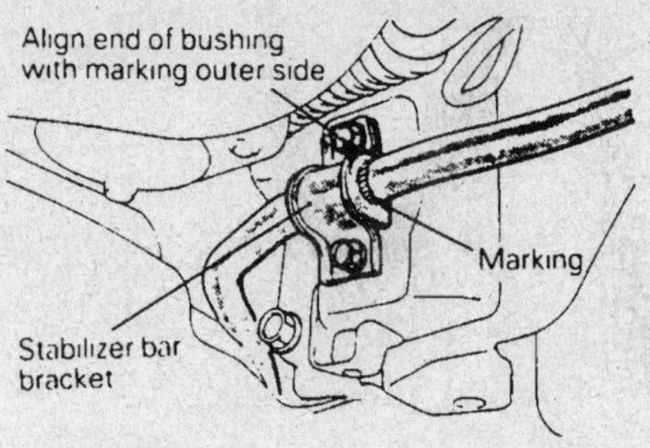
Align end of bushing
with marking outer side
Marking
Stabilizer bar
bracket
MT2029100018000X

Fig. 35 Stabilizer bar bracket position. 3000GT

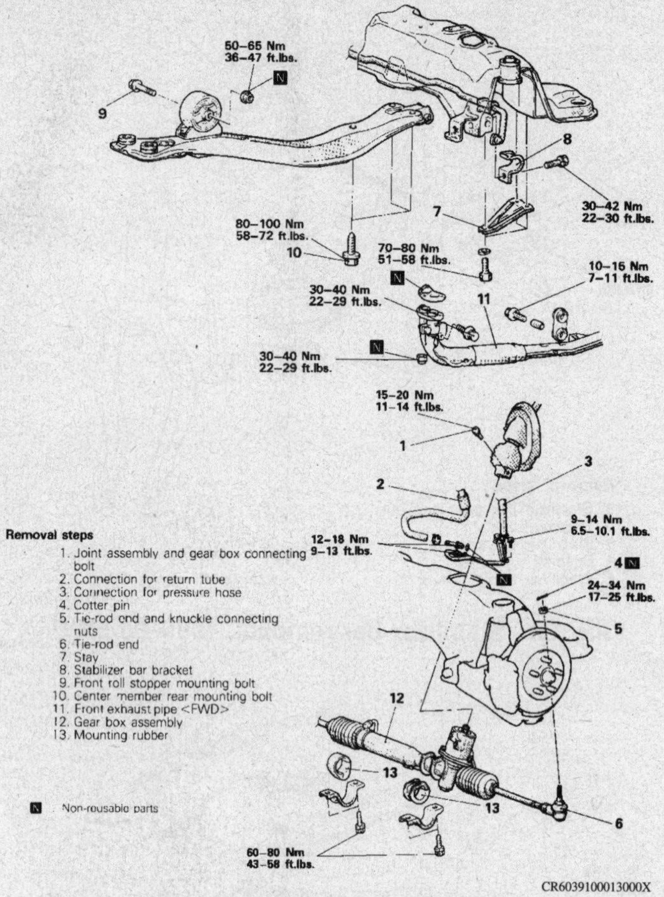
50–65 Nm
36–47 ft.lbs.
9
8
30–42 Nm
22–30 ft.lbs.
7
80–100 Nm
58–72 ft.lbs.
10
70–80 Nm
51–58 ft.lbs.
10–15 Nm
7–11 ft.lbs.
30–40 Nm
22–29 ft.lbs.
11
30–40 Nm
22–29 ft.lbs.
15–20 Nm
11–14 ft.lbs.
1
3
2
Removal steps
1. Joint assembly and gear box connecting bolt
2. Connection for return tube
3. Connection for pressure hose
4. Cotter pin
5. Tie-rod end and knuckle connecting nuts
6. Tie-rod end
7. Stay
8. Stabilizer bar bracket
9. Front roll stopper mounting bolt
10. Center member rear mounting bolt
11. Front exhaust pipe <FWD>
12. Gear box assembly
13. Mounting rubber
12–18 Nm
9–13 ft.lbs.
9–14 Nm
6.5–10.1 ft.lbs.
4
24–34 Nm
17–25 ft.lbs.
5
12
13
13
6
Non-reusable parts
60–80 Nm
43–58 ft.lbs.
CR6039100013000X

Fig. 36 Power steering rack & pinion removal. Eclipse

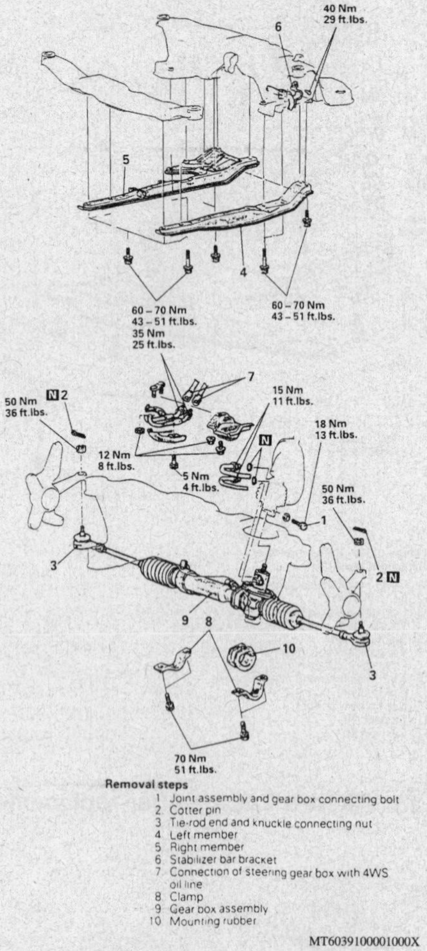
40 Nm
29 ft.lbs.
6
5
4
60 – 70 Nm
43 – 51 ft.lbs.
35 Nm
25 ft.lbs.
60 – 70 Nm
43 – 51 ft.lbs.
7
50 Nm
36 ft.lbs.
2
15 Nm
11 ft.lbs.
18 Nm
13 ft.lbs.
12 Nm
8 ft.lbs.
5 Nm
4 ft.lbs.
50 Nm
36 ft.lbs.
1
3
2
9
8
10
3
70 Nm
51 ft.lbs.
Removal steps
1. Joint assembly and gear box connecting bolt
2. Cotter pin
3. Tie-rod end and knuckle connecting nut
4. Left member
5. Right member
6. Stabilizer bar bracket
7. Connection of steering gear box with 4WS oil line
8. Clamp
9. Gear box assembly
10. Mounting rubber
MT6039100001000X

Fig. 37 Power steering gear replacement 3000GT

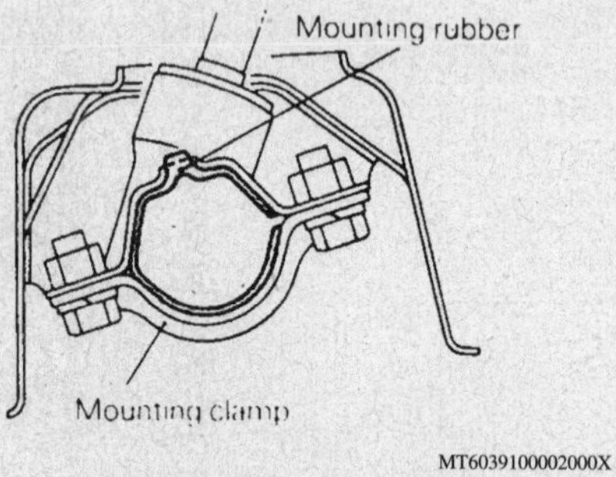
Mounting rubber
Mounting clamp
MT6039100002000X

Fig. 38 Rubber mount installation. 3000GT

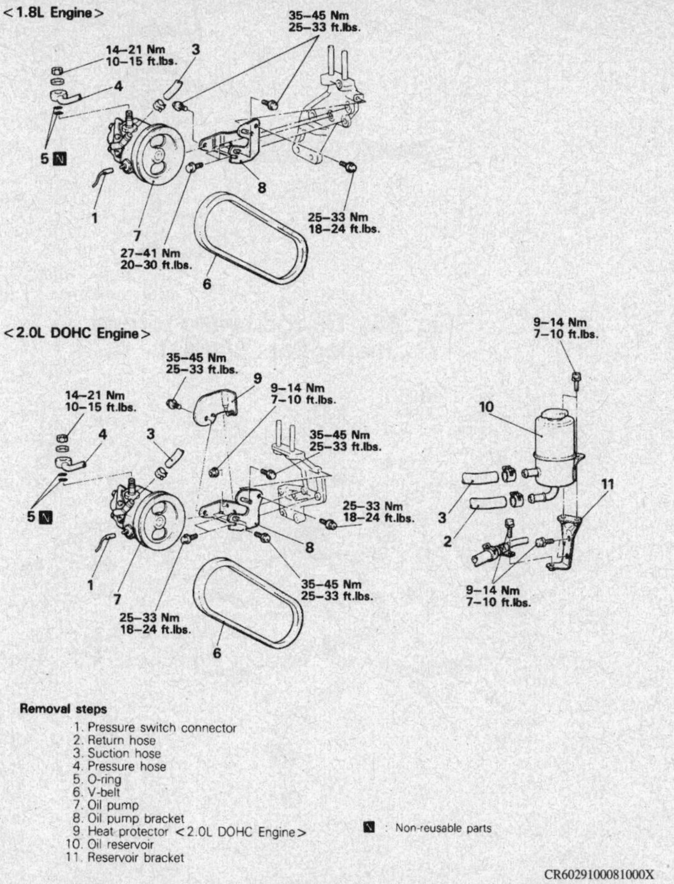
<1.8L Engine>
35–45 Nm
25–33 ft.lbs.
14–21 Nm
10–15 ft.lbs.
25–33 Nm
18–24 ft.lbs.
27–41 Nm
20–30 ft.lbs.
<2.0L DOHC Engine>
35–45 Nm
25–33 ft.lbs.
9–14 Nm
7–10 ft.lbs.
14–21 Nm
10–15 ft.lbs.
35–45 Nm
25–33 ft.lbs.
25–33 Nm
18–24 ft.lbs.
35–45 Nm
25–33 ft.lbs.
25–33 Nm
18–24 ft.lbs.
9–14 Nm
7–10 ft.lbs.
9–14 Nm
7–10 ft.lbs.
Removal steps
1. Pressure switch connector
2. Return hose
3. Suction hose
4. Pressure hose
5. O-ring
6. V-belt
7. Oil pump
8. Oil pump bracket
9. Heat protector <2.0L DOHC Engine>
10. Oil reservoir
11. Reservoir bracket
N : Non-reusable parts
CR6029100081000X

Fig. 39 Power steering pump removal. 1993–94 Eclipse

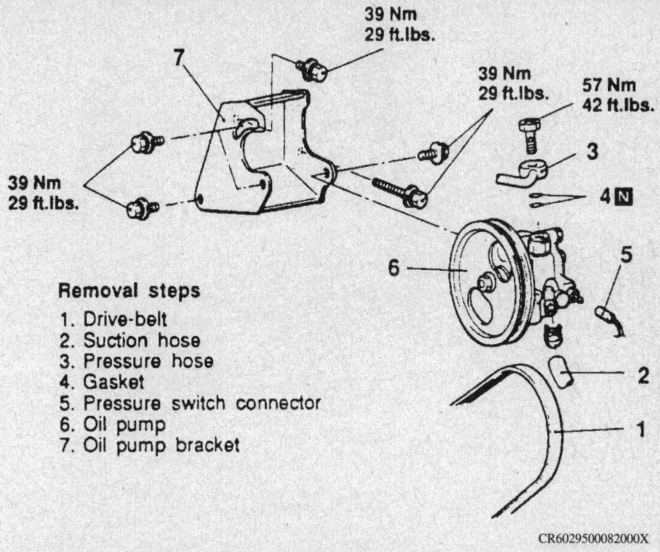
39 Nm
29 ft.lbs.
39 Nm
29 ft.lbs.
57 Nm
42 ft.lbs.
39 Nm
29 ft.lbs.
Removal steps
1. Drive-belt
2. Suction hose
3. Pressure hose
4. Gasket
5. Pressure switch connector
6. Oil pump
7. Oil pump bracket
CR6029500082000X

Fig. 40 Power steering pump removal. 1995–96 Eclipse less turbo

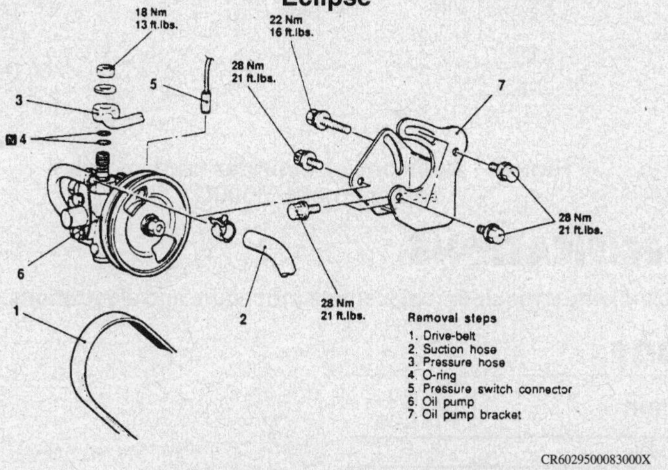
18 Nm
13 ft.lbs.
22 Nm
16 ft.lbs.
28 Nm
21 ft.lbs.
28 Nm
21 ft.lbs.
28 Nm
21 ft.lbs.
Removal steps
1. Drive-belt
2. Suction hose
3. Pressure hose
4. O-ring
5. Pressure switch connector
6. Oil pump
7. Oil pump bracket
CR6029500083000X

Fig. 41 Power steering pump removal. 1995–96 Eclipse w/turbocharged engine

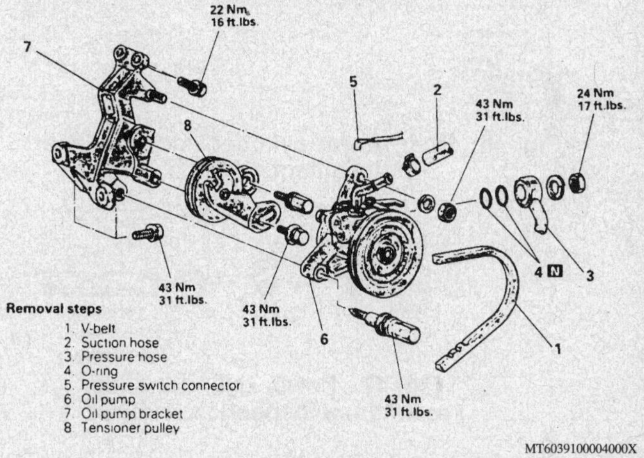
22 Nm
16 ft.lbs.
43 Nm
31 ft.lbs.
24 Nm
17 ft.lbs.
43 Nm
31 ft.lbs.
43 Nm
31 ft.lbs.
43 Nm
31 ft.lbs.
Removal steps
1. V-belt
2. Suction hose
3. Pressure hose
4. O-ring
5. Pressure switch connector
6. Oil pump
7. Oil pump bracket
8. Tensioner pulley
MT6039100004000X

Fig. 42 Front power steering pump replacement. 3000GT

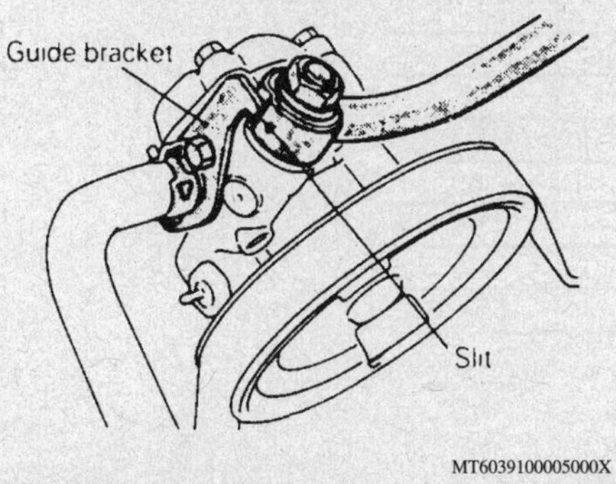
Guide bracket
Slit
MT6039100005000X

Fig. 43 Pressure hose installation

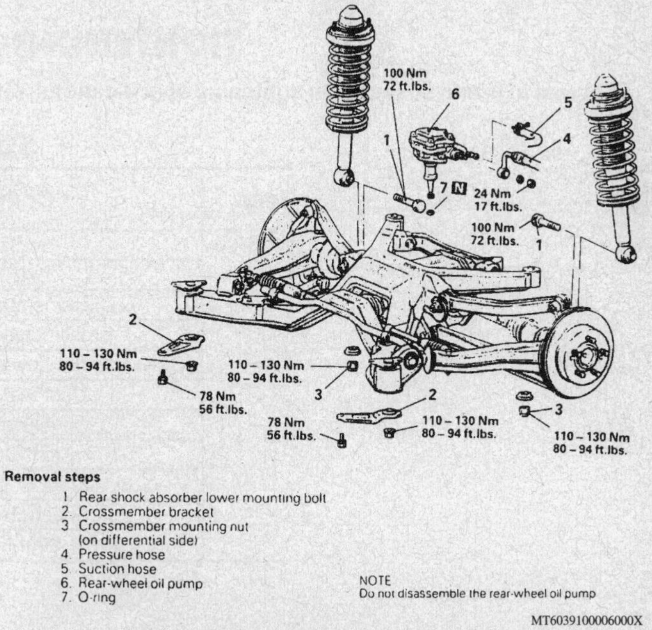
100 Nm
72 ft.lbs.
24 Nm
17 ft.lbs.
100 Nm
72 ft.lbs.
110 – 130 Nm
80 – 94 ft.lbs.
110 – 130 Nm
80 – 94 ft.lbs.
78 Nm
56 ft.lbs.
78 Nm
56 ft.lbs.
110 – 130 Nm
80 – 94 ft.lbs.
110 – 130 Nm
80 – 94 ft.lbs.
Removal steps
1. Rear shock absorber lower mounting bolt
2. Crossmember bracket
3. Crossmember mounting nut (on differential side)
4. Pressure hose
5. Suction hose
6. Rear-wheel oil pump
7. O-ring
NOTE
Do not disassemble the rear-wheel oil pump
MT6039100006000X

Fig. 44 Rear power steering pump replacement. 3000GT

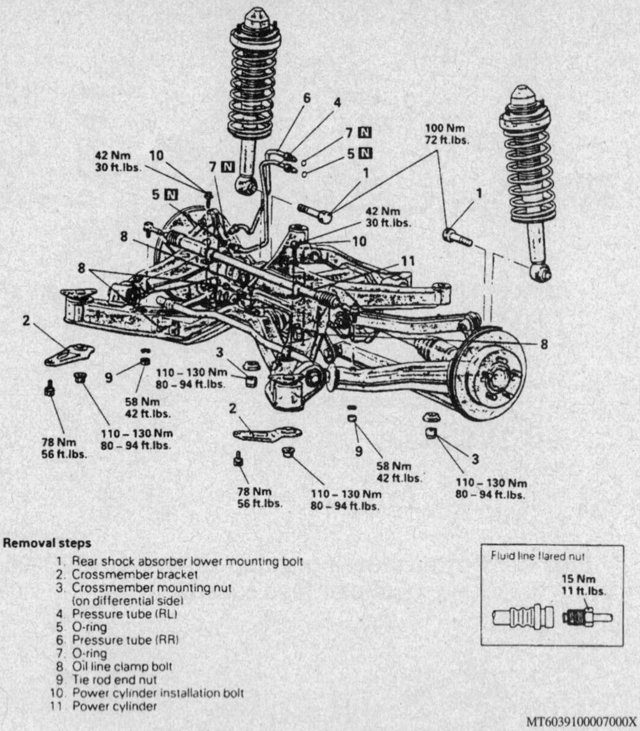
42 Nm
30 ft.lbs.
100 Nm
72 ft.lbs.
42 Nm
30 ft.lbs.
110 – 130 Nm
80 – 94 ft.lbs.
58 Nm
42 ft.lbs.
78 Nm
56 ft.lbs.
Removal steps
1. Rear shock absorber lower mounting bolt
2. Crossmember bracket
3. Crossmember mounting nut (on differential side)
4. Pressure tube (RL)
5. O-ring
6. Pressure tube (RR)
7. O-ring
8. Oil line clamp bolt
9. Tie rod end nut
10. Power cylinder installation bolt
11. Power cylinder
Fluid line flared nut
15 Nm
11 ft.lbs.
MT6039100007000X

Fig. 45 Rear power cylinder (steering gear) replacement. 3000GT

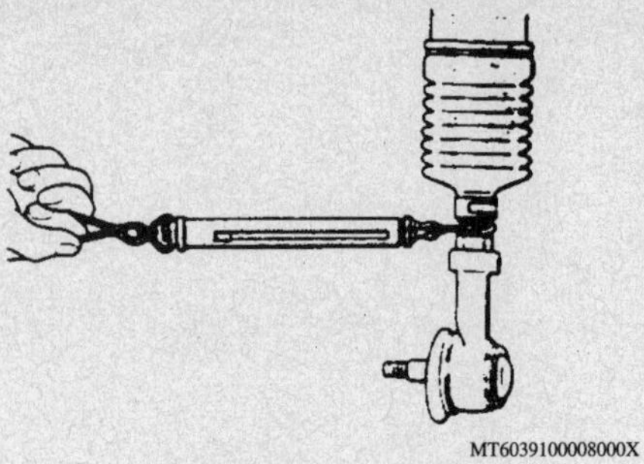
MT6039100008000X

Fig. 46 Tie rod swing torque inspection. 3000GT

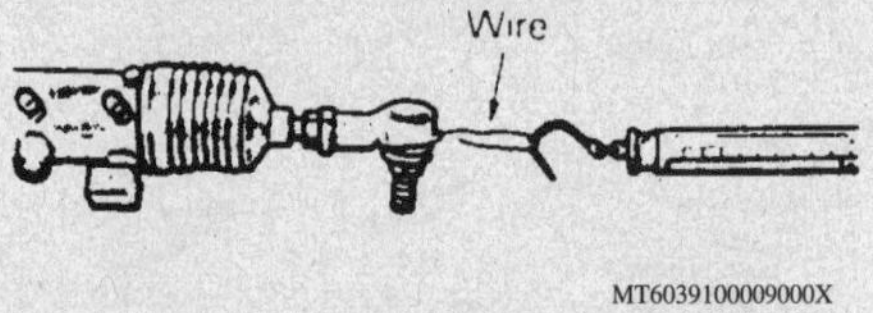
Wire
MT6039100009000X

Fig. 47 Power cylinder slide resistance inspection. 3000GT

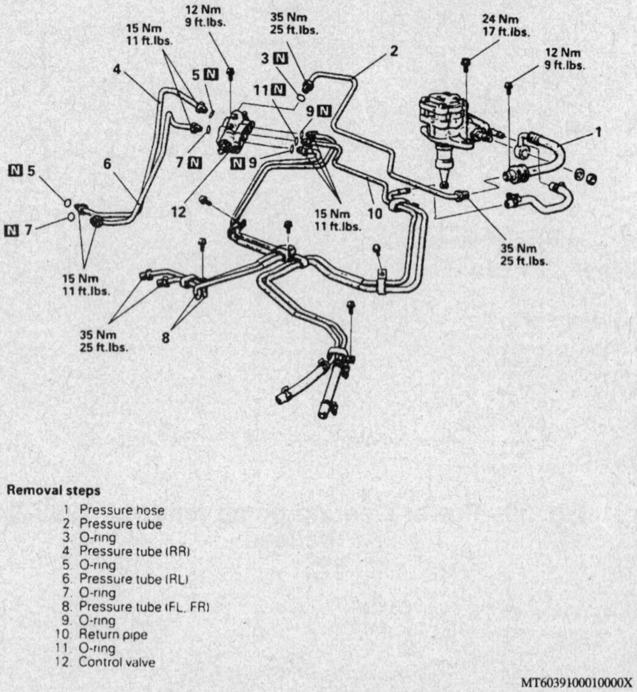
12 Nm
9 ft.lbs.
15 Nm
11 ft.lbs.
35 Nm
25 ft.lbs.
24 Nm
17 ft.lbs.
Removal steps
1. Pressure hose
2. Pressure tube
3. O-ring
4. Pressure tube (RR)
5. O-ring
6. Pressure tube (RL)
7. O-ring
8. Pressure tube (FL, FR)
9. O-ring
10. Return pipe
11. O-ring
12. Control valve
MT6039100010000X

Fig. 48 Rear power cylinder control valve replacement. 3000GT

TIGHTENING SPECIFICATIONS

For rear axle and suspension tightening specifications, refer to individual repair or replacement procedure and illustrations.

3000GT

Year	Component	Torque/ Ft. Lbs.
1993–96	Air Bag Module	4
	Axle Shaft Nut	145–188
	Crossmember Attaching Bolt	43–51
	Crossmember Attaching Nut	58–72
	Crossmember Lower Plate Self-Locking Nut	65
	Dust Plate Bolt (AWD)	7
	Driveshaft Nut	145-188
	Front Brake Caliper	65
	Front Roll Stopper Bolt	43–51
	Front Speed Sensor Attaching Bolt	9
	Front Strut Lower Mount Bolt	65–76

Continued

Year	Component	Torque/ Ft. Lbs.
1993–96	Front Strut Piston Rod Nut	56
	Hub Nut	145-188
	Inner Shaft Bracket Bolt	33
	Lower Ball Joint Nut	43–52
	Lower Ball Joint To Steering Knuckle Nut	43–52
	Lower Control Arm Clamp Long Bolt	72–87
	Lower Control Arm Clamp Mounting Nut	72
	Lower Control Arm Clamp Nut	29
	Lower Control Arm Clamp Short Bolt	65①
	Lower Control Arm Nut	72–87①
	Power Steering Gearbox Line Fittings (4WS)	25
	Power Steering Line Fitting	11
	Power Steering Line Inner Bracket (4WS)	4
	Power Steering Line Outer Bracket (4WS)	8
	Power Steering Pump Bracket Lower Bolt	31
	Power Steering Pump Bracket Upper Bolt	16
	Power Steering Pump Plug	18–22
	Power Steering Pump Pressure Hose Nut	17
	Power Steering Pump Tensioner Pulley	31
	Power Steering Pump To Bracket	31
	Power Steering Rack Bracket Attaching Bolts	51
	Power Steering Rack To Steering Column Linkage	13
	Steering Column Shaft Joint	13
	Steering Column Support	8
	Steering Wheel	29
	Stabilizer Bar Bracket Bolt	26
	Stabilizer Link Nut	29
	Tie Rod End Attaching Nut	21-36
	Tie Rod End Locking Nut	36-40
	Wheel Lug Nuts	87-101

① — Tighten temporarily, tighten to specifications when vehicle is unladen.

ECLIPSE

Year	Component	Torque/ Ft. Lbs.
1993–94	Axle Nut	144-188
	Caliper Assembly Mounting Bolt	58-72
	Center Bearing Bracket	26-33
	Center Member To Body	58-72
	Driveshaft Nut	144-188
	End Plug	36-51
	Feed Tubes	9-13
	Front Exhaust Pipe Clamp	22-29
	Front Roll Stopper Bracket To Center Member	29-36
	Front Speed Sensor Bracket	7-10
	Front Toothed Rotor	7-10
	Gearbox To Bracket To Crossmember	43-58
	Heat Protector Installation Nut	7-10
	Hub Nut	144-188
	Joint Assembly	11-14
	Knuckle To Ball Joint	43-52
	Knuckle To Strut Assembly	80-101
	Lower Arm Clamp To Crossmember (Nut)	25-34

Continued

Year	Component	Torque/ Ft. Lbs.
1993–94	Lower Arm Clamp To Crossmember (Bolt)	58-72
	Lower Arm To Crossmember	72-87
	Oil Pump To Bracket	25-33
	Oil Reservoir Bracket Installation Bolt	7-10
	Oil Reservoir Installation Bolt	7-10
	Pinion And Valve Assembly To Self-Locking Nut	14-22
	Pressure Hose To Gearbox	9-13
	Pressure Hose To Oil Pump	10-15
	Return Tube To Gearbox	9-13
	Stabilizer Bar Bracket	22-30
	Stabilizer Link	25-33
	Stay To Crossmember	51-58
	Strut Top End Nut	43-51
	Strut Upper Mounting Nut	29-39
	Terminal Assembly To Pump Body	18-22
	Tie Rod End Ball Joint	17-25
	Tie Rod End To Rack	58-72
	Wheel Lug Nuts	87-101
1995-96	Axle Nut	145-188
	Caliper Assembly Mounting Bolt	36-43
	Compression Lower Arm	51-60
	Dampener To Strut Collar	75
	Dampener Pivot	64
	Driveshaft Nut	145-188
	Dust Shield	6.5
	Hub Assembly To Knuckle	65
	Driveshaft Nut	145-188
	Knuckle To Ball Joint	21
	Knuckle To Compression Lower Arm	43-52
	Knuckle Upper Mounting	21
	Lateral Lower Arm To Crossmember	71-85
	Lateral Lower Arm Ball Joint	60
	P. S. Oil Pump To Bracket	21-29
	Stabilizer Bar Bracket	28
	Stabilizer Link To Dampener	28
	Stay To Crossmember	51-58
	Strut Top End Nut	16
	Strut Lower Mounting	64
	Strut Upper Mounting Nut	32
	Tie Rod End Ball Joint	21
	Upper Arm Shaft Assembly	62
	Upper Arm Pivot	41
	Upper Arm To Knuckle	20
	Wheel Lug Nuts	88-108

Wheel Alignment

INDEX

	Page No.
Front Wheel Alignment	24-109
Camber	24-109
Caster	24-109
Toe-In	24-109
Preliminary Inspection	24-109
Rear Wheel Alignment	24-109
Camber	24-109
Toe-In	24-109
Vehicle Ride Height	24-109
Wheel Alignment Specifications	24-3

PRELIMINARY INSPECTION

1. Ensure tires are inflated to correct pressure, then check for uneven wear.
2. Check front wheel bearings, suspension arm and ball joints for damage and replace as necessary, to correct improper alignment due to faulty components.
3. Check steering gear and shocks for damage and replace as necessary.
4. Rock vehicle back and forth, then bounce it up and down to settle vehicle prior to alignment.
5. Ensure vehicle is unloaded and on a suitable alignment rack in accordance with manufacturer's instructions. **When measuring, equipment is attached directly to outer end of driveshaft and front wheels are on turntables. Apply brake to prevent vehicle movement.**

FRONT WHEEL ALIGNMENT

CAMBER

Eclipse

Camber is preset during production and is not adjustable. If camber is out of specification, replace bent or damaged components as necessary.

3000GT

1. Install wheel alignment gauge attachment tool No. MB991004, or equivalent. Tighten to front driveshaft nut specification.
2. To adjust, turn upper bolt on strut lower mount. One graduation is equivalent to about 1/3° camber.

CASTER

Caster has been preset during production and is not adjustable.

TOE-IN

1. Adjust toe-in by loosening clips and turning left and right tie rod turnbuckles equally in opposite directions. Refer to **Fig. 1.**
2. To increase toe-out, turn left turnbuckle toward front of vehicle and right turnbuckle toward rear of vehicle. To increase toe-in, turn turnbuckles in other direction.
3. Toe-in adjustment should be 0.24 inch for each half turn of left and right tie rods.

REAR WHEEL ALIGNMENT

CAMBER

ECLIPSE

1993-94 FWD

Camber and toe-in have been preset during production and cannot be adjusted. If camber is out of specification, replace bent or damaged components as necessary.

1995-96 FWD Models

Camber and toe-in have been preset during production and cannot be adjusted. If camber is out of specification, replace bent or damaged components as necessary.

AWD Models

1. Measure camber with a camber/caster/kingpin gauge.
2. Adjust camber by moving mounting bolt located on crossmember side of upper arm. One graduation is equivalent to about 1/4° in camber, **Fig. 2.**

3000GT

FWD Models

1. Make adjustment with crossmember side assist link mounting bolt loosened.
2. Adjust camber by turning lower arm mounting bolt (crossmember side). One graduation is equivalent to about 1/4° in camber.
3. If camber is adjusted, ensure toe-in is also adjusted.

AWD Models

1. Measure camber with a camber/caster/kingpin gauge.
2. Adjust camber by moving mounting bolt located on crossmember side of lower arm. One graduation is equivalent to about 1/5° in camber, **Fig. 3.**

TOE-IN

ECLIPSE

1993-94 FWD Models

Rear toe-in is preset during production and cannot adjusted. If rear toe-in is out of specification, replace bent or damaged components as necessary.

1993-94 AWD Models

1. Adjust rear toe-in by moving mounting bolts located on crossmember side of the trailing arm.
2. Make adjustment by moving left and right bolts equally. One graduation changes toe by approximately 0.08 inch, **Fig. 4.**

1995-96 Models

1. Adjust rear toe-in by moving mounting bolts located on crossmember side of the trailing arm.
2. Make adjustment by moving left and right bolts equally. One graduation changes toe by approximately 0.05 inch.

3000GT

FWD MODELS

Adjust rear toe-in by turning the crossmember side assist link mounting bolts on both sides the same amount. One graduation changes toe by approximately 0.19 inch.

AWD MODELS

1. Adjust rear toe-in by moving mounting bolts located on crossmember side of the trailing arm.
2. Make adjustment by moving left and right bolts equally. One graduation changes toe by approximately 0.08 inch, **Fig. 5.**

VEHICLE RIDE HEIGHT

There is no provision for adjustment of vehicle ride height on these vehicles. If ride height is not satisfactory, check for damaged or modified suspension components.

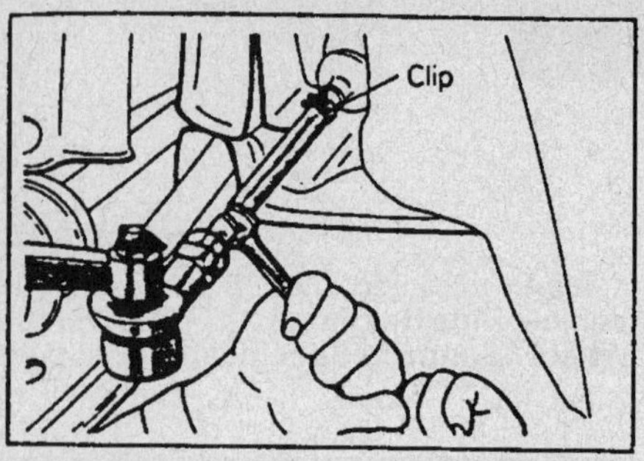
Clip
MT2049100019000X

Fig. 1 Front toe-in adjustment

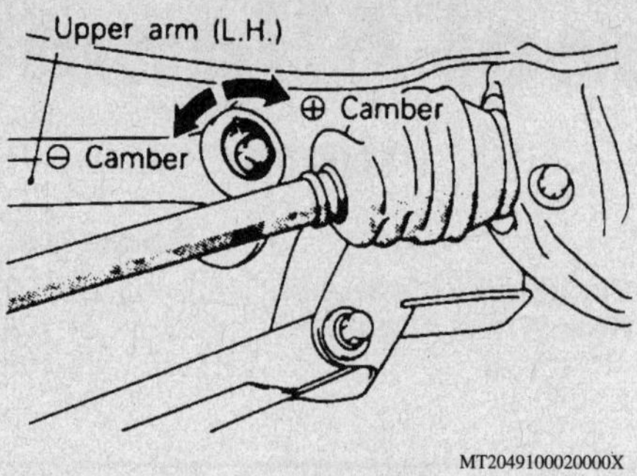
Upper arm (L.H.)
⊕ Camber
⊖ Camber
MT2049100020000X

Fig. 2 Rear camber adjustment. Eclipse AWD

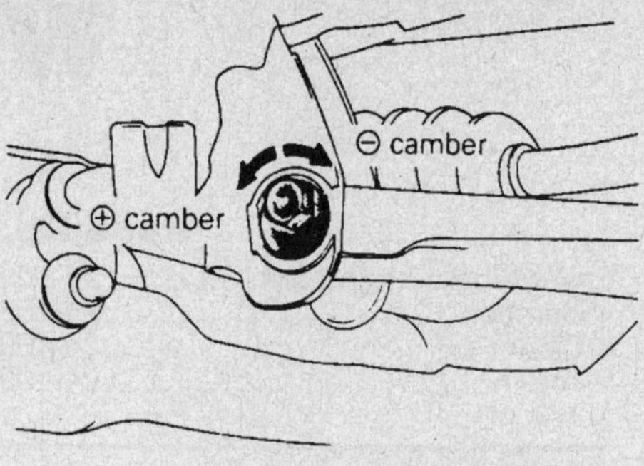
⊖ camber
⊕ camber
MT2049100021000X

Fig. 3 Rear camber adjustment. 3000GT AWD

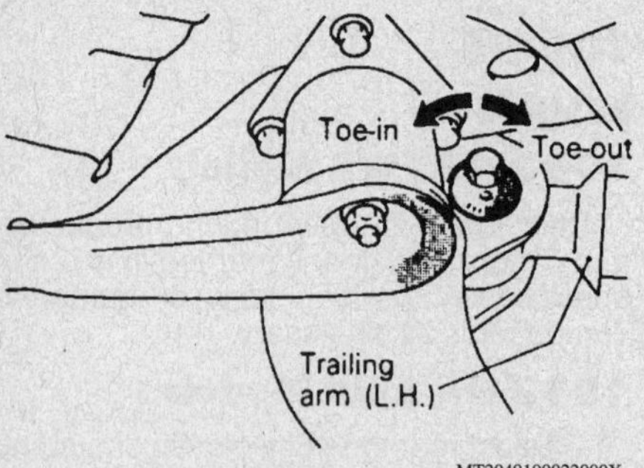
Toe-in
Toe-out
Trailing arm (L.H.)
MT2049100022000X

Fig. 4 Rear toe-in adjustment. 1993-94 Eclipse AWD

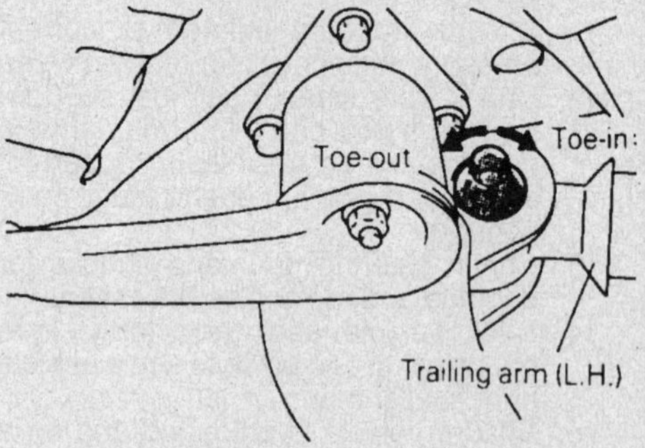
Toe-out
Toe-in
Trailing arm (L.H.)
MT2049100023000X

Fig. 5 Rear toe-in adjustment. 3000GT AWD

MITSUBISHI EXPO

INDEX OF SERVICE OPERATIONS

	Page No.
AIR BAG SYSTEM PRECAUTIONS	0-8
AUTOMATIC TRANSMISSIONS/ TRANSAXLES	29-1
BRAKES	
Anti-Lock Brakes	29-1
Disc Brakes	29-1
Drum Brakes	29-1
Hydraulic Brake Systems	29-1
Power Brake Units	29-1
CLUTCH & MANUAL TRANSAXLE	
Adjustments	25-35
Clutch, Replace	25-35
Hydraulic System Service	25-35
Tightening Specifications	25-39
Transaxle, Replace	25-36
ELECTRICAL	
Air Bags	29-1
Air Conditioning	29-1
Alternator, Replace	25-4
Alternators	29-1
Blower Motor, Replace	25-6
Combination Switch, Replace	25-5
Cooling Fans	29-1
Cruise Control	29-1
Dash Gauges	29-1
Dash Panels	29-1
Distributor, Replace	25-4
Evaporator Core, Replace	25-6
Fuel Pump Relay Location	25-4
Fuse Panel & Flasher Location	25-4
Heater Core, Replace	25-6
Ignition Lock, Replace	25-4
Ignition Switch, Replace	25-4
Instrument Cluster, Replace	25-5
Neutral Safety Switch, Replace	25-5
Passive Restraints	29-1
Precautions	25-4
Radio, Replace	25-5
Relay Center Location	25-4
Speed Controls	29-1
Starter, Replace	25-4
Steering Columns	29-1
Steering Wheel, Replace	25-5
Wiper Motor, Replace	25-5
Wiper Switch, Replace	25-5
Wiper Systems	29-1
ELECTRICAL SYMBOL IDENTIFICATION	0-139
FRONT SUSPENSION & STEERING	
Ball Joint, Replace	25-44
Control Arm, Replace	25-45
Manual Steering Gears	29-1
Power Steering	29-1
Power Steering Gear, Replace	25-45
Power Steering Pump, Replace	25-45
Precautions	25-43
Stabilizer Bar, Replace	25-45
Strut, Replace	25-44
Technical Service Bulletins	25-46
Tightening Specifications	25-47
Wheel Hub & Steering Knuckle, Replace	25-43
FRONT WHEEL DRIVE AXLES	29-1
REAR AXLE & SUSPENSION	
Coil Spring, Replace	25-39
Control Arm, Replace	25-39
Differential Carrier, Replace	25-39
Rear Crossmember, Replace	25-39
Shock Absorber, Replace	25-39
Stabilizer Bar, Replace	25-39
Tightening Specifications	25-43
SERVICE REMINDER & WARNING LAMP RESET PROCEDURES	0-10
SPECIFICATIONS	
Fluid Capacities & Cooling System Data	25-3
Front Wheel Alignment Specifications	25-3
General Engine Specifications	25-2
Lubricant Data	25-3
Rear Wheel Alignment Specifications	25-3
Tune Up Specifications	25-2
VEHICLE IDENTIFICATION	0-1
VEHICLE LIFT POINTS	0-34
VEHICLE MAINTENANCE SCHEDULES	0-69
WHEEL ALIGNMENT	
Front Wheel Alignment	25-47
Preliminary Inspection	25-47
Rear Wheel Alignment	25-47
Vehicle Ride Height	25-47
Wheel Alignment Specifications	25-3
WIRE COLOR CODE IDENTIFICATION	0-144
1.8L ENGINE	
Belt Tension Data	25-12
Camshaft, Replace	25-10
Compression Pressure	25-7
Cooling System Bleed	25-12
Crankshaft Seal, Replace	25-12
Cylinder Head, Replace	25-8
Engine Rebuilding Specifications	29-1
Engine, Replace	25-7
Exhaust Manifold, Replace	25-8
Front Cover, Replace	25-8
Fuel Filter, Replace	25-14
Fuel Pump, Replace	25-14
Intake Manifold, Replace	25-8
Main & Rod Bearings	25-11
Oil Pan, Replace	25-12
Oil Pump, Replace	25-12
Piston & Rod Assembly	25-11
Precautions	25-7
Radiator, Replace	25-13
Rocker Arms, Replace	25-8
Technical Service Bulletins	25-14
Thermostat, Replace	25-13
Tightening Specifications	25-17
Timing Belt, Replace	25-8
Valve Adjustment	25-8
Valve Arrangement	25-8
Valve Clearance Specifications	25-8
Water Pump, Replace	25-13
2.4L ENGINE	
Balance Shaft Belt, Replace	25-25
Belt Tension Data	25-30
Camshaft, Replace	25-25
Compression Pressure	25-18
Cooling System Bleed	25-30
Cylinder Head, Replace	25-20
Engine Rebuilding Specifications	29-1
Engine, Replace	25-19
Exhaust Manifold, Replace	25-20
Front Cover, Replace	25-23
Fuel Filter, Replace	25-31
Fuel Pump, Replace	25-31
Intake Manifold, Replace	25-20
Main & Rod Bearings	25-28
Oil Pan, Replace	25-29
Oil Pump, Replace	25-29
Piston & Rod Assembly	25-28
Precautions	25-18
Radiator, Replace	25-31
Rocker Arms, Replace	25-21
Silent Shaft, Replace	25-28
Technical Service Bulletins	25-31
Thermostat, Replace	25-30
Tightening Specifications	25-33
Timing Belt, Replace	25-23
Valve Adjustment	25-21
Valve Arrangement	25-20
Valve Clearance Specifications	25-21
Water Pump, Replace	25-30

Specifications

GENERAL ENGINE SPECIFICATIONS

Year	Engine Liters	Fuel System	Bore & Stroke	Compression Ratio	Maximum Net H.P. @ RPM	Maximum Torque Ft. Lbs. @ RPM
1993–96	1.8L	Multi-Point Fuel Injection	3.19 X 3.50	9.5	113 @ 6000	116 @ 4500
	2.4L	Multi-Point Fuel Injection	3.41 X 3.94	9.5	136 @ 5500	145 @ 4250

TUNE UP SPECIFICATIONS

Year	Engine	Spark Plug Gap, Inch	Ignition Timing			Idle Speed, RPM				Fuel Pump Pressure, psi	Valve Lash	
						Curb②		Fast				
			Firing Order	Timing, °BTDC①	Timing Mark Location	Man. Trans.	Auto. Trans.	Man. Trans.	Auto. Trans.		Intake	Exhaust
1993–94	1.8L/4	.041	1-3-4-2	5①	Pulley	700	700N	②	②	47.6	④	④
	2.4L	.041	1-3-4-2	5①	Pulley	750	750N	②	②	47.6	④	④
1995–96	1.8L/4	.041	1-3-4-2	5①	③	700	700N	②	②	47.6	④	④
	2.4L	.041	1-3-4-2	5①	③	750	750N	②	②	47.6	④	④

BTDC — Before Top Dead Center.

① — With a jumper wire connected between ground & ignition timing adjustment connector. On 1.8L models, refer to **Fig. A.** On 2.4L models refer to **Figs. B and C.**

② — Controlled by idle speed control servo.

③ — Equipped w/crankshaft position sensor.

④ — Equipped w/hydraulic lifters no adjustment required.

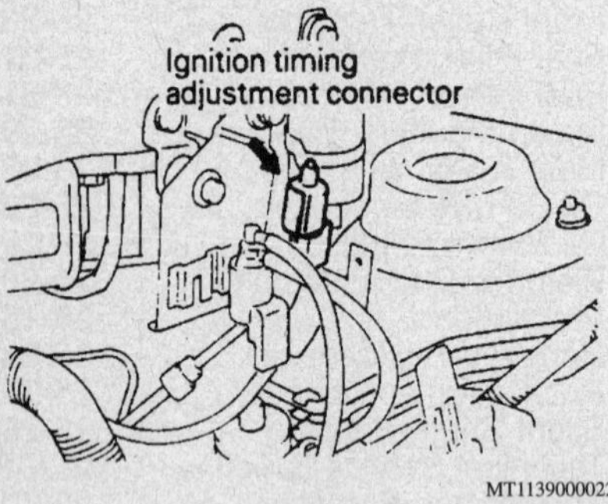
Ignition timing adjustment connector
MT1139000022000X

Fig. A

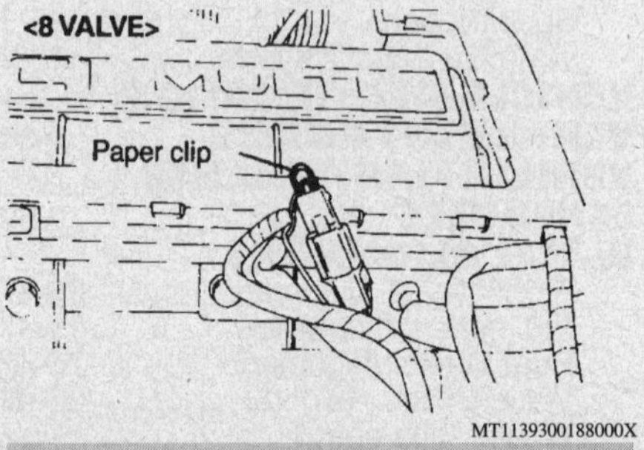
<8 VALVE>
Paper clip
MT1139300188000X

Fig. B

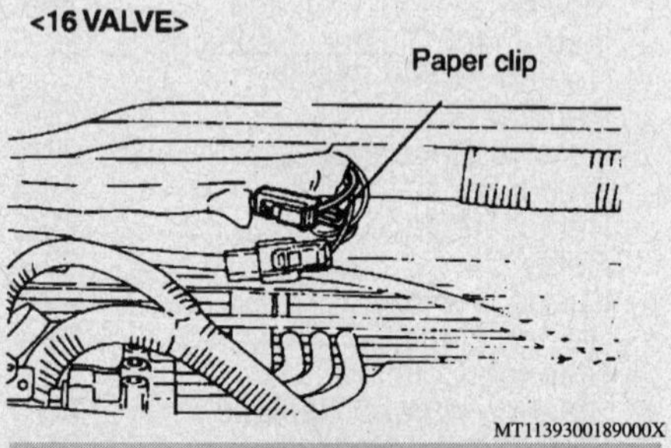
<16 VALVE>
Paper clip
MT1139300189000X

Fig. C

FRONT WHEEL ALIGNMENT SPECIFICATIONS

Year	Model	Caster Angle, Deg.		Camber Angle, Deg.		Toe, Inch①	Ball Joint Inspection Inch Lbs.
		Limits	Desired	Limits	Desired		
1993–96	FWD	+1½ to +2⅚	+2⅙	−⅙ to + ⅚	+⅓	−.12 to +.12	17–78②
	AWD	+1 5/12 to +2¾	+2 1/12	+⅙ to +1⅙	+⅔	−.12 to +.12	17–78②

AWD — All wheel drive
FWD — Front wheel drive
① — Toe-in (+); toe-out (-).
② — Breakaway torque measurement using tool No. MB990326, or equivalent.

REAR WHEEL ALIGNMENT SPECIFICATIONS

Year	Camber Angle, Deg.		Toe-In, Inch①
	Limits	Desired	
1993–96	−1 to 0	− ½	−0 to +.20

① — Toe-in (+); toe-out (-).

FLUID CAPACITIES & COOLING SYSTEM DATA

Year	Engine	Coolant Capacity, Qts.	Radiator Cap Relief Pressure, Lbs.	Thermo. Opening Temp., °F	Fuel Tank, Gals.	Engine Oil Refill, Qts. ①	Transaxle Oil		Transfer Case Oil, Pts.	Rear Drive Axle Oil, Pts.
							5 Speed, Pts.	Auto. Trans., Qts. ②		
1993	1.8L FWD	6.3	13	④	③	4	3.8	6.4	—	—
	1.8L AWD	6.3	13	④	③	4	4.8	6.9	1.2	1.48
	2.4L FWD	6.8	13	⑤	③	⑥	4.8	6.4	—	—
	2.4L AWD	6.8	13	⑤	③	⑥	4.8	6.9	1.2	1.48
1994	1.8L FWD	6.3	13	180	③	4	3.8	6.4	—	—
	1.8L AWD	6.3	13	180	③	4	4.8	6.9	1.2	1.48
	2.4L FWD	6.8	13	⑤	③	⑥	4.8	6.4	—	—
	2.4L AWD	6.8	13	⑤	③	⑥	4.8	6.9	1.2	1.48
1995–96	1.8L	6.3	13	180	③	4	3.8	6.4	—	—
	2.4L FWD	6.8	13	⑤	③	4.5	4.8	6.4	—	—
	2.4L AWD	6.8	13	⑤	③	4.5	4.8	6.9	1.2	1.48

AWD — All wheel drive
FWD — Front wheel drive
① — Includes filter.
② — Approximate, make final check with dipstick.
③ — Expo, 15.9 gals.; Expo LRV, 14.5 gals.
④ — Federal, 170°F; Calif., 180°F.
⑤ — 8-valve engine, 190°F; 16-valve engine, 180°F.
⑥ — 8-valve engine, 4 qts.; 16-valve engine, 4.5 qts.

LUBRICANT DATA

Year	Lubricant Type					
	Transaxle		Transfer Case	Rear Axle	Power Steering	Brake System
	Manual	Automatic				
1993–96	75W-90 GL-4/5	Dia ATF SP	75W-90 GL-4/5	GL-5	Dexron II/IIE/III	DOT 3

Electrical

NOTE: On Air Bag Equipped Models, Refer To "Air Bag System Precautions" Located In Front Of This Manual For System Disarming & Arming Procedures.

INDEX

	Page No.
Air Bags	29-1
Air Conditioning	29-1
Alternator, Replace	25-4
1.8L Engine	25-4
2.4L Engine	25-4
Alternators	29-1
Blower Motor, Replace	25-6
Combination Switch, Replace	25-5
Cooling Fans	29-1
Cruise Control	29-1
Dash Gauges	29-1
Dash Panels	29-1
Distributor, Replace	25-4
Evaporator Core, Replace	25-6
Fuel Pump Relay Location	25-4
Fuse Panel & Flasher Location	25-4
Heater Core, Replace	25-6
Ignition Lock, Replace	25-4
Ignition Switch, Replace	25-4
Instrument Cluster, Replace	25-5
Neutral Safety Switch, Replace	25-5
Passive Restraints	29-1
Precautions	25-4
Air Bag Systems	25-4
Radio, Replace	25-5
Relay Center Location	25-4
Speed Controls	29-1
Starter, Replace	25-4
Steering Columns	29-1
Steering Wheel, Replace	25-5
Wiper Motor, Replace	25-5
Front	25-5
Rear	25-5
Wiper Switch, Replace	25-5
Front	25-5
Rear	25-6
Wiper Systems	29-1

PRECAUTIONS

AIR BAG SYSTEMS

Refer to "Air Bag System Precautions" in front of this manual for system disarming and arming procedures.

FUSE PANEL & FLASHER LOCATION

Fuse panel is located under lefthand side of instrument panel, left of steering column. Hazard flasher unit is located above fuse panel.

FUEL PUMP RELAY LOCATION

The fuel pump relay, also known as multi-port fuel injection relay, is located under the righthand side of the I/P, **Fig. 1.**

RELAY CENTER LOCATION

Main relay centers are located on righthand side of engine compartment and behind lower lefthand side of instrument panel.

STARTER

REPLACE

1. Disconnect battery ground cable.
2. Raise and support vehicle.
3. Disconnect starter electrical connections.
4. Remove starter bolts and starter.
5. Reverse procedure to install.

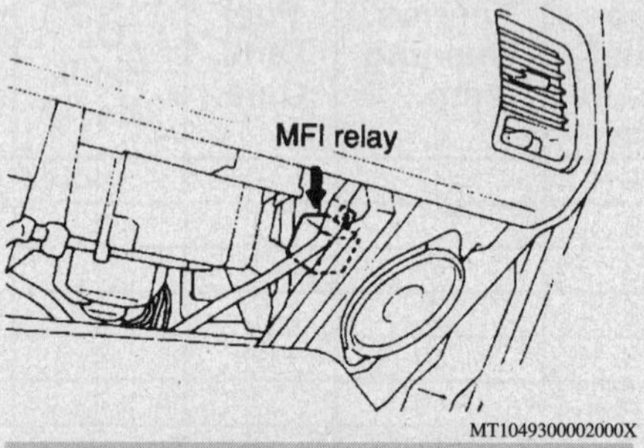

MFI relay
MT1049300002000X

Fig. 1 Fuel pump relay location. Expo

ALTERNATOR

REPLACE

1.8L ENGINE

1. Disconnect battery ground cable.
2. Loosen alternator adjusting nut, push alternator toward engine and remove drive belt.
3. Disconnect alternator electrical connections.
4. Remove alternator brace assembly.
5. Remove alternator.
6. Reverse procedure to install.

2.4L ENGINE

1. Disconnect battery ground cable.
2. Remove alternator harness connector lock bolt, then harness connector.
3. Remove alternator pivot bolt, then alternator.
4. Remove drive belt, water pump pulley bolt, then both water pump pulleys.
5. Remove alternator brace, then alternator.
6. Reverse procedure to install.

DISTRIBUTOR

REPLACE

1. Disconnect battery ground cable.
2. Remove spark plug cables.
3. Disconnect distributor electrical connections.
4. Rotate engine to position piston for No. 1 cylinder at top dead center.
5. Remove distributor retainer bolt then distributor.
6. Reverse procedure to install, noting following:
   a. Ensure piston for No. 1 cylinder is at top dead center.
   b. Align distributor housing and gear mating marks, **Figs. 2 and 3,** then install distributor on engine.

IGNITION LOCK

REPLACE

1. Disconnect hood lock release handle.
2. Remove instrument panel undercover.
3. Remove steering column lower cover.
4. Remove instrument cluster hood and upper column cover.
5. Remove steering wheel as outlined under "Steering Wheel, Replace."
6. Using a hacksaw, cut special bolts used to secure steering lock, **Fig. 4.**
7. Reverse procedure to install, noting following:
   a. Temporarily install steering lock bracket and steering lock on steering column.
   b. Ensure proper operation of steering lock.
   c. Tighten special bolts until heads twist off.

IGNITION SWITCH

REPLACE

1. Disconnect hood lock release handle.

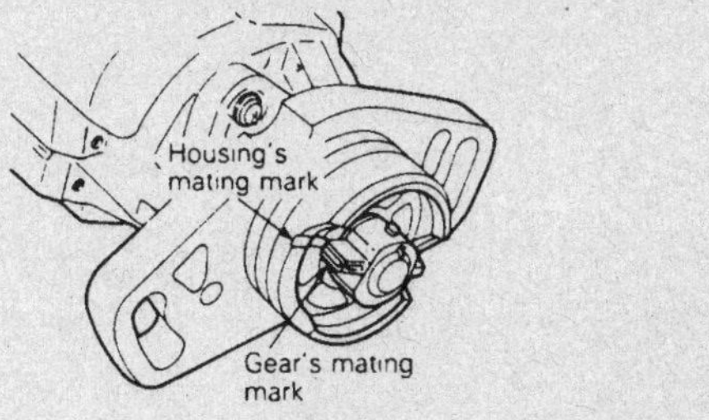
Housing's
mating mark
Gear's mating
mark
MT1119100002000X

Fig. 2 Distributor housing mating marks. 1.8L & 2.4L 16-valve engine

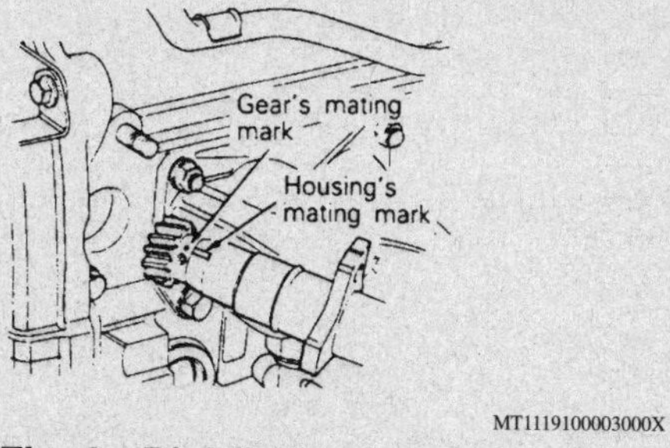
Gear's mating
mark
Housing's
mating mark
MT1119100003000X

Fig. 3 Distributor housing mating marks. 2.4L 8-valve engine

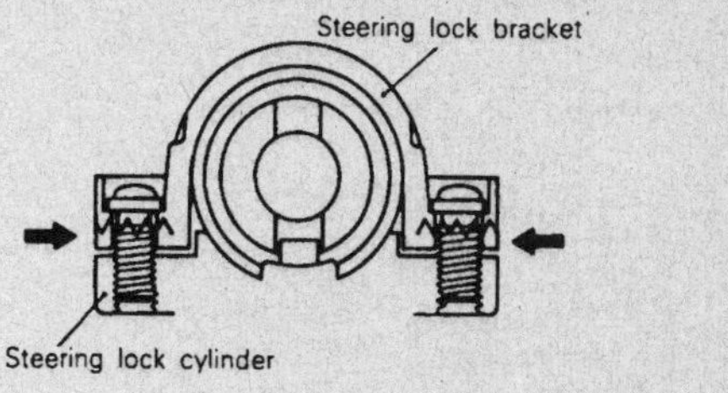
Steering lock bracket
Steering lock cylinder
MT1119100004000X

Fig. 4 Steering lock special bolts

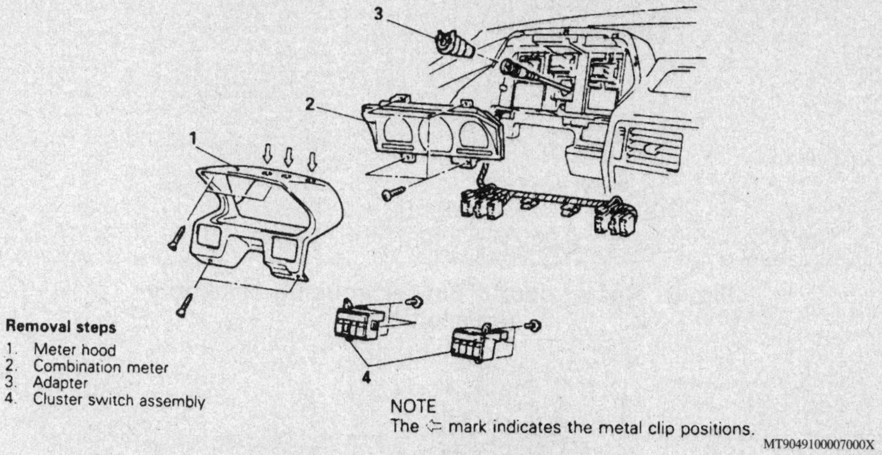
3
2
1
4
Removal steps
1. Meter hood
2. Combination meter
3. Adapter
4. Cluster switch assembly
NOTE
The ⇦ mark indicates the metal clip positions.
MT9049100007000X

Fig. 5 Cluster switch removal

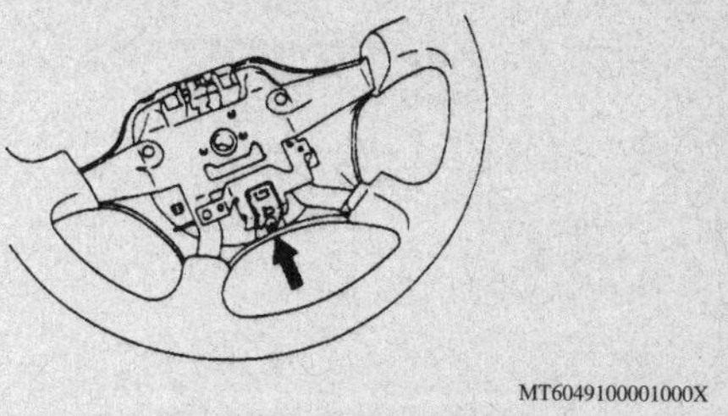
MT6049100001000X

Fig. 6 Spring holder installation

2. Remove instrument panel undercover, then steering column lower cover.
3. Remove instrument cluster hood and upper column cover.
4. Insert ignition key into cylinder and turn to ACC position.
5. Using a small Phillips screwdriver, or equivalent, push lockpin of steering lock cylinder inward, then pull steering lock cylinder outward.
6. Disconnect key reminder switch.
7. Remove ignition switch segment.
8. Reverse procedure to install.

NEUTRAL SAFETY SWITCH

REPLACE

1. Disconnect battery ground cable.
2. **On models with manual transmission,** disconnect switch electrical connections, then remove switch from transmission.
3. **On models with automatic transmission,** proceed as follows:
   a. Disconnect transmission gear selector cable from transmission.
   b. Disconnect position switch electrical connections.
   c. Remove manual control lever, then switch.
4. **On all models,** reverse procedure to install.

COMBINATION SWITCH

REPLACE

1. Remove instrument cluster hood, **Fig. 5.**
2. Remove cluster switch retaining screws.
3. Pull cluster switch toward rear of vehicle and disconnect electrical connectors.
4. Remove switch from vehicle.
5. Reverse procedure to install.

STEERING WHEEL

REPLACE

1. Remove horn pad assembly.
2. Remove spring holder.
3. Remove steering wheel using a suitable steering wheel puller. **Do not hammer on steering column to remove it, doing so may damage collapsible mechanism.**
4. Reverse procedure to install, noting following:
   a. Install spring clip as shown in **Fig. 6.**
   b. Press downward on horn pad to install it on steering wheel.

INSTRUMENT CLUSTER

REPLACE

1. Remove instrument cluster hood, **Fig. 5.**
2. Remove instrument cluster retaining screws.
3. Pull instrument cluster rearward and remove adapter lock, **Fig. 7.**
4. Pull speedometer cable slightly into passenger compartment and remove rear side of adapter from cable.
5. After turning adapter so that notched section is aligned with tab on cable, remove adapter by sliding it backwards.
6. Reverse procedure to install.

RADIO

REPLACE

1. Remove ashtray and center trim panel.
2. Remove radio bracket retaining bolts.
3. Pull radio assembly slightly into passengers compartment and disconnect electrical and antenna connections.
4. Remove radio from vehicle.
5. Reverse procedure to install.

WIPER MOTOR

REPLACE

FRONT

1. Disconnect battery ground cable.
2. Remove wiper blades and arm assemblies.
3. Remove front deck garnish.
4. Loosen wiper motor assembly bolts, then remove wiper motor assembly.
5. Disconnect wiper linkage and motor electrical connections.
6. Remove wiper motor assembly.
7. Reverse procedure to install.

REAR

1. Disconnect battery ground cable.
2. Remove wiper blades and arm assemblies.
3. Remove liftgate interior trim panel.
4. Disconnect wiper electrical connections, then remove wiper motor assembly.
5. Reverse procedure to install.

WIPER SWITCH

REPLACE

FRONT

Refer to "Column Switch, Replace" for windshield wiper switch replacement.

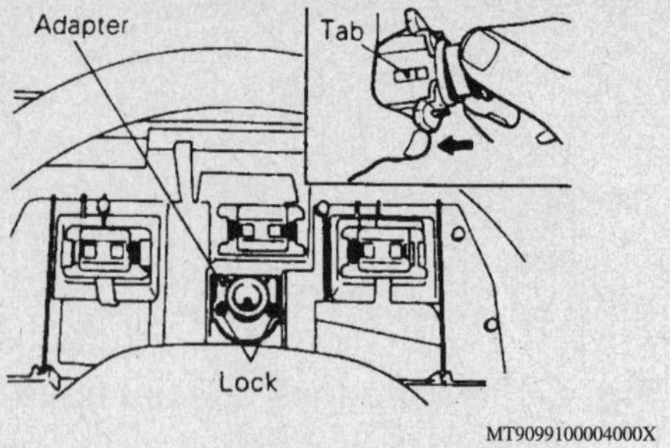

Adapter
Tab
Lock
MT9099100004000X

Fig. 7 Speedometer cable adapter lock

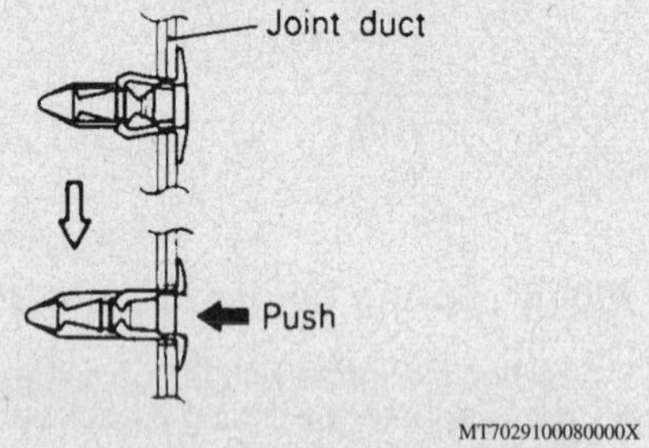

Joint duct
Push
MT7029100080000X

Fig. 9 Retainer clip removal

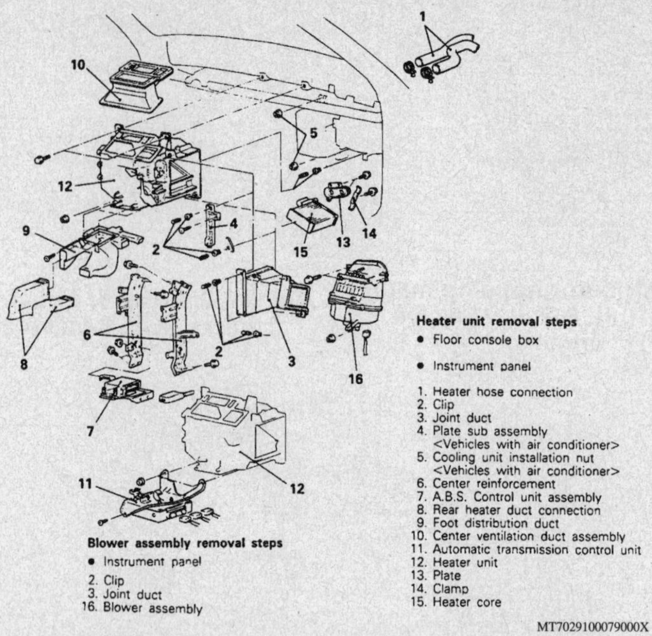

Heater unit removal steps
• Floor console box
• Instrument panel
1. Heater hose connection
2. Clip
3. Joint duct
4. Plate sub assembly <Vehicles with air conditioner>
5. Cooling unit installation nut <Vehicles with air conditioner>
6. Center reinforcement
7. A.B.S. Control unit assembly
8. Rear heater duct connection
9. Foot distribution duct
10. Center ventilation duct assembly
11. Automatic transmission control unit
12. Heater unit
13. Plate
14. Clamp
15. Heater core
Blower assembly removal steps
• Instrument panel
2. Clip
3. Joint duct
16. Blower assembly
MT7029100079000X

Fig. 8 Heater core & blower housing assembly replacement

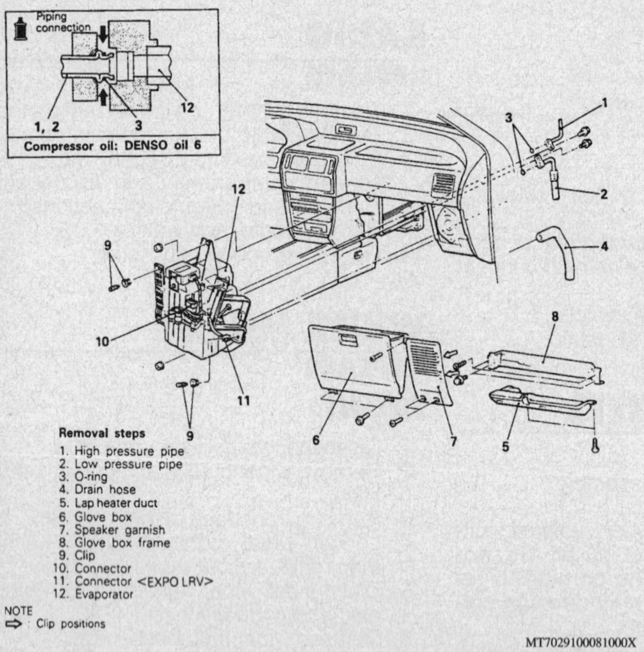

Piping connection
Compressor oil: DENSO oil 6
Removal steps
1. High pressure pipe
2. Low pressure pipe
3. O-ring
4. Drain hose
5. Lap heater duct
6. Glove box
7. Speaker garnish
8. Glove box frame
9. Clip
10. Connector
11. Connector <EXPO LRV>
12. Evaporator
NOTE
⇨ : Clip positions
MT7029100081000X

Fig. 10 Evaporator housing replacement

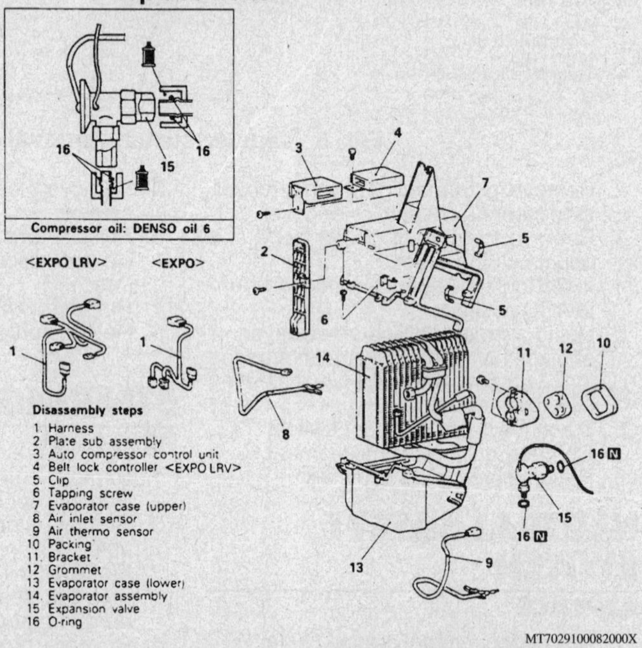

Compressor oil: DENSO oil 6
<EXPO LRV>
<EXPO>
Disassembly steps
1. Harness
2. Plate sub assembly
3. Auto compressor control unit
4. Belt lock controller <EXPO LRV>
5. Clip
6. Tapping screw
7. Evaporator case (upper)
8. Air inlet sensor
9. Air thermo sensor
10. Packing
11. Bracket
12. Grommet
13. Evaporator case (lower)
14. Evaporator assembly
15. Expansion valve
16. O-ring
MT7029100082000X

Fig. 11 Evaporator housing disassembly

REAR

Refer to "Combination Switch, Replace" for rear window wiper switch replacement.

BLOWER MOTOR

REPLACE

1. Remove passengers lap heater duct.
2. Remove glove compartment.
3. Disconnect and remove blower resistor.
4. Remove speaker garnish and glove compartment frame.
5. Disconnect then remove blower motor assembly.
6. Reverse procedure to install.

HEATER CORE

REPLACE

1. Drain cooling system into a suitable container.
2. Remove floor console and instrument panel as outlined under "Dash Panel Service."
3. Remove blower motor housing assembly and heater core assembly in numbered sequence shown in **Fig. 8,** pushing in center of joint duct clip for removal, **Fig. 9.**
4. Reverse procedure to install.

EVAPORATOR CORE

REPLACE

1. Discharge and recover refrigerant system.
2. Remove evaporator housing assembly in numbered sequence shown in **Fig. 10,** pushing in center of joint duct clip for removal, **Fig. 9.**
3. Disassemble evaporator housing assembly in numbered sequence shown in **Fig. 11,** noting following:
   a. Remove housing clips using a suitable flat blade screwdriver.
   b. Loosen expansion valve flare nut using two wrenches.
4. Reverse procedure to install.

1.8L Engine

NOTE: On Air Bag Equipped Models, Refer To "Air Bag System Precautions" Located In Front Of This Manual For System Disarming & Arming Procedures.

NOTE: Prior To Performing Any Service Operations Listed In This Section, Consult The "Technical Service Bulletins" Section For Related Information.

INDEX

Page No.

Belt Tension Data 25-12
Camshaft, Replace 25-10
Compression Pressure 25-7
Cooling System Bleed 25-12
Crankshaft Seal, Replace 25-12
  Rear 25-12
Cylinder Head, Replace 25-8
  Installation 25-8
  Removal 25-8
Engine Rebuilding Specifications 29-1
Engine, Replace 25-7
Exhaust Manifold, Replace 25-8
Front Cover, Replace 25-8
Fuel Filter, Replace 25-14
Fuel Pump, Replace 25-14
Intake Manifold, Replace 25-8
Main & Rod Bearings 25-11
Oil Pan, Replace 25-12
Oil Pump, Replace 25-12
  Inspection 25-12
  Installation 25-12
  Removal 25-12
Piston & Rod Assembly 25-11
Precautions 25-7
  Air Bag Systems 25-7
  Fuel System Pressure Relief 25-7
Radiator, Replace 25-13
Rocker Arms, Replace 25-8
Technical Service Bulletins 25-14
  Fuel Starvation 25-14
  Idle Vibration 25-14
Thermostat, Replace 25-13
Tightening Specifications 25-17
Timing Belt, Replace 25-8
  Installation 25-9
  Removal 25-8
Valve Adjustment 25-8
Valve Arrangement 25-8
Valve Clearance Specifications .. 25-8
Water Pump, Replace 25-13

PRECAUTIONS

AIR BAG SYSTEMS

Refer to "Air Bag System Precautions" in front of this manual for system disarming and arming procedures.

FUEL SYSTEM PRESSURE RELIEF

1. Remove grommet below floor and disconnect fuel pump connector.
2. Start engine and allow engine to runout of fuel.
3. Crank engine two or three times to release remaining fuel pressure.
4. Place ignition switch to Off position.
5. After fuel system repairs are completed, connect fuel pump electrical connections.

COMPRESSION PRESSURE

Ensure engine oil, starter motor and battery are in satisfactory condition. When checking compression, engine coolant should be at normal operating temperature, spark plugs should be removed and throttle valve should be wide open. For correct compression pressures at engine cranking speed, refer to compression pressure chart, **Fig. 1.** Difference between cylinders should not exceed 14 psi.

Engine	Model	Year	Compression Pressure Minimum, psi
1.8L/4	Expo	1993–96	151

Fig. 1 Compression pressure chart

ENGINE

REPLACE

1. Release fuel system pressure as outlined under "Precautions."
2. Disconnect battery ground cable.
3. Mark hood hinge bolt location on hood, then remove hood.
4. Drain cooling system into an approved container.
5. Remove transaxle assembly as outlined under "Transaxle, Replace" in "Clutch & Manual Transaxle"section for models with manual transaxle or in "Automatic Transaxle" unit repair section for models with automatic transaxle.
6. Remove radiator assembly.
7. Remove engine assembly in numbered sequence shown in **Fig. 2,** noting following:
   a. Remove power steering pump with hoses attached, then support aside.
   b. Remove air conditioner compressor with hoses attached, then support aside.
   c. Support engine using a suitable jack stand.
   d. Remove engine hanger tool used when transaxle was removed.
   e. Support engine using a chain and suitable engine lifting device.
   f. Raise engine slightly to remove weight off mounts then remove engine mounts.
   g. Ensure all electrical and hose connections are disconnected then raise engine assembly out of vehicle.
   h. **Always insert a piece of wood between engine hanger assembly and front deck. Do not pinch hood weatherstrip between front deck and piece of wood.**
8. Reverse procedure to install, noting following:
   a. Using a floor jack and a piece of wood, support engine on oil pan, then install engine mount bracket while adjusting position of engine.

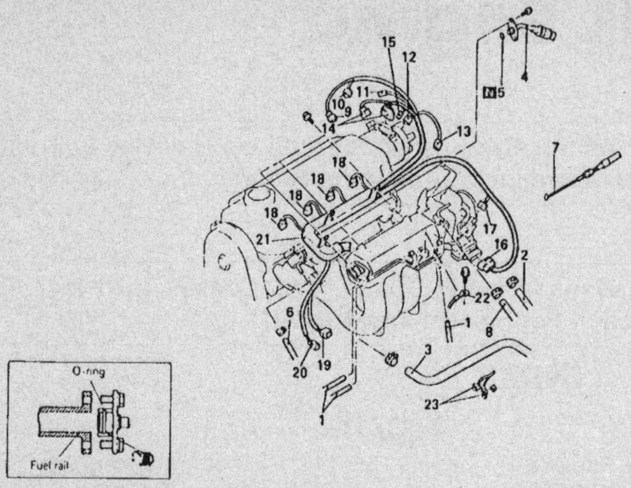
O-ring
Fuel rail

Removal steps

1. Vacuum hose connection
2. Heater hose connection (Thermostat housing → heater unit)
3. Heater hose connection (Heater unit → Water inlet pipe)
4. Fuel high pressure hose connection
5. O-ring
6. Fuel return hose connection
7. Accelerator cable connection
8. Brake booster vacuum hose connection
9. Air conditioning engine coolant temperature switch connector <Up to 1993 models>
10. Oxygen sensor connector <1992 models, 1993 models for Federal>
11. Oil pressure switch connector
12. Water temperature gauge unit connector
13. Engine coolant temperature sensor connector
14. Distributor connector
15. Condenser connector
16. Idle air control connector
17. TPS connector
18. Injector connector
19. Oxygen sensor connector <1993 models for California, From 1994 models>
20. EGR temperature sensor connector <All models for California, From 1994 models for Federal>
21. Control harness assembly
22. Ground wire
23. Generator harness connection

MT1069100102010X

Fig. 2 Engine replacement (Part 1 of 2)

b. Remove engine lifting device allowing engine hanger tool to support engine until transaxle is installed.

INTAKE MANIFOLD

REPLACE

1. Release fuel system pressure as outlined under "Precautions."
2. Disconnect battery ground cable.
3. Drain cooling system into an approved container.
4. Remove intake manifold in numbered sequence shown in **Fig. 3,** removing fuel delivery pipe leaving injectors and pressure regulator intact. **Do not drop injector when removing delivery pipe.**
5. Reverse procedure to install.

EXHAUST MANIFOLD

REPLACE

1. Disconnect battery ground cable.
2. Replace exhaust manifold in numbered sequence shown in **Fig. 4.**
3. Reverse procedure to install.

CYLINDER HEAD

REPLACE

REMOVAL

1. Release fuel system pressure as outlined under "Precautions."
2. Disconnect battery ground cable.
3. Drain cooling system into an approved container.
4. Remove cylinder head and gasket in numbered sequence shown in **Fig. 5,** noting following:
   a. Rotate engine so No. 1 cylinder is at top dead center on compression stroke and align camshaft timing mark, **Fig. 6.**
   b. Tie camshaft sprocket and timing belt together so that position of camshaft sprocket will not move with respect to timing belt, **Fig. 7.**
   c. Remove camshaft sprocket as outlined under "Timing Belt, Replace."
   d. Loosen cylinder head bolts in two or three steps in numbered sequence shown in **Fig. 8. Use care not to damage plug guide, as plug guides cannot be replaced.**
5. Inspect cylinder head gasket surface for flatness by using a straightedge.

INSTALLATION

Reverse numbered sequence shown in **Fig. 5** to install, noting following:

1. Clean cylinder gasket surface on both cylinder head and engine block.
2. Place cylinder head gasket on cylinder block with identification mark facing upward on intake side, **Fig. 9.**
3. Measure cylinder head bolts and ensure bolts are less than 3.795 inches long.
4. Apply a small amount of oil to cylinder head bolt threads and to bolt washer. **Ensure cylinder head bolt is installed as shown in Fig. 10.**
5. Tighten cylinder head bolts in numbered sequence shown in **Fig. 11** in five steps as follows:
   a. **Torque** bolts to 54 ft. lbs.
   b. Completely loosen bolts.
   c. **Torque** bolts to 15 ft. lbs.
   d. Turn bolts 90° (1/4 turn).
   e. Turn bolts an additional 90° (1/4 turn).
6. Loosen water inlet pipe bolt, apply sealant to thermostat case, **Figs. 12 and 13.**
7. Apply a small amount of water to O-ring of water inlet pipe and press thermostat case assembly onto water inlet pipe.
8. Install thermostat case assembly mounting bolt and tighten water inlet pipe bolt.
9. Install thermostat so jiggle valve is at top.

VALVE ARRANGEMENT

Intake valves are located on RH side of cylinder head and exhaust valves are located on LH side of cylinder head.

VALVE CLEARANCE SPECIFICATIONS

Valve stem to guide clearance with the engine hot is .008 for intake and .0012 inch for exhaust.

VALVE ADJUSTMENT

1. Disconnect battery ground cable.
2. Remove valve cover assembly as outlined under "Cylinder Head, Replace."
3. Position No. 1 cylinder at top dead center on compression stroke.
4. Adjust valve clearance at points shown in **Fig. 14** as follows:
   a. Loosen adjusting screw locknut.
   b. Using feeler gauge, adjust intake valve clearance to 0.008 inch and exhaust valve clearance to 0.012 inch by turning adjusting screw.
   c. While holding adjusting screw, tighten adjusting screw locknut.
5. Rotate engine crankshaft clockwise one complete turn to position No. 4 cylinder at top dead center on compression stroke.
6. Repeat Step 4 for points shown in **Fig. 15.**
7. Install valve cover.

ROCKER ARMS

REPLACE

Refer to "Camshaft, Replace" for rocker arm replacement procedure.

FRONT COVER

REPLACE

Refer to "Oil Pump, Replace" for front cover replacement procedure.

TIMING BELT

REPLACE

REMOVAL

1. Disconnect battery ground cable, then remove engine undercover.

2. **On 1993 models,** remove cooling system condenser tank.
3. **On all models,** remove air conditioning and power steering line clamp, **Fig. 16.**
4. Remove power steering and air conditioning drive belt, then alternator drive belt.
5. Stop crankshaft pulley from turning using crankshaft pulley holder, then remove crankshaft bolt, washer and pulley.
6. Remove upper and lower timing belt covers, then flange.
7. If belt is to be reused, mark rotational direction for installation.
8. Turn crankshaft clockwise to align each timing mark and set No. 1 cylinder at compression top dead center (TDC), **Fig. 6.**
9. Loosen timing belt tensioner bolt, then press tensioner fully back clockwise using a screwdriver.
10. Temporarily tighten timing belt tensioner bolt and remove timing belt.
11. Loosen tensioner bolt and move tensioner as close to engine mount as possible with screwdriver, then tighten bolt.

INSTALLATION

1. Ensure camshaft and crankshaft timing marks are aligned, **Fig. 6.**
2. Ensure tension side of belt is taut while installing timing belt over crankshaft, water pump and camshaft sprockets, then tensioner pulley.
3. Apply counterclockwise pressure (reverse of normal rotational direction) to camshaft sprocket and check that belt is fully tensioned, then ensure timing marks are properly aligned.
4. Loosen timing belt tensioner belt approximately ½ turn and allow tensioner spring to tension belt.
5. Rotate crankshaft clockwise two turns, then check timing marks.
6. Ensure timing belt is properly seated on sprockets, then tighten tensioner bolt to specifications.
7. Grasp timing belt with thumb and undercover with index finger and apply light pressure, Check clearance, **Fig. 17,** "A"between belt and undercover. Clearance should be approximately 1.18 inches.
8. Install crankshaft flange with flanged side out, **Fig. 18.**
9. Install timing belt upper and lower covers, then tighten bolts to specifications, **Fig. 19.** A bolts: 0.24 x 0.71 inch and B bolts: 0.24 x 1.18 inches.
10. Apply engine oil to bearing surface and thread section of crankshaft bolt, then install crankshaft bolt and tighten to specifications.
11. Install alternator drive belt, then air conditioning and power steering pump drive belt.
12. Install clamp attaching air conditioning and power steering lines to engine mount.
13. Install cooling system condenser tank.
14. Install engine undercover.
15. Connect battery ground cable.

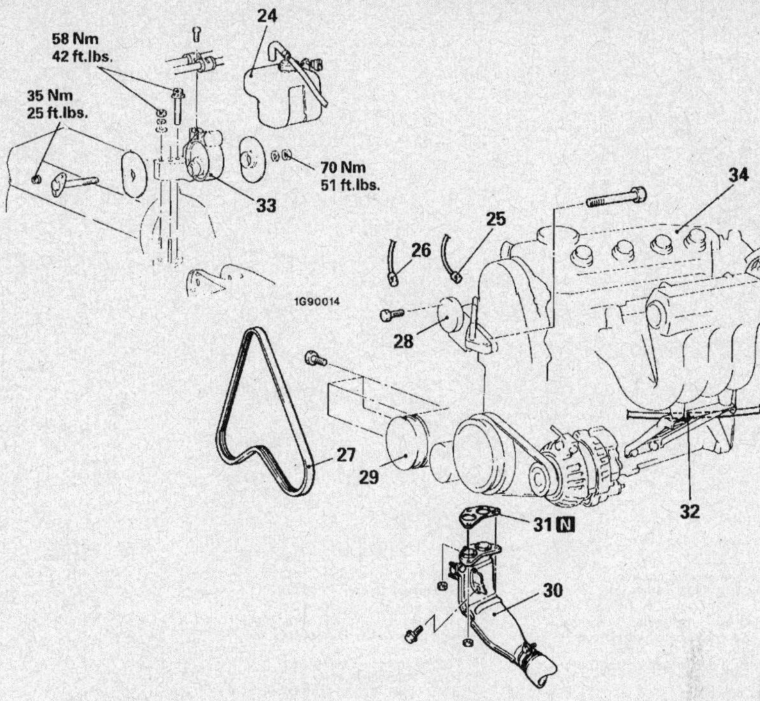

58 Nm
42 ft.lbs.
35 Nm
25 ft.lbs.
70 Nm
51 ft.lbs.
1G90014
24
33
34
25
26
28
27
29
31 N
32
30

Removal steps

24. Condense tank
25. Power steering pressure switch connector
26. Air conditioning compressor connector
27. V-ribbed belt
28. Power steering oil pump connection
29. Air conditioning compressor connection
30. Front exhaust pipe connection
31. Gasket
32. Starter and generator harness clamp
33. Engine mount bracket
34. Engine assembly

MT1069100102020X

Fig. 2 Engine replacement (Part 2 of 2)

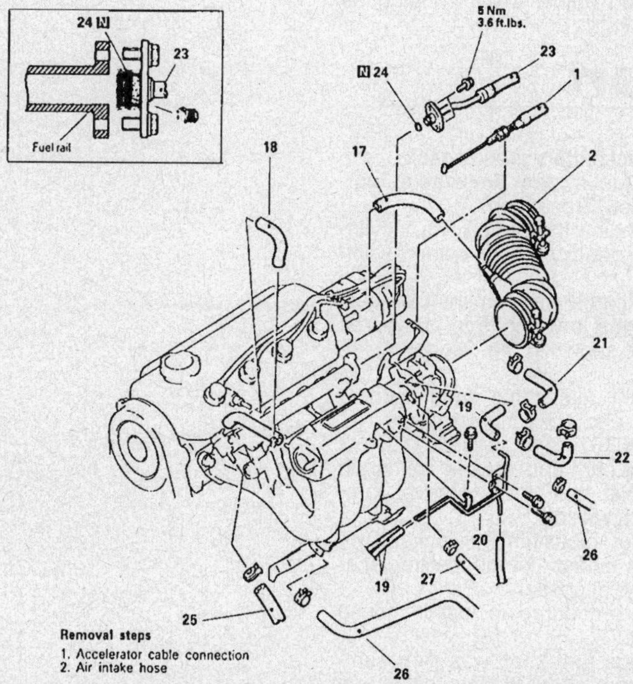

24 N
23
Fuel rail
5 Nm
3.6 ft.lbs.
N 24
Removal steps
1. Accelerator cable connection
2. Air intake hose

MT1059100016010X

Fig. 3 Intake manifold replacement (Part 1 of 2)

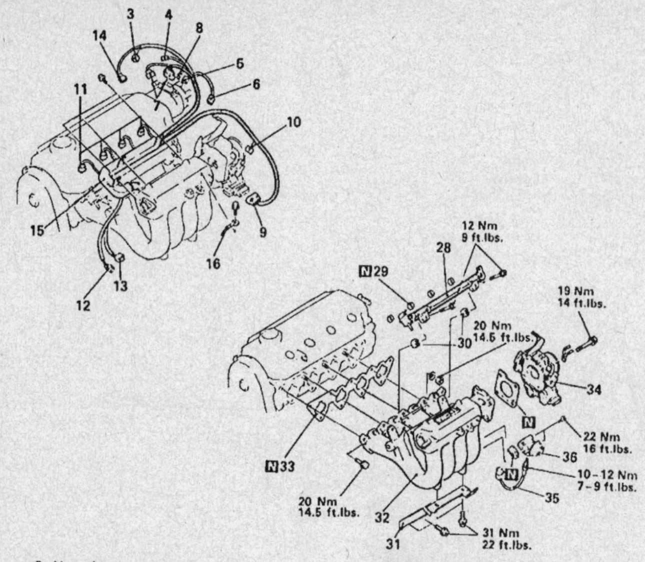
12 Nm
9 ft.lbs.
19 Nm
14 ft.lbs.
20 Nm
14.5 ft.lbs.
22 Nm
16 ft.lbs.
10-12 Nm
7-9 ft.lbs.
20 Nm
14.5 ft.lbs.
31 Nm
22 ft.lbs.

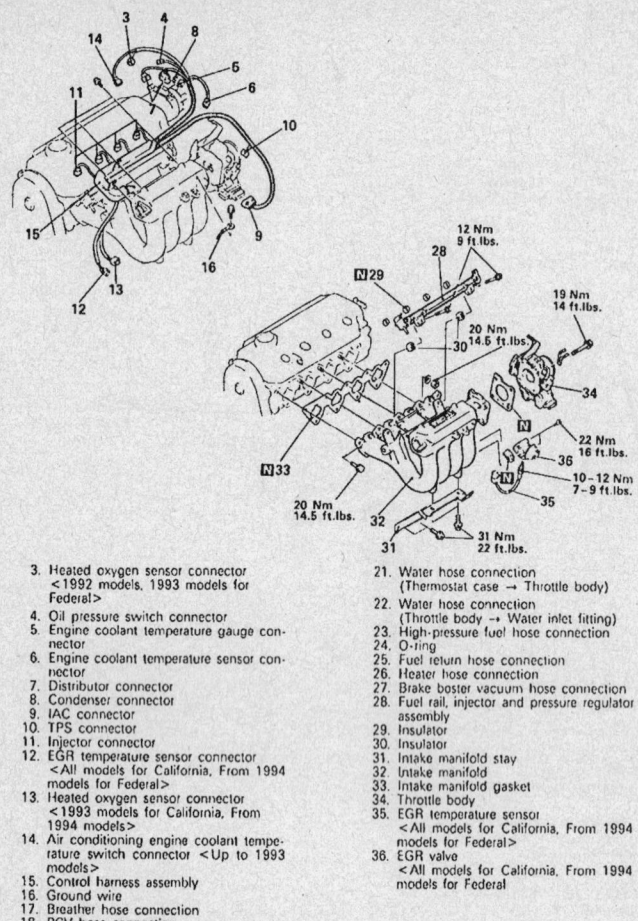

3. Heated oxygen sensor connector <1992 models, 1993 models for Federal>
4. Oil pressure switch connector
5. Engine coolant temperature gauge connector
6. Engine coolant temperature sensor connector
7. Distributor connector
8. Condenser connector
9. IAC connector
10. TPS connector
11. Injector connector
12. EGR temperature sensor connector <All models for California, From 1994 models for Federal>
13. Heated oxygen sensor connector <1993 models for California, From 1994 models>
14. Air conditioning engine coolant temperature switch connector <Up to 1993 models>
15. Control harness assembly
16. Ground wire
17. Breather hose connection
18. PCV hose connection
19. Vacuum hose connection
20. Vacuum pipe
21. Water hose connection (Thermostat case → Throttle body)
22. Water hose connection (Throttle body → Water inlet fitting)
23. High-pressure fuel hose connection
24. O-ring
25. Fuel return hose connection
26. Heater hose connection
27. Brake boster vacuum hose connection
28. Fuel rail, injector and pressure regulator assembly
29. Insulator
30. Insulator
31. Intake manifold stay
32. Intake manifold
33. Intake manifold gasket
34. Throttle body
35. EGR temperature sensor <All models for California, From 1994 models for Federal>
36. EGR valve <All models for California, From 1994 models for Federal

MT1059100016020X

Fig. 3 Intake manifold replacement (Part 2 of 2)

16. Check and adjust ignition timing as necessary.

CAMSHAFT

REPLACE

1. Disconnect battery ground cable.
2. Release fuel system pressure as outlined under "Precautions."
3. Rotate engine to position No. 1 cylinder at top dead center on compression stroke.
4. Remove camshaft, camshaft oil seal rocker arms and shafts in numbered sequence shown in **Fig. 20,** noting following:
   a. Prevent camshaft from turning using end yoke holder, tools No. MB990767 and MD998719, or equivalent, and loosen camshaft sprocket bolt, then remove camshaft sprocket.
   b. Do not disassemble rocker arm shafts unless component replacement is necessary.
5. Reverse procedure to install, noting following:
   a. If rocker arm shaft was disassembled, temporarily tighten rocker arm shaft bolt so all rocker arms on inlet side do not push valves. Install rocker arm shaft spring from above

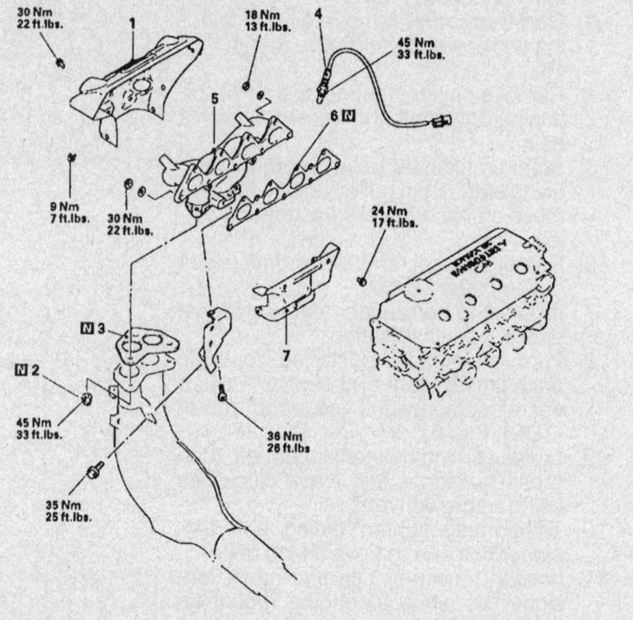
30 Nm
22 ft.lbs.
18 Nm
13 ft.lbs.
45 Nm
33 ft.lbs.
9 Nm
7 ft.lbs.
30 Nm
22 ft.lbs.
24 Nm
17 ft.lbs.
45 Nm
33 ft.lbs.
36 Nm
26 ft.lbs
35 Nm
25 ft.lbs.

Removal steps

1. Exhaust manifold cover A
2. Self-locking nut
3. Gasket
4. Oxygen sensor <Except vehicles for California since 1993>
5. Exhaust manifold
6. Exhaust manifold gasket
7. Exhaust manifold cover B <Except vehicles for California since 1993>

MT1079100008000X

Fig. 4 Exhaust manifold replacement

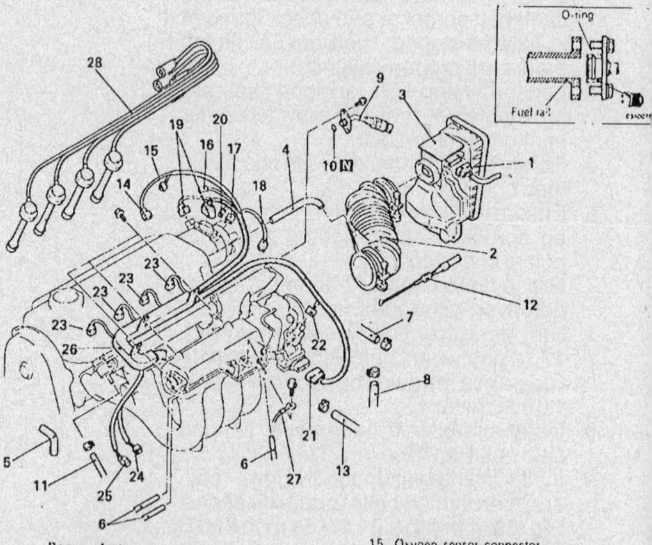
O-ring
Fuel rail

Removal steps

1. Volume air flow sensor connector
2. Air intake hose
3. Air cleaner case cover
4. Breather hose connection
5. PCV hose
6. Vacuum hose connection
7. Water hose connection (Thermostat case → throttle body)
8. Water hose connection (Throttle body → water inlet fitting)
9. Fuel high pressure hose connection
10. O-ring
11. Fuel return hose connection
12. Accelerator cable connection
13. Brake booster vacuum hose connection
14. Air conditioning engine coolant temperature switch connector <Up to 1993 models>
15. Oxygen sensor connector <1992 models, 1993 models for Federal>
16. Oil pressure switch connector
17. Water temperature gauge unit connector
18. Engine coolant temperature sensor connector
19. Distributor connector
20. Condenser connector
21. Idle air control connector
22. TPS connector
23. Injector connector
24. Oxygen sensor connector <1993 models for California, From 1994 models>
25. EGR temperature sensor connector <All models for California, From 1994 models for Federal>
26. Control harness assembly
27. Ground wire
28. Spark plug cable

MT1069100103010X

Fig. 5 Cylinder head replacement (Part 1 of 2)

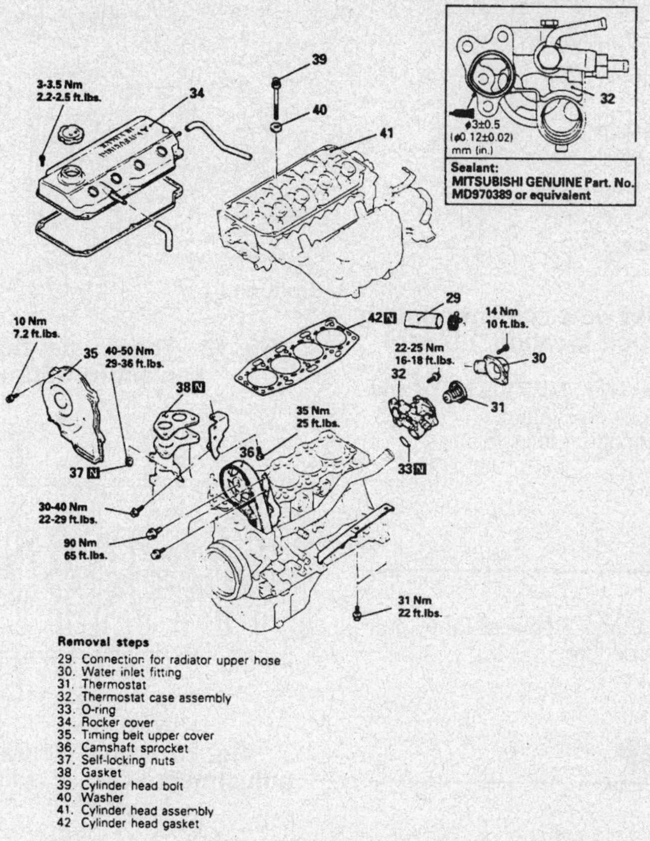
3-3.5 Nm
2.2-2.5 ft.lbs.
34
39
40
41
32
ϕ3±0.5
(ϕ0.12±0.02)
mm (in.)
Sealant:
MITSUBISHI GENUINE Part. No.
MD970389 or equivalent
29
42
14 Nm
10 ft.lbs.
10 Nm
7.2 ft.lbs.
35
40-50 Nm
29-36 ft.lbs.
22-25 Nm
16-18 ft.lbs.
30
32
38
31
35 Nm
25 ft.lbs.
36
33
37
30-40 Nm
22-29 ft.lbs.
90 Nm
65 ft.lbs.
31 Nm
22 ft.lbs.
Removal steps
29. Connection for radiator upper hose
30. Water inlet fitting
31. Thermostat
32. Thermostat case assembly
33. O-ring
34. Rocker cover
35. Timing belt upper cover
36. Camshaft sprocket
37. Self-locking nuts
38. Gasket
39. Cylinder head bolt
40. Washer
41. Cylinder head assembly
42. Cylinder head gasket
MT1069100103020X

Fig. 5 Cylinder head replacement (Part 2 of 2)

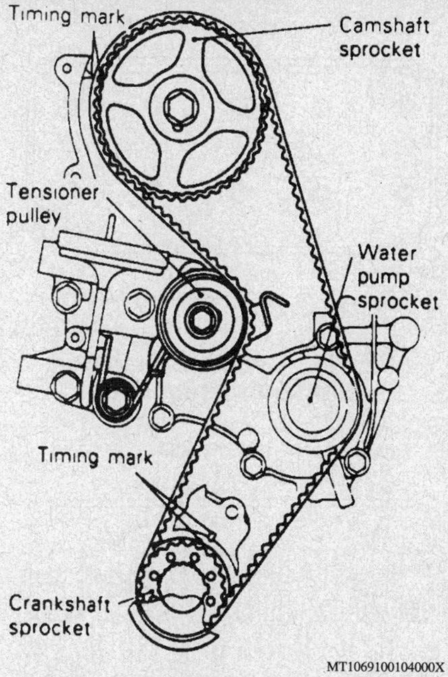
Timing mark
Camshaft sprocket
Tensioner pulley
Water pump sprocket
Timing mark
Crankshaft sprocket
MT1069100104000X

Fig. 6 Engine timing marks

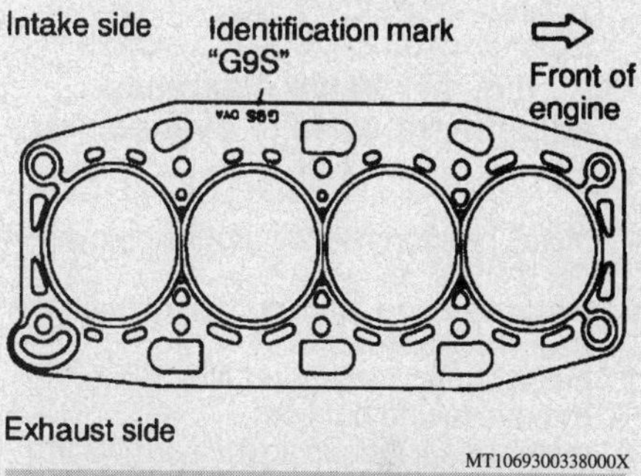
Intake side
Identification mark "G9S"
Front of engine
Exhaust side
MT1069300338000X

Fig. 9 Cylinder head gasket identification mark. 1.8L engine

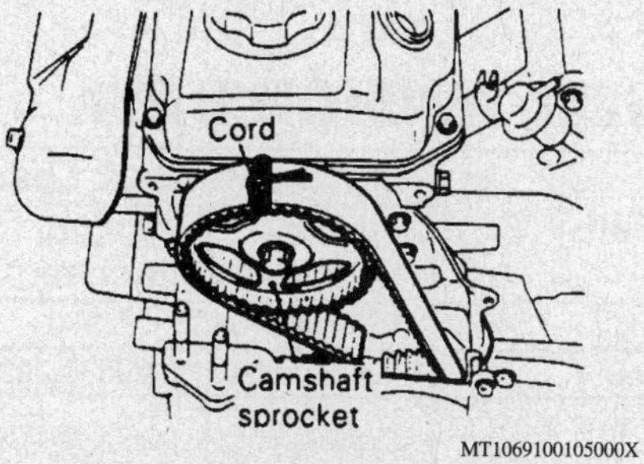
Cord
Camshaft sprocket
MT1069100105000X

Fig. 7 Camshaft sprocket secured position

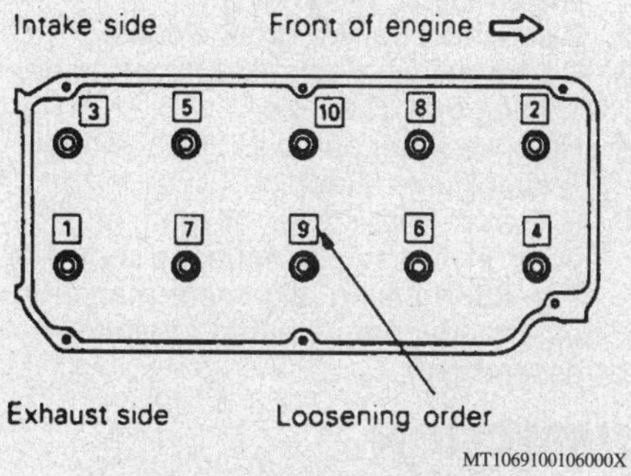
Intake side
Front of engine
3
5
10
8
2
1
7
9
6
4
Exhaust side
Loosening order
MT1069100106000X

Fig. 8 Cylinder head bolt loosening sequence

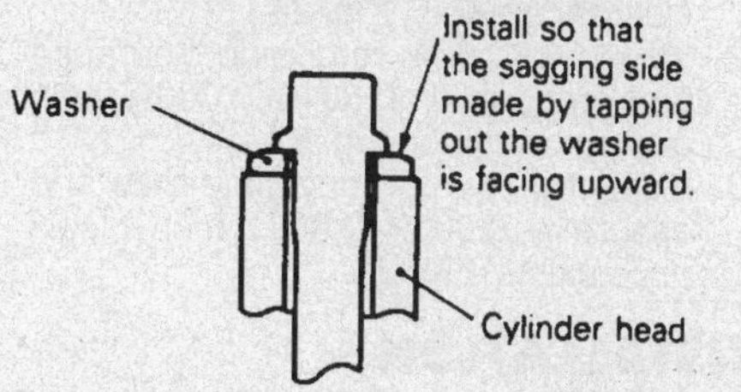
Washer
Install so that the sagging side made by tapping out the washer is facing upward.
Cylinder head
MT1069100107000X

Fig. 10 Cylinder head bolt washer installation

and position at right angle to plug guide, **Fig. 21.**

b. Tighten rocker arm shaft bolts to specification.
c. Using seal installation tool, No. MD998713-01, or equivalent, install camshaft seal.
d. Install distributor as outlined under "Distributor, Replace" in "Electrical" section.
e. Adjust timing belt tension as outlined under "Timing Belt, Replace."
f. Adjust valve clearance as outlined under "Valve Adjustment."

PISTON & ROD ASSEMBLY

1. Release fuel system pressure as outlined under "Precautions."
2. Disconnect battery ground cable.
3. Remove engine as outlined under "Engine, Replace."
4. Remove timing belt as outlined under "Timing Belt, Replace."
5. Remove water pump as outlined under "Water Pump, Replace."
6. Remove cylinder head as outlined under "Cylinder Head, Replace."
7. Remove oil pan as outlined under "Oil Pump, Replace."
8. Remove piston and connecting rod in numbered sequence shown in **Fig. 22,** marking large end of each connecting rod with cylinder number.
9. Reverse procedure to install, noting following:
   a. Arrange piston ring oil gaps and piston as shown in **Fig. 23.**
   b. Use suitable thread protectors on connection rod studs prior to installation.
   c. Mate each connecting rod marking with appropriate cylinder.
   d. Install connecting rod bearing cap on connecting rod.
   e. Coat threads lightly with oil.
   f. Install both nuts finger tight.
   g. Alternately tighten each nut to specifications.

MAIN & ROD BEARINGS

When servicing crankshaft bearings refer to **Fig. 24.**

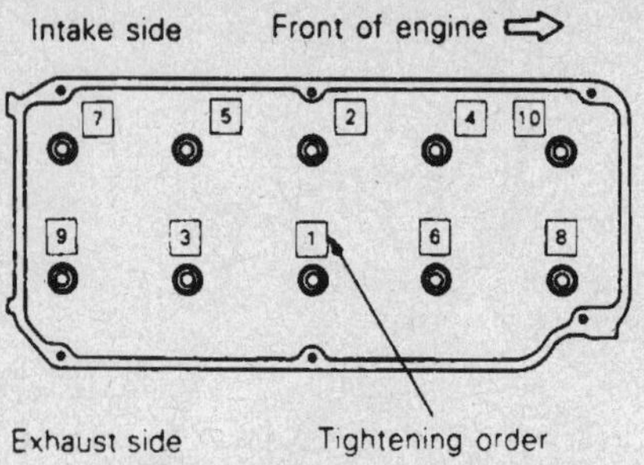
Intake side
Front of engine
7
5
2
4
10
9
3
1
6
8
Exhaust side
Tightening order

MT1069100108000X

Fig. 11 Cylinder head bolt tightening sequence

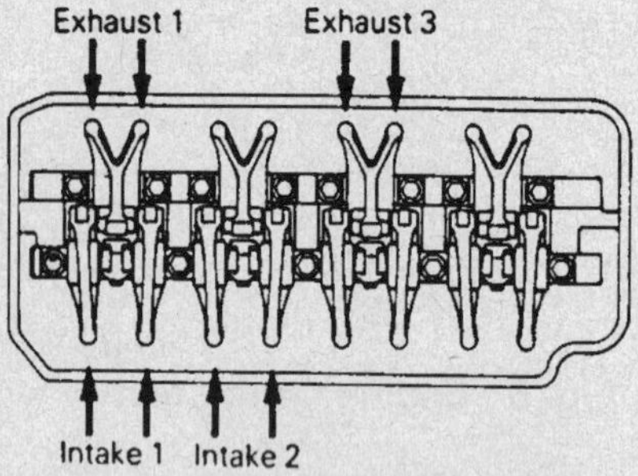
Exhaust 1
Exhaust 3
Intake 1
Intake 2

MT1069100111000X

Fig. 14 Valve clearance adjustment w/No. 1 cylinder at TDC

1. Install bearing with oil groove on cylinder block side.
2. Install bearing with no oil groove on bearing cap side.
3. Install thrust bearing to No. 3 bearing (groove facing outside).
4. Install bearing caps so their arrows are positioned toward timing belt side.
5. Measure each bearing cap bolt and ensure bolt is less than 2.79 inches long.
6. Tighten bearing cap bolts to specification.
7. Ensure crankshaft turns freely and endplay is 0.0020–0.0098 inch.
8. Replace rear main oil seal as outlined under "Crankshaft Seal, Replace."

CRANKSHAFT SEAL

REPLACE

REAR

1. Remove transaxle assembly as outlined under "Transaxle, Replace" in "Clutch & Manual Transaxle" section for models with manual transaxle or in "Automatic Transaxle" unit repair section for models with automatic transaxle.
2. Remove flywheel or driveplate from rear of crankshaft.
3. Remove rear engine place and inspection cover.
4. Remove rear main oil seal case and oil seal.
5. Drive out old oil seal using suitable seal removal tool.
6. Install rear main oil seal using seal in-

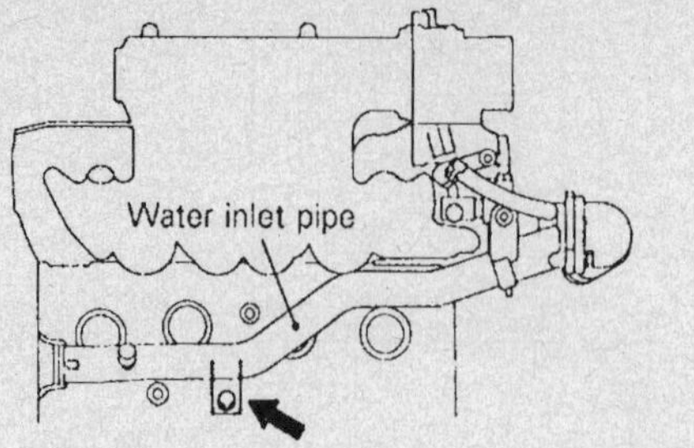
Water inlet pipe

MT1069100109000X

Fig. 12 Inlet water pipe mounting bolt location

staller tools, No. MB990938-01 and MD998776, or equivalent.

7. Reverse procedure to install.

OIL PAN

REPLACE

Refer to "Oil Pump, Replace" for oil pan replacement procedure.

OIL PUMP

REPLACE

REMOVAL

1. Release fuel system pressure as outlined under "Precautions."
2. Disconnect battery ground cable.
3. Remove timing belt as outlined under "Timing Belt, Replace."
4. Remove water pump as outlined under "Water Pump, Replace."
5. Remove front case, oil pan and oil pump in numbered sequence shown in **Fig. 25,** marking alignment marks on outer and inner oil pump rotors for reassembly.

INSPECTION

1. Inspect oil pump rotor tip clearance and ensure a 0.0024–0.0071 inch clearance exists, **Fig. 26.**
2. Inspect oil pump rotor side clearance and ensure a 0.0016–0.0039 inch clearance exists, **Fig. 27.**
3. Inspect oil pump body clearance and ensure a 0.0039–0.0071 inch clearance exists, **Fig. 28.**

INSTALLATION

Reverse numbered sequence shown in **Fig. 25** to install, noting following:

1. Apply engine oil to oil pump rotors.
2. Install oil pump rotors into pump body, aligning marks made during disassembly.
3. Apply sealant to oil pump case cover.
4. Install seal into oil pump case using seal installer tool, No. MD998717-01, or equivalent.

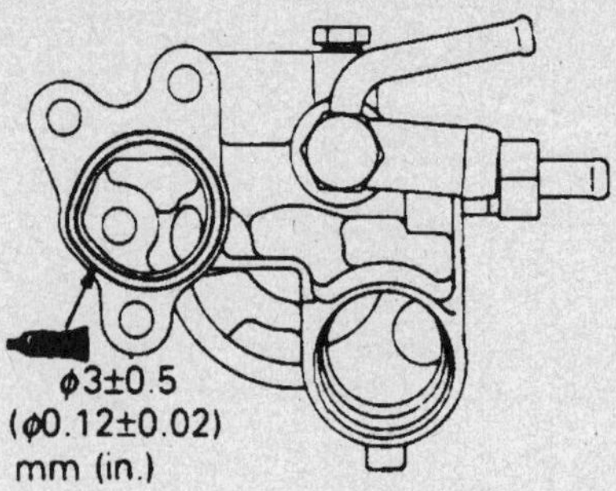
ϕ3±0.5
(ϕ0.12±0.02)
mm (in.)

MT1069100110000X

Fig. 13 Thermostat housing sealant location

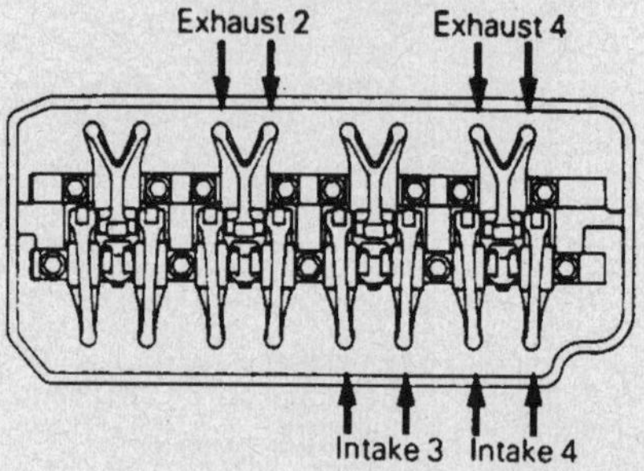
Exhaust 2
Exhaust 4
Intake 3
Intake 4

MT1069100112000X

Fig. 15 Valve clearance adjustment w/No. 1 cylinder at BDC

5. Apply a 0.16 inch diameter bead of sealant to oil pan flange as shown, **Fig. 29.**

BELT TENSION DATA

Belt	Deflection At 22 Lbs.	
	New, Inches	Used, Inches①
Alt.	0.280–0.340	0.370
A/C	0.217–0.236	0.268–0.299
Power Steering	0.295–0.354	0.374–0.453

① — Belt used for 5 minutes or more.

COOLING SYSTEM BLEED

1. Remove air bleed bolt from on top of thermostat housing, **Fig. 30.**
2. Fill coolant system through air bleed bolt hole until full.
3. Install air bleed bolt.
4. Slowly pour coolant into radiator until radiator is full and fill reservoir tank to FULL line.
5. Install radiator cap, start engine and allow to idle.
6. After thermostat has opened, perform 3000 RPM racing three times.
7. Stop engine and allow to cool completely. **Failure to allow engine to fully cool may result in personal injury.**
8. Open radiator cap, if coolant level has dropped repeat Steps 4 through 8.

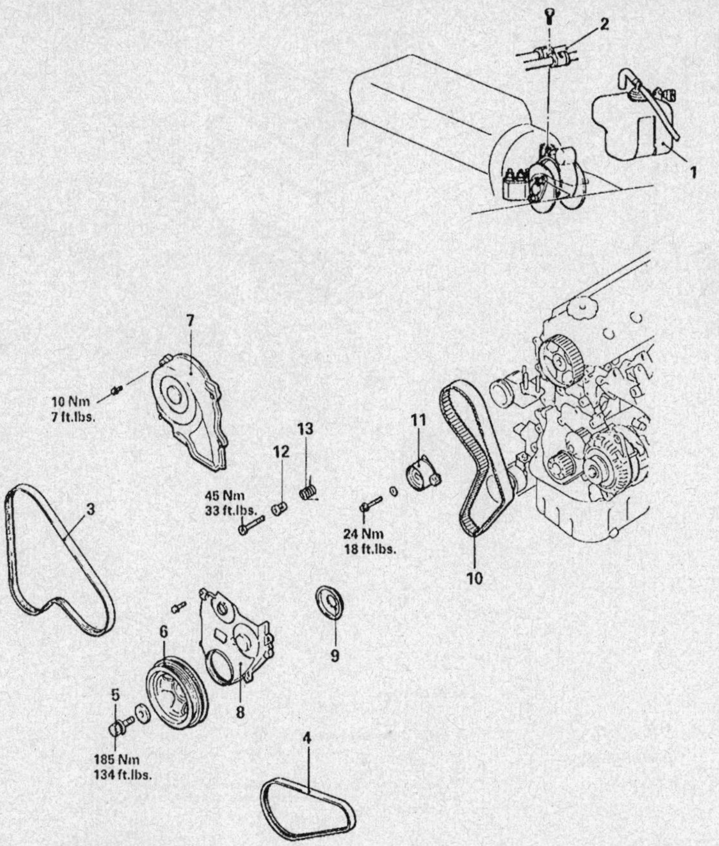
10 Nm
7 ft.lbs.
45 Nm
33 ft.lbs.
24 Nm
18 ft.lbs.
185 Nm
134 ft.lbs.

Removal steps

1. Condense tank
2. Clamp section of Air conditioner and Power steering hose
3. Drive belt (Power steering, Air conditioner)
4. Drive belt (Alternator)
5. Crankshaft bolt
6. Crankshaft pulley
7. Timing belt upper cover
8. Timing belt lower cover
9. Flange
- Adjustment of timing belt tension
10. Timing belt
11. Timing belt tensioner
12. Tensioner spacer
13. Tensioner spring

MT1069100113000X

Fig. 16 Exploded view of timing belt

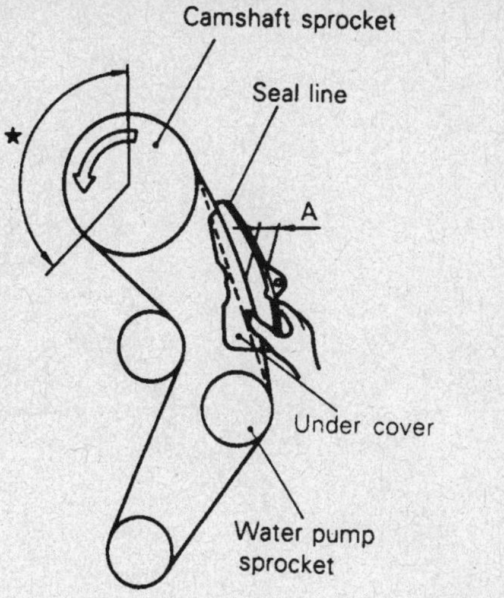
Camshaft sprocket
Seal line
A
Under cover
Water pump
sprocket

MT1069100115000X

Fig. 17 Timing belt tension inspection

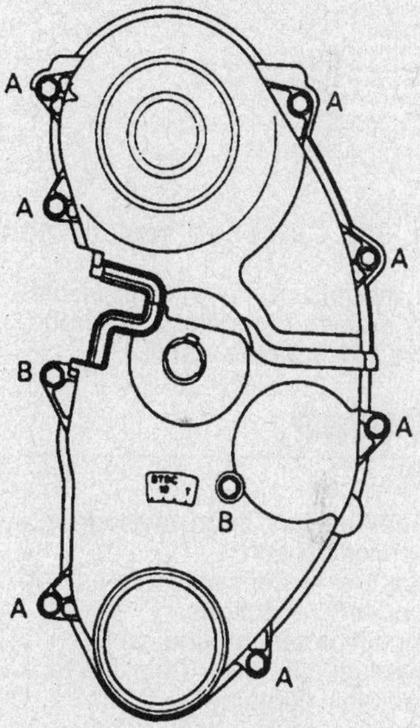
A
B

MT1069100117000X

Fig. 19 Timing belt cover bolt locations

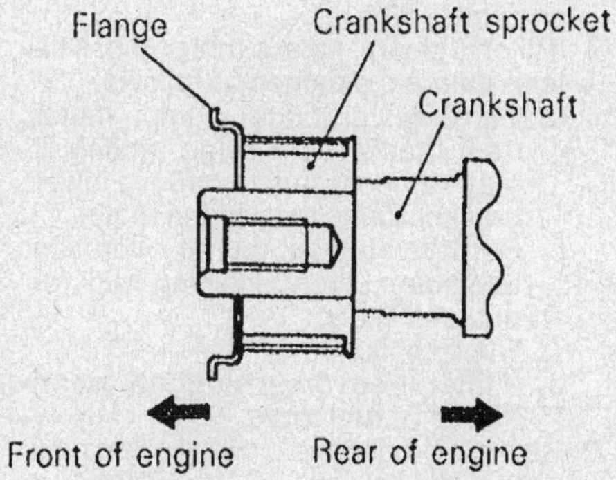
Flange
Crankshaft sprocket
Crankshaft
Front of engine
Rear of engine

MT1069100116000X

Fig. 18 Flange installation

9. Replace radiator cap and check for coolant system leaks.

THERMOSTAT

REPLACE

1. Disconnect battery ground cable.
2. Drain coolant into an approved container.
3. Disconnect upper radiator hose from thermostat housing.
4. Remove thermostat housing.
5. Install thermostat with jiggle valve at top, **Fig. 31.**
6. Reverse procedure to install, bleeding coolant system after installation is complete.

WATER PUMP

REPLACE

1. Disconnect battery ground cable.
2. Remove timing belt as outlined under "Timing Belt, Replace."
3. Remove timing belt rear cover.
4. Remove water pump mounting bolts, then water pump, **Fig. 32.**
5. Reverse procedure to install, noting bolt length position shown in **Fig. 33.**

RADIATOR

REPLACE

1. Drain engine coolant, then remove drain plug and radiator cap.
2. Remove overflow tube and reserve tank, then upper and lower radiator hoses.
3. **On models equipped with automatic transaxle,** remove ATF cooler hose, then plug hose and radiator nipple.
4. **On models equipped with air conditioning,** disconnect condenser fan connector.
5. **On all models,** disconnect radiator fan connector, then remove upper insulator and radiator assembly.
6. Remove resistor.
7. **On models equipped with air conditioning,** remove condenser fan motor assembly.
8. **On 1993 models,** disconnect engine coolant temperature switch connector.
9. **On all models,** remove radiator fan motor assembly.
10. **On 1993 models,** remove engine coolant temperature switch.

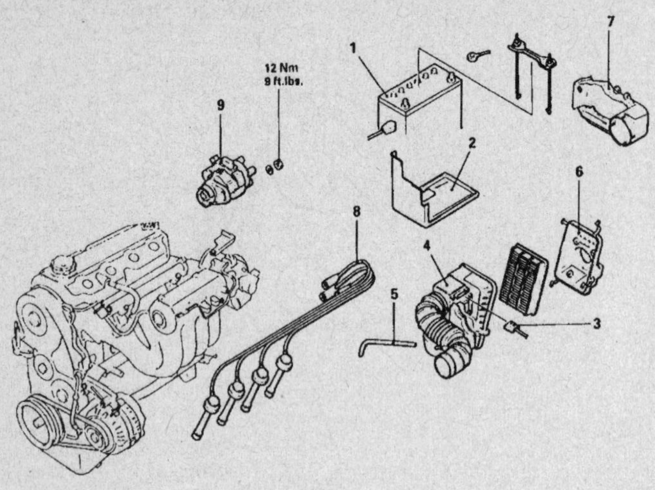
12 Nm
9 ft.lbs.
1
2
3
4
5
6
7
8
9

Removal steps
1. Battery
2. Battery cover
3. Volume air flow sensor connector
4. Air cleaner case cover assembly
5. Breather hose connection
6. Air cleaner case
7. Air intake duct
8. Spark plug cable
9. Distributor

MT1069100118010X

Fig. 20 Camshaft replacement (Part 1 of 2)

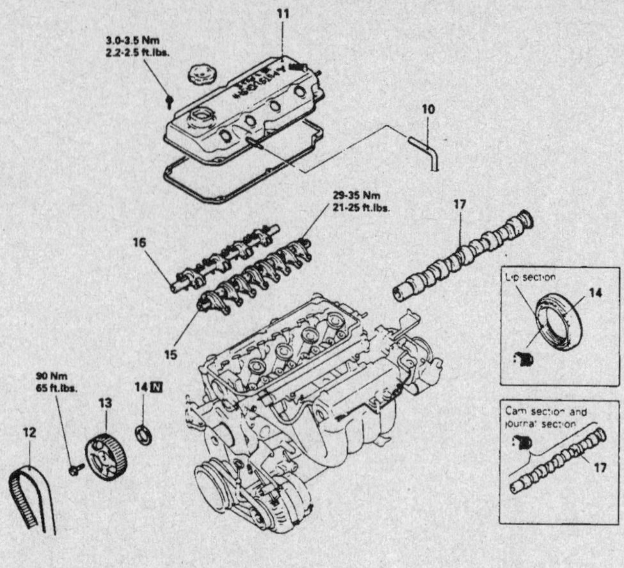
3.0-3.5 Nm
2.2-2.5 ft.lbs.
29-35 Nm
21-25 ft.lbs.
90 Nm
65 ft.lbs.
Lip section
Cam section and journal section
10
11
12
13
14
15
16
17

Removal steps
10. PCV hose connection
11. Rocker cover
- Valve clearance adjustment
12. Timing belt
13. Camshaft sprocket
14. Camshaft oil seal
15. Rocker arms and rocker arm shaft assembly (Intake side)
16. Rocker arms and rocker arm shaft assembly (Exhaust side)
17. Camshaft

MT1069100118020X

Fig. 20 Camshaft replacement (Part 2 of 2)

11. **On all models,** remove lower insulator, fan, radiator fan motor and shroud.
12. Reverse procedure to install.

FUEL PUMP

REPLACE

This procedure has been revised by a technical service bulletin.

1. Release fuel system pressure as outlined under "Precautions."
2. Disconnect battery ground cable.
3. Remove fuel cap, then drain fuel tank into a suitable container.
4. Disconnect return, high pressure, vapor and filler hoses.
5. Disconnect fuel gauge unit and electric fuel pump electrical connections.
6. **On AWD models,** remove rear propeller shaft.
7. **On all models,** support fuel tank and remove fuel tank supports.
8. Lower fuel tank from vehicle.
9. Remove fuel pump from fuel tank.
10. Reverse procedure to install.

FUEL FILTER

REPLACE

This procedure has been revised by a technical service bulletin.

1. Release fuel system pressure as outlined under "Precautions."
2. Remove air cleaner and intake hose.
3. Holding fuel filter with a spanner, remove eye bolt and high-pressure fuel hose. **As there will be some pressure remaining in fuel pipe line, cover it with a rag to prevent fuel from spraying out.**

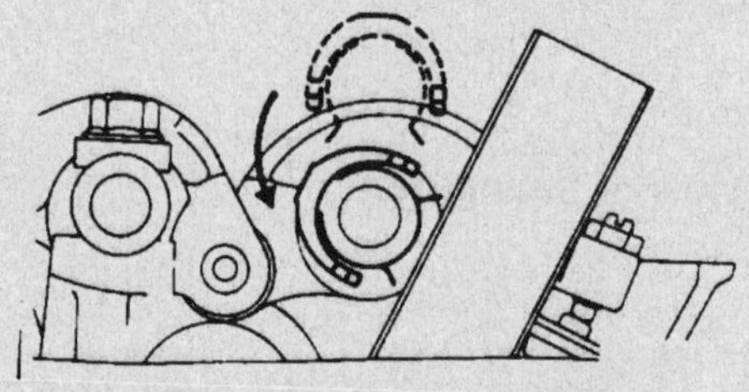

MT1069100120000X

Fig. 21 Rocker shaft spring installation

4. Loosen flare nut then disconnect fuel main pipe connection.
5. Remove fuel filter, **Figs. 34 and 35.**
6. Reverse procedure to install.

TECHNICAL SERVICE BULLETINS

FUEL STARVATION

Fuel starvation can occur when in-tank fuel filter is clogged, typically by contaminated fuel.

To correct problem, proceed as follows:

1. Activate fuel pump with scan tool, then measure pump's supply voltage.
2. If voltage is less than 8 volts, inspect and repair fuel pump wiring harness.
3. If voltage is 8 volts or more, check system fuel pressure.
4. If system fuel pressure is within specifications, check system for other starvation problems. Specification is 38 psi at curb idle with fuel pressure regulator vacuum hose attached and 47–50 psi with hose disconnected.
5. If fuel system pressure is not within specifications, remove fuel pump as described in "Fuel Pump, Replace" and check filter.
6. If filter is clean, replace fuel pump. If filter is clogged, proceed as follows:
   a. Carefully dislodge pump motor from bracket. On some models it may be necessary to remove lower bracket clamp to dislodge motor.
   b. Remove rubber pump vibration dampener, then retaining clip (or nut) and filter.
   c. Replace filter.
   d. **If filter is severely clogged, clean inside of fuel tank.**
7. Reverse procedure to install using new gasket.

IDLE VIBRATION

Some models (mostly equipped with automatic transaxles) may vibrate excessively at idle.

Radiator may be transmitting engine vibration through frame because mounting brackets are not centered on posts. To correct problem, proceed as follows:

1. Examine upper radiator mounting brackets. Brackets should be centered on post and radiator should move freely.
2. If brackets are not center, remove upper brackets and ensure bottom

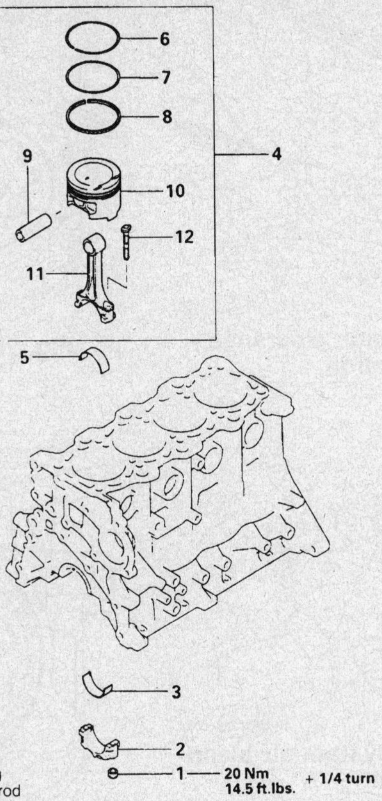

6
7
8
9
10
4
12
11
5
3
2
1
20 Nm
14.5 ft.lbs.
+ 1/4 turn

Removal steps

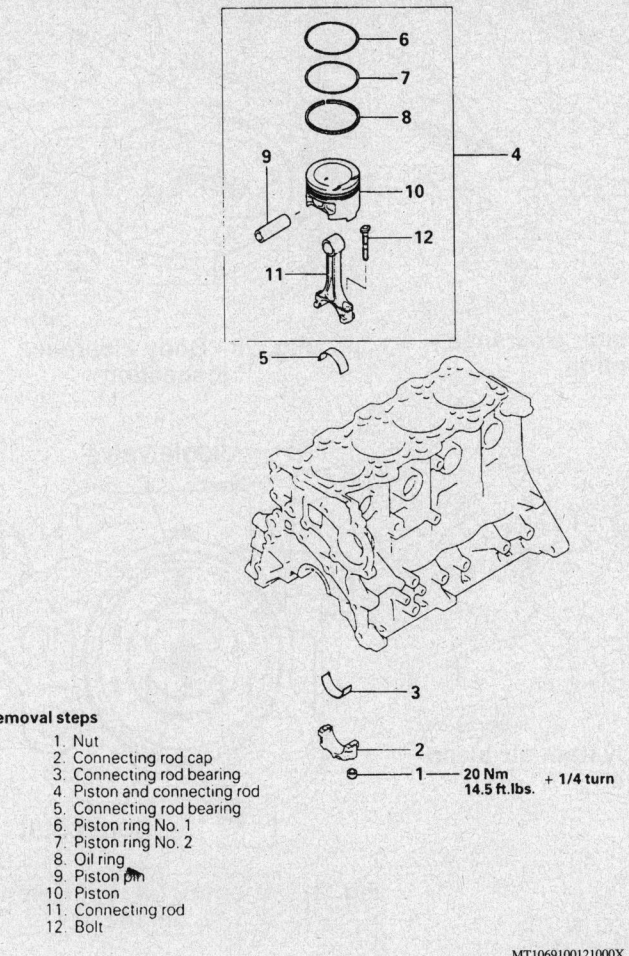

1. Nut
2. Connecting rod cap
3. Connecting rod bearing
4. Piston and connecting rod
5. Connecting rod bearing
6. Piston ring No. 1
7. Piston ring No. 2
8. Oil ring
9. Piston pin
10. Piston
11. Connecting rod
12. Bolt

MT1069100121000X

Fig. 22 Exploded view of piston & connecting rod

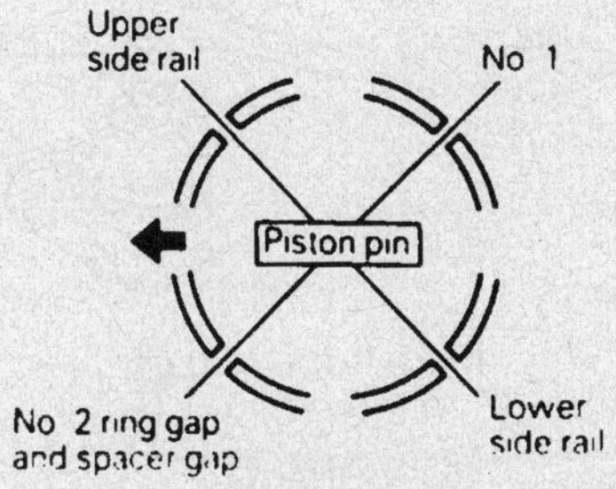

Upper
side rail
No 1
Piston pin
No 2 ring gap
and spacer gap
Lower
side rail

MT1069100122000X

Fig. 23 Piston pin & ring installation

mounting posts are seating in lower brackets.

3. Center upper brackets over posts and tighten bolts to specifications.
4. Measure clearance between upper brackets and radiator top. Standard clearance is .0394 inch or more.

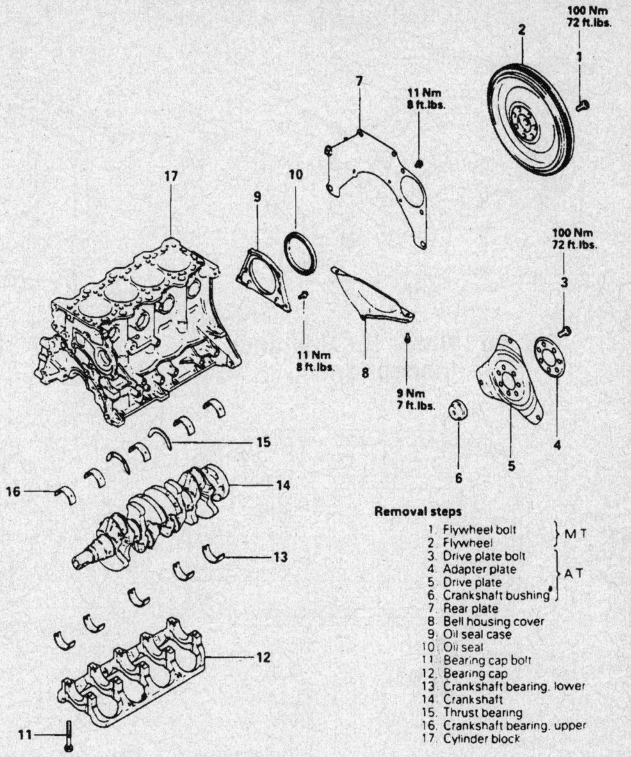

100 Nm
72 ft.lbs.
2
1
7
11 Nm
8 ft.lbs.
17
10
9
100 Nm
72 ft.lbs.
3
11 Nm
8 ft.lbs.
8
9 Nm
7 ft.lbs.
15
16
14
6
5
4
13
12
11

Removal steps

1. Flywheel bolt } M T
2. Flywheel
3. Drive plate bolt } A T
4. Adapter plate
5. Drive plate
6. Crankshaft bushing
7. Rear plate
8. Bell housing cover
9. Oil seal case
10. Oil seal
11. Bearing cap bolt
12. Bearing cap
13. Crankshaft bearing, lower
14. Crankshaft
15. Thrust bearing
16. Crankshaft bearing, upper
17. Cylinder block

MT1069100123000X

Fig. 24 Exploded view of crankshaft

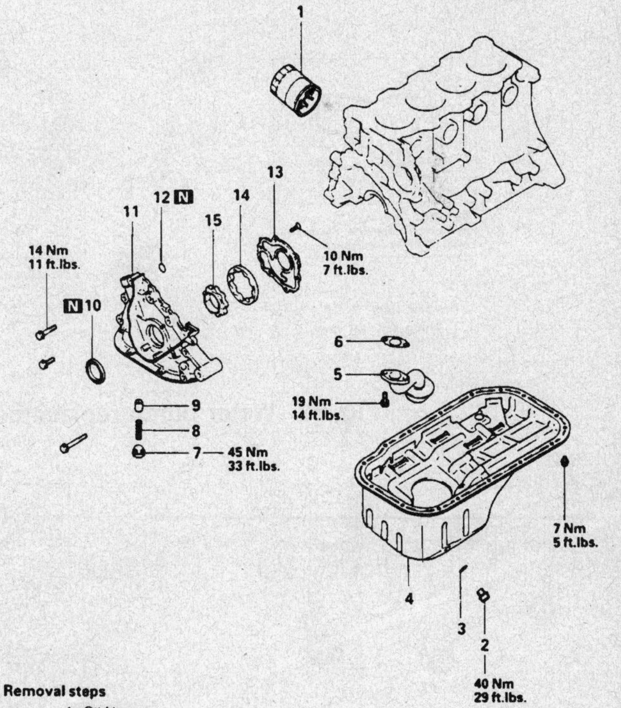

1
13
12 N
14
11
15
14 Nm
11 ft.lbs.
10 Nm
7 ft.lbs.
N 10
6
5
19 Nm
14 ft.lbs.
9
8
7
45 Nm
33 ft.lbs.
7 Nm
5 ft.lbs.
4
3
2
40 Nm
29 ft.lbs.

Removal steps

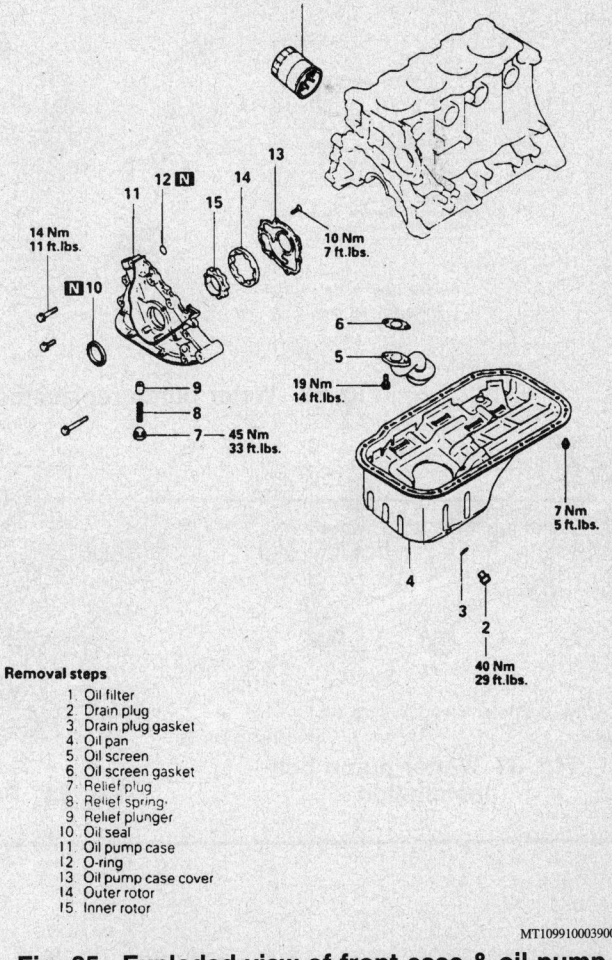

1. Oil filter
2. Drain plug
3. Drain plug gasket
4. Oil pan
5. Oil screen
6. Oil screen gasket
7. Relief plug
8. Relief spring
9. Relief plunger
10. Oil seal
11. Oil pump case
12. O-ring
13. Oil pump case cover
14. Outer rotor
15. Inner rotor

MT1099100039000X

Fig. 25 Exploded view of front case & oil pump

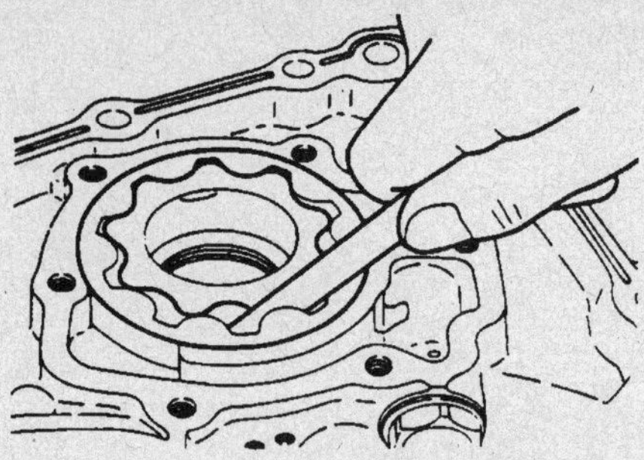
MT1099100040000X

Fig. 26 Rotor tip clearance inspection

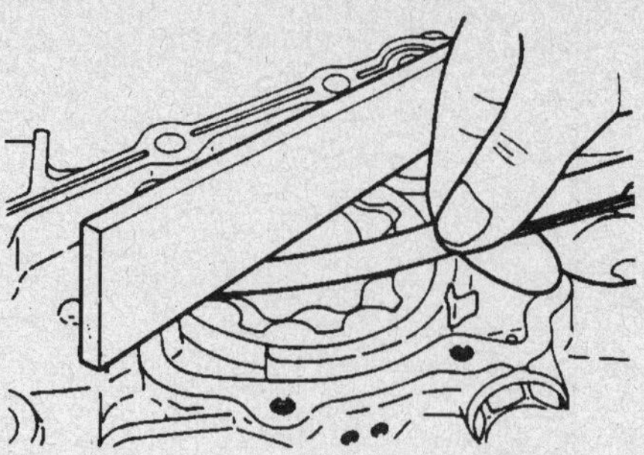
MT1099100041000X

Fig. 27 Rotor side clearance inspection

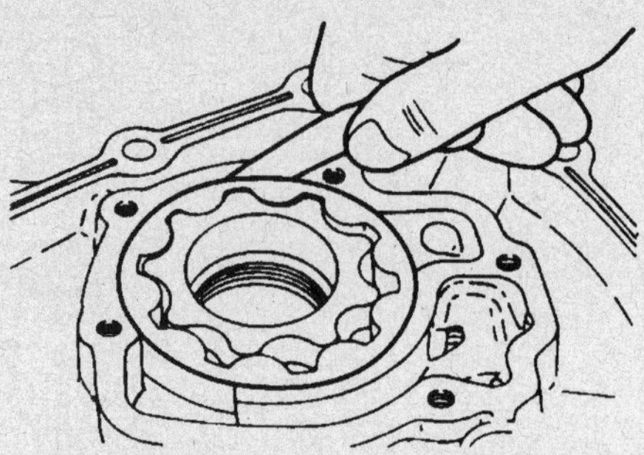
MT1099100042000X

Fig. 28 Body clearance inspection

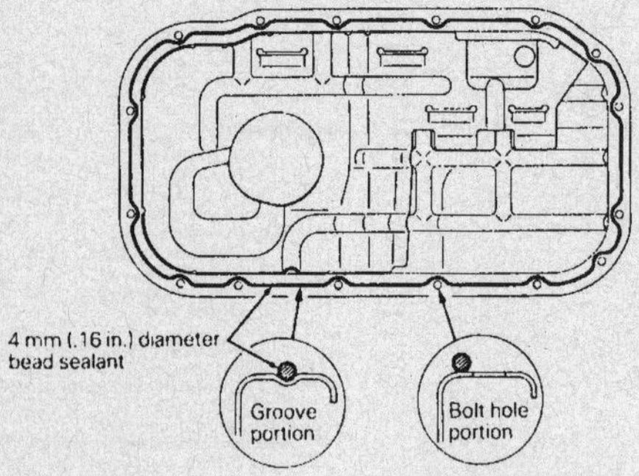
4 mm (.16 in.) diameter bead sealant
Groove portion
Bolt hole portion
MT1099100043000X

Fig. 29 Oil pan sealant location

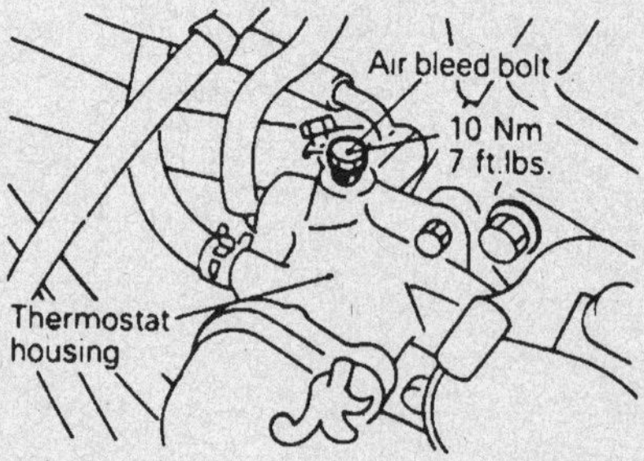
Air bleed bolt
10 Nm
7 ft.lbs.
Thermostat housing
MT1089100016000X

Fig. 30 Cooling system air bleed bolt

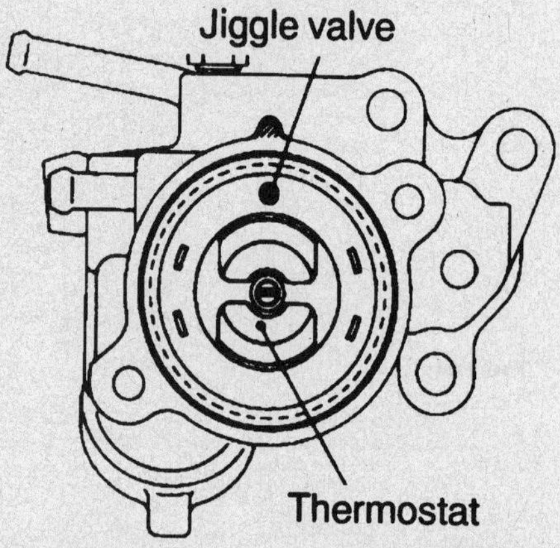
Jiggle valve
Thermostat
MT1069300341000X

Fig. 31 Thermostat replacement. 1.8L engine

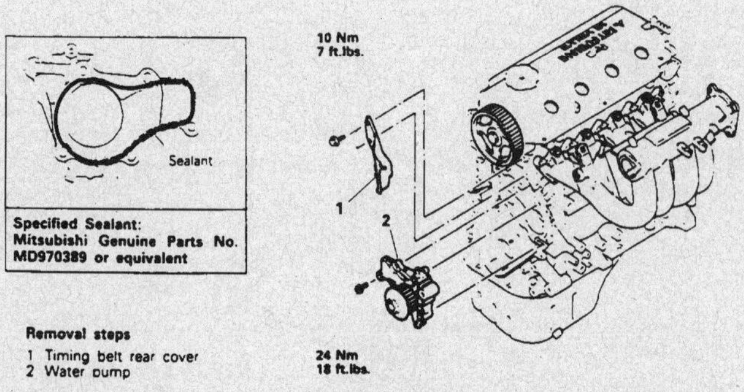
Sealant
Specified Sealant:
Mitsubishi Genuine Parts No. MD970389 or equivalent
10 Nm
7 ft.lbs.
1
2
Removal steps
1 Timing belt rear cover
2 Water pump
24 Nm
18 ft.lbs.
MT1089100014000X

Fig. 32 Water pump replacement

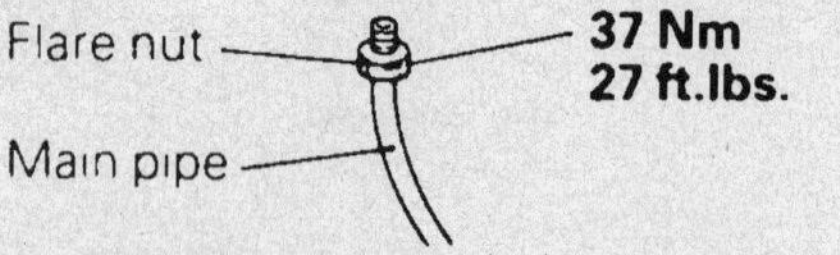
Eye bolt
30 Nm
22 ft.lbs.
Gasket
Spanner holding section
Flare nut
37 Nm
27 ft.lbs.
Main pipe
MT1029100011000X

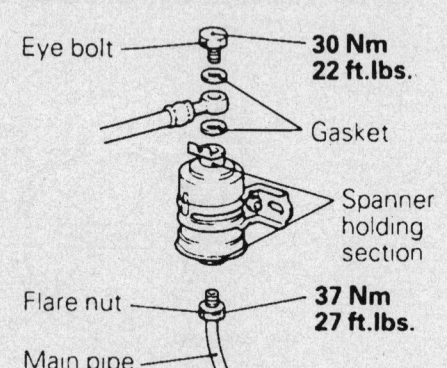

Fig. 35 Fuel filter installation

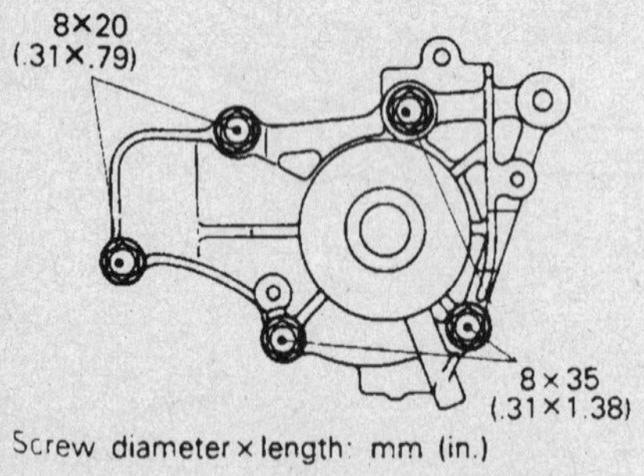
8×20
(.31×.79)
8×35
(.31×1.38)
Screw diameter×length: mm (in.)
MT1089100015000X

Fig. 33 Water pump bolt installation

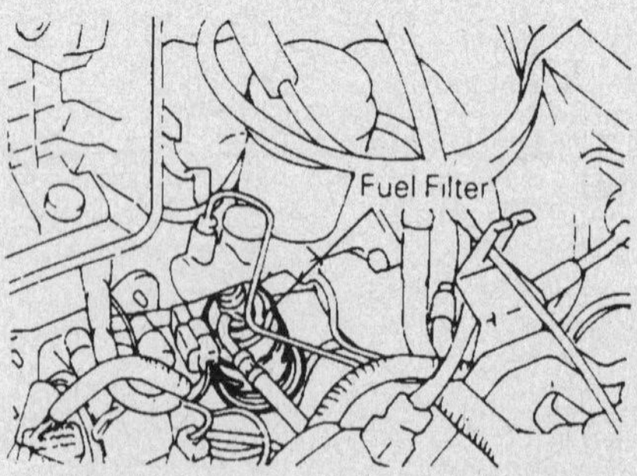
Fuel Filter
MT1029100010000X

Fig. 34 Fuel filter location

TIGHTENING SPECIFICATIONS

Year	Component	Torque/Ft. Lbs.
1993–96	Adjusting Screw Locknut	7
	Alternator Brace Bolt	17
	Alternator Brace Mounting Bolt	36
	Alternator Pivot Nut	33
	Bellhousing Cover Mounting Bolt	7
	Camshaft Sprocket Bolt	65
	Connecting Rod Cap Nut	②
	Crankshaft Bearing Cap Bolt	③
	Crankshaft Bolt	134
	Cylinder Head Bolt	①
	Distributor Mounting Nut	9
	Driveplate Bolt	72
	EGR Temperature Sensor (California)	8
	EGR Valve Mounting Bolt (California)	9
	Engine Coolant Temperature Gauge Unit	8
	Engine Coolant Temperature Sensor	22
	Engine Hanger Mounting Bolt	9
	Engine Support Bracket Left Mounting Bolt	36
	Exhaust Manifold Bracket Mounting Bolt	26
	Exhaust Manifold Cover "A" Mounting Bolt	22
	Exhaust Manifold Cover "B" Mounting Bolt	17
	Exhaust Manifold Mounting Nut	22
	Flywheel Bolt	72
	Fuel Delivery Pipe Mounting Bolt	9
	Fuel High Pressure Hose Union	25
	Fuel Pressure Regulator Bolt	7
	Fuel Pump Nut	1.8
	Fuel Tank Drain Bolt	4
	Fuel Tank Mounting Nut	17
	Intake Manifold Mounting Bolt	14.5
	Intake Manifold Mounting Nut	14.5
	Intake Manifold Stay Mounting Bolt	22
	Oil Drain Plug	29
	Oil Level Gauge Guide Mounting Bolt	8
	Oil Pan Mounting Bolt	5
	Oil Pressure Switch	7
	Oil Pump Case Mounting Bolt	11
	Oil Screen	14
	Oil Seal Case Mounting Bolt	8
	Oxygen Sensor	33
	Rear Plate Mounting Bolt	8
	Relief Plug	35
	Rocker Arm Shaft Mounting Bolt	23
	Rocker Cover Mounting Bolt	2.4
	Spark Plug	18
	Thermostat Housing Mounting Bolt	18
	Throttle Body Mounting Bolt	14
	Throttle Position Sensor Bolt	1.4
	Timing Belt Cover Mounting Bolt	7
	Timing Belt Tensioner Bolt	18

Continued

TIGHTENING SPECIFICATIONS—Continued

Year	Component	Torque/Ft. Lbs.
1993–96	Timing Belt Tensioner Spring Bolt	33
	Water Outlet Fitting Mounting Bolt	14
	Water Pipe Mounting Bolt	10
	Water Pump Mounting Bolt	18

① — Refer to "Cylinder Head, Replace" for procedure.
② — 14.5 ft. lbs. plus 90° (1/4 turn).
③ — 18 ft. lbs. plus 90° (1/4 turn).

2.4L Engine

NOTE: On Air Bag Equipped Models, Refer To "Air Bag System Precautions" Located In Front Of This Manual For System Disarming & Arming Procedures.

NOTE: Prior To Performing Any Service Operations Listed In This Section, Consult The "Technical Service Bulletins" Section For Related Information.

INDEX

	Page No.
Balance Shaft Belt, Replace	25-25
8–Valve Engine	25-25
16–Valve Engine	25-26
Belt Tension Data	25-30
Camshaft, Replace	25-25
Compression Pressure	25-18
Cooling System Bleed	25-30
Cylinder Head, Replace	25-20
Engine Rebuilding Specifications	29-1
Engine, Replace	25-19
Exhaust Manifold, Replace	25-20
Front Cover, Replace	25-23
Fuel Filter, Replace	25-31
Fuel Pump, Replace	25-31
Intake Manifold, Replace	25-20
Main & Rod Bearings	25-28
Oil Pan, Replace	25-29
Oil Pump, Replace	25-29
Inspection	25-29
Installation	25-30
Removal	25-29
Piston & Rod Assembly	25-28
Replacement	25-28
Precautions	25-18
Air Bag Systems	25-18
Fuel System Pressure Relief	25-18
Radiator, Replace	25-31
Rocker Arms, Replace	25-21
Installation	25-22
Removal	25-21
Silent Shaft, Replace	25-28
Technical Service Bulletins	25-31
Fuel Starvation	25-31
Idle Vibration	25-31
Thermostat, Replace	25-30
Tightening Specifications	25-33
Timing Belt, Replace	25-23
8-Valve Engine	25-23
16-Valve Engine	25-24
Valve Adjustment	25-21
Valve Arrangement	25-20
Front To Rear	25-21
Valve Clearance Specifications	25-21
Water Pump, Replace	25-30

PRECAUTIONS

AIR BAG SYSTEMS

Refer to "Air Bag System Precautions" in front of this manual for system disarming and arming procedures.

FUEL SYSTEM PRESSURE RELIEF

1. Remove grommet below floor and disconnect fuel pump connector.
2. Start engine and allow engine to runout of fuel.
3. Crank engine two or three times to release remaining fuel pressure.
4. Place ignition switch to Off position.
5. After fuel system repairs are completed, connect fuel pump electrical connections.

Engine	Model	Year	Compression Pressure Minimum, psi
2.4L①	Expo	1993–96	119
2.4L②	Expo	1993–96	139

① — 8 Valve Engine. ② — 16 Valve Engine.

Fig. 1 Compression pressure chart

COMPRESSION PRESSURE

Ensure engine oil, starter motor and battery are in satisfactory condition. When checking compression, engine coolant should be at normal operating temperature, spark plugs should be removed and throttle valve should be wide open. For correct compression pressures at engine cranking speed, refer to compression pressure chart, **Fig. 1.** Difference between cylinders should not exceed 14 psi.

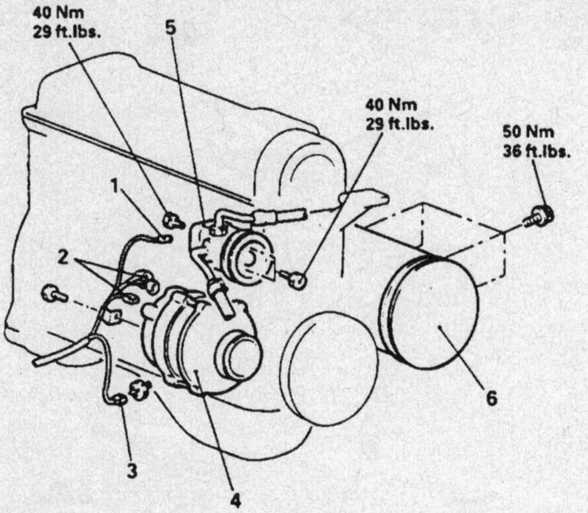
40 Nm
29 ft.lbs.
40 Nm
29 ft.lbs.
50 Nm
36 ft.lbs.

Removal steps

1. Power steering oil pressure switch connector
2. Alternator harness connector
3. Oil pressure switch connector
4. Alternator
5. Power steering oil pump connection
6. Air conditioner compressor connection (Vehicles with air conditioner)
   Removal of transaxle assembly

MT1069100124010X

Fig. 2 Engine assembly removal (Part 1 of 3). 8 valve engine

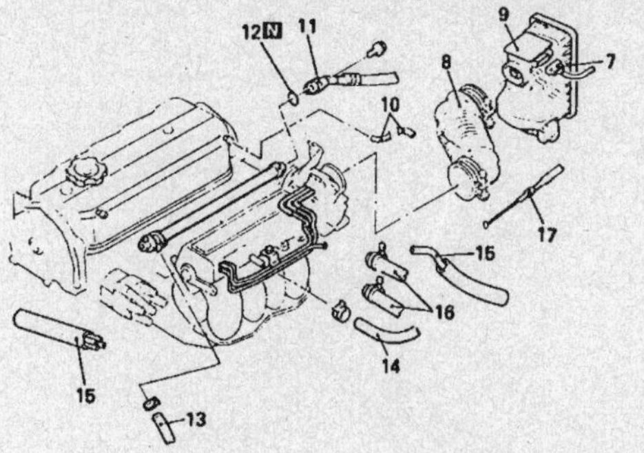

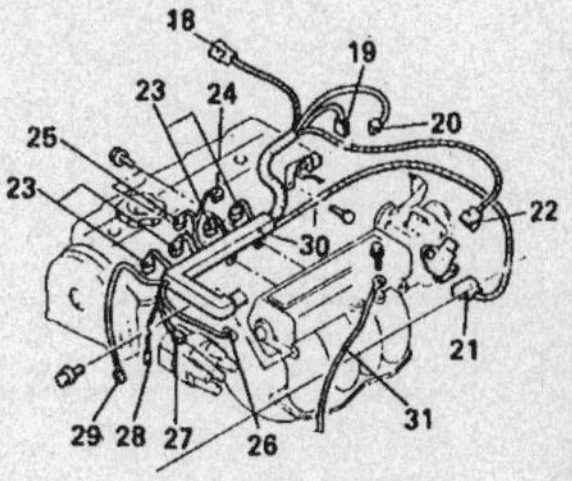

Removal steps

7. Volume air flow sensor connector
8. Air intake hose
9. Air cleaner case cover
10. Breather hose connection
11. Fuel hight pressure hose connection
12. O-ring
13. Fuel return hose connection
14. Brake booster vacuum hose connection
15. Vacuum hose connection
16. Heater hose connection
17. Accelerator cable connection
18. Oxygen sensor connector
19. Water temperature gauge unit connector
20. Engine coolant temperature sensor connector
21. Idle air control connector
22. TPS connector
23. Injector connector
24. EGR temperature sensor connector <California>
25. Ignition power transistor connector
26. Ignition coil connector
27. Distributor connector
28. Condenser connector
29. Air conditioning compressor connector
30. Control harness assembly
31. Ground wire

MT1069100124020X

Fig. 2 Engine assembly removal (Part 2 of 3). 8 valve engine

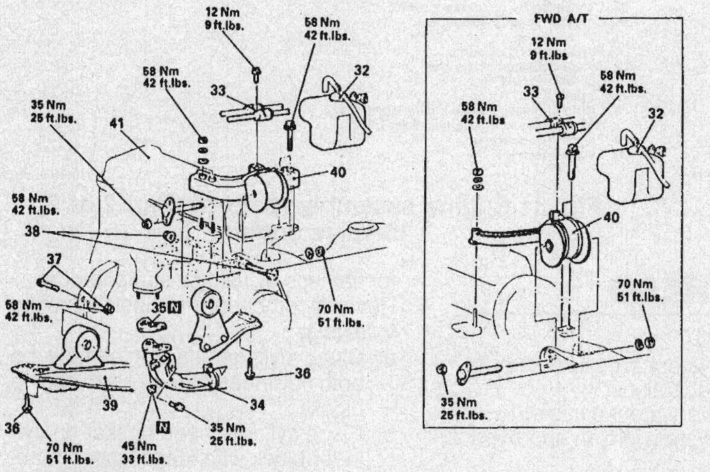
12 Nm
9 ft.lbs.
58 Nm
42 ft.lbs.
35 Nm
25 ft.lbs.
70 Nm
51 ft.lbs.
45 Nm
33 ft.lbs.
FWD A/T

Removal steps

32. Condense tank
33. Power steering hose and air conditioning hose clamp part
34. Front exhaust pipe connection
35. Gasket
36. Center member mounting bolt <FWD>
37. Front roll stopper connection <FWD>
38. Rear roll stopper connection <FWD>
39. Center member assembly
40. Engine mount bracket
41. Engine assembly

MT1069100124030X

Fig. 2 Engine assembly removal (Part 3 of 3). 8-valve engine

ENGINE

REPLACE

1. Release fuel system pressure as outlined under "Precautions."
2. Disconnect battery ground cable.
3. Mark hood hinge bolt location on hood, then remove hood.
4. Drain cooling system into a suitable container.
5. Remove radiator assembly.
6. **On models with 16-valve engine,** remove transaxle assembly as outlined under "Transaxle, Replace" in "Clutch & Manual Transaxle" section for models with manual transaxle or in "Automatic Transaxle" unit repair section for models with automatic transaxle.
7. **On all models,** remove power steering pump and air conditioner compressor without disconnecting hoses, then support aside.
8. Remove engine assembly in numbered sequence shown in **Figs. 2 and 3,** noting following:
   a. **On FWD models,** set engine hanger tool No. MB991191, or equivalent, on body to support engine assembly. **Always insert a piece of wood between engine hanger assembly and front deck, ensuring not to pinch hood weatherstrip.**
   b. **On FWD models,** remove center member mounting bolt.
   c. **On AWD models,** when transaxle assembly is removed, center member assembly has also been removed.
   d. Support engine using a floor jack and remove engine hanger assembly.
   e. Support engine using a chain and suitable engine lifting device.
   f. Raise engine slightly to remove weight off mounts then remove engine mounts.
   g. Ensure all electrical and hose connections are disconnected then raise engine assembly out of vehicle.
   h. **Always insert a piece of wood**

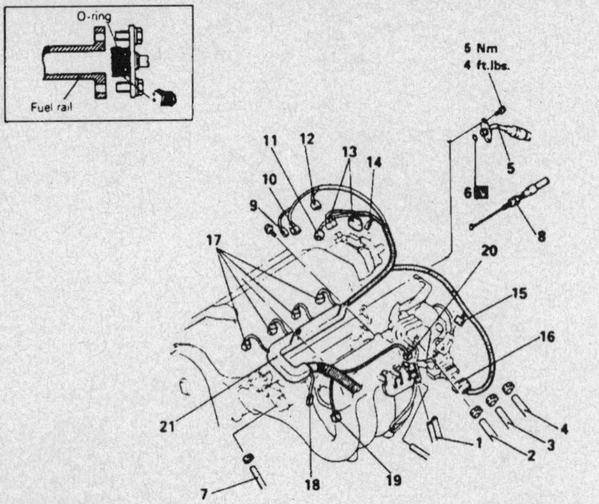
O-ring
Fuel rail
5 Nm
4 ft.lbs.

Removal steps

1. Vacuum hose connection
2. Brake booster vacuum hose connection
3. Heater hose connection (cylinder head → heater unit)
4. Heater hose connection (Heater unit → water inlet pipe)
5. Fuel high pressure hose connection
6. O-ring
7. Fuel return hose connection
8. Accelerator cable connection
9. Engine coolant temperature gauge unit connector
10. Engine coolant temperature sensor connector
11. Oxygen sensor connector <1993 models for Federal>
12. Air conditioning engine coolant temperature switch connector <1993 models>
13. Distributor connector
14. Condenser connector
15. TPS connector
16. IAC connector
17. Injector connector
18. Air conditioning compressor connector
19. Oxygen sensor connector <1993 models for California. From 1994 models>
20. EGR temperature sensor connector <1993 models for California. From 1994 models>
21. Control harness

MT1069100125010X

Fig. 3 Engine assembly removal (Part 1 of 2). 16-valve engine

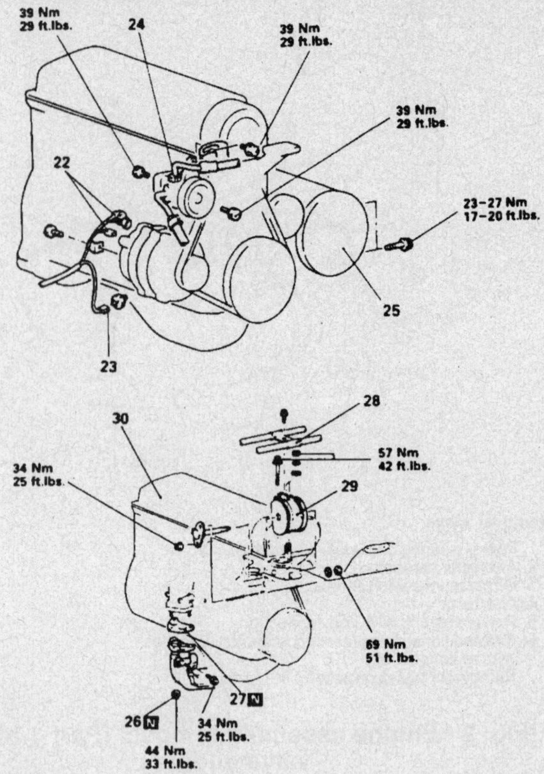
39 Nm
29 ft.lbs.
39 Nm
29 ft.lbs.
39 Nm
29 ft.lbs.
23-27 Nm
17-20 ft.lbs.
34 Nm
25 ft.lbs.
57 Nm
42 ft.lbs.
69 Nm
51 ft.lbs.
34 Nm
25 ft.lbs.
44 Nm
33 ft.lbs.

Removal steps

22. Connection for generator
23. Connection for oil pressure switch
- Drive belt tension adjustment

24. Power steering oil pump
25. Air conditioning compressor
26. Self-locking nuts
27. Gasket
28. Clamp of pressure hose (Power steering) and high pressure hose (Air conditioning)
29. Engine mount bracket
30. Engine assembly

MT1069100125020X

Fig. 3 Engine assembly removal (Part 2 of 2). 16-valve engine

between engine hanger assembly and front deck. Also, do not pinch hood weatherstrip between front deck and piece of wood.

9. Reverse procedure to install, noting following:
   a. Using a floor jack and a piece of wood, support engine on oil pan then install engine mount bracket while adjusting position of engine.
   b. Remove engine lifting device as allow engine hanger tool to support engine until transaxle is installed.

INTAKE MANIFOLD

REPLACE

1. Release fuel system pressure as outlined under "Precautions."
2. Disconnect battery ground cable.
3. Drain cooling system into an approved container.
4. Remove intake manifold in numbered sequence shown in **Fig.4,** removing fuel delivery pipe but leaving injectors and pressure regulator intact. **Do not drop injector when removing delivery pipe.**
5. Reverse procedure to install.

EXHAUST MANIFOLD

REPLACE

1. Disconnect battery ground cable.
2. Replace exhaust manifold in numbered sequence shown in **Fig. 5.**
3. Reverse procedure to install.

CYLINDER HEAD

REPLACE

1. Release fuel system pressure as outlined under "Precautions."
2. Disconnect battery ground cable.
3. Drain cooling system into an approved container.
4. Remove cylinder head and gasket in numbered sequence shown in **Figs. 6 and 7,** noting following:
   a. Place a wooden block against engine oil pan and on a suitable floor jack, then raise engine to remove weight from engine mount.
   b. Remove engine mount bracket.
   c. Rotate engine so No. 1 cylinder is at top dead center on compression stroke and align camshaft timing mark, **Fig. 8.**
   d. Tie camshaft sprocket and timing belt together so that position of camshaft sprocket will not move with respect to timing belt, **Fig. 9.**
   e. Remove camshaft sprocket as outlined under "Timing Belt, Replace."
   f. Loosen cylinder head bolts in two or three steps in numbered sequence shown in **Figs. 10 and 11.**
5. Inspect cylinder head gasket surface for flatness by using a straightedge.
6. Reverse procedure to install, noting following:
   a. Clean cylinder gasket surface on both cylinder head and engine block.
   b. Place cylinder head gasket on cylinder block with identification mark facing upward, **Figs. 12 and 13. Cylinder head gasket must be installed with identification mark properly positioned for oil passage hole alignment.**
   c. Apply a small amount of oil to cylinder head bolt threads and to bolt washer. **Ensure cylinder head bolt is installed as shown in Fig. 14.**
   d. **On 8–valve models, torque** cylinder head bolts in three steps to 76–83 ft. lbs., using numbered sequences, **Fig. 10.**
   e. **On 16–valve models, torque** bolts to 54 ft. lbs., using sequence, **Fig. 15.** Completely loosen bolts and **torque** bolts to 15 ft. lbs. in sequence. Turn bolts 90° (1/4 turn), then turn bolts an additional 90° (1/4 turn).

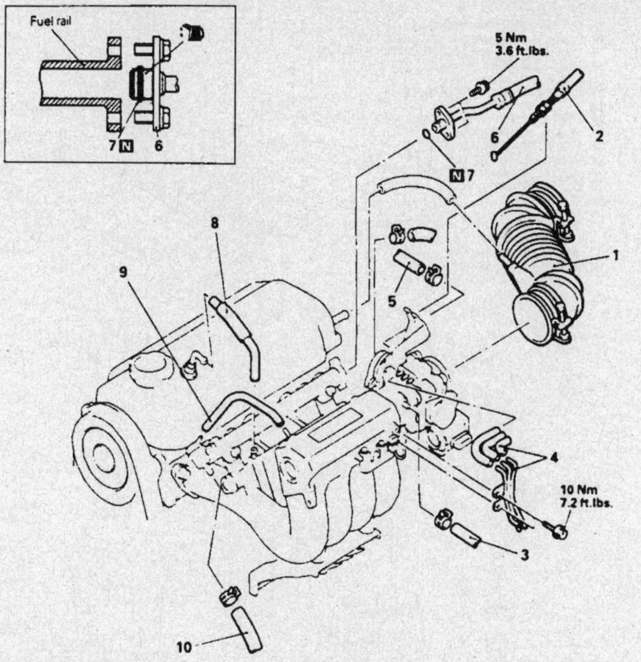
Fuel rail
5 Nm
3.6 ft.lbs.
10 Nm
7.2 ft.lbs.

Removal steps

1. Air intake hose
2. Connection for accelerator cable
3. Connection for brake booster vacuum hose
4. Connection for vacuum pipe and hose assembly
5. Connection for water hose
6. Connection for fuel high pressure hose
7. O-ring
8. PCV hose
9. Connection for vacuum hose
10. Connection for fuel return hose

MT1059300018010X

Fig. 4 Intake manifold removal (Part 1 of 2). 1993–95

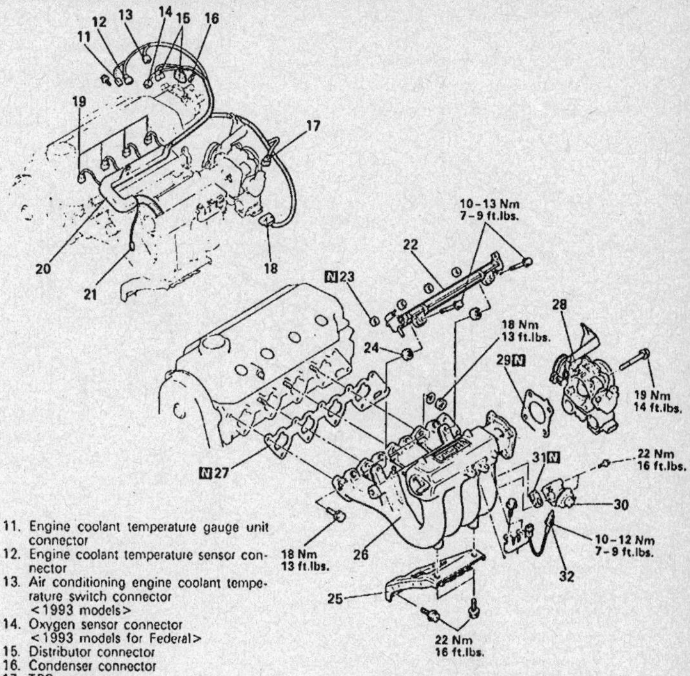
10-13 Nm
7-9 ft.lbs.
18 Nm
13 ft.lbs.
19 Nm
14 ft.lbs.
22 Nm
16 ft.lbs.
10-12 Nm
7-9 ft.lbs.
18 Nm
13 ft.lbs.
22 Nm
16 ft.lbs.

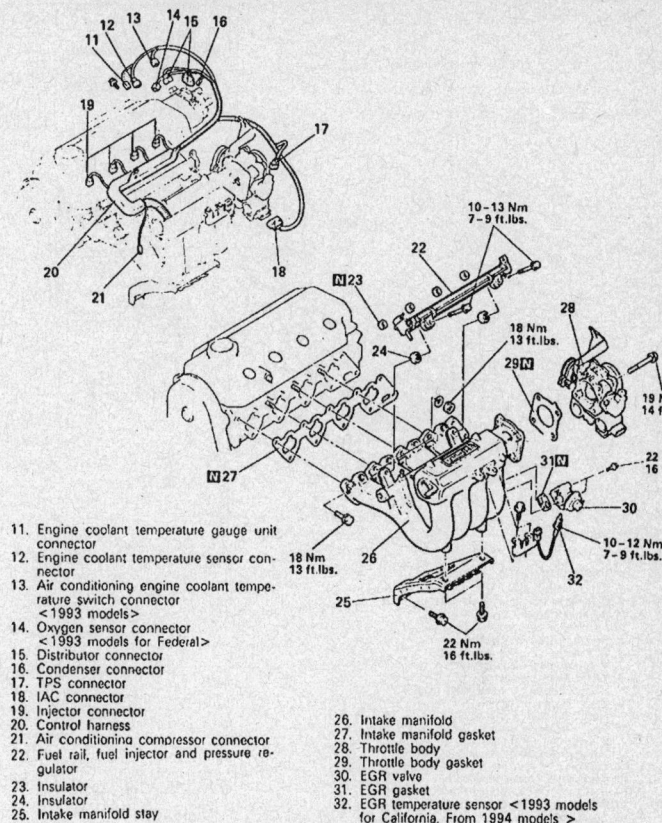

11. Engine coolant temperature gauge unit connector
12. Engine coolant temperature sensor connector
13. Air conditioning engine coolant temperature switch connector <1993 models>
14. Oxygen sensor connector <1993 models for Federal>
15. Distributor connector
16. Condenser connector
17. TPS connector
18. IAC connector
19. Injector connector
20. Control harness
21. Air conditioning compressor connector
22. Fuel rail, fuel injector and pressure regulator
23. Insulator
24. Insulator
25. Intake manifold stay
26. Intake manifold
27. Intake manifold gasket
28. Throttle body
29. Throttle body gasket
30. EGR valve
31. EGR gasket
32. EGR temperature sensor <1993 models for California, From 1994 models >

MT1059300018020X

Fig. 4 Intake manifold removal (Part 2 of 2). 1993–95

VALVE ARRANGEMENT

FRONT TO REAR

I-E-E-I-I-E-E-I

VALVE CLEARANCE SPECIFICATIONS

Valve stem to guide clearance with engine cool for SOHC engine is .0008–.0024 inch and DOHC engine is .0008–.0020 inch for intake valves and .0020–.0035 inch for exhaust valves.

VALVE ADJUSTMENT

These engines use hydraulic auto-lash adjusters. No adjustments are required.

ROCKER ARMS

REPLACE

REMOVAL

1. Release fuel system pressure as outlined under "Precautions."
2. Disconnect battery ground cable.
3. Remove timing belt as outlined under "Timing Belt, Replace."
4. Replace camshaft, camshaft oil seal, rocker arms and rocker arm shafts in

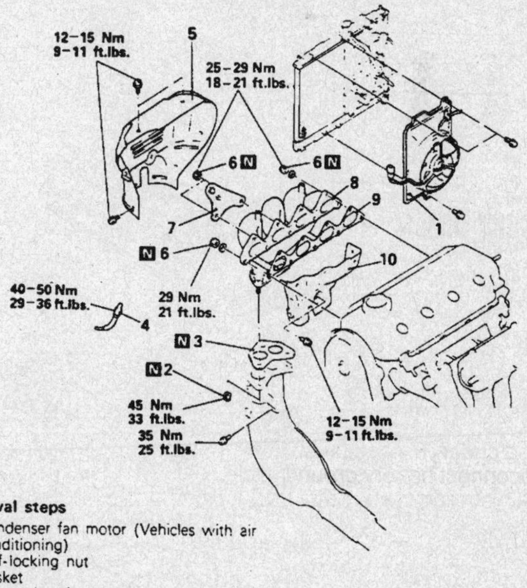
12-15 Nm
9-11 ft.lbs.
25-29 Nm
18-21 ft.lbs.
40-50 Nm
29-36 ft.lbs.
29 Nm
21 ft.lbs.
45 Nm
33 ft.lbs.
35 Nm
25 ft.lbs.
12-15 Nm
9-11 ft.lbs.

Removal steps

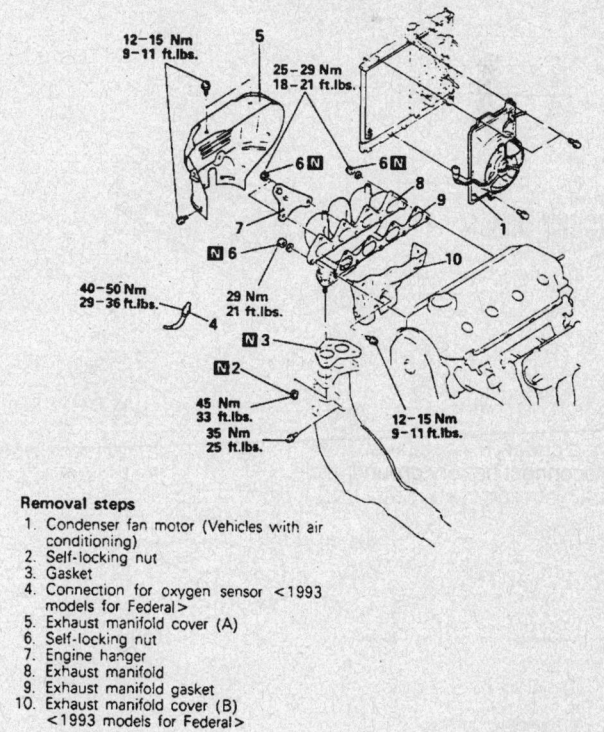

1. Condenser fan motor (Vehicles with air conditioning)
2. Self-locking nut
3. Gasket
4. Connection for oxygen sensor <1993 models for Federal>
5. Exhaust manifold cover (A)
6. Self-locking nut
7. Engine hanger
8. Exhaust manifold
9. Exhaust manifold gasket
10. Exhaust manifold cover (B) <1993 models for Federal>

MT1079300010000X

Fig. 5 Exhaust manifold removal. 1993–95

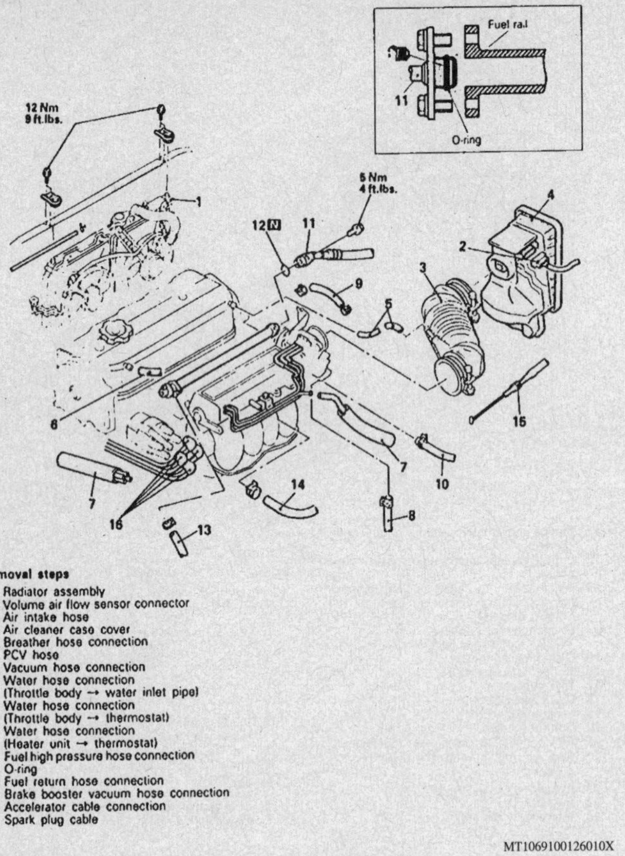
Fuel rail
O-ring
12 Nm
9 ft.lbs.
5 Nm
4 ft.lbs.
Removal steps
1. Radiator assembly
2. Volume air flow sensor connector
3. Air intake hose
4. Air cleaner case cover
5. Breather hose connection
6. PCV hose
7. Vacuum hose connection
8. Water hose connection
(Throttle body → water inlet pipe)
9. Water hose connection
(Throttle body → thermostat)
10. Water hose connection
(Heater unit → thermostat)
11. Fuel high pressure hose connection
12. O-ring
13. Fuel return hose connection
14. Brake booster vacuum hose connection
15. Accelerator cable connection
16. Spark plug cable
MT1069100126010X

Fig. 6 Cylinder head & gasket removal (Part 1 of 3). 8-valve engine

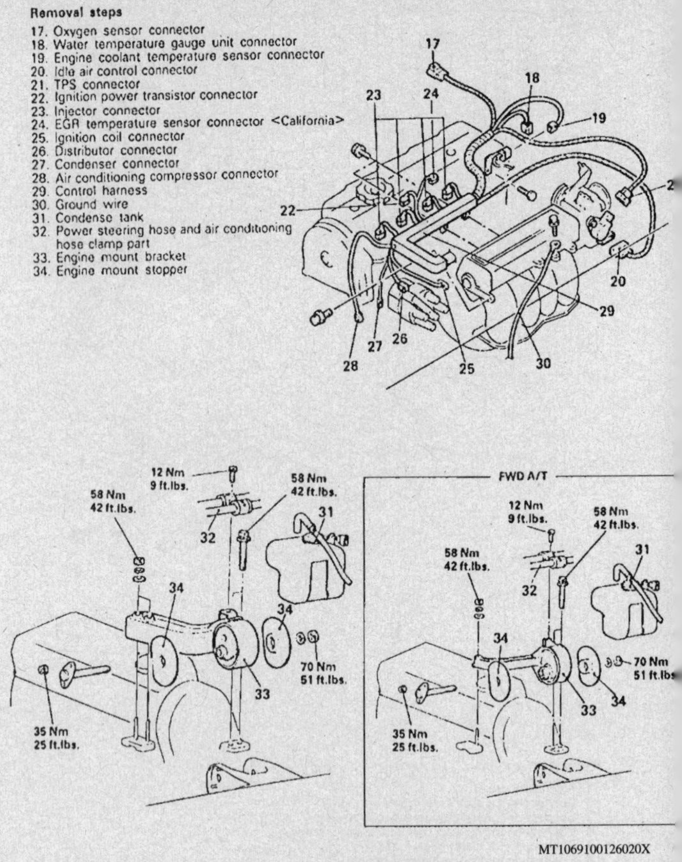
Removal steps
17. Oxygen sensor connector
18. Water temperature gauge unit connector
19. Engine coolant temperature sensor connector
20. Idle air control connector
21. TPS connector
22. Ignition power transistor connector
23. Injector connector
24. EGR temperature sensor connector <California>
25. Ignition coil connector
26. Distributor connector
27. Condenser connector
28. Air conditioning compressor connector
29. Control harness
30. Ground wire
31. Condense tank
32. Power steering hose and air conditioning hose clamp part
33. Engine mount bracket
34. Engine mount stopper
12 Nm
9 ft.lbs.
58 Nm
42 ft.lbs.
70 Nm
51 ft.lbs.
35 Nm
25 ft.lbs.
FWD A/T
MT1069100126020X

Fig. 6 Cylinder head & gasket removal (Part 2 of 3). 8-valve engine

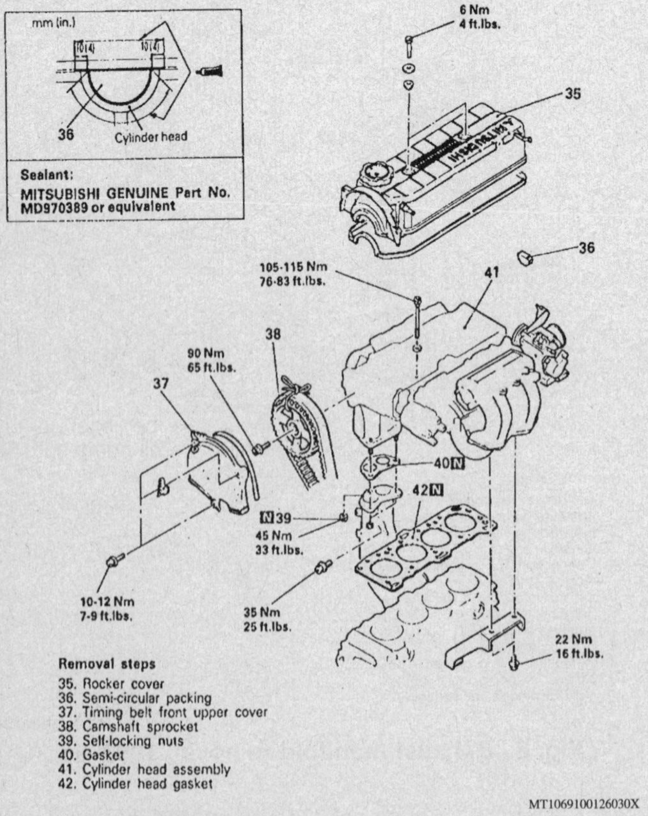
mm (in.)
Cylinder head
Sealant:
MITSUBISHI GENUINE Part No. MD970389 or equivalent
6 Nm
4 ft.lbs.
105-115 Nm
76-83 ft.lbs.
90 Nm
65 ft.lbs.
45 Nm
33 ft.lbs.
10-12 Nm
7-9 ft.lbs.
35 Nm
25 ft.lbs.
22 Nm
16 ft.lbs.
Removal steps
35. Rocker cover
36. Semi-circular packing
37. Timing belt front upper cover
38. Camshaft sprocket
39. Self-locking nuts
40. Gasket
41. Cylinder head assembly
42. Cylinder head gasket
MT1069100126030X

Fig. 6 Cylinder head & gasket removal (Part 3 of 3). 8-valve engine

numbered sequence shown in **Fig. 16,** installing auto-lash adjuster holder, tool No. MD998443, or equivalent, prior to removal of rocker arm and rocker shaft assembly, to ensure auto-lash adjuster is not allowed to fall.

INSTALLATION

1. Bleed auto-lash adjuster as follows:
   a. Immerse lash adjuster in clean diesel fuel.
   b. While lightly pushing down inner steel ball with a small wire, move plunger up and down several times to bleed air.
   c. Remove small wire and press plunger. If plunger is hard to depress, lash adjuster is operating normal, proceed to Step e.
   d. If plunger can be easily depressed, repeat Steps a through c. If plunger is still loose, replace lash adjuster.
   e. **After bleeding hold adjuster upright to prevent diesel fuel from spilling out,** set lash adjuster on leak down tester, tool No. MD998440, or equivalent.
   f. After plunger has depressed 0.008–0.020 inch, measure time taken for plunger to drop an additional 0.04 inch. If plunger drops 0.04 inch in 4–20 seconds, lash adjuster is operating correctly.
2. Reverse numbered sequence shown in **Fig. 16** to complete installation, noting following:
   a. Insert rocker arm shaft into front

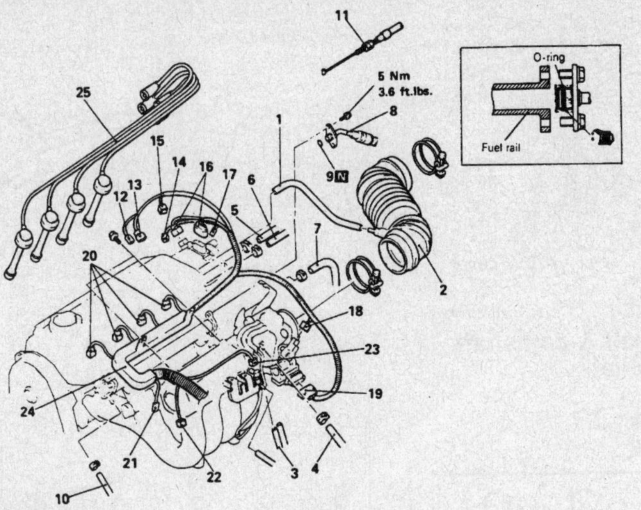
O-ring
Fuel rail
5 Nm
3.6 ft.lbs.

Removal steps

1. Breather hose
2. Air intake hose
3. Vacuum hose connection
4. Brake booster vacuum hose connection
5. Water hose connection (cylinder head → throttle body)
6. Heater hose connection (cylinder head → heater unit)
7. Water hose connection (throttle body → water inlet pipe)
8. Fuel high pressure hose connection
9. O-ring
10. Fuel return hose connection
11. Accelerator cable connection
12. Engine coolant temperature gauge unit connector
13. Engine coolant temperature sensor connector
14. Oxygen sensor connector <1993 models for Federal>
15. Air conditioning engine coolant temperature switch connector <1993 models>
16. Distributor connector
17. Condenser connector
18. TPS connector
19. IAC connector
20. Injector connector
21. Air conditioning compressor connector
22. Oxygen sensor connector <1993 models for California. From 1994 models>
23. EGR temperature sensor connector <1993 models for California. From 1994 models>
24. Control harness
25. Spark plug cable

MT1069100127010X

Fig. 7 Cylinder head & gasket removal (Part 1 of 2). 16-valve engine

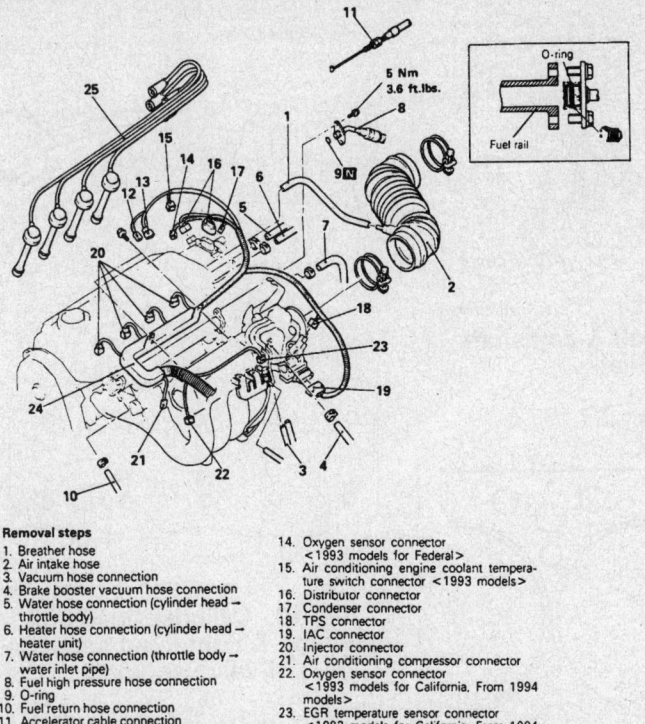

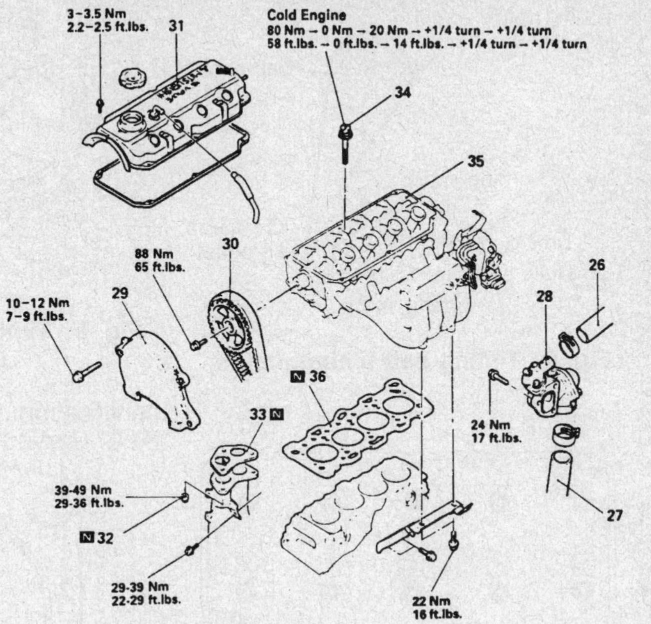
3-3.5 Nm
2.2-2.5 ft.lbs.
Cold Engine
80 Nm → 0 Nm → 20 Nm → +1/4 turn → +1/4 turn
58 ft.lbs. → 0 ft.lbs. → 14 ft.lbs. → +1/4 turn → +1/4 turn
88 Nm
65 ft.lbs.
10-12 Nm
7-9 ft.lbs.
24 Nm
17 ft.lbs.
39-49 Nm
29-36 ft.lbs.
29-39 Nm
22-29 ft.lbs.
22 Nm
16 ft.lbs.

26. Connection for radiator upper hose
27. Connection for radiator lower hose
28. Water inlet fitting, thermostat and thermostat case assembly
29. Timing belt upper cover
30. Camshaft sprocket
31. Rocker cover
32. Self-locking nuts
33. Gasket
34. Cylinder head bolt
35. Cylinder head assembly
36. Cylinder head gasket

MT1069100127020X

Fig. 7 Cylinder head & gasket removal (Part 2 of 2). 16-valve engine

bearing cap so notch on shaft faces up. Do not tighten at this time.

b. Install wave washer with raise side toward front bearing cap.
c. Install rocker arm marked "1-3" for cylinders 1 and 3 and rockers marked "2-4" for cylinders 2 and 4.
d. Identify bearing caps 2, 3 and 4 as shown in **Fig. 17.**
e. Install bearing caps with front marks pointing to camshaft sprocket side of engine.
f. Bleed auto-lash adjuster as outlined under Step 1, then insert adjuster into rocker arm securing with lash adjuster holder, tool No. MD998443-01, or equivalent.
g. Install camshaft oil seal using seal installation tools, No. MD998306-01 and MD998307-01, or equivalent.
h. Apply sealant to outer circumference of circular packing then install on cylinder head.

FRONT COVER

REPLACE

Refer to "Oil Pump, Replace" for front cover replacement procedure.

TIMING BELT

REPLACE

With the timing belt removed, avoid turning the camshaft or crankshaft. If movement is required, exercise extreme caution to avoid valve damage caused by piston contact.

8-VALVE ENGINE

Removal

1. Release fuel system pressure as outlined under "Precautions."
2. Disconnect battery ground cable and remove engine undercover, then remove coolant reservoir and air conditioning/power steering hose clamp, **Fig. 18.**
3. Support engine with wooden block between engine oil pan and a suitable floor jack, then remove engine mount and stopper.
4. Remove alternator and power steering pump drive belts, then tension pulley bracket and air conditioning drive belt.
5. Remove water pump, power steering and crankshaft pulleys, then upper and lower covers.
6. Turn crankshaft clockwise and align camshaft timing mark, **Fig. 8.**
7. Loosen timing belt tensioner bolts, **Fig. 19.**
8. Move timing belt tensioner toward water pump then temporarily tighten bolts.
9. Mark engine rotational direction on timing belt, then remove belt.
10. Remove tension spacer and spring, then timing belt tensioner.

Installation

1. Install tensioner spring, spacer and tensioner assembly. Keep tensioner spring in free position, **Fig. 20.**
2. Temporarily tighten bolts with tensioner pressed toward water pump.
3. Rotate engine to place No. 1 cylinder at top dead center and align timing marks.
4. Remove plug from LH side of cylinder block and insert a screwdriver with a shaft diameter of .31 inch. If screwdriver can be inserted 2.36 inches or more, alignment is correct.
5. If screwdriver can be inserted only .79–.98 inch, rotate oil pump sprocket one revolution and realign timing marks. Then check to ensure screwdriver can be inserted 2.36 inches or more. This check is performed to ensure silent shaft and oil pump sprocket are properly positioned. Leave screwdriver inserted in hole until after timing belt has been installed.
6. Install timing belt onto crankshaft, oil pump and camshaft sprockets, in order, ensuring tension side of belt does not slacken.
7. Loosen tensioner bolts and allow tensioner spring to force tensioner against belt, then ensure timing marks are aligned.
8. Remove screwdriver from silent shaft

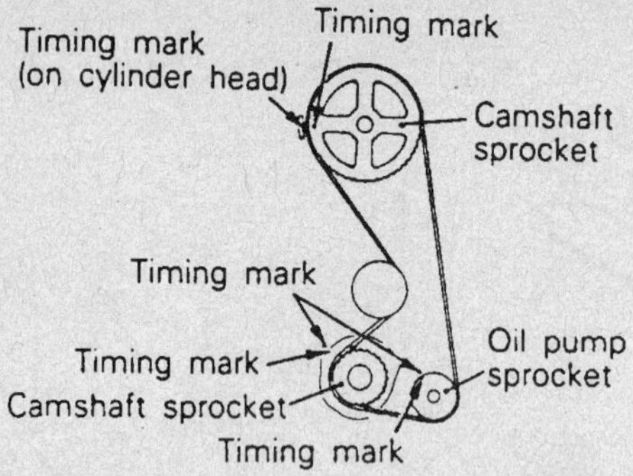
Timing mark
(on cylinder head)
Timing mark
Camshaft
sprocket
Timing mark
Timing mark
Camshaft sprocket
Oil pump
sprocket
Timing mark
MT1069100128000X

Fig. 8 Timing belt timing marks

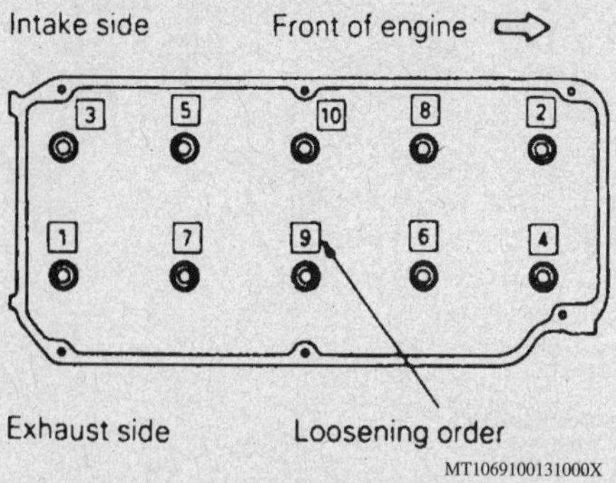
Intake side
Front of engine
3
5
10
8
2
1
7
9
6
4
Exhaust side
Loosening order
MT1069100131000X

Fig. 11 Cylinder head bolt loosening sequence. 16-valve engine

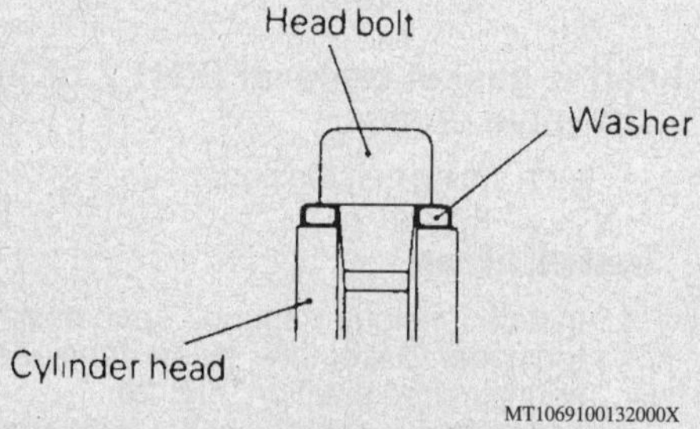
Head bolt
Washer
Cylinder head
MT1069100132000X

Fig. 14 Cylinder head bolt washer installation

alignment hole.

9. Turn crankshaft clockwise 15° (two teeth), **Fig. 21.**
10. Apply pressure on timing belt tensioner to ensure belt is properly seated in all sprockets and in area marked "A," **Fig. 22,** then tighten bolt "A" and "B," in order.
11. Grasp center timing belt center and check clearance between outside of belt and cover, **Fig. 23.** Standard clearance is .55 inch.
12. Install timing belt cover bolts in correct location, **Fig. 24,** and tighten to specifications.
13. Install crankshaft, power steering and water pump pulleys, then air conditioning drive belt and tension pulley bracket.
14. Install power steering pump and alternator drive belts, then engine mount stopper.
15. Install engine mount and air conditioning/power steering hose clamp, then condense tank.

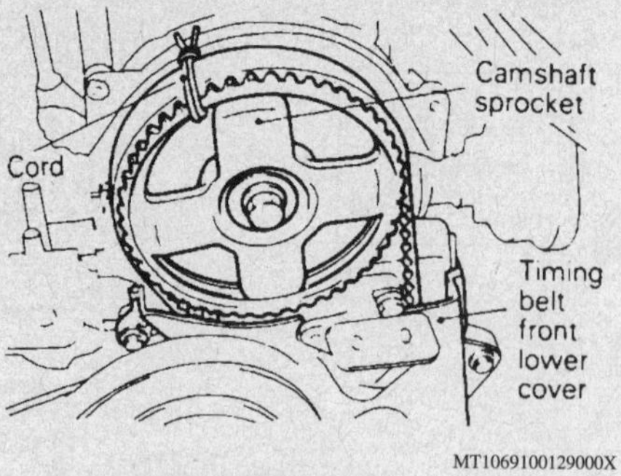
Cord
Camshaft
sprocket
Timing
belt
front
lower
cover
MT1069100129000X

Fig. 9 Timing belt & camshaft sprocket

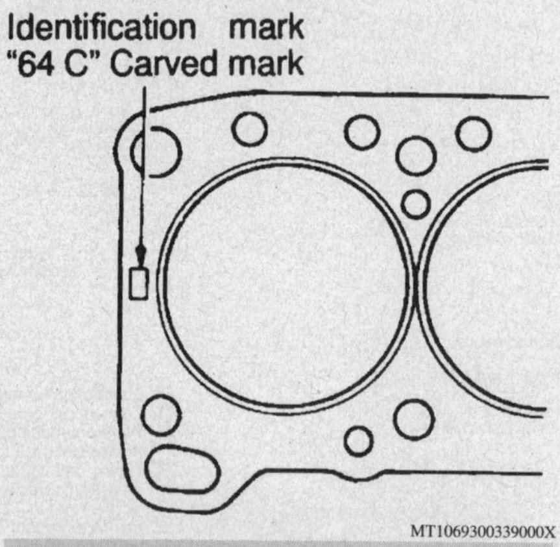
Identification mark
"64 C" Carved mark
MT1069300339000X

Fig. 12 Cylinder head gasket identification mark. 8-valve engine

16. Install engine undercover and connect battery ground cable.

16-VALVE ENGINE

Removal

1. Relieve fuel system pressure as described under "Precautions," then disconnect battery ground cable and remove engine under cover.
2. Remove coolant reservoir tank, **Fig. 25.**
3. Support engine with suitable jack and wooden block under oil pan, and remove right hand engine mount.
4. Remove alternator and power steering pump drive belts, then tensioner pulley bracket.
5. Remove air conditioning drive belt, then water pump and crankshaft pulleys.
6. **On 1995 FWD California models,** remove crankshaft position sensor bracket.
7. **On all models,** remove upper and lower covers.
8. Rotate crankshaft clockwise and align timing marks, then remove auto tensioner, **Fig. 26.**
9. Mark directional rotation on timing belt and remove. **Keep timing belt, sprocket and tensioner free of oil and water; do not wash or lubricate these parts.**
10. Remove tensioner pulley and arm, then idle pulley, **Fig. 27.**
11. Remove camshaft sprocket.

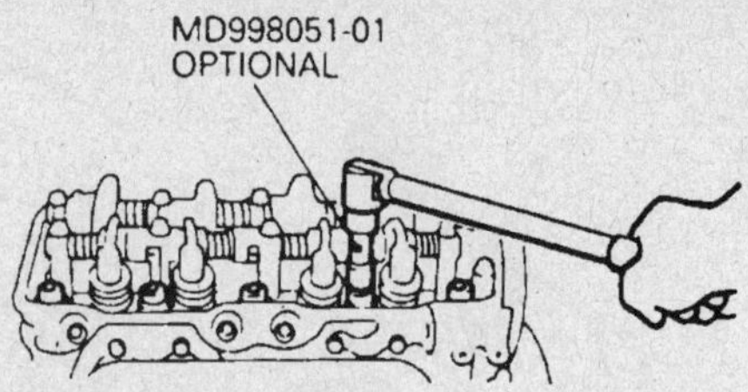
MD998051-01
OPTIONAL

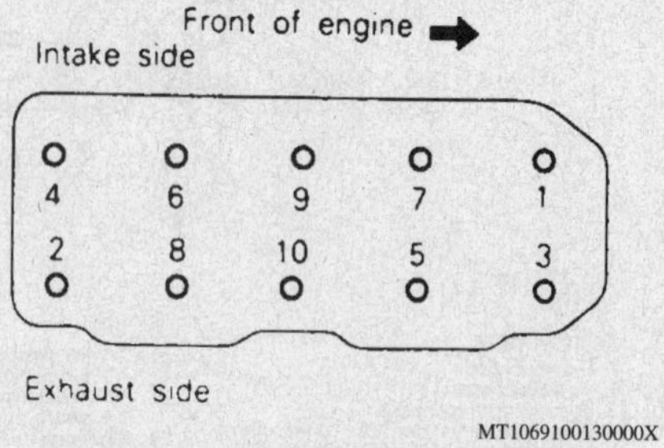
Front of engine
Intake side
4
6
9
7
1
2
8
10
5
3
Exhaust side
MT1069100130000X

Fig. 10 Cylinder head bolt loosening & tightening sequence. 8-valve engine

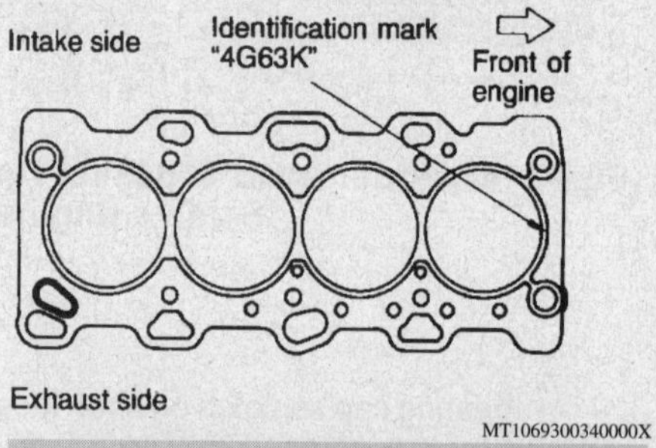
Intake side
Identification mark
"4G63K"
Front of
engine
Exhaust side
MT1069300340000X

Fig. 13 Cylinder head gasket identification mark. 16–valve engine

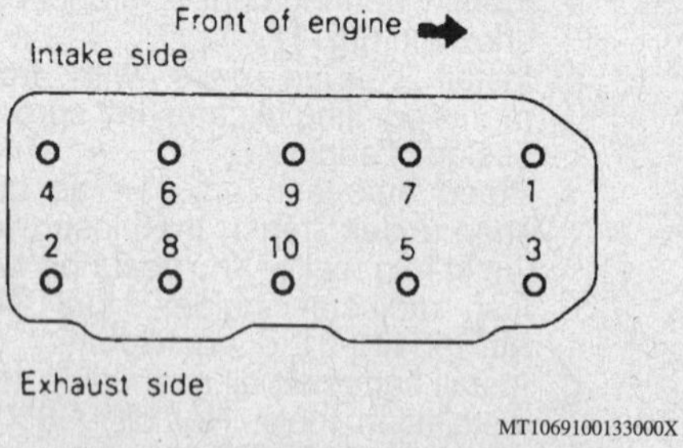
Front of engine
Intake side
4
6
9
7
1
2
8
10
5
3
Exhaust side
MT1069100133000X

Fig. 15 Cylinder head bolt tightening sequence. 16-valve engine

Installation

1. Install crankshaft sprocket flange with raised side facing out, then install crankshaft sprocket and idle pulley.
2. Measure auto-tensioner plunger protrusion. Protrusion from housing should be .47 inch. If plunger is fully extended, proceed as follows:
   a. Keep auto-tensioner level and place in vice with soft jaws. If plug at bottom protrudes, keep it from

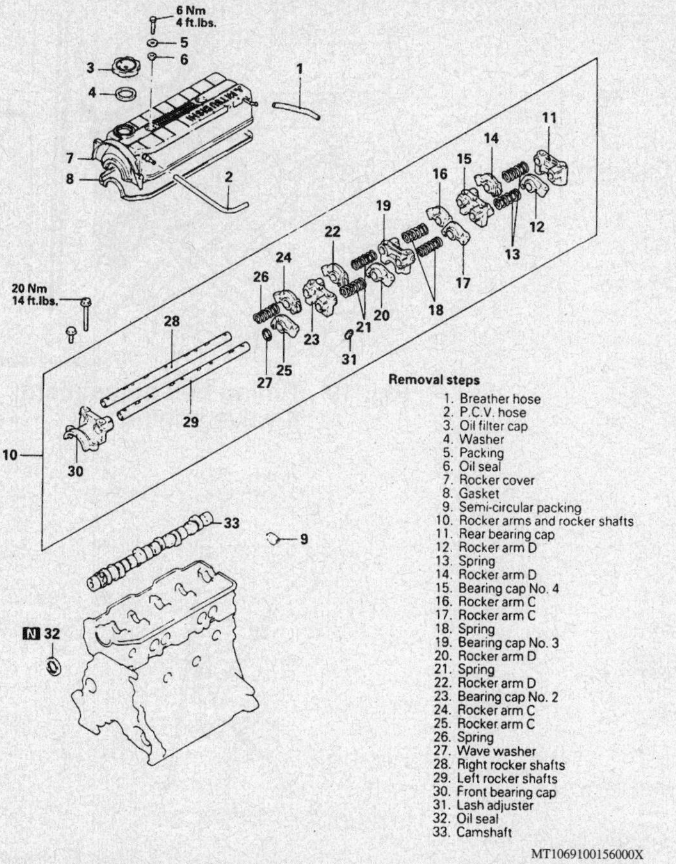
6 Nm
4 ft.lbs.
20 Nm
14 ft.lbs.
Removal steps
1. Breather hose
2. P.C.V. hose
3. Oil filter cap
4. Washer
5. Packing
6. Oil seal
7. Rocker cover
8. Gasket
9. Semi-circular packing
10. Rocker arms and rocker shafts
11. Rear bearing cap
12. Rocker arm D
13. Spring
14. Rocker arm D
15. Bearing cap No. 4
16. Rocker arm C
17. Rocker arm C
18. Spring
19. Bearing cap No. 3
20. Rocker arm D
21. Spring
22. Rocker arm D
23. Bearing cap No. 2
24. Rocker arm C
25. Rocker arm C
26. Spring
27. Wave washer
28. Right rocker shafts
29. Left rocker shafts
30. Front bearing cap
31. Lash adjuster
32. Oil seal
33. Camshaft
MT1069100156000X

Fig. 16 Exploded view of rocker arms & camshaft

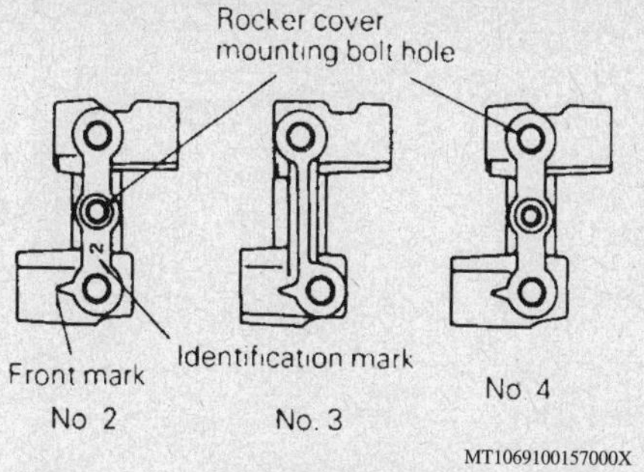
Rocker cover
mounting bolt hole
Front mark
Identification mark
No. 2
No. 3
No. 4
MT1069100157000X

Fig. 17 Camshaft bearing caps identification

touching vice with washer.

b. Slowly compress plunger with vise pressure until hole in plunger aligns with housing hole.
c. Hole plunger in place by inserting .055 inch pin or wire through aligned holes.

3. Remove auto-tensioner from vice and install. **Do not remove securing pin or wire.**
4. Install tensioner arm, then install tensioner pulley on arm.
5. Position tensioner pulley shaft pinhole to left of center bolt and finger-tighten bolt.
6. Ensure crankshaft and camshaft timing marks are aligned, **Fig. 26.**
7. With oil pump sprocket timing marks aligned, remove cylinder block plug and insert .31 inch diameter Phillips screwdriver through hole, **Fig. 28.** If screwdriver can be insert 2.4 inches or more, alignment is correct.
8. If screwdriver can only be inserted 0.8–1.0 inch, rotate oil pump sprocket one revolution and realign timing marks. Ensure screwdriver can be inserted 2.4 inches or more.
9. Ensure oil pump sprocket is properly aligned and leave screwdriver in hole until after timing belt has been installed.
10. Install timing belt around crankshaft and oil pump sprockets, then idler pulley camshaft sprocket and tensioner pulley. **Hold belt so there is no slack on tension side and apply counterclockwise force on camshaft sprocket to aid tension. Ensure all timing marks remain aligned.**
11. Carefully position timing belt tensioner pulley against belt and tighten center bolt.
12. Rotate crankshaft pulley ¼ turn counterclockwise, then turn clockwise and align crankshaft and camshaft timing marks.
13. Loosen tensioner pulley retaining bolt, position special socket tools, **Fig. 29,** and **torque** to 2.6 ft. lbs., then tighten retaining bolt to specifications while holding pulley in position.
14. Install special set screw tool No. MD998738, or equivalent, through left hand engine support bracket, **Fig. 30.** Engine may need to be raised slightly to install set screw tool.
15. Tighten set screw tool until it contacts tensioner arm, then tighten tool slightly more.
16. Remove auto-tensioner retaining pin or wire, then remove set screw tool.
17. Rotate crankshaft clockwise two turns and allow to sit for 15 minutes, then measure auto-tensioner plunger protrusion from housing dimension "A", **Fig. 31.** Distance should be .15–.18 inch. If not within specifications, adjust belt tension. Install rear cover rubber plug.
18. Install lower and upper covers, **Fig. 32,** and tighten to specifications.
19. **On 1995 FWD California models,** install crankshaft position sensor bracket.
20. **On all models,** install crankshaft and water pump pulleys, then tighten bolts to specifications.
21. Install air conditioning drive belt, then tension pulley bracket.
22. Install power steering pump and alternator drive belts, and adjust belt tensions.
23. Install right hand engine mount and tighten bolts to specifications, then remove jack and wood block.
24. Install engine coolant reservoir and fill to proper lever, then install under covers and battery ground cable.
25. Check and adjust ignition timing.

CAMSHAFT

REPLACE

Refer to "Rocker Arms, Replace" for camshaft replacement procedure.

BALANCE SHAFT BELT

REPLACE

8-VALVE ENGINE

Removal

1. Remove timing belt as described in "Timing Belt, Replace," **Fig. 33.**
2. Use an old ribbed belt and belt holder tool to prevent crankshaft from turning, and remove crankshaft sprocket bolt, crankshaft pulley and sprocket.
3. Remove flange and tensioner.
4. Mark rotational direction of engine on timing belt and remove.

Installation

1. Align crankshaft and balance shaft sprockets timing marks, **Fig. 34,** then install timing belt. **There should be no slack.**
2. Temporarily install tensioner with pulley center to left and above installation bolt center and flange faces front of engine, **Fig. 35.**
3. Holding tensioner up, exert tension until tension side of belt is taut, then tighten tensioner bolt, **Fig. 36. Do not allow tensioner pulley to rotate when tightening bolt.**
4. Apply finger pressure to center of belt's tension side and measure deflection, **Fig. 37.** Deflection should be .20–.28 inch.

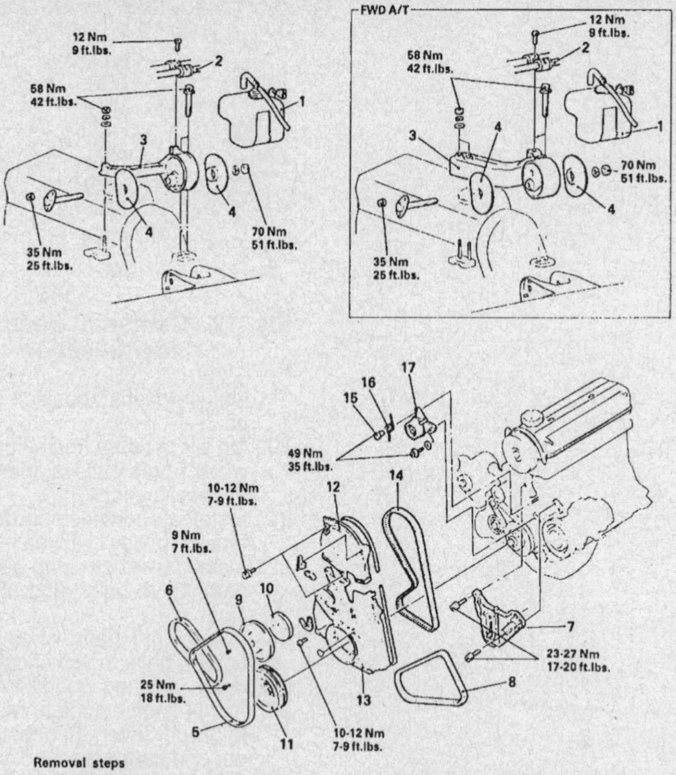
FWD A/T
12 Nm
9 ft.lbs.
58 Nm
42 ft.lbs.
70 Nm
51 ft.lbs.
35 Nm
25 ft.lbs.
49 Nm
35 ft.lbs.
10-12 Nm
7-9 ft.lbs.
9 Nm
7 ft.lbs.
25 Nm
18 ft.lbs.
23-27 Nm
17-20 ft.lbs.
Removal steps
1. Condense tank
2. Power steering hose and air conditioning hose clamp part
3. Engine mount bracket
4. Engine mount stopper
5. Drive belt (Generator)
6. Drive belt (Power steering oil pump)
7. Tension pulley bracket
8. Drive belt (Air conditioning compressor)
9. Water pump pulley
10. Water pump pulley for power steering
11. Crankshaft pulley
12. Timing belt front upper cover
13. Timing belt front lower cover
• Adjustment of timing belt tension
14. Timing belt
15. Tension spacer
16. Tension spring
17. Timing belt tensioner
MT1069100135000X

Fig. 18 Timing belt replacement. 8-valve engine

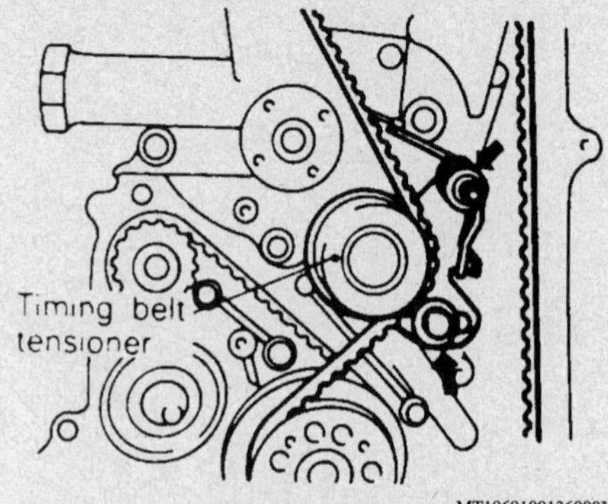
Timing belt
tensioner
MT1069100136000X

Fig. 19 Timing belt adjustment. 8-valve engine

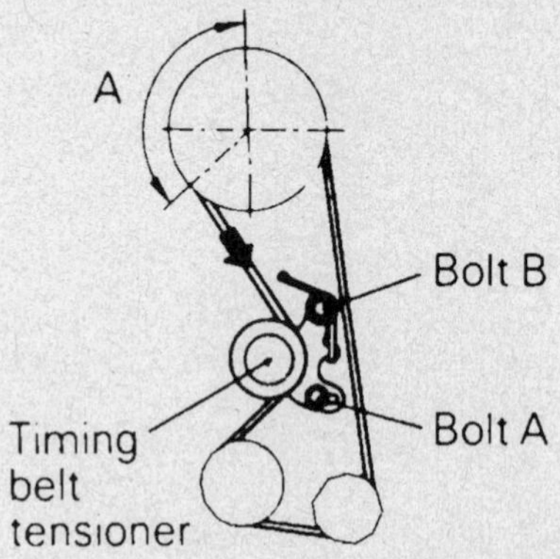
A
Bolt B
Bolt A
Timing
belt
tensioner
MT1069100145000X

Fig. 22 Tensioner belt tightening sequence. 8-valve engine

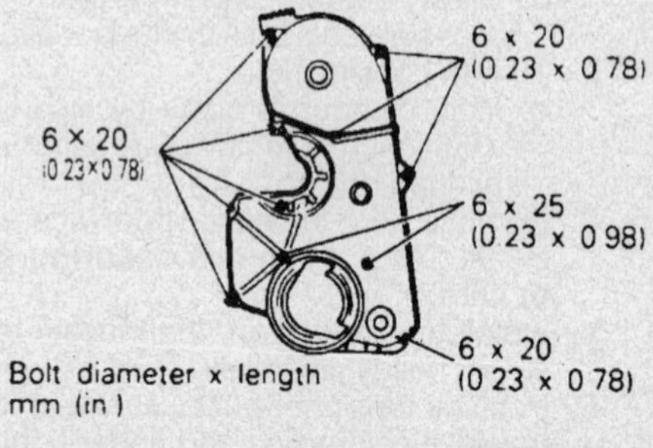
6 × 20
(0 23 × 0 78)
6 × 20
(0 23×0 78)
6 × 25
(0 23 × 0 98)
6 × 20
(0 23 × 0 78)
Bolt diameter × length
mm (in)
MT1069100147000X

Fig. 24 Timing belt cover bolt installation. 8-valve engine

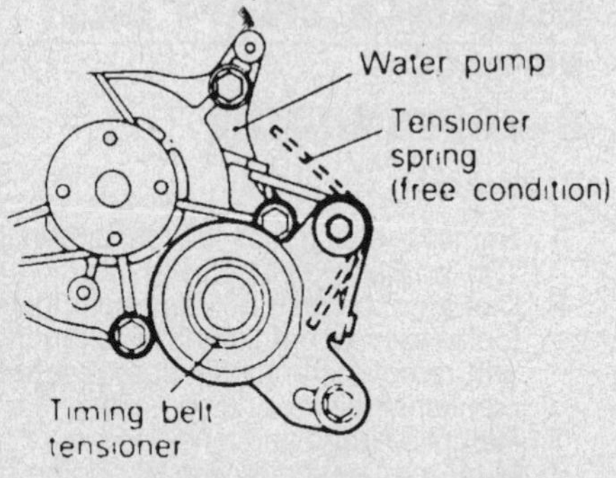
Water pump
Tensioner
spring
(free condition)
Timing belt
tensioner
MT1069100143000X

Fig. 20 Timing belt tensioner "Free" position. 8-valve engine

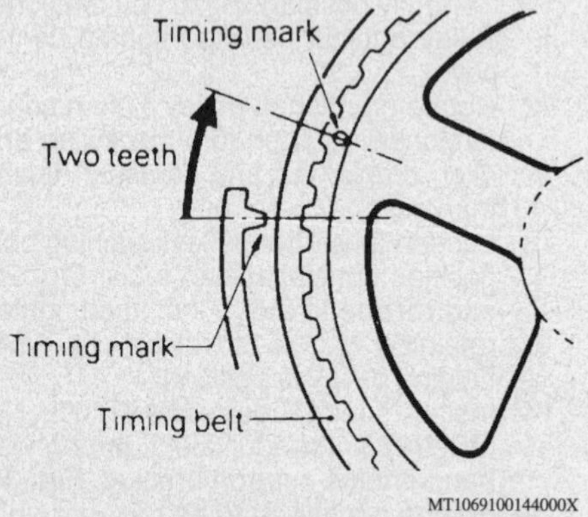
Timing mark
Two teeth
Timing mark
Timing belt
MT1069100144000X

Fig. 21 Camshaft 15° rotation. 8-valve engine

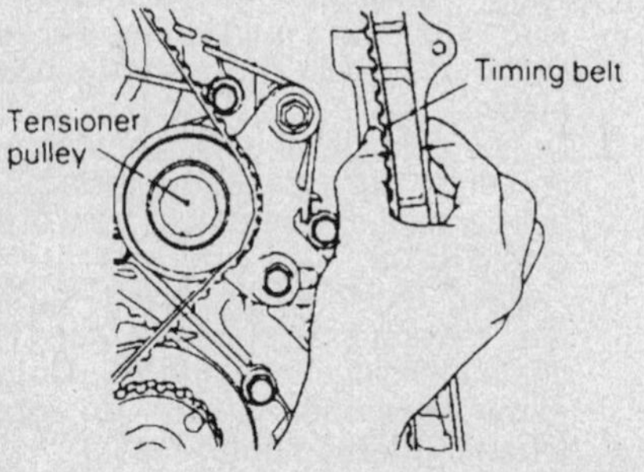
Timing belt
Tensioner
pulley
MT1069100146000X

Fig. 23 Belt tension inspection. 8-valve engine

5. Install crankshaft flange, **Fig. 38,** then install crankshaft sprocket and pulley, and tighten crankshaft bolt to specifications.

16-VALVE ENGINE

Removal

1. Remove timing belt as described in **Timing Belt, Replace.**
2. Remove cylinder block plug and insert .31 inch diameter Phillips screwdriver through hole to block left balance shaft, **Fig. 28,** then remove oil pump sprocket nut and sprocket.
3. Remove crankshaft sprocket bolt, washer and sprocket, then remove crankshaft flange, **Fig. 27.**
4. **On 1995 FWD California models,** remove crankshaft sensing blade.
5. **On all models,** remove balance shaft belt tensioner, then mark rotational direction on belt and remove. **Keep timing belt, sprocket and tensioner free of oil and water; do not wash or lubricate these parts.**
6. Remove right balance shaft sprocket and spacer, crankshaft sprocket and key, then engine support bracket and timing belt under cover.

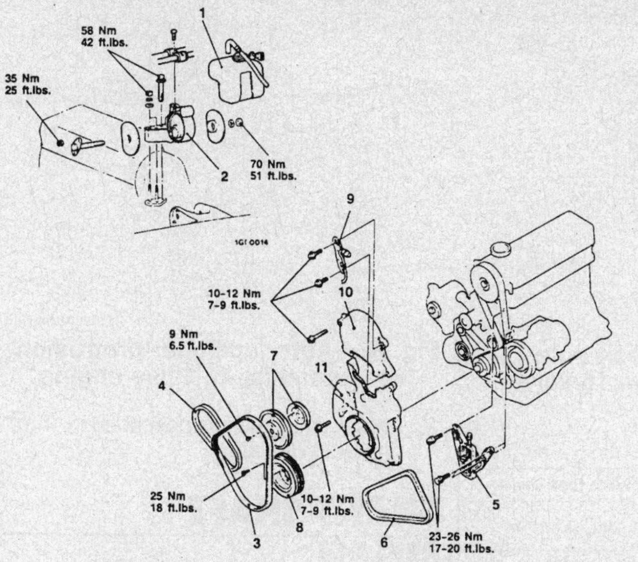
58 Nm
42 ft.lbs.
35 Nm
25 ft.lbs.
70 Nm
51 ft.lbs.
10-12 Nm
7-9 ft.lbs.
9 Nm
6.5 ft.lbs.
25 Nm
18 ft.lbs.
10-12 Nm
7-9 ft.lbs.
23-26 Nm
17-20 ft.lbs.

1. Condense tank
2. Engine mount bracket
3. Drive belt (generator)
4. Drive belt (power steering)
5. Tensioner pulley bracket
6. Drive belt (air conditioning)
7. Water pump pulley
8. Crankshaft pulley
9. Crankshaft position sensor bracket <FWD-Vehicles for California - 1995 models>
10. Timing belt front upper cover
11. Timing belt front lower cover

Installation steps

11. Timing belt front lower cover
10. Timing belt front upper cover
9. Crankshaft position sensor bracket <FWD-Vehicles for California - 1995 models>
8. Crankshaft pulley
7. Water pump pulley
6. Drive belt (air conditioning)
5. Tension pulley bracket
4. Drive belt (power steering)
3. Drive belt (generator)
• Drive belt tension adjustment

2. Engine mount bracket
1. Condense tank

MT1069100148000A

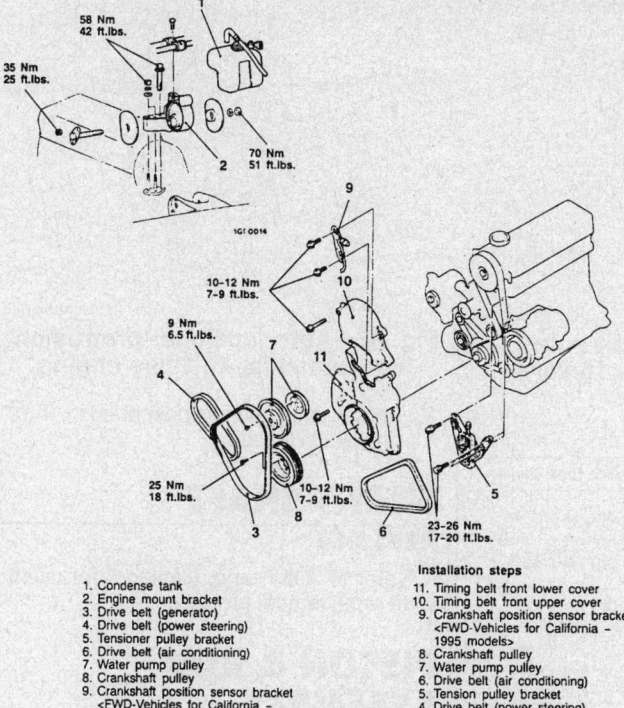

Fig. 25 Timing belt replacement. 16-valve engine

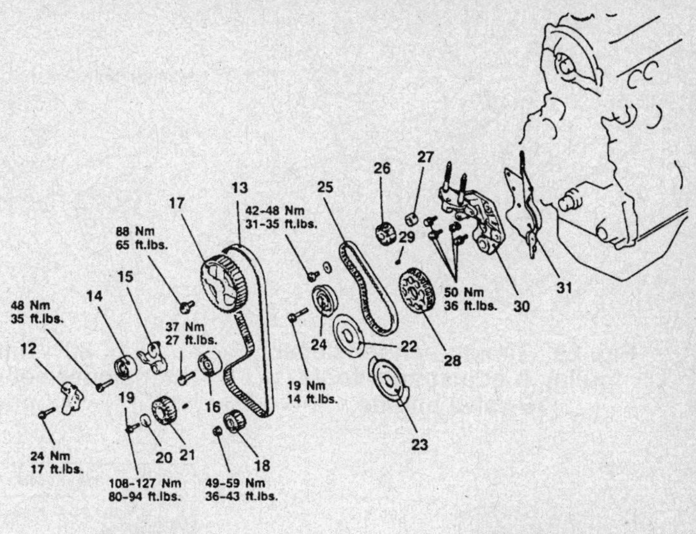
88 Nm
65 ft.lbs.
42-48 Nm
31-35 ft.lbs.
48 Nm
35 ft.lbs.
37 Nm
27 ft.lbs.
50 Nm
36 ft.lbs.
19 Nm
14 ft.lbs.
24 Nm
17 ft.lbs.
108-127 Nm
80-94 ft.lbs.
49-59 Nm
36-43 ft.lbs.

Removal steps

12. Auto tensioner
13. Timing belt
14. Tensioner pulley
15. Tensioner arm
16. Idle pulley
17. Camshaft sprocket
18. Oil pump sprocket
19. Crankshaft sprocket bolt
20. Special washer
21. Crankshaft sprocket
22. Flange <Except FWD-Vehicles for California - 1995 models>
23. Crankshaft sensing blade <FWD-Vehicles for California - 1995 models>
24. Timing belt tensioner "B"
25. Timing belt "B"
26. Right counterbalance shaft sprocket
27. Spacer
28. Crankshaft sprocket "B"
29. Key
30. Engine support bracket
31. Timing belt under cover

Installation steps

31. Timing belt under cover
30. Engine support bracket
29. Key
28. Crankshaft sprocket "B"
27. Spacer
26. Right counterbalance shaft sprocket
24. Timing belt tensioner "B"
25. Timing belt "B"
• Timing belt "B" tension adjustment
23. Crankshaft sensing blade <FWD-Vehicles for California - 1995 models>
22. Flange <Except FWD-Vehicles for California - 1995 models>
21. Crankshaft sprocket
20. Special washer
19. Crankshaft sprocket bolt
18. Oil pump sprocket
17. Camshaft sprocket
16. Idle pulley
12. Auto tensioner
15. Tensioner arm
14. Tensioner pulley
13. Timing belt
• Timing belt tension adjustment

MT1069100150000A

Fig. 27 Timing & balance shaft replacement. 16-valve engine

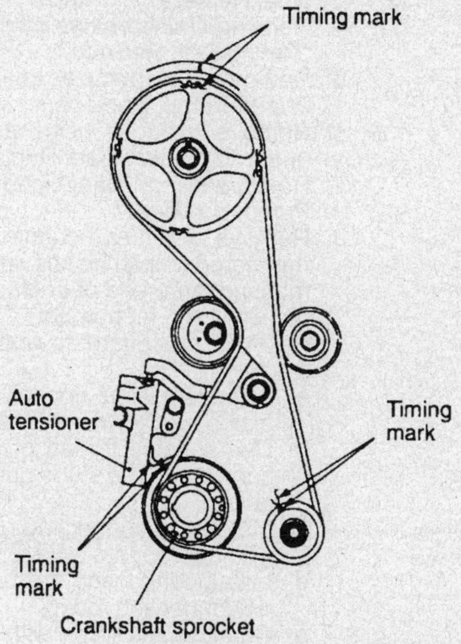
Timing mark
Auto tensioner
Timing mark
Timing mark
Crankshaft sprocket

MT1069300333000X

Fig. 26 Timing belt alignment. 16-valve engine

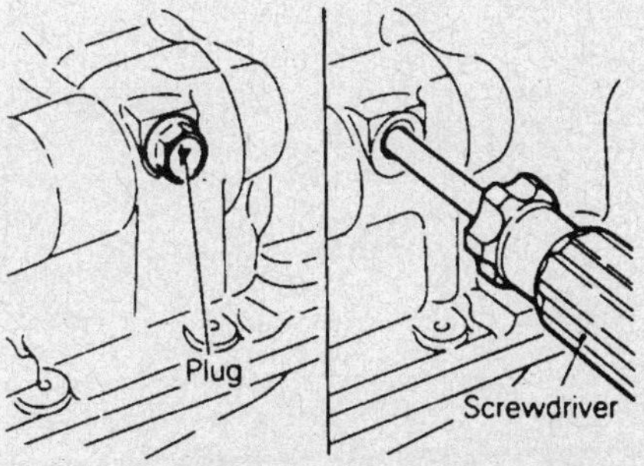
Plug
Screwdriver

MT1069100149000X

Fig. 28 Silent shaft blocking plug. 16-valve engine

Installation

1. Install timing belt under cover, then install engine support bracket, apply sealant to center bolt and tighten all bolts to specifications.
2. Install crankshaft sprocket, **Fig. 39.**
3. Apply thin coat of engine oil to outer inside diameter of space and install with chamfered end facing oil seal, **Fig. 40.**
4. Install right hand balance shaft sprocket.
5. Ensure balance shaft and crankshaft sprockets are properly aligned, **Fig. 41,** then fit balance shaft timing belt over crankshaft and balance shaft sprockets. **There should be no belt slack.**
6. Temporarily install tensioner with center of pulley to left and above installation bolt center, then temporarily install pulley with flange toward front of engine.
7. Hold tensioner up so that tension side of belt is taut and tighten tensioner bolt, then measure belt tension side deflection. Standard deflection is .20–.28 inch.
8. **On 1995 FWD California models,** install crankshaft sensing blade, **Fig. 42.**
9. **On all models,** install crankshaft flange, **Fig. 43.**

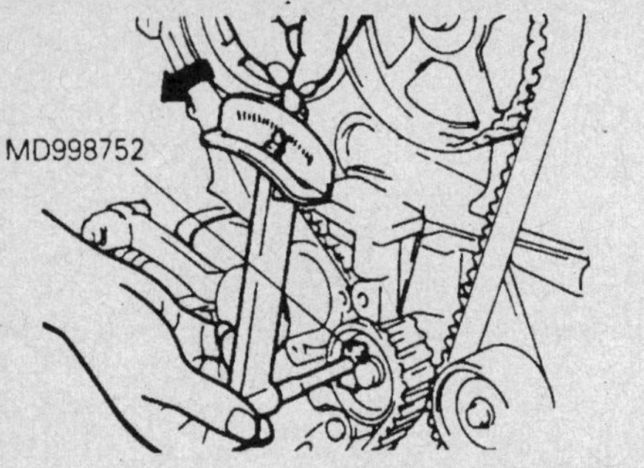
MD998752

MT1069100152000X

Fig. 29 Timing belt tensioner pulley & adjustment tools. 16-valve engine

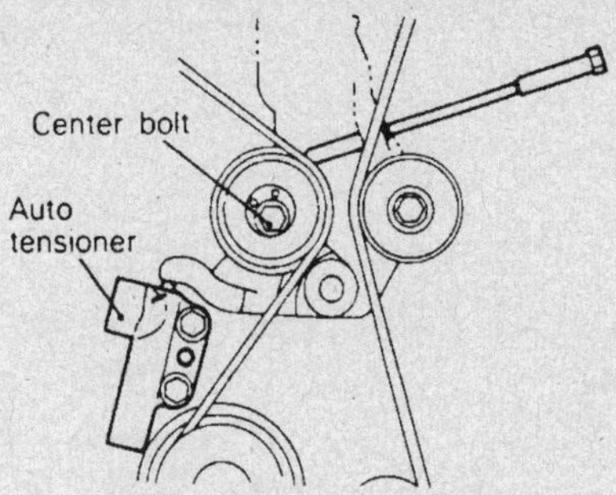
Center bolt
Auto tensioner

MT1069100153000X

Fig. 30 Timing belt auto tensioner set screw. 16-valve engine

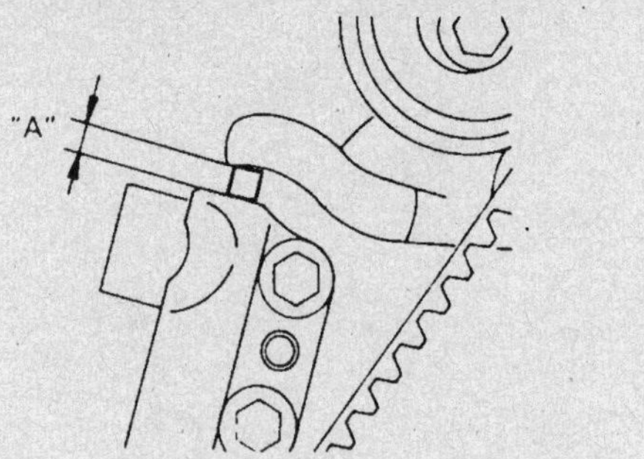
"A"

MT1069100154000X

Fig. 31 Auto tensioner protrusion measurement. 16-valve engine

10. Install timing belt as described in "Timing Belt, Replace."

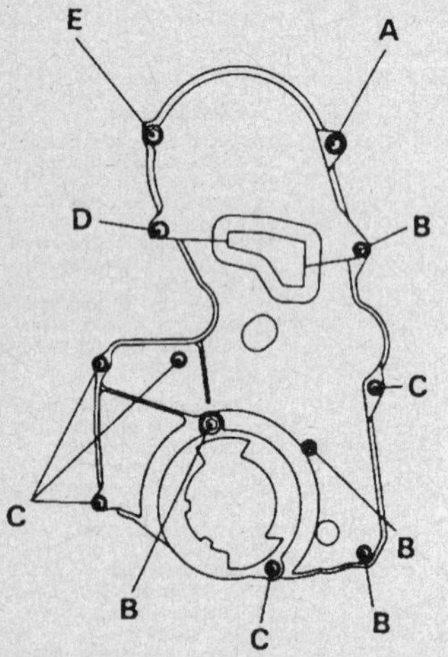
E
A
D
B
C
C
B
B
C
B

MT1069100155010X

Fig. 32 Timing belt cover bolt locations (Part 1 of 2). 16-valve engine

	1993 models	From 1994 models
A	6 × 20 (24 × .78) or 6 × 18 (24 × .71)	8 × 28 (.31 × 1.10)
B	6 × 22 (24 × .87) or 6 × 25 (24 × .98)	6 × 25 (24 × .98)
C	6 × 18 (24 × .71)	6 × 18 (24 × .71)
D	6 × 28 (24 × 1.10) or 6 × 25 (24 × .98)	8 × 35 (.31 × 1.38)
E	6 × 50 (24 × 1.97)	8 × 50 (.31 × 1.97)

Bolt diameter × length mm(in)

MT1069100155020X

Fig. 32 Timing belt cover bolt locations (Part 2 of 2). 16-valve engine

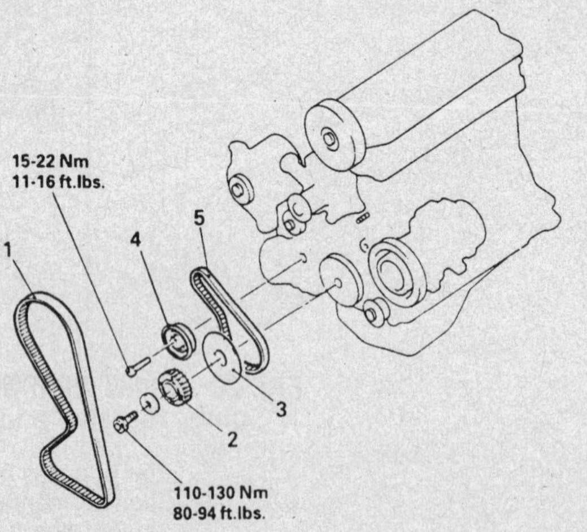
15-22 Nm
11-16 ft.lbs.
1
4
5
3
2
110-130 Nm
80-94 ft.lbs.

Removal steps
1. Timing belt
2. Crankshaft sprocket
3. Flange
4. Timing belt B tensioner
5. Timing belt B

MT1069100137000X

Fig. 33 Exploded view of balance shaft belt. 8-valve engine

SILENT SHAFT

REPLACE

Refer to "Oil Pump, Replace" for silent shaft replacement procedure.

PISTON & ROD ASSEMBLY

REPLACEMENT

1. Release fuel system pressure as outlined under "Precautions."
2. Disconnect battery ground cable.
3. Remove engine as outlined under "Engine, Replace."
4. Remove timing belt as outlined under "Timing Belt, Replace."
5. Remove water pump as outlined under "Water Pump, Replace."
6. Remove cylinder head as outlined under "Cylinder Head, Replace."
7. Remove oil pan as outlined under "Oil Pump, Replace."
8. Remove piston and connecting rod in numbered sequence shown in **Fig. 44,** marking large end of each connecting rod with cylinder number.
9. Reverse procedure to install, noting following:
   a. Arrange piston ring oil gaps and piston as shown in **Fig. 45.**
   b. Use suitable thread protectors on connecting rod studs prior to installation.
   c. Mate each connecting rod marking with appropriate cylinder.
   d. Install connecting rod bearing cap on connecting rod.
   e. Coat threads lightly with oil.
   f. Install both nuts finger tight.
   g. Alternately tighten each nut to specifications.

MAIN & ROD BEARINGS

When servicing crankshaft bearings refer to **Fig. 46.**

1. Install bearing with oil groove on cylinder block side.
2. Install bearing with no oil groove on bearing cap side.

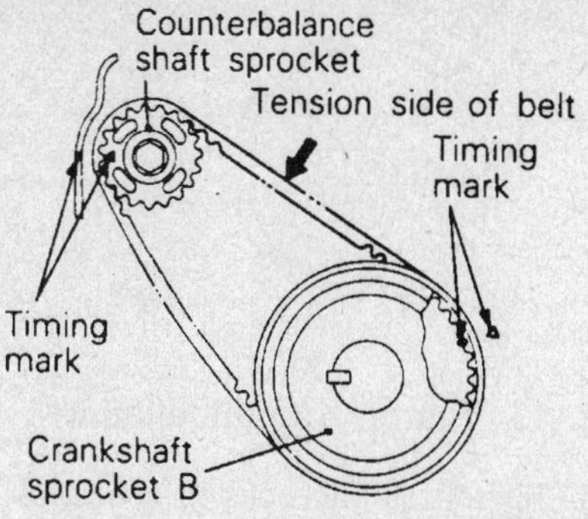
Counterbalance shaft sprocket
Tension side of belt
Timing mark
Timing mark
Crankshaft sprocket B
MT1069100138000X

Fig. 34 Crankshaft & balance shaft sprocket alignment. 8-valve engine

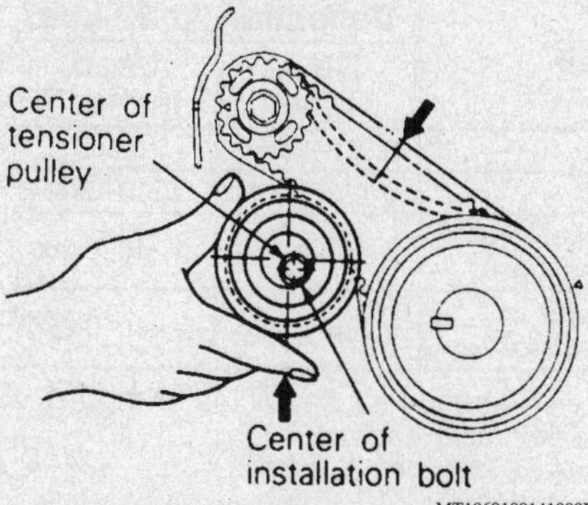
Center of tensioner pulley
Center of installation bolt
MT1069100141000X

Fig. 37 Balance shaft belt tension check. 8-valve engine

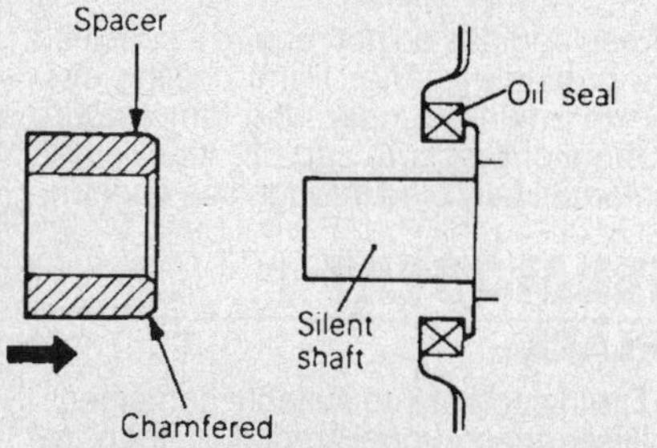
Spacer
Oil seal
Silent shaft
Chamfered
MT1069100151000X

Fig. 40 Balance shaft sprocket spacer orientation. 16-valve engine

3. Install bearing caps so their arrows are positioned on timing belt side.
4. Tighten bearing cap bolts to specifications.
5. Ensure crankshaft turns freely and endplay is 0.0020–0.0071 inch.
6. Force oil separator into oil seal case so that oil hole in separator is directed downward.

OIL PAN

REPLACE

Refer to "Oil Pump, Replace" for oil pan replacement procedure.

OIL PUMP

REPLACE

REMOVAL

1. Release fuel system pressure as out-

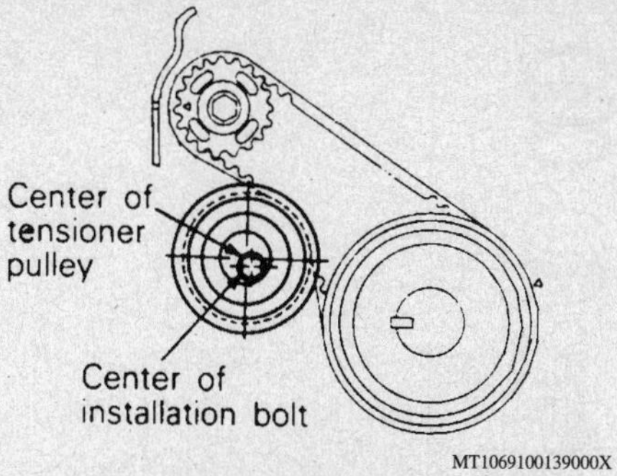
Center of tensioner pulley
Center of installation bolt
MT1069100139000X

Fig. 35 Tensioner pulley starting position. 8-valve engine

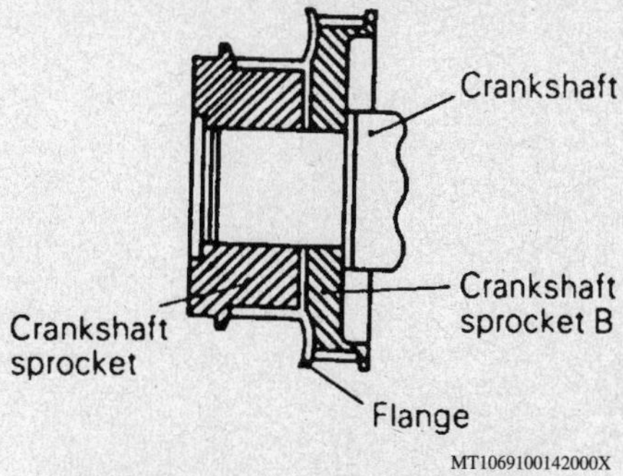
Crankshaft
Crankshaft sprocket B
Crankshaft sprocket
Flange
MT1069100142000X

Fig. 38 Crankshaft flange installation. 8 valve engine

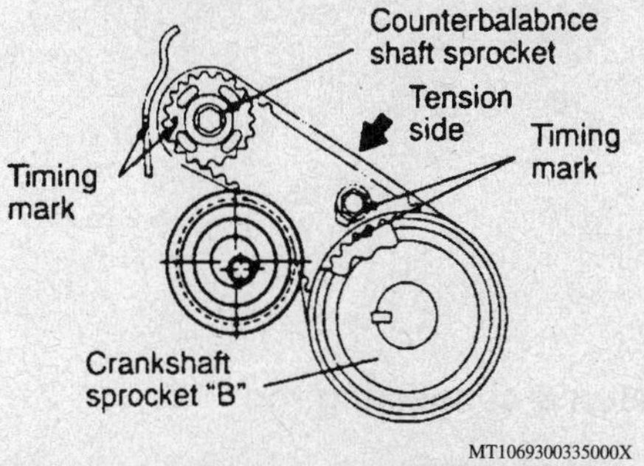
Counterbalabnce shaft sprocket
Tension side
Timing mark
Timing mark
Crankshaft sprocket "B"
MT1069300335000X

Fig. 41 Balance shaft belt timing marks. 16-valve engine

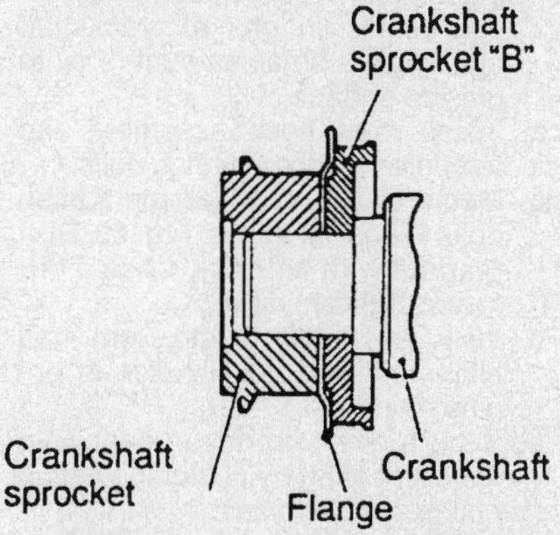
Crankshaft sprocket "B"
Crankshaft sprocket
Crankshaft
Flange
MT1069300337000X

Fig. 43 Crankshaft flange installation. 16-valve engine

lined under "Precautions."

2. Disconnect battery ground cable.
3. Remove timing belt as outlined under "Timing Belt, Replace."

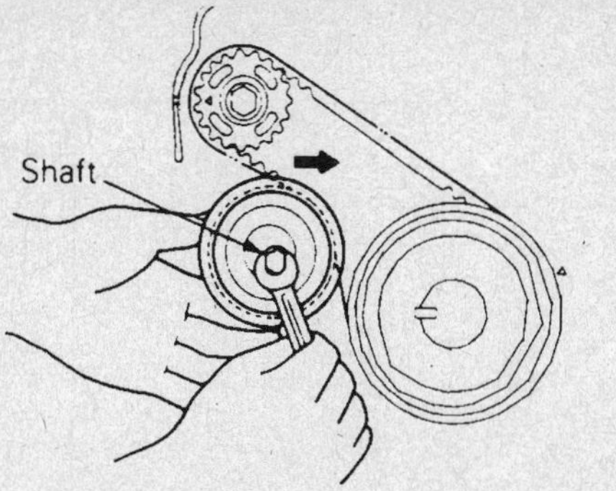
Shaft
MT1069100140000X

Fig. 36 Balance shaft belt adjustment. 8-valve engine

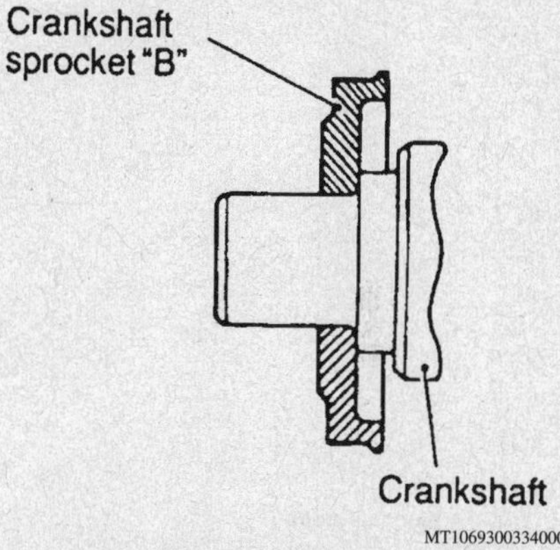
Crankshaft sprocket "B"
Crankshaft
MT1069300334000X

Fig. 39 Balance shaft sprocket installation. 16-valve engine

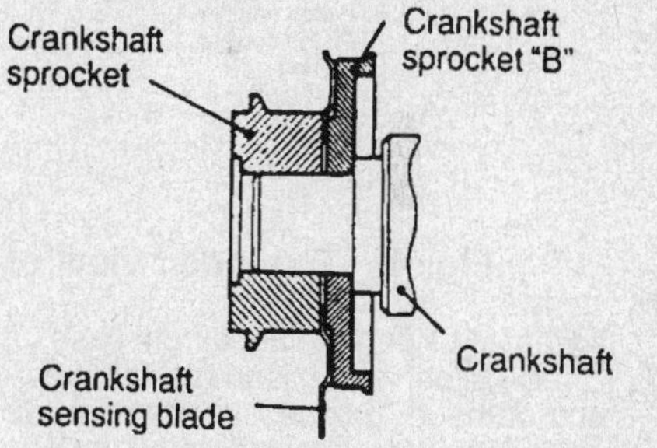
Crankshaft sprocket
Crankshaft sprocket "B"
Crankshaft
Crankshaft sensing blade
MT1069500336000X

Fig. 42 Crankshaft sensing blade installation. 16-valve engine

4. Remove balance shaft belt as described in "Balance Shaft Belt, Replace."
5. Remove components in numbered sequence shown in **Fig. 47,** noting following:
   a. Remove oil pan by driving oil pan remover tool around pan.
   b. Remove plug on side of cylinder block and insert a screwdriver into hole to prevent silent shaft from turning.
   c. Loosen oil pump sprocket flange nut.
   d. With silent shaft locked, remove flange bolt.

INSPECTION

1. Check gear contacting surface of front case and oil pump cover for step wear.

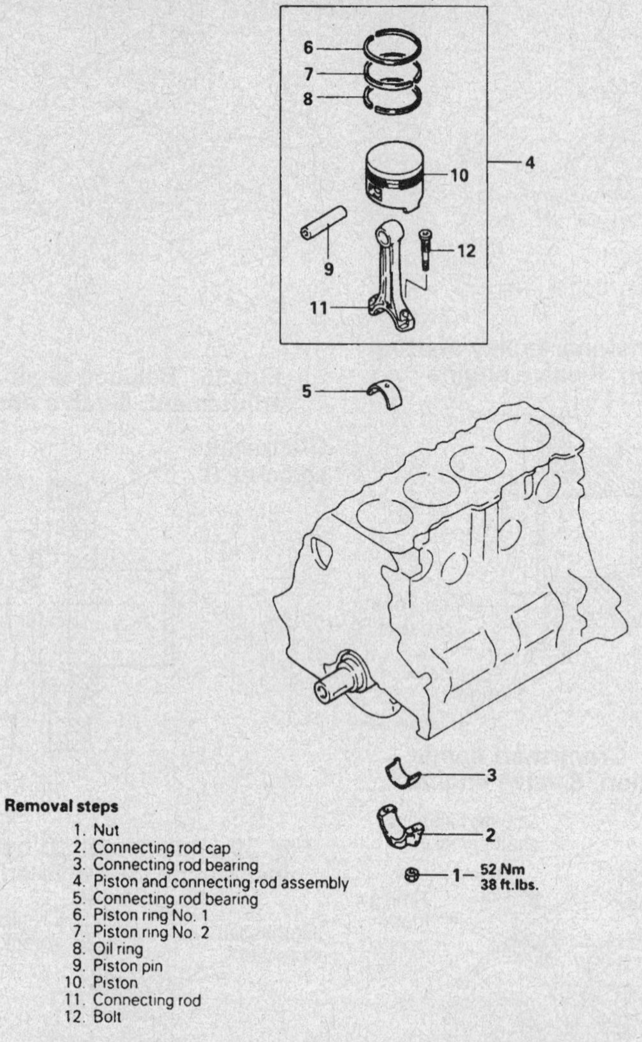
6
7
8
10
4
9
12
11
5
3
2
1
52 Nm
38 ft.lbs.
Removal steps
1. Nut
2. Connecting rod cap
3. Connecting rod bearing
4. Piston and connecting rod assembly
5. Connecting rod bearing
6. Piston ring No. 1
7. Piston ring No. 2
8. Oil ring
9. Piston pin
10. Piston
11. Connecting rod
12. Bolt
MT1069100158000X

Fig. 44 Exploded view of piston & connecting rod

If wear is evident, replace front case.

2. Check silent shaft journals for wear and damage. If excessive damage or wear is evident, check bearing. If necessary, replace silent shaft and/or bearing.
3. Inspect oil pump as follows:
   a. Assemble oil pump gear in front case and rotate gear to ensure smooth rotation with no looseness.
   b. Ensure no ridge wear exists on contact surface between front case and gear surface of oil pump cover.
   c. Ensure side clearance is 0.0031–0.0055 inch for drive gear and 0.0024–0.0047 inch for driven gear.

INSTALLATION

Reverse numbered sequence shown in **Fig. 47** to install, noting following:

1. Install silent shaft and water pump seal using suitable seal installer tool.
2. Install crankshaft front seal using seal installer, tool No. MD998375-01, or equivalent.
3. Apply engine oil amply to gears and line up alignment marks, **Fig. 48.**
4. Coat threads of oil pressure switch/gauge unit with 3M sealant, No. 8660, or equivalent.
5. Install front case as follows:
   a. Install crankshaft front oil seal guide, tool No. MD998285-01, or equivalent, on end of crankshaft and apply a small amount of oil to outside surface.
   b. Install front case assembly and temporarily tighten flange bolts.
   c. Mount oil filter bracket and tighten bolts to specifications, **Fig. 49. Bolt marked with asterisk 1 has a different tighten value.**
   d. Insert a screwdriver into silent shaft alignment hole on RH side of engine block.
   e. Secure oil pump driven gear onto left silent shaft by tightening flange bolt to specifications.
   f. Install new O-ring in groove of front case at plug position and install plug. Tighten to specifications.
   g. Lock silent shaft as outlined under Step d.
   h. Tighten flange bolt to specifications.
   i. Apply a 0.16 inch bead of sealant to oil pan as shown in **Fig. 50.**

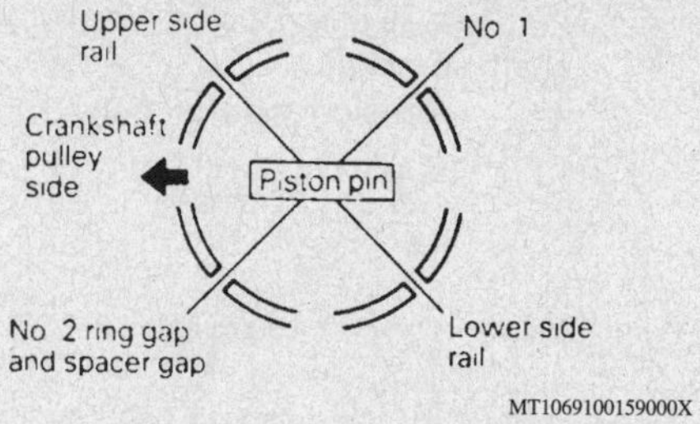
Upper side rail
No 1
Crankshaft pulley side
Piston pin
No 2 ring gap and spacer gap
Lower side rail
MT1069100159000X

Fig. 45 Piston ring installation

   j. Tighten oil pan bolts to specifications.

BELT TENSION DATA

Belt	Deflection At 22 Lbs.	
	New, Inches	Used, Inches①
Alt.	0.300–0.350	0.400
A/C	0.170–0.190	0.210–0.024
Power Steering②	0.180–0.260	0.240–0.350
Power Steering③	0.180–0.220	0.240–0.280

① — Belt used for 5 minutes or more.
② — 8-valve engine.
③ — 16-valve engine.

COOLING SYSTEM BLEED

These engines do not require a specified bleed procedure. After filling cooling system, run engine to operating temperature with radiator/pressure cap off. Air will then be automatically bled through cap opening.

THERMOSTAT

REPLACE

1. Drain coolant into suitable container.
2. Disconnect upper radiator, then remove thermostat housing attaching bolts.
3. Remove thermostat housing, then thermostat.
4. Reverse procedure to install, tightening attaching bolts to specifications.

WATER PUMP

REPLACE

1. Disconnect battery ground cable.
2. Drain cooling system into an approved container.
3. Remove timing belts as outlined under "Timing Belt, Replace."
4. Remove alternator brace, **Fig. 51.**
5. Remove water pump built and water pump.
6. Remove water pump gasket and O-ring.
7. Reverse procedure to install, noting following:
   a. Coat O-ring with water to ease installation.
   b. Install water pump bolts in correct location, **Fig. 52.**

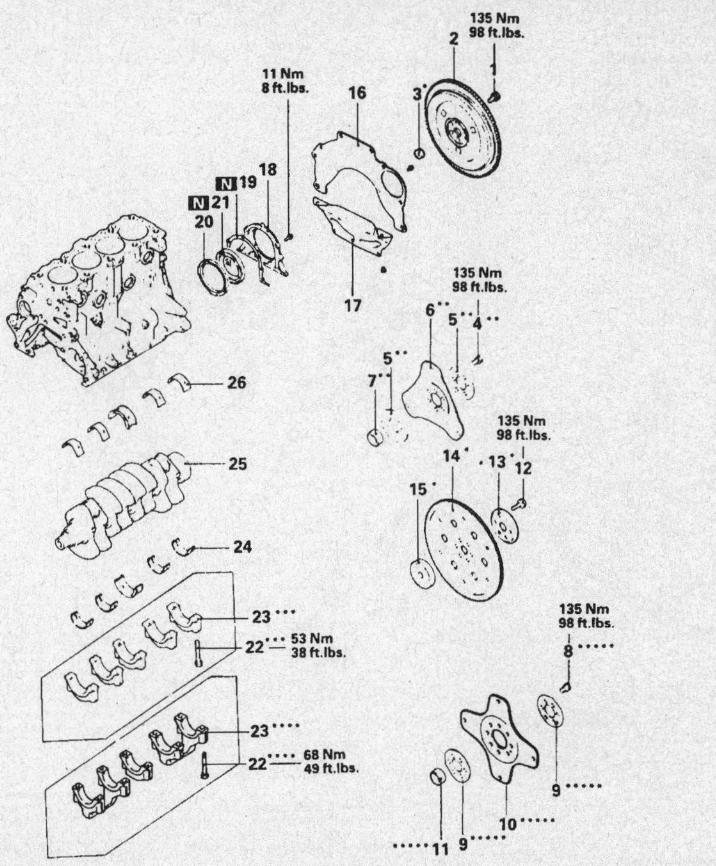
135 Nm
98 ft.lbs.
11 Nm
8 ft.lbs.
135 Nm
98 ft.lbs.
135 Nm
98 ft.lbs.
135 Nm
98 ft.lbs.
53 Nm
38 ft.lbs.
68 Nm
49 ft.lbs.

Removal steps

1. Flywheel bolt
2. Flywheel
3. Ball bearing*
4. Drive plate bolt**
5. Adapter plate**
6. Drive plate**
7. Crankshaft bushing**
8. Drive plate bolt
9. Adapter plate
10. Drive plate
11. Crankshaft bushing
12. Drive plate bolt*
13. Adapter plate*
14. Drive plate*
15. Crankshaft adapter*
16. Rear plate
17. Bell housing cover
18. Oil seal case
19. Gasket
20. Oil separator
21. Oil seal
22. Bearing cap bolt
23. Bearing cap
24. Crankshaft bearing (lower)
25. Crankshaft
26. Crankshaft bearing (upper)

NOTE
* : Rear wheel drive
** : Front wheel drive
*** : SOHC
**** : DOHC
***** : DOHC Turbo for ECLIPSE

MT1069100160000X

Fig. 46 Exploded view of crankshaft

RADIATOR

REPLACE

Service radiator as described in "1.8L engine."

FUEL PUMP

REPLACE

This procedure has been revised by a technical service bulletin.

1. Release fuel system pressure as outlined under "Precautions."
2. Disconnect battery ground cable.
3. Remove fuel cap, then drain fuel tank into a suitable container.
4. Disconnect return, high pressure, vapor and filler hoses.
5. Disconnect fuel gauge unit and electric fuel pump electrical connections.
6. **On AWD models,** remove rear propeller shaft.
7. **On all models,** support fuel tank then remove fuel tank supports.
8. Lower fuel tank from vehicle, then remove fuel pump from fuel tank.
9. Reverse procedure to install.

FUEL FILTER

REPLACE

This procedure has been revised by a technical service bulletin.

1. Release fuel system pressure as outlined under "Precautions."
2. Remove air cleaner and intake hose.
3. Holding fuel filter with a spanner, remove eye bolt and high-pressure fuel hose. **As there will be some pressure remaining in fuel pipe line, cover it with a rag to prevent fuel from spraying out.**
4. Loosen flare nut then disconnect fuel main pipe connection.
5. Remove fuel filter, **Figs. 53 and 54.**
6. Reverse procedure to install.

TECHNICAL SERVICE BULLETINS

FUEL STARVATION

Fuel starvation can occur when in-tank fuel filter is clogged, typically by contaminated fuel.

To correct problem, proceed as follows:

1. Activate fuel pump with scan tool, then measure pump's supply voltage.
2. If voltage is less than 8 volts, inspect and repair fuel pump wiring harness.
3. If voltage is 8 volts or more, check system fuel pressure.
4. If system fuel pressure is within specifications, check system for other starvation problems. Specification is 38 psi at curb idle with fuel pressure regulator vacuum hose attached and 47–50 psi with hose disconnected.
5. If fuel system pressure is not within specifications, remove fuel pump as described in "Fuel Pump, Replace" and check filter.
6. If filter is clean, replace fuel pump. If filter is clogged, proceed as follows:
   a. Carefully dislodge pump motor from bracket. On some models it may be necessary to remove lower bracket clamp to dislodge motor.
   b. Remove rubber pump vibration dampener, then retaining clip (or nut) and filter.
   c. Replace filter.
   d. **If filter is severely clogged, clean inside of fuel tank.**
7. Reverse procedure to install using new gasket.

IDLE VIBRATION

Some models (mostly equipped with automatic transaxles) may vibrate excessively at idle.

Radiator may be transmitting engine vibration through frame because mounting brackets are not centered on posts. To correct problem, proceed as follows:

1. Examine upper radiator mounting brackets. Brackets should be centered on post and radiator should move freely.
2. If brackets are not center, remove upper brackets and ensure bottom mounting posts are seating in lower brackets.
3. Center upper brackets over posts and tighten bolts to specifications.
4. Measure clearance between upper brackets and radiator top. Standard clearance is .0394 inch or more.

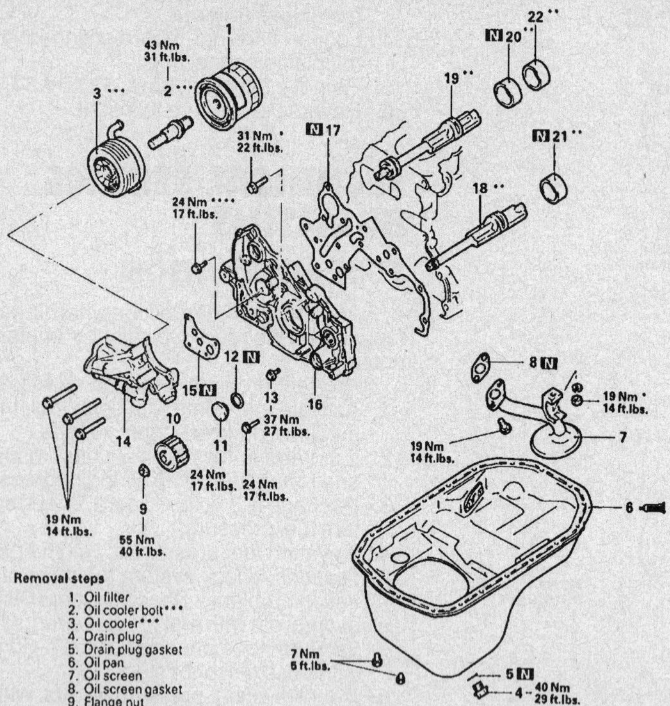
43 Nm
31 ft.lbs.
31 Nm *
22 ft.lbs.
24 Nm ****
17 ft.lbs.
19 Nm *
14 ft.lbs.
19 Nm
14 ft.lbs.
37 Nm
27 ft.lbs.
24 Nm
17 ft.lbs.
55 Nm
40 ft.lbs.
7 Nm
5 ft.lbs.
40 Nm
29 ft.lbs.

Removal steps

1. Oil filter
2. Oil cooler bolt***
3. Oil cooler***
4. Drain plug
5. Drain plug gasket
6. Oil pan
7. Oil screen
8. Oil screen gasket
9. Flange nut
10. Oil pump sprocket**
11. Plug
12. O-ring
13. Flange bolt
14. Oil filter bracket
15. Oil filter bracket gasket
16. Front case
17. Front case gasket
18. Silent shaft, left**
19. Silent shaft, right**
20. Silent shaft, front bearing**
21. Silent shaft, rear bearing, left**
22. Silent shaft, rear bearing, right**

NOTE
* : DOHC
** : Engine with silent shafts
*** : Engine with turbocharger
**** : Engine without silent shafts
***** : Engine with air-cooling type oil cooler

MT1099100044010X

Fig. 47 Oil pump, front case, silent shaft & oil pan replacement (Part 1 of 2)

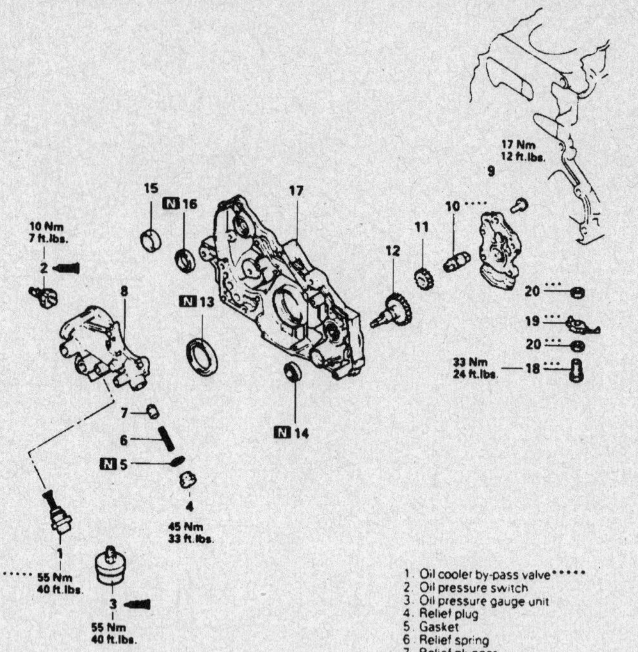
17 Nm
12 ft.lbs.
10 Nm
7 ft.lbs.
33 Nm
24 ft.lbs.
45 Nm
33 ft.lbs.
55 Nm
40 ft.lbs.
55 Nm
40 ft.lbs.

1. Oil cooler by-pass valve*****
2. Oil pressure switch
3. Oil pressure gauge unit
4. Relief plug
5. Gasket
6. Relief spring
7. Relief plunger
8. Oil filter bracket
9. Oil pump cover
10. Oil pump shaft****
11. Oil pump driven gear
12. Oil pump drive gear
13. Crankshaft front oil seal
14. Oil pump oil seal
15. Plug****
16. Silent shaft oil seal**
17. Front case
18. Check valve
19. Oil jet
20. Gasket

NOTE
* DOHC
** Engine with silent shafts
*** Engine with turbocharger
**** Engine without silent shafts
***** Engine with air-cooling type oil cooler

MT1099100044020X

Fig. 47 Oil pump, front case, silent shaft & oil pan replacement (Part 2 of 2)

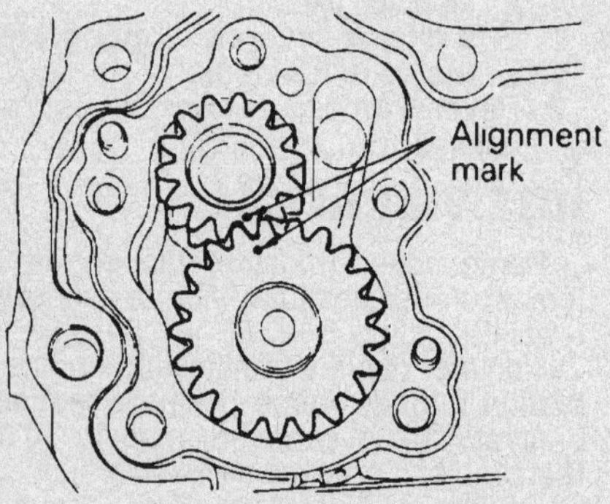
Alignment
mark

MT1099100045000X

Fig. 48 Oil pump gear alignment marks

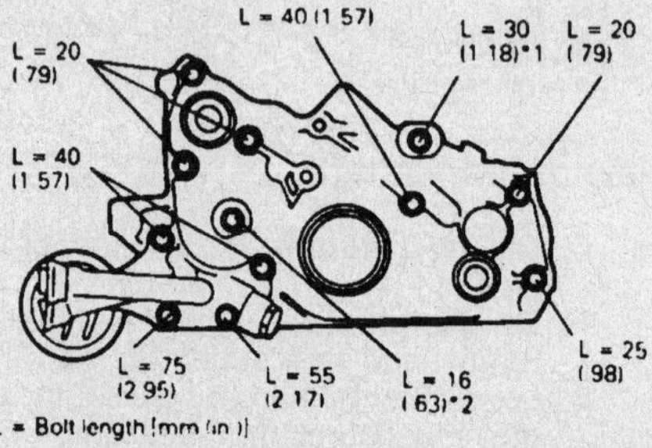
L = 40 (1.57)
L = 20
(.79)
L = 30
(1.18)*1
L = 20
(.79)
L = 40
(1.57)
L = 75
(2.95)
L = 55
(2.17)
L = 16
(.63)*2
L = 25
(.98)
L = Bolt length (mm (in.))

MT1099100046000X

Fig. 49 Oil filter bracket bolt location

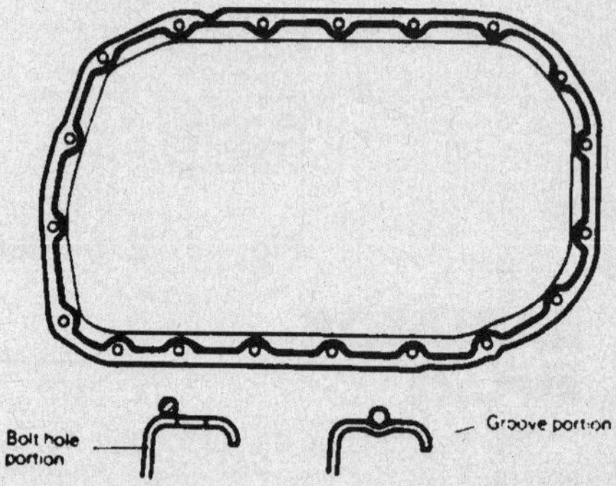
Bolt hole
portion
Groove portion

MT1099100047000X

Fig. 50 Oil pan sealant location

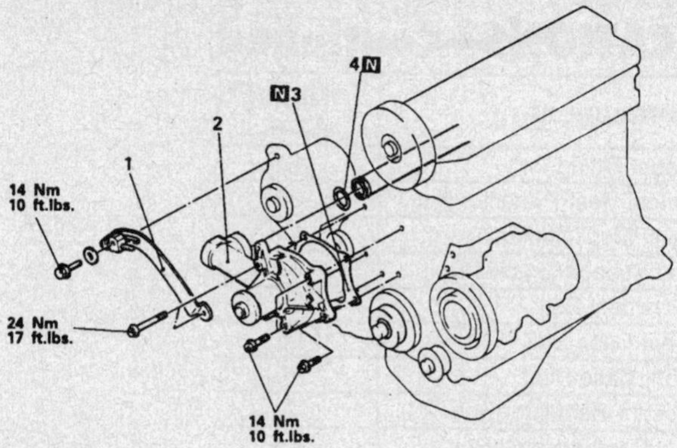
14 Nm
10 ft.lbs.
24 Nm
17 ft.lbs.
14 Nm
10 ft.lbs.
1
2
N3
4N

Removal steps
1. Alternator brace
2. Water pump
3. Water pump gasket
4. O-ring

MT1089100017000X

Fig. 51 Exploded view of water pump

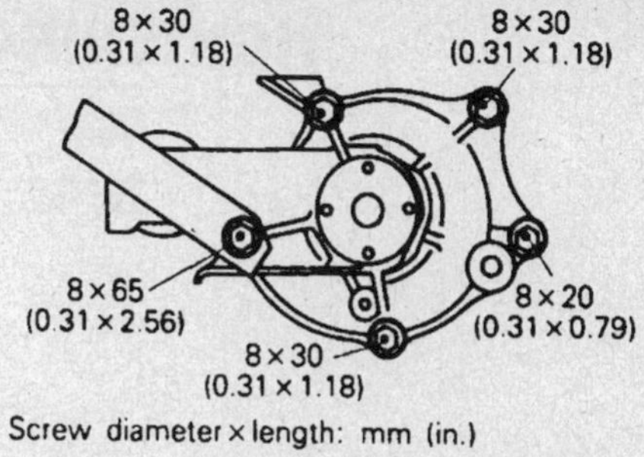
8×30
(0.31×1.18)
8×30
(0.31×1.18)
8×65
(0.31×2.56)
8×20
(0.31×0.79)
8×30
(0.31×1.18)
Screw diameter×length: mm (in.)

MT1089100018000X

Fig. 52 Water pump bolt location

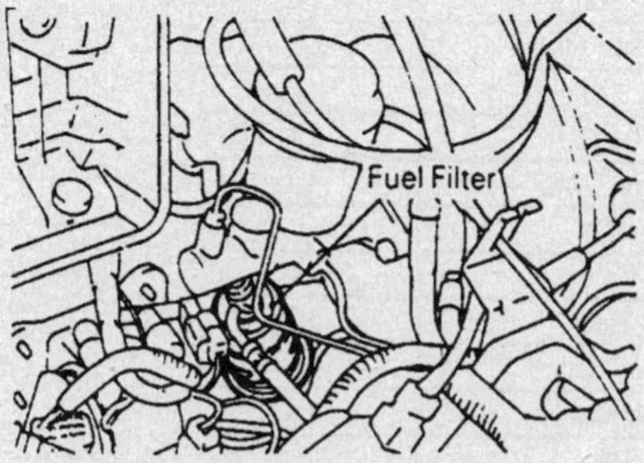
Fuel Filter

MT1029100012000X

Fig. 53 Fuel filter location

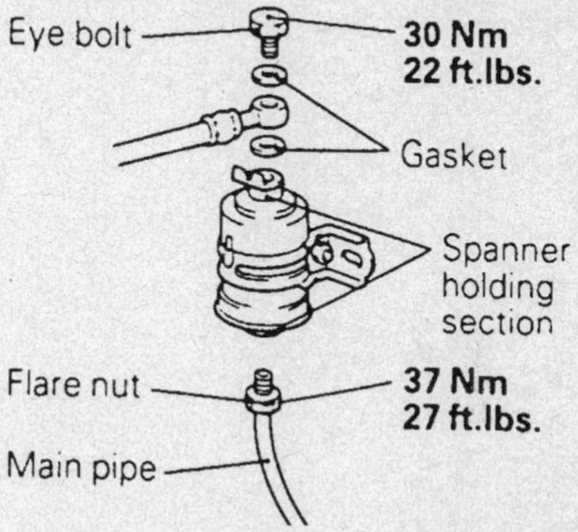
Eye bolt
30 Nm
22 ft.lbs.
Gasket
Spanner holding section
Flare nut
37 Nm
27 ft.lbs.
Main pipe

MT1029100013000X

Fig. 54 Fuel filter installation

TIGHTENING SPECIFICATIONS

Year	Component	Torque/Ft. Lbs.
1993–96	Air Intake Plenum Bolt & Nut	13
	Air Intake Plenum Stay Bolt	13
	Air Outlet Fitting Bolt	14
	Alternator Mounting Bolt	17
	Alternator Brace Bolt	10
	Alternator Pivot Nut	17
	Camshaft Bearing Cap Bolt	⑤
	Camshaft Sprocket Bolt	65
	Connecting Rod Cap Nut	38
	Cooling Fan Bolt	8
	Crankshaft Bearing Cap Bolt	38
	Crankshaft Pulley Bolt	18
	Crankshaft Sprocket Bolt	87
	Cylinder Head Bolts	⑦⑧
	Distributor Nut	8
	Driveplate Bolt	98
	EGR Valve Bolt	14
	Engine Coolant Temperature Gauge Unit	8
	Engine Coolant Temperature Sensor	22
	Engine Support Bracket Bolt	33
	Engine Support Bracket Bolt (Front)	43
	Engine Support Bracket Bolt (Left)	26

Continued

TIGHTENING SPECIFICATIONS—Continued

Year	Component	Torque/Ft. Lbs.
1993–96	Exhaust Fitting Bolt	43
	Exhaust Manifold Heat Protector Bolt	③
	Exhaust Manifold Nut	13
	Exhaust Pipe Support Bracket Bolt	26
	Flywheel Bolt	98
	Front Case Bolt	⑥
	Front Case Plug	17
	Fuel Pressure Regulator Bolt	7
	Idle Speed Control Servo Bolt	2.5
	Ignition Coil Bolt	10
	Intake Manifold Bolt & Nut	13
	Intake Manifold Stay Bolt	16
	Oil Cooler Bolt	31
	Oil Cooler By-Pass Valve	40
	Oil Delivery Body	8
	Oil Filter Bracket Bolt	14
	Oil Level Gauge Guise Bolt	②
	Oil Pan Bolt	5
	Oil Pan Drain Plug	29
	Oil Pressure Gauge Unit	40
	Oil Pressure Switch	7
	Oil Pump Check Valve	24
	Oil Pump Cover Bolt	12
	Oil Pump Sprocket Nut	40
	Oil Screen Bolt & Nut	14
	Oil Seal Case Bolt	8
	Power Transistor Bolt	10
	Relief Plug	33
	Rocker Cover Bolt	4
	Roll Stopper Bracket Bolt (Front)	47
	Roll Stopper Bracket Bolt (Rear)	87
	Silent Shaft Flange Bolt (Left)	27
	Silent Shaft Sprocket Bolt (Right)	33
	Spark Plug	18
	Tensioner Bolt	35
	Tensioner Spacer	35
	Tensioner "B" Bolt	14
	Thermostat Case Nut	13
	Throttle Body Bolt	14
	Throttle Position Sensor Bolt	1.4
	Timing Belt Tensioner Pulley Center Bolt	35
	Timing Belt Upper Cover Bolts	8
	Water Inlet Pipe Bolt	10
	Water Outlet Fitting Bolt	14
	Water Pipe Bolt	④
	Water Pipe 'A' & 'B' Eye Bolt	31

Continued

TIGHTENING SPECIFICATIONS—Continued

Year	Component	Torque/Ft. Lbs.
1993–96	Water Pipe 'A' Bolt	8
	Water Pipe 'B' Flare Nut	33
	Water Pump Bolt	17
	Water Pump Pulley Bolt	①

① — Less cooling fan, 7 ft. lbs; w/cooling fan, 8 ft. lbs.
② — 8 mm bolts, 10 ft. lbs; 10 mm bolts, 43 ft. lbs.
③ — 6 mm bolts, 7 ft. lbs.; 8 mm bolts, 10 ft. lbs.; 10 mm bolts, 22 ft. lbs.
④ — 6 mm bolts, 8 ft. lbs.; 8 mm bolts, 10 ft. lbs.
⑤ — 8 mm x 25 mm bolts, 17 ft. lbs.; 8 mm x 65 mm bolts, 14 ft. lbs.
⑥ — 8 mm bolts, 17 ft. lbs.; 10 mm bolts, 22 ft. lbs.
⑦ — 8-valve engine, refer to "Cylinder Head, Replace" for procedure.
⑧ — 16-valve engine, refer to "Cylinder Head, Replace" for procedure.

Clutch & Manual Transaxle

INDEX

	Page No.
Adjustments	25-35
Clutch Interlock Switch	25-35
Clutch Pedal	25-35
Clutch, Replace	25-35
Hydraulic System Service	25-35
Clutch Hydraulic Control Component, Replace	25-35
Tightening Specifications	25-39
Transaxle, Replace	25-36
AWD Models	25-36
FWD Models	25-36

ADJUSTMENTS

CLUTCH PEDAL

1. Measure clutch pedal height (A) and clutch pedal freeplay (B), **Fig. 1.**
2. Clutch pedal height should be 7.68–7.87 inches.
3. Clutch pedal clevis pin play should be 0.04–0.12 inch.
4. If clutch pedal height and freeplay are not within specifications, adjust as follows:
   a. **On models less cruise control,** turn adjusting bolt to adjust pedal to correct height.
   b. **On models with cruise control,** disconnect clutch switch, then turn clutch switch to adjust pedal to correct height.
   c. **On all models,** turn clutch master cylinder pushrod to adjust clutch pedal clevis pin play, **Fig. 2.**
   d. After completing adjustments, measure clutch pedal freeplay and clutch pedal floor clearance, **Fig. 3.** freeplay should be 0.24–0.51 inch and floor clearance should be 1.77 inches or more.
5. If clutch pedal freeplay and floor clearance is not within specifications, result is either air in hydraulic system or a faulty clutch master cylinder, clutch or interlock switch.

CLUTCH INTERLOCK SWITCH

1. Block front wheels, apply parking brake and place transaxle into 5th gear.
2. After adjusting clutch pedal, check clutch interlock as follows:
   a. Engine should not start even if ignition switch is turned to Start position with clutch pedal not depressed. If engine starts, check interlock switch and harness.
   b. Engine should start after clutch pedal has been fully depressed and ignition switch has been turned to Start position. If engine starts before clutch pedal is fully depressed, adjust clutch interlock.
3. Loosen clutch interlock switch locknut, depress clutch pedal six inches and adjust clearance to 0.14 inch, **Fig. 4.**
4. Connect ohmmeter to clutch interlock switch terminals No. 1 and No. 2, **Fig. 5.**
5. With clutch pedal fully depressed no continuity should exist at terminals, **Fig. 5.**
6. With clutch pedal released, continuity should exist between terminals No. 1 and No. 2., **Fig. 5.**

HYDRAULIC SYSTEM SERVICE

CLUTCH HYDRAULIC CONTROL COMPONENT, REPLACE

1. Disconnect battery ground cable.
2. Drain clutch fluid from bleeder screw into a suitable container.
3. Remove clutch control components in numbered sequence shown in **Fig. 6.**
4. Reverse procedure to install, adjusting clutch pedal as outlined under "Adjustments."

CLUTCH

REPLACE

1. Remove transaxle as outlined under "Manual Transaxle, Replace."
2. Remove clutch cover, disc and related components in numbered sequence shown in **Fig. 7.**
3. Reverse procedure to install, noting following:
   a. Apply Mitsubishi grease part No. 0101011, or equivalent, on contact points of release fork shown in **Fig. 8.**

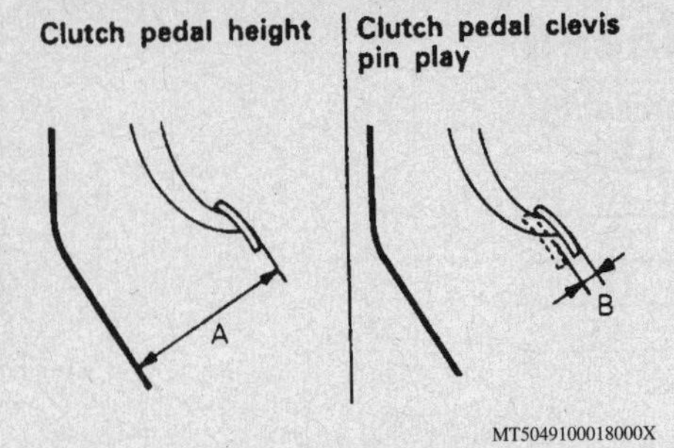
Clutch pedal height
Clutch pedal clevis pin play
A
B
MT5049100018000X

Fig. 1 Clutch pedal height & clevis pin freeplay

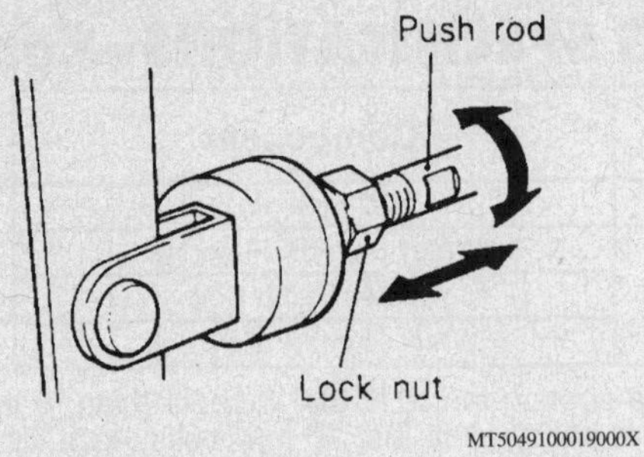
Push rod
Lock nut
MT5049100019000X

Fig. 2 Clevis pin adjustment

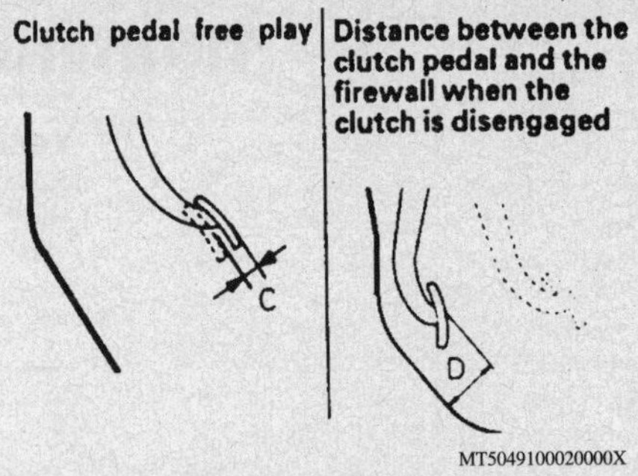
Clutch pedal free play
Distance between the clutch pedal and the firewall when the clutch is disengaged
C
D
MT5049100020000X

Fig. 3 Clutch pedal freeplay & floor clearance

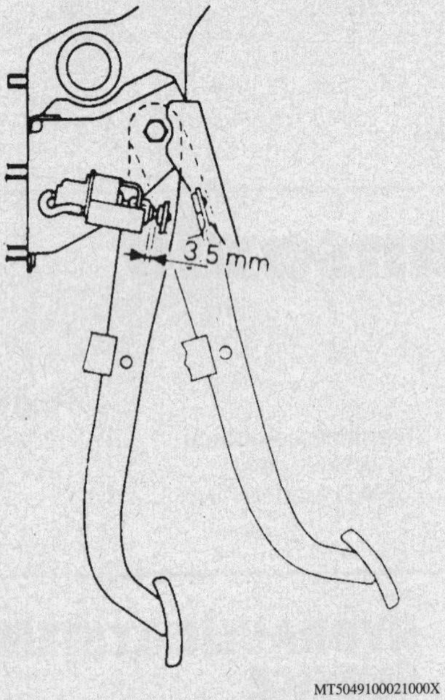
3.5 mm
MT5049100021000X

Fig. 4 Clutch interlock switch adjustment

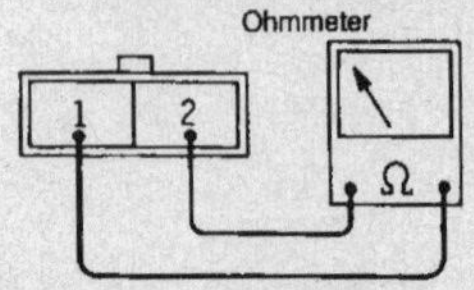
Ohmmeter
1
2
Ω

Pedal position	Terminal No.	
	1	2
Fully depressed		
Released	O—	—O

MT5049100063000X

Fig. 5 Clutch interlock switch continuity test

b. Apply Mitsubishi grease part No. 0101011, or equivalent, to inside surface of release bearing.
c. Apply Mitsubishi grease part No. 0101011, or equivalent, to clutch disc splines, then install clutch disc and cover using suitable alignment tool.

TRANSAXLE

REPLACE

FWD MODELS

1. Remove air cleaner assembly.
2. Disconnect battery ground cable.
3. Remove transaxle in numbered sequence shown in **Fig. 9,** noting following:
   a. Remove starter motor assembly with cables attached, then support aside.
   b. **On F5M22 transaxles,** support engine, using engine support hanger tool No. MB991191, or equivalent, to remove weight off transaxle mounting bolts.
   c. **On F5M31 transaxles,** use a suitable floor jack to raise transaxle assembly until no weight is applied on transaxle mounting bolts.
   d. **On all transaxles,** remove transaxle mounting bolt.
   e. Loosen tie rod end nut then disconnect tie rod end using steering linkage puller tool No. MB991113-01, or equivalent.
   f. Loosen lower ball joint nut then disconnect ball joint using steering linkage puller tool No. MB991113-01, or equivalent.
   g. Remove driveshafts as outlined in "Drive Axles "section.
   h. Disconnect clutch hydraulic cylinder leaving hoses attached.
   i. Support transaxle using a suitable jack stand, then move transaxle assembly to right and lower from vehicle.
4. Reverse procedure to install, ensuring stabilizer bar bolt protrusion is 0.3–0.4 inch, **Fig. 10.**

AWD MODELS

1. Remove air cleaner assembly.
2. Disconnect battery ground cable.
3. Remove transaxle in numbered sequence shown in **Fig. 11,** noting following:
   a. Remove starter motor assembly with cables attached, then support aside.
   b. Support engine, using engine support hanger tool No. MB991191, or equivalent, to remove weight off transaxle mounting bolts.
   c. Remove transaxle mounting bolt.
   d. Loosen tie rod end nut then disconnect tie rod end using steering linkage puller tool No. MB991113-01, or equivalent.
   e. Loosen lower ball joint nut then disconnect ball joint using steering linkage puller tool No. MB991113-01, or equivalent.
   f. Remove driveshafts as outlined in "Drive Axles"section.
   g. Disconnect clutch hydraulic cylinder leaving hoses attached.
   h. Remove propeller shaft.
   i. Remove transfer case assembly and cover opening to prevent oil discharge or entry of foreign material.
   j. Support transaxle using a suitable jack stand, then move transaxle assembly to right and lower from vehicle.
4. Reverse procedure to install, installing driveshafts as outlined in "Drive Axles" section.

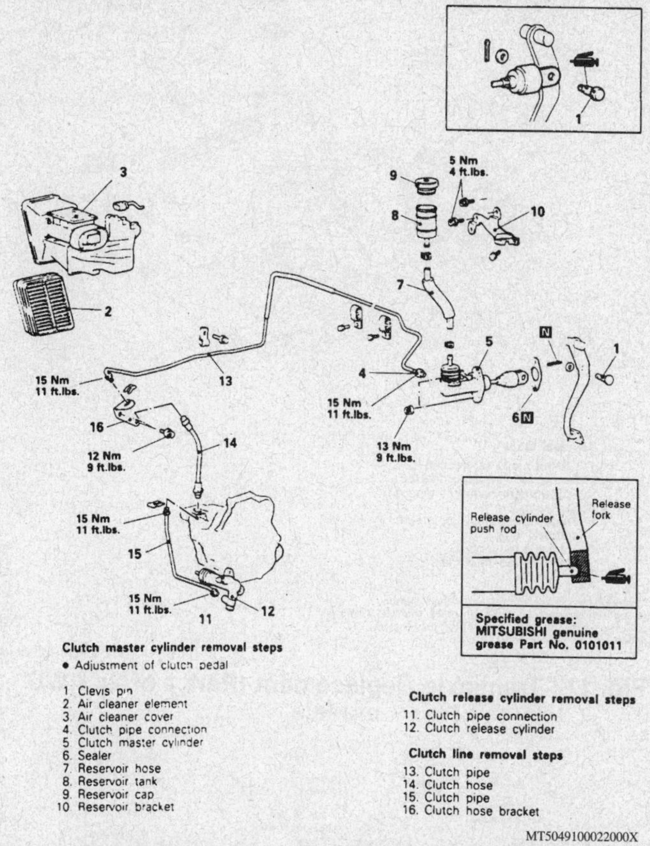
5 Nm
4 ft.lbs.
15 Nm
11 ft.lbs.
12 Nm
9 ft.lbs.
13 Nm
9 ft.lbs.
Release cylinder push rod
Release fork
Specified grease:
MITSUBISHI genuine grease Part No. 0101011
Clutch master cylinder removal steps
• Adjustment of clutch pedal
1. Clevis pin
2. Air cleaner element
3. Air cleaner cover
4. Clutch pipe connection
5. Clutch master cylinder
6. Sealer
7. Reservoir hose
8. Reservoir tank
9. Reservoir cap
10. Reservoir bracket
Clutch release cylinder removal steps
11. Clutch pipe connection
12. Clutch release cylinder
Clutch line removal steps
13. Clutch pipe
14. Clutch hose
15. Clutch pipe
16. Clutch hose bracket
MT5049100022000X

Fig. 6 Exploded view of clutch control components

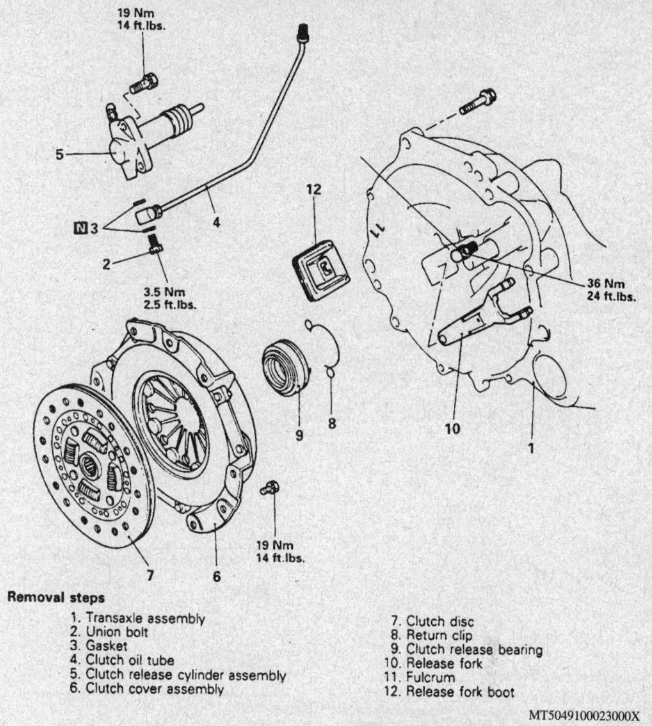
19 Nm
14 ft.lbs.
3.5 Nm
2.5 ft.lbs.
36 Nm
24 ft.lbs.
19 Nm
14 ft.lbs.
Removal steps
1. Transaxle assembly
2. Union bolt
3. Gasket
4. Clutch oil tube
5. Clutch release cylinder assembly
6. Clutch cover assembly
7. Clutch disc
8. Return clip
9. Clutch release bearing
10. Release fork
11. Fulcrum
12. Release fork boot
MT5049100023000X

Fig. 7 Exploded view of clutch assembly

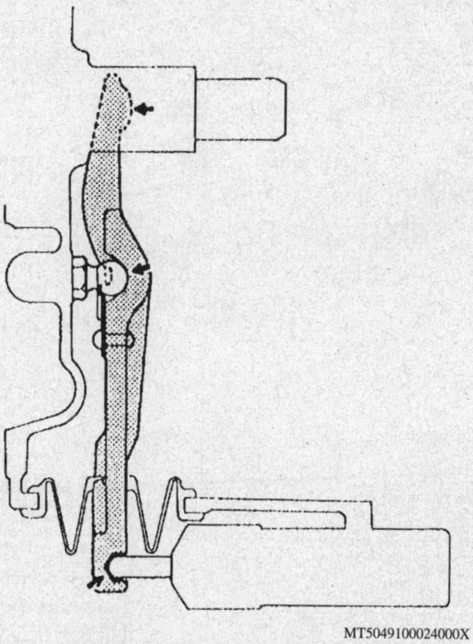
MT5049100024000X

Fig. 8 Release fork grease application

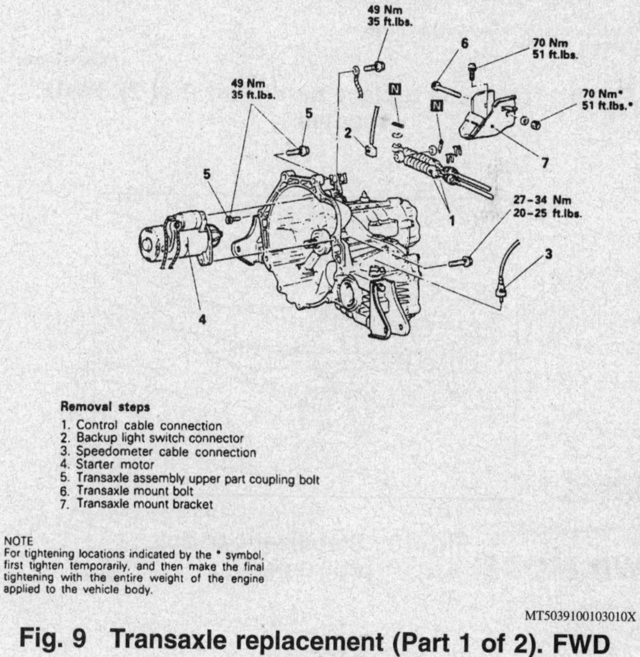
49 Nm
35 ft.lbs.
49 Nm
35 ft.lbs.
70 Nm
51 ft.lbs.
70 Nm*
51 ft.lbs.*
27-34 Nm
20-25 ft.lbs.
Removal steps
1. Control cable connection
2. Backup light switch connector
3. Speedometer cable connection
4. Starter motor
5. Transaxle assembly upper part coupling bolt
6. Transaxle mount bolt
7. Transaxle mount bracket
NOTE
For tightening locations indicated by the * symbol, first tighten temporarily, and then make the final tightening with the entire weight of the engine applied to the vehicle body.
MT5039100103010X

Fig. 9 Transaxle replacement (Part 1 of 2). FWD models

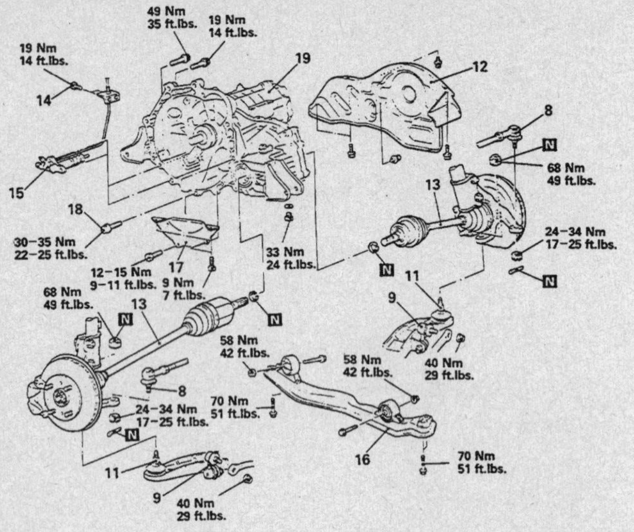
49 Nm
35 ft.lbs.
19 Nm
14 ft.lbs.
19 Nm
14 ft.lbs.
68 Nm
49 ft.lbs.
30-35 Nm
22-25 ft.lbs.
12-15 Nm
9-11 ft.lbs.
9 Nm
7 ft.lbs.
33 Nm
24 ft.lbs.
24-34 Nm
17-25 ft.lbs.
58 Nm
42 ft.lbs.
58 Nm
42 ft.lbs.
40 Nm
29 ft.lbs.
70 Nm
51 ft.lbs.
24-34 Nm
17-25 ft.lbs.
70 Nm
51 ft.lbs.
40 Nm
29 ft.lbs.

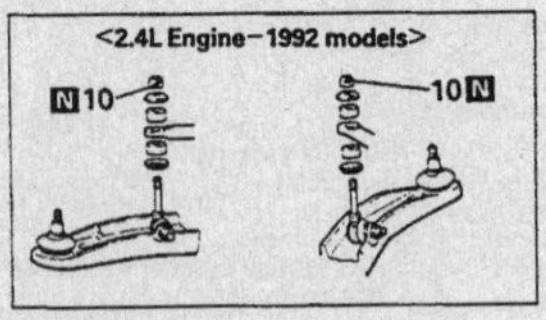
<2.4L Engine-1992 models>

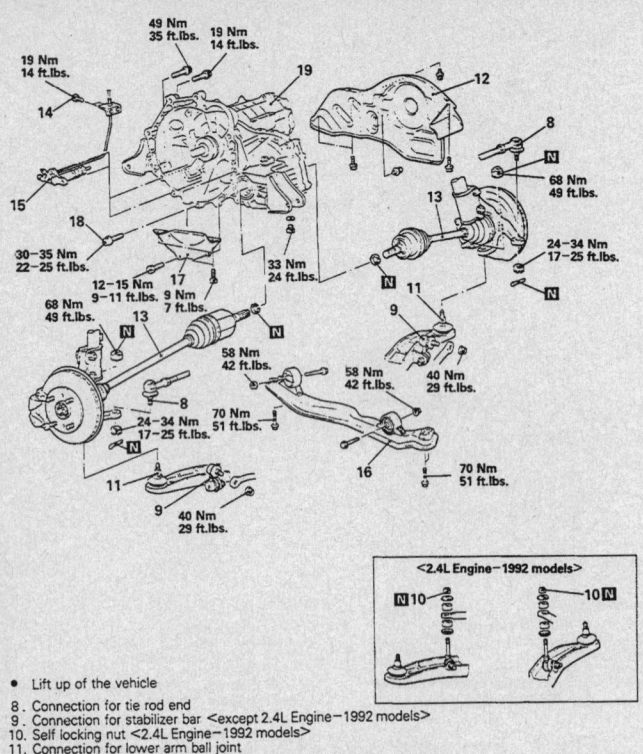

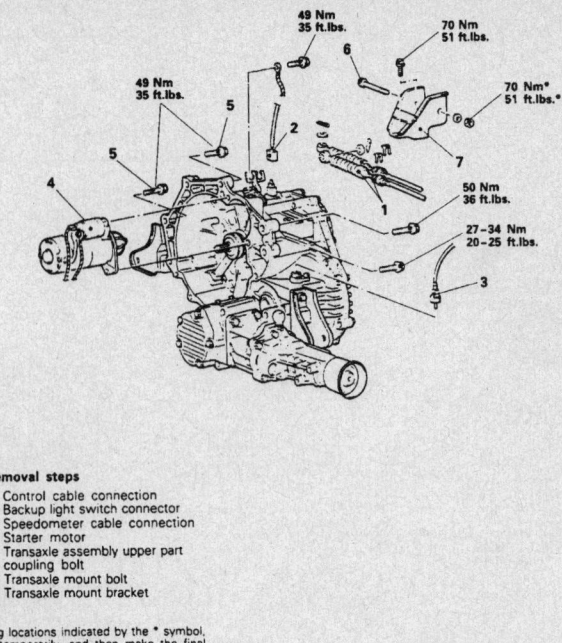

- Lift up of the vehicle

8. Connection for tie rod end
9. Connection for stabilizer bar <except 2.4L Engine-1992 models>
10. Self locking nut <2.4L Engine-1992 models>
11. Connection for lower arm ball joint
12. Under cover (RH)
- Draining of the transaxle oil
13. Drive shaft connection
14. Clutch oil line bracket bolt
15. Connection for release cylinder
16. Center member <except 2.4L Engine-1992 models>
17. Bell housing cover
18. Transaxle assembly lower part coupling bolts
19. Transaxle assembly

MT5039100103020X

Fig. 9 Transaxle replacement (Part 2 of 2). FWD models

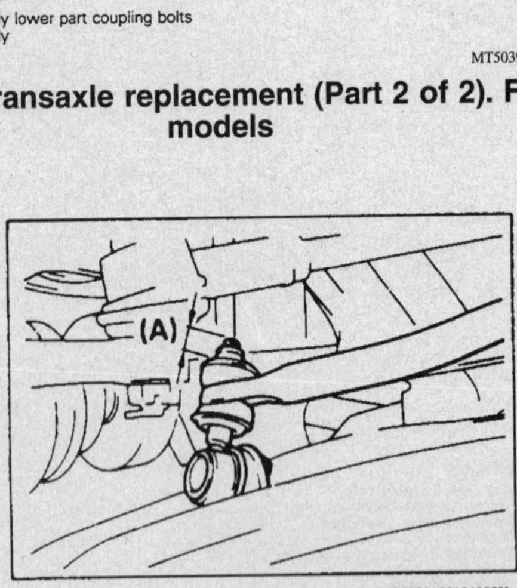
(A)

MT5039100104000X

Fig. 10 Stabilizer bar bolt protrusion

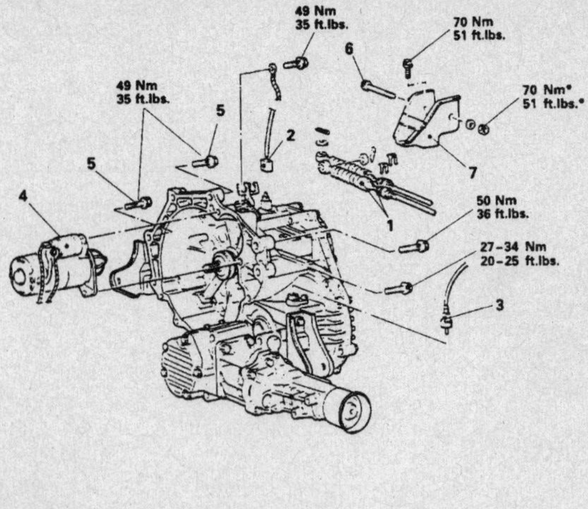
49 Nm
35 ft.lbs.
70 Nm
51 ft.lbs.
49 Nm
35 ft.lbs.
70 Nm*
51 ft.lbs.*
50 Nm
36 ft.lbs.
27-34 Nm
20-25 ft.lbs.

Removal steps

1. Control cable connection
2. Backup light switch connector
3. Speedometer cable connection
4. Starter motor
5. Transaxle assembly upper part coupling bolt
6. Transaxle mount bolt
7. Transaxle mount bracket

NOTE
For tightening locations indicated by the * symbol, first tighten temporarily, and then make the final tightening with the entire weight of the engine applied to the vehicle body.

MT5039100105010X

Fig. 11 Transaxle Replacement (Part 1 of 2). AWD models

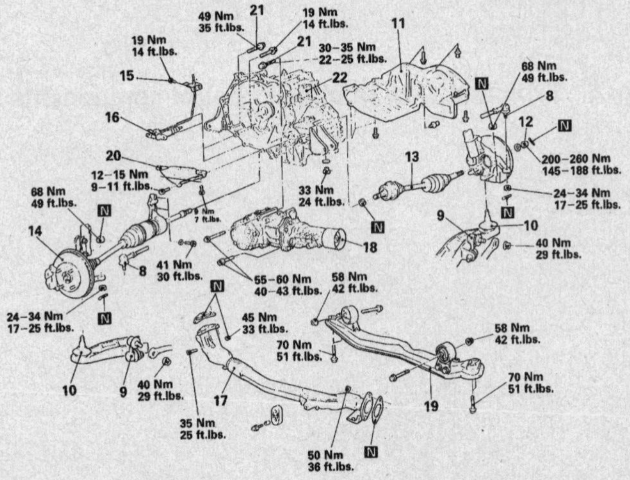
49 Nm
35 ft.lbs.
19 Nm
14 ft.lbs.
19 Nm
14 ft.lbs.
30-35 Nm
22-25 ft.lbs.
68 Nm
49 ft.lbs.
200-260 Nm
145-188 ft.lbs.
12-15 Nm
9-11 ft.lbs.
68 Nm
49 ft.lbs.
33 Nm
24 ft.lbs.
24-34 Nm
17-25 ft.lbs.
40 Nm
29 ft.lbs.
41 Nm
30 ft.lbs.
55-60 Nm
40-43 ft.lbs.
58 Nm
42 ft.lbs.
24-34 Nm
17-25 ft.lbs.
45 Nm
33 ft.lbs.
70 Nm
51 ft.lbs.
58 Nm
42 ft.lbs.
40 Nm
29 ft.lbs.
70 Nm
51 ft.lbs.
35 Nm
25 ft.lbs.
50 Nm
36 ft.lbs.

- Lifting up of the vehicle

8. Connection for tie rod end
9. Connection for stabilizer bar
10. Connection for lower arm ball joint
- Draining of the transaxle oil
11. Under cover (RH)
12. Drive shaft nut (RH)
13. Drive shaft (RH)
14. Connection for drive shaft and inner shaft
15. Clutch oil line bracket bolts
16. Connection for clutch release cylinder
17. Front exhaust pipe
18. Transfer assembly
19. Center member
20. Bell housing cover
21. Transaxle assembly lower part coupling bolts
22. Transaxle assembly

Transfer assembly removal steps

17. Front exhaust pipe
18. Transfer assembly

MT5039100105020X

Fig. 11 Transaxle Replacement (Part 2 of 2). AWD models

TIGHTENING SPECIFICATIONS

For tightening specifications, refer to individual repair procedure or illustrations.

Year	Component	Torque/ Ft. Lbs.
1993–96	Clutch Cover Bolts	14
	Clutch Hose Bracket Bolt	9
	Clutch Master Cylinder Nuts	9
	Clutch Oil Tube Union Bolt	2.5
	Clutch Release Cylinder Bolts	14
	Pipe Fitting Nuts	11
	Release Fork Bolt	24
	Reservoir Bracket Bolts	4
	Transaxle Coupling Bolts	①
	Transaxle Mount Bolts	51

① — Refer to "Transaxle, Replace" for procedure

Rear Axle & Suspension

INDEX

	Page No.
Coil Spring, Replace	25-39
Control Arm, Replace	25-39
Lower	25-39
Differential Carrier, Replace	25-39
Rear Crossmember, Replace	25-39
Shock Absorber, Replace	25-39
Stabilizer Bar, Replace	25-39
Tightening Specifications	25-43

DIFFERENTIAL CARRIER

REPLACE

1. Disconnect battery ground cable.
2. Raise and support vehicle.
3. Remove differential carrier and/or support member in numbered sequence shown in **Fig. 1,** noting following:
   a. Remove nuts and bolts from driveshaft and companion flange then support driveshaft aside.
   b. Using slide hammer tool No. MB990211-01, or equivalent, remove companion shaft from differential carrier.
   c. Mark propeller shaft location for reference during assembly.
   d. Remove propeller shaft bolts, then support propeller shaft aside.
   e. Support differential carrier bolts using a suitable jack then remove differential carrier support bolts.
   f. Disconnect main muffler from center exhaust pipe. Support muffler with wire from frame.
4. Reverse procedure to install, noting following:
   a. Install mount stopper as shown in **Fig. 2.**
   b. Install companion shaft into differential carrier using care not to damage oil seal.
   c. Identify RH and LH companion shafts prior to installation, **Fig. 3.**

SHOCK ABSORBER

REPLACE

1. Disconnect battery ground cable.
2. Support lower arm using suitable jack.
3. Remove and disassemble shock absorber in numbered sequence shown in **Fig. 4.**
4. Reverse procedure to assemble and install.

COIL SPRING

REPLACE

1. Raise and support vehicle.
2. Remove rear stabilizer bar as outlined under "Stabilizer Bar, Replace."
3. Remove shock absorber as outlined under "Shock Absorber, Service."
4. Disconnect driveshaft from differential carrier and support aside.
5. Disconnect speed sensor clamp bolt.
6. Lower jack used to support lower arm and remove coil spring.
7. Remove spring seat.
8. Reverse procedure to install, ensuring coil spring seat properly into spring seat grooves.

CONTROL ARM

REPLACE

LOWER

1. Remove stabilizer bar as outlined under "Stabilizer Bar, Replace."
2. Remove shock absorber as outlined under "Shock Absorber, Service."
3. Remove coil spring as outlined under "Coil Spring, Replace."
4. Replace lower arm assembly in numbered sequence shown in **Figs. 5 and 6,** not removing AWD models rear hub assembly except when replacing bearing.

REAR CROSSMEMBER

REPLACE

1. Remove stabilizer bar as outlined under "Stabilizer Bar, Replace."
2. Remove shock absorber as outlined under "Shock Absorber, Service."
3. Make mating marks on lower arm shaft assembly and crossmember.
4. Remove coil spring as outlined under "Coil Spring, Replace."
5. **On AWD models,** mark then remove propeller shaft.
6. **On all models,** replace suspension crossmember in numbered sequence shown in **Figs. 7 and 8.**
7. Reverse procedure to install, ensuring coil spring is properly seated.

STABILIZER BAR

REPLACE

1. Raise and support vehicle.
2. Remove stabilizer bar link nut.

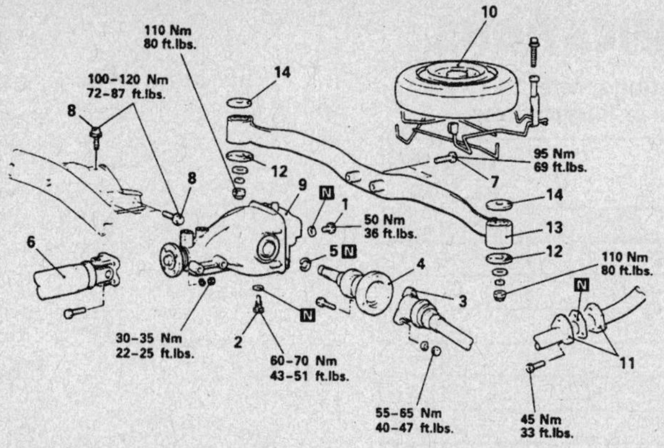
110 Nm
80 ft.lbs.
100–120 Nm
72–87 ft.lbs.
95 Nm
69 ft.lbs.
50 Nm
36 ft.lbs.
110 Nm
80 ft.lbs.
30–35 Nm
22–25 ft.lbs.
60–70 Nm
43–51 ft.lbs.
55–65 Nm
40–47 ft.lbs.
45 Nm
33 ft.lbs.

Differential carrier removal steps

1. Filler plug
2. Drain plug
3. Drive shaft connection
4. Companion shaft
5. Circlip
6. Propeller shaft connection
7. Bolts
8. Bolts
9. Differential Carrier

Differential support member removal steps

7. Bolts
10. Spare tyre
11. Connection for main muffler and center exhaust pipe
12. Differential mount lower stopper
13. Differential support member
14. Differential mount upper stopper

Caution
If the thread section of the mounting bolts and nuts for the drive shaft and propeller shaft and the companion shaft have any oil or grease on them, there is a possibility that they may loosen, even if they are tightened to the specified torque, so the threads should always be cleaned before tightening.

MT3019100003000X

Fig. 1 Exploded view of differential carrier

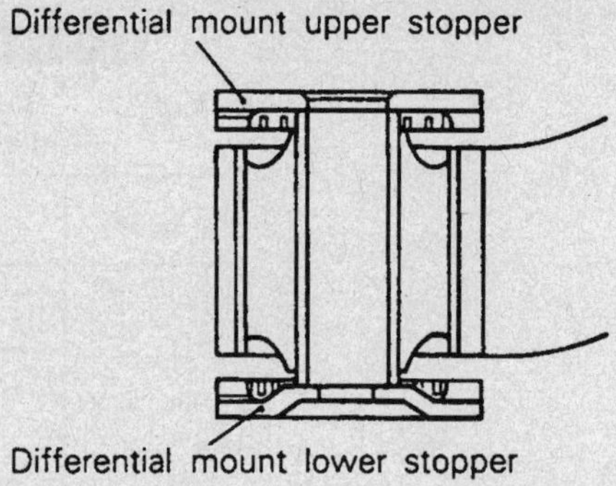
Differential mount upper stopper
Differential mount lower stopper

MT3019100031000X

Fig. 2 Differential mount stoppers

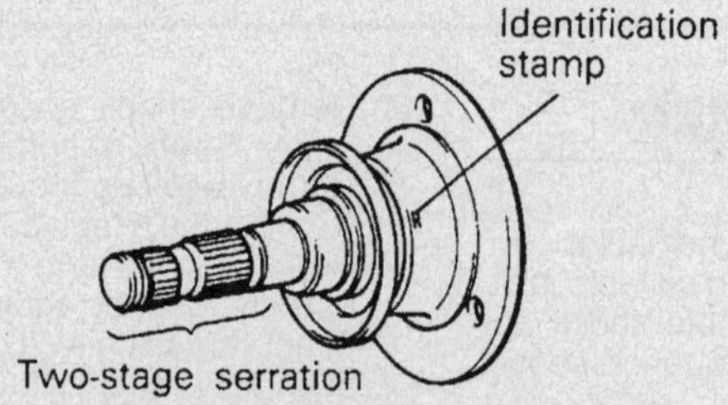
Identification stamp
Two-stage serration

MT3019100032000X

Fig. 3 Companion shaft identification mark

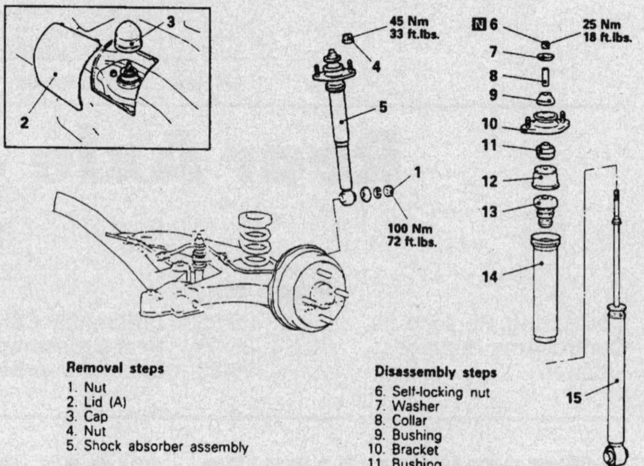
45 Nm
33 ft.lbs.
25 Nm
18 ft.lbs.
100 Nm
72 ft.lbs.

Removal steps

1. Nut
2. Lid (A)
3. Cap
4. Nut
5. Shock absorber assembly

Disassembly steps

6. Self-locking nut
7. Washer
8. Collar
9. Bushing
10. Bracket
11. Bushing
12. Cup assembly
13. Bump stopper
14. Dust cover
15. Shock absorber

MT2039100043000X

Fig. 4 Exploded view of shock absorber

3. Remove stabilizer bar link bolt, spacer joint cups, rubber bushing and collar.
4. Support stabilizer bar and remove frame mount bracket bolts and bushings.
5. Remove stabilizer bar from vehicle.
6. Reverse procedure to install, noting following:
   a. Position stabilizer bar by aligning painted section as shown, **Fig. 9.**
   b. Protrusion of stabilizer link bolt should be 0.98–1.06 inches, **Fig. 10.**

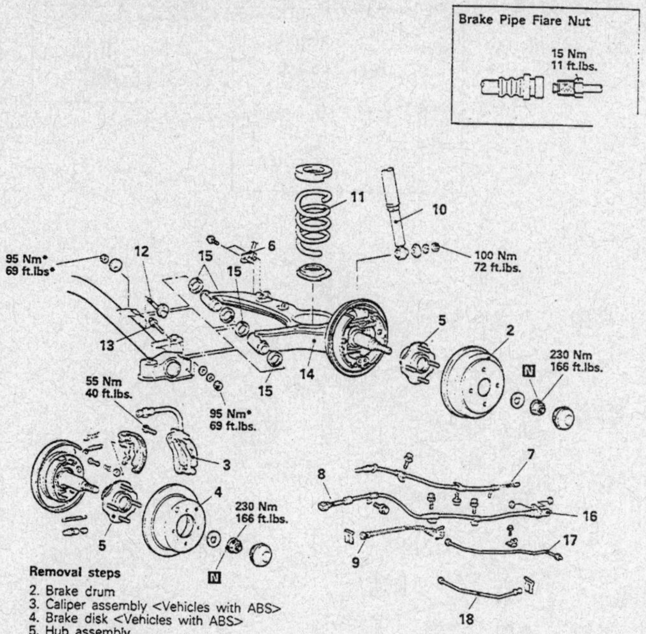
Brake Pipe Flare Nut
15 Nm
11 ft.lbs.
95 Nm*
69 ft.lbs*
55 Nm
40 ft.lbs.
95 Nm*
69 ft.lbs.
100 Nm
72 ft.lbs.
230 Nm
166 ft.lbs.
230 Nm
166 ft.lbs.
N

Removal steps

2. Brake drum
3. Caliper assembly <Vehicles with ABS>
4. Brake disk <Vehicles with ABS>
5. Hub assembly
6. Link bracket <EXPO>
7. Connection for parking brake cable and brake shoe

8. Rear sensor connector <Vehicles with ABS>
9. Brake hose
10. Shock absorber
11. Coil spring
12. Shaft assembly
13. Flange bolt
14. Lower arm assembly
15. Stopper
16. Rear speed sensor <Vehicles with ABS>
17. Brake pipe
18. Brake pipe <Vehicles with ABS>

NOTE
*Indicates parts which should be temporarily tightened, and then fully tightened with the vehicle in the unladen condition.

Caution
(1) For vehicles with ABS, be careful not to damage the rotor teeth when removing the hub assembly.
(2) For vehicles with ABS, when removing the speed sensor, be careful that the end of the pole piece does not touch any other component.

MT2039100044000X

Fig. 5 Exploded view of lower arm. FWD models

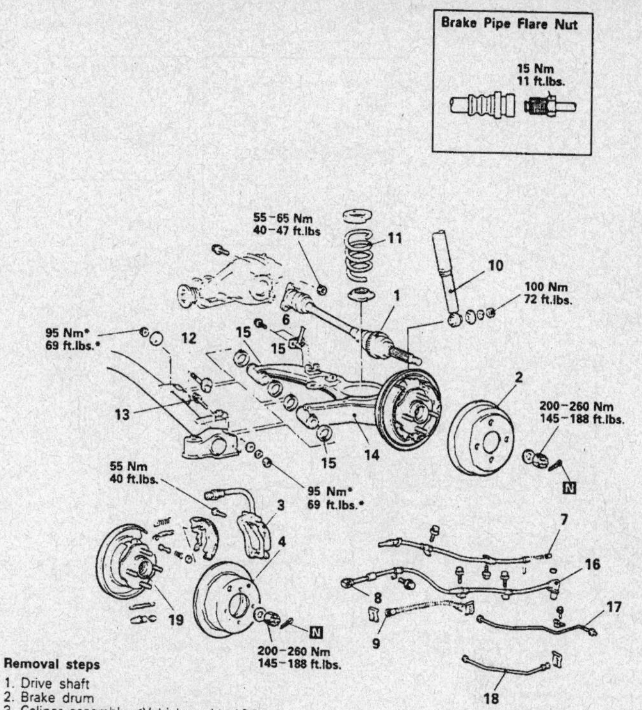
Brake Pipe Flare Nut
15 Nm
11 ft.lbs.
55-65 Nm
40-47 ft.lbs
100 Nm
72 ft.lbs.
95 Nm*
69 ft.lbs.*
200-260 Nm
145-188 ft.lbs.
55 Nm
40 ft.lbs.
95 Nm*
69 ft.lbs.*
200-260 Nm
145-188 ft.lbs.
N

Removal steps

1. Drive shaft
2. Brake drum
3. Caliper assembly <Vehicles with ABS>
4. Brake disk <Vehicles with ABS>
6. Link bracket <EXPO>
7. Connection for parking brake cable and brake shoe

8. Rear sensor connector <Vehicles with ABS>
9. Brake hose
10. Shock absorber
11. Coil spring
12. Shaft assembly
13. Flange bolt
14. Lower arm assembly
15. Stopper
16. Rear speed sensor <Vehicles with ABS>
17. Brake pipe
18. Brake pipe <Vehicles with ABS>
19. Hub assembly

NOTE
*Indicates parts which should be temporarily tightened, and then fully tightened with the vehicles in the unladen condition.

Caution
(1) For vehicles with ABS, be careful not to damage the rotor teeth when removing the drive shaft.
(2) For vehicles with ABS, when removing the speed sensor, be careful that the end of the pole piece does not touch any other component.

MT2039100045000X

Fig. 6 Exploded view of lower arm. AWD models

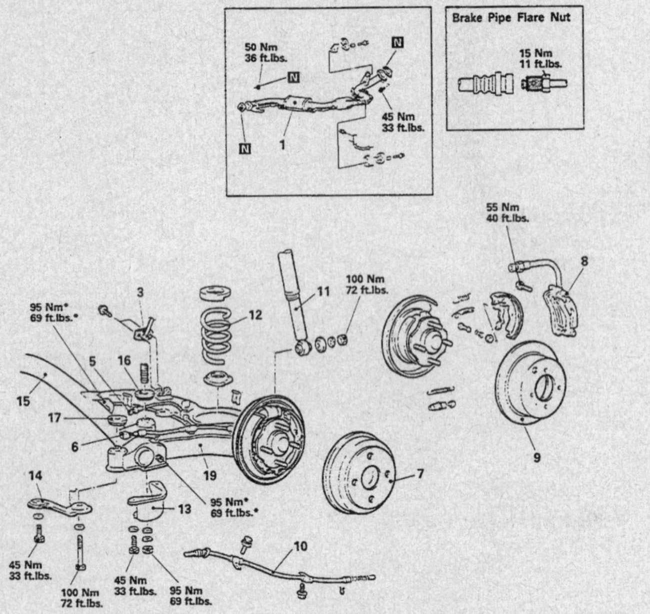

50 Nm
36 ft.lbs.
45 Nm
33 ft.lbs.
Brake Pipe Flare Nut
15 Nm
11 ft.lbs.
55 Nm
40 ft.lbs.
100 Nm
72 ft.lbs.
95 Nm*
69 ft.lbs.*
95 Nm*
69 ft.lbs.*
45 Nm
33 ft.lbs.
100 Nm
72 ft.lbs.
45 Nm
33 ft.lbs.
95 Nm
69 ft.lbs.

Removal steps
- Lift supporting point
1. Center exhaust pipe
3. Link bracket <EXPO>
5. Brake hose
6. Rear sensor connector <Vehicles with ABS>
7. Brake drum
8. Caliper assembly <Vehicles with ABS>
9. Brake disk <Vehicles with ABS>
10. Parking brake cable
11. Shock absorber
12. Coil spring
13. Crossmember bracket
14. Lower stopper
15. Suspension crossmember assembly
16. Upper stopper
17. Upper stopper
19. Lower arm assembly

NOTE
*Indicates parts which should be temporarily tightened, and then fully tightened with the vehicles in the unladen condition.

MT2039100046000X

Fig. 7 Exploded view of suspension crossmember. FWD models

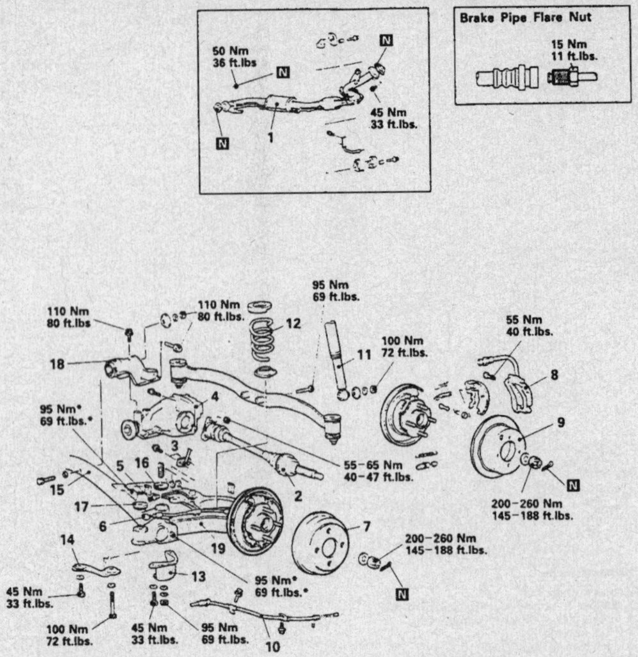

50 Nm
36 ft.lbs
45 Nm
33 ft.lbs.
Brake Pipe Flare Nut
15 Nm
11 ft.lbs.
95 Nm
69 ft.lbs.
110 Nm
80 ft.lbs
110 Nm
80 ft.lbs.
100 Nm
72 ft.lbs.
55 Nm
40 ft.lbs.
95 Nm*
69 ft.lbs.*
55–65 Nm
40–47 ft.lbs.
200–260 Nm
145–188 ft.lbs.
200–260 Nm
145–188 ft.lbs.
95 Nm*
69 ft.lbs.*
45 Nm
33 ft.lbs.
100 Nm
72 ft.lbs.
45 Nm
33 ft.lbs.
95 Nm
69 ft.lbs.

Removal steps
- Lift supporting point
1. Center exhaust pipe
2. Drive shaft
3. Link bracket <EXPO>
4. Differential carrier
5. Brake hose
6. Rear sensor connector <Vehicles with ABS>
7. Brake drum
8. Caliper assembly <Vehicles with ABS>
9. Brake disk <Vehicles with ABS>
10. Parking brake cable
11. Shock absorber
12. Coil spring
13. Crossmember bracket
14. Lower stopper
15. Suspension crossmember assembly
16. Upper stopper
17. Upper stopper
18. Bracket assembly
19. Lower arm assembly

Caution
For vehicles with ABS, be careful not to damage the rotor teeth when removing the drive shaft.

NOTE
*Indicates parts which should be temporarily tightened, and then fully tightened with the vehicles in the unladen condition.

MT2039100047000X

Fig. 8 Exploded view of suspension crossmember. AWD models

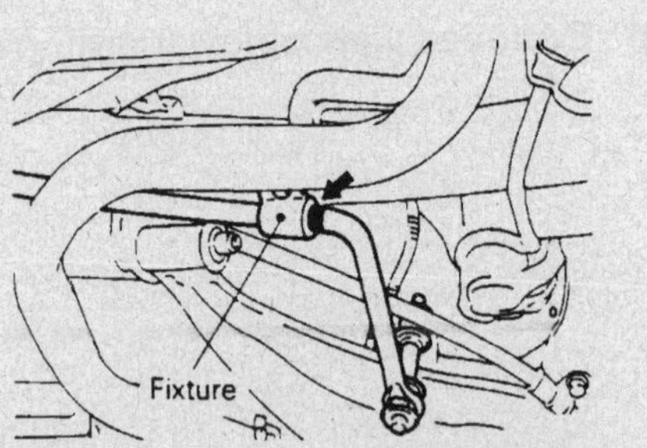

Fixture

MT2039100048000X

Fig. 9 Mounting stabilizer bar

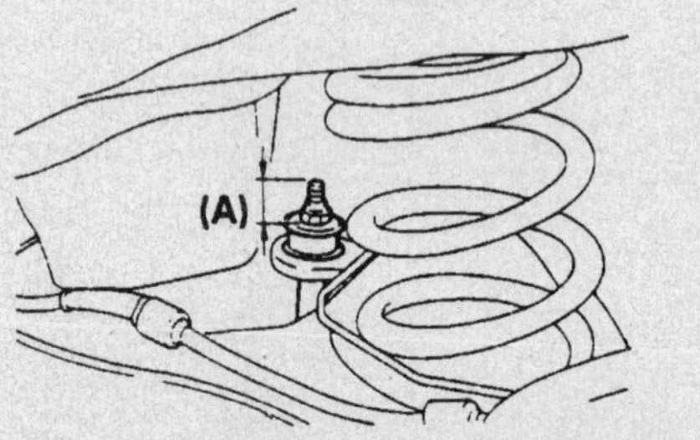

(A)

MT2039100049000X

Fig. 10 Stabilizer bar bolt protrusion

TIGHTENING SPECIFICATIONS

For tightening specifications, refer to individual repair procedure or illustrations.

Year	Component	Torque/ Ft. Lbs.
1993–96	Axle Nut, AWD	145–188
	Axle Nut, FWD	166
	Brake Caliper Mounting Bolts	40
	Crossmember Bracket Bolt	33
	Crossmember Bracket Nut	69
	Differential Carrier Mounting Bolts	①
	Driveshaft Connection Nuts	40–47
	Driveshaft Nut, AWD	145–188
	Driveshaft Nut, FWD	166
	Hub Nut, AWD	145–188
	Hub Nut, FWD	166
	Lower Arm Mounting Bolts	69
	Lower Stop Bolt, Front	33
	Lower Stop Bolt, Rear	72
	Shock Absorber Dust Cover Nut	18
	Shock Absorber Mounting Nuts, Lower	72
	Shock Absorber Mounting Nuts, Upper	33
	Wheel Bearing Nut, AWD	145–188
	Wheel Bearing Nut, FWD	166

① — Refer to "Differential Carrier, Replace" for procedure.

Front Suspension & Steering

NOTE: On Air Bag Equipped Models, Refer To "Air Bag System Precautions" Located In The Front Of This Manual For System Disarming & Arming Procedures.

NOTE: Prior To Performing Any Service Operations Listed In This Section, Consult The "Technical Service Bulletins" Section For Related Information.

INDEX

	Page No.
Ball Joint, Replace	25-44
Control Arm, Replace	25-45
Lower	25-45
Manual Steering Gears	29-1
Power Steering	29-1
Power Steering Gear, Replace	25-45
Power Steering Pump, Replace	25-45
Precautions	25-43
Air Bag Systems	25-43
Stabilizer Bar, Replace	25-45
Strut, Replace	25-44
Technical Service Bulletins	25-46
Front Suspension Rattle Or Popping Noise	25-46
Tightening Specifications	25-47
Wheel Hub & Steering Knuckle, Replace	25-43

PRECAUTIONS

AIR BAG SYSTEMS

Refer to "Air Bag System Precautions" in the front of this manual for system disarming and arming procedures.

WHEEL HUB & STEERING KNUCKLE

REPLACE

Replace hub, knuckle and bearing in numbered sequence shown in **Figs. 1 and 2,** noting following:

1. Remove caliper and suspend with wire, then remove driveshaft nut using end yoke holder, tool No. MB990767-01, or equivalent.

2. Disconnect ball joint and tie rod end using steering linkage puller, tool No. MB990635-01, or equivalent. **Loosen but do not remove ball joint and tie rod end nuts until knuckle is ready to be removed.**
3. Using a suitable axle shaft puller, press driveshaft from front hub.
4. Ensure driveshaft nut and washer are installed in direction shown in **Fig. 3.**
5. Temporarily install speed sensor to knuckle, if equipped, then insert a suitable thickness gauge between sensor pole piece and rotor toothed surface, **Fig. 4,** and tighten speed sensor at a position where clearance is 0.012–0.035 inch. **If clearance cannot be obtained, check for improper installation of rotor.**
6. Remove hub by attaching front hub remover/installer, tool No. MB990998-01 and knuckle arm bridge, tool No. MB991355, or equivalent, to knuckle and hub. Secure knuckle in vise, then tighten nut of front hub remover/installer to remove hub, or hub and rotor from knuckle.
7. Remove wheel bearing inner race from front hub using side bearing puller, tool No. MB990810-01, or equivalent. First, crush oil seal in two places to allow tabs of side bearing puller clearance to get under inner race.
8. Drive wheel bearing out using knuckle arm bridge, tool No. MB991355 remover/installer disc, tool No. MB990932-01 and handle, tool No. MB990938-01, or equivalent.
9. Fill wheel bearing with multi-purpose grease and apply a thin coating to knuckle and bearing contact surfaces, then press in wheel bearing using rear suspension bushing base, tool No. MB990890-01 and rear suspension arbor, tool No. MB990883-01, or equivalent.
10. Drive oil seal into knuckle using lower arm bushing arbor, tool No. MB990947-01 and rear suspension bushing base, tool No. MB990847-01, or equivalent. Apply multi-purpose grease to lip of oil seal and surfaces of oil seal which contact front hub.
11. Use front hub remover/installer, tool No. MB990998-01, or equivalent, to mount hub, or hub and rotor onto knuckle. **Torque**nut of hub remover/installer to 145–188 ft. lbs. while rotating hub to seat bearing. Leave hub remover/installer in place while taking measurements described in Steps 12 and 13.
12. Measure wheel bearing starting torque using hub remover/installer and a suitable inch pound torque wrench. Starting **torque**must be 16 inch lbs. or less and bearing must not feel rough when rotated.
13. Measure hub endplay using hub remover/installer and a suitable dial indicator, endplay must be within 0.002 inch. If starting torque and endplay are not within limits specified, bearing, hub and/or knuckle may have been incorrectly installed. Repeat disassembly and assembly procedures.

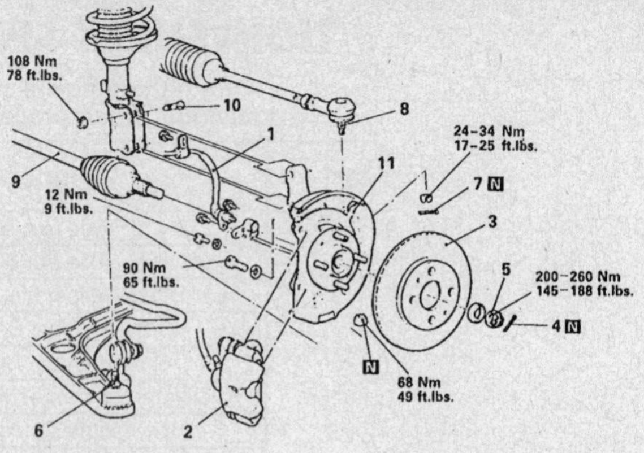
108 Nm
78 ft.lbs.
12 Nm
9 ft.lbs.
90 Nm
65 ft.lbs.
24–34 Nm
17–25 ft.lbs.
200–260 Nm
145–188 ft.lbs.
68 Nm
49 ft.lbs.

Removal steps

1. Front speed sensor <Vehicle with ABS>
2. Caliper assembly
3. Brake disc
4. Cotter pin
5. Drive shaft nut
6. Connection for lower arm ball joint
7. Cotter pin
8. Connection for tie rod end
9. Drive shaft
10. Front strut mounting bolt
11. Hub and knuckle

Caution
Be careful when handling the pole piece at the tip of the speed sensor and the toothed edge of the rotor so as not to damage them by striking against other parts.

MT2049100024000X

Fig. 1 Hub, knuckle & bearing replacement

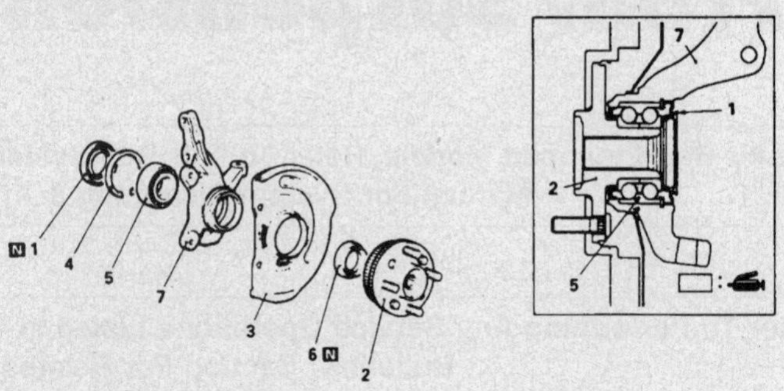

Disassembly steps

1. Inner oil seal
2. Hub
3. Dust cover
4. Snap ring
5. Wheel bearing
6. Outer oil seal
7. Knuckle

Reassembly steps

7. Knuckle
5. Wheel bearing
4. Snap ring
6. Outer oil seal
3. Dust cover
2. Hub
- Wheel bearing starting torque check
- Hub end play check
1. Inner oil seal

MT2049100025000X

Fig. 2 Servicing hub, knuckle & bearing

14. Apply multi-purpose grease to lip and install driveshaft side oil seal into knuckle using rear suspension bushing base, tool No. MB990890-01 and rear suspension arbor, tool No. MB990883-01, or equivalent. Drive seal in until it contacts snap ring.

BALL JOINT

REPLACE

Refer to "Control Arm, Replace" for ball joint replacement procedure.

STRUT

REPLACE

Remove, install, disassemble and assemble strut assembly in numbered sequence shown in **Figs. 5 and 6,** noting following:

1. Secure lower arm assembly with wire, then disconnect strut assembly from knuckle.
2. Hold spring upper seat using spring seat holder MB991176, or equivalent,

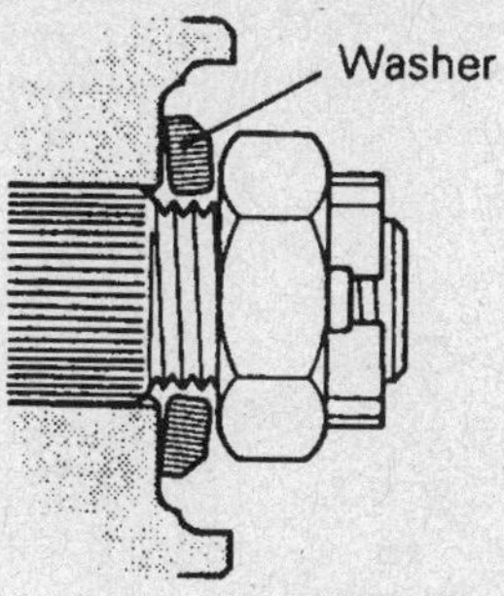
Washer

MT2049100026000X

Fig. 3 Driveshaft nut & washer installation

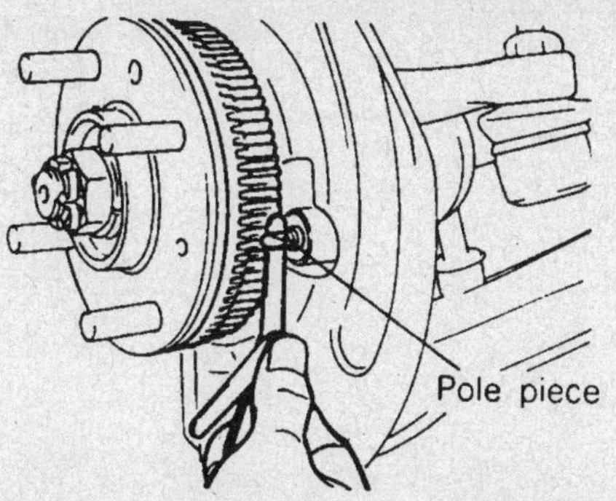
Pole piece

MT2049100027000X

Fig. 4 Speed sensor pole piece clearance check. Models w/ABS

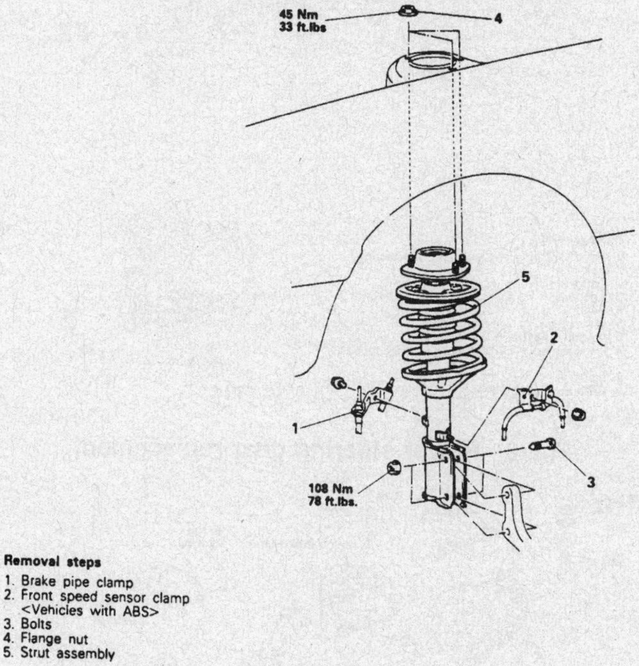
45 Nm
33 ft.lbs
4
5
2
1
3
108 Nm
78 ft.lbs.
Removal steps
1. Brake pipe clamp
2. Front speed sensor clamp <Vehicles with ABS>
3. Bolts
4. Flange nut
5. Strut assembly

MT2029100020000X

Fig. 5 Strut assembly replacement

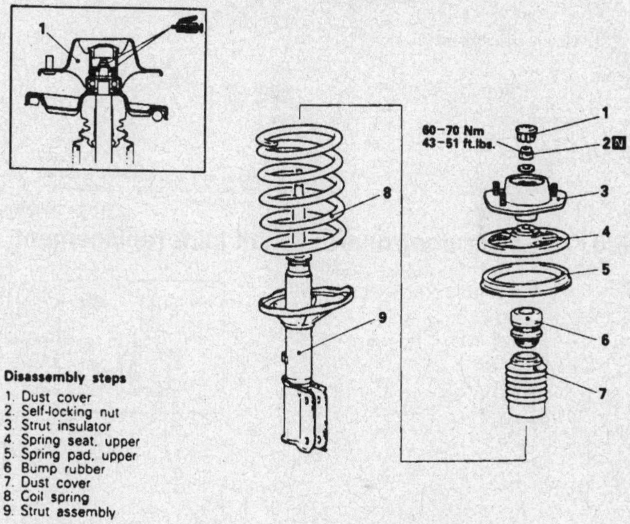
1
60-70 Nm
43-51 ft.lbs.
1
2
3
4
5
6
7
8
9
Disassembly steps
1. Dust cover
2. Self-locking nut
3. Strut insulator
4. Spring seat, upper
5. Spring pad, upper
6. Bump rubber
7. Dust cover
8. Coil spring
9. Strut assembly

MT2029100021000X

Fig. 6 Servicing strut assembly

then loosen, but do not remove self-locking nut.

3. Using spring compressor body and arm set, tools No. MB991237 and MB991238 or their equivalents, compress coil spring and remove self-locking nut.
4. Line up holes in strut assembly spring lower seat with hole in spring upper seat. **This is more easily accomplished using a piece of pipe .394 x 11.82 inches.**
5. Correctly align both ends of coil spring with grooves in spring seat.
6. Apply multi-purpose grease to bearing portion of strut insulator. **Do not allow grease to adhere to insulator's rubber portion.**

CONTROL ARM

REPLACE

LOWER

Replace lower control arm and ball joint in numbered sequence shown in **Fig. 7.**

Disconnect knuckle from lower arm ball joint using steering linkage puller MB991113-01, or equivalent. **Loosen but do not remove ball joint nut until lower control arm is ready to be removed.**

STABILIZER BAR

REPLACE

This procedure has been revised by a technical service bulletin.

Replace stabilizer bar in numbered sequence shown in **Fig. 8**, noting following:

1. **On LRV and AWD models,** remove propeller shaft, then disconnect front exhaust pipe and secure with wire. **Do not bend flexible joint of pipe excessively or damage to interior may result.**
2. When installing bar, align left edge of marking on stabilizer bar with edge of stabilizer bush, then tighten mounting bolt.
3. **On FWD models,** remove tie rod end using steering linkage puller, tool No. MB991113-01, or equivalent.

POWER STEERING GEAR

REPLACE

Replace power steering gearbox in numbered sequence shown in **Fig. 9.** Disconnect tie rod ends using steering linkage puller, tool No. MB991113-01, or equivalent.

POWER STEERING PUMP

REPLACE

Replace power steering pump in numbered sequence shown in **Fig. 10,** noting following:

1. Before disconnecting pressure and suction hoses, place a rag over alternator to prevent fluid leaking into alternator.
2. When connecting pressure hose, install so that notched part contacts suction connector.

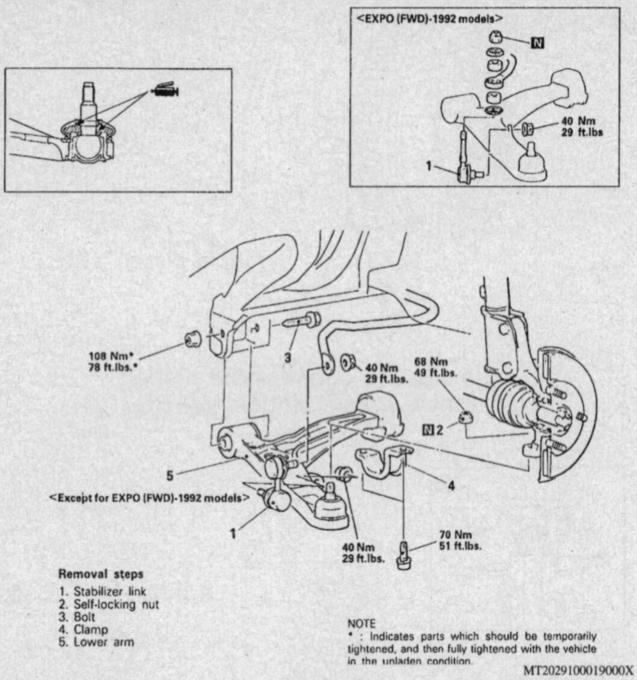
<EXPO (FWD)-1992 models>
40 Nm
29 ft.lbs
108 Nm*
78 ft.lbs.*
40 Nm
29 ft.lbs.
68 Nm
49 ft.lbs.
<Except for EXPO (FWD)-1992 models>
70 Nm
51 ft.lbs.
40 Nm
29 ft.lbs.
Removal steps
1. Stabilizer link
2. Self-locking nut
3. Bolt
4. Clamp
5. Lower arm
NOTE
* : Indicates parts which should be temporarily tightened, and then fully tightened with the vehicle in the unladen condition.
MT2029100019000X

Fig. 7 Lower control arm & ball joint replacement

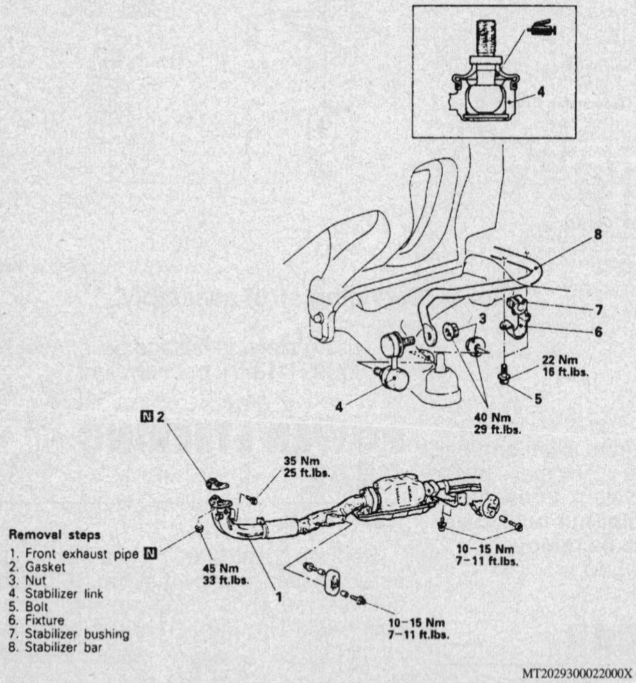
22 Nm
16 ft.lbs.
40 Nm
29 ft.lbs.
35 Nm
25 ft.lbs.
45 Nm
33 ft.lbs.
10–15 Nm
7–11 ft.lbs.
10–15 Nm
7–11 ft.lbs.
Removal steps
1. Front exhaust pipe
2. Gasket
3. Nut
4. Stabilizer link
5. Bolt
6. Fixture
7. Stabilizer bushing
8. Stabilizer bar
MT2029300022000X

Fig. 8 Stabilizer bar replacement. Expo LRV, Expo AWD & 1993–95 Expo FWD

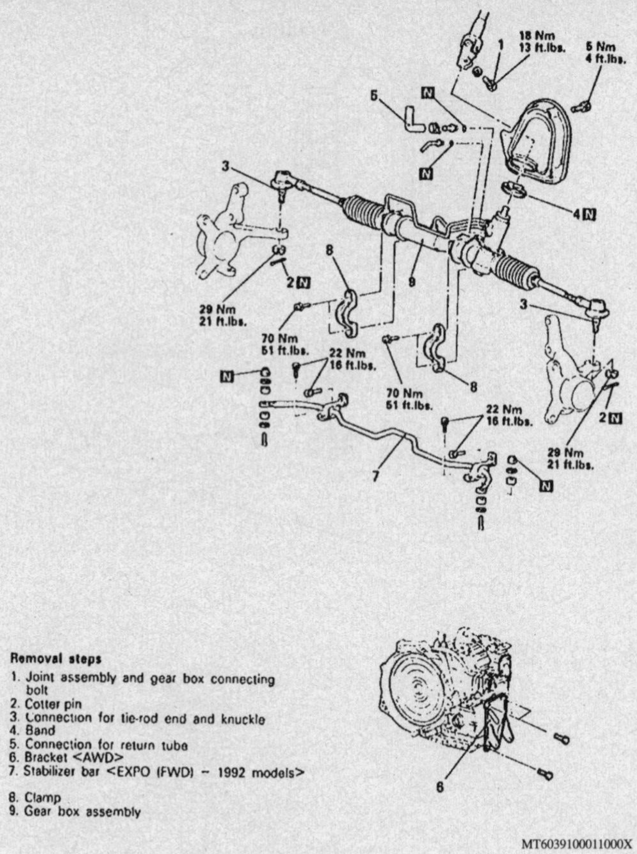
18 Nm
13 ft.lbs.
5 Nm
4 ft.lbs.
29 Nm
21 ft.lbs.
70 Nm
51 ft.lbs.
22 Nm
16 ft.lbs.
70 Nm
51 ft.lbs.
22 Nm
16 ft.lbs.
29 Nm
21 ft.lbs.
Removal steps
1. Joint assembly and gear box connecting bolt
2. Cotter pin
3. Connection for tie-rod end and knuckle
4. Band
5. Connection for return tube
6. Bracket <AWD>
7. Stabilizer bar <EXPO (FWD) – 1992 models>
8. Clamp
9. Gear box assembly
MT6039100011000X

Fig. 9 Power steering gear replacement

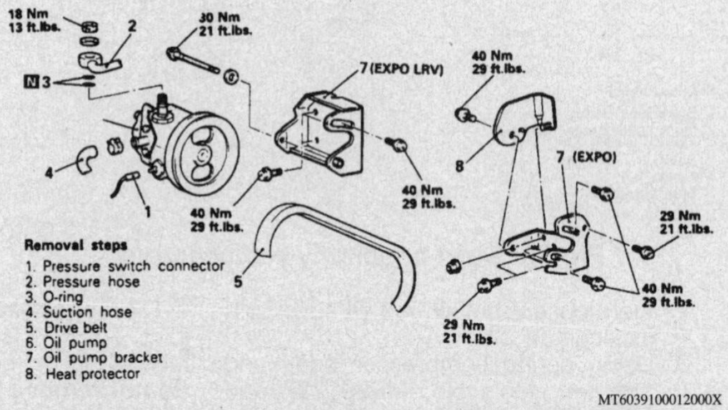
18 Nm
13 ft.lbs.
30 Nm
21 ft.lbs.
7 (EXPO LRV)
40 Nm
29 ft.lbs.
7 (EXPO)
40 Nm
29 ft.lbs.
40 Nm
29 ft.lbs.
29 Nm
21 ft.lbs.
40 Nm
29 ft.lbs.
29 Nm
21 ft.lbs.
Removal steps
1. Pressure switch connector
2. Pressure hose
3. O-ring
4. Suction hose
5. Drive belt
6. Oil pump
7. Oil pump bracket
8. Heat protector
MT6039100012000X

Fig. 10 Power steering pump replacement

TECHNICAL SERVICE BULLETINS

FRONT SUSPENSION RATTLE OR POPPING NOISE

1993

Some 1993 Expo and Expo LRV front suspensions may rattle or have popping noise.

This problem may be caused by corrosion in one or more on stabilizer link ball joints. To correct this problem, proceed as follows:

1. Raise and support vehicle, then inspect all stabilizer link ball joint dust boots.
2. Replace link is cracks or other damage is found in dust boots.
3. If dust boots are not damage, remove link as described in "Stabilizer Bar, Replace," then check starting torque of ball joint stud.
4. Standard starting torque is 15–28 ft. lbs. If any ball joint is not within specifications, replace link.

TIGHTENING SPECIFICATIONS

For tightening specifications, refer to individual repair procedure or illustrations.

Year	Component	Torque/ Ft. Lbs.
1993–96	Axle Nut	145–188
	Driveshaft Nut	145–188
	Hub Nut	145–188
	Lower Arm Bracket Nuts	49
	Lower Arm Mounting Bolts	78
	Power Steering Pump Bracket Bolts	①
	Stabilizer Link Bracket Bolts	16
	Stabilizer Link Nuts	29
	Steering Gear Box Bracket Bolts	51
	Strut Flange Nuts	33
	Strut Pinch Bolts	78
	Strut Shaft Nut	43–51
	Wheel Bearing Nut	145–188

① — Refer to "Power Steering Pump, Replace" for procedure.

Wheel Alignment

INDEX

Page No.

Front Wheel Alignment 25-47
Camber 25-47
Caster 25-47
Toe-In 25-47

Page No.

Preliminary Inspection 25-47
Rear Wheel Alignment 25-47
Camber 25-47

Page No.

Toe-In 25-47
Vehicle Ride Height 25-47
Wheel Alignment Specifications . 25-3

PRELIMINARY INSPECTION

1. Ensure tires are inflated to correct pressure, then check for uneven wear.
2. Check front wheel bearings, suspension arm and ball joints for damage and replace components as necessary to eliminate improper alignment.
3. Check steering gear for damage and adjust as necessary.
4. Check shocks for damage and replace as necessary.
5. Rock vehicle backward and forward and jounce it up and down to settle vehicle prior to alignment.
6. Ensure vehicle is unloaded and on a suitable alignment rack according manufacturer's instructions. **When measuring equipment is attached directly to outer end of driveshaft and front wheels are on turntables, apply brake to prevent vehicle movement.**

FRONT WHEEL ALIGNMENT

CAMBER

Camber is preset during production and is not adjustable. If camber is out of specification, replace bent or damaged components.

CASTER

Caster is preset during production and is not adjustable.

TOE-IN

1. Adjust toe-in by loosening clips and turning left and right tie rod turnbuckles equally in opposite directions. Refer to **Fig. 1.**
2. To increase toe-out, turn left turnbuckle toward front of vehicle and right turnbuckle toward rear of vehicle. To increase toe-in, turn turnbuckles in other direction.
3. Amount of toe-in adjustment is 0.24 inch for each half turn of left and right tie rods.

REAR WHEEL ALIGNMENT

CAMBER

Rear camber is preset to specifications and cannot be adjusted. If camber is out of specification, bent or damaged components must be replaced.

TOE-IN

1. Turn mounting bolts, located inside lower arms, equally to left and right sides. **Fig. 2.**
2. Toe adjustment changes approximately 0.08 inch for every scale gradation.

VEHICLE RIDE HEIGHT

There is no provision for adjustment of vehicle ride height on these vehicles. If ride height is not satisfactory, check for damaged or modified suspension components.

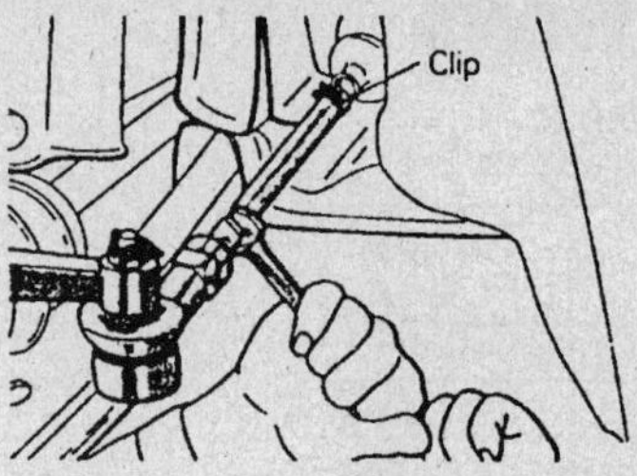
Clip
MT2049100028000X

Fig. 1 Front toe-in adjustment

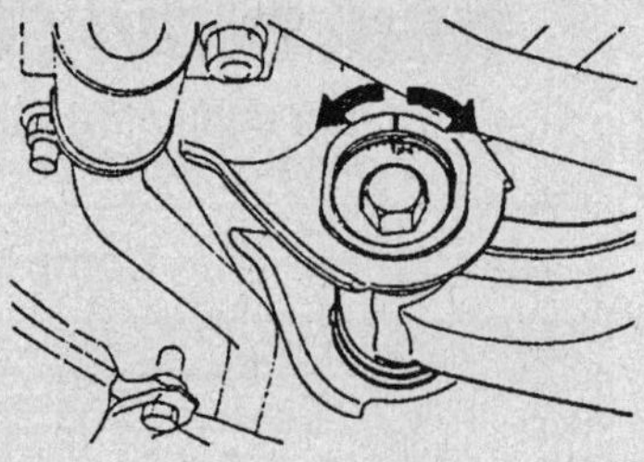
MT2049100029000X

Fig. 2 Rear toe-in adjustment

MITSUBISHI GALANT

INDEX OF SERVICE OPERATIONS

Page No.

AIR BAG SYSTEM PRECAUTIONS 0-8
AUTOMATIC TRANSMISSIONS/ TRANSAXLES 29-1
BRAKES
- Anti-Lock Brakes 29-1
- Disc Brakes 29-1
- Drum Brakes 29-1
- Hydraulic Brake Systems 29-1
- Power Brake Units 29-1

CLUTCH & MANUAL TRANSAXLE
- Adjustments 26-53
- Clutch, Replace 26-53
- Hydraulic System Service 26-53
- Tightening Specifications 26-56
- Transaxle, Replace 26-54

ELECTRICAL
- Air Bags 29-1
- Air Conditioning 29-1
- Alternators 29-1
- Blower Motor, Replace 26-6
- Combination Switch, Replace . 26-5
- Cooling Fans 29-1
- Cruise Control 29-1
- Dash Gauges 29-1
- Dash Panels 29-1
- Distributor, Replace 26-4
- Evaporator Core, Replace 26-7
- Fuel Pump Relay Location 26-4
- Fuse Panel & Flasher Location 26-4
- Heater Core, Replace 26-7
- Ignition Lock, Replace 26-4
- Ignition Switch, Replace 26-4
- Instrument Cluster, Replace 26-5
- Neutral Safety Switch, Replace 26-5
- Passive Restraints 29-1
- Precautions 26-4
- Radio, Replace 26-5
- Relay Center Location 26-4
- Speed Controls 29-1
- Starter Motors 29-1
- Starter, Replace 26-4
- Steering Columns 29-1
- Steering Wheel, Replace 26-5
- Wiper Motor, Replace 26-5
- Wiper Switch, Replace 26-6
- Wiper Systems 29-1

ELECTRICAL SYMBOL IDENTIFICATION 0-139
FRONT SUSPENSION & STEERING
- Ball Joint, Replace 26-93
- Control Arm, Replace 26-67
- Hub Service 26-65
- Manual Steering Gears 29-1
- Power Steering 29-1
- Power Steering Gear, Replace 26-67
- Power Steering Pump, Replace 26-68
- Precautions 26-64
- Rear Power Cylinder, Replace 26-70
- Rear Power Cylinder Control Valve, Replace 26-71
- Shock Absorber, Replace 26-67
- Stabilizer Bar, Replace 26-67
- Strut, Replace 26-65
- Strut Service 26-65
- Tightening Specifications 26-71
- Wheel Bearing, Adjust 26-64
- Wheel Hub & Steering Knuckle, Replace 26-64

FRONT WHEEL DRIVE AXLES 29-1
REAR AXLE & SUSPENSION
- Coil Spring, Replace 26-58
- Control Arm, Replace 26-58
- Hub & Bearing Service 26-56
- Knuckle, Replace 26-58
- Lateral Rod, Replace 26-59
- Rear Suspension, Replace 26-56
- Shock Absorber, Replace 26-57
- Stabilizer Bar, Replace 26-59
- Tightening Specifications 26-63
- Torsion Bar, Replace 26-59
- Trailing Arm, Replace 26-58
- Wheel Bearing, Adjust 26-56

SERVICE REMINDER & WARNING LAMP RESET PROCEDURES 0-10
SPECIFICATIONS
- Fluid Capacities & Cooling System Data 26-3
- Front Wheel Alignment Specifications 26-3
- General Engine Specifications 26-2
- Lubricant Data 26-4
- Rear Wheel Alignment Specifications 26-3
- Tune Up Specifications 26-2

VEHICLE IDENTIFICATION . 0-1
VEHICLE LIFT POINTS 0-34
VEHICLE MAINTENANCE SCHEDULES 0-69
WHEEL ALIGNMENT
- Front Wheel Alignment 26-74
- Preliminary Inspection 26-74
- Rear Wheel Alignment 26-74
- Technical Service Bulletins 26-74
- Vehicle Ride Height 26-74
- Wheel Alignment Specifications 26-3

WIRE COLOR CODE IDENTIFICATION 0-144
2.0L DOHC ENGINE
- Compression Pressures 26-34
- Engine Rebuilding Specifications 29-1
- Engine, Replace 26-34
- Precautions 26-34
- Radiator, Replace 26-34
- Technical Service Bulletins 26-36
- Thermostat, Replace 26-36
- Tightening Specifications 26-36

2.0L SOHC ENGINE
- Belt Tension Data 26-19
- Camshaft, Replace 26-15
- Compression Pressures 26-10
- Cooling System Bleed 26-19
- Crankshaft, Replace 26-18
- Cylinder Head, Replace 26-11
- Engine Mount, Replace 26-10
- Engine Rebuilding Specifications 29-1
- Engine, Replace 26-10
- Exhaust Manifold, Replace 26-11
- Front Cover, Replace 26-13
- Fuel Filter, Replace 26-19
- Fuel Pump, Replace 26-19
- Intake Manifold, Replace 26-11
- Oil Pan, Replace 26-18
- Oil Pump, Replace 26-19
- Piston & Rod Assembly 26-17
- Precautions 26-10
- Radiator, Replace 26-19
- Rocker Arms, Replace 26-12
- Silent Shaft, Replace 26-16
- Technical Service Bulletins 26-20
- Thermostat, Replace 26-19
- Tightening Specifications 26-32
- Timing Belt, Replace 26-13
- Valve Adjustment 26-12
- Valve Clearance Specifications 26-12
- Valves & Springs, Replace 26-12
- Water Pump, Replace 26-19

2.4L ENGINE
- Belt Tension Data 26-44
- Camshaft, Replace 26-43
- Compression Pressures 26-38
- Cooling System Bleed 26-44
- Crankshaft Rear Oil Seal, Replace 26-44
- Crankshaft Seal, Replace 26-44
- Cylinder Head, Replace 26-39
- Engine Mount, Replace 26-38
- Engine Rebuilding Specifications 29-1
- Engine, Replace 26-39
- Exhaust Manifold, Replace 26-39
- Fuel Filter, Replace 26-47
- Fuel Pump, Replace 26-47
- Hydraulic Lash Adjusters 26-40
- Intake Manifold, Replace 26-39
- Oil Pan, Replace 26-44
- Precautions 26-38
- Radiator, Replace 26-47
- Rocker Arms, Replace 26-41
- Technical Service Bulletins 26-48
- Thermostat, Replace 26-44
- Tightening Specifications 26-52
- Timing Belt, Replace 26-41
- Valve Adjustment 26-40
- Valve Clearance Specifications 26-40
- Water Pump, Replace 26-47

Specifications

GENERAL ENGINE SPECIFICATIONS

Year	Engine Liters	Fuel System	Bore & Stroke	Compression Ratio	Maximum Net H.P. @ RPM	Maximum Torque Ft. Lbs. @ RPM	Normal Oil Pressure, Psi.
1993	2.0L SOHC	MFI	3.35 x 3.46	8.5	121 @ 6000	120 @ 4750	11.4③
	2.0L DOHC	MFI	3.35 x 3.46	9.0	144 @ 6000	134 @ 4500	11.4③
1994	2.4L SOHC	MFI	3.41 x 3.94	9.5	141 @ 5500	148 @ 3000	11.4③
	2.4L DOHC	MFI	3.41 x 3.94	10.0	160 @ 6000	160 @ 4250	11.4③
1995–96	2.4L SOHC①	MFI	3.41 x 3.94	9.5	141 @ 5500	148 @ 3000	11.4③
	2.4L SOHC②	MFI	3.41 x 3.94	9.5	138 @ 5500	148 @ 3000	11.4③

DOHC — Dual Overhead Cam
MFI — Multi-Point Fuel Injection
SOHC — Single Overhead Cam

① — Federal models.

② — California models.

③ — Minimum at idle speed with oil temperature between 167 to 194 degrees F.

TUNE UP SPECIFICATIONS

Year & Engine⑤	Spark Plug Gap, Inch	Ignition Timing,			Idle Speed, RPM				Fuel Pump Pressure, psi	Valve Lash	
		Firing Order Fig.⑤	Timing °BTDC⑥	Timing Mark Loc.	Curb②		Fast			Intake	Exhaust
					Man. Trans.	Auto. Trans.	Man. Trans.	Auto. Trans.			
1993											
2.0L SOHC	.041	A	5	Pulley	750	750N	④	④	47.6	①	①
2.0L DOHC	.041	A	5	Pulley	750	750N	④	④	47.6	①	①
1994											
2.4L SOHC	.041	A	5	Pulley	750	750N	④	④	47.6	①	①
2.4L DOHC	.041	A	5	Pulley	800	800N	④	④	47.6	①	①
1995–96											
2.4L SOHC	.041	A	5	③	750	750N	④	④	47.6	①	①

BTDC — Before Top Dead Center.
N — Neutral.
① — Hydraulic lifters, no adjustment required.

② — When adjusting idle speed, set parking brake & chock drive wheels.

③ — Equipped w/crankshaft position sensor.

④ — Controlled by idle speed control servo.

⑤ — Cylinder numbering from front of engine to rear, 1, 2, 3, 4. Firing order, 1–3–4–2.

⑥ — With jumper wire connected between ignition timing adjustment connector & ground. Refer to Figs. B through D.

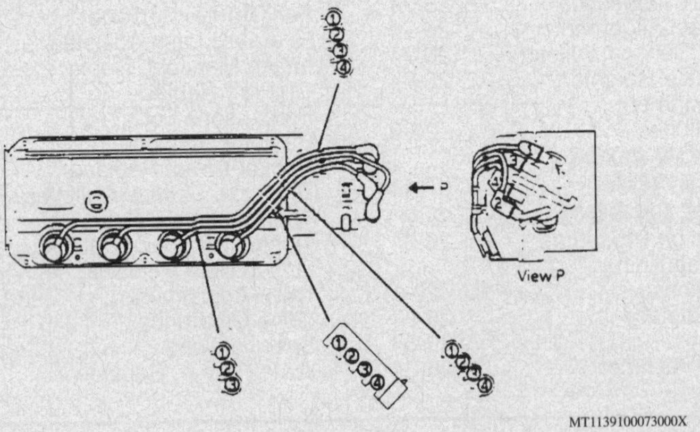
View P
MT1139100073000X
Fig. A

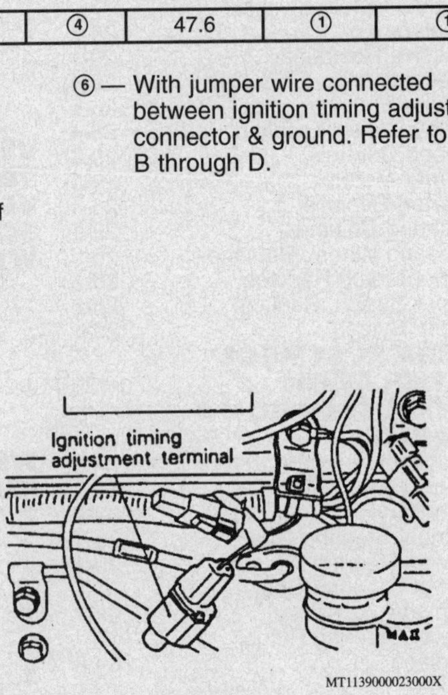
Ignition timing adjustment terminal
MT1139000023000X
Fig. B

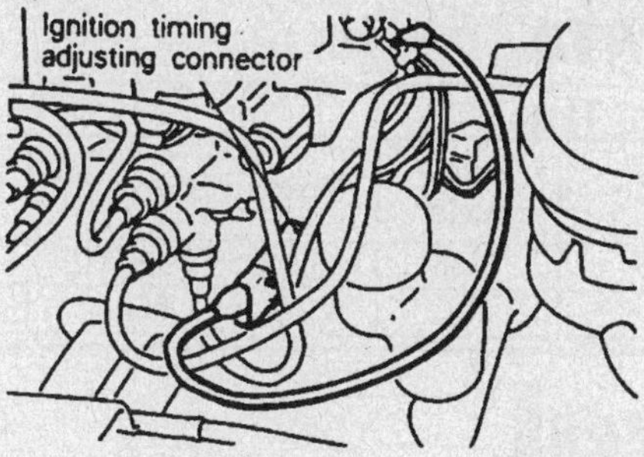
Ignition timing
adjusting connector
MT1139000024000X

Fig. C

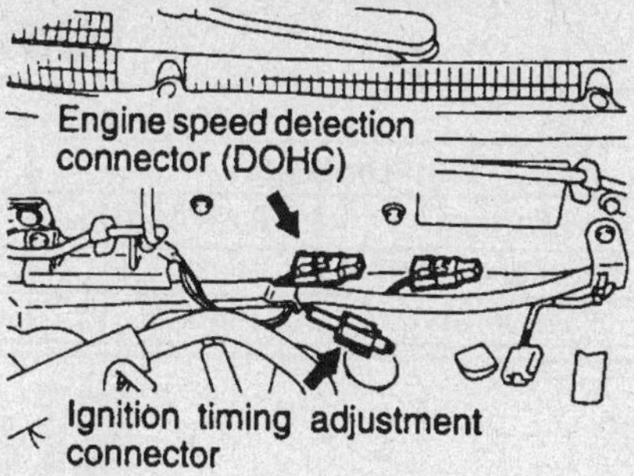
Engine speed detection
connector (DOHC)
Ignition timing adjustment
connector
MT1139000025000X

Fig. D

FRONT WHEEL ALIGNMENT SPECIFICATIONS

Year	Model	Caster Angle, Deg.		Camber Angle, Deg.		Toe, Inch①	Ball Joint Inspection, Inch Lbs.	
		Limits	Desired	Limits	Desired		Upper	Lower
1993	Galant	+1 ½ to +2 ½	+2	−2/15 to +13/15	+11/30	−.12 to +.12	3–13②	4–22②
1994–96	Galant	+2 5/6 to +5 5/6	+4 ⅓	−½ to +½	0	−.12 to +.12	3–13②	4–22②

① — Toe-in (+); toe-out (-).
② — Breakaway measurement using special service tool No. MB990326, or equivalent.

REAR WHEEL ALIGNMENT SPECIFICATIONS

Year	Model	Camber Angle, Deg.		Toe, Inch①	Ball Joint Inspection, Inch Lbs.	
		Limits	Desired		Upper	Lower
1993	Galant	−1 ¼ to −¼	−¾	−.12 to +.12	—	1–23②
1994–96	Galant	−1 5/6 to −5/6	−1 ⅓	0 to +.24	—	1–23②

① — Toe-in (+); toe-out (-).
② — Breakaway measurement using tool No. MB990326, or equivalent.

FLUID CAPACITIES & COOLING SYSTEM DATA

Year	Engine	Coolant Capacity, Qts.		Radiator Cap Relief Pressure, Lbs.	Thermo. Opening Temp., °F	Fuel Tank, Gals.	Engine Oil Refill, Qts. ①	Transmission Oil	
		Less A/C	With A/C					5 Speed, Pts.	Auto. Trans., Qts. ②
1993	2.0L SOHC	7.6	7.6	13	③	15.9	4.2	3.8	6.4
1994	2.4L SOHC	7.4	7.4	13	180	16.9	4.5	4.4	6.3
	2.4L DOHC	7.4	7.4	13	180	16.9	4.5	4.4	7.9
1995–96	2.4L	7.4	7.4	13	180	16.9	4.5	4.4	6.3

DOHC — Dual Overhead Cam.
SOHC — Single Overhead Cam.
① — Includes filter.

② — Approximate, make final check with dipstick.

③ — 8 valve engine, 190°F; 16 valve engine, 180°F.

LUBRICANT DATA

Year	Lubricant Type					
	Transmission		Transfer Case	Rear Axle	Power Steering	Brake System
	Manual	Automatic				
1993	75/85W GL-4/5	Dia ATF SP	75/85W GL-4/5	GL-5	Mitsubishi Plus ATF	DOT 3
1994–96	75W-90 GL-4	Dia ATF SP	—	—	Dexron II/IIE/III	DOT 3 or 4

Electrical

NOTE: On Air Bag Equipped Models, Refer To "Air Bag System Precautions" Located In The Front Of This Manual For System Disarming & Arming Procedures.

INDEX

	Page No.
Air Bags	29-1
Air Conditioning	29-1
Alternators	29-1
Blower Motor, Replace	26-6
1993	26-6
1994–96	26-7
Combination Switch, Replace	26-5
1993	26-5
1994–96	26-5
Cooling Fans	29-1
Cruise Control	29-1
Dash Gauges	29-1
Dash Panels	29-1
Distributor, Replace	26-4
Evaporator Core, Replace	26-7
Fuel Pump Relay Location	26-4
Fuse Panel & Flasher Location	26-4
Heater Core, Replace	26-7
Ignition Lock, Replace	26-4
Ignition Switch, Replace	26-4
1993	26-4
1994–96	26-5
Instrument Cluster, Replace	26-5
1993	26-5
1994–96	26-5
Neutral Safety Switch, Replace	26-5
Passive Restraints	29-1
Precautions	26-4
Air Bag Systems	26-4
Radio, Replace	26-5
Relay Center Location	26-4
Speed Controls	29-1
Starter Motors	29-1
Starter, Replace	26-4
Steering Columns	29-1
Steering Wheel, Replace	26-5
Wiper Motor, Replace	26-5
Wiper Switch, Replace	26-6
Wiper Systems	29-1

PRECAUTIONS

AIR BAG SYSTEMS

Refer to "Air Bag System Precautions" in the front of this manual for system disarming and arming procedures.

FUSE PANEL & FLASHER LOCATION

The fuse panel is located behind the lefthand side of the instrument panel. The centralized junction box is mounted on the righthand wheelhouse in the engine compartment. The turn signal and hazard flasher is located behind the lower lefthand side of the instrument panel.

FUEL PUMP RELAY LOCATION

The fuel pump relay (multi-point fuel injection MFI relay), is located on the lefthand side of the center console, **Figs. 1 and 2.**

RELAY CENTER LOCATION

The main relay center is located on top of the righthand wheelhouse in the engine compartment.

STARTER

REPLACE

1. Disconnect battery ground cable.
2. Remove air cleaner assembly.
3. **On models with electronically controlled suspension,** remove ECS compressor assembly.
4. **On all models,** disconnect starter cables.
5. Remove starter mounting bolts, then the starter.
6. Reverse procedure to install. **Torque** starter mounting bolts to 20–25 ft. lbs.

DISTRIBUTOR

REPLACE

1. Rotate crankshaft to No. 1 cylinder TDC, then remove spark plug cables.
2. Remove high tension cable from ignition coil.
3. Scribe alignment marks on distributor housing, then remove distributor.
4. Reverse procedure to install, noting the following:
   a. Ensure No. 1 cylinder is still at TDC.
   b. Align distributor housing and gear mating marks.
   c. Install distributor with housing and gear mating marks aligned as shown, **Figs. 3 and 4.**

IGNITION LOCK

REPLACE

1. Remove steering column shrouds.
2. Cut attaching bolts at steering lock bracket side using a suitable hacksaw, then remove bolts.
3. Remove ignition switch electrical connectors, then the lock assembly.
4. Reverse procedure to install, noting the following:
   a. Temporarily install ignition lock in alignment with column boss and check for proper switch operation.
   b. Steering lock bracket should be replaced when installing new ignition switch.
   c. Install special ignition lock attaching bolts and tighten until heads twist off.

IGNITION SWITCH

REPLACE

1993

1. Remove column shrouds and disconnect switch electrical connectors.
2. Remove switch attaching screws, then separate lock cylinder from switch as follows:
   a. Insert key in lock cylinder and turn to ACC position.
   b. Using a small screwdriver, push in

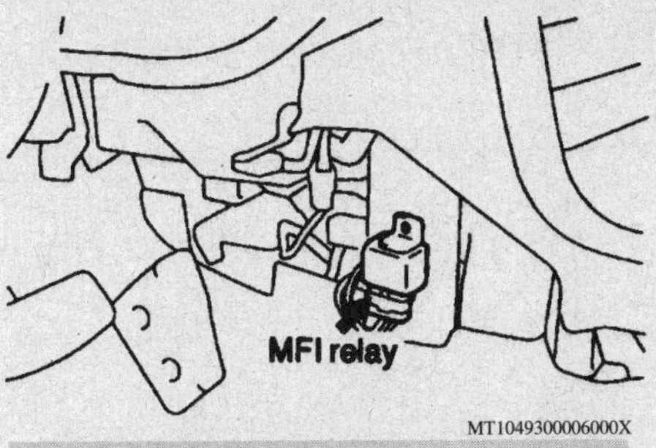
MFI relay
MT1049300006000X

Fig. 1 Fuel pump relay location. 1993–95

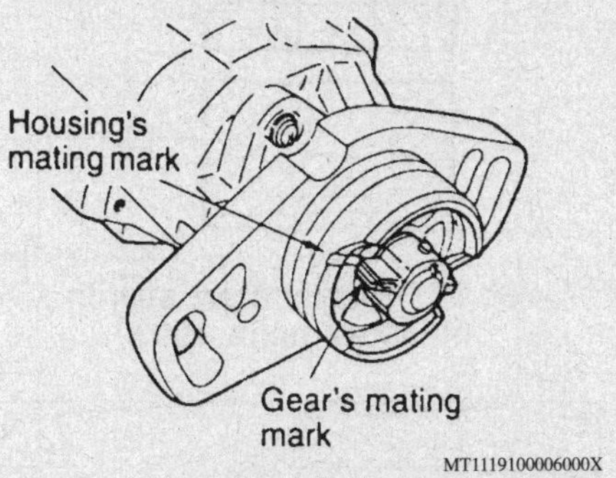
Housing's mating mark
Gear's mating mark
MT1119100006000X

Fig. 4 Distributor gear alignment. 2.4L engine

lock cylinder lockpin, **Fig. 5,** then remove lock cylinder.
3. Reverse procedure to install.

1994–96

Remove ignition switch in numbered sequence shown in **Fig. 6.**

NEUTRAL SAFETY SWITCH

REPLACE

1. Disconnect all switch connections, then remove switch from transaxle.
2. Reverse procedure to install, then adjust switch as follows:
   a. Place selector lever and manual control lever in Neutral position.
   b. Rotate switch body, ensuring manual control lever hole and switch body hole are aligned, **Figs. 7 and 8.**
   c. **Torque** mounting bolts of the park/neutral position switch body to 7–9 ft. lbs. **Do not drop switch body.**
   d. Loosen nut as shown, **Fig. 9,** then lightly pull end of transaxle control cable in "F" direction by hand. **Torque** to 7–10 ft. lbs.
   e. With selector lever in Neutral position, ensure neutral start switch operates and functions on transaxle side in range which corresponds to each position of selector lever.

COMBINATION SWITCH

REPLACE

1993

1. Disconnect battery ground cable.

MFI relay and
fuel pump relay
MT1049600007000X

Fig. 2 Fuel pump relay location. 1996

2. Remove horn pad, then steering wheel attaching nut.
3. Remove steering wheel using a suitable puller. Refer to procedure outlined under "Steering Wheel, Replace."
4. Remove knee protector, if equipped.
5. Remove upper and lower column covers.
6. Disconnect combination switch electrical connectors.
7. Remove combination switch attaching screws, then the switch from steering shaft.
8. Reverse procedure to install.

1994–96

1. Refer to numbered sequence in **Fig. 6** when replacing combination switch.
2. Reverse procedure to install.

STEERING WHEEL

REPLACE

1. Remove horn pad attaching screws, then the horn pad. On some 1993 models there are no horn pad attaching screws. To remove, push horn pad upward.
2. Remove steering wheel attaching nut.
3. Scribe mating marks on steering shaft and steering wheel for installation reference.
4. Using a suitable steering wheel puller, remove steering wheel. **Do not hammer on steering wheel to remove. Damage to the collapsible mechanism may occur.**
5. Reverse procedure to install, noting the following:
   a. Align mating marks on steering shaft and steering wheel.
   b. **Torque** steering wheel attaching nut to 30 ft. lbs.

INSTRUMENT CLUSTER

REPLACE

1993

1. Disconnect battery ground cable.
2. Remove instrument cluster meter bezel attaching screws, then the cluster hood.
3. Remove instrument cluster attaching screws, **Fig. 10,** then pull cluster slightly forward and disconnect speedometer cable and electrical connectors.

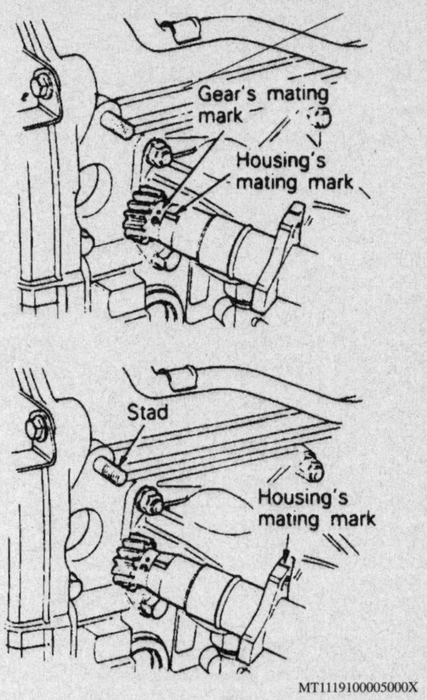
Gear's mating mark
Housing's mating mark
Stad
Housing's mating mark
MT1119100005000X

Fig. 3 Distributor installation. 2.0L engine

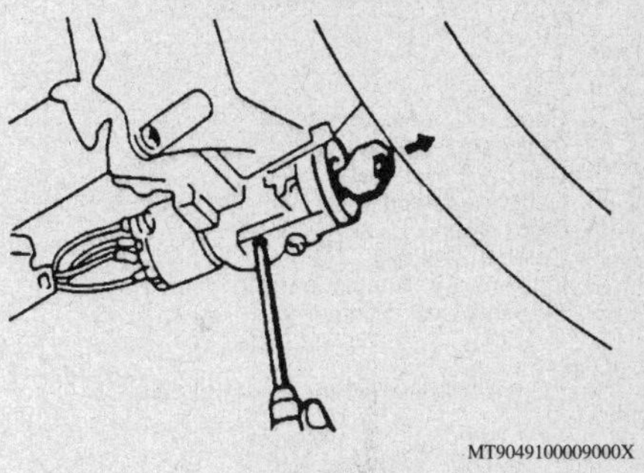
MT9049100009000X

Fig. 5 Lock cylinder removal. 1993

4. Remove instrument cluster from instrument panel.
5. Reverse procedure to install.

1994–96

1. Refer to numbered sequence in **Fig. 11** when replacing instrument cluster.
2. Reverse procedure to install.

RADIO

REPLACE

1. Disconnect battery ground cable.
2. Pry off radio panel using a suitable tool.
3. **On models with electronically controlled suspension,** remove ECS indicator.
4. **On all models,** remove radio bracket attaching screws, then disconnect antenna and radio electrical connector.
5. Remove radio.
6. Reverse procedure to install.

WIPER MOTOR

REPLACE

1. Disconnect battery ground cable.
2. Remove front deck and inlet garnish panels.

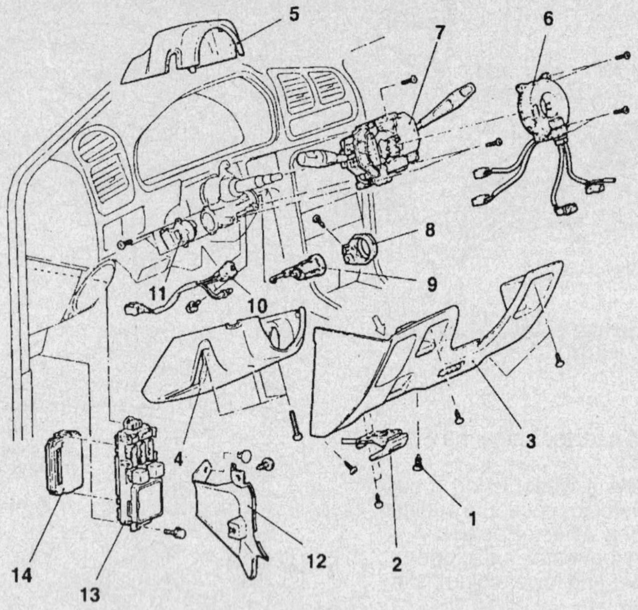
5
7
6
8
9
11
10
4
3
1
12
2
14
13

Steering lock cylinder removal steps
- Steering wheel

1. Clip
2. Hood lock release handle
3. Instrument under cover
4. Column cover lower
5. Column cover upper
6. Clock spring
7. Column switch
8. Ignition key illumination ring or ring cover
9. Steering lock cylinder

NOTE
The ⇦ mark indicates the sheet metal clip position.

Key reminder switch segment or key hole illumination light removal steps

4. Column cover lower
5. Column cover upper
10. Key reminder switch segment or key hole illumination light

Ignition switch segment removal steps

4. Column cover lower
5. Column cover upper
11. Ignition switch segment

BUZZER-ECU or ETACS-ECU removal steps

12. Cowl side trim (LH)
13. Junction block
14. BUZZER-ECU or ETACS-ECU

MT9049400008000X

Fig. 6 Ignition switch & combination switch replacement. 1994–96

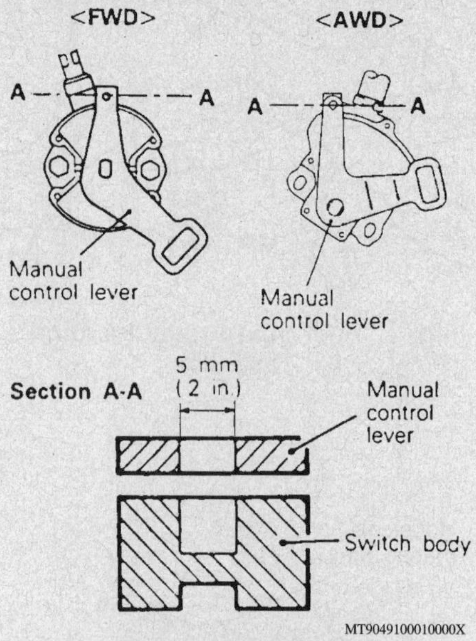
<FWD>
<AWD>
A
A
Manual control lever
Manual control lever
Section A-A
5 mm (2 in.)
Manual control lever
Switch body
MT9049100010000X

Fig. 7 Neutral start switch measurement. 1993

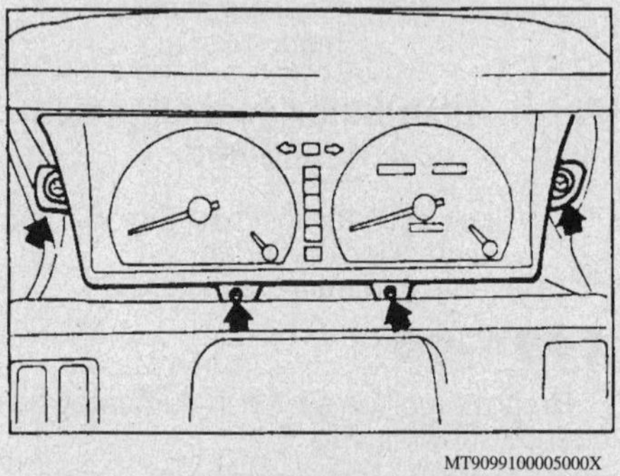
MT9099100005000X

Fig. 10 Instrument cluster attaching screw locations. 1993

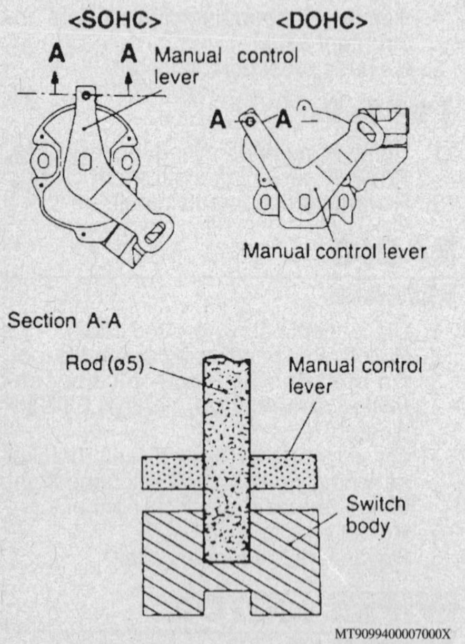
<SOHC>
<DOHC>
A
A
Manual control lever
Manual control lever
Section A-A
Rod (ø5)
Manual control lever
Switch body
MT9099400007000X

Fig. 8 Neutral start switch measurement. 1994–96

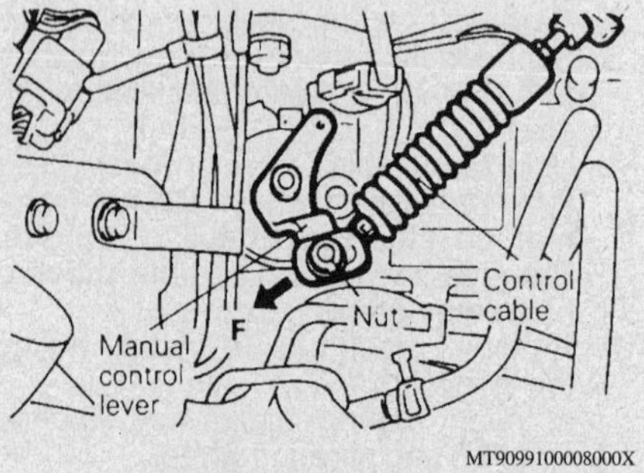
Control cable
Nut
F
Manual control lever
MT9099100008000X

Fig. 9 Manual control lever nut removal

3. Remove linkage mounting bolts.
4. Remove wiper motor attaching bolts, then pull wiper motor slightly and disconnect motor and linkage assembly.
5. Remove wiper motor with linkage from vehicle. **Mark position of crank arm to wiper motor, if necessary to remove.**
6. Reverse procedure to install.

WIPER SWITCH

REPLACE

Refer to "Column Switch, Replace" for wiper switch replacement procedure.

BLOWER MOTOR

REPLACE

1993

1. Disconnect battery ground cable.
2. Remove glove compartment stopper, then the glove compartment.
3. Remove undercover, then the foot shower duct.
4. Disconnect MPI control relay and glove compartment switch connectors.
5. Remove glove compartment frame.
6. Disconnect ventilation tube from blower assembly.
7. Remove blower motor attaching bolts, then the blower motor.
8. Reverse procedure to install.

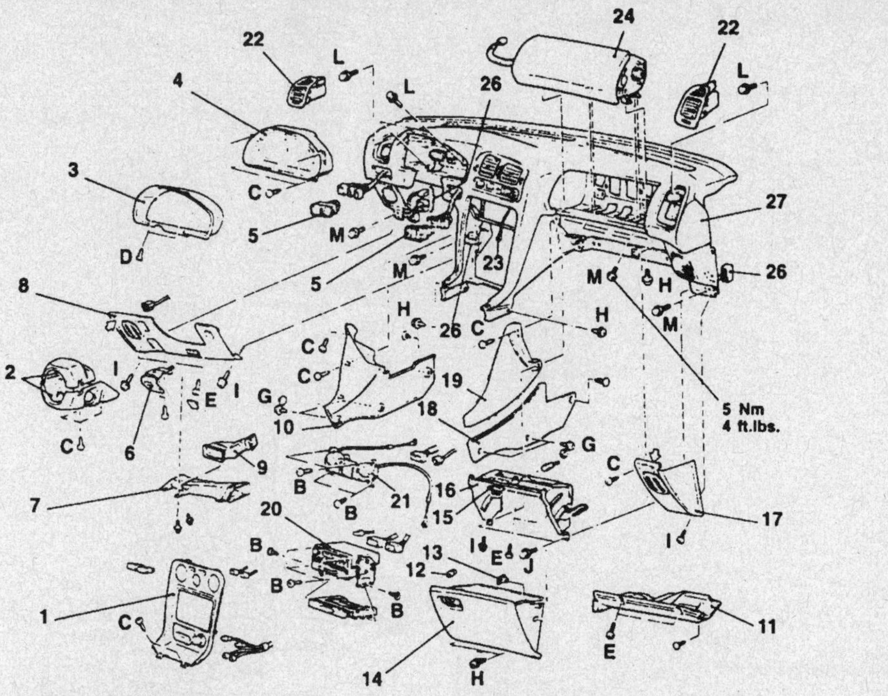
5 Nm
4 ft.lbs.

Removal steps

1. Center console panel
2. Column cover
3. Meter bezel
4. Combination meter
5. Instrument panel switch
6. Hood lock release handle
7. Shower foot duct
8. Instrument under cover
9. Lap cooler duct B
10. Side cover B
11. Under cover
12. Stopper
13. Catcher
14. Glove box
15. Glove box striker
16. Glove box cover
17. Corner panel
18. Side cover lower A
19. Side cover upper A
20. Radio and tape player, box, and cup holder
21. Heater control assembly
22. Side air outlet assembly
23. Cool air bypass damper lever cable connection
24. Passenger-side air bag module assembly
25. Steering column assembly installation bolts
26. Harness connector
27. Instrument panel assembly

MT9099400006000X

Fig. 11 Exploded view of instrument panel & cluster. 1994–96

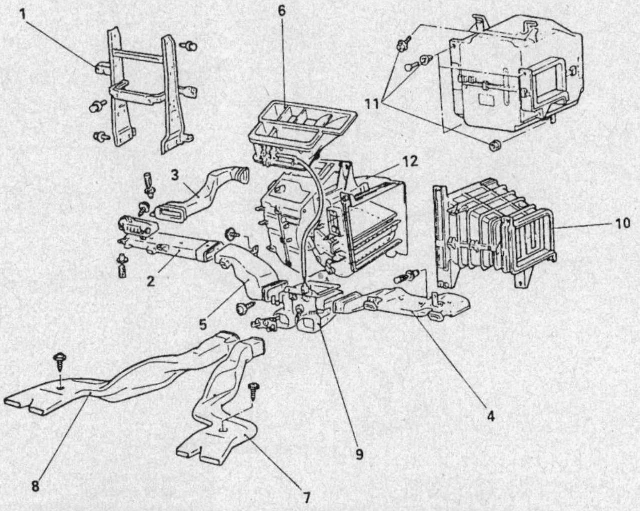

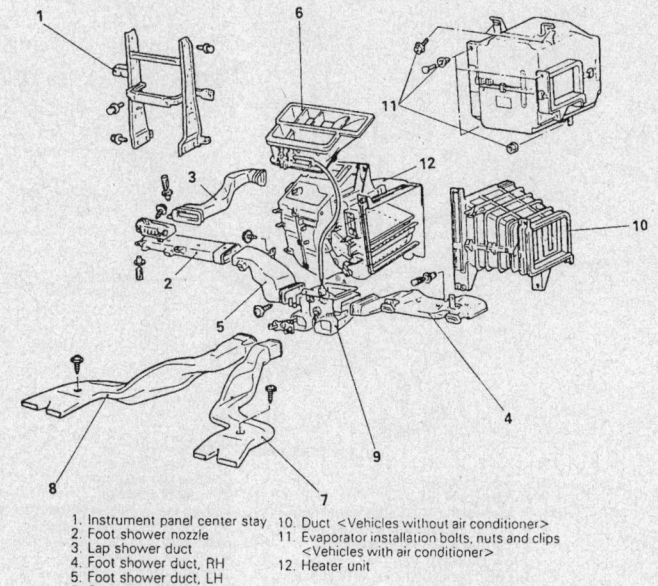

1. Instrument panel center stay
2. Foot shower nozzle
3. Lap shower duct
4. Foot shower duct, RH
5. Foot shower duct, LH
6. Center duct
7. Rear heater duct, B
8. Rear heater duct, C
9. Foot distribution duct
10. Duct <Vehicles without air conditioner>
11. Evaporator installation bolts, nuts and clips <Vehicles with air conditioner>
12. Heater unit

MT7029100083000X

Fig. 12 Exploded view of heater unit. 1993

1994-96

1. Remove instrument panel lower cover.
2. **On models with A/C,** remove automatic compressor ECM.
3. **On all models,** remove blower motor attaching bolts, then the blower motor.
4. Reverse procedure to install.

HEATER CORE

REPLACE

Remove heater unit components in order as shown, **Figs. 12 and 13,** noting the following:

1. Disconnect battery ground cable.
2. Drain cooling system into appropriate container.
3. Remove front seats and floor console as shown in **Figs. 14 through 17.**
4. Remove instrument panel as outlined under "Dash Panel Service."
5. **On models with A/C,** remove bolts and nuts attaching evaporator assembly to heater unit, then pull evaporator assembly out of heater unit.
6. **On all models,** remove heater unit from vehicle.
7. To prevent bolts from falling into blower assembly, set air selection damper to outside air induction position.
8. **On 1993 models,** remove plate from heater unit, **Fig. 18.**
9. **On all models,** remove heater core from heater unit.
10. Reverse procedure to install.

EVAPORATOR CORE

REPLACE

1. Discharge refrigerant from system as outlined in "Air Conditioning."
2. Disconnect evaporator inlet pipe and suction hose. **Plug openings to prevent contamination.**
3. Remove components in numbered sequences shown in **Figs. 19 and 20.**
4. Reverse procedure to install, recharge A/C system with refrigerant as outlined in "Air Conditioning" section.

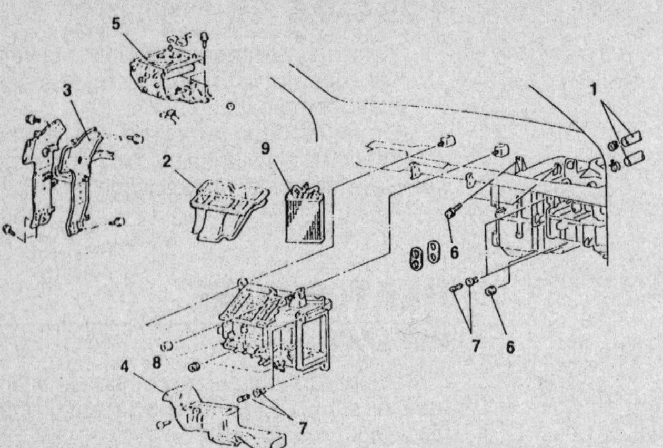

Removal steps

- Instrument panel

1. Heater hose connection
2. Center ventilation duct
3. Center reinforcement
4. Foot distribution duct
5. ECM bracket
6. Evaporator installation bolt and nut
7. Clip
8. Heater unit
9. Heater core

MT7029400084000X

Fig. 13 Exploded view of heater unit. 1994–96

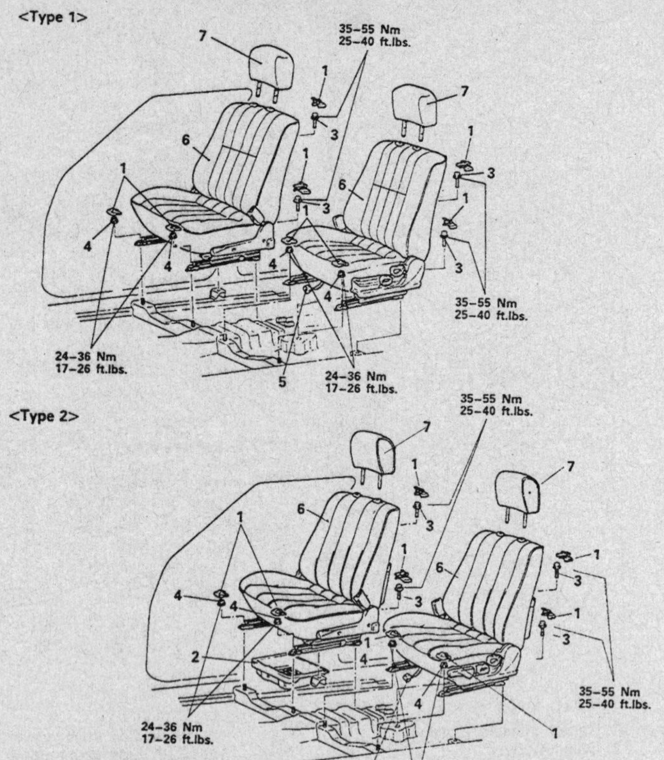
<Type 1>
35–55 Nm
25–40 ft.lbs.
24–36 Nm
17–26 ft.lbs.
<Type 2>

1. Seat anchor covers
2. Seat under tray
3. Seat mounting bolts (rear)
4. Seat mounting nuts (front)
5. Connection for seat belt switch wiring harness
6. Front seat assembly
7. Headrestraints

MT7029100085000X

Fig. 14 Front seat removal. 1993

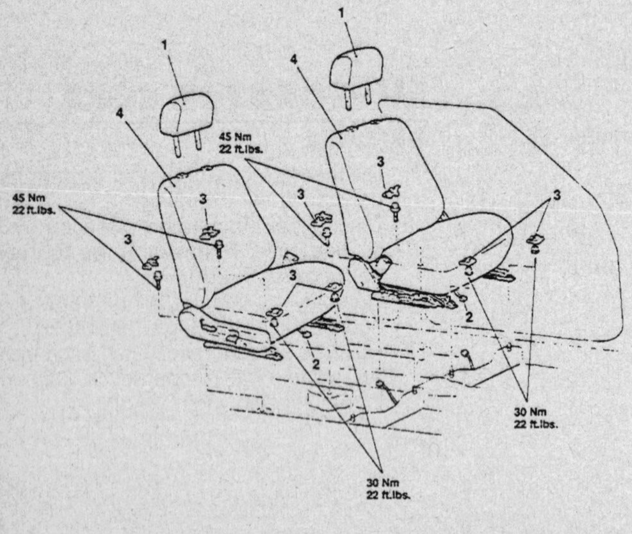
45 Nm
22 ft.lbs.
30 Nm
22 ft.lbs.

Headrestraint removal

1. Headrestraint

Front seat assembly removal steps

2. Harness connector
3. Seat anchor cover
4. Front seat assembly

NOTE
After provisionally tightening the seat assembly mounting nuts and bolts in every installation location, fully tighten them to the specified torque.

MT7029400086000X

Fig. 15 Front seat removal. 1994–96

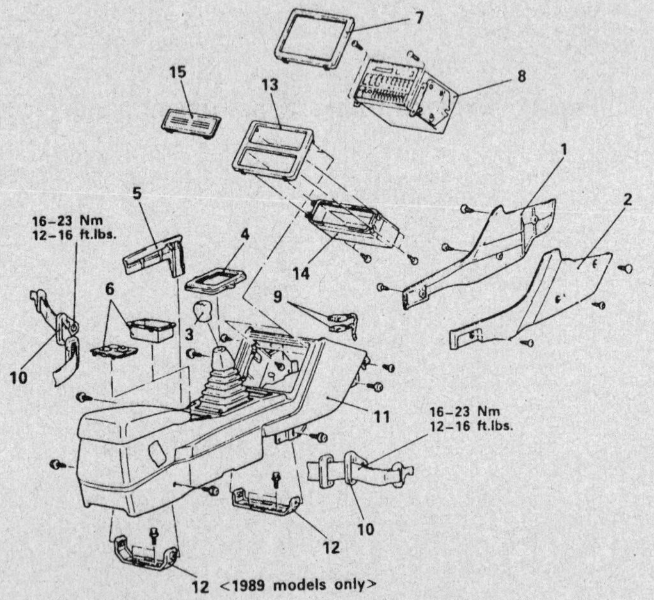
16–23 Nm
12–16 ft.lbs.
12 <1989 models only>

1. Side cover (A)
2. Side cover (B)
3. Manual transaxle shift lever knob
4. Automatic transaxle spacer
5. Parking brake side panel
6. Switch panel or box
7. Radio panel (Vehicles with audio)
8. Audio
9. Coupling of the audio and body wiring harness
10. Guide ring <1990 models>
11. Console box assembly
12. Console box bracket
13. Radio panel (Vehicles without audio)
14. Box (Vehicles without audio)
15. Radio plug (vehicles without audio)

MT7029100087000X

Fig. 16 Floor console removal. 1993

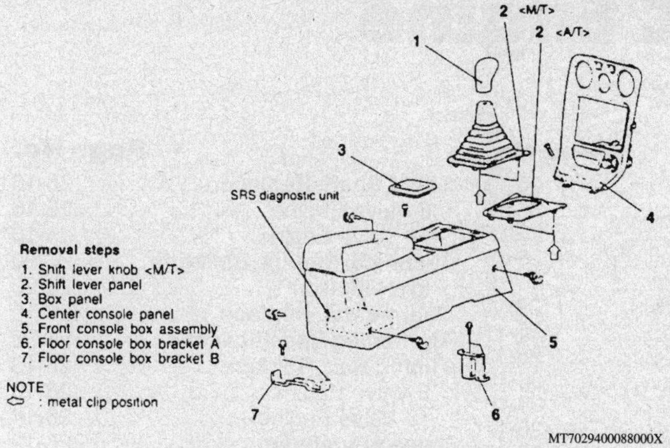
2 <M/T>
2 <A/T>
SRS diagnostic unit
Removal steps
1. Shift lever knob <M/T>
2. Shift lever panel
3. Box panel
4. Center console panel
5. Front console box assembly
6. Floor console box bracket A
7. Floor console box bracket B
NOTE
: metal clip position
MT7029400088000X

Fig. 17 Floor console removal. 1994–96

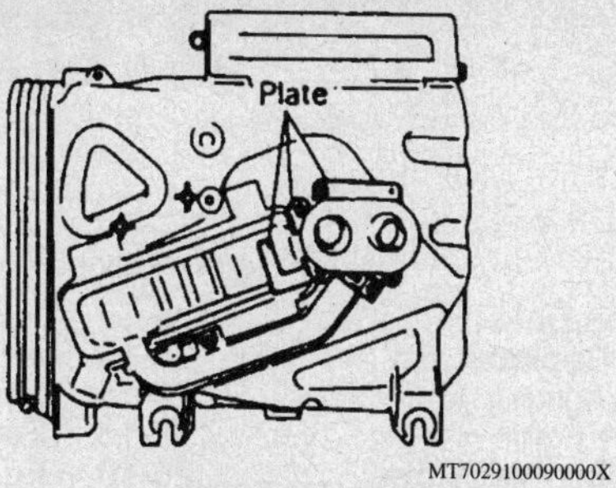
Plate
MT7029100090000X

Fig. 18 Heater core plate removal. 1993

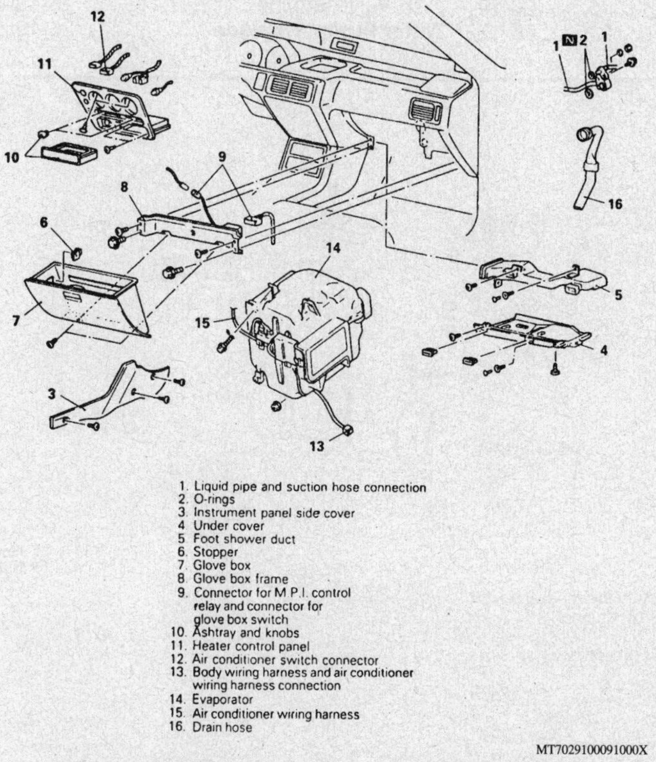
1. Liquid pipe and suction hose connection
2. O-rings
3. Instrument panel side cover
4. Under cover
5. Foot shower duct
6. Stopper
7. Glove box
8. Glove box frame
9. Connector for M.P.I. control relay and connector for glove box switch
10. Ashtray and knobs
11. Heater control panel
12. Air conditioner switch connector
13. Body wiring harness and air conditioner wiring harness connection
14. Evaporator
15. Air conditioner wiring harness
16. Drain hose
MT7029100091000X

Fig. 19 Evaporator core replacement. 1993

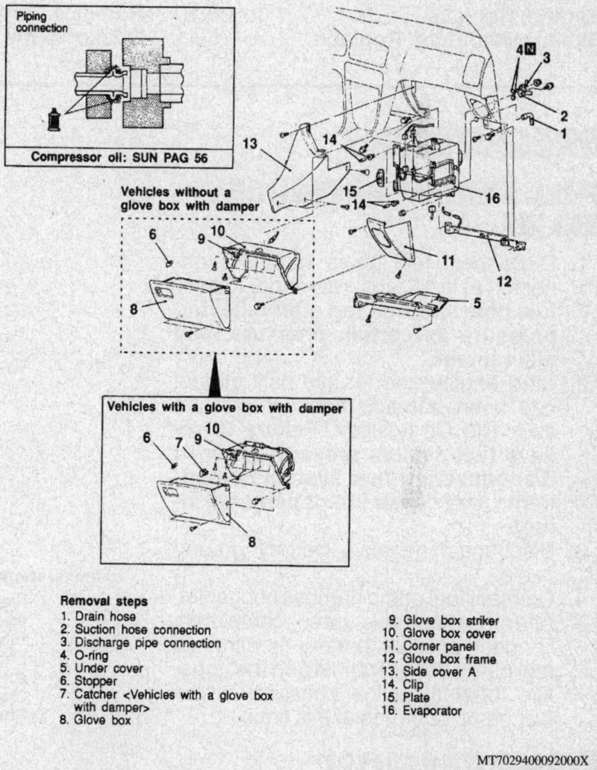
Piping connection
Compressor oil: SUN PAG 56
Vehicles without a glove box with damper
Vehicles with a glove box with damper
Removal steps
1. Drain hose
2. Suction hose connection
3. Discharge pipe connection
4. O-ring
5. Under cover
6. Stopper
7. Catcher <Vehicles with a glove box with damper>
8. Glove box
9. Glove box striker
10. Glove box cover
11. Corner panel
12. Glove box frame
13. Side cover A
14. Clip
15. Plate
16. Evaporator
MT7029400092000X

Fig. 20 Evaporator core replacement. 1994–96

2.0L SOHC Engine

INDEX

	Page No.
Belt Tension Data	26-19
Camshaft, Replace	26-15
8 Valve Engine	26-15
16 Valve Engine	26-16
Compression Pressures	26-10
Cooling System Bleed	26-19
Crankshaft, Replace	26-18
8 Valve Engine	26-18
16 Valve Engine	26-18
Cylinder Head, Replace	26-11
8 Valve Engine	26-11
16 Valve Engine	26-12
Engine Mount, Replace	26-10
Engine Rebuilding Specifications	29-1
Engine, Replace	26-10
Exhaust Manifold, Replace	26-11
8 Valve Engine	26-11
16 Valve Engine	26-11
Front Cover, Replace	26-13
Fuel Filter, Replace	26-19
Fuel Pump, Replace	26-19
Intake Manifold, Replace	26-11
8 Valve Engine	26-11
16 Valve Engine	26-11
Oil Pan, Replace	26-18
Oil Pump, Replace	26-19
Piston & Rod Assembly	26-17
8 Valve Engine	26-17
16 Valve Engine	26-17
Precautions	26-10
Fuel System Pressure Relief	26-10
Radiator, Replace	26-19
Rocker Arms, Replace	26-12
Silent Shaft, Replace	26-16
8 Valve Engine	26-16
16 Valve Engine	26-16
Technical Service Bulletins	26-20
Idle Vibration	26-20
Thermostat, Replace	26-19
Tightening Specifications	26-32
Timing Belt, Replace	26-13
8 Valve Engine	26-13
16 Valve Engine	26-14
Valve Adjustment	26-12
Valve Clearance Specifications	26-12
Valves & Springs, Replace	26-12
8 Valve Engine	26-12
16 Valve Engine	26-13
Water Pump, Replace	26-19

PRECAUTIONS

FUEL SYSTEM PRESSURE RELIEF

1. Disconnect fuel pump harness connector at fuel tank rear side. **Cover fuel pipe line with rag after relieving pressure as certain pressure may still remain.**
2. Start engine and let idle until all fuel has been burned, then turn ignition switch to Off position. **Failure to relieve fuel system pressure prior to disconnecting fuel system components may cause fire or personal injury.**
3. Disconnect negative battery ground cable.
4. Connect fuel pump harness connector.
5. After repairs have been completed, connect positive battery terminal to fuel pump drive terminal and the negative terminal to the chassis. Ensure fuel pump operates at this time.

COMPRESSION PRESSURES

Ensure engine oil, starter motor and battery are in satisfactory condition. When checking compression, engine coolant should be at normal operating temperature, spark plugs should be removed and throttle valve should be wide open. On 8–valve engines, minimum compression pressure is 125 psi. On 16–valve engines, minimum compression pressure is 139 psi. Difference between cylinders should not exceed 14 psi.

ENGINE MOUNT

REPLACE

1. Raise engine slightly and suspend to remove weight from mounts.

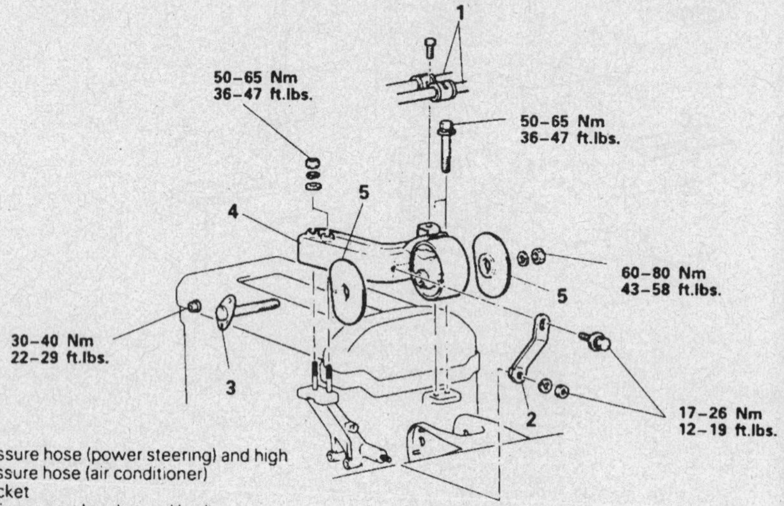

1
50–65 Nm
36–47 ft.lbs.
50–65 Nm
36–47 ft.lbs.
4
5
60–80 Nm
43–58 ft.lbs.
5
30–40 Nm
22–29 ft.lbs.
3
2
17–26 Nm
12–19 ft.lbs.

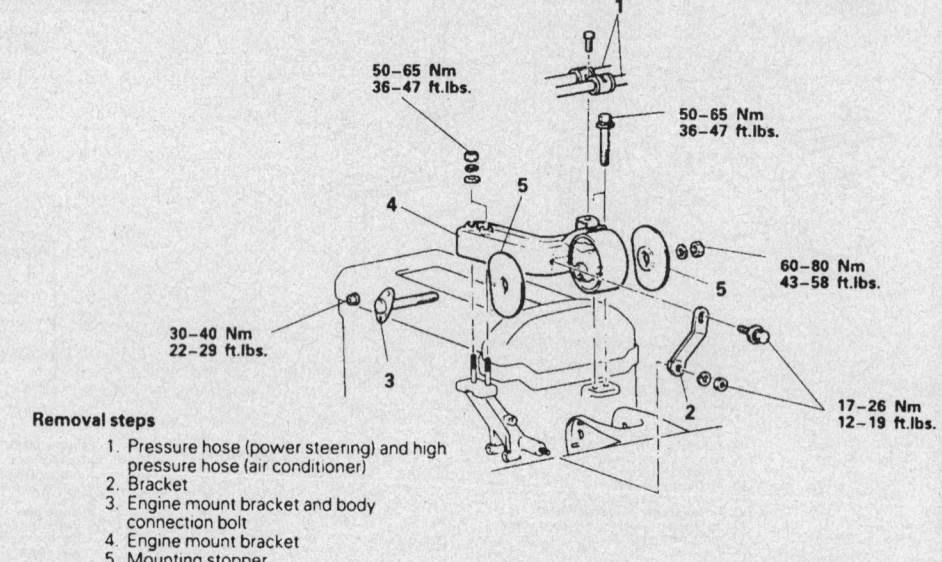

Removal steps

1. Pressure hose (power steering) and high pressure hose (air conditioner)
2. Bracket
3. Engine mount bracket and body connection bolt
4. Engine mount bracket
5. Mounting stopper

MT1069100161000X

Fig. 1 Engine mount replacement

2. Remove pressure hose (power steering) and high pressure hose (A/C), **Fig. 1**.
3. Remove engine mount bracket and body connection bolt.
4. Remove engine mount bracket and mounting stopper.
5. Reverse procedure to install.

ENGINE

REPLACE

1. Release fuel pressure as outlined under "Precautions."
2. Disconnect battery ground cable.
3. Scribe reference marks between hood and hood hinges, then remove hood.
4. Drain cooling system into appropriate container as follows:
   a. Place temperature control lever in Hot position.
   b. Carefully remove radiator cap.
   c. Remove radiator drain plug.
5. **On models with automatic transaxle,** remove transaxle assembly as outlined under "Transaxle, Replace" in "Automatic Transaxle" section.
6. **On models with manual transaxle,** remove transaxle assembly as outlined under "Transaxle, Replace" in "Clutch & Manual Transaxle" section.
7. **On all models,** remove radiator as outlined under "Radiator, Replace."
8. **On 8 valve engine models,** remove

engine components in order as shown, **Fig. 2.**

9. **On 16 valve engine models,** remove engine components in order as shown, **Fig. 3.**
10. **On all models,** note the following during engine removal:
    a. Remove oil pump with hoses attached and support aside with suitable wire.
    b. Disconnect A/C compressor connectors, then remove compressor with hoses attached from compressor bracket and support aside with suitable wire.
    c. Using a suitable engine hoist, slightly raise engine, then remove engine mount bracket.
    d. Ensure all cables, connectors and hoses are disconnected, then remove engine from engine compartment.
11. Reverse procedure to install.

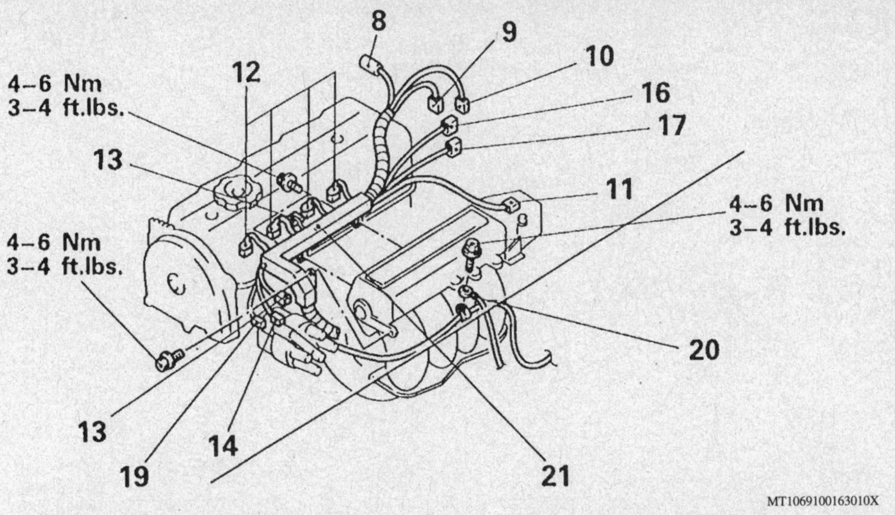
8
9
10
12
16
17
4–6 Nm
3–4 ft.lbs.
13
11
4–6 Nm
3–4 ft.lbs.
4–6 Nm
3–4 ft.lbs.
20
13
14
19
21
MT1069100163010X

Fig. 2 Engine assembly removal (Part 1 of 2). 8 valve engine

INTAKE MANIFOLD

REPLACE

8 VALVE ENGINE

1. Release fuel pressure as outlined under "Precautions."
2. Disconnect battery ground cable.
3. Remove intake manifold, noting the following:
    a. Chalk mating marks on radiator upper hose and hose clamp, then remove hose, **Fig. 4.**
    b. Remove fuel rail fuel injector and pressure regulator. **Do not drop injector when removing fuel rail.**
    c. Inspect intake manifold and intake manifold plenum for defects and cracks, replace as necessary.
    d. Inspect load of drain port, ensuring cooling water and jet air passages are not clogged.
    e. Measure deflection of installation surface with straightedge and feeler gauge, deflection should be 0.006–0.012 inch.
4. Reverse procedure to install, noting the following
    a. Align mating marks on upper radiator hose and hose clamp, then install.
    b. Apply pressure as shown, **Fig. 5,** to ensure clamp is seated correctly.

16 VALVE ENGINE

1. Release fuel pressure as outlined under "Precautions."
2. Disconnect battery ground cable.
3. Remove intake manifold, noting the following:
    a. Chalk mating marks on radiator upper hose and hose clamp, then remove hose, **Fig. 6.**
    b. Remove fuel rail fuel injector and pressure regulator. **Do not drop injector when removing fuel rail.**
    c. Inspect intake manifold for defects and cracks, replace as necessary.
    d. Inspect vacuum outlet port, water or gas passages are not clogged.
    e. Measure deflection of installation surface with straightedge and feeler gauge, deflection should be 0.006–0.012 inch.
4. Reverse procedure to install.

EXHAUST MANIFOLD

REPLACE

8 VALVE ENGINE

1. Release fuel pressure as outlined under "Precautions."
2. Disconnect battery ground cable.
3. Remove exhaust manifold in numbered sequence shown in **Fig. 7.**
4. Disconnect oxygen sensor connector, then install oxygen sensor tool No. MD998703, or equivalent, on oxygen sensor, **Fig. 8.**
5. Inspect exhaust manifold and manifold gasket for cracking, flaking or damage.
6. Reverse procedure to install.

16 VALVE ENGINE

1. Release fuel pressure as outlined under "Precautions."
2. Disconnect battery ground cable.
3. Remove exhaust manifold in numbered sequence shown in **Fig. 9.**
4. Disconnect oxygen sensor connector, then install oxygen sensor tool No. MD998703, or equivalent, on oxygen sensor, **Fig. 10.**
5. Inspect exhaust manifold and manifold gasket for cracking, flaking or damage.
6. Reverse procedure to install.

CYLINDER HEAD

REPLACE

8 VALVE ENGINE

1. Release fuel pressure as outlined under "Precautions."
2. Disconnect battery ground cable, then drain cooling system into appropriate container.
3. Remove air cleaner, if necessary, then disconnect control cables from throttle lever and bracket.
4. Disconnect upper radiator hose and engine mounting bracket, **Fig. 11.**
5. Disconnect spark plug wires.
6. Remove power steering pump attaching bolts and drive belt, then position pump aside.
7. Mark and disconnect electrical connectors and vacuum hoses, release harness clamps, then position harness aside.
8. Remove timing belt upper cover, then the rocker arm cover.
9. Rotate crankshaft in normal direction of rotation until No. 1 cylinder is at top dead center and camshaft and crankshaft timing marks are aligned.
10. Place a chalk mark between timing belt and camshaft sprocket, then remove camshaft sprocket bolt.
11. Separate sprocket from camshaft, leaving belt in place on sprocket. Secure sprocket and belt on lower timing cover. Ensure sprocket does not disengage from belt and fall, and maintain tension on belt to maintain proper timing. **Do not rotate crankshaft after sprocket is removed from camshaft.**
12. Remove cylinder head attaching bolts in sequence shown, **Fig. 12.** Loosen bolts evenly in three steps, to prevent cylinder head warpage, then remove cylinder head and gasket. Take care not to dislodge camshaft sprocket during cylinder head removal.
13. Check cylinder head gasket surface for squareness, using a suitable straightedge and feeler gauge. Place a straightedge across cylinder head, then check for warpage with feeler gauge. If clearance exceeds 0.008 inch in any direction, replace or lightly machine cylinder head. **If machining, do not remove more than 0.008 inch from gasket surface.**
14. Reverse procedure to install, noting the following:
    a. Clean both cylinder head and cylinder block gasket surfaces.
    b. Install gasket with identification mark toward cylinder head, **Fig. 13.**

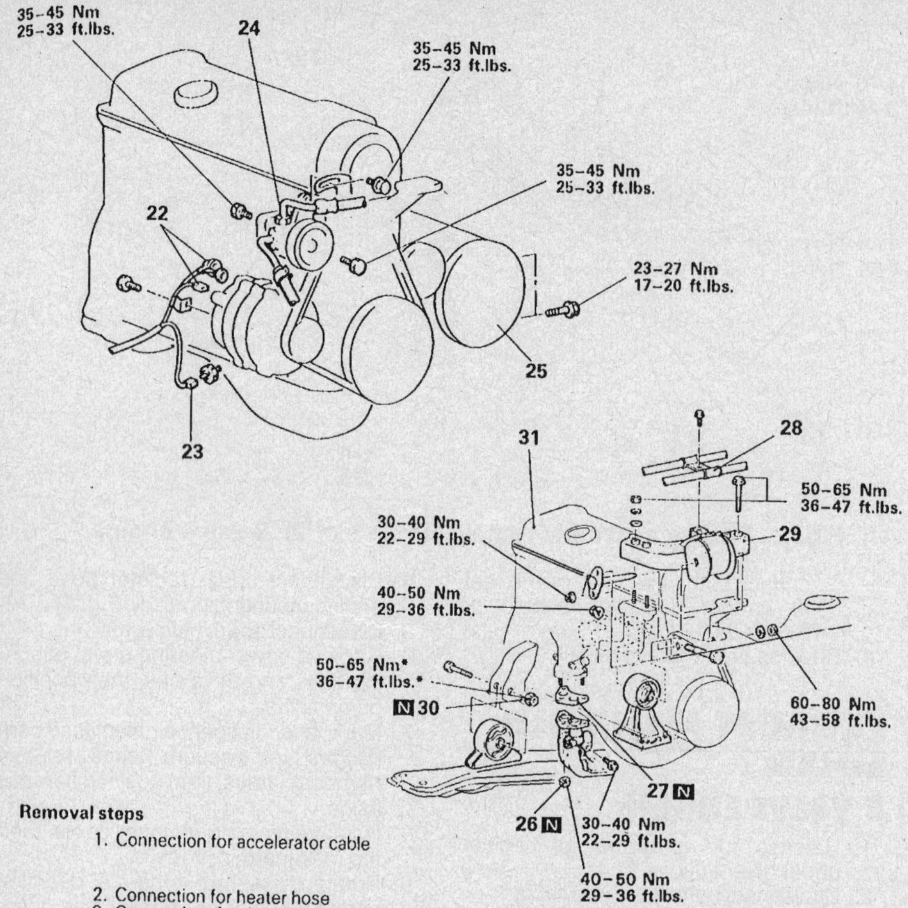
35-45 Nm
25-33 ft.lbs.
24
35-45 Nm
25-33 ft.lbs.
35-45 Nm
25-33 ft.lbs.
22
23-27 Nm
17-20 ft.lbs.
25
23
31
28
50-65 Nm
36-47 ft.lbs.
30-40 Nm
22-29 ft.lbs.
29
40-50 Nm
29-36 ft.lbs.
50-65 Nm*
36-47 ft.lbs.*
N 30
60-80 Nm
43-58 ft.lbs.
27 N
26 N
30-40 Nm
22-29 ft.lbs.
40-50 Nm
29-36 ft.lbs.

Removal steps

1. Connection for accelerator cable
2. Connection for heater hose
3. Connection for brake booster vacuum hose
4. Connection for fuel high pressure hose
5. O-ring
6. Connection for fuel return hose
7. Connection for vacuum hose
8. Connection for oxygen sensor
9. Connection for engine coolant temperature gauge unit
10. Connection for engine coolant temperature sensor
11. Connection for ISC
12. Connection for injector
13. Connection for EGR temperature sensor (California vehicles only)
14. Connection for ignition power transistor
15. Connection for condenser
16. Connection for TPS
17. Connection for idle speed control motor position sensor
18. Connection for distributor
19. Connection for crankshaft position sensor
20. Connection for ground cable
21. Control wiring harness
22. Connection for generator
23. Connection for oil pressure switch
24. Power steering oil pump
25. Air conditioning compressor
26. Self-locking nuts
27. Gasket
28. Clamp of pressure hose (Power steering) and high pressure hose (Air conditioning)
29. Engine mount bracket
30. Self locking nut
31. Engine assembly

NOTE
For tightening locations indicated by the • symbol, first tighten temporarily, and then make the final tightening with the entire weight of the engine applied to the vehicle body.

MT1069100163020X

Fig. 2 Engine assembly removal (Part 2 of 2). 8 valve engine

c. Install cylinder head bolts and tighten to specifications in sequence, **Fig. 14.**
d. Install intake and exhaust manifolds and gaskets. Tighten bolts to specification.

16 VALVE ENGINE

1. Release fuel pressure as outlined under "Precautions."
2. Disconnect battery ground cable.
3. Drain cooling system and engine oil into appropriate containers.
4. Rotate crankshaft in forward (right) direction and align timing mark, **Fig. 15. Crankshaft must always be rotated in the forward direction only.**
5. Tie camshaft sprocket and timing belt ensuring position of camshaft sprocket will not move with respect to timing belt.
6. Remove camshaft sprocket with timing belt attached. **Ensure crankshaft is not rotated after camshaft sprocket removal.**
7. Loosen bolts in order as shown, **Fig. 16,** then remove cylinder head assembly.
8. Reverse procedure to install, noting the following:
   a. Using a scraper, remove remaining gasket material from cylinder block.
   b. Position cylinder head gasket on top of cylinder head block ensuring identification mark is facing upwards, as shown, **Fig. 17. Ensure gasket is installed properly or malfunctions may occur.**
   c. Install cylinder head assembly and cylinder head bolts ensuring shank length of each bolt meets the limit. If limit exceeds 3.91 inches, replace bolt.
   d. Apply engine oil to threaded part of bolt and washer, then in order as shown, **Fig. 18, torque** bolts to 58 ft. lbs.
   e. Loosen water inlet pipe, then apply sealant, No. MD970389, or equivalent, to thermostat case assembly.
   f. Apply small amount of water to O-ring of water inlet pipe, then press thermostat case assembly onto water inlet pipe.
   g. Install thermostat case assembly mounting bolt, then tighten water inlet pipe to specification.

VALVE CLEARANCE SPECIFICATIONS

These engines use hydraulic auto-lash adjusters. No adjustments are required.

VALVE ADJUSTMENT

These engines use hydraulic auto-lash adjusters. No adjustments are required.

ROCKER ARMS

REPLACE

Refer to "Camshaft, Replace" for rocker arm replacement procedure.

VALVES & SPRINGS

REPLACE

8 VALVE ENGINE

1. Remove cylinder head as outlined under "Cylinder Head, Replace."
2. Using a suitable valve spring compressor, remove intake valve retainer lock, marking relative position of each to facilitate installation, **Fig. 19.**
3. Remove valve spring retainer, then the valve spring.
4. Remove valve spring seat, then the intake valves.
5. Remove and discard valve stem seals, then the intake valve guides and seats.
6. Using a suitable valve spring compressor, remove exhaust valve retainer lock, mark position of each for installation reference.
7. Remove valve spring retainer, then the valve spring.
8. Remove valve spring seat, then the exhaust valves.
9. Remove and discard valve stem seals, then the exhaust valve guides and seats.
10. Check each valve for wear and damage or defects in valve head and stem. Replace valve if unable to repair.
11. If stem tip has been pitted, grind stem tip slightly. Also grind valve face slightly.

12. Check stem to guide clearance. Refer to "Valves & Valve Springs" in the "Engine Rebuilding Specifications " section. If clearance is not within specification, replace valve and/or valve guide as necessary.
13. Replace valve if margin of face has decreased to less than the specified values, **Fig. 20.** Refer to "Valves & Valve Springs" in the "Engine Rebuilding Specifications" section.
14. If improper contact with valve seat is evident, reseat valve.
15. Check valve seat for evidence of overheating and improper contact with valve face, and replace as necessary.
16. Check free height of each valve spring. Refer to "Valves & Valve Springs" in the "Engine Rebuilding Specifications" section. If spring free height is not as specified, replace as necessary.
17. Test spring for squareness. Refer to "Valves & Valve Springs" in the "Engine Rebuilding Specifications " section. If spring squareness exceeds specified value, replace spring.
18. Reverse procedure to assemble, noting the following:
    a. Apply engine oil to each valve. Insert valves into guides, using care not to damage seal.
    b. Valve spring should be installed with identification color side directed toward valve spring retainer.
    c. Using a suitable valve spring compressor, compress spring and install retainer lock.

16 VALVE ENGINE

1. Remove cylinder head as outlined in "Cylinder Head, Replace."
2. Remove cylinder head bolts and retainer lock, **Fig. 21.** Keep removed parts in order according to the cylinder number and location for installation purposes.
3. Remove valve stem seal and discard.
4. Using a straightedge and thickness gauge, measure cylinder head gasket surface for flatness. Measurement should be 0.0020 inch and no greater than 0.008 inch. If greater, correct to meet specification.
5. Measure valve face for correct contact. Valve seat contact should be 0.039 inch (intake side) and 0.079 inch (exhaust side). If margin exceeds 0.020 inch (intake side) and 0.028 inch (exhaust side), replace valve.
6. Measure free height of spring. Free height should be 2.008 inch. If less than 1.969 inch, replace valve spring.
7. Measure squareness of spring. Spring inclination should be 2° or less. If greater than 4°, replace valve spring.
8. Measure clearance between valve guide and valve stem. Clearance should be 0.0008–0.0020 inch (intake side) and 0.0012–0.0028 inch (exhaust side). If greater than 0.004 inch (intake side) and 0.006 inch (exhaust side), replace valve guide and/or valve.
9. Reverse procedure to install, noting the following:
    a. Install valve spring seat, then the new valve stem seal. Ensure stem seal is installed correctly to avoid oil leaks.
    b. Install valve spring with white end toward spring retainer.
    c. Install retainer lock. **To avoid damaging retainer and stem seal, do not compress valve spring excessively.**
    d. Install cylinder head gasket without using a sealant.

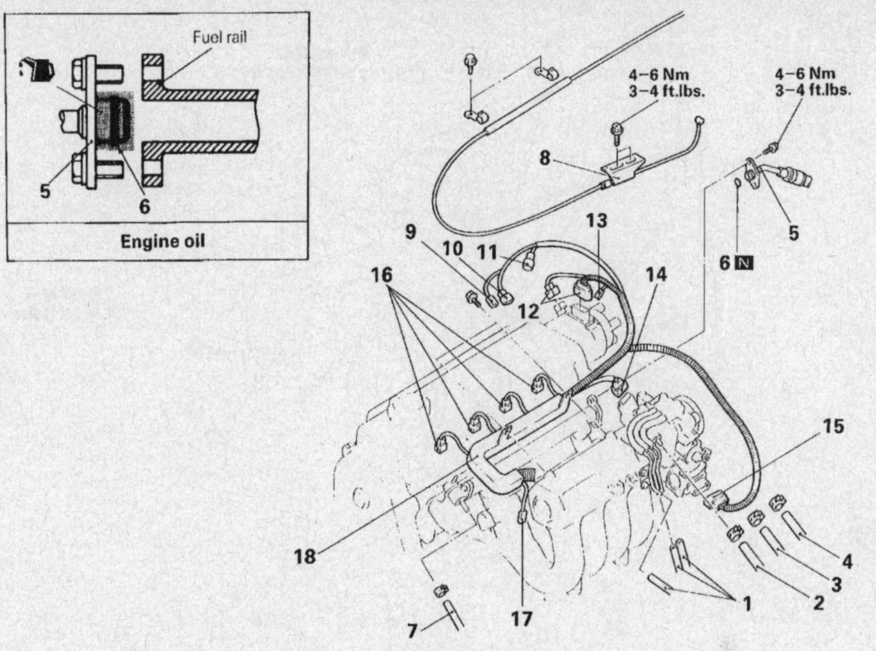
Fuel rail
5
6
Engine oil
4-6 Nm
3-4 ft.lbs.
4-6 Nm
3-4 ft.lbs.
8
9
10
11
12
13
14
16
6
5
15
18
4
3
2
1
7
17

Removal steps

1. Vacuum hose connection
2. Brake booster vacuum hose connection
3. Heater hose connection (cylinder head → heater unit)
4. Heater hose connection (Heater unit – water inlet pipe)
5. Fuel high pressure hose connection
6. O-ring
7. Fuel return hose connection
8. Accelerator cable connection
9. Engine coolant temperature gauge unit connector
10. Engine coolant temperature sensor connector
11. Oxygen sensor connector
12. Distributor connector
13. Condenser connector
14. TPS connector
15. IAC connector
16. Injector connector
17. Air conditioning compressor connector
18. Control harness

MT1069100164010X

Fig. 3 Engine assembly removal (Part 1 of 2). 16 valve engine

FRONT COVER

REPLACE

Refer to "Silent Shaft, Replace" for front cover replacement procedure.

TIMING BELT

REPLACE

With the timing belt removed, avoid turning the camshaft or crankshaft. If movement is required, exercise extreme caution to avoid valve damage caused by piston contact.

8 VALVE ENGINE

Refer to **Fig. 22** when removing and installing the timing belt.

1. Raise and support vehicle.
2. Place a suitable jack under engine with a wooden block between jack and oil pan, then raise engine enough to remove engine mount bracket.
3. Turn crankshaft clockwise and align timing marks, **Fig. 23.**
4. Mark timing belt to indicate direction of normal rotation for installation purposes.
5. Loosen bolt and tension spacer of the timing belt tensioner.
6. Move timing belt tensioner to water pump side, then loosely tighten bolt ensuring tensioner does not return.
7. Remove timing belt. If being reused, use chalk to mark direction of rotation for installation purposes.
8. **Water or oil on the belt can seriously reduce belt life, ensure timing belt sprocket and tensioner stay clean and dry. Do not wash belt and replace any parts that have become too dirty.**
9. Remove plug on side of cylinder block.
10. Insert a Phillips screwdriver to block left silent shaft, then remove oil pump sprocket nut and oil pump sprocket, **Fig. 24.**
11. Mark on back of timing belt "B" indicating direction of rotation for installation purposes. **Water or oil on the belt can seriously reduce belt life, ensure**

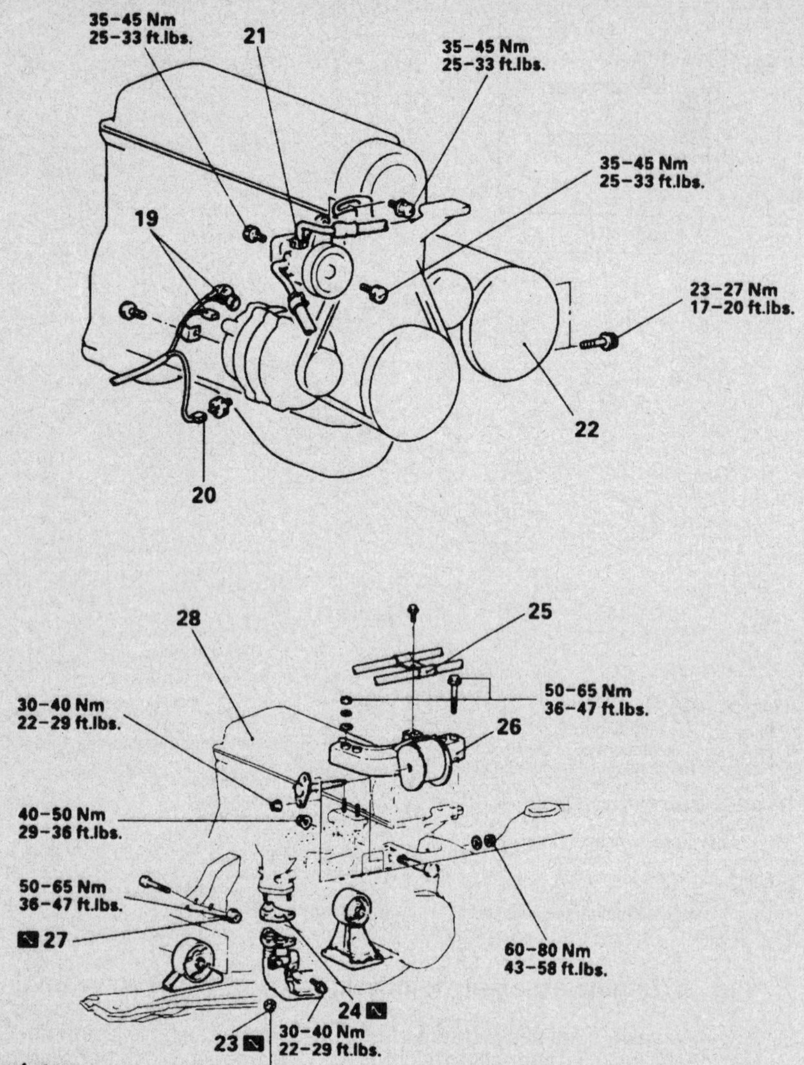
35-45 Nm
25-33 ft.lbs.
21
35-45 Nm
25-33 ft.lbs.
35-45 Nm
25-33 ft.lbs.
19
23-27 Nm
17-20 ft.lbs.
22
20
28
25
30-40 Nm
22-29 ft.lbs.
50-65 Nm
36-47 ft.lbs.
26
40-50 Nm
29-36 ft.lbs.
50-65 Nm
36-47 ft.lbs.
27
60-80 Nm
43-58 ft.lbs.
24
30-40 Nm
22-29 ft.lbs.
23
40-50 Nm
29-36 ft.lbs.

Removal steps

19. Connection for generator
20. Connection for oil pressure switch
21. Power steering oil pump
22. Air conditioning compressor
23. Self-locking nuts
24. Gasket
25. Clamp of pressure hose (Power steering) and high pressure hose (Air conditioning)
26. Engine mount bracket
27. Self locking nut
28. Engine assembly

MT1069100164020X

Fig. 3 Engine assembly removal (Part 2 of 2). 16 valve engine

timing belt sprocket and tensioner stay clean and dry. Do not try to clean parts and replace any parts that have become too dirty.

12. Inspect timing belts closely for hardening, cracks, discoloration, missing teeth or abnormal wear. Normal belt should have clear-cut sides as if cut by a sharp knife.
13. Turn tensioner pulleys to check for binding, excessive play or unusual noise and replace if necessary.
14. Reverse procedure to install, noting the following:
    a. Install crankshaft sprocket "B" while noting direction of rotation, **Fig. 25.**
    b. Apply thin coat of engine oil to outer diameter of spacer, then install with chamfered end facing oil seal, **Fig. 26.** If spacer is installed incorrectly, oil seal may be damaged.
    c. Ensure crankshaft sprocket "B" and silent shaft sprocket timing marks are aligned, then fit belt "B"over crankshaft sprocket "B" and silent shaft sprocket, **Fig. 27.** There should be no slack in belt.
    d. Position timing belt "B" ensure center of tensioner pulley is to the left and above the center of the installation bolt, then attach tensioner pulley with flange toward front of engine, **Fig. 28.**
    e. Holding timing belt "B" tensioner in direction of arrow, place pressure on belt until taut, then tighten bolt to fix tensioner. **Do not allow tensioner pulley shaft to rotate with bolt, this will cause excessive tension on belt.**
    f. Depress belt at point "A" tension should be 0.20–0.28 inch, if not, adjust, **Fig. 29.**
    g. Install flange noting direction of rotation, then the tensioner spring, spacer and timing belt tensioner, **Fig. 30.**
    h. Ensure timing marks of camshaft sprocket, crankshaft sprocket and oil pump sprockets are aligned, **Fig. 31.**
    i. When aligning timing mark of oil pump sprocket, remove plug of cylinder block, then insert a Phillips screwdriver into plug hole. If shaft of screwdriver cannot be inserted at least 2.36 inches into cylinder block, rotate sprocket one turn and insert screwdriver. Do not remove screwdriver until timing belt is completely installed, **Fig. 32.**
    j. With tension side of belt taut, install timing belt (noting direction of rotation) onto crankshaft sprocket, oil pump sprocket and camshaft sprocket in that order.
15. Adjust timing belt tension, noting the following:
    a. Loosen tensioner mounting bolt, then ensure each sprockets timing mark is aligned.
    b. Turn crankshaft clockwise by two teeth of camshaft sprocket, **Fig. 33. Do not rotate crankshaft counterclockwise or place pressure on belt to check amount of tension.**
    c. Applying force on tensioner in direction of rotation, ensure no portion of belt raises out, then place belt on camshaft sprocket, ensure belt teeth on sprocket are fully engaged.
    d. Tighten tensioner installation bolt, then the tensioner spacer. **Always tighten bolt first.**
    e. Ensure clearance between outside of the belt and cover is 0.55 inch.
    f. Install timing belt upper and lower covers, noting attaching bolts differ in size, **Fig. 34.**

16 VALVE ENGINE

Refer to **Fig. 35,** for removal and installation of timing belt assembly.

1. Raise and support vehicle.
2. Place a suitable jack under engine with a wooden block between jack and oil pan, then raise engine enough to remove engine mount bracket.
3. Turn crankshaft clockwise and align timing marks of camshaft sprocket and upper surface of cylinder head. Ensure No. 1 cylinder is at top dead center and dowel pin of camshaft sprocket is on upper side, **Fig. 36.**

4. Remove timing belt. If being reused, use chalk to mark direction of rotation for installation purposes.
5. **Water or oil on the belt can seriously reduce belt life, ensure timing belt sprocket and tensioner stay clean and dry. Do not wash belt and replace any parts that are too dirty.**
6. Rotate crankshaft in forward direction and align timing mark. **Crankshaft always must be rotated in a forward direction, Fig. 37.**
7. Tie camshaft sprocket and timing belt with a wire ensuring position of camshaft sprocket will not move with respect to timing belt.
8. Using removal tool, remove camshaft sprocket with timing belt attached. **After removal be sure not to rotate crankshaft.**
9. Remove plug on cylinder block, then insert a Phillips screwdriver to block left silent shaft, **Fig. 24.**
10. Remove oil pump sprocket nut and oil pump sprocket.
11. Mark on back of timing belt "B" indicating direction of rotation for installation reference. **Water or oil on the belt can seriously reduce belt life, ensure timing belt sprocket and tensioner stay clean and dry. Do not wash belt and replace any parts that have become too dirty.**
12. Inspect timing belts closely for hardening, cracks, discoloration, missing teeth or abnormal wear. Normal belt should have clear-cut sides as if cut by a sharp knife.
13. Turn tensioner and idler pulleys to check for binding, excessive play, unusual noise or a grease leak, replace as necessary.
14. Inspect auto tensioner for possible leaks, replace as necessary.
15. Inspect rod end for wear or damage, replace as necessary.
16. Measure rod protrusion, protrusion should be 0.47 inch. If not, replace auto tensioner, **Fig. 38.**
17. Using a soft jawed vise, push in auto tensioner rod. If rod can be easily removed, replace auto tensioner.
18. Reverse procedure to install, noting the following:
    a. Apply 3M ATD sealant, No. 8660, or equivalent, to bolt shown, **Fig. 39,** and tighten to specification.
    b. Install crankshaft sprocket "B" noting direction of rotation, **Fig. 25.**
    c. Apply thin coat of engine oil to outer diameter of spacer, then install with chamfered end facing oil seal, **Fig. 26.** If spacer is installed incorrectly, oil seal may be damaged, resulting in oil leaks.
    d. Ensure crankshaft sprocket "B" timing mark and silent shaft sprocket timing mark are aligned, fit belt "B" over crankshaft sprocket "B" and silent shaft sprocket leaving no slack.
    e. Position timing belt "B," ensure center of tensioner pulley is to the left and above the center of the installation bolt, then attach tensioner pulley with flange toward front of engine, **Fig. 28.**

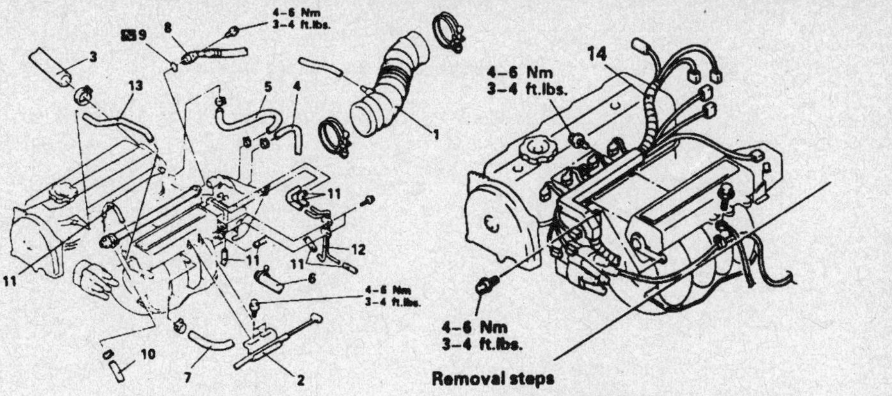
4-6 Nm
3-4 ft.lbs.
4-6 Nm
3-4 ft.lbs.
4-6 Nm
3-4 ft.lbs.

Removal steps

1. Air intake hose
2. Connection for accelerator cable
3. Connection for radiator upper hose
4. Connection for water by-pass hose
5. Water hose
6. Connection for heater hose
7. Connection for brake booster vacuum hose
8. Connection for fuel high pressure hose
9. O-ring
10. Connection for fuel return hose
11. Connection for vacuum hoses
12. Vacuum pipe
13. PCV hose
14. Connection for control harness

MT1059100019010X

Fig. 4 Intake manifold removal (Part 1 of 2). 8 valve engine

f. Holding timing belt "B" tensioner in direction of arrow, place pressure on belt until taut, then tighten bolt to fix tensioner. **Do not allow tensioner pulley shaft to rotate with bolt, this will cause excessive tension on belt.**
g. Depress belt at point "A" to ensure tension is 0.20–0.28 inch, if not, adjust, **Fig. 29.**
h. Install flange noting direction of rotation, then the crankshaft sprocket, **Fig 30. If flange is installed in wrong direction, a broken timing belt could result.**
i. If auto tensioner is in fully extended position, reset, then install. **Leave wire installed in auto tensioner.**
j. Install tensioner pulley on tensioner arm, then tighten center bolt.
k. Ensure timing marks of camshaft, crankshaft and oil pump sprockets are aligned, **Fig 40.**
l. Remove plug on cylinder block, then insert a Phillips screwdriver into plug hole. Ensure shaft of screwdriver can be inserted at least 2.4 inches or more, if not, rotate oil pump sprocket by one turn until measurement is reached. Do not remove screwdriver until timing belt is completely attached.
m. Install timing belt (noting direction of rotation) onto tensioner pulley, crankshaft sprocket, oil pump sprocket, idler pulley and camshaft sprocket in this order.
n. Gently raise tensioner pulley as shown, **Fig. 40,** and temporarily tighten center bolt.

19. Adjust timing belt tension, noting the following:
    a. After turning crankshaft a 1/4 turn counterclockwise, turn clockwise to move No. 1 cylinder top dead center.
    b. Loosen center bolt, then using gauge tool No. MD998752-01, or equivalent, and torque wrench (0–2.2 ft. lbs.), **torque** bolt to 1.88–2.03 ft. lbs.
    c. Screw gauge tool into engine left support bracket until end is screwed into tensioner arm, then remove set wire attached to auto tensioner and tool.
    d. Rotate crankshaft two complete turns clockwise and leave for 15 minutes, then measure auto tensioner protrusion "A" is 0.15–0.18 inch, **Fig. 41.**
    e. If out of specification, repeat steps a through d until specification is obtained.
    f. Install rubber plug to timing belt rear cover.
    g. Install timing belt front upper and lower covers, noting attaching bolts differ in size, **Fig. 42.**

CAMSHAFT

REPLACE

8 VALVE ENGINE

1. Release fuel pressure as outlined under "Precautions."
2. Disconnect battery ground cable.
3. Using lash adjuster holding tool No. MD998443-01, or equivalent, to hold auto-lash in place, remove rocker arm and shaft assembly, **Fig. 43. Do not disassemble rocker arm and shaft assembly.**
4. Remove camshaft from vehicle.
5. Reverse procedure to install, noting the following:

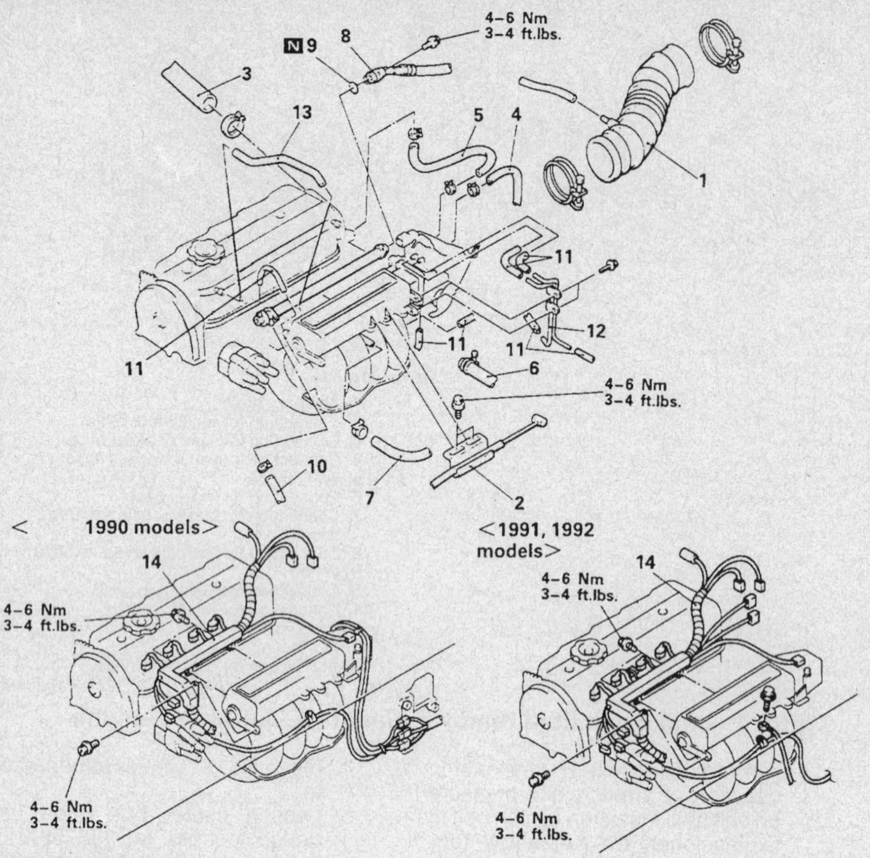

4-6 Nm
3-4 ft.lbs.
N 9
8
3
13
5
4
1
11
11
11
12
11
6
4-6 Nm
3-4 ft.lbs.
10
7
2
<1990 models>
<1991, 1992 models>
14
4-6 Nm
3-4 ft.lbs.
14
4-6 Nm
3-4 ft.lbs.
4-6 Nm
3-4 ft.lbs.
4-6 Nm
3-4 ft.lbs.

Removal steps

1. Air intake hose
2. Connection for accelerator cable
3. Connection for radiator upper hose
4. Connection for water by-pass hose
5. Water hose
6. Connection for heater hose
7. Connection for brake booster vacuum hose
8. Connection for fuel high pressure hose
9. O-ring
10. Connection for fuel return hose
11. Connection for vacuum hoses
12. Vacuum pipe
13. PCV hose
14. Connection for control harness

MT1059100019020X

Fig. 4 Intake manifold removal (Part 2 of 2). 8 valve engine

a. Apply coat of engine oil to camshaft journal and cams, then install in cylinder head.
b. Position rocker arm and shaft assembly on cylinder head and tighten bearing cap bolt.
c. Connect camshaft oil seal guide tool No. MD998307-01, or equivalent, to end of camshaft and apply engine oil to outer diameter of guide tool.
d. Using camshaft oil seal installer, press in oil seal, **Fig. 44.**

16 VALVE ENGINE

1. Release fuel pressure as outlined under "Precautions."
2. Disconnect battery ground cable.
3. Using end yoke holder, remove camshaft sprocket.
4. Using lash adjuster holding tool No. MD998443-01, or equivalent, to hold auto-lash in place, remove rocker arm and shaft assembly, **Fig. 43. Do not disassemble rocker arm and shaft assembly.**
5. Remove rocker arms and rocker arm shaft assembly from both the intake side and exhaust side, **Fig. 45,** then remove camshaft from vehicle.
6. Reverse procedure to install, noting the following:
   a. Temporarily tighten rocker shaft bolt, ensuring rocker arms on inlet valve side do not push on valves.
   b. Fit rocker shaft spring into position from above, ensuring it is at a right angle to plug guide. **Install rocker shaft spring before installing rocker arm and rocker arm shaft on exhaust side.**
   c. Remove lash adjuster holding tool, then ensure rocker shaft notch faces proper direction, **Fig. 46.**
   d. Using camshaft oil seal installer tool No. MD998713-01, or equivalent, install camshaft seal.

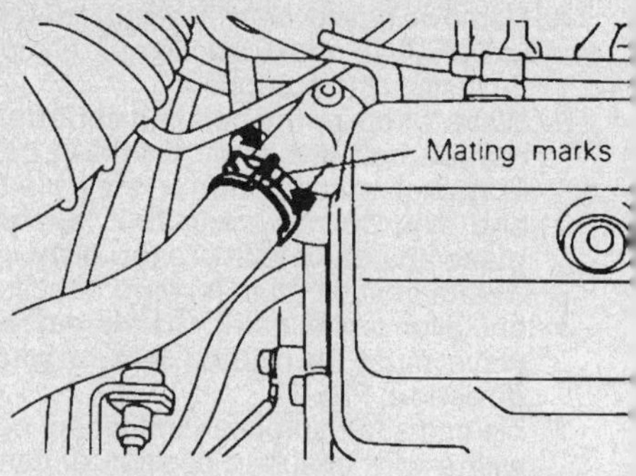

Mating marks

MT1059100020000X

Fig. 5 Radiator hose mating marks. 8 valve engine

SILENT SHAFT

REPLACE

8 VALVE ENGINE

Refer to **Fig. 47** when removing silent shaft, oil pump and front case. Keep silent shaft in position by inserting a screwdriver through plug hole in left side of cylinder block and remove oil pump driven gear securing bolt.

1. Check gear contacting surface of front case and oil pump cover for step wear. If wear is evident, replace front case.
2. Check silent shaft journals for wear and damage. If excessive damage or wear is evident, check bearing. If necessary, replace silent shaft and/or bearing.
3. Reverse procedure to install, noting the following:
   a. Install silent shaft in cylinder block.
   b. Install oil pump drive and driven gears in front case, ensuring gear timing marks are aligned, **Fig. 48.**
   c. Using small end of oil seal guide tool No. MD998375-01, or equivalent, install crankshaft front oil seal, **Fig. 49. If crankshaft front oil seal is already mounted to front case, use oil seal guide for protection of oil seal.**
   d. Install front case, then insert a screwdriver through plug hole in left side of cylinder block to keep shaft in position, **Fig. 50.** Tighten bolt to specification.
   e. Install oil filter bracket assembly and gasket, then tighten front case bolts and oil filter bracket bolts to specification.
   f. Install plug cap, then the oil screen and gasket. Clean gasket surfaces of cylinder block and oil pan.
   g. Install oil pan gasket, if equipped, using a small amount of suitable gasket sealant. If no gasket is used, apply a 0.16 inch wide bead of suitable sealant to entire circumference of oil pan flange.
   h. Install oil pan and tighten bolts to specification. Note difference in bolt length as shown in **Fig. 51.**

16 VALVE ENGINE

Refer to **Fig. 52,** when removing silent shaft, oil pump and front case. Keep silent shaft in position by inserting a screwdriver through plug hole in left side of cylinder block and remove oil pump driven gear securing bolt.

1. Inspect oil holes for clogging and clean if necessary.
2. Inspect left silent shaft front bearing section for wear, damage and seizure and replace as necessary.
3. Inspect front case for cracks or other damage and replace as necessary.
4. Inspect oil seal lip for wear, damage or deterioration and replace as necessary.
5. Inspect journal for seizure, damage or contact with bearing, replace as necessary.
6. Inspect silent shaft oil clearance. Clearance should be as follows:
   a. Front- Right (0.0012–0.0024 inch).
   b. Front- Left (0.0008–0.0020 inch).
   c. Rear- Right and left (0.0020–0.0036 inch).
   d. If clearance is out of specification, replace silent shaft bearing, silent shaft or front case assembly as necessary.
7. Position oil pump gear to front case and rotate to ensure smooth rotation with no looseness. Ensure there is no ridge wear on contact surface between front case and gear surface of oil pump cover.
8. Measure side clearance. Clearance should be 0.0031–0.0055 inch (drive gear) and 0.0024–0.0047 inch (driven gear).
9. Ensure oil cooler bypass valve moves smoothly on engines with air cooling type oil cooler.
10. Reverse procedure to install, noting the following:
    a. Using oil seal installer tool No. MD998375-01, or equivalent, install crankshaft front oil seal into front case.
    b. Apply engine oil amply to gears and align mating marks, then install oil pump drive and driven gear.
    c. Coat threads of oil pressure gauge unit and oil pressure switch with 3M ATD sealant, No. 8660, or equivalent, and install in that order avoiding overtightening.
    d. Apply engine oil to outer surface of right silent shaft rear bearing, then install ensuring oil hole of bearing is aligned with oil hole of cylinder block.
    e. Apply engine oil to left silent shaft rear bearing outer surface and bearing hole in cylinder block and install. Left bearing has no oil holes.
    f. Using bearing installer tools, No. MD9987373-01 and No. MB990938-01, or equivalent, install silent shaft front bearing .
    g. Install front case assembly through a new front case gasket, then temporarily tighten flange bolts.
    h. Insert a Phillips screwdriver into a hole in the left side of cylinder block to lock silent shaft. Tighten flange bolt to specification.
    i. Install new O-ring to groove of front case, then the plug and tighten to specifications.

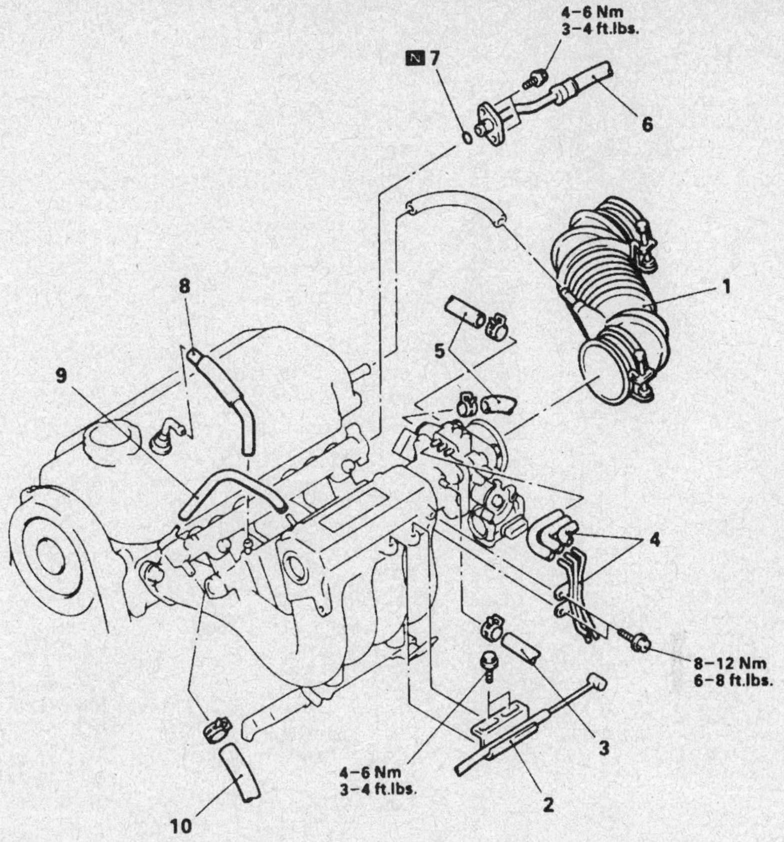
4-6 Nm
3-4 ft.lbs.
N 7
6
1
8
5
9
4
8-12 Nm
6-8 ft.lbs.
3
4-6 Nm
3-4 ft.lbs.
2
10
Removal steps
1 Air intake hose
2 Connection for accelerator cable
3 Connection for brake booster vacuum hose
4 Connection for vacuum pipe and hose assembly
5 Connection for water hose
6 Connection for fuel high pressure hose
7 O-ring
8 PCV hose
9 Connection for vacuum hose
10 Connection for fuel return hose
MT1059100021010X

Fig. 6 Intake manifold removal (Part 1 of 2). 16 valve engine

PISTON & ROD ASSEMBLY

8 VALVE ENGINE

Refer to **Fig. 53** when removing piston and rod assembly. Keep all components, such as connecting rod caps and bearings, in proper order for installation.

1. Reverse procedure to install, noting the following:
   a. Pistons and rings are available in standard sizes and oversizes of 0.010, 0.020, 0.030 and 0.039 inch. Oversize pins are not available.
   b. The piston and rod is assembled with the indented arrow on the piston and the embossed numeral on the rod facing toward front of engine, **Fig. 54.**
   c. Position each piston ring gap as far apart as possible.
   d. Ensure each piston and rod are installed in the same cylinder bore as removed.
   e. Ensure connecting rod caps and bearings are placed on proper connecting rods, then tighten bolts to specification.

16 VALVE ENGINE

Refer to **Fig. 55** when removing piston and rod assembly. Keep all components, such as connecting rod caps and bearings, in proper order for installation.

1. Inspect piston, piston ring and piston pin for wear or damage and replace as necessary.
2. Reverse procedure to install, noting the following:
   a. Install piston pin and ensure piston moves smoothly. **Due to production tolerance variations, it is**

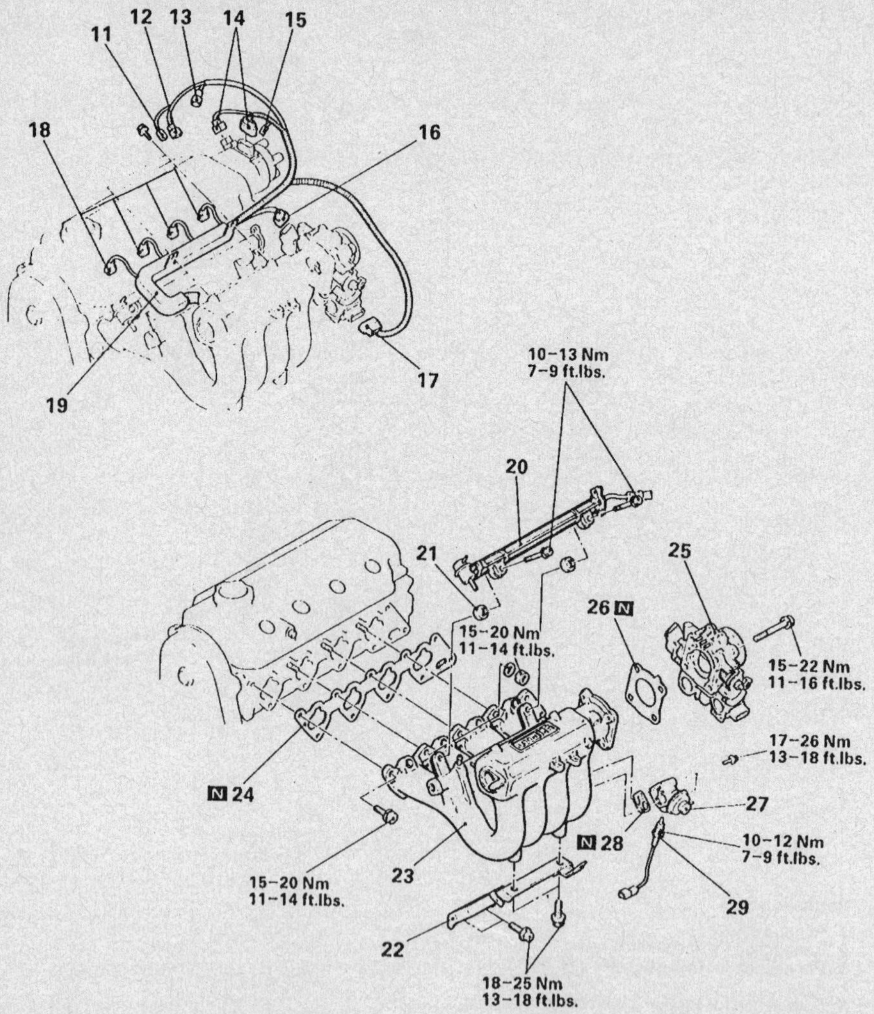

11
12
13
14
15
16
17
18
19
20
21
22
23
N 24
25
26 N
27
N 28
29
10–13 Nm
7–9 ft.lbs.
15–20 Nm
11–14 ft.lbs.
15–22 Nm
11–16 ft.lbs.
17–26 Nm
13–18 ft.lbs.
10–12 Nm
7–9 ft.lbs.
15–20 Nm
11–14 ft.lbs.
18–25 Nm
13–18 ft.lbs.

11. Engine coolant temperature gauge unit connector
12. Engine coolant temperature sensor connector
13. Oxygen sensor connector
14. Distributor connector
15. Condenser connector
16. TPS connector
17. IAC connector
18. Injector connector
19. Control harness
20. Fuel rail, injector and pressure regulator assembly
21. Insulator
22. Intake manifold stay
23. Intake manifold
24. Intake manifold gasket
25. Throttle body
26. Throttle body gasket
27. EGR valve
28. EGR gasket
29. EGR temperature sensor <Vehicles for California>

MT1059100021020X

Fig. 6 Intake manifold removal (Part 2 of 2). 16 valve engine

necessary to visually inspect piston pin depth after installation to verify piston pin is centered.

b. Install oil ring into piston ring groove, then the upper and lower side rails. Do not use piston ring expander when installing side rail.
c. Using piston ring expander, install Nos. 1 and 2 piston rings with marks on crown side facing up.
d. Apply engine oil on outer surface of piston, piston ring and oil ring, then arrange piston ring and oil ring gaps as shown, **Fig. 56.**
e. Install connecting rod bearings and rod cap. Ensure connecting rod big end side clearance measures 0.0039–0.0098 inch but does not exceed 0.016 inch.
f. Apply engine oil to threads of connecting rod cap nuts, then install and tighten to specifications.

CRANKSHAFT

REPLACE

8 VALVE ENGINE

Refer to **Fig. 57,** when removing crankshaft and main bearings.

1. Measure main bearing clearance. Refer to "Crankshaft, Bearings & Connecting Rods" in the "Engine Rebuilding Specifications" section. If clearance is not within specification, replace bearing.
2. Check crankshaft journals for damage or wear. If necessary, replace crankshaft or machine journal.
3. Reverse procedure to install, noting the following:
   a. Install main upper bearing on cylinder block, **Fig. 58** and lower bearing on main bearing caps.
   b. Install crankshaft and apply engine oil to journals.
   c. Caps should be installed with arrows facing forward and in proper number order, **Fig. 59.**
   d. Tighten main bearing cap bolts to specification and check to ensure crankshaft rotates freely and has proper endplay.
   e. Using crankshaft rear oil seal installer tool No. MD998376-01, or equivalent, install seal in case.
   f. Install oil separator into case with 0.16 inch diameter oil hole in lowermost position.
   g. Install new oil seal case gasket and oil seal case assembly.
   h. Install rear plate to cylinder block.
   i. **On manual transaxle models,** install flywheel and tighten bolts to specification, then check clutch mounting surface for runout.
   j. **On automatic transmission models,** install adapter plates and driveplate, then tighten bolts to specification.

16 VALVE ENGINE

Refer to **Fig. 60,** when removing crankshaft and main bearings.

1. Reverse procedure to install, noting the following:
   a. Measure width of crankshaft oil clearance. Clearance should be 0.0008–0.0020 inch and should not exceed 0.004 inch.
   b. Inspect cylinder block for scratches, rust or corrosion and replace as necessary.
   c. Using a straightedge and feeler gauge, measure block top for surface for warpage. Warpage should not exceed 0.004 inch.
   d. Inspect cylinder walls and cylinder bore for wear, scratches or seizure and replace as necessary.

OIL PAN

REPLACE

1. Drain engine oil into suitable container.
2. Remove oil pan mounting bolts, then tap general service tool between cylinder block and oil pan, **Fig. 61. Do not use a screwdriver, chisel or similar tool when removing oil pan.**
3. Inspect oil pan and oil screen for cracks, clogging or damage and replace as necessary.
4. Using a wire brush, scrape clean all surfaces of cylinder block and oil pan and ensure gasket is free of oil and dirt.
5. Reverse procedure to install. Apply sealant around surface of oil pan.

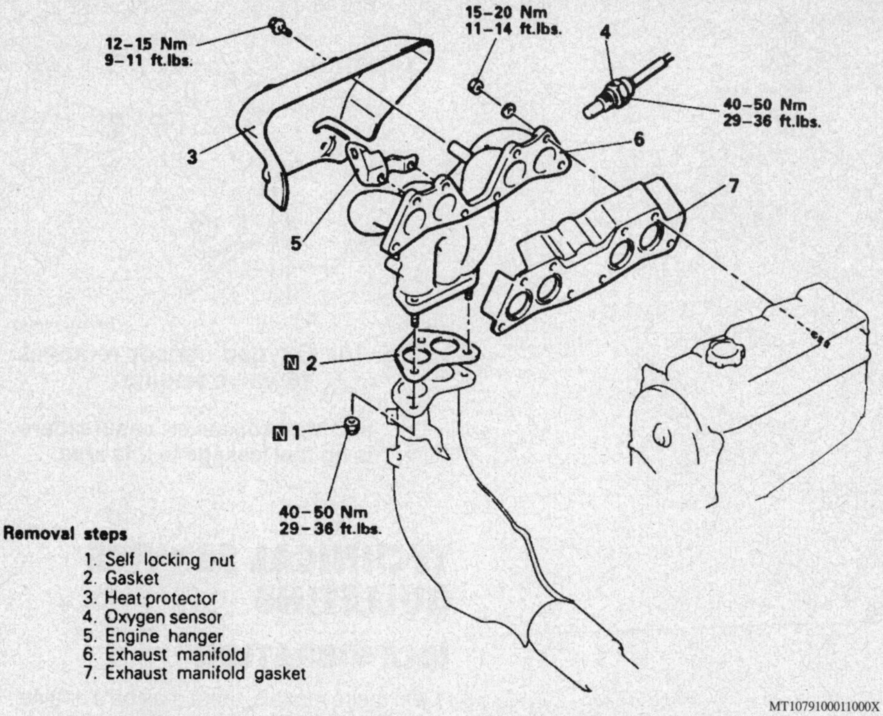
12-15 Nm
9-11 ft.lbs.
15-20 Nm
11-14 ft.lbs.
4
40-50 Nm
29-36 ft.lbs.
3
6
7
5
N 2
N 1
40-50 Nm
29-36 ft.lbs.
Removal steps
1. Self locking nut
2. Gasket
3. Heat protector
4. Oxygen sensor
5. Engine hanger
6. Exhaust manifold
7. Exhaust manifold gasket
MT1079100011000X

Fig. 7 Exhaust manifold removal. 8 valve engine

OIL PUMP

REPLACE

Refer to "Silent Shaft, Replace" for oil pump replacement procedure.

BELT TENSION DATA

Belt	Deflection @ 22 Lbs.	
	New Inches	Used Inches
Alt.	0.295–0.354	0.394
A/C	0.197–0.217	0.236–0.276
Power Steering	0.236–0.354	0.236–0.354

COOLING SYSTEM BLEED

These engines do not require a specified bleed procedure. After filling cooling system, run engine to operating temperature with radiator/pressure cap off. Air will then be automatically bled through the cap opening.

THERMOSTAT

REPLACE

1. Drain coolant into a suitable container.
2. Disconnect upper radiator hose, then remove thermostat housing attaching bolts.
3. Remove thermostat housing and thermostat.
4. Reverse procedure to install. Tighten thermostat housing bolts to specifications.

WATER PUMP

REPLACE

Remove water pump components in order as shown, **Fig. 62,** noting the following:

1. Disconnect battery ground cable.
2. Remove engine undercover.
3. When draining cooling system, place temperature control lever in Hot position.
4. To remove engine mount bracket, slightly raise and support engine to remove engine weight from mount.
5. Prior to removing water pump drive belt, loosen water pump attaching bolts.
6. Remove rocker cover, timing belt covers, timing belt and timing belt "B" as outlined under "Timing Belt, Replace."
7. Reverse procedure to install, noting the following:
   a. Coat outer diameter of O-ring with water to ease installation.
   b. Refer to bolt length chart, **Fig. 63,** when installing water pump attaching bolts.
   c. Install timing belt "B," timing belt, timing belt covers and rocker cover as outlined under "Timing Belt, Replace."

RADIATOR

REPLACE

1. Remove radiator components in order as shown, **Fig. 64,** noting the following:
   a. Prior to removing radiator hoses, mark hose clamps in relation to hoses for installation reference.
   b. After disconnecting transaxle cool-

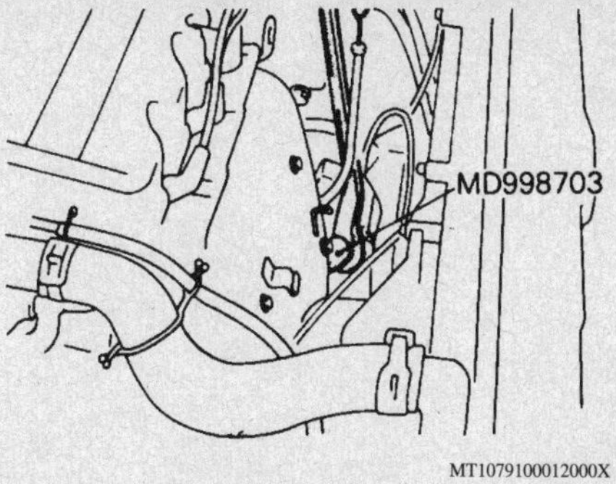
MD998703
MT1079100012000X

Fig. 8 Oxygen sensor removal. 8 valve engine

er lines plug or cover ends of lines to prevent entry of dirt or foreign material.

FUEL PUMP

REPLACE

1. Relieve fuel system pressure as outlined under "Precautions," then disconnect battery ground cable.
2. Raise and support rear of vehicle.
3. Remove left rear wheel, then loosen mounting band and lower fuel tank.
4. Remove fuel pump support, disconnect fuel lines, then remove pump.
5. Reverse procedure to install.

FUEL FILTER

REPLACE

1. Relieve fuel system pressure as outlined under "Precautions."
2. Remove eye bolt while holding fuel filter nut securely, **Fig. 65. Cover hose connection with rags to prevent splash of fuel caused by residual pressure left in fuel pipe line.**
3. Loosen main pipe flare nut while holding fuel filter nut securely.
4. Remove fuel filter mounting bolts, then the fuel filter from bracket.
5. Inspect hose and pipes for cracks, bends, deformation and clogging, replace as necessary.
6. Inspect evaporative emission canister and fuel filter for clogging or damage, replace as necessary.
7. Reverse procedure to install, noting the following:
   a. If fuel pipe has a stepped part, connect fuel hose to pipe securely up to stepped part.
   b. If fuel pipe does not have a stepped part, connect fuel hose to pipe securely so that it measures 0.8—1.0 inch.
   c. Temporarily install fuel filter to filter bracket, then insert main pipe at connector part of filter and manually screw in main pipe flare nut.
   d. Holding fuel filter nut, tighten fuel main pipe flare nut and eye bolt to specification, then the filter to the bracket.
   e. Install high pressure fuel hose and tighten securely. **High pressure is applied between the fuel pump**

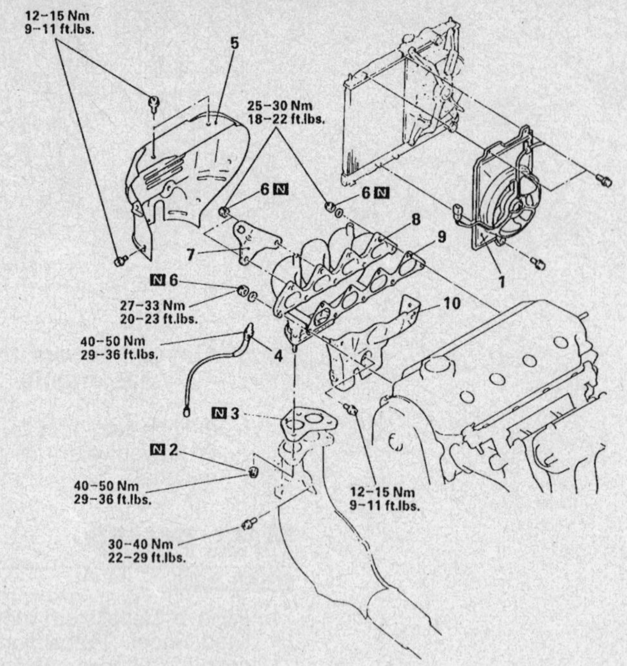
12-15 Nm
9-11 ft.lbs.
25-30 Nm
18-22 ft.lbs.
27-33 Nm
20-23 ft.lbs.
40-50 Nm
29-36 ft.lbs.
40-50 Nm
29-36 ft.lbs.
12-15 Nm
9-11 ft.lbs.
30-40 Nm
22-29 ft.lbs.

Removal steps

1. Condenser fan motor (Vehicles with air conditioning)
2. Self locking nut
3. Gasket
4. Oxygen sensor
5. Exhaust manifold cover (A)
6. Self locking nut
7. Engine hanger
8. Exhaust manifold
9. Exhaust manifold gasket
10. Exhaust manifold cover (B)

MT1079100013000X

Fig. 9 Exhaust manifold removal. 16 valve engine

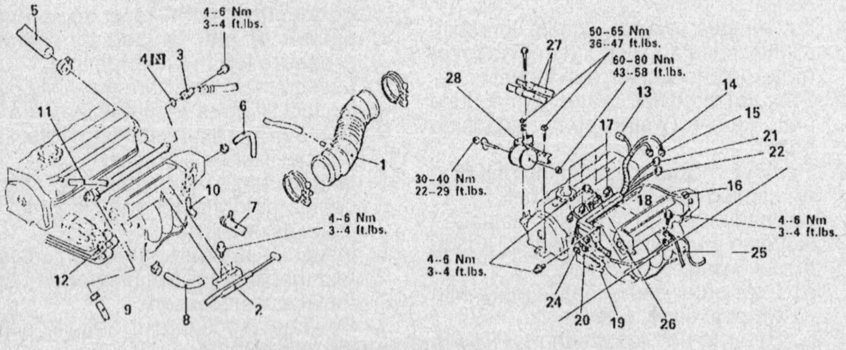
4-6 Nm
3-4 ft.lbs.
4-6 Nm
3-4 ft.lbs.
50-65 Nm
36-47 ft.lbs.
60-80 Nm
43-58 ft.lbs.
30-40 Nm
22-29 ft.lbs.
4-6 Nm
3-4 ft.lbs.
4-6 Nm
3-4 ft.lbs.

MT1069100190010X

Fig. 11 Cylinder head removal (Part 1 of 2). 8 valve engine

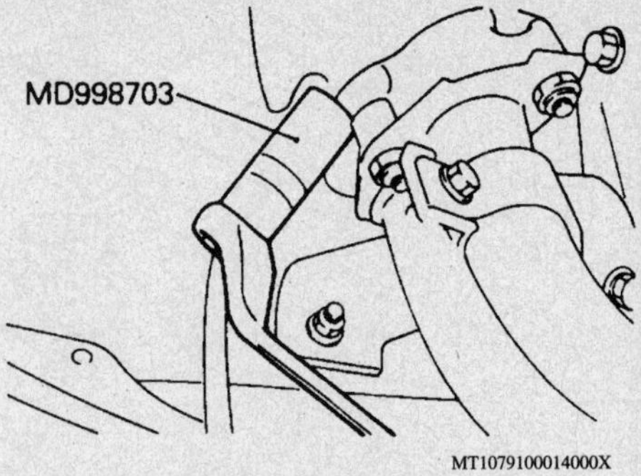
MD998703

MT1079100014000X

Fig. 10 Oxygen sensor removal. 16 valve engine

and injection mixer; ensure there is no fuel leakage in this area.

TECHNICAL SERVICE BULLETINS

IDLE VIBRATION

On these models, there may be a engine vibration at idle speed.

This condition may be caused by incorrectly positioned radiator mounts, which allow radiator vibrations to be transmitted through the frame to the passenger compartment. To correct this condition, proceed as follows:

1. Ensure upper radiator mount brackets are centered on mounting posts.
2. If not positioned correctly, remove brackets and ensure lower mount posts are seated in brackets.
3. Center upper brackets over posts, then **torque** bolts to 7–10 ft. lbs.
4. Clearance between upper brackets and radiator top should be 1/16 inch or more.

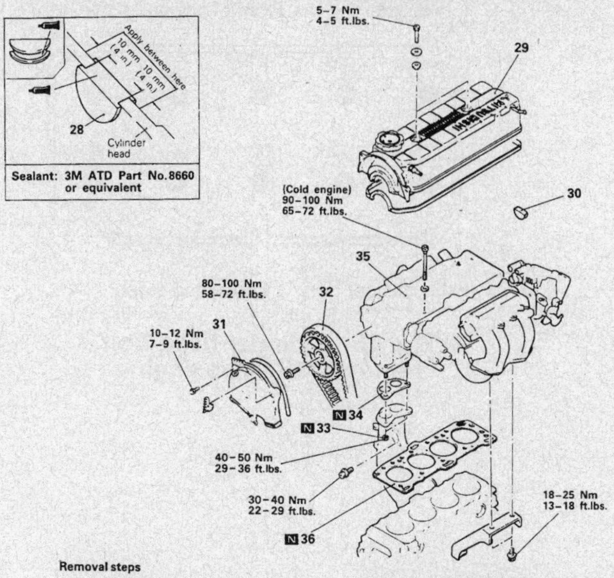
Apply between here
10 mm (4 in.)
10 mm (4 in.)
28
Cylinder head
Sealant: 3M ATD Part No.8660 or equivalent
5-7 Nm
4-5 ft.lbs.
29
(Cold engine)
90-100 Nm
65-72 ft.lbs.
30
35
80-100 Nm
58-72 ft.lbs.
32
31
10-12 Nm
7-9 ft.lbs.
34
33
40-50 Nm
29-36 ft.lbs.
30-40 Nm
22-29 ft.lbs.
18-25 Nm
13-18 ft.lbs.
36

Removal steps

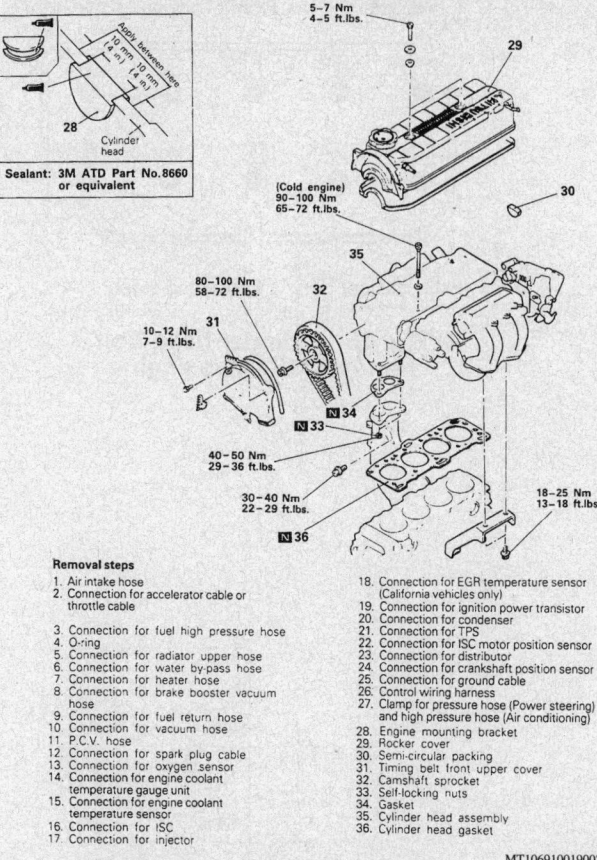

1. Air intake hose
2. Connection for accelerator cable or throttle cable
3. Connection for fuel high pressure hose
4. O-ring
5. Connection for radiator upper hose
6. Connection for water by-pass hose
7. Connection for heater hose
8. Connection for brake booster vacuum hose
9. Connection for fuel return hose
10. Connection for vacuum hose
11. P.C.V. hose
12. Connection for spark plug cable
13. Connection for oxygen sensor
14. Connection for engine coolant temperature gauge unit
15. Connection for engine coolant temperature sensor
16. Connection for ISC
17. Connection for injector
18. Connection for EGR temperature sensor (California vehicles only)
19. Connection for ignition power transistor
20. Connection for condenser
21. Connection for TPS
22. Connection for ISC motor position sensor
23. Connection for distributor
24. Connection for crankshaft position sensor
25. Connection for ground cable
26. Control wiring harness
27. Clamp for pressure hose (Power steering) and high pressure hose (Air conditioning)
28. Engine mounting bracket
29. Rocker cover
30. Semi-circular packing
31. Timing belt front upper cover
32. Camshaft sprocket
33. Self-locking nuts
34. Gasket
35. Cylinder head assembly
36. Cylinder head gasket

MT1069100190020X

Fig. 11 Cylinder head removal (Part 2 of 2). 8 valve engine

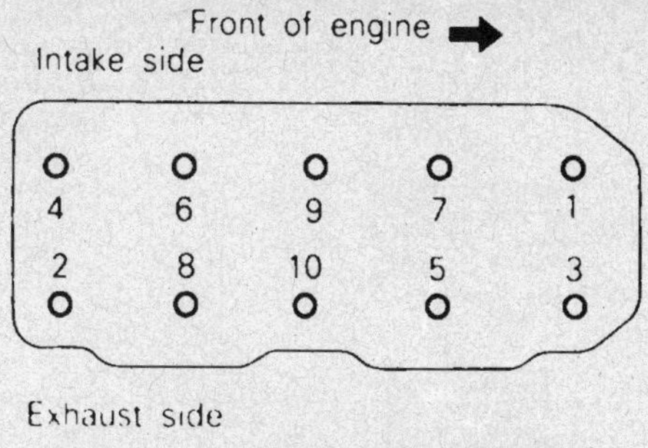
Front of engine
Intake side
4
6
9
7
1
2
8
10
5
3
Exhaust side

MT1069100191000X

Fig. 12 Cylinder head bolt removal. 8 valve engine

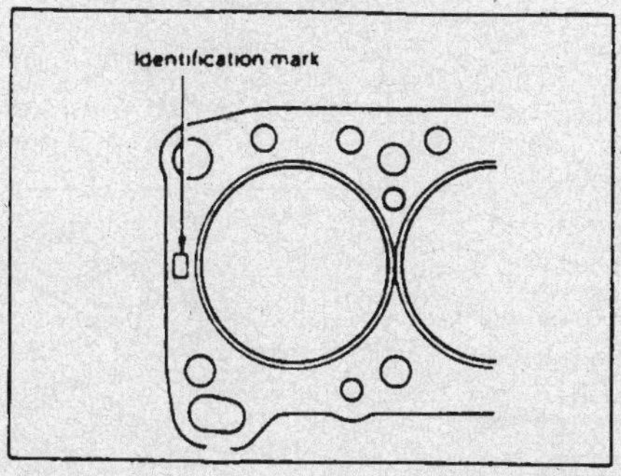
Identification mark

MT1069100192000X

Fig. 13 Cylinder head gasket identification mark. 8 valve engine

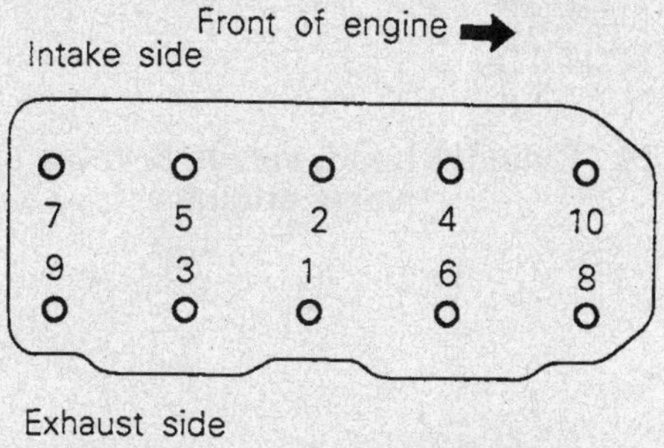
Front of engine
Intake side
7
5
2
4
10
9
3
1
6
8
Exhaust side

MT1069100193000X

Fig. 14 Cylinder head bolt installation. 8 valve engine

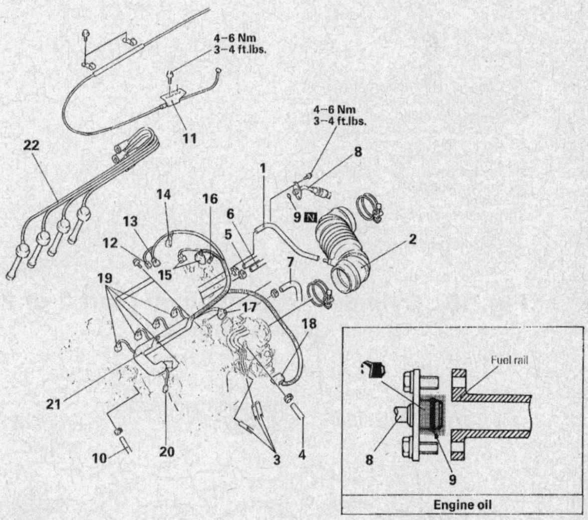
4-6 Nm
3-4 ft.lbs.
4-6 Nm
3-4 ft.lbs.
Fuel rail
Engine oil

Removal steps

1. Breather hose
2. Air intake hose
3. Vacuum hose connection
4. Brake booster vacuum hose connection
5. Water hose connection (cylinder head → throttle body)
6. Heater hose connection (cylinder head → heater unit)
7. Water hose connection (throttle body → water inlet pipe)
8. Fuel high pressure hose connection
9. O-ring
10. Fuel return hose connection
11. Accelerator cable connection
12. Engine coolant temperature gauge unit connector
13. Engine coolant temperature sensor connector
14. Oxygen sensor connector
15. Distributor connector
16. Condenser connector
17. TPS connector
18. IAC connector
19. Injector connector
20. Air conditioning compressor connector
21. Control harness
22. Spark plug cable

MT1069100194010X

Fig. 15 Cylinder head removal (Part 1 of 2). 16 valve engine

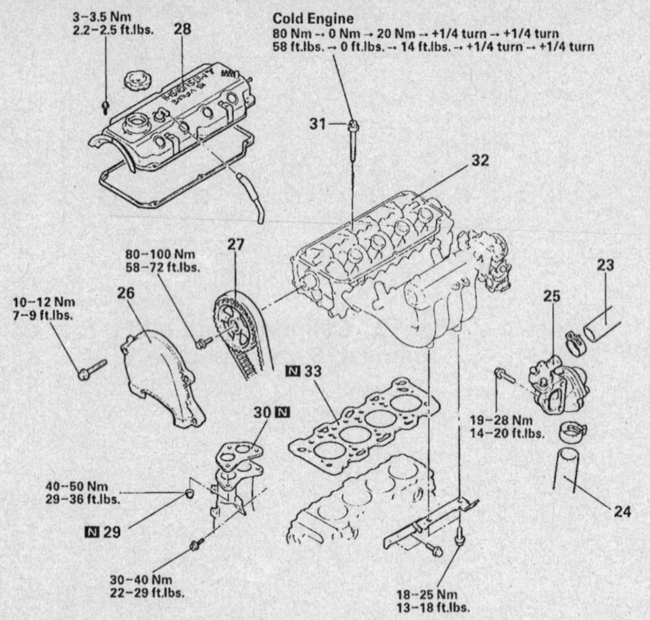
3–3.5 Nm
2.2–2.5 ft.lbs.
28
Cold Engine
80 Nm → 0 Nm → 20 Nm → +1/4 turn → +1/4 turn
58 ft.lbs. → 0 ft.lbs. → 14 ft.lbs. → +1/4 turn → +1/4 turn
31
32
80–100 Nm
58–72 ft.lbs.
27
10–12 Nm
7–9 ft.lbs.
26
23
25
33
30
19–28 Nm
14–20 ft.lbs.
40–50 Nm
29–36 ft.lbs.
29
24
30–40 Nm
22–29 ft.lbs.
18–25 Nm
13–18 ft.lbs.

23. Connection for radiator upper hose
24. Connection for radiator lower hose
25. Water inlet fitting, thermostat and thermostat case assembly
26. Timing belt upper cover
27. Camshaft sprocket
28. Rocker cover
29. Self-locking nuts
30. Gasket
31. Cylinder head bolt
32. Cylinder head assembly
33. Cylinder head gasket

MT1069100194020X

Fig. 15 Cylinder head removal (Part 2 of 2). 16 valve engine

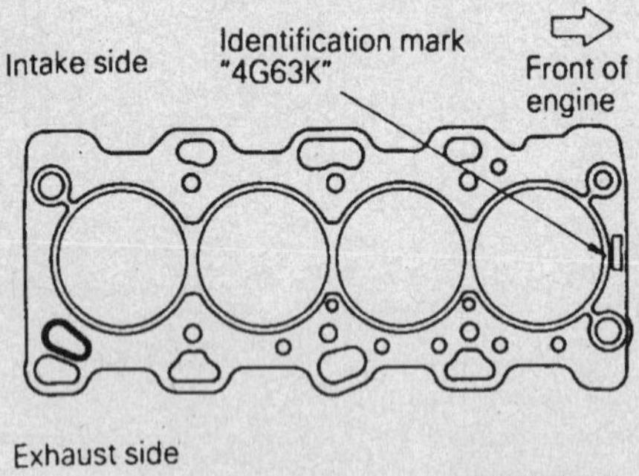
Intake side
Identification mark
"4G63K"
Front of
engine
Exhaust side

MT1069100196000X

Fig. 17 Cylinder head gasket identification mark. 16 valve engine

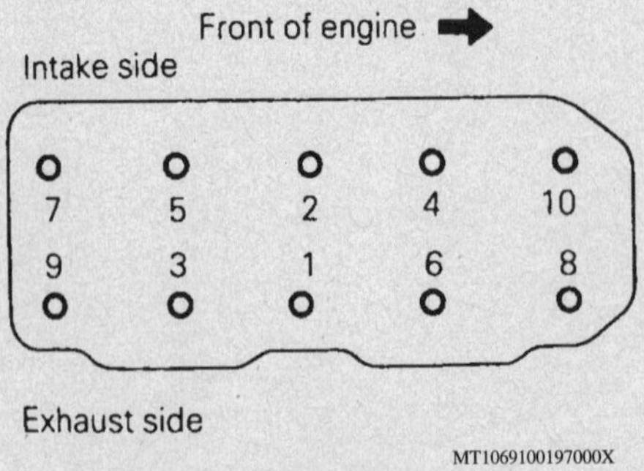
Front of engine
Intake side
7
5
2
4
10
9
3
1
6
8
Exhaust side

MT1069100197000X

Fig. 18 Cylinder head bolt installation. 16 valve engine

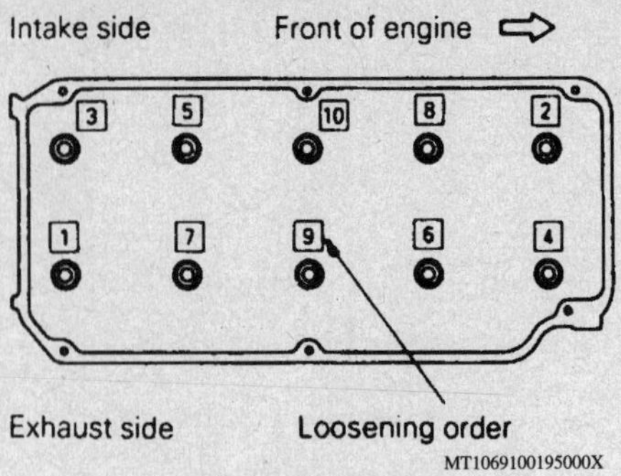
Intake side
Front of engine
3
5
10
8
2
1
7
9
6
4
Exhaust side
Loosening order

MT1069100195000X

Fig. 16 Cylinder head bolt removal. 16 valve engine

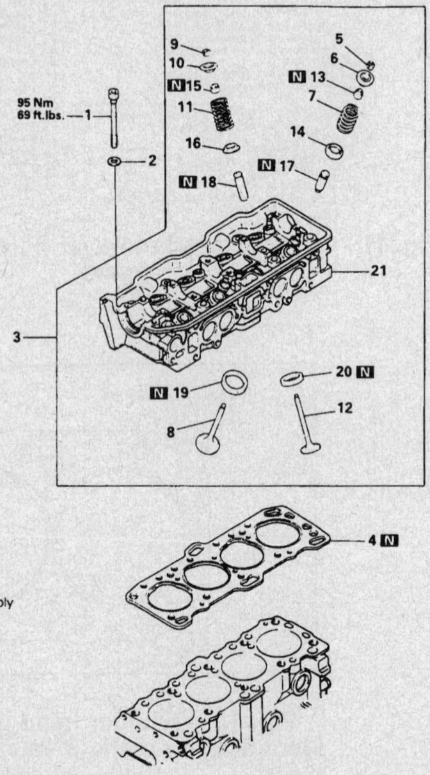
95 Nm
69 ft.lbs.
1
2
3
4
5
6
7
8
9
10
11
12
13
14
15
16
17
18
19
20
21

Removal steps

1. Cylinder head bolt
2. Washer
3. Cylinder head assembly
4. Gasket
5. Retainer lock
6. Valve spring retainer
7. Valve spring
8. Intake valve
9. Retainer lock
10. Valve spring retainer
11. Valve spring
12. Exhaust valve
13. Valve stem seal
14. Valve spring seat
15. Valve stem seal
16. Valve spring seat
17. Intake valve guide
18. Exhaust valve guide
19. Intake valve seat
20. Exhaust valve seat
21. Cylinder head

MT1069100198000X

Fig. 19 Cylinder head, valves & valve springs. 8 valve engine

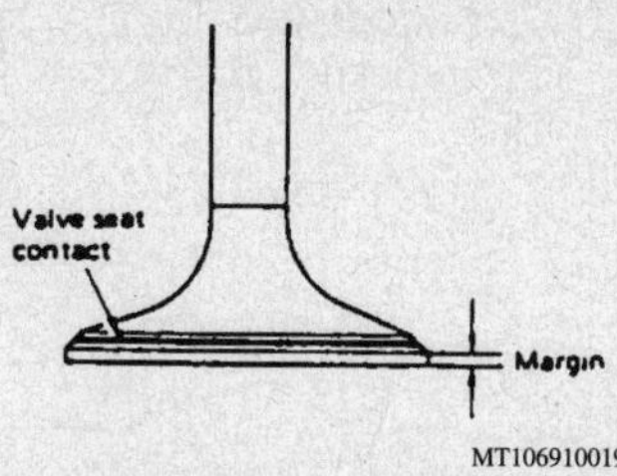
Valve seat contact
Margin

MT1069100199000X

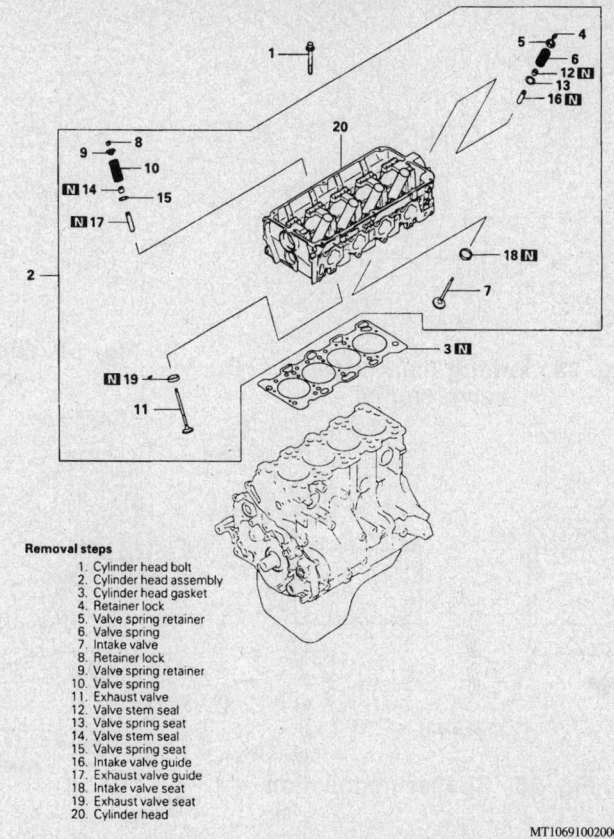

Fig. 20 Checking valve face margin. 8 valve engine

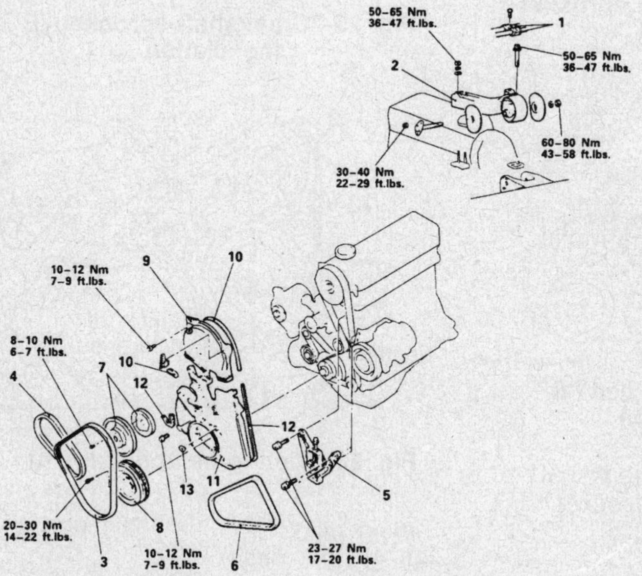
50–65 Nm
36–47 ft.lbs.
50–65 Nm
36–47 ft.lbs.
60–80 Nm
43–58 ft.lbs.
30–40 Nm
22–29 ft.lbs.
10–12 Nm
7–9 ft.lbs.
8–10 Nm
6–7 ft.lbs.
20–30 Nm
14–22 ft.lbs.
10–12 Nm
7–9 ft.lbs.
23–27 Nm
17–20 ft.lbs.

Removal steps

1. Clamp for pressure hose (power steering) and high pressure hose (air conditioning)
2. Engine mount bracket
3. Drive belt (generator)
4. Drive belt (power steering)
5. Tensioner pulley bracket
6. Drive belt (air conditioning)
7. Water pump pulley
8. Crankshaft pulley
9. Timing belt front upper cover
10. Gasket
11. Timing belt front lower cover
12. Gasket
13. Access cover
14. Crankshaft sprocket bolt
15. Special washer
16. Tensioner spacer
17. Tensioner spring
18. Timing belt tensioner
19. Spacer
20. Timing belt
21. Camshaft sprocket
22. Oil pump sprocket
23. Crankshaft sprocket
24. Flange
25. Timing belt tensioner "B"
26. Timing belt "B"
27. Right silent shaft sprocket
28. Spacer
29. Crankshaft sprocket "B"
30. Key
31. Timing belt under cover

MT1069100165010X

Fig. 22 Timing belt replacement (Part 1 of 2). 8 valve engine

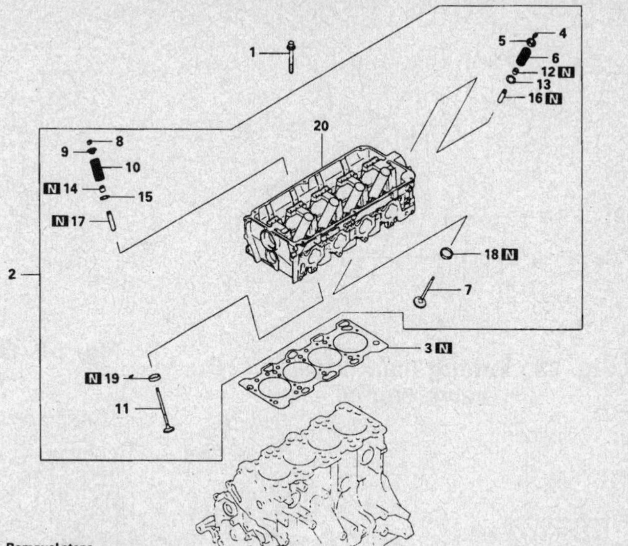

Removal steps

1. Cylinder head bolt
2. Cylinder head assembly
3. Cylinder head gasket
4. Retainer lock
5. Valve spring retainer
6. Valve spring
7. Intake valve
8. Retainer lock
9. Valve spring retainer
10. Valve spring
11. Exhaust valve
12. Valve stem seal
13. Valve spring seat
14. Valve stem seal
15. Valve spring seat
16. Intake valve guide
17. Exhaust valve guide
18. Intake valve seat
19. Exhaust valve seat
20. Cylinder head

MT1069100200000X

Fig. 21 Cylinder head, valves & valve springs. 16 valve engine

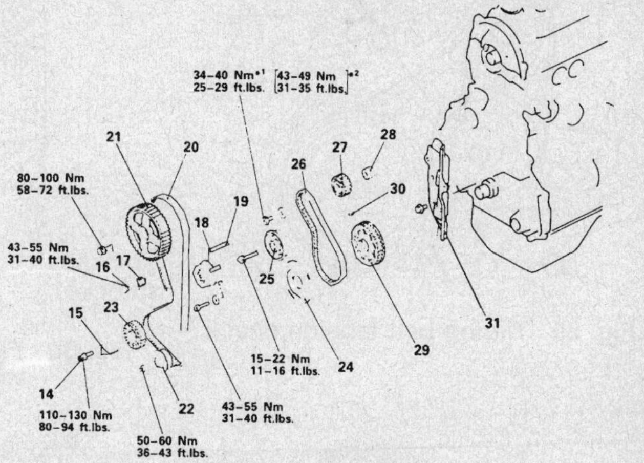
34–40 Nm*1
25–29 ft.lbs.
43–49 Nm *2
31–35 ft.lbs.
80–100 Nm
58–72 ft.lbs.
43–55 Nm
31–40 ft.lbs.
15–22 Nm
11–16 ft.lbs.
110–130 Nm
80–94 ft.lbs.
43–55 Nm
31–40 ft.lbs.
50–60 Nm
36–43 ft.lbs.

Installation steps

31. Timing belt under cover
30. Key
29. Crankshaft sprocket "B"
28. Spacer
27. Right silent shaft sprocket
25. Timing belt tensioner "B"
26. Timing belt "B"
    Adjustment of timing belt "B" tension
24. Flange
23. Crankshaft sprocket
22. Oil pump sprocket
21. Camshaft sprocket
19. Spacer
18. Timing belt tensioner
17. Tensioner spring
16. Tensioner spacer
20. Timing belt
    Adjustment of timing belt tension
15. Special washer
14. Crankshaft sprocket bolt
13. Access cover
12. Gasket
11. Timing belt front lower cover
10. Gasket
9. Timing belt front upper cover
8. Crankshaft pulley
7. Water pump pulley
6. Drive belt (air conditioning)
5. Tensioner pulley bracket
4. Drive belt (power steering)
3. Drive belt (generator)
2. Engine mount bracket
1. Clamp for pressure hose (power steering) and high pressure hose (air conditioning)

MT1069100165020X

Fig. 22 Timing belt replacement (Part 2 of 2). 8 valve engine

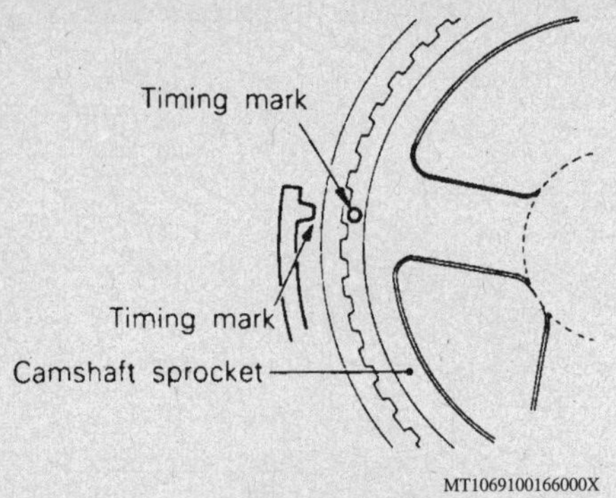
Timing mark
Timing mark
Camshaft sprocket
MT1069100166000X
Fig. 23 Timing mark locations. 8 valve engine

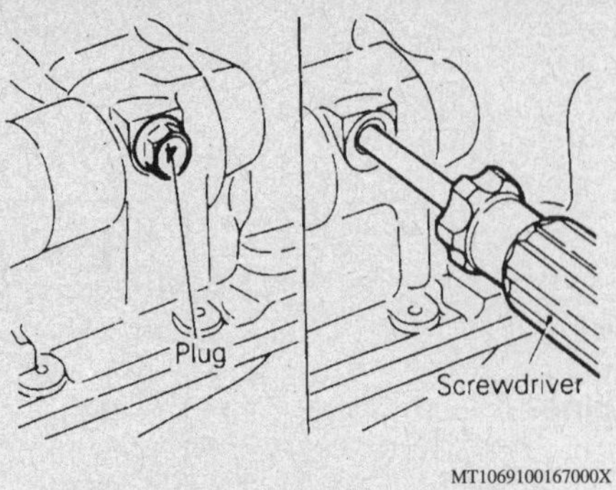
Plug
Screwdriver
MT1069100167000X
Fig. 24 Oil pump sprocket removal

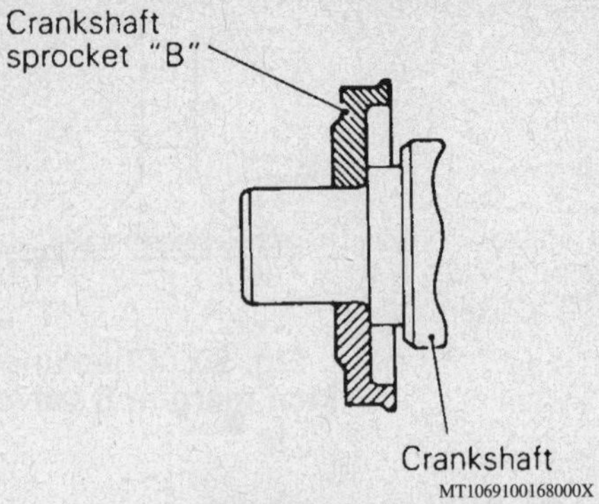
Crankshaft sprocket "B"
Crankshaft
MT1069100168000X
Fig. 25 Crankshaft sprocket "B" installation

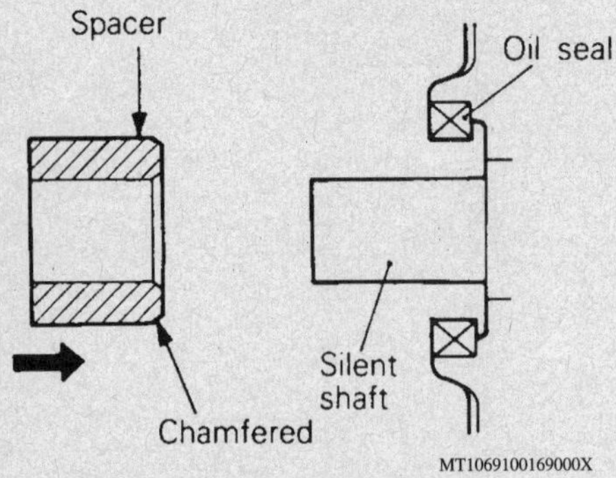
Spacer
Oil seal
Silent shaft
Chamfered
MT1069100169000X
Fig. 26 Spacer installation

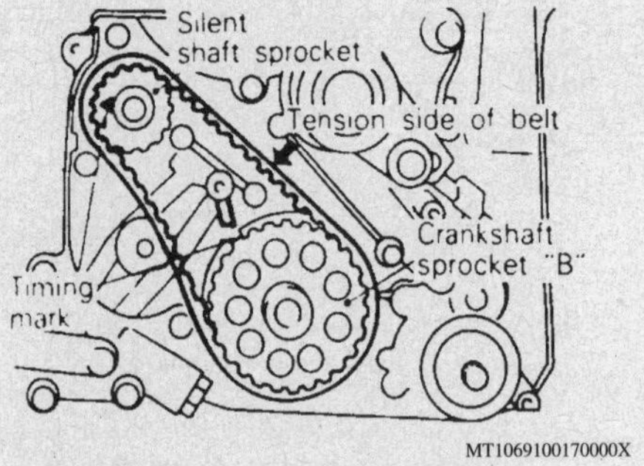
Silent shaft sprocket
Tension side of belt
Crankshaft sprocket "B"
Timing mark
MT1069100170000X
Fig. 27 Timing belt "B" installation

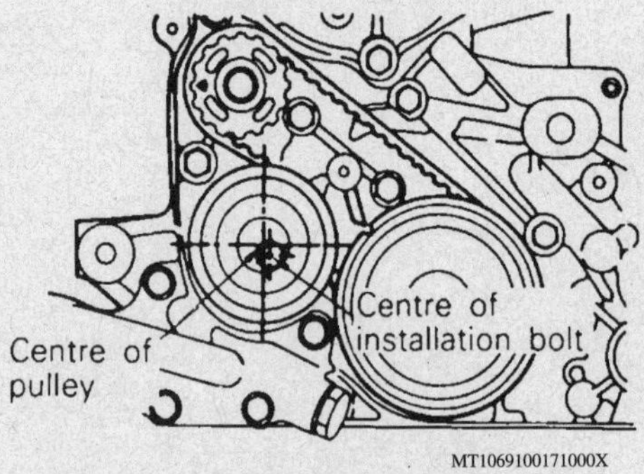
Centre of installation bolt
Centre of pulley
MT1069100171000X
Fig. 28 Timing belt adjustment

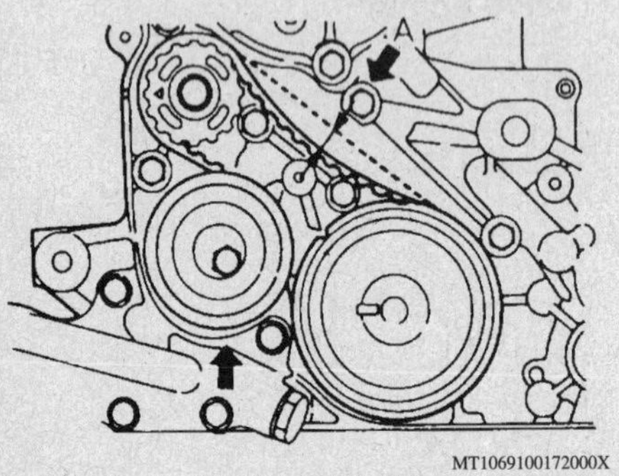
A
MT1069100172000X
Fig. 29 Timing belt tension check

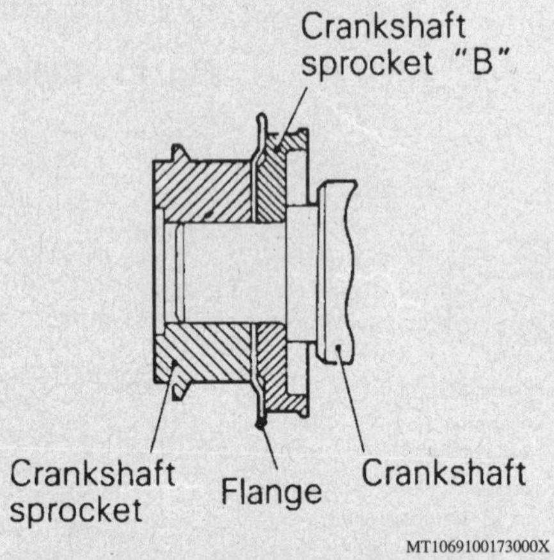
Crankshaft sprocket "B"
Crankshaft sprocket
Flange
Crankshaft
MT1069100173000X
Fig. 30 Flange installation. 8 valve engine

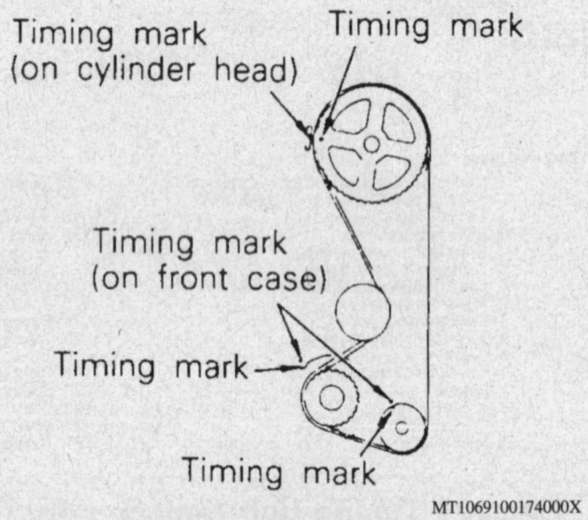
Timing mark (on cylinder head)
Timing mark
Timing mark (on front case)
Timing mark
Timing mark
MT1069100174000X
Fig. 31 Timing belt installation. 8 valve engine

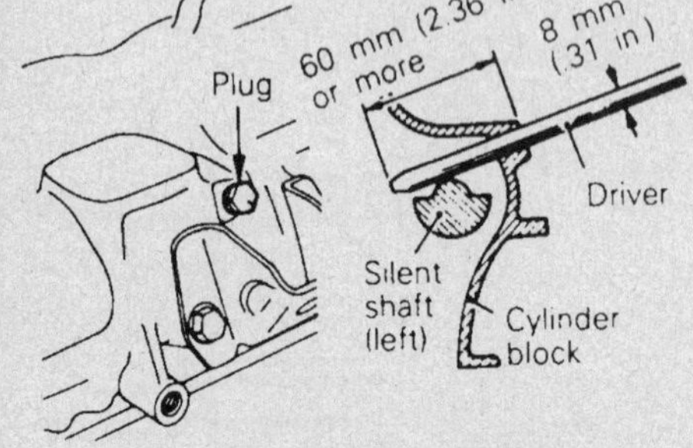
Plug
60 mm (2.36 in) or more
8 mm (.31 in)
Driver
Silent shaft (left)
Cylinder block
MT1069100175000X
Fig. 32 Oil pump sprocket installation. 8 valve engine

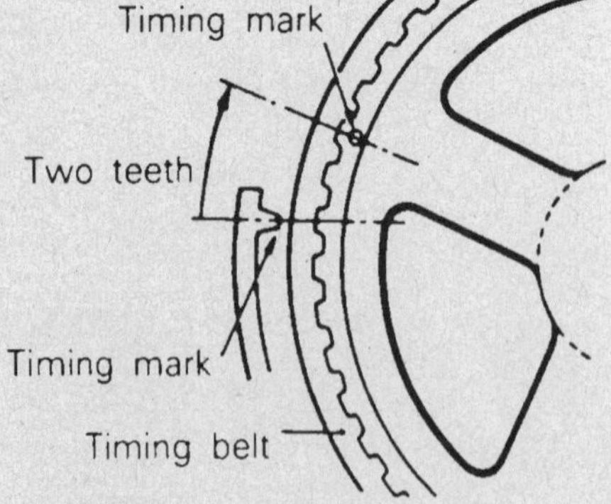
Timing mark
Two teeth
Timing mark
Timing belt
MT1069100176000X
Fig. 33 Timing mark alignment. 8 valve engine

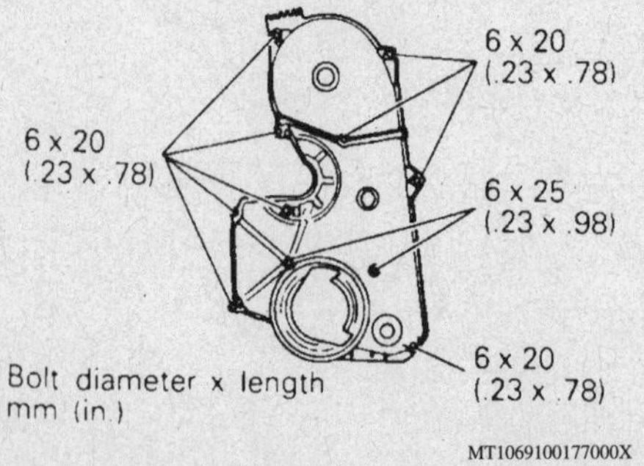
6 x 20 (.23 x .78)
6 x 20 (.23 x .78)
6 x 25 (.23 x .98)
6 x 20 (.23 x .78)
Bolt diameter x length mm (in.)
MT1069100177000X
Fig. 34 Timing belt upper & lower cover installation. 8 valve engine

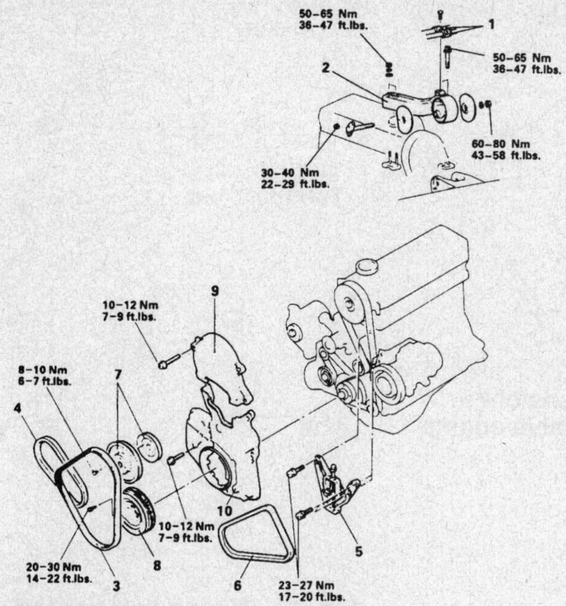

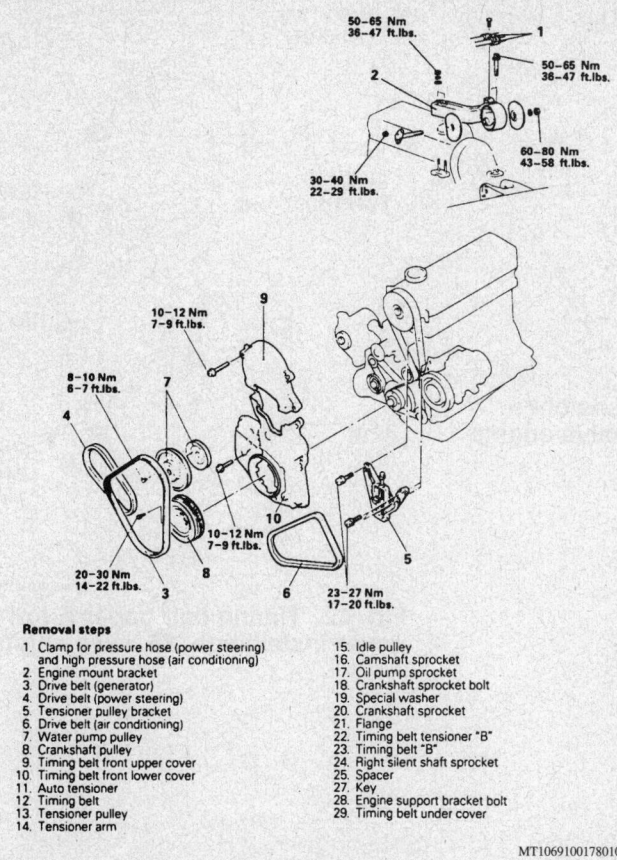

50–65 Nm
36–47 ft.lbs.
1
2
50–65 Nm
36–47 ft.lbs.
60–80 Nm
43–58 ft.lbs.
30–40 Nm
22–29 ft.lbs.
10–12 Nm
7–9 ft.lbs.
9
8–10 Nm
6–7 ft.lbs.
7
4
10–12 Nm
7–9 ft.lbs.
10
20–30 Nm
14–22 ft.lbs.
3
8
6
23–27 Nm
17–20 ft.lbs.
5

Removal steps

1. Clamp for pressure hose (power steering) and high pressure hose (air conditioning)
2. Engine mount bracket
3. Drive belt (generator)
4. Drive belt (power steering)
5. Tensioner pulley bracket
6. Drive belt (air conditioning)
7. Water pump pulley
8. Crankshaft pulley
9. Timing belt front upper cover
10. Timing belt front lower cover
11. Auto tensioner
12. Timing belt
13. Tensioner pulley
14. Tensioner arm
15. Idle pulley
16. Camshaft sprocket
17. Oil pump sprocket
18. Crankshaft sprocket bolt
19. Special washer
20. Crankshaft sprocket
21. Flange
22. Timing belt tensioner "B"
23. Timing belt "B"
24. Right silent shaft sprocket
25. Spacer
27. Key
28. Engine support bracket bolt
29. Timing belt under cover

MT1069100178010X

Fig. 35 Timing belt replacement (Part 1 of 2). 16 valve engine

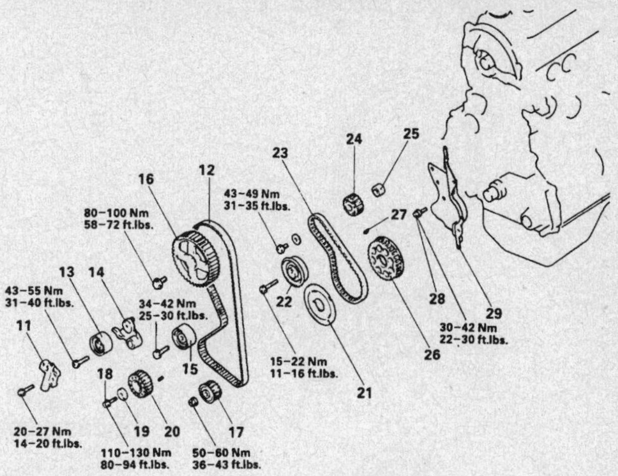

24
25
23
16
12
43–49 Nm
31–35 ft.lbs.
27
80–100 Nm
58–72 ft.lbs.
13
14
43–55 Nm
31–40 ft.lbs.
34–42 Nm
25–30 ft.lbs.
22
28
29
30–42 Nm
22–30 ft.lbs.
26
11
18
15
15–22 Nm
11–16 ft.lbs.
21
19
20
17
20–27 Nm
14–20 ft.lbs.
110–130 Nm
80–94 ft.lbs.
50–60 Nm
36–43 ft.lbs.

Installation steps

29. Timing belt under cover
28. Engine support bracket bolt
27. Key
26. Crankshaft sprocket "B"
25. Spacer
24. Right silent shaft sprocket
22. Timing belt tensioner "B"
23. Timing belt "B"
    Adjustment of timing belt "B" tension
21. Flange
20. Crankshaft sprocket
19. Special washer
18. Crankshaft sprocket bolt
17. Oil pump sprocket
16. Camshaft sprocket
15. Idle pulley
11. Auto tensioner
14. Tensioner arm
13. Tensioner pulley
12. Timing belt
    Adjustment of timing belt tension
10. Timing belt front lower cover
9. Timing belt front upper cover
8. Crankshaft pulley
7. Water pump pulley
6. Drive belt (air conditioning)
5. Tensioner pulley bracket
4. Drive belt (power steering)
3. Drive belt (generator)
2. Engine mount bracket
1. Clamp for pressure hose (power steering) and high pressure hose (air conditioning)

MT1069100178020X

Fig. 35 Timing belt replacement (Part 2 of 2). 16 valve engine

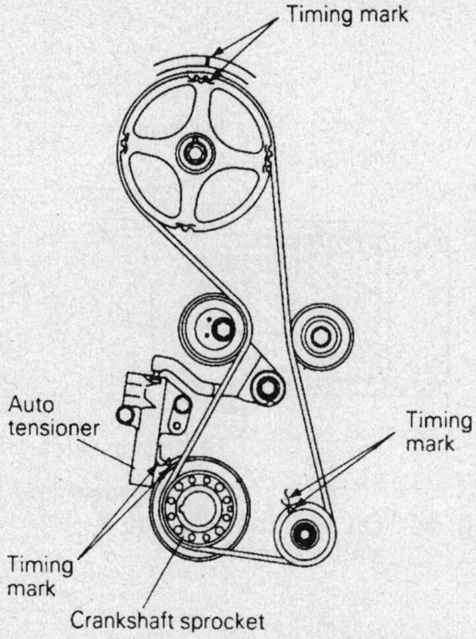

Timing mark
Auto tensioner
Timing mark
Timing mark
Crankshaft sprocket

MT1069100179000X

Fig. 36 Auto tensioner removal. 16 valve engine

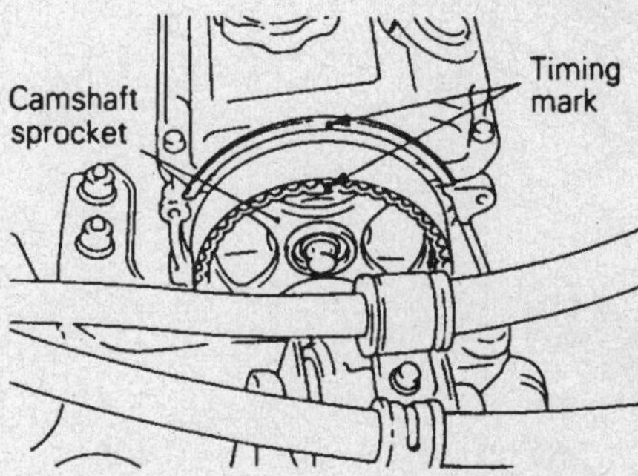

Camshaft sprocket
Timing mark

MT1069100180000X

Fig. 37 Crankshaft sprocket removal. 16 valve engine

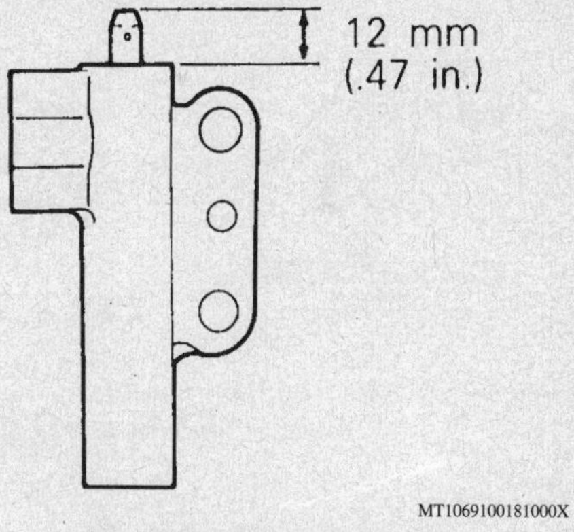

12 mm
(.47 in.)

MT1069100181000X

Fig. 38 Auto tensioner protrusion. 16 valve engine

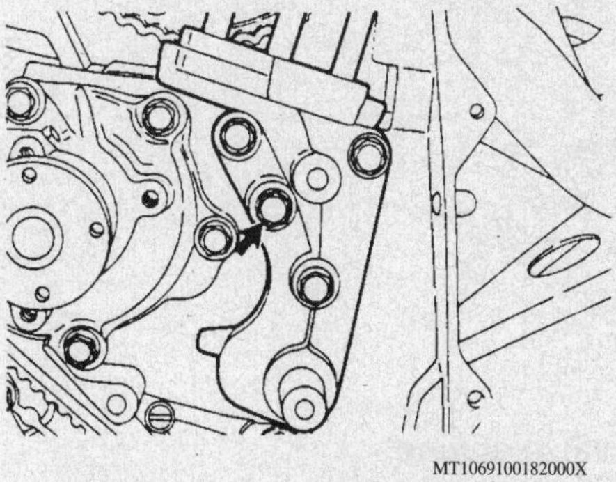

MT1069100182000X

Fig. 39 Auto tensioner bolt installation. 16 valve engine

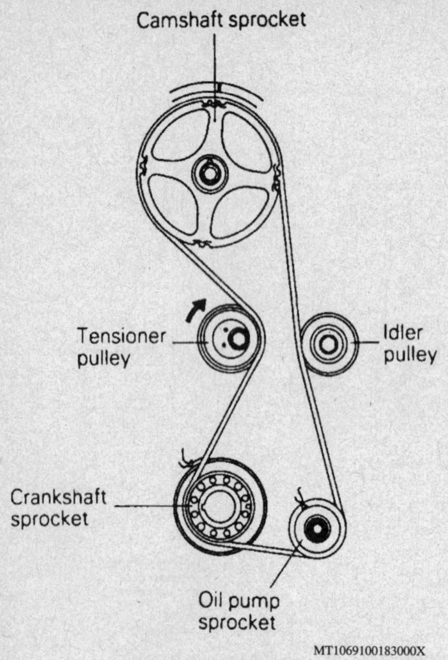
Camshaft sprocket
Tensioner pulley
Idler pulley
Crankshaft sprocket
Oil pump sprocket
MT1069100183000X

Fig. 40 Timing marks alignment. 16 valve engine

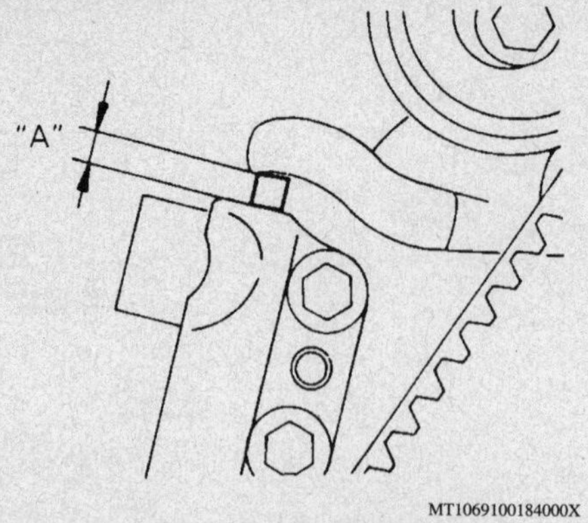
"A"
MT1069100184000X

Fig. 41 Auto tensioner measurement. 16 valve engine

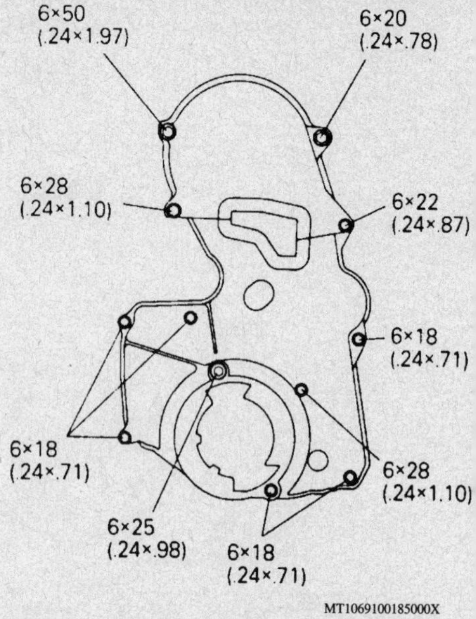
6×50 (.24×1.97)
6×20 (.24×.78)
6×28 (.24×1.10)
6×22 (.24×.87)
6×18 (.24×.71)
6×18 (.24×.71)
6×28 (.24×1.10)
6×25 (.24×.98)
6×18 (.24×.71)
MT1069100185000X

Fig. 42 Timing belt upper & lower cover installation. 16 valve engine

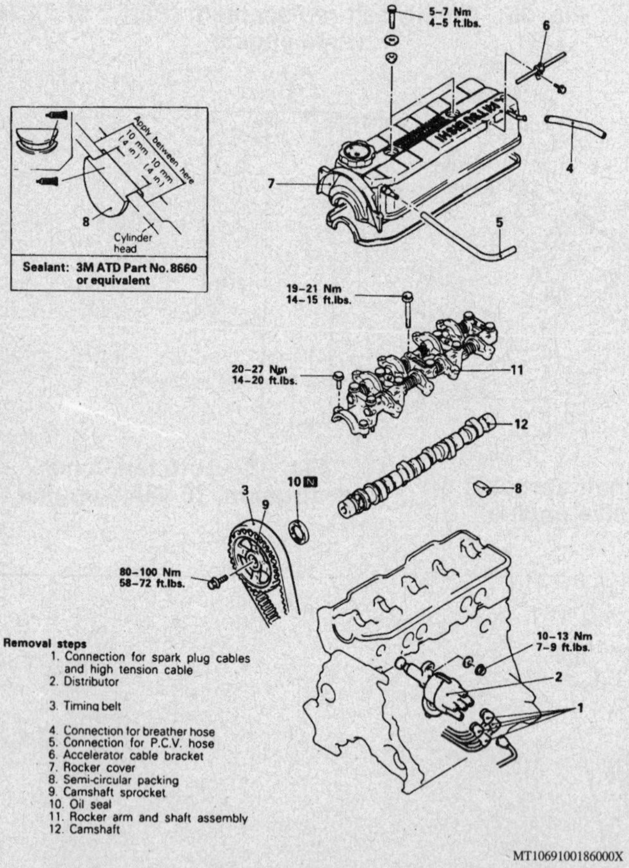
Apply between here
10 mm (4 in)
10 mm (4 in)
8
Cylinder head
Sealant: 3M ATD Part No. 8660 or equivalent
5–7 Nm 4–5 ft.lbs.
6
7
4
5
19–21 Nm 14–15 ft.lbs.
20–27 Nm 14–20 ft.lbs.
11
12
10
3
9
8
80–100 Nm 58–72 ft.lbs.
10–13 Nm 7–9 ft.lbs.
2
1
Removal steps
1. Connection for spark plug cables and high tension cable
2. Distributor
3. Timing belt
4. Connection for breather hose
5. Connection for P.C.V. hose
6. Accelerator cable bracket
7. Rocker cover
8. Semi-circular packing
9. Camshaft sprocket
10. Oil seal
11. Rocker arm and shaft assembly
12. Camshaft
MT1069100186000X

Fig. 43 Camshaft removal. 8 valve engine

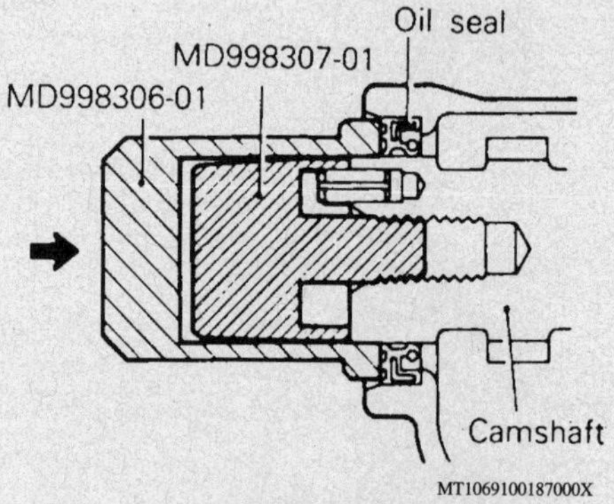
Oil seal
MD998307-01
MD998306-01
Camshaft
MT1069100187000X

Fig. 44 Oil seal installation. 8 valve engine

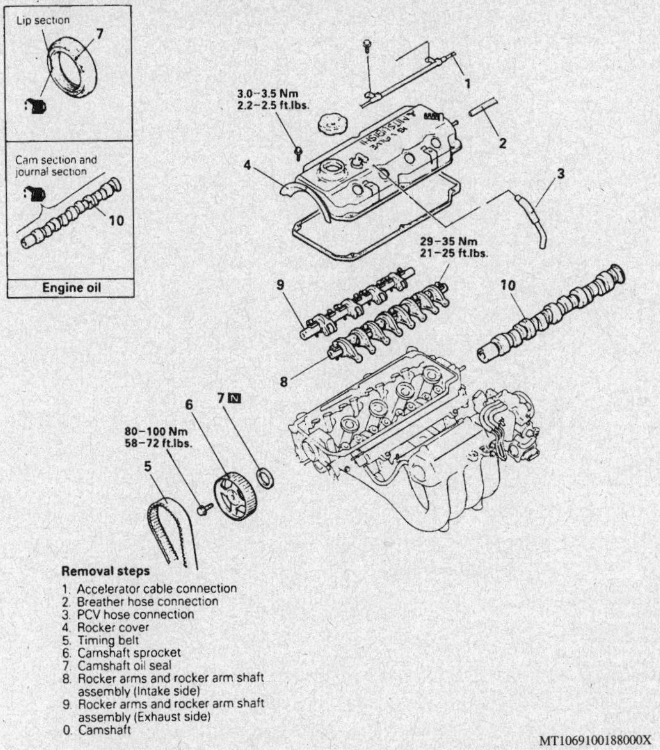
Lip section
7
Cam section and journal section
10
Engine oil
3.0–3.5 Nm
2.2–2.5 ft.lbs.
1
2
3
4
29–35 Nm
21–25 ft.lbs.
9
10
8
6
7
80–100 Nm
58–72 ft.lbs.
5
Removal steps
1. Accelerator cable connection
2. Breather hose connection
3. PCV hose connection
4. Rocker cover
5. Timing belt
6. Camshaft sprocket
7. Camshaft oil seal
8. Rocker arms and rocker arm shaft assembly (Intake side)
9. Rocker arms and rocker arm shaft assembly (Exhaust side)
0. Camshaft

MT1069100188000X

Fig. 45 Camshaft removal. 16 valve engine

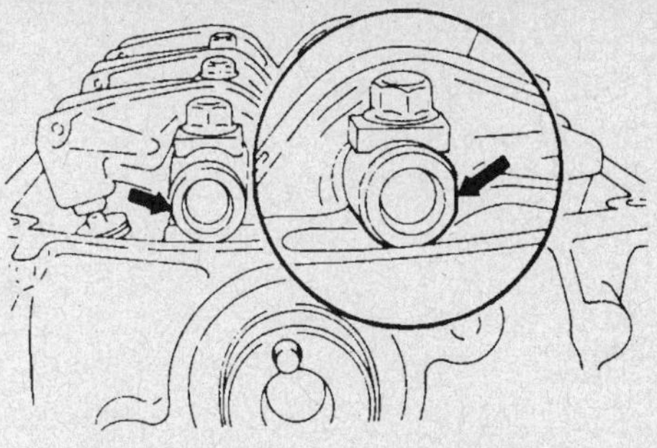

MT1069100189000X

Fig. 46 Rocker arm & shaft installation. 16 valve engine

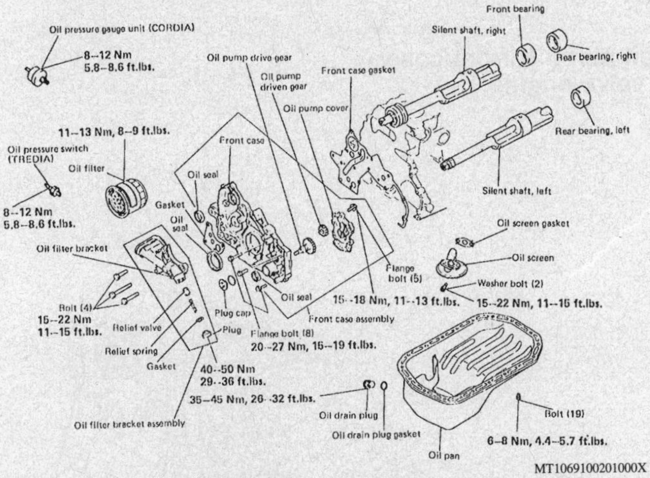
Oil pressure gauge unit (CORDIA)
8–12 Nm
5.8–8.6 ft.lbs.
Oil pump drive gear
Oil pump driven gear
Front case gasket
Oil pump cover
Front bearing
Silent shaft, right
Rear bearing, right
Rear bearing, left
Silent shaft, left
11–13 Nm, 8–9 ft.lbs.
Oil pressure switch (TREDIA)
Oil filter
Front case
Oil seal
Gasket
Oil seal
8–12 Nm
5.8–8.6 ft.lbs.
Oil filter bracket
Oil screen gasket
Oil screen
Washer bolt (2)
Flange bolt (5)
15–18 Nm, 11–13 ft.lbs.
15–22 Nm, 11–16 ft.lbs.
Bolt (4)
15–22 Nm
11–15 ft.lbs.
Relief valve
Relief spring
Gasket
Plug cap
Plug
Flange bolt (8)
20–27 Nm, 15–19 ft.lbs.
Front case assembly
40–50 Nm
29–36 ft.lbs.
35–45 Nm, 26–32 ft.lbs.
Oil drain plug
Oil drain plug gasket
Oil filter bracket assembly
Bolt (19)
6–8 Nm, 4.4–5.7 ft.lbs.
Oil pan

MT1069100201000X

Fig. 47 Silent shaft, oil pump & front case assembly. 8 valve engine

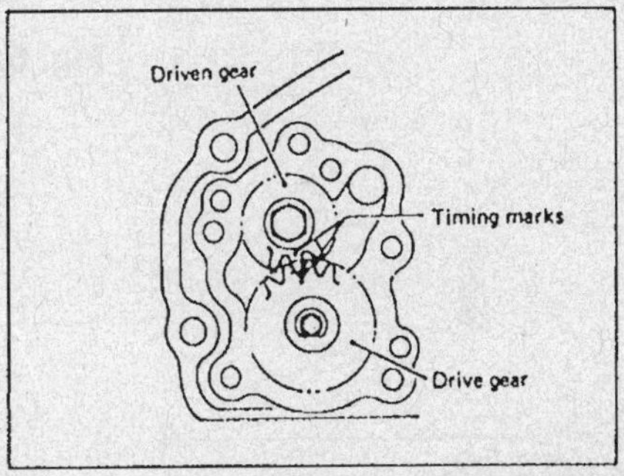
Driven gear
Timing marks
Drive gear

MT1069100202000X

Fig. 48 Oil pump gears timing marks. 8 valve engine

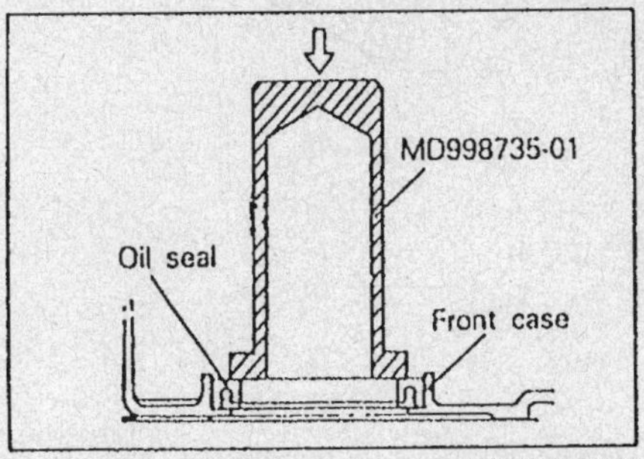
MD998735-01
Oil seal
Front case

MT1069100203000X

Fig. 49 Crankshaft front oil seal installation. 8 valve engine

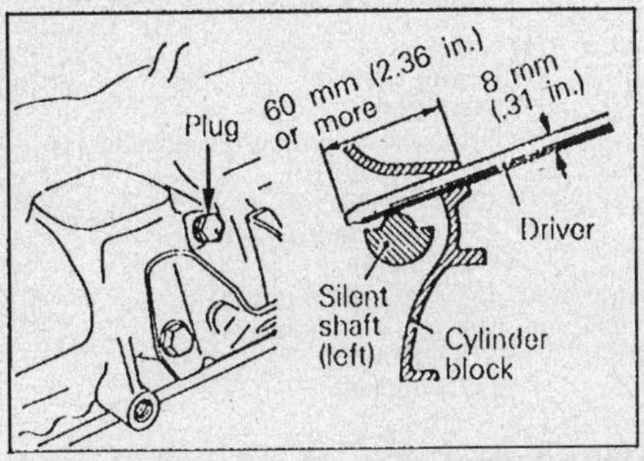
Plug
60 mm (2.36 in.) or more
8 mm (.31 in.)
Driver
Silent shaft (left)
Cylinder block

MT1069100204000X

Fig. 50 Securing silent shaft. 8 valve engine

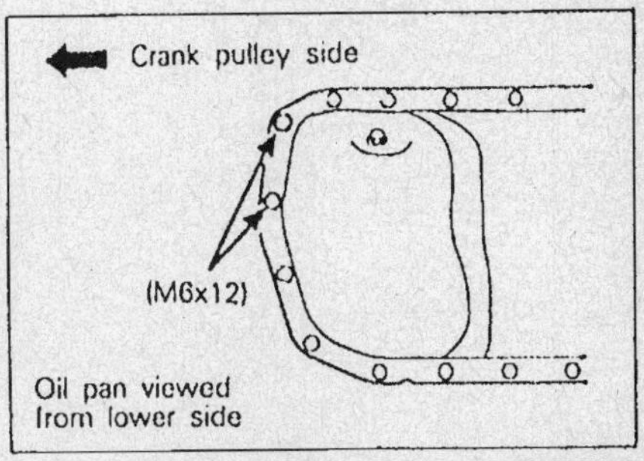
Crank pulley side
(M6x12)
Oil pan viewed from lower side

MT1069100205000X

Fig. 51 Oil pan bolt location. 8 valve engine

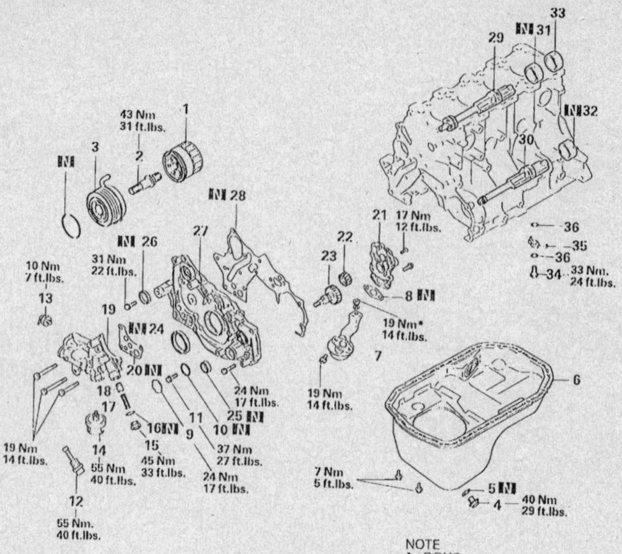
43 Nm
31 ft.lbs.
10 Nm
7 ft.lbs.
31 Nm
22 ft.lbs.
17 Nm
12 ft.lbs.
33 Nm
24 ft.lbs.
19 Nm*
14 ft.lbs.
24 Nm
17 ft.lbs.
19 Nm
14 ft.lbs.
37 Nm
27 ft.lbs.
45 Nm
33 ft.lbs.
55 Nm
40 ft.lbs.
7 Nm
5 ft.lbs.
40 Nm
29 ft.lbs.

NOTE
* : DOHC
** : Engine with turbocharger

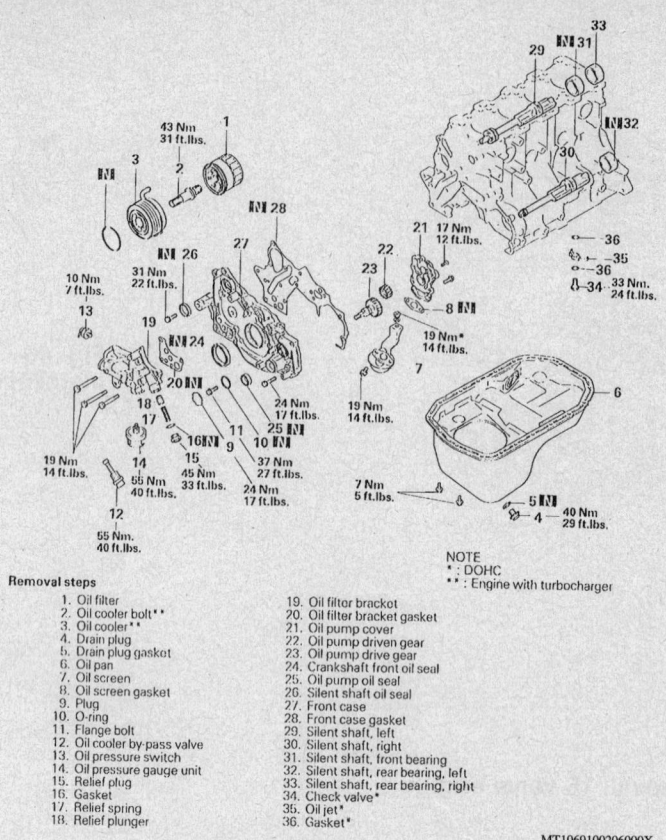

Removal steps

1. Oil filter
2. Oil cooler bolt**
3. Oil cooler**
4. Drain plug
5. Drain plug gasket
6. Oil pan
7. Oil screen
8. Oil screen gasket
9. Plug
10. O-ring
11. Flange bolt
12. Oil cooler by-pass valve
13. Oil pressure switch
14. Oil pressure gauge unit
15. Relief plug
16. Gasket
17. Relief spring
18. Relief plunger
19. Oil filter bracket
20. Oil filter bracket gasket
21. Oil pump cover
22. Oil pump driven gear
23. Oil pump drive gear
24. Crankshaft front oil seal
25. Oil pump oil seal
26. Silent shaft oil seal
27. Front case
28. Front case gasket
29. Silent shaft, left
30. Silent shaft, right
31. Silent shaft, front bearing
32. Silent shaft, rear bearing, left
33. Silent shaft, rear bearing, right
34. Check valve*
35. Oil jet*
36. Gasket*

MT1069100206000X

Fig. 52 Silent shaft, oil pump & front case assembly. 16 valve engine

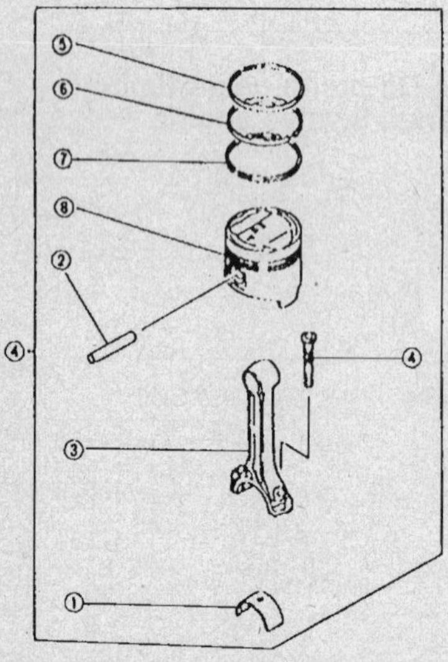

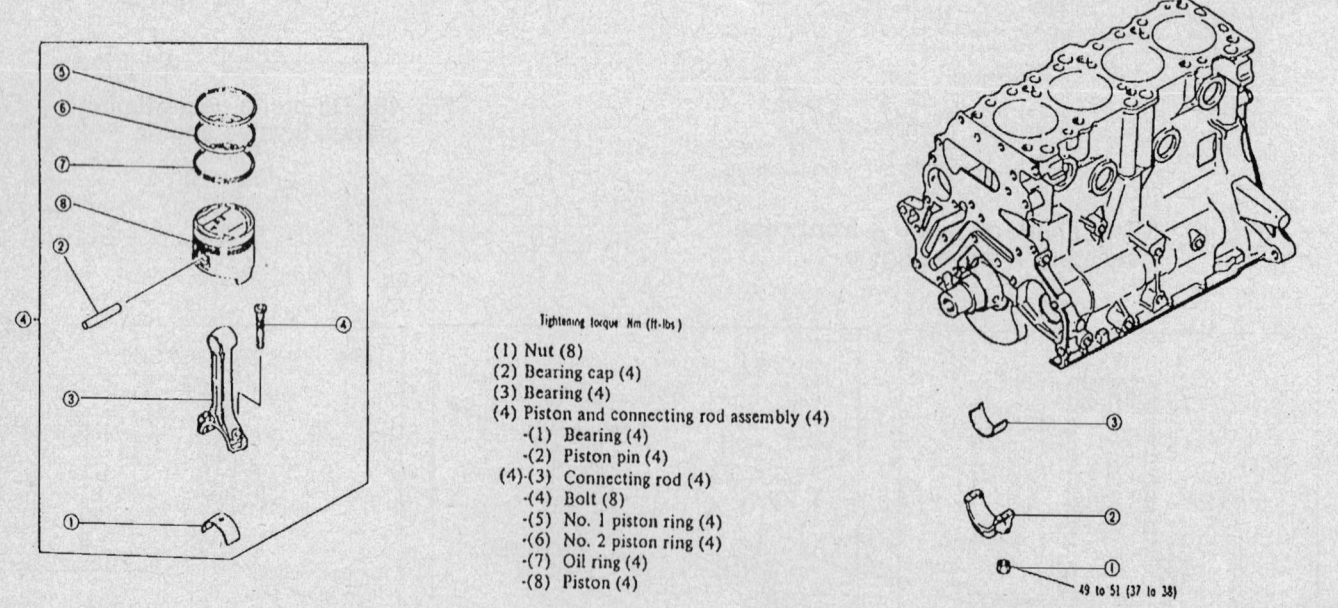

Tightening torque: Nm (ft-lbs)

(1) Nut (8)
(2) Bearing cap (4)
(3) Bearing (4)
(4) Piston and connecting rod assembly (4)
-(1) Bearing (4)
-(2) Piston pin (4)
(4)-(3) Connecting rod (4)
-(4) Bolt (8)
-(5) No. 1 piston ring (4)
-(6) No. 2 piston ring (4)
-(7) Oil ring (4)
-(8) Piston (4)

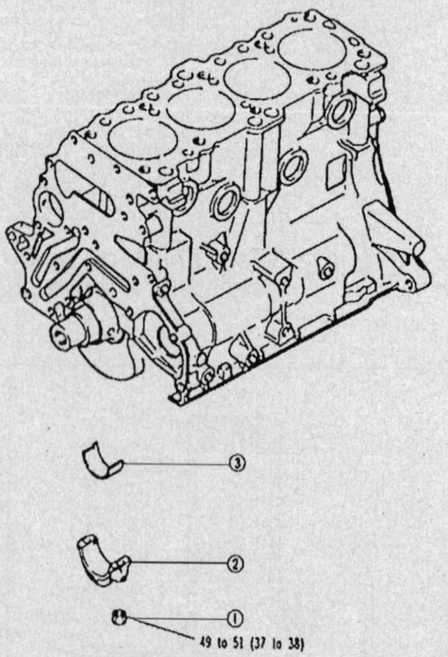
49 to 51 (37 to 38)

MT1069100207000X

Fig. 53 Exploded view of piston & rod assembly. 8 valve engine

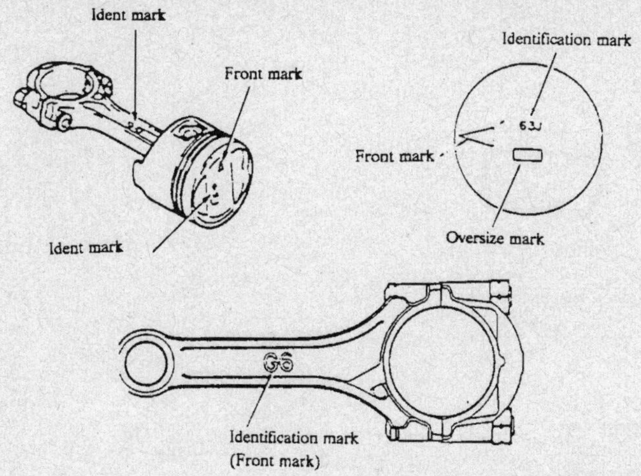
Ident mark
Front mark
Ident mark
Identification mark
Front mark
Oversize mark
Identification mark
(Front mark)
MT1069100208000X

Fig. 54 Piston assembly identification marks. 8 valve engine

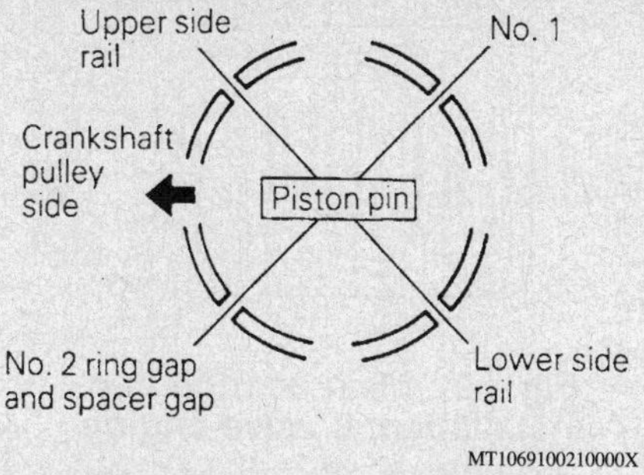
Upper side rail
No. 1
Crankshaft pulley side
Piston pin
No. 2 ring gap and spacer gap
Lower side rail
MT1069100210000X

Fig. 56 Piston & connecting rod installation. 16 valve engine

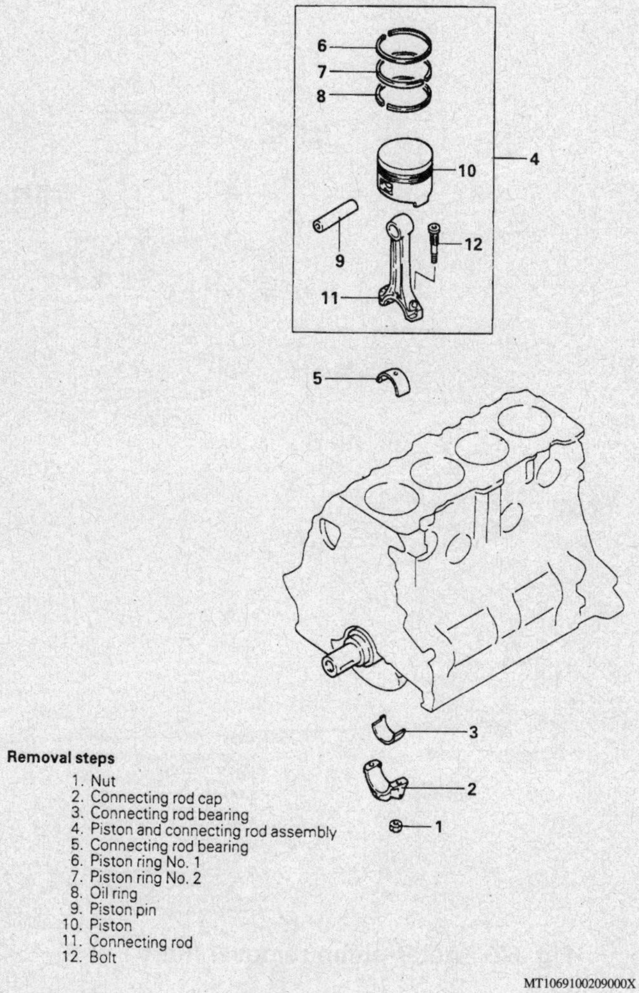
Removal steps
1. Nut
2. Connecting rod cap
3. Connecting rod bearing
4. Piston and connecting rod assembly
5. Connecting rod bearing
6. Piston ring No. 1
7. Piston ring No. 2
8. Oil ring
9. Piston pin
10. Piston
11. Connecting rod
12. Bolt
MT1069100209000X

Fig. 55 Exploded view of piston & rod assembly. 16 valve engine

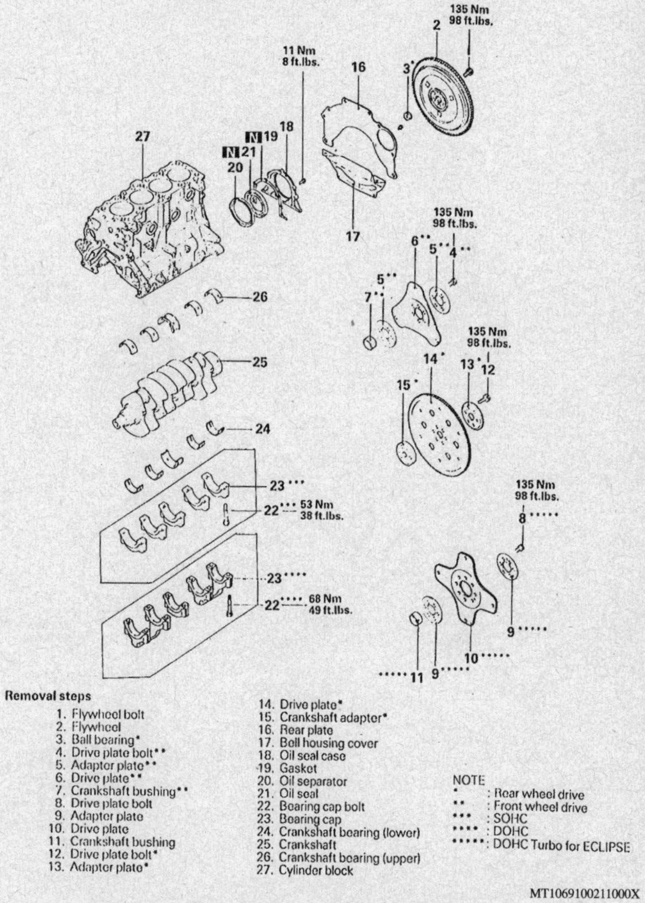
135 Nm 98 ft.lbs.
11 Nm 8 ft.lbs.
53 Nm 38 ft.lbs.
68 Nm 49 ft.lbs.
Removal steps
1. Flywheel bolt
2. Flywheel
3. Ball bearing*
4. Drive plate bolt**
5. Adaptor plate**
6. Drive plate**
7. Crankshaft bushing**
8. Drive plate bolt
9. Adapter plate
10. Drive plate
11. Crankshaft bushing
12. Drive plate bolt*
13. Adapter plate*
14. Drive plate*
15. Crankshaft adapter*
16. Rear plate
17. Bell housing cover
18. Oil seal case
19. Gasket
20. Oil separator
21. Oil seal
22. Bearing cap bolt
23. Bearing cap
24. Crankshaft bearing (lower)
25. Crankshaft
26. Crankshaft bearing (upper)
27. Cylinder block
NOTE
* : Rear wheel drive
** : Front wheel drive
*** : SOHC
**** : DOHC
*****: DOHC Turbo for ECLIPSE
MT1069100211000X

Fig. 57 Exploded view of crankshaft, flywheel & driveplate. 8 valve engine

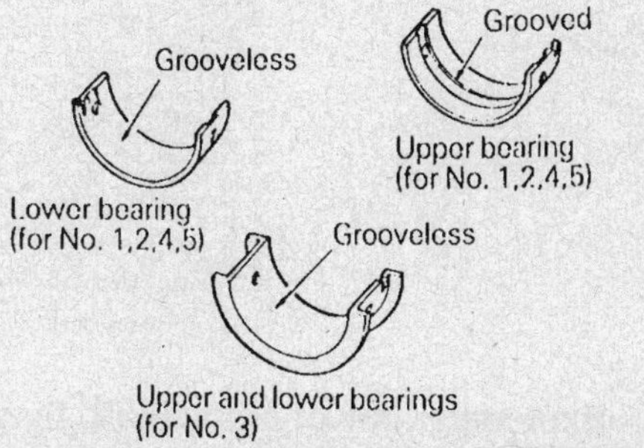
Grooved
Grooveless
Upper bearing (for No. 1,2,4,5)
Lower bearing (for No. 1,2,4,5)
Grooveless
Upper and lower bearings (for No. 3)
MT1069100212000X

Fig. 58 Main bearing insert identification. 8 valve engine

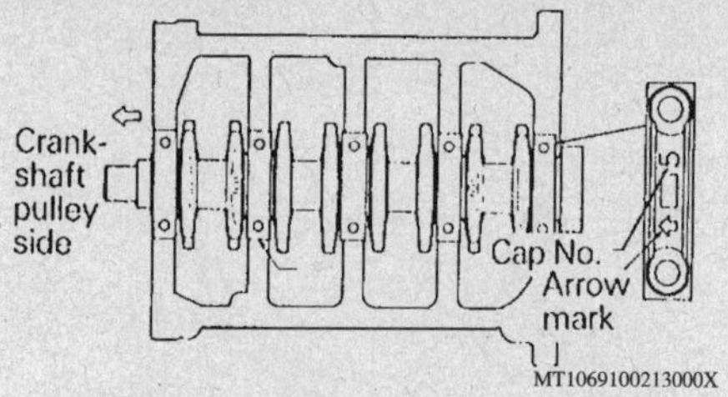
Crank-
shaft
pulley
side
Cap No.
Arrow
mark
MT1069100213000X

Fig. 59 Main bearing cap installation. 8 valve engine

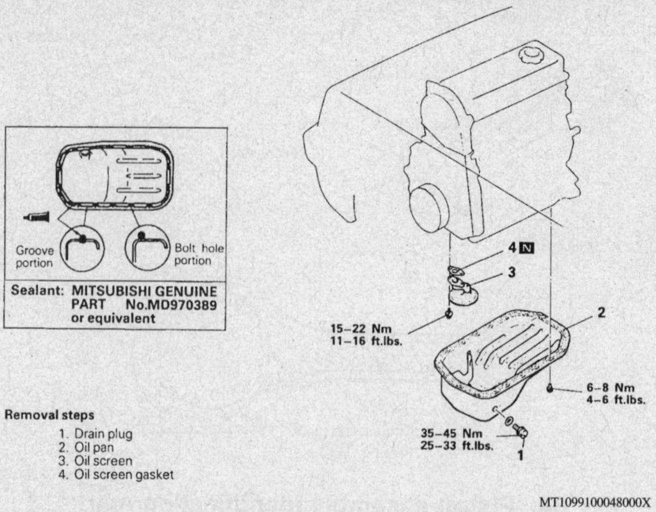
Groove
portion
Bolt hole
portion
Sealant: MITSUBISHI GENUINE PART No.MD970389 or equivalent
4 N
3
2
15–22 Nm
11–16 ft.lbs.
6–8 Nm
4–6 ft.lbs.
35–45 Nm
25–33 ft.lbs.
1
Removal steps
1. Drain plug
2. Oil pan
3. Oil screen
4. Oil screen gasket
MT1099100048000X

Fig. 61 Oil pan & screen replacement

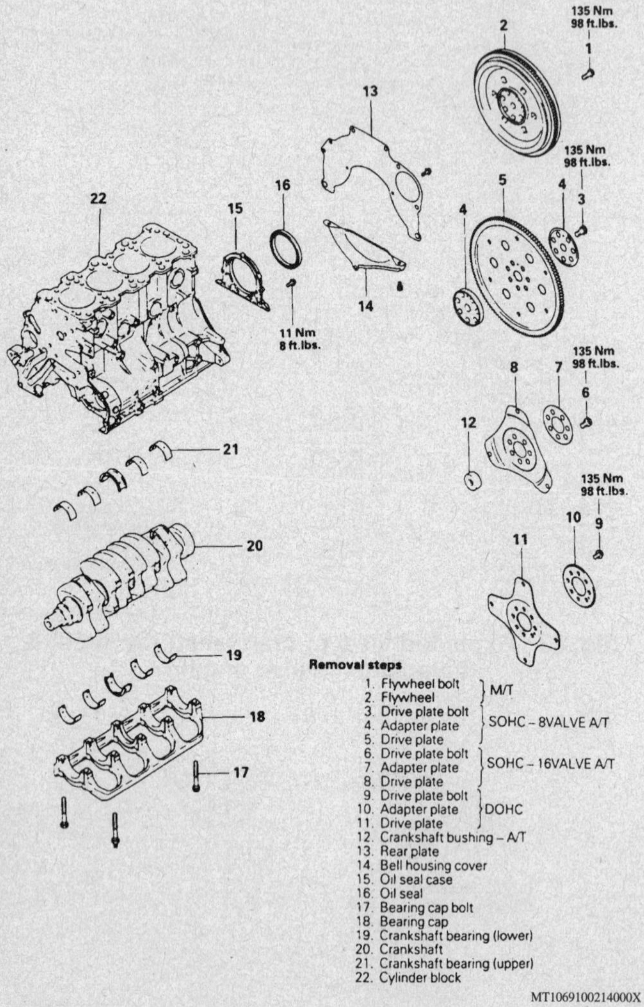
135 Nm
98 ft.lbs.
135 Nm
98 ft.lbs.
11 Nm
8 ft.lbs.
135 Nm
98 ft.lbs.
135 Nm
98 ft.lbs.
Removal steps
1. Flywheel bolt
2. Flywheel
M/T
3. Drive plate bolt
4. Adapter plate
5. Drive plate
SOHC – 8VALVE A/T
6. Drive plate bolt
7. Adapter plate
8. Drive plate
SOHC – 16VALVE A/T
9. Drive plate bolt
10. Adapter plate
11. Drive plate
DOHC
12. Crankshaft bushing – A/T
13. Rear plate
14. Bell housing cover
15. Oil seal case
16. Oil seal
17. Bearing cap bolt
18. Bearing cap
19. Crankshaft bearing (lower)
20. Crankshaft
21. Crankshaft bearing (upper)
22. Cylinder block
MT1069100214000X

Fig. 60 Exploded view of crankshaft, flywheel & drive plate. 16 valve engine

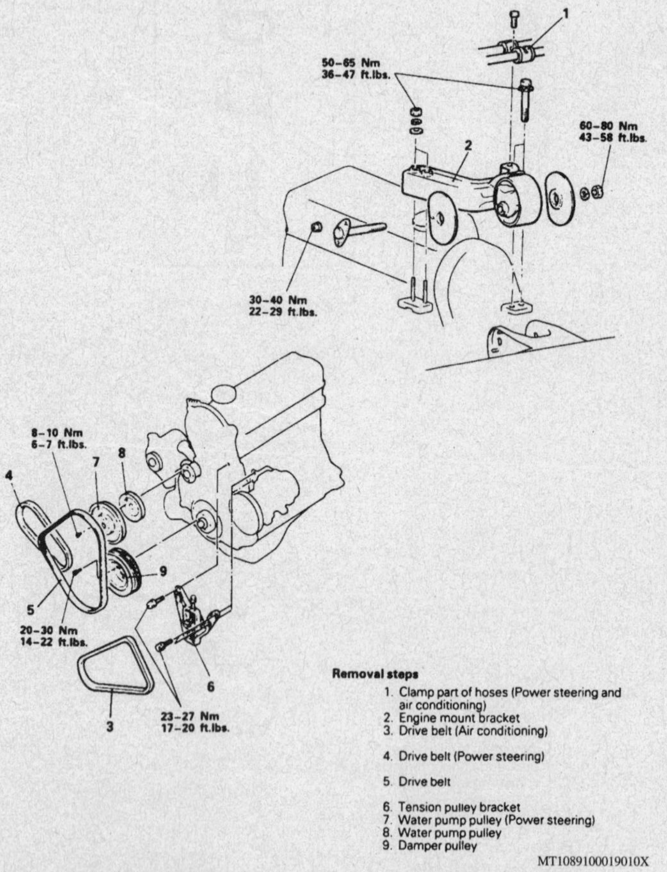
50–65 Nm
36–47 ft.lbs.
60–80 Nm
43–58 ft.lbs.
30–40 Nm
22–29 ft.lbs.
8–10 Nm
6–7 ft.lbs.
20–30 Nm
14–22 ft.lbs.
23–27 Nm
17–20 ft.lbs.
Removal steps
1. Clamp part of hoses (Power steering and air conditioning)
2. Engine mount bracket
3. Drive belt (Air conditioning)
4. Drive belt (Power steering)
5. Drive belt
6. Tension pulley bracket
7. Water pump pulley (Power steering)
8. Water pump pulley
9. Damper pulley
MT1089100019010X

Fig. 62 Water pump removal (Part 1 of 2)

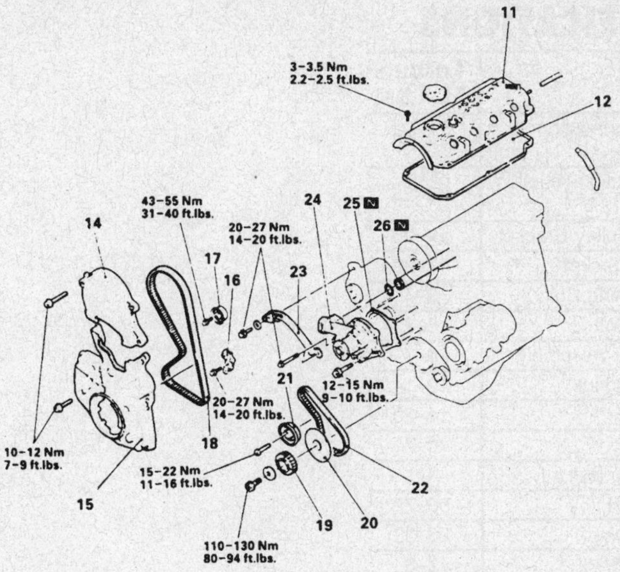
3-3.5 Nm
2.2-2.5 ft.lbs.
43-55 Nm
31-40 ft.lbs.
20-27 Nm
14-20 ft.lbs.
12-15 Nm
9-10 ft.lbs.
20-27 Nm
14-20 ft.lbs.
10-12 Nm
7-9 ft.lbs.
15-22 Nm
11-16 ft.lbs.
110-130 Nm
80-94 ft.lbs.

11. Rocker cover
12. Rocker cover gasket
14. Timing belt front upper cover
15. Timing belt front lower cover
16. Automatic tensioner
17. Tension pulley
18. Timing belt
19. Crankshaft sprocket
20. Flange B.)
21. Timing belt B tensioner
22. Timing belt B
23. Generator brace
24. Water pump
25. Water pump gasket
26. O-ring

MT108930001902BX

Fig. 62 Water pump removal (Part 2 of 2)

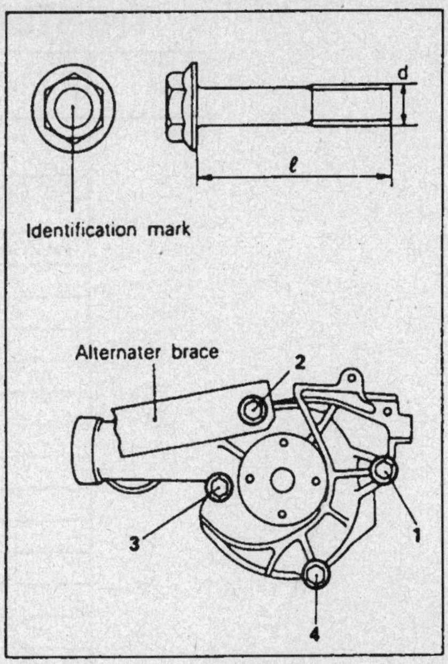
d
ℓ
Identification mark
Alternater brace

No.	Identification mark	Bolt diameter (d) x length (ℓ) mm (in.)	Torque Nm (ft.lbs.)
1	4	8 x 28 (.31 x 1.1)	12–15 (9–10)
2	7	8 x 70 (.31 x 2.76)	20–27 (15–19)
3	4	8 x 55 (.31 x 2.17)	12–15 (9–10)
4	4	8 x 28 (.31 x 1.1)	

MT1089100020000X

Fig. 63 Water pump attaching bolts

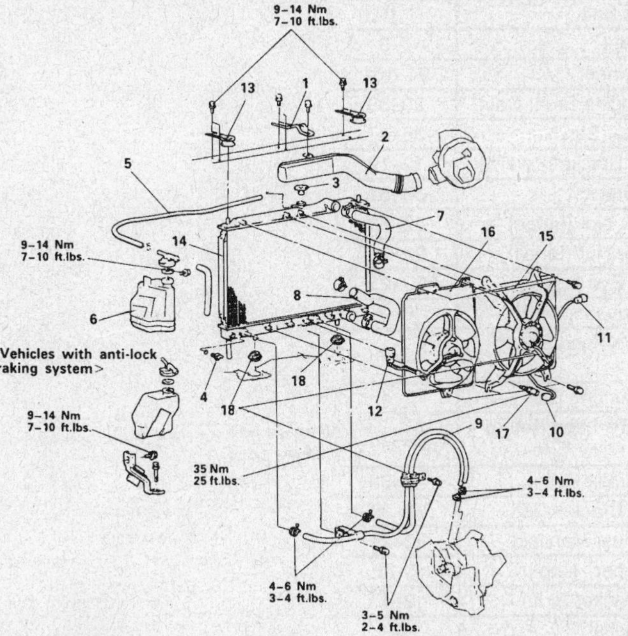
9-14 Nm
7-10 ft.lbs.
9-14 Nm
7-10 ft.lbs.
<Vehicles with anti-lock braking system>
9-14 Nm
7-10 ft.lbs.
35 Nm
25 ft.lbs.
4-6 Nm
3-4 ft.lbs.
4-6 Nm
3-4 ft.lbs.
3-5 Nm
2-4 ft.lbs.

Removal steps

1. Branch tube bracket <Non-Turbo>
2. Branch tube <Non-Turbo>
3. Radiator cap
4. Drain plug
5. Overflow tube
6. Reserve tank
7. Radiator upper hose
8. Radiator lower hose
9. Automatic transaxle oil cooler hoses <Vehicles with A/T>
10. Thermo sensor connector
11. Radiator fan motor connector
12. Condenser fan motor connector <Non-Turbo (FWD, AWD-M/T)-Vehicles with air conditioning>
13. Upper insulator
14. Radiator assembly
15. Radiator fan motor assembly
16. Condenser fan motor assembly <Non-Turbo (FWD, AWD-M/T)-Vehicles with air conditioning>
17. Thermo sensor
18. Lower insulator

MT1069100162000X

Fig. 64 Radiator replacement

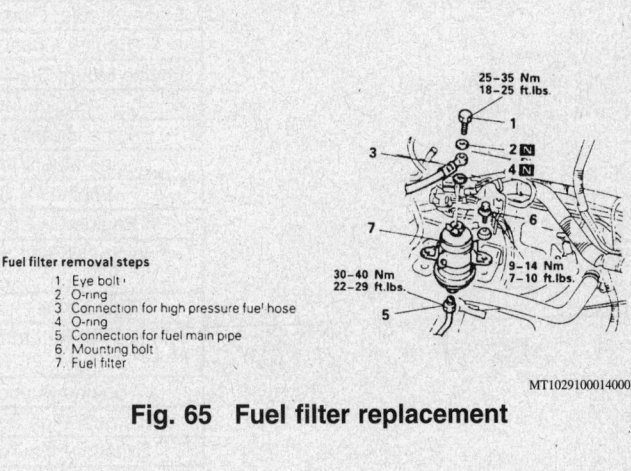

Fuel filter removal steps

1. Eye bolt
2. O-ring
3. Connection for high pressure fuel hose
4. O-ring
5. Connection for fuel main pipe
6. Mounting bolt
7. Fuel filter

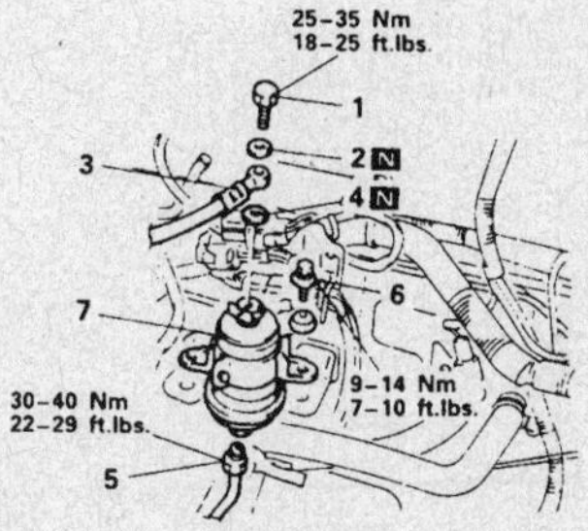
25-35 Nm
18-25 ft.lbs.
30-40 Nm
22-29 ft.lbs.
9-14 Nm
7-10 ft.lbs.

MT1029100014000X

Fig. 65 Fuel filter replacement

TIGHTENING SPECIFICATIONS

Year	Component	Torque/ Ft. Lbs.
1993	A/C Compressor Pipe Connection (Discharge Side)	14–18
	A/C Compressor Pipe Connection (Suction Side)	22–25
	A/C Compressor Tensioner Pulley Bracket	17–20
	A/C Compressor To Bracket	17–20
	Accelerator Cable Adjusting Bolt	3–4
	Air Cleaner Body Bolt	6–7
	Air Cleaner Body/Resonator Assembly	6–7
	Air Cleaner Mounting Nut	12–14
	Auto Tensioner	14–20
	Branch Tube Bolt	6–7
	Camshaft Bearing Cap Bolt	③
	Camshaft Sprocket	58–72
	Center Bearing Bracket	26–33
	Center Cover Bolt	2–3
	Centermember Installation Bolt	58–72
	Connecting Rod Cap Bolt	36–38
	Connecting Rod Cap Nut	15
	Control Wiring Harness Clamp Bolt	7–9
	Control Wiring Harness To Air Intake Manifold Or Air Intake Plenum	3–4
	Cooling Fan Mounting Nut	7–9
	Crankshaft Bearing Cap Bolt	36–40
	Crankshaft Angle Sensor Nut	7–9
	Crankshaft Pulley Bolt	14–22
	Crankshaft Rear Oil Seal Case Bolt	7–9
	Crankshaft Sprocket Bolt	58–72
	Cylinder Head Bolt	①
	Distributor Nut	7–9
	Driveplate/Flywheel	94–101
	Engine Cooler Pipe To Engine Front Case	29–33
	Engine Mount Bracket Bolt/Nut	36–47
	Engine Mount Bracket To Bracket Bolt/Nut	12–19
	Engine Mount Bracket	36–51
	Engine Mount Insulator Nut (Large)	43–58
	Engine Mount Insulator Nut (Small)	22–29
	Engine Oil Cooler Eye Bolt	22–25
	Engine Oil Cooler Mounting Nut	6–9
	Engine Oil Feed Hose To Feed/Return Tube	29–36
	Engine Oil Hose Mounting Bolt	2–4
	Engine Oil Return Hose To Feed/Return Tube	29–36
	Engine Support Bracket Bolts	29–36
	Exhaust Pipe Support Bracket Bolt	22–30
	Exhaust Pipe To Exhaust Manifold	22–29
	Exhaust Pipe To Rubber Hanger	7–11
	Eye Bolt (Oil Filter Bracket Side)	2–4
	Front Case Bolts	②
	Front Engine Mounting Insulator To Engine	9–14
	Front Engine Mounting Insulator/Insulator Stopper To Engine Mounting Bracket	22–29
	Front Engine Support Bracket Bolt	36–51
	Front Exhaust Pipe Clamp Bolt	22–29
	Front Exhaust Pipe To Engine	22–29

Continued

TIGHTENING SPECIFICATIONS—Continued

Year	Component	Torque/ Ft. Lbs.
1993	Front Insulator Stopper To Heat Protector	6–9
	Front Roll Stopper Bracket Bolt	40–54
	Front Roll Stopper Bracket To Centermember	29–36
	Front Roll Stopper Insulator Nut	36–47
	Fuel High Pressure Hose To Delivery Pipe	3–4
	Ground Cable To Intake Manifold	7–9
	Heat Protector To Exhaust Manifold	9–11
	Intake Manifold Bolts	11–14
	Intake Manifold Stay Bolt	13–18
	Left Engine Support Bracket Bolt	22–30
	Left Member Installation Bolt (Front)	58–72
	Left Member Installation Bolt (Rear)	51–58
	No. 2 Crossmember To Frame	29–36
	Oil Filter Bracket Bolt	11–16
	Oil Pan Bolts	4–6
	Oil Pan Drain Plug	25–33
	Oil Pan Nuts	3.5–5.0
	Oil Pressure Gauge Unit	6–9
	Oil Pressure Switch	6–9
	Oil Pump Cover Bolt	11–13
	Oil Pump Driven Gear Bolt	25–29
	Oil Pump Sprocket Nut	36–43
	Oil Return Pipe To Oil Pan	6–7
	Oil Screen Bolt/Nut	11–16
	Plug Case	14–20
	Power Steering Oil Pipe Connecting Nut	12–19
	Power Steering Oil Pump Mounting Bolt	18–24
	Power Steering Oil Pump To Bracket	25–33
	Radiator Mounting Bolt	6–8
	Radiator Shroud Mounting Bolt	2–4
	Rear Engine Mounting Insulator To No. 2 Crossmember	9–14
	Rear Engine Mounting Insulator To Transmission	14–17
	Rear Roll Stopper Bracket Bolt	80–94
	Rear Roll Stopper Bracket To Centermember	29–36
	Rear Roll Stopper Insulator	29–36
	Relief Plug	29–36
	Rocker Arm/Shaft Assembly Bolt (Large)	14–15
	Rocker Arm/Shaft Assembly Bolt (Small)	14–20
	Rocker Cover Bolt	2–3
	Silent Shaft Sprocket	31–35
	Thermostat Housing Bolts	12–14
	Throttle Body Stay	11–16
	Timing Belt Front Cover	7–9
	Timing Belt Idle Pulley Bolt	25–30
	Timing Belt Rear Left Cover (Lower)④	22–30
	Timing Belt Rear Left Cover (Upper)	7–9
	Timing Belt Rear Right Cover	7–9
	Timing Belt Tensioner Pulley Bolt	31–40
	Timing Belt Tensioner Spacer	31–40
	Timing Belt "B" Tensioner Bolt	11–16
	Transaxle Mount Bracket To Body	29–36
	Transaxle Mount Insulator	43–58

Continued

TIGHTENING SPECIFICATIONS—Continued

Year	Component	Torque/ Ft. Lbs.
1993	Water Pipe To Engine	10–14
	Water Pump Pulley Bolt	6–7

① — 8 valve engine, w/engine cold, torque to 65–72 ft. lbs. 16 valve engine, refer to "Cylinder Head, Replace" for procedure.
② — Except 0.12 inch (30 mm) long bolts, 14–20 ft. lbs.; 0.12 inch (30 mm) long bolts, 20–25 ft. lbs.
③ — 8 X 25 bolts, 15–19 ft. lbs.; 8 X 65 bolts, 14–15 ft. lbs.
④ — Also attaches to left engine support bracket.

2.0L DOHC Engine

NOTE: On Air Bag Equipped Models, Refer To "Air Bag System Precautions" Located In The Front Of This Manual For System Disarming & Arming Procedures.

NOTE: For Procedures Not Found In This Section, Refer To The Eclipse & 3000GT Engine Section In The Mitsubishi Chapter.

INDEX

	Page No.
Compression Pressures	26-34
Engine Rebuilding Specifications	29-1
Engine, Replace	26-34
Precautions	26-34
Fuel System Pressure Relief	26-34
Radiator, Replace	26-34
Technical Service Bulletins	26-36
Idle Vibration	26-36
Thermostat, Replace	26-36
Tightening Specifications	26-36

PRECAUTIONS

FUEL SYSTEM PRESSURE RELIEF

1. Disconnect fuel pump harness connector at the fuel tank rear side. **Cover fuel pipe line with rag after relieving pressure as some residual pressure may remain.**
2. Start engine and let it idle until it stalls from fuel starvation, then turn ignition switch to Off position. **Failure to relieve fuel system pressure prior to disconnecting fuel system components may cause fire or personal injury.**
3. Disconnect negative battery ground cable.
4. Connect fuel pump harness connector.
5. After repairs have been completed, connect positive battery terminal to fuel pump drive terminal and the negative terminal to the chassis. Ensure fuel pump operates at this time.

COMPRESSION PRESSURES

Ensure engine oil, starter motor and battery are in satisfactory condition. When checking compression, engine coolant should be at normal operating temperature, spark plugs should be removed and throttle valve should be wide open. Minimum compression pressure at engine cranking speed is 159 psi and difference between cylinders should not exceed 14 psi.

ENGINE

REPLACE

1. Relieve fuel system pressure as outlined under "Precautions."
2. Disconnect battery ground cable.
3. Scribe reference marks between hood and hood hinges, then remove hood.
4. Drain cooling system as follows:
   a. Place temperature control lever in Hot position.
   b. Carefully remove radiator cap.
   c. Remove radiator drain plug.
5. Remove radiator as outlined under "Radiator, Replace. "
6. Remove transaxle assembly. On models with automatic transaxle, refer to procedure outlined under "Transaxle, Replace"in the "Automatic Transmission" section. On models with manual transaxle, refer to procedure outlined under "Transaxle, Replace" in the "Clutch & Manual Transaxle " section.
7. Remove engine components in order as shown, **Fig. 1,** noting the following:
   a. Remove power steering pump from bracket with hoses attached, then secure pump aside with a piece of wire.
   b. Remove A/C compressor from bracket with hoses attached, then compressor pump aside with a piece of wire.
   c. Using a suitable engine hoist, slightly raise engine, then remove engine mount bracket.
   d. Ensure all cables, connectors and hoses are disconnected, then remove engine from engine compartment.
8. Reverse procedure to install.

RADIATOR

REPLACE

1. Remove radiator components in order as shown, **Fig. 2,** noting the following:
   a. Prior to removing radiator hoses, mark hose clamps in relation to hoses for installation reference.
   b. After disconnecting transaxle cooler lines, plug or cover ends of lines to prevent entry of dirt or foreign material.

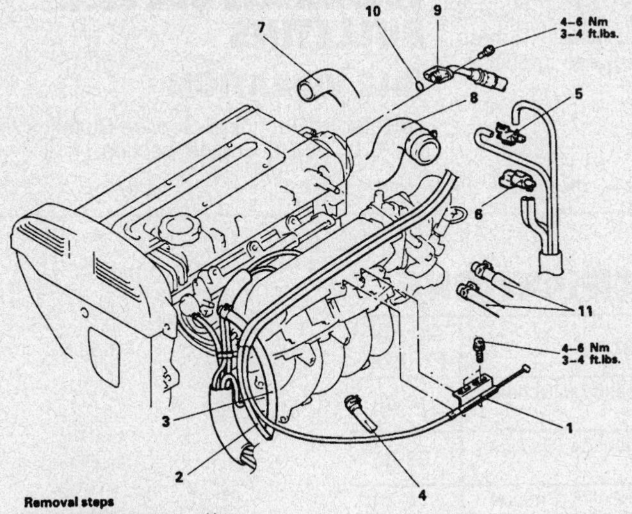
4-6 Nm
3-4 ft.lbs.
4-6 Nm
3-4 ft.lbs.

Removal steps

1. Connection for accelerator cable or throttle cable
2. Connection for throttle cable (Auto-cruise control)
3. Connection for fuel return hose
4. Connection for brake booster vacuum hose
5. Connection for fuel pressure solenoid valve (Turbo)
6. Connection for EGR solenoid valve (Turbo: California)
7. Connection for air hose A (Turbo)
8. Connection for air hose D (Turbo)
9. Connection for fuel high pressure hose
10. O-ring
11. Connection for heater hoses

MT1069100216010X

Fig. 1 Engine assembly (Part 1 of 3)

<From 1991 models>

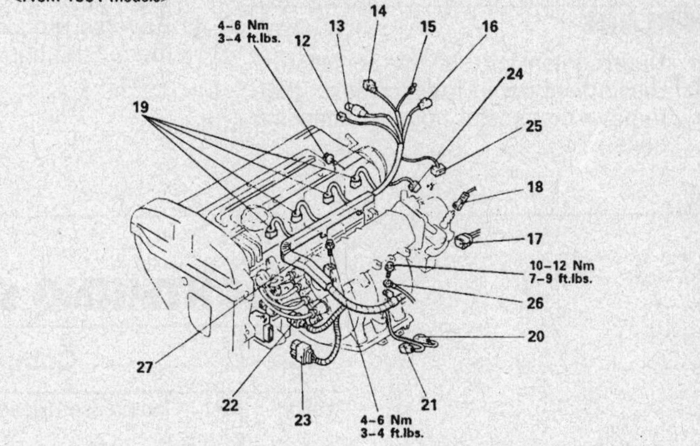
4-6 Nm
3-4 ft.lbs.
10-12 Nm
7-9 ft.lbs.
4-6 Nm
3-4 ft.lbs.

12. Connection for engine coolant temperature switch
13. Connection for oxygen sensor
14. Connection for engine coolant temperature sensor
15. Connection for engine coolant temperature gauge unit
16. Connection for engine coolant temperature switch (for air conditioner)
17. Connection for ISC motor
18. Connection for idle switch
19. Connection for fuel injectors
20. Connection for EGR temperature sensor (California vehicles only)
21. Connection for detonation sensor (Turbo)
22. Connection for ignition coil
23. Connection for power transistor
24. Connection for throttle position sensor
25. Connection for crank angle sensor
26. Connection for ground cable
27. Control wiring harness

MT1069100216020X

Fig. 1 Engine assembly (Part 2 of 3)

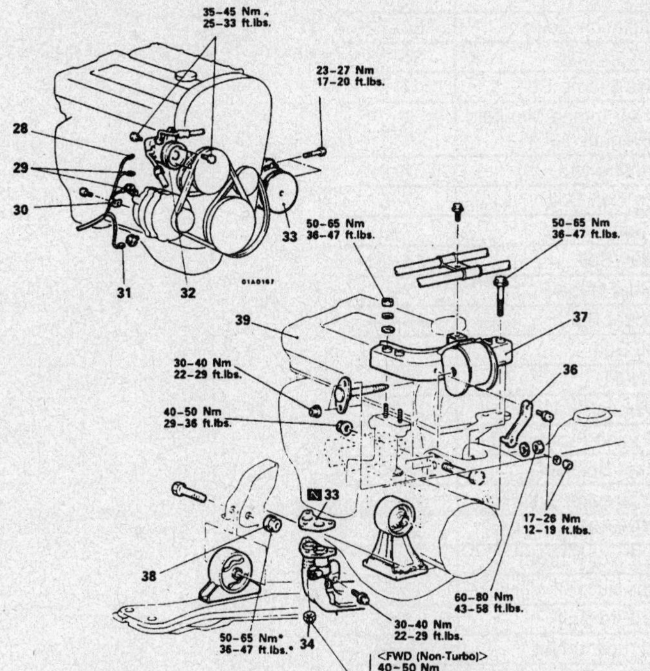
35-45 Nm
25-33 ft.lbs.
23-27 Nm
17-20 ft.lbs.
50-65 Nm
36-47 ft.lbs.
50-65 Nm
36-47 ft.lbs.
30-40 Nm
22-29 ft.lbs.
40-50 Nm
29-36 ft.lbs.
17-26 Nm
12-19 ft.lbs.
60-80 Nm
43-58 ft.lbs.
30-40 Nm
22-29 ft.lbs.
50-65 Nm*
36-47 ft.lbs.*
<FWD (Non-Turbo)>
40-50 Nm
29-36 ft.lbs.
<AWD (Non-Turbo)>
30-40 Nm
22-29 ft.lbs.
<Turbo>
40-60 Nm
29-43 ft.lbs.

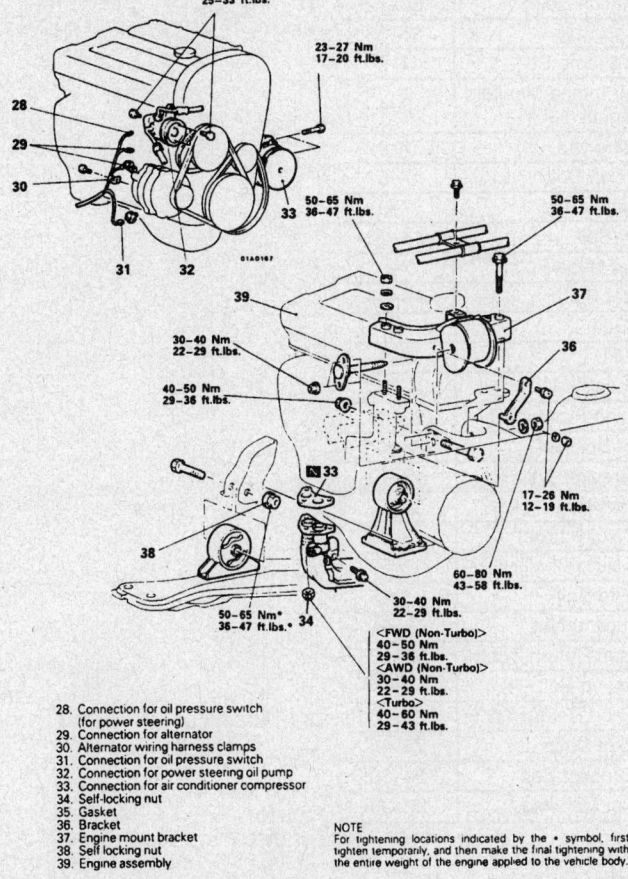

28. Connection for oil pressure switch (for power steering)
29. Connection for alternator
30. Alternator wiring harness clamps
31. Connection for oil pressure switch
32. Connection for power steering oil pump
33. Connection for air conditioner compressor
34. Self-locking nut
35. Gasket
36. Bracket
37. Engine mount bracket
38. Self locking nut
39. Engine assembly

NOTE
For tightening locations indicated by the • symbol, first tighten temporarily, and then make the final tightening with the entire weight of the engine applied to the vehicle body.

MT1069100216030X

Fig. 1 Engine assembly (Part 3 of 3)

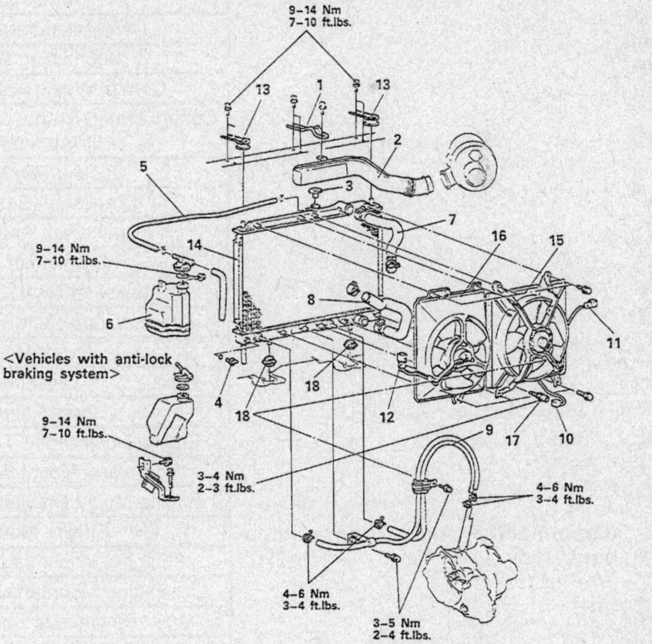
9-14 Nm
7-10 ft.lbs.
9-14 Nm
7-10 ft.lbs.
<Vehicles with anti-lock braking system>
9-14 Nm
7-10 ft.lbs.
3-4 Nm
2-3 ft.lbs.
4-6 Nm
3-4 ft.lbs.
4-6 Nm
3-4 ft.lbs.
3-5 Nm
2-4 ft.lbs.

Removal steps

1. Branch tube bracket <Non-Turbo>
2. Branch tube <Non-Turbo>
3. Radiator cap
4. Drain plug
5. Overflow tube
6. Reserve tank
7. Radiator upper hose
8. Radiator lower hose
9. Automatic transaxle oil cooler hoses <Vehicles with A/T>
10. Thermo sensor connector
11. Radiator fan motor connector
12. Condenser fan motor connector <Non-Turbo (FWD, AWD–M/T)–Vehicles with air conditioner>
13. Upper insulator
14. Radiator assembly
15. Radiator fan motor assembly
16. Condenser fan motor assembly <Non-Turbo (FWD, AWD–M/T)–Vehicles with air conditioner>
17. Thermo sensor
18. Lower insulator

MT1069100215000X

Fig. 2 Radiator assembly

THERMOSTAT

REPLACE

1. Drain coolant into suitable container.
2. Disconnect upper radiator hose, then remove thermostat housing attaching bolts.
3. Remove thermostat housing, then thermostat.
4. Reverse procedure to install. Tighten thermostat housing bolts to specifications.

TECHNICAL SERVICE BULLETINS

IDLE VIBRATION

Refer to "Technical Service Bulletins" in the "2.0L SOHC Engine" section.

TIGHTENING SPECIFICATIONS

Year	Component	Torque/ Ft. Lbs.
1993	A/C Compressor Pipe Connection (Discharge Side)	14–18
	A/C Compressor Pipe Connection (Suction Side)	22–25
	A/C Compressor Tensioner Pulley Bracket	17–20
	A/C Compressor To Bracket	17–20
	Accelerator Cable Adjusting Bolt	3–4
	Air Cleaner Body Bolt	6–7
	Air Cleaner Body/Resonator Assembly	6–7
	Air Cleaner Mounting Nut	12–14
	Auto Tensioner	14–20
	Branch Tube Bolt	6–7
	Camshaft Bearing Cap Bolt	④
	Camshaft Sprocket	58–72
	Center Bearing Bracket	26–33
	Center Cover Bolt	2–3
	Centermember Installation Bolt	58–72
	Connecting Rod Cap Bolt	36–38
	Control Wiring Harness Clamp Bolt	7–9
	Control Wiring Harness To Air Intake Manifold Or Air Intake Plenum	3–4
	Cooling Fan Mounting Nut	7–9
	Crankshaft Bearing Cap Bolt	47–51
	Crankshaft Angle Sensor Nut	7–9
	Crankshaft Pulley Bolt	14–22
	Crankshaft Rear Oil Seal Case Bolt	7–9
	Crankshaft Sprocket Bolt	80–94
	Cylinder Head Bolt	②
	Distributor Nut	7–9
	Driveplate/Flywheel	94–101
	Engine Cooler Pipe To Engine Front Case	29–33
	Engine Mount Bracket Bolt/Nut	36–47
	Engine Mount Bracket To Bracket Bolt/Nut	12–19
	Engine Mount Bracket	36–51
	Engine Mount Insulator Nut (Large)	43–58
	Engine Mount Insulator Nut (Small)	22–29
	Engine Oil Cooler Eye Bolt	22–25
	Engine Oil Cooler Mounting Nut	6–9
	Engine Oil Feed Hose To Feed/Return Tube	29–36
	Engine Oil Hose Mounting Bolt	2–4
	Engine Oil Return Hose To Feed/Return Tube	29–36
	Engine Support Bracket Bolts	29–36
	Exhaust Pipe Support Bracket Bolt	22–30
	Exhaust Pipe To Exhaust Manifold	22–29

Continued

TIGHTENING SPECIFICATIONS—Continued

Year	Component	Torque/ Ft. Lbs.
1993	Exhaust Pipe To Rubber Hanger	7–11
	Eye Bolt (Oil Filter Bracket Side)	2–4
	Feed/Return Tube To Oil Filter Bracket	29–33
	Front Case Bolts	③
	Front Engine Mounting Insulator To Engine	9–14
	Front Engine Mounting Insulator/Insulator Stopper To Engine Mounting Bracket	22–29
	Front Engine Support Bracket Bolt	36–51
	Front Exhaust Pipe Clamp Bolt	22–29
	Front Exhaust Pipe To Engine	22–29
	Front Insulator Stopper To Heat Protector	6–9
	Front Roll Stopper Bracket Bolt	40–54
	Front Roll Stopper Bracket To Centermember	29–36
	Fuel High Pressure Hose To Delivery Pipe	3–4
	Ground Cable To Intake Manifold	7–9
	Heat Protector To Exhaust Manifold	9–11
	Intake Manifold Bolts	11–14
	Intake Manifold Stay Bolt	18–22
	Left Engine Support Bracket Bolt	22–30
	Left Member Installation Bolt (Front)	58–72
	Left Member Installation Bolt (Rear)	51–58
	No. 2 Crossmember To Frame	29–36
	Oil Filter Bracket Bolt	11–16
	Oil Pan Bolts	4–6
	Oil Pan Drain Plug	25–33
	Oil Pan Nuts	3.5–5.0
	Oil Pressure Gauge Unit	6–9
	Oil Pressure Switch	6–9
	Oil Pump Cover Bolt	11–13
	Oil Pump Driven Gear Bolt	25–29
	Oil Pump Sprocket Nut	36–43
	Oil Return Pipe To Oil Pan	6–7
	Oil Screen Bolt/Nut	11–16
	Plug Case	14–20
	Power Steering Oil Pipe Connecting Nut	12–19
	Power Steering Oil Pump Mounting Bolt	18–24
	Power Steering Oil Pump To Bracket	25–33
	Radiator Mounting Bolt	6–8
	Radiator Shroud Mounting Bolt	2–4
	Rear Engine Mounting Insulator To No. 2 Crossmember	9–14
	Rear Engine Mounting Insulator To Transmission	14–17
	Rear Roll Stopper Bracket Bolt	80–94
	Rear Roll Stopper Bracket To Centermember	29–36
	Rear Roll Stopper Insulator	29–36
	Relief Plug	29–36
	Rocker Arm/Shaft Assembly Bolt (Large)	14–15
	Rocker Arm/Shaft Assembly Bolt (Small)	14–20
	Rocker Cover Bolt	2–3
	Silent Shaft Sprocket	31–35
	Thermostat Housing Bolts	12–14
	Throttle Body Stay	11–16
	Timing Belt Front Cover	7–9

Continued

TIGHTENING SPECIFICATIONS—Continued

Year	Component	Torque/ Ft. Lbs.
1993	Timing Belt Idle Pulley Bolt	25–30
	Timing Belt Rear Left Cover (Lower)①	22–30
	Timing Belt Rear Left Cover (Upper)	7–9
	Timing Belt Rear Right Cover	7–9
	Timing Belt Tensioner Pulley Bolt	31–40
	Timing Belt Tensioner Spacer	31–40
	Timing Belt "B" Tensioner Bolt	11–16
	Transaxle Mount Bracket To Body	29–36
	Transaxle Mount Insulator	43–58
	Water Pipe To Engine	10–14
	Water Pump Pulley Bolt	6–7

① — Also attaches to left engine support bracket.
② — With engine cold, 65–72 ft. lbs.; w/engine warm, 72–80 ft. lbs.
③ — Except 0.12 inch (30 mm) long bolts, 14–20 ft. lbs.; 0.12 inch (30 mm) long bolts, 20–25 ft. lbs.
④ — 8 X 25 bolts, 15–19 ft. lbs.; 8 X 65 bolts, 14–15 ft. lbs.

2.4L Engine

NOTE: On Air Bag Equipped Models, Refer To "Air Bag System Precautions" Located In The Front Of This Manual For System Disarming & Arming Procedures.

INDEX

	Page No.
Belt Tension Data	26-44
Camshaft, Replace	26-43
DOHC Engine	26-43
SOHC Engine	26-43
Compression Pressures	26-38
Cooling System Bleed	26-44
Crankshaft Rear Oil Seal, Replace	26-44
Crankshaft Seal, Replace	26-44
Cylinder Head, Replace	26-39
DOHC Engine	26-38
SOHC Engine	26-39
Engine Mount, Replace	26-38
Engine	26-38
Roll Stopper & Center Member	26-39
Transaxle	26-39
Engine Rebuilding Specifications	29-1
Engine, Replace	26-39
Exhaust Manifold, Replace	26-39
Fuel Filter, Replace	26-47
Fuel Pump, Replace	26-47
Hydraulic Lash Adjusters	26-40
Intake Manifold, Replace	26-39
Oil Pan, Replace	26-44
Precautions	26-38
Air Bag Systems	26-38
Fuel System Pressure Relief	26-38
Radiator, Replace	26-47
Rocker Arms, Replace	26-41
Technical Service Bulletins	26-48
Idle Vibration	26-48
Thermostat, Replace	26-44
Tightening Specifications	26-52
Timing Belt, Replace	26-41
DOHC Engine	26-42
SOHC Engine	26-41
Valve Adjustment	26-40
Valve Clearance Specifications	26-40
Water Pump, Replace	26-47

PRECAUTIONS

AIR BAG SYSTEMS

Refer to "Air Bag System Precautions" in the front of this manual for system disarming and arming procedures.

FUEL SYSTEM PRESSURE RELIEF

When service to any component necessitates working with the fuel system, fuel pressure in the system must be relieved. This is extremely important to reduce risk of personal injury, fire or explosion due to fuel spray and leakage. Relieve fuel system pressure as follows:

1. Remove rear seat cushion, then disconnect fuel pump wiring harness from floor wiring harness.
2. Start engine and allow all residual fuel in system to be consumed; when engine stalls, turn ignition switch to Off position.
3. Connect fuel pump wiring harness to floor wiring harness and install rear seat cushion, then continue with service.

COMPRESSION PRESSURES

Ensure engine oil, starter motor and battery are in satisfactory condition. When checking compression, engine coolant should be at normal operating temperature, spark plugs should be removed and throttle valve should be wide open. Minimum compression pressures at engine cranking speed is 145 psi on SOHC engines and 157 psi on DOHC engines. Difference between cylinders should not exceed 14 psi.

ENGINE MOUNT

REPLACE

ENGINE

1. Relieve fuel system pressure as outlined under "Precautions."
2. Using a suitable lifting device, raise engine and transaxle assembly slightly to alleviate pressure on engine mount.

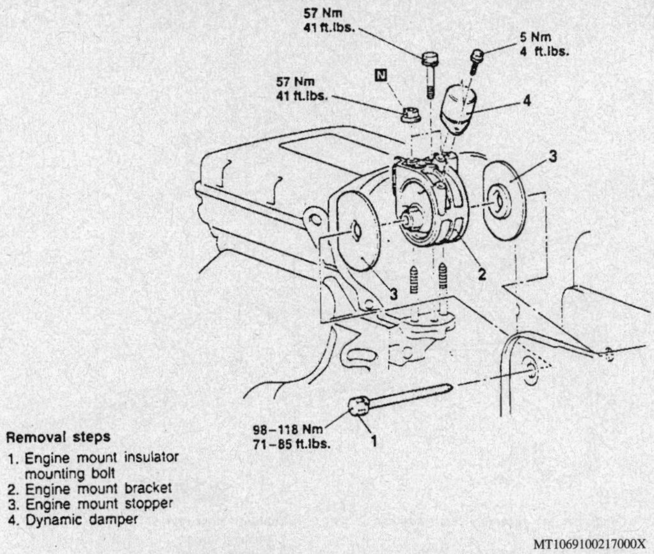
57 Nm
41 ft.lbs.
5 Nm
4 ft.lbs.
57 Nm
41 ft.lbs.
N
4
3
2
3
98–118 Nm
71–85 ft.lbs.
1
Removal steps
1. Engine mount insulator mounting bolt
2. Engine mount bracket
3. Engine mount stopper
4. Dynamic damper
MT1069100217000X

Fig. 1 Engine mount replacement

3. Remove engine mount in numbered sequence shown in **Fig. 1.**
4. Reverse procedure to install, noting the following:
   a. Position engine mount stopper as shown, **Fig. 2.**
   b. Tighten all bolts and nuts to specifications.

TRANSAXLE

1. Relieve fuel system pressure as outlined under "Precautions," then remove air cleaner assembly.
2. Using a suitable lifting device, raise engine and transaxle assembly slightly to alleviate pressure on transaxle mount.
3. Remove transaxle mount in numbered sequence shown in **Fig. 3.**
4. Reverse procedure to install. Tighten all bolts and nuts to specifications.

ROLL STOPPER & CENTER MEMBER

1. Relieve fuel system pressure as outlined under "Precautions."
2. Remove roll stopper and center member in numbered sequence shown in **Fig. 4.**
3. Reverse procedure to install. Tighten all bolts and nuts to specifications.

ENGINE

REPLACE

1. Relieve fuel system pressure as outlined under "Precautions," then scribe and remove hood.
2. Drain engine coolant into a suitable container, then remove transaxle as outlined under "Transaxle, Replace" in "Clutch & Manual Transaxle" or "Automatic Transaxle " section.
3. Remove radiator as outlined under "Radiator, Replace, " then the engine lower cover.
4. Remove engine assembly in numbered sequence shown in **Figs. 5 and 6,** noting the following:
   a. When removing power steering pump and A/C compressor, leave hoses attached and support aside.
   b. Ensure engine is supported when transaxle is removed. A block of wood placed between oil pan and a floor jack will suffice until a suitable engine lifting device can be installed.
5. Reverse procedure to install. Tighten all engine mounting bolts and nuts to specifications.

INTAKE MANIFOLD

REPLACE

1. Relieve fuel system pressure as outlined under "Precautions," then drain engine coolant into a suitable container.
2. Remove intake manifold in numbered sequence shown, **Figs. 7 and 8,** then inspect cylinder head mating surface for distortion using a straightedge and a feeler gauge. Distortion must be below .008 inch.
3. Reverse procedure to install. Tighten all bolts and nuts to specifications.

EXHAUST MANIFOLD

REPLACE

1. Relieve fuel system pressure as outlined under "Precautions."
2. Remove exhaust manifold in numbered sequence shown, **Fig. 9.**
3. Reverse procedure to install. Tighten all bolts and nuts to specifications.

CYLINDER HEAD

REPLACE

SOHC ENGINE

1. Relieve fuel system pressure as outlined under "Precautions," then drain engine coolant into a suitable container.
2. Drain engine oil into a suitable container and remove air intake hose.

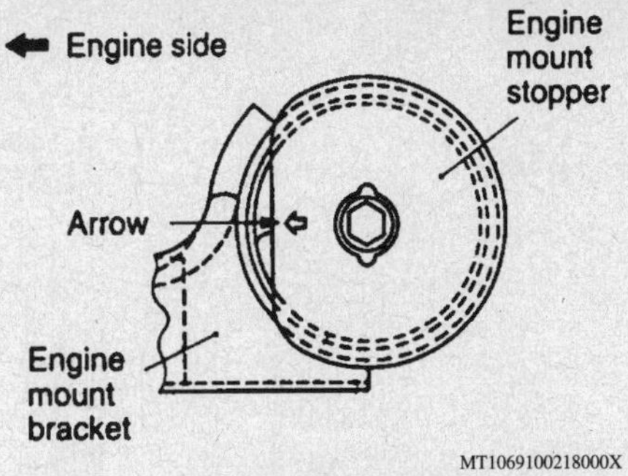
Engine side
Engine mount stopper
Arrow
Engine mount bracket
MT1069100218000X

Fig. 2 Engine mount stopper position

3. Remove cylinder head and gasket in numbered sequence shown in **Fig. 10,** noting the following:
   a. When removing camshaft sprocket, rotate crankshaft in direction of normal rotation until timing marks align, then secure timing belt to sprocket as shown in **Fig. 11** to maintain relative position of sprocket to belt.
   b. Remove sprocket with timing belt attached using special tools as shown, **Fig. 12. Do not rotate crankshaft with camshaft sprocket removed.**
   c. Loosen cylinder head bolts in two or three steps using loosening sequence shown, **Fig. 13. Avoid damaging plug guides during bolt removal.**
4. Reverse procedure to install, noting the following:
   a. Install cylinder head gasket as shown, **Fig. 14.**
   b. Before installing cylinder head bolts, measure length of each. Distance from bottom of bolt head to bottom of bolt should be 3.91 inches. Replace bolts if not within specification.
   c. Using sequence shown in **Fig. 15, torque** cylinder head bolts to 58 ft. lbs., then fully loosen bolts in sequence as shown in **Fig. 13.** Using tightening sequence shown in **Fig. 15,** tighten bolts in three steps; first step, **torque** bolts to 15 ft. lbs.; second step, ¼ turn; third step, an additional ¼ turn.

DOHC ENGINE

1. Relieve fuel system pressure as outlined under "Precautions," then drain engine coolant into a suitable container.
2. Drain engine oil into a suitable container and remove air intake hose, then remove timing belt upper cover and timing belt as outlined under "Timing Belt, Replace."
3. Remove cylinder head and gasket in numbered sequence shown, **Fig. 16.** Loosen cylinder head bolts in two or three steps using loosening sequence shown, **Fig. 17.**
4. Reverse procedure to install, noting the following:
   a. Position new gasket on block with

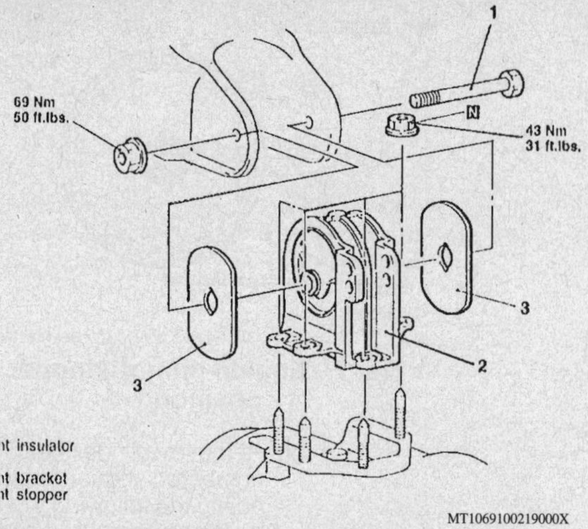
69 Nm
50 ft.lbs.
43 Nm
31 ft.lbs.
1
2
3

Removal steps
1. Transaxle mount insulator mounting bolt
2. Transaxle mount bracket
3. Transaxle mount stopper

MT1069100219000X

Fig. 3 Transaxle mount replacement

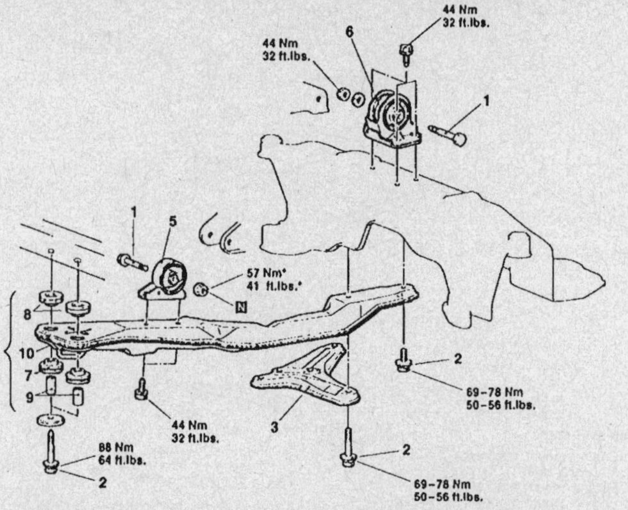
44 Nm
32 ft.lbs.
44 Nm
32 ft.lbs.
57 Nm*
41 ft.lbs.*
44 Nm
32 ft.lbs.
88 Nm
64 ft.lbs.
69-78 Nm
50-56 ft.lbs.
69-78 Nm
50-56 ft.lbs.

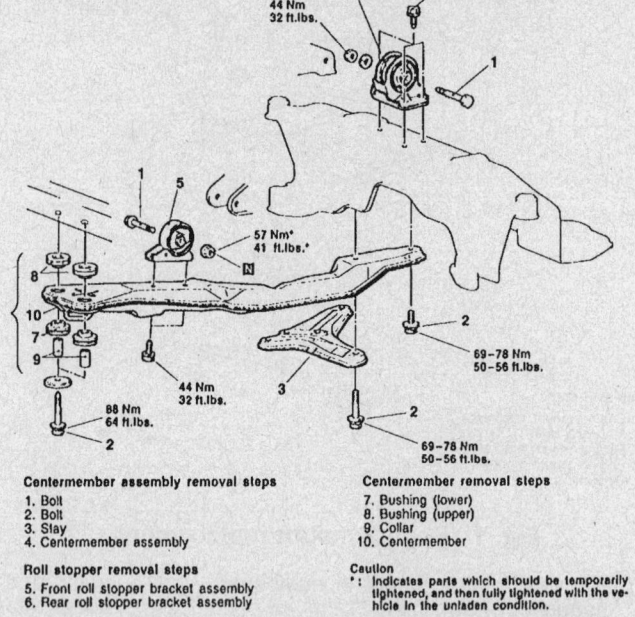

Centermember assembly removal steps
1. Bolt
2. Bolt
3. Stay
4. Centermember assembly

Roll stopper removal steps
5. Front roll stopper bracket assembly
6. Rear roll stopper bracket assembly

Centermember removal steps
7. Bushing (lower)
8. Bushing (upper)
9. Collar
10. Centermember

Caution
*: Indicates parts which should be temporarily tightened, and then fully tightened with the vehicle in the unladen condition.

MT1069100220000X

Fig. 4 Engine roll stopper & center member replacement

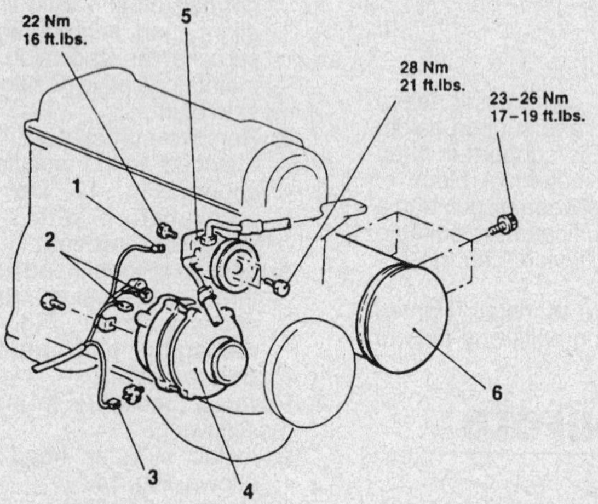
22 Nm
16 ft.lbs.
28 Nm
21 ft.lbs.
23-26 Nm
17-19 ft.lbs.

Removal steps
1. Power steering pressure switch connector
2. Genetator harness
3. Oil pressure switch connector
4. Genetator
5. Connection for power steering pump
6. Connection for A/C compressor

MT1069100221010X

Fig. 5 Engine assembly replacement (Part 1 of 3). SOHC engine

identification mark facing up, **Fig. 18.**

b. Before installing cylinder head bolts, measure length of each. Distance from bottom of bolt head to bottom of bolt should be 3.91 inches. Replace bolts if not within specification.
c. Using sequence shown in **Fig. 15, torque** cylinder head bolts to 58 ft. lbs., then fully loosen bolts by reversing tightening sequence. Using tightening sequence shown in **Fig. 15,** tighten bolts in three steps; first step, **torque** bolts to 15 ft. lbs.; second step, ¼ turn (90°); third step, an additional ¼ turn (90°).

VALVE CLEARANCE SPECIFICATIONS

Because this engine uses hydraulic valve lash adjusters, no adjustments are required

VALVE ADJUSTMENT

Because this engine uses hydraulic valve lash adjusters, no adjustments are required. If an abnormal rattling noise is heard from the lash adjusters refer to "Hydraulic Lash Adjusters" for testing and repair procedures.

HYDRAULIC LASH ADJUSTERS

Any air entering the high pressure chamber of the hydraulic lash adjuster can cause the adjuster to make a rattling noise. Use the following procedure to check and replace adjuster.

1. Check engine oil for any of the following conditions:
   a. If oil level is low, air will be sucked in from the oil strainer and will mix in the oil passage.
   b. If oil level is excessive, oil will be stirred by the crankshaft, causing a large amount of air mix in the oil.
   c. If oil is deteriorated, it will not easily separate from air and amount of air mixed in oil will increase.
2. If engine oil exhibits any of the above conditions, add or change engine oil as necessary.
3. Start engine and gently accelerate several times. If rattling noise stops, air is bled from high pressure chamber and adjuster is operating normally. If rattling noise does not stop, check lash adjusters as follows:
   a. Stop engine and remove rocker arm cover.
   b. Set No. 1 piston to top dead center of compression stroke.
   c. Push rocker arm as indicated in **Fig. 19.**
   d. Slowly rotate crankshaft 360° and push rocker arms indicated in **Fig. 20.**
   e. If rocker arm can be pushed easily, lash adjuster either has air in high pressure chamber or it is defective and should be replaced.

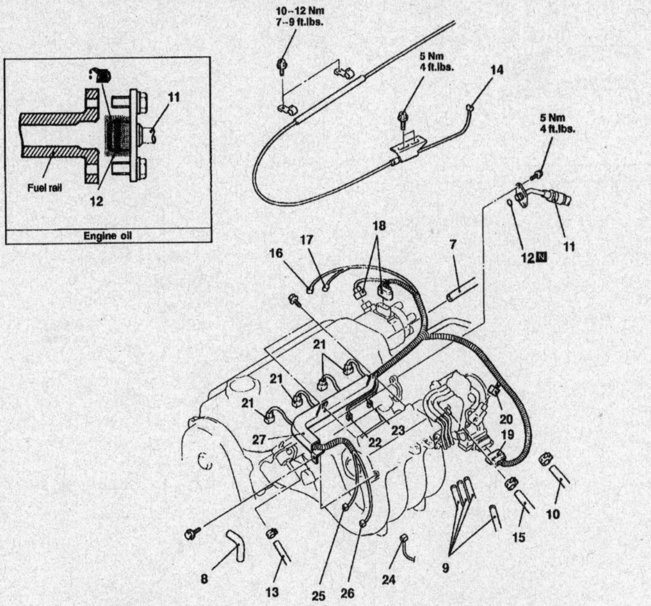
10–12 Nm
7–9 ft.lbs.
5 Nm
4 ft.lbs.
14
5 Nm
4 ft.lbs.
11
Fuel rail
12
Engine oil
18
17
16
7
12
11
21
21
21
20
19
27
22
23
10
15
8
13
25
26
24
9

7. Breather hose connection
8. PCV hose
9. Vacuum hose connection
10. Water hose connection
11. Fuel high-pressure hose connection
12. O-ring
13. Fuel return hose connection
14. Accelerator cable connection
15. Brake booster vacuum hose connection
16. Engine coolant temperature gauge unit connector
17. Engine coolant temperature sensor connector
18. Distributor connector
19. Idle speed control motor connector
20. Throttle position sensor connector
21. Injector connectors
22. Control wiring harness and heated oxygen sensor wiring harness connection
23. EGR temperature sensor connector
24. Heated oxygen sensor connector
25. Condenser connector
26. Refrigerant temperature switch connector
27. Control harness

MT1069100221020X

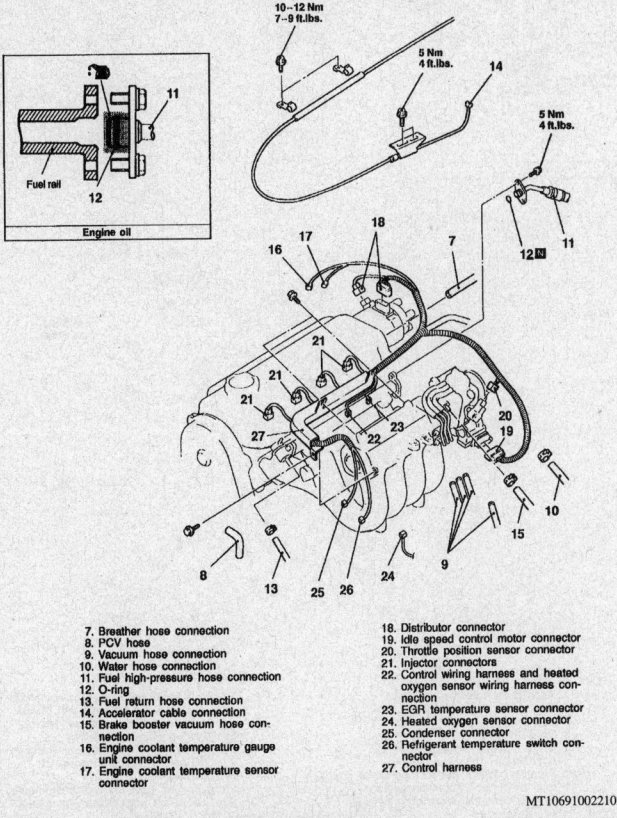

Fig. 5 Engine assembly replacement (Part 2 of 3). SOHC engine

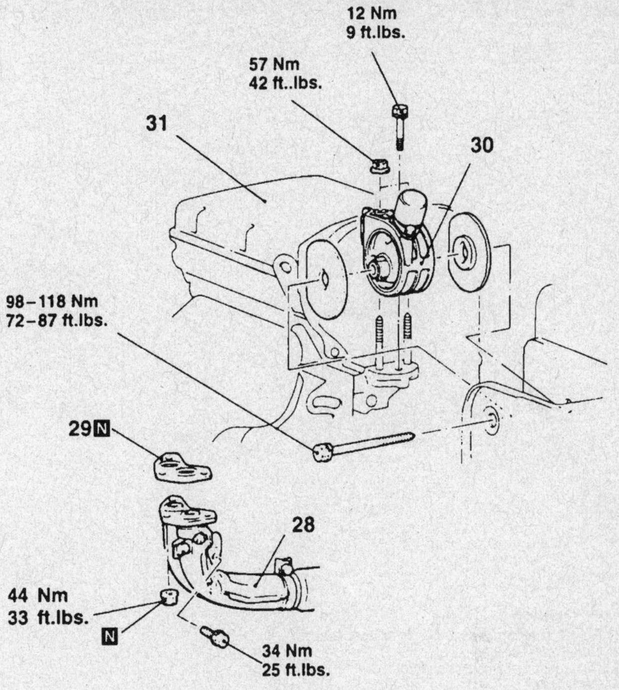
12 Nm
9 ft.lbs.
57 Nm
42 ft..lbs.
31
30
98–118 Nm
72–87 ft.lbs.
29
28
44 Nm
33 ft.lbs.
34 Nm
25 ft.lbs.

28. Front exhaust pipe connection
29. Gasket
30. Engine mount bracket
31. Engine assembly

MT1069100221030X

Fig. 5 Engine assembly replacement (Part 3 of 3). SOHC engine

4. To determine if the lash adjuster is defective, proceed as follows:
   a. Remove rocker arms as outlined under "Rocker Arms, Replace."
   b. Immerse lash adjuster in clean diesel fuel.
   c. Using a small wire, lightly push down inner steel ball four or five times, **Fig. 21.**
   d. Remove small wire and press plunger. If plunger is hard to press in, adjuster is normal. If plunger is easy to push in, lash adjuster is defective and must be replaced. **After air bleeding is complete, hold lash adjuster upright to prevent inside diesel fuel from spilling.**
   e. Air must be bled from new hydraulic lash adjusters prior to installation.

ROCKER ARMS

REPLACE

Refer to "Camshaft, Replace" for rocker arm replacement procedure.

TIMING BELT

REPLACE

SOHC ENGINE

1. Relieve fuel system pressure as outlined under "Precautions," then remove engine lower cover.
2. Remove timing belt in numbered sequence shown, **Fig. 22,** noting the following:
   a. When removing belt, turn crankshaft in direction of normal rotation to align timing marks, then loosen tensioner pulley center bolt and move pulley toward water pump.
   b. If timing belt is to be reused, mark direction of rotation for installation reference.
3. Remove timing belt "B" in numbered sequence shown, **Fig. 23,** noting the following:
   a. When removing crankshaft sprocket, secure flywheel or driveplate with holding tool No. MD998781, or equivalent, then use sprocket removal tool No. MD998778, or equivalent, to separate sprocket from shaft.
   b. If timing belt "B" is to be reused, mark direction of normal rotation on belt for installation reference.
4. Reverse procedure to install, noting the following:
   a. When installing timing belt "B," ensure crankshaft sprocket "B" timing mark and silent shaft sprocket timing mark are aligned, **Fig. 24,** then fit timing belt "B" over crankshaft sprocket "B" and silent shaft sprocket. There should be no slack in belt.
   b. To adjust timing belt "B" tension, temporarily secure tensioner such that center of pulley is offset from installation bolt as shown, **Fig. 25,** then attach tensioner pulley with flange toward front of engine. Hold tensioner up in direction of arrow, **Fig. 26,** then exert pressure on belt until tension side is taut. Tighten bolt to secure tensioner in place. **Do not allow tensioner pulley shaft to rotate with bolt.**
   c. Inspect timing belt "B" tension by pressing on belt at point A, **Fig. 25.** If deflection is not .20–.28 inch, adjust tension.
   d. When installing timing belt "B," ensure flange is installed as shown in **Fig. 27,**
   e. Before installing timing belt auto tensioner, use a vise to compress pushrod gently into cylinder until pin holes in cylinder and pushrod align, then insert set pin.
   f. When installing timing belt, align timing marks on camshaft, crankshaft and oil pump sprockets, then remove plug from cylinder block and insert suitable Phillips head screwdriver at least 2.36 inches into block, **Fig. 28,** to hold silent shaft in place. If screwdriver travels

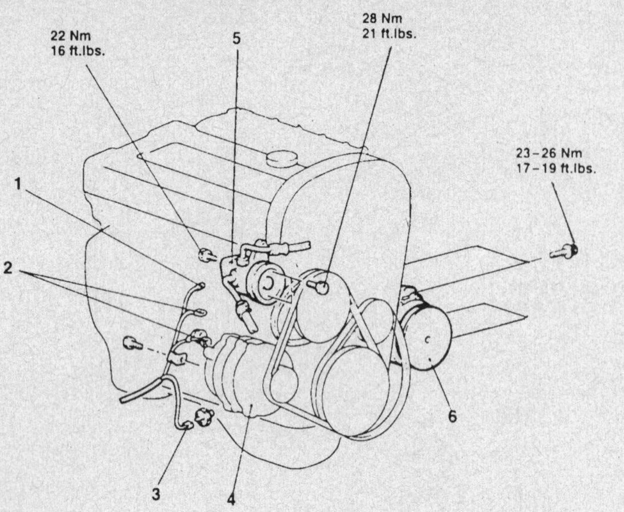
22 Nm
16 ft.lbs.
5
28 Nm
21 ft.lbs.
23–26 Nm
17–19 ft.lbs.
1
2
3
4
6

Removal steps
1. Power steering pressure switch connector
2. Generator harness
3. Oil pressure switch connector
4. Generator
5. Connection for power steering pump
6. Connection for A/C compressor

MT1069100222010X

Fig. 6 Engine assembly replacement (Part 1 of 3). DOHC engine

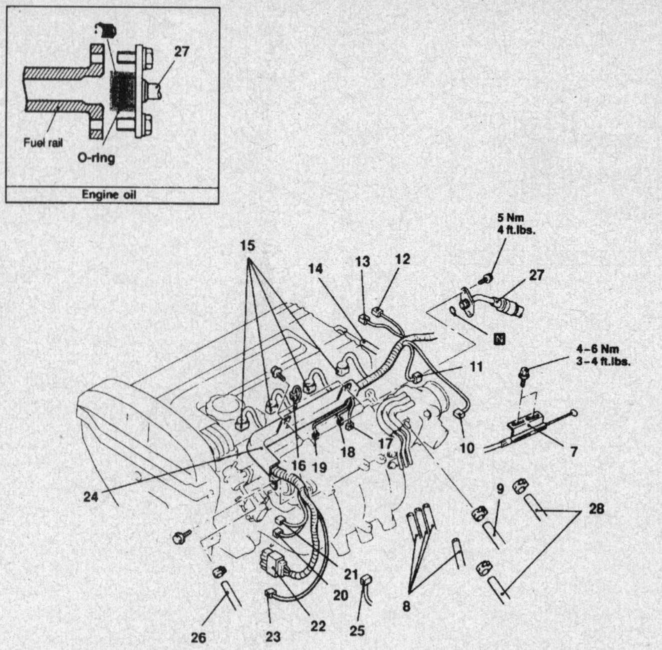
27
Fuel rail
O-ring
Engine oil
5 Nm
4 ft.lbs.
4–6 Nm
3–4 ft.lbs.
15
14
13
12
11
10
7
9
28
8
24
16
19
18
17
21
20
22
25
26
23

7. Accelerator cable connection
8. Vacuum hose
9. Brake booster vacuum hose connection
10. Throttle position sensor connector
11. Idle air control motor connector
12. Engine coolant temperature sensor connector
13. Engine coolant temperature gauge unit connector
14. Breather hose connection
15. Injector connectors
16. Ignition coil connector
17. EGR temperature sensor connector
18. Control wiring harness and oxygen sensor wiring harness connection
19. Knock sensor connector
20. Ignition power transistor connection
21. Refrigerant temperature switch connector
22. Camshaft position sensor connector
23. Crankshaft position sensor connector
24. Control wiring harness
25. Oxygen sensor connector
26. Fuel return hose connection
27. Fuel high-pressure hose connection
28. Heater hose connection

MT1069100222020X

Fig. 6 Engine assembly replacement (Part 2 of 3). DOHC engine

only .8–1 inch before contacting silent shaft, rotate sprocket once and realign timing mark, then insert screwdriver fully.

g. Position timing belt first over crankshaft sprocket, then over oil pump sprocket and, finally, over camshaft sprocket. There should be no slack in belt.
h. When preparing timing belt tensioner for belt tension adjustment, position tensioner pulley with pin holes at bottom, then press pulley against timing belt and tighten bolt only enough to secure pulley. Thread special tool through left engine support bracket as shown, **Fig. 29**, to exert pressure on tensioner pulley, then remove set pin and tighten center bolt to specifications. Remove tool.
i. To adjust timing belt tension, rotate crankshaft ¼ turn counterclockwise, then rotate clockwise until timing marks align. Loosen tensioner pulley bolt, then use tension adjustment tool No. MD998767, or equivalent, and a torque wrench to tighten bolt to specifications while applying 2.6 ft. lbs. of tension to belt. Finally, rotate crankshaft through two full clockwise revolutions, realign timing marks and measure auto tensioner protrusion as shown in **Fig. 30** (dimension "A") after leaving engine undisturbed for 15 minutes. If protrusion is not .150–.177 inch, repeat tension adjustment procedure.
j. When installing timing belt covers, refer to **Fig. 31** for proper bolt installation.

DOHC ENGINE

1. Relieve fuel system pressure as outlined under "Precautions," then remove engine lower cover.
2. Remove engine mount bracket as outlined under "Engine Mount, Replace," then remove timing belt in numbered sequence shown, **Fig. 32.**
3. Remove timing belt "B" in numbered sequence shown, **Fig. 33,** noting the following:
   a. When removing crankshaft sprocket, secure flywheel or driveplate with holding tool No. MD998781, or equivalent, then use sprocket removal tool No. MD998778, or equivalent, to separate sprocket from shaft.
   b. If timing belt "B" is to be reused, mark direction of normal rotation on belt for installation reference.
4. Reverse procedure to install, noting the following:
   a. When installing timing belt "B," ensure crankshaft sprocket "B" timing mark and silent shaft sprocket timing mark are aligned, **Fig. 24,** then fit timing belt "B" over crankshaft sprocket "B" and silent shaft sprocket. There should be no slack in belt.
   b. To adjust timing belt "B" tension, temporarily secure tensioner such that center of pulley is offset from installation bolt as shown, **Fig. 25,** then attach tensioner pulley with flange toward front of engine. Hold tensioner up in direction of arrow, **Fig. 26,** then exert pressure on belt until tension side is taut. Tighten bolt to secure tensioner in place. **Do not allow tensioner pulley shaft to rotate with bolt.**
   c. Inspect timing belt "B" tension by pressing on belt at point A, **Fig. 25.** If deflection is not .20–.28 inch, adjust tension.
   d. Ensure flange is installed as shown, **Fig. 27,** when installing timing belt "B."
   e. Before installing timing belt auto tensioner, use a vise to compress pushrod gently into cylinder until pin holes in cylinder and pushrod align, then insert set pin.
   f. When installing timing belt, align timing marks on camshaft, crankshaft and oil pump sprockets, then remove plug from cylinder block and insert suitable Phillips head screwdriver at least 2.36 inches into block, **Fig. 28,** to hold silent shaft in place. If screwdriver travels only .8–1 inch before contacting silent shaft, rotate sprocket once and realign timing mark, then insert screwdriver fully.

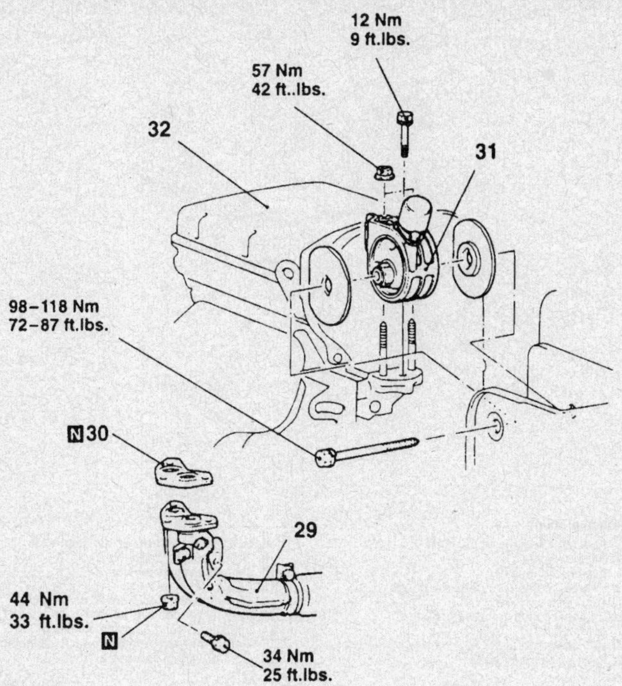
12 Nm
9 ft.lbs.
57 Nm
42 ft..lbs.
32
31
98–118 Nm
72–87 ft.lbs.
N 30
29
44 Nm
33 ft.lbs.
N
34 Nm
25 ft.lbs.

29. Front exhaust pipe connection
30. Gasket
31. Engine mount bracket
32. Engine assembly

MT1069100222030X

Fig. 6 Engine assembly replacement (Part 3 of 3). DOHC engine

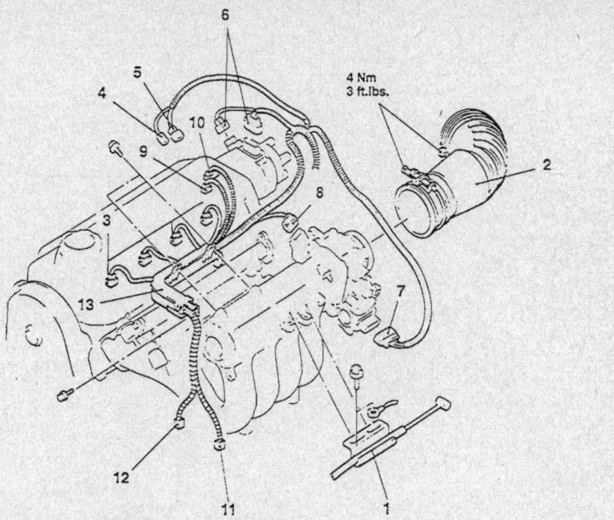
6
5
4
10
9
4 Nm
3 ft.lbs.
2
8
3
7
13
12
11
1

Removal steps
1. Accelerator cable connection
2. Air intake hose
3. Injector connector
4. Engine coolant temperature gauge connector
5. Engine coolant temperature sensor connector
6. Distributor connector
7. IAC connector
8. TPS connector
9. EGR temperature sensor connector
10. Heated oxygen sensor connector
11. Refrigerant temperature switch connector
12. Condenser connector
13. Control wiring harness

MT1059100023010X

Fig. 7 Intake manifold replacement (Part 1 of 2). SOHC engine

g. Install timing belt first over intake side camshaft sprocket, then over exhaust side camshaft sprocket and secure temporarily with binder clips as shown, **Fig. 34.** Align timing marks with cylinder head top surface, then position belt over idler pulley, crankshaft sprocket and, finally, over tensioner pulley.
h. When preparing timing belt tensioner for belt tension adjustment, position tensioner pulley with pin holes at bottom, then press pulley against timing belt and tighten bolt only enough to secure pulley. Thread special tool through left engine support bracket as shown, **Fig. 29,** to exert pressure on tensioner pulley, then remove set pin and tighten center bolt to specifications. Remove tool.
i. To adjust timing belt tension, rotate crankshaft ¼ turn counterclockwise, then rotate clockwise until timing marks align. Loosen tensioner pulley bolt, then use tension adjustment tool No. MD998767, or equivalent, and a torque wrench to tighten bolt to specifications while applying 2.6 ft. lbs. of tension to belt. Finally, rotate crankshaft through two full clockwise revolutions, realign timing marks and measure auto tensioner protrusion as shown in **Fig. 30** (dimension "A") after leaving engine undisturbed for 15 minutes. If protrusion is not .150–.177 inch, repeat tension adjustment procedure.
j. When installing timing belt covers, refer to **Fig. 35** for proper bolt installation.

CAMSHAFT

REPLACE

SOHC ENGINE

1. Relieve fuel system pressure as outlined under "Precautions," then remove battery and timing belt upper cover.
2. Remove camshaft and oil seal in numbered sequence shown, **Fig. 36,** noting the following:
   a. Use special tools to remove camshaft sprocket as shown, **Fig. 12.**
   b. Before removing rocker arm and shaft assembly, install valve lash adjuster holder tools No. MD998443, or equivalent, to prevent adjusters from falling out.
3. Reverse procedure to install, noting the following:
   a. When installing rocker arm and shaft assembly, temporarily tighten rocker shaft with bolt to prevent arms on intake side from pushing valves. Ensure rocker shaft springs are at right angles to plug guides.
   b. Ensure rocker shaft notches are positioned as shown, **Fig. 37.**
   c. Use seal installation tool No. MD998713, or equivalent, to install camshaft oil seal. Apply clean engine oil to oil seal lip prior to installation.
   d. When installing distributor, rotate crankshaft until No. 1 cylinder reaches camshaft position on compression stroke, then align mating marks on distributor housing and coupling key. Ensure distributor mounting stud bolt is aligned with slot in distributor flange.
   e. Tighten all bolts and nuts to specifications; inspect and adjust ignition timing as necessary.

DOHC ENGINE

1. Relieve fuel system pressure as outlined under "Precautions," then remove timing belt upper cover.
2. Remove camshafts in numbered sequence shown, **Fig. 38.** Remove camshaft bearing cap bolts in two or three steps; it may be necessary to tap camshaft end with a plastic hammer to remove bearing caps.
3. Reverse procedure to install, noting the following:
   a. Ensure camshafts are installed in their original positions.
   b. Camshaft dowel pins should be positioned as shown, **Fig. 39.**
   c. Tighten camshaft bearing cap bolts

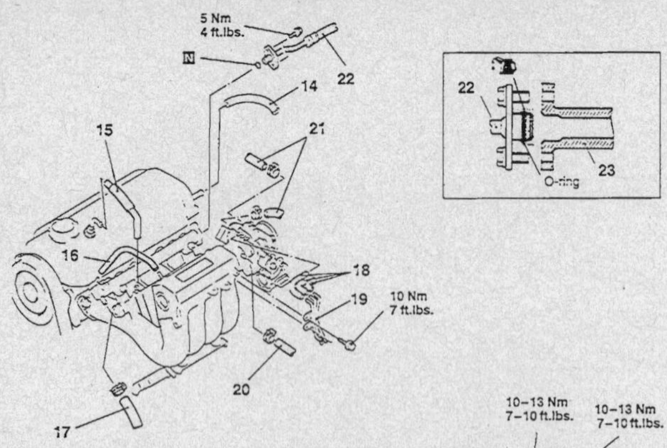
5 Nm
4 ft.lbs.
10 Nm
7 ft.lbs.
O-ring

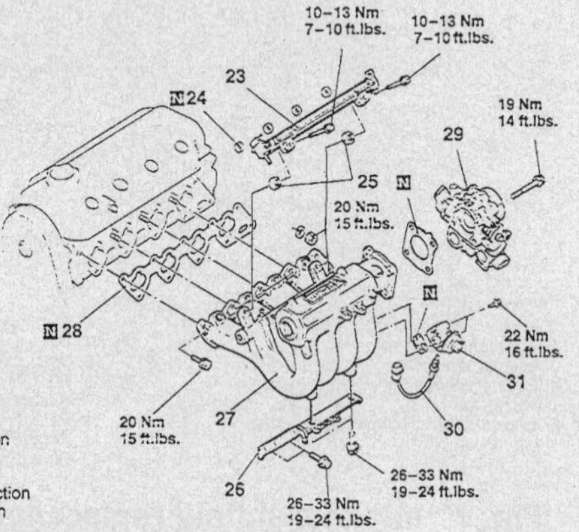
10–13 Nm
7–10 ft.lbs.
10–13 Nm
7–10 ft.lbs.
19 Nm
14 ft.lbs.
20 Nm
15 ft.lbs.
22 Nm
16 ft.lbs.
20 Nm
15 ft.lbs.
26–33 Nm
19–24 ft.lbs.
26–33 Nm
19–24 ft.lbs.

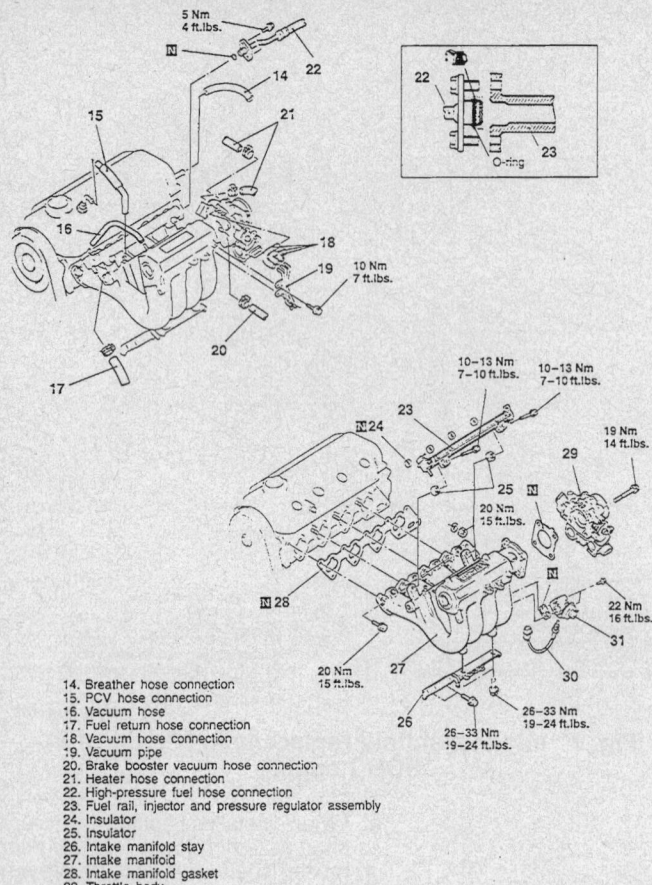

14. Breather hose connection
15. PCV hose connection
16. Vacuum hose
17. Fuel return hose connection
18. Vacuum hose connection
19. Vacuum pipe
20. Brake booster vacuum hose connection
21. Heater hose connection
22. High-pressure fuel hose connection
23. Fuel rail, injector and pressure regulator assembly
24. Insulator
25. Insulator
26. Intake manifold stay
27. Intake manifold
28. Intake manifold gasket
29. Throttle body
30. EGR temperature sensor
31. EGR valve

MT1059100023020X

Fig. 7 Intake manifold replacement (Part 2 of 2). SOHC engine

to specifications in two or three steps.

d. Install camshaft oil seals with seal installation tool No. MB998713, or equivalent.

CRANKSHAFT SEAL

REPLACE

1. Relieve fuel system pressure as outlined under "Precautions," then remove timing belt "B" as outlined under "Timing Belt, Replace."
2. Remove crankshaft front oil seal in numbered sequence shown, **Fig. 40.**
3. Reverse procedure to install. Apply clean engine oil to outer edge of seal lip before installation.

CRANKSHAFT REAR OIL SEAL

REPLACE

1. Relieve fuel system pressure as outlined under "Precautions," then remove transaxle as outlined in " Clutch & Manual Transaxle" or "Automatic Transaxle " section.
2. **On models with manual transaxle,** remove clutch cover and disc as outlined in "Clutch & Manual Transaxle " section.
3. **On all models,** remove oil pan as outlined under "Oil Pan, Replace."
4. Remove crankshaft rear oil seal in numbered sequence shown, **Fig. 41.**
5. Reverse procedure to install, noting the following:
   a. Apply clean engine oil to outer edge of seal lip.
   b. Use a suitable soft-faced hammer and seal installation tools No. MB990938 and MD998776, or equivalents, to install crankshaft rear oil seal.
   c. Tighten all bolts and nuts to specifications.

OIL PAN

REPLACE

1. Relieve fuel system pressure as outlined under "Precautions," then drain engine oil into a suitable container.
2. Remove dipstick tube and front exhaust pipe.
3. Remove oil pan and screen in numbered sequence shown, **Fig. 42.**

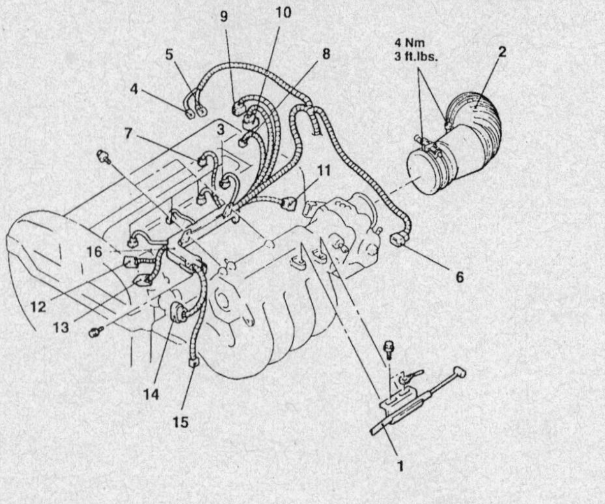
4 Nm
3 ft.lbs.

Removal steps

1. Accelerator cable connection
2. Air intake hose
3. Injector connector
4. Engine coolant temperature gauge connector
5. Engine coolant temperature sensor connector
6. IAC connector
7. Ignition coil connector
8. EGR temperature sensor connector
9. Knock sensor connector
10. Heated oxygen sensor
11. TPS connector
12. Camshaft position sensor connector
13. Crankshaft position sensor connector
14. Ignition power transistor connector
15. Refrigerant temperature switch connector
16. Control wiring harness

MT1059100024010X

Fig. 8 Intake manifold replacement (Part 1 of 2). DOHC engine

4. Reverse procedure to install.

BELT TENSION DATA

Belt	Deflection, Inch	
	New	Used
Alternator	.30–.35	.39
A/C	.22–.24	.26–.30
Power Steering	.18–.22	.24–.28

COOLING SYSTEM BLEED

This engine does not require a specified bleed procedure. After filling cooling system, start engine and remove radiator cap. Air will then be automatically bled through cap opening.

THERMOSTAT

REPLACE

1. Drain engine coolant into a suitable container, then disconnect lower radiator hose. **Mark hose position for installation reference.**
2. Remove water outlet fitting, then the thermostat.
3. Reverse procedure to install, noting the following:
   a. Ensure thermostat is installed with jiggle valve facing straight up and is aligned with mark on thermostat case.
   b. Tighten water outlet fitting bolts to specifications.

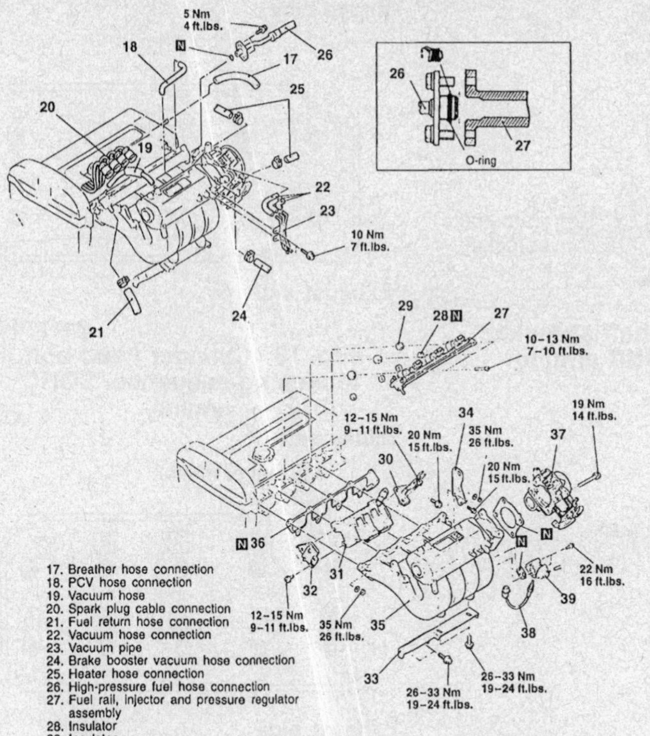
5 Nm
4 ft.lbs.
10 Nm
7 ft.lbs.
O-ring
10–13 Nm
7–10 ft.lbs.
12–15 Nm
9–11 ft.lbs.
20 Nm
15 ft.lbs.
35 Nm
26 ft.lbs.
19 Nm
14 ft.lbs.
22 Nm
16 ft.lbs.
26–33 Nm
19–24 ft.lbs.

17. Breather hose connection
18. PCV hose connection
19. Vacuum hose
20. Spark plug cable connection
21. Fuel return hose connection
22. Vacuum hose connection
23. Vacuum pipe
24. Brake booster vacuum hose connection
25. Heater hose connection
26. High-pressure fuel hose connection
27. Fuel rail, injector and pressure regulator assembly
28. Insulator
29. Insulator
30. Connector bracket
31. Ignition coil
32. Ignition power transistor
33. Intake manifold stay
34. Engine hanger
35. Intake manifold
36. Intake manifold gasket
37. Throttle body
38. EGR temperature sensor
39. EGR valve

MT1059100024020X

Fig. 8 Intake manifold replacement (Part 2 of 2). DOHC engine

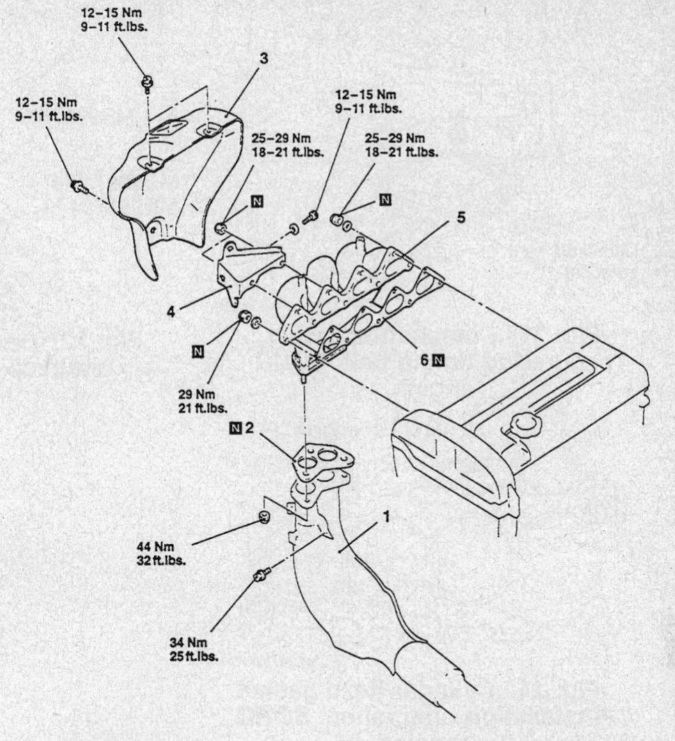
12–15 Nm
9–11 ft.lbs.
25–29 Nm
18–21 ft.lbs.
29 Nm
21 ft.lbs.
44 Nm
32 ft.lbs.
34 Nm
25 ft.lbs.

Removal steps

1. Front exhaust pipe connection
2. Gasket
3. Exhaust manifold cover
4. Engine hanger
5. Exhaust manifold
6. Exhaust manifold gasket

MT1079100015000X

Fig. 9 Exhaust manifold replacement

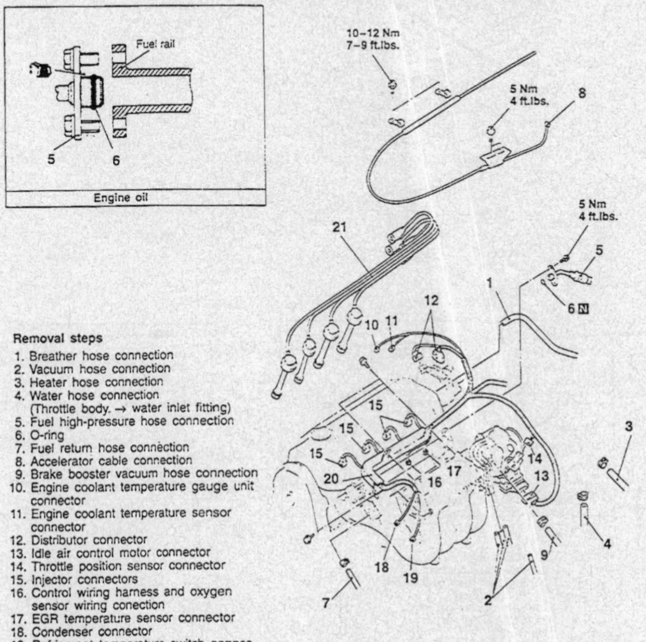
Fuel rail
Engine oil
10–12 Nm
7–9 ft.lbs.
5 Nm
4 ft.lbs.

Removal steps

1. Breather hose connection
2. Vacuum hose connection
3. Heater hose connection
4. Water hose connection (Throttle body. → water inlet fitting)
5. Fuel high-pressure hose connection
6. O-ring
7. Fuel return hose connection
8. Accelerator cable connection
9. Brake booster vacuum hose connection
10. Engine coolant temperature gauge unit connector
11. Engine coolant temperature sensor connector
12. Distributor connector
13. Idle air control motor connector
14. Throttle position sensor connector
15. Injector connectors
16. Control wiring harness and oxygen sensor wiring conection
17. EGR temperature sensor connector
18. Condenser connector
19. Refrigerant temperature switch connector
20. Control harness
21. Spark plug cable

MT1069100223010X

Fig. 10 Cylinder head replacement (Part 1 of 2). SOHC engine

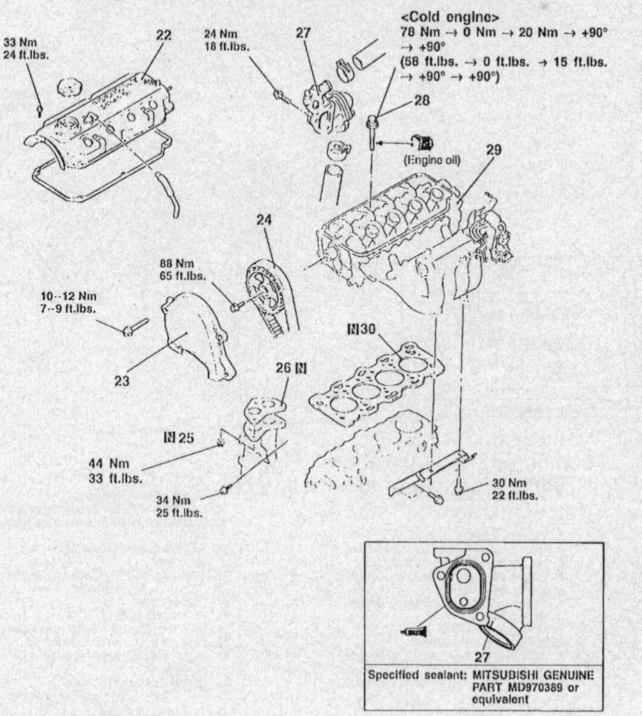
33 Nm
24 ft.lbs.
24 Nm
18 ft.lbs.
<Cold engine>
78 Nm → 0 Nm → 20 Nm → +90° → +90°
(58 ft.lbs. → 0 ft.lbs. → 15 ft.lbs. → +90° → +90°)
(Engine oil)
88 Nm
65 ft.lbs.
10–12 Nm
7–9 ft.lbs.
44 Nm
33 ft.lbs.
34 Nm
25 ft.lbs.
30 Nm
22 ft.lbs.
Specified sealant: MITSUBISHI GENUINE PART MD970389 or equivalent

22. Rocker cover
23. Timing belt upper cover
24. Camshaft sprocket
25. Self locking nut
26. Gasket
27. Thermostat case assembly
28. Cylinder head bolt
29. Cylinder head assembly
30. Cylinder head gasket

MT1069100223020X

Fig. 10 Cylinder head replacement (Part 2 of 2). SOHC engine

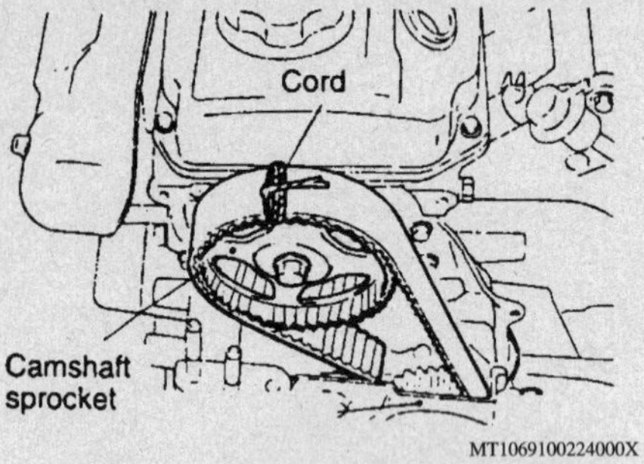
Cord
Camshaft sprocket
MT1069100224000X

Fig. 11 Camshaft sprocket secured to timing belt. SOHC engine

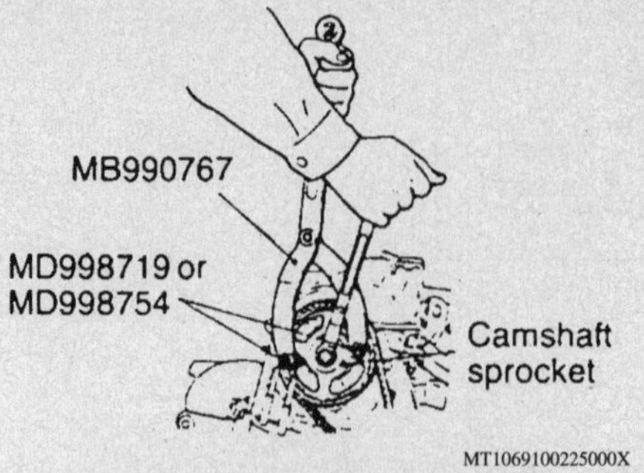
MB990767
MD998719 or
MD998754
Camshaft sprocket
MT1069100225000X

Fig. 12 Camshaft sprocket removal. SOHC engine

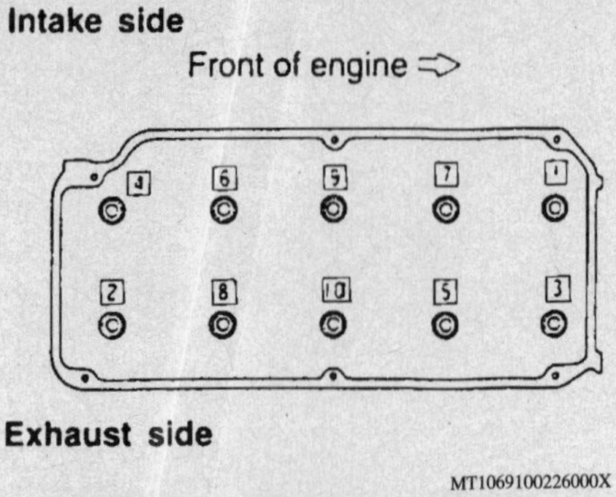
Intake side
Front of engine
4
6
9
7
1
2
8
10
5
3
Exhaust side
MT1069100226000X

Fig. 13 Cylinder head bolt loosening sequence. SOHC engine

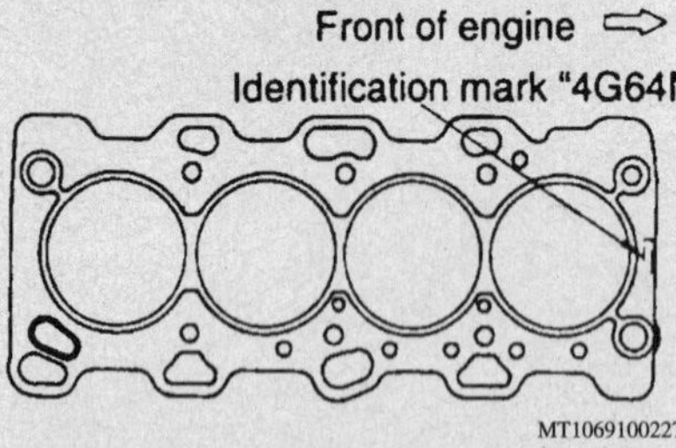
Front of engine
Identification mark "4G64N".
MT1069100227000X

Fig. 14 Cylinder head gasket installation orientation. SOHC engine

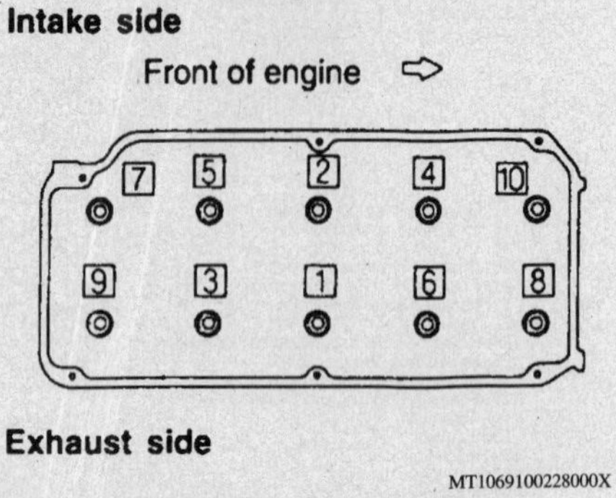
Intake side
Front of engine
7
5
2
4
10
9
3
1
6
8
Exhaust side
MT1069100228000X

Fig. 15 Cylinder head bolt tightening sequence

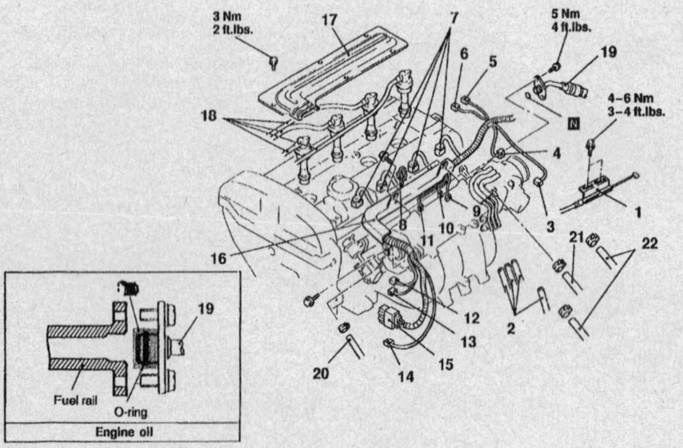
3 Nm
2 ft.lbs.
5 Nm
4 ft.lbs.
4-6 Nm
3-4 ft.lbs.
Fuel rail
O-ring
Engine oil

Removal steps
1. Accelerator cable connection
2. Vacuum hose
3. Throttle position sensor connector
4. Idle air control motor connector
5. Engine coolant temperature sensor connector
6. Engine coolant temperature gauge unit connector
7. Injector connectors
8. Ignition coil connector
9. EGR temperature sensor connector
10. Control wiring harness and oxygen sensor wiring harness connection
11. Knock sensor connector
12. Camshaft position sensor connector
13. Crankshaft position sensor connector
14. A/C refrigerant temperature switch connector
15. Ignition power transistor connection
16. Control wiring harness
17. Center cover
18. Spark plug cable
19. Fuel high-pressure hose connection
20. Fuel return hose connection
21. Brake booster vacuum hose connection
22. Heater hose connection

MT1069100229010X

Fig. 16 Cylinder head replacement (Part 1 of 2). DOHC engine

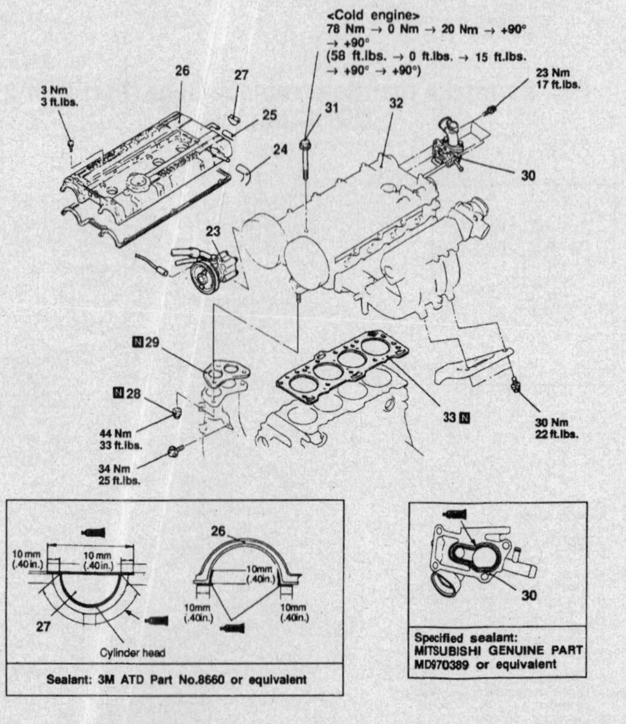
<Cold engine>
78 Nm → 0 Nm → 20 Nm → +90° → +90°
(58 ft.lbs. → 0 ft.lbs. → 15 ft.lbs. → +90° → +90°)
3 Nm
3 ft.lbs.
23 Nm
17 ft.lbs.
44 Nm
33 ft.lbs.
34 Nm
25 ft.lbs.
30 Nm
22 ft.lbs.
10 mm (.40 in.)
Cylinder head
Sealant: 3M ATD Part No.8660 or equivalent
Specified sealant: MITSUBISHI GENUINE PART MD970389 or equivalent

23. Power steering pump
24. PCV hose connection
25. Breather hose connection
26. Rocker cover
27. Semi-circular packing
28. Self locking nut
29. Gasket
30. Thermostat case assembly
31. Cylinder head bolt
32. Cylinder head assembly
33. Cylinder head gasket

MT1069100229020X

Fig. 16 Cylinder head replacement (Part 2 of 2). DOHC engine

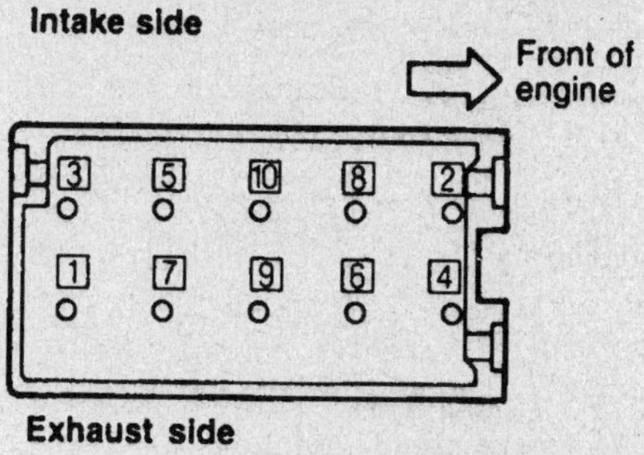
Intake side
Front of engine
3
5
10
8
2
1
7
9
6
4
Exhaust side

MT1069100230000X

Fig. 17 Cylinder head bolt loosening sequence. DOHC engine

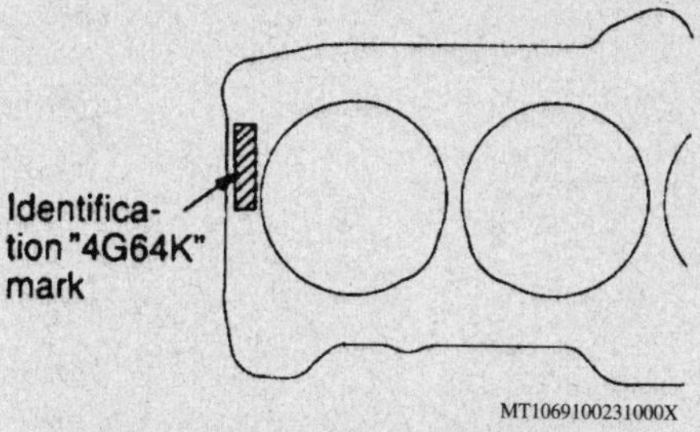
Identification "4G64K" mark

MT1069100231000X

Fig. 18 Cylinder head gasket identification mark. DOHC engine

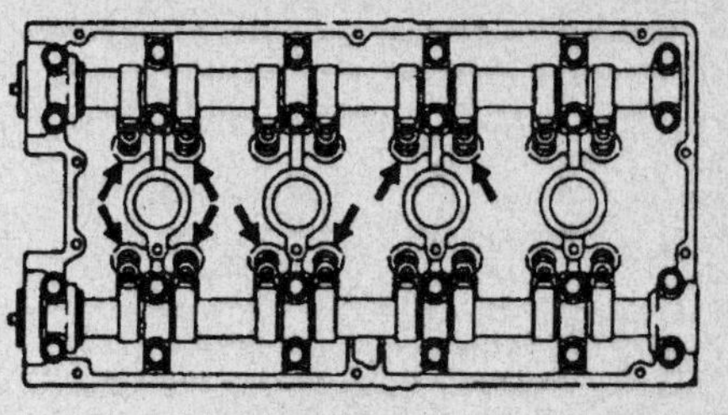

MT1069400327000X

Fig. 19 Checking hydraulic lash adjusters

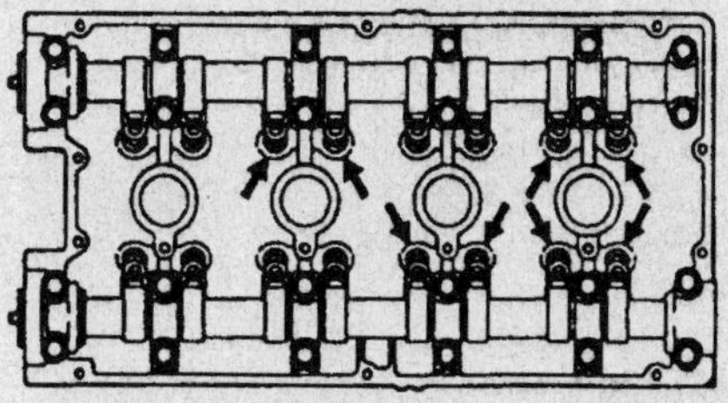

MT1069400328000X

Fig. 20 Checking hydraulic lash adjusters

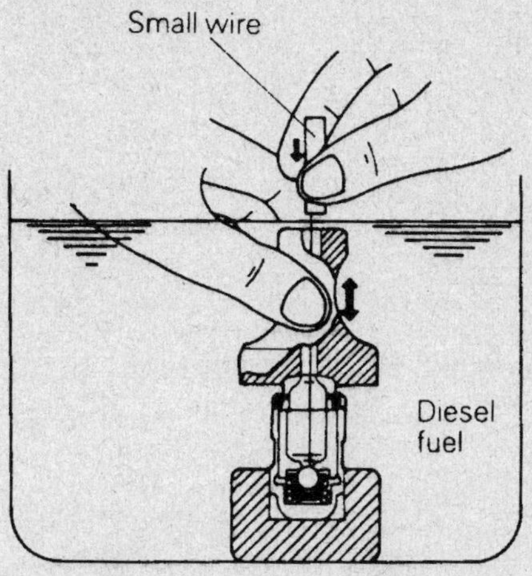
Small wire
Diesel fuel

MT1069400329000X

Fig. 21 Bleeding hydraulic lash adjuster

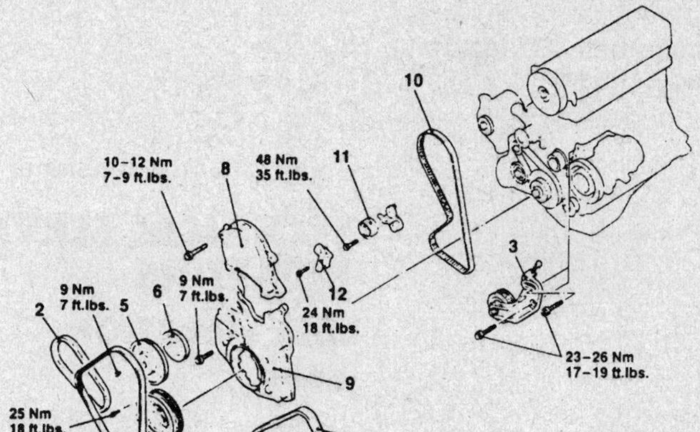
10-12 Nm
7-9 ft.lbs.
48 Nm
35 ft.lbs.
9 Nm
7 ft.lbs.
9 Nm
7 ft.lbs.
24 Nm
18 ft.lbs.
23-26 Nm
17-19 ft.lbs.
25 Nm
18 ft.lbs.

Removal steps

- Drive Belt Tension Adjustment

1. Drive belt (Generator)
2. Drive belt (Power steering)
3. Tensioner pulley bracket
4. Drive belt (A/C)
5. Water pump pulley
6. Power steering pulley
7. Crankshaft pulley
8. Timing belt front upper cover
9. Timing belt front lower cover

- Timing belt tension adjustment

10. Timing belt
11. Tension pulley
12. Auto tensioner

MT1069100232000X

Fig. 22 Timing belt replacement. SOHC engine

WATER PUMP

REPLACE

1. Relieve fuel system pressure as outlined under "Precautions," then drain engine coolant into a suitable container.
2. Remove timing belt as outlined under "Timing Belt, Replace."
3. Remove water pump in numbered sequence shown, **Fig. 43.**
4. Reverse procedure to install.

RADIATOR

REPLACE

1. Remove radiator drain plug and drain coolant.
2. Remove radiator cap, then the overflow tube.
3. Remove upper and lower coolant hoses from radiator.
4. **On models with automatic transaxle,** disconnect fluid cooler lines from radiator.
5. **On all models,** remove upper insulators, then the radiator assembly.
6. Remove condenser and radiator fan motor assemblies from radiator.
7. Remove shroud from radiator.
8. Reverse procedure to install.

FUEL PUMP

REPLACE

1. Relieve fuel system pressure as outlined under "Precautions," then remove rear seat cushion.
2. Remove fuel tank protector, then disconnect electrical connector from fuel gauge unit and pump assembly.
3. Remove pump and gauge unit assembly from fuel tank.
4. Reverse procedure to install. Tilt float to lefthand side when inserting assembly into fuel tank.

FUEL FILTER

REPLACE

Refer to **Fig. 44** throughout the following procedure.

1. Relieve fuel system pressure as outlined under "Precautions," then remove air intake hose.
2. Using a spanner wrench, hold fuel filter in place and remove eye bolt and high pressure hose.
3. With spanner wrench still attached to

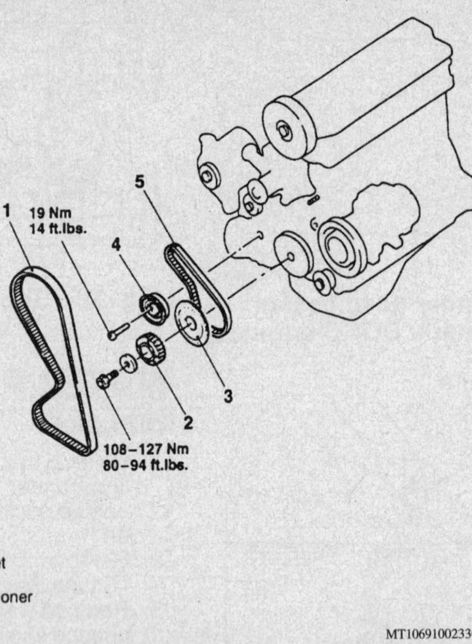
1
19 Nm
14 ft.lbs.
5
4
3
2
108–127 Nm
80–94 ft.lbs.
Removal steps
1. Timing belt
2. Crankshaft sprocket
3. Flange
4. Timing belt B tensioner
5. Timing belt B
MT1069100233000X

Fig. 23 Timing belt "B" replacement. SOHC engine

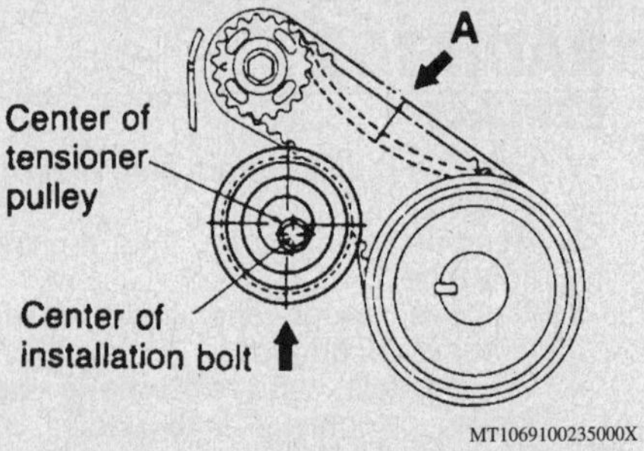
A
Center of tensioner pulley
Center of installation bolt
MT1069100235000X

Fig. 25 Timing belt "B" tensioner orientation & tension inspection point

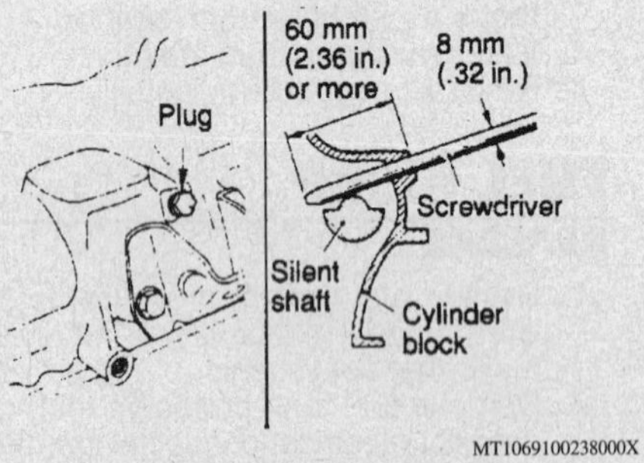
Plug
60 mm
(2.36 in.)
or more
8 mm
(.32 in.)
Screwdriver
Silent shaft
Cylinder block
MT1069100238000X

Fig. 28 Screwdriver installation in silent shaft access plug

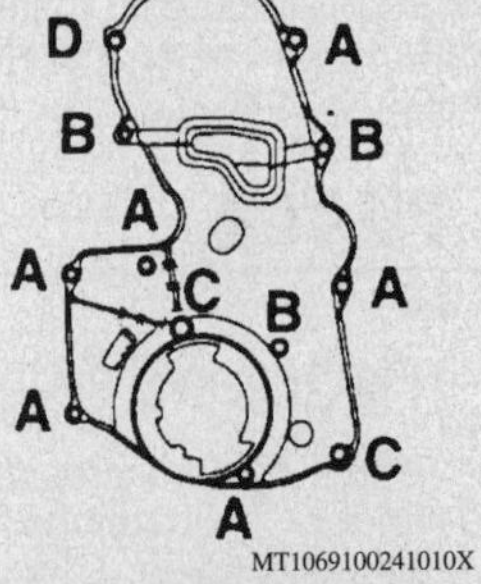
D
A
B
B
A
A
C
B
A
A
C
A
MT1069100241010X

Fig. 31 Timing belt cover bolt locations (Part 1 of 2). SOHC engine

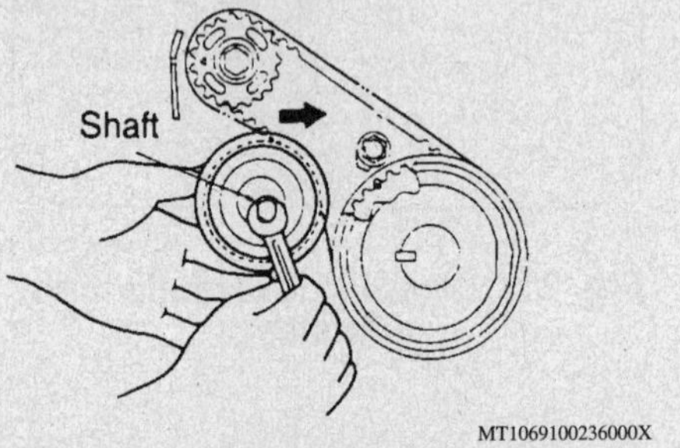
Shaft
MT1069100236000X

Fig. 26 Timing belt "B" tension adjustment

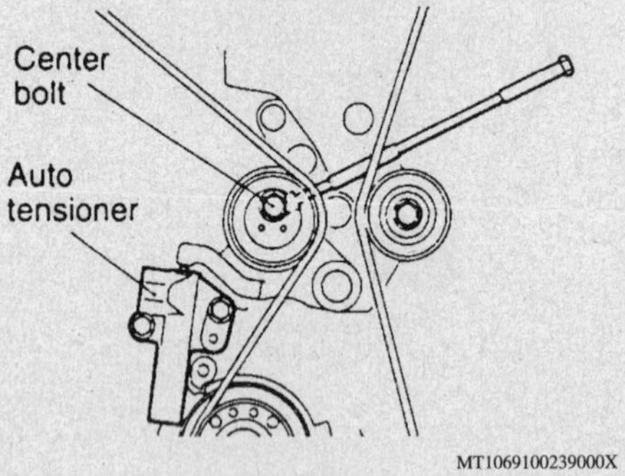
Center bolt
Auto tensioner
MT1069100239000X

Fig. 29 Tool installation & release of auto tensioner

filter, loosen flare nut, then disconnect main pipe and remove filter.

4. Reverse procedure to install, noting the following:
   a. Use a new filter gasket.
   b. Tighten all fittings to specifications.
   c. Inspect filter and fuel lines for leaks.

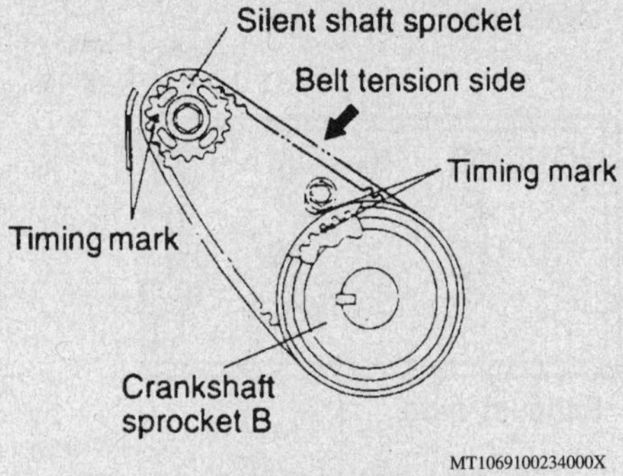
Silent shaft sprocket
Belt tension side
Timing mark
Timing mark
Crankshaft sprocket B
MT1069100234000X

Fig. 24 Timing belt "B" mark alignment

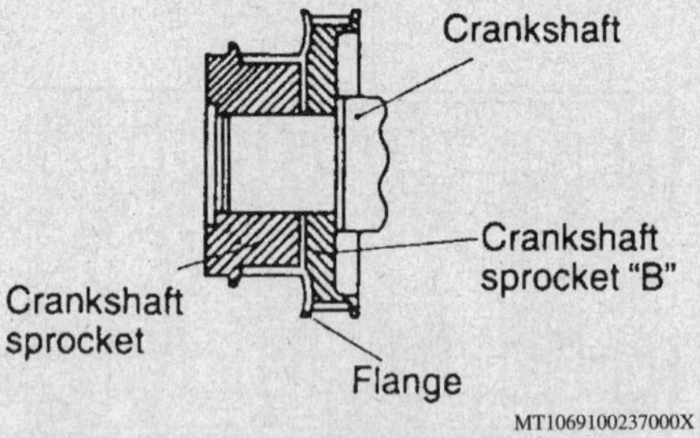
Crankshaft
Crankshaft sprocket "B"
Crankshaft sprocket
Flange
MT1069100237000X

Fig. 27 Timing belt "B" flange position

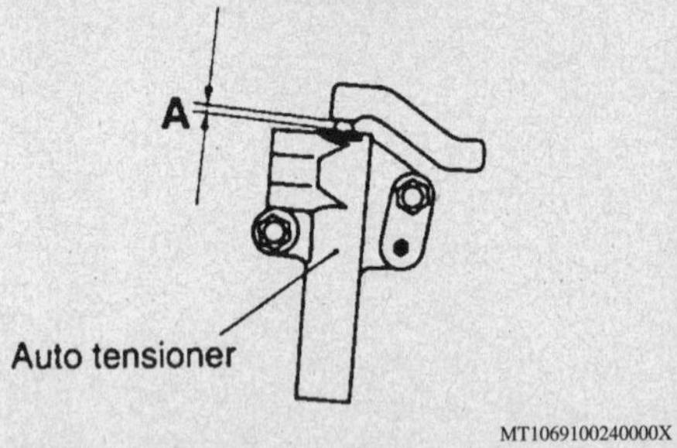
A
Auto tensioner
MT1069100240000X

Fig. 30 Auto tensioner protrusion

TECHNICAL SERVICE BULLETINS

IDLE VIBRATION

1994

On these models, there may be an idle speed vibration.

This condition may be caused by incorrectly positioned radiator mounts, which allow radiator vibrations to be transmitted through the frame to the passenger compartment. To correct this condition, proceed as follows:

1. Ensure upper radiator mount brackets are centered on mounting posts.
2. If not positioned correctly, remove brackets and ensure lower mount posts are seated in brackets.
3. Center upper brackets over posts, then **torque** bolts to 7–10 ft. lbs.
4. Clearance between upper brackets and radiator top should be 1⁄16 inch or more.

	Thread diameter × thread length mm (in.)	Bolt classification	Tightening torque Nm (ft.lbs.)
A	6 × 18 (.24 × .71)	Flange bolt	10–12 (7–9)
B	6 × 25 (.24 × .98)	Flange bolt	10–12 (7–9)
C	6 × 25 (.24 × .98)	Washer assembled bolt	8–10 (6–7)
D	6 × 50 (.24 × 1.97)	Flange bolt	10–12 (7–9)

MT1069100241020X

Fig. 31 Timing belt cover bolt locations (Part 2 of 2). SOHC engine

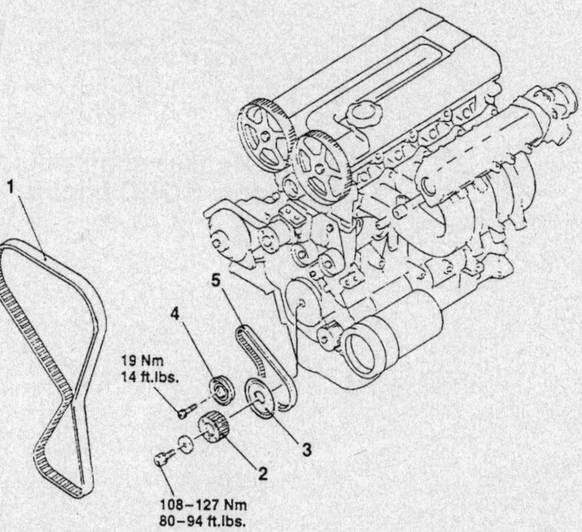
1
5
4
19 Nm
14 ft.lbs.
3
2
108–127 Nm
80–94 ft.lbs.

Removal steps

1. Timing belt
2. Crankshaft sprocket
3. Flange
4. Timing belt B tensioner
5. Timing belt B

MT1069100243000X

Fig. 33 Timing belt "B" replacement. DOHC engine

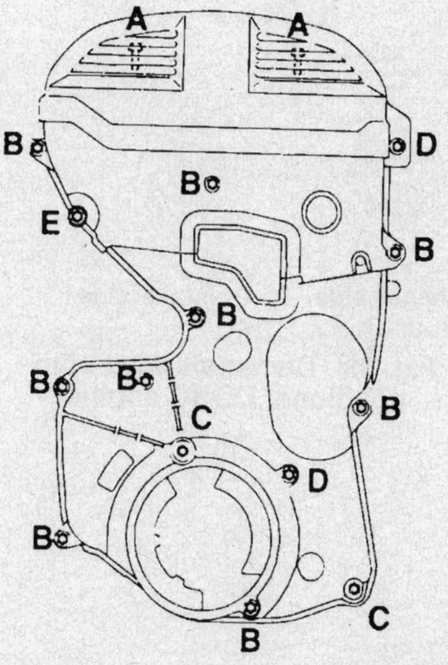
A
A
B
D
B
E
B
B
B
B
C
B
D
B
C
B

MT1069100245010X

Fig. 35 Timing belt cover bolt locations (Part 1 of 2). DOHC engine

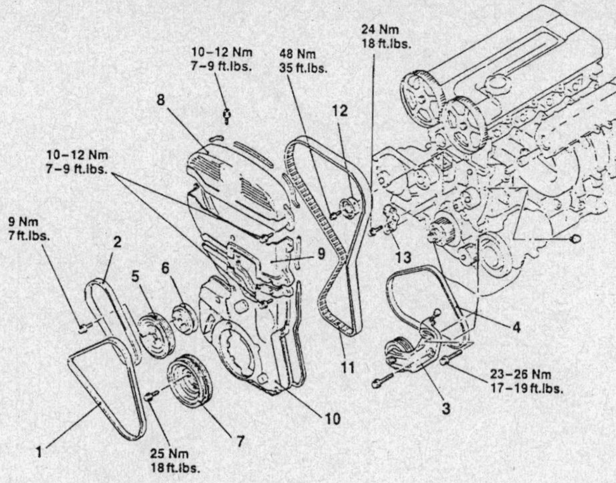
24 Nm
18 ft.lbs.
10–12 Nm
7–9 ft.lbs.
48 Nm
35 ft.lbs.
8
12
10–12 Nm
7–9 ft.lbs.
9 Nm
7 ft.lbs.
2
9
13
5
6
4
11
23–26 Nm
17–19 ft.lbs.
3
10
7
1
25 Nm
18 ft.lbs.

Removal steps

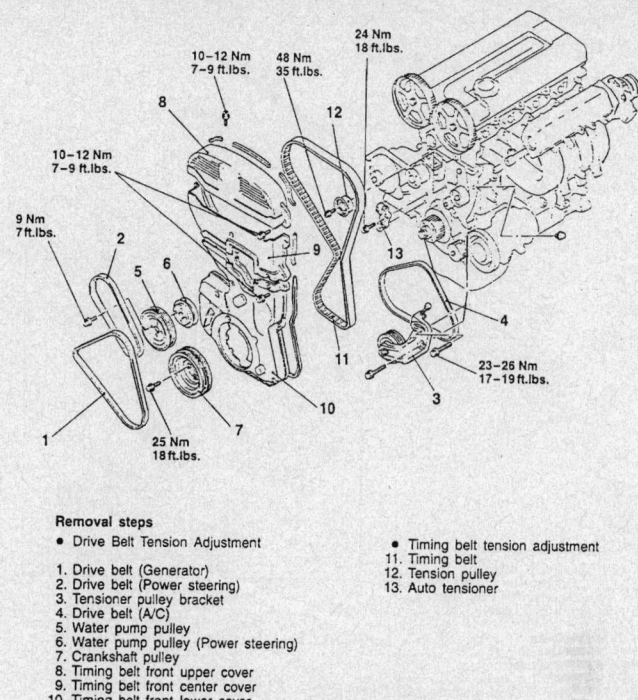

- Drive Belt Tension Adjustment

1. Drive belt (Generator)
2. Drive belt (Power steering)
3. Tensioner pulley bracket
4. Drive belt (A/C)
5. Water pump pulley
6. Water pump pulley (Power steering)
7. Crankshaft pulley
8. Timing belt front upper cover
9. Timing belt front center cover
10. Timing belt front lower cover

- Timing belt tension adjustment

11. Timing belt
12. Tension pulley
13. Auto tensioner

MT1069100242000X

Fig. 32 Timing belt replacement. DOHC engine

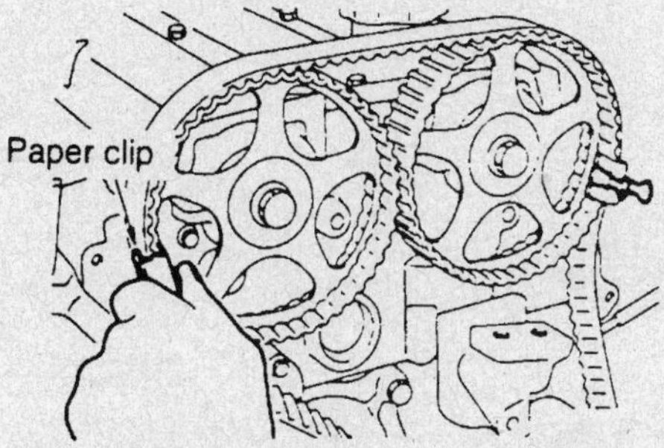
Paper clip

MT1069100244000X

Fig. 34 Timing belt installation over camshaft sprockets. DOHC engine

	Thread diameter × thread length mm (in.)	Bolt classification	Tightening torque Nm (ft.lbs.)
A	6 × 16 (.24 × .63)	Flange bolt	10–12 (7–9)
B	6 × 18 (.24 × .71)	Flange bolt	10–12 (7–9)
C	6 × 25 (.24 × .98)	Washer assembled bolt	8–10 (6–7)
D	6 × 25 (.24 × .98)	Flange bolt	10–12 (7–9)
E	6 × 45 (.24 × 1.77)	Flange bolt	10–12 (7–9)

MT1069100245020X

Fig. 35 Timing belt cover bolt locations (Part 2 of 2). DOHC engine

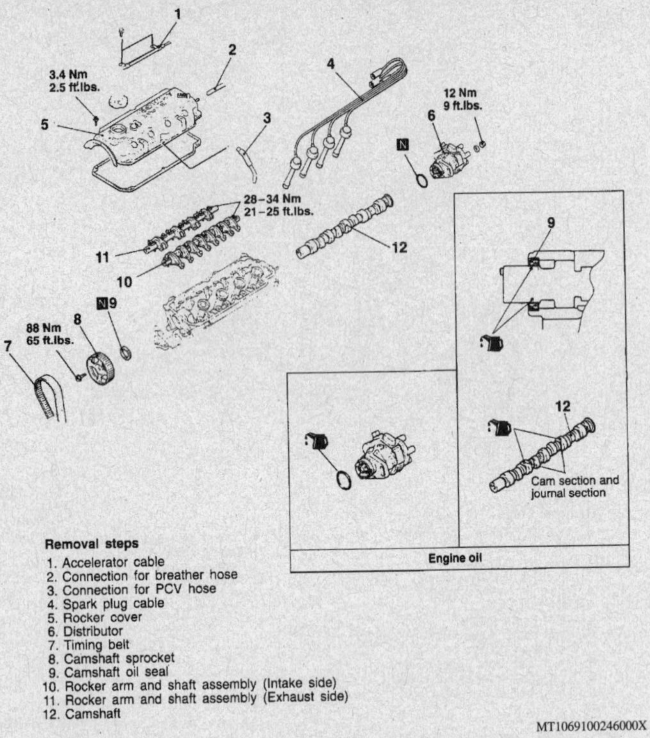
3.4 Nm
2.5 ft.lbs.
12 Nm
9 ft.lbs.
28–34 Nm
21–25 ft.lbs.
88 Nm
65 ft.lbs.
Cam section and journal section
Engine oil
Removal steps
1. Accelerator cable
2. Connection for breather hose
3. Connection for PCV hose
4. Spark plug cable
5. Rocker cover
6. Distributor
7. Timing belt
8. Camshaft sprocket
9. Camshaft oil seal
10. Rocker arm and shaft assembly (Intake side)
11. Rocker arm and shaft assembly (Exhaust side)
12. Camshaft
MT1069100246000X

Fig. 36 Camshaft replacement. SOHC engine

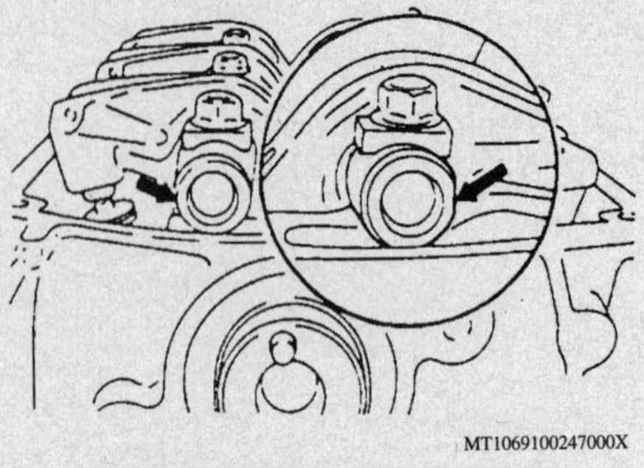
MT1069100247000X

Fig. 37 Rocker shaft notch positions. SOHC engine

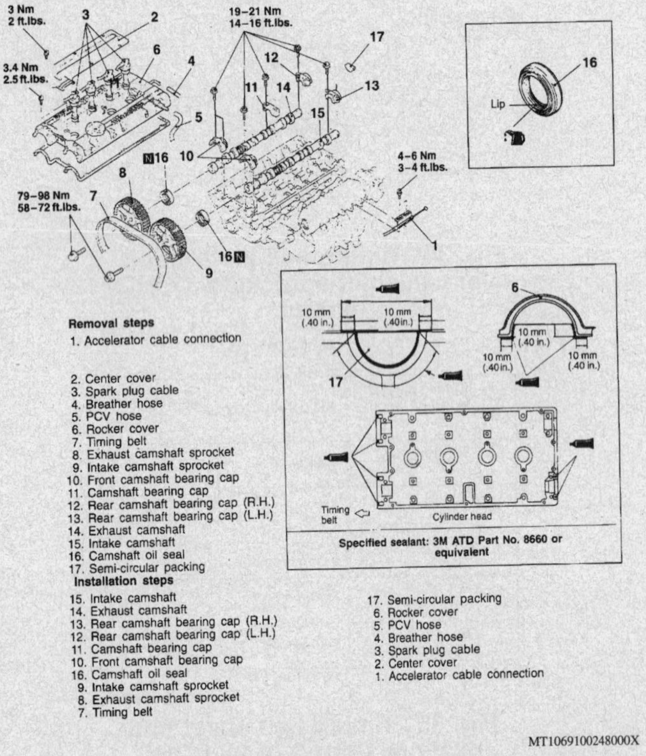
3 Nm
2 ft.lbs.
3.4 Nm
2.5 ft.lbs.
19–21 Nm
14–16 ft.lbs.
4–6 Nm
3–4 ft.lbs.
79–98 Nm
58–72 ft.lbs.
Lip
10 mm (.40 in.)
Timing belt
Cylinder head
Specified sealant: 3M ATD Part No. 8660 or equivalent
Removal steps
1. Accelerator cable connection
2. Center cover
3. Spark plug cable
4. Breather hose
5. PCV hose
6. Rocker cover
7. Timing belt
8. Exhaust camshaft sprocket
9. Intake camshaft sprocket
10. Front camshaft bearing cap
11. Camshaft bearing cap
12. Rear camshaft bearing cap (R.H.)
13. Rear camshaft bearing cap (L.H.)
14. Exhaust camshaft
15. Intake camshaft
16. Camshaft oil seal
17. Semi-circular packing
Installation steps
15. Intake camshaft
14. Exhaust camshaft
13. Rear camshaft bearing cap (R.H.)
12. Rear camshaft bearing cap (L.H.)
11. Camshaft bearing cap
10. Front camshaft bearing cap
16. Camshaft oil seal
9. Intake camshaft sprocket
8. Exhaust camshaft sprocket
7. Timing belt
17. Semi-circular packing
6. Rocker cover
5. PCV hose
4. Breather hose
3. Spark plug cable
2. Center cover
1. Accelerator cable connection
MT1069100248000X

Fig. 38 Camshaft replacement. DOHC engine

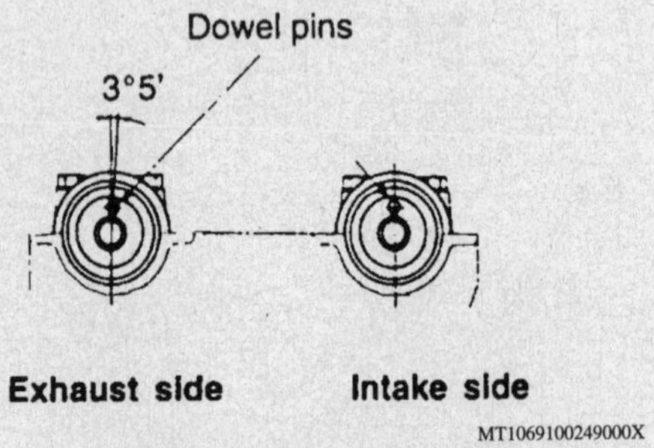
Dowel pins
3°5'
Exhaust side
Intake side
MT1069100249000X

Fig. 39 Camshaft dowel pin positions. DOHC engine

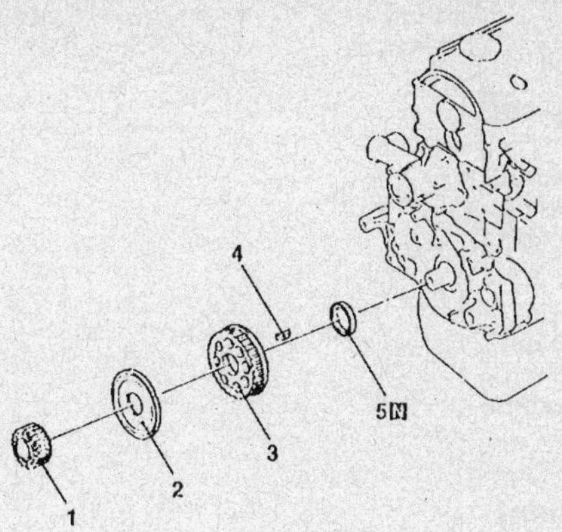
1
2
3
4
5N

Removal steps
1. Crankshaft sprocket
2. Flange
3. Crankshaft sprocket B
4. Key
5. Crankshaft front oil seal

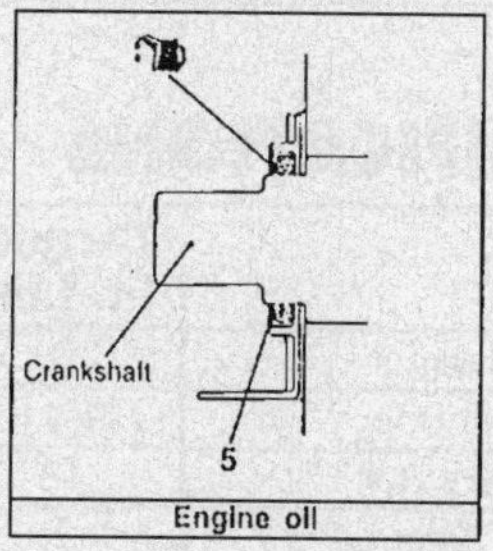
Crankshaft
5
Engine oil

MT1069100250000X

Fig. 40 Crankshaft front oil seal replacement

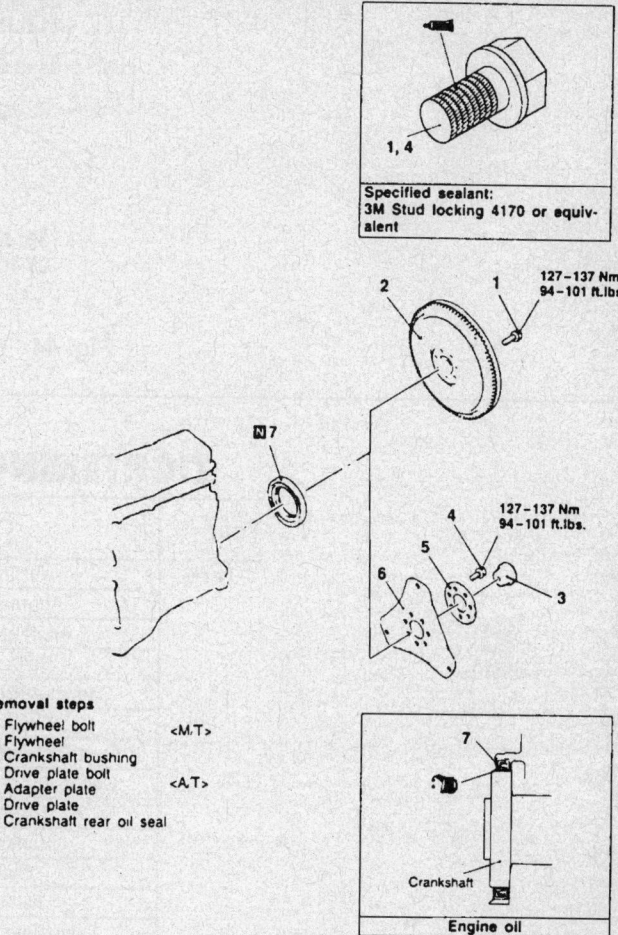

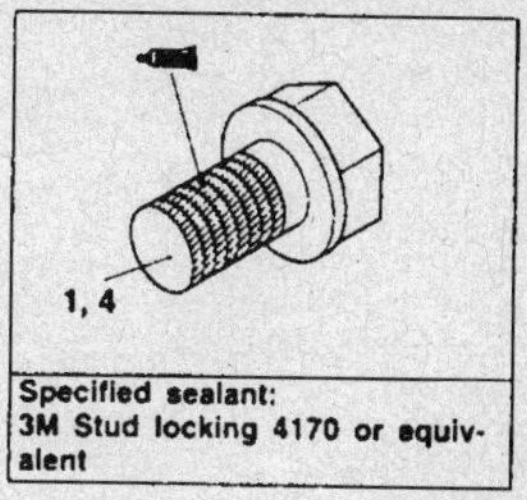
1, 4
Specified sealant:
3M Stud locking 4170 or equivalent

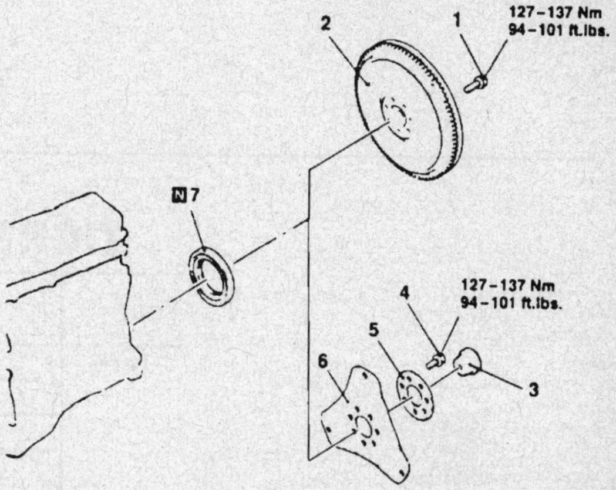
2
1
127-137 Nm
94-101 ft.lbs.
N 7
4
127-137 Nm
94-101 ft.lbs.
5
6
3

Removal steps
1. Flywheel bolt <M/T>
2. Flywheel
3. Crankshaft bushing
4. Drive plate bolt <A/T>
5. Adapter plate
6. Drive plate
7. Crankshaft rear oil seal

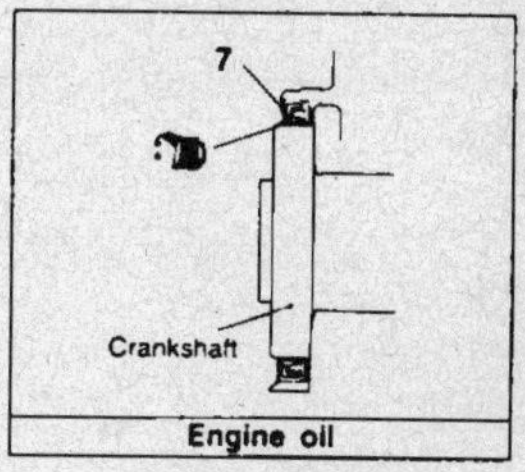
7
Crankshaft
Engine oil

MT1069100251000X

Fig. 41 Crankshaft rear oil seal replacement

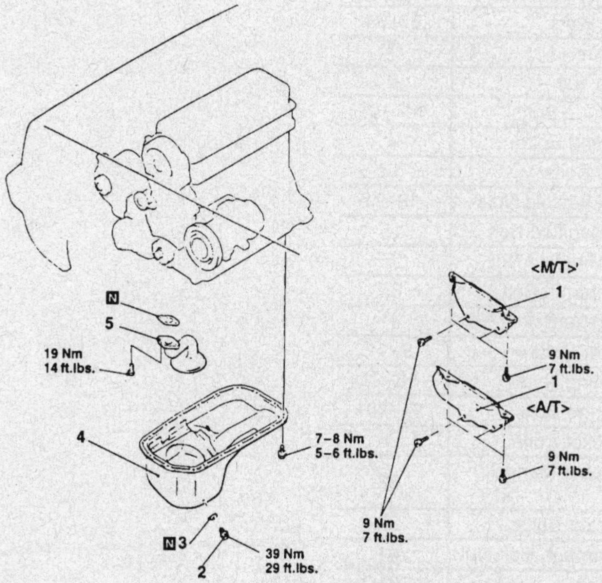
<M/T>
1
N
5
19 Nm
14 ft.lbs.
9 Nm
7 ft.lbs.
1
<A/T>
4
7-8 Nm
5-6 ft.lbs.
9 Nm
7 ft.lbs.
9 Nm
7 ft.lbs.
N 3
2
39 Nm
29 ft.lbs.

Removal steps
1. Bell housing cover
2. Drain plug
3. Gasket
4. Oil pan
5. Oil screen

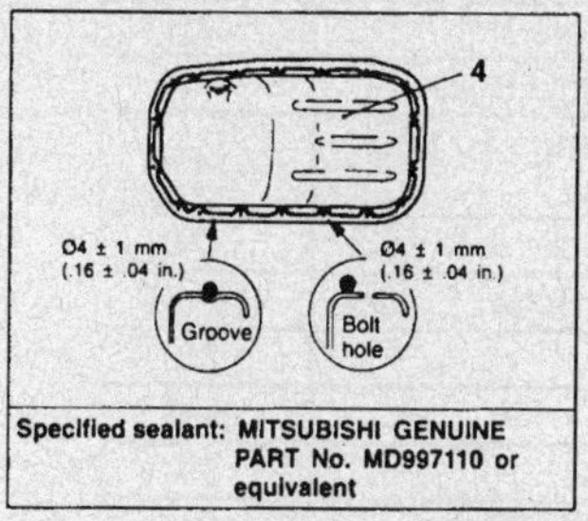
4
Ø4 ± 1 mm
(.16 ± .04 in.)
Ø4 ± 1 mm
(.16 ± .04 in.)
Groove
Bolt hole
Specified sealant: MITSUBISHI GENUINE PART No. MD997110 or equivalent

MT1099100049000X

Fig. 42 Oil pan & screen replacement

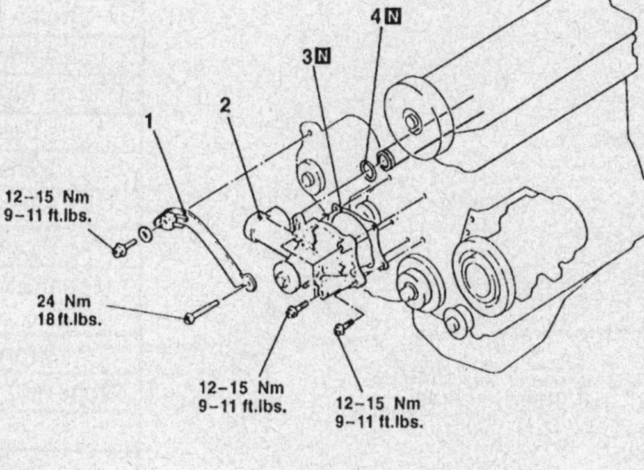
4N
3N
2
1
12-15 Nm
9-11 ft.lbs.
24 Nm
18 ft.lbs.
12-15 Nm
9-11 ft.lbs.
12-15 Nm
9-11 ft.lbs.

Removal steps
1. Generator brace
2. Water pump
3. Water pump gasket
4. O-ring

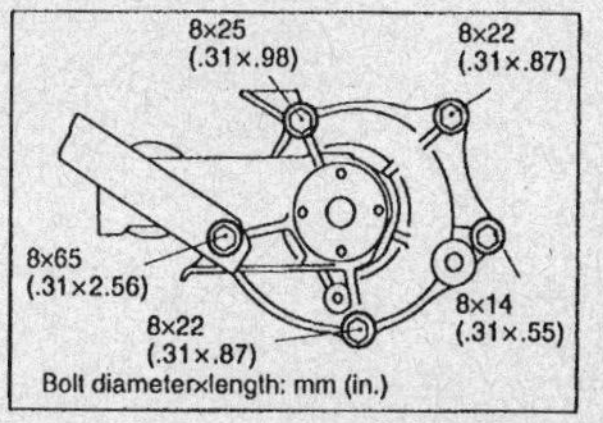
8x25
(.31x.98)
8x22
(.31x.87)
8x65
(.31x2.56)
8x14
(.31x.55)
8x22
(.31x.87)
Bolt diameterxlength: mm (in.)

MT1089100021000X

Fig. 43 Water pump replacement

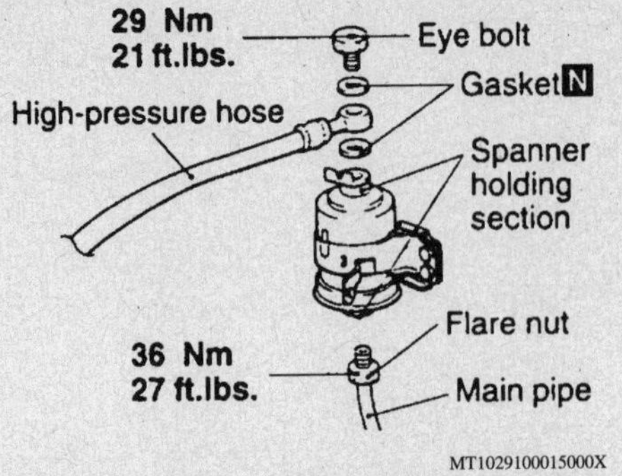
29 Nm
21 ft.lbs.
Eye bolt
Gasket N
High-pressure hose
Spanner holding section
Flare nut
36 Nm
27 ft.lbs.
Main pipe
MT1029100015000X

Fig. 44 Fuel filter replacement

TIGHTENING SPECIFICATIONS

Year	Component	Torque, Ft. Lbs.
1994–96	Air Intake Hose Clamp	3
	Alternator Adjustment Bolt	9–11
	Alternator Bracket Pivot Bolt	18
	Bellhousing Cover Bolts	7
	Camshaft Bearing Cap Bolts (DOHC)	14–16
	Camshaft Sprocket Bolt	65
	Center Member Attaching Bolts (Front)	64
	Center Member Attaching Bolts (Rear)	50–56
	Crankshaft Pulley Bolts	18
	Crankshaft Sprocket Bolts	80–94
	Cylinder Head Bolts	②
	Distributor Mounting Nut	9
	Driveplate To Output Flange Bolts	94–101
	Dynamic Damper Mounting Bolts	4
	EGR Valve Mounting Bolts	16
	Engine Hanger To Exhaust Manifold Nuts	18–21
	Engine Hanger To Intake Manifold Bolt	15
	Engine Hanger To Intake Manifold Nut	26
	Engine Mount Bracket Through Bolt	85
	Engine Mount Bracket To Engine Bolt & Nut	41
	Exhaust Manifold Cover Bolts	9–11
	Exhaust Manifold Mounting Nuts	18–21
	Flywheel To Output Flange Bolts	94–101
	Front Exhaust Pipe Bracket Bolts	25
	Front Exhaust Pipe To Exhaust Manifold Nuts	32
	Front Roll Stopper Bracket Bolts	32
	Front Roll Stopper Bracket Through Bolt Nut	41
	Fuel Filter Eye Bolt	21
	Fuel Filter Main Pipe Flare Nut	27
	Fuel Rail To Intake Manifold Bolts	7–10
	High Pressure Fuel Hose Flange To Fuel Rail Bolts	4
	Intake Manifold Mounting Bolts & Nuts	①
	Intake Manifold Stay Bolts	19–24
	Oil Drain Plug	29
	Oil Pan Bolts	5–6
	Oil Screen Bolts	14
	Power Steering Pump Pulley Bolts	21
	Rear Roll Stopper Bracket Bolts	32
	Rear Roll Stopper Bracket Through Bolt Nut	32
	Rocker Arm & Shaft Mounting Bolts	21–25

Continued

TIGHTENING SPECIFICATIONS—Continued

Year	Component	Torque, Ft. Lbs.
1994–96	Rocker Cover Bolts	3
	Thermostat Case To Engine Block Bolts	18
	Throttle Body Mounting Bolts	14
	Timing Belt Auto Tensioner Bolt	18
	Timing Belt Auto Tensioner Pulley Center Bolt	35
	Timing Belt "B" Tensioner Pulley Center Bolt	14
	Timing Belt Lower Cover Bolts	②
	Timing Belt Tensioner Pulley Bracket Bolts	17–19
	Timing Belt Upper Cover Bolts	②
	Transaxle Mount Bracket Nuts	31
	Transaxle Mount Bracket Through Bolt	50
	Vacuum Pipe Bracket To Intake Manifold Bolts	7
	Water Outlet Fitting	10
	Water Pump Bolts	9–11
	Water Pump Pulley Bolts (DOHC)	7

① — SOHC engine, 15 ft. lbs.; DOHC engine, 15 ft. lbs. (bolts), 26 ft. lbs. (nuts).
② — Refer to "Cylinder Head, Replace" for procedure.

Clutch & Manual Transaxle

INDEX

	Page No.
Adjustments	26-53
Clutch Pedal	26-53
Clutch, Replace	26-53
Hydraulic System Service	26-53
Clutch Master Cylinder, Replace	26-53
Clutch Release Cylinder, Replace	26-53
Tightening Specifications	26-56
Transaxle, Replace	26-54

ADJUSTMENTS

CLUTCH PEDAL

Refer to **Figs. 1 through 2** for clutch pedal removal and installation.

1. Measure clutch pedal height (A) and clutch pedal clevis pin play (B), **Fig. 3.** Pedal height should be 6.8–7.0 inches and pin play should be .04–.12 inch.
2. If either pedal height or pin play are not within specifications, adjust as follows:
   a. Thread bolt in or out until pedal height is correct, then secure by tightening locknut, **Figs. 4 and 5.** Disconnect clutch switch connector and turn the switch for standard clutch pedal height, then lock with the locknut.
   b. Turn pushrod, **Fig. 6,** to adjust clutch pedal clevis pin play to proper value, then secure pushrod with locknut. **When adjusting clutch pedal clevis pin play, ensure pushrod is not pushed toward the master cylinder.**
3. Ensure clutch pedal freeplay (C) is 0.2–0.5 inch and distance (D) between clutch pedal pad and firewall when clutch pedal is disengaged, **Fig. 7,** is 2.2 inches or more.
4. If clutch pedal freeplay (C) and distance (D) are not within specification, check for air in hydraulic system or a defective clutch or master cylinder assembly.

HYDRAULIC SYSTEM SERVICE

CLUTCH RELEASE CYLINDER, REPLACE

1993

Refer to **Fig. 8** and replace clutch release cylinder in numbered sequence as shown in **Fig. 9.**

1994–96

Refer to **Fig. 10** when replacing the clutch release cylinder.

CLUTCH MASTER CYLINDER, REPLACE

Refer to **Figs. 8 and 10** when replacing the clutch master cylinder.

CLUTCH

REPLACE

1. Remove transaxle as outlined under "Transaxle, Replace."
2. Insert clutch disc guide tool No. MD998126, or equivalent, into center hole to prevent dropping of clutch disc, then diagonally loosen bolts that hold clutch cover assembly to remove clutch cover assembly. **Do not clean clutch disc or release bearing with cleaning solvent.**
3. Remove snap ring, clevis pin and release cylinder assembly.
4. Remove return clip, then the release bearing.
5. Remove spring pins from clutch release fork and shaft using a suitable punch.
6. Install release shaft and packings, then the return spring and release fork.
7. Align lockpin holes of shift arm and control shaft, then using pin installer tool No. MD998245, or equivalent, drive in two new spring pins.
8. When installing spring pins ensure spring pin slot direction is at right angles to center line of control shaft.
9. Remove grease from clutch facing by

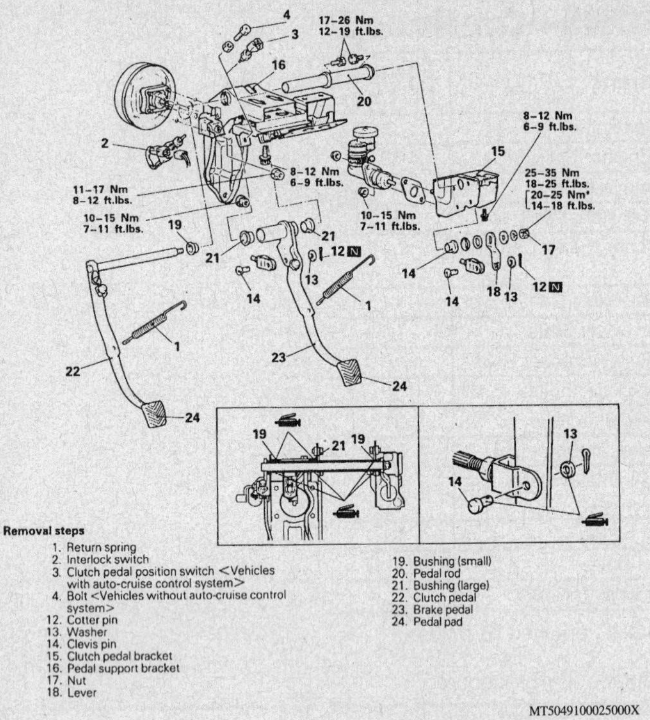
Removal steps
1. Return spring
2. Interlock switch
3. Clutch pedal position switch <Vehicles with auto-cruise control system>
4. Bolt <Vehicles without auto-cruise control system>
12. Cotter pin
13. Washer
14. Clevis pin
15. Clutch pedal bracket
16. Pedal support bracket
17. Nut
18. Lever
19. Bushing (small)
20. Pedal rod
21. Bushing (large)
22. Clutch pedal
23. Brake pedal
24. Pedal pad
MT5049100025000X

Fig. 1 Clutch pedal replacement. 1993

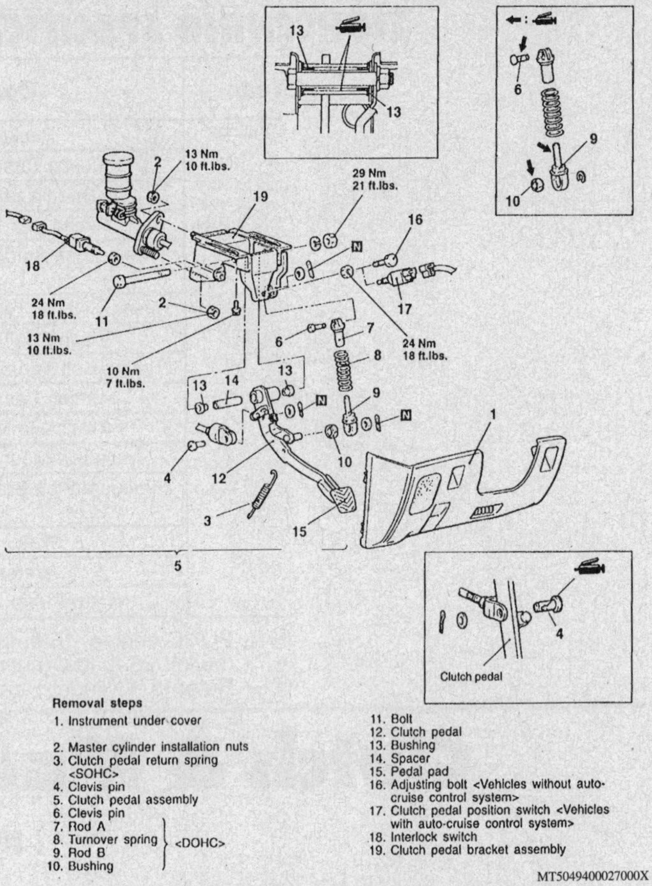
Removal steps
1. Instrument under cover
2. Master cylinder installation nuts
3. Clutch pedal return spring <SOHC>
4. Clevis pin
5. Clutch pedal assembly
6. Clevis pin
7. Rod A
8. Turnover spring <DOHC>
9. Rod B
10. Bushing
11. Bolt
12. Clutch pedal
13. Bushing
14. Spacer
15. Pedal pad
16. Adjusting bolt <Vehicles without auto-cruise control system>
17. Clutch pedal position switch <Vehicles with auto-cruise control system>
18. Interlock switch
19. Clutch pedal bracket assembly
Clutch pedal
MT5049400027000X

Fig. 2 Clutch pedal replacement. 1994–96

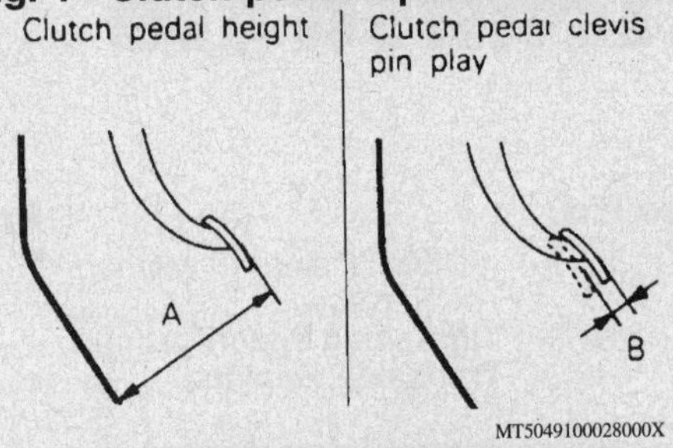
Clutch pedal height
Clutch pedal clevis pin play
A
B
MT5049100028000X

Fig. 3 Clutch pedal height & clevis pin play

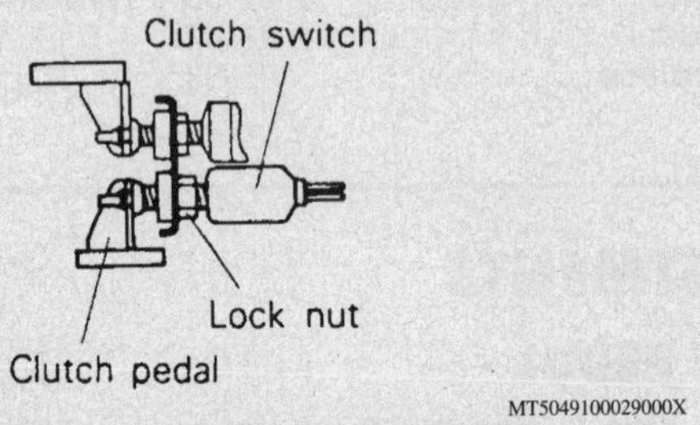
Clutch switch
Lock nut
Clutch pedal
MT5049100029000X

Fig. 4 Clutch start switch locknut location. 1993

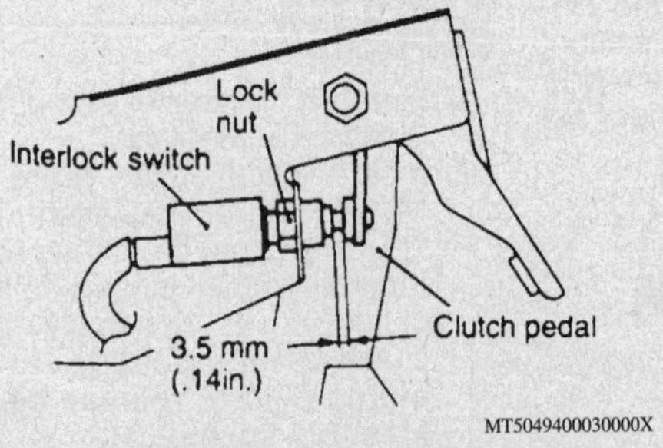
Lock nut
Interlock switch
Clutch pedal
3.5 mm
(.14in.)
MT5049400030000X

Fig. 5 Clutch start switch locknut location. 1994–96

wiping with clean cloth.

10. Apply small amount of grease to clutch disc spline and input shaft spline.
11. Using tool No. MD998126, or equivalent, install clutch disc and clutch cover assembly to flywheel. When installing clutch disc, make certain that surface with manufacturer's stamped mark is on pressure plate side.

TRANSAXLE

REPLACE

1. Drain transaxle oil and engine coolant into suitable container, then disconnect battery ground cable.
2. Remove air cleaner assembly.
3. Disconnect air flow sensor and purge control solenoid connectors.
4. Disconnect transaxle control cables and radiator hoses.
5. Disconnect engine wiring harness, back-up light switch and speedometer connections.
6. Remove transaxle mount bracket and air compressor.
7. Disconnect clutch release cylinder and clutch tube bracket, then remove starter.
8. Remove undercover panel, then the front wheel speed sensors.
9. Remove driveshafts as follows:
   a. Disconnect tie rod end and knuckle.
   b. Disconnect lower arm ball joint.
   c. Disconnect lefthand driveshaft from bearing bracket and suspend driveshaft with wire.
   d. Remove cotter pin and nut, then remove righthand driveshaft from hub and transaxle.

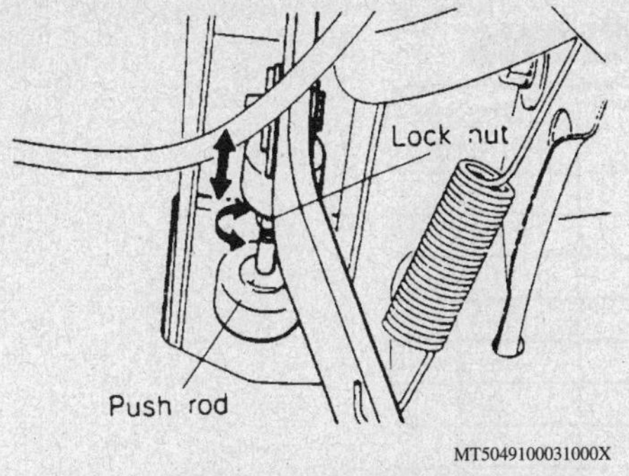
Lock nut
Push rod
MT5049100031000X

Fig. 6 Clutch pedal & clevis pin play adjustment

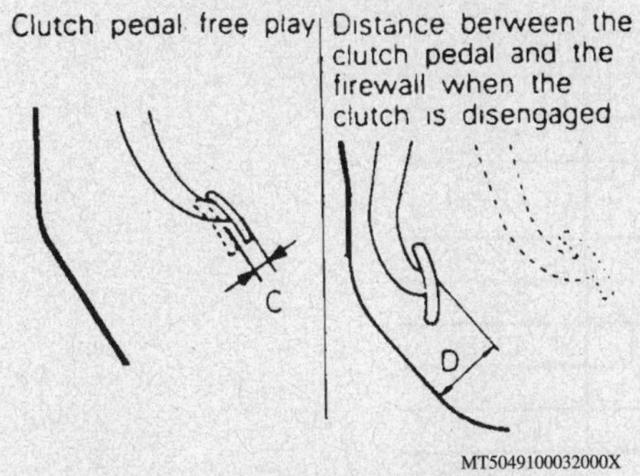
Clutch pedal free play
Distance between the clutch pedal and the firewall when the clutch is disengaged
C
D
MT5049100032000X

Fig. 7 Clutch pedal freeplay

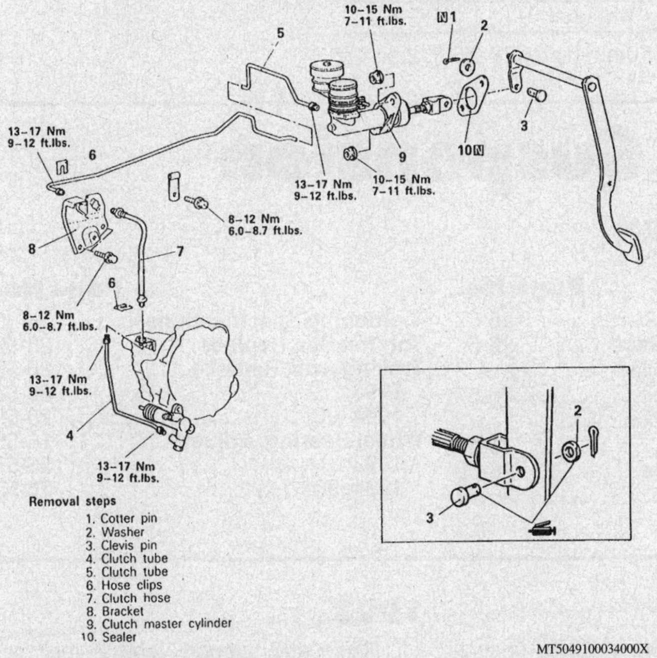
10-15 Nm
7-11 ft.lbs.
13-17 Nm
9-12 ft.lbs.
8-12 Nm
6.0-8.7 ft.lbs.
Removal steps
1. Cotter pin
2. Washer
3. Clevis pin
4. Clutch tube
5. Clutch tube
6. Hose clips
7. Clutch hose
8. Bracket
9. Clutch master cylinder
10. Sealer
MT5049100034000X

Fig. 8 Exploded view of clutch control system. 1993

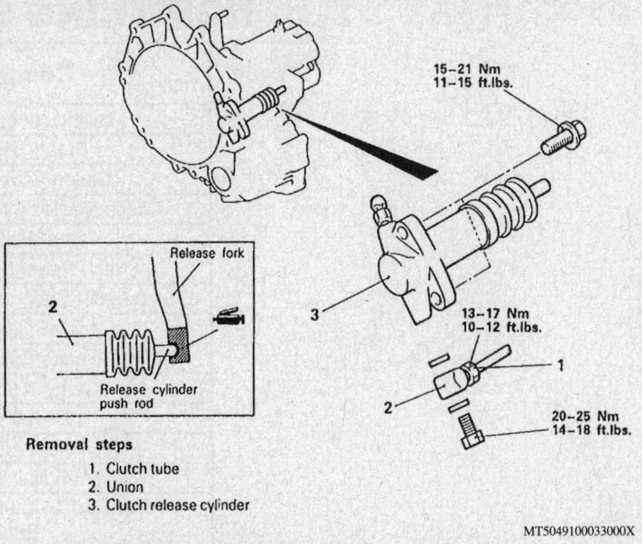
15-21 Nm
11-15 ft.lbs.
Release fork
Release cylinder push rod
13-17 Nm
10-12 ft.lbs.
20-25 Nm
14-18 ft.lbs.
Removal steps
1. Clutch tube
2. Union
3. Clutch release cylinder
MT5049100033000X

Fig. 9 Clutch release cylinder replacement. 1993

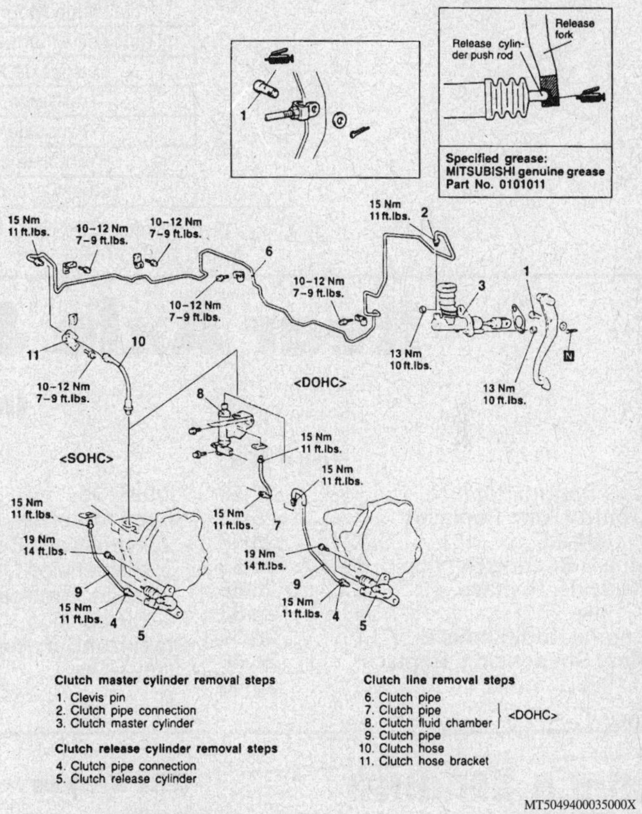
Release fork
Release cylinder push rod
Specified grease:
MITSUBISHI genuine grease
Part No. 0101011
15 Nm
11 ft.lbs.
10-12 Nm
7-9 ft.lbs.
13 Nm
10 ft.lbs.
19 Nm
14 ft.lbs.
<DOHC>
<SOHC>
Clutch master cylinder removal steps
1. Clevis pin
2. Clutch pipe connection
3. Clutch master cylinder
Clutch release cylinder removal steps
4. Clutch pipe connection
5. Clutch release cylinder
Clutch line removal steps
6. Clutch pipe
7. Clutch pipe
8. Clutch fluid chamber <DOHC>
9. Clutch pipe
10. Clutch hose
11. Clutch hose bracket
MT5049400035000X

Fig. 10 Exploded view of clutch control system. 1994–96

10. Remove bearing bracket and shaft assembly.
11. Remove front height sensor rod, then disconnect front exhaust pipe from engine.
12. Remove transaxle stay, then slide transaxle to the right and lower to remove.
13. Reverse procedure to install, noting the following:
    a. Tighten nuts and bolts to specification.
    b. Refill transaxle with suitable oil. Tighten filler and drain plugs to specification.

TIGHTENING SPECIFICATIONS

Year	Component	Torque/ Ft. Lbs.
1993–96	Bellhousing Cover Bolts	7–9
	Brake Booster Nut	8–12
	Clutch Cover Assembly	11–15
	Clutch Master Cylinder To Firewall	7–11
	Clutch Pedal Bracket	6–9
	Clutch Pedal Support Bracket	6–9
	Clutch Pedal Support Bracket To Firewall	7–11
	Clutch Release Cylinder	11–15
	Clutch Release Cylinder To Union Bolt	14–18
	Clutch Tube Bracket	6–9
	Driveshaft Nut	144–188
	Flywheel Attaching Bolt	98
	Lower Arm Ball Joint To Knuckle	43–52
	Pedal Rod To Clutch Pedal Support Bracket	12–19
	Tie Rod End To Knuckle	17–25
	Transaxle Mount Bracket To Body	29–36
	Transaxle Mount Bracket To Transaxle	43–58
	Transaxle Mounting Bolts	①
	Transaxle Oil Drain Plug	22–25
	Transaxle Oil Filler Plug	22–25
	Transaxle Stay To Engine	47–61
	Transaxle Case To Transaxle	40–43

① — 12mm bolts, 32–39 ft. lbs.; 10mm bolts, 22–25 ft. lbs.; 8mm bolts, 7–9 ft. lbs.

Rear Axle & Suspension

INDEX

	Page No.
Coil Spring, Replace	26-58
Control Arm, Replace	26-58
1994–96	26-58
Hub & Bearing Service	26-56
Knuckle, Replace	26-58
1994–96	26-58
Lateral Rod, Replace	26-59
Rear Suspension, Replace	26-56
1993	26-56
1994–96	26-57
Shock Absorber, Replace	26-57
Electronically Controlled Suspension	26-57
Less Electronically Controlled Suspension	26-57
Stabilizer Bar, Replace	26-59
1994–96	26-59
Tightening Specifications	26-63
Torsion Bar, Replace	26-59
Trailing Arm, Replace	26-58
1993	26-58
1994–96	26-59
Wheel Bearing, Adjust	26-56
1993	26-56
1994–96	26-56

HUB & BEARING SERVICE

Refer to **Figs. 1 through 3,** when replacing rear axle hub.

WHEEL BEARING

ADJUST

1993

Drum Brakes

Using a suitable spring scale, ensure rear hub rotary sliding **torque** is no more than 0.6 ft. lbs. when a new bearing is used or 0.5 ft. lbs. if an old bearing is used with drum brake pads removed.

Disc Brakes

Using a suitable spring scale, ensure rear hub rotary sliding **torque** is no more than 1.3 ft. lbs. with brake caliper assembly removed.

1994-96

Using a suitable spring scale, ensure rear hub rotary sliding resistance is no more than 3.9 lbs. with caliper or drum removed.

REAR SUSPENSION

REPLACE

Refer to **Figs. 4 through 6** for removal and installation of rear suspension.

1993

1. Raise and support vehicle, then remove rear wheels.
2. Disconnect parking brake cable from rear brake assembly and from the torsion axle and arm assembly.
3. Remove brake hose bracket from torsion axle and arm assembly.
4. Remove rear brake assembly and secure out of way.
5. Support torsion axle and arm assembly with a jack.
6. **On models with electronically controlled suspension,** disconnect height sensor rod from lateral rod.
7. **On all models,** remove lateral rod from body, refer to "Lateral Rod, Replace" procedure.

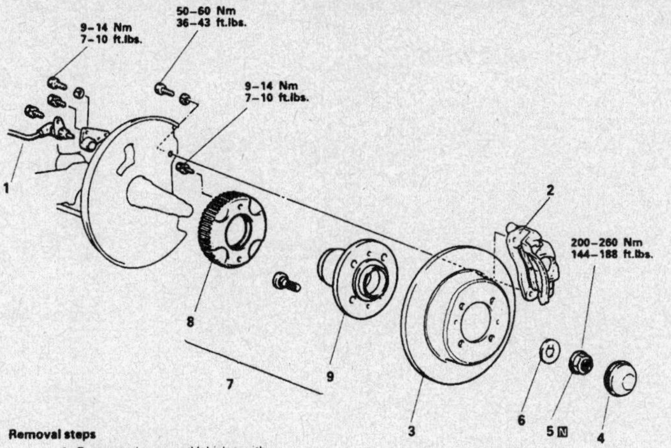
50-60 Nm
36-43 ft.lbs.
9-14 Nm
7-10 ft.lbs.
9-14 Nm
7-10 ft.lbs.
200-260 Nm
144-188 ft.lbs.

Removal steps

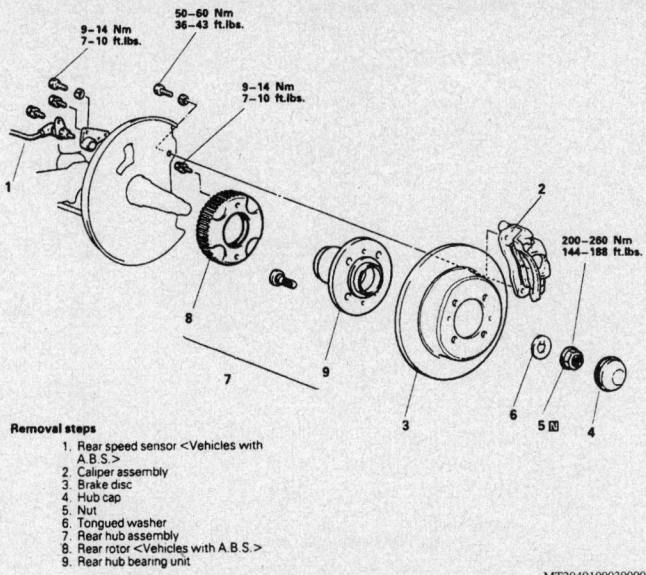

1. Rear speed sensor <Vehicles with A.B.S.>
2. Caliper assembly
3. Brake disc
4. Hub cap
5. Nut
6. Tongued washer
7. Rear hub assembly
8. Rear rotor <Vehicles with A.B.S.>
9. Rear hub bearing unit

MT2049100030000X

Fig. 1 Rear axle hub replacement. 1993 FWD w/rear disc brakes

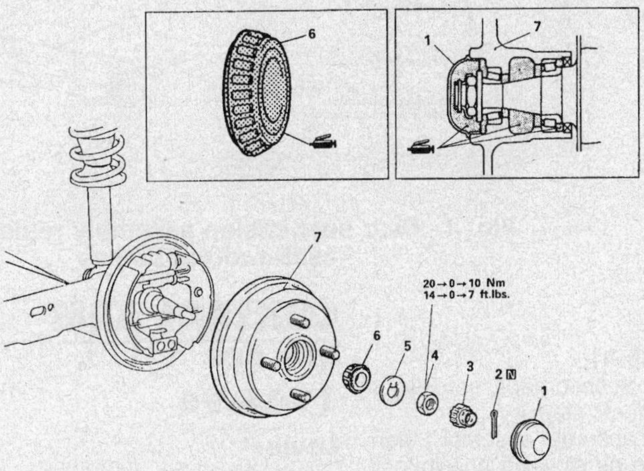
20→0→10 Nm
14→0→7 ft.lbs.

Removal steps

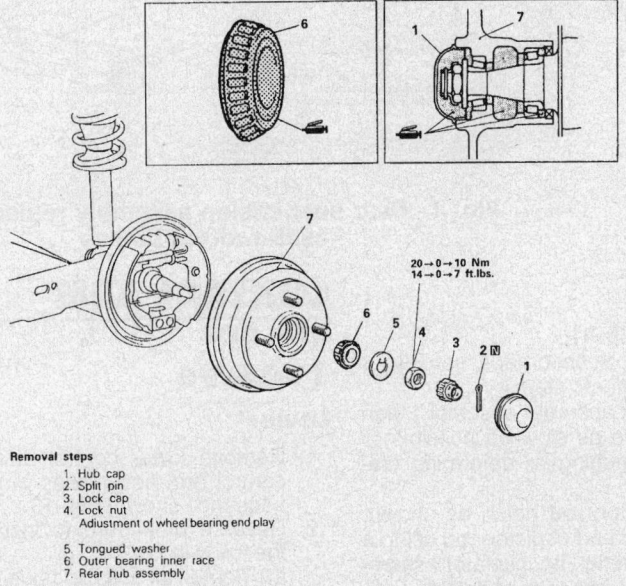

1. Hub cap
2. Split pin
3. Lock cap
4. Lock nut
   Adjustment of wheel bearing end play
5. Tongued washer
6. Outer bearing inner race
7. Rear hub assembly

MT2049100031000X

Fig. 2 Rear axle hub replacement. 1993 FWD w/rear drum brakes

8. Remove torsion axle and arm assembly from body, then disconnect top of shock absorber.
9. Lower jack, then remove rear suspension assembly from body.
10. Reverse procedure to install.

1994-96

1. Remove rear seat, then raise and support rear of vehicle and remove rear wheels, center exhaust pipe and shock absorber mounting nuts.
2. **On models with disc brakes,** remove brake caliper and rotor.
3. **On models with drum brakes,** remove brake drum and disconnect brake hose.
4. **On all models,** disconnect parking brake cable and rear speed sensor connector, then remove upper arm bracket mounting bolt.
5. Remove trailing arm mounting bolt, grommet and crossmember mounting nuts, then lower rear suspension assembly from vehicle.
6. Reverse procedure to install, noting the following:
   a. Bleed brake system as outlined in "Hydraulic Brake Systems" section.
   b. Adjust parking brake and inspect wheel alignment as necessary.
   c. Tighten all rear suspension assembly nuts and bolts to specifications in **Fig. 6.**

SHOCK ABSORBER

REPLACE

LESS ELECTRONICALLY CONTROLLED SUSPENSION

1. Raise and support vehicle.
2. Position jack under torsion axle and arm assembly, **Figs. 7 and 8.**
3. Remove shock absorber cap, shock absorber upper, then lower attaching nuts.
4. Remove shock absorber assembly from torsion axle and arm assembly.
5. Compress coil spring, then, while holding piston rod, remove piston rod attaching nut.
6. Remove washer, upper bushing (A), bracket, spring pad, upper bushing (B), collar, cup, dust cover, rubber bumper and coil spring from shock absorber.
7. Inspect rubber parts and coil springs for cracks, damage or deterioration and replace as necessary. **If coil spring replacement is necessary, be sure to use spring having the correct identification marks.**
8. Fully compress coil spring, then install spring into shock absorber.
9. Install dust cover on cup assembly.
10. Extend piston rod as far as possible, then install rubber bumper, cup assembly, collar, upper bushing (B), spring pad, bracket assembly, upper bushing (A) and washer.
11. Position bracket assembly as shown, **Fig. 8,** tighten piston rod attaching nut to specification, then remove spring compressor.
12. Install shock absorber assembly in torsion axle and arm assembly. Tighten lower attaching bolts to specification.
13. Install cap, then the shock absorber attaching nuts. Tighten upper attaching bolts to specification.
14. Install trunk compartment front trim, then remove jack from torsion axle and arm assembly.
15. Install rear wheels.

ELECTRONICALLY CONTROLLED SUSPENSION

1. Remove dust cover, **Figs. 9 through 11,** then disconnect and cap air tube from shock absorber. **Use caution not to bend air tube.**
2. Remove actuator from actuator bracket.
3. Remove adapter and snap ring, then the joint assembly from piston rod.
4. Remove O-ring and actuator bracket from piston rod.
5. Raise and support vehicle, then remove rear wheels.
6. Remove shock absorber assembly from torsion axle and arm assembly.
7. Remove shock absorber attaching nuts, then the shock absorber assembly from wheel housing. **Use caution not to damage piston rod.**
8. Check shock absorber assembly for air leaks as follows:

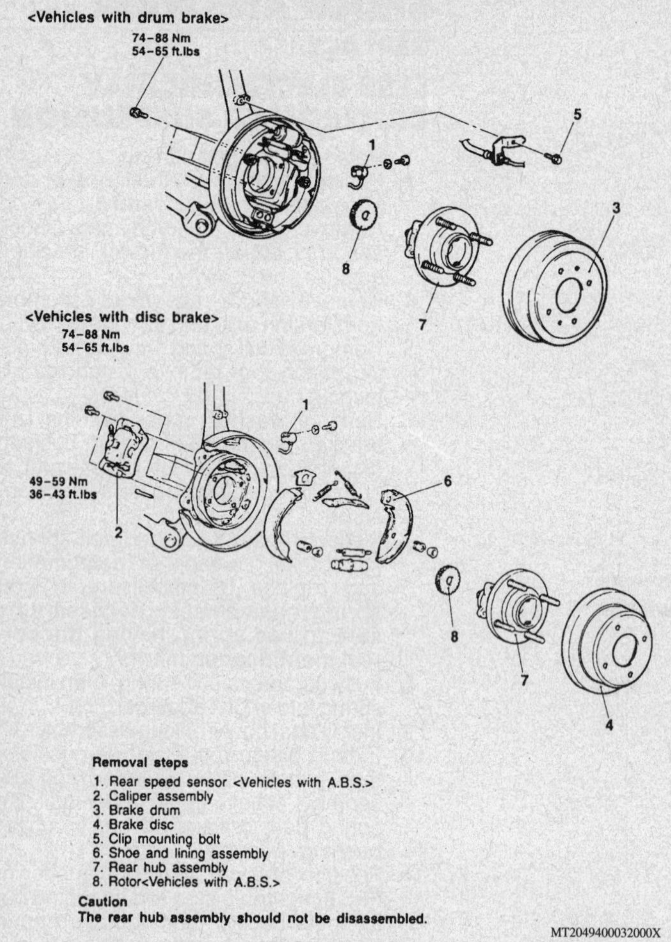
<Vehicles with drum brake>
74-88 Nm
54-65 ft.lbs
<Vehicles with disc brake>
74-88 Nm
54-65 ft.lbs
49-59 Nm
36-43 ft.lbs
Removal steps
1. Rear speed sensor <Vehicles with A.B.S.>
2. Caliper assembly
3. Brake drum
4. Brake disc
5. Clip mounting bolt
6. Shoe and lining assembly
7. Rear hub assembly
8. Rotor<Vehicles with A.B.S.>
Caution
The rear hub assembly should not be disassembled.
MT2049400032000X

Fig. 3 Rear axle hub replacement. 1994–96

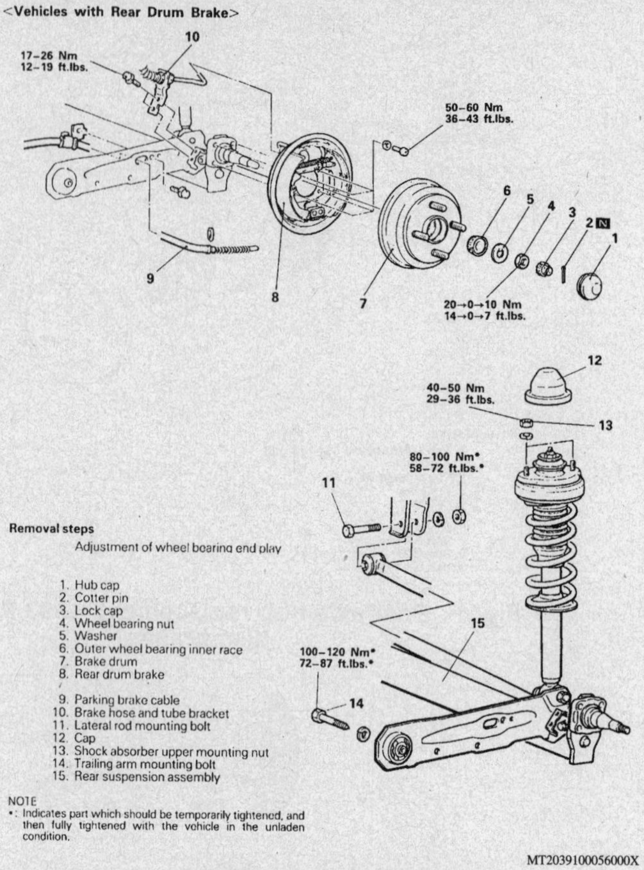
<Vehicles with Rear Drum Brake>
17-26 Nm
12-19 ft.lbs.
50-60 Nm
36-43 ft.lbs.
20→0→10 Nm
14→0→7 ft.lbs.
40-50 Nm
29-36 ft.lbs.
80-100 Nm*
58-72 ft.lbs.*
100-120 Nm*
72-87 ft.lbs.*
Removal steps
Adjustment of wheel bearing end play
1. Hub cap
2. Cotter pin
3. Lock cap
4. Wheel bearing nut
5. Washer
6. Outer wheel bearing inner race
7. Brake drum
8. Rear drum brake
9. Parking brake cable
10. Brake hose and tube bracket
11. Lateral rod mounting bolt
12. Cap
13. Shock absorber upper mounting nut
14. Trailing arm mounting bolt
15. Rear suspension assembly
NOTE
*: Indicates part which should be temporarily tightened, and then fully tightened with the vehicle in the unladen condition.
MT2039100056000X

Fig. 4 Rear suspension assembly replacement. 1993 w/drum brakes

a. Install joint assembly to shock absorber assembly and secure with snap ring.
b. Using air compressor for air supply, disconnect white air tube from solenoid valve, then connect tool No. MB991075, or equivalent, and inject 71 psi of air.
c. Submerse shock absorber assembly into a water tank and check for air leakage.
d. If air leakage is present, check sub-tank, O-ring and shock absorber assembly in that order. Repair as required.

9. Remove insulator attaching nut, then the insulator assembly, sub-tank, coil spring and lower spring pad.
10. Remove O-ring from sub-tank.
11. Check rubber parts, sub-tank and coil spring for damage, deterioration, deformation or cracks. Repair as required.
12. Install lower spring pad and coil spring on shock absorber. **When replacing coil spring, note that the left and right identification marks are different.**
13. Coat O-ring with specified grease, then install O-ring in sub-tank.
14. Install sub-tank, then the insulator assembly while temporarily tightening nut so installation angle of insulator assembly and lower bushing inner pipe is as shown, **Fig. 11.**
15. Recheck shock absorber assembly for air leaks. Refer to step 9.
16. Install shock absorber assembly, then lower vehicle as slow as possible to prevent damaging or deforming diaphragm.
17. Position piston rod notch as shown, **Fig. 11,** hold end of piston rod using a wrench, then tighten insulator assembly attaching nuts to specification.
18. Install actuator bracket, then tighten to specification.
19. Install O-ring on piston rod, the joint assembly, then secure with snap ring.
20. Install adapter and actuator, then connect air tubes.
21. Start engine and check for air leaks, then install dust cover.

COIL SPRING

REPLACE

1. Remove shock absorber assembly. Refer to procedure outlined under "Shock Absorber, Replace."
2. Disassemble shock absorber components in order as shown, **Fig. 12.**
3. Reverse procedure to install.

CONTROL ARM

REPLACE

1994–96

Lower

1. Remove lower control arm and toe control arm assemblies in numbered sequence shown, **Fig. 13.**
2. Reverse procedure to install, noting the following:
   a. Tighten all bolts and nuts to specifications, **Fig. 13.**
   b. Inspect and adjust rear wheel alignment as necessary.

KNUCKLE

REPLACE

1994–96

Refer to **Fig. 14** when replacing knuckle.

TRAILING ARM

REPLACE

1993

The trailing arm and torsion bar are removed as an assembly. Refer to "Torsion Bar, Replace" for replacement procedure.

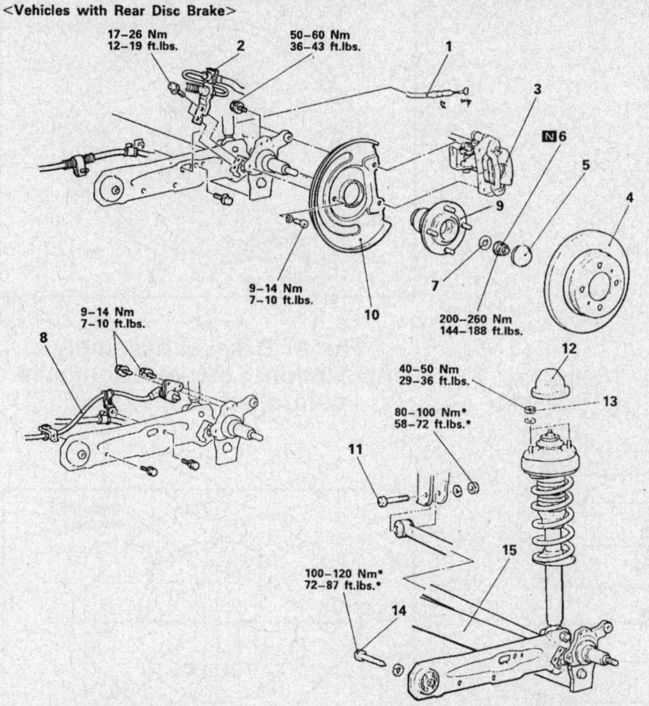
<Vehicles with Rear Disc Brake>
17–26 Nm
12–19 ft.lbs.
50–60 Nm
36–43 ft.lbs.
9–14 Nm
7–10 ft.lbs.
9–14 Nm
7–10 ft.lbs.
200–260 Nm
144–188 ft.lbs.
40–50 Nm
29–36 ft.lbs.
80–100 Nm*
58–72 ft.lbs.*
100–120 Nm*
72–87 ft.lbs.*

Removal steps

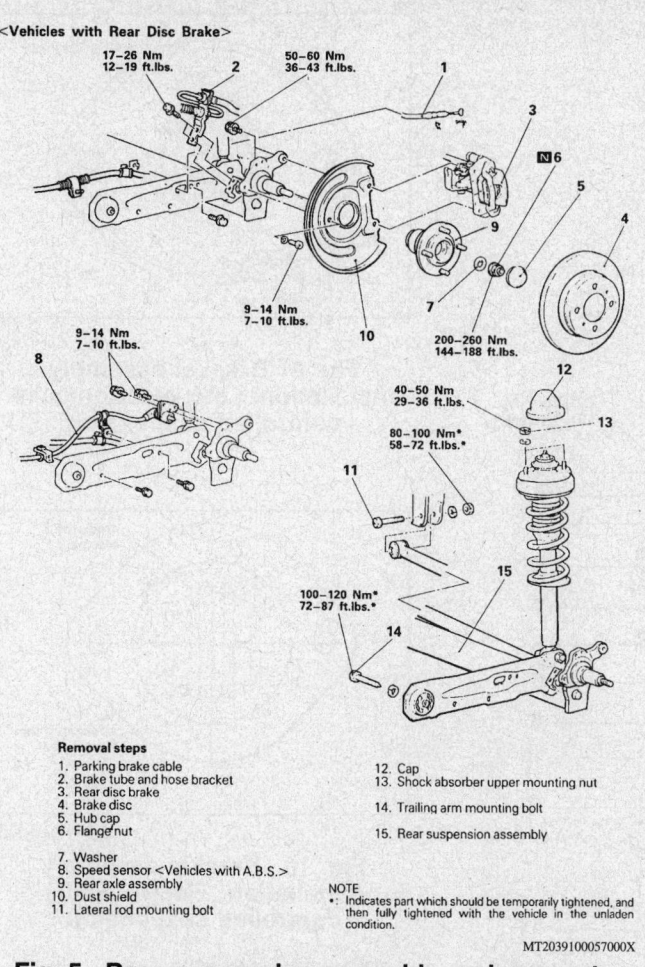

1. Parking brake cable
2. Brake tube and hose bracket
3. Rear disc brake
4. Brake disc
5. Hub cap
6. Flange nut
7. Washer
8. Speed sensor <Vehicles with A.B.S.>
9. Rear axle assembly
10. Dust shield
11. Lateral rod mounting bolt
12. Cap
13. Shock absorber upper mounting nut
14. Trailing arm mounting bolt
15. Rear suspension assembly

NOTE
*: Indicates part which should be temporarily tightened, and then fully tightened with the vehicle in the unladen condition.

MT2039100057000X

Fig. 5 Rear suspension assembly replacement. 1993 w/disc brakes

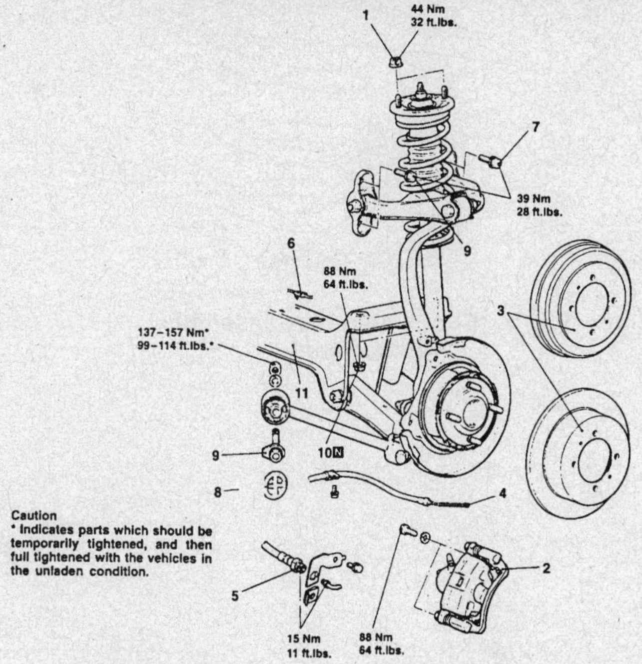
44 Nm
32 ft.lbs.
39 Nm
28 ft.lbs.
88 Nm
64 ft.lbs.
137–157 Nm*
99–114 ft.lbs.*
Caution
* Indicates parts which should be temporarily tightened, and then full tightened with the vehicles in the unladen condition.
15 Nm
11 ft.lbs.
88 Nm
64 ft.lbs.

Removal steps

1. Shock absorber mounting nuts
2. Brake caliper assembly <Vehicle with disc brake>
3. Brake disc <Vehicles with disc brake> or brake drum <Vehicles with drum brake>
4. Parking brake cable end
5. Brake hose connection <Vehicles with drum brake>
6. Rear speed sensor connector <Vehicles with ABS>
7. Upper arm bracket mounting bolt
8. Grommet
9. Trailing arm mounting bolt
10. Crossmember mounting self-locking nuts
11. Rear suspension assembly

MT2039400058000X

Fig. 6 Rear suspension assembly replacement. 1994–96

1994–96

1. Remove trailing arm assembly in numbered sequence shown, **Fig. 15.**
2. Reverse procedure to install, noting the following:
   a. Tighten all bolts and nuts to specifications, **Fig. 15.**
   b. Inspect and adjust rear wheel alignment as necessary.

STABILIZER BAR

REPLACE

1994–96

1. Remove stabilizer bar in numbered sequence shown in **Fig. 16.**
2. Reverse procedure to install. Tighten bolts and nuts to specifications.

TORSION BAR

REPLACE

1. Raise and support vehicle.
2. Remove torsion axle and arm assembly in numbered sequence shown in **Figs. 17 and 18,** noting the following:
   a. Raise up torsion axle and arm assembly. **Insert a wooden block between the jack and axle beam, do not allow jack to contact lateral rod.**
   b. Remove shock absorber mounting bolts and trailing arm mounting bolts.
   c. Lower jack slowly, then remove torsion axle and arm assembly.
3. Reverse procedure to install, noting the following:
   a. Install lateral rod mounting bolt from direction shown, **Fig. 19.**
   b. Adjust wheel bearing nut as outlined under "Wheel Bearings, Adjust."

LATERAL ROD

REPLACE

1. Raise and support vehicle, then remove rear wheels.
2. **On models with electronically controlled suspension,** disconnect height sensor rod from lateral rod.
3. **On all models,** remove lateral rod attaching nuts and bolts, then the lateral rod.
4. Reverse procedure to install. Tighten lateral rod attaching nuts and bolts to specifications.

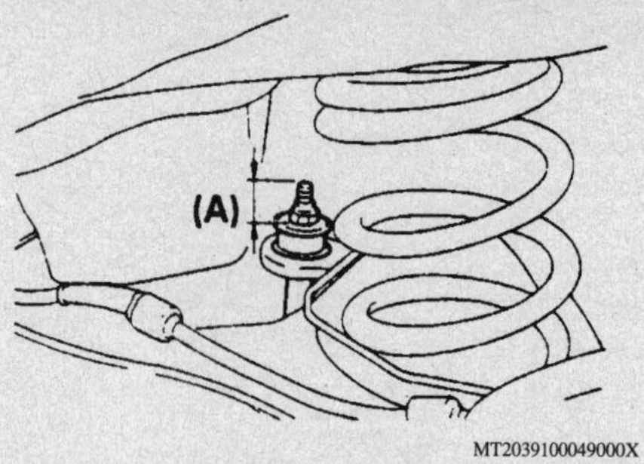
(A)
MT2039100049000X

Fig. 7 Shock absorber assembly replacement

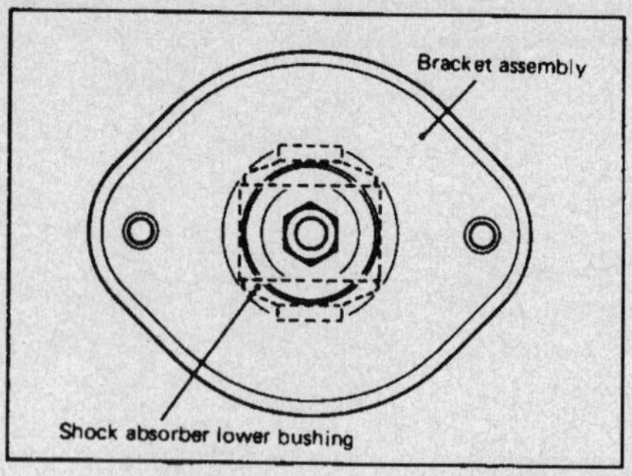
Bracket assembly
Shock absorber lower bushing
MT2039100050000X

Fig. 8 Bracket assembly installation. Less electronically controlled suspension

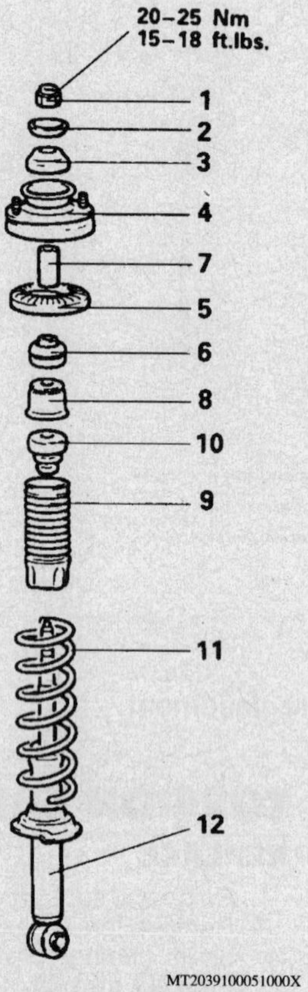
20–25 Nm
15–18 ft.lbs.
1
2
3
4
7
5
6
8
10
9
11
12
MT2039100051000X

Disassembly steps

1. Piston rod tightening nut
2. Washer
3. Upper bushing (A)
4. Bracket assembly
5. Spring pad
6. Upper bushing (B)
7. Collar
8. Cup assembly
9. Dust cover
10. Bump rubber
11. Coil spring
12. Shock absorber

Fig. 9 Shock absorber assembly replacement. Electronically controlled suspension

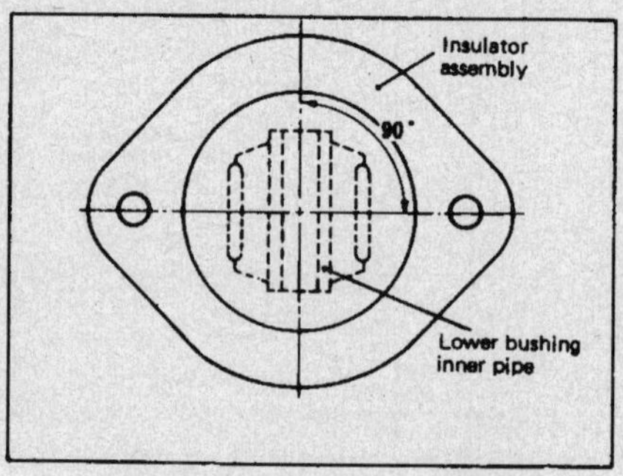
Insulator assembly
90°
Lower bushing inner pipe
MT2039100052000X

Fig. 10 Bracket assembly installation. Electronically controlled suspension

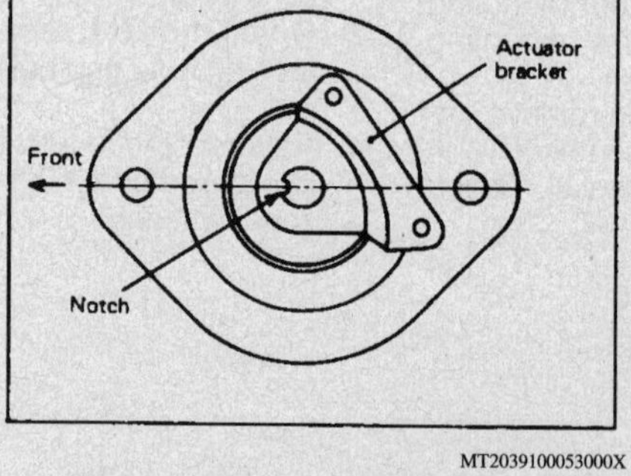
Actuator bracket
Front
Notch
MT2039100053000X

Fig. 11 Piston rod alignment. Electronically controlled suspension

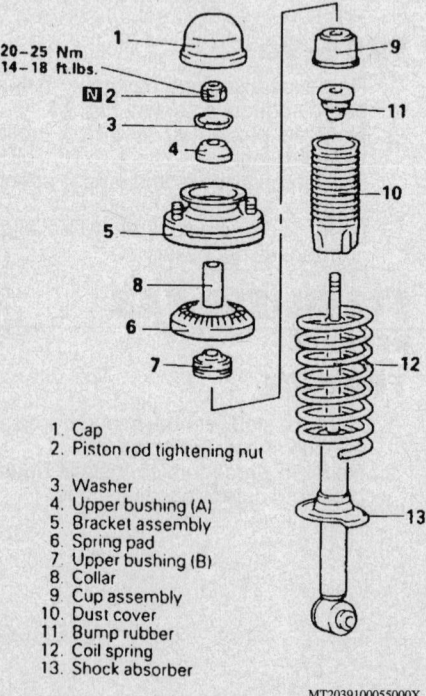

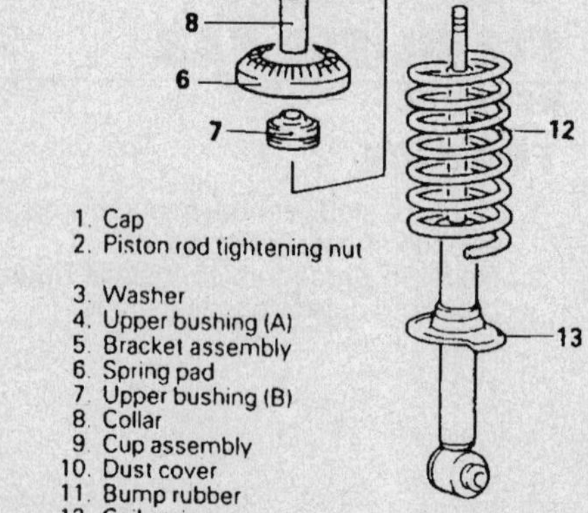
20–25 Nm
14–18 ft.lbs.
N 2
1
3
4
5
8
6
7
9
11
10
12
13

1. Cap
2. Piston rod tightening nut
3. Washer
4. Upper bushing (A)
5. Bracket assembly
6. Spring pad
7. Upper bushing (B)
8. Collar
9. Cup assembly
10. Dust cover
11. Bump rubber
12. Coil spring
13. Shock absorber

MT2039100055000X

Fig. 12 Coil spring replacement

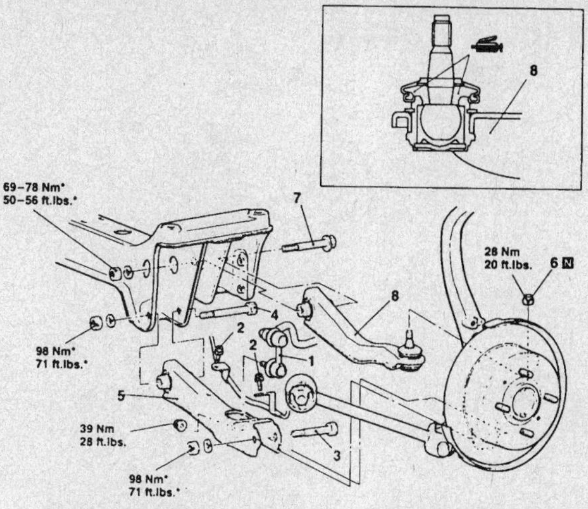
69–78 Nm*
50–56 ft.lbs.*
7
28 Nm
20 ft.lbs.
6 N
8
4
2
2
1
98 Nm*
71 ft.lbs.*
5
39 Nm
28 ft.lbs.
3
98 Nm*
71 ft.lbs.*

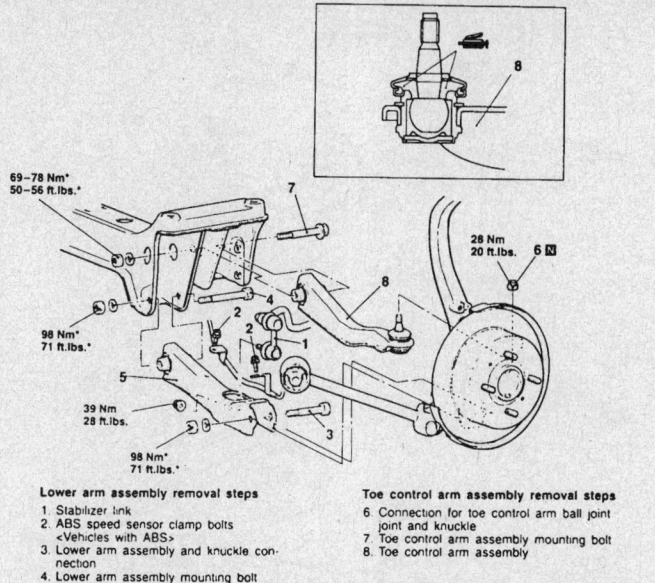

Lower arm assembly removal steps

1. Stabilizer link
2. ABS speed sensor clamp bolts <Vehicles with ABS>
3. Lower arm assembly and knuckle connection
4. Lower arm assembly mounting bolt
5. Lower arm assembly

Toe control arm assembly removal steps

6. Connection for toe control arm ball joint joint and knuckle
7. Toe control arm assembly mounting bolt
8. Toe control arm assembly

Caution
*** Indicates parts which should be temporarily tightened, and then fully tightened with the vehicle in the unladen condition.**

MT2039400070000X

Fig. 13 Lower control arm & toe control arm replacement. 1994–96

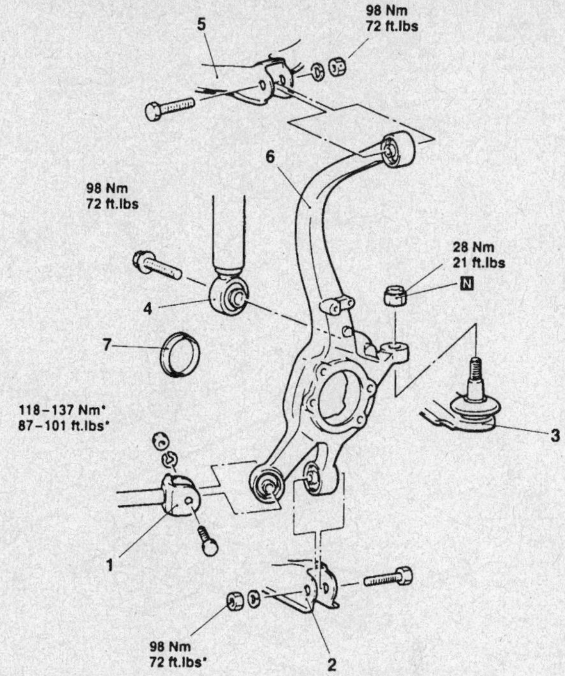
5
98 Nm
72 ft.lbs
6
98 Nm
72 ft.lbs
28 Nm
21 ft.lbs
N
4
7
118–137 Nm*
87–101 ft.lbs*
3
1
98 Nm
72 ft.lbs*
2

Removal steps

1. Connection for trailing arm
2. Connection for lower arm
3. Connection for toe control arm
4. Connection for shock absorber
5. Connection for upper arm
6. Knuckle
7. Hub cap <Vehicles without A.B.S.>

Caution
***: Indicates parts which should be temporarily tightened, and then fully tightened with the vehicle in the unladen condition.**

MT2039400071000X

Fig. 14 Knuckle replacement. 1994–96

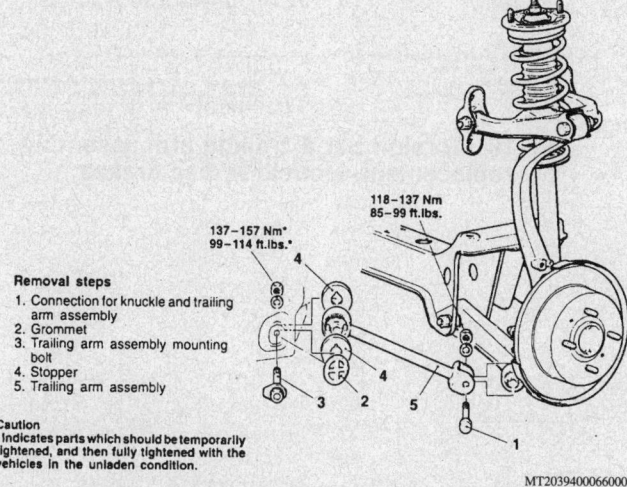

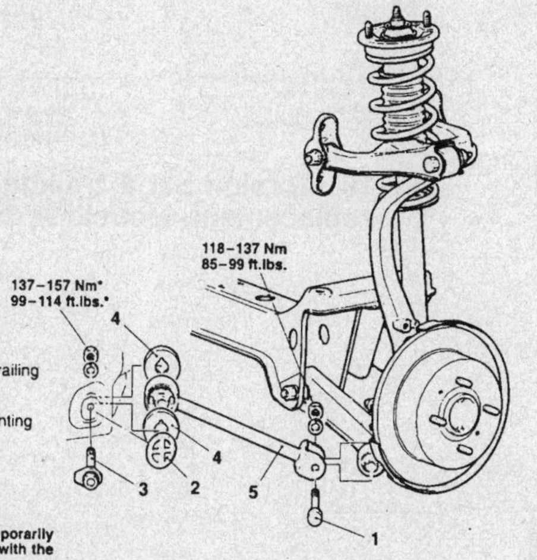
118–137 Nm
85–99 ft.lbs.
137–157 Nm*
99–114 ft.lbs.*
4
4
3
2
5
1

Removal steps

1. Connection for knuckle and trailing arm assembly
2. Grommet
3. Trailing arm assembly mounting bolt
4. Stopper
5. Trailing arm assembly

Caution
*** Indicates parts which should be temporarily tightened, and then fully tightened with the vehicles in the unladen condition.**

MT2039400066000X

Fig. 15 Trailing arm replacement. 1994–96

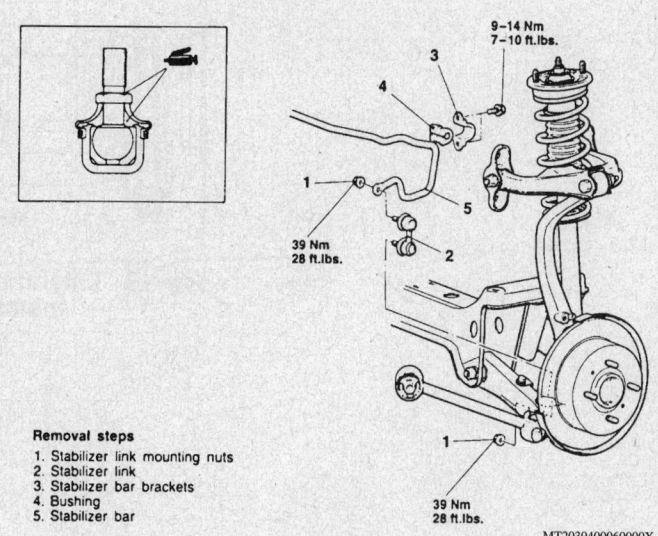

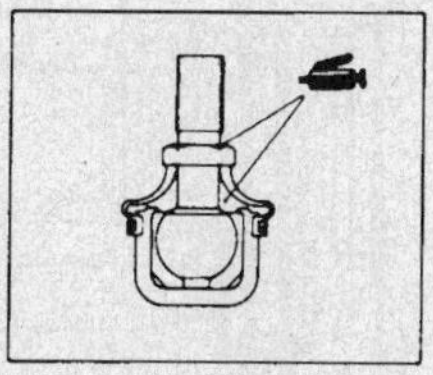

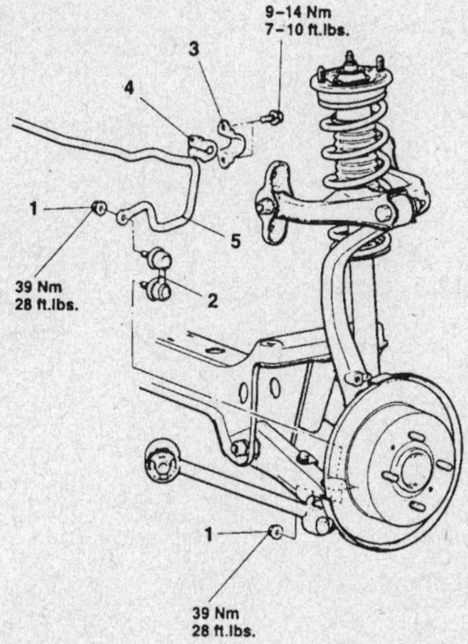
9–14 Nm
7–10 ft.lbs.
3
4
1
5
39 Nm
28 ft.lbs.
2
1
39 Nm
28 ft.lbs.

Removal steps

1. Stabilizer link mounting nuts
2. Stabilizer link
3. Stabilizer bar brackets
4. Bushing
5. Stabilizer bar

MT2039400060000X

Fig. 16 Stabilizer bar assembly replacement. 1994–96

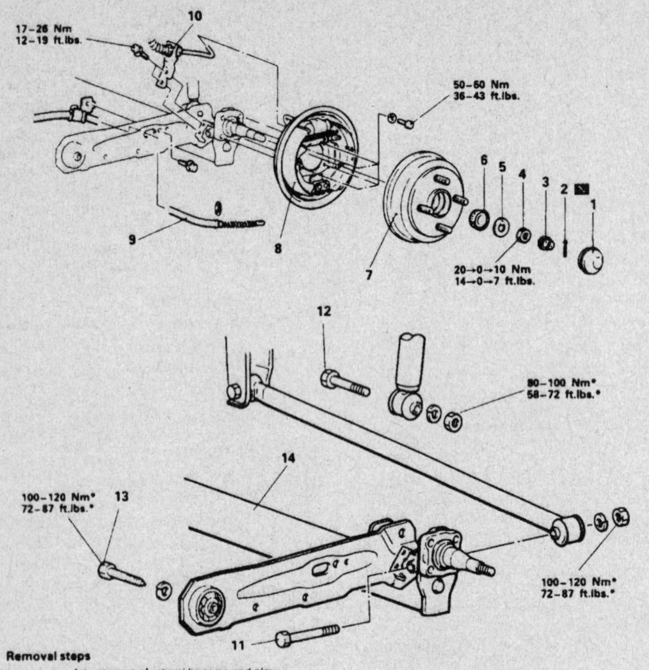

17-26 Nm
12-19 ft.lbs.
10
50-60 Nm
36-43 ft.lbs.
6
5
4
3
2
1
9
8
7
20→0→10 Nm
14→0→7 ft.lbs.
12
80-100 Nm*
58-72 ft.lbs.*
14
100-120 Nm*
72-87 ft.lbs.*
13
100-120 Nm*
72-87 ft.lbs.*
11

Removal steps

Adjustment of wheel bearing end play

Procedures)

1 Hub cap
2 Cotter pin
3 Cap
4 Wheel bearing nut
5 Washer
6 Outer wheel bearing inner race
7 Brake drum
8 Rear drum brake
9. Parking brake cable
10. Brake hose and tube bracket
11. Lateral rod mounting bolt
12. Shock absorber lower mounting bolt
13. Trailing arm mounting bolt
14. Torsion axle and arm assembly

• Indicates part which should be temporarily tightened, and then fully tightened with the vehicle in the unladen condition

MT2039100063000X

Fig. 17 Torsion bar & trailing arm assembly replacement. Models w/drum brakes

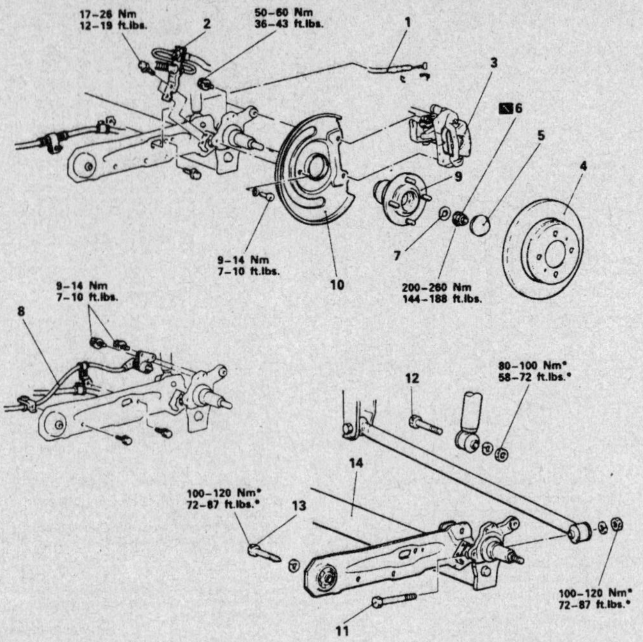

17-26 Nm
12-19 ft.lbs.
2
50-60 Nm
36-43 ft.lbs.
1
3
6
5
4
9
7
9-14 Nm
7-10 ft.lbs.
10
200-260 Nm
144-188 ft.lbs.
9-14 Nm
7-10 ft.lbs.
8
12
80-100 Nm*
58-72 ft.lbs.*
14
100-120 Nm*
72-87 ft.lbs.*
13
100-120 Nm*
72-87 ft.lbs.*
11

Removal steps

1. Parking brake cable
2. Brake tube and hose bracket
3. Rear disc brake
4. Brake disc
5. Hub cap
6. Flange nut
7. Washer
8. Speed sensor <Vehicles with A.B.S.>
9. Rear axle assembly
10. Dust shield
11. Lateral rod mounting bolt
12. Shock absorber lower mounting bolt
13. Trailing arm mounting bolt
14. Torsion axle and arm assembly

NOTE
• Indicates part which should be temporarily tightened, and then fully tightened with the vehicle in the unladen condition.

MT2039100064000X

Fig. 18 Torsion bar & trailing arm assembly replacement. Models w/disc brakes

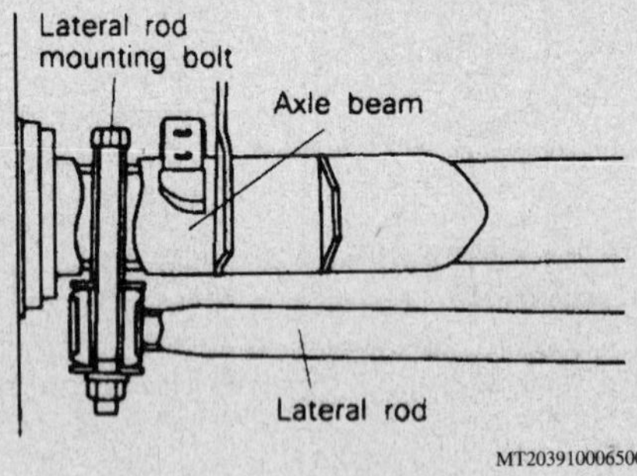

Lateral rod
mounting bolt
Axle beam
Lateral rod

MT2039100065000X

Fig. 19 Lateral rod mounting bolt installation

TIGHTENING SPECIFICATIONS

Year	Component	Torque/ Ft. Lbs
1993	Actuator Bracket To Shock Absorber	29–43
	Air Tube Flare Nut	6–7
	Bearing Cap Bolt	39–43
	Brake Assembly Mounting Bolt	36–43
	Brake Hose And Tube Bracket Mounting Bolt	12–19
	Brake Tube Bracket To Rear Shock Absorber	12–19
	Caliper Assembly Mounting Nut	36–43
	Center Exhaust Pipe To Front Exhaust Pipe Installation Nut	22–29
	Center Exhaust Pipe To Main Muffler Installation Nut	22–29
	Crossmember Bracket To Body	51–61
	Crossmember Bracket To Crossmember	80–84
	Dust Shield	7–10
	Filler Plug	29–43
	Hanger Installation Bolt	7–11
	Hook Installation Bolt	7–11
	Insulator Assembly Attaching Bolts	18–25
	Lateral Rod Mounting Bolt	72–87
	Lateral Rod Mounting Nut	58–72
	Lower Arm To Crossmember	65–80
	Lower Arm To Knuckle	43–52
	Piston Rod Tightening Nut	14–18
	Rear Brake Assembly Installation Bolt	36–43
	Rear Drum Brake Assembly To Axle Beam	36–43
	Rear Height Sensor Rod Locknut	7–10
	Rear Height Sensor Rod Mounting Bolt	12–19
	Rear Height Sensor Rod Mounting Nut	3.2–5.2
	Rear Hub To Rear Rotor	3–4
	Rear Speed Sensor Brackets	7–10
	Shock Absorber Installation Bolt	65–80
	Shock Absorber Installation Nut	29–36
	Shock Absorber Lower Mounting Nut	58–72
	Shock Absorber Upper Mounting Nut	18–25
	Speed Sensor	7–10
	Stabilizer Link To Stabilizer Bar	25–33
	Trailing Arm Mounting Bolt	72–87
	Trailing Arm To Crossmember	101–116
	Upper Arm To Crossmember	101–1116
	Upper Arm To Knuckle	43–52
	Upper Bushing To Piston Rod	14–18
	Wheel Bearing Locknut (Drum Brakes)	①
	Wheel Bearing Nut (Disc Brakes)	144–188
	Wheel Lug Nuts	65–80
	Brake Backing Plate Assembly Bolts	54–65
	Brake Hose To Brake Tube Fitting	11
	Caliper Bolts	36–43
	Crossmember Nuts	64

Continued

TIGHTENING SPECIFICATIONS—Continued

Year	Component	Torque/ Ft. Lbs
1993	Knuckle To Upper Arm Through Bolt Nut	72
	Lower Arm Assembly Mounting Bolt & Nut	71
	Lower Arm Assembly To Knuckle Bolt & Nut	71
	Shock Absorber Lower Mounting Bolt	72
	Shock Absorber Upper Mounting Nuts	32
	Stabilizer Bar Bracket Bolts	7–10
	Stabilizer Link Mounting Nuts	28
	Toe Control Arm Assembly Mounting Bolt & Nut	50–56
	Toe Control Arm Ball Joint Nut	20
	Trailing Arm Front Through Bolt Nut	99–114
	Trailing Arm To Knuckle Through Bolt Nut	85–99
	Upper Arm Bracket Bolts	28
	Wheel Lug Nuts	65–80

① — Torque to 14 ft. lbs., then to 0 ft. lbs., then retorque to 7 ft. lbs.

Front Suspension & Steering

NOTE: On Air Bag Equipped Models, Refer To "Air Bag System Precautions" Located In The Front Of This Manual For System Disarming & Arming Procedures.

INDEX

	Page No.
Ball Joint, Replace	26-65
Control Arm, Replace	26-67
Lower	26-67
Upper	26-67
Hub Service	26-65
1993	26-65
Manual Steering Gear	29-1
Power Steering	29-1
Power Steering Gear, Replace	26-67
1993	26-67
1994–96	26-67
Power Steering Pump, Replace	26-68
1993	26-68
1994–96	26-68
Precautions	26-64
Air Bag Systems	26-64
Rear Power Cylinder, Replace	26-70
Rear Power Cylinder Control Valve, Replace	26-71
Shock Absorber, Replace	26-67
1994–96	26-67
Stabilizer Bar, Replace	26-67
Strut, Replace	26-65
1993	26-65
Strut Service	26-65
1993	26-65
Tightening Specifications	26-71
Wheel Bearing, Adjust	26-64
Wheel Hub & Steering Knuckle, Replace	26-64
1993	26-64
1994–96	26-64

PRECAUTIONS

AIR BAG SYSTEMS

Refer to "Air Bag System Precautions" in the front of this manual for system disarming and arming procedures.

WHEEL BEARING

ADJUST

Bearing preload is preset to specified value by design and therefore cannot be adjusted.

WHEEL HUB & STEERING KNUCKLE

REPLACE

1993

1. Raise and support vehicle, then remove front wheels.
2. Disconnect brake caliper assembly and support using suitable wire.
3. Disconnect lower control arm ball joint from knuckle using a suitable tool.
4. Remove stabilizer bar from lower control arm.
5. Disconnect tie rod end from knuckle using a suitable tool.
6. Remove driveshaft from hub.
7. Remove hub and knuckle as an assembly from strut assembly.
8. Reverse procedure to install.

1994–96

1. Raise and support vehicle, then remove front wheels.
2. Remove hub assembly in numbered sequence shown, **Fig. 1.** Do not disconnect brake hose from caliper; support assembly aside, but do not allow caliper to hang by brake hose.
3. Remove knuckle in numbered sequence shown, **Fig. 2.** Use ball joint remover tool No. MB991113, or equivalent, to remove ball joints.

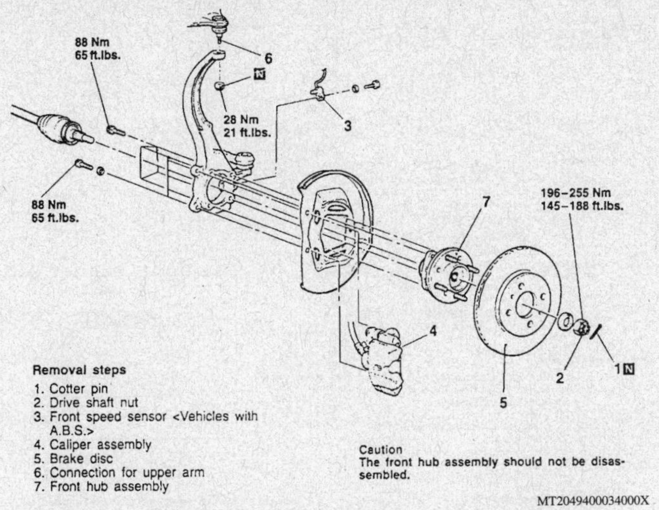
88 Nm
65 ft.lbs.
6
N
28 Nm
21 ft.lbs.
3
88 Nm
65 ft.lbs.
7
196–255 Nm
145–188 ft.lbs.
4
2
1 N
5
Removal steps
1. Cotter pin
2. Drive shaft nut
3. Front speed sensor <Vehicles with A.B.S.>
4. Caliper assembly
5. Brake disc
6. Connection for upper arm
7. Front hub assembly
Caution
The front hub assembly should not be disassembled.
MT2049400034000X

Fig. 1 Hub assembly replacement. 1994–96

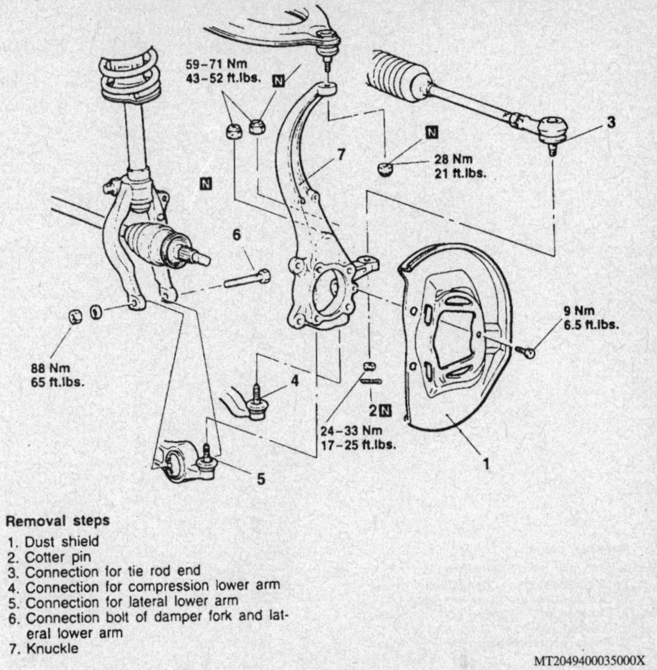
59–71 Nm
43–52 ft.lbs.
N
3
N
28 Nm
21 ft.lbs.
7
N
6
9 Nm
6.5 ft.lbs.
88 Nm
65 ft.lbs.
4
2 N
24–33 Nm
17–25 ft.lbs.
1
5
Removal steps
1. Dust shield
2. Cotter pin
3. Connection for tie rod end
4. Connection for compression lower arm
5. Connection for lateral lower arm
6. Connection bolt of damper fork and lateral lower arm
7. Knuckle
MT2049400035000X

Fig. 2 Knuckle replacement. 1994–96

4. Reverse procedure to install.

HUB SERVICE

1993

1. Attach tools No. MB990998-01 and MB991056, or equivalent, to knuckle and hub, then secure knuckle in vise.
2. Remove hub from knuckle by tightening nut of tool.
3. Remove outside bearing inner race from hub using tool No. MB990810-01, or equivalent.
4. Remove hub side oil seal from hub.
5. Remove brake disc from hub.
6. Remove driveshaft side oil seal from knuckle.
7. Remove snap ring from knuckle, then the wheel bearing using a suitable tool.
8. Pack wheel bearing with suitable grease.
9. Apply a thin coating of grease to knuckle and bearing contact surfaces.
10. With inside wheel bearing inner race removed, press in bearing using a suitable tool.
11. Install wheel bearing inner race to wheel bearing, then attach snap ring.
12. Drive hub side oil seal into knuckle using a suitable tool until it is flush with knuckle end surface.
13. Apply grease to lip of oil seal and surfaces of oil seal which contact hub.
14. Mount hub onto knuckle using tool No. MB990998-01, or equivalent. **Torque** nut to 145–187 ft. lbs.
15. Rotate hub to seat bearing, then check hub turning torque. Turning **torque** should be 16 inch lbs. or less.
16. Mount knuckle in vise, then check hub endplay using a suitable dial gauge. Endplay should be 0.008 inch.
17. If turning torque and hub endplay are not as specified, hub and/or knuckle may have been installed incorrectly. Repeat service procedures.
18. Apply grease to bearing and inside of knuckle, then drive driveshaft side oil seal into knuckle until it contacts snap ring.
19. Apply grease to lip of oil seal.

BALL JOINT

REPLACE

Refer to “Control Arm, Replace” for ball joint replacement procedure.

STRUT

REPLACE

1993

Less Electronically Controlled Suspension

1. Raise and support vehicle, then remove front wheel.
2. Remove brake hose bracket from strut assembly.
3. Disconnect strut assembly from knuckle arm.
4. Remove dust cover from strut assembly.
5. Hold piston rod with a suitable hex wrench, then remove strut assembly attaching nut using tool No. MB991038, or equivalent.
6. Remove stopper and stopper rubber insulator, then remove strut assembly from wheel house.
7. Reverse procedure to install.

Electronically Controlled Suspension

1. Raise and support vehicle, then remove front wheel.
2. Remove brake hose bracket from strut assembly.
3. Disconnect height sensor rod from lower control arm.
4. Disconnect strut assembly from knuckle arm, then support knuckle assembly with a suitable piece of wire.
5. Disconnect and cap air tube from strut assembly joint, then remove dust cover. Use caution not to bend air tube.
6. Remove strut assembly attaching nuts, then remove strut assembly from wheel house.
7. Reverse procedure to install.

STRUT SERVICE

1993

DISASSEMBLE

Less Electronically Controlled Suspension

1. Compress coil spring using tool No. MB990987, or equivalent.
2. Hold piston rod with suitable hex wrench, then remove piston rod attaching nut using tool No. MB991036, or equivalent.
3. Remove rubber insulator, support, spring seat, spring pad, rubber bumper, dust cover and coil spring from strut.
4. Remove bearing from support using a suitable brass rod.

Electronically Controlled Suspension

1. Attach tool No. MB991043, or equivalent, to strut assembly.
2. Remove snap ring using a suitable screwdriver, then the air joint from strut assembly.
3. Remove actuator bracket from strut assembly.
4. Remove insulator attaching nut, then the insulator from strut assembly.
5. Slowly loosen tool No. MB9901043, or equivalent, and remove sub-tank, coil spring and lower spring pad.
6. Remove O-ring from sub-tank.

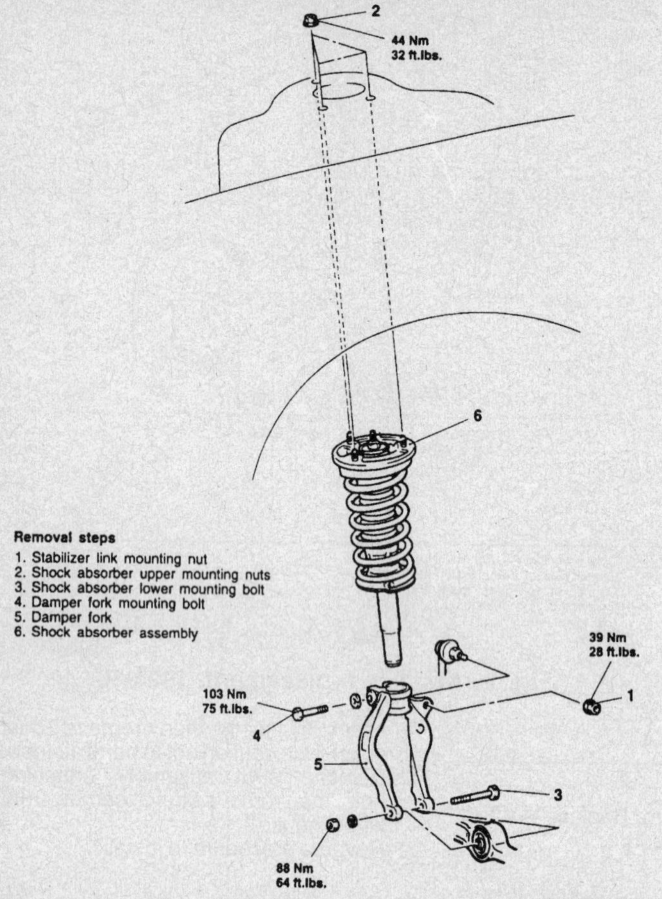
44 Nm
32 ft.lbs.
2
6
39 Nm
28 ft.lbs.
1
103 Nm
75 ft.lbs.
4
5
3
88 Nm
64 ft.lbs.
Removal steps
1. Stabilizer link mounting nut
2. Shock absorber upper mounting nuts
3. Shock absorber lower mounting bolt
4. Damper fork mounting bolt
5. Damper fork
6. Shock absorber assembly

MT2029400027000X

Fig. 3 Shock absorber replacement. 1994–96

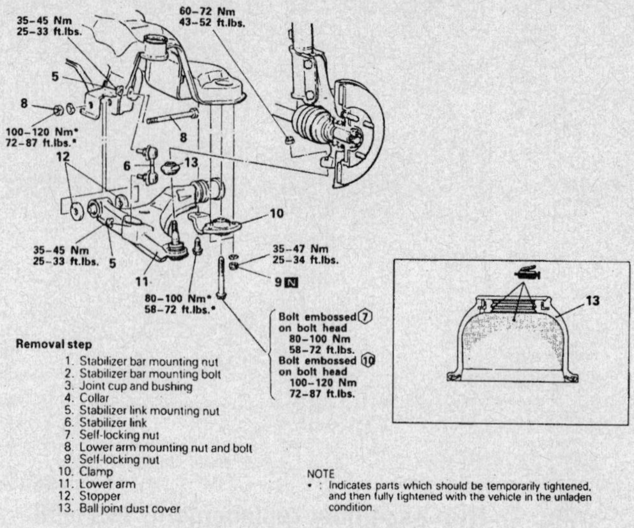
35–45 Nm
25–33 ft.lbs.
60–72 Nm
43–52 ft.lbs.
5
8
100–120 Nm*
72–87 ft.lbs.*
8
12
6
13
10
35–45 Nm
25–33 ft.lbs.
5
11
35–47 Nm
25–34 ft.lbs.
9 N
80–100 Nm*
58–72 ft.lbs.*
Bolt embossed (7) on bolt head
80–100 Nm
58–72 ft.lbs.
Bolt embossed (10) on bolt head
100–120 Nm
72–87 ft.lbs.
13
Removal step
1. Stabilizer bar mounting nut
2. Stabilizer bar mounting bolt
3. Joint cup and bushing
4. Collar
5. Stabilizer link mounting nut
6. Stabilizer link
7. Self-locking nut
8. Lower arm mounting nut and bolt
9. Self-locking nut
10. Clamp
11. Lower arm
12. Stopper
13. Ball joint dust cover
NOTE
* : Indicates parts which should be temporarily tightened, and then fully tightened with the vehicle in the unladen condition.

MT2029100024000X

Fig. 4 Exploded view of lower control arm & stabilizer bar. 1993

INSPECTION

Check all strut assembly components for wear or damage and replace as necessary.

ASSEMBLE

Coil springs have color marks to indicate coil spring identification and load classification. This identification mark indicates applicable vehicle model equipped with that particular coil spring. When replacing coil spring, be sure to use spring having appropriate identification mark.

Less Electronically Controlled Suspension

1. With support facing black retainer side of bearing, press bearing into support using suitable tool.
2. Compress spring using tool No. MB990987, or equivalent, then install spring into strut.
3. Extend piston rod as far as possible, then install dust cover, rubber bumper and spring pad.
4. Install spring upper seat onto piston rod and align D-shaped hole with notch in rod.
5. Install support on piston rod, then **torque**nut to 40–50 ft. lbs. using suitable tool.
6. Align both ends of coil spring with grooves in spring seat, then slowly loosen spring compressor. Ensure spring seat does not become twisted. **The upper and lower spring seats can be easily aligned by inserting a 0.4 inch diameter rod into holes in the seats.**
7. Install rubber insulator on strut assembly.

Electronically Controlled Suspension

1. Apply a coating of suitable grease to sub-tank O-ring, then install O-ring in sub-tank.
2. Install strut assembly lower spring pad, coil spring and sub-tank into tool No. MB991043, or equivalent. **Ensure larger outer diameter of coil spring is facing downward.**
3. Compress coil spring while aligning notched portion of piston rod to fit the D shape of sub-tank. Ensure lower edge of coil spring, spring pad and sub-tank are properly aligned.
4. Install insulator on strut assembly, then the insulator attaching nut. Tighten nut to specification.
5. Remove tool No. MB991043, or equivalent, and apply a coating of suitable grease to the insulator bearing channel.
6. Align notch of piston rod with D shape of actuator bracket.
7. Install actuator bracket to strut assembly, then the actuator bracket attaching nut. Tighten nut to specification.
8. Apply a coating of suitable grease to piston rod O-ring, then install O-ring on piston rod.
9. Install air joint on strut assembly, then using suitable pliers to pull piston rod upward, attach snap ring to piston rod.
10. Ensure joint turns smoothly, then check strut assembly for air leaks as follows:
    a. Disconnect white air tube (for HARD/SOFT mode switching) of front solenoid valve from reserve tank.
    b. Using air pressure gauge tool No. MB991075, or equivalent, and adapter A, connect white air tube to air tube at shutoff valve side of gauge.
    c. Using adapter D of air pressure gauge, connect air tube on other end of pressure gauge to joint of strut assembly. **To prevent moisture from getting into strut assembly, use air which has passed through reserve tank.**
    d. Disconnect air compressor electrical connector and apply battery voltage to operate air compressor.
    e. Submerse strut assembly into water tank and check for air leakage at an air pressure of about 71 psi.
    f. If air leakage is found, check sub-tank O-ring, sub-tank and strut assembly in that order, replace as necessary.
    g. Align adapter with notch in piston rod, then attach actuator.
    h. Exchange adapter D, connected to strut side, with adapter B and connect to joint part of actuator.
    i. Apply air at a pressure of 100 psi from joint part of actuator, then check to ensure there is no air leakage and system changes over to HARD mode.
    j. If air leak is found, repair as necessary.

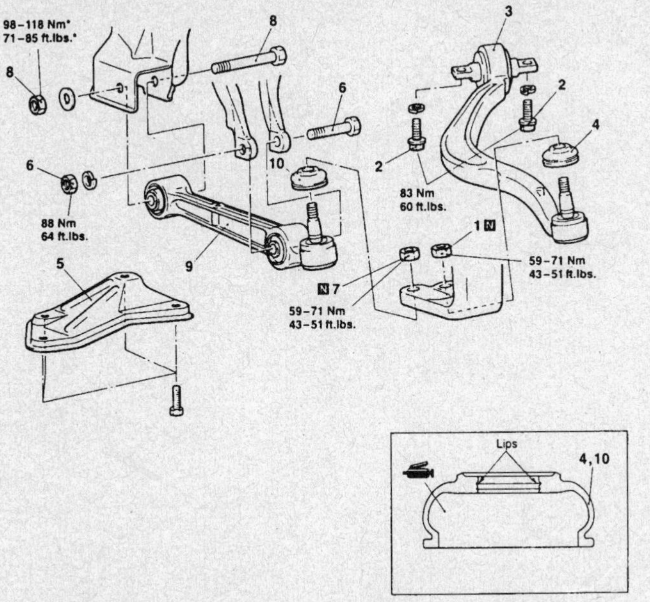
98–118 Nm*
71–85 ft.lbs.*
83 Nm
60 ft.lbs.
88 Nm
64 ft.lbs.
59–71 Nm
43–51 ft.lbs.
59–71 Nm
43–51 ft.lbs.
Lips
4,10
Compression lower arm assembly removal steps
1. Connection for compression lower arm ball joint and knuckle
2. Compression lower arm mounting bolt
3. Compression lower arm assembly
4. Dust cover
Lateral lower arm assembly removal steps
5. Stay
6. Shock absorber lower mounting bolt and nut
7. Connection for lateral lower arm ball joint and knuckle
8. Lateral lower arm mounting bolt and nut
9. Lateral lower arm assembly
10. Dust cover
Caution
*: Indicates parts which should be temporarily tightened, and then fully tightened with the vehicle in the unladen condition.
MT2029400025000X

Fig. 5 Lower control arm replacement. 1994–96

11. Reverse procedure to install.

SHOCK ABSORBER

REPLACE

1994–96

1. Raise and support vehicle, then remove front wheel.
2. Remove shock absorber in numbered sequence shown, **Fig. 3.**
3. Reverse procedure to install.

CONTROL ARM

REPLACE

LOWER

1993

1. Raise and support vehicle, then remove front wheels.
2. Disconnect stabilizer bar from lower control arm, **Fig. 4.**
3. **On models with electronically controlled suspension,** disconnect rod of height sensor from lower control arm if right side control arm is to be removed.
4. **On all models,** loosen ball joint stud nut, then disconnect ball joint from knuckle using a suitable tool.
5. Remove lower control arm from crossmember.
6. Inspect control arm and bushings, replacing as necessary.
7. Check ball joint starting torque. Starting **torque** should be 17–78 inch lbs. Replace ball joint as required.
8. Check ball joint dust cover for cracks and damage. If necessary, remove defective dust cover and replace with new cover using tool No. MB990800, or equivalent.
9. Reverse procedure to install noting the following:
   a. Refer to **Fig. 4** for tightening specifications.
   b. When installing ends of stabilizer bar to control arm, tighten self-locking attaching nut ensuring distance from base of nut to end of bolt is 0.63–0.70 inch.

1994–96

1. Raise and support vehicle, then remove front wheels.
2. Remove compression lower arm and/or lateral lower arm in numbered sequence shown, **Fig. 5.** Use ball joint remover tool No. MB991113, or equivalent, when disconnecting compression lower arm ball joint and knuckle.
3. Reverse procedure to install.

UPPER

1994–96

1. Raise and support front of vehicle.
2. Remove upper arm assembly in numbered sequence shown, **Fig. 6.**
3. Reverse procedure to install. Inspect and adjust wheel alignment as necessary.

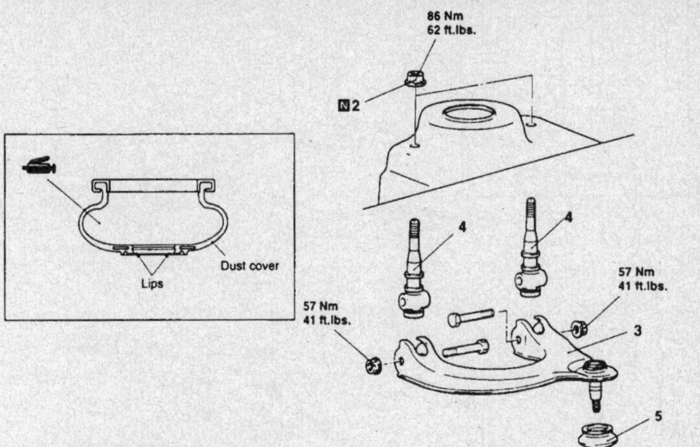
86 Nm
62 ft.lbs.
Dust cover
Lips
57 Nm
41 ft.lbs.
57 Nm
41 ft.lbs.
28 Nm
20 ft.lbs.
Removal steps
1. Connection for upper arm ball joint and knuckle
2. Self-locking nut for upper arm installation
3. Upper arm assembly
4. Upper arm shaft assembly
5. Dust cover
MT2029400026000X

Fig. 6 Upper control arm replacement. 1994–96

STABILIZER BAR

REPLACE

When replacing stabilizer bar refer to **Figs. 7 and 8** for removal and installation procedures.

POWER STEERING GEAR

REPLACE

1993

1. Raise and support front of vehicle, then remove front wheels.
2. **On models with electronically controlled suspension,** remove stabilizer bar.
3. **On all models,** disconnect tie rod from knuckle, using a suitable tool.
4. Drain power steering fluid into appropriate container, then disconnect and cap pressure and return hoses.
5. Disconnect joint assembly from gearbox, then the solenoid valve connector.
6. Remove center member rear attaching bolt and exhaust pipe hanger from crossmember.
7. Remove front roll stopper bolt, then disconnect and lower front end front exhaust pipe.
8. Remove stay at left side, then press rear side of center member downward.
9. Move rack to the right, then remove steering gear from crossmember.
10. Tilt steering gear downward, then remove from vehicle.
11. Reverse procedure to install.

1994–96

1. Drain power steering fluid as follows:
   a. Raise and support front of vehicle, then disconnect power steering fluid return hose.
   b. Connect a vinyl hose to return hose and drain fluid into a suitable container.

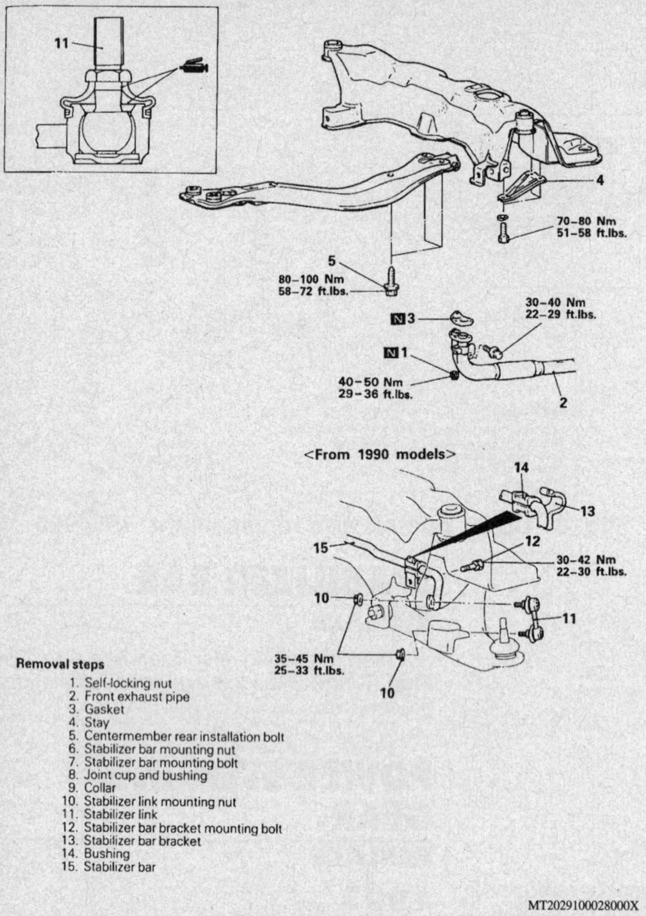

11
4
70–80 Nm
51–58 ft.lbs.
5
80–100 Nm
58–72 ft.lbs.
30–40 Nm
22–29 ft.lbs.
N 3
N 1
40–50 Nm
29–36 ft.lbs.
2
<From 1990 models>
14
13
12
15
30–42 Nm
22–30 ft.lbs.
10
11
35–45 Nm
25–33 ft.lbs.
10
Removal steps
1. Self-locking nut
2. Front exhaust pipe
3. Gasket
4. Stay
5. Centermember rear installation bolt
6. Stabilizer bar mounting nut
7. Stabilizer bar mounting bolt
8. Joint cup and bushing
9. Collar
10. Stabilizer link mounting nut
11. Stabilizer link
12. Stabilizer bar bracket mounting bolt
13. Stabilizer bar bracket
14. Bushing
15. Stabilizer bar
MT2029100028000X

Fig. 7 Stabilizer bar replacement. 1993

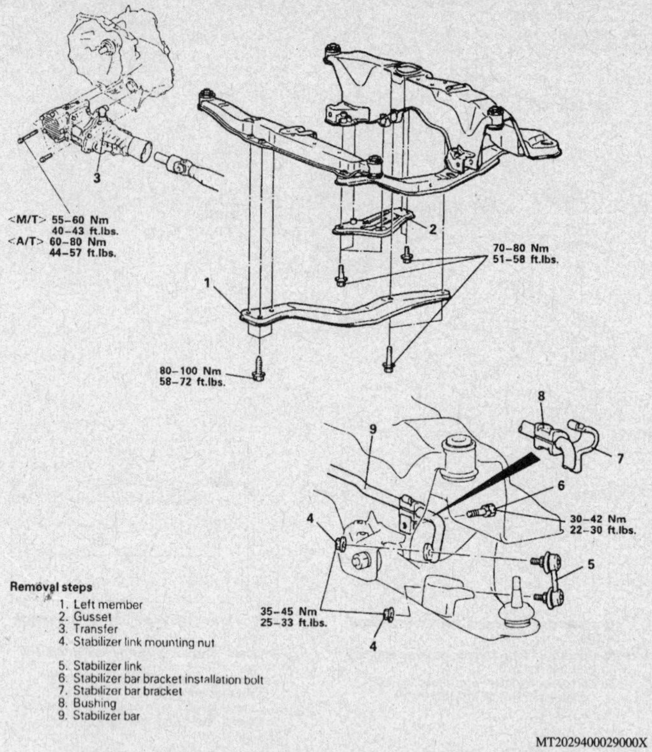

<M/T> 55–60 Nm
40–43 ft.lbs.
<A/T> 60–80 Nm
44–57 ft.lbs.
3
2
70–80 Nm
51–58 ft.lbs.
1
80–100 Nm
58–72 ft.lbs.
8
9
7
6
4
30–42 Nm
22–30 ft.lbs.
5
35–45 Nm
25–33 ft.lbs.
4
Removal steps
1. Left member
2. Gusset
3. Transfer
4. Stabilizer link mounting nut
5. Stabilizer link
6. Stabilizer bar bracket installation bolt
7. Stabilizer bar bracket
8. Bushing
9. Stabilizer bar
MT2029400029000X

Fig. 8 Stabilizer bar replacement. 1994–96

   c. Disconnect coil wire to prevent engine from starting, then crank engine intermittently while turning steering wheel back and forth between stops to purge remaining fluid from power steering circuit.
2. Remove stabilizer bar as outlined under "Stabilizer Bar, Replace," then remove power steering gear in numbered sequence shown, **Fig. 9,** noting the following:
   a. Use ball joint remover tool No. MB991113, or equivalent, when removing tie rod ends.
   b. In order to gain enough clearance to remove power steering gear from vehicle, it may be necessary to remove bolt from engine rear roll stopper bracket and lower rear of engine slightly.
3. Reverse procedure to install. Fill power steering fluid reservoir and bleed air from system as follows:
   a. Raise and support vehicle, then rotate oil pump pulley several times by hand and turn steering wheel back and forth between stops through 5 or 6 cycles.
   b. Disconnect coil wire to prevent engine from starting, then crank engine intermittently while turning steering wheel back and forth between stops. **Ensure reservoir is kept full during bleeding process. Do not attempt to bleed system with engine running.**
   c. After turning steering wheel from stop to stop 5 or 6 times, connect coil wire and start engine.
   d. Turn steering wheel from stop to stop until no bubbles appear in reservoir. Ensure fluid is not milky and fluid level does not diminish greatly when steering wheel is turned.

POWER STEERING PUMP

REPLACE

1993

Front

1. Drain power steering fluid into a suitable container.
2. Replace power steering pump in numbered sequence as shown, **Fig. 10,** noting the following:
   a. Turn pulley to align pulley hole with bolt position to remove mounting bolts.
   b. Connect so that hose covers 1 inch of pump tube.

Rear

1. Drain power steering fluid into a suitable container.
2. Remove main muffler assembly.
3. Replace rear power steering pump in numbered sequence as shown, **Fig. 11.**
4. Reverse procedure to install, noting the following:
   a. Bleed the power steering system as outlined under "Bleeding System" in the "Power Steering" section.
   b. Bleed the Four Wheel Steering (4WS) system as outlined under "Bleeding System" in the "Power Steering" section.

1994–96

1. Drain power steering fluid as follows:
   a. Raise and support front of vehicle, then disconnect power steering fluid return hose.
   b. Connect a vinyl hose to return hose and drain fluid into a suitable container.
   c. Disconnect coil wire to prevent engine from starting, then crank engine intermittently while turning steering wheel back and forth between stops to purge remaining fluid from power steering circuit.
2. Remove power steering pump in numbered sequence shown, **Fig. 12.**
3. Reverse procedure to install. Adjust pump drive belt tension as necessary.
4. Bleed air from power steering fluid as follows:
   a. Raise and support vehicle, then rotate oil pump pulley several times by hand and turn steering wheel back and forth between stops through 5 or 6 cycles.
   b. Disconnect coil wire to prevent engine from starting, then crank engine intermittently while turning

Removal steps

1. Joint assembly and gear box connecting bolt
2. Solenoid valve connector <Vehicles with EPS>
3. Cotter pin
4. Connection for tie-rod end and knuckle
5. Stay (L.H.)
6. Stay (R.H.)
7. Center member assembly
8. Clamp
9. Bolt
10. Gear box assembly

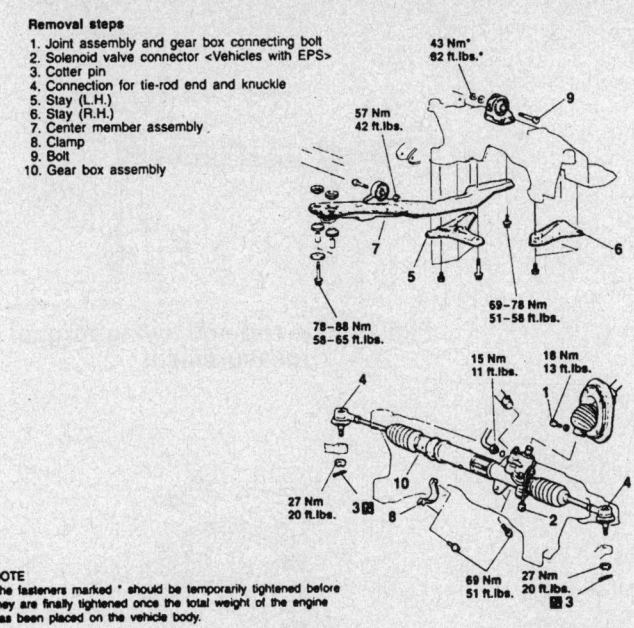

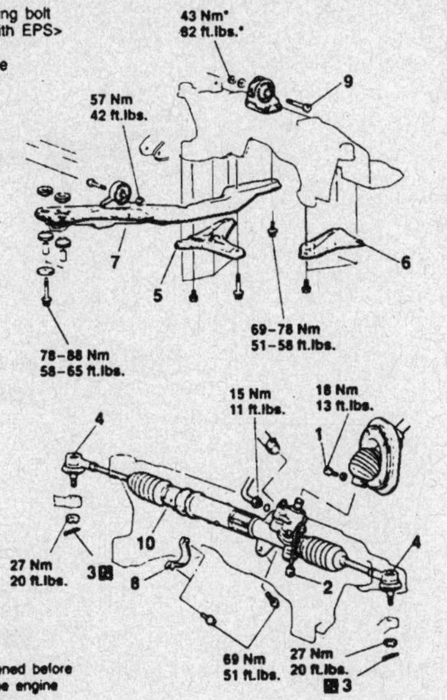
43 Nm*
62 ft.lbs.*
57 Nm
42 ft.lbs.
9
7
5
6
69-78 Nm
51-58 ft.lbs.
78-88 Nm
58-65 ft.lbs.
15 Nm
11 ft.lbs.
18 Nm
13 ft.lbs.
4
1
10
27 Nm
20 ft.lbs.
3
8
2
69 Nm
51 ft.lbs.
27 Nm
20 ft.lbs.

NOTE
The fasteners marked * should be temporarily tightened before they are finally tightened once the total weight of the engine has been placed on the vehicle body.

MT6039400013000X

Fig. 9 Power steering gear replacement. 1994–96

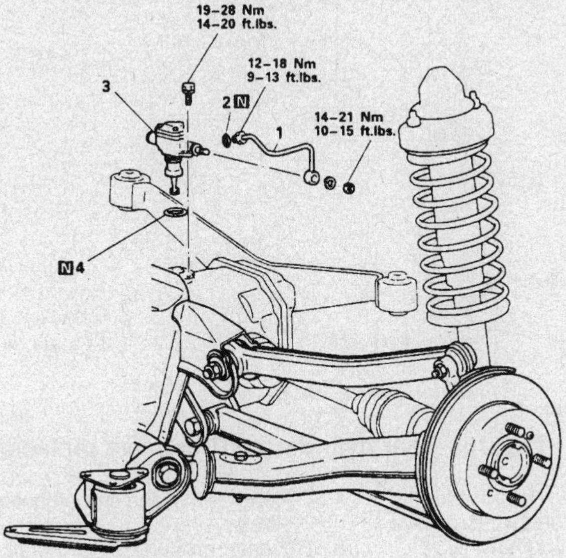
19-28 Nm
14-20 ft.lbs.
12-18 Nm
9-13 ft.lbs.
14-21 Nm
10-15 ft.lbs.
3
2
1
4

Removal steps

1. Feed tube
2. O-ring
3. Rear oil pump
4. O-ring

MT6039400015000X

Fig. 11 Power steering pump replacement. 1994–96

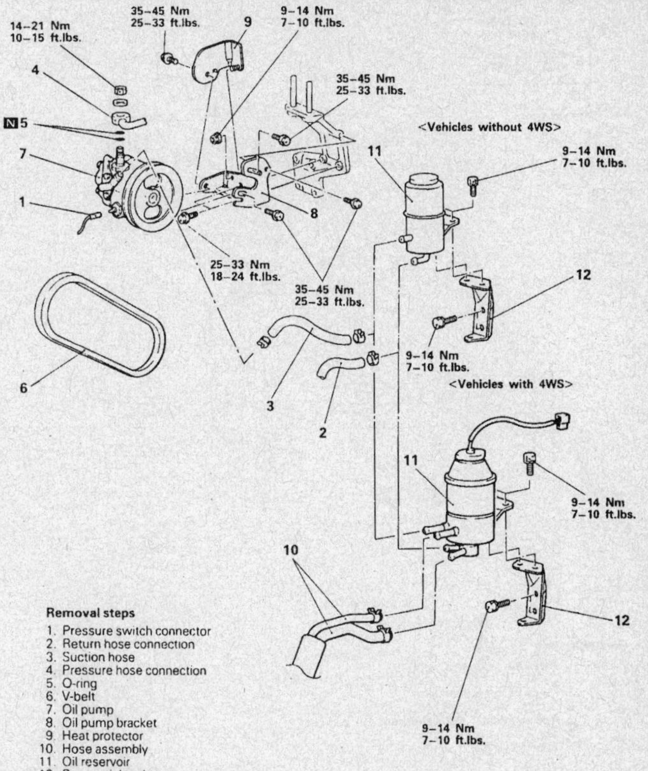
35-45 Nm
25-33 ft.lbs.
9-14 Nm
7-10 ft.lbs.
14-21 Nm
10-15 ft.lbs.
9
4
5
7
1
35-45 Nm
25-33 ft.lbs.
<Vehicles without 4WS>
11
9-14 Nm
7-10 ft.lbs.
8
25-33 Nm
18-24 ft.lbs.
35-45 Nm
25-33 ft.lbs.
12
6
9-14 Nm
7-10 ft.lbs.
<Vehicles with 4WS>
3
2
11
9-14 Nm
7-10 ft.lbs.
10
12
9-14 Nm
7-10 ft.lbs.

Removal steps

1. Pressure switch connector
2. Return hose connection
3. Suction hose
4. Pressure hose connection
5. O-ring
6. V-belt
7. Oil pump
8. Oil pump bracket
9. Heat protector
10. Hose assembly
11. Oil reservoir
12. Reservoir bracket

MT6039100014000X

Fig. 10 Front power steering pump replacement. 1993

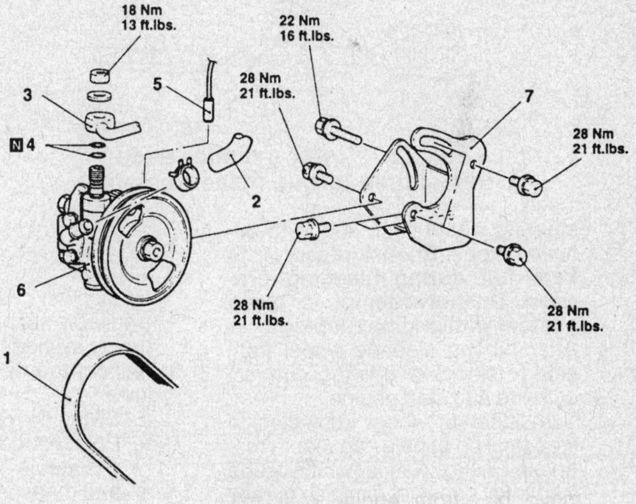
18 Nm
13 ft.lbs.
22 Nm
16 ft.lbs.
28 Nm
21 ft.lbs.
3
5
7
4
2
28 Nm
21 ft.lbs.
6
28 Nm
21 ft.lbs.
28 Nm
21 ft.lbs.
1

Removal steps

1. Drive-belt
2. Suction hose
3. Pressure hose
4. O-ring
5. Pressure switch connector
6. Oil pump
7. Oil pump bracket

MT6039100016000X

Fig. 12 Rear power steering pump replacement. 1993

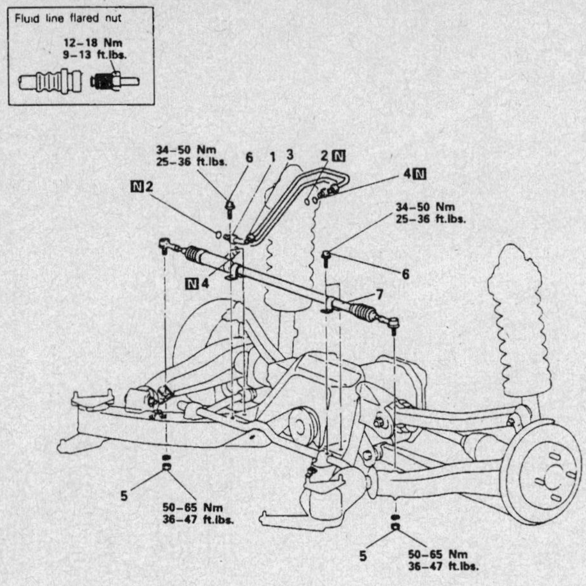
Fluid line flared nut
12-18 Nm
9-13 ft.lbs.
34-50 Nm
25-36 ft.lbs.
50-65 Nm
36-47 ft.lbs.

Removal steps

1. Pressure tube (rear right)
2. O-ring
3. Pressure tube (rear left)
4. O-ring
5. Power cylinder installation nut
6. Bolt
7. Power cylinder

MT6039100017000X

Fig. 13 Rear power cylinder replacement

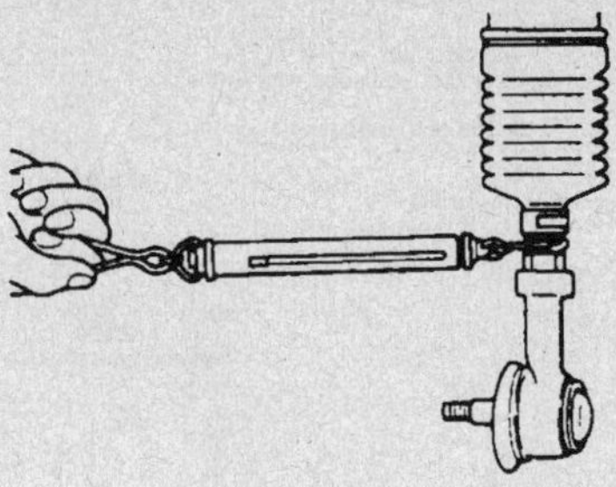

MT6039100018000X

Fig. 14 Tie rod end swing torque measurement

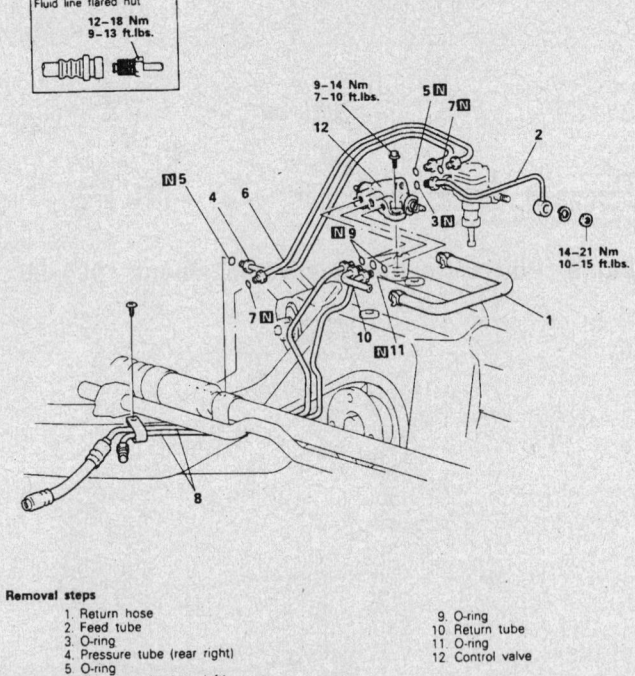

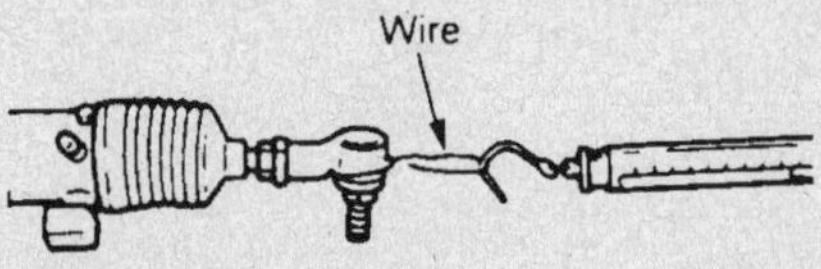
Wire

MT6039100019000X

Fig. 15 Power cylinder slide resistance torque measurement

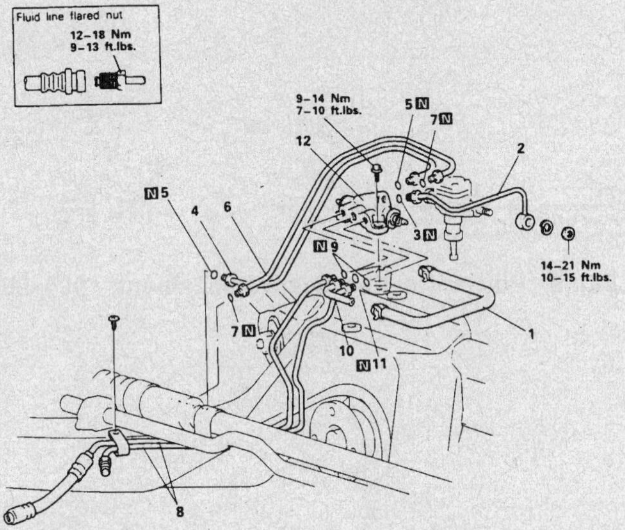
Fluid line flared nut
12-18 Nm
9-13 ft.lbs.
9-14 Nm
7-10 ft.lbs.
14-21 Nm
10-15 ft.lbs.

Removal steps

1. Return hose
2. Feed tube
3. O-ring
4. Pressure tube (rear right)
5. O-ring
6. Pressure tube (rear left)
7. O-ring
8. Pressure tube (front left, front right)
9. O-ring
10. Return tube
11. O-ring
12. Control valve

MT6039100020000X

Fig. 16 Rear cylinder control valve replacement

steering wheel back and forth between stops. **Ensure reservoir is kept full during bleeding process. Do not attempt to bleed system with engine running.**

c. After turning steering wheel from stop to stop 5 or 6 times, connect coil wire and start engine.

d. Turn steering wheel from stop to stop until no bubbles appear in reservoir. Ensure fluid is not milky and fluid level does not diminish greatly when steering wheel is turned.

REAR POWER CYLINDER

REPLACE

1. Raise and support vehicle.
2. Clean steering system piping using suitable steam cleaner, or equivalent.
3. Drain steering system fluid into a suitable container.
4. Remove main muffler assembly.
5. Remove rear power cylinder in numbered sequence as shown, **Fig. 13,** secure power cylinder on tie rod side with a suitable spanner wrench and remove power cylinder mounting nut.
6. Inspect the tie rod swing load as follows:
   a. Swing tie rod ten times vigorously.
   b. Point tie rod end down, then attach a suitable spring scale as shown and measure swing load, **Fig. 14.**
   c. If swing load is more than 12 lbs., replace the tie rod.
   d. If swing load is less than 2 lbs., the ball joint may be reused as long as it operates smoothly and is not loose.
7. Inspect power cylinder slide resistance as follows:
   a. Place piston in Neutral position.
   b. Wrap wire around tie rod end, then measure slide resistance using a suitable spring scale, **Fig. 15.**
   c. If slide resistance is more than 15 lbs., replace the power cylinder.
   d. If resistance is less than 15 lbs., the power cylinder may be reused as long as it slides smoothly and is not loose.
8. Reverse procedure to install, noting the following:
   a. Secure power cylinder to crossmember.
   b. Move power cylinder piston rod over its full stroke to determine its neutral position.
   c. Align tie rod ends and installation holes at trailing arm.
   d. When tie rod ends and the installation holes on the trailing arm do not meet, loosen tie rod end securing nut, then adjust the length. **The dust cover fastener clip should be removed for this.**
   e. The difference between lengths of left and right tie rods should be less than 0.039 inch. **The threads of the tie rod ends may be used as a guide.**
   f. Bleed the Four Wheel Steering (4WS) system as outlined under

"Bleeding System" in the "Power Steering Service"section.

REAR POWER CYLINDER CONTROL VALVE

REPLACE

1. Raise and support vehicle.
2. Clean steering system piping using suitable steam cleaner.
3. Drain steering system fluid into a suitable container.
4. Remove the rear suspension assembly as outlined under "Rear Suspension Assembly, Replace" in the "Rear Axle & Suspension" section.
5. Replace control valve and related components in numbered sequence as shown, **Fig. 16.**
6. Reverse procedure to install, then bleed the Four Wheel Steering (4WS) system as outlined under "Bleeding System" in the "Power Steering Service" section.

TIGHTENING SPECIFICATIONS

Year	Component	Torque/ Ft. Lbs
1993	Actuator Bracket To Strut Assembly	29–43
	Anchor Arm B	69–87
	Anchor Arm Locknut	29–36
	Automatic Free Wheeling Hub Cover	13–25
	Axle Nut	145–188
	Bearing Cap	40–47
	Bleeder Screw③	4–6
	Bracket To Differential Carrier	58–80
	Brake Tube Flare Nut	9–12
	Brake Tube To Front Brake	9–12
	Bump Stopper To Lower Arm	14–22
	Center Bearing Bracket To Engine Strut Assembly	26–33
	Center Member Rear Mounting Bolt	43–58
	Companion Flange To Drive Pinion	116–159
	Control Pipe To Pressure Tube③	22–29
	Control Valve To Crossmember	7–10
	Crossmember To Body	②
	Differential Case To Drive Gear	58–65
	Differential Cover To Differential Carrier	11–16
	Differential Mounting Brackets To Frame	58–80
	Disc Cover To Strut Assembly	6–9
	Drain Plug	43–51
	Driveshaft Nut	145–188
	Engine Mount Bracket To Crossmember	22–29
	Feed Tube To Rear Oil Pump③	10–15
	Filler Plug	29–43
	Flared Oil Line Nuts③	9–13
	Free Wheeling Hub Body Or Front Hub Assembly	36–43
	Front Anchor Arm To Upper Arm	51–69
	Front Hub To Brake Disc	36–43
	Front Propeller Shaft To Differential Carrier	36–43
	Front Shock Absorber To Crossmember	9–13
	Front Suspension Crossmember Mounting Bolts	72–87
	Housing Tube To Differential Carrier	58–72
	Hub Nut	145–188
	Insulator To Strut Assembly Nut	58–72
	Knuckle Arm To Ball Joint	43–52
	Knuckle Arm To McPherson Strut Assembly	58–72
	Knuckle Spindle To Slotted Nut	④
	Knuckle To Front Brake Assembly	58–72
	Knuckle To Front Brake Tube	36–43

Continued

TIGHTENING SPECIFICATIONS—Continued

Year	Component	Torque/ Ft. Lbs
1993	Knuckle To Strut Assembly	65–76
	Knuckle To Tie Rod Assembly	33
	LH Differential Mounting Bracket To Differential Carrier	58–72
	Lower Arm Ball Joint To Lower Arm	39–54
	Lower Arm Ball Joint	43–52
	Lower Arm Bushing B Mounting Nut	90–112
	Lower Arm Mounting Shaft Mounting Nut	69–87
	Lower Arm Rear Mounting Bolt	43–58
	Lower Arm Shaft Bolt	58–69
	Lower Arm Shaft	101–116①
	Lower Arm To Ball Joint	43–51
	Lower Arm To Suspension Crossmember	80–94
	Lower Ball Joint to Knuckle	87–130
	Pipe Clamp③	3–4
	Pipe To No. 1 Crossmember③	3–4
	Power Cylinder To Crossmember③	25–36
	Power Cylinder To Trailing Arm③	26–47
	Rear Oil Pump To Differential Carrier③	14–20
	Rear Roll Stopper Mounting Nut	33–43
	Rebound Stopper To Rebound Stopper Bracket	14–22
	Rebound Stopper To Upper Arm	6–9
	RH Differential Mounting Bracket To Housing Tube	58–72
	RH Driveshaft To Inner Shaft	36–43
	Spring Seat To Strut Assembly	29–36
	Stabilizer Bar Bracket	22—30
	Stabilizer Bar Mounting Bolt	12–19
	Stabilizer Bar To Lower Arm	7–14
	Stabilizer Link Mounting Nut	40–51
	Strut Assembly To Brake Assembly	58–72
	Strut Bar Bracket To Frame	25–33
	Strut Bar Locknut	54-61①
	Strut Bar To Lower Arm	43–51
	Strut Bar To Strut Bar Bracket Mounting Nut	54–61
	Strut Insulator To Body	18–25
	Strut Mounting Self Locking Nut	29–36
	Suspension Crossmember Mounting Bolts To Frame	57–72
	Suspension Crossmember To Body	87–116
	Suspension Crossmember To Steering Gearbox	51–65
	Tie Rod And Turnbuckle Locking Nut	36–40
	Tie Rod End Ball Joint	11–25
	Tie Rod End To Cylinder Assembly③	25–36
	Tie Rod End To Knuckle Arm	25–33
	Torsion Bar Adjusting Nut To Torsion Bar Locknut	29–36
	Undercover To Frame	7–9
	Under Skid Plate To side Frame	13–18
	Upper Arm Shaft To Crossmember	72–87
	Upper Ball Joint To Knuckle	43–65
	Wheel Lug Nuts	65–80

Continued

TIGHTENING SPECIFICATIONS—Continued

Year	Component	Torque/ Ft. Lbs
1994–96	Brake Dust Shield Mounting Bolts	7
	Caliper Mounting Bolts	65
	Compression Lower Arm Ball Joint Nut	43–51
	Compression Lower Arm Mounting Bolts	60
	Damper Fork Mounting Bolt	75
	Driveshaft Nut	145–188
	Hub Mounting Bolts	65
	Knuckle To Upper Arm Nut	21
	Lateral Lower Arm Ball Joint Nut	43–51
	Lateral Lower Arm Mounting Bolt Nut	71–85
	Lateral Lower Arm To Damper Fork Through Bolt Nut	65
	Power Steering Gear Fluid Fitting	11
1994–96	Power Steering Gear & Joint Connecting Bolt	13
	Power Steering Pump Adjustment Bolt	16
	Power Steering Pump Bracket Mounting Bolts	21
	Power Steering Pump Pressure Hose Nut	13
	Shock Absorber Lower Mounting Nut	64
	Shock Absorber Upper Mounting Nuts	32
	Stabilizer Bar Bracket Bolts	28
	Stabilizer Link Mounting Nut	28
	Tie Rod End Nut	17–25
	Upper Arm Pivot Shaft Mounting Bolts	62
	Upper Arm To Pivot Shaft Bolts	41
	Wheel Lug Nuts	65–80

① — Must be tightened while vehicle is unladen.

② — 58–72 ft. lbs., No. 7 embossed on bolt head; 72–87 ft. lbs., No. 10 embossed on bolt head.

③ — Four Wheel Steering System (4WS).

④ — Torque first to 22 ft. lbs., then back off completely and retorque to 8 ft. lbs.

Wheel Alignment

INDEX

Page No.		Page No.		Page No.	
Front Wheel Alignment	26-74	**Preliminary Inspection**	26-74	**Technical Service Bulletins**	26-74
Camber	26-74	**Rear Wheel Alignment**	26-74	Steering Drift To Right	26-74
Caster	26-74	Camber	26-74	**Vehicle Ride Height**	26-74
Toe-In	26-74	Toe-In	26-74	**Wheel Alignment Specifications**	26-3

PRELIMINARY INSPECTION

1. Ensure tires are inflated to correct pressure, then check for uneven wear.
2. Check front wheel bearings, suspension arm and ball joints for damage and replace components as necessary.
3. Check steering gear for damage and adjust as necessary.
4. Check shocks for damage and replace as necessary.
5. Rock vehicle backward and forward and bounce it upward and downward to settle vehicle prior to alignment.
6. Ensure vehicle is unloaded and on a suitable alignment rack according manufacturers' instructions. **When measuring equipment is attached directly to outer end of driveshaft and front wheels are on turntables, apply brake to prevent improper vehicle movement.**

FRONT WHEEL ALIGNMENT

CAMBER

Camber on these vehicles is preset to specifications and cannot be adjusted. If camber is out of specification, bent or damaged components must be replaced.

CASTER

Caster is preset to specifications and cannot be adjusted. If caster is out of specification, bent or damaged components must be replaced.

TOE-IN

1. Adjust toe-in by undoing clips and turning left and right tie rod turnbuckles by same amount in opposite directions, **Fig. 1.**
2. To increase toe-out, turn left turnbuckle toward front of vehicle and right turnbuckle toward rear of vehicle. To increase toe-in, turn turnbuckles in other direction. Toe-in is adjusted 0.24 inch for each half turn of left and right tie rods.
3. After adjusting toe-in, check that steering wheel turning angle is within specification.

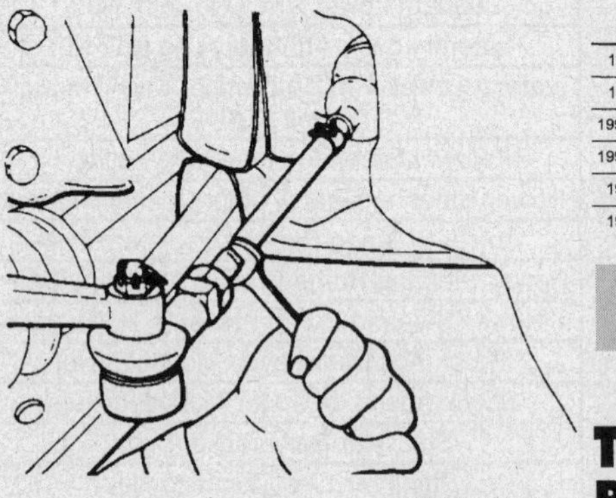

MT2049100036000X

Fig. 1 Front toe-in adjustment

REAR WHEEL ALIGNMENT

CAMBER

Camber and toe-in are preset to specifications and cannot be adjusted. If camber is out of specification, bent or damaged components must be replaced.

TOE-IN

Rear toe-in is preset to specifications and cannot adjusted. If rear toe-in is out of specification, bent or damaged components must be replaced.

VEHICLE RIDE HEIGHT

There is no provision for adjustment of vehicle ride height. If ride height is not satisfactory, inspect suspension for damaged or modified components.

VEHICLE	VEHICLE PRODUCTION DATES*	PART NAME	PART NUMBER
1994 Galant	02/93 Through 09/93	Lower Compression Arm, LH	MR223301
1994 Galant	02/93 Through 09/93	Lower Compression Arm, RH	MR223302
1994-95 Galant	From 10/93	Lower Compression Arm, LH	MR223121
1994-95 Galant	From 10/93	Lower Compression Arm, RH	MR223122
1995 Eclipse	Not Applicable	Lower Compression Arm, LH	MR223123
1995 Eclipse	Not Applicable	Lower Compression Arm, RH	MR223124

MTA069500001000X

Fig. 2 Lower compression arm replacement

TECHNICAL SERVICE BULLETINS

STEERING DRIFT TO RIGHT

1994-95

On some of these models built before March 16, 1995, VIN SE173922, steering may drift to the right. This condition may be more pronounced on roads with high crowns.

To correct this condition, proceed as follows:

1. Ensure cold tire inflation is correct: front, 32 psi; rear, 29 psi.
2. Perform front end alignment.
3. **On 1994 Galant models built before VIN RE030500,** record front camber readings .
4. **On all models,** road test vehicle at highway speeds. If drift is observed, switch front tires from one side to the other.
5. If drift is still present, install replacement front lower compression arms, **Fig. 2.**
6. Inspect toe reading and ensure steering wheel is centered, reset if needed.
7. **On 1994 Galant models built before VIN RE030500,**if drift is still exists, proceed as follows:
   a. Determine if adding 0.5° positive camber to lefthand wheel and 0.5° negative camber to righthand wheel will correct overall front camber reading to specification.
   b. If adding these values will achieve specified measurement, install replacement front upper control arm.

MITSUBISHI MIRAGE & PRECIS

INDEX OF SERVICE OPERATIONS

Page No.

AIR BAG SYSTEM PRECAUTIONS ... 0-8
AUTOMATIC TRANSMISSIONS/ TRANSAXLES ... 29-1
BRAKES
- Anti-Lock Brakes ... 29-1
- Disc Brakes ... 29-1
- Drum Brakes ... 29-1
- Hydraulic Brake Systems ... 29-1
- Power Brake Units ... 29-1

CLUTCH & MANUAL TRANSAXLE
- Adjustments ... 27-25
- Clutch, Replace ... 27-26
- Hydraulic System Service ... 27-25
- Tightening Specifications ... 27-27
- Transaxle, Replace ... 27-26

ELECTRICAL
- Air Bags ... 29-1
- Air Conditioning ... 29-1
- Alternators ... 29-1
- Blower Motor, Replace ... 27-8
- Coil Pack, Replace ... 27-5
- Cooling Fans ... 29-1
- Cruise Control ... 29-1
- Dash Gauges ... 29-1
- Dash Panels ... 29-1
- Distributor, Replace ... 27-5
- Evaporator Core, Replace ... 27-9
- Fuel Pump Relay Location ... 27-5
- Fuse Panel & Flasher Location ... 27-4
- Heater Core, Replace ... 27-8
- Ignition Lock, Replace ... 27-5
- Ignition Switch, Replace ... 27-5
- Instrument Cluster, Replace ... 27-6
- Multi-Function Switch, Replace ... 27-6
- Neutral Safety Switch, Replace ... 27-6
- Passive Restraints ... 29-1
- Precautions ... 27-4
- Radio, Replace ... 27-7
- Relay Center Location ... 27-5
- Speed Controls ... 29-1
- Starter Motors ... 29-1
- Starter, Replace ... 27-5
- Steering Columns ... 29-1
- Steering Wheel, Replace ... 27-6
- Wiper Motor, Replace ... 27-7
- Wiper Switch, Replace ... 27-8
- Wiper Systems ... 29-1

Page No.

ELECTRICAL SYMBOL IDENTIFICATION ... 0-139
FRONT SUSPENSION & STEERING
- Ball Joint, Replace ... 27-31
- Control Arm, Replace ... 27-32
- Hub Service ... 27-30
- Manual Steering Gear, Replace ... 27-34
- Manual Steering Gears ... 29-1
- Power Steering ... 29-1
- Power Steering Gear, Replace ... 27-33
- Stabilizer Bar, Replace ... 27-33
- Strut, Replace ... 27-31
- Strut Bar, Replace ... 27-33
- Strut Service ... 27-32
- Technical Service Bulletins ... 27-34
- Tightening Specifications ... 27-34
- Wheel Hub & Steering Knuckle, Replace ... 27-30

FRONT WHEEL DRIVE AXLES ... 29-1
REAR AXLE & SUSPENSION
- Coil Spring, Replace ... 27-29
- Control Arm, Replace ... 27-29
- Hub & Bearing, Replace ... 27-27
- Rear Suspension Service ... 27-27
- Shock Absorber, Replace ... 27-28
- Stabilizer Bar, Replace ... 27-29
- Strut, Replace ... 27-28
- Tightening Specifications ... 27-29
- Trailing Arm, Replace ... 27-29

SERVICE REMINDER & WARNING LAMP RESET PROCEDURES ... 0-10
SPECIFICATIONS
- Fluid Capacities & Cooling System Data ... 27-4
- Front Wheel Alignment Specifications ... 27-3
- General Engine Specifications ... 27-2
- Lubricant Data ... 27-4
- Rear Wheel Alignment Specifications ... 27-3
- Tune Up Specifications ... 27-2

VEHICLE IDENTIFICATION ... 0-1
VEHICLE LIFT POINTS ... 0-34
VEHICLE MAINTENANCE SCHEDULES ... 0-69

Page No.

WHEEL ALIGNMENT
- Front Wheel Alignment ... 27-36
- Preliminary Inspection ... 27-36
- Rear Wheel Alignment ... 27-36
- Vehicle Ride Height ... 27-36
- Wheel Alignment Specifications ... 27-3

WIRE COLOR CODE IDENTIFICATION ... 0-144
1.5L ENGINE
- Belt Tension Data ... 27-16
- Camshaft, Replace ... 27-14
- Compression Pressure ... 27-11
- Cooling System Bleed ... 27-16
- Crankshaft Rear Oil Seal, Replace ... 27-15
- Cylinder Head, Replace ... 27-12
- Engine, Replace ... 27-11
- Engine Mount, Replace ... 27-11
- Engine Rebuilding Specifications ... 29-1
- Exhaust Manifold, Replace ... 27-12
- Fuel Filter, Replace ... 27-16
- Fuel Pump, Replace ... 27-16
- Intake Manifold, Replace ... 27-12
- Main & Rod Bearings ... 27-15
- Oil Pan, Replace ... 27-15
- Oil Pump, Replace ... 27-15
- Piston & Rod Assembly ... 27-15
- Pistons, Pins & Rings ... 27-15
- Precautions ... 27-11
- Radiator, Replace ... 27-16
- Rocker Arms, Replace ... 27-13
- Technical Service Bulletins ... 27-16
- Thermostat, Replace ... 27-16
- Tightening Specifications ... 27-19
- Timing Belt, Replace ... 27-13
- Valve Adjustment ... 27-13
- Valve Clearance Specifications ... 27-13
- Valve Guides ... 27-13
- Water Pump, Replace ... 27-16

1.8L ENGINE
- Belt Tension Data ... 27-22
- Compression Pressure ... 27-21
- Engine, Replace ... 27-22
- Engine Rebuilding Specifications ... 29-1
- Precautions ... 27-21
- Radiator, Replace ... 27-22
- Tightening Specifications ... 27-24
- Timing Belt, Replace ... 27-22
- Valve Clearance Specifications ... 27-22

Specifications

GENERAL ENGINE SPECIFICATIONS

Year	Model	Engine Liters	Fuel System	Bore & Stroke	Compression Ratio	Maximum Net H.P. @ RPM	Maximum Torque Ft. Lbs. @ RPM
1993–94	Mirage	1.5L	Fuel Inj.	2.97 X 3.23	9.2	92 @ 6000	93 @ 3000
		1.8L	Fuel Inj.	3.19 X 3.50	9.5	113 @ 6000	116 @ 4500
	Precis	1.5L	Fuel Inj.	2.97 X 3.23	9.4	81 @ 5500	91 @ 3000
1995–96	Mirage	1.5L	Fuel Inj.	2.97 X 3.23	9.2	92 @ 6000	93 @ 3000
		1.8L	Fuel Inj.	3.19 X 3.50	9.5	113 @ 6000	116 @ 4500

TUNE UP SPECIFICATIONS

Year & Engine	Spark Plug Gap Inch	Firing Order①	Ignition Timing		Idle Speed, RPM②				Fuel Pressure, psi	Valve, Lash
					Curb		Fast			
			Timing, ° BTDC⑥	Timing Mark Location	Man. Trans.	Auto. Trans.	Man. Trans.	Auto. Trans.		
1993										
1.5L⑤	.041	2	5	Pulley	700	700N	③	③	48	⑧
1.5L④	.041	2	5	Pulley	750	750N	③	③	50	⑧
1.8L④	.041	3	5	Pulley	700	700N	③	③	50	⑨
1994										
1.5L⑤	.041	2	5	Pulley	825	825N	③	③	48	⑧
1.5L④	.041	2	5	Pulley	750	750N	③	③	48	⑧
1.8L④	.041	3	5	Pulley	700	700N	③	③	50	⑨
1995–96										
1.5L④	.041	2	5	⑦	750	750N	③	③	48	⑧
1.8L④	.041	3	5	⑦	700	700N	③	③	50	⑨

BTDC — Before Top Dead Center
N — Neutral
① — Cylinder numbering from front of engine to rear, 1, 2, 3, 4. Firing order, 1–3–4–2.
② — When adjusting idle speed, set parking brake & chock drive wheels.
③ — Controlled by idle speed control servo.
④ — Mirage.
⑤ — Precis.
⑥ — With jumper wire connected between ignition timing adjustment connector & ground. Refer to Figs. 4 through 6.
⑦ — Equipped w/crankshaft position sensor.
⑧ — Intake when hot, .0080 inch; intake when cold, .0040 inch; exhaust when hot, .0100 inch; exhaust when cold, .0070 inch.
⑨ — Intake when hot, .0080 inch; intake when cold, .0040 inch; exhaust when hot, .0120 inch; exhaust when cold, .0080 inch.

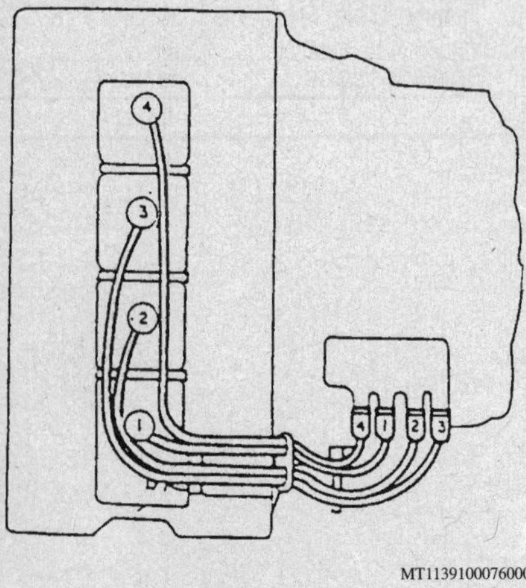
4
3
2
1
4 1 2 3

MT1139100076000X

Fig. A

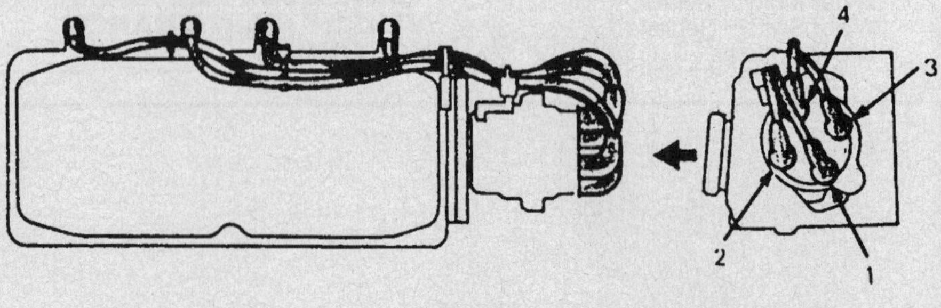
4
3
2
1

Fig. B

MT1139100077000X

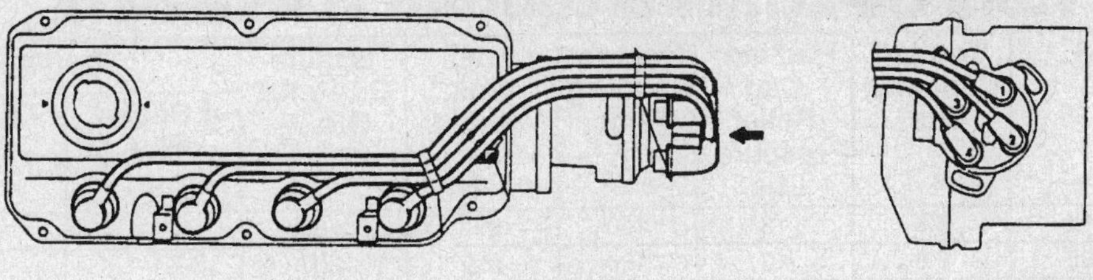

Fig. C

MT1139100078000X

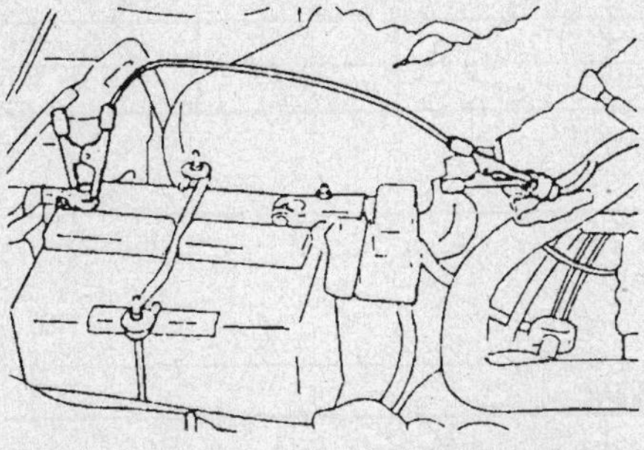

MT1139200080000X

Fig. D Ignition timing adjustment connector. 1993 Precis

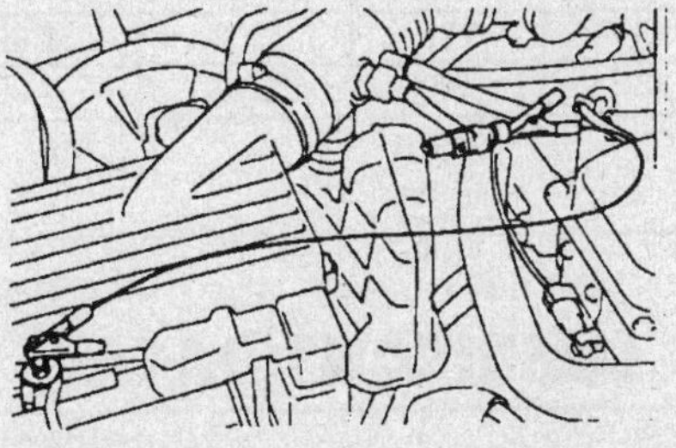

MT1139400033000X

Fig. E Ignition timing adjustment connector. 1994 Precis

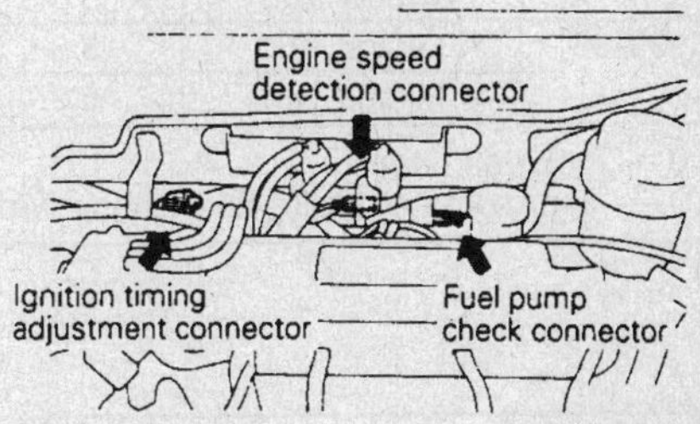
Engine speed detection connector
Ignition timing adjustment connector
Fuel pump check connector

MT1139300028000X

Fig. F Ignition timing adjustment connector. Mirage

FRONT WHEEL ALIGNMENT SPECIFICATIONS

Year	Model	Caster Angle, Deg.		Camber Angle, Deg.		Toe, Inch①	Kingpin Inclination, Deg.	Ball Joint Wear
		Limits	Desired	Limits	Desired			
1993–96	Mirage	—	+2 1/4	-1/2 to +1/2	0	-.12 to +.12	—	④
	Precis②	+ 8/15 to +1 8/15	+1 1/30	-1/2 to +1/2	0	-.08 to +.16	12 59/60	⑤
	Precis③	+1 1/6 to +2 1/6	+1 2/3	-1/2 to +1/2	0	-.08 to +.16	12 59/60	⑤

① — Toe-in (+); toe-out (-).
② — Manual steering.
③ — Power steering.

④ — Lower arm ball joint break away torque, 9–56 inch lbs.

⑤ — Lower arm ball joint break away torque, 26–87 inch lbs.

REAR WHEEL ALIGNMENT SPECIFICATIONS

Year	Model	Camber Angle, Deg.		Toe, Inch①
		Limits	Desired	
1993	Mirage	-1 1/4 to -1/12	-2/3	+.04 to +.20
	Precis	-1 to -1/6	-2/3	-.12 to +.24
1994	Mirage	-1 1/6 to -1/6	-2/3	+.04 to +.20
	Precis	-1 to -1/6	-2/3	-.12 to +.24
1995–96	Mirage	-1 1/6 to -1/6	-2/3	+.04 to +.20

① — Toe-in (+); toe-out (-).

FLUID CAPACITIES & COOLING SYSTEM DATA

Year	Model & Engine	Coolant Capacity, Qts.	Radiator Cap Relief Pressure, Lbs.	Thermo. Opening Temp. °F	Fuel Tank, Gals.	Engine Oil Refill, Qts. ①	Transmission Oil		
							4 Speed, Pts.	5 Speed, Pts.	Auto. Trans., Qts. ②
1993	Mirage 1.5L	5.3	13	190	13.2	3.60	—	3.8	6.30
	Mirage 1.8L	6.3	13	180	13.2	4.00	—	3.8	6.30
	Precis 1.5L	5.6	13	190	11.9	3.60	3.6	3.8	6.40
1994	Mirage 1.5L	5.3	13	190	13.2	3.50	—	3.8	6.30
	Mirage 1.8L	6.3	13	180	13.2	4.00	—	3.8	6.30
	Precis 1.5L	5.6	13	190	11.9	3.60	3.6	3.8	6.40
1995–96	Mirage 1.5L	5.3	13	190	13.2	3.50	—	3.8	6.30
	Mirage 1.8L	6.3	13	180	13.2	4.00	—	3.8	6.30

① — Includes filter.
② — Approximate; make final check w/dipstick.

LUBRICANT DATA

Year	Model	Lubricant Type			
		Transmission		Power Steering	Brake System
		Manual	Automatic		
1993–94	Precis	75W-90 GL-4/5	Mitsubishi Plus ATF	Dexron II/IIE/III	DOT 3
1993–96	Mirage	75W-90 GL-4/5	Dia ATF SP	Dexron II/IIE/III	DOT 3 or 4

Electrical

NOTE: On Air Bag Equipped Models, Refer To "Air Bag System Precautions" Located In The Front Of This Manual For System Disarming & Arming Procedures.

INDEX

	Page No.
Air Bags	29-1
Air Conditioning	29-1
Alternators	29-1
Blower Motor, Replace	27-8
Mirage	27-8
Precis	27-8
Coil Pack, Replace	27-5
Cooling Fans	29-1
Cruise Control	29-1
Dash Gauges	29-1
Dash Panels	29-1
Distributor, Replace	27-5
Evaporator Core, Replace	27-9
Mirage	27-9
Precis	27-10
Fuel Pump Relay Location	27-5
Mirage	27-5
Precis	27-5
Fuse Panel & Flasher Location	27-4
Mirage	27-4
Precis	27-4
Heater Core, Replace	27-8
Mirage	27-8
Precis	27-8
Ignition Lock, Replace	27-5
Mirage	27-5
Precis	27-5
Ignition Switch, Replace	27-5
Mirage	27-5
Precis	27-6
Instrument Cluster, Replace	27-6
Mirage	27-6
Precis	27-7
Multi-Function Switch, Replace	27-6
Neutral Safety Switch, Replace	27-6
Passive Restraints	29-1
Precautions	27-4
Air Bag Systems	27-4
Radio, Replace	27-7
Mirage	27-7
Precis	27-7
Relay Center Location	27-5
Speed Controls	29-1
Starter Motors	29-1
Starter, Replace	27-5
Steering Columns	29-1
Steering Wheel, Replace	27-6
Wiper Motor, Replace	27-7
Front	27-7
Rear	27-8
Wiper Switch, Replace	27-8
Front	27-8
Rear	27-8
Wiper Systems	29-1

PRECAUTIONS

AIR BAG SYSTEMS

Refer to "Air Bag System Precautions" in front of this manual for system disarming and arming procedures.

FUSE PANEL & FLASHER LOCATION

MIRAGE

Fuse panel is located on instrument panel to left of steering wheel. There is an A/C fuse located in front left corner of engine compartment, near power steering oil reservoir. Flashers are located on fuse panel.

PRECIS

Fuse panel is located under a cover on

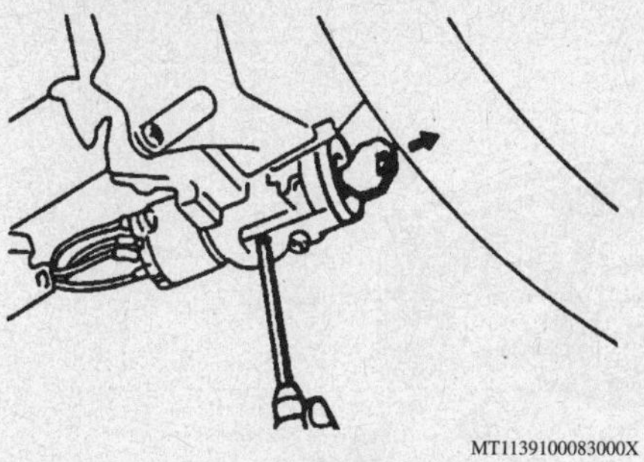
MT1139100083000X

Fig. 1 Lock cylinder removal. Mirage

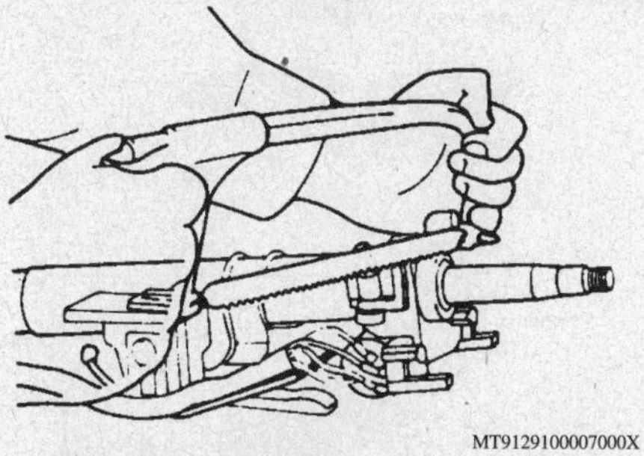
MT9129100007000X

Fig. 2 Ignition lock removal. Precis

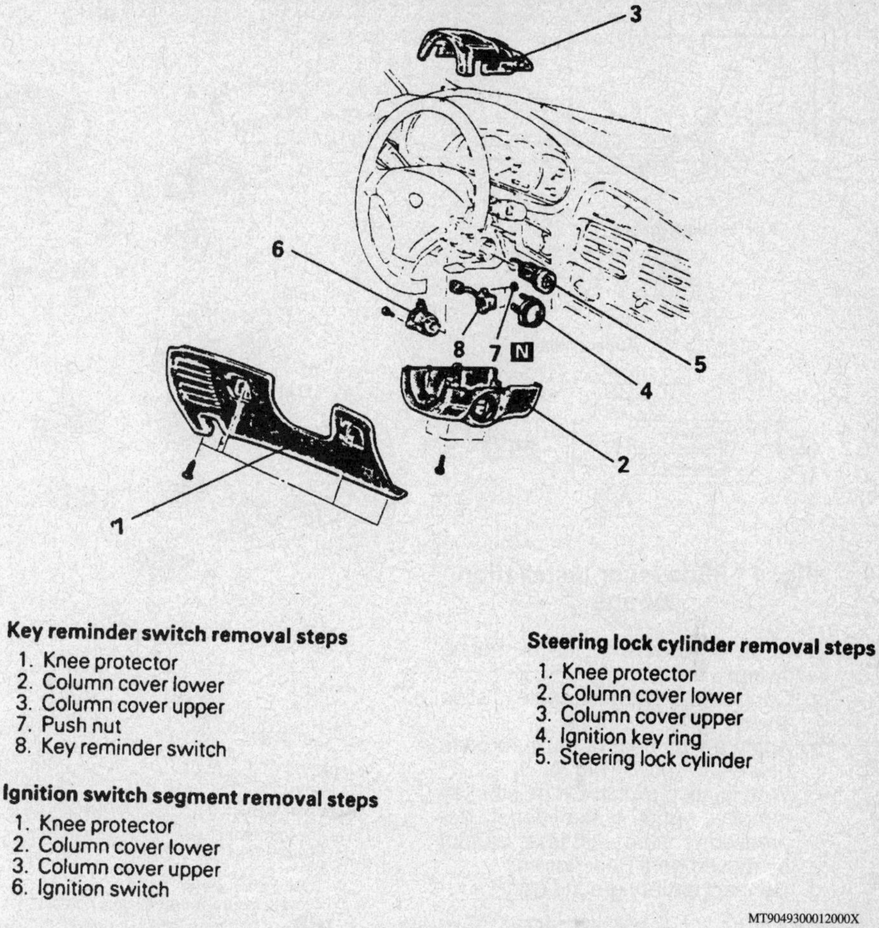
3
6
8
7
N
5
4
2
1
Key reminder switch removal steps
1. Knee protector
2. Column cover lower
3. Column cover upper
7. Push nut
8. Key reminder switch
Ignition switch segment removal steps
1. Knee protector
2. Column cover lower
3. Column cover upper
6. Ignition switch
Steering lock cylinder removal steps
1. Knee protector
2. Column cover lower
3. Column cover upper
4. Ignition key ring
5. Steering lock cylinder
MT9049300012000X

Fig. 3 Ignition switch replacement. Mirage

dash panel to left of steering wheel. Flashers are located under left corner of instrument panel.

FUEL PUMP RELAY LOCATION

MIRAGE

The multi-port fuel injection relay is located behind the center console.

PRECIS

The fuel injection relay is located behind the lefthand side of the instrument panel, at the fuel injection control module.

RELAY CENTER LOCATION

Main relay centers are located behind lefthand side of instrument panel and on righthand side of engine compartment.

STARTER

REPLACE

1. Disconnect battery ground cable.
2. Remove air cleaner assembly and intake manifold stay.
3. **On Precis models,** remove EGR valve (California models), then the speedometer cable.
4. **On all models,** remove starter cover.
5. Disconnect starter cables.
6. Remove starter mounting bolts, then the starter.
7. Reverse procedure to install. **Torque** starter mounting bolts to 22 ft. lbs.

DISTRIBUTOR

REPLACE

1. Remove distributor cap.
2. Rotate crankshaft until distributor rotor lines up with No. 1 spark plug wire on distributor cap.
3. Align notch on crankshaft with mark on timing indicator.
4. Remove distributor hold-down, then the distributor.
5. Reverse procedure to install, noting following:
   a. Align mark on distributor housing with mark on drive gear, then install distributor.
   b. With distributor installed, align mark on flange with center of mounting stud, then tighten distributor hold-down bolt.

COIL PACK

REPLACE

The ignition coil and ignition power transistor are built into the distributor assembly. For ignition coil replacement, refer to "Distributor, Replace".

IGNITION LOCK

REPLACE

MIRAGE

1. Remove knee protector and steering column shrouds.
2. Insert key into cylinder lock and turn to ACC position.
3. Using a Phillips head screwdriver or similar tool, push lockpin inward, **Fig. 1,** then remove cylinder lock.
4. Reverse procedure to install.

PRECIS

1. Disconnect battery ground cable.
2. Remove knee protector and steering column shrouds.
3. Remove steering wheel.
4. Cut groove in attaching bolt heads using a hacksaw, then remove bolts, **Fig. 2.**
5. Remove ignition key lock.
6. Reverse procedure to install.

IGNITION SWITCH

REPLACE

MIRAGE

Remove components in order as shown, **Fig. 3** noting following:

1. Disconnect battery ground cable.
2. Remove steering lock cylinder as follows:
   a. Insert key in lock cylinder and turn to ACC position.
   b. Using a small screwdriver, push lock cylinder lockpin in, **Fig. 1,** then remove lock cylinder.

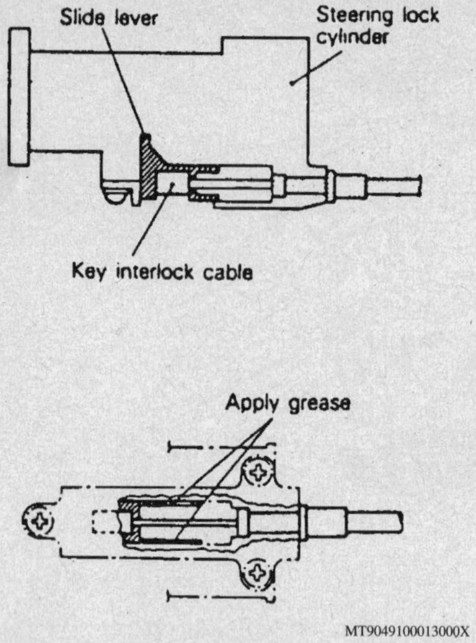
Slide lever
Steering lock cylinder
Key interlock cable
Apply grease
MT9049100013000X

Fig. 4 Slide lever installation. Mirage

3. Reverse procedure to install, noting following:
   a. Connect key interlock cable to slide lever, **Fig. 4.**
   b. Apply a light coat of multi-purpose grease as shown, **Fig. 4.**
   c. With ignition switch Off or with key removed and brake pedal depressed, ensure shift lever cannot be moved from Park position.
   d. Connect battery ground cable.

PRECIS

1. Disconnect battery ground cable.
2. Remove knee protector, if applicable.
3. Remove column shrouds, then disconnect switch electrical connectors.
4. Remove switch attaching screws, then the lock cylinder from switch as follows:
   a. Insert key in lock cylinder and turn to ACC position.
   b. Using a small screwdriver, push lock cylinder lockpin in, **Fig. 2,** then remove lock cylinder.
5. Reverse procedure to install.

NEUTRAL SAFETY SWITCH

REPLACE

1. Place selector lever in Neutral position.
2. Place manual control lever in Neutral position, then remove control lever retainer and lever.
3. Disconnect electrical harness, then remove switch retaining bolts and switch assembly.
4. Reverse procedure to install, noting following:
   a. With manual control lever in Neutral position, rotate switch body until wide end of manual control lever aligns with switch body flange.
   b. Hold switch body in position, then **torque** retaining bolts to 7–9 ft. lbs.

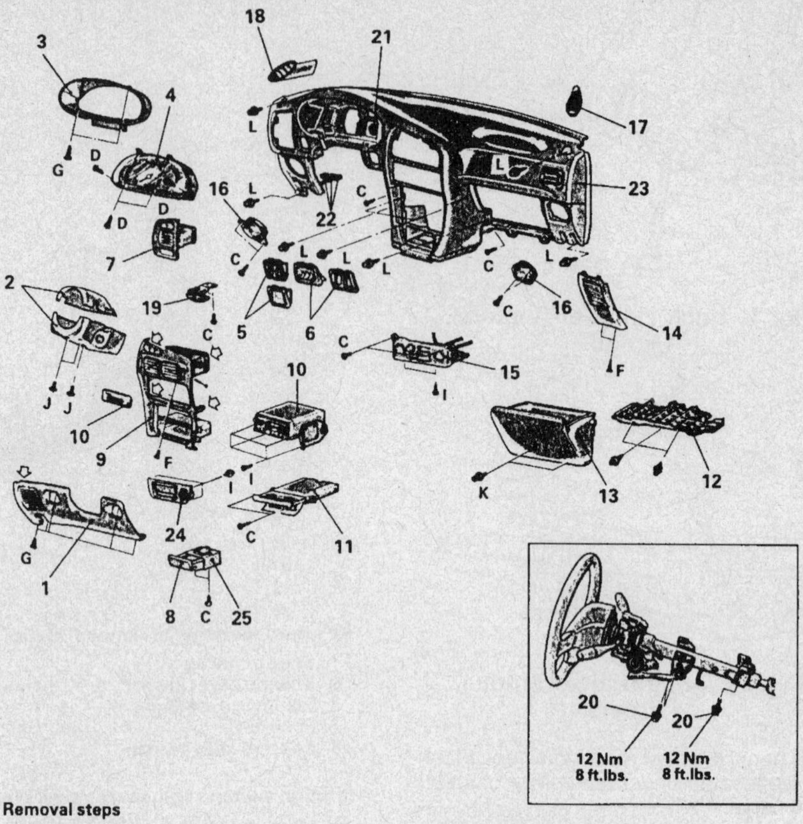
12 Nm
8 ft.lbs.
12 Nm
8 ft.lbs.

Removal steps

1. Knee protector
2. Column cover
3. Meter bezel
4. Combination meter
5. Remote control mirror switch, rheostat or plug
6. Coin box or rear wiper washer switch
7. Air outlet panel assembly
8. Ashtray
9. Air outlet center panel assembly
10. Radio and tape player or radio plug
11. Cup holder
12. Under cover
13. Glove box
14. Corner panel
15. Heater control assembly
16. Speaker
17. Side defroster grille (RH)
18. Side defroster grille (LH)
19. Hood lock release handle
20. Steering column assembly installation bolts
21. Adapter
22. Harness connector
23. Instrument panel assembly
24. Ashtray panel
25. Ashtray bracket

NOTE
⇦ : metal clip position

MT9099300011000X

Fig. 5 Instrument cluster replacement. Mirage

MULTI-FUNCTION SWITCH

REPLACE

1. Disconnect battery ground cable.
2. Remove steering wheel as outlined under "Steering Wheel, Replace."
3. **On models with tilt steering,** set tilt position of steering shaft to lowest position.
4. **On 1994–96 Mirage,** remove air bag clockspring.
5. **On all models,** disconnect column switch electrical connectors, then remove cable band.
6. Remove column switch attaching screws, then the column switch from steering shaft.
7. Reverse procedure to install.

STEERING WHEEL

REPLACE

1. **On 1994–96 Mirage,** carefully remove air bag module from steering wheel.
2. **On Precis and 1993 Mirage,** disconnect battery ground cable, then remove horn pad attaching screw(s) and horn pad.
3. **On all models,** remove steering wheel attaching nut.
4. Scribe mating marks on steering shaft and steering wheel for installation reference.
5. Using a suitable steering wheel puller, remove steering wheel. **Do not hammer on steering wheel to remove. Damage to collapsible mechanism may occur.**
6. Reverse procedure to install, noting following:
   a. Align mating marks on steering shaft and steering wheel.
   b. **Torque** steering wheel attaching nut to 25–33 ft. lbs.

INSTRUMENT CLUSTER

REPLACE

MIRAGE

1. Remove cool air bypass lever cable of

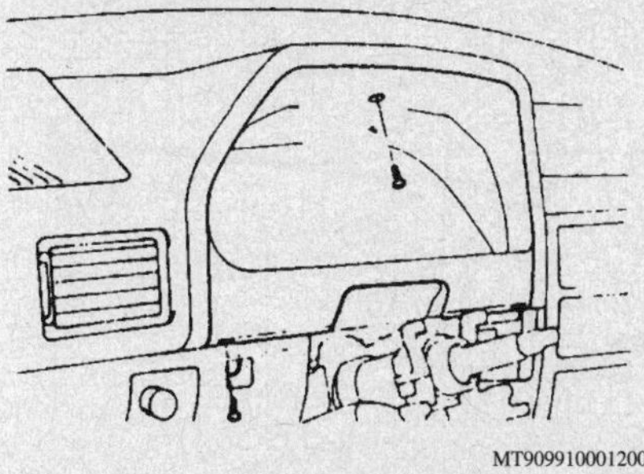
MT9099100012000X

Fig. 6 Instrument cluster fascia attaching screw locations. Precis

air outlet center panel assembly at heater unit side.
2. Remove air outlet center panel assembly mounting screws, then the air outlet center panel assembly.
3. Remove heater control assembly damper cables from heater unit and blower assembly.
4. Remove heater control assembly mounting screws.
5. Remove heater control assembly boss from center reinforcement (LH).
6. Remove heater control assembly from instrument panel as shown, **Fig. 5.**
7. Remove adapter lock from instrument panel.
8. Pull speedometer cable slightly into passenger compartment, then remove adapter.
9. Reverse procedure to install, noting following:
   a. After installing heater control assembly, connect each damper cable.
   b. Install air outlet center panel assembly to instrument panel, then turn cool air bypass lever of air outlet center panel assembly fully upward.
   c. Turn cool air bypass damper level at heater unit side fully downward, then install cool air bypass lever cable.

PRECIS

1. Disconnect battery ground cable.
2. Remove three instrument cluster attaching screws, then the fascia from instrument panel, **Fig. 6.**
3. Remove four instrument cluster retaining screws, **Fig. 7.**
4. Disconnect speedometer cable and all wire connectors from rear of cluster, then remove cluster from instrument panel.
5. Reverse procedure to install.

RADIO

REPLACE

On some models, radio fuse is located on rear of radio. If radio fuse is to be replaced it is necessary to remove radio.

MIRAGE

1. Disconnect battery ground cable.
2. Pry off center panel using a suitable tool, then remove panel from instrument panel.

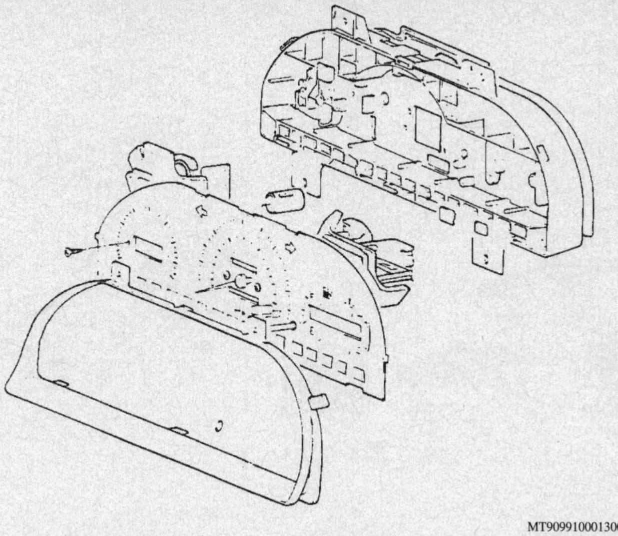
MT9099100013000X

Fig. 7 Instrument cluster retaining screw locations. Precis

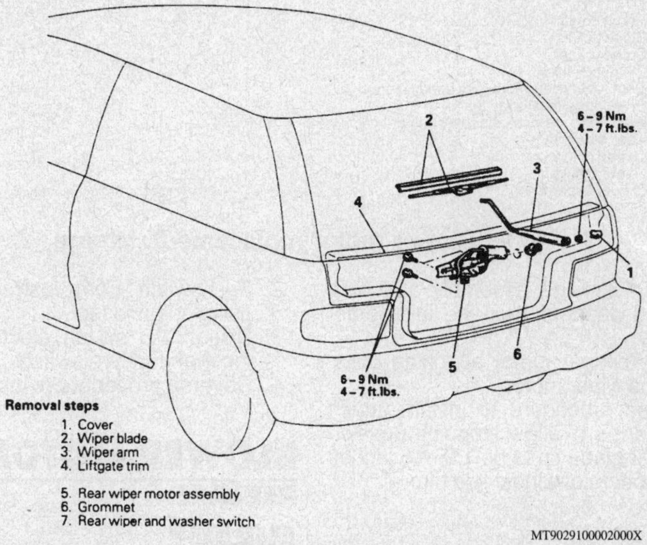
2
6 – 9 Nm
4 – 7 ft.lbs.
3
4
1
5
6
6 – 9 Nm
4 – 7 ft.lbs.
Removal steps
1. Cover
2. Wiper blade
3. Wiper arm
4. Liftgate trim
5. Rear wiper motor assembly
6. Grommet
7. Rear wiper and washer switch
MT9029100002000X

Fig. 8 Rear wiper motor installation. Mirage

3. Remove radio bracket attaching screws, then the radio bracket.
4. Pull radio outward enough to gain access to rear of radio.
5. Disconnect antenna lead wire and electrical connector, then remove radio.
6. Reverse procedure to install.

PRECIS

1. Disconnect battery ground cable.
2. Remove ashtray, then the two outer switches on center fascia panel.
3. Remove four center lower crash pad fascia panel attaching screws, then the panel.
4. Remove radio mounting screws.
5. Pull radio outward enough to gain access to rear of radio.
6. Disconnect antenna lead wire and electrical connector, then remove radio.
7. Reverse procedure to install.

WIPER MOTOR

REPLACE

FRONT

Mirage

1. Disconnect battery ground cable.
2. Remove pivot shaft attaching nuts, then push pivot shaft inward.
3. Remove wiper motor attaching bolts, then pull wiper motor slightly and disconnect motor and linkage assembly.
4. Remove wiper motor with linkage from vehicle. **Mark position of crank arm to wiper motor, if necessary to remove.**
5. Reverse procedure to install.

Precis

1. Disconnect battery ground cable.
2. Remove wiper arm and blade assembly.
3. Remove cowl top cover.

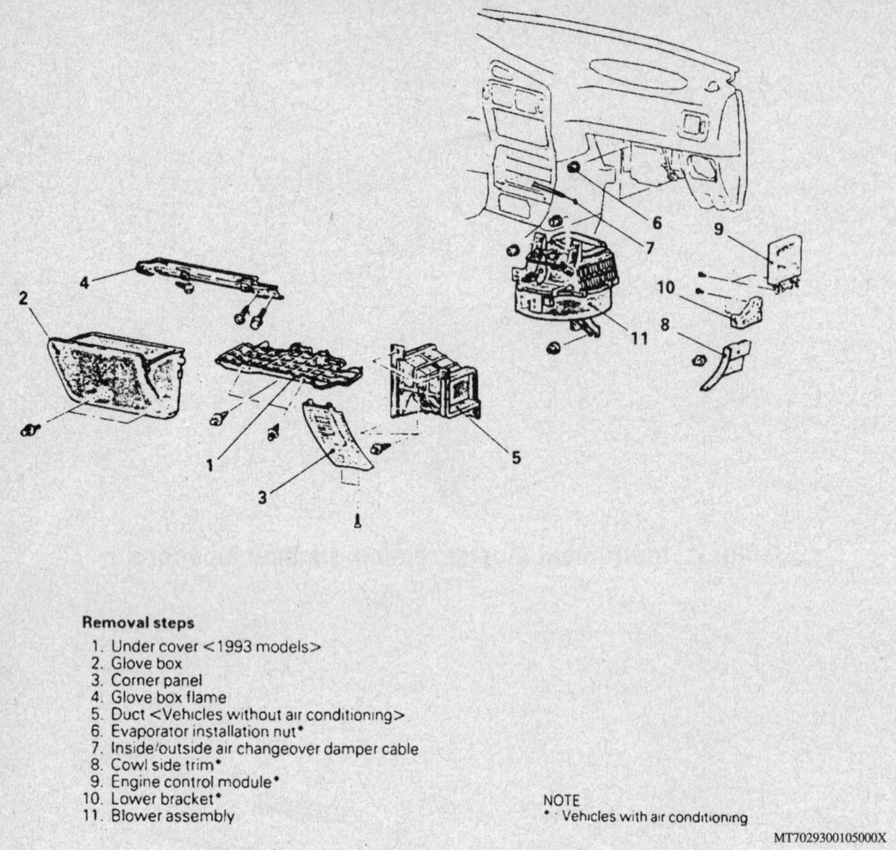
1
2
3
4
5
6
7
8
9
10
11
Removal steps
1. Under cover <1993 models>
2. Glove box
3. Corner panel
4. Glove box flame
5. Duct <Vehicles without air conditioning>
6. Evaporator installation nut*
7. Inside/outside air changeover damper cable
8. Cowl side trim*
9. Engine control module*
10. Lower bracket*
11. Blower assembly
NOTE
*: Vehicles with air conditioning
MT7029300105000X

Fig. 9 Blower motor replacement. Mirage

4. Remove linkage assembly attaching nut and washers, then the linkage assembly.
5. Remove wiper motor attaching bolts, then the wiper motor.
6. Reverse procedure to install. Attach wiper arms to allow stopping position of wiper blade tip to be 1.2–1.6 inches from bottom of windshield trim.

REAR

Mirage

When replacing rear wiper motor, refer to **Fig. 8** for removal and installation procedure.

Precis

1. Disconnect battery ground cable.
2. Remove rear wiper arm assembly.
3. Remove tailgate trim.
4. Remove wiper motor assembly attaching bolts, then the wiper motor assembly.
5. Reverse procedure to install.

WIPER SWITCH

REPLACE

FRONT

Refer to "Column Switch, Replace" procedure.

REAR

1. Disconnect battery ground cable.
2. Pry switch from instrument cluster using suitable tool.
3. Disconnect switch electrical connector, then remove switch.
4. Reverse procedure to install.

BLOWER MOTOR

REPLACE

MIRAGE

1. Disconnect battery ground cable.
2. Remove blower assembly in numbered sequence shown, **Fig. 9.**
3. Reverse procedure to install. Connect inside/outside air changeover damper cable as follows:
   a. Set instrument panel changeover lever to RECIRC position, then position blower motor damper lever to RECIRC position, **Fig. 10.**
   b. Connect cable to lever pin, **Fig. 10,** then pull outer cable in direction of arrow until all looseness is removed and secure with clip.

PRECIS

1. Disconnect battery ground cable.
2. Remove glove compartment housing cover assembly, then the lower crash pad assembly.
3. Disconnect resistor and blower motor electrical connectors.
4. Disconnect ventilation tube from blower motor.
5. Remove blower unit attaching bolts, **Fig. 11.**

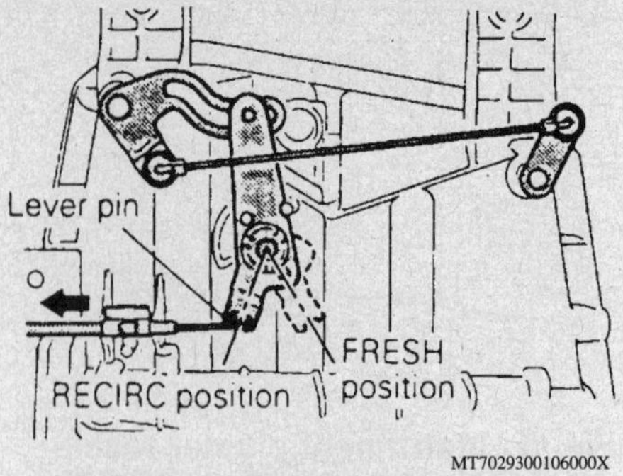
Lever pin
FRESH position
RECIRC position
MT7029300106000X

Fig. 10 Inside/outside air changeover cable connection. Mirage

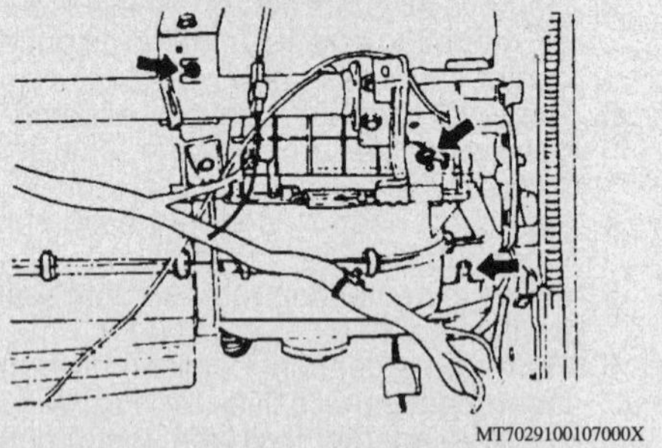
MT7029100107000X

Fig. 11 Blower unit attaching bolt locations. Precis

6. Pull blower unit out slightly, then disconnect recirculation vacuum connector.
7. Remove blower motor from blower unit.
8. Reverse procedure to install.

HEATER CORE

REPLACE

MIRAGE

Remove heater unit components in order as shown in, **Figs. 12 and 13,** noting the following:

1. Disconnect battery ground cable.
2. Drain cooling system into appropriate container.
3. Remove front seats and floor console, **Figs. 14 through 16,**then instrument panel as outlined under "Instrument Cluster, Replace."
4. **On models with A/C,** remove bolts and nuts attaching evaporator assembly to heater unit.
5. **On all models,** pull evaporator assembly outward, then remove heater unit.
6. Remove heater core fastening clips.
7. Remove heater core from heater unit. **Use caution not to damage heater core fins or pad part of heater core.**
8. Reverse procedure to install.

PRECIS

1. Disconnect battery ground cable.
2. Drain cooling system into appropriate container.
3. Disconnect heater hoses from heater core.
4. **On models with A/C,** disconnect

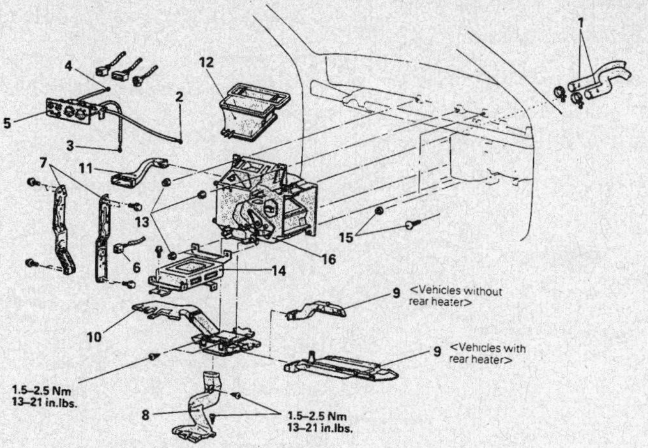
<Vehicles without rear heater>
<Vehicles with rear heater>
1.5–2.5 Nm
13–21 in.lbs.
1.5–2.5 Nm
13–21 in.lbs.

Removal steps

1. Connection for the heater hoses
2. Connection for the air selection control wire
3. Connection for the temperature control wire
4. Connection for the mode selection control wire
5. Heater control assembly
6. Connection of the connector [8P <1500> or 10P <1600>] for ECI control relay
7. Instrument panel center stay assembly
8. Rear heater duct A
9. Lap heater duct <vehicles without rear heater> or shower duct <vehicles with rear heater>
10. Foot duct
11. Lap duct
12. Center ventilation duct
13. Heater unit mounting nuts
14. ELC-4 A/T control unit
15. Evaporator mounting nuts, clips
16. Heater unit

MT7029100093000X

Fig. 12 Heater unit replacement. 1993 Mirage

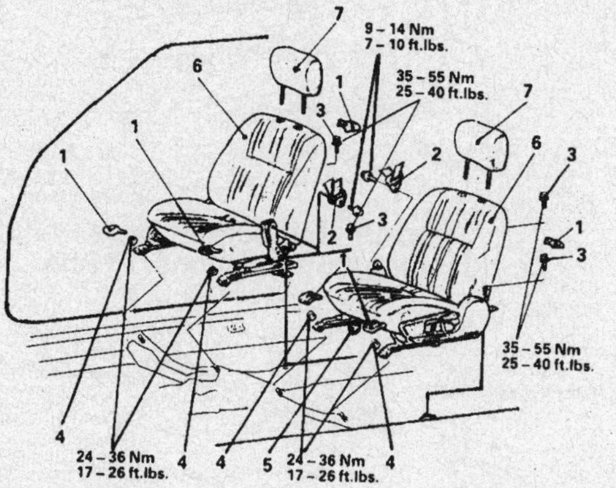
9 – 14 Nm
7 – 10 ft.lbs.
35 – 55 Nm
25 – 40 ft.lbs.
35 – 55 Nm
25 – 40 ft.lbs.
24 – 36 Nm
17 – 26 ft.lbs.
24 – 36 Nm
17 – 26 ft.lbs.

Removal steps

1. Seat anchor covers
2. Guide ring
3. Seat mounting bolts
4. Seat mounting nuts
5. Connection of seat belt switch wiring harness
6. Front seat assembly
7. Headrestraint

MT7029100095000X

Fig. 14 Front seat removal. Mirage

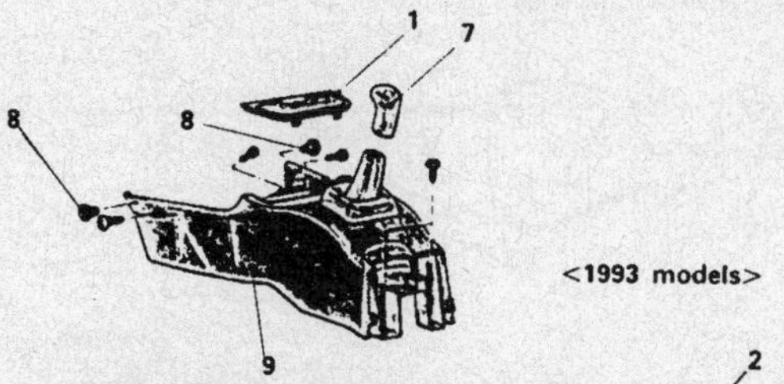

<1993 models>

Removal steps

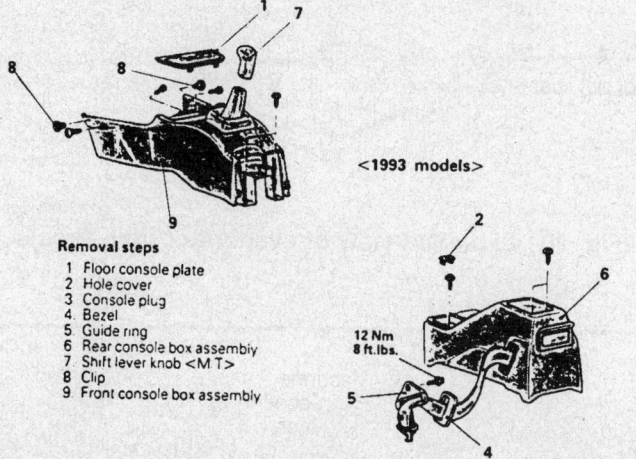

1. Floor console plate
2. Hole cover
3. Console plug
4. Bezel
5. Guide ring
6. Rear console box assembly
7. Shift lever knob <M/T>
8. Clip
9. Front console box assembly

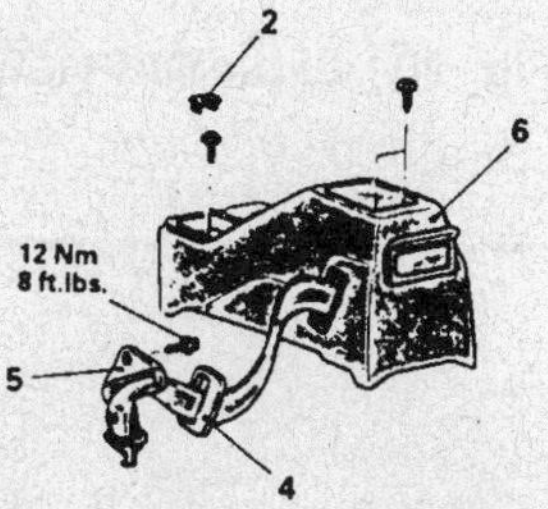
12 Nm
8 ft.lbs.

MT7029300097000X

Fig. 15 Floor console removal. 1993 Mirage

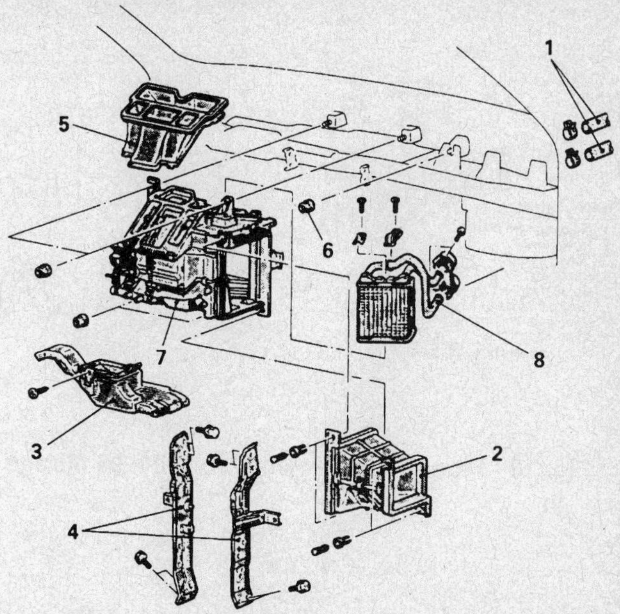

Removal steps

1. Heater hose connection
2. Joint duct <Vehicles without air conditioning>
3. Foot duct
4. Center reinforcement
5. Center ventilation duct
6. Evapolator installation nut <Vehicles with air conditioning>
7. Heater unit
8. Heater core

MT7029400094000X

Fig. 13 Heater unit & core replacement. 1994–96 Mirage

evaporator drain hose and discharge refrigerant from system. Disconnect suction and liquid lines from evaporator.

5. **On all models,** remove console assembly.
6. Remove glove compartment, main lower crash pad and lower crash pad center fascia panel assembly.
7. Remove heater control assembly.
8. Remove lower crash pad center skin.
9. Remove crash pad center support.
10. **On models with A/C,** remove evaporator assembly. Refer to procedure outlined under "Evaporator Core, Replace."
11. **On all models,** remove rear heating joint duct.
12. Remove heater unit assembly from vehicle.
13. Remove heater core from heater case, **Fig. 17.**
14. Reverse procedure to install.

EVAPORATOR CORE

REPLACE

MIRAGE

1. Disconnect battery ground cable.
2. Discharge A/C refrigerant into a suitable recovery device, then remove evaporator core in numbered sequence shown, **Fig. 18.**

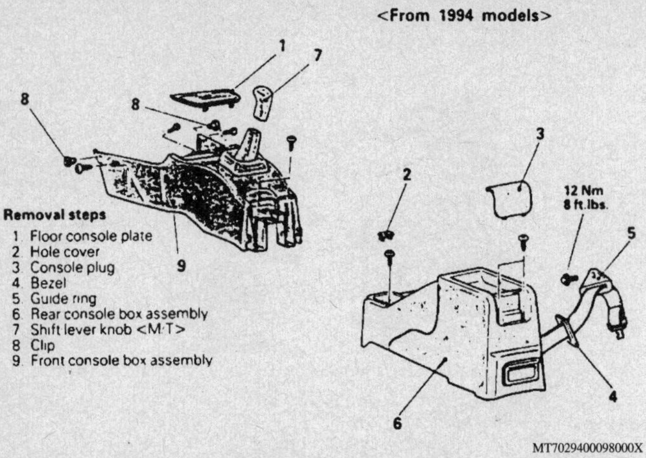
<From 1994 models>
Removal steps
1 Floor console plate
2 Hole cover
3 Console plug
4 Bezel
5 Guide ring
6 Rear console box assembly
7 Shift lever knob <M/T>
8 Clip
9 Front console box assembly
12 Nm
8 ft.lbs.
MT7029400098000X

Fig. 16 Floor console removal. 1994–96 Mirage

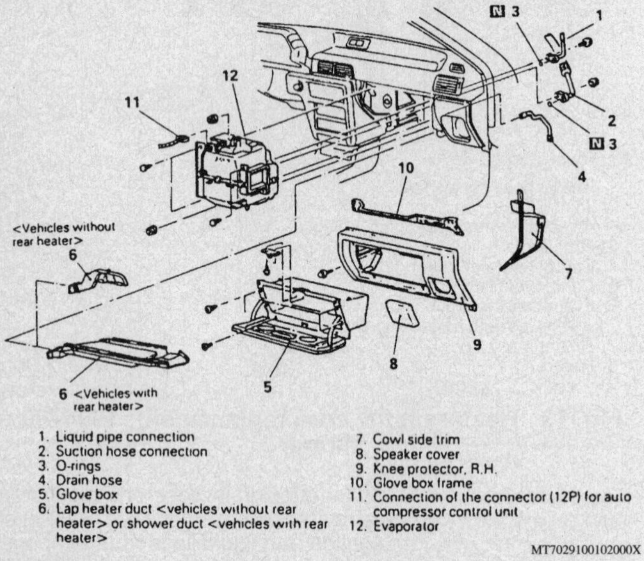
<Vehicles without rear heater>
6 <Vehicles with rear heater>
1. Liquid pipe connection
2. Suction hose connection
3. O-rings
4. Drain hose
5. Glove box
6. Lap heater duct <vehicles without rear heater> or shower duct <vehicles with rear heater>
7. Cowl side trim
8. Speaker cover
9. Knee protector, R.H.
10. Glove box frame
11. Connection of the connector (12P) for auto compressor control unit
12. Evaporator
MT7029100102000X

Fig. 18 Evaporator core replacement. Mirage

3. Reverse procedure to install.

PRECIS

1. Disconnect battery ground cable.
2. Discharge refrigerant from system into appropriate container.
3. Disconnect suction and liquid lines and plug openings to prevent contamination.
4. Remove grommet cover.
5. Remove console assembly, then the glove compartment assembly.
6. Remove main lower crash pad, lower crash pad center fascia panel and lower crash pad center skin.
7. Remove evaporator case attaching bolts, **Fig. 19,** then case.
8. Remove evaporator from evaporator case, **Fig. 20.**
9. Reverse procedure to install.

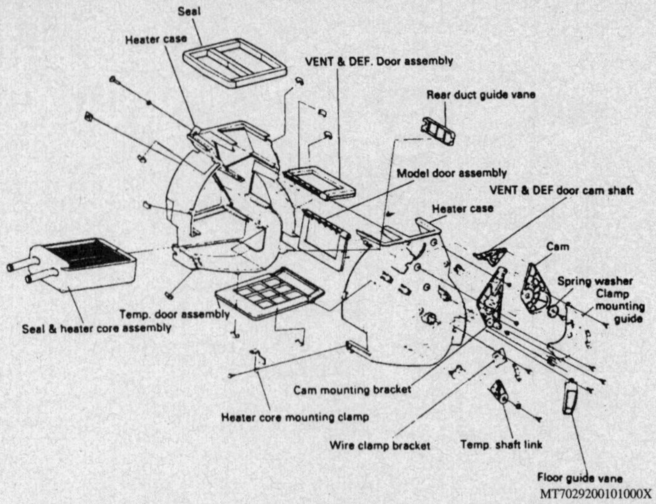
Seal
Heater case
VENT & DEF. Door assembly
Rear duct guide vane
Model door assembly
VENT & DEF door cam shaft
Heater case
Cam
Spring washer
Clamp
mounting
guide
Temp. door assembly
Seal & heater core assembly
Cam mounting bracket
Heater core mounting clamp
Wire clamp bracket
Temp. shaft link
Floor guide vane
MT7029200101000X

Fig. 17 Exploded view of heater unit (lever type). 1993 Precis

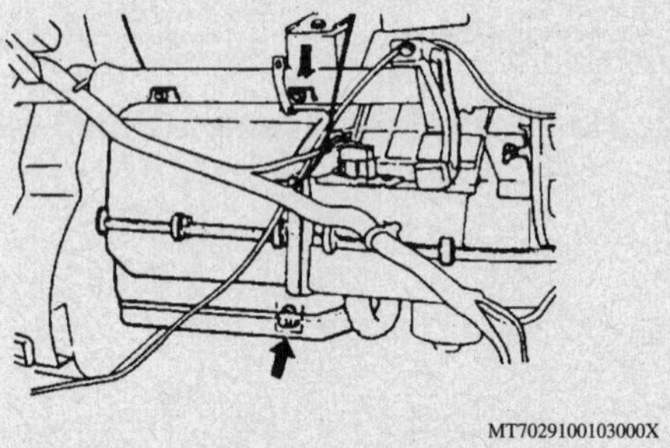
MT7029100103000X

Fig. 19 Evaporator case attaching bolt locations. Precis

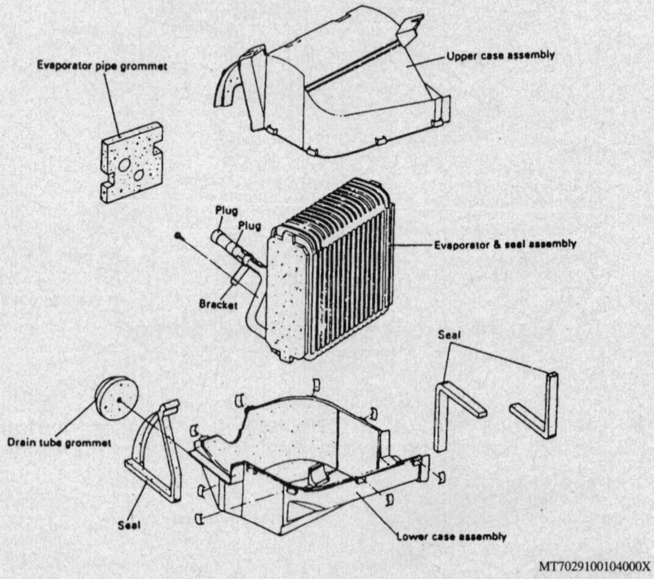
Evaporator pipe grommet
Upper case assembly
Plug
Plug
Evaporator & seal assembly
Bracket
Seal
Drain tube grommet
Seal
Lower case assembly
MT7029100104000X

Fig. 20 Exploded view of evaporator unit. Precis

1.5L Engine

NOTE: On Air Bag Equipped Models, Refer To "Air Bag System Precautions" Located In Front Of This Manual For System Disarming & Arming Procedures.

INDEX

	Page No.
Belt Tension Data	27-16
Camshaft, Replace	27-14
Installation	27-15
Removal	27-14
Compression Pressure	27-11
Cooling System Bleed	27-16
Crankshaft Rear Oil Seal, Replace	27-15
Cylinder Head, Replace	27-12
Mirage	27-12
Precis	27-13
Engine Mount, Replace	27-11
Engine Rebuilding Specifications	29-1
Engine, Replace	27-11
Mirage	27-12
Precis	27-11
Exhaust Manifold, Replace	27-12
Fuel Filter, Replace	27-16
Fuel Pump, Replace	27-16
Intake Manifold, Replace	27-12
Mirage	27-12
Precis	27-12
Main & Rod Bearings	27-15
Oil Pan, Replace	27-15
Oil Pump, Replace	27-15
Piston & Rod Assembly	27-15
Pistons, Pins & Rings	27-15
Precautions	27-11
Air Bag Systems	27-11
Fuel System Pressure Relief	27-11
Radiator, Replace	27-16
Mirage	27-16
Precis	27-16
Rocker Arms, Replace	27-13
Technical Service Bulletins	27-16
Fuel Starvation	27-16
Idle Vibration	27-17
Thermostat, Replace	27-16
Tightening Specifications	27-19
Timing Belt, Replace	27-13
Installation	27-14
Removal	27-13
Valve Adjustment	27-13
Valve Clearance Specifications	27-13
Valve Guides	27-13
Water Pump, Replace	27-16

PRECAUTIONS

AIR BAG SYSTEMS

Refer to "Air Bag System Precautions" in front of this manual for system disarming and arming procedures.

FUEL SYSTEM PRESSURE RELIEF

1. Disconnect fuel pump harness connector at rear side of fuel tank. **Cover fuel pipe line with rag after relieving pressure as residual pressure may still remain.**
2. Start engine and let idle until engine stops by itself, then turn ignition switch to Off. **Failure to relieve fuel system pressure prior to disconnecting fuel system components may cause fire or personal injury.**
3. Disconnect negative battery ground cable.
4. Connect fuel pump harness connector.
5. After repairs have been completed, connect positive battery terminal to fuel pump drive terminal and negative terminal to chassis. Ensure fuel pump operates at this time.

COMPRESSION PRESSURE

Standard compression pressure is 192 psi. Minimum compression pressure is 137 psi. Maximum difference between cylinders is 14 psi.

ENGINE MOUNT

REPLACE

1. Raise and support engine to reduce weight upon mounts.
2. Remove power steering pressure hose and A/C high pressure hose.
3. Remove engine mount bracket and body connection bolt.
4. Remove engine mount bracket and mounting stopper.
5. Reverse procedure to install.

ENGINE

REPLACE

PRECIS

1. Scribe and remove hood.
2. Relieve fuel system pressure as outlined under "Precautions."
3. Disconnect battery cables, then remove battery and battery tray.
4. Remove air cleaner and engine undercover.
5. Drain cooling system into a suitable container.
6. **On models with automatic transaxle,** disconnect transaxle cooling hoses from transaxle.
7. **On all models,** disconnect heater hoses, then the upper and lower radiator hoses.
8. Disconnect cooling fan motor and remove radiator.
9. Disconnect necessary vacuum hoses and engine/transaxle wiring. Mark vacuum hoses and electrical connectors for installation reference.
10. Disconnect accelerator cable and brake booster vacuum hose.
11. **On models with manual transaxle,** disconnect control cable or clutch tube.
12. **On models with automatic transaxle,** disconnect automatic transaxle control cable. **Handle control cable very carefully so as not to bend inner cable.**
13. **On all models,** disconnect speedometer cable.
14. **On models with power steering,** remove power steering pump and hoses as an assembly leaving hoses connected, then use wire to secure pump.
15. **On all models,** raise and support vehicle.
16. **On models with A/C,** remove compressor belt, then the compressor mounting bolts and compressor leaving refrigerant lines connected. Disconnect compressor wiring, then use wire to secure compressor and hose assembly.
17. **On models with manual transaxle,** remove shift control rod and extension rod from transaxle. Use wire to secure rods out of way.
18. **On all models,** disconnect front exhaust pipe from exhaust manifold.
19. Drain engine oil into appropriate container.
20. Disconnect stabilizer bar from lower control arm.
21. Loosen, but do not remove ball joint stud attaching nut, then disconnect ball joint from steering knuckle using puller tool No. MB991113, or equivalent.
22. Loosen, but do not remove tie rod end attaching nut, then disconnect tie rod end from steering knuckle using puller tool No. MB991113, or equivalent.
23. Drain transaxle oil into appropriate container.
24. **On models with driveshaft center bearing,** remove snap ring securing center bearing, then using plastic hammer, lightly tap double offset joint (DOJ) outer race to remove driveshaft from transaxle. Remove center bearing.

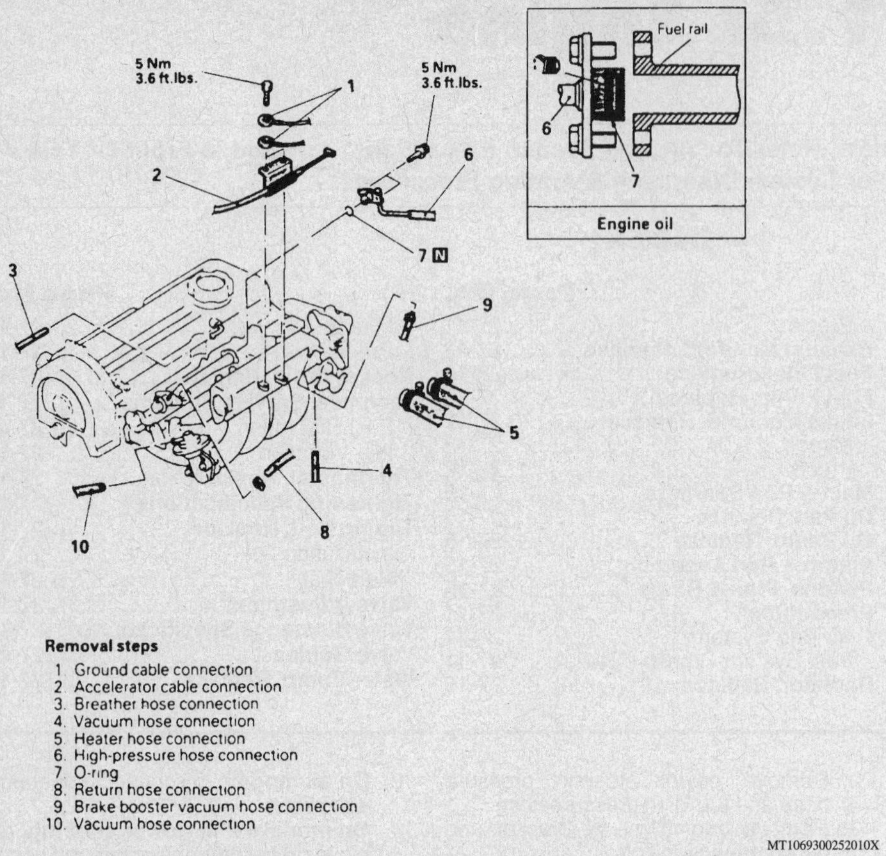
5 Nm
3.6 ft.lbs.
5 Nm
3.6 ft.lbs.
Fuel rail
Engine oil
Removal steps
1. Ground cable connection
2. Accelerator cable connection
3. Breather hose connection
4. Vacuum hose connection
5. Heater hose connection
6. High-pressure hose connection
7. O-ring
8. Return hose connection
9. Brake booster vacuum hose connection
10. Vacuum hose connection
MT1069300252010X

Fig. 1 Engine assembly replacement (Part 1 of 2). Mirage

25. **On models less driveshaft center bearing,** insert suitable pry bar between transaxle case and driveshaft, then pry driveshaft from transaxle case. **Do not insert pry bar too deep or oil seal will be damaged. Do not pull on drive axle or overextend CV joints, as joints will be damaged.**
26. **On all models,** cover transaxle holes to prevent entry of dirt and replace drive axle circlips.
27. Use wire to secure driveshafts out of way.
28. Attach suitable engine lifting device, then raise lift enough to exert tension upon equipment.
29. Remove front roll stopper insulator bolt, then the rear roll stopper insulator bolt.
30. Remove left mount insulator attaching nut. **Do not remove bolt.**
31. Raise engine/transaxle assembly enough to remove weight from mounts.
32. Remove blind cover from inside right fender shield, then the transaxle mount bracket bolt.
33. Remove left mount insulator bolt; then, while directing transaxle side down, remove engine/transaxle assembly from vehicle.
34. Remove starter motor.
35. **On models with automatic transaxle,** remove bolts securing torque converter to driveplate.
36. **On all models,** remove engine-to-transaxle attaching bolts, then separate transaxle from engine.
37. Reverse procedure to install.

MIRAGE

1. Relieve fuel system pressure as outlined under "Precautions," then scribe and remove hood.
2. Drain engine coolant into a suitable container, then remove transaxle as outlined in "Clutch & Manual Transaxle" or in "Automatic Transaxle" section.
3. Remove radiator, then the engine assembly in numbered sequence shown, **Fig. 1.** Support A/C compressor and power steering pump aside with hoses attached.
4. Reverse procedure to install. Tighten all bolts to specifications.

INTAKE MANIFOLD

REPLACE

MIRAGE

When replacing intake manifold, remove and install manifold in numbered sequence as shown, **Fig. 2.**

PRECIS

1. Remove air intake hose from throttle body, then the accelerator cable.
2. Remove coolant hoses, PCV hose, then the brake booster hose.
3. Relieve fuel system pressure as outlined under "Precautions," then disconnect high pressure fuel hose connector.
4. Remove surge fuel tank assembly, then disconnect fuel injector harness connector.
5. Remove delivery pipe with fuel injectors and pressure regulator as an assembly.
6. Remove insulator from intake manifold, then disconnect wiring harness connector between water temperature unit and water temperature sensor.
7. Remove thermostat housing and thermostat.
8. Remove distributor, ignition coil, then the intake manifold stay.
9. Remove intake manifold attaching bolts, then the intake manifold.
10. Reverse procedure to install.

EXHAUST MANIFOLD

REPLACE

When replacing exhaust manifold, remove and install manifold in numbered sequence as shown, **Fig. 3.**

CYLINDER HEAD

REPLACE

MIRAGE

1. Reduce fuel system pressure as outlined under "Precautions, " then drain engine coolant and oil into suitable containers.
2. Remove air intake hose.
3. Remove cylinder head and gasket in numbered sequence shown, **Fig. 4,** noting following:
   a. After timing belt upper cover is removed, rotate crankshaft in direction of normal rotation until timing marks align.
   b. Remove camshaft sprocket using sprocket remover tool Nos. MB990767 and MD998719, or equivalents.
   c. Remove cylinder head bolts in sequence shown, **Fig. 5,** in two or three steps.
4. Reverse procedure to install, noting following:
   a. Install new head gasket on block with "ICG"identification mark facing up.
   b. Tighten cylinder head bolts to specifications in sequence shown in, **Fig. 6,** in two or three steps.

PRECIS

1. Disconnect battery ground cable.
2. Remove breather hose, then the air cleaner.
3. Remove radiator and water hoses, fuel lines, then the vacuum hoses.
4. Remove ignition cables, distributor, then the surge tank.
5. Remove intake manifold, heat cowl, then the exhaust manifold assembly.
6. Remove timing belt cover, then move belt tensioner pulley toward water pump and secure.
7. Remove timing belt front camshaft

sprocket. **Do not remove timing belt from crankshaft sprocket.**

8. Remove rocker cover.
9. Remove cylinder head bolts using tool No. 09221–11001, or equivalent, as shown, **Fig. 5.** Loosen bolts evenly, in three steps to prevent cylinder head warpage.
10. Remove cylinder head and gasket. Ensure no gasket pieces fall into engine.
11. Reverse procedure to install, noting following:
    a. Do not apply sealer to cylinder head gasket. Install gasket with ID mark toward timing belt.
    b. Prior to installing cylinder head on engine, ensure crankshaft and camshaft timing marks are aligned.
    c. Tighten cylinder head bolts to specifications in sequence shown in, **Fig. 6.** Tighten bolts in two steps to ensure proper seating of cylinder head to cylinder block.
    d. Tighten intake and exhaust manifold nuts and bolts to specification.
    e. After cylinder head has been installed, adjust timing belt tension.
    f. Tighten rocker cover bolts to specification.

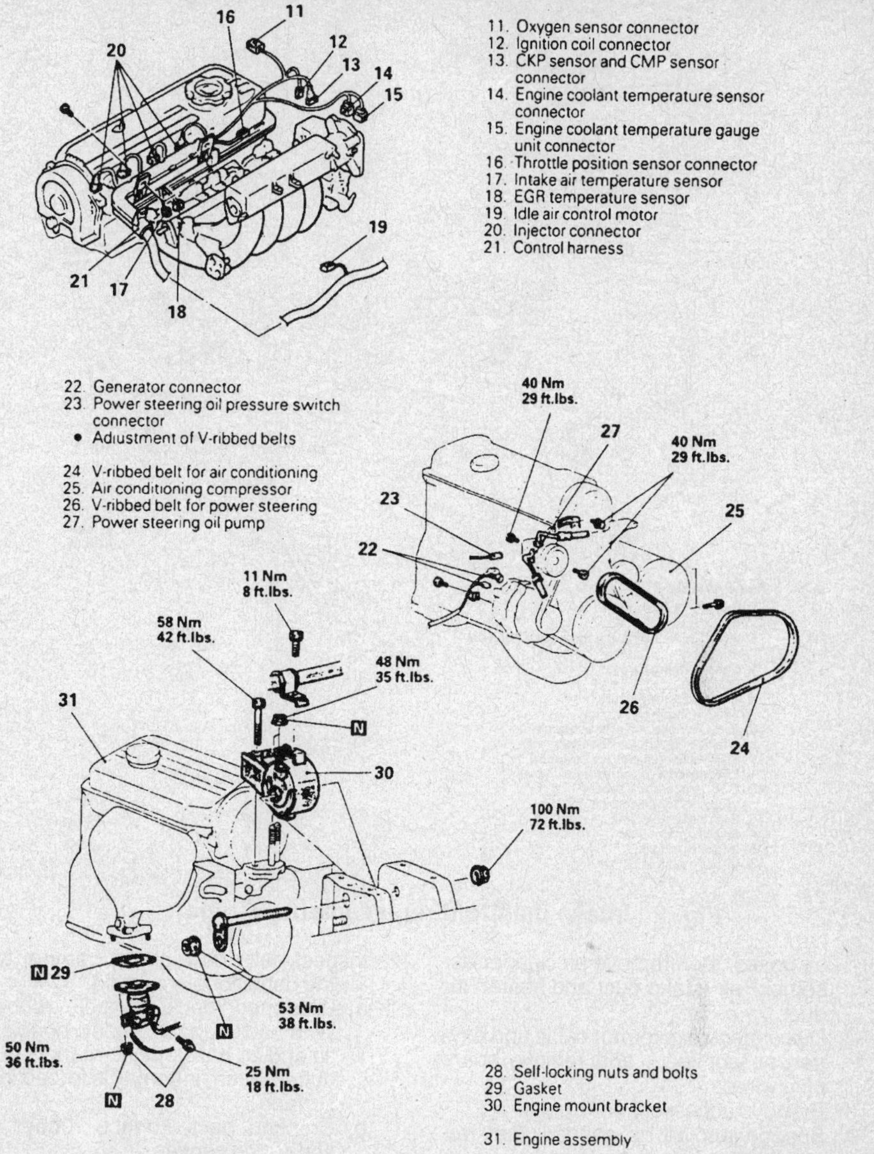
11. Oxygen sensor connector
12. Ignition coil connector
13. CKP sensor and CMP sensor connector
14. Engine coolant temperature sensor connector
15. Engine coolant temperature gauge unit connector
16. Throttle position sensor connector
17. Intake air temperature sensor
18. EGR temperature sensor
19. Idle air control motor
20. Injector connector
21. Control harness
22. Generator connector
23. Power steering oil pressure switch connector
• Adjustment of V-ribbed belts
24. V-ribbed belt for air conditioning
25. Air conditioning compressor
26. V-ribbed belt for power steering
27. Power steering oil pump
40 Nm 29 ft.lbs.
40 Nm 29 ft.lbs.
11 Nm 8 ft.lbs.
58 Nm 42 ft.lbs.
48 Nm 35 ft.lbs.
100 Nm 72 ft.lbs.
53 Nm 38 ft.lbs.
50 Nm 36 ft.lbs.
25 Nm 18 ft.lbs.
28. Self-locking nuts and bolts
29. Gasket
30. Engine mount bracket
31. Engine assembly
MT1069300252020X

Fig. 1 Engine assembly replacement (Part 2 of 2). Mirage

VALVE CLEARANCE SPECIFICATIONS

Year	Stem-To-Guide Clearance, Inch①	
	Intake	Exhaust
PRECIS		
1993–94	.0060	.0100
MIRAGE		
1993–96	.0080	.0100

① — Hot.

VALVE ADJUSTMENT

1. With engine at operating temperature, remove rocker arm cover.
2. Disconnect high tension lead from ignition coil.
3. While observing rocker arms on No. 4 cylinder, rotate crankshaft clockwise until exhaust valve is closing and intake valve is slightly open. Ensure timing mark on crankshaft pulley is aligned with "T" mark on lower timing cover case and No. 1 cylinder is at top dead center (TDC) compression stroke. Check and adjust valve clearance for both intake and exhaust valves of No. 1 cylinder, intake valve of No. 2 cylinder and exhaust valve of No. 3 cylinder. If valve clearance is not as specified, adjust valves as follows:
    a. Loosen rocker arm locknut.
    b. Turn adjusting screw while measuring clearance with a feeler gauge, **Fig. 7,** until screw contacts feeler gauge.
    c. Hold adjusting screw in place and tighten locknut to specifications.
4. Rotate crankshaft clockwise 360 degrees then check and adjust valve clearance for exhaust valve of No. 2 cylinder, intake valve of No. 3 cylinder and intake and exhaust valves of No. 4 cylinder.
5. After completing adjustment, install rocker arm cover and connect ignition coil high tension lead.
6. Tighten rocker arm cover bolts to specifications.

ROCKER ARMS

REPLACE

Refer to "Camshaft, Replace" for rocker arm and shaft replacement procedure.

VALVE GUIDES

1. Press old valve guide from cylinder head toward lower surface using a suitable pushrod and press.
2. Ream each valve guide bore in cylinder head to outer diameter of replacement valve guide, **Fig. 8.**Never use a valve guide of same size as removed guide.
3. Press fit new valve guide into top of cylinder head until a protrusion of .579–.602 inch is obtained.
4. Note that valve guides for intake and exhaust are of different lengths. Intake guides are 1.791 inches long; exhaust guides are 1.988 inches long.
5. After installation of new valve guides, insert valve and ensure it slides freely, then check for proper clearance. If clearance is not correct, ream valve guide until proper clearance is obtained. Refer to "Valve Specifications" for stem to guide clearance.

TIMING BELT

REPLACE

REMOVAL

1. Disconnect breather and secondary

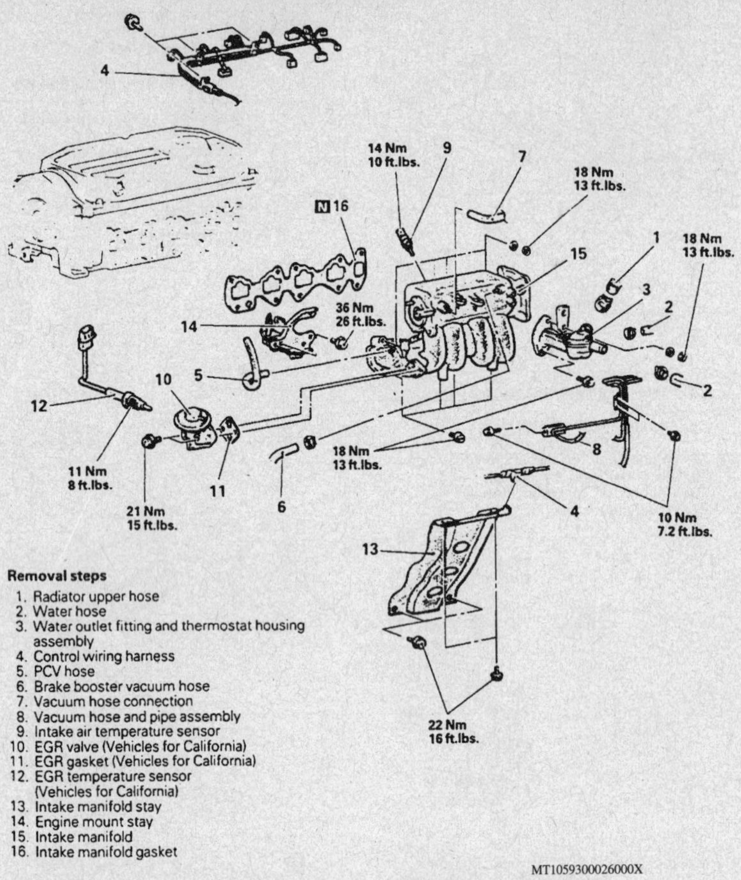

4
14 Nm
10 ft.lbs.
9
7
18 Nm
13 ft.lbs.
N 16
1
18 Nm
13 ft.lbs.
15
3
2
36 Nm
26 ft.lbs.
14
10
5
2
12
18 Nm
13 ft.lbs.
8
11 Nm
8 ft.lbs.
11
6
4
21 Nm
15 ft.lbs.
10 Nm
7.2 ft.lbs.
13
Removal steps
1. Radiator upper hose
2. Water hose
3. Water outlet fitting and thermostat housing assembly
4. Control wiring harness
5. PCV hose
6. Brake booster vacuum hose
7. Vacuum hose connection
8. Vacuum hose and pipe assembly
9. Intake air temperature sensor
10. EGR valve (Vehicles for California)
11. EGR gasket (Vehicles for California)
12. EGR temperature sensor (Vehicles for California)
13. Intake manifold stay
14. Engine mount stay
15. Intake manifold
16. Intake manifold gasket
22 Nm
16 ft.lbs.
MT1059300026000X

Fig. 2 Intake manifold replacement. Mirage

air hoses, then remove air cleaner assembly, air intake duct and heated air duct.

2. Disconnect accelerator cable and oxygen sensor lead, and remove spark plug wires.
3. Remove accessory drive belts.
4. Support engine as needed, then remove left engine mount bracket.
5. Remove power steering pump and water pump pulleys.
6. Remove rocker arm cover, gasket and packing, and upper timing belt cover.
7. After removing rocker cover, back off all valve adjusting screws until tip of each screw protrudes less than .08 inch from rocker arm. **This is essential to provide enough freeplay at camshaft to allow correct valve timing during timing belt installation.**
8. Remove damper pulley, crankshaft pulley and lower timing belt cover.
9. Rotate crankshaft in normal direction of rotation (clockwise) until timing marks are aligned, **Fig. 9,** loosen belt tensioner bolts and move timing belt tensioner fully toward water pump, then tighten bolts to hold tensioner.
10. Remove timing belt. If timing belt is to be reused, place an arrow mark indicating turning direction (direction of engine rotation) to ensure proper installation.
11. Remove camshaft sprocket, crankshaft sprocket and flange, and timing belt tensioner as needed.
12. Inspect belt and replace if any of following conditions are noted:
    a. Hardened back surface rubber. With back surface glossy, nonelastic and so hard that no mark is produced when fingernail is forced into surface.
    b. Cracked back surface rubber or separated canvas.
    c. Cracks at tooth bottom or side of belt.

INSTALLATION

1. Install flange and crankshaft sprocket as shown, **Fig. 10.**
2. Tighten crankshaft sprocket bolt to specification.
3. Install camshaft sprocket and tighten bolt to specification.
4. Install timing belt tensioner as follows:
    a. Mount tensioner, spring and spacer, then temporarily tighten pivot bolt.
    b. Temporarily tighten adjusting bolt, then install bottom end of spring into front case.
    c. Secure tensioner to position nearest water pump.
5. Ensure timing marks are aligned, **Fig. 9.**
6. Install timing belt over crankshaft sprocket, then the camshaft sprocket, keeping tension side of belt tight as belt is installed. If used belt is installed, ensure belt is installed in original direction.
7. Apply counterclockwise force to camshaft sprocket to tighten tension side of belt. Ensure timing marks remain aligned.
8. Install crankshaft pulley to prevent belt from slipping off sprocket, then adjust belt tension as follows:
    a. Loosen tensioner bolts to allow tensioner to bear against belt, then tighten adjusting bolt and pivot bolt. **Tighten adjusting bolt first to prevent tensioner from rotating away from belt.**
    b. Rotate crankshaft clockwise one full revolution, then realign crankshaft sprocket timing mark with pointer. **Crankshaft must be rotated smoothly, in clockwise direction. Do not apply any force other than spring force of tensioner to timing belt.**
    c. Loosen tensioner pivot and adjusting bolts, then tighten adjuster bolt and pivot bolt. **Tighten adjusting bolt first to prevent tensioner from rotating away from belt.**
    d. Check belt tension by holding belt as shown, **Fig. 11,** and applying thumb pressure to tension side of belt. Tension is correct when tooth of belt covers approximately 1/4 width of tensioner adjuster bolt.
    e. Rotate crankshaft clockwise, one full revolution and ensure timing marks line up.
9. Reverse remaining procedure to complete installation, then adjust valve clearances as outlined.

CAMSHAFT

REPLACE

REMOVAL

1. Disconnect battery ground cable.
2. Disconnect breather hose and secondary air hose.
3. Remove air cleaner and timing belt cover.
4. Rotate crankshaft in normal direction of rotation (clockwise) to bring No. 1 cylinder to top dead center (TDC) of compression stroke. No. 1 cylinder is at TDC compression stroke when mark on upper timing undercover is aligned with mark on camshaft sprocket, **Fig. 12.**
5. Move timing belt tensioner fully toward water pump assembly and temporarily secure it.
6. Remove camshaft sprocket attaching bolt, then detach sprocket from camshaft with timing belt attached. Position camshaft sprocket on lower belt cover or suspend sprocket and belt from hood to maintain proper timing alignment. **Do not rotate crankshaft after removing sprocket from camshaft.**
7. Remove rocker cover and note position of camshaft.
8. Remove rocker shaft assembly and cylinder head rear cover.
9. Remove camshaft thrust case tightening bolt, thrust case and camshaft. Remove assembly toward transaxle side

of cylinder head.

INSTALLATION

1. Check camshaft journals for wear. If journals are badly worn, replace camshaft.
2. Install camshaft thrust case and thrust plate to camshaft end and firmly tighten attaching bolt. Check camshaft endplay. Endplay should be .002–.008 inch. If endplay exceeds specified value, replace thrust case and recheck endplay.
3. If endplay is still not within specification, check rear end of camshaft journal for wear. If badly worn, replace camshaft.
4. Lubricate camshaft journal and thrust portions of camshaft with clean engine oil.
5. Insert camshaft into cylinder head and rotate camshaft to position noted during disassembly (TDC of compression stroke for No. 1 cylinder).
6. Insert camshaft thrust case with threaded hole facing upward. Align threaded hole with bolt hole in cylinder head. Install and firmly tighten attaching bolt.
7. Install rear gasket and cover. Firmly tighten bolts to specification.
8. Using guide tool No. MD998307 and seal installer tool No. MD998306, or equivalent, install camshaft oil seal. Lubricate external surface of seal completely with engine oil.
9. Ensure seal is completely seated.
10. Install camshaft sprocket and timing belt, and ensure timing marks are aligned, **Fig. 12.** Tighten camshaft sprocket bolt to specification.
11. **On Precis models,** install rocker arm and shaft assembly, **Fig. 13.** Both intake and exhaust rocker arms have identification marks stamped on side of rocker arm at valve end. Rocker arms marked 1 and 3 can be installed at cylinder locations 1 and 3. Rocker arms marked 2 and 4 can be installed at cylinder locations 2 and 4. Also note that rocker arm springs for exhaust rocker arms have a free length of 1.85 inches, while those for intake rocker arms have a free length of 3.03 inches. Tighten rocker arm shaft bolts to specification.
12. **On Mirage models,** install rocker arms with identification marks positioned as shown, **Fig. 14.**
13. **On all models,** position large chamfer end of rocker shaft toward timing belt side of engine.
14. Temporarily set valve clearances to cold engine clearance specifications.
15. Install gasket in rocker cover groove, then temporarily install rocker cover.
16. Start and operate engine at idle speed until normal operating temperature is reached and adjust valve clearances.
17. Install rocker cover.
18. Reverse procedure to install. Tighten rocker cover bolts to specifications.

PISTON & ROD ASSEMBLY

Piston and rod are assembled with indented arrow on piston and embossed numeral on rod facing toward front of engine, **Fig. 15.**

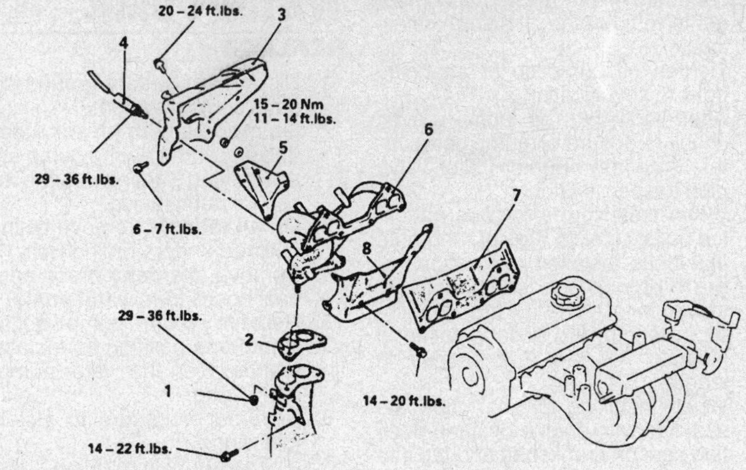
20 – 24 ft.lbs.
3
4
15 – 20 Nm
11 – 14 ft.lbs.
6
5
29 – 36 ft.lbs.
7
6 – 7 ft.lbs.
8
29 – 36 ft.lbs.
2
1
14 – 20 ft.lbs.
14 – 22 ft.lbs.

Removal steps

1. Self-locking nut
2. Gasket
3. Exhaust manifold cover (A)
4. Oxygen sensor
5. Engine hanger
6. Exhaust manifold
7. Exhaust manifold gasket
8. Exhaust manifold cover (B)

MT1079100016000X

Fig. 3 Exhaust manifold replacement

PISTONS, PINS & RINGS

Pistons and rings are available in standard size and oversizes of .010, .020, .030 and .039 inch. Oversize pins are not available.

MAIN & ROD BEARINGS

Main and rod bearings are available in undersizes of .010, .020 and .030 inch.

Main bearing caps are installed with arrows facing front of engine.

CRANKSHAFT REAR OIL SEAL

REPLACE

1. Remove transmission, clutch assembly and flywheel or flex plate, as equipped.
2. Remove rear oil seal case and separate: oil seal, case and separator, if equipped. **Fig. 16.**
3. Drive in oil seal from inside of case, **Fig. 17.** Ensure oil seal plate fits properly in inner contact surface of seal case, if equipped.
4. Install separator with oil hole facing bottom of case, if equipped.
5. Apply engine oil to oil seal lips.
6. Install oil seal case in cylinder block.

OIL PAN

REPLACE

On some models, it may be necessary to remove engine from vehicle to gain access to oil pan.

1. Raise and support vehicle, remove engine splash pan, if equipped, then drain crankcase into appropriate container.
2. Remove oil pressure sender unit, if necessary.
3. Remove oil pan bolts, then the oil pan using gasket cutter tool No. MD998727, or equivalent, to break seal of oil pan gasket.
4. Remove oil pump pickup, if necessary.
5. Reverse procedure to install, noting following:
   a. Tighten oil pump pickup bolts to specifications.
   b. Tighten oil pan bolts to specifications.

OIL PUMP

REPLACE

To remove oil pump pickup, refer to "Oil Pan, Replace."

1. Remove timing belt as outlined under "Timing Belt, Replace."
2. Remove oil pan and oil screen, then the front case.
3. Remove oil pump cover, then the inner and outer gears from front case. Mark outer gear surface facing timing case so it can be installed in same direction.
4. Remove relief valve plug, spring and valve.
5. Reverse procedure to install, noting following:

a. Lubricate oil pump internal components with engine oil before installing.
b. Tighten oil pump cover attaching bolts to specification.
c. After installing oil pump cover, check to ensure oil pump gears rotate smoothly. Tighten relief valve plug to specification.
d. When installing front case attaching bolts, refer to **Fig. 18,** and note that bolts installed in location "A" are 1.18 inches in length, bolts installed in location " B" are .79 inches in length and bolts installed in location "C" are 2.36 inches in length.
e. When installing oil seal, lubricate seal lips with engine oil, then position seal on crankshaft and tap into front case using seal installer tool No. MD998304, or equivalent.
f. Before installing oil pan, apply sealer at four front case and rear oil seal case to cylinder block mating surfaces.
g. Tighten front timing case attaching bolts and oil pan attaching bolts to specification.

BELT TENSION DATA

Model	Belt	Deflection, Inch①	
		New	Used②
Precis	Alternator	0.27–0.32	—
	A/C	0.32–0.40	—
	Power Steering	0.27–0.39	—
Mirage	Alternator	.22–.28	.31
	A/C	.20–.24	0.24–0.28
	Power Steering	.16–.22	0.22–0.30

① — Measurement at 22 lbs.
② — Used 5 minutes or more.

COOLING SYSTEM BLEED

These engines do not require a specified bleed procedure. After filling cooling system, run engine to operating temperature with radiator/pressure cap off. Air will then be automatically bled through cap opening.

THERMOSTAT

REPLACE

1. Drain engine coolant into suitable container.
2. Remove upper radiator hose from thermostat housing.
3. Remove thermostat housing attaching bolts, then the housing.
4. Remove thermostat gasket, then the thermostat.
5. Reverse procedure to install. Tighten bolts to specifications.

WATER PUMP

REPLACE

1. Disconnect battery ground cable and drain cooling system.
2. **On models with power steering,** remove power steering pump and bracket leaving hoses connected, and secure pump aside.
3. **On all models,** remove timing belt as outlined under "Timing Belt, Replace."
4. Remove alternator brace and disconnect hoses from water pump.
5. Remove water pump bolts, noting length and position for installation reference, then the water pump, gasket and O-ring.
6. Reverse procedure to install, noting following:
   a. **Torque** 28 mm pump bolts to 10 ft. lbs.
   b. **Torque** 65 mm pump bolt to 17 ft. lbs.
   c. Refer to **Fig. 19** for bolt length and position.

RADIATOR

REPLACE

MIRAGE

1. Drain engine coolant, then remove overflow and reserve tank.
2. Remove upper and lower radiator hoses.
3. **On models with automatic transaxle,** remove ATC cooler hose, then plug hose and nipple.
4. **On all models,** remove radiator fan motor connector, then the upper insulator.
5. Remove radiator and fan motor assembly, then the engine coolant temperature switch connector.
6. Remove radiator fan motor assembly and engine coolant temperature switch, then the lower insulator.
7. Reverse procedure to install.

PRECIS

1. Disconnect fan motor connection, then set heater control warm water flow knob to Hot position.
2. Drain coolant, then disconnect upper and lower hoses as well as overflow tube.
3. **On models with automatic transaxle,** disconnect ATF cooler hoses, then plug hoses and port.
4. **On all models,** remove radiator mounting bolts, then the radiator and fan motor.
5. Remove fan motor from radiator.
6. Reverse procedure to install.

FUEL PUMP

REPLACE

The following procedure has been revised by a Technical Service Bulletin.

1. Relieve fuel system pressure as outlined under "Precautions."
2. Remove fuel tank cap, raise and support rear of vehicle and drain fuel into suitable container.
3. Disconnect filler hose from tank, support tank with suitable jack and remove nuts securing tank straps.
4. Lower fuel tank, then mark and disconnect fuel hoses, vapor hoses and electrical connectors.
5. Remove nuts securing fuel pump assembly, then the fuel pump and gasket.
6. **On Precis models,** proceed as follows:
   a. Remove fuel pump filter and disconnect insulated wire connector.
   b. Using non-flame type soldering iron, disconnect second non-insulated connector.
   c. Remove pump from bracket. It may be necessary to bend bracket ears slightly to remove pump.
   d. Disconnect hose from pump and remove rubber insulator.
7. **On all models,** reverse procedure to install.

FUEL FILTER

REPLACE

Prior To Performing Any Service Operations Listed In This Section, Consult "Technical Service Bulletins"Section For Related Information.

1. Release fuel system pressure as outlined under "Precautions."
2. Remove air cleaner and air intake hose.
3. Hold fuel filter with spanner and remove eye bolt, **Fig. 20.** Cover fuel pipe line with rag to prevent remaining fuel from spraying out.
4. Hold fuel filter with spanner and loosen flare nut, then disconnect fuel main pipe connection.

TECHNICAL SERVICE BULLETINS

FUEL STARVATION

Fuel starvation can occur when the in-tank fuel filter is clogged, typically by contaminated fuel.

Use the following procedure to correct this problem.

1. Activate fuel pump with scan tool, then measure pump supply voltage.
2. If voltage is less than eight volts, inspect and repair fuel pump wiring harness.
3. If voltage is eight or more volts, check system fuel pressure.
4. Fuel system pressure should be 38 psi at curb idle with fuel pressure regulator vacuum hose attached and 47–50 psi with hose disconnected.
5. If system pressure is within specifications, check system for other starvation problems.
6. If fuel system pressure is not within specifications, remove fuel pump as outlined in "Fuel Pump, Replace" and check filter.
7. If filter is clean, replace fuel pump. If filter is clogged, replace filter as outlined in "Fuel Filter, Replace."

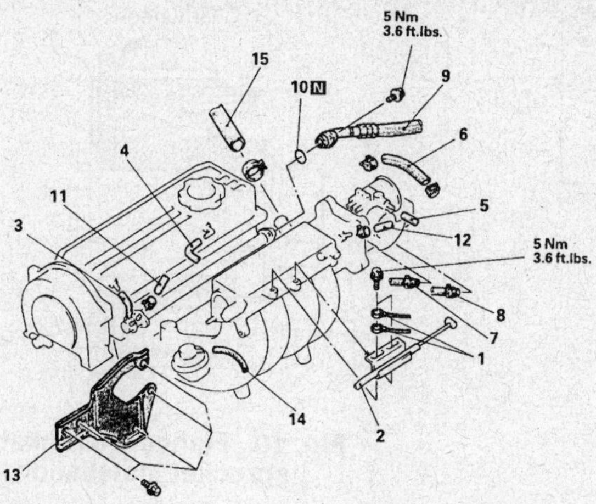
5 Nm
3.6 ft.lbs.
15
10 N
9
6
4
11
5
3
12
5 Nm
3.6 ft.lbs.
8
7
1
14
2
13

Removal steps

1. Ground cable connection
2. Accelerator cable connection
3. PCV hose connection
4. Breather hose connection
5. Vacuum hose connection
6. Water hose connection (Throttle body → thermostat housing)
7. Water hose connection (Throttle body → water inlet pipe)
8. Water hose connection (Heater unit → thermostat housing)
9. Fuel high-pressure hose connection
10. O-ring
11. Return hose connection
12. Brake booster vacuum hose connection
13. Engine mounting stay
14. Vacuum hose
15. Radiator upper hose

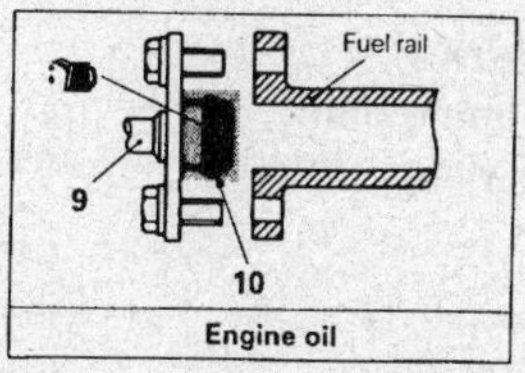
Fuel rail
9
10
Engine oil
MT1069300256010X

Fig. 4 Cylinder head replacement (Part 1 of 2). Mirage

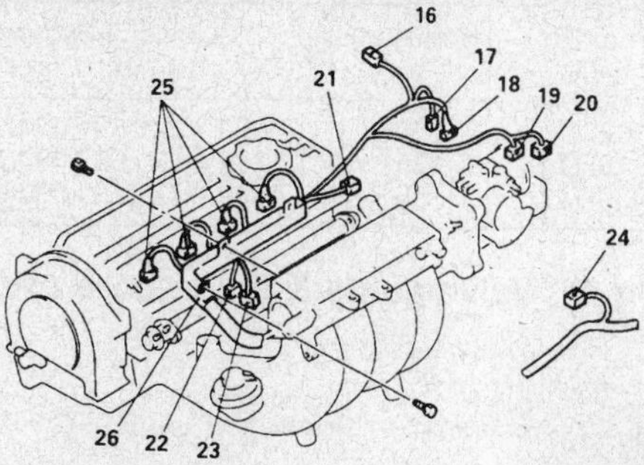
16
17
18
19
20
25
21
24
26
22
23

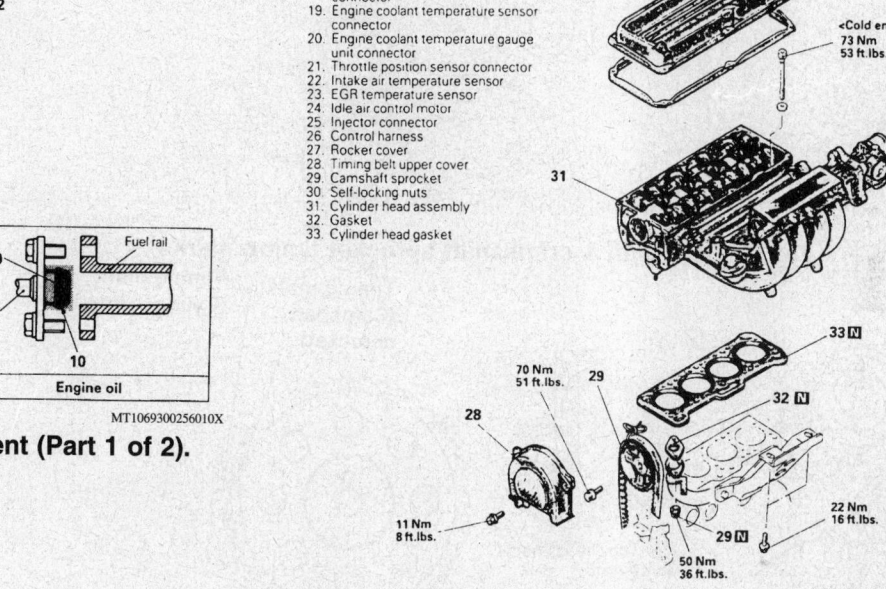

16. Oxygen sensor connector
17. Ignition coil connector
18. CKP sensor and CMP sensor connector
19. Engine coolant temperature sensor connector
20. Engine coolant temperature gauge unit connector
21. Throttle position sensor connector
22. Intake air temperature sensor
23. EGR temperature sensor
24. Idle air control motor
25. Injector connector
26. Control harness
27. Rocker cover
28. Timing belt upper cover
29. Camshaft sprocket
30. Self-locking nuts
31. Cylinder head assembly
32. Gasket
33. Cylinder head gasket

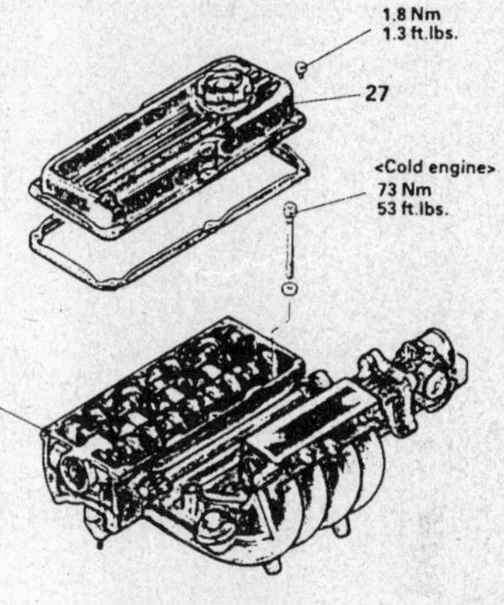
1.8 Nm
1.3 ft.lbs.
27
<Cold engine>
73 Nm
53 ft.lbs.
31

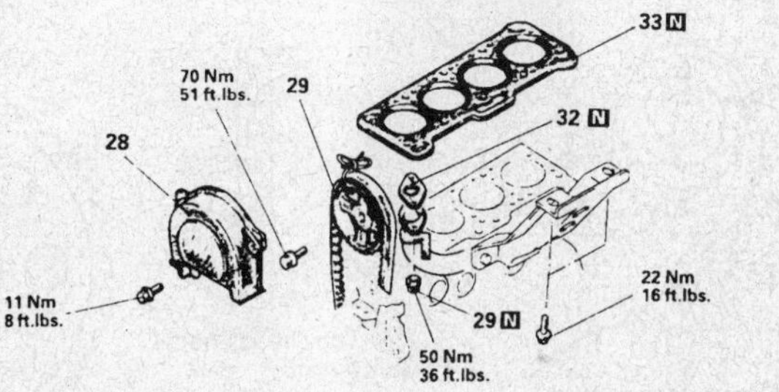
33 N
70 Nm
51 ft.lbs.
29
32 N
28
11 Nm
8 ft.lbs.
29 N
22 Nm
16 ft.lbs.
50 Nm
36 ft.lbs.
MT1069300256020X

Fig. 4 Cylinder head replacement (Part 2 of 2). Mirage

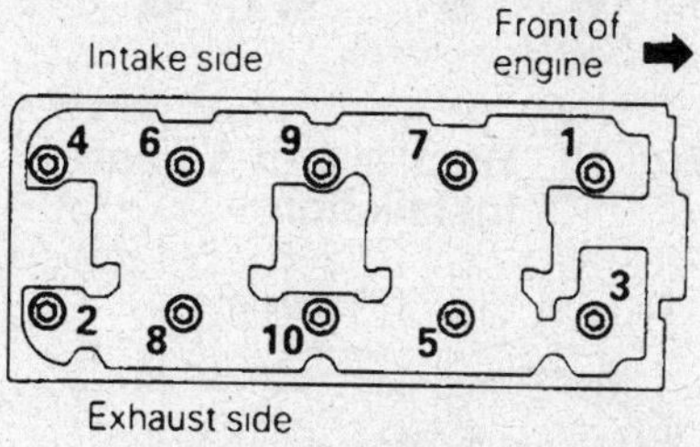
Intake side
Front of engine
4
6
9
7
1
3
2
8
10
5
Exhaust side
MT1069100254000X

Fig. 5 Cylinder head bolt loosening sequence

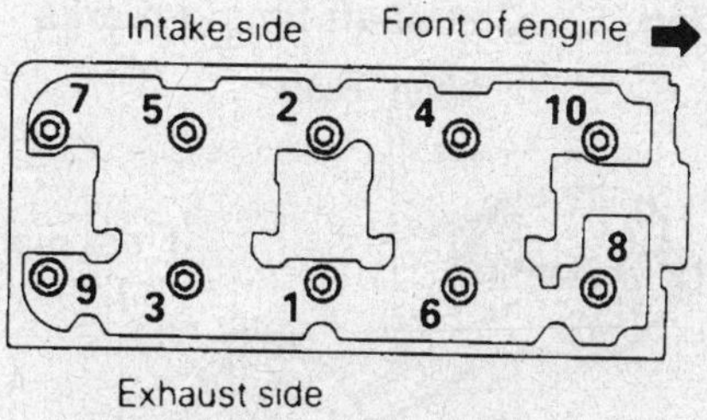
Intake side
Front of engine
7
5
2
4
10
8
9
3
1
6
Exhaust side
MT1069100255000X

Fig. 6 Cylinder head bolt tightening sequence

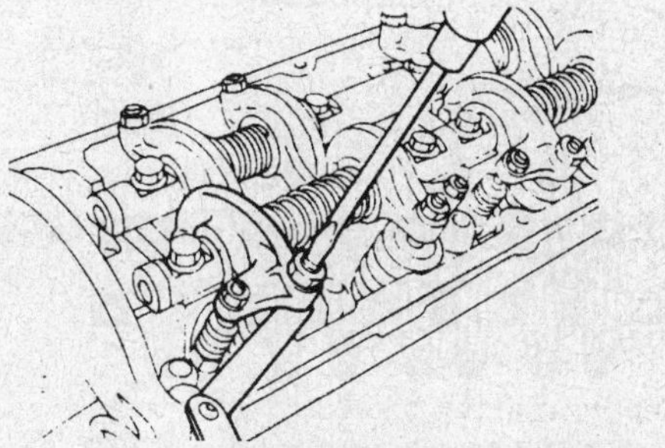
MT1069100260000X

Fig. 7 Valve clearance adjustment

8. **If filter is severely clogged, clean inside of fuel tank.**

IDLE VIBRATION

Mirage

Some of these models may vibrate excessively at idle.

This condition could be caused by an incorrectly mounted radiator. If the radiator mounting brackets are not centered on their posts, the radiator will transmit engine vibration through the frame. Use the following procedure to correct problem.

1. Examine upper radiator mounting brackets, brackets should be centered on post
2. If brackets are not centered, remove upper brackets. Ensure bottom mounting posts are in lower brackets.
3. Center upper brackets over posts and tighten bolts to specifications.
4. Measure clearance between upper brackets and radiator top. Standard clearance is .0394 inch or more.

Size mm (in.)	Size mark	Cylinder head hole size mm (in.)
0.05 (.002) O.S.	5	12.050 – 12.068 (.4744 – .4751)
0.25 (.010) O.S.	25	12.250 – 12.268 (.4823 – .4830)
0.50 (.020) O.S.	50	12.500 – 12.518 (.4921 – .4928)

MT1069100266000X

Fig. 8 Valve guide & guide bore oversizes

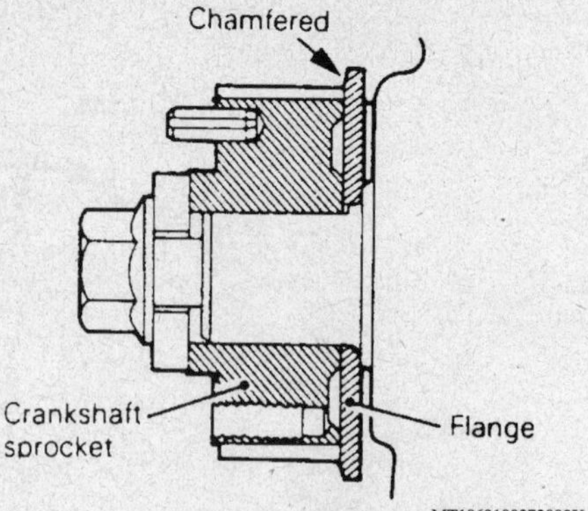
Chamfered
Crankshaft sprocket
Flange
MT1069100272000X

Fig. 10 Flange & crankshaft sprocket installation

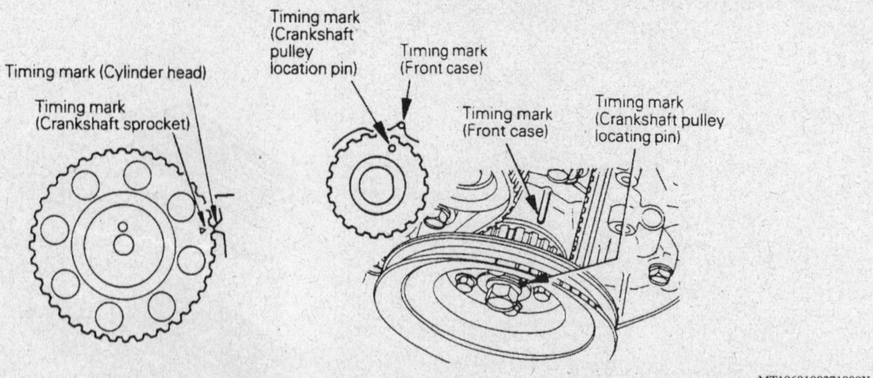
Timing mark (Crankshaft pulley location pin)
Timing mark (Front case)
Timing mark (Cylinder head)
Timing mark (Crankshaft sprocket)
Timing mark (Front case)
Timing mark (Crankshaft pulley locating pin)
MT1069100271000X

Fig. 9 Camshaft & crankshaft sprocket timing marks

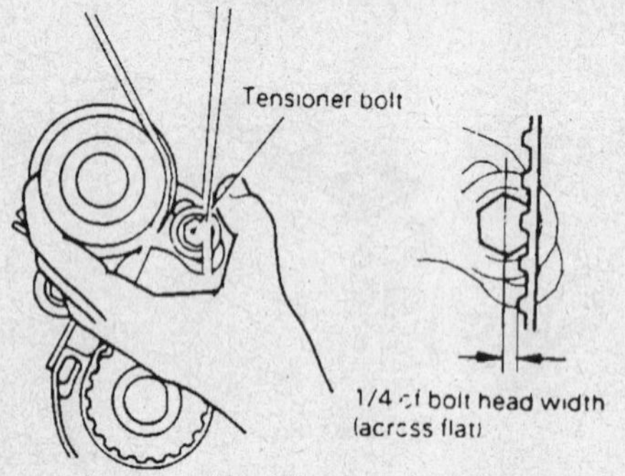
Tensioner bolt
1/4 of bolt head width (across flat)
MT1069100273000X

Fig. 11 Timing belt tension inspection

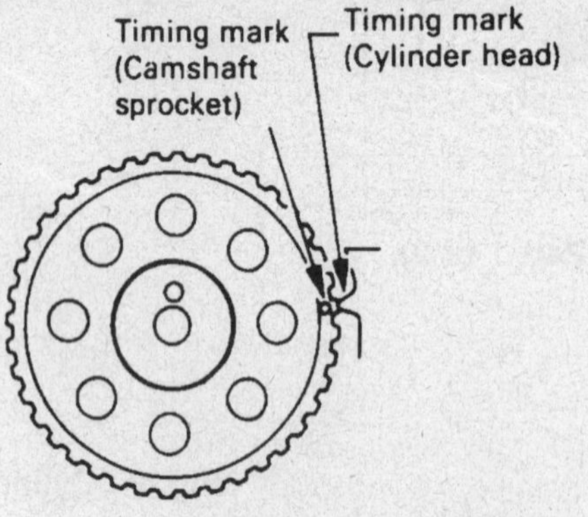
Timing mark (Camshaft sprocket)
Timing mark (Cylinder head)
MT1069100253000X

Fig. 12 Camshaft timing marks

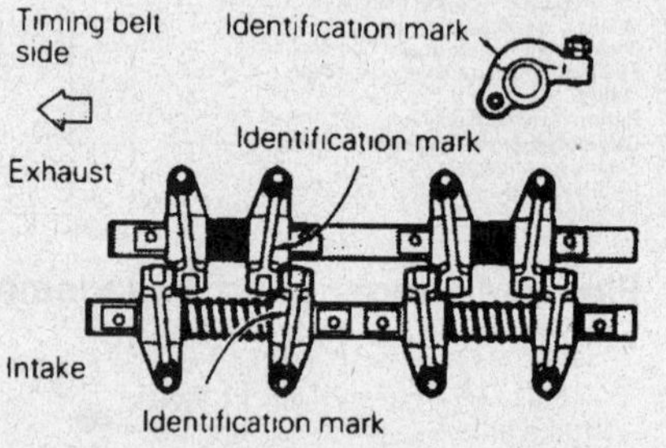
Timing belt side
Identification mark
Identification mark
Exhaust
Intake
Identification mark
MT1069100261000X

Fig. 13 Rocker arm & shaft installation

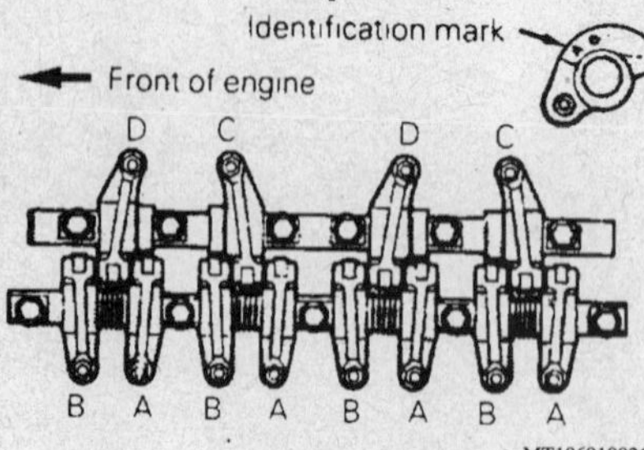
Identification mark
Front of engine
D C D C
B A B A B A B A
MT1069100262000X

Fig. 14 Rocker arm & shaft installation. Mirage

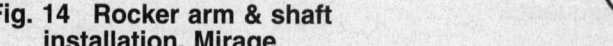

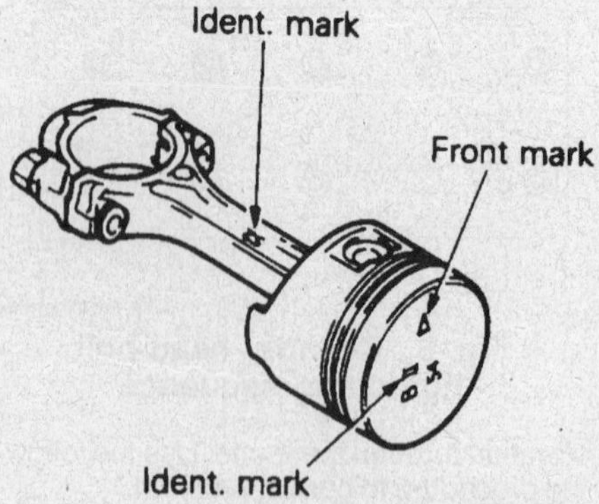
Ident. mark
Front mark
Ident. mark
MT1069100281000X

Fig. 15 Piston & rod assembly

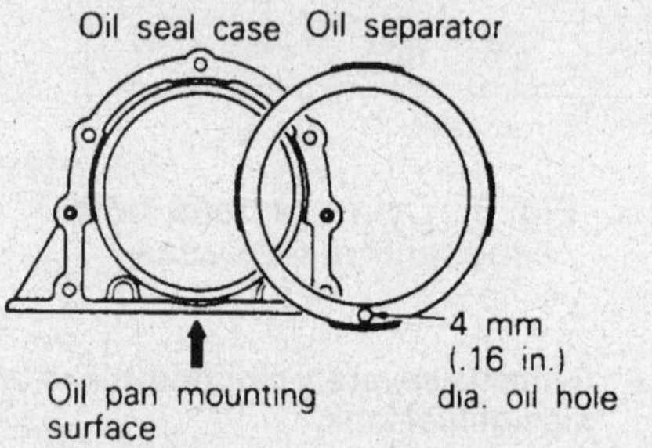
Oil seal case
Oil separator
Oil pan mounting surface
4 mm (.16 in.) dia. oil hole
MT1069100282000X

Fig. 16 Disassembled view of oil seal case & separator

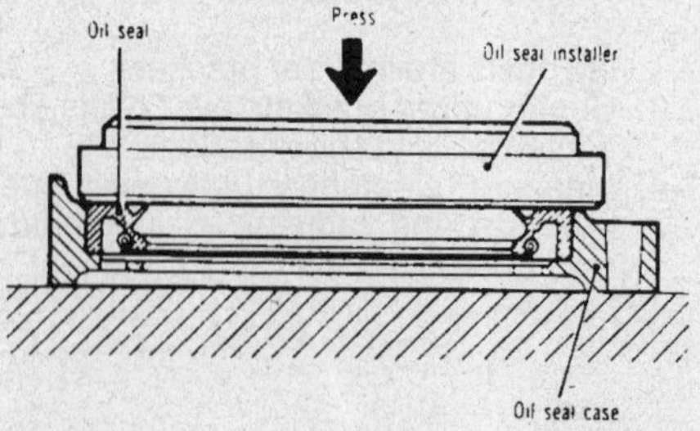
Oil seal
Press
Oil seal installer
Oil seal case
MT1069100283000X

Fig. 17 Rear seal installation

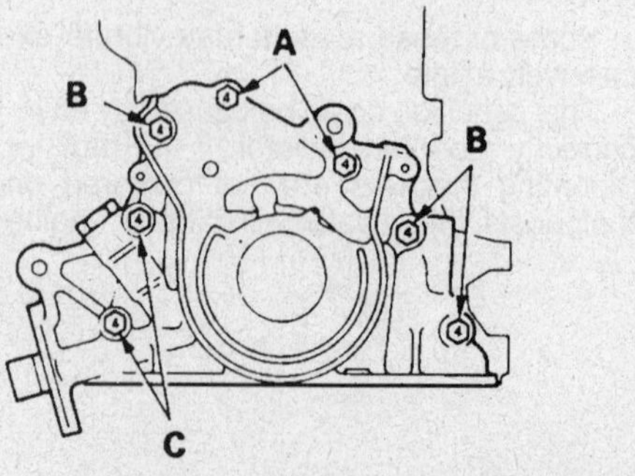
A
B
B
C
MT1069100268000X

Fig. 18 Front case cover bolt locations. 1.5L engine

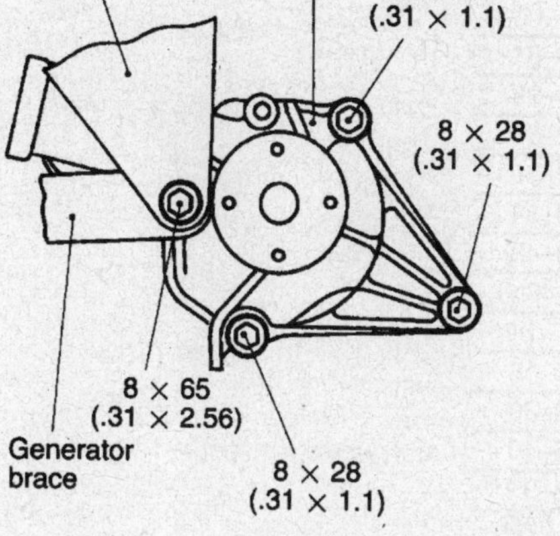
Power steering oil pump bracket
Water pump
8 × 28 (.31 × 1.1)
8 × 28 (.31 × 1.1)
8 × 65 (.31 × 2.56)
Generator brace
8 × 28 (.31 × 1.1)
Screw diameter × length: mm (in.)

MT1089600086000X

Fig. 19 Water pump bolt lengths & locations

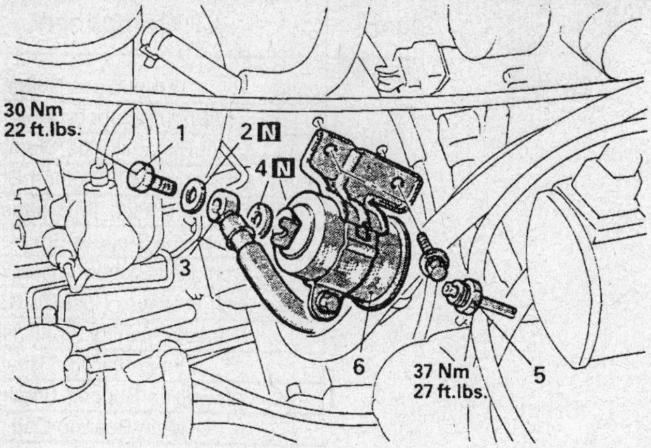
30 Nm
22 ft.lbs.
1
2 N
4 N
3
6
37 Nm
27 ft.lbs.
5

Removal steps

1. Eye bolt
2. Gasket
3. High-pressure fuel hose connection
4. Gasket
5. Fuel main pipe connection
6. Fuel filter

MT1029100016000X

Fig. 20 Fuel filter replacement

TIGHTENING SPECIFICATIONS

Year	Component	Torque/ Ft. Lbs.
1993–96	A/C Compressor To Bracket	17–20
	Accelerator Cable Adjusting Bolt	36-48④
	Ball Joint Attaching Nut	43–52
	Camshaft Bolts	14–20
	Camshaft Sprocket Bolt	47–54
	Connecting Rod Cap	①
	Control Wiring Harness Protector To Air Intake Plenum	36-48④
	Crankshaft Bearing Caps	36–39
	Crankshaft Pulley To Crankshaft Sprocket	9–11
	Crankshaft Sprocket Bolt	51–72
	Cylinder Head Bolts	51–54
	Distributor Mounting Nut	7–9
	Driveplate	94–101
	Engine Ground Cable Bolt	20–24
	Engine Mount Bracket Nut And Bolt	36–47
	Engine Mount Insulator Nut (Large)	65–80
	Engine Mount Insulator Nut (Small)	33–43
	Engine To Transaxle	②
	Exhaust Manifold Bolts/Nuts	11–14
	Flywheel	94–101

Continued

Year	Component	Torque/ Ft. Lbs.
1993–96	Front Case Bolt	7–11
	Front Engine Support Bracket Bolt	36–51
	Front Exhaust Pipe Clamp Bolt	14–22
	Front Exhaust Pipe Support Bracket Bolt	22–30
	Front Exhaust Pipe To Exhaust Manifold	22–29
	Front Roll Stopper Bracket Bolt	40–54
	Front Roll Stopper Insulator Nut	33–43
	Fuel High Pressure Hose To Delivery Pipe	36-48④
	Intake Manifold Bolts/Nuts	11–14
	Intake Manifold Stay	13–18
	Left Engine Support Bracket Bolt	22–30
	Main Bearing Cap	36–40
	Oil Filter	8–9
	Oil Pan Bolts	48-72④
	Oil Pan Drain Plug	25–33
	Oil Pressure Switch	11–16
	Oil Pump Cover Bolt	6–7
	Oil Screen	11–16
	Power Steering Oil Pump Brace Bolt	18–24
	Power Steering Oil Pump To Bracket	33–40
	Rear Plate Bolt	6–7
	Rear Roll Stopper Bracket Bolt	80–94
	Rear Roll Stopper Insulator Nut	33–43
	Relief Valve Plug	29–36
	Rocker Arm Shaft Bolt	14–20
	Rocker Cover Bolt	14-20④
	Roll Rod Bracket To Body Bolt	51–65
	Roll Rod To Engine Bolt	40–47
	Surge Tank To Intake Manifold Bolts And Nuts	11–14
	Thermostat Housing Attaching Bolts	12–14
	Tie Rod Attaching Nut	11–25
	Timing Belt Lower Cover	7–9
	Timing Belt Tensioner	14–20
	Timing Belt Upper Cover	7–9
	Transaxle Mounting Bolts	43–58
	Transaxle To Engine Mounting Bolts	②
	Valve Adjusting Screw Nut	9–13
	Water Pump Bolts	③
	Water Pump Pulley Bolt	6–7

① — Tighten in four steps: torque to 14.5 ft. lbs.; then back off; torque again to 14.5 ft. lbs.; then tighten an additional ¼ turn.

② — 8 mm bolts, 7–8 ft. lbs.; 10 mm bolts, 22–25 ft. lbs.; 12 mm bolts, 31–40 ft. lbs.

③ — Refer to "Water Pump, Replace" for procedure.

④ — Inch lbs.

1.8L Engine

NOTE: On Air Bag Equipped Models, Refer To "Air Bag System Precautions" Located In The Front Of This Manual For System Disarming & Arming Procedures.

NOTE: For Procedures Not Found In This Section, Refer To "1.8L Engine" Section in "Mitsubishi Expo."

INDEX

	Page No.
Belt Tension Data	27-22
Compression Pressure	27-21
Engine Rebuilding Specifications	29-1
Engine, Replace	27-22
Precautions	27-21
Air Bag Systems	27-21
Fuel System Pressure Relief	27-21
Radiator, Replace	27-22
Tightening Specifications	27-24
Timing Belt, Replace	27-22
Installation	27-22
Removal	27-22
Valve Clearance Specifications	27-22

PRECAUTIONS

AIR BAG SYSTEMS

Refer to "Air Bag System Precautions" in front of this manual for system disarming and arming procedures.

FUEL SYSTEM PRESSURE RELIEF

1. Disconnect fuel pump harness connector at fuel tank rear side. **Cover fuel pipe line with rag after relieving pressure as residual pressure may still remain.**
2. Start engine and let idle until engine stops, then turn ignition switch to Off. **Failure to relieve fuel system pressure prior to disconnecting fuel system components may cause fire or personal injury.**
3. Disconnect negative battery ground cable.
4. Connect fuel pump harness connector.
5. After repairs have been completed, connect positive battery terminal to fuel pump drive terminal and negative terminal to chassis. Ensure fuel pump operates at this time.

COMPRESSION PRESSURE

Standard compression pressure is 199 psi. Minimum compression pressure is 151 psi.

ENGINE

REPLACE

1. Release fuel system pressure as outlined under "Precautions."
2. Remove engine hood.
3. Drain engine coolant into appropriate container.
4. Remove transaxle assembly as outlined under "Transmission/Transaxle, Replace."

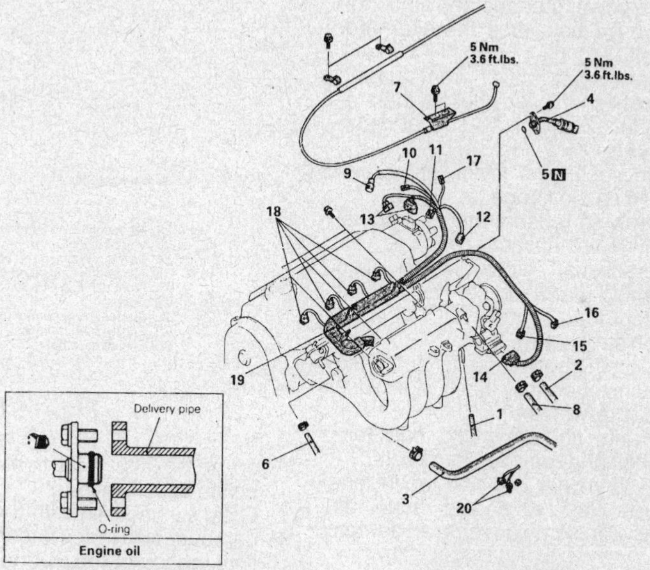

5 Nm
3.6 ft.lbs.
5 Nm
3.6 ft.lbs.
Delivery pipe
O-ring
Engine oil

Removal steps

1. Vacuum hose connection
2. Heater hose connection (Thermostat housing → heater unit)
3. Heater hose connection (Heater unit → Water inlet pipe)
4. Fuel high pressure hose connection
5. O-ring
6. Fuel return hose connection
7. Accelerator cable connection
8. Brake booster vacuum hose connection
9. Oxygen sensor connector
10. Oil pressure switch connector
11. Engine temperature gauge unit connector
12. Engine coolant temperature sensor connector
13. Distributor connector
14. Idle air control motor connector
15. Heated oxygen sensor connector (front) <Vehicles for California>
16. EGR temperature sensor connector <Vehicles for California>
17. Throttle position sensor connector
18. Injector connector
19. Control harness assembly
20. Generator harness connection

MT1069100284010X

Fig. 1 Engine replacement (Part 1 of 2)

5. Remove radiator assembly.
6. Remove power steering oil pump from bracket with hose attached, **Fig. 1.** Tie with a cord and place aside.
7. **On models with A/C,** disconnect A/C compressor connector and remove compressor from compressor bracket with hose attached.
8. **On all models,** connect engine assembly to engine hoist.
9. Place piece of wood between oil pan and jack, then after raising engine until no weight is on engine mount brackets, remove engine mount brackets.
10. After checking that all cables, hoses and harness connections are disconnected from engine, slowly remove engine assembly upward from engine compartment.
11. Reverse procedure to install, noting following:
    a. Ensure cables, harnesses and hose connections are clear of engine assembly.

b. Install engine mount brackets using engine support tool No. MZ203827, or equivalent, to support engine assembly while installing transaxle.

VALVE CLEARANCE SPECIFICATIONS

Year	Stem-To-Guide Clearance, Inch①	
	Intake	Exhaust
1993–96	.008	.012

① — Cold.

TIMING BELT

REPLACE

REMOVAL

1. Disconnect battery ground cable, then remove engine undercover.
2. Remove air conditioning and power steering line clamp, **Fig. 2.**
3. Remove power steering and air conditioning drive belt, then the alternator drive belt.
4. Stop crankshaft pulley from turning using crankshaft pulley holder, then remove crankshaft bolt, washer and pulley.
5. Remove upper and lower timing belt covers, then the flange.
6. If belt is to be reused, mark rotational direction for installation.
7. Turn crankshaft clockwise to align each timing mark and set No. 1 cylinder at top dead center (TDC) of compression stroke, **Fig. 3.**
8. Loosen timing belt tensioner bolt, then press tensioner fully back clockwise using a screwdriver.
9. Temporarily tighten timing belt tensioner bolt and remove timing belt.
10. Loosen tensioner bolt and move tensioner as close to engine mount as possible with screwdriver, then tighten bolt.

INSTALLATION

1. Ensure camshaft and crankshaft timing marks are aligned, **Fig. 3.**
2. Ensure tension side of belt is taut while installing timing belt over crankshaft, water pump and camshaft sprockets, then the tensioner pulley.
3. Apply counterclockwise pressure (reverse of normal rotational direction) to camshaft sprocket and check that belt is fully tensioned. Ensure timing marks are properly aligned.
4. Loosen timing belt tensioner belt approximately ½ turn and allow tensioner spring to tension belt.
5. Rotate crankshaft clockwise two turns, then check timing marks.
6. Ensure timing belt is properly seated on sprockets, then tighten tensioner bolt to specifications.
7. Grasp timing belt with thumb and undercover with index finger and apply light pressure, **Fig. 4.**Check clearance "A"between belt and undercover. Clearance should be approximately 1.18 inches.
8. Install crankshaft flange with flanged side out, **Fig. 5.**
9. Install timing belt upper and lower covers, then tighten bolts to specifications **Fig. 6.** A bolts: .24 x .71 inch and B bolts: .24 x 1.18 inches.
10. Apply engine oil to bearing surface and thread section of crankshaft bolt, then install crankshaft bolt and tighten to specifications.
11. Install alternator drive belt, then the air conditioning and power steering pump drive belt.
12. Install clamp attaching air conditioning and power steering lines to engine mount.
13. Connect battery ground cable.
14. Check and adjust ignition timing as necessary.

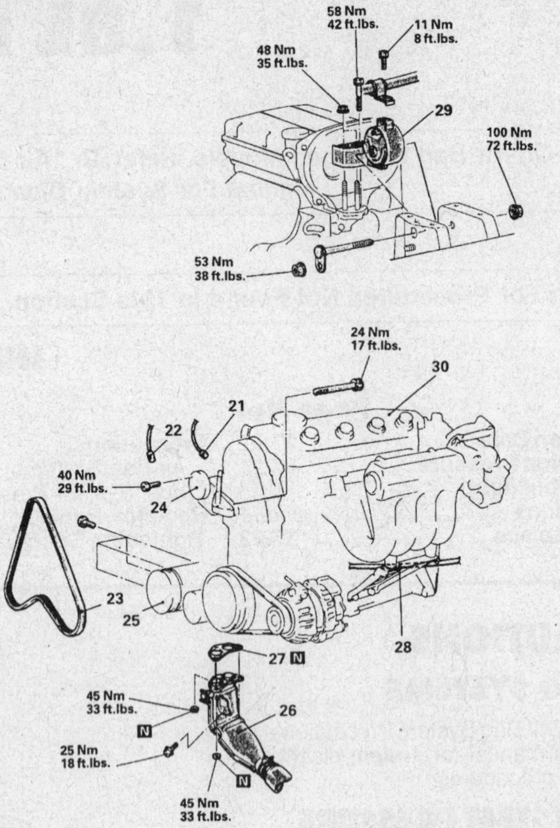
58 Nm
42 ft.lbs.
11 Nm
8 ft.lbs.
48 Nm
35 ft.lbs.
29
100 Nm
72 ft.lbs.
53 Nm
38 ft.lbs.
24 Nm
17 ft.lbs.
30
21
22
40 Nm
29 ft.lbs.
24
23
25
28
27 N
45 Nm
33 ft.lbs.
26
N
25 Nm
18 ft.lbs.
N
45 Nm
33 ft.lbs.

Removal steps

21. Power steering oil pressure switch connector
22. Air conditioning compressor connector
23. V-ribbed belt
24. Power steering oil pump connection
25. Air conditioning compressor connection
26. Front exhaust pipe connection
27. Gasket
28. Starter and generator harness clamp
29. Engine mount bracket
30. Engine assembly

MT1069100284020X

Fig. 1 Engine replacement (Part 2 of 2)

BELT TENSION DATA

Belt	Deflection @ 22 Lbs.	
	New Inches	Used Inches
Alternator	0.280–0.340	0.340–0.470
A/C	0.217–0.236	0.268–0.299
Power Steering	0.295–0.354	0.374–0.453

RADIATOR

REPLACE

Replace radiator as outlined under "Radiator, Replace " in the "1.5L Engine" section.

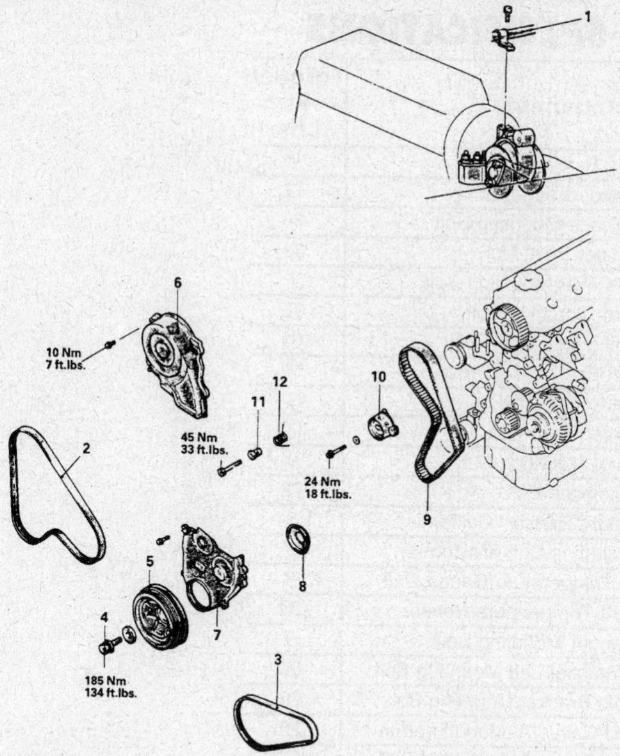
1
6
10 Nm
7 ft.lbs.
12
10
11
2
45 Nm
33 ft.lbs.
24 Nm
18 ft.lbs.
9
5
8
4
7
185 Nm
134 ft.lbs.
3

Removal steps

1. Clamp section hose of air conditioning
2. Drive belt (Power steering, Air conditioning)
3. Drive belt (Generator)
4. Crankshaft bolt
5. Crankshaft pulley
6. Timing belt upper cover
7. Timing belt lower cover
8. Flange
- Adjustment of timing belt tension
9. Timing belt
10. Timing belt tensioner
11. Tensioner spacer
12. Tensioner spring

MT1069100285000X

Fig. 2 Timing belt replacement

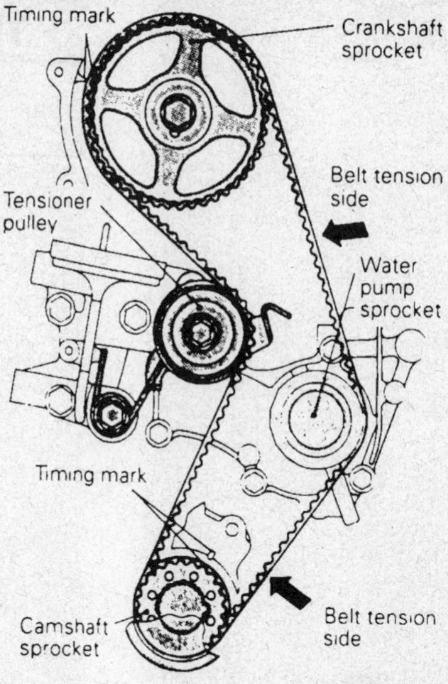
Timing mark
Crankshaft sprocket
Belt tension side
Tensioner pulley
Water pump sprocket
Timing mark
Camshaft sprocket
Belt tension side

MT1069100287000X

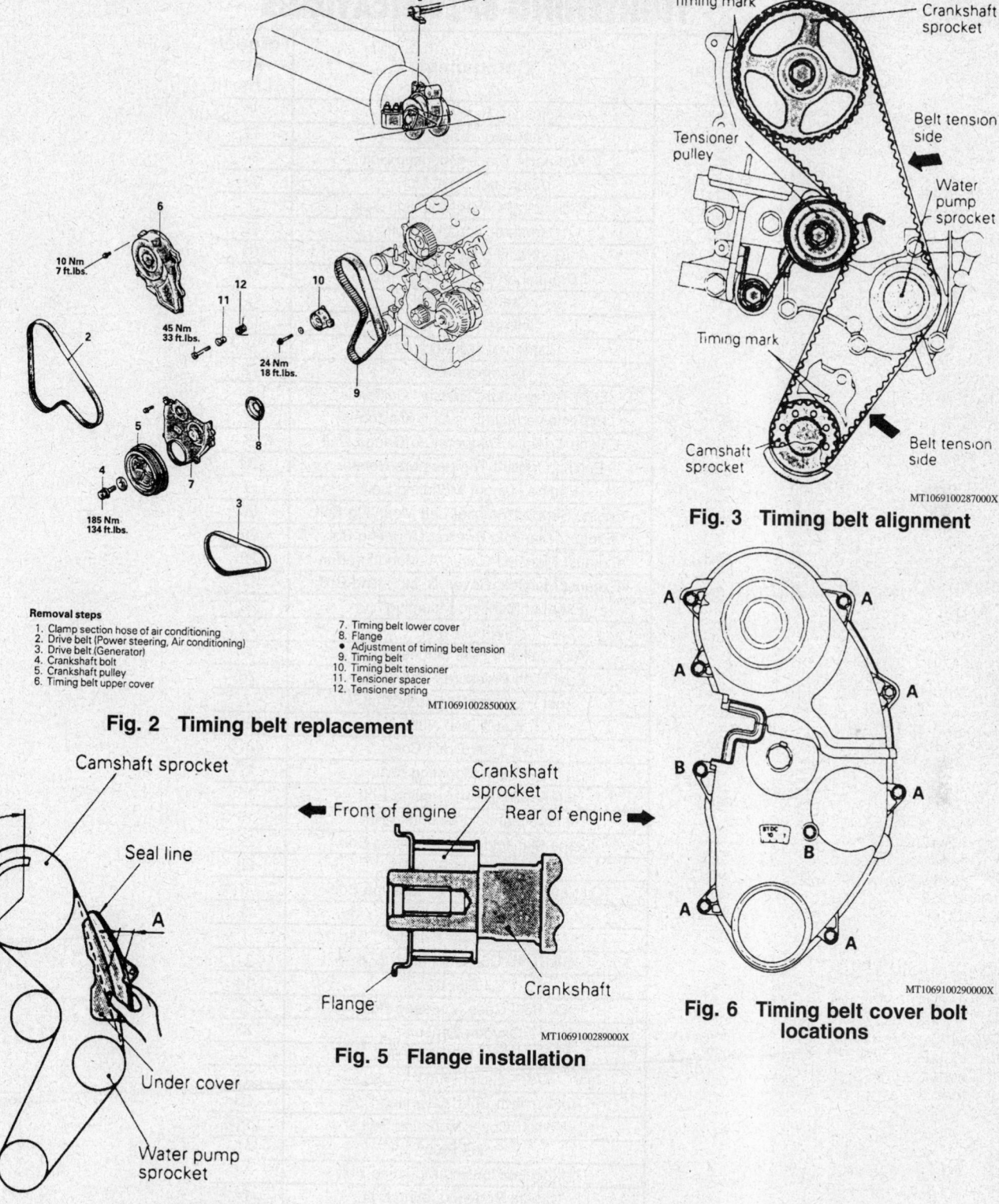

Fig. 3 Timing belt alignment

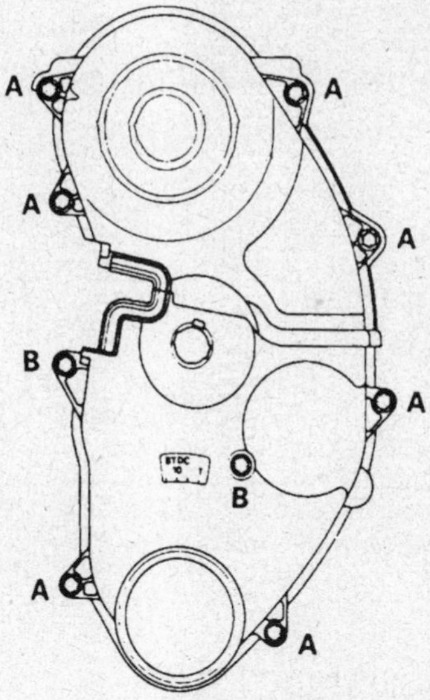
A
A
A
A
B
A
B
A
A

MT1069100290000X

Fig. 6 Timing belt cover bolt locations

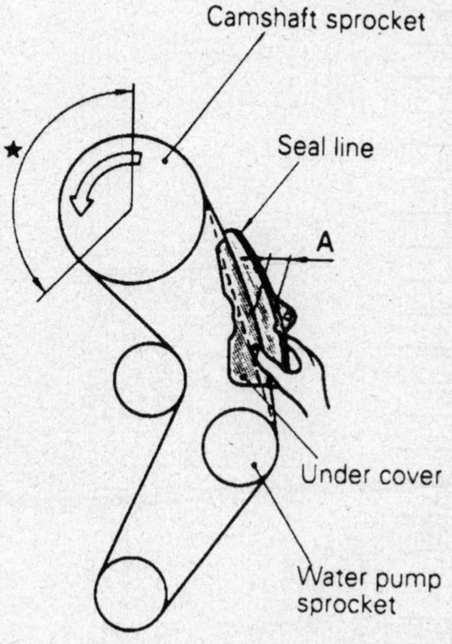
Camshaft sprocket
★
Seal line
A
Under cover
Water pump sprocket

MT1069100288000X

Fig. 4 Timing belt clearance

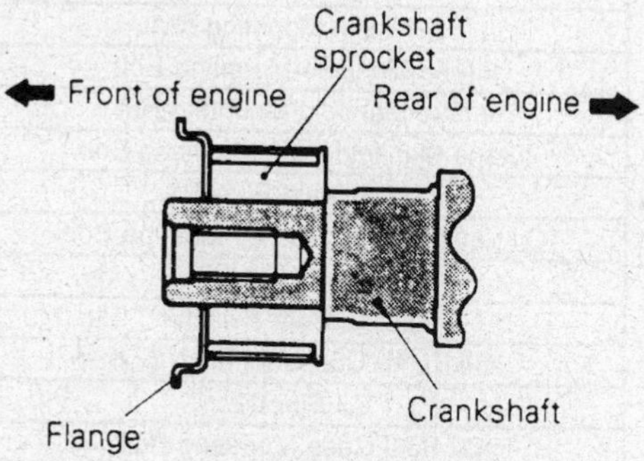
Crankshaft sprocket
Front of engine
Rear of engine
Flange
Crankshaft

MT1069100289000X

Fig. 5 Flange installation

TIGHTENING SPECIFICATIONS

Year	Component	Torque/ Ft. Lbs.
1993–96	Adjusting Screw Locknut	7
	Alternator Brace Bolt	17
	Alternator Brace Mounting Bolt	36
	Alternator Pivot Nut	33
	Bellhousing Cover Mounting Bolt	7
	Camshaft Sprocket Bolt	65
	Connecting Rod Cap Nut	②
	Crankshaft Bearing Cap Bolt	③
	Crankshaft Bolt	134
	Cylinder Head Bolt	①
	Distributor Mounting Nut	9
	Driveplate Bolt	72
	EGR Temperature Sensor (California)	8
	EGR Valve Mounting Bolt (California)	9
	Engine Coolant Temperature Gauge Unit	8
	Engine Coolant Temperature Sensor	22
	Engine Hanger Mounting Bolt	9
	Engine Support Bracket Left Mounting Bolt	36
	Exhaust Manifold Bracket Mounting Bolt	26
	Exhaust Manifold Cover 'A' Mounting Bolt	22
	Exhaust Manifold Cover 'B' Mounting Bolt	17
	Exhaust Manifold Mounting Nut	22
	Flywheel Bolt	72
	Fuel Delivery Pipe Mounting Bolt	9
	Fuel High Pressure Hose Union	25
	Fuel Pressure Regulator Bolt	7
	Fuel Pump Nut	22④
	Fuel Tank Drain Bolt	48④
	Fuel Tank Mounting Nut	17
	Intake Manifold Mounting Bolt	15
	Intake Manifold Mounting Nut	15
	Intake Manifold Stay Mounting Bolt	22
	Oil Drain Plug	29
	Oil Level Gauge Guide Mounting Bolt	8
	Oil Pan Mounting Bolt	5
	Oil Pressure Switch	7
	Oil Pump Case Mounting Bolt	11
	Oil Screen	14
	Oil Seal Case Mounting Bolt	8
	Oxygen Sensor	33
	Rear Plate Mounting Bolt	8
	Relief Plug	35
	Rocker Arm Shaft Mounting Bolt	23
	Rocker Cover Mounting Bolt	29④
	Spark Plug	18
	Thermostat Housing Mounting Bolt	18
	Throttle Body Mounting Bolt	14
	Throttle Position Sensor Bolt	17④
	Timing Belt Cover Mounting Bolt	7
	Timing Belt Tensioner Bolt	18
	Timing Belt Tensioner Spring Bolt	33
	Water Outlet Fitting Mounting Bolt	14
	Water Pipe Mounting Bolt	10
	Water Pump Mounting Bolt	18

① — Refer to "Cylinder Head, Replace" in "1.8L Engine" section of "Mitsubishi Expo."

②— 14.5 ft. lbs. plus 90° ¼ turn.
③— 18 ft. lbs. plus 90° ¼ turn.
④— Inch lbs.

Clutch & Manual Transaxle

INDEX

	Page No.
Adjustments	27-25
Clutch Pedal	27-25
Clutch, Replace	27-26
Hydraulic System Service	27-25
Clutch Release Cylinder, Replace	27-26
Clutch System Bleed	27-25
Tightening Specifications	27-27
Transaxle, Replace	27-26

ADJUSTMENTS

CLUTCH PEDAL

Cable Operated

1. Measure distance between upper surface of floor board and top of clutch pedal.
2. **On Mirage models,** pedal height should be 6.2–6.4 inches.
3. **On Precis models,** pedal height should be 7.4–7.6 inches.
4. **On all models,** if clutch pedal height is not as specified in step 1, check pedal stopper of pedal support member for deterioration and replace as necessary.
5. Measure clutch pedal freeplay "B," **Fig. 1.** Freeplay should be .8–1.2 inches.
6. If freeplay is not as specified in step 5, turn outer cable adjusting nut at bulkhead in engine compartment and adjust clutch cable freeplay "C" to .20–.25 inch, **Fig. 2.**
7. After adjusting pedal freeplay, depress clutch pedal several times, then with pedal fully depressed check clutch pedal to floor board clearance.
8. **On Mirage models,** clearance should be 3.1 inches or more.
9. **On Precis models,** clutch pedal stroke should equal 5.7 inches.
10. **On all models,** if clutch pedal clearance is not as specified in step 5 or if clutch pedal stroke is not as specified in step 6, clutch assembly is defective. Repair clutch assembly as required.

Hydraulic Operated

1. Measure clutch pedal height (A) and clutch pedal clevis pin play (B), **Fig. 3.**
2. Clutch pedal height (A) should be as follows:
   a. **On Mirage models,** 6.4–6.5 inches.
   b. **On Precis models,** 7.0 inches.
3. **On all models,** clevis pin play (B) should be .04–.12 inch.
4. If either (A) or (B) are not within correct range, adjust as follows:
   a. Turn and adjust bolt so pedal height is correct, then secure by tightening locknut, **Fig. 4.**
   b. Disconnect clutch switch connector and turn switch for standard clutch pedal height, then lock with locknut.

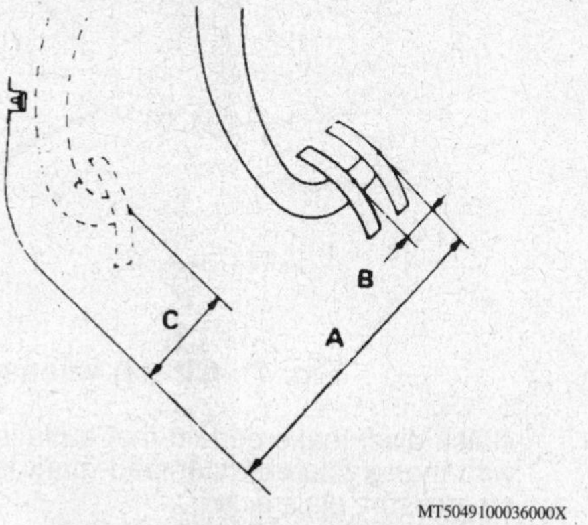

B
C
A
MT5049100036000X

Fig. 1 Clutch pedal height, freeplay & floorboard clearance measurement

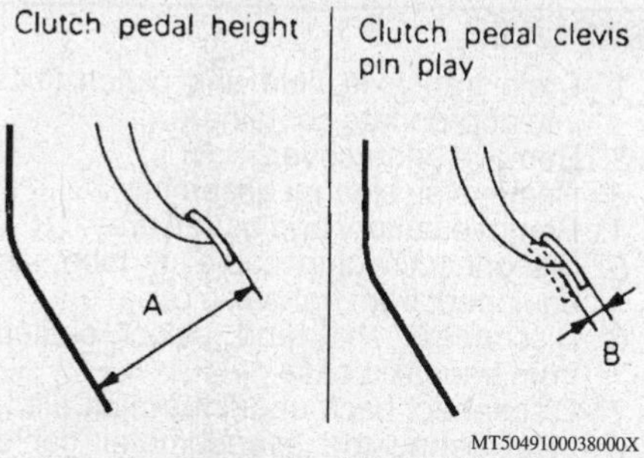

Clutch pedal height
Clutch pedal clevis pin play
A
B
MT5049100038000X

Fig. 3 Clutch pedal height & clevis pin play

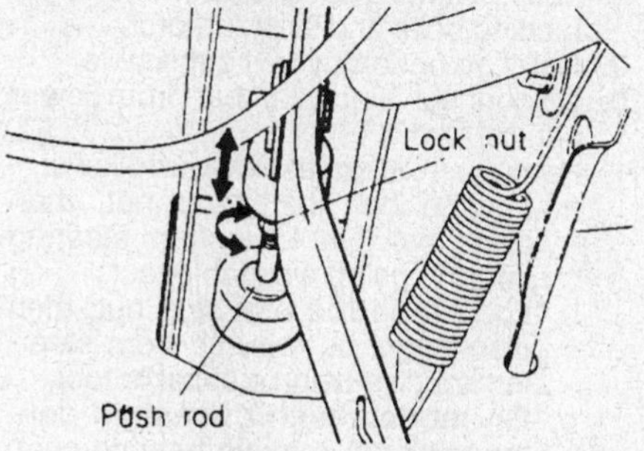

Lock nut
Push rod
MT5049100040000X

Fig. 5 Clutch pedal clevis pin play adjustment

   c. Turn pushrod, **Fig. 5,** to adjust clutch pedal clevis pin play to proper value, then secure pushrod with locknut. **When adjusting clutch pedal clevis pin play, ensure pushrod is not pushed toward master cylinder.**

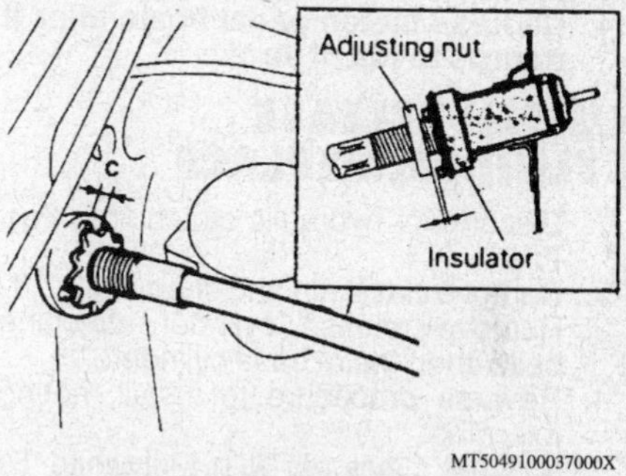

Adjusting nut
C
Insulator
MT5049100037000X

Fig. 2 Clutch pedal freeplay adjustment

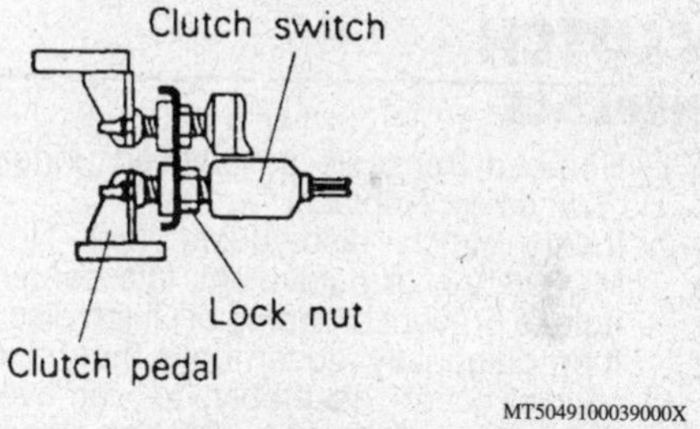

Clutch switch
Lock nut
Clutch pedal
MT5049100039000X

Fig. 4 Locknut location

5. After completing adjustments, ensure clutch pedal freeplay (C) is .2–.5 inch. In addition, confirm that distance (D) between clutch pedal pad and firewall when clutch pedal is disengaged, **Fig. 6,** is as follows:
   a. **On Mirage models,** 2.8 inches or more.
   b. **On Precis models,** 1.57 inches or more.
6. **On all models** if clutch pedal freeplay (C) and distance (D) are not within correct range, check for air in hydraulic system or a defective clutch or master cylinder assembly.

HYDRAULIC SYSTEM SERVICE

CLUTCH SYSTEM BLEED

1. Loosen bleeder screw at release cylinder.
2. Push pedal down slowly, when pedal is at bottom of pedal stroke tighten bleeder screw.

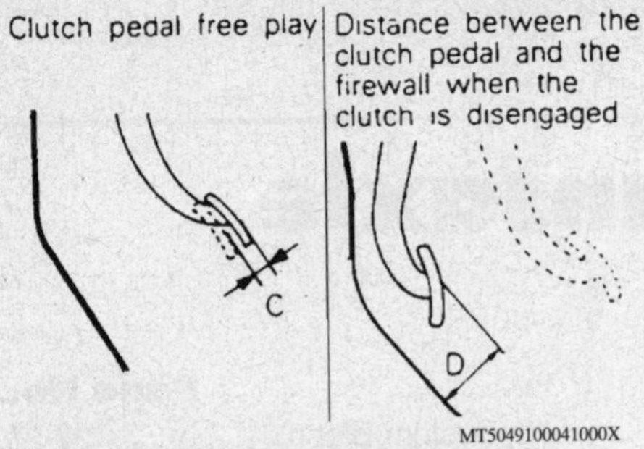
Clutch pedal free play
Distance between the clutch pedal and the firewall when the clutch is disengaged
C
D
MT5049100041000X

Fig. 6 Clutch pedal freeplay & distance to firewall when engaged

3. Repeat procedure until all air is expelled from system.
4. **Depress clutch pedal again after it returns to top of stroke.**

CLUTCH RELEASE CYLINDER, REPLACE

1. Disconnect hydraulic clutch line, **Fig. 7.**
2. Remove clevis pin and snap ring.
3. Remove release cylinder attaching bolts, then the release cylinder.
4. Reverse procedure to install, noting following:
   a. Coat clevis pin with Molywhite TA No. 2 grease, or equivalent, when installing.

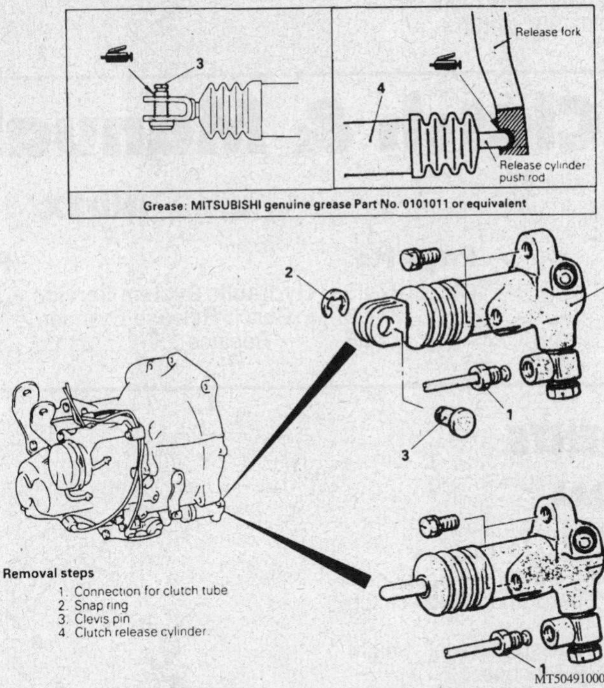
Release fork
Release cylinder push rod
Grease: MITSUBISHI genuine grease Part No. 0101011 or equivalent
Removal steps
1. Connection for clutch tube
2. Snap ring
3. Clevis pin
4. Clutch release cylinder
MT5049100042000X

Fig. 7 Clutch release cylinder replacement

CLUTCH

REPLACE

1. Remove transaxle as outlined under "Transaxle, Replace."
2. Insert clutch disc guide tool No. MD998126, or equivalent, into center hole to prevent dropping of clutch disc, then diagonally loosen bolts that hold clutch cover assembly to remove clutch cover assembly. **Do not clean clutch disc or release bearing with cleaning solvent.**
3. Remove snap ring, clevis pin and release cylinder assembly, if equipped.
4. Remove return clip, then the release bearing.
5. Remove spring pins from clutch release fork and shaft using a suitable punch.
6. Install release shaft and packings, then the return spring and release fork.
7. Align lockpin holes of shift arm and control shaft and, using tool No. MD998245, or equivalent, drive in two new spring pins.
8. When installing spring pins ensure spring pin slot direction is at right angles to center line of control shaft.
9. Remove grease from clutch facing by wiping with clean cloth.
10. Apply small amount of grease to clutch disc spline and input shaft spline.
11. Using tool No. MD998126, or equivalent, install clutch disc and clutch cover assembly to flywheel. When installing clutch disc, make certain that surface with manufacturer's stamped mark is on pressure plate side.

TRANSAXLE

REPLACE

1. Drain transaxle fluid and clutch fluid into appropriate containers.
2. Remove undercover.
3. Remove air cleaner assembly.
4. Remove battery and battery tray.
5. Disconnect clutch cable or tube, as equipped, from transaxle case.
6. Disconnect shift and select cables from transaxle case.
7. Disconnect back-up light switch electrical connector, speedometer cable and ground cable from transaxle case.
8. Disconnect starter motor wiring harness, then remove starter motor attaching bolts and starter motor.
9. Remove undercover, if applicable.
10. Disconnect stabilizer bar from lower control arm.
11. Remove front driveshafts as follows:
    a. Loosen ball joint stud nut, then break ball joint loose from steering knuckle using a suitable tool.
    b. Loosen tie rod end stud nut, then disconnect tie rod end from steering knuckle using a suitable tool.
    c. **On models with driveshaft center bearing,** remove bearing snap ring. Lightly tap tripod joint outer race to remove driveshaft from transaxle, then remove center bearing. **Do not insert pry bar between transaxle case and driveshaft or remove driveshaft from Birfield joint side.**
    d. **On models less driveshaft center bearing,** insert suitable pry bar between transaxle case and driveshaft, then pry driveshaft from transaxle. **Do not pull on driveshaft or insert pry bar deep enough to damage oil seal.**
    e. **On all models,** secure driveshaft to body.
12. Remove bellhousing cover attaching bolts and cover.
13. Support transaxle assembly with a suitable jack.
14. Remove transaxle mounting strut, then the mounting bracket bolt caps, bolts and brackets.
15. Carefully lower transaxle assembly from vehicle.
16. Reverse procedure to install, noting following:
    a. Tighten tie rod end stud nut, ball joint stud nut and transaxle mounting bracket to transaxle attaching bolts to specification.
    b. Tighten transaxle mounting bracket to body attaching bolts, bellhousing cover attaching bolts and starter motor attaching bolts to specification.
    c. Tighten filler and drain plugs, transaxle to engine attaching bolts, transaxle mounting strut to transaxle attaching bolts, and transaxle mounting strut to bracket attaching bolts to specification.

TIGHTENING SPECIFICATIONS

Year	Component	Torque/ Ft. Lbs.
1993–96	Ball Joint Stud Nut	43–52
	Back-Up Light Switch	22–25
	Bellhousing Cover Bolts	7–9
	Clutch Master Cylinder To Firewall	7–11
	Clutch To Flywheel	11–15
	Clutch Release Cylinder	11–16
	Drain Plug	22–25
	Filler Plug	22–25
	Flywheel	94–101
	Lower Arm Ball Joint	43–52
	Reservoir Band	48-60②
	Starter Motor	20–25
	Tie Rod End Nut	11–25
	Transaxle Mounting Bracket To Body	65–80
	Transaxle Mounting Bracket To Transaxle	43–58
	Transaxle Mounting Bolts	①
	Transaxle Mounting Stud To Transaxle	43–51
	Transaxle Mounting Stud To Bracket	33–43

① — .47 inch diameter bolt, 32–39 ft. lbs.; .39 inch diameter bolt, 22–25 ft. lbs.; .31 inch diameter bolt, 7–9 ft. lbs.
② — Inch lbs.

Rear Axle & Suspension

INDEX

	Page No.
Coil Spring, Replace	27-29
Precis	27-29
Control Arm, Replace	27-29
Mirage	27-29
Hub & Bearing, Replace	27-27
Mirage	27-27
Precis	27-27
Rear Suspension Service	27-27
Precis	27-27
Shock Absorber, Replace	27-28
Precis	27-28
Stabilizer Bar, Replace	27-29
Strut, Replace	27-28
Mirage	27-28
Tightening Specifications	27-29
Trailing Arm, Replace	27-29
Mirage	27-29

HUB & BEARING

REPLACE

MIRAGE

1. Raise and support vehicle, then remove rear wheel and rear speed sensor.
2. Disconnect parking brake cable, then remove caliper bolts and support caliper aside without disconnecting hydraulic tube.
3. Remove brake disc or drum, hub nut cap and flange nut, then slide hub assembly and rotor off axle.
4. Reverse procedure to install, noting following:
   a. Do not dismantle rear hub unit.
   b. Do not allow rotor teeth to be damaged in any way; ABS malfunction will result.
   c. When installing rear speed sensor, adjust clearance between pole piece and rotor teeth to .012–.035 inch.

PRECIS

1. Raise and support vehicle, then remove rear wheels.
2. Remove rear drum, oil seal and bearings; then, using a suitable drift, remove bearing races.
3. When replacing bearings, apply grease to bearing surface and install new bearing races, then the new oil seal.
4. Tighten bearing nut to specification.

REAR SUSPENSION SERVICE

PRECIS

Removal

1. Remove coil spring as outlined under "Coil Spring, Replace."
2. Disconnect brake hoses at suspension arm, then remove suspension assembly from body, **Fig. 1.**

Disassemble

Before disassembling, place alignment marks on suspension arms and components so they can be assembled in same position. On models with stabilizer bar, make alignment marks on stabilizer bar and stabilizer bracket.

1. Remove nuts on both ends of suspension arm, then the fixtures and rubber bushings.
2. Remove dust cover clamp and slide dust cover to right, being careful not to damage it.
3. Separate suspension arm into right and left arms.
4. Using screwdriver, remove bushing "A" from lefthand suspension arm, **Fig. 2.**
5. Using a drift punch, drive bushing "B" from lefthand suspension arm, **Fig. 3.**
6. Inspect all components for wear or damage and replace as necessary.

Assemble

1. Apply specified grease to inside of left

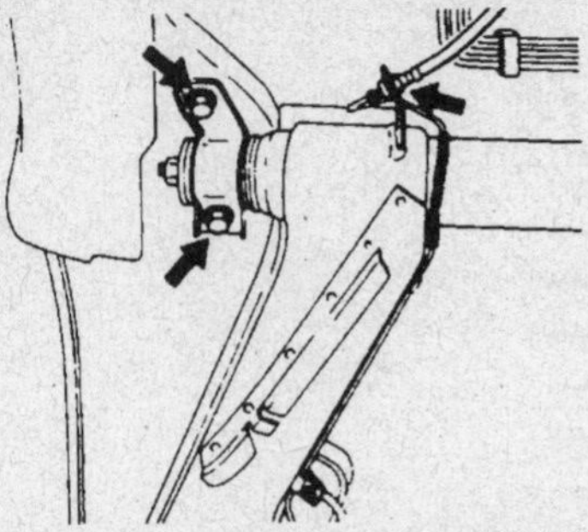
MT2039100074000X

Fig. 1 Suspension assembly removal. Precis

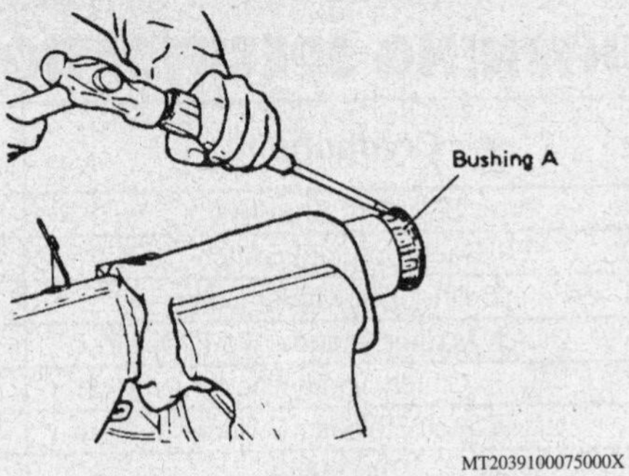
Bushing A
MT2039100075000X

Fig. 2 Bushing "A" removal. Precis

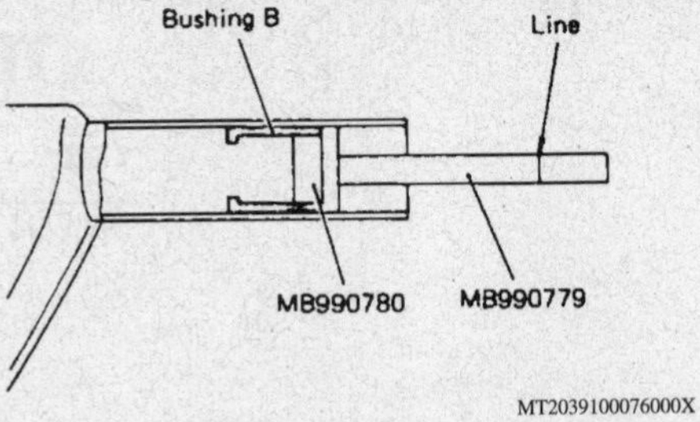
Bushing B
Line
MB990780
MB990779
MT2039100076000X

Fig. 3 Bushing "B" removal. Precis

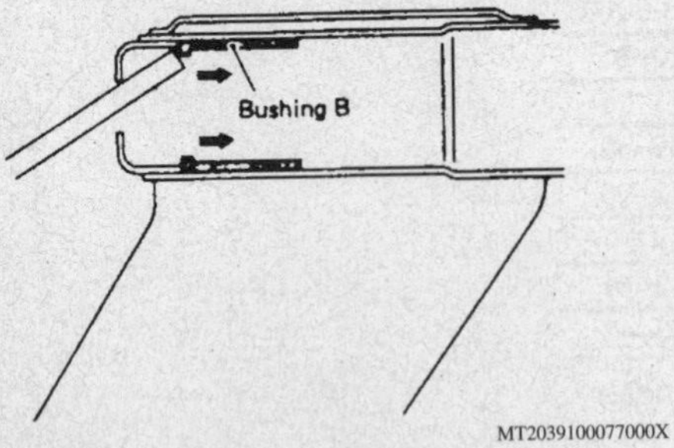
Bushing B
MT2039100077000X

Fig. 4 Bushing "B" installation. Precis

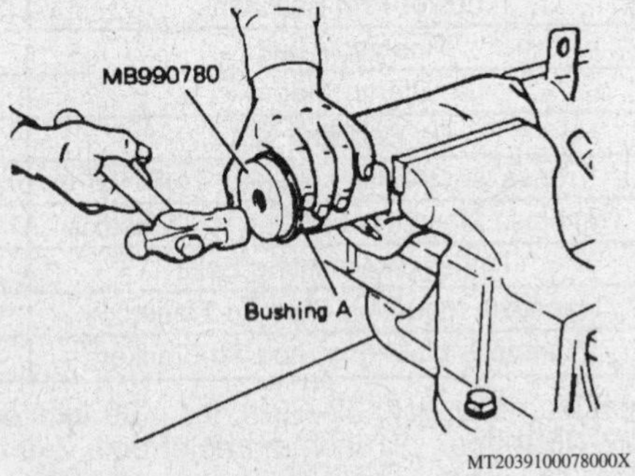
MB990780
Bushing A
MT2039100078000X

Fig. 5 Bushing "A" installation. Precis

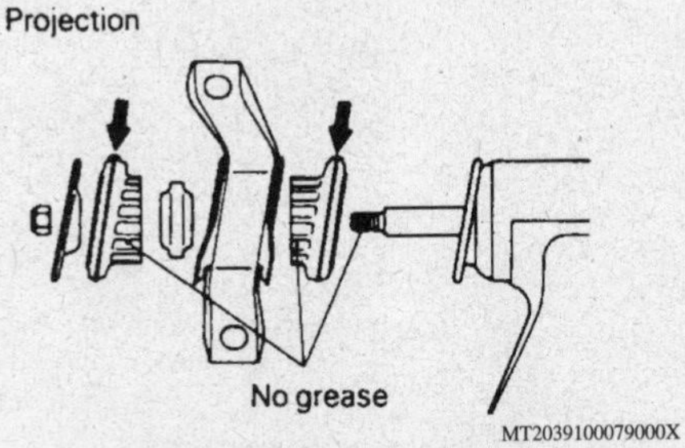
Projection
No grease
MT2039100079000X

Fig. 6 Washer & fixture installation. Precis

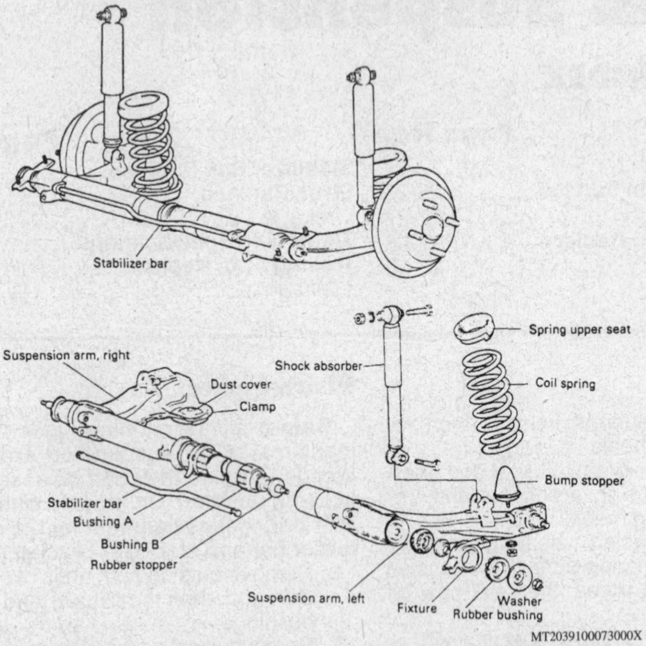
Stabilizer bar
Spring upper seat
Suspension arm, right
Shock absorber
Dust cover
Clamp
Coil spring
Bump stopper
Stabilizer bar
Bushing A
Bushing B
Rubber stopper
Suspension arm, left
Fixture
Washer
Rubber bushing
MT2039100073000X

Fig. 7 Coil spring rear suspension. Precis

suspension arm and on outer edge of right suspension arm. If dust cover was replaced, push new dust cover up to stopper positioned on right arm before applying grease.
2. Install rubber stopper on right suspension arm.
3. Apply specified grease to inner edges of bushings "A" and "B."
4. Using bar tool No. MB990779 and installer attachment tool No. MB990780, or equivalents, press fit bushing "B" into left suspension arm until bushing reaches bottom of suspension arm, **Fig. 4.**
5. Using installer attachment tool No. MB990780, or equivalent, install bushing "A" on left suspension arm, **Fig. 5.**
6. Wrap tape on threads of right suspension arm to prevent grease from getting on them and fit right and left suspension arms together, wiping away any grease that comes out.
7. After fitting suspension arms together, mount rubber bushings, fittings and washers, **Fig. 6.**
8. After aligning suspension arm and components according to alignment marks, tighten to specifications.
9. Pack specified grease in dust cover and lip, then secure with new clamp.

Installation

Reverse procedure to install, paying attention to different shapes of upper and lower spring seats. Ensure proper coil spring is being installed by painted identification mark on spring.

STRUT

REPLACE

MIRAGE

1. Remove quarter trim lid and strut upper flange self-locking nuts.
2. Remove two bolts to disconnect lower arm and trailing arm from lower end of strut assembly, then the strut.
3. Reverse procedure to install. Tighten bolts and nuts to specifications.

SHOCK ABSORBER

REPLACE

PRECIS

1. Raise rear of vehicle, then position jack stands under frame side rails.
2. Position jack under suspension arm to keep it raised.

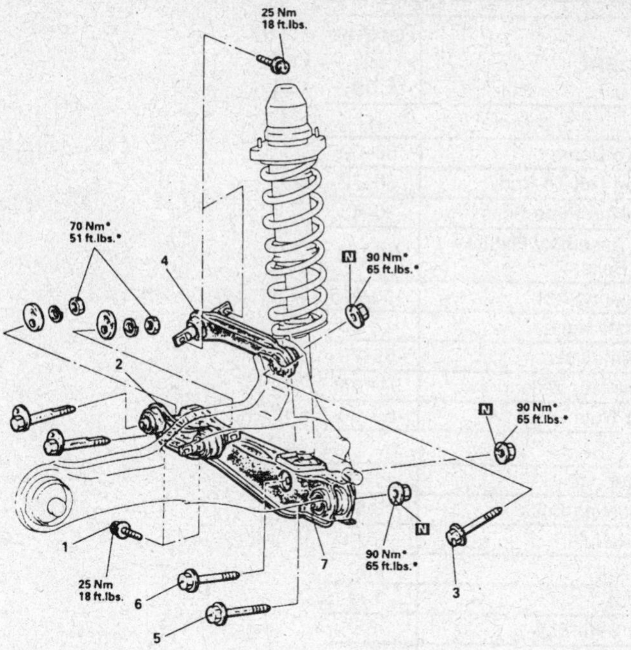
25 Nm
18 ft.lbs.
70 Nm*
51 ft.lbs.*
90 Nm*
65 ft.lbs.*
90 Nm*
65 ft.lbs.*
90 Nm*
65 ft.lbs.*
25 Nm
18 ft.lbs.
N
1
2
3
4
5
6
7

Control link removal steps
1. Control link and trailing arm connection
2. Control link

Upper link removal steps
3. Upper link and trailing arm connection
4. Upper link

Lower arm removal steps
1. Control link and trailing arm connection
5. Lower arm and trailing arm connection
6. Shock absorber assembly and lower arm connection
7. Lower arm

NOTE
*Indicates parts which should be temporarily tightened, and then fully tightened with the vehicles in the unladen condition.

MT2039300082000X

Fig. 8 Control arm replacement. Mirage

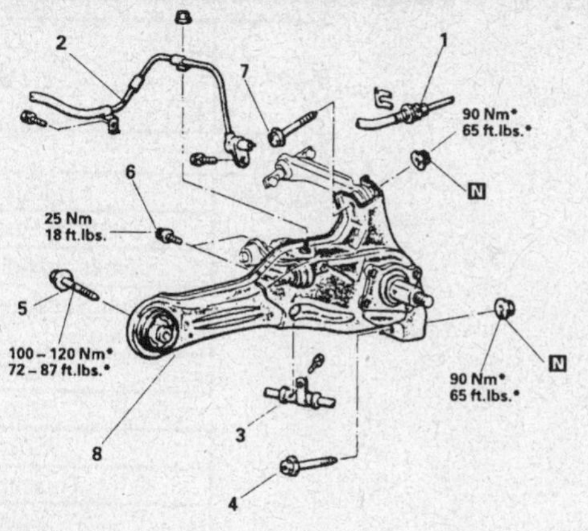
90 Nm*
65 ft.lbs.*
25 Nm
18 ft.lbs.
100 – 120 Nm*
72 – 87 ft.lbs.*
90 Nm*
65 ft.lbs.*
N
1
2
3
4
5
6
7
8

Removal steps
1. Brake hose
2. Rear speed sensor <Vehicles with ABS>
3. Parking brake cable
4. Lower arm and trailing arm connection
5. Trailing arm and body connection
6. Control link and trailing arm connection
7. Upper link and trailing arm connection
8. Trailing arm

NOTE
* Indicates parts which should be temporarily tightened, and then fully tightened with the vehicles in the unladen condition.

MT2039300083000X

Fig. 9 Trailing arm replacement. Mirage

3. Remove wheel and tire assembly.
4. Remove upper and lower shock absorber mounting bolts, then the shock absorber.
5. Reverse procedure to install, then tighten upper and lower mounting bolts to specification.

COIL SPRING
REPLACE
PRECIS

1. Raise rear of vehicle, then position jack stands under frame side rails to support body.
2. Remove wheel and tire assembly, then the rear brake drum assembly.
3. Disconnect muffler from exhaust pipe, then remove muffler assembly.
4. Position a jack under suspension arm, then raise suspension arm slightly.
5. Disconnect shock absorber from upper and lower mounting, **Fig. 7.**
6. Carefully lower jack to relieve spring tension, then remove coil spring, noting position of upper and lower spring seats.
7. Reverse procedure to install, then bleed brake system and adjust rear wheel bearings.

CONTROL ARM
REPLACE
MIRAGE

1. Remove control arms in numbered sequence shown, **Fig. 8.** Scribe mating marks on toe-in or camber adjustment bolts prior to removing control link and lower arm.
2. Reverse procedure to install. Inspect and adjust wheel alignment as necessary.

TRAILING ARM
REPLACE
MIRAGE

1. Remove rear brake assembly, then the hub as outlined under “Hub, Replace.”
2. Remove trailing arm in numbered sequence shown, **Fig. 9.** When removing speed sensor, do not allow pole piece to contact rotor teeth or other parts.
3. Reverse procedure to install, noting following:
   a. When installing rear speed sensor, adjust clearance between pole piece and rotor toothed surface to .012–.035 inch.
   b. Bleed brake system as necessary.

STABILIZER BAR
REPLACE

Refer to **Fig. 7** for stabilizer bar replacement procedure.

TIGHTENING SPECIFICATIONS

Year	Component	Torque/ Ft. Lbs.
PRECIS		
1993–94	Axle Nut	108-145
	Bumper Stopper To Suspension Arm	6-9
	Flange Nut	108-145
Hub Nut	108-145	

Continued

TIGHTENING SPECIFICATIONS—Continued

Year	Component	Torque/ Ft. Lbs.
PRECIS		
1993–94	Lateral Rod To Beam	58–72
	Lateral Rod Mounting Nut To Body	58–72
	Rear Spindle To Backing Plate Bolts	36–43
	Rear Suspension Arm Assembly Fixture Mounting Bolts	94-108
	Rear Wheel Bearing Nut	108-145
	Shock Absorber Nuts	47–58
	Suspension Arm Nuts	65–79
	Trailing Arm Mounting Bolts	94–108
	Wheel Lug Nuts	65–80
MIRAGE		
1993–96	Axle Nut	130
	Control Link Mounting Bolts	18
	Control Link Nuts	51
	Flange Nut	130
	Hub Nut	130
	Lower Arm To Strut Bolt	65
	Lower Arm To Trailing Arm Bolt	65
	Rotor To Hub Bolts	9
	Strut Cap Nut	18
	Strut Upper Flange Nuts	20
	Trailing Arm Front Mount Bolt	72–87
	Upper Link Mounting Bolts	18
	Upper Link To Trailing Arm Nut	65

Front Suspension & Steering

INDEX

Page No.

Ball Joint, Replace 27-31
Lower.............................. 27-31
Control Arm, Replace 27-32
Lower.............................. 27-32
Hub Service...................... 27-30
Mirage............................. 27-30
Precis 27-31
Manual Steering Gear, Replace .. 27-34
Mirage............................. 27-34
Precis 27-34
Manual Steering Gears 29-1
Power Steering 29-1
Power Steering Gear, Replace ... 27-33
Mirage............................. 27-33
Precis 27-33
Stabilizer Bar, Replace 27-33
Mirage............................. 27-33
Precis 27-33
Strut, Replace.................... 27-31
Mirage............................. 27-32
Precis 27-32
Strut Bar, Replace 27-33
Precis 27-33
Strut Service..................... 27-32
Assemble.......................... 27-32
Disassemble....................... 27-32
Inspection 27-32
Technical Service Bulletins 27-34
Front Suspension "Pop" Or "Squeak" 27-34
Tightening Specifications 27-34
Wheel Hub & Steering Knuckle, Replace 27-30
Mirage............................. 27-30
Precis 27-30

WHEEL HUB & STEERING KNUCKLE

REPLACE

MIRAGE

When replacing drive hub and knuckle assembly, refer to **Fig. 1.**

1. Raise and support vehicle, then remove front wheels.
2. Remove cotter pin, wheel bearing nut and washer.
3. Disconnect brake caliper assembly and support using suitable wire.
4. Disconnect lower control arm ball joint from knuckle using a suitable tool.
5. Disconnect tie rod end from knuckle using a suitable tool.
6. Remove driveshaft from hub, then the circlip.
7. Remove hub and knuckle as an assembly from strut assembly.
8. Reverse procedure to install.

PRECIS

1. Remove dust cover, cotter pin, driveshaft retaining nut and washer, then raise and support vehicle.
2. Remove wheel and tire assembly.
3. Remove brake caliper and support with suitable wire.
4. Remove ball joint stud retaining nut, then separate ball joint from steering knuckle.
5. Remove retaining nut, then separate tie rod from steering knuckle.
6. Remove driveshaft from hub.
7. Remove steering knuckle to strut retaining nuts and bolts, then the steering knuckle, brake disc, hub and bearings as an assembly.
8. Reverse procedure to install.

HUB SERVICE

MIRAGE

1. Attach tool Nos. MB990998-01 and

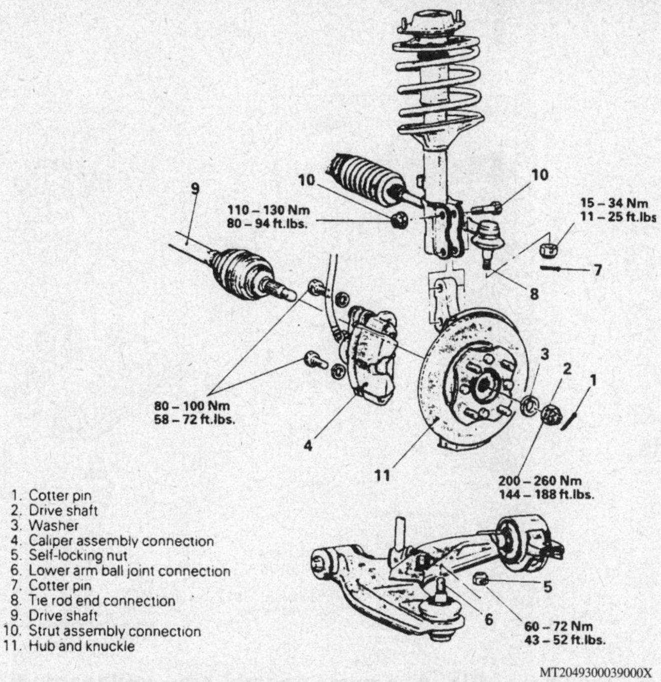
10
9
110 – 130 Nm
80 – 94 ft.lbs.
10
15 – 34 Nm
11 – 25 ft.lbs
7
8
3
2
1
80 – 100 Nm
58 – 72 ft.lbs.
4
11
200 – 260 Nm
144 – 188 ft.lbs.
1. Cotter pin
2. Drive shaft
3. Washer
4. Caliper assembly connection
5. Self-locking nut
6. Lower arm ball joint connection
7. Cotter pin
8. Tie rod end connection
9. Drive shaft
10. Strut assembly connection
11. Hub and knuckle
5
6
60 – 72 Nm
43 – 52 ft.lbs.
MT2049300039000X

Fig. 1 Axle hub replacement. Mirage

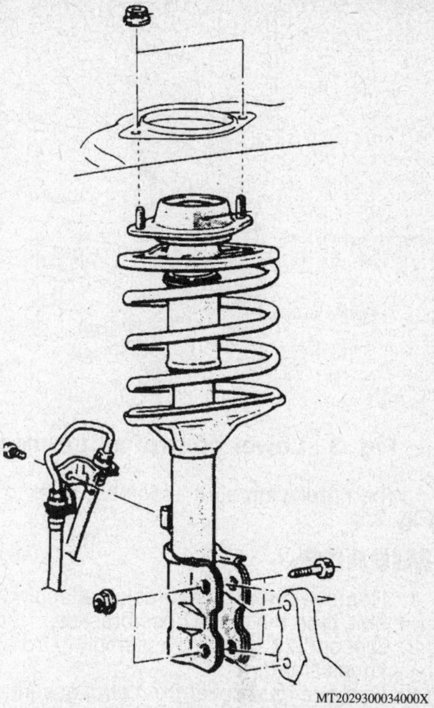
MT2029300034000X

Fig. 2 Strut replacement

MB991056, or equivalents, to knuckle and hub, then secure knuckle in vise.

2. Remove hub from knuckle by tightening nut of tool.
3. Remove dust cover, then the hub and disc assembly attaching bolts and nuts.
4. Remove brake disc, then the inner oil seal.
5. Remove inner bearing inner race, then the outer bearing inner race using suitable tools.
6. Remove outer oil seal, then the outer and inner bearing outer race using a suitable punch. **If either outer or inner race needs replacement, they should be replaced as a set.**
7. Install outer and inner bearing outer race using a suitable tool.
8. Pack outer and inner bearing inner race with suitable grease, then install bearings.
9. Drive outer oil seal into knuckle using a suitable tool until it is flush with knuckle end surface.
10. Apply suitable grease to lip and side lip of oil seal.
11. Install brake disc, then the hub and disc assembly attaching bolts and nuts. Tighten nuts to specification.
12. Install dust cover, then the inner bearing into knuckle.
13. Rotate hub to seat bearing, then check hub turning torque. Turning torque should be 11.3 inch lbs. or less.
14. Mount knuckle in vise, then check hub endplay using a suitable dial gauge. Endplay should be .008 inch.
15. If turning torque and hub endplay are not as specified, hub and/or knuckle may have been installed incorrectly. Repeat service procedures.
16. Install inner oil seal using suitable tool until it projects from knuckle to a height of .10 inch, then apply grease to lip of seal.

PRECIS

1. Using tools, No. 09517-21500 and 09517-21600 or equivalents, separate hub from steering knuckle.
2. Remove brake disc from hub.
3. Using tools, No. 09532-11000, 09532-11301 and 09517-21100 or equivalents, remove outer bearing inner race from hub.
4. Remove oil seal and inner bearing inner race from steering knuckle.
5. Drive bearing outer races from steering knuckle using suitable drift. **If either inner or outer races require replacement, they must be replaced as a set.**
6. Apply suitable grease to outer surface of bearing outer race, then drive race into steering knuckle.
7. Install brake disc to hub and tighten retaining bolts to specification.
8. Apply suitable grease to bearings and inside surface of hub, then position outer bearing inner race into steering knuckle.
9. Drive hub side oil seal into steering knuckle, then apply suitable grease to seal lip and hub contact areas.
10. Install inner bearing into knuckle.
11. Using tool No. 09517-21500, or equivalent, assemble hub to steering knuckle. **Torque** nut on tool to 144–188 ft. lbs., then rotate hub to seat bearing.
12. Measure bearing starting torque. Starting torque should be 11 inch lbs. If starting torque is 0 inch lbs., measure hub axial play. Axial play should be .004 inch with tool nut tightened to specification as in previous step.
13. If starting torque or hub axial play is not within specification, repeat service procedures.
14. Remove service tool, then apply suitable grease to bearing and inside surface of steering knuckle.
15. Drive driveshaft side oil seal into steering knuckle until it contacts bearing outer race, then apply suitable grease to lip of seal.

BALL JOINT

REPLACE

LOWER

Mirage

Refer to "Control Arm, Replace" for ball joint replacement procedure.

Precis

1. Disconnect strut bar from control arm.
2. Remove ball joint to control arm retaining nuts and bolts, then separate ball joint from control arm.
3. Remove ball joint stud nut, then separate ball joint from steering knuckle using suitable tool.
4. Install ball joint to control arm, then tighten retaining nuts and bolts to specification.
5. Install ball joint stud into steering knuckle, then tighten ball joint stud nut to specification.
6. Loosely install strut bar to control arm, then lower vehicle to floor. Tighten strut bar to control arm retaining nuts and bolts to specification.

STRUT

REPLACE

Prior to performing any service operations listed in this section, consult "Technical Service Bulletins"Section for related information.

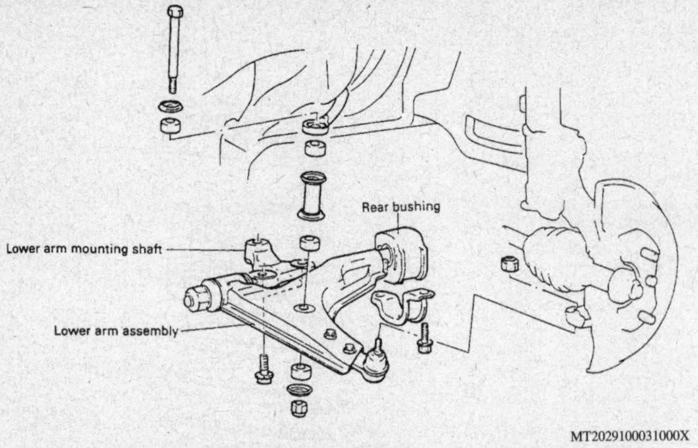
Rear bushing
Lower arm mounting shaft
Lower arm assembly
MT2029100031000X

Fig. 3 Lower control arm replacement. Precis

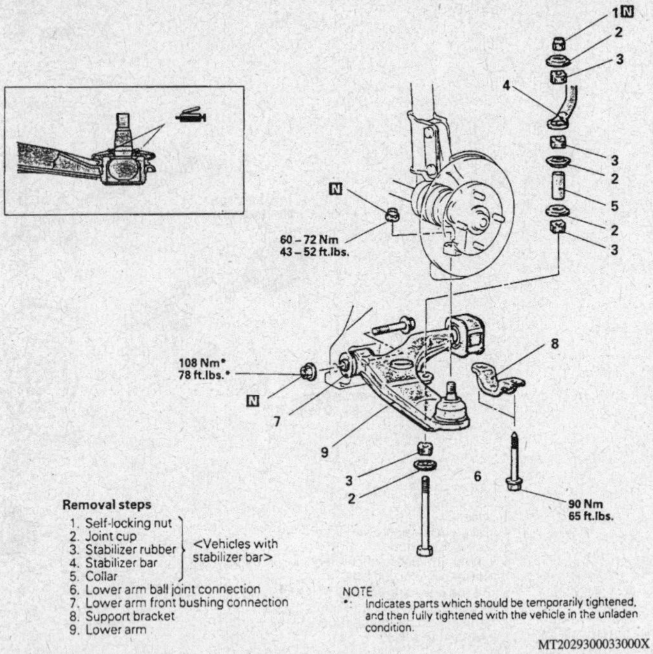
60 – 72 Nm
43 – 52 ft.lbs.
108 Nm*
78 ft.lbs.*
90 Nm
65 ft.lbs.
Removal steps
1. Self-locking nut
2. Joint cup
3. Stabilizer rubber
4. Stabilizer bar
5. Collar
<Vehicles with stabilizer bar>
6. Lower arm ball joint connection
7. Lower arm front bushing connection
8. Support bracket
9. Lower arm
NOTE
*: Indicates parts which should be temporarily tightened, and then fully tightened with the vehicle in the unladen condition.
MT2029300033000X

Fig. 4 Lower control arm replacement. Mirage

When replacing strut assembly, refer to **Fig. 2.**

MIRAGE

1. Remove brake hose bracket attaching bolt, then the brake hose bracket.
2. Disconnect strut assembly from knuckle arm.
3. Remove dust cover from strut assembly.
4. Hold piston rod with a suitable hex wrench, then remove strut assembly attaching nut using tool No. MB991036, or equivalent.
5. Remove stopper and stopper rubber insulator, then the strut assembly.
6. Reverse procedure to install. Tighten all bolts and nuts to specifications.

PRECIS

1. Raise and support vehicle, then remove front wheels.
2. Remove bolts securing brake hose and tube bracket. **Do not pry brake hose and tube away when removing it.**
3. Disconnect strut assembly from knuckle arm.
4. Remove strut insulator to strut house panel mounting nuts.
5. Remove strut assembly.
6. Reverse procedure to install. Tighten all bolts and nuts to specifications.

STRUT SERVICE

DISASSEMBLE

Precis

1. Using tool No. MB990987, or equivalent, compress coil spring.
2. Pry up insulator cap from insulator.
3. Using tool No. MB990775, or equivalent, hold spring seat and remove top end nut.
4. Remove strut insulator, spring seat, spring upper pad, bumper rubber, coil spring and spring lower pad from strut.

Mirage

Prior to performing any service operations listed in this section, consult "Technical Service Bulletins" Section for related information.

1. Remove rubber insulator.
2. Compress coil spring using spring compressor body tool No. MB991237 and arm set tool No. MB991238, or equivalents.
3. Hold piston rod with suitable Hex wrench, then remove piston rod attaching nut using tool No. MB991036, or equivalent.
4. Remove support, spring seat, coil spring and rubber bumper from strut.
5. Remove bearing from support using a suitable brass rod.

INSPECTION

Check all strut assembly components for wear or damage and replace as necessary.

ASSEMBLE

Coil springs have color marks to indicate coil spring identification and load classification. This identification mark indicates applicable vehicle model equipped with that particular coil spring. When replacing coil spring, be sure to use spring having appropriate identification mark.

Precis

1. Mount spring lower pad on strut.
2. Using tool No. MB990987, or equivalent, fully compress spring and install onto strut.
3. Extend piston rod as far as possible, then install bumper rubber and spring upper pad.
4. Mount spring upper seat onto piston rod, then align "D" shaped hole with notch in rod.
5. Using tool No. MB990775, or equivalent, hold spring seat and tighten strut insulator to specifications.
6. After aligning both ends of spring with grooves in spring seat, loosen tool No. MB990987, or equivalent.
7. Apply suitable grease to strut insulator bearing, being careful not to get any grease on rubber part of insulator.

Mirage

1. With support facing black retainer side of bearing, press bearing into support using suitable tool.
2. Compress spring using compressor tool No. MB990987, or equivalent, then install spring into strut.
3. Extend piston rod as far as possible, then install rubber bumper.
4. Install spring upper seat onto piston rod.
5. Install support on piston rod, then tighten nut to specification using suitable tool.
6. Align both ends of coil spring with grooves in spring seat, then slowly loosen spring compressor. Ensure spring seat does not become twisted.
7. Install rubber insulator on strut assembly.

CONTROL ARM

REPLACE

LOWER

Precis

When replacing lower control arm, refer to **Fig. 3.**

1. Disconnect strut bar from control arm.
2. Remove ball joint to control arm retaining nuts and bolts, then separate ball joint from control arm. **Do not separate ball joint from steering knuckle unless damage to ball joint or dust cover is evident.**
3. Remove control arm to crossmember retaining nut and bolt, then the control arm.

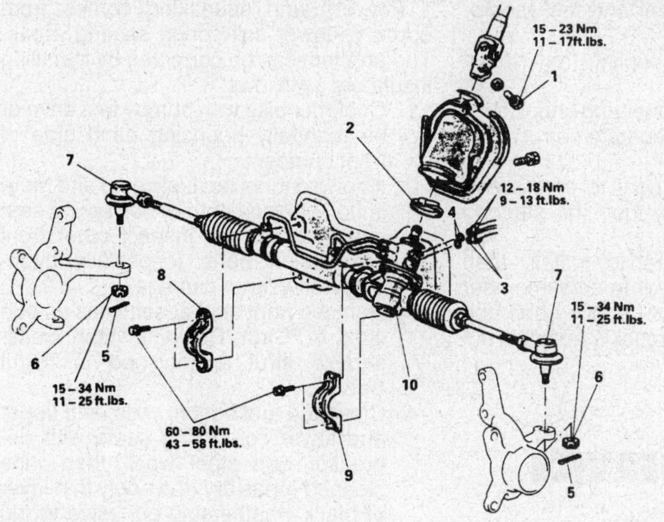
15 – 23 Nm
11 – 17ft.lbs.
12 – 18 Nm
9 – 13 ft.lbs.
15 – 34 Nm
11 – 25 ft.lbs.
15 – 34 Nm
11 – 25 ft.lbs.
60 – 80 Nm
43 – 58 ft.lbs.

1. Joint assembly and gear box connecting bolt
2. Band
3. Pressure tube and return tube
4. O-ring
5. Cotter pin
6. Tie rod end and knuckle connecting nut
7. Tie rod end
8. Gear housing clamp
9. Cylinder clamp
10. Gear box assembly

MT6039100022000X

Fig. 5 Power steering gear replacement. Mirage

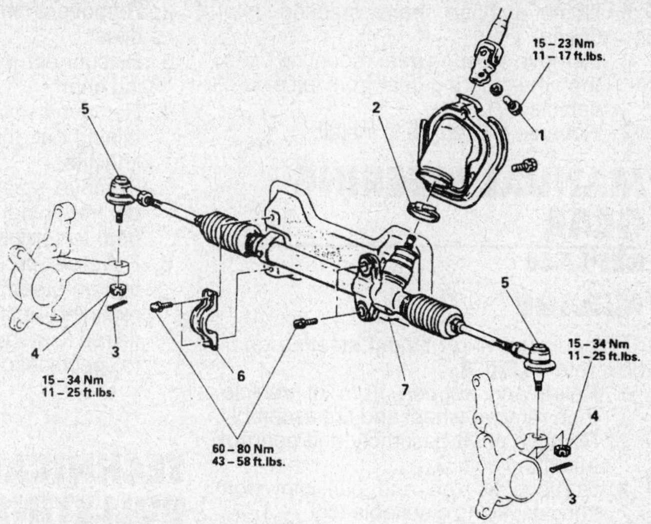
15 – 23 Nm
11 – 17 ft.lbs.
15 – 34 Nm
11 – 25 ft.lbs.
15 – 34 Nm
11 – 25 ft.lbs.
60 – 80 Nm
43 – 58 ft.lbs.

1. Joint assembly and gear box connecting bolt
2. Band
3. Split pin
4. Tie rod end and knuckle connecting nuts
5. Tie rod end
6. End housing clamp
7. Gear box assembly

MT6039100021000X

Fig. 6 Manual steering gear replacement. Mirage

4. Inspect control arm and bushings and replace as necessary.
5. Install control arm, then the retaining nut and bolt onto crossmember. Do not tighten nut at this time.
6. Install ball joint to control arm, then tighten retaining nuts and bolts to specification.
7. Loosely install strut bar.
8. Lower vehicle to floor, then tighten control arm to crossmember and strut bar to control arm retaining nuts and bolts to specification.

Mirage

1. Raise and support vehicle, then remove front wheel.
2. Remove lower arm in sequence shown, **Fig. 4.**
3. Reverse procedure to install, noting following:
   a. Tighten stabilizer bar mounting bolt self-locking nut until .87 inch of bolt protrudes above nut.
   b. Tighten all bolts and nuts to specifications.

STABILIZER BAR

REPLACE

MIRAGE

1. Raise and support vehicle.
2. Remove undercover attaching bolt, then the undercover.
3. Remove stabilizer bar to lower control arm attaching bolt and nut.
4. Remove joint cup, bushing and collar.
5. Remove fixture attaching bolts, then the upper and lower fixtures from stabilizer bar.
6. Remove stabilizer bar from vehicle.
7. Reverse procedure to install, noting following:
   a. Tighten fixture attaching bolts to specification.
   b. When installing ends of stabilizer bar to control arm, tighten self locking attaching nut so distance from base of nut to end of bolt is .83–.91 inch.

PRECIS

Prior to performing any service operations listed in this section, consult "Technical Service Bulletins"Section for related information.

1. Raise and support vehicle.
2. Disconnect stabilizer bar from lower arms and No. 1 crossmember and remove bar.
3. Disconnect strut bar at lower arm and No. 1 crossmember and remove bar.
4. Inspect stabilizer bar, strut bar and all bushings and replace as necessary. Strut bar bend should not exceed .12 inch.
5. Reverse procedure to install, noting following:
   a. Note white paint mark on lefthand side strut bar.
   b. Install locknut on strut bar so outer edge of nut is 3.17 inches from end of bar.
   c. Tighten strut bar locknut and strut bar to No. 1 crossmember nut, strut bar to lower arm bolt, stabilizer bar to No. 1 crossmember bolts, and stabilizer bar bracket bolts to specification. **Strut bar and stabilizer bar should be tightened to specification after vehicle is lowered to floor.**
   d. Check for correct wheel alignment.

STRUT BAR

REPLACE

PRECIS

Refer to "Stabilizer Bar, Replace." for strut bar replacement procedure.

POWER STEERING GEAR

REPLACE

MIRAGE

When replacing power steering gearbox, refer to **Fig. 5.**

1. Raise and support vehicle, then remove front wheels.
2. Disconnect return hose and drain power steering fluid into appropriate container.
3. Remove shaft assembly and gearbox attaching bolt.
4. Remove tie rod end ball joint from knuckle, using a suitable tool.
5. Remove power steering feed hose, then the dust cover band.
6. Remove gear housing clamp attaching bolts, then the gear housing clamps.
7. Remove gear housing mounting rubber, then the steering gear assembly.
8. Reverse procedure to install.

PRECIS

1. Raise and support vehicle.
2. Disconnect tie rod end from knuckle using tool No. 09568-31000, or equivalent.
3. Working from inside passenger compartment, disconnect shaft assembly from steering gear.
4. Drain power steering fluid into appropriate container, then disconnect hoses from steering gear.

5. Remove band from steering joint cover.
6. Remove steering gear mounting bolts, then the steering gear from left side of vehicle.
7. Reverse procedure to install.

MANUAL STEERING GEAR

REPLACE

MIRAGE

When removing manual steering gearbox, refer to **Fig. 6.**

1. Raise and support from of vehicle, then remove wheel and tire assembly.
2. Remove shaft assembly and gearbox attaching bolt.
3. Remove tie rod end ball joint from knuckle, using a suitable tool.
4. Remove dust cover band.
5. Remove gear housing clamp attaching bolts, then the gear housing clamps.
6. Remove gear housing mounting rubber, then the steering gear assembly.
7. Reverse procedure to install.

PRECIS

1. Raise and support vehicle.
2. Remove both wheel and tire assemblies.
3. Disconnect joint coupling from steering gear.
4. Remove tie rod to steering knuckle retaining nut, then separate tie rod from knuckle.
5. Remove steering gear to crossmember retaining nuts, then the steering gear assembly.
6. Reverse procedure to install, then tighten steering gear to crossmember retaining nuts, joint coupling bolt and tie rod to steering knuckle retaining nut to specification.

TECHNICAL SERVICE BULLETINS

FRONT SUSPENSION "POP" OR "SQUEAK"

1993–94 Mirage

Front suspensions may pop or squeak when driven over bumpy roads.

Popping and squeaking comes from upper or lower coil spring seating areas. The problem can be corrected by installing insulators as follows:

1. Confirm noise with bumpy test drive or by manually bouncing each side of front bumper.
2. If noise cannot be duplicated and there is no evidence of front coil spring seat rust or corrosion, inspect other front suspension parts (especially bushings) for wear or damage.
3. Remove front strut assemblies as outlined in "Strut, Replace," then disassemble strut as outlined in "Strut Service."
4. Clean top and bottom coils, and upper and lower coil spring seats with degreaser and steel wool, then wipe cleaned areas dry and apply thin layer of black weatherstrip adhesive to top and bottom coils.
5. Before adhesive dries, install insulators on top and bottom coils. Ensure each insulator end is flush with coil spring end.

TIGHTENING SPECIFICATIONS

Year	Component	Torque/ Ft. Lbs.
MIRAGE		
1993–96	Axle Nut	144-188
	Caliper To Knuckle	58-72
	Center Member Rear Mounting Bolt	43–58
	Driveshaft Nut	144–188
	Gearbox To Body	43–58
	Hub Nut	144-88
	Hub To Brake Disc	36–43
	Joint To Gearbox	11–17
	Knuckle To Strut Assembly	65–76
	Lower Arm Ball Joint	43–52
	Lower Arm Front Mounting Nut	69–87
	Lower Arm Rear Mounting Bolt	43–58
	Pressure Tube To Gearbox	9–13
	Rack Support Cover Locking Nut	36–51
	Rear Roll Stopper Mounting Nut	33–43
	Return Tube To Gearbox	9–13
	Stabilizer Bar Mounting Bolt	12–19
	Stabilizer Link Mounting Nut	40–51
	Strut Assembly To Knuckle	80–94
	Strut Top End Nut	43–51
	Strut Upper Mounting Nut	25–36
	Tie Rod End Ball Joint	11–25
	Tie Rod End Locknut	25–36
	Tie Rod End To Knuckle	11–25
	Tie Rod To Rack	58–72
	Wheel Lug Nut	65–80

Continued

TIGHTENING SPECIFICATIONS—Continued

Year	Component	Torque/ Ft. Lbs.
PRECIS		
1993–94	Axle Nut	144-188
	Ball Joint To Lower Arm Assembly	69-87
	Ball Joint Stud Nut To Steering Knuckle	43–52
	Brake Caliper To Steering Knuckle	69–87
	Control Arm To Crossmember	69–87
	Driveshaft Nut	144–188
	Gearbox Mounting Clamp	43–58
	Hub Nut	144-188
	Knuckle To Strut Assembly	54–65
	Lower Arm Ball Joint To Knuckle	43–52
	Lower Arm Mounting Bracket Bolt (to Floor)	43–58
	Lower Arm Mounting Shaft Bolt (to Floor)	116–137
	Lower Arm Mounting Shaft Mounting Nut	69–87
	Lower Arm To Strut Bar	69–87
	Rack Support Cover	5.1–8.7
	Rack Support Cover Locknut	36–51
	Stabilizer Bar Lower/Upper Bracket Mounting Bolt	12–19
	Stabilizer Bar To Crossmember	22–29
	Strut Bar To Control Arm	69–87
	Strut Insulator	43–50
	Strut Mounting Self Locking Nut	29–36
	Strut To Steering Knuckle	54–65
	Tie Rod End Ball	
	Joint Slotted Nut	11–25
	Tie Rod End Ball Joint To Knuckle	11–25
1993–94	Tie Rod End Locknut	36–40
	Tie Rod End To Knuckle	11–25
	Tie Rod To Rack	58–72
	Upper Strut Installation Nut	11–14
	Wheel Hub Nut	145–188

Wheel Alignment

INDEX

	Page No.
Front Wheel Alignment	27-36
Camber	27-36
Caster	27-36
Toe	27-36
Preliminary Inspection	27-36
Rear Wheel Alignment	27-36
Camber	27-36
Toe	27-36
Vehicle Ride Height	27-36
Wheel Alignment Specifications	27-3

PRELIMINARY INSPECTION

1. Ensure tires are inflated to correct pressure, then check for uneven wear.
2. Check front wheel bearings, suspension arm and ball joints for damage and replace as necessary, to eliminate improper alignment due to faulty components.
3. Check steering gear for damage and replace as necessary.
4. Check shocks for damage and replace as necessary.
5. Rock vehicle back and forth and bounce upward and downward to settle vehicle prior to alignment.
6. Ensure vehicle is unloaded and on a suitable alignment rack according to manufacturers' instructions. **When measuring equipment is attached directly to outer end of driveshaft and front wheels are on turntables, apply brake to prevent improper vehicle movement.**

FRONT WHEEL ALIGNMENT

CAMBER

Camber refers to the angle at which a wheel leans in or out, **Fig. 1.** Positive camber is when wheel leans outward and negative camber is when wheel leans inward.

Camber on these vehicles is preset to specification and cannot be adjusted. If camber is out of specification, bent or damaged components must be replaced.

CASTER

Caster angle refers the to angle at which wheel center deviates from vertical when viewed from side, **Fig. 2.** Caster is preset to specification and cannot be adjusted. If caster is out of specification, bent or damaged components must be replaced.

TOE

As viewed from above, wheels must be set so distances A and B, **Fig. 3,** measured at wheel rims and at axle height, are different at a given value. If distance A is smaller than distance B, setting is known as toe-in. If distance A is greater than distance B, setting is known as toe-out. toe setting is given in inches and refers to difference between A and B. If distances A and B are same, toe setting is 0.

1. Adjust toe-in by undoing clips and turning left and right tie rod turnbuckles by same amount in opposite directions.
2. To increase toe-out, turn left turnbuckle toward front of vehicle and right turnbuckle toward rear of vehicle. To increase toe-in, turn turnbuckles in opposite direction.
3. **On Precis models,** toe-in is adjusted .24 inch and .48 inch on Mirage for each half turn of left and right tie rods.
4. **On all models,** after adjusting toe-in, check that steering wheel turning angle is within specification.

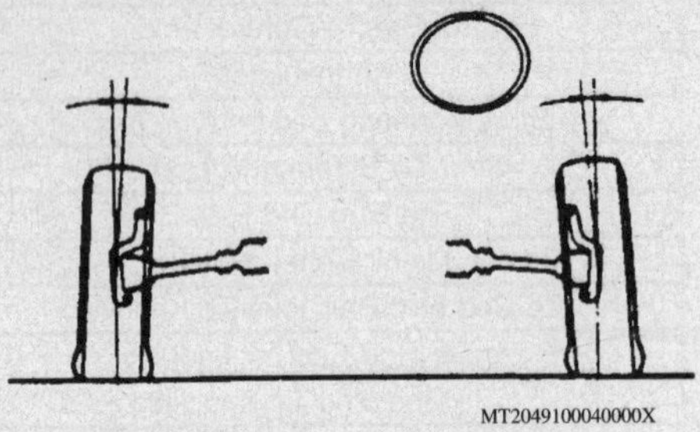
MT2049100040000X

Fig. 1 Camber setting

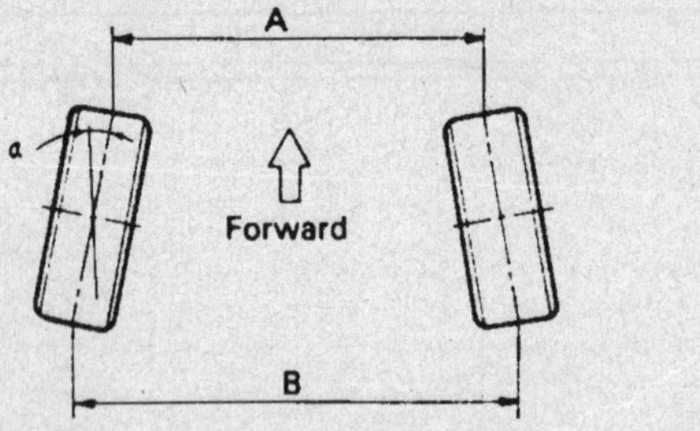
A
a
Forward
B
MT2049100041000X

Fig. 3 Toe setting

REAR WHEEL ALIGNMENT

CAMBER

Camber and toe-in are preset to specification and cannot be adjusted. If camber is out of specification, bent or damaged components must be replaced.

TOE

As viewed from above, wheels must be set so distances A and B, **Fig. 3,** measured at wheel rims and at axle height, are different at a given value. If distance A is smaller than distance B, setting is known as toe-in. If distance A is greater than distance B, setting is known as toe-out. Toe setting is given in inches and refers to difference between A and B. If distances A and B are same, toe setting is 0.

Rear toe-in is preset to specification and cannot be adjusted. If rear toe-in is out of specification, bent or damaged components must be replaced.

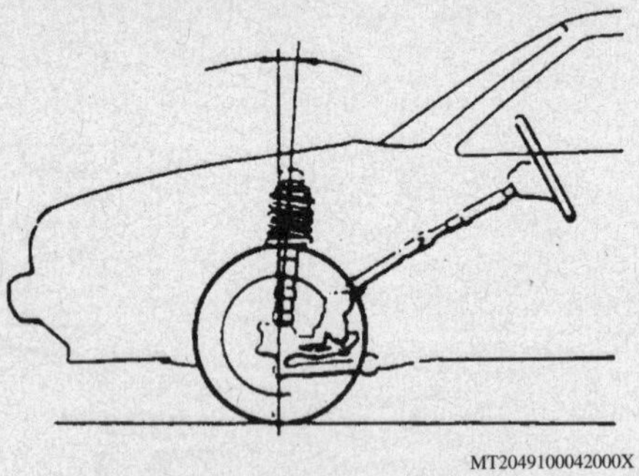
MT2049100042000X

Fig. 2 Caster setting

VEHICLE RIDE HEIGHT

There is no provision for adjustment of vehicle ride height. If ride height is not satisfactory, inspect suspension components for damage or modification.

MITSUBISHI LIGHT TRUCKS

INDEX OF SERVICE OPERATIONS

	Page No.
AIR BAG SYSTEM PRECAUTIONS	0-8
AUTOMATIC TRANSMISSIONS/ TRANSAXLES	29-1
BRAKES	
Anti-Lock Brakes	29-1
Disc Brakes	29-1
Drum Brakes	29-1
Hydraulic Brake Systems	29-1
Power Brake Units	29-1
CLUTCH & MANUAL TRANSMISSION	
Adjustments	28-34
Clutch, Replace	28-35
Hydraulic System Service	28-35
Tightening Specifications	28-37
Transfer Case, Replace	28-36
Transmission, Replace	28-35
ELECTRICAL	
Air Bags	29-1
Air Conditioning	29-1
Alternators	29-1
Blower Motor, Replace	28-7
Coil Pack, Replace	28-5
Column Switch, Replace	28-6
Cooling Fans	29-1
Cruise Control	29-1
Dash Gauges	29-1
Dash Panels	29-1
Distributor, Replace	28-5
Evaporator Core, Replace	28-8
Fuel Pump Relay Location	28-5
Fuse Panel & Flasher Location	28-5
Heater Core, Replace	28-7
Ignition Lock, Replace	28-6
Ignition Switch, Replace	28-6
Instrument Cluster, Replace	28-6
Neutral Safety Switch, Replace	28-6
Passive Restraints	29-1
Precautions	28-5
Radio, Replace	28-7
Relay Center Location	28-5
Speed Controls	29-1
Starter Motors	29-1
Starter, Replace	28-5
Steering Columns	29-1
Steering Wheel, Replace	28-6
Wiper Motor, Replace	28-7
Wiper Switch, Replace	28-7
Wiper Systems	29-1
ELECTRICAL SYMBOL IDENTIFICATION	0-139
FRONT SUSPENSION & STEERING	
Front Suspension Service	28-44
Hub Service	28-43
Manual Steering Gears	29-1
Manual Steering Gear, Replace	28-48
Power Steering	29-1
Power Steering Gear, Replace	28-47
Stabilizer Bar, Replace	28-47
Strut Bar, Replace	28-47
Tightening Specifications	28-48
Torsion Bar, Replace	28-46
FRONT WHEEL DRIVE AXLES	29-1
REAR AXLE & SUSPENSION	
Coil Spring, Replace	28-41
Control Arm, Replace	28-41
Differential Carrier, Replace	28-41
Lateral Rod, Replace	28-41
Leaf Spring, Replace	28-41
Rear Axle, Replace	28-39
Rear Axle Shaft, Replace	28-39
Shock Absorber, Replace	28-41
Stabilizer Bar, Replace	28-41
Tightening Specifications	28-43
SERVICE REMINDER & WARNING LAMP RESET PROCEDURES	0-10
SPECIFICATIONS	
Fluid Capacities & Cooling System Data	28-4
Front Wheel Alignment Specifications	28-3
General Engine Specifications	28-2
Lubricant Data	28-4
Rear Wheel Alignment Specifications	28-4
Tune Up Specifications	28-2
VEHICLE IDENTIFICATIONS	0-1
VEHICLE LIFT POINTS	0-34
VEHICLEMAINTENANCE SCHEDULES	0-69
WHEEL ALIGNMENT	
Front Wheel Alignment	28-50
Preliminary Inspection	28-50
Rear Wheel Alignment	28-50
Vehicle Ride Height	28-50
Wheel Alignment Specifications	28-3
WIRE COLOR CODE IDENTIRICATION	0-144
2.4L ENGINE	
Belt Tension Data	28-10
Compression Pressure	28-9
Cooling System Bleed	28-10
Engine Rebuilding Specifications	29-1
Engine, Replace	28-9
Fuel Filter, Replace	28-10
Fuel Pump, Replace	28-10
Precautions	28-9
Technical Service Bulletins	28-11
Thermostat, Replace	28-10
Tightening Specifications	28-12
Water Pump, Replace	28-10
3.0L ENGINE	
Belt Tension Data	28-17
Compression Pressure	28-14
Cooling System Bleed	28-17
Crankshaft Seal, Replace	28-16
Cylinder Head, Replace	28-15
Engine Mount, Replace	28-14
Engine Rebuilding Specifications	29-1
Engine, Replace	28-14
Exhaust Manifold, Replace	28-15
Fuel Filter, Replace	28-18
Fuel Pump, Replace	28-18
Intake Manifold, Replace	28-14
Oil Pan, Replace	28-16
Precautions	28-13
Radiator, Replace	28-18
Thermostat, Replace	28-17
Tightening Specifications	28-24
Timing Belt, Replace	28-15
Valve Adjustment	28-15
Water Pump, Replace	28-17
3.5L ENGINE	
Belt Tension Data	28-29
Compression Pressure	28-27
Cooling System Bleed	28-29
Crankshaft Seal, Replace	28-28
Cylinder Head, Replace	28-28
Engine Mount, Replace	28-27
Engine Oil Cooler, Replace	28-29
Engine Rebuilding Specifications	29-1
Engine, Replace	28-27
Exhaust Manifold, Replace	28-28
Fuel Filter, Replace	28-31
Fuel Pump, Replace	28-30
Intake Manifold, Replace	28-27
Oil Pan, Replace	28-29
Precautions	28-27
Radiator, Replace	28-30
Thermostat, Replace	28-30
Tightening Specifications	28-33
Timing Belt, Replace	28-28
Valve Adjustment	28-28
Water Pump, Replace	28-30

Specifications

GENERAL ENGINE SPECIFICATIONS

Year	Engine, Liters	Fuel System	Bore & Stroke	Compression Ratio	Maximum Net HP @ RPM	Maximum Torque, Ft. Lbs. @ RPM
1993	2.4L	Fuel Inj.	3.41 X 3.94	8.5	116 @ 5000	136 @ 3500
	3.0L	Fuel Inj.	3.59 X 2.99	8.9	151 @ 5000	174 @ 4000
1994–96	2.4L	Fuel Inj.	3.41 X 3.94	8.5	116 @ 5000	136 @ 3500
	3.0L①	Fuel Inj.	3.59 X 2.99	8.9	151 @ 5000	174 @ 4000
	3.0L②	Fuel Inj.	3.59 X 2.99	9.0	177 @ 5500	188 @ 4500
	3.5L	Fuel Inj.	3.66 X 3.38	9.5	215 @ 5000	228 @ 3000

① — 12 valve engine.
② — 24 valve engine.

TUNE UP SPECIFICATIONS

Year & Engine	Spark Plug Gap, Inch	Firing Order	Ignition Timing		Curb Idle Speed②		Fast Idle Speed		Fuel Pressure psi	Valve Lash
			Timing BTDC	Timing Mark Location	Man. Trans.	Auto. Trans.	Man. Trans.	Auto. Trans.		
1993										
2.4L	.041	A	5①	Pulley	750	750N	④	④	50	⑨
3.0L	.041	B	5①	Pulley	700	700N	④	④	50	⑨
1994										
2.4L	.041	A	5①	Pulley	750	750N	④	④	50	⑨
3.0L	.041	B	5①	Pulley	700	700N	④	④	50	⑨
3.5L	.041	G⑥	5①	⑦	—	700N	—	④	47.6	⑨
1995–96										
2.4L	.041	A	5①	⑦	750	750N	④	④	50	⑨
3.0L③	.041	⑥	5⑧	⑦	700	700N	④	④	50	⑨
3.0L⑤	.041	B	5①	⑦	700	700N	④	④	50	⑨
3.5L	.041	G⑥	5①	⑦	700	700N	④	④	47.6	⑨

BTDC — Before Top Dead Center.
N — Neutral.
① — With jumper wire connected between ignition timing adjustment connector and ground. Refer to Figs.C through F.
② — When adjusting idle speed, set parking brake & chock drive wheels.
③ — Montero.
④ — Controlled by idle speed control servo.
⑤ — Pickup.
⑥ — Cylinder numbering from front of engine to rear: right bank, 1, 3, 5; left bank, 2, 4, 6. Firing order: 1–2–3–4–5–6.
⑦ — Equipped w/crankshaft position sensor.
⑧ — Electronically controlled.
⑨ — Equipped with hydraulic valve lash adjusters.

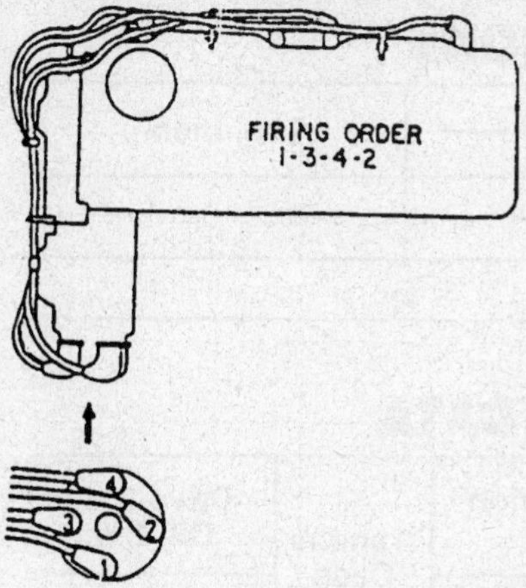
FIRING ORDER
1-3-4-2
MT1139100084000X

Fig. A

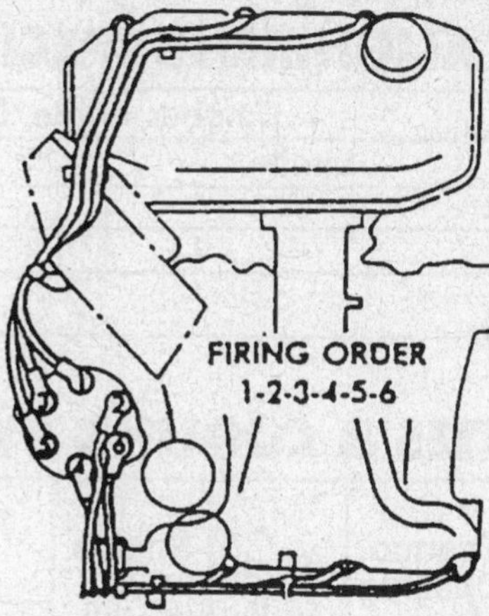
FIRING ORDER
1-2-3-4-5-6
MT1139100086000X

Fig. B

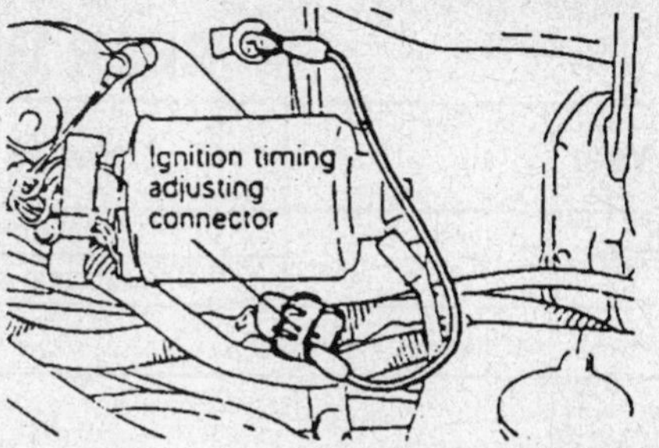
Ignition timing
adjusting
connector
MT1139100087000X

Fig. C Ignition timing adjustment connector. Montero w/3.0L engine

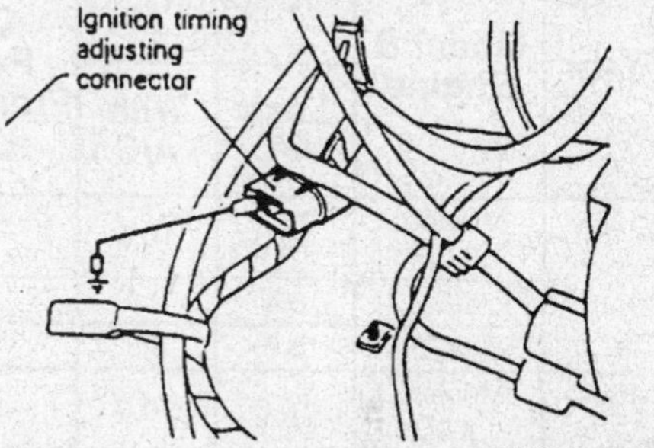
Ignition timing
adjusting
connector
MT1139100088000X

Fig. F Ignition timing adjustment connector. Pickup w/3.0L engine

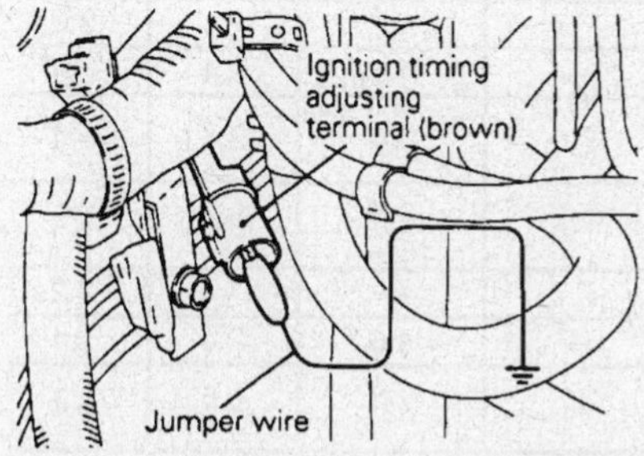
Ignition timing
adjusting
terminal (brown)
Jumper wire
MT1138800030000X

Fig. D Ignition timing adjustment connector. Montero w/3.5L engine

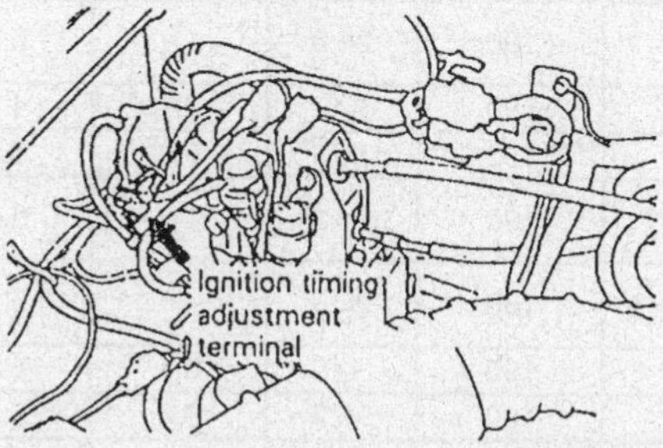
Ignition timing
adjustment
terminal
MT1139100089000X

Fig. E Ignition timing adjustment connector. Pickup w/2.4L engine

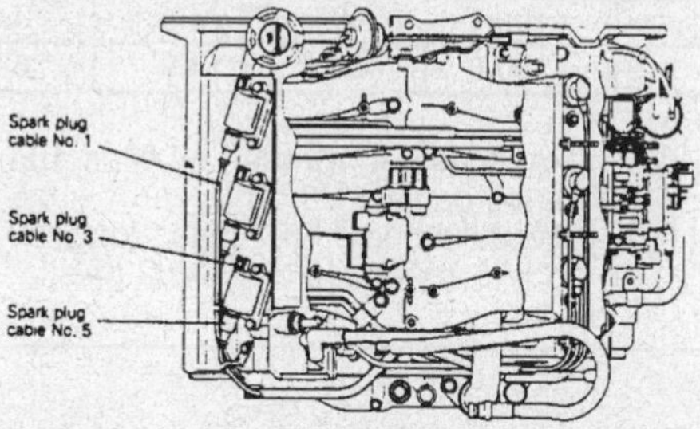
Spark plug
cable No. 1
Spark plug
cable No. 3
Spark plug
cable No. 5
MT1139400174000X

Fig. G

FRONT WHEEL ALIGNMENT SPECIFICATIONS

Year	Model	Caster Angle, Deg.		Camber Angle, Deg.		Toe, Inch①	Kingpin Inclination, Deg.	Ball Joint Wear
		Limits	Desired	Limits	Desired			
1993–96	Montero	+2 to +4	+3	+ ⅙ to +1 ⅙	+ ⅔	0 to +.28	14 13⁄15	②
	Pickup 2WD	+1 ½ to +3 ½	+2 ½	+ ⅙ to +1 ⅙	+ ⅔	+.08 to +.35	—	③
	Pickup 4WD	+1 to +3	+2	+ ½ to +1 ½	+1	+.08 to +.35	—	③

2WD — Two Wheel Drive.
4WD — Four Wheel Drive.
① — Toe-in (+); toe-out (-).
② — Upper ball joint starting torque, 7–30 inch lbs.; stabilizer link ball joint starting torque, 15–27 inch lbs.; lower ball joint end play, .012 maximum.
③ — Upper ball joint starting torque, 7–30 inch lbs.; lower ball joint end play, .020 maximum.

REAR WHEEL ALIGNMENT SPECIFICATIONS

Year	Model	Camber Angle, Deg. Limits	Camber Angle, Deg. Desired	Toe, Inch①
1993–96	Montero	—	0	0
	Pickup	—	0	0

①— Toe-in (+); toe-out (-).

FLUID CAPACITIES & COOLING SYSTEM DATA

Year	Model & Engine	Coolant Capacity, Qts.		Radiator Cap Relief Pressure, Lbs.	Thermo. Opening Temp., °F	Fuel Tank, Gals.	Engine Oil Refill, Qts.①	Transmission Oil		Transfer Case Oil, Pts.	Drive Axle Oil, Pts.	
		Less A/C	With A/C					5 Speed, Pts.	Auto. Trans., Qts. ②		Front	Rear
1993	Montero 3.0L	10.0	10.0	13	190	24.3	③	5.2	7.6	4.8	2.6	5.4
	Pickup 2.4L	6.4	6.4	13	190	④	5.1	4.8	7.7	—	—	3.2
	Pickup 3.0L	8.9	8.9	13	190	15.9	5.0	5.2	—	4.6	2.4	5.4
1994	Montero 3.0L	10.0	10.0	13	190	24.3	③	5.2	7.6	⑤	2.6	5.4
	Montero 3.5L	10.0	10.0	13	180	24.3	③	5.2	7.6	⑤	2.6	5.4
	Pickup 2.4L	6.4	6.4	13	190	④	5.1	4.8	7.7	—	—	3.2
	Pickup 3.0L	8.9	8.9	13	190	15.9	5.0	5.2	—	4.6	2.4	5.4
1995–96	Montero 3.0L	10.0	10.0	13	190	24.3	5.2	5.2	9.0	⑤	2.6	5.4
	Montero 3.5L	10.0	10.0	13	180	24.3	5.2	5.2	9.0	⑤	2.6	5.4
	Pickup 2.4L	6.3	6.4	13	190	④	4.0	4.8	7.7	—	—	3.2
	Pickup 3.0L	8.9	8.9	13	190	15.9	4.9	5.2	7.7	4.6	2.4	5.4

①— Includes filter, unless otherwise noted.
②— Approximate; make final check with dipstick.
③— Crankcase, 4 1/2 qts.; oil filter, 1/2 qt.; oil cooler, 1/2 qt.
④— Standard body, 13.7 gals.; long body & extended cab, 18.2 gals.
⑤— V4AW2 & V5MT1, 4.8 pts.; V4AW3, 5.2 pts.

LUBRICANT DATA

Year	Lubricant Type: Transmission Manual	Transmission Automatic	Transfer Case	Rear Axle	Power Steering	Brake System
1993–96	75W-90 GL-4	Dia ATF SP	75W-90 GL-4	GL-5①	Dexron II/IIE/III	DOT 3 or 4

①— With limited slip differential, use Mitsubishi part No. 8149630EX or equivalent.

Electrical

NOTE: On Air Bag Equipped Models, Refer To "Air Bag System Precautions" Located In The Front Of This Manual For System Disarming & Arming Procedures.

INDEX

	Page No.
Air Bags	29-1
Air Conditioning	29-1
Alternators	29-1
Blower Motor, Replace	28-7
Montero	28-7
Pickup	28-7
Coil Pack, Replace	28-5
2.4L Engine	28-5
3.0L Engine	28-5
3.5L Engine	28-5
Column Switch, Replace	28-6
Cooling Fans	29-1
Cruise Control	29-1
Dash Gauges	29-1
Dash Panels	29-1
Distributor, Replace	28-5
Evaporator Core, Replace	28-8
Montero	28-8
Pickup	28-8
Fuel Pump Relay Location	28-5
Montero	28-5
Pickup	28-5
Fuse Panel & Flasher Location	28-5
Heater Core, Replace	28-7
Montero	28-7
Pickup	28-8
Ignition Lock, Replace	28-6
Ignition Switch, Replace	28-6
Instrument Cluster, Replace	28-6
Montero	28-6
Pickup	28-6
Neutral Safety Switch, Replace	28-6
Montero	28-6
Pickup	28-6
Passive Restraints	29-1
Precautions	28-5
Air Bag Systems	28-5
Radio, Replace	28-7
Montero	28-7
Pickup	28-7
Relay Center Location	28-5
Speed Controls	29-1
Starter Motors	29-1
Starter, Replace	28-5
Steering Columns	29-1
Steering Wheel, Replace	28-6
Wiper Motor, Replace	28-7
Front	28-7
Rear	28-7
Wiper Switch, Replace	28-7
Front	28-7
Rear	28-7
Wiper Systems	29-1

PRECAUTIONS

AIR BAG SYSTEMS

Refer to "Air Bag System Precautions" in the front of this manual for system disarming and arming procedures.

FUSE PANEL & FLASHER LOCATION

On Montero, the fuse panel is located on side of left end of instrument panel. There is an A/C fuse located on evaporator and a headlight fuse located in front left corner of engine compartment. Flashers are located on the left kick panel.

On Pickup, the fuse panel is located on the instrument panel to the left of steering wheel. Flashers are located under the left corner of instrument panel.

FUEL PUMP RELAY LOCATION

MONTERO

The multi-port fuel injection (MFI) relay is located behind the righthand side of the instrument panel, right of the glove compartment.

PICKUP

The multi-port fuel injection (MFI) relay is located below the righthand side of the instrument panel, behind the right kick panel.

RELAY CENTER LOCATION

On Montero, the main relay centers are located on the upper lefthand side of the engine compartment and behind the lefthand side of the instrument panel.

On Pickup, the main relay center is located behind the lower lefthand corner of the instrument panel.

STARTER

REPLACE

1. Disconnect battery ground cable.
2. Remove air cleaner assembly, if necessary.
3. Remove intake manifold stay, if necessary.
4. Remove starter cover, if necessary.
5. Disconnect starter cables.
6. Remove starter mounting bolts, then the starter.
7. Reverse procedure to install, noting the following:
   a. Before mounting starter, clean mating surfaces of starter and engine.
   b. Install starter and **torque** mounting bolts to 20–25 ft. lbs.

DISTRIBUTOR

REPLACE

1. Remove distributor cap with spark plug wires attached.
2. Turn engine No. 1 cylinder to top dead center (TDC).
3. Disconnect distributor electrical connections.
4. Remove distributor retaining nut, then the distributor.
5. Reverse procedure to install, noting the following:
   a. Ensure engine No. 1 cylinder is at TDC.
   b. Align distributor housing and gear mating marks.
   c. Install distributor into engine while aligning groove cut of the distributor installation flange with center of retaining stud.

COIL PACK

REPLACE

2.4L ENGINE

The ignition coil is located on top of the engine, near the base of the distributor and is mounted with a screw.

3.0L ENGINE

12 Valve Engine

The ignition coil is located on top of the engine, near the base of the distributor and is mounted with a screw.

24 Valve Engine

The power transistor and ignition coil located on the top lefthand front of the engine and are mounted with a screws.

3.5L ENGINE

The ignition power transistor is located on top of intake manifold and is mounted with a screw. The secondary ignition coils are located on top of spark plugs on lefthand side of engine and may be replaced by hand.

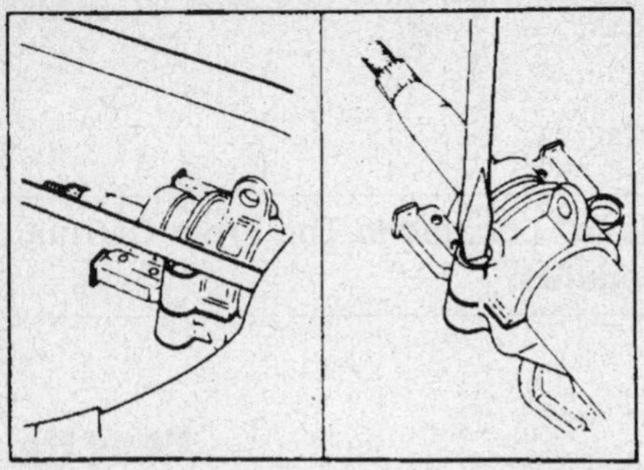
MT9129100008000X

Fig. 1 Ignition lock removal

IGNITION LOCK

REPLACE

1. **On Pickup and 1993 Montero,** disconnect battery ground cable.
2. **On all models,** remove steering column shrouds.
3. Cut groove in attaching bolt head using a suitable hacksaw, then remove bolts, **Fig. 1.**
4. Remove ignition switch electrical connectors, then the lock assembly.
5. Reverse procedure to install, noting the following:
   a. Temporarily install ignition lock in alignment with column boss and check for proper switch operation.
   b. Steering lock bracket should be replaced when installing new ignition switch.
   c. Install special ignition lock attaching bolts and tighten until heads twist off.

IGNITION SWITCH

REPLACE

1. **On Pickup and 1993 Montero,** disconnect battery ground cable.
2. **On all models,** remove knee protector, if necessary.
3. Remove column shrouds, then the switch electrical connectors.
4. Remove switch attaching screws, then remove lock cylinder from switch as follows:
   a. Insert key in lock cylinder and turn to ACC position.
   b. Using a small screwdriver, push lock cylinder lockpin in, **Fig. 2,** then remove lock cylinder.
5. Reverse procedure to install.

NEUTRAL SAFETY SWITCH

REPLACE

MONTERO

1. Remove neutral start switch attaching screws.
2. Disconnect switch electrical connector, then remove switch from vehicle.
3. Reverse procedure to install, then adjust as follows:
   a. Move selector lever to Neutral position.

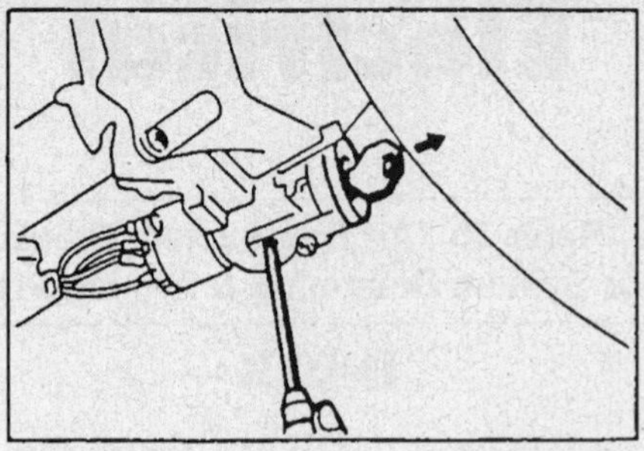
MT9049100014000X

Fig. 2 Lock cylinder removal

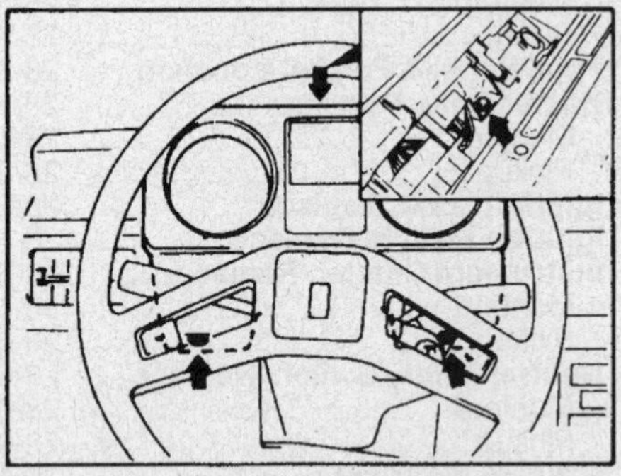
MT9099100014000X

Fig. 4 Instrument cluster mounting screw locations. Montero

   b. Loosen adjusting nut of control cable.
   c. Loosen park/neutral position switch mounting bolt.
   d. Turn park/neutral position switch so bosses on switch align with neutral position adjustment lever, **Fig. 3.**
   e. **Torque** switch mounting bolt to 4 ft. lbs.
   f. Gently pull end of transmission control cable toward front of vehicle and **torque** adjusting nut to 17 ft. lbs.
   g. Ensure selector lever is in Neutral position, then check each position of selector lever for proper operation.

PICKUP

1. Disconnect switch electrical connector, then remove switch from transmission case. Allow fluid to drain into a suitable container.
2. Move selector lever to Park and Neutral positions. Ensure switch operating lever fingers are centered in switch opening in transmission case.
3. Install switch using a new seal and **torque** to 25 ft. lbs.
4. Using a suitable ohmmeter, ensure continuity is present between center pin of switch and transmission case. **Continuity should exist only when transmission is in Park or Neutral.**
5. Add transmission fluid as required to fill transmission to proper level.

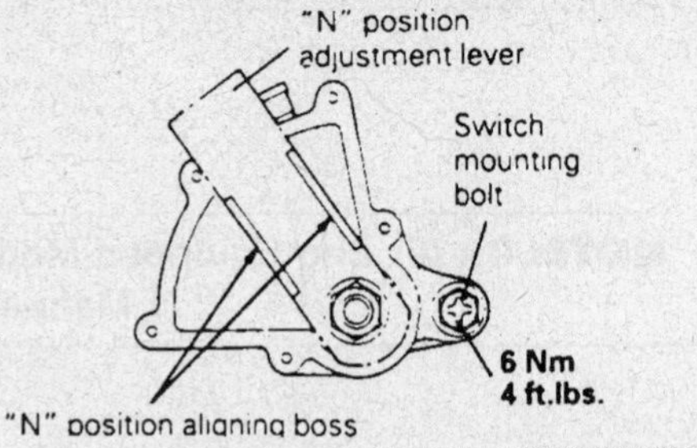
"N" position adjustment lever
Switch mounting bolt
6 Nm
4 ft.lbs.
"N" position aligning boss
MT9049200016000X

Fig. 3 Positioning selector lever. Montero

STEERING WHEEL

REPLACE

1. Remove horn pad attaching screw(s) and horn pad.
2. Remove steering wheel attaching nut.
3. Scribe mating marks on steering shaft and steering wheel for installation reference.
4. Using a suitable steering wheel puller, remove steering wheel. **Do not hammer on steering wheel to remove. Damage to the collapsible mechanism may occur.**
5. Reverse procedure to install, noting the following:
   a. Align mating marks on steering shaft and steering wheel.
   b. **Torque** steering wheel attaching nut to 25–36 ft. lbs.

INSTRUMENT CLUSTER

REPLACE

MONTERO

1. Disconnect battery ground cable.
2. Remove instrument cluster upper trim cover.
3. Remove attaching screws from bottom of instrument cluster, then the attaching bolt from upper part of cluster, **Fig. 4.**
4. Disconnect speedometer cable and all electrical connectors from rear of cluster, **Fig. 5,** then remove cluster.
5. Reverse procedure to install.

PICKUP

1. Disconnect battery ground cable.
2. Remove hazard warning switch and hole cover using a suitable trim tool.
3. Remove four instrument cluster bezel attaching screws, then remove bezel.
4. Remove four instrument cluster attaching screws.
5. Disconnect speedometer cable and all wire connectors from rear of cluster, then remove cluster from instrument panel.
6. Reverse procedure to install.

COLUMN SWITCH

REPLACE

1. Disconnect battery ground cable.
2. **On Montero models,** remove dash

MT9099100015000X

Fig. 5 Instrument cluster electrical connectors. Montero

panel lower cover.
3. **On all models,** remove steering wheel as outlined under "Steering Wheel, Replace."
4. **On models equipped with tilt steering,** set the tilt position of the steering shaft to the lowest position.
5. **On all models,** remove column upper and lower covers.
6. Disconnect column switch electrical connectors, then remove the cable band.
7. Remove column switch attaching screws, then the column switch from steering shaft.
8. Reverse procedure to install.

RADIO

REPLACE

On some models, the radio fuse is located on the rear of the radio. If radio fuse is to be replaced, it is necessary to remove the radio.

MONTERO

1. Disconnect battery ground cable.
2. Remove radio trim panel using suitable trim stick.
3. Remove radio bracket attaching screws, then the radio with cassette player, if equipped.
4. Disconnect antenna lead and electrical connectors from rear of radio.
5. Remove radio from instrument panel.
6. Reverse procedure to install.

PICKUP

1. Remove heater control lever knob.
2. Pry off center panel using a suitable tool, then remove panel from instrument panel.
3. Remove radio bracket attaching screws, then the radio bracket.
4. Pull radio outward enough to gain access to rear of radio.
5. Disconnect antenna lead wire and electrical connector, then remove radio.
6. Reverse procedure to install.

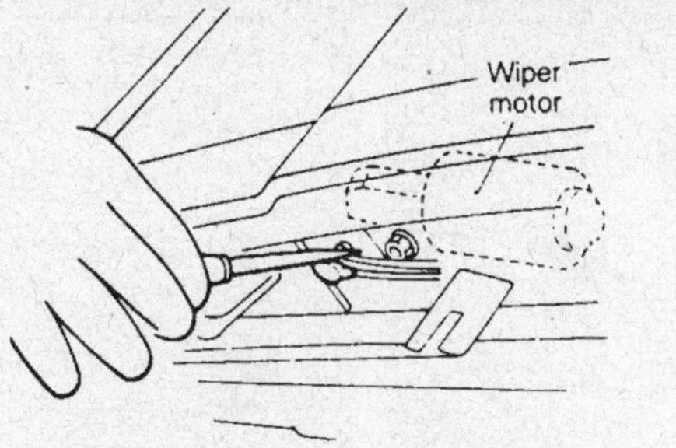
Wiper motor

MT9029100003000X

Fig. 6 Wiper linkage disconnection. Pickup

WIPER MOTOR

REPLACE

FRONT

Montero

1. Disconnect battery ground cable.
2. Remove wiper arms, then the arm shaft locknut and push shaft inward.
3. Remove bolts securing motor bracket to body, disconnect linkage, then remove wiper motor assembly. **Scribe marks on linkage for installation reference.**
4. Reverse procedure to install.

Pickup

1. Disconnect battery ground cable.
2. Remove wiper arms and blades.
3. Insert a trim stick into front deck garnish and pry off.
4. Using a suitable screwdriver, disconnect wiper linkage, **Fig. 6,** then remove wiper motor.
5. Reverse procedure to install.

REAR

1. Disconnect battery ground cable.
2. Remove spare wheel from rear door.
3. Raise wiper arm pivot cover, then remove pivot shaft locking nut.
4. Remove wiper arm and shield cap, **Fig. 7.**
5. Remove nut and collar.
6. Remove hatch trim.
7. Remove rear wiper motor bracket mounting nuts, then remove rear wiper motor assembly from hatch.
8. Reverse procedure to install.

WIPER SWITCH

REPLACE

FRONT

Refer to "Column Switch, Replace " procedure.

REAR

1. Disconnect battery ground cable.
2. Pry switch from instrument cluster using suitable tool.
3. Disconnect switch electrical connector, then remove switch.
4. Reverse procedure to install.

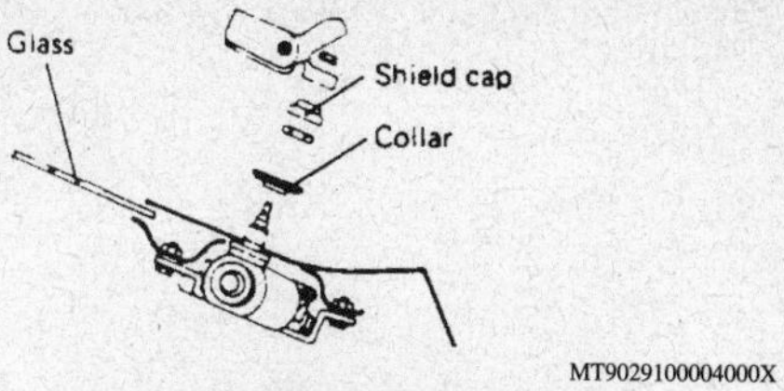
Glass
Shield cap
Collar

MT9029100004000X

Fig. 7 Rear wiper motor installation

BLOWER MOTOR

REPLACE

MONTERO

1. Disconnect battery ground cable.
2. Disconnect blower motor electrical connectors, then remove lower blower motor assembly attaching bolts.
3. Remove lap heater duct.
4. Remove glove compartment stopper and push glove compartment down.
5. Remove recirculation control wire, then the remaining blower motor attaching bolts.
6. Remove blower motor assembly.
7. Reverse procedure to install.

PICKUP

1. Disconnect battery ground cable.
2. Remove glove compartment stopper, then the glove compartment and frame.
3. Disconnect air selection control wire from blower assembly.
4. Remove duct, then disconnect blower motor electrical connector.
5. Remove bolts attaching blower assembly to heater housing.
6. Remove blower fan from blower motor.
7. Reverse procedure to install, noting the following:
   a. Place air selection lever in Outside Air position.
   b. Press air selection damper against stopper, then connect air selection control wire inner cable to end of air selection damper lever.
   c. Secure outer cable with clip.

HEATER CORE

REPLACE

MONTERO

1. Disconnect battery ground cable.
2. Place temperature control lever in Hot position, then drain cooling system into appropriate container.
3. Disconnect heater hoses from heater core, then plug heater core fittings to prevent coolant spillage.
4. Remove instrument panel as outlined under "Dash Panel Service" in the "Unit Repair" section.
5. Proceed as follows:
   a. Remove foot shower ducts and lap cooler duct, **Fig. 8.**
   b. **On models with A/C,** remove evaporator unit attaching nuts, then the heater unit.

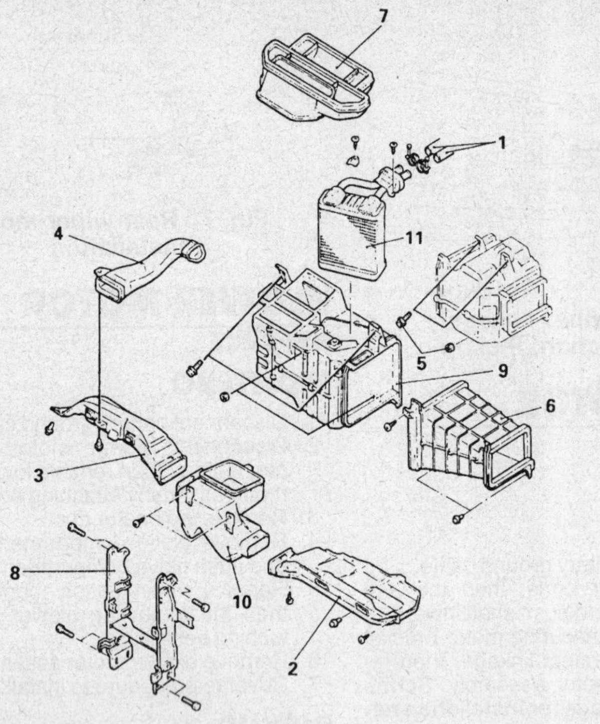
7
1
4
11
5
9
6
3
8
10
2

1. Connection for water hoses
2. Foot shower duct (RH)
3. Foot shower duct (LH)
4. Lap cooler duct A
5. Evaporator mounting bolt and nut <Vehicles with A/C>
6. Joint duct <Vehicles without A/C>
7. Center duct assembly
8. Center reinforcement
9. Heater unit
10. Foot distribution duct
11. Heater core

MT7029100108000X

Fig. 8 Heater unit replacement. Montero

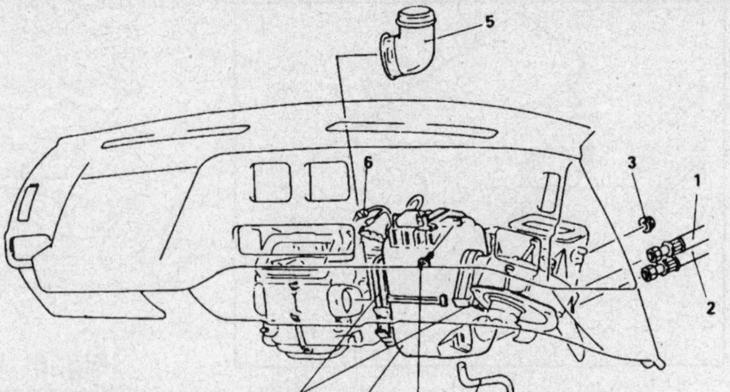
5
6
3
1
2
4
7
10
9
8

1. Liquid line connection
2. Suction line connection
3. Nut
4. Glove box
5. Defroster duct
6. Main harness connector connection
7. Duct joint
8. Drain line connection
9. Bolt
10. Evaporator

MT7029100109000X

Fig. 9 Evaporator core replacement. Pickup

c. **On models less A/C,** remove joint duct.
d. **On all models,** remove center duct, then the center reinforcement.
e. Remove heater unit, then the heater core.

6. Reverse procedure to install.

PICKUP

1. Disconnect battery ground cable.
2. Place temperature control lever in extreme right position.
3. Loosen radiator drain plug and drain cooling system into appropriate container.
4. Remove air filter, then remove hose clamps and disconnect heater hoses from heater core.
5. Remove dash panel as outlined under "Dash Panel Service " in the "Unit Repair" section.
6. Remove heater duct, then the center ventilator duct.
7. Remove defroster duct, then the center reinforcement.
8. Remove heater unit and grommet.
9. Separate heater core from heater unit.
10. Remove hose cover, joint hose clamp, joint hose and support plate from end of heater core.
11. Reverse procedure to install.

EVAPORATOR CORE

REPLACE

MONTERO

1. **On 1993 models,** disconnect battery ground cable.
2. **On all models,** discharge refrigerant from system into appropriate recovery device, then disconnect evaporator inlet pipe and suction hose. Plug openings to prevent contamination.
3. Remove drain hose.
4. Remove glove compartment stopper, then the glove compartment.
5. Remove speaker grille.
6. Remove lower frame and foot shower duct.
7. Disconnect air conditioner wiring harness.
8. Remove evaporator unit.
9. Remove air conditioner control unit.
10. Remove evaporator case halves retaining screws and clips.
11. Separate case halves, then remove air thermo sensor, air inlet sensor and expansion valve.
12. Remove high/low pressure extension pipe.
13. Remove evaporator assembly.
14. Reverse procedure to install. Rearm air bag system as described under "Precautions."

PICKUP

1. Disconnect battery ground cable.
2. Discharge refrigerant from system into appropriate container, then disconnect evaporator inlet pipe and suction hose. Plug openings to prevent contamination.
3. Remove nut, glove compartment and defroster duct, **Fig. 9.**
4. Disconnect main harness connector, duct joint and drain hose.
5. Remove bolt, then the evaporator.
6. Reverse procedure to install.

2.4L Engine

NOTE: On Air Bag Equipped Models, Refer To "Air Bag System Precautions" Located In The Front Of This Manual For System Disarming & Arming Procedures.

NOTE: For Procedures Not Found In This Section, Refer To The Engine Section Of The Mitsubishi Expo Chapter.

INDEX

	Page No.
Belt Tension Data	28-10
Compression Pressure	28-9
Cooling System Bleed	28-10
Engine Rebuilding Specifications	29-1
Engine, Replace	28-9
Fuel Filter, Replace	28-10
Fuel Pump, Replace	28-10
Precautions	28-9
Air Bag Systems	28-9
Fuel System Pressure Relief	28-9
Technical Service Bulletins	28-11
Underhood Exhaust Noise	28-11
Thermostat, Replace	28-10
Tightening Specifications	28-12
Water Pump, Replace	28-10

PRECAUTIONS

AIR BAG SYSTEMS

Refer to "Air Bag System Precautions" in the front of this manual for system disarming and arming procedures.

FUEL SYSTEM PRESSURE RELIEF

1. Disconnect fuel pump harness connector at the fuel tank rear side. **Cover fuel pipe line with rag after relieving pressure as certain pressure may still remain.**
2. Start engine and let idle until engine stops by itself, then turn ignition switch to Off. **Failure to relieve fuel system pressure prior to disconnecting fuel system components may cause fire or personal injury.**
3. Disconnect negative battery ground cable.
4. Connect fuel pump harness connector.
5. After repairs have been completed, connect positive battery terminal to fuel pump drive terminal and the negative terminal to the chassis. Ensure fuel pump operates at this time.

COMPRESSION PRESSURE

Compression pressure should be a minimum 171 psi with a maximum difference of 14 psi between cylinders.

ENGINE

REPLACE

1. Relieve fuel system pressure as described under "Precautions."
2. Scribe reference marks between hood and hood hinges, then remove hood.
3. Drain cooling system into an appropriate container as follows:
   a. Place temperature control lever in Hot position.
   b. Carefully remove radiator cap.
   c. Remove radiator drain plug.
4. Remove transmission assembly as outlined under "Transmission, Replace" in "Automatic Transmission/Transaxle" section or in "Clutch & Manual Transmission" section.
5. Remove radiator components in order as shown, **Fig. 1,** noting the following:
   a. Prior to removing radiator hoses, mark hose clamps in relation to hoses for installation reference.
   b. After disconnecting transmission cooler lines on models with automatic transmission, plug or cover ends of lines to prevent entry of dirt or foreign material.
6. Remove engine components in order as shown, **Fig. 2,** noting the following:
   a. Remove A/C compressor from bracket with hoses attached, then support compressor pump aside with a piece of wire.
   b. Remove power steering pump from bracket with hoses attached, then secure pump aside with a piece of wire.
   c. When disconnecting high pressure fuel hose, cover fuel pipe line with a shop towel. **Some residual fuel pressure may be present.**
   d. Ensure all cables, connectors and

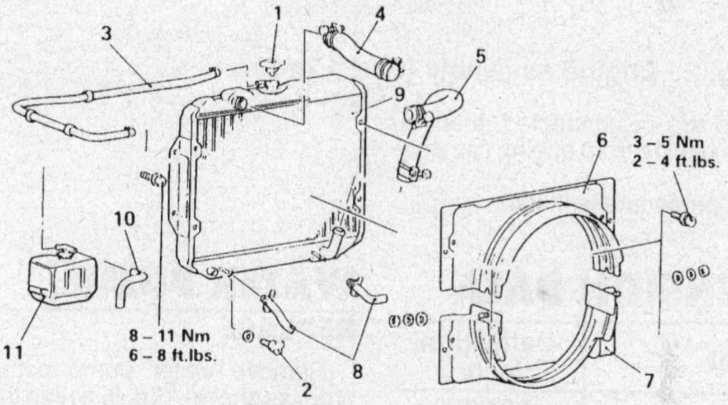

3
1
4
5
9
6
3 – 5 Nm
2 – 4 ft.lbs.
10
8 – 11 Nm
6 – 8 ft.lbs.
11
2
8
7

1. Radiator cap
2. Drain plug
3. Overflow hose
4. Radiator upper hose
5. Radiator lower hose
6. Radiator upper shroud
7. Radiator lower shroud
8. Automatic transmission oil cooler hose connection <A/T>
9. Radiator
10. Overflow tube
11. Reserve tank

MT1069100291000X

Fig. 1 Radiator assembly

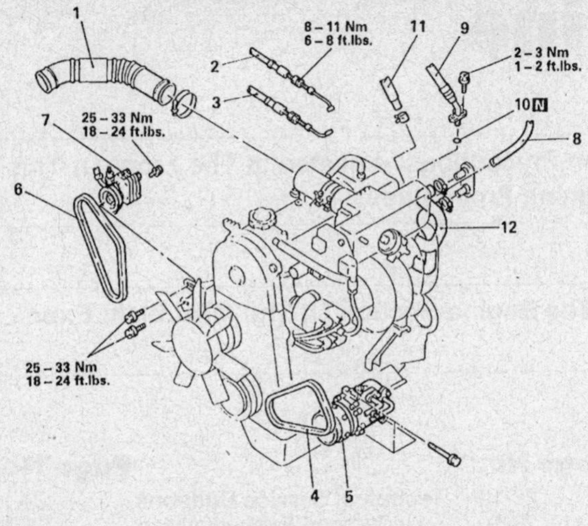
8 – 11 Nm
6 – 8 ft.lbs.
2 – 3 Nm
1 – 2 ft.lbs.
25 – 33 Nm
18 – 24 ft.lbs.
25 – 33 Nm
18 – 24 ft.lbs.

Removal Steps

1. Air cleaner duct
2. Accelerator cable connection
3. Throttle control cable connection
<A/T>
4. Air conditioning compressor drive belt
5. Compressor
6. Power steering oil pump drive belt
7. Power steering oil pump
8. Cruise control vacuum hose connection <Vehicles with cruise control>
9. High pressure fuel hose connection
10. O-ring
11. Fuel return hose connection
12. Water hose connection

MT1069100292010X

Fig. 2 Engine assembly (Part 1 of 2)

hoses are disconnected, then remove engine from engine compartment.

7. Reverse procedure to install.

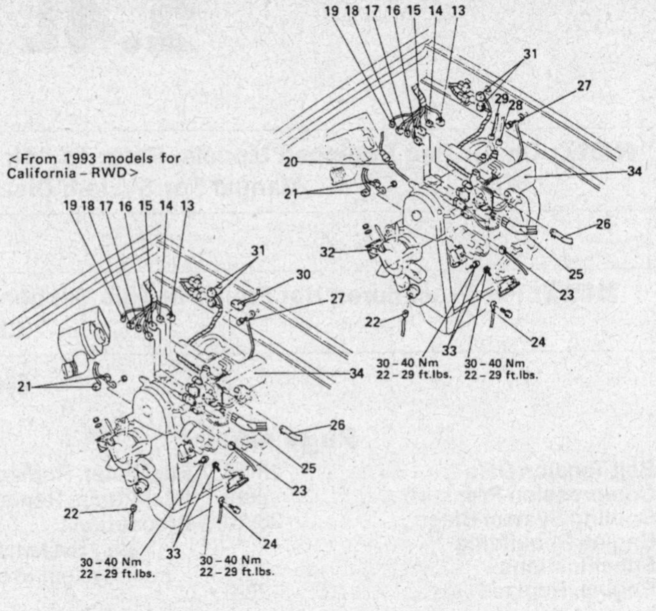
<From 1993 models for California – RWD>
30 – 40 Nm
22 – 29 ft.lbs.
30 – 40 Nm
22 – 29 ft.lbs.

Removal steps

13. Throttle position sensor connector
14. Ignition coil connector
15. Power transistor connector
16. EGR temperature sensor connector
17. Engine coolant temperature gauge unit connector
18. Engine coolant temperature sensor connector
19. Thermal switch connector <A/T>
20. Oxygen sensor connector
21. Generator connector
22. Oil pressure gauge unit connector
23. Air conditioning engine coolant temperature switch connector <A/C>
24. Ground cable connection
25. Emission control vacuum hose connection
26. Brake booster vacuum hose connection
27. Ground cable connection
28. Idle speed control motor connector
29. Idle speed control motor position sensor connector
30. Idle air control motor connector
31. Control wiring harness connector
32. Heat protector
33. Engine mounting bolt
34. Engine assembly

MT1069100292020X

Fig. 2 Engine assembly (Part 2 of 2)

BELT TENSION DATA

Component	Deflection, Inch①
Water Pump	0.27–0.39
Power Steering Pump	②
A/C Compressor	0.33–0.39

① — With 22 lbs. of force is applied.
② — 2WD, 0.23–0.35 4WD, 0.35–0.47

COOLING SYSTEM BLEED

These engines do not require a specified bleed procedure. After filling cooling system, run engine to operating temperature with radiator/pressure cap off. Air will then be automatically bled through cap opening.

THERMOSTAT

REPLACE

1. Drain cooling system into a appropriate container.
2. Disconnect upper radiator hose from thermostat housing.
3. Remove thermostat housing retaining bolts, thermostat housing and thermostat.
4. Reverse procedure to install, then ensure thermostat flange is correctly seated in the thermostat housing socket.

WATER PUMP

REPLACE

Remove water pump components in order as shown, **Fig. 3,** noting the following:

1. Disconnect battery ground cable.
2. Drain cooling system into appropriate container as follows:
   a. Place temperature control lever in Hot position.
   b. Carefully remove radiator cap.
   c. Remove radiator drain plug.
3. Prior to removing water pump drive belt, loosen water pump attaching bolts.
4. Remove timing belt covers and timing belts.
5. Reverse procedure to install, noting the following:
   a. Coat outer diameter of O-ring with water to ease installation.
   b. Refer to bolt chart, **Fig. 4,** when installing water pump attaching bolts.
   c. Install timing belts and timing belt covers.

FUEL PUMP

REPLACE

1. Disconnect battery ground cable.
2. Release fuel system pressure as described under "Precautions."
3. Drain fuel tank into a appropriate container.
4. Lower fuel tank using suitable jack.
5. Disconnect all electrical and hose connections.
6. Remove fuel pump/sending unit retaining nuts.
7. Remove fuel pump from fuel tank.
8. Reverse procedure to install, noting the following:
   a. Install check valve as shown, **Fig. 5.**
   b. Install overfill limiter valve with arrow pointing toward engine side fuel hose.
   c. Do not allow the main hose to become twisted when tightening.

FUEL FILTER

REPLACE

1. Disconnect battery ground cable.
2. Release fuel system pressure as described under "Precautions."
3. Drain fuel tank into a appropriate container.
4. Hold fuel filter with a wrench and remove eye bolt retaining fuel high pressure hose with an eye wrench, **Fig. 6.**
5. Inspect hose and pipes for cracks, damage or clogging and replace as necessary.
6. Inspect evaporative emission canister for clogging and replace as necessary.
7. Inspect check valve and fuel filter for clogging or damage and replace as necessary.
8. Remove protector of fuel filter, then disconnect fuel filter mounting bolt.

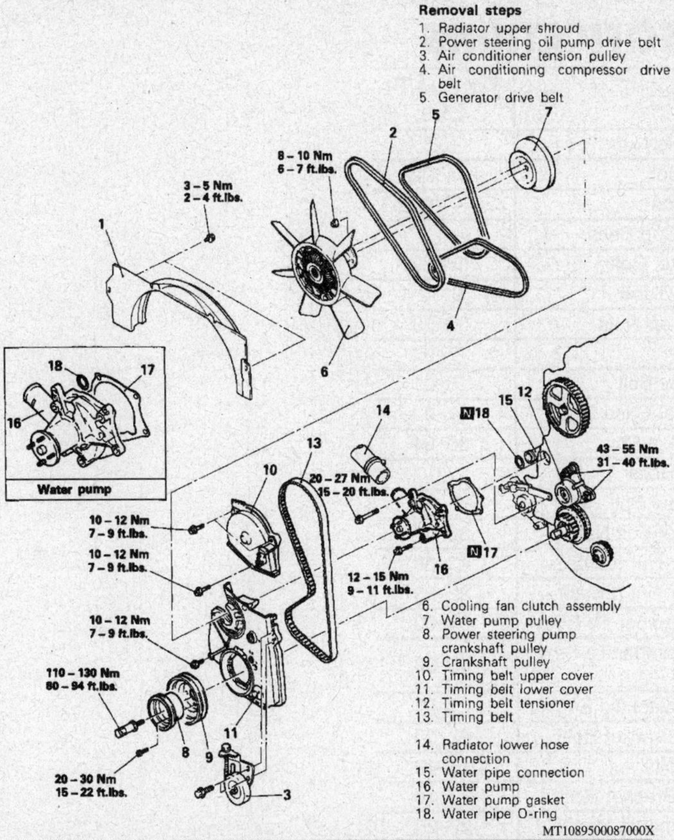

Removal steps
1. Radiator upper shroud
2. Power steering oil pump drive belt
3. Air conditioner tension pulley
4. Air conditioning compressor drive belt
5. Generator drive belt
6. Cooling fan clutch assembly
7. Water pump pulley
8. Power steering pump crankshaft pulley
9. Crankshaft pulley
10. Timing belt upper cover
11. Timing belt lower cover
12. Timing belt tensioner
13. Timing belt
14. Radiator lower hose connection
15. Water pipe connection
16. Water pump
17. Water pump gasket
18. Water pipe O-ring
8 – 10 Nm
6 – 7 ft.lbs.
3 – 5 Nm
2 – 4 ft.lbs.
Water pump
10 – 12 Nm
7 – 9 ft.lbs.
20 – 27 Nm
15 – 20 ft.lbs.
12 – 15 Nm
9 – 11 ft.lbs.
43 – 55 Nm
31 – 40 ft.lbs.
110 – 130 Nm
80 – 94 ft.lbs.
20 – 30 Nm
15 – 22 ft.lbs.
MT1089500087000X

Fig. 3 Water pump assembly

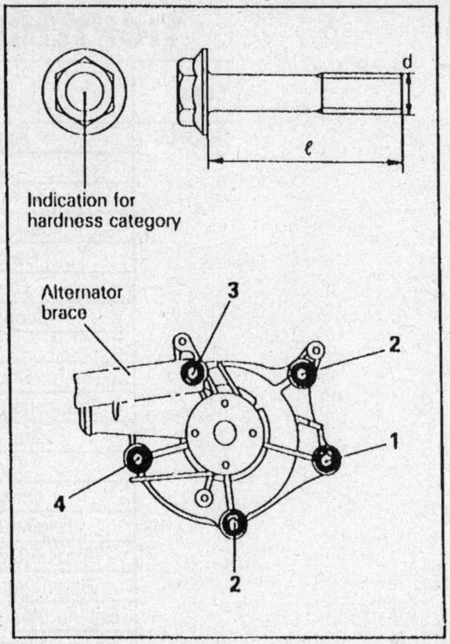

d
ℓ
Indication for hardness category
Alternator brace

No.	Hardness category (Head mark)	d × ℓ mm (in.)	Torque Nm (ft.lbs.)
1	4T	8×20 (.31×.79)	12 – 15 (9 – 11)
2	4T	8×30 (.31×1.18)	
3	7T	8×65 (.31×2.26)	20 – 27 (15 – 20)
4	4T	8×40 (.31×1.57)	12 – 15 (9 – 11)

MT1069100293000X

Fig. 4 Water pump attaching bolts

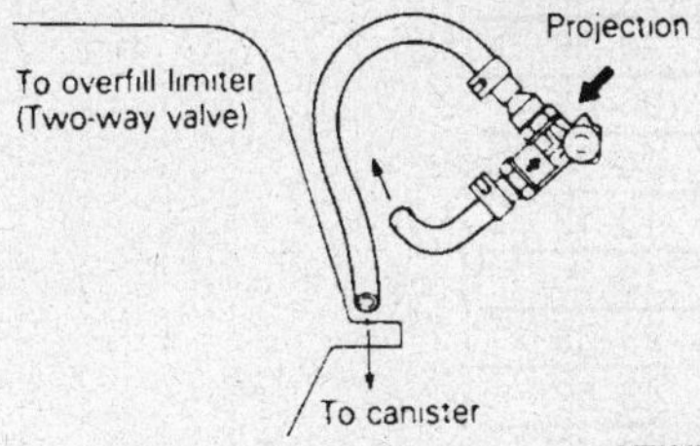

Projection
To overfill limiter (Two-way valve)
To canister
MT1069100294000X

Fig. 5 Check valve installation

9. Remove fuel filter and high pressure hose assembly.

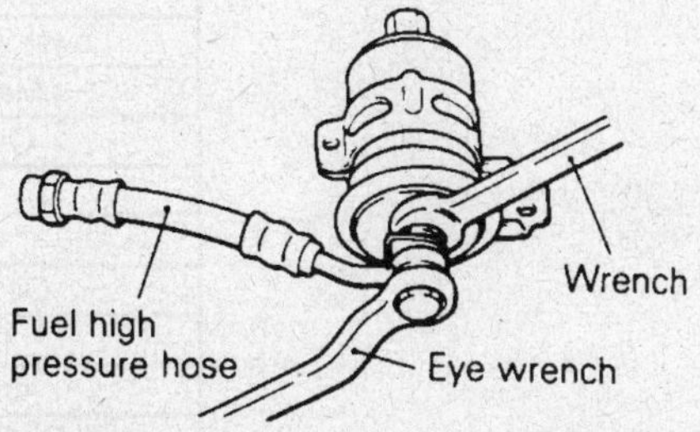

Wrench
Fuel high pressure hose
Eye wrench
MT1029100017000X

Fig. 6 Fuel filter replacement

TECHNICAL SERVICE BULLETINS

UNDERHOOD EXHAUST NOISE

1993-94 Pickup w/2.4L Engine

On these models built before September 1994, there may be underhood exhaust noise. This condition may be caused by exhaust manifold stud breakage. Soot may also appear at offending stud. To correct this condition, install replacement studs as needed (part No. MD321848), and replacement manifold gasket (part No. MD190962).

TIGHTENING SPECIFICATIONS

Year	Component	Torque/Ft. Lbs.
1993–96	Accelerator Cable Nut	6–8
	Air Cleaner Bolt	14–22
	Air Intake Pipe	7–9
	Camshaft Bearing Cap Bolts	②
	Camshaft Sprocket Bolt	58–72
	Clutch Hose To Tube	9–12
	Connecting Rod Cap Nuts	37–38
	Cooling Fan	7–9
	Crankshaft Pulley Bolt	15–21
	Crankshaft Rear Oil Seal Case Bolts	7–9
	Crankshaft Sprocket Bolt	80–94
	Cylinder Head Bolts	①
	Driveplate/Flywheel Bolt	94–101
	Engine Mount Bracket Bolt/Nut	36–47
	Engine Mount Insulator Nut (Large)	43–58
	Engine Mount Insulator Nut (Small)	22–29
	Engine Mounting Crossmember To Body	65–80
	Engine Mounting Crossmember To Strut Bar	65–90
	Engine Support Front Insulator To Engine	22–24
	Exhaust Pipe Support Bracket Bolt	22–30
	Front Case Bolts	15–19
	Front Engine Support Bracket Bolt	22–30
	Front Exhaust Pipe To Exhaust Manifold	22–29
	Front Exhaust Pipe To Under Catalytic Converter	36–50
	Front Exhaust Pipe Clamp Bolt	14–22
	Front Roll Stopper Bracket Bolt	29–36
	Front Roll Stopper Bracket Nut	36–47
	High Pressure Hose And Delivery Pipe	18–25
	Intake Manifold Stay Bolt	13–18
	Jet Valve	13–15
	Left Engine Support Bracket	29–36
	Lower Arm Ball Joint To Knuckle	43–52
	Main Bearing Cap Bolts	37–39
	Oil Filter Bracket Bolts	11–15
	Oil Pan Bolts	4–6
	Oil Pan Drain Plug	26–32
	Oil Pressure Gauge Unit	6–8
	Oil Pressure Switch	6–9
	Oil Pump Cover Bolts	11–13
	Oil Pump Driven Gear Bolt	25–28
	Oil Pump Sprocket Bolt/Nut	36–43
	Oil Screen Bolts	11–15
	Power Steering Oil Pump Bracket	14–20
	Power Steering Oil Pump Lower Bolt	14–20
	Power Steering Oil Pump Upper Bolt	18–24
	Power Steering Pressure Hose To Oil Pump	29–36
	Propeller Shaft	36–43
	Radiator Upper Shroud	2–4
	Rear Engine Insulator To Rear Engine Mounting Bracket	51–69
	Rear Roll Stopper Bracket Bolt	80–94

Continued

TIGHTENING SPECIFICATIONS—Continued

Year	Component	Torque/Ft. Lbs.
1993–96	Rear Roll Stopper Insulator Bolt	29–36
	Rear Roll Stopper Insulator Nut	22–29
	Relief Valve Plug	29–36
	Right Engine Support Bracket	29–36
	Right Silent Shaft Sprocket Bolt	25–28
	Rocker Arm Adjusting Nuts	6–7
	Rocker Arm Shaft Bolts	14–15
	Rocker Cover Bolts	4–5
	Silent Shaft Sprocket Bolt	31–35
	Strut Bar To Lower Arm	61–80
	Tensioner Spacer	32–39
	Tensioner "B" Bolt	11–15
	Tie Rod End To Knuckle	17–25
	Timing Belt Lower Cover Bolts	7–9
	Timing Belt Tensioner Bolt	30–40
	Timing Belt Upper Cover Bolts	7–9
	Transaxle Mount Bracket Bolt	29–36
	Transaxle Mount Insulator Nut	43–58
	Water Pump Pulley Bolt	5.8–7.2

① — With engine cold, 65–72 ft. lbs.; w/engine warm, 73–79 ft. lbs.
② — 8 X 25 bolts, 15–19 ft. lbs.; 8 X 65 bolts, 14–15 ft. lbs.

3.0L Engine

NOTE: On Air Bag Equipped Models, Refer To "Air Bag System Precautions" Located In The Front Of This Manual For System Disarming & Arming Procedures.

NOTE: For Procedures Not Found In This Section, Refer To The Engine Section of The Mitsubishi 3000GT Chapter.

INDEX

	Page No.
Belt Tension Data	28-17
Compression Pressure	28-14
Cooling System Bleed	28-17
Crankshaft Seal, Replace	28-16
Front	28-16
Rear	28-16
Cylinder Head, Replace	28-15
12 Valve Engine	28-15
24 Valve Engine	28-15
Engine Mount, Replace	28-14
Engine Rebuilding Specifications	29-1
Engine, Replace	28-14
Exhaust Manifold, Replace	28-15
Fuel Filter, Replace	28-18
Fuel Pump, Replace	28-18
Montero	28-18
Pickup	28-18
Intake Manifold, Replace	28-14
Oil Pan, Replace	28-16
Montero	28-17
Pickup	28-16
Precautions	28-13
Air Bag Systems	28-13
Fuel System Pressure Relief	28-13
Radiator, Replace	28-18
Thermostat, Replace	28-17
Tightening Specifications	28-24
Timing Belt, Replace	28-15
12 Valve Engine	28-15
24 Valve Engine	28-15
Valve Adjustment	28-15
Water Pump, Replace	28-17

PRECAUTIONS

AIR BAG SYSTEMS

Refer to "Air Bag System Precautions" in the front of this manual for system disarming and arming procedures.

FUEL SYSTEM PRESSURE RELIEF

Montero

1. Remove carpet from cargo compartment, then remove bolts from floor cover.
2. Disconnect fuel pump electrical connection.
3. Start engine and let idle until all residual fuel is consumed, then turn ignition

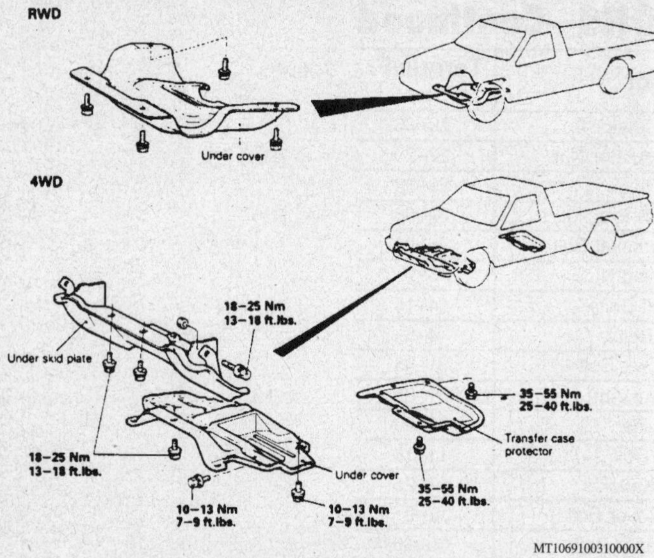
RWD
Under cover
4WD
18–25 Nm
13–18 ft.lbs.
Under skid plate
35–55 Nm
25–40 ft.lbs.
Transfer case protector
18–25 Nm
13–18 ft.lbs.
Under cover
35–55 Nm
25–40 ft.lbs.
10–13 Nm
7–9 ft.lbs.
10–13 Nm
7–9 ft.lbs.
MT1069100310000X

Fig. 1 Under guard components

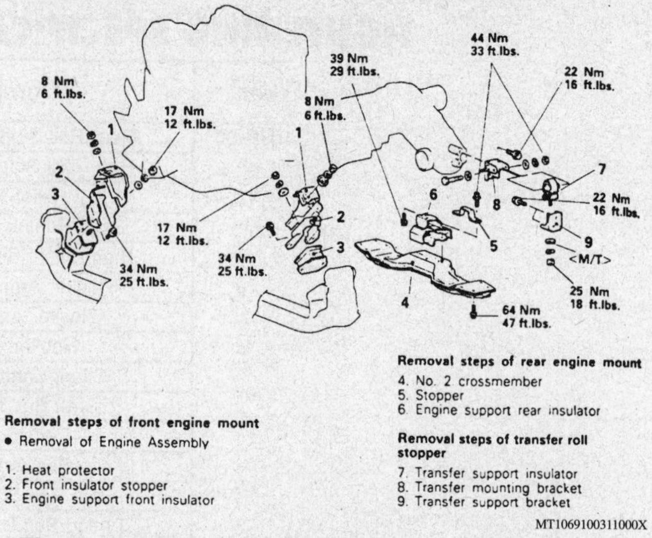
8 Nm
6 ft.lbs.
17 Nm
12 ft.lbs.
39 Nm
29 ft.lbs.
8 Nm
6 ft.lbs.
44 Nm
33 ft.lbs.
22 Nm
16 ft.lbs.
17 Nm
12 ft.lbs.
34 Nm
25 ft.lbs.
34 Nm
25 ft.lbs.
22 Nm
16 ft.lbs.
<M/T>
25 Nm
18 ft.lbs.
64 Nm
47 ft.lbs.
Removal steps of rear engine mount
4. No. 2 crossmember
5. Stopper
6. Engine support rear insulator
Removal steps of front engine mount
• Removal of Engine Assembly
1. Heat protector
2. Front insulator stopper
3. Engine support front insulator
Removal steps of transfer roll stopper
7. Transfer support insulator
8. Transfer mounting bracket
9. Transfer support bracket
MT1069100311000X

Fig. 2 Engine mount replacement. Montero w/12 valve engine

switch to Off position. **Failure to relieve fuel system pressure prior to disconnecting fuel system components may cause fire or personal injury.**

4. Disconnect battery ground cable.
5. Connect fuel pump electrical connection.
6. Install cargo compartment floor cover and bolts then install carpet. **Torque** bolts to 9 ft. lbs.
7. After repairs have been completed, connect battery cable and ensure fuel pump operates properly.

Pickup

1. Disconnect fuel pump harness connector at the fuel tank rear side. **Cover fuel pipe line with rag after relieving pressure as certain pressure may still remain.**
2. Start engine and let idle until engine stops by itself, then turn ignition switch to Off. **Failure to relieve fuel system pressure prior to disconnecting fuel system components may cause fire or personal injury.**
3. Disconnect negative battery ground cable.
4. Connect fuel pump harness connector.
5. After repairs have been completed, connect positive battery terminal to fuel pump drive terminal and the negative terminal to the chassis. Ensure fuel pump operates at this time.

COMPRESSION PRESSURE

Compression pressure should be a minimum 171 psi with a maximum difference of 14 psi between cylinders.

ENGINE MOUNT

REPLACE

1. Raise and support vehicle, then remove snow protection lower cover, undercover, skid plate, transfer case protector and cross shaft protector, **Fig. 1.**
2. Lower vehicle, then remove engine mounts in numbered sequence shown, **Figs. 2 through 5.**
3. Reverse procedure to install. Tighten all bolts and nuts to specifications, **Figs. 2 through 5.**

ENGINE

REPLACE

Refer to **Figs. 6 and 7** when replacing engine.

1. Relieve fuel system pressure as described under "Precautions."
2. Scribe hood hinge locations and remove hood.
3. Drain engine coolant, engine oil, transfer case fluid and transmission oil into appropriate containers.
4. **On models with manual transmission,** drain clutch hydraulic fluid into appropriate containers.
5. **On models equipped with A/C,** discharge refrigerant into appropriate container.
6. **On all models,** raise and support vehicle, then remove snow protection undercover, skid plate, transfer case protector and cross shaft protector, **Fig. 1.**
7. Remove transmission and transfer case assembly. Refer to "Transmission, Replace " in appropriate transmission section.
8. Disconnect radiator upper and lower hoses and overflow tube, then remove fan shroud.
9. **On models with automatic transmission,** remove oil cooler hose and tube assemblies.
10. **On all models,** remove radiator and bushings.
11. Disconnect front exhaust pipe from engine.
12. Remove air cleaner duct.
13. Remove engine drive belts.
14. Remove A/C compressor and position aside. **Leave compressor lines connected.**
15. Disconnect oil cooler hoses from engine.
16. Remove power steering pump, if equipped and position aside. **Leave pressure and return hoses connected.**
17. Disconnect fuel high pressure hose. **Cover fuel pipe line with a rag as fuel pressure may remain.**
18. Disconnect fuel return hose.
19. Disconnect vacuum hose, **Fig. 7.**
20. Disconnect water hoses from engine.
21. Disconnect electrical wiring and electrical sensors.
22. Remove ignition coil and power transistor assembly.
23. Disconnect purge hose and brake booster hose.
24. Disconnect accelerator cable, bracket, and cruise control cable, if equipped.
25. Remove heat protector, then the engine mounting bolts.
26. Connect suitable engine lifting equipment, ensure all cables, hoses and harness connectors are positioned aside, then remove engine assembly.
27. Reverse procedure to install.

INTAKE MANIFOLD

REPLACE

1. Relieve fuel system pressure as described under "Precautions," then drain engine coolant into a suitable container.
2. Remove intake manifold plenum, then the manifold in numbered sequence as shown, **Figs. 8 and 9.**
3. Reverse procedure to install, noting the following:
   a. **On 24 valve engines,** install intake manifold gaskets as shown, **Fig. 10.**
   b. **On 24 valve engines,** when installing intake manifold mounting nuts, first **torque** right bank nuts to 5 ft. lbs., then the left bank nuts to 14–

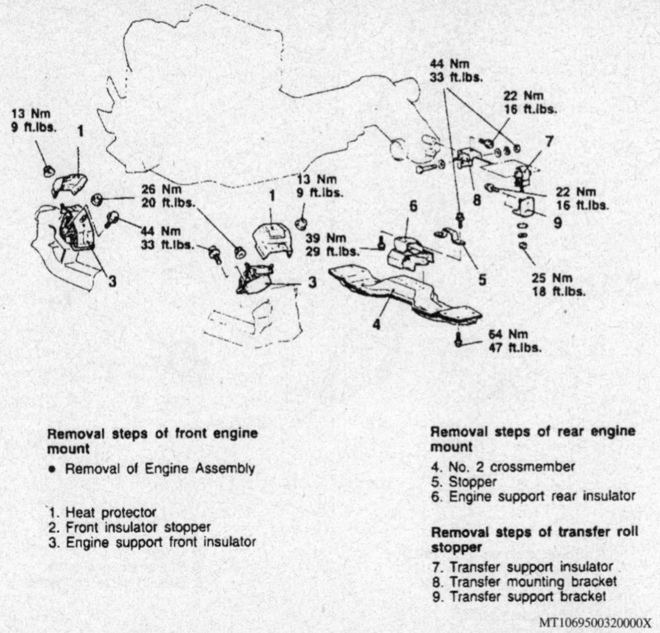
13 Nm
9 ft.lbs.
44 Nm
33 ft.lbs.
22 Nm
16 ft.lbs.
26 Nm
20 ft.lbs.
13 Nm
9 ft.lbs.
22 Nm
16 ft.lbs.
44 Nm
33 ft.lbs.
39 Nm
29 ft.lbs.
25 Nm
18 ft.lbs.
64 Nm
47 ft.lbs.
Removal steps of front engine mount
• Removal of Engine Assembly
1. Heat protector
2. Front insulator stopper
3. Engine support front insulator
Removal steps of rear engine mount
4. No. 2 crossmember
5. Stopper
6. Engine support rear insulator
Removal steps of transfer roll stopper
7. Transfer support insulator
8. Transfer mounting bracket
9. Transfer support bracket
MT1069500320000X

Fig. 3 Engine mount replacement. Montero w/24 valve engine & M/T

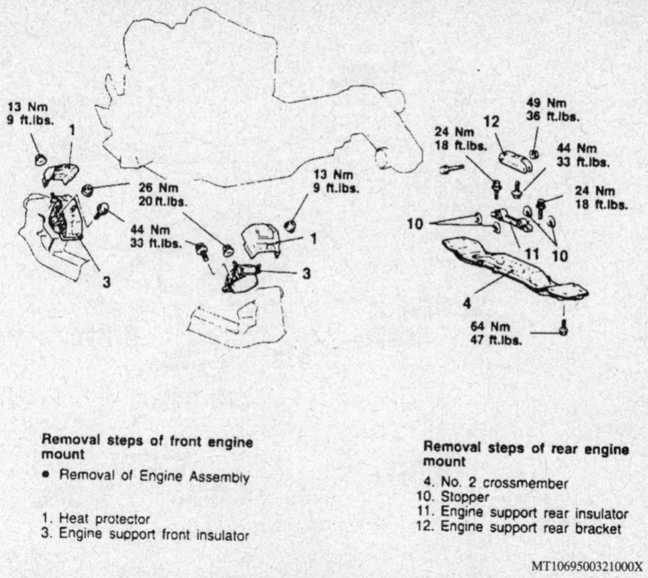
13 Nm
9 ft.lbs.
26 Nm
20 ft.lbs.
44 Nm
33 ft.lbs.
13 Nm
9 ft.lbs.
49 Nm
36 ft.lbs.
24 Nm
18 ft.lbs.
44 Nm
33 ft.lbs.
24 Nm
18 ft.lbs.
64 Nm
47 ft.lbs.
Removal steps of front engine mount
• Removal of Engine Assembly
1. Heat protector
3. Engine support front insulator
Removal steps of rear engine mount
4. No. 2 crossmember
10. Stopper
11. Engine support rear insulator
12. Engine support rear bracket
MT1069500321000X

Fig. 4 Engine mount replacement. Montero w/24 valve engine & A/T

17 ft. lbs. Finally, **torque** right bank nuts to 14–17 ft. lbs.

c. **On 12 valve engines,** install intake manifold mounting nuts and **torque** to 11–14 ft. lbs.

EXHAUST MANIFOLD

REPLACE

1. Relieve fuel system pressure as described under "Precautions."
2. **On Federal models,** remove front exhaust pipe.
3. **On California models,** remove warm up three way catalytic converter.
4. **On all models,** remove exhaust manifold in numbered sequence as shown, **Figs. 11 and 12.**
5. Reverse procedure to install. Tighten to specifications.

CYLINDER HEAD

REPLACE

12 VALVE ENGINE

Refer to **Fig. 13** for cylinder head replacement, noting the following:

1. Drain engine coolant into suitable container, then remove timing belt, intake manifold, skid plate and front exhaust pipe.
2. Remove cylinder head bolts in three steps in sequence shown in **Fig. 14,** using head bolt replacement tool No. MD998051-01, or equivalent.
3. Reverse procedure to install, noting the following:
   a. When installing cylinder head gasket, degrease gasket mounting surface, then lay gasket on cylinder block with ID mark at front top.
   b. Tighten cylinder head bolts to specifications, in three steps in sequence shown in **Fig. 14,** using head bolt replacement tool No. MD998051-01, or equivalent.

24 VALVE ENGINE

Refer to **Fig. 15,** when replacing the cylinder head noting the following:

1. Drain engine coolant into suitable container, then remove timing belt & intake manifold.
2. Remove cylinder head bolts in three steps in sequence shown in **Fig. 16,** using head bolt replacement tool No. MD998051-01, or equivalent.
3. Reverse procedure to install, noting the following:
   a. When installing cylinder head gasket, degrease gasket mounting surface, then lay gasket on cylinder block with ID mark at front top.
   b. Tighten cylinder head bolts to specifications, in three steps in sequence shown in **Fig. 16,** using head bolt replacement tool No. MD998051-01, or equivalent.
   c. Rinse mounting location of water pipe O-ring and water pipe with water then install. **Do not apply oil or grease to O-ring. Insert water pipe until its end bottoms.**
   d. Bend tabs of water passage gasket onto water passage, then install. Ensure gasket does not slip.

VALVE ADJUSTMENT

This engine uses automatic valve lash adjusters. No valve adjustment is required.

TIMING BELT

REPLACE

12 VALVE ENGINE

1. Drain engine coolant into suitable container.
2. Remove timing belt in numbered sequence as shown, **Fig. 17,** noting the following:
   a. When removing A/C compressor and power steering pump, leave hoses attached and support aside.
   b. Use pulley remover tool No. MB990767-01, or equivalent, to remove crankshaft pulley.
   c. Loosen timing belt tensioner bolt, then rotate tensioner counterclockwise.
   d. Remove timing belt. **Ensure direction of normal rotation is marked on belt if it is to be reused.**
3. Reverse procedure to install, noting the following:
   a. Align timing marks of camshaft sprockets and crankshaft sprocket to bring No. 1 cylinder to TDC as shown in **Fig. 18.**
   b. Route timing belt over crankshaft sprocket and RH side camshaft sprocket, then route timing belt over water pump pulley, LH side camshaft sprocket and timing belt tensioner.
   c. Ensure all timing marks are aligned, then install the flange.
   d. Loosen tensioner bolts and tighten timing belt, then using tool No. MD998716-01, or equivalent, rotate crankshaft two turns clockwise. **Do not rotate crankshaft counterclockwise.**
   e. Align timing marks and tighten tensioner bolts to specification.

24 VALVE ENGINE

1. Drain engine coolant into suitable container.
2. Remove timing belt in numbered sequence as shown, **Fig. 19,** noting the following:
   a. When removing A/C compressor and power steering pump, leave hoses attached and support aside.
   b. Use pulley remover tool No.

RWD

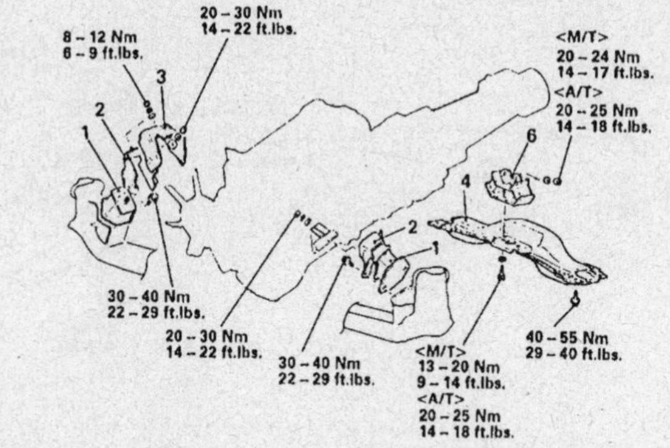
20 – 30 Nm
14 – 22 ft.lbs.
8 – 12 Nm
6 – 9 ft.lbs.
<M/T>
20 – 24 Nm
14 – 17 ft.lbs.
<A/T>
20 – 25 Nm
14 – 18 ft.lbs.
30 – 40 Nm
22 – 29 ft.lbs.
20 – 30 Nm
14 – 22 ft.lbs.
30 – 40 Nm
22 – 29 ft.lbs.
<M/T>
13 – 20 Nm
9 – 14 ft.lbs.
<A/T>
20 – 25 Nm
14 – 18 ft.lbs.
40 – 55 Nm
29 – 40 ft.lbs.

4WD

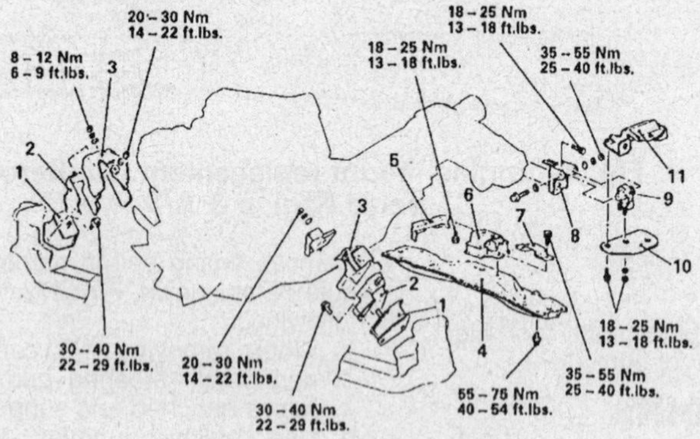
20 – 30 Nm
14 – 22 ft.lbs.
8 – 12 Nm
6 – 9 ft.lbs.
18 – 25 Nm
13 – 18 ft.lbs.
18 – 25 Nm
13 – 18 ft.lbs.
35 – 55 Nm
25 – 40 ft.lbs.
30 – 40 Nm
22 – 29 ft.lbs.
20 – 30 Nm
14 – 22 ft.lbs.
30 – 40 Nm
22 – 29 ft.lbs.
55 – 75 Nm
40 – 54 ft.lbs.
18 – 25 Nm
13 – 18 ft.lbs.
35 – 55 Nm
25 – 40 ft.lbs.

1. Engine support front insulator
2. Front insulator stopper
3. Heat protector
4. No. 2 crossmember
5. Heat protector
6. Engine support rear insulator
7. Stopper
8. Transfer mounting bracket
9. Transfer support insulator
10. Plate assembly
11. Transfer support bracket

MT1069100312000X

Fig. 5 Engine mount replacement. Pickup

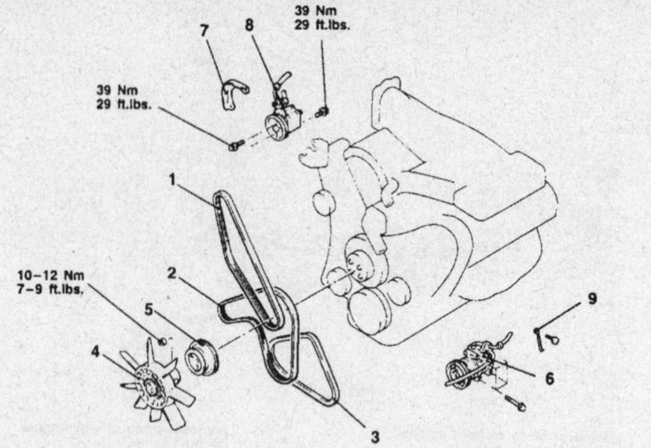
39 Nm
29 ft.lbs.
39 Nm
29 ft.lbs.
10–12 Nm
7–9 ft.lbs.

Removal Steps
1. Power steering drive belt
2. Generator drive belt
3. A/C drive belt
4. Cooling fan
5. Water pump pulley
6. A/C compressor
7. Cover
8. Power steering pump
9. Ground cable connection

MT1069500322010X

Fig. 6 Engine replacement (Part 1 of 2). Montero w/24 valve engine

MB990767-01, or equivalent, to remove crankshaft pulley.

c. Loosen timing belt tensioner bolt, then rotate tensioner counterclockwise.
d. Remove timing belt. **Ensure direction of normal rotation is marked on belt if it is to be reused.**

3. Reverse procedure to install, noting the following:
   a. If auto tensioner rod is fully extended, gently push rod into cylinder by clamping tensioner assembly in a soft jawed vise until set hole in rod aligns with hole in cylinder wall, then insert a stiff wire through set hole to keep rod in place.
   b. Align timing marks of camshaft sprockets and crankshaft sprocket to bring No. 1 cylinder to TDC as shown in **Fig. 20.**
   c. Route timing belt over crankshaft sprocket, idler pulley and LH side camshaft sprocket, then route timing belt over water pump pulley, RH side camshaft sprocket and timing belt tensioner. **RH side camshaft sprocket turns easily due to spring force applied and may cause personal injury if fingers are caught.**
   d. Turn RH side camshaft sprocket counterclockwise until tension side of timing belt is firmly stretched, then ensure all timing marks are aligned.
   e. Use tool No. MD998767, or equivalent, to push the tension pulley into timing belt, then temporarily tighten tensioner bolt.
   f. Using tool No. MD998769, or equivalent, rotate crankshaft ¼ turn clockwise, then turn crankshaft again until timing marks are aligned.
   g. Loosen tensioner bolt and apply 3.3 ft. lbs. of **torque** to timing belt, then tighten tensioner bolt.
   h. Remove setting wire from auto tensioner, then rotate crankshaft two turns and ensure timing marks are aligned.
   i. Wait five minutes and measure auto tensioner push rod protrusion. If protrusion is not .149–.177 inch, repeat steps "f" through "i."

CRANKSHAFT SEAL

REPLACE

FRONT

1. Remove timing belt as described under "Timing Belt, Replace," then remove crankshaft sprocket, position sensor, sensing blade and spacer.
2. Remove key from keyway, then separate oil seal from case as follows:
   a. Cut out a small portion of crankshaft oil seal lip.
   b. Cover tip of a suitable screwdriver with a cloth, then insert into seal cutout and pry away from oil pump case.
3. Reverse procedure to install. Drive seal in until flush with surface of oil pump case using seal installation tool No. MD998717, or equivalent.

REAR

1. Remove transmission assembly as described under "Transmission, Replace" in "Automatic Transmission/Transaxle" section, then remove outer adapter plate and driveplate.
2. Remove driveplate to output flange adapter, then remove oil seal from engine as follows:
   a. Cut out a small portion of crankshaft oil seal lip.
   b. Cover tip of a suitable screwdriver with a cloth, then insert into seal cutout and pry away from engine.
3. Reverse procedure to install. Drive seal in using seal installation tool No. MD998718-01, or equivalent.

OIL PAN

REPLACE

PICKUP

1. Remove relay rod from idler arm and steering gear box using tool No. MB990778-01, or equivalent, then drain engine oil into a suitable container.
2. Separate oil pan from engine.
3. Reverse procedure to install, noting the following:

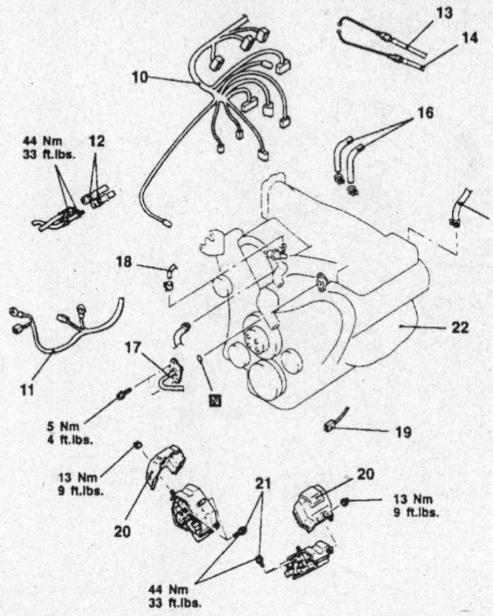
13
14
10
16
44 Nm
33 ft.lbs.
12
15
18
22
17
11
5 Nm
4 ft.lbs.
19
13 Nm
9 ft.lbs.
21
20
13 Nm
9 ft.lbs.
20
44 Nm
33 ft.lbs.

10. Engine control harness connection
11. Generator and starter harness connection
12. Engine oil cooler hose connection
13. Accelerator cable connection
14. Throttle cable connection
15. Brake booster vacuum hose connection
16. Heater hose connection
17. Fuel hose connection
18. Fuel return hose connection
19. Oil pressure switch harness connection
20. Heat protectors
21. Engine mounting bolt
22. Engine assembly

MT1069500322020X

Fig. 6 Engine replacement (Part 2 of 2). Montero w/24 valve engine

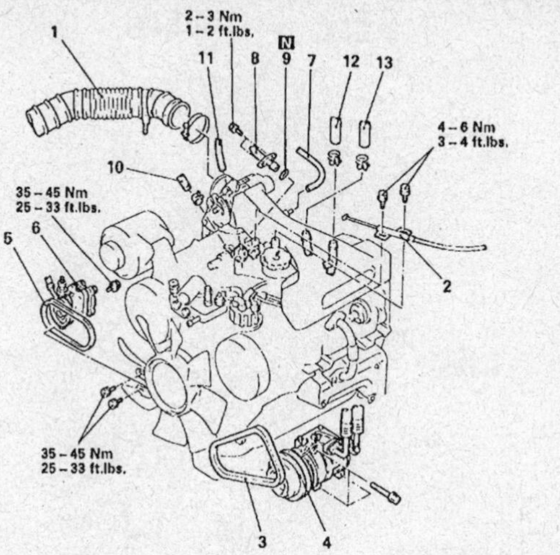
2–3 Nm
1–2 ft.lbs.
1
11
8
9
7
12
13
4–6 Nm
3–4 ft.lbs.
10
35–45 Nm
25–33 ft.lbs.
5
6
2
35–45 Nm
25–33 ft.lbs.
3
4

Removal Steps
1. Air cleaner duct
2. Accelerator cable connection
3. Air conditioner compressor drive belt
4. Compressor
5. Power steering oil pump drive belt
6. Power steering oil pump
7. Auto cruise control vacuum hose connection <Vehicles with auto cruise control>
8. High pressure fuel hose connection
9. O-ring
10. Fuel return hose connection
11. Vacuum hose connection
12. Water hose A connection
13. Water hose B connection

MT1069100313010X

Fig. 7 Engine replacement (Part 1 of 2). Pickup & Montero w/12 Valve engine

a. Ensure oil pan mating surfaces are clean, then apply Mitsubishi sealant No. MD970389 or equivalent in a continuous bead as shown, **Fig. 21.**
b. Install oil pan on engine block within 30 minutes of sealant application.
c. **Torque** oil pan mounting bolts to 4–5 ft. lbs.

MONTERO

12 Valve Engine

1. Remove skid plate, lower cover and front exhaust pipe, then drain engine oil into a suitable container.
2. Remove starter, then remove RH and LH transmission stay.
3. Remove mounting bolts and front suspension crossmember, then lower front axle as low as possible.
4. Separate oil pan from engine.
5. Reverse procedure to install, noting the following:
   a. Ensure oil pan mating surfaces are clean, then apply Mitsubishi sealant No. MD970389 or equivalent in a continuous bead as shown, **Fig. 21.**
   b. Install oil pan on engine block within 30 minutes of sealant application.
   c. **Torque** oil pan mounting bolts to 29 ft. lbs.

24 Valve Engine

Refer to "Oil Pan Replace" in the 3.5L engine section.

BELT TENSION DATA

Component	Deflection, Inch①	
	New	Used ②
Montero w/12-VALVE ENGINE		
Alternator	.26–.32	.35
Power Steering Pump	.32	.39
A/C Compressor	.20–.24	.26–.29
Montero w/24-VALVE ENGINE		
Alternator③	.22–.33	.31–.35
Power Steering Pump	.37–.45	.45–.53
A/C Compressor	.20–.24	.26–.30
Pickup		
Water Pump	.26–.32	.32–.39
Power Steering Pump	—	④
A/C Compressor	—	.33–.39

① — With 22 lbs. of force applied.

② — Used 5 minutes or more.

③ — Measured between water pump pulley & generator.

④ — 2WD, .23–.35; 4WD, .35–.47.

COOLING SYSTEM BLEED

This engine does not require a specified bleed procedure. After filling cooling system, run engine to operating temperature with radiator/pressure cap off. Air will then be automatically bled through cap opening.

THERMOSTAT

REPLACE

1. Drain cooling system into appropriate container.
2. Disconnect radiator hose from thermostat housing.
3. Remove thermostat housing retaining bolts, then the thermostat housing and thermostat.
4. Reverse procedure to install.

WATER PUMP

REPLACE

Remove water pump in numbered sequence as shown in **Figs. 22 and 23,** noting the following:

1. Drain cooling system into appropriate container.
2. Relieve fuel system pressure as described under "Precautions."
3. Reverse procedure to install, noting the following:

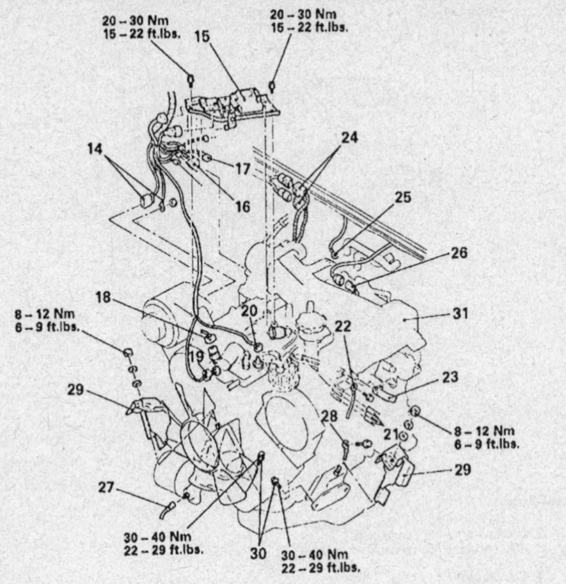

20 – 30 Nm
15 – 22 ft.lbs.
20 – 30 Nm
15 – 22 ft.lbs.
8 – 12 Nm
6 – 9 ft.lbs.
8 – 12 Nm
6 – 9 ft.lbs.
30 – 40 Nm
22 – 29 ft.lbs.
30 – 40 Nm
22 – 29 ft.lbs.

14. Alternator connector
15. Ignition coil and power transistor assembly
16. I.S.C. connector
17. Throttle position sensor connector
18. Engine coolant temperature switch connector <A/C>
19. Engine coolant temperature sensor connector
20. Engine coolant temperature gauge unit connector
21. Emission control vacuum hose connection
22. Ground cable connection
23. Brake booster vacuum hose connection
24. Control wiring harness connector
25. Ground cable connection
26. EGR temperature sensor connector
27. Oil pressure gauge unit connector
28. Ground cable connection
29. Heat protector
30. Engine mounting bolt
31. Engine assembly

MT1069100313020X

Fig. 7 Engine replacement (Part 2 of 2). Pickup & Montero w/12 Valve engine

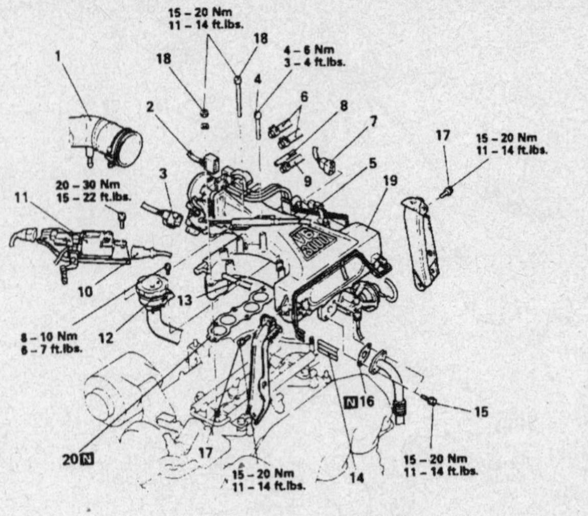

15 – 20 Nm
11 – 14 ft.lbs.
4 – 6 Nm
3 – 4 ft.lbs.
15 – 20 Nm
11 – 14 ft.lbs.
20 – 30 Nm
15 – 22 ft.lbs.
8 – 10 Nm
6 – 7 ft.lbs.
15 – 20 Nm
11 – 14 ft.lbs.
15 – 20 Nm
11 – 14 ft.lbs.

Removal steps

1. Air intake hose connection
2. Throttle position sensor connector
3. Idle air control motor connector
4. Accelerator cable adjusting bolt
5. Accelerator cable connection
6. Water hose connection
7. EGR temperature sensor connector
8. Vacuum hose connection
9. Brake booster vacuum hose connection
10. High tension cable connection
11. Ignition coil
12. Engine oil filler tube bracket
13. PCV hose connection
14. Vacuum hose connection
15. EGR pipe attaching bolt
16. Gasket
17. Bolt
18. Bolt and nut
19. Intake manifold plenum and throttle body
20. Intake manifold plenum gasket

MT1059500042010X

Fig. 8 Intake manifold replacement (Part 1 of 2). 12 valve engine

a. Coat O-ring with water to ease installation.
b. Tighten water pump attaching bolts to specifications.

RADIATOR

REPLACE

1. Drain engine coolant into suitable container, then remove engine under cover.
2. **On models equipped with 24 valve engines,** remove air cleaner case.
3. **On all models,** remove transmission oil cooler hose.
4. Remove radiator upper hose and radiator shroud, over flow hose and reserve tank.
5. Remove radiator lower hose, then radiator.
6. Reverse procedure to install.

FUEL PUMP

REPLACE

MONTERO

1. Remove drain plug from fuel tank and drain fuel into suitable container, then remove cargo compartment carpet.
2. Release fuel system pressure as described under "Precautions."
3. Remove floor cover, then packing.
4. Disconnect fuel pump electrical connection.
5. Disconnect high pressure fuel hose at body side main pipe connection, then at pump side connection.
6. Disconnect fuel return hose connection.
7. Remove fuel pump assembly.
8. Reverse procedure to install.

PICKUP

1. Disconnect battery ground cable.
2. Release fuel system pressure as described under "Precautions."
3. Drain fuel tank into a suitable container.
4. Lower fuel tank using suitable jack.
5. Disconnect all electrical and hose connections.
6. Remove fuel pump/sending unit retaining nuts.
7. Remove fuel pump from fuel tank.
8. Reverse procedure to install, noting the following:
   a. Install check valve as shown, **Fig. 24.**
   b. Install overfill limiter valve with arrow pointing toward engine side fuel hose.
   c. Do not allow the main hose to become twisted when tightening.

FUEL FILTER

REPLACE

1. Disconnect battery ground cable.
2. Release fuel system pressure as described under "Precautions."
3. Drain fuel tank into a suitable container.
4. Hold fuel filter with a wrench and remove eye bolt retaining fuel high pressure hose with an eye wrench, **Fig. 25.**
5. Inspect hose and pipes for cracks, damage or clogging and replace as necessary.
6. Inspect evaporative emission canister for clogging and replace as necessary.
7. Inspect check valve and fuel filter for clogging or damage and replace as necessary.
8. Remove protector of fuel filter, then disconnect fuel filter mounting bolt.
9. Remove fuel filter and high pressure hose assembly.
10. Reverse procedure to install.

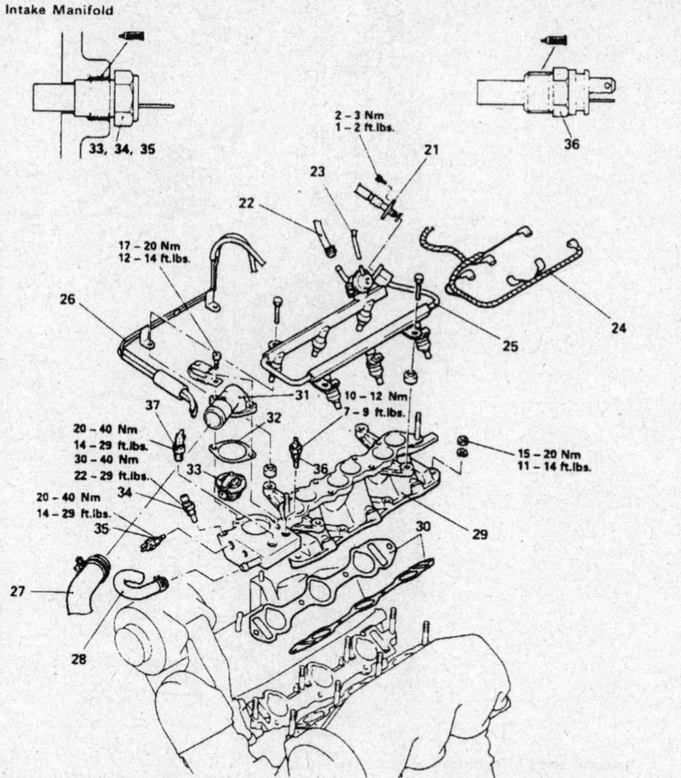
Intake Manifold
33, 34, 35
36
2 – 3 Nm
1 – 2 ft.lbs.
21
23
22
17 – 20 Nm
12 – 14 ft.lbs.
26
24
25
31
10 – 12 Nm
7 – 9 ft.lbs.
37
32
20 – 40 Nm
14 – 29 ft.lbs.
30 – 40 Nm
22 – 29 ft.lbs.
33
36
15 – 20 Nm
11 – 14 ft.lbs.
20 – 40 Nm
14 – 29 ft.lbs.
34
35
30
29
27
28

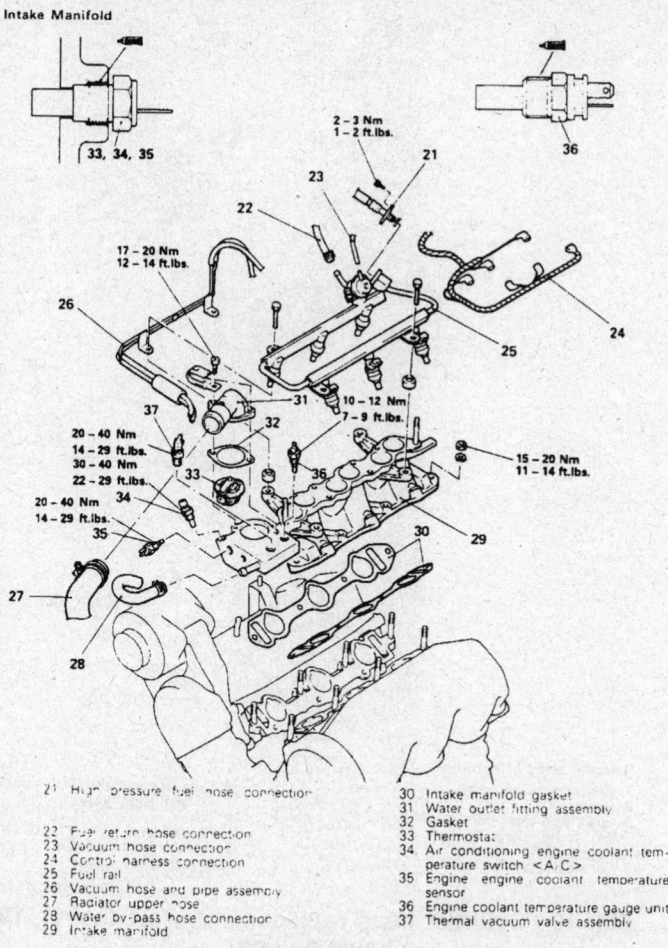

21 High pressure fuel hose connection
22 Fuel return hose connection
23 Vacuum hose connection
24 Control harness connection
25 Fuel rail
26 Vacuum hose and pipe assembly
27 Radiator upper hose
28 Water by-pass hose connection
29 Intake manifold
30 Intake manifold gasket
31 Water outlet fitting assembly
32 Gasket
33 Thermostat
34 Air conditioning engine coolant temperature switch <A/C>
35 Engine engine coolant temperature sensor
36 Engine coolant temperature gauge unit
37 Thermal vacuum valve assembly

MT1059500042020X

Fig. 8 Intake manifold replacement (Part 2 of 2). 12 valve engine

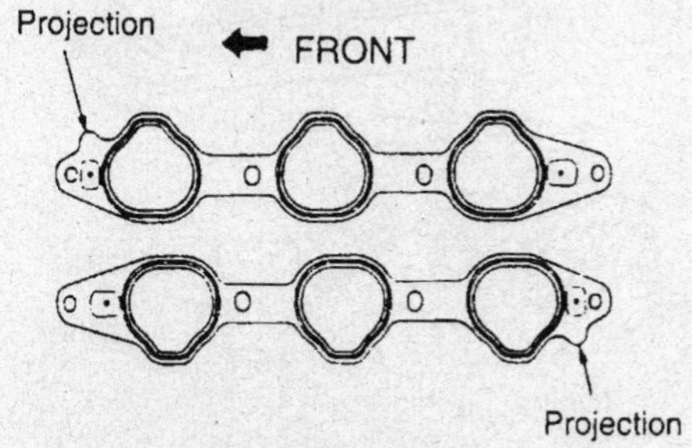
Projection
FRONT
Projection

MT1059500044000X

Fig. 10 Intake manifold gasket installation

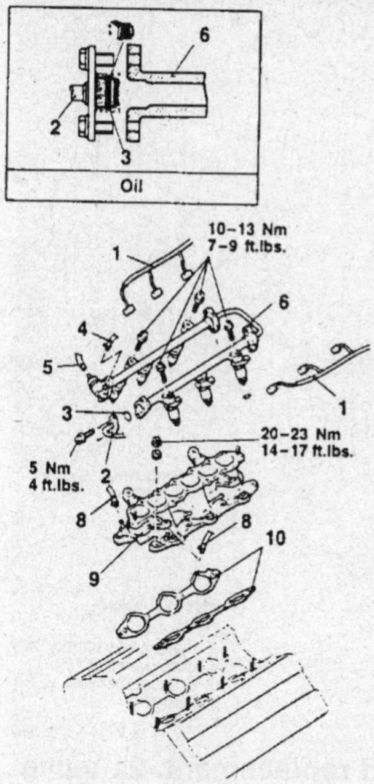
Oil
6
2
3
10–13 Nm
7–9 ft.lbs.
1
4
5
6
3
1
20–23 Nm
14–17 ft.lbs.
5 Nm
4 ft.lbs.
2
8
8
10
9

Removal steps

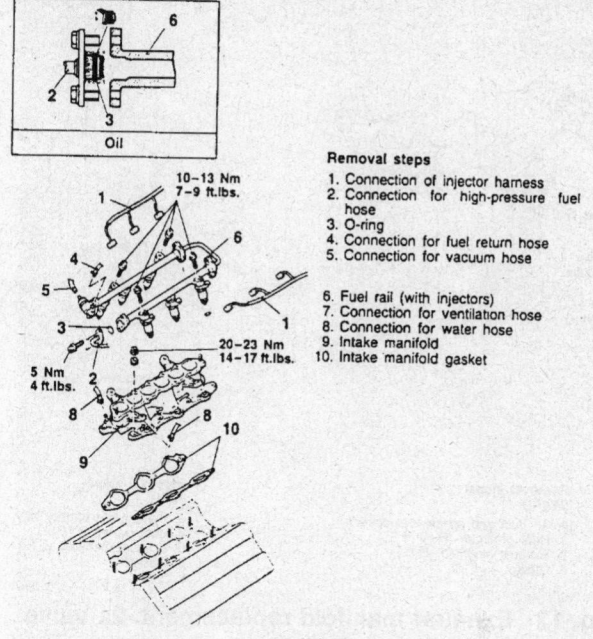

1. Connection of injector harness
2. Connection for high-pressure fuel hose
3. O-ring
4. Connection for fuel return hose
5. Connection for vacuum hose
6. Fuel rail (with injectors)
7. Connection for ventilation hose
8. Connection for water hose
9. Intake manifold
10. Intake manifold gasket

MT1059500043000X

Fig. 9 Intake manifold replacement. 24 valve engine

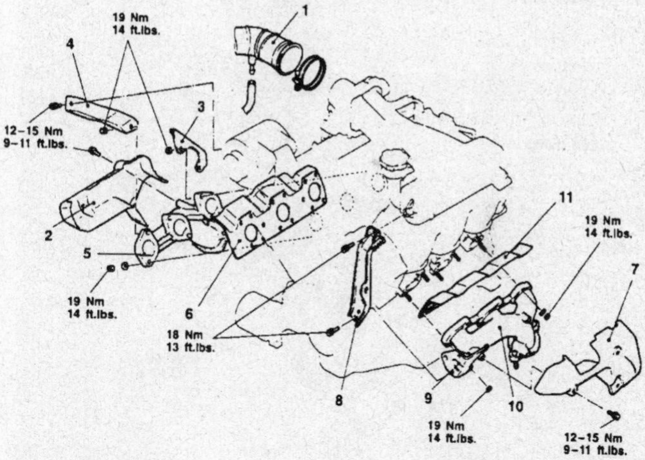
1
19 Nm
14 ft.lbs.
4
3
12–15 Nm
9–11 ft.lbs.
2
5
19 Nm
14 ft.lbs.
6
18 Nm
13 ft.lbs.
11
19 Nm
14 ft.lbs.
7
8
9
10
19 Nm
14 ft.lbs.
12–15 Nm
9–11 ft.lbs.

Removal steps (Right)

1. Air duct
2. Heat protector
3. Engine hanger
4. Generator stay
5. Exhaust manifold
6. Exhaust manifold gasket

Removal steps (Left)

7. Heat protector
8. Air intake plenum stay (front)
9. Bracket
10. Exhaust manifold
11. Exhaust manifold gasket

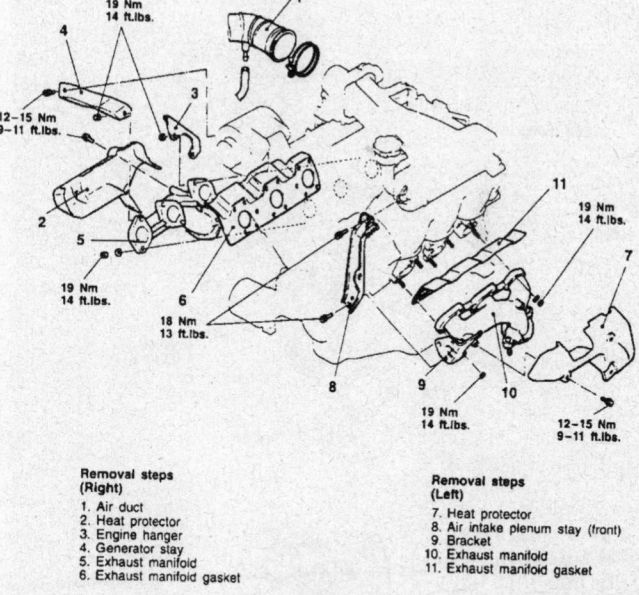

MT1079500019000X

Fig. 11 Exhaust manifold replacement. 12 valve engine

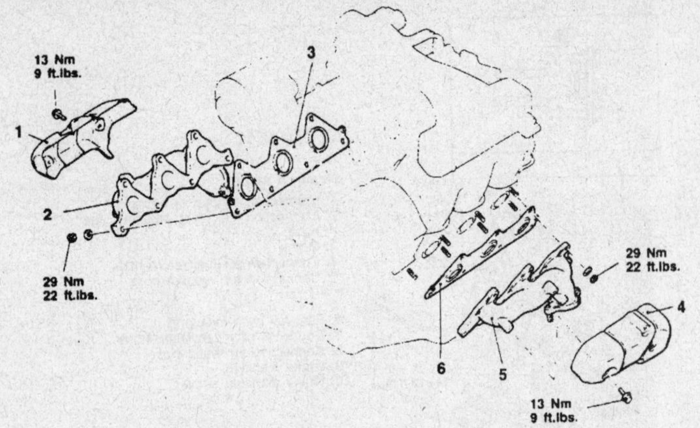
13 Nm
9 ft.lbs.
1
2
3
29 Nm
22 ft.lbs.
29 Nm
22 ft.lbs.
4
5
6
13 Nm
9 ft.lbs.

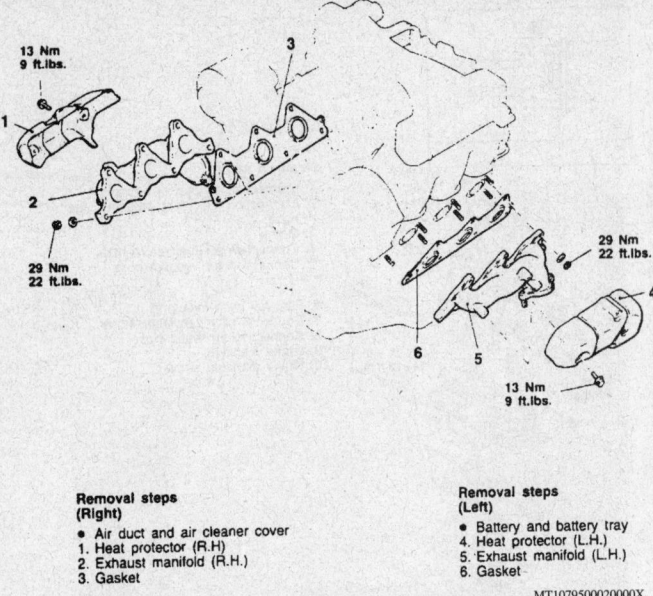

Removal steps (Right)
- Air duct and air cleaner cover
1. Heat protector (R.H)
2. Exhaust manifold (R.H.)
3. Gasket

Removal steps (Left)
- Battery and battery tray
4. Heat protector (L.H.)
5. Exhaust manifold (L.H.)
6. Gasket

MT1079500020000X

Fig. 12 Exhaust manifold replacement. 24 valve engine

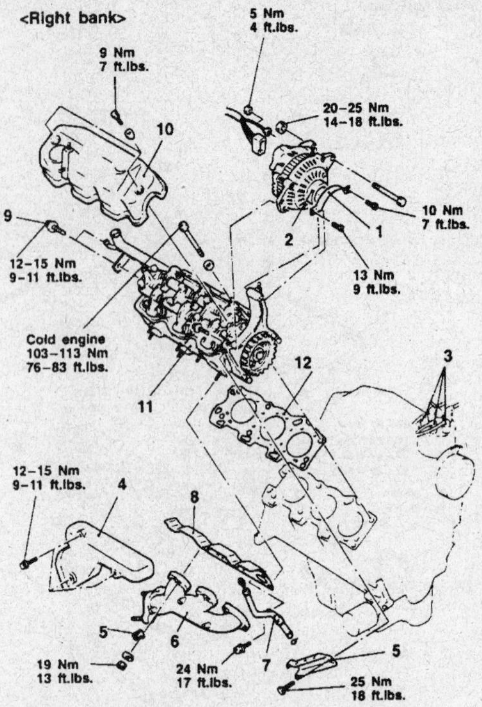
<Right bank>
5 Nm
4 ft.lbs.
9 Nm
7 ft.lbs.
10
20–25 Nm
14–18 ft.lbs.
9
10 Nm
7 ft.lbs.
2
1
12–15 Nm
9–11 ft.lbs.
13 Nm
9 ft.lbs.
Cold engine
103–113 Nm
76–83 ft.lbs.
12
3
11
12–15 Nm
9–11 ft.lbs.
4
8
5
6
19 Nm
13 ft.lbs.
24 Nm
17 ft.lbs.
7
5
25 Nm
18 ft.lbs.

Removal steps of right bank
1. Generator pulley cover
2. Generator
3. Spark plug cable connection (No. 1, No. 3 and No. 5)
4. Heat protector
5. Generator stay
6. Exhaust manifold (R.H.)
7. Oil level gage guide
9. Bolt
10. Rocker cover
11. Cylinder head assembly
12. Cylinder head gasket

MT1069500327010X

Fig. 13 Cylinder head replacement (Part 1 of 2). 12 valve engine

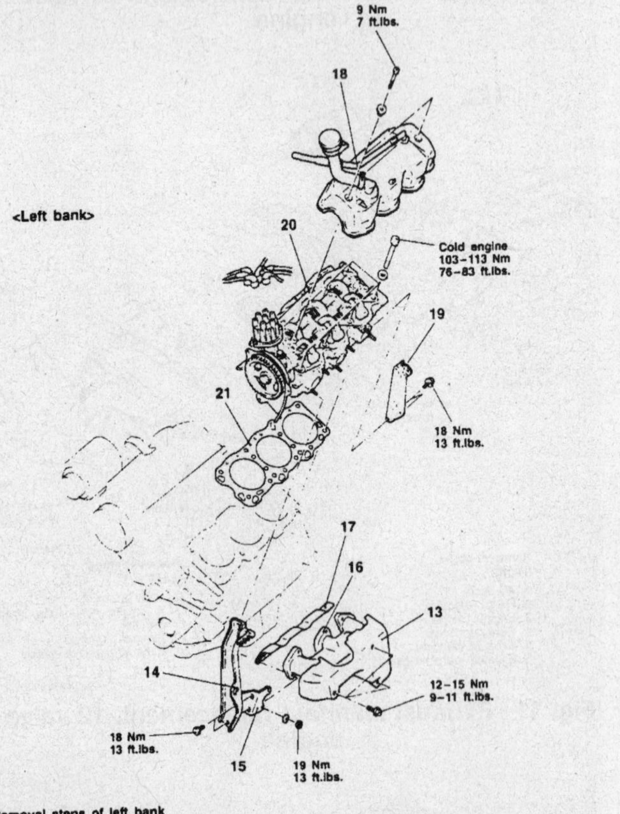
9 Nm
7 ft.lbs.
18
<Left bank>
20
Cold engine
103–113 Nm
76–83 ft.lbs.
19
21
18 Nm
13 ft.lbs.
17
16
13
14
12–15 Nm
9–11 ft.lbs.
18 Nm
13 ft.lbs.
15
19 Nm
13 ft.lbs.

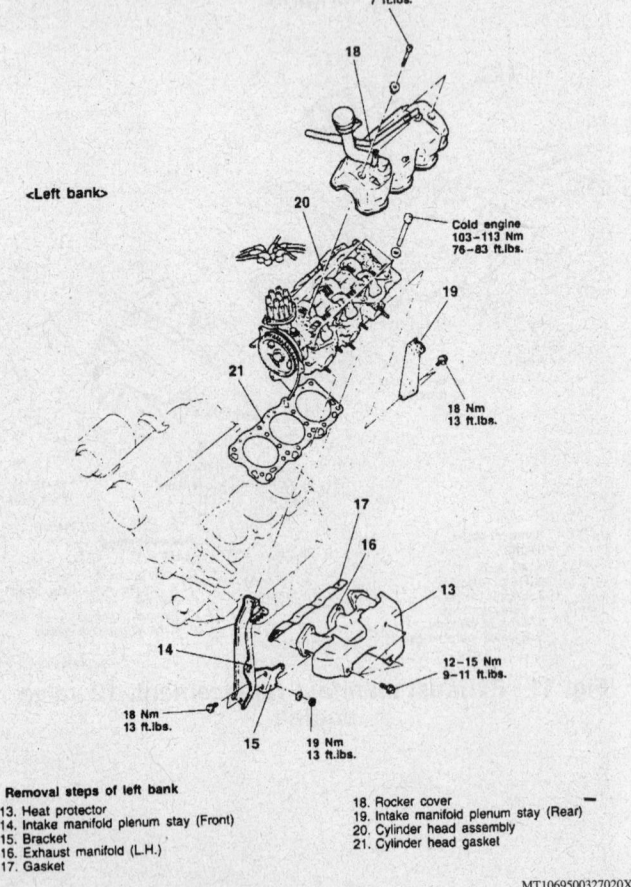

Removal steps of left bank
13. Heat protector
14. Intake manifold plenum stay (Front)
15. Bracket
16. Exhaust manifold (L.H.)
17. Gasket
18. Rocker cover
19. Intake manifold plenum stay (Rear)
20. Cylinder head assembly
21. Cylinder head gasket

MT1069500327020X

Fig. 13 Cylinder head replacement (Part 2 of 2). 12 valve engine

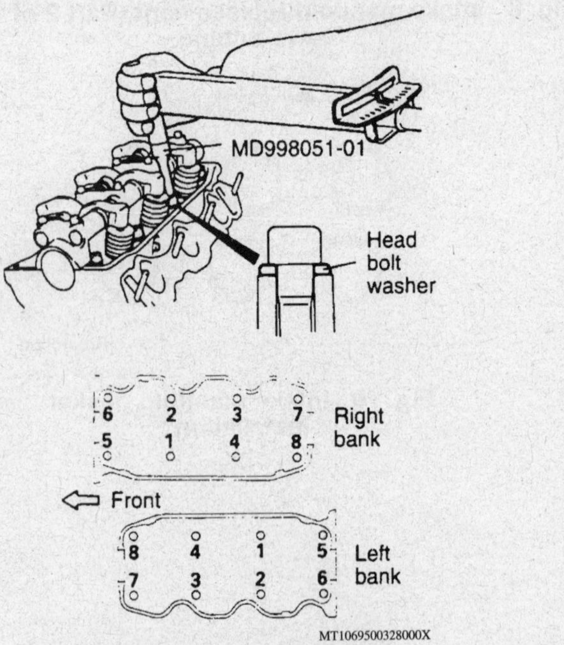
MD998051-01
Head bolt washer
6 2 3 7
5 1 4 8
Right bank
Front
8 4 1 5
7 3 2 6
Left bank

MT1069500328000X

Fig. 14 Cylinder head bolt sequence. 3.0L 12 valve engine

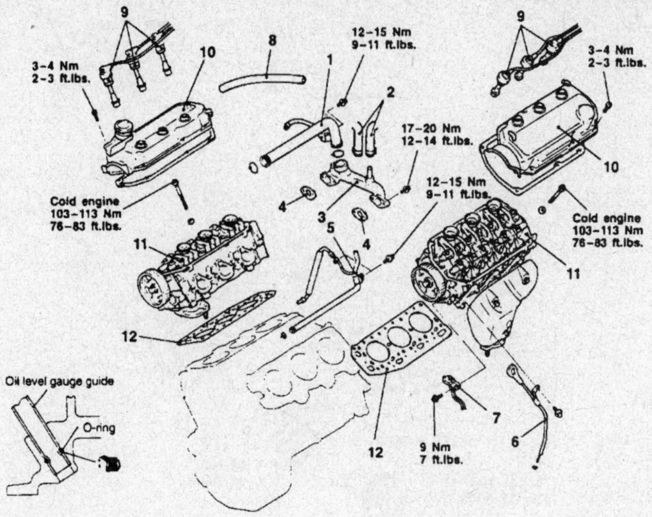
3-4 Nm
2-3 ft.lbs.
12-15 Nm
9-11 ft.lbs.
17-20 Nm
12-14 ft.lbs.
12-15 Nm
9-11 ft.lbs.
Cold engine
103-113 Nm
76-83 ft.lbs.
Cold engine
103-113 Nm
76-83 ft.lbs.
Oil level gauge guide
O-ring
9 Nm
7 ft.lbs.

Removal steps

1. Water outlet pipe
2. Heater hose
3. Water passage
4. Gasket
5. Water pipe and hose assembly
6. Oil level gage guide <Only left bank is removed>
7. Camshaft position sensor <Only left bank is removed>
8. Ventilation hose
9. Spark plug cable
10. Rocker cover
11. Cylinder head assembly
12. Cylinder head gasket

MT1069500329000X

Fig. 15 Cylinder head replacement. 24 valve engine

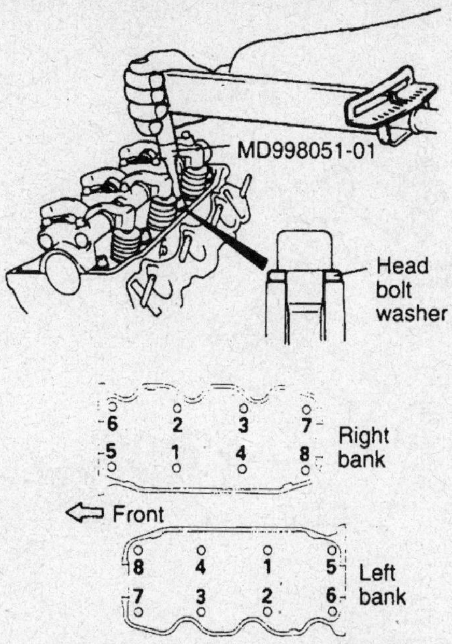
MD998051-01
Head
bolt
washer
6 2 3 7
5 1 4 8
Right
bank
Front
8 4 1 5
7 3 2 6
Left
bank

MT1069500330000X

Fig. 16 Cylinder head bolt sequence. 24 valve engine

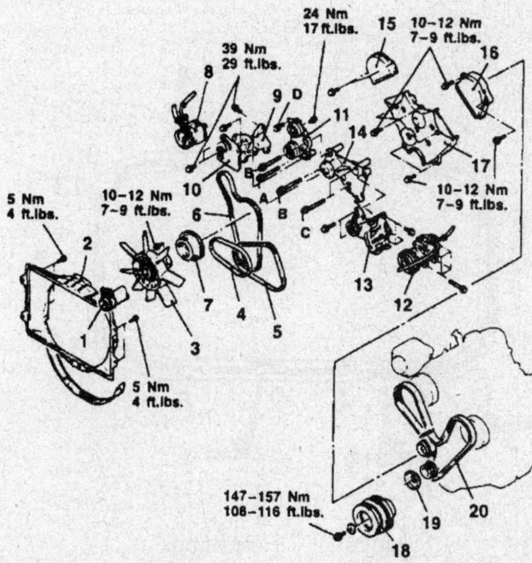
24 Nm
17 ft.lbs.
10-12 Nm
7-9 ft.lbs.
39 Nm
29 ft.lbs.
5 Nm
4 ft.lbs.
10-12 Nm
7-9 ft.lbs.
10-12 Nm
7-9 ft.lbs.
5 Nm
4 ft.lbs.
147-157 Nm
108-116 ft.lbs.

Symbol	Hardness category	d × ℓ mm (in.)	Torque Nm (ft.lbs.)	Note
A	7T	10 × 85 (.39 × 3.34)	42 (30)	
B		10 × 95 (.39 × 3.74)		
C		12 × 100 (.47 × 3.93)	75 (54)	
D		8 × 20 (.31 × .79)	16 (12)	

Removal steps

1. Radiator upper hose connection
2. Radiator shroud
3. Cooling fan clutch assembly
• *Adjustment of drive belt tension*

4. Drive belt (Power steering)
5. Drive belt <A/C>
6. Drive belt (Generator, *Cooling fan*)
7. Cooling fan pulley
8. Power steering oil pump
9. Oil pump bracket
10. Oil pump mounting bracket
11. Tension pulley bracket
12. Compressor <A/C>
13. Compressor bracket
14. *Cooling fan bracket assembly*
15. Timing belt cover outer (A)
16. Timing belt cover outer (B)
17. Timing belt cover outer (C)
18. *Crankshaft pulley*
19. Front flange
20. Timing belt

MT1069500323000X

Fig. 17 Timing belt replacement. 12 valve engine

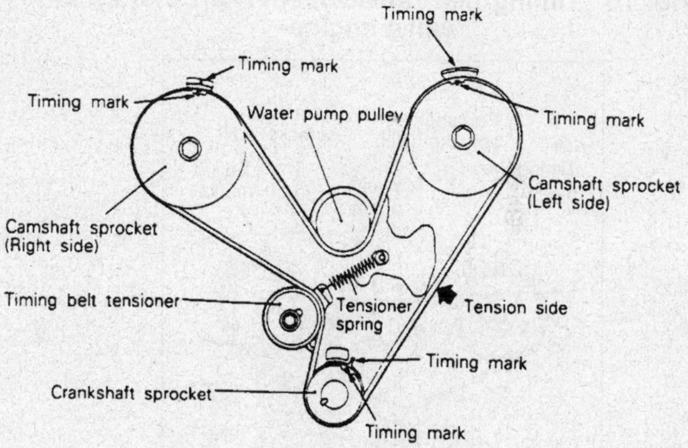
Timing mark
Timing mark
Timing mark
Water pump pulley
Timing mark
Camshaft sprocket
(Right side)
Camshaft sprocket
(Left side)
Timing belt tensioner
Tensioner
spring
Tension side
Timing mark
Crankshaft sprocket
Timing mark

MT1069500324000X

Fig. 18 Timing marks. 12 valve engine

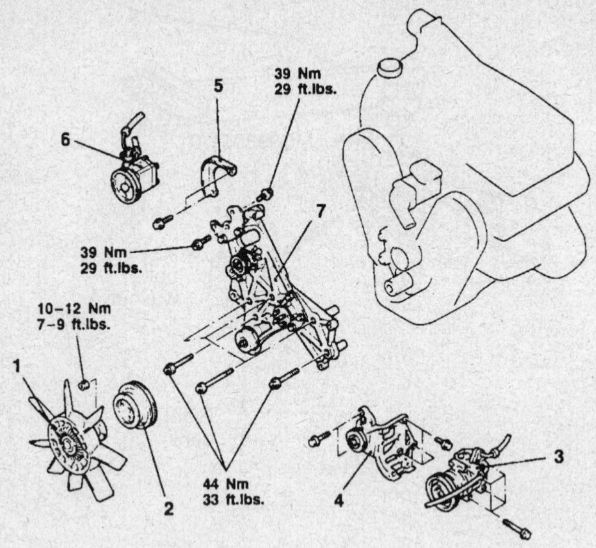
39 Nm
29 ft.lbs.
5
6
7
39 Nm
29 ft.lbs.
10–12 Nm
7–9 ft.lbs.
1
2
44 Nm
33 ft.lbs.
4
3

Removal steps

1. Cooling fan clutch assembly
2. Water pump pulley
3. Compressor <A/C>
4. Compressor bracket <A/C>
5. Cover
6. Power steering oil pump
7. Accessory mount

MT1069500325010X

Fig. 19 Timing belt replacement (Part 1 of 2). 24 valve engine

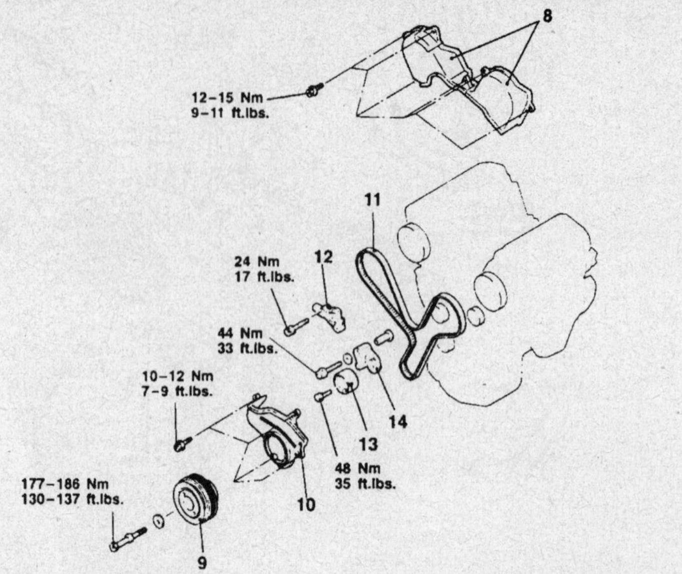
8
12–15 Nm
9–11 ft.lbs.
11
24 Nm
17 ft.lbs.
12
44 Nm
33 ft.lbs.
10–12 Nm
7–9 ft.lbs.
14
13
48 Nm
35 ft.lbs.
177–186 Nm
130–137 ft.lbs.
10
9

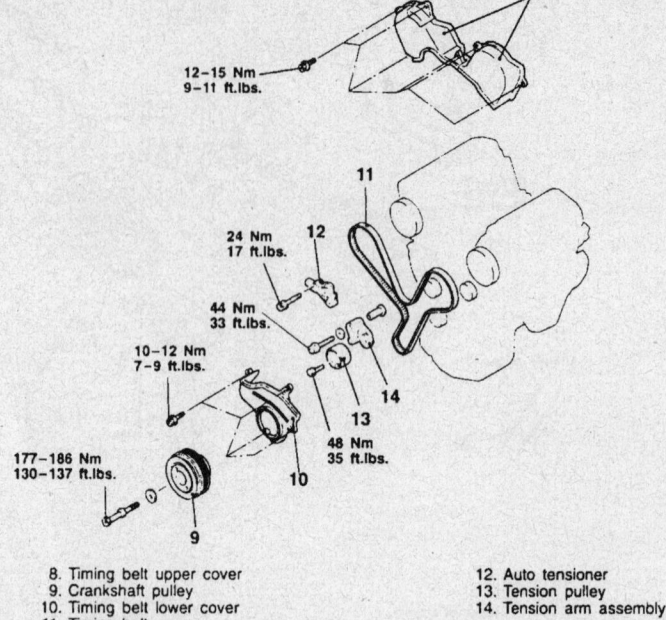

8. Timing belt upper cover
9. Crankshaft pulley
10. Timing belt lower cover
11. Timing belt
12. Auto tensioner
13. Tension pulley
14. Tension arm assembly

MT1069500325020X

Fig. 19 Timing belt replacement (Part 2 of 2). 24 valve engine

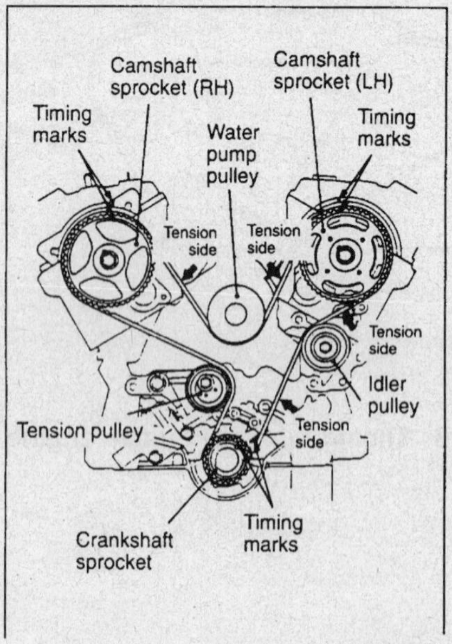
Camshaft sprocket (RH)
Camshaft sprocket (LH)
Timing marks
Water pump pulley
Timing marks
Tension side
Tension side
Tension side
Idler pulley
Tension pulley
Tension side
Crankshaft sprocket
Timing marks

MT1069500326000X

Fig. 20 Timing marks. 24 valve engine

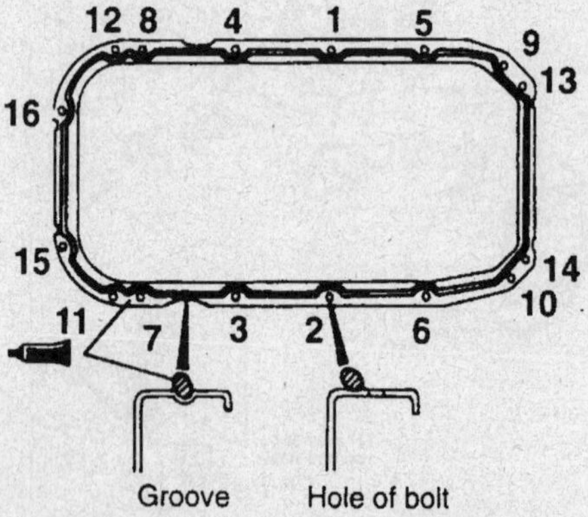
12 8
4
1
5
9
13
16
15
14
10
11
7
3
2
6
Groove
Hole of bolt

MT1099500059000X

Fig. 21 Oil pan sealant application & bolt tightening sequence

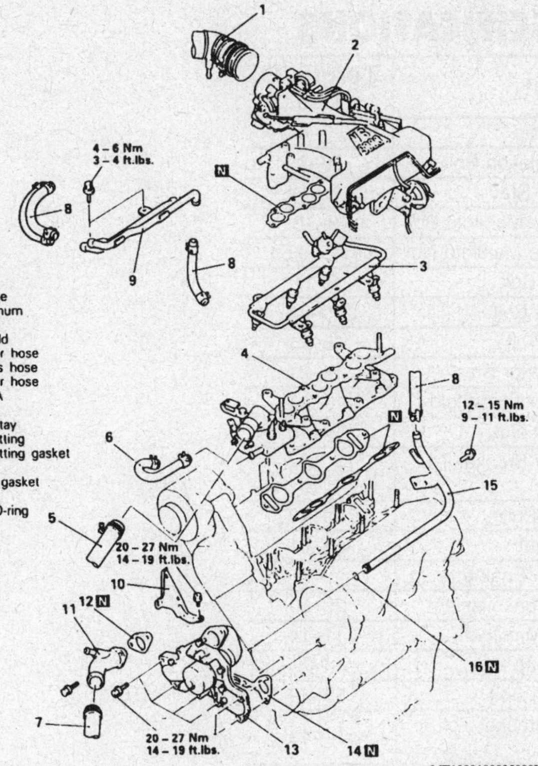
4 – 6 Nm
3 – 4 ft.lbs.
12 – 15 Nm
9 – 11 ft.lbs.
20 – 27 Nm
14 – 19 ft.lbs.
20 – 27 Nm
14 – 19 ft.lbs.

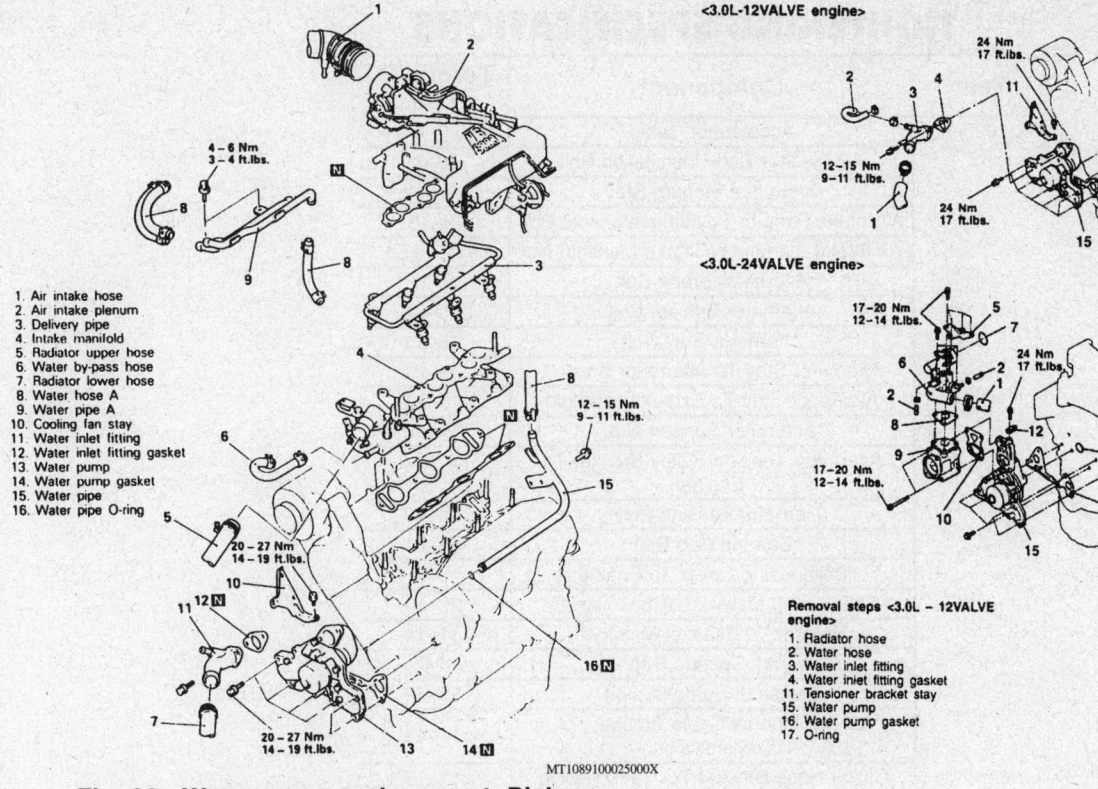

1. Air intake hose
2. Air intake plenum
3. Delivery pipe
4. Intake manifold
5. Radiator upper hose
6. Water by-pass hose
7. Radiator lower hose
8. Water hose A
9. Water pipe A
10. Cooling fan stay
11. Water inlet fitting
12. Water inlet fitting gasket
13. Water pump
14. Water pump gasket
15. Water pipe
16. Water pipe O-ring

MT1089100025000X

Fig. 22 Water pump replacement. Pickup

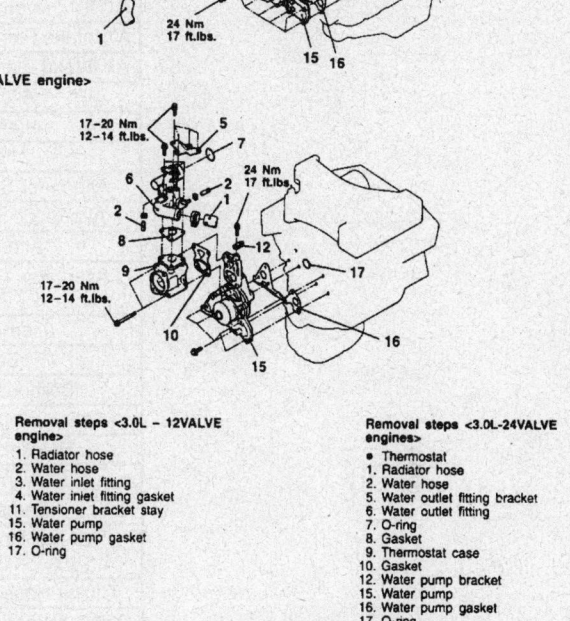

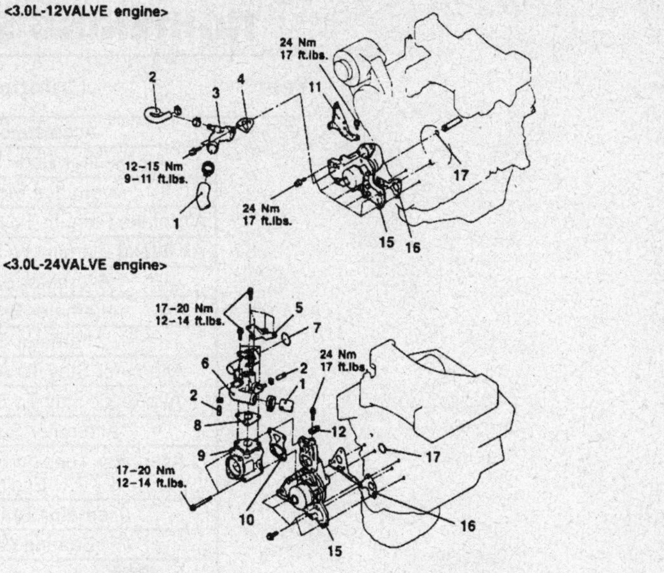
<3.0L-12VALVE engine>
24 Nm
17 ft.lbs.
12–15 Nm
9–11 ft.lbs.
24 Nm
17 ft.lbs.
<3.0L-24VALVE engine>
17–20 Nm
12–14 ft.lbs.
24 Nm
17 ft.lbs.
17–20 Nm
12–14 ft.lbs.

Removal steps <3.0L – 12VALVE engine>

1. Radiator hose
2. Water hose
3. Water inlet fitting
4. Water inlet fitting gasket
11. Tensioner bracket stay
15. Water pump
16. Water pump gasket
17. O-ring

Removal steps <3.0L-24VALVE engines>

- Thermostat
1. Radiator hose
2. Water hose
5. Water outlet fitting bracket
6. Water outlet fitting
7. O-ring
8. Gasket
9. Thermostat case
10. Gasket
12. Water pump bracket
15. Water pump
16. Water pump gasket
17. O-ring

MT1089500078000X

Fig. 23 Water pump replacement. Montero

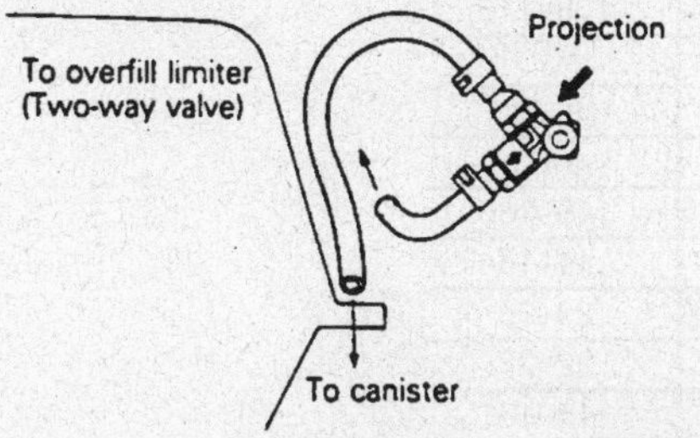
Projection
To overfill limiter
(Two-way valve)
To canister

MT1089100026000X

Fig. 24 Check valve installation. Pickup

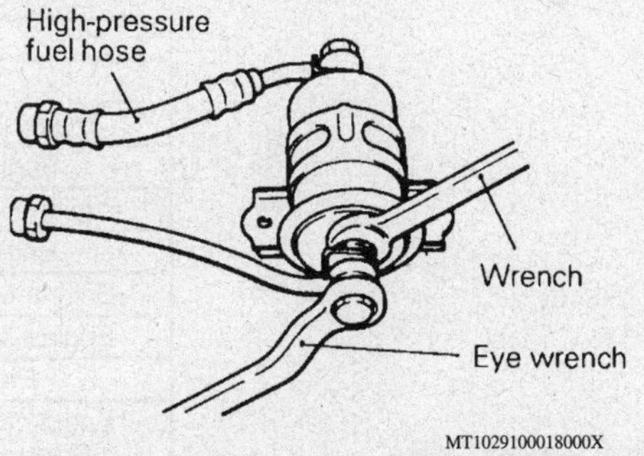
High-pressure
fuel hose
Wrench
Eye wrench

MT1029100018000X

Fig. 25 Fuel filter replacement

TIGHTENING SPECIFICATIONS

Year	Component	Torque/Ft. Lbs.
1993–96	Accelerator Cable	3–4
	Air Cleaner Body Installation Bolt	6–7
	Air Intake Plenum Stay	11–14
	Air Intake Plenum To Intake Manifold Bolt	9–10
	Air Intake Plenum To Intake Manifold Nut	7.5–9.5
	Alternator Brace Bolt	8–11
	Alternator Bracket Bolt	15–21
	Alternator Stay Bolt	15–21
	Alternator Stay To Alternator Bracket	14–21
	Alternator Stay To Exhaust Manifold	11–16
	Alternator Support Nut	14–18
	Alternator Tension Pulley Bracket To Engine	24–36
	Alternator Tension Pulley	29–43
	Bearing Cap Bolt	55–61
	Bellhousing Cover To Engine	6–7
	Bellhousing Cover To Transmission	22–30
	Bracket To Exhaust Manifold	11–14
	Camshaft Bearing Cap Bolt	⑩
	Camshaft Sprocket Bolt	58–72
	Clutch Control Cable Bracket To Transmission	11–16
	Clutch Hose Bracket To Transmission	11–16
	Clutch Release Cylinder To Transmission	11–16
	Connecting Rod Cap Nut	37–38
	Cooling Fan Bracket	③
	Cooling Fan To Cooling Fan Bracket	7–9
	Crankshaft Pulley	108–116
	Cylinder Head Bolt	①
	Distributor Adapter To Engine	9–10
	Distributor Adapter Bolt	9–11
	Driveshaft Nut	145–188
	EGR Pipe	11–14
	Engine Damper To Crossmember	29–36
	Engine Damper To Engine	22–28
	Engine Hanger To Exhaust Manifold	11–16
	Engine Mount Bracket Nut	44–57
	Engine Mount Insulator Nut (Large)	44–57
	Engine Mount Insulator Nut (Small)	22–28
	Engine Mount Insulator	22–29
	Engine Mounting Rear Insulator To Engine Support Rear Bracket⑥	11–18
	Engine Mounting Rear Insulator To Engine⑤	13–18
	Engine Oil Feed Hose Assembly To Engine Oil Cooler	22–25
	Engine Oil Return Hose Assembly To Engine Oil Cooler	22–25
	Engine Support Bracket (Left)	15–21
	Engine Support Bracket (Right)	②
	Engine Support Bracket	⑨
	Engine Support Rear Bracket To Engine⑥	13–18
	Engine To Engine Mounting Front Insulator	9–15
	Engine To Transmission Stay (Right)	⑦
	Exhaust Manifold To Engine	11–16
	Flywheel/Driveplate Bolt	53–55

Continued

TIGHTENING SPECIFICATIONS—Continued

Year	Component	Torque/Ft. Lbs.
1993–96	Front Exhaust Pipe To Exhaust Manifold	22–28
	Front Insulator Stopper To Frame	22–29
	Front Roll Stopper Bracket To Center member	29–36
	Front Roll Stopper Insulator Nut	37–47
	Front Suspension Crossmember To Differential	58–72
	Front Suspension Crossmember To Frame	72–87
	Fuel High Pressure Hose To Delivery Pipe	18–25
	Fuel Hose Clamp To Rear Cylinder Head	9–10
	Heat Protector To Engine Mount Insulator	6–9
	Heat Protector To Exhaust Manifold	9–11
	Heat Protector	4–7
	High Pressure Fuel Hose	④
	Ignition Coil Assembly Bolt	14–22
	Intake Manifold To Engine	11–14
	Lower Arm Ball Joint To Knuckle	44–52
	No. 2 Crossmember To Frame	40–54
	Oil Cooler Hose	29–32
	Oil Filter Bracket Bolt	9–11
	Oil Level Gauge Guide To Engine	14–21
	Oil Pan Bolt	4–6
	Oil Pan Drain Plug	26–32
	Oil Pressure Switch	6–9
	Oil Pump Bracket	25–33
	Oil Pump Case Bolt	9–10
	Oil Pump Cover Screw	6–9
	Oil Pump Mounting Bracket	25–33
	Oil Relief Valve Plug	29–36
	Oil Screen Bolt	11–15
	Plate To Frame	13–18
	Plate To Transfer Mounting Insulator	13–18
	Power Steering Oil Pump Bracket To Front Cylinder Head	13–18
	Power Steering Oil Pump To Bracket	13–18
	Power Steering Oil Pump	25–33
	Power Steering Pressure Hose To Oil Pump	29–36
	Radiator Shroud To Radiator	2–5
	Radiator Upper Shroud To Radiator Lower Shroud	6–8
	Rear Engine Support Member To Frame⑥	7–9
	Rear Engine Support Member To No. 2 Crossmember⑥	13–18
	Rear Plate Bolt	6–7
	Rear Roll Stopper Bracket To Crossmember	29–36
	Rear Roll Stopper Insulator Nut	22–29
	Rocker Arm And Shaft Assembly	14–15
	Rocker Cover Bolt	6–7
	Roll Stopper Bracket (A)	24–36
	Roll Stopper Bracket (B)	⑧

Continued

TIGHTENING SPECIFICATIONS—Continued

Year	Component	Torque/Ft. Lbs.
1993–96	Starter Bolt	20–25
	Support Plate To No. 2 Crossmember⑤	13–18
	Tension Adjusting Bolt	14–20
	Tension Pulley Bracket	24–36
	Tie Rod End To Knuckle	18–24
	Timing Belt Cover Bolt	7–9
	Timing Belt Tensioner Bolt	16–21
	Transmission Mount Bracket To Body	29–36
	Transmission Mount Bracket To Transaxle	44–57
	Transmission Mount Insulator Nut	44–57
	Transmission Mounting Plate	7.5–8.5
	Transmission Stay To Engine	47–61
	Transfer Mounting Bracket To Transfer	22–29
	Transmission Stay To Transmission Assembly	22–30
	Water Inlet Pipe To Front Cylinder Head	9–10
	Water Pump Bolts	14–20

①— Engine cold, 65–72 ft. lbs.; w/engine warm, 73–79 ft. lbs.

②— 10 X 22 mm (0.39 X 0.87 inch) bolts, 24–36 ft. lbs.; 12 X 22 mm (0.47 X 0.87 inch) & 12 X 32 mm (0.47 X 1.26 inch) bolts, 47–61 ft. lbs.

③— Except 12 X 100 mm (0.47 X 3.93 inch) bolts, 24–36 ft. lbs.; 12 X 100 mm (0.47 X 3.93 inch) bolts, 47–61 ft. lbs.

④— Montero, 7–9 ft. lbs.; Pickup, 12–24 inch lbs.

⑤— Models w/manual transmission.

⑥— Models w/automatic transmission.

⑦— 10 X 30 mm (0.39 X 1.18 inch) bolts, 24–36 ft. lbs.; 12 X 35 mm (0.47 X 1.37 inch) & 12 X 50 mm (0.47 X 1.96 inch) bolts, 47–61 ft. lbs.

⑧— 10 X 25 mm (0.39 X 0.98 inch) bolts, 24–36 ft. lbs.; 12 X 30 mm (0.47 X 1.18 inch) bolts, 47–61 ft. lbs.

⑨— 10 X 53 mm (0.39 X 2.09 inch) bolts, 47–54 ft. lbs.; 12 X 56 mm (0.47 X 2.20 inch) bolts, 76–83 ft. lbs.; 10 X 450 mm (0.39 X 1.57 inch) bolts, 26–36 ft. lbs.

⑩— Bearing cap bolts No. 2, 3 & 4 8 ft. lbs. Bearing caps front & rear, 14 ft. lbs.

3.5L Engine

NOTE: On Air Bag Equipped Models, Refer To "Air Bag System Precautions" Located In The Front Of This Manual For System Disarming & Arming Procedures.

INDEX

	Page No.
Belt Tension Data	28-29
Compression Pressure	28-27
Cooling System Bleed	28-29
Crankshaft Seal, Replace	28-28
Front	28-28
Rear	28-29
Cylinder Head, Replace	28-28
Engine Mount, Replace	28-27
Engine Oil Cooler, Replace	28-29
Engine Rebuilding Specifications	29-1
Engine, Replace	28-27
Exhaust Manifold, Replace	28-28
Fuel Filter, Replace	28-31
Fuel Pump, Replace	28-30
Intake Manifold, Replace	28-27
Oil Pan, Replace	28-29
Lower	28-29
Upper	28-29
Precautions	28-27
Air Bag Systems	28-27
Fuel System Pressure Relief	28-27
Radiator, Replace	28-30
Thermostat, Replace	28-30
Tightening Specifications	28-33
Timing Belt, Replace	28-28
Valve Adjustment	28-28
Water Pump, Replace	28-30

PRECAUTIONS

AIR BAG SYSTEMS

Refer to "Air Bag System Precautions" in the front of this manual for system disarming and arming procedures.

FUEL SYSTEM PRESSURE RELIEF

1. Remove carpet from cargo compartment, then remove bolts from floor cover.
2. Disconnect fuel pump electrical connection.
3. Start engine and let idle until all residual fuel is consumed, then turn ignition switch to Off position. **Failure to relieve fuel system pressure prior to disconnecting fuel system components may cause fire or personal injury.**
4. Disconnect battery ground cable.
5. Connect fuel pump electrical connection.
6. Install cargo compartment floor cover and bolts then install carpet. **Torque** bolts to 9 ft. lbs.
7. After repairs have been completed, connect battery cable and ensure fuel pump operates properly.

COMPRESSION PRESSURE

Compression pressure should be a minimum 171 psi with a maximum difference of 14 psi between cylinders.

ENGINE MOUNT

REPLACE

Refer to **Fig. 1** when replacing engine mounts.

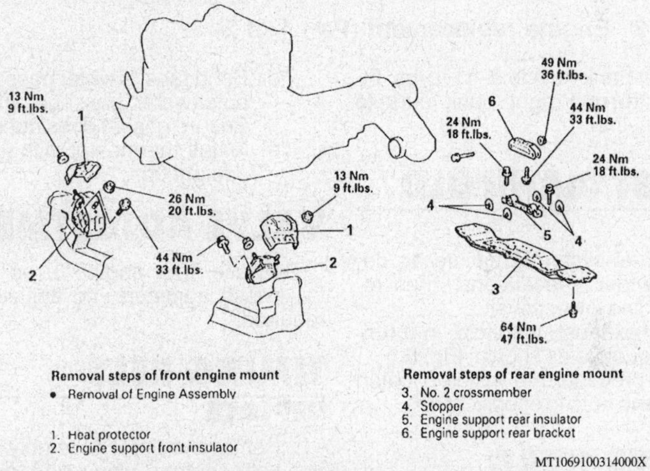

13 Nm
9 ft.lbs.
26 Nm
20 ft.lbs.
44 Nm
33 ft.lbs.
13 Nm
9 ft.lbs.
49 Nm
36 ft.lbs.
44 Nm
33 ft.lbs.
24 Nm
18 ft.lbs.
24 Nm
18 ft.lbs.
64 Nm
47 ft.lbs.
1
2
3
4
5
6
Removal steps of front engine mount
• Removal of Engine Assembly
1. Heat protector
2. Engine support front insulator
Removal steps of rear engine mount
3. No. 2 crossmember
4. Stopper
5. Engine support rear insulator
6. Engine support rear bracket
MT1069100314000X

Fig. 1 Engine mount replacement

ENGINE

REPLACE

1. Scribe and remove hood, then remove battery, tray and cruise control intermediate link.
2. Relieve fuel system pressure as described under "Precautions," then remove radiator assembly, skid plate, lower cover and front exhaust pipe.
3. Remove transmission and transfer assembly as described under "Transmission, Replace" in appropriate transmission section.
4. Remove engine assembly from vehicle in numbered sequence shown, **Fig. 2,** noting the following:
   a. When removing power steering pump and A/C compressor, leave hoses attached and support aside.
   b. When disconnecting oil cooler hose, use a spanner wrench or equivalent.
5. Reverse procedure to install.

INTAKE MANIFOLD

REPLACE

1. Relieve fuel system pressure as described under "Precautions," then drain engine coolant into a suitable container.
2. Remove intake manifold plenum, then the manifold in numbered sequence as shown, **Fig. 3.**
3. Reverse procedure to install, noting the following:
   a. Install intake manifold gaskets as shown, **Fig. 4.**
   b. When installing intake manifold mounting nuts, first **torque** right bank nuts to 2.2–3.6 ft. lbs., then

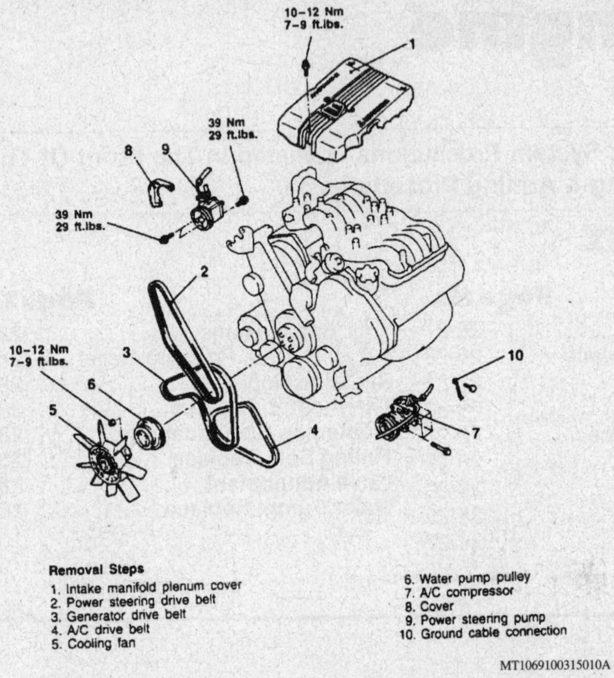
10–12 Nm
7–9 ft.lbs.
39 Nm
29 ft.lbs.
39 Nm
29 ft.lbs.
10–12 Nm
7–9 ft.lbs.
Removal Steps
1. Intake manifold plenum cover
2. Power steering drive belt
3. Generator drive belt
4. A/C drive belt
5. Cooling fan
6. Water pump pulley
7. A/C compressor
8. Cover
9. Power steering pump
10. Ground cable connection
MT1069100315010A

Fig. 2 Engine replacement (Part 1 of 2)

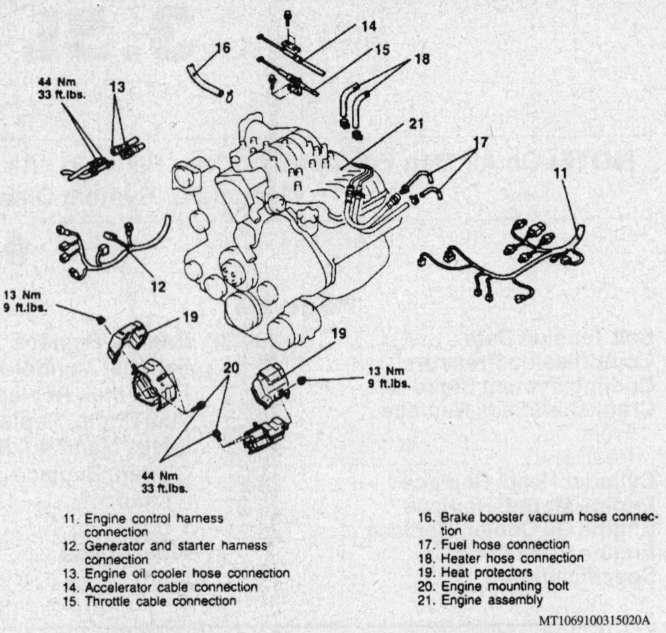
44 Nm
33 ft.lbs.
13 Nm
9 ft.lbs.
13 Nm
9 ft.lbs.
44 Nm
33 ft.lbs.
11. Engine control harness connection
12. Generator and starter harness connection
13. Engine oil cooler hose connection
14. Accelerator cable connection
15. Throttle cable connection
16. Brake booster vacuum hose connection
17. Fuel hose connection
18. Heater hose connection
19. Heat protectors
20. Engine mounting bolt
21. Engine assembly
MT1069100315020A

Fig. 2 Engine replacement (Part 2 of 2)

the left bank nuts to 9–11 ft. lbs. Finally, **torque** right bank nuts to 9–11 ft. lbs.

EXHAUST MANIFOLD

REPLACE

1. Relieve fuel system pressure as described under "Precautions," then remove engine lower cover.
2. Remove exhaust manifold in numbered sequence as shown, **Fig. 5.**
3. Reverse procedure to install. Tighten all bolts and nuts to specifications.

CYLINDER HEAD

REPLACE

Refer to **Fig. 6,** when replacing the cylinder head noting the following:

1. Drain engine coolant into suitable container, then remove timing belt, intake manifold & exhaust manifold.
2. Use replacement tool No. MD998051-01, or equivalent, to remove cylinder head bolts after loosening them in three steps in the sequence shown in **Fig. 7.**
3. Reverse procedure to install, noting the following:
   a. When installing cylinder head gasket, degrease gasket mounting surface, then lay gasket on cylinder block with ID mark at front top.
   b. Use replacement tool No. MD998051-01, or equivalent, to install cylinder head bolts in three steps in the sequence shown in **Fig. 7.**
   c. Rinse mounting location of water pipe O-ring and water pipe with water then install. **Do not apply oil or grease to O-ring. Insert water pipe until its end bottoms.**
   d. Bend tabs of water passage gasket onto water passage, then install. Ensure gasket does not slip.
   e. Install thermostat with jiggle valve straight up.

VALVE ADJUSTMENT

Because this engine uses automatic valve lash adjusters, no adjustments are required.

TIMING BELT

REPLACE

1. Remove radiator assembly, alternator, battery, tray, skid plate and engine lower cover.
2. Remove timing belt in numbered sequence as shown, **Fig. 8,** noting the following:
   a. When removing A/C compressor and power steering pump, leave hoses attached and support aside.
   b. Use pulley remover tool No. MB990767-01, or equivalent to remove crankshaft pulley.
   c. When removing timing belt, align timing marks as shown, **Fig. 9,** and ensure direction of normal rotation is marked on belt if it is to be reused.
3. Reverse procedure to install, noting the following:
   a. If auto tensioner rod is fully extended, gently push rod into cylinder by clamping tensioner assembly in a soft jawed vise until set hole in rod aligns with hole in cylinder wall, then insert a stiff wire through set hole to keep rod in place.
   b. When installing timing belt, install crankshaft pulley and turn crankshaft sprocket timing mark forward three teeth to move No. 1 piston slightly past top dead center. **Prevent piston from contacting valves during this procedure.**
   c. Align left camshaft sprocket with timing mark, then align right camshaft sprocket with timing mark and prevent rotation using suitable wrenches.
   d. When camshaft sprockets are aligned with timing marks, clamp timing belt over each sprocket using suitable binder clips, then slip belt over water pump pulley and idler pulley.
   e. After aligning crankshaft sprocket timing marks, rotate crankshaft counterclockwise slightly, then place timing belt over crankshaft sprocket and tensioner pulley.
   f. Position tensioner pulley pin hole at top, then press tensioner pulley onto timing belt and tighten set bolt until snug. Align crankshaft sprocket timing marks and ensure all timing marks are aligned, then remove binder clips from timing belt.
   g. To adjust timing belt tension, rotate crankshaft ¼ turn counterclockwise and then back to position where timing marks align, then loosen tensioner pulley center bolt. Using tensioner tool No. MD998767, or equivalent and a torque wrench, apply a **torque** of 7 ft. lbs. to timing belt while tightening pulley center bolt to specifications. Remove auto tensioner set pin and measure rod protrusion. If protrusion is not .149–.177 inch, repeat adjustment procedure.

CRANKSHAFT SEAL

REPLACE

FRONT

1. Remove timing belt as described

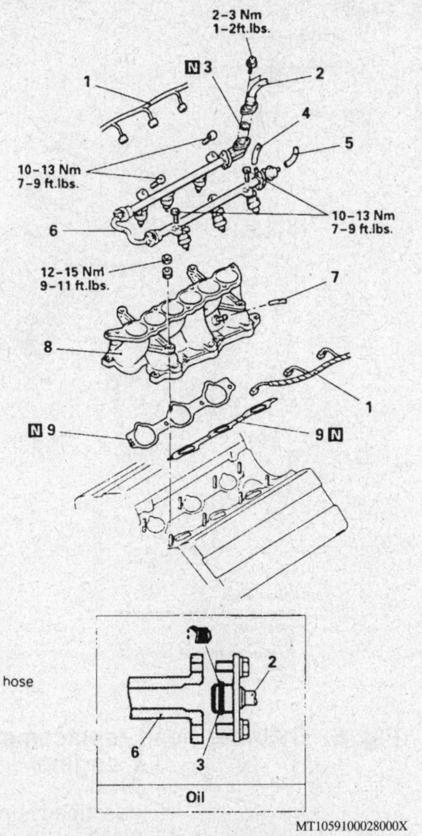
2-3 Nm
1-2ft.lbs.
N 3
2
1
4
5
10-13 Nm
7-9 ft.lbs.
6
10-13 Nm
7-9 ft.lbs.
12-15 Nm
9-11 ft.lbs.
7
8
1
N 9
9 N
2
6
3
Oil

Removal steps

1. Connection of injector harness
2. Connection for high-pressure fuel hose
3. O-ring
4. Connection for fuel return hose
5. Connection for vacuum hose
6. Fuel rail (with injectors)
7. Connection for ventilation hose
8. Intake manifold
9. Intake manifold gasket

MT1059100028000X

Fig. 3 Intake manifold replacement

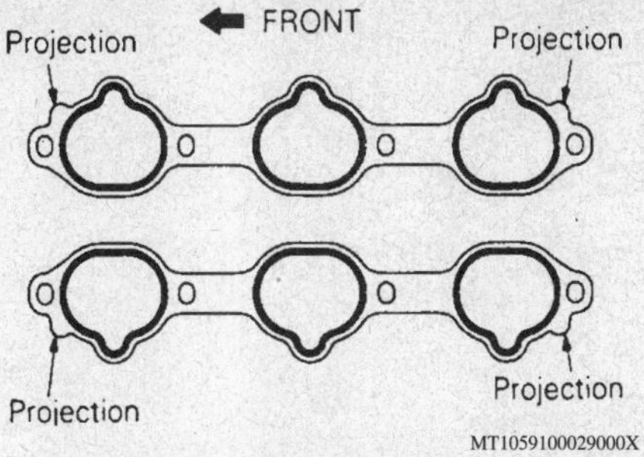
FRONT
Projection
Projection
Projection
Projection

MT1059100029000X

Fig. 4 Intake manifold gasket orientation

under "Timing Belt, Replace," then remove crankshaft sprocket, position sensor, sensing blade and spacer.

2. Remove key from keyway, then separate oil seal from case as follows:
   a. Cut out a small portion of crankshaft oil seal lip.
   b. Cover tip of a suitable screwdriver with a cloth, then insert into seal cutout and pry away from oil pump case.
3. Reverse procedure to install. Drive seal in until flush with surface of oil pump case using seal installation tool No. MD998717, or equivalent.

REAR

1. Remove transmission assembly as described under "Transmission, Replace" in appropriate transmission section, then remove outer adapter plate and driveplate.
2. Remove driveplate to output flange adapter, then remove oil seal from engine as follows:
   a. Cut out a small portion of crankshaft oil seal lip.
   b. Cover tip of a suitable screwdriver with a cloth, then insert into seal cutout and pry away from engine.
3. Reverse procedure to install. Drive seal in using seal installation tool No. MD998718-01, or equivalent.

OIL PAN

REPLACE

LOWER

1. Remove skid plate, lower cover and front exhaust pipe, then drain engine oil into a suitable container.
2. Separate oil pan from engine, noting the following:
   a. It may be necessary to free pan by placing a wooden block against it and tapping with a hammer.
   b. Do not attempt to remove pan using oil pan remover No. MD998727 or equivalent; damage to aluminum components may result.
3. Reverse procedure to install, noting the following:
   a. Ensure oil pan mating surfaces are clean, then apply Mitsubishi sealant No. MD970389 or equivalent in a continuous bead as shown, **Fig. 10.**
   b. Install oil pan on engine block within 30 minutes of sealant application.
   c. Tighten oil pan mounting bolts to specifications in sequence shown, **Fig. 10.**

UPPER

1. Remove lower oil pan as described in this section, then remove front differential carrier.
2. Remove upper oil pan in sequence as shown, **Fig. 11.**
3. Reverse procedure to install, noting the following:
   a. Clean upper oil pan mating surfaces, then apply Mitsubishi sealant No. MD970389 or equivalent in a continuous bead as shown, **Fig. 12.**
   b. Install upper oil pan on cylinder block within 30 minutes of sealant application.
   c. Tighten upper oil pan mounting bolts to specifications in sequence shown, **Fig. 12.**

ENGINE OIL COOLER

REPLACE

1. Remove radiator grille, then remove engine oil cooler in numbered sequence as shown, **Fig. 13.**
2. Reverse procedure to install, noting the following:
   a. Tighten return and feed hose eye bolts, **Fig. 14,** until snug, then install clamp so it touches hose crimps.
   b. Tighten return hose eye bolt to specifications, then place feed hose against stopper and tighten its eye bolt to specifications.

BELT TENSION DATA

Component	Inch Deflection①	
	New Belt	Used Belt②
Alternator	.22–.30③	.31–.35③
Power Steering Pump	.43–.51	.55–.63
A/C Compressor	.20–.24	.26–.30

① — With 22 lbs. of force applied.
② — Used 5 minutes or more.
③ — Measured between water pump pulley & generator.

COOLING SYSTEM BLEED

This engine does not require a specified bleed procedure. After filling cooling system, run engine to operating temperature with radiator/pressure cap off. Air will then be automatically bled through cap opening.

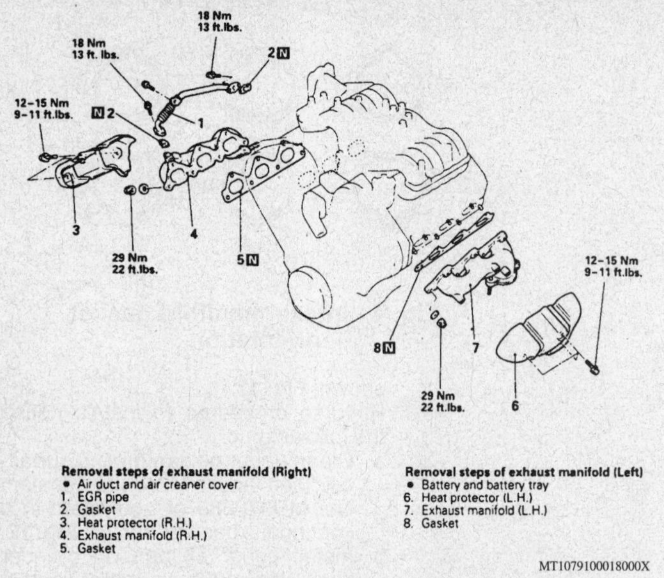
18 Nm
13 ft.lbs.
18 Nm
13 ft. lbs.
12-15 Nm
9-11 ft.lbs.
29 Nm
22 ft.lbs.
12-15 Nm
9-11 ft.lbs.
29 Nm
22 ft.lbs.
Removal steps of exhaust manifold (Right)
• Air duct and air creaner cover
1. EGR pipe
2. Gasket
3. Heat protector (R.H.)
4. Exhaust manifold (R.H.)
5. Gasket
Removal steps of exhaust manifold (Left)
• Battery and battery tray
6. Heat protector (L.H.)
7. Exhaust manifold (L.H.)
8. Gasket
MT1079100018000X

Fig. 5 Exhaust manifold replacement

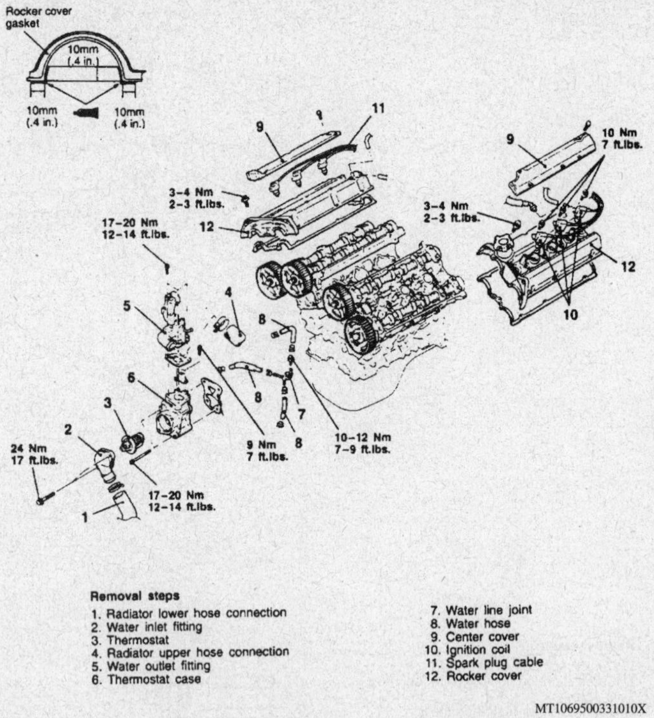
Rocker cover gasket
10mm (.4 in.)
10mm (.4 in.)
10mm (.4 in.)
3-4 Nm
2-3 ft.lbs.
17-20 Nm
12-14 ft.lbs.
10 Nm
7 ft.lbs.
3-4 Nm
2-3 ft.lbs.
24 Nm
17 ft.lbs.
9 Nm
7 ft.lbs.
10-12 Nm
7-9 ft.lbs.
17-20 Nm
12-14 ft.lbs.
Removal steps
1. Radiator lower hose connection
2. Water inlet fitting
3. Thermostat
4. Radiator upper hose connection
5. Water outlet fitting
6. Thermostat case
7. Water line joint
8. Water hose
9. Center cover
10. Ignition coil
11. Spark plug cable
12. Rocker cover
MT1069500331010X

Fig. 6 Cylinder head replacement (Part 1 of 2). 3.5L engine

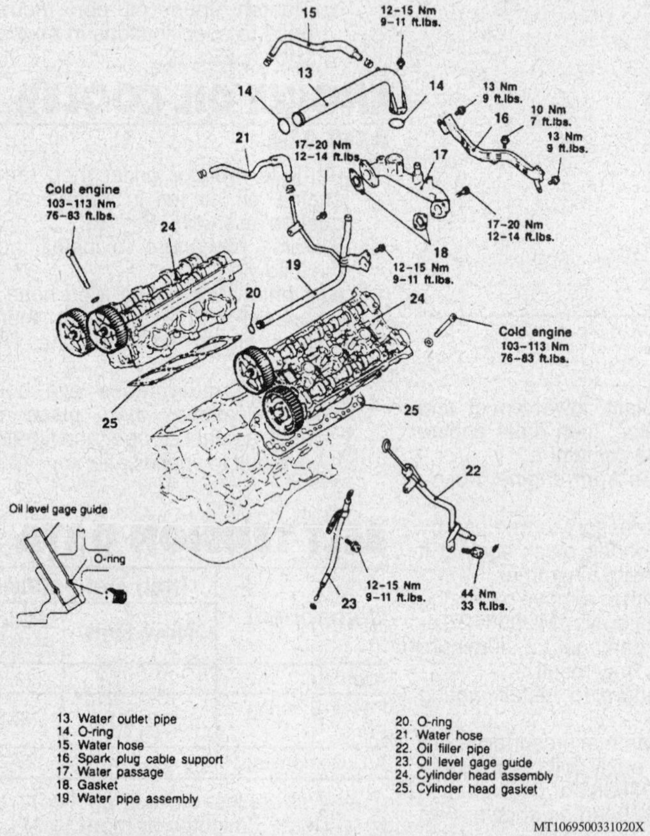
12-15 Nm
9-11 ft.lbs.
13 Nm
9 ft.lbs.
10 Nm
7 ft.lbs.
13 Nm
9 ft.lbs.
17-20 Nm
12-14 ft.lbs.
Cold engine
103-113 Nm
76-83 ft.lbs.
17-20 Nm
12-14 ft.lbs.
12-15 Nm
9-11 ft.lbs.
Cold engine
103-113 Nm
76-83 ft.lbs.
Oil level gage guide
O-ring
12-15 Nm
9-11 ft.lbs.
44 Nm
33 ft.lbs.
13. Water outlet pipe
14. O-ring
15. Water hose
16. Spark plug cable support
17. Water passage
18. Gasket
19. Water pipe assembly
20. O-ring
21. Water hose
22. Oil filler pipe
23. Oil level gage guide
24. Cylinder head assembly
25. Cylinder head gasket
MT1069500331020X

Fig. 6 Cylinder head replacement (Part 2 of 2). 3.5L engine

THERMOSTAT

REPLACE

1. Drain engine coolant into a suitable container, then disconnect lower radiator hose and remove water inlet fitting.
2. Remove thermostat from engine.
3. Reverse procedure to install, noting the following:
   a. Install thermostat with jiggle valve facing straight up.
   b. Tighten water inlet fitting mounting bolts to specifications.

WATER PUMP

REPLACE

1. Drain engine coolant into a suitable container, then remove timing belt as described under "Timing Belt, Replace."
2. Remove thermostat as described under "Thermostat, Replace," then remove water pump in numbered sequence as shown, **Fig. 15.**
3. Reverse procedure to install, noting the following:
   a. When installing O-ring, rinse mounting location with water. **Do not apply oil or grease to O-ring.**
   b. Tighten all bolts and nuts to specifications.

RADIATOR

REPLACE

1. Drain engine coolant into suitable container, then remove engine under cover.
2. Remove air cleaner case, then remove transmission oil cooler hose.
3. Remove radiator upper hose and radiator shroud, over flow hose and reserve tank.
4. Remove radiator lower hose, then radiator.
5. Reverse procedure to install.

FUEL PUMP

REPLACE

1. Relieve fuel system pressure as described under "Precautions, " then drain fuel tank into a suitable container.
2. Remove rear carpet, then remove fuel pump in numbered sequence shown, **Fig. 16.**
3. Reverse procedure to install. Tighten all bolts and fittings to specifications.

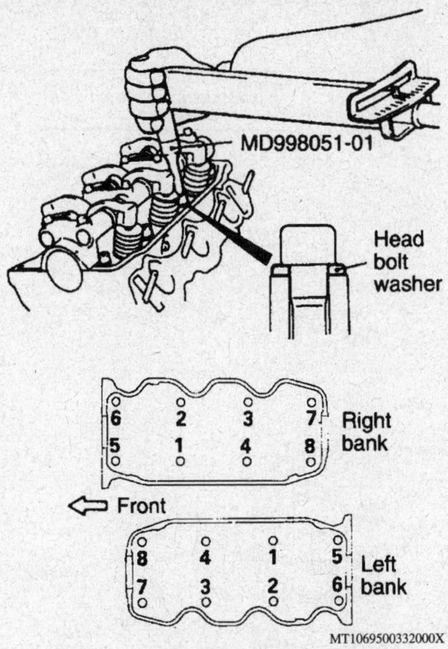
MD998051-01
Head bolt washer
6 2 3 7
5 1 4 8
Right bank
Front
8 4 1 5
7 3 2 6
Left bank
MT1069500332000X

Fig. 7 Cylinder head bolt loosening & tightening sequence. 3.5L engine

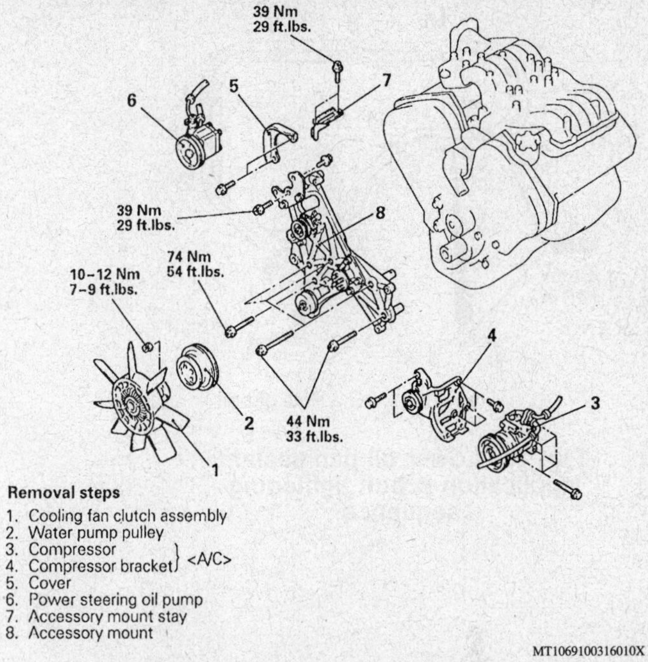
39 Nm
29 ft.lbs.
39 Nm
29 ft.lbs.
74 Nm
54 ft.lbs.
10–12 Nm
7–9 ft.lbs.
44 Nm
33 ft.lbs.
Removal steps
1. Cooling fan clutch assembly
2. Water pump pulley
3. Compressor
4. Compressor bracket
<A/C>
5. Cover
6. Power steering oil pump
7. Accessory mount stay
8. Accessory mount
MT1069100316010X

Fig. 8 Timing belt replacement (Part 1 of 2)

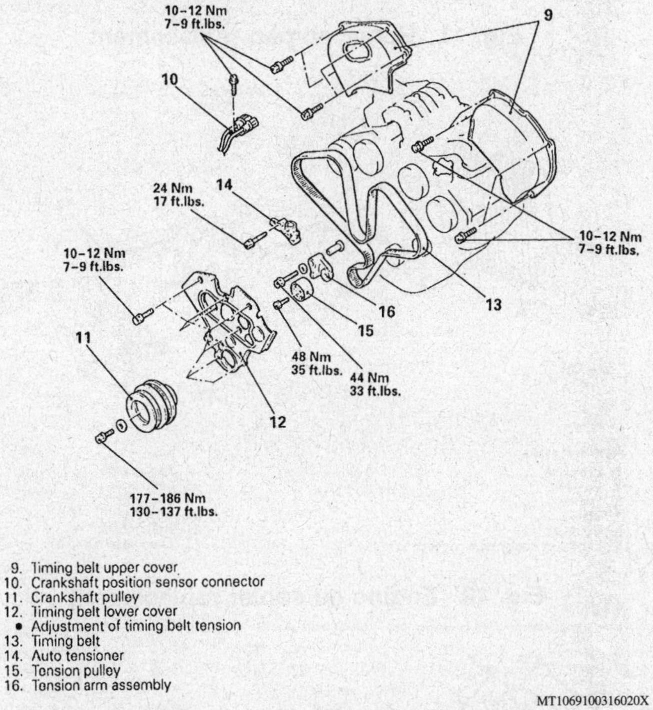
10–12 Nm
7–9 ft.lbs.
24 Nm
17 ft.lbs.
10–12 Nm
7–9 ft.lbs.
10–12 Nm
7–9 ft.lbs.
48 Nm
35 ft.lbs.
44 Nm
33 ft.lbs.
177–186 Nm
130–137 ft.lbs.
9. Timing belt upper cover
10. Crankshaft position sensor connector
11. Crankshaft pulley
12. Timing belt lower cover
• Adjustment of timing belt tension
13. Timing belt
14. Auto tensioner
15. Tension pulley
16. Tension arm assembly
MT1069100316020X

Fig. 8 Timing belt replacement (Part 2 of 2)

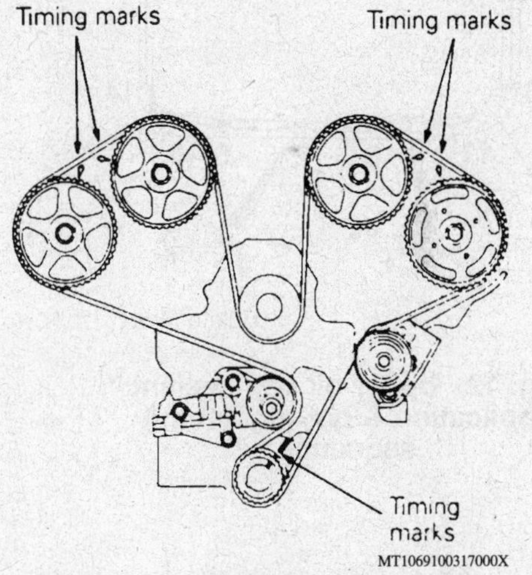
Timing marks
Timing marks
Timing marks
MT1069100317000X

Fig. 9 Timing mark alignment

FUEL FILTER

REPLACE

1. Disconnect battery ground cable.
2. Release fuel system pressure as described under "Precautions."
3. Drain fuel tank into a suitable container.
4. Hold fuel filter with a wrench and remove eye bolt retaining fuel high pressure hose with an eye wrench, **Fig. 17.**
5. Inspect hose and pipes for cracks, damage or clogging and replace as necessary.
6. Inspect evaporative emission canister for clogging and replace as necessary.
7. Inspect check valve and fuel filter for clogging or damage and replace as necessary.
8. Remove protector of fuel filter, then disconnect fuel filter mounting bolt.
9. Remove fuel filter and high pressure hose assembly.
10. Reverse procedure to install.

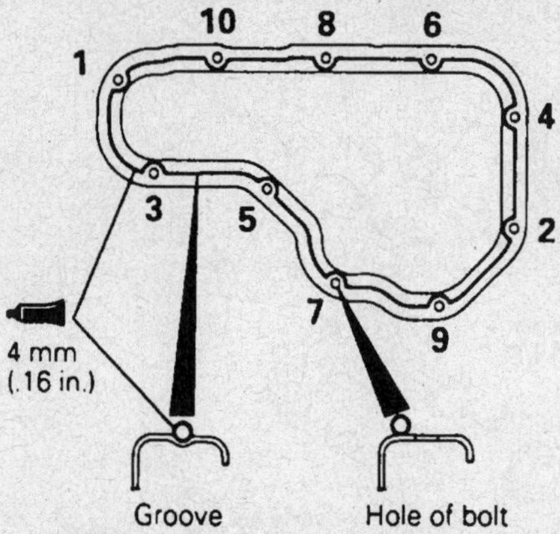
10
8
6
1
4
3
5
2
7
9
4 mm
(.16 in.)
Groove
Hole of bolt

MT1099100053000X

Fig. 10 Lower oil pan sealant application & bolt tightening sequence

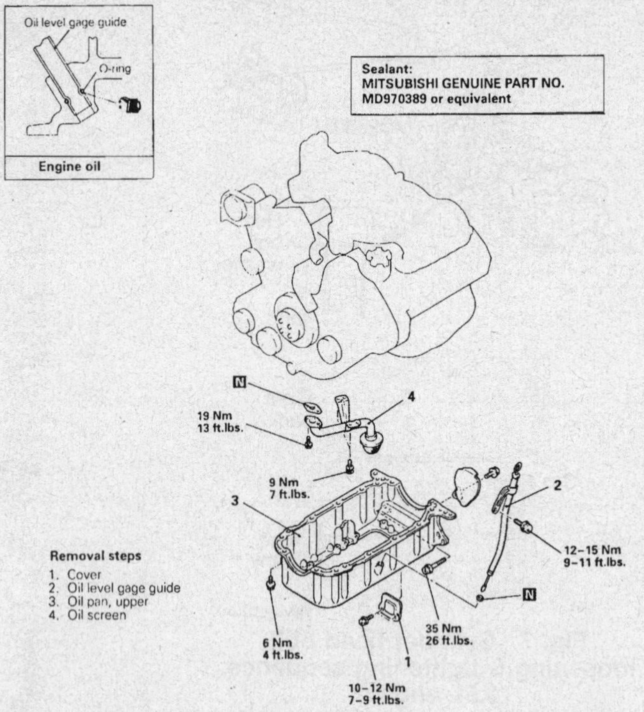
Oil level gage guide
O-ring
Engine oil
Sealant:
MITSUBISHI GENUINE PART NO.
MD970389 or equivalent
19 Nm
13 ft.lbs.
4
9 Nm
7 ft.lbs.
3
2
12–15 Nm
9–11 ft.lbs.
Removal steps
1. Cover
2. Oil level gage guide
3. Oil pan, upper
4. Oil screen
35 Nm
26 ft.lbs.
6 Nm
4 ft.lbs.
1
10–12 Nm
7–9 ft.lbs.

MT1099100054000X

Fig. 11 Upper oil pan replacement

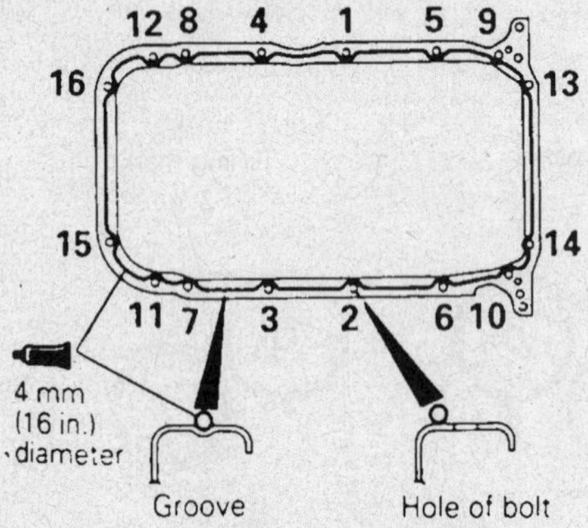
12 8 4 1 5 9
16
13
15
14
11 7 3 2 6 10
4 mm
(16 in.)
diameter
Groove
Hole of bolt

MT1099100055000X

Fig. 12 Upper oil pan sealant application & bolt tightening sequence

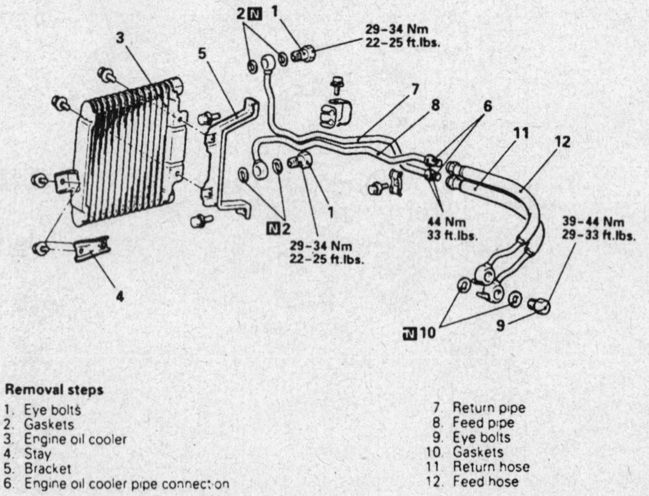
2
1
29–34 Nm
22–25 ft.lbs.
3
5
7
8
6
11
12
2
1
29–34 Nm
22–25 ft.lbs.
44 Nm
33 ft.lbs.
39–44 Nm
29–33 ft.lbs.
4
10
9
Removal steps
1. Eye bolts
2. Gaskets
3. Engine oil cooler
4. Stay
5. Bracket
6. Engine oil cooler pipe connection
7. Return pipe
8. Feed pipe
9. Eye bolts
10. Gaskets
11. Return hose
12. Feed hose

MT1099100056000X

Fig. 13 Engine oil cooler replacement

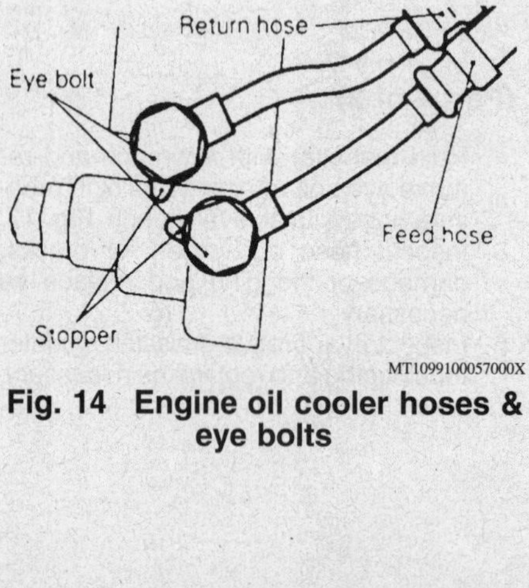
Return hose
Eye bolt
Feed hose
Stopper

MT1099100057000X

Fig. 14 Engine oil cooler hoses & eye bolts

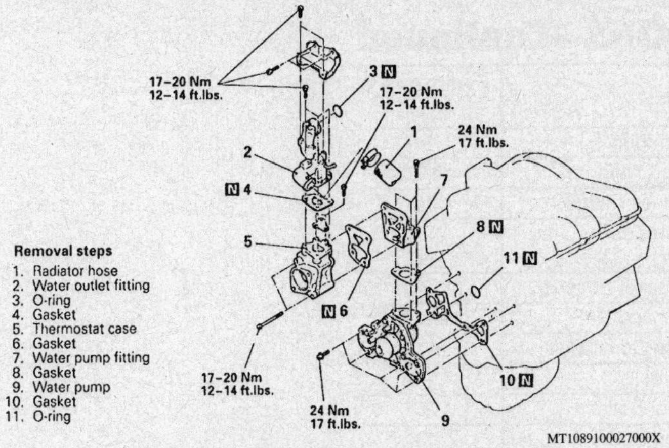
17-20 Nm
12-14 ft.lbs.
3 N
17-20 Nm
12-14 ft.lbs.
1
24 Nm
17 ft.lbs.
2
N 4
7
8 N
5
11 N
N 6
17-20 Nm
12-14 ft.lbs.
10 N
24 Nm
17 ft.lbs.
9
Removal steps
1. Radiator hose
2. Water outlet fitting
3. O-ring
4. Gasket
5. Thermostat case
6. Gasket
7. Water pump fitting
8. Gasket
9. Water pump
10. Gasket
11. O-ring
MT1089100027000X

Fig. 15 Water pump replacement

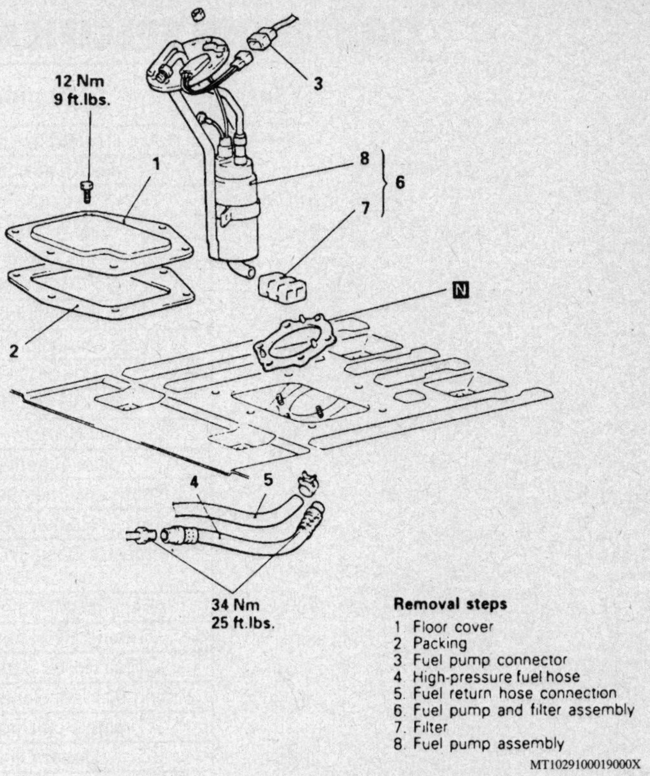
12 Nm
9 ft.lbs.
3
1
8
6
7
N
2
4
5
34 Nm
25 ft.lbs.
Removal steps
1. Floor cover
2. Packing
3. Fuel pump connector
4. High-pressure fuel hose
5. Fuel return hose connection
6. Fuel pump and filter assembly
7. Filter
8. Fuel pump assembly
MT1029100019000X

Fig. 16 Fuel pump replacement

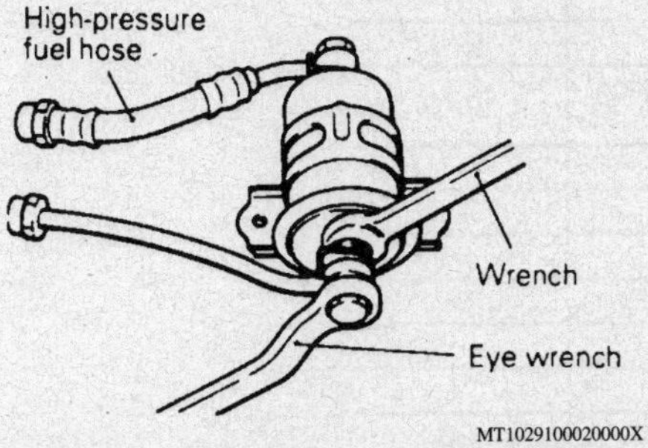
High-pressure
fuel hose
Wrench
Eye wrench
MT1029100020000X

Fig. 17 Fuel filter replacement

TIGHTENING SPECIFICATIONS

Year	Component	Torque/Ft. Lbs.
1994–96	Camshaft Sprocket Bolt	65
	Cooling Fan To Water Pump Pulley Bolts	7–9
	Crankshaft Position Sensor Bracket Bolt	7
	Crankshaft Pulley Bolt	130–137
	Dipstick Tube Bracket Bolt	9–11
	EGR Pipe Flange Bolts	13
	Engine Mount Bolts	33
	Engine Mount Heat Protector Nuts	9
	Engine Mount Nuts	20
	Engine Oil Cooler Hose Fittings	33
	Engine Oil Cooler Hose To Cooler Eye Bolts	22–25
	Engine Oil Cooler Hose To Engine Eye Bolts	29–33
	Engine Oil Drain Plug	29
	Engine Rear Support Insulator To Crossmember Bolts	18
	Engine Support Rear Bracket Nut	36
	Engine Support Rear Bracket To Engine Bolt	33
	Exhaust Manifold Heat Protector Bolts	9–11
	Exhaust Manifold Mounting Nuts	22
	Fuel Gauge Sending Unit Mounting Nuts	2
	Fuel Pump Floor Access Cover Bolts	9
	Fuel Pump Mounting Nuts	2
	Fuel Rail Mounting Bolts	7–9

Continued

TIGHTENING SPECIFICATIONS—Continued

Year	Component	Torque/Ft. Lbs.
1994–96	Fuel Tank Drain Plug	14
	Fuel Tank Support Nuts	18–22
	High Pressure Fuel Hose Fittings	25
	High Pressure Fuel Hose To Fuel Rail Flange Bolts	1–2
	Ignition Coil Wire Bracket Bolts	7
	Intake Manifold Mounting Nuts	9–11
	Intake Manifold Plenum Cover Bolt	7–9
	Lower Oil Pan Bolts	7–9
	Oil Screen Bracket Bolts	7
	Oil Screen Flange Bolts	13
	Power Steering Pump Bolts	29
	Rear Crossmember Mounting Bolts	47
	Rocker Cover Bolts	2–3
	Thermostat Case To Water Pump Fitting Bolts	12–14
	Timing Belt Auto Tensioner Bolt	17
	Timing Belt Lower Cover Bolts	7–9
	Timing Belt Tension Arm Bolts	33
	Timing Belt Tensioner Pulley Center Bolt	35
	Timing Belt Upper Cover Bolts	7–9
	Upper Oil Pan Bolts	4
	Upper Oil Pan To Transmission Bolts	26
	Water Outlet Fitting To Thermostat Case Bolts	12–14
	Water Pump Mounting Bolts	17

Clutch & Manual Transmission

INDEX

	Page No.
Adjustments	28-34
Clutch Pedal	28-34
Clutch, Replace	28-35
Montero	28-35
Pickup	28-35
Hydraulic System Service	28-35
Clutch Slave Cylinder, Replace	28-35
Tightening Specifications	28-37
Transfer Case, Replace	28-36
Transmission, Replace	28-35
Montero	28-36
Pickup	28-35

ADJUSTMENTS

CLUTCH PEDAL

Cable Operated

1. Measure clutch pedal height as shown, **Fig. 1.** Clutch pedal height should be 6.5–6.7 inches. If clutch pedal height is not as specified, rotate pedal stopper until specified dimension is obtained.
2. Measure clutch pedal freeplay by lightly depressing on clutch pedal until light resistance is felt. Clutch pedal freeplay should be 0.8–1.4 inches. If clutch pedal freeplay is not as specified, pull clutch cable lightly at toe board, then rotate adjusting nut until adjusting nut to insulator clearance, **Fig. 2,** is 0.12–0.16 inch.
3. Check clutch pedal height and freeplay after making adjustments.
4. Measure distance between face of clutch pedal and floor board, with clutch pedal depressed. Distance should be 2.4 inches or more.

Hydraulically Operated

1. Measure clutch pedal height (A) and clutch pedal freeplay (B), **Fig. 3.** Clutch pedal height should be as follows:
   a. **On Pickup,** 6.5–6.7 inches.
   b. **On Montero,** 7.3–7.5 inches.
2. **On all models,** clutch pedal freeplay should be as follows:
   a. **On Montero,** 0.04–0.12 inch.
   b. **On Pickup with 2.4L engine,** 0.8–1.4 inch.
   c. **On Pickup with 3.0L engine,** 0.31–0.67 inch.
3. **On all models,** if clutch pedal height and freeplay are not within specification, adjust as follows:
   a. Back off pedal stopper bolt until it does not contact pedal arm, **Fig. 4.**
   b. Loosen pushrod locknut, then adjust pedal height to specified value by turning the pushrod, **Fig. 4.**
   c. Turn pedal stopper bolt until it comes into contact with pedal arm, then tighten the locknut.
4. After above adjustment is completed, depress clutch pedal and check the clutch pedal to floorboard clearance (C), **Fig. 3.** Pedal to floorboard clearance should be 2.4 inches or more on Pickup or 1.4 inches or more on Montero.
5. If clutch pedal to floorboard clearance is less than specified value, check for

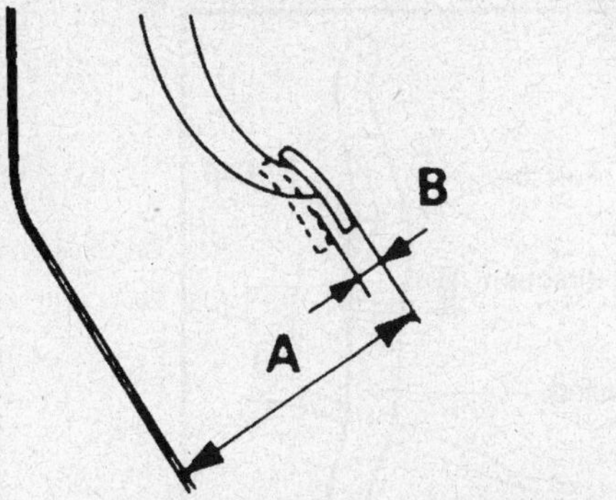
B
A

MT5049100043000X

Fig. 1 Clutch pedal height adjustment. Pickup

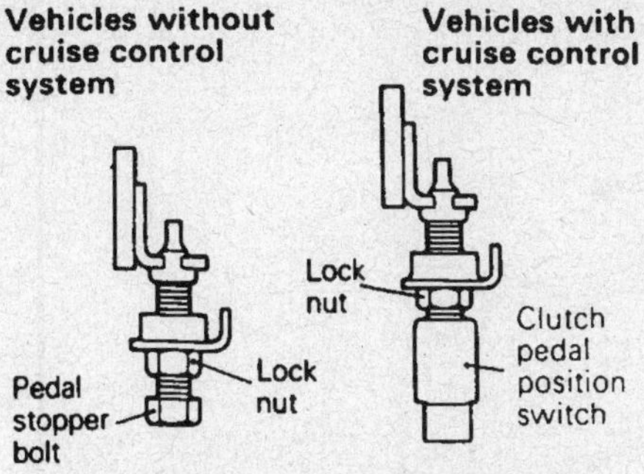
Vehicles without cruise control system
Vehicles with cruise control system
Lock nut
Lock nut
Pedal stopper bolt
Clutch pedal position switch

MT5049100044000X

Fig. 2 Clutch pedal freeplay adjustment. Pickup

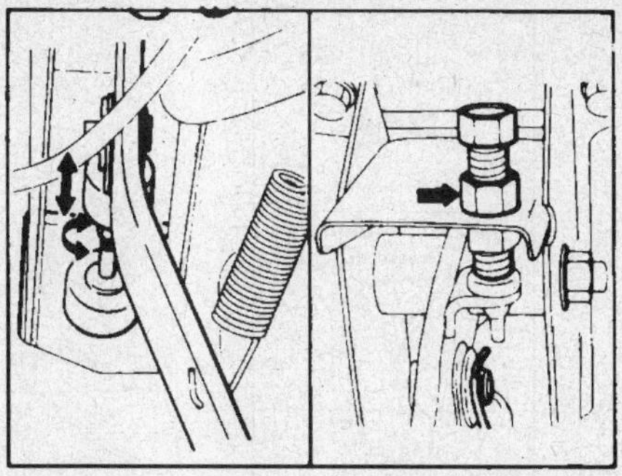

MT5049100045000X

Fig. 3 Clutch pedal height, freeplay & floorboard clearance

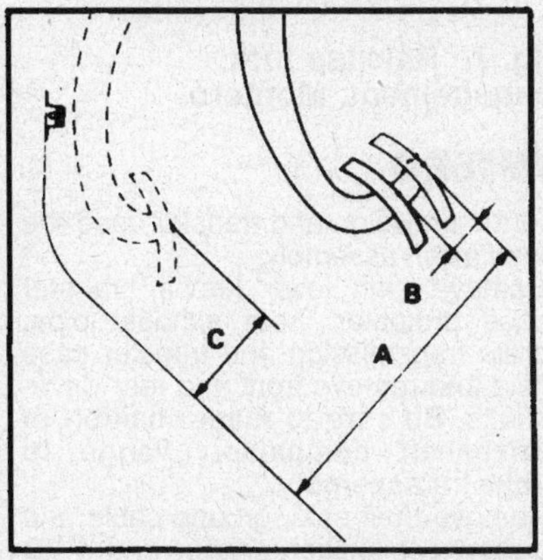
B
C
A

MT5049100046000X

Fig. 4 Clutch pedal height & freeplay adjustment

air in hydraulic system or defective clutch assembly.

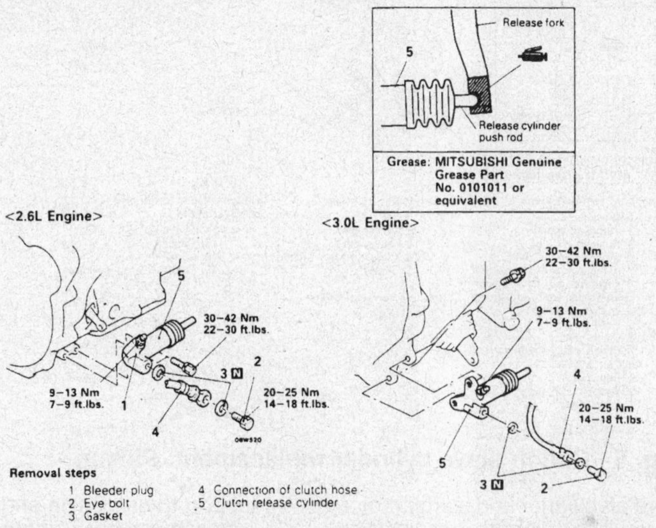
Release fork
5
Release cylinder push rod
Grease: MITSUBISHI Genuine Grease Part No. 0101011 or equivalent
<2.6L Engine>
<3.0L Engine>
30–42 Nm 22–30 ft.lbs.
9–13 Nm 7–9 ft.lbs.
20–25 Nm 14–18 ft.lbs.
Removal steps
1 Bleeder plug
2 Eye bolt
3 Gasket
4 Connection of clutch hose
5 Clutch release cylinder

MT5049100047000X

Fig. 5 Clutch slave cylinder replacement. Montero

HYDRAULIC SYSTEM SERVICE

CLUTCH SLAVE CYLINDER, REPLACE

Replace clutch slave cylinder in sequence as shown, **Figs. 5 and 6.**

CLUTCH

REPLACE

PICKUP

1. Remove transmission and transfer case assembly, if applicable, as outlined under "Transmission, Replace."
2. Insert suitable tool into center hole to prevent dropping clutch disc, then diagonally loosen bolts holding clutch cover assembly and remove assembly.
3. Remove clutch disc and tool.
4. Remove two return clips on transmission side, then the release bearing.
5. Remove shift arm spring pin and control lever shaft assembly with 3⁄16 inch punch, then remove clutch shift arm, two felt packing and two return springs.
6. Apply grease to inside surface of bushing and oil seal lips and apply engine oil to two felt packing.
7. Insert clutch control lever and shaft assembly into transmission case from left, then install clutch shift arm, two felt packing, and two return springs onto shaft.
8. Align lockpin holes on shift arm and control shaft, then drive in two spring pins. Ensure spring pin slot direction is at right angles to control shaft.
9. Apply ample amount of rubber grease to outer surface of piston and piston cup and insert them in release cylinder, then install pushrod and rubber boot.
10. Install release cylinder assembly to transmission case.
11. Fill groove of bearing inside diameter with grease.
12. Install release bearing to transmission front bearing retainer, then install return clips.
13. Rub grease in clutch disc spline and transmission main gear spline.
14. Using suitable tool, install clutch disc and clutch cover assembly on flywheel. When installing clutch disc, make certain that surface with manufacturer's stamped mark is on pressure plate side.
15. Install transmission.

MONTERO

1. Remove transmission and transfer case assembly as outlined under "Transmission, Replace."
2. Insert tool No. MB998127, or equivalent, in center hole to prevent dropping of clutch disc.
3. Diagonally loosen bolts that hold clutch cover assembly and remove assembly.
4. Slide release fork in direction of arrow, **Fig. 7**, to disengage fulcrum from clip.
5. Pack release fork fulcrum hole and release cylinder pushrod hole with grease.
6. Pack grease in groove on release bearing inside diameter.
7. Clean clutch facing and pressure plate with clean cloth.
8. Lightly grease clutch disc spline and main drive gear spline of transmission.
9. Using tool, No. MB998127 or equivalent, install clutch disc and clutch cover assembly on flywheel. When installing clutch disc, make certain that surface with manufacturer's stamped mark is on pressure plate side.

TRANSMISSION

REPLACE

PICKUP

On 4WD models, the transmission and transfer case are removed as an assembly.

1. Disconnect battery ground cable.

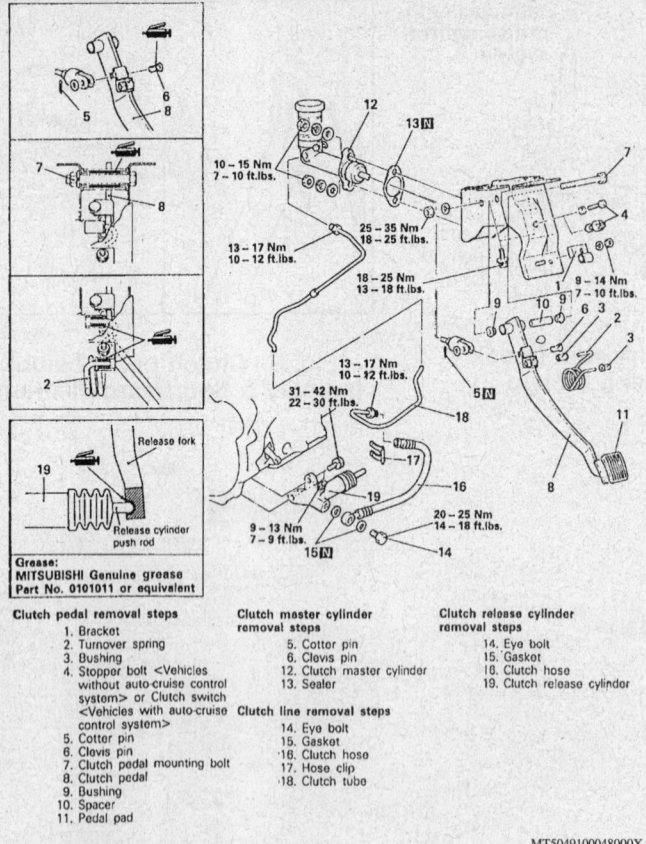

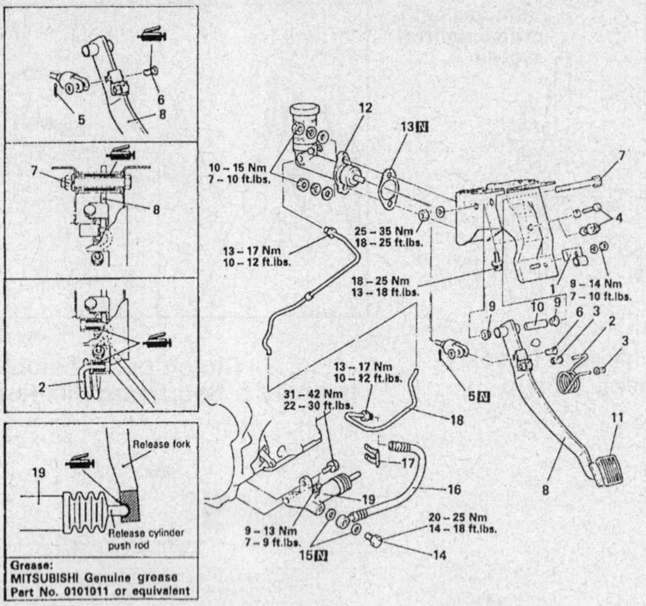
Release fork
Release cylinder push rod
Grease:
MITSUBISHI Genuine grease
Part No. 0101011 or equivalent
10 – 15 Nm
7 – 10 ft.lbs.
13 – 17 Nm
10 – 12 ft.lbs.
25 – 35 Nm
18 – 25 ft.lbs.
18 – 25 Nm
13 – 18 ft.lbs.
9 – 14 Nm
7 – 10 ft.lbs.
13 – 17 Nm
10 – 12 ft.lbs.
31 – 42 Nm
22 – 30 ft.lbs.
20 – 25 Nm
14 – 18 ft.lbs.
9 – 13 Nm
7 – 9 ft.lbs.

Clutch pedal removal steps
1. Bracket
2. Turnover spring
3. Bushing
4. Stopper bolt <Vehicles without auto-cruise control system> or Clutch switch <Vehicles with auto-cruise control system>
5. Cotter pin
6. Clevis pin
7. Clutch pedal mounting bolt
8. Clutch pedal
9. Bushing
10. Spacer
11. Pedal pad

Clutch master cylinder removal steps
5. Cotter pin
6. Clevis pin
12. Clutch master cylinder
13. Sealer

Clutch line removal steps
14. Eye bolt
15. Gasket
16. Clutch hose
17. Hose clip
18. Clutch tube

Clutch release cylinder removal steps
14. Eye bolt
15. Gasket
16. Clutch hose
19. Clutch release cylinder

MT5049100048000X

Fig. 6 Clutch slave cylinder replacement. Pickup

2. Remove air cleaner and starter motor.
3. Remove two upper transmission mounting bolts from bellhousing.
4. **On models with a console box,** remove lock screws and lift up console box.
5. **On models less a console box,** remove backbone carpet.
6. **On all models,** remove attaching screws and lift out dust cover retaining plate.
7. Turn up dust cover and remove control housing attaching bolts from extension housing, then remove control lever assembly.
8. Raise and support vehicle, then drain transmission oil and transfer case oil into appropriate containers.
9. Remove propeller shaft and disconnect speedometer cable.
10. Disconnect back-up light switch harness and, on 4WD models, the 4WD indicator light switch harness.
11. Disconnect front exhaust pipe.
12. **On models with cable operated clutch,** disconnect clutch cable from clutch control lever.
13. **On models with hydraulic operated clutch,** disconnect clutch slave cylinder, leaving hoses attached.
14. Support rear of engine with suitable jack.
15. **On 4WD models,** disconnect plate and remove transfer case mounting bracket.
16. **On all models,** using suitable jack, support transmission and remove No. 2 crossmember. **Transmission supporting area should be as wide as possible.**
17. Remove bellhousing cover, then the remaining transmission mounting bolts.
18. Withdraw transmission from engine, being careful not to twist front end of main drive gear.
19. Lower jack and remove transmission/transfer case assembly from under vehicle.
20. **On 4WD models,** remove transfer case to transmission bolts and nuts, then the transfer case.
21. **On all models,** reverse procedure to install, noting the following:
    a. Tighten bolts to specifications.
    b. When installing control lever assembly on RWD models, place gearshift lever in 2nd on 4 speed transmission, or in 1st speed position on 5 speed transmission.
    c. When installing gearshift lever assembly on 4WD models, set transmission gearshift lever to Neutral position and transfer case gearshift lever to 4H position.
    d. Ensure bellhousing cover is not bent.
    e. Install dust cover onto tunnel hole, then install retaining plate with attaching screws.
    f. Adjust clutch and fill transmission to specification with suitable fluid.

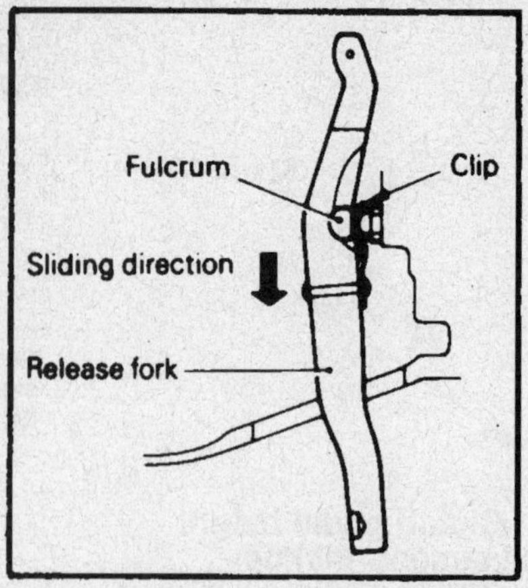
Fulcrum
Clip
Sliding direction
Release fork

MT5049100049000X

Fig. 7 Release fork disengagement. Montero

MONTERO

The transmission and transfer case are removed as an assembly.

1. Remove shift lever knobs, transfer case protector, front exhaust pipe, drain transmission and transfer case fluid and remove front and rear driveshafts. **Be sure to mark position of driveshaft companion flange to yoke for assembly.**
2. Remove dust seal, ground cable and disconnect oxygen sensor and 4WD indicator connectors at transfer case remove ground cable at transfer case.
3. Disconnect speedometer cable, back-up light switch connector and clutch release cylinder. Leave hoses attached to clutch release cylinder and suspend with wire.
4. Remove starter cover and motor, then remove left and right side transmission stays. Care must be taken to install bolt in correct position.
5. Remove bellhousing cover, then support transfer case with a suitable jack and remove the transfer mounting bracket.
6. Remove crossmember mount retaining bolts, crossmember, and mount.
7. Support transmission and transfer assembly with suitable jack, move assembly rearward carefully, tilt front of transmission downward slightly and remove assembly from vehicle.
8. Reverse procedure to install, noting the following:
    a. Place a piece of wood under engine oil pan, between pan and crossmember, to tilt engine toward rear.
    b. Ensure to center engine and transmission before mating them together.

TRANSFER CASE

REPLACE

The transmission and transfer case are removed as an assembly. Refer to procedure outlined under "Transmission, Replace."

TIGHTENING SPECIFICATIONS

Year	Component	Torque/Ft. Lbs.
1993–96	Adapter Cover Bolts	17 ③
	Adapter Part Poppet Spring Installation Screw Plug④	35
	Adapter Part Side Poppet Spring Installation Screw Plug④	22–30
	Adapter To Transfer Case Mounting Bolts And Nuts	22–30
	Back Light Switch	22–30
	Bellhousing Attaching Bolts	7–9
	Bleeder Plug	7–9
	Brake Pedal To Pedal Support③	18–25
	Chain Cover Bolt	22–30
	Clutch Cover Assembly To Flywheel	11–15
	Clutch Flare Nut	10–12
	Clutch Housing Mounting Bolts	86
	Clutch Master Cylinder To Firewall①	5–7
	Clutch Master Cylinder To Firewall③	7–10
	Clutch Pedal Bracket①	13–18
	Clutch Pedal To Pedal Bracket①	18–25
	Clutch Release Cylinder Mounting Bolts⑥	40–54
	Clutch Release Cylinder Mounting Bolt①	22–29
	Control Housing Bolt	11–15
	Control Housing To Cover	7–9
	Engine Mounting Rear Insulator To No. 2 Crossmember	13–18
	Engine Mounting Rear Insulator To Transmission	13–18
	Exhaust Pipe Mounting Bracket Mounting Bolts	15–20
	Extension Housing And Transmission Case Connection Bolt	11–15
	Eye Bolt	14–18
	Flywheel Bolt	54
	Front Exhaust Pipe Mounting Bolt	15–22
	Fulcrum	22–30
	Neutral Return Plunger Plug	35
	No. 2 Crossmember To Frame⑨	40–54
	No. 2 Crossmember Mounting Bolts⑧	29–36
	Oil Drain Plug⑪	43
	Oil Filler & Drain Plug④	17
	Oil Filler & Drain Plug⑩	22–25
	Oil Filler Drain Plug①	40–61
	Oil Filler Plug⑪	22—25
	Pedal Support Member Mounting Bolt③	6–9
	Plugs	15
	Power Take-Off Cover Bolts	14
	Pulse Generator Bolt	7–9
	Pulse Rotor Bolt	11–15
	Rear Cover Bolt⑤	5–7
	Rear Cover Bolt⑦	11–15
	Rear Engine Support Insulator To Transmission⑥	13–18
	Rear Engine Support Insulator To Transmission⑧	14—17
	Release Cylinder To Transmission Case	22–30

Continued

TIGHTENING SPECIFICATIONS—Continued

Year	Component	Torque/Ft. Lbs.
1993–96	Reservoir Band	4–5
	Seal Plug	22–30
	Select Plunger Plug	22–25
	Shift Knob⑥	11–15
	Shift Knob⑧	3.3–5.4
	Side Cover Bolt	5–7
	Slotted Nut	15–43
	Speedometer Sleeve Clamp Bolt⑧	7–9
	Speedometer Sleeve Clamp Bolt⑩	11–15
	Starter Motor Mounting Bolt②	20–25
	Starting Motor Mounting Bolts⑧	16–23
	Stopper Bracket Assembly Attaching Bolt	11–15
	Stopper Plate To Control Housing⑥	13–18
	Stopper Plate To Control Housing⑧	5–8
	Transfer Adapter And Transmission Case Coupling Bolt	11–15
	Transfer Case Adapter To Transmission Case Mounting Bolts	30
	Transfer Mounting Bracket To Transmission	13–18
	Transfer Mounting Bracket Mounting Bolts	13–18
	Transfer Mounting Bracket To Pipe	25–40
	Transmission Case And Clutch Housing	86
	Transmission Case And Lower Case	17
	Transmission Case And Transfer Adapter	30
	Transmission Case PTO Cover	14
	Transmission To Engine (A)⑨	47–61
	Transmission To Engine (B)⑨	58–72
	Transmission To Engine⑪	32–39
	Transmission To Exhaust Pipe Mounting Bracket	15–20
	Transmission To Transmission Stay	22–30
	Undercover Attaching Bolt	5–7
	4WD Indicator Light Switch	22

① — Montero.

② — Models except 2WD Pickup.

③ — Pickup.

④ — Montero 4WD.

⑤ — Montero transfer case assembly.

⑥ — Pickup 4WD.

⑦ — Pickup transfer case assembly.

⑧ — Pickup 2WD.

⑨ — 4WD models.

⑩ — Transfer case.

⑪ — 2WD models.

Rear Axle & Suspension

INDEX

	Page No.
Coil Spring, Replace	28-41
Control Arm, Replace	28-41
Lower	28-41
Differential Carrier, Replace	28-41
Lateral Rod, Replace	28-41
Leaf Spring, Replace	28-41
Rear Axle, Replace	28-39
Montero	28-39
Rear Axle Shaft, Replace	28-39
Installation	28-40
Removal	28-39
Shock Absorber, Replace	28-41
Stabilizer Bar, Replace	28-41
Tightening Specifications	28-43

REAR AXLE

REPLACE

MONTERO

1. Disconnect battery ground cable.
2. Raise and support vehicle.
3. Support rear axle using suitable jack stands.
4. Remove rear axle assembly in numbered sequence as shown, **Fig. 1,** noting the following:
   a. Make alignment marks on flange yoke of rear propeller shaft and flange of differential.
   b. After supporting axle assembly by floor jack, remove lower arm assembly.
   c. Remove rear axle assembly toward the rear of the vehicle. **Use care not to allow axle to fall.**
5. Reverse procedure to install, noting the following:
   a. Install lateral rod bolt from the axle housing side.
   b. Install lower arm washers as shown **Fig. 2.**
   c. After installing stabilizer bar bracket, ensure amount of projection of stabilizer bar bolt is 0.59–0.67 inch.
   d. Align propeller shaft mating marks made during disassembly.

REAR AXLE SHAFT

REPLACE

REMOVAL

1. Raise and support rear of vehicle, then remove rear wheel and brake drum and disconnect brake hose from wheel cylinder.
2. Disconnect bearing case from axle housing end, **Figs. 3 and 4.**
3. Remove brake backing plate, if equipped, bearing case, and axle shaft as an assembly, using slide hammer and adapter tool, No. MB990211-01 and axle puller tool, No. MB990241-01 or equivalent, to remove axle shaft if necessary.
4. Remove O-ring and wheel bearing preload shims.
5. Using slide hammer and adapter tool, No. MB990211-01 and seal removal tool, No. MB990212 or equivalent, remove oil seal.
6. **On Pickup,** proceed as follows:
   a. Remove wheel bearing by first removing lock washer, then using locknut spanner wrench tool, No. MB990785-01 or equivalent, remove the locknut.
   b. Remove washers, then reinsert

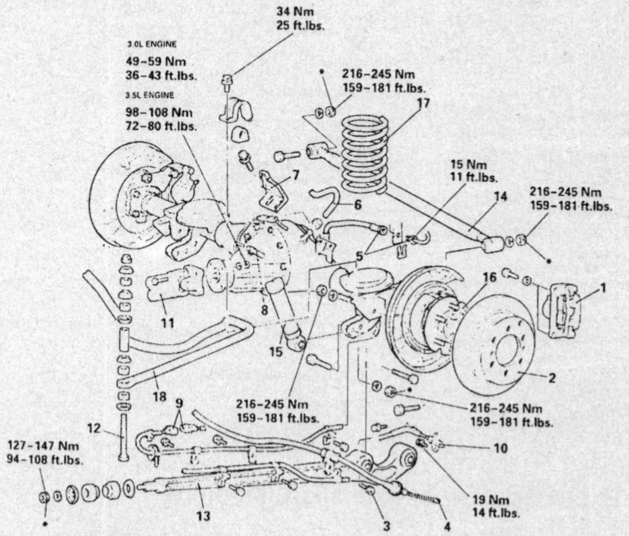

34 Nm
25 ft.lbs.
3.0L ENGINE
49-59 Nm
36-43 ft.lbs.
3.5L ENGINE
98-108 Nm
72-80 ft.lbs.
216-245 Nm
159-181 ft.lbs.
15 Nm
11 ft.lbs.
216-245 Nm
159-181 ft.lbs.
216-245 Nm
159-181 ft.lbs.
216-245 Nm
159-181 ft.lbs.
127-147 Nm
94-108 ft.lbs.
19 Nm
14 ft.lbs.

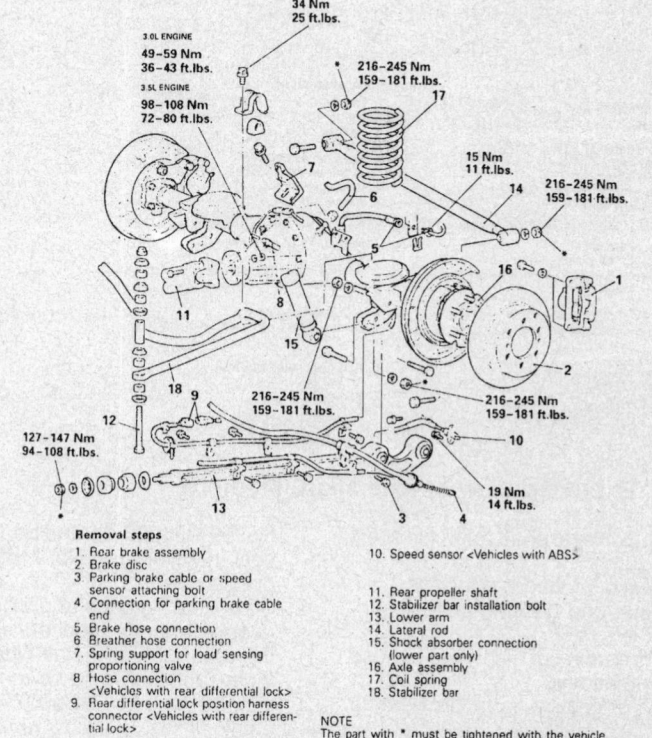

Removal steps

1. Rear brake assembly
2. Brake disc
3. Parking brake cable or speed sensor attaching bolt
4. Connection for parking brake cable end
5. Brake hose connection
6. Breather hose connection
7. Spring support for load sensing proportioning valve
8. Hose connection <Vehicles with rear differential lock>
9. Rear differential lock position harness connector <Vehicles with rear differential lock>
10. Speed sensor <Vehicles with ABS>
11. Rear propeller shaft
12. Stabilizer bar installation bolt
13. Lower arm
14. Lateral rod
15. Shock absorber connection (lower part only)
16. Axle assembly
17. Coil spring
18. Stabilizer bar

NOTE
The part with * must be tightened with the vehicle lowered to the ground.

MT3039100008000X

Fig. 1 Axle assembly replacement. Montero

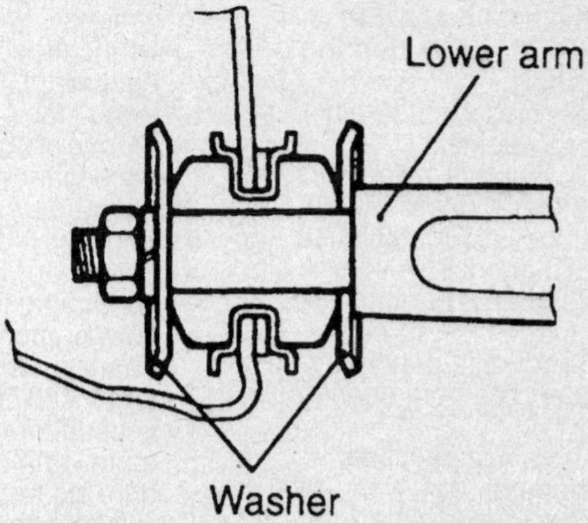

Lower arm
Washer

MT3039500056000X

Fig. 2 Lower arm washer installation. Montero

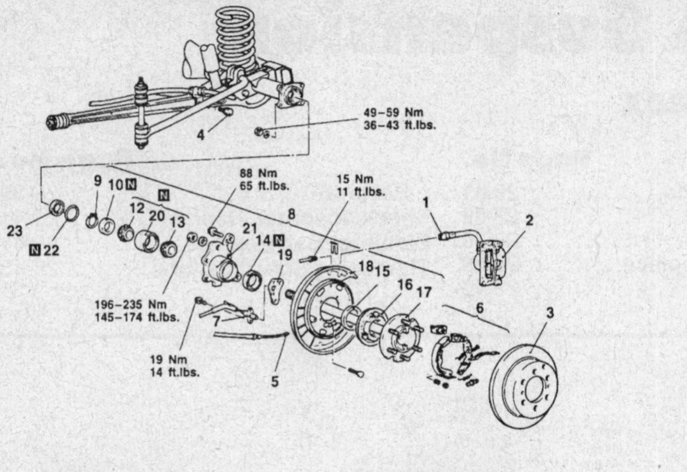
49-59 Nm
36-43 ft.lbs.
88 Nm
65 ft.lbs.
15 Nm
11 ft.lbs.
196-235 Nm
145-174 ft.lbs.
19 Nm
14 ft.lbs.

Removal steps

1. Connection for brake pipe
2. Rear brake assembly
3. Brake disc
4. Parking brake cable attaching bolt
5. Parking cable end
6. Parking brake assembly
7. Speed sensor <Vehicles with ABS>
8. Axle shaft assembly
9. Snap ring
10. Retainer
11. Axle shaft sub assembly (Parts from step 13 to step 17)
12. Bearing inner race (inner)
13. Bearing inner race (outer)
14. Oil seal
15. Dust cover <Vehicles without ABS>
16. Rotor assembly <Vehicles with ABS>
17. Axle shaft
18. Backing plate
19. Speed sensor bracket <Vehicles with ABS>
20. Bearing outer race
21. Bearing case
22. O-ring
23. Oil seal

Installation steps

23. Oil seal
22. O-ring
21. Bearing case
20. Bearing outer race
19. Sped sensor bracket <Vehicles with ABS>
18. Backing plate
17. Axle shaft
16. Rotor assembly <Vehicles with ABS>
15. Dust cover <Vehicles with ABS>
13. Bearing inner race (outer)
14. Oil seal
12. Bearing inner race (inner)
10. Retainer
9. Snap ring
8. Axle shaft assembly
7. Speed sensor <Vehicles with ABS>

6. Parking brake assembly

5. Parking cable end
3. Brake disc
2. Rear brake assembly
1. Connection for brake pipe

MT3039100006000X

Fig. 3 Exploded view of axle shaft. Montero

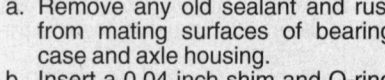

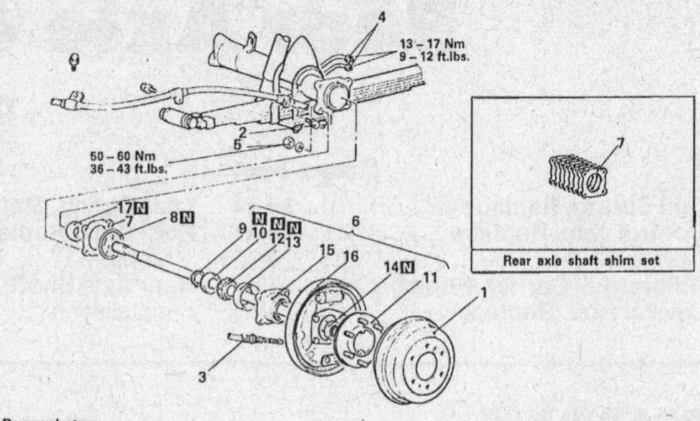
13-17 Nm
9-12 ft.lbs.
50-60 Nm
36-43 ft.lbs.
Rear axle shaft shim set

Removal steps

1. Brake drum
2. Parking brake cable attaching bolts
3. Connection for parking brake cable and rear brake assembly

4. Brake tube connection
5. Nut
Adjustment of rear axle shaft end play
6. Rear axle shaft assembly (with parking brake cable)
7. Shim
8. O-ring
9. Snap ring
10. Retainer ring
11. Rear axle shaft
12. Bearing inner race
13. Bearing outer race
14. Oil seal
15. Bearing case
16. Backing plate
17. Oil seal

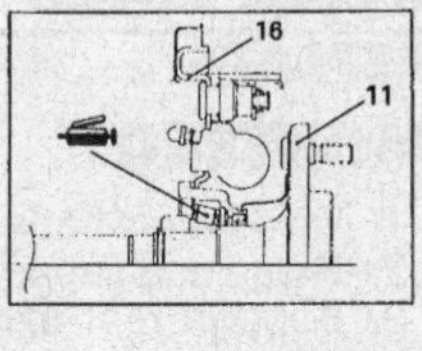

MT3039100007000X

Fig. 4 Exploded view of axle shaft. Pickup

locknut on axle shaft approximately three turns.

7. **On Montero,** proceed as follows:
   a. Remove one backing plate retaining bolt.
   b. Push bearing case down to expose bearing retainer.
   c. Apply protective tape on bearing case.
   d. Secure axle shaft assembly then, using suitable grinder, shave off a point of the bearing retainer until thickness is about 0.08 inch, **Fig. 5. Use care not to damage bearing case or axle shaft.**
   e. Using a suitable chisel, cut retainer ring and remove retainer.
8. **On all models,** install rear axle bearing case removal tool, No. MB990787 or equivalent, as shown, **Fig. 6.** Install nuts and washers diagonally.
9. Remove wheel bearing by turning nuts evenly.
10. Using hammer and drift punch, remove bearing outer race from bearing case.
11. Remove oil seal from bearing case.
12. Check all components for wear or damage and check axle shaft for runout.

INSTALLATION

1. After applying specified grease to outer surface of wheel bearing outer race and lip of new oil seal, drive them into bearing case using handle tool, No. MB990938-01 and bearing and oil seal installer tool, No. MB990937-01, or equivalent.
2. Slide bearing case and wheel bearing over axle shaft, lubricate wheel bearing rollers, then install wheel bearing inner race with axle bearing remover/installer tool, No. MB990799, or equivalent.
3. **On Pickup,** proceed as follows:
   a. Install washer, lock washer and locknut, tighten locknut to specifications with locknut spanner wrench tool, No. MB990785-01, or equivalent.
   b. Bend tab on lock washer into groove on locknut, tightening nut as necessary to align tab and groove.
4. **On all models,** install bearing retainer as follows:
   a. Press on bearing retainer while confirming that 11,023 lbs. of pressure or more is needed to start the bearing retainer on the axle shaft and 17,637 lbs. of pressure or more is used for the final pressure input.
   b. Install retainer snap ring, and measure clearance (A) as shown **Fig. 7** is less than 0.0065 inch.
5. Lubricate lip of new oil seal, then using oil seal installer tool, No. MB990930-01 and handle tool No. MB990938, or equivalent, drive oil seal into axle housing.
6. Adjust axial play of rear axle shaft as follows:
   a. Remove any old sealant and rust from mating surfaces of bearing case and axle housing.
   b. Insert a 0.04 inch shim and O-ring into left side of axle housing and apply semi-drying sealer to mating surface of bearing case.
   c. Insert left side axle shaft assembly into left side of axle housing, then tighten bearing case to specifications.
   d. Insert right side axle shaft assembly into right side axle housing without using shim or O-ring, then **torque** bearing case to 4 ft. lbs. Measure gap between bearing case and axle housing.
   e. Loosen nut and separate right side axle shaft assembly from axle housing.
   f. Using a shim with thickness equal to that of measured gap and a shim with thickness of 0.0020–0.0079 inch, insert shims and O-ring into axle housing, then apply semi-drying sealant to mating surface of bearing case.
   g. Insert right side axle shaft assembly into right side axle housing, then tighten bearing case to specifications.
   h. Using dial indicator, check that axial play of axle shaft is 0.002–0.008 inch. If not, adjust shim thickness.
7. Lubricate bearing case and axle housing end.
8. Attach brake assembly, with wheel cylinder, to axle housing.
9. Insert O-ring between axle housing end and bearing case, then apply semi-drying sealant to bearing case.
10. Tighten bearing case to specifications.
11. Connect brake line to wheel cylinder,

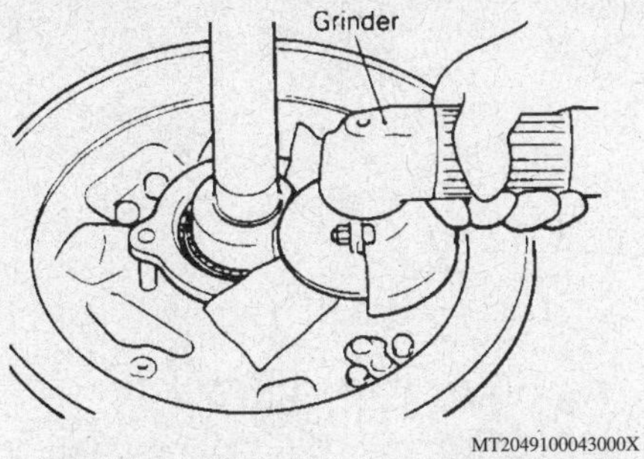
Grinder
MT2049100043000X

Fig. 5 Bearing retainer removal

then install rear brake drum and wheel.

DIFFERENTIAL CARRIER

REPLACE

1. Drain gear oil into appropriate container.
2. Remove parking brake cable adjusting nuts, then disconnect parking brake cables.
3. Raise and support vehicle, then remove wheel and tire assembly.
4. Remove brake drum, then the axle shaft assembly as previously described.
5. Disconnect rear propeller shaft from differential assembly.
6. Remove differential carrier.
7. Reverse procedure to install.

SHOCK ABSORBER

REPLACE

1. Raise rear of vehicle, then position jackstands under frame side sills.
2. Disconnect variable shock absorbers actuator, if equipped.
3. Remove wheel and tire assembly, then disconnect shock absorbers at upper and lower mountings, then remove from vehicle.
4. Reverse procedure to install, noting the following:
   a. Tighten shock absorber attaching nuts to specification.
   b. **On models with variable shock absorbers,** tighten nuts so dimension "A" is 0.04–0.08 inch and dimension "B" is 0.06–0.10 inch, **Fig. 8.**

COIL SPRING

REPLACE

1. Disconnect battery ground cable.
2. Raise and support vehicle.
3. Support rear axle using suitable jack stand.
4. Remove coil spring in numbered sequence as shown **Fig. 9,** while slowly lowering jack supporting axle housing to remove coil spring.
5. Reverse procedure to install.

LEAF SPRING

REPLACE

1. Loosen rear wheel lug nuts, then jack up rear of vehicle with jack placed under differential.

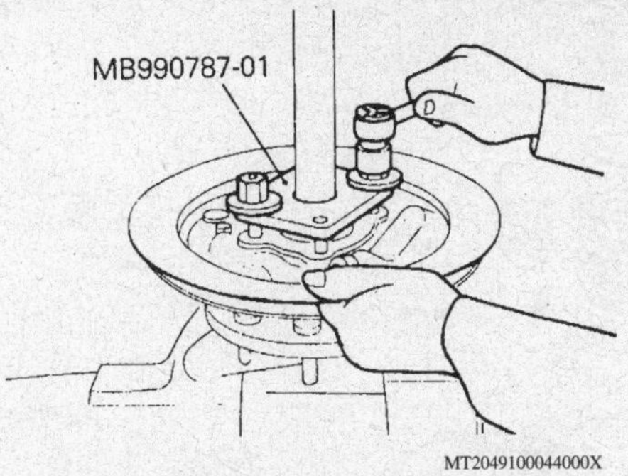
MB990787-01
MT2049100044000X

Fig. 6 Wheel bearing removal

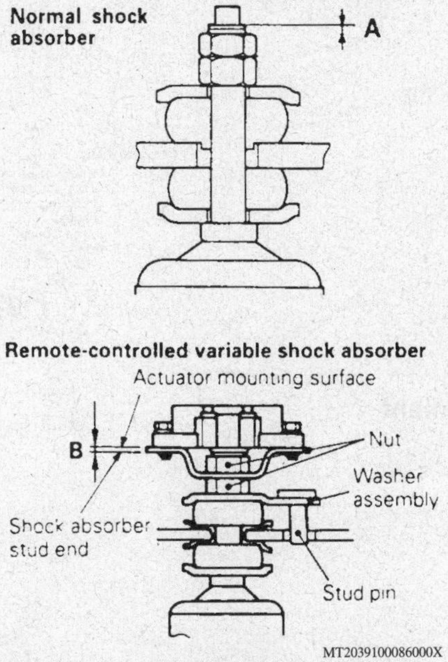
Normal shock absorber
A
Remote-controlled variable shock absorber
Actuator mounting surface
B
Nut
Washer assembly
Shock absorber stud end
Stud pin
MT2039100086000X

Fig. 8 Variable shock absorber actuator installation

2. Remove rear wheels and support vehicle on axle stands placed forward of rear spring front bracket, with jack still applying slight upward pressure on axle assembly, **Fig. 10.**
3. Make mating marks on rear propeller shaft flange yoke and companion flange of differential case to facilitate installation, then remove propeller shaft. Remove adjusting nuts, then disconnect parking brake cables.
4. Loosen joint between brake hose and brake line and pull out stops to disconnect brake hose.
5. Disconnect rear cable of parking brake at balancer.
6. **On 4WD models,** disconnect breather hose.
7. **On all models,** disconnect shock absorbers at lower end.
8. Remove spring U-bolts, then the spring seats.
9. Remove spring shackle pin nuts, then the shackle plate. **Be careful not to drop axle housing from jack.**
10. Remove axle housing by slowly lowering jack.
11. Reverse procedure to install, noting the following:
    a. Align match marks when installing

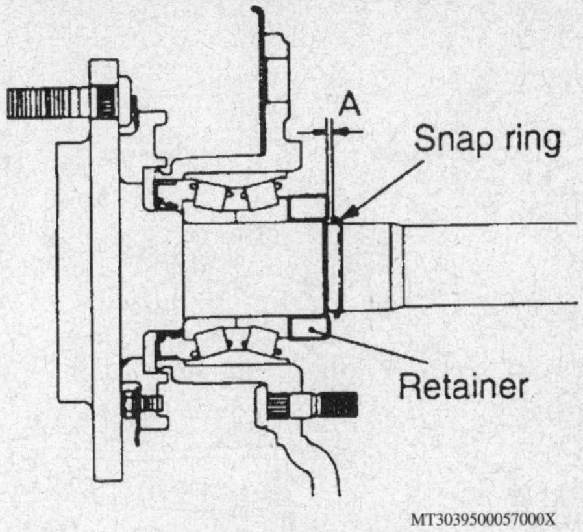
A
Snap ring
Retainer
MT3039500057000X

Fig. 7 Axle bearing retainer snap ring clearance

propeller shaft. Install spring support so distance between hole on load sensing proportioning valve lever and spring support hole is 6.77–6.93 inch.
    b. Bleed rear brake system.

CONTROL ARM

REPLACE

LOWER

1. Disconnect battery ground cable.
2. Raise and support vehicle.
3. Support rear axle using suitable jack stand.
4. Replace lower arm in numbered sequence as shown **Fig. 11,** installing lower arm front bushing as shown **Fig. 12.**

STABILIZER BAR

REPLACE

1. Disconnect battery ground cable.
2. Raise and support vehicle.
3. Remove rear stabilizer bar in numbered sequence as shown **Fig. 13.**
4. Reverse procedure to install.

LATERAL ROD

REPLACE

1. Disconnect battery ground cable.
2. Raise and support vehicle.
3. Disconnect shock absorber lower mounting bolt.
4. Disconnect left brake cable attaching bolt.
5. Remove rear differential lock position harness attaching bolt.
6. Disconnect rear anti-lock brake sensor (ABS) sensor attaching bolt.
7. Disconnect lower arm, then remove arm from vehicle.
8. Reverse procedure to install.

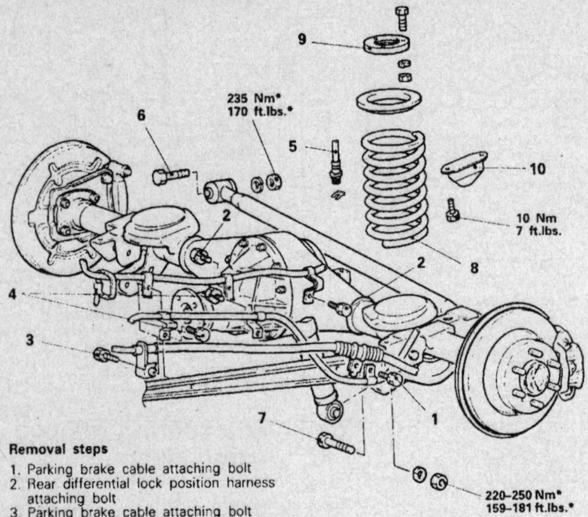
235 Nm*
170 ft.lbs.*
10 Nm
7 ft.lbs.
220-250 Nm*
159-181 ft.lbs.*

Removal steps

1. Parking brake cable attaching bolt
2. Rear differential lock position harness attaching bolt
3. Parking brake cable attaching bolt
4. Rear sensor attaching bolt (Vehicles with A.B.S.)
5. Brake hose connection
6. Lateral rod mounting bolt (body side only)
7. Shock absorber mounting bolt (lower side only)
8. Coil spring
9. Rear spring pad
10. Helper rubber

NOTE
*: Indicates part which should be temporarily tightened, and then fully tightened with the vehicle in the unladen condition.

MT2039100088000X

Fig. 9 Coil spring replacement

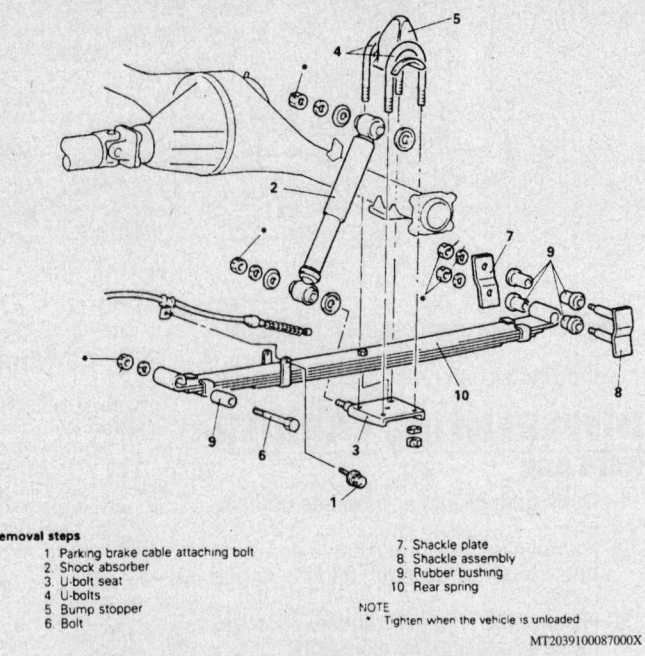

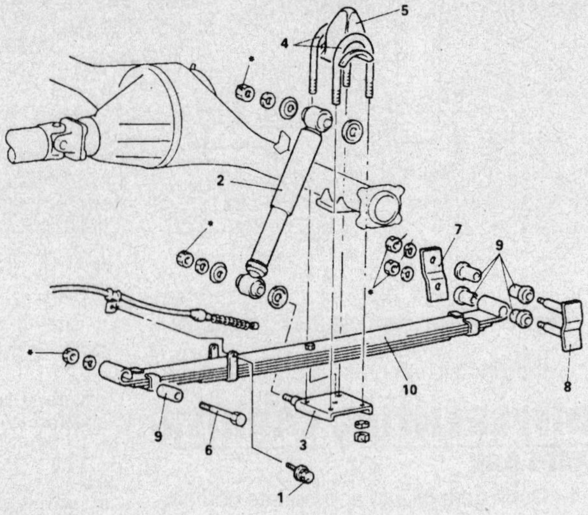

Removal steps

1. Parking brake cable attaching bolt
2. Shock absorber
3. U-bolt seat
4. U-bolts
5. Bump stopper
6. Bolt
7. Shackle plate
8. Shackle assembly
9. Rubber bushing
10. Rear spring

NOTE
*: Tighten when the vehicle is unloaded

MT2039100087000X

Fig. 10 Leaf spring replacement

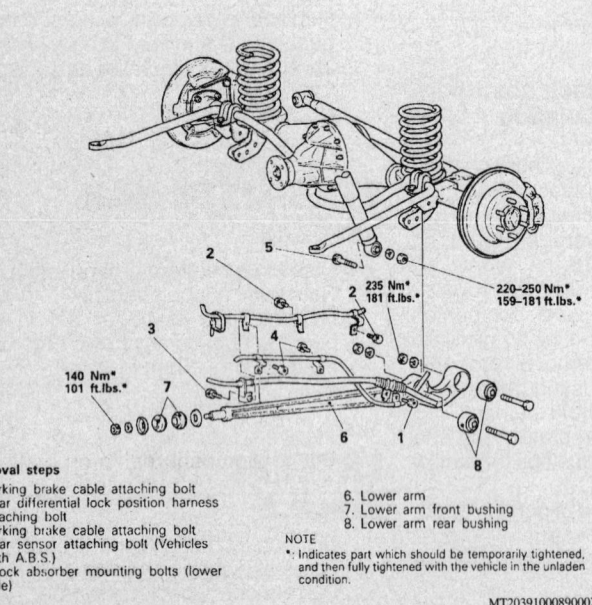

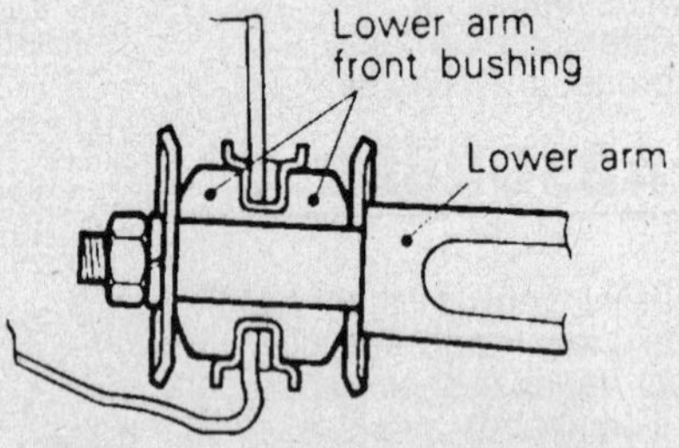
Lower arm
front bushing
Lower arm

MT2039100090000X

Fig. 12 Lower arm bushing installation

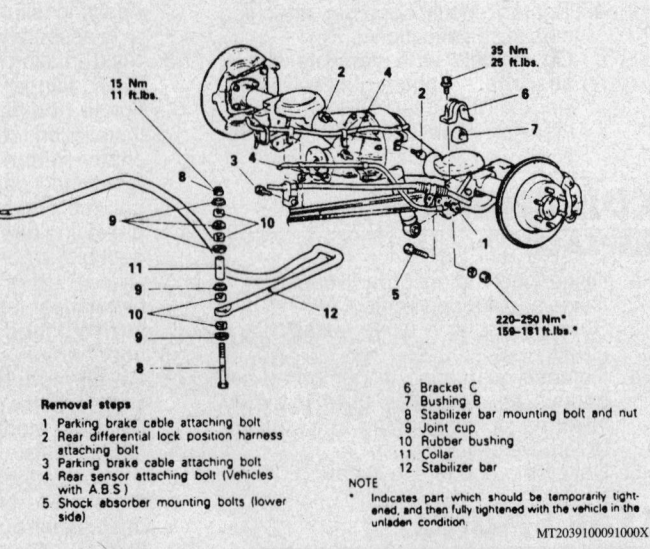

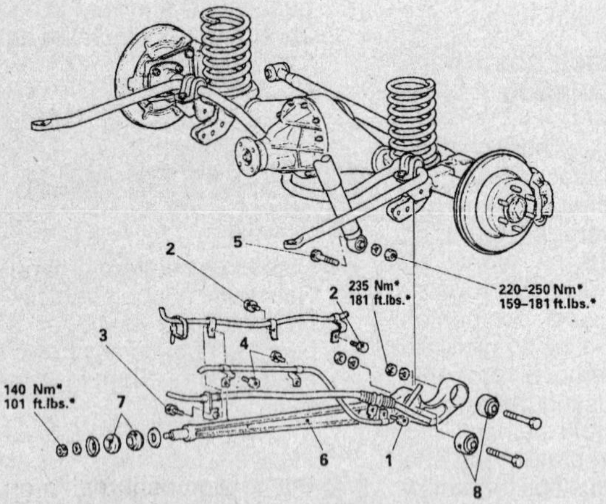
235 Nm*
181 ft.lbs.*
220-250 Nm*
159-181 ft.lbs.*
140 Nm*
101 ft.lbs.*

Removal steps

1. Parking brake cable attaching bolt
2. Rear differential lock position harness attaching bolt
3. Parking brake cable attaching bolt
4. Rear sensor attaching bolt (Vehicles with A.B.S.)
5. Shock absorber mounting bolts (lower side)
6. Lower arm
7. Lower arm front bushing
8. Lower arm rear bushing

NOTE
*: Indicates part which should be temporarily tightened, and then fully tightened with the vehicle in the unladen condition.

MT2039100089000X

Fig. 11 Lower arm replacement

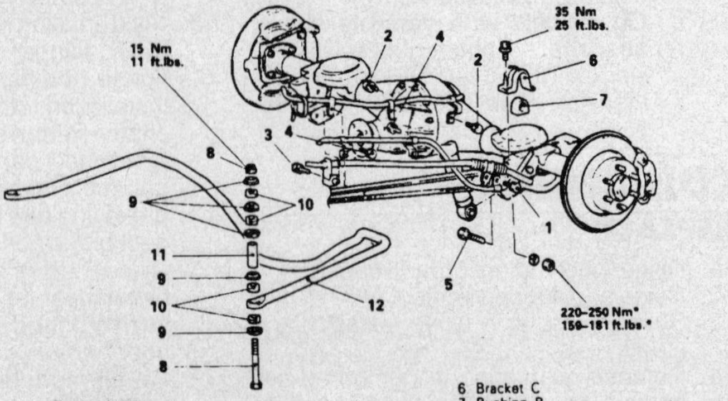
35 Nm
25 ft.lbs.
15 Nm
11 ft.lbs.
220-250 Nm*
159-181 ft.lbs.*

Removal steps

1. Parking brake cable attaching bolt
2. Rear differential lock position harness attaching bolt
3. Parking brake cable attaching bolt
4. Rear sensor attaching bolt (Vehicles with A.B.S.)
5. Shock absorber mounting bolts (lower side)
6. Bracket C
7. Bushing B
8. Stabilizer bar mounting bolt and nut
9. Joint cup
10. Rubber bushing
11. Collar
12. Stabilizer bar

NOTE
*: Indicates part which should be temporarily tightened, and then fully tightened with the vehicle in the unladen condition.

MT2039100091000X

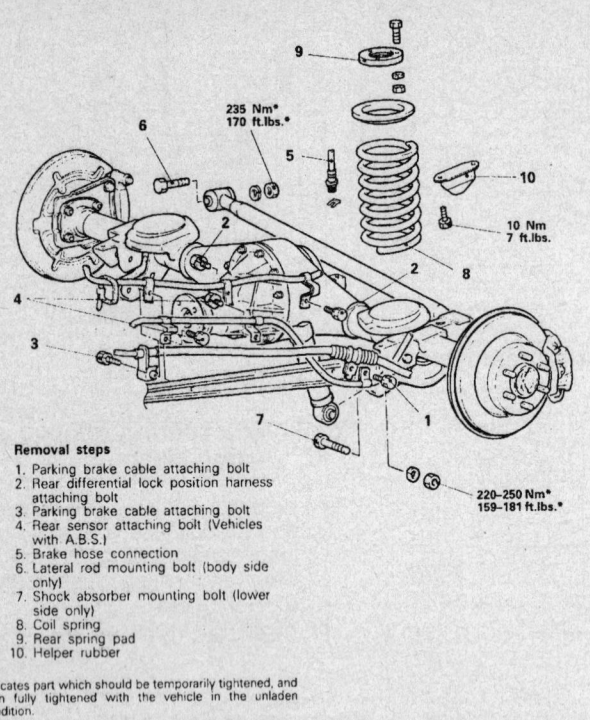

Fig. 13 Stabilizer bar replacement

TIGHTENING SPECIFICATIONS

Year	Component	Torque/ Ft. Lbs.
1993–96	Axle Bumper To Body	6–9
	Bearing Case To Axle Housing	36–43
	Brake Line Flare Nut	9–12
	Differential Carrier To Axle Housing	④
	Drain Plug	36–51
	Filler Plug	29–43
	Front Pin Assembly Mounting Bolt	10–14
	Front Pin Assembly Mounting Nut	33–43
	Lateral Rod Mounting Bolt	72–87
	Lateral Rod Mounting Nut	80–94
	Leaf Spring Front Mounting Bolt	87–116
	Lower Control Arm To Axle Housing	137–159
	Lower Control Arm To Body	94–108
	Propeller Shaft	36–43
	Rear Axle Bearing Locknut	130–159
	Shackle Assembly Mounting Nut	33–43
	Shock Absorber Mounting Nut	②
	Stabilizer Bar To Axle Housing	22–29
	U-Bolt Mounting Nut	①
	Wheel Lug Nuts	③

① — Montero, 61–80 ft. lbs.; Pickup, 72–87 ft. lbs.
② — Montero: upper, 11 ft. lbs.; lower, 65–76 ft. lbs.; Pickup: upper, 9–13 ft. lbs.; lower, 7–10 ft. lbs.
③ — Montero, 72–87 ft. lbs.; Pickup, 87–101 ft. lbs.
④ — Montero w/3.0L, 29–40 ft. lbs.; RWD Pickup, 18–22 ft. lbs.; 4WD Pickup, 29–40 ft. lbs.

Front Suspension & Steering

INDEX

	Page No.
Front Suspension Service	28-44
Montero & 4WD Pickup	28-44
2WD Pickup	28-46
Hub Service	28-43
Montero & 4WD Pickup	28-43
Manual Steering Gear, Replace	28-48
Pickup	28-48
Manual Steering Gears	29-1
Power Steering	29-1
Power Steering Gear, Replace	28-47
Montero	28-47
Pickup	28-48
Stabilizer Bar, Replace	28-47
Montero & 4WD Pickup	28-47
2WD Pickup	28-47
Strut Bar, Replace	28-47
2WD Pickup	28-47
Tightening Specifications	28-48
Torsion Bar, Replace	28-46

HUB SERVICE

MONTERO & 4WD PICKUP

REMOVAL

1. Remove wheel and tire assembly, then the brake caliper assembly with brake hose connected. **Suspend caliper assembly from frame using a wire hook to prevent damage to brake hose.**
2. **On models with automatic freewheeling hubs,**proceed as follows:
   a. Remove automatic freewheeling hub cover. When cover cannot be loosened by hand, protect cover with shop towel to prevent damage, then loosen cover using a suitable oil filter wrench.
   b. Remove O-ring from hub cover, then the snap ring and spacer.
   c. Remove automatic freewheeling hub using tool, No. MD998360 or equivalent, **Fig. 1.**
3. **On models with manual freewheeling hubs,** proceed as follows:
   a. Place hub in free position, then remove freewheeling hub cover.
   b. Remove snap ring attaching freewheeling hub body to driveshaft.
   c. Remove freewheeling hub to front hub attaching bolts, then the freewheeling hub assembly, **Fig. 1.**
4. **On all models,** remove lock washer, then the hub locknut using tool, No. MB990954, or equivalent **Fig. 2.**
5. Pull front hub with brake disc from knuckle, using care not to drop outer wheel bearing inner race.
6. Remove grease from inside front hub, then using a suitable drift, drive bearing races from hub.
7. Place alignment marks on brake disc and hub, then separate hub and disc as necessary.
8. Inspect all components for wear and damage. Measure spindle bearing seating area diameter, **Fig. 3.** Diameter should be 1.7805–1.7812 inches.

DISASSEMBLE

Automatic Freewheeling Hub

1. Remove cover, then the O-ring.
2. Remove housing, then depress brake "B" and remove C-ring.
3. Remove brakes "B" and "A," then the brake spring.
4. Remove housing snap ring, then using tool, No. MB990811-01 or equivalent,

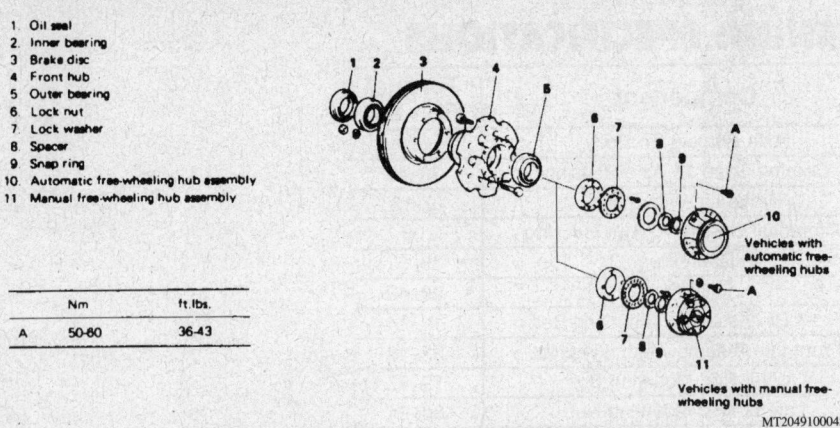

1. Oil seal
2. Inner bearing
3. Brake disc
4. Front hub
5. Outer bearing
6. Lock nut
7. Lock washer
8. Spacer
9. Snap ring
10. Automatic free-wheeling hub assembly
11. Manual free-wheeling hub assembly

	Nm	ft.lbs.
A	50-60	36-43

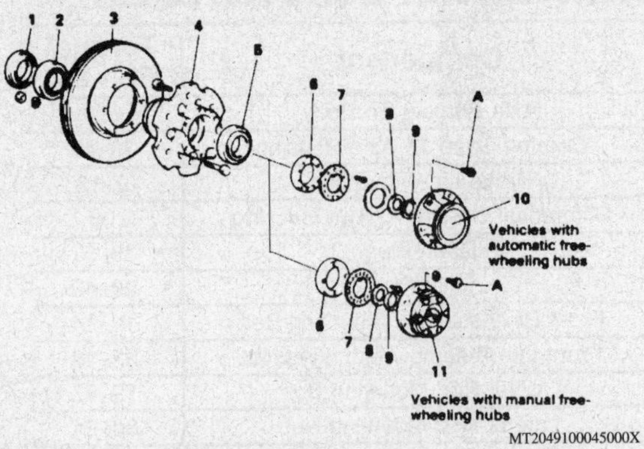

Vehicles with automatic free-wheeling hubs
Vehicles with manual free-wheeling hubs
MT2049100045000X

Fig. 1 Exploded view of front axle hub

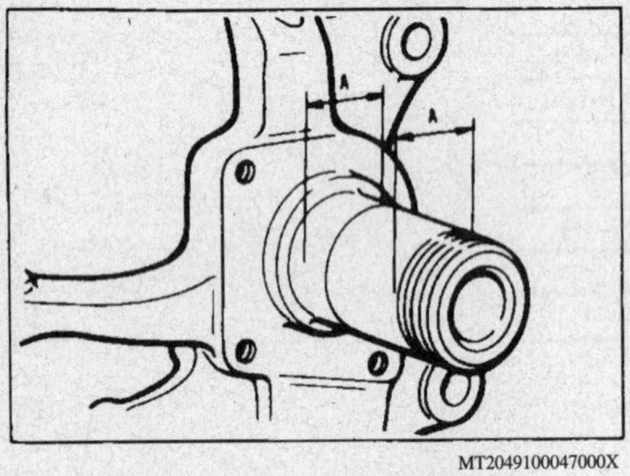

MT2049100047000X

Fig. 3 Spindle inspection

depress drive gear and remove retainer and C-ring.

5. Using tool, No. MB990811-01 or equivalent and a suitable press, remove drive gear, slide gear and return spring.
6. Remove retainer "B," then the retainer bearing.
7. Remove drive gear snap ring and discard.
8. Remove retainer "A," then the drive gear.
9. Depress cam, then remove slide gear C-ring.
10. Remove cam, then the spring holder, shift spring and slide gear.

Manual Freewheeling Hub

1. Remove snap ring and inner hub from freewheeling hub body using a suitable screwdriver, **Fig. 4.**
2. Remove snap ring from inner hub with snap ring pliers.

ASSEMBLE

Automatic Freewheeling Hub

Reverse disassembly procedure to assemble, noting the following:

1. Apply suitable grease to mounting surfaces of all components.
2. Pack groove in brake "B," groove around outside of retainer and both sides of bearing with suitable grease.
3. Install return spring with smaller coil diameter side toward spring seat.

Manual Freewheeling Hub

Reverse disassembly procedure to assemble, noting the following:

1. Apply suitable grease to outer surface of freewheeling hub ring, inner hub and clutch and inside of freewheeling hub body.

INSTALLATION

1. Apply grease to wheel bearing outer races, then using a suitable drift, drive outer races into front hub.
2. Pack inner and outer bearings with suitable grease. Apply grease to oil seal lip.
3. Evenly coat inner wall of front hub with grease.
4. Position inner bearing and oil seal on hub, then install oil seal using tool, No. MB990985 or equivalent.
5. If removed, install brake disc on front hub, **Fig. 1,** tightening attaching bolts alternately and evenly to 36–44 ft. lbs. After assembling, check brake disc runout. Brake disc runout should not exceed 0.006 inch.
6. Carefully install front hub on steering knuckle spindle.
7. Install outer bearing on spindle, then install and **torque** spindle nut to 94–145 ft. lbs. Loosen spindle nut and retighten to 18 ft. lbs., then back-off and install lock washer. **If hole in lock washer is not aligned with hole in spindle nut, then nut may be loosened up to an additional 20° to obtain proper alignment.**
8. Measure force required to rotate front hub, using a suitable spring scale, **Fig. 5.** The force required to rotate front hub assembly should be between 0.9–3.1 lbs. on Pickup or 0.9–4.1 lbs. on Montero. If not within specification, readjust bearings as described in step 7.
9. Apply grease to inner surface of freewheeling hub body assembly.
10. Apply semi-dry sealant to front hub surface to which the freewheeling hub body assembly is attached.
11. Install freewheeling hub body assembly on front hub, then tighten attaching bolts to specification.
12. Install freewheeling hub cover and tighten to specification.
13. Install brake caliper assembly.

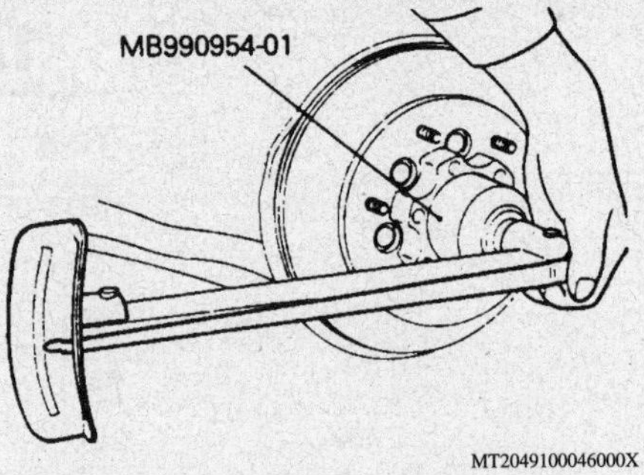

MB990954-01
MT2049100046000X

Fig. 2 Spindle nut removal

FRONT SUSPENSION SERVICE

MONTERO & 4WD PICKUP

Replacement

1. Raise and support vehicle.
2. Detach dust covers from anchor arm assembly and anchor arm.
3. Scribe alignment mark on torsion bar to line up with mark on anchor arm.
4. Loosen adjusting nut and remove torsion bar from anchor arm. It may be necessary to remove anchor arm assembly to remove torsion bar.
5. Detach stabilizer bar from lower arm.
6. Remove shock absorber.
7. Remove cotter pin and slotted nut from tie rod end and upper and lower ball joint studs.
8. Using tool, No. MB990635 or equivalent, disconnect tie rod from knuckle.
9. Using tools, No. MB990635 and No. MB990809 or equivalent, loosen connection between ball joint and knuckle, tapping knuckle with plastic mallet.
10. After upper ball joint has been removed from knuckle, disconnect lower ball joint. Slotted nut should be temporarily tightened to upper ball joint. **When knuckle is removed, be careful not to damage Birfield joint boots.**
11. Disconnect knuckle from ball joint.
12. Remove bolts connecting upper arm shaft to arm post of side frame, then the upper arm assembly, retaining camber adjusting shims.
13. Remove lower arm assembly.
14. Reverse procedure to install, noting the following:
    a. Install camber adjusting shims between upper arm shaft and arm post of side frame, then install bolt connecting upper arm shaft to arm post of side frame as shown, **Fig. 6,** and tighten to specification.
    b. Assemble lower arm to bracket of side frame. Do not tighten at this time.
    c. Assemble knuckle to upper and lower ball joints, then tighten to specification.
    d. Attach shock absorber to arm post of side frame with double nuts. Tighten first nut, ensuring distance between bottom of nut and end of strut is 0.81 inch, then tighten to specification.

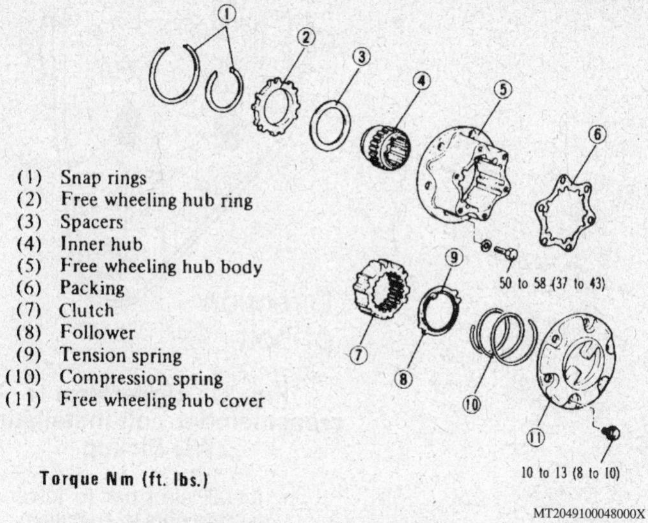
(1) Snap rings
(2) Free wheeling hub ring
(3) Spacers
(4) Inner hub
(5) Free wheeling hub body
(6) Packing
(7) Clutch
(8) Follower
(9) Tension spring
(10) Compression spring
(11) Free wheeling hub cover
Torque Nm (ft. lbs.)
50 to 58 (37 to 43)
10 to 13 (8 to 10)
MT2049100048000X

Fig. 4 Manual freewheeling hub components

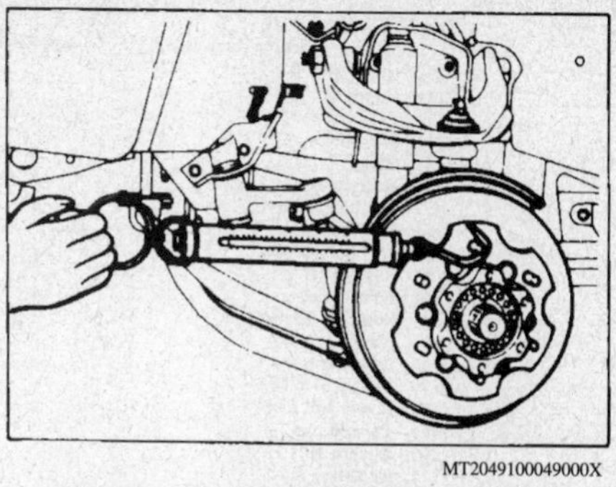
MT2049100049000X

Fig. 5 Front hub assembly bearing adjustment

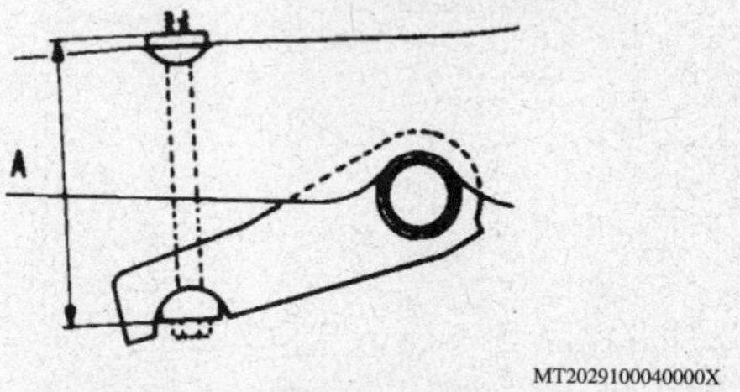
A
MT2029100040000X

Fig. 8 Torsion bar adjusting nut installation. Montero & 4WD Pickup

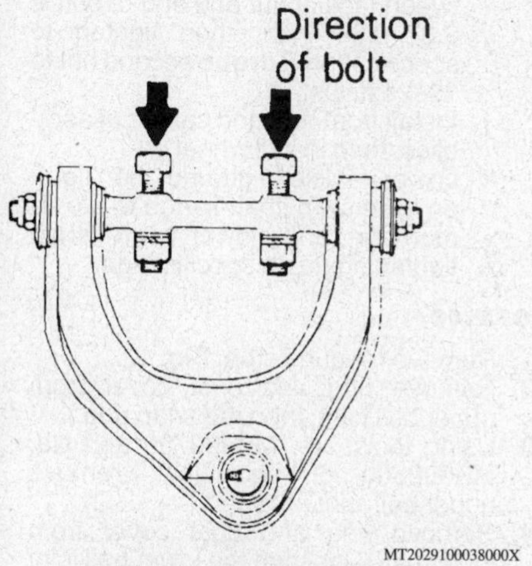
Direction
of bolt
MT2029100038000X

Fig. 6 Upper arm to crossmember bolt installation. Montero & 4WD Pickup

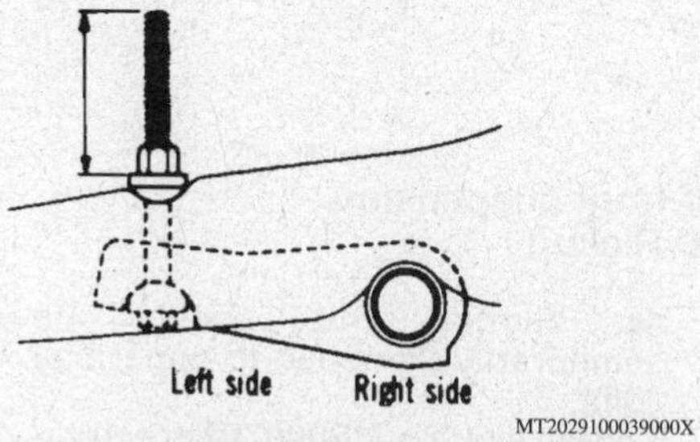
Left side
Right side
MT2029100039000X

Fig. 7 Torsion bar & anchor arm installation. Montero & 4WD Pickup

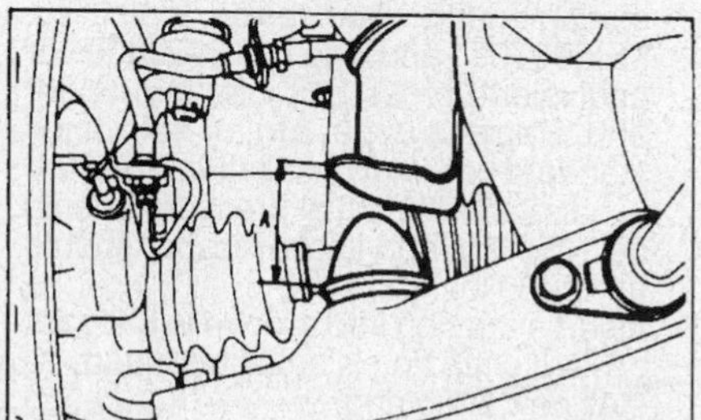
MT2029100041000X

Fig. 9 Distance between bump stop & bump stop bracket. Montero & 4WD Pickup

e. Apply suitable grease to torsion bar serrations, anchor arms serrations, inside of dust boot and anchor bolt thread.
f. Left and right torsion bars are marked for identification.
g. Face end of torsion bar with identification mark forward and align mark on anchor arm with mating mark on torsion bar when torsion bar is inserted in anchor arm. If installing new torsion bar, align serration painted white with mark on anchor arm.
h. When torsion bar and anchor arm are assembled, and rebound stop is in contact with side frame, dimension "A," **Fig. 7,** should be 5.52–5.82 inches for left side and 5.32–5.62 inch for right side on Pickup or 5.43–5.73 inches for left side and 5.04–5.35 inches for right side on Montero.
i. Tighten adjusting nut, ensuring dimension, **Fig. 8,** is 3.0 inches for left side and 2.7 inches for right side on Pickup, and 2.17 inches for left side and 2.68 inches for right side on Montero.
j. Install stabilizer bar to lower arm, ensuring distance between bottom of nut and end of bolt is 0.63–0.71 inch
k. Install front hub and caliper assemblies, then inspect driveshaft play in axial direction. Install wheel.
l. With vehicle lowered to ground, tighten to specification.
m. Measure distance "A" **Fig. 9.** If distance is not 3.1 inches, tighten adjusting nut of anchor bolt to obtain correct distance. When tightening adjusting nuts, ensure anchor bolt protrusion does not exceed 3.5 inches on left side or 3.3 inches on right side.

Service

1. Remove knuckle oil seal and spacer, **Fig. 10.**
2. Drive out needle bearing by tapping needles uniformly.
3. Remove rebound stop.
4. Remove ring, dust cover and snap ring from upper ball joint.
5. Using tools, No. MB990799 and No. MB990800 or equivalent, remove upper ball joint.
6. Remove lower ball joint from lower arm.
7. Remove ring and dust cover from lower ball joint.
8. Using tools, No. MB990883 and No. MB990957 or equivalent, remove bushing "B" from lower arm.
9. Using tool, No. MB990958 or equivalent, remove bushing "A" from front suspension crossmember bracket. When removing LH bushing, detach differential carrier.
10. Inspect all components and replace as necessary.
11. Apply suitable grease to roller surface of needle bearing.
12. Using tool, No. MB990956 or equivalent, press in needle bearing until it is flush with knuckle end face.
13. Install spacer into knuckle with smaller inside diameter side toward needle bearing.
14. Using tool, No. MB990985 or equivalent, press in oil seal.
15. Pack suitable grease inside oil seal and on lip.
16. Line up mating marks on upper ball joint with that on upper arm.
17. Using tools, No. MB990799 and No.

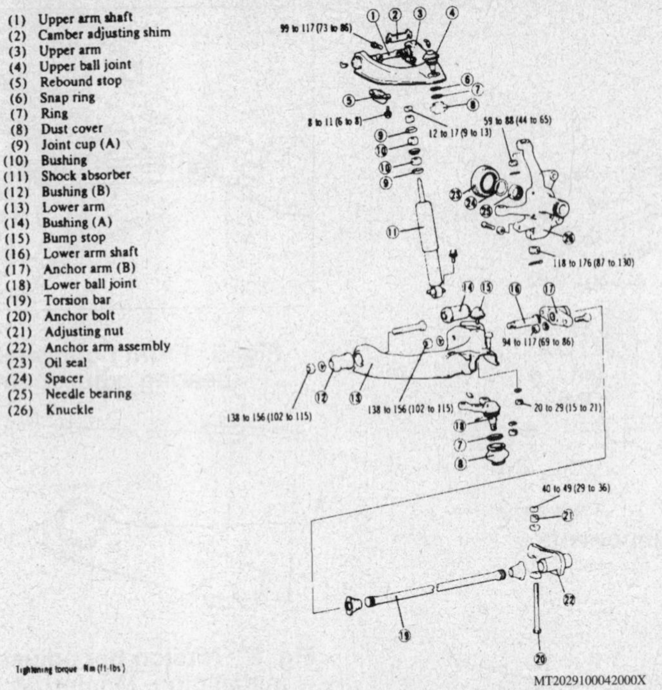
(1) Upper arm shaft
(2) Camber adjusting shim
(3) Upper arm
(4) Upper ball joint
(5) Rebound stop
(6) Snap ring
(7) Ring
(8) Dust cover
(9) Joint cup (A)
(10) Bushing
(11) Shock absorber
(12) Bushing (B)
(13) Lower arm
(14) Bushing (A)
(15) Bump stop
(16) Lower arm shaft
(17) Anchor arm (B)
(18) Lower ball joint
(19) Torsion bar
(20) Anchor bolt
(21) Adjusting nut
(22) Anchor arm assembly
(23) Oil seal
(24) Spacer
(25) Needle bearing
(26) Knuckle
MT2029100042000X

Fig. 10 Exploded view of front suspension. Montero & 4WD Pickup

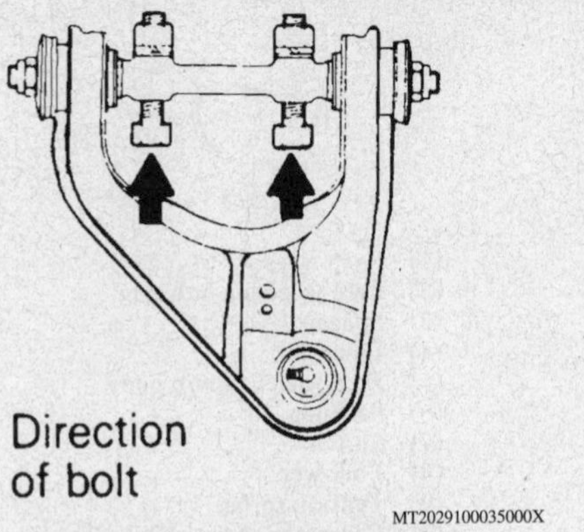
Direction of bolt
MT2029100035000X

Fig. 11 Upper arm to crossmember bolt installation. 2WD Pickup

MB990800 or equivalent, press ball joint into upper arm.
18. Insert snap ring into groove in ball joint case. If snap ring is loose, replace as necessary.
19. Install dust cover and ring and fit to groove of ball joint.
20. Assemble ball joint to lower arm and tighten to specification.
21. Install dust cover with embossed portion facing forward, then install ring into groove of ball joint case.
22. Coat bushing "B" and lower arm with soap solution, then press bushing into lower arm, using tools, No. MB990883 and No. MB990957 or equivalent. Press in bushing, ensuring both ends of bushing protrude from lower arm by same amount.
23. Using tool, No. MB990958 or equivalent, press in busing "A" with collar of bushing facing forward.

2WD PICKUP

Replace

1. Raise and support vehicle.
2. Remove front wheel and caliper assembly, then the front hub assembly.
3. Loosen adjusting nut at tip of strut bar, then disconnect stabilizer and strut bars from lower control arm.
4. Remove shock absorber.
5. Using tool, No. MB990792 or equivalent, compress coil spring.
6. Remove cotter pin and slotted nut from upper and lower ball joint studs.
7. Using tool, No. MB990635 or equivalent, loosen connection between ball joint and knuckle, tapping knuckle with plastic mallet. **After disconnecting upper ball joint from knuckle, disconnect lower ball joint from knuckle. Slotted nut should be temporarily tightened to upper ball joint.**
8. Loosen tool, No. MB990792 or equivalent, remove coil spring and disconnect knuckle from ball joint.
9. Remove lower arm shaft and lower arm.
10. Remove bolts connecting upper arm shaft to crossmember, then remove upper arm as an assembly. Retain camber adjusting shims.
11. Reverse procedure to install, noting the following:
    a. Install camber adjusting shims between upper arm shaft and crossmember. Install bolts connecting upper arm shaft to crossmember in direction shown, **Fig. 11,** then tighten to specification.
    b. Install lower arm shaft to crossmember, leaving nut to lower arm shaft loose. After completion of front suspension installation and with vehicle lowered to ground, tighten to specification.
    c. When installing front spring, insert spring seat between coil spring upper end and crossmember, and place other end in groove of lower arm.
    d. Coil springs have identification marks inscribed. Ensure springs are paired and that they are proper springs for vehicle.
    e. Using tool, No. MB990792 or equivalent, compress springs until lower arm is brought to level position.
    f. Assemble knuckle with upper and lower ball joints, then tighten to specification.
    g. Install shock absorber and tighten to specification.
    h. Install strut bar to lower arm and tighten nuts to specification.
    i. When installing ends of stabilizer bar, tighten first nut so distance between face of nut and end of bolt is 0.87–0.94 inch, then tighten to specification. **Torque** second nut to 19–25 ft. lbs.
    j. Install front hub and caliper assemblies, then install wheel.
    k. Lower vehicle to ground, then tighten lower arm shaft flange to crossmember and lower arm shaft tightening nut to specification.

Service

1. Remove rebound stop, **Fig. 12.**
2. Remove ring and dust cover from upper ball joint, then the snap ring.
3. Using tools, No. MB990799 and No. MB990800 or equivalent, remove upper ball joint.
4. Remove ring and dust cover from lower ball joint, then the lower ball joint from lower arm.
5. Inspect all components and replace as necessary.
6. Line up upper ball joint to upper arm mating marks, then using tools, No. MB990799 and No. MB990800 or equivalent, press ball joint into upper arm. Replace upper arm or ball joint if standard ball joint installation pressure is not obtained. Initial pressure should be 1550 lbs. and final pressure should be 11000 lbs.
7. Insert snap ring into groove in ball joint case. If snap ring is not tightly fitted, install new snap ring.
8. Install dust cover and ring and fit to groove of ball joint.
9. Turn upper arm shaft to obtain specified dimension, **Fig. 13.**
10. Assemble lower ball joint to lower arm and tighten to specification.
11. Install dust cover with embossed portion facing front of vehicle, then install ring into groove of ball joint case.

TORSION BAR

REPLACE

1. Remove torsion bar locknut.

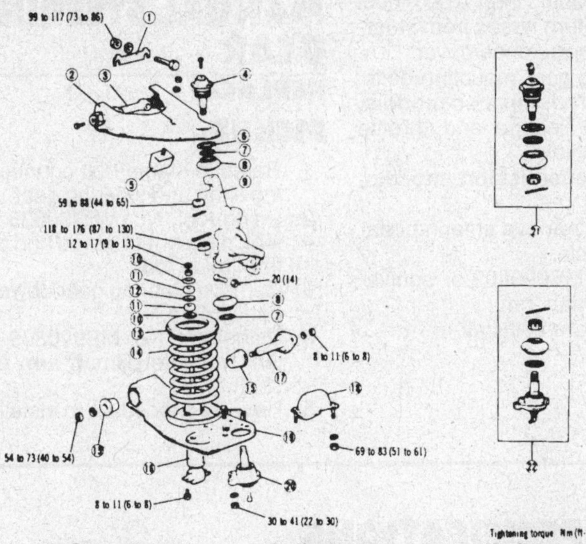
99 to 117 (73 to 86)
59 to 88 (44 to 65)
118 to 176 (87 to 130)
12 to 17 (9 to 13)
20 (14)
8 to 11 (6 to 8)
69 to 83 (51 to 61)
54 to 73 (40 to 54)
8 to 11 (6 to 8)
30 to 41 (22 to 30)
Tightening torque Nm (ft-lbs)

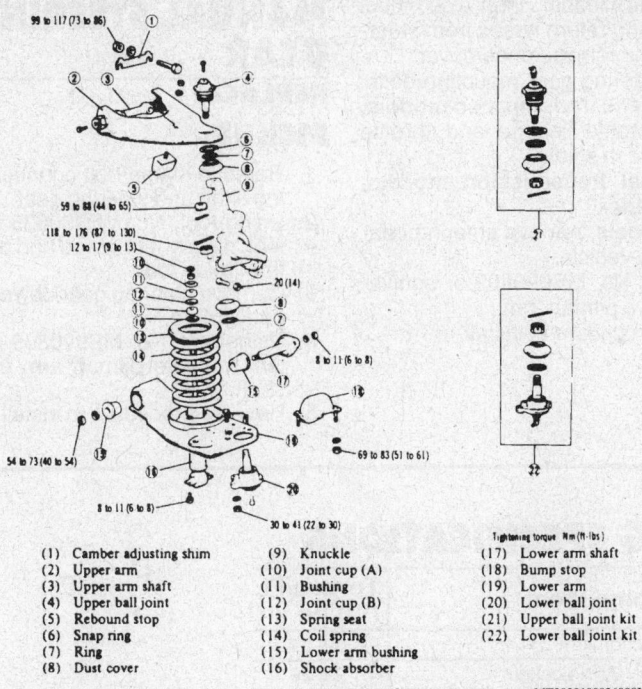

(1) Camber adjusting shim
(2) Upper arm
(3) Upper arm shaft
(4) Upper ball joint
(5) Rebound stop
(6) Snap ring
(7) Ring
(8) Dust cover
(9) Knuckle
(10) Joint cup (A)
(11) Bushing
(12) Joint cup (B)
(13) Spring seat
(14) Coil spring
(15) Lower arm bushing
(16) Shock absorber
(17) Lower arm shaft
(18) Bump stop
(19) Lower arm
(20) Lower ball joint
(21) Upper ball joint kit
(22) Lower ball joint kit

MT2029100036000X

Fig. 12 Exploded view of front suspension. 2WD Pickup

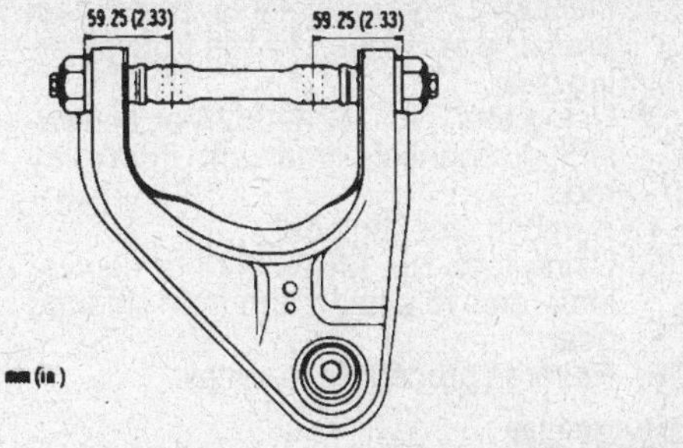
59.25 (2.33)
59.25 (2.33)
mm (in.)

MT2029100037000X

Fig. 13 Upper arm shaft to caster adjustment. 2WD Pickup

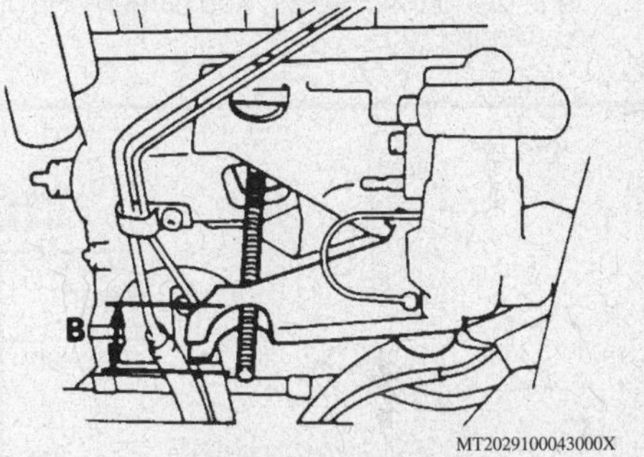
B

MT2029100043000X

Fig. 14 Anchor bolt installation measurement

2. Measure distance "A" from end of anchor bolt to outer edge of nut, then remove torsion bar adjusting nut. If torsion bar is to be reused, when reinstalling nut ensure distance "A" equals the value found prior to removal of nut.
3. Remove seat-holding nut, anchor bolt and nuts.
4. Remove torsion bar assembly.
5. Move the dust covers of the front and rear anchor arms and make mating marks on the anchor arms and the torsion bar. Remove the anchor arms from the torsion bar.
6. Reverse procedure to install, noting the following:
   a. When installing torsion bar, note that the marked end of the bar is to be installed toward the rear of the vehicle.
   b. Apply suitable grease to the torsion bar serrations and dust covers.
   c. If torsion bar is to be reused, reinstall anchor arms, ensuring they line up with mating marks.
   d. Apply suitable grease to threaded part of anchor bolt.
   e. When using a new torsion bar, perform the following prior to installing torsion bar adjusting nut. Offset the torsion bar's and rear anchor arm's phase so value of projection "B," **Fig. 14,** of the anchor bolt (from the rear anchor arm) is 1.42 inches. As a temporary adjustment of vehicle height, tighten torsion bar adjusting nut until amount of projection of anchor bolt is 2.48 inches.

STABILIZER BAR

REPLACE

MONTERO & 4WD PICKUP

1. Remove stabilizer bar from lower arm and stabilizer link assembly.
2. Inspect stabilizer bar, bushings, and stabilizer link assembly and replace as necessary.
3. Install stabilizer bar, noting the following:
   a. When installing stabilizer link assembly to No. 1 crossmember, tighten self locking nut, ensuring distance from base of nut to top of stud is 0.24–0.31 inch.
   b. When installing ends of stabilizer bar to lower arms, tighten self-locking nuts, ensuring distance from base of nut to end of bolt is 0.24–0.31 inch.
   c. Tighten stabilizer bracket attaching nuts to specification.

2WD PICKUP

1. Disconnect strut bar at lower control arm.
2. Disconnect strut bar at strut bar bracket and slide bar out.
3. Disconnect stabilizer bar at stabilizer bracket and at stabilizer links and remove bar.
4. Inspect stabilizer bar, strut bar and bushings, then replace as necessary.
5. Reverse procedure to install, noting the following:
   a. LH strut bar is marked with an "L."
   b. Strut bar bushings for front side and rear side are different. Bushing with convex surface is installed on front side.
   c. When installing strut bar to strut bar bracket, distance between face of innermost nut and end of strut bar should be 2.9 inches. Tighten top end nut to specification after vehicle is lowered to ground. Check caster adjustment and correct as necessary, then adjust distance between nut face and bar end as necessary.
   d. When installing stabilizer bar to links, tighten first nut, ensuring distance between top of nut and end of bolt is 0.87–0.94 inch
   e. Tighten stabilizer bracket attaching bolts to specification.

STRUT BAR

REPLACE

2WD PICKUP

Refer to "Stabilizer Bar, Replace" for strut bar replacement procedure.

POWER STEERING GEAR

REPLACE

MONTERO

1. Remove clamp bolt that connects steering shaft to steering gear mainshaft.
2. Using tools, No. MB990716 and

MB990717 or equivalents, disconnect pressure and return hoses from steering gear.
3. Using tool, No. MB990635 or equivalent, disconnect pitman arm from relay rod.
4. Remove steering gear.
5. Using tool, No. MB990915 or equivalent, remove pitman arm from steering gear.
6. Reverse procedure to install.

PICKUP

1. Disconnect steering shaft from input worm shaft.
2. Using tool, No. MB990635 or equivalent, disconnect tie rod and pitman arm from relay rod.
3. Remove air cleaner, then disconnect pressure and return hoses from steering gear and remove undercover.
4. Loosen steering gear mounting bolts.
5. **On automatic transmission models,** remove throttle linkage and throttle linkage splash shield.
6. **On manual transmission models,** remove starter.
7. **On all models,** remove steering gear from below vehicle.
8. Using tool, No. MB990809 or equivalent, remove pitman arm.
9. Reverse procedure to install.

MANUAL STEERING GEAR

REPLACE

PICKUP

1. Remove clamp bolt connecting steering shaft and steering gear.
2. Using tool, No. MB990635 or equivalent, disconnect tie rod and pitman arm from relay rod.
3. Remove steering gear downward from body frame.
4. Using tool, No. MB990809 or equivalent, remove pitman arm from cross shaft.
5. Reverse procedure to install.

TIGHTENING SPECIFICATIONS

Year	Component	Torque/Ft. Lbs.
1993–96	Anchor Arm "B"	69–87
	Anchor Arm Locknut	29–36
	Automatic Free Wheeling Hub Cover	13–25
	Axle Nut	144–188
	Bearing Cap	40–47
	Bracket To Differential Carrier	58–80
	Brake Tube Flare Nut	9–12
	Brake Tube To Front Brake	9–12
	Bump Stop To Lower Arm	14–22
	Center Bearing Bracket To Engine Strut Assembly	26–33
	Center Member Rear Mounting Bolt	43–58
	Companion Flange To Drive Pinion	116–159
	Differential Case To Drive Gear	58–65
	Differential Cover To Differential Carrier	11–16
	Differential Mounting Brackets To Frame	58–80
	Disc Cover To Strut Assembly	6–9
	Drain Plug	43–51
	Driveshaft Nut	144–188
	Engine Mount Bracket To Crossmember	22–29
	Filler Plug	29–43
	Freewheeling Hub Body Or Front Hub Assembly	36–43
	Freewheeling Hub Cover	7–10④
	Front Anchor Arm To Upper Arm	51–69
	Front Hub To Brake Disc	36–43
	Front Propeller Shaft To Differential Carrier	36–43
	Front Shock Absorber To Crossmember	9–13
	Front Shock Absorber To Lower Arm②	11–16
	Front Suspension Crossmember Mounting Bolts	72–87
	Housing Tube To Differential Carrier	58–72
	Hub Nut	144–188
	Knuckle Arm To Ball Joint	43–52
	Knuckle Arm To McPherson Strut Assembly	58–72
	Knuckle Spindle To Slotted Nut	⑦
	Knuckle To Front Brake Assembly	58–72
	Knuckle To Front Brake Tube	36–43

Continued

TIGHTENING SPECIFICATIONS—Continued

Year	Component	Torque/Ft. Lbs.
1993–96	Knuckle To Tie Rod Assembly	33
	Left Differential Mounting Bracket To Differential Carrier	58–72
	Lower Arm Ball Joint	43–52
	Lower Arm Bushing "B" Mounting Nut	90–112
	Lower Arm Mounting Shaft Mounting Nut	69–87
	Lower Arm Rear Mounting Bolt	43–58
	Lower Arm Shaft①	101–116
	Lower Arm Shaft Bolt	58–69
	Lower Arm Shaft Flange	6–8
	Lower Arm To Ball Joint⑤	22–30
	Lower Arm To Ball Joint⑥	39–54
	Lower Arm To Suspension Crossmember	80–94
	Lower Ball Joint to Knuckle	87–130
	Rear Roll Stopper Mounting Nut	33–43
	Rebound Stop To Rebound Stop Bracket	14–22
	Rebound Stop To Upper Arm	6–9
	Right Differential Mounting Bracket To Housing Tube	58–72
	Right Driveshaft To Inner Shaft	36–43
	Shock Absorber Ring Nut	101–108
	Spring Seat To Strut Assembly	29–36
	Stabilizer Bar Bracket	6–9
	Stabilizer Bar Mounting Bolt	12–19
	Stabilizer Bar To Lower Arm	7–14
	Stabilizer Link Mounting Nut	40–51
	Strut Assembly To Brake Assembly	58–72
	Strut Bar Bracket To Frame	25–33
	Strut Bar Locknut①	54–61
	Strut Bar To Lower Arm	43–51
	Strut Bar To Strut Bar Bracket Mounting Nut	54–61
	Strut Insulator To Body	18–25
	Strut Mounting Self Locking Nut	29–36
	Suspension Crossmember Mounting Bolts To Frame	3–4
	Suspension Crossmember To Body	87–116
	Suspension Crossmember To Steering Gearbox	51–65
	Tie Rod And Turnbuckle Locking Nut	36–40
	Tie Rod End Ball Joint	11–25
	Tie Rod End To Knuckle Arm	25–33
	Torsion Bar Adjusting Nut To Torsion Bar Locknut	29–36
	Transfer Assembly	40–43
	Undercover To Frame	7–9
	Under Skid Plate To side Frame	13–18
	Upper Arm Shaft To Crossmember	72–87
	Upper Ball Joint To Knuckle	43–65
	Wheel Lug Nuts	③

①— Must be tightened while vehicle is unladen.
②— Montero.
③— Montero, 72–87 ft. lbs.; Pickup, 87–101 ft. lbs.
④— Inch lbs.
⑤— 2WD
⑥— 4WD
⑦— Three steps; torque to 22 ft. lbs., back off to 0 ft. lbs., then a final torque of 8 ft. lbs.

Wheel Alignment

INDEX

	Page No.
Front Wheel Alignment	28-50
Camber	28-50
Caster	28-50
Toe-In	28-50
Preliminary Inspection	28-50
Rear Wheel Alignment	28-50
Camber	28-50
Toe-In	28-50
Vehicle Ride Height	28-50
Wheel Alignment Specifications	28-3
Front	28-3
Rear	28-4

PRELIMINARY INSPECTION

1. Ensure tires are inflated to correct pressure, then check for uneven wear.
2. Inspect front wheel bearings, suspension arm and ball joints for damage and replace as necessary.
3. Inspect steering gear for damage and adjust as necessary.
4. Inspect shocks for damage and replace as necessary.
5. Rock vehicle backward and forward and bounce it upward and downward to settle vehicle prior to alignment.
6. Ensure vehicle is unloaded and on a suitable alignment rack according to manufacturers' instructions. **When measuring equipment is attached directly to outer end of driveshaft and front wheels are on turntables, apply brake to prevent improper vehicle movement.**

FRONT WHEEL ALIGNMENT

CAMBER

Montero & 4WD Pickup

Adjust camber by adjusting number of shims between upper arm shaft and arm post of side frame. A 0.039 inch adjustment of shim thickness provides approximately 13 minutes adjustment of camber, **Fig. 1.**

2WD Pickup

1. Hold upper arm shaft to crossmember bolt and remove nut from engine compartment side.
2. Adjust number of shims between upper arm shaft and crossmember. A total of approximately 0.16 inch of shim thickness is standard camber. A 0.039 inch adjustment of shim thickness provides approximately 13 minutes adjustment of camber.

CASTER

Adjustment of caster on these vehicles is made by turning the eccentrics on upper arm shaft. A half turn of upper arm shaft will cause 0.049 inch fore or aft movement of upper arm shaft, resulting in 3 ¾° caster adjustment.

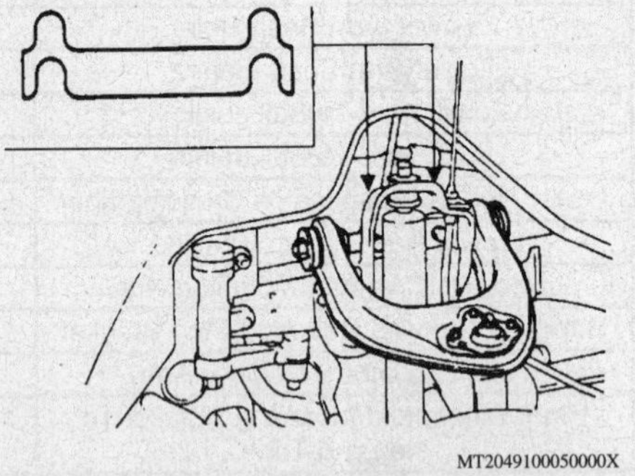
MT2049100050000X

Fig. 1 Front camber adjustment. Montero & 4WD Pickup

TOE-IN

Montero & 4WD Pickup

1. Adjust toe-in by turning left and right tie rod turnbuckles equal amounts in opposite directions, **Fig. 2.**
2. Toe-in on left wheel is reduced by turning tie rod toward front of vehicle or increased by turning tie rod toward rear of vehicle. Toe-in on right wheel is reduced by turning tie rod toward rear of vehicle or increased by turning tie rod toward front of vehicle. A half turn of turnbuckles changes toe-in approximately 0.3 inch.

2WD Pickup

1. Adjust toe-in by turning left tie rod turnbuckle. Toe-in is increased by turning tie rod toward front of vehicle or decreased by turning tie rod toward rear of vehicle. One complete turn of turnbuckle changes toe-in adjustment by approximately 0.3 inch

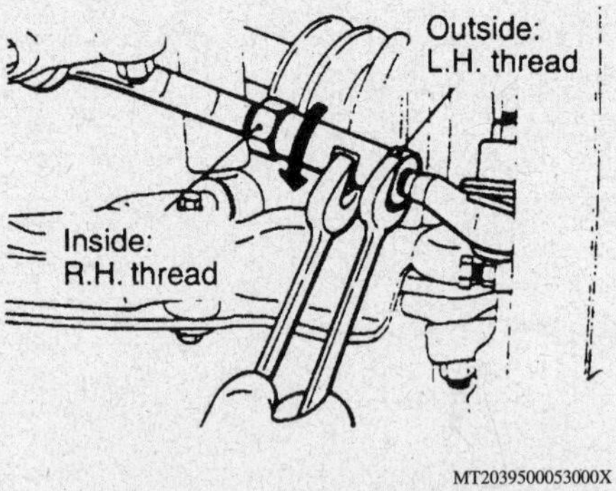
Outside:
L.H. thread
Inside:
R.H. thread
MT2039500053000X

Fig. 2 Front toe-in adjustment. Montero & 4WD Pickup

2. After adjusting toe-in, check difference in length of left and right tie rods. If difference is greater than 0.2 inch, remove right tie rod and adjust length until difference is reduced to 0.2 inch or less. "L" stamped on outer surface of tie rod indicates LH thread.

REAR WHEEL ALIGNMENT

CAMBER

Rear camber is preset to specification and cannot be adjusted. If camber is out of specification, bent or damaged components must be replaced.

TOE-IN

Rear toe-in is preset to specification and cannot be adjusted. If rear toe-in is out of specification, bent or damaged components must be replaced.

VEHICLE RIDE HEIGHT

There is no provision for adjustment of vehicle ride height on these models. If ride height is not satisfactory, inspect suspension components for damage or modification.

MITSUBISHI UNIT REPAIR

TABLE OF CONTENTS

	Page No.
AIR BAG SYSTEM	29-65
AIR CONDTITIONING	29-1
ALL-WHEEL DRIVE AXLES	29-294
ALTERNATORS	29-27
ANTI-LOCK BRAKES	29-155
AUTOMATIC TRANSMISSIONS/TRANSAXLES	29-250
COOLING FANS	29-9
DASH GAUGES	29-20
DASH PANEL SERVICE	29-78
DISC BRAKES	29-119
DRIVE AXLES	29-305
DRUM BRAKES	29-142
ENGINE REBUILDING SPECIFICATIONS	29-310
FOUR WHEEL STEERING	29-116
FRONT WHEEL DRIVE AXLES	29-287
HYDRAULIC BRAKE SYSTEM	29-146
MANUAL STEERING GEARS	29-89
POWER BRAKE UNITS	29-154
POWER STEERING	29-93
SPEED CONTROL SYSTEMS	29-33
STARTER MOTORS	29-23
STEERING COLUMNS	29-86
WIPER SYSTEMS	29-53

Air Conditioning

NOTE: On Air Bag Equipped Models, Refer To "Air Bag System Precautions" Located In The Front Of This Manual For System Disarming & Arming Procedures.

NOTE: Prior To Performing Any Service Operations Listed In This Section, Consult The "Technical Service Bulletins" Section For Related Information.

INDEX

	Page No.
A/C Specifications	29-6
Belt Tension	29-7
Charging System	29-6
Discharging System	29-4
Leak Test	29-2
Electronic Leak Detectors	29-3
Flame Type (Halide) Leak Detectors	29-4
Fluid Leak Detectors	29-4
Oil Charge	29-6
Performance Test	29-2
Except Precis	29-2
Precis	29-2
Precautions	29-1
Air Bag Systems	29-1
Refrigerant	29-1
System Evacuation	29-4
Charging Station	29-6
Vacuum Pump	29-4
Technical Service Bulletins	29-8
A/C Inoperative	29-8
A/C Whooping	29-8
A/C Odor	29-8
Troubleshooting	29-2
Sight Glass Refrigerant Level	29-2

PRECAUTIONS

AIR BAG SYSTEMS

Refer to "Air Bag System Precautions" in the front of this manual for system disarming and arming procedures.

REFRIGERANT

R-12 Systems

R-12 is a Freon refrigerant that is odorless and colorless both as a gas and as a liquid. Since it boils (vaporizes) at –21.7°F, it will usually be in its vapor state while being handled during repairs. However, if a portion of the liquid coolant should come in contact with the hands or face, the momentary –22°F refrigerant temperature can cause serious injury. **Use of an approved R-12 recovery device is required when it is necessary to discharge the A/C system for any reason.**

Protective goggles should be worn when opening any refrigerant lines. If liquid coolant does touch the eyes, bathe eyes quickly in cold water, then apply a bland disinfectant oil. See an eye doctor.

When checking a system for leaks with a torch type leak detector, do not breathe vapors coming from the flame. Do not discharge the refrigerant in an area of a live flame. A poisonous phosgene gas is produced when R-12 is burned. While the small amount of gas produced by a leak detector is not harmful unless inhaled directly at the flame.

Never allow the temperature of refrigerant drums to exceed 125°F. The resultant increase in temperature will cause a corresponding increase in pressure, which may cause the safety plug to release or the drum to burst.

If it is necessary to heat a drum of refrigerant when charging a system, the drum should be placed in water that is no hotter than 125°F. Never use a blow

Garage ambient temperature °C (°F)	21 (70)	26.7 (80)	32.2 (90)	37.8 (100)	43.3 (110)
Discharge air temperature °C (°F)	0.0 – 3.0 (32.0 – 37.4)	0.0 – 3.0 (32.0 – 37.4)	0.0 – 4.0 (32.0 – 39.2)	0.0 – 4.0 (32.0 – 39.2)	0.0 – 4.0 (32.0 – 39.2)
Compressor discharge pressure kPa (psi)	650 – 700 (92.5 – 99.6)	740 – 790 (105.3 – 112.4)	980 – 1.020 (139.4 – 145.1)	1.150 – 1.200 (163.6 – 170.7)	1.320 – 1.370 (187.7 – 194.9)
Compressor suction pressure kPa (psi)	130 – 190 (18.5 – 27.5)	130 – 190 (18.5 – 27.5)	130 – 190 (18.5 – 27.5)	130 – 190 (18.5 – 27.5)	130 – 190 (18.5 – 27.5)

MT7029100183000X

Fig. 1 A/C performance chart. Diamante

Garage ambient temperature °C (°F)	21 (70)	26.7 (80)	32.2 (90)	37.8 (100)	43.3 (110)
Discharge air temperature °C (°F)	2.0–8.0 (35.6–46.4)	2.0–8.0 (35.6–46.4)	2.0–8.0 (35.6–46.4)	4.0–11.0 (39.2–51.8)	6.0–14.0 (42.8–57.2)
Compressor discharge pressure kPa (psi)	900–1,300 (128–186)	1,000–1,400 (142–199)	1,100–1,500 (156–212)	1,300–1,700 (186–242)	1,500–1,900 (212–270)
Compressor suction pressure kPa (psi)	50–150 (7.1–21.3)	80–180 (11.4–25.6)	100–200 (14.2–28.4)	130–230 (18.5–32.7)	150–250 (21.3–35.6)

MT7029100111000X

Fig. 2 A/C performance chart. 1993–94 Eclipse

torch or other open flame. If possible, a pressure release mechanism should be attached before the drum is heated.

When connecting and disconnecting service gauges in the A/C system, ensure the gauge hand valves are fully closed and the compressor service valves, if equipped, are in the back-seated (fully counterclockwise) position. Do not disconnect gauge hoses from service port adapters, if used, while gauges are connected to the A/C system. To disconnect hoses, always remove the adapter from the service port. Do not disconnect the hoses from the gauge manifold while connected to A/C system, as refrigerant will be rapidly discharged.

After disconnecting gauge lines, check the valve areas to be sure service valves are correctly seated and Schraeder valves, if used, are not leaking.

R-134a Systems

R-134a is a hydrofluorocarbon refrigerant designed to protect the earth's ozone layer. **However, use of an approved R-134a recovery device is required when it is necessary to discharge the A/C system for any reason.** While this transparent, colorless refrigerant is not flammable or explosive, it is dangerous because its rapid evaporation rate causes it to freeze anything it contacts. **For this reason, it is extremely important to wear protective goggles and clothing to prevent refrigerant from contacting skin and eyes.**

If R-134a refrigerant does enter the eyes, it is best to rinse them with a few drops of sterile mineral oil and plenty of cold water. Contact a physician even if irritation ceases.

Do not expose R-134a refrigerant to temperatures above 104°F as pressure may increase beyond system or container capacity. It is also important to keep R-134a containers upright while charging the A/C system to prevent the liquid portion of the refrigerant from entering the system.

Do not allow R-134a refrigerant to come into contact with finished or bright metal surfaces. The metal will tarnish and, if exposed to moisture, corrode.

TROUBLESHOOTING

SIGHT GLASS REFRIGERANT LEVEL

1. Clean refrigerant level sight glass, then start engine.
2. Push A/C button to operate compressor, place blower switch to high position and move temperature lever to the extreme left.
3. Allow system to operate for several minutes, then check sight glass as follows:
   a. If sight glass is clear, magnetic clutch is engaged, compressor discharge line is warm and compressor inlet line is cool, the system has a full charge.
   b. If sight glass is clear, magnetic clutch is engaged and there is no difference in temperature between compressor inlet and discharge lines, the system has lost some refrigerant.
   c. If sight glass is clear and magnetic clutch is disengaged, clutch is defective or system is out of refrigerant.
   d. If foam or bubbles are present in sight glass, system could be low on refrigerant. **Occasional foam or bubbles are normal when temperature is above 110°F or below 70°F.**
4. Allow engine to run at 1500 RPM, then block airflow through condenser to increase compressor discharge pressure to 206–220 psi. If foam or bubbles are still present in sight glass, system is low on refrigerant. **The refrigerant system should not be low on charge unless there is a leak. Repair leak as required, then repeat test.**

PERFORMANCE TEST

EXCEPT PRECIS

Before performing this test a visual inspection of system should be made to ensure system is operating efficiently and correctly. Move vehicle out of direct sunlight.

1. Connect suitable tachometer and manifold gauge set, then start engine.
2. Press A/C button, then reset the control buttons to the maximum cooling position in manual mode as follows:
   a. Place mode selection button in face position.
   b. Place temperature control button in maximum cooling position.
   c. Place air selection button in recirculation position.
   d. Place blower switch in high speed position.
3. Run engine at 1000 RPM with A/C clutch engaged.
4. **On models equipped with R-12 refrigerant,** engine should be warmed up with doors, windows and hood open.
5. **On models equipped with R-134a refrigerant,** engine should be warmed up with doors and windows closed.
6. **On all models,** insert suitable thermometer in left center A/C outlet and operated engine for approximately 20 minutes.
7. Note discharge air temperature and refer to A/C performance temperature chart, **Figs. 1 through 12.** If clutch cycles, take reading before clutch disengages.

PRECIS

1. Place A/C controls on maximum A/C (recirculating air) and blower on high speed.
2. Run engine for ten minutes at 1500 RPM to stabilize system.
3. System must be tested in a ambient temperature of 70–80°F.
4. Connect manifold gauge set.
5. As soon as system is stabilized, record high and low pressure reading.
6. Determine clutch cycle time.
7. Record clutch off time in seconds.
8. Record clutch on time in seconds.
9. Record center register discharge temperature.
10. Determine and record ambient temperature.
11. Compare test reading with applicable chart, **Figs. 13 and 14.**
12. If test reading falls within acceptable range, system is operating normally.
13. If test reading falls outside acceptable range, refer to refrigerant system and clutch cycle timing evaluation chart, **Fig. 15.**
14. After servicing and correcting a refrigerant system problem, repeat this procedure to ensure proper operation of the A/C system. In ambient temperatures above 100°F, compressor clutch will not normally cycle off and, in many instances, clutch will not cycle off when temperatures are above 90°F.

LEAK TEST

Testing the refrigerant system for leaks is one of the most important phases of troubleshooting. One or more of the methods outlined will prove useful in detecting leaks or checking connections if service is performed. Before beginning any leak test, attach a manifold gauge set and note pressure. If little or no pressure is indicated, a partial charge must be supplied. Inspect all connections, compressor head gasket, oil filler plug and compressor shaft seal for leaks.

R-12 leak detectors will not detect R-134a leaks. For R-134a systems, an electronic type leak detector is recommended.

Garage ambient temperature °C (°F)	20 (68)	25 (77)	35 (95)	40 (104)
Discharge air temperature °C (°F)	2.5–5.0 (37–41)	3.0–6.0 (37–43)	3.5–7.5 (38–46)	4.0–8.0 (39–46)
Compressor high pressure kPa (psi)	700–900 (101.6–130.6)	740–1,100 (107.4–159.6)	750–1,350 (108.8–195.4)	960–1,570 (139.3–227.8)
Compressor low pressure kPa (psi)	140 (20.3)	140–210 (20.3–30.5)	140–220 (20.3–31.9)	150–230 (21.8–33.4)

MT7029500184000X

Fig. 3 A/C performance chart. 1995–96 Eclipse

Garage ambient temperature °C (°F)	21 (70)	26.7 (80)	32.2 (90)	37.8 (100)	43.3 (110)
Discharge air temperature °C (°F)	2.5–7.5 (36.5–45.5)	2.5–8.0 (36.5–46.5)	3.0–8.0 (37.4–46.5)	3.5–8.0 (38.3–46.5)	3.5–8.0 (38.3–46.5)
Compressor discharge pressure kPa (psi)	850–900 (121.0–128.1)	1,000–1,070 (142.3–152.3)	1,100–1,150 (156.5–163.6)	1,250–1,320 (177.9–187.8)	1,350–1,400 (192.1–199.2)
Compressor suction pressure kPa (psi)	130–310 (18.5–27.0)	140–310 (19.9–27.0)	140–320 (19.9–28.5)	160–320 (22.8–28.5)	165–320 (23.5–29.9)

MT7029100112000X

Fig. 4 A/C performance chart. 1993 Expo

Garage ambient temperature °C (°F)	20 (68)	25 (77)	35 (95)	45 (113)
Discharge air temperature °C (°F)	10.8 (51.4)	16.8 (62.2)	23.5 (74.3)	24.3 (95.7)
Compressor discharge pressure kPa (psi)	1,030 (149)	1,128 (164)	1,393 (202)	1,736 (252)
Compressor suction pressure kPa (psi)	178 (26)	184 (27)	196 (28)	210 (30)

MT7029500185000X

Fig. 5 A/C performance chart. 1994–95 Expo

Garage ambient temperature °C (°F)	21 (70)	26.7 (80)	32.2 (90)	37.8 (100)	43.3 (110)
Discharge air temperature °C (°F)	2.8–4.4 (37–40)	3.3–5.0 (38–41)	3.9–5.6 (39–42)	4.4–7.2 (40–45)	4.4–7.8 (40–46)
Compressor discharge pressure kPa (psi)	758–1,310 (110–190)	896–1,517 (130–220)	1,103–1,793 (160–260)	1,310–1,999 (190–290)	1,517–2,206 (220–320)
Evaporator suction pressure kPa (psi)	131–165 (19–24)	138–179 (20–26)	145–186 (21–27)	152–193 (22–28)	159–200 (23–29)

MT7029100113000X

Fig. 6 A/C performance chart. Pickup & 1993 Galant

Garage ambient temperature °C (°F)	20 (68)	25 (77)	35 (95)	40 (104)
Discharge air temperature °C (°F)	2.5–5.0 (37–41)	3.0–6.0 (37–43)	3.5–7.5 (38–46)	4.0–8.0 (39–46)
Compressor high pressure kPa (psi)	700–900 (101.6–130.6)	740–1,100 (107.4–159.6)	750–1,350 (108.8–195.4)	960–1,570 (139.3–227.8)
Compressor low pressure kPa (psi)	140 (20.3)	140–210 (20.3–30.5)	140–220 (20.3–31.9)	150–230 (21.8–33.4)

MT7029400114000X

Fig. 7 A/C performance chart. 1994–95 Galant

Garage ambient temperature °C (°F)	20 (68)	25 (77)	35 (95)	40 (104)
Discharge air temperature °C (°F)	2.5–4.5 (37–40)	2.5–4.5 (33–40)	4.0–6.5 (39–44)	6.5–9.0 (44–48)
Compressor high pressure kPa (psi)	765–960 (111.0–139.3)	765–960 (111.0–139.3)	1,325–1,420 (192.2–206.0)	1,570–1,765 (227.8–256.1)
Compressor low pressure kPa (psi)	40–135 (5.8–19.6)	40–135 (5.8–19.6)	80–175 (11.6–25.4)	155–255 (22.5–37.0)

MT7029600187000X

Fig. 8 A/C performance chart. 1996 Galant

Garage ambient temperature °C (°F)	21 (70)	26.7 (80)	32.2 (90)	37.8 (100)	43.3 (110)
Discharge air temperature °C (°F)	2.5 – 5.0 (36.5 – 41.0)	3.0 – 5.5 (37.4 – 41.9)	3.0 – 6.0 (37.4 – 42.8)	3.5 – 7.5 (38.3 – 45.5)	3.5 – 8.0 (38.3 – 46.4)
Compressor discharge pressure kPa (psi)	650 – 890 (92.5 – 126.6)	740 – 1,040 (105.3 – 147.9)	750 – 1,130 (106.7 – 160.7)	950 – 1,320 (135.1 – 187.7)	1,150 – 1,410 (163.6 – 200.5)
Compressor suction pressure kPa (psi)	140 – 210 (19.9 – 29.9)	140 – 210 (19.9 – 29.9)	140 – 210 (19.9 – 29.9)	150 – 220 (21.3 – 31.3)	150 – 220 (21.3 – 31.3)

MT7029300115000X

Fig. 9 A/C performance chart. Mirage

Garage ambient temperature °C (°F)	21 (70)	26.7 (80)	32.2 (90)	37.8 (100)	43.3 (110)
Discharge air temperature °C (°F)	3.0–6.0 (37.4–42.8)	3.0–7.0 (37.4–44.6)	3.5–7.5 (38.3–45.5)	4.0–8.0 (39.2–46.4)	4.5–8.5 (40.1–47.3)
Compressor discharge pressure kPa (psi)	980–1,230 (139.4–174.9)	1,050–1,300 (149.3–184.9)	1,130–1,380 (160.7–196.3)	1,270–1,580 (180.6–224.7)	1,330–1,740 (189.2–247.5)
Compressor suction pressure kPa (psi)	120–220 (17.1–31.3)	120–230 (17.1–32.7)	130–240 (18.5–34.1)	150–270 (21.3–38.4)	170–280 (24.2–39.8)

MT7029100116000X

Fig. 10 A/C performance chart. 1993–95 Montero

Garage ambient temperature °C (°F)	21 (70)	26.7 (80)	32.2 (90)	37.8 (100)	43.3 (110)
Discharge air temperature °C (°F)	3.0–6.0 (37.4–42.8)	3.0–7.0 (37.4–44.4)	3.5–7.5 (38.3–45.5)	4.0–8.0 (39.2–46.4)	4.5–8.5 (40.1–47.3)
Compressor discharge pressure kPa (psi)	961–1,402 (139–203)	1,029–1,471 (149–213)	1,108–1,549 (161–225)	1,245–1,745 (181–253)	1,304–1,902 (189–276)
Compressor suction pressure kPa (psi)	98–216 (14–31)	98–226 (14–33)	108–235 (16–34)	137–265 (20–38)	157–275 (23–40)

MT7029600188000X

Fig. 11 A/C performance chart. 1996 Montero

Garage ambient temperature °C (°F)	21 (70)	26.7 (80)	32.2 (90)	37.8 (100)	43.3 (110)
Discharge air temperature °C (°F)	0.0 – 3.0 (32.0 – 37.4)	1.0 – 4.0 (33.8 – 39.2)	1.0 – 4.0 (33.8 – 39.2)	1.0 – 4.0 (33.8 – 39.2)	2.0 – 5.0 (35.6 – 41.0)
Compressor discharge pressure kPa (psi)	690 – 740 (98.1 – 105.3)	780 – 830 (110.9 – 118.1)	870 – 920 (123.7 – 130.9)	1,080 – 1,130 (153.6 – 160.7)	1,210 – 1,260 (172.1 – 179.2)
Compressor suction pressure kPa (psi)	130 – 190 (18.5 – 27.5)	130 – 190 (18.5 – 27.5)	130 – 190 (18.5 – 27.5)	130 – 190 (18.5 – 27.5)	130 – 190 (18.5 – 27.5)

MT7029100117000X

Fig. 12 A/C performance chart. 3000GT

ELECTRONIC LEAK DETECTORS

The following procedure has been revised by a Technical Service Bulletin.

There are a number of electronic leak detectors available to perform leak tests. It is necessary to obtain a detector conforming to SAE J1627 requirements. Refer to the operating instructions for the unit being used and follow these general procedures:

1. To ensure accuracy of test results, perform test only when ambient temperature is at least 60°F and compressor drive belt tension is correct.
2. Ensure system pressure is at least 50 psi before beginning test. If necessary, add refrigerant until proper pressure is reached. In most cases, this will require no more than four ounces of refrigerant.
3. If area to be tested is excessively dirty, clean it with a dry shop towel and compressed air prior to testing. **Do not use cleaning agents; a false detector reading may result.**
4. Move detector probe one to two inches per second in areas of suspected leaks, approximately ¼ inch from surface. **Do not allow probe tip to touch any surfaces or to become contaminated by dirt or moisture.**
5. Position probe below test points, as refrigerant gas is heavier than air.
6. Inspect service access gauge port valve fittings, particularly when valve caps are missing, as dirt accumulations can destroy sealing area of valve core when manifold gauge set is attached. Replace missing valve caps after cleaning valve core area. **Valve caps should only be finger tightened. Using pliers to tighten valve caps may distort sealing surface of valve.**
7. Thoroughly inspect bulkhead evaporator fittings, as O-rings in these fittings are a common source of leakage.
8. Leak test A/C evaporator as follows:
   a. Run A/C on highest setting for 15 seconds, then turn system off and wait for refrigerant to accumulate in evaporator case. Refer to leak detector instructions for accumulation time.
   b. After accumulation time has elapsed, insert leak detector probe into evaporator drain tube (if no condensation is present). Probe may also be inserted through a heater vent close to evaporator case.
   c. Listen for leak detector alarm. If

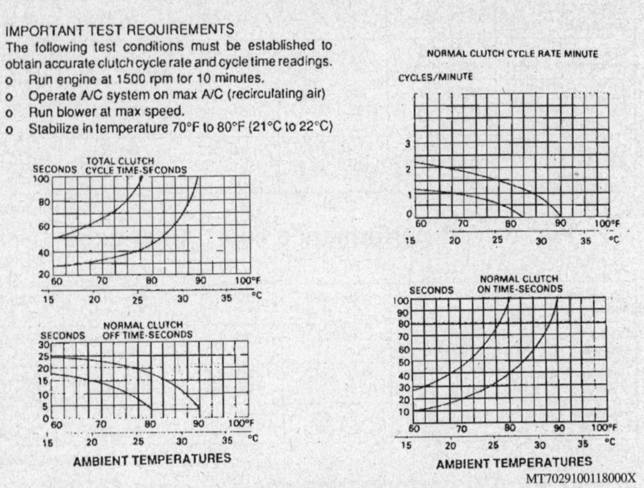
IMPORTANT TEST REQUIREMENTS
The following test conditions must be established to obtain accurate clutch cycle rate and cycle time readings.
o Run engine at 1500 rpm for 10 minutes.
o Operate A/C system on max A/C (recirculating air)
o Run blower at max speed.
o Stabilize in temperature 70°F to 80°F (21°C to 22°C)
TOTAL CLUTCH CYCLE TIME-SECONDS
SECONDS
NORMAL CLUTCH CYCLE RATE MINUTE
CYCLES/MINUTE
NORMAL CLUTCH OFF TIME-SECONDS
NORMAL CLUTCH ON TIME-SECONDS
AMBIENT TEMPERATURES
MT7029100118000X

Fig. 13 A/C clutch cycling timing rates chart. Precis

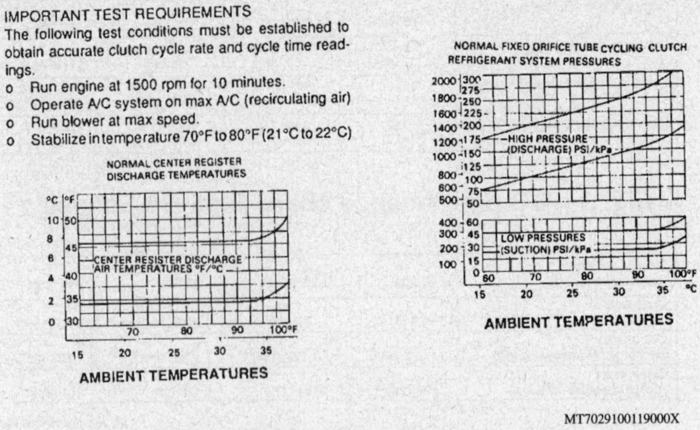
IMPORTANT TEST REQUIREMENTS
The following test conditions must be established to obtain accurate clutch cycle rate and cycle time readings.
o Run engine at 1500 rpm for 10 minutes.
o Operate A/C system on max A/C (recirculating air)
o Run blower at max speed.
o Stabilize in temperature 70°F to 80°F (21°C to 22°C)
NORMAL CENTER REGISTER DISCHARGE TEMPERATURES
CENTER RESISTER DISCHARGE AIR TEMPERATURES °F/°C
NORMAL FIXED ORIFICE TUBE CYCLING CLUTCH REFRIGERANT SYSTEM PRESSURES
HIGH PRESSURE (DISCHARGE) PSI/kPa
LOW PRESSURES (SUCTION) PSI/kPa
AMBIENT TEMPERATURES
MT7029100119000X

Fig. 14 A/C pressure temperature chart. Precis

High (Discharge) pressure	Low (suction) pressure	Clutch cycle time: Rate	ON	OFF	Component-Causes
High	High	Continuous run			Condenser-Inadequate Airflow
High	Normal to high	Continuous run			Engine overheating
Normal to High	Normal	Continuous run			Air in system refrigerant overcharge(a) Humidity or ambient temp very high(b)
Normal	High	Continuous run			Fixed orifice tube-Missing. O-rings Leaking/Missing
Normal	High	Slow	Long	Long	Clutch cycling switch-High Cut-in
Normal	Normal	Slow or no cycle	Long or continuous	Normal or no cycle	Moisture in refrigerant system. Excessive refrigerant oil.
		Fast	Short	Short	Clutch cycling switch- Low Cut-in or High Cut-Out
Normal	Low	Slow	Long	Long	Clutch cycling switch- Low Cut-Out
Normal to low	High	Continuous run			Compessor-Low Performance
Normal to low	Normal to high	Continuous run			A/C suction line-Partially Restricted or Plugged(c)
Normal to low	Normal	Fast	Short	Normal	Evaporator-Low Airflow
			Short to very short	Normal to long	Condenser, fixed orifice tube, or A/C liquid line-Partially Restricted or Plugged
			Short to very short	Short to very short	Low refrigerant charge
			Short to very short	Long	Evaporator core-Partially Restricted or Plugged
Normal to low	Low	Continuous run			A/C suction line-Partially Restricted or Plugged (d). Clutch cycling switch-Sticking Closed

MT7029100186010X

Fig. 15 Refrigerant system clutch cycle timing evaluation chart (Part 1 of 2). Precis

alarm sounds, a leak exists at evaporator.

9. Check for leaks in manifold gauge set and hoses, as well as in remainder of system.

FLAME TYPE (HALIDE) LEAK DETECTORS

When using flame type detectors, avoid inhaling fumes produced by burning refrigerant. Do not use this type of detector where concentrations of combustible gases, dusts or vapors may exist.

1. Adjust detector flame as low as possible to obtain maximum sensitivity. Ensure copper element is cherry red and is not burned away. Flame will be almost colorless.
2. Slowly move detector along areas of suspected leaks. A slight leak will cause flame to change to a bright yellow or green color; a significant leak will be indicated by a brilliant blue flame. Position detector below areas being tested, as refrigerant gas is heavier than air. **Dust in pickup hose may cause a change in flame color. If this is not remedied, a false diagnosis may result. Store leak detector in a clean place and ensure hose is free of dust before leak testing.**
3. Check for leaks in manifold gauge set and hoses, as well as in remainder of system.
4. Use a suitable small fan to ventilate areas where leak detector indicates refrigerant constantly. These areas are contaminated with refrigerant and must be ventilated before leak can be pinpointed.

FLUID LEAK DETECTORS

Apply leak detector solution around joints to be tested. A cluster of bubbles will form immediately if there is a leak. A white foam that forms after a short while will indicate an extremely small leak. In some confined areas, such as sections of the evaporator and condenser, electronic leak detectors will be more useful.

DISCHARGING SYSTEM

R-134a systems require the use of special service equipment designed specifically to be compatible with them. R-12 service equipment cannot be used on R-134a systems. Recovery and recycling stations must also be compatible with the type of refrigerant in use; a station will be contaminated if it is used in conjunction with an incompatible refrigerant.

Refrigerant recovery and recycling stations allow the retention and reuse of refrigerant after contaminants and moisture have been removed. When using such a station, follow the manufacturer's operating instructions, noting the following:

1. **Use extreme caution and observe all safety and service precautions related to the use of refrigerants.**
2. Connect refrigerant recycling station hose(s) to vehicle A/C service port(s) and recovery station inlet fitting. Use hoses equipped with shutoff devices or check valves located within 12 inches of hose ends to minimize introduction of air into recycling station and to minimize amount of refrigerant released when hose ends are disconnected.
3. Turn recycling station on to begin recovery process. Allow station to pump refrigerant from A/C system until station pressure gauge indicates vacuum.
4. After vehicle A/C system has been evacuated, close station inlet valve, if equipped.
5. Turn station off. Some stations may be shut off automatically by a low pressure switch.
6. Allow vehicle A/C system to remain closed for approximately two minutes. Observe vacuum level indicated on gauge. If pressure does not rise, disconnect recycling station hose(s).
7. If system pressure rises, repeat recovery steps until vacuum level remains stable for two minutes.
8. Service A/C system as necessary, then evacuate and recharge A/C system.

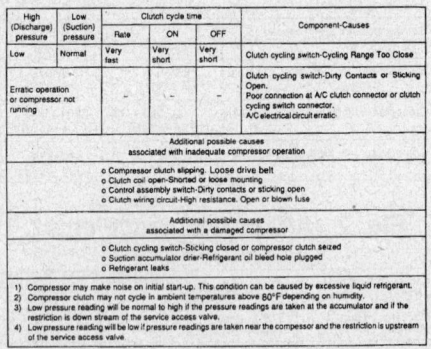

High (Discharge) pressure	Low (Suction) pressure	Clutch cycle time: Rate	ON	OFF	Component-Causes
Low	Normal	Very fast	Very short	Very short	Clutch cycling switch-Cycling Range Too Close
Erratic operation or compressor not running		-	-	-	Clutch cycling switch-Dirty Contacts or Sticking Open. Poor connection at A/C clutch connector or clutch cycling switch connector. A/C electrical circuit erratic
Additional possible causes associated with inadequate compressor operation					
o Compressor clutch slipping. Loose drive belt o Clutch coil open-Shorted or loose mounting o Control assembly switch-Dirty contacts or sticking open o Clutch wiring circuit-High resistance. Open or blown fuse					
Additional possible causes associated with a damaged compressor					
o Clutch cycling switch-Sticking closed or compressor clutch seized o Suction accumulator drier-Refrigerant oil bleed hole plugged o Refrigerant leaks					
1) Compressor may make noise on initial start-up. This condition can be caused by excessive liquid refrigerant. 2) Compressor clutch may not cycle in ambient temperatures above 80°F depending on humidity. 3) Low pressure reading will be normal to high if the pressure readings are taken at the accumulator and if the restriction is down stream of the service access valve. 4) Low pressure reading will be low if pressure readings are taken near the compessor and the restriction is upstream of the service access valve.					

MT7029100186020X

Fig. 15 Refrigerant system clutch cycle timing evaluation chart (Part 2 of 2). Precis

SYSTEM EVACUATION

VACUUM PUMP

Vacuum pumps suitable for removing air and moisture from A/C systems are commercially available. The system pump down specification used as a reference point is 28–29½ inches Hg vacuum. However, this reading can be attained at or near sea level only. For each 1000 feet of altitude at which this operation is performed,

Model	Compressor Type	Oil Charge (Fl. Oz.) When Changing Component				
		Compressor	Condenser	Evaporator	Lines	Receiver Drier
1993						
Diamante	FX105VS	⑤	.30	2.40	.30	.20
Diamante Wagon	10PA17C	⑤	.30	2.40	.30	.20
Eclipse	10PA17	⑤	.60	1.00	.30	.30
Expo	10PA15	⑤	1.00	2.00	.30	.30
Galant	FX105V	⑤	.50	1.70	.30	.20
Mirage	FX105V	⑤	.50	1.70	.30	.20
Montero	10PA15	⑤	1.00	2.00	.30	.30
Pickup	FX80	⑤	.50	1.70	.30	.30
Precis	SD709	⑤	1.00	3.00	—	1.00
3000GT	FX105VS	⑤	.20	2.40	.30	.20
1994						
Diamante③	FX105VS	⑤	.50	2.00	.30	.30
Diamante④	MSC105	⑤	.50	2.00	.30	.30
Diamante Wagon④	10PA17C	⑤	.30	2.40	.30	.20
Eclipse	10PA17	⑤	.60	1.00	.30	.30
Expo	10PA17C	⑤	1.30	1.30	.30	.30
Galant	AX105VS	⑤	1.20	2.30	.40	.40
Mirage	FX105V	⑤	.50	2.00	.30	.30
Montero	10PA15	⑤	1.00	2.00	.30	.30
Pickup	MSC90C	⑤	.50	2.00	.30	.30
3000GT③	FX105VS	⑤	.20	2.40	.30	.20
3000GT④	MSC105	⑤	.50	2.00	.30	.30
1995						
Diamante	MSC105	⑤	.50	2.00	.30	.30
Diamante Wagon	10PA17C	⑤	.30	2.40	.30	.20
Eclipse ⑥	10PA17	⑤	.60	1.00	.30	.30
Eclipse⑦	MSC105CVS	⑤	.50	2.00	.30	.30
Expo	10PA17C	⑤	1.30	1.30	.30	.30
Galant	MSC105CVS	⑤	.50	2.00	.30	.30
Mirage	FX105V	⑤	.50	2.00	.30	.30
Montero	10PA15	⑤	1.00	2.00	.30	.30
Pickup	MSC90C	⑤	.50	2.00	.30	.30
3000GT	MSC105	⑤	.50	2.00	.30	.30
1996						
Diamante	MSC105	⑤	.50	2.00	.30	.30
Eclipse①	MSC105CVS	⑤	.51	2.03	.34	.34
Eclipse②	10PA17C	⑤	1.35	1.35	.34	.34
Galant	MSC105CVS	⑤	.50	2.00	.30	.30
Mirage	FX105V	⑤	.50	2.00	.30	.30
Montero	10PA15	⑤	1.40	1.40	.30	.30
Pickup	MSC90C	⑤	.50	2.00	.30	.30
3000GT	MSC105	⑤	.50	2.00	.30	.30

① — 2.0L turbocharged engine & 2.4L engine.
② — 2.0L non-turbocharged engine.
③ — With R-12 refrigerant system.
④ —With R-134a refrigerant system.
⑤ — To determine correct oil charge, measure amount of oil drained from old compressor, then adjust new compressor oil charge to match.
⑥ — Non-turbo.
⑦ — Turbo.

Fig. 16 Oil charge specifications chart

the reading will be one inch of vacuum higher. For example, at an elevation of 5000 feet, only 23–24½ inches Hg vacuum can be obtained. **The system refrigerant must be completely recovered before it can be evacuated. Damage to the vacuum pump will result if pressurized refrigerant is allowed to enter.**

1. Connect vacuum pump to gauge manifold. With gauges connected to system, remove vacuum hose connector

cap and connect gauge manifold center hose to vacuum pump connector. Place high and low side compressor service valve, if used, in middle position and open high and low side gauge manifold hand valves.
2. Operate vacuum pump for at least 30 minutes to remove air and moisture. Observe compound gauge to ensure system pumps down into vacuum. System should reach 28–29½ inches Hg vacuum within five minutes. If system does not pump down, inspect all connections and leak test if necessary.
3. Close gauge manifold hand valves and shut off vacuum pump.
4. Evaluate system's ability to hold vacuum pressure. Observe compound gauge and ensure needle does not rise at a rate exceeding one inch Hg vacuum every four or five minutes. If gauge rises at too rapid a rate, supply partial charge and leak test, then recover refrigerant as described under "Discharging System."
5. If system holds vacuum, charge with refrigerant.

CHARGING STATION

A vacuum pump is built into the charging station and is designed to withstand repeated and prolonged use without damage. Complete moisture removal from the system is possible only with a vacuum pump constructed for that purpose.

The system refrigerant must be completely recovered before it can be evacuated. Damage to the vacuum pump will result if pressurized refrigerant is allowed to enter.

1. Connect hose to vacuum pump if system refrigerant was recovered through charging station.
2. Open charging station low side gauge hand valve.
3. Connect station to 110V current.
4. Activate vacuum pump according to station manufacturer's instructions.
5. Evacuate system with vacuum pump until low pressure gauge reads at least 28 inches Hg vacuum. Continue evacuating system for an additional 15 minutes for routine system service or 20–30 minutes if any components have been replaced.
6. Close low side gauge hand valve, then turn off vacuum pump.
7. Evaluate system's ability to hold vacuum. Observe low side gauge and ensure needle does not rise at a rate exceeding one inch Hg vacuum every four to five minutes. If low side gauge indication rises at too rapid a rate, supply a partial charge and leak test, then evacuate system again.
8. If system holds vacuum, charge with refrigerant.

CHARGING SYSTEM

Use instructions provided with charging station. Follow these procedures to prevent charging station from being exposed accidentally to the vehicle's high-side system pressure:

1. Do not connect high pressure line to A/C system.
2. Always keep high pressure valve closed on charging station.
3. Perform all evacuation and charging through receiver/drier low-side pressure service fitting.

OIL CHARGE

When replacing an A/C component, refer to the oil charge specifications chart, **Fig. 16,** for oil charge specifications.

A/C SPECIFICATIONS

Year	Model	Refrigerant		Compressor Oil Viscosity	Total System Oil Capacity, Oz.	Compressor Oil Level, Inches	Compressor Clutch Air Gap, Inch
		Capacity, Lbs.	Type				
1993	Diamante Sedan	2.31	R-12	①	5.40	②	.010–.020
	Diamante Wagon	1.75	R-12	①	5.40	②	.010–.020
	Eclipse	2.06	R-12	⑥	2.70	②	.014–.026
	Expo	1.87	R-12	⑤	2.70	②	.014–.026
	Galant	2.06	R-12	①	5.06–5.78	②	.015–.023
	Mirage	1.63–1.88	R-12	①	4.39	②	.016–.026
	Montero	1.75	R-12	⑤	6.00	②	.014–.026
	Pickup	1.88	R-12	①	4.39–5.06	②	.015–.024
	Precis	1.90–2.00	R-12	⑧	8.10	②	.016–.032
	3000GT	1.81	R-12	①	5.40	②	.010–.020
1994	Diamante Sedan	1.74	R-134a	⑦	5.70	②	.020–.030
	Diamante Wagon	1.74	R-134a	⑦	4.70	②	.010–.020
	Eclipse	2.06	R-12	⑥	2.70	②	.014–.026
	Expo	1.68	R-134a	④	⑫	②	.014–.026
	Galant	1.72	R-134a	⑦	5.10–5.70	②	.016–.025
	Mirage	1.63–1.88	R-134a	⑨	4.40–5.10	②	.016–.026
	Montero	1.43	R-134a	⑦	3.40	②	.014–.026
	Pickup	1.63–1.75	R-134a	⑦	4.10–4.80	②	.015–.024
	3000GT	1.72	R-134a	⑦	5.40	②	.010–.020

Continued

A/C SPECIFICATIONS—Continued

Year	Model	Refrigerant		Compressor Oil Viscosity	Total System Oil Capacity, Oz.	Compressor Oil Level, Inches	Compressor Clutch Air Gap, Inch
		Capacity, Lbs.	Type				
1995	Diamante Sedan	1.74	R-134a	⑦	5.70	②	.020–.030
	Diamante Wagon	1.74	R-134a	⑦	4.70	②	.010–.020
	Eclipse	1.63	R-134a	④	③	②	.016–.026
	Expo	1.68	R-134a	④	⑫	②	.014–.026
	Galant	1.52	R-134a	⑦	5.72	②	.020–.030
	Mirage	1.63–1.88	R-134a	⑨	4.40–5.10	②	.016–.026
	Montero	1.43	R-134a	⑦	3.40	②	.014–.026
	Pickup	1.63–1.75	R-134a	⑦	4.10–4.80	②	.015–.024
	3000GT	1.72	R-134a	⑦	5.40	②	.010–.020
1996	Diamante	1.63–1.74	R-134a	⑨	5.70	②	.010–.020
	Eclipse⑩	1.54–1.63	R-134a	⑨	5.70–6.40	②	.016–.026
	Eclipse⑪	1.54–1.63	R-134a	④	2.70–4.10	②	.014–.026
	Galant	1.44–1.52	R-134a	⑨	5.70–6.40	②	.016–.024
	Mirage	1.63–1.88	R-134a	⑨	4.40–5.10	②	.016–.026
	Montero	1.31–1.44	R-134a	④	2.70	②	.014–.026
	Pickup	1.63–1.75	R-134a	⑨	4.10–4.80	②	.015–.024
	3000GT	1.63–1.75	R-134a	⑨	5.40	②	.010–.020

① — Freol S-83, Suniso 5GS or equivalent.
② — Oil level inches cannot be checked.
③ — With turbo, 6.4 oz.; less turbo, 4.1 oz.
④ — DENSO Oil 8 or equivalent.
⑤ — DENSO Oil 6 or equivalent.
⑥ — DENSO Oil 6, Suniso 5GS or equivalent.
⑦ — Special Polyalkalene Glycol (PAG) lubricant required.
⑧ — Suniso 5GS or equivalent.
⑨ — SUN PAG 56 or equivalent.
⑩ — 2.0L turbocharged engine & 2.4L engine.
⑪ — 2.0L non-turbocharged engine.
⑫ — 1.8L engine, 3.40–4.80 oz.; 2.4L engine, 2.00–3.40 oz.

BELT TENSION

Model	Engine	A/C Compressor Belt Deflection, Inch
1993		
Diamante	3.0L SOHC	.24–.32
	3.0L DOHC	.16–.20
Eclipse	1.8L	.24–.28
	2.0L	.24–.28
Expo	1.8L	.27–.30
	2.4L	.21–.24
Galant	2.0L	.24–.28
Mirage	1.5L	.24–.28
	1.6L	.27–.30
Montero	3.0L	.20–.24
Pickup	2.4L & 3.0L	.33–.39
Precis	1.5L	.31
3000GT	3.0L	.16–22
1994–95		
Diamante	3.0L	.28–.37
Eclipse	1.8L	.32–.43
	2.0L	.24–.32
Expo	1.8L	.22–.32
	2.4L	.14–.22
Galant	2.4L	.22–.32

Continued

BELT TENSION—Continued

Model	Engine	A/C Compressor Belt Deflection, Inch
1994–95		
Mirage	1.5L	.24–.28
	1.8L	.27–.30
Montero	3.0L	.20–.29
	3.5L	.20–.30
Pickup	2.4L & 3.0L	.33–.39
3000GT	3.0L	.16–.22
1996		
Diamante	3.0L	.28–.37
Eclipse	2.0L Non-Turbo	.39–.43
	2.0L Turbo & 2.4L	.26–.30
Galant	2.4L	.32
Mirage	1.5L	.24–.28
	1.8L	.27–.30
Montero	3.0L	.26–.29
	3.5L	.26–.30
Pickup	2.4L & 3.0L	.33–.39
3000GT	3.0L	.16–.22

TECHNICAL SERVICE BULLETINS

A/C WHOOPING

1994-95 Galant

On these models built before March 10, 1995, VIN SE168854, the air conditioning system may make a whooping noise in high temperatures with high humidity, usually when the A/C is turned on immediately after engine start-up.

This condition may be caused by the expansion valve. To correct this condition, install replacement expansion valve (part No. MR240612). **Refer to MOTOR'S AIR CONDITIONER & HEATER MANUAL for expansion valve replacement procedure.**

A/C INOPERATIVE

1994 Galant

On these models built before VIN RE024687, the A/C compressor may fail to start and run.

This condition may be caused by a broken wire at the B-13 connector. To correct this condition, proceed as follows:

1. Inspect for broken or frayed wire at the B-13 connector. **Refer to MOTOR'S IMPORTED COMPONENT LOCATOR MANUAL for location.**
2. Repair wiring as needed.
3. **On models equipped with SOHC engine,** install connector with tie strap to No. 1 fuel injector wire.
4. **On models equipped with DOHC engine,** install connector with tie strap to ignition's power transistor harness.

AIR CONDITIONING ODOR

An A/C odor may be created when condensation forms in and around the A/C evaporator. The condensation eventually mixes with airborne pollutants to form growths of bacteria and/or fungi. This produces an unpleasant or musty odor when the blower is turned on.

To remove this odor and prevent new bacteria growth, Mitsubishi Air Conditioner Treatment should be applied. This treatment kills bacteria and fungi growths inside the A/C system and leaves a protective film that guards against new growth for at least one year.

The A/C treatment is applied to the evaporator core through the fresh air inlet. This is done using compressed air, an air gun and the product's applicator nozzle. Use treatment from case part No. A993ZC1X01 and nozzle/adapter kit part No. A993ZC1X02.

Cooling Fans

INDEX

Page No.

Cooling Fans 29-9
Clutch Cooling Fans 29-19

Electric Cooling Fans

INDEX

Page No.

Component Diagnosis & Testing 29-9
Condenser Fan Motor........... 29-10
Condenser Fan Motor Relay 29-13
Condenser Fan Motor Resistor.. 29-13
Engine Coolant Temperature Switch 29-13
Radiator Fan Motor 29-9
Radiator Fan Motor Relay....... 29-11
Radiator Fan Motor Resistor 29-10
Thermo Sensor 29-12
Component Replacement........ 29-14
Troubleshooting 29-9
Both Fans Do Not Operate...... 29-9
Both Fans Do Not Operate In High Speed Mode Only 29-9
Both Fans Do Not Operate In Low Speed Mode Only 29-9
Condenser Fan Only Does Not Operate 29-9

TROUBLESHOOTING

BOTH FANS DO NOT OPERATE

DIAMANTE

Inspect fusible link No. 4.

ECLIPSE

1993

Inspect sub-fusible link No. 3.

CONDENSER FAN ONLY DOES NOT OPERATE

DIAMANTE

Inspect dedicated fuse No. 7.

ECLIPSE

1993

Inspect dedicated fuse No. 5.

BOTH FANS DO NOT OPERATE IN LOW SPEED MODE ONLY

DIAMANTE

1. **On 1993 models,** proceed as follows:
   a. If A/C compressor clutch does not engage, inspect A/C control unit output.
   b. If A/C compressor clutch engages, inspect resistor, radiator and condenser fan (LO) relays, thermo sensor (LO) and A/C control unit connector C-71 terminal 60 output voltage.
2. **On 1994–96 models,** proceed as follows:
   a. **On models equipped with DOHC engine,** if compressor clutch does not engage, check for output from A/C belt lock controller.

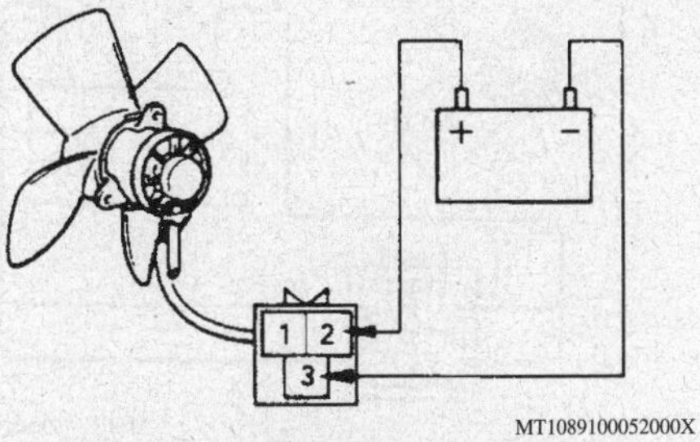
+
−
1 2
3
MT1089100052000X

Fig. 1 Radiator fan motor inspection. Mirage

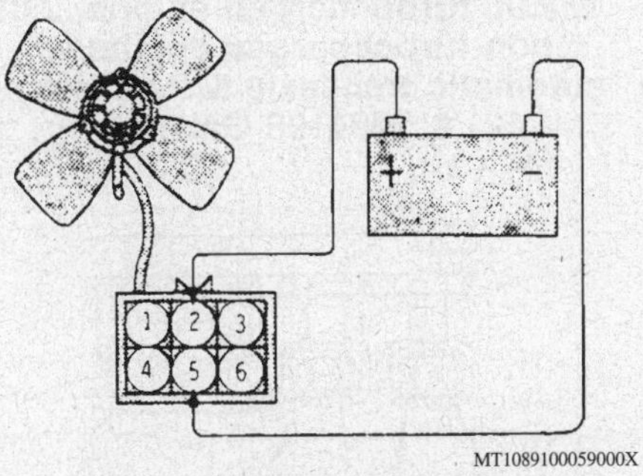
+
−
1 2 3
4 5 6
MT1089100059000X

Fig. 3 Radiator fan motor inspection. 1993 Diamante, Eclipse & 3000GT

   b. **On models equipped with SOHC engine,** if compressor clutch does not engage, check for output from A/C control.
   c. **On all models,** if compressor clutch engages, inspect condenser fan motor (LO) relay.

ECLIPSE

1993

1. If A/C compressor clutch does not engage, check for A/C control unit output.
2. If A/C compressor clutch engages, in-

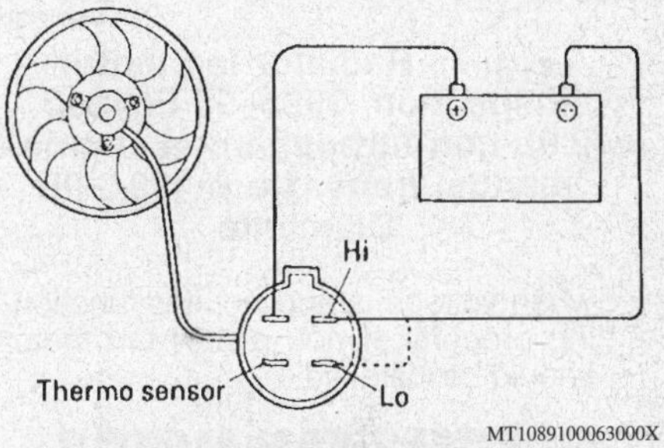
Hi
Thermo sensor
Lo
MT1089100063000X

Fig. 2 Radiator fan motor inspection. Precis

spect resistor.

BOTH FANS DO NOT OPERATE IN HIGH SPEED MODE ONLY

DIAMANTE

1. **On 1993 models,** proceed as follows:
   a. Inspect radiator and condenser fan motor (HI) relays and thermo sensor (HI).
   b. Inspect A/C control unit connector C-71 terminal 60 output voltage.
2. **On 1994–96 models,** check Engine Control Module (ECM).

COMPONENT DIAGNOSIS & TESTING

RADIATOR FAN MOTOR

DIAMANTE, ECLIPSE, EXPO, GALANT, MIRAGE, PRECIS & 3000GT

1. Apply battery voltage between fan motor connector terminals, **Figs. 1 through 8.**
2. If fan motor runs smoothly and quietly

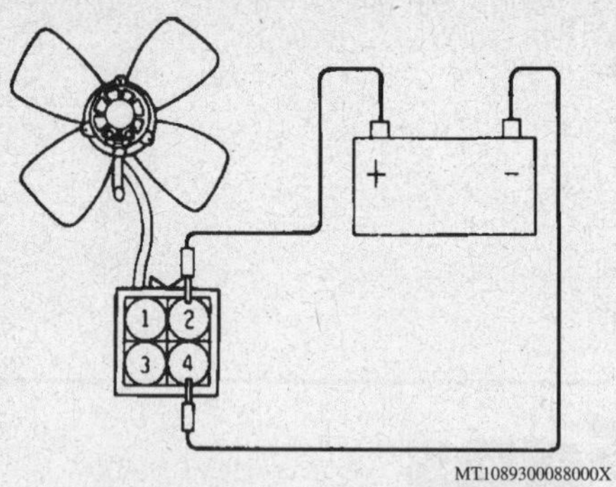
1
2
3
4
+
-
MT1089300088000X

Fig. 4 Radiator fan motor inspection. 1993 Expo, 1994 Eclipse & 1994–96 3000GT

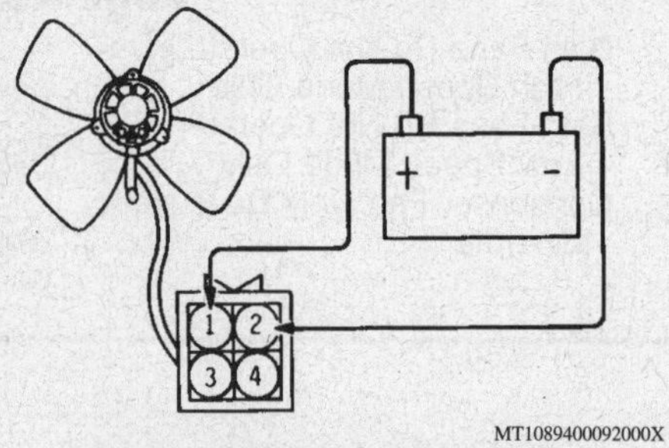
1
2
3
4
+
-
MT1089400092000X

Fig. 7 Radiator fan motor inspection. 1995–96 Eclipse w/2.0L non-turbocharged engine & manual transaxle & 1994–96 Diamante

when voltage is applied, it is functioning properly; if not, a new fan motor should be installed.

CONDENSER FAN MOTOR

DIAMANTE

1. Apply battery voltage to terminal 3 and battery ground to terminal 4, **Fig. 9.**
2. If motor runs smoothly and quietly, operation is satisfactory; if not, a new motor should be installed.

3000GT & 1993-94 ECLIPSE

1. Disconnect fan motor connector.
2. Apply battery positive voltage to terminal 3 and battery ground to terminal 4, **Figs. 10 and 11.** Motor should operate smoothly.
3. If results are not as indicated, a new motor should be installed.

1995-96 ECLIPSE

1. Apply battery voltage to motor connector terminal 1 while grounding terminal 4, **Fig. 12.** Condenser fan motor should operate smoothly and quietly.
2. Apply battery voltage to motor connector terminal 3 while grounding terminal 2. Condenser fan motor should again operate smoothly, but at a higher speed.
3. If results are not as indicated, a new fan motor should be installed.

EXPO

1. Disconnect condenser fan motor connection.

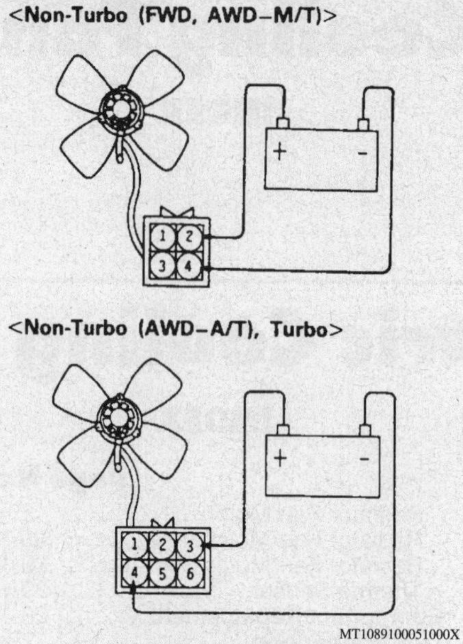
<Non-Turbo (FWD, AWD–M/T)>
1
2
3
4
+
-
<Non-Turbo (AWD–A/T), Turbo>
1
2
3
4
5
6
+
-
MT1089100051000X

Fig. 5 Radiator fan motor inspection. 1993 Galant

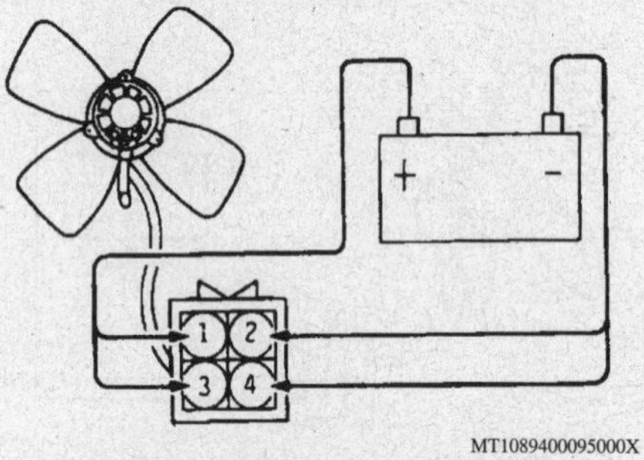
1
2
3
4
+
-
MT1089400095000X

Fig. 8 Radiator fan motor inspection. 1995–96 Eclipse w/2.0L turbocharged engine, 2.0L non-turbocharged engine w/ automatic transaxle & 2.4L engine & 1994–96 Galant

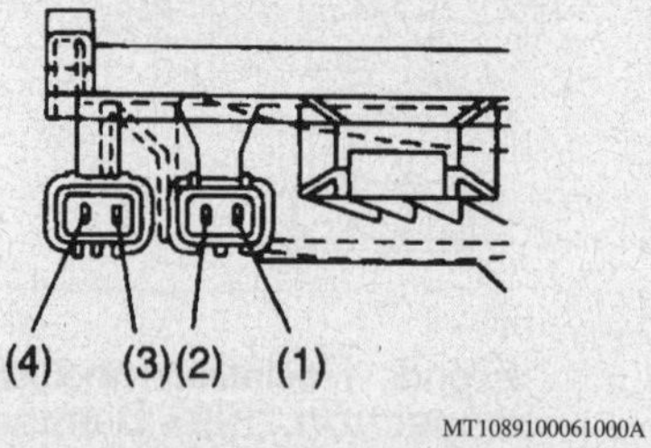
(4)
(3)(2)
(1)
MT1089100061000A

Fig. 10 Condenser fan motor terminal identification. 3000GT

2. Connect battery positive to terminal 3 and battery ground to terminal 1, **Fig. 13.** Motor should operate smoothly.

GALANT

1993

1. Disconnect fan motor connector, then apply battery positive voltage to terminal 2 and battery ground to terminal 4, **Fig. 14.** Motor should operate smoothly.

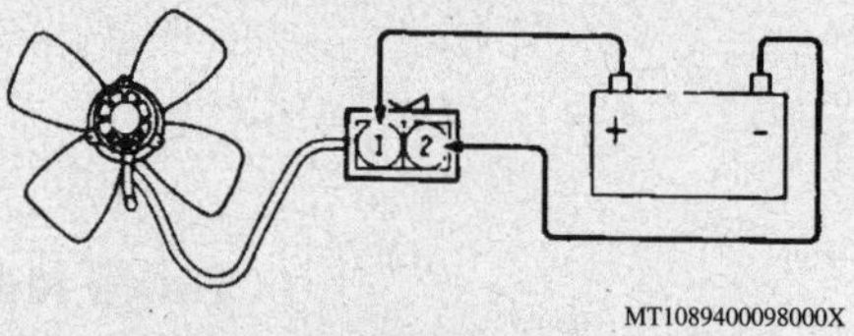
1
2
+
-
MT1089400098000X

Fig. 6 Radiator fan motor inspection. 1994–95 Expo

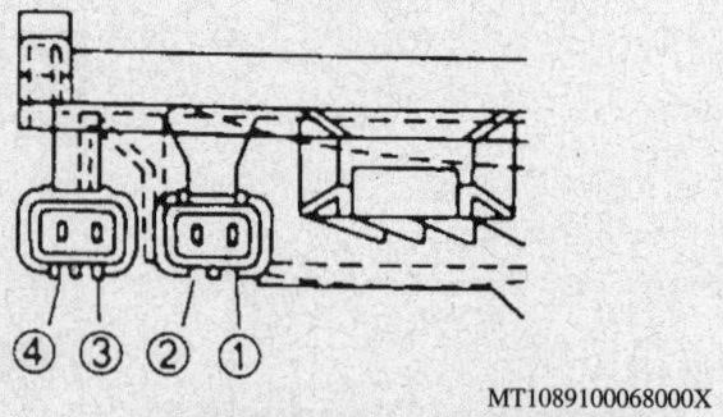
④ ③ ② ①
MT1089100068000X

Fig. 9 Condenser fan motor terminal identification. Diamante

2. If results are not as indicated, a new fan motor should be installed.

1994-96

1. Connect battery (+) to gray connector terminal 1, **Fig. 15,** while grounding terminal 2; motor should operate smoothly and quietly at low speed.
2. Connect battery (+) to black connector terminal 1, **Fig. 15,** while grounding terminal 2; motor should operate smoothly and quietly at high speed.
3. If results are not as indicated, a new fan motor should be installed.

MIRAGE

1. Connect battery (+) to condenser fan motor connector terminal 2 while grounding terminal 1, **Fig. 16.**
2. If fan motor runs smoothly and quietly, operation is satisfactory; if not, a new fan motor should be installed.

MONTERO

1. Apply battery (+) voltage to condenser fan motor connector terminal 2, **Fig. 17,** while grounding terminal 1.
2. If condenser fan motor runs smoothly and quietly, operation is satisfactory; if not, a new motor should be installed.

PRECIS

Connect an ohmmeter to condenser motor terminal, **Fig. 18,** and ensure continuity exists between motor terminals (+) and (-). If it does not, replace motor.

RADIATOR FAN MOTOR RESISTOR

GALANT

1993

1. Disconnect radiator fan motor connector, then measure resistance between terminals, **Fig. 19.**
2. If resistance is .26–.32 ohms, resistor is satisfactory; if not, a new resistor should be installed.

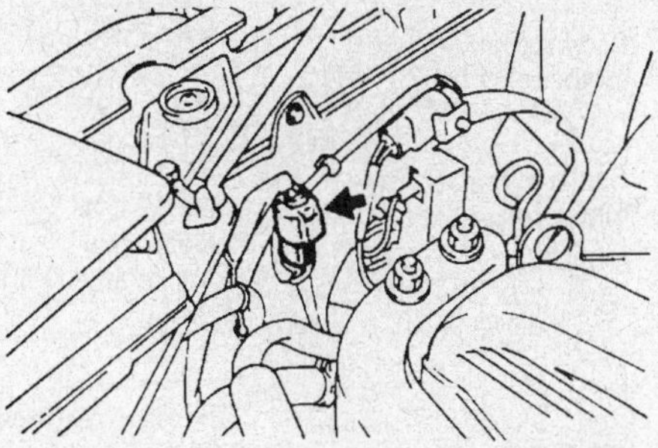

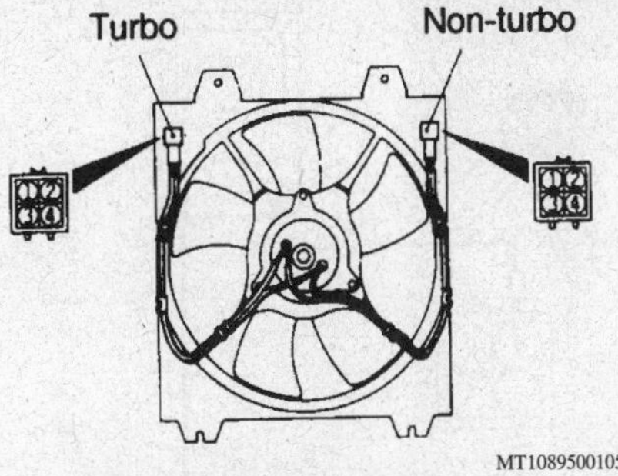
Turbo
Non-turbo
MT1089500105000X

Fig. 12 Condenser fan motor terminal identification. 1995–96 Eclipse

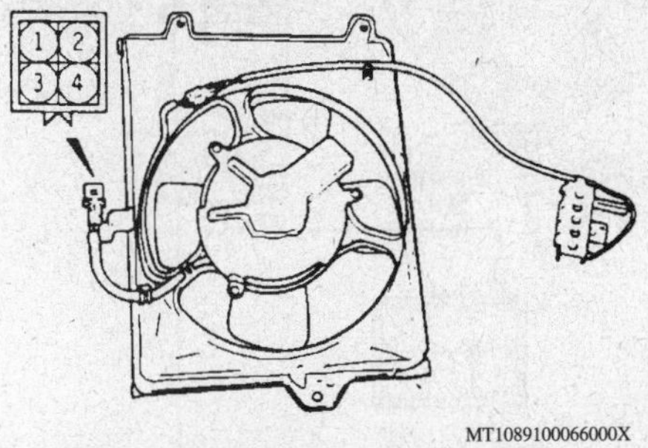
MT1089100066000X

Fig. 13 Condenser fan motor terminal identification. Expo

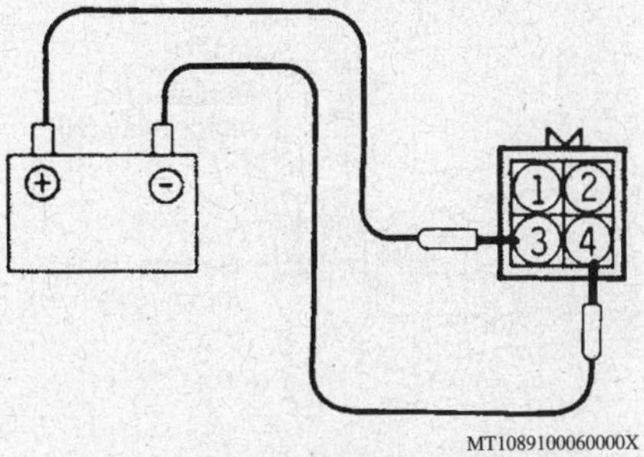
MT1089100060000X

Fig. 11 Condenser fan motor inspection. 1993–94 Eclipse

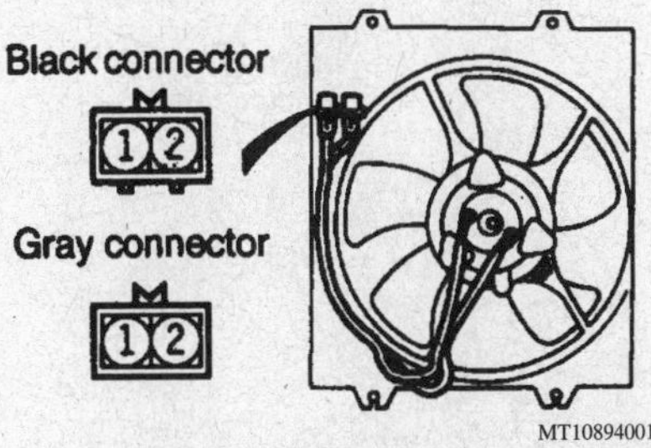
Black connector
Gray connector
MT1089400106000X

Fig. 15 Condenser fan motor terminal identification. 1994–96 Galant

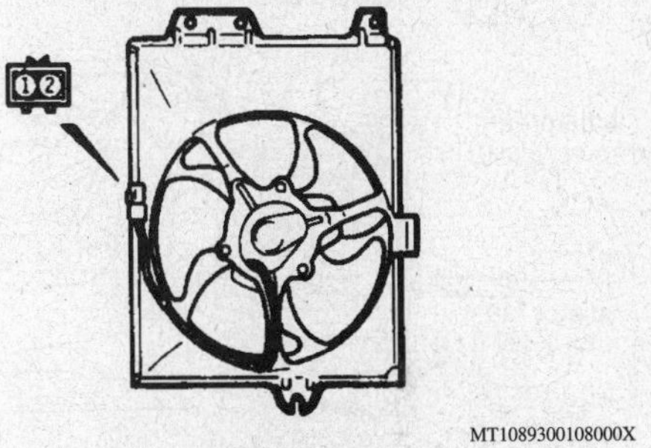
MT1089300108000X

Fig. 16 Condenser fan motor terminal identification. Mirage

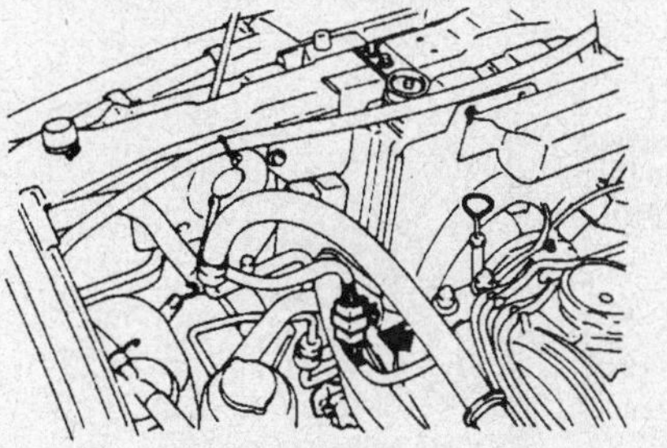

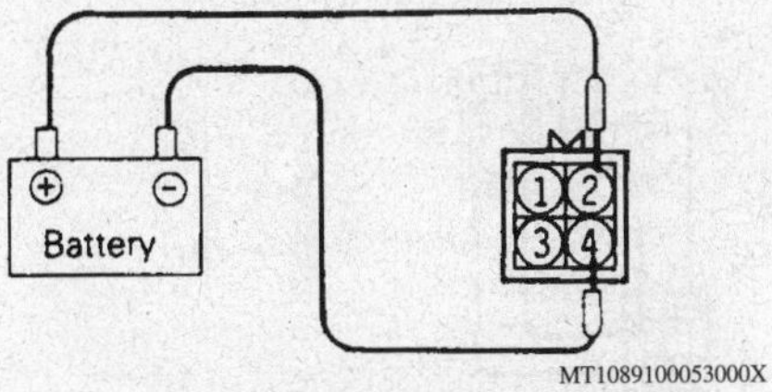
Battery
MT1089100053000X

Fig. 14 Condenser fan motor terminal identification. 1993 Galant

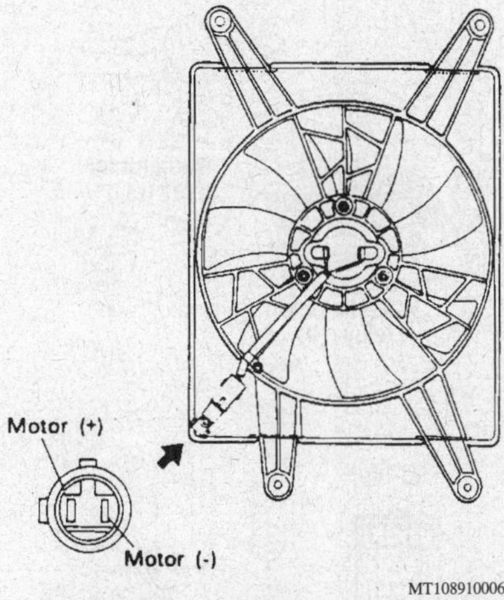
Motor (+)
Motor (-)
MT1089100064000X

Fig. 18 Condenser fan motor terminal identification. Precis

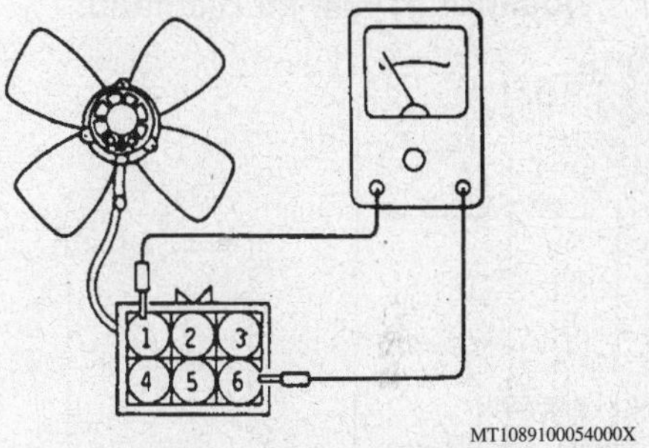
MT1089100054000X

Fig. 19 Resistor inspection. 1993 Galant

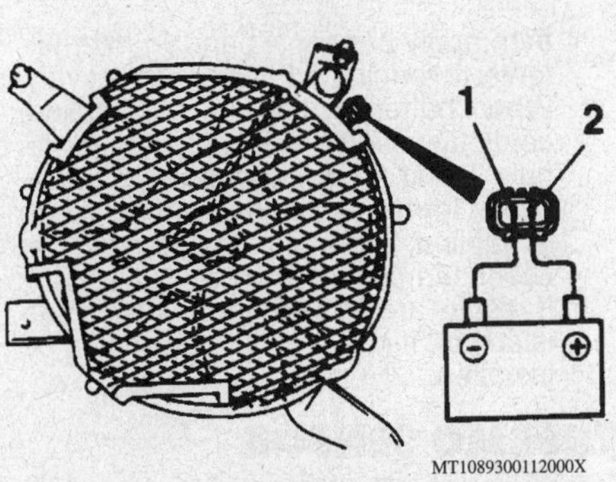
1
2
MT1089300112000X

Fig. 17 Condenser fan motor inspection. Montero

3000GT

1. Disconnect radiator fan motor connector, then measure resistance between terminals, **Figs. 20 and 21.**
2. If resistance is .29–.35 ohms, resistor is satisfactory; if not, a new resistor should be installed.

RADIATOR FAN MOTOR RELAY

DIAMANTE, 3000GT & 1993-94 ECLIPSE

1. Remove relay from relay box at right-hand side of engine compartment, **Figs. 22 through 25.**
2. Check for continuity between terminals with battery (+) and (-) applied intermittently to terminals 2 and 4 respectively, **Fig. 26.**
3. When battery voltage is applied, continuity should exist between terminals 1 and 3 but should not exist when voltage is removed. Continuity should also exist between terminals 2 and 4 when voltage is removed.
4. If results are as indicated, relay is satisfactory; if not, a new relay should be installed.

EXPO, MIRAGE & 1994-96 GALANT

1. Remove relay from engine compartment relay box, **Figs. 27 through 29.**
2. Check for continuity between terminals with battery (+) and (-) applied intermittently to terminals 1 and 3 respectively, **Fig. 30.**
3. When battery voltage is applied, continuity should exist between terminals 1 and 3 and between terminals 4 and 5; when voltage is removed, continuity should exist only between terminals 1 and 3.

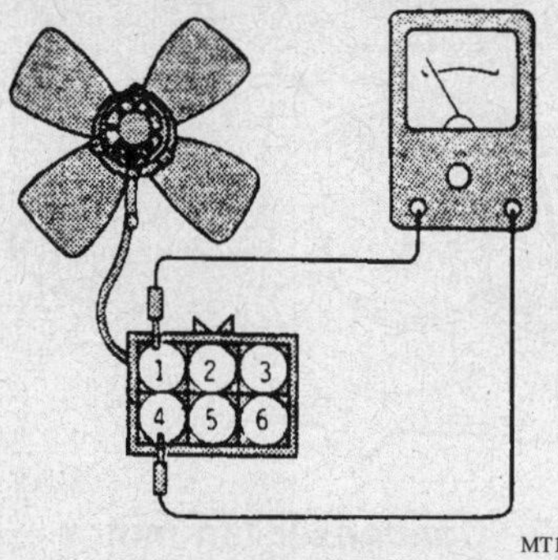
1
2
3
4
5
6
MT1089100057000X

Fig. 20 Resistor inspection. 1993 3000GT

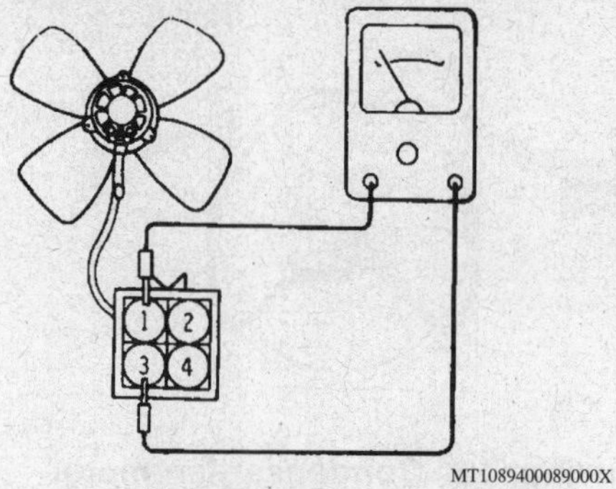
1
2
3
4
MT1089400089000X

Fig. 21 Resistor inspection. 1994–96 3000GT

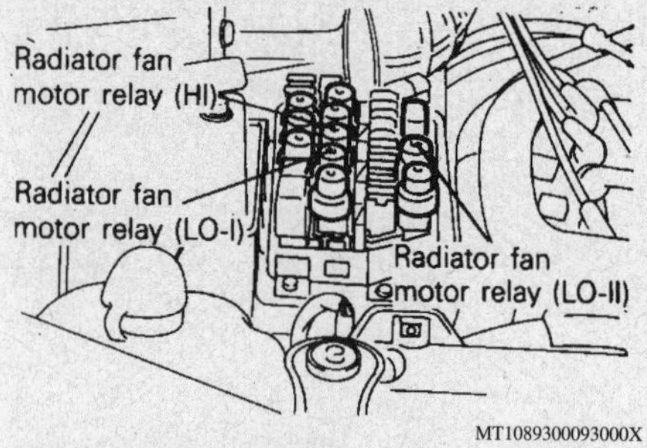
Radiator fan motor relay (HI)
Radiator fan motor relay (LO-I)
Radiator fan motor relay (LO-II)
MT1089300093000X

Fig. 22 Radiator fan motor relay location. 1993 Diamante

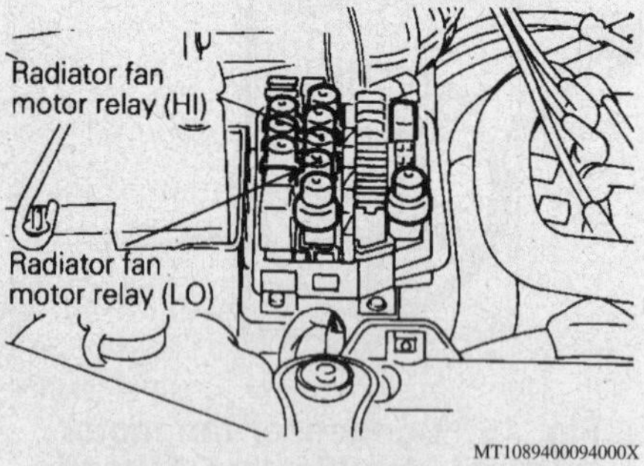
Radiator fan motor relay (HI)
Radiator fan motor relay (LO)
MT1089400094000X

Fig. 23 Radiator fan motor relay location. 1994–96 Diamante

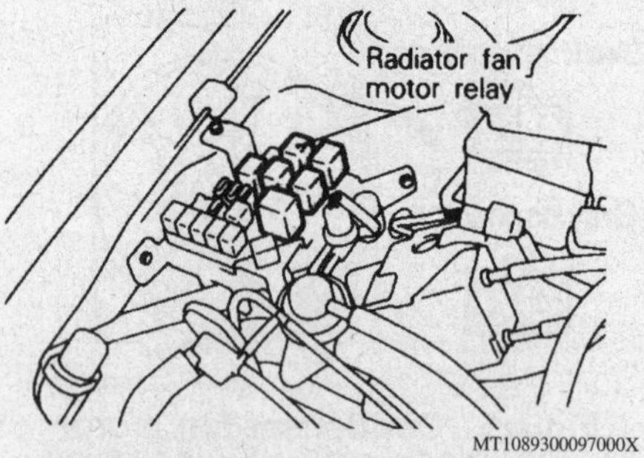
Radiator fan motor relay
MT1089300097000X

Fig. 24 Radiator fan motor relay location. 1993–94 Eclipse

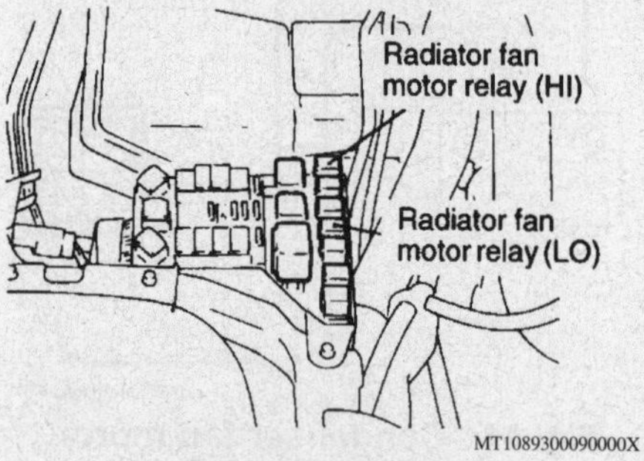
Radiator fan motor relay (HI)
Radiator fan motor relay (LO)
MT1089300090000X

Fig. 25 Radiator fan motor relay location. 3000GT

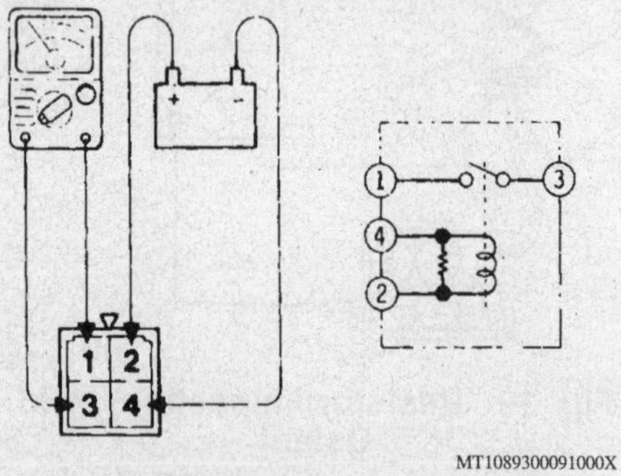
1
2
3
4
MT1089300091000X

Fig. 26 Radiator fan motor relay inspection. Diamante, 3000GT & 1993–94 Eclipse

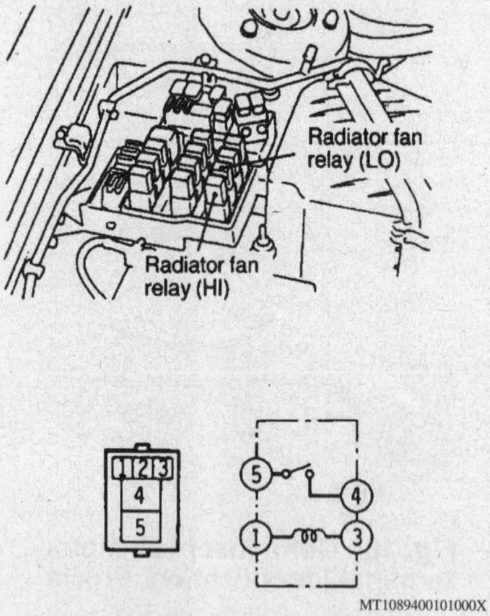
Radiator fan relay (LO)
Radiator fan relay (HI)
1
2
3
4
5
MT1089400101000X

Fig. 27 Radiator fan motor relay location. 1994–96 Galant

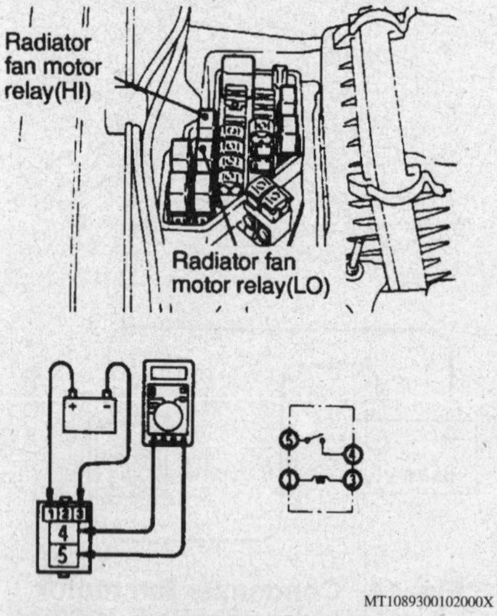
Radiator fan motor relay(HI)
Radiator fan motor relay(LO)
1
2
3
4
5
MT1089300102000X

Fig. 28 Radiator fan motor relay location. Expo

4. If results are as indicated, relay is satisfactory; if not, a new relay should be installed.

1993 GALANT

1. Remove relay from engine compartment relay box, **Fig. 31.**
2. Check for continuity between terminals with battery (-) and (+) applied intermittently to terminals 1 and 2 respectively, **Fig. 32.**
3. When battery voltage is applied, continuity should exist between terminals 3 and 4 but should not exist when voltage is removed. Continuity should also exist between terminals 1 and 2 when voltage is removed.
4. If results are as indicated, relay is satisfactory; if not, a new relay should be installed.

1995-96 ECLIPSE

1. Remove relay from relay box, **Fig. 33,**

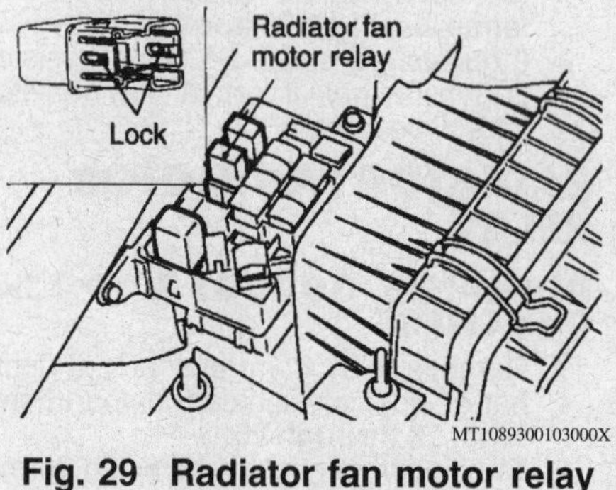
Radiator fan motor relay
Lock
MT1089300103000X

Fig. 29 Radiator fan motor relay location. Mirage

then apply battery (+) and (-) intermittently to terminals 1 and 3 respectively.

2. When battery voltage is not applied, continuity should exist between terminals 1 and 3 but should not exist between terminals 4 and 5; when voltage is applied, continuity should exist between terminals 4 and 5.
3. If results are as indicated, relay is satisfactory; if not, a new relay should be installed.

THERMO SENSOR

DIAMANTE, EXPO, GALANT, MIRAGE, PRECIS & 3000GT

1. Immerse sensing end of sensor in hot

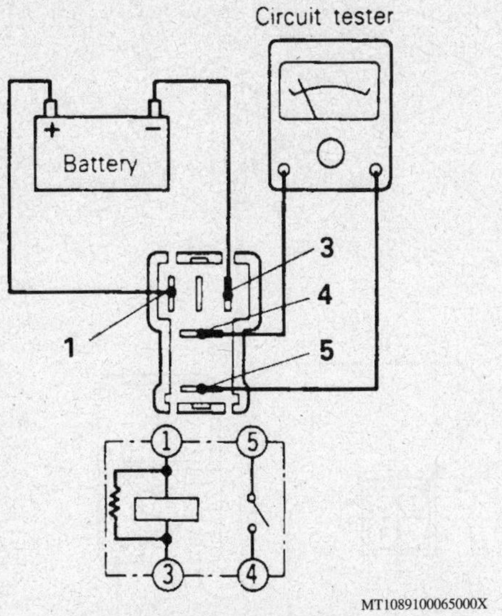
Circuit tester
Battery
+
−
1
3
4
5
MT1089100065000X

Fig. 30 Radiator fan motor relay inspection. Expo, Mirage & 1994–96 Galant

water with a suitable circuit tester connected to sensor terminals, **Fig. 34.**

2. Moderate water temperature while monitoring continuity.
3. **On Diamante and 3000GT models,** if condenser fan sensor is being tested, results should be as follows:
   a. **On Diamante models,** continuity should exist when temperature is 205–219°F but should not exist at or below 198°F.
   b. **On 3000GT models,** continuity should exist when temperature is 196–210°F but should not exist at or below 189°F.
4. **On all models,** if radiator fan sensor is being tested, results should be as follows:
   a. **On Mirage models with 1.5L engine and Diamante, Eclipse and Galant models,** continuity should exist when temperature is 180–190°F but should not exist at or below 172°F.
   b. **On Mirage models with 1.8L engine and Expo models,** continuity should exist when temperature is 178–190°F but should not exist at or below 171°F.
   c. **On 3000GT models,** continuity should exist when temperature is 178–192°F but should not exist at or below 171°F.
5. **On all models,** if results are as indicated, sensor operation is satisfactory; if not, a new sensor should be installed.

ENGINE COOLANT TEMPERATURE SWITCH

Refer to "Thermo Sensor" in this section for inspection procedure.

CONDENSER FAN MOTOR RESISTOR

DIAMANTE

1. Measure resistance between terminals 1 and 2, **Fig. 9;** resistance should be .29 ohms.

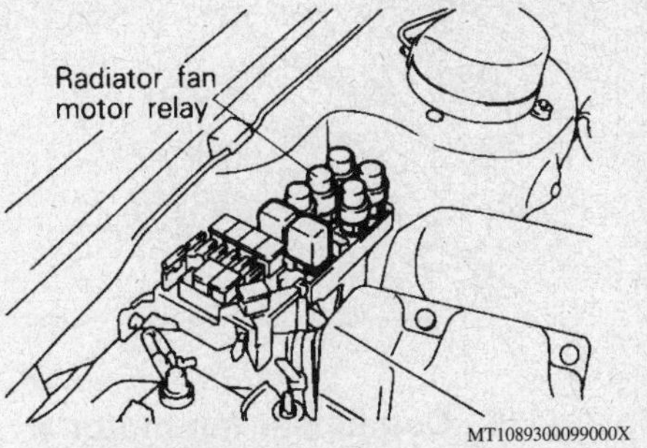
Radiator fan motor relay
MT1089300099000X

Fig. 31 Radiator fan motor relay location. 1993 Galant

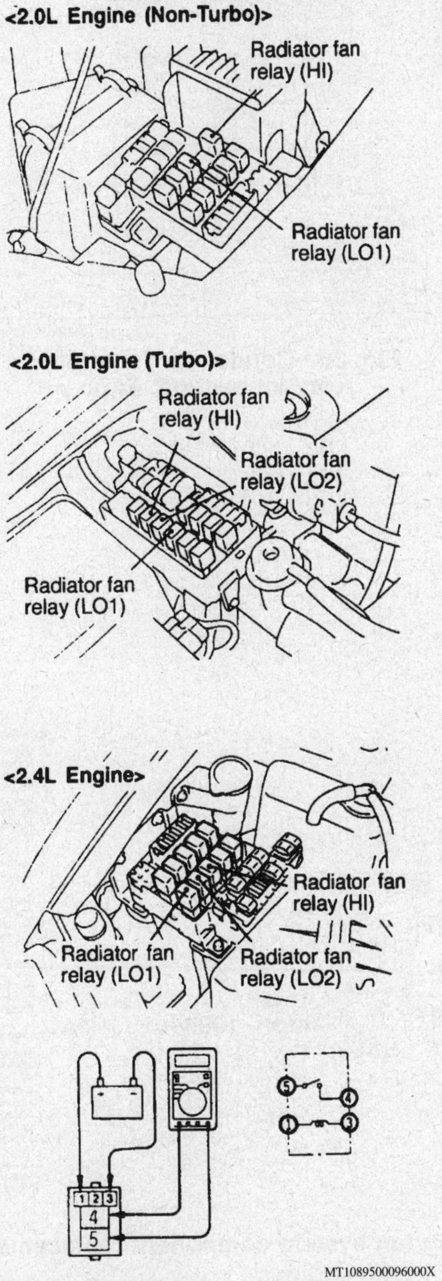
<2.0L Engine (Non-Turbo)>
Radiator fan relay (HI)
Radiator fan relay (LO1)
<2.0L Engine (Turbo)>
Radiator fan relay (HI)
Radiator fan relay (LO2)
Radiator fan relay (LO1)
<2.4L Engine>
Radiator fan relay (HI)
Radiator fan relay (LO1)
Radiator fan relay (LO2)
MT1089500096000X

Fig. 33 Radiator fan motor relay location & inspection. 1995–96 Eclipse

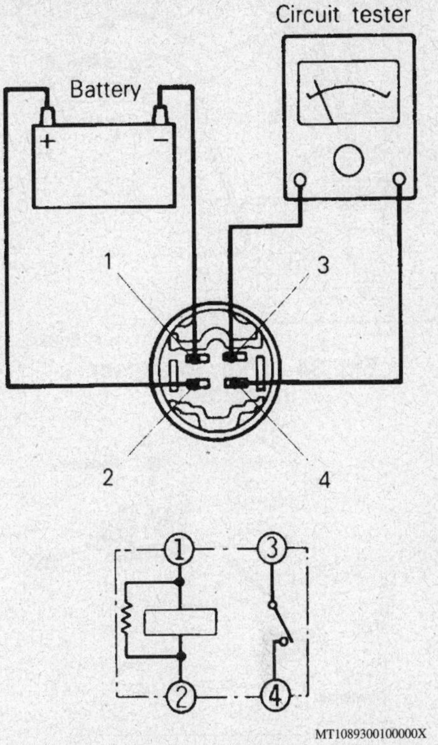
Circuit tester
Battery
+
−
1
2
3
4
MT1089300100000X

Fig. 32 Radiator fan motor relay inspection. 1993 Galant

2. If resistance is as indicated, resistor is satisfactory; if not, a new resistor should be installed.

ECLIPSE

1993-94

1. Disconnect condenser fan motor resistor connector, **Fig. 35,** then connect a suitable ohmmeter to connector terminals, **Fig. 36.**
2. If resistance is .26–.32 ohms, resistor is satisfactory; if not, a new resistor should be installed.

EXPO

1. Using a suitable ohmmeter, measure resistance between terminals 2 and 4, **Fig. 13.**
2. If resistance is .29 ohms, resistor is satisfactory; if not, a new resistor should be installed.

MIRAGE

1.8L Engine

1. Disconnect resistor connector, then use a suitable ohmmeter to measure resistance between terminals 1 and 3 and between terminals 2 and 4, **Fig. 37.**
2. If resistance is .45 ohm, resistor is satisfactory; if not, a new resistor should be installed.

CONDENSER FAN MOTOR RELAY

EXPO

Test condenser fan motor relay as shown in **Fig. 38.**

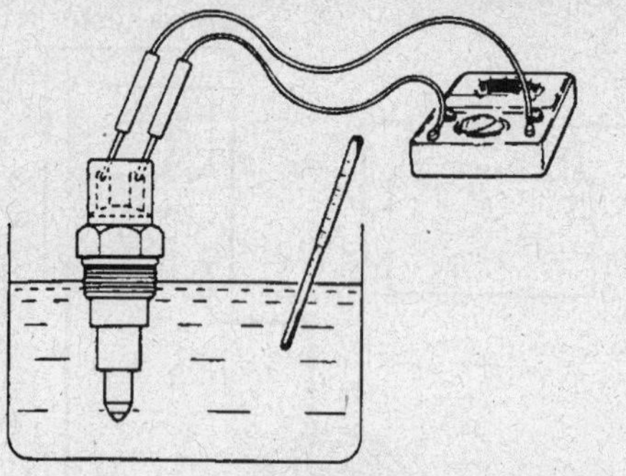

MT1089100049000X

Fig. 34 Thermo sensor inspection

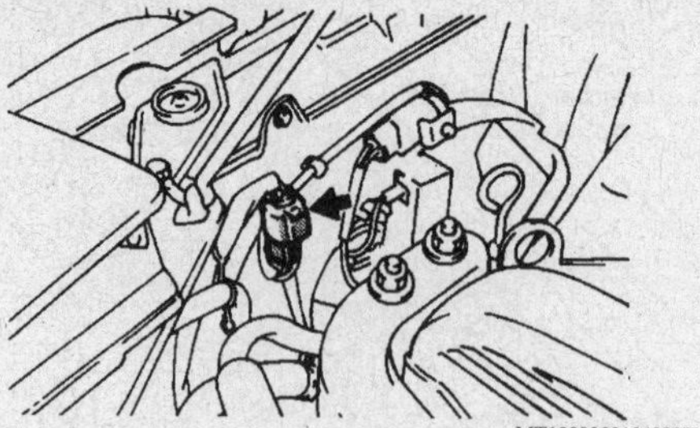

MT1089300104000X

Fig. 35 Condenser fan motor & resistor connector location. 1993–94 Eclipse

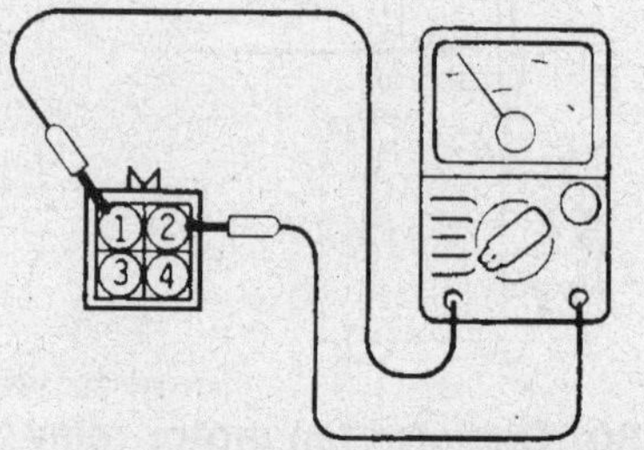

MT1089100056000X

Fig. 36 Condenser fan motor resistor inspection. 1993–94 Eclipse

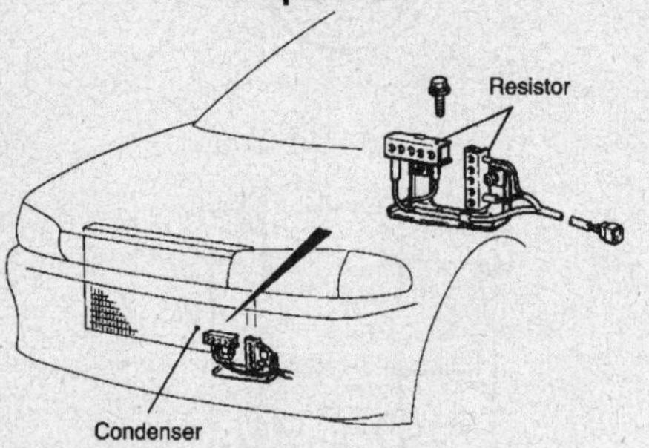
Resistor
Condenser

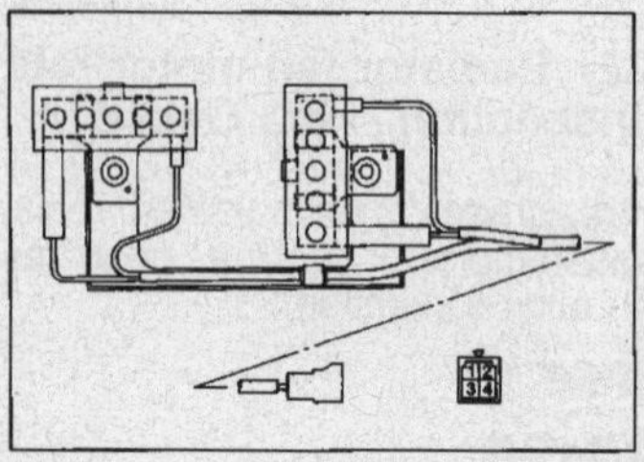

MT1089300107000X

Fig. 37 Condenser fan resistor location & terminal identification. Mirage w/1.8L engine

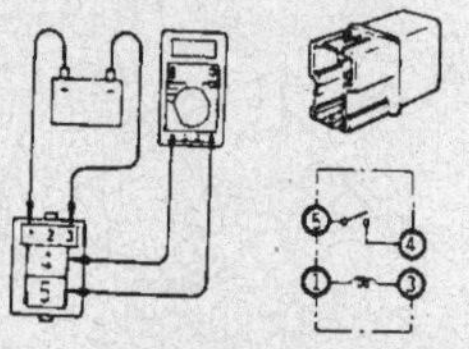

Terminal / Battery voltage	1	3	4	5
Continuity no voltage	O—	—O		
Continuity with voltage	O—	—O	O—	—O

MT1089100067000X

Fig. 38 Condenser fan motor relay inspection. Expo

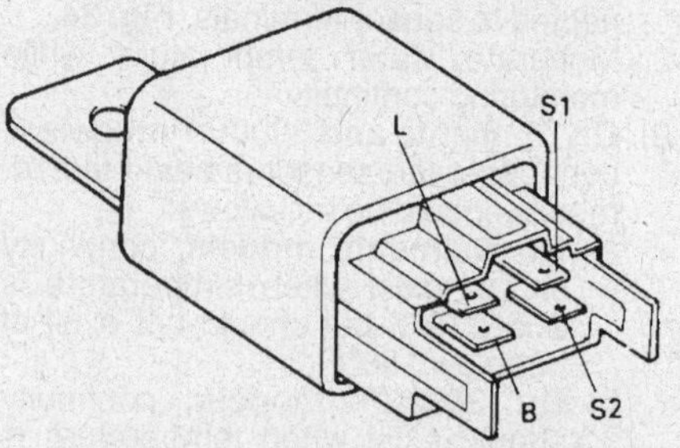
L
S1
B
S2

MT1089100062000X

Fig. 39 Condenser fan motor relay inspection. Precis

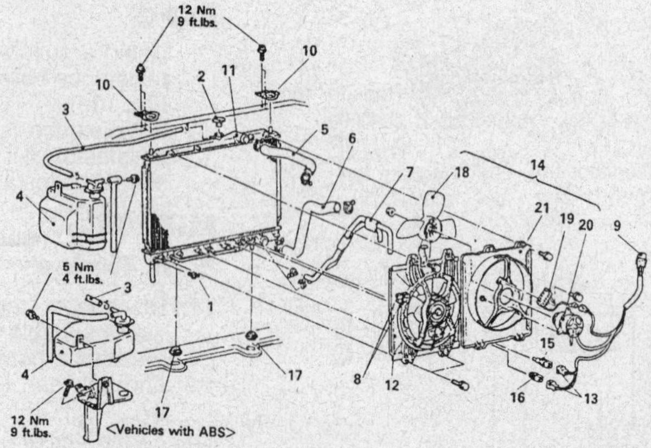
12 Nm
9 ft.lbs.
5 Nm
4 ft.lbs.
12 Nm
9 ft.lbs.
<Vehicles with ABS>

Removal steps of radiator

1. Drain plug
2. Radiator cap
3. Overflow hose
4. Reserve tank
5. Radiator upper hose
6. Radiator lower hose
7. Automatic transaxle oil cooler hoses (Radiator side)
8. Condenser fan motor connector
9. Radiator fan motor connector
10. Upper insulator
11. Radiator assembly
12. Condenser fan motor assembly
13. Thermo sensor connector
14. Radiator fan motor assembly
15. Thermo sensor (For radiator fan)
16. Thermo sensor (For condenser fan)
17. Lower insulator
18. Fan
19. Resistor
20. Radiator fan motor
21. Shroud

Removal steps of radiator fan motor assembly

1. Drain plug
2. Radiator cap
5. Radiator upper hose
8. Condenser fan motor connector
9. Radiator fan motor connector
12. Condenser fan motor assembly
13. Thermo sensor connector
14. Radiator fan motor assembly
18. Fan
19. Resistor
20. Radiator fan motor
21. Shroud

MT1089100069000X

Fig. 40 Cooling fan system component replacement. Diamante

PRECIS

1. Connect an ohmmeter as shown in **Fig. 39.** No continuity should exist between terminals L and B.
2. Apply battery voltage between terminals S1 and S2; continuity should now exist between terminals L and B.

COMPONENT REPLACEMENT

Refer to **Figs. 40 through 51** for component replacement.

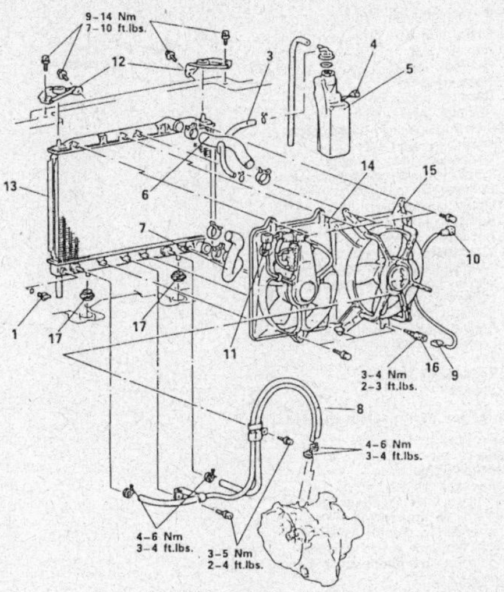
9-14 Nm
7-10 ft.lbs.
3-4 Nm
2-3 ft.lbs.
4-6 Nm
3-4 ft.lbs.
4-6 Nm
3-4 ft.lbs.
3-5 Nm
2-4 ft.lbs.

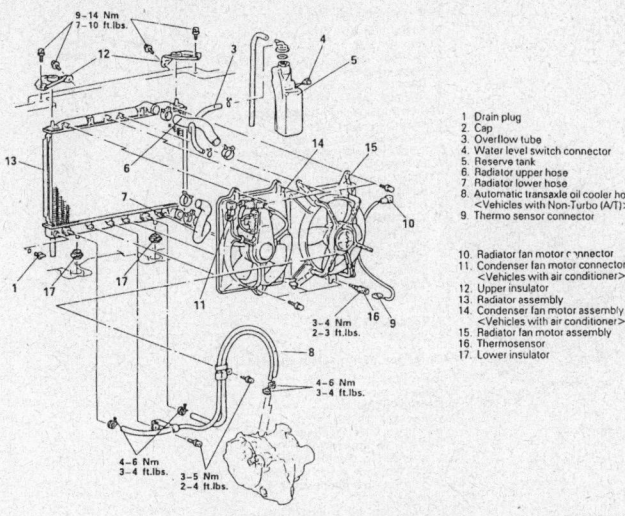

1. Drain plug
2. Cap
3. Overflow tube
4. Water level switch connector
5. Reserve tank
6. Radiator upper hose
7. Radiator lower hose
8. Automatic transaxle oil cooler hoses <Vehicles with Non-Turbo (A/T)>
9. Thermo sensor connector
10. Radiator fan motor connector
11. Condenser fan motor connector <Vehicles with air conditioner>
12. Upper insulator
13. Radiator assembly
14. Condenser fan motor assembly <Vehicles with air conditioner>
15. Radiator fan motor assembly
16. Thermosensor
17. Lower insulator

MT1089100070000X

Fig. 41 Cooling fan system component replacement. 1993–94 Eclipse

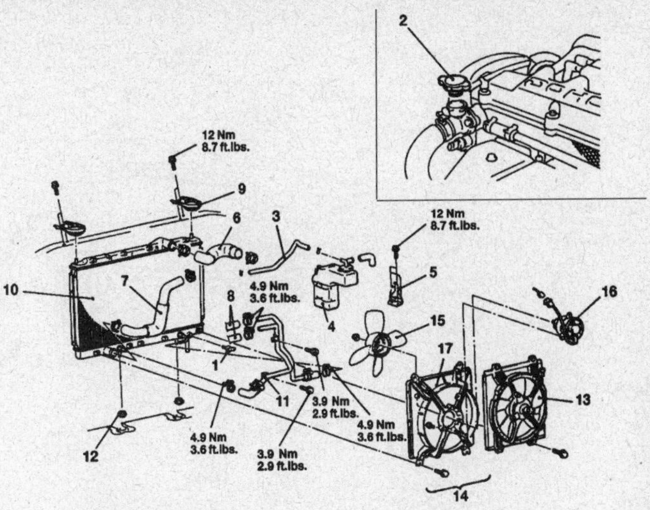
12 Nm
8.7 ft.lbs.
12 Nm
8.7 ft.lbs.
4.9 Nm
3.6 ft.lbs.
3.9 Nm
2.9 ft.lbs.
4.9 Nm
3.6 ft.lbs.
4.9 Nm
3.6 ft.lbs.
3.9 Nm
2.9 ft.lbs.

Radiator removal steps

1. Drain plug
2. Radiator cap
3. Overflow tube
4. Reserve tank
5. Reserve tank bracket
6. Radiator upper hose
7. Radiator lower hose
8. Transaxle fluid cooler hose connection <Vehicles with A/T>
9. Upper insulator
10. Radiator assembly
11. Transaxle fluid cooler hose and pipe assembly <Vehicles with A/T>
12. Lower insulator
13. Condenser fan motor assembly <Vehicles with A/C>
14. Radiator fan motor assembly
15. Fan
16. Radiator fan motor
17. Shroud

Radiator fan motor removal steps

11. Transaxle fluid cooler hose and pipe assembly <Vehicles with A/T>
14. Radiator fan motor assembly
15. Fan
16. Radiator fan motor
17. Shroud

MT1089500109000X

Fig. 42 Cooling fan system component replacement. 1995–96 Eclipse w/2.0L non-turbocharged engine

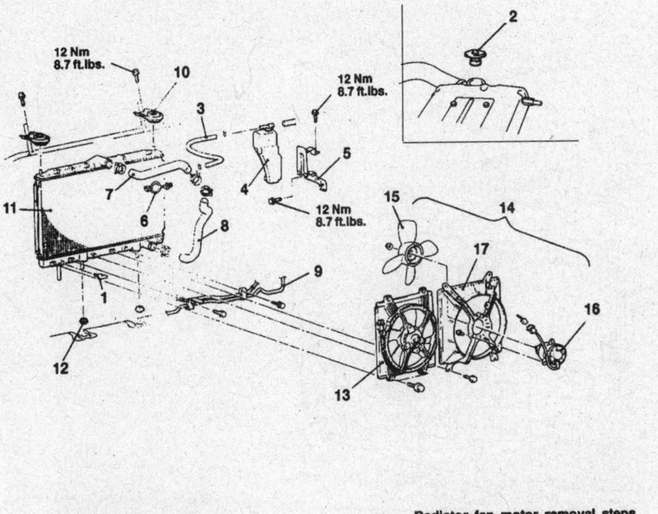
12 Nm
8.7 ft.lbs.
12 Nm
8.7 ft.lbs.
12 Nm
8.7 ft.lbs.

Radiator removal steps

1. Drain plug
2. Radiator cap
3. Overflow tube
4. Reserve tank
5. Reserve tank bracket
6. Clip
7. Radiator upper hose
8. Radiator lower hose
9. Transaxle fluid cooler hose and pipe assembly <Vehicles with A/T>
10. Upper insulator
11. Radiator assembly
12. Lower insulator
13. Condenser fan motor assembly <Vehicles with A/C>
14. Radiator fan motor assembly
15. Fan
16. Radiator fan motor
17. Shroud

Radiator fan motor removal steps

4. Reserve tank
9. Transaxle fluid cooler hose and pipe assembly <Vehicles with A/T>
14. Radiator fan motor assembly
15. Fan
16. Radiator fan motor
17. Shroud

MT108950011000X

Fig. 43 Cooling fan system component replacement. 1995–96 Eclipse w/2.0L turbocharged engine

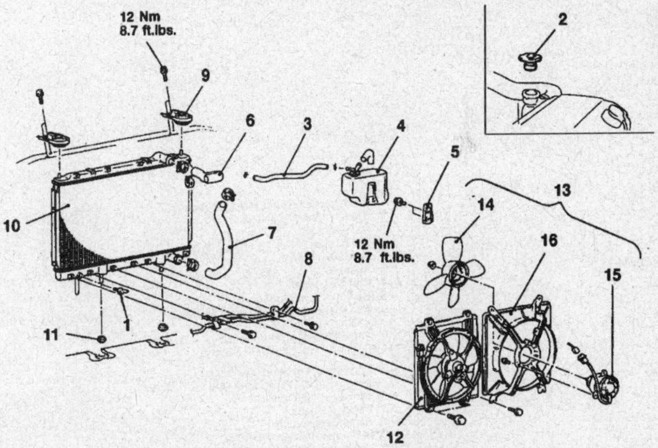
12 Nm
8.7 ft.lbs.
12 Nm
8.7 ft.lbs.

Radiator removal steps

1. Drain plug
2. Radiator cap
3. Overflow tube
4. Reserve tank
5. Reserve tank bracket
6. Radiator upper hose
7. Radiator lower hose
8. Transaxle fluid cooler hose and pipe assembly <Vehicles with A/T>
9. Upper insulator
10. Radiator assembly
11. Lower insulator
12. Condenser fan motor assembly <Vehicles with A/C>
13. Radiator fan motor assembly
14. Fan
15. Radiator fan motor
16. Shroud

Radiator fan motor removal steps

4. Reserve tank
8. Transaxle fluid cooler hose and pipe assembly <Vehicle with A/T>
13. Radiator fan motor assembly
14. Fan
15. Radiator fan motor
16. Shroud

MT1089600111000X

Fig. 44 Cooling fan system component replacement. 1996 Eclipse w/2.4L engine

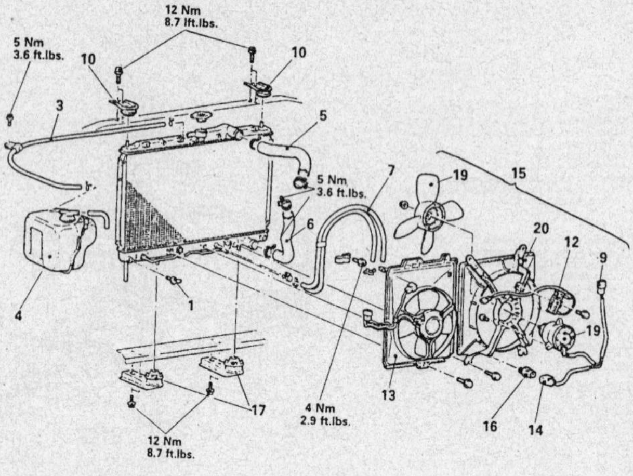
12 Nm
8.7 ft.lbs.
5 Nm
3.6 ft.lbs.
5 Nm
3.6 ft.lbs.
4 Nm
2.9 ft.lbs.
12 Nm
8.7 ft.lbs.

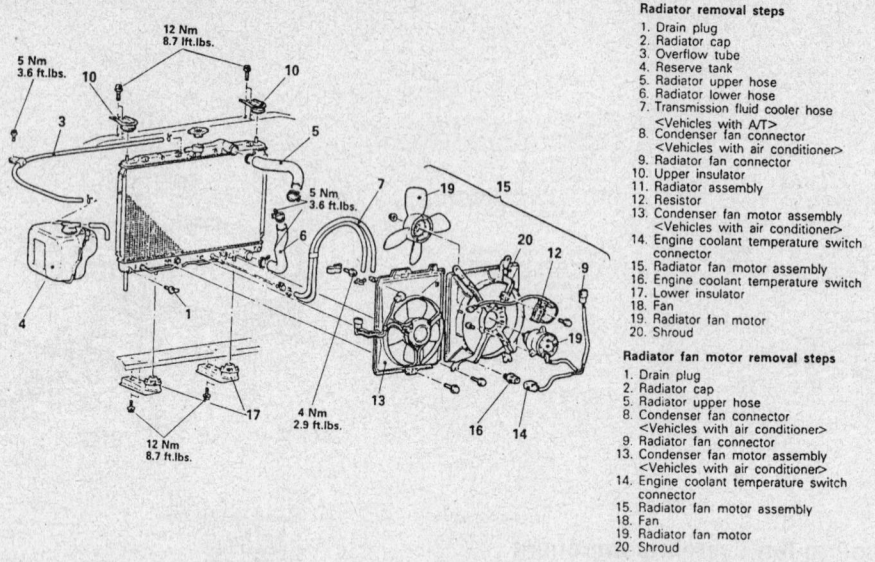

Radiator removal steps

1. Drain plug
2. Radiator cap
3. Overflow tube
4. Reserve tank
5. Radiator upper hose
6. Radiator lower hose
7. Transmission fluid cooler hose <Vehicles with A/T>
8. Condenser fan connector <Vehicles with air conditioner>
9. Radiator fan connector
10. Upper insulator
11. Radiator assembly
12. Resistor
13. Condenser fan motor assembly <Vehicles with air conditioner>
14. Engine coolant temperature switch connector
15. Radiator fan motor assembly
16. Engine coolant temperature switch
17. Lower insulator
18. Fan
19. Radiator fan motor
20. Shroud

Radiator fan motor removal steps

1. Drain plug
2. Radiator cap
5. Radiator upper hose
8. Condenser fan connector <Vehicles with air conditioner>
9. Radiator fan connector
13. Condenser fan motor assembly <Vehicles with air conditioner>
14. Engine coolant temperature switch connector
15. Radiator fan motor assembly
18. Fan
19. Radiator fan motor
20. Shroud

MT1089100071000X

Fig. 45 Cooling fan system component replacement. Expo

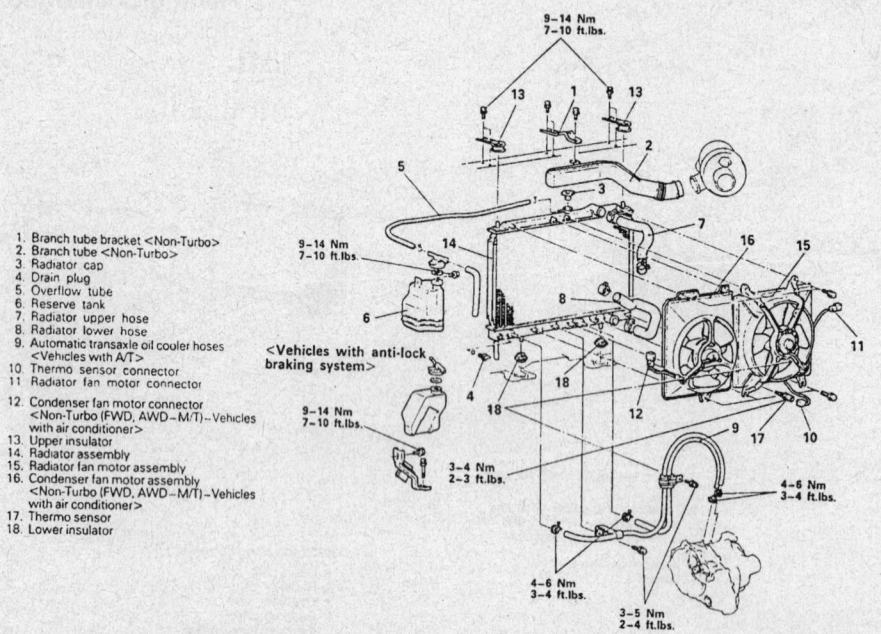

1. Branch tube bracket <Non-Turbo>
2. Branch tube <Non-Turbo>
3. Radiator cap
4. Drain plug
5. Overflow tube
6. Reserve tank
7. Radiator upper hose
8. Radiator lower hose
9. Automatic transaxle oil cooler hoses <Vehicles with A/T>
10. Thermo sensor connector
11. Radiator fan motor connector
12. Condenser fan motor connector <Non-Turbo (FWD, AWD-M/T)-Vehicles with air conditioner>
13. Upper insulator
14. Radiator assembly
15. Radiator fan motor assembly
16. Condenser fan motor assembly <Non-Turbo (FWD, AWD-M/T)-Vehicles with air conditioner>
17. Thermo sensor
18. Lower insulator

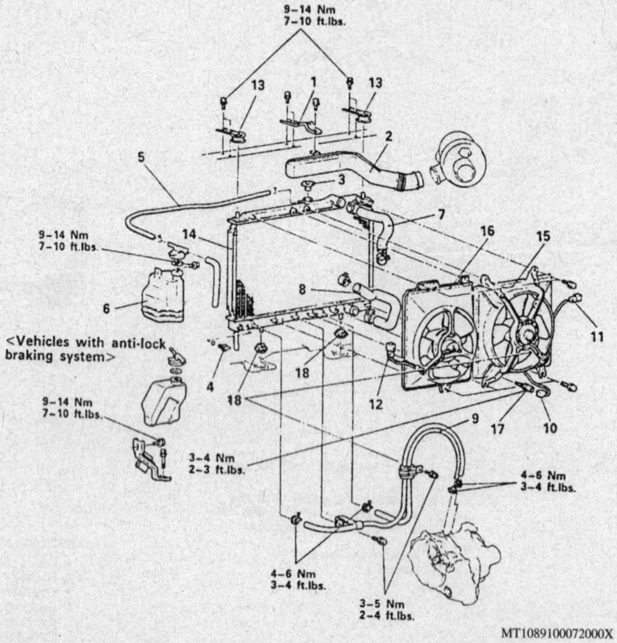
9-14 Nm
7-10 ft.lbs.
9-14 Nm
7-10 ft.lbs.
<Vehicles with anti-lock braking system>
9-14 Nm
7-10 ft.lbs.
3-4 Nm
2-3 ft.lbs.
4-6 Nm
3-4 ft.lbs.
4-6 Nm
3-4 ft.lbs.
3-5 Nm
2-4 ft.lbs.

MT1089100072000X

Fig. 46 Cooling fan system component replacement. 1993 Galant

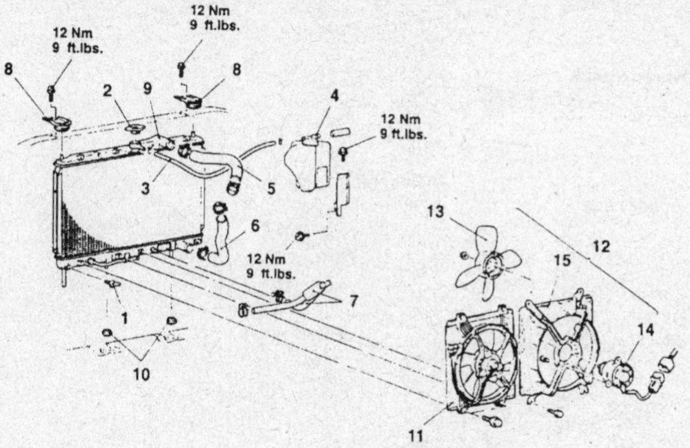
12 Nm
9 ft.lbs.
12 Nm
9 ft.lbs.
12 Nm
9 ft.lbs.
12 Nm
9 ft.lbs.

Radiator removal steps

1. Drain plug
2. Radiator cap
3. Overflow tube
4. Reserve tank
5. Radiator upper hose
6. Radiator lower hose
7. Transaxle fluid cooler hose connection <Vehicles with A/T>
8. Upper insulator
9. Radiator assembly
10. Lower insulator
11. Condenser fan motor assembly <Vehicles with A/C>
12. Radiator fan motor assembly
13. Fan
14. Radiator fan motor
15. Shroud

Radiator fan motor removal steps

1. Drain plug
2. Radiator cap
5. Radiator upper hose
11. Condenser fan motor assembly <Vehicles with A/C>
12. Radiator fan motor assembly
13. Fan
14. Radiator fan motor
15. Shroud

MT1089400073000X

Fig. 47 Cooling fan system component replacement. 1994–96 Galant

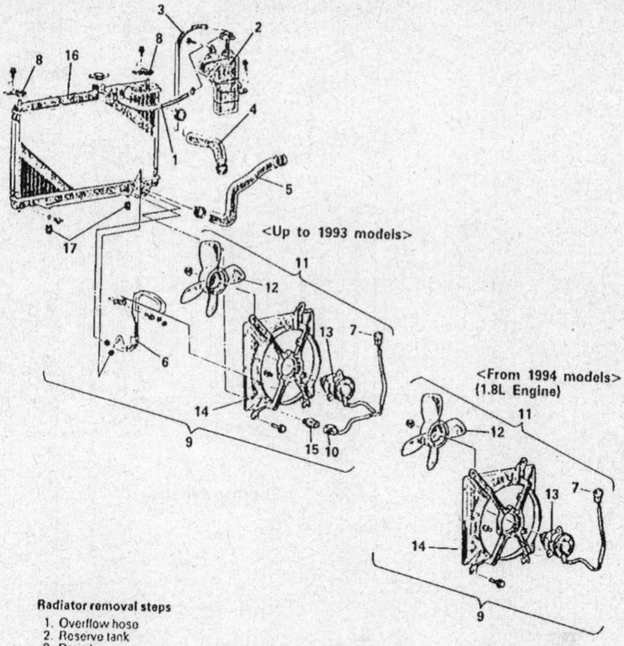
<Up to 1993 models>
<From 1994 models>
(1.8L Engine)

Radiator removal steps

1. Overflow hose
2. Reserve tank
3. Drain hose
4. Radiator upper hose
5. Radiator lower hose
6. Transmission fluid cooler hose <A/T>
7. Radiator fan motor connector
8. Upper insulator
9. Radiator and radiator fan motor assembly
10. Engine coolant temperature switch connector (Up to 1993 models)
11. Radiator fan motor assembly
15. Engine coolant temperature switch (Up to 1993 models)
16. Radiator
17. Lower insulator

Radiator fan motor removal steps

1. Overflow hose
4. Radiator upper hose
6. Transmission fluid cooler hose <A/T>
7. Radiator fan motor connector
10. Engine coolant temperature switch connector (Up to 1993 models)
11. Radiator fan motor assembly
12. Fan
13. Radiator fan motor
14. Shroud

MT1089300075000X

Fig. 48 Cooling fan system component replacement. Mirage

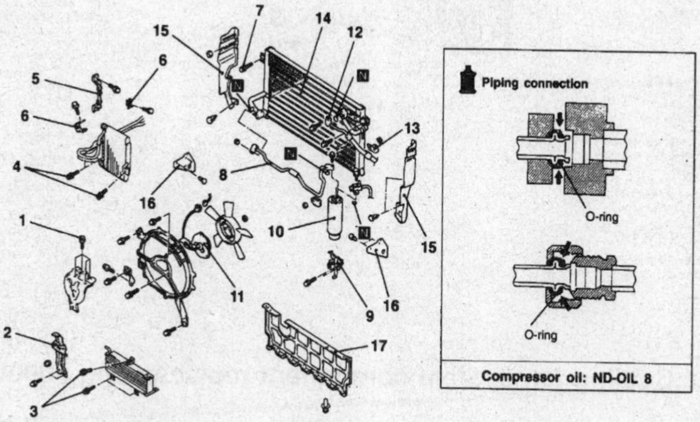
Piping connection
O-ring
O-ring
Compressor oil: ND-OIL 8

Removal steps

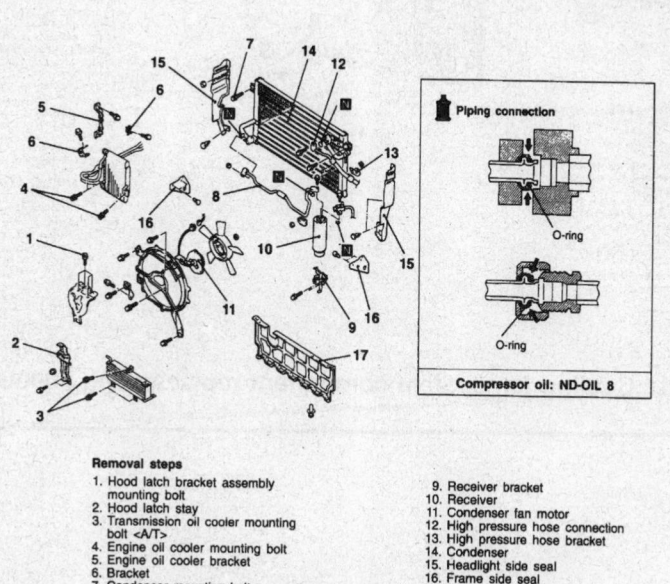

1. Hood latch bracket assembly mounting bolt
2. Hood latch stay
3. Transmission oil cooler mounting bolt <A/T>
4. Engine oil cooler mounting bolt
5. Engine oil cooler bracket
6. Bracket
7. Condenser mounting bolt
8. High pressure pipe A
9. Receiver bracket
10. Receiver
11. Condenser fan motor
12. High pressure hose connection
13. High pressure hose bracket
14. Condenser
15. Headlight side seal
16. Frame side seal
17. Under seal

MT1089300113000X

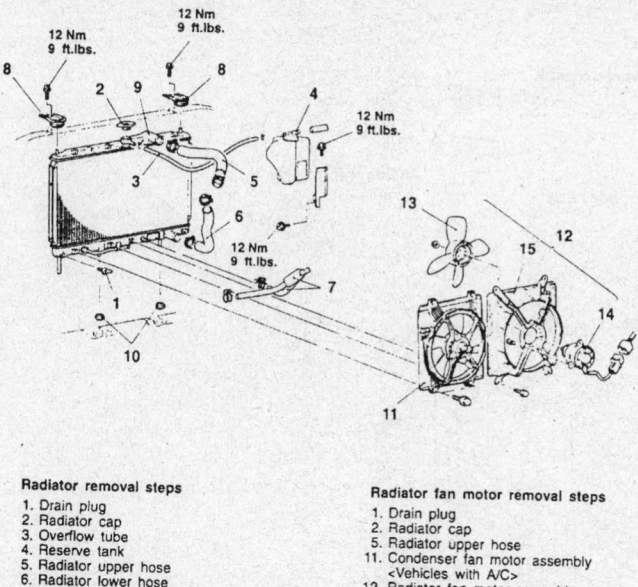

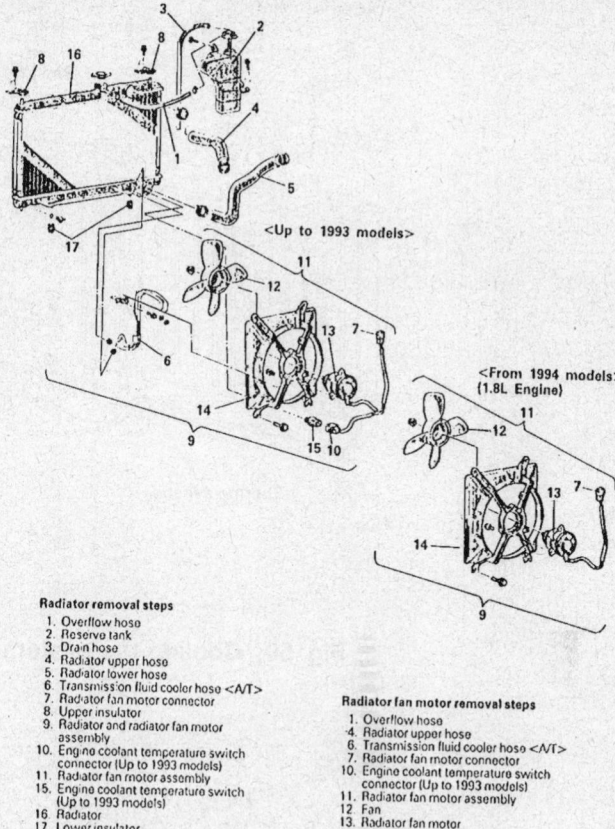

Fig. 49 Condenser & condenser fan replacement. Montero

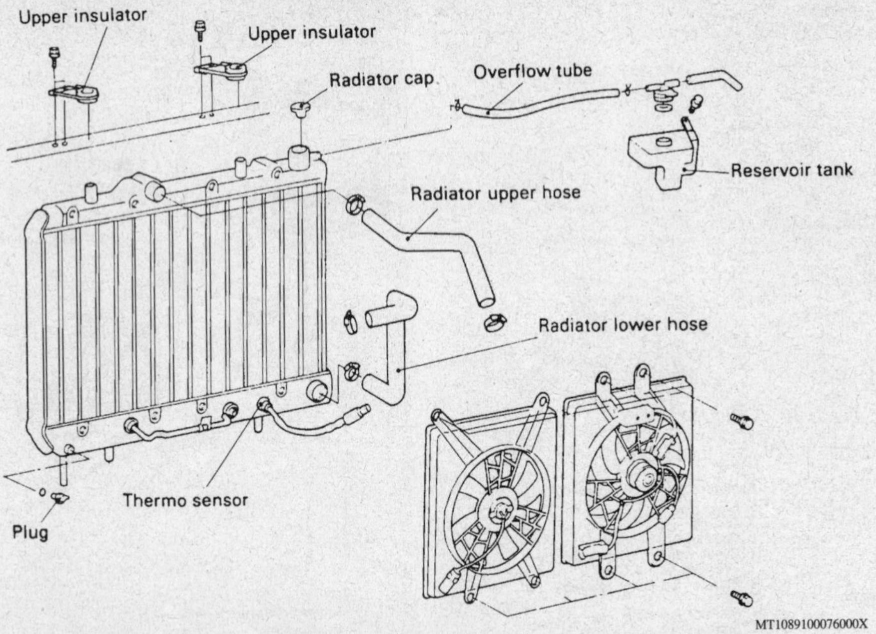
Upper insulator
Upper insulator
Radiator cap
Overflow tube
Reservoir tank
Radiator upper hose
Radiator lower hose
Thermo sensor
Plug
MT1089100076000X

Fig. 50 Cooling fan system component replacement. Precis

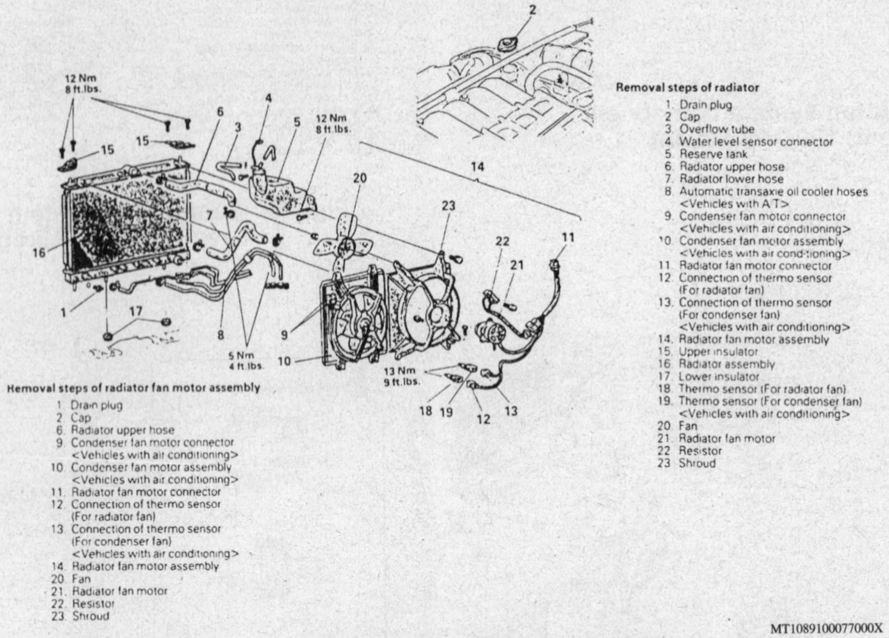
12 Nm
8 ft.lbs.
12 Nm
8 ft.lbs.
5 Nm
4 ft.lbs.
13 Nm
9 ft.lbs.
Removal steps of radiator
1. Drain plug
2. Cap
3. Overflow tube
4. Water level sensor connector
5. Reserve tank
6. Radiator upper hose
7. Radiator lower hose
8. Automatic transaxle oil cooler hoses <Vehicles with A/T>
9. Condenser fan motor connector <Vehicles with air conditioning>
10. Condenser fan motor assembly <Vehicles with air conditioning>
11. Radiator fan motor connector
12. Connection of thermo sensor (For radiator fan)
13. Connection of thermo sensor (For condenser fan) <Vehicles with air conditioning>
14. Radiator fan motor assembly
15. Upper insulator
16. Radiator assembly
17. Lower insulator
18. Thermo sensor (For radiator fan)
19. Thermo sensor (For condenser fan) <Vehicles with air conditioning>
20. Fan
21. Radiator fan motor
22. Resistor
23. Shroud
Removal steps of radiator fan motor assembly
1. Drain plug
2. Cap
6. Radiator upper hose
9. Condenser fan motor connector <Vehicles with air conditioning>
10. Condenser fan motor assembly <Vehicles with air conditioning>
11. Radiator fan motor connector
12. Connection of thermo sensor (For radiator fan)
13. Connection of thermo sensor (For condenser fan) <Vehicles with air conditioning>
14. Radiator fan motor assembly
20. Fan
21. Radiator fan motor
22. Resistor
23. Shroud
MT1089100077000X

Fig. 51 Cooling fan system component replacement. 3000GT

Viscous Clutch Cooling Fans

INDEX

	Page No.
Component Replacement........	29-19
Component Service..............	29-19
Inspection	29-19

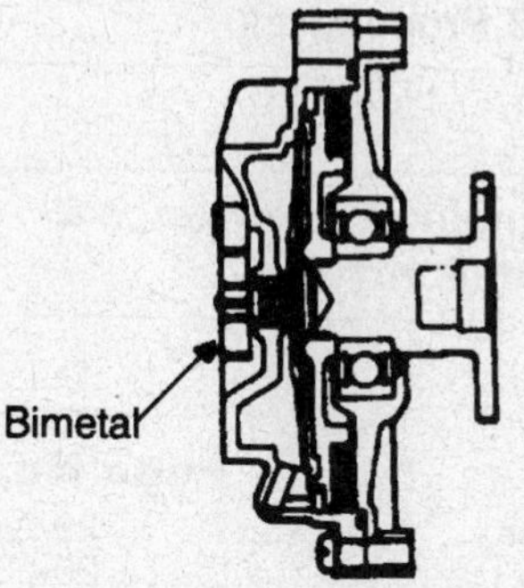
Bimetal
MT1089300114000X

Fig. 1 Fan clutch

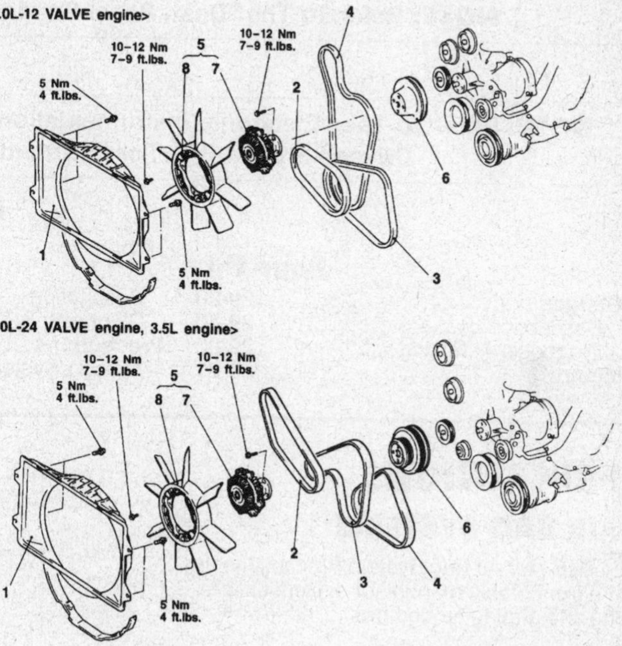
<3.0L-12 VALVE engine>
<3.0L-24 VALVE engine, 3.5L engine>

Removal steps
<3.0L-12 VALVE engine>
1. Shroud
2. Drive belt (Power steering)
3. Drive belt (Air conditioning)
4. Drive belt (Generator)
5. Cooling fan and fan clutch assembly
6. Pulley
7. Fan clutch
8. Cooling fan

Removal steps <3.0L-24 VALVE engine, 3.5L engine>
1. Shroud
2. Drive belt (Power steering)
3. Drive belt (Generator)
4. Drive belt (Air conditioning)
5. Cooling fan and fan clutch assembly
6. Pulley
7. Fan clutch
8. Cooling fan

MT1089300115000X

Fig. 2 Cooling fan component replacement. Montero

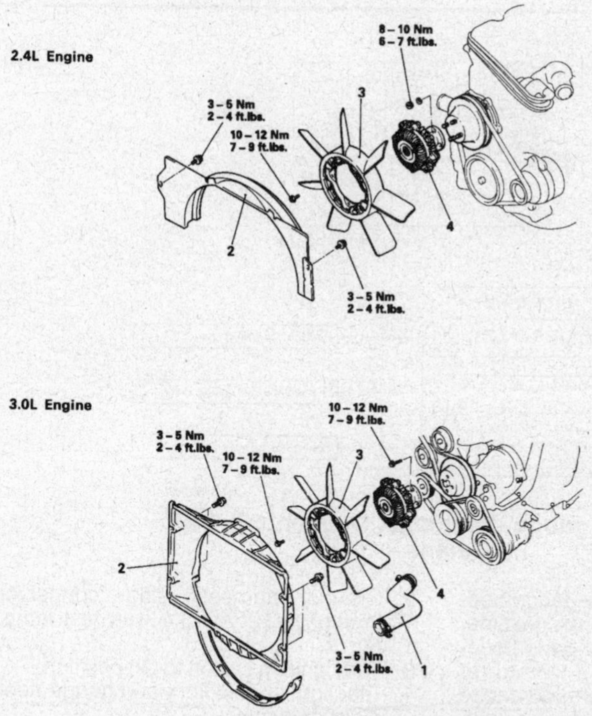
2.4L Engine
3.0L Engine

Removal steps
1. Radiator upper hose
2. Radiator upper shroud <2.4L Engine>
Radiator shroud <3.0L Engine>
3. Cooling fan
4. Fan clutch

MT1089300116000X

Fig. 3 Cooling fan component replacement. Pickup

COMPONENT SERVICE

INSPECTION

Cooling Fan

1. Inspect fan blades for cracks or other signs of damage.
2. Inspect fan hub and bolt hole areas for cracks or other signs of damage.
3. Replace cooling fan if any portion appears to be cracked or otherwise damaged.

Fan Clutch

1. Inspect fan clutch for fluid leaks at case joints and seals. **Fluid loss will result in decreased fan rotation and engine overheating.**
2. Rotate fan by hand. If moderate resistance is noted, fan clutch operation is satisfactory; if little or no resistance is felt, fan clutch should be replaced.
3. Inspect bi-metal strip, **Fig. 1,** for signs of damage.

COMPONENT REPLACEMENT

Refer to **Figs. 2 and 3** when replacing the cooling fan or any related components.

Dash Gauges

NOTE: On Air Bag Equipped Models, Refer To "Air Bag System Precautions" Located In The Front Of This Manual For System Disarming & Arming Procedures.

NOTE: Refer To The "Dash Panel Service" Section For Dash Panel Removal Procedures.

NOTE: Refer To The "Electronic Instrumentation" Section In MOTOR'S "Imported Engine Performance & Driveability Manual" For Information Related To Electronic Instrumentation.

INDEX

	Page No.		Page No.		Page No.
Gauges	29-20	Description	29-21	**Speedometer**	29-22
Description	29-20	Diagnosis & Testing	29-21	Inspection	29-22
Diagnosis & Testing	29-20	**Precautions**	29-20	**Warning Lamps**	29-21
Meters	29-21	Air Bag Systems	29-20	Description	29-21

PRECAUTIONS

AIR BAG SYSTEMS

Refer to "Air Bag System Precautions" in the front of this manual for system disarming and arming procedures.

GAUGES

DESCRIPTION

FUEL GAUGE

When the ignition key is placed in the On position, power is supplied to the fuel gauge. When the fuel tank is full, the fuel gauge unit's resistance is very low and current flow is high, causing the indicator to reside in the Full or "F" range. A low fuel level generates high resistance at the unit and reduces current flow to the gauge, causing the indicator to move toward the Empty or "E" range.

COOLANT TEMPERATURE GAUGE

When the ignition key is placed in the On position, power is supplied to the coolant temperature gauge. When the coolant temperature is high, the temperature gauge unit's resistance is very low and current flow is high, causing the indicator to reside in the Hot or "H" range. A low coolant temperature generates high resistance at the unit and reduces current flow to the gauge, causing the indicator to move toward the Cool or "C" range.

OIL PRESSURE GAUGE

When the ignition key is placed in the On position, power is supplied to the oil pressure gauge. When the oil pressure is high, the gauge's internal contacts remain closed for a longer period of time. This allows more current to flow and causes the gauge needle to swing toward the high pressure side. When the pressure is low, the gauge contacts open in a short period of time to reduce current flow in the circuit and cause the needle to swing toward the low pressure side.

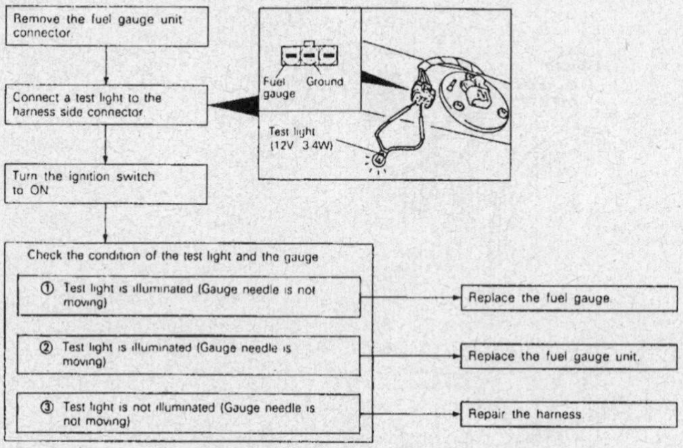

Remove the fuel gauge unit connector.
Connect a test light to the harness side connector.
Turn the ignition switch to ON
Check the condition of the test light and the gauge
① Test light is illuminated (Gauge needle is not moving)
② Test light is illuminated (Gauge needle is moving)
③ Test light is not illuminated (Gauge needle is not moving)
Replace the fuel gauge.
Replace the fuel gauge unit.
Repair the harness.
Fuel gauge
Ground
Test light (12V 3.4W)

MT9099100016000X

Fig. 1 Fuel gauge diagnosis. Diamante & 1996 Galant

DIAGNOSIS & TESTING

FUEL GAUGE

Diamante, Expo, Mirage, Montero, 3000GT, 1994-96 Galant & 1995-96 Eclipse

Refer to **Figs. 1 through 6** for fuel gauge diagnosis.

1993 Galant & 1993-94 Eclipse

1. Disconnect electrical connector from fuel gauge unit in fuel tank.
2. Ground harness side connector through a 12 volt 3.4 watt test lamp, **Fig. 7.**
3. Turn ignition switch to On position.
4. Test light should light and gauge needle should move.
5. If test light lights and needle does not move, replace fuel gauge.
6. If light does not light and needle does not move, check for a blown fuse or a broken wire.

Pickup

1. Disconnect electrical connector from fuel gauge unit in fuel tank.
2. Ground harness side connector through a 12 volt 3.4 watt test lamp.
3. Turn ignition switch to On position.
4. Test light should light and gauge needle should move.
5. If test light lights and needle does not move, replace fuel gauge.

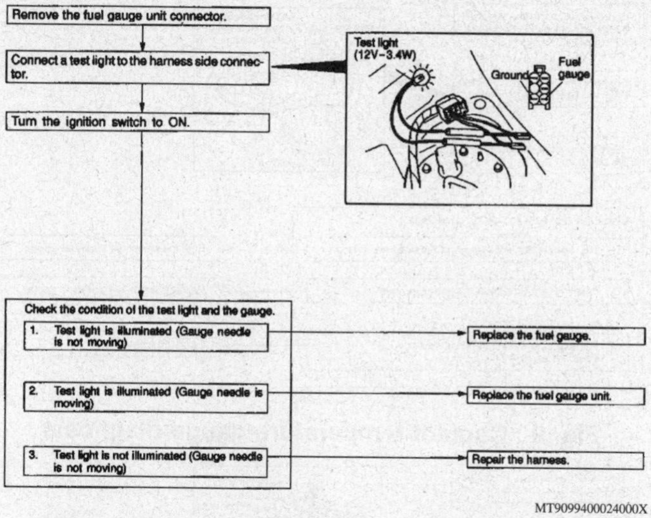
Remove the fuel gauge unit connector.
Connect a test light to the harness side connector.
Turn the ignition switch to ON.
Test light (12V–3.4W)
Ground
Fuel gauge
Check the condition of the test light and the gauge.
1. Test light is illuminated (Gauge needle is not moving)
Replace the fuel gauge.
2. Test light is illuminated (Gauge needle is moving)
Replace the fuel gauge unit.
3. Test light is not illuminated (Gauge needle is not moving)
Repair the harness.
MT9099400024000X

Fig. 2 Fuel gauge diagnosis. 1994–95 Galant

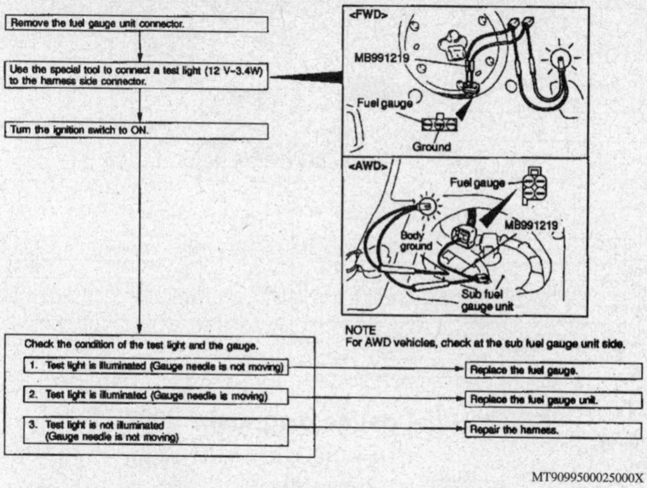
Remove the fuel gauge unit connector.
Use the special tool to connect a test light (12 V–3.4W) to the harness side connector.
Turn the ignition switch to ON.
<FWD>
MB991219
Fuel gauge
Ground
<AWD>
Fuel gauge
MB991219
Body ground
Sub fuel gauge unit
NOTE
For AWD vehicles, check at the sub fuel gauge unit side.
Check the condition of the test light and the gauge.
1. Test light is illuminated (Gauge needle is not moving)
Replace the fuel gauge.
2. Test light is illuminated (Gauge needle is moving)
Replace the fuel gauge unit.
3. Test light is not illuminated (Gauge needle is not moving)
Repair the harness.
MT9099500025000X

Fig. 3 Fuel gauge diagnosis. 1995–96 Eclipse

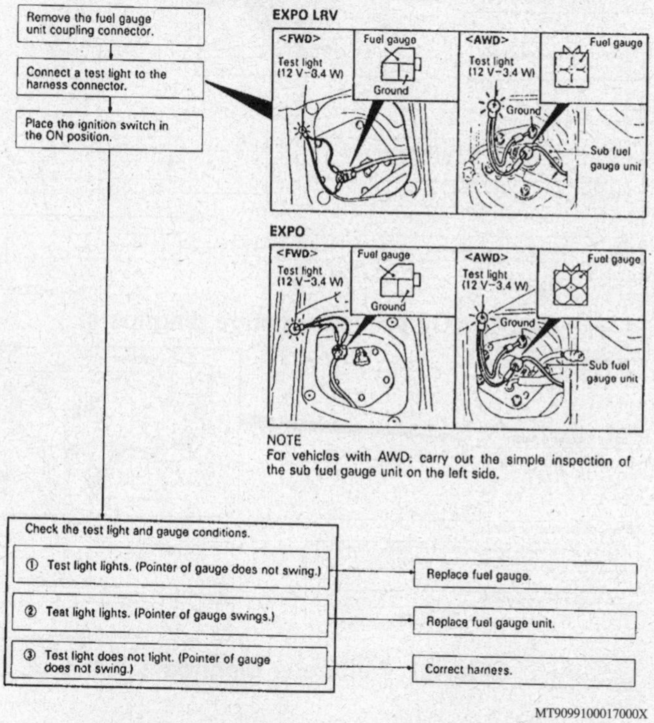
Remove the fuel gauge unit coupling connector.
Connect a test light to the harness connector.
Place the ignition switch in the ON position.
EXPO LRV
<FWD>
Fuel gauge
Test light (12 V–3.4 W)
Ground
<AWD>
Test light (12 V–3.4 W)
Fuel gauge
Ground
Sub fuel gauge unit
EXPO
<FWD>
Fuel gauge
Test light (12 V–3.4 W)
Ground
<AWD>
Test light (12 V–3.4 W)
Fuel gauge
Ground
Sub fuel gauge unit
NOTE
For vehicles with AWD, carry out the simple inspection of the sub fuel gauge unit on the left side.
Check the test light and gauge conditions.
① Test light lights. (Pointer of gauge does not swing.)
Replace fuel gauge.
② Test light lights. (Pointer of gauge swings.)
Replace fuel gauge unit.
③ Test light does not light. (Pointer of gauge does not swing.)
Correct harness.
MT9099100017000X

Fig. 4 Fuel gauge diagnosis. Expo

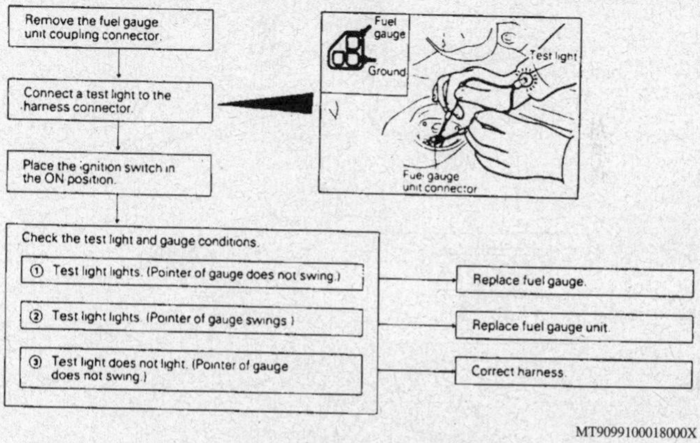
Remove the fuel gauge unit coupling connector.
Connect a test light to the harness connector.
Place the ignition switch in the ON position.
Fuel gauge
Ground
Test light
Fuel gauge unit connector
Check the test light and gauge conditions.
① Test light lights. (Pointer of gauge does not swing.)
Replace fuel gauge.
② Test light lights. (Pointer of gauge swings.)
Replace fuel gauge unit.
③ Test light does not light. (Pointer of gauge does not swing.)
Correct harness.
MT9099100018000X

Fig. 5 Fuel gauge diagnosis. Mirage & Montero

6. If light does not light and needle does not move, check for a blown fuse or a broken wire.

Precis

1. Disconnect electrical connector from fuel gauge unit in fuel tank.
2. Ground harness side connector terminal 2 through a 12 volt 3.4 watt test lamp, **Fig. 8.**
3. Turn ignition switch to On position.
4. Test light should light and gauge needle should move.
5. If test light lights and needle does not move, replace fuel gauge.
6. If light does not light and needle does not move, check for a blown fuse or a broken wire.

COOLANT TEMPERATURE GAUGE

Refer to **Fig. 9** for coolant temperature gauge diagnosis.

OIL PRESSURE GAUGE

Refer to **Fig. 10** for oil pressure gauge diagnosis.

METERS

DESCRIPTION

Voltmeter

When the ignition key is placed in the On position, power is supplied to the voltmeter. The meter should indicate approximately 12 volts until the engine is started and the charging system begins to operate. If the charging system is functioning properly, the meter should indicate 12–16 volts while the engine is running.

DIAGNOSIS & TESTING

Voltmeter

Refer to **Fig. 11** for voltmeter diagnosis and testing procedures.

WARNING LAMPS

DESCRIPTION

Oil Pressure Warning Lamp

The oil pressure warning lamp illuminates when the ignition key is placed in the On position, but will go out after the engine has started unless a problem exists in the oil circulation system. The lamp will also light during driving if oil fails to circulate properly or if pressure drops.

Brake Warning Lamp

The brake warning lamp illuminates when the ignition key is placed in the On position, but will go out after the engine has started. However, if the parking brake is applied or if the brake fluid level is low, the lamp will remain lit.

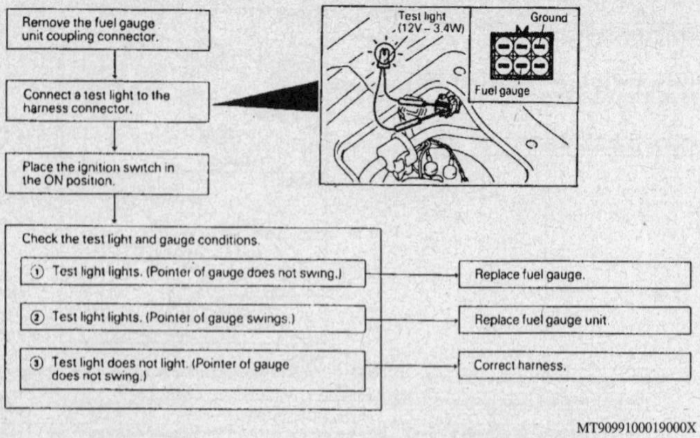
Remove the fuel gauge unit coupling connector.
Connect a test light to the harness connector.
Place the ignition switch in the ON position.
Check the test light and gauge conditions.
① Test light lights. (Pointer of gauge does not swing.)
② Test light lights. (Pointer of gauge swings.)
③ Test light does not light. (Pointer of gauge does not swing.)
Replace fuel gauge.
Replace fuel gauge unit.
Correct harness.
Test light (12V – 3.4W)
Ground
Fuel gauge

MT9099100019000X

Fig. 6 Fuel gauge diagnosis. 3000GT

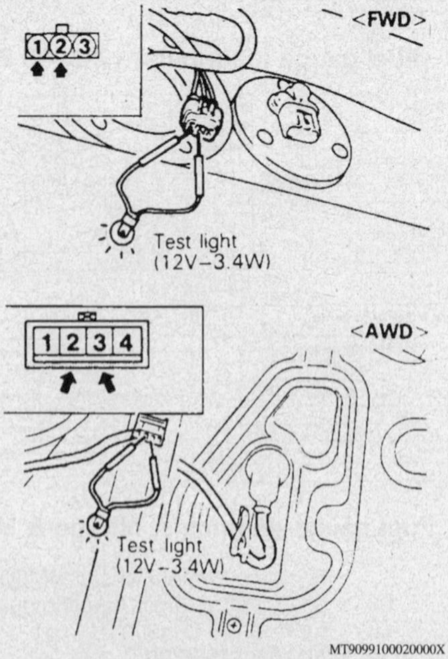
<FWD>
1 2 3
Test light (12V–3.4W)
<AWD>
1 2 3 4
Test light (12V–3.4W)

MT9099100020000X

Fig. 7 Fuel gauge harness terminal identification. 1993 Galant & 1993–94 Eclipse

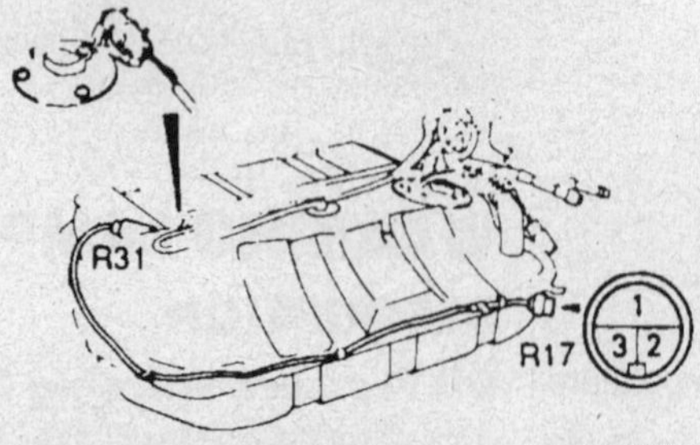
R31
R17
1
3 2

MT9099100021000X

Fig. 8 Fuel gauge harness terminal identification. Precis

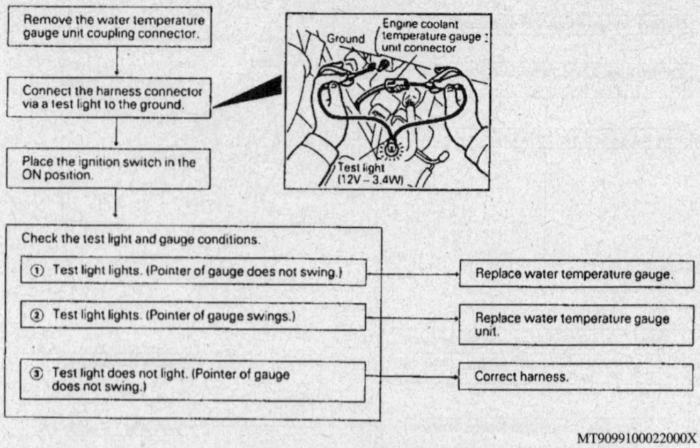
Remove the water temperature gauge unit coupling connector.
Connect the harness connector via a test light to the ground.
Place the ignition switch in the ON position.
Check the test light and gauge conditions.
① Test light lights. (Pointer of gauge does not swing.)
② Test light lights. (Pointer of gauge swings.)
③ Test light does not light. (Pointer of gauge does not swing.)
Replace water temperature gauge.
Replace water temperature gauge unit.
Correct harness.
Ground
Engine coolant temperature gauge unit connector
Test light (12V – 3.4W)

MT9099100022000X

Fig. 9 Coolant temperature gauge diagnosis

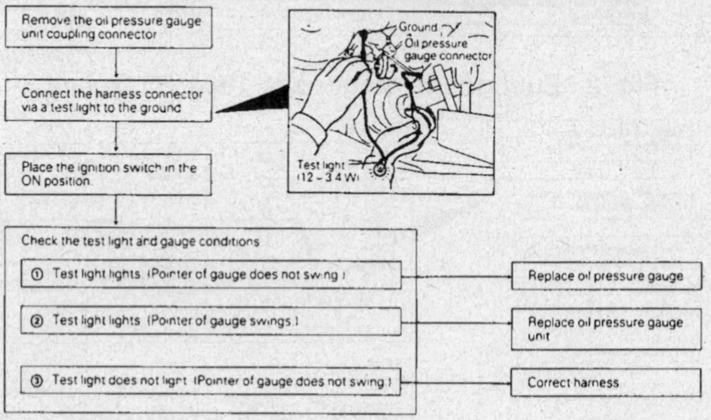
Remove the oil pressure gauge unit coupling connector
Connect the harness connector via a test light to the ground
Place the ignition switch in the ON position.
Check the test light and gauge conditions
① Test light lights (Pointer of gauge does not swing.)
② Test light lights (Pointer of gauge swings.)
③ Test light does not light (Pointer of gauge does not swing.)
Replace oil pressure gauge
Replace oil pressure gauge unit
Correct harness
Ground
Oil pressure gauge connector
Test light (12 – 3.4 W)

MT9099100023000X

Fig. 10 Oil pressure gauge diagnosis

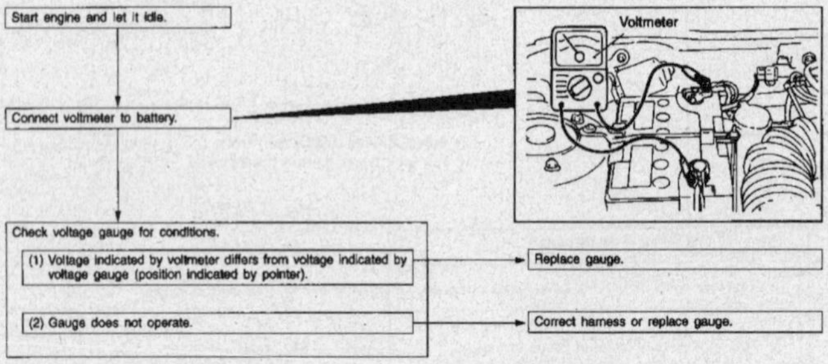
Start engine and let it idle.
Connect voltmeter to battery.
Check voltage gauge for conditions.
(1) Voltage indicated by voltmeter differs from voltage indicated by voltage gauge (position indicated by pointer).
(2) Gauge does not operate.
Replace gauge.
Correct harness or replace gauge.
Voltmeter

MT9099300026000X

Fig. 11 Voltmeter diagnosis

Low Fuel Warning Lamp

The low fuel lamp illuminates when the fuel level in the tank falls below a specific level.

Seat Belt Warning Lamp

The seat belt warning lamp illuminates for six seconds after the ignition key has been placed in the On position, regardless of whether the drivers seat belt has been fastened.

Four Wheel Steering Oil Level Warning Lamp

The four wheel steering oil level warning lamp illuminates when the power steering oil level in the reservoir tank is low.

SPEEDOMETER

INSPECTION

A speedometer test drum and related equipment are required for completion of the following procedure.

1. Ensure tire pressures are correct, then position vehicle on speedometer test drum.
2. **On models equipped with Traction Control (TCL),** place TCL switch in Off position.
3. **On all models,** set parking brake, then secure vehicle as required by speedometer test equipment. **Failure to do so may allow vehicle to move unexpectedly during testing.**
4. Simulate a range of vehicle speeds,

noting the following:

a. **Do not operate clutch suddenly or change indicated speed rapidly during testing.**

b. When standard indication reaches 20 mph, allowable indication range is 19–22 mph; at 40 mph, allowable range is 38–44 mph; at 60 mph, allowable range is 57–66 mph; at 80 mph, allowable range is 76–88 mph; at 100 mph, allowable range is 94–110 mph.

Starter Motors

INDEX

	Page No.
Description	29-23
Automatic Transmission/Transaxle	29-23
Manual Transmission/Transaxle	29-23
Diagnosis & Testing	29-23
Free Running Test	29-24
Magnetic Switch Hold-In Test	29-24
Magnetic Switch Pull-In Test	29-24
Magnetic Switch Return Test	29-25
Pinion Gap Inspection	29-23
Starter & Theft Alarm Starter Relay Tests	29-25
General Information	29-23
Starter Specifications	29-27
Troubleshooting	29-23

GENERAL INFORMATION

The starting system includes the battery, starter motor, magnet switch, ignition switch, Park/Neutral Position (PNP) switch (on models equipped with an automatic transmission), starter or PNP switch relays, connecting wires and battery cables.

When the ignition switch is turned to the Start position, current flows to energize the solenoid windings of the starter motor. As a result, the solenoid plunger and clutch shift lever (on reduction drive units) operate to cause the clutch pinion to engage with the flywheel ring gear, **Figs. 1 through 3.** At the same time, the magnet switch contacts close to energize the starter motor windings.

The overrunning running clutch pinion gear prevents damage that could be caused by overrunning the starter armature when the engine is started. When the engine is started, the ignition switch must be turned back to the On position to prevent damage to the starter motor or ring gear.

DESCRIPTION

MANUAL TRANSMISSION/ TRANSAXLE

The interlock or clutch switch contact is switched Off when the clutch pedal is depressed, when the ignition switch is turned to the Start position, electricity flows to the starter or inhibitor relay and the starter motor. The contact of the starter is switched On and the starter motor is activated.

If the ignition switch is turned to the Start position without depressing the clutch pedal, electricity flows to the starter or inhibitor relay (coil), the interlock switch (contacts) and to ground. This results in that the contacts of the starter relay are switched Off and the power to the starter motor is interrupted.

AUTOMATIC TRANSMISSION/ TRANSAXLE

when the ignition switch is turned to the Start position while the gear selector is in "P" or "N" position, the contact (magnetic switch) of the starter is switched On and the starter motor is activated.

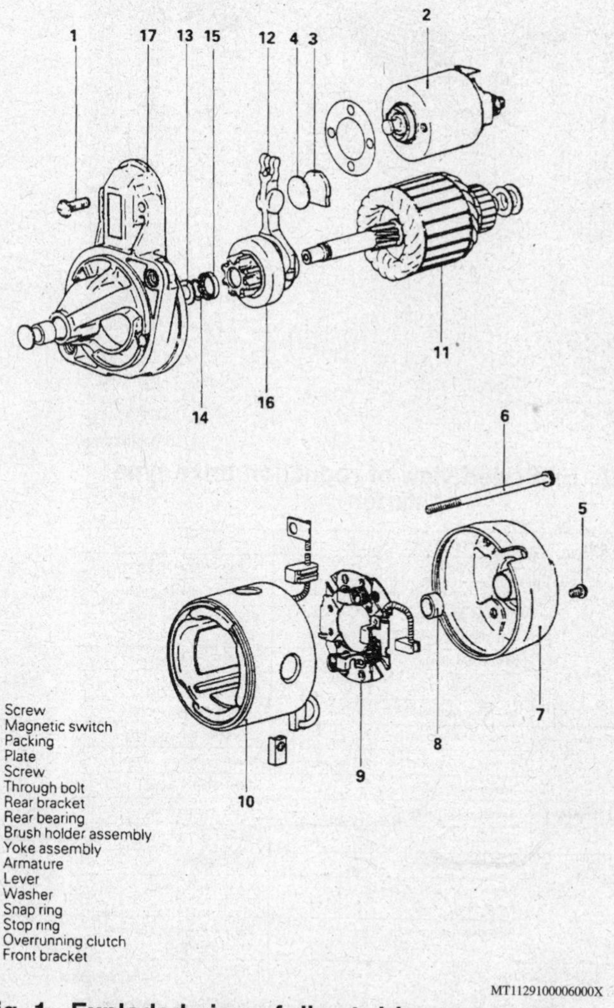

1
17
13
15
12
4
3
2
11
14
16
6
5
7
8
9
10
1. Screw
2. Magnetic switch
3. Packing
4. Plate
5. Screw
6. Through bolt
7. Rear bracket
8. Rear bearing
9. Brush holder assembly
10. Yoke assembly
11. Armature
12. Lever
13. Washer
14. Snap ring
15. Stop ring
16. Overrunning clutch
17. Front bracket
MT1129100006000X

Fig. 1 Exploded view of direct drive type starter. Except Precis

TROUBLESHOOTING

Refer to **Fig. 4** when troubleshooting the starting system.

DIAGNOSIS & TESTING

PINION GAP INSPECTION

1. Disconnect field coil wire from "M" terminal of magnetic switch, **Fig. 5.**
2. Connect a 12 volt battery between "S" and "M" terminals. **This test must be**

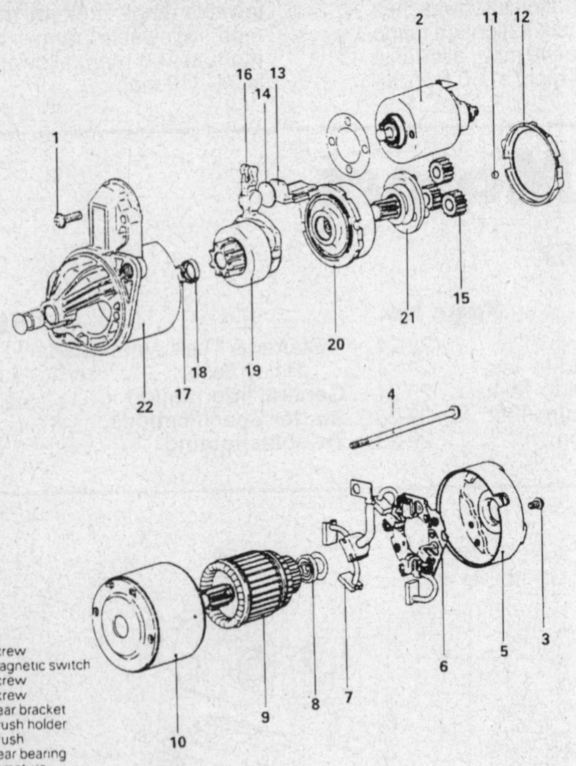

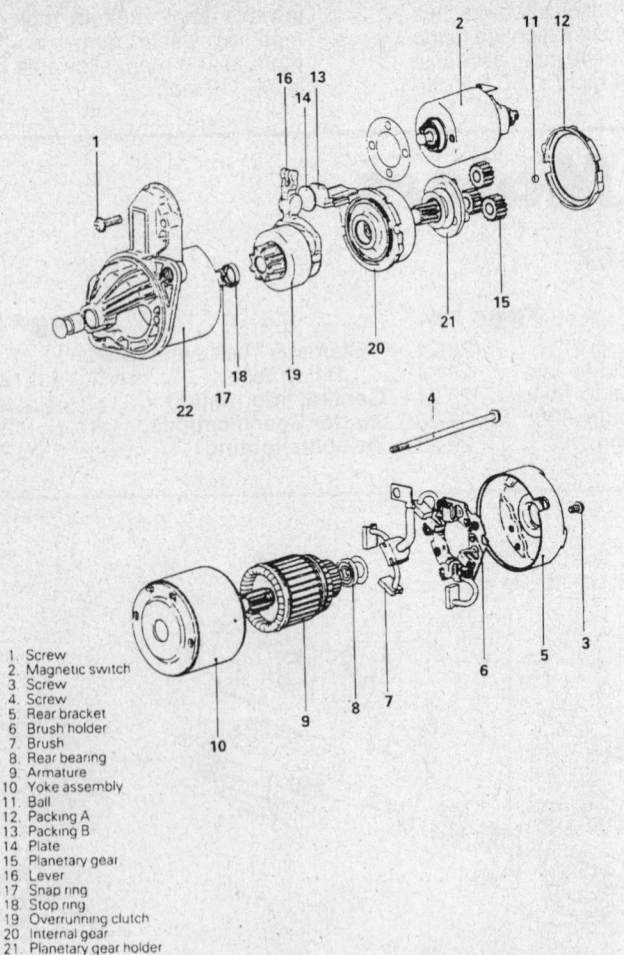

1. Screw
2. Magnetic switch
3. Screw
4. Screw
5. Rear bracket
6. Brush holder
7. Brush
8. Rear bearing
9. Armature
10. Yoke assembly
11. Ball
12. Packing A
13. Packing B
14. Plate
15. Planetary gear
16. Lever
17. Snap ring
18. Stop ring
19. Overrunning clutch
20. Internal gear
21. Planetary gear holder
22. Front bracket

MT1129100007000X

Fig. 2 Exploded view of reduction drive type starter

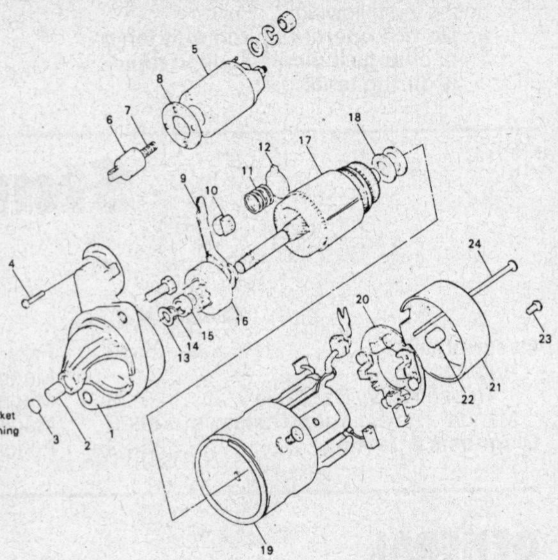

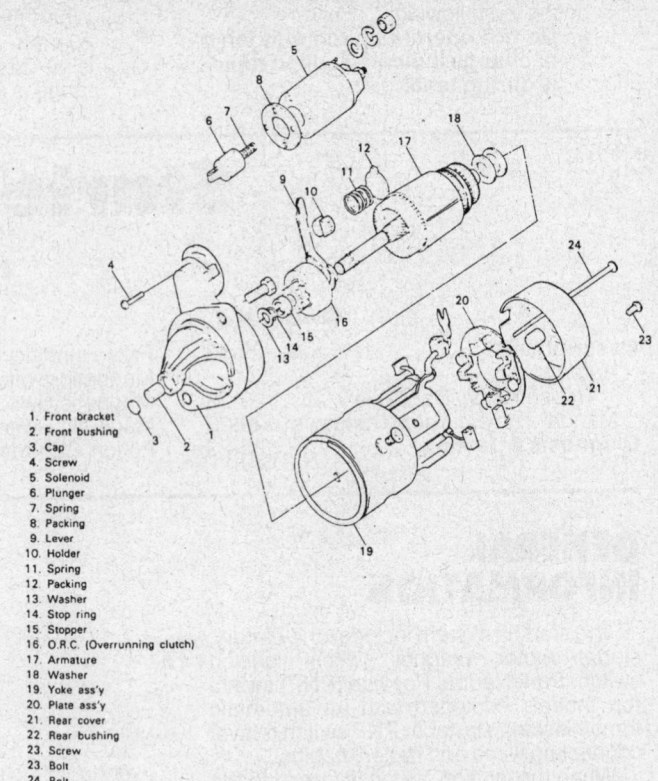

1. Front bracket
2. Front bushing
3. Cap
4. Screw
5. Solenoid
6. Plunger
7. Spring
8. Packing
9. Lever
10. Holder
11. Spring
12. Packing
13. Washer
14. Stop ring
15. Stopper
16. O.R.C. (Overrunning clutch)
17. Armature
18. Washer
19. Yoke ass'y
20. Plate ass'y
21. Rear cover
22. Rear bushing
23. Screw
23. Bolt
24. Bolt

MT1129100008000X

Fig. 3 Exploded view of direct drive type starter. Precis

Probable condition	Probable cause	Remedy
Engine will not crank.	Battery charge low	Charge or replace battery.
	Battery cables loose, corroded or worn	Repair or replace cables.
	Inhibitor switch faulty (Vehicle with automatic transaxle only)	Adjust or replace switch.
	Fusible link blown	Replace fusible link.
	Starter motor faulty	Repair starter motor.
	Ignition switch faulty	Replace ignition switch.
Engine cranks slowly	Battery charge low	Charge or replace battery.
	Battery cables loose, corroded or worn	Repair or replace cables.
	Starter motor faulty	Repair starter motor.
Starter keeps running.	Starter motor faulty	Repair starter motor.
	Ignition switch faulty	Replace ignition switch.
Starter spins but engine will not crank.	Short in wiring	Repair wiring.
	Pinion gear teeth broken or starter motor faulty	Repair starter motor.
	Ring gear teeth broken	Replace flywheel ring gear or torque converter.

MT1129100009000X

Fig. 4 Starting system troubleshooting chart

performed in less than 10 seconds to prevent coil from burning out.

3. Measure pinion gap with a suitable feeler gauge, **Fig. 6.**
4. If pinion gap is not as specified under "Starter Specifications," adjust by adding or removing gaskets between magnetic switch and front bracket.

MAGNETIC SWITCH PULL-IN TEST

1. Disconnect field coil wire from "M" terminal of magnetic switch, **Fig. 5.**
2. Connect a 12 volt battery between "S" and "M" terminals. **This test must be performed in less than 10 seconds to prevent coil from burning out.**
3. If pinion moves out, then pull-in coil is operating correctly. If pinion does not move out, replace magnetic switch.

MAGNETIC SWITCH HOLD-IN TEST

1. Disconnect field coil wire from "M" terminal of magnetic switch, **Fig. 5.**
2. Connect a 12 volt battery between "S" terminal and body ground, **Fig. 7. This test must be performed in less than ten seconds to prevent coil from burning out.**
3. If pinion remains out, magnetic switch is operating correctly. If pinion moves in, hold-in circuit is open and the magnetic switch must be replaced.

FREE RUNNING TEST

1. Place starter in a suitable soft jawed vise.
2. Connect a fully charged 12 volt battery, ammeter and voltmeter to starter motor as shown in **Fig. 8** using a suitable 0–100 amperage ammeter, voltmeter and carbon pile rheostat.
3. Rotate carbon pile rheostat to full resistance position.
4. Adjust rheostat until battery voltage shown on the voltmeter matches free running test voltage listed under "Starter Specifications."
5. Confirm that the maximum amperage is as indicated under "Starter Specifications" chart in this section, ensuring

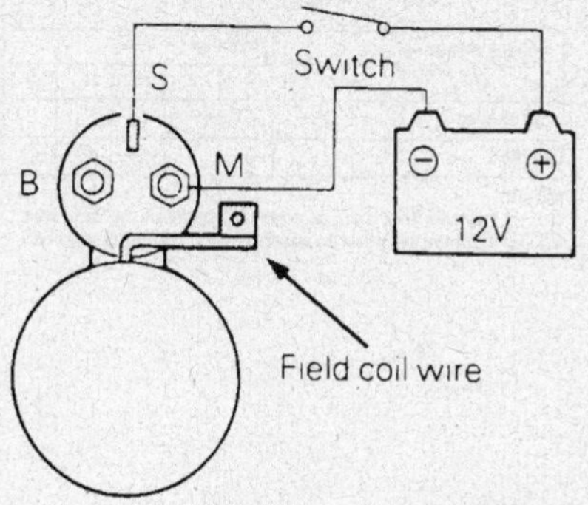
Switch
S
B
M
12V
Field coil wire
MT1129100010000X

Fig. 5 Magnetic switch inspection

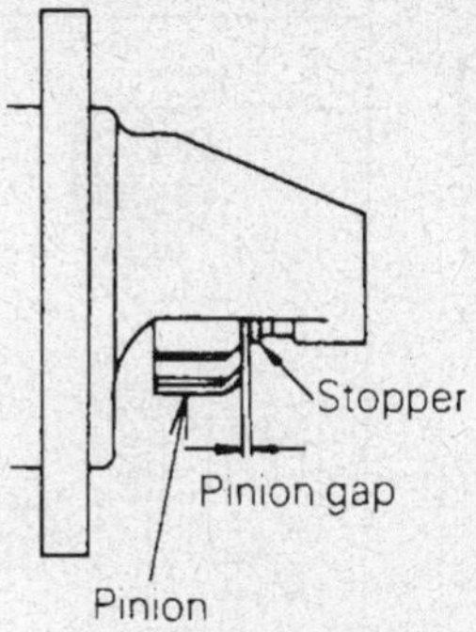
Stopper
Pinion gap
Pinion
MT1129100011000X

Fig. 6 Pinion gap inspection

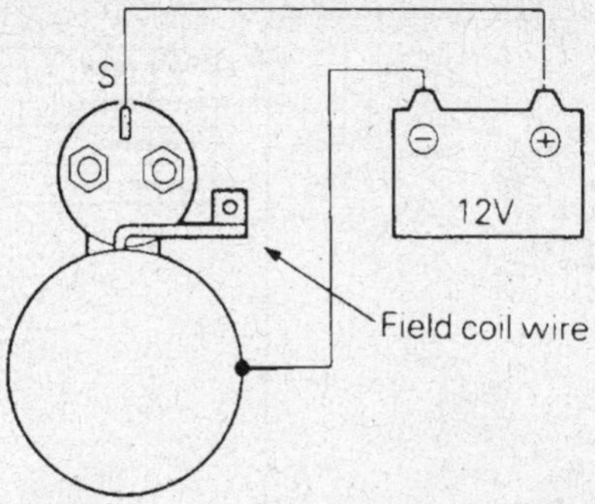
S
12V
Field coil wire
MT1129100012000X

Fig. 7 Magnetic switch hold-in function inspection

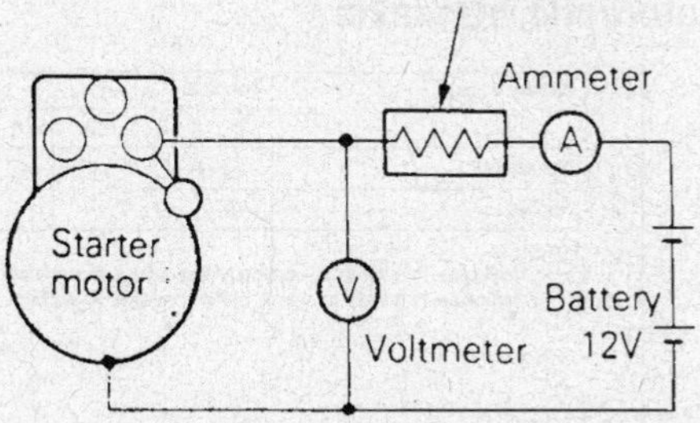
Carbon-pile rheostat
Ammeter
Starter motor
Battery 12V
Voltmeter
MT1129100013000X

Fig. 8 Free running test connections

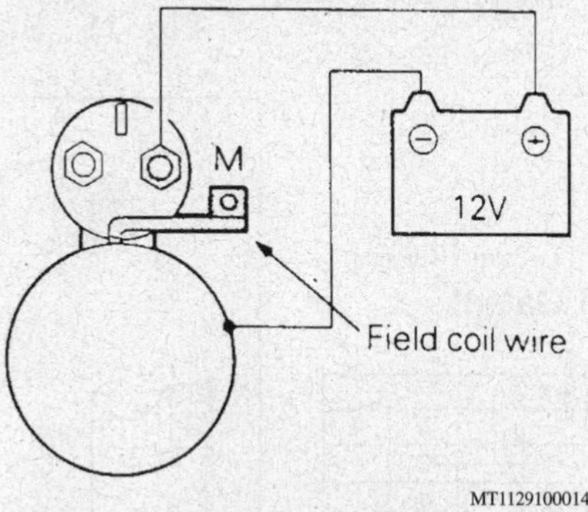
M
12V
Field coil wire
MT1129100014000X

Fig. 9 Magnetic switch return function inspection

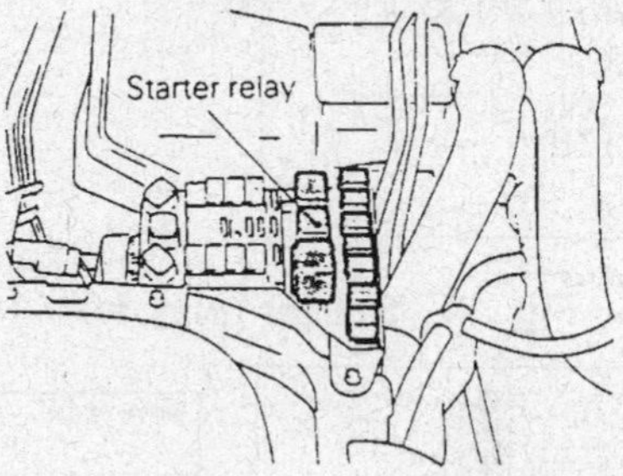
Starter relay

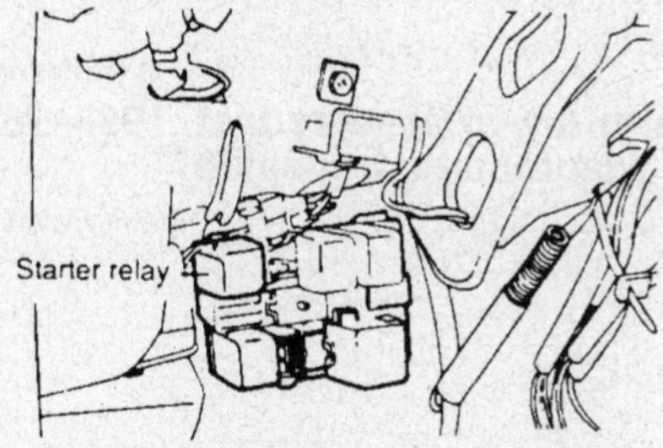

Condition \ Terminal	S_1 [1]	S_2 [3]	L [2]	B [4]
When de-energized	O———	———O		
When energized	O———	———O	O———	———O

MT1129100016000X

Fig. 11 Starter relay test. Precis

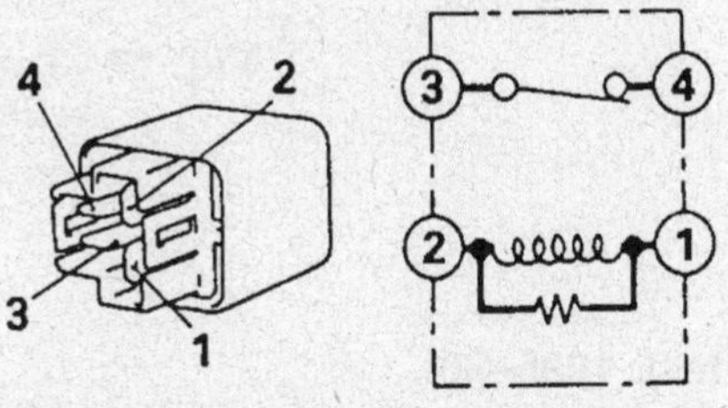

Power is supplied	3–4 terminals	No continuity
Power is not supplied	3–4 terminals	Continuity
	1–2 terminals	Continuity

MT1129200017000X

Fig. 12 Starter relay test. Diamante, Montero, Pickup, 1995–96 Eclipse w/manual transaxle & 1993–94 Eclipse

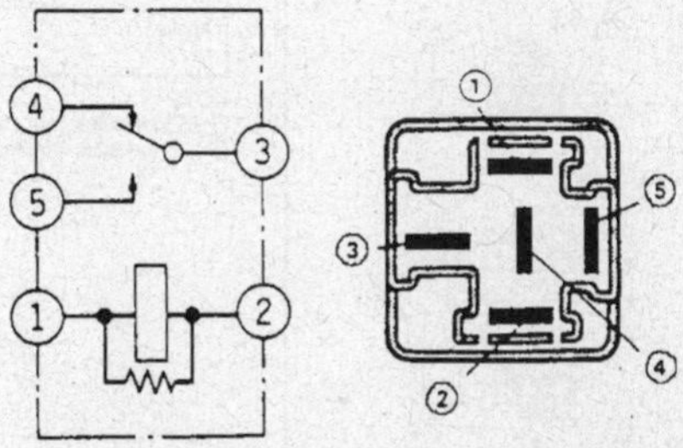

Power is supplied	3-4 terminals	No continuity
	3-5 terminals	Continuity
Power is not supplied	3-4 terminals	Continuity
	3-5 terminals	No continuity
	1-2 terminals	Continuity

MT1129100015000X

Fig. 10 Starter relay test. Expo, Mirage & 3000GT

starter motor turns smoothly and freely.

MAGNETIC SWITCH RETURN TEST

1. Disconnect field coil wire from "M" terminal of magnetic switch, **Fig. 9.**
2. Connect a 12 volt battery between "M" terminal and body ground. **This test must be performed in less than ten seconds to prevent coil from burning out.**
3. Pull pinion out and release. If pinion quickly returns to its original position, magnetic switch is operating correctly. If pinion does not return, replace magnetic switch.

STARTER & THEFT ALARM STARTER RELAY TESTS

For relay testing, refer to **Figs. 10 through 18.**

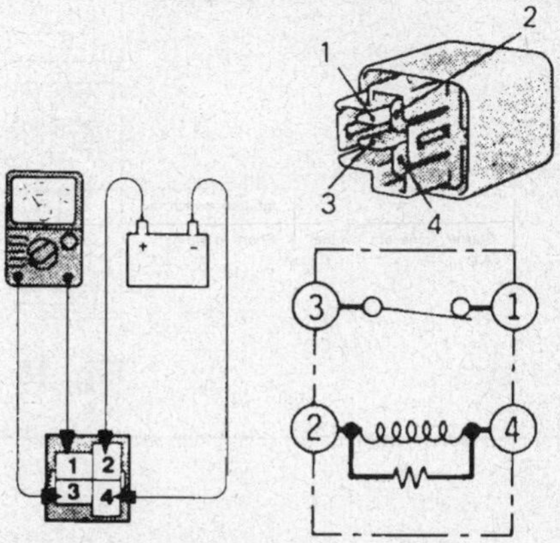

Power is supplied	1–3 terminals	No continuity
Power is not supplied	1–3 terminals	Continuity
	2–4 terminals	Continuity

MT1129200018000X

Fig. 13 Starter relay test. 1993 Galant

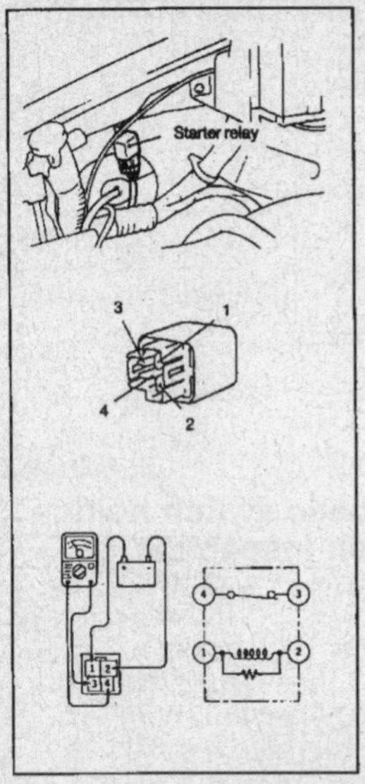
Starter relay

Battery voltage	Terminal No.			
Battery voltage	1	2	3	4
Not supplied	○—	—○		
Supplied	⊕- - -	- - -⊖	○—	—○

MT1129400039000X

Fig. 14 Starter relay test. 1994–96 Galant

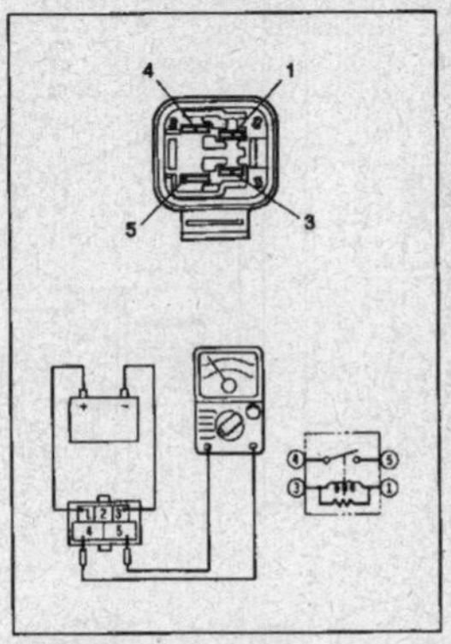

Battery voltage	Terminal				
	1	2	3	4	5
Not applied	○—	—	—○		
Applied	⊕- - -	- - -	- - -⊖	○—	—○

NOTE
○—○ indicates that there is continuity between the terminals.
⊕- -⊖ indicates terminals to which battery voltage is applied.

MT1129500035000X

Fig. 15 Starter relay test. 1995–96 Eclipse w/ automatic transaxle

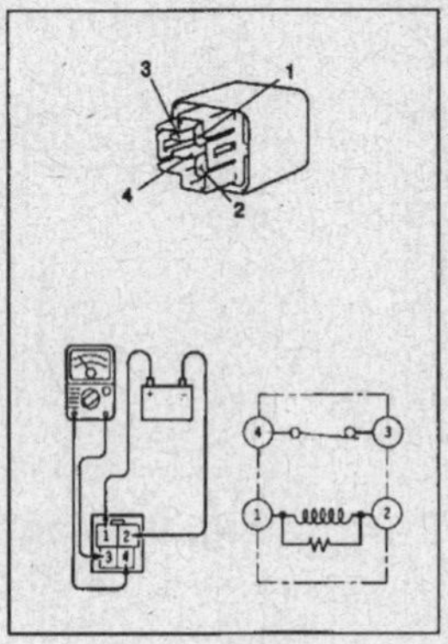

Battery voltage	Terminal			
	1	2	3	4
Not applied	○—	—○	○—	—○
Applied	⊕- - -	- - -⊖		

NOTE
○—○ indicates that there is continuity between the terminals.
⊕- -⊖ indicates terminals to which battery voltage is applied.

MT1129500037000X

Fig. 17 Theft alarm & starter relay test. 1995–96 Eclipse w/automatic transaxle

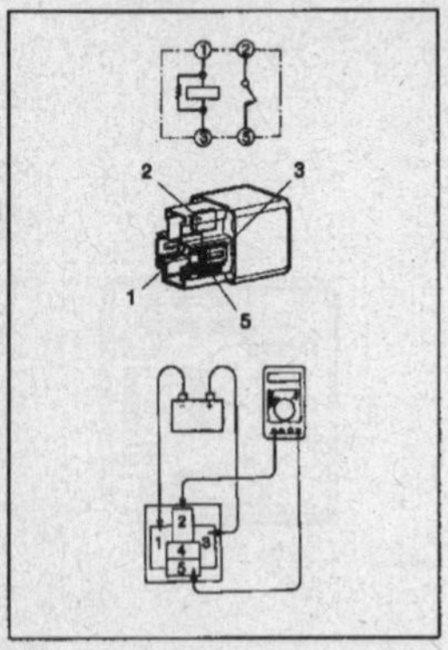

Battery voltage	Terminal			
	1	2	3	5
Not applied	○—	—	—○	
Applied	⊖- - -	- - - / ○—	- - -⊕ / —	—○

NOTE
○—○ indicates that there is continuity between the terminals.
⊕- -⊖ indicates terminals to which battery voltage is applied.

MT1129500036000X

Fig. 16 Theft alarm & starter relay test. 1995–96 Eclipse w/manual transaxle

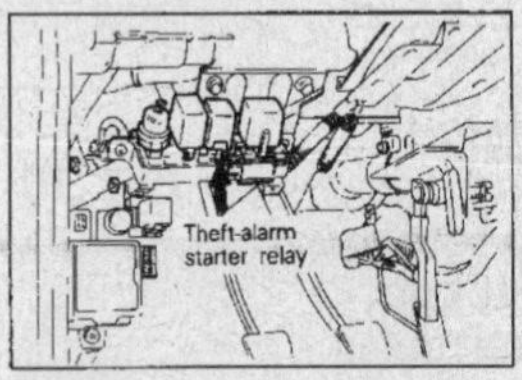
Theft-alarm
starter relay

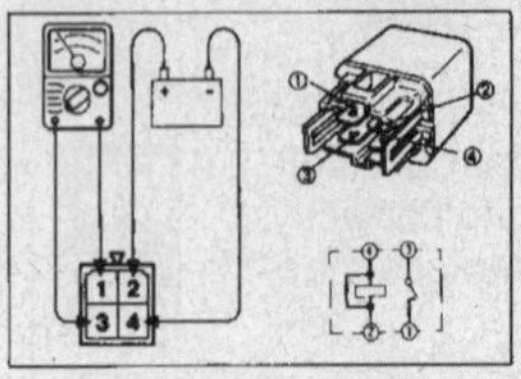

(1) Remove the theft-alarm starter relay from the indoor relay box.
(2) Connect battery to terminal 2 and check continuity between terminals with terminal 4 grounded.

Power is supplied	1–3 terminals	Continuity
Power is not supplied	1–3 terminals	No continuity
	2–4 terminals	Continuity

MT1129300038000X

Fig. 18 Theft alarm & starter relay test. 1993 Galant

STARTER SPECIFICATIONS

Model	Year	Drive Type	Output, kW	Pinion Gap, Inch	Commutator		Free Speed Test		
					Runout, Inch	Diameter, Inch	Terminal Voltage	Max. Current, Amps	Min. RPM
Diamante	1993–96	Reduction	1.20	.020–.079	.0020	1.158	11.0	90	3000
Eclipse	1993–94	Direct③	.90	.020–.079	.0020	1.260	11.5	60	6600
		Reduction④	1.20	.020–.079	.0020	1.158	11.0	90	3000
	1995–96	Direct⑤	.95	—	—	—	—	—	—
		Reduction⑥	1.20	.020–.079	.0020	1.158	11.0	90	3000
Expo	1993–95	Reduction①③	1.00	.020–.079	.0020	1.158	11.0	90	3000
		Reduction⑦	1.20	.020–.079	.0020	1.158	11.0	90	3000
		Direct⑧	.90	.020–.079	.0020	1.260	11.5	60	6600
Galant	1993–96	Reduction	1.20	.020–.079	.0020	1.158	11.0	90	3000
Mirage	1993–96	Direct⑪	.70	.020–.079	.0020	1.260	11.5	60	6600
		Direct⑫	.90	.020–.079	.0020	1.260	11.5	60	6600
		Reduction⑬	1.00	.020–.079	.0020	1.158	11.0	90	3000
Montero	1993–96	Reduction	1.20	.020–.079	.0020	1.157	11.0	90	3000
Pickup	1993–96	Direct⑨	.90	.020–.079	.0020	1.260	11.5	60	6600
		Reduction⑩	1.20	.020–.079	.0020	1.157	11.0	90	3000
Precis	1993	Direct①	.90	.020–.079	—	—	11.5	60	6600
		Direct②	.70	.020–.079	—	—	11.5	60	6500
3000GT	1993–96	Reduction	1.20	.020–.079	.0020	1.158	11.0	90	3000

① — Automatic transaxle.
② — Manual transaxle.
③ — 1.8L engine.
④ — 2.0L engine.
⑤ — 2.0L non-turbocharged engine.
⑥ — 2.0L turbocharged engine & 2.4L engine.
⑦ — 2.4L 8 valve engine w/automatic transaxle & 2.4L 16 valve engine.
⑧ — 1.8L & 2.4L 8 valve engines w/manual transaxle.
⑨ — 2.4L engine w/manual transmission.
⑩ — 2.4L engine w/automatic transmission & 3.0L engine.
⑪ — 1.5L engine w/manual transaxle.
⑫ — 1.5L engine w/automatic transaxle & 1.8L engine w/manual transaxle.
⑬ — 1.8L engine w/automatic transaxle.

Alternators

INDEX

Page No.

Application Chart 29-27
Mitsubishi Alternators 29-28
Melco & Mando Alternators 29-31

Application Chart

Model	Alternator
Except Precis	Mitsubishi
Precis	Melco
	Mando

Mitsubishi Alternators

INDEX

	Page No.		Page No.		Page No.
Alternator Specifications	29-29	Bench Tests	29-29	**General Information**	29-28
Diagnosis & Testing	29-28	In-Vehicle Tests	29-28	**Troubleshooting**	29-28

GENERAL INFORMATION

When the ignition switch is turned to the On position and before the engine starts, current flows through the charging indicator light then to the alternator and ground, causing the charging light to illuminate.

Once the engine starts, battery voltage is applied to the alternator "S" or "R" terminal. The battery voltage imposed on this terminal is monitored by the IC voltage regulator, and according to the voltage detected the IC voltage regulator regulates the alternator field coil current, thus controlling the alternator current.

Once the alternator starts alternator starts generating current, a slightly higher voltage than battery voltage is applied to terminal "L." This prevents current from flowing to the charging indicator light and the light goes off.

At alternator terminal "B," a load current proportional to the battery voltage is produced and is sent to any load. The alternator relay provides charge to the battery even when the charging indicator light bulb is burnt out.

TROUBLESHOOTING

1. If charging indicator light does not illuminate when Ignition switch is turned to On position (before engine starts), check charge indicator lamp bulb.
2. If charging indicator light fails to go off once engine starts, check drive belt tension and IC voltage regulator.
3. If battery is discharged or overcharged, check IC voltage regulator.
4. If charging warning light illuminates dimly, check diode inside combination meter for a short.

DIAGNOSIS & TESTING

IN-VEHICLE TESTS

ALTERNATOR OUTPUT WIRE VOLTAGE DROP TEST

This test judges whether or not the wiring between alternator "B" terminal and battery positive terminal is sound by voltage drop method.

1. Refer to **Fig. 1** when preparing the charging system as follows:
   a. Turn ignition switch to Off position.
   b. disconnect battery ground cable.
   c. Disconnect alternator output lead from alternator terminal "B."
   d. Connect a 0–100 DC ammeter in series to terminal "B" and the disconnected output lead. Connect positive lead of meter to terminal "B" and negative lead to disconnected output wire.
   e. Connect positive lead of a digital voltmeter to alternator terminal "B" and negative lead to battery positive terminal.
   f. Connect battery ground cable.
2. Start engine.
3. Turn headlights and small lights On or Off and adjust engine speed so that ammeter reads 20 amps and read value on voltmeter under this condition.
4. If voltmeter indicates maximum value of .2 volts, system is operating correctly.
5. If voltmeter indicates a value that is larger than the standard value, poor wiring is suspected between terminal "B" and battery positive terminal.
6. After completion of test, set engine speed at idle, turn Off lights and ignition switch.
7. Disconnect battery ground.
8. Disconnect ammeter and voltmeter then reconnect alternator output wire and connect battery ground cable.

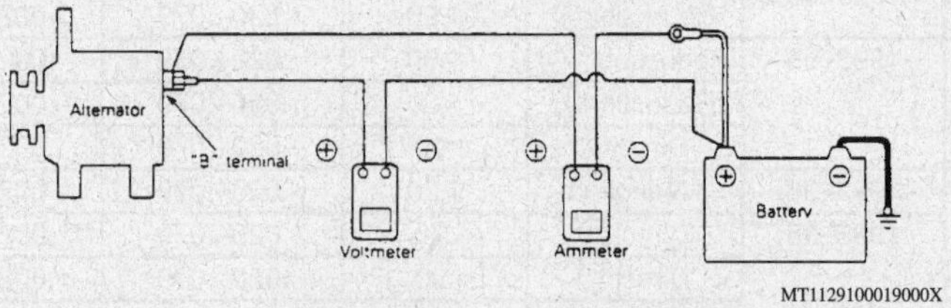

Alternator
"B" terminal
Voltmeter
Ammeter
Battery
MT1129100019000X

Fig. 1 Voltage drop test

OUTPUT CURRENT TEST

This test judges whether or not the alternator gives an output current that is equivalent to the normal output.

1. Ensure battery condition is in sound state and that the tension of the alternator drive belt is correct as outlined under "Drive Belt Tension" in the appropriate engine section.
2. Refer to **Fig. 2** when preparing the charging system as follows:
   a. Turn ignition switch to Off position.
   b. Disconnect battery ground cable.
   c. Disconnect alternator output wire from terminal "B."
   d. Connect a 0–100 DC ammeter positive lead to terminal "B" and the negative lead to the disconnected output wire. **Tighten all connections using suitable bolt and nut as a heavy current will flow. Do not relay on clips.**
   e. Connect a 0–20 voltmeter positive lead to alternator terminal "B" and negative lead to a sound ground.
   f. Connect an engine tachometer then the battery ground cable.
3. Ensure voltmeter reads same voltage as battery.
4. Turn headlights On and start engine.
5. Set headlight on high beam and heater blower switch on high, quickly increase engine speed to 2500 RPM and read maximum output current indicated on ammeter.
6. Calculate output limit value. Limit value is equal to 70% of output rating listed under "Alternator Specifications" in this section.
7. Ammeter reading must be higher than limit value. If reading is lower and output wire is satisfactory, replace alternator.
8. Normal output current value is shown in nameplate attached to alternator. The output current value changed with electrical load and temperature. therefore the normal output current may not be obtained if the vehicle electrical load, at time of test, is small. In such a case, discharge battery by leaving headlights on or by using another vehicle's lights to increase load.
9. After completion of test, set engine speed at idle and turn off lights and ignition switch.
10. Disconnect battery ground cable.
11. Disconnect ammeter and voltmeter then reconnect alternator output wire and connect battery ground cable.

REGULATED VOLTAGE TEST

The purpose of this test is to check that the electronic voltage regulator controls the voltage correctly.

1. Prepare charging system, **Fig. 3,** as follows:
   a. Ensure battery condition is good and alternator drive belt tension is correct. Refer to "Belt Tension Data" in appropriate engine section.
   b. Turn ignition switch to Off position.
   c. Disconnect battery ground cable.

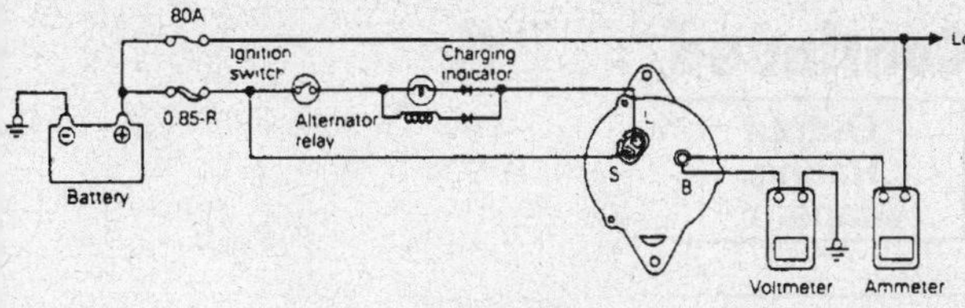
80A
Ignition switch
Charging indicator
Load
0.85-R
Alternator relay
Battery
L
S
B
Voltmeter
Ammeter
MT1129100020000X

Fig. 2 Output current test

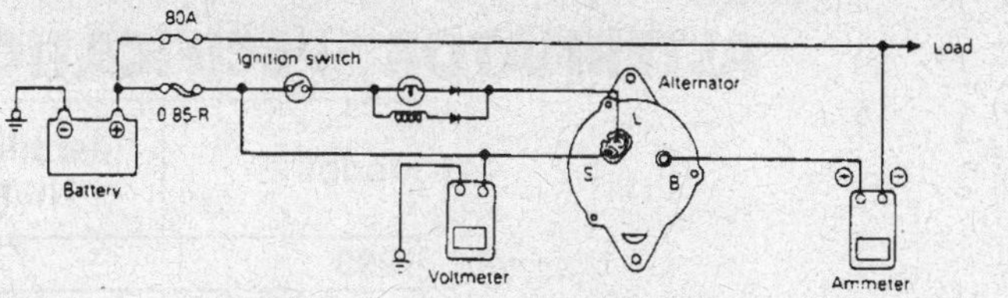
80A
Ignition switch
Load
Alternator
0.85-R
Battery
L
S
B
Voltmeter
Ammeter
MT1129100021000X

Fig. 3 Regulated voltage test

Voltage regulator ambient temperature °C (°F)	Regulating voltage V
−20 (−4)	14.2−15.4
20 (68)	13.9−14.9
60 (140)	13.4−14.6
80 (176)	13.1−14.5

MT1129100022000X

Fig. 4 Regulated voltage table

d. Connect the positive lead of a digital voltmeter to terminal "S" of the alternator and the negative lead to a sound ground or battery ground terminal.
e. Disconnect alternator output wire from terminal "B."
f. Connect the positive lead of a 0–100 ammeter to terminal "B" and the negative lead to the disconnected output wire.
g. Connect an engine tachometer and then the battery ground cable.

2. Turn ignition switch to On position. If voltmeter reads zero volts, there is a open circuit in wire between alternator terminal "S" and battery positive terminal.
3. Start engine. Keep all electrical components Off.
4. run engine at 2500 RPM and read voltmeter when output current drops to 10 amps or less.
5. If voltmeter reading agrees with the value shown in **Fig. 4,** the voltage regulator is functioning correctly. If reading is other than standard value, replace the voltage regulator.
6. After completion of test, set engine speed at idle, turn Off ignition switch.
7. Disconnect battery ground.
8. Disconnect ammeter and voltmeter then reconnect alternator output wire and connect battery ground cable.

BENCH TESTS

ROTOR

1. Check rotor for continuity. Ensure there is continuity between slip rings.
2. If resistance is not 3–5 ohms, a short exists in rotor. If no continuity exists or if there is a short, replace rotor assembly.
3. Ensure there is no continuity between slip ring and core. If continuity exists, replace rotor assembly.

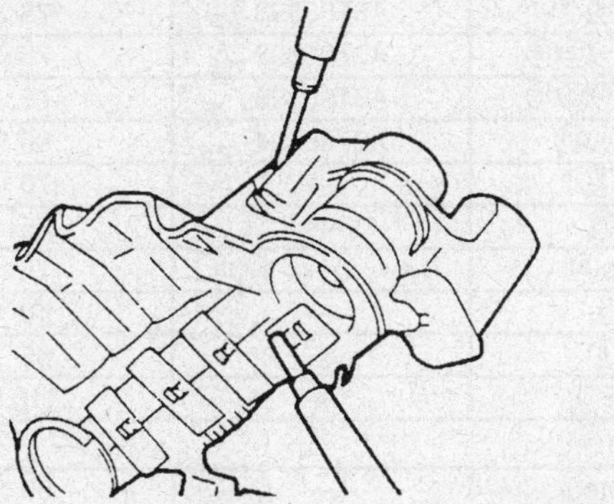
MT1129100023000X

Fig. 5 Positive rectifier test

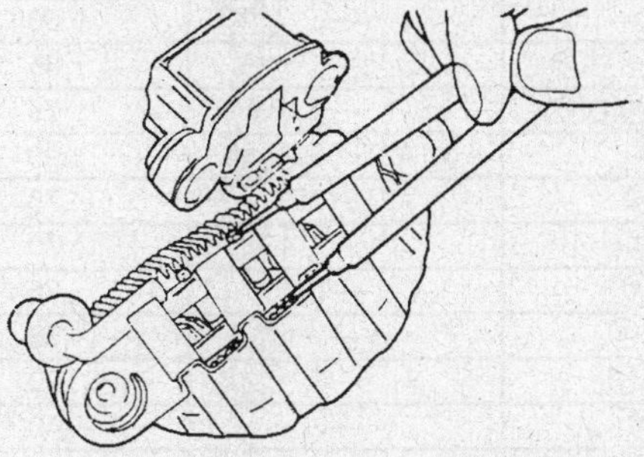
MT1129100025000X

Fig. 7 Diode trio test

STATOR

1. Ensure continuity exists between coil leads. Replace stator if no continuity exists.
2. Ensure there is no continuity between coil and core. Replace stator is continuity exists.

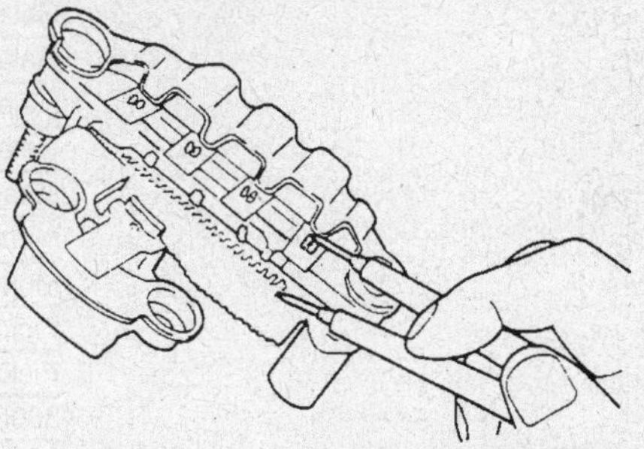
MT1129100024000X

Fig. 6 Negative rectifier test

RECTIFIERS

Positive Rectifier Test

Ensure continuity exists in only one direction between positive rectifier and stator coil lead, **Fig. 5.** If continuity exists in both directions, diode is shorted and rectifier must be replaced.

Negative Rectifier Test

Ensure continuity exists in only one direction between negative rectifier and stator coil lead, **Fig. 6.** If continuity exists in both directions, diode is shorted and rectifier must be replaced.

Diode Trio Test

Ensure continuity exists in only one direction between both ends of each diode, **Fig. 7.** If continuity exists in both directions, diode is faulty and heat sink assembly must be replaced.

ALTERNATOR SPECIFICATIONS

Model	Identification Number	Output Rating, Amps①⑪
1993		
Diamante	—	90
Eclipse⑨⑰	—	65
Eclipse⑩⑱	—	75
Expo⑲	—	60

Continued

ALTERNATOR SPECIFICATIONS—Continued

Model	Identification Number	Output Rating, Amps①⑪
1993		
Expo⑥⑨⑭③	—	65
Expo⑤⑥⑦⑩	—	75
Galant⑮	A3T03393	75
Galant⑨⑫⑯	A3T03392	75
Galant⑨⑬⑯	A3T03393	75
Galant⑯⑩	A3T45694	90
Mirage②	—	70
Mirage⑲	—	75
Montero⑧	—	75
Pickup⑥	—	40
Pickup⑧	—	65
3000GT	—	110
1994		
Diamante	—	90
Eclipse⑰⑨	—	65
Eclipse⑩⑱	—	75
Expo⑲	—	60
Expo⑥⑨⑭③	—	65
Expo⑤⑥⑦⑩	—	75
Galant⑮	A2T80591	90
Galant⑯	A2T61791	75
Mirage②	—	70
Mirage⑲	—	75
Montero⑧	—	75
Montero④	—	90
Pickup⑥	—	40
Pickup⑧	—	65
3000GT	—	110
1995		
Diamante	—	90
Eclipse	—	90
Expo⑲	—	60
Expo⑥⑨⑭③	—	65
Expo⑤⑥⑦⑩	—	75
Galant⑮	A2T80591	90
Galant⑯	A2T61791	75
Mirage②	—	70
Mirage⑲	—	75
Montero⑧	—	75
Montero④	—	90
Pickup⑥	—	40
Pickup⑧	—	65
3000GT	—	110
1996		
Diamante	—	90
Eclipse	A002T81292	90
Galant	A2TA0891	90
Mirage②	—	70
Mirage⑲	—	75
Montero⑧⑳	—	75
Montero⑧㉑	—	90
Montero④	—	90
Pickup⑥	—	40
Pickup⑧	—	65

Continued

ALTERNATOR SPECIFICATIONS—Continued

Model	Identification Number	Output Rating, Amps①⑪
1996		
3000GT	—	95

① — At 12 volts.
② — 1.5L engine.
③ — 8 valve engine.
④ — 3.5L engine.
⑤ — Includes California models w/manual transaxle.
⑥ — 2.4L engine.
⑦ — 16 valve engine.
⑧ — 3.0L engine.
⑨ — Manual transaxle.
⑩ — Automatic transaxle.
⑪ — Internal voltage regulator.
⑫ — FWD models.
⑬ — AWD models.
⑭ — Except California models.
⑮ — SOHC engine.
⑯ — DOHC engine.
⑰ — Non-turbocharged engine.
⑱ — Turbocharged engine.
⑲ — 1.8L engine.
⑳ — 12 valve engine.
㉑ — 24 valve engine.

Melco & Mando Alternators

INDEX

	Page No.
Alternator Specifications	29-33
Application Chart	29-31
Diagnosis & Testing	29-31
Bench Tests	29-32
In-Vehicle Tests	29-31
General Information	29-31
Troubleshooting	29-31

APPLICATION CHART

Model	Identification Number	Type
Precis	A2T09493	Melco
	AB175015	Mando

GENERAL INFORMATION

The Melco and Mando alternators have six built-in diodes, three positive and three negative. Each rectifies AC current to DC Current, and DC current is supplied from the alternator "B" terminal. The charging voltage is regulated by a built-in electronic voltage regulator.

TROUBLESHOOTING

When troubleshooting Melco and Mando alternators, refer to **Fig. 1.**

DIAGNOSIS & TESTING

IN-VEHICLE TESTS

Alternator Output Wire Voltage Drop Test

This test checks whether or not the wiring between the alternator "B" terminal and the battery (+) terminal is sound by the voltage drop method.

1. Turn ignition switch to off, then disconnect battery ground cable.
2. Disconnect output lead from alternator "B" terminal.
3. Connect voltmeter and ammeter as follows:
   a. Connect a DC ammeter in series to the "B" terminal and disconnected output lead, then connect the positive lead of the ammeter to the "B" terminal and the negative lead to the disconnected output wire as shown is **Fig. 2.**
   b. Connect a digital voltmeter between alternator "B" terminal and the battery positive terminal. Connect the positive lead wire of the voltmeter to "B" terminal and the negative lead wire to the battery positive terminal as shown in **Fig. 2.**
4. Start engine, turn on headlamps and adjust engine speed so that the ammeter reads 20 amps.
5. Read voltmeter. Standard value is 0.2 volts maximum. If reading is higher than 0.2 volts, check the following:
   a. Check wiring from alternator "B" terminal to battery positive terminal fusible link.
   b. Check for loose connections.
   c. Check color change of wire caused by overheated wiring harness.
6. Correct problem, then test system again.

Output Current Test

1. Before performing the output current test check and repair if necessary the following:
   a. Check to make sure battery is in good condition. The battery should be partially discharged, with a fully charged battery the test will not conducted properly due to an insufficient load.
   b. Check condition and tension of the alternator belt.

Symptom	Probable cause	Remedy
Charging warning indicator does not light with ignition switch "ON" and engine off.	Fuse blown.	Check fuses.
	Light burned out.	Replace light.
	Wiring connection loose.	Tighten loose connections.
	Electronic voltage regulator faulty.	Replace voltage regulator.
Charging warning indicator does not go out with engine running. (Battery requires frequent recharging).	Drive belt loose or worn.	Adjust tension or replace drive belt.
	Battery cables loose, corroded or worn.	Repair or replace cables.
	Fuse blown.	Check fuses.
	Fusible link blown.	Replace fusible link.
	Electronic voltage regulator or alternator faulty.	Test alternator.
	Wiring faulty.	Repair wiring.
Discharge battery.	Drive belt loose or worn.	Adjust tension or replace drive belt.
	Wiring connection loose or open circuit.	Tighten loose connection or repair wiring.
	Fusible link blown.	Replace fusible link.
	Poor grounding.	Repair.
	Electronic voltage regulator or alternator faulty.	Test alternator.
Overcharge	Battery life.	Replace battery.
	Electronic voltage regulator faulty.	Replace voltage regulator.
	Voltage sensing wire faulty.	Repair wire.

MT1129100026000X

Fig. 1 Troubleshooting chart

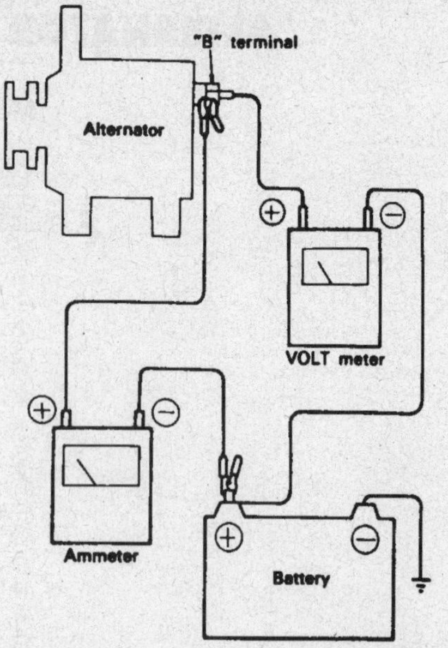
"B" terminal
Alternator
VOLT meter
Ammeter
Battery

MT1129100027000X

Fig. 2 Alternator output wire voltage drop test

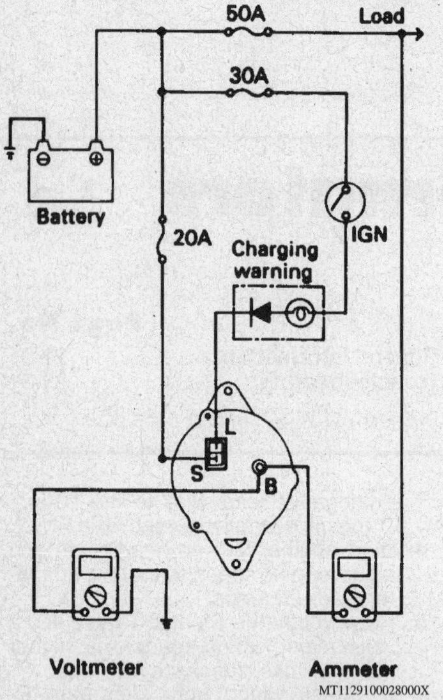
50A
Load
30A
Battery
20A
IGN
Charging warning
L
S
B
Voltmeter
Ammeter

MT1129100028000X

Fig. 3 Output current test

2. Turn ignition off, then disconnect battery ground cable.
3. Disconnect output lead from alternator "B" terminal.
4. Connect ammeter and voltmeter as follows:
   a. Connect a DC ammeter in series between the "B" terminal and the disconnected output wire. Be sure negative lead of ammeter is connected to disconnected output wire as shown in **Fig. 3.**
   b. Connect a digital voltmeter between alternator "B" terminal and ground. Connect the positive lead wire of the voltmeter to the alternator "B" terminal and the negative lead wire to ground **Fig. 3.**
5. Connect tachometer, then reconnect battery ground cable.
6. Voltmeter should read battery voltage. If voltmeter reads 0 volts check for a open in the wire between the alternator "B" terminal and battery negative terminal, a blown fusible link, or a poor ground.
7. Start engine, turn headlamps on, place blower on high speed.
8. Set engine speed to 2500 RPM and read ammeter; ammeter reading must be higher than 52.5 amps.

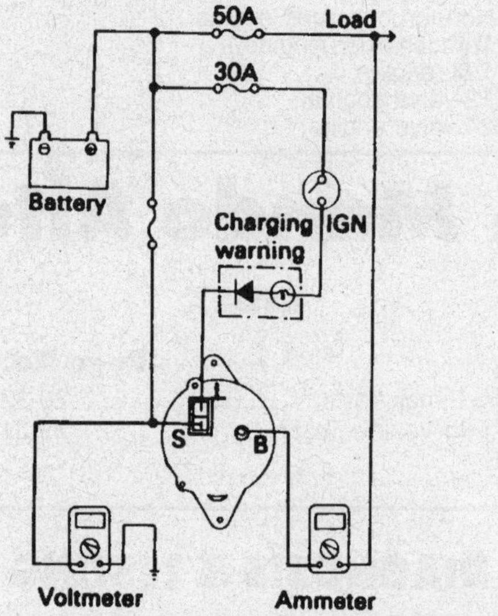
50A
Load
30A
Battery
Charging warning
IGN
S
B
Voltmeter
Ammeter

MT1129100029000X

Fig. 4 Regulated voltage test

Regulated Voltage Test

1. Before performing regulated voltage test check battery to insure that it has a full charge, and check condition and tension of alternator belt.
2. Turn ignition off, then disconnect battery ground cable.
3. Connect a digital voltmeter between alternator "S" terminal and ground. Connect voltmeter positive lead to alternator "S" terminal and negative lead to ground, **Fig. 4.**
4. Disconnect the alternator output wire at "B" terminal.
5. Connect a DC ammeter in series between "B" terminal and disconnected output wire. Connect the ammeter negative wire to disconnected output wire.
6. Turn ignition switch to On position and ensure voltmeter is reading battery voltage. If reading is 0 volts, check for an open wire between alternator "S" terminal and battery positive, or blown fusible link.
7. Start engine and run at 2500 RPM, then read voltmeter when alternator output current drops to 10 amps or less.
8. Voltmeter reading should be within specifications as shown in **Fig. 5.** If reading is not as indicated, alternator or regulator is faulty.

Voltage regulator ambient temperature °C(°F)	Regulating voltage V	
	75A alternator	65A alternator
−20 (−4)	14.2—15.4	14.4—15.6
20 (68)	13.9—14.9	14.2—15.2
60 (140)	13.4—14.6	13.8—15.1
80 (176)	13.1—14.5	13.6—15.0

MT1129100030000X

Fig. 5 Regulator voltage specifications

BENCH TESTS

Rotor

1. Check for continuity between slip rings. If resistance is low or there is no continuity, replace rotor. Resistance value is approximately 3.1 ohms.
2. Check rotor for ground by checking continuity between slip ring and rotor core. If continuity exists, replace rotor assembly.

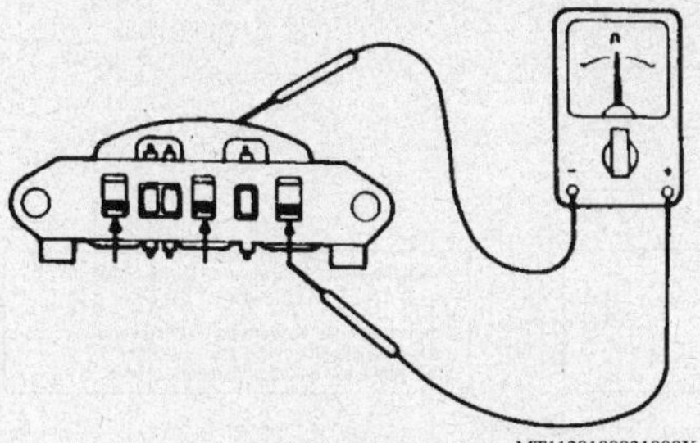
MT1129100031000X
Fig. 6 Positive rectifier inspection

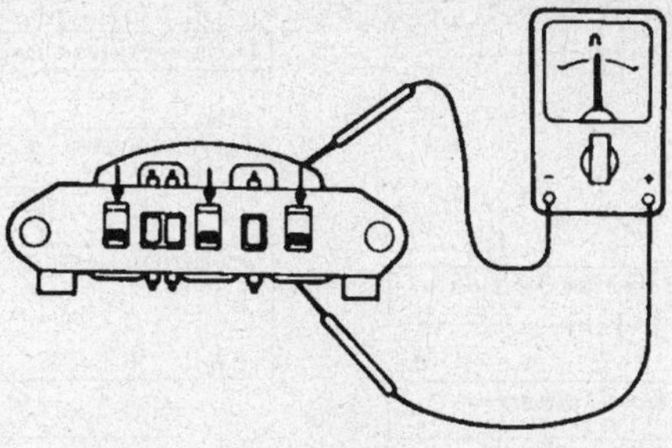
MT1129100032000X
Fig. 7 Negative rectifier inspection

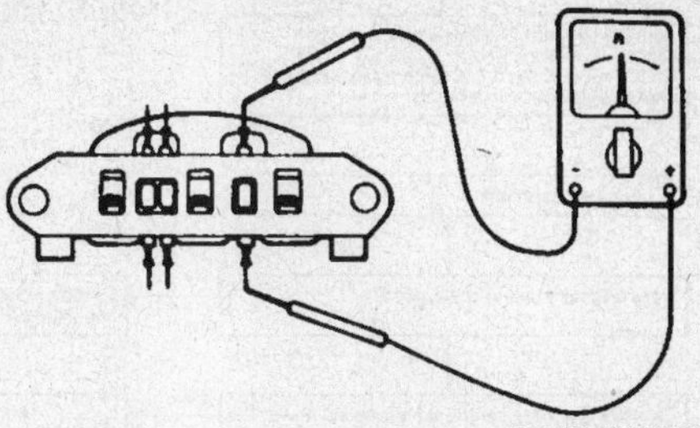
MT1129100033000X
Fig. 8 Diode trio inspection

Stator Coil

1. Check for continuity between coil leads. If there is no continuity, replace stator assembly.
2. Check for a ground by checking continuity between coil lead and core of stator assembly. If continuity exists, replace stator assembly.

Positive Rectifier

Check continuity between positive rectifier and stator coil lead terminal with an ohmmeter as shown in **Fig. 6.** Ohmmeter should read continuity in only one direction. If continuity exists in both directions, a diode is shorted and the rectifier assembly must be replaced.

Negative Rectifier

Check continuity between negative rectifier and stator coil lead terminal with an ohmmeter as shown in **Fig. 7.** Ohmmeter should read continuity in only one direction. If continuity exists in both directions, a diode is shorted and the rectifier assembly must be replaced.

Diode Trio Test

Check continuity of the three diodes by connecting an ohmmeter to both ends of each diode as shown in **Fig. 8.** Diodes should have continuity in one direction only. If diode has continuity in both directions, replace diode heat sink assembly.

ALTERNATOR SPECIFICATIONS

Type	Identification Number	Rated Output, Amps①②
Melco	A2T09493	75
Mando	AB175015	75

① — At 12 volts.
② — Internal voltage regulator.

Speed Control Systems

NOTE: On Air Bag Equipped Models, Refer To "Air Bag System Precautions" Located In The Front Of This Manual For System Disarming & Arming Procedures.

INDEX

	Page No.
Adjustments	29-33
Auto Cruise Control Cable	29-34
Speed Control Cable	29-33
Component Diagnosis & Testing	29-35
Clutch Switch	29-35
Park/Neutral Position (PNP) Switch	29-36
Speed Control Actuator	29-36
Electrical Type	29-36
Vacuum Type	29-37
Stop Lamp/Brake Switch	29-35
Component Replacement	29-37
Precautions	29-33
Air Bag Systems	29-33
System Diagnosis & Testing	29-35
Auto Cruise Control Signal Circuit Inspection	29-35
Troubleshooting	29-33

PRECAUTIONS

AIR BAG SYSTEMS

Refer to "Air Bag System Precautions" in the front of this manual for system disarming and arming procedures.

TROUBLESHOOTING

Refer to **Figs. 1 through 7** when troubleshooting the speed control system.

ADJUSTMENTS

SPEED CONTROL CABLE

EXPO, MIRAGE, 1993 GALANT & 1993-94 ECLIPSE

1. Turn all accessories off, warm up engine until specified idle speed is reached, then turn engine off.
2. Remove air cleaner, then depress accelerator pedal completely, ensuring throttle valve operates smoothly from full close to full open.
3. Remove actuator cover.
4. **On models equipped with automatic transaxle or SOHC engine,** turn ignition switch to On position for 15 seconds, ensuring throttle lever returns.
5. **On all models,** check the inner cable (throttle valve side) for too much or too little slack. Cable deflection should measure .04–.08 inch. If not within specified limits, adjust as follows:
   a. Loosen the adjustment bolts at the air intake plenum side and free

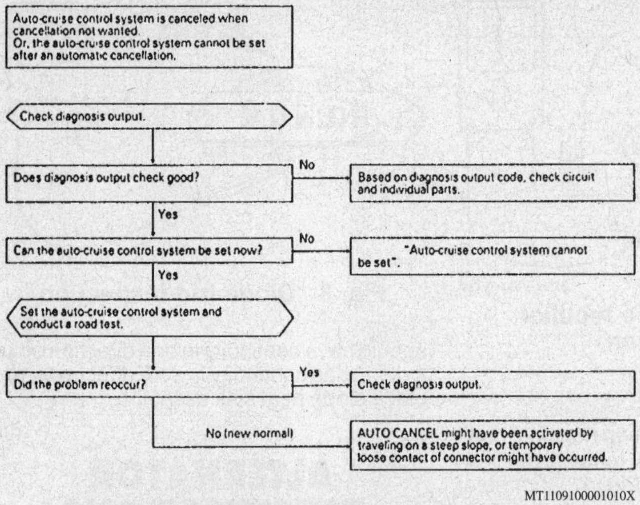
Auto-cruise control system is canceled when cancellation not wanted.
Or, the auto-cruise control system cannot be set after an automatic cancellation.
Check diagnosis output.
Does diagnosis output check good?
No
Based on diagnosis output code, check circuit and individual parts.
Yes
Can the auto-cruise control system be set now?
No
"Auto-cruise control system cannot be set".
Yes
Set the auto-cruise control system and conduct a road test.
Did the problem reoccur?
Yes
Check diagnosis output.
No (new normal)
AUTO CANCEL might have been activated by traveling on a steep slope, or temporary loose contact of connector might have occurred.
MT1109100001010X

Fig. 1 Troubleshooting (Part 1 of 4). Mirage

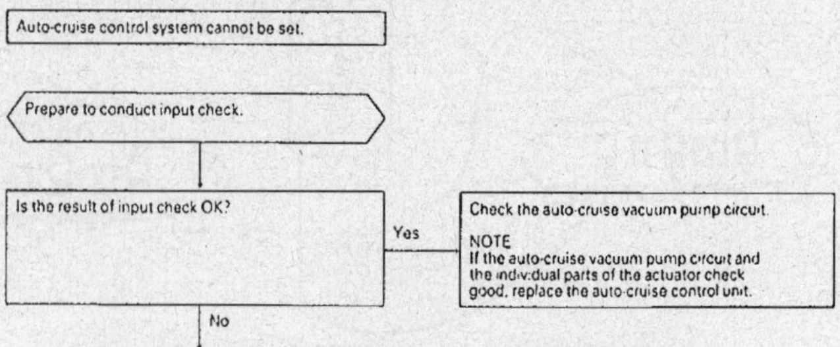
Auto-cruise control system cannot be set.
Prepare to conduct input check.
Is the result of input check OK?
Yes
Check the auto-cruise vacuum pump circuit.
NOTE
If the auto-cruise vacuum pump circuit and the individual parts of the actuator check good, replace the auto-cruise control unit.
No

Check results	Probable cause	Remedy
Even if an attempt is made to enter data, no code appears.	Open circuit in auto-cruise control unit power supply circuit	Replace control switch or repair harness.
	Open circuit in control switch circuit	
	Defective auto-cruise control unit	Replace auto-cruise control unit.
Code No. 21 remains even though SET switch is set to OFF.	SET switch ON malfunction	Replace the control switch.
Code No. 22 remains even though RESUME switch is set to OFF.	RESUME switch ON malfunction	Replace the control switch.
Code No. 23 does not appear when brake pedal is depressed.	Defective stop light switch circuit	Replace stop light switch or repair harness.
Code No. 23 does not disappear when brake pedal is released.		
Code No. 26 does not disappear when clutch pedal is released. <M/T>	Defective clutch switch circuit	Replace clutch switch or repair harness.
Code No. 26 does not disappear when SELECT lever is placed in a position other than "N" and "P". <A/T>	Defective inhibitor switch circuit	Replace inhibitor switch or repair harness.
Code No. 25 does not appear when vehicle is traveling at less than 40 km/h (25 mph).	Defective vehicle speed sensor circuit	Check or repair vehicle speed sensor circuit.
Code No. 25 does not disappear or code No. 24 does not appear when vehicle speed is increased to more than approximately 40 km/h (25 mph).		

MT1109100001020X

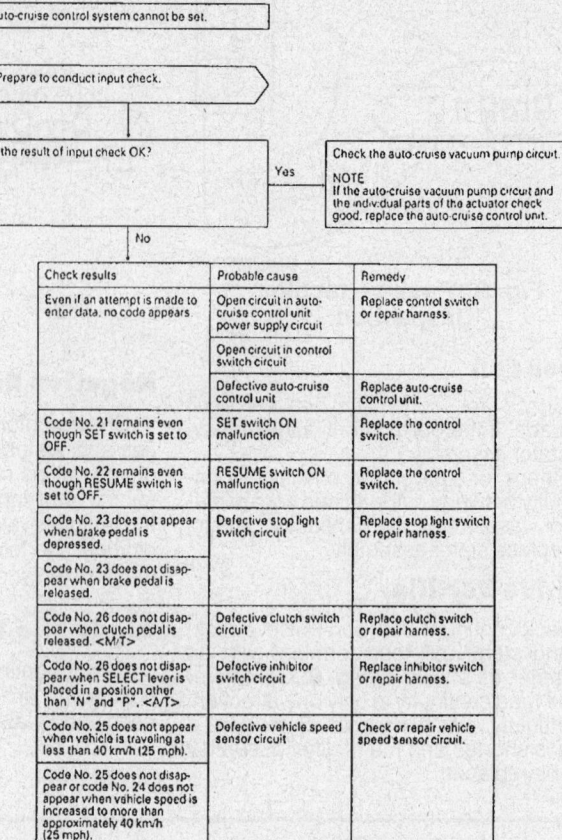

Fig. 1 Troubleshooting (Part 2 of 4). Mirage

inner cable, **Fig. 8.** Adjust cable to specified limits. **Excessive cable deflection will cause vehicle speed to drop; excessive cable tension will cause idle speed to increase.**

b. After adjustment of the cable, ensure throttle lever contacts idle position switch.

6. Adjust cable (accelerator pedal side) as follows:
   a. Loosen cable locknut.
   b. Adjust inner cable deflection to 0–.04 inch on models with manual transaxle or .08–.12 inch on models with automatic transaxle, then tighten adjusting bolt, **Fig. 9,** or locknut, **Fig. 10. Use caution not to decrease play in cable B (throttle valve side).**
   c. Ensure throttle lever travels distance shown in **Fig. 11.**
   d. Ensure throttle valve fully opens and closes when operating accelerator pedal.
   e. Install air cleaner.

1995-96 ECLIPSE

2.0L Non-Turbocharged Engine

Hold link (C), **Fig. 12,** where it contacts link (B), then secure the speed control cable in position.

MONTERO

1993-95

1. Turn all accessories off, warm up engine until specified idling speed is reached, then turn engine off.
2. Remove air cleaner, then depress accelerator pedal completely, ensuring throttle valve operates smoothly from full close to full open.
3. Remove actuator cover.
4. Adjust cable B as follows:
   a. Connect cable B to the actuator shown in **Fig. 13.**
   b. Loosen adjusting bolts. Slide the outer cable so that cable deflection measures .04–.08 inch, **Fig. 14. Ensure throttle link contacts the stopper.**
5. Adjust cable A as follows:
   a. Connect cable A to the dimensions shown in **Fig. 15.**
   b. Adjust cable A deflection at point G to 0–.04 inch, **Fig. 16.**
   c. Ensure throttle link moves, when the actuator link is turned .04–.08 inch, then check for free movement when accelerator pedal is fully opened and closed.
   d. Install actuator cover.

PICKUP

1. Turn all accessories off, warm up engine until specified idling speed is reached, then turn engine off.
2. Remove air cleaner, then depress the accelerator pedal down, ensuring throttle valve operates smoothly from full close to full open.
3. Remove actuator cover.
4. Loosen locknuts of the cables and let inner cables sag.
5. Contact lever P to stopper, then turn adjusting nut to lengthen outer cable, until just before the lever P begins to operate. **Fig. 17.**
6. Turn back adjusting nut ½ turn, then tighten locking nut. Deflection of cable A should be between 0–.04 inch.
7. Turn adjusting nut of cable B at carburetor or throttle body for a distance of 0–.08 inch between levers C and P, **Fig. 18.**

AUTO CRUISE CONTROL CABLE

DIAMANTE & 1996 MONTERO

1. Inspect cables for sharp bends and straighten as necessary.
2. Fully depress accelerator pedal to ensure throttle lever moves smoothly from closed to open position.
3. Determine point at which intermediate link (A), **Figs. 19 and 20,** contacts link (B), then unscrew adjusting nut (A) approximately one full turn in this position.
4. Ensure inner cable play is .04–.08 inch, then secure cable with locknut.

3000GT, 1995-96 ECLIPSE W/2.0L TURBOCHARGED ENGINE & 2.4L ENGINE & 1994-96 GALANT

1. Determine position at which intermediate link (C), **Fig. 21,** touches link (B). At this contact point, loosen adjusting nut approximately one turn.
2. Ensure inner cable play is .04–.08

Trouble symptom	Probable cause	Remedy
• The set vehicle speed varies greatly upward or downward. • "Hunching" (repeated alternating acceleration and deceleration) occurs after setting is made	Malfunction of the vehicle speed sensor circuit	Repair the vehicle speed sensor system, or replace the part.
	Malfunction of the speedometer cable or speedometer drive gear	
	Auto-cruise vacuum pump circuit poor contact	Repair the auto-cruise vacuum pump system, or replace the part.
	Malfunction of the auto-cruise vacuum pump	
	Malfunction of the auto cruise control unit	Replace the auto cruise control unit.
The auto cruise control system is not canceled when the brake pedal is depressed	Brake switch (for auto-cruise control) malfunction (short-circuit)	Repair the harness or replace the stop light switch.
	Auto-cruise vacuum pump drive circuit short-circuit	Repair the harness or replace the auto cruise vacuum pump
	Malfunction of the auto-cruise control unit	Replace the auto-cruise control unit
The auto cruise control system is not canceled when the clutch pedal is depressed <M/T> (It is canceled, however, when the brake pedal is depressed.)	Damaged or disconnected wiring of clutch switch input circuit	Repair the harness, or repair or replace the clutch switch.
	Clutch switch improper installation (won't switch ON)	
	Malfunction of the auto-cruise control unit	Replace the auto-cruise control unit.
The auto-cruise control system is not canceled when the shift lever is moved to the "N" position <A/T> (It is canceled, however, when the brake pedal is depressed.)	Damaged or disconnected wiring of inhibitor switch input circuit	Repair the harness, or repair or replace the inhibitor switch.
	Improper adjustment of inhibitor switch	
	Malfunction of the auto-cruise control unit	Replace the auto-cruise control unit.
Cannot decelerate by using the SET switch.	Temporary damaged or disconnected wiring of SET switch input circuit	Repair the harness or replace the SET switch.
	Auto-cruise vacuum pump circuit poor contact	Repair the harness or replace the auto-cruise vacuum pump and actuator.
	Malfunction of the auto-cruise vacuum pump and actuator (including blocking of negative pressure passage)	
	Malfunction of the auto-cruise control unit	Replace the auto-cruise control unit.

MT1109100001030X

Fig. 1 Troubleshooting (Part 3 of 4). Mirage

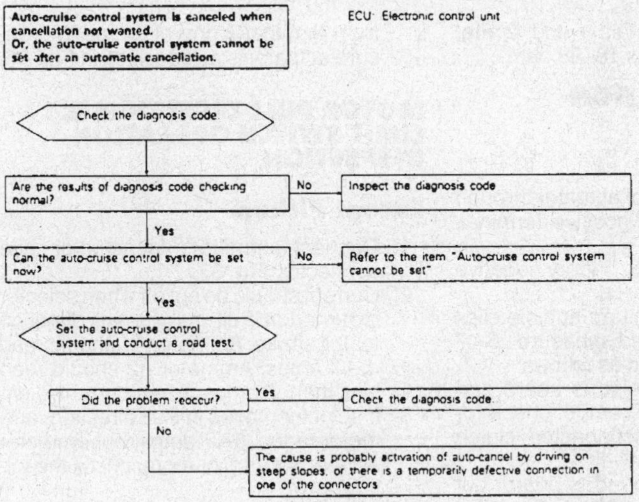
Auto-cruise control system is canceled when cancellation not wanted.
Or, the auto-cruise control system cannot be set after an automatic cancellation.
ECU: Electronic control unit
Check the diagnosis code.
Are the results of diagnosis code checking normal?
No
Inspect the diagnosis code
Yes
Can the auto-cruise control system be set now?
No
Refer to the item "Auto-cruise control system cannot be set"
Yes
Set the auto-cruise control system and conduct a road test.
Did the problem reoccur?
Yes
Check the diagnosis code.
No
The cause is probably activation of auto-cancel by driving on steep slopes, or there is a temporarily defective connection in one of the connectors
MT1109100002010X

Fig. 2 Troubleshooting (Part 1 of 4). 1993–95 Montero

Trouble symptom	Probable cause	Remedy
Cannot accelerate or resume speed by using the RESUME switch.	Open or short circuit in RESUME switch circuit in control switch	Replace the control switch.
	Auto-cruise vacuum pump circuit poor contact	Repair the harness or replace the auto-cruise vacuum pump and actuator.
	Malfunction of the auto-cruise vacuum pump and actuator (including air leaks from negative pressure passage)	
	Malfunction of the auto-cruise control unit	Replace the auto-cruise control unit.
Auto-cruise control system can be set while traveling at a vehicle speed of less than 40 km/h (25 mph), or there is no automatic cancellation at that speed	Malfunction of the vehicle speed sensor circuit	Repair the vehicle speed sensor system, or replace the part.
	Malfunction of the speedometer cable or the speedometer drive gear	
	Malfunction of the auto-cruise control unit	Replace the auto-cruise control unit.
The auto-cruise control switch indicator light does not illuminate. (But auto-cruise control system is normal.)	Damaged or disconnected bulb of auto-cruise control switch indicator	Repair the harness or replace the control switch.
	Harness damaged or disconnected	
Malfunction of control function by ON/OFF switching of 4 A/T accelerator switch (Non-operation of damper clutch, 2nd gear hold, etc.)	Malfunction of circuit related to accelerator switch OFF function	Repair the harness or replace the part.
	Malfunction of the auto-cruise control unit	
Overdrive is not canceled during fixed speed driving. <A/T>	Malfunction of circuit related to overdrive cancellation, or malfunction of auto-cruise control unit	Repair the harness or replace the part.
No shift to overdrive during manual driving <A/T>		
The auto-cruise control indicator light does not illuminate (But auto-cruise control system is normal.)	Damaged or disconnected bulb of indicator light	Repair the harness or replace the bulb.
	Harness damaged or disconnected	

MT1109100001040X

Fig. 1 Troubleshooting (Part 4 of 4). Mirage

inch, then secure cable with locknut.

SYSTEM DIAGNOSIS & TESTING

Auto Cruise Control Signal Circuit Inspection

Refer to **Figs. 22 through 26** for test procedure.

COMPONENT DIAGNOSIS & TESTING

Stop Lamp/Brake Switch

1. Disconnect electrical connector from switch.
2. Check for continuity between terminals of switch, **Figs. 27 and 28.**

Clutch Switch

1. Disconnect electrical connector from switch.
2. Check for continuity between terminals when clutch pedal is depressed.

Auto-cruise control system cannot be set.

Prepare to conduct input checking.

Are the results of all input checks normals?

Yes — Check the motor-driven vacuum pump circuit.

No:

Check results	Probable cause	Remedy
Code 21 remains even though SET switch is set to OFF.	SET switch ON malfunction	Replace the control switch.
	SET switch input line short-circuit	Repair the harness.
Code 22 remains even though RESUME switch is set to OFF.	RESUME switch ON malfunction	Replace the control switch.
	RESUME switch input line short-circuit	Repair the harness.
Code 23 remains even if the stop light switch is turned OFF by releasing the brake pedal.	Malfunction of stop light switch circuit.	Replace stop light switch or repair harness.
Code 25 remains, and code 24 does not appear, even though vehicle speed reaches approximately 40 km/h (25 mph) or higher.	Malfunction of the vehicle-speed sensor circuit (damaged or disconnected wiring, or short-circuit)	Check or repair the vehicle speed sensor circuit.
Code 26 remains even if the clutch switch is turned OFF by releasing the clutch pedal. <M/T>	Malfunction of clutch switch circuit.	Replace clutch switch or repair harness.
Code 26 remains even if the selector lever is moved to anything but N, P. <A/T>	Malfunction of inhibitor switch circuit.	Replace inhibitor switch or repair harness.
Code 27 remains even though CANCEL switch is set to OFF.	Malfunction of CANCEL switch circuit.	Replace the control switch or repair harness.
Code 28 remains even if the accelerator is released.	Malfunction of throttle position sensor circuit.	Replace the sensor or repair harness.
Code 29 remains even though the idle switch is set to ON.	Malfunction of idle switch circuit	Replace the switch or repair harness.

MT1109100002020X

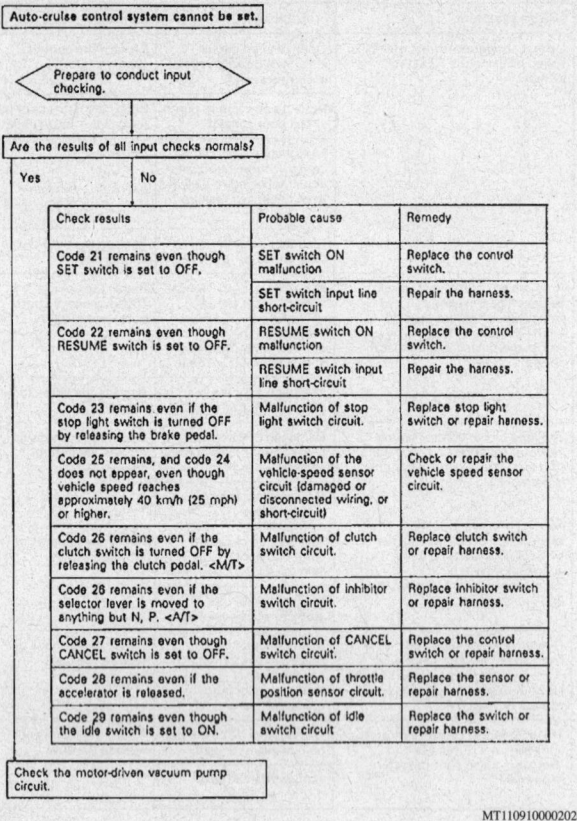

Fig. 2 Troubleshooting (Part 2 of 4). 1993–95 Montero

Trouble symptom	Probable cause	Remedy
• The set vehicle speed varies greatly upward or downward. • "Hunching" (repeated alternating acceleration and deceleration) occurs after setting is made.	Malfunction of the vehicle speed sensor circuit	Repair the vehicle speed sensor system, or replace the part.
	Malfunction of the speedometer cable or speedometer drive gear	
	Motor-driven vacuum pump circuit poor contact	Repair the motor-driven vacuum pump or replace the part
	Malfunction of the motor-driven vacuum pump	
	Malfunction of the ECU	Replace the ECU
The auto-cruise control system is not canceled when the brake pedal is depressed	Damaged or disconnected wiring of the stop light switch input circuit or stop light switch (for auto-cruise control) poor contact (short circuit)	Repair the harness or replace the stop light switch.
	Motor-driven vacuum pump drive circuit short-circuit	Repair the harness or replace the motor-driven vacuum pump
	Malfunction of the ECU	Replace the ECU
The auto-cruise control system is not canceled when the clutch pedal is depressed. <M/T> (It is canceled, however, when the brake pedal is depressed.)	Damaged or disconnected wiring of clutch switch input circuit	Repair the harness, or repair or replace the clutch switch
	Clutch switch improper installation (won't switch ON)	
	Malfunction of the ECU	Replace the ECU
The auto-cruise control system is not canceled when the selector lever is moved to the "N" position. <A/T> (It is canceled, however, when the brake pedal is depressed.)	Damaged or disconnected wiring of inhibitor switch input circuit	Repair the harness, or repair or replace the inhibitor switch
	Improper adjustment of inhibitor switch	
	Malfunction of the ECU	Replace the ECU

MT1109100002030X

Fig. 2 Troubleshooting (Part 3 of 4). 1993–95 Montero

Park/Neutral Position (PNP) Switch

1. Disconnect electrical connector from switch.
2. Place selector lever in the N, then P ranges to check switch. Check continuity between terminals as shown in **Figs. 29 and 30.**

Speed Control Actuator

ELECTRICAL TYPE

CONTINUITY INSPECTION

Except Pickup

1. Disconnect electrical connector.
2. Measure clutch coil resistance between terminals 1 and 2, **Fig. 31.** Standard value is 20 ohms.

Pickup

1. Disconnect electrical connector.
2. Measure resistance value of clutch coil, between terminals 1 and 2, **Fig. 31.** Standard value is 45–65 ohms.
3. Measure resistance value of clutch coil, between terminals 1 and 3, **Fig. 31.** Standard value is 25–35 ohms.
4. Measure resistance value of clutch coil, between terminals 1 and 4, **Fig. 31.** Standard value is 18–28 ohms.

ACTUATOR OPERATION INSPECTION

Except Pickup

1. Connect terminal 1 of actuator through ammeter to battery positive terminal, **Fig. 32.**
2. Connect terminal 2 to battery negative terminal.
3. Solenoid should emit an audible click and ammeter should measure .5–.7 amps. If not, proceed as follows:
   a. If no solenoid noise is heard and ammeter reads 0 amps, check for damaged or disconnected clutch coil wiring.
   b. If no solenoid sound is heard, but ammeter reads infinite, check for clutch coil short circuit.

Pickup

1. Disconnect actuator, then connect battery voltage and an ammeter, **Fig. 33.**
2. Apply 16 inches vacuum to actuator. Ensure actuator operation is as specified in **Fig. 34.**
3. Disconnect wire from terminal 2 and ensure actuator is as specified in **Fig. 35.**
4. Disconnect wire on terminal 2 then from terminal 3 one at a time and ensure actuator is as specified in **Fig. 36.**

MOTOR PULL DIRECTION & LIMIT SWITCH OPERATION INSPECTION

Except Pickup

1. Connect ammeters to actuator side connector, **Fig. 37.**
2. Current should be cut off when selector is turned in Pull (fully open) direction for full stroke. Ammeter A1 should read .5–.7 amps. Ammeter A2 should read less than .5 amps, when current is on.
3. If selector moves in Pull direction, ammeter reads .5–.7 amps, but ammeter A2 reads 1 amp or more, check the following:
   a. Improper gear backlash, burning between shaft and metal, or insufficient thrust clearance.
4. If selector does not move, ammeter A1 reads .5–.7 amps and ammeter A2 reads 1 amp or more, check the following:
   a. Burned shaft or motor, or foreign material caught between gears.
5. If selector does not move, ammeter A1 reads .3–.7 amps and ammeter A2 reads 0.0 amps, check the following:
   a. Damaged or disconnected internal

Trouble symptom	Probable cause	Remedy
Cannot decelerate by using the SET switch	Temporary damaged or disconnected wiring of SET switch input circuit	Repair the harness or replace the control switch.
	Motor-driven vacuum pump circuit poor contact	Repair the harness or replace the motor-driven vacuum pump.
	Malfunction of the auto-cruise actuator	
	Malfunction of the ECU	Replace the ECU.
Cannot accelerate or resume speed by using the RESUME switch	Damaged or disconnected wiring, or short-circuit, of RESUME switch input circuit	Repair the harness or replace the control switch.
	Motor-driven vacuum pump circuit poor contact	Repair the harness or replace the motor-driven vacuum pump.
	Malfunction of the motor-driven vacuum pump	
	Malfunction of the ECU	Replace the ECU.
Auto-cruise control system can be set while traveling at a vehicle speed of less than 40 km/h (25 mph), or there is no automatic cancellation at that speed.	Malfunction of the vehicle-speed sensor circuit	Repair the vehicle-speed sensor system, or replace the part.
	Malfunction of the speedometer cable or the speedometer drive gear	
	Malfunction of the ECU	Replace the ECU.
The indicator light of the main switch does not illuminate (But auto-cruise control system is normal.)	Damaged or disconnected bulb of indicator light or malfunction of the main switch	Repair the harness or replace the main switch.
	Harness damaged or disconnected	
Overdrive is not canceled during fixed speed driving <A/T>	Malfunction of circuit related to overdrive cancelation, or malfunction of ECU	Repair the harness or replace the part.
No shift to overdrive during manual driving <A/T>		

MT1109100002040X

Fig. 2 Troubleshooting (Part 4 of 4). 1993–95 Montero

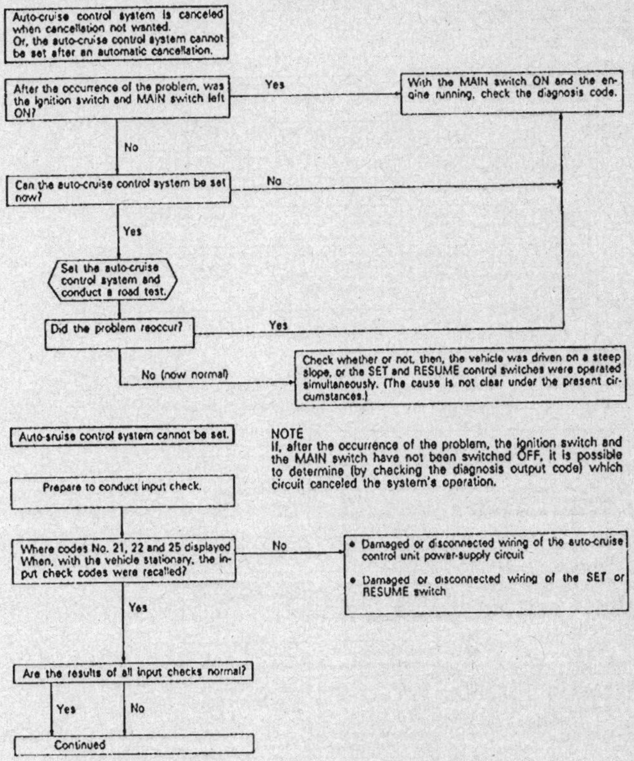
Auto-cruise control system is canceled when cancellation not wanted.
Or, the auto-cruise control system cannot be set after an automatic cancellation.
After the occurrence of the problem, was the ignition switch and MAIN switch left ON?
Yes
With the MAIN switch ON and the engine running, check the diagnosis code.
No
Can the auto-cruise control system be set now?
No
Yes
Set the auto-cruise control system and conduct a road test.
Did the problem reoccur?
Yes
No (now normal)
Check whether or not, then, the vehicle was driven on a steep slope, or the SET and RESUME control switches were operated simultaneously. (The cause is not clear under the present circumstances.)
Auto-sruise control system cannot be set.
NOTE
If, after the occurrence of the problem, the ignition switch and the MAIN switch have not been switched OFF, it is possible to determine (by checking the diagnosis output code) which circuit canceled the system's operation.
Prepare to conduct input check.
Where codes No. 21, 22 and 25 displayed When, with the vehicle stationary, the input check codes were recalled?
No
• Damaged or disconnected wiring of the auto-cruise control unit power-supply circuit
• Damaged or disconnected wiring of the SET or RESUME switch
Yes
Are the results of all input checks normal?
Yes
No
Continued

!T1109100003010X

Fig. 3 Troubleshooting (Part 1 of 3). Pickup

lead wire or motor wiring, poor contact of limit switch, or open diode.

6. With selector stroke in the intermediate level, disconnect connection to terminal 1, then cut the current flow to the clutch coil.
7. If selector does not return to original position, even if current is cut to the clutch coil, check for clutch plate remaining engaged with clutch.

MOTOR RELEASE DIRECTION & LIMIT SWITCH OPERATION INSPECTION

Except Pickup

1. Connect ammeters to actuator side connector, **Fig. 38.**
2. Turn selector in the Release (fully closed), direction. Current should be cut off, ammeter A1 should read .5–.7 amps, ammeter A2 should read less than .5 amps when current is on.
3. If the selector moves in the Release direction, ammeter reads .5–.7 amps, but ammeter A2 reads 1 amp or more, check the following:
   a. Improper gear backlash, burning between shaft and metal, or insufficient thrust clearance.
4. If selector does not move, ammeter A1 reads .5–.7 amps, but ammeter A2 reads 1 amp or more, check the following:
   a. Burned shaft or motor, or foreign material caught between gears.
5. If selector does not move, ammeter A1 reads .30007 amps and ammeter A2 reads 0.0 amps, check the following:
   a. Damaged or disconnected internal lead wire or motor wiring, poor limit switch contact, or open diode.

VACUUM TYPE

1. Remove actuator.
2. Apply vacuum to actuator and ensure holder moves more than 1.38 inches. In addition, ensure there is no change in position of holder when vacuum is maintained.
3. Install actuator and inspect and adjust cruise control cable.

COMPONENT REPLACEMENT

Refer to numbered sequences shown in **Figs. 39 through 49** for component replacement.

Continued

Yes / No

No:

Check results	Probable cause	Remedy
Code No 21 remains even though SET switch is set to OFF.	SET switch ON malfunction	Replace the control switch.
	SET switch input line short-circuit	Repair the harness.
Code No. 22 remains even though RESUME switch is set to OFF.	RESUME switch ON malfunction	Replace the control switch.
	RESUME switch input line short-circuit	Repair the harness.
Code No. 23 remains even though CANCEL switch is set to OFF.	Malfunction of the CANCEL circuit (ON malfunction)	Check or repair each CANCEL circuit.
Code No 25 does not disappear, and code No. 24 does not appear, even though vehicle speed reaches approximately 40 km/h (25 mph) or higher.	Malfunction of the vehicle-speed sensor circuit (damaged or disconnected wiring, or short-circuit)	Check or repair the vehicle speed sensor circuit.

Yes: Check the actuator circuit?

NOTE
If the results of the check of the actuator circuit and of the actuator itself reveal no abnormal condition, replace the auto-cruise control unit.

Symptom	Probable cause	Remedy
• The set vehicle speed varies greatly upward or downward. • "Hunching" (repeated alternating acceleration and deceleration) occurs after setting is made.	Malfunction of the vehicle speed sensor circuit	Repair the vehicle-speed sensor system, or replace the part.
	Malfunction of the speedometer cable or speedometer drive gear	
	Malfunction of the vacuum circuit	Repair vacuum system, or replace the part.
	Actuator circuit poor contact	Repair the actuator system, or replace the part.
	Malfunction of the actuator	
	Malfunction of the Auto-cruise control unit	Replace the auto-cruise control unit.
The auto-cruise control system is not canceled when the brake pedal is depressed.	Damaged or disconnected wiring of the stop light switch input circuit; brake switch (for auto-cruise control) malfunction (short-circuit)	Repair the harness or replace the stop light switch.
	Actuator drive circuit short-circuit	Repair the harness or replace the actuator.
	Malfunction of the auto-cruise control unit	Replace the auto-cruise control unit

MT1109100003020X

Fig. 3 Troubleshooting (Part 2 of 3). Pickup

Symptom	Probable cause	Remedy
The auto-cruise control system is not canceled when the clutch pedal is depressed. (It is canceled, however, when the brake pedal is depressed.)	Damaged or disconnected wiring of clutch switch input circuit	Repair the harness, or repair or replace the clutch switch.
	Clutch switch improper installation (won't switch ON)	
	Malfunction of the auto-cruise control unit	Replace the auto-cruise control unit.
Cannot decelerate by using the SET switch	Temporary damaged or disconnected wiring of SET switch input circuit	Repair the harness or replace the SET switch
	Actuator circuit poor contact	Repair the harness or replace the actuator
	Malfunction of the actuator	
	Malfunction of the auto-cruise control unit	Replace the auto-cruise control unit
Cannot accelerate or resume speed by using the RESUME switch	Damaged or disconnected wiring, or short-circuit, of RESUME switch input circuit	Repair the harness or replace the RESUME switch.
	Actuator circuit poor contact	Repair the harness or replace the actuator
	Malfunction of the actuator	
	Malfunction of the auto-cruise control unit	Replace the auto-cruise control unit
Auto-cruise control system can be set while traveling at a vehicle speed of less than 40 km/h (25 mph), or there is no automatic cancelation at that speed	Malfunction of the vehicle speed sensor circuit	Repair the vehicle speed sensor system, or replace the part
	Malfunction of the speedometer cable or the speedometer drive gear	
	Malfunction of the auto-cruise control unit	Replace the auto-cruise control unit

MT1109100003030X

Fig. 3 Troubleshooting (Part 3 of 3). Pickup

Auto-cruise control system is canceled when cancellation not wanted.
Or, the auto-cruise control system cannot be set after an automatic cancellation.

ECU: Electronic control unit

Can the auto-cruise control system be set now?
- No → Check the diagnosis code
- Yes → Set the auto-cruise control system and conduct a road test.

Did the problem reoccur?
- Yes → Check the diagnosis code
- No (new normal) → Check whether or not, then, the vehicle was driven on a steep slope.

MT1109100004010X

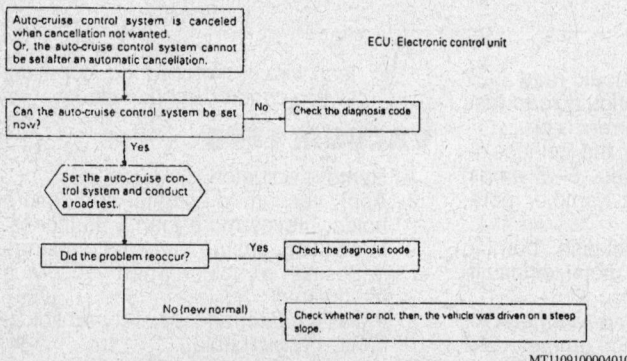

Fig. 4 Troubleshooting (Part 1 of 4). 1993 Galant & 1993–94 Eclipse

Auto-cruise control system cannot be set.

Prepare to conduct input check.

Where codes No. 21, 22, 23, 25 and 26, displayed when, with the vehicle stationary, the input check codes were recalled?
- No →
  - Damaged or disconnected wiring of the ECU power-supply circuit
  - Damaged or disconnected wiring of the SET or RESUME switch
  - Damaged or disconnected wiring of the stop light switch, clutch pedal position switch or park/neutral position switch
- Yes ↓

Are the results of all input checks normals?

Yes / No

No:

Check results	Probable cause	Remedy
Code 21 remains even though SET switch is set to OFF.	SET switch ON malfunction	Replace the control switch.
	SET switch input line short-circuit	Repair the harness.
Code 22 remains even though RESUME switch is set to OFF.	RESUME switch ON malfunction	Replace the control switch.
	RESUME switch input line short-circuit	Repair the harness.
Code 23 is not canceled even if the stop light switch is turned OFF by releasing the brake pedal.	Malfunction of stop light switch circuit.	Replace stop light switch or repair harness.
Code 25 does not disappear, and code 24 does not appear, even though vehicle speed reaches approximately 40 km/h (25 mph) or higher.	Malfunction of the vehicle-speed sensor circuit (damaged or disconnected wiring, or short-circuit)	Check or repair the vehicle speed sensor circuit.
Code 26 is not canceled even if the clutch pedal position switch is turned OFF by releasing the clutch pedal.	Malfunction of clutch pedal position switch circuit.	Replace clutch pedal position switch or repair harness.
Code 26 is not canceled even if the select lever is moved to anything but N, P <A/T>.	Malfunction of park/neutral position switch circuit	Replace park/neutral position switch or repair harness.

Yes: Check the auto-cruise vacuum pump circuit.

NOTE
If the results of the check of the auto-cruise vacuum pump circuit and of the auto-cruise vacuum pump and actuator itself reveal no abnormal condition, replace the electronic control unit (ECU).

MT1109100004020X

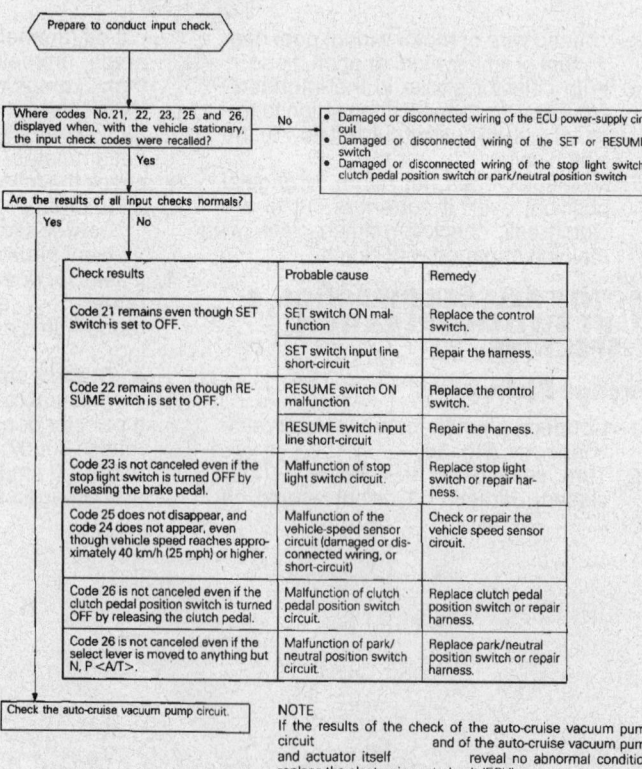

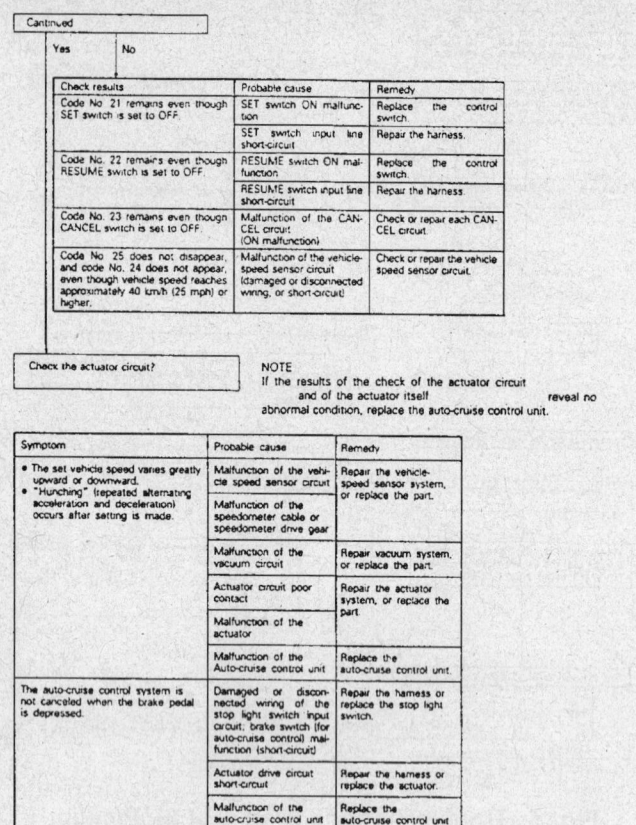

Fig. 4 Troubleshooting (Part 2 of 4). 1993 Galant & 1993–94 Eclipse

Trouble symptom	Probable cause	Remedy
• The set vehicle speed varies greatly upward or downward. • "Hunching" (repeated alternating acceleration and deceleration) occurs after setting is made.	Malfunction of the vehicle speed sensor circuit	Repair the vehicle speed sensor system, or replace the part.
	Malfunction of the speedometer cable or speedometer drive gear	
	Auto-cruise vacuum pump circuit poor contact	Repair the auto-cruise vacuum pump system, or replace the part.
	Malfunction of the auto-cruise vacuum pump	
	Malfunction of the auto-cruise control unit	Replace the auto-cruise control unit.
The auto-cruise control system is not canceled when the brake pedal is depressed.	Brake switch (for auto-cruise control) malfunction (short-circuit)	Repair the harness or replace the stop light switch.
	Auto-cruise vacuum pump drive circuit short-circuit	Repair the harness or replace the auto-cruise vacuum pump.
	Malfunction of the auto-cruise control unit	Replace the auto-cruise control unit.
The auto-cruise control system is not canceled when the clutch pedal is depressed. <M.T> (It is canceled, however, when the brake pedal is depressed.)	Damaged or disconnected wiring of clutch switch input circuit	Repair the harness, or repair or replace the clutch switch.
	Clutch switch improper installation (won't switch ON)	
	Malfunction of the auto-cruise control unit	Replace the auto-cruise control unit.
The auto-cruise control system is not canceled when the shift lever is moved to the "N" position. <A/T> (It is canceled, however, when the brake pedal is depressed.)	Damaged or disconnected wiring of inhibitor switch input circuit	Repair the harness, or repair or replace the inhibitor switch.
	Improper adjustment of inhibitor switch	
	Malfunction of the auto-cruise control unit	Replace the auto-cruise control unit.
Cannot decelerate by using the SET switch.	Temporary damaged or disconnected wiring of SET switch input circuit	Repair the harness or replace the SET switch.
	Auto-cruise vacuum pump circuit poor contact	Repair the harness or replace the auto-cruise vacuum pump and actuator.
	Malfunction of the auto-cruise vacuum pump and actuator (including blocking of negative pressure passage)	
	Malfunction of the auto-cruise control unit	Replace the auto-cruise control unit.

MT1109100004030X

Fig. 4 Troubleshooting (Part 3 of 4). 1993–94 Eclipse

Trouble symptom	Probable cause	Check chart No.	Remedy
Cannot accelerate or resume speed by using the RESUME switch.	Damaged or disconnected wiring, or short-circuit, of RESUME switch input circuit	No. 3	Repair the harness or replace the RESUME switch.
	Auto cruise vacuum pump circuit poor contact	No. 5	Repair the harness or replace the auto-cruise vacuum pump and actuator.
	Malfunction of the auto-cruise vacuum pump and actuator (including air leak from negative pressure passage)		
	Malfunction of the ECU	--	Replace the ECU.
Auto-cruise control system can be set while traveling at a vehicle speed of less than 40 km/h (25 mph), or there is no automatic cancellation at that speed.	Malfunction of the vehicle-speed sensor circuit	No. 4	Repair the vehicle-speed sensor system, or replace the part.
	Malfunction of the speedometer cable or the speedometer drive gear		
	Malfunction of the ECU	–	Replace the ECU.
The indicator light of combination meter does not illuminate. (But auto-cruise control system is normal.)	Damaged or disconnected bulb of indicator light	--	Repair the harness or replace the bulb.
	Harness damaged or disconnected		
Malfunction of control function by ON/OFF switching of ELC 4 A/T accelerator switch (Non-operation of damper clutch, 2nd gear hold, etc.)	Malfunction of circuit related to accelerator switch OFF function	No. 9	Repair the harness or replace the part.
	Malfunction of the ECU		
Overdrive is not canceled during fixed speed driving. <A/T>	Malfunction of circuit related to overdrive cancellation, or malfunction of ECU	No. 10	Repair the harness or replace the part.
No shift to overdrive during manual driving. <A/T>			

MT1109100004040X

Fig. 4 Troubleshooting (Part 4 of 4). 1993 Galant & 1993–94 Eclipse

Trouble symptom	Probable cause	Remedy
• The set vehicle speed varies greatly upward or downward. • "Hunching" (repeated alternating acceleration and deceleration) occurs after setting is made.	Malfunction of the vehicle speed sensor circuit	Repair the vehicle speed sensor system, or replace the part.
	Malfunction of the speedometer cable or speedometer drive gear	
	Auto-cruise vacuum pump circuit poor contact	Repair the auto-cruise vacuum pump or replace the part.
	Malfunction of the auto-cruise vacuum pump	
	Malfunction of the ECU	Replace the ECU.
The auto-cruise control system is not canceled when the brake pedals is depressed.	Damaged or disconnected wiring of the stop light switch input circuit; brake switch (for auto-cruise control) malfunction (short-circuit)	Repair the harness or replace the stop light switch.
	Auto-cruise vacuum pump drive circuit short-circuit.	Repair the harness or replace the auto-cruise vacuum pump.
	Malfunction of the ECU	Replace the ECU.
The auto-cruise control system is not canceled when the clutch pedal is depressed. (vehicles with a manual transaxle) (It is canceled, however, when the brake pedal is depressed.)	Damaged or disconnected wiring of clutch pedal position switch input circuit	Repair the harness, or repair or replace the clutch pedal position switch.
	Clutch pedal position switch improper installation (won't switch ON)	
	Malfunction of the ECU	Replace the ECU.
The auto-cruise control system is not canceled when the shift lever is moved to the "N" position. (vehicles with an automatic transaxle) (It is canceled, however, when the brake pedal is depressed.)	Damaged or disconnected wiring of park/neutral position switch input circuit	Repair the harness, or repair or replace the park/neutral position switch.
	Improper adjustment of park/neutral position switch	
	Malfunction of the ECU	Replace the ECU.
Cannot decelerate by using the SET switch	Temporary damaged or disconnected wiring of SET switch input circuit	Repair the harness or replace the SET switch.
	Auto-cruise vacuum pump circuit poor contact	Repair the harness or replace the auto-cruise vacuum pump and actuator.
	Malfunction of the auto-cruise vacuum pump and actuator (including clogging of negative pressure passage)	
	Malfunction of the ECU	Replace the ECU.

MT110910000403AX

Fig. 4 Troubleshooting (Part 3 of 4). 1993 Galant

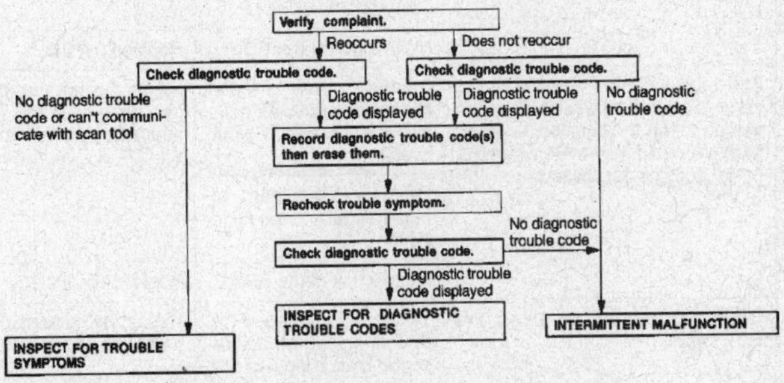

Verify complaint.
Reoccurs
Does not reoccur
Check diagnostic trouble code.
Check diagnostic trouble code.
No diagnostic trouble code or can't communicate with scan tool
Diagnostic trouble code displayed
Diagnostic trouble code displayed
No diagnostic trouble code
Record diagnostic trouble code(s) then erase them.
Recheck trouble symptom.
No diagnostic trouble code
Check diagnostic trouble code.
Diagnostic trouble code displayed
INSPECT FOR DIAGNOSTIC TROUBLE CODES
INTERMITTENT MALFUNCTION
INSPECT FOR TROUBLE SYMPTOMS

NOTE
Before carrying out trouble diagnosis, check all the following items.
1. Is the vacuum hose correctly installed and undamaged?
2. Are the auto-cruise, accelerator, and throttle cables routed correctly?
3. Do the link assembly and cables move smoothly?
4. Is the play of each cable within its standard value?

MT1109400043000X

Fig. 5 Troubleshooting. 1994–96 Galant, 1995–96 Eclipse & 1996 Montero

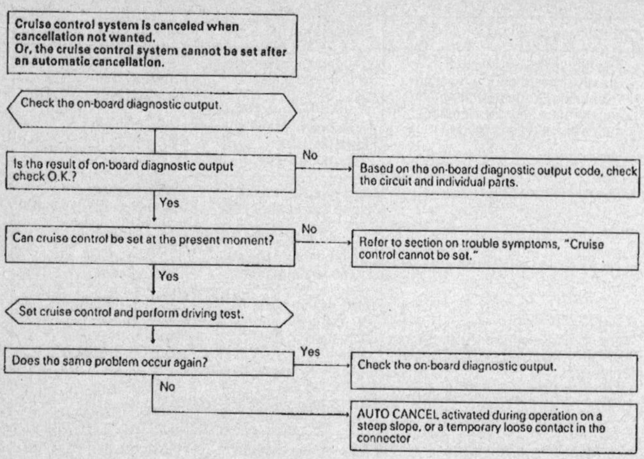

Cruise control system is canceled when cancellation not wanted.
Or, the cruise control system cannot be set after an automatic cancellation.
Check the on-board diagnostic output.
Is the result of on-board diagnostic output check O.K.?
No
Based on the on-board diagnostic output code, check the circuit and individual parts.
Yes
Can cruise control be set at the present moment?
No
Refer to section on trouble symptoms, "Cruise control cannot be set."
Yes
Set cruise control and perform driving test.
Does the same problem occur again?
Yes
Check the on-board diagnostic output.
No
AUTO CANCEL activated during operation on a steep slope, or a temporary loose contact in the connector

MT1109100005010X

Fig. 6 Troubleshooting (Part 1 of 4). Expo & 3000GT

Trouble symptom	Probable cause	Remedy
• The set vehicle speed varies greatly upward or downward. • "Hunting" (repeated alternating acceleration and deceleration) occurs after setting is made.	Malfunction of the vehicle speed sensor circuit	Repair the vehicle speed sensor system, or replace the part.
	Malfunction of the speedometer cable or speedometer drive gear <Up to 1993 models (Non turbo)>	
	Vacuum pump assembly circuit poor contact	Repair the actuator system, or replace the part.
	Malfunction of the vacuum pump assembly (including air leaks from negative pressure passage)	
	Malfunction of the ECU	Replace the ECU.
The cruise control system is not canceled when the brake pedal is depressed.	Brake switch (for cruise control) malfunction (short-circuit)	Repair the harness or replace the stop light switch.
	Vacuum pump assembly drive circuit short-circuit	Repair the harness or replace the vacuum pump assembly.
	Malfunction of the ECU	Replace the ECU.
The cruise control system is not canceled when the clutch pedal is depressed. <M/T> (It is canceled, however, when the brake pedal is depressed.)	Damaged or disconnected wiring of clutch switch input circuit	Repair the harness, or repair or replace the clutch switch.
	Clutch switch improper installation (won't switch ON)	
	Malfunction of the ECU	Replace the ECU.
The cruise control system is not canceled when the shift lever is moved to the "N" position. – <A/T> (It is canceled, however, when the brake pedal is depressed.)	Damaged or disconnected wiring of park/neutral position switch input circuit.	Repair the harness, or repair or replace the park/neutral position switch.
	Improper adjustment of park/neutral position switch	
	Malfunction of the ECU	Replace the ECU.
Cannot decelerate by using the SET switch.	Temporary damaged or disconnected wiring of control switch input circuit	Repair the harness or replace the control switch.
	Vacuum pump assembly circuit poor contact	Repair the harness or replace the vacuum pump assembly.
	Malfunction of the vacuum pump assembly	
	Malfunction of the ECU	Replace the ECU.

NOTE
ECU: Electronic control unit

MT1109100005030A

Fig. 6 Troubleshooting (Part 3 of 4). Expo & 3000GT

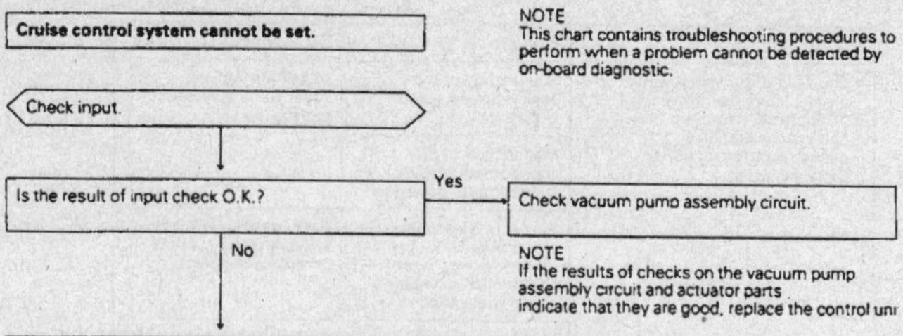

Cruise control system cannot be set.
NOTE
This chart contains troubleshooting procedures to perform when a problem cannot be detected by on-board diagnostic.
Check input.
Is the result of input check O.K.?
Yes
Check vacuum pump assembly circuit.
No
NOTE
If the results of checks on the vacuum pump assembly circuit and actuator parts indicate that they are good, replace the control uni

Result of check	Probable cause	Remedy
None of the codes appear even if input operations are performed.	Open circuit in control unit power supply circuit.	Replace main switch or repair harness.
	Open circuit in control switch circuit	Replace control switch or repair harness.
	Defective control unit	Replace control unit.
Even when SET switch is set to OFF, code No. 21 does not go away.	SET switch ON malfunction	Replace the control switch.
Even when RESUME switch is set to OFF, code No. 22 does not go away.	RESUME switch ON malfunction	Replace control switch.
Even when CANCEL switch is set to OFF, code No. 27 does not go away.	CANCEL switch ON malfunction	Replace control switch.
Even when brake pedal is depressed, code No. 23 is not displayed.	Defective stop light switch circuit	Replace stop light switch or repair harness.
Even when brake pedal is released, code No. 23 does not go away.		
Even when clutch pedal is released, code No. 26 does not go away. <M/T>	Defective clutch pedal position switch circuit	Replace clutch pedal position switch or repair harness.
Even when select lever is placed in any position other than "N" and "P", code No. 26 does not go away. <A/T>	Defective park/neutral position switch circuit	Replace park/neutral position switch or repair harness.
Code No. 25 is not displayed even when vehicle speed is less than about 40 km/h (25 mph).	Defective vehicle speed sensor circuit	Check and repair vehicle speed sensor circuit.
Even when vehicle speed is increased to more than about 40 km/h (25 mph), code No. 25 does not go away. Code No. 24 is not displayed, either.		

MT1109100005020X

Fig. 6 Troubleshooting (Part 2 of 4). Expo & 3000GT

Trouble symptom	Probable cause	Remedy
Cannot accelerate or resume speed by using the RESUME switch.	Open or short circuit in RESUME switch circuit in control switch	Replace the control switch.
	Vacuum pump assembly circuit poor contact	Repair the harness or replace the vacuum pump assembly.
	Malfunction of the vacuum pump assembly (including air leaks from negative pressure passage)	
	Malfunction of the ECU	Replace the ECU
Even when CANCEL switch is set to ON, cruise control is not canceled (Cruise control, however, is canceled when brake pedal is depressed.)	Open or short circuit in CANCEL switch circuit in control switch	Replace the control switch
	Malfunction of the ECU	Replace the ECU
The cruise control system can be set while traveling at a vehicle speed of less than 40 km/h (25 mph), or there is no automatic cancellation at that speed	Malfunction of the vehicle-speed sensor circuit	Repair the vehicle speed sensor system, or replace the part.
	Malfunction of the speedometer cable or the speedometer drive gear <Non turbo>	
	Malfunction of the ECU	Replace the ECU.
The cruise control indicator light of the combination meter does not illuminate (But cruise control system is normal)	Damaged or disconnected bulb of indicator light	Repair the harness or replace the light bulb.
	Harness damaged or disconnected	
	Malfunction of the ECU	Replace the ECU.
Cruise control ON indicator light does not come on. (However, cruise control is functional.)	Burned-out indicator light bulb	Repair the harness or replace the main switch.
	Open or short circuit in harness	
Malfunction of control function by ON/OFF switching of ELC 4 A/T accelerator switch (Non-operation of damper clutch, 2nd gear hold, etc.)	Malfunction of circuit related to accelerator switch OFF function	Repair the harness or replace the part.
	Malfunction of the ECU	
Overdrive is not canceled during fixed speed driving <A/T>	Malfunction of circuit related to overdrive cancellation, or malfunction of ECU	Repair the harness or replace the part.
No shift to overdrive during manual driving <A/T>		

MT1109100005040X

Fig. 6 Troubleshooting (Part 4 of 4). Expo & 3000GT

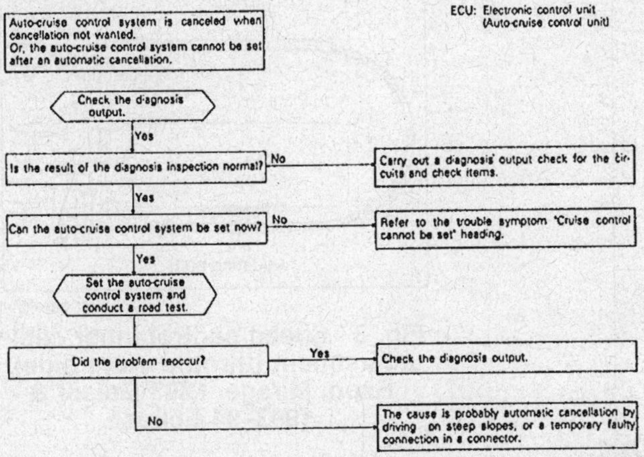
ECU: Electronic control unit
(Auto-cruise control unit)
Auto-cruise control system is canceled when cancellation not wanted.
Or, the auto-cruise control system cannot be set after an automatic cancellation.
Check the diagnosis output.
Yes
Is the result of the diagnosis inspection normal?
No
Carry out a diagnosis output check for the circuits and check items.
Yes
Can the auto-cruise control system be set now?
No
Refer to the trouble symptom "Cruise control cannot be set" heading.
Yes
Set the auto-cruise control system and conduct a road test.
Did the problem reoccur?
Yes
Check the diagnosis output.
No
The cause is probably automatic cancellation by driving on steep slopes, or a temporary faulty connection in a connector.

MT1109100006010X

Fig. 7 Troubleshooting (Part 1 of 5). Diamante

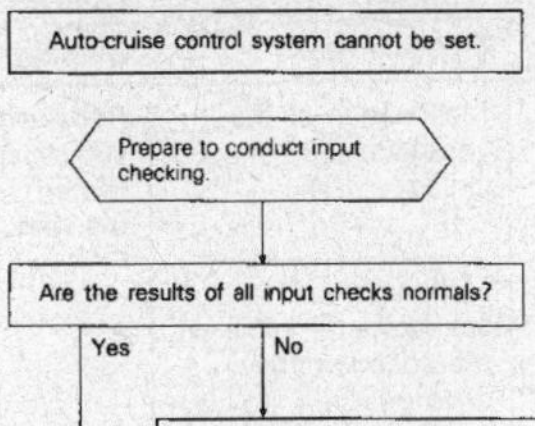
Auto-cruise control system cannot be set.
Prepare to conduct input checking.
Are the results of all input checks normals?
Yes
No

Check results	Probable cause	Remedy
Code 21 remains even though SET switch is set to OFF.	SET switch ON malfunction	Replace the control switch.
	SET switch input line short-circuit	Repair the harness.
Code 22 remains even though RESUME switch is set to OFF.	RESUME switch ON malfunction	Replace the control switch.
	RESUME switch input line short-circuit	Repair the harness.
Code 23 is not canceled even if the stop light switch is turned OFF by releasing the brake pedal.	Malfunction of stop light switch circuit.	Replace stop light switch or repair harness.
Code 25 does not disappear, and code 24 does not appear, even though vehicle speed reaches approximately 40 km/h (25 mph) or higher.	Malfunction of the vehicle speed sensor circuit (damaged or disconnected wiring, or short-circuit)	Check or repair the vehicle speed sensor circuit.
Code 26 is not canceled even if the selector lever is moved to anything but N, P	Malfunction of park/neutral position switch circuit.	Replace inhibitor switch or repair harness.
Code 27 remains even when the CANCEL switch is set to OFF.	Malfunction of CANCEL switch circuit	Replace the control switch or repair the harness.
Code 28 remains even when the accelerator pedal is released.	Malfunction of throttle position sensor circuit or accelerator position sensor circuit.	Replace the sensor or repair the harness.
Code 29 remains even when closed throttle position switch is set to ON.	Malfunction of closed throttle position switch circuit.	Replace the switch or repair the harness.

Check the auto-cruise vacuum pump circuit.

NOTE
If the results of the check of the auto-cruise vacuum pump circuit and the auto-cruise vacuum pump and/or actuator themselves reveal no abnormal condition, replace the electronic control unit (ECU).

MT1109100006020X

Fig. 7 Troubleshooting (Part 2 of 5). Diamante

Trouble symptom	Probable cause	Remedy
• The set vehicle speed varies gratly upward or downward. • "Hunching" (repeated alternating acceleration and deceleration) occurs after setting is made.	Malfunction of the vehicle speed sensor circuit	Repair the vehicle speed sensor system, or replace the part.
	Malfunction of the speedometer cable or speedometer drive gear	
	Auto-cruise vacuum pump circuit poor contact	Repair auto-cruise vacuum pump assembly or replace the part.
	Malfunction of the ECU	Replace the ECU.
The auto-cruise control system is not canceled when the brake pedal is depressed.	Damaged or disconnected wiring of the stop light switch input circuit: brake switch (for auto-cruise control) malfunction (short-circuit)	Repair the harness or replace the stop light switch.
	Auto-cruise vacuum pump drive circuit short-circuit	Repair the harness or replace the auto-cruise vacuum pump.
	Malfunction of the ECU	Replace the ECU

NOTE
ECU: Electronic control unit

MT1109100006030X

Fig. 7 Troubleshooting (Part 3 of 5). Diamante

Trouble symptom	Probable cause	Remedy
The auto-cruise control system is not canceled when the selector lever is moved to the "N". position. (Vehicles with an automatic transaxle) (It is canceled, however, when the brake pedal is depressed.)	Damaged or disconnected wiring of park/neutral position switch input circuit	Repair the harness, or repair or replace the park/neutral position switch
	Improper adjustment of park/neutral position switch	
	Malfunction of the ECU	Replace the ECU.
Cannot decelerate by using the SET switch	Temporary damaged or disconnected wiring of SET switch input circuit	Repair the harness or replace the auto-cruise control switch.
	Auto-cruise vacuum pump circuit poor contact	Repair the harness or replace the auto-cruise vacuum pump.
	Malfunction of the vacuum pump assembly (including air leaks from negative pressure passage)	
	Malfunction of the ECU	Replace the ECU.
Cannot accelerate or resume speed by using the RESUME switch.	Damaged or disconnected wiring, or short-circuit, of RESUME switch input circuit	Repair the harness or replace the auto-cruise control switch.
	Auto-cruise vacuum pump circuit poor contact	Repair the harness or replace the auto-cruise vacuum pump.
	Malfunction of the vacuum pump assembly (including air leaks from negative pressure passage)	
	Malfunction of the ECU	Replace the ECU.
Cruise control does not cancel even when the CANCEL switch is set to ON. (However, it is cancelled when the brake pedal is depressed.)	Broken wire in the CANCEL switch circuit inside the control switch	Repair the harness or replace the auto-cruise control switch.
	Malfunction of the ECU	Replace the ECU.

MT1109100006040X

Fig. 7 Troubleshooting (Part 4 of 5). Diamante

Trouble symptom	Probable cause	Remedy
Auto-cruise control system can be set while traveling at a vehicle speed of less than 40 km/h (25 mph), or there is no automatic cancellation at that speed	Malfunction of the vehicle-speed sensor circuit	Repaire the vehicle-speed sensor system, or replace the part.
	Malfunction of the speedometer cable or the speedometer drive gear	
	Malfunction of the ECU	Replace the ECU.
The indicator lamp of the main switch does not illuminate. (But auto-cruise control system is normal.)	Damaged or disconnected bulb of indicator lamp Malfunction of the main switch	Repair the harness or replace the main switch.
	Harness damaged or disconnected	
Malfunction of control function by ON/OFF switching of ELC 4 A/T accelerator switch (Non-operation of damper clutch, 2nd gear hold, etc.)	Malfunction of circuit related to accelerator switch OFF function	Repair the harness or replace the part.
	Malfunction of the ECU	Replace the ECU
Overdrive is not canceled during fixed speed driving.	Malfunction of circuit related to overdrive cancelation, or malfunction of ECU	Repair the harness or replace the part.
No shift to overdrive during manual driving		

MT1109100006050X

Fig. 7 Troubleshooting (Part 5 of 5). Diamante

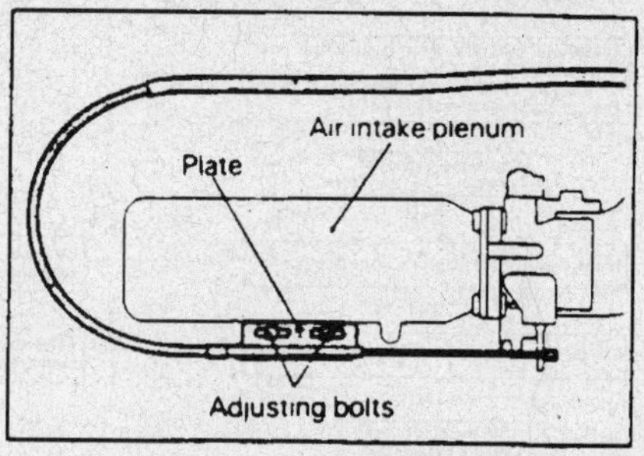
Air intake plenum
Plate
Adjusting bolts
MT1109100007000X

Fig. 8 Speed control inner cable adjustment (throttle valve side). Expo, Mirage, 1993 Galant & 1993–94 Eclipse

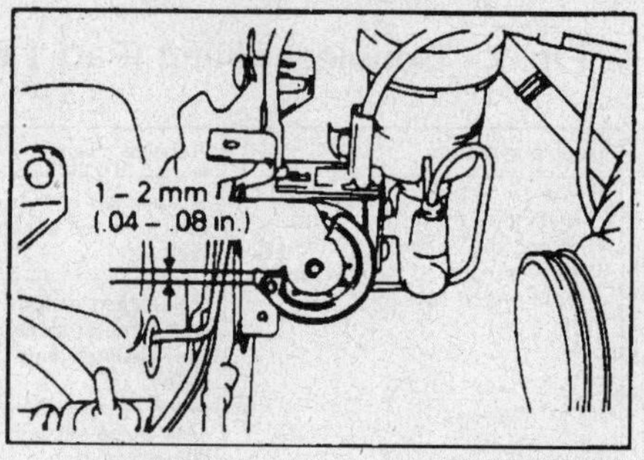
1 – 2 mm
(.04 – .08 in.)
MT1109100010000X

Fig. 11 Throttle lever measurement. Expo, Mirage, 1993–94 Eclipse & 1993 Galant

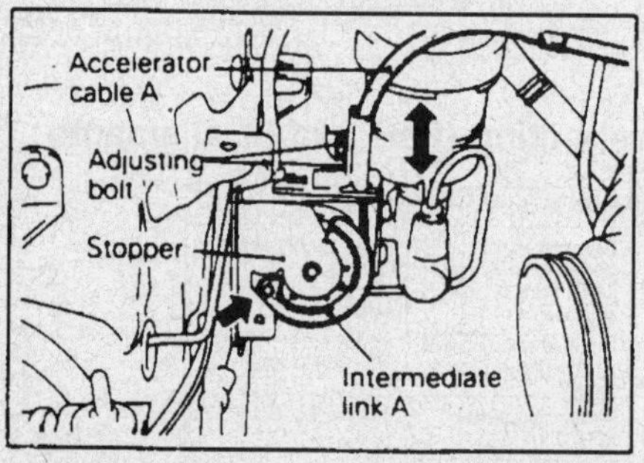
Accelerator cable A
Adjusting bolt
Stopper
Intermediate link A
MT1109100008000X

Fig. 9 Speed control inner cable adjustment (accelerator pedal side). Mirage

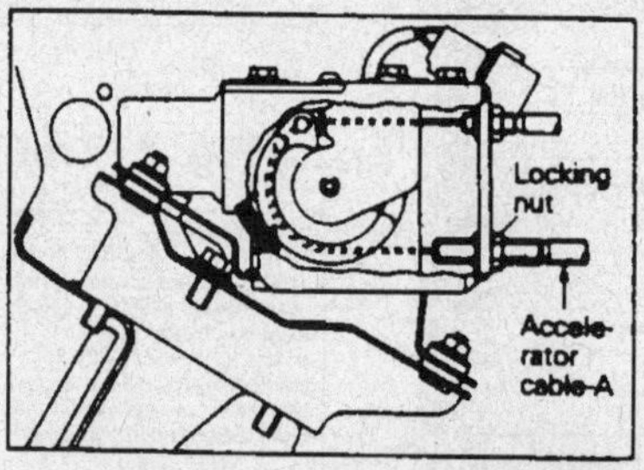
Locking nut
Accelerator cable-A
MT1109100009000X

Fig. 10 Speed control inner cable adjustment (accelerator pedal side). 1993–94 Eclipse & 1993 Galant

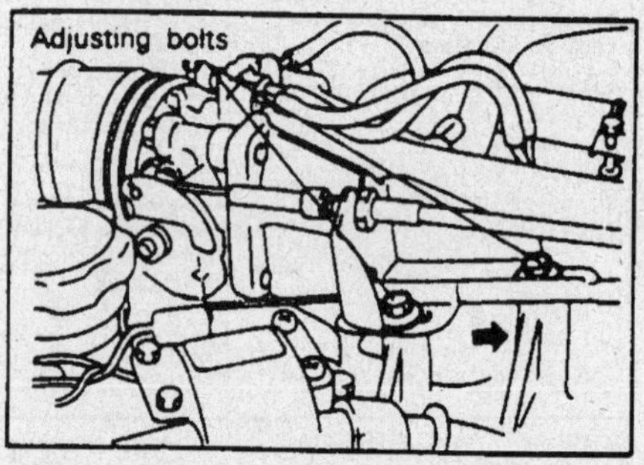
Adjusting bolts
MT1109100012000X

Fig. 14 Speed control outer cable freeplay adjustment. 1993–95 Montero

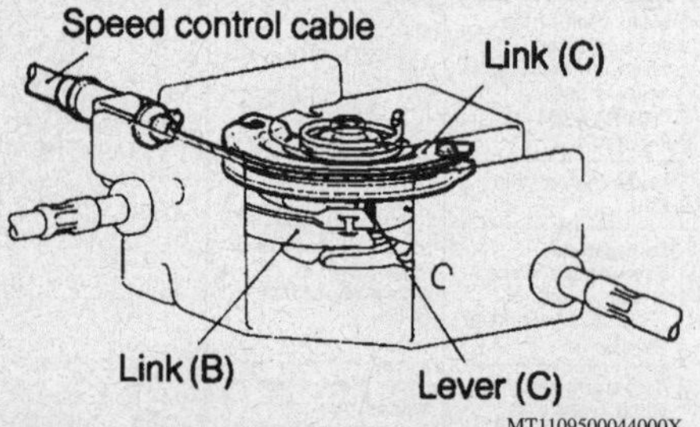
Speed control cable
Link (C)
Link (B)
Lever (C)
MT1109500044000X

Fig. 12 Speed control cable adjustment. 1995–96 Eclipse w/2.0L non-turbocharged engine

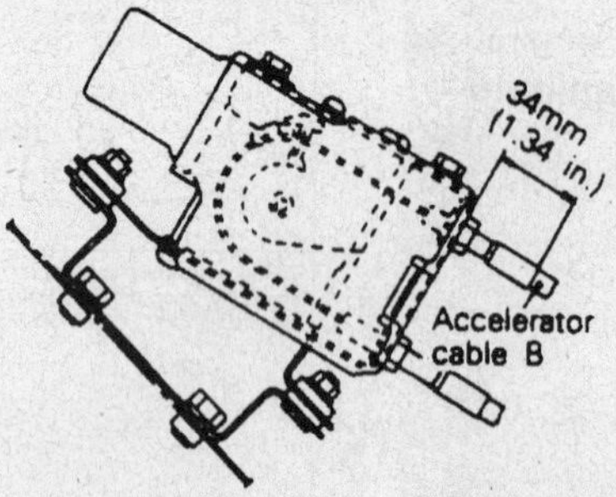
34mm
(1.34 in.)
Accelerator cable B
MT1109100011000X

Fig. 13 Speed control cable A measurement. 1993–95 Montero

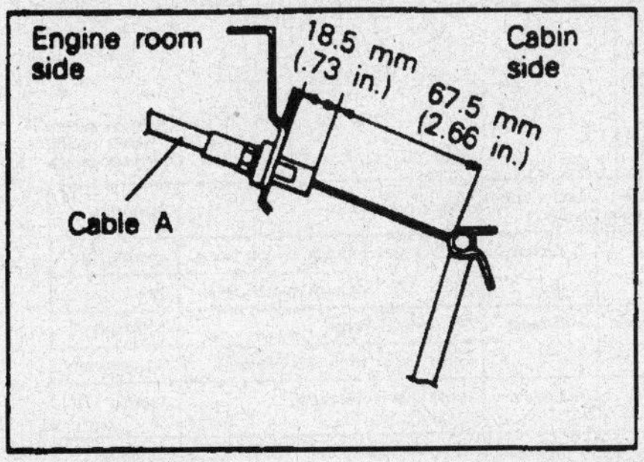
Engine room side
18.5 mm (.73 in.)
Cabin side
67.5 mm (2.66 in.)
Cable A
MT1109100013000X

Fig. 15 Speed control outer cable measurement. 1993–95 Montero

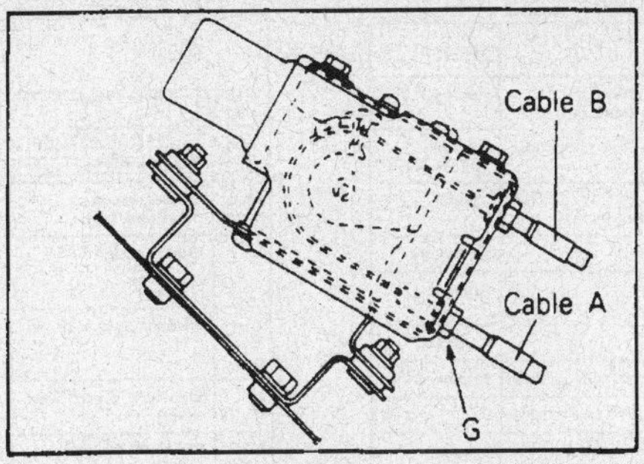
Cable B
Cable A
G
MT1109100014000X

Fig. 16 Speed control cable freeplay adjustment. 1993–95 Montero

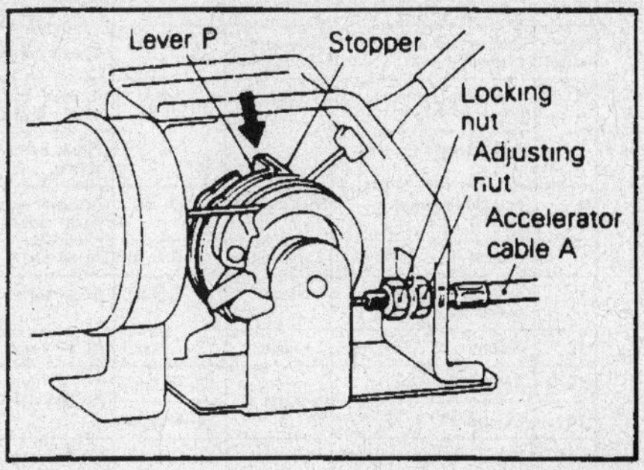
Lever P
Stopper
Locking nut
Adjusting nut
Accelerator cable A
MT1109100015000X

Fig. 17 Speed control outer cable freeplay adjustment. Pickup

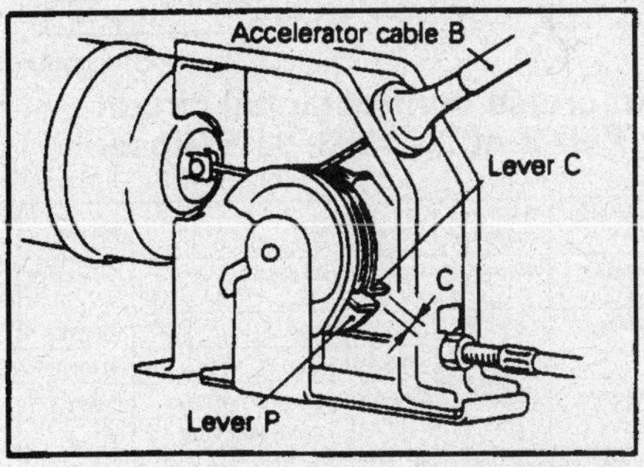
Accelerator cable B
Lever C
C
Lever P
MT1109100016000X

Fig. 18 Speed control cable B freeplay adjustment. Pickup

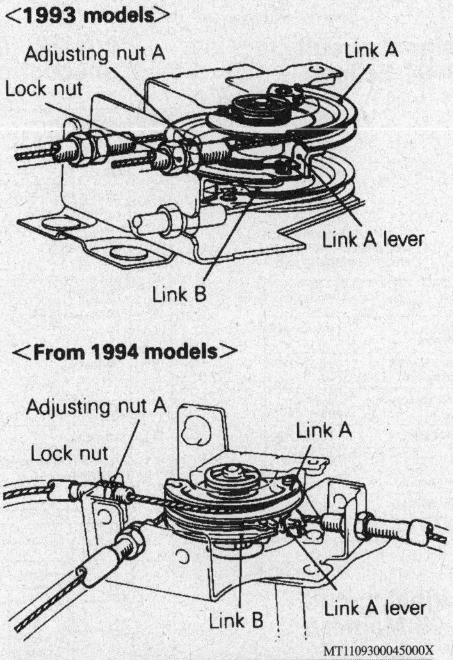
<1993 models>
Adjusting nut A
Link A
Lock nut
Link A lever
Link B
<From 1994 models>
Adjusting nut A
Link A
Lock nut
Link B
Link A lever
MT1109300045000X

Fig. 19 Auto cruise control cable adjustment. Diamante

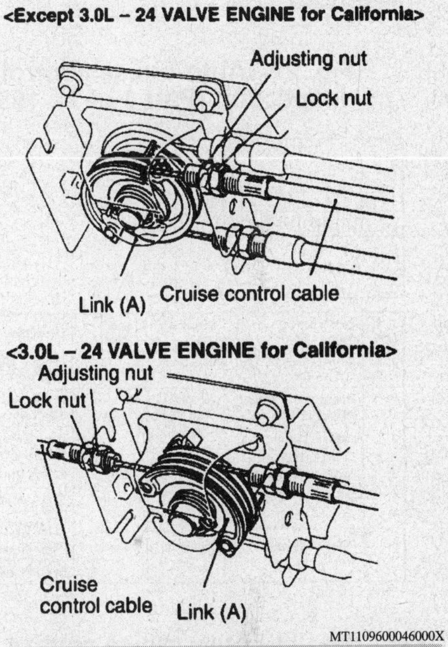
<Except 3.0L – 24 VALVE ENGINE for California>
Adjusting nut
Lock nut
Link (A)
Cruise control cable
<3.0L – 24 VALVE ENGINE for California>
Adjusting nut
Lock nut
Cruise control cable
Link (A)
MT1109600046000X

Fig. 20 Auto cruise control cable adjustment. 1996 Montero

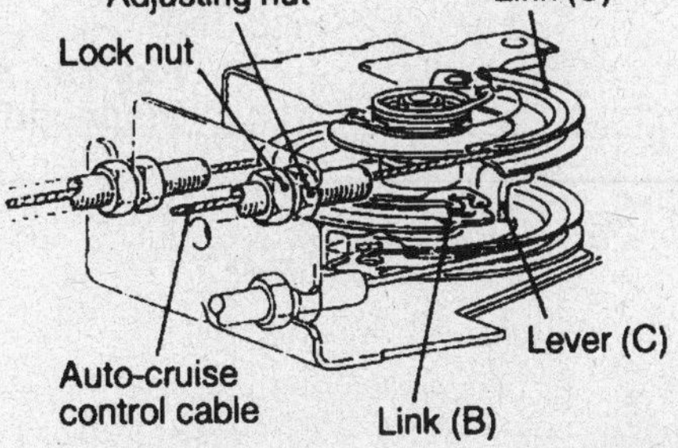
Adjusting nut
Link (C)
Lock nut
Lever (C)
Auto-cruise control cable
Link (B)
MT1109400046000X

Fig. 21 Auto cruise control cable adjustment. 3000GT, 1995–96 Eclipse w/2.0L turbocharged engine & 2.4L Engine & 1994–96 Galant

Terminal	Connection or measured part	Measurement item	Tester connection	Check conditions	Standard
8	Stop light switch (for auto-cruise control cancellation) and actuator (clutch)	Voltage	8–Ground	IG S/W ON, Main S/W ON (Don't press brake pedal.)	Approx. 12V
				Press brake pedal after checking above.	Approx. 12V → 0V
9, 20	Actuator (motor)	Resistance	9→20	Actuator selector (Fully closed position)	Approx. 12Ω
10	Ground	Continuity	10–Ground	At all times	Continuity
11	Stop light switch power supply side	Voltage	11–Ground	At all times	Approx. 12V
12	Ground	Continuity	12–Ground	At all times	Continuity
13	4WD control unit	Voltage	13–Ground	IG S/W ON: OD S/W ON position	Approx. 12V
14	OD switch		14–Ground	OD S/W OFF position	0V
15	Vehicle speed sensor	Voltage	15–Ground	With the ignition key at the ON position, slowly turn the speedometer cable.	4 voltage changes/cable rotation
16	Accelerator switch	Voltage	16–Ground	IG S/W ON (Accelerator pedal free)	Approx. 12V
				Press accelerator pedal after checking above.	Approx. 12V → 0V
17*2	Self-diagnosis	–	–	–	–

MT1109100031010X

Fig. 22 Auto cruise control signal circuit inspection (Part 1 of 2). 1993–94 Eclipse

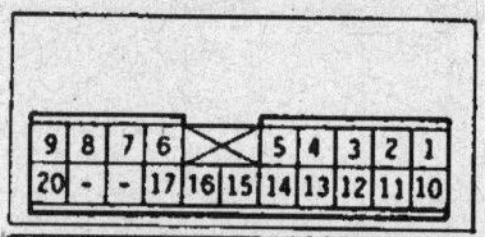

9 8 7 6 5 4 3 2 1
20 - - 17 16 15 14 13 12 11 10

IG S/W: Ignition switch
MAIN S/W: MAIN switch
OD S/W: Overdrive switch

Terminal	Connection or measured part	Measurement item	Tester connection	Check conditions		Standard
1	Clutch switch	Voltage	1–Ground	IG S/W ON	Clutch switch ON	Approx. 12V
					Clutch switch OFF	0V
2	Inhibitor switch (P, N)	Continuity	2–Ground	"P" or "N" range		Continuity
				Other than "P" or "N" range		No continuity
3	Stop light switch load side	Voltage	3–Ground	Press the brake pedal.		Approx. 12V
4	RESUME switch	Continuity	4–Ground	RESUME switch ON (Turn)		Continuity
				RESUME switch OFF (Release)		No continuity
5	SET switch	Continuity	5–Ground	SET switch ON (Press)		Continuity
				SET switch OFF (Release)		No continuity
6	Power supply (IG_2)	Voltage	6–Ground	IG switch ON		Approx. 12V
7	Power supply (Main)	Voltage	7–Ground	IG S/W ON, Main S/W ON		Approx. 12V

MT1109100031020X

Fig. 22 Auto cruise control signal circuit inspection (Part 2 of 2). 1993–94 Eclipse

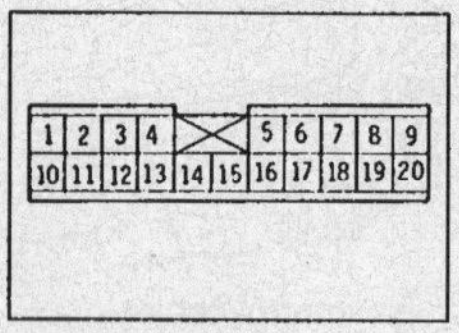

1 2 3 4 5 6 7 8 9
10 11 12 13 14 15 16 17 18 19 20

IG S/W : Ignition switch
MAIN S/W : MAIN switch
OD S/W : Overdrive switch

Terminal	Connection or measured part	Measurement item	Tester connection	Check conditions	Standard
1, 10	Actuator (motor)	Resistance	9–*120	Actuator selector (Fully closed position)	Approx. 12Ω
2	Stop light switch (for auto-cruise control cancellation) and actuator (clutch)	Voltage	8-Ground	IG S/W ON, MAIN S/W ON (Don't press brake pedal.)	Approx. 12V
				Press brake pedal after checking above.	Approx. 12V → 0V
3	Power supply (MAIN)	Voltage	7-Ground	IG S/W ON, MAIN S/W ON	Approx. 12V
5	SET switch	Continuity	5-Ground	SET switch ON (Press)	Continuity
				SET switch OFF (Release)	No continuity
6	RESUME switch	Continuity	4-Ground	RESUME switch ON (Turn)	Continuity
				RESUME switch OFF (Release)	No continuity

MT1109100029010X

Fig. 23 Auto cruise control signal circuit inspection (Part 1 of 2). 1993–95 Montero

Terminal	Connection or measured part	Measurement item	Tester connection	Check conditions		Standard
7	Stop light switch load side	Voltage	3-Ground	Press the brake pedal.		Approx. 12V
8	Inhibitor switch (P, N)	Continuity	2-Ground	"P" or "N" range		Continuity
				Other than "P" or "N" range		No continuity
9	Clutch switch	Voltage	1-Ground	IG S/W ON	Clutch switch ON	Approx. 12V
					Clutch switch OFF	0V
13*2	Self-diagnosis	—	—	—		—
15	Vehicle speed sensor	Voltage	15-Ground	With the ignition key at the ON position, slowly turn the speedometer cable.		4 voltage changes/cable rotation
16*2	OD switch	Voltage	14-Ground	IG S/W ON	OD S/W ON position	Approx. 12V
					OD S/W OFF position	0V
17	Overdrive solenoid	Continuity	13-Ground	At all times		Continuity
18	Ground	Continuity	12-Ground	At all times		Continuity
19	Stop light switch power supply side	Voltage	11-Ground	At all times		Approx. 12V
20	Ground	Continuity	10-Ground	At all times		Continuity

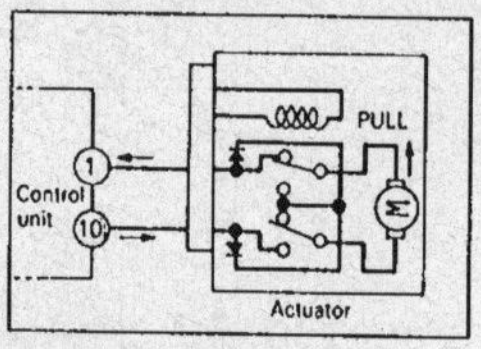

PULL
Control unit
1
10
Actuator

NOTE

1. As shown by the *1 symbol, the limit switch within the actuator will become as shown in the figure at the left if the actuator selector is at the fully closed position when the resistance between terminals No. 1 and No. 10 is measured; for that reason, after checking the polarity of the tester, the tester's probe should be connected so that current flows from the No.10 terminal to the No. 1 terminal.
2. For terminals No. 13 and 16 indicated by the *2 symbol, it is necessary to check individual terminal voltages with the auto-cruise control unit's harness connector connected and with the ignition switch ON.
   (1) The No. 13 terminal is normal if the self-diagnosis code can be confirmed.
   (2) The No. 16 terminal is normal if there is approximately 12V with the auto-cruise control system not functioning and the overdrive switch switched ON.

MT1109100029020X

Fig. 23 Auto cruise control signal circuit inspection (Part 2 of 2). 1993–95 Montero

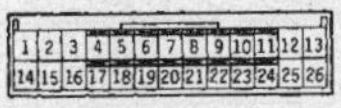
1 2 3 4 5 6 7 8 9 10 11 12 13
14 15 16 17 18 19 20 21 22 23 24 25 26

Terminal No.	Check item	Check conditions		Normal condition
1	Clutch pedal position switch input <M/T>	When pedal is not depressed	When clutch pedal position switch is OFF	Battery positive voltage
		When pedal is depressed	When clutch pedal position switch is ON	0V
	Park/neutral position switch input <A/T>	When selector lever is in a position other than N range	When park/neutral position switch is OFF	Battery positive voltage
		When selector lever is in N range	When park/neutral position switch is ON	0V
2	ECU power supply	When ignition switch is ON		Battery positive voltage
3	Power supply for OD signal control <A/T>	When ignition switch is ON		Battery positive voltage
4	Closed throttle position switch output	When accelerator pedal is depressed	When closed throttle position switch is OFF	4.5–5.5V
		When accelerator pedal is not depressed	When closed throttle position switch is ON	0V
5	Throttle position sensor input	When accelerator pedal is fully depressed		4.0–5.5V
		When accelerator pedal is released		0.5–0.7V
6	Ground	At all times		Continuity
8	Ground	At all times		Continuity
10	OD control output <A/T>	When OD switch is ON		Battery positive voltage
		When OD switch is OFF		0V
11	OD switch input <A/T>	When OD switch is ON		Battery positive voltage
		When OD switch is OFF		0V
12	Auto-cruise vacuum pump release valve and control valve input	When driving at constant speed using the SET switch	Release valve closed	0V
13			Control valve closed	0V
12		When accelerating with the RESUME switch while driving at constant speed	Release valve closed	0V
13			Release valve closed	0V
12		When decelerating with the SET switch while driving at constant speed	Release valve closed	0V
13			Control valve open	Battery positive voltage
12		When canceling constant-speed driving with the CANCEL switch	Release valve open	Battery positive voltage
13			Control valve open	Battery positive voltage

MT1109500151010X

Fig. 24 Auto cruise control signal circuit inspection (Part 1 of 2). 1995–96 Eclipse & 1996 Montero

Terminal No.	Check item	Check conditions		Normal condition
14	Ground	At all times		Continuity
15	Stop light switch input	When brake pedal is depressed	When stop light switch is ON	Battery positive voltage
		When brake pedal is not depressed	When stop light switch is OFF	0V
16	ECU backup power supply	At all times		Battery positive voltage
18	Auto-cruise control switch input	When SET switch is pressed	When SET switch is ON	3V
		When SET switch is not pressed	When SET switch is OFF	0V
		When RESUME switch is pressed	When RESUME switch is ON	6V
		When RESUME switch is not pressed	When RESUME switch is OFF	0V
		When CANCEL switch is pressed	When CANCEL switch is ON	Battery positive voltage
		When CANCEL switch is not pressed	When CANCEL switch is OFF	0V
19	Vehicle speed sensor input	When vehicle is moved forwards and backwards, sensor turns ON and OFF repeatedly.	When sensor is ON	0V
			When sensor is OFF	4.5 V or more
20	ACC power supply	When ignition switch is in ACC position		Battery positive voltage
23	Indicator input (inside combination meter)	When driving at constant speed	When indicator is illuminated	0V
		When constant-speed driving is cancelled	When indicator is switched off	Battery positive voltage
24	Diagnosis control input	When ignition switch is ON		4V or more
25	Surge absorption circuit terminal	When auto-cruise main switch is ON		Battery positive voltage
26	Auto-cruise vacuum pump motor input	When driving at constant speed using the SET switch	Motor stopped	Battery positive voltage
		When accelerating with the RESUME switch while driving at constant speed	Motor running	0V
		When decelerating with the SET switch while driving at constant speed	Motor stopped	Battery positive voltage
		When cancelling constant-speed driving with the CANCEL switch	Motor stopped	Battery positive voltage

MT1109500151020X

Fig. 24 Auto cruise control signal circuit inspection (Part 2 of 2). 1995–96 Eclipse & 1996 Montero

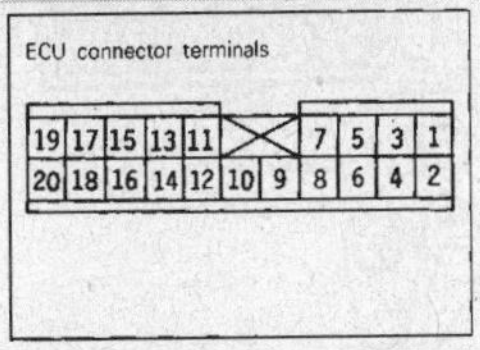
ECU connector terminals
19 17 15 13 11 7 5 3 1
20 18 16 14 12 10 9 8 6 4 2

IG S/W: Ignition switch
MAIN S/W: Main switch
OD S/W: Overdrive switch

Terminal	Connection or measured part	Measurement item	Tester connection	Check conditions	Standard
1	Actuator (motor)	Resistance	1→*1 2	Actuator selector (Fully closed position)	Approx. 12Ω
2					
3	Stop light switch (for auto-cruise control cancellation) and actuator (clutch)	Voltage	3–Ground	IG S/W ON, Main S/W ON (Don't press brake pedal.)	System voltage
				Press brake pedal after checking above.	System voltage →0V
5	Power supply (MAIN)	Voltage	5–Ground	IG S/W ON, Main S/W ON	System voltage
6	None	–	–	–	–
7	Power supply (IG_2)	Voltage	7–Ground	IG S/W ON	System voltage
8*2	Self-diagnosis	–	–	–	–
9	Accelerator pedal switch	Voltage	9–Ground	IG S/W ON (Accelerator pedal free)	System voltage
				Press accelerator pedal after checking above.	System voltage →0V
10	Vehicle speed sensor	Voltage	10–Ground	With the ignition key at the ON position, slowly turn the speedometer cable.	4 voltage changes/ cable rotation
11	SET switch	Continuity	11–Ground	SET switch ON (Press)	Continuity
				SET switch OFF (Release)	No continuity
12	OD switch	Voltage	12–Ground	IG S/W ON OD S/W ON position	System voltage
				OD S/W OFF position	0V
13	RESUME switch	Continuity	13–Ground	RESUME switch ON (Turn)	Continuity
				RESUME switch OFF (Release)	No continuity
14	4 A/T control unit	–	–	–	–
15	Stop light switch load side	Voltage	15–Ground	Press the brake pedal	System voltage
16	Ground	Continuity	16–Ground	At all times	Continuity

MT1109100030010X

Fig. 25 Auto cruise control signal circuit inspection (Part 1 of 2). 1993 Galant

Terminal	Connection of measured part	Measurement item	Tester connection	Check conditions		Standard
17	Park/neutral position switch (P, N)	Continuity	17–Ground	"P" or "N" range		Continuity
				Other than "P" or "N" range		No continuity
18	Stop light switch power supply side	Voltage	18–Ground	At all times		Battery positive voltage
19	Clutch pedal position switch	Voltage	19–Ground	IG S/W ON	Clutch pedal position switch ON	Battery positive voltage
					Clutch pedal position switch OFF	0V
20	Ground	Continuity	20–Ground	At all times		Continuity

MT1109100030020X

Fig. 25 Auto cruise control signal circuit inspection (Part 2 of 2). 1993 Galant

1 2 3 4 5 6 7 8 9 10 11 12 13
14 15 16 17 18 19 20 21 22 23 24 25 26

Terminal No.	Check item	Check conditions		Normal condition
1	Clutch pedal position switch input <M/T>	When pedal is not depressed	When clutch pedal position switch is OFF	Battery positive voltage
		When pedal is depressed	When clutch pedal position switch is ON	0V
	Park/neutral position switch input <A/T>	When select lever is in a position other than N range	When park/neutral position switch is OFF	5V
		When select lever is in N range	When park/neutral position switch is ON	0V
2	ECU power supply	When ignition switch is ON		Battery positive voltage
3	Power supply for OD signal control <A/T>	–		Battery positive voltage
4	Closed throttle position switch output	When accelerator pedal is depressed	When idle switch is OFF	4.5–5.5V
		When accelerator pedal is not depressed	When idle switch is ON	0V
5	Throttle position sensor input	When accelerator pedal is fully depressed		4.0–5.5V
		When accelerator pedal is released		0.5–0.7V
6	Ground	–		Continuity
8	Ground	–		Continuity
10	OD control output <A/T>	When OD switch is ON		Battery positive voltage
		When OD switch is OFF		0V
11	OD switch input <A/T>	When OD switch is ON		Battery positive voltage
		When OD switch is OFF		0V
12	Auto-cruise vacuum pump release valve and control valve input	When driving at constant speed using the SET switch	Release valve closed	0V
13			Control valve closed	0V
12		When accelerating with the RESUME switch while driving at constant speed	Release valve closed	0V
13			Release valve closed	0V
12		When decelerating with the SET switch while driving at constant speed	Release valve closed	0V
13			Control valve open	Battery positive voltage
12		When cancelling constant-speed driving with the CANCEL switch	Release valve open	Battery positive voltage
13			Control valve open	Battery positive voltage
14	Ground	–		Continuity

MT1109400152010X

Fig. 26 Auto cruise control signal circuit inspection (Part 1 of 2). 1994–96 Galant

Terminal No.	Check item	Check conditions		Normal condition
15	Stop light switch input	When brake pedal is depressed	When stop light switch is ON	Battery positive voltage
		When brake pedal is not depressed	When stop light switch is OFF	0V
16	ECU backup power supply	–		Battery positive voltage
18	Auto-cruise control switch input	When SET switch is pressed	When SET switch is ON	3V
		When SET switch is not pressed	When SET switch is OFF	0V
		When RESUME switch is pressed	When RESUME switch is ON	6V
		When RESUME switch is not pressed	When RESUME switch is OFF	0V
		When CANCEL switch is pressed	When CANCEL switch is ON	Battery positive voltage
		When CANCEL switch is not pressed	When CANCEL switch is OFF	0V
19	Vehicle speed sensor input	When vehicle is moved forwards and backwards, sensor turns ON and OFF repeatedly.	When sensor is ON	0V
			When sensor is OFF	4.5 V or more
20	ACC power supply	When ignition switch is in ACC position		Battery positive voltage
23	Indicator input (inside combination meter)	When driving at constant speed	When indicator is illuminated	0V
		When constant-speed driving is cancelled	When indicator is switched off	Battery positive voltage
24	Diagnosis control input	When ignition switch is ON		4V or more
26	Auto-cruise vacuum pump motor input	When driving at constant speed using the SET switch	Motor stopped	Battery positive voltage
		When accelerating with the RESUME switch while driving at constant speed	Motor running	0V
		When decelerating with the SET switch while driving at constant speed	Motor stopped	Battery positive voltage
		When cancelling constant-speed driving with the CANCEL switch	Motor stopped	Battery positive voltage

MT1109400152020X

Fig. 26 Auto cruise control signal circuit inspection (Part 2 of 2). 1994–96 Galant

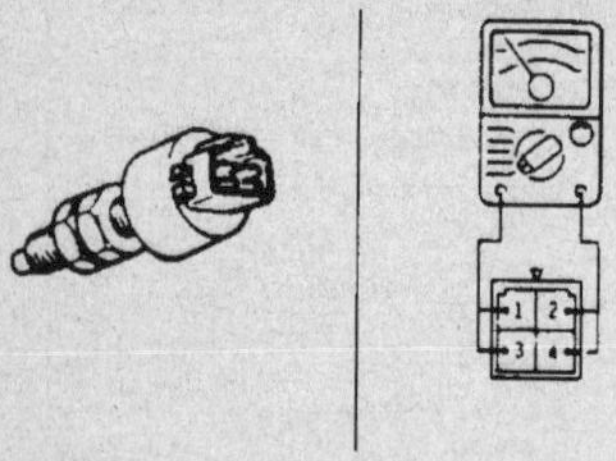
1 2
3 4

MT1109100017000X

Fig. 27 Stop lamp/brake switch terminal identification

O–O :Continuity

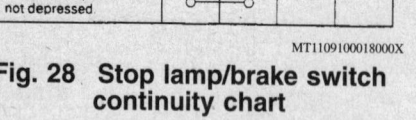

Measurement conditions \ Switch / Terminal	Brake switch 1	Brake switch 4	Stop light switch 2	Stop light switch 3
When brake pedal depressed.			O–	–O
When brake pedal not depressed	O–	–O		

MT1109100018000X

Fig. 28 Stop lamp/brake switch continuity chart

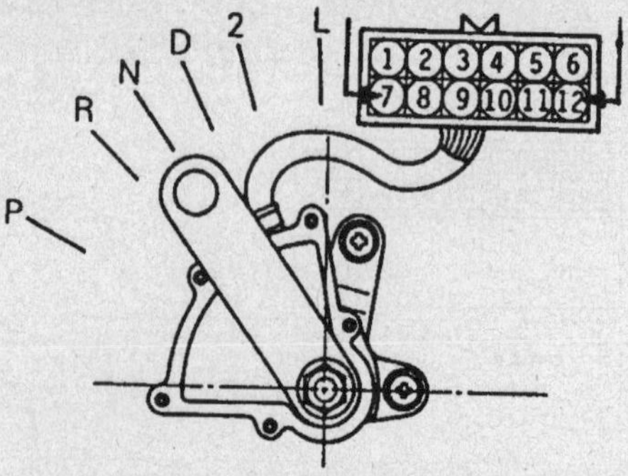
P
R
N
D
2
L
1 2 3 4 5 6
7 8 9 10 11 12

MT1109200019000X

Fig. 29 PNP switch N & P position inspection. Montero

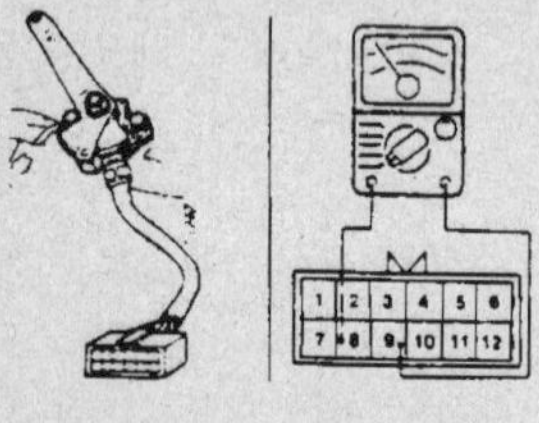
1 2 3 4 5 6
7 8 9 10 11 12

MT1109100020000X

Fig. 30 PNP switch N & P position inspection. Diamante, Eclipse, Expo, Galant, Mirage, Pickup & 3000GT

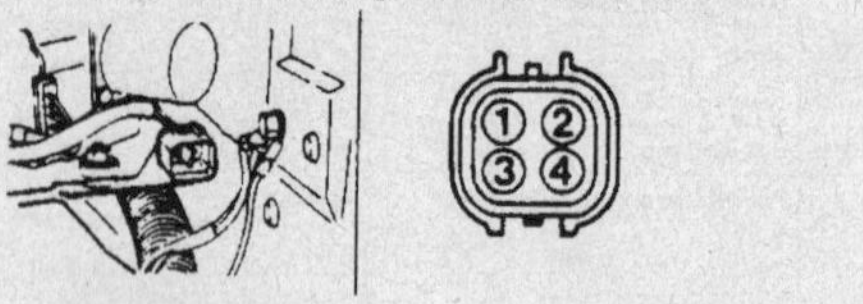
1 2
3 4

MT1109100021000X

Fig. 31 Actuator inspection

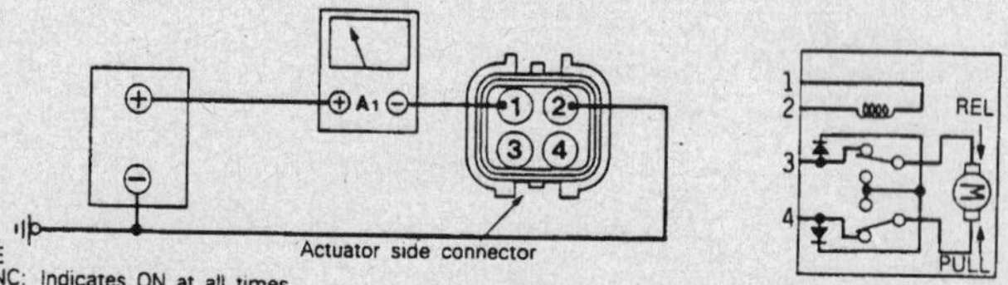
A1
1 2
3 4
Actuator side connector
1
2
3
4
REL
PULL
M
Actuator

NOTE
(1) NC: Indicates ON at all times.
(2) NO: Indicates OFF at all times.

MT1109100022000X

Fig. 32 Actuator circuit inspection. Except Pickup

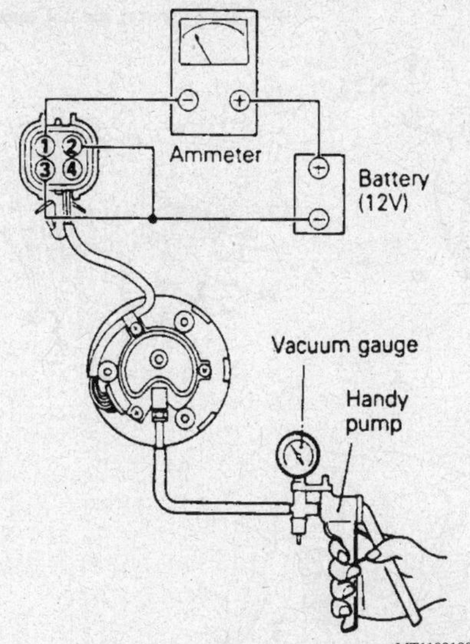

Ammeter
1 2
3 4
Battery (12V)
Vacuum gauge
Handy pump

MT1109100023000X

Fig. 33 Actuator operation inspection. Pickup

Judgement		Probable cause
Normal	Abnormal	
Holder keeps its position • Gauge negative pressure reading constant • Ammeter: 0.5 – 0.6A	Holder returns to initial position • Gauge reading constant • Ammeter: 0.5 – 0.6A	Leaks from VENT1 or VENT2 valve seal (foreign matter caught in valve, etc.)
	Holder returns to initial position • Gauge reading: 0 mmHg. (0 in. Hg.) • Ammeter: 0.5 – 0.6A	VAC valve and VENT valves both sealing poorly

MT1109100025000X

Fig. 35 Actuator operation inspection (VAC solenoids off). Pickup

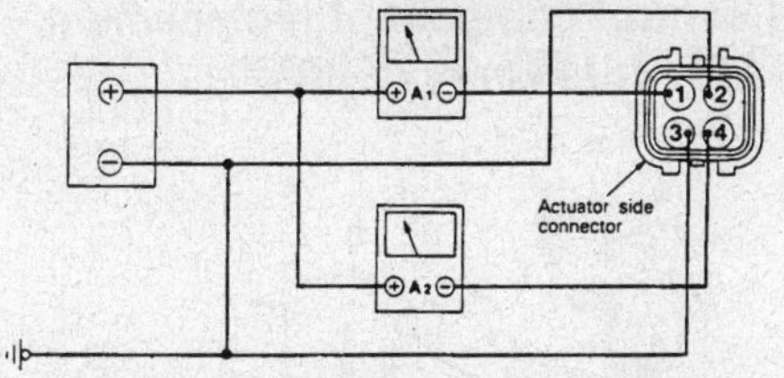

A1
A2
1 2
3 4
Actuator side connector

MT1109100027000X

Fig. 37 Motor pull direction & limit switch operation. Except Pickup

Judgement		Probable cause
Normal	Abnormal	
Holder moves in PULL direction • Gage indicates negative pressure • Ammeter indicates 1.5A or less	Holder does not move in PULL direction • Ammeter: 0A	Open circuit in lead wire Open circuit in valve solenoid coil
	Holder does not move in PULL direction • Ammeter: 0.7 – 1.5A • No gauge indication	Faulty solenoid valve in actuator (foreign matter caught inside)
	Holder does not move in PULL direction • Ammeter: 0.5 – 0.6A • Gauge gives indication	Open circuit in VAC side solenoid or valve remaining closed
	Holder once moves in PULL direction but soon moves back • Ammeter: 0.4 – 0.5A	Open circuit in VENT1 or VENT2 solenoid

MT1109100024000X

Fig. 34 Actuator operation inspection (VAC, VENT1, VENT2 solenoids on). Pickup

Judgement		Probable cause
Normal	Abnormal	
Holder returns to initial position • Gauge negative pressure reading remains as (2) • Ammeter: 0.2 – 0.4A	Holder does not return to initial position • Gauge negative pressure reading remaining as (2)	• VENT valve binding • Atmosphere section filter completely loaded

MT1109100026000X

Fig. 36 Actuator operation inspection (VAC or VENT1, VENT2 solenoids off). Pickup

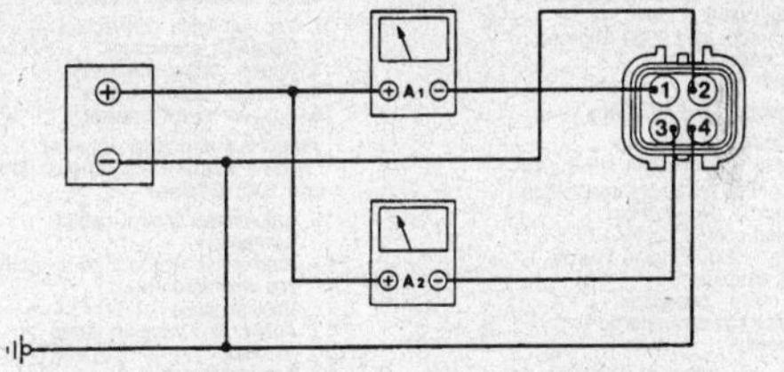

A1
A2
1 2
3 4

MT1109100028000X

Fig. 38 Motor release direction & limit switch operation. Except Pickup

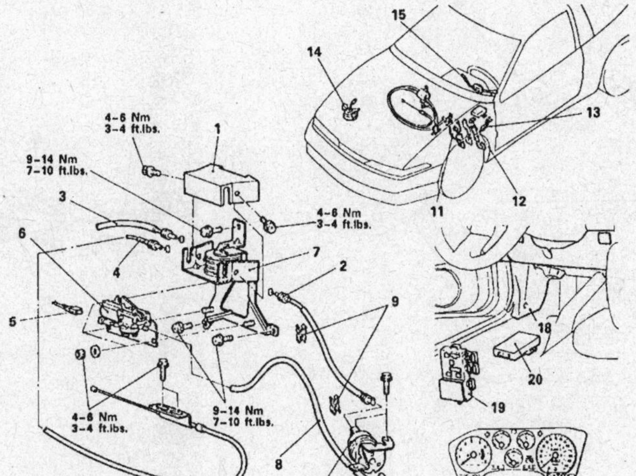

4-6 Nm
3-4 ft.lbs.
9-14 Nm
7-10 ft.lbs.
4-6 Nm
3-4 ft.lbs.
4-6 Nm
3-4 ft.lbs.
9-14 Nm
7-10 ft.lbs.
1
2
3
4
5
6
7
8
9
10
11
12
13
14
15
16
17
18
19
20

Removal steps of actuator

1. Link protector
2. Auto-cruise control cable
3. Accelerator cable
4. Throttle cable
5. Auto-cruise control vacuum pump connector
6. Auto-cruise control vacuum pump
7. Link assembly
8. Vacuum hose
9. Clip
10. Auto-cruise control actuator

Removal steps of sensor and switches

11. Accelerator switch <A/T>
12. Stop light switch
13. Clutch pedal position switch <M/T>
14. Park/Neutral position switch <A/T>
15. Auto-cruise control switch
16. Vehicle speed sensor
17. Auto-cruise control indicator light

Removal steps of control unit

18. Cowl side trim
19. Junction block
20. Auto-cruise control unit

MT1109100032000X

Fig. 39 Speed control component replacement. 1993–94 Eclipse

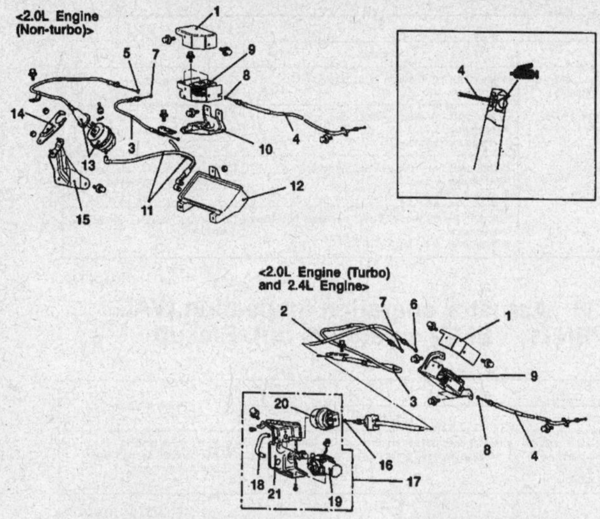

<2.0L Engine (Non-turbo)>
<2.0L Engine (Turbo) and 2.4L Engine>

Auto-cruise control cable, throttle cable and accelerator cable removal steps

1. Link protector
- Auto-cruise control cable adjustment
2. Auto-cruise control cable <2.0L Engine (Turbo) and 2.4L Engine>
3. Throttle cable
4. Accelerator cable

Link assembly removal steps

1. Link protector
- Auto-cruise control cable adjustment
5. Speed control assembly connection <2.0L Engine (Non-turbo)>
6. Auto-cruise control cable connection <2.0L Engine (Turbo) and 2.4L Engine>
7. Throttle cable connection
8. Accelerator cable connection
9. Link assembly
10. Link bracket <2.0L Engine (Non-turbo)>

Reservoir assembly and speed control assembly removal steps <2.0L Engine (Non-turbo)>

11. Vacuum hose connection
12. Reservoir assembly
13. Speed control assembly
14. Actuator upper bracket
15. Actuator lower bracket

Vacuum pump and actuator removal steps <2.0L Engine (Turbo) and 2.4L Engine>

16. Auto-cruise control cable connection
17. Auto-cruise vacuum pump and actuator assembly
18. Vacuum hose
19. Auto-cruise vacuum pump
20. Actuator
21. Actuator bracket

MT1109500154010X

Fig. 40 Speed control component replacement (Part 1 of 3). 1995–96 Eclipse

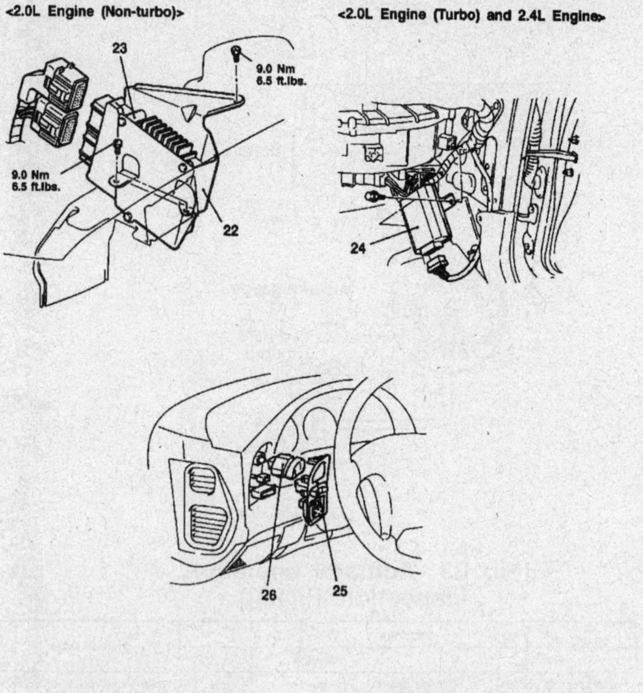

<2.0L Engine (Non-turbo)>
<2.0L Engine (Turbo) and 2.4L Engine>
9.0 Nm
6.5 ft.lbs.
9.0 Nm
6.5 ft.lbs.

Powertrain control module removal steps <2.0L Engine (Non-turbo)>

- Air cleaner
22. Powertrain control module bracket
23. Powertrain control module

Auto-cruise control – ECU removal steps <2.0L Engine (Turbo) and 2.4L Engine>

- Cowl side trim
24. Auto-cruise control-ECU

Auto-cruise control main switch removal steps

25. Instrument panel switch
26. Auto-cruise control main switch

MT1109500154020X

Fig. 40 Speed control component replacement (Part 2 of 3). 1995–96 Eclipse

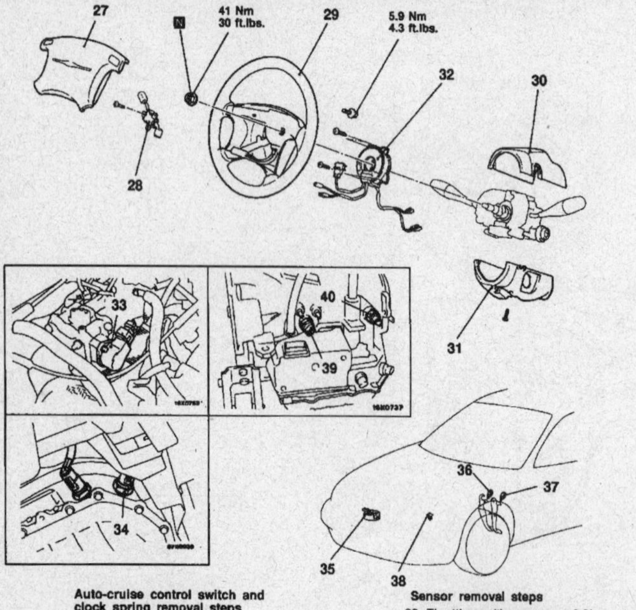

41 Nm
30 ft.lbs.
5.9 Nm
4.3 ft.lbs.

Auto-cruise control switch and clock spring removal steps

27. Air bag module
28. Auto-cruise control switch
29. Steering wheel
30. Steering column upper cover
31. Steering column lower cover
- Instrument under cover
32. Clock spring

Sensor removal steps

33. Throttle position sensor <2.0L Engine (Turbo) and 2.4L Engine>
34. Transaxle range switch <2.0L Engine (Non-turbo) – A/T>
35. Park/neutral position switch <2.0L Engine (Turbo) – A/T and 2.4L Engine – A/T>
36. Stop light switch
37. Clutch pedal position switch <2.0L Engine (Turbo) – M/T and 2.4L Engine – M/T>
38. Vehicle speed sensor <Except 2.0L Engine (Non-turbo) – A/T>
39. Input speed sensor <2.0L Engine (Non-turbo) – A/T>
40. Output speed sensor <2.0L Engine (Non-turbo) – A/T>

MT1109500154030X

Fig. 40 Speed control component replacement (Part 3 of 3). 1995–96 Eclipse

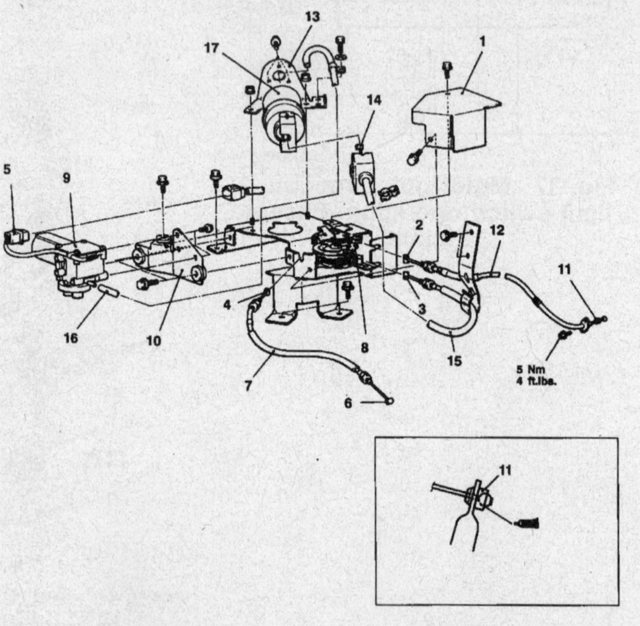

5 Nm
4 ft.lbs.

Removal steps

- Cruise control cables adjustment
1. Link protector
2. Accelerator cable and link assembly connection
3. Cruise control cable and link assembly connection
4. Throttle cable link assembly connection
5. Vacuum pump connector
6. Throttle cable and throttle body connection
7. Throttle cable
8. Link assembly
9. Vacuum pump
10. Pump bracket
11. Bush connection
12. Accelerator cable
13. Actuator bracket
14. Cruise control cable and actuator connection
15. Cruise control cable
16. Vacuum hose
17. Actuator

MT1109300153010X

Fig. 41 Speed control component replacement (Part 1 of 2). Expo

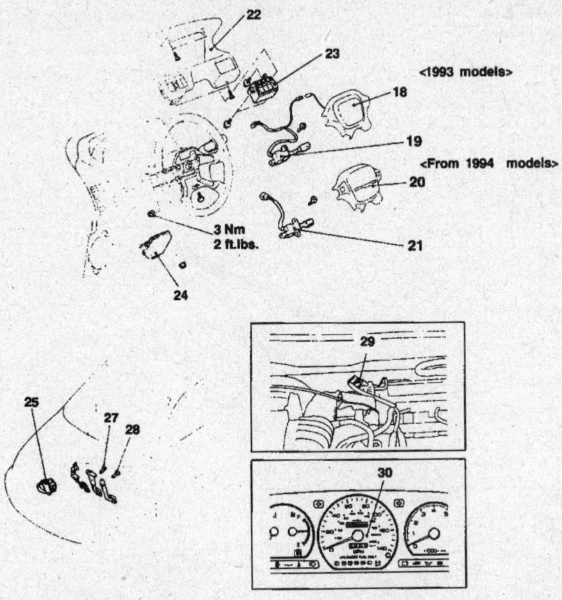

<1993 models>
<From 1994 models>
3 Nm
2 ft.lbs.

Control switch and control unit removal steps

18. Horn pad <1993 models>
19. Control switch <1993 models>
20. Air bag module <From 1994 models>
21. Control switch <From 1994 models>
22. Meter hood
23. Main switch (Cluster switch assembly)
- Instrument under cover
24. Control unit

Sensor and switches removal steps

25. Park/neutral position switch
27. Stop light switch
28. Clutch pedal position switch <M/T>
29. Throttle position sensor (with built-in closed throttle position switch)
30. Vehicle speed sensor

MT1109300153020X

Fig. 41 Speed control component replacement (Part 2 of 2). Expo

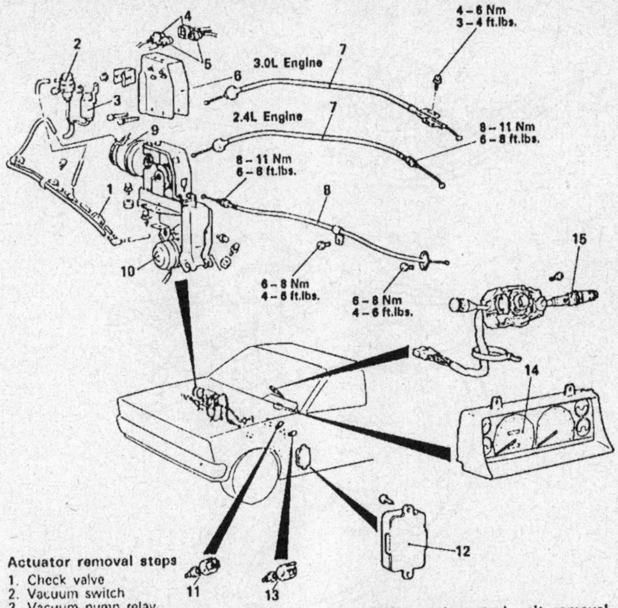

4 – 6 Nm
3 – 4 ft.lbs.
3.0L Engine
2.4L Engine
8 – 11 Nm
6 – 8 ft.lbs.
6 – 8 Nm
4 – 6 ft.lbs.

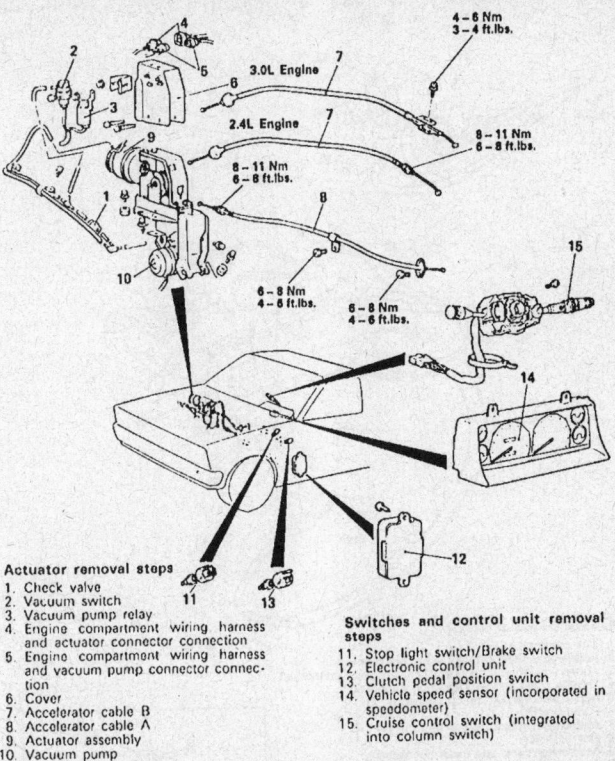

Actuator removal steps

1. Check valve
2. Vacuum switch
3. Vacuum pump relay
4. Engine compartment wiring harness and actuator connector connection
5. Engine compartment wiring harness and vacuum pump connector connection
6. Cover
7. Accelerator cable B
8. Accelerator cable A
9. Actuator assembly
10. Vacuum pump

Switches and control unit removal steps

11. Stop light switch/Brake switch
12. Electronic control unit
13. Clutch pedal position switch
14. Vehicle speed sensor (incorporated in speedometer)
15. Cruise control switch (integrated into column switch)

MT1109100033000X

Fig. 42 Speed control component replacement. Pickup

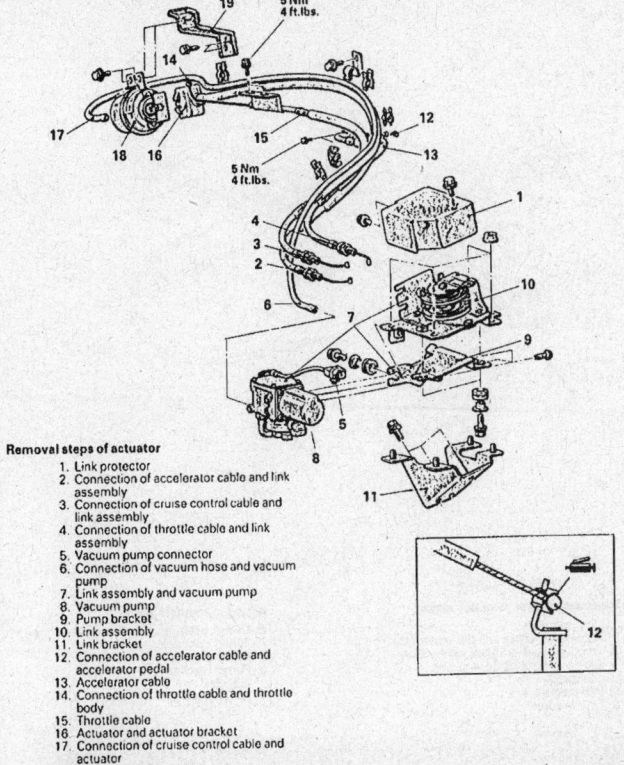

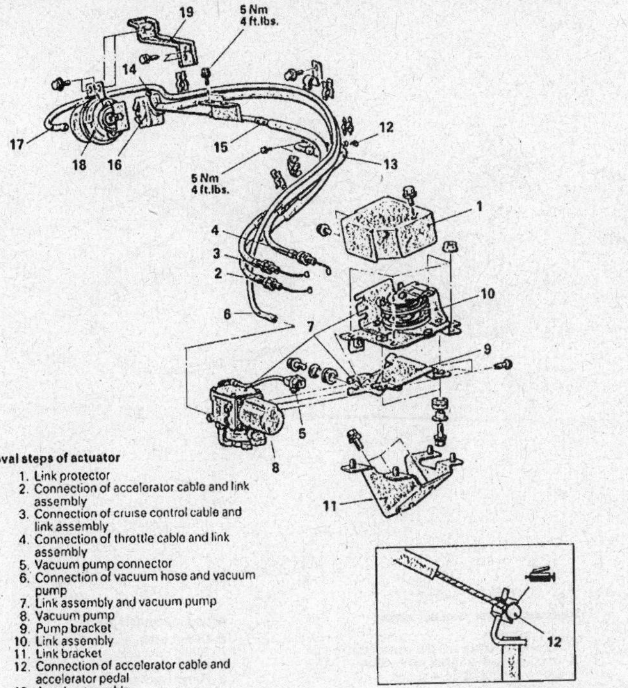

5 Nm
4 ft.lbs.

Removal steps of actuator

1. Link protector
2. Connection of accelerator cable and link assembly
3. Connection of cruise control cable and link assembly
4. Connection of throttle cable and link assembly
5. Vacuum pump connector
6. Connection of vacuum hose and vacuum pump
7. Link assembly and vacuum pump
8. Vacuum pump
9. Pump bracket
10. Link assembly
11. Link bracket
12. Connection of accelerator cable and accelerator pedal
13. Accelerator cable
14. Connection of throttle cable and throttle body
15. Throttle cable
16. Actuator and actuator bracket
17. Connection of cruise control cable and actuator
18. Actuator
19. Actuator bracket

MT1109100034010X

Fig. 43 Speed control component replacement (Part 1 of 2). 3000GT

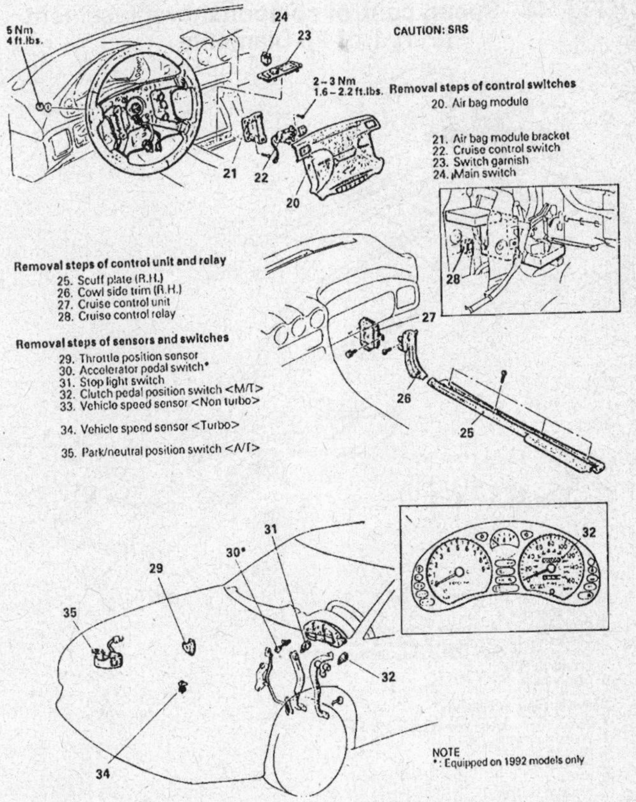

5 Nm
4 ft.lbs.
CAUTION: SRS
2 – 3 Nm
1.6 – 2.2 ft.lbs.
Removal steps of control switches
20. Air bag module
21. Air bag module bracket
22. Cruise control switch
23. Switch garnish
24. Main switch
Removal steps of control unit and relay
25. Scuff plate (R.H.)
26. Cowl side trim (R.H.)
27. Cruise control unit
28. Cruise control relay
Removal steps of sensors and switches
29. Throttle position sensor
30. Accelerator pedal switch*
31. Stop light switch
32. Clutch pedal position switch <M/T>
33. Vehicle speed sensor <Non turbo>
34. Vehicle speed sensor <Turbo>
35. Park/neutral position switch <A/T>
NOTE
*: Equipped on 1992 models only

MT1109100034020X

Fig. 43 Speed control component replacement (Part 2 of 2). 3000GT

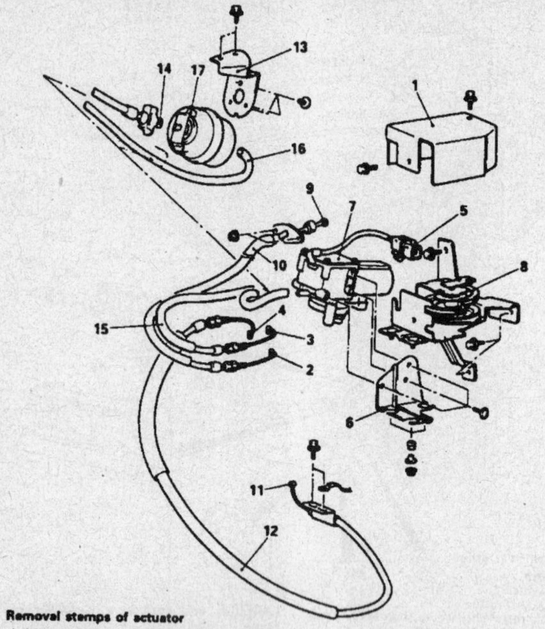

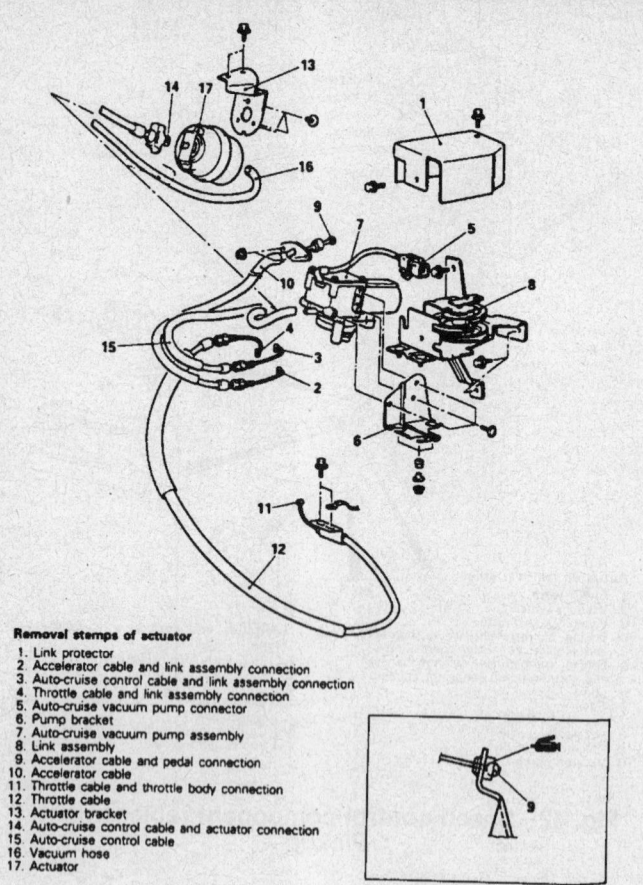

Removal stemps of actuator

1. Link protector
2. Accelerator cable and link assembly connection
3. Auto-cruise control cable and link assembly connection
4. Throttle cable and link assembly connection
5. Auto-cruise vacuum pump connector
6. Pump bracket
7. Auto-cruise vacuum pump assembly
8. Link assembly
9. Accelerator cable and pedal connection
10. Accelerator cable
11. Throttle cable and throttle body connection
12. Throttle cable
13. Actuator bracket
14. Auto-cruise control cable and actuator connection
15. Auto-cruise control cable
16. Vacuum hose
17. Actuator

MT1109100036010X

Fig. 44 Speed control component replacement (Part 1 of 2). Diamante

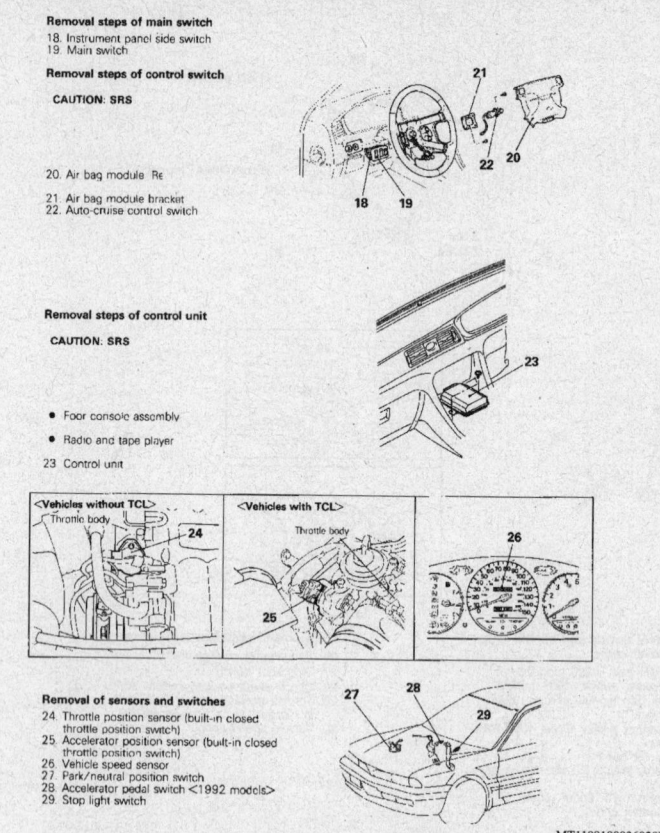

Removal steps of main switch

18. Instrument panel side switch
19. Main switch

Removal steps of control switch

CAUTION: SRS

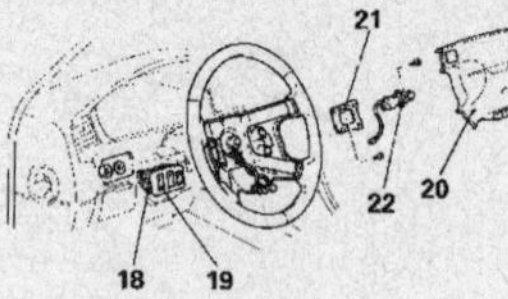

20. Air bag module Re
21. Air bag module bracket
22. Auto-cruise control switch

Removal steps of control unit

CAUTION: SRS

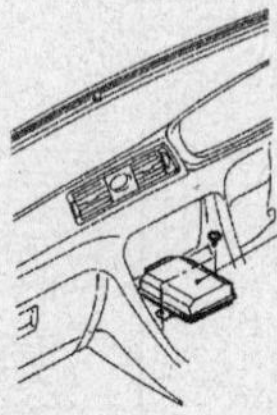

- Foor console assembly
- Radio and tape player

23. Control unit

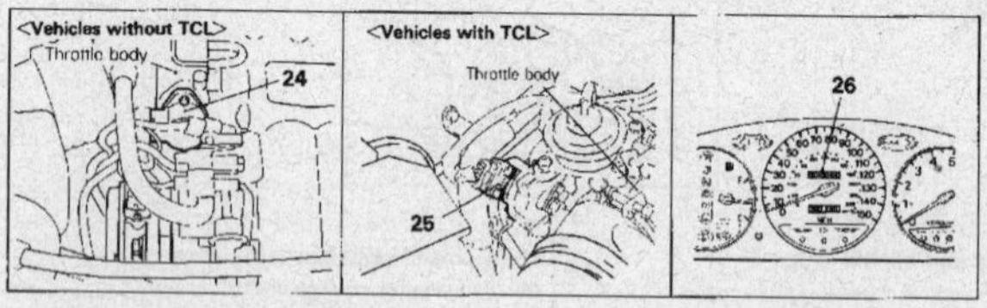
<Vehicles without TCL>
Throttle body
<Vehicles with TCL>
Throttle body

Removal of sensors and switches

24. Throttle position sensor (built-in closed throttle position switch)
25. Accelerator position sensor (built-in closed throttle position switch)
26. Vehicle speed sensor
27. Park/neutral position switch
28. Accelerator pedal switch <1992 models>
29. Stop light switch

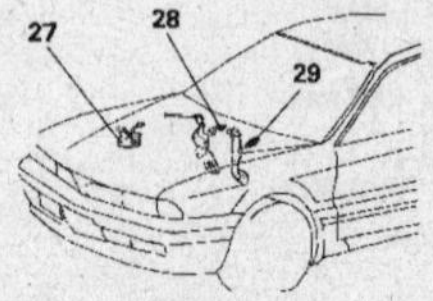

MT1109100036020X

Fig. 44 Speed control component replacement (Part 2 of 2). Diamante

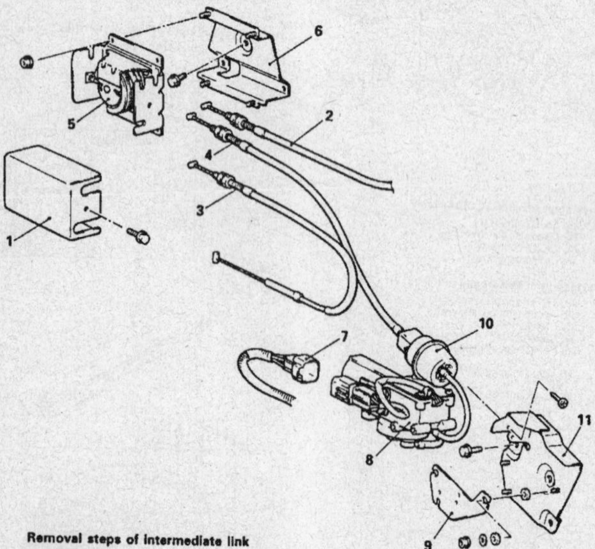

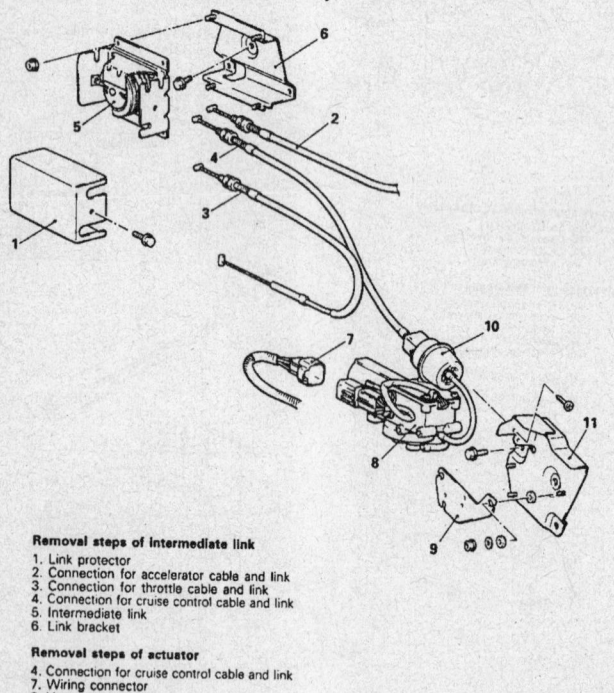

Removal steps of intermediate link

1. Link protector
2. Connection for accelerator cable and link
3. Connection for throttle cable and link
4. Connection for cruise control cable and link
5. Intermediate link
6. Link bracket

Removal steps of actuator

4. Connection for cruise control cable and link
7. Wiring connector
8. Vacuum pump
9. Pump bracket
10. Actuator
11. Actuator bracket

MT1109200037010X

Fig. 45 Speed control component replacement (Part 1 of 2). Montero except 1996 w/3.0L 24 valve engine & California emissions

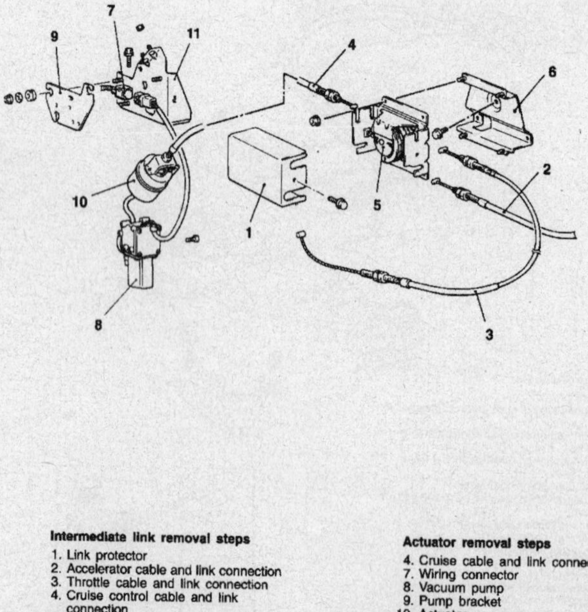

Intermediate link removal steps

1. Link protector
2. Accelerator cable and link connection
3. Throttle cable and link connection
4. Cruise control cable and link connection
5. Intermediate link
6. Link bracket

Actuator removal steps

4. Cruise cable and link connection
7. Wiring connector
8. Vacuum pump
9. Pump bracket
10. Actuator
11. Actuator bracket

MT110920003701AX

Fig. 45 Speed control component replacement (Part 1 of 2). 1996 Montero w/3.0L 24 valve engine & California emissions

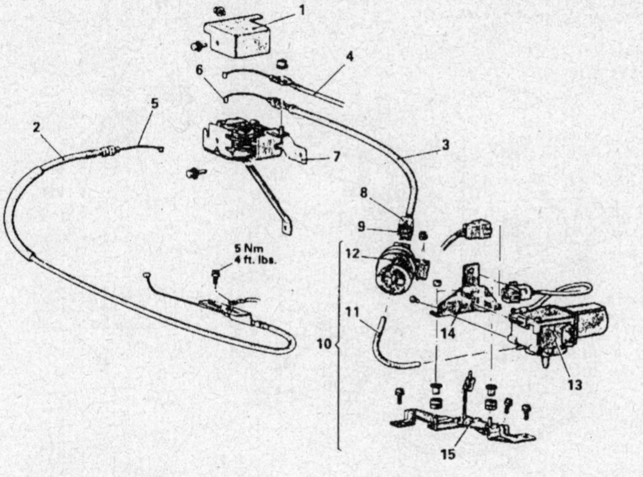
1
4
6
5
2
3
7
8
9
12
5 Nm
4 ft. lbs.
11
10
14
13
15

Throttle cable and auto-cruise control cable removal steps
1. Link protector
2. Throttle cable
3. Auto-cruise control cable

Link assembly removal steps
1. Link protector
4. Accelerator cable connection
5. Throttle cable connection
6. Auto-cruise control cable connection
7. Link assembly

Actuator removal steps
8. Cover
9. Auto-cruise control cable connection
10. Actuator and pump assembly (Part No. 11–15)
11. Vacuum hose
12. Actuator
13. Vacuum pump
14. Pump bracket
15. Actuator and pump bracket

MT1109300039010X

Fig. 46 Speed control component replacement (Part 1 of 3). Mirage

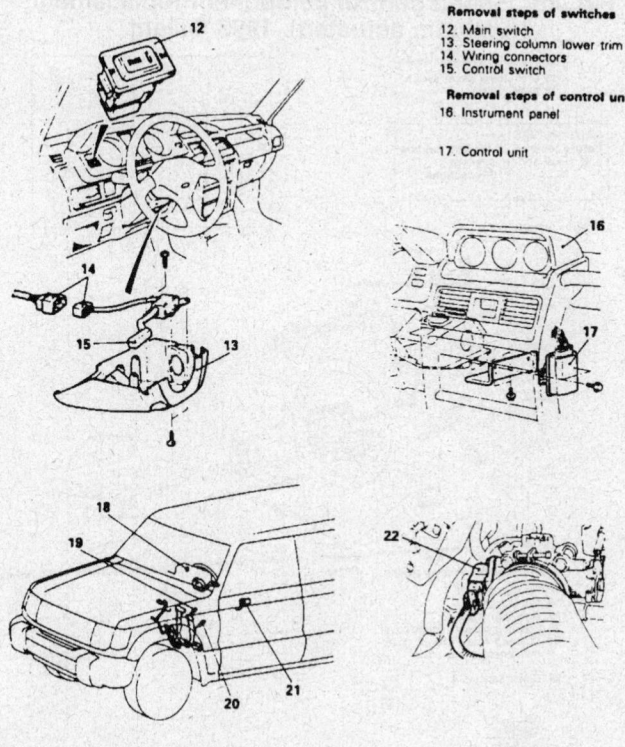

Removal steps of switches
12. Main switch
13. Steering column lower trim
14. Wiring connectors
15. Control switch

Removal steps of control unit
16. Instrument panel

17. Control unit

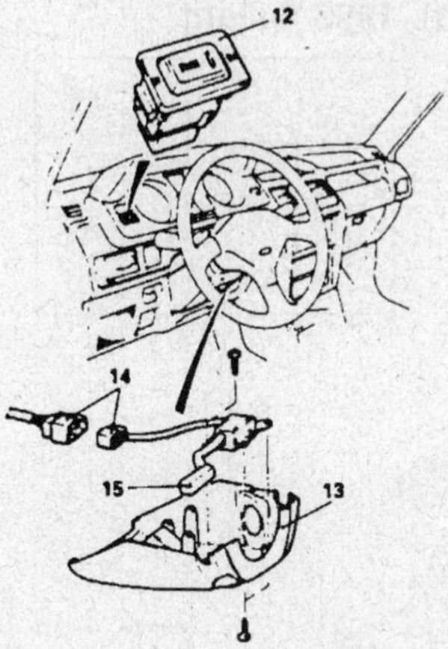
12
14
15
13

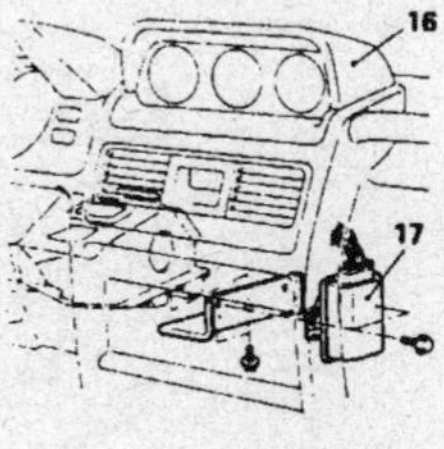
16
17

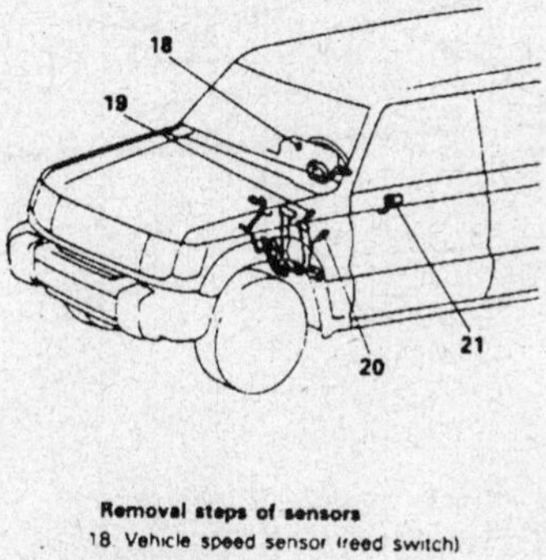
18
19
20
21

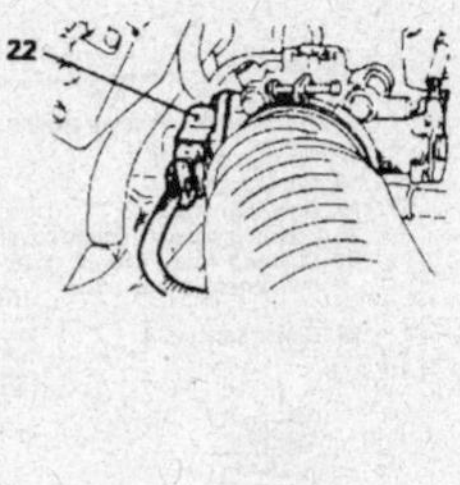
22

Removal steps of sensors
18. Vehicle speed sensor (reed switch)

19. Stop light switch
20. Clutch pedal position switch <M/T>
21. Park/Neutral position switch <A/T>
22. TPS (Throttle position sensor)

MT1109200037020X

Fig. 45 Speed control component replacement (Part 2 of 2). Montero

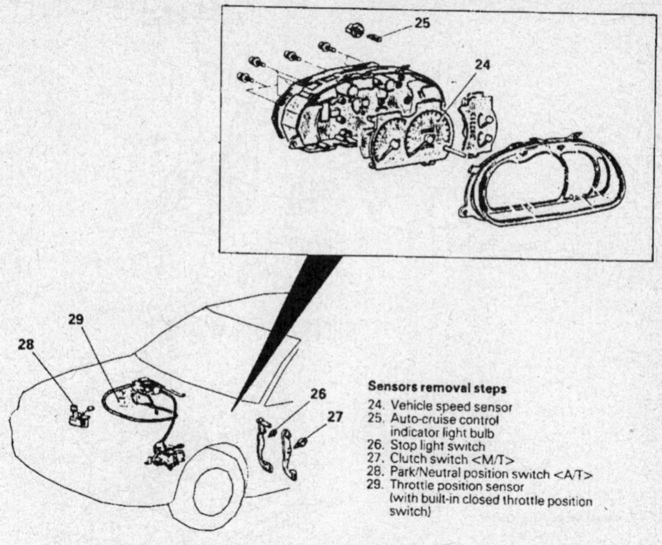
25
24
29
28
26
27

Sensors removal steps
24. Vehicle speed sensor
25. Auto-cruise control indicator light bulb
26. Stop light switch
27. Clutch switch <M/T>
28. Park/Neutral position switch <A/T>
29. Throttle position sensor (with built-in closed throttle position switch)

MT1109300039020X

Fig. 46 Speed control component replacement (Part 2 of 3). Mirage

Auto-cruise control unit removal
16. Auto-cruise control unit

Auto-cruise control switch removal steps
17. Horn pad
18. Spring holder
19. Auto-cruise control switch

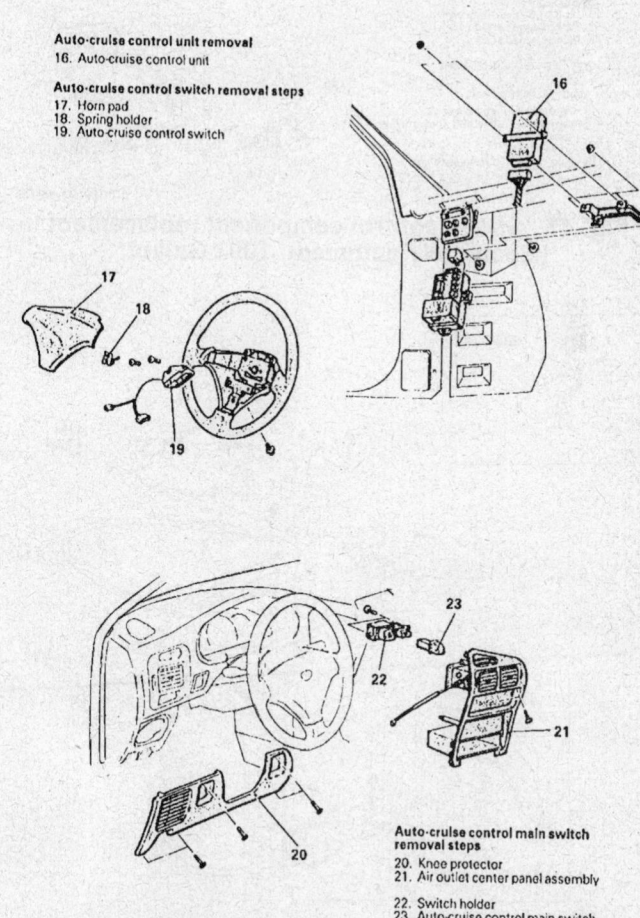

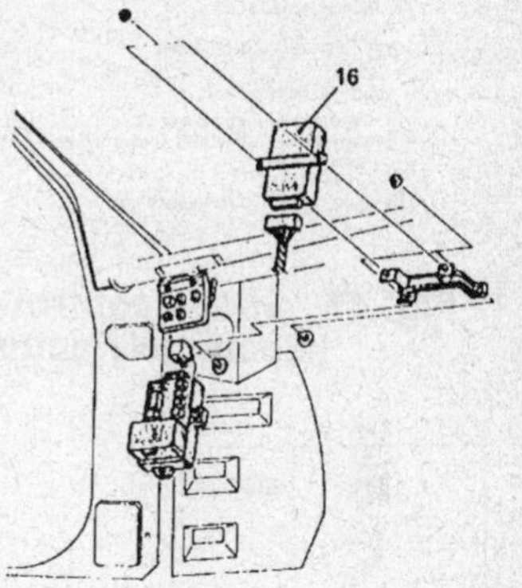
16

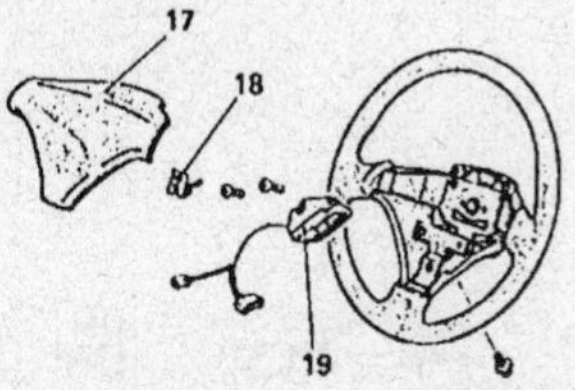
17
18
19

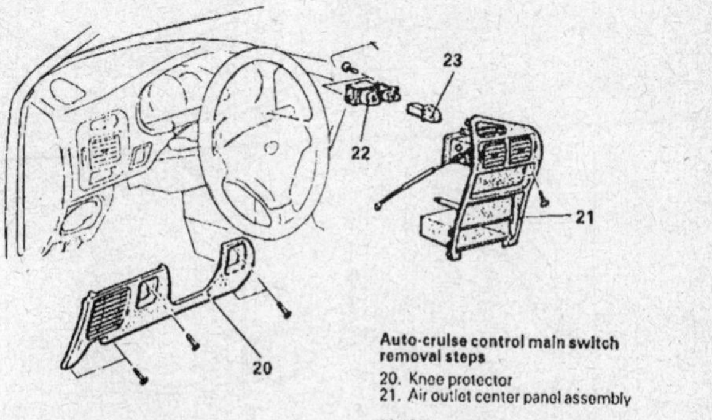
23
22
21
20

Auto-cruise control main switch removal steps
20. Knee protector
21. Air outlet center panel assembly

22. Switch holder
23. Auto-cruise control main switch

MT1109300039030X

Fig. 46 Speed control component replacement (Part 3 of 3). Mirage

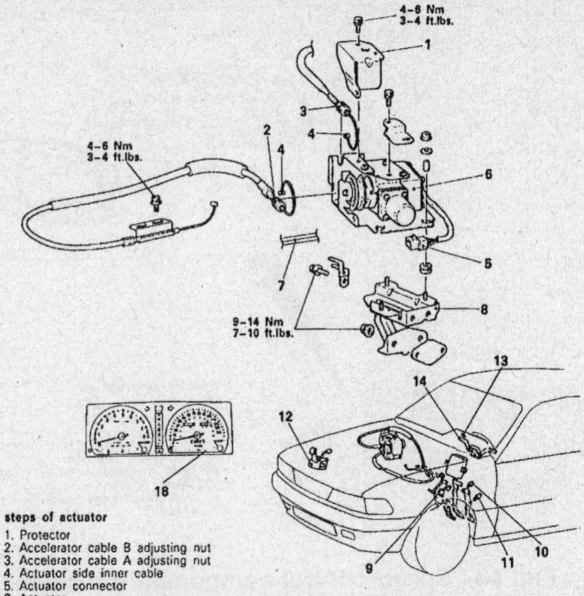
4-6 Nm
3-4 ft.lbs.
4-6 Nm
3-4 ft.lbs.
9-14 Nm
7-10 ft.lbs.

Removal steps of actuator

1. Protector
2. Accelerator cable B adjusting nut
3. Accelerator cable A adjusting nut
4. Actuator side inner cable
5. Actuator connector
6. Actuator
7. Air hoses
   <ACTIVE-Electronic Control Suspension>
8. Bracket

Removal steps of sensor and switches

9. Accelerator switch <A/T>
10. Stop light switch
11. Clutch pedal position switch <M/T>
12. Park/neutral position switch <A/T>
13. Vehicle speed sensor

14. Auto-cruise control switch

Removal steps of control unit

15. Instrument under cover
16. Lap shower duct and foot shower nozzle
17. Control unit
18. Auto-cruise control indicator light

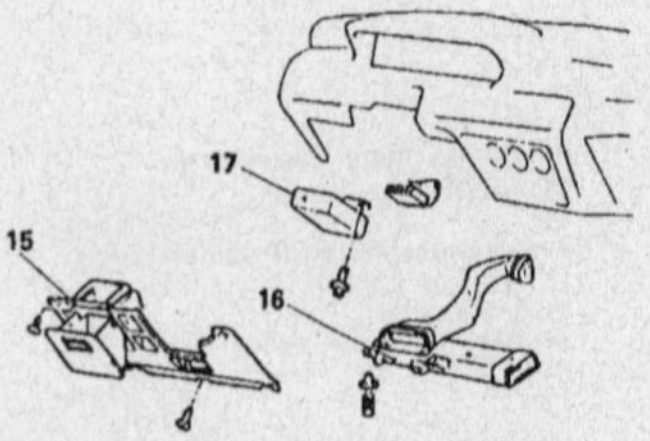

MT1109100040000X

Fig. 47 Speed control component replacement (electrically actuated). 1993 Galant

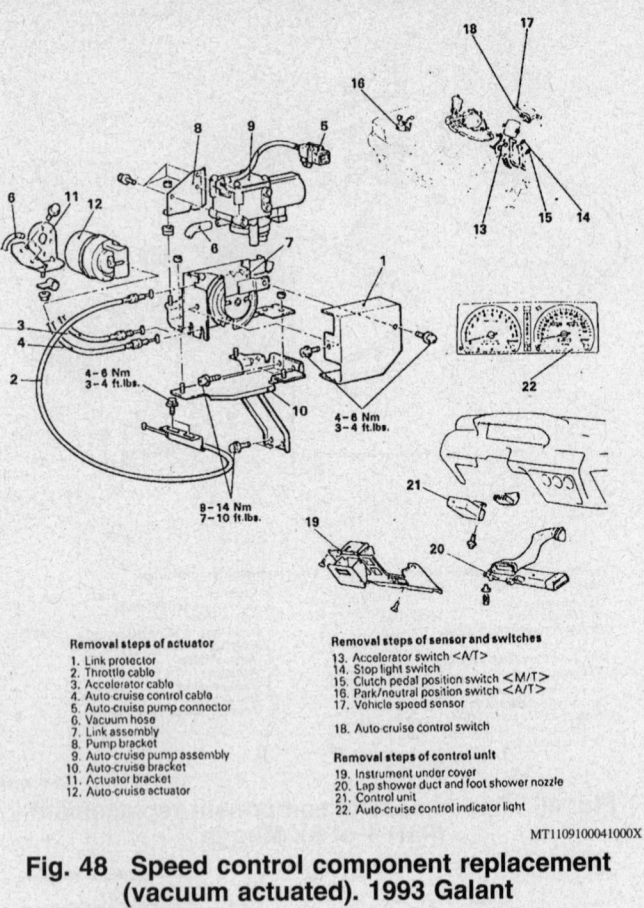

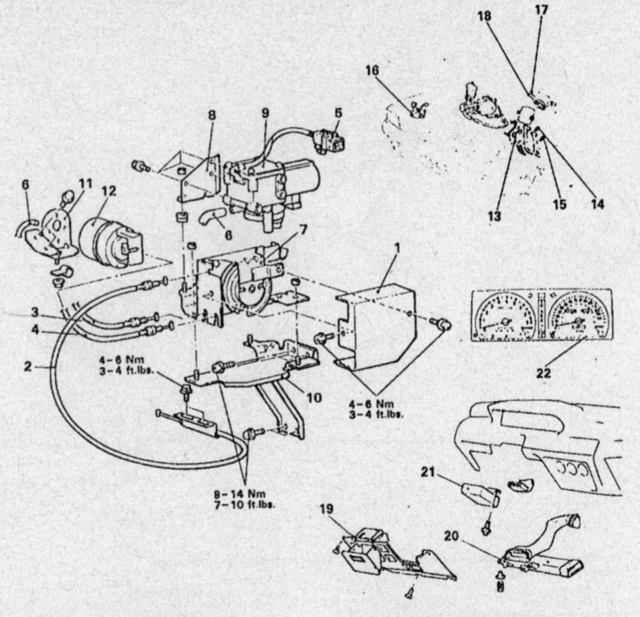
4-6 Nm
3-4 ft.lbs.
9-14 Nm
7-10 ft.lbs.
4-6 Nm
3-4 ft.lbs.

Removal steps of actuator

1. Link protector
2. Throttle cable
3. Accelerator cable
4. Auto-cruise control cable
5. Auto-cruise pump connector
6. Vacuum hose
7. Link assembly
8. Pump bracket
9. Auto-cruise pump assembly
10. Auto-cruise bracket
11. Actuator bracket
12. Auto-cruise actuator

Removal steps of sensor and switches

13. Accelerator switch <A/T>
14. Stop light switch
15. Clutch pedal position switch <M/T>
16. Park/neutral position switch <A/T>
17. Vehicle speed sensor

18. Auto-cruise control switch

Removal steps of control unit

19. Instrument under cover
20. Lap shower duct and foot shower nozzle
21. Control unit
22. Auto-cruise control indicator light

MT1109100041000X

Fig. 48 Speed control component replacement (vacuum actuated). 1993 Galant

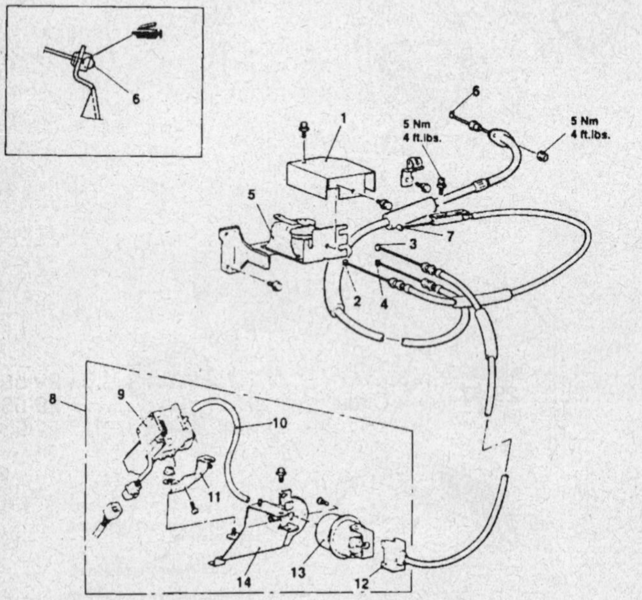
5 Nm
4 ft.lbs.
5 Nm
4 ft.lbs.

Link assembly removal steps

1. Link protector
2. Throttle cable connection
3. Auto-cruise control cable connection
4. Accelerator cable connection
5. Link assembly
6. Accelerator cable connection
7. Throttle cable connection

Actuator removal steps

8. Auto-cruise actuator assembly
9. Auto-cruise vacuum pump assembly
10. Vacuum hose
11. Pump bracket
12. Auto-cruise control cable connection
13. Actuator
14. Actuator bracket

MT1109400042010X

Fig. 49 Speed control component replacement (Part 1 of 3). 1994–96 Galant

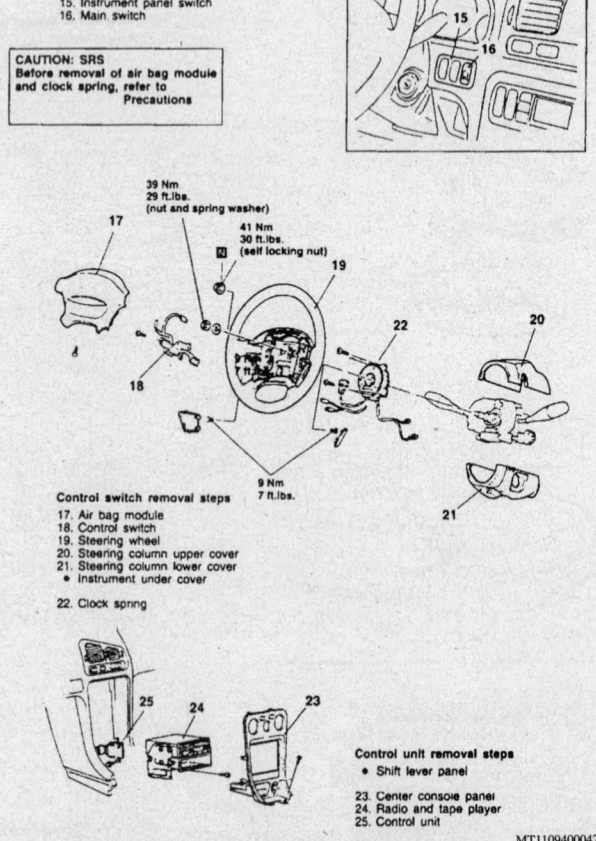

Main switch removal steps

15. Instrument panel switch
16. Main switch

CAUTION: SRS
Before removal of air bag module and clock spring, refer to Precautions

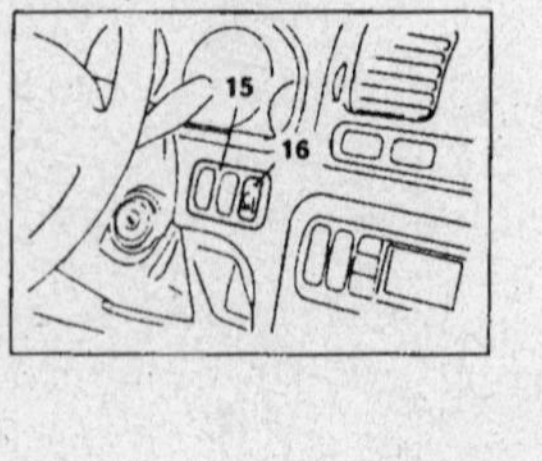

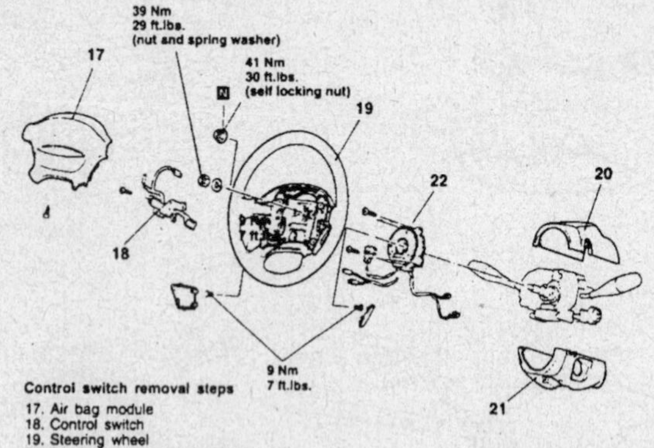
39 Nm
29 ft.lbs.
(nut and spring washer)
41 Nm
30 ft.lbs.
(self locking nut)
9 Nm
7 ft.lbs.

Control switch removal steps

17. Air bag module
18. Control switch
19. Steering wheel
20. Steering column upper cover
21. Steering column lower cover
  • Instrument under cover

22. Clock spring

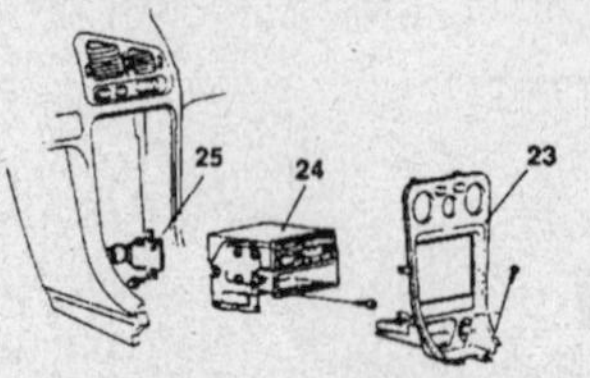

Control unit removal steps

• Shift lever panel

23. Center console panel
24. Radio and tape player
25. Control unit

MT1109400042020X

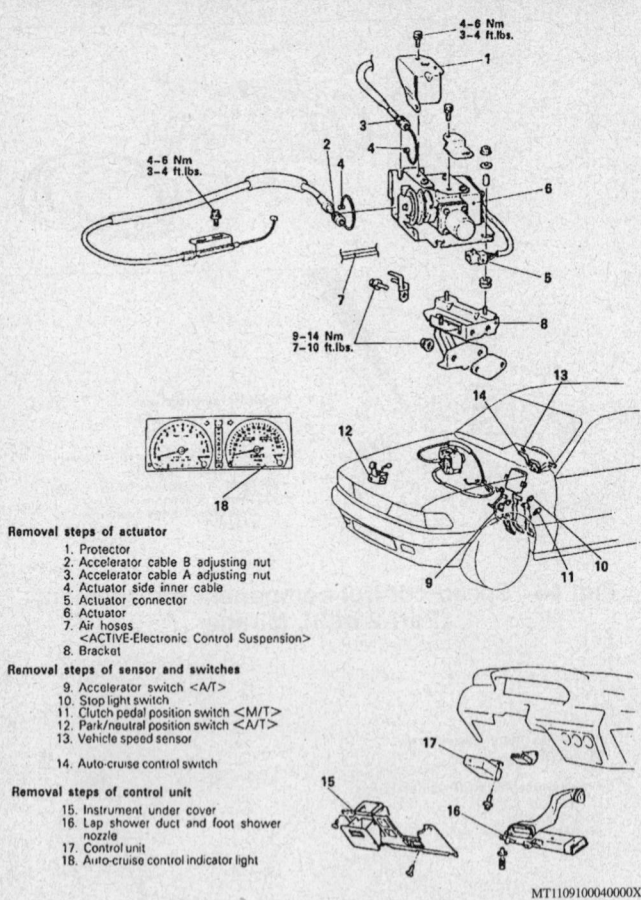

Fig. 49 Speed control component replacement (Part 2 of 3). 1994–96 Galant

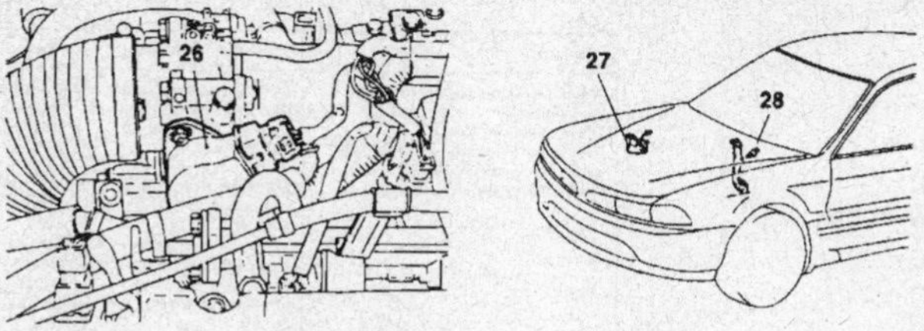
26
27
28

Sensor removal steps
26. Throttle position sensor
27. Park/neutral position switch
28. Stop light switch

MT1109400042030X

Fig. 49 Speed control component replacement (Part 3 of 3). 1994–96 Galant

Wiper Systems

NOTE: On Air Bag Equipped Models, Refer To "Air Bag System Precautions" Located In The Front Of This Manual For System Disarming & Arming Procedures.

NOTE: Prior To Performing Any Service Operations Listed In This Section, Consult The "Technical Service Bulletins" Section For Related Information.

INDEX

	Page No.
Component Diagnosis & Testing	29-57
Diamante	29-60
Washer Fluid Level Sensor	29-61
Washer Motor	29-61
Wiper & Washer Switch	29-60
Wiper Motor	29-60
Wiper Relay	29-61
Eclipse	29-58
Front Wiper & Washer Switch	29-59
Front Wiper Motor	29-58
Rear Wiper & Washer Switch	29-59
Rear Wiper Motor	29-59
Washer Motor	29-59
Expo	29-61
Front Intermittent Wiper Relay	29-61
Front Wiper & Washer Switch	29-61
Front Wiper Motor	29-61
Rear Intermittent Wiper Relay	29-62
Rear Wiper & Washer Switch	29-62
Rear Wiper Motor	29-61
Washer Motor	29-61
Galant	29-58
Intermittent Wiper Relay	29-58
Washer Motor	29-58
Wiper & Washer Switch	29-58
Wiper Motor	29-58
Wiper Relay	29-58
Mirage	29-59
Front Wiper & Washer Switch	29-59
Front Wiper Motor	29-59
Rear Wiper & Washer Switch	29-60
Rear Wiper Motor	29-59
Montero	29-57
Front Wiper Motor	29-57
Intermittent Wiper Relay	29-57
Rear Washer Motor	29-57
Rear Wiper & Washer Switch	29-57
Rear Wiper Motor	29-57
Washer Motor	29-57
Wiper & Washer Switch	29-57
Pickup	29-57
Wiper Motor	29-57
Precis	29-57
Front Wiper Motor	29-57
Rear Wiper & Washer Switch	29-58
3000GT	29-62
Front Wiper & Washer Switch	29-62
Front Wiper Motor	29-62
Front Wiper Relay	29-62
Rear Intermittent Wiper Relay	29-64
Rear Wiper & Washer Switch	29-63
Rear Wiper Motor	29-62
Description	29-53
Washer Operation	29-54
Wiper Automatic Stop	29-54
Wiper Intermittent Operation	29-54
Wiper Operation	29-54
Precautions	29-53
Air Bag Systems	29-53
System Diagnosis & Testing	29-55
Diamante	29-57
Input Signal	29-57
Eclipse	29-56
1995–96	29-56
Galant	29-55
1993	29-55
1994–96	29-55
3000GT	29-56
Circuit Tests	29-56
Technical Service Bulletins	29-64
Front Washer Nozzle Leakage	29-64
Troubleshooting	29-54
Front Wiper System	29-54
Rear Wiper System	29-55

PRECAUTIONS

AIR BAG SYSTEMS

Refer to "Air Bag System Precautions" in the front of this manual for system disarming and arming procedures.

DESCRIPTION

Two wiper systems are utilized on these vehicles: a manual system and an ETACS controlled system. The manual system is controlled by a dash or column mounted switch. On all models with the ETACS system except the 3000GT, the system utilizes a vehicle speed response type intermittent wiper system, mist wiper action and washer interlock. The 3000GT uses an electronically controlled intermittent wiper system.

Problem	Probable cause(s)	Checking procedure	Remedy
The wipers don't operate when the wiper switch is set to the "INT" position. (The wipers do operate, however, when the wiper switch is set to the "1" (low speed) position.)	Damage or disconnection of the wiring of the wiper switch ("INT") input circuit.	If a malfunction is discovered as a result of the checking of the input, conduct check of the individual part and circuit.	Repair the wiring harness, or replace the column switch.
	Damage or disconnection of the wiring of the wiper switch ("INT").		
	Damage or disconnection of the wiring of the ignition switch input circuit.	If a malfunction is discovered as a result of the checking of the input, conduct check of the individual part and circuit.	Repair the wiring harness.
	Damage or disconnection of the wiring of the wiper relay activation circuit.	Conduct check of the individual part and circuit.	Repair the wiring harness, or replace the column switch.
	Malfunction of the wiper relay.		
	Malfunction of the electronic control unit.	-	Replace the electronic control unit.
The wipers don't stop when the wiper switch is OFF. (This problem occurs at the low speed of the wipers.) NOTE If the wipers continue operating (without stopping) at the "2" position (high speed) of the wiper switch, there is a short-circuit in the circuit at the wiper motor high-speed side.	Short-circuit in the wiper switch ("INT") input circuit.	If a malfunction is discovered as a result of the checking of the input conduct check of the individual part and circuit.	Repair the wiring harness, or replace the column switch.
	Short-circuit in the wiper switch ("INT").		
	Short-circuit in the wiper relay activation circuit.	Conduct check of the individual part and circuit.	Repair the wiring harness.
	Malfunction of the electronic control unit.	-	Replace the electronic control unit.
When the wiper switch is set to the "INT" position, the wipers operate continuously at low speed, not intermittent operation. (The wipers stop, however, when the wiper switch is set to "OFF".)	Short-circuit in the wiper switch ("INT") input circuit.	If a malfunction is discovered as a result of the checking of the input conduct check of the individual part and circuit.	Repair the wiring harness, or replace the column switch.
	Short-circuit in the wiper switch ("INT").		
	Malfunction of the electronic control unit.	-	Replace the electronic control unit.
The intermittent time does not change when the intermittent variable volume switch setting is changed.	Damage or disconnection of the wiring of the intermittent variable volume switch input circuit.	If a malfunction is discovered as a result of the checking of the input conduct check of the individual part and circuit.	Repair the wiring harness, or replace the column switch.
	Damage or disconnection of the wiring of the intermittent variable volume switch.		
	Malfunction of the electronic control unit.	-	Replace the electronic control unit.

MT9029100005010X

Fig. 1 Wiper system troubleshooting chart (Part 1 of 2). 3000GT

WIPER OPERATION

Front

When the wiper switch is at the "LO" position and ignition switch is in On position, current flows through the wiper motor low speed brush, wiper switch and ground. The wipers then operate at low speed. When the wiper switch is at the "HI" position and ignition switch is in On position, current flows through the wiper motor high speed brush, wiper switch and ground. The wipers then operate at high speed.

Rear

With the rear wiper switch in the On position, current flows through the wiper switch, rear wiper motor and ground causing the rear wiper to operate.

WIPER AUTOMATIC STOP

Front

When the wiper switch is turned to the "OFF" position, current flows through the wiper motor low speed brush, wiper switch, intermittent control relay, wiper motor cam contacts and ground. This allows the wiper motor to continue operating until the blades return to the park (auto stop) position. When the blades reach the park position, the wiper motor contacts open and current flow to ground is interrupted, causing the wipers to stop.

Rear

With the wiper switch set to the "OFF" position, current flows through the wiper motor cam contacts, wiper switch, and ground causing the wiper to operate until the wiper returns to the park (auto stop) position. When the blades reach the park position, the wiper motor contacts open, which interrupts the current flow and causes the wiper motor to stop.

WIPER INTERMITTENT OPERATION

Front

With the ignition switch turned to the On position and the wiper switch set to the "INT" position, current flows through the intermittent relay, wiper switch and ground, causing the intermittent relay contacts to open and close repeatedly. When the contacts are closed, current flows through the low speed brush, wiper switch, intermittent wiper control relay and ground, causing the wiper to operate. The operation of the wiper opens the relay contacts and causes current to flow through the wiper motor cam contacts and ground. The wipers will operate until they return to the park position.

Rear

With the ignition switch turned to the On position and the wiper switch set to the "INT" position, current flows through the intermittent relay, wiper switch and ground, causing the intermittent relay contacts to open and close repeatedly. When the contacts are closed, current flows through the wiper motor, wiper switch, intermittent wiper control relay and ground, causing the wiper to operate. This operation causes the relay contacts to open and current flows through the wiper motor cam contacts and ground. The wiper will operate until it returns to the park position.

WASHER OPERATION

Front

With the washer switch turned to the On position, current flows through the intermittent wiper relay and ground, causing the intermittent wiper relay internal contacts to close. Once closed, current flows through the intermittent wiper relay contacts, wiper switch, wiper motor and ground, causing the wipers to operate.

Rear

When the rear washer switch is turned to the On position, current flows through the rear washer switch, washer motor and ground, causing the washer to operate.

TROUBLESHOOTING

FRONT WIPER SYSTEM

LESS ETACS SYSTEM

Wipers Do Not Operate

1. Ensure fuse is not blown.
2. Ensure proper ground connection.

Wipers Do Not Operate At High Or Low Speed

Check wiper switch.

Wipers Do Not Operate In Intermittent Mode

Check intermittent wiper relay terminal voltage.

Wipers Fail To Stop

Check wiper motor.

Interval Period Will Not Adjust

1. Check interval adjustment switch.
2. Check intermittent wiper relay.

Washer Does Not Work

1. If wiper still operates when attempting to activate washer, check washer motor.
2. If wiper does not operate when attempting to activate washer, check washer switch.

Wipers Do Not Operate In Coordination With Washer

Check intermittent wiper relay.

WITH ETACS SYSTEM

Refer to **Figs. 1 and 2** when troubleshooting the ETACS wiper system.

Problem	Probable cause(s)	Checking procedure	Remedy
The wipers do not function when the washer switch is switched ON for 0.6 second or longer. (With the wiper switch at the "INT" position, however, intermittent operation of the wipers is normal, and the washer function is normal.)	Damage or disconnection of the wiring of the washer switch input circuit.	If a malfunction is discovered as a result of the checking of the input conduct check of the individual part and circuit.	Repair the wiring harness, or replace the column switch.
	Damage or disconnection of the wiring of the washer switch.		
	Malfunction of the electronic control unit.	–	Replace the electronic control unit.
The wipers do not function when the washer switch is switched ON for less than 0.6 second. (The wipers and washer do function, however, when the washer switch is switched ON for 0 6 second or longer.)	Malfunction of the electronic control unit.	–	Replace the electronic control unit.

NOTE
"ECU" (electronic control unit) indicates the ETACS unit.

MT9029100005020X

Fig. 1 Wiper system troubleshooting chart (Part 2 of 2). 3000GT

Problem	Probable cause (s)	Checking procedure	Remedy
The wipers don't operate when the wiper switch is set to the "AUTO" position. (The wipers do operate, however, when the wiper switch is set to the "1" (low speed) position.)	Damage or disconnection of the wiring of the wiper switch (AUTO) input circuit.	If a malfunction is discovered as a result of the checking of the input, conduct check of the individual part and circuit	Repair the wiring harness, or replace the column switch.
	Damage or disconnection of the wiring of the wiper switch ("AUTO").		
	Damage or disconnection of the wiring of the ignition switch input circuit.	If a malfunction is discovered as a result of the checking of the input, conduct check of the individual part and circuit.	Repair the wiring harness.
	Damage or disconnection of the wiring of the wiper relay activation circuit.	Conduct check of the individual part and circuit.	Repair the wiring harness, or replace the wiper relay.
	Malfunction of the wiper relay.		
	Malfunction of the electronic control unit.	—	Replace the electronic control unit.
The wipers don't stop when the wiper switch is switched OFF. (This problem occurs at the low speed of the wipers.) NOTE If the wipers continue operating (without stopping) at the "2" position (high speed) of the wiper switch, there is a short-circuit in the circuit at the wiper motor high-speed side.	Short-circuit in the wiper switch ("AUTO") input circuit.	If a malfunction is discovered as a result of the checking of the input, conduct check of the individual part and circuit	Repair the wiring harness, or replace the column switch.
	Short-circuit in the wiper switch ("AUTO").		
	Short-circuit in the wiper relay activation circuit.	Conduct check of the individual part and circuit.	Repair the wiring harness.
	Malfunction of the electronic control unit.	—	Replace the electronic control unit.
When the wiper switch is set to the "AUTO" position, the wipers operate continuously at low speed, not intermittent operation. (The wipers stop, however, when the wiper switch is set to "OFF".)	Short-circuit in the wiper switch ("AUTO") input circuit.	If a malfunction is discovered as a result of the checking of the input, conduct check of the individual part and circuit	Repair the wiring harness, or replace the column switch.
	Short-circuit in the wiper switch ("AUTO").		
	Malfunction of the electronic control unit.	—	Replace the electronic control unit.

MT9029100006010X

Fig. 2 Wiper system troubleshooting chart (Part 1 of 2). 1993 Galant

REAR WIPER SYSTEM

WIPER DOES NOT OPERATE

If washer also does not operate, proceed as follows:

1. Check fuse.
2. Check for ground connection.

WIPER DOES NOT OPERATE IN INTERMITTENT MODE

Check intermittent wiper relay terminal voltage.

WIPER FAILS TO STOP

Check wiper motor.

SYSTEM DIAGNOSIS & TESTING

Galant

1993

INPUT CHECK

Connect a multi-use tester between the ETACS terminal and ground as shown in **Fig. 3.** With ignition switch at the "ACC" position select the special test of the tester. The buzzer of the tester should sound one time when each switch or sensor is activated. If the buzzer does not sound there is a problem in that switch, sensor, or wiring of that circuit.

CIRCUIT TESTS

Power Supply & Ground Circuit

1. Ensure battery voltage is present at ECU connector 36 at all times.
2. Ensure continuity exists between ECU connector terminal 29 and ground at all times.
3. Ensure continuity exists between ECU connector terminal 30 and ground at all times. **Fig. 4.**

Ignition Switch Input Circuit

1. Ensure terminal voltage is zero volts at ECU connector 7 with ignition switch in "OFF" position and battery voltage is present in "ACC" position, **Fig. 4.**

A/INT Switch Input Circuit

1. Ensure terminal voltage is 5 volts at ECU connector 10 with wiper switch in "OFF" position and zero volts in "AUTO" position.
2. Ensure no continuity exists between ECU connector terminal 10 and ground with wiper switch in "OFF" position.
3. Ensure continuity exists between ECU connector terminal 10 and ground, with wiper switch in "AUTO" position, **Fig. 4.**

Intermittent Variable Volume Switch Input Circuit

1. Ensure terminal voltage is 0–2.5 volts at ECU connector terminal 1.
2. Ensure continuity between intermittent variable volume switch connector terminal 1 and ground. Resistance should be 0–1000 ohms, and should change with movement of the intermittent variable volume, **Fig. 4.**

Vehicle Speed Sensor Input Circuit

1. Ensure terminal voltage is zero volts at ECU connector terminal 4 to ground with vehicle speed sensor On.
2. Ensure terminal voltage is 8 volts at ECU connector terminal 4 to ground with vehicle speed sensor off, **Fig. 4.**
3. Connect ohmmeter between ECU connector terminal 4 and ground, then check conditions as follows:
   a. Raise and support front end of vehicle.
   b. Rotate tires in a forward direction.
   c. Continuity should exist as wheels are rotating.

Wiper Relay Activation Circuit

1. Ensure terminal voltage is zero volts at ECU connector terminal 27, with wiper and ignition switch Off.
2. Ensure battery voltage is present at ECU connector terminal 27, with wiper switch "OFF" and ignition switch in "ACC" position, **Fig. 4.**

Washer Switch Input Circuit

1. Ensure terminal voltage is zero volts at ECU connector terminal 35, with washer switch in Off position and ignition switch in Accessory position.
2. Ensure battery voltage is present at ECU connector terminal 4 with washer switch in On position and ignition switch in Accessory position, **Fig. 4.**

1994–96

INTERMITTENT WIPER SYSTEM

1. Select intermittent wiper operation while measuring voltage at steering column switch terminal 7, **Fig. 5.** Voltage should alternate between zero and battery voltage.

Problem	Probable cause (s)	Checking procedure	Remedy
The intermittent time does not change when the intermittent variable volume switch setting is changed. (The vehicle speed is a constant speed.)	Damage or disconnection of the wiring of the intermittent variable volume switch input circuit.	If a malfunction is discovered as a result of the checking of the input conduct check of the individual part and circuit.	Repair the wiring harness, or replace the column switch.
	Damage or disconnection of the wiring of the intermittent variable volume switch.		
	Malfunction of the electronic control unit.		Replace the electronic control unit.
The wipers' intermittent time does not change according to changes in the vehicle speed. (The intermittent variable volume switch setting is fixed.)	Damage or disconnection of the wiring of the vehicle-speed sensor input circuit, or a short-circuit.	If a malfunction is discovered as a result of the checking of the input conduct check of the individual part and circuit.	Repair the wiring harness, or replace the vehicle-speed sensor.
	Malfunction of the vehicle-speed sensor.		
	Malfunction of the electronic control unit.	—	Replace the electronic control unit.

MIST WIPERS/WASHER-INTERLOCKED WIPERS

Problem	Probable cause (s)	Checking procedure	Remedy
The wipers do not function when the washer switch is switched ON for 0.6 second or longer. (With the wiper switch at the "AUTO" position, however, intermittent operation of the wipers is normal, and the washer function is normal.)	Damage or disconnection of the wiring of the washer switch input circuit	If a malfunction is discovered as a result of the checking of the input conduct check of the individual part and circuit.	Repair the wiring harness, or replace the washer switch.
	Damage or disconnection of the wiring of the washer switch.		
	Malfunction of the electronic control unit.	—	Replace the electronic control unit.
The wipers do not function when the washer switch is switched ON for less than 0.6 second (The wipers and washer do function, however, when the washer switch is switched ON for 0.6 second or longer.)	Malfunction of the electronic control unit	—	Replace the electronic control unit.

NOTE
The "ECU" (electronic control unit) indicates the ETACS control unit.

MT9029100006020X

Fig. 2 Wiper system troubleshooting chart (Part 2 of 2). 1993 Galant

2. If voltage remains at zero, inspect intermittent wiper relay or switch. Replace as necessary.
3. If voltage indication remains at battery voltage, inspect intermittent wiper relay. Replace as necessary.

Eclipse

1995–96

INTERMITTENT WIPER SYSTEM

Refer to "Galant" in this section for intermittent wiper system inspection procedure.

3000GT

Connect a multi-use tester or voltmeter between the ETACS terminal and ground as shown in **Fig. 6.** The buzzer of the tester should sound or the needle of the voltmeter should move when each switch or sensor is activated. If the buzzer does not sound or the voltmeter does not move there is a problem in that switch or switch input circuit.

CIRCUIT TESTS

POWER SUPPLY & GROUND CIRCUIT TEST

1. Ensure terminal voltage is zero volts at ECU connector 14, with ignition switch in "OFF" position and battery voltage is present in "ACC" position, **Fig. 7.**

A/INT SWITCH INPUT CIRCUIT TEST

1. Ensure terminal voltage is 5 volts at

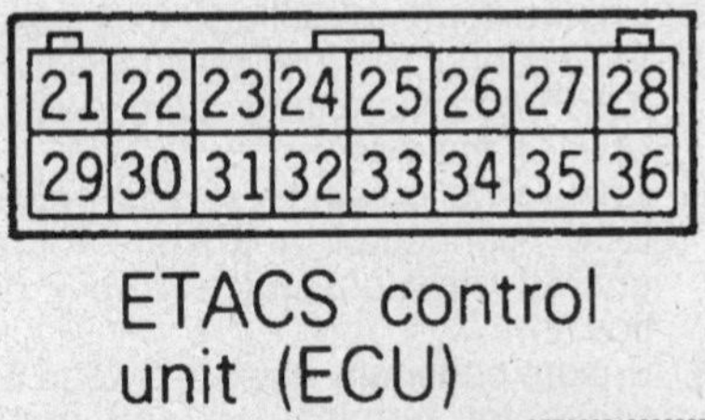
21 22 23 24 25 26 27 28
29 30 31 32 33 34 35 36
ETACS control unit (ECU)

MT9029100008000X

Fig. 4 ETACS control unit terminal identification. 1993 Galant

ECU connector 9 without anti-theft system or connector 11 with anti-theft system, with wiper switch in "OFF" position and zero volts in "INT " position.
2. Ensure no continuity exists between ECU connector terminal 9 without anti-theft system or connector 11 with anti-theft system and ground, with wiper switch in "OFF" position.
3. Ensure continuity exists between ECU connector terminal 9 without anti-theft system or connector 11 with anti-theft system and ground, with wiper switch in "INT" position, **Fig. 7.**

INTERMITTENT VARIABLE VOLUME SWITCH INPUT CIRCUIT

1. Ensure terminal voltage is 0–2.5 volts at ECU connector terminal 13 without anti-theft system or connector 15 with anti-theft system.
2. Ensure continuity between intermittent variable volume switch connector terminal 13 without anti-theft system or

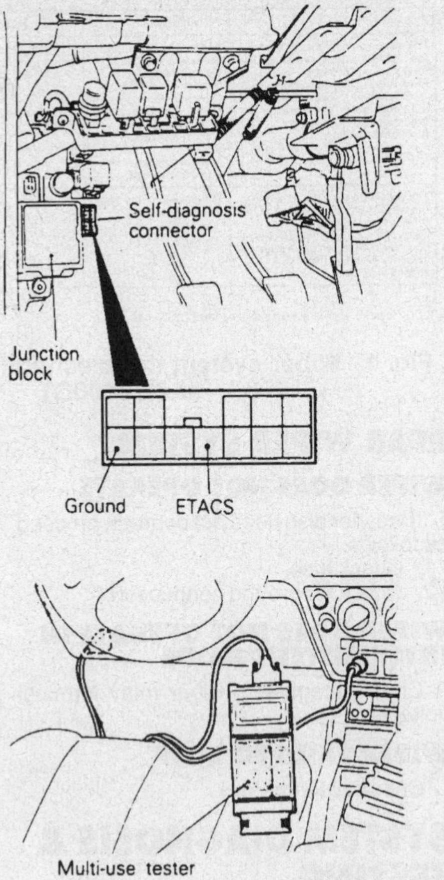
Self-diagnosis connector
Junction block
Ground
ETACS
Multi-use tester

MT9029100007000X

Fig. 3 ETACS diagnosis connector. 1993 Galant

connector 15 with anti-theft system and ground. Resistance should be 0–1000 ohms, and should change with movement of the intermittent variable volume, **Fig. 7.**

WIPER RELAY ACTIVATION CIRCUIT

1. Ensure terminal voltage is zero volts at ECU connector terminal 4 without anti-theft system or connector 6 with anti-theft system, with wiper and ignition switch Off.
2. Ensure battery voltage is present at ECU connector terminal 4 without anti-theft system or connector 6 with anti-theft system with wiper switch "OFF" and ignition switch in "ACC" position, **Fig. 7.**

WASHER SWITCH INPUT CIRCUIT TEST

1. Ensure terminal voltage is zero volts at ECU connector terminal 58 without anti-theft system or connector 60 with anti-theft system, with washer switch Off and ignition switch in the "ACC" position.
2. Ensure battery voltage is present at ECU connector terminal 58 without anti-theft system or connector 60 with anti-theft system with washer switch On and ignition switch is the "ACC" position, **Fig. 7.**

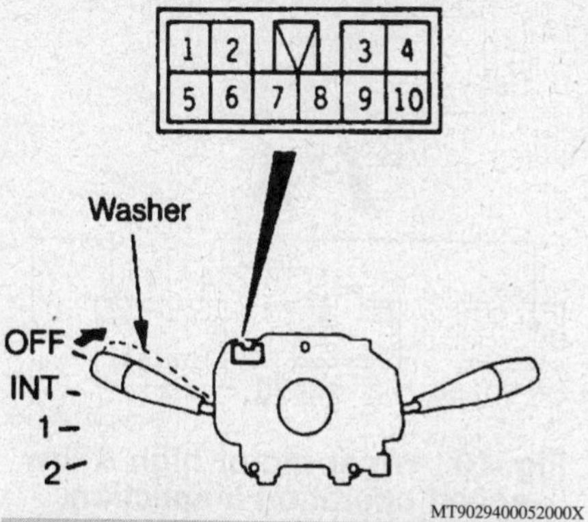
1 2 3 4
5 6 7 8 9 10
Washer
OFF
INT
1
2
MT9029400052000X

Fig. 5 Wiper & washer switch terminal identification. 1994–96 Galant & 1995–96 Eclipse

Diamante

INPUT SIGNAL

Connect a multi-use tester or voltmeter between the ETACS terminal and ground as shown in **Fig. 8.** The buzzer of the tester should sound or the needle of the voltmeter should move the switch is activated. If the buzzer does not sound or the voltmeter does not move there is a problem in that switch or switch input circuit.

COMPONENT DIAGNOSIS & TESTING

Pickup

WIPER MOTOR

Refer to **Fig. 9** for connector terminal identification.

1. To check low speed operation, connect battery positive to terminal 3 and battery negative to terminal 1. Motor should operate at low speed.
2. To check high speed operation, connect battery positive to terminal 3 and battery negative to terminal 2. Motor should operate at high speed.
3. To check auto stop function operation, proceed as follows:
   a. Connect battery positive to terminal 3 and battery negative to terminal 1, then run wipers at low speed. When terminal 3 is disconnected, motor should stop.
   b. Connect terminals 1 and 4, then connect B+ to terminal 3 and battery ground to wiper motor bracket. Wiper motor should start to run, then stop.

Montero

FRONT WIPER MOTOR

1. Connect battery positive to wiper motor as shown in **Fig. 10** and check operation of motor at high and low speeds.

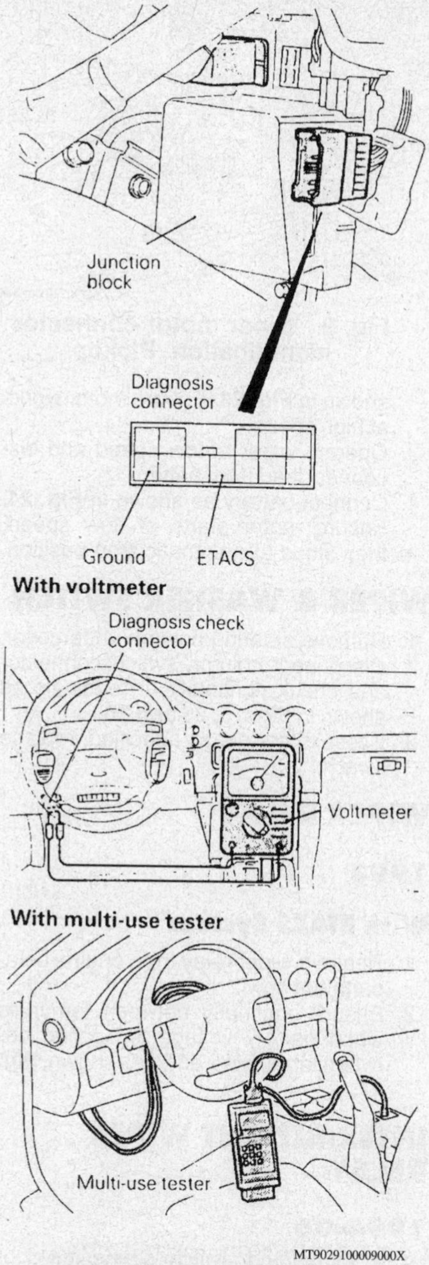
Junction block
Diagnosis connector
Ground
ETACS
With voltmeter
Diagnosis check connector
Voltmeter
With multi-use tester
Multi-use tester
MT9029100009000X

Fig. 6 ETACS diagnosis connector. 3000GT

2. With motor running at low speed, disconnect battery to stop motor.
3. Reconnect battery as shown in **Fig. 11,** then ensure motor starts to run at low speed and stops at automatic stop position.

WIPER & WASHER SWITCH

Disconnect column switch connector and ensure continuity exists between terminals as shown in **Figs. 12 through 14.**

INTERMITTENT WIPER RELAY

1. With column switch connected, turn ignition switch to ACC position.
2. **On models without variable intermittent controls,** wipers should cycle at approximately 3–6 second intervals.

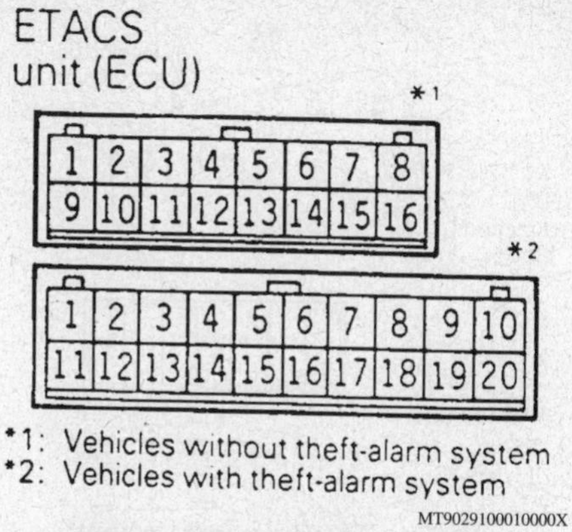
ETACS unit (ECU)
*1
1 2 3 4 5 6 7 8
9 10 11 12 13 14 15 16
*2
1 2 3 4 5 6 7 8 9 10
11 12 13 14 15 16 17 18 19 20
*1: Vehicles without theft-alarm system
*2: Vehicles with theft-alarm system
MT9029100010000X

Fig. 7 ETACS control unit terminal identification. 3000GT

3. **On models with variable intermittent controls,** wipers should cycle approximately every three seconds on "fast" or 12 seconds on "slow."

WASHER MOTOR

1. Ensure washer reservoir is full.
2. With battery connected as shown in **Fig. 15,** washer motor should operate properly.

REAR WIPER & WASHER SWITCH

Operate switch and check continuity between terminals as shown in **Figs. 13, 16 and 17.**

REAR WIPER MOTOR

1. Disconnect wiper motor connector.
2. Connect battery positive to terminal 3 as shown in **Fig. 18.** Motor should operate.
3. With wiper motor running, disconnect battery ground to stop motor.
4. Reconnect battery as shown in **Fig. 19.** Motor should start to run, then stop in auto stop position.

REAR WASHER MOTOR

1. Ensure washer reservoir is full.
2. With battery connected as shown in **Fig. 15,** washer should operate properly.

Precis

FRONT WIPER MOTOR

Refer to **Fig. 20** for connector terminal identification.

1. Connect B+ to terminal 1 and battery ground to terminal 5; ensure motor operates at low speed.
2. Connect B+ to terminal 1 and battery ground to terminal 2; ensure motor operates at high speed.
3. Operate motor at low speed, then stop motor with wipers at any point except auto stop position by disconnecting terminal 5.
4. Connect terminal 5 to terminal 6 and B+ to terminal 1.
5. Ensure wipers stop at auto stop position after motor operates again.

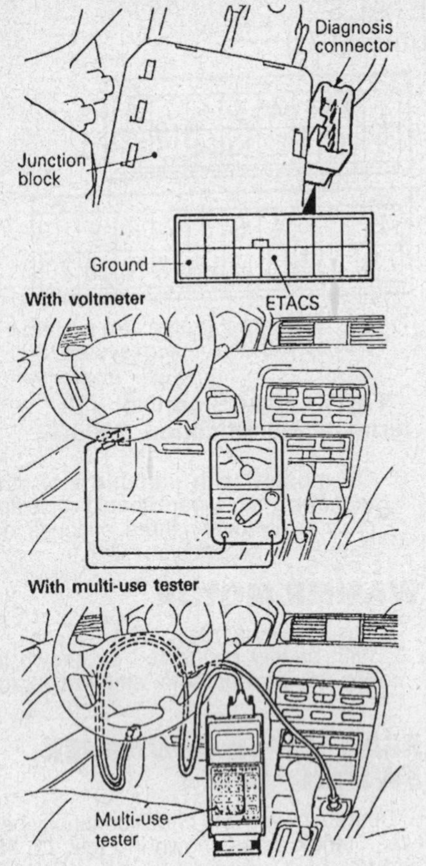
Diagnosis connector
Junction block
Ground
ETACS
With voltmeter
With multi-use tester
Multi-use tester
MT9029100011000X

Fig. 8 ETACS diagnosis connector. Diamante

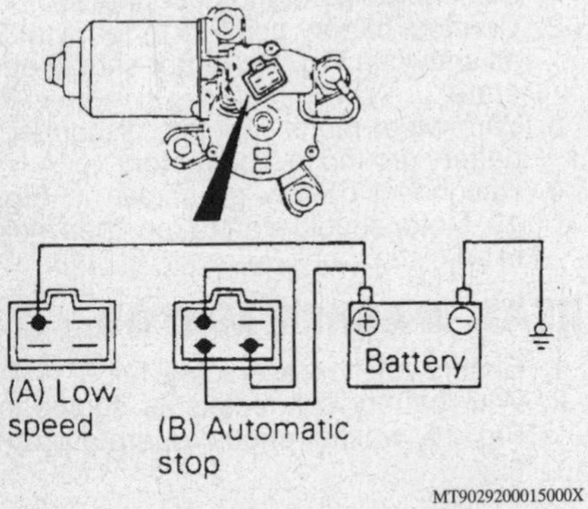
Battery
(A) Low speed
(B) Automatic stop
MT9029200015000X

Fig. 11 Front wiper motor auto stop operation inspection. Montero

REAR WIPER & WASHER SWITCH

Connect B+ to terminal 1 and battery ground to terminal 4, **Fig. 21.** Ensure motor operates.

Galant

WIPER MOTOR

1. Connect battery to wiper motor as shown in **Fig. 22.** Ensure motor works at low speed.
2. Connect battery to wiper motor as

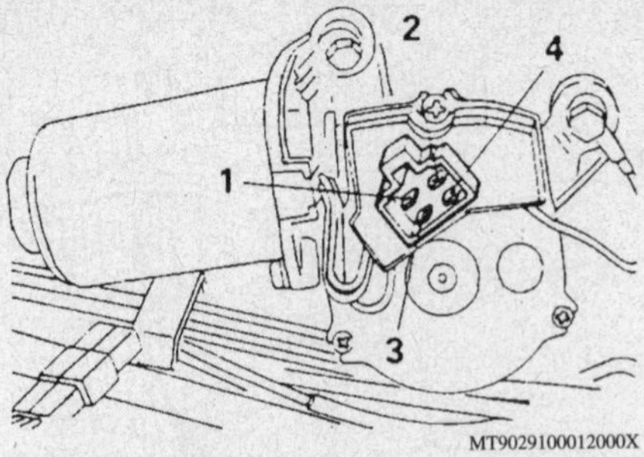
1
2
3
4
MT9029100012000X

Fig. 9 Wiper motor connector identification. Pickup

shown in **Fig. 23.** Ensure motor works at high speed.
3. Operate wiper at low speed and disconnect lead from battery.
4. Connect battery as shown in **Fig. 24.** Ensure motor starts on low speed, then stops at automatic stop position.

WIPER & WASHER SWITCH

1. Remove steering column undercover.
2. Disconnect column switch connector and check continuity at terminals as shown in **Figs. 5, 25 and 26.**
3. If results are not as specified, replace switch.

WIPER RELAY

1993

With ETACS System

1. Remove wiper relay from engine compartment cowl.
2. Ensure continuity between terminals when battery voltage is applied between terminals 2 and 5 as shown, **Fig. 27.**

INTERMITTENT WIPER RELAY

1994–96

1. With column switch connector connected, place ignition switch in Accessory position.
2. Set wiper switch to intermittent function and note operation time. When set to fastest speed, wipers should cycle at three second intervals; at slowest speed, wipers should cycle at approximately 12 second intervals.
3. If results are not as specified, replace relay.

WASHER MOTOR

1994–96

1. Fill washer tank with water, then disconnect motor connector.
2. Apply battery voltage to motor terminals, **Fig. 28.**
3. If a strong spray of water is emitted from ducts, motor operation is satisfactory; if not, replace motor.

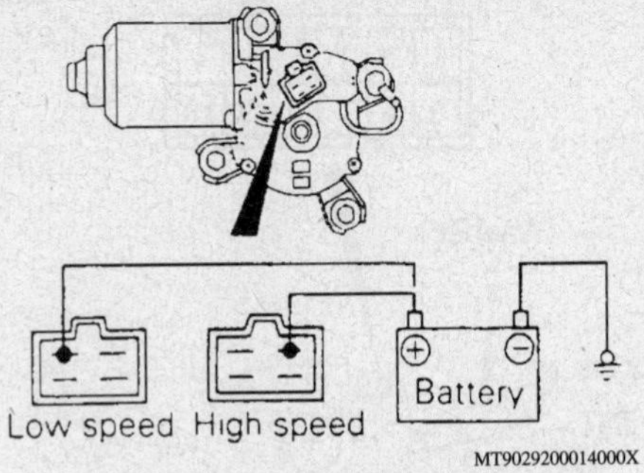
Low speed
High speed
Battery
MT9029200014000X

Fig. 10 Wiper motor high & low speed operation inspection. Montero

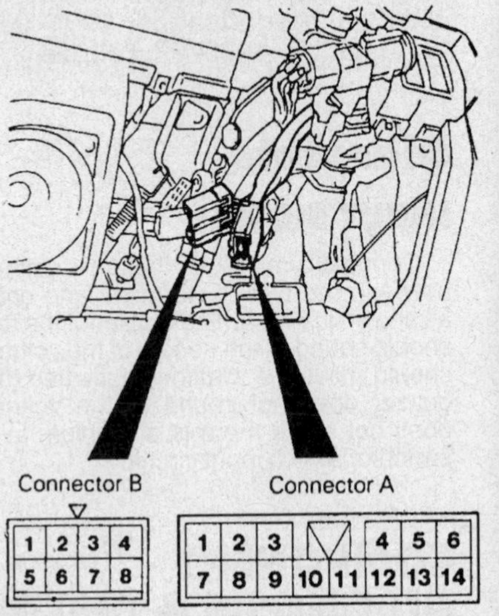
Connector B
Connector A
1 2 3 4
5 6 7 8
1 2 3 4 5 6
7 8 9 10 11 12 13 14

Switch position	Terminal (Connector)	A: 5	B: 3	B: 4	B: 7	B: 8
Wiper switch	OFF		O	—	O	
	1 (LO)		O	—	—	O
	2 (HI)			O	—	O
Washer switch	ON	O	—	—	—	O

NOTE
O—O indicates that there is continuity between the terminals.

MT9029200016000X

Fig. 12 Front wiper & washer switch inspection. 1993–95 Montero

Eclipse

FRONT WIPER MOTOR

1993–94

1. Connect battery to wiper motor as shown in **Fig. 22.** Ensure motor works at low speed.
2. Connect battery to wiper motor as shown in **Fig. 23.** Ensure motor works at high speed.
3. Operate wiper at low speed and disconnect lead from battery.
4. Connect battery as shown in **Fig. 24.** Ensure motor starts on low speed, then stops at automatic stop position.

1995–96

Do not remove motor and link assembly for inspection purposes.

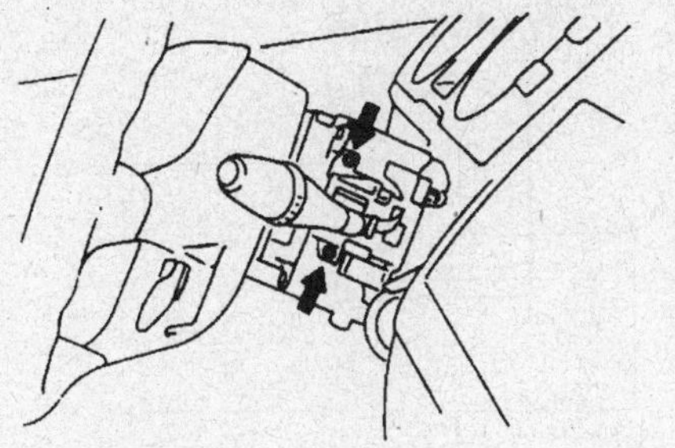

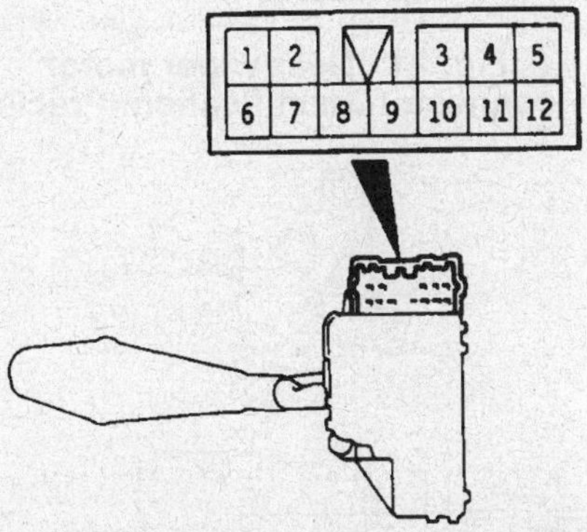
1
2
3
4
5
6
7
8
9
10
11
12

MT9029600053000X

Fig. 13 Wiper & washer switch terminal identification. 1996 Montero

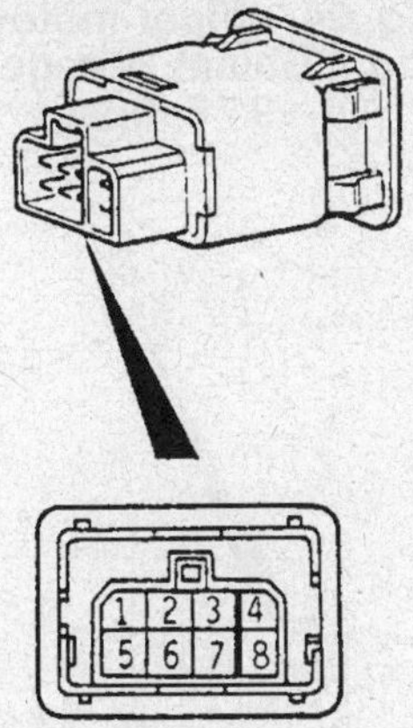
1
2
3
4
5
6
7
8

Switch position		Terminal 1	2	3	4	5	6	7	8
Wiper switch	ON		O	—	—	—	—	O	
	OFF				O	—	—	O	
	INT				O	—	—	O	
		O	—	—	—	—	O		
Washer switch	ON		O	O					
	OFF								
Illumination light						O	—	(lamp)	O

NOTE
O—O indicates that there is continuity between the terminals.

MT9029200018000X

Fig. 16 Rear wiper & washer switch inspection. 1993–95 Montero

1. Connect battery to wiper motor terminals, **Fig. 29,** for low and high speed operation. Ensure motor operates at each speed when battery voltage is applied.
2. To inspect stop position operation, proceed as follows:
   a. Run wiper motor at low speed, then remove battery voltage supply and stop motor.
   b. Reconnect battery, **Fig. 29;** ensure motor runs at low speed until it reaches its automatic stop position.

Switch position		Terminal 6	7	8	9	10
Wiper switch	OFF		O	O		
	1 (LO)			O	—	O
	2 (HI)				O	O
Washer switch	ON	O	—	—	—	O

MT9029600054000X

Fig. 14 Front wiper & washer switch inspection. 1996 Montero

Switch position		Terminal 2	3	4	10
Wiper switch	OFF				
	INT		O	—	O
	ON			O	O
Washer switch	ON	O	—	—	O

MT9029600055000X

Fig. 17 Rear wiper & washer switch inspection. 1996 Montero

FRONT WIPER & WASHER SWITCH

1993-94

1. Remove column cover and knee protector.
2. Disconnect and operate column switch and ensure continuity between terminals as shown, **Fig. 30.**
3. If results are not as specified, replace switch.

1995-96

Refer to "Galant" in this section for switch inspection procedure.

REAR WIPER MOTOR

Do not remove the wiper motor for testing purposes.

1. Connect battery as shown in **Figs. 31 and 32** and ensure proper low and high speed operation.
2. Connect jumper and battery as shown in **Figs. 32 and 33.** Ensure motor starts to run, then stops in automatic stop position.

REAR WIPER & WASHER SWITCH

Disconnect switch, then ensure continuity exists between terminals as shown in **Figs. 34 through 36.**

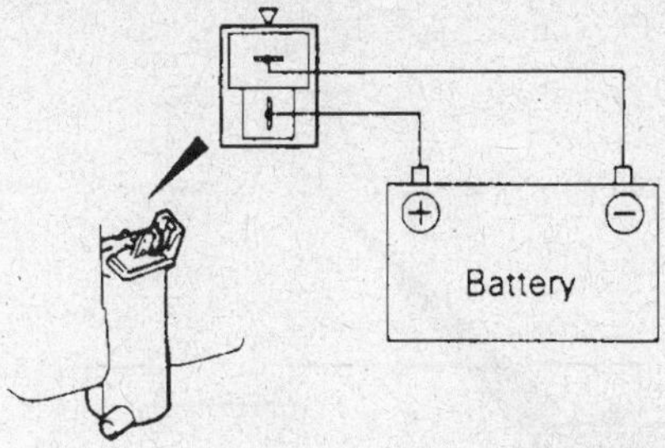
Battery

MT9029100017000X

Fig. 15 Washer motor inspection

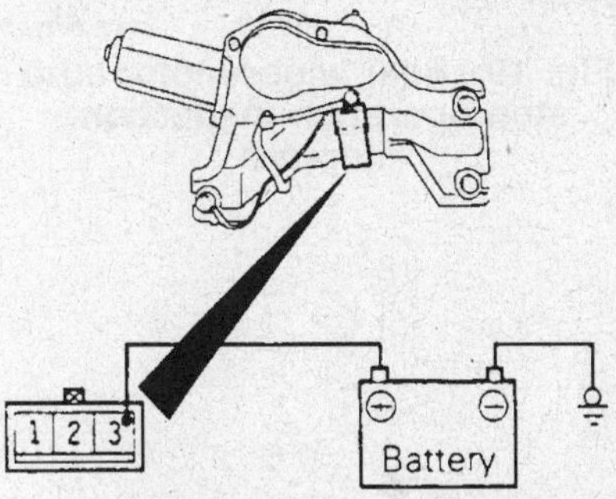
1
2
3
Battery

MT9029200019000X

Fig. 18 Rear wiper motor inspection. Montero

WASHER MOTOR

1995-96

Refer to "Galant" in this section for washer motor inspection procedure.

Mirage

FRONT WIPER MOTOR

1. Connect battery to wiper motor as shown in **Fig. 22.** Ensure motor works at low speed.
2. Connect battery to wiper motor as shown in **Fig. 23.** Ensure motor works at high speed.
3. Operate wipers at low speed and disconnect lead from battery.
4. Connect battery as shown in **Fig. 24.** Ensure motor starts on low speed, then stops at automatic stop position.

FRONT WIPER & WASHER SWITCH

1. Remove column cover and knee protector.
2. Disconnect switch connector and ensure continuity between terminals as shown in **Fig. 37.**
3. If results are not as specified, replace switch.

REAR WIPER MOTOR

1. Connect battery as shown in **Fig. 38** and ensure rear wiper motor operates properly.
2. Connect jumper and battery as shown in **Fig. 39.** Ensure motor starts to run, then stops in automatic stop position.

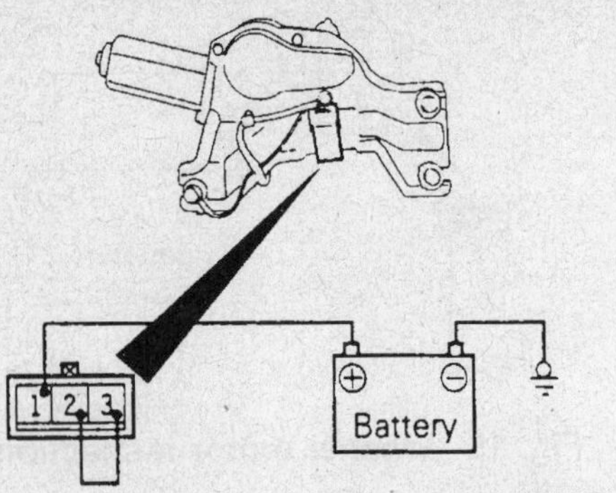
1 2 3
Battery
MT9029200020000X

Fig. 19 Rear wiper motor auto stop operation inspection. Montero

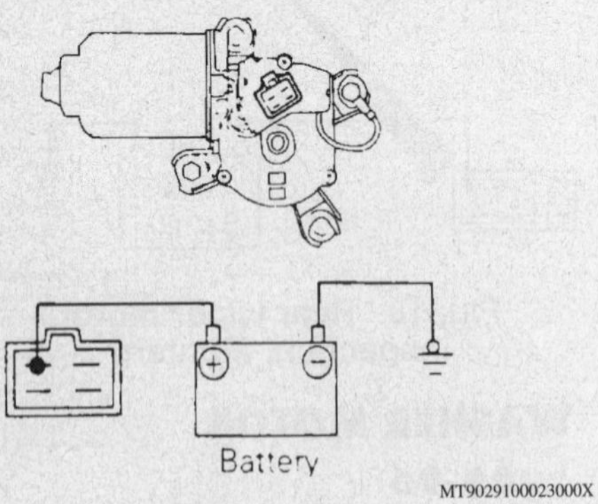
Battery
MT9029100023000X

Fig. 22 Low speed wiper motor operation. Galant, Mirage & 1993–94 Eclipse

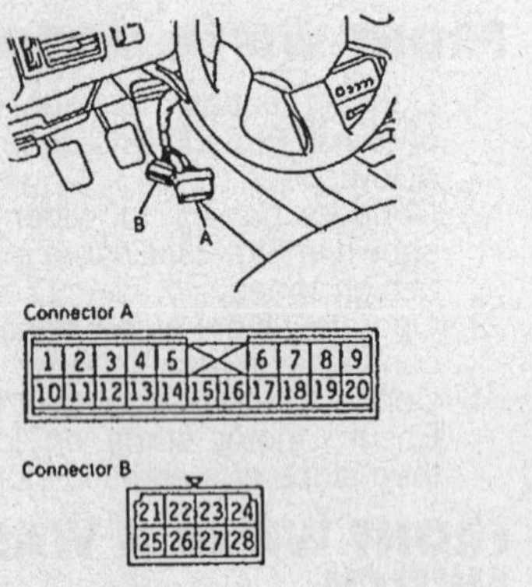
B
A
Connector A
1 2 3 4 5 6 7 8 9
10 11 12 13 14 15 16 17 18 19 20
Connector B
21 22 23 24
25 26 27 28

Switch position		Terminal 5	7	13	17	23	24	27	28
Wiper switch	"OFF"					O		O	
	"INT"*1					O		O	
	"AUTO"*2			O	O	O		O	
	LO					O			O
	HI						O		O
Intermittent variable volume switch*2		O		O					
Washer switch	ON		O						O

NOTE
(1) O—O indicates that there is continuity between the terminals.
(2) The *1 symbol indicates models equipped with the intermittent wipers.
(3) The *2 symbol indicates models equipped with the ETACS.

MT9029100026000X

Fig. 25 Wiper & washer switch continuity chart. 1993 Galant

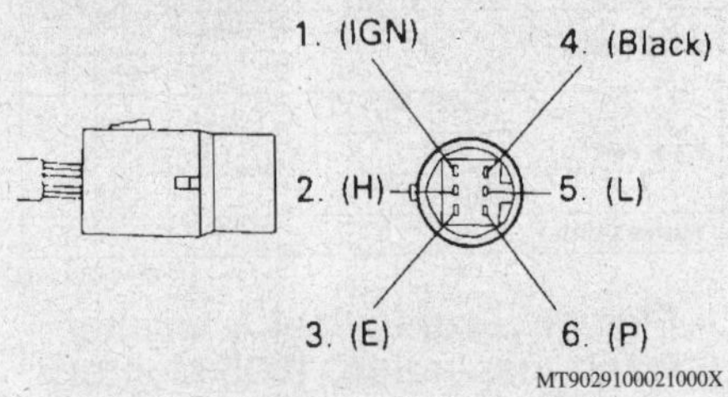
1. (IGN)
4. (Black)
2. (H)
5. (L)
3. (E)
6. (P)
MT9029100021000X

Fig. 20 Wiper motor connector identification. Precis

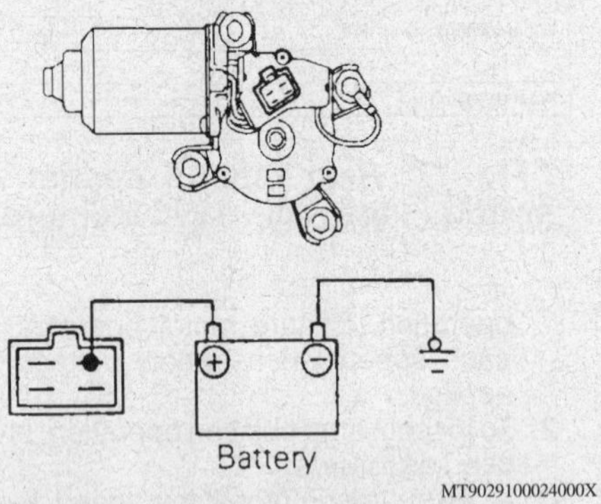
Battery
MT9029100024000X

Fig. 23 High speed wiper motor operation. Galant, Mirage & 1993–94 Eclipse

Switch position		Terminal No. 5	6	7	8	9
Wiper switch	OFF		O	O		
	1 (LO)			O		O
	2 (HI)				O	O
Washer switch	ON	O				O

MT9029400056000X

Fig. 26 Wiper & washer switch continuity chart. 1994–96 Galant & 1995–96 Eclipse

REAR WIPER & WASHER SWITCH

Operate switch and check for continuity between terminal as shown in **Fig. 40.** If results are not as specified, replace switch.

Diamante

WIPER MOTOR

1. To check low and high speed operation of wiper motor, connect battery as shown in **Fig. 41.**
2. To check wiper automatic stop position, run motor at low speed and disconnect battery, then connect jumper wire and battery as shown in **Fig. 42.** Motor should run at low speed, then stop in auto stop position.

WIPER & WASHER SWITCH

1. Disconnect column switch connector.
2. Operate switch and ensure continuity exists between terminals as shown in **Fig. 43.**

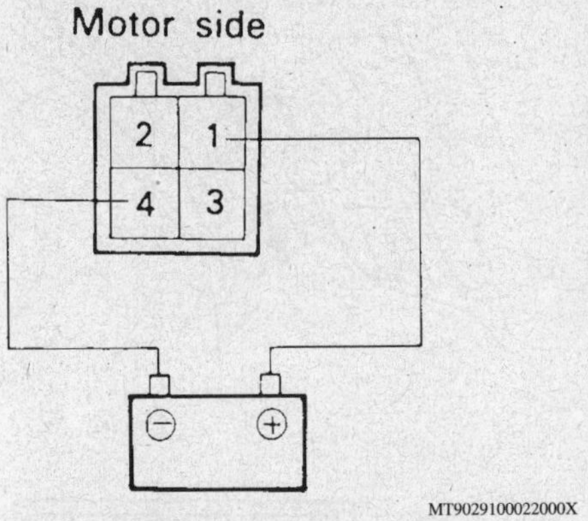
Motor side
2
1
4
3
MT9029100022000X

Fig. 21 Rear wiper motor connector identification. Precis

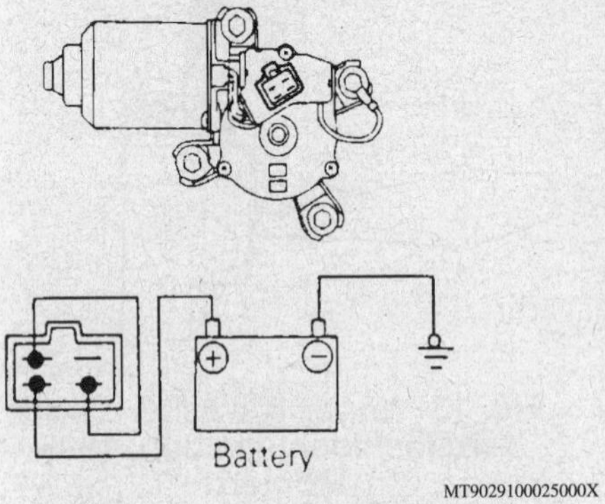
Battery
MT9029100025000X

Fig. 24 Wiper motor stop position. Galant, Mirage & 1993–94 Eclipse

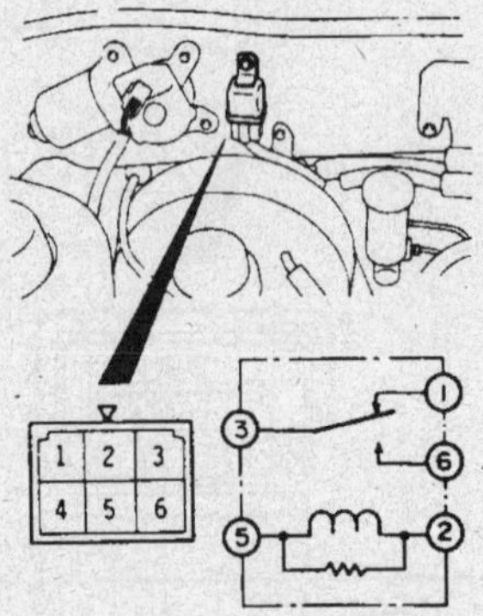
1 2 3
4 5 6

Status	Terminal 1	2	3	4	5	6
During no current flow		O			O	
	O		O			
During current flow		⊕			⊖	
			O			O

NOTE
(1) O—O indicates that there is continuity between the terminals
(2) ⊕ ⊖ indicates terminals to which battery voltage is applied

MT9029100027000X

Fig. 27 Wiper relay continuity chart. Galant w/ETACS

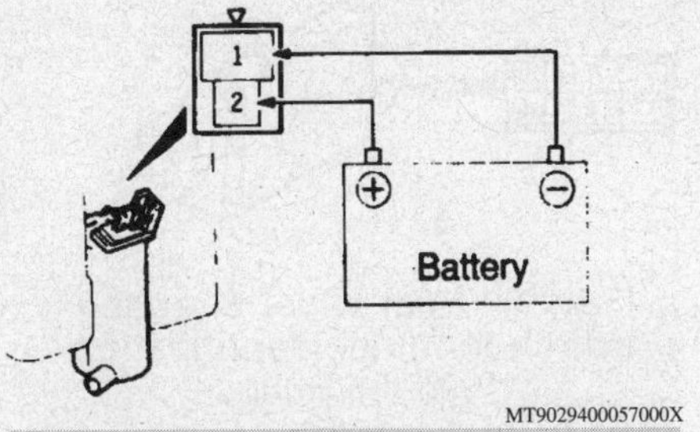
1
2
Battery

MT9029400057000X

Fig. 28 Washer motor inspection. 1994–96 Galant & 1995–96 Eclipse

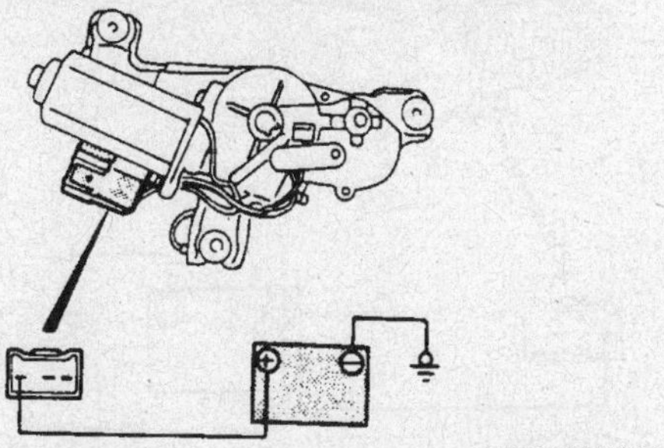

MT9029100029000X

Fig. 31 Rear wiper operation inspection. 1993–94 Eclipse

3. If results are not as specified, replace switch.

WIPER RELAY

Refer to **Fig. 44** for terminal identification when checking wiper relay.

1. Turn column switch to Off or AUTO position. Ensure continuity exists between terminals 3 and 10 and between terminals 1 and 12. Ensure no continuity exists between terminal 3 and 12.
2. Connect B+ to terminal 12 and battery negative to terminal 1, then ensure battery voltage is present at terminal 3.

WASHER MOTOR

1. Ensure washer reservoir is full.
2. With battery connected as shown in **Fig. 15,** washer motor should operate properly.

WASHER FLUID LEVEL SENSOR

1. Remove washer fluid level sensor from washer tank.
2. Connect circuit tester to connector of washer fluid lever sensor.
3. When float is raised, no continuity should exist. When float is lowered, continuity should exist.

Expo

FRONT WIPER MOTOR

1. Connect battery positive to wiper motor as shown in **Fig. 10** and ensure correct operation of motor at high and low speeds.
2. With motor running at low speed, disconnect battery to stop motor.
3. Reconnect battery as shown in **Fig. 11.** Ensure motor starts to run at low speed, then stops at automatic stop position.

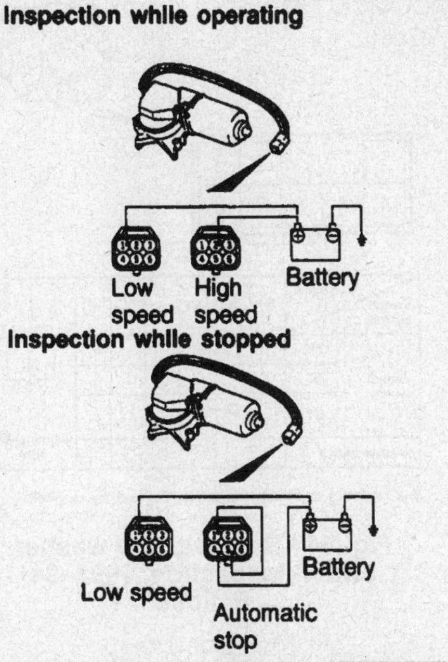
Inspection while operating
Low speed
High speed
Battery
Inspection while stopped
Low speed
Battery
Automatic stop

MT9029500058000X

Fig. 29 Front wiper motor inspection. 1995–96 Eclipse

FRONT WIPER & WASHER SWITCH

1. Disconnect column switch connector and check continuity between terminals as shown in **Fig. 45.**
2. If results are not as specified, replace switch.

FRONT INTERMITTENT WIPER RELAY

1. With column switch connected, turn ignition switch to ACC position.
2. Place wiper switch at INT position, then check voltage between terminal 3 and ground. Voltage should alternate from zero to battery voltage.
3. If results are not as specified, replace relay.

WASHER MOTOR

1. Ensure washer reservoir is full.
2. With battery connected as shown in **Fig. 46,** washer motor should operate properly.

REAR WIPER MOTOR

1. Connect battery positive to wiper motor as shown in **Fig. 47** and ensure motor operates correctly.
2. With motor running at low speed, disconnect battery to stop motor.
3. Reconnect battery as shown in **Fig. 48.** Motor should start to run, then stop at automatic stop position.

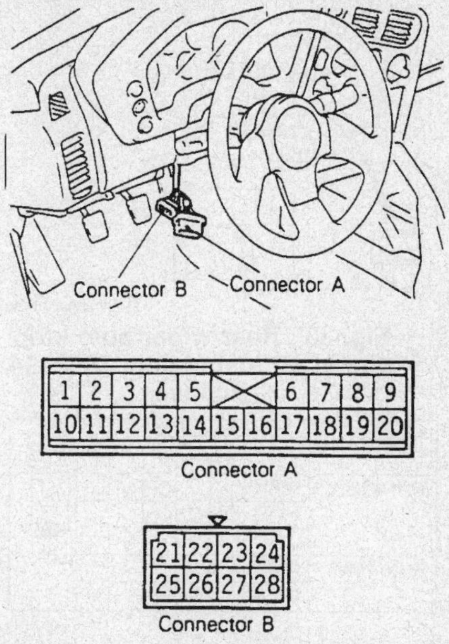
Connector B
Connector A
1
2
3
4
5
6
7
8
9
10
11
12
13
14
15
16
17
18
19
20
Connector A
21
22
23
24
25
26
27
28
Connector B

Switch position		23	24	27	28
Wiper switch	OFF	O—		—O	
	INT	O—		—O	
	LO	O—			—O
	HI		O—		—O

NOTE
O—O indicates that there is continuity between the terminals.

WASHER SWITCH

Switch position	7	28
OFF		
ON	O—	—O

NOTE
O—O indicates that there is continuity between the terminals.

MT9029100028000X

Fig. 30 Front wiper & washer switch connector identification. Eclipse

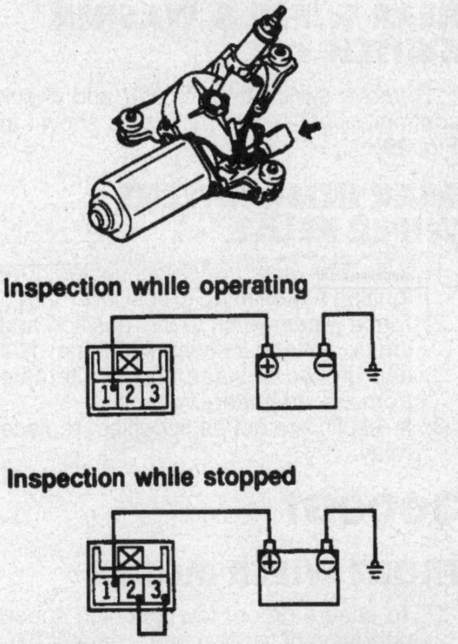
Inspection while operating
1
2
3
Inspection while stopped
1
2
3

MT9029500059000X

Fig. 32 Rear wiper operation inspection. 1995–96 Eclipse

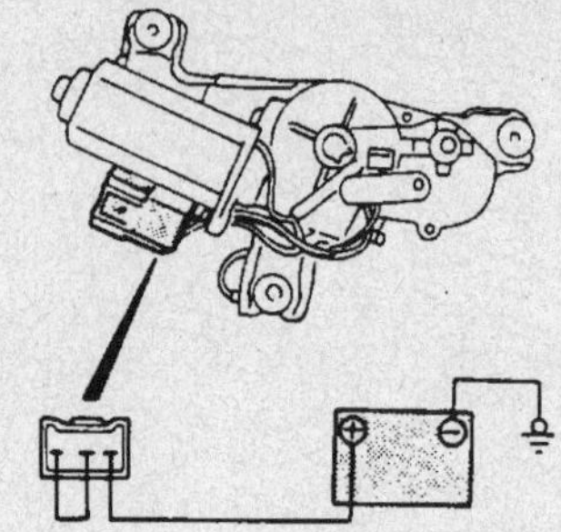

MT9029100030000X

Fig. 33 Rear wiper auto stop operation inspection. 1993–94 Eclipse

Switch position		Terminal No. 3	7	5	6	8	1	4
Wiper switch	OFF			O	O		ILL	ILL
	INT	O	O	O	O			
	LO		O	—	O			
Washer switch	OFF							
	ON		O	—	—	O		

MT9029500061000X

Fig. 36 Rear wiper & washer switch inspection. 1995–96 Eclipse

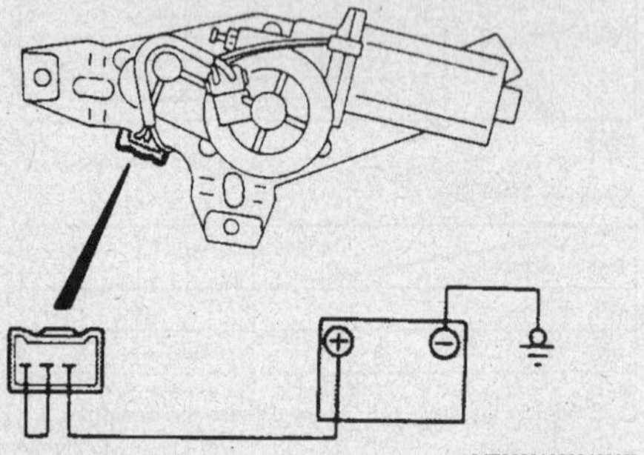

MT9029100034000X

Fig. 39 Rear wiper automatic stop operation inspection. Mirage

REAR WIPER & WASHER SWITCH

Remove switch from cluster and check continuity between terminals as shown in **Fig. 49.**

REAR INTERMITTENT WIPER RELAY

1. With rear wiper switch connected, turn ignition switch to ACC position.
2. Place wiper switch to INT position and check voltage between terminal five and ground. Voltage should alternate from zero to battery voltage.
3. If results are not as specified, replace relay.

3000GT

FRONT WIPER MOTOR

1. To ensure proper low and high speed operation of wiper motor, connect battery as shown in **Fig. 50.**
2. To check motor automatic stop position, run motor at low speed, then disconnect battery and connect jumper wire and battery as shown in **Fig. 50.**

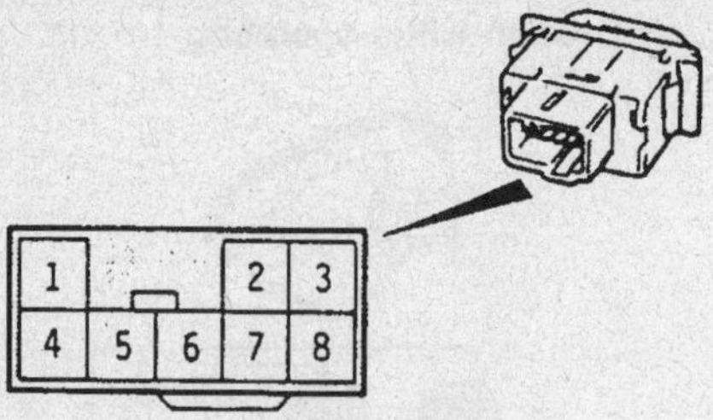
1
2
3
4
5
6
7
8

Switch position \ Terminal		2	4	5	6	7	8	3	1
Wiper switch	OFF		O	O				Illumination light	Illumination light
	ON			O	O				
	INT	O	O	O	—	—	O		
Washer switch					O	O			

NOTE
O—O indicates that there is continuity between the terminals.

MT9029100031000X

Fig. 34 Rear wiper & washer switch inspection. 1993–94 Eclipse

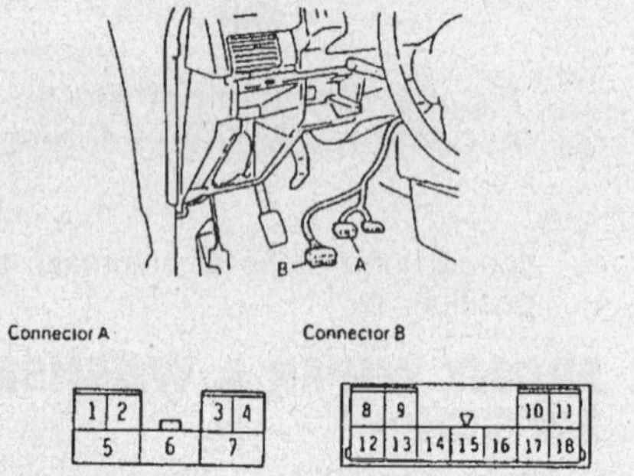
B
A
Connector A
Connector B
1
2
3
4
5
6
7
8
9
10
11
12
13
14
15
16
17
18

Switch position \ Terminal	10	17	18	4	14
OFF		O	O	O	- - O
INT*		O O	— O	O O	 - - O
1		O	—	O O	 - - O
2	O	—	—	O O	 - - O

NOTE
(1) O—O indicates that there is continuity between the terminals.
(2) The * symbol indicates models equipped with intermittent wipers.
(3) O·O Indicates continuity when the washer switch is in the ON state.

MT9029100032000X

Fig. 37 Front wiper & washer switch continuity chart. Mirage

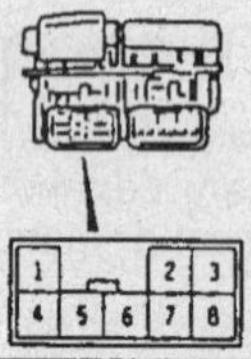
1
2
3
4
5
6
7
8

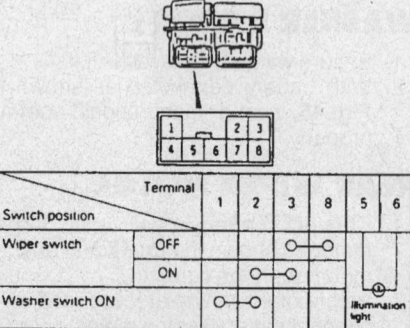

Switch position \ Terminal		1	2	3	8	5	6
Wiper switch	OFF			O	O	Illumination light	Illumination light
	ON		O	O			
Washer switch ON		O	O				

NOTE
O—O indicates that there is continuity between the terminals.

MT9029100035000X

Fig. 40 Rear wiper & washer switch continuity chart. Mirage

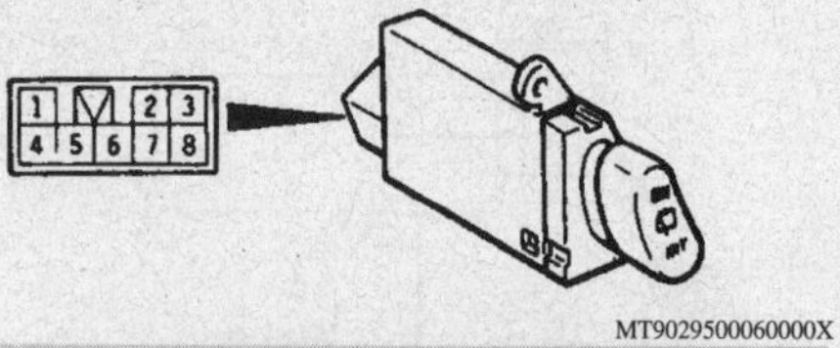
1
2
3
4
5
6
7
8

MT9029500060000X

Fig. 35 Rear wiper & washer switch terminal identification. 1995–96 Eclipse

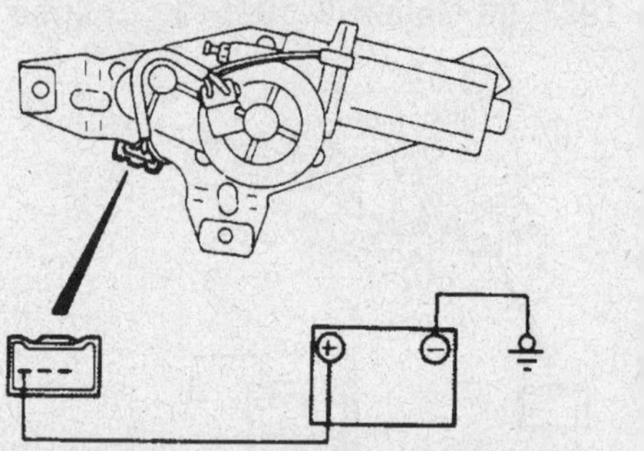

MT9029100033000X

Fig. 38 Rear wiper low speed operation inspection. Mirage

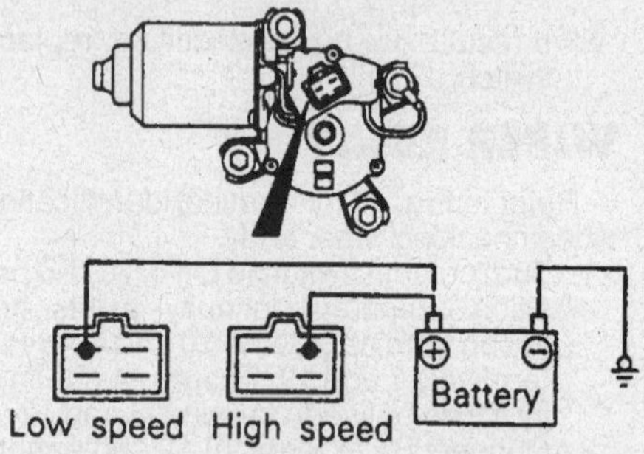
Low speed
High speed
Battery

MT9029100036000X

Fig. 41 Wiper motor high & low speed operation inspection. Diamante

FRONT WIPER & WASHER SWITCH

1. Remove knee protector and column cover.
2. Disconnect switch connector.
3. Operate switch and ensure continuity between terminals as shown in **Fig. 51.**

FRONT WIPER RELAY

Refer to **Fig. 52** for terminal identification when checking wiper relay.

1. Ensure continuity exists between terminals 5 and 11, and 6 and 10. Ensure no continuity exists between terminal 6 and 11.
2. Connect battery positive to terminal 5 and battery negative to terminal 11, ensure battery voltage is at terminal 6.

REAR WIPER MOTOR

1. Connect battery as shown in **Fig. 53** ensure proper motor operation.
2. Connect jumper and battery as shown

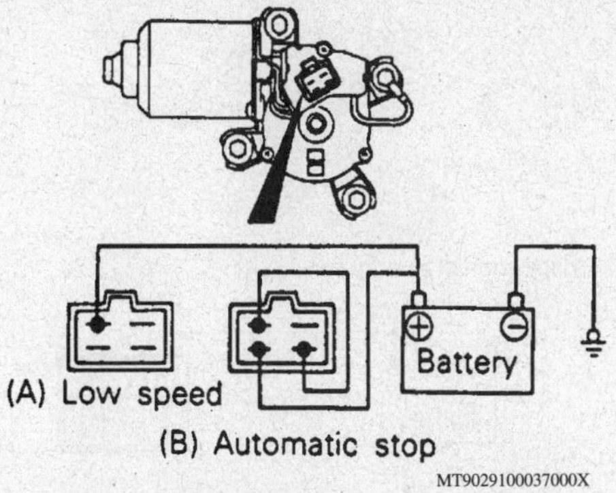
Battery
(A) Low speed
(B) Automatic stop
MT9029100037000X

Fig. 42 Wiper motor in auto stop operation inspection. Diamante

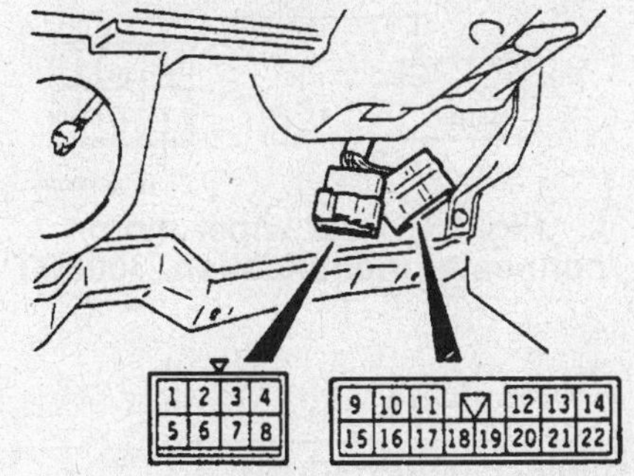
1 2 3 4
5 6 7 8
9 10 11 12 13 14
15 16 17 18 19 20 21 22

Switch position		Terminal 3	4	7	8	13	22
Wiper switch	OFF	○	—	○			
	LO	○	—	—	○		
	HI		○	—	○		
	INT	○	—	○	○	—	○
Washer switch	ON				○	○	

NOTE
○—○ indicates that there is continuity between the terminals.
MT9029100040000X

Fig. 45 Wiper & washer switch inspection. Expo

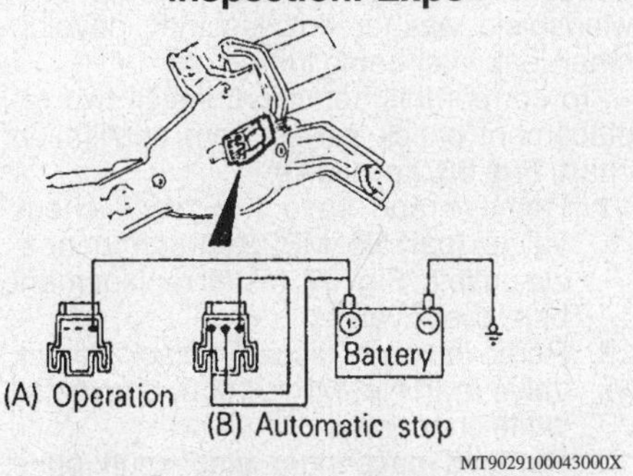
Battery
(A) Operation
(B) Automatic stop
MT9029100043000X

Fig. 48 Rear wiper auto stop operation inspection. Expo

in **Fig. 53,** ensure motor starts to run, then stops in automatic stop position.

REAR WIPER & WASHER SWITCH

1. Remove switch from knee pad protector.
2. Operate switch and check continuity between terminal as shown in **Fig. 54.**
3. If results are not as specified, replace switch.

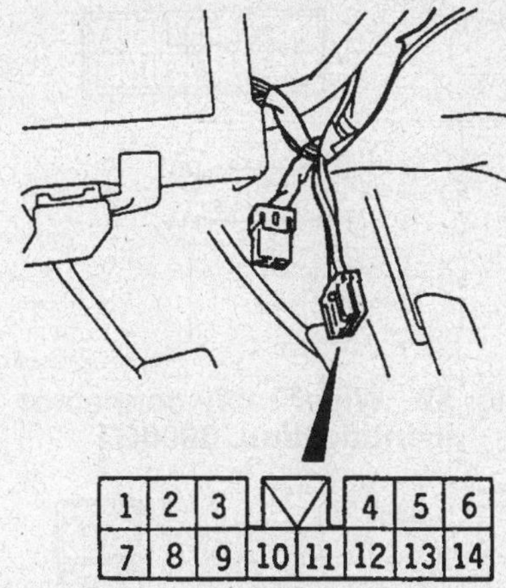
1 2 3 4 5 6
7 8 9 10 11 12 13 14

Switch position		Terminal 3	4	7	8	9	10	11	12
Wiper switch	OFF	○	—	—	—	—	○		
	AUTO				○	—	—	○	
		○	—	—	—	—	○		
	1 (LO)	○	—	—	—	—	—	—	○
	2 (HI)					○	—	—	○
Variable intermittent wiper control switch			○	—	○				
Washer switch	ON			○	—	—	—	—	○

NOTE
○—○ indicates that there is continuity between the terminals.
MT9029100038000X

Fig. 43 Wiper & washer switch inspection. Diamante

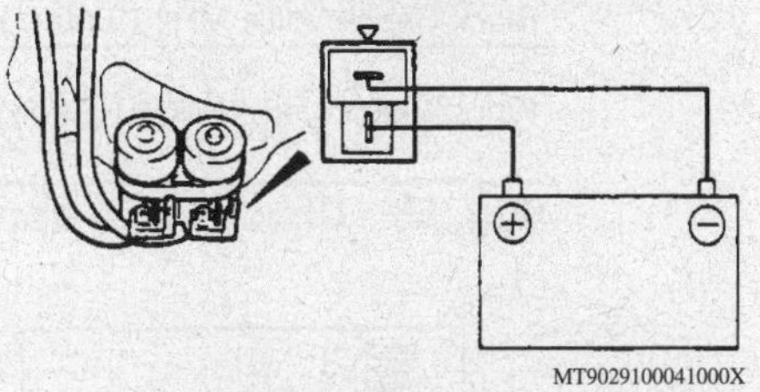
MT9029100041000X

Fig. 46 Washer pump inspection. Expo

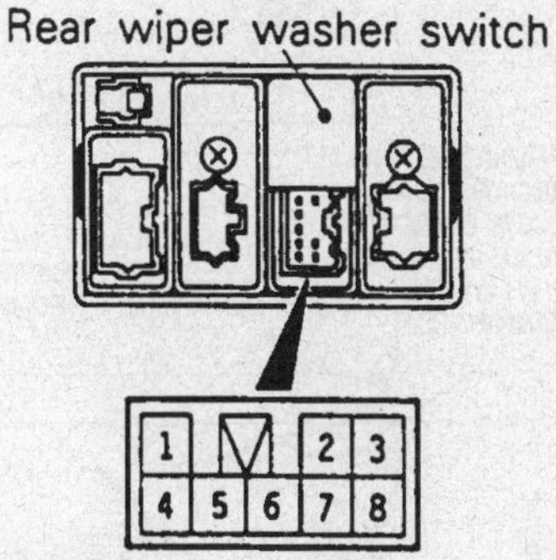
Rear wiper washer switch
1 2 3
4 5 6 7 8

Switch position		Terminal 1	4	5	7	8
Wiper switch	OFF		○	○		
	ON			○	—	○
	INT		○	○		
		○	—	—	—	○
Washer switch					○	○

NOTE
○—○ indicates that there is continuity between the terminals.
MT9029100044000X

Fig. 49 Rear wiper & washer switch inspection. Expo

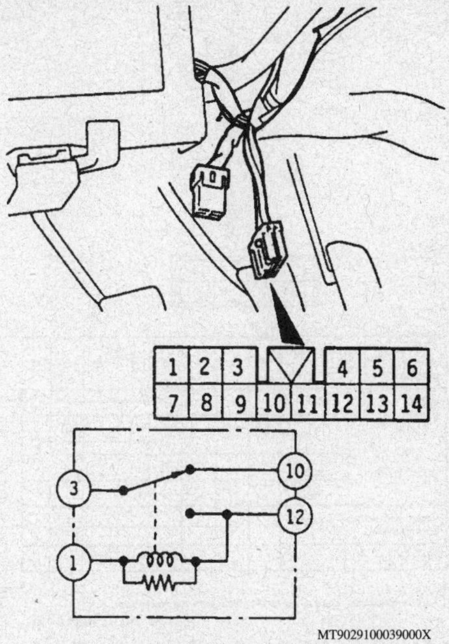
1 2 3 4 5 6
7 8 9 10 11 12 13 14
3
10
12
1
MT9029100039000X

Fig. 44 Wiper relay inspection. Diamante

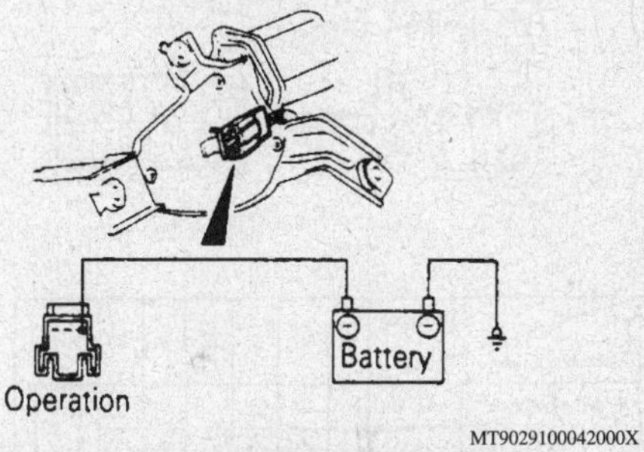
Battery
Operation
MT9029100042000X

Fig. 47 Rear wiper operation inspection. Expo

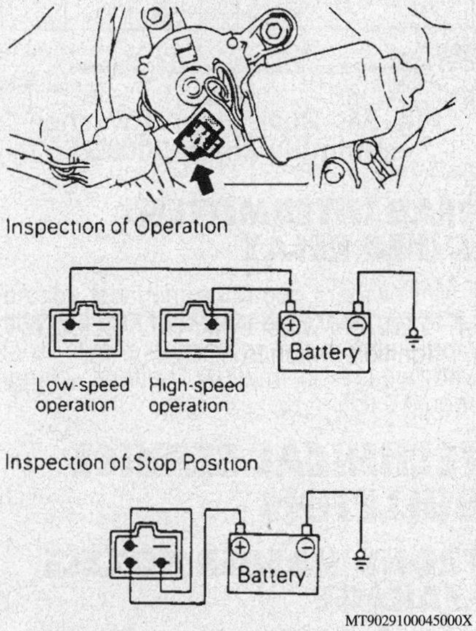
Inspection of Operation
Battery
Low-speed operation
High-speed operation
Inspection of Stop Position
Battery
MT9029100045000X

Fig. 50 Front wiper motor connector identification. 3000GT

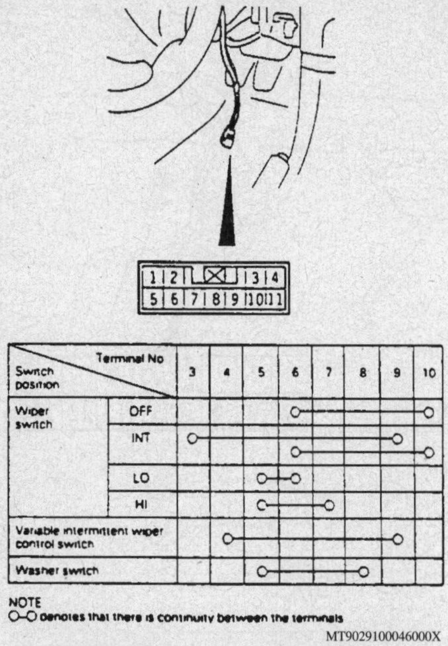
Terminal No
Switch position
Wiper switch
OFF
INT
LO
HI
Variable intermittent wiper control switch
Washer switch
NOTE
O–O denotes that there is continuity between the terminals
MT9029100046000X

Fig. 51 Wiper & washer switch continuity chart. 3000GT

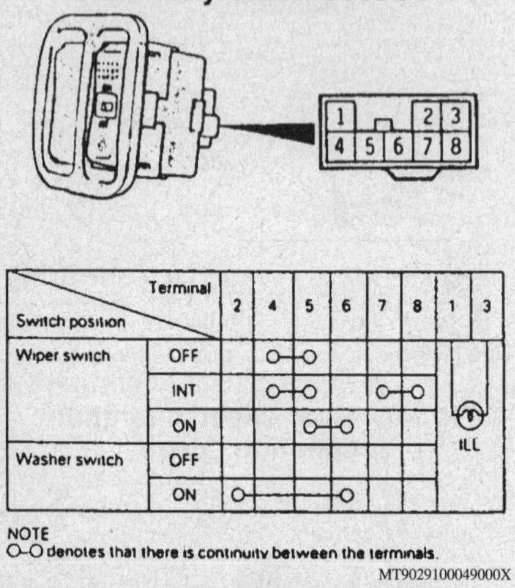
Terminal
Switch position
Wiper switch
OFF
INT
ON
Washer switch
OFF
ON
ILL
NOTE
O–O denotes that there is continuity between the terminals.
MT9029100049000X

Fig. 54 Rear wiper & washer continuity chart. 3000GT

REAR INTERMITTENT WIPER RELAY

With wipers operating, connect voltmeter to terminal 2 as shown in **Fig. 55.** With wipers stationary, no voltage should exist; with wipers in motion, battery voltage should exist.

TECHNICAL SERVICE BULLETINS

FRONT WASHER NOZZLE LEAKAGE

1995 Eclipse

On these models built before Oct. 12, 1994, VIN SE083033 and equipped with

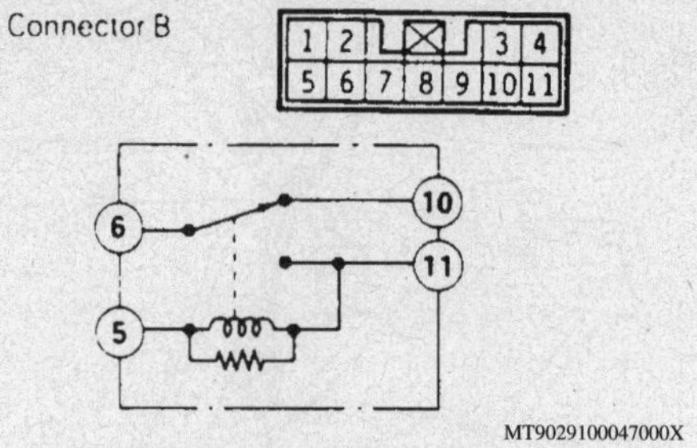
Connector B
MT9029100047000X

Fig. 52 Wiper relay connector identification. 3000GT

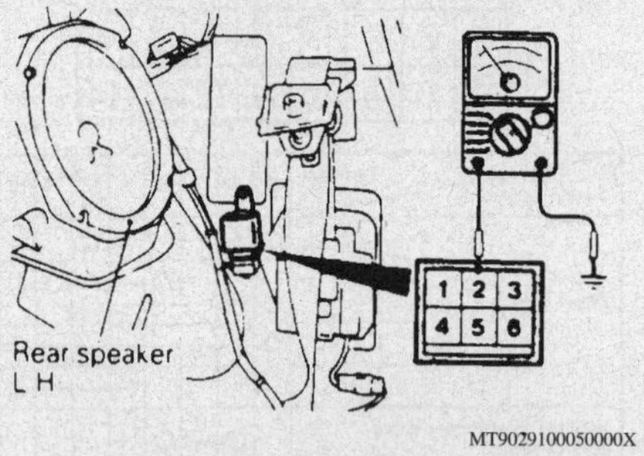
Rear speaker
L H
MT9029100050000X

Fig. 55 Intermittent relay connector identification. 3000GT

Original Description & Quantity	Replacement Part No. & Quantity
Black Check Valve MB229708 (2)	Blue Check Valve MB171570 (2)
Black Check Valve MR191060 (1)	White Connector MB083730 (1)
White Check Valve MR191059 (1)	Black Check Valve MB229708 Saved From Disassembly Procedure (2)

Fig. 56 Check valve application chart. 1995 Eclipse

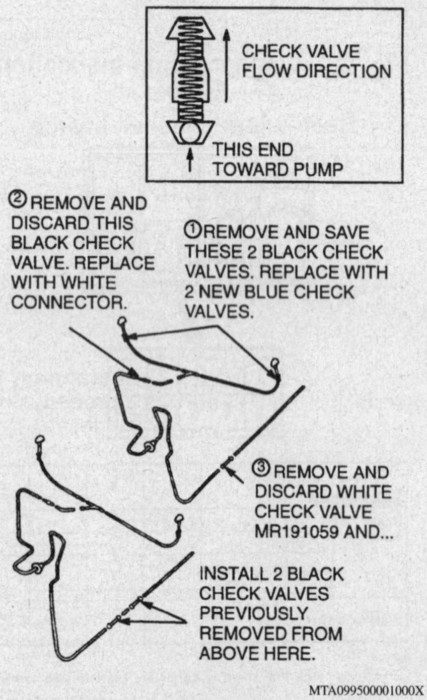
CHECK VALVE FLOW DIRECTION
THIS END TOWARD PUMP
②REMOVE AND DISCARD THIS BLACK CHECK VALVE. REPLACE WITH WHITE CONNECTOR.
①REMOVE AND SAVE THESE 2 BLACK CHECK VALVES. REPLACE WITH 2 NEW BLUE CHECK VALVES.
③REMOVE AND DISCARD WHITE CHECK VALVE MR191059 AND...
INSTALL 2 BLACK CHECK VALVES PREVIOUSLY REMOVED FROM ABOVE HERE.
MTA099500001000X

Fig. 57 Check valves. 1995 Eclipse

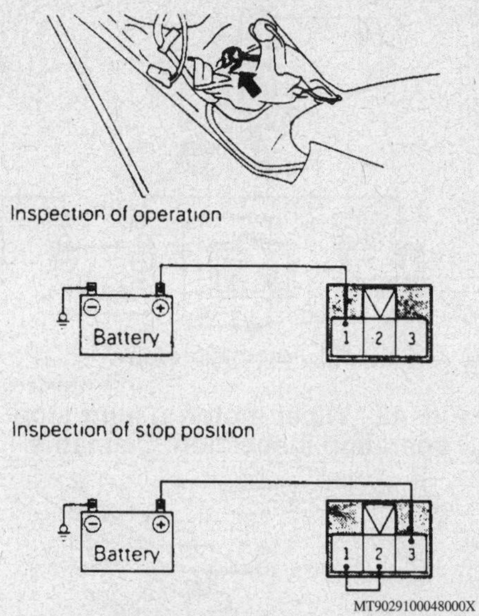
Inspection of operation
Battery
Inspection of stop position
Battery
MT9029100048000X

Fig. 53 Rear wiper motor connector identification. 3000GT

turbocharged engine, either or both front windshield washer nozzles may develop small leak after being turned off.

To correct this condition, install two replacement check valves from application chart, **Fig. 56,** as follows:

1. Remove and save two black check valves (part No. MB229708) from nozzle outlets, **Fig. 57.** Install replacement blue check valves.
2. Remove and discard black check valve (part No. MR191060) and install white connector.
3. Remove passenger side scuff plate and discard white check valve, then replace with two black check valves saved in earlier step. **Install with ball sides toward washer pump.**

Air Bag System

NOTE: Electrical Symbol & Wire Color Code Identification Located In The Front Of This Manual May Be Used As An Aid When Using Wiring Circuits Found In This Section.

INDEX

	Page No.
Air Bag System Disarming & Arming	29-65
Arming	29-65
Disarming	29-65
Collision Inspection	29-67
Repair Procedure	29-68
SRS Diagnosis Unit Memory Inspection	29-67
Component Locations	29-67
Component Service	29-68
Air Bag Module Disposal Procedures	29-71
Air Bag Module Replacement	29-68
Clockspring Replacement	29-68
Front Impact Sensor Replacement	29-70
Post Installation Inspection	29-70
SRS Diagnosis Unit (SDU) Replacement	29-68
Description & Operation	29-65
Diamante, Eclipse, Galant, Montero & 3000GT	29-65
Expo & Mirage	29-65
Diagnosis & Testing	29-67
Precautions	29-65
Scheduled Maintenance	29-65
Air Bag Module	29-66
Clockspring	29-67
Front Impact Sensor Inspection	29-66
Front Wiring Harness & Body Wiring Harness	29-67
SRS Diagnosis Unit (SDU) Inspection	29-66
SRS Warning Lamp Inspection	29-65
Steering Wheel, Column & Intermediate Joint	29-67
Tightening Specifications	29-77

AIR BAG SYSTEM DISARMING & ARMING

Disarming

1. Turn ignition switch to Lock position.
2. Disconnect and isolate battery ground cable.
3. **Wait at least 60 seconds after disconnection before performing repair procedures.** The SRS is designed to retain enough deployment voltage for a short time even after battery has been disconnected.

Arming

1. Ensure no one is inside vehicle.
2. Connect battery ground cable and start engine.
3. Ensure SRS warning lamp lights for approximately seven seconds, then goes off and remains off for at least 45 seconds.
4. If lamp operates as described, SRS is functioning properly.
5. If lamp does not operate as described, an SRS malfunction is indicated. Diagnose and repair as necessary.

DESCRIPTION & OPERATION

DIAMANTE, ECLIPSE, GALANT, MONTERO & 3000GT

The Supplemental Restraint System (SRS) consists of left and right front impact sensors, drivers and front passengers air bag modules, and the SRS diagnosis unit, which contains a safing impact sensor.

The air bags will deploy when the safing sensor and either or both impact sensors simultaneously activate while the ignition is turned On. This is designed to occur in frontal or near frontal impacts of moderate to severe force.

EXPO & MIRAGE

The Supplemental Restraint System (SRS) consists of drivers and front passengers air bag modules, as well as an SRS diagnosis unit with safing impact and analog G sensors.

Air bags will deploy when the safing sensor activates. This is designed to occur in frontal or near frontal impacts of moderate to severe force when the ignition switch is in the On position.

PRECAUTIONS

It is necessary to disarm the Supplemental Restraint System (SRS) prior to servicing any systems or components that may cause an air bag to deploy unexpectedly. Failure to do so may result in serious injury and vehicle damage. Refer to "Air Bag System Disarming & Arming" in this section for procedures.

1. Do not use any electrical test equipment on or near SRS components, except those specified in procedures.
2. **Never use analog ohmmeters or other powered test instruments on air bag units.**
3. **Do not disconnect any SRS components, fuses or connectors until battery ground cable has been disconnected for at least 60 seconds** to avoid storing false diagnostic trouble codes in the SRS Electronic Control Unit (ECU).
4. Always replace clockspring when replacing a deployed air bag module.
5. **Never attempt to repair following components:**
   a. Front impact sensors.
   b. SRS Diagnosis Unit (SDU).
   c. Clockspring.
   d. Air bag module.
   e. If any of these components are diagnosed as faulty, they should be replaced as outlined under "Component Service."
6. Do not attempt to repair SRS wiring harness connectors. Replace harness if any connectors are diagnosed as faulty. If wires are diagnosed as faulty, replace or repair harness according to tables shown in **Figs. 1 through 7.**
7. After disconnecting battery cable, wait 60 seconds or more before beginning repair procedures.
8. SRS components should not be subjected to heat over 200°F. Remove front impact sensors, SRS diagnosis unit, air bag module and clockspring before drying or baking vehicle after painting.
9. Do not paint air bag to correct cosmetic flaws. Replacement is necessary to correct such flaws.
10. Inspect SRS warning lamp operation to ensure system is functioning properly when service is complete.

SCHEDULED MAINTENANCE

SRS WARNING LAMP INSPECTION

When the ignition switch is turned to the On position or the engine is started, the SRS warning lamp will light for about seven seconds, then go Off. If the lamp operates as specified, the system is functioning properly. If the lamp stays lit more than seven seconds or lights when driving, a system malfunction or condition is indicated. Refer to "Diagnosis and Testing."

SDU Terminal No.	Harness Connector (No. of Terminals, Color)	Destination of Harness	Corrective Action
1	2 pins, red	Clock spring	Replace clock spring.
2			
3	No connection	–	–
4			
5	2 pins, green	Body wiring harness → Air bag module (passenger's side)	Correct or replace body wiring harness
6			
7	14 pins, red	Body wiring harness	–
8			
9		Body wiring harness → Diagnosis check pin	Correct or replace control wiring, instrument panel wiring harness or body wiring harness.
10		Body wiring harness → Control wiring harness → Ignition switch (ST)	
11		Body wiring harness → Multi-purpose fuse No. 11	
12		Body wiring harness → Multi-purpose fuse No. 18	
13		Body wiring harness → Instrument panel wiring harness → SRS warning light	
14			
15		Body wiring harness → Front wiring harness → Front impact sensor (R.H.) – positive (+) terminal	Replace the sensor cable*
16		Body wiring harness → Front wiring harness → Front impact sensor (L.H.) – positive (+) terminal	
17		Body wiring harness → Front wiring harness → Front impact sensor (L.H.) – negative (–) terminal	
18		Body wiring harness → Front wiring harness → Front impact sensor (R.H.) – negative (–) terminal	
19		Body wiring harness → Junction block → Body wiring harness → Ground	Correct or replace body wiring harness.
20			

NOTE
(1) The sensor cable marked with * is available as service part.
(2) The sensor cable used as a replacement part is routed along the body wiring harness.

MT8019400084000X

Fig. 1 SRS wire service chart. Diamante, Galant & 3000GT

SDU Terminal No.	Harness Connector (No. of Terminals, Color)	Destination of Harness	Corrective Action
1	2 pins, red	Body wiring harness → Clock spring	Correct or replace each wiring harness Replace clock spring
2			
3 and 4	–	–	–
5	2 pins, green	Body wiring harness → Air bag module (Passenger's side)	Correct or replace each wiring harness
6			
9	14 pins, red	Body wiring harness → Data link connector	Correct or replace each wiring harness
10		Body wiring harness → Control wiring harness → Body wiring harness → Ignition switch (ST)	
11		Body wiring harness → Junction block	
12		Body wiring harness → Junction block	
13		Body wiring harness → Instrument panel wiring harness → SRS warning light	
14			
15		Body wiring harness → Front wiring harness → Front impact sensor (LH)	Replace with sensor cable*
16			
17		Body wiring harness → Front wiring harness → Front impact sensor (RH)	
18			
19		Body wiring harness → Ground	Correct or replace body wiring harness
20			

MT8019400085000X

Fig. 2 SRS wire service chart. 1995 Eclipse

SRS-ECU Terminal No.	Harness Connector (No. of Terminals, Color)	Destination of Harness	Corrective Action
1 to 4	21 pins, yellows	–	–
5		Body wiring harness → Clock spling → Air bag module (Driver's side)	Correct or replace body wiring harness Replace clock spring
6			
7		Body wiring harness → Air bag module (Front passenger's side)	Correct or replace body wiring harness
8			
9, 10		–	–
11		Body wiring harness → Data link connector	Correct or replace body wiring harness
12		–	–
13		Body wiring harness → Junction block (fuse No.3)	Correct or replace body wiring harness
14		Body wiring harness → Junction block (fuse No.8)	
15		Body wiring harness → Instrument panel wiring harness → SRS warning light	
16 to 19		–	–
20		Body wiring harness → Ground	Correct or replace body wiring harness
21			

MT8019600176000X

Fig. 3 SRS wire service chart. 1996 Eclipse

Harness Connector (No. of Terminals, Color)	SRS-ECU Terminal No.	Destination of Harness	Corrective Action
2 pins, red	1 to 2	Body wiring harness → Clock spring → Air bag module (Driver's side)	Replace clock spring. Correct or replace body wiring harness
2 pins, green	5 to 6	Body wiring harness → Air bag module (Front passenger's side)	Correct or replace body wiring harness
14 pins, red	7 to 8	–	–
	9	Body wiring harness → Data link connector	Correct or replace body wiring harness
	10	–	–
	11	Body wiring harness → Junction block	Correct or replace body wiring harness
	12	Body wiring harness → Junction block	
	13	Body wiring harness → SRS warning light	
	14		
	15 to 18	–	–
	19	Body wiring harness → Junction block → Body wiring harness → Ground	Correct or replace body wiring harness
	20		

MT8019400086000X

Fig. 4 SRS wire service chart. Expo & 1993–95 Mirage

FRONT IMPACT SENSOR INSPECTION

1. Remove righthand and lefthand front splash shields or extensions.
2. Ensure arrow mark on sensor is facing front of vehicle.
3. Inspect sensor frame mounting location condition and ensure it is free from deformities or rust. **SRS may not activate properly if an impact sensor is not installed properly.**
4. Inspect sensor for dents, cracks, deformities or rust.
5. Inspect sensor harnesses for binds, connectors for damage and terminals for deformities.

SRS DIAGNOSIS UNIT (SDU) INSPECTION

1. Inspect case and brackets for dents, cracks, deformities, or rust. **SRS may not activate properly if SDU is improperly installed.**
2. Inspect SDU connectors for damaged or deformed terminals.
3. Inspect lock lever for damage or rust.

AIR BAG MODULE

Drivers

1. Remove module as described under "Component Service."
2. Inspect pad cover for dents, cracks or deformities.
3. Inspect hooks and connector for deformities and binding harness.
4. Inspect air bag inflator case for damage.
5. Install air bag module to steering wheel to inspect fit and alignment.

Passengers

1. Remove module as described under "Component Service."
2. Inspect cover for dents, cracks and deformities.
3. Inspect connector for deformed terminal and binding harness.

Harness Connector (No. of Terminals, Color)	SRS-ECU Terminal No.	Destination of Harness	Corrective Action
21 pins	1 to 4	–	–
	5 to 6	Body wiring harness → Clock spring → Air bag module (Driver's side)	Replace clock spring. Correct or replace body wiring harness
	7 to 8	Body wiring harness → Air bag module (Front passenger's side)	Correct or replace body wiring harness
	9 to 10	–	–
	11	Body wiring harness → Data link connector	Correct or replace body wiring harness
	12	–	–
	13	Body wiring harness → Junction block (fuse No. 7)	Correct or replace body wiring harness
	14	Body wiring harness → Junction block (fuse No. 2)	
	15	Body wiring harness → SRS warning light	
	16 to 19	–	–
	20	Body wiring harness → Junction block → Body wiring harness → Ground	Correct or replace body wiring harness
	21		

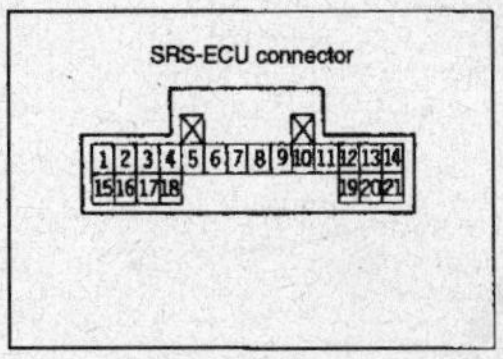
SRS-ECU connector
1 2 3 4 5 6 7 8 9 10 11 12 13 14
15 16 17 18 19 20 21

MT8019600181000X

Fig. 5 SRS wire service chart. 1996 Mirage

SDU Terminal No.	Harness Connector (No. of Terminals, Color)	Destination of Harness	Corrective Action
1	2 pins, red	Dash wiring harness → Clock spring	Correct or replace each wiring harness Replace clock spring
2			
13	14 pins, red	Dash wiring harness → Diagnosis connector	Correct or replace each wiring harness
14		Dash wiring harness → Control wiring harness → Dash wiring harness → Ignition switch (ST)	
15		Dash wiring harness → Junction block (fuse No. 18)	
16		Dash wiring harness → Junction block (fuse No. 12)	
17		Dash wiring harness → Instrument panel wiring harness → SRS warning light	
18			
20		Dash wiring harness → Front wiring harness → Front impact sensor (LH)	Replace with sensor cable*
21			
19		Dash wiring harness → Front wiring harness → Front impact sensor (RH)	
22			
23		Dash wiring harness → Ground	Correct or replace dash wiring harness
24			

NOTE
(1) The sensor cable marked with* is available as service part.
(2) The sensor cable used as a replacement part is routed along the front wiring harness.

MT8019200173000X

Fig. 6 SRS wire service chart. 1995 Montero

SDU Terminal No.	Harness Connector (No. of Terminals, Color)	Destination of Harness	Corrective Action
1	2 pins, red	Dash wiring harness → Clock spring	Correct or replace each wiring harness Replace clock spring
2			
3 and 4	Unused terminals	–	–
5	2 pins, green	Dash wiring harness → Front passenger's air bag module	Correct or replace each wiring harness
6			
11 and 12	14 pins, red	–	–
13	14 pins, red	Dash wiring harness → Diagnosis connector	Correct or replace each wiring harness
14		Dash wiring harness → Control wiring harness → Dash wiring harness → Ignition switch (ST)	
15		Dash wiring harness → Junction block (fuse No. 18)	
16		Dash wiring harness → Junction block (fuse No. 12)	
17		Dash wiring harness → Instrument panel wiring harness → SRS warning light	
18			
20		Dash wiring harness → Front wiring harness → Front impact sensor (LH)	Correct or replace with sensor cable*
21			
19		Dash wiring harness → Front wiring harness → Front impact sensor (RH)	
22			
23		Dash wiring harness → Ground	Correct or replace dash wiring harness
24			

NOTE
(1) The sensor cable marked with* is available as service part.
(2) The sensor cable used as a replacement part is routed along the front wiring harness and front wiring harness.

MT8019600174000X

Fig. 7 SRS wire service chart. 1996 Montero

4. Inspect inflator case for damage.

CLOCKSPRING

1. Remove clockspring as described under "Component Service."
2. Inspect connectors, protective tube and terminals for damage and deformities.
3. Visually inspect case and gears for damage.

STEERING WHEEL, COLUMN & INTERMEDIATE JOINT

1. Inspect wiring harness, connectors and terminals for damage and deformities.
2. Install air bag module to inspect fit and alignment.
3. Inspect steering wheel for noise, binding, difficult operation or excessive freeplay.

FRONT WIRING HARNESS & BODY WIRING HARNESS

1. Inspect harness connectors for damaged or deformed terminals.
2. Inspect harness for any crimps or binding.
3. Inspect harness wiring for any fraying or damage.
4. Replace harness or connectors if they show any signs of damage.

COMPONENT LOCATIONS

Refer to **Figs. 8 through 16** for SRS component locations.

DIAGNOSIS & TESTING

Refer to MOTOR's Air Bag Manual for complete air bag system diagnosis and testing information.

COLLISION INSPECTION

On vehicles which have experienced an air bag system deployment, certain air bag components must be replaced. To determine which components require replacement, refer to MOTOR's Air Bag Manual.

SRS DIAGNOSIS UNIT MEMORY INSPECTION

Perform the following steps to inspect and service the SRS after a collision, whether or not an air bag has been deployed:

1. Connect scan tool to diagnostic check connector.
2. Read all displayed DTCs. **If battery power supply has been disconnected or disrupted by collision, scan tool cannot communicate with SRS diagnosis unit. Inspect, and if necessary, repair body wiring harness before proceeding further.**
3. Read service data, then erase DTCs.
4. Read and record all DTCs displayed after 45 seconds. Refer to "Diagnosis and Testing" for DTC diagnosis.

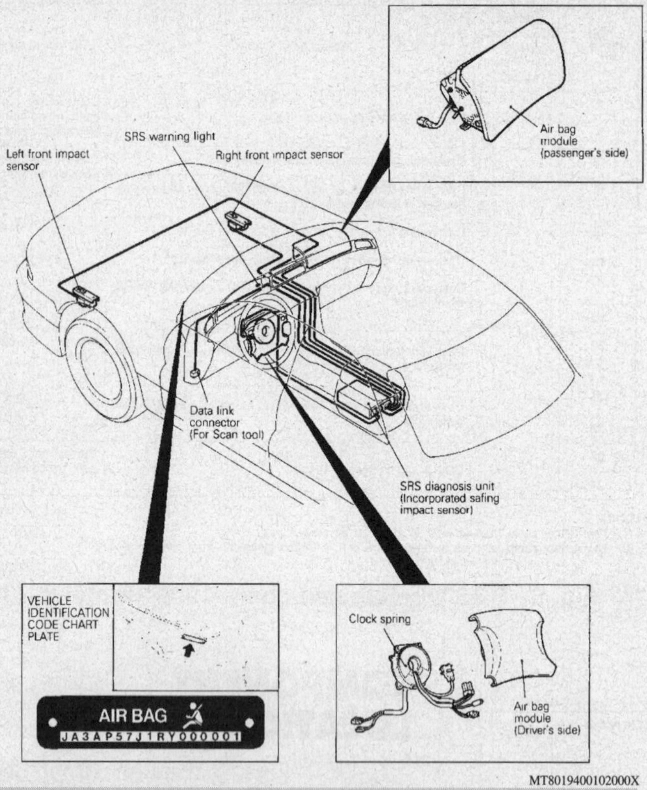
Air bag module (passenger's side)
SRS warning light
Left front impact sensor
Right front impact sensor
Data link connector (For Scan tool)
SRS diagnosis unit (Incorporated safing impact sensor)
VEHICLE IDENTIFICATION CODE CHART PLATE
AIR BAG
JA3AP57J1RY000001
Clock spring
Air bag module (Driver's side)
MT8019400102000X

Fig. 8 SRS component locations. Diamante

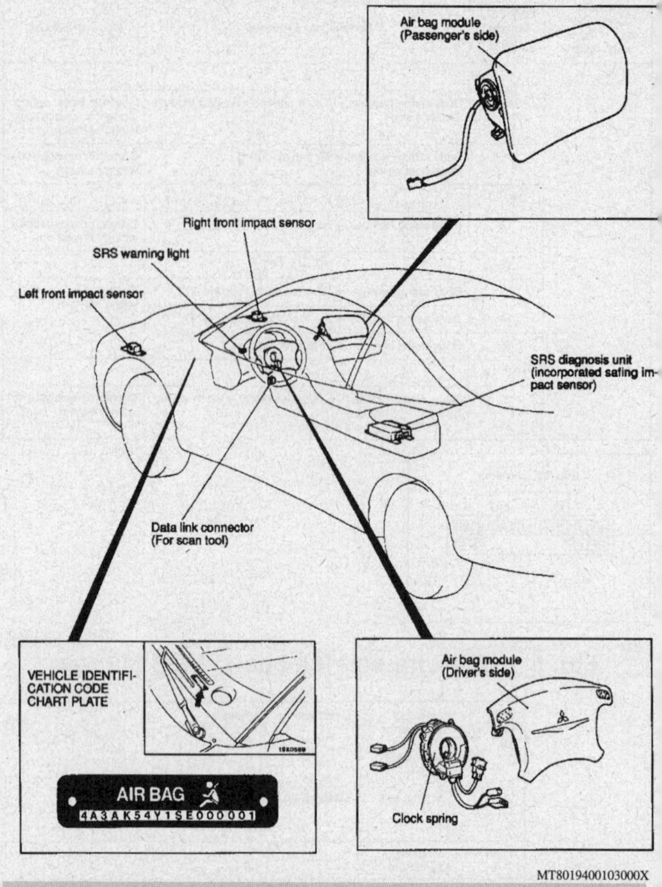
Air bag module (Passenger's side)
Right front impact sensor
SRS warning light
Left front impact sensor
SRS diagnosis unit (incorporated safing impact sensor)
Data link connector (For scan tool)
VEHICLE IDENTIFICATION CODE CHART PLATE
AIR BAG
4A3AK54Y1SE000001
Air bag module (Driver's side)
Clock spring
MT8019400103000X

Fig. 9 SRS component locations. 1995 Eclipse

REPAIR PROCEDURE

Air Bag(s) Deployed In Collision

1. Inspect clockspring for any visible damage such as dents, cracks or deformation, and replace as necessary.
2. Inspect wiring harness built into steering wheel and connectors for damage and terminals for deformities.
3. Inspect steering wheel, column and intermediate joint for noise, binding, difficult operation and excessive freeplay.
4. Inspect harness for binding, connectors for damage and poor connections, and terminals for deformities.

Air Bag(s) Did Not Deploy

Inspect SRS components as described under "Scheduled Maintenance" for visible damage such as dents, cracks or deformities and replace as necessary.

COMPONENT SERVICE

AIR BAG MODULE REPLACEMENT

DRIVER

1. Set front wheels in straight ahead position, then remove ignition key.
2. Remove air bag module mounting nut from rear side of steering wheel, **Figs. 17 through 23.**
3. Spread air bag connector lock by pressing toward outer side with screwdriver, then disconnect clockspring connector.
4. Remove air bag module.
5. Remove clockspring.
6. Reverse procedure to install. **Ensure clockspring mating marks are properly aligned.**

PASSENGER

1. Remove glove compartment.
2. **On Expo models,** remove knee protector bracket.
3. **On Montero models,** remove right-hand foot shower duct.
4. **On 3000GT models,** remove cross pipe cover.
5. **On all models,** remove air bag module, **Figs. 24 through 30.**
6. Reverse procedure to install.

CLOCKSPRING REPLACEMENT

1. Remove air bag module as described under "Air Bag Module Replacement."
2. Use steering wheel puller to remove steering wheel. **Do not hammer on wheel.**
3. **On Diamante and 3000GT models,** remove knee protector.
4. **On Expo models,** remove hook lock release handle and instrument panel undercover.
5. **On all models,** remove lower steering column cover.
6. **On Expo models,** remove meter hood and steering column upper cover.
7. **On 3000GT models,** remove floor console, then the clockspring and SRS diagnostic unit connection.
8. **On all models,** remove clockspring and body wiring harness connection, then the clockspring.
9. Reverse procedure to install, noting the following:
   a. Align mating marks on clockspring neutral position indicator. Place front wheels in straight–ahead position, then install clockspring to steering column. **If mating marks are not properly aligned, steering wheel may not turn completely, or flat cable in clockspring may be severed.**
   b. After securing steering wheel, turn from lock to lock to verify normal operation.

SRS DIAGNOSIS UNIT (SDU) REPLACEMENT

1. **On Diamante models,** remove floor console switch panel.
2. **On Eclipse models,** remove manual transaxle shift lever knob, ashtray, inner box and center console panel.
3. **On Expo models,** remove side covers, manual transaxle shift lever knob, floor console switch panel and armrest assembly.
4. **On Mirage models,** remove hole

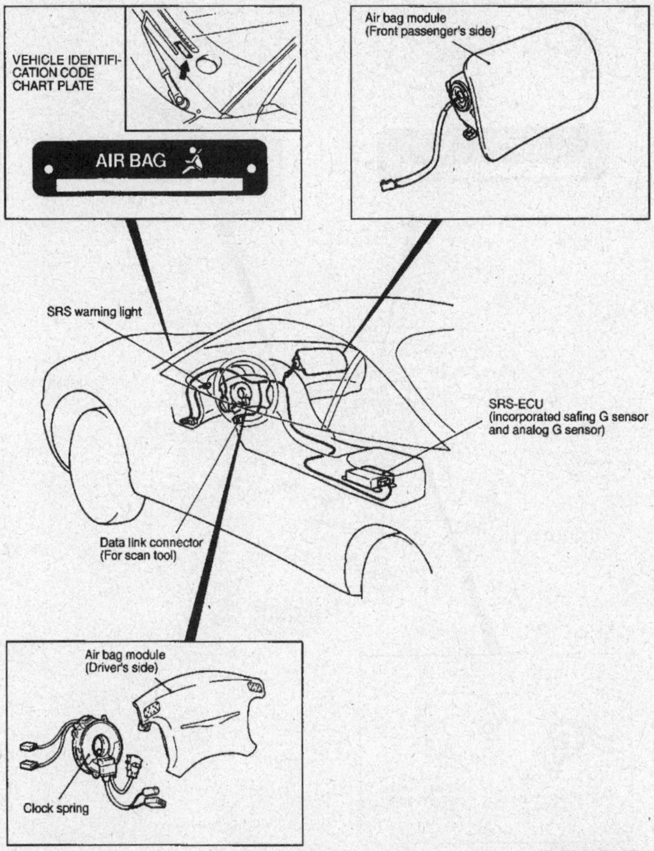
VEHICLE IDENTIFICATION CODE CHART PLATE
AIR BAG
Air bag module (Front passenger's side)
SRS warning light
SRS-ECU (incorporated safing G sensor and analog G sensor)
Data link connector (For scan tool)
Air bag module (Driver's side)
Clock spring
MT8019600186000X

Fig. 10 SRS component locations. 1996 Eclipse

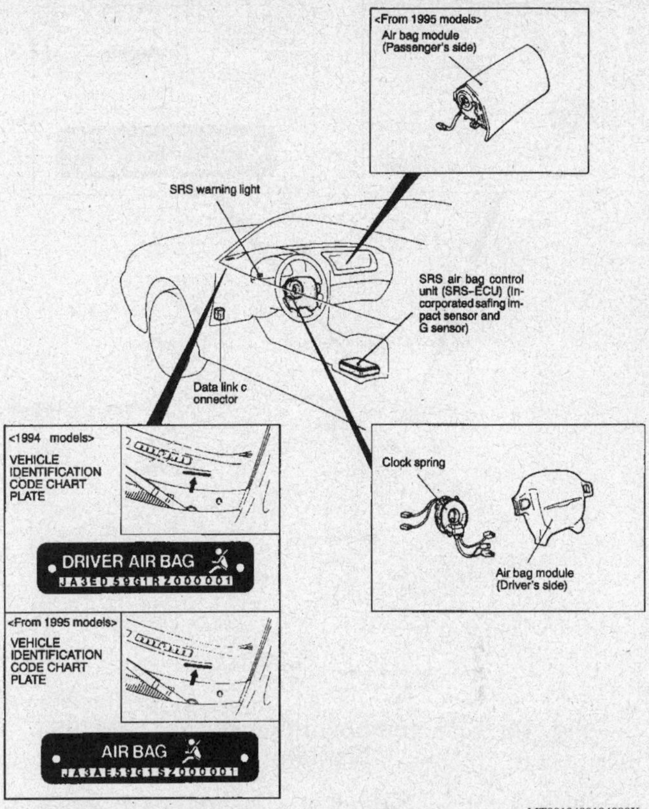
<From 1995 models>
Air bag module (Passenger's side)
SRS warning light
SRS air bag control unit (SRS-ECU) (Incorporated safing impact sensor and G sensor)
Data link connector
<1994 models>
VEHICLE IDENTIFICATION CODE CHART PLATE
DRIVER AIR BAG
<From 1995 models>
VEHICLE IDENTIFICATION CODE CHART PLATE
AIR BAG
Clock spring
Air bag module (Driver's side)
MT8019400104000X

Fig. 11 SRS component locations. Expo

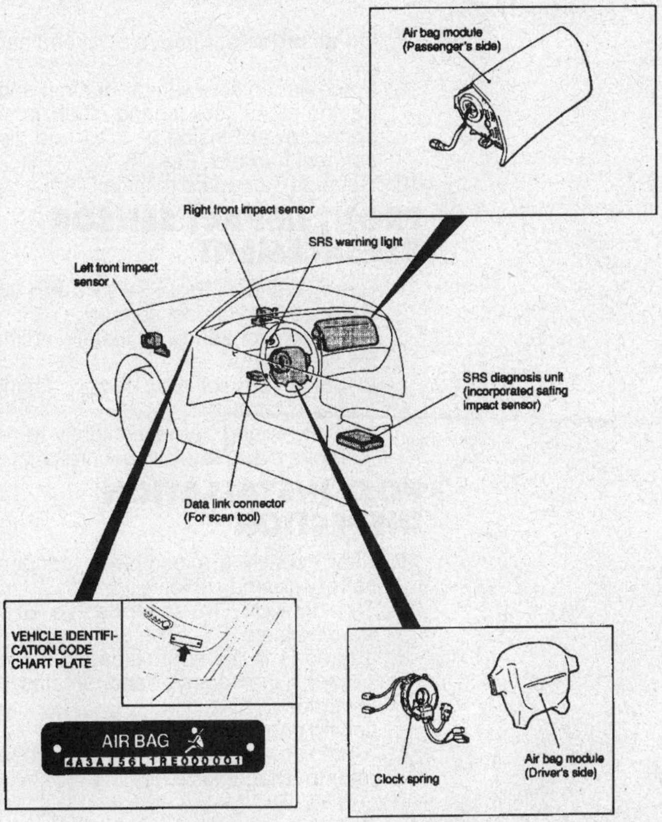
Air bag module (Passenger's side)
Right front impact sensor
SRS warning light
Left front impact sensor
SRS diagnosis unit (incorporated safing impact sensor)
Data link connector (For scan tool)
VEHICLE IDENTIFICATION CODE CHART PLATE
AIR BAG
Clock spring
Air bag module (Driver's side)
MT8019400105000X

Fig. 12 SRS component locations. Galant

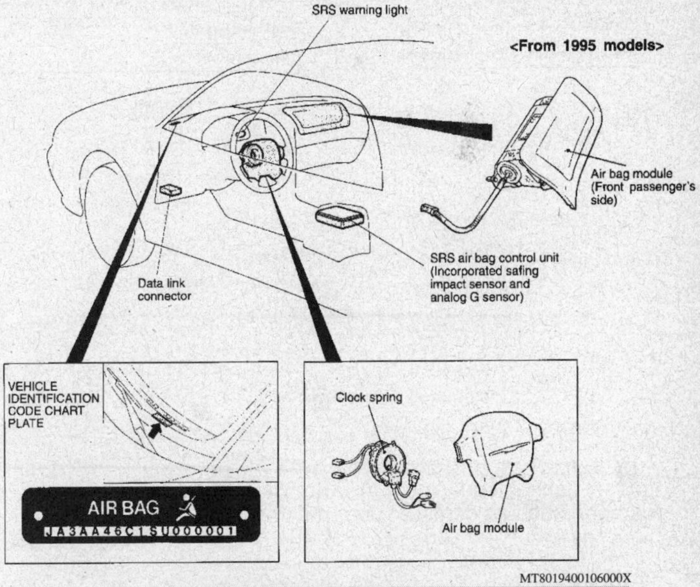
SRS warning light
<From 1995 models>
Air bag module (Front passenger's side)
SRS air bag control unit (Incorporated safing impact sensor and analog G sensor)
Data link connector
VEHICLE IDENTIFICATION CODE CHART PLATE
AIR BAG
Clock spring
Air bag module
MT8019400106000X

Fig. 13 SRS component locations. Mirage

cover, console plug, bezel and guide ring.

5. **On all models,** remove floor console, **Figs. 31 through 37.**
6. **On 1994 Expo models,** remove retractor assembly.
7. **On 3000GT models,** remove cup holder, console plug and rear console assembly.

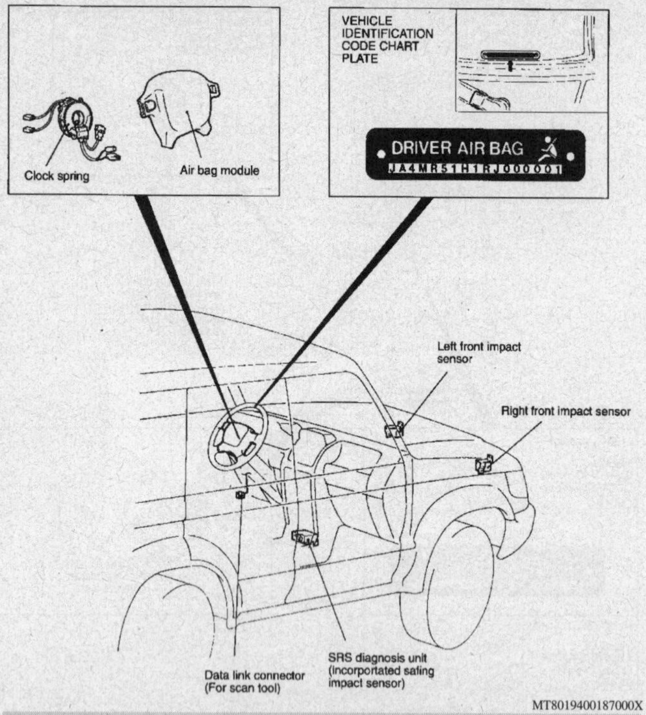
Clock spring
Air bag module
VEHICLE IDENTIFICATION CODE CHART PLATE
DRIVER AIR BAG
JA4MR51H1RJ000001
Left front impact sensor
Right front impact sensor
Data link connector (For scan tool)
SRS diagnosis unit (incorporated safing impact sensor)
MT8019400187000X

Fig. 14 SRS component locations. 1994–95 Montero

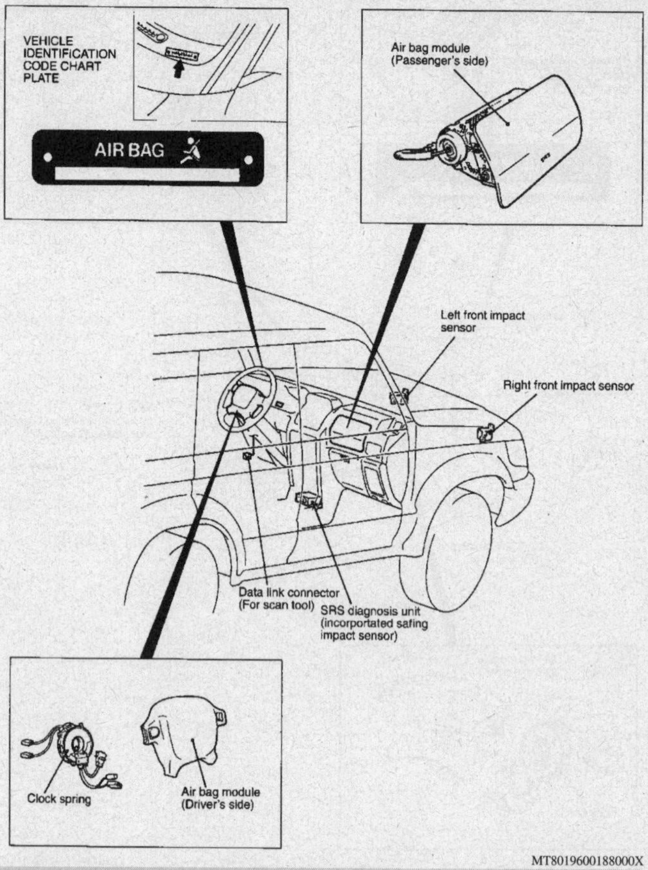
VEHICLE IDENTIFICATION CODE CHART PLATE
AIR BAG
Air bag module (Passenger's side)
Left front impact sensor
Right front impact sensor
Data link connector (For scan tool)
SRS diagnosis unit (incorporated safing impact sensor)
Clock spring
Air bag module (Driver's side)
MT8019600188000X

Fig. 15 SRS component locations. 1996 Montero

Name	Symbol	Name	Symbol
Data link connector <From 1994 models>	D	Front impact sensor	A
Data link connector <Up to 1993 models>	C	SRS diagnosis unit	B

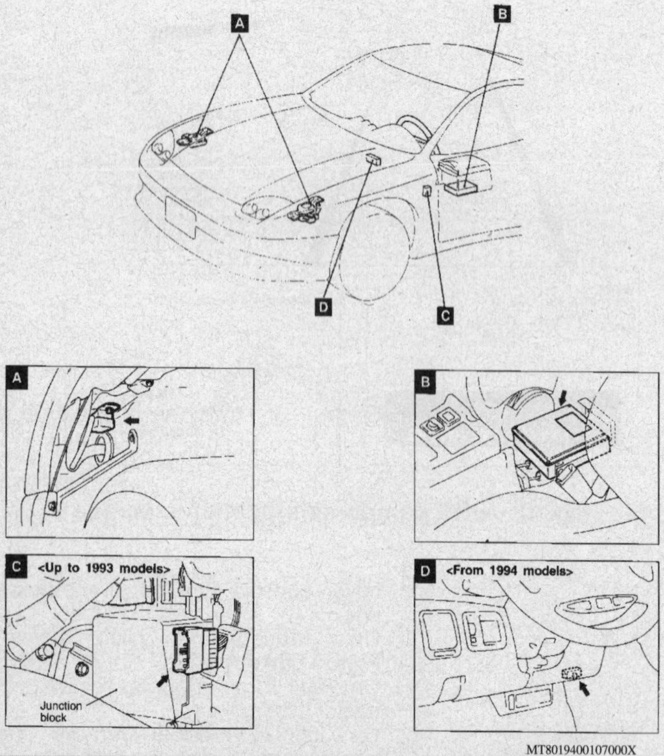
A
B
C
D
<Up to 1993 models>
Junction block
<From 1994 models>
MT8019400107000X

Fig. 16 SRS component locations. 3000GT

8. **On all models,** remove SDU and harness.
9. Place flat tip screwdriver against connector metal lock spring, then push spring toward inside of SDU and disconnect harness, **Fig. 38.**
10. Reverse procedure to install.

FRONT IMPACT SENSOR REPLACEMENT

1. Remove shield, **Figs. 39 through 43.**
2. Remove front impact sensor.
3. Reverse procedure to install, noting following:
   a. Install sensor with arrow facing front of vehicle.
   b. Bend wiring harness slightly to remove slack, and clip securely.

POST INSTALLATION INSPECTION

1. After repairs are complete, connect battery ground cable.
2. Turn ignition On and observe SRS warning lamp.
3. If lamp is lit for approximately seven seconds, then goes off and remains off for at least 45 seconds, SRS is functioning properly.
4. If lamp does not perform as described, refer to "Diagnosis & Testing."

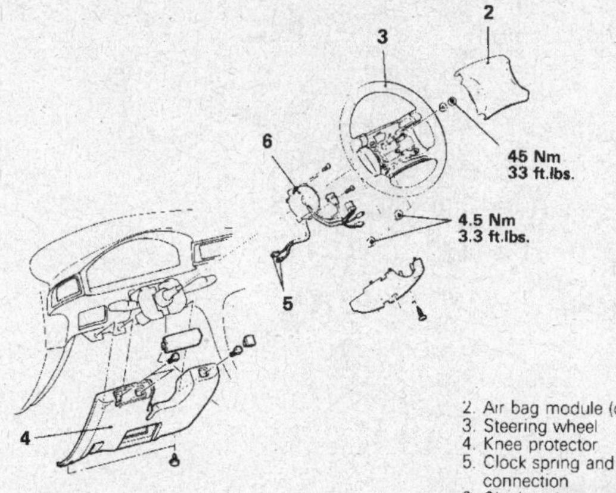
2
3
6
45 Nm
33 ft.lbs.
4.5 Nm
3.3 ft.lbs.
5
4

2. Air bag module (driver's side)
3. Steering wheel
4. Knee protector
5. Clock spring and body wiring harness connection
6. Clock spring

MT8019400172000X

Fig. 17 Driver air bag & clockspring replacement. Diamante

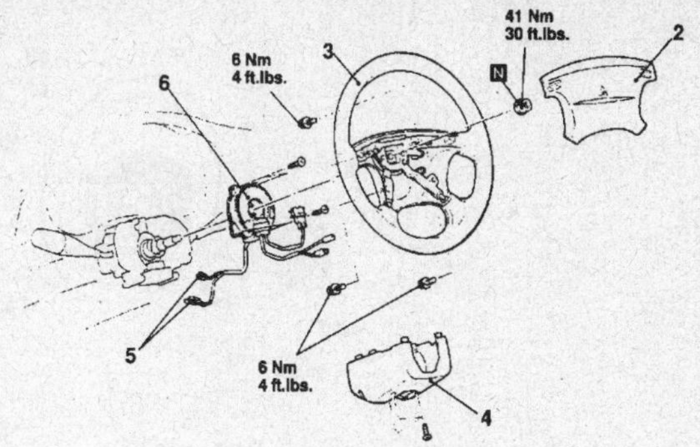
41 Nm
30 ft.lbs.
2
6 Nm
4 ft.lbs.
3
6
N
5
6 Nm
4 ft.lbs.
4

2. Air bag module
3. Steering wheel
4. Column cover lower
5. Clock spring and body wiring harness connection
6. Clock spring

MT8019400148000X

Fig. 18 Driver air bag & clockspring replacement. Eclipse

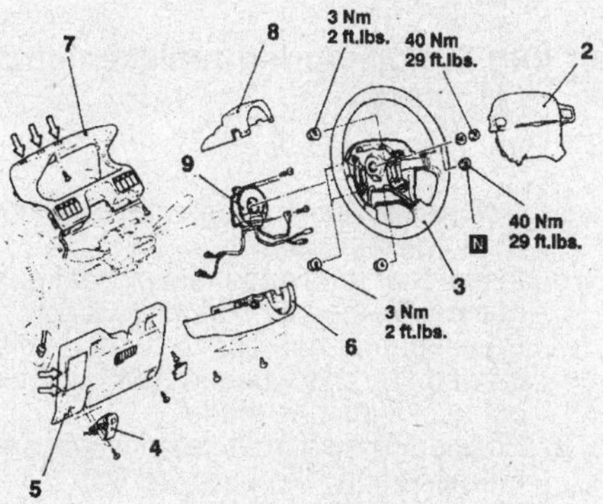
3 Nm
2 ft.lbs.
40 Nm
29 ft.lbs.
7
8
2
9
40 Nm
N
29 ft.lbs.
3
3 Nm
2 ft.lbs.
6
4
5

2. Air bag module
3. Steering wheel
4. Hook lock release handle
5. Instrument panel under cover
6. Steering column cover lower
7. Meter hood
8. Steering cloumn cover upper
9. Clock spring

MT8019400149000X

Fig. 19 Driver air bag & clockspring replacement. Expo

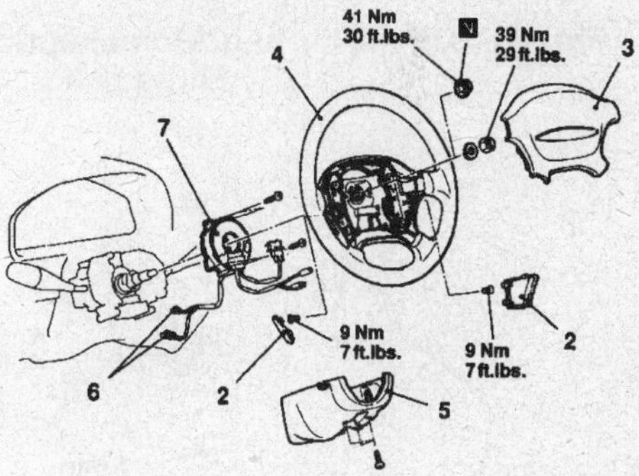
41 Nm
30 ft.lbs.
N
39 Nm
29 ft.lbs.
3
4
7
9 Nm
7 ft.lbs.
9 Nm
7 ft.lbs.
2
6
2
5

2. Steering wheel lower cover
3. Air bag module (Driver's side)
4. Steering wheel
5. Column cover lower
6. Clock spring and body wiring harness connection
7. Clock spring

MT8019400150000X

Fig. 20 Driver air bag & clockspring replacement. Galant

AIR BAG MODULE DISPOSAL PROCEDURES

Before scrapping a vehicle equipped with an air bag system, or prior to disposing of an air bag module, the module must be deployed. If vehicle is to be scrapped, deploy air bag(s) inside vehicle. If vehicle is to continue in service, air bags must be removed and deployed outside vehicle.

UNDEPLOYED AIR BAG MODULE DISPOSAL

Deployment Inside Vehicle

1. Open windows and doors of vehicle.
2. Disconnect and remove battery from vehicle. **Wait at least 60 seconds after disconnection before performing any further steps. SRS is designed to retain enough deployment voltage for a short time even after battery has been disconnected.**
3. Remove lower steering column cover.
4. Disconnect clockspring red two-pin connector from body wiring connector.
5. Remove glove compartment and outer case, then disconnect passengers air bag module red two-pin connector from body wiring harness.
6. Connect two 20 ft. long wires to the two leads of SRS air bag adapter harness "A" tool No. MB686560, or equivalent. Cover connections with tape. **Other ends of two wires should be connected to each other to prevent unwanted deployment.**
7. Connect adapter harness "A" to clockspring connector.
8. Connect harness "A" to passenger red two-pin connector and pass deployment wires out of vehicle.
9. From as far away as possible, in a shielded position, disconnect the two wires from each other. **Read following cautions before proceeding:**
   a. **Ensure no people, animals, equipment or objects are in or near vehicle before deploying air bag in this manner. Wear safety glasses and protective gloves.**
   b. Connect the two wires to a fully charged 12 volt battery. Deployment should occur.
   c. **Inflator will be quite hot immediately after deployment. Wait 30 minutes to allow air bag to cool.**
   d. **Do not inhale gas from air bag.**
   e. **Dispose of air bag as outlined**

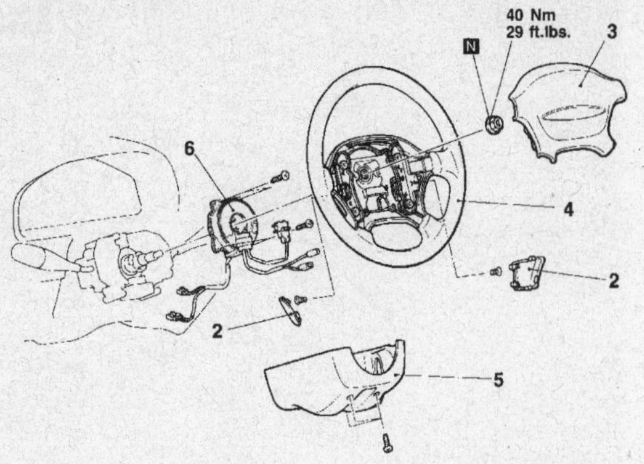
40 Nm
29 ft.lbs.
N
3
6
4
2
2
5

2. Cover
3. Air bag module
4. Steering wheel
5. Lower column cover
6. Clock spring

MT8019400151000X

Fig. 21 Driver air bag & clockspring replacement. Mirage

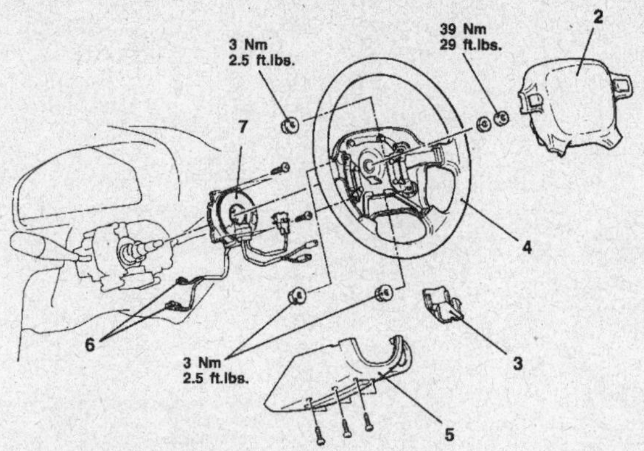
3 Nm
2.5 ft.lbs.
39 Nm
29 ft.lbs.
2
7
4
6
3 Nm
2.5 ft.lbs.
3
5

Clock spring removal steps
- Post-installation inspection

2. Air bag module (Driver's side)
3. Cap
4. Steering wheel
5. Column cover lower
6. Clock spring and body wiring harness connection
7. Clock spring

MT8019200215000X

Fig. 22 Driver air bag & clockspring replacement. Montero

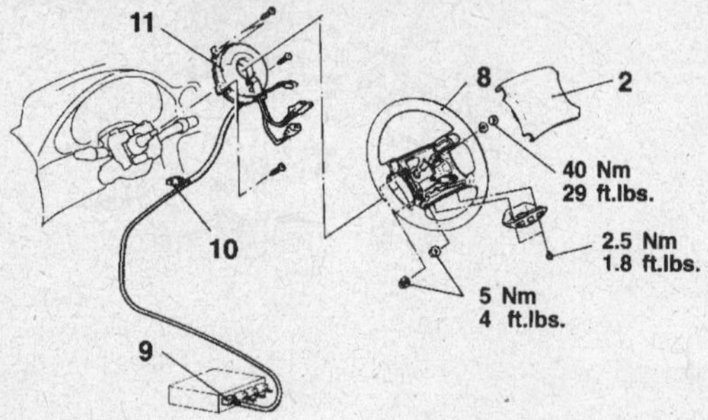
11
8
2
40 Nm
29 ft.lbs.
10
2.5 Nm
1.8 ft.lbs.
5 Nm
4 ft.lbs.
9

2. Air bag module (Driver's side)
8. Steering wheel

9. Clock spring and SRS diagnosis unit connection
10. Clock spring and body wiring harness connection
11. Clock spring

MT8019400152000X

Fig. 23 Driver air bag & clockspring replacement. 3000GT

under "Deployed Air Bag Module Disposal."

Deployment Outside Vehicle

1. Disconnect and remove battery from vehicle. **Wait at least 60 seconds after disconnection before performing any further steps. SRS is designed to retain enough deployment voltage for a short time even after battery has been disconnected.**
2. Remove air bag module as described in "Air Bag Module, Replace."
3. Connect two 20 ft. long wires to the two leads of SRS drivers air bag adapter harness "B" tool No. MB628919, or equivalent, or passengers air bag adapter harness "A" tool No. MB686560, or equivalent, and cover connections with tape. **Other ends of two wires should be connected to each other to prevent unexpected deployment.**
4. Place air bag module with pad cover facing upward in a flat, spacious area at least 20 feet away from any people, animals, equipment or other objects.
5. Connect adapter harness "B" to air bag module connector.
6. Install four nuts and bolts on rear side of module, then tie with thick wire.
7. Pass adapter harness "B" under a discarded tire and wheel assembly, then connect to air bag module.
8. Position air bag module on wheel and tire assembly, then secure with wires attached to bolt holes. Ensure module is facing upward, **Fig. 44. Leave some space below wheel for deployment wires.**
9. Place three tires without rims on top of tire and wheel assembly with air bag module attached.
   a. **Do not perform deployment outside if a strong wind is blowing. Even in a slight breeze, the air bag should be deployed downwind from battery.**
   b. **Ensure no people, animals, equipment or objects are nearby.** Module will jump upward several feet into the air.
10. From as far away as possible, in a shielded position, disconnect two connected wires from each other and connect them to a fully charged 12 volt battery, **Fig. 45.**
11. **Inflator will be quite hot immediately after deployment. Wait 30 minutes to allow air bag to cool.**
12. **Do not inhale gas from air bag.**
13. **Dispose of air bag as outlined under "Deployed Air Bag Module Disposal."**

DEPLOYED AIR BAG MODULE DISPOSAL

After deployment, the air bag module should be placed in a sealed plastic bag and disposed of in same manner as any

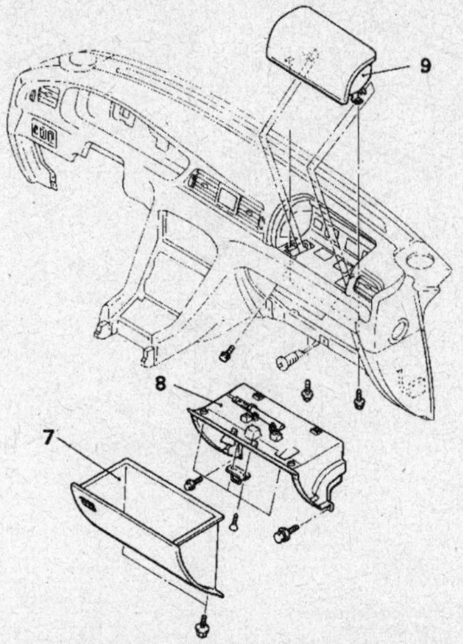
9
8
7

7. Glove box
8. Glove box outer case
9. Air bag module (passenger's side)

MT8019400153000X

Fig. 24 Passenger air bag replacement. Diamante

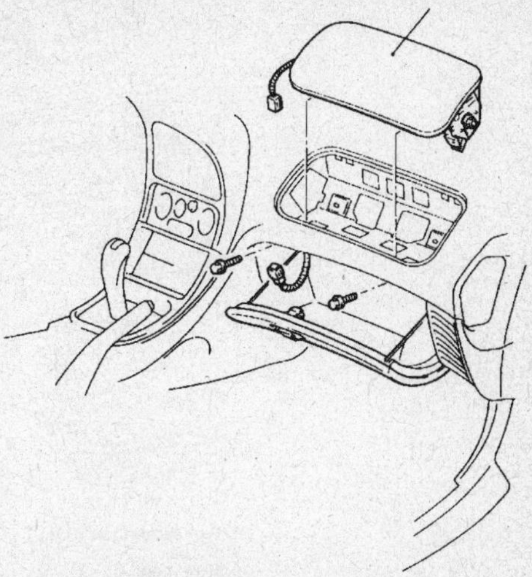

MT8019400154000X

Fig. 25 Passenger air bag replacement. Eclipse

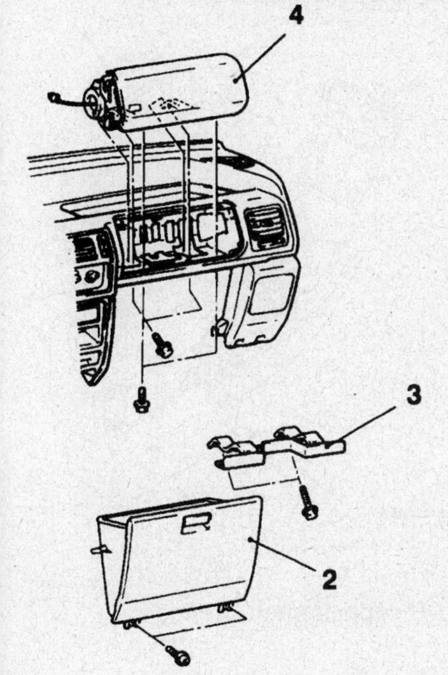
4
3
2

2. Glove box
3. Kneeprotector bracket
4. Air bag module

MT8019400155000X

Fig. 26 Passenger air bag replacement. Expo

other scrap parts, except that the following points should be carefully noted during disposal:

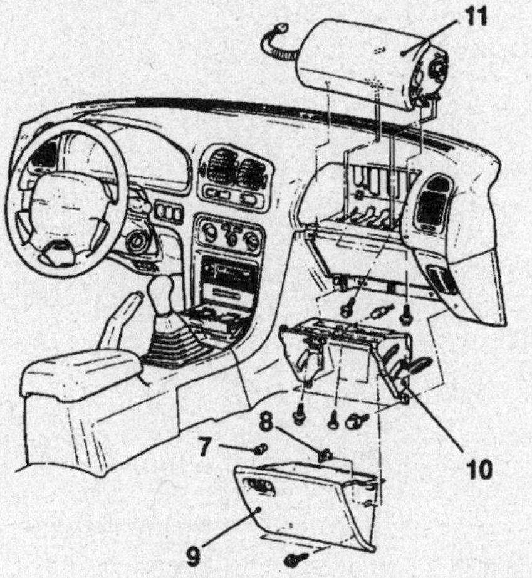
11
8
7
10
9

8. Catcher
9. Glove box
10. Glove box cover
11. Air bag module

MT8019400156000X

Fig. 27 Passenger air bag replacement. Galant

1. **Inflator will be quite hot immediately after deployment. Wait 30 minutes to allow air bag to cool.**
2. Do not put water or oil on air bag after deployment.
3. There may be material adhered to module that could irritate eyes and/or skin. Wear gloves and safety glasses when handling a deployed air bag. **If material comes in contact with eyes and/or skin, rinse affected area immediately with a large amount of**

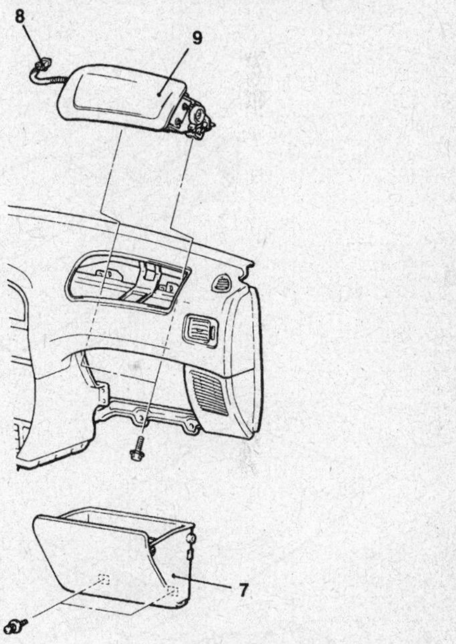
8
9
7

7. Glove box
8. Air bag module and body wiring harness connection
9. Air bag module

MT8019400157000X

Fig. 28 Passenger air bag replacement. Mirage

clear water. Seek medical attention if any irritation develops.

4. Place deployed air bag in a hermetically sealed container and discard it.

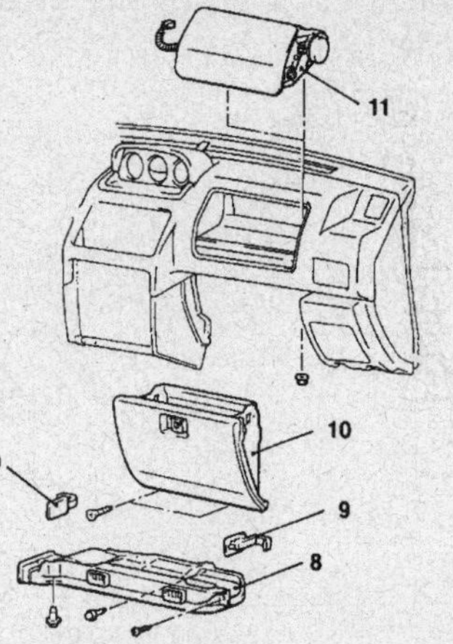
11
10
9
9
8

8. Foot shower duct (R.H.)
9. Stopper
10. Glove box
11. Air bag module (Passenger's side)

MT8019600216000X

Fig. 29 Passenger air bag replacement. Montero

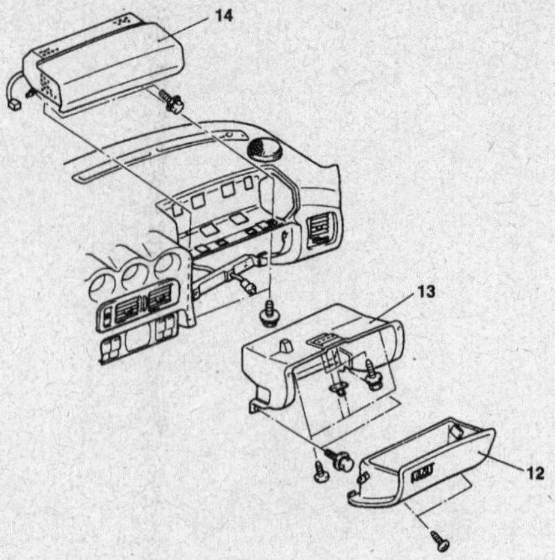
14
13
12

12. Glove box assembly
13. Cross pipe cover
14. Air bag module (passenger's side)

MT8019400158000X

Fig. 30 Passenger air bag replacement. 3000GT

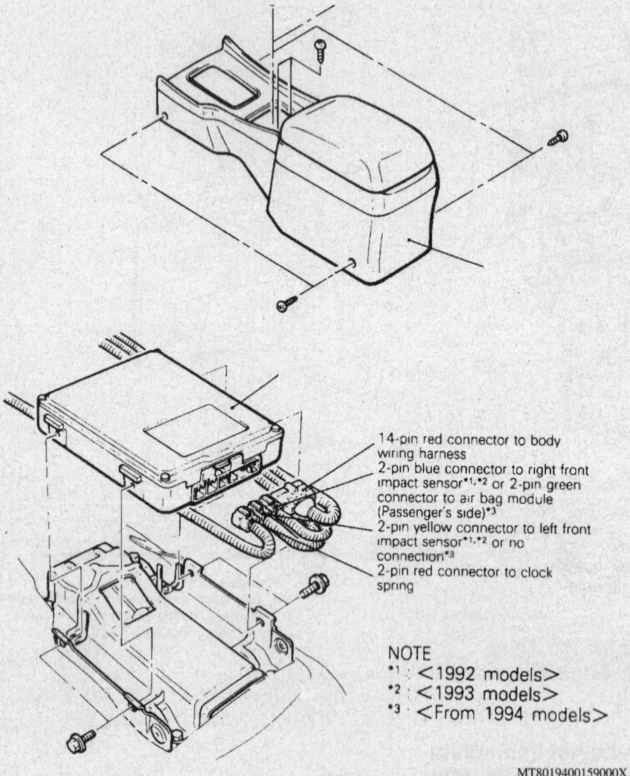
14-pin red connector to body wiring harness
2-pin blue connector to right front impact sensor*1,*2 or 2-pin green connector to air bag module (Passenger's side)*3
2-pin yellow connector to left front impact sensor*1,*2 or no connection*3
2-pin red connector to clock spring
NOTE
*1 : <1992 models>
*2 : <1993 models>
*3 : <From 1994 models>

MT8019400159000X

Fig. 31 SDU replacement. Diamante

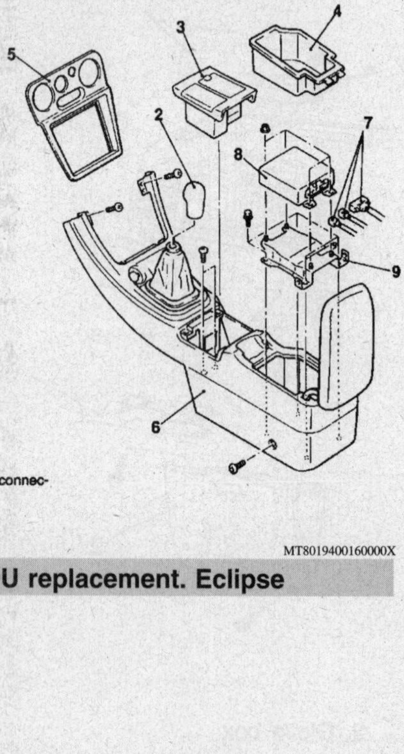
5
3
4
2
8
7
9
6

2. Shift lever knob <M/T>
3. Ashtray
4. Inner box
5. Center console panel
6. Floor console assembly
7. SRS diagnosis unit and harness connector connection
8. SRS diagnosis unit (SDU)
9. Bracket

MT8019400160000X

Fig. 32 SDU replacement. Eclipse

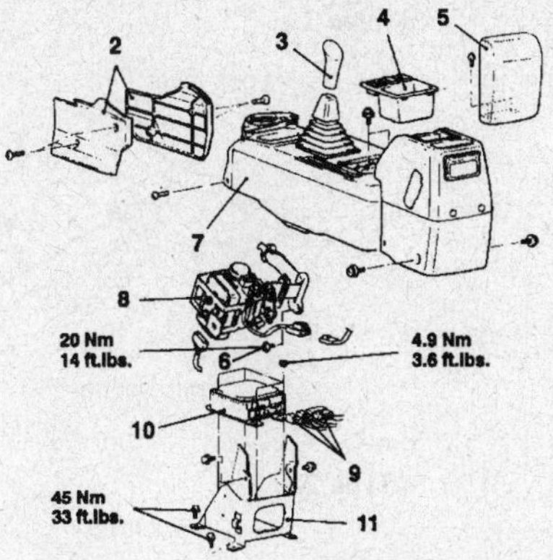
2
3
4
5
7
8
20 Nm
14 ft.lbs.
6
4.9 Nm
3.6 ft.lbs.
10
9
45 Nm
33 ft.lbs.
11

2. Side cover
3. Shift lever knob <M/T>
4. Floor console switch panel
5. Armrest assembly
6. Bolts
7. Floor console assembly
8. Retractor assembly <1994 models>
9. Connection of the SRS-ECU and harness connector
10. SRS air bag control unit (SRS-ECU)
11. Bracket

MT8019400161000X

Fig. 33 SDU replacement. Expo

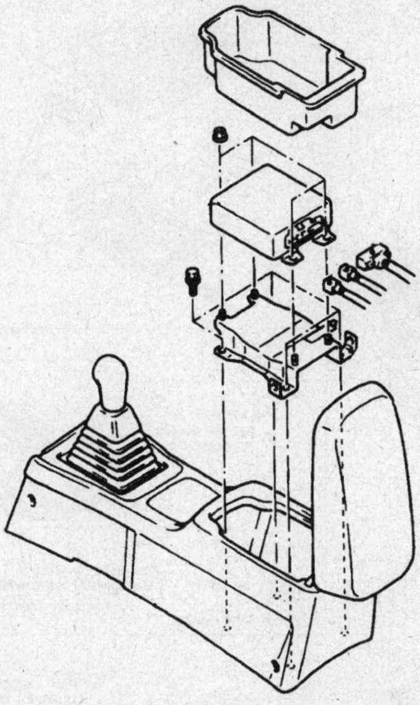

MT8019400162000X

Fig. 34 SDU replacement. Galant

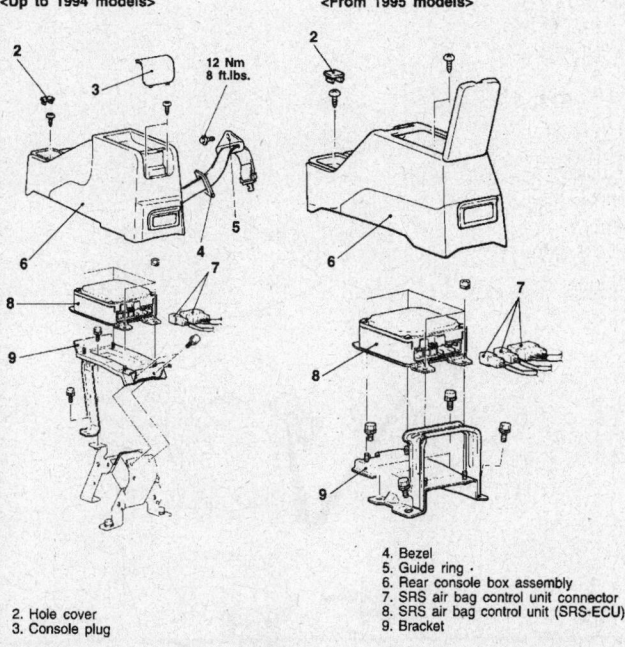

<Up to 1994 models> <From 1995 models>

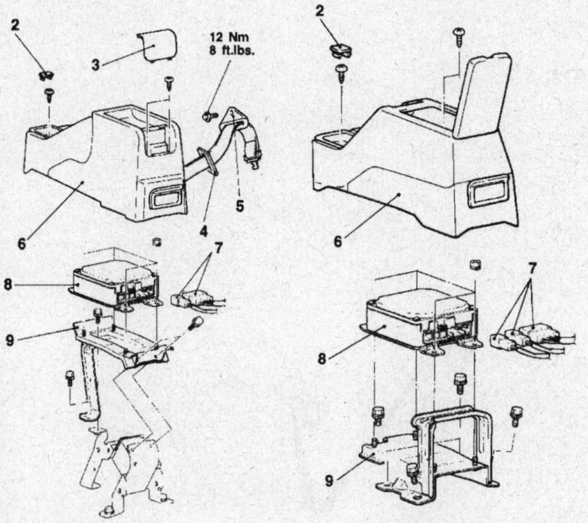
2
3
12 Nm
8 ft.lbs.
5
4
6
7
8
9
2
6
7
8
9

2. Hole cover
3. Console plug
4. Bezel
5. Guide ring ·
6. Rear console box assembly
7. SRS air bag control unit connector
8. SRS air bag control unit (SRS-ECU)
9. Bracket

MT8019400163000X

Fig. 35 SDU replacement. Mirage

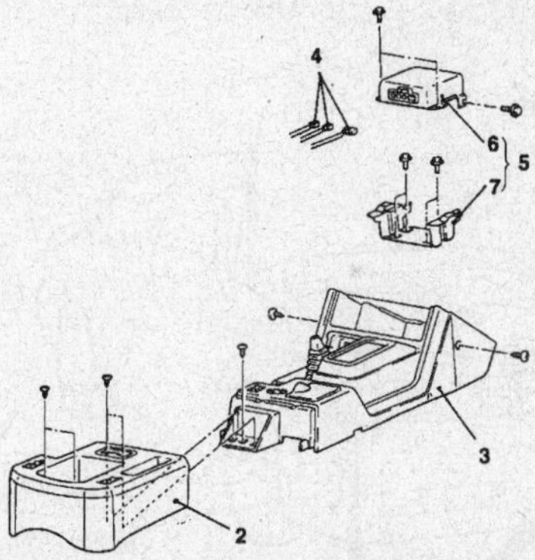
4
6
5
7
3
2

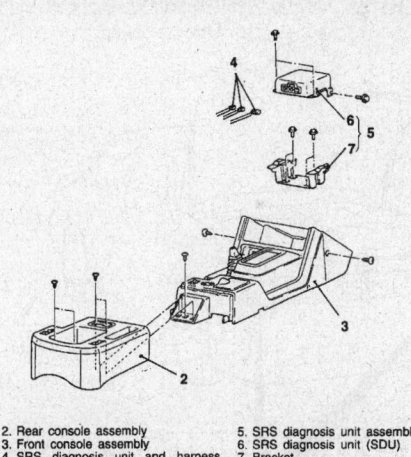

2. Rear console assembly
3. Front console assembly
4. SRS diagnosis unit and harness connector connection
5. SRS diagnosis unit assembly
6. SRS diagnosis unit (SDU)
7. Bracket

MT8019200217000X

Fig. 36 SDU replacement. Montero

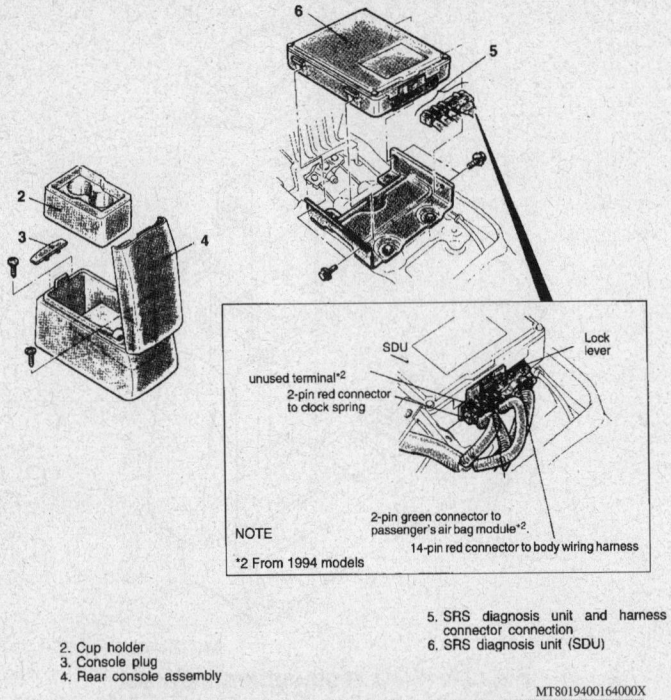

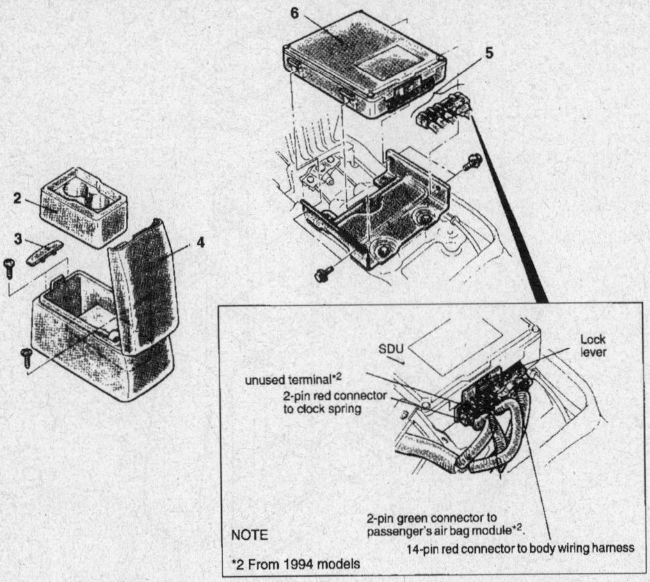
6
5
2
3
4
SDU
Lock lever
unused terminal*2
2-pin red connector to clock spring
2-pin green connector to passenger's air bag module*2.
14-pin red connector to body wiring harness
NOTE
*2 From 1994 models

2. Cup holder
3. Console plug
4. Rear console assembly
5. SRS diagnosis unit and harness connector connection
6. SRS diagnosis unit (SDU)

MT8019400164000X

Fig. 37 SDU replacement. 3000GT

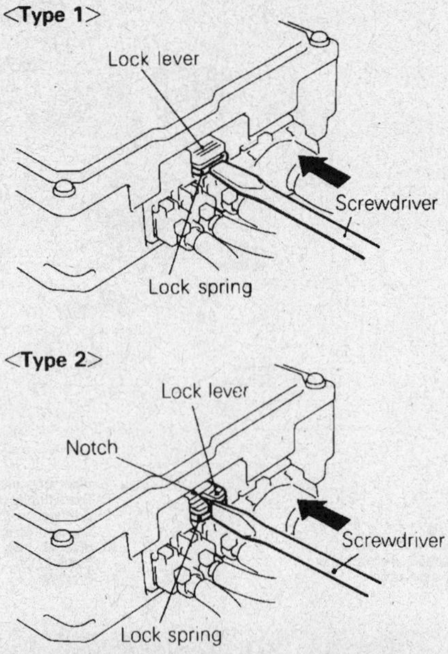
<Type 1>
Lock lever
Screwdriver
Lock spring
<Type 2>
Lock lever
Notch
Screwdriver
Lock spring

MT8019400165000X

Fig. 38 SDU harness

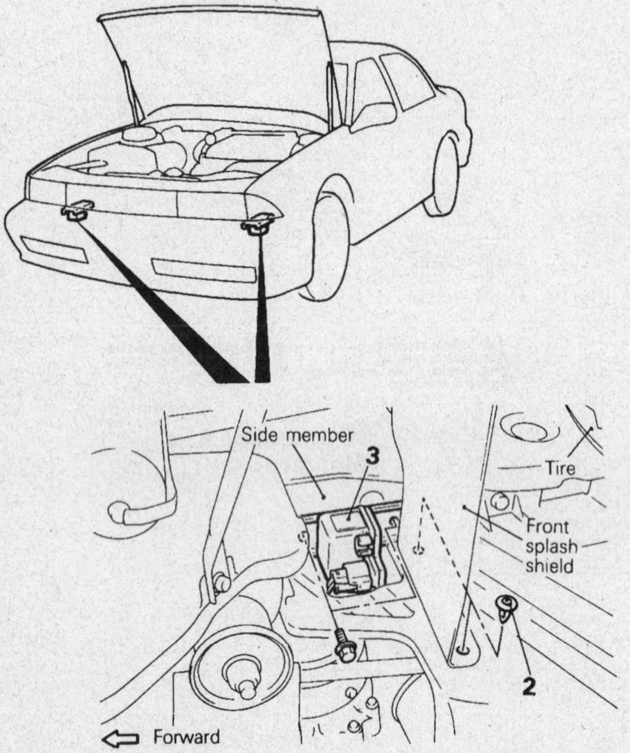
Side member
3
Tire
Front splash shield
2
Forward

2. Front splash shield attaching clips
3. Front impact sensor

MT8019400166000X

Fig. 39 Front sensor replacement. Diamante

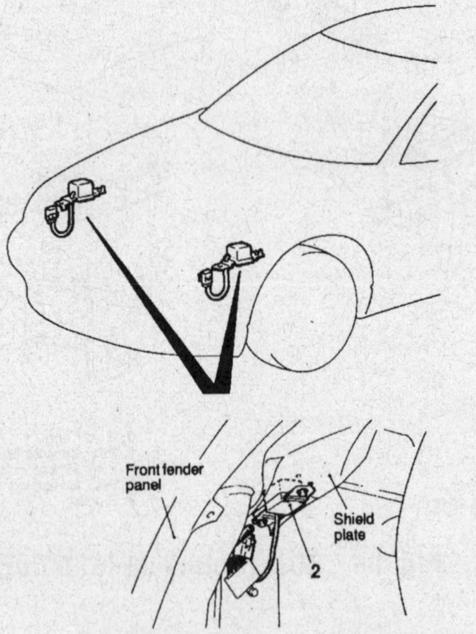
Front fender panel
Shield plate
2

2. Front impact sensor

MT8019400167000X

Fig. 40 Front sensor replacement. Eclipse

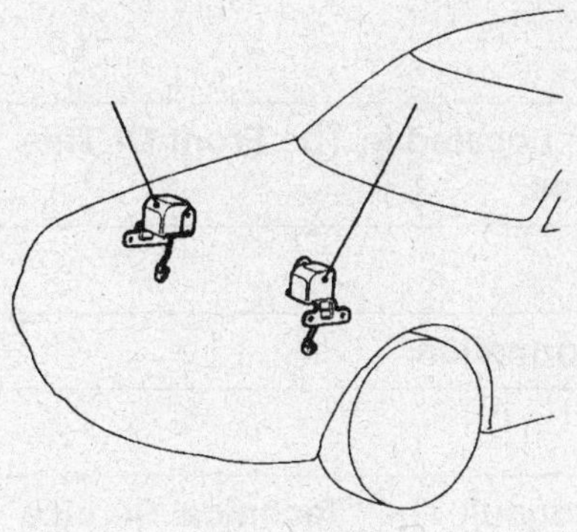
2. Front impact sensor
MT8019400168000X

Fig. 41 Front sensor replacement. Galant

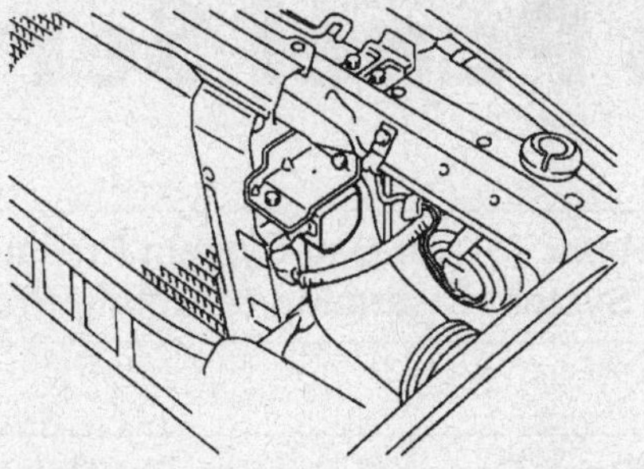
MT8019200218000X

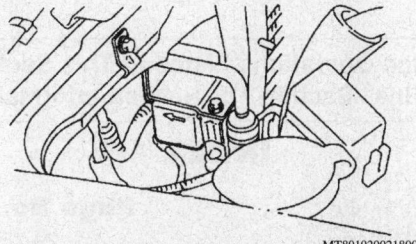

Fig. 42 Front sensor replacement. Montero

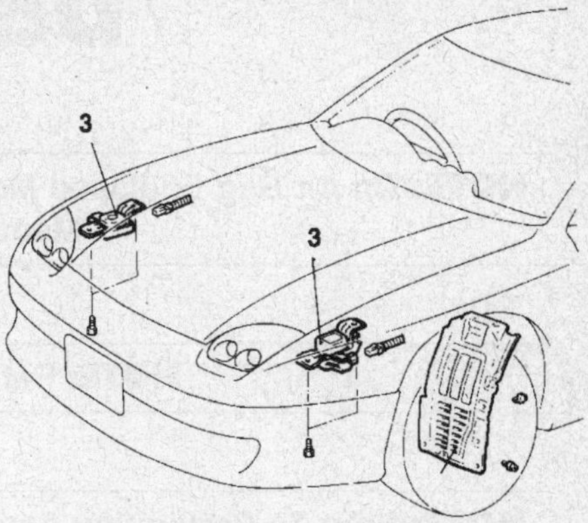
3
3
3. Front impact sensor
MT8019400169000X

Fig. 43 Front sensor replacement. 3000GT

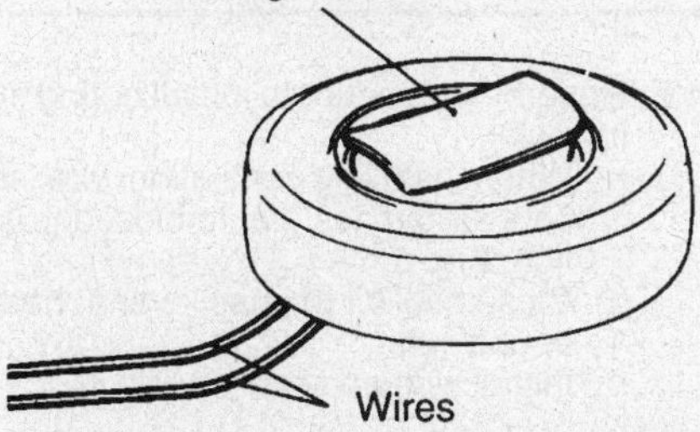
Air bag module
Wires
MT8019400170000X

Fig. 44 Air bag module deployment position

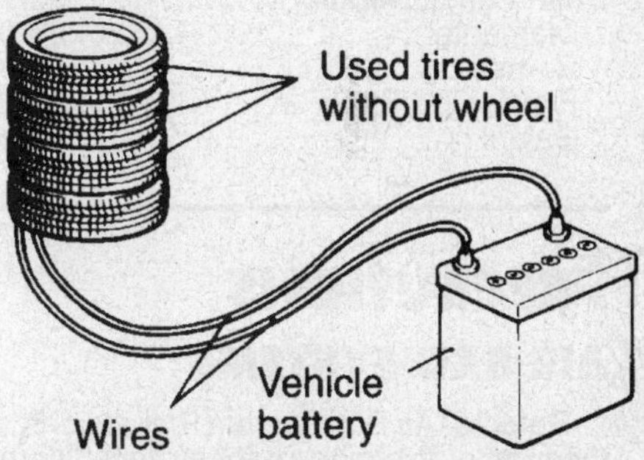
Used tires
without wheel
Vehicle
battery
Wires
MT8019400171000X

Fig. 45 Air bag module deployment

TIGHTENING SPECIFICATIONS

Component	Torque/Ft. Lbs.
Drivers Air Bag Module Nuts (Except 1995–96 Montero)	4
Drivers Air Bag Module Nuts (1995–96 Montero)	30①
Steering Wheel	29

① — Inch lbs.

Dash Panel Service

NOTE: On Air Bag Equipped Models, Refer To "Air Bag System Precautions" Located In The Front Of This Manual For System Disarming & Arming Procedures.

NOTE: Refer To "Dash Gauges" Section For Related Information.

NOTE: Prior To Performing Any Service Operations Listed In This Section, Consult The "Technical Service Bulletins" Section For Related Information.

INDEX

	Page No.
Dash Panel, Replace	29-78
Diamante	29-82
Eclipse	29-80
Expo	29-83
Galant	29-80
Mirage	29-78
Montero	29-78
Pickup	29-79
Precis	29-78
3000GT	29-82
Precautions	29-78
Air Bag Systems	29-78
Technical Service Bulletins	29-84
Dashboard Center Ticking	29-84

PRECAUTIONS

AIR BAG SYSTEMS

Refer to "Air Bag System Precautions" in the front of this manual for system disarming and arming procedures.

DASH PANEL

REPLACE

MIRAGE

1. Disconnect battery ground cable.
2. Remove dash panel in numbered sequence as shown, **Fig. 1,** noting the following:
   a. Remove cool air bypass lever cable of the air outlet center panel assembly at the heater unit side.
   b. Remove the air outlet center panel assembly mounting screws, then the air outlet center panel assembly.
   c. Remove the adapter lock from the instrument panel then pull speedometer cable slightly into the passenger compartment and remove the adapter.
3. Reverse procedure to install, noting the following:
   a. Install air outlet center panel assembly to instrument panel.
   b. Turn cool air bypass lever of air outlet center panel assembly fully upward.
   c. Turn cool air bypass damper lever at the heater unit side fully downward and install the cool air bypass lever cable.

MONTERO

1. Disconnect battery ground cable.
2. Remove floor console as follows:
   a. Remove switch panel, suspension control switch and rear console harness connector, **Fig. 2.**
   b. Remove side panel (A), then the rear console assembly.
   c. **On models with manual transmission,** remove shift knob.
   d. **On all models,** remove transfer shift lever, then floor console harness connector.
   e. Remove front console assembly. On models with automatic transmissions, set selector lever to "L" position when removing console assembly.
3. Remove hood lock release and fuel filler door lock release handle, then instrument under and corner covers **Fig. 3.**
4. Remove glove compartment stopper, then the glove compartment assembly.
5. Remove center panel (A), heater control assembly, then radio.
6. Remove meter hood, meter bezel, then combination meter.
7. Disconnect speedometer cable at transmission, remove lock of speedometer cable adapter from instrument panel. **Fig. 4.**
8. Pull cable slightly toward vehicle interior, then remove speedometer cable adapter.
9. Remove column cover, clock if equipped, side defroster garnish, then door mirror control switch.
10. Remove front speakers, rheostat, rear wiper and washer switch, then door lock switch.
11. Remove ventilation control wire, then harness connector.
12. Remove steering column attaching bolts, then panel assembly.
13. Reverse procedure to install noting the following:
    a. When installing ventilation wire, set cool air bypass dial to closed position, **Fig. 5.**
    b. Close cool air bypass lever at heater unit side.
    c. Install wire and secure with clip.

PRECIS

1. Disconnect battery ground cable.
2. Remove steering wheel.
3. Remove steering column upper and lower shroud, **Fig. 6.**
4. Remove hood release handle retaining screws, then the hood release handle.
5. Remove center bezel assembly.
6. Remove left side lower crash pad retaining screws, then pull crash pad outward and disconnect electrical connector.
7. Remove glove compartment.
8. Remove right side lower crash pad retaining screws, then pull crash pad outward and disconnect electrical connectors.
9. Disconnect instrument panel to dash panel electrical connector.
10. Remove cluster housing assembly.
11. Disconnect cluster housing switch electrical connector and remove illumination lamp.
12. Remove cluster assembly retaining screws, then pull cluster assembly outward and disconnect speedometer cable and cluster assembly electrical connectors.
13. Disconnect heater control wire from heater and blower assembly.
14. Remove instrument panel to heater bracket retaining bolts.
15. Remove instrument panel retaining

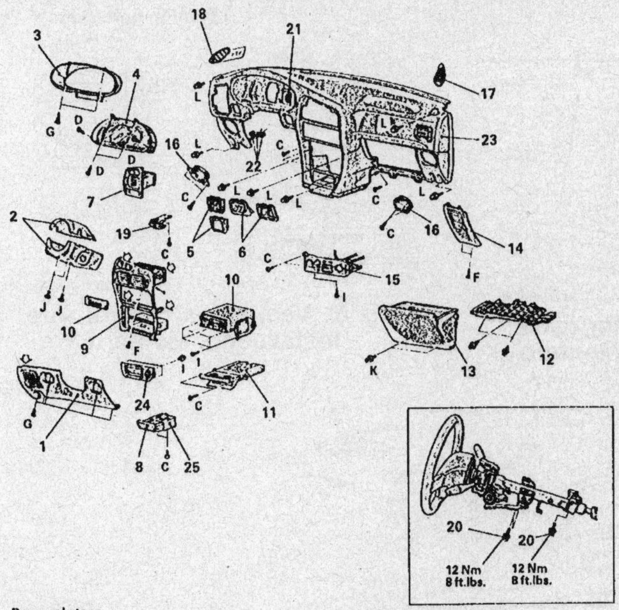
12 Nm
8 ft.lbs.
12 Nm
8 ft.lbs.

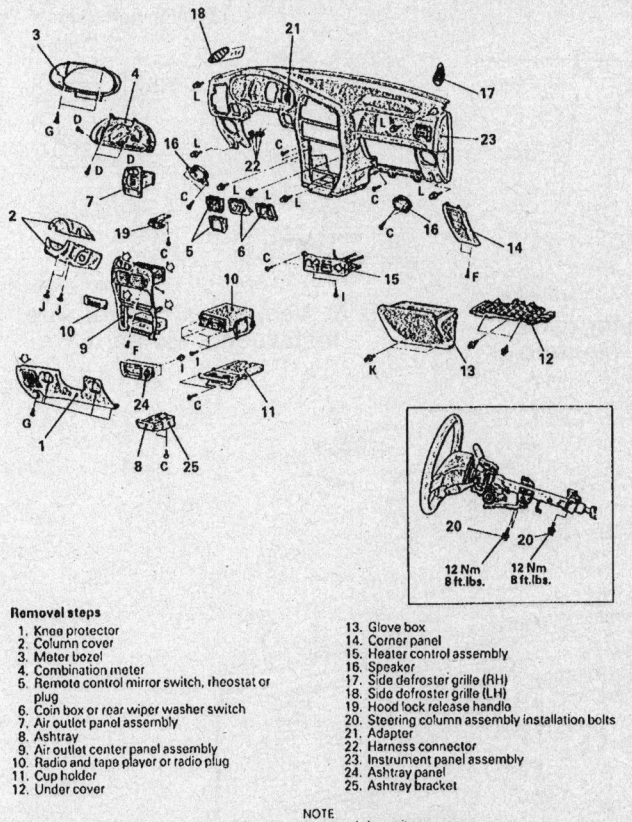

Removal steps

1. Knee protector
2. Column cover
3. Meter bezel
4. Combination meter
5. Remote control mirror switch, rheostat or plug
6. Coin box or rear wiper washer switch
7. Air outlet panel assembly
8. Ashtray
9. Air outlet center panel assembly
10. Radio and tape player or radio plug
11. Cup holder
12. Under cover
13. Glove box
14. Corner panel
15. Heater control assembly
16. Speaker
17. Side defroster grille (RH)
18. Side defroster grille (LH)
19. Hood lock release handle
20. Steering column assembly installation bolts
21. Adapter
22. Harness connector
23. Instrument panel assembly
24. Ashtray panel
25. Ashtray bracket

NOTE
⇦ : metal clip position

MT9149300002000X

Fig. 1 Exploded view of instrument panel. Mirage

bolt covers from top of instrument panel.

16. Remove front speaker grilles and speakers.
17. Remove instrument panel retaining bolts, then the instrument panel.
18. Reverse procedure to install, noting the following:
    a. Set tube in clamp groove and cable in cam pin.
    b. Move control knob to cam pin lowest position, then set knob to the DEF position.
    c. Secure heater clamp.
    d. Remove clamp from COOL-WARM mounting boss.
    e. Set tube into clamp, then insert cable to the COOL—WARM lever pin at the highest position (warm mode) and set control knob to the DEF position.
    f. Secure tube to the heater holder.
    g. Remove clamp from FRESH—RECIRC mounting boss.
    h. Move tube to the FRESH—RECIRC lever pin and put tube inside clamp.
    i. Move lever fully backward, then secure control knob to the RECIRC position.

PICKUP

1. Disconnect battery ground cable.
2. Remove hazard warning flasher switch, **Fig. 7.**
3. Remove meter hood hole cover.
4. Tilt steering column down, then re-

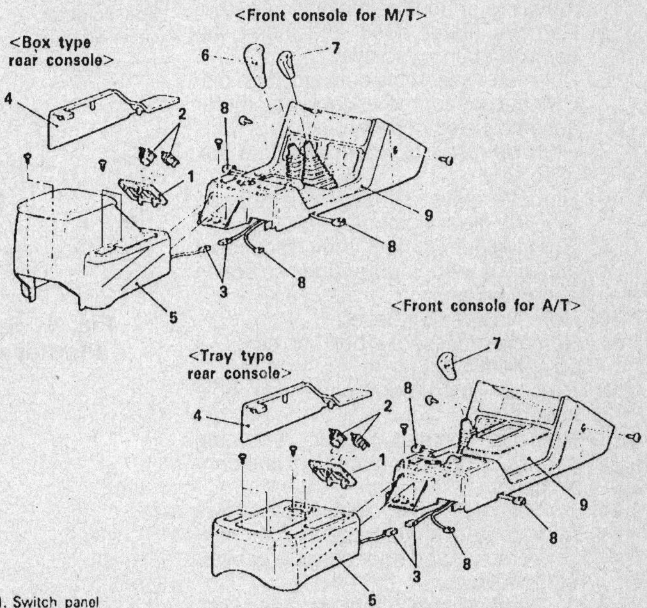
<Front console for M/T>
<Box type rear console>
<Front console for A/T>
<Tray type rear console>

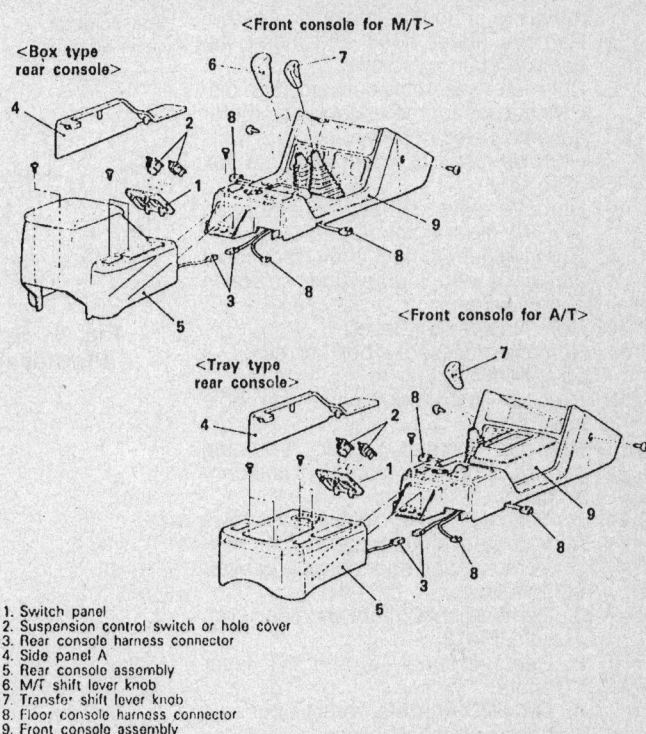

1. Switch panel
2. Suspension control switch or hole cover
3. Rear console harness connector
4. Side panel A
5. Rear console assembly
6. M/T shift lever knob
7. Transfer shift lever knob
8. Floor console harness connector
9. Front console assembly

MT9149200003000X

Fig. 2 Exploded view of floor console. Montero

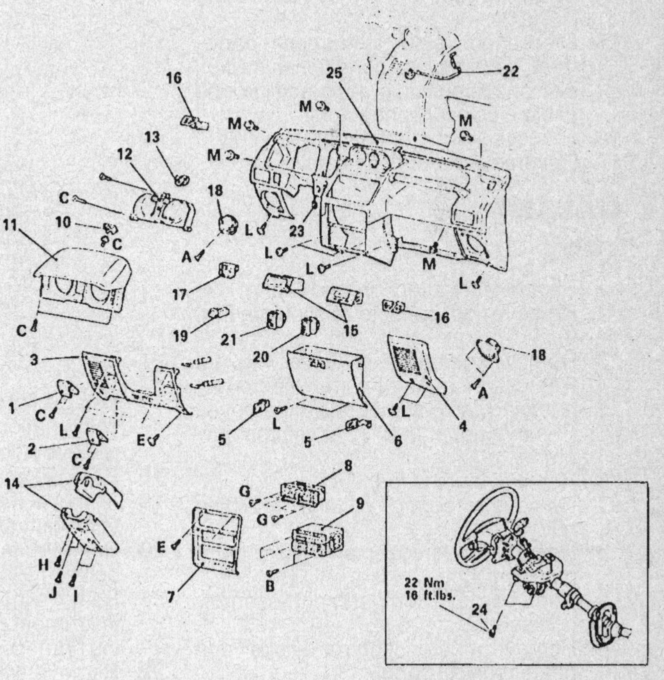
22 Nm
16 ft.lbs.

1. Hood lock release handle
2. Fuel filler door lock release handle
3. Instrument under cover
4. Instrument corner cover
5. Glove box stopper
6. Glove box assembly
7. Center panel A
8. Heater control assembly
9. Radio and tape player
10. Meter hood plug
11. Meter bezel assembly
12. Combination meter
13. Speedometer cable adapter
14. Column cover
15. Clock or clock plug
16. Side defroster garnish
17. Door mirror control switch
18. Front speaker
19. Rheostat
20. Rear wiper and washer switch
21. Door lock switch
22. Ventilation control wire
23. Harness connector
24. Steering column installation bolts
25. Instrument panel assembly

MT9149200004000X

Fig. 3 Exploded view of instrument panel. Montero

move meter hood retaining screws.
5. Remove meter hood and meter assembly retaining screws.
6. Pull meter assembly outward, then disconnect speedometer cable and meter assembly electrical connectors.
7. Remove fuse box cover and fuse box assembly.
8. Remove glove compartment stopper, then the glove compartment.
9. Remove defrost duct, then disconnect air, mode and temperature selection control wires.
10. Remove speaker bezel.
11. Remove accessory box, or clock, if equipped.
12. Remove instrument panel top hole covers.
13. Remove center cover retaining screws, center reinforcement and center cover.
14. Remove console retaining screws from center reinforcement, floor console bracket and floor console assembly as follows:
    a. Remove shift knob and floor console, **Fig. 8.**
    b. Remove panel (A) and shift lever boots.
    c. **On 4WD models,** remove console box and console cover.
    d. Remove console mounting bracket.
    e. **On all models,** remove accessory box.
15. Disconnect side instrument panel, front harness, air conditioner switch, air conditioner unit, radio and ground cable electrical connectors.
16. Remove instrument panel assembly.
17. Reverse procedure to install.

GALANT

1993

1. Disconnect battery ground cable.
2. Remove floor console as shown in **Fig. 9.**
3. Remove knee protector cover, **Fig. 10.**
4. Remove instrument panel undercover retaining screws, then the undercover.
5. Remove upper and lower column covers.
6. Remove lap and foot duct.
7. Remove steering column retaining bolts.
8. Remove undercover and glove compartment stop.
9. Remove glove compartment assembly and ashtray.
10. Remove heater control knobs and heater control panel.
11. Remove trip counter reset knob.
12. Remove meter bezel.
13. Remove combination meter assembly retaining screws, then turn top of meter outward.
14. **On models equipped with automatic position indicator,** remove combination meter after removing meter harness electrical connector.
15. **On all models,** disconnect speedometer cable at transaxle.
16. Slightly pull speedometer cable, then turn adapter to left or right to release lock and remove adapter.

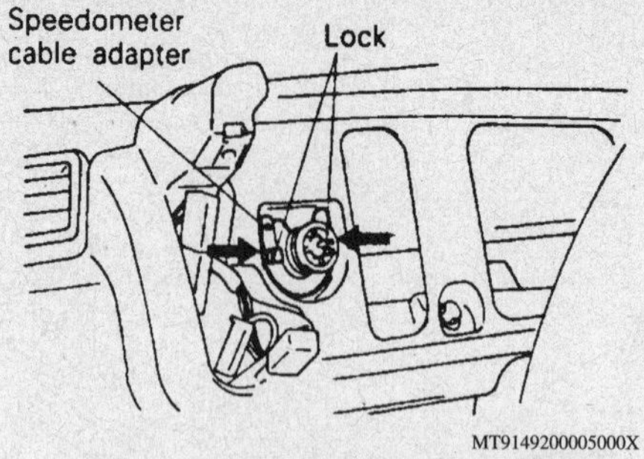
Speedometer cable adapter
Lock
MT9149200005000X

Fig. 4 Speedometer cable adapter removal. Montero

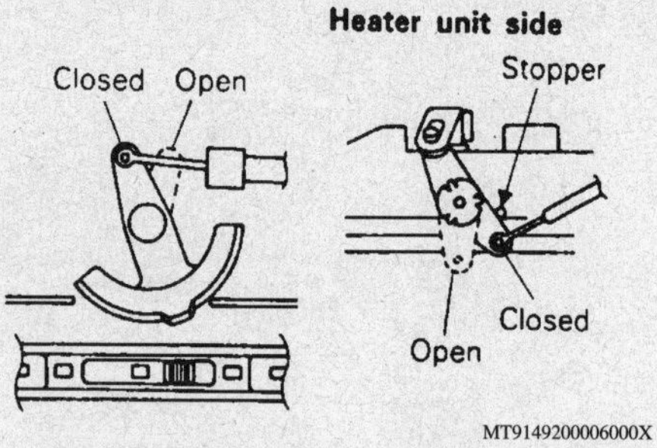
Heater unit side
Closed
Open
Stopper
Closed
Open
MT9149200006000X

Fig. 5 Ventilation control wire installation. Montero

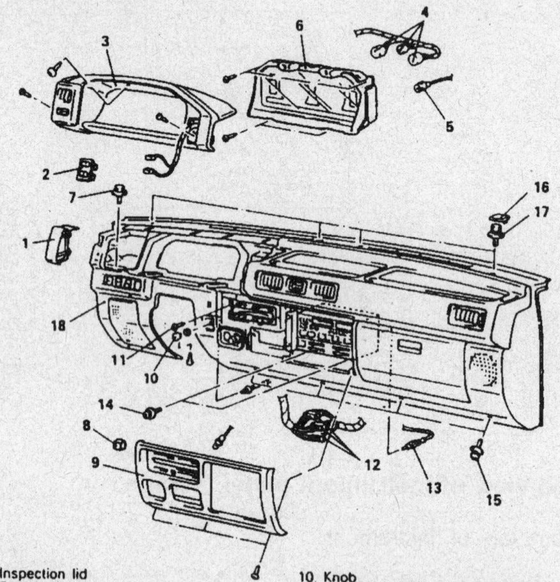
1
2
3
4
5
6
7
8
9
10
11
12
13
14
15
16
17
18

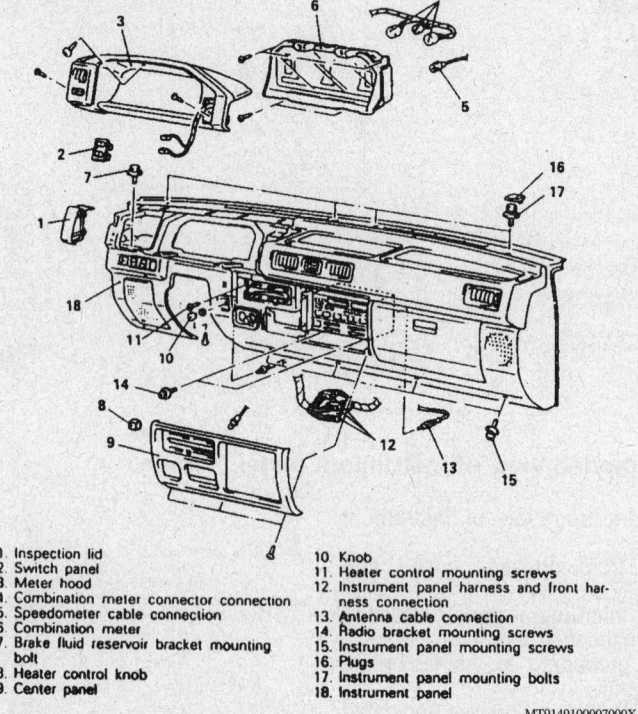

1. Inspection lid
2. Switch panel
3. Meter hood
4. Combination meter connector connection
5. Speedometer cable connection
6. Combination meter
7. Brake fluid reservoir bracket mounting bolt
8. Heater control knob
9. Center panel
10. Knob
11. Heater control mounting screws
12. Instrument panel harness and front harness connection
13. Antenna cable connection
14. Radio bracket mounting screws
15. Instrument panel mounting screws
16. Plugs
17. Instrument panel mounting bolts
18. Instrument panel

MT9149100007000X

Fig. 6 Exploded view of instrument panel. Precis

17. Using a flat tip screwdriver, open tab of combination meter wiring harness and remove from vehicle.
18. Remove speaker grilles and clock.
19. Remove heater control assembly retaining screws.
20. Remove instrument panel retaining bolts.
21. Remove instrument panel-to-body and instrument panel-to-junction block wiring harness couplers.
22. Remove MPI control relay to control wiring harness coupling.
23. Remove instrument panel assembly.
24. Reverse procedure to install.

1994–96

1. Remove dash panel in numbered sequence shown, **Fig. 11.**
2. Reverse procedure to install, noting the following:
    a. Connect cool air bypass damper lever cable by turning lever on air outlet fully upward, then positioning lever on heater unit fully downward and fitting cable over connection point.

ECLIPSE

1993–94

1. Disconnect battery ground cable.
2. Remove center console as follows:
    a. Remove side panel hole covers, **Fig. 12.**
    b. Remove side cover (A) and (B).
    c. **On models with manual transaxle,** remove manual shift lever knob.
    d. **On all models,** remove cup holder and carpet.
    e. Disconnect console electrical harness connector.
    f. Disconnect (PWR/ECONOMY, ECO) changeover switch electrical connector.
    g. Remove guide ring and shoulder belt.
    h. Remove console assembly.
3. Remove knee protector hole covers, **Fig. 13.**

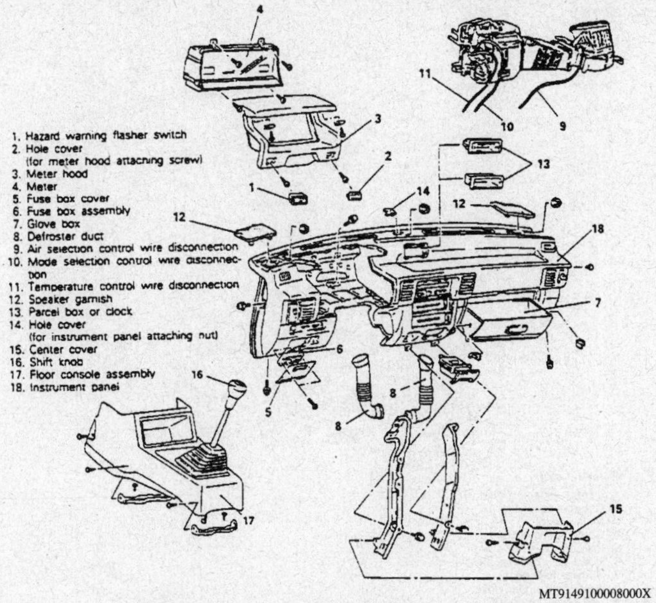
1. Hazard warning flasher switch
2. Hole cover (for meter hood attaching screw)
3. Meter hood
4. Meter
5. Fuse box cover
6. Fuse box assembly
7. Glove box
8. Defroster duct
9. Air selection control wire disconnection
10. Mode selection control wire disconnection
11. Temperature control wire disconnection
12. Speaker garnish
13. Parcel box or clock
14. Hole cover (for instrument panel attaching nut)
15. Center cover
16. Shift knob
17. Floor console assembly
18. Instrument panel
MT9149100008000X

Fig. 7 Exploded view of instrument panel. Pickup

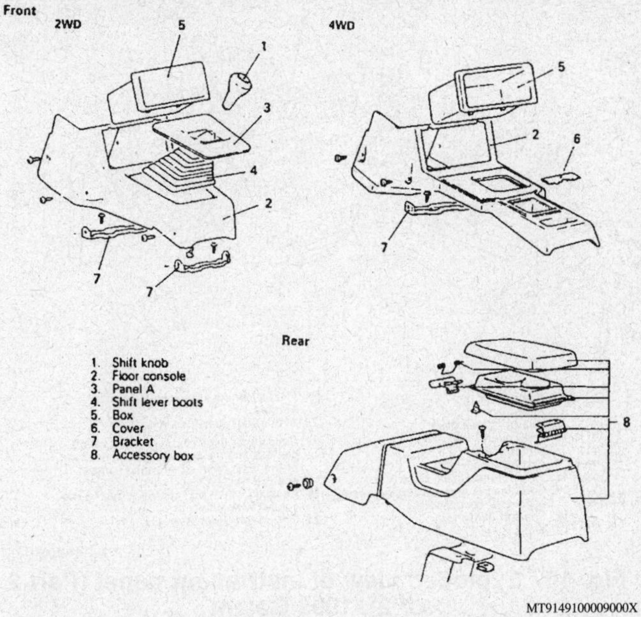
Front
2WD
4WD
Rear
1. Shift knob
2. Floor console
3. Panel A
4. Shift lever boots
5. Box
6. Cover
7. Bracket
8. Accessory box
MT9149100009000X

Fig. 8 Exploded view of console assembly. Pickup

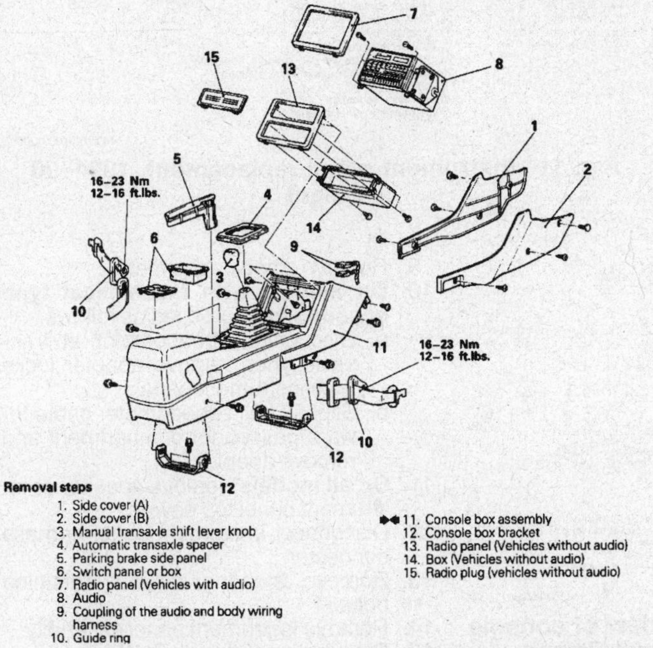
16–23 Nm
12–16 ft.lbs.
16–23 Nm
12–16 ft.lbs.
Removal steps
1. Side cover (A)
2. Side cover (B)
3. Manual transaxle shift lever knob
4. Automatic transaxle spacer
5. Parking brake side panel
6. Switch panel or box
7. Radio panel (Vehicles with audio)
8. Audio
9. Coupling of the audio and body wiring harness
10. Guide ring
11. Console box assembly
12. Console box bracket
13. Radio panel (Vehicles without audio)
14. Box (Vehicles without audio)
15. Radio plug (vehicles without audio)
MT9149100010000A

Fig. 9 Floor console removal. 1993 Galant

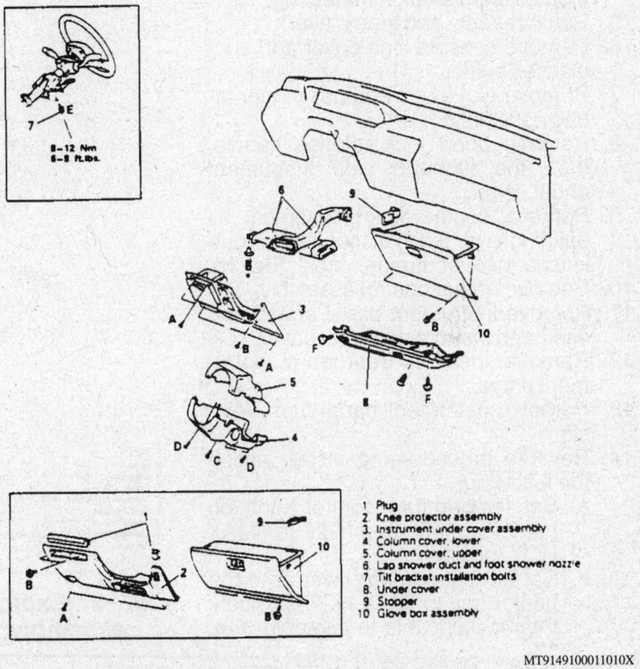
8–12 Nm
6–9 ft.lbs.
1 Plug
2. Knee protector assembly
3. Instrument under cover assembly
4. Column cover, lower
5. Column cover, upper
6. Lap shower duct and foot shower nozzle
7 Tilt bracket installation bolts
8. Under cover
9. Stopper
10 Glove box assembly
MT9149100011010X

Fig. 10 Exploded view of instrument panel (Part 1 of 2). 1993 Galant

4. Remove knee protector assembly and hood lock release handle.
5. Remove steering column upper and lower covers.
6. Remove instrument panel cover (A).
7. Remove cluster panel (A) and radio panel.
8. Remove radio and center air outlet assembly.
9. Remove dial knob (A) and cluster panel assembly (B).
10. Remove glove compartment stopper and glove compartment assembly.
11. Remove combination meter.
12. Disconnect speedometer cable at transaxle, then slightly pull cable outward from inside vehicle.
13. Release speedometer lock by turning to the right or left, then remove speedometer cable adapter.
14. Remove speaker bezel.
15. Remove bracket from center of instrument panel.
16. Remove heater control assembly retaining screw.
17. Remove lap cooler duct and left side shower duct.
18. Remove steering column retaining bolt.
19. Remove instrument panel retaining screw and bolt.
20. Remove instrument panel assembly.
21. Reverse procedure to install.

1995-96

1. Disconnect battery ground cable.
2. Remove steering wheel as outlined in "Electrical " section of "Eclipse" chassis section.
3. Remove center console assembly as follows:
   a. Remove center console panel, **Fig. 14.**
   b. Remove ashtray and cup holder assembly.
   c. **On models with manual transaxle,** remove shift knob.
   d. **On all models,** remove center console assembly.

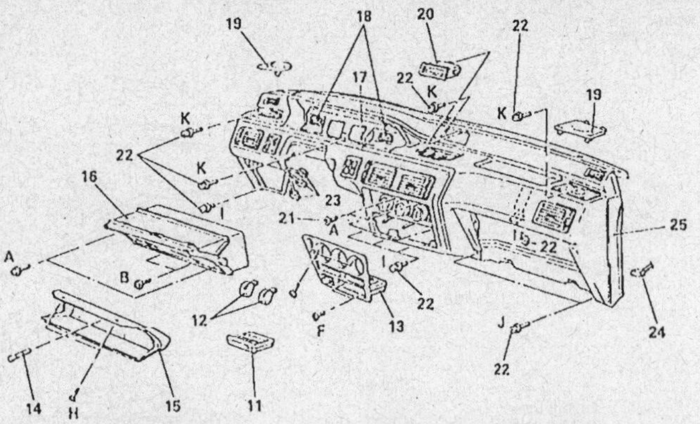
5 Nm
4 ft.lbs.

11. Ashtray
12. Knob
13. Heater control panel
14. Trip counter reset knob
15. Meter bezel
16. Combination meter
17. Speedometer cable adapter
18. Combination meter wiring harness connector connections
19. Speaker garnishes
20. Clock
21. Heater control assembly installation screws
22. Instrument panel mounting bolts
23. Coupling of the instrument panel wiring harness and the body wiring harness, and of the instrument panel wiring harness and the junction block
24. Coupling of the MPI control relay and the control wiring harness
25. Instrument panel assembly

MT9149100011020X

Fig. 10 Exploded view of instrument panel (Part 2 of 2). 1993 Galant

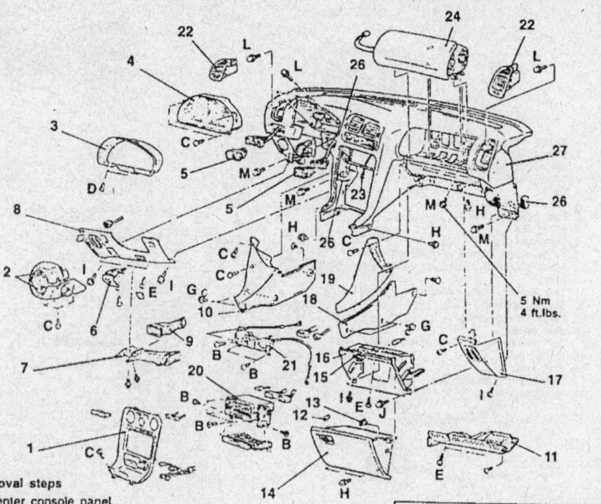

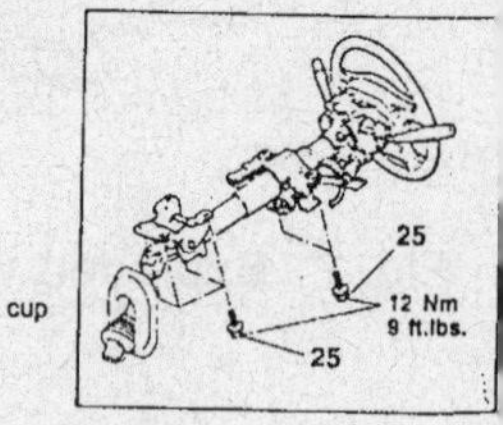
12 Nm
9 ft.lbs.

Removal steps
1. Center console panel
2. Column cover
3. Meter bezel
4. Combination meter
5. Instrument panel switch
6. Hood lock release handle
7. Shower foot duct
8. Instrument under cover
9. Lap cooler duct B
10. Side cover B
11. Under cover
12. Stopper
13. Catcher
14. Glove box
15. Glove box striker
16. Glove box cover
17. Corner panel
18. Side cover lower A
19. Side cover upper A
20. Radio and tape player, box, and cup holder
21. Heater control assembly
22. Side air outlet assembly
23. Cool air bypass damper lever cable connection
24. Passenger-side air bag module assembly
25. Steering column assembly installation bolts
26. Harness connector
27. Instrument panel assembly

MT9149400012000X

Fig. 11 Instrument panel replacement. 1994–96 Galant

4. Remove combination meter bezel, then the combination meter, **Fig. 15.**
5. Remove radio and tape player.
6. Remove console side cover and sunglasses holder.
7. Remove glove box and passenger air bag assembly.
8. Remove hood lock release handle, then the lefthand side instrument under cover.
9. Remove center outlet assembly by pushing lever pin to disconnect air outlet changeover damper cable, **Fig. 16.**
10. Remove heater control assembly.
11. Remove instrument panel switch and righthand instrument under cover.
12. Remove speakers from top of instrument panel.
13. Remove instrument panel from vehicle.
14. Reverse procedure to install, noting the following:
    a. Set temperature control knob on heater control assembly to "MAX HOT" position.
    b. Set air mix damper lever at top of heater unit to "MAX HOT" position, then install cable to lever pin, **Fig. 17.**
    c. Push outer cable in direction of arrow as shown in **Fig. 17,** ensure there is no looseness in cable, then secure it with clip.
    d. Set knob for air outlet changeover on heater control assembly to the "DEF" position.
    e. Set air outlet changeover damper lever of heater unit to the "DEF" position, then install cable to lever pin, **Fig. 16.**

3000GT

1. Remove console assembly as follows:
    a. Remove cup holder and console plug, **Fig. 18.**
    b. Remove rear console assembly.
    c. Remove radio panel and radio.
    d. Remove switch trim panel C and console side cover.
    e. Remove front console trim panel.
    f. **On models with manual transaxle,** remove shift lever knob.
    g. **On all models,** remove front console assembly.
2. Remove hood release handle and rheostat, **Fig. 19.**
3. Remove switch trim panel B and knee protector assembly.
4. Remove steering column cover.
5. Remove glove compartment striker, glove compartment and cross pipe cover.
6. Using a flat tip screwdriver, remove center air outlet assembly.
7. Remove heater control assembly retaining screws.
8. Remove meter bezel.

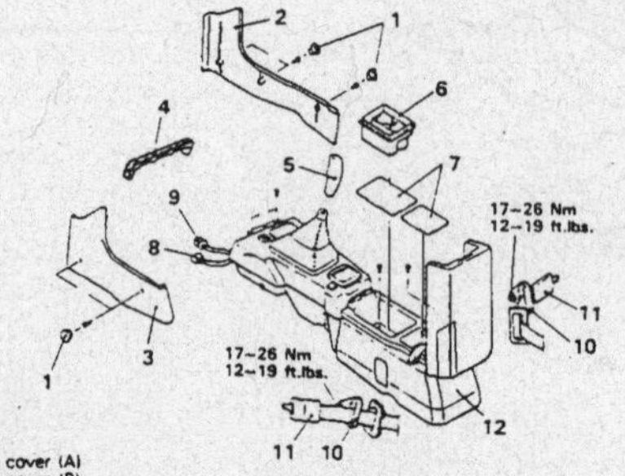
17–26 Nm
12–19 ft.lbs.
17–26 Nm
12–19 ft.lbs.

1. Plug
2. Side cover (A)
3. Side cover (B)
4. Cover (B)
5. Manual transaxle shift lever knob
6. Cup holder
7. Carpet
8. Connection for floor console wiring harness
9. POWER (PWR)/ECONOMY (ECO) changeover switch connector <A/T>
10. Guide ring
11. Shoulder belt
12. Floor console assembly

MT9149100013000X

Fig. 12 Exploded view of console assembly. 1993–94 Eclipse

9. Remove combination meter.
10. **On models with mechanical type speedometer,** proceed as follows:
    a. Disconnect speedometer at transaxle, then remove adapter locks from instrument panel.
    b. Slightly pull speedometer cable toward passenger compartment and remove adapter.
11. **On all models,** remove speaker or instrument panel top covers.
12. Disconnect instrument panel harness connector.
13. Remove steering column retaining bolts.
14. Remove instrument panel assembly.
15. Reverse procedure to install.

DIAMANTE

1. Disconnect battery ground cable.
2. Remove ashtray from floor console, floor console attaching screws, then console assembly.
3. Remove plug, knee protector and support bracket, then column cover, **Fig. 20.**
4. Remove glove compartment striker, glove compartment, then glove compartment outer case.
5. Remove undercover attaching screw, audio panel, then radio and tape player.
6. Remove heater control panel assembly, cup holder, then speakers.
7. Remove meter bezel, combination meter.
8. Disconnect speedometer cable at

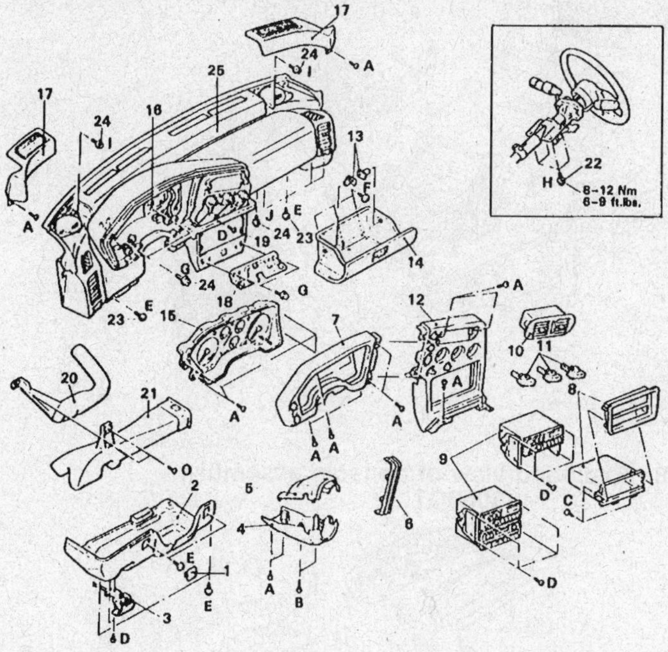
8-12 Nm
6-9 ft.lbs.

Removal steps

1. Plug
2. Knee protecter assembly
3. Hood lock release handle
4. Column cover lower
5. Column cover upper
6. Cover (A)
7. Cluster panel assembly (A)
8. Radio panel
9. Radio or radio and tape player
10. Center air outlet assembly
11. Dial knob (A)
12. Cluster panel assembly (B)
13. Stopper
14. Glove box assembly
15. Combination meter
16. Speedometer cable adapter
17. Speaker garnishe
18. Bracket
19. Heater control assembly installation screw
20. Lap cooler duct
21. Shower duct (L.H.)
22. Steering shaft mounting bolt
23. Instrument panel mounting screw
24. Instrument panel mounting bolt
25. Instrument panel assembly

MT9149100014000X

Fig. 13 Exploded view of instrument panel. 1993–94 Eclipse

NOTE
(1) ⇦ Metal clip position
(2) ⬅ Resin clip position

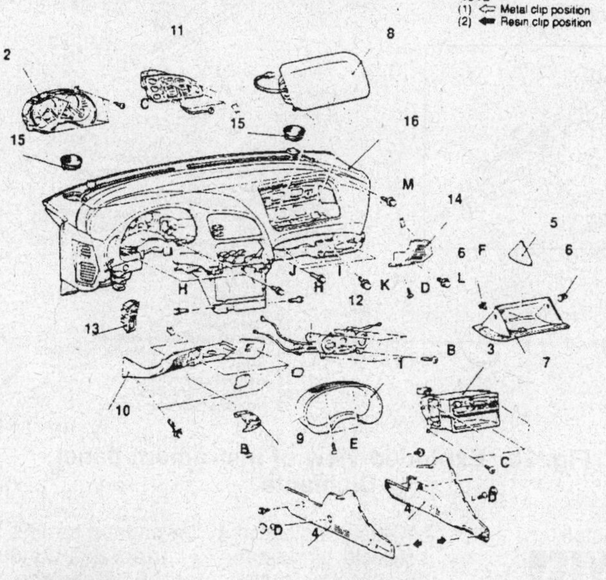

Removal steps

1. Meter bezel
2. Combination meter
3. Radio and tape player, and box
4. Console side cover
5. Sunglasses holder
6. Stopper
7. Glove box
8. Passenger's side air bag module assembly
9. Hood lock release handle
10. Instrument under cover L.H
11. Center air outlet assembly
12. Heater control assembly
13. Instrument panel switch
14. Instrument under cover R.H
15. Front speaker
16. Instrument panel assembly

MT9149500024000X

Fig. 15 Exploded view of instrument panel. 1995–96 Eclipse

Removal steps

1. Center console panel
2. Ashtray and cupholder assembly
3. Ashtray
4. Cup holder
5. Shift lever knob <M/T>
6. Floor console assembly
7. Ashtray illumination light bracket

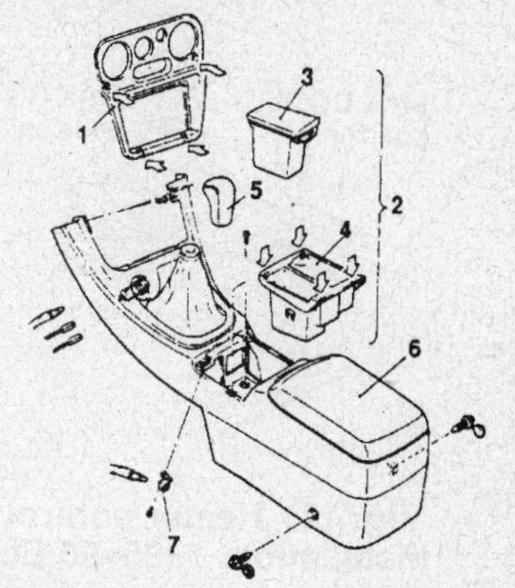

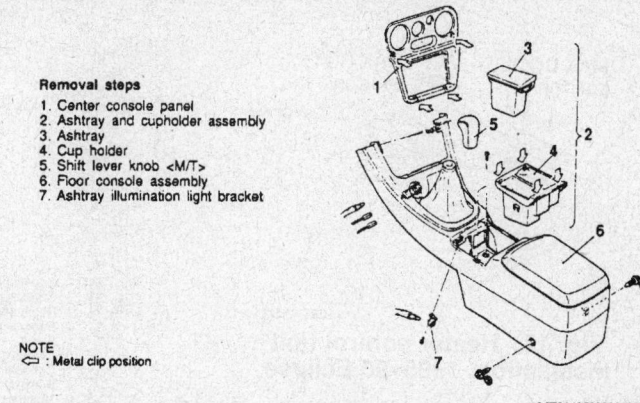

NOTE
⇦ : Metal clip position

MT9149500023000X

Fig. 14 Exploded view of center console assembly. 1995–96 Eclipse

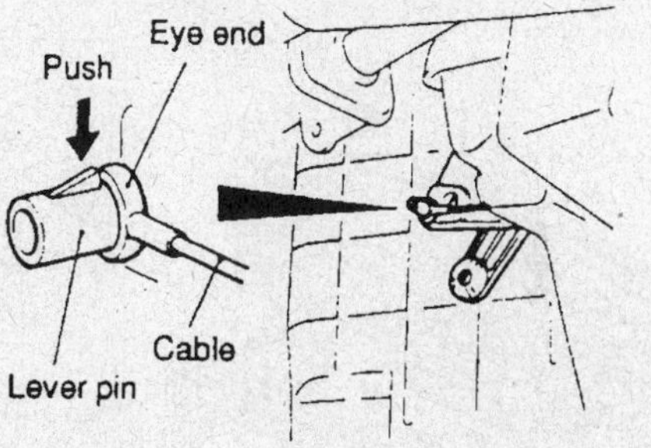
Eye end
Push
Cable
Lever pin

MT9149500025000X

Fig. 16 Air outlet changeover damper cable. 1995–96 Eclipse

transmission, remove lock of speedometer cable adapter from instrument panel. **Fig. 21.**

9. Pull cable slightly toward vehicle interior, then remove speedometer cable adapter.
10. Remove steering column attaching bolts, then disconnect harness connector.
11. Remove glove compartment light switch, then instrument panel assembly.
12. Reverse procedure to install.

EXPO

1. Disconnect battery ground cable.
2. Remove floor console side cover attaching screws, then the side covers, **Fig. 22.**
3. **On models equipped with manual transaxle,** remove shift knob.
4. **On all models,** remove floor console switch panel.
5. Remove seat belt guide bolt.
6. Remove console attaching bolts, then console.
7. Remove hood lock release handle, then knee protector plug, **Fig. 23.**
8. Remove instrument undercover, lower frame, then foot, lap and lap heater duct.
9. Remove glove compartment, speaker garnish, then glove compartment frame.
10. Remove meter hood, then combination meter.
11. Remove adapter as follows:
    a. Remove adapter lock, **Fig. 24.**

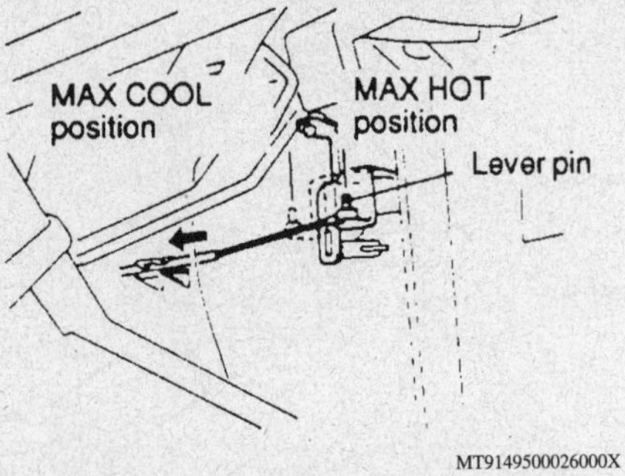
MAX COOL position
MAX HOT position
Lever pin
MT9149500026000X

Fig. 17 Heater control unit installation. 1995–96 Eclipse

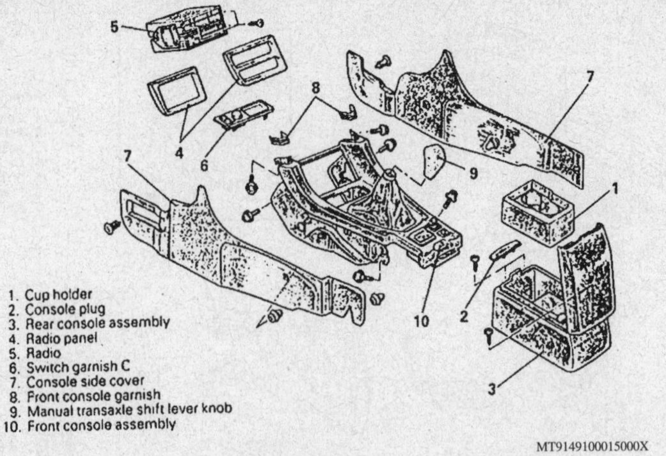
1. Cup holder
2. Console plug
3. Rear console assembly
4. Radio panel
5. Radio
6. Switch garnish C
7. Console side cover
8. Front console garnish
9. Manual transaxle shift lever knob
10. Front console assembly
MT9149100015000X

Fig. 18 Exploded view of console assembly. 3000GT

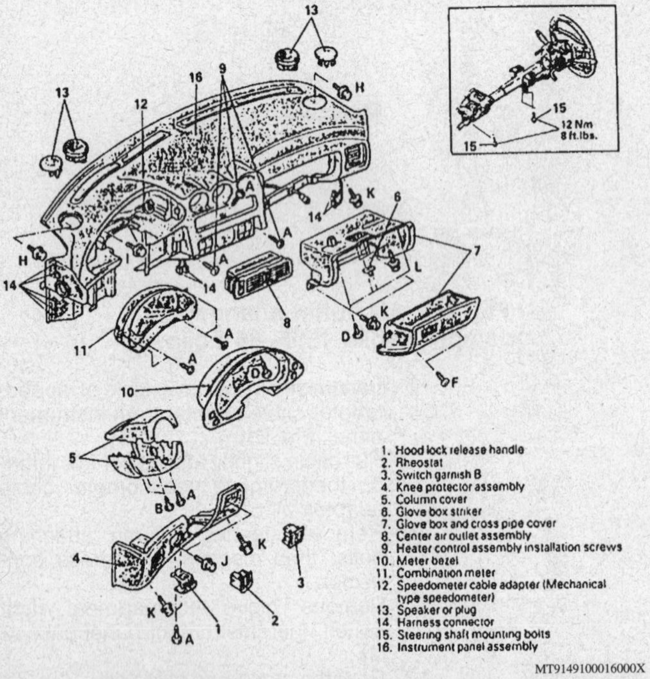
12 Nm
8 ft.lbs.
1. Hood lock release handle
2. Rheostat
3. Switch garnish B
4. Knee protector assembly
5. Column cover
6. Glove box striker
7. Glove box and cross pipe cover
8. Center air outlet assembly
9. Heater control assembly installation screws
10. Meter bezel
11. Combination meter
12. Speedometer cable adapter (Mechanical type speedometer)
13. Speaker or plug
14. Harness connector
15. Steering shaft mounting bolts
16. Instrument panel assembly
MT9149100016000X

Fig. 19 Exploded view of instrument panel. 3000GT

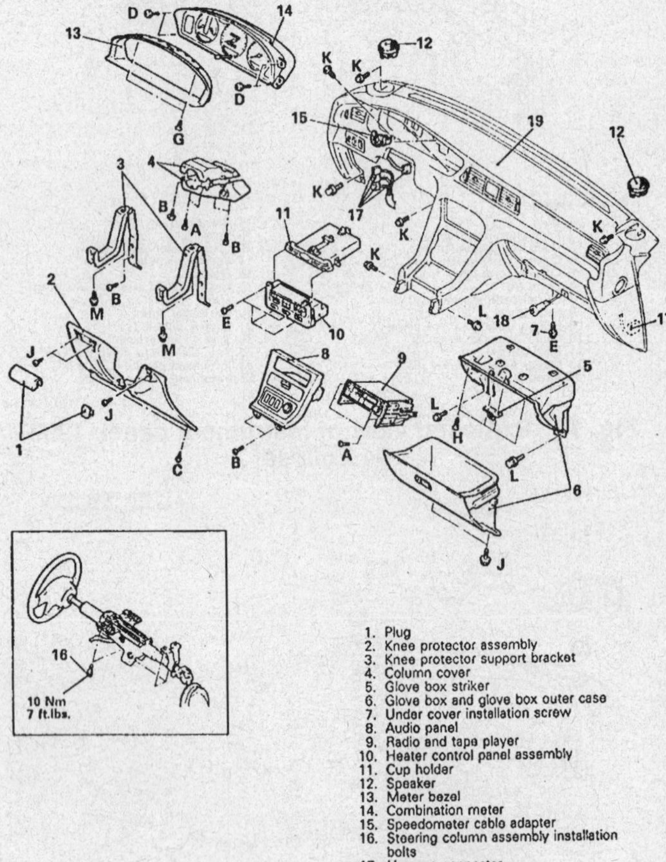
10 Nm
7 ft.lbs.
1. Plug
2. Knee protector assembly
3. Knee protector support bracket
4. Column cover
5. Glove box striker
6. Glove box and glove box outer case
7. Under cover installation screw
8. Audio panel
9. Radio and tape player
10. Heater control panel assembly
11. Cup holder
12. Speaker
13. Meter bezel
14. Combination meter
15. Speedometer cable adapter
16. Steering column assembly installation bolts
17. Harness connector
18. Glove box light switch
19. Instrument panel assembly
MT9149100017000X

Fig. 20 Exploded view of instrument panel. Diamante

b. Pull speedometer cable slightly into interior compartment, then remove the rear of the adapter from cable.
c. Turn adapter so that notched section is aligned with tab on cable section, remove adapter by sliding it in reverse direction, **Fig. 24.**

12. Remove ashtray, center panel, then radio or radio and tape player.
13. Remove center air outlet assembly as follows:
    a. Remove clip on lower section of center outlet assembly, **Fig. 25.**
    b. Insert small tipped screw driver in between fins, remove clip on top section while pulling lock spring toward inside.
    c. Remove center air outlet assembly.
14. Remove heater control assembly, clock, then disconnect harness assembly.
15. Remove instrument panel assembly.
16. Reverse procedure to install.

TECHNICAL SERVICE BULLETINS

DASHBOARD CENTER TICKING

1993 Diamante Wagon

On these models, there may be ticking sound from center of dashboard.

This condition may be caused by EGR solenoid vibrations. To correct this condition, install replacement EGR solenoid bracket (part No. AW339449). Use old bracket's bolts and washers to mount replacement, then **torque** to 17 ft. lbs.

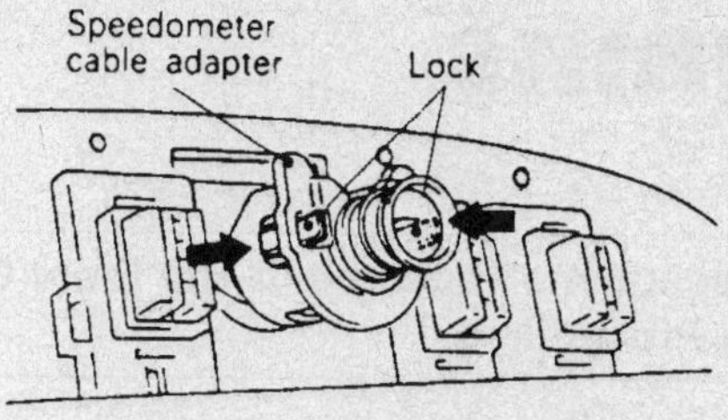
Speedometer cable adapter
Lock

MT9149100018000X

Fig. 21 Speedometer cable adapter removal. Diamante

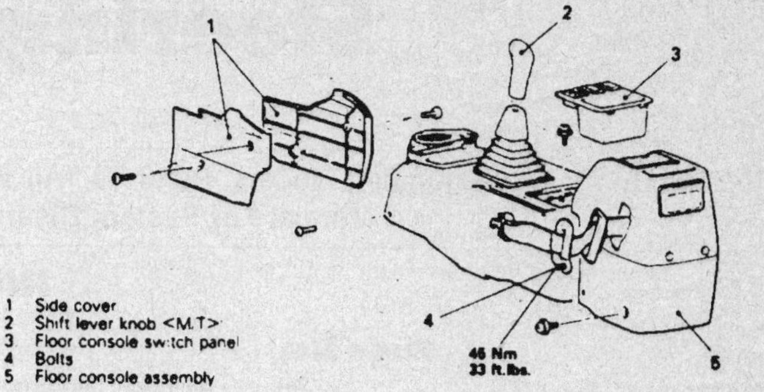
1 Side cover
2 Shift lever knob <M.T>
3 Floor console switch panel
4 Bolts
5 Floor console assembly
46 Nm
33 ft.lbs.

MT9149100019000X

Fig. 22 Exploded view of floor console. Expo

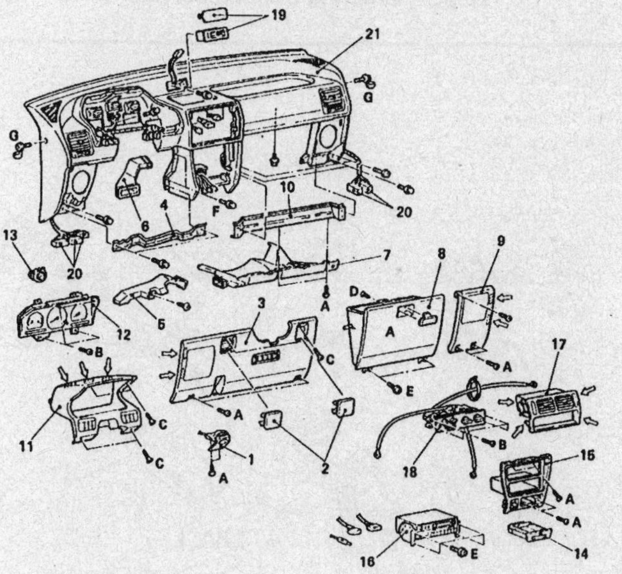

1. Hood lock release handle
2. Knee pro plug
3. Instrument under cover
4. Lower frame
5. Foot duct
6. Lap duct
7. Lap heater duct
8. Glove box
9. Speaker garnish
10. Glove box frame
11. Meter hood
12. Combination meter
13. Adapter
14. Ashtray
15. Center panel
16. Radio or radio and tape player
17. Center air outlet assembly
18. Heater control assembly
19. Clock or plug
20. Harness connector
21. Instrument panel assembly

NOTE
⇦ : metal clip position

MT9149100020000X

Fig. 23 Exploded view of instrument panel. Expo

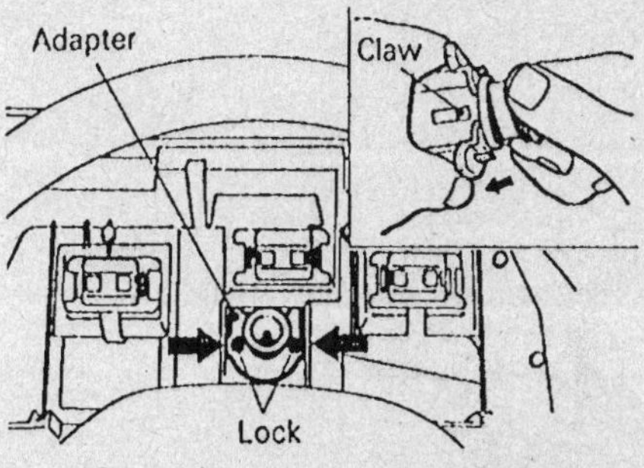
Adapter
Claw
Lock

MT9149100021000X

Fig. 24 Speedometer cable adapter removal. Expo

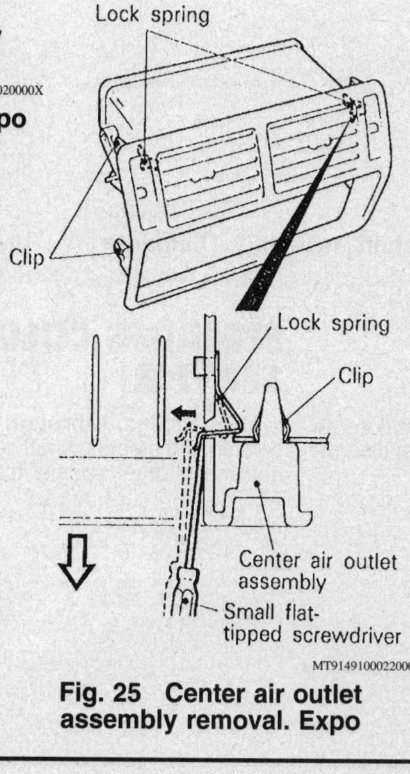
Lock spring
Clip
Lock spring
Clip
Center air outlet assembly
Small flat-tipped screwdriver

MT9149100022000X

Fig. 25 Center air outlet assembly removal. Expo

Steering Columns

NOTE: On Air Bag Equipped Models, Refer To "Air Bag System Precautions" Located In The Front Of This Manual For System Disarming & Arming Procedures.

INDEX

	Page No.
Precautions	29-86
Air Bag Systems	29-86
Steering Column Service	29-86

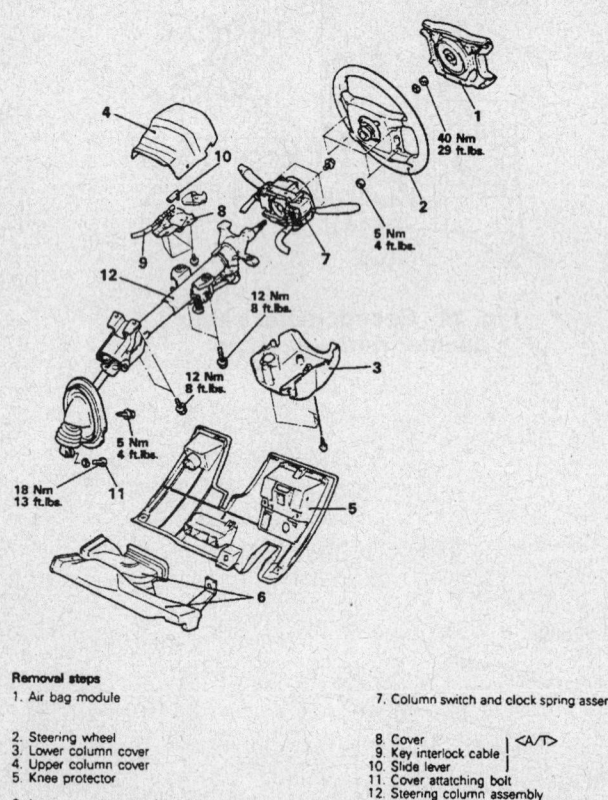

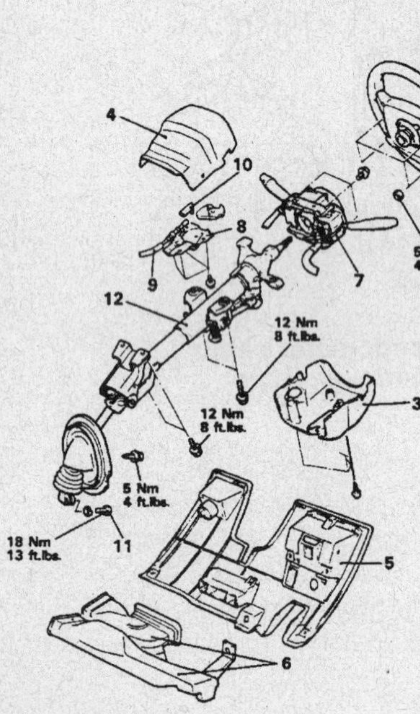

40 Nm
29 ft.lbs.
5 Nm
4 ft.lbs.
12 Nm
8 ft.lbs.
12 Nm
8 ft.lbs.
5 Nm
4 ft.lbs.
18 Nm
13 ft.lbs.

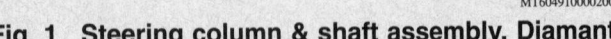

Removal steps

1. Air bag module
2. Steering wheel
3. Lower column cover
4. Upper column cover
5. Knee protector
6. Lap cooler duct and foot shower duct
7. Column switch and clock spring assembly
8. Cover <A/T>
9. Key interlock cable <A/T>
10. Slide lever <A/T>
11. Cover attaching bolt
12. Steering column assembly

MT6049100002000X

Fig. 1 Steering column & shaft assembly. Diamante

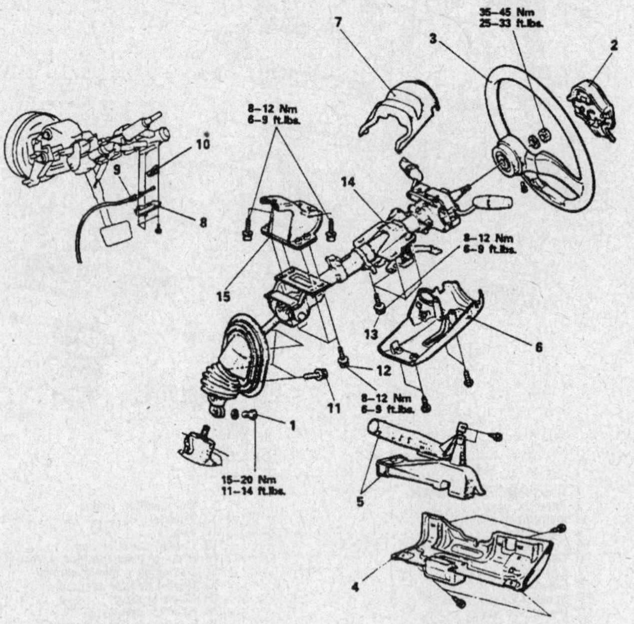

35–45 Nm
25–33 ft.lbs.
8–12 Nm
6–9 ft.lbs.
8–12 Nm
6–9 ft.lbs.
8–12 Nm
6–9 ft.lbs.
15–20 Nm
11–14 ft.lbs.

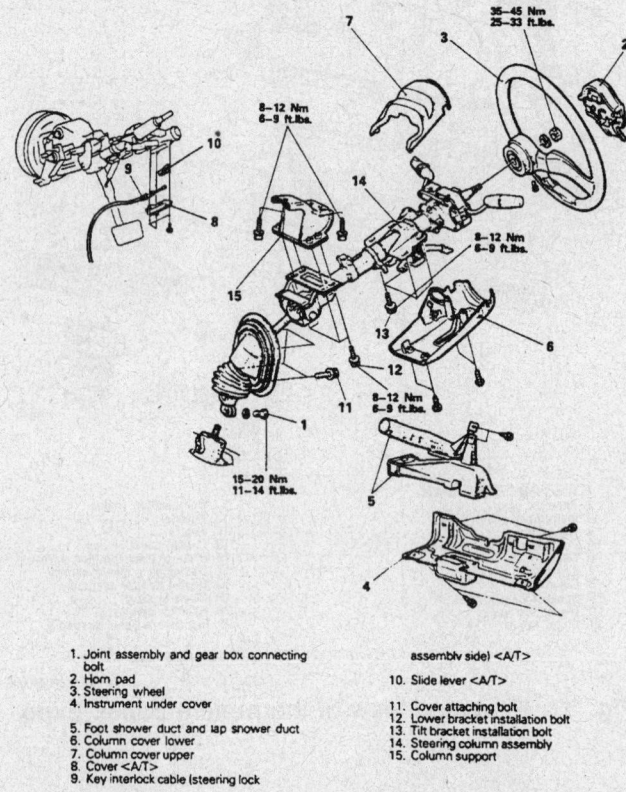

1. Joint assembly and gear box connecting bolt
2. Horn pad
3. Steering wheel
4. Instrument under cover
5. Foot shower duct and lap shower duct
6. Column cover lower
7. Column cover upper
8. Cover <A/T>
9. Key interlock cable (steering lock assembly side) <A/T>
10. Slide lever <A/T>
11. Cover attaching bolt
12. Lower bracket installation bolt
13. Tilt bracket installation bolt
14. Steering column assembly
15. Column support

MT6049100003000X

Fig. 2 Steering column & shaft assembly. 1993–94 Eclipse

PRECAUTIONS

AIR BAG SYSTEMS

Refer to "Air Bag System Precautions" in the front of this manual for system disarming and arming procedures.

STEERING COLUMN SERVICE

Refer to **Figs. 1 through 12** for steering column and steering shaft service. On Galant and Mirage models, the steering column and shaft cannot be disassembled. If column and shaft are found to be defective on the above models, they should be replaced as an assembly.

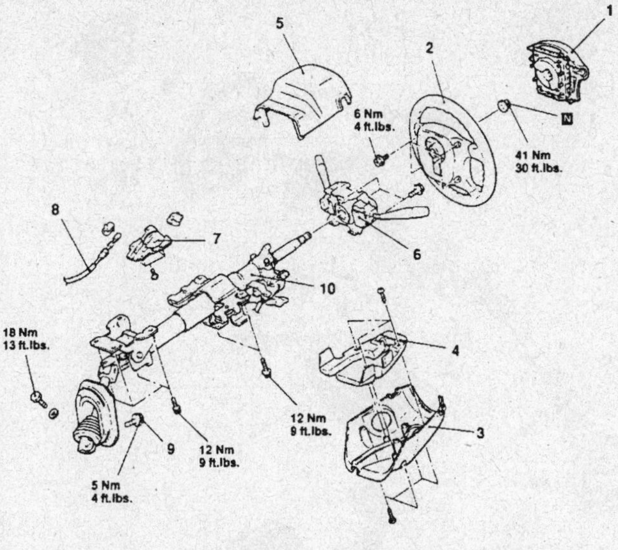
6 Nm
4 ft.lbs.
41 Nm
30 ft.lbs.
18 Nm
13 ft.lbs.
12 Nm
9 ft.lbs.
12 Nm
9 ft.lbs.
5 Nm
4 ft.lbs.

Removal steps

1. Air bag module
2. Steering wheel
3. Lower column cover
4. Column pad
5. Upper column cover
6. Clock spring and column switch assembly
7. Cover
8. Key interlock cable
9. Retainer attachment bolt
10. Steering column assembly

MT6049500018000X

Fig. 3 Steering column & shaft assembly. 1995–96 Eclipse

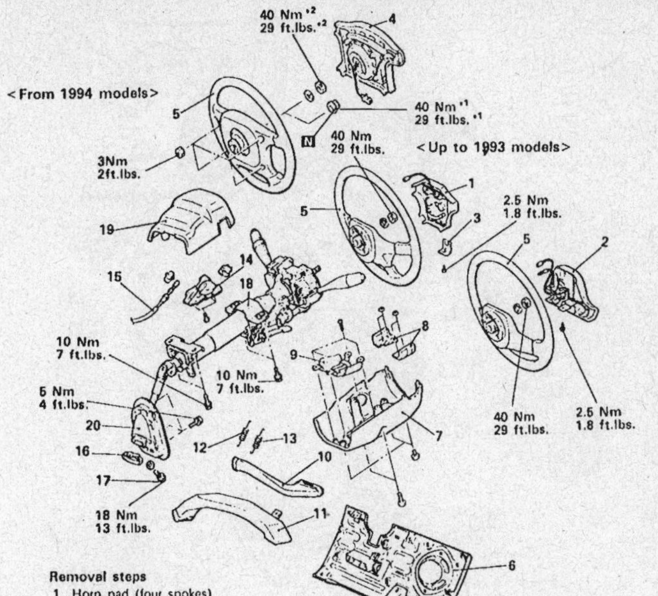
40 Nm *2
29 ft.lbs.*2
<From 1994 models>
40 Nm *1
29 ft.lbs. *1
40 Nm
29 ft.lbs.
<Up to 1993 models>
3Nm
2ft.lbs.
2.5 Nm
1.8 ft.lbs.
10 Nm
7 ft.lbs.
10 Nm
7 ft.lbs.
5 Nm
4 ft.lbs.
40 Nm
29 ft.lbs.
2.5 Nm
1.8 ft.lbs.
18 Nm
13 ft.lbs.

Removal steps

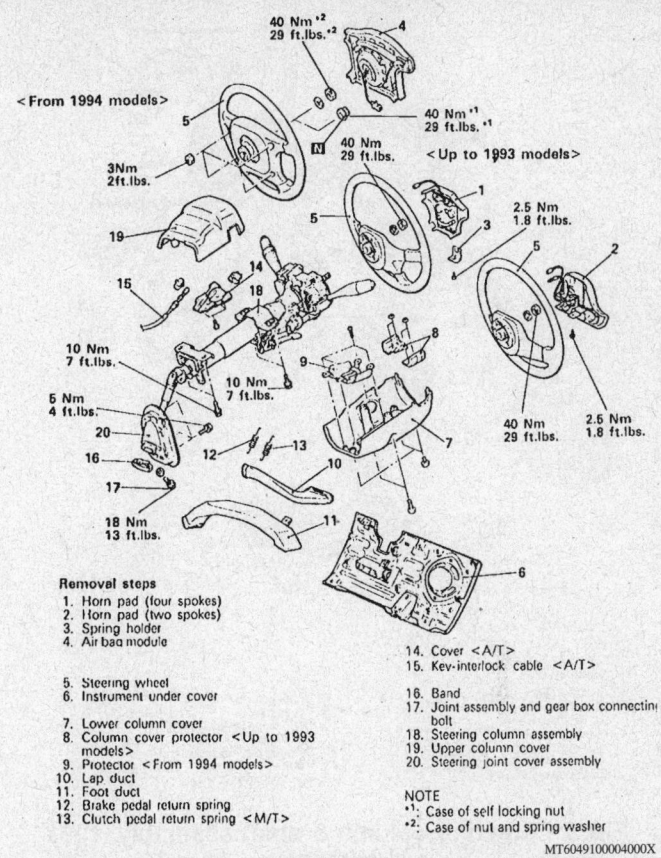

1. Horn pad (four spokes)
2. Horn pad (two spokes)
3. Spring holder
4. Air bag module
5. Steering wheel
6. Instrument under cover
7. Lower column cover
8. Column cover protector <Up to 1993 models>
9. Protector <From 1994 models>
10. Lap duct
11. Foot duct
12. Brake pedal return spring
13. Clutch pedal return spring <M/T>
14. Cover <A/T>
15. Key-interlock cable <A/T>
16. Band
17. Joint assembly and gear box connecting bolt
18. Steering column assembly
19. Upper column cover
20. Steering joint cover assembly

NOTE
*1: Case of self locking nut
*2: Case of nut and spring washer

MT6049100004000X

Fig. 4 Steering column & shaft assembly. Expo

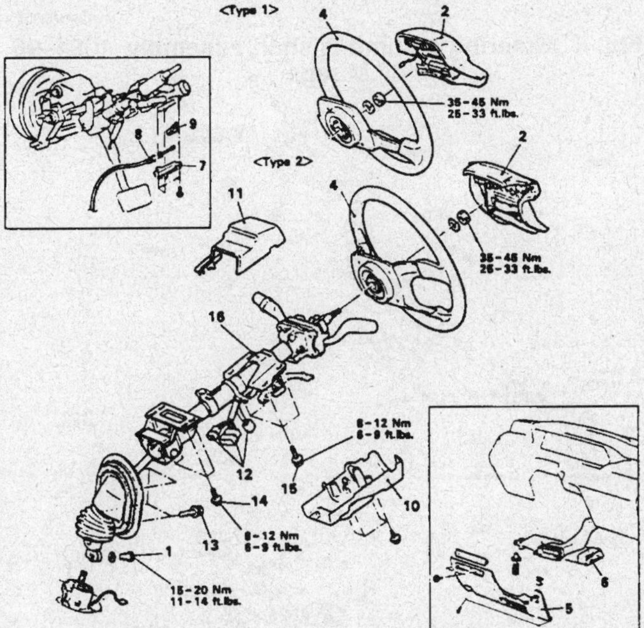
<Type 1>
35–45 Nm
25–33 ft.lbs.
<Type 2>
35–45 Nm
25–33 ft.lbs.
8–12 Nm
6–9 ft.lbs.
8–12 Nm
6–9 ft.lbs.
15–20 Nm
11–14 ft.lbs.

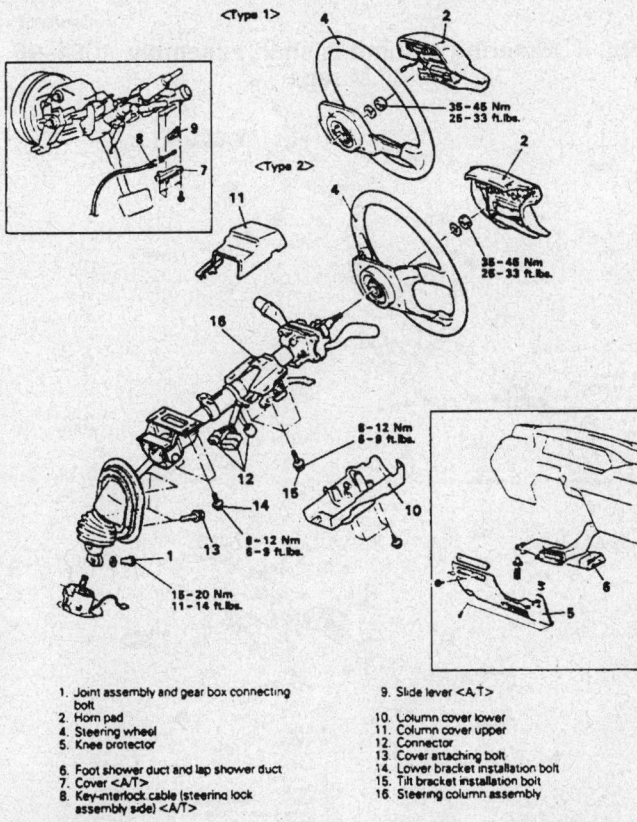

1. Joint assembly and gear box connecting bolt
2. Horn pad
4. Steering wheel
5. Knee protector
6. Foot shower duct and lap shower duct
7. Cover <A/T>
8. Key-interlock cable (steering lock assembly side) <A/T>
9. Slide lever <A/T>
10. Column cover lower
11. Column cover upper
12. Connector
13. Cover attaching bolt
14. Lower bracket installation bolt
15. Tilt bracket installation bolt
16. Steering column assembly

MT6049200009000X

Fig. 5 Steering column & shaft assembly. 1993 Galant

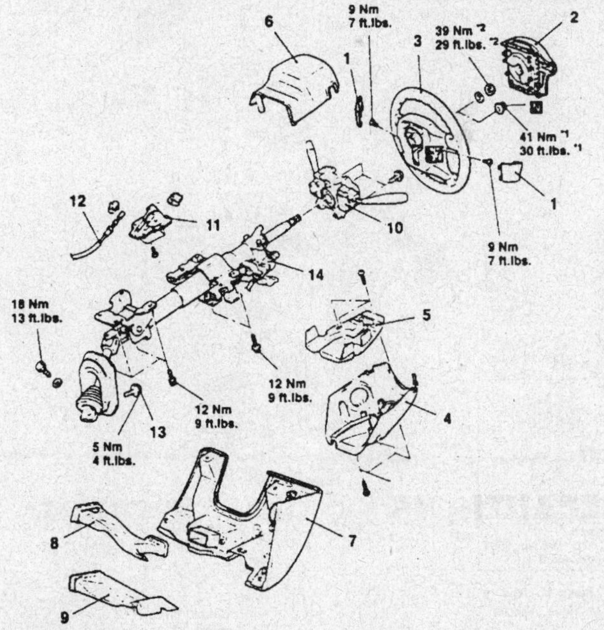
9 Nm
7 ft.lbs.
39 Nm *2
29 ft.lbs. *2
41 Nm *1
30 ft.lbs. *1
9 Nm
7 ft.lbs.
18 Nm
13 ft.lbs.
12 Nm
9 ft.lbs.
12 Nm
9 ft.lbs.
5 Nm
4 ft.lbs.

Removal steps

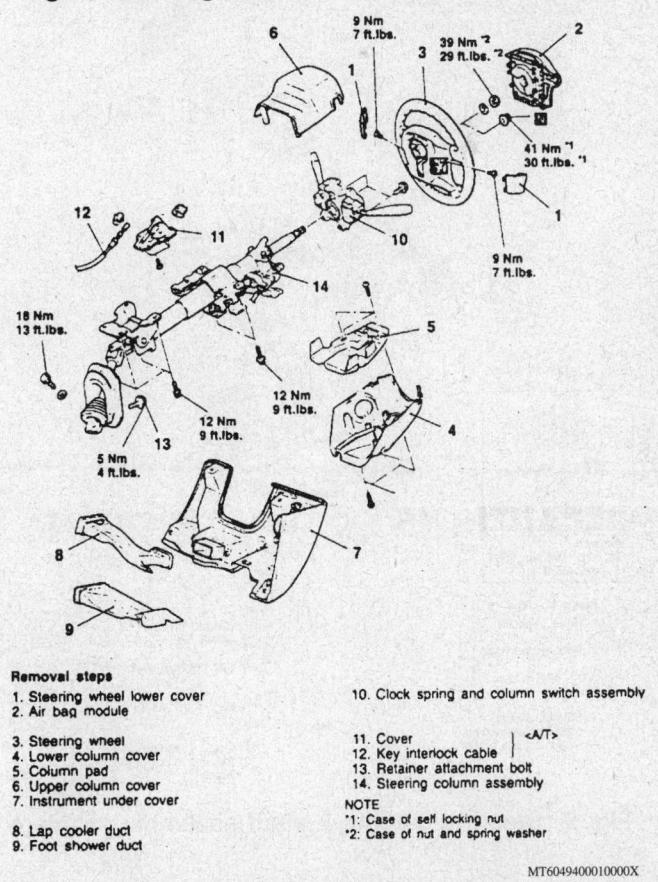

1. Steering wheel lower cover
2. Air bag module
3. Steering wheel
4. Lower column cover
5. Column pad
6. Upper column cover
7. Instrument under cover
8. Lap cooler duct
9. Foot shower duct
10. Clock spring and column switch assembly
11. Cover <A/T>
12. Key interlock cable <A/T>
13. Retainer attachment bolt
14. Steering column assembly

NOTE
*1: Case of self locking nut
*2: Case of nut and spring washer

MT6049400010000X

Fig. 6 Steering column & shaft assembly. 1994–96 Galant

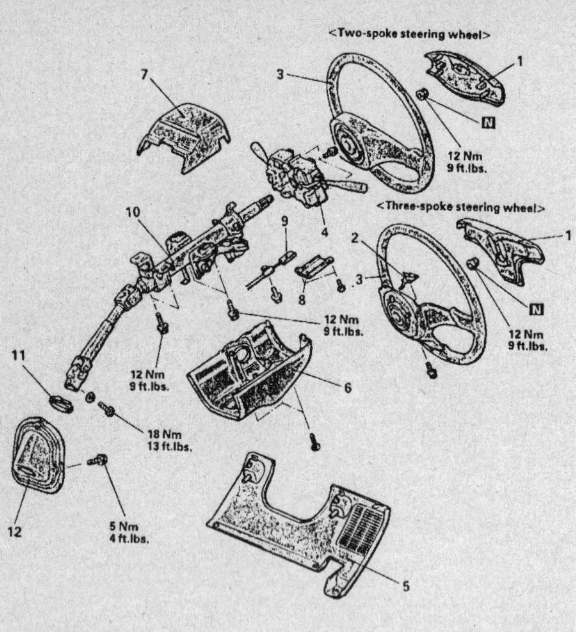
<Two-spoke steering wheel>
<Three-spoke steering wheel>
12 Nm
9 ft.lbs.
18 Nm
13 ft.lbs.
5 Nm
4 ft.lbs.
N

Removal steps

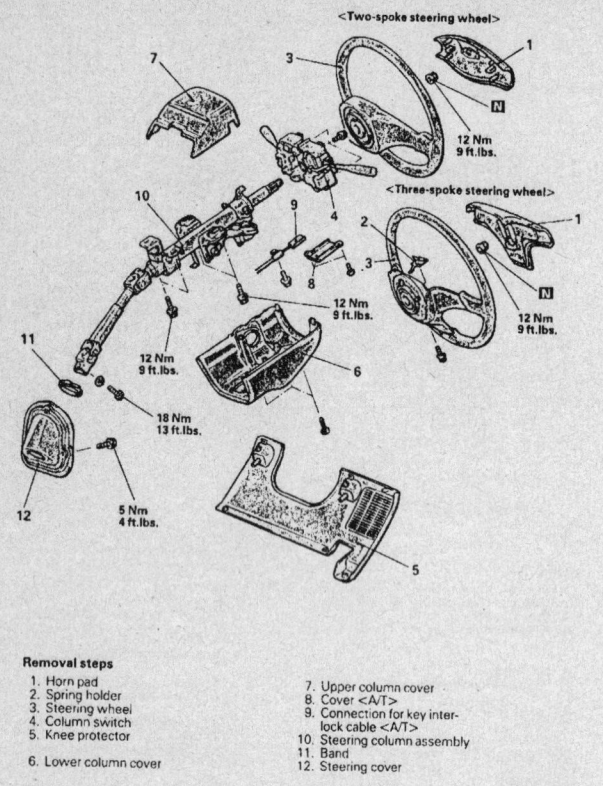

1. Horn pad
2. Spring holder
3. Steering wheel
4. Column switch
5. Knee protector
6. Lower column cover
7. Upper column cover
8. Cover <A/T>
9. Connection for key interlock cable <A/T>
10. Steering column assembly
11. Band
12. Steering cover

MT6049300012000X

Fig. 7 Steering column & shaft assembly. 1993 Mirage

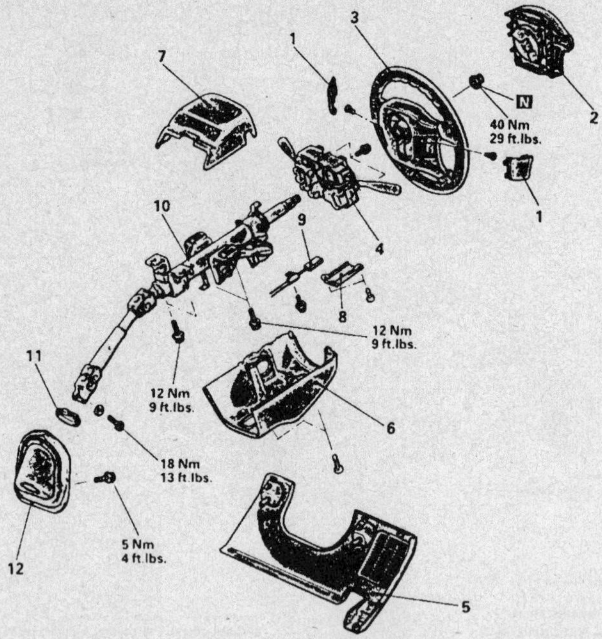
40 Nm
29 ft.lbs.
12 Nm
9 ft.lbs.
18 Nm
13 ft.lbs.
5 Nm
4 ft.lbs.
N

Removal steps

1. Cover
2. Air bag module
3. Steering wheel
4. Column switch assembly
5. Knee protector
6. Lower column cover
7. Upper column cover
8. Cover <A/T>
9. Connection for key interlock cable <A/T>
10. Steering column assembly
11. Band
12. Steering cover

MT6049400013000X

Fig. 8 Steering column & shaft assembly. 1994–96 Mirage

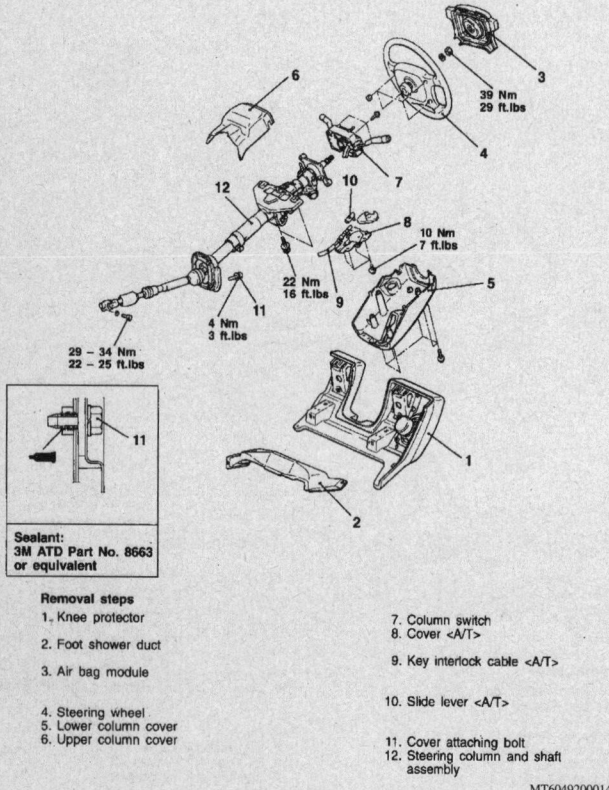

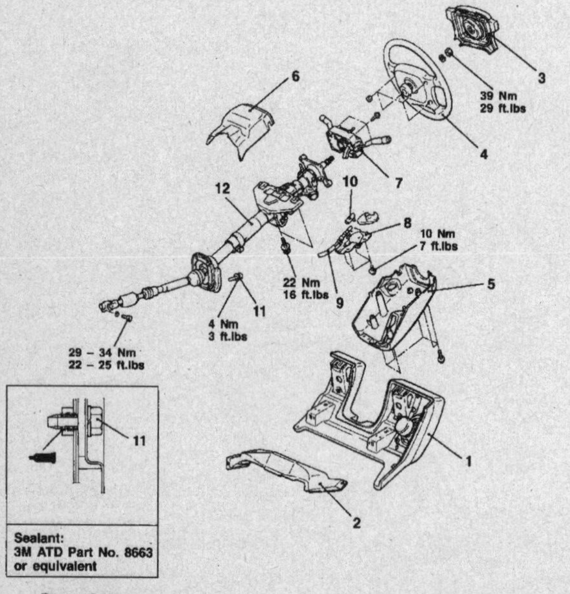
39 Nm
29 ft.lbs
10 Nm
7 ft.lbs
22 Nm
16 ft.lbs
4 Nm
3 ft.lbs
29 – 34 Nm
22 – 25 ft.lbs
Sealant:
3M ATD Part No. 8663
or equivalent

Removal steps

1. Knee protector
2. Foot shower duct
3. Air bag module
4. Steering wheel
5. Lower column cover
6. Upper column cover
7. Column switch
8. Cover <A/T>
9. Key interlock cable <A/T>
10. Slide lever <A/T>
11. Cover attaching bolt
12. Steering column and shaft assembly

MT6049200014000A

Fig. 9 Steering column & shaft assembly. Montero

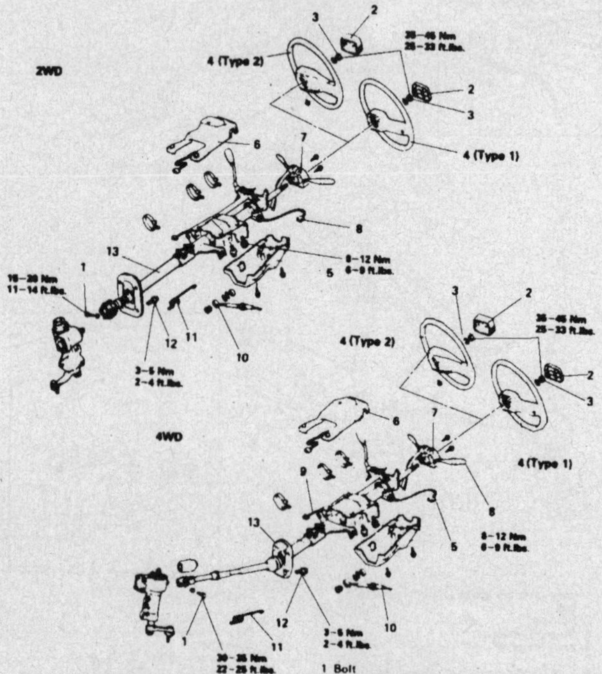
2WD
4WD
4 (Type 2)
4 (Type 1)
35–45 Nm
25–33 ft.lbs.
8–12 Nm
6–9 ft.lbs.
3–5 Nm
2–4 ft.lbs.

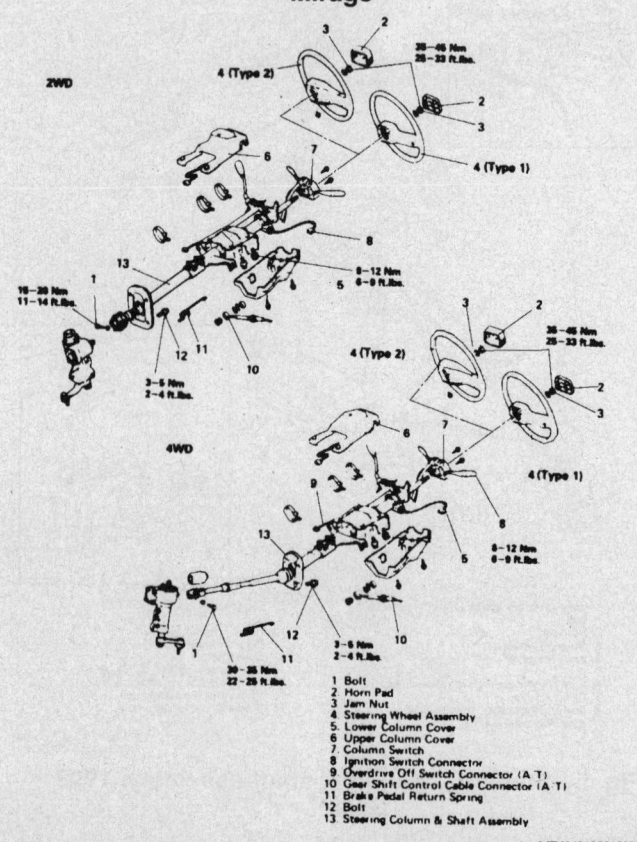

1. Bolt
2. Horn Pad
3. Jam Nut
4. Steering Wheel Assembly
5. Lower Column Cover
6. Upper Column Cover
7. Column Switch
8. Ignition Switch Connector
9. Overdrive Off Switch Connector (A/T)
10. Gear Shift Control Cable Connector (A/T)
11. Brake Pedal Return Spring
12. Bolt
13. Steering Column & Shaft Assembly

MT6049100015000X

Fig. 10 Steering column & shaft assembly. Pickup

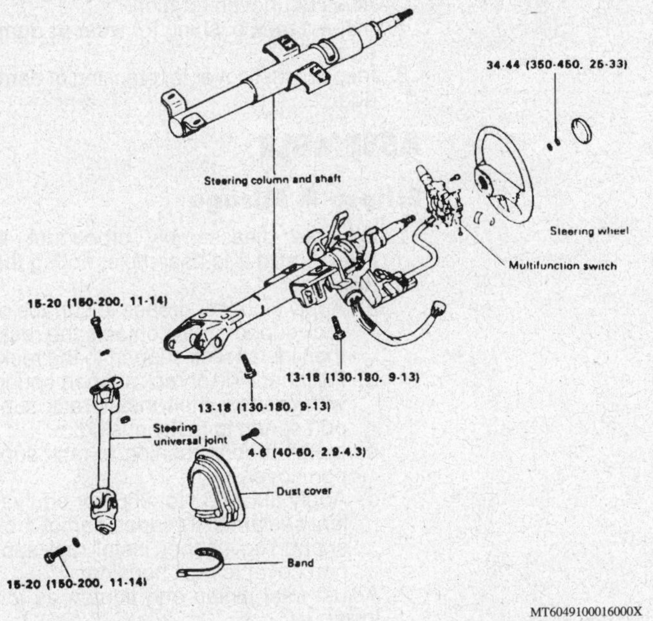
34-44 (350-450, 25-33)
Steering column and shaft
Steering wheel
Multifunction switch
15-20 (150-200, 11-14)
13-18 (130-180, 9-13)
13-18 (130-180, 9-13)
Steering universal joint
4-6 (40-60, 2.9-4.3)
Dust cover
Band
15-20 (150-200, 11-14)
MT6049100016000X

Fig. 11 Steering column & shaft assembly. Precis

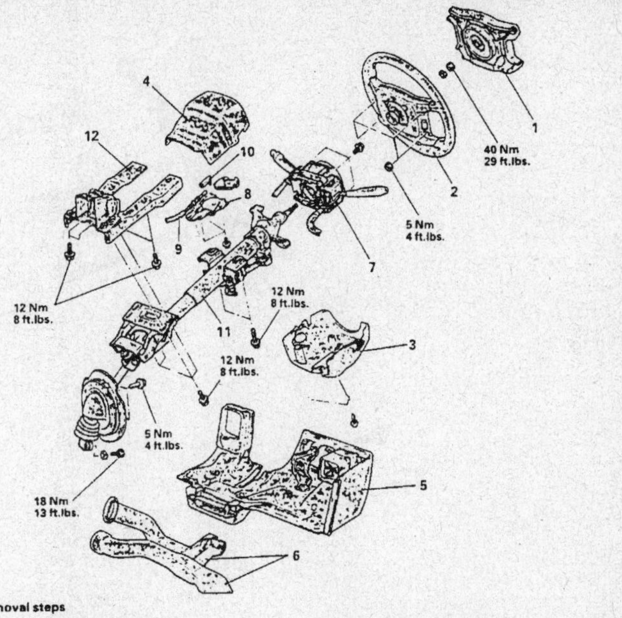
40 Nm
29 ft.lbs.
5 Nm
4 ft.lbs.
12 Nm
8 ft.lbs.
12 Nm
8 ft.lbs.
12 Nm
8 ft.lbs.
5 Nm
4 ft.lbs.
18 Nm
13 ft.lbs.

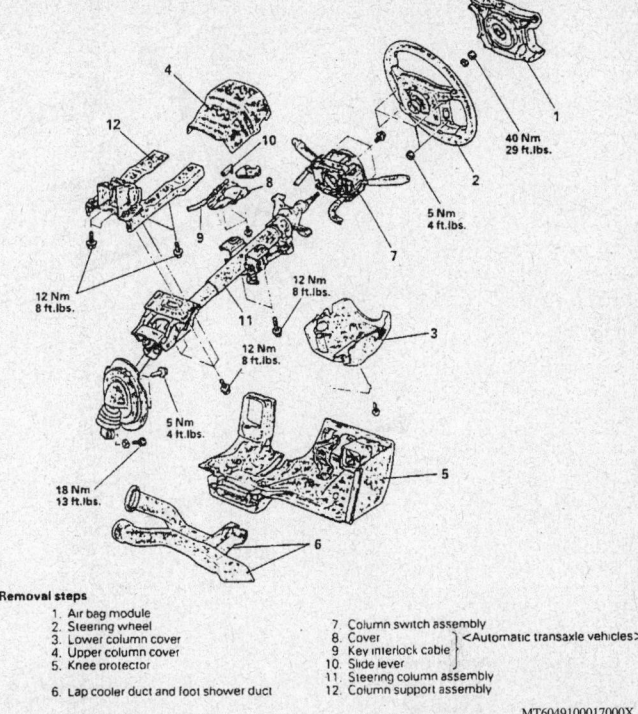

Removal steps

1. Air bag module
2. Steering wheel
3. Lower column cover
4. Upper column cover
5. Knee protector
6. Lap cooler duct and foot shower duct
7. Column switch assembly
8. Cover <Automatic transaxle vehicles>
9. Key interlock cable <Automatic transaxle vehicles>
10. Slide lever
11. Steering column assembly
12. Column support assembly

MT6049100017000X

Fig. 12 Steering column & shaft assembly. 3000GT

Manual Steering Gears

NOTE: On Air Bag Equipped Models, Refer To "Air Bag System Precautions" Located In The Front Of This Manual For System Disarming & Arming Procedures.

INDEX

	Page No.
Precautions	29-89
Air Bag Systems	29-89
Steering Gear Service	29-89
Assemble	29-90
Disassemble	29-89
Inspection	29-90
Tightening Specifications	29-92

PRECAUTIONS

AIR BAG SYSTEMS

Refer to "Air Bag System Precautions" in the front of this manual for system disarming and arming procedures.

STEERING GEAR SERVICE

DISASSEMBLE

Eclipse & Mirage

1. Disassemble steering gear in numbered sequence as shown, **Figs. 1 and 2,** noting the following:
   a. Remove tie rod end snap ring, then the dust cover.
   b. Cut and remove band securing bellow.
   c. Remove bellow securing clip, then the bellow from tie rod.
   d. Unstake tab washer which attaches tie rod and rack, then remove tie rod from rack.
   e. Remove rack from gear housing in direction shown, **Fig. 3,** to avoid damaging gearbox bushing.

Pickup

1. Remove jam nut; then, using tool No. MB990809-01, or equivalent, separate pitman arm from steering gear, **Fig. 4.** Drain lubricant.
2. Remove dust cover attaching bolts, then the dust cover.
3. Remove breather plug.
4. Remove adjusting cover locknut, then the attaching bolts with washers.
5. Remove side cover, then the packing.
6. Remove cross shaft, then the adjusting cover cap.
7. Remove adjusting cover locknut, then the adjusting cover.
8. Remove end cover retaining bolts, then the end cover.
9. Remove adjusting shims and retain to facilitate assembly.
10. Remove bearing (16), then the mainshaft assembly.
11. Remove second bearing (18), then the oil seal (19).
12. Separate oil seal (20) from gearbox housing.

Precis

Before disassembly, note rack starting force and pinion preload torque in straight ahead position for reference at reassembly.

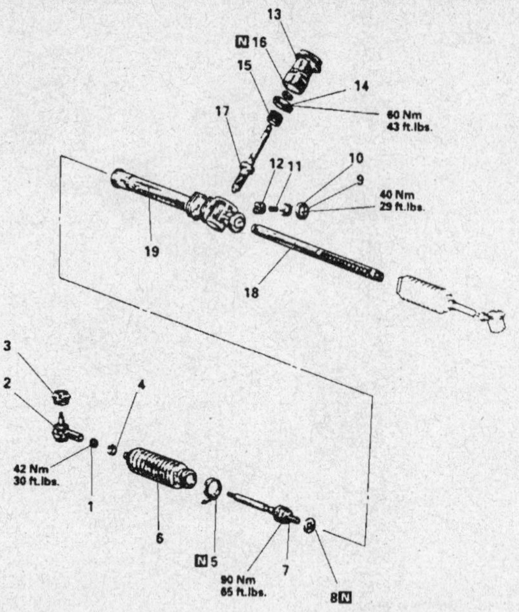
13
16
15
14
17
60 Nm
43 ft.lbs.
12
11
10
9
40 Nm
29 ft.lbs.
19
18
3
2
4
42 Nm
30 ft.lbs.
1
6
5
7
90 Nm
65 ft.lbs.
8

Disassembly steps

1 Tie-rod end locking nut
2 Tie-rod end
3 Dust cover
4 Bellows clip
5 Bellows band
6 Bellows
7 Tie-rod
8 Tab washer
• Adjustment of total pinion preload
9 Locking nut
10. Rack support cover
11. Rack support spring
12 Rack support
13 Joint cover
14 Locking nut
15 Top cover
16 Oil seal
17 Pinion
18 Rack
19 Gear housing

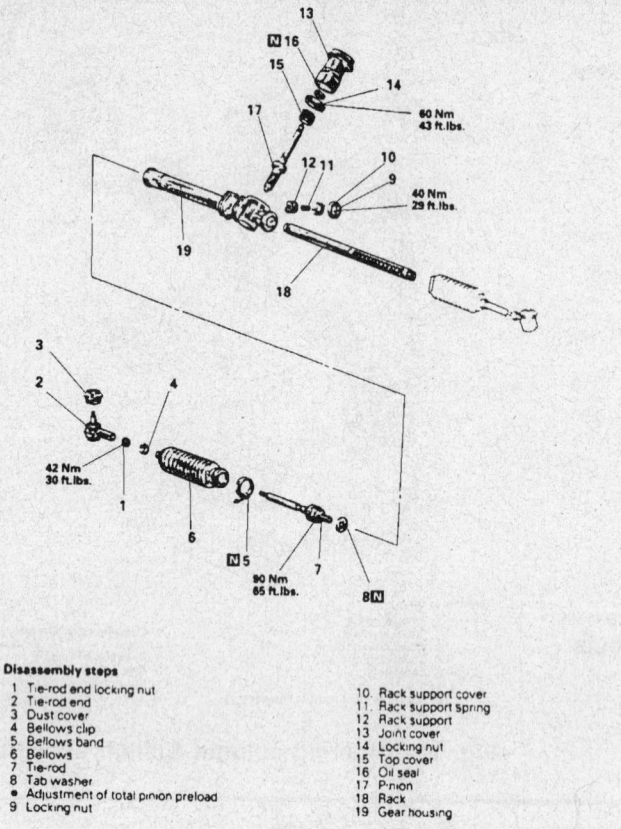

MT6039100023000X

Fig. 1 Exploded view of manual steering gear. Mirage

1. Wrap a shop towel around center portion of steering, gear, then mount gear in a soft-jawed vise.
2. Cut nylon bellows band, then remove bellows from left tie rod.
3. Unstake left tie rod end nut using a chisel, then remove tie rod from rack assembly.
4. Remove yoke plug locknut, **Fig. 5;** then, using tool No. 09565-21100, or equivalent, remove yoke plug.
5. Remove yoke spring, cushion rubber and support yoke from gearbox.
6. Remove and discard oil seal.
7. Remove snap ring, then the pinion and bearing assembly.
8. Remove pinion bearing retainer snap ring; then, using tool No. 09565-21000, or equivalent, and a suitable press, press bearing from pinion.
9. Cut bellows band, then remove bellows from right tie rod.
10. Unstake right tie rod end nut, then move rack fully toward housing. Carefully position toothed portion of rack in a suitable vise and remove tie rod.
11. Remove rack from left side of gear housing to prevent damage to bushing, **Fig. 3.**

INSPECTION

Eclipse & Mirage

Check all steering gear components and repair or replace as necessary.

1. Check rack support for uneven wear.
2. Check rack support spring for deterioration.
3. Check cushion rubber for cracking.
4. Check rack and pinion for worn or damaged tooth surfaces.
5. Check ball bearings and needle roller bearings for uneven rotation.
6. Check ball joint dust cover for cracks.

Pickup

1. Check ball nut for smooth rotation and endplay.
2. Check bearing for seizure and discoloration, then for a rough rolling surface.
3. Check oil seal for cracks and damage.
4. Check mainshaft and cross shaft tooth surfaces for wear and damage.
5. Check pitman arm for wear and damage.

Precis

Check all steering gear components and repair or replace as necessary.

1. Inspect support yoke for damage or uneven wear.
2. Inspect yoke spring for deterioration and free length. Free length should be .55 inch.
3. Inspect rubber spring for cracking or deterioration.
4. Check mounting rubber for wear or damage.
5. Inspect rack and pinion for damage or worn tooth surfaces.
6. Check bearings for wear, damage, noise or uneven rotation.
7. Inspect rack bushing for wear or damage.
8. Inspect dust cover for cracking or damage.

ASSEMBLE

Eclipse & Mirage

1. Reverse disassembly procedure in **Figs. 1 and 2** to assemble, noting the following:
   a. Apply a coat of grease to surface of rack support that contacts the rack, then install rack support to the rack.
   b. Fill inner side of rack support spring with grease, then install rack support spring to rack housing.
   c. Install rubber cushion to rack support cover.
   d. Apply 3M ATD No. 8663 or equivalent sealant to threaded part of rack support cover, then install rack support cover to rack housing.
2. Adjust total pinion and tighten as follows:
   a. Position rack at its center then **torque** rack support cover to 11 ft. lbs.
   b. From neutral position, rotate pinion shaft clockwise one complete turn within 4–6 seconds using socket tool No. MB991006-01, or equivalent.
   c. Loosen rack support cover 30–60° and adjust pinion **torque** to 5–11 inch lbs. from 0–90° and to 2–9 inch lbs. from 90° to rack stop.
   d. If specified value cannot be reached, check rack support cover and components.
   e. After adjustment, tighten support cover locknut.

Pickup

1. Adjust position of gear housing as to allow level installation of mainshaft. Press oil seals into housing using tool No. MB990925, or equivalent, then apply lubricant.
2. Apply lubricant to tooth and sliding surfaces of mainshaft and bearings, then install them into gear housing.
3. Install bearing (16).
4. Apply sealant to adjusting shims of same thickness as removed during disassembly, then install adjusting shims and end cover into gear housing and tighten attaching bolts. Measure mainshaft starting torque using tool No. MB990228-01, or equivalent, **Fig. 6.** Starting **torque** should be 3–5 inch lbs. If measured torque is not as specified, remove shims and add shims to reduce starting torque or remove shims to increase starting torque. Tighten attaching bolts to specifications.
5. Install adjusting cover, then apply sealant to base of threads on adjusting bolt. Temporarily tighten locknut with chamfered end facing downward. Place center portion of cross shaft in a vise, then measure starting torque. Starting **torque** should be 3.4–6.9 inch

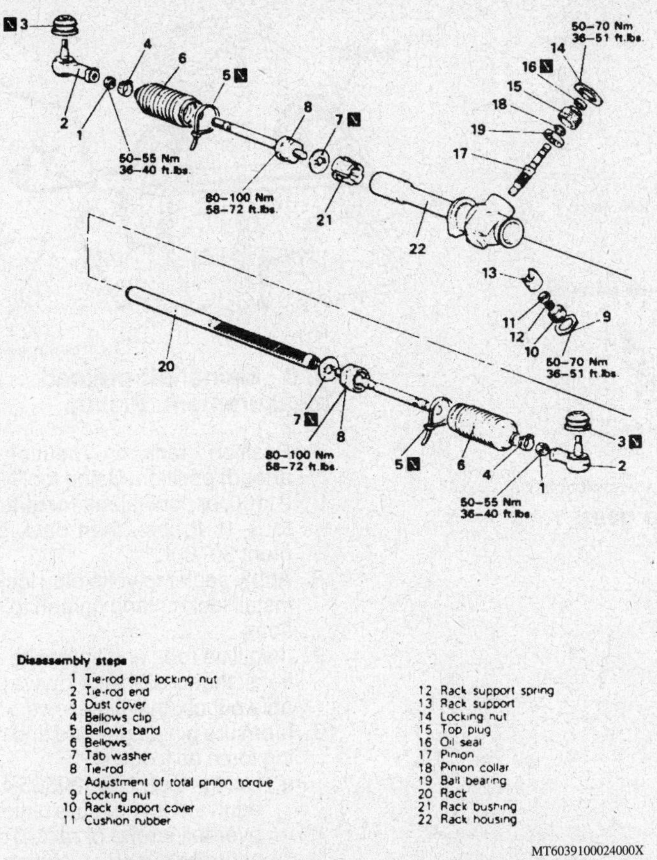
50–70 Nm
36–51 ft.lbs.
50–55 Nm
36–40 ft.lbs.
80–100 Nm
58–72 ft.lbs.
Disassembly steps
1 Tie-rod end locking nut
2 Tie-rod end
3 Dust cover
4 Bellows clip
5 Bellows band
6 Bellows
7 Tab washer
8 Tie-rod
Adjustment of total pinion torque
9 Locking nut
10 Rack support cover
11 Cushion rubber
12 Rack support spring
13 Rack support
14 Locking nut
15 Top plug
16 Oil seal
17 Pinion
18 Pinion collar
19 Ball bearing
20 Rack
21 Rack bushing
22 Rack housing
MT6039100024000X

Fig. 2 Exploded view of manual steering gear. Eclipse

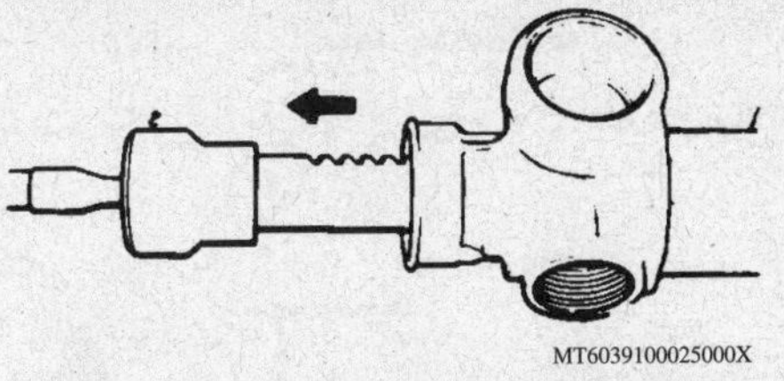
MT6039100025000X

Fig. 3 Rack removal from gear housing

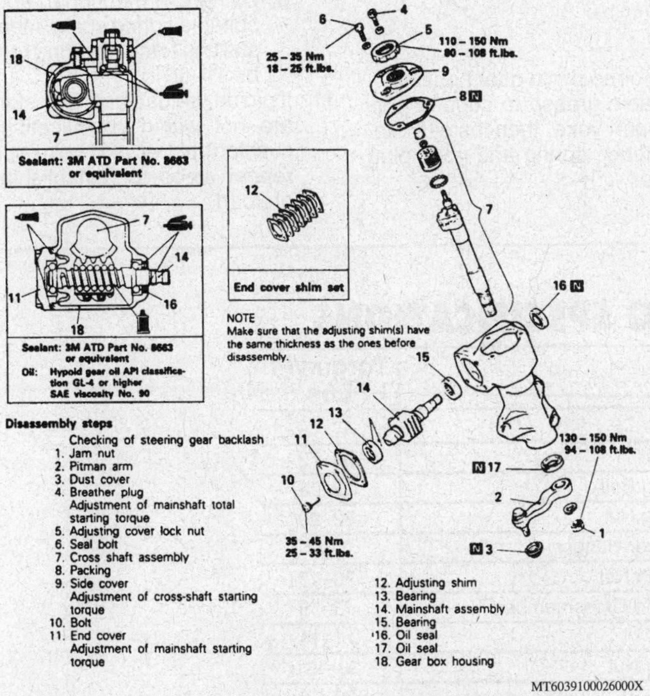
Sealant: 3M ATD Part No. 8663 or equivalent
Sealant: 3M ATD Part No. 8663 or equivalent
Oil: Hypoid gear oil API classification GL-4 or higher SAE viscosity No. 90
End cover shim set
NOTE
Make sure that the adjusting shim(s) have the same thickness as the ones before disassembly.
25–35 Nm
18–25 ft.lbs.
110–150 Nm
80–108 ft.lbs.
130–150 Nm
94–108 ft.lbs.
35–45 Nm
25–33 ft.lbs.
Disassembly steps
Checking of steering gear backlash
1. Jam nut
2. Pitman arm
3. Dust cover
4. Breather plug
Adjustment of mainshaft total starting torque
5. Adjusting cover lock nut
6. Seal bolt
7. Cross shaft assembly
8. Packing
9. Side cover
Adjustment of cross-shaft starting torque
10. Bolt
11. End cover
Adjustment of mainshaft starting torque
12. Adjusting shim
13. Bearing
14. Mainshaft assembly
15. Bearing
16. Oil seal
17. Oil seal
18. Gear box housing
MT6039100026000X

Fig. 4 Exploded view of manual steering gear. Pickup

lbs. If measured torque is not as specified, adjust by rotating adjusting bolt as necessary.

6. Install cross shaft assembly into gear housing with mainshaft ball nut at center of gear housing, in a straight ahead position.
7. After adjustment, retain adjusting cover using tool No. MB990914, or equivalent, then **torque** locknut to 18–25 ft. lbs.
8. Apply sealant to component threads, except breather plug mounting hole. Apply grease to annular bearing of cross shaft, then temporarily screw in adjusting cover using tool No. MB990914, or equivalent.
9. Install adjusting cover locknut using tool Nos. MB991149 and MB990914, or equivalents.
10. Adjust mainshaft total starting torque as follows:
    a. Rotate cross shaft approximately 36° to ensure proper fit between teeth, then with mainshaft in Neutral position (straight ahead), measure combined starting torque of mainshaft using tool No. MB990228-01, or equivalent.
    b. Starting **torque** should be 7.7–8.6 inch lbs.
    c. If starting torque is not as specified, rotate adjusting cover in or out as necessary.
11. Install adjusting cover locknut, then **torque** to 80–108 ft. lbs.
12. Install breather plug, then the dust cover.
13. Install pitman arm and align mating marks. Install jam nut and **torque** to 94–108 ft. lbs.
14. Adjust steering gear backlash with mainshaft, cross shaft and pitman arm in neutral position as follows:
    a. Inject a small amount of gear oil through the breather plug hole to lubricate bearings and shaft gear teeth.
    b. Move pitman arm 3–5 times in each direction to ensure is properly meshed with gear teeth.
    c. Using a dial indicator, **Fig. 7,** measure steering gear backlash at the pitman arm. If reading exceeds .02 inch, replace mainshaft.

Precis

1. Using tool No. 09565-21000, or equivalent, and a suitable press, press bearing onto pinion, then install bearing retainer snap ring.
2. Apply suitable grease to rack, pinion, housing bushing, roller bearing and all sliding surfaces. **Ensure air passage in housing bushing is not blocked with grease before continuing assembly procedure.**
3. Insert rack into gear housing from left side, then install and mesh pinion gear with rack teeth. Wipe away excessive grease.

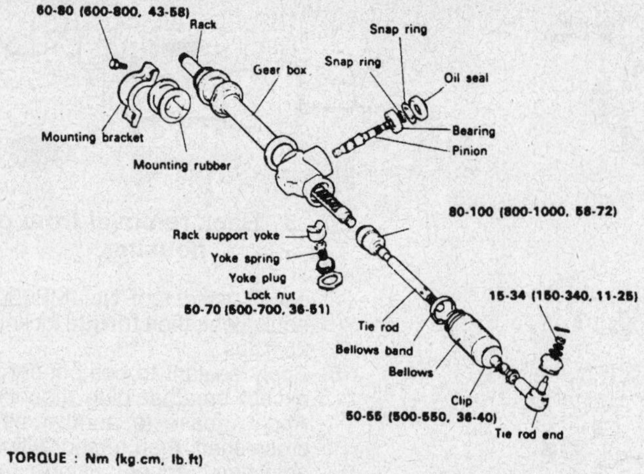
60-80 (600-800, 43-58)
Rack
Snap ring
Snap ring
Gear box
Oil seal
Mounting bracket
Mounting rubber
Bearing
Pinion
80-100 (800-1000, 58-72)
Rack support yoke
Yoke spring
Yoke plug
Lock nut
50-70 (500-700, 36-51)
15-34 (150-340, 11-25)
Tie rod
Bellows band
Bellows
Clip
50-55 (500-550, 36-40)
Tie rod end
TORQUE : Nm (kg.cm, lb.ft)

MT6039100027000X

Fig. 5 Exploded view of manual steering gear. Precis

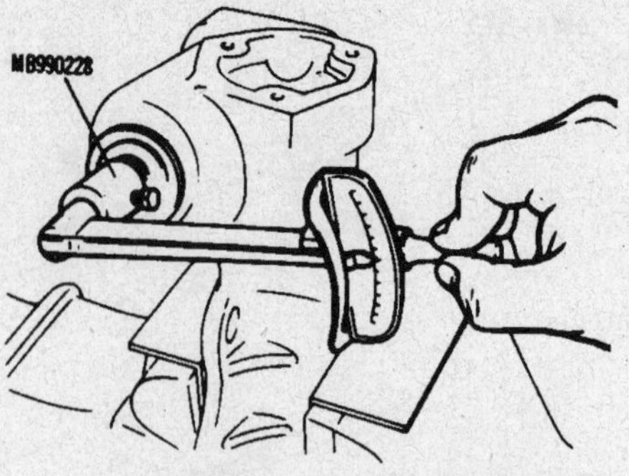
MB990228

MT6039100028000X

Fig. 6 Mainshaft preload measurement. Pickup

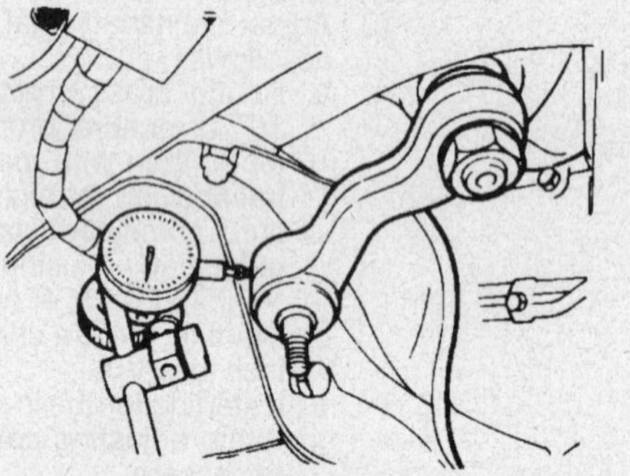

MT6039100029000X

Fig. 7 Steering gear backlash measurement. Pickup

4. Select and install snap ring which will minimize pinion endplay. Snap rings are available in .063 inch (blue), .066 inch (white) and .069 inch (yellow) thicknesses.
5. Apply suitable grease to seal lips, then install new oil seal into gear housing.
6. Apply suitable grease to cupped portion of support yoke, then install yoke, cushion rubber, spring and yoke plug into gearbox.
7. Position rack in neutral (straight ahead) position. Using tool No. 09565-21100, or equivalent, **torque** yoke plug to 5–11 ft. lbs., then back off adjustment 30–60°.
8. Apply sealer to yoke plug locknut, then install locknut and tighten to specifications.
9. Install tie rods and tighten to specifications, then stake rack keyway with suitable punch. Install bellows.
10. Measure pinion preload and rack starting force as follows:
    a. Using tool No. 09565-11000, or equivalent, measure pinion preload over full stroke of rack. Turn pinion at a rate of one revolution for every four to six seconds. Preload should be .3–.8 ft. lbs.
    b. Using tool mentioned above and a suitable spring scale, measure rack starting force. Starting force should be 11–66 lbs.
11. If pinion preload and rack starting force are not within specification, replace cushion rubber and yoke spring, then repeat steps for establishing correct preload.

TIGHTENING SPECIFICATIONS

Component	Torque/Ft. Lbs.
ECLIPSE	
Center Member To Body	58–72
Front Exhaust Pipe Mounting Bolt	22–29
Front Exhaust Pipe Mounting Nut	22–29
Front Exhaust Pipe To Rubber Hanger	7–11
Front Roll Stopper Installation Nut	36–47
Gearbox Mounting Bracket To Crossmember	43–58
Joint Assembly To Gearbox	11–14
Rack Support Cover Locking Nut	36–51
Stabilizer Bar Bracket	22–30
Stay To Crossmember	51–58
Tie Rod End To Knuckle	17–25
Tie Rod End Locknut	36–40
Tie Rod To Rack	58–72
Top Plug Locking Nut	36–51

Continued

TIGHTENING SPECIFICATIONS—Continued

Component	Torque/Ft. Lbs.
MIRAGE	
Gearbox To Body	43–58
Joint To Gearbox	11–17
Rack Support Cover Locking Nut	36–51
Tie Rod End To Knuckle	11–25
Tie Rod End Locknut	25–36
Tie Rod To Rack	58–72
Top Cover Locking Nut	36–51
PICKUP	
Adjusting Cover Locknut	80–108
End Cover	25–33
Gearbox Installation	25–40
Gearbox To Column Shaft Assembly	11–14
Idler Arm Support To Frame	25–29
Idler Arm To Idler Arm Support	29–43
Locknut	18–25
Pitman Arm	94–108
Pitman Arm To Relay Rod	25–33
Relay Rod To Idler Arm	25–33
Relay Rod To Pitman Arm	25–33
Side Cover	18–25
Tie Rod End To Knuckle	25–33
Tie Rod End To Pipe	47–58
Tie Rod End To Relay Rod	33
PRECIS	
Tie Rods	58–72
Yoke Plug Locknut	36–51

Power Steering

NOTE: On Air Bag Equipped Models, Refer To "Air Bag System Precautions" Located In The Front Of This Manual For System Disarming & Arming Procedures.

NOTE: For Procedures Not Found In This Section, Refer To The "Four Wheel Steering" Section.

INDEX

Page No.

Diagnosis & Testing 29-94
Electronic Power Steering (EPS) System Component Testing 29-97
Electronic Power Steering (EPS) System Diagnosis...... 29-97
Oil Pressure Switch Test........ 29-96
Oil Pump Pressure Tests........ 29-94
Maintenance 29-94
Fluid Change 29-94
Power Steering Pressure Specifications 29-94
Power Steering System Service . 29-97
Component Service.............29-100
Power Steering Gear 29-100
Power Steering Pump..........29-106
Diamante, Eclipse, Expo, Galant, Mirage, Precis & 3000GT 29-97
Montero & Pickup.............. 29-98
Power Steering System Bleed .. 29-97
Precautions...................... 29-94
Air Bag Systems................. 29-94
Tightening Specifications 29-109
Troubleshooting................. 29-94

POWER STEERING PRESSURE SPECIFICATIONS

Year	Model	Pump Pressure, psi		Retention Pressure, psi
		Gauge Valve Closed①	Gauge Valve Open①	
1993	Diamante	1067–1166	114–142	1067–1166
	Eclipse	1067–1166	114–142	1067–1166
	Expo	1067–1166	114–142	1067–1166
	Galant	1067–1166	114–142	1067–1166
	Mirage	1351–1451	114–142	1351–1451
	Montero	②	114–142	②
	Pickup	1067–1166	114–142	1067–1166
	Precis	923	—	—
	3000GT	1067–1166	114–142	1067–1166
1994	Diamante	1067–1166	114–142	1067–1166
	Eclipse	1067–1166	114–142	1067–1166
	Expo	1067–1166	114–142	1067–1166
	Galant	1209–1309	114–142	1209–1309
	Mirage	1351–1451	114–142	1351–1451
	Montero	②	114–142	②
	Pickup	1067–1166	114–142	1067–1166
	3000GT	1067–1166	114–142	1067–1166
1995	Diamante	1067–1166	114–142	1067–1166
	Eclipse	1209–1309	114–142	1209–1309
	Expo	1067–1166	114–142	1067–1166
	Galant	1209–1309	114–142	1209–1309
	Mirage	1351–1451	114–142	1351–1451
	Montero	②	114–142	②
	Pickup	1067–1166	114–142	1067–1166
	3000GT	1067–1166	114–142	1067–1166
1996	Diamante	1067–1166	114–142	1067–1166
	Eclipse	1209–1309	114–142	1209–1309
	Galant	1209–1309	114–142	1209–1309
	Mirage	1351–1451	114–142	1351–1451
	Montero	③	114–142	③
	Pickup	1067–1166	114–142	1067–1166
	3000GT	1067–1166	114–142	1067–1166

① — With special tool installed; refer to text.
② — 3.0L 12-valve engine, 1067–1166 psi; 3.0L 24-valve & 3.5L engines, 1209–1309 psi.
③ — 3.0L 12-valve engine, 1067–1166 psi; 3.0L 24-valve & 3.5L engines, 1205–1305 psi.

PRECAUTIONS

AIR BAG SYSTEMS

Refer to "Air Bag System Precautions" in the front of this manual for system disarming and arming procedures.

MAINTENANCE

FLUID CHANGE

1. Raise and support vehicle.
2. Disconnect return hose.
3. Connect a vinyl hose to return hose to drain oil into a suitable container.
4. Disconnect ignition coil high tension cable.
5. Rotate engine using starter motor and turn steering wheel from stop to stop to drain fluid from system. **Do not crank engine longer than ten seconds at a time.**
6. Connect return hose, fill reservoir with fluid and bleed air from system as outlined under "Power Steering System Service."

TROUBLESHOOTING

Refer to **Figs. 1 through 4** for troubleshooting procedures.

DIAGNOSIS & TESTING

OIL PUMP PRESSURE TESTS

DIAMANTE, ECLIPSE, EXPO, GALANT, MONTERO, MIRAGE & 3000GT

The following procedures require the use of oil pressure gauge assembly tool No. MB990662, or equivalent. All models except 1995–96 Eclipse with 2.0L non-turbocharged engine require power steering oil pressure gauge pump side adapter tool No. MB990993-01 and power steering oil pressure gauge hose side adapter tool No. MB990994-01, or equivalents; 1995–96 Eclipse models equipped with 2.0L non-turbocharged engine require power steering oil pressure gauge pump side adapter tool No. MB991548 and power steering oil pressure gauge hose side adapter tool No. MB991549, or equivalents.

Oil Pump Relief Pressure Inspection

1. Disconnect pressure hose from oil pump, then connect special tools as shown, **Fig. 5**.
2. Bleed air from system as outlined under "Power Steering System Service," then turn steering wheel from stop to stop until fluid temperature in reservoir is 122–140°F.
3. Start engine and run at 900–1100 RPM.
4. Fully close shutoff valve and ensure oil pump relief pressure is as specified in

Symptom	Probable cause	Remedy
Steering operation is "hard" (at low speed and in all gears), or there is notable torque unevenness when the steering wheel is turned	Loose drive belt	Adjust
	Insufficient fluid	Replenish
	Fluid leakage	Retighten or replace
	Twisted or damaged hoses	Correct the routing or replace
	No increase in oil pump pressure	Repair or replace (oil pump, gear box)
	Incorrect mounting of the steering gear box on the crossmember	Retighten
	Twisted firewall cover with steering shaft	
	Improper front wheel alignment	Adjust
	Damaged drive belt	Replace
	Excessive friction around steering linkage	
	Pinion and valve malfunction (seal damage, etc)	
	Rack piston seal damage	
	Malfunction of ball joint (s) (excessive swinging torque or starting torque)	
The steering wheel does not return properly	Incorrect front wheel alignment	Adjust
	Friction of steering shaft joint and/or body grommet	Correct or replace
	Rough turning of tie rod end and/or ball joint	Apply grease or replace
	Excessive turning resistance of tie rod ball joint	Replace
	Gear sliding or rotating part if damaged	
	Bent rack	
	Incorrect installation of gear box cross-member	Replace
		Retighten

MT6029100001010X

Fig. 1 Troubleshooting chart (Part 1 of 2). Expo

Symptom	Probable cause	Remedy
Lack of driving stability	Loosened steering linkage ball joint	Retighten or replace
	Malfunction of ball joint (s) (insufficient swinging torque or starting torque)	Replace
	Loose installation of gear box and cross-member	Retighten
Drifts to one side	Tires (Assuming that the tire inflation pressure, tire wear, front alignment, and front wheels are all normal)	Rotate
Abnormal noise (hissing sound, whistling sound)	Air in system due to insufficient fluid	Replenish or bleed air
	Air trapped in pipes	Retighten or replace or bleed air
	Crushed suction hose	Replace
Abnormal noise (creaking sound, squeaking sound)	Slipping drive belt	Adjust or replace
	Damaged drive belt	Replace
	Burned out oil pump	
Abnormal noise (rattling sound, clunking sound)	Loose gear box bracket mounting	Retighten
	Loose oil pump bracket and/or oil pump mounting bolts	
	Loose steering linkage or ball joint	
	Play in steering linkage or ball joint	Replace
	Interference between chassis and piping	Repair

MT6029100001020X

Fig. 1 Troubleshooting chart (Part 2 of 2). Expo

Symptom	Probable cause	Remedy
Excessive play of steering wheel	Loose rack support cover	Retighten
	Loose steering gear mounting bolts	Retighten
	Loose or worn stud of tie-rod end	Retighten or replace as necessary
Steering wheel operation is hard (Improper power assist)	Drive belt slippage	Check
	Damaged drive belt	Replace
	Low fluid level	Refill
	Air in the fluid	Bleed
	Twisted or damaged hoses	Correct the routing or replace
	Improper oil pump pressure	Repair or replace oil pump
	Sticky flow control valve	Replace
	Excessive internal oil pump leakage	Replace damaged parts
	Excessive oil leaks from rack & pinion in gear box	Replace damaged parts
	Bent or damaged gear box or valve body seal ring	Replace ·

MT6029100002010X

Fig. 2 Troubleshooting chart (Part 1 of 2). Mirage

Symptom	Probable cause	Remedy
Steering wheel does not return properly	Excessive turning resistance of tie-rod ball joint	Replace
	Excessively tightened rack support cover	Adjust
	Rough turning of inner tie-rod and/or ball joint	Replace
	Worn steering shaft joint and/or body grommet	Correct or replace
	Bent rack	Replace
	Damaged pinion bearing	Replace
	Twisted or damaged hoses	Reroute or replace
	Damaged flow control valve	Replace
	Damaged oil pump input shaft bearing	Replace
Noise	Hissing Noise in Steering Gear There is some noise in all power steering systems. One of the most common is a hissing sound when the steering wheel is turned and the car is not moving. This noise will be most evident when turning the wheel while the brakes are applied. There is no relationship between this noise and steering performance. Do not replace the valve unless the "hissing" noise is extremely objectionable. A replacement valve will also have a slight noise, and is not always a cure for the condition.	
Rattling or chucking noise in rack & pinion	Pressure hose touching other parts of vehicle	Reroute
	Loose gear box mounting bolts	Retighten
	Loose tie-rod end ball joint	Retighten
	Worn tie-rod end ball joint	Replace
Groaning noise in oil pump	Low fluid level	Refill
	Air in the fluid	Bleed
	Loose pump mounting bolts	Retighten

MT6029100002020X

Fig. 2 Troubleshooting chart (Part 2 of 2). Mirage

"Power Steering Pressure Specifications" chart. **Do not leave shutoff valve closed for more than ten seconds, as damage or injury may occur.**

5. If pressure is not within specified range, service oil pump as outlined under "Power Steering System Service."
6. Remove special tools and bleed system as outlined under " System Service."

No Load Pressure Inspection

1. Disconnect pressure hose from oil pump then connect special tools as shown, **Fig. 5.**
2. Bleed air from system as outlined under "Power Steering System Service," then turn steering wheel from stop to stop until fluid temperature in reservoir is 122–140°F.
3. Start engine and run at 900–1100 RPM.
4. Check hydraulic pressure and ensure it is as specified in the "Power Steering Pressure Specifications" chart.
5. If pressure is not within specification, probable causes include a clogged pressure line or faulty steering gearbox. Check and repair as necessary.
6. Remove special tools and bleed system as outlined under "Power Steering System Service."

Steering Gear Retention Hydraulic Pressure Inspection

1. Disconnect pressure hose from oil pump then connect special tools as shown, **Fig. 5.**
2. Bleed air from system as outlined under "Power Steering System Service," then turn steering wheel from stop to stop until fluid temperature in reservoir is 122–140°F.
3. Start engine and run at 900–1100 RPM.
4. Fully close, then fully open shutoff valve.
5. Turn steering wheel from stop to stop, then ensure retention pressure is as specified in "Power Steering Pressure Specifications " chart.
6. If pressure is not as specified, service steering gearbox and repeat steps for establishing correct retention pressure.
7. Remove special tools and bleed system.

PICKUP

1. Disconnect pressure hose from pump and install special tools as shown, **Fig. 6.**

Symptom	Probable cause	Remedy
Excessive play of steering wheel	Excessive play in steering gear box	Repair
	Loose steering gear mounting bolts	Retighten
	Loose or worn stud of tie rod end	Retighten or replace as necessary
Steering wheel operation is hard (insufficient power assist)	Loose belt	Adjust the belt tension
	Damaged belt	Replace the belt
	Low fluid level	Refill with fluid
	Air in fluid line	Bleed the system
	Twisted or damage hoses	Correct the hose routing or replace the hoses
	Fluid leakage	Repair or replace
	Malfunction of gear box	Check and replace the gear box if necessary
	Malfunction of oil pump	Check the oil pump pressure and repair oil pump
Rattling noise	Loose installation of oil pump or gear box	Retighten the oil pump or gear box
	Loose oil pump pulley nut	Retighten the oil pump pulley nut
	Interference around column or between pressure hose and other parts	Correct or replace the pressure hose and the parts around the column
	Abnormal noise inside of gear box and oil pump	Replace the gear box or oil pump

MT6029100003010X

Fig. 3 Troubleshooting chart (Part 1 of 2). Montero & Pickup

Symptom	Probable cause	Remedy
Excessive play of steering wheel	Loose rack support cover	Retighten
	Loose steering gear mounting bolts	Retighten
	Loose or worn tie-rod end	Retighten or replace as necessary
Steering wheel operation is heavy (Insufficient power assist)	V-belt slippage	Check
	Damaged V-belt	Replace
	Low fluid level	Replenish
	Air in the fluid	Bleed air
	Twisted or damaged hoses	Correct the routing or replace
	Insufficient oil pump pressure	Repair or replace the oil pump
	Sticky flow control valve	Replace
	Excessive internal oil pump leakage	Replace damaged parts
	Excessive oil leaks from rack and pinion in gear box	Replace damaged parts
	Distorted or damaged gear box or valve body seal ring	Replace
The steering wheel does not return properly	Excessive turning resistance of tie-rod end	Replace
	Excessively tightened rack support cover	Adjust
	Rough turning or inner tie-rod and/or ball joint	Replace
	Loose mounting of gear box to gear box mounting bracket	Retighten
	Worn steering shaft joint and/or body grommet	Correct or replace
	Distorted rack	Replace
	Damaged pinion bearing	Replace
	Twisted or damaged hoses	Reroute or replace
	Damaged oil pressure control valve	Replace
	Damaged oil pump input shaft bearing	Replace
Noise	**Hissing Noise In Steering Gear** There is some noise in all power steering systems. One of the most common is a hissing sound when the steering wheel is turned and the car is not moving. This noise will be most evident when turning the wheel while the brakes are applied. There is no relationship between this noise and steering performance. Do not replace the valve unless the "hissing" noise is extremely objectionable. A replacement valve will also have a slight noise, and is not always a cure for the condition.	

MT6029100004010X

Fig. 4 Troubleshooting chart (Part 1 of 2). Precis

Symptom	Probable cause	Remedy
Shrill noise	Air sucked into oil pump	Check the oil level and hose clips, bleed the system or replace the oil pump
	Oil pump seizure	Replace the oil pump
Squealing noise	Loose belt	Adjust the belt deflection
	Oil pump seizure	Replace the oil pump
Hissing noise	Air sucked into oil pump	Check the oil level and hose clips, bleed the system
	Damage to the olive of the gear box port section	Replace the gear box
	Malfunction of return hose	Replace the hose
Whistling noise	Malfunction of gear box port section	Replace the gear box
Droning noise	Loose mounting bolt on oil pump or oil pump bracket	Retighten the pump bracket or pump mounting bolt
	Poor condition of oil pump body*	Replace the oil pump
Squeaking noise	Malfunction of steering stopper contact	Check and adjust the steering stopper
	Interference of wheel with vehicle body	Adjust the steering angle
	Malfunction of gear box	Replace the gear box
Vibration**	Air suction	Bleed the system
	Malfunction of gear box	Replace the gear box
Oil leakage from hose connection	Improperly tightened flare nut Incorrectly inserted hose Improperly clamped hose	Check, and repair or replace
Oil leakage from hose assembly	Damaged or clogged hose Hose connector malfunction	Replace
Oil leakage from reservoir	Improperly welded pipe	Weld the pipes or replace
	Overflow	Bleed the system or adjust the oil level
Oil leakage from oil pump	Malfunction oil pump housing	Replace the oil pump
	Malfunction of O-ring and/or oil seal	Replace the O-ring and oil seal
Oil leakage from gear box	Malfunction of gear box housing (including leakage from air hole)	Replace the gear box
	Malfunction of O-ring and/or oil seal	Replace the O-ring and oil seal

NOTE
* A slight "beat noise" is produced by the oil pump; this is not a malfunction. (This noise occurs particularly when a stationary steering effort is made.)
** A slight vibration may be felt when the stationary steering effort is made due to the condition of the road surface. To check whether the vibration actually exists or not, test-drive the vehicle on a dry concrete or asphalt surface. Moreover, a very slight amount of vibration is not a malfunction.

MT6029100003020X

Fig. 3 Troubleshooting chart (Part 2 of 2). Montero & Pickup

Symptom	Probable cause	Remedy
Rattling or chucking noise in rack and pinion	Interference with hoses from vehicle body	Reroute
	Loose gear box bracket	Retighten
	Loose tie-rod end and/or ball joint	Retighten
	Worn tie-rod end and/or ball joint	Replace
Noise in the oil pump	Low fluid level	Replenish
	Air in the fluid	Bleed air
	Loose pump mounting bolts	Retighten

NOTE
A slight "grinding noise" may be heard immediately after the engine is started in extremely cold whether condition (below -20°C): This is due to power steering fluid characteristics in extreme cold conditions and is not a malfunction.

MT6029100004020X

Fig. 4 Troubleshooting chart (Part 2 of 2). Precis

2. Bleed power steering system as outlined under "Power Steering System Service."
3. Start engine and raise engine temperature to 131°F.
4. Raise engine idle to 1000 RPM.
5. Close shutoff valve completely and read pressure. Pressure should read as specified in "Power Steering Pressure Specifications" chart. **Do not keep valve closed for more than ten seconds.**
6. If pressure is not within specification, replace pump.
7. Open shutoff valve completely and read pressure. Pressure should read as specified in "Power Steering Pressure Specifications " chart.
8. If pressure is not within specification, check for clogged hoses.
9. With the shutoff valve open, turn steering wheel from stop to stop and measure maximum oil pressure.
10. If pressure is not as specified in "Power Steering Pressure Specifications" chart, replace power steering gearbox.

PRECIS

1. Disconnect pressure hose, then connect pressure gauge tool Nos. 09572-33100 and 09572-21200, or equivalents, **Fig. 7.**
2. Bleed air from system as outlined under "Power Steering System Service."
3. Start engine and turn steering wheel from stop to stop until fluid temperature reaches 122°F.
4. Increase engine speed to 1000 RPM.
5. Close the shutoff valve and read system pressure. Pressure with valve closed should be as specified in "Power Steering Pressure Specifications" chart. **Do not allow valve to be closed for more than ten seconds.**
6. Remove gauge tools and bleed system as outlined under "Power Steering System Service."

OIL PRESSURE SWITCH TEST

The following procedures require the use of oil pressure gauge assembly tool No. MB990662, or equivalent. All models except 1995–96 Eclipse with 2.0L non-turbocharged engine require power steering oil pressure gauge pump side adapter tool No. MB990993-01 and power steering oil pressure gauge hose side adapter tool No. MB990994-01, or equivalents; 1995–96 Eclipse models equipped with 2.0L non-turbocharged engine require power steering oil pressure gauge pump side adapter tool No. MB991548 and power steering oil pressure gauge hose side adapter tool No. MB991549, or equivalents.

1. Disconnect pressure hose from oil

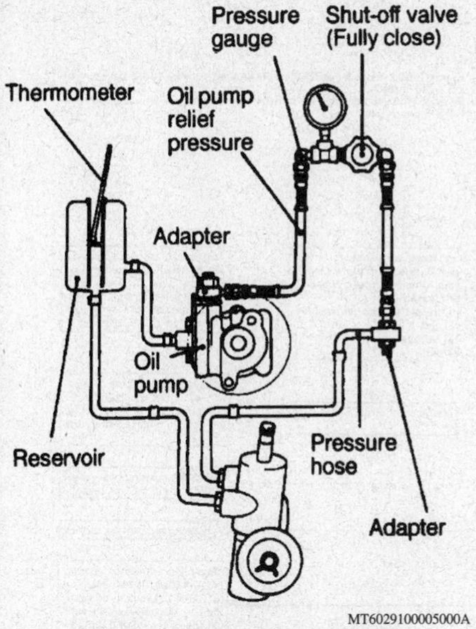
Pressure gauge
Shut-off valve (Fully close)
Thermometer
Oil pump relief pressure
Adapter
Oil pump
Reservoir
Pressure hose
Adapter
MT6029100005000A

Fig. 5 Pressure gauge installation. Diamante, Eclipse, Expo, Galant, Montero, Mirage & 3000GT

pump, then connect special tools as shown, **Fig. 8.**

2. Bleed air from system as outlined under "Power Steering System Service," then turn steering wheel from stop to stop until fluid temperature in reservoir is 122–140°F.
3. Start engine and allow to idle.
4. Disconnect connector of pressure switch and place an ohmmeter in position.
5. Gradually close shutoff valve and increase hydraulic pressure, then record switch activation pressure.
6. Pressure should be 213–284 psi when switch activates.
7. Gradually open shutoff valve and decrease hydraulic pressure and record pressure when switch deactivates.
8. Pressure should be 100–171 psi when switch deactivates.
9. Replace switch if not as specified.
10. Remove special tools and bleed system as outlined under "Power Steering System Service."

ELECTRONIC POWER STEERING (EPS) SYSTEM DIAGNOSIS

GALANT

Refer to **Fig. 9** for EPS system diagnostic procedures and **Fig. 10** for symptom charts.

DIAMANTE

Refer to **Fig. 11** for EPS system diagnostic procedures and **Fig. 12** for symptom charts.

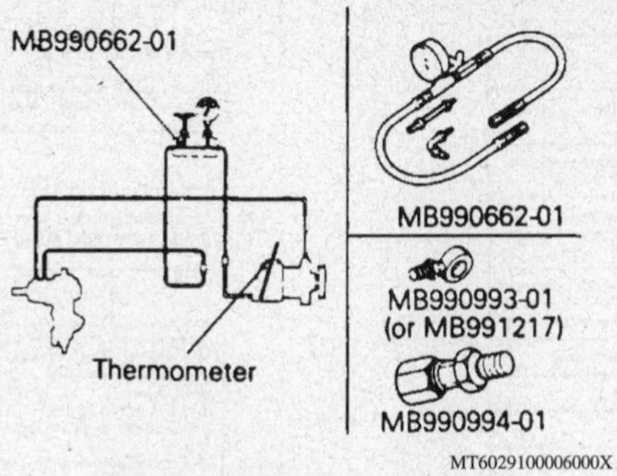
MB990662-01
Thermometer
MB990662-01
MB990993-01 (or MB991217)
MB990994-01
MT6029100006000X

Fig. 6 Pressure gauge installation. Pickup

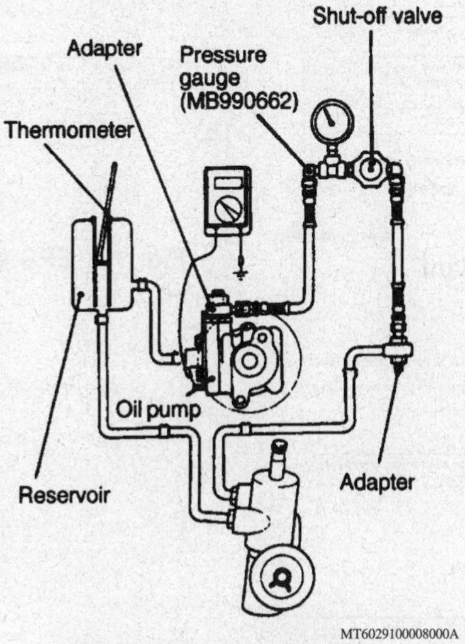
Shut-off valve
Adapter
Pressure gauge (MB990662)
Thermometer
Oil pump
Reservoir
Adapter
MT6029100008000A

Fig. 8 Pressure gauge & ohmmeter installation

ELECTRONIC POWER STEERING (EPS) SYSTEM COMPONENT TESTING

DIAMANTE & GALANT

EPS Solenoid Continuity Inspection

Check for continuity between solenoid valve terminals with the connector disconnected.

EPS Solenoid Current Inspection

1. If dummy speed oscillator tool No. MB991139, or equivalent, is to be used, proceed as follows:
   a. Set speed selection switch to zero mph.
   b. Turn cruise control main switch to off, then start engine and allow to idle.
   c. Set vehicle speed to 6–12 mph and ensure monitor light is flashing.
   d. If light remains illuminated and

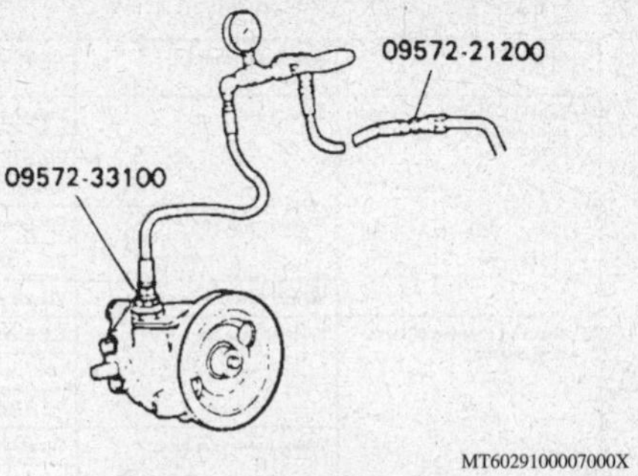
09572-21200
09572-33100
MT6029100007000X

Fig. 7 Pressure gauge installation. Precis

does not flash, move vehicle forward 1.0–1.3 feet.

2. If multi-use tester tool No. MB991341, or equivalent, is used, proceed as follows:
   a. Connect multi-use tester to self diagnostic connector and cigarette lighter.
   b. Input simulated vehicle speed, using vehicle speed signal function.
   c. If simulated vehicle speed cannot be input, a message will be displayed on testers display to move vehicle forward .98–1.31 feet.
3. Disconnect EPS solenoid valve wiring harness connector and connect a voltmeter between the two connectors as shown, **Fig. 13. Do not ground the solenoid terminal.**
4. Ensure solenoid current is .9–1.1 amps with vehicle at 0 mph, **Figs. 14 and 15.**
5. If current does not decrease as simulated speed increases, check EPS control.
6. **On models equipped with four speed automatic transmission,** there will be a three speed hold caused by the fail safe function when multi-use tester is used. Therefore, disconnect the battery ground cable for ten seconds. **Never drive vehicle with the tester connected.**

ELECTRONIC POWER STEERING (EPS) MODE SELECTOR SWITCH TEST

Diamante & Galant

Refer to **Fig. 16** for a continuity test of the EPS mode selector switch.

POWER STEERING SYSTEM SERVICE

POWER STEERING SYSTEM BLEED

DIAMANTE, ECLIPSE, EXPO, GALANT, MIRAGE, PRECIS & 3000GT

1. Raise and support vehicle.

Symptom	Malfunction system	Check items
1. Steering effort remains light at moderate and high speeds	Control unit	Steering effort (full turn simulated by tester)
		E.P.S. solenoid current relative to vehicle speed change
	Steering gear box	E.P.S. solenoid activation
		P.C.V. activation
	Vehicle speed sensor	Vehicle speed sensor operation
2. Required steering effort is always great	Steering gear box	E.P.S. solenoid valve continuity
		E.P.S. solenoid activation
		P.C.V. activation
	Wiring harness or fuse	Fuse blown or not
		E.P.S. solenoid harness
	Control unit	*Fail-safe system activation
		Each harness continuity, and control unit power supply circuit
		Control unit activation
3. No change of the steering effort characteristic when the E.P.S. mode-select switch is used	E.P.S. mode-select switch	Continuity of E.P.S. mode-select switch
	Control unit	Each harness continuity, and control unit power supply circuit
		Control unit activation

NOTE
(1) For checking procedures for each problem, refer to the flow-chart type of troubleshooting guide
(2) To release the fail-safe system where indicated by the * symbol, set the ignition switch to the "ACC" or "LOCK" position, and then start the engine once again.
(3) P.C.V. = Pressure control valve

MT6029100009000X

Fig. 9 EPS diagnosis. Galant

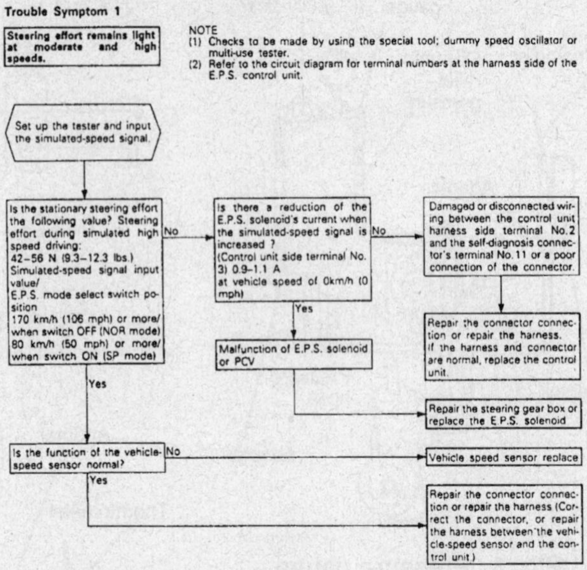
Trouble Symptom 1
Steering effort remains light at moderate and high speeds.
NOTE
(1) Checks to be made by using the special tool; dummy speed oscillator or multi-use tester.
(2) Refer to the circuit diagram for terminal numbers at the harness side of the E.P.S. control unit.
Set up the tester and input the simulated-speed signal.
Is the stationary steering effort the following value? Steering effort during simulated high speed driving: 42–56 N (9.3–12.3 lbs.) Simulated-speed signal input value/ E.P.S. mode select switch position 170 km/h (106 mph) or more/ when switch OFF (NOR mode) 80 km/h (50 mph) or more/ when switch ON (SP mode)
No
Yes
Is there a reduction of the E.P.S. solenoid's current when the simulated-speed signal is increased ? (Control unit side terminal No. 3) 0.9–1.1 A at vehicle speed of 0km/h (0 mph)
Damaged or disconnected wiring between the control unit harness side terminal No.2 and the self-diagnosis connector's terminal No.11 or a poor connection of the connector.
Malfunction of E.P.S. solenoid or PCV
Repair the connector connection or repair the harness. If the harness and connector are normal, replace the control unit.
Repair the steering gear box or replace the E.P.S. solenoid
Is the function of the vehicle-speed sensor normal?
Vehicle speed sensor replace
Repair the connector connection or repair the harness (Correct the connector, or repair the harness between the vehicle-speed sensor and the control unit.)

MT6029100010010X

Fig. 10 EPS symptom charts (Part 1 of 3). Galant

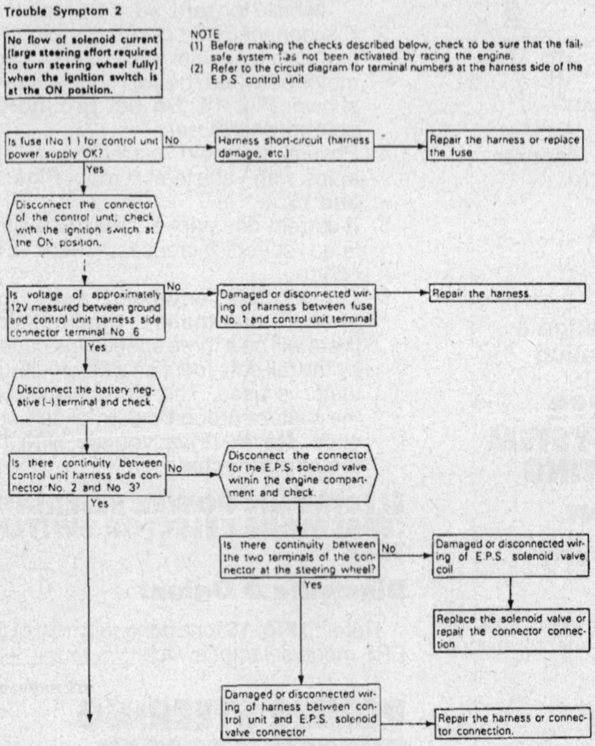
Trouble Symptom 2
No flow of solenoid current (large steering effort required to turn steering wheel fully) when the ignition switch is at the ON position.
NOTE
(1) Before making the checks described below, check to be sure that the fail-safe system has not been activated by racing the engine.
(2) Refer to the circuit diagram for terminal numbers at the harness side of the E.P.S. control unit.
Is fuse (No.1) for control unit power supply OK?
Harness short-circuit (harness damage, etc.)
Repair the harness or replace the fuse
Disconnect the connector of the control unit; check with the ignition switch at the ON position.
Is voltage of approximately 12V measured between ground and control unit harness side connector terminal No. 6
Damaged or disconnected wiring of harness between fuse No. 1 and control unit terminal
Repair the harness.
Disconnect the battery negative (–) terminal and check.
Is there continuity between control unit harness side connector No. 2 and No. 3?
Disconnect the connector for the E.P.S. solenoid valve within the engine compartment and check.
Is there continuity between the two terminals of the connector at the steering wheel?
Damaged or disconnected wiring of E.P.S. solenoid valve coil
Replace the solenoid valve or repair the connector connection
Damaged or disconnected wiring of harness between control unit and E.P.S. solenoid valve connector
Repair the harness or connector connection.

MT6029100010020X

Fig. 10 EPS symptom charts (Part 2 of 3). Galant

2. Manually turn oil pump several complete turns.
3. Turn steering wheel from stop to stop.
4. Disconnect ignition coil high tension cable.
5. Rotate engine using starter motor and turn steering wheel from stop to stop for 15 to 20 seconds, refilling fluid in reservoir as necessary. **Only bleed system while cranking engine. Never bleed system with engine running.**
6. Connect ignition coil cable, then start engine and allow to idle.
7. Turn steering wheel from stop to stop until no air bubbles appear in fluid in reservoir.
8. Confirm fluid is not milky and fluid level does not change significantly when steering wheel is turned from stop to stop.
9. Ensure fluid level does not change by more than .2 inch when engine is turned off.
10. If fluid level change is more than specified, all air has not been bled from system. Leave steering system undisturbed for several minutes, then repeat bleed procedure.

MONTERO & PICKUP

1. Fill power steering reservoir, then raise and support front of vehicle so that front wheels clear floor.
2. Remove ignition coil high tension cable.
3. Rotate engine using starter motor and turn steering wheel from stop to stop for 15 to 20 seconds refilling fluid in reservoir as necessary. **Only bleed system while cranking engine. Never bleed system with engine running.**
4. Lower front of vehicle.
5. Connect one end of a vinyl hose to the breather plug on the gearbox and place the other end into a suitable container.
6. Start engine and allow to idle.
7. Keeping reservoir full, loosen breather plug and turn steering wheel from stop to stop until no air can be seen in vinyl hose.
8. After completion, tighten breather plug and check fluid.
9. When turning steering wheel from stop to stop, ensure fluid level does not

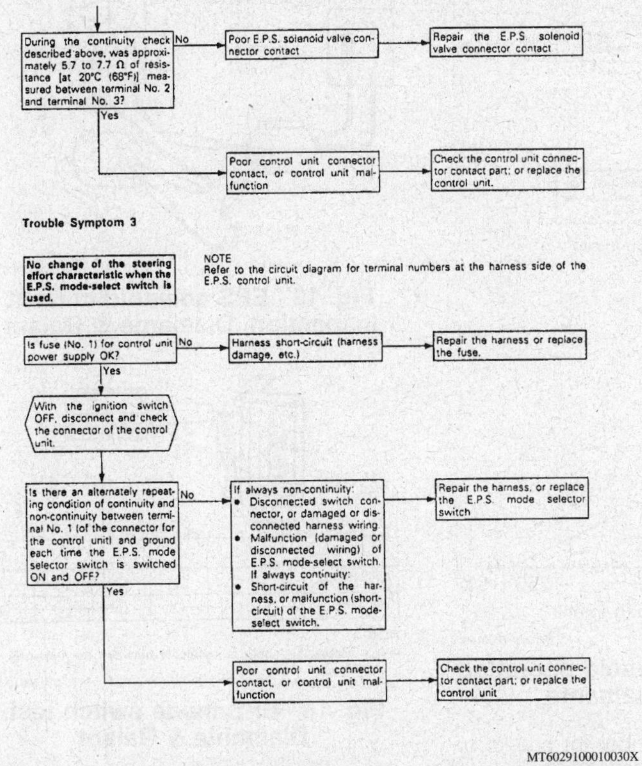
During the continuity check described above, was approximately 5.7 to 7.7 Ω of resistance [at 20°C (68°F)] measured between terminal No. 2 and terminal No. 3?
No
Poor E.P.S. solenoid valve connector contact
Repair the E.P.S. solenoid valve connector contact
Yes
Poor control unit connector contact, or control unit malfunction
Check the control unit connector contact part; or replace the control unit.
Trouble Symptom 3
No change of the steering effort characteristic when the E.P.S. mode-select switch is used.
NOTE
Refer to the circuit diagram for terminal numbers at the harness side of the E.P.S. control unit.
Is fuse (No. 1) for control unit power supply OK?
No
Harness short-circuit (harness damage, etc.)
Repair the harness or replace the fuse.
Yes
With the ignition switch OFF, disconnect and check the connector of the control unit.
Is there an alternately repeating condition of continuity and non-continuity between terminal No. 1 (of the connector for the control unit) and ground each time the E.P.S. mode selector switch is switched ON and OFF?
No
If always non-continuity:
• Disconnected switch connector, or damaged or disconnected harness wiring.
• Malfunction (damaged or disconnected wiring) of E.P.S. mode-select switch.
If always continuity:
• Short-circuit of the harness, or malfunction (short-circuit) of the E.P.S. mode-select switch.
Repair the harness, or replace the E.P.S. mode selector switch
Yes
Poor control unit connector contact, or control unit malfunction
Check the control unit connector contact part; or repalce the control unit
MT6029100010030X

Fig. 10 EPS symptom charts (Part 3 of 3). Galant

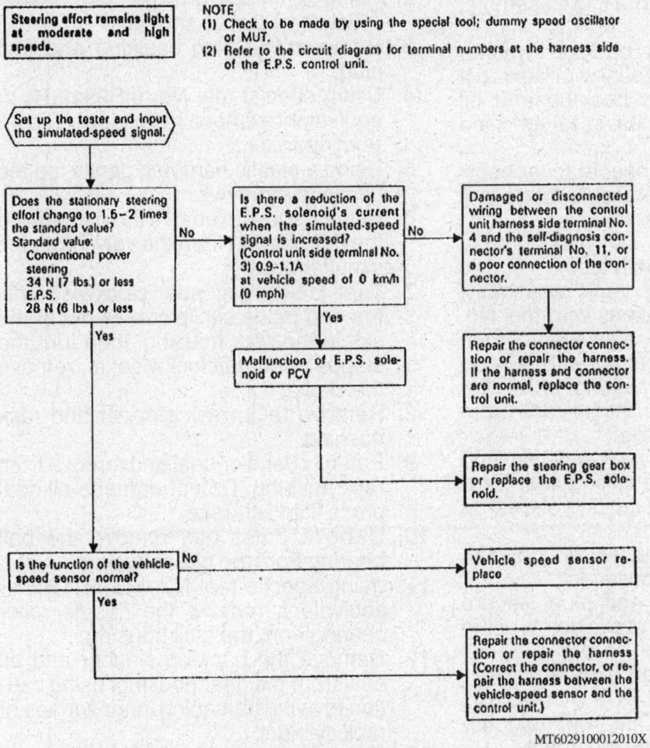
Steering effort remains light at moderate and high speeds.
NOTE
(1) Check to be made by using the special tool; dummy speed oscillator or MUT.
(2) Refer to the circuit diagram for terminals at the harness side of the E.P.S. control unit.
Set up the tester and input the simulated-speed signal.
Does the stationary steering effort change to 1.5–2 times the standard value?
Standard value:
Conventional power steering
34 N (7 lbs.) or less
E.P.S.
28 N (6 lbs.) or less
No
Is there a reduction of the E.P.S. solenoid's current when the simulated-speed signal is increased?
(Control unit side terminal No. 3) 0.9–1.1A
at vehicle speed of 0 km/h (0 mph)
No
Damaged or disconnected wiring between the control unit harness side terminal No. 4 and the self-diagnosis connector's terminal No. 11, or a poor connection of the connector.
Repair the connector connection or repair the harness. If the harness and connector are normal, replace the control unit.
Yes
Malfunction of E.P.S. solenoid or PCV
Repair the steering gear box or replace the E.P.S. solenoid.
Yes
Is the function of the vehicle-speed sensor normal?
No
Vehicle speed sensor replace
Yes
Repair the connector connection or repair the harness (Correct the connector, or repair the harness between the vehicle-speed sensor and the control unit.)
MT6029100012010X

Fig. 12 EPS symptom charts (Part 1 of 3). Diamante

Trouble symptom	Trouble area	Inspection item
Steering wheel movement is heavy (When ignition key is turned to ON, no current flows through the solenoid.)	Steering gear and linkage	Solenoid valve continuity
		Solenoid or PCV operation is faulty.
	Harness or fuse	Blown fuse
		Remove the control unit connector and check the continuity in the solenoid harness (between terminals No. 2 and No. 3).
	Control unit	Turn the ignition key momentarily to ACC or LOCK and check if the fail-safe function is operating.
		Check for continuity in each harness and for abnormalities in the control unit power circuit.
While driving at medium or high speed, steering remains light.	Control unit	Use a tester to check the stationary steering effort.
		Check the solenoid current in relation to changes in vehicle speed.
	Steering gear and linkage	Solenoid or PCV operation.

NOTE
(1) For checking procedures for each problem, refer to the flow-chart type of troubleshooting guide on the following page.
(2) P C V = Pressure control valve

MT6029100011000X

Fig. 11 EPS diagnosis. Diamante

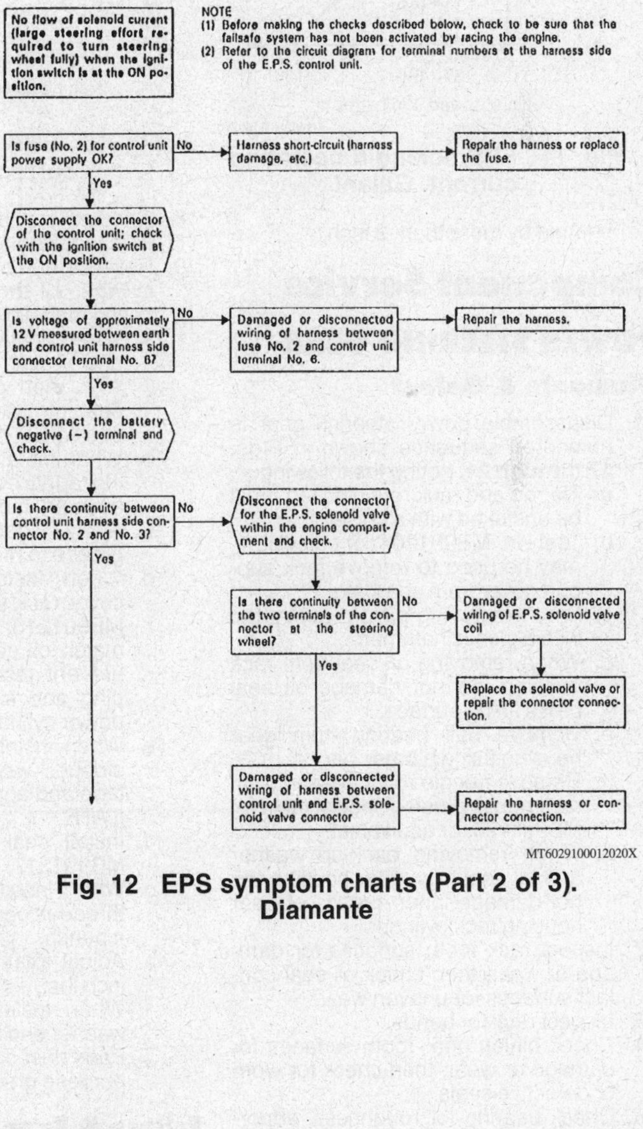
No flow of solenoid current (large steering effort required to turn steering wheel fully) when the ignition switch is at the ON position.
NOTE
(1) Before making the checks described below, check to be sure that the failsafe system has not been activated by racing the engine.
(2) Refer to the circuit diagram for terminal numbers at the harness side of the E.P.S. control unit.
Is fuse (No. 2) for control unit power supply OK?
No
Harness short-circuit (harness damage, etc.)
Repair the harness or replace the fuse.
Yes
Disconnect the connector of the control unit; check with the ignition switch at the ON position.
Is voltage of approximately 12 V measured between earth and control unit harness side connector terminal No. 6?
No
Damaged or disconnected wiring of harness between fuse No. 2 and control unit terminal No. 6.
Repair the harness.
Yes
Disconnect the battery negative (−) terminal and check.
Is there continuity between control unit harness side connector No. 2 and No. 3?
No
Disconnect the connector for the E.P.S. solenoid valve within the engine compartment and check.
Yes
Is there continuity between the two terminals of the connector at the steering wheel?
No
Damaged or disconnected wiring of E.P.S. solenoid valve coil
Replace the solenoid valve or repair the connector connection.
Yes
Damaged or disconnected wiring of harness between control unit and E.P.S. solenoid valve connector
Repair the harness or connector connection.
MT6029100012020X

Fig. 12 EPS symptom charts (Part 2 of 3). Diamante

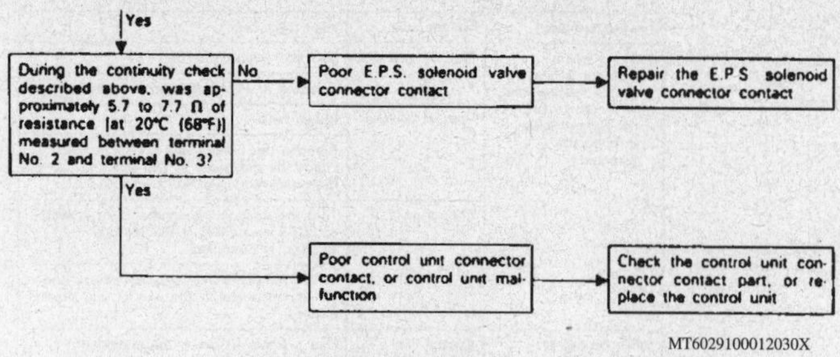
Yes
During the continuity check described above, was approximately 5.7 to 7.7 Ω of resistance [at 20°C (68°F)] measured between terminal No. 2 and terminal No. 3?
No
Poor E.P.S. solenoid valve connector contact
Repair the E.P.S. solenoid valve connector contact
Yes
Poor control unit connector contact, or control unit malfunction
Check the control unit connector contact part, or replace the control unit
MT6029100012030X

Fig. 12 EPS symptom charts (Part 3 of 3). Diamante

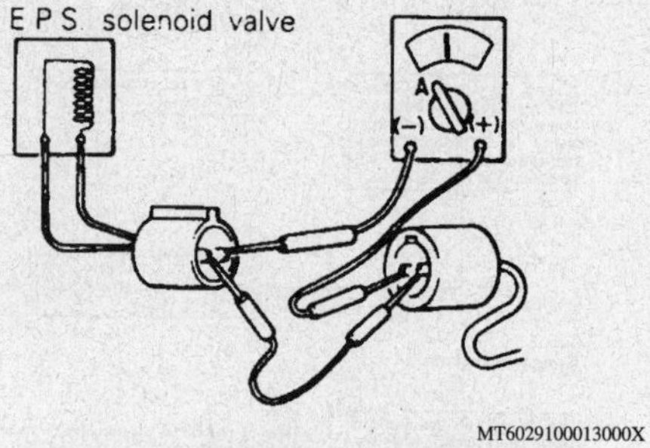
E.P.S. solenoid valve
A
(-)
(+)
MT6029100013000X

Fig. 13 EPS solenoid current inspection. Diamante & Galant

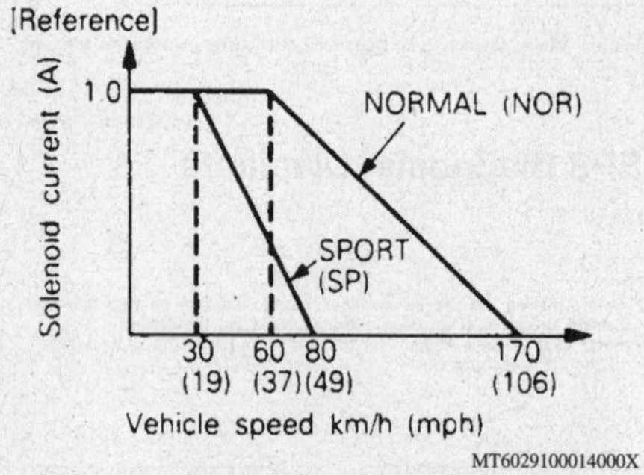
[Reference]
Solenoid current (A)
1.0
NORMAL (NOR)
SPORT (SP)
30 (19)
60 (37)
80 (49)
170 (106)
Vehicle speed km/h (mph)
MT6029100014000X

Fig. 14 EPS solenoid operating current. Galant

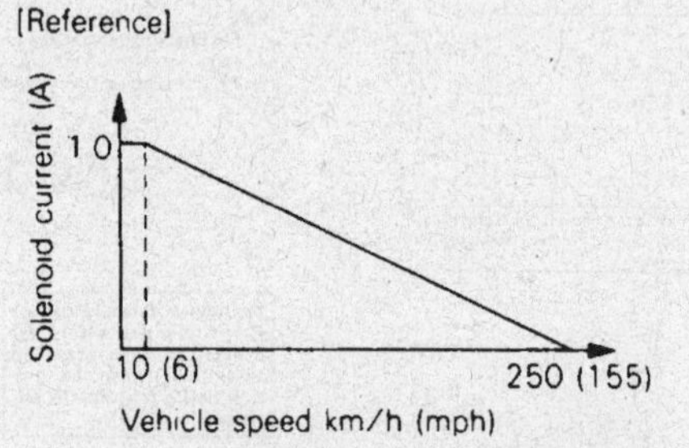
[Reference]
Solenoid current (A)
1.0
10 (6)
250 (155)
Vehicle speed km/h (mph)
MT6029100015000X

Fig. 15 EPS solenoid operating current. Diamante

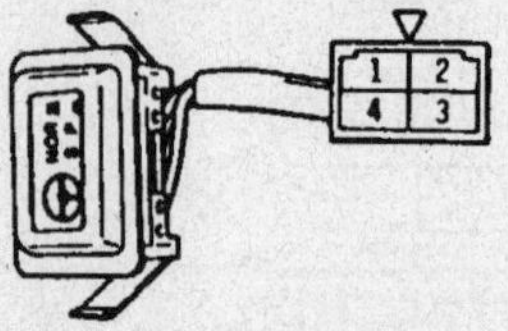
1 2
4 3

	1	2	3	–	4
OFF (NOR)	o	o	o—	—⊙—	—o
ON (SP)	o—	—o	o—	—⊙—	—o

NOTE
o–o indicates that there is continuity between the terminals.

MT6029100016000X

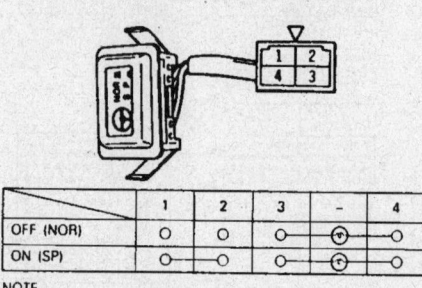

Fig. 16 EPS mode switch test. Diamante & Galant

change by more than .2 inch.

Component Service

POWER STEERING GEAR

Diamante & Galant

1. Disassemble power steering gear in numbered sequence shown in **Figs. 17 through 21,** noting the following:
   a. Tie rod and rack retaining tab must be unstaked with a chisel.
   b. Tool No. MB991204, or equivalent, may be used to remove rack support cover from gearbox.
   c. When removing pinion, gently tap with a plastic hammer.
   d. When removing oil seal from rack bushing, do not damage oil seal press fitting surface.
   e. Remove ball bearing from gear housing using a brass bar.
   f. Remove needle roller bearing from rack housing using special tool No. MB991120, or equivalent.
   g. When removing back-up washer and oil seal from gear housing, do not damage inner surface of gear housing rack cylinder.
2. Inspect rack tooth surfaces for damage or wear, then check oil seal contact surfaces for uneven wear.
3. Inspect rack for bends.
4. Check pinion gear tooth surfaces for damage or wear, then check for worn or defective seals.
5. Check bearing for roughness, abnormal noise and excessive play during operation.
6. Check needle roller bearings for roller slip-off.
7. Check rack housing cylinder inner surface for damage.
8. Check mounting rubber for cracks or damage. Replace as required.
9. Reverse numbered sequence shown in **Figs. 17 through 21** to assemble, noting the following:
   a. When installing back-up washer and oil seal, coat seal with Dexron II ATF, then press back-up and oil seal into rack housing to specified position.
   b. When installing needle roller bearing, apply even pressure to prevent housing damage.
   c. Apply coating of multipurpose grease to rack tooth face.
   d. When installing rack assembly, cover rack serrations with tool No. MB991213, or equivalent, then match oil seal center with rack to prevent retainer spring from slipping and slowly insert rack from power cylinder side.
   e. When installing rack bushing and stopper, wrap rack end with vinyl tape and apply a coating of Dexron II ATF.
   f. Install seal rings using tool No. MB991317, or equivalent.
   g. When installing end plug, secure threaded portion at two points using a punch.
   h. Adjust total pinion **torque** to 5–11 inch lbs.
   i. When installing tie rod, fold tab washer end into tie rod notch.
   j. Pack dust cover interior with multipurpose grease.

Eclipse & Expo

Disassemble power steering gear in numbered sequence shown in **Figs. 22 and 23,** noting the following:

1. Using a screwdriver, remove dust cover from tie rod end. Loosen, then remove boot retaining band.
2. Using a chisel, unstake tab washer which fixes tie rod and rack.
3. Remove end plug caulking and end plug.
4. Using special tool No. MB991204, or equivalent, remove rack support cover from gearbox.
5. Using a plastic hammer, gently tap the pinion to remove it.
6. Using a socket, remove the oil seal and the ball bearing from the valve housing simultaneously.
7. Turn the rack stopper clockwise until the end of the circlip comes out of the slot in the rack housing, then turn the stopper counterclockwise to remove the circlip.
8. Remove rack, rack stopper and rack bushing.
9. Partially bend oil seal and remove from rack bushing. Do not damage oil seal press fitting surface.
10. Using a brass bar, remove the ball bearing from the gear housing.
11. Using special tool No. MB991120, or equivalent, remove the needle roller bearing from the rack housing.
12. Remove the back-up washer and oil seal from the gear housing, using caution to avoid damaging inner surface of rack cylinder.
13. Inspect the rack tooth surfaces for damage or wear, then the oil seal contact surfaces for uneven wear.
14. Inspect the rack for bends.
15. Check the pinion gear tooth surfaces for damage or wear, then check for worn or defective seal.
16. Check bearing for roughness or abnormal noise during operation, check the bearing for play.

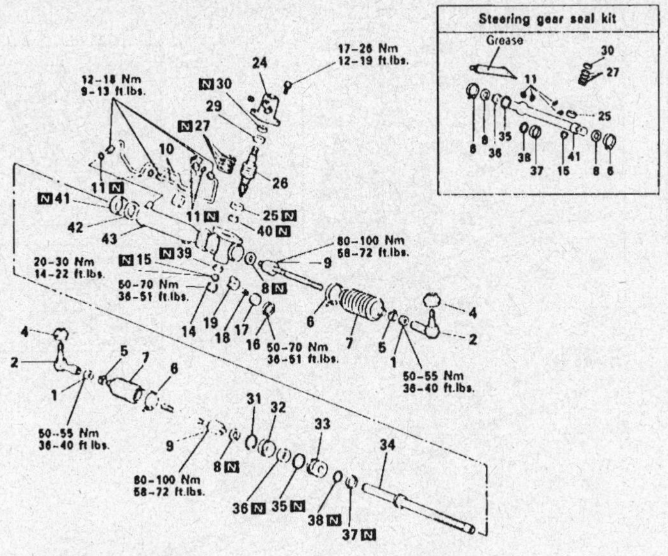
Steering gear seal kit
Grease
17-26 Nm
12-19 ft.lbs.
12-18 Nm
9-13 ft.lbs.
80-100 Nm
58-72 ft.lbs.
20-30 Nm
14-22 ft.lbs.
50-70 Nm
36-51 ft.lbs.
50-70 Nm
36-51 ft.lbs.
50-55 Nm
36-40 ft.lbs.
50-55 Nm
36-40 ft.lbs.
80-100 Nm
58-72 ft.lbs.

Disassembly steps

1. Tie-rod end locking nut
2 Tie-rod end

4 Dust cover
5 Bellow clip
6 Bellow band
7 Bellows
8 Tab washer
9 Tie-rod
10 Feed tube
11. O-ring
Adjustment of total pinion torque
14. End plug
15. Self-locking nut
16. Locking nut
17. Rack support cover
18 Rack support spring
19. Rack support
24. Valve housing
25 Oil seal
26 Pinion and valve assembly
27. Seal ring
29. Ball bearing
30. Oil seal
31. Circlip
32. Rack stopper
33. Rack bushing
34. Rack
35. O-ring
36. Oil seal
37. Seal ring
38. O-ring
39. Ball bearing
40. Needle roller bearing
41. Oil seal
42. Back-up washer
43. Rack housing

MT6029100017000X

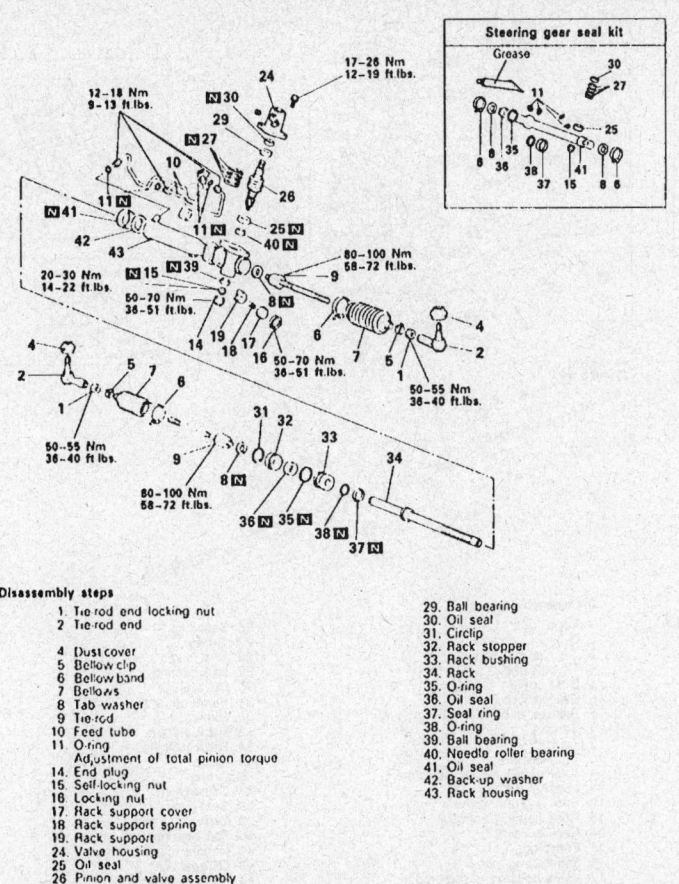

Fig. 17 Exploded view of power steering gear. Diamante & 1993 Galant w/conventional steering gear

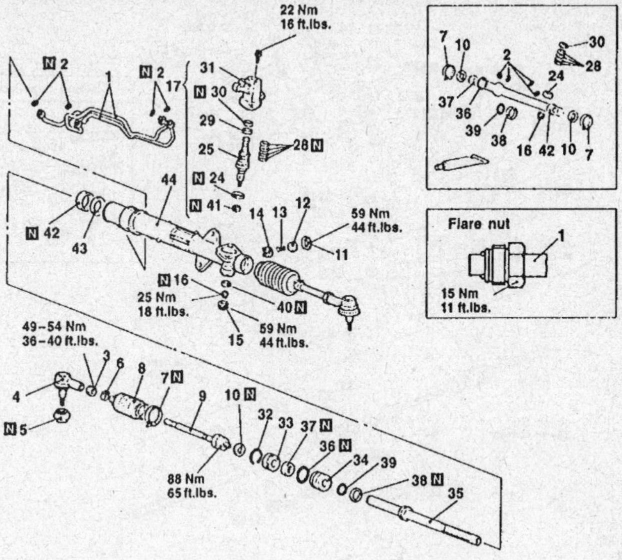
22 Nm
16 ft.lbs.
59 Nm
44 ft.lbs.
Flare nut
15 Nm
11 ft.lbs.
25 Nm
18 ft.lbs.
49-54 Nm
36-40 ft.lbs.
59 Nm
44 ft.lbs.
88 Nm
65 ft.lbs.

Disassembly steps

1. Feed tube
2. O-ring
3. Tie rod end locking nut
4. Tie rod end
5. Dust cover
6. Bellows clip
7. Bellows band
8. Bellows
9. Tie rod
10. Tab washer
• Total pinion torque adjustment
11. Locking nut
12. Rack support cover
13. Rack support spring
14. Rack support
15. End plug
16. Self-locking nut
17. Valve housing assembly
24. Oil seal
25. Pinion and valve assembly
26. Seal ring
27. O-ring
28. Seal ring
29. Ball bearing
30. Oil seal
31. Valve housing
32. Circlip
33. Rack stopper
34. Rack bushing
35. Rack
36. O-ring
37. Oil seal
38. Seal ring
39. O-ring
40. Ball bearing
41. Needle roller bearing
42. Oil seal
43. Back-up washer
44. Rack housing

MT6029400018000X

Fig. 18 Exploded view of power steering gear. 1994–96 Galant w/conventional steering gear

17. Check the needle roller for bearings for roller slip-off.
18. Check the cylinder inner surface of the rack housing for damage.
19. Check mounting rubber for cracks or damage. Replace as required.
20. Reverse numbered sequence shown in **Fig. 22** to assemble steering gear, noting the following:
    a. When installing back-up washer and oil seal, coat seal with Dexron II ATF and press washer and seal into rack housing to specified position.
    b. **On 1995–96 Eclipse models,** it will be necessary to use installer tool No. MB991199, guide tool No. MB991099 and bar tool No. MB991197, or equivalents, to install back-up washer and oil seal.
    c. **On all models,** when installing needle roller bearing, press evenly as valve housing is aluminum.
    d. **On 1995–96 Eclipse models,** it will be necessary to use installer tool Nos. MB990938 and MB991202, or equivalents, to install needle roller and ball bearings.
    e. **On all models,** when installing oil seal and O-ring, press fit oil seal until it reaches rack bush end.
    f. Apply coating of multipurpose grease to rack tooth face.
    g. When installing rack assembly, cover rack serrations with tool No. MB991213, or equivalent, then match oil seal center with rack to prevent retainer spring from slipping and slowly insert rack from power cylinder side.
    h. When installing rack bushing and stopper, wrap rack end with vinyl tape and apply a coating of Dexron II ATF.
    i. Install seal rings using tool No. MB991317, or equivalent.
    j. When installing end plug, secure threaded portion at two points using a punch.
    k. **On Expo and 1993–94 Eclipse models,** adjust total pinion **torque** to 5–11 inch lbs.
    l. **On 1995–96 Eclipse models,** adjust total pinion **torque** to 6–12 inch lbs.
    m. **On all models,** when installing tie rod, fold tab washer end into tie rod notch.
    n. Pack dust cover interior with multipurpose grease.

Mirage & 3000GT

1. Disassemble steering gear in numbered sequence shown in **Figs. 24 and 25,** noting the following:
    a. Unstake tie rod end tab washer.
    b. Using socket tool No. MB990607, or equivalent, remove rack support cover.
    c. Using a plastic hammer, lightly tap on pinion shaft to remove.
    d. Turn rack stopper clockwise until end of circlip is visible.
    e. Turn rack stopper counterclockwise to remove circlip, **Fig. 26.**
    f. Remove rack slowly, **Fig. 27.**
    g. Remove oil seal using suitable oil seal remover tool.
    h. Remove ball bearing using brass bar tool No. MB990939, or equivalent.
    i. Remove needle roller bearing using bearing tool No. MB991120, or equivalent.
    j. Remove oil seal from housing using a piece of pipe.
2. Reverse numbered sequence shown in **Figs. 24 and 25** to assemble, noting the following:
    a. Using rack installer tool No. MB991212, or equivalent, press back-up washer and oil seal into rack housing.
    b. Install needle roller bearing using bearing installation tool No. MB991120, or equivalent.
    c. Apply a coat of multipurpose

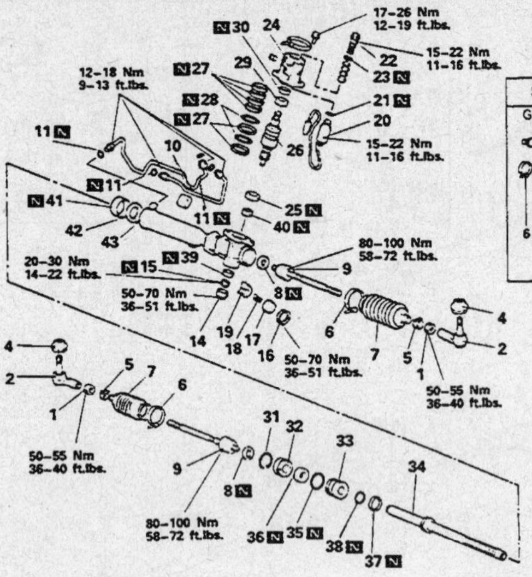
17–26 Nm
12–19 ft.lbs.
15–22 Nm
11–16 ft.lbs.
12–18 Nm
9–13 ft.lbs.
Steering gear seal kit
Grease
80–100 Nm
58–72 ft.lbs.
20–30 Nm
14–22 ft.lbs.
50–70 Nm
36–51 ft.lbs.
50–55 Nm
36–40 ft.lbs.

Disassembly steps

1. Tie-rod end locking nut
2. Tie-rod end

4. Dust cover
5. Bellow clip
6. Bellow band
7. Bellows
8. Tab washer
9. Tie-rod
10. Feed tube
11. O-ring
Adjustment of total pinion torque
14. End plug
15. Self-locking nut
16. Locking nut
17. Rack support cover
18. Rack support spring
19. Rack support
20. Solenoid valve
21. O-ring
22. P.C.V. cap assembly
23. O-ring
24. Valve housing
25. Oil seal
26. Pinion and valve assembly
27. Seal ring
28. O-ring
29. Ball bearing
30. Oil seal
31. Circlip
32. Rack stopper
33. Rack bushing
34. Rack
35. O-ring
36. Oil seal
37. Seal ring
38. O-ring
39. Ball bearing
40. Needle roller bearing
41. Oil seal
42. Back-up washer
43. Rack housing

MT6029100019000X

Fig. 19 Exploded view of power steering gear. 1993 Galant w/electronic steering gear

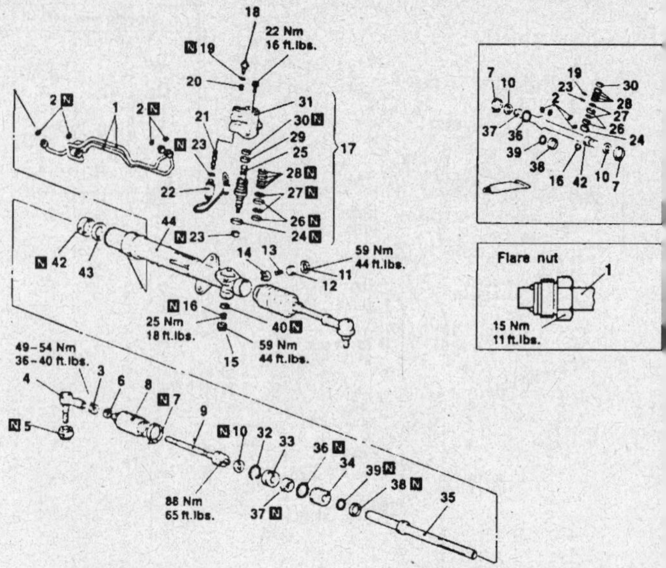
22 Nm
16 ft.lbs.
59 Nm
44 ft.lbs.
Flare nut
15 Nm
11 ft.lbs.
25 Nm
18 ft.lbs.
49–54 Nm
36–40 ft.lbs.
88 Nm
65 ft.lbs.

Disassembly steps

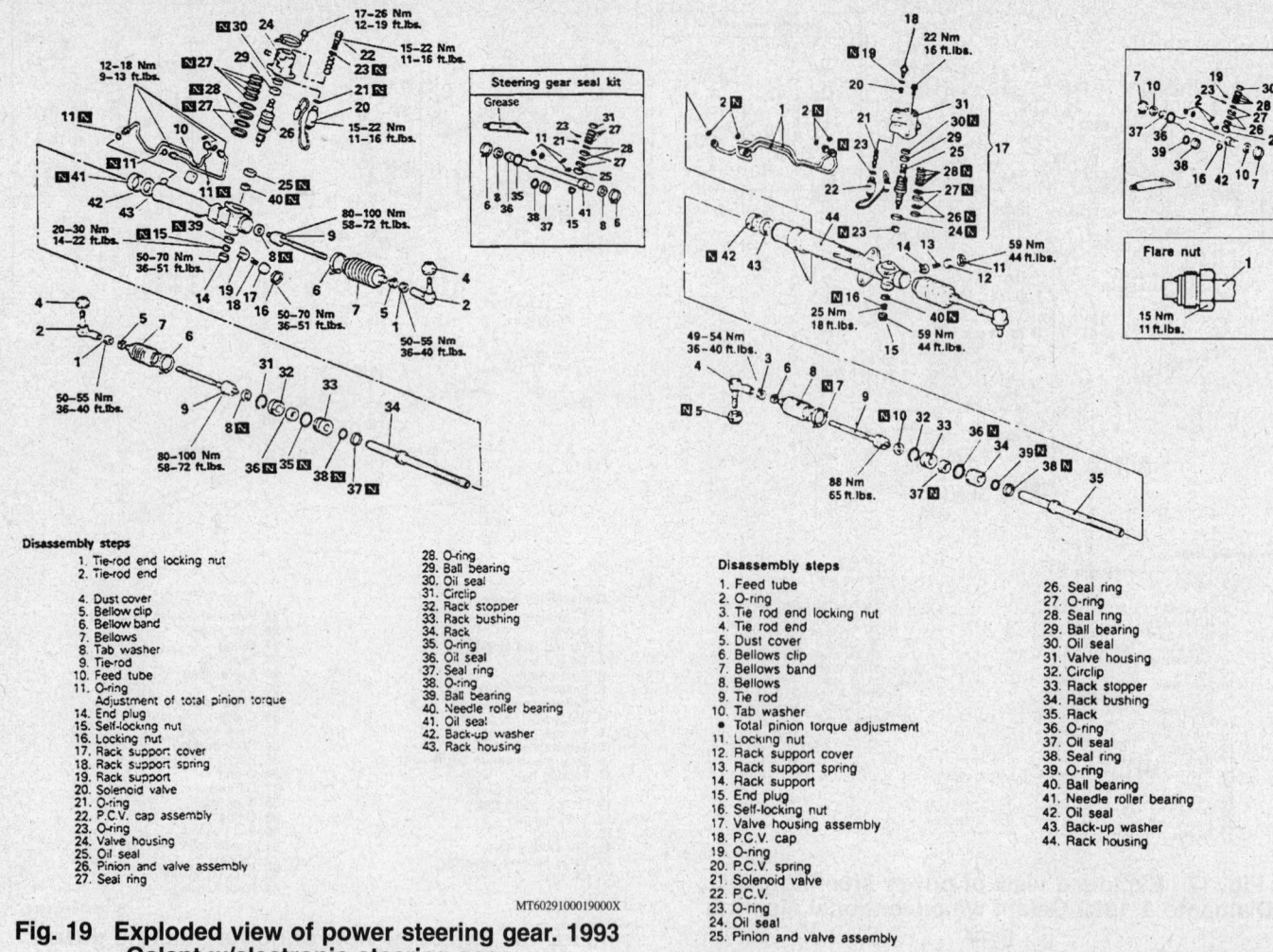

1. Feed tube
2. O-ring
3. Tie rod end locking nut
4. Tie rod end
5. Dust cover
6. Bellows clip
7. Bellows band
8. Bellows
9. Tie rod
10. Tab washer
• Total pinion torque adjustment
11. Locking nut
12. Rack support cover
13. Rack support spring
14. Rack support
15. End plug
16. Self-locking nut
17. Valve housing assembly
18. P.C.V. cap
19. O-ring
20. P.C.V. spring
21. Solenoid valve
22. P.C.V.
23. O-ring
24. Oil seal
25. Pinion and valve assembly
26. Seal ring
27. O-ring
28. Seal ring
29. Ball bearing
30. Oil seal
31. Valve housing
32. Circlip
33. Rack stopper
34. Rack bushing
35. Rack
36. O-ring
37. Oil seal
38. Seal ring
39. O-ring
40. Ball bearing
41. Needle roller bearing
42. Oil seal
43. Back-up washer
44. Rack housing

MT6029400020000X

Fig. 20 Exploded view of power steering gear. 1994–96 Galant w/electronic steering gear

grease to rack teeth face. **Do not close vent hose in rack with grease.**

d. Cover rack serrations with special rack installer tool, apply Dexron II ATF fluid to tool.
e. Align oil seal center with rack to prevent retainer spring from slipping and slowly insert rack from power cylinder side.
f. Wrap vinyl tape around end of rack, and install rack bushing and stopper.
g. Insert circlip to rack stopper through cylinder hole. Turn rack stopper clockwise and insert circlip firmly, **Fig. 28.**
h. Apply multipurpose grease to pinion gear and housing, wrap tape around serrated part.
i. Use seal ring installer tool No. MB991317, or equivalent, to install seal ring, then install pinion and valve assembly into valve housing.
j. Install valve housing seal using suitable seal installation tool and allow seal upper surface to project outward .040 inch, **Fig. 29.**
k. Apply 3M ATD sealant part No. 8663, or equivalent, to end plug threads, then install end plug securing in place using a suitable punch.
l. To adjust total pinion torque, center rack, then use torque wrench socket tool No. MB990607, or equivalent, to **torque** rack support cover to 11 ft. lbs. Then, from neutral position, rotate pinion shaft clockwise one turn within four to six seconds. Loosen rack support cover 30–60° and adjust **torque** to 5–11 inch lbs., then lock rack support cover with locknut.

Montero & Pickup

1. Disassemble power steering gear in numbered sequence shown in **Figs. 30 and 31,** noting the following:
   a. Remove pitman arm using removal tool No. MB990809-01, or equivalent.
   b. Position mainshaft and cross shaft in straight ahead position, then tap bottom of cross shaft lightly with a plastic hammer to remove the cross shaft and side cover.
   c. **Do not remove packing unless fluid is leaking from threads of adjusting bolt.**
   d. **On Pickup models,** remove valve housing locknut using housing nut wrench tool No. MB990852-01, or equivalent, then remove rack piston from mainshaft by turning it clockwise. **Use care not to lose 26 balls inside rack piston.** Remove top cover and mainshaft from valve housing by using spanner wrench tool No. MB990201-01, or equivalent, then install top cover on valve housing and remove top cover bearing and seal using suitable bearing removal tool.
   e. **On Montero models,** remove rack piston from mainshaft by turning it counterclockwise. **Use care not to lose 26 balls inside rack piston.** Remove locknut using spanner wrench tool No. MB991367, or equivalent, and guide mainshaft out while pressing bearing race so balls do not drop out, then remove valve housing oil seal and bearing using a suitable bearing removal tool.
2. **On all models,** reverse numbered sequence shown in **Figs. 30 and 31** to assemble power steering gear, noting the following:
   a. Apply grease to bearing surface of

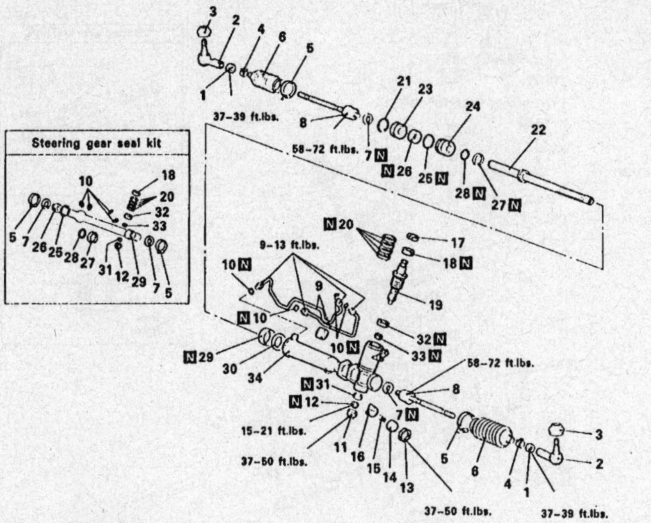
Steering gear seal kit
37-39 ft.lbs.
58-72 ft.lbs.
9-13 ft.lbs.
15-21 ft.lbs.
37-50 ft.lbs.
37-50 ft.lbs.
37-39 ft.lbs.

1. Tie-rod end locking nuts
2. Tie-rod ends
3. Dust covers
4. Bellows clips
5. Bellows bands
6. Bellows
7. Tab washers
8. Tie-rods
9. Feed tubes
10. O-rings
Adjustment of total pinion torque
11. End plug
12. Self-locking nut
13. Locking nut
14. Rack support cover
15. Rack support spring
16. Rack support
17. Snap ring
18. Oil seal
19. Pinion and valve assembly
20. Seal rings
21. Circlip
22. Rack
23. Rack stopper
24. Rack bushing
25. O-ring
26. Oil seal
27. Seal rings
28. O-ring
29. Oil seal
30. Back up washer
31. Ball bearing
32. Oil seal
33. Needle roller bearing
34. Rack housing

MT6029100022000X

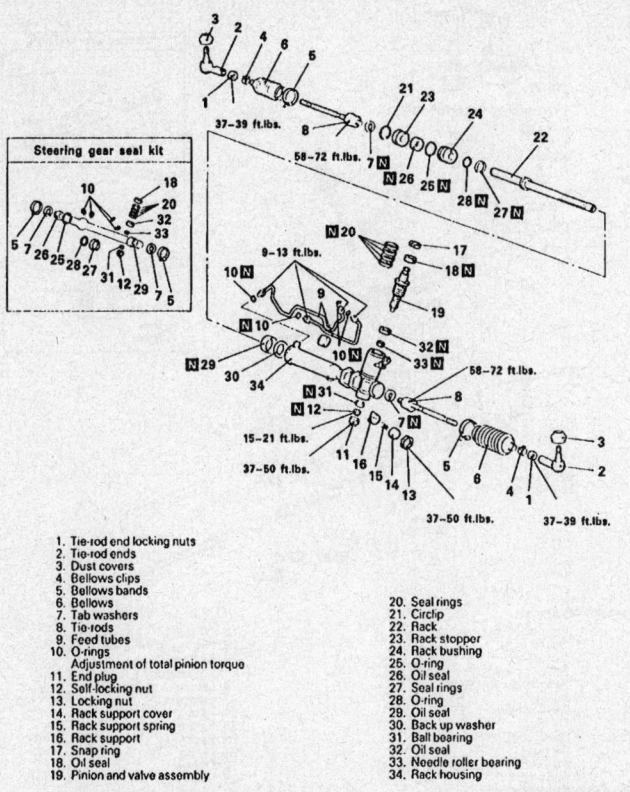

Fig. 21 Exploded view of power steering gear. Diamante w/electronic steering gear

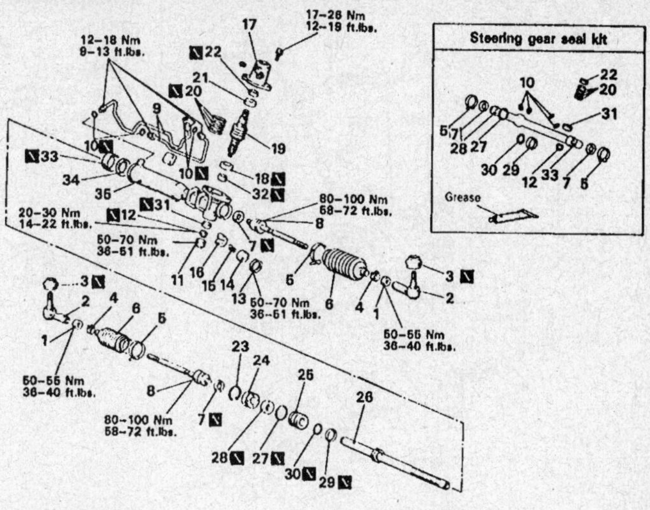
Steering gear seal kit
Grease
17-26 Nm
12-19 ft.lbs.
12-18 Nm
9-13 ft.lbs.
20-30 Nm
14-22 ft.lbs.
50-70 Nm
36-51 ft.lbs.
80-100 Nm
58-72 ft.lbs.
50-55 Nm
36-40 ft.lbs.

Disassembly steps
1. Tie rod end locking nut
2. Tie rod end
3. Dust cover
4. Bellows clip
5. Bellows band
6. Bellow
7. Tab washer
8. Tie rod
9. Feed tube
10. O-ring
Adjustment of total pinion torque
11. End plug
12. Self-locking nut
13. Locking nut
14. Rack support cover
15. Rack support spring
16. Rack support
17. Valve housing
18. Oil seal
19. Pinion and valve assembly
20. Seal ring
21. Ball bearing
22. Oil seal
23. Circlip
24. Rack stopper
25. Rack bushing
26. Rack
27. O-ring
28. Oil seal
29. Seal ring
30. O-ring
31. Ball bearing
32. Needle roller bearing
33. Oil seal
34. Back-up washer
35. Rack housing

MT6029100023000X

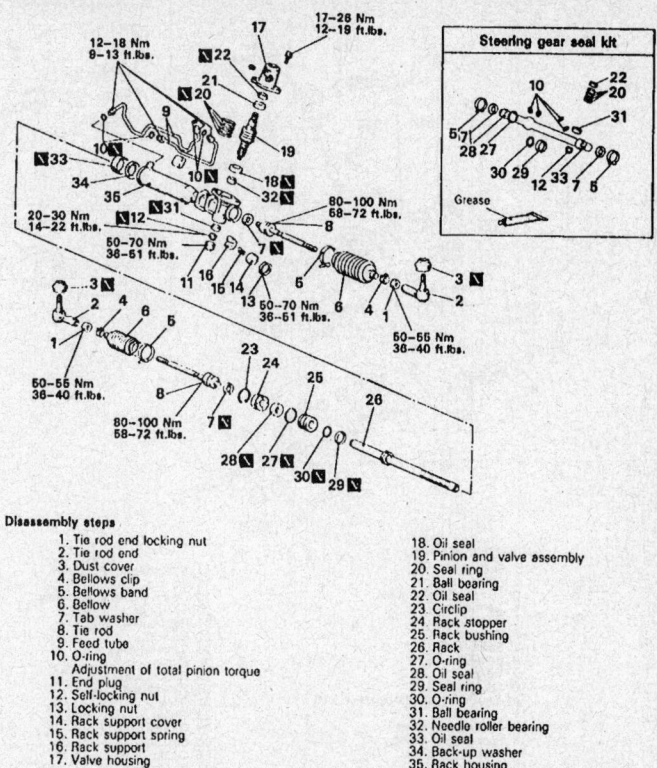

Fig. 22 Exploded view of power steering gear. Expo & 1993–94 Eclipse

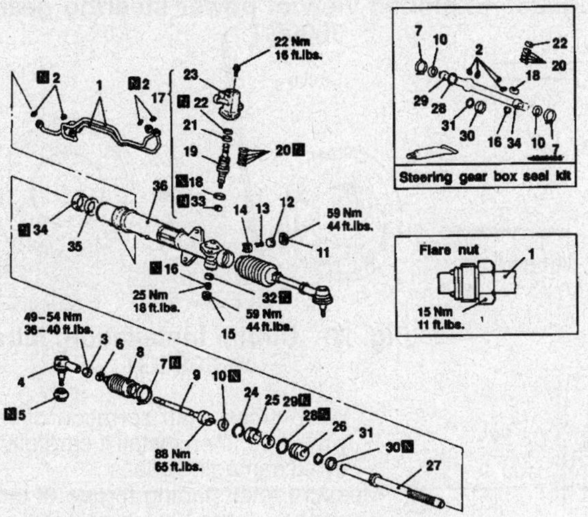
22 Nm
16 ft.lbs.
Steering gear box seal kit
Flare nut
15 Nm
11 ft.lbs.
59 Nm
44 ft.lbs.
25 Nm
18 ft.lbs.
59 Nm
44 ft.lbs.
49-54 Nm
36-40 ft.lbs.
88 Nm
65 ft.lbs.

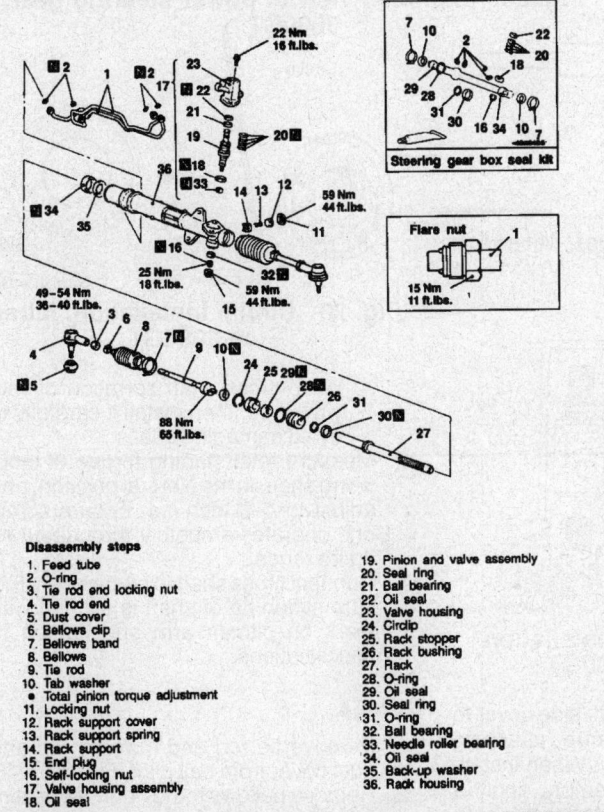

Disassembly steps
1. Feed tube
2. O-ring
3. Tie rod end locking nut
4. Tie rod end
5. Dust cover
6. Bellows clip
7. Bellows band
8. Bellows
9. Tie rod
10. Tab washer
• Total pinion torque adjustment
11. Locking nut
12. Rack support cover
13. Rack support spring
14. Rack support
15. End plug
16. Self-locking nut
17. Valve housing assembly
18. Oil seal
19. Pinion and valve assembly
20. Seal ring
21. Ball bearing
22. Oil seal
23. Valve housing
24. Circlip
25. Rack stopper
26. Rack bushing
27. Rack
28. O-ring
29. Oil seal
30. Seal ring
31. O-ring
32. Ball bearing
33. Needle roller bearing
34. Oil seal
35. Back-up washer
36. Rack housing

MT6029500050000X

Fig. 23 Exploded view of power steering gear. 1995–96 Eclipse

side cover needle bearing and install the 33 rollers.

b. Apply grease to bottom of side cover, then position new O-ring on the cover.
c. Install adjusting bolt and plate into slot on top of cross shaft. Install plate with chamfered side toward cross shaft mating surface.
d. Adjust cross shaft endplay to 0–.002 inch, using spacers as necessary.
e. Install side cover onto cross shaft, tighten with adjusting bolt, then tighten locknut temporarily.
f. Apply thin coat of grease to gear housing U-packing and oil seal, then press them into housing using tool Nos. MB990938 and MB990926, or equivalents.
g. Apply thin coat of grease to lip of valve housing oil seal, then press it into housing.
h. Press ball bearing into top cover, then install thrust plate, needle roller bearing and second thrust plate into cover. **Install the thinner of the two thrust plates on top cover side.**
i. Install, then temporarily tighten top cover.
j. Using tool No. MB990853, or equivalent, and a spring scale, **torque** top cover to 14–19 lbs., then loosen cover completely. Rotate input worm shaft and check for smooth operation.
k. Measure starting torque using tool No. MB990228, or equivalent,

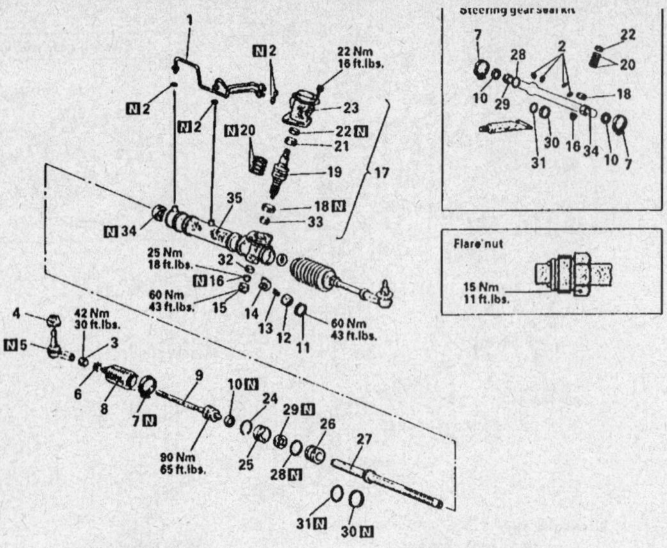
Steering gear seal kit
Flare nut
15 Nm
11 ft.lbs.
22 Nm
16 ft.lbs.
25 Nm
18 ft.lbs.
60 Nm
43 ft.lbs.
42 Nm
30 ft.lbs.
90 Nm
65 ft.lbs.

Disassembly steps

1. Feed pipe
2. O-ring
3. Tie-rod end locking nut
4. Tie-rod end
5. Dust cover
6. Bellows clip
7. Bellows band
8. Bellows
9. Tie-rod
10. Tab washer
• Adjustment of total pinion preload
11. Locking nut
12. Rack support cover
13. Rack support spring
14. Rack support
15. End plug
16. Self-locking nut
17. Valve housing assembly
18. Oil seal
19. Pinion and valve assembly
20. Seal ring
21. Ball bearing
22. Oil seal
23. Valve housing
24. Circlip
25. Rack stopper
26. Rack bushing
27. Rack
28. O-ring
29. Oil seal
30. Seal ring
31. O-ring
32. Ball bearing
33. Needle roller bearing
34. Oil seal
35. Rack housing

MT6029100024000X

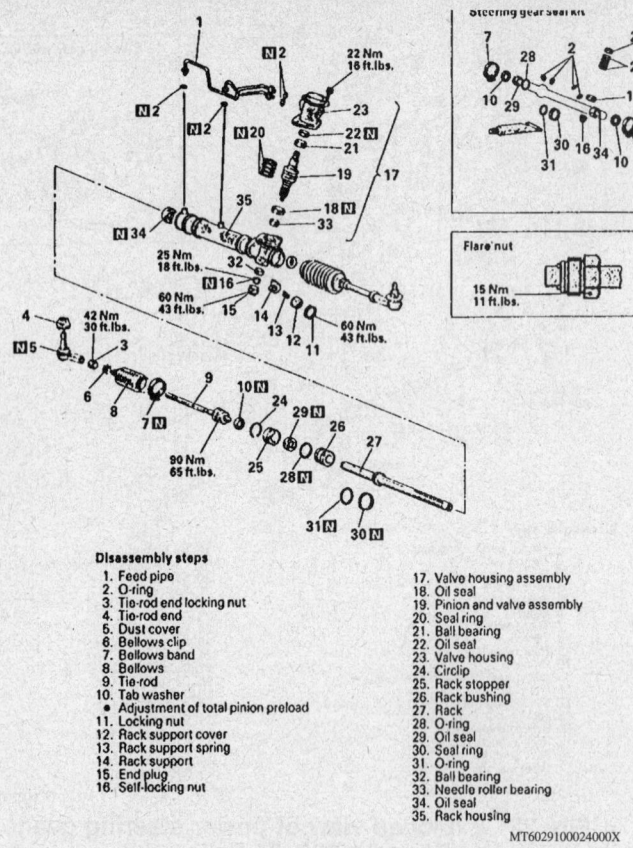

Fig. 24 Exploded view of power steering gear. Mirage

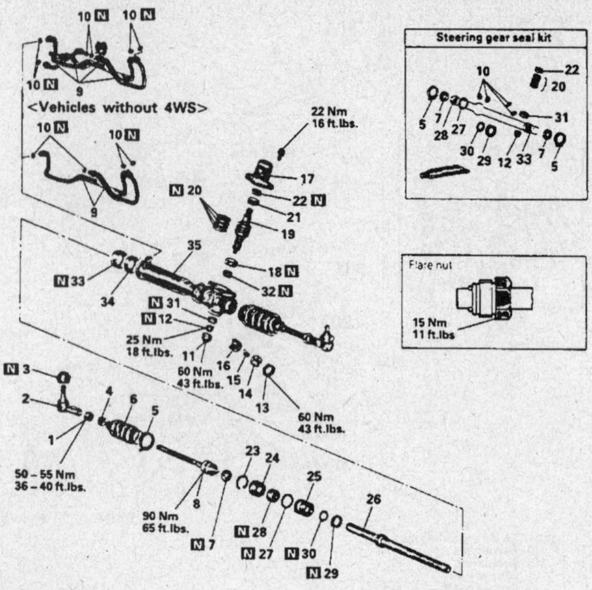
<Vehicles without 4WS>
Steering gear seal kit
Flare nut
15 Nm
11 ft.lbs
22 Nm
16 ft.lbs.
25 Nm
18 ft.lbs.
60 Nm
43 ft.lbs.
50 – 55 Nm
36 – 40 ft.lbs.
90 Nm
65 ft.lbs.

Disassembly steps

1. Tie rod end locking nuts
2. Tie rod ends
3. Dust shield
4. Bellows clips
5. Bellows bands
6. Bellows
7. Tab washers
8. Tie rods
9. Feed tubes
10. O-rings
Adjustment of total pinion torque
11. End plug
12. Self-locking nut
13. Locking nut
14. Rack support cover
15. Rack support spring
16. Rack support
17. Valve housing
18. Oil seal
19. Pinion and valve assembly
20. Seal rings
21. Ball bearing
22. Oil seal
23. Circlip
24. Rack stopper
25. Rack bushing
26. Rack
27. O-ring
28. Oil seal
29. Seal rings
30. O-ring
31. Ball bearing
32. Needle roller bearing
33. Oil seal
34. Back-up washer
35. Rack housing

MT6029100025000X

Fig. 25 Exploded view of power steering gear. 3000GT

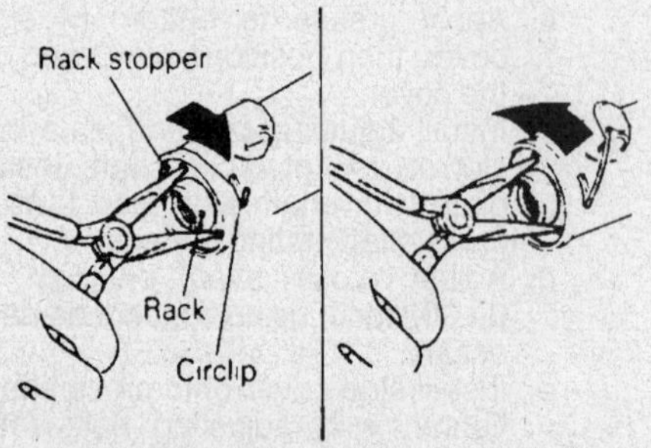
Rack stopper
Rack
Circlip

MT6029100026000X

Fig. 26 Circlip removal. Mirage & 3000GT

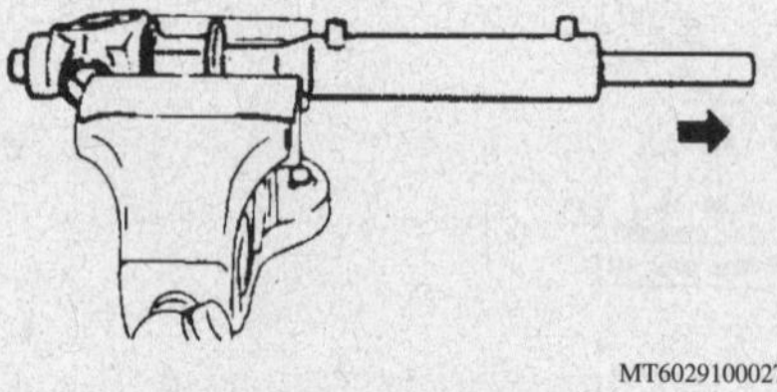

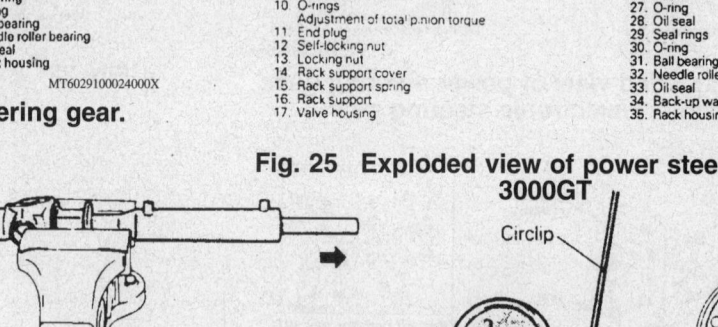

MT6029100027000X

Fig. 27 Rack removal. Mirage & 3000GT

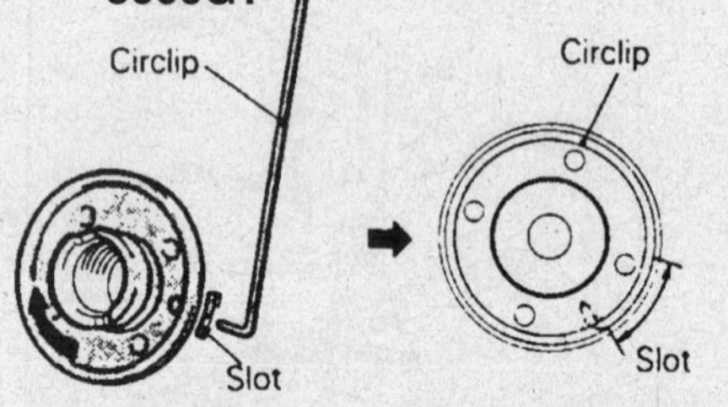
Circlip
Circlip
Slot
Slot

MT6029100028000X

Fig. 28 Circlip installation. Mirage & 3000GT

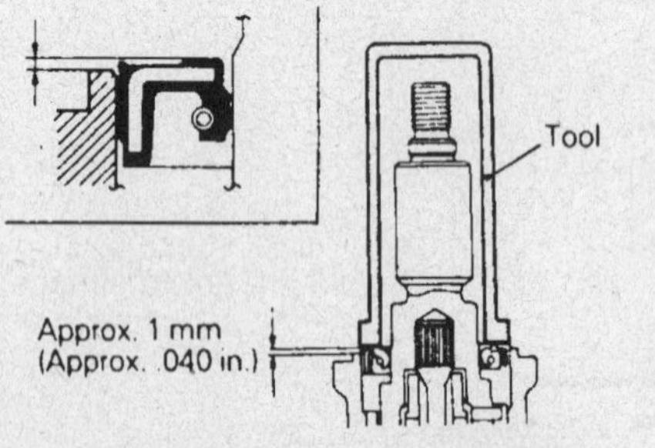
Tool
Approx. 1 mm
(Approx. .040 in.)

MT6029100029000X

Fig. 29 Oil seal installation. Mirage & 3000GT

while turning input worm shaft and note the value.

l. Tighten top cover until starting **torque** of input worm shaft is 1.8–2.7 inch lbs., more than value measured in preceding step.
m. Install valve housing nut, then **torque** to 131–166 ft. lbs.
n. Measure starting torque again while turning input worm shaft. Preload should measure 2–6 inch lbs. If not, loosen valve housing nut and repeat steps for establishing correct preload.
o. Secure gear housing in a vise, then install screw unit.
p. Install valve housing attaching bolts, then **torque** to 33–39 ft. lbs. Rotate input worm shaft to move rack piston to the Neutral position.
q. Install cross shaft with side cover to gear housing. **Torque** attaching bolts to 33–39 ft. lbs. When installing cross shaft assembly, apply a thin coat of Dexron II to rack piston teeth and shaft and multi-purpose grease to lip of oil seal. **Do not rotate side cover when installing.** Wrap cross shaft serration of with vinyl tape, then install it carefully to avoid damaging seal.

3. Measure total starting torque of input worm shaft, in the Neutral position, and adjust to 4–8 inch lbs. Ensure screw unit operates smoothly throughout its entire range.
4. Connect cross shaft to pitman arm. Ensure slit on tip of shaft is aligned with mark on pitman arm and tighten to specifications.

Precis

1. Remove tie rod end from tie rod and dust cover from ball joint, **Fig. 32.**
2. Remove bellows band, then the retaining clip.
3. Pull bellows out toward tie rod. **Check for rust on rack when bellows are replaced.**

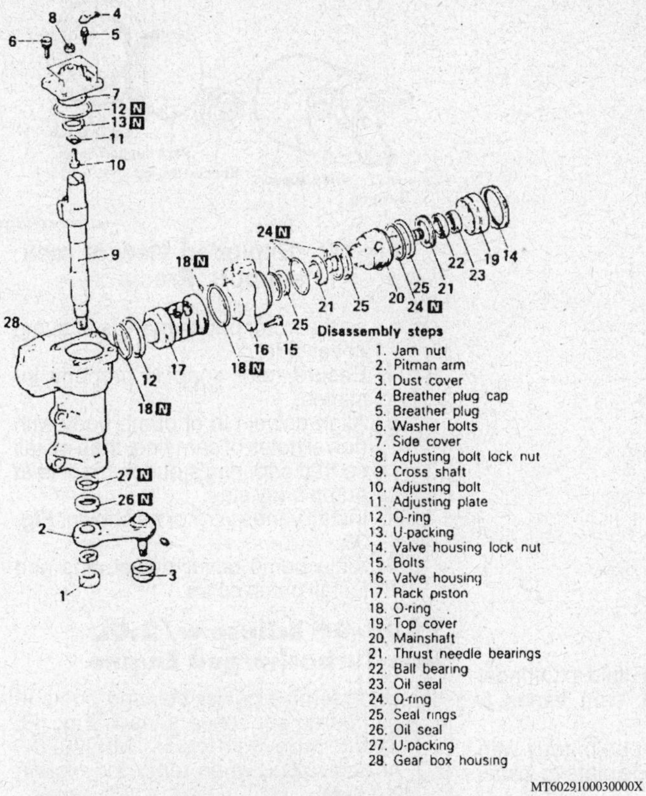
Disassembly steps
1. Jam nut
2. Pitman arm
3. Dust cover
4. Breather plug cap
5. Breather plug
6. Washer bolts
7. Side cover
8. Adjusting bolt lock nut
9. Cross shaft
10. Adjusting bolt
11. Adjusting plate
12. O-ring
13. U-packing
14. Valve housing lock nut
15. Bolts
16. Valve housing
17. Rack piston
18. O-ring
19. Top cover
20. Mainshaft
21. Thrust needle bearings
22. Ball bearing
23. Oil seal
24. O-ring
25. Seal rings
26. Oil seal
27. U-packing
28. Gear box housing
MT6029100030000X

Fig. 30 Exploded view of power steering gear. Pickup

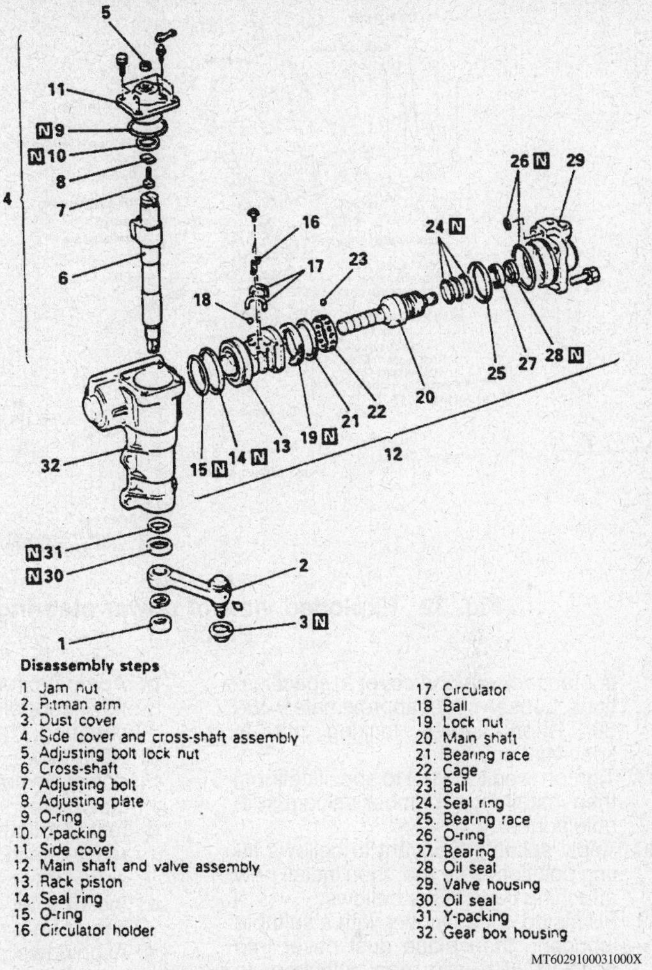
Disassembly steps
1. Jam nut
2. Pitman arm
3. Dust cover
4. Side cover and cross-shaft assembly
5. Adjusting bolt lock nut
6. Cross-shaft
7. Adjusting bolt
8. Adjusting plate
9. O-ring
10. Y-packing
11. Side cover
12. Main shaft and valve assembly
13. Rack piston
14. Seal ring
15. O-ring
16. Circulator holder
17. Circulator
18. Ball
19. Lock nut
20. Main shaft
21. Bearing race
22. Cage
23. Ball
24. Seal ring
25. Bearing race
26. O-ring
27. Bearing
28. Oil seal
29. Valve housing
30. Oil seal
31. Y-packing
32. Gear box housing
MT6029100031000X

Fig. 31 Exploded view of steering gear. Montero

4. Remove feed tube from gear housing; then, while slowly moving rack, drain fluid from gear housing.
5. Remove end plug; then, with piston turned clockwise until rack is locked, remove self locking nut.
6. Chisel tab washer off of rack, then remove tie rod from rack. **Use care to avoid twisting tie rod when removing from rack.**
7. Remove rack support cover locking nut, then use yoke plug socket 09565-21100 or equivalent to remove rack support cover.
8. Remove rack support spring, rack support and bushing from gearbox.
9. Remove valve body housing attaching bolts.
10. Rotate rack stopper clockwise until end circlip is removed from slot in gear housing, then turn rack counterclockwise and remove circlip.
11. Remove O-ring and oil seal from rack bushing, then separate oil seal from rack bushing.
12. Remove valve body from housing using a soft hammer.
13. Using pinion bearing remover tool No. 09565-21000, or equivalent, remove oil seal and ball bearing from valve body housing.
14. Remove ball bearing from gear housing, using a suitable drift. **Ensure not to damage the pinion valve cylinder inside of gear housing.**
15. Remove needle bearing from gear housing.
16. Using oil seal guide tool No. 09573-21200 and bar tool No. 09555-21000, or equivalents, remove back washer and oil seal from gear housing.
17. Check rack for excessive wear or damaged tooth surfaces.
18. Inspect all oil seal contact surfaces for damage.
19. Check bearing for seizure, abnormal noise and excessive play.
20. Inspect dust cover for cracking or other damage.
21. Apply suitable oil to entire surface of oil seal for rack.
22. Using bearing installer tool No. 09432-21600, or equivalent, install back-up washer and oil seal in gear housing.
23. Apply suitable lubricant to surface of needle bearing. Place inscribed side of bearing in bearing installer tool No. 09432-21600, or equivalent, and insert it into gear housing until tool bottoms. **Note direction of needle bearing.**
24. Apply suitable lubricant to ball bearing, then install bearing, using a valve stem oil seal installer tool No. 09222-21100, or equivalent. **Ensure to use a new ball bearing.**
25. Apply lubricant to rack bushing oil seal surface, then insert seal into rack bushing using countershaft bearing installer tool No. 09434-14200, or equivalent.
26. Insert rack bushing O-ring, then apply a suitable lubricant to rack teeth. **Do not plug vent hole in rack with grease.**
27. Insert rack into gear housing, then install rack bushing and rack stopper.
28. Push rack stopper until circlip groove is aligned with notched hole in housing, then insert circlip while turning rack stopper, **Ensure circlip end is not visible through notched hole of rack housing.**
29. Using bearing installer, install oil seal and ball bearing to valve body.
30. Apply suitable lubricant to pinion valve assembly, then install to gear housing.
31. Using a countershaft bearing installer or equivalent, install the seal to valve body housing.
32. Install valve body assembly with the seal ring to gearbox, then the new tab washer and tie rod. Caulk tab washer end at two points to the tie rod.
33. Rotate pinion fully clockwise, then tighten new self-locking nut.
34. Apply suitable sealant to threaded section of end plug, then tighten to specifications.
35. Stake end plug at two points using a suitable punch, then install bushing, rack support, spring, and support cover as shown, **Fig. 33.** Apply suitable lubricant to threaded section of rack support prior to installation.
36. Place rack at center position, then

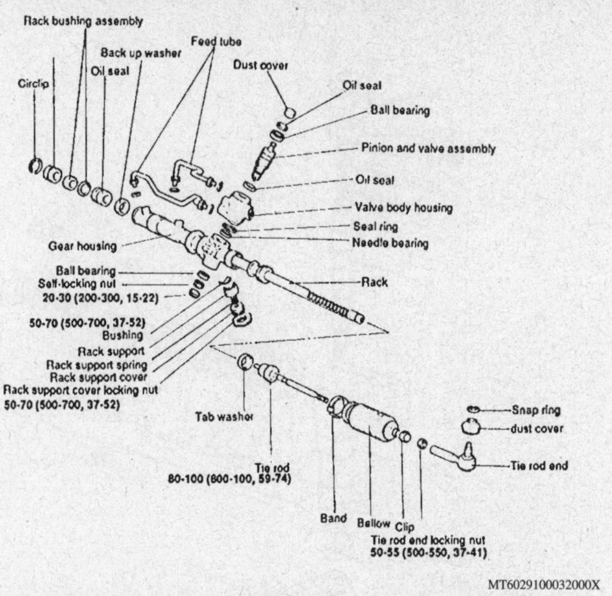
Rack bushing assembly
Feed tube
Back up washer
Oil seal
Dust cover
Circlip
Oil seal
Ball bearing
Pinion and valve assembly
Oil seal
Valve body housing
Seal ring
Needle bearing
Gear housing
Ball bearing
Self-locking nut
20-30 (200-300, 15-22)
Rack
50-70 (500-700, 37-52)
Bushing
Rack support
Rack support spring
Rack support cover
Rack support cover locking nut
50-70 (500-700, 37-52)
Tab washer
Snap ring
dust cover
Tie rod end
Tie rod
80-100 (800-100, 59-74)
Band
Bellow
Clip
Tie rod end locking nut
50-55 (500-550, 37-41)
MT6029100032000X

Fig. 32 Exploded view of power steering gear. Precis

tighten rack support cover to specifications. Loosen cover approximately 30–60°, then tighten locking nut to specifications.

37. Tighten feed tube nut to specifications, then install mount rubber using a suitable adhesive.
38. Apply suitable lubricant to bellows fitting position of tie rod, then install new attaching band to the bellows.
39. Fill inside of dust cover with a suitable lubricant, then place dust cover into position with clip ring attached to groove at tie rod end.
40. Install tie rods until free length of left and right rods are 6.1–6.2 inch, **Fig. 34.**

POWER STEERING PUMP

Diamante & Galant

1. Disassemble power steering pump in numbered sequence shown in **Figs. 35 and 36,** using a plastic hammer to remove pulley by lightly tapping rotor side of pulley shaft.
2. Inspect flow control spring for wear.
3. Inspect shaft for signs of wear and bending.
4. Check groove of rotor vane for "stepped" wear.
5. Check contact surface of cam ring and vanes for "stepped" wear.
6. Check for broken vanes.
7. Install vane in rotor then measure gap between vane and rotor groove. Gap should not exceed .0024 inch.
8. Place a dial indicator at end of pulley shaft, **Fig. 37.**
9. Move pulley assembly up and down and measure freeplay. Freeplay should not exceed .004 inch.
10. Reverse numbered sequence shown in **Figs. 35 and 36** to assemble power steering pump, noting the following:
    a. Install spring in oil pump body with larger diameter end at terminal assembly side.
    b. Apply Dexron II ATF fluid to O-rings, flow control valve, cam vanes & cam ring.
    c. Align dowel pin of pump body with dowel pin hole of side plate to install side plate.
    d. Install rotor to pulley assembly with rotor punch mark at pump cover side.
    e. Install rotor snap ring and ensure snap ring is properly countersunk.
    f. Align dowel pin cutouts in side plate with dowel pin holes of cam ring then install cam ring with punch mark toward pump body side.
    g. Install vanes on rotor as shown in **Fig. 38.**

Expo, Mirage, 3000GT, 1995–96 Eclipse w/2.0L Turbocharged Engine & 2.4L Engine & 1993–94 Eclipse

1. Disassemble power steering pump in numbered sequence shown in **Fig. 39.**
2. Measure gap between vane and rotor. Gap limit is .0024 inch.
3. Using a dial gauge at the end of the pump shaft, move pulley up and down and ensure movement is less than .004 inch.
4. Reverse numbered sequence shown in **Fig. 39** to assemble, noting the following:
    a. Install piston rod spring into pump body with larger diameter end at terminal assembly side.
    b. Apply Dexron II ATF to O-rings, flow control valve, rotor vanes and cam ring prior to installation.
    c. Drive pulley shaft oil seal into pump body using suitable seal installation tool.
    d. Align dowel pin of pump body with dowel pin hole of side plate to install side plate.
    e. Install rotor onto pulley assembly so that rotor punch mark is at pump cover side.
    f. Ensure rotor snap is properly installed.
    g. Align dowel pin of pump body with dowel holes of cam ring, then install so that cam ring's punch mark is at pump body side.
    h. Install vanes in rotor as shown, **Fig. 38.**
    i. Align pump cover dowel pins and install pump cover.

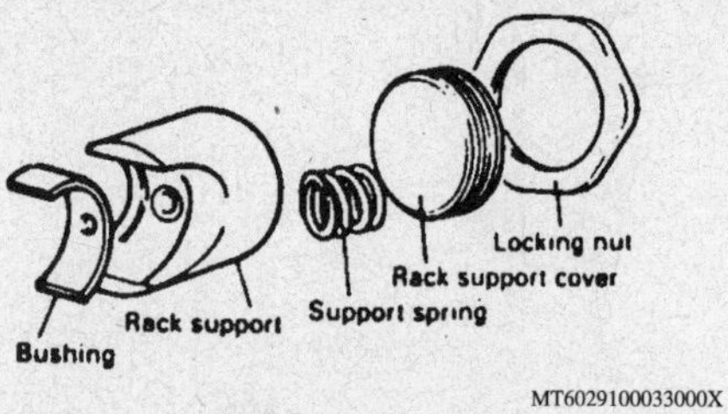
Locking nut
Rack support cover
Support spring
Rack support
Bushing
MT6029100033000X

Fig. 33 Exploded view of rack support. Precis

1995–96 Eclipse w/2.0L Non-Turbocharged Engine

1. Disassemble power steering pump in numbered sequence shown, **Fig. 40.** Secure pulley with tool No. MB990767, or equivalent, when removing mounting nuts.
2. Reverse numbered sequence to reassemble, noting the following:
    a. Install oil seal using installation tool Nos. MB990938 and MB991203, or equivalents.
    b. Apply Dexron II ATF to all O-rings prior to installation.
    c. Install rotor on shaft with punch mark at pump cover side.
    d. Install cam ring with punch mark facing pump cover.
    e. Install rotor vanes with rounded edges facing cam ring.
    f. Secure pulley with tool No. MB990767 and spacer tool No. MD998719, or equivalents, when installing pulley locknut.
3. Inspect flow control valve for clogging, shaft for damage or excessive wear, rotor and vane groove for "stepped" wear and vanes for damage.
4. Measure clearance between shaft and oil pump body using a suitable micrometer and caliper gauge as follows:
    a. Measure inside diameter of oil pump body bore, then measure outside diameter of shaft.
    b. Subtract shaft diameter from oil pump body bore diameter to obtain clearance measurement. Clearance should not exceed .0276 inch.

Montero

1. Disassemble power steering pump in numbered sequence shown in **Fig. 41.**
2. Reverse numbered sequence shown in **Fig. 41** to assemble, noting the following:
    a. Install flow control valve spring with larger diameter end at terminal side.
    b. Line up dowel pin hole with dowel

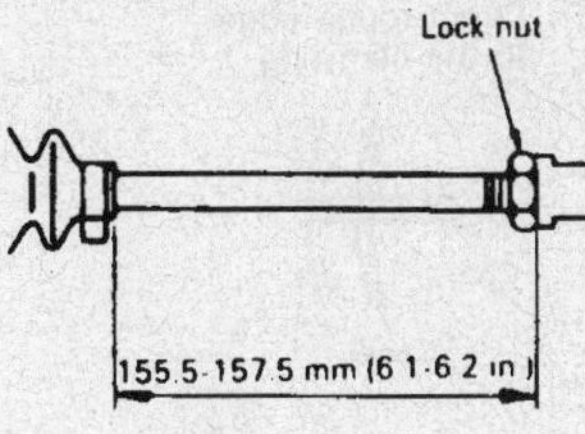
Lock nut
155.5-157.5 mm (6.1-6.2 in.)

MT6029100034000X

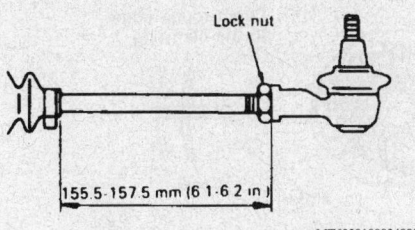

Fig. 34 Tie rod length adjustment. Precis

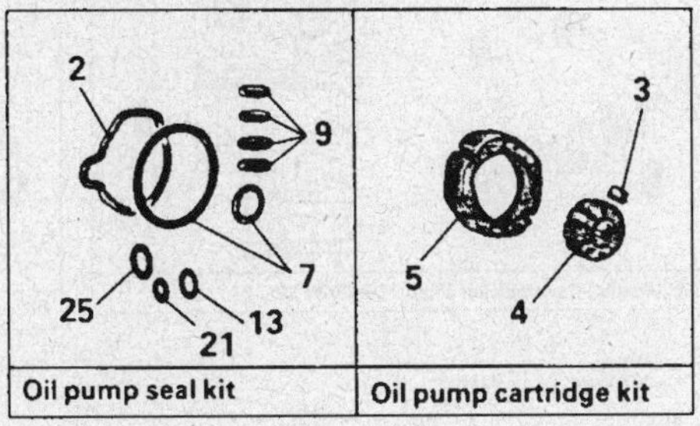
Oil pump seal kit
Oil pump cartridge kit

<DOHC Engine>

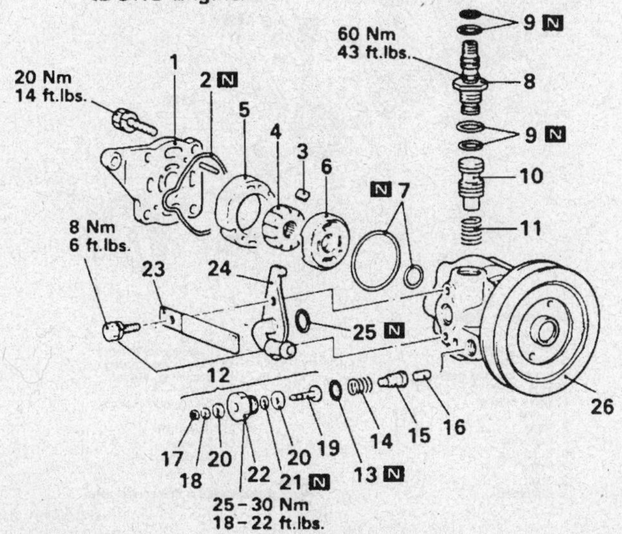
60 Nm
43 ft.lbs.
20 Nm
14 ft.lbs.
8 Nm
6 ft.lbs.
25–30 Nm
18–22 ft.lbs.

Disassembly steps

1. Pump cover
2. O-ring
3. Vanes
4. Rotor
5. Cam ring
6. Side plate
7. O-ring
8. Connector
9. O-ring
10. Flow control valve
11. Flow control spring
12. Terminal assembly
13. O-ring
14. Spring
15. Plunger
16. Piston rod
17. Snap ring
18. Terminal
19. Washer
20. Insulator
21. O-ring
22. Plug
23. Clip
24. Suction connector
25. O-ring
26. Oil pump body and Pulley assembly

Caution
Do not disassemble the flow control valve.

MT6029400036000X

Fig. 36 Exploded view of power steering pump. 1994–96 Diamante w/DOHC engine

pin in bump body when installing side plate.

c. Install rotor with punch mark at pump cover side.

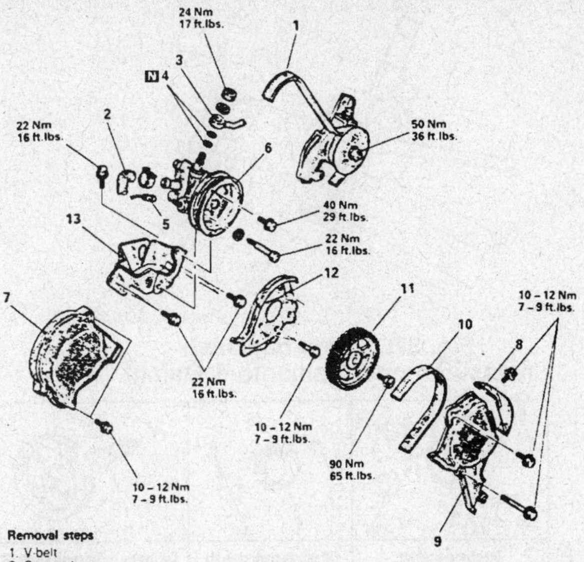
24 Nm
17 ft.lbs.
22 Nm
16 ft.lbs.
50 Nm
36 ft.lbs.
40 Nm
29 ft.lbs.
22 Nm
16 ft.lbs.
10 – 12 Nm
7 – 9 ft.lbs.
22 Nm
16 ft.lbs.
10 – 12 Nm
7 – 9 ft.lbs.
90 Nm
65 ft.lbs.
10 – 12 Nm
7 – 9 ft.lbs.

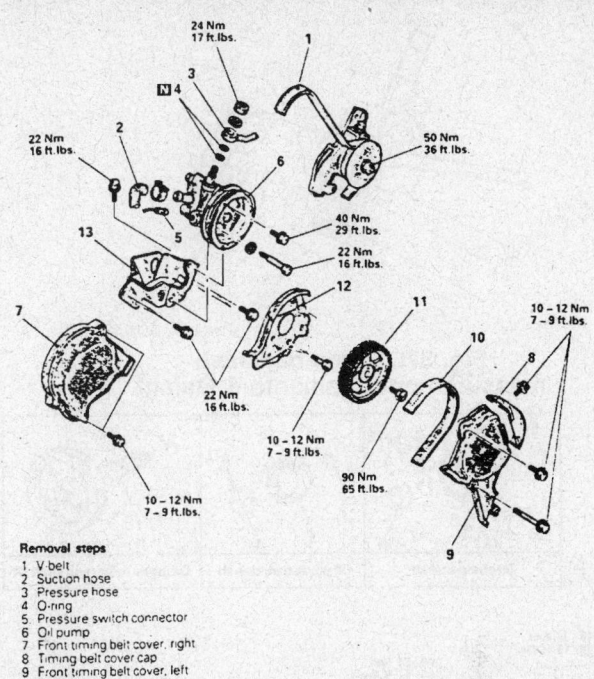

Removal steps

1. V-belt
2. Suction hose
3. Pressure hose
4. O-ring
5. Pressure switch connector
6. Oil pump
7. Front timing belt cover, right
8. Timing belt cover cap
9. Front timing belt cover, left
10. Timing belt
11. Camshaft sprocket
12. Rear timing belt cover, left
13. Oil pump bracket

MT6029100035000X

Fig. 35 Exploded view of power steering pump. Galant, 1993 Diamante & 1994–96 Diamante w/SOHC engine

d. Ensure rotor snap ring is properly installed.
e. Install cam ring with the punch mark facing the side plate.
f. Install vanes as shown in **Fig. 38.**

Pickup & Precis

1. Disassemble power steering pump in numbered sequence shown in **Fig. 42.**
2. Reverse numbered sequence shown in **Fig. 42** to assemble, noting the following:
   a. If flow control valve is to be replaced, match identification mark on housing with mark on valve.
   b. Install flow control spring, flow control valve and connector to pump body.
   c. Install rotor with the countersunk portion toward pump cover side.
   d. Ensure rotor snap ring is installed correctly.
   e. Install vanes in rotor as shown in **Fig. 38.**
   f. Align dowel pin with dowel pin holes when installing cam ring with punch mark at pump body side.

MT6029100037000X

Fig. 37 Pump backlash measurement. Diamante & Galant

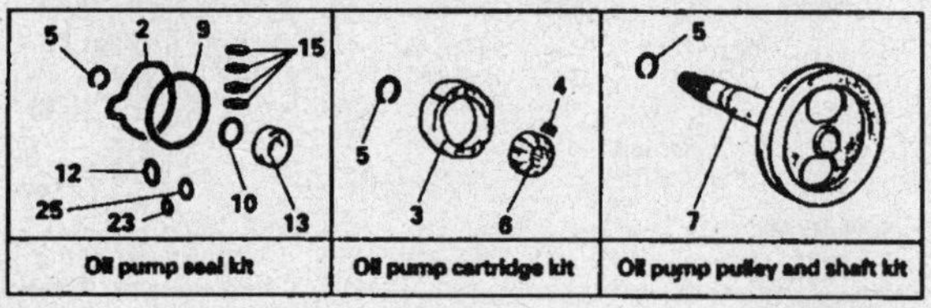
Oil pump seal kit
Oil pump cartridge kit
Oil pump pulley and shaft kit

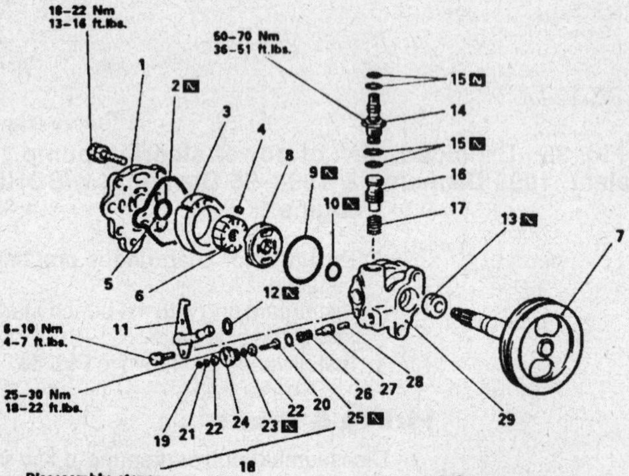
18–22 Nm
13–16 ft.lbs.
50–70 Nm
36–51 ft.lbs.
6–10 Nm
4–7 ft.lbs.
25–30 Nm
18–22 ft.lbs.

Disassembly steps

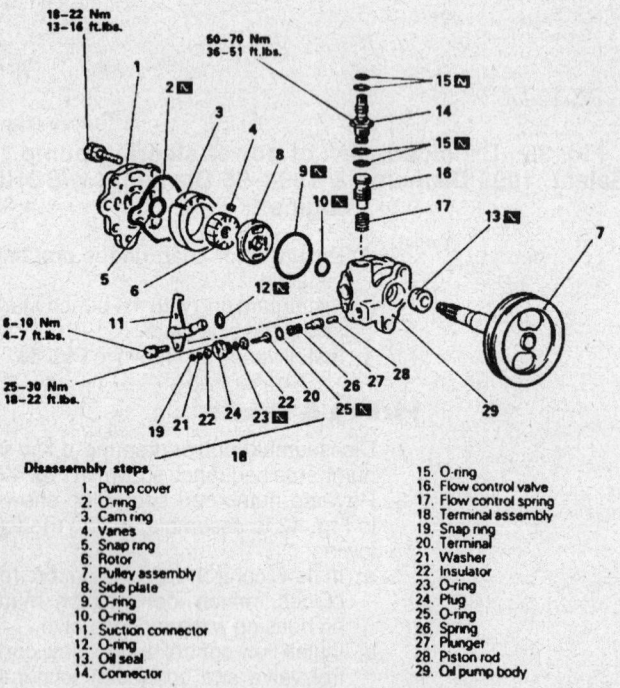

1. Pump cover
2. O-ring
3. Cam ring
4. Vanes
5. Snap ring
6. Rotor
7. Pulley assembly
8. Side plate
9. O-ring
10. O-ring
11. Suction connector
12. O-ring
13. Oil seal
14. Connector
15. O-ring
16. Flow control valve
17. Flow control spring
18. Terminal assembly
19. Snap ring
20. Terminal
21. Washer
22. Insulator
23. O-ring
24. Plug
25. O-ring
26. Spring
27. Plunger
28. Piston rod
29. Oil pump body

MT6029100039000X

Fig. 39 Exploded view of steering pump. Expo, Mirage, 3000GT, 1995–96 Eclipse w/2.0L turbocharged engine & 2.4L engine & 1993–94 Eclipse

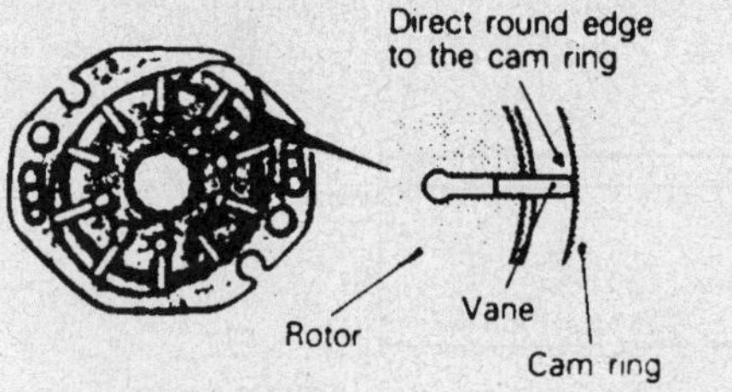
Direct round edge to the cam ring
Rotor
Vane
Cam ring

MT6029100038000X

Fig. 38 Rotor vane orientation

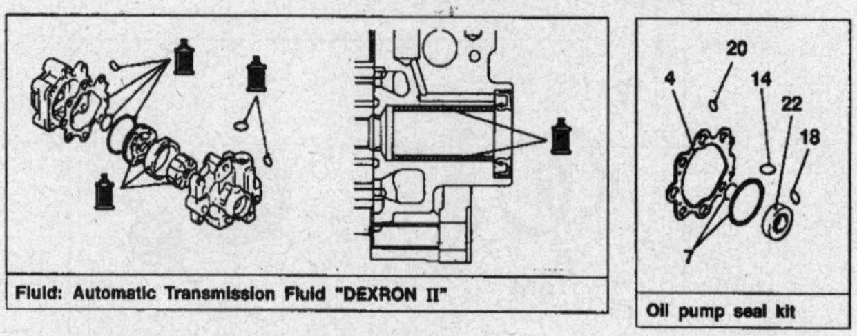
Fluid: Automatic Transmission Fluid "DEXRON II"
Oil pump seal kit

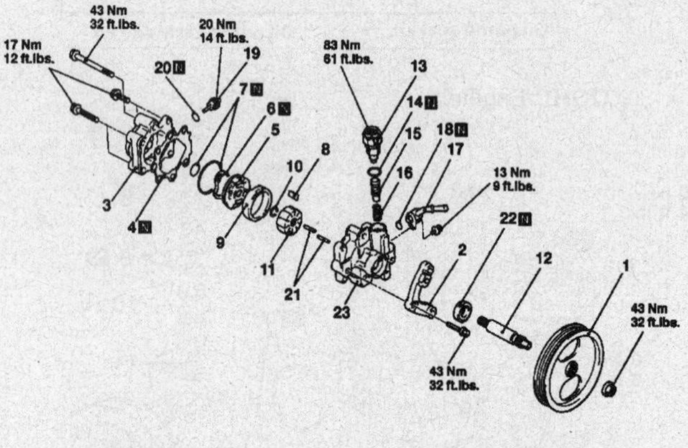
43 Nm
32 ft.lbs.
20 Nm
14 ft.lbs.
17 Nm
12 ft.lbs.
83 Nm
61 ft.lbs.
13 Nm
9 ft.lbs.
43 Nm
32 ft.lbs.
43 Nm
32 ft.lbs.

Disassembly steps

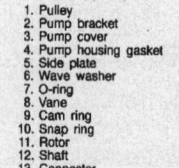

1. Pulley
2. Pump bracket
3. Pump cover
4. Pump housing gasket
5. Side plate
6. Wave washer
7. O-ring
8. Vane
9. Cam ring
10. Snap ring
11. Rotor
12. Shaft
13. Connector
14. O-ring
15. Flow control valve
16. Flow control spring
17. Suction connector
18. O-ring
19. Oil pressure switch
20. O-ring
21. Dowel pin
22. Oil seal
23. Oil pump body

Caution
Do not disassemble the flow control valve.

MT6029500051000X

Fig. 40 Exploded view of power steering pump. 1995–96 Eclipse w/2.0L non-turbocharged engine

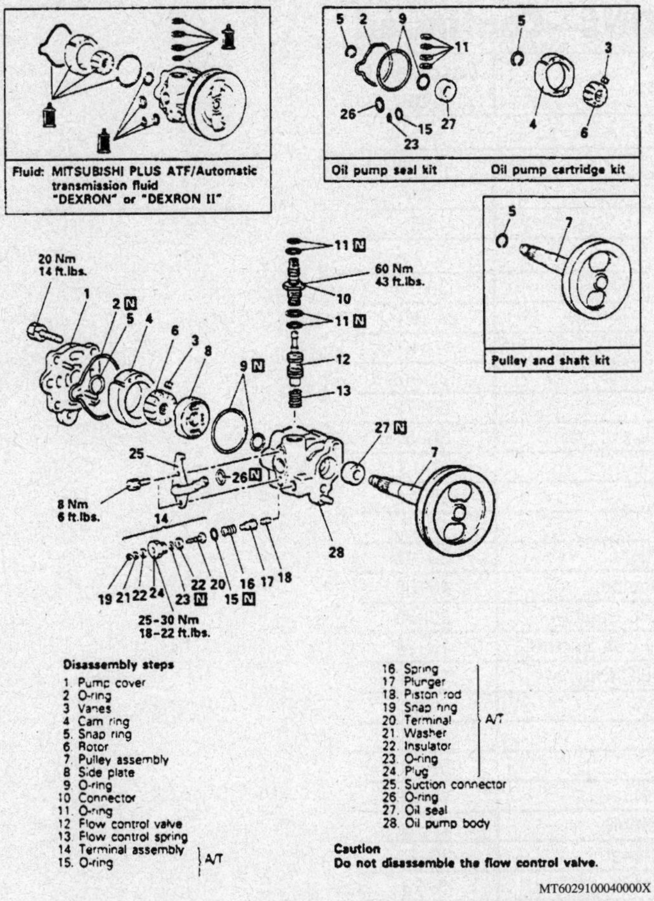
Fluid: MITSUBISHI PLUS ATF/Automatic transmission fluid "DEXRON" or "DEXRON II"
Oil pump seal kit
Oil pump cartridge kit
Pulley and shaft kit
20 Nm
14 ft.lbs.
60 Nm
43 ft.lbs.
8 Nm
6 ft.lbs.
25-30 Nm
18-22 ft.lbs.
Disassembly steps
1. Pump cover
2. O-ring
3. Vanes
4. Cam ring
5. Snap ring
6. Rotor
7. Pulley assembly
8. Side plate
9. O-ring
10. Connector
11. O-ring
12. Flow control valve
13. Flow control spring
14. Terminal assembly } A/T
15. O-ring
16. Spring
17. Plunger
18. Piston rod
19. Snap ring
20. Terminal } A/T
21. Washer
22. Insulator
23. O-ring
24. Plug
25. Suction connector
26. O-ring
27. Oil seal
28. Oil pump body
Caution
Do not disassemble the flow control valve.
MT6029100040000X

Fig. 41 Exploded view of power steering pump. Montero

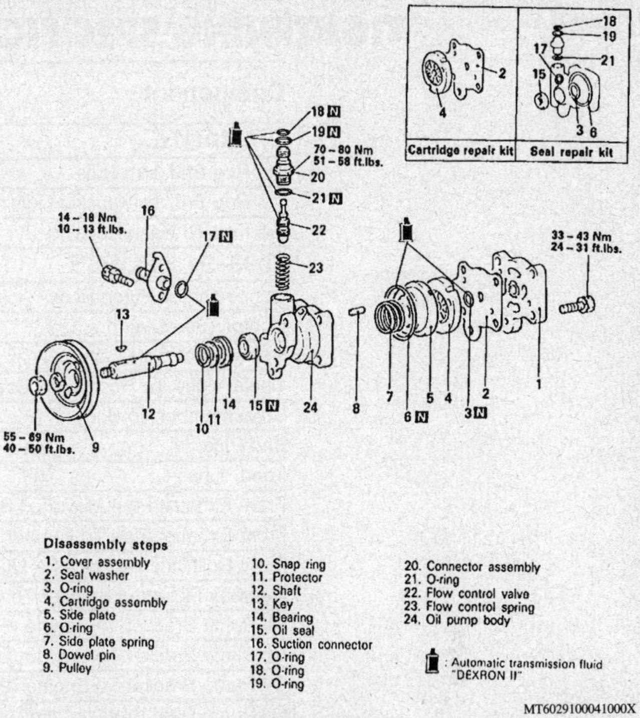
Cartridge repair kit
Seal repair kit
70 – 80 Nm
51 – 58 ft.lbs.
14 – 18 Nm
10 – 13 ft.lbs.
33 – 43 Nm
24 – 31 ft.lbs.
55 – 69 Nm
40 – 50 ft.lbs.
Disassembly steps
1. Cover assembly
2. Seal washer
3. O-ring
4. Cartridge assembly
5. Side plate
6. O-ring
7. Side plate spring
8. Dowel pin
9. Pulley
10. Snap ring
11. Protector
12. Shaft
13. Key
14. Bearing
15. Oil seal
16. Suction connector
17. O-ring
18. O-ring
19. O-ring
20. Connector assembly
21. O-ring
22. Flow control valve
23. Flow control spring
24. Oil pump body
: Automatic transmission fluid "DEXRON II"
MT6029100041000X

Fig. 42 Exploded view of power steering pump. Pickup

TIGHTENING SPECIFICATIONS

Component	Torque/Ft. Lbs.
DIAMANTE	
Control Valve Bolts	8
Crossmember Mounting Bolts	43–51
Flow Connector Fitting To Power Steering Pump Body	43
Hose Bracket Bolts	7
Joint Assembly Clamp Bolt	13
Oil Reservoir Mounting Bracket Mounting Bolts	8
Oil Reservoir To Mounting Bracket Bolts	8
PCV Assembly	13
Pinion & Valve Nut	18
Power Steering Gearbox Mounting Clamp Bolts	51
Power Steering Pump Bracket Bolts	16
Power Steering Pump Rear Cover Bolts	14
Power Steering Pump Terminal Fitting	18–22
Pressure Hose To Power Steering Pump Fitting	17
Pressure Tube To Pressure Hose Fitting	25
Rack Support Nut	43
Stabilizer Bar Bracket Bolts	29
Steering Shaft End Plug	43
Steering Shaft Flange To Gearbox Bolts	16
Suction Connector To Power Steering Pump Bolts	6

Continued

TIGHTENING SPECIFICATIONS—Continued

Component	Torque/Ft. Lbs.
DIAMANTE	
Tie Rod End Jam Nuts	36–39
Tie Rod End To Knuckle Nuts	21
Tie Rod To Rack Housing	65
1993–94 ECLIPSE	
Connector To Pump Body	36–51
Cooler Tube Clamp	24–36①
Cooler Tube To Body	7–10
Cooler Tube To Hood Lock Stay	29–43
Crossmember To Body	58–72
End Plug	36–51
Feed Tubes	9–13
Front Exhaust Pipe Mounting Bolt	22–29
Front Exhaust Pipe To Rubber Hanger	7–11
Front Roll Stopper Insulator Nut	36–47
Gearbox Mounting Bracket To Crossmember	43–58
Oil Pump Bracket To Engine (Front, 1.8L Engine)	20–30
Oil Pump Bracket To Engine (LH Side, 1.8L Engine)	18–24
Oil Pump Bracket To Engine (2.0L DOHC Engine)	18–24
Oil Pump Heat Protector Nut	7–10
Oil Reservoir Bracket Bolt	7–10
Oil Reservoir Bolt	7–10
Pinion & Valve Assembly Self Locking Nut	14–22
Power Steering Gearbox To Joint Assembly	11–14
Power Steering Oil Pump To Pump Bracket	25–33
Power Steering Pressure Hose To Gearbox	9–13
Power Steering Pressure Hose To Oil Pump	10–15
Power Steering Return Tube To Gearbox	9–13
Pressure Hose Bracket	7—10
Pressure Hose To Body	7–10
Pressure Hose To Oil Pump	10–15
Pressure Hose To Pressure Tube	22–29
Pressure Tube To Gearbox	9–13
Pump Cover To Pump Body	13–16
Rack Support Cover Locking Nut	36–51
Return Tube To Body	7–10
Return Tube To Gearbox	9–13
Stabilizer Bar Bracket	22–30
Stay To Crossmember	51–58
Steering Column Tube Clamp	48–60①
Steering Shaft Joint Assembly	11–14
Steering Wheel Column Support	6–9
Steering Wheel Locknut	25–33
Steering Wheel Shaft Lower Bracket	6–9
Steering Wheel Tilt Bracket Bolt	6–9
Suction Connector To Pump Body	48–84①
Terminal Assembly To Pump Body	18–22
Tie Rod End Locknut	36–40

Continued

TIGHTENING SPECIFICATIONS—Continued

Component	Torque/Ft. Lbs.
1993–94 ECLIPSE	
Tie Rod End To Knuckle	17–25
Tie Rod To Rack	58–72
Valve Housing Bolts	12–19
1995–96 ECLIPSE	
Center Member To Crossmember	58–65
Center Member To Support	51–58
Cooler Tube Bracket	34①
End Plug	44
End Plug Self-Locking Nut	18
Feed Tube Flare Nut	11
Gearbox Retaining Clamps	51
Oil Pump Adjusting Bolt③	29
Oil Pump Adjusting Bolt④	16
Oil Pump Bracket To Engine③	29
Oil Pump Bracket To Engine④	21
Oil Pump Cover③	②
Oil Pump Cover④	13
Oil Pump Flow Control Valve Connector③	61
Oil Pump Flow Control Valve Connector④	51–58
Oil Pump Pulley③	32
Oil Pump Pulley④	45
Pinion & Valve Assembly	16
Pipe Connections To Gearbox	11
Power Steering Hose Brackets	8
Power Steering Oil Pressure Switch	14
Pressure Hose To Oil Pump③	42
Pressure Hose To Oil Pump④	13
Rack Support Cover Locknut	44
Steering Shaft Joint To Gearbox	13
Suction Connector To Oil Pump③	9
Suction Connector To Oil Pump④	12
Tie Rod End Jam Nut	36–40
Tie Rod End To Knuckle	18–24
EXPO	
Flow Connector Fitting To Power Steering Pump Body	43
Hose Bracket Bolts	9
Joint Assembly Clamp Bolt	13
Oil Reservoir Mounting Bracket Mounting Bolts	9
Oil Reservoir To Mounting Bracket Bolts	9
Power Steering Gearbox Mounting Clamp Bolts	51
Power Steering Pump Adjustment Bolt	29
Power Steering Pump Bracket Mounting Bolts	29
Power Steering Pump Pivot Bolt	21
Power Steering Pump Rear Cover Bolts	14
Power Steering Pump Terminal Plug	18–22
Pressure Hose To Power Steering Pump Fitting	13
Stabilizer Bar Bracket Bolts	16
Steering Shaft End Plug	43
Steering Shaft Flange To Gearbox Bolts	16
Tie Rod End Jam Nut	38
Tie Rod End To Knuckle Ball Joint Nuts	21
Tie Rod To Rack Housing	65
1993 GALANT	
EPS Solenoid Valve	11–16
Flow Connector Fitting To Power Steering Pump Body	36–51

Continued

TIGHTENING SPECIFICATIONS—Continued

Component	Torque/Ft. Lbs.
1993 GALANT	
Four Wheel Steering Oil Line Fittings	22–29
Hose Bracket Bolts	7–10
Joint Assembly Clamp Bolt	11–14
Oil Reservoir Mounting Bracket Mounting Bolts	7–10
Oil Reservoir To Mounting Bracket Bolts	7–10
PCV Cap Assembly	11–16
Pinion & Valve Nut	14–22
Power Steering Gearbox Mounting Clamp Bolts	43–58
Power Steering Pump Bracket Bolts	25–33
Power Steering Pump Bracket Nut	7–10
Power Steering Pump Rear Cover Bolts	13–16
Power Steering Pump Terminal Plug	18–22
Pressure Hose To Power Steering Pump Nut	10–15
Pressure Tube Fitting	9–13
Pressure Tube To Pressure Hose Fitting	22–29
Rack Support Nut	36–51
Return Tube Fitting	9–13
Stabilizer Bar Bracket Bolts	22–30
Steering Shaft End Plug	36–51
Steering Shaft Flange To Gearbox Bolts	12–19
Suction Connector To Power Steering Pump Bolts	48–84①
Tie Rod End Jam Nuts	36–40
Tie Rod End To Knuckle Nuts	17–25
Tie Rod To Rack Housing	58–72
1994–96 GALANT	
Center Member To Crossmember	58–65
Center Member To Support	51–58
End Plug	44
End Plug Self-Locking Nut	18
Feed Tube Flare Nut	11
Flow Control Valve Connector	51–58
Gearbox Retaining Clamps	51
Oil Pump Adjusting Bolt	16
Oil Pump Bracket To Engine	21
Oil Pump Cover	13
Oil Pump Pivots	21
Oil Pump Pressure Hose	13
Oil Pump Pulley	45
Pinion & Valve Assembly	16
Pipe Connections To Gearbox	11
Pipe Connections To Hoses	25
Power Steering Hose Brackets	9
Power Steering Oil Pressure Switch	15
Rack Support Locknut	44
Suction Connector To Oil Pump	12
Steering Shaft Joint To Gearbox	13
Tie Rod End To Knuckle	18–24
Tie Rod End Jam Nut	36–40
Tie Rod To Rack	65
MIRAGE	
End Plug	43
End Plug Self-Locking Nut	18
Feed Tube Flare Nut	9
Flow Control Valve Connector	43
Gearbox Retaining Clamps	51

Continued

TIGHTENING SPECIFICATIONS—Continued

Component	Torque/Ft. Lbs.
MIRAGE	
Oil Pump Adjusting Bolt	29
Oil Pump Bracket To Engine⑤	16
Oil Pump Bracket To Engine⑥	29
Oil Pump Cover	14
Oil Pump Pivot	17
Oil Pump To Oil Pump Bracket	29
Oil Reservoir	48①
Power Steering Hose Brackets	9
Pressure Pipe To Gearbox	11
Pressure Pipe To Oil Pump	13
Rack Support Cover Locking Nut	43
Return Pipe To Gearbox	11
Steering Shaft Grommet	48①
Steering Shaft Joint To Gearbox	13
Suction Connector To Oil Pump	6
Terminal Assembly To Oil Pump	18–22
Tie Rod End Jam Nut	30
Tie Rod End To Knuckle	11–25
Tie Rod To Rack	65
Valve Housing	16
MONTERO	
Flow Connector Fitting To Power Steering Pump Body	43
Hose Bracket Bolts	9
Idler Arm Support Mounting Nuts	40–47
Idler Arm To Support Nut	101
Joint Assembly Clamp Bolt	22–25
Oil Reservoir Mounting Nuts	9
Outer Tie Rod End To Inner Tie Rod End Jam Nuts	53
Pitman Arm To Power Steering Gearbox Nut	108–123
Power Steering Gearbox Adjusting Bolt Locknut	27
Power Steering Gearbox Mounting Nuts	40–47
Power Steering Gearbox Side Cover Bolts	36
Power Steering Pump Bracket Mounting Bolts	29
Power Steering Pump Rear Cover Bolts	14
Power Steering Pump Terminal Plug	18–22
Pressure Hose Fitting At Gearbox	11
Pressure Hose Fitting At Pump	14
Pressure Pipe To Pressure Hose Fitting	25
Relay Rod To Idler Arm Ball Joint Nut	33
Relay Rod To Inner Tie Rod End Ball Joint Nut	33
Relay Rod To Pitman Arm Nut	33
Return Hose Fitting	11
Suction Connector To Power Steering Pump Body Bolts	6
PICKUP	
Breather Pipe To Engine	6–9
Breather Plug	24–48①
Column Shaft Assembly To Steering Gearbox (2WD)	11–14
Column Tube Clamp Bolt	36–48①
Dash Panel Cover	24–48①
Idler Arm Support To Frame	25–29
Idler Arm To Idler Arm Support	29–43
Joint Assembly To Steering Gearbox (4WD)	22–25
Locknut Less Special Tool	130–166
Locknut w/Special Tool	98–127

Continued

TIGHTENING SPECIFICATIONS—Continued

Component	Torque/Ft. Lbs.
PICKUP	
Oil Pump Body To Oil Pump Bracket (2WD)	18–24
Oil Pump Body To Oil Pump Bracket (4WD)	25–33
Oil Pump Bracket (RH Front, 2WD)	12–19
Oil Pump Bracket (RH Front, 4WD)	18–24
Oil Pump Bracket (RH Rear)	12–19
Oil Pump Bracket To Engine (Front)	18–24
Oil Pump Connector Assembly	51–58
Oil Pump Cover (2WD w/2.0L Engine)	13–16
Oil Pump To Pressure Hose	12–19
Oil Pump Reservoir Assembly	7–10
Oil Pump Suction Connector (2WD w/2.0L Engine)	48–84①
Pitman Arm	94–108
Pitman Arm To Relay Rod	33
Power Gearbox	40–47
Power Steering Adjusting Bolt Locknut	22–33
Power Steering Gearbox Side Cover	22–33
Power Steering Gearbox To Pressure Hose	9–13
Power Steering Gearbox To Return Hose	9–13
Power Steering Valve Housing	33–40
Pressure Hose Clip	7–10
Pressure Hose Gearbox Side	9–14
Pressure Hose To Oil Pump Side	12–19
Pressure Tube Flare Nut (2WD)	9–14
Relay Arm To Idler Arm	33
Relay Rod To Pitman Arm	33
Return Hose Clip	7–10
Return Hose Or Tube	9–14
Socket Assembly To Yoke (2WD)	14–18
Steering Wheel Locknut	25–33
Tie Rod End To Knuckle	33
Tie Rod End To Pipe (2WD)	36–40
Tie Rod End To Pipe (4WD)	47–58
Tie Rod End To Relay Rod	33
Tilt Bracket Bolts	6–9
Tube Clip (4WD)	7–10
Tube Stay	7–10
PRECIS	
Dust Cover Mounting Bolt	36–48①
End Plug	36–51
Feed Tube	9–13
Gearbox Mounting Clamp	43–58
Oil Cooler Tube Mounting Clip	6–9
Oil Pump Adjust Bolt	18–24
Oil Pump Bracket Mounting Bolt	14–20
Oil Pump Reservoir Mounting Bolt	6–9
Pinion Gear And Joint	11–14
Rack Support Cover	5–9
Rack Support Cover Locking Nut	36–51
Self Locking Nut	14–22
Steering Column & Shaft Assembly Mounting Bracket	9–13
Steering Hose Clamp	24–48①
Steering Pressure Hose Clip	6–9
Steering Pressure Hose Mounting Nut To Oil Pump	12–17
Steering Pressure Hose To Gearbox	9–13

Continued

TIGHTENING SPECIFICATIONS—Continued

Component	Torque/Ft. Lbs.
PRECIS	
Steering Return Hose Mounting Clamp To Oil Pump Suction Connector	24–48①
Steering Shaft & Joint	11–14
Steering Wheel & Shaft	25–33
Tie Rod End Locknut	36–40
Tie Rod End Ball Joint Slotted Nut	11–25
Tie Rod To Rack	56–72
Valve Body Housing To Rack Housing Assembly	14–22
3000GT	
Cooler Tube Clamps	48①
Gearbox Assembly Clamps	51
Joint Assembly & Gearbox Connecting Bolt	13
LH Member Installation Bolts	43–51
Oil Pump Bracket Lower Bolt	31
Oil Pump Bracket Upper Bolt	16
Oil Pump To Bracket Lower Bolt	31
Oil Pump To Bracket Upper Nut	31
Oil Reservoir Mounting Bolts	8
Pressure Hose To Oil Pump	17
Pressure Tube To Pressure Hose Connector	25
Return Hose To Cooler Tube Clamps	8
RH Member Installation Bolts	43–51
Stabilizer Bar Bracket	29
Steering Column Support Assembly	8
Steering Column To Joint Assembly	13
Steering Gearbox Clamp	51
Steering Wheel Locknut	29
Tie Rod End & Knuckle Connecting Nut	36
Tubing Clamp	48①
Tubing Connectors To Gearbox	11
Tubing Hold-Down Clamp	8

① — Inch lbs.

② — Long bolt, 32 ft. lbs.; short bolts, 12 ft. lbs.

③ — 2.0L non-turbocharged engine.

④ — 2.0L turbocharged engine & 2.4L engine.

⑤ — 1.5L engine.

⑥ — 1.8L engine.

Four Wheel Steering

NOTE: On Air Bag Equipped Models, Refer To "Air Bag System Precautions" Located In The Front Of This Manual For System Disarming & Arming Procedures.

NOTE: For Procedures Not Found In This Section, Refer To The "Power Steering" Section.

INDEX

	Page No.
Description	29-116
Diagnosis & Testing	29-116
Functional Inspection	29-116
Rear Oil Pump Discharge Flow Volume Inspection	29-116
Power Steering Pressure Specifications	29-116
Precautions	29-116
Air Bag Systems	29-116
System Service	29-116
4WS System Bleed	29-116
Rear Power Cylinder (Steering Gear) Service	29-117
Rear Power Steering Pump Service	29-117
Tightening Specifications	29-118
Troubleshooting	29-116

POWER STEERING PRESSURE SPECIFICATIONS

Model	Disp., Qts. @ mph	Relief Set Pressure, psi
Diamante	1.06 @ 31	569
3000GT	1.06 @ 31	569

PRECAUTIONS

AIR BAG SYSTEMS

Refer to "Air Bag System Precautions" in the front of this manual for system disarming and arming procedures.

DESCRIPTION

The Four Wheel Steering (4WS) system is designed to improve handling under a variety of conditions by adding steering control to the vehicle's rear wheels. A conventional steering gear is utilized to control front wheel steering; the addition of a vane type rear oil pump and hydraulic double action power cylinder allows full four wheel steering control. The power cylinder acts as a rear wheel steering gear.

TROUBLESHOOTING

Refer to **Fig. 1** when troubleshooting the Four Wheel Steering (4WS) system.

Malfunction symptom	Malfunctioning system	Inspection item
4WS does not operate	Power cylinder	Tie rod swing torque
		Power cylinder slide resistance
	Rear oil pump	Flow volume check
	Control valve	
Poor steering feeling Feeling of friction in steering Poor steering return	Steering gears and linkage	Rack cracks or deformation
Steering wheel efforts excessive	Control valve	Oil leakage from control valve joint
	Power cylinder	Oil leakage from piston rod
	Oil line	Pressure hose breakage
	Oil reservoir	Oil reservoir deformation or oil leakage
Rear wheels cannot be steered Poor rear wheels return Hydraulic pressure for rear wheel is constantly high	Control valve	Stuck control valve spool
	Power cylinder	Stuck power cylinder
	Rear oil pump	Relief valve remains open
Long rear wheel steering delay Poor steering response Poor steering return	Power cylinder	Excessive power cylinder friction
		Looseness in power cylinder tie rod ball joint
		Ball joint dust cover cracks
Poor rear wheel steering response Poor rear wheel steering range	Control valve	Oil leakage from control valve spool
	Power cylinder	Oil leakage from power cylinder
	Rear oil pump	Extreme oil pump internal wear
Poor steerability (extreme tire wear)	Power cylinder	Tie rod length improperly adjusted after toe-in adjustment

MT6029100042000X

Fig. 1 4WS system troubleshooting chart

DIAGNOSIS & TESTING

FUNCTIONAL INSPECTION

1. Raise and support vehicle.
2. Start engine, place transaxle in Drive range and raise indicated vehicle speed to 50 mph. **Ensure vehicle is properly supported and secured for this step. Use extreme caution when working around moving wheels.**
3. Quickly turn steering wheel from stop to stop, ensuring rear wheels steer in same direction as front wheels.

REAR OIL PUMP DISCHARGE FLOW VOLUME INSPECTION

1. Disconnect pressure hose from rear oil pump and install power steering oil pressure gauge adapter tool No. MB990993-01, or equivalent, **Fig. 2.**
2. Connect a suitable rubber hose to tool and place other end into a two quart graduated container.
3. Raise and support vehicle.
4. Start engine and place transaxle in Drive position, then slowly raise indicated vehicle speed to 31 mph and hold, measuring discharge flow volume for 30 seconds, **Fig. 3. Ensure vehicle is properly supported and secured for this step. Use extreme caution when working around moving wheels.**
5. If the discharge flow volume is not as specified in "Power Steering Pressure Specifications" chart, rear oil pump should be replaced.

SYSTEM SERVICE

4WS SYSTEM BLEED

1. Bleed air from power steering system as outlined in the "Power Steering" section.
2. Raise and support vehicle just off ground.
3. Start engine and allow to idle.
4. Loosen bleeder screw on left side of

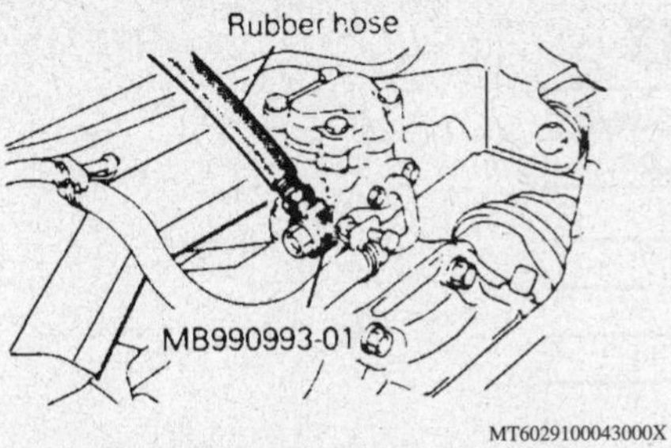
Rubber hose
MB990993-01
MT6029100043000X

Fig. 2 Adapter tool connection

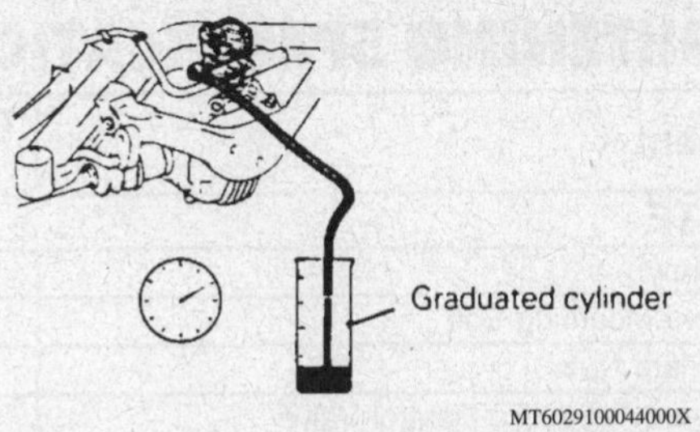
Graduated cylinder
MT6029100044000X

Fig. 3 Flow volume measurement

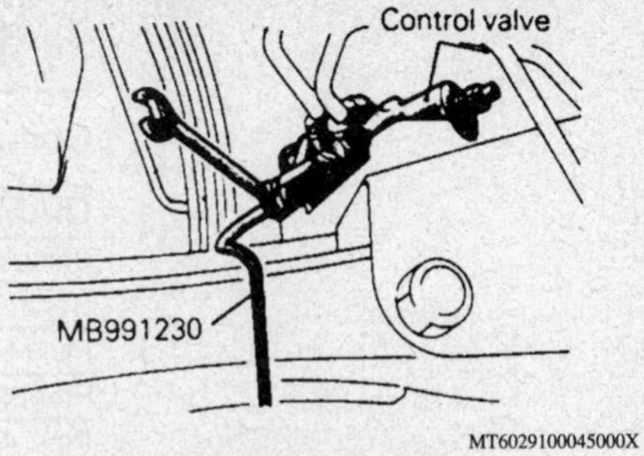
Control valve
MB991230
MT6029100045000X

Fig. 4 4WS system bleed

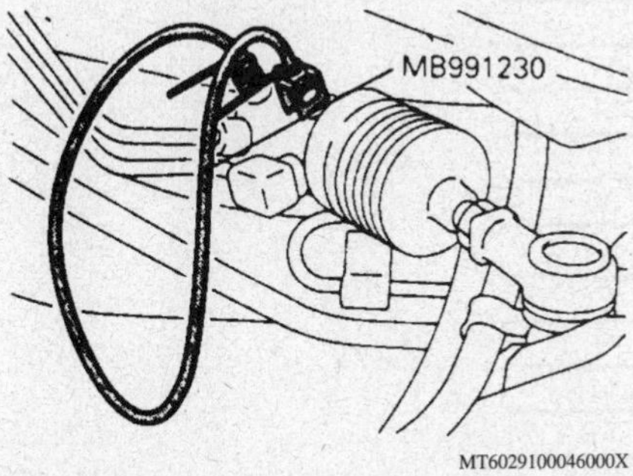
MB991230
MT6029100046000X

Fig. 5 Rear power cylinder bleed

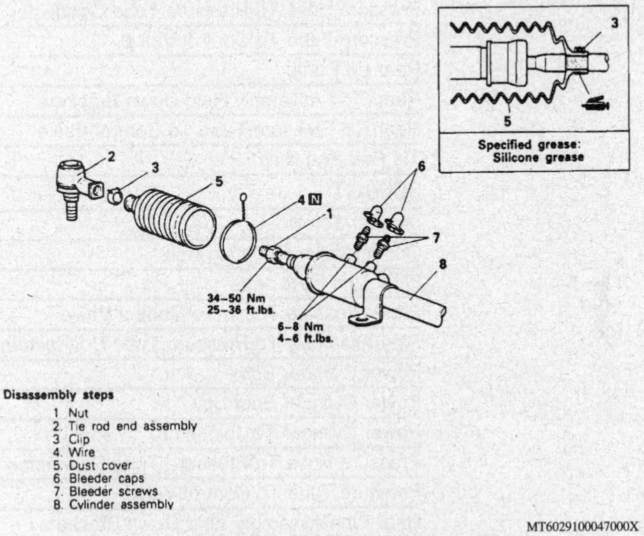
Specified grease:
Silicone grease
34–50 Nm
25–36 ft.lbs.
6–8 Nm
4–6 ft.lbs.
Disassembly steps
1. Nut
2. Tie rod end assembly
3. Clip
4. Wire
5. Dust cover
6. Bleeder caps
7. Bleeder screws
8. Cylinder assembly
MT6029100047000X

Fig. 6 Rear power cylinder service

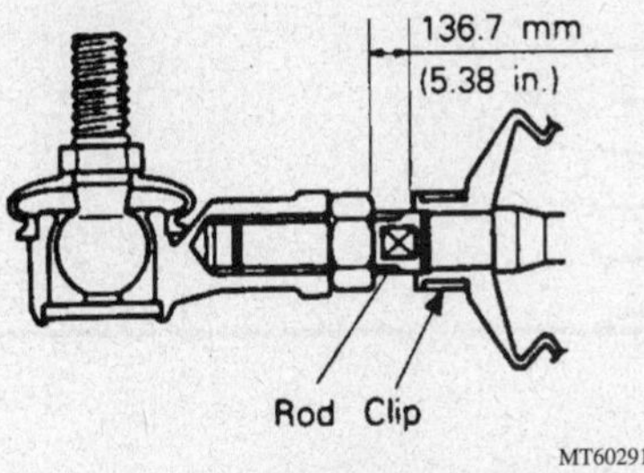
136.7 mm
(5.38 in.)
Rod
Clip
MT6029100048000X

Fig. 7 Tie rod installation. Diamante

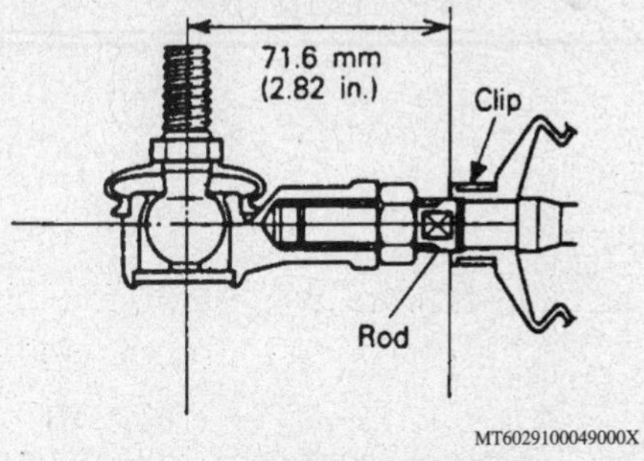
71.6 mm
(2.82 in.)
Clip
Rod
MT6029100049000X

Fig. 8 Tie rod installation. 3000GT

control valve and install air bleeder set tool No. MB991230, or equivalent, on bleeder screw, **Fig. 4.**

5. Turn steering wheel to left stop, then immediately return it to center position. Air will be discharged with fluid. **Ensure reservoir is kept filled.**
6. Repeat preceding step two or three times until all air is bled from system.
7. Repeat preceding bleed steps using right side bleeder screw.
8. Turn ignition switch to Off position.
9. Install air bleeder tool on rear power cylinder, **Fig. 5.**
10. Start engine, place transaxle in Drive position and raise indicated vehicle speed to 43–50 mph to circulate fluid. **Ensure vehicle is properly supported and secured for this step. Use extreme caution when working around moving wheels.**
11. Reduce indicated vehicle speed to 19–25 mph, turn steering wheel from stop to stop. Air will be bleed into reservoir at this time. When steering wheel is at each stop air will circulate inside special hose.
12. Repeat preceding step several times until no more air is seen in reservoir.

REAR POWER CYLINDER (STEERING GEAR) SERVICE

Service rear power cylinder (steering gear) in numbered sequence shown in **Fig. 6,** positioning tie rod end as shown in **Figs. 7 and 8.**

REAR POWER STEERING PUMP SERVICE

The rear power steering pump is not serviceable and must be replaced if inoperative.

TIGHTENING SPECIFICATIONS

Component	Torque/Ft. Lbs.
DIAMANTE	
Bleeder Screw	7
Control Valve Mounting Bolt	8
Fluid Line Flare Nuts	11
Front Pressure Tubes To Control Valve	11
Pipe Assembly To Pressure Tube Connectors	25
Power Cylinder Bolt	30
Pressure Hose To Pressure Tube Connector	11
Pressure Tube To Control Valve	11
Rear Oil Pump	17
Rear Pipe Assembly Hold-Down Brackets	9
Rear RH Pressure Tube To Control Valve	11
Tie Rod End Nuts	30
3000GT	
Bleeder Screw	7
Control Valve Mounting Bolt	9
Fluid Line Flare Nuts	11
Front Pressure Tubes To Control Valve	11
Pipe Assembly To Pressure Tube Connectors	25
Power Cylinder Bolt	30
Power Cylinder Boot Bolt	30
Power Cylinder To Joint Nut	30
Pressure Hose To Pressure Tube Connector	25
Pressure Tube To Control Valve	25
Rear Pipe Assembly Hold Down Brackets	9
Rear RH Pressure Tube To Control Valve	11
Tie Rod End Nuts	42

Disc Brakes

TABLE OF CONTENTS

	Page No.		Page No.
DIAMANTE & 3000GT	29-131	MONTERO & PICKUP	29-136
ECLIPSE, EXPO & GALANT	29-123	PRECIS	29-140
MIRAGE	29-119		

Mirage

INDEX

	Page No.		Page No.		Page No.
Adjustments	29-122	**Caliper Service**	29-120	Rotor Specifications	29-122
Parking Brake	29-122	Overhaul & Inspection	29-120	**Rotor, Replace**	29-121
Application Chart	29-119	Replacement	29-120	Front	29-121
Brake Pad Service	29-119	**Disc Brake Specifications**	29-122	Rear............................	29-122
Replacement	29-119	Caliper Specifications	29-122	**Tightening Specifications**	29-123
Brake System Bleed	29-119				

APPLICATION CHART

Year	Model	Caliper No.
FRONT		
1993–94	2 Door	MR31S
	4 Door	MR34V
1995–96	2 Door 1.5L	MR31S
	2 Door 1.8L	MR34V
	4 Door	MR34V
REAR		
1993–96	All	AD30P

BRAKE SYSTEM BLEED

The hydraulic brake system must be bled if air has entered the system. This could be caused by an open in the system, or replacement of a hydraulic system component. Symptoms include loss of brake operation, and a low or spongy brake pedal.

On models with ABS, use a suitable filter when adding fluid to reservoir tank.

1. Ensure master cylinder reservoir is full. Add suitable brake fluid as needed, and securely reinstall the master cylinder cap.
2. Raise and support vehicle.
3. Position a drain pan under the wheel being bled.
4. Have an assistant depress the brake pedal with a slow even pressure and hold it. **Do not press brake pedal to the end of the master cylinder stroke. This may cause damage to the master cylinder.**
5. Using a suitable wrench, open the bleeder valve one full turn. Watch for air bubbles in the fluid, and listen for air escaping from the system.
6. With the brake pedal still depressed, close the bleeder valve.
7. Have the assistant pump the brake pedal several times. **Pressing brake pedal to the end of the master cylinder stroke, this may cause damage to the master cylinder.**
8. Repeat preceding bleed steps until all air is removed from the hydraulic system. **While bleeding the system, recheck brake fluid supply in the master cylinder often. Do not allow the master cylinder to run dry.**
9. After system bleed, proceed as follows:
   a. Ensure the master cylinder reservoir is full. Add suitable brake fluid as needed.
   b. Lower the vehicle and ensure brake pedal is firm and braking operation is satisfactory.

BRAKE PAD SERVICE

REPLACEMENT

Front

1. Raise and support vehicle then remove wheel.
2. Remove guide/slide pins, **Figs. 1 and 2.**
3. Lift caliper assembly and support to frame suing suitable wire. **Guide pin is coated with special grease. Be careful not to remove grease and ensure no dirt adheres to pin.**
4. Remove inner & outer shims, anti-squeak shims and pad assembly.
5. Measure hub torque with pad removed to measure brake drag after pad installation, **Fig. 3.**
6. Securely attach pad clip to caliper support.
7. Press piston into cylinder. **Ensure piston boot does not become caught during installation.**
8. Lower caliper body and install lower guide pin, tightening to specification.
9. Check brake drag as follows:
   a. Start engine and hold brake pedal down for five seconds.
   b. Stop engine.
   c. Turn brake disc forward ten times.
   d. Check brake drag. If the difference between brake drag and hub torque measured in this procedure exceeds 4.4 lbs., disassemble piston and clean. Check piston and caliper for corrosion or worn parts.

Rear

1. Raise and support vehicle and remove wheel.
2. Loosen parking brake cable from inside vehicle then disconnect parking

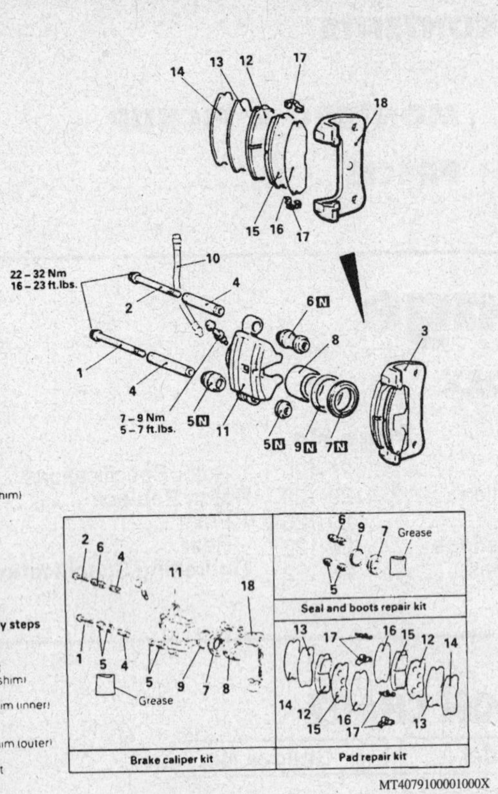
22 - 32 Nm
16 - 23 ft.lbs.
7 - 9 Nm
5 - 7 ft.lbs.
Grease
Seal and boots repair kit
Brake caliper kit
Pad repair kit
MT4079100001000X

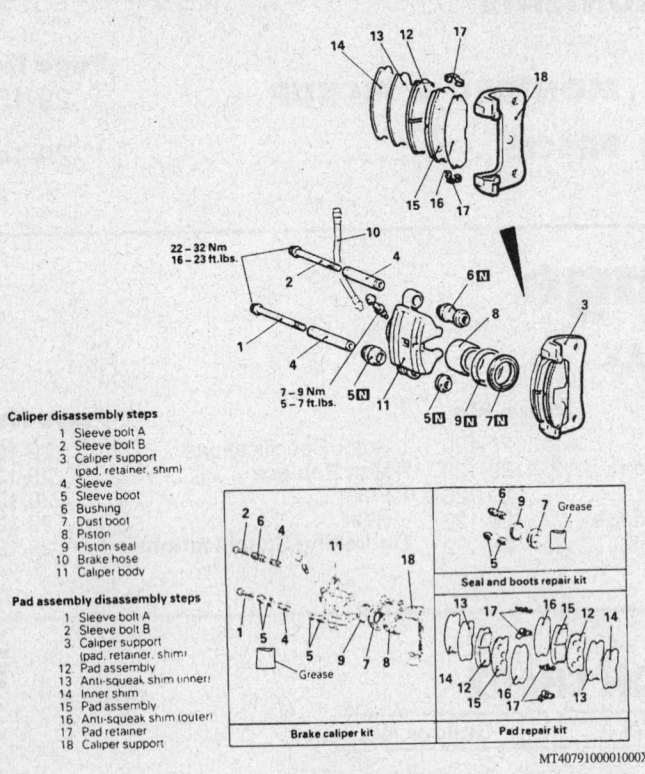

Caliper disassembly steps

1. Sleeve bolt A
2. Sleeve bolt B
3. Caliper support (pad, retainer, shim)
4. Sleeve
5. Sleeve boot
6. Bushing
7. Dust boot
8. Piston
9. Piston seal
10. Brake hose
11. Caliper body

Pad assembly disassembly steps

1. Sleeve bolt A
2. Sleeve bolt B
3. Caliper support (pad, retainer, shim)
12. Pad assembly
13. Anti-squeak shim (inner)
14. Inner shim
15. Pad assembly
16. Anti-squeak shim (outer)
17. Pad retainer
18. Caliper support

Fig. 1 Exploded view of front disc brake assembly. MR31S

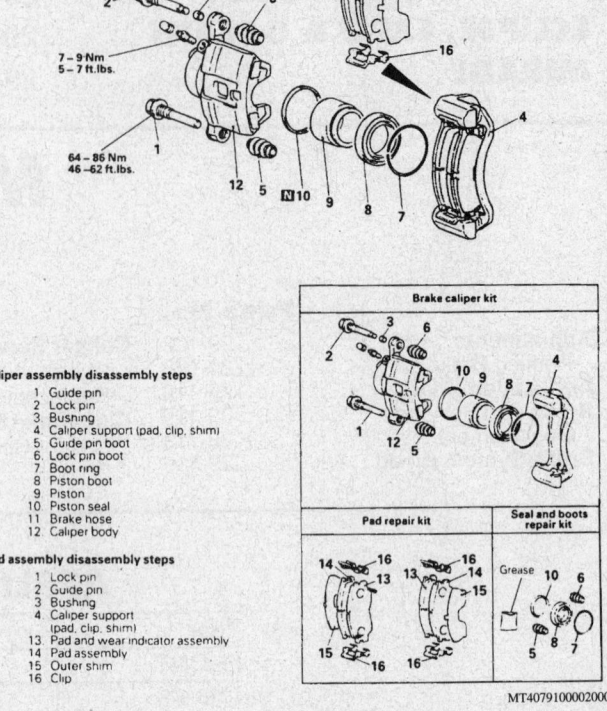

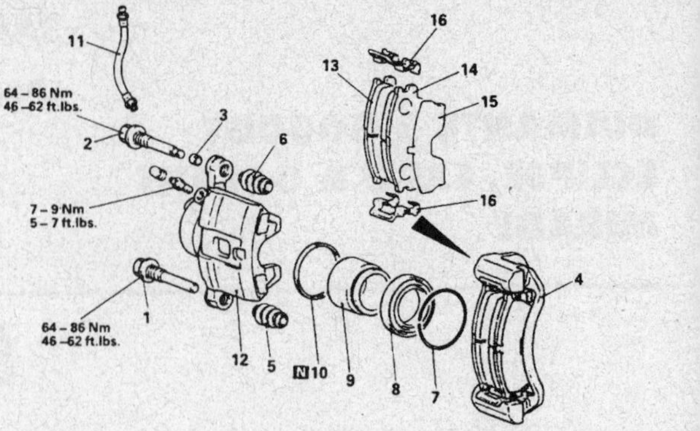
64 - 86 Nm
46 - 62 ft.lbs.
7 - 9 Nm
5 - 7 ft.lbs.
64 - 86 Nm
46 - 62 ft.lbs.

Caliper assembly disassembly steps

1. Guide pin
2. Lock pin
3. Bushing
4. Caliper support (pad, clip, shim)
5. Guide pin boot
6. Lock pin boot
7. Boot ring
8. Piston boot
9. Piston
10. Piston seal
11. Brake hose
12. Caliper body

Pad assembly disassembly steps

1. Lock pin
2. Guide pin
3. Bushing
4. Caliper support (pad, clip, shim)
13. Pad and wear indicator assembly
14. Pad assembly
15. Outer shim
16. Clip

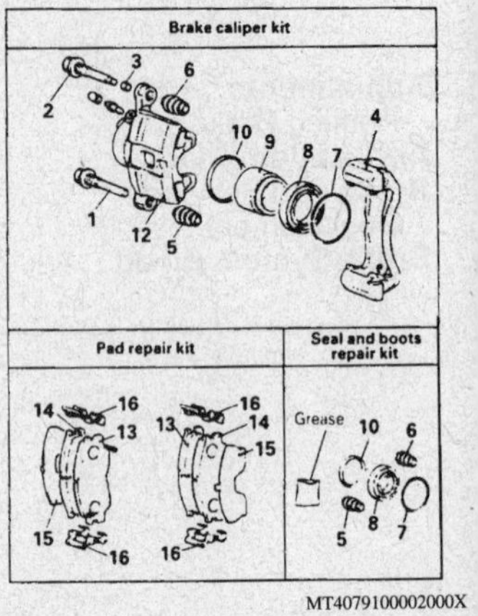
Brake caliper kit
Pad repair kit
Seal and boots repair kit
Grease
MT4079100002000X

Fig. 2 Exploded view of front disc brake assembly. MR34V

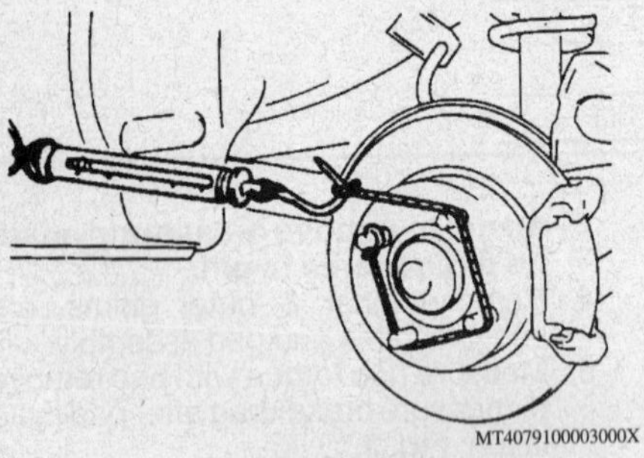
MT4079100003000X

Fig. 3 Measuring hub & brake drag torque

brake cable end on rear brake assembly.

3. Remove lower lockpin, **Fig. 4.**
4. Lift caliper assembly and secure to frame using suitable wire.
5. Remove outer shim and pad assembly.
6. Remove pad clips "C" and "B."
7. Measure hub torque with pad removed to be able to measure brake drag torque after installation, **Fig. 3.**
8. Attach pad clip to caliper support.
9. Clean piston surface then use rear disc brake piston driver tool No. MB990652, or equivalent, to thread piston into cylinder. **Ensure the stopper grove of piston correctly fits to projection on pads rear surface.**
10. Install pads and shims onto caliper assembly.
11. Lower caliper assembly and install lockpin. **Ensure piston boot does not become caught when lowering the caliper into place.**
12. Check brake drag torque as follows:
    a. Start engine and hold brake pedal down for five seconds.
    b. Stop engine and turn disc rotor froward ten times.
    c. If difference between brake drag torque and hub torque exceeds 4.4 lbs., disassemble piston and clean piston. Check for corrosion, wear or damaged on brake caliper components.

CALIPER SERVICE

REPLACEMENT

Front

1. Raise and support vehicle, then remove wheel.
2. Disconnect and cap brake hose.
3. Remove sleeve bolts, sleeves, boot pins and bushings, then the caliper body from torque member.
4. Reverse procedure to install, noting the following:
    a. Replace bushing and pin boot.
    b. Tighten sleeve bolts to specifications.
    c. Bleed brake system as outlined in "Brake System Bleed."

Rear

1. Raise and support vehicle, then remove wheel.
2. Disconnect and cap brake hose.
3. Disconnect parking brake cable.
4. Remove upper and lower guide pin then the caliper assembly.
5. Reverse procedure to install, noting the following:
    a. Replace bushing and pin boot.
    b. Tighten sleeve bolts to specifications.
    c. Bleed brake system as outlined in "Brake System Bleed."

OVERHAUL & INSPECTION

Front

1. Place rag in front of piston, then remove piston and dust boot by applying compressed air through brake hose fitting hole. **Keep fingers clear of front of piston.**
2. Remove piston seal. Use caution not to scratch the cylinder walls.
3. Check cylinder and piston for wear, damage and/or corrosion. Repair or replace as required.
4. Check caliper body and sleeve for wear. Replace as required.
5. Apply suitable brake fluid to the cylinder walls.
6. Apply an even coat of suitable grease to the new piston seal, then install seal in cylinder.
7. Install piston into cylinder. Use caution not to twist piston seal.
8. Apply suitable grease to dust boot, then install boot on piston and cylinder.

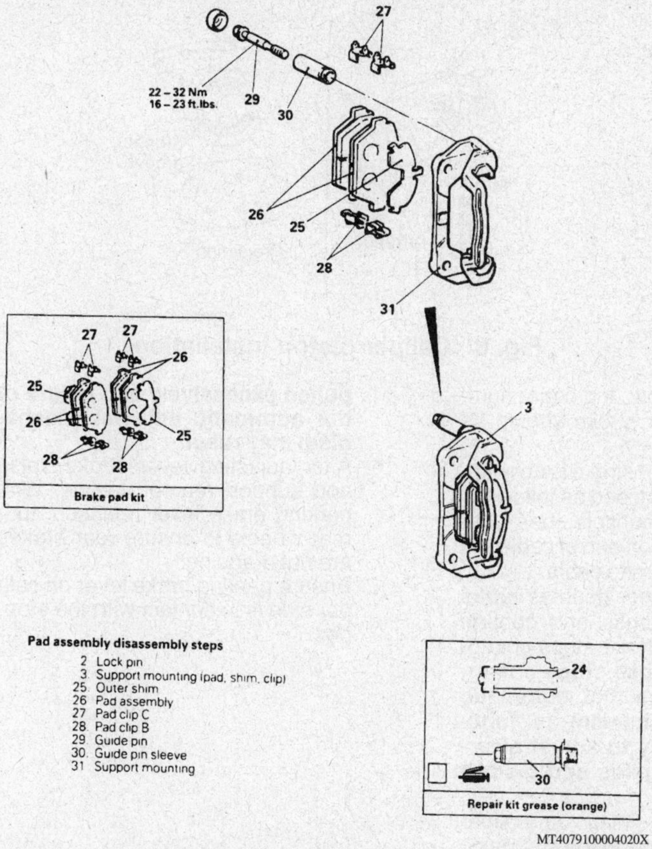
22 – 32 Nm
16 – 23 ft.lbs.
Brake pad kit
Repair kit grease (orange)
Pad assembly disassembly steps
2. Lock pin
3. Support mounting (pad, shim, clip)
25. Outer shim
26. Pad assembly
27. Pad clip C
28. Pad clip B
29. Guide pin
30. Guide pin sleeve
31. Support mounting
MT4079100004020X

Fig. 4 Exploded view of rear disc brake assembly (Part 2 of 2)

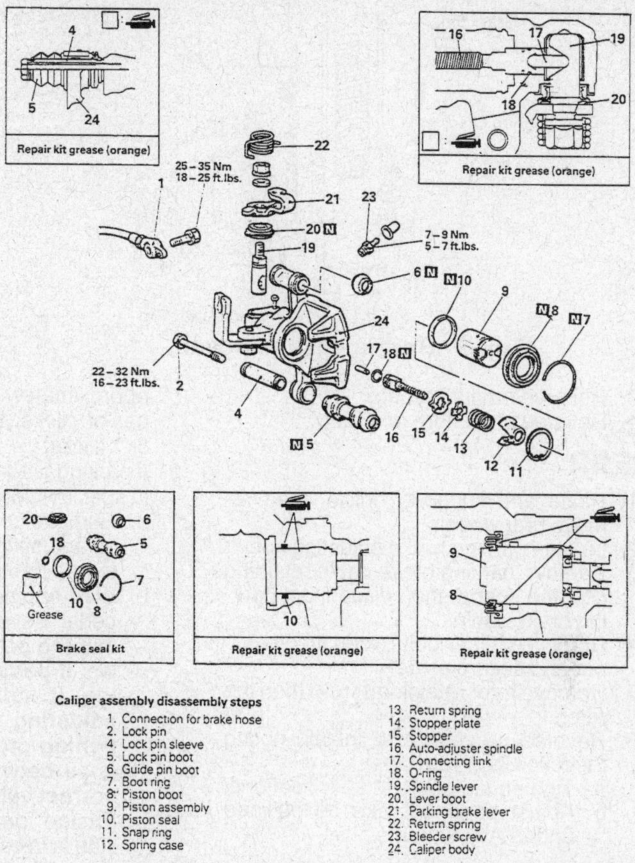
Repair kit grease (orange)
25 – 35 Nm
18 – 25 ft.lbs.
7 – 9 Nm
5 – 7 ft.lbs.
22 – 32 Nm
16 – 23 ft.lbs.
Brake seal kit
Grease
Caliper assembly disassembly steps
1. Connection for brake hose
2. Lock pin
4. Lock pin sleeve
5. Lock pin boot
6. Guide pin boot
7. Boot ring
8. Piston boot
9. Piston assembly
10. Piston seal
11. Snap ring
12. Spring case
13. Return spring
14. Stopper plate
15. Stopper
16. Auto-adjuster spindle
17. Connecting link
18. O-ring
19. Spindle lever
20. Lever boot
21. Parking brake lever
22. Return spring
23. Bleeder screw
24. Caliper body
MT4079100004010X

Fig. 4 Exploded view of rear disc brake assembly (Part 1 of 2)

Rear

1. Remove caliper.
2. Disassemble caliper in numbered sequence, **Fig. 4,** noting the following:
   a. Use rear disc brake piston driver tool No. MB990652, or equivalent, to remove piston from caliper assembly.
   b. Remove piston seal with fingers. **Do not use a screwdriver or other tool to prevent damage to cylinder inner surface.**
   c. Use a .75 inch diameter steel pipe to press the spring case into the caliper body, then remove snap ring from caliper body using suitable snap ring pliers, **Fig. 5.**
3. Reverse numbered sequence, **Fig. 4** when assembling caliper, noting the following:
   a. Use a .75 inch diameter steel pipe to press the spring case into the caliper body, then install snap ring into caliper body using suitable snap ring pliers. **Attach snap ring to caliper body with opening facing the bleeder.**
   b. Push piston into caliper using piston driver tool and align groove, **Fig. 6.**
   c. When installing brake pads, pins in pad must be placed in grooves in piston.

ROTOR

REPLACE

FRONT

1. Raise and support vehicle, then remove wheel.
2. Remove caliper as described under "Caliper Service" and secure aside. **Do not allow caliper to hang from brake hose.**

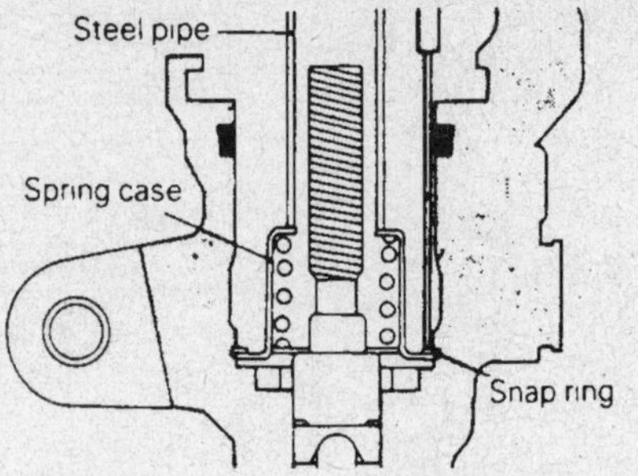
Steel pipe
Spring case
Snap ring
MT4079100005000X

Fig. 5 Spring case removal

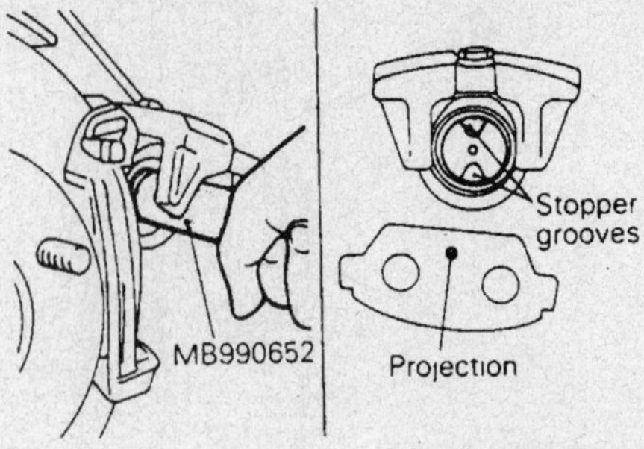
Stopper grooves
MB990652
Projection
MT4079100006000X

Fig. 6 Caliper piston installation

3. Remove rotor from hub.
4. Reverse procedure to install.

REAR

1. Raise and support vehicle, then remove rear wheels.
2. Loosen parking brake adjusting nut.
3. Remove parking brake cable retaining clip and spring, then disconnect parking brake cable.
4. Remove caliper bolts, then lift off caliper and secure aside.
5. Remove rotor retaining screw, then the rotor.
6. Reverse procedure to install, noting the following:
   a. Tighten fasteners to specifications.
   b. Adjust parking brake as outlined under "Adjustments."

ADJUSTMENTS

PARKING BRAKE

1. Pull parking brake lever with a force of approximately 45 lbs. and count number of clicks. Lever stroke should be 5–7 clicks.
2. If parking brake lever stroke is not within specifications, proceed as follows:
   a. Remove center console, then loosen adjusting nut on end of cable rod to free parking brake cable.
   b. With engine idling, depress brake pedal several times and confirm that the pedal stroke stops changing. **If pedal stroke stops changing, it indicates that automatic adjusting mechanism is functioning properly to adjust clearance between pads and disc to correct value.**
   c. Ensure parking lever on caliper side is in contact with the stopper.
   d. Turn adjusting nut to adjust parking brake lever stroke to specified range. **If number of brake lever notches engaged are less than specified value, cable has been pulled excessively and failure of the automatic adjuster mechanism may result.**
   e. After adjusting lever stroke, raise and support rear of vehicle. With parking brake lever released, turn rear wheels to ensure rear brakes are not dragging.
   f. Ensure parking brake lever on caliper side is in contact with the stopper.

DISC BRAKE SPECIFICATIONS

CALIPER SPECIFICATIONS

Caliper Model	Caliper Bore Diameter, Inch
FRONT	
MR31S	2.0100
MR34V	2.1250
REAR	
All	1.1875

ROTOR SPECIFICATIONS

Rotor Type	Nominal Thickness, Inch	Minimum Refinish Thickness, Inch	Lateral Runout (T.I.R.), Inch
FRONT			
Solid Rotor	.510	.450	.003
Ventilated Rotor	.710	.650	.003
REAR			
All	.370	.330	.003

TIGHTENING SPECIFICATIONS

Component	Torque/Ft. Lbs.
Bleeder Screw	5–7
Caliper Brake Line Hollow Bolt	22
Caliper Mounting Bolt	65
Flared Brake Line Nuts	9–12
Front Brake Assembly Mounting Bolt	58–72
Guide Pin (M-R31S Type)	61–69
Guide Pin (M-R34V Type)	27–36
Guide Pin (M-R46V Type)	46–62
Lockpin (M-R31S and M-R34V Type)	27–36
Lockpin (M-R46V)	46–62
Wheel Bearing Nut	108–145

Eclipse, Expo & Galant

INDEX

	Page No.
Adjustments	29-127
Parking Brake	29-127
Application Chart	29-123
Brake Pad Service	29-124
Replacement	29-124
Brake System Bleed	29-124
Caliper Service	29-124
Overhaul & Inspection	29-125
Replacement	29-124
Disc Brake Specifications	29-128
Caliper Specifications	29-128
Rotor Specifications	29-128
Parking Brake Service	29-127
Adjustment	29-127
Overhaul	29-127
Rotor, Replace	29-127
Tightening Specifications	29-129

APPLICATION CHART

Year	Model	Caliper No.
FRONT		
1993–94	Eclipse FWD Turbo	MR46V
	Eclipse AWD Turbo	MR56W
	Eclipse Non-Turbo	MR44V
	Expo	MR46V
	Galant SOHC	MR44V
	Galant DOHC	MR46V
1995	Eclipse FWD	MR46V
	Eclipse AWD	MR56W
	Expo	MR46V
	Galant	MR46V
1996	Eclipse FWD	MR46V
	Eclipse AWD	MR56W
	Galant	MR46V
REAR		
1993	Eclipse FWD Turbo	AD30P
	Eclipse AWD Turbo	AD35P
	Eclipse Non-Turbo	AD30P
	Expo	MR45S
	Galant	AD35P
1994	Eclipse FWD Turbo	AD30P
	Eclipse AWD Turbo	AD35P
	Eclipse Non-Turbo	AD30P
	Expo	MR45S
	Galant	MR45S

Continued

APPLICATION CHART—Continued

Year	Model	Caliper No.
REAR		
1995	Eclipse	MR45S
	Expo	MR45S
	Galant	MR45S
1996	Eclipse	MR45S

BRAKE SYSTEM BLEED

The hydraulic brake system must be bled if air has entered the system. This condition may be caused by low fluid level, a hydraulic fluid leak, the opening of a hydraulic line or replacement of a hydraulic system component. Symptoms include a loss of basic brake operation and/or a low or spongy brake pedal.

On models equipped with ABS, use a suitable filter when adding fluid to reservoir tank.

1. Ensure master cylinder reservoir is full. Add suitable brake fluid as needed, and securely reinstall the master cylinder cap.
2. Raise and support vehicle.
3. Position a drain pan under the wheel being bled.
4. Have an assistant depress the brake pedal with a slow even pressure and hold it. **Do not depress brake pedal fully to the end of the master cylinder stroke. This may cause damage to the master cylinder.**
5. Using a suitable wrench, open the bleeder valve one full turn. Watch for air bubbles in the fluid, and listen for air escaping from the system.
6. With the brake pedal still depressed, close the bleeder valve.
7. Have the assistant pump the brake pedal several times. **Do not depress brake pedal fully to the end of the master cylinder stroke, this may cause damage to the master cylinder.**
8. Repeat preceding bleed steps until all air is removed from the hydraulic system. **While bleeding the system, recheck brake fluid supply in the master cylinder often so as not to allow the master cylinder to run dry.**
9. Upon completion of hydraulic system bleeding, proceed as follows:
   a. Ensure the master cylinder reservoir is full. Add suitable brake fluid as needed, and securely reinstall the master cylinder cap.
   b. Lower the vehicle. Ensure brake pedal is firm and braking operation is satisfactory.

BRAKE PAD SERVICE

REPLACEMENT

Front

1. Raise and support vehicle, then remove wheel.
2. Remove lower lockpin, **Figs. 1 and 2,** and lift caliper body upward, then support caliper with wire. **Lockpin is coated with special grease. Use caution not to remove grease and ensure no dirt adheres to pin.**
3. Remove inner shim(s), anti-squeak shim and pad assemblies from support mounting.
4. Remove pad clips.
5. Measure hub torque with pad removed to aid in measuring brake drag torque after pad installation, **Fig. 3.**
6. Install pad clips, pad assemblies, inner shim(s) and anti-squeak shim onto the support mounting.
7. Apply a coating of suitable grease to the pad and anti-squeak shim contact surface and to the anti-squeak shim and inner shim contact surface. **Ensure grease does not come in contact with brake pad assemble.**
8. Lower caliper body into position, then install lower lockpin tightening to specification.
9. Check brake drag torque as follows:
   a. Start engine and hold brake pedal down for five seconds.
   b. Stop engine and turn brake rotor forward ten turns.
   c. Check brake drag using suitable tool.
   d. If the difference between brake drag torque and hub torque exceeds 3 ft. lbs., disassemble caliper assembly, clean and check for corrosion, worn or damaged parts.
10. Install wheel.

Rear

1. Raise and support vehicle, then remove wheel.
2. Remove parking brake cable.
3. Remove lower lockpin, **Figs. 4 and 5,** and lift caliper body upward, then support caliper with wire. **Lockpin is coated with special grease. Use caution not to remove grease and ensure no dirt adheres to pin.**
4. Remove outer shim and pad assembly from caliper support.
5. Remove pad clips.
6. Measure hub torque with pad removed to aid in measuring brake drag torque after pad installation, **Fig. 9.**
7. Press piston into cylinder using a suitable tool. Ensure stopper grooves in rear of piston are in the vertical position.
8. Install pad clips, then the pad and shim as an assembly onto the caliper support. Pins on back side of brake pad must be placed in grooves of piston.
9. Lower caliper body into position, then install lower lockpin tightening to specification.
10. With engine running, forcefully depress brake pedal five to six times and ensure the stroke of the parking brake lever is .078 inch or less, **Fig. 6.**
11. Check brake drag torque as follows:
    a. Start engine and hold brake pedal down for five seconds.
    b. Stop engine and turn brake rotor forward ten turns.
    c. Check brake drag using suitable tool.
    d. If the difference between brake drag torque and hub torque exceeds 3 ft. lbs., disassemble caliper assembly, clean and check for corroded, worn or damaged parts.
12. Install wheel.

CALIPER SERVICE

REPLACEMENT

FRONT

1. Raise and support vehicle, then remove wheel.
2. Disengage strut brake hose clips, then disconnect brake hose.
3. Remove lockpins, then the caliper assembly.
4. Reverse procedure to install, noting the following:
   a. Replace pin boots.
   b. **On models equipped with MR44V and MR46V calipers,** install guide and lockpin so identification mark on pin matches mark on caliper body, **Fig. 7.**
   c. **On all models,** bleed brake system as outlined under "Brake System Bleed."

REAR

1. Raise and support vehicle, then remove rear wheel.
2. Disconnect parking brake cable from caliper assembly.
3. Disconnect brake hoses and brake tubes.
4. Remove lockpins from caliper assembly, noting position for installation reference.
5. Remove caliper assembly to adapter attaching bolts.
6. Remove caliper assembly.
7. Reverse procedure to install, noting the following:
   a. Install lockpins into original position using marks on pin head and marks on caliper body.
   b. Tighten bolts to specifications.

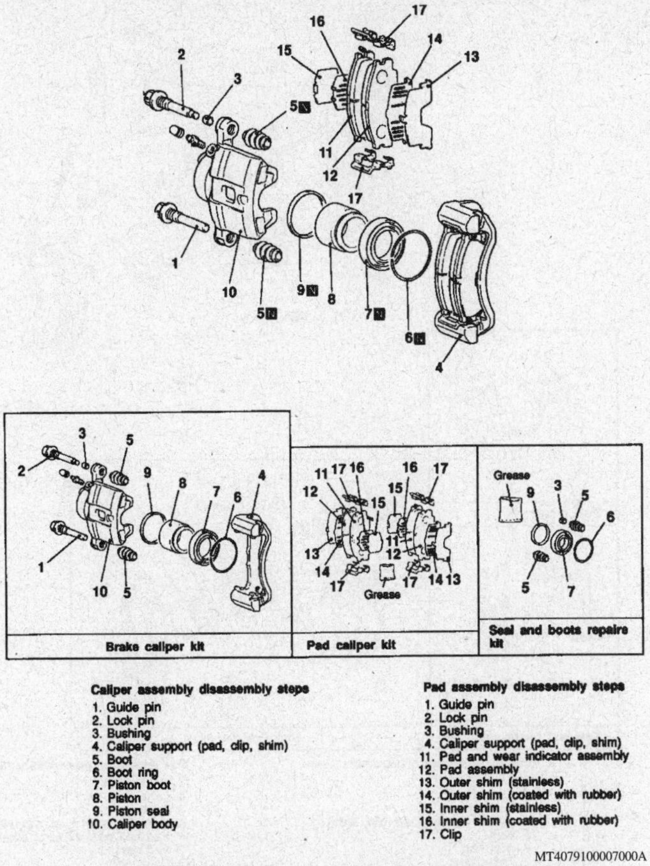
Brake caliper kit
Pad caliper kit
Seal and boots repairs kit
Grease
Caliper assembly disassembly steps
1. Guide pin
2. Lock pin
3. Bushing
4. Caliper support (pad, clip, shim)
5. Boot
6. Boot ring
7. Piston boot
8. Piston
9. Piston seal
10. Caliper body
Pad assembly disassembly steps
1. Guide pin
2. Lock pin
3. Bushing
4. Caliper support (pad, clip, shim)
11. Pad and wear indicator assembly
12. Pad assembly
13. Outer shim (stainless)
14. Outer shim (coated with rubber)
15. Inner shim (stainless)
16. Inner shim (coated with rubber)
17. Clip
MT4079100007000A

Fig. 1 Exploded view of MR44V & MR46V disc brake assemblies

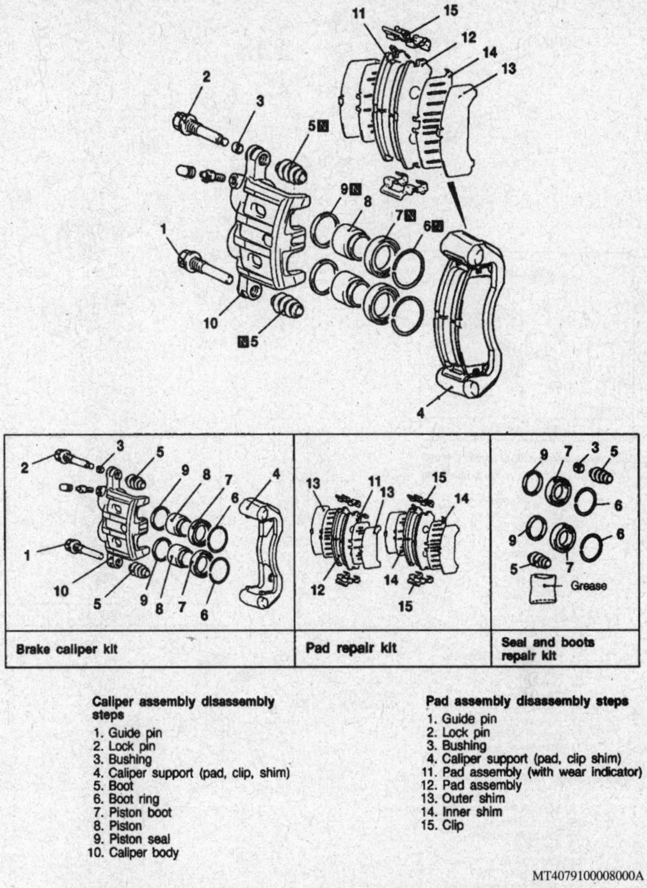
Brake caliper kit
Pad repair kit
Seal and boots repair kit
Grease
Caliper assembly disassembly steps
1. Guide pin
2. Lock pin
3. Bushing
4. Caliper support (pad, clip, shim)
5. Boot
6. Boot ring
7. Piston boot
8. Piston
9. Piston seal
10. Caliper body
Pad assembly disassembly steps
1. Guide pin
2. Lock pin
3. Bushing
4. Caliper support (pad, clip shim)
11. Pad assembly (with wear indicator)
12. Pad assembly
13. Outer shim
14. Inner shim
15. Clip
MT4079100008000A

Fig. 2 Exploded view of MR56W disc brake assembly

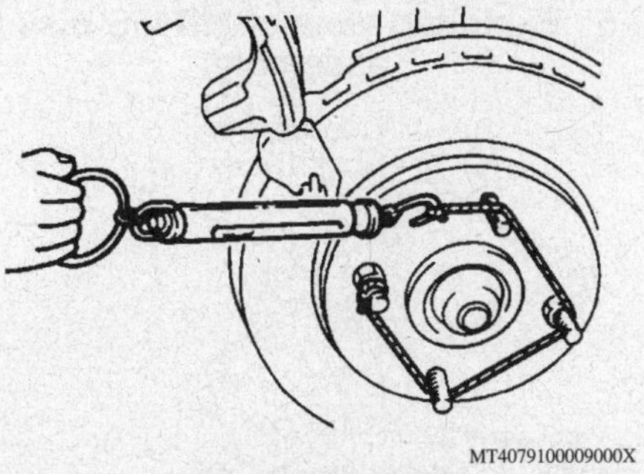
MT4079100009000X

Fig. 3 Hub and brake drag torque measurement

c. Bleed brake system as outlined under "Brake System Bleed."

OVERHAUL & INSPECTION

FRONT

1. Remove boot ring.
2. Place rag in front of piston, then remove piston and dust boot by applying compressed air through brake hose fitting hole. Keep fingers clear of front of piston.
3. Remove piston seal. Use caution not to scratch the cylinder walls.
4. Remove sleeve and boot from caliper body.
5. Check cylinder and piston for wear, damage and/or corrosion. Repair or replace as required.
6. Check caliper body and sleeve for wear. Replace as required.
7. Apply suitable brake fluid to the cylinder walls.
8. Apply an even coat of suitable grease to the new piston seal, then install seal in cylinder.
9. Install piston into cylinder. Use caution not to twist piston seal.
10. Apply suitable grease to dust boot, then install boot on piston.
11. Attach piston boot onto cylinder with the boot ring.
12. Apply suitable grease to sliding parts of caliper body and sleeves, guide pin and lockpin boot.

REAR

AD30P & AD35P Calipers

1. Remove boot ring from caliper body, then the piston boot.
2. Twist piston out of caliper body using suitable tool.
3. Press spring case into caliper body using a .75 inch diameter steel pipe, then remove snap ring from caliper body using a suitable tool.
4. Remove spring case, return spring, washer and stopper from caliper body.
5. Pull auto-adjuster spindle out of caliper body and remove connecting link at the same time.
6. Remove O-ring from auto-adjuster spindle. Use caution not to scratch cylinder walls.
7. Remove piston seal from caliper body.
8. Disconnect return spring, then remove parking brake lever attaching nut.
9. Pull parking brake lever and spindle lever out of caliper body, then remove lever boot.
10. Pull sleeve, boot and lid out of the caliper body.
11. Remove guide pin and sleeve from caliper support.
12. Check connecting link and spindle for wear or damage. Replace as required.
13. Check caliper body, spindle lever shaft and piston for cracks or rust. Repair or replace as required.
14. Apply suitable grease to new piston seal and cylinder walls, then install piston seal into cylinder.
15. Apply suitable grease to bearing, spindle lever shaft, boot lever, connecting

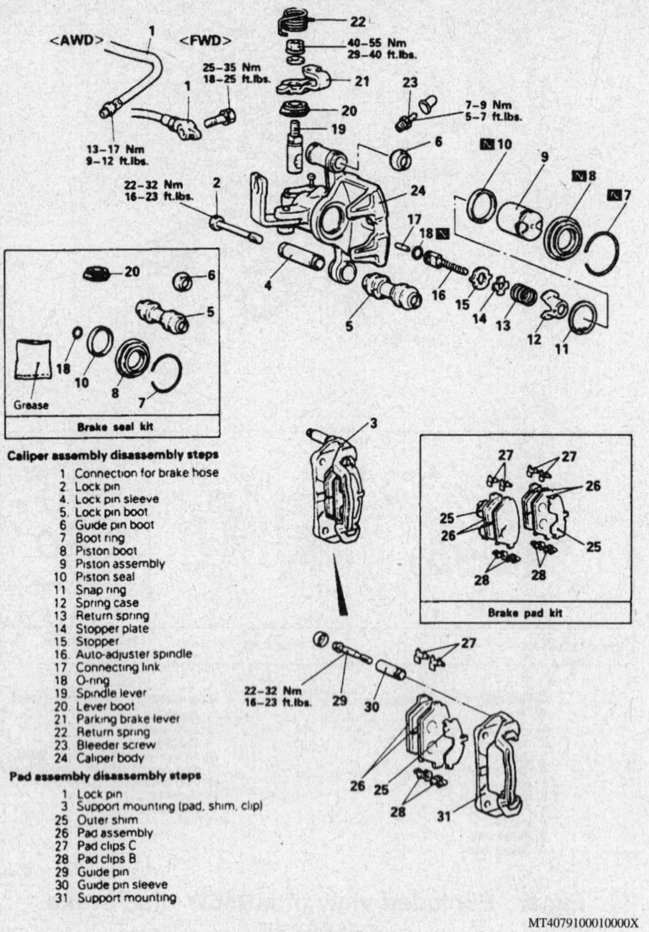

<AWD>
<FWD>
25–35 Nm
18–25 ft.lbs.
40–55 Nm
29–40 ft.lbs.
7–9 Nm
5–7 ft.lbs.
13–17 Nm
9–12 ft.lbs.
22–32 Nm
16–23 ft.lbs.
Grease
Brake seal kit
Brake pad kit
Caliper assembly disassembly steps
1 Connection for brake hose
2 Lock pin
4. Lock pin sleeve
5. Lock pin boot
6 Guide pin boot
7 Boot ring
8 Piston boot
9 Piston assembly
10 Piston seal
11 Snap ring
12 Spring case
13 Return spring
14 Stopper plate
15 Stopper
16 Auto-adjuster spindle
17 Connecting link
18 O-ring
19 Spindle lever
20 Lever boot
21 Parking brake lever
22 Return spring
23 Bleeder screw
24 Caliper body
Pad assembly disassembly steps
1 Lock pin
3 Support mounting (pad, shim, clip)
25 Outer shim
26 Pad assembly
27 Pad clips C
28 Pad clips B
29 Guide pin
30 Guide pin sleeve
31 Support mounting
MT4079100010000X

Fig. 4 Exploded view of AD30P & AD35P disc brake assemblies

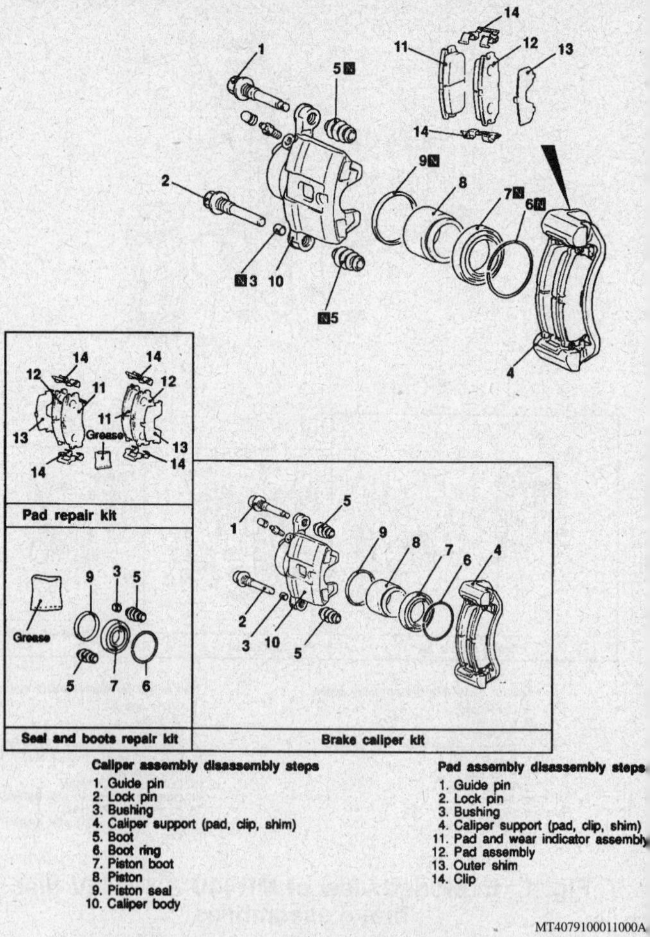

Pad repair kit
Grease
Seal and boots repair kit
Brake caliper kit
Caliper assembly disassembly steps
1. Guide pin
2. Lock pin
3. Bushing
4. Caliper support (pad, clip, shim)
5. Boot
6. Boot ring
7. Piston boot
8. Piston
9. Piston seal
10. Caliper body
Pad assembly disassembly steps
1. Guide pin
2. Lock pin
3. Bushing
4. Caliper support (pad, clip, shim)
11. Pad and wear indicator assembly
12. Pad assembly
13. Outer shim
14. Clip
MT4079100011000A

Fig. 5 Exploded view of MR45S disc brake assembly

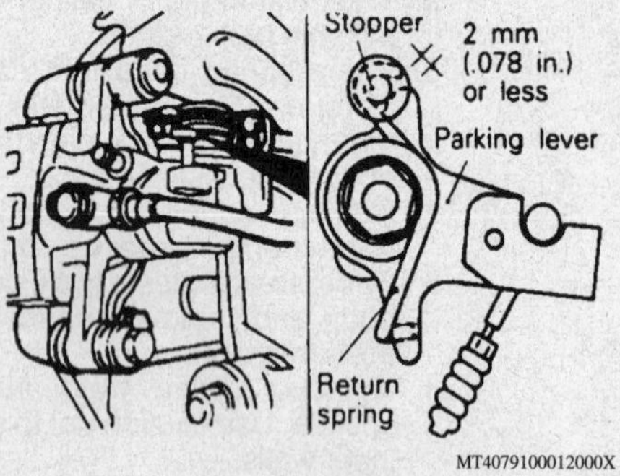

Stopper
2 mm
(.078 in.)
or less
Parking lever
Return spring
MT4079100012000X

Fig. 6 Parking brake adjustment. Eclipse & Galant

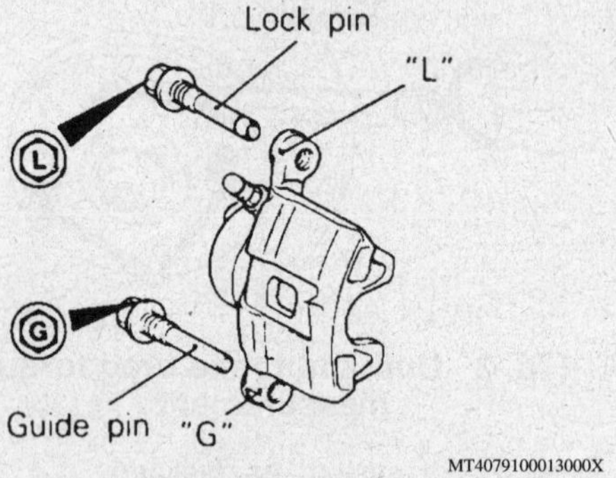

Lock pin
"L"
Guide pin
"G"
MT4079100013000X

Fig. 7 Caliper bolt location

link, auto-adjuster spindle and caliper body.

16. Align hole in bearing with hole in connecting link.
17. Press dust boot into caliper body, then install shaft with groove facing hole in bearing.
18. Install connecting link from cylinder side.
19. Install O-ring on auto-adjuster spindle, then coat it with suitable brake fluid.
20. Install auto-adjuster spindle, then the stopper, spring washer, spring and spring case into caliper body.
21. Press in spring case using a suitable .75 inch diameter pipe, then install snap ring in caliper body and remove pipe. **Install snap ring in caliper body with opening facing bleeder.**
22. Twist piston in cylinder using a suitable tool.
23. Apply suitable grease to piston boot mounting grooves in caliper body and piston, then install piston boot and boot ring.
24. Install guide pin and sleeve into caliper support.
25. Apply suitable grease to sliding part of sleeve, caliper body, boot mounting groove and lid mounting.
26. Press in lid until edges are in contact with caliper body.
27. Attach caliper support to caliper assembly.

MR45S Caliper

1. Remove boot ring.
2. Place rag in front of piston, then remove piston and dust boot by applying compressed air through brake hose fitting hole. Keep fingers clear of front of piston.
3. Remove piston seal. Use caution not to scratch the cylinder walls.
4. Remove sleeve and boot from caliper body.
5. Check cylinder and piston for wear, damage and/or corrosion. Repair or replace as required.

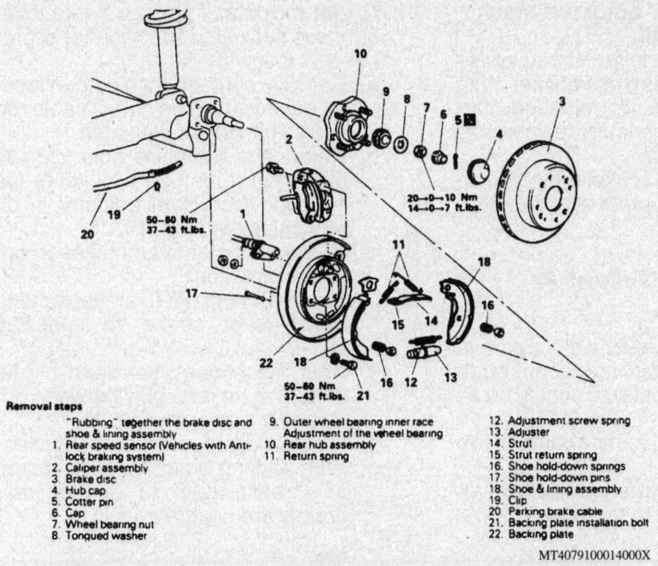
20→0→10 Nm
14→0→7 ft.lbs.
50–60 Nm
37–43 ft.lbs.
50–60 Nm
37–43 ft.lbs.
Removal steps
"Rubbing" together the brake disc and shoe & lining assembly
1. Rear speed sensor (Vehicles with Anti-lock braking system)
2. Caliper assembly
3. Brake disc
4. Hub cap
5. Cotter pin
6. Cap
7. Wheel bearing nut
8. Tongued washer
9. Outer wheel bearing inner race
Adjustment of the wheel bearing
10. Rear hub assembly
11. Return spring
12. Adjustment screw spring
13. Adjuster
14. Strut
15. Strut return spring
16. Shoe hold-down springs
17. Shoe hold-down pins
18. Shoe & lining assembly
19. Clip
20. Parking brake cable
21. Backing plate installation bolt
22. Backing plate
MT4079100014000X

Fig. 8 Exploded view of parking brake assembly. Expo

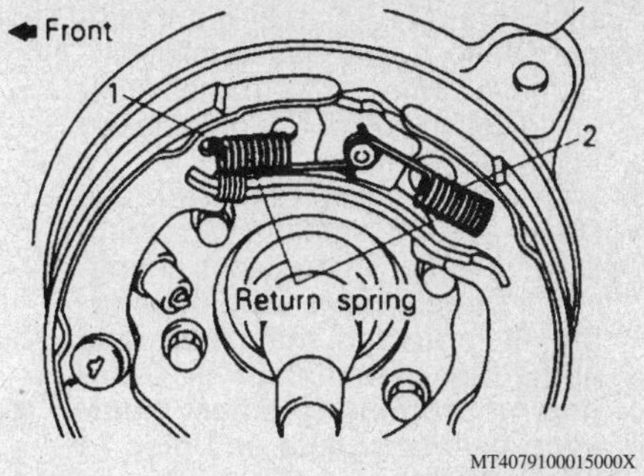
Front
Return spring
MT4079100015000X

Fig. 9 Return spring installation. Expo

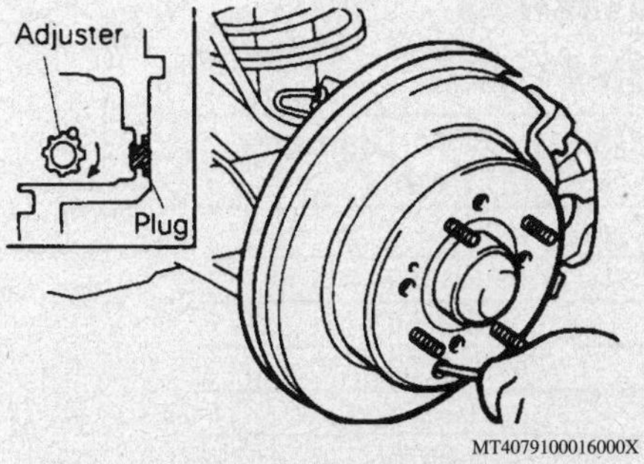
Adjuster
Plug
MT4079100016000X

Fig. 10 Parking brake adjuster rotation. Expo, 1994–95 Galant & 1995–96 Eclipse

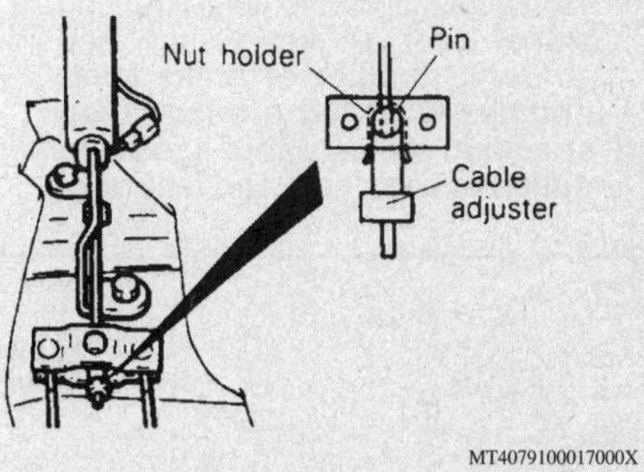
Nut holder
Pin
Cable adjuster
MT4079100017000X

Fig. 11 Parking brake cable adjuster freeplay inspection. Expo & 1995–96 Eclipse

6. Check caliper body and sleeve for wear. Replace as required.
7. Apply suitable brake fluid to the cylinder walls.
8. Apply an even coat of suitable grease to the new piston seal, then install seal in cylinder.
9. Install piston into cylinder. Use caution not to twist piston seal.
10. Apply suitable grease to dust boot, then install boot on piston.
11. Attach piston boot onto cylinder with the boot ring.
12. Apply suitable grease to sliding parts of caliper body and sleeves, guide pin and lockpin boot.

ROTOR

REPLACE

1. Raise and support vehicle, then remove wheel.
2. Separate caliper from adapter as described under "Brake Pad Service." **It is not necessary to disconnect brake hose from caliper; suspend caliper aside with suitable wire to prevent brake hose damage.**
3. Remove rotor assembly from hub.
4. Reverse procedure to install.

PARKING BRAKE SERVICE

OVERHAUL

Expo

1. Raise and support vehicle and remove rear wheels.
2. Separate caliper from adapter as described under "Brake Pad Service." **It is not necessary to disconnect brake hose from caliper; suspend caliper aside with suitable wire to prevent brake hose damage.**
3. Disassemble parking brakes in numbered sequence, **Fig. 8,** noting the following:
   a. **When removing the speed sensor from knuckle, use care not to hit pole piece at its tip against the rotor teeth or other parts.**
   b. Remove parking brake clips.
   c. Disconnect parking brake cable from parking brake lever of shoe and lining assembly using suitable pliers.
   d. Remove parking brake cable from backing plate.
4. Reverse numbered sequence in **Fig. 8** to assemble parking brakes, noting the following:
   a. Install return springs, **Fig. 9.**
   b. When installing brake disc, ensure there is no corrosion or oil on parking brake drum.
5. Adjust rear wheel bearing as follows:
   a. Inspect play of bearing while vehicle is raised and supported.
   b. If any play is noted, remove hub cap, split pin and lock cap then loosen locknut.
   c. **Torque** bearing nut to 14 ft. lbs.
   d. Turn hub 180° and then return it to its original position. Repeat this step several times.
   e. Completely loosen locknut, then **torque** locknut to 7 ft. lbs.
   f. Repeat hub rotation step, turning hub in same direction.
   g. **Torque** locknut to 7 ft. lbs.
   h. Install lock cap and cotter pin.
   i. Seat bearing by rotating hub as described in preceding steps.
   j. After securing wheel nuts, Ensure rotary sliding resistance is .6 ft. lbs. when a new bearing is used or .05 ft. lbs. if bearing is reused.

ADJUSTMENT

Refer to "Adjustments" in this section for parking brake adjustment procedures.

ADJUSTMENTS

PARKING BRAKE

1993–94 Eclipse & 1993 Galant

1. Pull parking brake lever with a force of approximately 45 lbs. and count number of clicks. Lever stroke should be five to seven clicks.

2. If parking brake lever stroke is not within specifications, proceed as follows:
   a. Remove center console, then loosen adjusting nut on end of cable rod to free parking brake cable.
   b. With engine idling, depress brake pedal several times and confirm that the pedal stroke stops changing. **If pedal stroke stops changing, it indicates that automatic adjusting mechanism is functioning properly to adjust clearance between pads and disc to correct value.**
   c. Ensure parking lever on caliper side is in contact with the stopper.
   d. Turn adjusting nut to adjust parking brake lever stroke to specified range. **If number of brake lever notches engaged are less than specified value, cable has been pulled excessively and failure of the automatic adjuster mechanism may result.**
   e. After adjusting lever stroke, raise and support rear of vehicle. With parking brake lever released, turn rear wheels to ensure rear brakes are not dragging.
   f. Ensure parking brake lever on caliper side is in contact with the stopper.

Expo, 1994–95 Galant & 1995–96 Eclipse

1. Pull parking brake lever with a force of approximately 45 lbs. and count number of clicks. Lever stroke should be as follows:
2. **On Expo models,** lever should move four to six clicks.
3. **On Eclipse and Galant models,** lever should move three to five clicks.
4. **On all models,** if parking brake lever stroke is not within specifications, proceed as follows:
   a. Remove center console, then loosen adjusting nut on end of cable rod to free parking brake cable.
   b. Remove adjustment hole plug in disc rotor, then use a suitable flat screwdriver to turn adjuster in direction shown, **Fig. 10.**
   c. Return adjuster five notches in opposite direction.
   d. Turn adjusting nut to adjust parking brake lever stroke to specified range.
   e. After adjustment has been made, ensure there is no play between adjusting nut and pin, **Fig. 11.**
   f. Raise and support rear of vehicle.
   g. With parking brake lever released, turn rear wheel to ensure rear brakes are not dragging.

DISC BRAKE SPECIFICATIONS

CALIPER SPECIFICATIONS

Model	Year	Caliper Bore Diameter, Inch
FRONT		
Eclipse Non-Turbo	1993–94	2.1250
	1995–96	2.3750
Eclipse FWD Turbo	1993–96	2.3750
Eclipse AWD Turbo①	1993–94	1.6250
	1995–96	1.6875
Expo	1993–95	2.3750
Galant SOHC	1993	2.1250
	1994–96	2.3750
Galant DOHC	1993–95	2.3750
REAR		
Eclipse FWD	1993–94	1.1875
	1995–96	1.3750
Eclipse AWD	1993–94	1.3750
	1995	1.5000
	1996	1.3750
Expo	1993–95	1.3750
Galant	1993–95	1.3750

① — Two piston caliper.

ROTOR SPECIFICATIONS

Year	Model	Nominal Thickness, Inch	Minimum Refinish Thickness, Inch	Lateral Runout (T.I.R.), Inch
FRONT				
1993	Eclipse	.940	.882	.0031
	Expo	.940	.880	.0031
	Galant	.940	.882	.0031
1994	Eclipse	.940	.882	.0031
	Expo	.940	.880	.0031
	Galant	.940	.880	.0031

Continued

ROTOR SPECIFICATIONS

Year	Model	Nominal Thickness, Inch	Minimum Refinish Thickness, Inch	Lateral Runout (T.I.R.), Inch
FRONT				
1995	Eclipse	.940	.880	.0031
	Expo	.940	.880	.0031
	Galant	.940	.880	.0031
1996	Eclipse	.940	.880	.0031
	Galant	.940	.880	.0031
REAR				
1993	Eclipse	.390	.331	.0031
	Expo	.390	.331	.0031
	Galant	.390	.331	.0031
1994	Eclipse	.390	.331	.0031
	Expo	.390	.331	.0031
	Galant	.390	.330	.0031
1995	Eclipse AWD	.790	.720	.0031
	Eclipse FWD	.390	.330	.0031
	Expo	.390	.331	.0031
	Galant	.390	.330	.0031
1996	Eclipse	.390	.330	.0031

TIGHTENING SPECIFICATIONS

Component	Torque/Ft. Lbs.
1993–94 ECLIPSE	
Axle Nut	116–159
Bleeder Screw	5–7
Brake Hose Bracket Bolts	12–19
Driveshaft Nut	116–159
Dust Shield To Axle Beam	7–10
Fitting	11–13
Flared Brake Line Nuts	9–12
Front Disc Brake Assembly	58–72
Front Guide Pin	64–86
Front Lockpin	64–86
Hub Nut	116–159
Lever Assembly A Nut	14–18
Lever Assembly B Nut	14–18
Nipple Screw	12–24③
Piston Stopper	12–24③
Rear Brake Hose To Caliper Body	18–25
Rear Disc Brake Assembly	35–43
Rear Guide Pin	16–23
Rear Lockpin	16–23
Spindle Lever To Parking Brake Lever	29–40
Turn Over Spring Bolt	12–19
Wheel Bearing Nut	144–188
1995–96 ECLIPSE	
Bleeder Screw	6
Brake Hose To Front Caliper	11
Brake Hose To Rear Caliper	⑤
Caliper Body To Caliper Support	54
Front Caliper To Backing Plate	65
Rear Caliper To Backing Plate	36–43

Continued

TIGHTENING SPECIFICATIONS—Continued

Component	Torque/Ft. Lbs.
1995–96 ECLIPSE	
Rear Hub To Knuckle	54–65
EXPO	
Bleeder Screw	6
Brake Line To Caliper	11
Brake Line To Wheel Cylinder	11
Front Caliper Mounting Bolts	65
Front Caliper Sliding Bolts	54
Rear Axle Nut①	17
Rear Axle Nut②	166
Rear Caliper Sliding Bolts	32
Wheel Cylinder Mounting Bolts	7
1993 GALANT	
Axle Nut	116–159
Backing Plate To Axle Beam	36–43
Bleeder Screw	5–7
Bracket A Installation Bolts	12–19
Brake Hose Bracket Installation Bolts	12–19
Brake Hose To Caliper Body (Rear)	18–25
Driveshaft Nut	116–159
Driveshaft To Companion Flange	16–23
Dust Shield To Axle Beam	7–10
Fitting	11–13
Flared Brake Line Nuts	9–12
Front Disc Brake Assembly Installation Bolts	58–72
Guide Pin (Front)	42–62
Guide Pin (Rear)	16–23
Hub Nut	116–159
Lever Assembly Nut	14–18
Lockpin (Front)	42–62
Lockpin (Rear)	16–23
Nipple Screw	12–24③
Parking Brake Lever Installation Nut	29–40
Piston Stopper Bolt	12–24③
Rear Brake Assembly Installation Bolt	36–43
Rear Disc Brake Assembly Installation Bolts	36–43
Rear Speed Sensor Installation Bolt	7–10
Rotor To Front Hub	7–10
Rotor To Rear Hub	7–10
Speed Sensor Bracket Installation Bolt	7–10
Wheel Bearing Nut	144–188
1994–96 GALANT	
Bleeder Screw	6
Brake Hose To Caliper	22
Caliper Body To Caliper Support	54
Front Caliper To Backing Plate	65
Rear Caliper To Backing Plate④	36–43
Rear Hub To Knuckle④	54–65

① — Rear drum brakes.
② — Rear disc brakes.
③ — Inch lbs.
④ — 1994–95.
⑤ — 1995, 22 ft. lbs.; 1996, 11 ft. lbs.

Diamante & 3000GT

INDEX

Page No.		Page No.		Page No.	
Adjustments	29-133	**Caliper Service**	29-131	Rotor Specifications	29-135
Parking Brake	29-133	Inspection	29-132	**Parking Brake Service**	29-132
Brake Pad Service	29-131	Replacement	29-131	Adjustment	29-133
Replacement	29-131	**Disc Brake Specifications**	29-134	Overhaul	29-132
Brake System Bleed	29-131	Caliper Specifications	29-134	**Tightening Specifications**	29-135

BRAKE SYSTEM BLEED

The hydraulic brake system must be bled if air has entered the system. Air may enter due to low fluid level, a hydraulic fluid leak, the opening of a hydraulic line or replacement of a hydraulic system component. Symptoms include loss of brake operation and/or a low or spongy brake pedal.

On models equipped with ABS, use a suitable filter when adding fluid to reservoir tank.

1. Ensure master cylinder reservoir is full. Add suitable brake fluid as needed, and securely reinstall the master cylinder cap.
2. Raise and support vehicle.
3. Position a drain pan under the wheel being bled.
4. Have an assistant depress the brake pedal with a slow even pressure and hold it. **Do not depress brake pedal fully to the end of the master cylinder stroke. This may cause damage to the master cylinder.**
5. Using a suitable wrench, open the bleeder valve one full turn. Watch for air bubbles in the fluid, and listen for air escaping from the system.
6. With the brake pedal still depressed, close the bleeder valve.
7. Have the assistant pump the brake pedal several times. **Do not depress brake pedal fully to the end of the master cylinder stroke, this may cause damage to the master cylinder.**
8. Repeat steps 4 through 7 until all air is removed from the hydraulic system. **While bleeding the system, recheck brake fluid supply in the master cylinder often so as not to allow the master cylinder to run dry.**
9. Upon completion of hydraulic system bleeding, proceed as follows:
   a. Ensure the master cylinder reservoir is full. Add suitable brake fluid as needed, and securely reinstall the master cylinder cap.
   b. Lower the vehicle. Ensure brake pedal is firm and braking operation is satisfactory.

BRAKE PAD SERVICE

REPLACEMENT

FRONT

FWD

1. Raise and support vehicle, then remove wheel.
2. Remove lower guide pin and pivot caliper assembly up and support using suitable wire.
3. Remove brake pads, pad clips and outer shim, **Fig. 1.**
4. Measure rotating torque of hub with brake pads removed using a suitable spring scale, **Fig. 2.**
5. Clean piston surface and push into caliper using suitable tool. **Ensure piston boot does not become wedged.**
6. Install pad clips and pads onto caliper.
7. Lower caliper assembly and install lower guide pin.
8. Check brake drag as follows:
   a. Start engine and hold brake pedal down for five seconds.
   b. Stop engine and turn brake rotor forward ten turns.
   c. Check brake drag using suitable tool.
   d. If the difference between brake drag torque and hub torque exceeds 3 ft. lbs., disassemble caliper assembly, clean and check for corrosion, worn or damaged parts.

AWD

1. Raise and support vehicle and remove wheel.
2. Remove pad pin clip and while holding cross spring with hand, remove pad pins, **Fig. 3.**
3. Using a suitable screwdriver, remove pads and shims.
4. Measure rotating torque of hub with brake pads removed using a suitable spring scale, **Fig. 2.**
5. Clean piston surface and push into caliper using suitable tool. **Ensure piston boot does not become wedged.**
6. Apply repair kit grease to both sides of inner shims. **Ensure grease does not come in contact with frictional surface of brake pads, grease should never squeeze out from around shim.**
7. Check brake drag as follows:
   a. Start engine and hold brake pedal down for five seconds.
   b. Stop engine and turn brake rotor forward ten turns.
   c. Check brake drag using suitable tool.
   d. If the difference between brake drag torque and hub torque exceeds 3 ft. lbs., disassemble caliper assembly, clean and check for corrosion, worn or damaged parts.

REAR

1. Loosen parking brake cable from interior end of cable and disconnect parking brake cable from rear brake caliper assembly.
2. Remove lower lockpin. Lift caliper assembly and support with suitable wire. **Do not smear grease on lockpin and ensure it is free of dirt.**
3. Remove outer shim, pad assembly, pad clip and inner shims, **Figs. 4 through 6.**
4. Measure rotating torque of hub with brake pads removed using a suitable spring scale, **Fig. 2.** On models with Viscous Coupling Unit (VCU) equipped Limited Slip Differential (LSD), disengage the driveshaft and companion flange.
5. Clean piston surface and push into caliper using suitable tool. **Ensure piston boot does not become wedged.**
6. Attach pad clip and pads to caliper support.
7. Check brake drag as follows:
   a. Start engine and hold brake pedal down for five seconds.
   b. Stop engine and turn brake rotor forward ten turns.
   c. Check brake drag using suitable tool.
   d. If the difference between brake drag torque and hub torque exceeds 3 ft. lbs., disassemble caliper assembly, clean and check for corrosion, worn or damaged parts.

CALIPER SERVICE

REPLACEMENT

1. Disconnect and plug brake hose.
2. Remove upper and lower caliper mounting bolts.
3. Remove caliper assembly; then, if necessary, separate from brake pads as outlined under "Brake Pad Service."
4. Reverse procedure to install, noting the following:
   a. Measure brake drag torque as outlined under "Brake Pad Service."
   b. Tighten brake hose fitting to specifications.
   c. Bleed brake system as outlined under "Brake System Bleed."

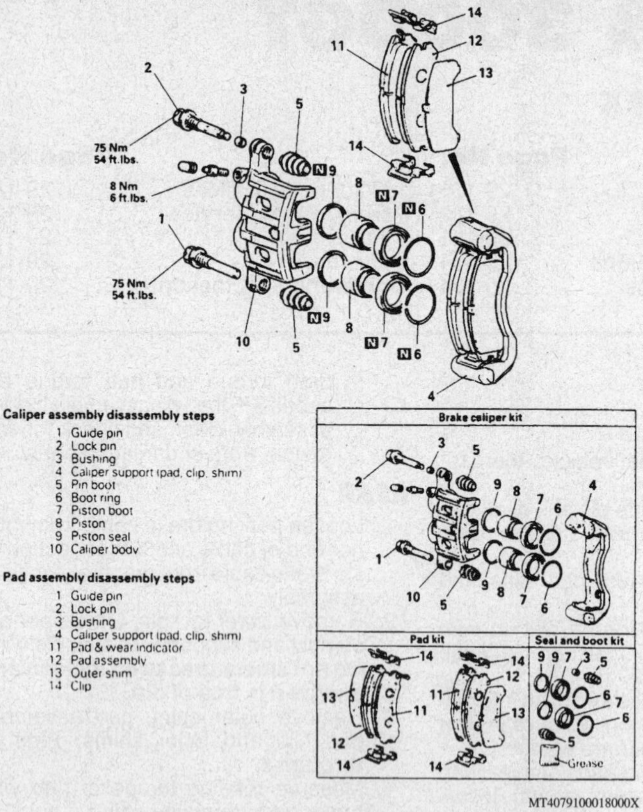
75 Nm
54 ft.lbs.
8 Nm
6 ft.lbs.
75 Nm
54 ft.lbs.
Caliper assembly disassembly steps
1 Guide pin
2 Lock pin
3 Bushing
4 Caliper support (pad, clip, shim)
5 Pin boot
6 Boot ring
7 Piston boot
8 Piston
9 Piston seal
10 Caliper body
Pad assembly disassembly steps
1 Guide pin
2 Lock pin
3 Bushing
4 Caliper support (pad, clip, shim)
11 Pad & wear indicator
12 Pad assembly
13 Outer shim
14 Clip
Brake caliper kit
Pad kit
Seal and boot kit
Grease
MT4079100018000X

Fig. 1 Exploded view of front disc brake caliper. FWD models

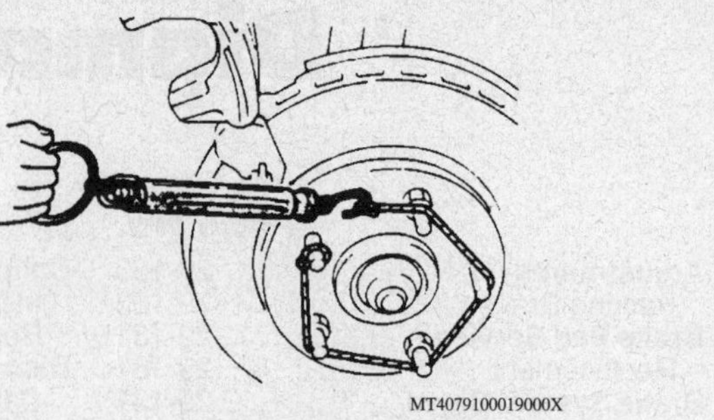
MT4079100019000X

Fig. 2 Hub and brake drag torque measurement

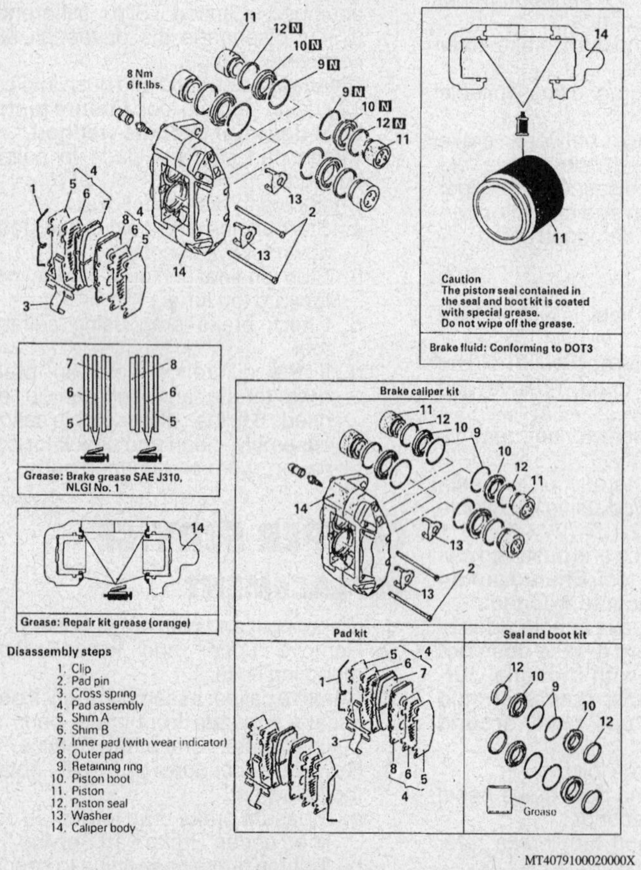
8 Nm
6 ft.lbs.
Caution
The piston seal contained in the seal and boot kit is coated with special grease.
Do not wipe off the grease.
Brake fluid: Conforming to DOT3
Grease: Brake grease SAE J310, NLGI No. 1
Grease: Repair kit grease (orange)
Brake caliper kit
Pad kit
Seal and boot kit
Grease
Disassembly steps
1. Clip
2. Pad pin
3. Cross spring
4. Pad assembly
5. Shim A
6. Shim B
7. Inner pad (with wear indicator)
8. Outer pad
9. Retaining ring
10. Piston boot
11. Piston
12. Piston seal
13. Washer
14. Caliper body
MT4079100020000X

Fig. 3 Exploded view of front disc brake caliper. AWD models

INSPECTION

Front

1. Raise and support vehicle and remove wheel.
2. Remove brake caliper.
3. Disassemble caliper assembly in numbered sequence shown in **Figs. 1 and 3,** noting the following:
   a. Remove pistons by placing a hammer handle in caliper to keep pistons even then send compressed air to break hose opening. **Use care not to pinch fingers when removing pistons. Send compressed air gradually. If one piston is removed, the others will not be able to be removed.**
   b. Remove piston seal with finger.
   c. Clean piston surface and inner cylinder with alcohol or specified brake fluid.
4. Reverse numbered sequence in **Figs. 1 and 3** to assemble caliper. On FWD models, match guide and lockpins identification marks with marks on caliper body when installing.

Rear

1. Raise and support vehicle and remove wheel.
2. Remove brake caliper.
3. Disassemble caliper assembly in numbered sequence shown in **Figs. 4 through 6,** noting the following:
   a. Protect caliper body with shop towel. Blow compressed air through brake hose opening to remove piston boot and piston.
   b. Remove piston seal using finger.
   c. Clean piston and inner cylinder using alcohol or brake fluid.
4. Reverse numbered sequence in **Figs. 4 through 6** to assemble caliper. On AWD models, match guide and lockpins identification marks with marks on caliper body when installing.

PARKING BRAKE SERVICE

OVERHAUL

1. Raise and support vehicle, then remove rear wheels.
2. Remove rear disc caliper from adapter as outlined under "Brake Pad Service."

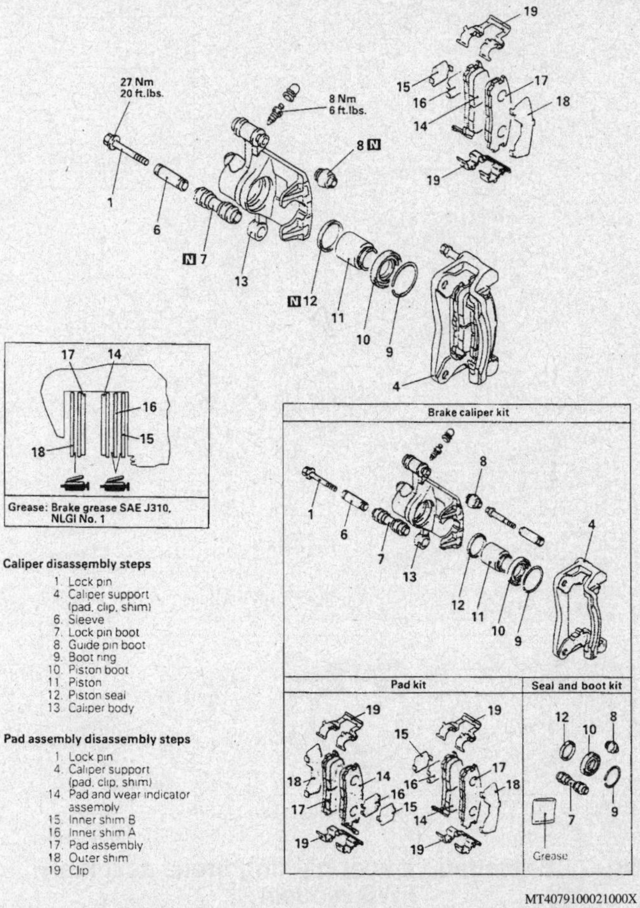
27 Nm
20 ft.lbs.
8 Nm
6 ft.lbs.
Grease: Brake grease SAE J310, NLGI No. 1
Brake caliper kit
Pad kit
Seal and boot kit
Grease
MT4079100021000X

Caliper disassembly steps
1. Lock pin
4. Caliper support (pad, clip, shim)
6. Sleeve
7. Lock pin boot
8. Guide pin boot
9. Boot ring
10. Piston boot
11. Piston
12. Piston seal
13. Caliper body

Pad assembly disassembly steps
1. Lock pin
4. Caliper support (pad, clip, shim)
14. Pad and wear indicator assembly
15. Inner shim B
16. Inner shim A
17. Pad assembly
18. Outer shim
19. Clip

Fig. 4 Exploded view of rear disc brake caliper. FWD models except Diamante Wagon

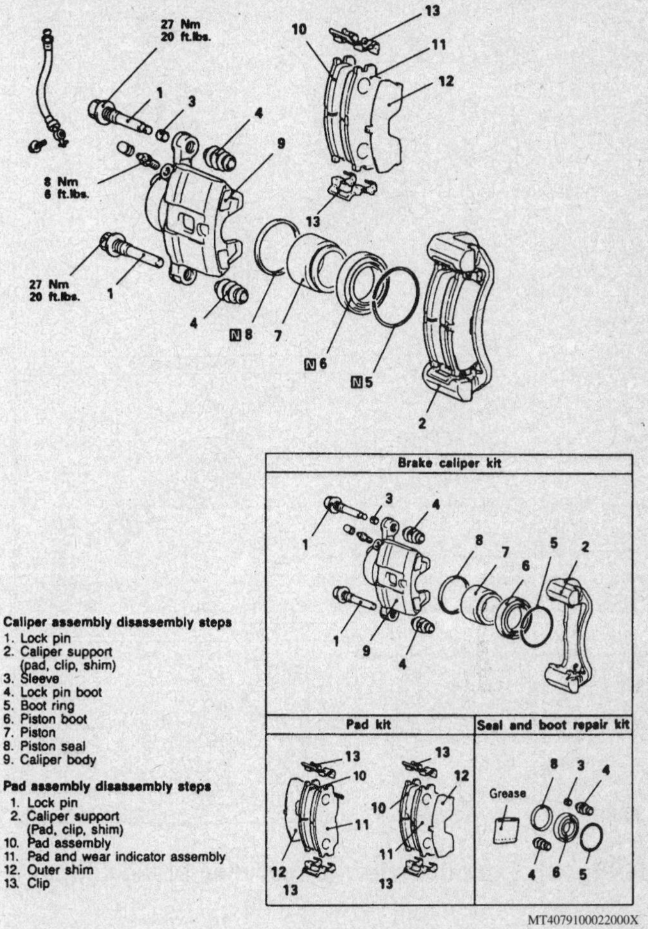
27 Nm
20 ft.lbs.
8 Nm
6 ft.lbs.
Brake caliper kit
Pad kit
Seal and boot repair kit
Grease
MT4079100022000X

Caliper assembly disassembly steps
1. Lock pin
2. Caliper support (pad, clip, shim)
3. Sleeve
4. Lock pin boot
5. Boot ring
6. Piston boot
7. Piston
8. Piston seal
9. Caliper body

Pad assembly disassembly steps
1. Lock pin
2. Caliper support (Pad, clip, shim)
10. Pad assembly
11. Pad and wear indicator assembly
12. Outer shim
13. Clip

Fig. 5 Exploded view of rear disc brake caliper. Diamante Wagon

3. Disassemble parking brakes in numbered sequence shown in **Figs. 7 and 8,** noting the following:
   a. **When removing speed sensor from knuckle, use care not to hit pole piece at its tip against the rotor teeth or other parts.**
   b. Using axle shaft holding tool No. MB990767-01, or equivalent, secure axle shaft and remove companion flange self locking nut.
   c. Using axle shaft puller tool Nos. MB990211-01 and MB990241-01, or equivalents, remove axle shaft from trailing arm.
4. Reverse numbered sequence shown in **Figs. 7 and 8** to assemble parking brakes, noting the following:
   a. Install shoe on anchor spring, **Fig. 9. Each shoe to anchor spring has a unique spring load and spring marked "a" is painted for identification.** Figure shown is for left wheel.
   b. Install adjuster facing left adjusting bolt to vehicle front and right adjusting bolt to vehicle rear.
   c. Secure axle shaft using special tool and install companion flange self locking nut.
   d. **On FWD models,** after tightening flange nut to specifications, align with spindle's indentation and crimp, **Fig. 10.**
   e. **On all models,** insert a .008–.028 inch feeler gauge between speed sensor pole piece and rotor teeth and tighten speed sensor in position where gap is within this range over entire circumference.

ADJUSTMENT

Refer to "Adjustments" for parking brake adjustment procedures.

ADJUSTMENTS

PARKING BRAKE

1. Pull parking brake lever with a force of approximately 45 lbs. and count number of clicks. Lever stroke should be three to five clicks.
2. If parking brake lever stroke is not within specifications, proceed as follows:
   a. Remove cup holder and plug then loosen the adjusting nut on parking brake cable end so cable becomes free.
   b. With engine idling, depress brake pedal several times and confirm that the pedal stroke stops changing. **If pedal stroke stops changing, it indicates that automatic adjusting mechanism is functioning properly to adjust clearance between pads and disc to correct value.**
   c. Disconnect driveshaft and companion flange.
   d. Remove rotor adjusting hole plug and turn adjuster in direction shown in **Fig. 11,** until brake is slightly applied.
   e. Turn adjuster five notches in opposite direction to obtain the .0075 inch shoe to drum clearance.
   f. Turn parking brake cable adjusting nut to obtain a lever stroke of three to five clicks.
   g. After adjustment, ensure there is no play between the adjuster nut and pin.
   h. After adjustments have been made, ensure parking brake operates properly.

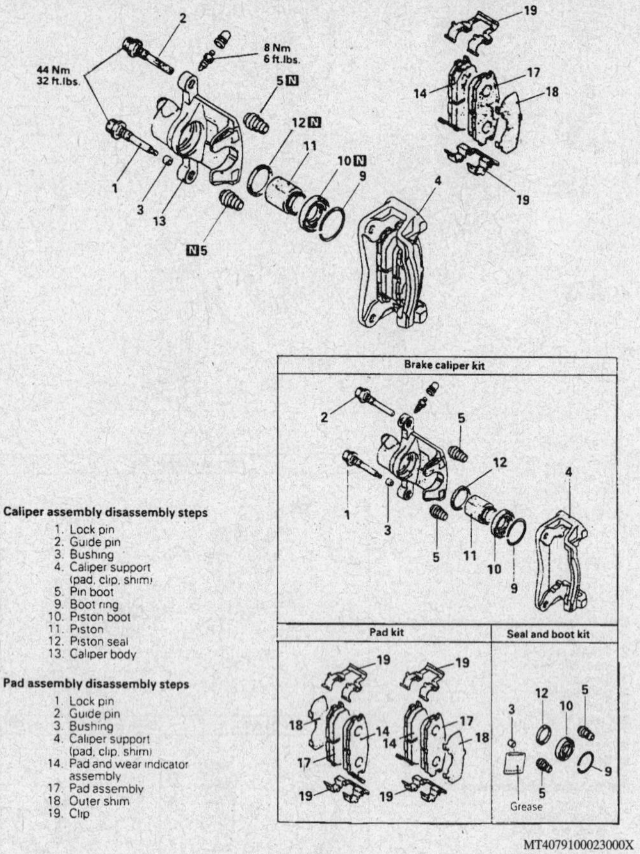
44 Nm
32 ft.lbs.
8 Nm
6 ft.lbs.
Brake caliper kit
Pad kit
Seal and boot kit
Grease
Caliper assembly disassembly steps
1. Lock pin
2. Guide pin
3. Bushing
4. Caliper support (pad, clip, shim)
5. Pin boot
9. Boot ring
10. Piston boot
11. Piston
12. Piston seal
13. Caliper body
Pad assembly disassembly steps
1. Lock pin
2. Guide pin
3. Bushing
4. Caliper support (pad, clip, shim)
14. Pad and wear indicator assembly
17. Pad assembly
18. Outer shim
19. Clip
MT4079100023000X

Fig. 6 Exploded view of rear disc brake caliper. AWD models

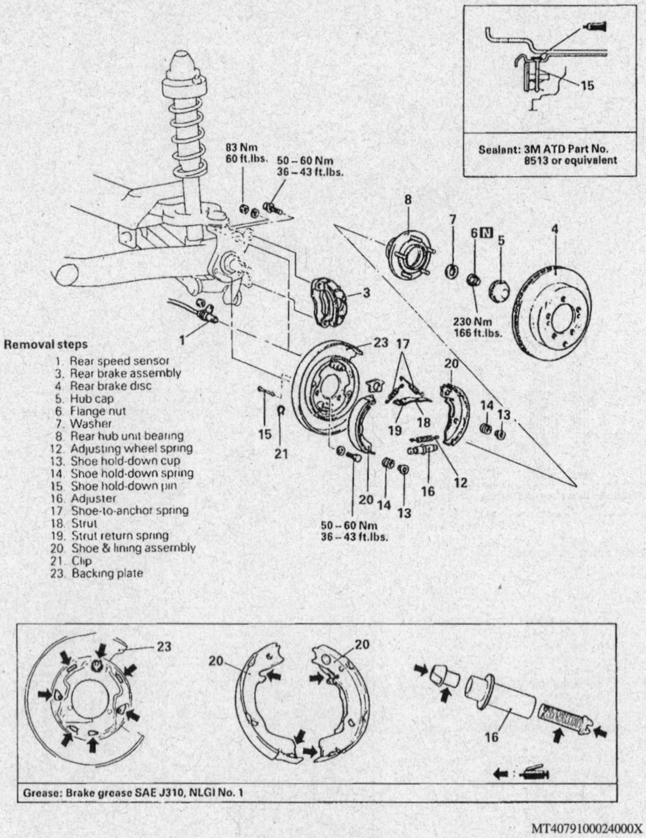
Sealant: 3M ATD Part No. 8513 or equivalent
83 Nm
60 ft.lbs.
50 – 60 Nm
36 – 43 ft.lbs.
230 Nm
166 ft.lbs.
Removal steps
1. Rear speed sensor
3. Rear brake assembly
4. Rear brake disc
5. Hub cap
6. Flange nut
7. Washer
8. Rear hub unit bearing
12. Adjusting wheel spring
13. Shoe hold-down cup
14. Shoe hold-down spring
15. Shoe hold-down pin
16. Adjuster
17. Shoe-to-anchor spring
18. Strut
19. Strut return spring
20. Shoe & lining assembly
21. Clip
23. Backing plate
Grease: Brake grease SAE J310, NLGI No. 1
MT4079100024000X

Fig. 7 Exploded view of parking brake assembly. FWD models

DISC BRAKE SPECIFICATIONS

CALIPER SPECIFICATIONS

Model	Caliper Bore Dia., Inch
FRONT	
Diamante	1.6875①
3000GT AWD	②
3000GT FWD	1.6825①
REAR	
Diamante Sedan	1.3750
Diamante Wagon	1.5000
3000GT AWD	1.5000
3000GT FWD	1.3750

① — Two piston caliper.
② — Four piston caliper, two at 1.5938 inch and two at 1.6875 inch.

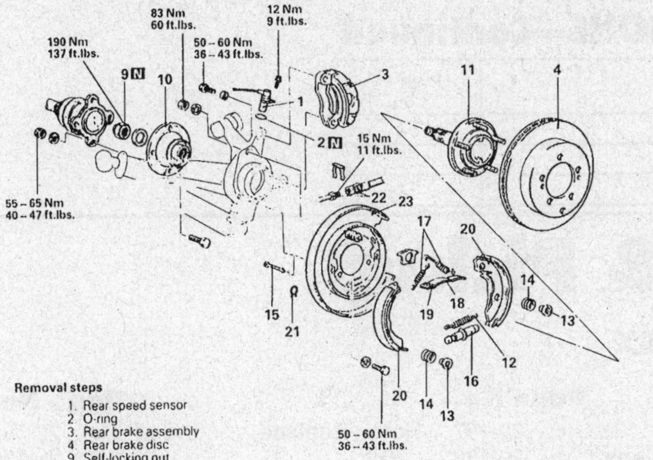
83 Nm
60 ft.lbs.
12 Nm
9 ft.lbs.
190 Nm
137 ft.lbs.
50 – 60 Nm
36 – 43 ft.lbs.
15 Nm
11 ft.lbs.
55 – 65 Nm
40 – 47 ft.lbs.
50 – 60 Nm
36 – 43 ft.lbs.

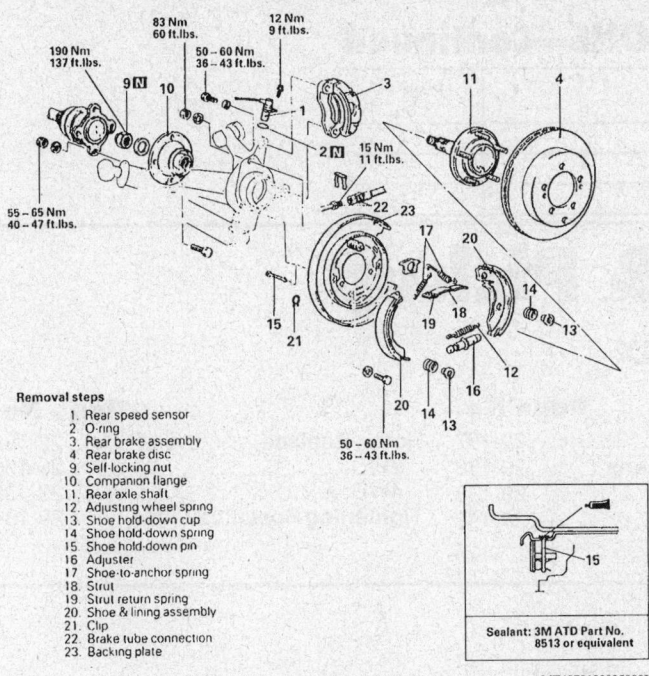

Removal steps
1. Rear speed sensor
2. O-ring
3. Rear brake assembly
4. Rear brake disc
9. Self-locking nut
10. Companion flange
11. Rear axle shaft
12. Adjusting wheel spring
13. Shoe hold-down cup
14. Shoe hold-down spring
15. Shoe hold-down pin
16. Adjuster
17. Shoe-to-anchor spring
18. Strut
19. Strut return spring
20. Shoe & lining assembly
21. Clip
22. Brake tube connection
23. Backing plate

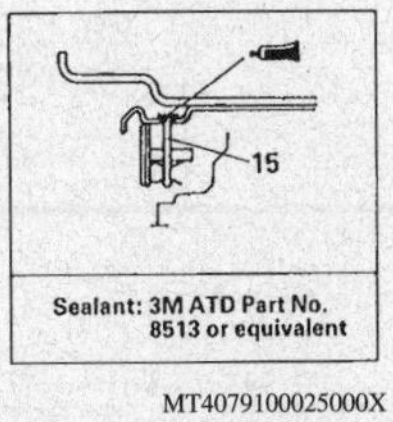
15
Sealant: 3M ATD Part No. 8513 or equivalent
MT4079100025000X

Fig. 8 Exploded view of parking brake assembly. AWD models

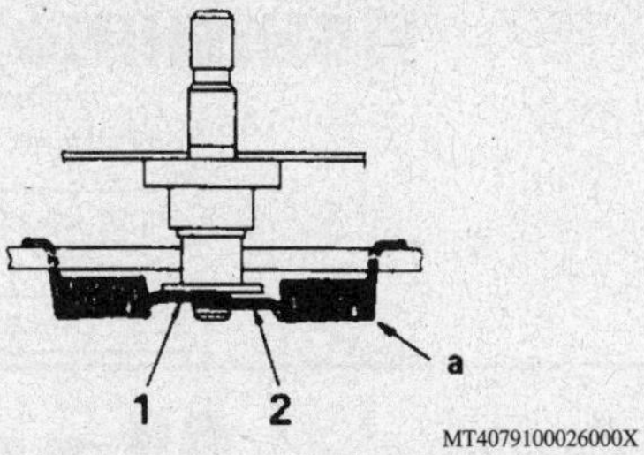
1
2
a
MT4079100026000X

Fig. 9 Shoe installation

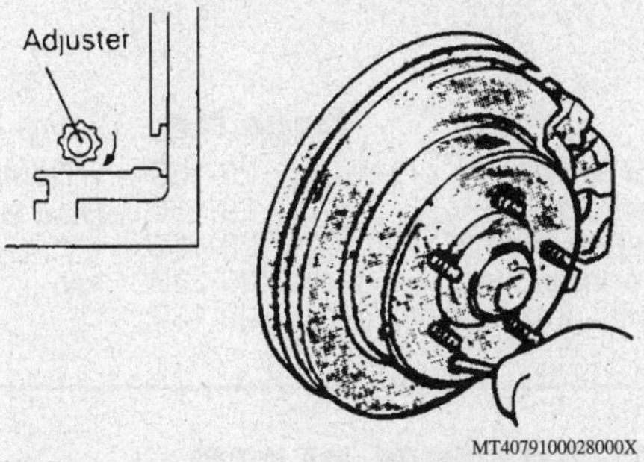
Adjuster
MT4079100028000X

Fig. 11 Parking brake adjustment

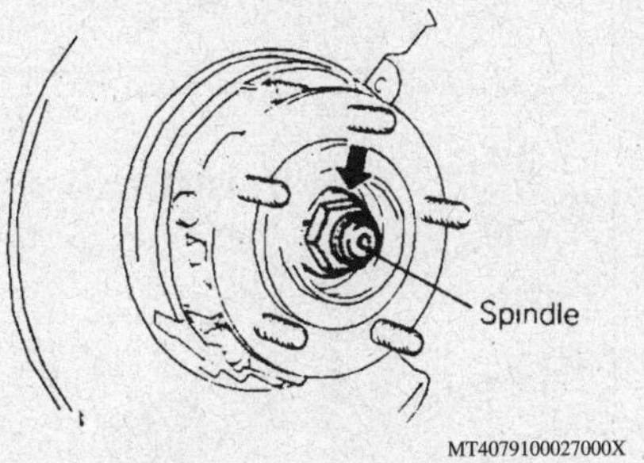
Spindle
MT4079100027000X

Fig. 10 Flange nut installation. FWD models

ROTOR SPECIFICATIONS

Model	Nominal Thickness, Inch	Minimum Refinish Thickness, Inch	Lateral Runout (T.I.R.), Inch
FRONT			
Diamante	.940	.880	.0028
3000GT FWD	.940	.880	.0040
3000GT AWD	1.180	1.120	.0040
REAR			
Diamante Sedan	.710	.650	.0031
Diamante Wagon	.790	.720	.0031
3000GT FWD	.710	.650	.0031
3000GT AWD	.790	.720	.0031

TIGHTENING SPECIFICATIONS

Component	Torque/Ft. Lbs.
Bleeder Screws	6
Brake Rotor	36–43

Continued

TIGHTENING SPECIFICATIONS—Continued

Component	Torque/Ft. Lbs.
Caliper Lockpin	54
Caliper Mounting Bolts	65
Flared Brake Line Nuts	11

Montero & Pickup

INDEX

	Page No.
Brake Pad Service	29-136
Replacement	29-136
Brake System Bleed	29-136
Caliper Service	29-137
Overhaul & Inspection	29-137
Replacement	29-137
Disc Brake Specifications	29-138
Caliper Specifications	29-138
Rotor Specifications	29-138
Rotor, Replace	29-138
2WD	29-138
4WD	29-138
Tightening Specifications	29-139

BRAKE SYSTEM BLEED

The hydraulic brake system must be bled if air has entered the system. Air may enter due to low fluid level, a hydraulic fluid leak, opening of a hydraulic line or replacement of a hydraulic system component. Symptoms include loss of brake operation and/or a low or spongy brake pedal.

On models with ABS, use a suitable filter when adding fluid to reservoir tank.

1. Ensure master cylinder reservoir is full. Add suitable brake fluid as needed, and securely reinstall the master cylinder cap.
2. Raise and support vehicle.
3. Position a drain pan under the wheel being bled.
4. Have an assistant depress the brake pedal with a slow even pressure and hold it. **Do not depress brake pedal fully to the end of the master cylinder stroke. This may cause damage to the master cylinder.**
5. Using a suitable wrench, open the bleeder valve one full turn. Watch for air bubbles in the fluid, and listen for air escaping from the system.
6. With the brake pedal still depressed, close the bleeder valve.
7. Have the assistant pump the brake pedal several times. **Do not depress brake pedal fully to the end of the master cylinder stroke, as this may cause damage to the master cylinder.**
8. Repeat preceding bleed steps until all air is removed from the hydraulic system. **While bleeding the system, recheck brake fluid supply in the master cylinder often so as not to allow the master cylinder to run dry.**
9. Upon completion of hydraulic system bleeding, proceed as follows:
   a. Ensure the master cylinder reservoir is full. Add suitable brake fluid as needed, and securely reinstall the master cylinder cap.
   b. Lower the vehicle. Ensure brake pedal is firm and braking operation is proper.

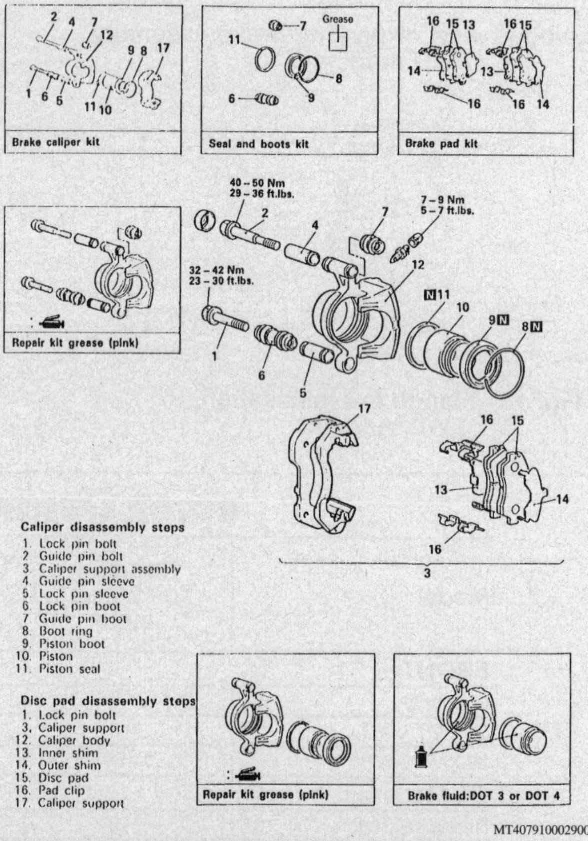

Brake caliper kit
Seal and boots kit
Grease
Brake pad kit
40 – 50 Nm
29 – 36 ft.lbs.
7 – 9 Nm
5 – 7 ft.lbs.
32 – 42 Nm
23 – 30 ft.lbs.
Repair kit grease (pink)
Caliper disassembly steps
1. Lock pin bolt
2. Guide pin bolt
3. Caliper support assembly
4. Guide pin sleeve
5. Lock pin sleeve
6. Lock pin boot
7. Guide pin boot
8. Boot ring
9. Piston boot
10. Piston
11. Piston seal
Disc pad disassembly steps
1. Lock pin bolt
3. Caliper support
12. Caliper body
13. Inner shim
14. Outer shim
15. Disc pad
16. Pad clip
17. Caliper support
Repair kit grease (pink)
Brake fluid:DOT 3 or DOT 4
MT4079100029000X

Fig. 1 Exploded view of disc brake assembly. Pickup

BRAKE PAD SERVICE

REPLACEMENT

1. Raise and support vehicle, then remove front wheel.
2. Remove lockpin bolt, **Figs. 1 through 3.**
3. Lift up caliper body, using the guide pin bolt as a fulcrum. Use wire to suspend the caliper.
4. Remove inner and outer shims, pad assemblies, and pad clips from caliper support.

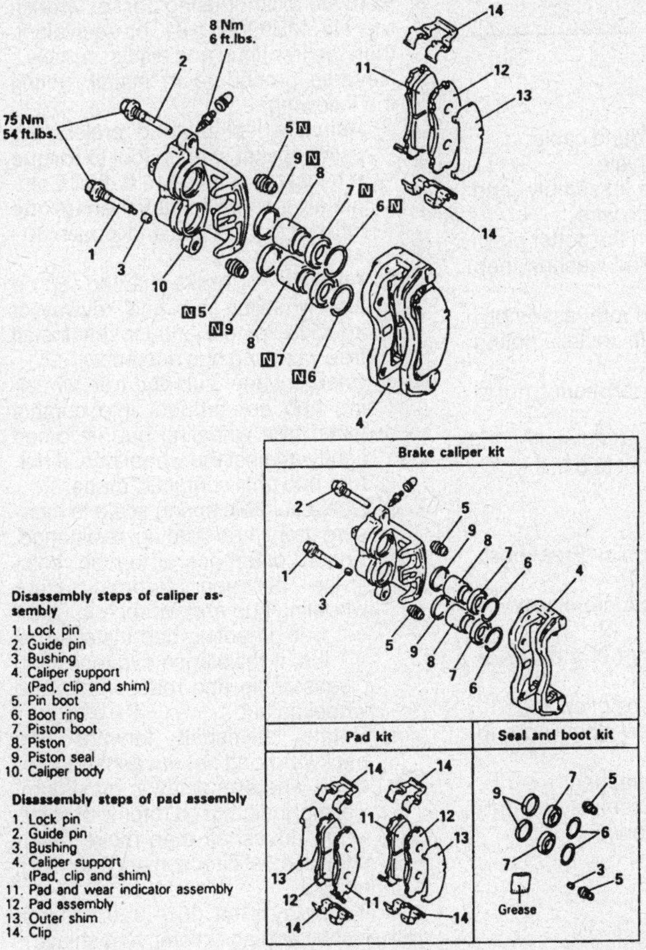
8 Nm
6 ft.lbs.
75 Nm
54 ft.lbs.
Brake caliper kit
Pad kit
Seal and boot kit
Grease

Disassembly steps of caliper assembly
1. Lock pin
2. Guide pin
3. Bushing
4. Caliper support (Pad, clip and shim)
5. Pin boot
6. Boot ring
7. Piston boot
8. Piston
9. Piston seal
10. Caliper body

Disassembly steps of pad assembly
1. Lock pin
2. Guide pin
3. Bushing
4. Caliper support (Pad, clip and shim)
11. Pad and wear indicator assembly
12. Pad assembly
13. Outer shim
14. Clip

MT4079200030000X

Fig. 2 Exploded view of front disc brake assembly. Montero

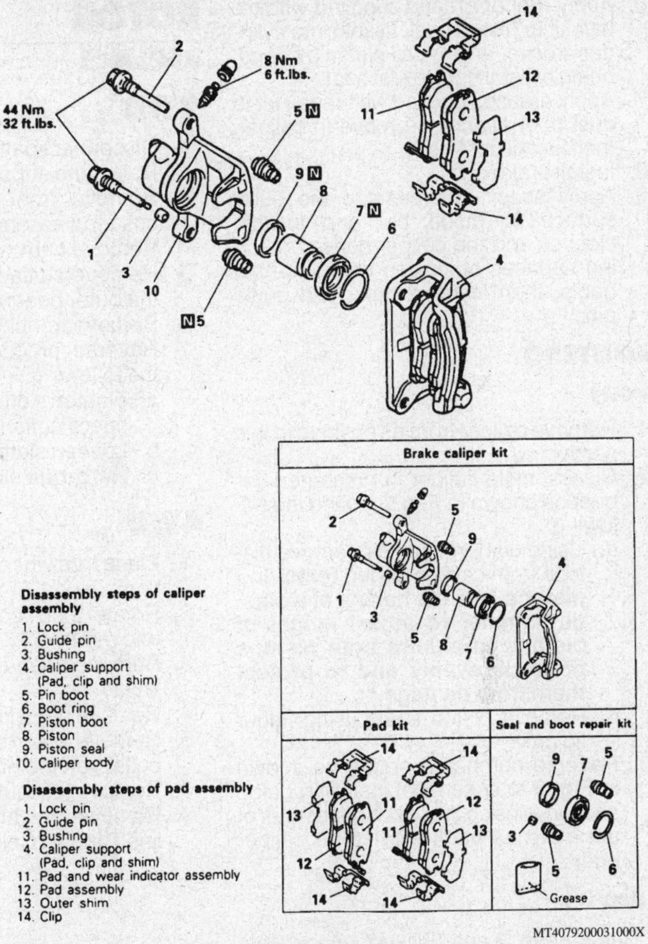
44 Nm
32 ft.lbs.
8 Nm
6 ft.lbs.
Brake caliper kit
Pad kit
Seal and boot repair kit
Grease

Disassembly steps of caliper assembly
1. Lock pin
2. Guide pin
3. Bushing
4. Caliper support (Pad, clip and shim)
5. Pin boot
6. Boot ring
7. Piston boot
8. Piston
9. Piston seal
10. Caliper body

Disassembly steps of pad assembly
1. Lock pin
2. Guide pin
3. Bushing
4. Caliper support (Pad, clip and shim)
11. Pad and wear indicator assembly
12. Pad assembly
13. Outer shim
14. Clip

MT4079200031000X

Fig. 3 Exploded view of rear disc brake assembly. Montero

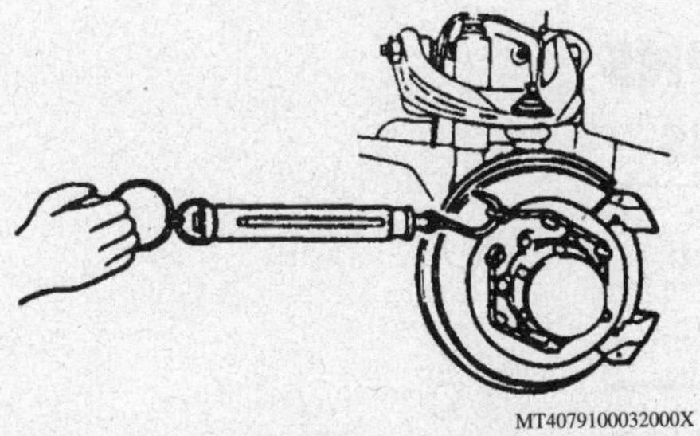

MT4079100032000X

Fig. 4 Hub & brake drag torque measurement

5. Measure hub torque using a suitable spring scale to determine brake drag torque after pan installation, **Fig. 4.**
6. Inspect all components, replacing as necessary.
7. Clean exposed part of piston, then compress piston.
8. Reverse procedure to install, ensuring that pad clips, shims, and pads are properly installed.
9. Measure brake drag torque as follows:
   a. Start engine and hold brake pedal down for five seconds.
   b. Stop engine and turn brake rotor forward ten turns.
   c. Check brake drag using suitable tool.
   d. **On Pickup models,** it will be necessary to disassemble caliper assembly, clean and check for corrosion, worn or damaged parts if difference between brake drag torque and hub torque exceeds 3 ft. lbs.
   e. **On Montero models,** it will be necessary to disassemble caliper assembly, clean and check for corrosion, worn or damaged parts if difference between front brake drag torque and hub torque exceeds 4 ft. lbs. or difference between rear brake drag torque and hub torque exceeds 13 ft. lbs.
10. **On all models,** install wheel.

CALIPER SERVICE

REPLACEMENT

1. Raise and support vehicle, then remove front wheel.
2. Disconnect brake hose.
3. Remove caliper from vehicle.
4. Reverse procedure to install, noting the following:
   a. Tighten brake hose to specifications.
   b. Bleed brake system as outlined under "Brake System Bleed."

OVERHAUL & INSPECTION

PICKUP

1. Remove dust boot.
2. Cover inner side of caliper with rag, then slowly inject compressed air through brake hose fitting to push out piston.
3. Remove piston seal, being careful not to damage cylinder.
4. Clean all metal parts and piston seal with brake fluid and clean dust boot with alcohol.
5. Check components for wear or damage, replacing as necessary. Use new piston seal, dust boot, and boot ring.

6. Apply rubber grease supplied with repair kit to piston seal, fit seal into cylinder groove, and install piston by hand, being careful not to twist seal.
7. Apply grease supplied with repair kit to dust boot attaching groove in caliper, then install dust boot.
8. Install brake pad.
9. Apply specified grease to the outer surface of guide pin and lockpin sleeves and the caliper body contacting surfaces of lockpin and guide pin boots, then install lockpin and guide pin.

MONTERO

Front

1. Remove caliper from as outlined in this section.
2. Disassemble caliper in numbered sequence shown in **Fig. 2,** noting the following:
   a. Using compressed air, remove pistons from caliper. **When removing pistons, use the handle of a plastic hammer to adjust height of pistons to ensure both pistons protrude evenly and to protect them from damage.**
   b. Remove piston seals using finger tip only.
3. Reverse numbered sequence shown in **Fig. 2** to assemble, installing guide and lockpins so that each head mark of pin matches mark located on caliper body.

Rear

Refer to **Fig. 3** and "Pickup" under "Caliper Service " for service procedures.

ROTOR

REPLACE

2WD

1. Disconnect battery ground cable.
2. Raise and support vehicle.
3. Remove front brake assembly and suspend assembly with wire.
4. Remove hub cap, then the cotter pin.
5. Remove slotted nut and washer, then the outer bearing.
6. Remove front hub and rotor assembly.
7. Reverse procedure to install, noting the following:
   a. Tighten slotted wheel bearing nut to specifications.
   b. Loosen slotted nut completely.
   c. **Retorque** slotted nut to 6 ft. lbs.

4WD

1. Place free wheeling hub in "Free" position.
2. Rotate hub cover counterclockwise and remove.
3. Remove snap ring from end of driveshaft.
4. Remove adjusting shims (if equipped).
5. Remove automatic free wheeling hub bolts then the hub.
6. Remove locknut lock washer.
7. Remove disc brake assembly as outlined under "Caliper Service."
8. Remove locknut using socket wrench tool No. MB990954-01, or equivalent, then the front hub and disc assembly.
9. Reverse procedure to install, noting the following:
   a. Adjust wheel bearing preload by using socket wrench tool to **torque** the locknut to 94–145 ft. lbs. Completely loosen locknut, then **torque** locknut to 18 ft. lbs. and loosen 30–40°.
   b. Align key of brake marked "B" on free wheeling hub and keyway of knuckle spindle and loosely install free wheeling hub assembly.
   c. Ensure wheel hub and free wheeling hub are brought into contact when free wheeling hub is forced lightly against the wheel hub. If not, turn hub until contact is made.
   d. Use a suitable spring scale to measure front hub turning resistance. Ensure difference of turning resistance between automatic free wheeling hub and wheel hub (without free wheeling hub installed) is 3.1 lbs. If resistance exceeds limit, disassemble and reassemble free wheeling hub.
   e. Rotate driveshaft forward and backward and set driveshaft to position where endplay is maximum. Set dial indicator on rotor with pointer on driveshaft then move driveshaft in axial direction and measure endplay.
   f. If endplay is not .008–.020 inch, adjust by adding or removing shims.

DISC BRAKE SPECIFICATIONS

CALIPER SPECIFICATIONS

Model	Caliper Bore Diameter, Inch
FRONT	
Montero	1.6875①
Pickup	2.2500
REAR	
Montero	1.6875

① — Two piston caliper.

ROTOR SPECIFICATIONS

Model	Nominal Thickness, Inch	Minimum Refinish Thickness, Inch	Lateral Runout (T.I.R.), Inch
FRONT			
Montero	.940	.882	.004
Pickup	—	.803	.006
REAR			
Montero	.710	.646	.003

TIGHTENING SPECIFICATIONS

Component	Torque/Ft. Lbs.
MONTERO	
Bleeder Screw	5–7
Brake Booster To Pedal Support	6–9
Brake Line Flare Nut	9–12
Brake Pedal Shaft	18–25
Caliper Attaching Bolts (Front)	65
Caliper Attaching Bolts (Rear)	65
Guide Pin Bolt	29–36
Lockpin Bolt	23–30
Master Cylinder To Booster	6–9
Master Cylinder To Brake Line Connector	18–25
Mounting Support To Knuckle	58–72
Pedal Support Member Attaching Bolt	13–18
Piston Stopper	1–2
Reservoir Stopper Bolt	1–2
Speed Sensor Bolt	14
Wheel Bearing Nut	①
Wheel Cylinder To Backing Plate	13–15
PICKUP	
Bleeder Screw	5–7
Brake Line Flare Nut	9–12
Caliper Support Mounting Bolt	58–72
Fitting	11–13
Guide Pin Bolt	29–36
Lockpin Bolt	23–30
Master Cylinder To Brake Booster	6–9
Master Cylinder To Brake Line Connector	18–25
Piston Stopper	1–2
Wheel Bearing Nut	①
Wheel Cylinder To Backing Plate	13–15

① — On 2WD models, torque to 22 ft. lbs., then loosen and torque back to 6 ft. lbs.; on 4WD models, torque to 94–145 ft. lbs., then loosen and torque back to 18 ft. lbs.

Precis

INDEX

	Page No.
Brake Pad Service	29-140
Replacement	29-140
Brake System Bleed	29-140
Caliper Service	29-140
Assemble	29-140
Disassemble	29-140
Installation	29-140
Removal	29-140
Disc Brake Specifications	29-141
Caliper Specifications	29-141
Rotor Specifications	29-141
Rotor, Replace	29-141
Tightening Specifications	29-141

BRAKE SYSTEM BLEED

The hydraulic brake system must be bled if air has entered the system. This condition may be caused by low fluid level, a hydraulic fluid leak, opening of a hydraulic line or replacement of a hydraulic system component. Symptoms include loss of brake operation and/or a low or spongy brake pedal.

On models equipped with ABS, use a suitable filter when adding fluid to reservoir tank.

1. Ensure master cylinder reservoir is full. Add suitable brake fluid as needed, and securely reinstall the master cylinder cap.
2. Raise and support vehicle.
3. Position a drain pan under the wheel being bled.
4. Have an assistant depress the brake pedal with a slow even pressure and hold it. **Do not depress brake pedal fully to the end of the master cylinder stroke. This may cause damage to the master cylinder.**
5. Using a suitable wrench, open the bleeder valve one full turn. Watch for air bubbles in the fluid, and listen for air escaping from the system.
6. With the brake pedal still depressed, close the bleeder valve.
7. Have the assistant pump the brake pedal several times. **Do not depress brake pedal fully to the end of the master cylinder stroke, this may cause damage to the master cylinder.**
8. Repeat preceding bleed steps until all air is removed from the hydraulic system. **While bleeding the system, recheck brake fluid supply in the master cylinder often so as not to allow the master cylinder to run dry.**
9. Upon completion of hydraulic system bleeding, proceed as follows:
   a. Ensure the master cylinder reservoir is full. Add suitable brake fluid as needed, and securely reinstall the master cylinder cap.
   b. Lower the vehicle. Ensure brake pedal is firm and braking operation is satisfactory.

BRAKE PAD SERVICE

REPLACEMENT

1. Raise and support vehicle, then remove wheel/tire assembly.

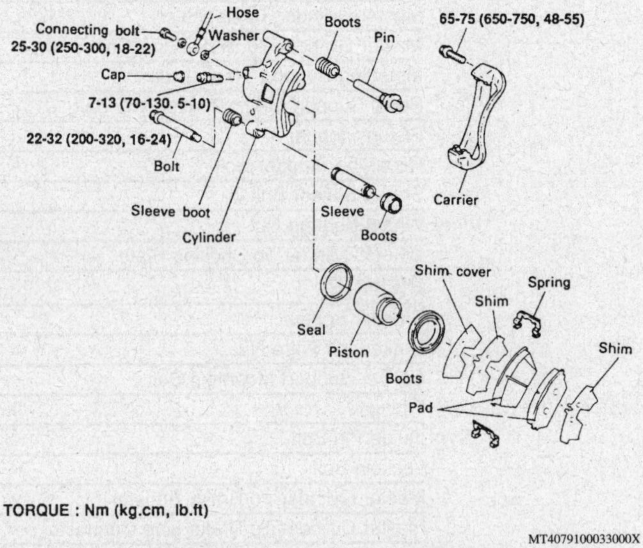

Hose
Connecting bolt
25-30 (250-300, 18-22)
Washer
Boots
Pin
65-75 (650-750, 48-55)
Cap
7-13 (70-130. 5-10)
22-32 (200-320, 16-24)
Bolt
Sleeve boot
Cylinder
Sleeve
Boots
Carrier
Shim cover
Spring
Shim
Seal
Piston
Boots
Shim
Pad
TORQUE : Nm (kg.cm, lb.ft)
MT4079100033000X

Fig. 1 Exploded view of disc brake assembly

2. Remove lower bolt and caliper assembly, **Fig. 1.** Position assembly aside using suitable wire. **Do not disconnect brake hose or allow caliper to hang by hose.**
3. Remove brake pads and shim.
4. Reverse procedure to install, noting the following:
   a. Install new brake pads and attach shim to the outer pad.
   b. Tighten lower bolt to specifications.
   c. Bleed brake system as outlined under "Brake System Bleed."

CALIPER SERVICE

REMOVAL

1. Remove brake pads as described previously.
2. Disconnect and cap brake line(s).
3. Remove caliper attaching bolts and caliper assembly from steering knuckle.

DISASSEMBLE

1. Remove sleeve, sleeve boot and pin boots, **Fig. 1.**
2. Protect fingers with shop towel, then blow piston from caliper bore with compressed air.
3. Remove piston boot, then pry piston seal from caliper bore using a suitable screwdriver.

ASSEMBLE

1. Clean all components with suitable cleaner.
2. Inspect caliper bore, piston and carrier for damage or excessive wear.
3. Apply rubber grease to new piston seal, then install piston seal in caliper bore.
4. Assemble the piston and piston boots as follows:
   a. Apply rubber grease to cylinder inner face, sliding surface of piston and piston boots.
   b. Install piston boots on piston.
   c. Insert piston boots to inner groove of caliper and slide piston into caliper.
5. Assemble sliding components as follows:
   a. Apply rubber grease to sliding surface of sleeve and pin, sliding bore of caliper, pin boots and sleeve boots.
   b. Insert boots into grooves of cylinder.

INSTALLATION

1. Install caliper assembly and attaching bolts on steering knuckle. Tighten caliper to steering knuckle attaching bolts to specifications.
2. Connect brake line(s) and assemble brake pads in caliper as outlined under

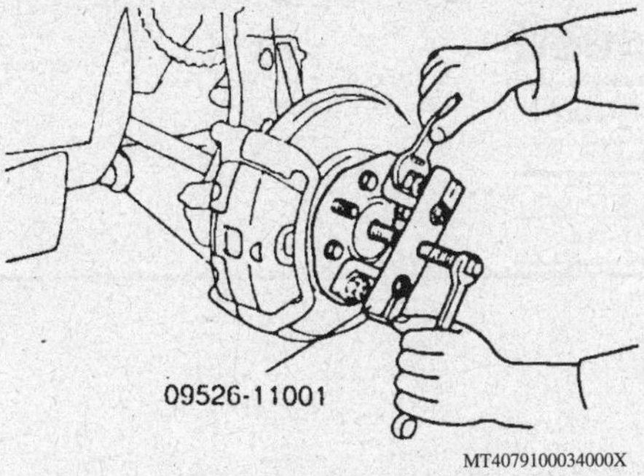
09526-11001
MT4079100034000X

Fig. 2 Axle separation from hub

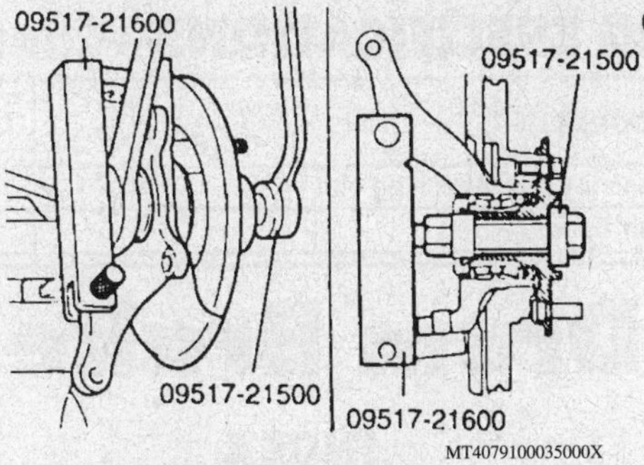
09517-21600
09517-21500
09517-21500
09517-21600
MT4079100035000X

Fig. 3 Hub removal

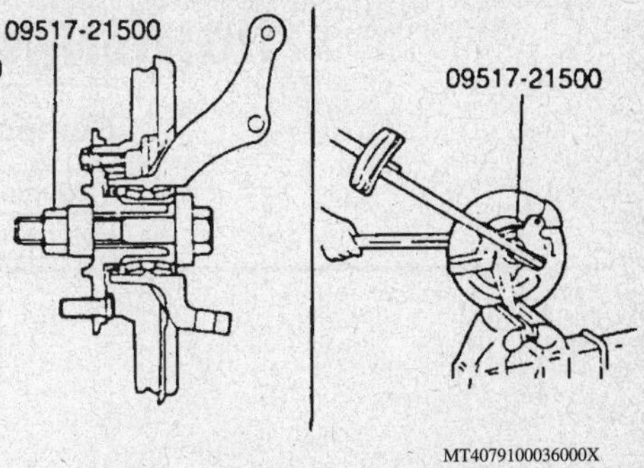
09517-21500
09517-21500
MT4079100036000X

Fig. 4 Hub installation

"Brake Pad Service," then bleed brake system as outlined under "Brake System Bleed."

ROTOR

REPLACE

1. Raise and support vehicle, then remove wheels.
2. Remove caliper as outlined under "Caliper Service."
3. Remove drive axle nut, then disconnect tie rod and ball joint using separator tool No. 09568–31000, or equivalent.
4. Separate drive axle from hub using pusher tool No. 09526–11001, or equivalent, **Fig. 2.**
5. Remove hub and knuckle from strut as an assembly.
6. Place knuckle in a vise, then use puller tool Nos. 09517–21600 and 09517–21500, or equivalents, **Fig. 3,** to remove hub from knuckle. **Do not use a hammer to remove hub. Bearing damage will result.**
7. Remove bolts, then separate rotor from hub.
8. Reverse procedure to install, noting the following:
   a. **Torque** rotor to hub bolts to 37–44 ft. lbs.
   b. Use puller tool No. 09517–21500, or equivalent, to install hub into knuckle, **Fig. 4. Torque** tool to 167 ft. lbs.
   c. With tool No. 09517–21500, or equivalent, installed and tightened to specification, turning **torque** of rotor should not exceed 11 inch lbs. Axial play should not exceed 0.0043 inch.
   d. **Torque** drive axle nut to 148–192 ft. lbs.
   e. **Torque** hub to knuckle bolts to 66–77 ft. lbs.

DISC BRAKE SPECIFICATIONS

CALIPER SPECIFICATIONS

Year	Caliper Bore Diameter, Inch
1993	2.1260

ROTOR SPECIFICATIONS

Nominal Thickness, Inch	Minimum Refinish Thickness, Inch	Lateral Runout (T.I.R.), Inch
.750	.669	.006

TIGHTENING SPECIFICATIONS

Component	Torque/Ft. Lbs.
Axle Nut	148–192
Backing Plate Attaching Bolt	36–43
Bleeder Screw	5.1–6.5
Brake Booster Hose Fitting To Manifold	5.8–6.5
Brake Booster Mounting Nuts	5.8–6.5
Brake Hose Flare Nut	9–12
Brake Hose To Caliper	18–22
Caliper Assembly To Knuckle	47–54
Caliper Guide Rod Bolt	16–23
Caliper Pin Bolt	25–32
Driveshaft Nut	148–192
Hub Nut	148–192
Hub To Knuckle Bolts	66–77
Master Cylinder To Booster Attaching Nuts	5.8–6.5

Continued

TIGHTENING SPECIFICATIONS—Continued

Component	Torque/Ft. Lbs.
Proportioning Valve Attaching Nut	5.8–8.7
Rotor Hub Bolts	37–44

Drum Brakes

INDEX

Page No.	Page No.	Page No.
Adjustments 29-142	Service Brakes 29-142	**Drum Brake Specifications** 29-144
Parking Brake 29-142	**Brake Service** 29-142	**Tightening Specifications** 29-144

BRAKE SERVICE

For drum brake service procedures, refer to **Figs. 1 through 6.**

ADJUSTMENTS

SERVICE BRAKES

Rear brakes should be adjusted after rear brake service or before adjusting parking brake. These brakes have self-adjusting shoe mechanisms that maintain correct brake lining to drum clearances at all times. The automatic self-adjusting mechanism operates whenever the parking brake lever is applied on all models except the Duo-Servo type. These contain a self-adjusting mechanism which operates when the brakes are applied as the vehicle is moving rearward.

PARKING BRAKE

Montero & Precis

1. Pull parking brake lever with force of approximately 45 lbs., noting the following:
   a. **On Montero models,** lever stroke should be four to six notches.
   b. **On Precis models,** lever stroke should be five to seven notches.
2. **On all models,** if lever stroke is not as indicated, pull parking brake lever repeatedly to adjust shoe clearance, then adjust parking brake lever stroke by turning cable adjusting nut.
3. Raise and support rear of vehicle and, with parking brake lever released, turn rear wheels to ensure rear brakes are not dragging.

Eclipse & Galant

1. Pull parking brake lever with a force of approximately 45 lbs. and count number of clicks. Lever stroke should be five to seven clicks.
2. If parking brake lever stroke is not within specifications, proceed as follows:
   a. Remove center console, then loosen adjusting nut to end of cable rod to free parking brake cable.
   b. With engine idling, depress brake pedal several times and confirm that the pedal stroke stops changing. **If pedal stroke stops changing, it indicates that automatic adjusting mechanism is functioning properly to adjust clearance between drum and shoe assembly to correct value.**
   c. Turn adjusting nut to adjust parking brake lever stroke to specified range. **If number of brake lever notches engaged is less than specified value, cable has been pulled excessively and failure of the automatic adjuster mechanism may result.**
   d. After adjusting lever stroke, raise and support rear of vehicle. With parking brake lever released, turn rear wheels to ensure rear brakes are not dragging.

Mirage

1. Pull parking brake lever with a force of approximately 45 lbs. and count number of clicks. Lever stroke should be five to seven clicks.
2. If parking brake lever stroke is not within specifications, proceed as follows:
   a. Remove center console, then with parking brake lever released, loosen cable adjuster locknut.
   b. After slacking off parking brake cable locknut, tighten cable adjuster locknut to take up slack in cable. **Excessive pulling of cable may result in failure of the automatic adjuster mechanism.**
   c. Pull parking brake lever repeatedly while depressing brake pedal until no more clicks are heard from the automatic adjuster mechanism.
   d. Adjust parking brake lever to the specified stroke, then secure with locknut.
   e. After adjusting lever stroke, raise and support rear of vehicle. With parking brake lever released, turn rear wheels to ensure rear brakes are not dragging.

Pickup

1. Adjust rear brake shoe clearance.
2. **On RWD models,** adjust turnbuckle so that lever stroke is 16–17 notches with pulling force of 66 lbs.
3. **On 4WD models,** turn adjusting nut to obtain lever stroke as described in preceding step.
4. **On all models,** ensure rear parking brake cable is not taut.
5. **On RWD models,** ensure balancer is almost parallel with center line of vehicle.
6. **On 4WD models,** ensure joint and equalizer are at right angles to each other.
7. **On all models,** if, after above adjustments, stroke is not 16–17 notches, rear brake automatic adjusters are malfunctioning. Correct as necessary.

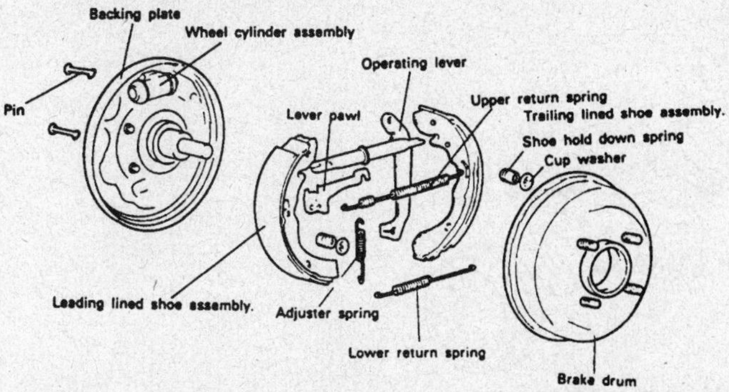
Backing plate
Wheel cylinder assembly
Pin
Operating lever
Lever pawl
Upper return spring
Trailing lined shoe assembly.
Shoe hold down spring
Cup washer
Leading lined shoe assembly.
Adjuster spring
Lower return spring
Brake drum

MT4089100001000X

Fig. 1 Exploded view of drum brake assembly. Precis

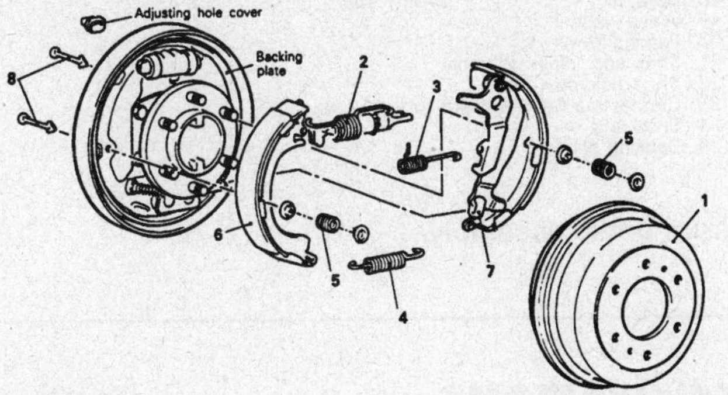
Adjusting hole cover
Backing plate

1. Brake drum
2. Shoe return spring with brake shoe adjuster
3. Adjusting spring
4. Shoe retainer spring
5. Shoe hold-down spring
6. Shoe and lining assembly
7. Shoe and lever assembly
8. Shoe hold-down pin

MT4089100004000X

Fig. 3 Exploded view of drum brake assembly. Pickup

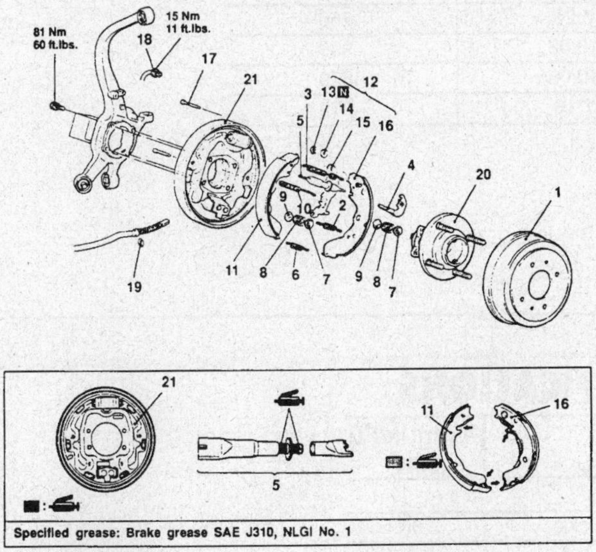
81 Nm
60 ft.lbs.
15 Nm
11 ft.lbs.
Specified grease: Brake grease SAE J310, NLGI No. 1

Removal steps

1. Brake drum
2. Lever return spring
3. Shoe-to-lever spring
4. Adjuster lever
5. Auto adjuster assembly
6. Retainer spring
7. Shoe hold-down cup
8. Shoe hold-down spring
9. Shoe hold-down cup
10. Shoe-to-shoe spring
11. Shoe and lining assembly
12. Shoe and lever assembly
13. Retainer
14. Wave washer
15. Parking lever
16. Shoe and lining assembly
17. Shoe hold-down pin
18. Connection for the brake pipe
19. Snap ring
20. Rear hub assembly
21. Backing plate

MT4089400007000X

Fig. 5 Exploded view of drum brake assembly. Eclipse & 1994–96 Galant

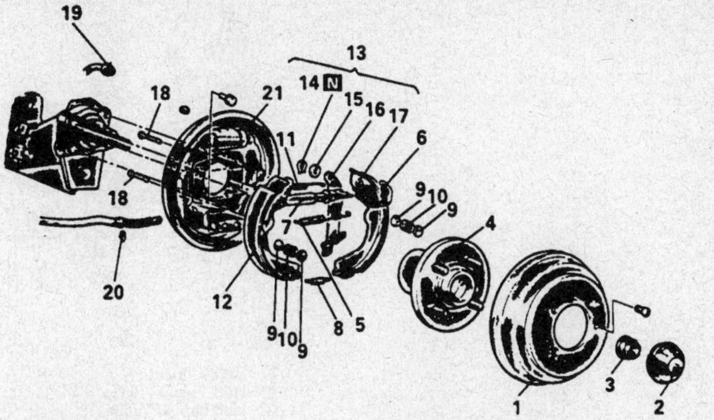

1. Brake drum
   Adjustment of shoe outside diameter
2. Hub cap
3. Wheel bearing nut
4. Rear hub assembly
5. Shoe to lever spring
6. Adjuster lever
7. Auto adjuster assembly
8. Retainer spring
9. Shoe hold down cups
10. Shoe hold down springs
11. Shoe to shoe spring
12. Shoe and lining assembly
13. Shoe and lining and pin assembly
14. Retainer
15. Wave washer
16. Parking lever
17. Shoe and lining assembly
18. Shoe hold down pins
19. Brake tube
20. Snap ring
21. Backing plate

MT4089100003000X

Fig. 2 Exploded view of drum brake assembly. Mirage

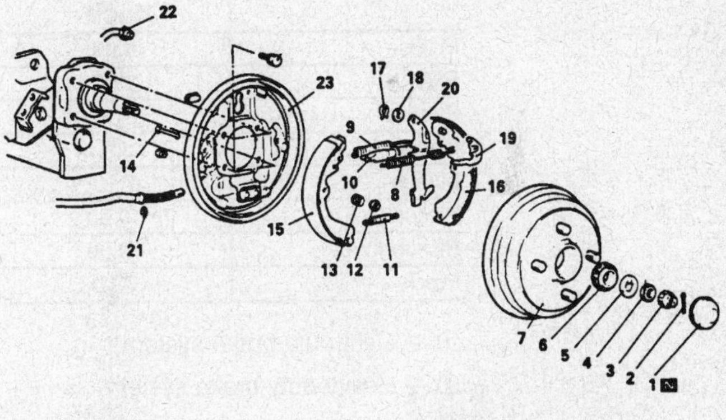

1. Hub cap
2. Cotter pin
3. Lock cap
4. Wheel bearing nut
5. Tongued washer
6. Outer bearing inner race
7. Brake drum
8. Shoe-to-lever spring
9. Shoe-to-shoe spring
10. Auto adjuster assembly
11. Retainer spring
12. Shoe hold down cups
13. Shoe hold down springs
14. Shoe hold down pins
15. Shoe and lining assembly
16. Shoe and lever assembly
17. Retainer
18. Wahser
19. Auto adjuster lever
20. Parking brake lever
21. Snap ring
22. Brake tube
23. Backing plate

MT4089100005000X

Fig. 4 Exploded view of drum brake assembly. 1993 Galant

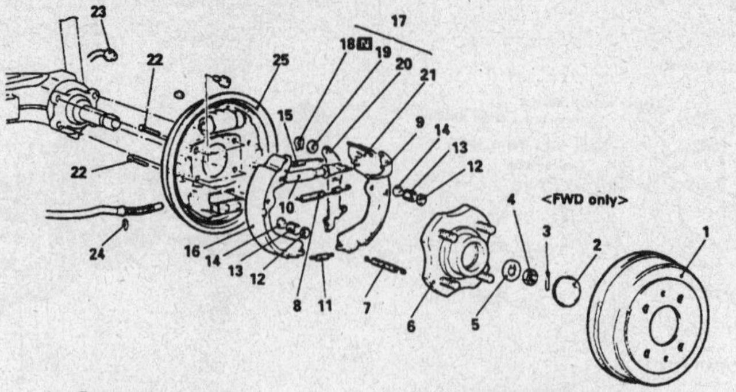
<FWD only>

1. Brake drum
2. Hub cap <2WD>
3. Hub cap <FWD>
4. Split pin <AWD>
5. Washer
6. Rear hub washer
7. Lever return spring <EXPO LRV (AWD), EXPO>
8. Shoe-to-lever spring
9. Adjuster lever
10. Auto adjuster assembly
11. Retainer
12. Shoe hold-down cup
13. Shoe hold-down spring
14. Shoe hold-down cup
15. Shoe-to-shoe spring
16. Shoe and lining assembly
17. Shoe and lever assembly
18. Retainer
19. Wave washer
20. Parking lever
21. Shoe and lining assembly
22. Shoe hold-down pin
23. Connection for the brake tube
24. Snap ring
25. Backing plate

MT4089100006000X

Fig. 6 Exploded view of drum brake assembly. Expo

DRUM BRAKE SPECIFICATIONS

Model	Brake Drum Inside Dia., Inch	Maximum Refinish Dia., Inch	Rear Wheel Cylinder Bore, Inch
Eclipse	8.00	8.10	.813
Expo①	8.00	8.10	—
Expo②	9.00	9.10	—
Galant	③	④	.750
Mirage	7.10	7.20	.750
Pickup 2WD	10.00	10.08	.930
Pickup 4WD	10.00	10.08	.870
Precis	7.10	7.16	.813

① — Light duty brake system.

② — Heavy duty brake system.

③ — 1993, 8.00 inch; 1994–96, 9.00 inch.

④ — 1993, 8.10 inch; 1994–96, 9.10 inch.

TIGHTENING SPECIFICATIONS

Year	Component	Torque/Ft. Lbs.
ECLIPSE		
1995–96	Backing Plate To Knuckle	60
	Bleeder Screw	6
	Flared Brake Line Nuts	11
	Wheel Cylinder Bolt	7
EXPO		
1993–95	Bleeder Screw	6
	Brake Line To Wheel Cylinder	11
	Rear Axle Nut	17
	Wheel Cylinder Mounting Bolts	7

Continued

TIGHTENING SPECIFICATIONS—Continued

Year	Component	Torque/Ft. Lbs.
GALANT		
1993	Backing Plate To Axle Beam	36–43
	Bleeder Screw	5–7
	Flared Brake Line Nuts	9–12
	Rear Brake Assembly Installation Bolt	36–43
	Wheel Bearing Nut	7
	Wheel Cylinder Installation Bolt	6–9
1994–96	Backing Plate To Knuckle	60
	Bleeder Screw	6
	Flared Brake Line Nuts	11
	Wheel Cylinder Bolt	7
MIRAGE		
1993–96	Backing Plate & Rear Axle Beam	36–43
	Bleeder Screw	5–7
	Flared Brake Line Nuts	9–12
	Rear Drum Brake Wheel Cylinder & Backing Plate	6–9
	Wheel Bearing Nut	108–145
MONTERO		
1993–96	Bleeder Screw	5–7
	Brake Line Flare Nut	9–12
	Wheel Cylinder To Backing Plate	13–15
PICKUP		
1993–96	Bleeder Screw	5–7
	Brake Line Flare Nut	9–12
	Wheel Cylinder To Backing Plate	13–15
PRECIS		
1993	Backing Plate Attaching Bolt	36–43
	Bleeder Screw	5.1–6.5
	Brake Hose Flare Nut	9–12
	Proportioning Valve Attaching Nut	5.8–8.7
	Wheel Cylinder Attaching Bolt	8.7–13

Hydraulic Brake Systems

NOTE: On Air Bag Equipped Models, Refer To "Air Bag System Precautions" Located In The Front Of This Manual For System Disarming & Arming Procedures.

INDEX

	Page No.
Adjustments	29-146
Brake Booster Pushrod	29-146
Brake System Bleed	29-148
Hydraulic System Bleed	29-148
Master Cylinder Bleed	29-148
Component Replacement	29-146
Master Cylinder	29-146
Wheel Cylinder	29-147
Component Service	29-147
Master Cylinder	29-147
Wheel Cylinder	29-147
Diagnosis & Testing	29-146
Proportioning Valve	29-146
Hydraulic Brake System Specifications	29-150
Precautions	29-146
Air Bag Systems	29-146
Tightening Specifications	29-151

PRECAUTIONS

AIR BAG SYSTEMS

Refer to "Air Bag System Precautions" in the front of this manual for system disarming and arming procedures.

DIAGNOSIS & TESTING

PROPORTIONING VALVE

Except Pickup & 1993 Montero

1. Connect two pressure gauges to proportioning valve, one to the output side and one to the input side, **Fig. 1.**
2. Bleed system after connecting gauges.
3. Depress brake pedal and ensure measured values are within specifications shown in "Hydraulic Brake System Specifications" chart at end of this section.

Pickup & 1993 Montero

1. Check load proportioning valve spring length with vehicle on flat ground.
2. Press load sensor lever and measure distance between spring ends, **Fig. 2.**
3. **On all models except 1993 Montero,** distance should be between 6.93–7.05 inch.
4. **On 1993 Montero models,** distance should be 8.8–9.0 inches. Adjust spring support if not within specifications, **Fig. 3.**
5. **On all models,** connect two pressure gauges to proportioning valve, one to the output side and one to the input side, **Fig. 4.**
6. Bleed system after connecting gauges, then remove load sensor spring.
7. Depress brake pedal and ensure measured values are within specifications as shown in "Hydraulic Brake System Specifications" chart at the end of this section.
8. Install load sensor spring, then supply load to rear of vehicle so that distance between load sensing proportioning valve lever hole and hole for support come to midpoint of standard value range with lever slightly pressed in, **Fig. 2.**
9. **On Pickup models except 2WD with heavy duty suspension,** output pressure should be 299–583 psi at an input pressure of 1991 psi.
10. **On 2WD Pickup models with heavy duty suspension,** output pressure should be 512–683 psi at an input pressure of 1991 psi.
11. **On 1993 Montero models,** with input at pressure at 1422, output should be between 873–1001 psi, or at a input pressure of 2560, output pressure should be between 1129–1314 psi.
12. **On all models,** after checking load sensing proportioning valve, adjust spring length as necessary.

ADJUSTMENTS

BRAKE BOOSTER PUSHROD

1. Remove master cylinder as outlined under "Component Replacement," then proceed as follows:
   a. Measure distance between master cylinder end face and piston, **Fig. 5.** Position a square (straight scale) against edge of master cylinder, then measure and subtract thickness of the square to determine dimension B.
   b. Find dimension C by measuring distance between brake booster mounting surface and the end face, **Fig. 6.**
   c. Measure distance between master cylinder mounting surface and the pushrod end, **Fig. 7.** Find dimension D by subtracting the square's thickness from the measurement taken.
   d. Find brake booster to primary piston clearance dimension A, **Fig. 8,** using the formula A = B–C–D. Refer to **Fig. 9** for proper clearance specifications.
   e. If dimension A is not as specified, adjust brake booster pushrod as shown, **Fig. 10.**

COMPONENT REPLACEMENT

MASTER CYLINDER

Except Diamante & 1995-96 Eclipse

1. Disconnect brake fluid sensor electrical connector from master cylinder reservoir.
2. Position a drain pan under master cylinder.
3. **On models with separately mounted reservoir,** disconnect reservoir hoses from the master cylinder.
4. **On all models,** disconnect brake lines from the master cylinder. Plug all lines and fittings.
5. Remove master cylinder to brake booster attaching nuts.
6. Pull master cylinder outward and away from brake booster.
7. Reverse procedure to install, noting the following:
   a. Prior to master cylinder installation, adjust brake booster pushrod as described under "Adjustments" in this section.
   b. Bleed master cylinder and hydraulic system as described under "Brake System Bleed" in this section.

Diamante

1. Position a drain pan under master cylinder.
2. Remove brake line connectors, then brake lines.
3. Remove proportioning valve.
4. **On models with ABS brakes,** remove connector assembly.
5. **On all models,** remove master cylinder attaching bolts, then the master cylinder.
6. Reverse procedure to install, noting the following:
   a. Prior to master cylinder installation, adjust brake booster pushrod as described under "Adjustments."
   b. Bleed hydraulic system as described under "Brake System Bleed."

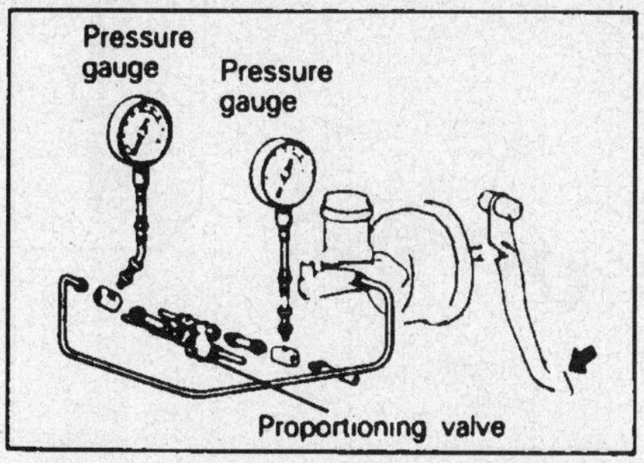
Pressure gauge
Pressure gauge
Proportioning valve

MT4099100012000X

Fig. 1 Proportioning valve pressure gauge test connection

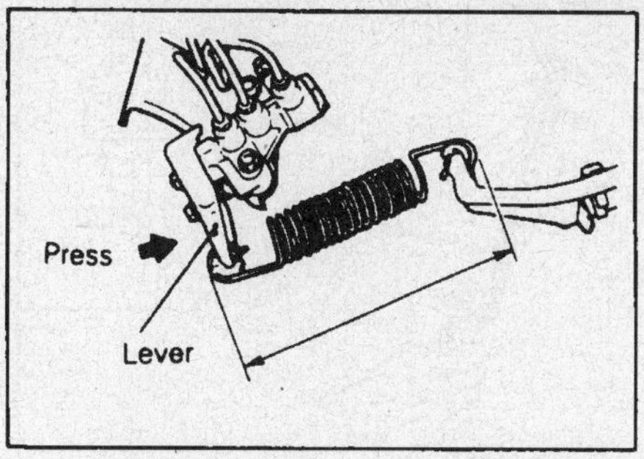
Press
Lever

MT4099100013000X

Fig. 2 Load sensing proportioning valve spring. Expo, Pickup & 1993 Montero

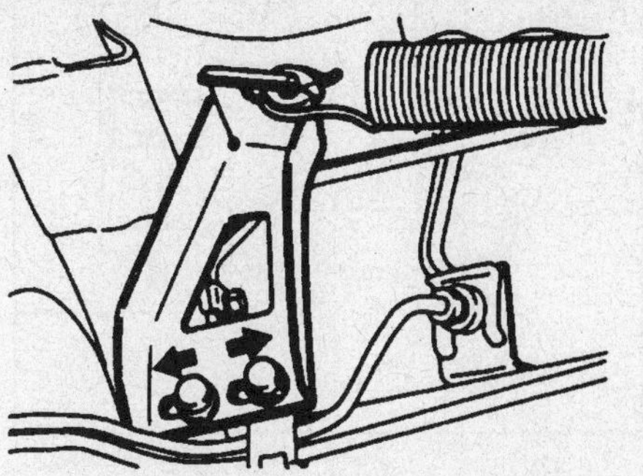

MT4099200014000X

Fig. 3 Spring support bracket. 1993 Montero

1995–96 Eclipse

1. Drain brake fluid from reservoir.
2. **On models equipped with manual transaxle,** remove clutch fluid reservoir bracket.
3. **On models equipped with 2.0L nonturbocharged engine,** remove battery, relay assembly mounting bolts and washer tank mounting bolts.
4. **On models equipped with 2.0L turbocharged engine and 2.4L engine,** remove center member assembly mounting bolts, engine mount bracket, A/C compressor mounting bolts, A/C high pressure hose clamp mounting bolts and power steering pressure hose, pipe and return pipe clamp mounting bolts.
5. **On all models,** remove brake fluid reservoir from mounting bracket, then disconnect brake tubes at master cylinder.
6. Remove bolts securing master cylinder to power booster, then remove cylinder from vehicle.
7. Reverse procedure to install, noting the following:
   a. Adjust brake booster pushrod clearance as outlined under "Adjustments."
   b. Bleed master cylinder and brake system as outlined under "Brake System Bleed."

WHEEL CYLINDER

Removal

1. Remove wheel, drum and brake shoes.
2. Loosen brake line fitting at wheel cylinder. Do not pull metal line away from cylinder.
3. Remove screw holding cylinder to backing plate.
4. Separate wheel cylinder from brake line and backing plate by pulling cylinder outward and away from backing plate.

Installation

1. Wipe end of hydraulic line to remove any foreign matter.
2. Position wheel cylinder to backing plate. Install brake line to cylinder and start connecting fitting.
3. Secure wheel cylinder to backing plate, then complete tightening of brake line fitting.

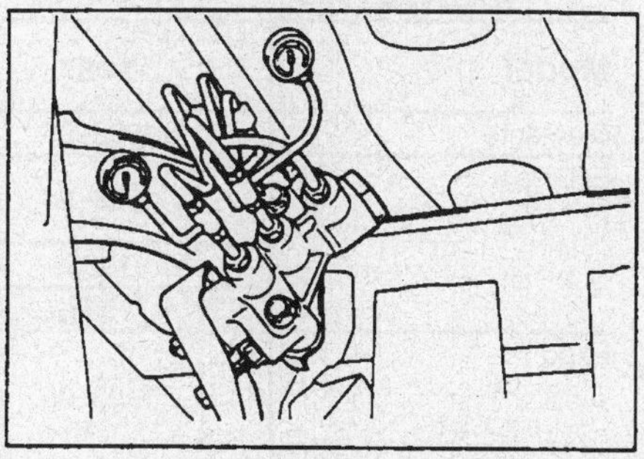

MT4099200015000X

Fig. 4 Load sensing proportioning valve. Pickup & 1993 Montero

4. Install brake shoes, drum and wheel.
5. Bleed system as outlined under "Brake System Bleed."

COMPONENT SERVICE

MASTER CYLINDER

OVERHAUL

1. Disassemble master cylinder in numbered sequence shown, **Figs. 11 and 12.** Note the position of all parts as they are removed for proper installation.
2. **On models equipped with attached reservoir master cylinder,** remove reservoir screw and cap, brake fluid sensor, float, then the reservoir, **Fig. 11.**
3. **On models equipped with separately mounted reservoir,** remove nipple, **Fig. 12.**
4. Use a wooden stick or dowel to depress primary piston into cylinder bore.
5. **On all models except Precis,** with pushrod depressed, remove piston stopper bolt, then the piston stopper ring.
6. **On Precis models,** remove snap ring.
7. **On all models,** release pushrod, then remove piston assemblies. If secondary piston assembly is stuck in the bore, apply a light amount of compressed air to the secondary outlet port until piston assembly works free.
8. Reverse procedure to assemble, noting the following:
   a. **On models equipped with separate reservoir,** when replacing nipples, make sure primary and secondary nipples are installed properly, **Fig. 13.**
   b. **On all models,** use all parts contained in repair kit.
   c. Coat all components with clean brake fluid.

CLEANING & INSPECTION

Examine reservoirs for foreign matter and check all passages for restrictions. If there is any indication of contamination or evidence of corrosion, service the hydraulic system as needed, then flush the entire system as outlined under "Brake System Bleed."

When disassembled, wash all parts in denatured alcohol or clean brake fluid. Use an air hose to blow out all passages, orifices and valve holes. Air dry and place parts on clean paper or lint-free cloth.

1. Check components for wear, damage, or corrosion. Replace as needed.
2. Check master cylinder bore for scoring, rust or pitting. Replace as necessary.

WHEEL CYLINDER

OVERHAUL

Note position of all parts as they are removed for proper installation, **Fig. 14.**

Disassemble

1. Remove boots, piston, cups and spring from wheel cylinder.
2. Wipe cylinder walls with denatured alcohol or clean brake fluid.
3. Examine cylinder bore. A scored bore may be honed, unless bore diameter will be increased by more than .005 inch. Replace as necessary.
4. Check pistons for wear or damage. Replace as necessary.

Assemble

1. Before assembling, wash hands with soap and water so as not to contaminate rubber parts.
2. Use all parts contained in repair kit. Lubricate cylinder walls and rubber parts with clean brake fluid.
3. Carefully install spring, cups, pistons and boots in housing.

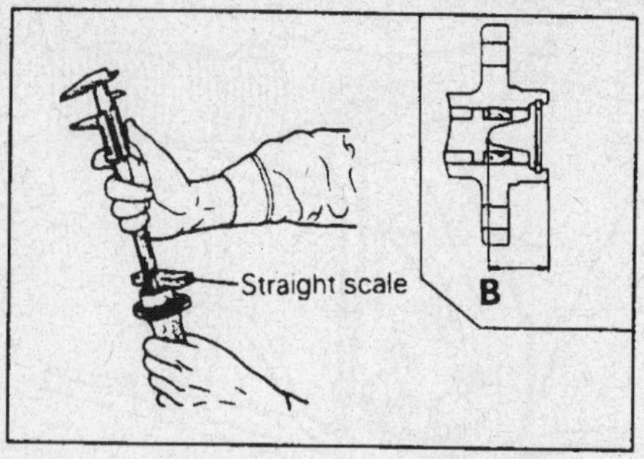

Straight scale
B

MT4099100007000X

Fig. 5 Distance B measurement between master cylinder end face & piston

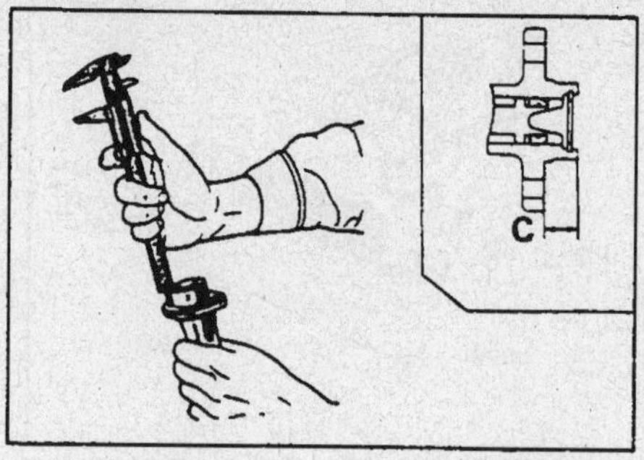

C

MT4099100008000X

Fig. 6 Distance C measurement between brake booster mounting on master cylinder & end face

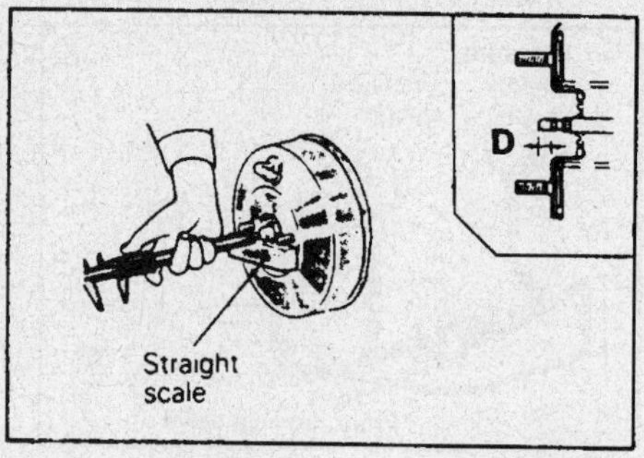

D
Straight scale

MT4099100009000X

Fig. 7 Distance D measurement between master cylinder mounting surface & pushrod end

Model	Year	Booster Size, Inches	Pushrod Clearance, Inch
Diamante	1993–96	—	.0260–.0330
Eclipse	1993–94	7 & 8	.0200–.0280
		9	.0310–.0390
	1995	All	.0255–.0334⑥
	1996	All	.0260–.0340
Expo	1993–95	7	.0200–.0280
		8	.0200–.0310
		9	.0240–.0390
Galant	1993	7 & 8②	.0200–.0280
		9①	.0310–.0390
	1994–95	7 & 8③⑤	.0160–.0240
		8 & 9②	.0160–.0240
		9④	.0240–.0310
	1996	7 & 8⑤	.0160–.0240
		9④	.0240–.0310
Mirage	1993–96	7	.0160–.0240
		8	.0180–.0260
Montero	1993–96	—	.0260–.0350
Pickup	1993–96	—	.0040–.0200
Precis	1993	—	—
3000GT	1993–96	7 & 8	.0220–.0300
		9	.0260–.0330

① — DOHC engine less ABS & SOHC engine.
② — DOHC engine w/ABS.
③ — DOHC engine less ABS.
④ — SOHC engine less ABS.
⑤ — SOHC engine w/ABS.
⑥ — Revised by a Technical Service Bulletin.

Fig. 9 Brake booster rod adjustment specifications

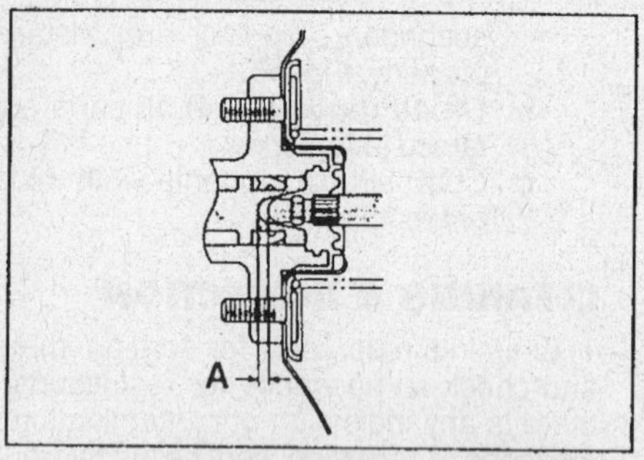

A

MT4099100010000X

Fig. 8 Brake booster to primary piston clearance dimension A

BRAKE SYSTEM BLEED

MASTER CYLINDER BLEED

1. If master cylinder has been replaced or overhauled and reservoir is empty, proceed as follows:
   a. Fill reservoir with clean brake fluid, then disconnect brake lines at master cylinder.
   b. Depress pedal slowly and hold pedal in depressed position.
   c. Place fingers over outlet port, then release brake pedal.
   d. Repeat above steps several times. Refill reservoir suitable brake fluid.

HYDRAULIC SYSTEM BLEED

The hydraulic brake system must be bled if air has entered the system. This condition may be precipitated by low fluid level, a hydraulic fluid leak, the opening of a hydraulic line or replacement of a hydraulic system component. Symptoms include a loss of brake operation and/or a low or spongy brake pedal.

1. Ensure master cylinder reservoir is full. Add suitable brake fluid as needed, and securely reinstall the master cylinder cap.
2. Raise and support vehicle.
3. Position a drain pan under the wheel being bled.
4. Have an assistant depress the brake pedal with a slow even pressure and hold it. **Do not depress brake pedal fully to the end of the master cylinder stroke. This may cause damage to the master cylinder.**
5. Using a suitable wrench, open the bleeder valve one full turn. Watch for air bubbles in the fluid, and listen for air escaping from the system.
6. With the brake pedal still depressed, close the bleeder valve.
7. Have the assistant pump the brake pedal several times. **Do not depress brake pedal fully to the end of the master cylinder stroke, this may cause damage to the master cylinder.**
8. Repeat preceding bleed steps until all air is removed from the hydraulic system. **While bleeding the system, recheck brake fluid supply in the master cylinder often so as not to allow the master cylinder to run dry.**
9. Upon completion of hydraulic system bleeding, proceed as follows:
   a. Ensure the master cylinder reservoir is full. Add suitable brake fluid as needed, and securely reinstall the master cylinder cap.
   b. Lower the vehicle. Ensure brake pedal is firm and braking operation is proper.

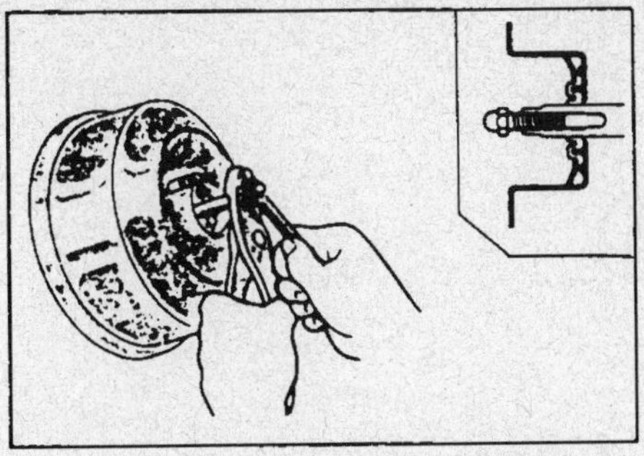

MT4099100011000X

Fig. 10 Brake booster pushrod adjustment

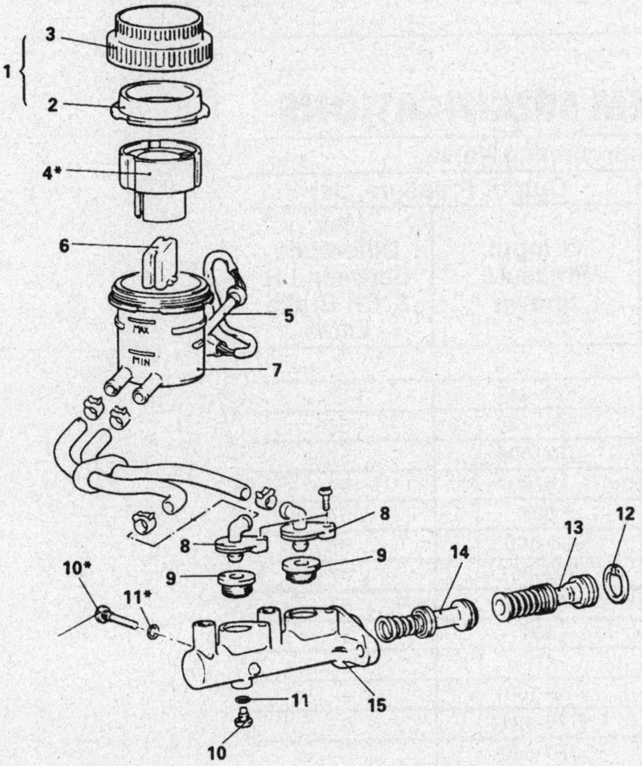
1
2
3
4*
5
6
7
8
9
10*
11*
11
10
12
13
14
15
MAX
MIN

1. Reservoir cap assembly
2. Diaphragm
3. Reservoir cap
4. Filter
5. Brake fluid level sensor
6. Float
7. Reservoir
8. Nipple
9. Reservoir seal
10. Piston stopper bolt
11. Gasket
12. Piston stopper ring
13. Primary piston assembly
14. Secondary piston assembly
15. Master cylinder body

NOTE
* : <Vehicles with ABS>

MT4099100004000X

Fig. 12 Exploded view of master cylinder. Separate reservoir

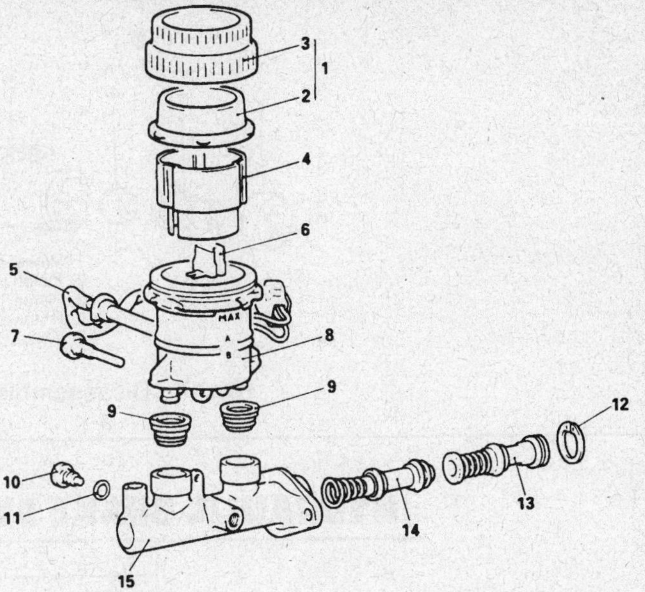
1
2
3
4
5
6
7
8
9
10
11
12
13
14
15
MAX

1. Reservoir cap assembly
2. Diaphragm
3. Reservoir cap
4. Filter <Vehicles with ABS>
5. Brake fluid level sensor
6. Float
7. Reservoir stopper bolt
8. Reservoir tank
9. Reservoir seal
10. Piston stopper bolt
11. Gasket
12. Stopper ring
13. Primary piston assembly
14. Secondary piston assembly
15. Master cylinder body

MT4099100002000X

Fig. 11 Exploded view of master cylinder. Attached reservoir

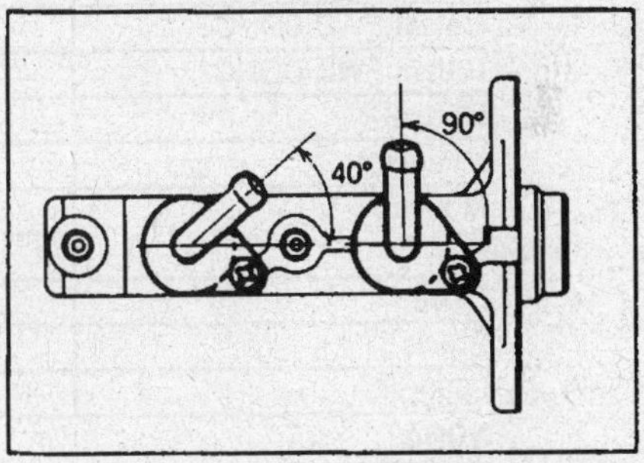
90°
40°

MT4099100005000X

Fig. 13 Brake fluid nipple orientation

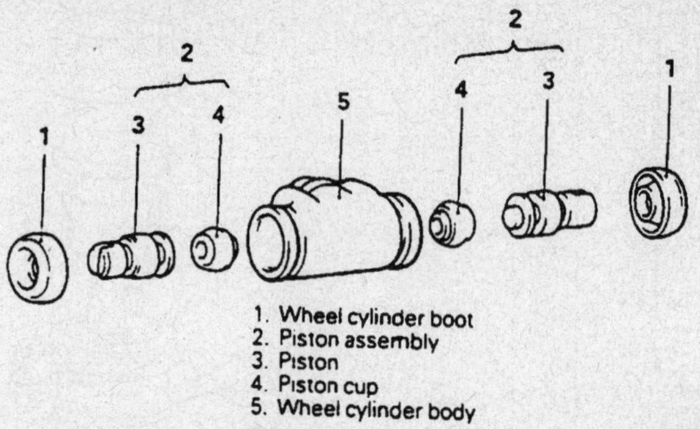
1
2
3
4
5
1. Wheel cylinder boot
2. Piston assembly
3. Piston
4. Piston cup
5. Wheel cylinder body
MT4099100006000X

Fig. 14 Disassembled view of wheel cylinder

HYDRAULIC BRAKE SYSTEM SPECIFICATIONS

Model	Proportioning Valve		
	Input Pressure, psi	Output Pressure, psi	
		@ Input Pressure Shown	Max. Difference Between LH & RH Brake Lines
1993			
Diamante	1138	676–747	57
Eclipse AWD	1095	661–732	57
Eclipse FWD	1163	732–804	57
Expo AWD	1067	676	57
Expo FWD	996	604	57
Galant AWD	1309	931–1003	57
Galant FWD SOHC	1163	789–861	57
Galant FWD DOHC	1095	661–732	57
Mirage②	996	604	57
Mirage①	1067	676	57
Montero	1422	873–1001	—
	2560	1129–1314	—
Pickup	1991	370–540	—
Precis	1931	950	—
3000GT	1138	744–815	57
1994			
Diamante	1138	676–747	57
Eclipse AWD	1095	661–732	57
Eclipse FWD	1163	732–804	57
Expo AWD	1067	676	57
Expo FWD	996	604	57
Galant	996	604	57
Mirage②	996	604	57
Mirage①	1067	676	57
Montero	1422	873–1001	—
	2560	1129–1314	—
Pickup	1991	370–540	—
3000GT	1138	744–815	57
1995			
Diamante	1138	676–747	57
Eclipse AWD②	996	533–604	57
Eclipse AWD①	925	498–569	57
Eclipse FWD②	925	462–533	57
Eclipse FWD①	996	569–640	57

Continued

HYDRAULIC BRAKE SYSTEM SPECIFICATIONS—Continued

Model	Proportioning Valve		
	Input Pressure, psi	Output Pressure, psi	
		@ Input Pressure Shown	Max. Difference Between LH & RH Brake Lines
1995			
Expo AWD	1067	676	57
Expo FWD	996	604	57
Galant	996	604	57
Mirage②	996	604	57
Mirage①	1067	676	57
Montero	1422	873–1001	—
	2560	1129–1314	—
Pickup	1991	370–540	—
3000GT	1138	744–815	57
1996			
Diamante	1138	676–747	57
Eclipse②	925	462–533	57
Eclipse①	996	569–640	57
Galant	996	604	57
Mirage②	996	604	57
Mirage①	1067	676	57
Montero	1422	873–1001	—
	2560	1129–1314	—
Pickup	1991	370–540	—
3000GT	1138	744–815	57

AWD: All Wheel Drive

FWD: Front Wheel Drive

DOHC: Dual Overhead Cam

SOHC: Single Overhead Cam

2WD: Two Wheel Drive

4WD: Four Wheel Drive

① — With ABS.

② — Less ABS.

TIGHTENING SPECIFICATIONS

Year	Component	Torque/Ft. Lbs.
DIAMANTE		
1993–96	Bleeder Screw	6
	Brake Booster To Pedal Support Bracket	10
	Brake Pedal Support Bolt	22
	Brake Pedal Support Bracket	7
	Flared Line Fittings	11
	Master Cylinder To Brake Booster	7
	Piston Stopper Bolt	24①
	Vacuum Hose Fitting	11–13

Continued

TIGHTENING SPECIFICATIONS—Continued

Year	Component	Torque/Ft. Lbs.
ECLIPSE		
1993–96	Bleeder Screw	5–7
	Brake Booster Nuts	8–12
	Brake Hose Bracket Bolts	12–19
	Flared Brake Line Nuts	9–12
	Master Cylinder To Brake Booster	6–9
	Nipple Screw	12–24①
	Pedal Rod To Clutch Pedal Bracket	12–19
	Pedal Rod To Pedal Support Bracket	12–19
	Pedal Support Bracket Bolts	6–9
	Pedal Support Nut	7–11
	Piston Stopper Bolt	12–24①
	Vacuum Hose Fitting	11–13
	Wheel Cylinder	7
EXPO		
1993–95	Bleeder Screw	6
	Brake Booster	7
	Brake Line To Wheel Cylinder	11
	Master Cylinder	7
	Wheel Cylinder	7
GALANT		
1993	Bleeder Screw	5–7
	Bracket A Installation Bolts	12–19
	Brake Booster	8–12
	Brake Hose Bracket	12–19
	Clutch Master Cylinder	7–11
	Clutch Pedal	14–18
	Flared Brake Line Nuts	9–12
	Hydraulic Unit Mounting Bolts	12–19
	Lever Assembly (A) Nut	14–18
	Lever Assembly (B) Nut	14–18
	Master Cylinder To Brake Booster	6–9
	Nipple Screw	1–2
	Parking Brake Lever	29–40
	Pedal Rod To Clutch Pedal Bracket	12–19
	Pedal Rod To Pedal Support Bracket	12–19
	Pedal Support Bracket Bolts	6–9
	Pedal Support Bracket Nuts	7–11
	Piston Stopper Bolt	1–2
	Reserve Tank Bracket (Upper)	7–10
	Reservoir	12–24①
	Vacuum Hose Fitting	11–13
	Wheel Cylinder	6–9
1994–96	Bleeder Screw	6
	Brake Booster	10
	Brake Hose Bracket	12–19
	Brake Pedal Shaft	23
	Flared Brake Line Nuts	11
	Hydraulic Unit	12–19
	Master Cylinder To Brake Booster	7
	Parking Brake Lever	29–40
	Pedal Support Bracket Installation Nut	7
	Vacuum Hose Fitting	11–13
	Wheel Cylinder Bolt	7

Continued

TIGHTENING SPECIFICATIONS—Continued

Year	Component	Torque/Ft. Lbs.
MIRAGE		
1993–96	Bleeder Screw	5–7
	Brake Booster & Pedal Support Member (Right Side)	8–12
	Flared Brake Line Nuts	9–12
	Master Cylinder	6–9
	Pedal Support Member	12–15
	Piston Stopper Bolt	12–24①
	Reservoir	12–24①
	Sleeve Bolt	16–23
	Vacuum Hose Fitting	11–13
MONTERO		
1993–96	Bleeder Screw	5–7
	Brake Booster To Pedal Support	6–9
	Brake Line Flare Nut	9–12
	Brake Pedal Shaft	18–25
	Master Cylinder To Brake Booster	6–9
	Master Cylinder To Brake Line Connector	18–25
	Pedal Support Member	13–18
	Piston Stopper	12–24①
	Reservoir Stopper Bolt	12–24①
PICKUP		
1993–96	Bleeder Screw	5–7
	Brake Booster To Pedal Support Member	6–9
	Brake Line Flare Nut	9–12
	Brake Pedal Shaft	18–25
	Master Cylinder To Brake Booster	6–9
	Master Cylinder To Brake Line Connector	18–25
	Piston Stopper	12–24①
	Reservoir Stopper Belt	12–24①
	Vacuum Hose Fitting	11–13
PRECIS		
1993	Bleeder Screw	5–7
	Brake Booster	6–7
	Brake Booster Hose Fitting To Manifold	6–7
	Brake Hose Flare Nut	9–12
	Master Cylinder To Brake Booster	6–7
	Proportioning Valve	6–9
3000GT		
1993–96	Bleeder Screw	6
	Brake Booster	10
	Brake Pedal Support Bolt	22
	Brake Pedal Support Bracket	9
	Flared Brake Line Fittings	11
	Master Cylinder To Brake Booster	7
	Vacuum Hose Fitting	11–13

① — Inch lbs.

Power Brake Units

INDEX

Page No.		Page No.		Page No.	
Description	29-154	Overhaul	29-154	Replacement	29-154
Power Brake Unit Service	29-154	Pushrod Adjustment	29-154	**Troubleshooting**	29-154

DESCRIPTION

The power brake unit is a vacuum assist diaphragm assembly which multiplies the force exerted on the master cylinder piston in order to increase the hydraulic pressure delivered to the wheel calipers. This effectively decreases the effort necessary to attain sufficient stopping performance.

Vacuum assist units are powered by the opposition of engine vacuum to atmospheric pressure. A piston, cylinder and flexible diaphragm utilize this energy to provide brake assistance. The diaphragm is balanced with engine vacuum until the brake pedal is depressed, allowing atmospheric pressure to unbalance the unit and apply force to the brake system.

The basic brake system will operate even if the power unit fails, although more effort is required at the pedal to achieve the same amount of braking performance attainable with a functional power assist unit.

TROUBLESHOOTING

1. Run engine for two minutes, then turn engine off. Depress brake pedal slowly several times.
2. Pedal should go down farther the first time and rise gradually the second and third time, **Fig. 1.** If pedal height remains the same booster is faulty.
3. With engine off, depress brake pedal several times, **Fig. 1.** There should be no change in pedal stroke.

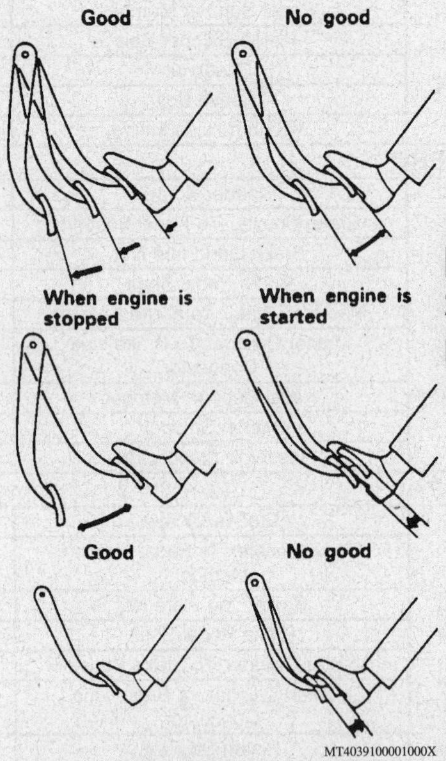

Good
No good
When engine is stopped
When engine is started
Good
No good
MT4039100001000X

Fig. 1 Brake booster functional inspection

4. With brake pedal depressed, start engine. Pedal should go down slightly, if no change in pedal, booster is faulty.
5. With engine running and brake pedal depressed, stop engine.
6. If after 30 seconds there is no change in pedal movement, the booster is in good condition, **Fig. 1.** If pedal rises booster is faulty.

POWER BRAKE UNIT SERVICE

REPLACEMENT

1. Remove master cylinder as outlined in "Hydraulic Brake Systems" section.
2. Disconnect vacuum hose from power brake booster.
3. Remove pin connecting power brake rod with pedal.
4. Remove booster attaching nuts and remove booster.
5. Reverse procedure to install.

OVERHAUL

These units cannot be overhauled and must be replaced in the event of a malfunction.

PUSHROD ADJUSTMENT

Refer to "Adjustments" in "Hydraulic Brake Systems" section, for pushrod adjustment procedures.

Anti-Lock Brakes

NOTE: On Air Bag Equipped Models, Refer To "Air Bag System Precautions" Located In The Front Of This Manual For System Disarming & Arming Procedures.

NOTE: Wire Color Code Identification & Electrical Symbol Identification Located In The Front Of This Manual May Be Used As An Aid When Using Wiring Circuits Found In This Section.

INDEX

	Page No.
Description	29-155
Diagnosis & Testing	29-156
Accessing Diagnostic Trouble Codes	29-156
Diamante	29-158
Expo, 1993 Galant, 1993–94 Eclipse & 1993–95 3000GT	29-156
Mirage	29-158
Montero	29-160
Pickup	29-161
1994–96 Galant	29-157
1995–96 Eclipse AWD	29-157
1995–96 Eclipse FWD & 1996 3000GT	29-157
Clearing Diagnostic Trouble Codes	29-162
Diamante & Mirage	29-162
Eclipse, Expo & 3000GT	29-162
Galant & Montero	29-162
Pickup	29-162
Diagnostic Trouble Code Interpretation	29-161
Diamante	29-161
Expo, 1993 Galant, 1993–94 Eclipse & 1993–95 3000GT	29-161
Mirage	29-161
Montero	29-161
Pickup	29-161
1994–96 Galant	29-161
1995 Eclipse	29-161
1996 3000GT	29-161
1996 Eclipse	29-161
Diagnostic Chart Index	29-204
Precautions	29-155
Air Bag Systems	29-155
System Service	29-162
Brake System Bleed	29-162
Component Replacement	29-162
Brake Fluid Pressure Switch	29-162
Electronic Control Unit & Power Relay	29-162
Front Speed Sensor	29-162
G-Sensor	29-163
Hydraulic Unit	29-163
Modulator	29-164
Rear Speed Sensor	29-164
Troubleshooting	29-155
General Malfunction Diagnosis	29-155
Transient Malfunction Diagnosis	29-155

PRECAUTIONS

AIR BAG SYSTEMS

Refer to "Air Bag System Precautions" in the front of this manual for system disarming and arming procedures.

DESCRIPTION

The Anti-Lock Braking System (ABS) prevents wheels from locking up when braking, regardless of the surface conditions. This allows the vehicle to stop in a shorter distance and allows the driver to maintain directional control of the vehicle during heavy braking.

During normal braking conditions, the ABS operates like a conventional diagonally split hydraulic power assist system. During heavy braking, however, each wheel's braking pressure is modulated according to its speed. To maintain stability, both rear wheels receive the same signal.

TROUBLESHOOTING

Refer to **Figs. 1 through 31** for ABS wiring diagrams.

GENERAL MALFUNCTION DIAGNOSIS

Except Pickup

Problems related to the Anti-Lock Brake System (ABS) can generally be classified as electrical or hydraulic.

For problems in the electrical system, a self-diagnostic function is built into the Electronic Control Unit (ECU), allowing the ABS warning lamp to illuminate as a warning to the driver in the event of an abnormality. In this instance, inspections can be performed with a voltmeter, Multi-Use Tester (MUT), oscilloscope or the ABS warning lamp.

Problems with the hydraulic system can be located in the same manner as ordinary brakes. It is, however, necessary to determine whether the problem is related to ordinary brake components or to the components related to the ABS.

Refer to "Diagnosis & Testing" for diagnostic test procedures.

Pickup

Refer to **Figs. 32 and 33** for troubleshooting procedures.

TRANSIENT MALFUNCTION DIAGNOSIS

In electronic control systems, momentary problems can occur in electronic circuits and input and output signals, and this can result in temporary trouble symptoms or a diagnostic trouble code being recorded by means of ECU on-board diagnostics. If the cause of the problem is continuous, the location of the abnormality can be discovered by checking according to the diagnosis chart classified by trouble symptoms. However, the symptoms of some transient problems may return to normal by themselves, so there is a possibility that the cause of the problem will be unclear.

The causes of problems in vehicles with temporary malfunctions include vibration, heat and excessive electrical resistance. By performing an inspection according to the following simulation method, the trouble symptom can be recreated.

1. If main cause is possibly vibration, perform the following:
   a. Gently shake connector up, down, right and left.
   b. Gently shake wiring harness up, down, right and left.
   c. Gently rock each sensor by hand.
   d. Gently shake other moving parts.
2. If any wires or connections break during inspection, replace with new ones.
3. The vehicle speed sensors are particularly subject to intermittently poor contacts due to movement of suspension while driving, so it is desirable that a driving test be conducted while monitoring sensor signals.
4. If main cause is probably heat, use a hair dryer to heat suspected component. **Do not heat component above 176°F.**
5. If main cause is probably excessive electrical resistance, turn all electrical switches, including headlights and rear defogger, to On positions.

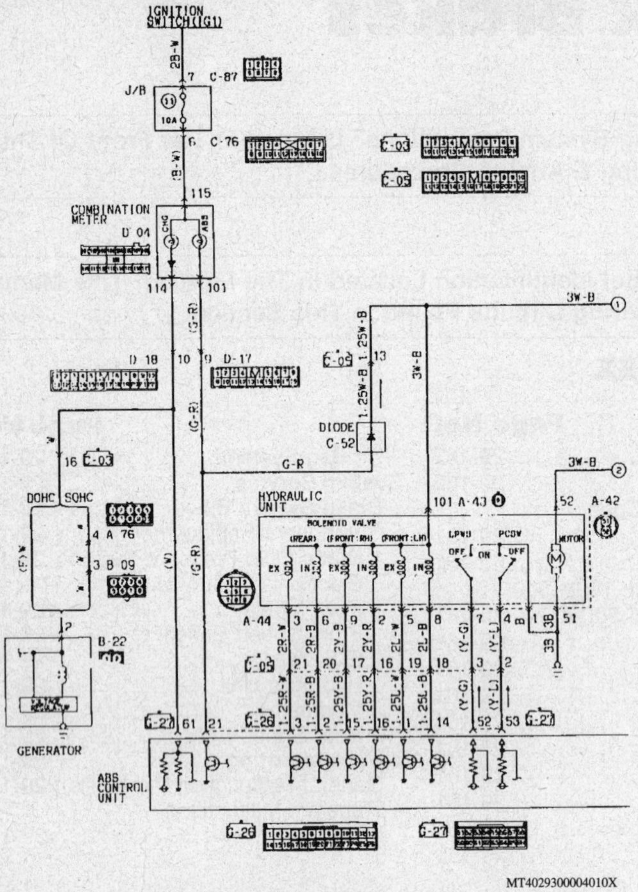
IGNITION SWITCH(IG1)
J/B
COMBINATION METER
DOHC SOHC
GENERATOR
DIODE C-52
HYDRAULIC UNIT
SOLENOID VALVE
ABS CONTROL UNIT
MT4029300004010X

Fig. 1 Anti-lock brake system wiring diagram (Part 1 of 3). 1993 Diamante

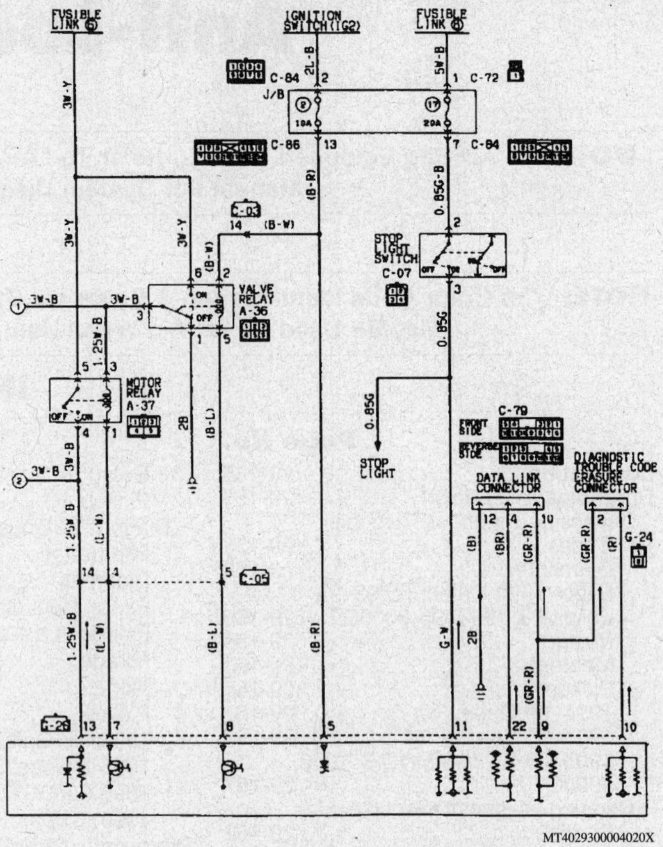
FUSIBLE LINK ⑤
IGNITION SWITCH(IG2)
FUSIBLE LINK ⑤
VALVE RELAY A-36
MOTOR RELAY A-37
STOP LIGHT SWITCH C-07
STOP LIGHT
DATA LINK CONNECTOR
DIAGNOSTIC TROUBLE CODE ERASURE CONNECTOR
MT4029300004020X

Fig. 1 Anti-lock brake system wiring diagram (Part 2 of 3). 1993 Diamante

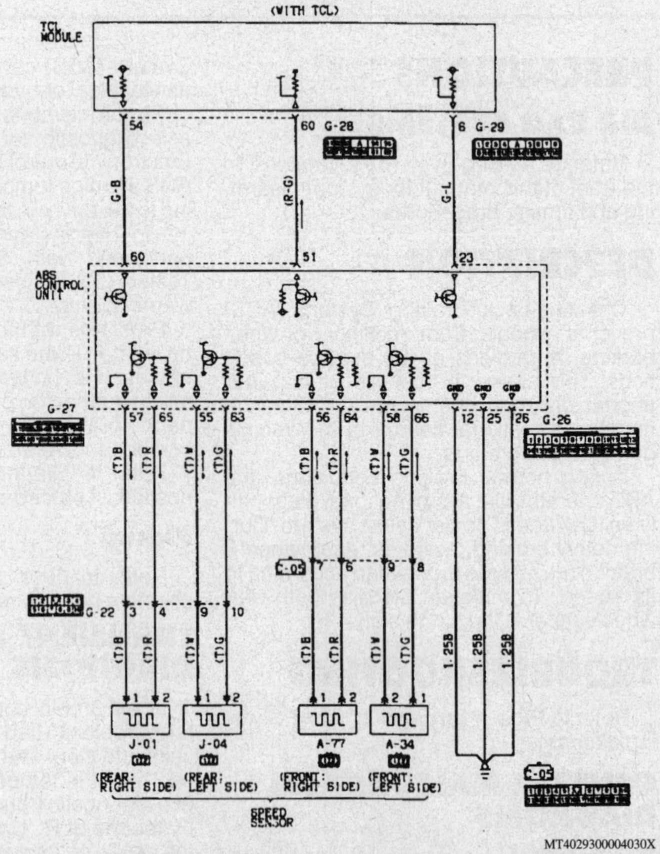
(WITH TCL)
TCL MODULE
ABS CONTROL UNIT
(REAR: RIGHT SIDE)
(REAR: LEFT SIDE)
(FRONT: RIGHT SIDE)
(FRONT: LEFT SIDE)
SPEED SENSOR
MT4029300004030X

Fig. 1 Anti-lock brake system wiring diagram (Part 3 of 3). 1993 Diamante

DIAGNOSIS & TESTING

Accessing Diagnostic Trouble Codes

EXPO, 1993 GALANT, 1993-94 ECLIPSE & 1993-95 3000GT

USING ABS WARNING LAMP

Refer to **Figs. 34 through 39** for ABS warning lamp diagnostic procedures.

USING MULTI-USE TESTER (MUT)

1. With ignition switch in Off position, connect MUT through adapter harness, then turn ignition switch to On position and select ABS. **In MUT mode, ABS does not function.**
2. The ABS warning lamp should light when in MUT mode. If access is not possible, check ECU power circuit and harness between ECU and diagnosis check terminal.
3. Read and record diagnostic trouble code output.
4. Clear diagnostic trouble codes once from memory.
5. If memory can be cleared, trouble is either intermittent or appears only when driving.

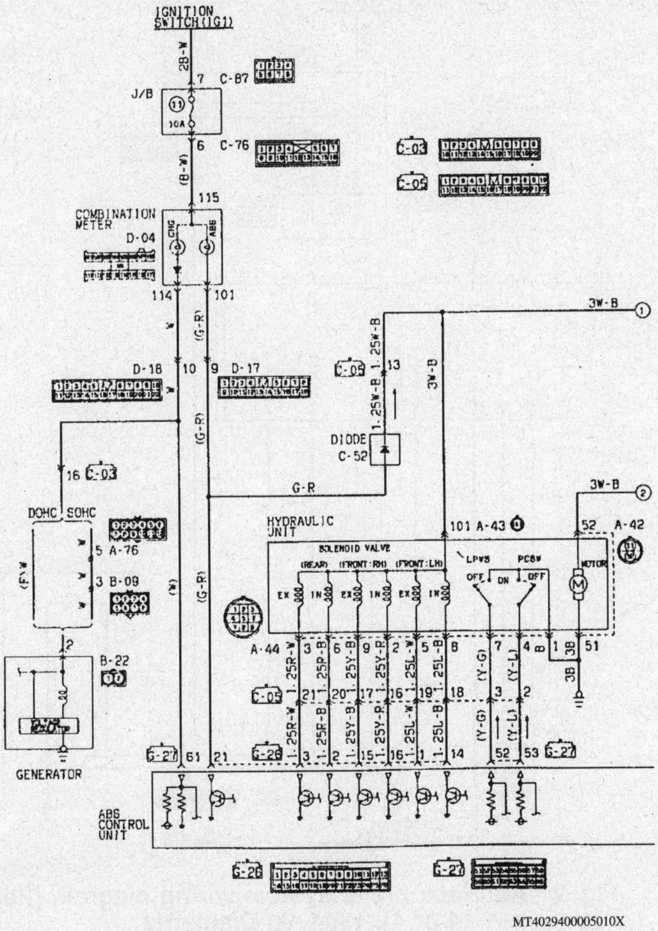
IGNITION SWITCH (IG1)
C-87
J/B
10A
C-76
C-03
C-05
COMBINATION METER
D-04
D-18
D-17
DIODE C-52
G-R
3W-B
DOHC SOHC
A-76
B-09
B-22
GENERATOR
HYDRAULIC UNIT
SOLENOID VALVE
LPWS
PCSW
MOTOR
A-43
A-42
A-44
ABS CONTROL UNIT
C-26
C-27
MT4029400005010X

Fig. 2 Anti-lock brake system wiring diagram (Part 1 of 4). 1994–96 Diamante

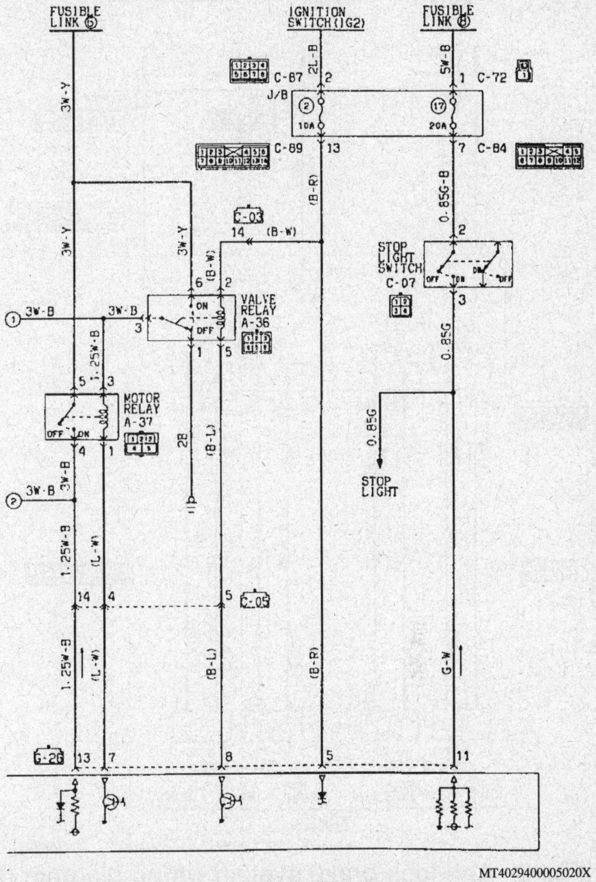
FUSIBLE LINK 5
IGNITION SWITCH (IG2)
FUSIBLE LINK 8
C-87
J/B
10A
20A
C-72
C-89
C-84
C-03
STOP LIGHT SWITCH C-07
VALVE RELAY A-36
MOTOR RELAY A-37
STOP LIGHT
C-05
C-26
MT4029400005020X

Fig. 2 Anti-lock brake system wiring diagram (Part 2 of 4). 1994–96 Diamante

6. If memory cannot be cleared, ECU is currently detecting trouble and ABS ECU is in fail safe mode.
7. When diagnostic trouble codes cannot be cleared, or when ABS ECU goes into fail safe during another test drive and diagnostic trouble codes are output, proceed to "Diagnostic Trouble Code Interpretation" for further information pertaining to specific diagnostic trouble codes.

1994–96 GALANT

USING SCAN TOOL

Connect scan tool to data link connector, located below the lefthand side of the instrument panel, and observe diagnostic trouble code output. Proceed to "Diagnostic Trouble Code Interpretation" for further information regarding specific diagnostic trouble code output.

USING ABS WARNING LAMP

1. Place ignition switch in On position, then depress brake pedal intermittently to cycle stop lamp switch off and on at one second intervals, noting the following:
   a. Begin cycling within three seconds after ignition switch is placed in On position.
   b. **If more than three seconds elapses after ignition switch is placed in On position or if cycling interval exceeds one second, system will return to normal mode and no diagnostic trouble codes will be output until ignition switch is turned to Off position, then back to On position.**
2. Note ABS warning lamp flash pattern, then refer to **Fig. 40** for an example of warning lamp diagnostic trouble code output.
3. Proceed to "Diagnostic Trouble Code Interpretation" for further information regarding specific diagnostic trouble code output.

1995–96 ECLIPSE AWD

If using a scan tool, turn the ignition switch to the Off position and connect a suitable diagnostic scan tool to the Data Link Connector (DLC). The DLC is located under the lefthand side of the instrument panel, **Fig. 41.**

If an analog voltmeter is to be used to access diagnostic trouble codes, use special harness tool, **Fig. 42,** to connect it between the DLC diagnostic output and ground terminals. Specific diagnostic trouble codes are indicated by sweeps of the voltmeter needle as follows:

1. Following an initial pause of approximately three seconds, needle will begin to indicate "tens" digit of diagnostic trouble code. This digit will be represented by 1.5 second sweeps.
2. A two second pause will follow "tens" digit indication, then "ones" digit will be indicated by sweeps of approximately .5 seconds each. These will be separated from one another by .5 second pauses.

After obtaining any diagnostic trouble codes, proceed to "Diagnostic Trouble Code Interpretation" for diagnostic trouble code identification and diagnosis. The "Diagnostic Chart Index" may also be helpful in identifying diagnostic trouble codes and in locating diagnostic charts.

1995–96 ECLIPSE FWD & 1996 3000GT

If using a scan tool, turn the ignition switch to the Off position and connect a suitable diagnostic scan tool to the Data Link Connector (DLC). The DLC is located under the lefthand side of the instrument panel, **Fig. 41.**

When using the ABS warning lamp, ground terminal No. 1 of the DLC with a fused jumper, **Fig. 41.** Refer to the example of ABS warning lamp operation shown in **Fig. 40** to determine which diagnostic trouble codes, if any, are present.

After obtaining any diagnostic trouble codes, proceed to "Diagnostic Trouble

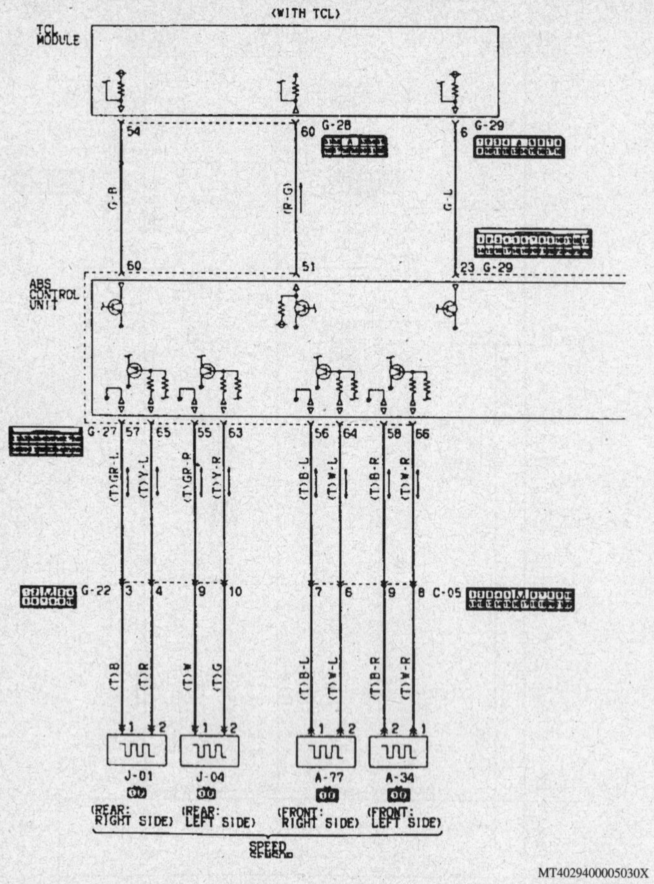

(WITH TCL)
TCL MODULE
ABS CONTROL UNIT
(REAR: RIGHT SIDE)
(REAR: LEFT SIDE)
(FRONT: RIGHT SIDE)
(FRONT: LEFT SIDE)
SPEED SENSOR
MT4029400005030X

Fig. 2 Anti-lock brake system wiring diagram (Part 3 of 4). 1994–96 Diamante

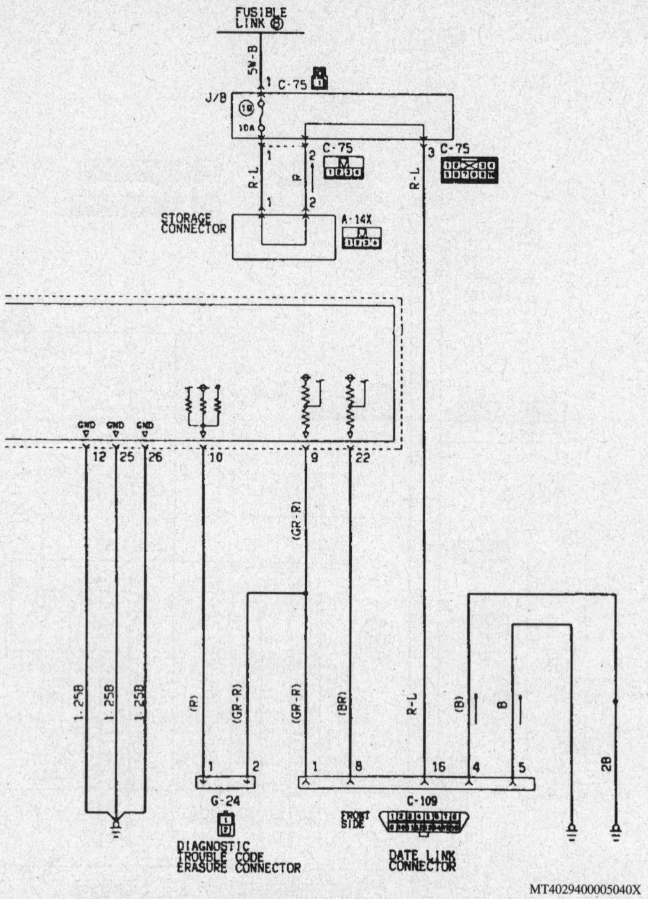

FUSIBLE LINK
J/B
STORAGE CONNECTOR
DIAGNOSTIC TROUBLE CODE ERASURE CONNECTOR
DATE LINK CONNECTOR
MT4029400005040X

Fig. 2 Anti-lock brake system wiring diagram (Part 4 of 4). 1994–96 Diamante

Code Interpretation" for diagnostic trouble code identification and diagnosis. The "Diagnostic Chart Index " may also be helpful in identifying diagnostic trouble codes and in locating diagnostic charts.

DIAMANTE

USING ABS WARNING LAMP

Refer to **Figs. 43 through 49** for diagnostic procedures.

USING VOLTMETER

1. With engine idling, read and note voltage output pattern between ABS terminal and ground of diagnostic check connector, **Fig. 50.**
2. Erase diagnostic trouble code memory.
3. If memory can be erased, then problem is intermittent or can only be detected while driving.
4. If memory cannot be erased, function is being stopped by a problem that is currently displaying a diagnostic trouble code.
5. If diagnostic trouble codes cannot be erased, or if ABS function is stopped by a repeated driving test and a diagnostic trouble code output, proceed to "Diagnostic Trouble Code Interpretation" for further information regarding diagnosis of specific diagnostic trouble codes.
6. Diagnostic Trouble Codes 16, 35 and 37 are output according to vehicle condition, even when ABS system is normal. These diagnostic trouble codes are output only for a current problem, and if vehicle condition returns to normal, diagnostic trouble codes will become normal.

USING MULTI-USE TESTER (MUT)

1. With engine idling, connect MUT tester to check connector, **Fig. 50,** then select ABS system.
2. Read and note diagnostic trouble code output.
3. Attempt to erase diagnostic trouble code memory.
4. If memory can be erased, then problem is intermittent or can only be detected while driving.
5. If memory cannot be erased, function is being stopped by a problem that is currently displaying a diagnostic trouble code.
6. If diagnostic trouble codes cannot be erased, or if ABS function is stopped by a repeated driving test and a diagnostic trouble code output, proceed to "Diagnostic Trouble Code Interpretation" for further information regarding diagnosis of specific diagnostic trouble codes.
7. Diagnostic Trouble Codes 16, 35 and 37 are output according to vehicle condition, even when ABS system is normal. These diagnostic trouble codes are output only for a current problem and if vehicle condition returns to normal, diagnostic trouble codes will also return to normal.

MIRAGE

USING ABS WARNING LAMP

Refer to **Figs. 51 through 59** for diagnostic procedures.

USING VOLTMETER

1. **On 1993 models,** proceed as follows:
   a. With engine idling, read and note voltage output pattern between ABS terminal and diagnostic check connector ground, **Figs. 60 and 61.**
   b. Erase diagnostic trouble codes from memory.
   c. If memory can be erased, then problem is intermittent or can only be detected while driving.
   d. If memory cannot be erased, function is being stopped by a problem that is currently displaying a diagnostic trouble code.
   e. If diagnostic trouble codes cannot be erased, or if ABS function is stopped by a repeated driving test and a diagnostic trouble code output, proceed to "Diagnostic Trouble Code Interpretation" for further information regarding analysis and repair of malfunctions generating specific diagnostic trouble codes.

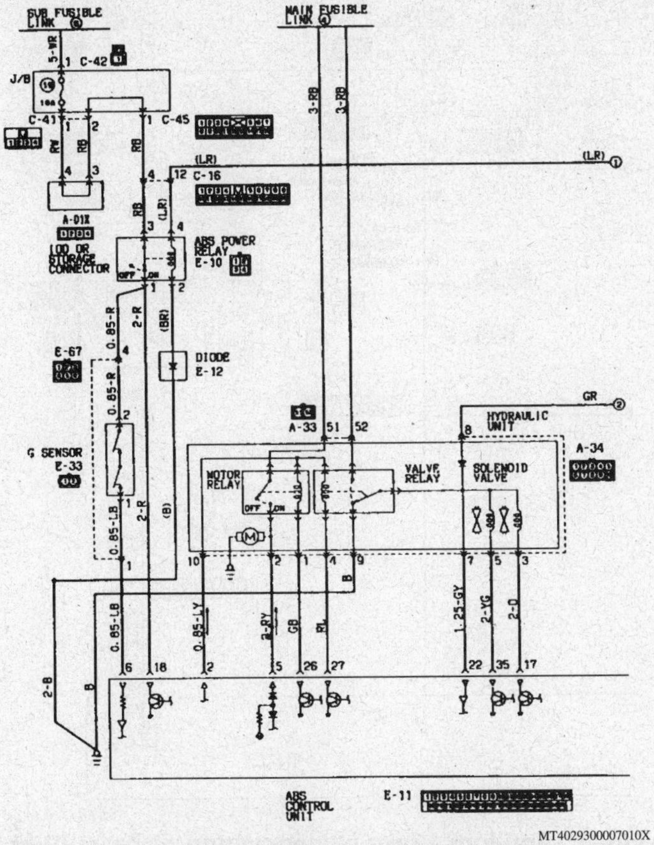
SUB FUSIBLE LINK
MAIN FUSIBLE LINK
J/B
A-01X
LOD OR STORAGE CONNECTOR
ABS POWER RELAY E-10
DIODE E-12
G SENSOR E-33
HYDRAULIC UNIT
MOTOR RELAY
VALVE RELAY
SOLENOID VALVE
A-34
A-33
ABS CONTROL UNIT
E-11
MT4029300007010X

Fig. 3 Anti-lock brake system wiring diagram (Part 1 of 3). 1993–94 Eclipse AWD

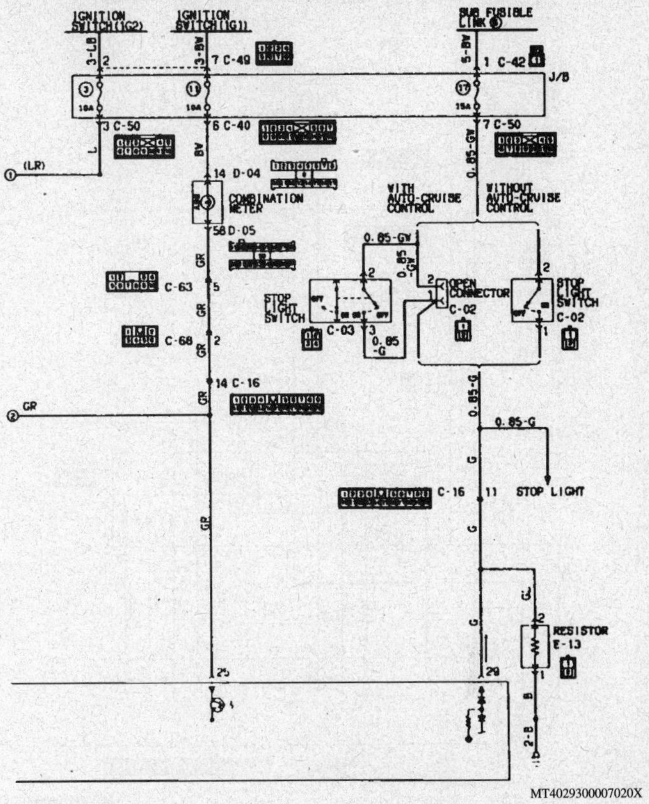
IGNITION SWITCH (IG2)
IGNITION SWITCH (IG1)
SUB FUSIBLE LINK
J/B
COMBINATION METER
WITH AUTO-CRUISE CONTROL
WITHOUT AUTO-CRUISE CONTROL
STOP LIGHT SWITCH
OPEN CONNECTOR
STOP LIGHT
RESISTOR E-13
MT4029300007020X

Fig. 3 Anti-lock brake system wiring diagram (Part 2 of 3). 1993–94 Eclipse AWD

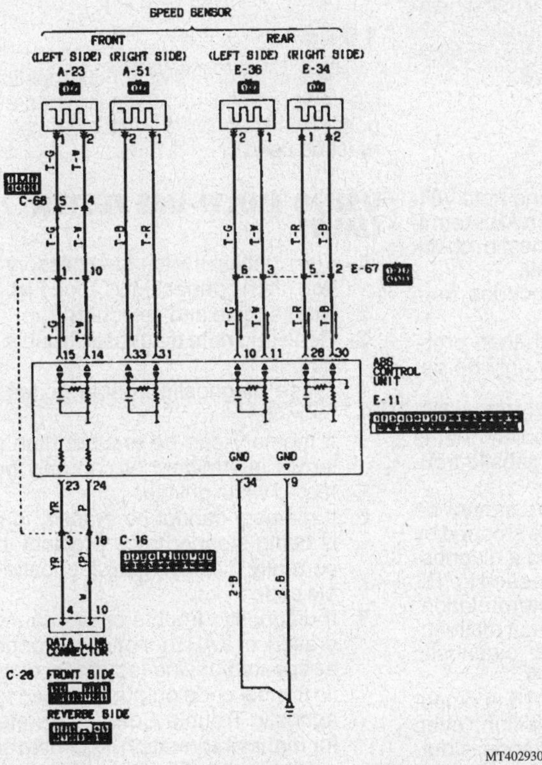
SPEED SENSOR
FRONT
REAR
(LEFT SIDE) (RIGHT SIDE)
(LEFT SIDE) (RIGHT SIDE)
A-23 A-51 E-36 E-34
ABS CONTROL UNIT
E-11
GND
DATA LINK CONNECTOR
C-26 FRONT SIDE
REVERSE SIDE
MT4029300007030X

Fig. 3 Anti-lock brake system wiring diagram (Part 3 of 3). 1993–94 Eclipse AWD

f. Diagnostic Trouble Codes 16 and 35 are output according to vehicle condition, even when ABS system is normal. These diagnostic trouble codes are output only for a current problem, and if vehicle condition returns to normal, diagnostic trouble codes will become normal.

2. **On 1994–96 models,** proceed as follows:
   a. Connect voltmeter to terminal 8 (diagnostic output terminal) and terminal 4 or 5 (ground terminals) of data link connector via special harness tool, **Fig. 62.**
   b. Observe voltmeter deflection pattern, **Fig. 61,** to obtain diagnostic trouble code.

USING MULTI-USE TESTER (MUT)

1. Turn ignition switch to Accessory position, then connect MUT tool, **Fig. 63.**
2. Start engine and select ABS function on scan tool.
3. Read and note diagnostic trouble code output.
4. Erase diagnostic trouble codes from memory.
5. If memory can be erased, then problem is intermittent or can only be detected while driving.
6. If memory cannot be erased, function is being stopped by a problem that is currently displaying a diagnostic trouble code.
7. If diagnostic trouble codes cannot be erased, or if ABS function is stopped by

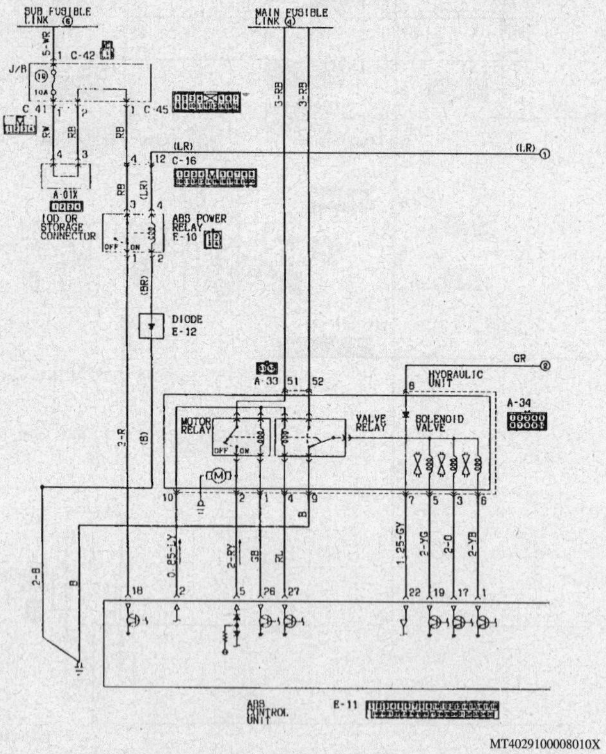
SUB FUSIBLE LINK
MAIN FUSIBLE LINK
IOD OR STORAGE CONNECTOR
ABS POWER RELAY E-10
DIODE E-12
HYDRAULIC UNIT
MOTOR RELAY
VALVE RELAY
SOLENOID VALVE
ABS CONTROL UNIT
MT4029100008010X

Fig. 4 Anti-lock brake system wiring diagram (Part 1 of 3). 1993–94 Eclipse FWD

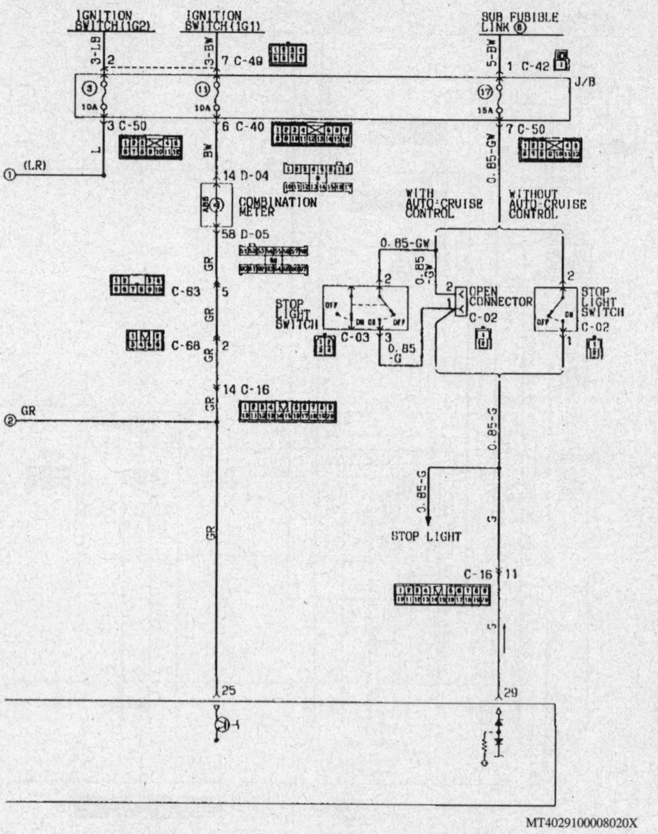
IGNITION SWITCH (IG2)
IGNITION SWITCH (IG1)
SUB FUSIBLE LINK
COMBINATION METER
WITH AUTO-CRUISE CONTROL
WITHOUT AUTO-CRUISE CONTROL
STOP LIGHT SWITCH
OPEN CONNECTOR
STOP LIGHT
MT4029100008020X

Fig. 4 Anti-lock brake system wiring diagram (Part 2 of 3). 1993–94 Eclipse FWD

a repeated driving test and a diagnostic trouble code output, proceed to "Diagnostic Trouble Code Interpretation" for further information regarding analysis and repair of malfunctions generating specific diagnostic trouble codes.

8. Diagnostic Trouble Codes 16 and 35 are output according to vehicle condition, even when ABS system is normal. These diagnostic trouble codes are output only for a current problem, and if vehicle condition returns to normal, diagnostic trouble codes will automatically be erased.

MONTERO

USING ABS WARNING LAMP

1993–95

Refer to **Figs. 64 through 68** for diagnostic procedures.

1996

1. With ignition switch in Off position, remove valve relay, **Fig. 69,** then use special harness tool to ground data link connector terminal 1, **Fig. 70.**
2. Place ignition switch in On position, then observe flashes of ABS warning lamp. Diagnostic trouble code is indicated by flash pattern, **Fig. 71.**
3. If any diagnostic trouble codes are output, proceed to "Diagnostic Trouble Code Interpretation" for analysis and correction of malfunctions related to specific diagnostic trouble codes.
4. To diagnose trouble symptoms indicated by warning lamp without using diagnostic trouble codes, proceed to trouble symptom inspection procedures, **Figs. 72 through 78.**

USING VOLTMETER

1993–95

1. With engine idling, read and note voltage output pattern between ABS terminal and ground of diagnostic check connector, **Figs. 79 and 80.**
2. Erase diagnostic trouble codes from memory.
3. If memory can be erased, then problem is intermittent or can only be detected while driving.
4. If memory cannot be erased, function is being stopped by a problem that is currently displaying a diagnostic trouble code.
5. If diagnostic trouble codes cannot be erased, or if ABS function is stopped by a repeated driving test and a diagnostic trouble code output, proceed to "Diagnostic Trouble Code Interpretation" for analysis and correction of malfunctions related to specific diagnostic trouble codes.
6. Diagnostic Trouble Code 16 is output according to vehicle condition, even when ABS is normal. This code is output only for a current problem, and if vehicle condition returns to normal, diagnostic trouble code output will also return to normal.

1996

There is no provision for diagnostic trouble code retrieval using a voltmeter; a diagnostic scan tool or the ABS warning lamp must be used.

USING MULTI-USE TESTER (MUT)

1. Turn ignition switch to Accessory position, then connect MUT tool, **Fig. 81.**
2. Start engine and select ABS.
3. Read and note diagnostic trouble code output.
4. Erase diagnostic trouble codes from memory.
5. If memory can be erased, then problem is intermittent or can only be detected while driving.
6. If memory cannot be erased, function is being stopped by a problem that is currently displaying a diagnostic trouble code.
7. If diagnostic trouble codes cannot be erased, or if ABS function is stopped by a repeated driving test and a diagnostic trouble code output, proceed to "Diagnostic Trouble Code Interpretation" for further information regarding analysis and correction of malfunctions related to specific diagnostic trouble codes.

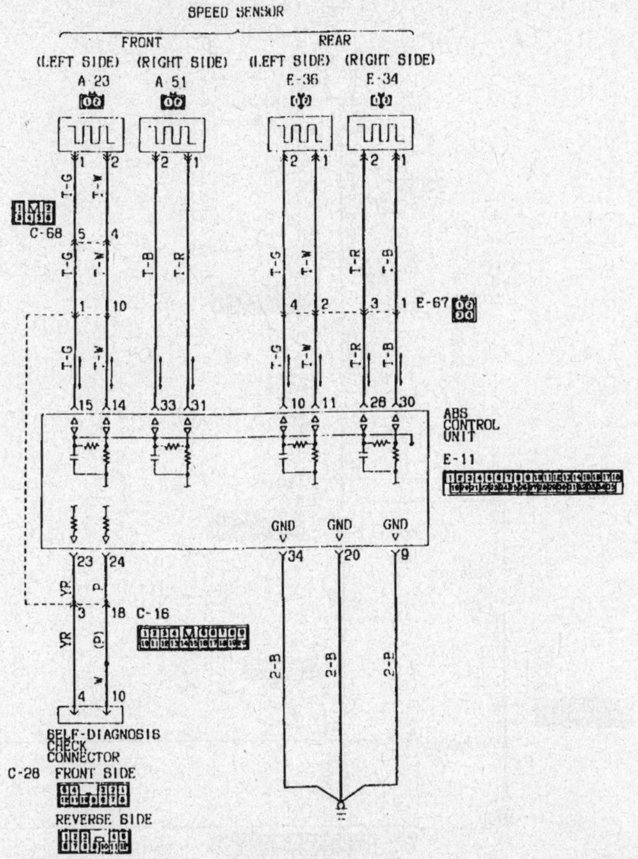
SPEED SENSOR
FRONT
REAR
(LEFT SIDE)
(RIGHT SIDE)
(LEFT SIDE)
(RIGHT SIDE)
A-23
A-51
E-36
E-34
C-68
E-67
ABS CONTROL UNIT
E-11
GND
C-16
SELF-DIAGNOSIS CHECK CONNECTOR
C-28
FRONT SIDE
REVERSE SIDE
MT4029100008030X

Fig. 4 Anti-lock brake system wiring diagram (Part 3 of 3). 1993–94 Eclipse FWD

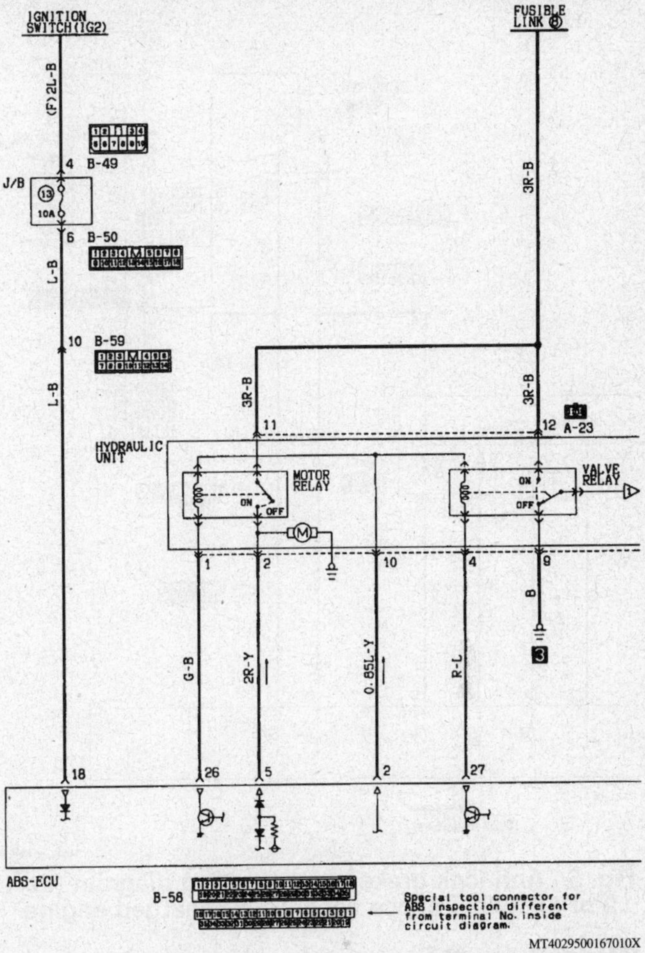
IGNITION SWITCH(IG2)
FUSIBLE LINK ⑧
J/B
B-49
B-50
B-59
HYDRAULIC UNIT
MOTOR RELAY
VALVE RELAY
A-23
ABS-ECU
B-58
Special tool connector for ABS inspection different from terminal No. inside circuit diagram.
MT4029500167010X

Fig. 5 Anti-lock brake system wiring diagram (Part 1 of 5). 1995 Eclipse w/non-turbocharged engine

PICKUP

1. Turn ignition switch to Off position.
2. Connect Multi-Use Tester (MUT) or voltmeter to diagnostic connector, **Fig. 82.**
3. Turn ignition switch to On position.
4. Read diagnostic trouble codes, then proceed to "Diagnostic Trouble Code Interpretation" for further information regarding analysis and correction of malfunctions related to specific diagnostic trouble codes.
5. Disconnect MUT or voltmeter.

Diagnostic Trouble Code Interpretation

Refer to **Figs. 1 through 31** for ABS wiring diagrams when following diagnostic procedures found in this section. The "Diagnostic Chart Index" may be helpful in identifying diagnostic trouble codes and in locating diagnostic charts.

EXPO, 1993 GALANT, 1993–94 ECLIPSE & 1993–95 3000GT

Refer to **Figs. 83 through 126** for diagnostic flowcharts corresponding to specific diagnostic trouble codes.

1995 ECLIPSE

Refer to **Figs. 127 through 138** for diagnostic flowcharts corresponding to specific diagnostic trouble codes.

If the anti-lock brake system or ABS warning lamp is operating abnormally and there are no trouble codes present, refer to **Figs. 139 through 147** for symptom diagnosis.

1996 ECLIPSE

AWD MODELS

Refer to **Figs. 148 through 154** for diagnostic flowcharts corresponding to specific diagnostic trouble codes.

FWD MODELS

Refer to **Figs. 155 through 162** for diagnostic flowcharts corresponding to specific diagnostic trouble codes.

1994–96 GALANT

Refer to **Figs. 163 through 178** for diagnostic flowcharts corresponding to specific diagnostic trouble codes.

1996 3000GT

Refer to **Figs. 179 through 187** for diagnostic flowcharts corresponding to specific diagnostic trouble codes.

DIAMANTE

Refer to **Figs. 188 through 197** for diagnostic flowcharts corresponding to specific diagnostic trouble codes.

MIRAGE

Refer to **Figs. 198 through 209** for diagnostic flowcharts corresponding to specific diagnostic trouble codes.

MONTERO

1993–95

Refer to **Figs. 210 through 220** for diagnostic flowcharts corresponding to specific diagnostic trouble codes.

1996

Refer to **Figs. 221 through 233** for diagnostic flowcharts corresponding to specific diagnostic trouble codes.

PICKUP

Refer to **Fig. 234** to interpret diagnostic trouble code output.

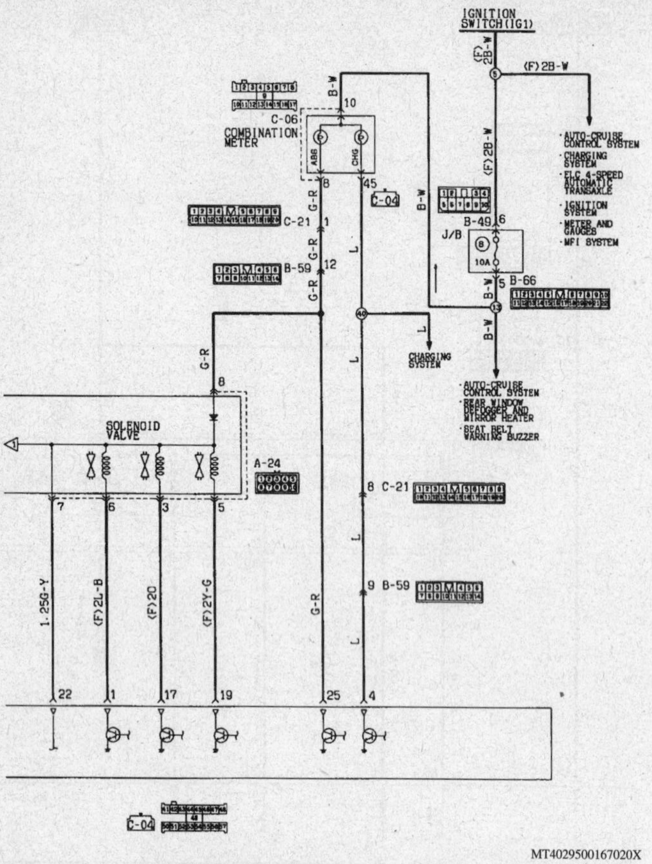
IGNITION SWITCH(IG1)
COMBINATION METER
C-06
C-21
B-59
B-49
J/B
B-66
C-04
AUTO-CRUISE CONTROL SYSTEM
CHARGING SYSTEM
IGNITION SYSTEM
METER AND GAUGES
MFI SYSTEM
SOLENOID VALVE
A-24
MT4029500167020X

Fig. 5 Anti-lock brake system wiring diagram (Part 2 of 5). 1995 Eclipse w/non-turbocharged engine

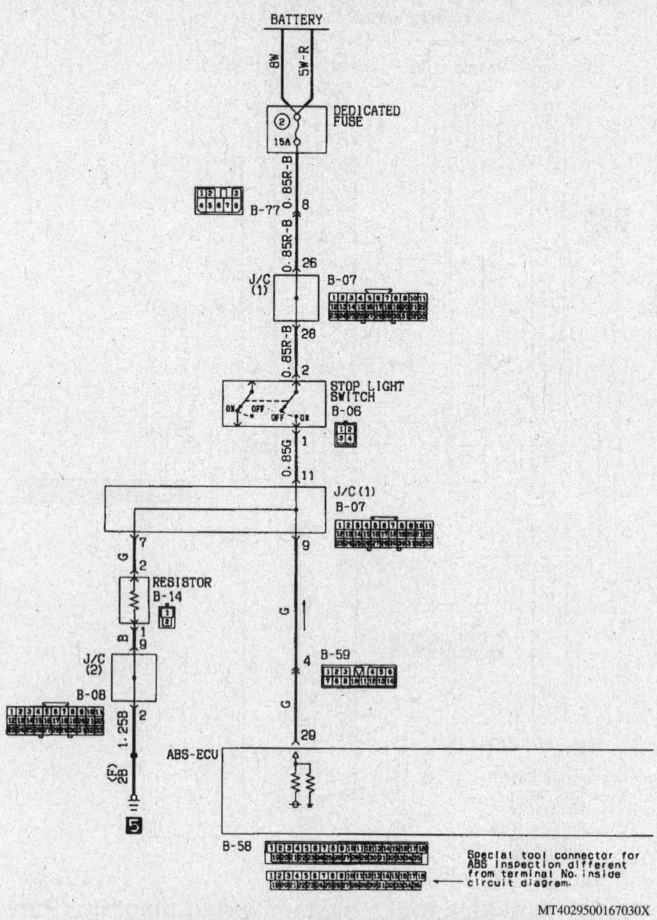
BATTERY
DEDICATED FUSE
B-77
J/C (1)
B-07
STOP LIGHT SWITCH
B-06
RESISTOR
B-14
J/C (2)
B-08
B-59
ABS-ECU
B-58
Special tool connector for ABS inspection different from terminal No. inside circuit diagram.
MT4029500167030X

Fig. 5 Anti-lock brake system wiring diagram (Part 3 of 5). 1995 Eclipse w/non-turbocharged engine

Clearing Diagnostic Trouble Codes

DIAMANTE & MIRAGE

LESS MULTI-USE TESTER (MUT)

1. Connect two diagnostic trouble code memory erasure connector terminals.
2. Turn ignition switch to On position.
3. **On Diamante models,** turn ignition switch to Off position after one second or more.
4. **On Mirage models,** turn ignition switch to Off position after seven seconds or more.
5. **On all models,** disconnect two diagnostic trouble code memory erasure connector terminals, then turn ignition switch to On position and ensure diagnostic trouble code(s) have been cleared.

WITH MULTI-USE TESTER (MUT)

Erase diagnostic trouble codes following scan tool manufacturer's instructions.

ECLIPSE, EXPO & 3000GT

To erase diagnostic trouble codes, use the Multi-Use Tester (MUT) and follow manufacturer's instructions for erasure.

GALANT & MONTERO

To erase diagnostic trouble codes, use the Multi-Use Tester (MUT) or disconnect the battery ground cable for ten seconds or more.

PICKUP

To erase diagnostic trouble codes, disconnect battery ground cable for ten seconds or more.

SYSTEM SERVICE

Brake System Bleed

1. Bleed brake master cylinder as follows:
   a. Fill master cylinder reservoir with DOT 3 or DOT 4 brake fluid, then depress brake pedal fully and plug master cylinder outlet fitting.
   b. With fitting opening plugged, release brake pedal. Perform this operation several times to fill master cylinder with brake fluid and purge all air.
2. Start engine and bleed air from hydraulic lines. Refer to **Figs. 235 through 237** for hydraulic line bleed sequence. **Ensure master cylinder reservoir is kept full during bleed procedure.**
3. Ensure brake pedal feels firm when applied. Check and fill master cylinder reservoir as necessary.

Component Replacement

BRAKE FLUID PRESSURE SWITCH

AWD MODELS

1. Disconnect pressure switch electrical connector.
2. Remove brake line connection.
3. Remove pressure switch from side of hydraulic unit.
4. Reverse procedure to install.

ELECTRONIC CONTROL UNIT & POWER RELAY

1. Remove ECU electrical connector mounting screws, then the ECU.
2. Remove ABS power relay, located under lefthand side of instrument panel.
3. Reverse procedure to install.

FRONT SPEED SENSOR

EXCEPT PICKUP

1. Remove front toothed rotor.
2. Remove front speed sensor connector.
3. Remove front speed sensor and bracket.
4. Temporarily install sensor into knuckle.

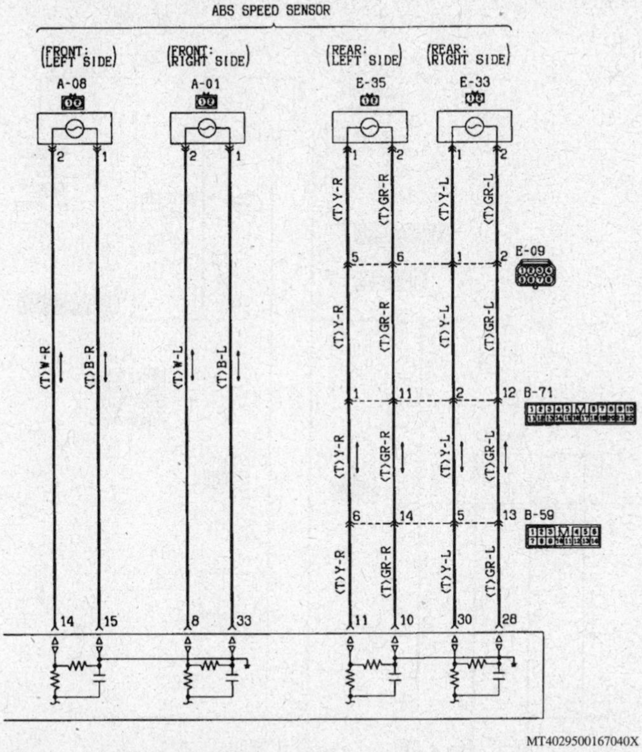

ABS SPEED SENSOR
(FRONT: LEFT SIDE)
(FRONT: RIGHT SIDE)
(REAR: LEFT SIDE)
(REAR: RIGHT SIDE)
A-08
A-01
E-35
E-33
E-09
B-71
B-59
(T)Y-R
(T)GR-R
(T)Y-L
(T)GR-L
(T)W-R
(T)B-R
(T)W-L
(T)B-L
MT4029500167040X

Fig. 5 Anti-lock brake system wiring diagram (Part 4 of 5). 1995 Eclipse w/non-turbocharged engine

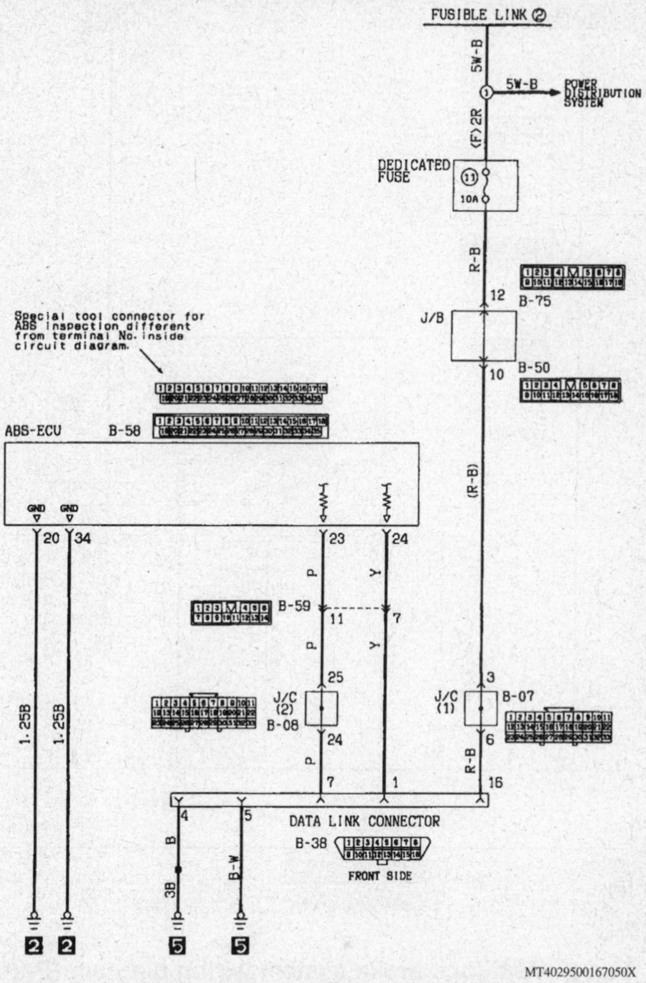

FUSIBLE LINK ②
5W-B
POWER DISTRIBUTION SYSTEM
(F)2R
DEDICATED FUSE
10A
R-B
B-75
J/B
B-50
Special tool connector for ABS inspection different from terminal No. inside circuit diagram.
ABS-ECU
B-58
GND
(R-B)
B-59
J/C (2)
B-08
J/C (1)
B-07
1.25B
DATA LINK CONNECTOR
B-38
FRONT SIDE
B-W
3B
MT4029500167050X

Fig. 5 Anti-lock brake system wiring diagram (Part 5 of 5). 1995 Eclipse w/non-turbocharged engine

5. Secure clip so white-painted portion is non twisted.
6. Insert a feeler gauge between speed sensor pole piece and rotor toothed surface.
7. Tighten front speed sensor bracket and toothed rotor attaching bolts.
8. **On all models except Montero, 1994–96 Galant and 1995–96 Eclipse,** ensure a gap of .012–.035 inch exists between pole piece and rotor. If this gap cannot be reached, rotor may be improperly installed.
9. **On Montero models,** ensure a gap of .008–.039 inch exists between pole piece and rotor. If this gap cannot be reached, rotor may be improperly installed.
10. **On 1994–96 Galant & 1995–96 Eclipse models,** ensure a gap of 1.11–1.12 inch exists between sensor installation surface and rotor toothed surface.

PICKUP

1. Disconnect electrical connector to speed sensor.
2. Remove speed sensor to rear axle attaching bolt, then the speed sensor.
3. Reverse procedure to install.

G-SENSOR

1. Disconnect G-sensor electrical connections.
2. Remove G-sensor bracket and G-sensor.
3. Reverse procedure to install.

HYDRAULIC UNIT

The hydraulic unit must never be disassembled, subjected to impact or turned upside down. Do not loosen bolts.

GALANT

1993

1. Remove dust shield, engine coolant reservoir and bracket.
2. Remove brake hose and tube connections.
3. Remove relay box cover and connector.
4. Remove forward bracket mounting bolts, then the bracket.
5. Remove hydraulic unit.
6. Reverse procedure to install. **Torque** all bolts except upper coolant reservoir bolt to 12–19 ft. lbs. and upper coolant reservoir bolt to 7–10 ft lbs.

1994–96

1. Drain brake fluid from reservoir and remove air intake hose.
2. Remove hydraulic unit in numbered sequence, **Fig. 238. Exercise caution during removal; unit is heavy and must be handled carefully.**
3. Reverse procedure to install, noting the following:
   a. Ensure brake lines are connected to proper ports, **Fig. 239.**
   b. Bleed brake system as outlined under "Brake System Bleed" in this section.

ECLIPSE

1993–94

1. Disconnect brake tube connection.
2. Remove relay box cover.
3. Disconnect hydraulic unit harness connection.
4. Remove hydraulic unit nuts and lift out hydraulic unit.
5. Remove bracket, valve relay and motor relay from hydraulic unit.
6. Reverse procedure to install. Bleed brake system as outlined under "Brake System Bleed" in this section.

1995–96

1. Drain brake fluid from reservoir, then remove lefthand splash shield and headlamp.
2. **On models equipped with 2.0L non-turbocharged engine,** remove air cleaner assembly, Engine Control Module (ECM), relay box bracket and power steering oil reservoir mounting bolts.

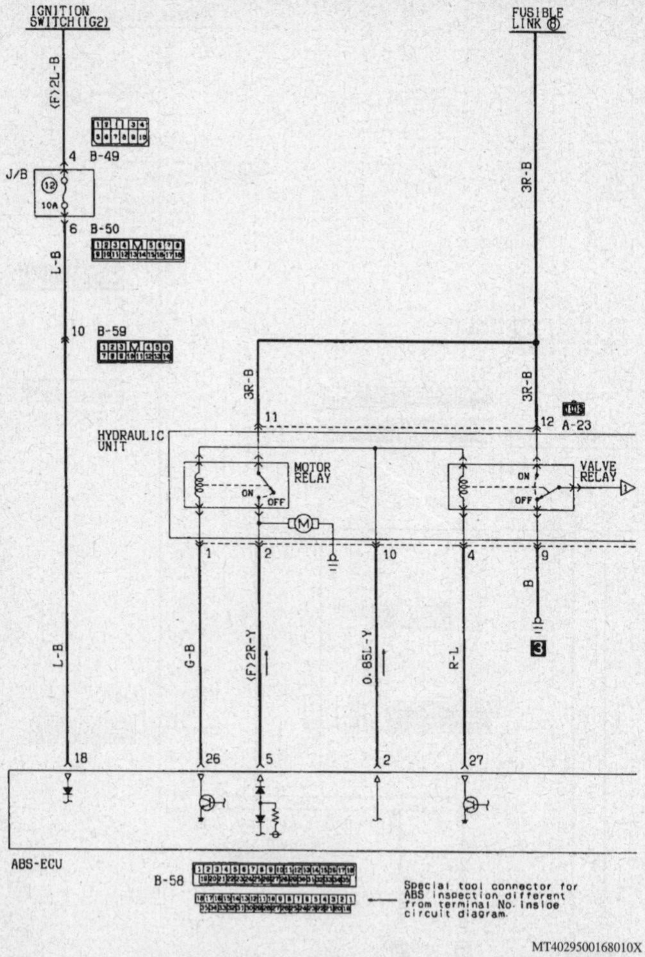
IGNITION SWITCH(IG2)
FUSIBLE LINK 6
(F)2L-B
B-49
J/B
10A
B-50
L-B
B-59
3R-B
HYDRAULIC UNIT
MOTOR RELAY
VALVE RELAY
ON
OFF
A-23
B
G-B
(F)2R-Y
0.85L-Y
R-L
ABS-ECU
B-58
Special tool connector for ABS inspection different from terminal No. inside circuit diagram.
MT4029500168010X

Fig. 6 Anti-lock brake system wiring diagram (Part 1 of 5). 1995 Eclipse AWD w/turbocharged engine

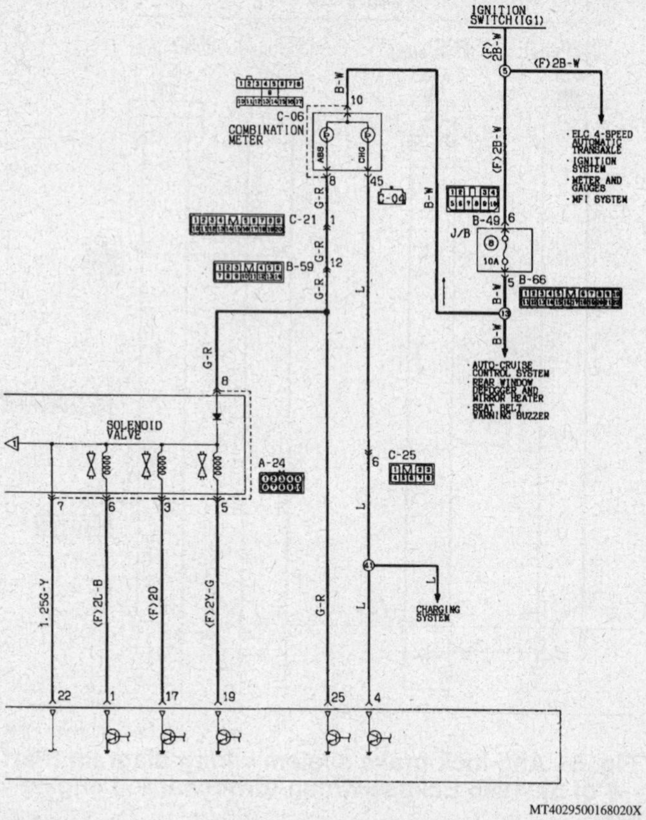
IGNITION SWITCH(IG1)
(F)2B-W
B-W
C-06
COMBINATION METER
ABS
CHG
C-04
C-21
G-R
B-59
L
ELC 4-SPEED AUTOMATIC TRANSAXLE
IGNITION SYSTEM
METER AND GAUGES
MFI SYSTEM
B-49
J/B
10A
B-66
AUTO-CRUISE CONTROL SYSTEM
REAR WINDOW DEFOGGER AND MIRROR HEATER
SEAT BELT WARNING BUZZER
SOLENOID VALVE
A-24
C-25
1.25G-Y
(F)2L-B
(F)2O
(F)2Y-G
CHARGING SYSTEM
MT4029500168020X

Fig. 6 Anti-lock brake system wiring diagram (Part 2 of 5). 1995 Eclipse AWD w/turbocharged engine

3. **On models equipped with 2.0L turbocharged engine and 2.4L engine,** remove power steering pressure and return pipe clamp mounting bolts.
4. **On all models,** remove hydraulic unit from vehicle in numbered sequence, **Fig. 240. Exercise caution when removing unit; it is heavy and must be handled carefully.**
5. Reverse procedure to install, noting the following:
   a. Ensure brake pipes are connected to proper ports, **Fig. 241.**
   b. Bleed brake system as outlined under "Brake System Bleed" in this section.

MIRAGE

Remove hydraulic unit in numbered sequence as shown in **Fig. 242,** keeping brake pipes in order when installing, **Fig. 243. Brake system must be bled as described under "Brake System Bleed" in this section.**

MONTERO

Remove the hydraulic relay and unit in numbered sequence shown in **Fig. 244. Brake system must be bled as described under "Brake System Bleed" in this section.**

DIAMANTE

1. Remove the hydraulic relay unit in numbered sequence as shown in **Fig. 245,** pushing the unit rearward so that it does not come in contact with the piping on the A/C receiver.
2. Reverse numbered sequence to install. **Brake system must be bled as outlined under "Brake System Bleed" in this section.**

EXPO

1. Disconnect brake tune connection.
2. Remove relay box cover.
3. Disconnect hydraulic unit harness connection.
4. Remove hydraulic unit nuts and lift out hydraulic unit.
5. Remove bracket, valve relay and motor relay from hydraulic unit.
6. Reverse procedure to install. Bleed brake system as outlined under "Brake System Bleed."

3000GT

1. Remove splash shield, then disconnect and remove relay box.
2. Remove hydraulic unit in numbered sequence shown in **Fig. 246,** noting the following:
   a. When removing brake tubes, pull up relay box with harness attached and insert a suitable wrench under relay box.
   b. Remove hydraulic unit along with bracket from wheelhouse.
3. Reverse procedure to install, noting the following:
   a. Ensure ground cable is properly attached.
   b. Bleed brake system as outlined under "Brake System Bleed" in this section.

MODULATOR

PICKUP

1. Disconnect brake tubes.
2. Remove filter spacer, air filter and washer.
3. Disconnect vacuum hose.
4. Remove modulator to bracket attaching screws, then the modulator.
5. Reverse procedure to install.

REAR SPEED SENSOR

EXCEPT PICKUP

1. Remove rear toothed rotor.
2. Remove rear speed sensor connector.
3. Remove rear speed sensor.
4. Temporarily install speed sensor in backing plate.
5. Secure clip so white-painted portion is non twisted.
6. Insert a feeler gauge between speed sensor pole piece and rotor toothed surface.
7. Tighten rear toothed rotor attaching bolts.

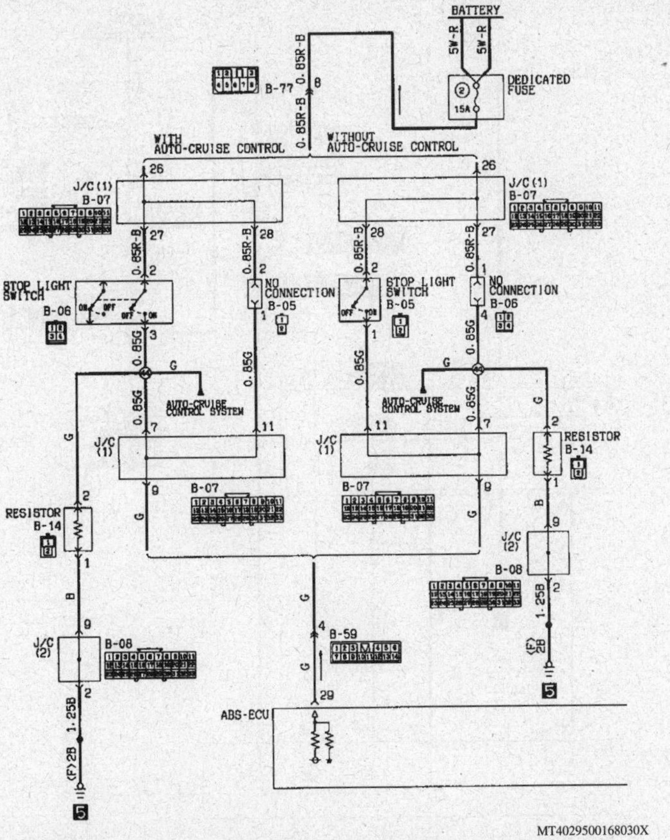

BATTERY
DEDICATED FUSE
B-77
WITH AUTO-CRUISE CONTROL
WITHOUT AUTO-CRUISE CONTROL
J/C (1) B-07
STOP LIGHT SWITCH B-06
NO CONNECTION B-05
STOP LIGHT SWITCH B-05
NO CONNECTION B-06
AUTO-CRUISE CONTROL SYSTEM
RESISTOR B-14
J/C (2) B-08
B-59
ABS-ECU
MT4029500168030X

Fig. 6 Anti-lock brake system wiring diagram (Part 3 of 5). 1995 Eclipse AWD w/turbocharged engine

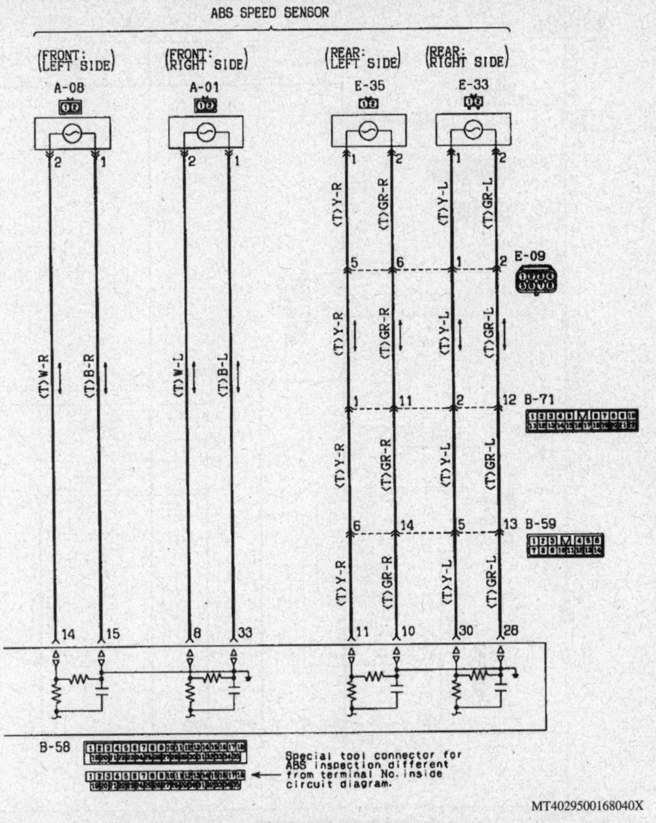

ABS SPEED SENSOR
(FRONT: LEFT SIDE)
(FRONT: RIGHT SIDE)
(REAR: LEFT SIDE)
(REAR: RIGHT SIDE)
A-08
A-01
E-35
E-33
E-09
B-71
B-59
B-58
Special tool connector for ABS inspection different from terminal No. inside circuit diagram.
MT4029500168040X

Fig. 6 Anti-lock brake system wiring diagram (Part 4 of 5). 1995 Eclipse AWD w/turbocharged engine

8. **On all models except Montero, 3000GT, 1994–95 Galant and 1995–96 Eclipse,** ensure a gap of .012–.035 inch exists between pole piece and rotor.
9. **On 3000GT models,** ensure a gap of .008–.028 inch exists between pole piece and rotor.
10. **On 1994–96 Galant and 1995–96 Eclipse models,** ensure a gap of 1.11–1.12 inch exists between sensor mounting surface and rotor.
11. **On all models,** slowly spin rotor one full revolution to ensure sensor pole piece does not come in contact with rotor.

PICKUP

1. Disconnect electrical connector to speed sensor.
2. Remove speed sensor to rear axle attaching bolt, then the speed sensor.
3. Reverse procedure to install.

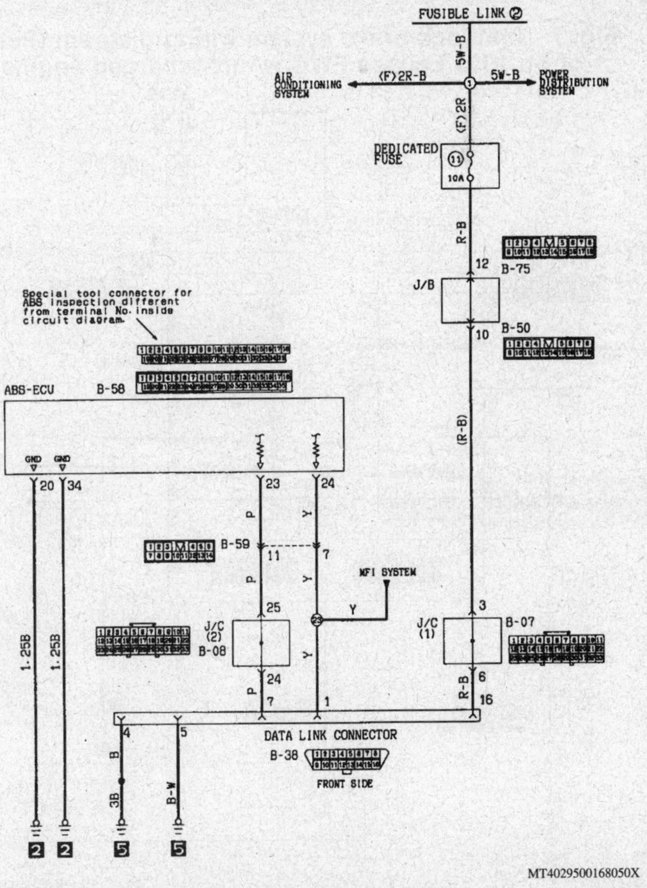

FUSIBLE LINK ②
AIR CONDITIONING SYSTEM
POWER DISTRIBUTION SYSTEM
DEDICATED FUSE
B-75
J/B
B-50
Special tool connector for ABS inspection different from terminal No. inside circuit diagram.
ABS-ECU
B-58
B-59
MFI SYSTEM
J/C (2) B-08
J/C (1) B-07
DATA LINK CONNECTOR
B-38
FRONT SIDE
MT4029500168050X

Fig. 6 Anti-lock brake system wiring diagram (Part 5 of 5). 1995 Eclipse AWD w/turbocharged engine

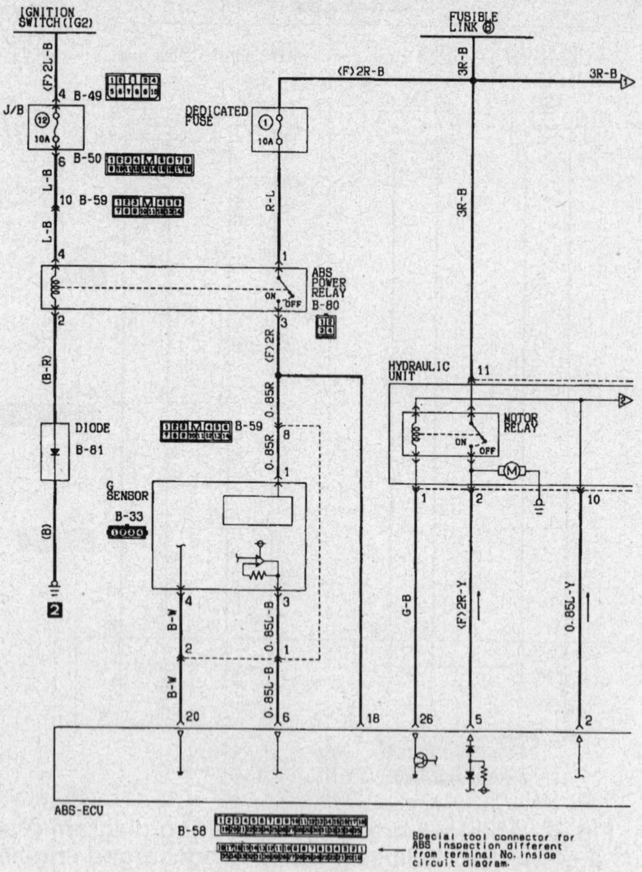
IGNITION SWITCH (IG2)
FUSIBLE LINK ⑧
(F)2L-B
B-49
J/B
10A
B-50
L-B
B-59
(F)2R-B
3R-B
DEDICATED FUSE
R-L
ABS POWER RELAY
B-80
ON
OFF
(B-R)
(F)2R
0.85R
DIODE
B-81
G SENSOR
B-33
(B)
HYDRAULIC UNIT
MOTOR RELAY
G-B
(F)2R-Y
0.85L-Y
B-W
0.85L-B
ABS-ECU
B-58
Special tool connector for ABS inspection different from terminal No. inside circuit diagram.
MT4029500169010X

Fig. 7 Anti-lock brake system wiring diagram (Part 1 of 5). 1995 Eclipse FWD w/turbocharged engine

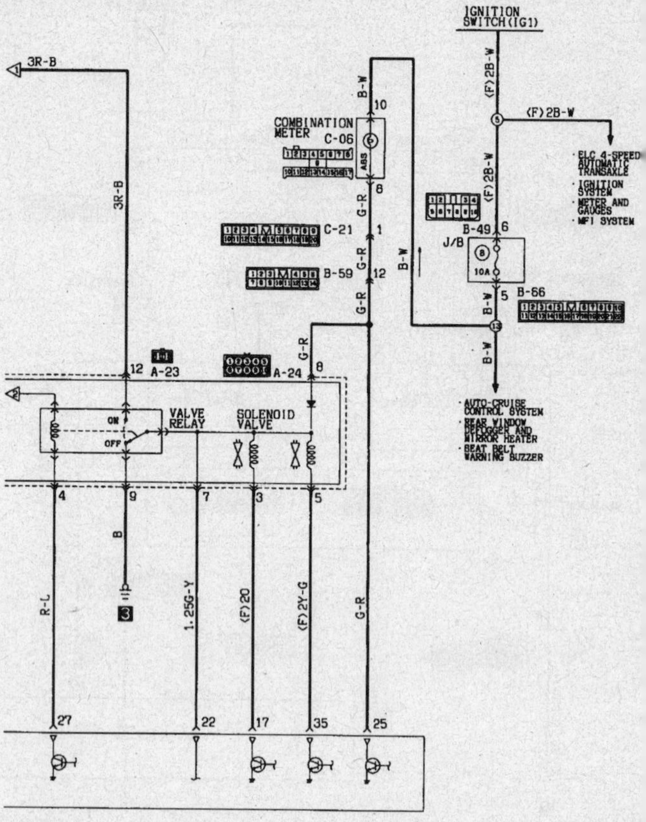
3R-B
IGNITION SWITCH (IG1)
(F)2B-W
COMBINATION METER
C-06
ABS
G-R
C-21
B-59
B-49
J/B
10A
B-66
B-W
ELC 4-SPEED AUTOMATIC TRANSAXLE
IGNITION SYSTEM
METER AND GAUGES
MFI SYSTEM
AUTO-CRUISE CONTROL SYSTEM
REAR WINDOW DEFOGGER AND MIRROR HEATER
SEAT BELT WARNING BUZZER
A-23
A-24
VALVE RELAY
SOLENOID VALVE
ON
OFF
R-L
B
1.25G-Y
(F)2G
(F)2Y-G
MT4029500169020X

Fig. 7 Anti-lock brake system wiring diagram (Part 2 of 5). 1995 Eclipse FWD w/turbocharged engine

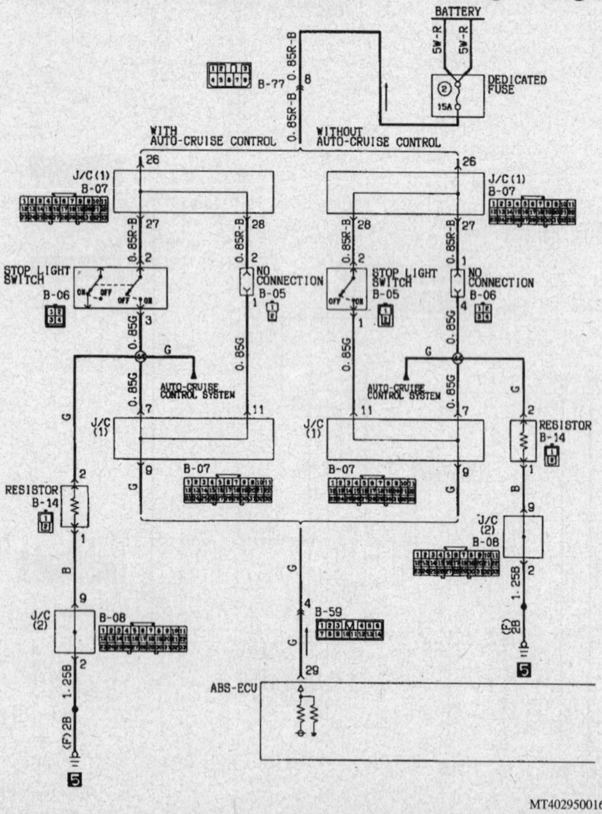
BATTERY
5W-R
DEDICATED FUSE
15A
0.85R-B
B-77
WITH AUTO-CRUISE CONTROL
WITHOUT AUTO-CRUISE CONTROL
J/C (1)
B-07
STOP LIGHT SWITCH
B-06
NO CONNECTION
B-05
0.85G
G
AUTO-CRUISE CONTROL SYSTEM
RESISTOR
B-14
B
J/C (2)
B-08
1.25B
(F)2B
B-59
ABS-ECU
MT4029500169030X

Fig. 7 Anti-lock brake system wiring diagram (Part 3 of 5). 1995 Eclipse FWD w/turbocharged engine

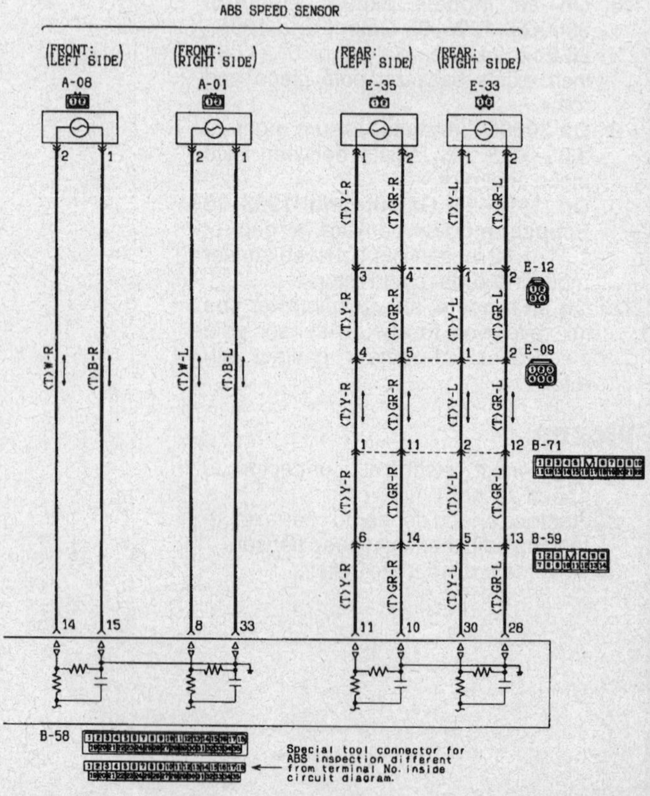
ABS SPEED SENSOR
(FRONT: LEFT SIDE)
(FRONT: RIGHT SIDE)
(REAR: LEFT SIDE)
(REAR: RIGHT SIDE)
A-08
A-01
E-35
E-33
(T)W-R
(T)B-R
(T)W-L
(T)B-L
(T)Y-R
(T)GR-R
(T)Y-L
(T)GR-L
E-12
E-09
B-71
B-59
B-58
Special tool connector for ABS inspection different from terminal No. inside circuit diagram.
MT4029500169040X

Fig. 7 Anti-lock brake system wiring diagram (Part 4 of 5). 1995 Eclipse FWD w/turbocharged engine

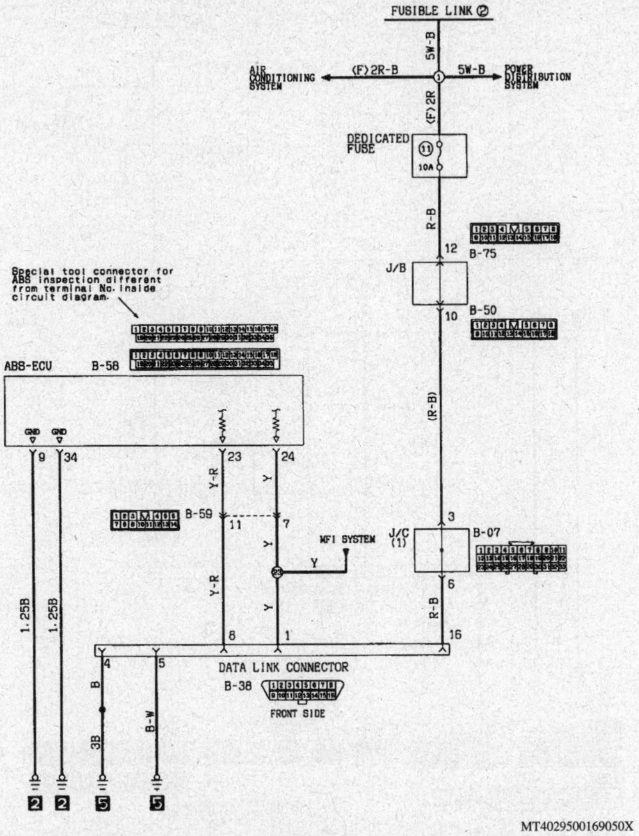
FUSIBLE LINK ②
5W-B
AIR CONDITIONING SYSTEM
(F)2R-B
5W-B
POWER DISTRIBUTION SYSTEM
(F)2R
DEDICATED FUSE
10A
R-B
12
B-75
J/B
10
B-50
Special tool connector for ABS inspection different from terminal No. inside circuit diagram.
ABS-ECU
B-58
GND
GND
9
34
23
24
Y-R
Y
B-59
11
7
MFI SYSTEM
J/C (1)
3
B-07
6
(R-B)
R-B
16
1.25B
1.25B
8
1
DATA LINK CONNECTOR
B-38
FRONT SIDE
4
5
B
3B
B-W
MT4029500169050X

Fig. 7 Anti-lock brake system wiring diagram (Part 5 of 5). 1995 Eclipse FWD w/turbocharged engine

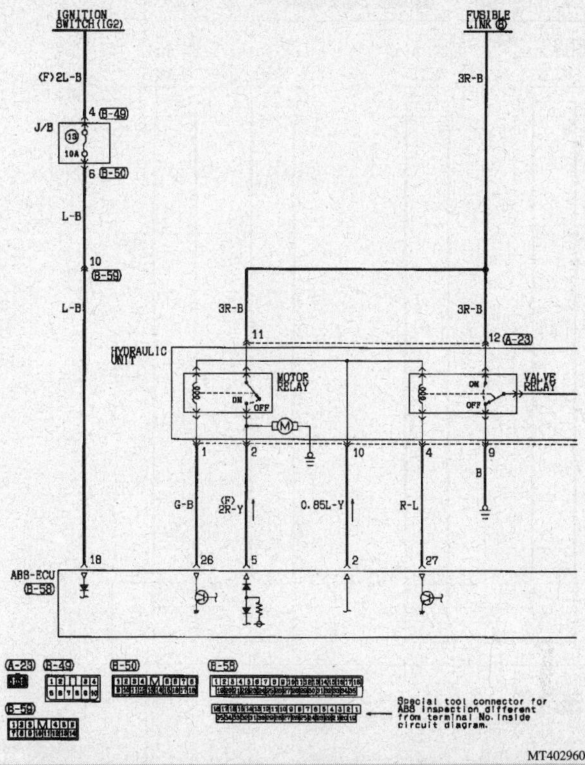
IGNITION SWITCH(IG2)
FUSIBLE LINK ⑤
(F)2L-B
3R-B
4 B-49
J/B
10A
6 B-50
L-B
10
B-59
L-B
3R-B
3R-B
11
12 A-23
HYDRAULIC UNIT
MOTOR RELAY
ON
OFF
VALVE RELAY
ON
OFF
1
2
10
4
9
B
G-B
(F) 2R-Y
0.85L-Y
R-L
ABS-ECU
B-58
18
26
5
2
27
A-23
B-49
B-50
B-58
B-59
Special tool connector for ABS inspection different from terminal No. inside circuit diagram.
MT4029600201010X

Fig. 8 Anti-lock brake system wiring diagram (Part 1 of 5). 1996 Eclipse w/2.0L non-turbocharged engine

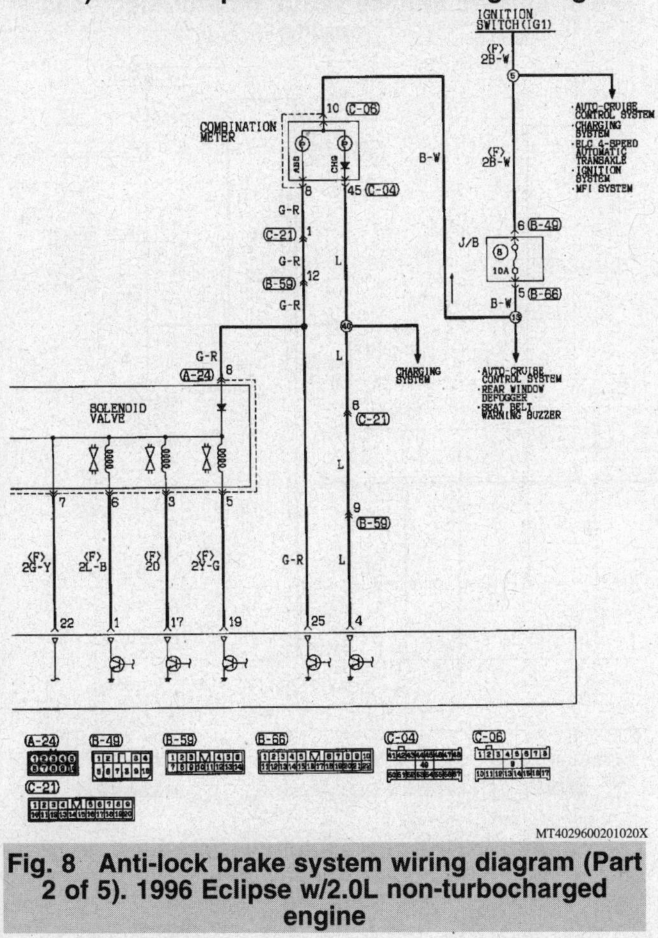
IGNITION SWITCH(IG1)
(F) 2B-W
AUTO-CRUISE CONTROL SYSTEM
CHARGING SYSTEM
ELC 4-SPEED AUTOMATIC TRANSAXLE
IGNITION SYSTEM
MFI SYSTEM
COMBINATION METER
10 C-06
ABS
CHG
B-W
(F) 2B-W
8
45 C-04
G-R
C-21
1
G-R
L
J/B
6 B-49
10A
5 B-66
B-59
12
B-W
G-R
CHARGING SYSTEM
AUTO-CRUISE CONTROL SYSTEM
REAR WINDOW DEFOGGER
SEAT BELT WARNING BUZZER
G-R
A-24
8
SOLENOID VALVE
L
8
C-21
L
9
B-59
7
6
3
5
(F) 2G-Y
(F) 2L-B
(F) 2G
(F) 2Y-G
G-R
L
22
1
17
19
25
4
A-24
B-49
B-59
B-66
C-04
C-06
C-21
MT4029600201020X

Fig. 8 Anti-lock brake system wiring diagram (Part 2 of 5). 1996 Eclipse w/2.0L non-turbocharged engine

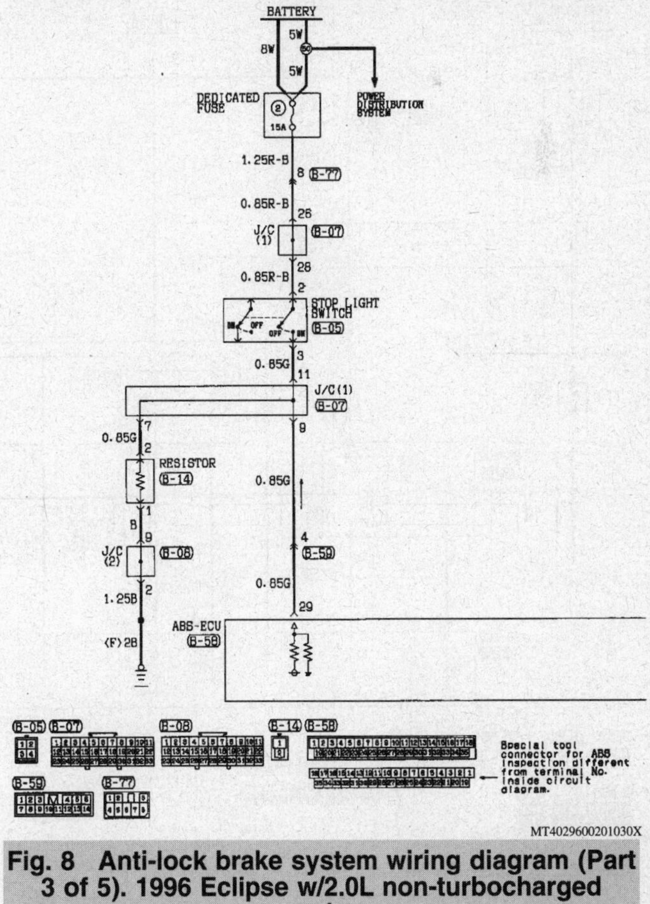
BATTERY
5W
8W
5W
POWER DISTRIBUTION SYSTEM
DEDICATED FUSE
15A
1.25R-B
8 B-77
0.85R-B
26
J/C (1)
B-07
28
0.85R-B
2
STOP LIGHT SWITCH
B-05
ON
OFF
3
0.85G
11
J/C(1)
B-07
7
9
0.85G
2
RESISTOR
B-14
0.85G
1
B
9
4
B-59
J/C (2)
B-08
2
0.85G
1.25B
29
ABS-ECU
B-58
(F) 2B
B-05
B-07
B-08
B-14
B-58
Special tool connector for ABS inspection different from terminal No. inside circuit diagram.
B-59
B-77
MT4029600201030X

Fig. 8 Anti-lock brake system wiring diagram (Part 3 of 5). 1996 Eclipse w/2.0L non-turbocharged engine

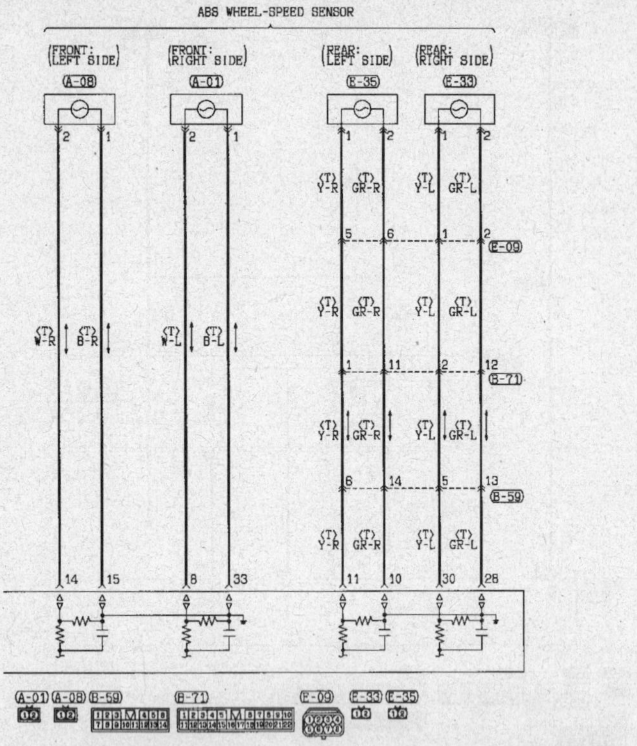
ABS WHEEL-SPEED SENSOR
(FRONT: LEFT SIDE)
(FRONT: RIGHT SIDE)
(REAR: LEFT SIDE)
(REAR: RIGHT SIDE)

MT4029600201040X

Fig. 8 Anti-lock brake system wiring diagram (Part 4 of 5). 1996 Eclipse w/2.0L non-turbocharged engine

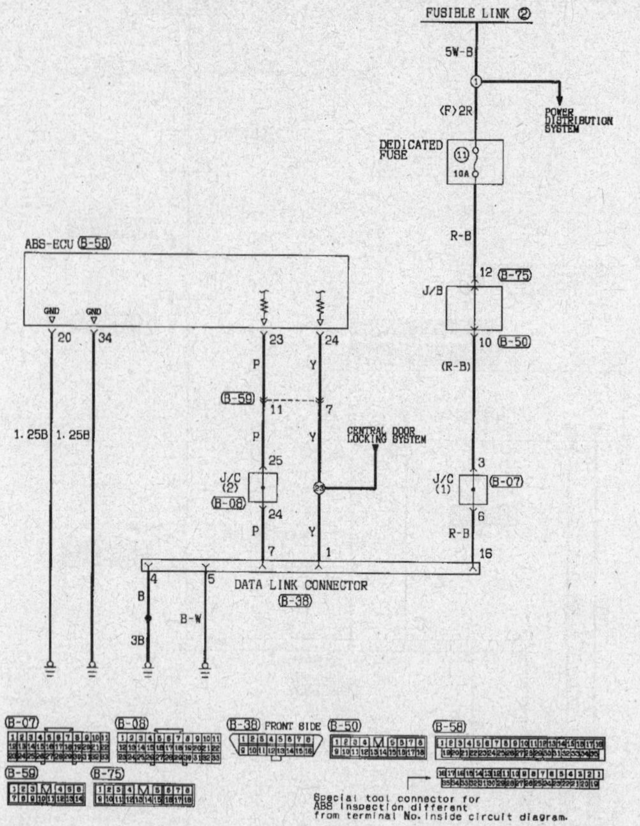
FUSIBLE LINK ②
POWER DISTRIBUTION SYSTEM
DEDICATED FUSE
ABS-ECU (B-58)
CENTRAL DOOR LOCKING SYSTEM
DATA LINK CONNECTOR (B-38)
Special tool connector for ABS inspection different from terminal No. inside circuit diagram.

MT4029600201050X

Fig. 8 Anti-lock brake system wiring diagram (Part 5 of 5). 1996 Eclipse w/2.0L non-turbocharged engine

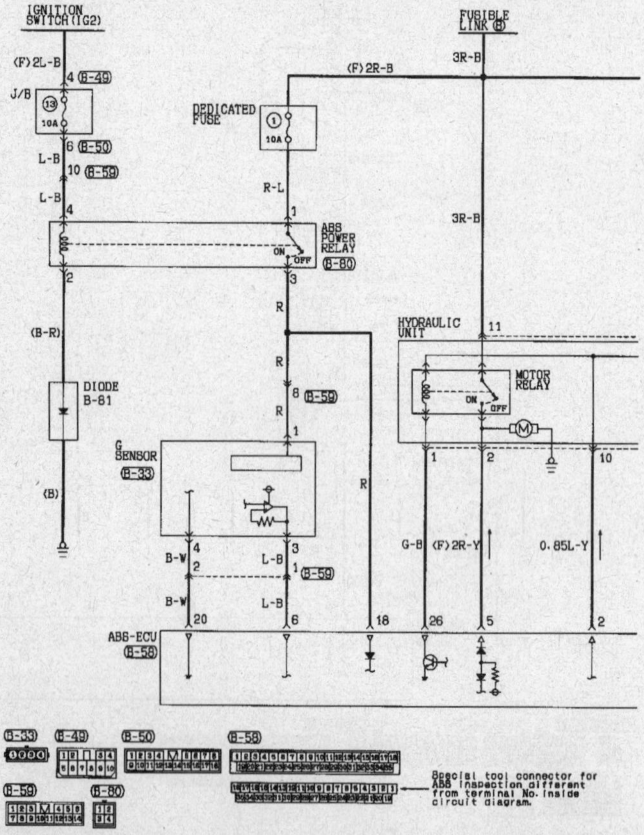
IGNITION SWITCH (IG2)
FUSIBLE LINK ⑧
DEDICATED FUSE
ABS POWER RELAY (B-80)
HYDRAULIC UNIT
MOTOR RELAY
DIODE B-81
G SENSOR (B-33)
ABS-ECU (B-58)
Special tool connector for ABS inspection different from terminal No. inside circuit diagram.

MT4029600202010X

Fig. 9 Anti-lock brake system wiring diagram (Part 1 of 5). 1996 Eclipse AWD w/2.0L turbocharged engine

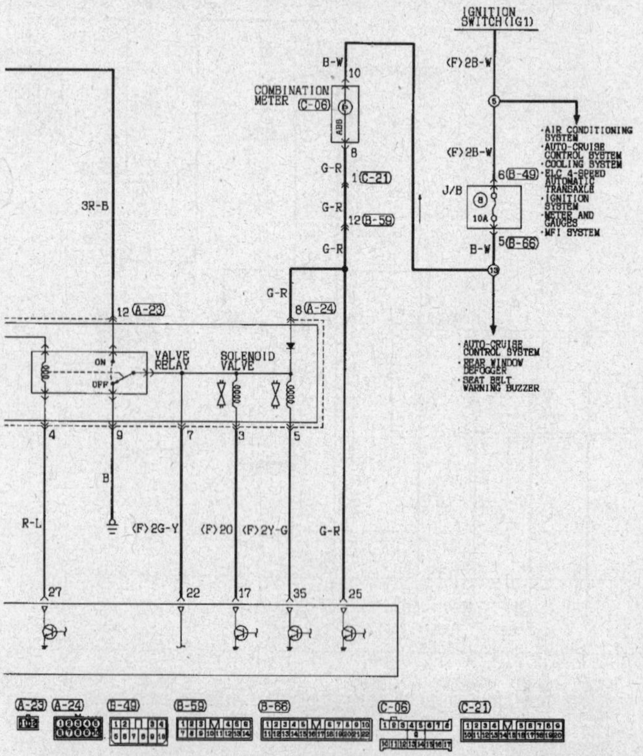
IGNITION SWITCH (IG1)
COMBINATION METER (C-06)
·AIR CONDITIONING SYSTEM
·AUTO-CRUISE CONTROL SYSTEM
·COOLING SYSTEM
·ELC 4-SPEED AUTOMATIC TRANSAXLE
·IGNITION SYSTEM
·METER AND GAUGES
·MFI SYSTEM
VALVE RELAY
SOLENOID VALVE
·AUTO-CRUISE CONTROL SYSTEM
·REAR WINDOW DEFOGGER
·SEAT BELT WARNING BUZZER

MT4029600202020X

Fig. 9 Anti-lock brake system wiring diagram (Part 2 of 5). 1996 Eclipse AWD w/2.0L turbocharged engine

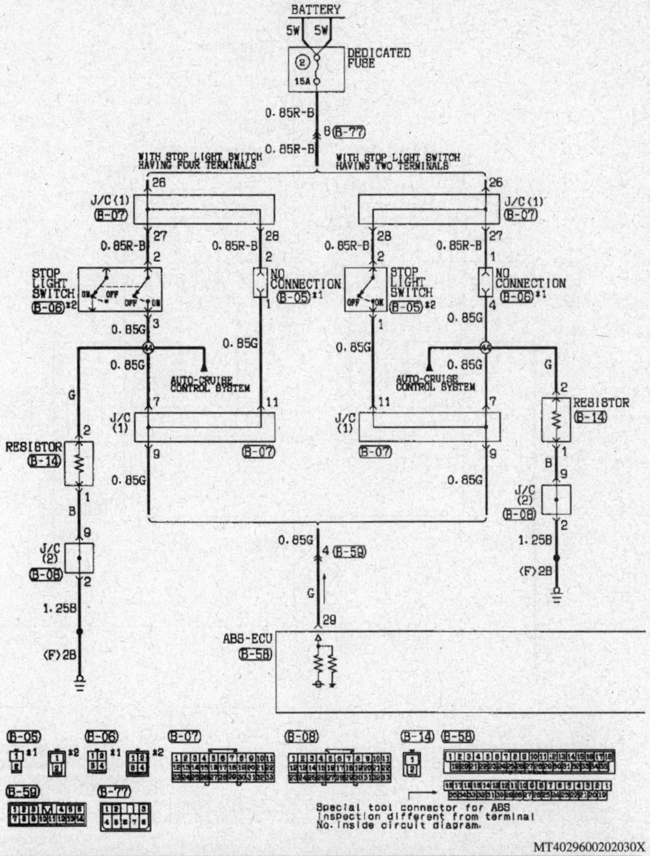
BATTERY
DEDICATED FUSE
WITH STOP LIGHT SWITCH HAVING FOUR TERMINALS
WITH STOP LIGHT SWITCH HAVING TWO TERMINALS
STOP LIGHT SWITCH
NO CONNECTION
AUTO-CRUISE CONTROL SYSTEM
RESISTOR
ABS-ECU
Special tool connector for ABS inspection different from terminal No. inside circuit diagram.
MT4029600202030X

Fig. 9 Anti-lock brake system wiring diagram (Part 3 of 5). 1996 Eclipse AWD w/2.0L turbocharged engine

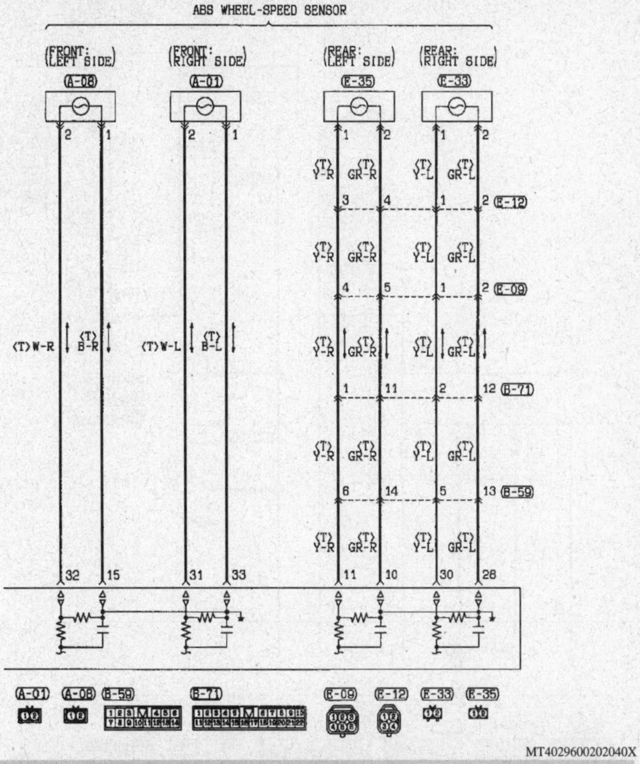
ABS WHEEL-SPEED SENSOR
(FRONT: LEFT SIDE)
(FRONT: RIGHT SIDE)
(REAR: LEFT SIDE)
(REAR: RIGHT SIDE)
MT4029600202040X

Fig. 9 Anti-lock brake system wiring diagram (Part 4 of 5). 1996 Eclipse AWD w/2.0L turbocharged engine

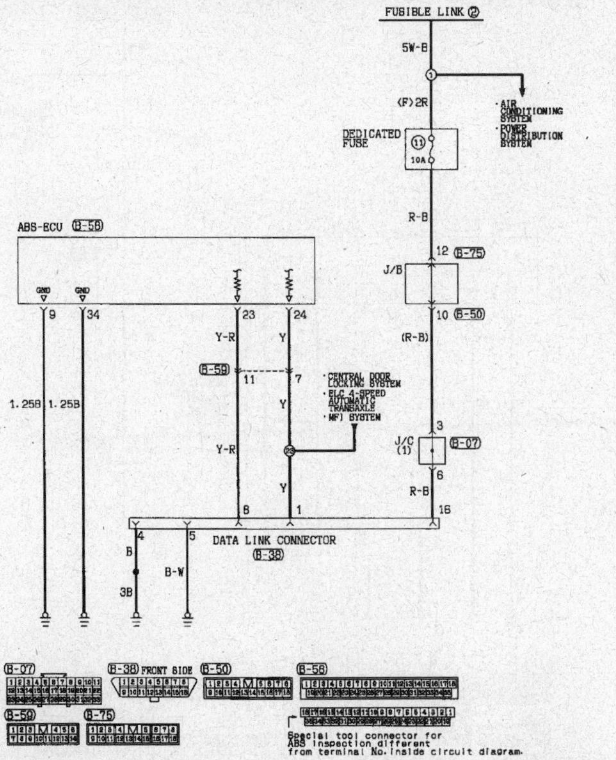
FUSIBLE LINK ②
DEDICATED FUSE
AIR CONDITIONING SYSTEM
POWER DISTRIBUTION SYSTEM
ABS-ECU
CENTRAL DOOR LOCKING SYSTEM
ELC 4-SPEED AUTOMATIC TRANSAXLE
MFI SYSTEM
DATA LINK CONNECTOR
FRONT SIDE
Special tool connector for ABS inspection different from terminal No. inside circuit diagram.
MT4029600202050X

Fig. 9 Anti-lock brake system wiring diagram (Part 5 of 5). 1996 Eclipse AWD w/2.0L turbocharged engine

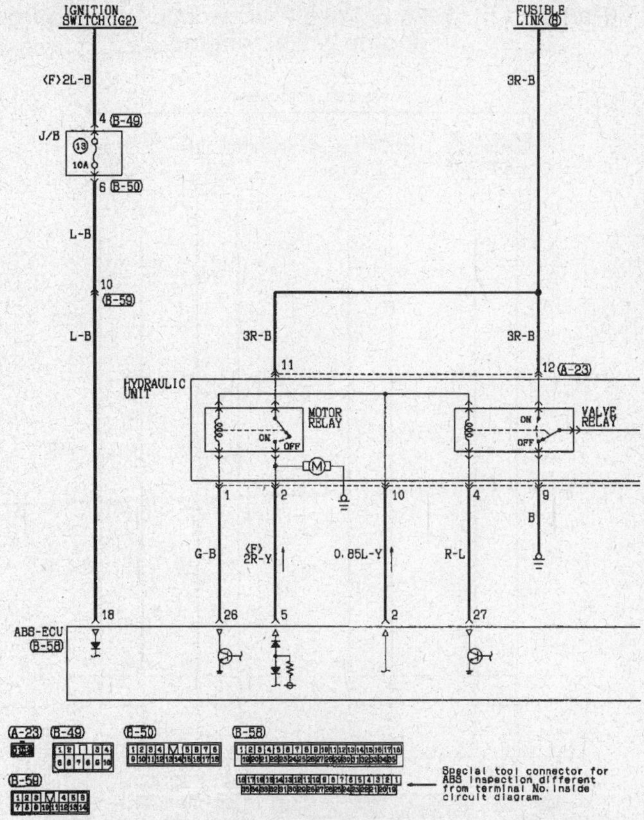
IGNITION SWITCH (IG2)
FUSIBLE LINK ⑥
HYDRAULIC UNIT
MOTOR RELAY
VALVE RELAY
ABS-ECU
Special tool connector for ABS inspection different from terminal No. inside circuit diagram.
MT4029600203010X

Fig. 10 Anti-lock brake system wiring diagram (Part 1 of 5). 1996 Eclipse FWD w/2.0L turbocharged engine & 2.4L engine

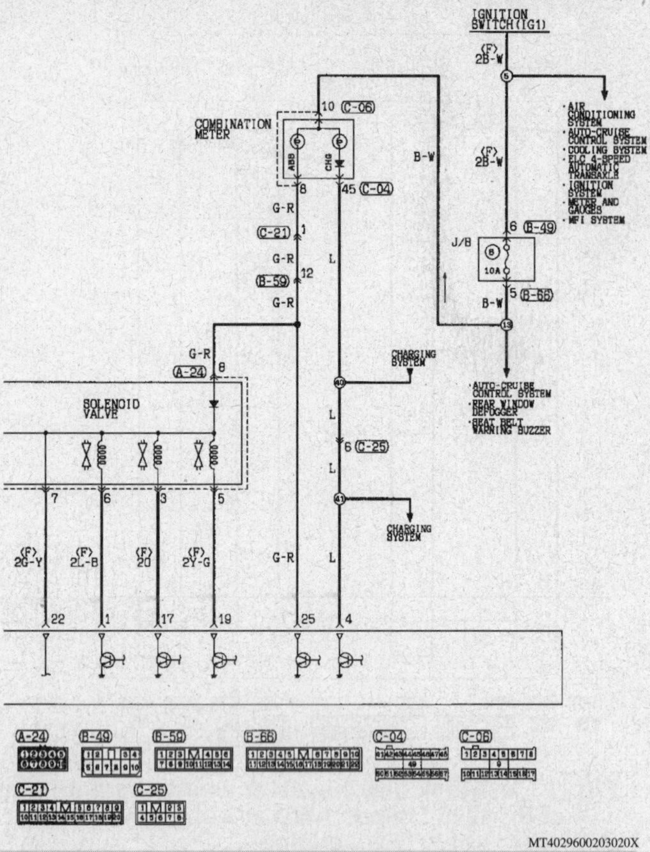
IGNITION SWITCH(IG1)
COMBINATION METER
AIR CONDITIONING SYSTEM
AUTO-CRUISE CONTROL SYSTEM
COOLING SYSTEM
ELC 4-SPEED AUTOMATIC TRANSAXLE
IGNITION SYSTEM
METER AND GAUGES
MFI SYSTEM
J/B
CHARGING SYSTEM
AUTO-CRUISE CONTROL SYSTEM
REAR WINDOW DEFOGGER
SEAT BELT WARNING BUZZER
SOLENOID VALVE
MT4029600203020X

Fig. 10 Anti-lock brake system wiring diagram (Part 2 of 5). 1996 Eclipse FWD w/2.0L turbocharged engine & 2.4L engine

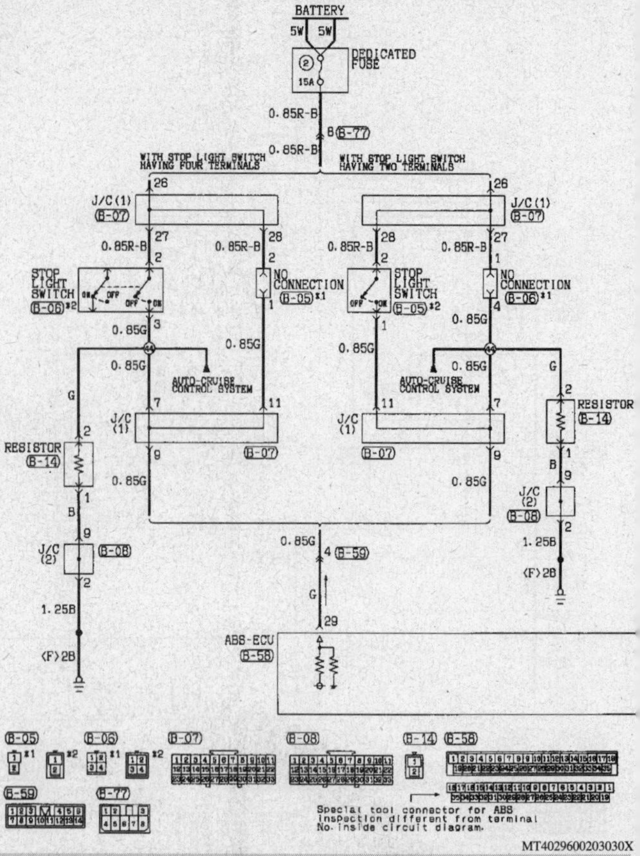
BATTERY
DEDICATED FUSE
WITH STOP LIGHT SWITCH HAVING FOUR TERMINALS
WITH STOP LIGHT SWITCH HAVING TWO TERMINALS
STOP LIGHT SWITCH
NO CONNECTION
AUTO-CRUISE CONTROL SYSTEM
RESISTOR
ABS-ECU
Special tool connector for ABS inspection different from terminal No. inside circuit diagram.
MT4029600203030X

Fig. 10 Anti-lock brake system wiring diagram (Part 3 of 5). 1996 Eclipse FWD w/2.0L turbocharged engine & 2.4L engine

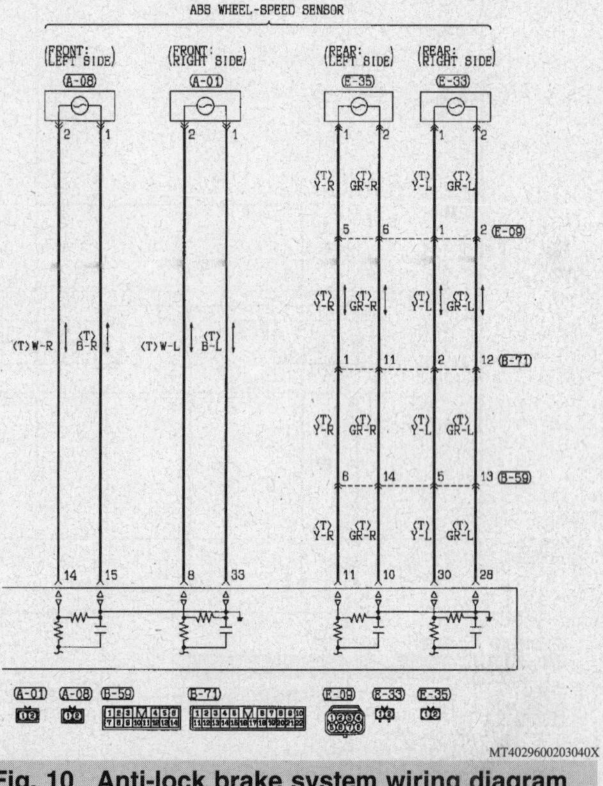
ABS WHEEL-SPEED SENSOR
(FRONT: LEFT SIDE)
(FRONT: RIGHT SIDE)
(REAR: LEFT SIDE)
(REAR: RIGHT SIDE)
MT4029600203040X

Fig. 10 Anti-lock brake system wiring diagram (Part 4 of 5). 1996 Eclipse FWD w/2.0L turbocharged engine & 2.4L engine

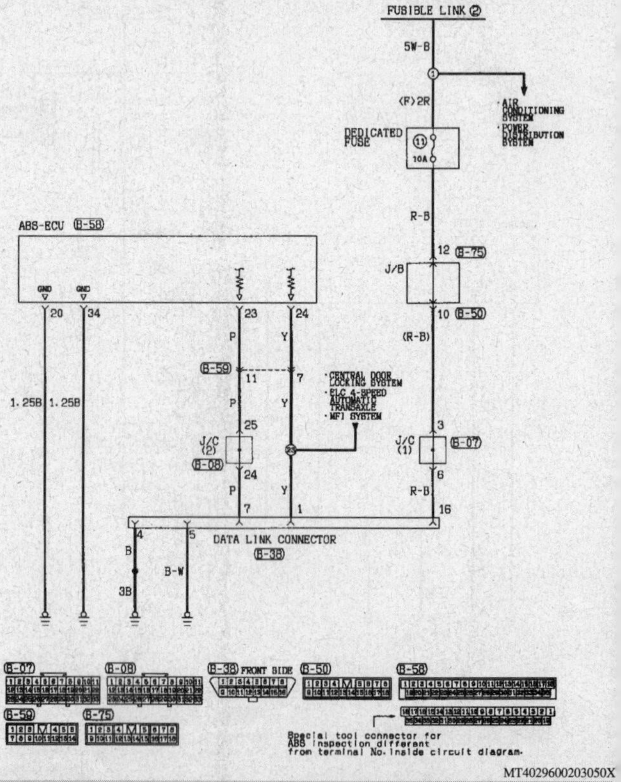
FUSIBLE LINK ②
AIR CONDITIONING SYSTEM
POWER DISTRIBUTION SYSTEM
DEDICATED FUSE
ABS-ECU
J/B
CENTRAL DOOR LOCKING SYSTEM
ELC 4-SPEED AUTOMATIC TRANSAXLE
MFI SYSTEM
DATA LINK CONNECTOR
FRONT SIDE
Special tool connector for ABS inspection different from terminal No. inside circuit diagram.
MT4029600203050X

Fig. 10 Anti-lock brake system wiring diagram (Part 5 of 5). 1996 Eclipse FWD w/2.0L turbocharged engine & 2.4L engine

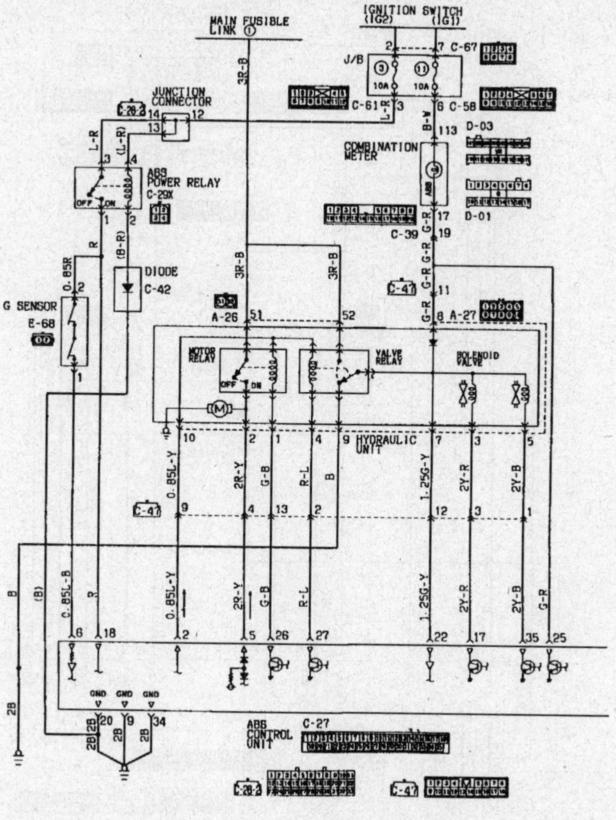
MAIN FUSIBLE LINK ①
IGNITION SWITCH (IG2) (IG1)
J/B
JUNCTION CONNECTOR
ABS POWER RELAY C-29X
COMBINATION METER
DIODE C-42
G SENSOR E-68
MOTOR RELAY
VALVE RELAY
SOLENOID VALVE
HYDRAULIC UNIT
ABS CONTROL UNIT C-27
GND GND GND

MT4029300010010X

Fig. 11 Anti-lock brake system wiring diagram (Part 1 of 2). 1993 Expo AWD

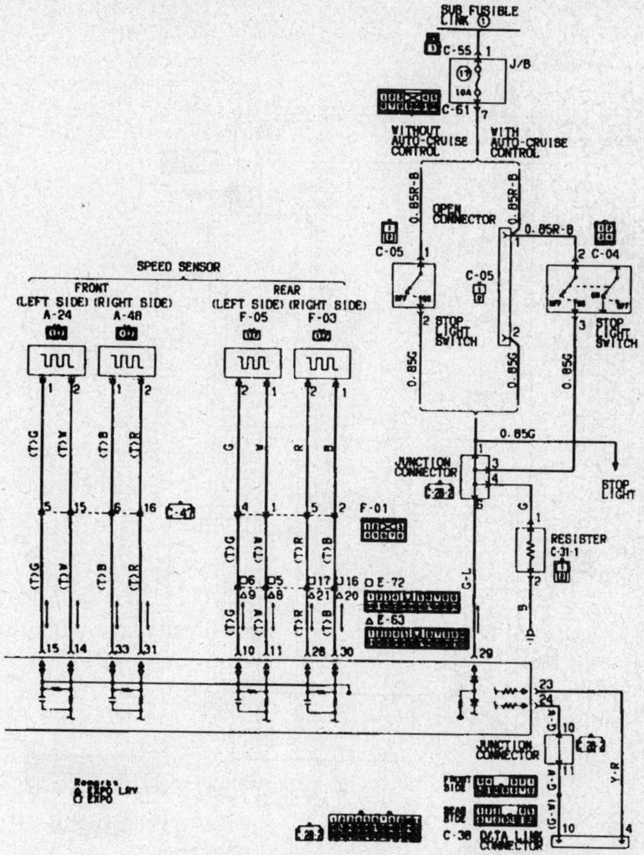
SUB FUSIBLE LINK ①
J/B
WITHOUT AUTO-CRUISE CONTROL
WITH AUTO-CRUISE CONTROL
OPEN CONNECTOR
STOP LIGHT SWITCH
SPEED SENSOR
FRONT (LEFT SIDE) (RIGHT SIDE) A-24 A-48
REAR (LEFT SIDE) (RIGHT SIDE) F-05 F-03
JUNCTION CONNECTOR
STOP LIGHT
RESISTER
DATA LINK CONNECTOR
Remarks
△: EXPO LRV
□: EXPO

MT4029300010020X

Fig. 11 Anti-lock brake system wiring diagram (Part 2 of 2). 1993 Expo AWD

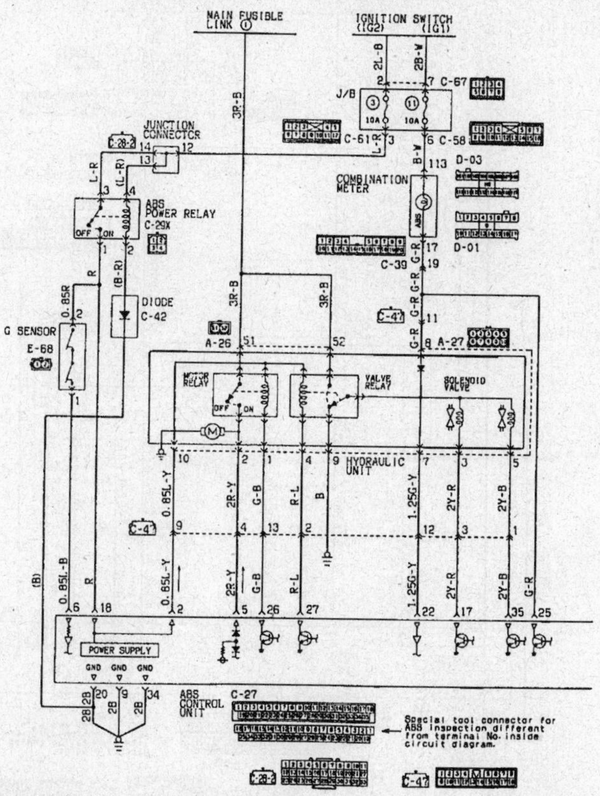
MAIN FUSIBLE LINK ①
IGNITION SWITCH (IG2) (IG1)
J/B
JUNCTION CONNECTOR
ABS POWER RELAY C-29X
COMBINATION METER
DIODE C-42
G SENSOR E-68
MOTOR RELAY
VALVE RELAY
SOLENOID VALVE
HYDRAULIC UNIT
POWER SUPPLY
ABS CONTROL UNIT C-27
Special tool connector for ABS inspection different from terminal No. inside circuit diagram.

MT4029400011010X

Fig. 12 Anti-lock brake system wiring diagram (Part 1 of 3). 1994–95 Expo AWD

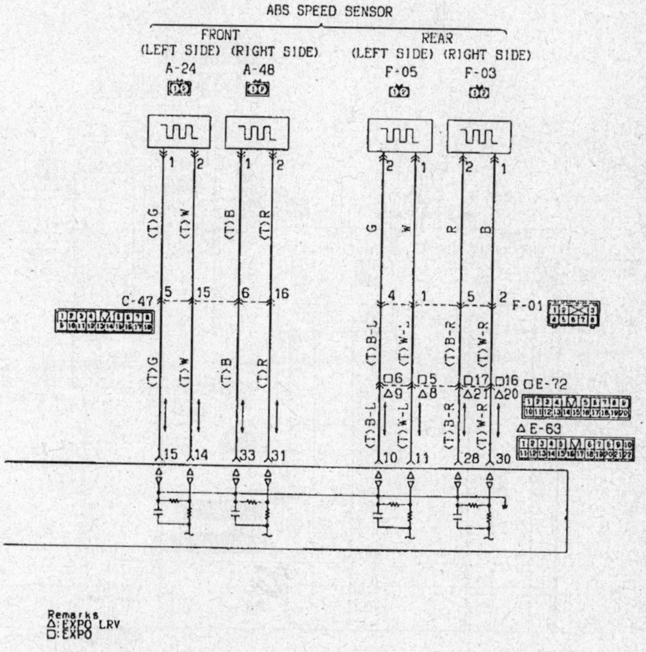
ABS SPEED SENSOR
FRONT (LEFT SIDE) (RIGHT SIDE) A-24 A-48
REAR (LEFT SIDE) (RIGHT SIDE) F-05 F-03
C-47
F-01
E-72
E-63
Remarks
△: EXPO LRV
□: EXPO

MT4029400011020X

Fig. 12 Anti-lock brake system wiring diagram (Part 2 of 3). 1994–95 Expo AWD

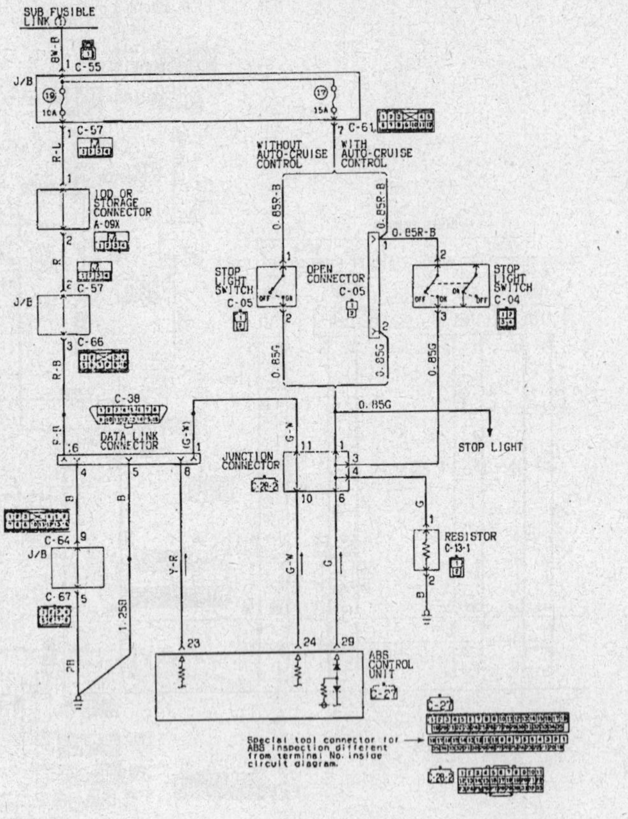
SUB FUSIBLE LINK
J/B
C-55
C-57
C-61
WITHOUT AUTO-CRUISE CONTROL
WITH AUTO-CRUISE CONTROL
IOD OR STORAGE CONNECTOR A-09X
STOP LIGHT SWITCH C-05
OPEN CONNECTOR C-05
STOP LIGHT SWITCH C-04
C-66
C-38
DATA LINK CONNECTOR
JUNCTION CONNECTOR
STOP LIGHT
C-64
C-67
RESISTOR C-13-1
ABS CONTROL UNIT
Special tool connector for ABS inspection different from terminal No. inside circuit diagram.

MT4029400011030X

Fig. 12 Anti-lock brake system wiring diagram (Part 3 of 3). 1994–95 Expo AWD

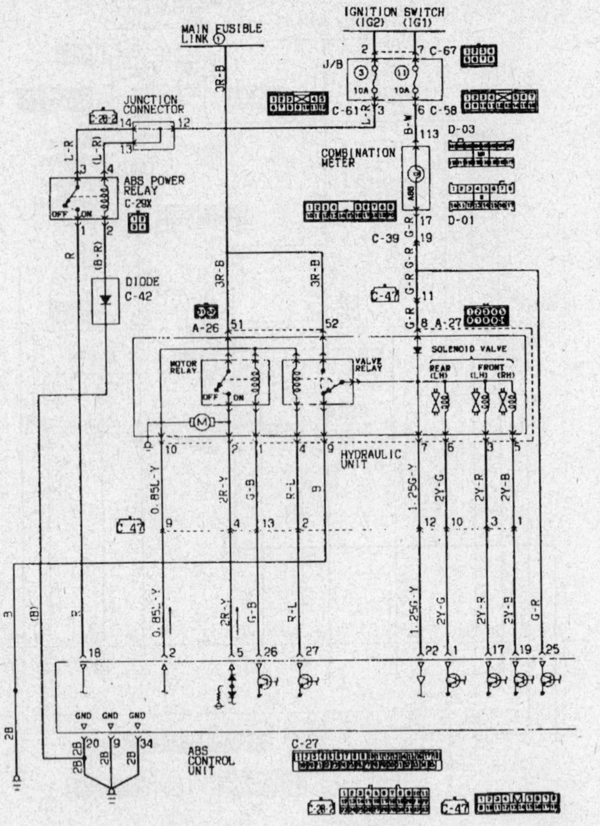
MAIN FUSIBLE LINK
IGNITION SWITCH (IG2) (IG1)
J/B
C-67
JUNCTION CONNECTOR
C-61
C-58
COMBINATION METER
D-03
D-01
ABS POWER RELAY C-29X
C-39
DIODE C-42
A-26
A-27
MOTOR RELAY
VALVE RELAY
SOLENOID VALVE
REAR (LH)
FRONT (LH) (RH)
HYDRAULIC UNIT
GND GND GND
ABS CONTROL UNIT
C-27

MT4029300013010X

Fig. 13 Anti-lock brake system wiring diagram (Part 1 of 2). 1993 Expo FWD

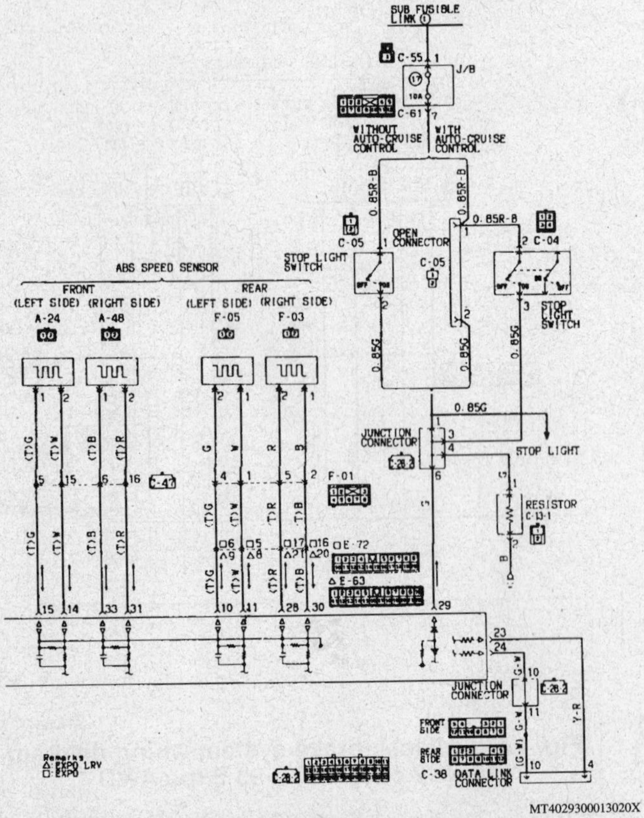
SUB FUSIBLE LINK
C-55
J/B
C-61
WITHOUT AUTO-CRUISE CONTROL
WITH AUTO-CRUISE CONTROL
C-05
OPEN CONNECTOR
C-04
STOP LIGHT SWITCH
ABS SPEED SENSOR
FRONT
REAR
(LEFT SIDE) (RIGHT SIDE)
A-24
A-48
F-05
F-03
JUNCTION CONNECTOR
STOP LIGHT
F-01
RESISTOR C-13-1
E-72
E-63
FRONT SIDE
REAR SIDE
C-38 DATA LINK CONNECTOR
Remarks
Δ: EXPO LRV
□: EXPO

MT4029300013020X

Fig. 13 Anti-lock brake system wiring diagram (Part 2 of 2). 1993 Expo FWD

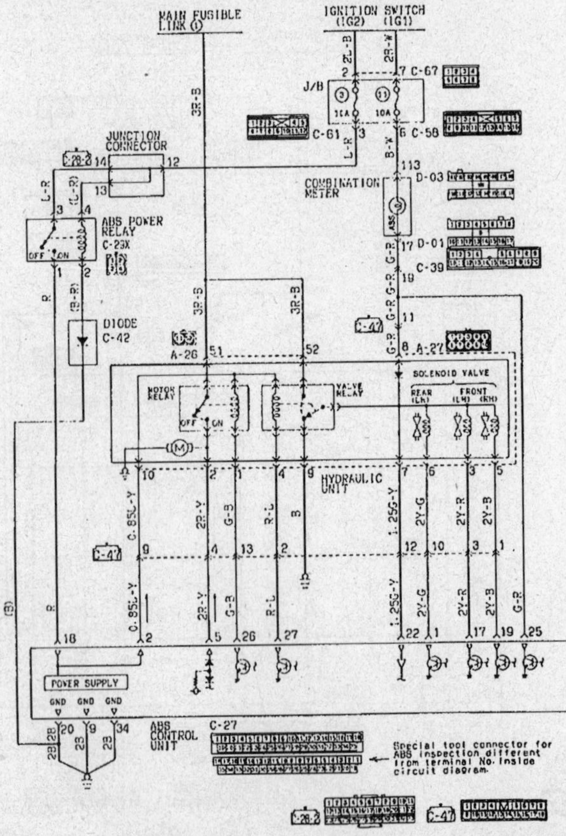
MAIN FUSIBLE LINK
IGNITION SWITCH (IG2) (IG1)
J/B
C-67
JUNCTION CONNECTOR
C-61
C-58
COMBINATION METER
D-03
D-01
C-39
ABS POWER RELAY C-23X
DIODE C-42
A-26
A-27
MOTOR RELAY
VALVE RELAY
SOLENOID VALVE
REAR (LH)
FRONT (LH) (RH)
HYDRAULIC UNIT
POWER SUPPLY
GND GND GND
ABS CONTROL UNIT
C-27
Special tool connector for ABS inspection different from terminal No. inside circuit diagram.

MT4029400014010X

Fig. 14 Anti-lock brake system wiring diagram (Part 1 of 3). 1994–95 Expo FWD

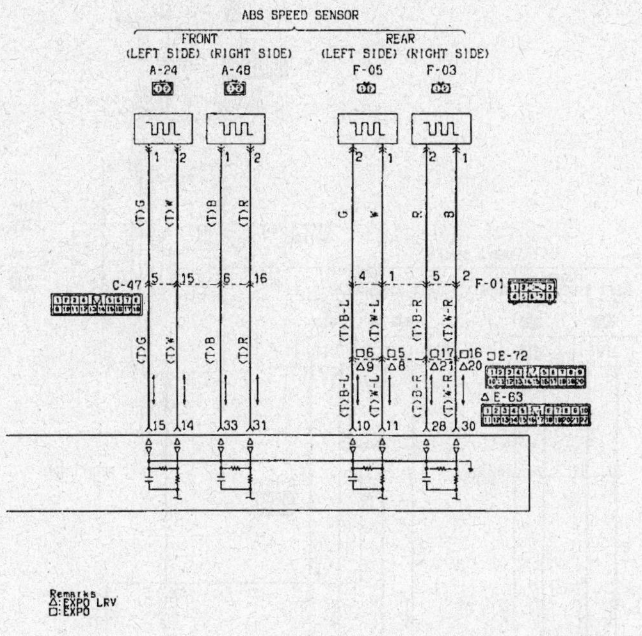
ABS SPEED SENSOR
FRONT
REAR
(LEFT SIDE) (RIGHT SIDE)
(LEFT SIDE) (RIGHT SIDE)
A-24
A-48
F-05
F-03
C-47
F-01
E-72
E-63
Remarks
△:EXPO LRV
□:EXPO

MT4029400014020X

Fig. 14 Anti-lock brake system wiring diagram (Part 2 of 3). 1994–95 Expo FWD

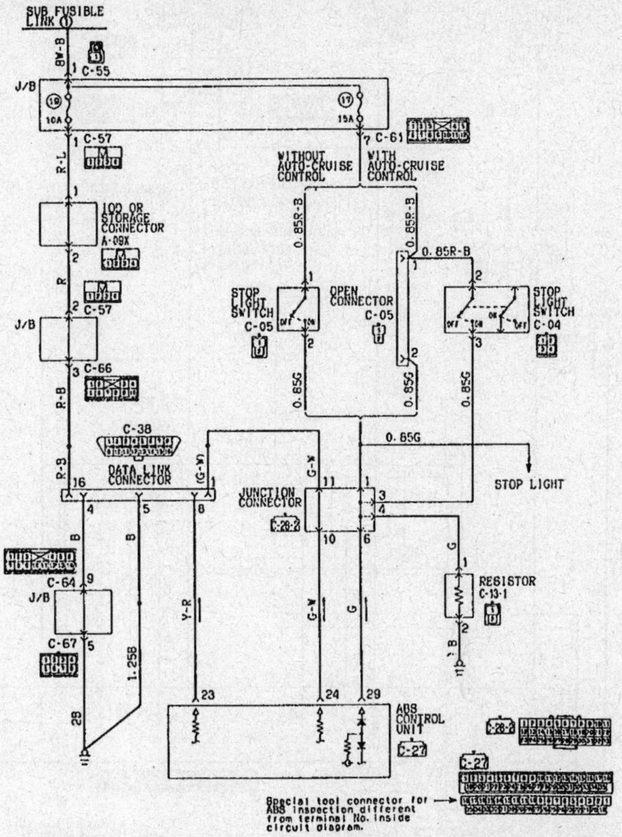
SUB FUSIBLE LINK ①
J/B
C-55
C-57
C-61
WITHOUT AUTO-CRUISE CONTROL
WITH AUTO-CRUISE CONTROL
IOD OR STORAGE CONNECTOR
A-09X
STOP LIGHT SWITCH
C-05
OPEN CONNECTOR
C-04
C-66
C-38
DATA LINK CONNECTOR
JUNCTION CONNECTOR
STOP LIGHT
RESISTOR
C-13-1
C-64
C-67
ABS CONTROL UNIT
C-27
Special tool connector for ABS inspection different from terminal No. inside circuit diagram.

MT4029400014030X

Fig. 14 Anti-lock brake system wiring diagram (Part 3 of 3). 1994–95 Expo FWD

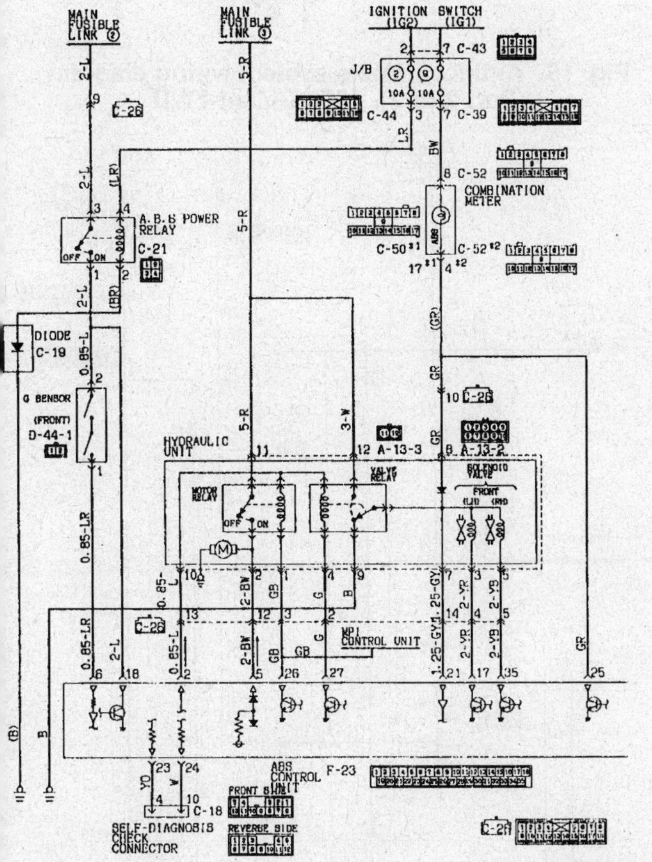
MAIN FUSIBLE LINK ②
MAIN FUSIBLE LINK ③
IGNITION SWITCH
(IG2)
(IG1)
J/B
C-43
C-44
C-39
C-52
COMBINATION METER
A.B.S POWER RELAY
C-21
C-50
DIODE
C-19
G SENSOR
(FRONT)
D-44-1
HYDRAULIC UNIT
A-13-3
A-13-2
MPI CONTROL UNIT
ABS CONTROL UNIT
F-23
C-18
SELF-DIAGNOSIS CHECK CONNECTOR

MT4029200018010X

Fig. 15 Anti-lock brake system wiring diagram (Part 1 of 2). 1993 Galant AWD

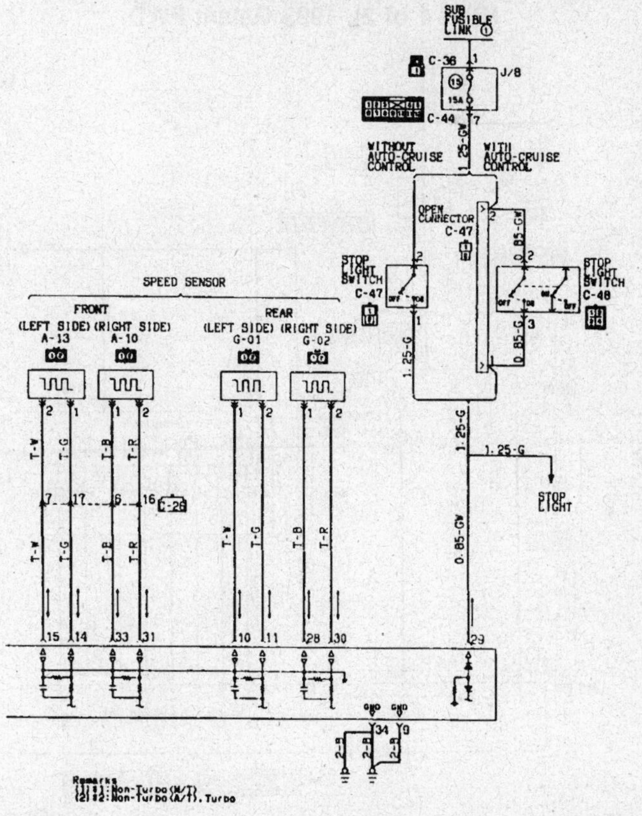
SUB FUSIBLE LINK ①
C-36
J/B
C-44
WITHOUT AUTO-CRUISE CONTROL
WITH AUTO-CRUISE CONTROL
OPEN CONNECTOR
C-47
STOP LIGHT SWITCH
C-48
SPEED SENSOR
FRONT
REAR
(LEFT SIDE) (RIGHT SIDE)
(LEFT SIDE) (RIGHT SIDE)
A-13
A-10
G-01
G-02
STOP LIGHT

MT4029200018020X

Fig. 15 Anti-lock brake system wiring diagram (Part 2 of 2). 1993 Galant AWD

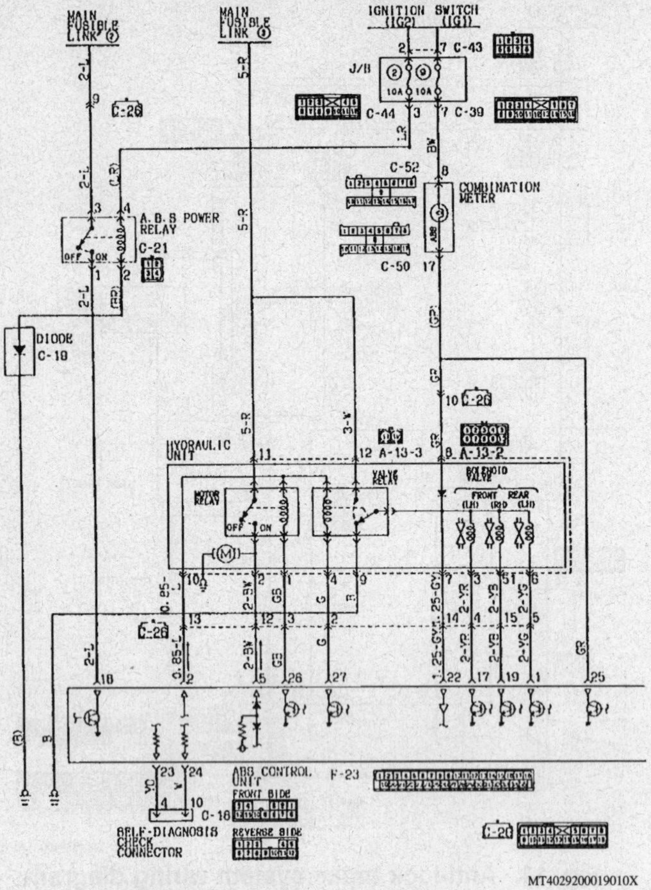
MAIN FUSIBLE LINK ②
MAIN FUSIBLE LINK ④
IGNITION SWITCH (IG2) (IG1)
J/B
COMBINATION METER
A.B.S POWER RELAY
C-21
DIODE
C-19
HYDRAULIC UNIT
VALVE RELAY
SOLENOID VALVE
MOTOR RELAY
ABS CONTROL UNIT
FRONT SIDE
REVERSE SIDE
SELF-DIAGNOSIS CHECK CONNECTOR
MT4029200019010X

Fig. 16 Anti-lock brake system wiring diagram (Part 1 of 2). 1993 Galant FWD

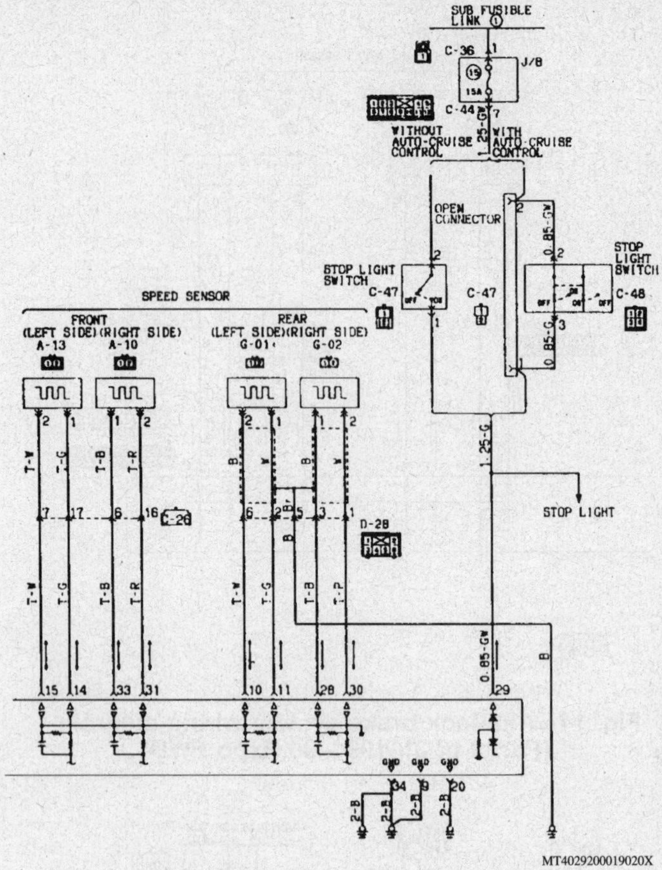
SUB FUSIBLE LINK ①
J/B
WITHOUT AUTO-CRUISE CONTROL
WITH AUTO-CRUISE CONTROL
OPEN CONNECTOR
STOP LIGHT SWITCH
STOP LIGHT SWITCH
SPEED SENSOR
FRONT
(LEFT SIDE)(RIGHT SIDE)
REAR
(LEFT SIDE)(RIGHT SIDE)
STOP LIGHT
MT4029200019020X

Fig. 16 Anti-lock brake system wiring diagram (Part 2 of 2). 1993 Galant FWD

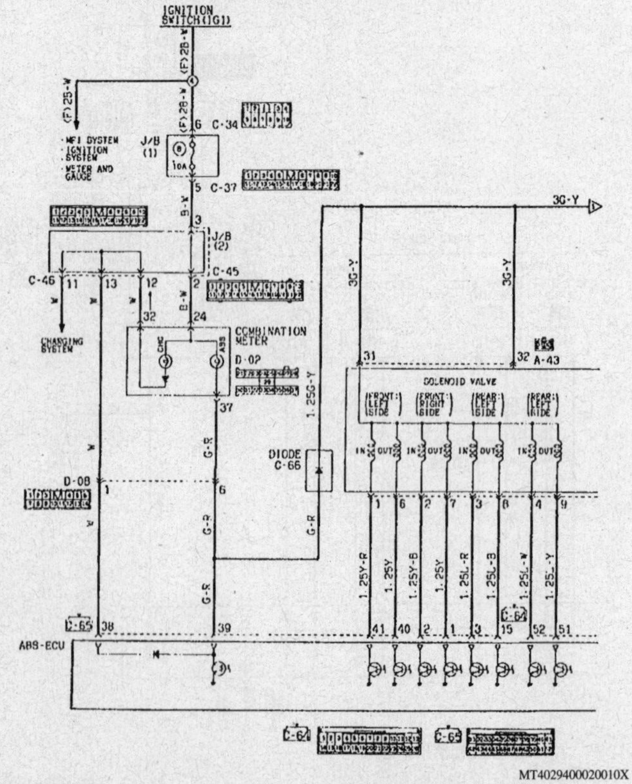
IGNITION SWITCH(IG1)
J/B (1)
·MFI SYSTEM ·IGNITION SYSTEM ·METER AND GAUGE
J/B (2)
CHARGING SYSTEM
COMBINATION METER
DIODE C-66
SOLENOID VALVE
ABS-ECU
MT4029400020010X

Fig. 17 Anti-lock brake system wiring diagram (Part 1 of 4). 1994–95 Galant

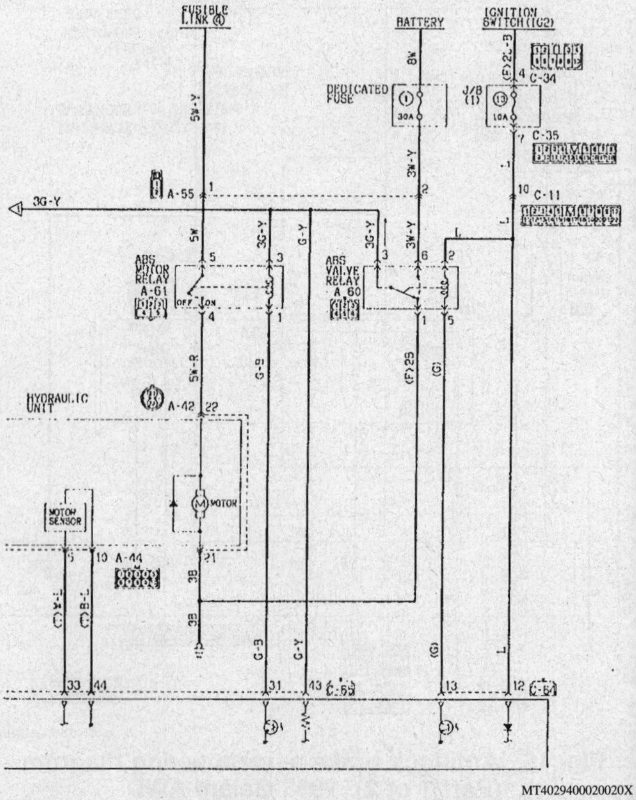
FUSIBLE LINK ④
BATTERY
IGNITION SWITCH(IG2)
DEDICATED FUSE
ABS MOTOR RELAY A-61
ABS VALVE RELAY A-60
HYDRAULIC UNIT
MOTOR SENSOR
MOTOR
MT4029400020020X

Fig. 17 Anti-lock brake system wiring diagram (Part 2 of 4). 1994–95 Galant

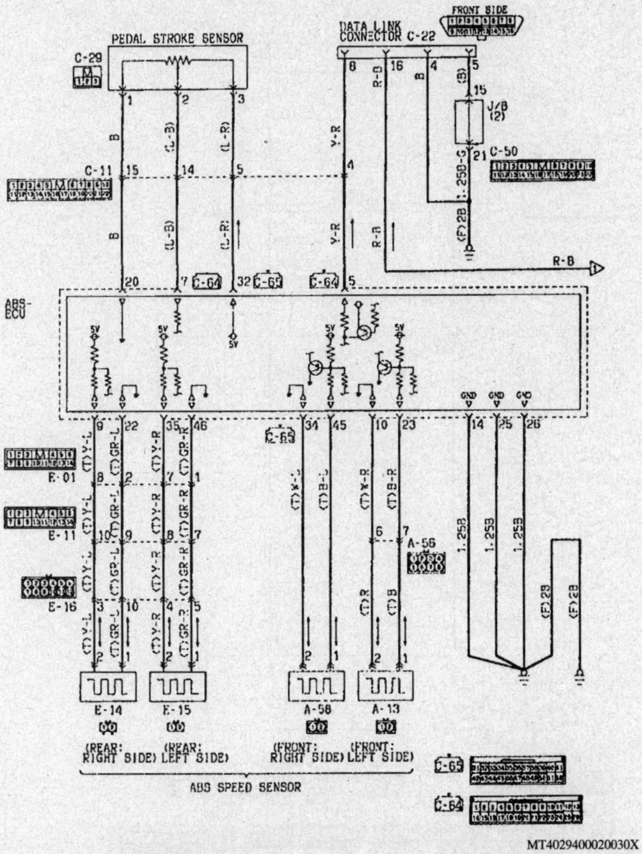
PEDAL STROKE SENSOR
DATA LINK CONNECTOR C-22
FRONT SIDE
ABS-ECU
ABS SPEED SENSOR
(REAR: RIGHT SIDE)
(REAR: LEFT SIDE)
(FRONT: RIGHT SIDE)
(FRONT: LEFT SIDE)
MT4029400020030X

Fig. 17 Anti-lock brake system wiring diagram (Part 3 of 4). 1994–95 Galant

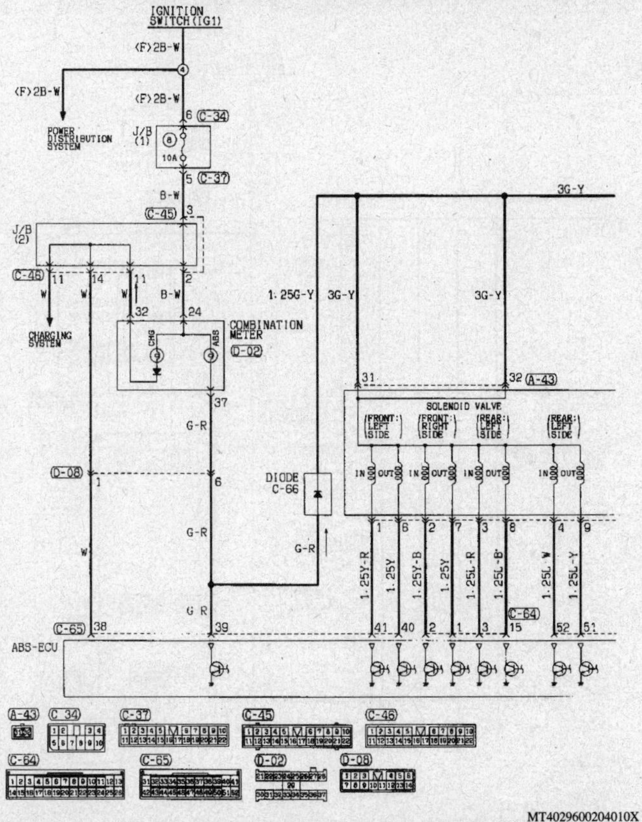
IGNITION SWITCH (IG1)
POWER DISTRIBUTION SYSTEM
CHARGING SYSTEM
COMBINATION METER
DIODE C-66
SOLENOID VALVE
(FRONT: LEFT SIDE)
(FRONT: RIGHT SIDE)
(REAR: RIGHT SIDE)
(REAR: LEFT SIDE)
ABS-ECU
MT4029600204010X

Fig. 18 Anti-lock brake system wiring diagram (Part 1 of 4). 1996 Galant

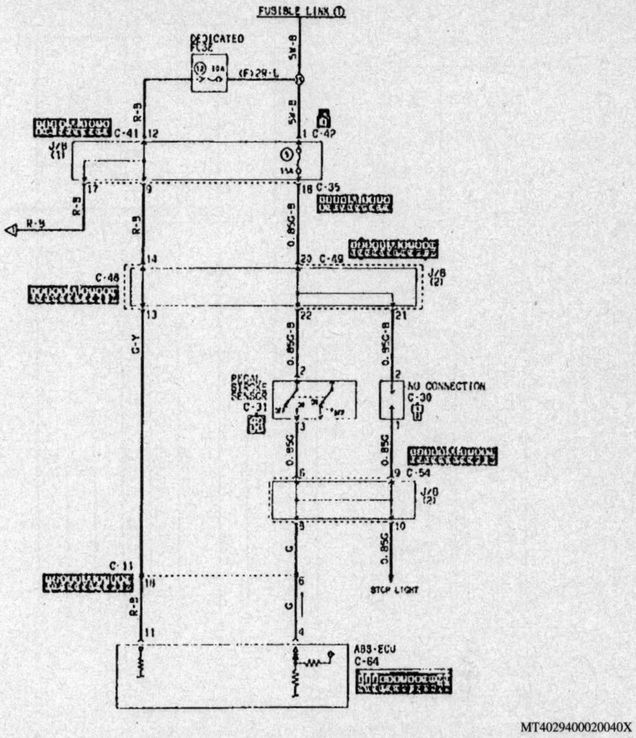
FUSIBLE LINK ①
DEDICATED FUSE
NO CONNECTION
STOP LIGHT
ABS-ECU C-64
MT4029400020040X

Fig. 17 Anti-lock brake system wiring diagram (Part 4 of 4). 1994–95 Galant

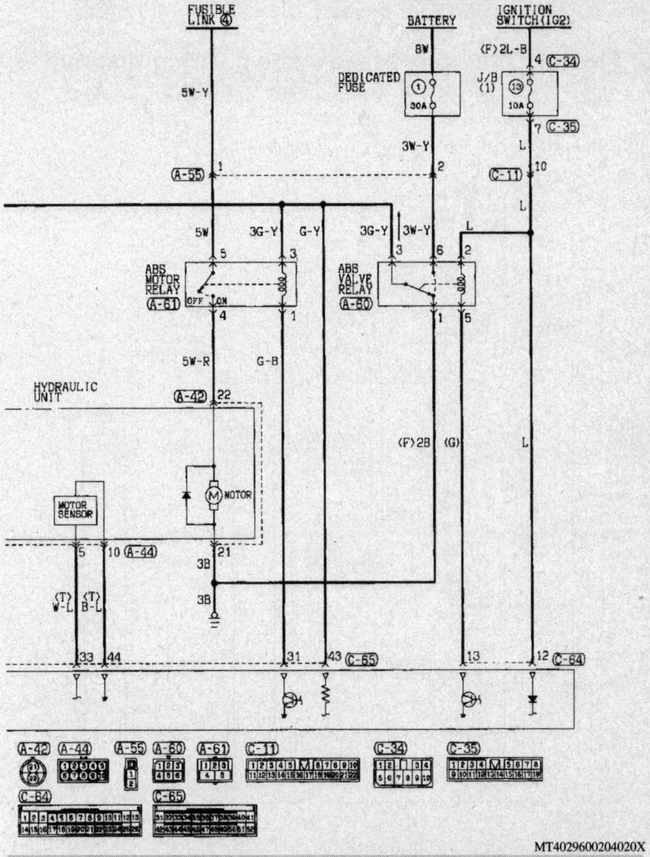
FUSIBLE LINK ④
BATTERY
IGNITION SWITCH (IG2)
DEDICATED FUSE
ABS MOTOR RELAY
ABS VALVE RELAY
HYDRAULIC UNIT
MOTOR SENSOR
MOTOR
MT4029600204020X

Fig. 18 Anti-lock brake system wiring diagram (Part 2 of 4). 1996 Galant

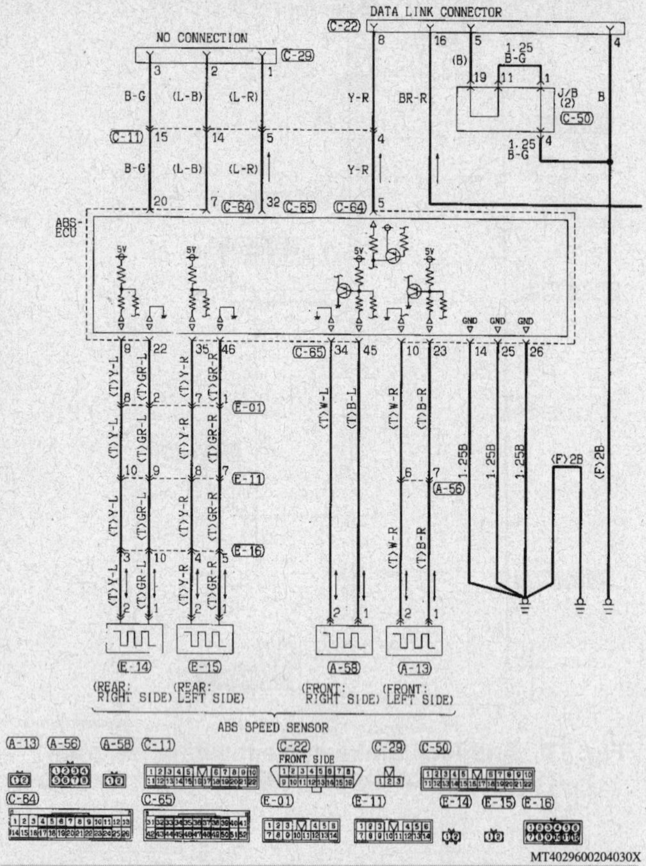
DATA LINK CONNECTOR
NO CONNECTION
ABS-ECU
ABS SPEED SENSOR
(REAR: RIGHT SIDE)
(REAR: LEFT SIDE)
(FRONT: RIGHT SIDE)
(FRONT: LEFT SIDE)
FRONT SIDE
MT4029600204030X

Fig. 18 Anti-lock brake system wiring diagram (Part 3 of 4). 1996 Galant

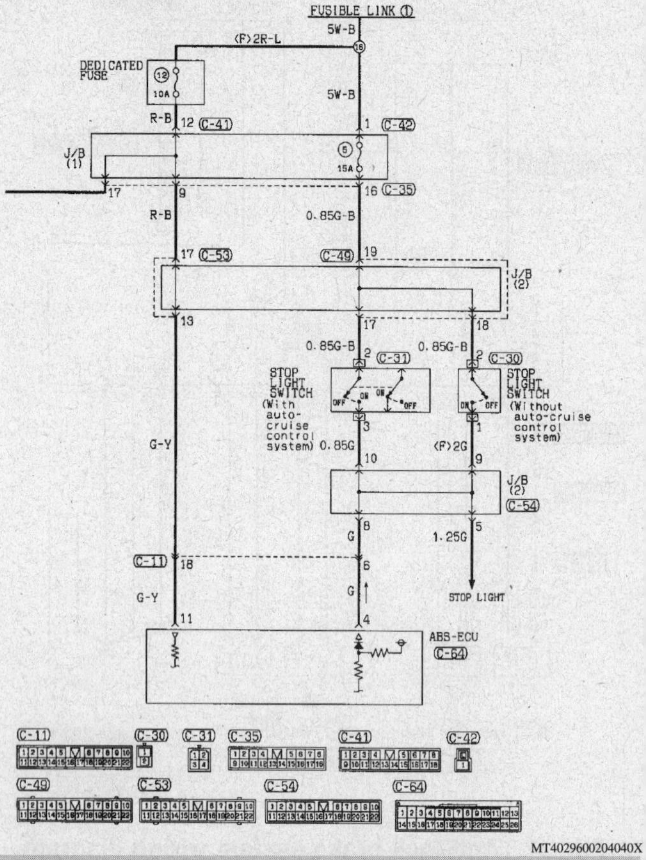
FUSIBLE LINK ①
DEDICATED FUSE
STOP LIGHT SWITCH (With auto-cruise control system)
STOP LIGHT SWITCH (Without auto-cruise control system)
STOP LIGHT
ABS-ECU
MT4029600204040X

Fig. 18 Anti-lock brake system wiring diagram (Part 4 of 4). 1996 Galant

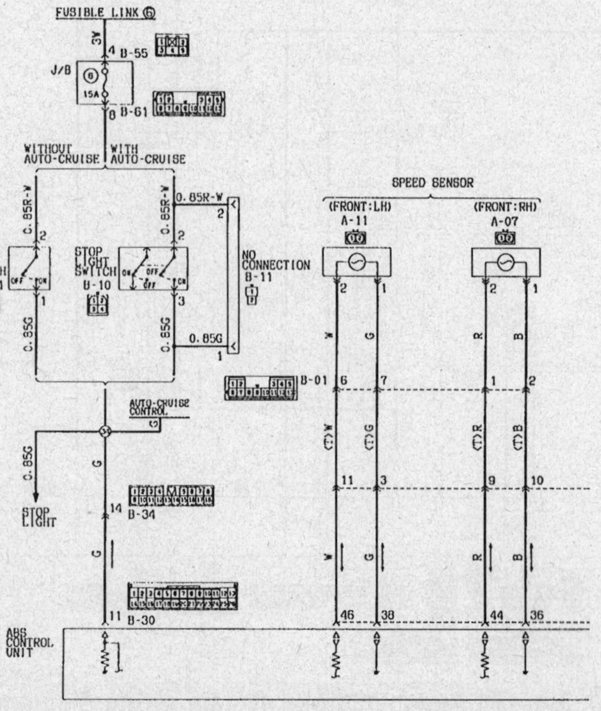
FUSIBLE LINK ⑥
WITHOUT AUTO-CRUISE
WITH AUTO-CRUISE
STOP LIGHT SWITCH
NO CONNECTION
SPEED SENSOR
(FRONT: LH)
(FRONT: RH)
AUTO-CRUISE CONTROL
STOP LIGHT
ABS CONTROL UNIT
MT4029300023010X

Fig. 19 Anti-lock brake system wiring diagram (Part 1 of 4). 1993 Mirage

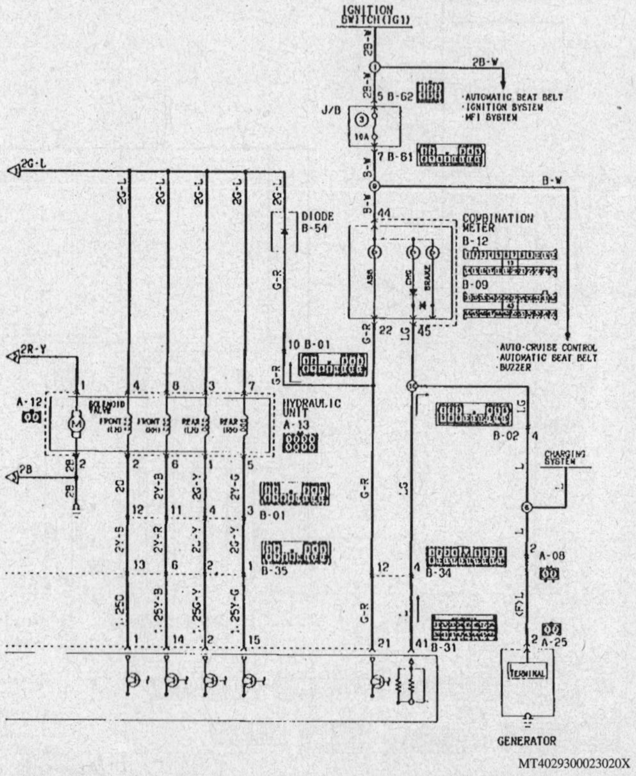
IGNITION SWITCH (IG1)
DIODE
COMBINATION METER
HYDRAULIC UNIT
CHARGING SYSTEM
GENERATOR
MT4029300023020X

Fig. 19 Anti-lock brake system wiring diagram (Part 2 of 4). 1993 Mirage

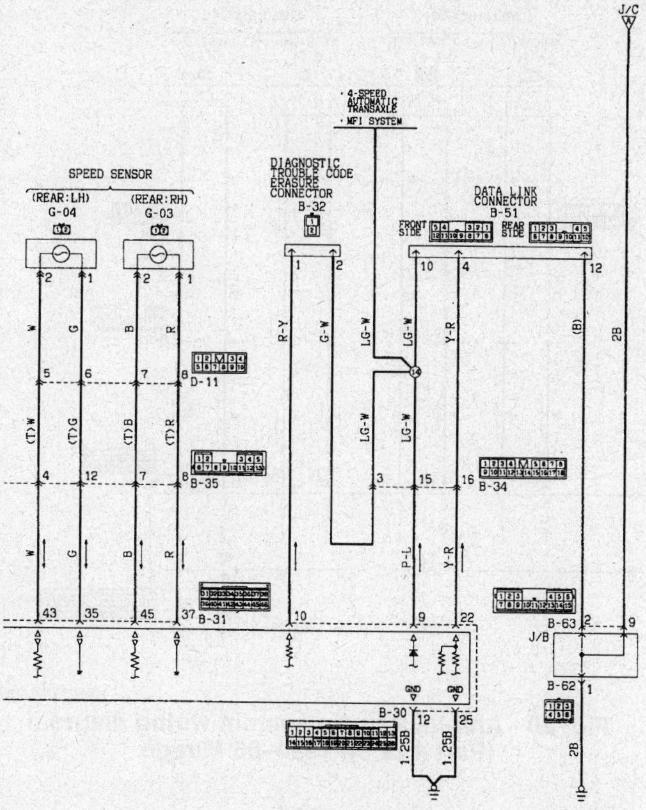
J/C
4-SPEED AUTOMATIC TRANSAXLE
MFI SYSTEM
SPEED SENSOR
(REAR:LH) G-04
(REAR:RH) G-03
DIAGNOSTIC TROUBLE CODE ERASURE CONNECTOR B-32
DATA LINK CONNECTOR B-51
FRONT SIDE
REAR SIDE
D-11
B-35
B-34
B-31
B-63
J/B
B-62
B-30
GND

MT4029300023030X

Fig. 19 Anti-lock brake system wiring diagram (Part 3 of 4). 1993 Mirage

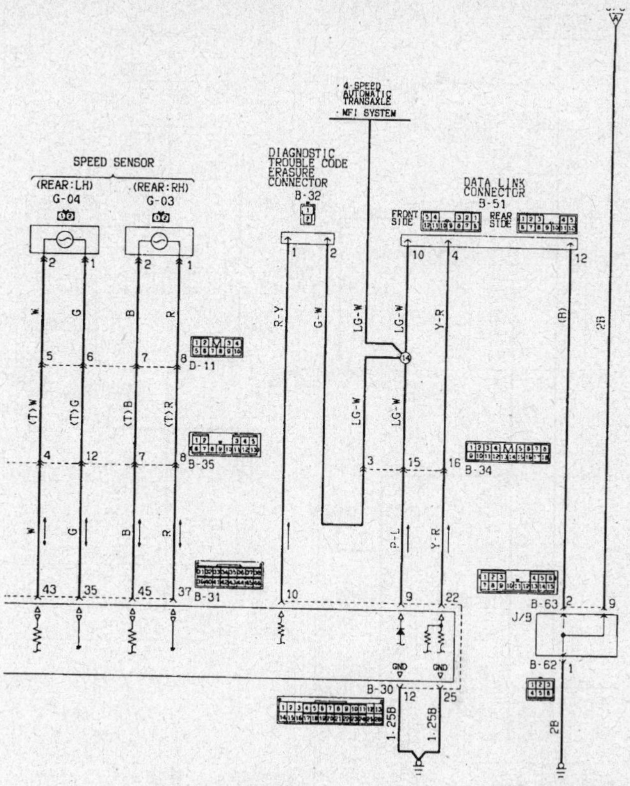
4-SPEED AUTOMATIC TRANSAXLE
MFI SYSTEM
SPEED SENSOR
(REAR:LH) G-04
(REAR:RH) G-03
DIAGNOSTIC TROUBLE CODE ERASURE CONNECTOR B-32
DATA LINK CONNECTOR B-51
FRONT SIDE
REAR SIDE
D-11
B-35
B-34
B-31
B-63
J/B
B-62
B-30
GND

MT4029300023040X

Fig. 19 Anti-lock brake system wiring diagram (Part 4 of 4). 1993 Mirage

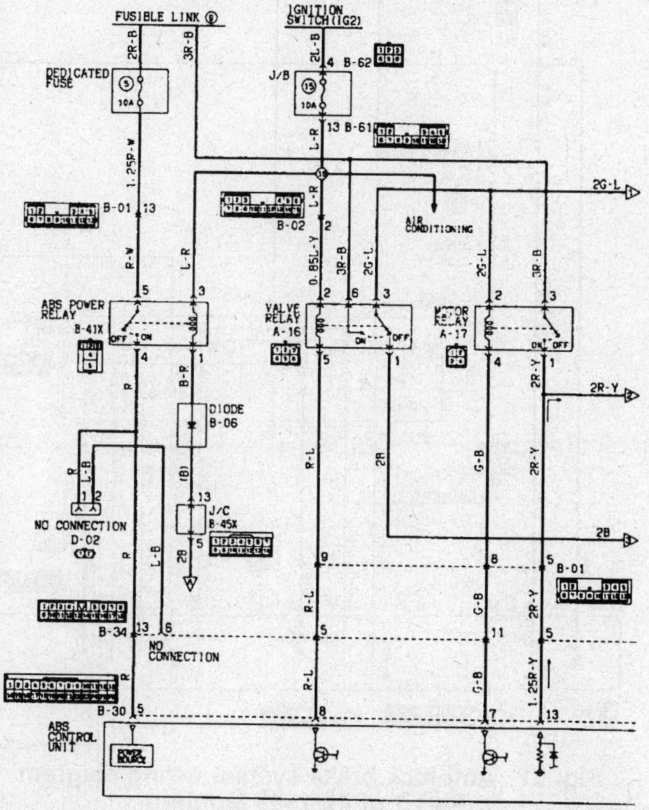
FUSIBLE LINK
IGNITION SWITCH (IG2)
DEDICATED FUSE
J/B
B-62
B-61
B-01
B-02
AIR CONDITIONING
ABS POWER RELAY
B-41X
VALVE RELAY A-16
MOTOR RELAY A-17
DIODE B-06
NO CONNECTION D-02
J/C B-45X
B-34
NO CONNECTION
B-30
ABS CONTROL UNIT
POWER SOURCE

MT4029400024010X

Fig. 20 Anti-lock brake system wiring diagram (Part 1 of 5). 1994–96 Mirage

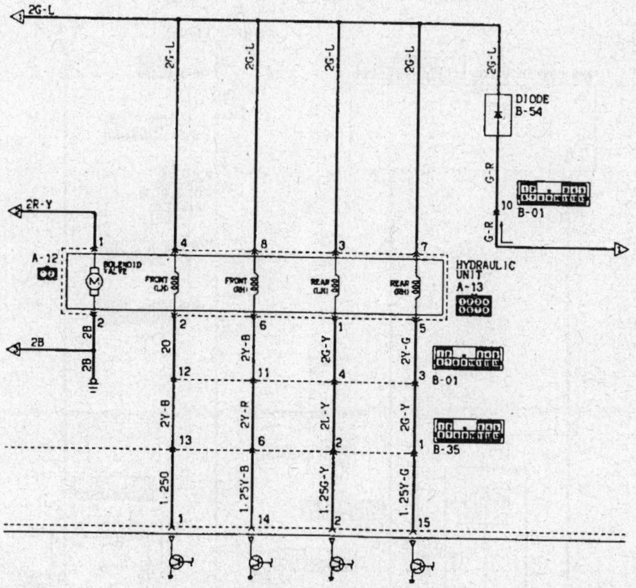
DIODE B-54
B-01
A-12
SOLENOID VALVE
FRONT (LH)
FRONT (RH)
REAR (LH)
REAR (RH)
HYDRAULIC UNIT A-13
B-35

MT4029400024020X

Fig. 20 Anti-lock brake system wiring diagram (Part 2 of 5). 1994–96 Mirage

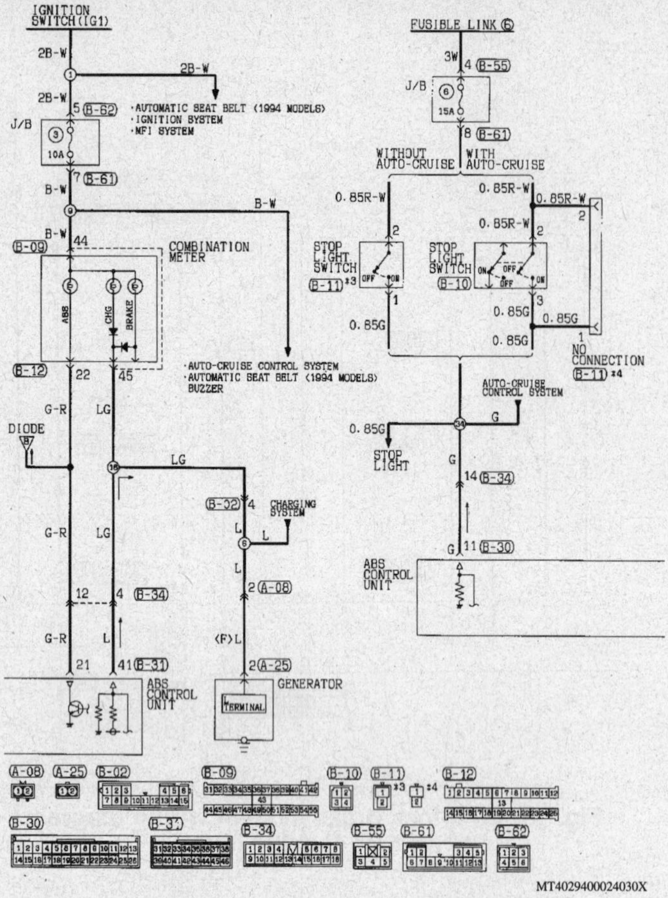
IGNITION SWITCH (IG1)
J/B
·AUTOMATIC SEAT BELT (1994 MODELS)
·IGNITION SYSTEM
·MFI SYSTEM
COMBINATION METER
·AUTO-CRUISE CONTROL SYSTEM
·AUTOMATIC SEAT BELT (1994 MODELS)
BUZZER
DIODE
CHARGING SYSTEM
ABS CONTROL UNIT
GENERATOR
TERMINAL
FUSIBLE LINK ⑥
WITHOUT AUTO-CRUISE
WITH AUTO-CRUISE
STOP LIGHT SWITCH
NO CONNECTION
AUTO-CRUISE CONTROL SYSTEM
STOP LIGHT
MT4029400024030X

Fig. 20 Anti-lock brake system wiring diagram (Part 3 of 5). 1994–96 Mirage

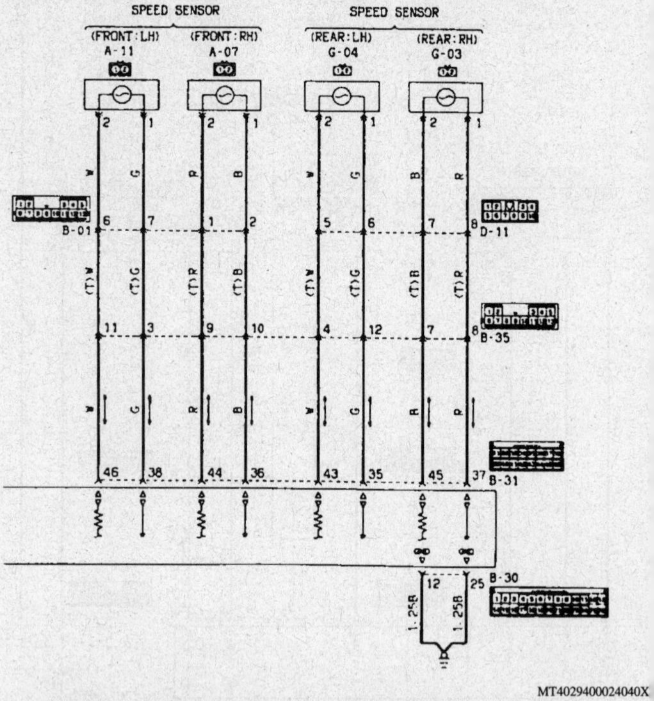
SPEED SENSOR
(FRONT: LH) A-11
(FRONT: RH) A-07
SPEED SENSOR
(REAR: LH) G-04
(REAR: RH) G-03
B-01
D-11
B-35
B-31
B-30
MT4029400024040X

Fig. 20 Anti-lock brake system wiring diagram (Part 4 of 5). 1994–96 Mirage

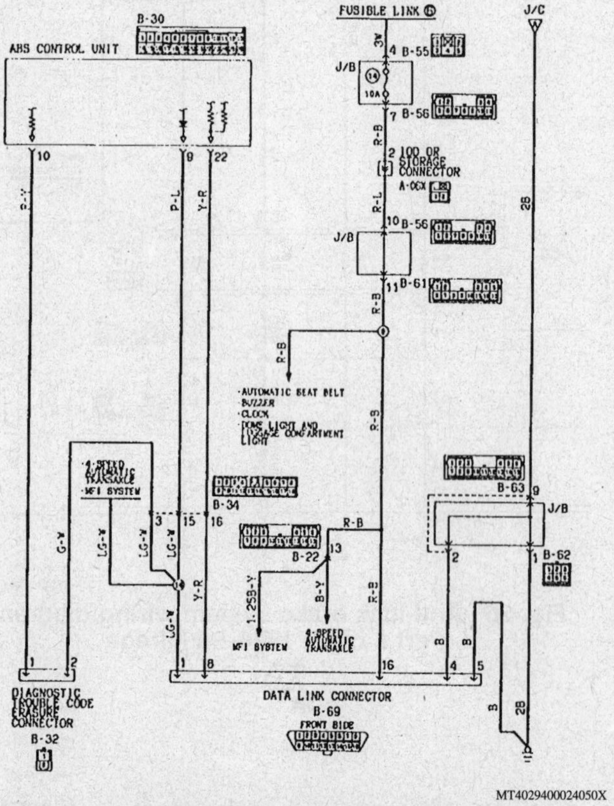
ABS CONTROL UNIT
B-30
FUSIBLE LINK ⑥
J/C
J/B
100 OR STORAGE CONNECTOR
·AUTOMATIC SEAT BELT
·BUZZER
·CLOCK
4-SPEED AUTOMATIC TRANSAXLE
·MFI SYSTEM
MFI SYSTEM
DIAGNOSTIC TROUBLE CODE ERASURE CONNECTOR
B-32
DATA LINK CONNECTOR
B-69
FRONT SIDE
MT4029400024050X

Fig. 20 Anti-lock brake system wiring diagram (Part 5 of 5). 1994–96 Mirage

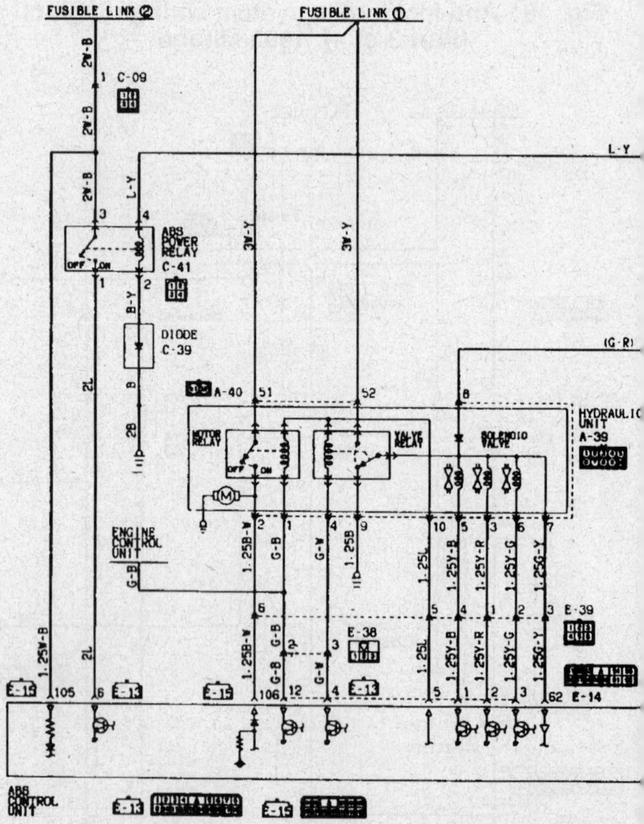
FUSIBLE LINK ②
FUSIBLE LINK ①
C-09
ABS POWER RELAY
C-41
DIODE
C-39
A-40
MOTOR RELAY
VALVE RELAY
SOLENOID VALVE
HYDRAULIC UNIT
A-39
ENGINE CONTROL UNIT
E-38
E-39
E-14
ABS CONTROL UNIT
MT4029100021010X

Fig. 21 Anti-lock brake system wiring diagram (Part 1 of 4). 1993 Montero

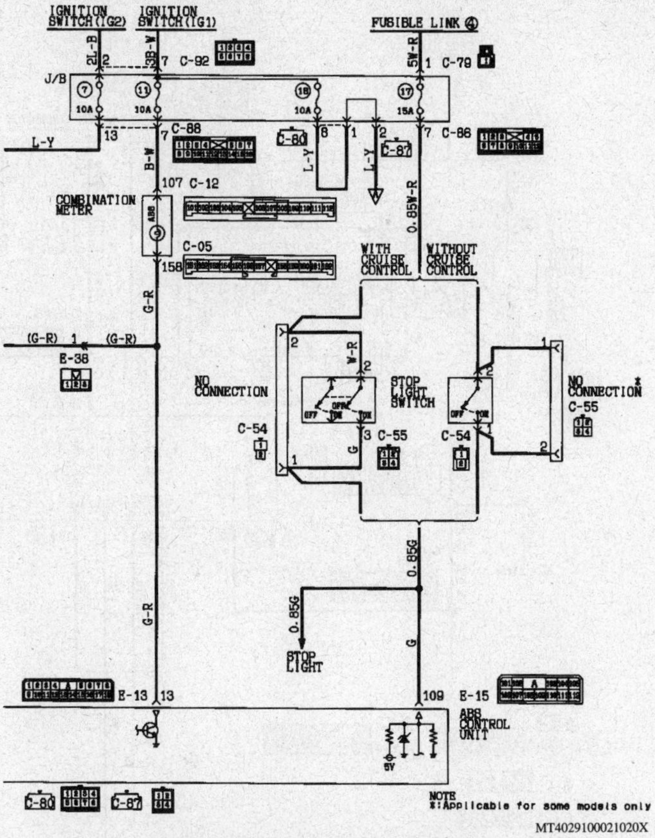
IGNITION SWITCH(IG2)
IGNITION SWITCH(IG1)
FUSIBLE LINK ④
J/B
L-Y
COMBINATION METER
C-05
WITH CRUISE CONTROL
WITHOUT CRUISE CONTROL
NO CONNECTION
STOP LIGHT SWITCH
C-54
C-55
E-38
STOP LIGHT
E-13
E-15
ABS CONTROL UNIT
NOTE
*:Applicable for some models only
MT4029100021020X

Fig. 21 Anti-lock brake system wiring diagram (Part 2 of 4). 1993 Montero

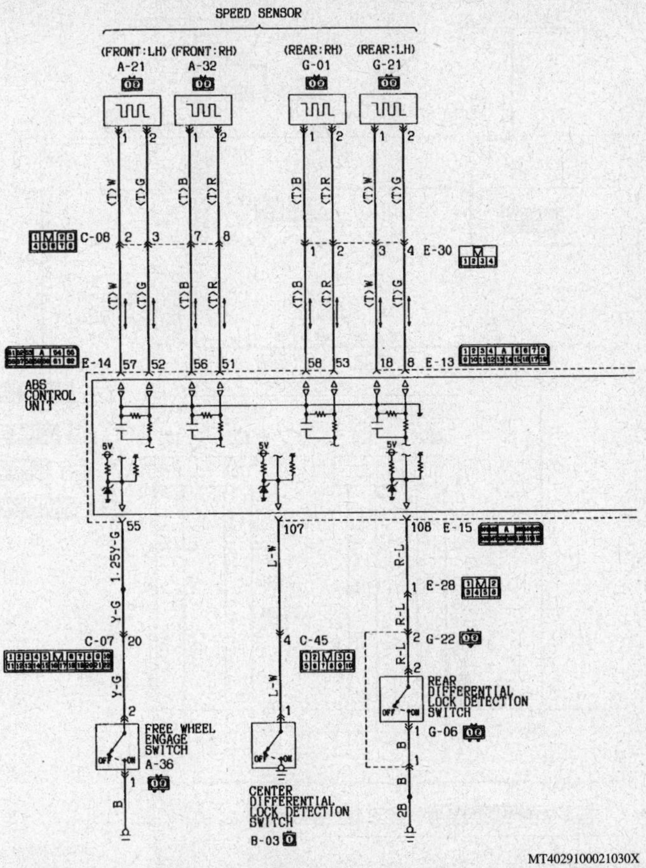
SPEED SENSOR
(FRONT:LH) A-21
(FRONT:RH) A-32
(REAR:RH) G-01
(REAR:LH) G-21
C-08
E-30
E-14
E-13
ABS CONTROL UNIT
E-15
E-28
G-22
REAR DIFFERENTIAL LOCK DETECTION SWITCH
G-06
C-07
C-45
FREE WHEEL ENGAGE SWITCH
A-36
CENTER DIFFERENTIAL LOCK DETECTION SWITCH
B-03
MT4029100021030X

Fig. 21 Anti-lock brake system wiring diagram (Part 3 of 4). 1993 Montero

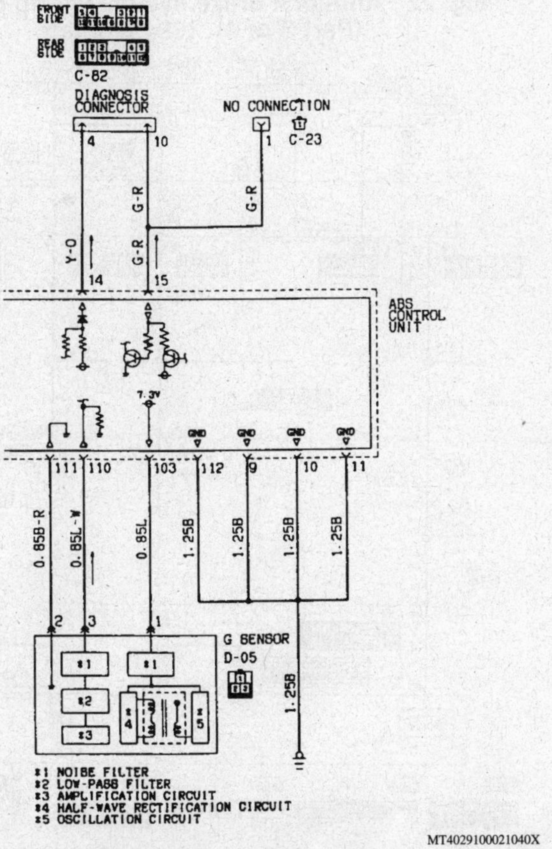
FRONT SIDE
REAR SIDE
C-82
DIAGNOSIS CONNECTOR
NO CONNECTION
C-23
ABS CONTROL UNIT
G SENSOR
D-05
*1 NOISE FILTER
*2 LOW-PASS FILTER
*3 AMPLIFICATION CIRCUIT
*4 HALF-WAVE RECTIFICATION CIRCUIT
*5 OSCILLATION CIRCUIT
MT4029100021040X

Fig. 21 Anti-lock brake system wiring diagram (Part 4 of 4). 1993 Montero

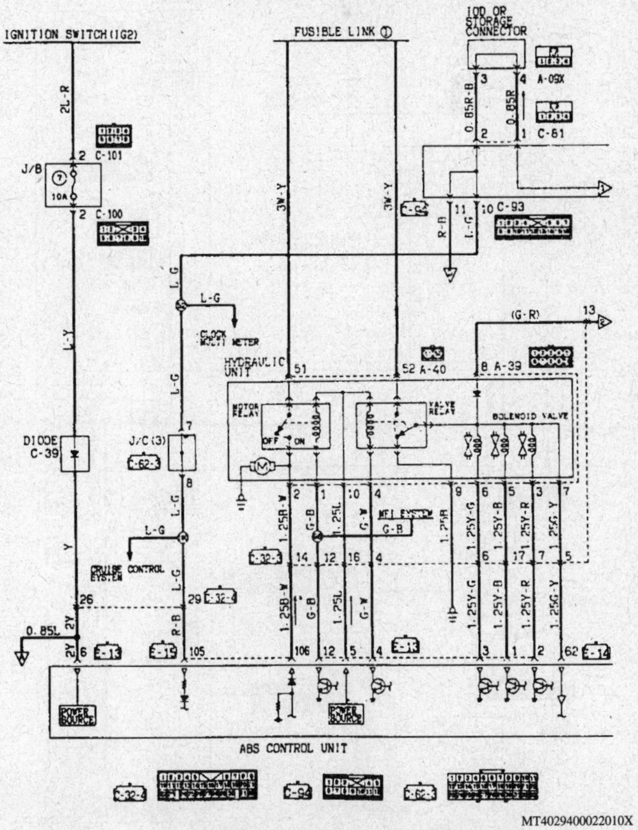
IGNITION SWITCH(IG2)
FUSIBLE LINK ①
IOD OR STORAGE CONNECTOR
A-09X
C-81
C-101
J/B
C-100
C-93
HYDRAULIC UNIT
A-40
A-39
MOTOR RELAY
VALVE RELAY
SOLENOID VALVE
DIODE C-39
J/C(3)
MFI SYSTEM
CRUISE CONTROL SYSTEM
POWER SOURCE
ABS CONTROL UNIT
MT4029400022010X

Fig. 22 Anti-lock brake system wiring diagram (Part 1 of 4). 1994 Montero

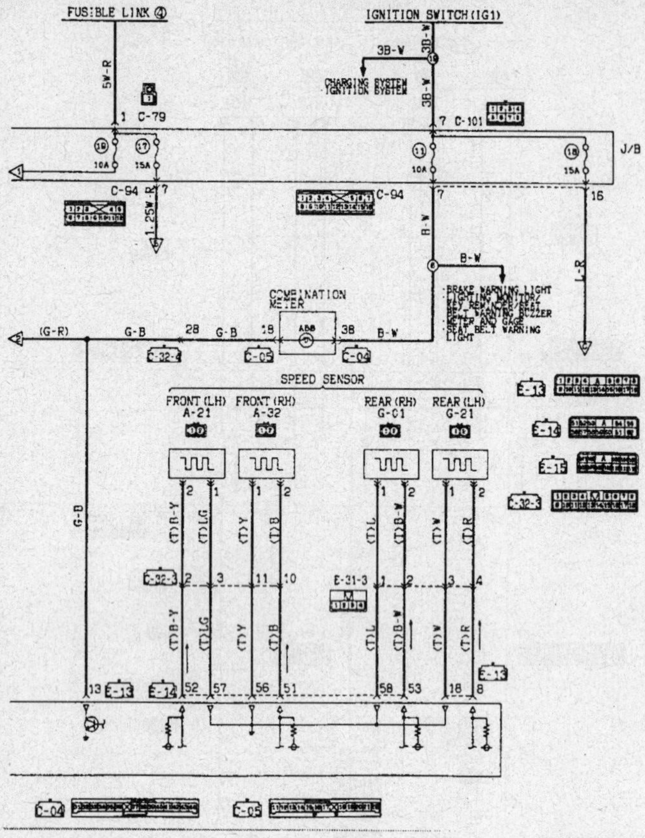
FUSIBLE LINK ④
IGNITION SWITCH (IG1)
CHARGING SYSTEM
IGNITION SYSTEM
C-79
C-101
J/B
C-94
COMBINATION METER
BRAKE WARNING LIGHT
LIGHTING MONITOR/
KEY REMINDER/SEAT
BELT WARNING BUZZER
METER AND GAGE
SEAT BELT WARNING
LIGHT
SPEED SENSOR
FRONT (LH)
A-21
FRONT (RH)
A-32
REAR (RH)
G-01
REAR (LH)
G-21
E-31-3
MT4029400022020X

Fig. 22 Anti-lock brake system wiring diagram (Part 2 of 4). 1994 Montero

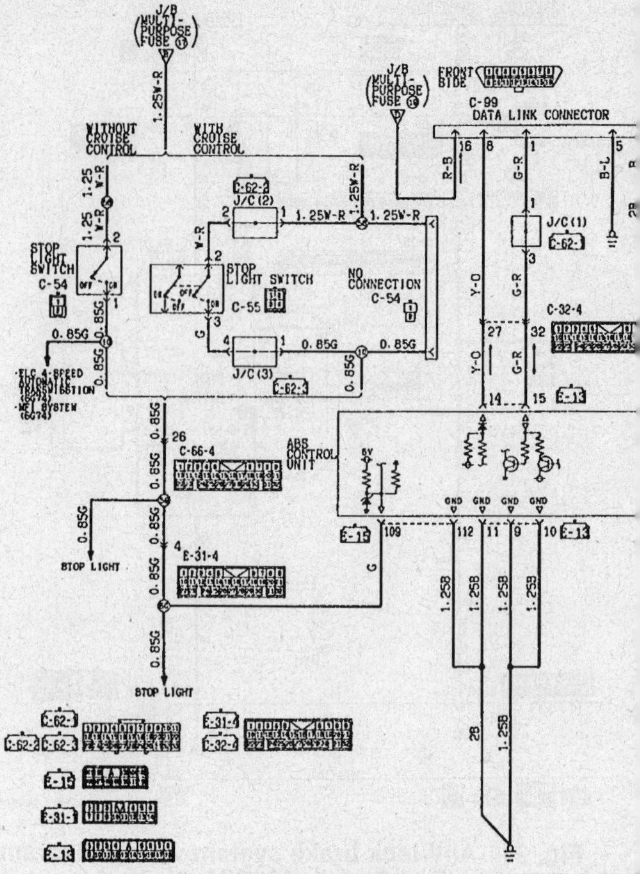
J/B
MULTI-PURPOSE FUSE
WITHOUT CRUISE CONTROL
WITH CRUISE CONTROL
J/B
MULTI-PURPOSE FUSE
FRONT SIDE
C-99
DATA LINK CONNECTOR
J/C(1)
C-62-2
J/C(2)
STOP LIGHT SWITCH
C-54
STOP LIGHT SWITCH
C-55
NO CONNECTION
C-54
C-32-4
J/C(3)
C-62-3
ELC 4-SPEED AUTOMATIC TRANSMISSION SYSTEM
MPI SYSTEM
C-66-4
ABS CONTROL UNIT
E-31-4
STOP LIGHT
STOP LIGHT
MT4029400022030X

Fig. 22 Anti-lock brake system wiring diagram (Part 3 of 4). 1994 Montero

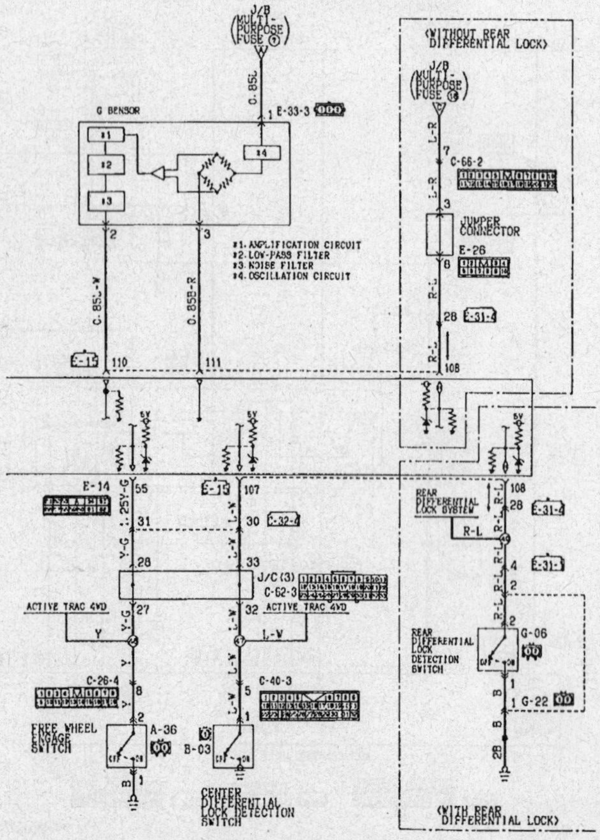
J/B
MULTI-PURPOSE FUSE
E-33-3
G SENSOR
#1 AMPLIFICATION CIRCUIT
#2 LOW-PASS FILTER
#3 NOISE FILTER
#4 OSCILLATION CIRCUIT
(WITHOUT REAR DIFFERENTIAL LOCK)
C-66-2
JUMPER CONNECTOR
E-26
E-14
J/C(3)
C-62-3
ACTIVE TRAC 4WD
ACTIVE TRAC 4WD
REAR DIFFERENTIAL LOCK SYSTEM
REAR DIFFERENTIAL LOCK DETECTION SWITCH
G-06
G-22
C-26-4
C-40-3
FREE WHEEL ENGAGE SWITCH
A-36
B-03
CENTER DIFFERENTIAL LOCK DETECTION SWITCH
(WITH REAR DIFFERENTIAL LOCK)
MT4029400022040X

Fig. 22 Anti-lock brake system wiring diagram (Part 4 of 4). 1994 Montero

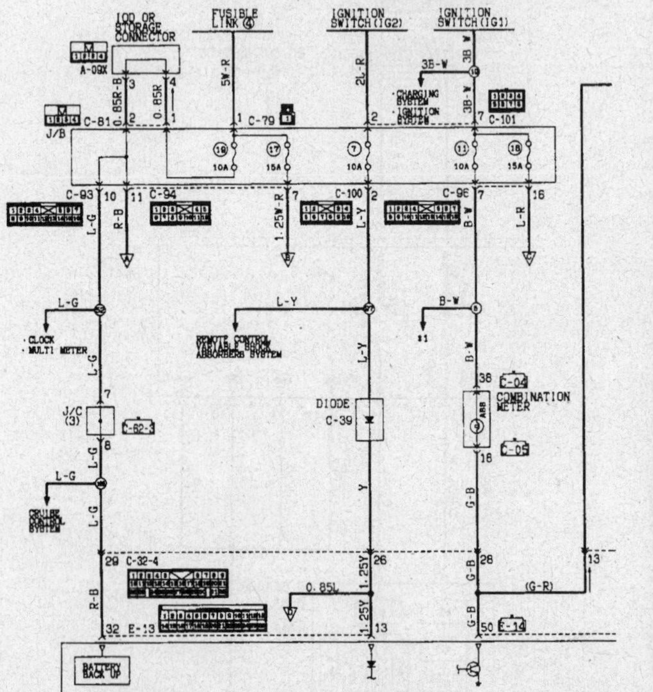
IOD OR STORAGE CONNECTOR
A-09X
FUSIBLE LINK ④
IGNITION SWITCH (IG2)
IGNITION SWITCH (IG1)
CHARGING SYSTEM
IGNITION SYSTEM
C-101
J/B
C-81
C-79
C-93
C-94
C-100
C-96
CLOCK
MULTI METER
REMOTE CONTROL VARIABLE SHOCK ABSORBERS SYSTEM
J/C (3)
C-62-3
DIODE
C-39
COMBINATION METER
CRUISE CONTROL SYSTEM
C-32-4
E-13
BATTERY BACK-UP
#1
BRAKE WARNING LIGHT
LIGHTING MONITOR/
KEY REMINDER/SEAT
BELT WARNING BUZZER
METER AND GAGE
SEAT BELT WARNING
LIGHT
MT4029500176010X

Fig. 23 Anti-lock brake system wiring diagram (Part 1 of 6). 1995–96 Montero

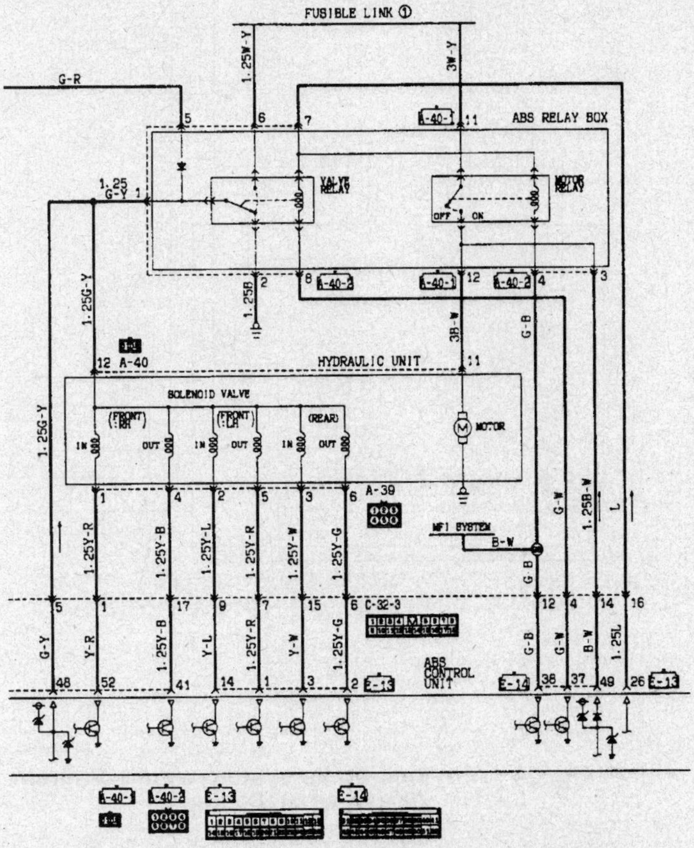
FUSIBLE LINK ①
ABS RELAY BOX
VALVE RELAY
MOTOR RELAY
HYDRAULIC UNIT
SOLENOID VALVE
MOTOR
MFI SYSTEM
ABS CONTROL UNIT

MT4029500176020X

Fig. 23 Anti-lock brake system wiring diagram (Part 2 of 6). 1995–96 Montero

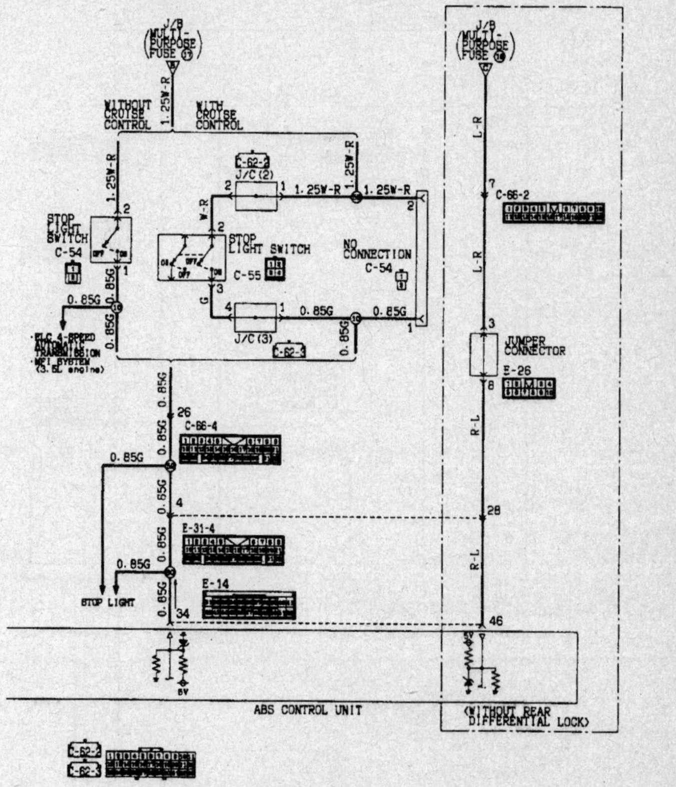
J/B MULTI-PURPOSE FUSE
WITHOUT CRUISE CONTROL
WITH CRUISE CONTROL
STOP LIGHT SWITCH
NO CONNECTION
JUMPER CONNECTOR
STOP LIGHT
ABS CONTROL UNIT
<WITHOUT REAR DIFFERENTIAL LOCK>

MT4029500176030X

Fig. 23 Anti-lock brake system wiring diagram (Part 3 of 6). 1995–96 Montero

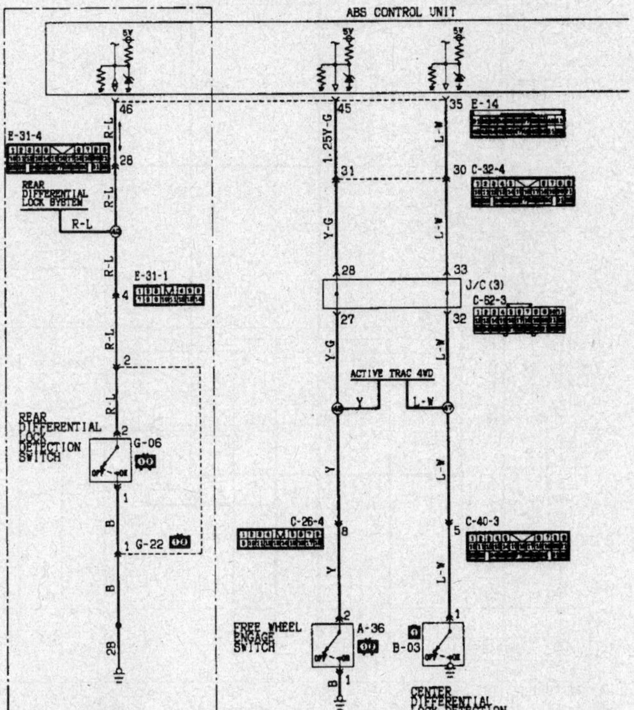
ABS CONTROL UNIT
REAR DIFFERENTIAL LOCK SYSTEM
REAR DIFFERENTIAL LOCK DETECTION SWITCH
ACTIVE TRAC 4WD
FREE WHEEL ENGAGE SWITCH
CENTER DIFFERENTIAL LOCK DETECTION SWITCH
<WITH REAR DIFFERENTIAL LOCK>

MT4029500176040X

Fig. 23 Anti-lock brake system wiring diagram (Part 4 of 6). 1995–96 Montero

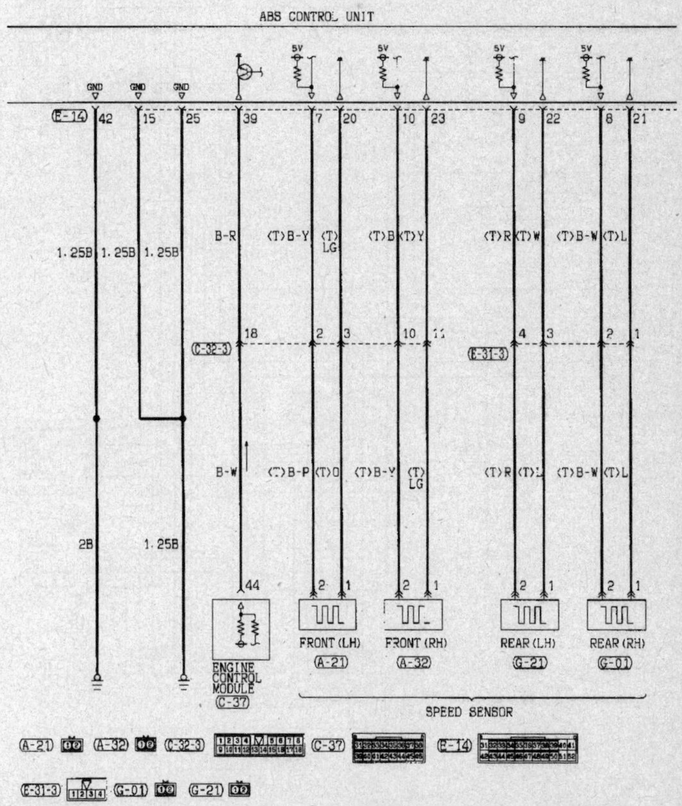
ABS CONTROL UNIT
ENGINE CONTROL MODULE
FRONT (LH)
FRONT (RH)
REAR (LH)
REAR (RH)
SPEED SENSOR

MT4029500176050A

Fig. 23 Anti-lock brake system wiring diagram (Part 5 of 6). 1995–96 Montero

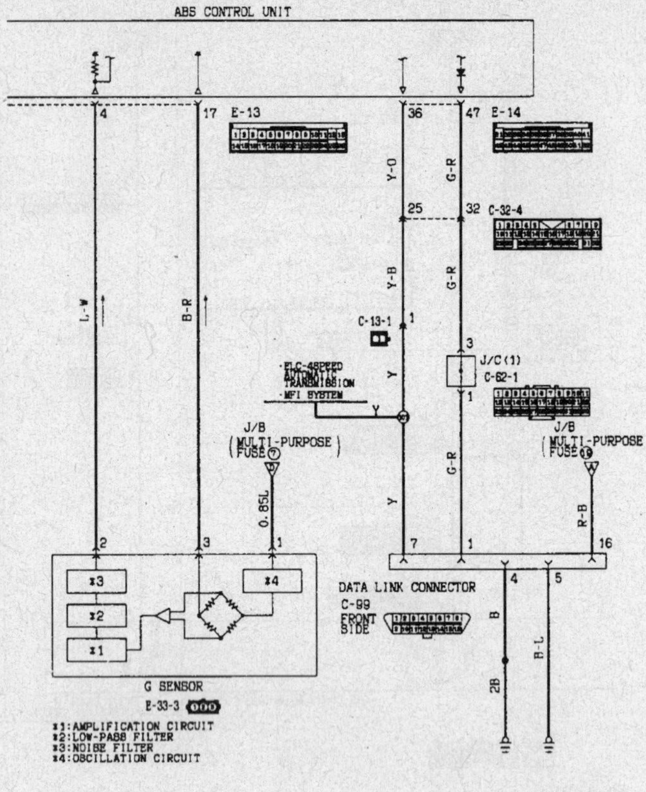
ABS CONTROL UNIT
E-13
E-14
C-32-4
C-13-1
J/C(1)
C-62-1
ELC-4SPEED AUTOMATIC TRANSMISSION
MFI SYSTEM
J/B (MULTI-PURPOSE FUSE ⑦)
J/B (MULTI-PURPOSE FUSE ⑯)
DATA LINK CONNECTOR
C-99
FRONT SIDE
G SENSOR
E-33-3
*1:AMPLIFICATION CIRCUIT
*2:LOW-PASS FILTER
*3:NOISE FILTER
*4:OSCILLATION CIRCUIT
MT4029500176060X

Fig. 23 Anti-lock brake system wiring diagram (Part 6 of 6). 1995–96 Montero

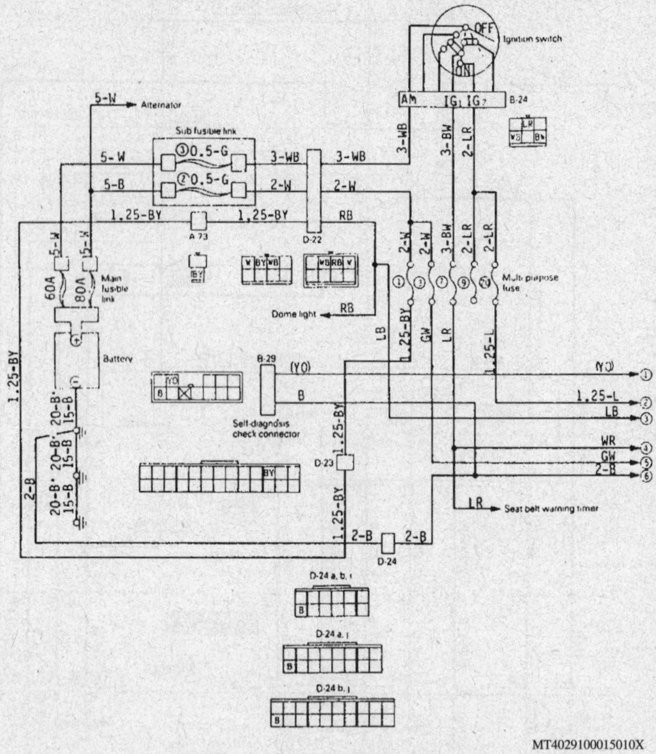
Ignition switch
Alternator
Sub fusible link
Main fusible link
Battery
Dome light
Multi-purpose fuse
Self-diagnosis check connector
Seat belt warning timer
MT4029100015010X

Fig. 24 Anti-lock brake system wiring diagram (Part 1 of 2). Pickup

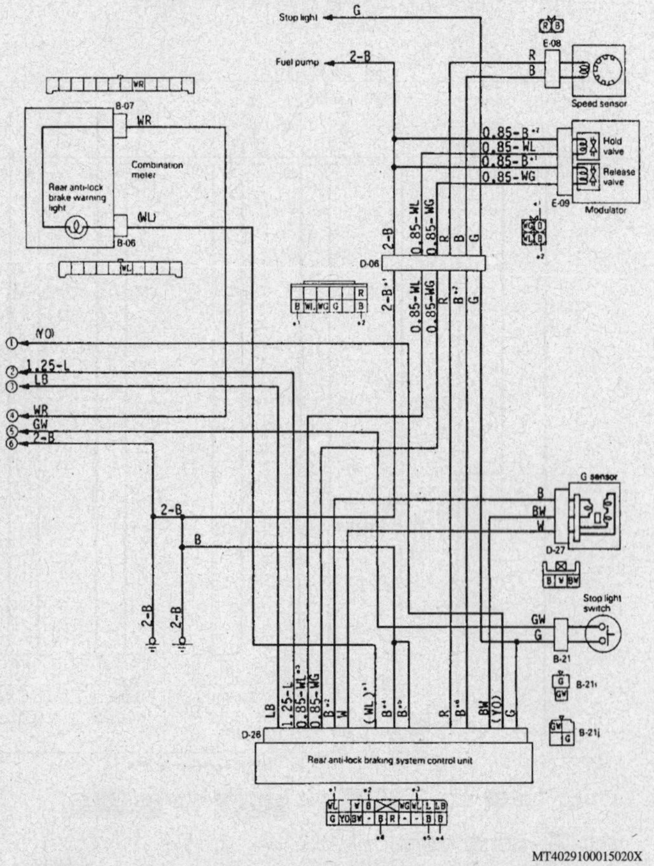
Stop light
Fuel pump
Speed sensor
Hold valve
Release valve
Modulator
Combination meter
Rear anti-lock brake warning light
G sensor
Stop light switch
Rear anti-lock braking system control unit
MT4029100015020X

Fig. 24 Anti-lock brake system wiring diagram (Part 2 of 2). Pickup

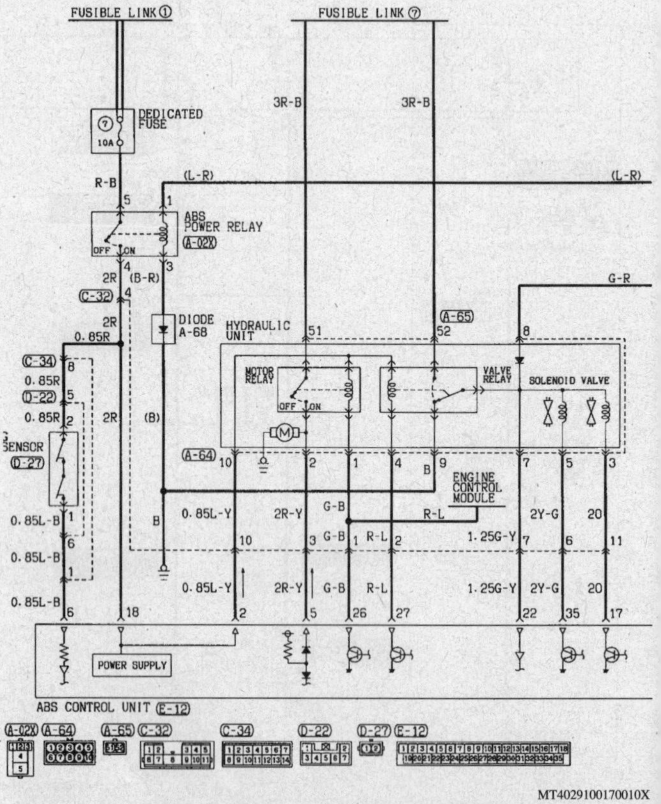
FUSIBLE LINK ①
FUSIBLE LINK ⑦
DEDICATED FUSE
ABS POWER RELAY
DIODE A-68
HYDRAULIC UNIT
MOTOR RELAY
VALVE RELAY
SOLENOID VALVE
ENGINE CONTROL MODULE
POWER SUPPLY
ABS CONTROL UNIT
MT4029100170010X

Fig. 25 Anti-lock brake system wiring diagram (Part 1 of 3). 1993 3000GT AWD

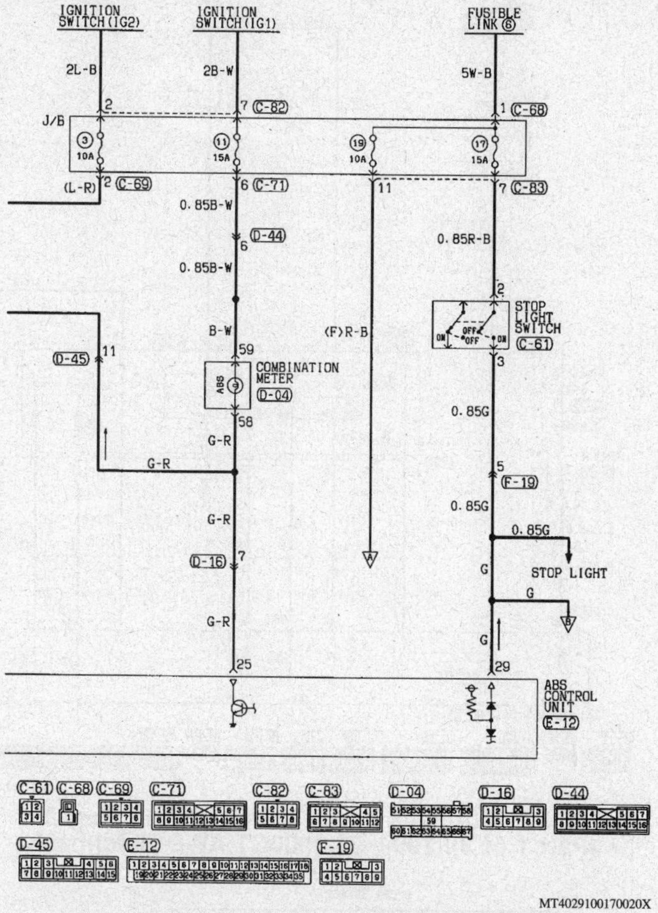
IGNITION SWITCH (IG2)
IGNITION SWITCH (IG1)
FUSIBLE LINK ⑥
J/B
STOP LIGHT SWITCH
COMBINATION METER
STOP LIGHT
ABS CONTROL UNIT
MT4029100170020X

Fig. 25 Anti-lock brake system wiring diagram (Part 2 of 3). 1993 3000GT AWD

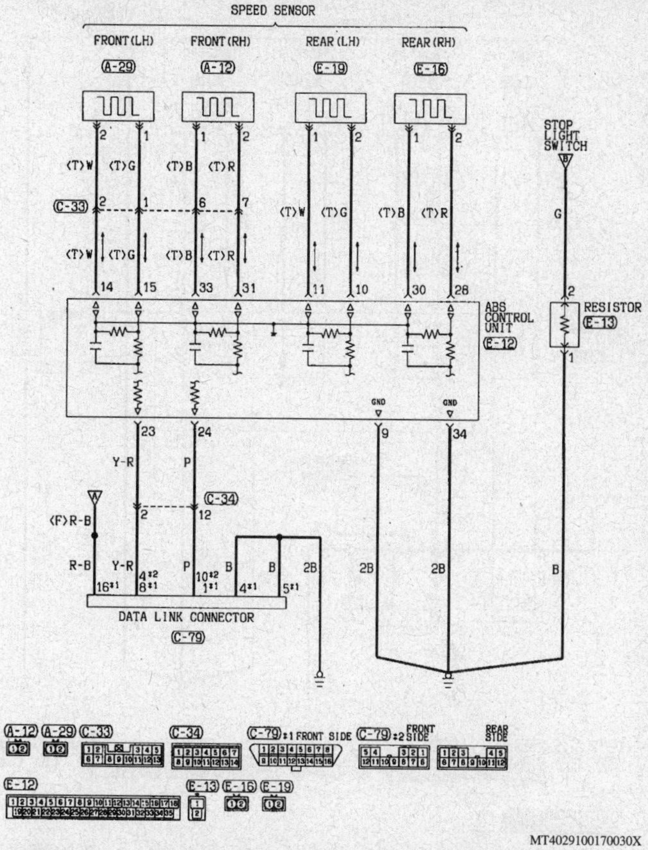
SPEED SENSOR
FRONT (LH)
FRONT (RH)
REAR (LH)
REAR (RH)
STOP LIGHT SWITCH
ABS CONTROL UNIT
RESISTOR
DATA LINK CONNECTOR
MT4029100170030X

Fig. 25 Anti-lock brake system wiring diagram (Part 3 of 3). 1993 3000GT AWD

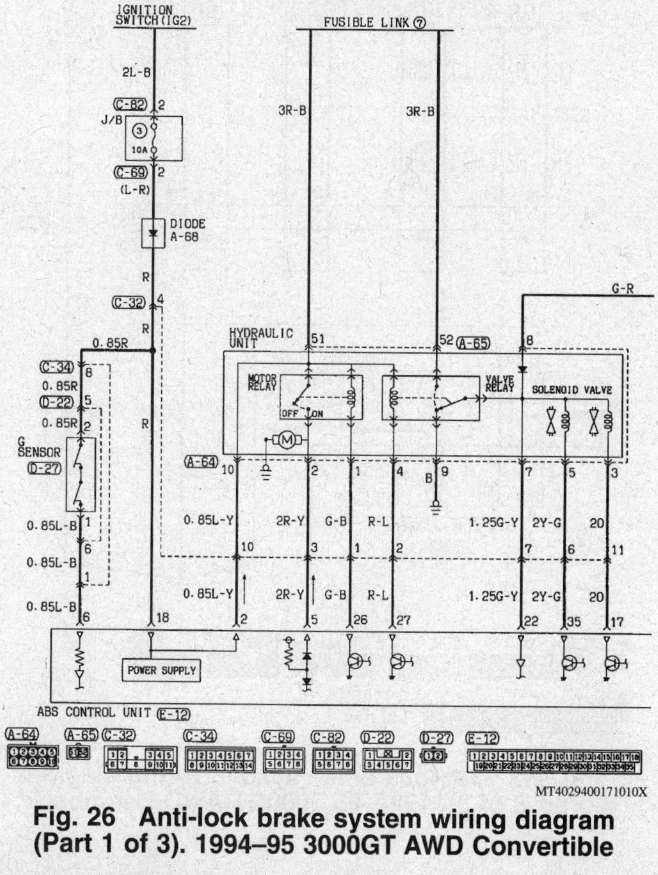
IGNITION SWITCH (IG2)
FUSIBLE LINK ⑦
J/B
DIODE A-68
G SENSOR
HYDRAULIC UNIT
MOTOR RELAY
VALVE RELAY
SOLENOID VALVE
POWER SUPPLY
ABS CONTROL UNIT
MT4029400171010X

Fig. 26 Anti-lock brake system wiring diagram (Part 1 of 3). 1994–95 3000GT AWD Convertible

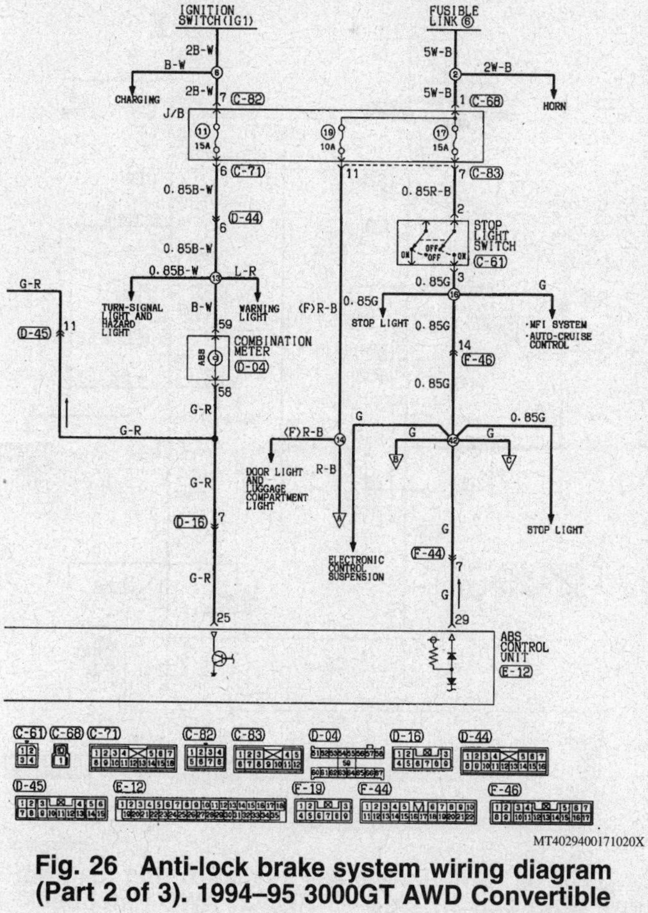
IGNITION SWITCH (IG1)
FUSIBLE LINK ⑥
CHARGING
HORN
J/B
STOP LIGHT SWITCH
TURN-SIGNAL LIGHT AND HAZARD LIGHT
WARNING LIGHT
STOP LIGHT
MFI SYSTEM
AUTO-CRUISE CONTROL
COMBINATION METER
DOOR LIGHT AND LUGGAGE COMPARTMENT LIGHT
ELECTRONIC CONTROL SUSPENSION
ABS CONTROL UNIT
MT4029400171020X

Fig. 26 Anti-lock brake system wiring diagram (Part 2 of 3). 1994–95 3000GT AWD Convertible

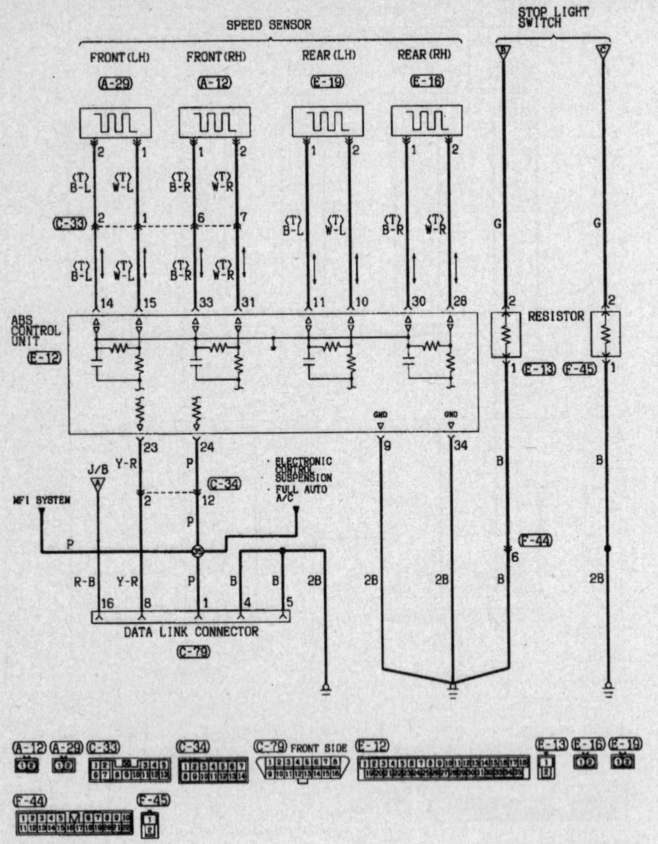
SPEED SENSOR
FRONT(LH)
FRONT(RH)
REAR(LH)
REAR(RH)
STOP LIGHT SWITCH
RESISTOR
ABS CONTROL UNIT
MFI SYSTEM
ELECTRONIC CONTROL SUSPENSION
FULL AUTO A/C
DATA LINK CONNECTOR
FRONT SIDE

MT4029400171030X

Fig. 26 Anti-lock brake system wiring diagram (Part 3 of 3). 1994–95 3000GT AWD Convertible

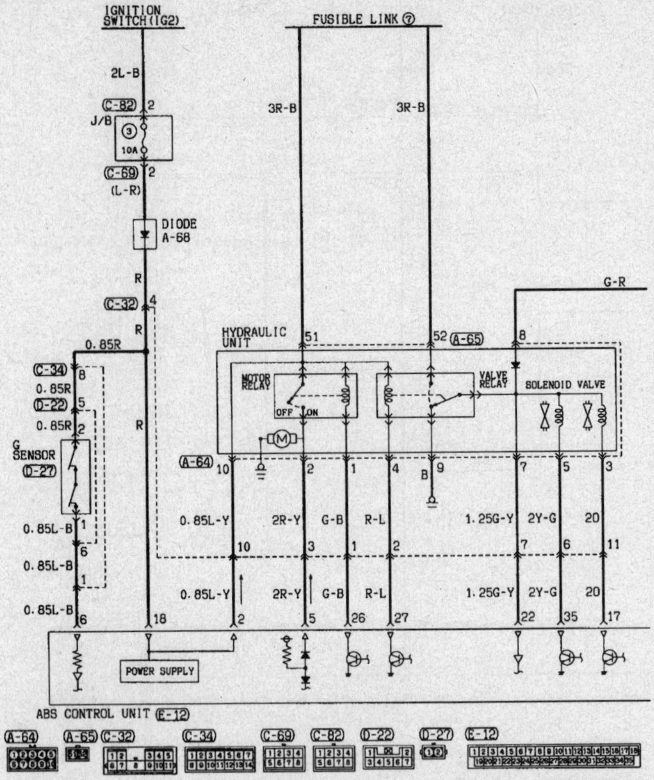
IGNITION SWITCH(IG2)
FUSIBLE LINK ⑦
DIODE A-68
HYDRAULIC UNIT
MOTOR RELAY
VALVE RELAY
SOLENOID VALVE
G SENSOR
POWER SUPPLY
ABS CONTROL UNIT

MT4029400172010X

Fig. 27 Anti-lock brake system wiring diagram (Part 1 of 3). 1994–95 3000GT AWD Hatchback

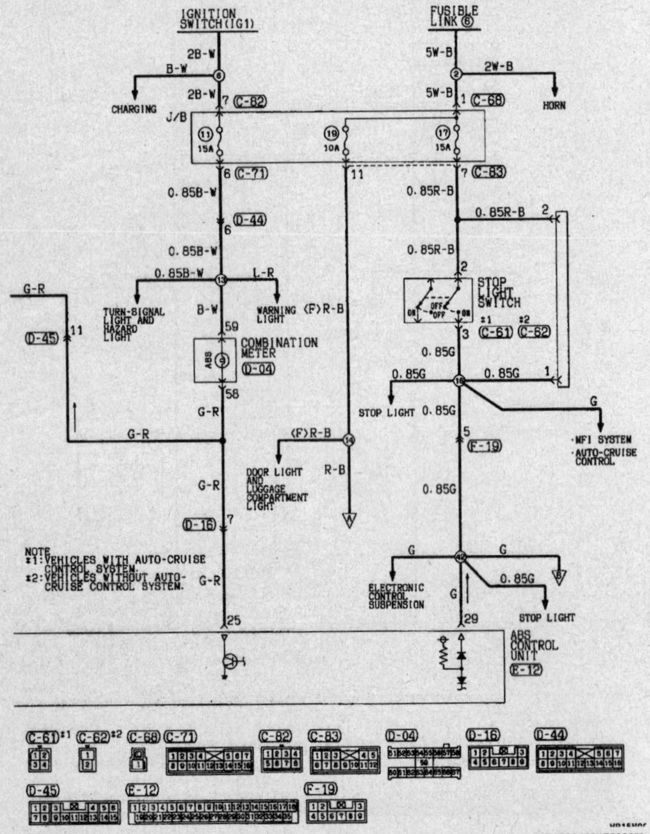
IGNITION SWITCH(IG1)
FUSIBLE LINK ⑥
CHARGING
HORN
TURN-SIGNAL LIGHT AND HAZARD LIGHT
WARNING LIGHT
COMBINATION METER
STOP LIGHT SWITCH
STOP LIGHT
MFI SYSTEM
AUTO-CRUISE CONTROL
DOOR LIGHT AND LUGGAGE COMPARTMENT LIGHT
ELECTRONIC CONTROL SUSPENSION
ABS CONTROL UNIT
NOTE
*1: VEHICLES WITH AUTO-CRUISE CONTROL SYSTEM.
*2: VEHICLES WITHOUT AUTO-CRUISE CONTROL SYSTEM.

MT4029400172020X

Fig. 27 Anti-lock brake system wiring diagram (Part 2 of 3). 1994–95 3000GT AWD Hatchback

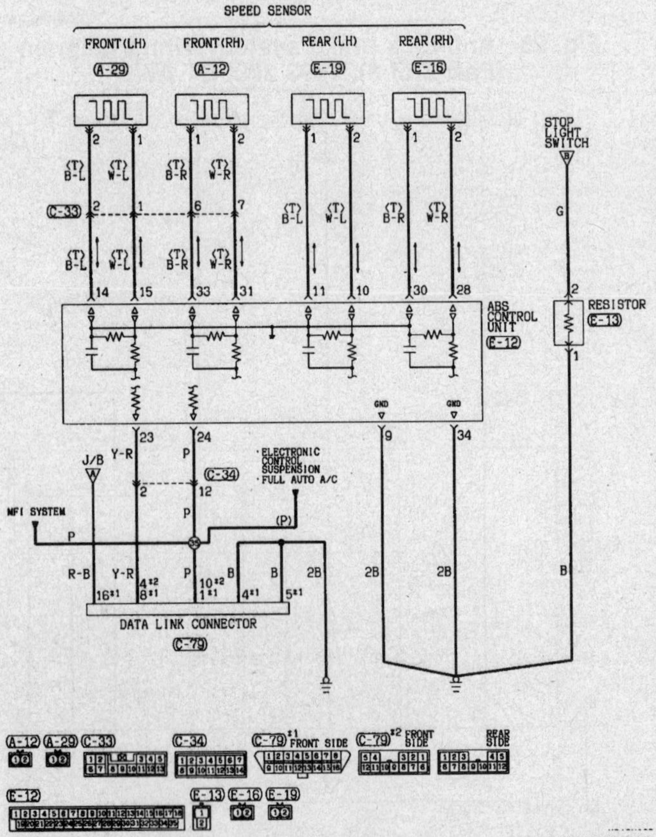
SPEED SENSOR
FRONT(LH)
FRONT(RH)
REAR(LH)
REAR(RH)
STOP LIGHT SWITCH
RESISTOR
ABS CONTROL UNIT
MFI SYSTEM
ELECTRONIC CONTROL SUSPENSION
FULL AUTO A/C
DATA LINK CONNECTOR
FRONT SIDE
REAR SIDE

MT4029400172030X

Fig. 27 Anti-lock brake system wiring diagram (Part 3 of 3). 1994–95 3000GT AWD Hatchback

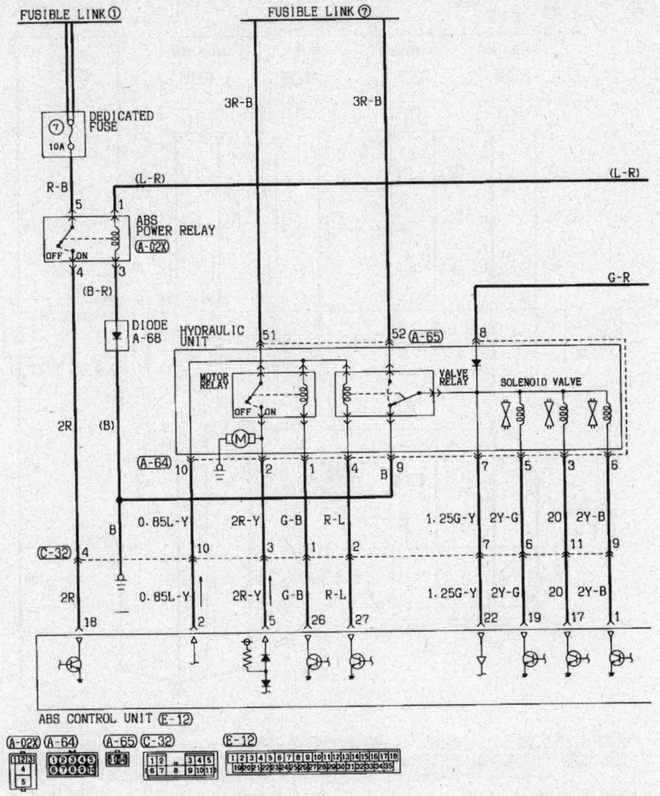
FUSIBLE LINK①
FUSIBLE LINK⑦
DEDICATED FUSE
ABS POWER RELAY
A-02X
DIODE A-68
HYDRAULIC UNIT
A-65
MOTOR RELAY
VALVE RELAY
SOLENOID VALVE
A-64
C-32
ABS CONTROL UNIT E-12

MT4029100173010X

Fig. 28 Anti-lock brake system wiring diagram (Part 1 of 3). 1993 3000GT FWD

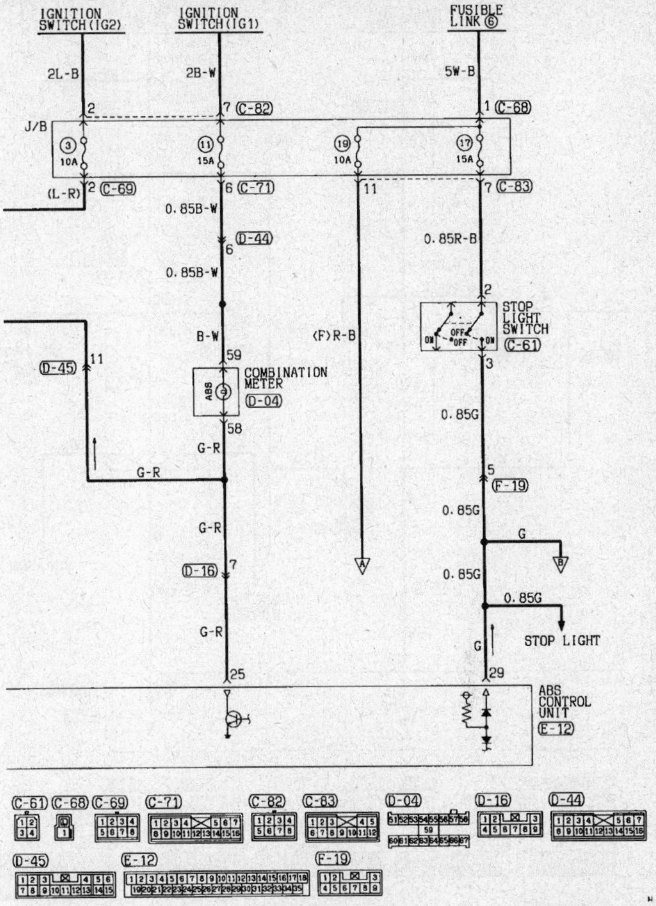
IGNITION SWITCH (IG2)
IGNITION SWITCH (IG1)
FUSIBLE LINK⑥
J/B
C-82
C-68
C-69
C-71
C-83
D-44
D-45
STOP LIGHT SWITCH
C-61
COMBINATION METER
D-04
F-19
D-16
STOP LIGHT
ABS CONTROL UNIT
E-12

MT4029100173020X

Fig. 28 Anti-lock brake system wiring diagram (Part 2 of 3). 1993 3000GT FWD

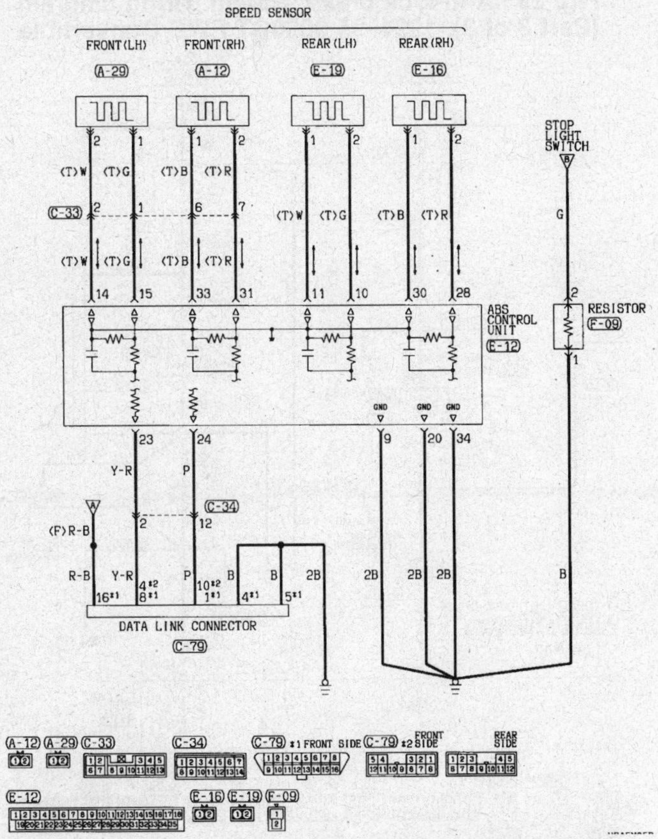
SPEED SENSOR
FRONT(LH)
FRONT(RH)
REAR(LH)
REAR(RH)
A-29
A-12
E-19
E-16
STOP LIGHT SWITCH
C-33
ABS CONTROL UNIT
E-12
RESISTOR
F-09
GND
C-34
DATA LINK CONNECTOR
C-79
*1 FRONT SIDE
*2 FRONT SIDE
REAR SIDE

MT4029100173030X

Fig. 28 Anti-lock brake system wiring diagram (Part 3 of 3). 1993 3000GT FWD

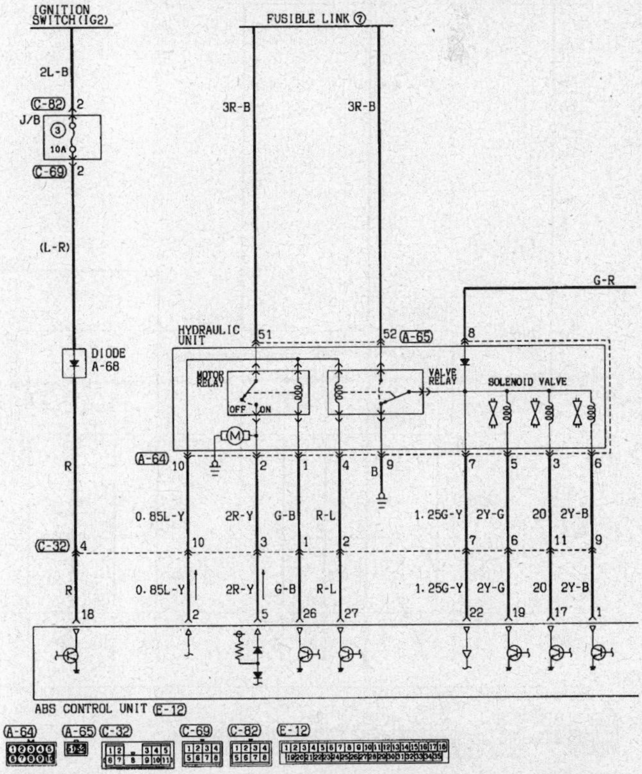
IGNITION SWITCH (IG2)
FUSIBLE LINK⑦
C-82
J/B
C-69
DIODE A-68
HYDRAULIC UNIT
A-65
MOTOR RELAY
VALVE RELAY
SOLENOID VALVE
A-64
C-32
ABS CONTROL UNIT E-12

MT4029400174010X

Fig. 29 Anti-lock brake system wiring diagram (Part 1 of 3). 1994–95 3000GT FWD Convertible

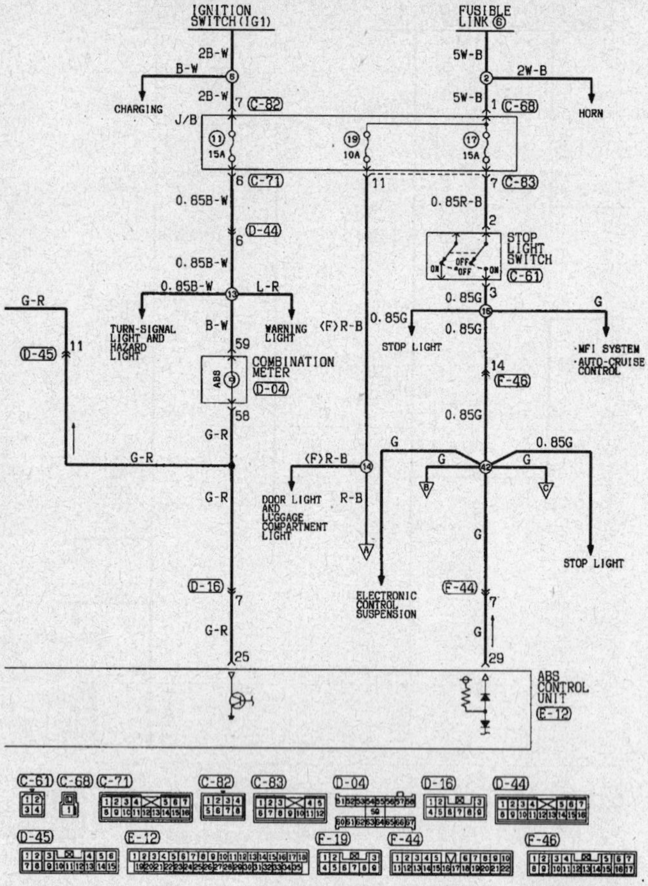

IGNITION SWITCH (IG1)
FUSIBLE LINK ⑥
2B-W
B-W
5W-B
2W-B
CHARGING
HORN
J/B
15A
10A
0.85B-W
0.85R-B
STOP LIGHT SWITCH
TURN-SIGNAL LIGHT AND HAZARD LIGHT
WARNING LIGHT
COMBINATION METER
STOP LIGHT
·MFI SYSTEM
·AUTO-CRUISE CONTROL
DOOR LIGHT AND LUGGAGE COMPARTMENT LIGHT
ELECTRONIC CONTROL SUSPENSION
ABS CONTROL UNIT

MT4029400174020X

Fig. 29 Anti-lock brake system wiring diagram (Part 2 of 3). 1994–95 3000GT FWD Convertible

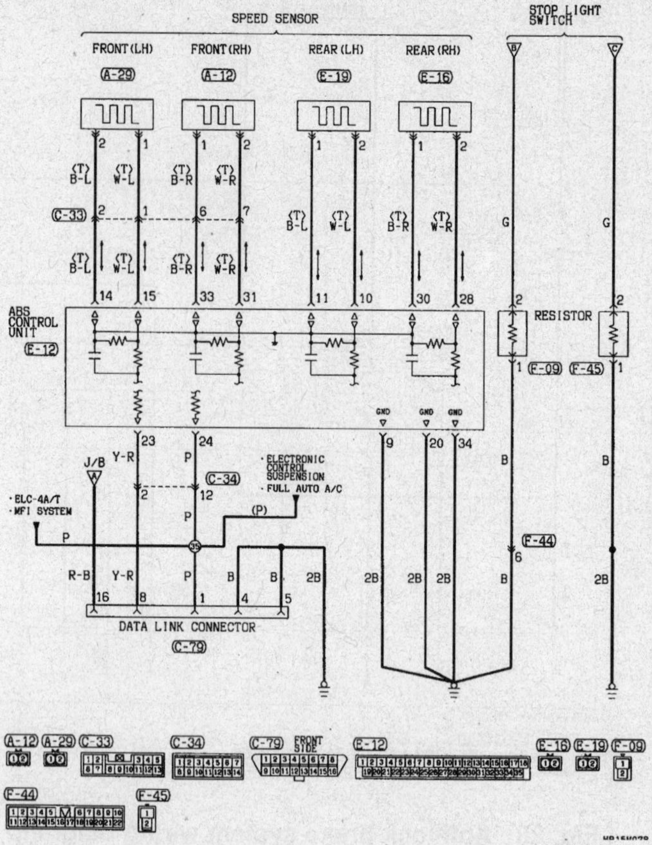

SPEED SENSOR
STOP LIGHT SWITCH
FRONT (LH)
FRONT (RH)
REAR (LH)
REAR (RH)
ABS CONTROL UNIT
RESISTOR
·ELECTRONIC CONTROL SUSPENSION
·FULL AUTO A/C
·ELC-4A/T
·MFI SYSTEM
DATA LINK CONNECTOR

MT4029400174030X

Fig. 29 Anti-lock brake system wiring diagram (Part 3 of 3). 1994–95 3000GT FWD Convertible

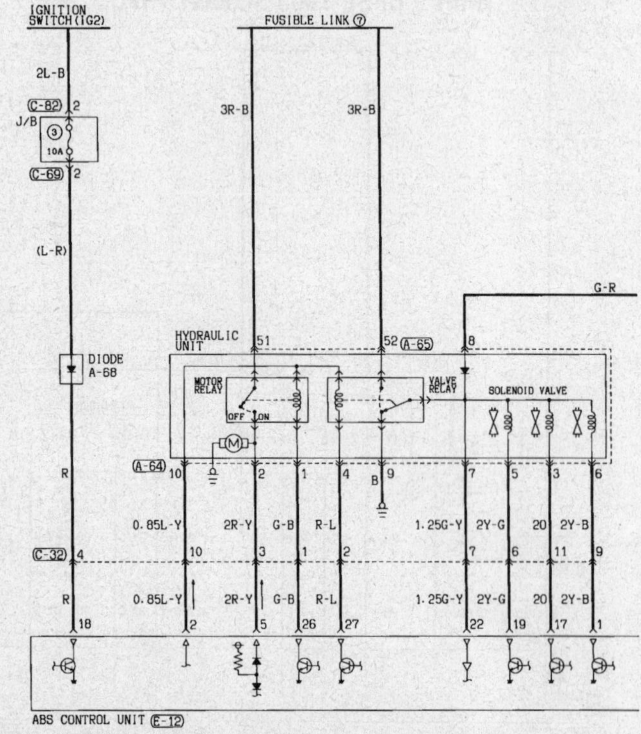

IGNITION SWITCH (IG2)
FUSIBLE LINK ⑦
J/B
10A
DIODE A-68
HYDRAULIC UNIT
MOTOR RELAY
VALVE RELAY
SOLENOID VALVE
ABS CONTROL UNIT

MT4029400175010X

Fig. 30 Anti-lock brake system wiring diagram (Part 1 of 3). 1994–95 3000GT FWD Hatchback

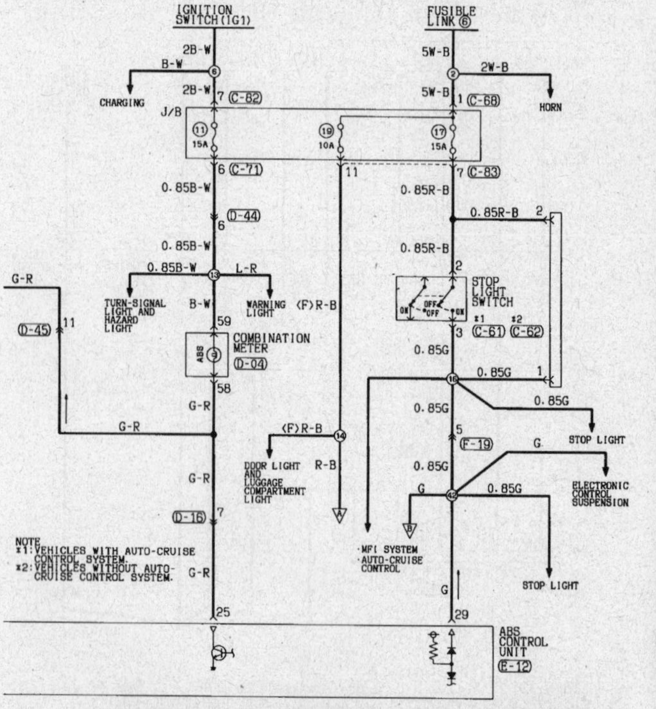

IGNITION SWITCH (IG1)
FUSIBLE LINK ⑥
CHARGING
HORN
J/B
STOP LIGHT SWITCH
TURN-SIGNAL LIGHT AND HAZARD LIGHT
WARNING LIGHT
COMBINATION METER
STOP LIGHT
ELECTRONIC CONTROL SUSPENSION
DOOR LIGHT AND LUGGAGE COMPARTMENT LIGHT
·MFI SYSTEM
·AUTO-CRUISE CONTROL
NOTE
*1: VEHICLES WITH AUTO-CRUISE CONTROL SYSTEM.
*2: VEHICLES WITHOUT AUTO-CRUISE CONTROL SYSTEM.
ABS CONTROL UNIT

MT4029400175020X

Fig. 30 Anti-lock brake system wiring diagram (Part 2 of 3). 1994–95 3000GT FWD Hatchback

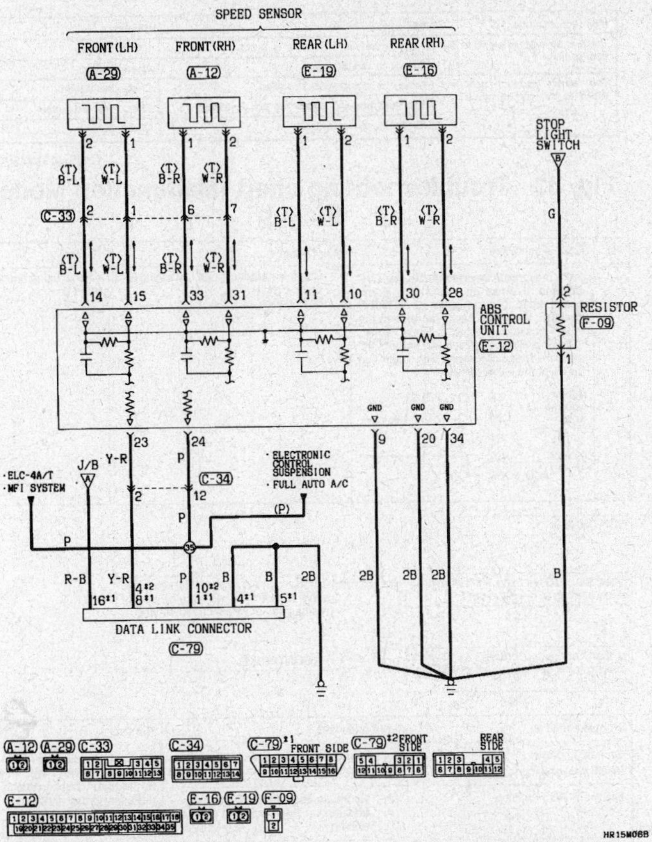
SPEED SENSOR
FRONT (LH)
FRONT (RH)
REAR (LH)
REAR (RH)
STOP LIGHT SWITCH
RESISTOR
ABS CONTROL UNIT
ELECTRONIC CONTROL SUSPENSION
FULL AUTO A/C
ELC-4A/T
MFI SYSTEM
DATA LINK CONNECTOR
FRONT SIDE
REAR SIDE
HR15M08B

MT4029400175030X

Fig. 30 Anti-lock brake system wiring diagram (Part 3 of 3). 1994–95 3000GT FWD Hatchback

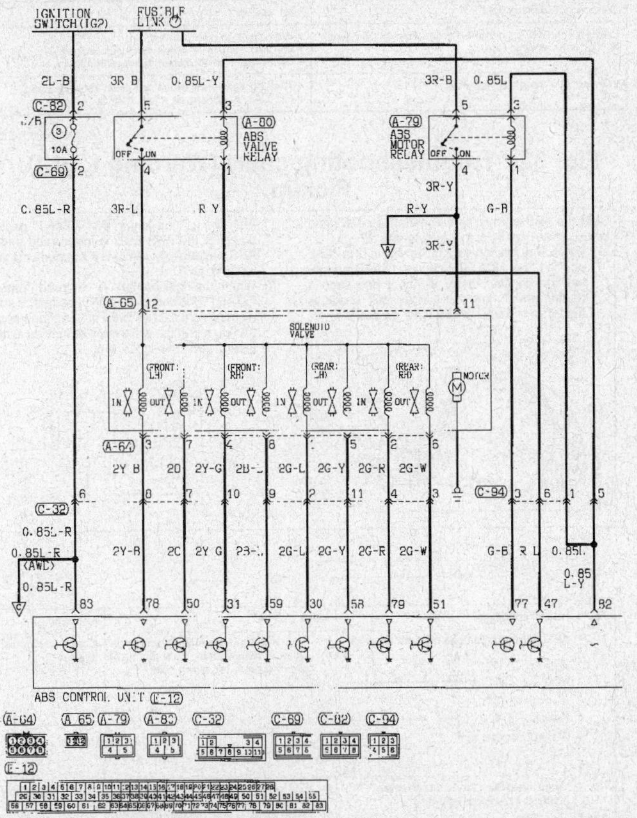
IGNITION SWITCH (IG2)
FUSIBLE LINK
ABS VALVE RELAY
ABS MOTOR RELAY
SOLENOID VALVE
MOTOR
ABS CONTROL UNIT

MT4029600205010X

Fig. 31 Anti-lock brake system wiring diagram (Part 1 of 3). 1996 3000GT

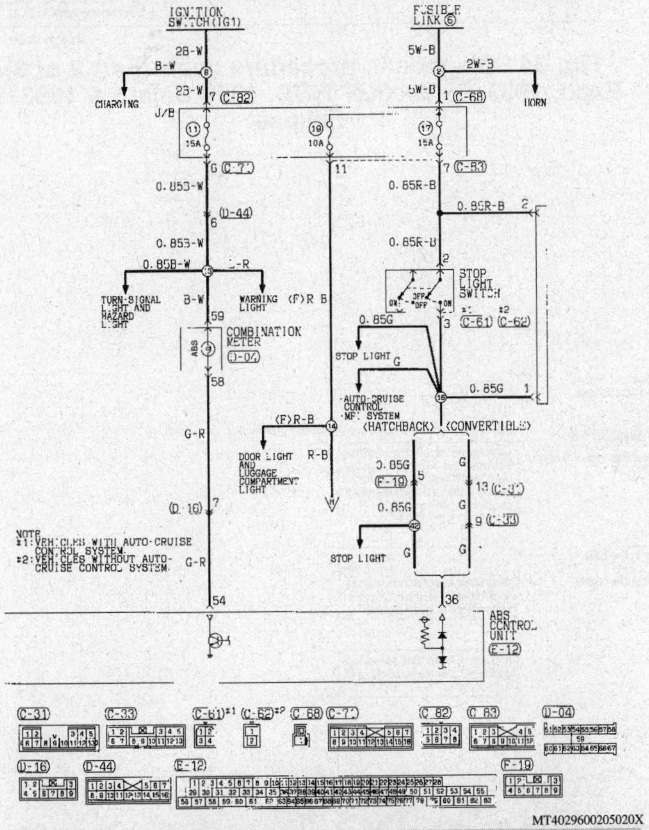
IGNITION SWITCH (IG1)
FUSIBLE LINK
CHARGING
HORN
TURN-SIGNAL LIGHT AND HAZARD LIGHT
WARNING LIGHT
COMBINATION METER
STOP LIGHT SWITCH
STOP LIGHT
AUTO-CRUISE CONTROL
MFI SYSTEM
(HATCHBACK)
(CONVERTIBLE)
DOOR LIGHT AND LUGGAGE COMPARTMENT LIGHT
NOTE
*1: VEHICLES WITH AUTO-CRUISE CONTROL SYSTEM
*2: VEHICLES WITHOUT AUTO-CRUISE CONTROL SYSTEM
ABS CONTROL UNIT

MT4029600205020X

Fig. 31 Anti-lock brake system wiring diagram (Part 2 of 3). 1996 3000GT

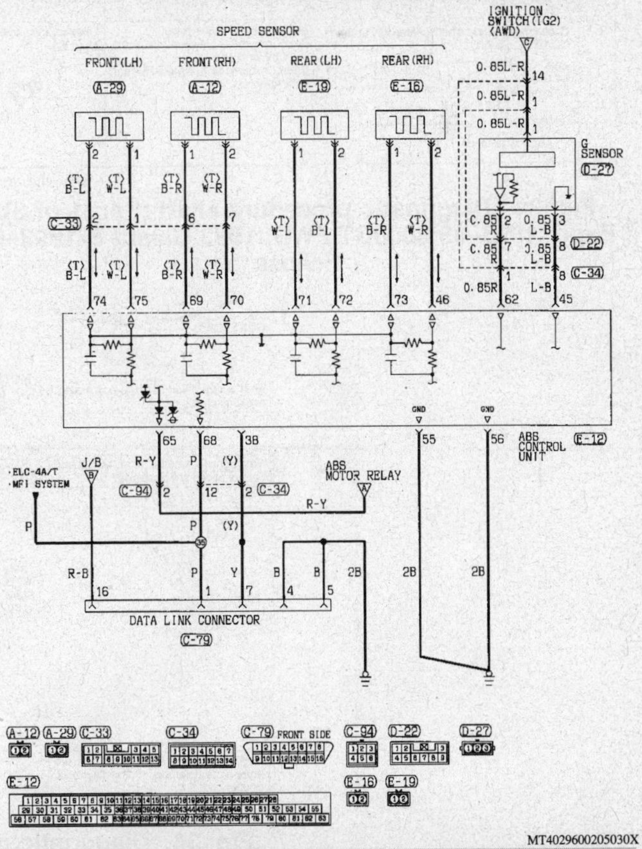
IGNITION SWITCH (IG2) (AWD)
SPEED SENSOR
FRONT (LH)
FRONT (RH)
REAR (LH)
REAR (RH)
G SENSOR
ABS CONTROL UNIT
ELC-4A/T
MFI SYSTEM
ABS MOTOR RELAY
DATA LINK CONNECTOR
FRONT SIDE

MT4029600205030X

Fig. 31 Anti-lock brake system wiring diagram (Part 3 of 3). 1996 3000GT

Condition of warning light	Main causes
Warning light will not come on even when ignition switch is "ON" with engine stop.	• Warning light bulb has run out. • Warning light drive circuit has been broken. • Control unit power circuit has been broken.
Warning light keeps on lighting	• Warning light drive circuit has been short-circuited. • Fail safe is working as a result of self-check.

MT4029100001000X

Fig. 32 Troubleshooting chart (Warning Light). Pickup

Malfunction mode	Malfunction cause	Remedy
There is no input of signal in the control unit.	Harness between sensors is broken.	Check harness.
	Sensor is out of order.	Check sensor.
The sensor outputs abnormal signal to the control unit.	Sensor is not properly installed.	Check installation.
	Specified tire and wheel are not installed.	Check tire and wheel.
	Sensor is out of order.	Check sensor.

MT4029100002000X

Fig. 33 Troubleshooting chart (Malfunction Mode). Pickup

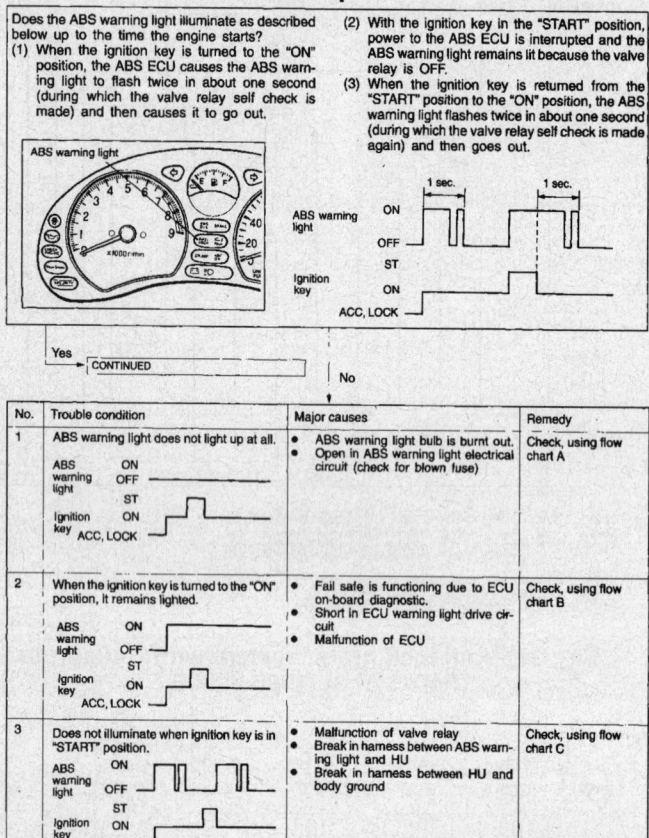

Does the ABS warning light illuminate as described below up to the time the engine starts?

(1) When the ignition key is turned to the "ON" position, the ABS ECU causes the ABS warning light to flash twice in about one second (during which the valve relay self check is made) and then causes it to go out.

(2) With the ignition key in the "START" position, power to the ABS ECU is interrupted and the ABS warning light remains lit because the valve relay is OFF.

(3) When the ignition key is returned from the "START" position to the "ON" position, the ABS warning light flashes twice in about one second (during which the valve relay self check is made again) and then goes out.

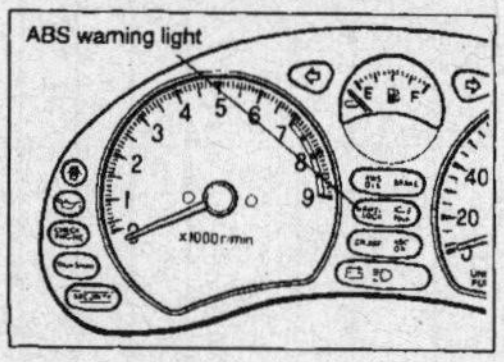
ABS warning light

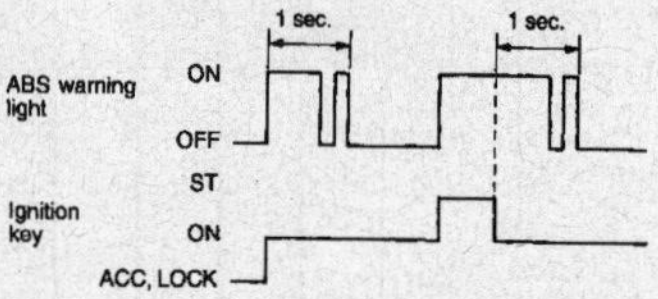
1 sec.
1 sec.
ABS warning light
ON
OFF
ST
Ignition key
ON
ACC, LOCK

Yes → CONTINUED

No ↓

No.	Trouble condition	Major causes	Remedy
1	ABS warning light does not light up at all. 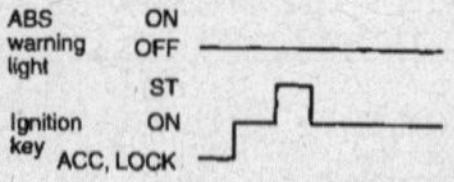	• ABS warning light bulb is burnt out. • Open in ABS warning light electrical circuit (check for blown fuse)	Check, using flow chart A
2	When the ignition key is turned to the "ON" position, it remains lighted. 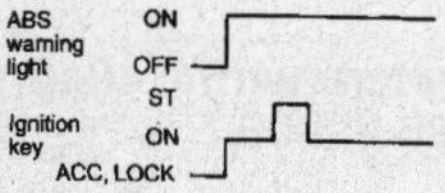	• Fail safe is functioning due to ECU on-board diagnostic. • Short in ECU warning light drive circuit • Malfunction of ECU	Check, using flow chart B
3	Does not illuminate when ignition key is in "START" position. 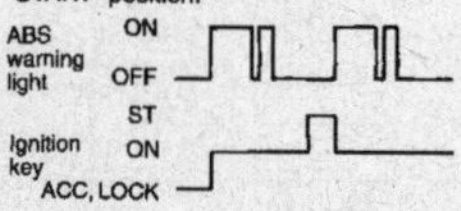	• Malfunction of valve relay • Break in harness between ABS warning light and HU • Break in harness between HU and body ground	Check, using flow chart C

MT4029100200010A

Fig. 34 Diagnostic procedure chart (Part 1 of 3). Expo, 1993–95 3000GT FWD, 1993 Galant & 1993–94 Eclipse

No.	Trouble condition	Major causes	Remedy
4	After the ignition key is turned to the "ON" position, it blinks once and then illuminates when it is turned to the "START" position. When the key is returned to the "ON" position, the light blinks again. (Blinking with the ignition key in the "ON" position is synchronized with operation noise of the valve relay.) 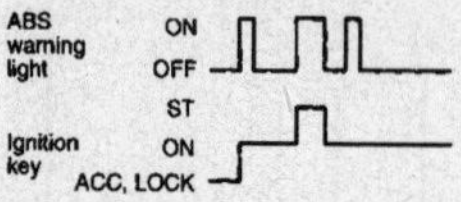	• Break in harness for ECU warning light drive circuit • Malfunction of ECU	Check, using flow chart D

CONTINUED

Does the ABS warning light illuminate when starting to drive the car?
- Yes → Trouble with the motor relay, solenoid valve [due to self test at start-up or malfunction of wheel speed sensor] → CONTINUED
- No → Is there one-sided braking, insufficient braking force or malfunction of ABS operation?
  - No → CONTINUED
  - Yes ↓

Trouble condition	Major causes	Remedy
One-sided braking Insufficient braking force	• Hydraulic line in HU is clogged. • Mechanical lock of HU solenoid valve	Check HU operation and, if necessary, replace HU. If HU is normal, check structural parts for normal braking.
Decline in ABS function	• Hydraulic line in HU is clogged. • Malfunction in HU solenoid valve operation	
ABS sometimes functions even when there is no sudden braking. (ABS operation vibration is transmitted.)	• Insufficient wheel speed sensor output voltage (sensor malfunction, too large a gap between sensor rotor, missing rotor teeth) • Malfunction of ABS ECU	Check wheel speed sensor and, if necessary, replace sensor, adjust gap or replace rotor. If tests indicate that there are no mechanical or electrical failures, replace the ECU.

MT4029100200020A

Fig. 34 Diagnostic procedure chart (Part 2 of 3). Expo, 1993–95 3000GT FWD, 1993 Galant & 1993–94 Eclipse

CONTINUED

After a test drive*, use on-board diagnostic to check

NOTE
*: Drive at 19 mph or higher for more than 30 seconds.

No diagnostic trouble codes output and normal codes are displayed?
- No — No on-board diagnostic output / No — Diagnostic trouble codes are output → Check and repair the harness between the ABS ECU serial/on-board diagnostic output terminals and the diagnosis check connector.
- (Diagnostic trouble codes are output) → There was trouble in the past. NOTE Store diagnostic trouble codes in the memory. → Make the diagnostic trouble code reoccur to discover the main cause of intermittent or other trouble. → If trouble does not reappear, watch vehicle movements until it reappears.
- Yes → All ABS functions are normal. (Nor are there stored memory of past diagnostic trouble code.)

MT4029100200030A

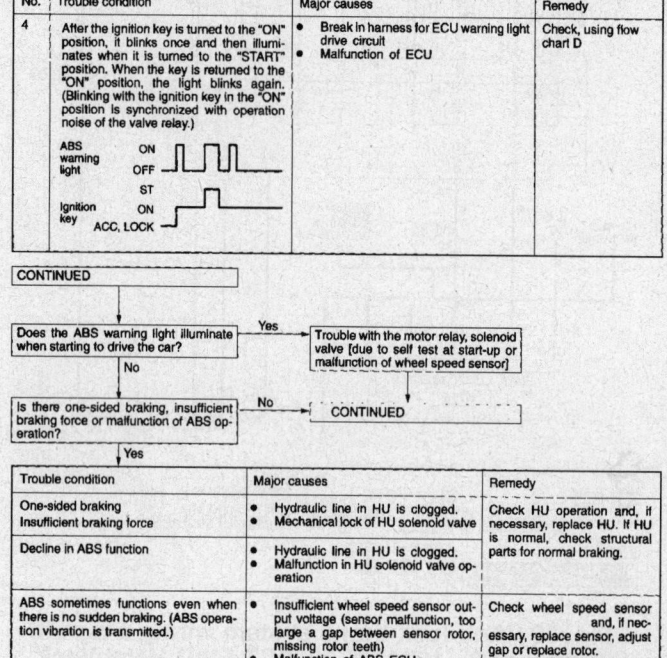

Fig. 34 Diagnostic procedure chart (Part 3 of 3). Expo, 1993–95 3000GT FWD, 1993 Galant & 1993–94 Eclipse

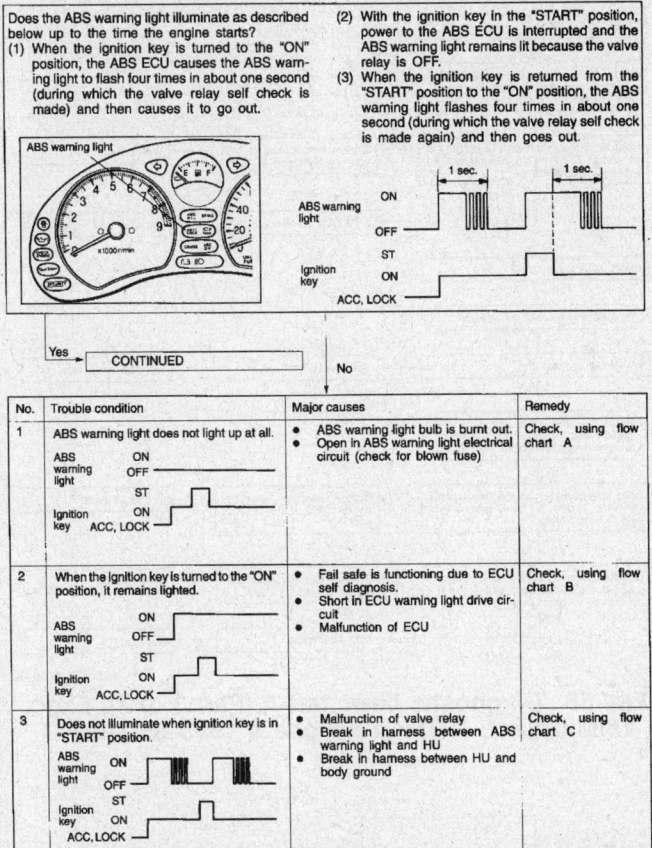

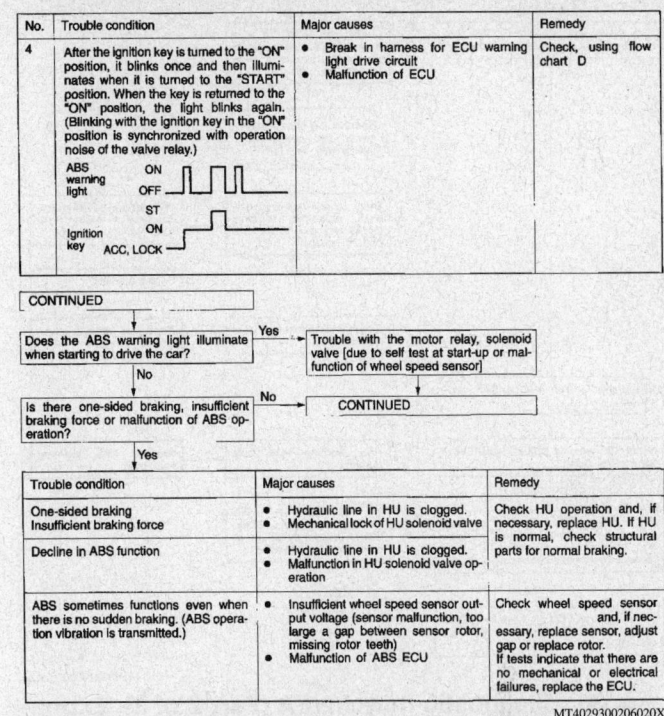

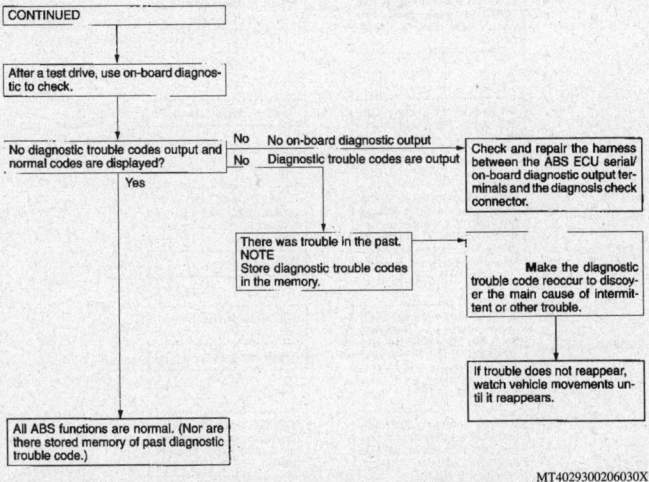

Does the ABS warning light illuminate as described below up to the time the engine starts?

(1) When the ignition key is turned to the "ON" position, the ABS ECU causes the ABS warning light to flash four times in about one second (during which the valve relay self check is made) and then causes it to go out.

(2) With the ignition key in the "START" position, power to the ABS ECU is interrupted and the ABS warning light remains lit because the valve relay is OFF.

(3) When the ignition key is returned from the "START" position to the "ON" position, the ABS warning light flashes four times in about one second (during which the valve relay self check is made again) and then goes out.

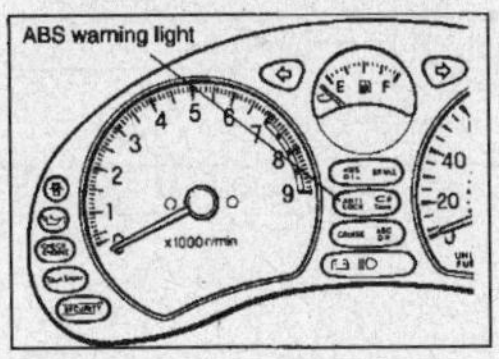
ABS warning light
x1000r/min

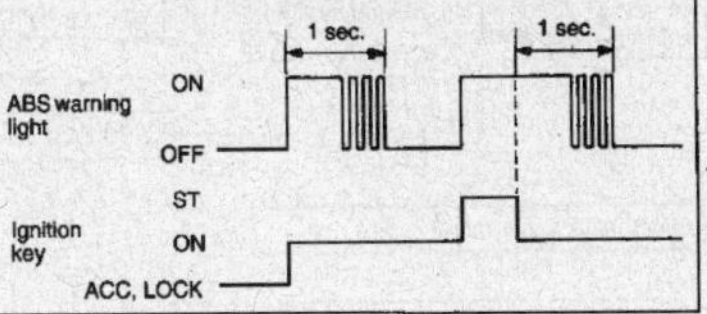
1 sec.
1 sec.
ABS warning light
ON
OFF
ST
Ignition key
ON
ACC, LOCK

Yes → CONTINUED

No ↓

No.	Trouble condition	Major causes	Remedy
1	ABS warning light does not light up at all. (ABS warning light: ON/OFF; Ignition key: ST/ON/ACC, LOCK)	• ABS warning light bulb is burnt out. • Open in ABS warning light electrical circuit (check for blown fuse)	Check, using flow chart A
2	When the ignition key is turned to the "ON" position, it remains lighted. (ABS warning light: ON/OFF; Ignition key: ST/ON/ACC, LOCK)	• Fail safe is functioning due to ECU self diagnosis. • Short in ECU warning light drive circuit • Malfunction of ECU	Check, using flow chart B
3	Does not illuminate when ignition key is in "START" position. (ABS warning light: ON/OFF; Ignition key: ST/ON/ACC, LOCK)	• Malfunction of valve relay • Break in harness between ABS warning light and HU • Break in harness between HU and body ground	Check, using flow chart C

MT4029300206010X

Fig. 35 Diagnostic procedure chart (Part 1 of 3). 1993–95 3000GT AWD

No.	Trouble condition	Major causes	Remedy
4	After the ignition key is turned to the "ON" position, it blinks once and then illuminates when it is turned to the "START" position. When the key is returned to the "ON" position, the light blinks again. (Blinking with the ignition key in the "ON" position is synchronized with operation noise of the valve relay.) (ABS warning light: ON/OFF; Ignition key: ST/ON/ACC, LOCK)	• Break in harness for ECU warning light drive circuit • Malfunction of ECU	Check, using flow chart D

CONTINUED

Does the ABS warning light illuminate when starting to drive the car? — Yes → Trouble with the motor relay, solenoid valve [due to self test at start-up or malfunction of wheel speed sensor] → CONTINUED

No ↓

Is there one-sided braking, insufficient braking force or malfunction of ABS operation? — No → CONTINUED

Yes ↓

Trouble condition	Major causes	Remedy
One-sided braking Insufficient braking force	• Hydraulic line in HU is clogged. • Mechanical lock of HU solenoid valve	Check HU operation and, if necessary, replace HU. If HU is normal, check structural parts for normal braking.
Decline in ABS function	• Hydraulic line in HU is clogged. • Malfunction in HU solenoid valve operation	
ABS sometimes functions even when there is no sudden braking. (ABS operation vibration is transmitted.)	• Insufficient wheel speed sensor output voltage (sensor malfunction, too large a gap between sensor rotor, missing rotor teeth) • Malfunction of ABS ECU	Check wheel speed sensor and, if necessary, replace sensor, adjust gap or replace rotor. If tests indicate that there are no mechanical or electrical failures, replace the ECU.

MT4029300206020X

Fig. 35 Diagnostic procedure chart (Part 2 of 3). 1993–95 3000GT AWD

CONTINUED

↓

After a test drive, use on-board diagnostic to check.

↓

No diagnostic trouble codes output and normal codes are displayed?

- No — No on-board diagnostic output → Check and repair the harness between the ABS ECU serial/on-board diagnostic output terminals and the diagnosis check connector.
- No — Diagnostic trouble codes are output → There was trouble in the past. NOTE Store diagnostic trouble codes in the memory. → Make the diagnostic trouble code reoccur to discover the main cause of intermittent or other trouble. → If trouble does not reappear, watch vehicle movements until it reappears.
- Yes → All ABS functions are normal. (Nor are there stored memory of past diagnostic trouble code.)

MT4029300206030X

Fig. 35 Diagnostic procedure chart (Part 3 of 3). 1993–95 3000GT AWD

A ABS warning light does not light at all.

[Explanation]

When it does not light up at all, there is a strong possibility that there is trouble with ABS warning light or with power to the light.

[Hint]

If other warning lights do not light up either, fuse is probably blown.

MT4029100026010X

Fig. 36 Diagnostic flowchart A (Part 1 of 3). Expo, 1993 Galant, 1993–94 Eclipse & 1993–95 3000GT

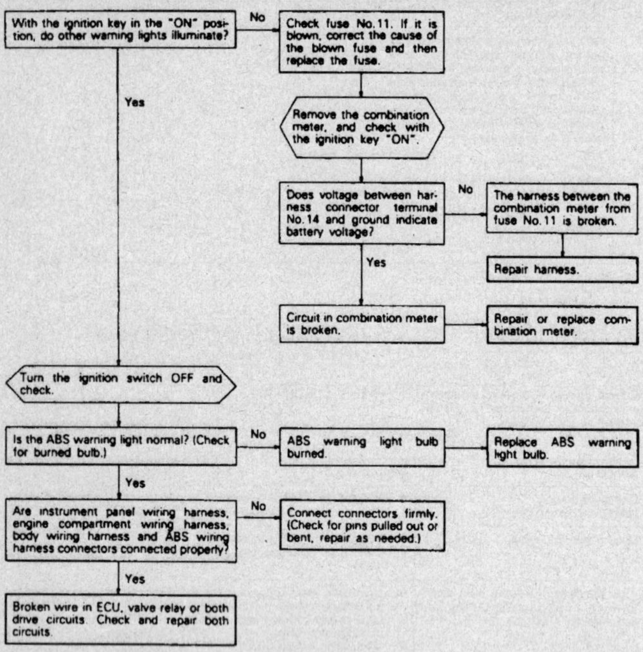
With the ignition key in the "ON" position, do other warning lights illuminate?
No
Check fuse No.11. If it is blown, correct the cause of the blown fuse and then replace the fuse.
Yes
Remove the combination meter, and check with the ignition key "ON".
Does voltage between harness connector terminal No.14 and ground indicate battery voltage?
No
The harness between the combination meter from fuse No.11 is broken.
Repair harness.
Yes
Circuit in combination meter is broken.
Repair or replace combination meter.
Turn the ignition switch OFF and check.
Is the ABS warning light normal? (Check for burned bulb.)
No
ABS warning light bulb burned.
Replace ABS warning light bulb.
Yes
Are instrument panel wiring harness, engine compartment wiring harness, body wiring harness and ABS wiring harness connectors connected properly?
No
Connect connectors firmly. (Check for pins pulled out or bent, repair as needed.)
Yes
Broken wire in ECU, valve relay or both drive circuits. Check and repair both circuits.
MT4029100026020X

Fig. 36 Diagnostic flowchart A (Part 2 of 3). Expo, 1993 Galant, 1993–94 Eclipse & 1993–95 3000GT

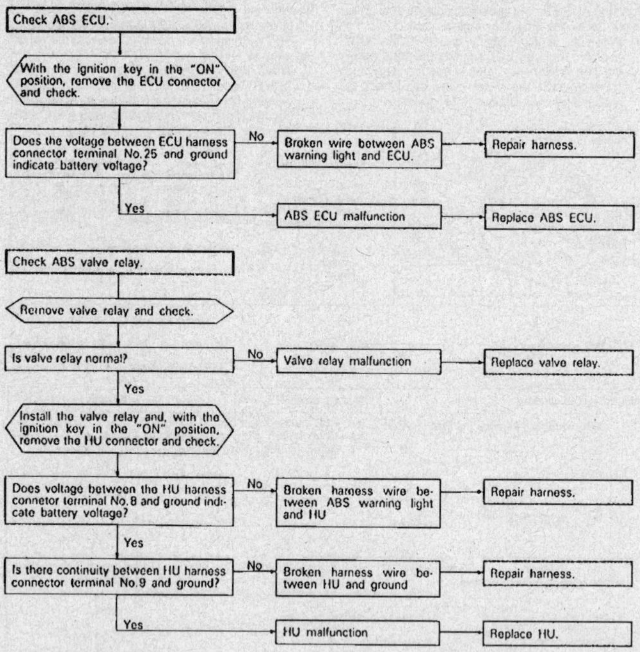
Check ABS ECU.
With the ignition key in the "ON" position, remove the ECU connector and check.
Does the voltage between ECU harness connector terminal No.25 and ground indicate battery voltage?
No
Broken wire between ABS warning light and ECU.
Repair harness.
Yes
ABS ECU malfunction
Replace ABS ECU.
Check ABS valve relay.
Remove valve relay and check.
Is valve relay normal?
No
Valve relay malfunction
Replace valve relay.
Yes
Install the valve relay and, with the ignition key in the "ON" position, remove the HU connector and check.
Does voltage between the HU harness connetor terminal No.8 and ground indicate battery voltage?
No
Broken harness wire between ABS warning light and HU
Repair harness.
Yes
Is there continuity between HU harness connector terminal No.9 and ground?
No
Broken harness wire between HU and ground
Repair harness.
Yes
HU malfunction
Replace HU.
MT402910026030X

Fig. 36 Diagnostic flowchart A (Part 3 of 3). Expo, 1993 Galant, 1993–94 Eclipse & 1993–95 3000GT

B	ABS warning light illuminated after the engine is started and remains on.

[Explanation]

This is the symptom when the ABS ECU does not power up due to broken ECU power circuit, etc., when the fail safe function operates and isolates the system or when the warning light drive circuit is short circuited.

[Hint]

Check the on-board diagnostic output and if there is no output voltage or if the ST and ABS ECU cannot communicate, there is a good possibility that power is not flowing to the ECU.

Caution

- **If there is no output of diagnostic trouble codes, there is a good possibility that the fail safe is functioning.**

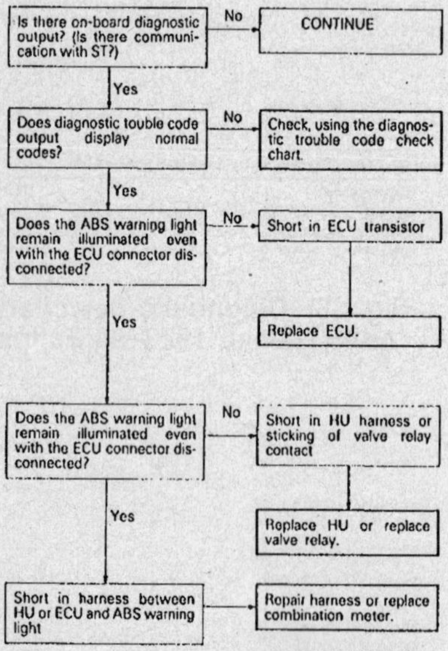
Is there on-board diagnostic output? (Is there communication with ST?)
No
CONTINUE
Yes
Does diagnostic touble code output display normal codes?
No
Check, using the diagnostic trouble code check chart.
Yes
Does the ABS warning light remain illuminated even with the ECU connector disconnected?
No
Short in ECU transistor
Replace ECU.
Yes
Does the ABS warning light remain illuminated even with the ECU connector disconnected?
No
Short in HU harness or sticking of valve relay contact
Replace HU or replace valve relay.
Yes
Short in harness between HU or ECU and ABS warning light
Repair harness or replace combination meter.
MT4029100027010X

Fig. 37 Diagnostic flowchart B (Part 1 of 2). Expo, 1993 Galant, 1993–94 Eclipse & 1993–95 3000GT

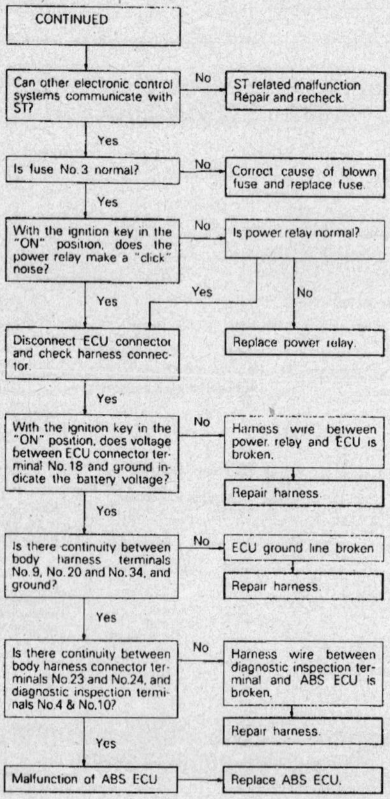
CONTINUED
Can other electronic control systems communicate with ST?
No
ST related malfunction Repair and recheck.
Yes
Is fuse No.3 normal?
No
Correct cause of blown fuse and replace fuse.
Yes
With the ignition key in the "ON" position, does the power relay make a "click" noise?
No
Is power relay normal?
Yes
No
Replace power relay.
Yes
Disconnect ECU connector and check harness connector.
Yes
With the ignition key in the "ON" position, does voltage between ECU connector terminal No.18 and ground indicate the battery voltage?
No
Harness wire between power relay and ECU is broken.
Repair harness.
Yes
Is there continuity between body harness terminals No.9, No.20 and No.34, and ground?
No
ECU ground line broken
Repair harness.
Yes
Is there continuity between body harness connector terminals No.23 and No.24, and diagnostic inspection terminals No.4 & No.10?
No
Harness wire between diagnostic inspection terminal and ABS ECU is broken.
Repair harness.
Yes
Malfunction of ABS ECU
Replace ABS ECU.
MT4029100027020X

Fig. 37 Diagnostic flowchart B (Part 2 of 2). Expo, 1993 Galant, 1993–94 Eclipse & 1993–95 3000GT

C	ABS warning light does not illuminate when ignition key is in "START" position.

[Explanation]

The ABS ECU uses the IG2 power source which is turned off in the "START" position. The ABS warning light uses the IG1 power source which is not turned off even in the "START" position. Consequently, in the "START" position, power is off and the ECU turns the valve relay OFF. If the warning light does not illuminate at this time, there is trouble in the warning light circuit on the valve relay side.

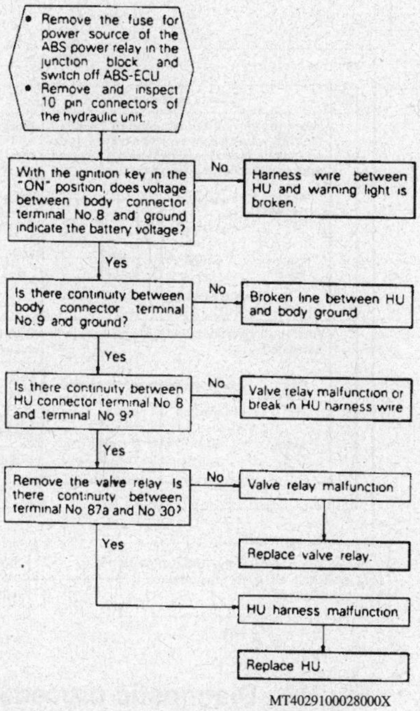

• Remove the fuse for power source of the ABS power relay in the junction block and switch off ABS-ECU
• Remove and inspect 10 pin connectors of the hydraulic unit.
With the ignition key in the "ON" position, does voltage between body connector terminal No.8 and ground indicate the battery voltage?
No
Harness wire between HU and warning light is broken.
Yes
Is there continuity between body connector terminal No.9 and ground?
No
Broken line between HU and body ground
Yes
Is there continuity between HU connector terminal No 8 and terminal No 9?
No
Valve relay malfunction or break in HU harness wire
Yes
Remove the valve relay. Is there continuity between terminal No 87a and No 30?
No
Valve relay malfunction
Yes
Replace valve relay.
HU harness malfunction
Replace HU.
MT4029100028000X

Fig. 38 Diagnostic flowchart C. Expo, 1993 Galant, 1993–94 Eclipse & 1993–95 3000GT

D	ABS warning light blinks once after the ignition key is turned to the "ON" position. It illuminates in the "START" position and blinks once again when turned to the "ON" position.

[Explanation]

When power flows, the ABS ECU turns on the warning light for approximately 1 sec. while it performs a valve relay test. If there is a break in the harness between the ECU and the warning light, the light illuminates only when the valve relay is off in the valve relay test, etc.

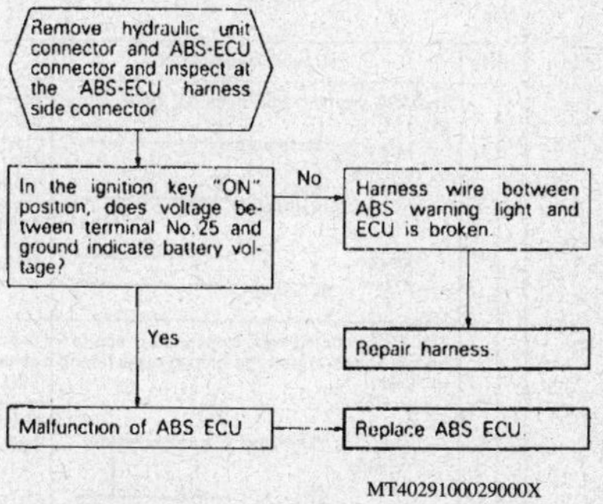

Remove hydraulic unit connector and ABS-ECU connector and inspect at the ABS-ECU harness side connector
In the ignition key "ON" position, does voltage between terminal No.25 and ground indicate battery voltage?
No
Harness wire between ABS warning light and ECU is broken.
Yes
Repair harness.
Malfunction of ABS ECU
Replace ABS ECU.
MT4029100029000X

Fig. 39 Diagnostic flowchart D. Expo, 1993 Galant, 1993–94 Eclipse & 1993–95 3000GT

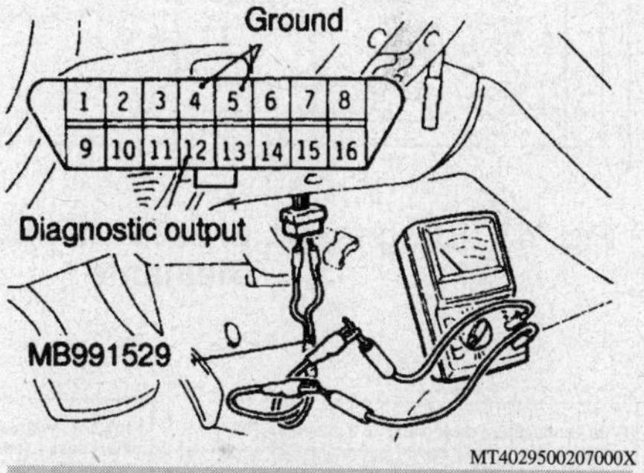

Ground
1 2 3 4 5 6 7 8
9 10 11 12 13 14 15 16
Diagnostic output
MB991529
MT4029500207000X

Fig. 42 Voltmeter diagnostic trouble code retrieval. 1995–96 Eclipse

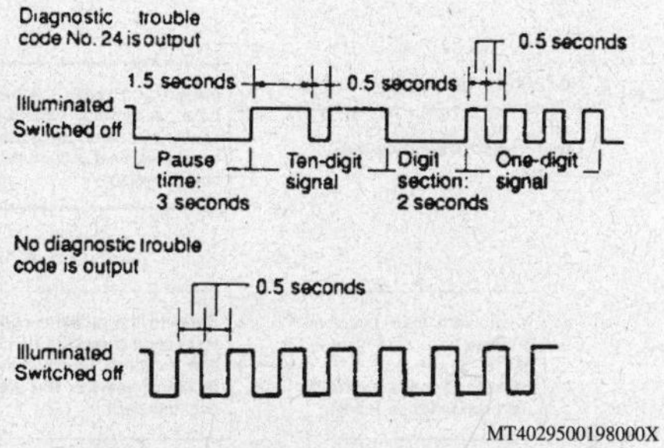

Diagnostic trouble code No. 24 is output
0.5 seconds
1.5 seconds
0.5 seconds
Illuminated
Switched off
Pause time: 3 seconds
Ten-digit signal
Digit section: 2 seconds
One-digit signal
No diagnostic trouble code is output
0.5 seconds
Illuminated
Switched off
MT4029500198000X

Fig. 40 ABS warning lamp diagnostic trouble code retrieval

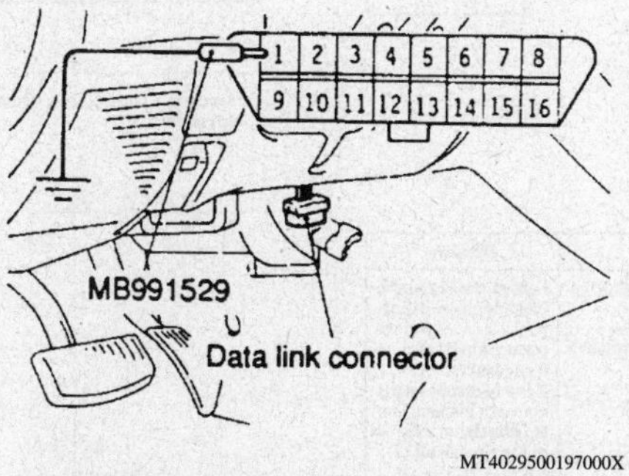

1 2 3 4 5 6 7 8
9 10 11 12 13 14 15 16
MB991529
Data link connector
MT4029500197000X

Fig. 41 Data link connector. 1995–96 Eclipse & 1996 3000GT

When the ignition key is turned to "ON", does the ABS warning light illuminate?

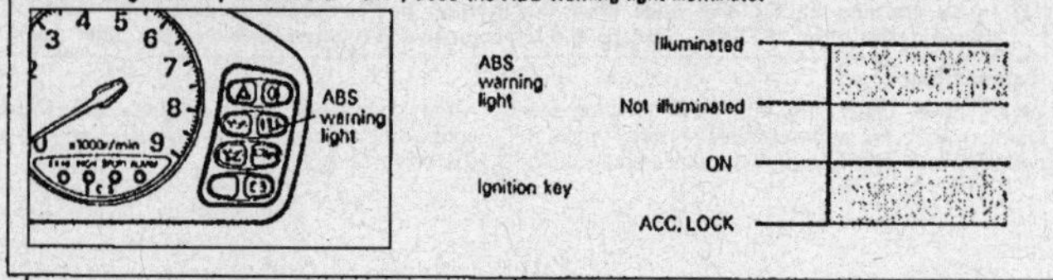
ABS
warning
light
Illuminated
Not illuminated
ON
Ignition key
ACC, LOCK

Yes / No

No.	Trouble symptom	Main cause	Remedy
1	The ABS warning light does not illuminate at all. (ABS warning light: Illuminated / Not illuminated; Ignition key: ON / ACC, LOCK)	Broken wire in the warning light power circuit (including blown fuse).	Inspect according to Chart A
		Warning light bulb failure.	
		Broken wire in two warning light drive circuits (both bulb relay and ABS-ECU).	
2	The ABS warning light switches off approximately 1 second after the ignition key is turned to "ON". (ABS warning light: Illuminated / Not illuminated; Ignition key: ON / ACC, LOCK)	Broken harness wire between the generator L terminal and the ABS-ECU.	Inspect according to Chart B
		Interface inside the ABS-ECU is faulty.	
3	The ABS warning light illuminates twice, but after that it remains switched off. (ABS warning light: Illuminated / Not illuminated; Ignition key: ON / ACC, LOCK)	Broken harness wire between the ABS warning light and the ABS-ECU.	Inspect according to Chart C
		Interface inside the ABS-ECU is faulty.	

MT4029100094010X

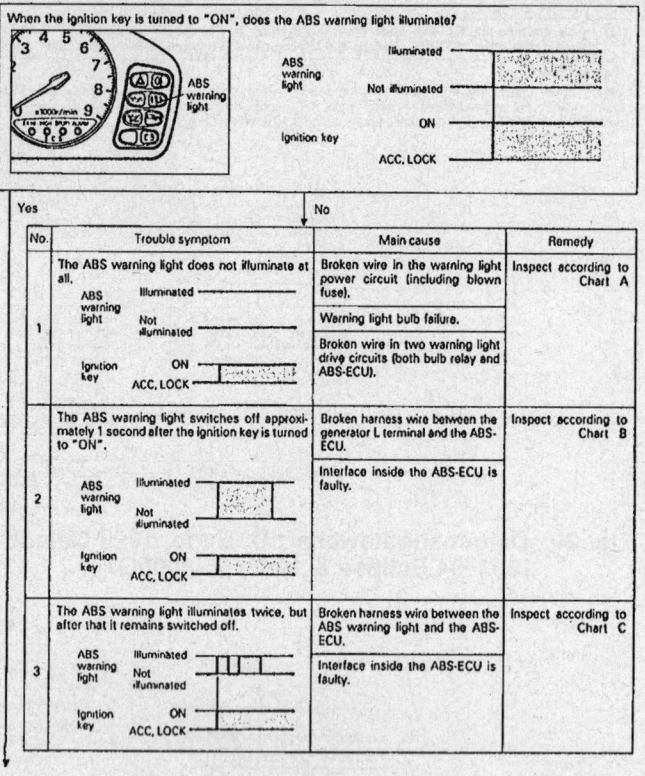

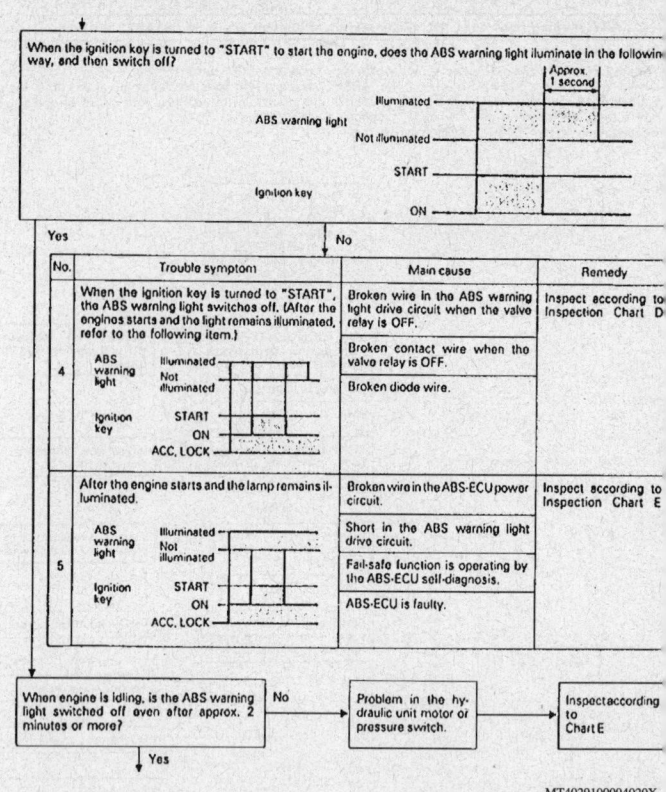

Fig. 43 Diagnostic procedure chart (Part 1 of 4). Diamante

When the ignition key is turned to "START" to start the engine, does the ABS warning light illuminate in the following way, and then switch off?

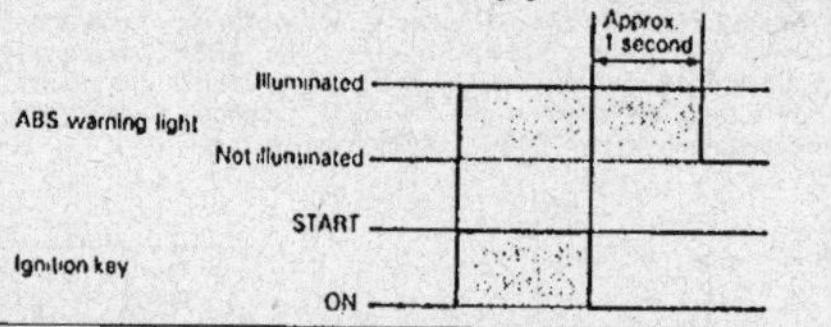
Approx.
1 second
Illuminated
ABS warning light
Not illuminated
START
Ignition key
ON

Yes / No

No.	Trouble symptom	Main cause	Remedy
4	When the ignition key is turned to "START", the ABS warning light switches off. (After the engines starts and the light remains illuminated, refer to the following item.) (ABS warning light: Illuminated / Not illuminated; Ignition key: START / ON / ACC, LOCK)	Broken wire in the ABS warning light drive circuit when the valve relay is OFF.	Inspect according to Inspection Chart D
		Broken contact wire when the valve relay is OFF.	
		Broken diode wire.	
5	After the engine starts and the lamp remains illuminated. (ABS warning light: Illuminated / Not illuminated; Ignition key: START / ON / ACC, LOCK)	Broken wire in the ABS-ECU power circuit.	Inspect according to Inspection Chart E
		Short in the ABS warning light drive circuit.	
		Fail-safe function is operating by the ABS-ECU self-diagnosis.	
		ABS-ECU is faulty.	

When engine is idling, is the ABS warning light switched off even after approx. 2 minutes or more?
- No → Problem in the hydraulic unit motor or pressure switch. → Inspect according to Chart E
- Yes ↓

MT4029100094020X

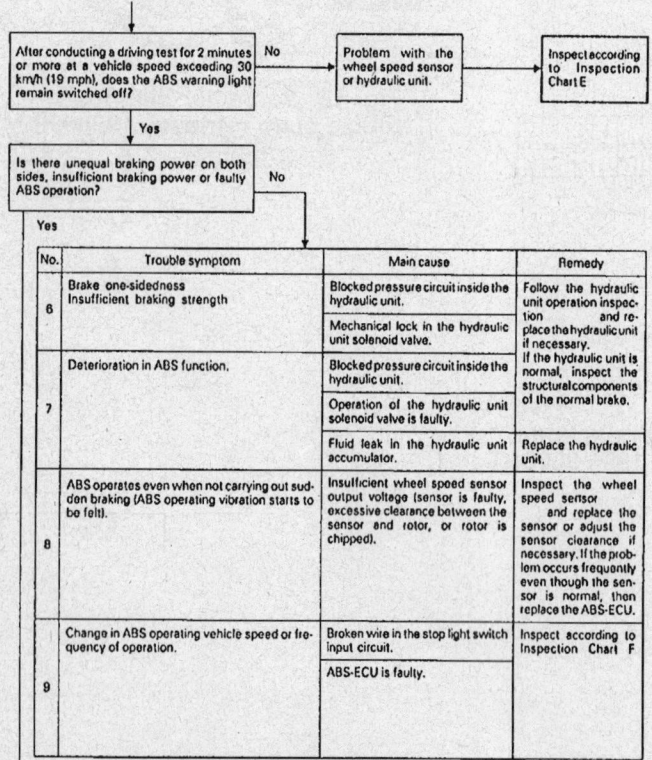

Fig. 43 Diagnostic procedure chart (Part 2 of 4). Diamante

After conducting a driving test for 2 minutes or more at a vehicle speed exceeding 30 km/h (19 mph), does the ABS warning light remain switched off?
- No → Problem with the wheel speed sensor or hydraulic unit. → Inspect according to Inspection Chart E
- Yes ↓

Is there unequal braking power on both sides, insufficient braking power or faulty ABS operation?
- No ↓
- Yes ↓

No.	Trouble symptom	Main cause	Remedy
6	Brake one-sidedness Insufficient braking strength	Blocked pressure circuit inside the hydraulic unit.	Follow the hydraulic unit operation inspection and replace the hydraulic unit if necessary. If the hydraulic unit is normal, inspect the structural components of the normal brake.
		Mechanical lock in the hydraulic unit solenoid valve.	
7	Deterioration in ABS function.	Blocked pressure circuit inside the hydraulic unit.	
		Operation of the hydraulic unit solenoid valve is faulty.	
		Fluid leak in the hydraulic unit accumulator.	Replace the hydraulic unit.
8	ABS operates even when not carrying out sudden braking (ABS operating vibration starts to be felt).	Insufficient wheel speed sensor output voltage (sensor is faulty, excessive clearance between the sensor and rotor, or rotor is chipped).	Inspect the wheel speed sensor and replace the sensor or adjust the sensor clearance if necessary. If the problem occurs frequently even though the sensor is normal, then replace the ABS-ECU.
9	Change in ABS operating vehicle speed or frequency of operation.	Broken wire in the stop light switch input circuit.	Inspect according to Inspection Chart F
		ABS-ECU is faulty.	

MT4029100094030X

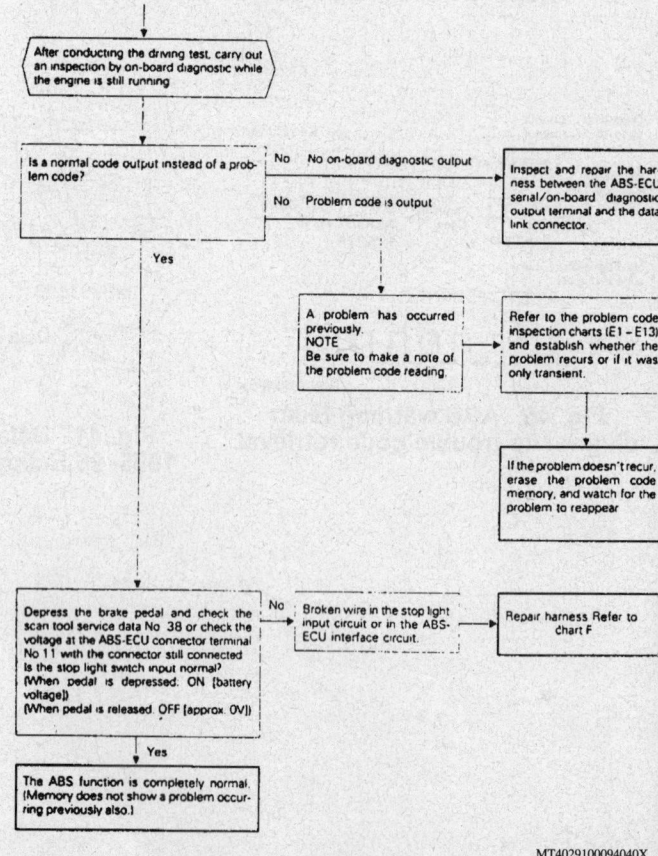

Fig. 43 Diagnostic procedure chart (Part 3 of 4). Diamante

After conducting the driving test, carry out an inspection by on-board diagnostic while the engine is still running

Is a normal code output instead of a problem code?
- No — No on-board diagnostic output → Inspect and repair the harness between the ABS-ECU serial/on-board diagnostic output terminal and the data link connector.
- No — Problem code is output → A problem has occurred previously. NOTE Be sure to make a note of the problem code reading. → Refer to the problem code inspection charts (E1 – E13) and establish whether the problem recurs or if it was only transient. → If the problem doesn't recur, erase the problem code memory, and watch for the problem to reappear
- Yes ↓

Depress the brake pedal and check the scan tool service data No 38 or check the voltage at the ABS-ECU connector terminal No 11 with the connector still connected Is the stop light switch input normal? (When pedal is depressed: ON [battery voltage]) (When pedal is released. OFF [approx. 0V])
- No → Broken wire in the stop light input circuit or in the ABS-ECU interface circuit. → Repair harness Refer to chart F
- Yes ↓

The ABS function is completely normal. (Memory does not show a problem occurring previously also.)

MT4029100094040X

Fig. 43 Diagnostic procedure chart (Part 4 of 4). Diamante

A	When ignition key is turned to "ON", ABS warning light does not illuminate

Comment: When power is supplied to the ABS-ECU, the valve relay changes from OFF to ONOFFON by the initial check, and thus even if there is a problem with the light illumination circuit that is driven by the ABS-ECU, the light will illuminate twice when the valve relay is OFF. Accordingly, there is a strong possibility that the problem is in the light bulb or in the power supply to the light.

Hint: When other warning lights also do not illuminate, the cause is probably a blown fuse.

MT4029100095010X

Fig. 44 Diagnostic flowchart A (Part 1 of 3). Diamante

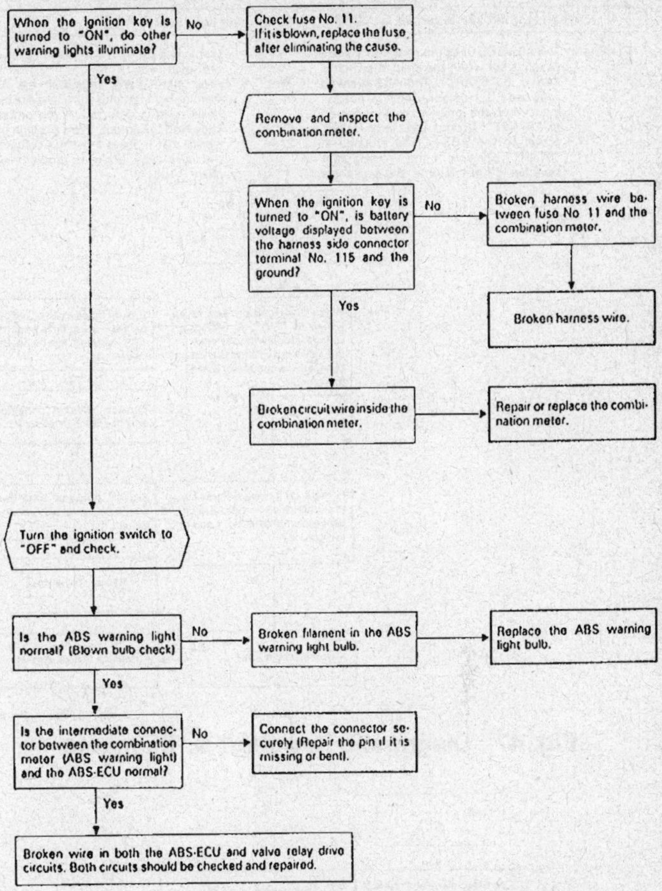
When the ignition key is turned to "ON", do other warning lights illuminate?
No
Check fuse No. 11. If it is blown, replace the fuse after eliminating the cause.
Yes
Remove and inspect the combination meter.
When the ignition key is turned to "ON", is battery voltage displayed between the harness side connector terminal No. 115 and the ground?
No
Broken harness wire between fuse No 11 and the combination meter.
Broken harness wire.
Yes
Broken circuit wire inside the combination meter.
Repair or replace the combination meter.
Turn the ignition switch to "OFF" and check.
Is the ABS warning light normal? (Blown bulb check)
No
Broken filament in the ABS warning light bulb.
Replace the ABS warning light bulb.
Yes
Is the intermediate connector between the combination meter (ABS warning light) and the ABS-ECU normal?
No
Connect the connector securely (Repair the pin if it is missing or bent).
Yes
Broken wire in both the ABS-ECU and valve relay drive circuits. Both circuits should be checked and repaired.

MT4029100095020X

Fig. 44 Diagnostic flowchart A (Part 2 of 3). Diamante

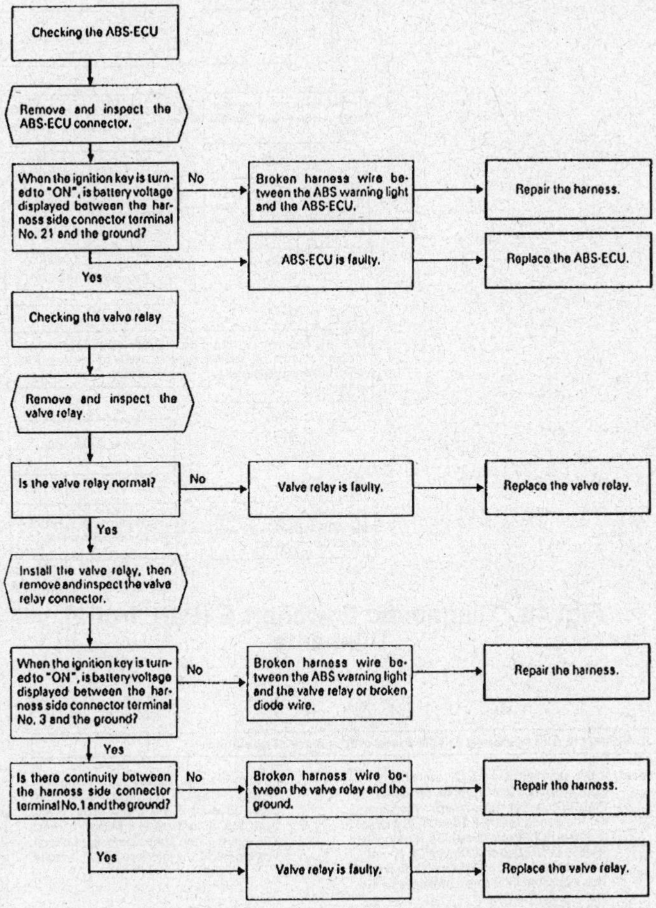
Checking the ABS-ECU
Remove and inspect the ABS-ECU connector.
When the ignition key is turned to "ON", is battery voltage displayed between the harness side connector terminal No. 21 and the ground?
No
Broken harness wire between the ABS warning light and the ABS-ECU.
Repair the harness.
ABS-ECU is faulty.
Replace the ABS-ECU.
Yes
Checking the valve relay
Remove and inspect the valve relay.
Is the valve relay normal?
No
Valve relay is faulty.
Replace the valve relay.
Yes
Install the valve relay, then remove and inspect the valve relay connector.
When the ignition key is turned to "ON", is battery voltage displayed between the harness side connector terminal No. 3 and the ground?
No
Broken harness wire between the ABS warning light and the valve relay or broken diode wire.
Repair the harness.
Yes
Is there continuity between the harness side connector terminal No. 1 and the ground?
No
Broken harness wire between the valve relay and the ground.
Repair the harness.
Yes
Valve relay is faulty.
Replace the valve relay.

MT4029100095030X

Fig. 44 Diagnostic flowchart A (Part 3 of 3). Diamante

C	The ABS warning light illuminates twice after the ignition key is turned to "ON", but after that it remains switched off

Comment: The ABS-ECU causes the ABS warning light to illuminate during the initial check. The valve relay changes from OFF to OFF→ON by the initial check, and if there is a broken wire in the light drive circuit from the ABS-ECU, the light will illuminate when the valve relay is OFF. Accordingly, if the ignition key is "ON", and the light illuminates twice and then switches off, there is a problem in the ABS-ECU drive circuit.

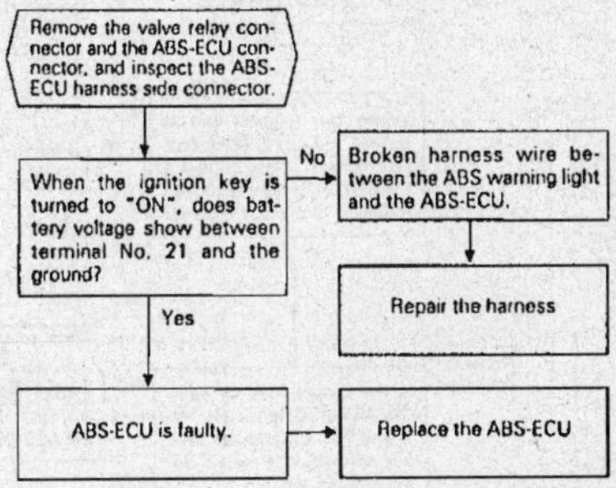
Remove the valve relay connector and the ABS-ECU connector, and inspect the ABS-ECU harness side connector.
When the ignition key is turned to "ON", does battery voltage show between terminal No. 21 and the ground?
No
Broken harness wire between the ABS warning light and the ABS-ECU.
Repair the harness
Yes
ABS-ECU is faulty.
Replace the ABS-ECU

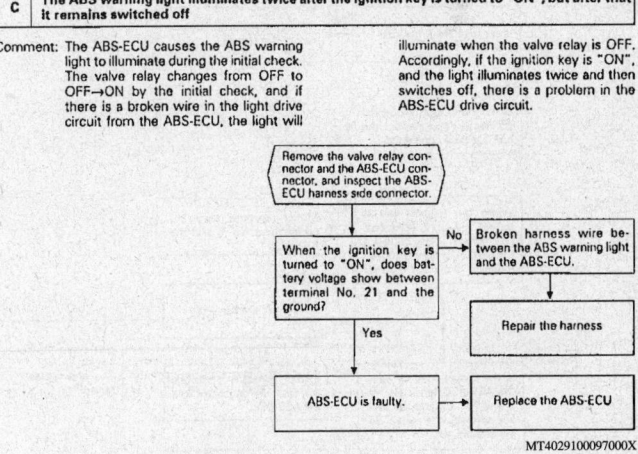

MT4029100097000X

Fig. 46 Diagnostic flowchart C. Diamante

D	When ignition key is turned to "START", ABS warning light switches off

Comment: The ABS-ECU uses the power to the IG2 which is cut when the ignition switch is turned to "START". The ABS warning light uses IG1 power which is not cut even when the ignition switch is turned to "START". Accordingly, because the power to the ABS-ECU is stopped in "START" position, if the warning light switches off at this time, the cause is a problem in the light illumination circuit in the valve relay.

Hint: After starting the engine, if the ABS warning light remains illuminated, a diagnosis code is detected. If the problem code No.51 is output, there is a high possibility that there is a melted contact in the valve relay. (Refer to problem code chart E-10.)

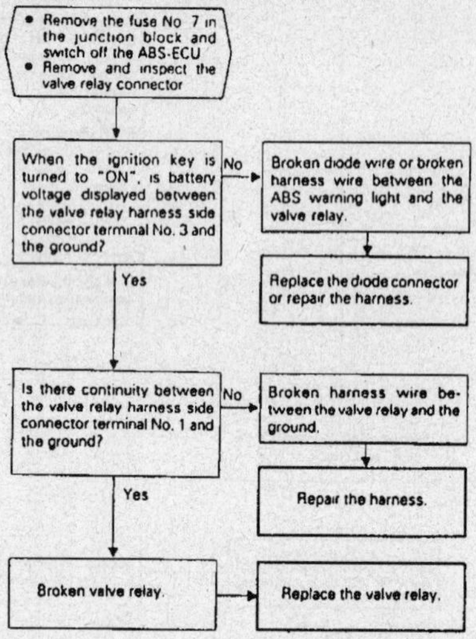

• Remove the fuse No. 7 in the junction block and switch off the ABS-ECU
• Remove and inspect the valve relay connector
When the ignition key is turned to "ON", is battery voltage displayed between the valve relay harness side connector terminal No. 3 and the ground?
No
Broken diode wire or broken harness wire between the ABS warning light and the valve relay.
Replace the diode connector or repair the harness.
Yes
Is there continuity between the valve relay harness side connector terminal No. 1 and the ground?
No
Broken harness wire between the valve relay and the ground.
Repair the harness.
Yes
Broken valve relay.
Replace the valve relay.

MT4029100098000X

Fig. 47 Diagnostic flowchart D. Diamante

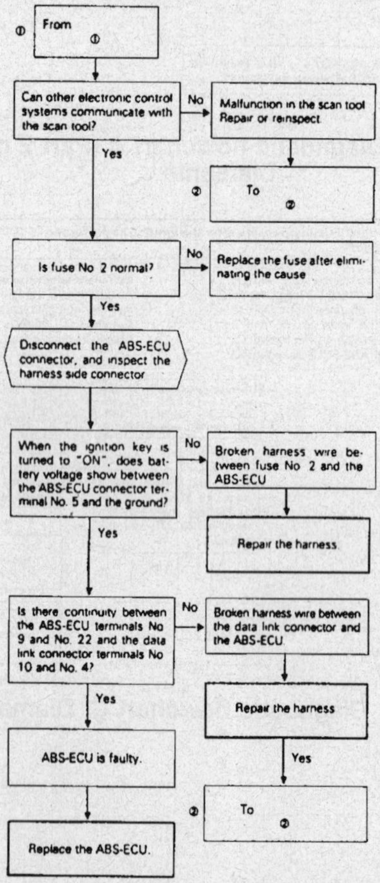

① From ①
Can other electronic control systems communicate with the scan tool?
No
Malfunction in the scan tool Repair or reinspect
② To ②
Yes
Is fuse No. 2 normal?
No
Replace the fuse after eliminating the cause
Yes
Disconnect the ABS-ECU connector, and inspect the harness side connector
When the ignition key is turned to "ON", does battery voltage show between the ABS-ECU connector terminal No. 5 and the ground?
No
Broken harness wire between fuse No. 2 and the ABS-ECU
Repair the harness.
Yes
Is there continuity between the ABS-ECU terminals No. 9 and No. 22 and the data link connector terminals No. 10 and No. 4?
No
Broken harness wire between the data link connector and the ABS-ECU.
Repair the harness
Yes
ABS-ECU is faulty.
Yes
② To ②
Replace the ABS-ECU.

MT4029100099020X

Fig. 48 Diagnostic flowchart E (Part 2 of 2). Diamante

E	Even after the engine is stated, the ABS warning light remains illuminated

Comment: This symptom occurs when the ABS-ECU is not functioning due to a broken wire, etc., in the ABS-ECU power circuit, when the fail-safe function is operating to isolate the system, or when there is a isolate the system, or when there is a short in the warning light drive circuit.

Hint: Check the on-board diagnostic output and if there is no output voltage, or the scan tool and the ABS-ECU cannot communicate, then there is a high possil that power is not being supplied to ABS-ECU.

Caution

If a problem code is output, there is a h possibility that the fail-safe function is operati In this case, to check if there is a current proble the memory should be temporarily erased, the engine should be restarted.

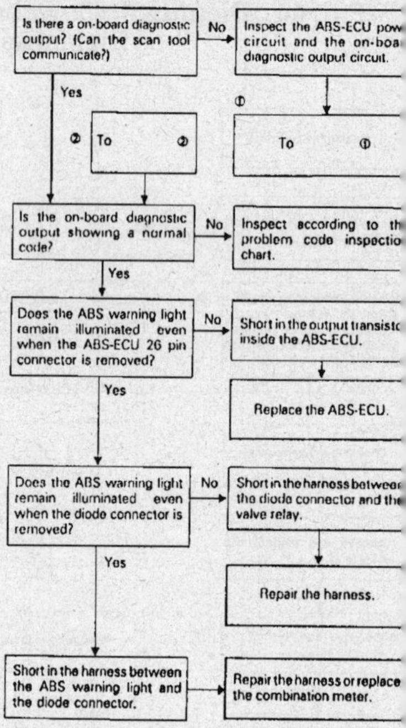

Is there a on-board diagnostic output? (Can the scan tool communicate?)
No
Inspect the ABS-ECU pow circuit and the on-boa diagnostic output circuit.
①
To ①
Yes
② To ②
Is the on-board diagnostic output showing a normal code?
No
Inspect according to th problem code inspectio chart.
Yes
Does the ABS warning light remain illuminated even when the ABS-ECU 26 pin connector is removed?
No
Short in the output transistc inside the ABS-ECU.
Replace the ABS-ECU.
Yes
Does the ABS warning light remain illuminated even when the diode connector is removed?
No
Short in the harness betweer the diode connector and the valve relay.
Repair the harness.
Yes
Short in the harness between the ABS warning light and the diode connector.
Repair the harness or replace the combination meter.

MT4029100099010

Fig. 48 Diagnostic flowchart E (Part 1 of 2). Diamante

F	Change in ABS operating vehicle speed or frequency of operation

Comment: If the stop light switch ON signal is not input even once after the engine is started, the ABS control commences when the vehicle speed reaches 15 km/h (9 mph) or above. (Control is possible if the signal is input even once and the vehicle speed is approximately 6 km/h (4 mph) or above.) This symptom indicates a broken wire in the stop light switch.

Hint: When the stop light is illuminating normally, if the scan tool service data shows No. 38 even if the brake pedal is depressed, then there is a broken harness wire in the stop light switch input circuit, or the ABS-ECU interface circuit is faulty.

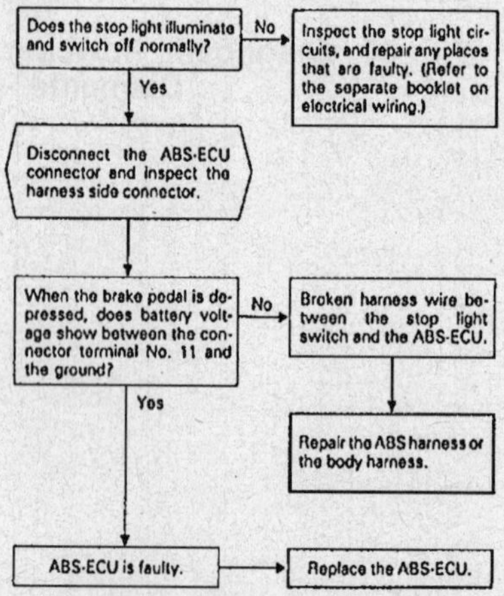

Does the stop light illuminate and switch off normally?
No
Inspect the stop light circuits, and repair any places that are faulty. (Refer to the separate booklet on electrical wiring.)
Yes
Disconnect the ABS-ECU connector and inspect the harness side connector.
When the brake pedal is depressed, does battery voltage show between the connector terminal No. 11 and the ground?
No
Broken harness wire between the stop light switch and the ABS-ECU.
Repair the ABS harness or the body harness.
Yes
ABS-ECU is faulty.
Replace the ABS-ECU.

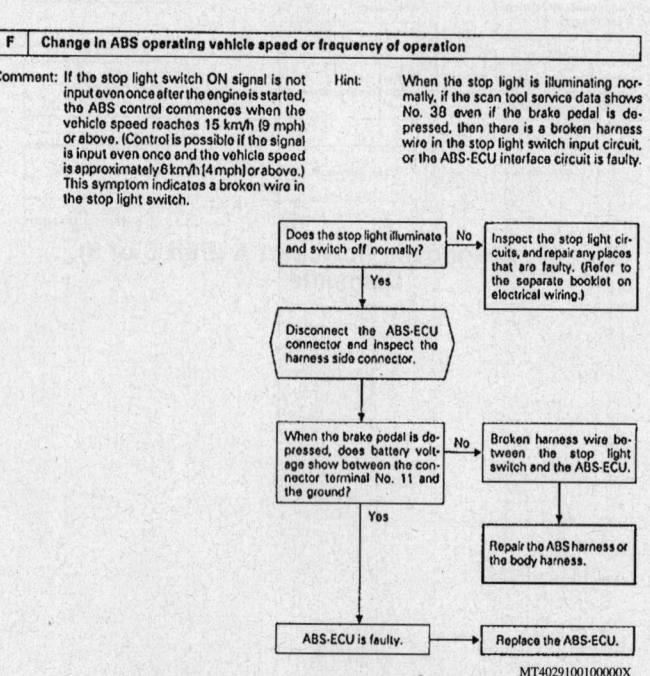

MT4029100100000X

Fig. 49 Diagnostic flowchart F. Diamante

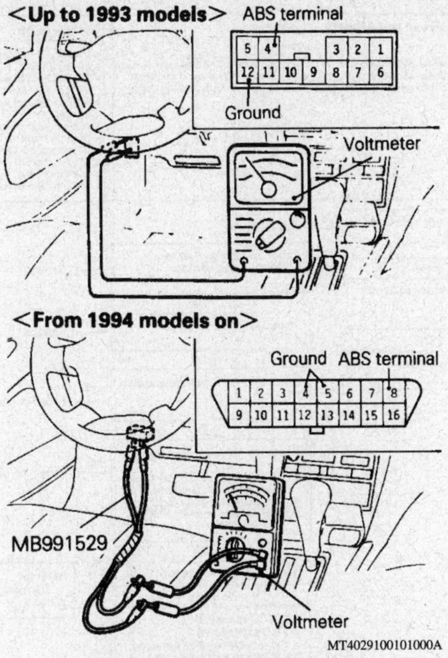
<Up to 1993 models>
ABS terminal
5 4 3 2 1
12 11 10 9 8 7 6
Ground
Voltmeter
<From 1994 models on>
Ground
ABS terminal
1 2 3 4 5 6 7 8
9 10 11 12 13 14 15 16
MB991529
Voltmeter

MT4029100101000A

Fig. 50 Diagnostic check connector. Diamante

Trouble symptom			Inspection procedure No.
When the ignition key is turned to "ON" (engine stopped), the ABS warning light does not illuminate.	ABS warning light	Illuminated / Not illuminated	1
	Ignition key	ON / ACC, LOCK	
After the engine starts, the light remains illuminated.	ABS warning light	Illuminated / Not illuminated	2
	Ignition key	START / ON / ACC, LOCK	
The ABS warning light switches off approximately 1.5 second after the ignition key is turned to "ON". (Engine not running)	ABS warning light	Illuminated / Not illuminated	3
	Ignition key	ON / ACC, LOCK	
After the ignition key is turned to "ON", the ABS warning light illuminates twice, but after that it remains switched off.	ABS warning light	Illuminated / Not illuminated	4
	Ignition key	ON / ACC, LOCK	
When the ignition key is turned to "START", the ABS warning light switches off.	ABS warning light	Illuminated / Not illuminated	5
	Ignition key	START / ON / ACC, LOCK	
Faulty ABS operation	Unequal braking power on both sides		6
	Insufficient braking power		
	ABS operates under normal braking conditions		
	ABS operates before vehicle stops under normal braking conditions		
	Large brake pedal vibration when ABS operates		
	Large amount of skidding when ABS operates (ABS does not operate properly)		7
No on-board diagnostic output (no communication with scan tool)*1			8
No communication with scan tool*2	Impossible for all systems		9
	Impossible only for ABS		10

NOTE
*1: 1993 models
*2: From 1994 models

MT4029100114000A

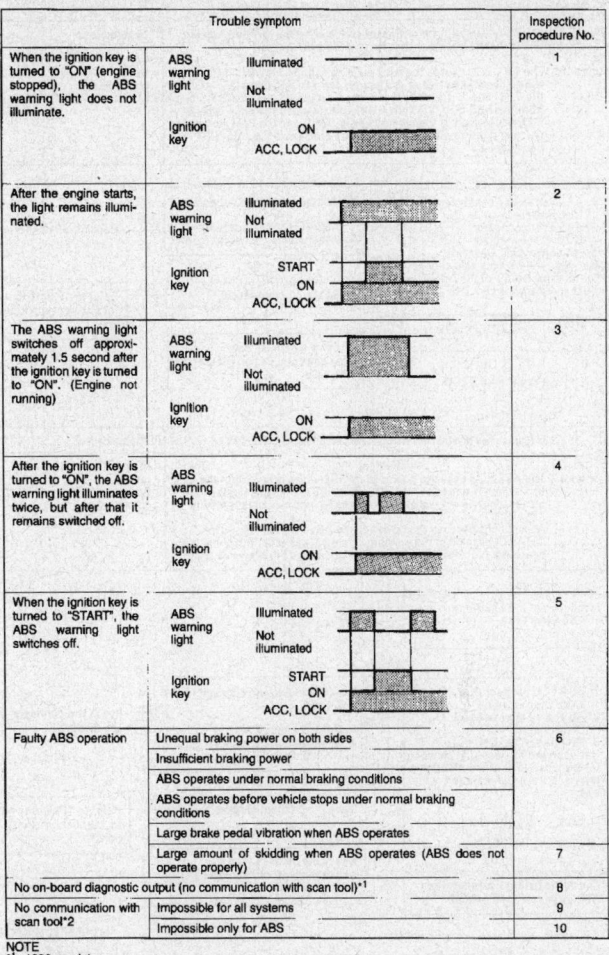

Fig. 51 Trouble symptom inspection chart. Mirage

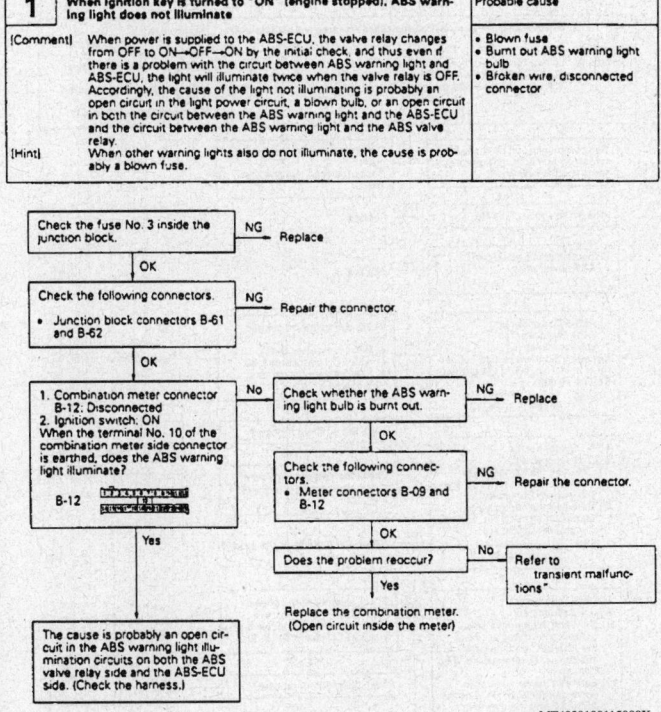

1 When ignition key is turned to "ON" (engine stopped), ABS warning light does not illuminate	Probable cause
[Comment] When power is supplied to the ABS-ECU, the valve relay changes from OFF to ON→OFF→ON by the initial check, and thus even if there is a problem with the circuit between ABS warning light and ABS-ECU, the light will illuminate twice when the valve relay is OFF. Accordingly, the cause of the light not illuminating is probably an open circuit in the light power circuit, a blown bulb, or an open circuit in both the circuit between the ABS warning light and the ABS-ECU and the circuit between the ABS warning light and the ABS valve relay. [Hint] When other warning lights also do not illuminate, the cause is probably a blown fuse.	• Blown fuse • Burnt out ABS warning light bulb • Broken wire, disconnected connector

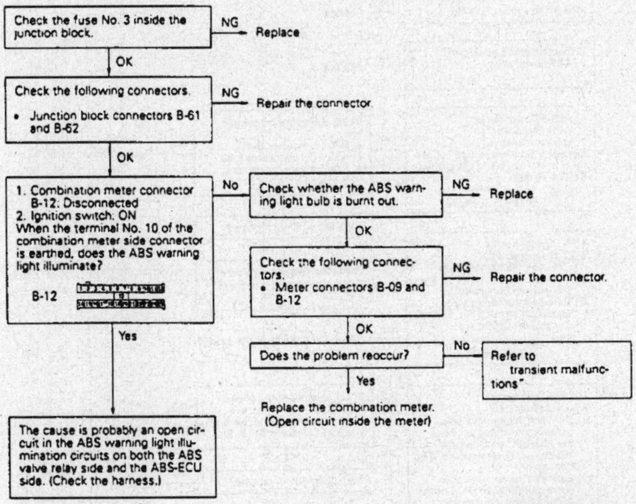
Check the fuse No. 3 inside the junction block.
NG
Replace
OK
Check the following connectors.
• Junction block connectors B-61 and B-62
NG
Repair the connector.
OK
1. Combination meter connector B-12: Disconnected
2. Ignition switch: ON
When the terminal No. 10 of the combination meter side connector is earthed, does the ABS warning light illuminate?
B-12
No
Check whether the ABS warning light bulb is burnt out.
NG
Replace
OK
Check the following connectors.
• Meter connectors B-09 and B-12
NG
Repair the connector.
OK
Does the problem reoccur?
No
Refer to transient malfunctions"
Yes
Replace the combination meter. (Open circuit inside the meter)
Yes
The cause is probably an open circuit in the ABS warning light illumination circuits on both the ABS valve relay side and the ABS-ECU side. (Check the harness.)

MT4029100115000X

Fig. 52 Symptom inspection chart 1. Mirage

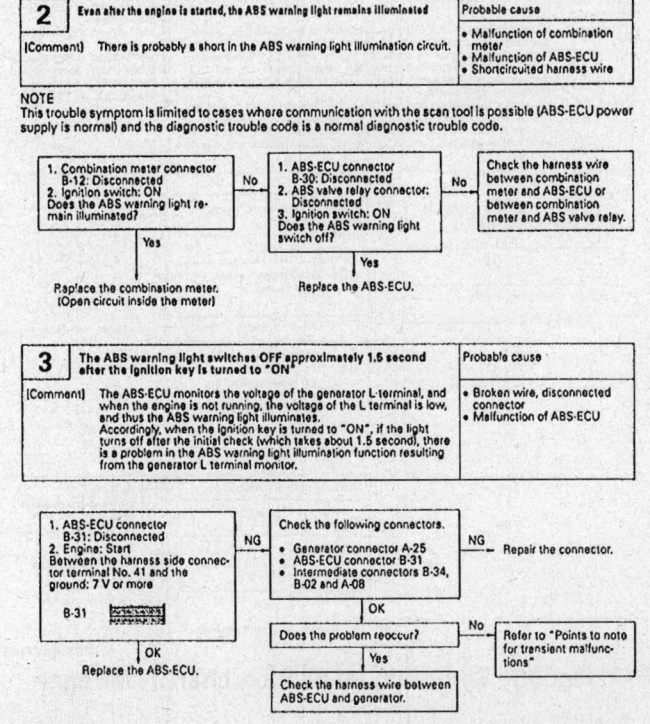

2 Even after the engine is started, the ABS warning light remains illuminated	Probable cause
[Comment] There is probably a short in the ABS warning light illumination circuit.	• Malfunction of combination meter • Malfunction of ABS-ECU • Shortcircuited harness wire

NOTE
This trouble symptom is limited to cases where communication with the scan tool is possible (ABS-ECU power supply is normal) and the diagnostic trouble code is a normal diagnostic trouble code.

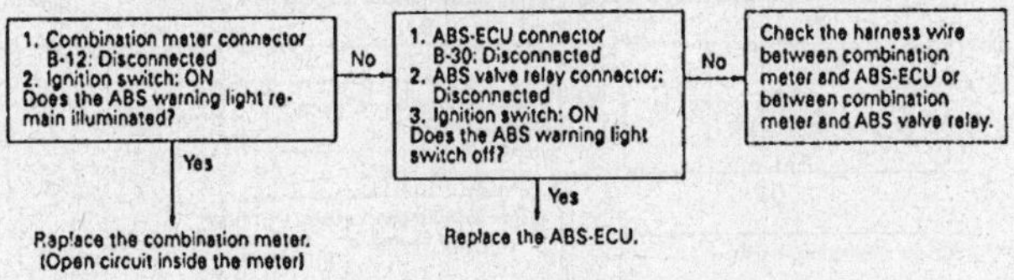
1. Combination meter connector B-12: Disconnected
2. Ignition switch: ON
Does the ABS warning light remain illuminated?
No
1. ABS-ECU connector B-30: Disconnected
2. ABS valve relay connector: Disconnected
3. Ignition switch: ON
Does the ABS warning light switch off?
No
Check the harness wire between combination meter and ABS-ECU or between combination meter and ABS valve relay.
Yes
Replace the combination meter. (Open circuit inside the meter)
Yes
Replace the ABS-ECU.

3 The ABS warning light switches OFF approximately 1.5 second after the ignition key is turned to "ON"	Probable cause
[Comment] The ABS-ECU monitors the voltage of the generator L-terminal, and when the engine is not running, the voltage of the L terminal is low, and thus the ABS warning light illuminates. Accordingly, when the ignition key is turned to "ON", if the light turns off after the initial check (which takes about 1.5 second), there is a problem in the ABS warning light illumination function resulting from the generator L terminal monitor.	• Broken wire, disconnected connector • Malfunction of ABS-ECU

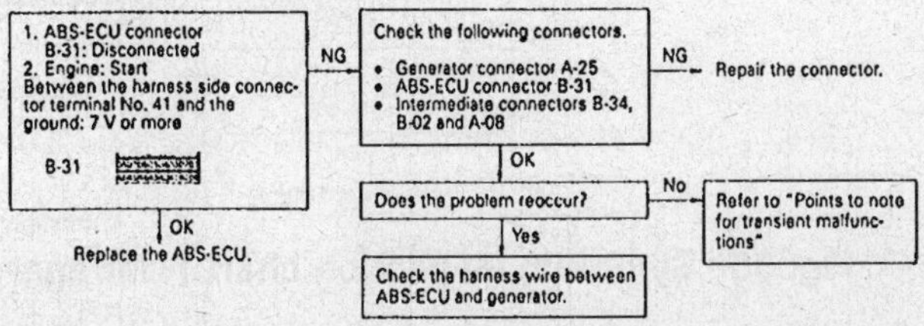
1. ABS-ECU connector B-31: Disconnected
2. Engine: Start
Between the harness side connector terminal No. 41 and the ground: 7 V or more
B-31
NG
Check the following connectors.
• Generator connector A-25
• ABS-ECU connector B-31
• Intermediate connectors B-34, B-02 and A-08
NG
Repair the connector.
OK
Does the problem reoccur?
No
Refer to "Points to note for transient malfunctions"
Yes
Check the harness wire between ABS-ECU and generator.
OK
Replace the ABS-ECU.

MT4029100116000X

Fig. 53 Symptom inspection charts 2 & 3. Mirage

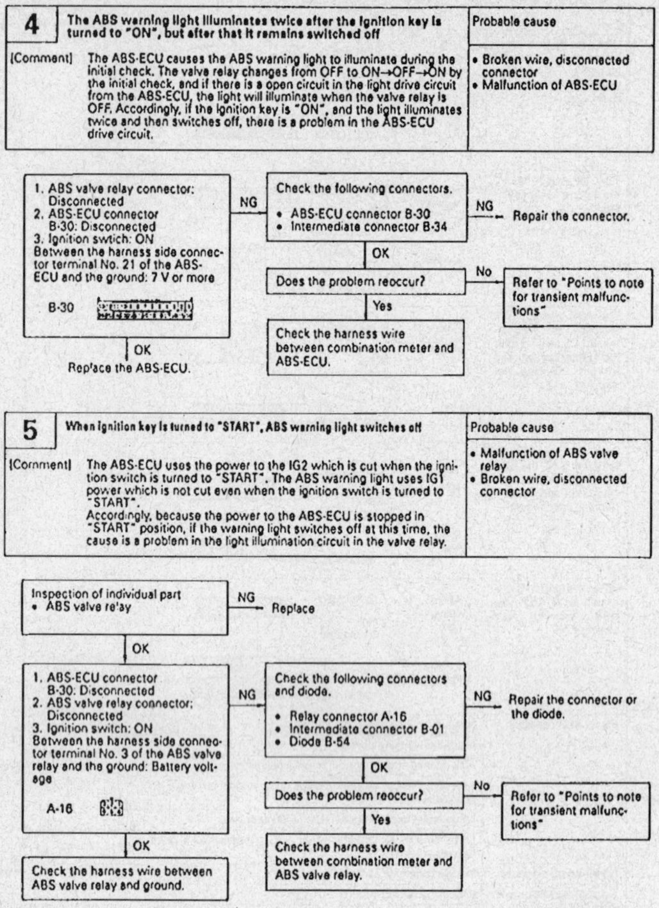
4
The ABS warning light illuminates twice after the ignition key is turned to "ON", but after that it remains switched off
Probable cause
[Comment] The ABS-ECU causes the ABS warning light to illuminate during the initial check. The valve relay changes from OFF to ON→OFF→ON by the initial check, and if there is a open circuit in the light drive circuit from the ABS-ECU, the light will illuminate when the valve relay is OFF. Accordingly, if the ignition key is "ON", and the light illuminates twice and then switches off, there is a problem in the ABS-ECU drive circuit.
• Broken wire, disconnected connector
• Malfunction of ABS-ECU
1. ABS valve relay connector: Disconnected
2. ABS-ECU connector B-30: Disconnected
3. Ignition swtich: ON
Between the harness side connector terminal No. 21 of the ABS-ECU and the ground: 7 V or more
B-30
NG
Check the following connectors.
• ABS-ECU connector B-30
• Intermediate connector B-34
NG
Repair the connector.
OK
Does the problem reoccur?
No
Refer to "Points to note for transient malfunctions"
Yes
Check the harness wire between combination meter and ABS-ECU.
OK
Replace the ABS-ECU.
5
When ignition key is turned to "START", ABS warning light switches off
Probable cause
[Comment] The ABS-ECU uses the power to the IG2 which is cut when the ignition switch is turned to "START". The ABS warning light uses IG1 power which is not cut even when the ignition switch is turned to "START".
Accordingly, because the power to the ABS-ECU is stopped in "START" position, if the warning light switches off at this time, the cause is a problem in the light illumination circuit in the valve relay.
• Malfunction of ABS valve relay
• Broken wire, disconnected connector
Inspection of individual part
• ABS valve relay
NG
Replace
OK
1. ABS-ECU connector B-30: Disconnected
2. ABS valve relay connector: Disconnected
3. Ignition switch: ON
Between the harness side connector terminal No. 3 of the ABS valve relay and the ground: Battery voltage
A-16
NG
Check the following connectors and diode.
• Relay connector A-16
• Intermediate connector B-01
• Diode B-54
NG
Repair the connector or the diode.
OK
Does the problem reoccur?
No
Refer to "Points to note for transient malfunctions"
Yes
Check the harness wire between combination meter and ABS valve relay.
OK
Check the harness wire between ABS valve relay and ground.
MT4029100117000X

Fig. 54 Symptom inspection chart 4 & 5. Mirage

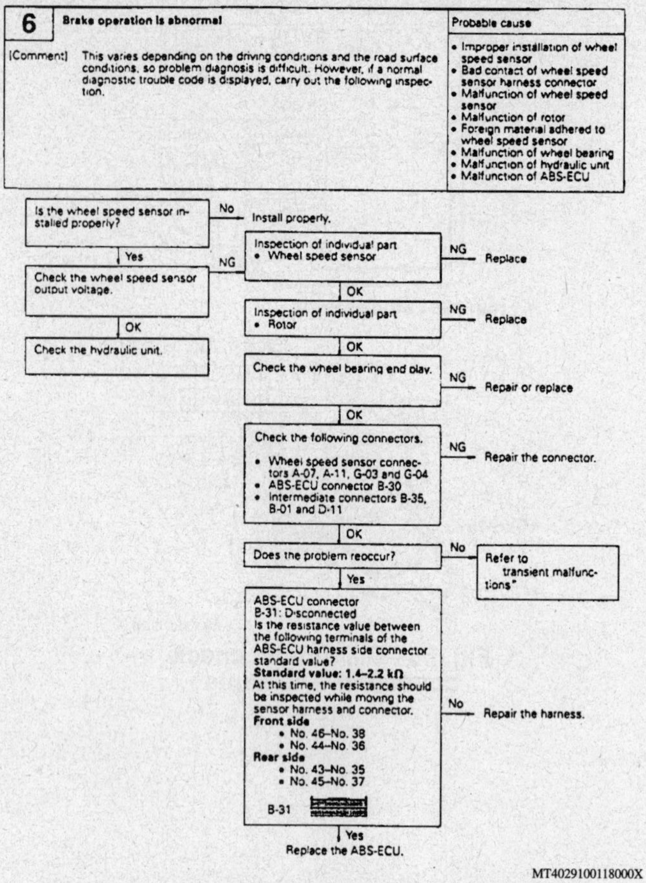
6
Brake operation is abnormal
Probable cause
[Comment] This varies depending on the driving conditions and the road surface conditions, so problem diagnosis is difficult. However, if a normal diagnostic trouble code is displayed, carry out the following inspection.
• Improper installation of wheel speed sensor
• Bad contact of wheel speed sensor harness connector
• Malfunction of wheel speed sensor
• Malfunction of rotor
• Foreign material adhered to wheel speed sensor
• Malfunction of wheel bearing
• Malfunction of hydraulic unit
• Malfunction of ABS-ECU
Is the wheel speed sensor installed properly?
No
Install properly.
Yes
Check the wheel speed sensor output voltage.
NG
OK
Check the hydraulic unit.
Inspection of individual part
• Wheel speed sensor
NG
Replace
OK
Inspection of individual part
• Rotor
NG
Replace
OK
Check the wheel bearing end play.
NG
Repair or replace
OK
Check the following connectors.
• Wheel speed sensor connectors A-07, A-11, G-03 and G-04
• ABS-ECU connector B-30
• Intermediate connectors B-35, B-01 and D-11
NG
Repair the connector.
OK
Does the problem reoccur?
No
Refer to transient malfunctions"
Yes
ABS-ECU connector B-31: Disconnected
Is the resistance value between the following terminals of the ABS-ECU harness side connector standard value?
Standard value: 1.4–2.2 kΩ
At this time, the resistance should be inspected while moving the sensor harness and connector.
Front side
• No. 46–No. 38
• No. 44–No. 36
Rear side
• No. 43–No. 35
• No. 45–No. 37
B-31
No
Repair the harness.
Yes
Replace the ABS-ECU.
MT4029100118000X

Fig. 55 Symptom inspection chart 6. Mirage

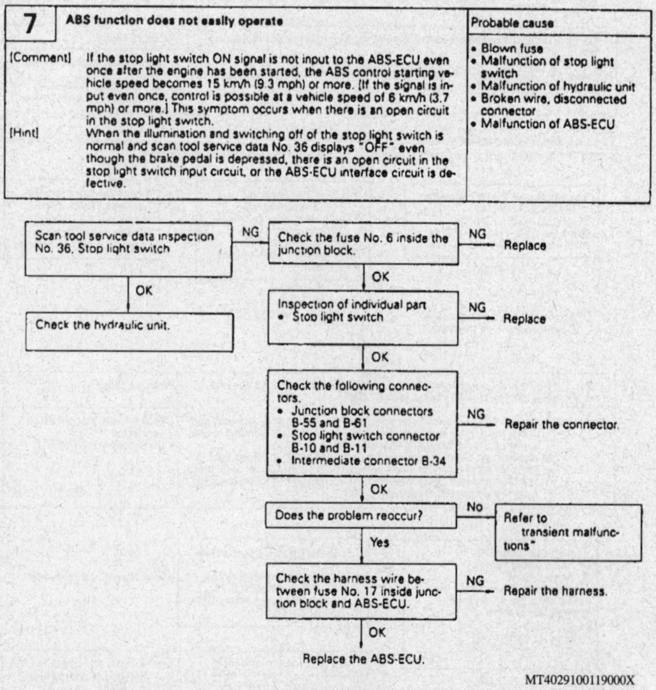
7
ABS function does not easily operate
Probable cause
[Comment] If the stop light switch ON signal is not input to the ABS-ECU even once after the engine has been started, the ABS control starting vehicle speed becomes 15 km/h (9.3 mph) or more. [If the signal is input even once, control is possible at a vehicle speed of 6 km/h (3.7 mph) or more.] This symptom occurs when there is an open circuit in the stop light switch.
[Hint] When the illumination and switching off of the stop light switch is normal and scan tool service data No. 36 displays "OFF" even though the brake pedal is depressed, there is an open circuit in the stop light switch input circuit, or the ABS-ECU interface circuit is defective.
• Blown fuse
• Malfunction of stop light switch
• Malfunction of hydraulic unit
• Broken wire, disconnected connector
• Malfunction of ABS-ECU
Scan tool service data inspection No. 36. Stop light switch
NG
Check the fuse No. 6 inside the junction block.
NG
Replace
OK
Check the hydraulic unit.
OK
Inspection of individual part
• Stop light switch
NG
Replace
OK
Check the following connectors.
• Junction block connectors B-55 and B-61
• Stop light switch connector B-10 and B-11
• Intermediate connector B-34
NG
Repair the connector.
OK
Does the problem reoccur?
No
Refer to transient malfunctions"
Yes
Check the harness wire between fuse No. 17 inside junction block and ABS-ECU.
NG
Repair the harness.
OK
Replace the ABS-ECU.
MT4029100119000X

Fig. 56 Symptom inspection chart 7. Mirage

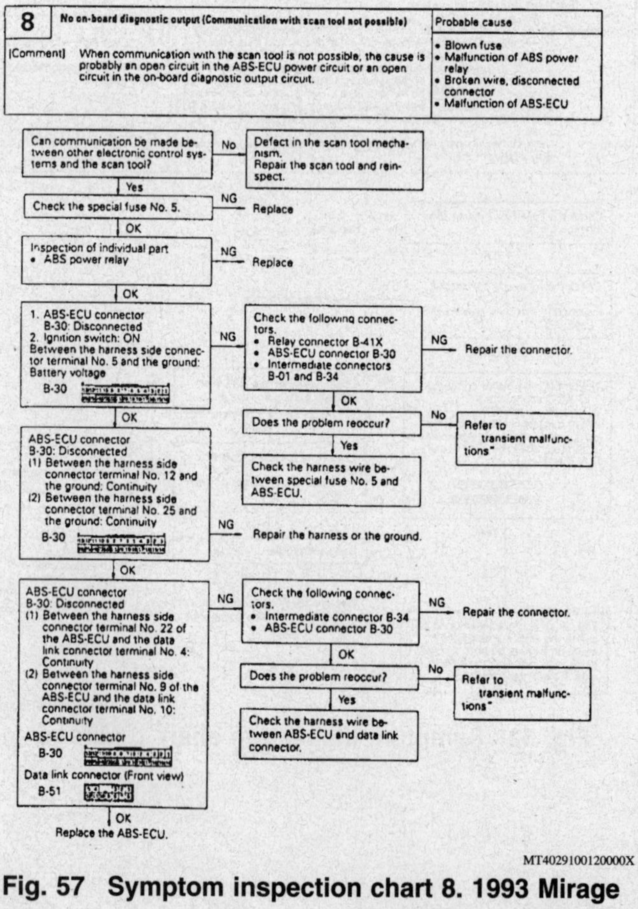
8
No on-board diagnostic output (Communication with scan tool not possible)
Probable cause
[Comment] When communication with the scan tool is not possible, the cause is probably an open circuit in the ABS-ECU power circuit or an open circuit in the on-board diagnostic output circuit.
• Blown fuse
• Malfunction of ABS power relay
• Broken wire, disconnected connector
• Malfunction of ABS-ECU
Can communication be made between other electronic control systems and the scan tool?
No
Defect in the scan tool mechanism.
Repair the scan tool and reinspect.
Yes
Check the special fuse No. 5.
NG
Replace
OK
Inspection of individual part
• ABS power relay
NG
Replace
OK
1. ABS-ECU connector B-30: Disconnected
2. Ignition switch: ON
Between the harness side connector terminal No. 5 and the ground: Battery voltage
B-30
NG
Check the following connectors.
• Relay connector B-41X
• ABS-ECU connector B-30
• Intermediate connectors B-01 and B-34
NG
Repair the connector.
OK
Does the problem reoccur?
No
Refer to transient malfunctions"
Yes
Check the harness wire between special fuse No. 5 and ABS-ECU.
OK
ABS-ECU connector B-30: Disconnected
(1) Between the harness side connector terminal No. 12 and the ground: Continuity
(2) Between the harness side connector terminal No. 25 and the ground: Continuity
B-30
NG
Repair the harness or the ground.
OK
ABS-ECU connector B-30: Disconnected
(1) Between the harness side connector terminal No. 22 of the ABS-ECU and the data link connector terminal No. 4: Continuity
(2) Between the harness side connector terminal No. 9 of the ABS-ECU and the data link connector terminal No. 10: Continuity
ABS-ECU connector
B-30
Data link connector (Front view)
B-51
NG
Check the following connectors.
• Intermediate connector B-34
• ABS-ECU connector B-30
NG
Repair the connector.
OK
Does the problem reoccur?
No
Refer to transient malfunctions"
Yes
Check the harness wire between ABS-ECU and data link connector.
OK
Replace the ABS-ECU.
MT4029100120000X

Fig. 57 Symptom inspection chart 8. 1993 Mirage

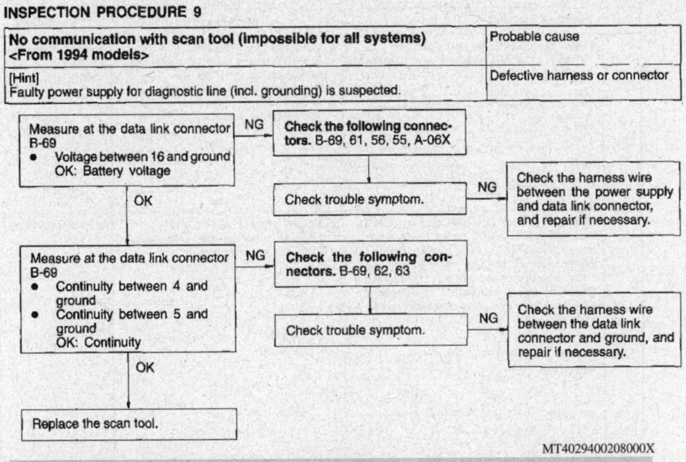
INSPECTION PROCEDURE 9
No communication with scan tool (impossible for all systems) <From 1994 models>
Probable cause
[Hint]
Faulty power supply for diagnostic line (incl. grounding) is suspected.
Defective harness or connector
Measure at the data link connector B-69
• Voltage between 16 and ground
OK: Battery voltage
NG
Check the following connectors. B-69, 61, 56, 55, A-06X
Check trouble symptom.
NG
Check the harness wire between the power supply and data link connector, and repair if necessary.
OK
Measure at the data link connector B-69
• Continuity between 4 and ground
• Continuity between 5 and ground
OK: Continuity
NG
Check the following connectors. B-69, 62, 63
Check trouble symptom.
NG
Check the harness wire between the data link connector and ground, and repair if necessary.
OK
Replace the scan tool.
MT4029400208000X

Fig. 58 Symptom inspection chart 9. 1994–96 Mirage

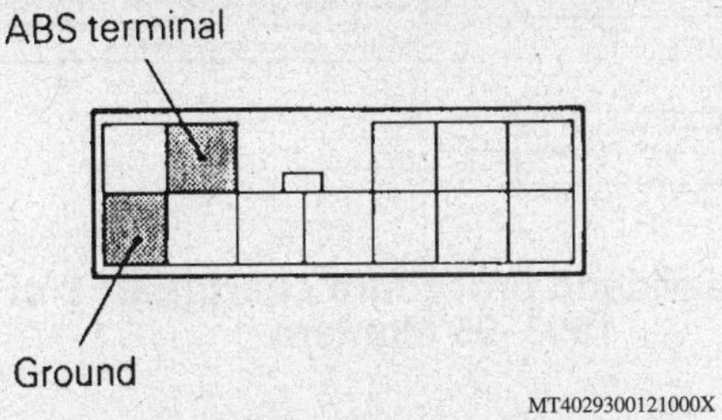
ABS terminal
Ground
MT4029300121000X

Fig. 60 Data link connector. 1993 Mirage

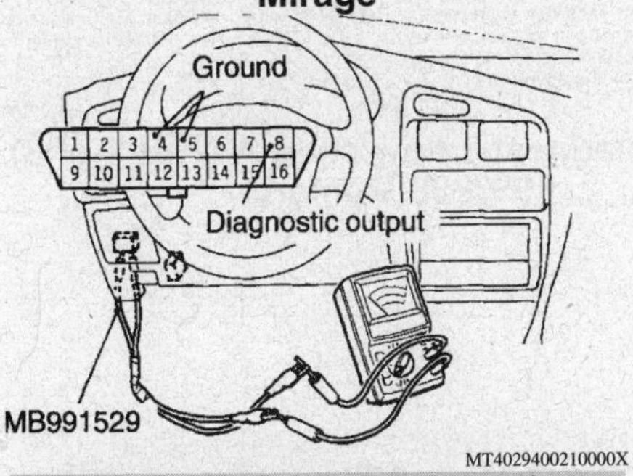
Ground
1 2 3 4 5 6 7 8
9 10 11 12 13 14 15 16
Diagnostic output
MB991529
MT4029400210000X

Fig. 62 Data link connector. 1994–96 Mirage

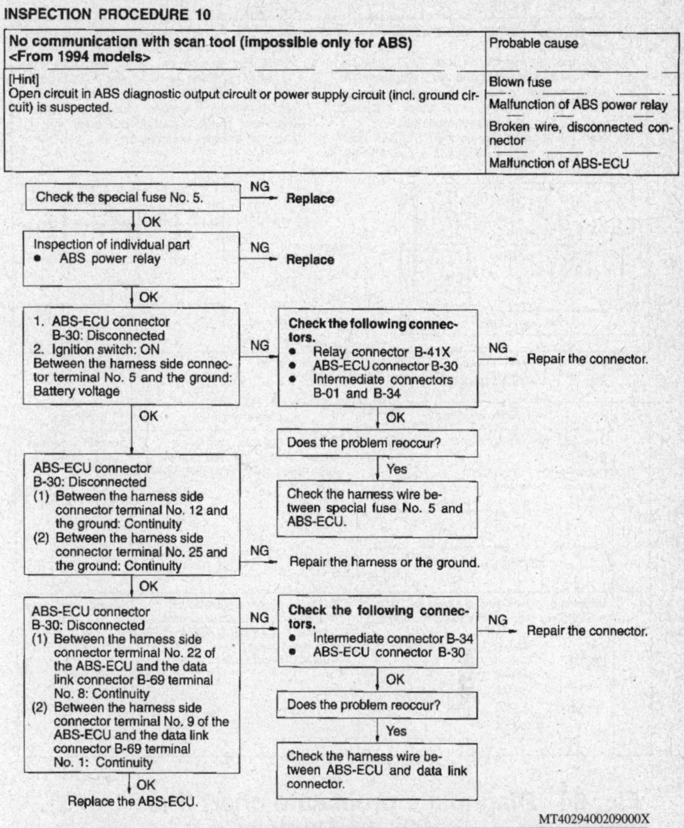
INSPECTION PROCEDURE 10
No communication with scan tool (impossible only for ABS) <From 1994 models>
Probable cause
[Hint]
Open circuit in ABS diagnostic output circuit or power supply circuit (incl. ground circuit) is suspected.
Blown fuse
Malfunction of ABS power relay
Broken wire, disconnected connector
Malfunction of ABS-ECU
Check the special fuse No. 5.
NG
Replace
OK
Inspection of individual part
• ABS power relay
NG
Replace
OK
1. ABS-ECU connector B-30: Disconnected
2. Ignition switch: ON
Between the harness side connector terminal No. 5 and the ground: Battery voltage
NG
Check the following connectors.
• Relay connector B-41X
• ABS-ECU connector B-30
• Intermediate connectors B-01 and B-34
NG
Repair the connector.
OK
Does the problem reoccur?
Yes
Check the harness wire between special fuse No. 5 and ABS-ECU.
OK
ABS-ECU connector
B-30: Disconnected
(1) Between the harness side connector terminal No. 12 and the ground: Continuity
(2) Between the harness side connector terminal No. 25 and the ground: Continuity
NG
Repair the harness or the ground.
OK
ABS-ECU connector
B-30: Disconnected
(1) Between the harness side connector terminal No. 22 of the ABS-ECU and the data link connector B-69 terminal No. 8: Continuity
(2) Between the harness side connector terminal No. 9 of the ABS-ECU and the data link connector B-69 terminal No. 1: Continuity
NG
Check the following connectors.
• Intermediate connector B-34
• ABS-ECU connector B-30
NG
Repair the connector.
OK
Does the problem reoccur?
Yes
Check the harness wire between ABS-ECU and data link connector.
OK
Replace the ABS-ECU.
MT4029400209000X

Fig. 59 Symptom inspection chart 10. 1994–96 Mirage

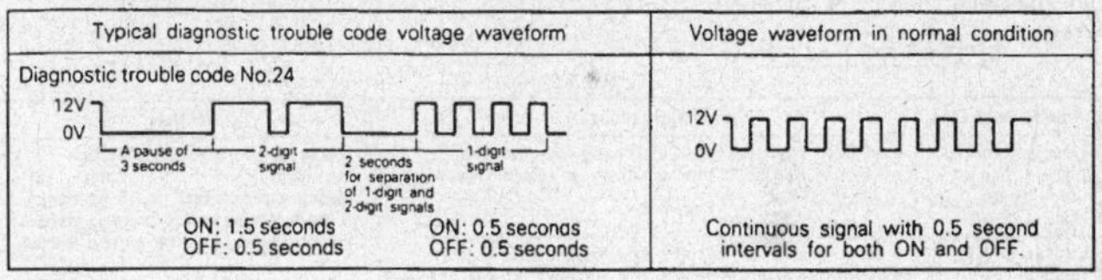
Typical diagnostic trouble code voltage waveform
Voltage waveform in normal condition
Diagnostic trouble code No.24
12V
0V
A pause of 3 seconds
2-digit signal
2 seconds for separation of 1-digit and 2-digit signals
1-digit signal
ON: 1.5 seconds
OFF: 0.5 seconds
ON: 0.5 seconds
OFF: 0.5 seconds
Continuous signal with 0.5 second intervals for both ON and OFF.

NOTE
The voltage waveform corresponding to the same code No. as used when using the scan tool is displayed for each of the other diagnostic items.

MT4029100122000X

Fig. 61 Voltmeter diagnostic trouble code display. Mirage

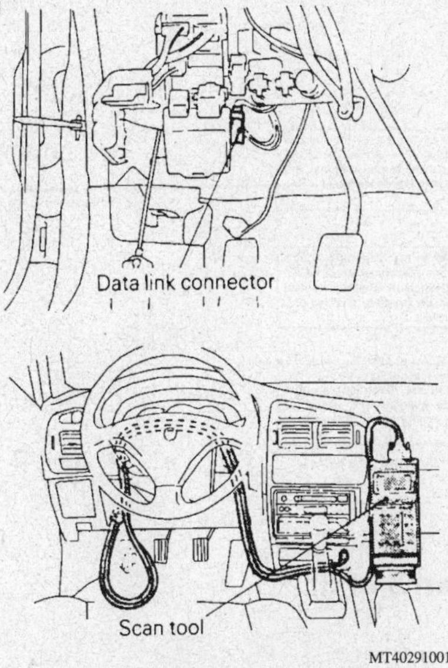
Data link connector
Scan tool
MT4029100136000X

Fig. 63 Diagnostic scan tool connection. Mirage

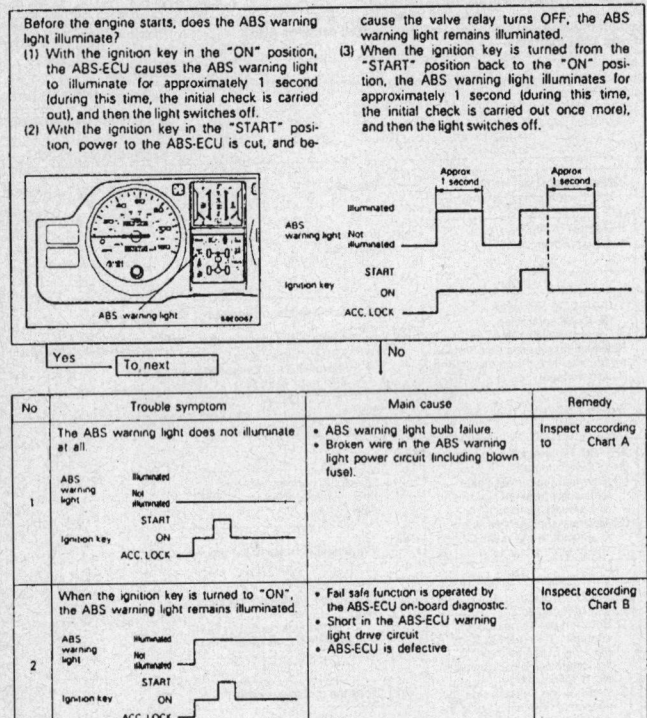

Before the engine starts, does the ABS warning light illuminate?
(1) With the ignition key in the "ON" position, the ABS-ECU causes the ABS warning light to illuminate for approximately 1 second (during this time, the initial check is carried out), and then the light switches off.
(2) With the ignition key in the "START" position, power to the ABS-ECU is cut, and because the valve relay turns OFF, the ABS warning light remains illuminated.
(3) When the ignition key is turned from the "START" position back to the "ON" position, the ABS warning light illuminates for approximately 1 second (during this time, the initial check is carried out once more), and then the light switches off.

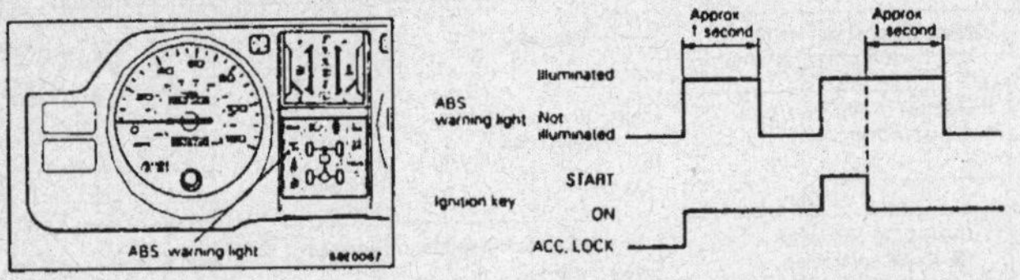
ABS warning light
Approx 1 second
Approx 1 second
Illuminated
ABS warning light
Not illuminated
START
Ignition key
ON
ACC. LOCK

Yes → To next

No ↓

No	Trouble symptom	Main cause	Remedy
1	The ABS warning light does not illuminate at all. 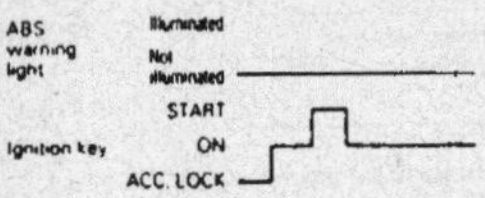	• ABS warning light bulb failure. • Broken wire in the ABS warning light power circuit (including blown fuse).	Inspect according to Chart A
2	When the ignition key is turned to "ON", the ABS warning light remains illuminated. 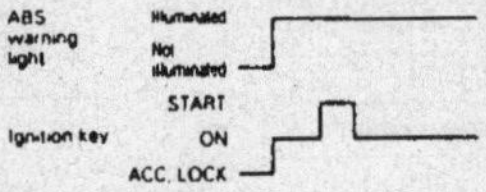	• Fail safe function is operated by the ABS-ECU on-board diagnostic. • Short in the ABS-ECU warning light drive circuit • ABS-ECU is defective	Inspect according to Chart B

MT4029100137010X

Fig. 64 Diagnostic procedure chart (Part 1 of 3). 1993–95 Montero

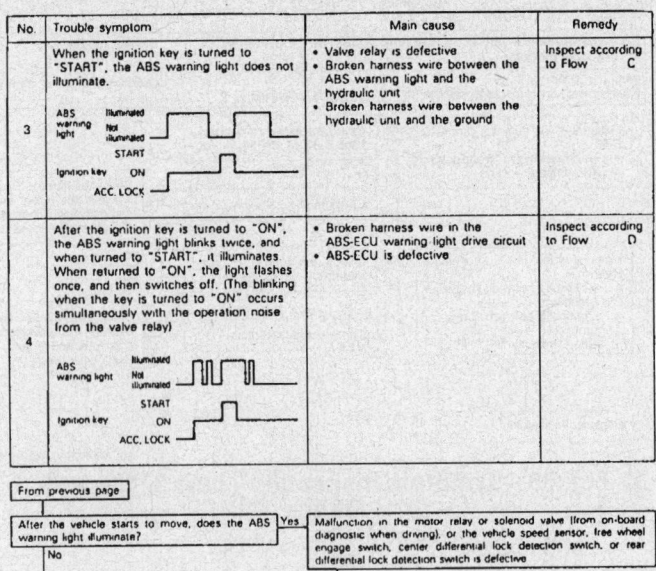

No.	Trouble symptom	Main cause	Remedy
3	When the ignition key is turned to "START", the ABS warning light does not illuminate. 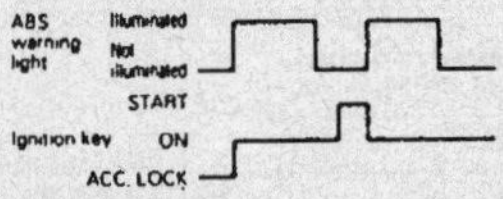	• Valve relay is defective • Broken harness wire between the ABS warning light and the hydraulic unit • Broken harness wire between the hydraulic unit and the ground	Inspect according to Flow C
4	After the ignition key is turned to "ON", the ABS warning light blinks twice, and when turned to "START", it illuminates. When returned to "ON", the light flashes once, and then switches off. (The blinking when the key is turned to "ON" occurs simultaneously with the operation noise from the valve relay) 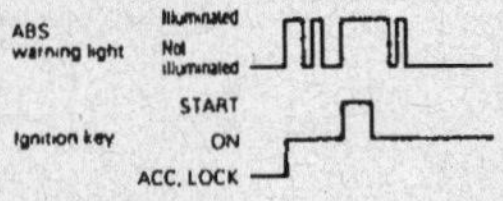	• Broken harness wire in the ABS-ECU warning light drive circuit • ABS-ECU is defective	Inspect according to Flow D

From previous page

After the vehicle starts to move, does the ABS warning light illuminate?
- Yes → Malfunction in the motor relay or solenoid valve (from on-board diagnostic when driving), or the vehicle speed sensor, free wheel engage switch, center differential lock detection switch, or rear differential lock detection switch is defective → To next
- No → Is there unequal braking power on both sides, insufficient braking power or defective ABS operation?
  - No → To next
  - Yes ↓

MT4029100137020X

Fig. 64 Diagnostic procedure chart (Part 2 of 3). 1993–95 Montero

From previous

Trouble symptom	Main cause	Remedy
Unequal braking power Insufficient braking power	• Blocked pressure circuit inside the hydraulic unit. • Mechanical lock in the hydraulic unit solenoid valve.	Follow the hydraulic unit operation inspection and replace the hydraulic unit if necessary. If the hydraulic unit is normal, inspect the components of the normal brake.
Decline in ABS function	• Blocked pressure circuit inside the hydraulic unit. • Operation of the hydraulic unit solenoid valve is defective.	
ABS operates even when not carrying out sudden braking (ABS operating vibration starts to be felt).	• Insufficient wheel speed sensor output voltage (sensor is defective, excessive clearance between the sensor and rotor, or rotor is chipped). • ABS-ECU is defective	Inspect the wheel speed sensor (refer to P.35-50), and replace the sensor or adjust the sensor clearance if necessary. If the problem occurs frequently even though the sensor is normal, then replace the ABS-ECU.

From previous

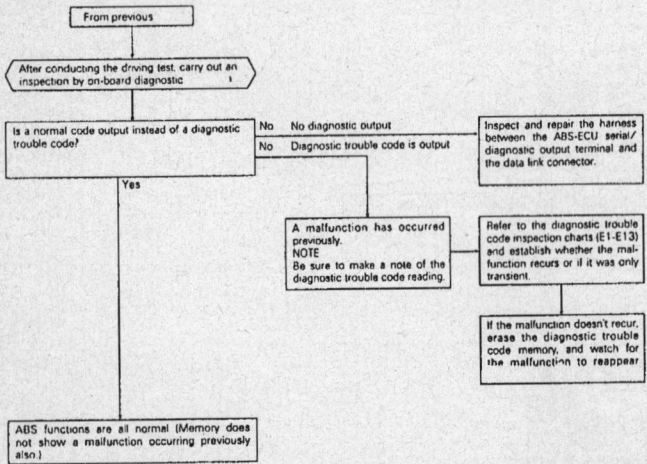

After conducting the driving test, carry out an inspection by on-board diagnostic

Is a normal code output instead of a diagnostic trouble code?
- No — No diagnostic output → Inspect and repair the harness between the ABS-ECU serial/diagnostic output terminal and the data link connector.
- No — Diagnostic trouble code is output → A malfunction has occurred previously. NOTE Be sure to make a note of the diagnostic trouble code reading. → Refer to the diagnostic trouble code inspection charts (E1-E13) and establish whether the malfunction recurs or if it was only transient. → If the malfunction doesn't recur, erase the diagnostic trouble code memory, and watch for the malfunction to reappear
- Yes → ABS functions are all normal (Memory does not show a malfunction occurring previously also.)

MT4029100137030X

Fig. 64 Diagnostic procedure chart (Part 3 of 3). 1993–95 Montero

A	ABS warning light does not illuminate at all

[Comment] When the light does not illuminate at all, there is a strong possibility that there is a malfunction of the ABS warning light or the power supply.

(Hint) If other warning light also do not illuminate, it is probably a blown fuse.

MT4029100138010X

Fig. 65 Diagnostic flow chart A (Part 1 of 3). 1993–95 Montero

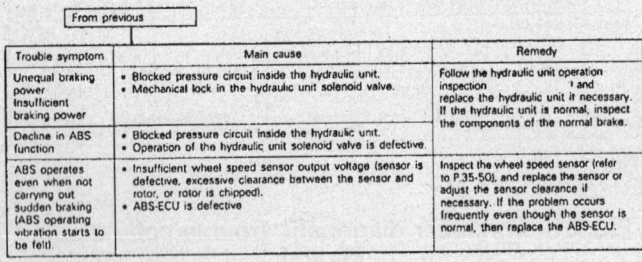

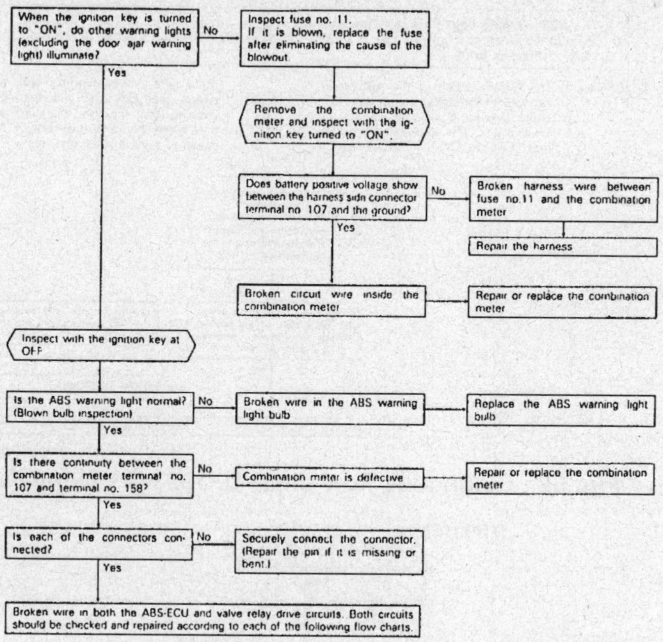
When the ignition key is turned to "ON", do other warning lights (excluding the door ajar warning light) illuminate?
No
Inspect fuse no. 11. If it is blown, replace the fuse after eliminating the cause of the blowout.
Remove the combination meter and inspect with the ignition key turned to "ON".
Does battery positive voltage show between the harness side connector terminal no. 107 and the ground?
No
Broken harness wire between fuse no.11 and the combination meter
Repair the harness
Yes
Broken circuit wire inside the combination meter
Repair or replace the combination meter
Yes
Inspect with the ignition key at OFF
Is the ABS warning light normal? (Blown bulb inspection)
No
Broken wire in the ABS warning light bulb
Replace the ABS warning light bulb
Yes
Is there continuity between the combination meter terminal no. 107 and terminal no. 158?
No
Combination meter is defective
Repair or replace the combination meter
Yes
Is each of the connectors connected?
No
Securely connect the connector. (Repair the pin if it is missing or bent.)
Yes
Broken wire in both the ABS-ECU and valve relay drive circuits. Both circuits should be checked and repaired according to each of the following flow charts.

MT4029100138020X

Fig. 65 Diagnostic flow chart A (Part 2 of 3). 1993–95 Montero

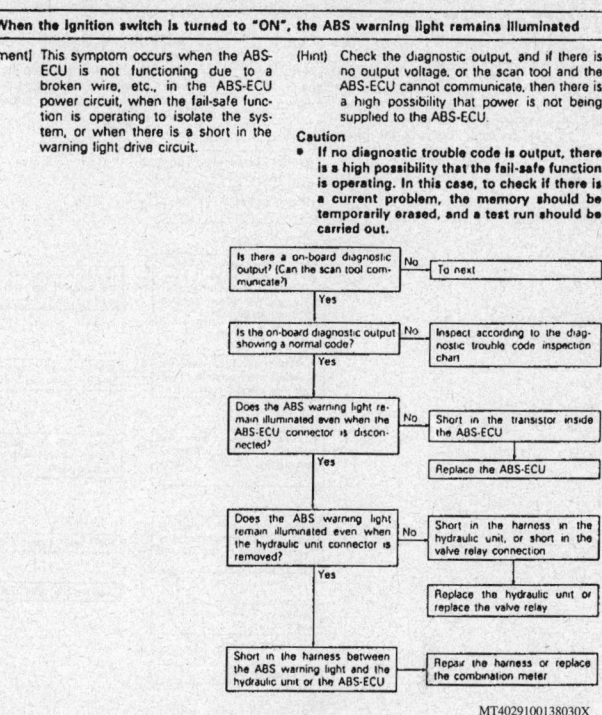

B	When the ignition switch is turned to "ON", the ABS warning light remains illuminated

[Comment] This symptom occurs when the ABS-ECU is not functioning due to a broken wire, etc., in the ABS-ECU power circuit, when the fail-safe function is operating to isolate the system, or when there is a short in the warning light drive circuit.

(Hint) Check the diagnostic output, and if there is no output voltage, or the scan tool and the ABS-ECU cannot communicate, then there is a high possibility that power is not being supplied to the ABS-ECU.

Caution

- **If no diagnostic trouble code is output, there is a high possibility that the fail-safe function is operating. In this case, to check if there is a current problem, the memory should be temporarily erased, and a test run should be carried out.**

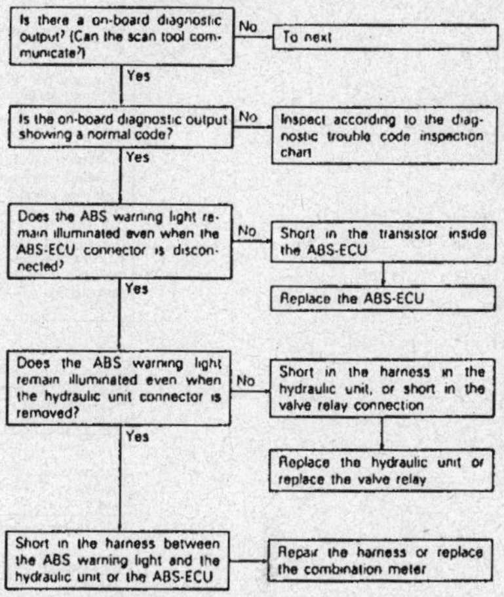
Is there a on-board diagnostic output? (Can the scan tool communicate?)
No
To next
Yes
Is the on-board diagnostic output showing a normal code?
No
Inspect according to the diagnostic trouble code inspection chart
Yes
Does the ABS warning light remain illuminated even when the ABS-ECU connector is disconnected?
No
Short in the transistor inside the ABS-ECU
Replace the ABS-ECU
Yes
Does the ABS warning light remain illuminated even when the hydraulic unit connector is removed?
No
Short in the harness in the hydraulic unit, or short in the valve relay connection
Replace the hydraulic unit or replace the valve relay
Yes
Short in the harness between the ABS warning light and the hydraulic unit or the ABS-ECU
Repair the harness or replace the combination meter

MT4029100138030X

Fig. 65 Diagnostic flow chart A (Part 3 of 3). 1993–95 Montero

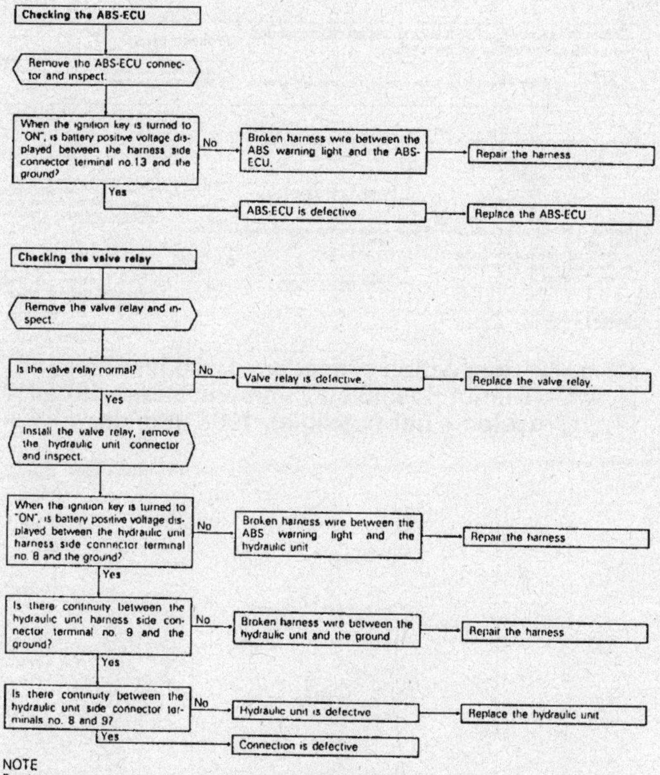
Checking the ABS-ECU
Remove the ABS-ECU connector and inspect.
When the ignition key is turned to "ON", is battery positive voltage displayed between the harness side connector terminal no.13 and the ground?
No
Broken harness wire between the ABS warning light and the ABS-ECU.
Repair the harness
Yes
ABS-ECU is defective
Replace the ABS-ECU
Checking the valve relay
Remove the valve relay and inspect.
Is the valve relay normal?
No
Valve relay is defective.
Replace the valve relay.
Yes
Install the valve relay, remove the hydraulic unit connector and inspect.
When the ignition key is turned to "ON", is battery positive voltage displayed between the hydraulic unit harness side connector terminal no. 8 and the ground?
No
Broken harness wire between the ABS warning light and the hydraulic unit
Repair the harness
Yes
Is there continuity between the hydraulic unit harness side connector terminal no. 9 and the ground?
No
Broken harness wire between the hydraulic unit and the ground
Repair the harness
Yes
Is there continuity between the hydraulic unit side connector terminals no. 8 and 9?
No
Hydraulic unit is defective
Replace the hydraulic unit
Yes
Connection is defective

NOTE
For inspection sections marked by *, pay attention to the polarity of the diodes.

MT4029100139010X

Fig. 66 Diagnostic flow chart B (Part 1 of 2). 1993–95 Montero

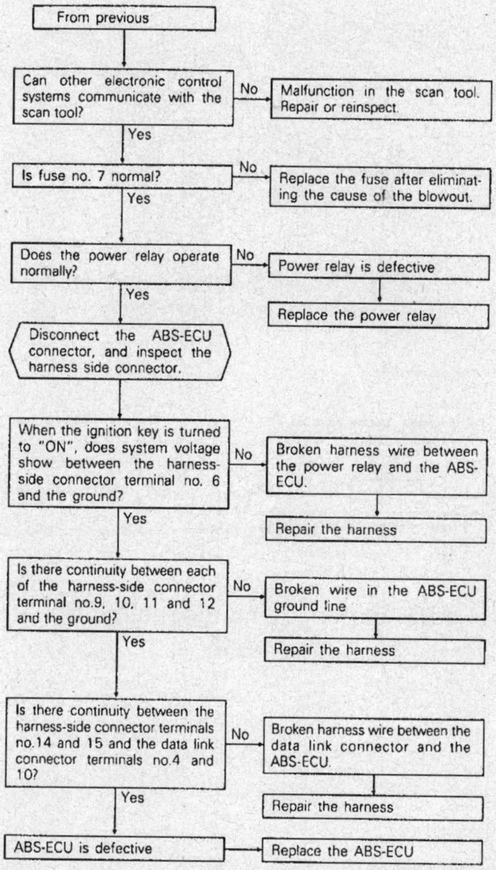
From previous
Can other electronic control systems communicate with the scan tool?
No
Malfunction in the scan tool. Repair or reinspect.
Yes
Is fuse no. 7 normal?
No
Replace the fuse after eliminating the cause of the blowout.
Yes
Does the power relay operate normally?
No
Power relay is defective
Replace the power relay
Yes
Disconnect the ABS-ECU connector, and inspect the harness side connector.
When the ignition key is turned to "ON", does system voltage show between the harness-side connector terminal no. 6 and the ground?
No
Broken harness wire between the power relay and the ABS-ECU.
Repair the harness
Yes
Is there continuity between each of the harness-side connector terminal no.9, 10, 11 and 12 and the ground?
No
Broken wire in the ABS-ECU ground line
Repair the harness
Yes
Is there continuity between the harness-side connector terminals no.14 and 15 and the data link connector terminals no.4 and 10?
No
Broken harness wire between the data link connector and the ABS-ECU.
Repair the harness
Yes
ABS-ECU is defective
Replace the ABS-ECU

MT4029100139020X

Fig. 66 Diagnostic flow chart B (Part 2 of 2). 1993–95 Montero

C	When ignition key is turned to "START", ABS warning light switches off

[Comment] The ABS-ECU uses the power to the IG2 which is cut when the ignition switch is turned to "START". The ABS warning light uses IG1 power which is not cut even when the ignition switch is turned to "START". Accordingly, because the power to the ABS-ECU is stopped in "START" position, the valve relay turns OFF. At this time, if the warning light does not illuminate, the cause is a problem in the light illumination circuit in the valve relay.

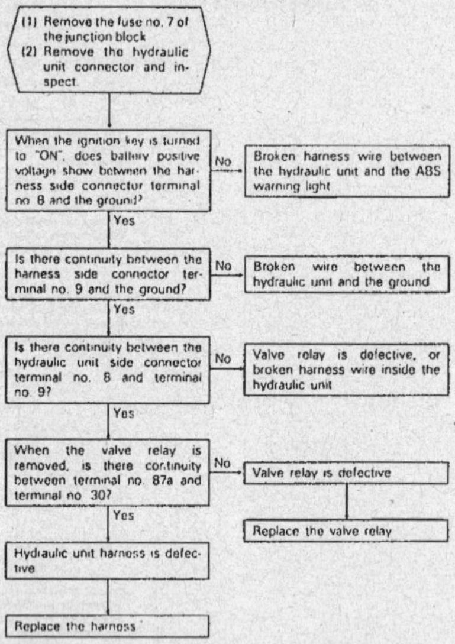
(1) Remove the fuse no. 7 of the junction block
(2) Remove the hydraulic unit connector and inspect.
When the ignition key is turned to "ON", does battery positive voltage show between the harness side connector terminal no. 8 and the ground?
No
Broken harness wire between the hydraulic unit and the ABS warning light
Yes
Is there continuity between the harness side connector terminal no. 9 and the ground?
No
Broken wire between the hydraulic unit and the ground
Yes
Is there continuity between the hydraulic unit side connector terminal no. 8 and terminal no. 9?
No
Valve relay is defective, or broken harness wire inside the hydraulic unit
Yes
When the valve relay is removed, is there continuity between terminal no. 87a and terminal no. 30?
No
Valve relay is defective
Replace the valve relay
Yes
Hydraulic unit harness is defective
Replace the harness

NOTE
For inspection sections marked by *, pay attention to the polarity of the diodes.

MT4029100140000X

Fig. 67 Diagnostic flow chart C. 1993–95 Montero

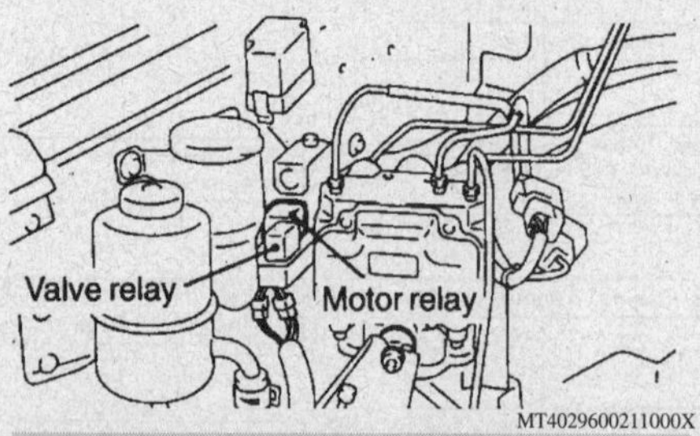
Valve relay
Motor relay

MT4029600211000X

Fig. 69 ABS valve & motor relays. 1996 Montero

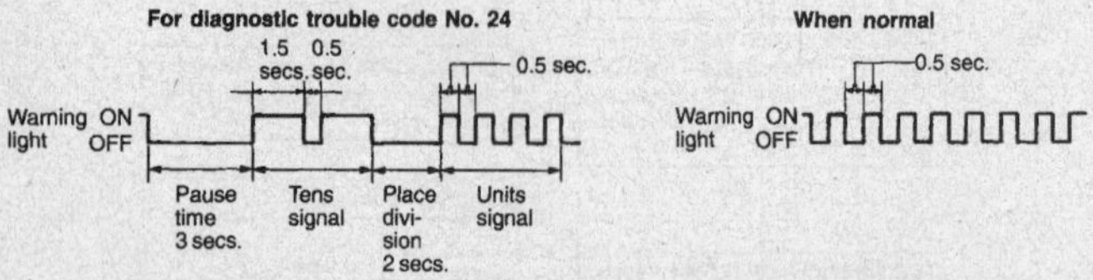
For diagnostic trouble code No. 24
1.5 secs.
0.5 sec.
0.5 sec.
Warning light ON OFF
Pause time 3 secs.
Tens signal
Place division 2 secs.
Units signal
When normal
0.5 sec.
Warning light ON OFF

MT4029300213000X

Fig. 71 ABS warning lamp diagnostic trouble code output

D	The ABS warning light flashes twice after the ignition key is turned to "ON". The light illuminates when the ignition key is turned to "START", and when the key is returned to "ON", it flashes once.

[Comment] The ABS-ECU causes the ABS warning light to illuminate during the initial check (approx. 1 second). During the initial check, the valve relay changes from OFF to ON→OFF→ON, and if there is a broken harness wire between the ABS-ECU and the ABS warning light, the light will illuminate only when the valve relay is OFF because of a valve relay test, etc.

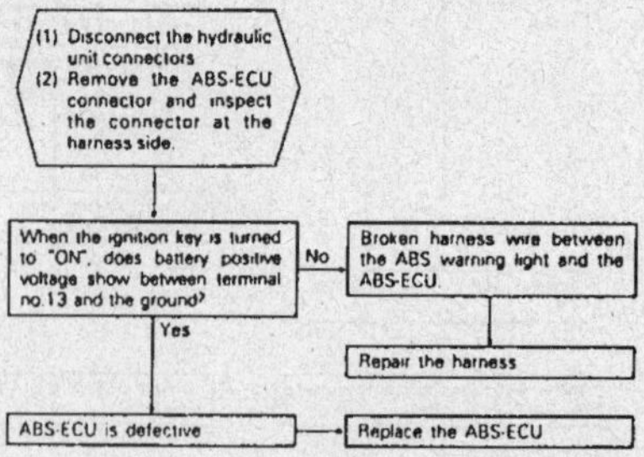
(1) Disconnect the hydraulic unit connectors
(2) Remove the ABS-ECU connector and inspect the connector at the harness side.
When the ignition key is turned to "ON", does battery positive voltage show between terminal no. 13 and the ground?
No
Broken harness wire between the ABS warning light and the ABS-ECU.
Repair the harness
Yes
ABS-ECU is defective
Replace the ABS-ECU

MT4029100141000X

Fig. 68 Diagnostic flow chart D. 1993–95 Montero

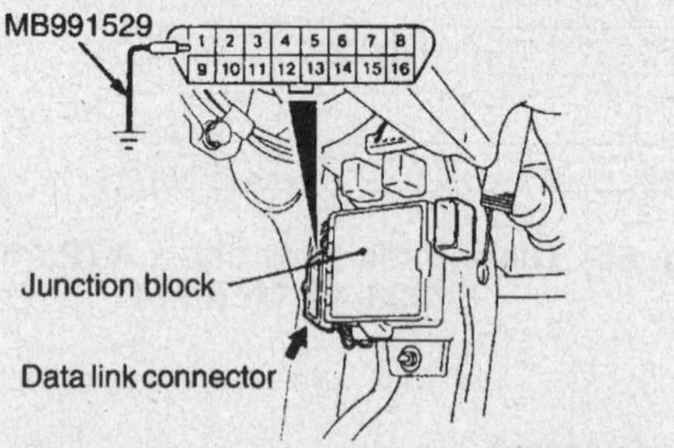
MB991529
1 2 3 4 5 6 7 8
9 10 11 12 13 14 15 16
Junction block
Data link connector

MT4029600212000X

Fig. 70 Data link connector. 1996 Montero

Communication with MUT-II is not possible. (Communication with all system is not possible.)	Probable cause
[Comment] The reason is probably a defect in the power supply system (including earth) for the diagnosis line.	• Malfunction of connector • Malfunction of harness

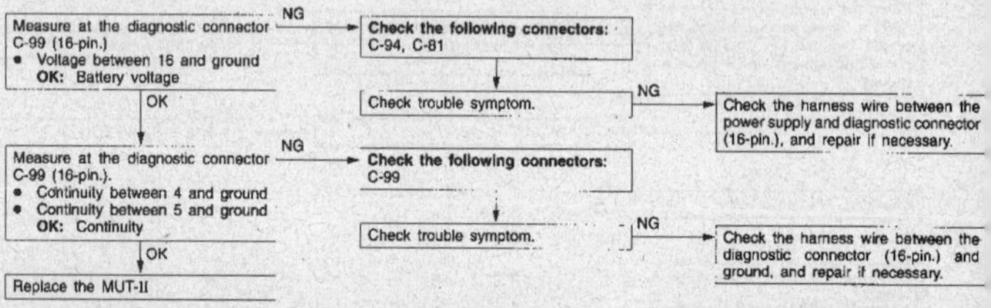
Measure at the diagnostic connector C-99 (16-pin.)
• Voltage between 16 and ground
OK: Battery voltage
NG
Check the following connectors: C-94, C-81
Check trouble symptom.
NG
Check the harness wire between the power supply and diagnostic connector (16-pin.), and repair if necessary.
OK
Measure at the diagnostic connector C-99 (16-pin.).
• Continuity between 4 and ground
• Continuity between 5 and ground
OK: Continuity
NG
Check the following connectors: C-99
Check trouble symptom.
NG
Check the harness wire between the diagnostic connector (16-pin.) and ground, and repair if necessary.
OK
Replace the MUT-II

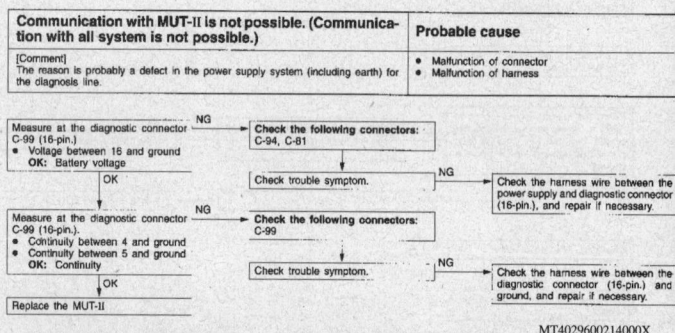

MT4029600214000X

Fig. 72 Inspection procedure 1: Communication w/MUT-II not possible (Communication with all systems not possible). 1996 Montero

Communication with MUT-II is not possible. (Communication with ABS only is not possible.)	Probable cause
[Comment] When communication with the MUT-II is not possible, the cause is probably an open circuit in the ABS-ECU power circuit or an open circuit in the diagnosis output circuit.	• Blown fuse • Malfunction of wiring harness or connecter • Malfunction of ABS-ECU

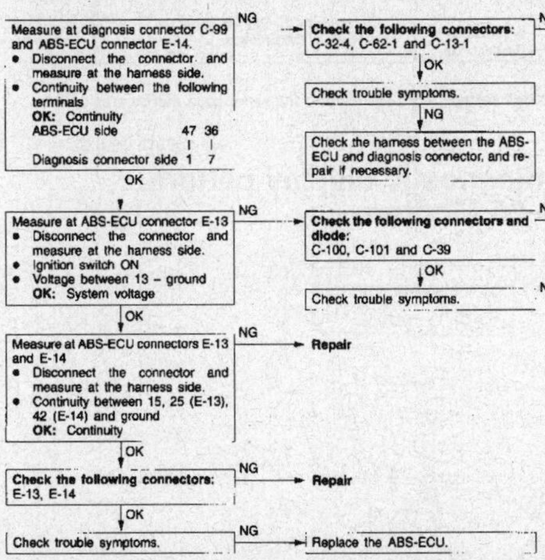
Measure at diagnosis connector C-99 and ABS-ECU connector E-14.
• Disconnect the connector and measure at the harness side.
• Continuity between the following terminals
OK: Continuity
ABS-ECU side 47 36
Diagnosis connector side 1 7
NG
Check the following connectors: C-32-4, C-62-1 and C-13-1
NG
Repair
OK
Check trouble symptoms.
NG
Check the harness between the ABS-ECU and diagnosis connector, and repair if necessary.
OK
Measure at ABS-ECU connector E-13
• Disconnect the connector and measure at the harness side.
• Ignition switch ON
• Voltage between 13 – ground
OK: System voltage
NG
Check the following connectors and diode: C-100, C-101 and C-39
NG
Repair
OK
Check trouble symptoms.
NG
Check the harness between fuse No. 13 inside the junction block and ABS-ECU, and repair if necessary.
OK
Measure at ABS-ECU connectors E-13 and E-14
• Disconnect the connector and measure at the harness side.
• Continuity between 15, 25 (E-13), 42 (E-14) and ground
OK: Continuity
NG
Repair
OK
Check the following connectors: E-13, E-14
NG
Repair
OK
Check trouble symptoms.
NG
Replace the ABS-ECU.

MT4029600215000X

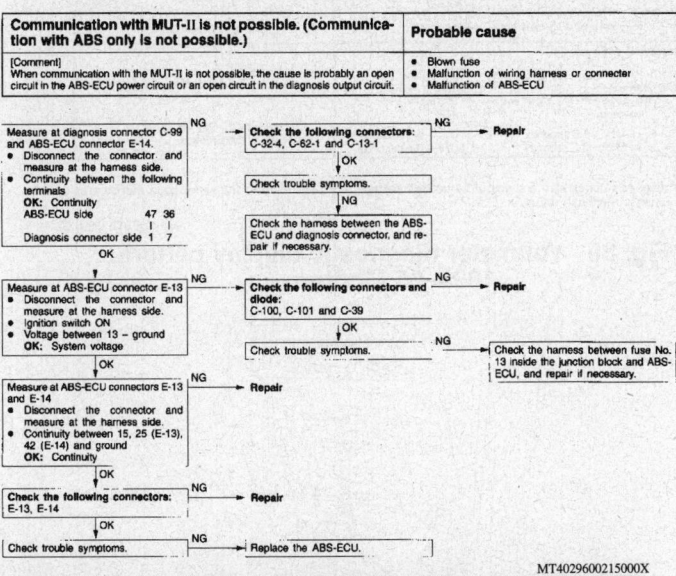

Fig. 73 Inspection procedure 2: Communication w/MUT-II not possible (Can communicate w/systems other than ABS). 1996 Montero

Even after the engine is started, the ABS warning light remains illuminated.	Probable cause
[Comment] A short-circuit in the ABS warning light illumination circuit may be present.	• Malfunction of combination meter • Malfunction of ABS-ECU • Malfunction of wiring harness

NOTE

This trouble symptom is limited to cases where communication with the MUT-II is possible (ABS-ECU power supply is normal) and the diagnosis code is a normal diagnosis code.

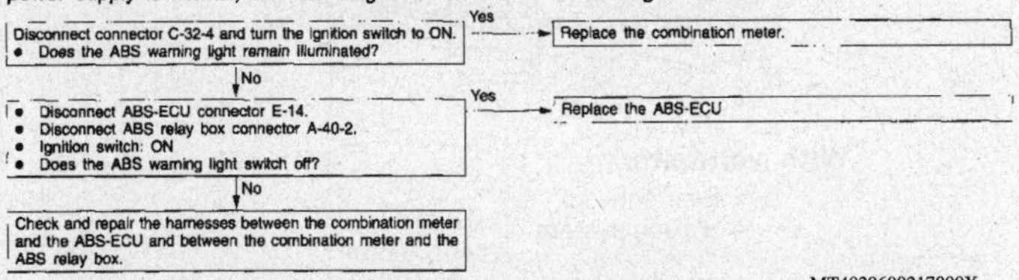
Disconnect connector C-32-4 and turn the ignition switch to ON.
• Does the ABS warning light remain illuminated?
Yes
Replace the combination meter.
No
• Disconnect ABS-ECU connector E-14.
• Disconnect ABS relay box connector A-40-2.
• Ignition switch: ON
• Does the ABS warning light switch off?
Yes
Replace the ABS-ECU
No
Check and repair the harnesses between the combination meter and the ABS-ECU and between the combination meter and the ABS relay box.

MT4029600217000X

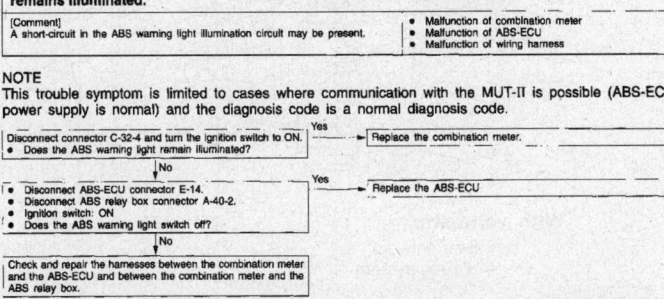

Fig. 75 Inspection procedure 4: ABS warning lamp remains lit after engine is started. 1996 Montero

The ABS warning light flashes twice after the ignition key is turned to "ON". The light illuminates when the ignition key is turned to "START", and when the key is returned to "ON", it flashes once.	Probable cause
[Comment] The ABS-ECU causes the ABS warning light to illuminate during the initial check (approx. 1 second). During the initial check, the valve relay turns from off to on, off and back to on again, and if there is a open circuit in the harness between the ABS-ECU and the ABS warning light, the light will illuminate only when the valve relay is OFF because of a valve relay test, etc.	• Malfunction of wiring harness or connector • Malfunction of ABS-ECU

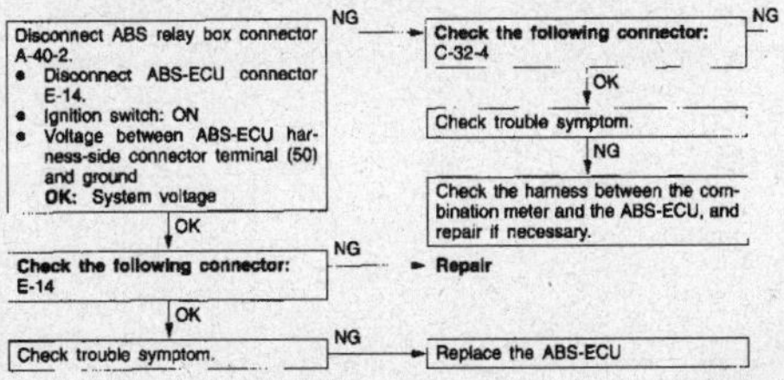
Disconnect ABS relay box connector A-40-2.
• Disconnect ABS-ECU connector E-14.
• Ignition switch: ON
• Voltage between ABS-ECU harness-side connector terminal (50) and ground
OK: System voltage
NG
Check the following connector: C-32-4
NG
Repair
OK
Check trouble symptom.
NG
Check the harness between the combination meter and the ABS-ECU, and repair if necessary.
OK
Check the following connector: E-14
NG
Repair
OK
Check trouble symptom.
NG
Replace the ABS-ECU

MT4029600219000X

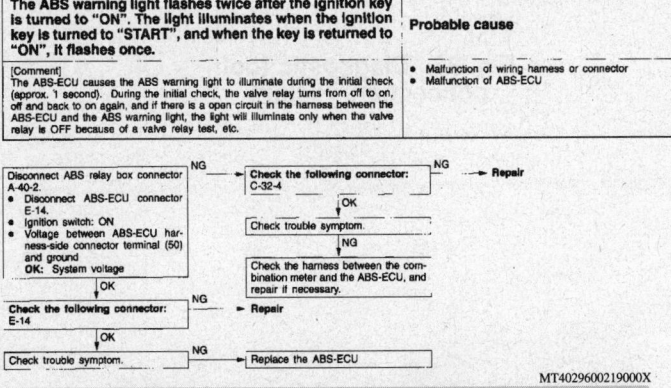

Fig. 77 Inspection procedure 6: ABS warning lamp flashes abnormally. 1996 Montero

When ignition key is turned to "ON" (engine stopped), ABS warning light does not illuminate	Probable cause
[Comment] When power is supplied to the ABS-ECU, the valve relay turns from off to on, off and back to on again as an initial check. Because of this, the ABS warning light will illuminate twice when the valve relay is off even if there is a problem with the circuit between the ABS warning light and the ABS-ECU. Accordingly, if the light does not illuminate, the cause is probably one of the following items. An open circuit in the light power supply circuit A blown light bulb An open circuit in both the circuit between the ABS warning light and the ABS-ECU and in the circuit between the ABS warning light and the valve relay	• Blown fuse • Burnt out ABS warning light bulb • Malfunction of wiring harness or connector

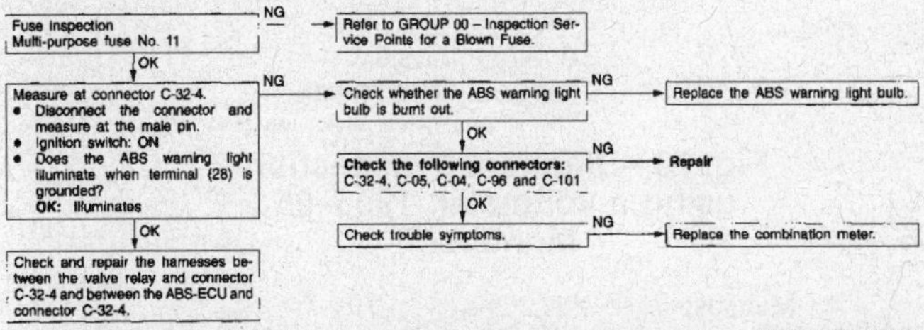
Fuse inspection
Multi-purpose fuse No. 11
NG
Refer to GROUP 00 – Inspection Service Points for a Blown Fuse.
OK
Measure at connector C-32-4.
• Disconnect the connector and measure at the male pin.
• Ignition switch: ON
• Does the ABS warning light illuminate when terminal (28) is grounded?
OK: Illuminates
NG
Check whether the ABS warning light bulb is burnt out.
NG
Replace the ABS warning light bulb.
OK
Check the following connectors: C-32-4, C-05, C-04, C-96 and C-101
NG
Repair
OK
Check trouble symptoms.
NG
Replace the combination meter.
OK
Check and repair the harnesses between the valve relay and connector C-32-4 and between the ABS-ECU and connector C-32-4.

MT4029600216000X

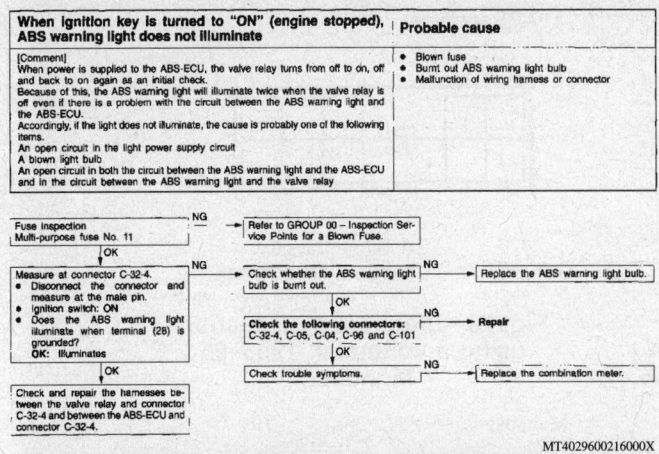

Fig. 74 Inspection procedure 3: ABS warning lamp does not light at key On, engine off. 1996 Montero

When ignition key is turned to "START", ABS warning light does not illuminate.	Probable cause
[Comment] The ABS-ECU uses the power supply which is turned off when the ignition switch is turned to START. The ABS warning light uses the power supply which is not turned off when the ignition switch is turned to START. Accordingly, when the ignition switch is at START, the power supply to the ABS-ECU is turned off and the valve relay is also turned off. So, when the ABS warning light does not illuminate at this time, the light illumination circuit in the valve relay system is defective.	• Malfunction of wiring harness or connector • Malfunction of ABS relay box

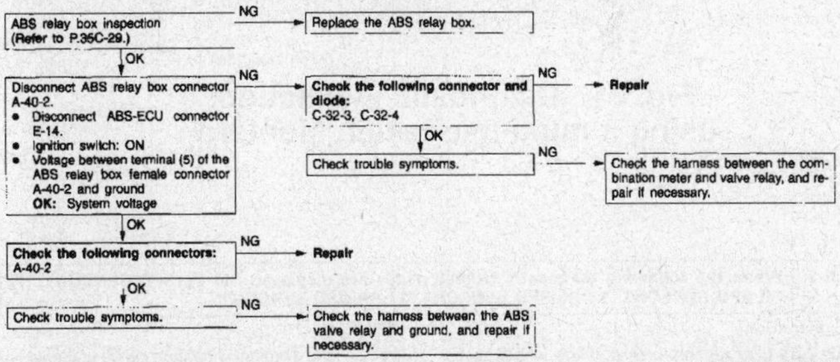
ABS relay box inspection
(Refer to P.35C-29.)
NG
Replace the ABS relay box.
OK
Disconnect ABS relay box connector A-40-2.
• Disconnect ABS-ECU connector E-14.
• Ignition switch: ON
• Voltage between terminal (5) of the ABS relay box female connector A-40-2 and ground
OK: System voltage
NG
Check the following connector and diode: C-32-3, C-32-4
NG
Repair
OK
Check trouble symptoms.
NG
Check the harness between the combination meter and valve relay, and repair if necessary.
OK
Check the following connectors: A-40-2
NG
Repair
OK
Check trouble symptoms.
NG
Check the harness between the ABS valve relay and ground, and repair if necessary.

MT4029600218000X

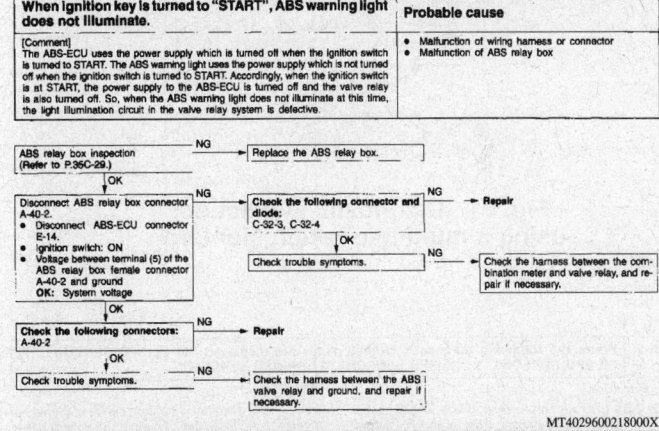

Fig. 76 Inspection procedure 5: ABS warning lamp does not light w/key in Start position. 1996 Montero

Brake operation is abnormal	Probable cause
[Comment] This varies depending on the driving conditions and the road surface conditions, so problem diagnosis is difficult. However, if a normal diagnosis code is displayed, carry out the following inspection.	• Improper installation of wheel speed sensor • Incorrect sensor harness contact • Foreign material adhering to wheel speed sensor • Malfunction of wheel speed sensor • Malfunction of rotor • Malfunction of wheel bearing • Malfunction of hydraulic unit • Malfunction of ABS-ECU

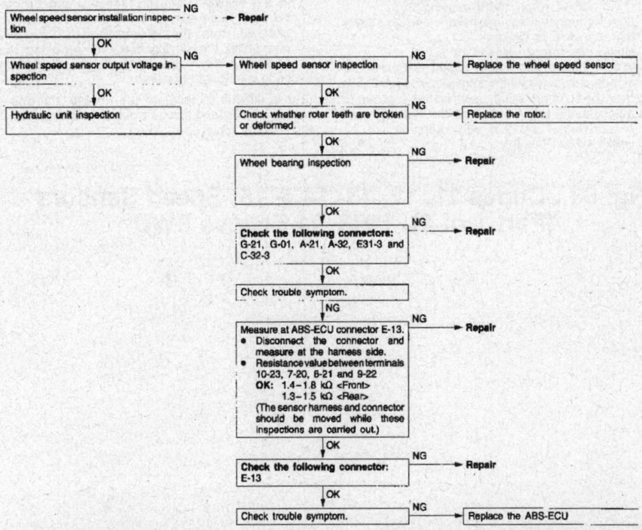
Wheel speed sensor installation inspection
NG
Repair
OK
Wheel speed sensor output voltage inspection
OK
Hydraulic unit inspection
NG
Wheel speed sensor inspection
NG
Replace the wheel speed sensor
OK
Check whether roter teeth are broken or deformed.
NG
Replace the rotor.
OK
Wheel bearing inspection
NG
Repair
OK
Check the following connectors: G-21, G-01, A-21, A-32, E31-3 and C-32-3
NG
Repair
OK
Check trouble symptom.
NG
Measure at ABS-ECU connector E-13.
• Disconnect the connector and measure at the harness side.
• Resistance value between terminals 10-23, 7-20, 8-21 and 9-22
OK: 1.4–1.8 kΩ <Front>
1.3–1.5 kΩ <Rear>
(The sensor harness and connector should be moved while these inspections are carried out.)
NG
Repair
OK
Check the following connector: E-13
NG
Repair
OK
Check trouble symptom.
NG
Replace the ABS-ECU

MT4029600220000X

Fig. 78 Inspection procedure 7: Brake operation is abnormal. 1996 Montero

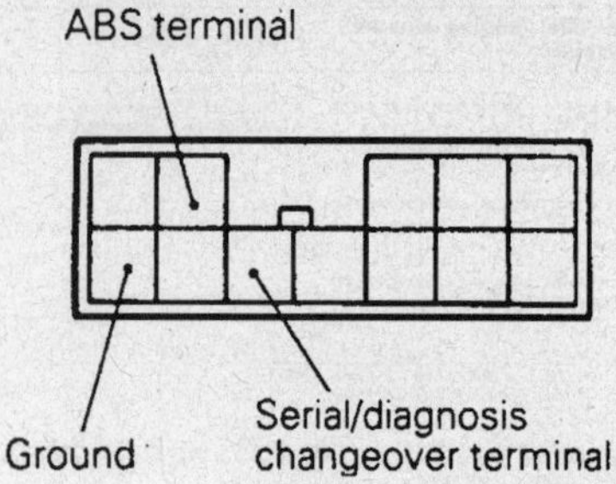
ABS terminal
Ground
Serial/diagnosis
changeover terminal

MT4029100142000X

Fig. 79 Diagnostic inspection using a voltmeter. 1993–95 Montero

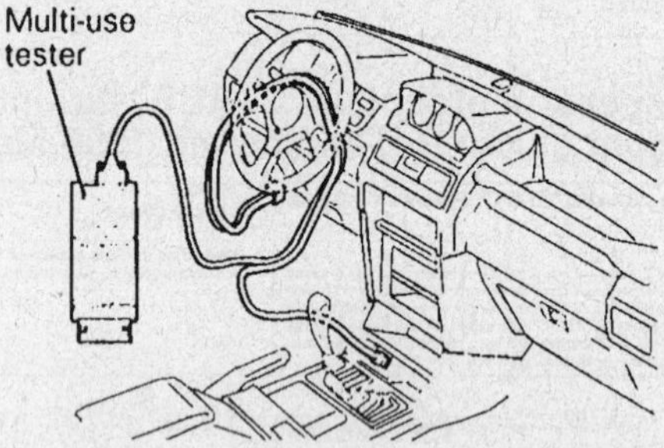
Multi-use
tester

MT4029100156000X

Fig. 81 Diagnostic inspection using a multi-use tester. Montero

E-1	When the following diagnostic trouble codes are displayed "11 FL SPD SENSOR" "12 FR SPD SENSOR" "13 RL SPD SENSOR" "14 RR SPD SENSOR"

[Explanation]

The ABS ECU detects breaks in the wheel speed sensor wire. This diagnostic trouble code is output if the wheel speed sensor signal is not input (or short circuited) or if its output is low when starting to drive or while driving.

[Hint]

In addition to a broken wire/short circuit in the wheel speed sensor, also check whether the sensor gap is too large, rotor teeth are missing, sensor harness wire is temporarily broken, or sensor harness and body connector are not properly inserted.

E-2	When diagnostic trouble code "15 SENSOR FAULT" is displayed

[Explanation]

This diagnostic trouble code is output when there is an abnormality (other than broken wire or short circuit) in the wheel speed sensor output signal while driving.

[Hint]

The following can be considered as the cause of the wheel speed sensor output abnormality.

- Distortion of rotor, teeth missing
- Low frequency noise interference when sensor harness wire is broken
- Noise interference in sensor signal
- When the sensor output signal is below the standard value or when amplitude modulation is over the standard value, using an oscilloscope to measure the wave shape of the wheel speed sensor output signal is very effective.
- Loose wheel bearing
- Temporarily broken wire in sensor harness
- Sensor harness and body connector are not properly inserted.

NOTE

(1) If contact is poor, check the sensor cable by bending and lightly stretching it.

(2) If there is currently no trouble and if abnormality in the displayed sensor circuit cannot be discovered since values are normal even when checked, turn the ignition switch OFF and re-execute the driving test. Try replacing the ABS ECU only if the same diagnostic trouble code is output at this time.

(If it is difficult to recreate the trouble, there is a possibility of speed sensor trouble recurring even if the ECU is replaced.)

MT4029100032010X

Fig. 83 Codes 11, 12, 13, 14 & 15: Speed Sensors (Part 1 of 2). 1993–94 Eclipse FWD

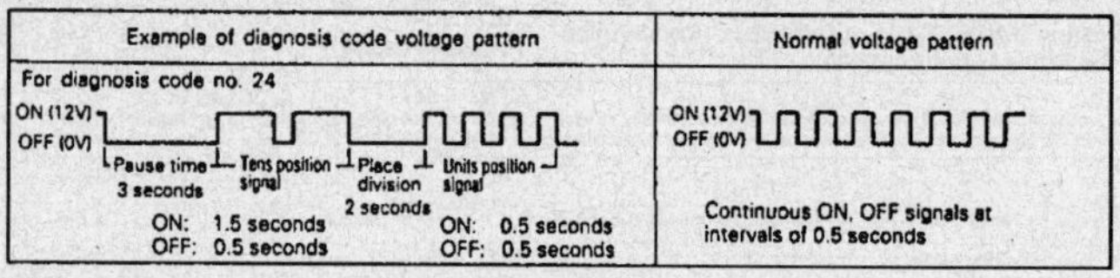
Example of diagnosis code voltage pattern
Normal voltage pattern
For diagnosis code no. 24
ON (12V)
OFF (0V)
Pause time
3 seconds
Tens position signal
Place division
2 seconds
Units position signal
ON: 1.5 seconds
OFF: 0.5 seconds
ON: 0.5 seconds
OFF: 0.5 seconds
ON (12V)
OFF (0V)
Continuous ON, OFF signals at intervals of 0.5 seconds

NOTE

Other diagnosis codes also are output as voltage patterns corresponding to the same code numbers as when using a multi-use tester.

MT4029100143000X

Fig. 80 Voltmeter diagnostic display pattern. 1993–95 Montero

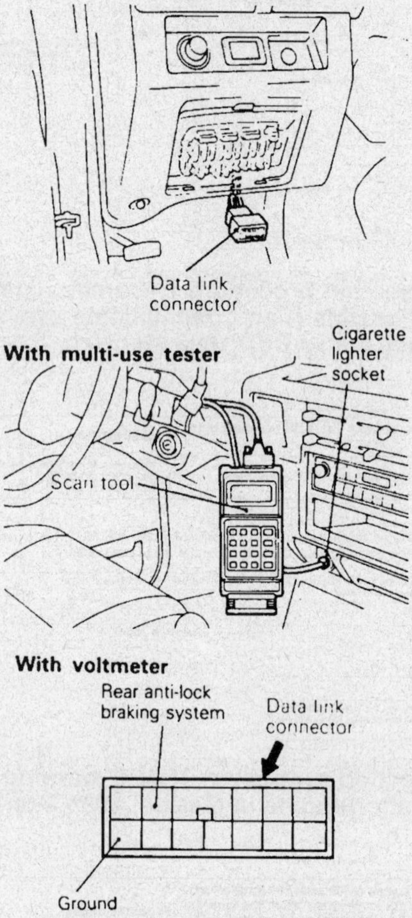
Data link
connector
With multi-use tester
Cigarette
lighter
socket
Scan tool
With voltmeter
Rear anti-lock
braking system
Data link
connector
Ground

MT4029100157000X

Fig. 82 Diagnostic tool connection. Pickup

Check flow connected with wheel speed sensor

NOTE:
When checking with an oscilloscope, first measure voltage variations in the wheel speed sensor output.

- Is the resistance value of the wheel speed sensor part, which the displayed diagnostic trouble code indicates, normal? **Standard value: 0.8–1.2 kΩ**
  - No → Malfunction of wheel speed sensor → Replace wheel speed sensor.
  - Yes ↓
- Is the resistance value with the ECU connector normal?
  - No → Harness wire for wheel speed sensor circuit is broken. → Repair harness.
  - Yes ↓

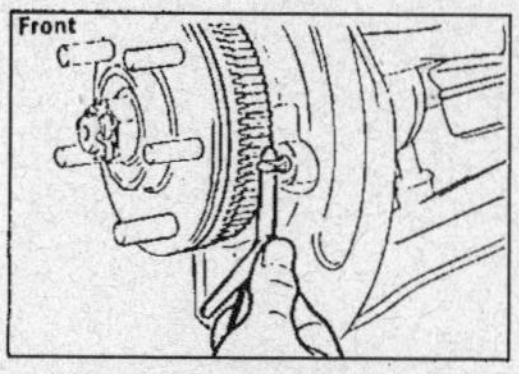
Front

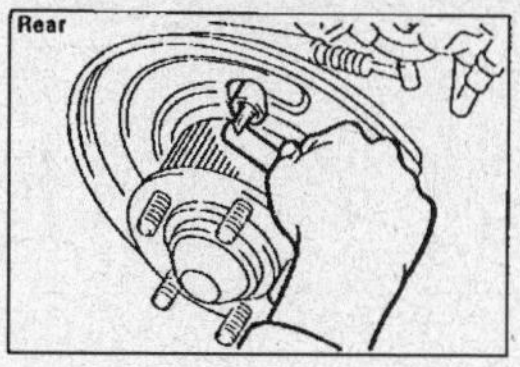
Rear

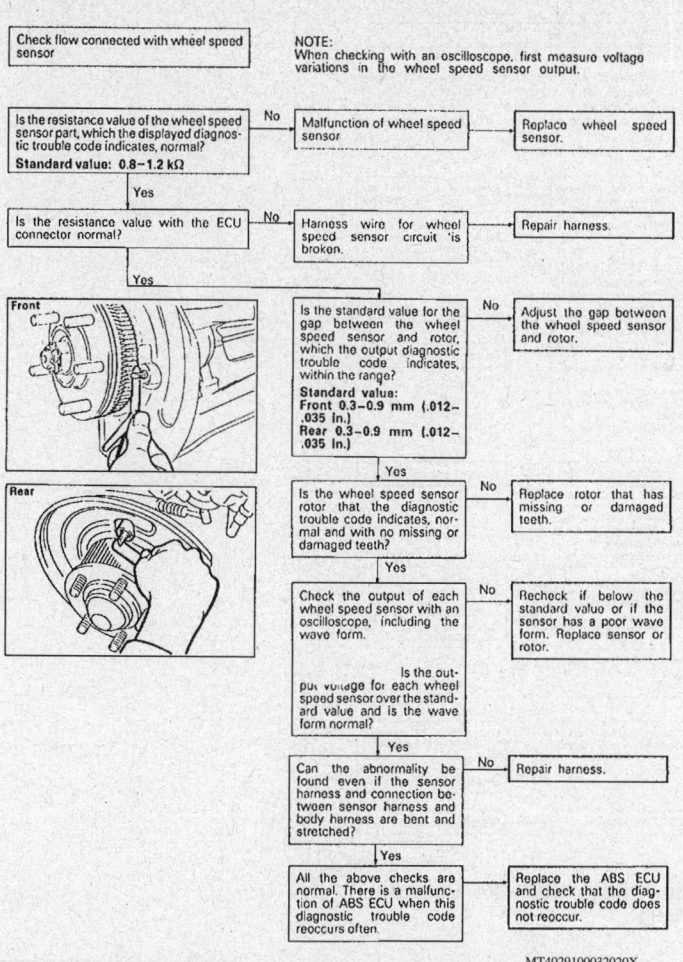

- Is the standard value for the gap between the wheel speed sensor and rotor, which the output diagnostic trouble code indicates, within the range? **Standard value: Front 0.3–0.9 mm (.012–.035 in.) Rear 0.3–0.9 mm (.012–.035 in.)**
  - No → Adjust the gap between the wheel speed sensor and rotor.
  - Yes ↓
- Is the wheel speed sensor rotor that the diagnostic trouble code indicates, normal and with no missing or damaged teeth?
  - No → Replace rotor that has missing or damaged teeth.
  - Yes ↓
- Check the output of each wheel speed sensor with an oscilloscope, including the wave form. Is the output voltage for each wheel speed sensor over the standard value and is the wave form normal?
  - No → Recheck if below the standard value or if the sensor has a poor wave form. Replace sensor or rotor.
  - Yes ↓
- Can the abnormality be found even if the sensor harness and connection between sensor harness and body harness are bent and stretched?
  - No → Repair harness.
  - Yes ↓
- All the above checks are normal. There is a malfunction of ABS ECU when this diagnostic trouble code reoccurs often. → Replace the ABS ECU and check that the diagnostic trouble code does not reoccur.

MT4029100032020X

Fig. 83 Codes 11, 12, 13, 14 & 15: Speed Sensors (Part 2 of 2). 1993–94 Eclipse FWD

E-4	When diagnostic trouble codes "41 SOL V FRONT L", "42 SOL V FRONT R" OR "43 SOL V REAR" are displayed

[Explanation]

The ABS ECU normally monitors the solenoid valve drive circuit.
If no current flows in the solenoid even if the ECU turns the solenoid ON or if it continues to flow even when turned OFF, the ECU determines the solenoid coil wire is broken/short circuited or the harness is broken short circuited and then these diagnostic trouble codes are output.

- Remove HU 10P connector and check with the HU side connector.
- Is the resistance value for the solenoid valve, that the displayed diagnostic trouble code indicates, within the range of the standard values? **Standard value: 3.0–3.2 Ω**
  - No → Replace HU.
  - Yes ↓
- Connect HU 10P connector, disconnect ECU connector and check.
- Is the solenoid valve resistance value, that the output diagnostic trouble code displays, within the range of the standard values when measured at the ECU connector? **Standard value: 3.0–3.2 Ω**
  - No → The harness wire for the solenoid valve circuit whose resistance value is outside the range of the standard value is broken or short circuited. → Repair ABS harness.
  - Yes ↓
- Malfunction of ABS ECU → Replace ABS ECU.

MT4029100034000X

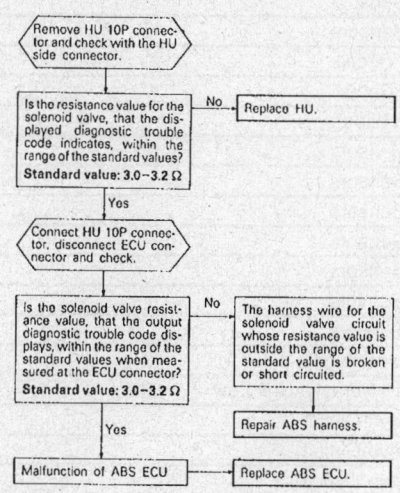

Fig. 85 Codes 41, 42 & 43: Solenoid Valves. 1993–94 Eclipse FWD

E-3	When diagnostic trouble code "22 STOP SW" is displayed

[Explanation]

The ABS ECU outputs this diagnostic trouble code in the following cases.

- Stop light switch may remain on for more than 15 minutes without the ABS functions.
- The harness wire for the stop light switch may be open.

[Hint]

If the stop light operates normal, the ABS harness wire for the stop light switch input circuit to the ECU is broken or there is a malfunction in the ABS ECU.

- Do the stop lights light up and go out normally?
  - No → Check the stop light related circuit and repair problem spots.
  - Yes ↓
- Disconnect the ABS ECU connector and inspect at the harness side connector.
- When the brake pedal is pressed forcefully, does the voltage between connector terminal No. 29 and ground indicate battery voltage?
  - No → Harness wire between stop light switch and ABS ECU is broken. → Repair harness.
  - Yes ↓
- Malfunction of ABS ECU → Replace ABS ECU.

MT4029100033000X

Fig. 84 Code 22: Stop Switch. 1993–94 Eclipse FWD

E-5	When diagnostic trouble code "51 VALVE RLY" is displayed

[Explanation]

When the ignition switch is turned ON, the ABS ECU switches the valve relay OFF and ON for an initial check, compares the voltage of the signal to the valve relay and valve power monitor line voltage to check whether the valve relay operation is normal. In addition, normally it monitors whether or not there is power in the valve power monitor line since the valve relay is normally ON. Then, if the supply of power to the valve power monitor line is interrupted, this diagnostic trouble code will output.

- Remove and check the valve relay.
- When the valve relay is checked, are the following conditions found?
  No. 85–No. 86: resistance value 60–120 Ω
  No. 30–No. 87a: continuity
  No. 30–No. 87: No continuity
  When battery voltage is applied between terminals No. 86 and No. 85 grounded.
  No. 30–No. 87: continuity
  No. 30–No. 87a: no continuity
  - No → Valve relay malfunction → Replace valve relay.
  - Yes ↓
- Install the valve relay and remove the HU connector.
- With the ignition key "ON", does the voltage between the connector terminal No. 52 and ground indicate battery voltage?
  - No → HU power harness wire is broken? → Repair harness.
  - Yes ↓
- Connect the HU harness and remove the ECU connector.
- Does resistance between body connector terminal No. 2 and terminal No. 27 indicate 60–120 ohm?
  - No → Malfunction of harness between HU and ECU → Repair harness.
  - Yes ↓
- Is there continuity between body connector terminal No. 22 and ground?
  - No → Repair harness.
  - Yes ↓
- ABS ECU malfunction → Replace ABS ECU.

MT4029100035000X

Fig. 86 Code 51: Valve Relay. 1993–94 Eclipse FWD

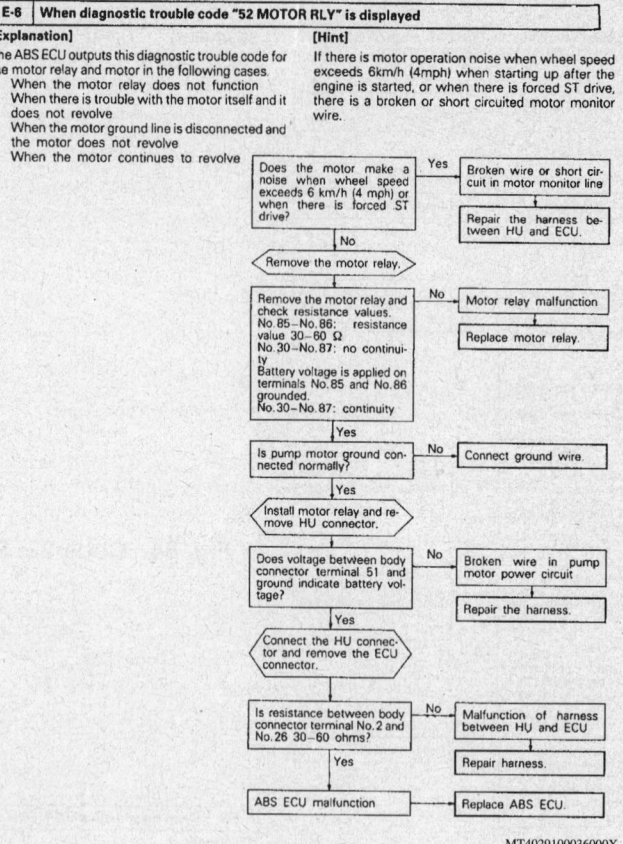

E-6	When diagnostic trouble code "52 MOTOR RLY" is displayed

[Explanation]

The ABS ECU outputs this diagnostic trouble code for the motor relay and motor in the following cases.

- When the motor relay does not function
- When there is trouble with the motor itself and it does not revolve
- When the motor ground line is disconnected and the motor does not revolve
- When the motor continues to revolve

[Hint]

If there is motor operation noise when wheel speed exceeds 6km/h (4mph) when starting up after the engine is started, or when there is forced ST drive, there is a broken or short circuited motor monitor wire.

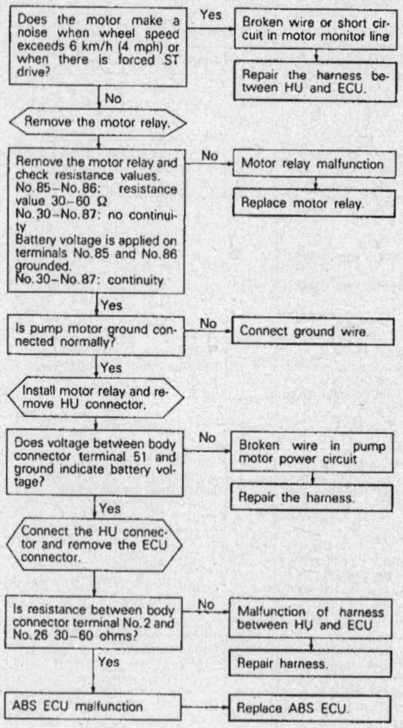
Does the motor make a noise when wheel speed exceeds 6 km/h (4 mph) or when there is forced ST drive?
Yes
Broken wire or short circuit in motor monitor line
Repair the harness between HU and ECU.
No
Remove the motor relay.
Remove the motor relay and check resistance values. No.85–No.86: resistance value 30–60 Ω No.30–No.87: no continuity Battery voltage is applied on terminals No.85 and No.86 grounded. No.30–No.87: continuity
No
Motor relay malfunction
Replace motor relay.
Yes
Is pump motor ground connected normally?
No
Connect ground wire.
Yes
Install motor relay and remove HU connector.
Does voltage between body connector terminal 51 and ground indicate battery voltage?
No
Broken wire in pump motor power circuit
Repair the harness.
Yes
Connect the HU connector and remove the ECU connector.
Is resistance between body connector terminal No.2 and No.26 30–60 ohms?
No
Malfunction of harness between HU and ECU
Repair harness.
Yes
ABS ECU malfunction
Replace ABS ECU.

MT4029100036000X

Fig. 87 Code 52: Motor Relay. 1993–94 Eclipse FWD

DIAGNOSTIC CHART INDEX

Code	Description	Page No.	Fig. No.
DIAMANTE			
Code 11	Wheel Speed Sensors	29-234	188
Code 12	Wheel Speed Sensors	29-234	188
Code 13	Wheel Speed Sensors	29-234	188
Code 14	Wheel Speed Sensors	29-234	188
Code 15	Speed Sensor Circuit	29-234	189
Code 15	Speed Sensor Circuit	29-234	189
Code 16	Power Supply Voltage	29-235	190
Code 21	Wheel Speed Sensors	29-234	188
Code 22	Wheel Speed Sensors	29-234	188
Code 23	Wheel Speed Sensors	29-234	188
Code 24	Wheel Speed Sensors	29-234	188
Code 25	Wheel Speed Sensors	29-234	188
Code 31	Wheel Speed Sensors	29-234	188
Code 32	Wheel Speed Sensors	29-234	188
Code 35	Generator Output Voltage	29-235	190
Code 37	Power Source Pressure For Hydraulic Unit Low	29-235	191
Code 41	Solenoid Valve Drive Circuit	29-235	192
Code 42	Solenoid Valve Drive Circuit	29-235	192
Code 43	Solenoid Valve Drive Circuit	29-235	192
Code 44	Solenoid Valve Drive Circuit	29-235	192
Code 45	Solenoid Valve Drive Circuit	29-235	192
Code 46	Solenoid Valve Drive Circuit	29-235	192

Continued

DIAGNOSTIC CHART INDEX—Continued

Code	Description	Page No.	Fig. No.
DIAMANTE			
Code 51	Valve Relay Drive Circuit	29-235	193
Code 52	Valve Relay Off & Motor Monitor Low	29-236	194
Code 53	Valve Relay Off & Motor Monitor Low	29-236	194
Code 54	Motor Relay	29-236	195
Code 61	Hydraulic Unit	29-236	196
Code 62	Hydraulic Unit Or Wheel Speed Sensor	29-237	197
1993–94 ECLIPSE AWD			
Code 11	Speed Sensors	29-210	88
Code 12	Speed Sensors	29-210	88
Code 13	Speed Sensors	29-210	88
Code 14	Speed Sensors	29-210	88
Code 15	Speed Sensors	29-210	88
Code 21	G Sensor	29-211	89
Code 22	Stop Switch	29-211	90
Code 41	Solenoid Valves	29-211	91
Code 42	Solenoid Valves	29-211	91
Code 43	Solenoid Valves	29-211	91
Code 51	Valve Relay	29-211	92
1993–94 ECLIPSE FWD			
Code 11	Speed Sensors	29-202	83
Code 12	Speed Sensors	29-202	83
Code 13	Speed Sensors	29-202	83
Code 14	Speed Sensors	29-202	83
Code 15	Speed Sensors	29-202	83
Code 22	Stop Switch	29-203	84
Code 41	Solenoid Valves	29-203	85
Code 42	Solenoid Valves	29-203	85
Code 43	Solenoid Valves	29-203	85
Code 51	Valve Relay	29-203	86
Code 52	Motor Relay	29-204	87
1995 ECLIPSE AWD			
Code 11	Wheel Speed Sensors (Open Or Short Circuit)	29-222	127
Code 12	Wheel Speed Sensors (Open Or Short Circuit)	29-222	127
Code 13	Wheel Speed Sensors (Open Or Short Circuit)	29-222	127
Code 14	Wheel Speed Sensors (Open Or Short Circuit)	29-222	127
Code 15	Wheel Speed Sensor System	29-222	128
Code 16	Power Supply System	29-222	129
Code 21	G-Sensor System	29-222	130
Code 22	Stop Light Switch System	29-222	132
Code 41	Solenoid Valve System	29-223	134
Code 42	Solenoid Valve System	29-223	134
Code 43	Solenoid Valve System	29-223	134
Code 51	Valve Relay System	29-223	136
Code 52	Motor Relay (Motor System)	29-223	137
1995 ECLIPSE FWD			
Code 11	Wheel Speed Sensors (Open Or Short Circuit)	29-222	127
Code 12	Wheel Speed Sensors (Open Or Short Circuit)	29-222	127
Code 13	Wheel Speed Sensors (Open Or Short Circuit)	29-222	127
Code 14	Wheel Speed Sensors (Open Or Short Circuit)	29-222	127
Code 15	Wheel Speed Sensor System	29-222	128
Code 16	Power Supply System	29-222	129
Code 21	Wheel Speed Sensor (Excessive Gap)	29-222	131
Code 22	Wheel Speed Sensor (Excessive Gap)	29-222	131
Code 23	Wheel Speed Sensor (Excessive Gap)	29-222	131

Continued

DIAGNOSTIC CHART INDEX—Continued

Code	Description	Page No.	Fig. No.
1995 ECLIPSE FWD			
Code 24	Wheel Speed Sensor (Excessive Gap)	29-222	131
Code 38	Stop Light Switch System	29-223	133
Code 41	Solenoid Valve System	29-223	135
Code 42	Solenoid Valve System	29-223	135
Code 43	Solenoid Valve System	29-223	135
Code 51	Valve Relay System	29-223	136
Code 53	Motor Relay (Motor System)	29-224	138
1996 ECLIPSE AWD			
Code 11	Wheel Speed Sensor Open Circuit	29-225	148
Code 12	Wheel Speed Sensor Open Circuit	29-225	148
Code 13	Wheel Speed Sensor Open Circuit	29-225	148
Code 14	Wheel Speed Sensor Open Circuit	29-225	148
Code 15	Wheel Speed Sensor System	29-226	149
Code 21	G-Sensor System	29-226	150
Code 22	Stop Light Switch System	29-226	151
Code 41	Solenoid Valve System	29-226	152
Code 42	Solenoid Valve System	29-226	152
Code 43	Solenoid Valve System	29-226	152
Code 51	Valve Relay System	29-226	153
Code 52	Motor Relay, Motor System	29-227	154
1996 ECLIPSE FWD			
Code 11	Wheel Speed Sensor Open Circuit	29-227	155
Code 12	Wheel Speed Sensor Open Circuit	29-227	155
Code 13	Wheel Speed Sensor Open Circuit	29-227	155
Code 14	Wheel Speed Sensor Open Circuit	29-227	155
Code 15	Wheel Speed Sensor System	29-227	156
Code 16	Power Supply System	29-227	157
Code 21	Wheel Speed Sensor Excessive Gap Or Short Circuit	29-227	158
Code 22	Wheel Speed Sensor Excessive Gap Or Short Circuit	29-227	158
Code 23	Wheel Speed Sensor Excessive Gap Or Short Circuit	29-227	158
Code 24	Wheel Speed Sensor Excessive Gap Or Short Circuit	29-227	158
Code 38	Stop Light Switch System	29-228	159
Code 41	Solenoid Valve System	29-228	160
Code 42	Solenoid Valve System	29-228	160
Code 43	Solenoid Valve System	29-228	160
Code 51	Valve Relay System	29-228	161
Code 53	Motor Relay, Motor System	29-228	162
EXPO AWD			
Code 11	Speed Sensors	29-213	99
Code 12	Speed Sensors	29-213	99
Code 13	Speed Sensors	29-213	99
Code 14	Speed Sensors	29-213	99
Code 15	Speed Sensors	29-213	99
Code 21	G Sensor	29-214	100
Code 22	Stop Lamp Switch	29-214	101
Code 41	Solenoid Valves	29-214	102
Code 42	Solenoid Valves	29-214	102
Code 43	Solenoid Valves	29-214	102
Code 51	Valve Relay	29-215	103
Code 52	Motor Relay	29-215	104
EXPO FWD			
Code 11	Speed Sensors	29-212	94
Code 12	Speed Sensors	29-212	94
Code 13	Speed Sensors	29-212	94

Continued

DIAGNOSTIC CHART INDEX—Continued

Code	Description	Page No.	Fig. No.
EXPO FWD			
Code 14	Speed Sensors	29-212	94
Code 15	Speed Sensors	29-212	94
Code 22	Stop Lamp Switch	29-212	95
Code 41	Solenoid Valves	29-213	96
Code 42	Solenoid Valves	29-213	96
Code 43	Solenoid Valves	29-213	96
Code 51	Valve Relay	29-213	97
Code 52	Motor Relay	29-213	98
1993 GALANT AWD			
Code 11	Speed Sensors	29-217	110
Code 12	Speed Sensors	29-217	110
Code 13	Speed Sensors	29-217	110
Code 14	Speed Sensors	29-217	110
Code 15	Speed Sensors	29-217	110
Code 21	G Sensor	29-217	111
Code 22	Stop Switch	29-217	112
Code 41	Solenoid Valves	29-218	113
Code 42	Solenoid Valves	29-218	113
Code 43	Solenoid Valves	29-218	113
Code 51	Valve Relay	29-218	114
Code 52	Motor Relay	29-218	115
1993 GALANT FWD			
Code 11	Speed Sensors	29-215	105
Code 12	Speed Sensors	29-215	105
Code 13	Speed Sensors	29-215	105
Code 14	Speed Sensors	29-215	105
Code 15	Speed Sensors	29-215	105
Code 22	Stop Switch	29-216	106
Code 41	Solenoid Valves	29-216	107
Code 42	Solenoid Valves	29-216	107
Code 43	Solenoid Valves	29-216	107
Code 51	Valve Relay	29-216	108
Code 52	Motor Relay	29-216	109
1994–96 GALANT			
Code 11	Speed Sensors (Open Circuit)	29-228	163
Code 12	Speed Sensors (Open Circuit)	29-228	163
Code 13	Speed Sensors (Open Circuit)	29-228	163
Code 14	Speed Sensors (Open Circuit)	29-228	163
Code 16	Power Supply System	29-229	164
Code 21	Speed Sensors (Short Circuit)	29-229	165
Code 22	Speed Sensors (Short Circuit)	29-229	165
Code 23	Speed Sensors (Short Circuit)	29-229	165
Code 24	Speed Sensors (Short Circuit)	29-229	165
Code 25	Speed Sensors (Excessive Gap)	29-229	166
Code 26	Speed Sensors (Excessive Gap)	29-229	166
Code 27	Speed Sensors (Excessive Gap)	29-229	166
Code 28	Speed Sensors (Excessive Gap)	29-229	166
Code 31	Pedal Stroke Sensor Circuit System (1994–95)	29-229	167
Code 32	Pedal Stroke Sensor Abnormality (1994–95)	29-229	168
Code 33	Stop Light Switch System	29-229	169
Code 34	Pedal Stroke Sensor & Pump System (1994–95)	29-230	170
Code 35	Wheel Speed Sensor Pulse Processing	29-230	171
Code 36	Wheel Speed Sensor Pulse Processing	29-230	171
Code 37	Wheel Speed Sensor Pulse Processing	29-230	171
Code 38	Wheel Speed Sensor Pulse Processing	29-230	171

Continued

DIAGNOSTIC CHART INDEX—Continued

Code	Description	Page No.	Fig. No.
1994–96 GALANT			
Code 41	Solenoid Valve	29-230	172
Code 42	Solenoid Valve	29-230	172
Code 43	Solenoid Valve	29-230	172
Code 44	Solenoid Valve	29-230	172
Code 45	Solenoid Valve	29-230	172
Code 46	Solenoid Valve	29-230	172
Code 47	Solenoid Valve	29-230	172
Code 48	Solenoid Valve	29-230	172
Code 51	Valve Relay ON Impossible (1994–95)	29-230	173
	Valve Relay ON Impossible (1996)	29-231	174
Code 52	Valve Relay OFF Impossible	29-231	175
Code 53	Motor Relay, Motor ON Impossible (1994–95)	29-231	176
	Motor Relay, Motor ON Impossible (1996)	29-231	177
Code 54	Motor Relay, Motor OFF Impossible	29-232	178
MIRAGE			
Code 11	Speed Sensors (Open Circuit)	29-237	198
Code 12	Speed Sensors (Open Circuit)	29-237	198
Code 13	Speed Sensors (Open Circuit)	29-237	198
Code 14	Speed Sensors (Open Circuit)	29-237	198
Code 15	Speed Sensors (Open Circuit)	29-237	198
Code 16	Drop Of Battery Voltage & Drop Of Generator Output Voltage	29-238	202
Code 21	Speed Sensors (Short Circuit)	29-237	199
Code 22	Speed Sensors (Short Circuit)	29-237	199
Code 23	Speed Sensors (Short Circuit)	29-237	199
Code 24	Speed Sensors (Short Circuit)	29-237	199
Code 25	Open Circuit In Both Rear Wheel Speed Sensors	29-238	200
Code 31	Front Wheel Speed Sensor Rotors	29-238	201
Code 32	Front Wheel Speed Sensor Rotors	29-238	201
Code 35	Drop Of Battery Voltage & Drop Of Generator Output Voltage	29-238	202
Code 41	Solenoid Valves	29-238	203
Code 42	Solenoid Valves	29-238	203
Code 43	Solenoid Valves	29-238	203
Code 44	Solenoid Valves	29-238	203
Code 51	Valve Relay No. 1	29-239	204
Code 52	Valve Relay No. 2	29-239	205
Code 53	Motor Relay No. 1	29-239	206
Code 54	Motor Relay No. 2	29-239	207
Code 55	Motor Sticking	29-240	208
Code 62	Hydraulic Unit	29-240	209
1993–95 MONTERO			
Code 11	Speed Sensor Circuits	29-240	210
Code 12	Speed Sensor Circuits	29-240	210
Code 13	Speed Sensor Circuits	29-240	210
Code 14	Speed Sensor Circuits	29-240	210
Code 16	ECU Power Voltage	29-241	211
Code 21	Speed Sensor Circuits	29-240	210
Code 22	Speed Sensor Circuits	29-240	210
Code 23	Speed Sensor Circuits	29-240	210
Code 24	Speed Sensor Circuits	29-240	210
Code 25	Free Wheel Engage Switch	29-241	212
Code 26	Center Differential Lock Detection Switch	29-242	213
Code 27	Rear Differential Lock Detection Switch	29-242	214
Code 31	G Sensor Power Voltage	29-242	215
Code 32	G Sensor Output Voltage	29-243	216
Code 33	Stop Light Switch	29-243	217

Continued

DIAGNOSTIC CHART INDEX—Continued

Code	Description	Page No.	Fig. No.
1993–95 MONTERO			
Code 41	Solenoid Valves	29-244	218
Code 43	Solenoid Valves	29-244	218
Code 45	Solenoid Valves	29-244	218
Code 53	Motor Relay	29-244	220
1996 MONTERO			
Code 11	Wheel Speed Sensor Open Circuit	29-244	221
Code 12	Wheel Speed Sensor Open Circuit	29-244	221
Code 13	Wheel Speed Sensor Open Circuit	29-244	221
Code 14	Wheel Speed Sensor Open Circuit	29-244	221
Code 15	Wheel Speed Sensor Defective Output Signal	29-245	222
Code 16	Power Supply System	29-245	223
Code 21	Wheel Speed Sensor Short Circuit	29-245	224
Code 22	Wheel Speed Sensor Short Circuit	29-245	224
Code 23	Wheel Speed Sensor Short Circuit	29-245	224
Code 24	Wheel Speed Sensor Short Circuit	29-245	224
Code 25	Free Wheel Engage Switch	29-245	225
Code 26	Center Differential Lock Detection Switch	29-245	226
Code 27	Rear Differential Lock Detection Switch (w/Rear Differential Lock)	29-245	227
	Rear Differential Lock Detection Switch (Less Rear Differential Lock)	29-246	228
Code 32	G-Sensor System	29-246	229
Code 33	Stop Light Switch System	29-246	230
Code 41	Solenoid Valve	29-246	231
Code 42	Solenoid Valve	29-246	231
Code 43	Solenoid Valve	29-246	231
Code 51	Valve Relay	29-246	232
Code 53	Motor Relay & Motor Operation	29-247	233
PICKUP			
—	Diagnostic Trouble Codes	29-247	234
1993–95 3000GT AWD			
Code 11	Speed Sensors	29-220	121
Code 12	Speed Sensors	29-220	121
Code 13	Speed Sensors	29-220	121
Code 14	Speed Sensors	29-220	121
Code 15	Speed Sensors	29-220	121
Code 21	G Sensor	29-220	122
Code 22	Stop Lamp Switch	29-221	123
Code 41	Solenoid Valves	29-221	124
Code 42	Solenoid Valves	29-221	124
Code 43	Solenoid Valves	29-221	124
Code 51	Valve Relay	29-221	125
Code 52	Motor Relay	29-221	126
1993–95 3000GT FWD			
Code 11	Speed Sensors	29-218	116
Code 12	Speed Sensors	29-218	116
Code 13	Speed Sensors	29-218	116
Code 14	Speed Sensors	29-218	116
Code 15	Speed Sensors	29-218	116
Code 22	Stop Lamp Switch	29-219	117
Code 41	Solenoid Valves	29-219	118
Code 42	Solenoid Valves	29-219	118
Code 43	Solenoid Valves	29-219	118
Code 51	Valve Relay	29-219	119
Code 52	Motor Relay	29-220	120

Continued

DIAGNOSTIC CHART INDEX—Continued

Code	Description	Page No.	Fig. No.
1996 3000GT			
Code 11	Wheel Speed Sensor System Open Circuit	29-232	179
Code 12	Wheel Speed Sensor System Open Circuit	29-232	179
Code 13	Wheel Speed Sensor System Open Circuit	29-232	179
Code 14	Wheel Speed Sensor System Open Circuit	29-232	179
Code 15	Wheel Speed Sensor System Output Signal Abnormal	29-232	180
Code 16	ABS ECU Power Supply System Voltage Abnormally Low Or High	29-232	181
Code 21	Wheel Speed Sensor System Shorted	29-232	182
Code 22	Wheel Speed Sensor System Shorted	29-232	182
Code 23	Wheel Speed Sensor System Shorted	29-232	182
Code 24	Wheel Speed Sensor System Shorted	29-232	182
Code 26	G-Sensor System Open, Shorted Or Signal Abnormal	29-232	183
Code 38	Stop Light Switch System Open Circuit Or ON Trouble	29-233	184
Code 41	Solenoid Valve Systems	29-233	185
Code 42	Solenoid Valve Systems	29-233	185
Code 43	Solenoid Valve Systems	29-233	185
Code 44	Solenoid Valve Systems	29-233	185
Code 45	Solenoid Valve Systems	29-233	185
Code 46	Solenoid Valve Systems	29-233	185
Code 47	Solenoid Valve Systems	29-233	185
Code 48	Solenoid Valve Systems	29-233	185
Code 51	ABS Valve Relay System	29-233	186
Code 53	HU Pump Motor Or ABS Motor Relay System	29-233	187

E-1	When the following diagnostic trouble codes are displayed "11 FL SPD SENSOR" "12 FR SPD SENSOR" "13 RL SPD SENSOR" "14 RR SPD SENSOR"

[Explanation]

The ABS ECU detects breaks in the wheel speed sensor wire. This diagnostic trouble code is output if the wheel speed sensor signal is not input (or short circuited) or if its output is low when starting to drive or while driving.

[Hint]

In addition to a broken wire/short circuit in the wheel speed sensor, also check whether the sensor gap is too large, rotor teeth are missing, sensor harness wire is temporarily broken, or sensor harness and body connector are not properly inserted.

E-2	When diagnostic trouble code "15 SENSOR FAULT" is displayed

[Explanation]

This diagnostic trouble code is output when there is an abnormality (other than broken wire or short circuit) in the wheel speed sensor output signal while driving.

[Hint]

The following can be considered as the cause of the wheel speed sensor output abnormality.

- Distortion of rotor, teeth missing
- Low frequency noise interference when sensor harness wire is broken
- Noise interference in sensor signal
- When the sensor output signal is below the standard value or when amplitude modulation is over the standard value, using an oscilloscope to measure the wave shape of the wheel speed sensor output signal is very effective.
- Loose wheel bearing
- Temporarily broken wire in sensor harness
- Sensor harness and body connector are not properly inserted.

NOTE

(1) If contact is poor, check the sensor cable by bending and lightly stretching it.

(2) If there is currently no trouble and if abnormality in the displayed sensor circuit cannot be discovered since values are normal even when checked, turn the ignition switch OFF and re-execute the driving test. Try replacing the ABS ECU only if the same diagnostic trouble code is output at this time.

(If it is difficult to recreate the trouble, there is a possibility of speed sensor trouble recurring even if the ECU is replaced.)

MT4029100037010X

Fig. 88 Codes 11, 12, 13, 14 & 15: Speed Sensors (Part 1 of 2). 1993–94 Eclipse AWD

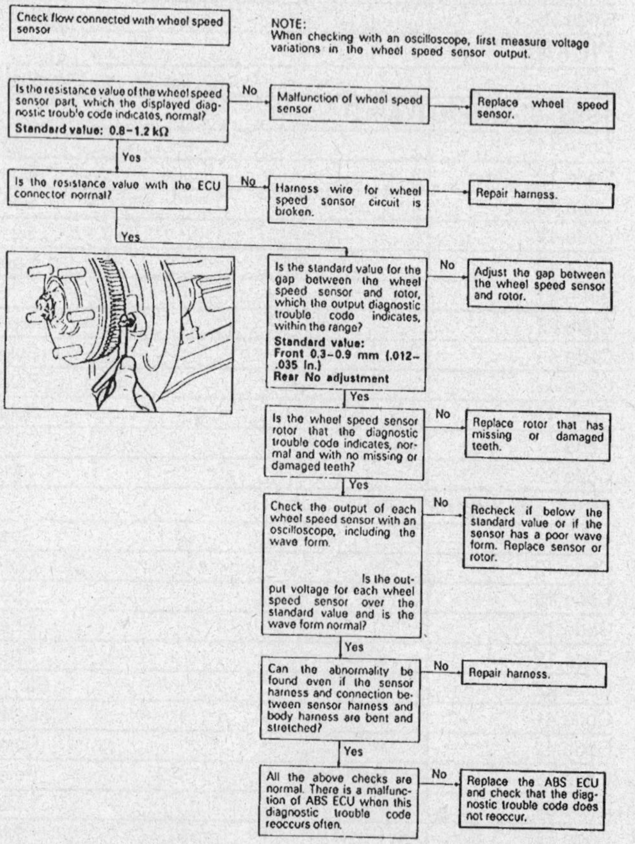
Check flow connected with wheel speed sensor
NOTE:
When checking with an oscilloscope, first measure voltage variations in the wheel speed sensor output.
Is the resistance value of the wheel speed sensor part, which the displayed diagnostic trouble code indicates, normal?
Standard value: 0.8–1.2 kΩ
No
Malfunction of wheel speed sensor
Replace wheel speed sensor.
Yes
Is the resistance value with the ECU connector normal?
No
Harness wire for wheel speed sensor circuit is broken.
Repair harness.
Yes
Is the standard value for the gap between the wheel speed sensor and rotor, which the output diagnostic trouble code indicates, within the range?
Standard value:
Front 0.3–0.9 mm (.012–.035 In.)
Rear No adjustment
No
Adjust the gap between the wheel speed sensor and rotor.
Yes
Is the wheel speed sensor rotor that the diagnostic trouble code indicates, normal and with no missing or damaged teeth?
No
Replace rotor that has missing or damaged teeth.
Yes
Check the output of each wheel speed sensor with an oscilloscope, including the wave form.
Is the output voltage for each wheel speed sensor over the standard value and is the wave form normal?
No
Recheck if below the standard value or if the sensor has a poor wave form. Replace sensor or rotor.
Yes
Can the abnormality be found even if the sensor harness and connection between sensor harness and body harness are bent and stretched?
No
Repair harness.
Yes
All the above checks are normal. There is a malfunction of ABS ECU when this diagnostic trouble code reoccurs often.
No
Replace the ABS ECU and check that the diagnostic trouble code does not reoccur.

MT4029100037020X

Fig. 88 Codes 11, 12, 13, 14 & 15: Speed Sensors (Part 2 of 2). 1993–94 Eclipse AWD

E-3	When diagnostic trouble code "21 G SENSOR" is displayed

[Explanation]

The ABS ECU outputs this diagnostic trouble code in the following cases.

- OFF trouble turning G sensor OFF (It is judged that the G sensor continues to be OFF for more than approximately 13 seconds except when the vehicle is stopped or when there is stop light switch input.
- When there is a broken wire or short circuit in the harness for the G sensor system.

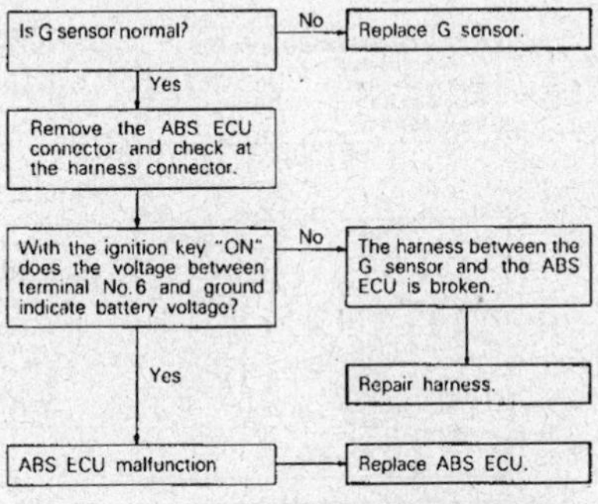
Is G sensor normal?
No
Replace G sensor.
Yes
Remove the ABS ECU connector and check at the harness connector.
With the ignition key "ON" does the voltage between terminal No.6 and ground indicate battery voltage?
No
The harness between the G sensor and the ABS ECU is broken.
Yes
Repair harness.
ABS ECU malfunction
Replace ABS ECU.

MT4029100040000X

Fig. 89 Code 21: G-Sensor. 1993–94 Eclipse AWD

E-4	When diagnostic trouble code "22 STOP SW" is displayed

[Explanation]

The ABS ECU outputs this diagnostic trouble code in the following cases.

- Stop light switch may remain on for more than 15 minutes without the ABS functions.
- The harness wire for the stop light switch may be open.

[Hint]

If the stop light operates normal, the ABS harness wire for the stop light switch input circuit to the ECU is broken or there is a malfunction in the ABS ECU.

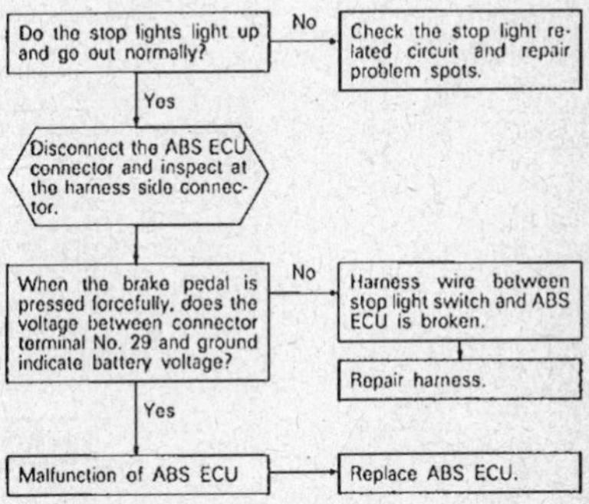
Do the stop lights light up and go out normally?
No
Check the stop light related circuit and repair problem spots.
Yes
Disconnect the ABS ECU connector and inspect at the harness side connector.
When the brake pedal is pressed forcefully, does the voltage between connector terminal No. 29 and ground indicate battery voltage?
No
Harness wire between stop light switch and ABS ECU is broken.
Repair harness.
Yes
Malfunction of ABS ECU
Replace ABS ECU.

MT4029100041000X

Fig. 90 Code 22: Stop Switch. 1993–94 Eclipse AWD

E-5	When diagnostic trouble codes "41 SOL V FRONT L", "42 SOL V FRONT R" OR "43 SOL V DRIFT" are displayed

[Explanation]

The ABS ECU normally monitors the solenoid valve drive circuit.

If no current flows in the solenoid even if the ECU turns the solenoid ON or if it continues to flow even when turned OFF, the ECU determines the solenoid coil wire is broken/short circuited or the harness is broken short circuited and then these diagnostic trouble codes are output.

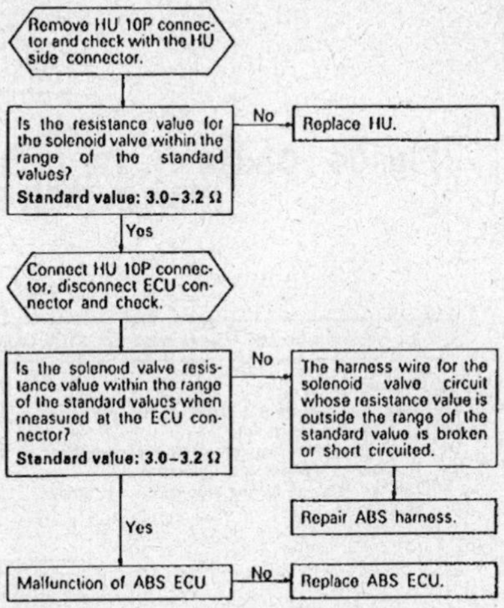
Remove HU 10P connector and check with the HU side connector.
Is the resistance value for the solenoid valve within the range of the standard values?
Standard value: 3.0–3.2 Ω
No
Replace HU.
Yes
Connect HU 10P connector, disconnect ECU connector and check.
Is the solenoid valve resistance value within the range of the standard values when measured at the ECU connector?
Standard value: 3.0–3.2 Ω
No
The harness wire for the solenoid valve circuit whose resistance value is outside the range of the standard value is broken or short circuited.
Repair ABS harness.
Yes
Malfunction of ABS ECU
No
Replace ABS ECU.

MT4029100042000X

Fig. 91 Codes 41, 42 & 43: Solenoid Valves. 1993–94 Eclipse AWD

E-6	When diagnostic trouble code "51 VALVE RLY" is displayed

[Explanation]

When the ignition switch is turned ON, the ABS ECU switches the valve relay OFF and ON for an initial check, compares the voltage of the signal to the valve relay and valve power monitor line voltage to check whether the valve relay operation is normal. In addition, normally it monitors whether or not there is power in the valve power monitor line since the valve relay is normally ON. Then, if the supply of power to the valve power monitor line is interrupted, this diagnostic trouble code will output.

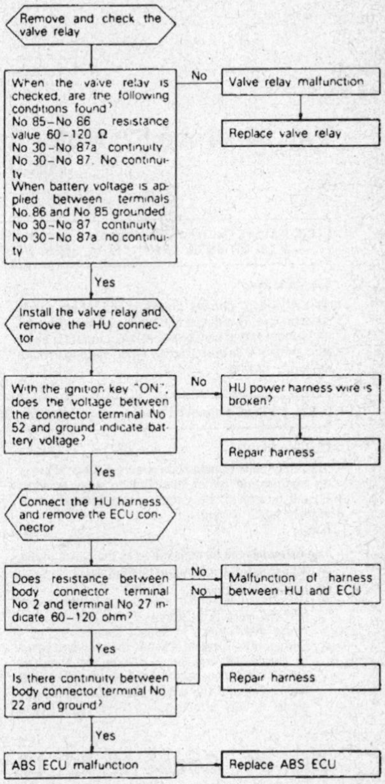
Remove and check the valve relay
When the valve relay is checked, are the following conditions found?
No 85–No 66 resistance value 60–120 Ω
No 30–No 87a continuity
No 30–No 87 No continuity
When battery voltage is applied between terminals No.86 and No 85 grounded
No 30–No 87 continuity
No 30–No 87a no continuity
No
Valve relay malfunction
Replace valve relay
Yes
Install the valve relay and remove the HU connector
With the ignition key "ON", does the voltage between the connector terminal No 52 and ground indicate battery voltage?
No
HU power harness wire is broken?
Repair harness
Yes
Connect the HU harness and remove the ECU connector
Does resistance between body connector terminal No 2 and terminal No 27 indicate 60–120 ohm?
No
No
Malfunction of harness between HU and ECU
Yes
Is there continuity between body connector terminal No 22 and ground?
Repair harness
Yes
ABS ECU malfunction
Replace ABS ECU

MT4029100043000X

Fig. 92 Code 51: Valve Relay. 1993–94 Eclipse AWD

E-7	When diagnostic trouble code "52 MOTOR RLY" is displayed

[Explanation]

The ABS ECU outputs this diagnostic trouble code for the motor relay and motor in the following cases.

- When the motor relay does not function
- When there is trouble with the motor itself and it does not revolve
- When there is trouble with the motor itself and it the motor does not revolve
- When the motor continues to revolve

[Hint]

If there is motor operation noise when wheel speed exceeds 6km/h (4mph) when starting up after the engine is started, or when there is forced ST drive, there is a broken or short circuited motor monitor wire.

- Does the motor make a noise when wheel speed exceeds 6 km/h (4 mph) or when there is forced ST drive?
  - Yes → Broken wire or short circuit in motor monitor line → Repair the harness between HU and ECU.
  - No ↓
- Remove the motor relay
- Remove the motor relay and check resistance values. No.85–No.86: resistance value 30–60 Ω. No 30–No.87: no continuity. Battery voltage is applied on terminals No 86 and No 85 grounded. No 30–No.87: continuity
  - No → Motor relay malfunction → Replace motor relay
  - Yes ↓
- Is pump motor ground connected normally?
  - No → Connect ground wire.
  - Yes ↓
- Install motor relay and remove HU connector
- Does voltage between body connector terminal 51 and ground indicate battery voltage?
  - No → Broken wire in pump motor power circuit → Repair the harness.
  - Yes ↓
- Connect the HU connector and remove the ECU connector
- Is resistance between body connector terminal No 2 and No 26 30–60 ohms?
  - No → Malfunction of harness between HU and ECU → Repair harness.
  - Yes ↓
- ABS ECU malfunction → Replace ABS ECU.

MT4029100044000X

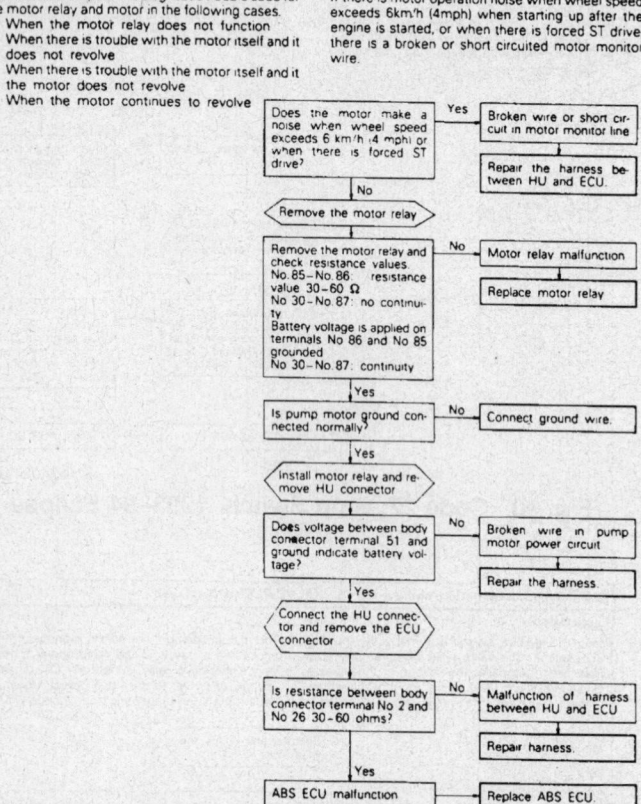

Fig. 93 Code 52: Motor Relay. 1993–94 Eclipse AWD

E-1	When the following diagnostic trouble codes are displayed "11 FL SNSR. OPEN" "12 FR SNSR. OPEN" "13 RL SNSR. OPEN" "14 RR SNSR. OPEN"

[Explanation]

The ABS ECU detects breaks in the wheel speed sensor wire. This diagnostic trouble code is output if the wheel speed sensor signal is not input (or short circuited) or if its output is low when starting to drive or while driving.

[Hint]

In addition to a broken wire/short circuit in the wheel speed sensor, also check whether the sensor gap is too large, sensor harness wire is broken, or sensor harness and body connector are not properly connected.

E-2	When diagnostic trouble code "15 VEH. SPD. SNSR." is displayed

[Explanation]

This diagnostic trouble code is output when there is an abnormality (other than broken wire or short circuit) in any of the wheel speed sensor output signals while driving.

[Hint]

The following can be considered as the cause of the wheel speed sensor output abnormality.

- Distortion of rotor, teeth missing
- Low frequency noise interference when sensor harness wire is broken
- Noise interference in sensor signal
- Sensor output signal is below the standard value or amplitude modulation is over the standard value. Using an oscilloscope to measure the wave shape of the wheel speed sensor output signal is very effective.
- Broken sensor harness
- Poor connection of connector

NOTE

(1) If contact is poor, check the sensor cable by bending and lightly stretching it.

(2) Except for the case where a fault condition exists in the system, but the inspection results are normal; if an abnormality cannot be found in the sensor circuit displayed as abnormal, erase the diagnostic trouble code and turn the ignition switch to OFF once, and then test-drive again. If the same diagnostic trouble code is output, replace the ABS ECU. If the trouble does not occur anymore, the problem is likely to be with the ABS ECU.
(If the trouble is in the speed sensor circuit, but is difficult to recreate, it will recur even after the ABS ECU has been replaced.)

MT4029100045010X

Fig. 94 Codes 11, 12, 13, 14 & 15: Speed Sensors (Part 1 of 2). Expo FWD

Check flow connected with wheel speed sensor

NOTE
When checking with an oscilloscope, first measure voltage variations in the wheel speed sensor output.

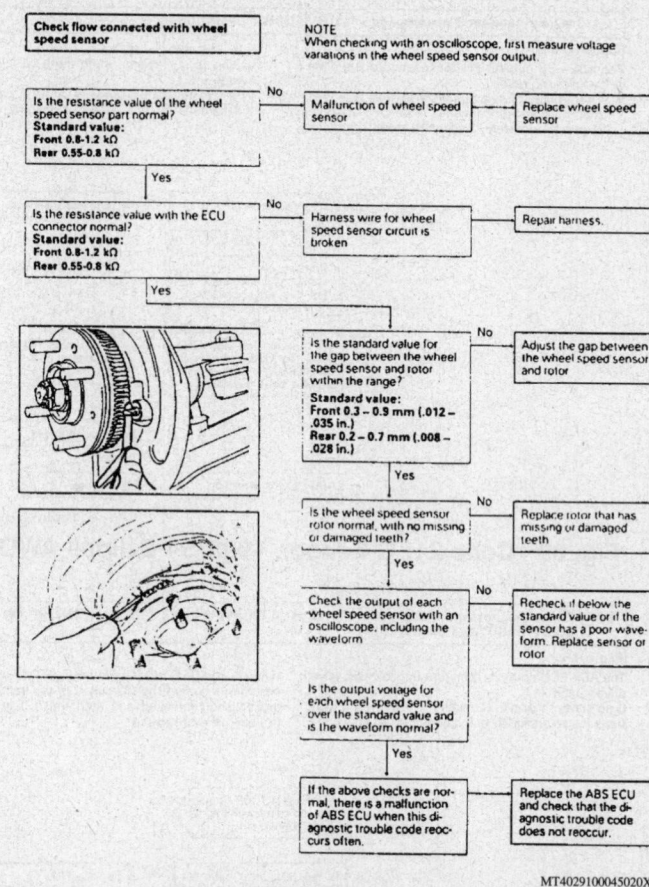

- Is the resistance value of the wheel speed sensor part normal? **Standard value: Front 0.8-1.2 kΩ Rear 0.55-0.8 kΩ**
  - No → Malfunction of wheel speed sensor → Replace wheel speed sensor
  - Yes ↓
- Is the resistance value with the ECU connector normal? **Standard value: Front 0.8-1.2 kΩ Rear 0.55-0.8 kΩ**
  - No → Harness wire for wheel speed sensor circuit is broken → Repair harness.
  - Yes ↓

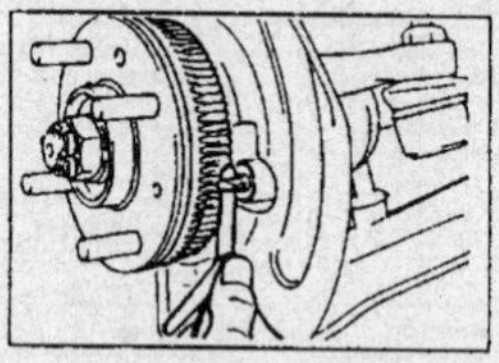

- Is the standard value for the gap between the wheel speed sensor and rotor within the range? **Standard value: Front 0.3 – 0.9 mm (.012 – .035 in.) Rear 0.2 – 0.7 mm (.008 – .028 in.)**
  - No → Adjust the gap between the wheel speed sensor and rotor
  - Yes ↓
- Is the wheel speed sensor rotor normal, with no missing or damaged teeth?
  - No → Replace rotor that has missing or damaged teeth
  - Yes ↓
- Check the output of each wheel speed sensor with an oscilloscope, including the waveform. Is the output voltage for each wheel speed sensor over the standard value and is the waveform normal?
  - No → Recheck if below the standard value or if the sensor has a poor waveform. Replace sensor or rotor
  - Yes ↓
- If the above checks are normal, there is a malfunction of ABS ECU when this diagnostic trouble code reoccurs often. → Replace the ABS ECU and check that the diagnostic trouble code does not reoccur.

MT4029100045020X

Fig. 94 Codes 11, 12, 13, 14 & 15: Speed Sensors (Part 2 of 2). Expo FWD

E-3	When diagnostic trouble code "22 STOP LAMP SW" is displayed

[Explanation]

The ABS ECU outputs this diagnostic trouble code in the following cases.

- Stop light switch may remain on for more than 15 minutes without ABS operation.
- The harness wire for the stop light switch may be open.

[Hint]

If the stop light operates normal, the harness for the stop light switch input circuit is broken or there is malfunction in the ABS ECU.

- Do the stop lights light up and go out normally?
  - No → Check the stop light related circuit and repair problem spots.
  - Yes ↓
- Disconnect the ABS ECU connector and inspect at the harness side connector.
- When the brake pedal is pressed forcefully, does the voltage between connector terminal No. 29 and ground indicate battery voltage?
  - No → Harness wire between stop light switch and ABS ECU is broken. → Repair harness.
  - Yes ↓
- Malfunction of ABS ECU → Replace ABS ECU.

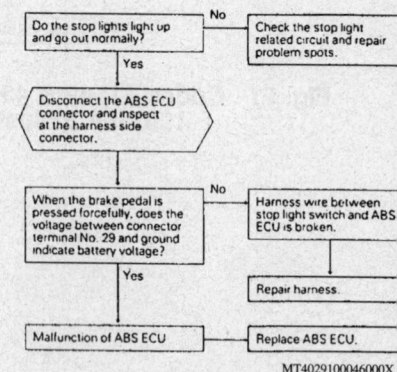

MT4029100046000X

Fig. 95 Code 22: Stop Lamp Switch. Expo FWD

E-4	When diagnostic trouble codes "41 FL SOL. VALVE", "42 FR SOL. VALVE" or "43 REAR SOL. V." are displayed.

[Explanation]

The ABS ECU normally monitors the solenoid valve drive circuit.
If no current flows in the solenoid even if the ECU turns the solenoid ON or if it continues to flow even when turned OFF, the ECU determines the solenoid coil wire is broken/short-circuited or the harness is broken/short-circuited, and then these diagnostic trouble codes are output.

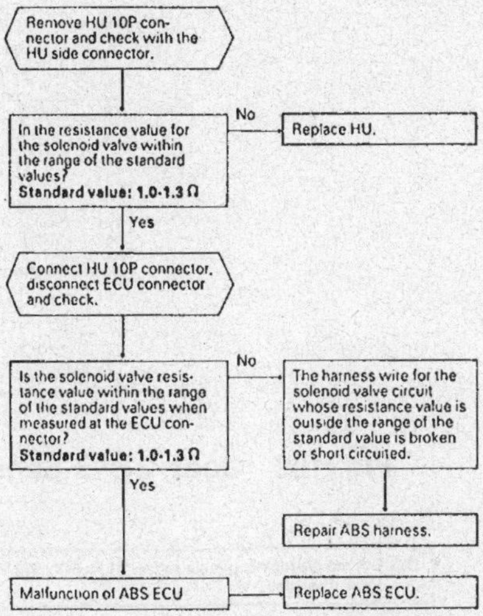

Remove HU 10P connector and check with the HU side connector.
In the resistance value for the solenoid valve within the range of the standard values?
Standard value: 1.0-1.3 Ω
No
Replace HU.
Yes
Connect HU 10P connector, disconnect ECU connector and check.
Is the solenoid valve resistance value within the range of the standard values when measured at the ECU connector?
Standard value: 1.0-1.3 Ω
No
The harness wire for the solenoid valve circuit whose resistance value is outside the range of the standard value is broken or short circuited.
Repair ABS harness.
Yes
Malfunction of ABS ECU
Replace ABS ECU.

MT4029100047000X

Fig. 96 Codes 41, 42 & 43: Solenoid Valves. Expo FWD

E-5	When diagnostic trouble code "51 VALVE RELAY" is displayed

[Explanation]

When the ignition switch is turned ON, the ABS ECU switches the valve relay OFF and ON for an initial check, compares the voltage of the signal to the valve relay and valve power monitor line voltage to check whether the valve relay operation is normal. In addition, normally it monitors whether or not there is power in the valve power monitor line since the valve relay is normally ON. Then, if the supply of power to the valve power monitor line is interrupted, this diagnostic trouble code will be output.

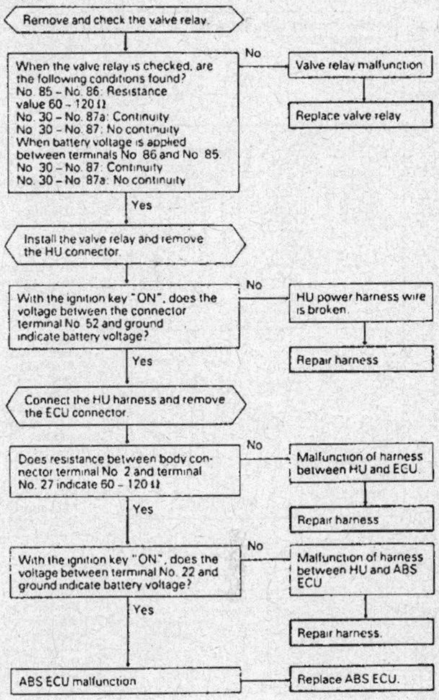

Remove and check the valve relay.
When the valve relay is checked, are the following conditions found?
No. 85 – No. 86: Resistance value 60 – 120 Ω
No. 30 – No. 87a: Continuity
No. 30 – No. 87: No continuity
When battery voltage is applied between terminals No. 86 and No. 85.
No. 30 – No. 87: Continuity
No. 30 – No. 87a: No continuity
No
Valve relay malfunction
Replace valve relay
Yes
Install the valve relay and remove the HU connector.
With the ignition key "ON", does the voltage between the connector terminal No. 52 and ground indicate battery voltage?
No
HU power harness wire is broken.
Repair harness
Yes
Connect the HU harness and remove the ECU connector.
Does resistance between body connector terminal No. 2 and terminal No. 27 indicate 60 – 120 Ω
No
Malfunction of harness between HU and ECU.
Repair harness
Yes
With the ignition key "ON", does the voltage between terminal No. 22 and ground indicate battery voltage?
No
Malfunction of harness between HU and ABS ECU
Repair harness.
Yes
ABS ECU malfunction
Replace ABS ECU.

MT4029100048000X

Fig. 97 Code 51: Valve Relay. Expo FWD

E-6	When diagnostic trouble code "52 MOTOR RELAY" is displayed

[Explanation]

The ABC-ECU outputs this diagnostic trouble code when the motor relay and motor are as follows:

- When the motor relay is ON and no signal is input to the motor monitor line (motor does not operate, etc.)
- When the motor relay is OFF and signals enter the motor monitor line for a period of approximately 5 seconds or more (motor operates continuously, etc.)
- When motor does not operate

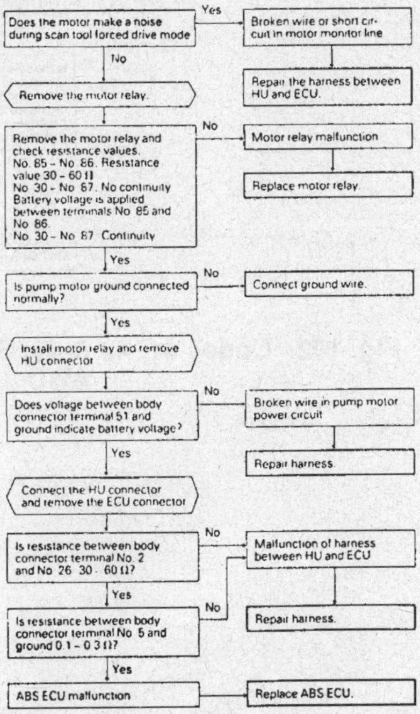

Does the motor make a noise during scan tool forced drive mode
Yes
Broken wire or short circuit in motor monitor line
Repair the harness between HU and ECU.
No
Remove the motor relay.
Remove the motor relay and check resistance values.
No. 85 – No. 86. Resistance value 30 – 60 Ω
No. 30 – No. 87. No continuity
Battery voltage is applied between terminals No. 85 and No. 86.
No. 30 – No. 87 Continuity
No
Motor relay malfunction
Replace motor relay.
Yes
Is pump motor ground connected normally?
No
Connect ground wire.
Yes
Install motor relay and remove HU connector
Does voltage between body connector terminal 51 and ground indicate battery voltage?
No
Broken wire in pump motor power circuit
Repair harness.
Yes
Connect the HU connector and remove the ECU connector
Is resistance between body connector terminal No. 2 and No. 26 30 - 60 Ω?
No
Malfunction of harness between HU and ECU
Repair harness.
Yes
Is resistance between body connector terminal No. 5 and ground 0.1 – 0.3 Ω?
No
Yes
ABS ECU malfunction
Replace ABS ECU.

MT4029100049000X

Fig. 98 Code 52: Motor Relay. Expo FWD

E-1	When the following diagnostic trouble codes are displayed "11 FL SNSR. OPEN" "12 FR SNSR. OPEN" "13 RL SNSR. OPEN" "14 RR SNSR. OPEN"

[Explanation]

The ABS ECU detects breaks in the wheel speed sensor wire. This diagnostic trouble code is output if the wheel speed sensor signal is not input (or short circuited) or if its output is low when starting to drive or while driving.

[Hint]

In addition to a broken wire/short circuit in the wheel speed sensor, also check whether the sensor gap is too large, sensor harness wire is broken, or sensor harness and body connector are not properly connected.

E-2	When diagnostic trouble code "15 VEH. SPD. SNSR." is displayed

[Explanation]

This diagnostic trouble code is output when there is an abnormality (other than broken wire or short circuit) in any of the wheel speed sensor output signals while driving.

[Hint]

The following can be considered as the cause of the wheel speed sensor output abnormality.

- Distortion of rotor, teeth missing
- Low frequency noise interference when sensor harness wire is broken
- Noise interference in sensor signal
- Sensor output signal is below the standard value or amplitude modulation is over the standard value. Using an oscilloscope to measure the wave shape of the wheel speed sensor output signal is very effective.
- Broken sensor harness
- Poor connection of connector

NOTE

(1) If contact is poor, check the sensor cable by bending and lightly stretching it.

(2) Except for the case where a fault condition exists in the system, but the inspection results are normal; if an abnormality cannot be found in the sensor circuit displayed as abnormal, erase the diagnostic trouble code and turn the ignition switch to OFF once, and then test-drive again. If the same diagnostic trouble code is output, replace the ABS ECU. If the trouble does not occur anymore, the problem is likely to be with the ABS ECU.
(If the trouble is in the speed sensor circuit, but is difficult to recreate, it will recur even after the ABS ECU has been replaced.)

MT4029100050010X

Fig. 99 Codes 11, 12, 13, 14 & 15: Speed Sensors (Part 1 of 2). Expo AWD

Check flow connected with wheel speed sensor

NOTE
Check speed sensor harness and connector connection and then observe with oscilloscope.

Is the resistance value of the wheel speed sensor part normal? **Standard value: 0.8 – 1.2 kΩ**
- No → Malfunction of wheel speed sensor → Replace wheel speed sensor
- Yes ↓

Is the resistance value at the ECU connector normal? **Standard value: 0.8 – 1.2 kΩ**
- No → Harness wire for wheel speed sensor circuit is broken → Repair harness.
- Yes ↓

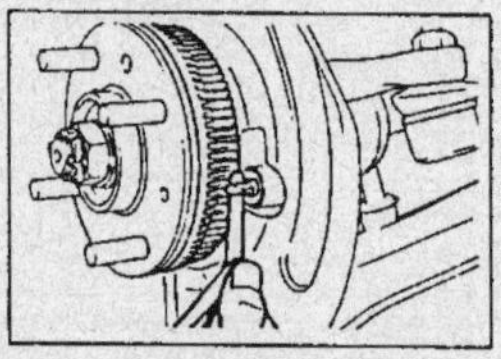

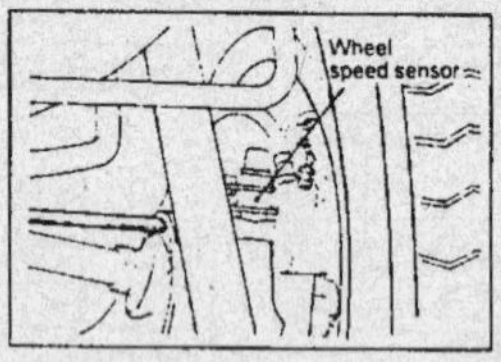
Wheel speed sensor

Is the front wheel speed sensor-to-rotor clearance normal? **Standard value: 0.3 – 0.9 mm (.012 – .035 in.)**
- No → Adjust the gap between the wheel speed sensor and rotor.
- Yes ↓

Are there any abnormalities such as a loose rear speed sensor mounting bolt?
- No → Retighten or correct abnormalities.
- Yes ↓

Is the rear speed sensor mounting surface-to-rotor tooth flank (all around) distance normal? **Standard value: 0.3 – 0.9 mm (.012 – .035 in.)**
- No → Adjust the gap between the wheel speed sensor and rotor.
- Yes ↓

Is the wheel speed sensor rotor normal, with no missing or damaged teeth?
- No → Replace rotor that has missing or damaged teeth.
- Yes ↓

Check the output of each wheel speed sensor with an oscilloscope, including the waveform. Is the output voltage for each wheel speed sensor over the standard value and is the waveform normal?
- No → Recheck if below the standard value or if the sensor has a poor waveform. Replace sensor or rotor.
- Yes ↓

If the above checks are normal, there is a malfunction of ABS ECU when this diagnostic trouble code reoccurs often. → Replace the ABS ECU and check that the diagnostic trouble code does not reoccur.

MT4029100050020X

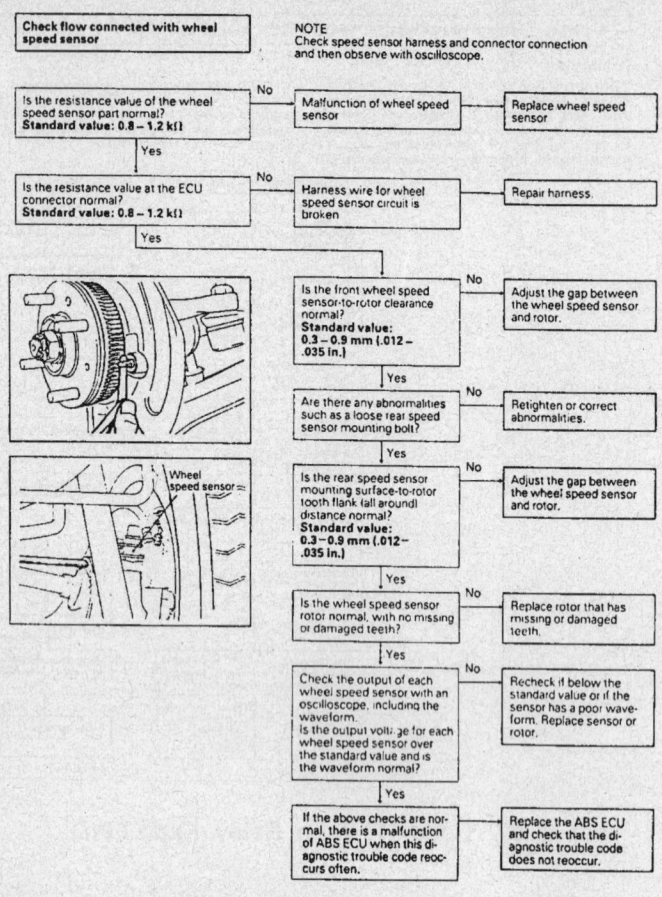

Fig. 99 Codes 11, 12, 13, 14 & 15: Speed Sensors (Part 2 of 2). Expo AWD

E-4	When diagnostic trouble code "22 STOP LAMP SW" is displayed

[Explanation]

The ABS-ECU outputs this diagnostic trouble code in the following cases.
- Stop light switch remains on for more than 15 minutes while the ABS is not functioning.
- The harness wire for the stop light switch may be open.

[Hint]

If the stop light operates normal, the harness for the stop light switch input circuit is broken or there is a malfunction in the ABS-ECU.

Do the stop lights light up and go out normally?
- No → Check the stop light related circuit and repair problem spots.
- Yes ↓

Disconnect the ABS-ECU connector and inspect at the harness side connector.

When the brake pedal is pressed forcefully, does the voltage between connector terminal No. 29 and ground indicate battery voltage?
- No → Harness wire between stop light switch and ABS-ECU is broken. → Repair harness.
- Yes ↓

Malfunction of ABS-ECU → Replace ABS-ECU

MT4029100052000X

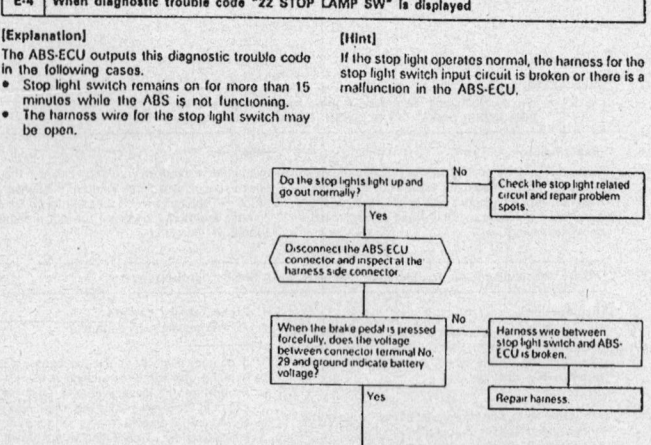

Fig. 101 Code 22: Stop Lamp Switch. Expo AWD

E-3	When diagnostic trouble code "21 G SNSR." is displayed

[Explanation]

The ABS-ECU outputs this diagnostic trouble code in the following cases.
- G sensor OFF trouble (It is judged that the G sensor continues to be OFF for more than approximately 13 seconds except when the vehicle is stopped or when there is stop light switch input.)
- When there is a broken wire or short circuit in the harness for the G sensor system.

Is G sensor normal?
- No → Replace G sensor
- Yes ↓

Remove the ABS-ECU connector and check at the harness connector.

With the ignition key "ON", does the voltage between terminal No. 6 and ground indicate battery voltage?
- No → The harness between the G sensor and the ABS ECU is broken → Repair harness.
- Yes ↓

ABS-ECU malfunction → Replace ABS-ECU.

MT4029100051000X

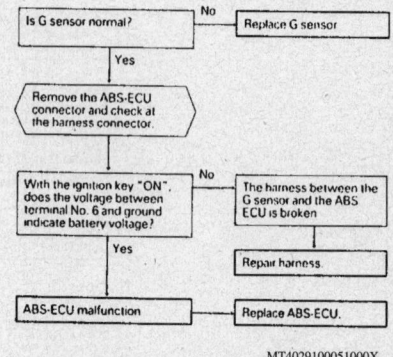

Fig. 100 Code 21: G Sensor. Expo AWD

E-5	When diagnostic trouble codes "41 FL SOL. VALVE", "42 FR SOL. VALVE" or "43 VALVE DRIFT are displayed.

[Explanation]

The ABS-ECU normally monitors the solenoid valve drive circuit.
If no current flows in the solenoid even if the ECU turns the solenoid ON or if it continues to flow even when turned OFF, the ECU determines the solenoid coil wire is broken/short-circuited or t harness is broken/short-circuited, and then the diagnostic trouble codes are output.
ABS-ECU controls the solenoid valve current and the current value of the solenoid valves differs fro each other in the same mode, solenoid valve dr error is produced and the ABS-ECU goes into t failsafe mode.

Remove HU 10P connector and check with the HU side connector.

In the resistance value for the solenoid valve within the range of the standard values? **Standard value: 1.0-1.3 Ω**
- No → Replace HU.
- Yes ↓

Connect HU 10P connector, disconnect ECU connector and check.

Is the solenoid valve resistance value within the range of the standard values when measured at the ECU connector? **Standard value: 1.0-1.3 Ω**
- No → The harness wire for the solenoid valve circuit whose resistance value is outside the range of the standard value is broken or short circuited. → Repair harness.
- Yes ↓

Malfunction of ABS-ECU → Replace ABS-ECU.

MT4029100053000X

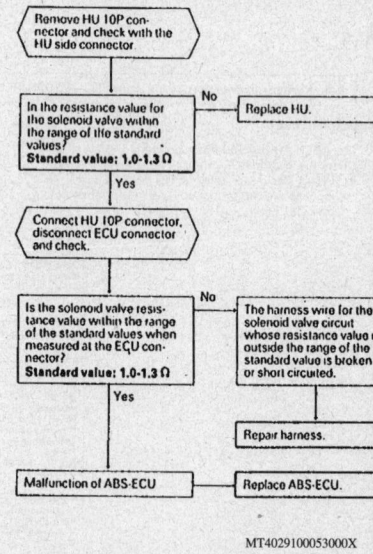

Fig. 102 Codes 41, 42 & 43: Solenoid Valves. Expo AWD

E-6 When diagnostic trouble code "51 VALVE RELAY" is displayed

[Explanation]

When the ignition switch is turned ON, the ABS ECU switches the valve relay OFF and ON for an initial check, compares the voltage of the signal to the valve relay and valve power monitor line voltage to check whether the valve relay operation is normal. In addition, normally it monitors whether or not there is power in the valve power monitor line since the valve relay is normally ON. If the supply of power to the valve power monitor line is interrupted, this diagnostic trouble code will be output.

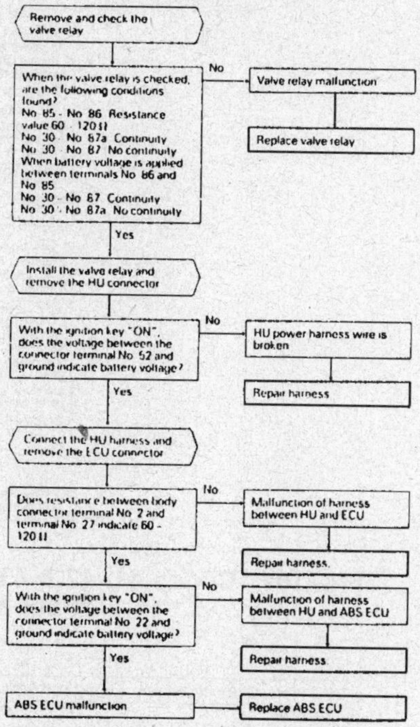

Remove and check the valve relay
When the valve relay is checked, are the following conditions found?
No 85 - No 86 Resistance value 60 - 120 Ω
No 30 - No 87a Continuity
No 30 - No 87 No continuity
When battery voltage is applied between terminals No 86 and No 85
No 30 - No 87 Continuity
No 30 - No 87a No continuity
No
Valve relay malfunction
Replace valve relay
Yes
Install the valve relay and remove the HU connector
With the ignition key "ON", does the voltage between the connector terminal No 52 and ground indicate battery voltage?
No
HU power harness wire is broken
Repair harness
Yes
Connect the HU harness and remove the ECU connector
Does resistance between body connector terminal No 2 and terminal No 27 indicate 60 - 120 Ω
No
Malfunction of harness between HU and ECU
Repair harness.
Yes
With the ignition key "ON", does the voltage between the connector terminal No 22 and ground indicate battery voltage?
No
Malfunction of harness between HU and ABS ECU
Repair harness.
Yes
ABS ECU malfunction
Replace ABS ECU

MT4029100054000X

Fig. 103 Code 51: Valve Relay. Expo AWD

E-7 When diagnostic trouble code "52 MOTOR RELAY" is displayed

[Explanation]

The ABC-ECU outputs this diagnostic trouble code when the motor relay and motor are as follows.

- When the motor relay is ON and no signal is input to the motor monitor line (motor does not operate, etc.)
- When the motor relay is OFF and signals enter the motor monitor line for a period of approximately 5 seconds or more (motor operates continuously, etc.)
- When motor does not oporate

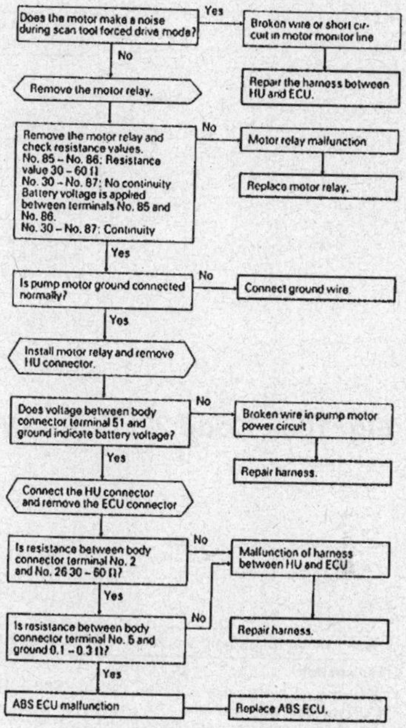

Does the motor make a noise during scan tool forced drive mode?
Yes
Broken wire or short circuit in motor monitor line
Repair the harness between HU and ECU.
No
Remove the motor relay.
Remove the motor relay and check resistance values.
No. 85 – No. 86: Resistance value 30 – 60 Ω
No. 30 – No. 87: No continuity
Battery voltage is applied between terminals No. 85 and No. 86.
No. 30 – No. 87: Continuity
No
Motor relay malfunction
Replace motor relay.
Yes
Is pump motor ground connected normally?
No
Connect ground wire.
Yes
Install motor relay and remove HU connector.
Does voltage between body connector terminal 51 and ground indicate battery voltage?
No
Broken wire in pump motor power circuit
Repair harness.
Yes
Connect the HU connector and remove the ECU connector
Is resistance between body connector terminal No. 2 and No. 26 30 – 60 Ω?
No
Malfunction of harness between HU and ECU
Repair harness.
Yes
Is resistance between body connector terminal No. 5 and ground 0.1 – 0.3 Ω?
No
Yes
ABS ECU malfunction
Replace ABS ECU.

MT4029100055000X

Fig. 104 Code 52: Motor Relay. Expo AWD

E-1 When the following diagnostic trouble codes are displayed "11 FL SPD SENSOR" "12 FR SPD SENSOR" "13 RL SPD SENSOR" "14 RR SPD SENSOR"

[Explanation]

The ABS ECU detects breaks in the wheel speed sensor wire. This diagnostic trouble code is output if the wheel speed sensor signal is not input (or short circuited) or if its output is low when starting to drive or while driving.

[Hint]

In addition to a broken wire/short circuit in the wheel speed sensor, also check whether the sensor gap is too large, rotor teeth are missing, sensor harness wire is temporarily broken, or sensor harness and body connector are not properly inserted.

E-2 When diagnostic trouble code "15 SENSOR FAULT" is displayed

[Explanation]

This diagnostic trouble code is output when there is an abnormality (other than broken wire or short circuit) in the wheel speed sensor output signal while driving.

[Hint]

The following can be considered as the cause of the wheel speed sensor output abnormality.

- Distortion of rotor, teeth missing
- Low frequency noise interference when sensor harness wire is broken
- Noise interference in sensor signal
- When the sensor output signal is below the standard value or when amplitude modulation is over the standard value, using an oscilloscope to measure the wave shape of the wheel speed sensor output signal is very effective.
- Loose wheel bearing
- Temporarily broken wire in sensor harness
- Sensor harness and body connector are not properly inserted.

NOTE

(1) If contact is poor, check the sensor cable by bending and lightly stretching it.

(2) If there is currently no trouble and if abnormality in the displayed sensor circuit cannot be discovered since values are normal even when checked, turn the ignition switch OFF and re-execute the driving test. Try replacing the ABS ECU only if the same diagnostic trouble code is output at this time.

(If it is difficult to recreate the trouble, there is a possibility of speed sensor trouble recurring even if the ECU is replaced.)

MT4029100056010X

Fig. 105 Codes 11, 12, 13, 14 & 15: Speed Sensors (Part 1 of 2). 1993 Galant FWD

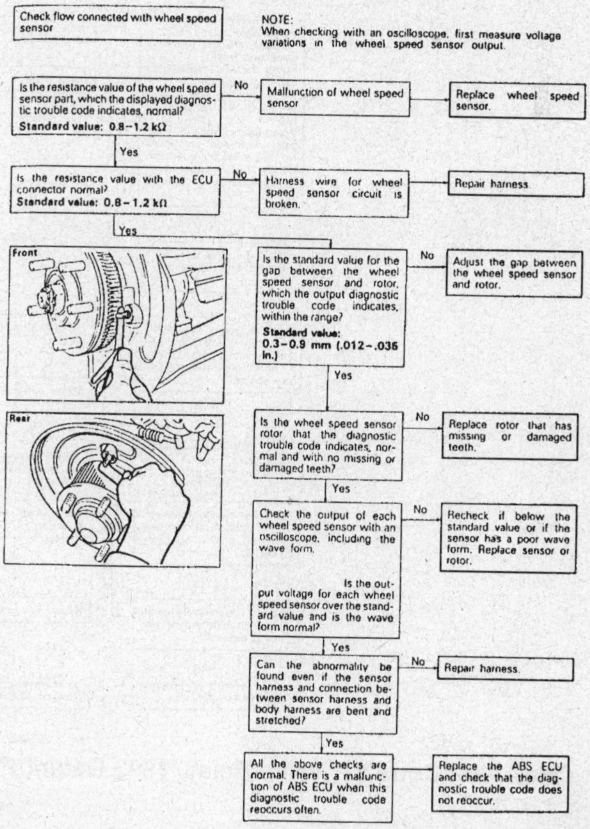

Check flow connected with wheel speed sensor
NOTE:
When checking with an oscilloscope, first measure voltage variations in the wheel speed sensor output.
Is the resistance value of the wheel speed sensor part, which the displayed diagnostic trouble code indicates, normal?
Standard value: 0.8–1.2 kΩ
No
Malfunction of wheel speed sensor
Replace wheel speed sensor.
Yes
Is the resistance value with the ECU connector normal?
Standard value: 0.8 – 1.2 kΩ
No
Harness wire for wheel speed sensor circuit is broken.
Repair harness.
Yes
Front
Rear
Is the standard value for the gap between the wheel speed sensor and rotor, which the output diagnostic trouble code indicates, within the range?
Standard value:
0.3–0.9 mm (.012–.036 in.)
No
Adjust the gap between the wheel speed sensor and rotor.
Yes
Is the wheel speed sensor rotor that the diagnostic trouble code indicates, normal and with no missing or damaged teeth?
No
Replace rotor that has missing or damaged teeth.
Yes
Check the output of each wheel speed sensor with an oscilloscope, including the wave form.
Is the output voltage for each wheel speed sensor over the standard value and is the wave form normal?
No
Recheck if below the standard value or if the sensor has a poor wave form. Replace sensor or rotor.
Yes
Can the abnormality be found even if the sensor harness and connection between sensor harness and body harness are bent and stretched?
No
Repair harness.
Yes
All the above checks are normal. There is a malfunction of ABS ECU when this diagnostic trouble code reoccurs often.
Replace the ABS ECU and check that the diagnostic trouble code does not reoccur.

MT4029100056020X

Fig. 105 Codes 11, 12, 13, 14 & 15: Speed Sensors (Part 2 of 2). 1993 Galant FWD

E-3	When diagnostic trouble code "22 STOP SW" is displayed

[Explanation]

The ABS ECU outputs this diagnostic trouble code in the following cases.

- Stop light switch may remain on for more than 15 minutes without the ABS functions.
- The harness wire for the stop light switch may be open.

[Hint]

If the stop light operates normal, the ABS harness wire for the stop light switch input circuit to the ECU is broken or there is a malfunction in the ABS ECU.

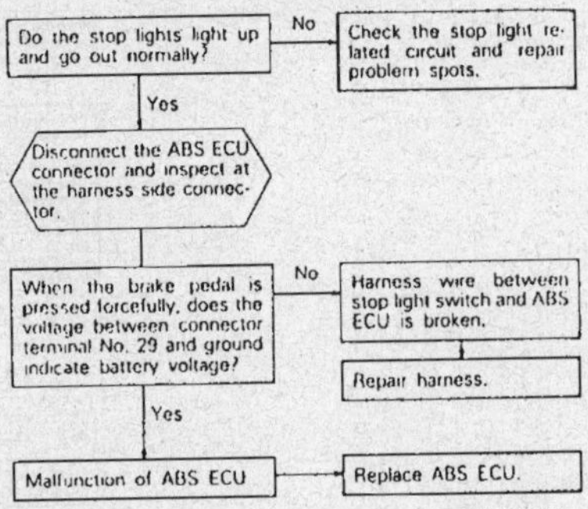

Do the stop lights light up and go out normally?
No
Check the stop light related circuit and repair problem spots.
Yes
Disconnect the ABS ECU connector and inspect at the harness side connector.
When the brake pedal is pressed forcefully, does the voltage between connector terminal No. 29 and ground indicate battery voltage?
No
Harness wire between stop light switch and ABS ECU is broken.
Repair harness.
Yes
Malfunction of ABS ECU
Replace ABS ECU.

MT4029100057000X

Fig. 106 Code 22: Stop Switch. 1993 Galant FWD

E-4	When diagnostic trouble codes "41 SOL V FRONT L", "42 SOL V FRONT R" OR "43 SOL V REAR" are displayed

[Explanation]

The ABS ECU normally monitors the solenoid valve drive circuit.
If no current flows in the solenoid even if the ECU turns the solenoid ON or if it continues to flow even when turned OFF, the ECU determines the solenoid coil wire is broken/short circuited or the harness is broken short circuited and then these diagnostic trouble codes are output.

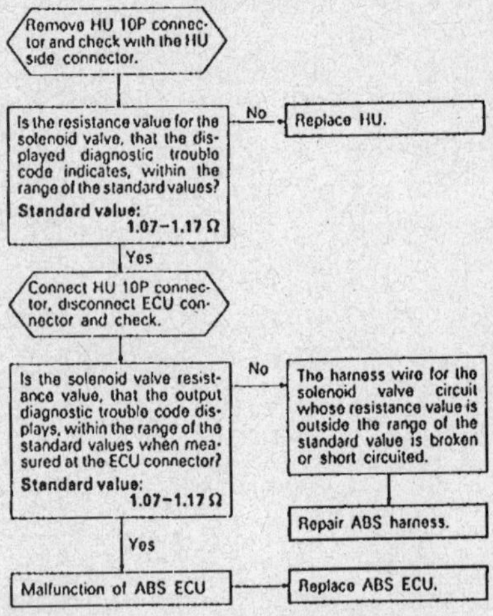

Remove HU 10P connector and check with the HU side connector.
Is the resistance value for the solenoid valve, that the displayed diagnostic trouble code indicates, within the range of the standard values?
Standard value:
1.07–1.17 Ω
No
Replace HU.
Yes
Connect HU 10P connector, disconnect ECU connector and check.
Is the solenoid valve resistance value, that the output diagnostic trouble code displays, within the range of the standard values when measured at the ECU connector?
Standard value:
1.07–1.17 Ω
No
The harness wire for the solenoid valve circuit whose resistance value is outside the range of the standard value is broken or short circuited.
Repair ABS harness.
Yes
Malfunction of ABS ECU
Replace ABS ECU.

MT4029100058000X

Fig. 107 Codes 41, 42 & 43: Solenoid Valves. 1993 Galant FWD

E-5	When diagnostic trouble code "51 VALVE RLY" is displayed

[Explanation]

When the ignition switch is turned ON, the ABS ECU switches the valve relay OFF and ON for an initial check, compares the voltage of the signal to the valve relay and valve power monitor line voltage to check whether the valve relay operation is normal. In addition, normally it monitors whether or not there is power in the valve power monitor line since the valve relay is normally ON. Then, if the supply of power to the valve power monitor line is interrupted, this diagnostic trouble code will output.

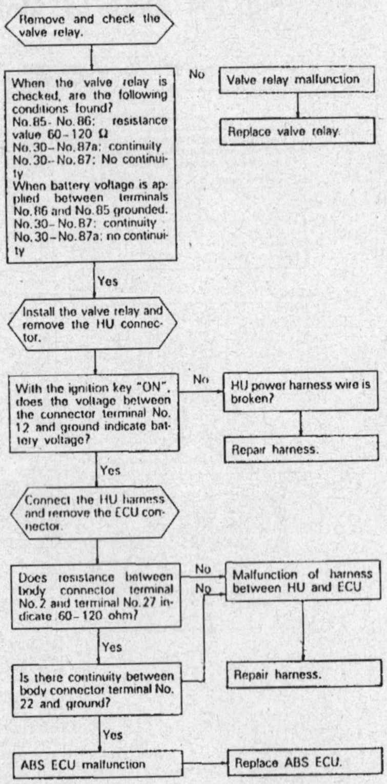

Remove and check the valve relay.
When the valve relay is checked, are the following conditions found?
No.85–No.86: resistance value 60–120 Ω
No.30–No.87a: continuity
No.30–No.87: No continuity
When battery voltage is applied between terminals No.86 and No.85 grounded.
No.30–No.87: continuity
No.30–No.87a: no continuity
No
Valve relay malfunction
Replace valve relay.
Yes
Install the valve relay and remove the HU connector.
With the ignition key "ON", does the voltage between the connector terminal No. 12 and ground indicate battery voltage?
No
HU power harness wire is broken?
Repair harness.
Yes
Connect the HU harness and remove the ECU connector.
Does resistance between body connector terminal No.2 and terminal No.27 indicate 60–120 ohm?
No
No
Malfunction of harness between HU and ECU
Yes
Is there continuity between body connector terminal No. 22 and ground?
Repair harness.
Yes
ABS ECU malfunction
Replace ABS ECU.

MT4029100059000X

Fig. 108 Code 51: Valve Relay. 1993 Galant FWD

E-6	When diagnostic trouble code "52 MOTOR RLY" is displayed

[Explanation]

The ABS ECU outputs this diagnostic trouble code for the motor relay and motor in the following cases.

- When the motor relay does not function
- When there is trouble with the motor itself and it does not revolve
- When the motor ground line is disconnected and the motor does not revolve
- When the motor continues to revolve

[Hint]

If there is motor operation noise when wheel speed exceeds 6km/h (4mph) when starting up after the engine is started, or when there is forced scan tool drive, there is a broken or short circuited motor monitor wire.

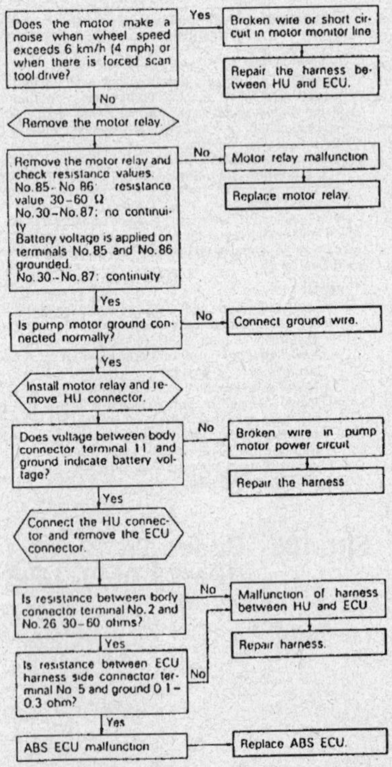

Does the motor make a noise when wheel speed exceeds 6 km/h (4 mph) or when there is forced scan tool drive?
Yes
Broken wire or short circuit in motor monitor line
Repair the harness between HU and ECU.
No
Remove the motor relay.
Remove the motor relay and check resistance values.
No.85–No.86: resistance value 30–60 Ω
No.30–No.87: no continuity
Battery voltage is applied on terminals No.85 and No.86 grounded.
No.30–No.87: continuity
No
Motor relay malfunction
Replace motor relay.
Yes
Is pump motor ground connected normally?
No
Connect ground wire.
Yes
Install motor relay and remove HU connector.
Does voltage between body connector terminal 11 and ground indicate battery voltage?
No
Broken wire in pump motor power circuit
Repair the harness
Yes
Connect the HU connector and remove the ECU connector.
Is resistance between body connector terminal No.2 and No.26 30–60 ohms?
No
Malfunction of harness between HU and ECU
Repair harness.
Yes
Is resistance between ECU harness side connector terminal No. 5 and ground 0.1–0.3 ohm?
No
Yes
ABS ECU malfunction
Replace ABS ECU.

MT4029100060000X

Fig. 109 Code 52: Motor Relay. 1993 Galant FWD

E-1 When the following diagnostic trouble codes are displayed "11 FL SPD SENSOR" "12 FR SPD SENSOR" "13 RL SPD SENSOR" "14 RR SPD SENSOR"

[Explanation]

The ABS ECU detects breaks in the wheel speed sensor wire. This diagnostic trouble code is output if the wheel speed sensor signal is not input (or short circuited) or if its output is low when starting to drive or while driving.

[Hint]

In addition to a broken wire/short circuit in the wheel speed sensor, also check whether the sensor gap is too large, rotor teeth are missing, sensor harness wire is temporarily broken, or sensor harness and body connector are not properly inserted.

E-2 When diagnostic trouble code "15 SENSOR FAULT" is displayed

[Explanation]

This diagnostic trouble code is output when there is an abnormality (other than broken wire or short circuit) in the wheel speed sensor output signal while driving.

[Hint]

The following can be considered as the cause of the wheel speed sensor output abnormality.

- Distortion of rotor, teeth missing
- Low frequency noise interference when sensor harness wire is broken
- Noise interference in sensor signal
- When the sensor output signal is below the standard value or when amplitude modulation is over the standard value, using an oscilloscope to measure the wave shape of the wheel speed sensor output signal is very effective.
- Loose wheel bearing
- Temporarily broken wire in sensor harness
- Sensor harness and body connector are not properly inserted.

NOTE

(1) If contact is poor, check the sensor cable by bending and lightly stretching it.

(2) If there is currently no trouble and if abnormality in the displayed sensor circuit cannot be discovered since values are normal even when checked, turn the ignition switch OFF and re-execute the driving test. Try replacing the ABS ECU only if the same diagnostic trouble code is output at this time.

(If it is difficult to recreate the trouble, there is a possibility of speed sensor trouble recurring even if the ECU is replaced.)

MT4029100061010X

Fig. 110 Codes 11, 12, 13, 14 & 15: Speed Sensors (Part 1 of 2). 1993 Galant AWD

Check flow connected with wheel speed sensor

NOTE:
When checking with an oscilloscope, first measure voltage variations in the wheel speed sensor output.

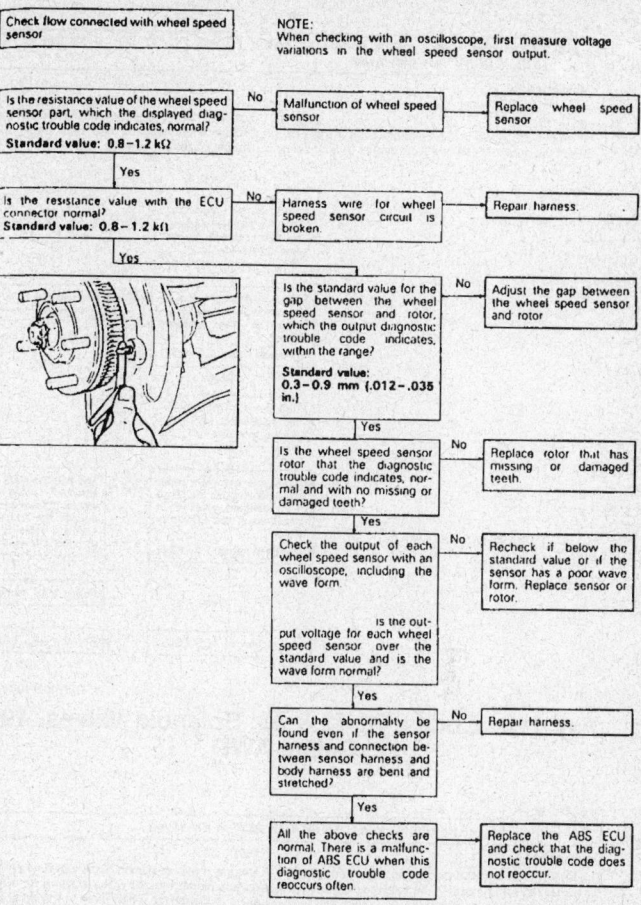

- Is the resistance value of the wheel speed sensor part, which the displayed diagnostic trouble code indicates, normal? **Standard value: 0.8–1.2 kΩ**
  - No → Malfunction of wheel speed sensor → Replace wheel speed sensor
  - Yes ↓
- Is the resistance value with the ECU connector normal? **Standard value: 0.8–1.2 kΩ**
  - No → Harness wire for wheel speed sensor circuit is broken. → Repair harness.
  - Yes ↓

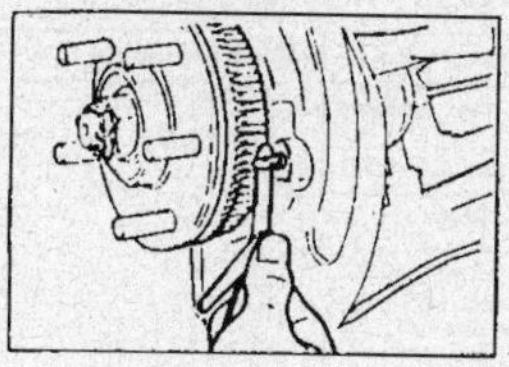

- Is the standard value for the gap between the wheel speed sensor and rotor, which the output diagnostic trouble code indicates, within the range? **Standard value: 0.3–0.9 mm (.012–.035 in.)**
  - No → Adjust the gap between the wheel speed sensor and rotor
  - Yes ↓
- Is the wheel speed sensor rotor that the diagnostic trouble code indicates, normal and with no missing or damaged teeth?
  - No → Replace rotor that has missing or damaged teeth.
  - Yes ↓
- Check the output of each wheel speed sensor with an oscilloscope, including the wave form. Is the output voltage for each wheel speed sensor over the standard value and is the wave form normal?
  - No → Recheck if below the standard value or if the sensor has a poor wave form. Replace sensor or rotor.
  - Yes ↓
- Can the abnormality be found even if the sensor harness and connection between sensor harness and body harness are bent and stretched?
  - No → Repair harness.
  - Yes ↓
- All the above checks are normal. There is a malfunction of ABS ECU when this diagnostic trouble code reoccurs often. → Replace the ABS ECU and check that the diagnostic trouble code does not reoccur.

MT4029100061020X

Fig. 110 Codes 11, 12, 13, 14 & 15: Speed Sensors (Part 2 of 2). 1993 Galant AWD

E-3 When diagnostic trouble code "21 G SENSOR" is displayed

[Explanation]

The ABS ECU outputs this diagnostic trouble code in the following cases.

- OFF trouble turning G sensor OFF (It is judged that the G sensor continues to be OFF for more than approximately 13 seconds except when the vehicle is stopped or when there is stop light switch input.
- When there is a broken wire or short circuit in the harness for the G sensor system.

- Is G sensor normal?
  - No → Replace G sensor.
  - Yes ↓
- Remove the ABS ECU connector and check at the harness connector.
- With the ignition key "ON" does the voltage between terminal No 6 and ground indicate battery voltage?
  - No → The harness between the G sensor and the ABS ECU is broken. → Repair harness.
  - Yes ↓
- ABS ECU malfunction → Replace ABS ECU.

MT4029100062000X

Fig. 111 Code 21: G Sensor. 1993 Galant AWD

E-4 When diagnostic trouble code "22 STOP SW" is displayed

[Explanation]

The ABS ECU outputs this diagnostic trouble code in the following cases.

- Stop light switch may remain on for more than 15 minutes without the ABS functions.
- The harness wire for the stop light switch may be open.

[Hint]

If the stop light operates normal, the ABS harness wire for the stop light switch input circuit to the ECU is broken or there is a malfunction in the ABS ECU.

- Do the stop lights light up and go out normally?
  - No → Check the stop light related circuit and repair problem spots.
  - Yes ↓
- Disconnect the ABS ECU connector and inspect at the harness side connector.
- When the brake pedal is pressed forcefully, does the voltage between connector terminal No. 29 and ground indicate battery voltage?
  - No → Harness wire between stop light switch and ABS ECU is broken. → Repair harness.
  - Yes ↓
- Malfunction of ABS ECU → Replace ABS ECU.

MT4029100063000X

Fig. 112 Code 22: Stop Switch. 1993 Galant AWD

E-5	When diagnostic trouble codes "41 SOL V FRONT L", "42 SOL V FRONT R" OR "43 SOL V DRIFT" are displayed

[Explanation]

The ABS ECU normally monitors the solenoid valve drive circuit.
If no current flows in the solenoid even if the ECU turns the solenoid ON or if it continues to flow even when turned OFF, the ECU determines the solenoid coil wire is broken/short circuited or the harness is broken short circuited and then these diagnostic trouble codes are output.

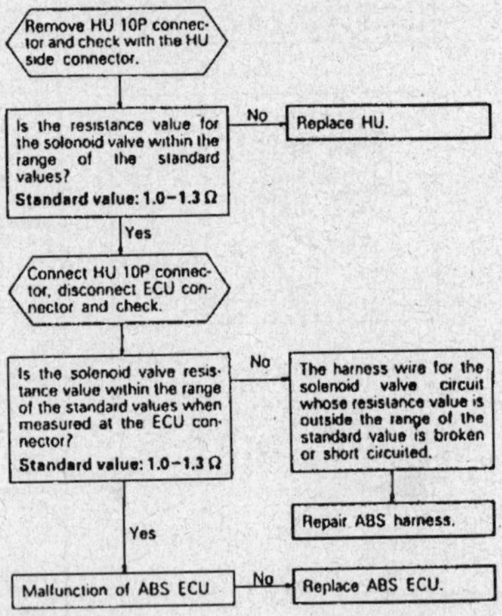

Remove HU 10P connector and check with the HU side connector.
Is the resistance value for the solenoid valve within the range of the standard values?
Standard value: 1.0–1.3 Ω
No
Replace HU.
Yes
Connect HU 10P connector, disconnect ECU connector and check.
Is the solenoid valve resistance value within the range of the standard values when measured at the ECU connector?
Standard value: 1.0–1.3 Ω
No
The harness wire for the solenoid valve circuit whose resistance value is outside the range of the standard value is broken or short circuited.
Repair ABS harness.
Yes
Malfunction of ABS ECU
No
Replace ABS ECU.

MT4029100064000X

Fig. 113 Codes 41, 42 & 43: Solenoid Valves. 1993 Galant AWD

E-7	When diagnostic trouble code "52 MOTOR RLY" is displayed

[Explanation]

The ABS ECU outputs this diagnostic trouble code for the motor relay and motor in the following cases.

- When the motor relay does not function
- When there is trouble with the motor itself and it does not revolve
- When there is trouble with the motor itself and it the motor does not revolve
- When the motor continues to revolve

[Hint]

If there is motor operation noise when wheel speed exceeds 6km/h (4mph) when starting up after the engine is started, or when there is forced scan tool drive, there is a broken or short circuited motor monitor wire.

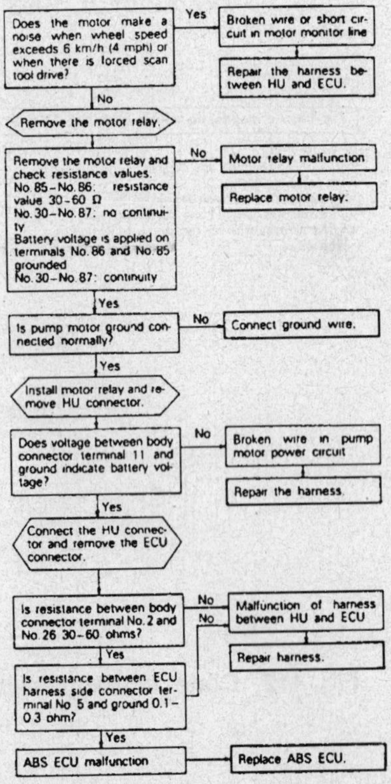

Does the motor make a noise when wheel speed exceeds 6 km/h (4 mph) or when there is forced scan tool drive?
Yes
Broken wire or short circuit in motor monitor line
Repair the harness between HU and ECU.
No
Remove the motor relay.
Remove the motor relay and check resistance values.
No. 85–No. 86: resistance value 30–60 Ω
No. 30–No. 87: no continuity
Battery voltage is applied on terminals No. 86 and No. 85 grounded
No. 30–No. 87: continuity
No
Motor relay malfunction
Replace motor relay.
Yes
Is pump motor ground connected normally?
No
Connect ground wire.
Yes
Install motor relay and remove HU connector.
Does voltage between body connector terminal 11 and ground indicate battery voltage?
No
Broken wire in pump motor power circuit
Repair the harness.
Yes
Connect the HU connector and remove the ECU connector.
Is resistance between body connector terminal No. 2 and No. 26 30–60 ohms?
No
No
Malfunction of harness between HU and ECU
Repair harness.
Yes
Is resistance between ECU harness side connector terminal No. 5 and ground 0.1–0.3 ohm?
Yes
ABS ECU malfunction
Replace ABS ECU.

MT4029100066000X

Fig. 115 Code 52: Motor Relay. 1993 Galant AWD

E-6	When diagnostic trouble code "51 VALVE RLY" is displayed

[Explanation]

When the ignition switch is turned ON, the ABS ECU switches the valve relay OFF and ON for an initial check, compares the voltage of the signal to the valve relay and valve power monitor line voltage to check whether the valve relay operation is normal. In addition, normally it monitors whether or not there is power in the valve power monitor line since the valve relay is normally ON. Then, if the supply of power to the valve power monitor line is interrupted, this diagnostic trouble code will output.

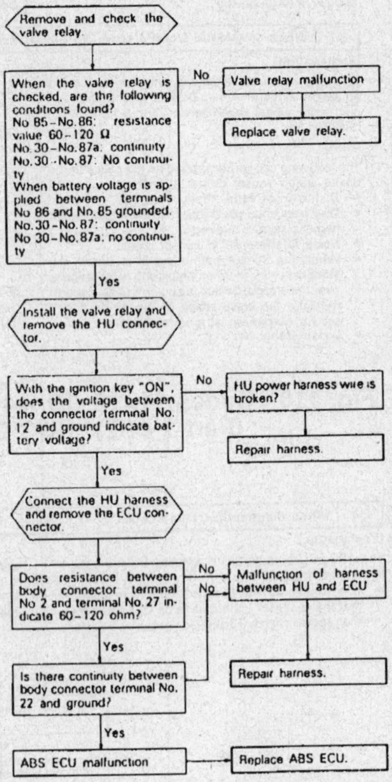

Remove and check the valve relay.
When the valve relay is checked, are the following conditions found?
No 85–No. 86: resistance value 60–120 Ω
No. 30–No. 87a: continuity
No. 30–No. 87: No continuity
When battery voltage is applied between terminals No 86 and No. 85 grounded.
No. 30–No. 87: continuity
No 30–No. 87a: no continuity
No
Valve relay malfunction
Replace valve relay.
Yes
Install the valve relay and remove the HU connector.
With the ignition key "ON", does the voltage between the connector terminal No. 12 and ground indicate battery voltage?
No
HU power harness wire is broken?
Repair harness.
Yes
Connect the HU harness and remove the ECU connector.
Does resistance between body connector terminal No 2 and terminal No. 27 indicate 60–120 ohm?
No
No
Malfunction of harness between HU and ECU
Repair harness.
Yes
Is there continuity between body connector terminal No. 22 and ground?
Yes
ABS ECU malfunction
Replace ABS ECU.

MT4029100065000X

Fig. 114 Code 51: Valve Relay. 1993 Galant AWD

E-1	When the following diagnostic trouble codes are displayed "11 FL SNSR. OPEN" "12 FR SNSR. OPEN" "13 RL SNSR. OPEN" "14 RR SNSR. OPEN"

[Explanation]

The ABS ECU detects breaks in the wheel speed sensor wire. This trouble code is output if the wheel speed sensor signal is not input (or short circuited) or if its output is low when starting to drive or while driving.

[Hint]

In addition to a broken wire/short circuit in the whe speed sensor, also check whether the sensor gap too large, sensor harness wire is broken, or sens harness and body connector are not properly co nected.

E-2	When diagnostic trouble code "15 VEH. SPD. SNSR." is displayed

[Explanation]

This trouble code is output when there is an abnormality (other than broken wire or short circuit) in any of the wheel speed sensor output signals while driving.

[Hint]

The following can be considered as the cause of the wheel speed sensor output abnormality.

- Distortion of rotor, teeth missing
- Low frequency noise interference when sensor harness wire is broken
- Noise interference in sensor signal
- Sensor output signal is below the standard value or amplitude modulation is over the standard value. Using an oscilloscope to measure the wave shape of the wheel speed sensor output signal is very effective.
- Broken sensor harness
- Poor connection of connector

NOTE

(1) If contact is poor, check the sensor cable bending and lightly stretching it.

(2) Except for the case where a fault conditi exists in the system, but the inspection resu are normal; if an abnormality cannot be found the sensor circuit displayed as abnormal, era the diagnostic trouble code and turn the igniti switch to OFF once, and then test-drive* aga If the same diagnostic trouble code is outp replace the ABS ECU. If the trouble does r occur anymore, the problem is likely to be w the ABS ECU.
(If the trouble is in the speed sensor circuit, b is difficult to recreate, it will recur even after t ABS ECU has been replaced.)

(3) *: Drive at 19 mph or higher for more than seconds.

MT4029100067010X

Fig. 116 Codes 11, 12, 13, 14 & 15: Speed Sensors (Part 1 of 2). 1993–95 3000GT FWD

Check flow connected with wheel speed sensor

NOTE
When checking with an oscilloscope, first measure voltage variations in the wheel speed sensor output.

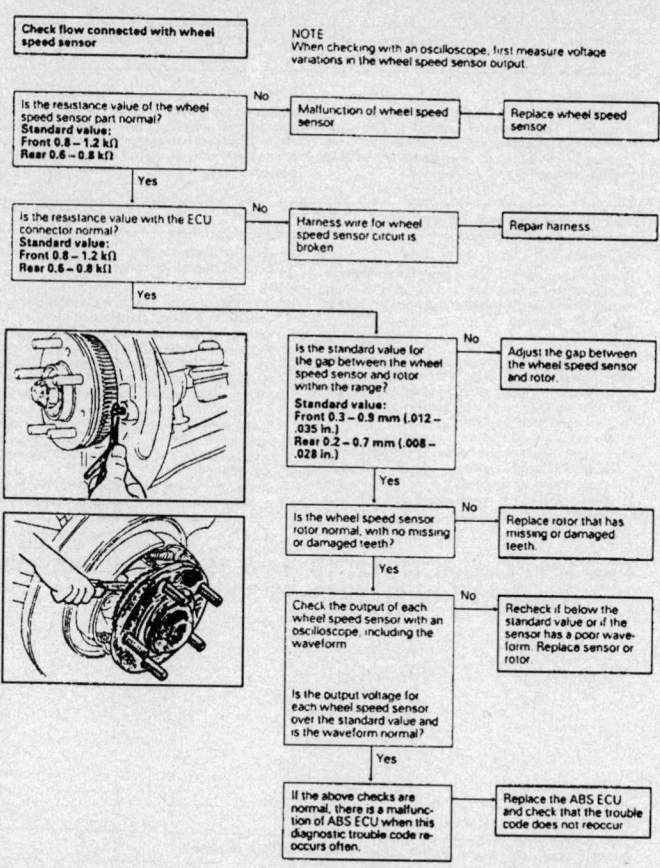

- Is the resistance value of the wheel speed sensor part normal? **Standard value: Front 0.8 – 1.2 kΩ Rear 0.6 – 0.8 kΩ**
  - No → Malfunction of wheel speed sensor → Replace wheel speed sensor
  - Yes ↓
- Is the resistance value with the ECU connector normal? **Standard value: Front 0.8 – 1.2 kΩ Rear 0.6 – 0.8 kΩ**
  - No → Harness wire for wheel speed sensor circuit is broken → Repair harness.
  - Yes ↓
- Is the standard value for the gap between the wheel speed sensor and rotor within the range? **Standard value: Front 0.3 – 0.9 mm (.012 – .035 in.) Rear 0.2 – 0.7 mm (.008 – .028 in.)**
  - No → Adjust the gap between the wheel speed sensor and rotor.
  - Yes ↓
- Is the wheel speed sensor rotor normal, with no missing or damaged teeth?
  - No → Replace rotor that has missing or damaged teeth.
  - Yes ↓
- Check the output of each wheel speed sensor with an oscilloscope, including the waveform. Is the output voltage for each wheel speed sensor over the standard value and is the waveform normal?
  - No → Recheck if below the standard value or if the sensor has a poor waveform. Replace sensor or rotor.
  - Yes ↓
- If the above checks are normal, there is a malfunction of ABS ECU when this diagnostic trouble code reoccurs often. → Replace the ABS ECU and check that the trouble code does not reoccur

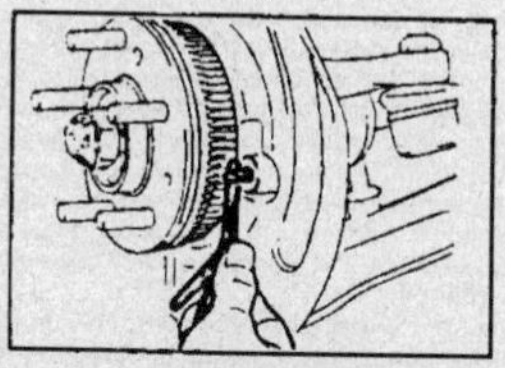

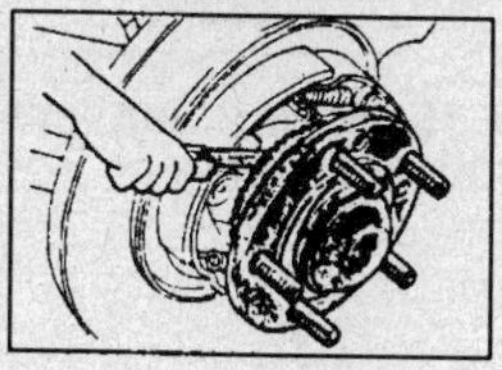

MT4029100067020X

Fig. 116 Codes 11, 12, 13, 14 & 15: Speed Sensors (Part 2 of 2). 1993–95 3000GT FWD

E-4 When diagnostic trouble codes "41 FL SOL. VALVE", "42 FR SOL. VALVE" or "43 REAR SOL. V." are displayed.

[Explanation]

The ABS ECU normally monitors the solenoid valve drive circuit.
If no current flows in the solenoid even if the ECU turns the solenoid ON or if it continues to flow even when turned OFF, the ECU determines the solenoid coil wire is broken/short-circuited or the harness is broken/short-circuited, and then these diagnostic trouble codes are output.

- Remove HU 10P connector and check with the HU side connector.
- Is the resistance value for the solenoid valve within the range of the standard values? **Standard value: 1.1 – 1.3 Ω**
  - No → Replace HU.
  - Yes ↓
- Connect HU 10P connector, disconnect ECU connector and check.
- Is the solenoid valve resistance value within the range of the standard values when measured at the ECU connector? **Standard value: 1.1 – 1.3 Ω**
  - No → The harness wire for the solenoid valve circuit whose resistance value is outside the range of the standard value is broken or short circuited. → Repair ABS harness.
  - Yes ↓
- Malfunction of ABS ECU → Replace ABS ECU.

MT4029100069000X

Fig. 118 Codes 41, 42 & 43: Solenoid Valves. 1993–95 3000GT FWD

E-3 When diagnostic trouble code "22 STOP LAMP SW" is displayed

[Explanation]

The ABS ECU outputs this diagnostic trouble code in the following cases.

- Stop light switch may remain on for more than 15 minutes without ABS operation.
- The harness wire for the stop light switch may be open.

[Hint]

If the stop light operates normal, the harness for the stop light switch input circuit is broken or there is a malfunction in the ABS ECU.

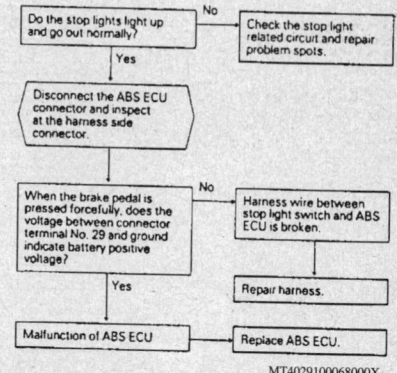

- Do the stop lights light up and go out normally?
  - No → Check the stop light related circuit and repair problem spots.
  - Yes ↓
- Disconnect the ABS ECU connector and inspect at the harness side connector.
- When the brake pedal is pressed forcefully, does the voltage between connector terminal No. 29 and ground indicate battery positive voltage?
  - No → Harness wire between stop light switch and ABS ECU is broken. → Repair harness.
  - Yes ↓
- Malfunction of ABS ECU → Replace ABS ECU.

MT4029100068000X

Fig. 117 Code 22: Stop Lamp Switch. 1993–95 3000GT FWD

E-5 When diagnostic trouble code "51 VALVE RELAY" is displayed

[Explanation]

When the ignition switch is turned ON, the ABS ECU switches the valve relay OFF and ON for an initial check, compares the voltage of the signal to the valve relay and valve power monitor line voltage to check whether the valve relay operation is normal. In addition, normally it monitors whether or not there is power in the valve power monitor line since the valve relay is normally ON. Then, if the supply of power to the valve power monitor line is interrupted, this diagnostic trouble code will be output.

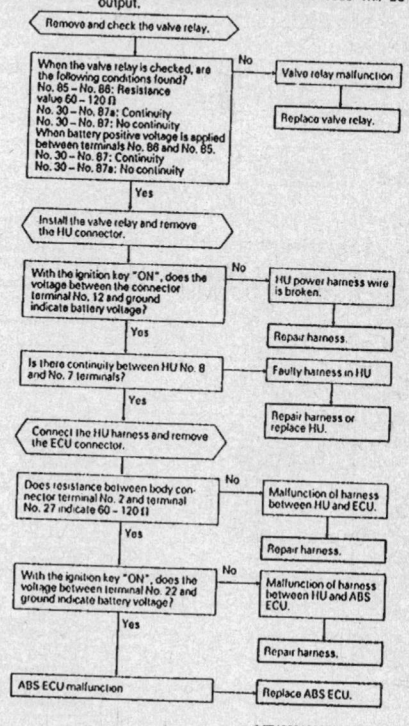

- Remove and check the valve relay.
- When the valve relay is checked, are the following conditions found? No. 85 – No. 86: Resistance value 60 – 120 Ω; No. 30 – No. 87a: Continuity; No. 30 – No. 87: No continuity; When battery positive voltage is applied between terminals No. 86 and No. 85. No. 30 – No. 87: Continuity; No. 30 – No. 87a: No continuity
  - No → Valve relay malfunction → Replace valve relay.
  - Yes ↓
- Install the valve relay and remove the HU connector.
- With the ignition key "ON", does the voltage between the connector terminal No. 12 and ground indicate battery voltage?
  - No → HU power harness wire is broken. → Repair harness.
  - Yes ↓
- Is there continuity between HU No. 8 and No. 7 terminals?
  - → Faulty harness in HU → Repair harness or replace HU.
  - Yes ↓
- Connect the HU harness and remove the ECU connector.
- Does resistance between body connector terminal No. 2 and terminal No. 27 indicate 60 – 120 Ω
  - No → Malfunction of harness between HU and ECU. → Repair harness.
  - Yes ↓
- With the ignition key "ON", does the voltage between terminal No. 22 and ground indicate battery voltage?
  - No → Malfunction of harness between HU and ABS ECU. → Repair harness.
  - Yes ↓
- ABS ECU malfunction → Replace ABS ECU.

MT4029100070000X

Fig. 119 Code 51: Valve Relay. 1993–95 3000GT FWD

E-6 When diagnostic trouble code "52 MOTOR RELAY" is displayed

[Explanation]

The ABS ECU outputs this diagnostic trouble code for the motor relay and motor in the following cases.

- When the motor relay does not function
- When there is trouble with the motor itself and it does not revolve
- When the motor ground line is disconnected and the motor does not revolve
- When the motor continues to revolve

[Hint]

If there is motor operation noise during scan tool forced drive mode, there is a broken or short circuited motor monitor wire.

- Does the motor make a noise during scan tool forced drive mode
  - Yes → Broken wire or short circuit in motor monitor line → Repair the harness between HU and ECU.
  - No → Remove the motor relay.
- Remove the motor relay and check resistance values: No. 85 – No. 86 Resistance value 30 – 60 Ω; No. 30 – No. 87 No continuity; Battery positive voltage is applied between terminals No. 85 and No. 86. No. 30 – No. 87: Continuity
  - No → Motor relay malfunction → Replace motor relay.
  - Yes → Is pump motor ground connected normally?
- Is pump motor ground connected normally?
  - No → Connect ground wire.
  - Yes → Install motor relay and remove HU connector.
- Does voltage between body connector terminal 11 and ground indicate battery positive voltage?
  - No → Broken wire in pump motor power circuit → Repair harness
  - Yes → Connect the HU connector and remove the ECU connector
- Is resistance between body connector terminal No. 2 and No. 26: 30 – 60 Ω?
  - No → Malfunction of harness between HU and ECU
  - Yes → Is resistance between body connector terminal No. 5 and ground 0.1 – 0.3 Ω?
- Is resistance between body connector terminal No. 5 and ground 0.1 – 0.3 Ω?
  - No → Repair harness.
  - Yes → ABS ECU malfunction → Replace ABS ECU.

MT4029100071000X

Fig. 120 Code 52: Motor Relay. 1993–95 3000GT FWD

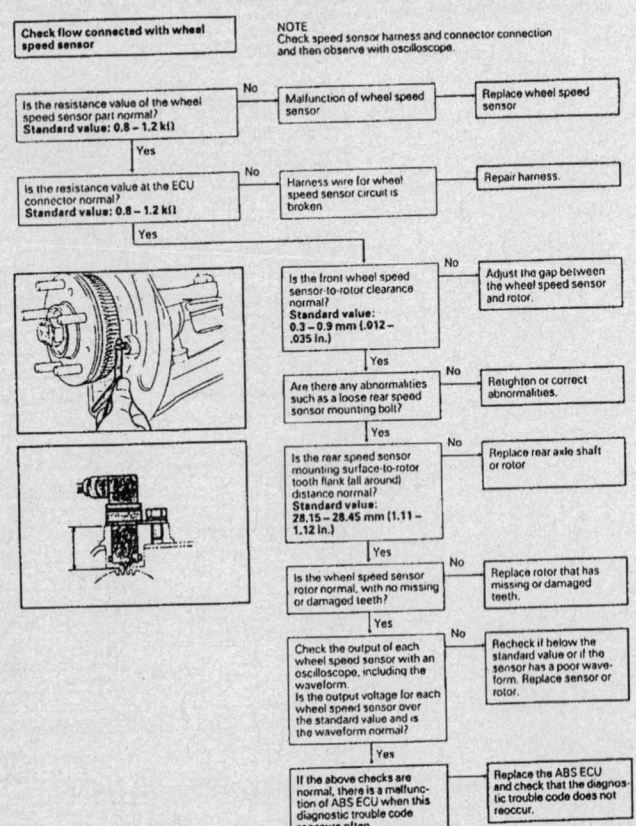

Check flow connected with wheel speed sensor

NOTE
Check speed sensor harness and connector connection and then observe with oscilloscope.

- Is the resistance value of the wheel speed sensor part normal? **Standard value: 0.8 – 1.2 kΩ**
  - No → Malfunction of wheel speed sensor → Replace wheel speed sensor
  - Yes → Is the resistance value at the ECU connector normal?
- Is the resistance value at the ECU connector normal? **Standard value: 0.8 – 1.2 kΩ**
  - No → Harness wire for wheel speed sensor circuit is broken → Repair harness.
  - Yes → Is the front wheel speed sensor-to-rotor clearance normal?

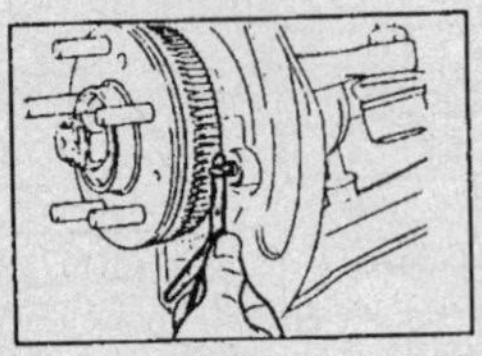

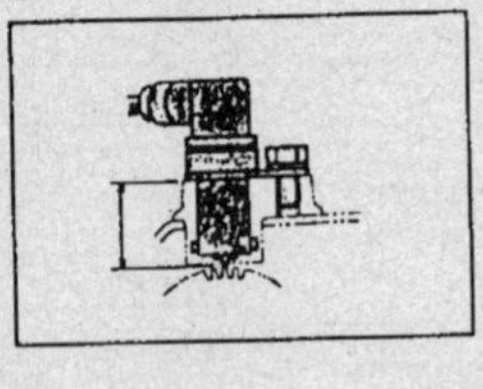

- Is the front wheel speed sensor-to-rotor clearance normal? **Standard value: 0.3 – 0.9 mm (.012 – .035 in.)**
  - No → Adjust the gap between the wheel speed sensor and rotor.
  - Yes → Are there any abnormalities such as a loose rear speed sensor mounting bolt?
- Are there any abnormalities such as a loose rear speed sensor mounting bolt?
  - No → Retighten or correct abnormalities.
  - Yes → Is the rear speed sensor mounting surface-to-rotor tooth flank (all around) distance normal?
- Is the rear speed sensor mounting surface-to-rotor tooth flank (all around) distance normal? **Standard value: 28.15 – 28.45 mm (1.11 – 1.12 in.)**
  - No → Replace rear axle shaft or rotor
  - Yes → Is the wheel speed sensor rotor normal, with no missing or damaged teeth?
- Is the wheel speed sensor rotor normal, with no missing or damaged teeth?
  - No → Replace rotor that has missing or damaged teeth.
  - Yes → Check the output of each wheel speed sensor with an oscilloscope, including the waveform.
- Check the output of each wheel speed sensor with an oscilloscope, including the waveform. Is the output voltage for each wheel speed sensor over the standard value and is the waveform normal?
  - No → Recheck if below the standard value or if the sensor has a poor waveform. Replace sensor or rotor.
  - Yes → If the above checks are normal, there is a malfunction of ABS ECU when this diagnostic trouble code reoccurs often. → Replace the ABS ECU and check that the diagnostic trouble code does not reoccur.

MT4029100072020X

Fig. 121 Codes 11, 12, 13, 14 & 15: Speed Sensors (Part 2 of 2). 1993–95 3000GT AWD

E-1 When the following diagnostic trouble codes are displayed "11 FL SNSR. OPEN" "12 FR SNSR. OPEN" "13 RL SNSR. OPEN" "14 RR SNSR. OPEN"

[Explanation]

The ABS ECU detects breaks in the wheel speed sensor wire. This diagnostic trouble code is output if the wheel speed sensor signal is not input (or short circuited) or if its output is low when starting to drive or while driving.

[Hint]

In addition to a broken wire/short circuit in the wheel speed sensor, also check whether the sensor gap is too large, sensor harness wire is broken, or sensor harness and body connector are not properly connected.

E-2 When diagnostic trouble code "15 VEH. SPD. SNSR." is displayed

[Explanation]

This diagnostic trouble code is output when there is an abnormality (other than broken wire or short circuit) in any of the wheel speed sensor output signals while driving.

[Hint]

The following can be considered as the cause of the wheel speed sensor output abnormality.

- Distortion of rotor, teeth missing
- Low frequency noise interference when sensor harness wire is broken
- Noise interference in sensor signal
- Sensor output signal is below the standard value or amplitude modulation is over the standard value. Using an oscilloscope to measure the wave shape of the wheel speed sensor output signal is very effective.
- Broken sensor harness
- Poor connection of connector

NOTE

(1) If contact is poor, check the sensor cable by bending and lightly stretching it.

(2) Except for the case where a fault condition exists in the system, but the inspection results are normal; if an abnormality cannot be found in the sensor circuit displayed as abnormal, erase the diagnostic trouble code and turn the ignition switch to OFF once, and then test-drive again. If the same diagnostic trouble code is output, replace the ABS ECU. If the trouble does not occur anymore, the problem is likely to be with the ABS ECU.
(If the trouble is in the speed sensor circuit, but is difficult to recreate, it will recur even after the ABS ECU has been replaced.)

MT4029100072010X

Fig. 121 Codes 11, 12, 13, 14 & 15: Speed Sensors (Part 1 of 2). 1993–95 3000GT AWD

E-3 When diagnostic trouble code "21 G SNSR." is displayed

[Explanation]

The ABS-ECU outputs this diagnostic trouble code in the following cases.

- G sensor OFF trouble (It is judged that the G sensor continues to be OFF for more than approximately 13 seconds except when the vehicle is stopped or when there is stop light switch input.)
- When there is a broken wire or short circuit in the harness for the G sensor system.

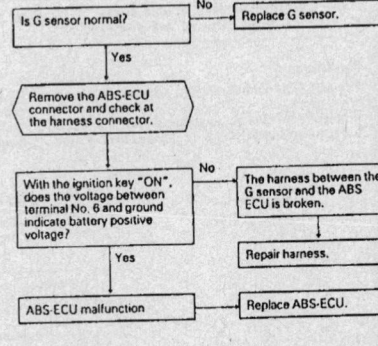

- Is G sensor normal?
  - No → Replace G sensor.
  - Yes → Remove the ABS-ECU connector and check at the harness connector.
- With the ignition key "ON", does the voltage between terminal No. 6 and ground indicate battery positive voltage?
  - No → The harness between the G sensor and the ABS ECU is broken. → Repair harness.
  - Yes → ABS-ECU malfunction → Replace ABS-ECU.

MT4029100073000X

Fig. 122 Code 21: G Sensor. 1993–95 3000GT AWD

E-4 | When diagnostic trouble code "22 STOP LAMP SW" is displayed

[Explanation]

The ABS-ECU outputs this diagnostic trouble code in the following cases.

- Stop light switch remains on for more than 15 minutes while the ABS is not functioning.
- The harness wire for the stop light switch may be open.

[Hint]

If the stop light operates normal, the harness for the stop light switch input circuit is broken or there is a malfunction in the ABS-ECU.

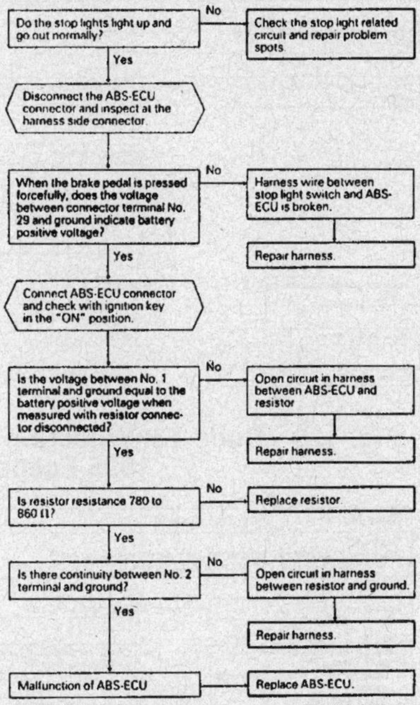

Do the stop lights light up and go out normally?
No
Check the stop light related circuit and repair problem spots.
Yes
Disconnect the ABS-ECU connector and inspect at the harness side connector.
When the brake pedal is pressed forcefully, does the voltage between connector terminal No. 29 and ground indicate battery positive voltage?
No
Harness wire between stop light switch and ABS-ECU is broken.
Yes
Repair harness.
Connect ABS-ECU connector and check with ignition key in the "ON" position.
Is the voltage between No. 1 terminal and ground equal to the battery positive voltage when measured with resistor connector disconnected?
No
Open circuit in harness between ABS-ECU and resistor
Yes
Repair harness.
Is resistor resistance 780 to 860 Ω?
No
Replace resistor.
Yes
Is there continuity between No. 2 terminal and ground?
No
Open circuit in harness between resistor and ground.
Yes
Repair harness.
Malfunction of ABS-ECU
Replace ABS-ECU.

MT4029100074000X

Fig. 123 Code 22: Stop Lamp Switch. 1993-95 3000GT AWD

E-6 | When diagnostic trouble code "51 VALVE RELAY" is displayed

[Explanation]

When the ignition switch is turned ON, the ABS ECU switches the valve relay OFF and ON for an initial check, compares the voltage of the signal to the valve relay and valve power monitor line voltage to check whether the valve relay operation is normal. In addition, normally it monitors whether or not there is power in the valve power monitor line since the valve relay is normally ON. If the supply of power to the valve power monitor line is interrupted, this diagnostic trouble code will be output.

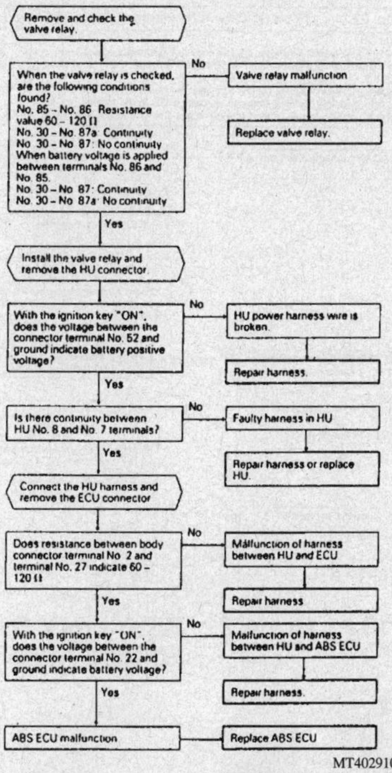

Remove and check the valve relay.
When the valve relay is checked, are the following conditions found?
No. 85 – No. 86: Resistance value 60 – 120 Ω
No. 30 – No. 87a: Continuity
No. 30 – No. 87: No continuity
When battery voltage is applied between terminals No. 86 and No. 85.
No. 30 – No. 87: Continuity
No. 30 – No. 87a: No continuity
No
Valve relay malfunction
Replace valve relay.
Yes
Install the valve relay and remove the HU connector.
With the ignition key "ON", does the voltage between the connector terminal No. 52 and ground indicate battery positive voltage?
No
HU power harness wire is broken.
Repair harness.
Yes
Is there continuity between HU No. 8 and No. 7 terminals?
No
Faulty harness in HU
Repair harness or replace HU.
Yes
Connect the HU harness and remove the ECU connector
Does resistance between body connector terminal No. 2 and terminal No. 27 indicate 60 – 120 Ω
No
Malfunction of harness between HU and ECU
Repair harness
Yes
With the ignition key "ON", does the voltage between the connector terminal No. 22 and ground indicate battery voltage?
No
Malfunction of harness between HU and ABS ECU
Repair harness.
Yes
ABS ECU malfunction
Replace ABS ECU

MT4029100076000X

Fig. 125 Code 51: Valve Relay. 1993-95 3000GT AWD

E-5 | When diagnostic trouble codes "41 FL SOL. VALVE", "42 FR SOL. VALVE" or "43 VALVE DRIFT" are displayed.

[Explanation]

The ABS-ECU normally monitors the solenoid valve drive circuit.

If no current flows in the solenoid even if the ECU turns the solenoid ON or if it continues to flow even when turned OFF, the ECU determines the solenoid coil wire is broken/short-circuited or the harness is broken/short-circuited, and then these diagnostic trouble codes are output.

ABS-ECU controls the solenoid valve current and if the current value of the solenoid valves differs from each other in the same mode, solenoid valve drift error is produced and the ABS-ECU goes into the failsafe mode.

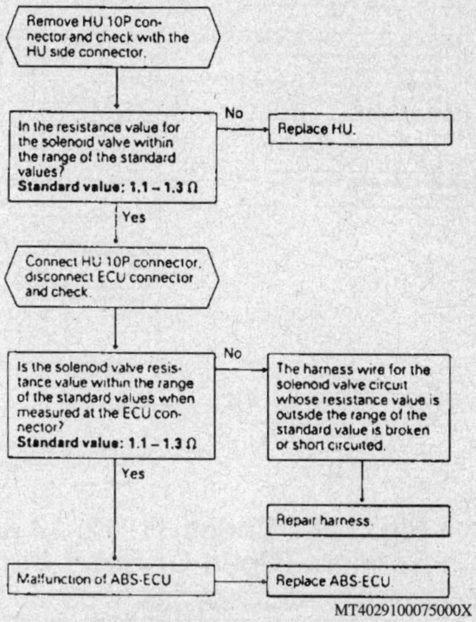

Remove HU 10P connector and check with the HU side connector.
In the resistance value for the solenoid valve within the range of the standard values?
Standard value: 1.1 – 1.3 Ω
No
Replace HU.
Yes
Connect HU 10P connector, disconnect ECU connector and check.
Is the solenoid valve resistance value within the range of the standard values when measured at the ECU connector?
Standard value: 1.1 – 1.3 Ω
No
The harness wire for the solenoid valve circuit whose resistance value is outside the range of the standard value is broken or short circuited.
Repair harness.
Yes
Malfunction of ABS-ECU
Replace ABS-ECU.

MT4029100075000X

Fig. 124 Codes 41, 42 & 43: Solenoid Valves. 1993-95 3000GT AWD

E-7 | When diagnostic trouble code "52 MOTOR RELAY" is displayed

[Explanation]

The ABS ECU outputs this diagnostic trouble code for the motor relay and motor in the following cases.

- When the motor relay does not function
- When there is trouble with the motor itself and it does not revolve
- When the motor ground is disconnected and the motor does not revolve
- When the motor continues to revolve

[Hint]

If there is motor operation noise during scan tool forced drive mode, there is a broken or short circuited motor monitor wire.

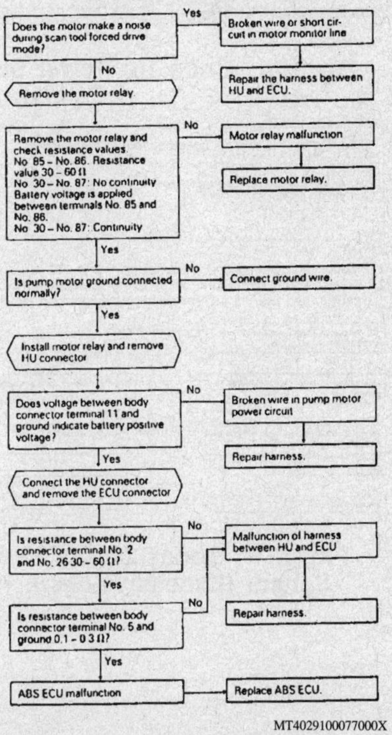

Does the motor make a noise during scan tool forced drive mode?
Yes
Broken wire or short circuit in motor monitor line
Repair the harness between HU and ECU.
No
Remove the motor relay.
Remove the motor relay and check resistance values.
No. 85 – No. 86: Resistance value 30 – 60 Ω
No. 30 – No. 87: No continuity
Battery voltage is applied between terminals No. 85 and No. 86.
No. 30 – No. 87: Continuity
No
Motor relay malfunction
Replace motor relay.
Yes
Is pump motor ground connected normally?
No
Connect ground wire.
Yes
Install motor relay and remove HU connector
Does voltage between body connector terminal 11 and ground indicate battery positive voltage?
No
Broken wire in pump motor power circuit
Repair harness.
Yes
Connect the HU connector and remove the ECU connector
Is resistance between body connector terminal No. 2 and No. 26 30 – 60 Ω?
No
Malfunction of harness between HU and ECU
Repair harness.
Yes
Is resistance between body connector terminal No. 5 and ground 0.1 – 0.3 Ω?
No
Yes
ABS ECU malfunction
Replace ABS ECU.

MT4029100077000X

Fig. 126 Code 52: Motor Relay. 1993-95 3000GT AWD

INSPECTION PROCEDURE CLASSIFIED BY DIAGNOSTIC TROUBLE CODES

Code No. 11, 12, 13, 14	Wheel speed sensor open circuit or short + wire	Probable cause
[Comment] The ABS-ECU detects breaks in the wheel speed sensor wire. This diagnostic trouble code is output if the wheel speed sensor signal is not input (or short circuited) or if its output is low when starting to drive or while driving. In addition to an open or short circuit in the wheel speed sensor, also check whether the sensor gap is too large, sensor harness wire is broken, or sensor harness and body connector are not properly connected.		• Malfunction of wheel speed sensor. • Malfunction of wiring harness or connector. • Malfunction of rotor. • Malfunction of ABS-ECU

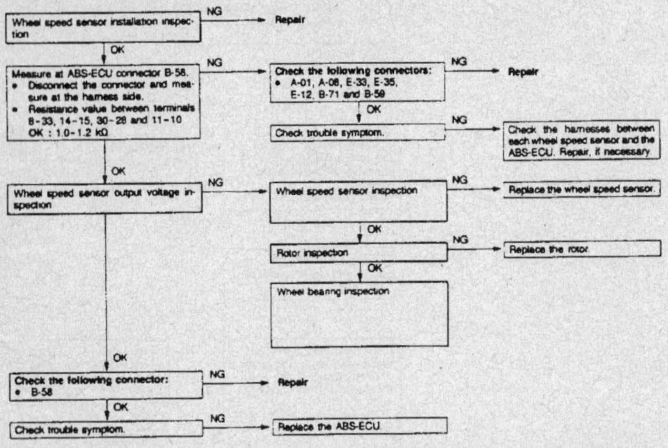
Wheel speed sensor installation inspection
NG
Repair
OK
Measure at ABS-ECU connector B-58.
• Disconnect the connector and measure at the harness side.
• Resistance value between terminals 8-33, 14-15, 30-28 and 11-10
OK : 1.0-1.2 kΩ
NG
Check the following connectors:
• A-01, A-08, E-33, E-35, E-12, B-71 and B-59
NG
Repair
OK
Check trouble symptom.
NG
Check the harnesses between each wheel speed sensor and the ABS-ECU. Repair, if necessary.
OK
Wheel speed sensor output voltage inspection
NG
Wheel speed sensor inspection
NG
Replace the wheel speed sensor.
OK
Rotor inspection
NG
Replace the rotor.
OK
Wheel bearing inspection
OK
Check the following connector:
• B-58
NG
Repair
OK
Check trouble symptom.
NG
Replace the ABS-ECU.

MT4029500177000X

Fig. 127 Codes 11, 12, 13 & 14: Wheel Speed Sensors (Open Or Short Circuit). 1995 Eclipse

Code No. 16	Power supply system	Probable cause
[Comment] This diagnostic trouble code is output when the ABS-ECU power voltage is outside the standard value. Furthermore, if the voltage returns to normal, this diagnostic trouble code will not be output.		• Malfunction of wiring harness or connector. • Malfunction of battery or generator. • Malfunction of ABS-ECU.

Caution

If the battery voltage drops during inspection, this code will be output as a current problem, and correct diagnostic of the problem cannot be made.
Before carrying out the following inspection, check the battery condition, and recharge it if necessary.

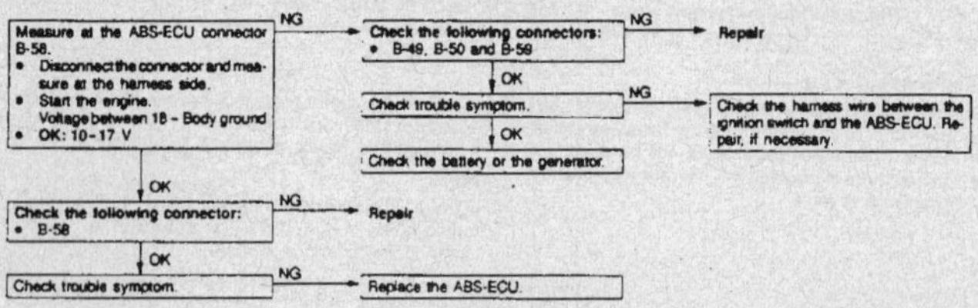
Measure at the ABS-ECU connector B-58.
• Disconnect the connector and measure at the harness side.
• Start the engine.
Voltage between 18 – Body ground
• OK: 10-17 V
NG
Check the following connectors:
• B-49, B-50 and B-59
NG
Repair
OK
Check trouble symptom.
NG
Check the harness wire between the ignition switch and the ABS-ECU. Repair, if necessary.
OK
Check the battery or the generator.
OK
Check the following connector:
• B-58
NG
Repair
OK
Check trouble symptom.
NG
Replace the ABS-ECU.

MT4029500199000X

Fig. 129 Code 16: Power Supply System. 1995 Eclipse

Code No. 21, 22, 23, 24	Wheel speed sensor excessive gap	Probable cause
[Comment] These diagnostic trouble codes are output when the detection speed of the wheel speed sensors is below the standard value.		• Improper installation of wheel speed sensor. • Malfunction of wheel speed sensor (intermittent open circuit or short circuit). • Malfunction of rotor (chipped tooth or rotor not installed). • Noise interference in wheel speed sensor. • Malfunction of ABS-ECU.

NOTE
1. Momentary interruptions within approximately 100 ms are not detected.
2. To inspect the twisted pair wires in the wheel speed sensor, check if there is any damage to the cables, and flex the cables to check for any open circuits.

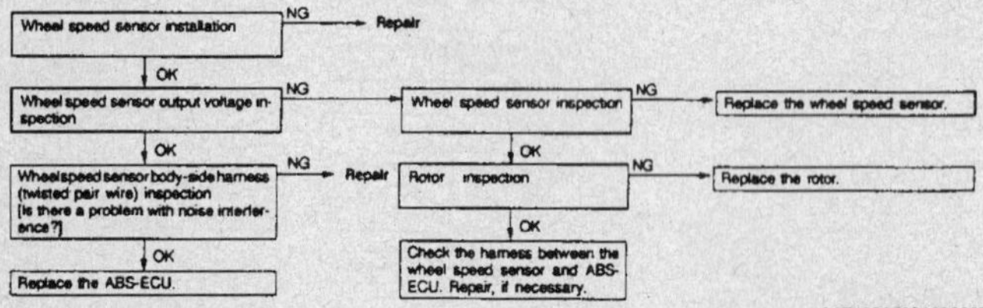
Wheel speed sensor installation
NG
Repair
OK
Wheel speed sensor output voltage inspection
NG
Wheel speed sensor inspection
NG
Replace the wheel speed sensor.
OK
Wheelspeed sensor body-side harness (twisted pair wire) inspection
[Is there a problem with noise interference?]
NG
Repair
OK
Rotor inspection
NG
Replace the rotor.
OK
Check the harness between the wheel speed sensor and ABS-ECU. Repair, if necessary.
OK
Replace the ABS-ECU.

MT4029500180000X

Fig. 131 Codes 21, 22, 23 & 24: Wheel Speed Sensor (Excessive Gap). 1995 Eclipse FWD

Code No. 15	Wheel speed sensor system	Probable cause
[Comment] This diagnostic trouble code is output when there is an abnormality (other than broken wire or short circuit) in any of the wheel speed sensor output signals while driving. The following can be considered as the cause of the wheel speed sensor output abnormality. • Distortion of rotor, teeth missing • Low frequency noise interference when sensor harness wire is broken • Noise interference in sensor signal • Sensor output signal is below the standard value or amplitude modulation is over the standard value. Using an oscilloscope to measure the wave shape of the wheel speed sensor output signal is very effective. • Broken sensor harness • Poor connection of connector		• Malfunction of wheel speed sensor. • Malfunction of wiring harness. • Malfunction of rotor. • Malfunction of wheel bearing. • Malfunction of ABS-ECU.

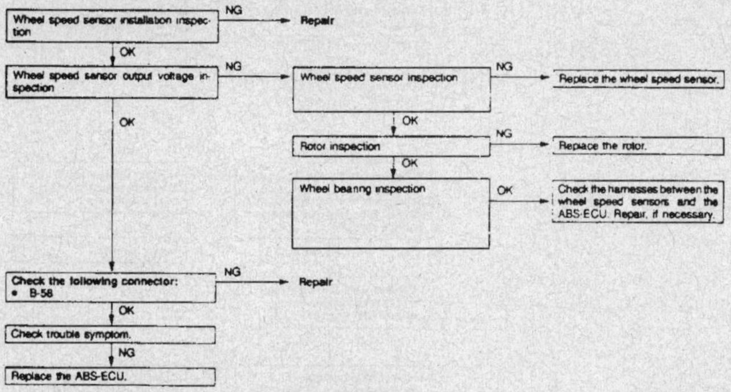
Wheel speed sensor installation inspection
NG
Repair
OK
Wheel speed sensor output voltage inspection
NG
Wheel speed sensor inspection
NG
Replace the wheel speed sensor.
OK
Rotor inspection
NG
Replace the rotor.
OK
Wheel bearing inspection
OK
Check the harnesses between the wheel speed sensors and the ABS-ECU. Repair, if necessary.
OK
Check the following connector:
• B-58
NG
Repair
OK
Check trouble symptom.
NG
Replace the ABS-ECU.

MT4029500178000X

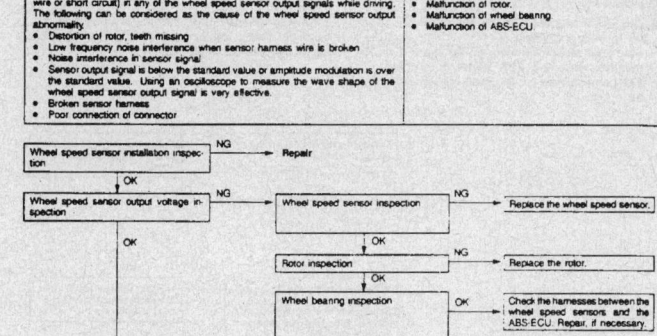

Fig. 128 Code 15: Wheel Speed Sensor System. 1995 Eclipse

Code No. 21	G-sensor system	Probable cause
[Comment] The ABS-ECU outputs this diagnostic trouble code in the following cases • When there is an open or short circuit in the harness for the G-sensor system.		• Malfunction of G-sensor. • Malfunction of wiring harness or connector. • Malfunction of ABS-ECU

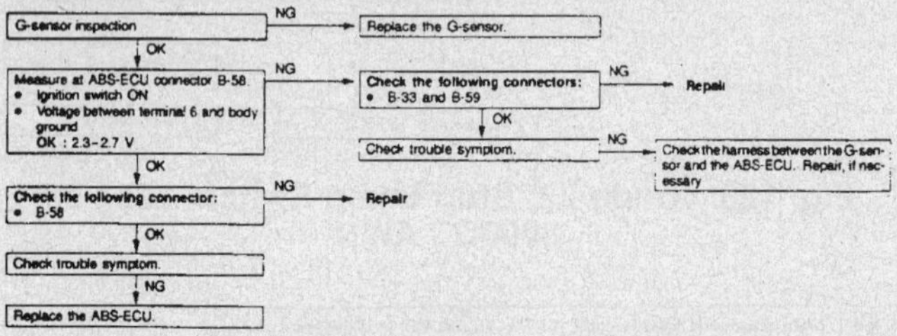
G-sensor inspection
NG
Replace the G-sensor.
OK
Measure at ABS-ECU connector B-58.
• Ignition switch ON
• Voltage between terminal 6 and body ground
OK : 2.3-2.7 V
NG
Check the following connectors:
• B-33 and B-59
NG
Repair
OK
Check trouble symptom.
NG
Check the harness between the G-sensor and the ABS-ECU. Repair, if necessary
OK
Check the following connector:
• B-58
NG
Repair
OK
Check trouble symptom.
NG
Replace the ABS-ECU.

MT4029500179000X

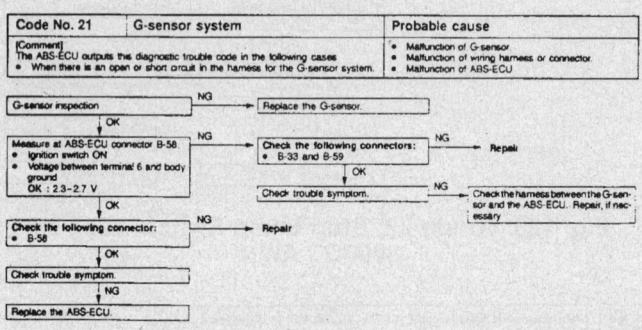

Fig. 130 Code 21: G-Sensor System. 1995 Eclipse AWD

Code No. 22	Stop light switch system	Probable cause
[Comment] The ABS-ECU outputs this diagnostic trouble code in the following cases. • Stoplight switch remains on for more than 15 minutes while the ABS is not functioning. • The harness wire for the stop light switch may be open. If the stop light operates normally, there is an open circuit in the harness for the stop light switch input circuit is broken or there is a malfunction in the ABS-ECU.		• Malfunction of stop light switch. • Malfunction of harness or connector. • Malfunction of ABS-ECU.

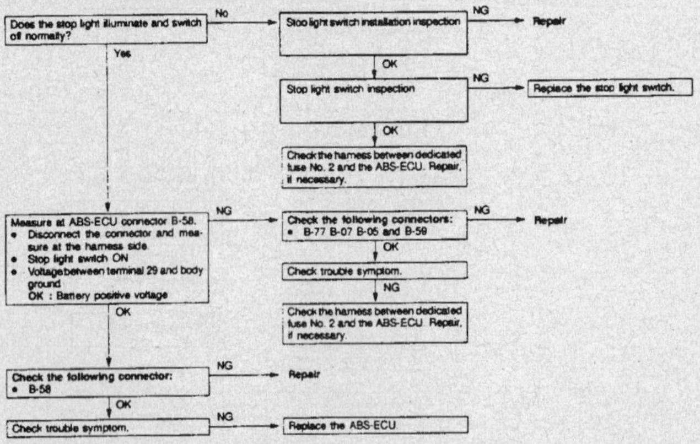
Does the stop light illuminate and switch off normally?
No
Stop light switch installation inspection
NG
Repair
OK
Stop light switch inspection
NG
Replace the stop light switch.
OK
Check the harness between dedicated fuse No. 2 and the ABS-ECU. Repair, if necessary.
Yes
Measure at ABS-ECU connector B-58.
• Disconnect the connector and measure at the harness side.
• Stop light switch ON
• Voltage between terminal 29 and body ground
OK : Battery positive voltage
NG
Check the following connectors:
• B-77 B-07 B-05 and B-59
NG
Repair
OK
Check trouble symptom.
NG
Check the harness between dedicated fuse No. 2 and the ABS-ECU. Repair, if necessary.
OK
Check the following connector:
• B-58
NG
Repair
OK
Check trouble symptom.
NG
Replace the ABS-ECU.

MT4029500181000X

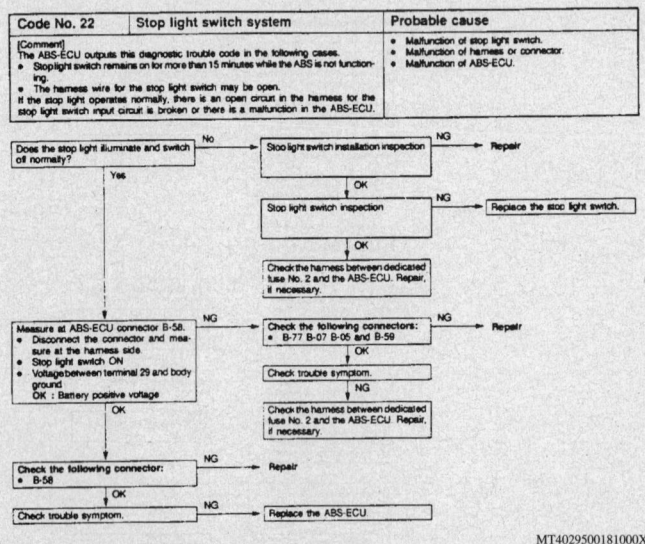

Fig. 132 Code 22: Stop Light Switch System. 1995 Eclipse AWD

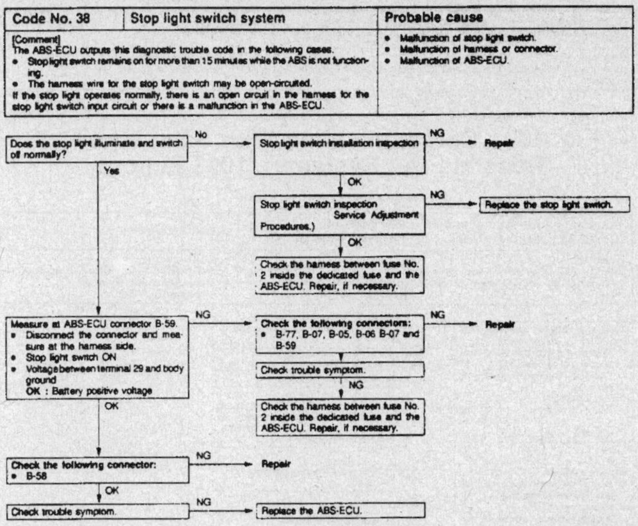
Code No. 38
Stop light switch system
Probable cause
[Comment]
The ABS-ECU outputs this diagnostic trouble code in the following cases.
• Stop light switch remains on for more than 15 minutes while the ABS is not functioning.
• The harness wire for the stop light switch may be open-circuited.
If the stop light operates normally, there is an open circuit in the harness for the stop light switch input circuit or there is a malfunction in the ABS-ECU.
• Malfunction of stop light switch.
• Malfunction of harness or connector.
• Malfunction of ABS-ECU.
Does the stop light illuminate and switch off normally?
No
Yes
Stop light switch installation inspection
NG
Repair
OK
Stop light switch inspection Service Adjustment Procedures.)
Replace the stop light switch.
Check the harness between fuse No. 2 inside the dedicated fuse and the ABS-ECU. Repair, if necessary.
Measure at ABS-ECU connector B-59.
• Disconnect the connector and measure at the harness side.
• Stop light switch ON
• Voltage between terminal 29 and body ground
OK : Battery positive voltage
Check the following connectors:
• B-77, B-07, B-05, B-06 B-07 and B-59
Check trouble symptom.
Check the harness between fuse No. 2 inside the dedicated fuse and the ABS-ECU. Repair, if necessary.
Check the following connector:
• B-58
Check trouble symptom.
Replace the ABS-ECU.
MT4029500182000X

Fig. 133 Code 38: Stop Light Switch System. 1995 Eclipse FWD

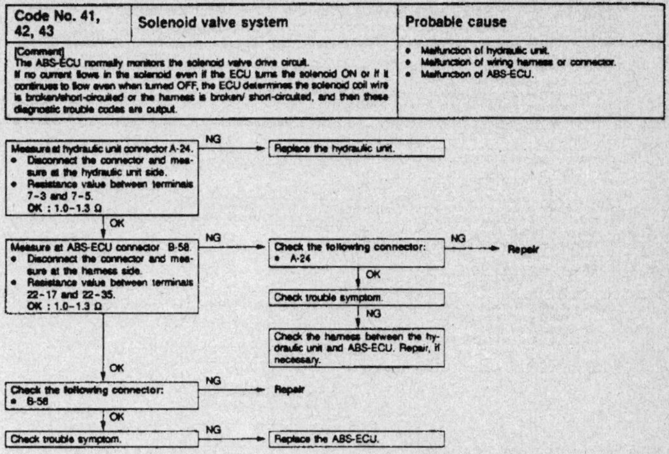
Code No. 41, 42, 43
Solenoid valve system
Probable cause
[Comment]
The ABS-ECU normally monitors the solenoid valve drive circuit.
If no current flows in the solenoid even if the ECU turns the solenoid ON or if it continues to flow even when turned OFF, the ECU determines the solenoid coil wire is broken/short-circuited or the harness is broken/ short-circuited, and then these diagnostic trouble codes are output.
• Malfunction of hydraulic unit.
• Malfunction of wiring harness or connector.
• Malfunction of ABS-ECU.
Measure at hydraulic unit connector A-24.
• Disconnect the connector and measure at the hydraulic unit side.
• Resistance value between terminals 7-3 and 7-5.
OK : 1.0-1.3 Ω
NG
Replace the hydraulic unit.
OK
Measure at ABS-ECU connector B-58.
• Disconnect the connector and measure at the harness side.
• Resistance value between terminals 22-17 and 22-35.
OK : 1.0-1.3 Ω
Check the following connector:
• A-24
Repair
Check trouble symptom.
Check the harness between the hydraulic unit and ABS-ECU. Repair, if necessary.
Check the following connector:
• B-58
Repair
Check trouble symptom.
Replace the ABS-ECU.
MT4029500183000X

Fig. 134 Codes 41, 42 & 43: Solenoid Valve System. 1995 Eclipse AWD

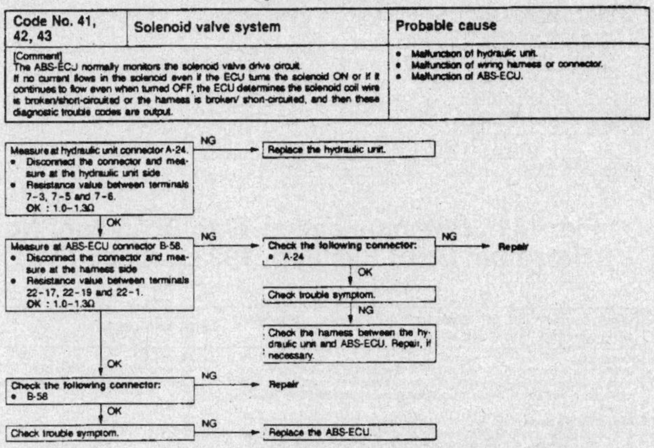
Code No. 41, 42, 43
Solenoid valve system
Probable cause
[Comment]
The ABS-ECU normally monitors the solenoid valve drive circuit.
If no current flows in the solenoid even if the ECU turns the solenoid ON or if it continues to flow even when turned OFF, the ECU determines the solenoid coil wire is broken/short-circuited or the harness is broken/ short-circuited, and then these diagnostic trouble codes are output.
• Malfunction of hydraulic unit.
• Malfunction of wiring harness or connector.
• Malfunction of ABS-ECU.
Measure at hydraulic unit connector A-24.
• Disconnect the connector and measure at the hydraulic unit side.
• Resistance value between terminals 7-3, 7-5 and 7-8.
OK : 1.0-1.3Ω
NG
Replace the hydraulic unit.
OK
Measure at ABS-ECU connector B-58.
• Disconnect the connector and measure at the harness side.
• Resistance value between terminals 22-17, 22-19 and 22-1.
OK : 1.0-1.3Ω
Check the following connector:
• A-24
Repair
Check trouble symptom.
Check the harness between the hydraulic unit and ABS-ECU. Repair, if necessary.
Check the following connector:
• B-58
Repair
Check trouble symptom.
Replace the ABS-ECU.
MT4029500184000X

Fig. 135 Codes 41, 42 & 43: Solenoid Valve System. 1995 Eclipse FWD

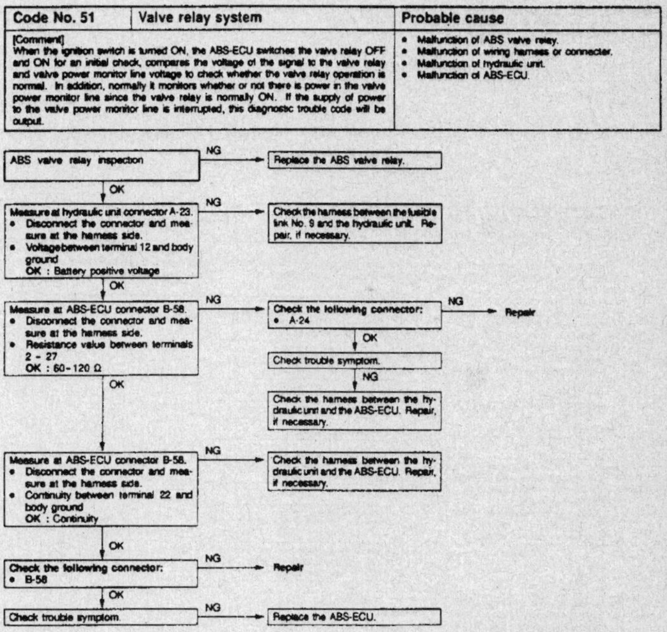
Code No. 51
Valve relay system
Probable cause
[Comment]
When the ignition switch is turned ON, the ABS-ECU switches the valve relay OFF and ON for an initial check, compares the voltage of the signal to the valve relay and valve power monitor line voltage to check whether the valve relay operation is normal. In addition, normally it monitors whether or not there is power in the valve power monitor line since the valve relay is normally ON. If the supply of power to the valve power monitor line is interrupted, this diagnostic trouble code will be output.
• Malfunction of ABS valve relay.
• Malfunction of wiring harness or connecter.
• Malfunction of hydraulic unit.
• Malfunction of ABS-ECU.
ABS valve relay inspection
NG
Replace the ABS valve relay.
OK
Measure at hydraulic unit connector A-23.
• Disconnect the connector and measure at the harness side.
• Voltage between terminal 12 and body ground
OK : Battery positive voltage
Check the harness between the fusible link No. 9 and the hydraulic unit. Repair, if necessary.
Measure at ABS-ECU connector B-58.
• Disconnect the connector and measure at the harness side.
• Resistance value between terminals 2 - 27
OK : 60-120 Ω
Check the following connector:
• A-24
Repair
Check trouble symptom.
Check the harness between the hydraulic unit and the ABS-ECU. Repair, if necessary.
Measure at ABS-ECU connector B-58.
• Disconnect the connector and measure at the harness side.
• Continuity between terminal 22 and body ground
OK : Continuity
Check the harness between the hydraulic unit and the ABS-ECU. Repair, if necessary.
Check the following connector:
• B-58
Repair
Check trouble symptom.
Replace the ABS-ECU.
MT4029500185000X

Fig. 136 Code 51: Valve Relay System. 1995 Eclipse

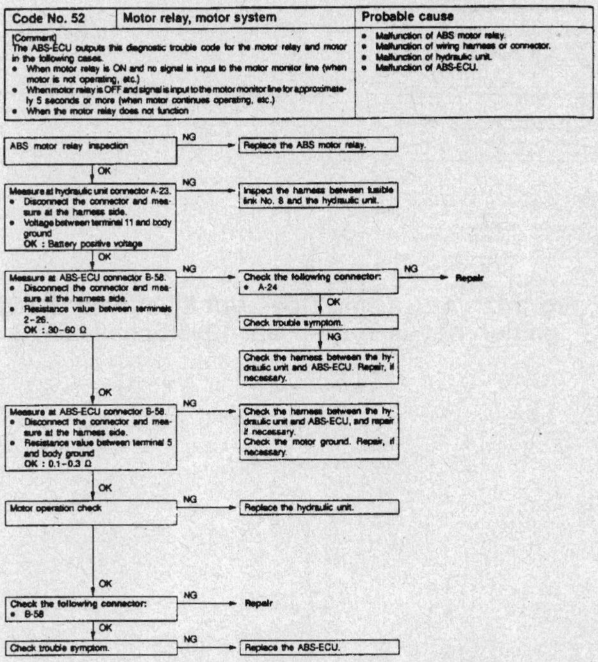
Code No. 52
Motor relay, motor system
Probable cause
[Comment]
The ABS-ECU outputs this diagnostic trouble code for the motor relay and motor in the following cases.
• When motor relay is ON and no signal is input to the motor monitor line (when motor is not operating, etc.)
• When motor relay is OFF and signal is input to the motor monitor line for approximately 5 seconds or more (when motor continues operating, etc.)
• When the motor relay does not function
• Malfunction of ABS motor relay.
• Malfunction of wiring harness or connector.
• Malfunction of hydraulic unit.
• Malfunction of ABS-ECU.
ABS motor relay inspection
NG
Replace the ABS motor relay.
OK
Measure at hydraulic unit connector A-23.
• Disconnect the connector and measure at the harness side.
• Voltage between terminal 11 and body ground
OK : Battery positive voltage
Inspect the harness between fusible link No. 8 and the hydraulic unit.
Measure at ABS-ECU connector B-58.
• Disconnect the connector and measure at the harness side.
• Resistance value between terminals 2-26.
OK : 30-60 Ω
Check the following connector:
• A-24
Repair
Check trouble symptom.
Check the harness between the hydraulic unit and ABS-ECU. Repair, if necessary.
Measure at ABS-ECU connector B-58.
• Disconnect the connector and measure at the harness side.
• Resistance value between terminal 5 and body ground
OK : 0.1-0.3 Ω
Check the harness between the hydraulic unit and ABS-ECU, and repair if necessary.
Check the motor ground. Repair, if necessary.
Motor operation check
Replace the hydraulic unit.
Check the following connector:
• B-58
Repair
Check trouble symptom.
Replace the ABS-ECU.
MT4029500186000X

Fig. 137 Code 52: Motor Relay (Motor System). 1995 Eclipse AWD

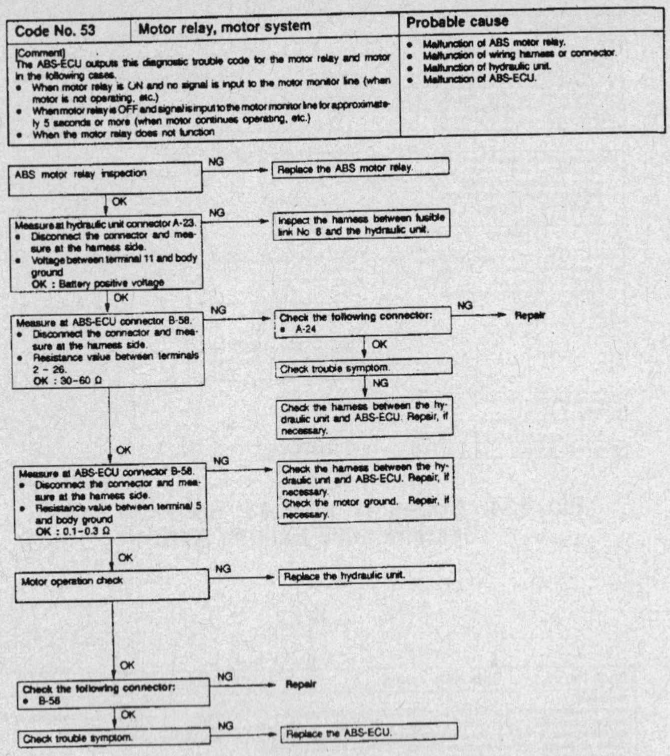
Code No. 53
Motor relay, motor system
Probable cause
[Comment]
The ABS-ECU outputs this diagnostic trouble code for the motor relay and motor in the following cases.
• When motor relay is ON and no signal is input to the motor monitor line (when motor is not operating, etc.)
• When motor relay is OFF and signal is input to the motor monitor line for approximately 5 seconds or more (when motor continues operating, etc.)
• When the motor relay does not function
• Malfunction of ABS motor relay.
• Malfunction of wiring harness or connector.
• Malfunction of hydraulic unit.
• Malfunction of ABS-ECU.
ABS motor relay inspection
NG
Replace the ABS motor relay.
OK
Measure at hydraulic unit connector A-23.
• Disconnect the connector and measure at the harness side.
• Voltage between terminal 11 and body ground
OK : Battery positive voltage
Inspect the harness between fusible link No. 8 and the hydraulic unit.
Measure at ABS-ECU connector B-58.
• Disconnect the connector and measure at the harness side.
• Resistance value between terminals 2 - 26.
OK : 30-60 Ω
Check the following connector:
• A-24
Repair
Check trouble symptom.
Check the harness between the hydraulic unit and ABS-ECU. Repair, if necessary.
Measure at ABS-ECU connector B-58.
• Disconnect the connector and measure at the harness side.
• Resistance value between terminal 5 and body ground
OK : 0.1-0.3 Ω
Check the harness between the hydraulic unit and ABS-ECU. Repair, if necessary.
Check the motor ground. Repair, if necessary.
Motor operation check
Replace the hydraulic unit.
Check the following connector:
• B-58
Repair
Check trouble symptom.
Replace the ABS-ECU.
MT4029500187000X

Fig. 138 Code 53: Motor Relay (Motor System). 1995 Eclipse FWD

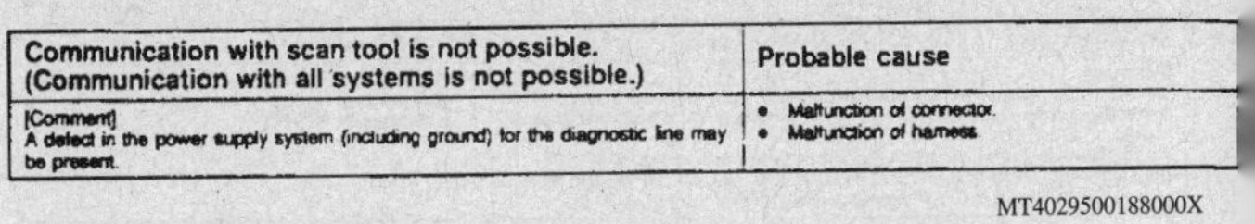
Communication with scan tool is not possible. (Communication with all systems is not possible.)
Probable cause
[Comment]
A defect in the power supply system (including ground) for the diagnostic line may be present.
• Malfunction of connector.
• Malfunction of harness.
MT4029500188000X

Fig. 139 Communication With Scan Tool Not Possible (All Systems). 1995 Eclipse

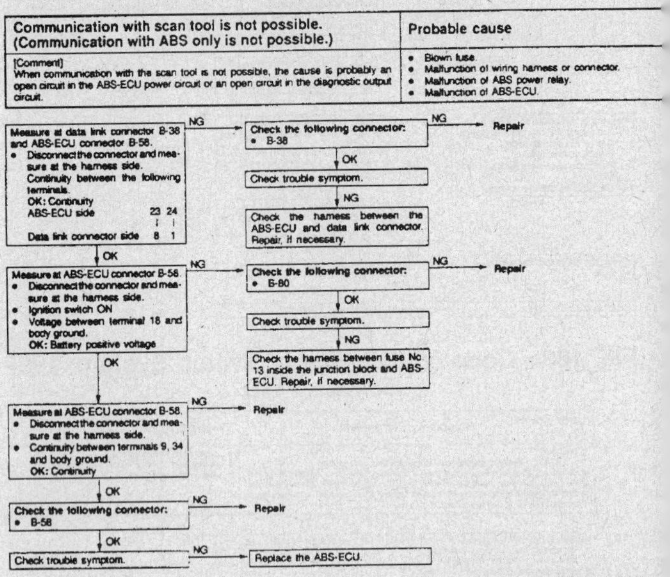
Communication with scan tool is not possible. (Communication with ABS only is not possible.)
Probable cause
[Comment]
When communication with the scan tool is not possible, the cause is probably an open circuit in the ABS-ECU power circuit or an open circuit in the diagnostic output circuit.
• Blown fuse.
• Malfunction of wiring harness or connector.
• Malfunction of ABS power relay.
• Malfunction of ABS-ECU.
Measure at data link connector B-38 and ABS-ECU connector B-58.
• Disconnect the connector and measure at the harness side.
Continuity between the following terminals.
OK: Continuity
ABS-ECU side 23 24
Data link connector side 8 1
Check the following connector:
• B-38
Repair
Check trouble symptom.
Check the harness between the ABS-ECU and data link connector. Repair, if necessary.
Measure at ABS-ECU connector B-58.
• Disconnect the connector and measure at the harness side.
• Ignition switch ON
• Voltage between terminal 18 and body ground.
OK: Battery positive voltage
Check the following connector:
• B-80
Check trouble symptom.
Check the harness between fuse No. 13 inside the junction block and ABS-ECU. Repair, if necessary.
Measure at ABS-ECU connector B-58.
• Disconnect the connector and measure at the harness side.
• Continuity between terminals 9, 34 and body ground.
OK: Continuity
Repair
Check the following connector:
• B-58
Check trouble symptom.
Replace the ABS-ECU.
MT4029500190000X

Fig. 141 Communication With Scan Tool Not Possible (ABS System). 1995 Eclipse FWD

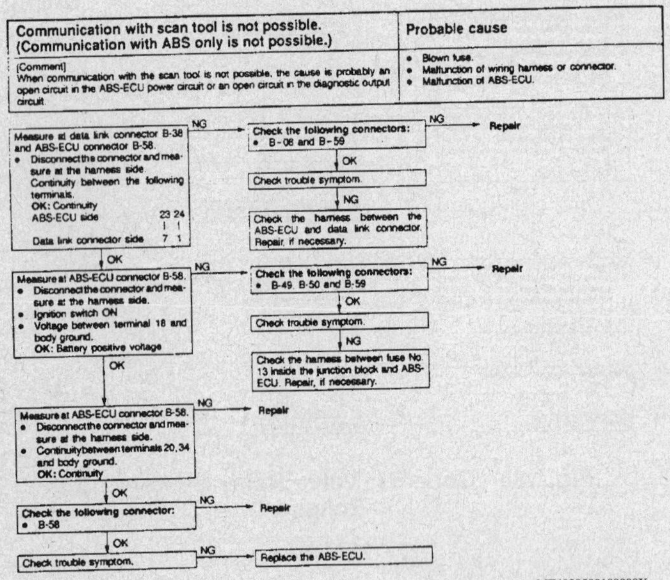
Communication with scan tool is not possible. (Communication with ABS only is not possible.)
Probable cause
[Comment]
When communication with the scan tool is not possible, the cause is probably an open circuit in the ABS-ECU power circuit or an open circuit in the diagnostic output circuit.
• Blown fuse.
• Malfunction of wiring harness or connector.
• Malfunction of ABS-ECU.
Measure at data link connector B-38 and ABS-ECU connector B-58.
• Disconnect the connector and measure at the harness side.
Continuity between the following terminals.
OK: Continuity
ABS-ECU side 23 24
Data link connector side 7 1
Check the following connectors:
• B-08 and B-59
Repair
Check trouble symptom.
Check the harness between the ABS-ECU and data link connector. Repair, if necessary.
Measure at ABS-ECU connector B-58.
• Disconnect the connector and measure at the harness side.
• Ignition switch ON
• Voltage between terminal 18 and body ground.
OK: Battery positive voltage
Check the following connectors:
• B-49, B-50 and B-59
Check trouble symptom.
Check the harness between fuse No. 13 inside the junction block and ABS-ECU. Repair, if necessary.
Measure at ABS-ECU connector B-58.
• Disconnect the connector and measure at the harness side.
• Continuity between terminals 20, 34 and body ground.
OK: Continuity
Repair
Check the following connector:
• B-58
Check trouble symptom.
Replace the ABS-ECU.
MT4029500189000X

Fig. 140 Communication With Scan Tool Not Possible (ABS System). 1995 Eclipse AWD

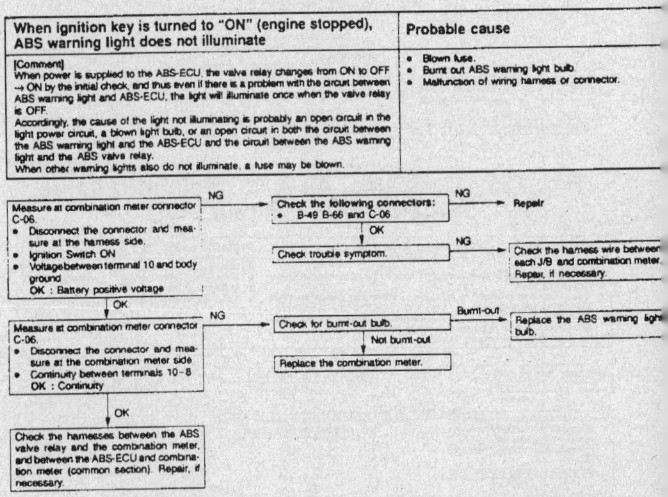
When ignition key is turned to "ON" (engine stopped), ABS warning light does not illuminate
Probable cause
[Comment]
When power is supplied to the ABS-ECU, the valve relay changes from ON to OFF → ON by the initial check, and thus even if there is a problem with the circuit between ABS warning light and ABS-ECU, the light will illuminate once when the valve relay is OFF.
Accordingly, the cause of the light not illuminating is probably an open circuit in the light power circuit, a blown light bulb, or an open circuit in both the circuit between the ABS warning light and the ABS-ECU and the circuit between the ABS warning light and the ABS valve relay.
When other warning lights also do not illuminate, a fuse may be blown.
• Blown fuse.
• Burnt out ABS warning light bulb.
• Malfunction of wiring harness or connector.
Measure at combination meter connector C-06.
• Disconnect the connector and measure at the harness side.
• Ignition Switch ON
• Voltage between terminal 10 and body ground
OK : Battery positive voltage
Check the following connectors:
• B-49 B-66 and C-06
Repair
Check trouble symptom.
Check the harness wire between each J/B and combination meter. Repair, if necessary.
Measure at combination meter connector C-06.
• Disconnect the connector and measure at the combination meter side
• Continuity between terminals 10-8
OK : Continuity
Check for burnt-out bulb.
Burnt-out
Replace the ABS warning light bulb.
Not burnt-out
Replace the combination meter.
Check the harnesses between the ABS valve relay and the combination meter, and between the ABS-ECU and combination meter (common section). Repair, if necessary.
MT4029500191000X

Fig. 142 ABS Lamp Does Not Illuminate When Ignition Key Is Turned On. 1995 Eclipse AWD

When ignition key is turned to "ON" (engine stopped), ABS warning light does not illuminate	Probable cause
[Comment] When power is supplied to the ABS-ECU, the valve relay changes from ON to OFF → ON by the initial check, and thus even if there is a problem with the circuit between ABS warning light and ABS-ECU, the light will illuminate once when the valve relay is OFF. Accordingly, the cause of the light not illuminating is probably an open circuit in the light power circuit, a blown light bulb, or an open circuit in both the circuit between the ABS warning light and the ABS-ECU and the circuit between the ABS warning light and the ABS valve relay. When other warning lights also do not illuminate, a fuse may be present.	• Blown fuse. • Burnt out ABS warning light bulb. • Malfunction of wiring harness or connector.

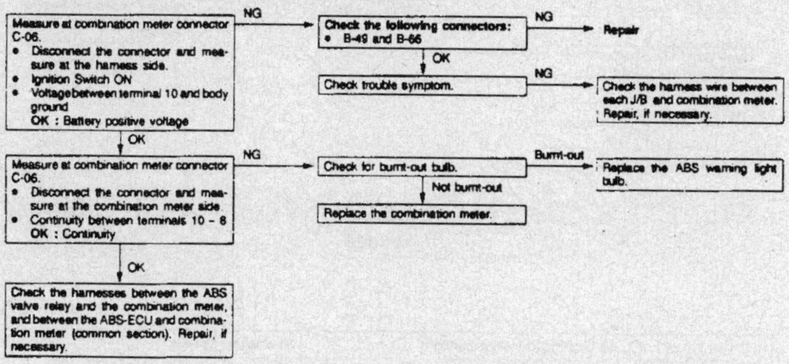

Measure at combination meter connector C-06.
• Disconnect the connector and measure at the harness side.
• Ignition Switch ON
• Voltage between terminal 10 and body ground
OK : Battery positive voltage
NG
Check the following connectors:
• B-49 and B-66
NG
Repair
OK
Check trouble symptom.
NG
Check the harness wire between each J/B and combination meter. Repair, if necessary.
OK
Measure at combination meter connector C-06.
• Disconnect the connector and measure at the combination meter side.
• Continuity between terminals 10 - 8
OK : Continuity
NG
Check for burnt-out bulb.
Burnt-out
Replace the ABS warning light bulb.
Not burnt-out
Replace the combination meter.
OK
Check the harnesses between the ABS valve relay and the combination meter, and between the ABS-ECU and combination meter (common section). Repair, if necessary.
MT4029500192000X

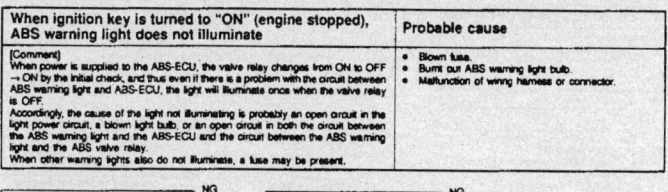

Fig. 143 ABS Lamp Does Not Illuminate When Ignition Key Is Turned On. 1995 Eclipse FWD

When ignition key is turned to "START", ABS warning light does not illuminate.	Probable cause
[Comment] The ABS-ECU uses the power to the IG2 which is cut when the ignition switch is turned to "START". The ABS warning light uses IG1 power which is not cut even when the ignition switch is turned to "START". Accordingly, because the power to the ABS-ECU is stopped in "START" position, if the warning light does not illuminate at this time, the cause is a problem in the light illumination circuit in the valve relay.	• Malfunction of wiring harness or connector. • Malfunction of hydraulic unit.

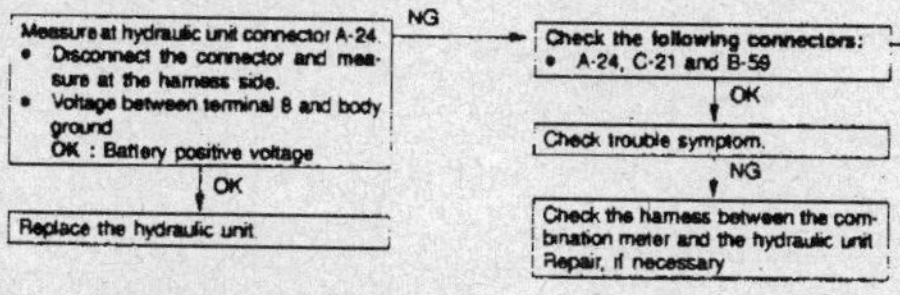

Measure at hydraulic unit connector A-24.
• Disconnect the connector and measure at the harness side.
• Voltage between terminal 8 and body ground
OK : Battery positive voltage
NG
Check the following connectors:
• A-24, C-21 and B-59
NG
Repair
OK
Check trouble symptom.
NG
Check the harness between the combination meter and the hydraulic unit. Repair, if necessary
OK
Replace the hydraulic unit
MT4029500194000X

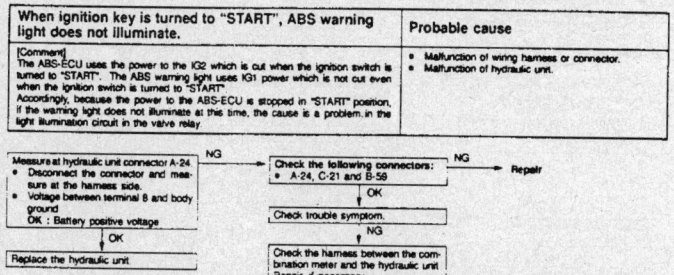

Fig. 145 ABS Lamp Does Not Illuminate When Ignition Is Turned To Start. 1995 Eclipse

Break operation is abnormal	Probable cause
[Comment] This varies depending on the driving conditions and the road surface conditions, so problem diagnosis is difficult. However, if a normal diagnostic trouble code is displayed, carry out the following inspection.	• Malfunction of wheel speed sensor. • Malfunction of rotor. • Malfunction of wheel bearing. • Malfunction of hydraulic unit. • Malfunction of ABS-ECU.

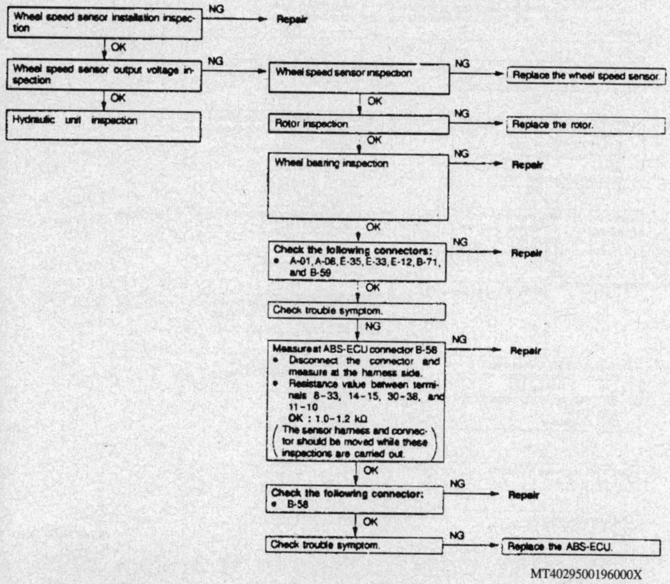

Wheel speed sensor installation inspection
NG
Repair
OK
Wheel speed sensor output voltage inspection
NG
Wheel speed sensor inspection
NG
Replace the wheel speed sensor.
OK
Hydraulic unit inspection
OK
Rotor inspection
NG
Replace the rotor.
OK
Wheel bearing inspection
NG
Repair
OK
Check the following connectors:
• A-01, A-08, E-35, E-33, E-12, B-71, and B-59
NG
Repair
OK
Check trouble symptom.
NG
Measure at ABS-ECU connector B-58
• Disconnect the connector and measure at the harness side.
• Resistance value between terminals 8-33, 14-15, 30-38, and 11-10
OK : 1.0-1.2 kΩ
The sensor harness and connector should be moved while these inspections are carried out.
NG
Repair
OK
Check the following connector:
• B-58
NG
Repair
OK
Check trouble symptom.
NG
Replace the ABS-ECU.
MT4029500196000X

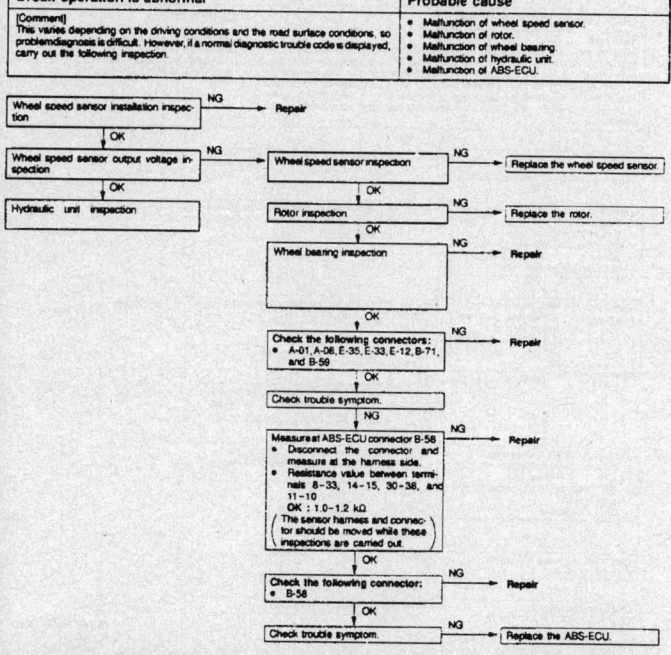

Fig. 147 Brake Operation Is Abnormal. 1995 Eclipse

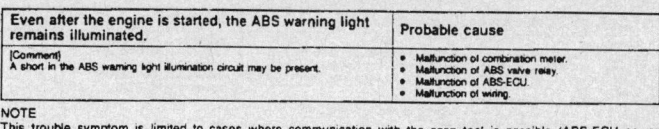

Even after the engine is started, the ABS warning light remains illuminated.	Probable cause
[Comment] A short in the ABS warning light illumination circuit may be present.	• Malfunction of combination meter. • Malfunction of ABS valve relay. • Malfunction of ABS-ECU. • Malfunction of wiring.

NOTE
This trouble symptom is limited to cases where communication with the scan tool is possible (ABS-ECU power supply is normal) and the diagnostic trouble code is a normal diagnostic trouble code.

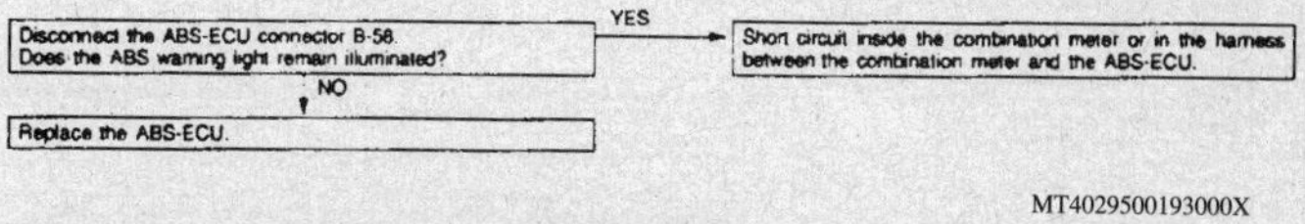

Disconnect the ABS-ECU connector B-58.
Does the ABS warning light remain illuminated?
YES
Short circuit inside the combination meter or in the harness between the combination meter and the ABS-ECU.
NO
Replace the ABS-ECU.
MT4029500193000X

Fig. 144 ABS Lamp Remains On When Engine Is Started. 1995 Eclipse

The ABS warning light flashes once after the ignition key is turned to "ON". The light illuminates when the ignition key is turned to "START", and when the key is returned to "ON", it flashes once.	Probable cause
[Comment] When power flows, the ABS-ECU turns on the warning light for approximately 1 second while it performs a valve relay test. If there is a break in the harness between the ECU and the warning light illuminates only when the valve relay is off in the valve relay test, etc.	• Malfunction of wiring harness or connector. • Malfunction of ABS-ECU.

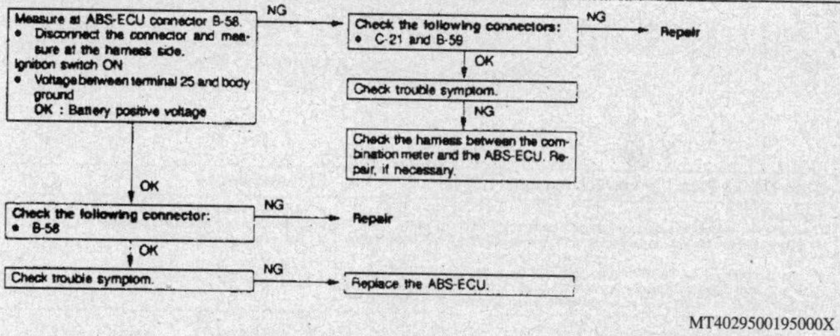

Measure at ABS-ECU connector B-58.
• Disconnect the connector and measure at the harness side.
Ignition switch ON
• Voltage between terminal 25 and body ground
OK : Battery positive voltage
NG
Check the following connectors:
• C-21 and B-59
NG
Repair
OK
Check trouble symptom.
NG
Check the harness between the combination meter and the ABS-ECU. Repair, if necessary.
OK
Check the following connector:
• B-58
NG
Repair
OK
Check trouble symptom.
NG
Replace the ABS-ECU.
MT4029500195000X

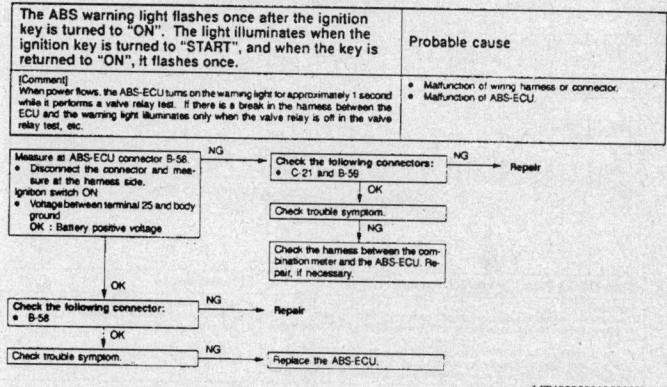

Fig. 146 ABS Lamp Flashes Once After Ignition Key Is Turned To On. 1995 Eclipse

Code No. 11, 12, 13, 14 Wheel speed sensor open circuit	Probable cause
[Comment] The ABS-ECU detects breaks in the wheel speed sensor wire.	• Malfunction of wheel speed sensor • Malfunction of wiring harness or connector • Malfunction of ABS-ECU

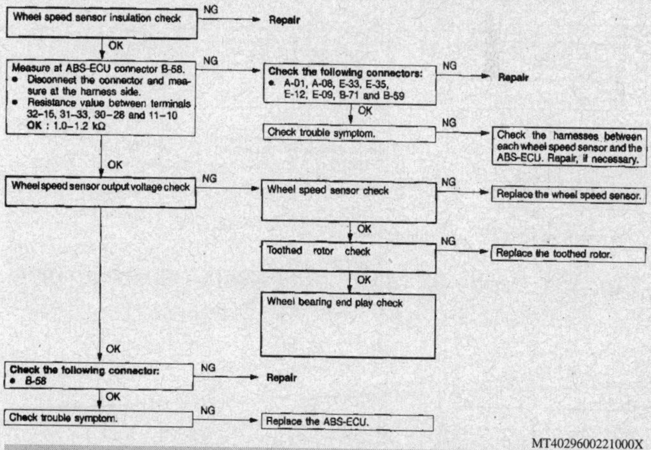

Wheel speed sensor insulation check
NG
Repair
OK
Measure at ABS-ECU connector B-58.
• Disconnect the connector and measure at the harness side.
• Resistance value between terminals 32-15, 31-33, 30-28 and 11-10
OK : 1.0-1.2 kΩ
NG
Check the following connectors:
• A-01, A-08, E-33, E-35, E-12, E-09, B-71 and B-59
NG
Repair
OK
Check trouble symptom.
NG
Check the harnesses between each wheel speed sensor and the ABS-ECU. Repair, if necessary.
OK
Wheel speed sensor output voltage check
NG
Wheel speed sensor check
NG
Replace the wheel speed sensor.
OK
Toothed rotor check
NG
Replace the toothed rotor.
OK
Wheel bearing end play check
OK
Check the following connector:
• B-58
NG
Repair
OK
Check trouble symptom.
NG
Replace the ABS-ECU.
MT4029600221000X

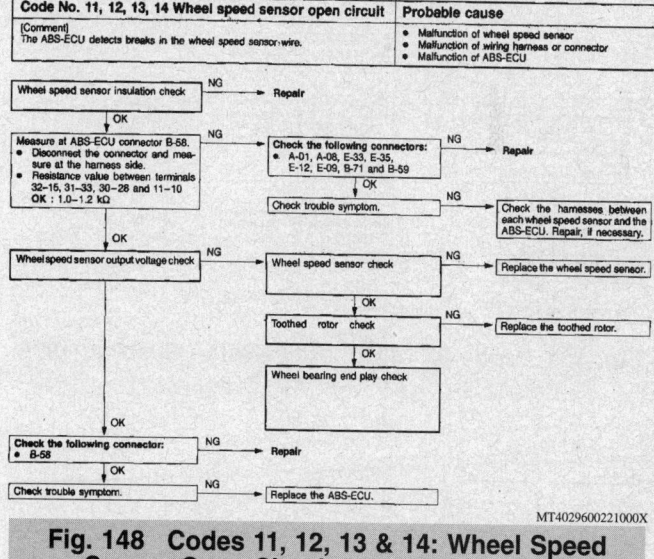

Fig. 148 Codes 11, 12, 13 & 14: Wheel Speed Sensor Open Circuit. 1996 Eclipse AWD

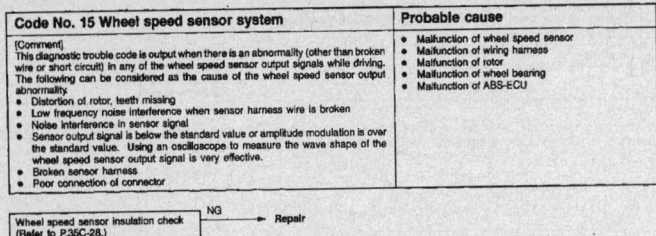

Code No. 15 Wheel speed sensor system	Probable cause
[Comment] This diagnostic trouble code is output when there is an abnormality (other than broken wire or short circuit) in any of the wheel speed sensor output signals while driving. The following can be considered as the cause of the wheel speed sensor output abnormality. • Distortion of rotor, teeth missing • Low frequency noise interference when sensor harness wire is broken • Noise interference in sensor signal • Sensor output signal is below the standard value or amplitude modulation is over the standard value. Using an oscilloscope to measure the wave shape of the wheel speed sensor output signal is very effective. • Broken sensor harness • Poor connection of connector	• Malfunction of wheel speed sensor • Malfunction of wiring harness • Malfunction of rotor • Malfunction of wheel bearing • Malfunction of ABS-ECU

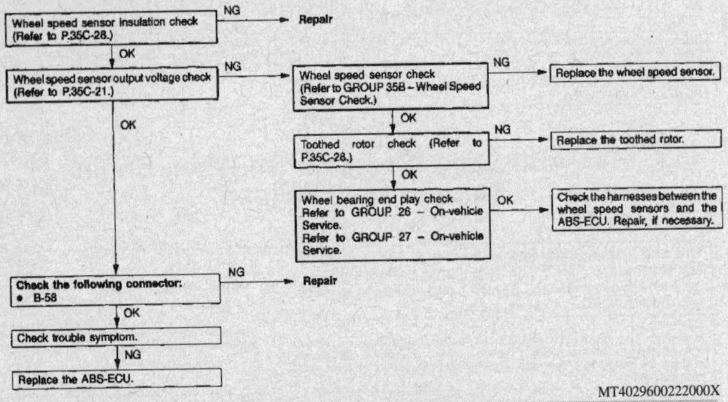

Wheel speed sensor insulation check (Refer to P.35C-28.)
NG
Repair
OK
Wheel speed sensor output voltage check (Refer to P.35C-21.)
NG
Wheel speed sensor check (Refer to GROUP 35B – Wheel Speed Sensor Check.)
NG
Replace the wheel speed sensor.
OK
Toothed rotor check (Refer to P.35C-28.)
NG
Replace the toothed rotor.
OK
Wheel bearing end play check Refer to GROUP 26 – On-vehicle Service. Refer to GROUP 27 – On-vehicle Service.
OK
Check the harnesses between the wheel speed sensors and the ABS-ECU. Repair, if necessary.
OK
Check the following connector:
• B-58
NG
Repair
OK
Check trouble symptom.
NG
Replace the ABS-ECU.
MT4029600222000X

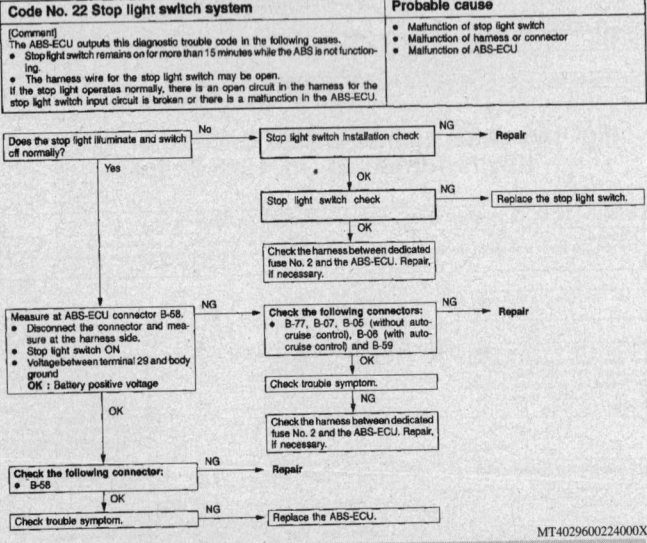

Fig. 149 Code 15: Wheel Speed Sensor System. 1996 Eclipse AWD

Code No. 22 Stop light switch system	Probable cause
[Comment] The ABS-ECU outputs this diagnostic trouble code in the following cases. • Stop light switch remains on for more than 15 minutes while the ABS is not functioning. • The harness wire for the stop light switch may be open. If the stop light operates normally, there is an open circuit in the harness for the stop light switch input circuit is broken or there is a malfunction in the ABS-ECU.	• Malfunction of stop light switch • Malfunction of harness or connector • Malfunction of ABS-ECU

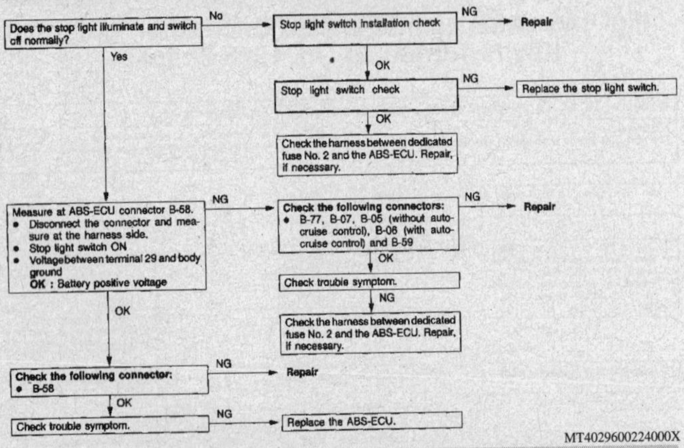

Does the stop light illuminate and switch off normally?
No
Stop light switch installation check
NG
Repair
OK
Stop light switch check
NG
Replace the stop light switch.
OK
Check the harness between dedicated fuse No. 2 and the ABS-ECU. Repair, if necessary.
Yes
Measure at ABS-ECU connector B-58.
• Disconnect the connector and measure at the harness side.
• Stop light switch ON
• Voltage between terminal 29 and body ground
OK : Battery positive voltage
NG
Check the following connectors:
• B-77, B-07, B-05 (without auto-cruise control), B-06 (with auto-cruise control) and B-59
NG
Repair
OK
Check trouble symptom.
NG
Check the harness between dedicated fuse No. 2 and the ABS-ECU. Repair, if necessary.
OK
Check the following connector:
• B-58
NG
Repair
OK
Check trouble symptom.
NG
Replace the ABS-ECU.
MT4029600224000X

Fig. 151 Code 22: Stop Light Switch System. 1996 Eclipse AWD

Code No. 21 G-sensor system	Probable cause
[Comment] The ABS-ECU outputs this diagnostic trouble code in the following cases. • When there is an open or short circuit in the harness for the G-sensor system.	• Malfunction of G-sensor • Malfunction of wiring harness or connector • Malfunction of ABS-ECU

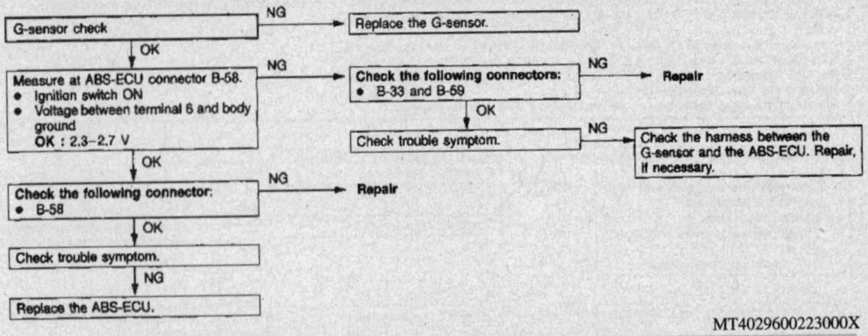

G-sensor check
NG
Replace the G-sensor.
OK
Measure at ABS-ECU connector B-58.
• Ignition switch ON
• Voltage between terminal 6 and body ground
OK : 2.3–2.7 V
NG
Check the following connectors:
• B-33 and B-59
NG
Repair
OK
Check trouble symptom.
NG
Check the harness between the G-sensor and the ABS-ECU. Repair, if necessary.
OK
Check the following connector:
• B-58
NG
Repair
OK
Check trouble symptom.
NG
Replace the ABS-ECU.
MT4029600223000X

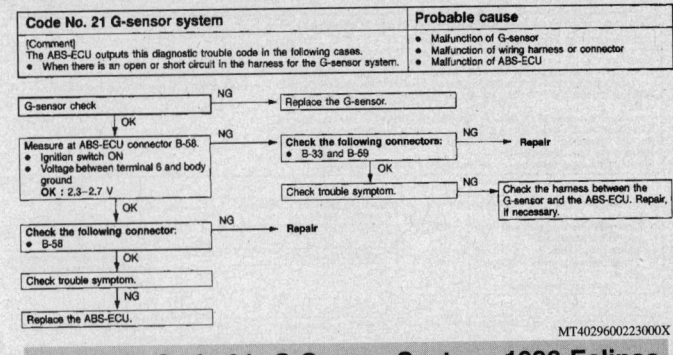

Fig. 150 Code 21: G-Sensor System. 1996 Eclipse AWD

Code No. 41, 42, 43 Solenoid valve system	Probable cause
[Comment] The ABS-ECU normally monitors the solenoid valve drive circuit. If no current flows in the solenoid even if the ECU turns the solenoid ON or if it continues to flow even when turned OFF, the ECU determines the solenoid coil wire is broken/short-circuited or the harness is broken/ short-circuited, and then these diagnostic trouble codes are output.	• Malfunction of hydraulic unit • Malfunction of wiring harness or connector • Malfunction of ABS-ECU

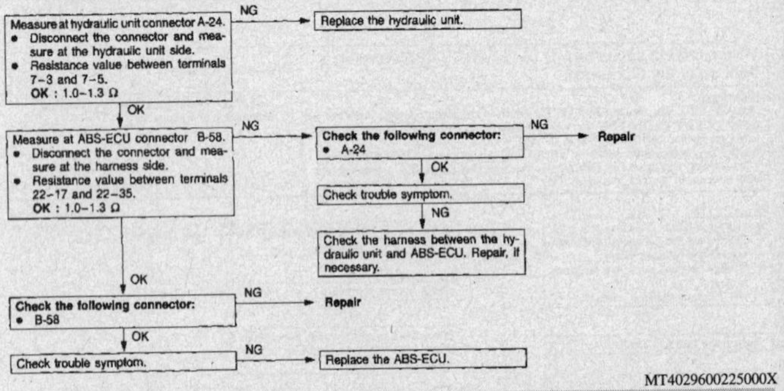

Measure at hydraulic unit connector A-24.
• Disconnect the connector and measure at the hydraulic unit side.
• Resistance value between terminals 7–3 and 7–5.
OK : 1.0–1.3 Ω
NG
Replace the hydraulic unit.
OK
Measure at ABS-ECU connector B-58.
• Disconnect the connector and measure at the harness side.
• Resistance value between terminals 22–17 and 22–35.
OK : 1.0–1.3 Ω
NG
Check the following connector:
• A-24
NG
Repair
OK
Check trouble symptom.
NG
Check the harness between the hydraulic unit and ABS-ECU. Repair, if necessary.
OK
Check the following connector:
• B-58
NG
Repair
OK
Check trouble symptom.
NG
Replace the ABS-ECU.
MT4029600225000X

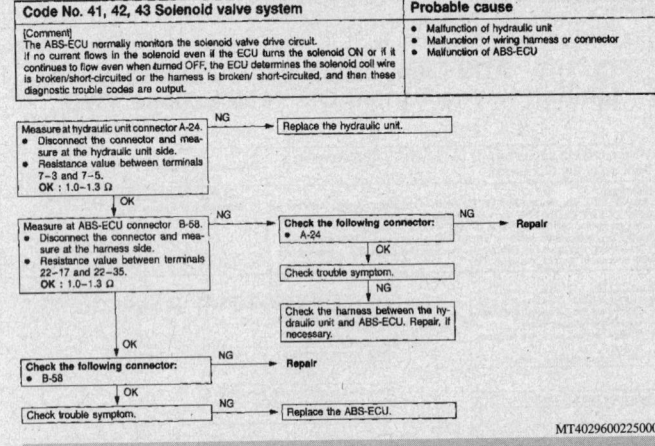

Fig. 152 Codes 41, 42 & 43: Solenoid Valve System. 1996 Eclipse AWD

Code No. 51 Valve relay system	Probable cause
[Comment] When the ignition switch is turned ON, the ABS-ECU switches the valve relay OFF and ON for an initial check, compares the voltage of the signal to the valve relay and valve power monitor line voltage to check whether the valve relay operation is normal. In addition, normally it monitors whether or not there is power in the valve power monitor line since the valve relay is normally ON. If the supply of power to the valve power monitor line is interrupted, this diagnostic trouble code will be output.	• Malfunction of ABS valve relay • Malfunction of wiring harness or connecter • Malfunction of hydraulic unit • Malfunction of ABS-ECU

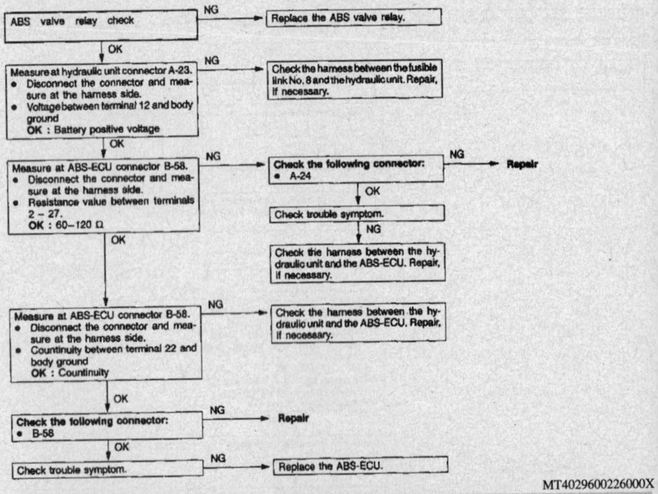

ABS valve relay check
NG
Replace the ABS valve relay.
OK
Measure at hydraulic unit connector A-23.
• Disconnect the connector and measure at the harness side.
• Voltage between terminal 12 and body ground
OK : Battery positive voltage
NG
Check the harness between the fusible link No. 8 and the hydraulic unit. Repair, if necessary.
OK
Measure at ABS-ECU connector B-58.
• Disconnect the connector and measure at the harness side.
• Resistance value between terminals 2 – 27.
OK : 60–120 Ω
NG
Check the following connector:
• A-24
NG
Repair
OK
Check trouble symptom.
NG
Check the harness between the hydraulic unit and the ABS-ECU. Repair, if necessary.
OK
Measure at ABS-ECU connector B-58.
• Disconnect the connector and measure at the harness side.
• Countinuity between terminal 22 and body ground
OK : Countinuity
NG
Check the harness between the hydraulic unit and the ABS-ECU. Repair, if necessary.
OK
Check the following connector:
• B-58
NG
Repair
OK
Check trouble symptom.
NG
Replace the ABS-ECU.
MT4029600226000X

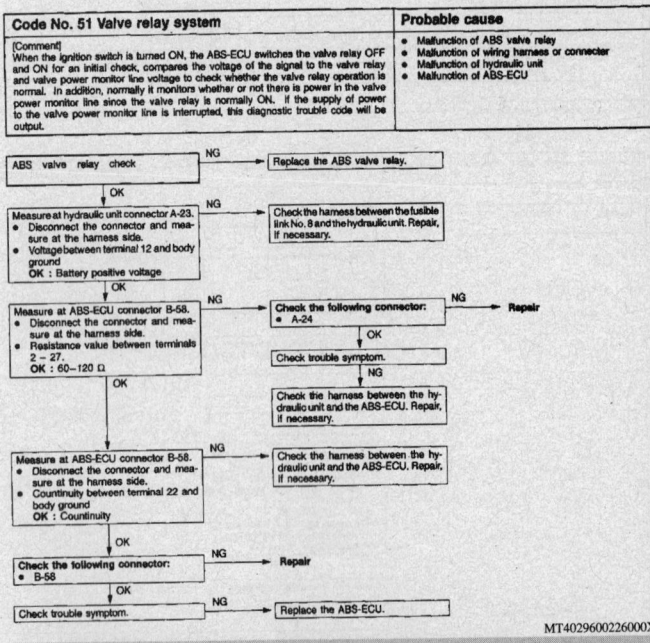

Fig. 153 Code 51: Valve Relay System. 1996 Eclipse AWD

Code No. 52 Motor relay, motor system	Probable cause
[Comment] The ABS-ECU outputs this diagnostic trouble code for the motor relay and motor in the following cases. • When motor relay is ON and no signal is input to the motor monitor line (when motor is not operating, etc.) • When motor relay is OFF and signal is input to the motor monitor line for approximately 5 seconds or more (when motor continues operating, etc.) • When the motor relay does not function	• Malfunction of ABS motor relay • Malfunction of wiring harness or connector • Malfunction of hydraulic unit • Malfunction of ABS-ECU

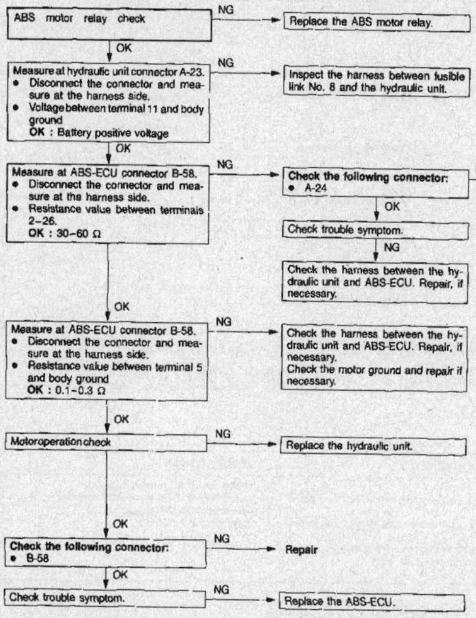
ABS motor relay check
NG
Replace the ABS motor relay.
OK
Measure at hydraulic unit connector A-23.
• Disconnect the connector and measure at the harness side.
• Voltage between terminal 11 and body ground
OK : Battery positive voltage
NG
Inspect the harness between fusible link No. 8 and the hydraulic unit.
OK
Measure at ABS-ECU connector B-58.
• Disconnect the connector and measure at the harness side.
• Resistance value between terminals 2–26.
OK : 30–60 Ω
NG
Check the following connector:
• A-24
NG
Repair
OK
Check trouble symptom.
NG
Check the harness between the hydraulic unit and ABS-ECU. Repair, if necessary.
OK
Measure at ABS-ECU connector B-58.
• Disconnect the connector and measure at the harness side.
• Resistance value between terminal 5 and body ground
OK : 0.1–0.3 Ω
NG
Check the harness between the hydraulic unit and ABS-ECU. Repair, if necessary.
Check the motor ground and repair if necessary.
OK
Motoroperation check
NG
Replace the hydraulic unit.
OK
Check the following connector:
• B-58
NG
Repair
OK
Check trouble symptom.
NG
Replace the ABS-ECU.
MT4029600227000X

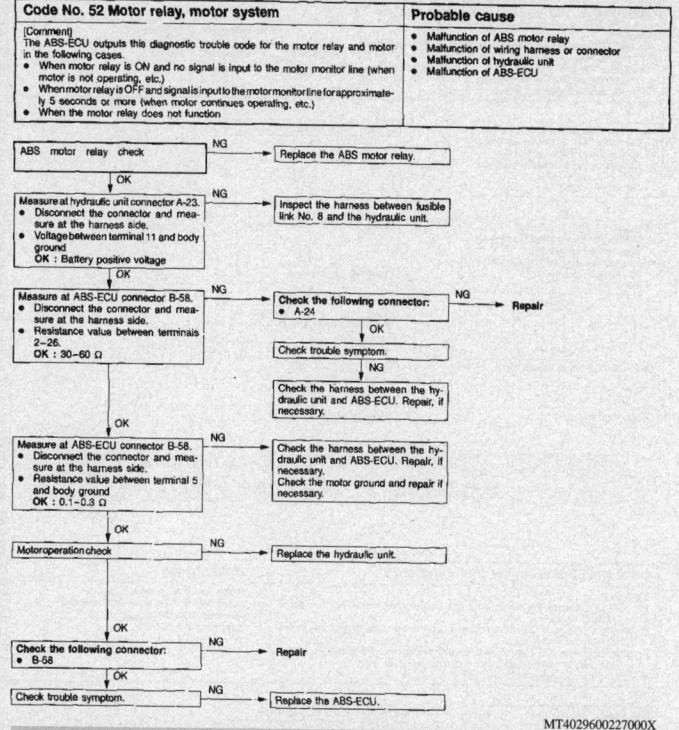

Fig. 154 Code 52: Motor Relay, Motor System. 1996 Eclipse AWD

Code No. 15 Wheel speed sensor system	Probable cause
[Comment] This diagnostic trouble code is output when there is a malfunction (other than broken wire or short circuit) in any of the wheel speed sensor output signals while driving. The following can be considered as the cause of the wheel speed sensor output malfunction. • Distortion of rotor, teeth missing • Low frequency noise interference when sensor harness wire is broken • Noise interference in sensor signal • Sensor output signal is below the standard value or amplitude modulation is over the standard value. Using an oscilloscope to measure the wave shape of the wheel speed sensor output signal is very effective. • Broken sensor harness • Poor connection of connector	• Malfunction of wheel speed sensor • Malfunction of wiring harness • Malfunction of rotor • Malfunction of wheel bearing • Malfunction of ABS-ECU

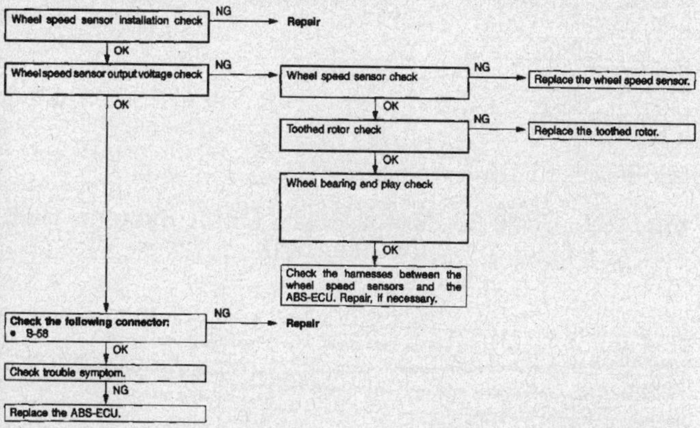
Wheel speed sensor installation check
NG
Repair
OK
Wheel speed sensor output voltage check
NG
Wheel speed sensor check
NG
Replace the wheel speed sensor.
OK
Toothed rotor check
NG
Replace the toothed rotor.
OK
Wheel bearing and play check
OK
Check the harnesses between the wheel speed sensors and the ABS-ECU. Repair, if necessary.
OK
Check the following connector:
• B-58
NG
Repair
OK
Check trouble symptom.
NG
Replace the ABS-ECU.
MT4029600229000X

Fig. 156 Code 15: Wheel Speed Sensor System. 1996 Eclipse FWD

Code No. 11, 12, 13, 14 Wheel speed sensor open circuit	Probable cause
[Comment] The ABS-ECU detects breaks in the wheel speed sensor wire	• Malfunction of wheel speed sensor • Malfunction of wiring harness or connector • Malfunction of ABS-ECU

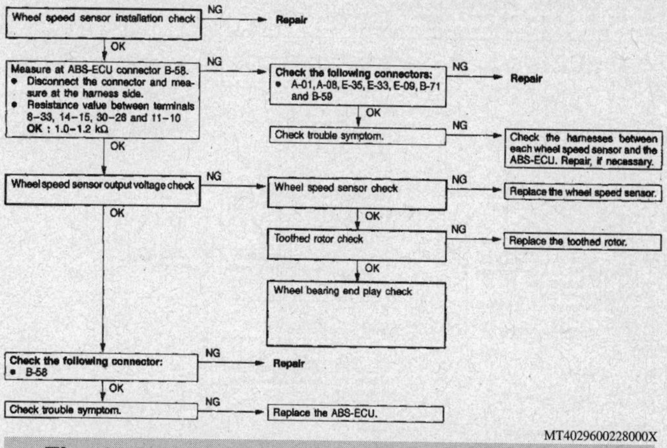
Wheel speed sensor installation check
NG
Repair
OK
Measure at ABS-ECU connector B-58.
• Disconnect the connector and measure at the harness side.
• Resistance value between terminals 8–33, 14–15, 30–28 and 11–10
OK : 1.0–1.2 kΩ
NG
Check the following connectors:
• A-01, A-08, E-35, E-33, E-09, B-71 and B-59
NG
Repair
OK
Check trouble symptom.
NG
Check the harnesses between each wheel speed sensor and the ABS-ECU. Repair, if necessary.
OK
Wheel speed sensor output voltage check
NG
Wheel speed sensor check
NG
Replace the wheel speed sensor.
OK
Toothed rotor check
NG
Replace the toothed rotor.
OK
Wheel bearing end play check
OK
Check the following connector:
• B-58
NG
Repair
OK
Check trouble symptom.
NG
Replace the ABS-ECU.
MT4029600228000X

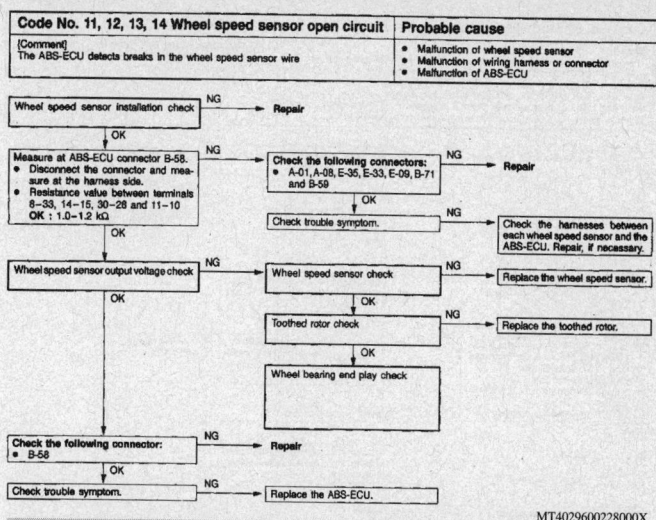

Fig. 155 Codes 11, 12, 13 & 14: Wheel Speed Sensor Open Circuit. 1996 Eclipse FWD

Code No. 16 Power supply system	Probable cause
[Comment] This diagnostic trouble code is output when the ABS-ECU power voltage is outside the standard value. Furthermore, if the voltage returns to normal, this diagnostic trouble code will not be output.	• Malfunction of wiring harness or connector. • Malfunction of battery or generator • Malfunction of ABS-ECU

Caution

If the battery voltage drops during check, this code will be output as a current problem, and correct diagnostic of the problem cannot be made.
Before carrying out the following check, check the battery condition, and recharge it if necessary.

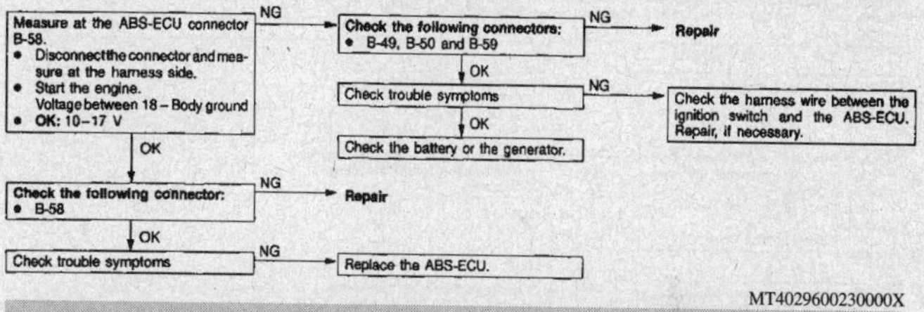
Measure at the ABS-ECU connector B-58.
• Disconnect the connector and measure at the harness side.
• Start the engine.
Voltage between 18 – Body ground
• OK: 10–17 V
NG
Check the following connectors:
• B-49, B-50 and B-59
NG
Repair
OK
Check trouble symptoms
NG
Check the harness wire between the ignition switch and the ABS-ECU. Repair, if necessary.
OK
Check the battery or the generator.
OK
Check the following connector:
• B-58
NG
Repair
OK
Check trouble symptoms
NG
Replace the ABS-ECU.
MT4029600230000X

Fig. 157 Code 16: Power Supply System. 1996 Eclipse FWD

Code No. 21, 22, 23, 24 Wheel speed sensor excessive gap or short circuit	Probable cause
[Comment] These diagnostic trouble codes are output when the detection speed of the wheel speed sensors is below the standard value.	• Improper installation of wheel speed sensor • Malfunction of wheel speed sensor (intermittent open circuit or short circuit) • Malfunction of rotor (chipped tooth or rotor not installed) • Noise interference in wheel speed sensor • Malfunction of ABS-ECU

NOTE
1. Momentary interruptions within approximately 100 ms are not detected.
2. To inspect the twisted pair wires in the wheel speed sensor, check if there is any damage to the cables, and flex the cables to check for any open circuits.

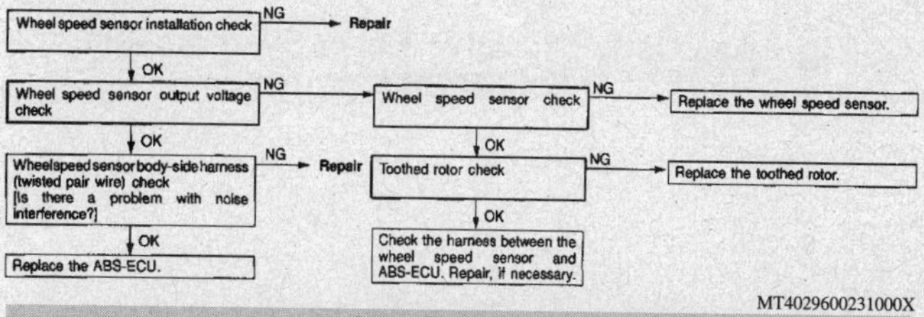
Wheel speed sensor installation check
NG
Repair
OK
Wheel speed sensor output voltage check
NG
Wheel speed sensor check
NG
Replace the wheel speed sensor.
OK
Wheelspeed sensor body-side harness (twisted pair wire) check
[Is there a problem with noise interference?]
NG
Repair
OK
Replace the ABS-ECU.
OK
Toothed rotor check
NG
Replace the toothed rotor.
OK
Check the harness between the wheel speed sensor and ABS-ECU. Repair, if necessary.
MT4029600231000X

Fig. 158 Codes 21, 22, 23 & 24: Wheel Speed Sensor Excessive Gap Or Short Circuit. 1996 Eclipse FWD

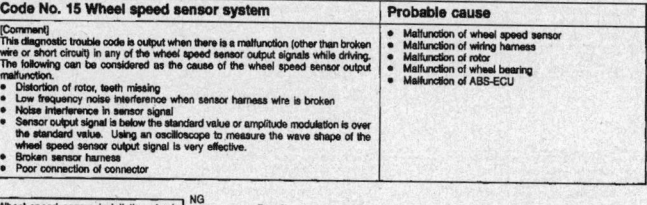

Code No. 38 Stop light switch system	Probable cause
[Comment] The ABS-ECU outputs this diagnostic trouble code in the following cases. • Stop light switch remains on for more than 15 minutes while the ABS is not functioning. • The harness wire for the stop light switch may be open-circuited. If the stop light operates normally, there is an open circuit in the harness for the stop light switch input circuit or there is a malfunction in the ABS-ECU.	• Malfunction of stop light switch • Malfunction of harness or connector • Malfunction of ABS-ECU

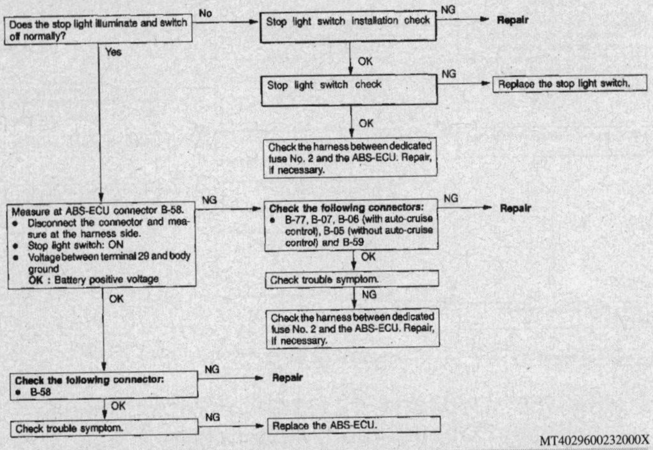
Does the stop light illuminate and switch off normally?
No
Yes
Stop light switch installation check
NG
Repair
OK
Stop light switch check
NG
Replace the stop light switch.
OK
Check the harness between dedicated fuse No. 2 and the ABS-ECU. Repair, if necessary.
Measure at ABS-ECU connector B-58.
• Disconnect the connector and measure at the harness side.
• Stop light switch: ON
• Voltage between terminal 29 and body ground
OK : Battery positive voltage
NG
Check the following connectors:
• B-77, B-07, B-06 (with auto-cruise control), B-05 (without auto-cruise control) and B-59
NG
Repair
OK
Check trouble symptom.
NG
Check the harness between dedicated fuse No. 2 and the ABS-ECU. Repair, if necessary.
OK
Check the following connector:
• B-58
NG
Repair
OK
Check trouble symptom.
NG
Replace the ABS-ECU.
MT4029600232000X

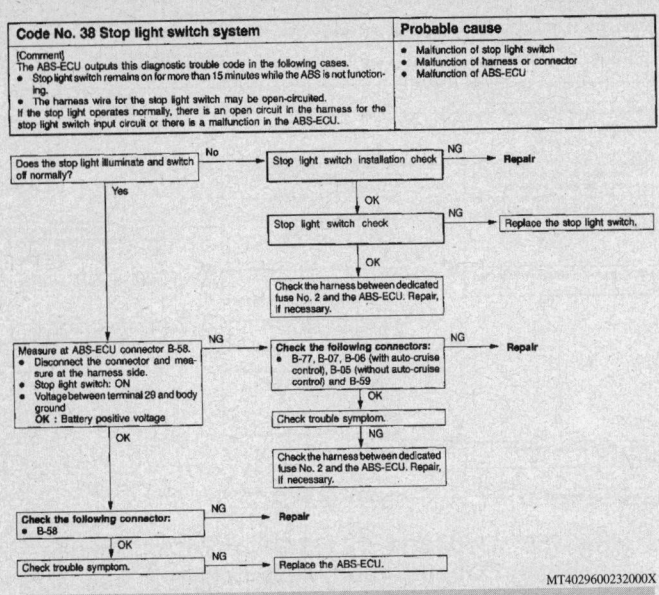

Fig. 159 Code 38: Stop Light Switch System. 1996 Eclipse FWD

Code No. 51 Valve relay system	Probable cause
[Comment] When the ignition switch is turned ON, the ABS-ECU switches the valve relay OFF and ON for an initial check, compares the voltage of the signal to the valve relay and valve power monitor line voltage to check whether the valve relay operation is normal. In addition, normally it monitors whether or not there is power in the valve power monitor line since the valve relay is normally ON. If the supply of power to the valve power monitor line is interrupted, this diagnostic trouble code will be output.	• Malfunction of ABS valve relay • Malfunction of wiring harness or connecter • Malfunction of hydraulic unit • Malfunction of ABS-ECU

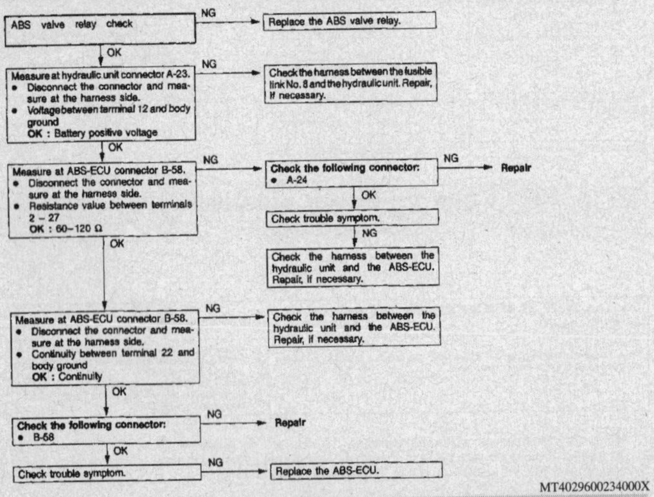
ABS valve relay check
NG
Replace the ABS valve relay.
OK
Measure at hydraulic unit connector A-23.
• Disconnect the connector and measure at the harness side.
• Voltage between terminal 12 and body ground
OK : Battery positive voltage
NG
Check the harness between the fusible link No. 8 and the hydraulic unit. Repair, if necessary.
OK
Measure at ABS-ECU connector B-58.
• Disconnect the connector and measure at the harness side.
• Resistance value between terminals 2 – 27
OK : 60–120 Ω
NG
Check the following connector:
• A-24
NG
Repair
OK
Check trouble symptom.
NG
Check the harness between the hydraulic unit and the ABS-ECU. Repair, if necessary.
OK
Measure at ABS-ECU connector B-58.
• Disconnect the connector and measure at the harness side.
• Continuity between terminal 22 and body ground
OK : Continuity
NG
Check the harness between the hydraulic unit and the ABS-ECU. Repair, if necessary.
OK
Check the following connector:
• B-58
NG
Repair
OK
Check trouble symptom.
NG
Replace the ABS-ECU.
MT4029600234000X

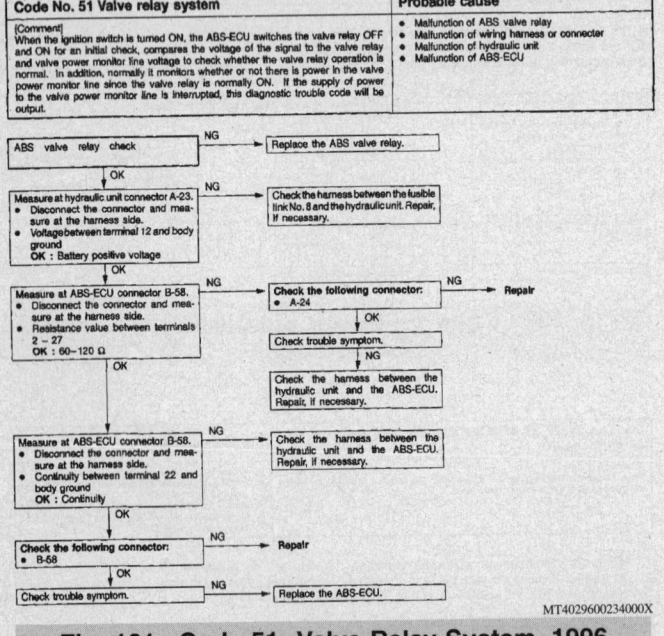

Fig. 161 Code 51: Valve Relay System. 1996 Eclipse FWD

Code No. 41, 42, 43 Solenoid valve system	Probable cause
[Comment] The ABS-ECU normally monitors the solenoid valve drive circuit. If no current flows in the solenoid even if the ECU turns the solenoid ON or if it continues to flow even when turned OFF, the ECU determines the solenoid coil wire is broken/short-circuited or the harness is broken/ short-circuited, and then these diagnostic trouble codes are output.	• Malfunction of hydraulic unit • Malfunction of wiring harness or connector • Malfunction of ABS-ECU

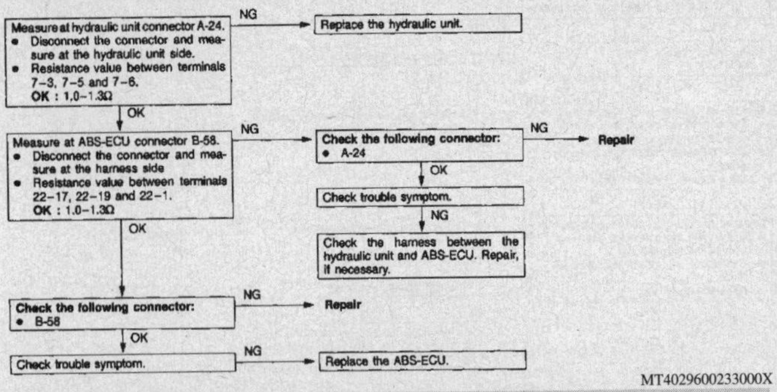
Measure at hydraulic unit connector A-24.
• Disconnect the connector and measure at the hydraulic unit side.
• Resistance value between terminals 7–3, 7–5 and 7–6.
OK : 1.0–1.3Ω
NG
Replace the hydraulic unit.
OK
Measure at ABS-ECU connector B-58.
• Disconnect the connector and measure at the harness side
• Resistance value between terminals 22–17, 22–19 and 22–1.
OK : 1.0–1.3Ω
NG
Check the following connector:
• A-24
NG
Repair
OK
Check trouble symptom.
NG
Check the harness between the hydraulic unit and ABS-ECU. Repair, if necessary.
OK
Check the following connector:
• B-58
NG
Repair
OK
Check trouble symptom.
NG
Replace the ABS-ECU.
MT4029600233000X

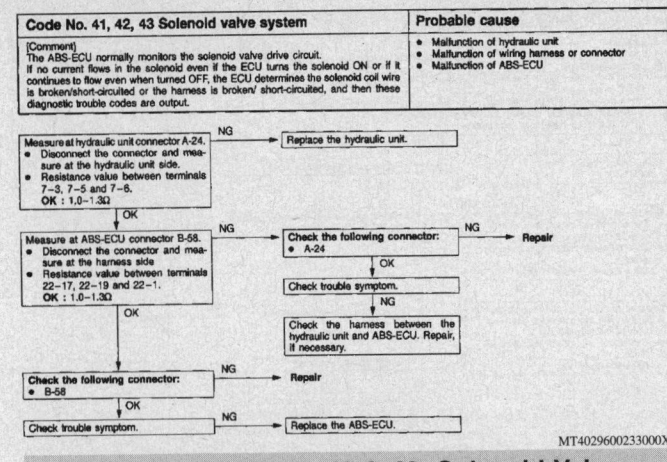

Fig. 160 Codes 41, 42 & 43: Solenoid Valve System. 1996 Eclipse FWD

Code No. 53 Motor relay, motor system	Probable cause
[Comment] The ABS-ECU outputs this diagnostic trouble code for the motor relay and motor in the following cases. • When motor relay is ON and no signal is input to the motor monitor line (when motor is not operating, etc.) • When motor relay is OFF and signal is input to the motor monitor line for approximately 5 seconds or more (when motor continues operating, etc.) • When the motor relay does not function	• Malfunction of ABS motor relay • Malfunction of wiring harness or connector • Malfunction of hydraulic unit • Malfunction of ABS-ECU

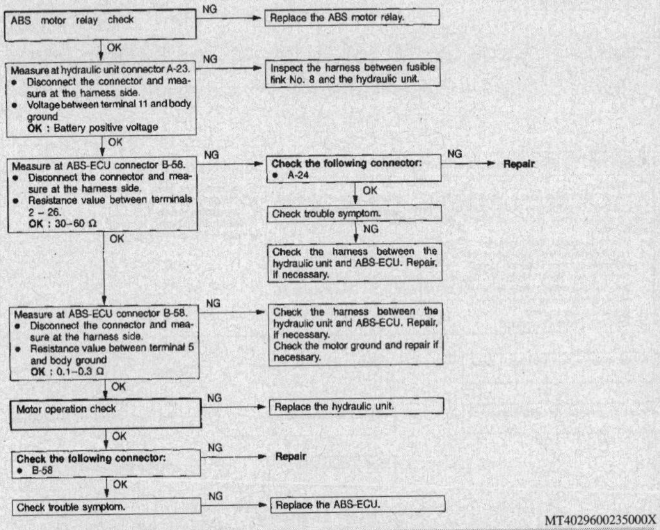
ABS motor relay check
NG
Replace the ABS motor relay.
OK
Measure at hydraulic unit connector A-23.
• Disconnect the connector and measure at the harness side.
• Voltage between terminal 11 and body ground
OK : Battery positive voltage
NG
Inspect the harness between fusible link No. 8 and the hydraulic unit.
OK
Measure at ABS-ECU connector B-58.
• Disconnect the connector and measure at the harness side.
• Resistance value between terminals 2 – 26.
OK : 30–60 Ω
NG
Check the following connector:
• A-24
NG
Repair
OK
Check trouble symptom.
NG
Check the harness between the hydraulic unit and ABS-ECU. Repair, if necessary.
OK
Measure at ABS-ECU connector B-58.
• Disconnect the connector and measure at the harness side.
• Resistance value between terminal 5 and body ground
OK : 0.1–0.3 Ω
NG
Check the harness between the hydraulic unit and ABS-ECU. Repair, if necessary.
Check the motor ground and repair if necessary.
OK
Motor operation check
NG
Replace the hydraulic unit.
OK
Check the following connector:
• B-58
NG
Repair
OK
Check trouble symptom.
NG
Replace the ABS-ECU.
MT4029600235000X

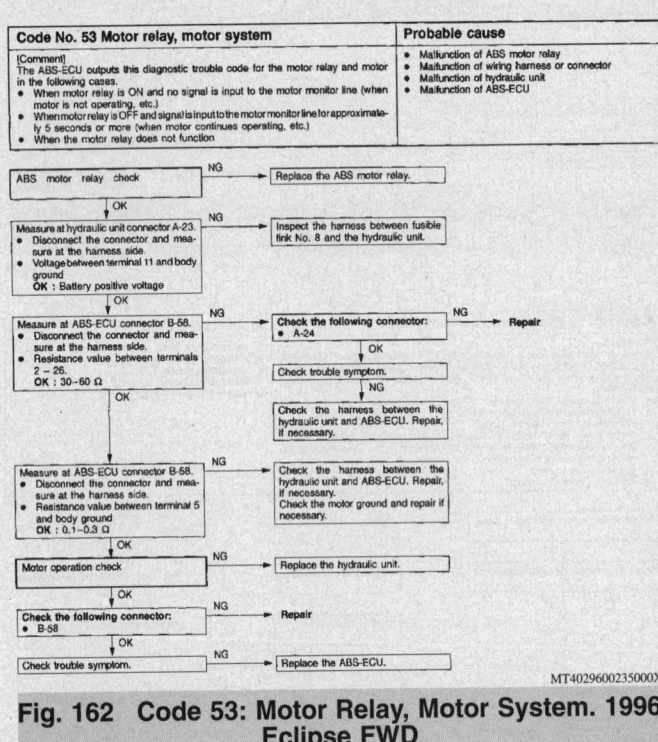

Fig. 162 Code 53: Motor Relay, Motor System. 1996 Eclipse FWD

Code No. 11, 12, 13, 14	Wheel speed sensor open circuit	Probable cause
[Comment] These codes are displayed when the sensor with the open circuit can be distinguished.		• Malfunction of wheel speed sensor (Open circuit) • Malfunction of wiring harness or connector • Malfunction of ABS-ECU

Caution
Because diagnostic trouble code No. 12 is also used when incorrect assembly of the ABS-ECU is detected, if code No. 12 is output immediately after replacing the ABS-ECU, first check the part number of the ABS-ECU.

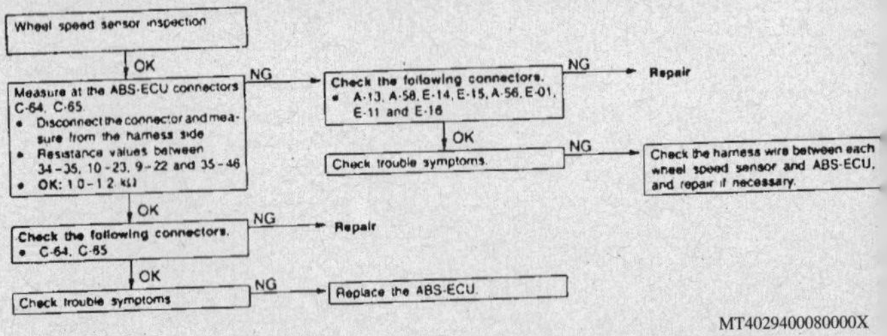
Wheel speed sensor inspection
OK
Measure at the ABS-ECU connectors C-64, C-65.
• Disconnect the connector and measure from the harness side
• Resistance values between 34–35, 10–23, 9–22 and 35–46
• OK: 1.0–1.2 kΩ
NG
Check the following connectors.
• A-13, A-58, E-14, E-15, A-56, E-01, E-11 and E-16
NG
Repair
OK
Check trouble symptoms.
NG
Check the harness wire between each wheel speed sensor and ABS-ECU, and repair if necessary.
OK
Check the following connectors.
• C-64, C-65
NG
Repair
OK
Check trouble symptoms
NG
Replace the ABS-ECU.
MT4029400080000X

Fig. 163 Codes 11, 12, 13 & 14: Speed Sensors (Open Circuit). 1994–96 Galant

Code No. 16	Power supply system	Probable cause
[Comment] This diagnostic trouble code is output when the ABS-ECU power voltage is outside the standard value. Furthermore, if the voltage returns to normal this diagnostic trouble code will not be output.		• Malfunction of wiring harness or connector. • Malfunction of battery or alternator • Malfunction of ABS-ECU

Caution

If the battery voltage drops during inspection, this code will be output as a current problem, and correct diagnostic of the problem cannot be made.
Before carrying out the following inspection, check the battery condition, and recharge it if necessary.

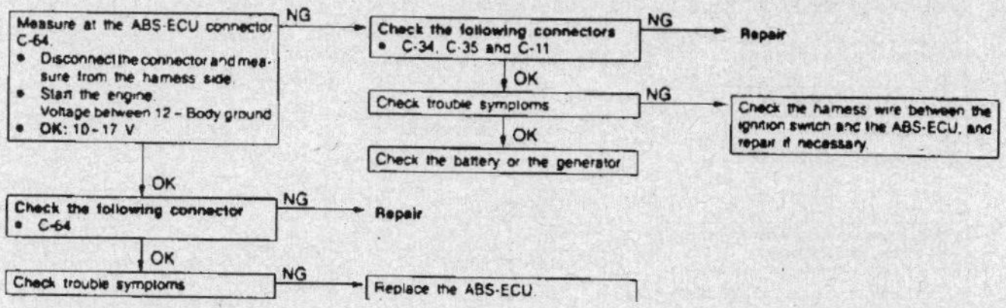
Measure at the ABS-ECU connector C-64.
• Disconnect the connector and measure from the harness side.
• Start the engine.
Voltage between 12 – Body ground
• OK: 10 – 17 V
NG
Check the following connectors
• C-34, C-35 and C-11
NG
Repair
OK
Check trouble symptoms
NG
Check the harness wire between the ignition switch and the ABS-ECU, and repair if necessary.
OK
Check the battery or the generator
OK
Check the following connector
• C-64
NG
Repair
OK
Check trouble symptoms
NG
Replace the ABS-ECU.

MT4029400081000X

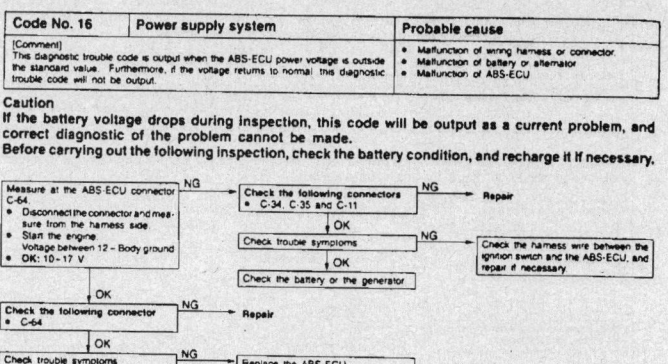

Fig. 164 Code 16: Power Supply System. 1994–96 Galant

Code No. 21, 22, 23, 24	Wheel speed sensor short circuit	Probable cause
[Comment] These codes are displayed when the sensor with the short circuited can be distinguished.		• Malfunction of wheel speed sensor (short at (+) side or layer short) • Malfunction of wiring harness • Malfunction of ABS-ECU

NOTE
Short circuit is not detected when IG power voltage drops.

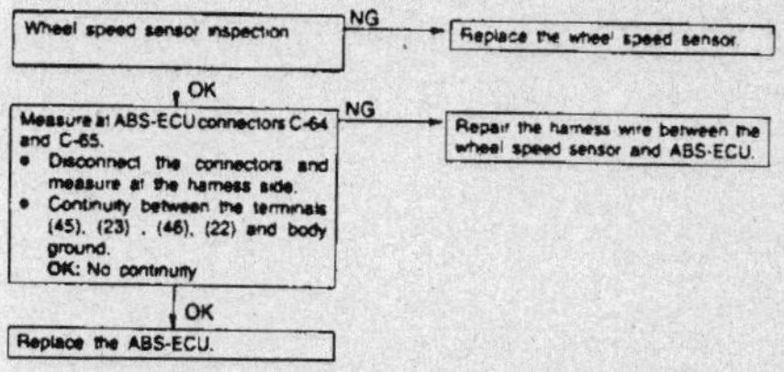
Wheel speed sensor inspection
NG
Replace the wheel speed sensor.
OK
Measure at ABS-ECU connectors C-64 and C-65.
• Disconnect the connectors and measure at the harness side.
• Continuity between the terminals (45), (23), (46), (22) and body ground.
OK: No continuity
NG
Repair the harness wire between the wheel speed sensor and ABS-ECU.
OK
Replace the ABS-ECU.

MT4029400082000X

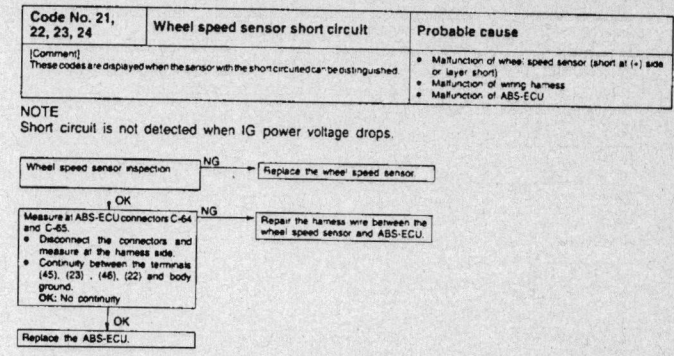

Fig. 165 Codes 21, 22, 23 & 24: Speed Sensors (Short Circuit). 1994–96 Galant

Code No. 25, 26, 27, 28 Wheel speed sensor excessive gap	Probable cause
[Comment] These diagnostic trouble codes are output when the detection speed of the wheel speed sensors is below the standard value.	• Improper installation of wheel speed sensor • Malfunction of wheel speed sensor (intermittent open circuit or short circuit) • Malfunction of rotor (chipped tooth or rotor not installed) • Noise interference in wheel speed sensor • Malfunction of ABS-ECU

NOTE
1. Momentary interruptions within approximately 100 ms are not detected.
2. To inspect the twisted pair wires in the wheel speed sensor, check if there is any damage to the cables, and flex the cables to check for any open circuits.

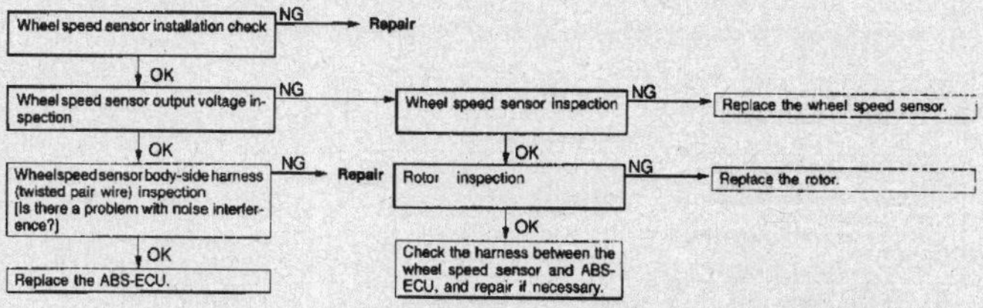
Wheel speed sensor installation check
NG
Repair
OK
Wheel speed sensor output voltage inspection
NG
Wheel speed sensor inspection
NG
Replace the wheel speed sensor.
OK
Wheel speed sensor body-side harness (twisted pair wire) inspection
[Is there a problem with noise interference?]
NG
Repair
Rotor inspection
NG
Replace the rotor.
OK
Check the harness between the wheel speed sensor and ABS-ECU, and repair if necessary.
OK
Replace the ABS-ECU.

MT4029400083000A

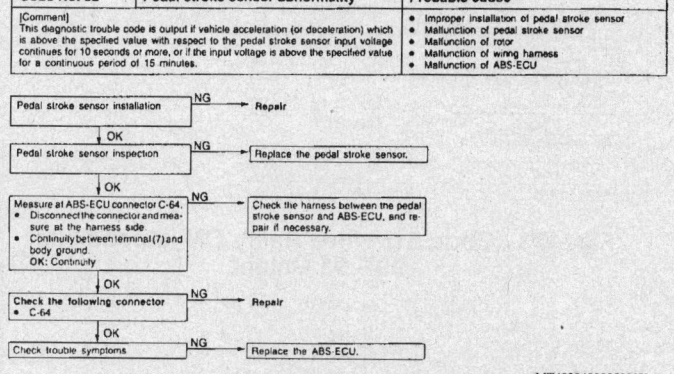

Fig. 166 Codes 25, 26, 27 & 28: Speed Sensors (Excessive Gap). 1994–96 Galant

Code No. 31	Pedal stroke sensor circuit system	Probable cause
[Comment] This diagnostic trouble code is output if the pedal stroke sensor supply voltage or input voltage is outside the specified value.		• Malfunction of wiring harness or connector • Malfunction of pedal stroke sensor • Malfunction of ABS-ECU

NOTE
1. Diagnostic trouble code No. 31 may be output if an OFF malfunction in the stop light switch (remains OFF) is detected while the brake pedal is depressed.
2. Short circuit is not detected when IG power voltage drops.

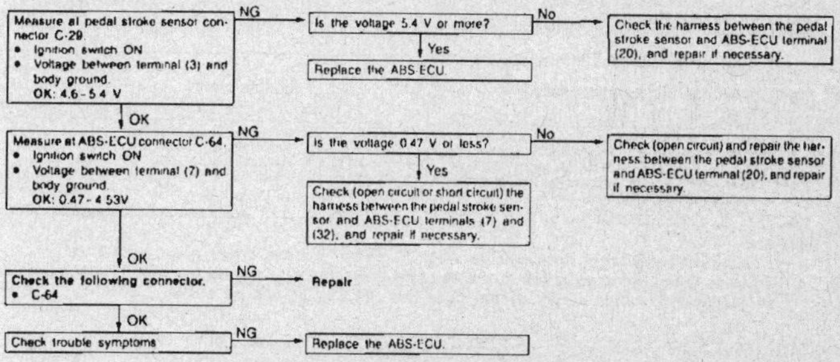
Measure at pedal stroke sensor connector C-29.
• Ignition switch ON
• Voltage between terminal (3) and body ground.
OK: 4.6 - 5.4 V
NG
Is the voltage 5.4 V or more?
No
Check the harness between the pedal stroke sensor and ABS-ECU terminal (20), and repair if necessary.
Yes
Replace the ABS-ECU.
OK
Measure at ABS-ECU connector C-64.
• Ignition switch ON
• Voltage between terminal (7) and body ground.
OK: 0.47 - 4.53V
NG
Is the voltage 0.47 V or less?
No
Check (open circuit) and repair the harness between the pedal stroke sensor and ABS-ECU terminal (20), and repair if necessary.
Yes
Check (open circuit or short circuit) the harness between the pedal stroke sensor and ABS-ECU terminals (7) and (32), and repair if necessary.
OK
Check the following connector.
• C-64
NG
Repair
OK
Check trouble symptoms
NG
Replace the ABS-ECU.

MT4029400084000X

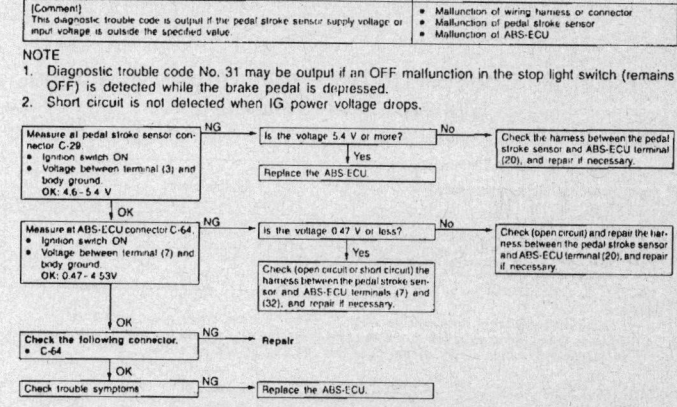

Fig. 167 Code 31: Pedal Stroke Sensor Circuit System. 1994–95 Galant

Code No. 32	Pedal stroke sensor abnormality	Probable cause
[Comment] This diagnostic trouble code is output if vehicle acceleration (or deceleration) which is above the specified value with respect to the pedal stroke sensor input voltage continues for 10 seconds or more, or if the input voltage is above the specified value for a continuous period of 15 minutes.		• Improper installation of pedal stroke sensor • Malfunction of pedal stroke sensor • Malfunction of rotor • Malfunction of wiring harness • Malfunction of ABS-ECU

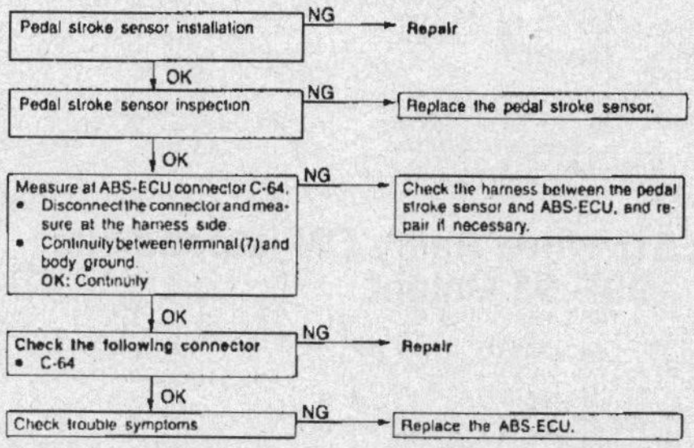
Pedal stroke sensor installation
NG
Repair
OK
Pedal stroke sensor inspection
NG
Replace the pedal stroke sensor.
OK
Measure at ABS-ECU connector C-64.
• Disconnect the connector and measure at the harness side.
• Continuity between terminal (7) and body ground.
OK: Continuity
NG
Check the harness between the pedal stroke sensor and ABS-ECU, and repair if necessary.
OK
Check the following connector
• C-64
NG
Repair
OK
Check trouble symptoms
NG
Replace the ABS-ECU.

MT4029400085000X

Fig. 168 Code 32: Pedal Stroke Sensor Abnormality. 1994–95 Galant

Code No. 33	Stop light switch system	Probable cause
[Comment] This diagnostic trouble code is output if it is judged to be an open circuit when the stop light switch is ON for a continuous period of 15 minutes or more, or if it is judged to be a short circuit when the pedal stroke sensor output voltage is above the specified value and the switch is OFF for a constant period of time		• Malfunction of wiring harness or connector • Malfunction of pedal stroke sensor (ON or OFF malfunction of stop light switch) • Malfunction of ABS-ECU

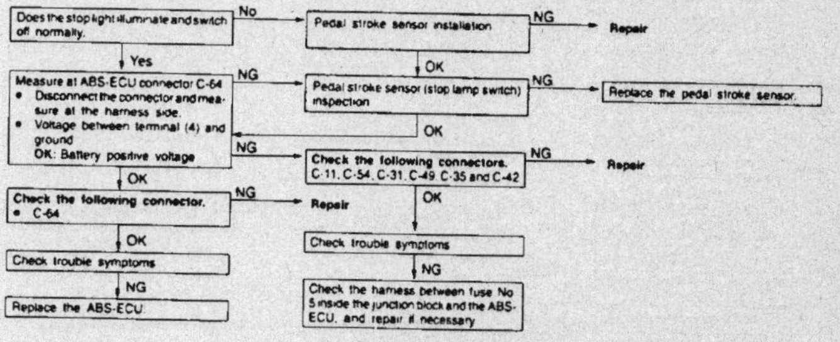
Does the stop light illuminate and switch off normally.
No
Pedal stroke sensor installation
NG
Repair
Yes
OK
Measure at ABS-ECU connector C-64
• Disconnect the connector and measure at the harness side.
• Voltage between terminal (4) and ground
OK: Battery positive voltage
NG
Pedal stroke sensor (stop lamp switch) inspection
NG
Replace the pedal stroke sensor.
OK
NG
Check the following connectors.
C-11, C-54, C-31, C-49, C-35 and C-42
NG
Repair
OK
Check the following connector.
• C-64
NG
Repair
OK
Check trouble symptoms
OK
Check trouble symptoms
NG
Replace the ABS-ECU
NG
Check the harness between fuse No 5 inside the junction block and the ABS-ECU, and repair if necessary

MT4029400086000X

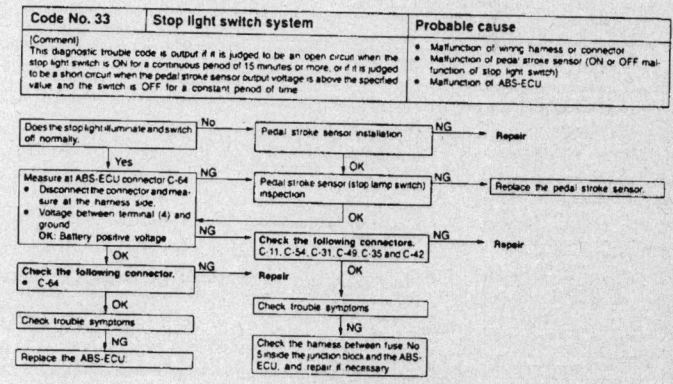

Fig. 169 Code 33: Stop Light Switch System. 1994–96 Galant

Code No. 34 Pedal stroke sensor and pump system	Probable cause
[Comment] This diagnostic trouble code is output if a motor pump ON instruction has been given but the output voltage of the pedal stroke sensor does not change.	• Malfunction of hydraulic unit • Malfunction of pedal stroke sensor • Malfunction of wiring harness or connector • Malfunction of ABS-ECU

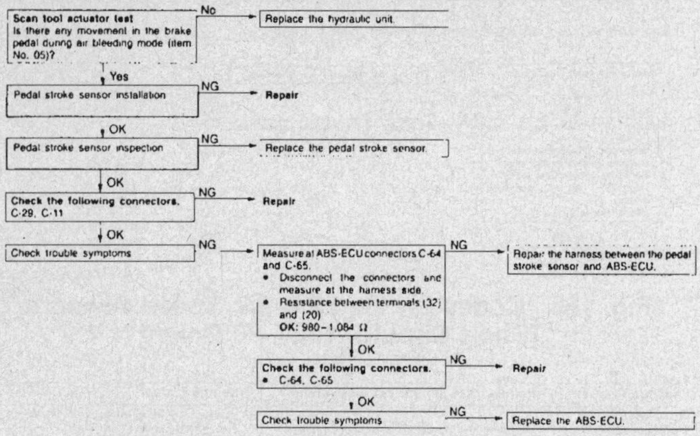
Scan tool actuator test
Is there any movement in the brake pedal during air bleeding mode (item No. 05)?
No
Replace the hydraulic unit.
Yes
Pedal stroke sensor installation
NG
Repair
OK
Pedal stroke sensor inspection
NG
Replace the pedal stroke sensor.
OK
Check the following connectors.
C-29, C-11
NG
Repair
OK
Check trouble symptoms
NG
Measure at ABS-ECU connectors C-64 and C-65.
• Disconnect the connectors and measure at the harness side.
• Resistance between terminals (32) and (20)
OK: 980 – 1,084 Ω
NG
Repair the harness between the pedal stroke sensor and ABS-ECU.
OK
Check the following connectors.
• C-64, C-65
NG
Repair
OK
Check trouble symptoms
NG
Replace the ABS-ECU.

MT4029400087000X

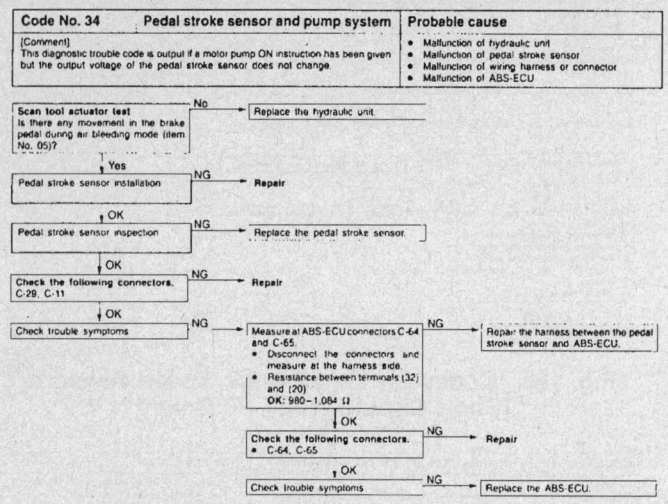

Fig. 170 Code 34: Pedal Stroke Sensor & Pump System. 1994–95 Galant

Code No. 41, 42, 43, 44, 45, 46, 47, 48,	Solenoid valve	Probable cause
[Comment] The ABS-ECU normally monitors the solenoid valve drive circuit. If there is no current flowing to the solenoid even when the solenoid is ON, or the current continues to flow to the solenoid even when the solenoid is OFF, the ABS-ECU diagnostic a open circuit or short in the solenoid coil or a open circuit or short in the harness, and this diagnostic trouble code is output.		• Malfunction of wiring harness • Malfunction of hydraulic unit • Malfunction of ABS-ECU

Caution

- **A valve malfunction is not detected when IG power voltage drops (less than 9 V).**
- **If power is not being supplied to the solenoid valve because connector A-43 is disconnected, all diagnostic trouble codes except code Nos. 41 and 46 will be output.**

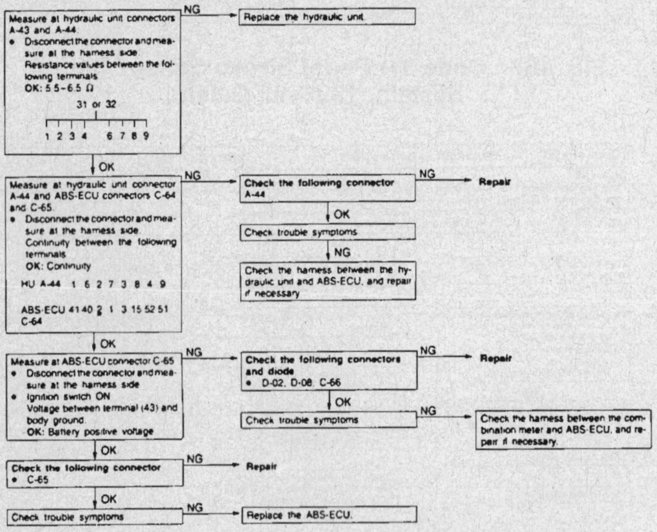
Measure at hydraulic unit connectors A-43 and A-44.
• Disconnect the connector and measure at the harness side.
Resistance values between the following terminals
OK: 5.5 – 6.5 Ω
31 or 32
1 2 3 4 6 7 8 9
NG
Replace the hydraulic unit.
OK
Measure at hydraulic unit connector A-44 and ABS-ECU connectors C-64 and C-65.
• Disconnect the connector and measure at the harness side.
Continuity between the following terminals
OK: Continuity
HU A-44 1 6 2 7 3 8 4 9
ABS-ECU C-64 41 40 2 1 3 15 52 51
NG
Check the following connector
A-44
NG
Repair
OK
Check trouble symptoms
NG
Check the harness between the hydraulic unit and ABS-ECU, and repair if necessary
OK
Measure at ABS-ECU connector C-65
• Disconnect the connector and measure at the harness side
• Ignition switch ON
Voltage between terminal (43) and body ground.
OK: Battery positive voltage
NG
Check the following connectors and diode
• D-02, D-08, C-66
NG
Repair
OK
Check trouble symptoms
NG
Check the harness between the combination meter and ABS-ECU, and repair if necessary.
OK
Check the following connector
• C-65
NG
Repair
OK
Check trouble symptoms
NG
Replace the ABS-ECU.

MT4029400089000X

Fig. 172 Codes 41, 42, 43, 44, 45, 46, 47 & 48: Solenoid Valve. 1994–96 Galant

Code No. 35, 36, 37, 38	Wheel speed sensor pulse processing	Probable cause
[Comment] These diagnostic trouble codes are output if a sensor pulse corresponding to a vehicle speed of 300 km/h (186 mph) or more is input to the wheel speed signal circuit due to ignition noise or excessive axle vibration.		• Malfunction of wiring harness • Malfunction of wheel speed sensor • Malfunction of rotor • Malfunction of wheel bearing • Noise interference in wheel speed signal • Malfunction of ABS-ECU

NOTE

To inspect the twisted pair wires in the wheel speed sensors, check if there is any damage to the cable and flex the cables to check for any open circuits.

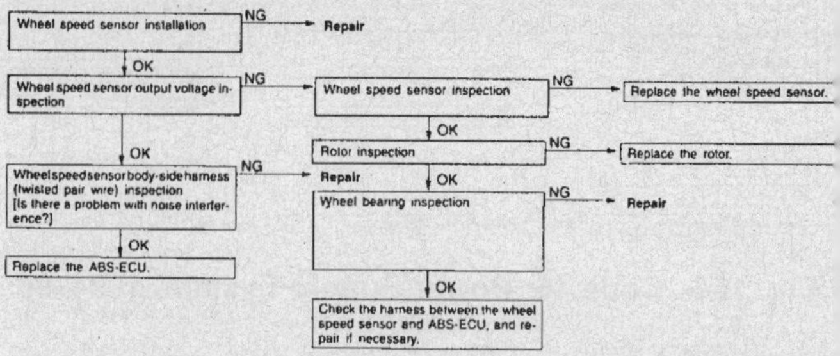
Wheel speed sensor installation
NG
Repair
OK
Wheel speed sensor output voltage inspection
NG
Wheel speed sensor inspection
NG
Replace the wheel speed sensor.
OK
Rotor inspection
NG
Replace the rotor.
OK
Wheel bearing inspection
NG
Repair
OK
Check the harness between the wheel speed sensor and ABS-ECU, and repair if necessary.
OK
Wheel speed sensor body-side harness (twisted pair wire) inspection
[Is there a problem with noise interference?]
NG
Repair
OK
Replace the ABS-ECU.

MT4029400088000X

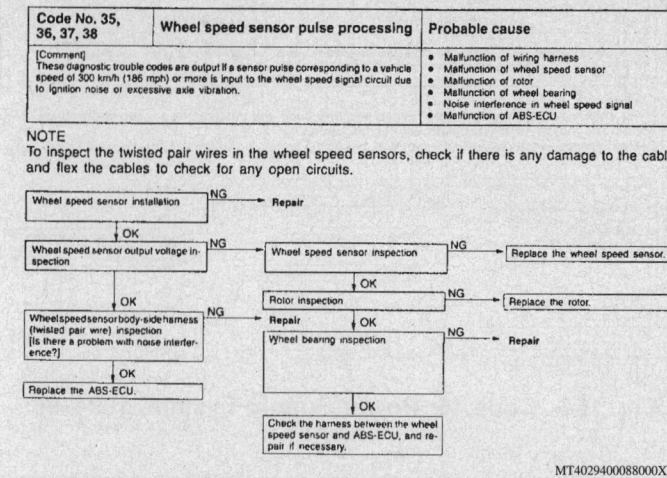

Fig. 171 Codes 35, 36, 37 & 38: Wheel Speed Sensor Pulse Processing. 1994–96 Galant

Code No. 51	Valve relay ON Impossible	Probable cause
[Comment] During the initial check when the ignition switch is turned to "ON", if power is not being supplied to the solenoid when the valve relay is ON, the ABS-ECU diagnostic an OFF problem in the valve relay (not turned ON), and outputs this malfunction code.		• Malfunction of ABS valve relay • Malfunction of wiring harness or connector • Malfunction of ABS-ECU

NOTE

A valve malfunction is not detected when IG power voltage drops (less than 9 V).

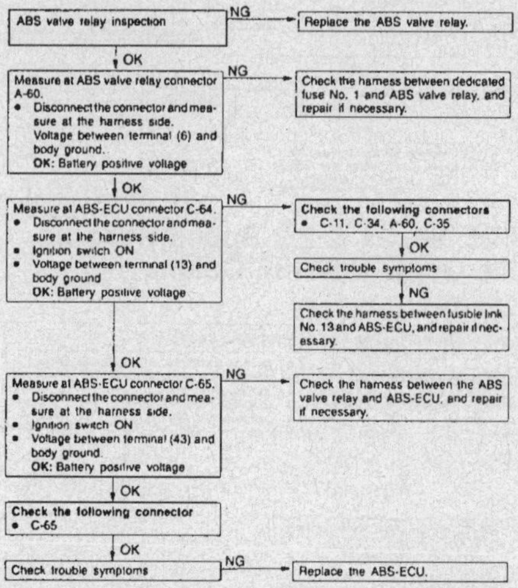
ABS valve relay inspection
NG
Replace the ABS valve relay.
OK
Measure at ABS valve relay connector A-60.
• Disconnect the connector and measure at the harness side.
Voltage between terminal (6) and body ground.
OK: Battery positive voltage
NG
Check the harness between dedicated fuse No. 1 and ABS valve relay, and repair if necessary.
OK
Measure at ABS-ECU connector C-64.
• Disconnect the connector and measure at the harness side.
• Ignition switch ON
• Voltage between terminal (13) and body ground
OK: Battery positive voltage
NG
Check the following connectors
• C-11, C-34, A-60, C-35
OK
Check trouble symptoms
NG
Check the harness between fusible link No. 13 and ABS-ECU, and repair if necessary.
OK
Measure at ABS-ECU connector C-65.
• Disconnect the connector and measure at the harness side.
• Ignition switch ON
• Voltage between terminal (43) and body ground.
OK: Battery positive voltage
NG
Check the harness between the ABS valve relay and ABS-ECU, and repair if necessary.
OK
Check the following connector
• C-65
OK
Check trouble symptoms
NG
Replace the ABS-ECU.

MT4029400090000X

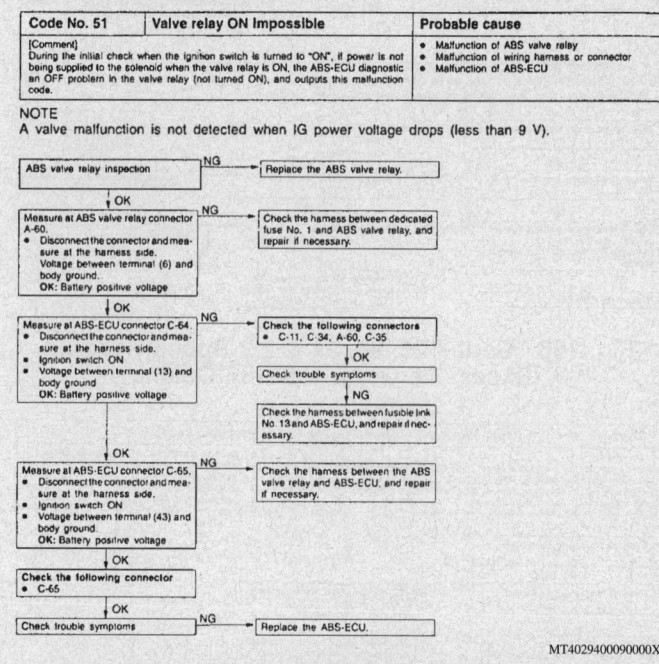

Fig. 173 Code 51: Valve Relay ON Impossible. 1994–95 Galant

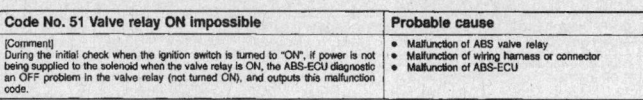

Code No. 51 Valve relay ON impossible	Probable cause
[Comment] During the initial check when the ignition switch is turned to "ON", if power is not being supplied to the solenoid when the valve relay is ON, the ABS-ECU diagnostic an OFF problem in the valve relay (not turned ON), and outputs this malfunction code.	• Malfunction of ABS valve relay • Malfunction of wiring harness or connector • Malfunction of ABS-ECU

NOTE
A valve malfunction is not detected when IG power voltage drops (less than 9 V).

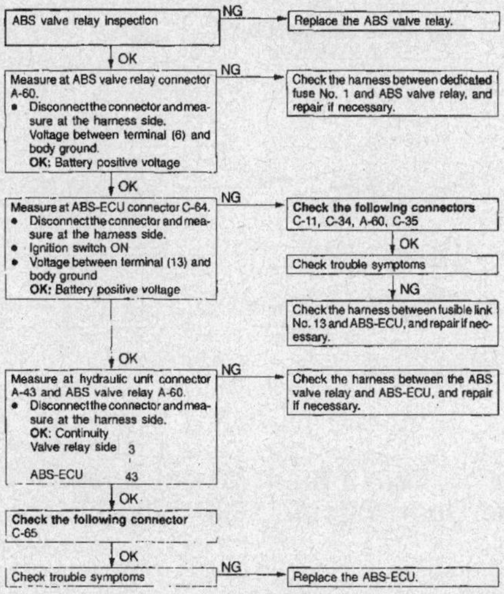

ABS valve relay inspection
NG
Replace the ABS valve relay.
OK
Measure at ABS valve relay connector A-60.
• Disconnect the connector and measure at the harness side.
Voltage between terminal (6) and body ground.
OK: Battery positive voltage
NG
Check the harness between dedicated fuse No. 1 and ABS valve relay, and repair if necessary.
OK
Measure at ABS-ECU connector C-64.
• Disconnect the connector and measure at the harness side.
• Ignition switch ON
• Voltage between terminal (13) and body ground
OK: Battery positive voltage
NG
Check the following connectors C-11, C-34, A-60, C-35
OK
Check trouble symptoms
NG
Check the harness between fusible link No. 13 and ABS-ECU, and repair if necessary.
OK
Measure at hydraulic unit connector A-43 and ABS valve relay A-60.
• Disconnect the connector and measure at the harness side.
OK: Continuity
Valve relay side 3
ABS-ECU 43
NG
Check the harness between the ABS valve relay and ABS-ECU, and repair if necessary.
OK
Check the following connector C-65
OK
Check trouble symptoms
NG
Replace the ABS-ECU.

MT4029600236000X

Fig. 174 Code 51: Valve Relay ON Impossible. 1996 Galant

Code No. 53	Motor relay, motor ON impossible	Probable cause
[Comment] This diagnostic trouble code is output if a motor relay ON instruction has been given but the motor revolution sensor signal has not risen above 150 Hz.		• Malfunction of ABS motor relay • Malfunction of wiring harness or connector • Malfunction of hydraulic unit • Malfunction of ABS-ECU

Caution
Because force-driving of the motor by means of the actuator test will drain the battery, the engine should be started and left to run for a while after testing is completed.

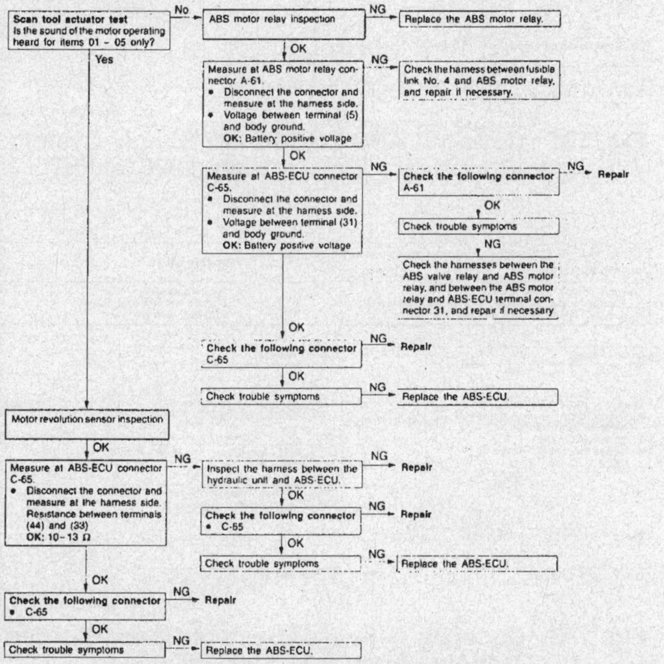

Scan tool actuator test
Is the sound of the motor operating heard for items 01 – 05 only?
No
ABS motor relay inspection
NG
Replace the ABS motor relay.
OK
Measure at ABS motor relay connector A-61.
• Disconnect the connector and measure at the harness side.
• Voltage between terminal (5) and body ground.
OK: Battery positive voltage
NG
Check the harness between fusible link No. 4 and ABS motor relay, and repair if necessary.
OK
Measure at ABS-ECU connector C-65.
• Disconnect the connector and measure at the harness side.
• Voltage between terminal (31) and body ground.
OK: Battery positive voltage
NG
Check the following connector A-61
NG
Repair
OK
Check trouble symptoms
NG
Check the harnesses between the ABS valve relay and ABS motor relay, and between the ABS motor relay and ABS-ECU terminal connector 31, and repair if necessary
OK
Check the following connector C-65
NG
Repair
OK
Check trouble symptoms
NG
Replace the ABS-ECU.
Yes
Motor revolution sensor inspection
OK
Measure at ABS-ECU connector C-65.
• Disconnect the connector and measure at the harness side.
Resistance between terminals (44) and (33)
OK: 10 – 13 Ω
NG
Inspect the harness between the hydraulic unit and ABS-ECU.
NG
Repair
OK
Check the following connector
• C-65
NG
Repair
OK
Check trouble symptoms
NG
Replace the ABS-ECU.
OK
Check the following connector
• C-65
NG
Repair
OK
Check trouble symptoms
NG
Replace the ABS-ECU.

MT4029400092000X

Fig. 176 Code 53: Motor Relay, Motor ON Impossible. 1994–95 Galant

Code No. 52	Valve relay OFF impossible	Probable cause
[Comment] During the initial check when the ignition switch is turned to "ON", if power is being supplied to the solenoid when the valve relay is OFF, the ABS-ECU diagnostic a melted relay contact or a short in the valve relay drive circuit, and this diagnostic trouble code is output.		• Malfunction of ABS valve relay • Malfunction of wiring harness (Short circuited) • Malfunction of ABS-ECU

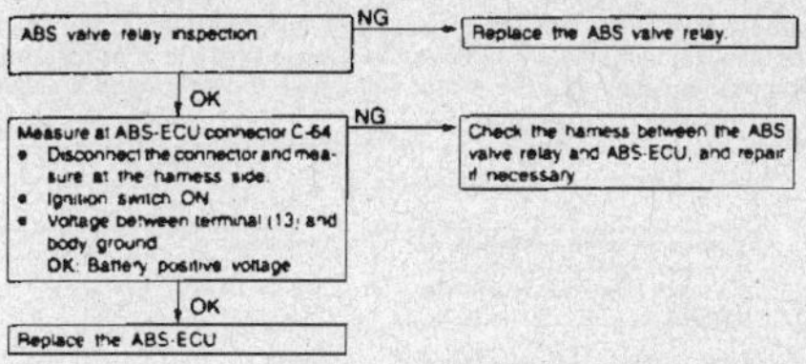

ABS valve relay inspection
NG
Replace the ABS valve relay.
OK
Measure at ABS-ECU connector C-64
• Disconnect the connector and measure at the harness side.
• Ignition switch ON
• Voltage between terminal (13) and body ground
OK: Battery positive voltage
NG
Check the harness between the ABS valve relay and ABS-ECU, and repair if necessary
OK
Replace the ABS-ECU

MT4029400091000X

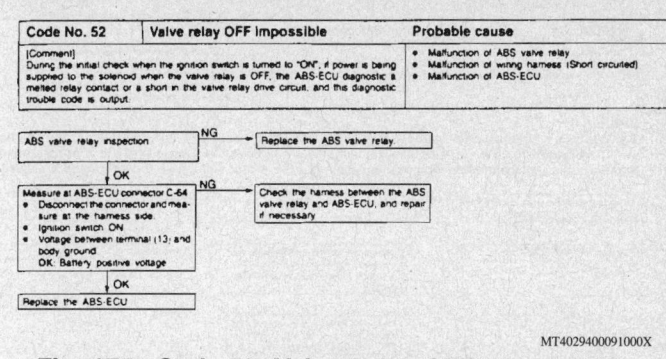

Fig. 175 Code 52: Valve Relay OFF Impossible. 1994–96 Galant

Code No. 53 Motor relay, motor ON impossible	Probable cause
[Comment] This diagnostic trouble code is output if a motor relay ON instruction has been given but the motor revolution sensor signal has not risen above 150 Hz.	• Malfunction of ABS motor relay • Malfunction of wiring harness or connector • Malfunction of hydraulic unit • Malfunction of ABS-ECU

Caution
Because force-driving of the motor by means of the actuator test will drain the battery, the engine should be started and left to run for a while after testing is completed.

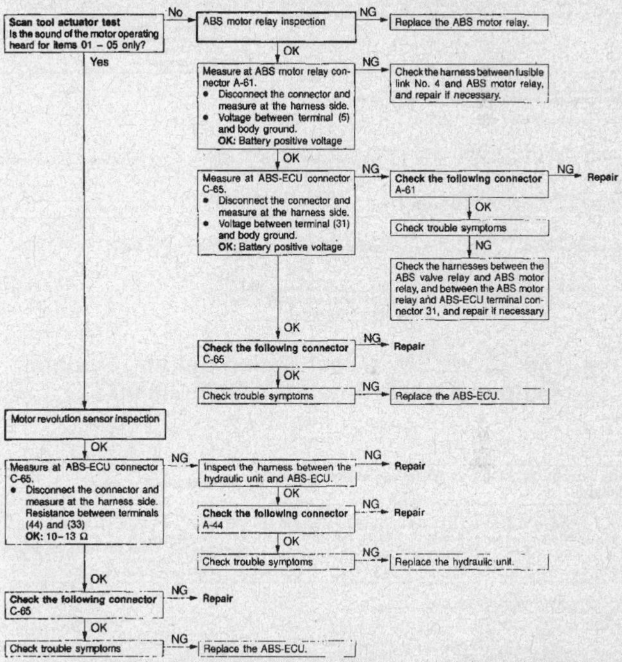

Scan tool actuator test
Is the sound of the motor operating heard for items 01 – 05 only?
No
ABS motor relay inspection
NG
Replace the ABS motor relay.
OK
Measure at ABS motor relay connector A-61.
• Disconnect the connector and measure at the harness side.
• Voltage between terminal (5) and body ground.
OK: Battery positive voltage
NG
Check the harness between fusible link No. 4 and ABS motor relay, and repair if necessary.
OK
Measure at ABS-ECU connector C-65.
• Disconnect the connector and measure at the harness side.
• Voltage between terminal (31) and body ground.
OK: Battery positive voltage
NG
Check the following connector A-61
NG
Repair
OK
Check trouble symptoms
NG
Check the harnesses between the ABS valve relay and ABS motor relay, and between the ABS motor relay and ABS-ECU terminal connector 31, and repair if necessary
OK
Check the following connector C-65
NG
Repair
OK
Check trouble symptoms
NG
Replace the ABS-ECU.
Yes
Motor revolution sensor inspection
OK
Measure at ABS-ECU connector C-65.
• Disconnect the connector and measure at the harness side.
Resistance between terminals (44) and (33)
OK: 10 – 13 Ω
NG
Inspect the harness between the hydraulic unit and ABS-ECU.
NG
Repair
OK
Check the following connector A-44
NG
Repair
OK
Check trouble symptoms
NG
Replace the hydraulic unit.
OK
Check the following connector C-65
NG
Repair
OK
Check trouble symptoms
NG
Replace the ABS-ECU.

MT4029600237000X

Fig. 177 Code 53: Motor Relay, Motor ON Impossible. 1996 Galant

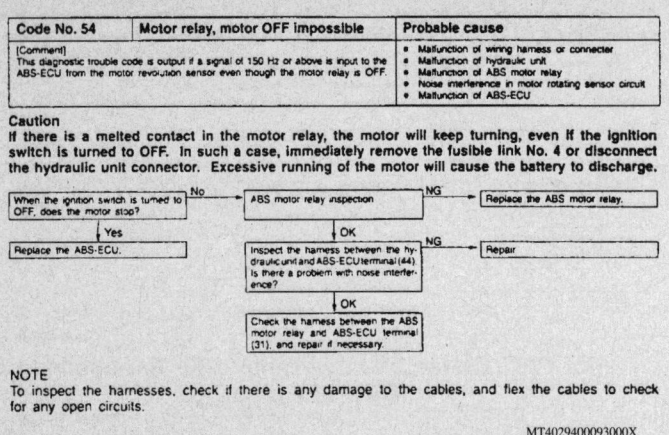

Code No. 54	Motor relay, motor OFF impossible	Probable cause
[Comment] This diagnostic trouble code is output if a signal of 150 Hz or above is input to the ABS-ECU from the motor revolution sensor even though the motor relay is OFF.		• Malfunction of wiring harness or connecter • Malfunction of hydraulic unit • Malfunction of ABS motor relay • Noise interference in motor rotating sensor circuit • Malfunction of ABS-ECU

Caution
If there is a melted contact in the motor relay, the motor will keep turning, even if the ignition switch is turned to OFF. In such a case, immediately remove the fusible link No. 4 or disconnect the hydraulic unit connector. Excessive running of the motor will cause the battery to discharge.

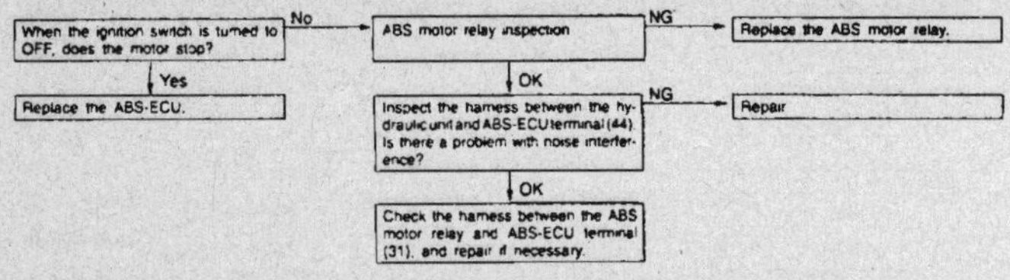
When the ignition switch is turned to OFF, does the motor stop?
No
Yes
Replace the ABS-ECU.
ABS motor relay inspection
NG
Replace the ABS motor relay.
OK
Inspect the harness between the hydraulic unit and ABS-ECU terminal (44). Is there a problem with noise interference?
NG
Repair
OK
Check the harness between the ABS motor relay and ABS-ECU terminal (31), and repair if necessary.

NOTE
To inspect the harnesses, check if there is any damage to the cables, and flex the cables to check for any open circuits.

MT4029400093000X

Fig. 178 Code 54: Motor Relay, Motor OFF Impossible. 1994–96 Galant

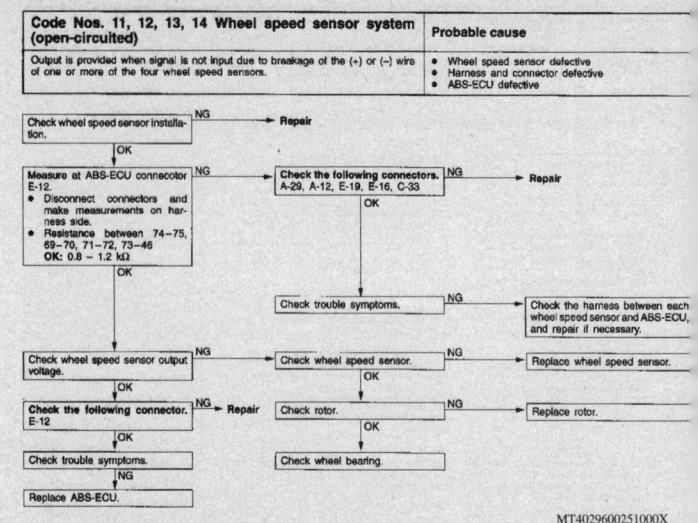

Code Nos. 11, 12, 13, 14 Wheel speed sensor system (open-circuited)	Probable cause
Output is provided when signal is not input due to breakage of the (+) or (–) wire of one or more of the four wheel speed sensors.	• Wheel speed sensor defective • Harness and connector defective • ABS-ECU defective

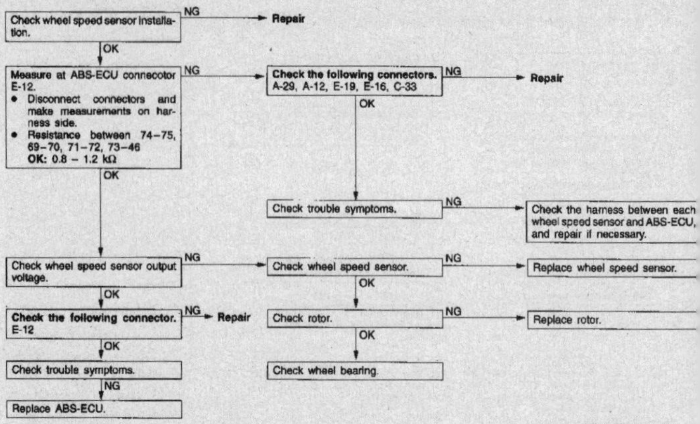
Check wheel speed sensor installation.
NG
Repair
OK
Measure at ABS-ECU connector E-12.
• Disconnect connectors and make measurements on harness side.
• Resistance between 74–75, 69–70, 71–72, 73–46
OK: 0.8 – 1.2 kΩ
NG
Check the following connectors. A-29, A-12, E-19, E-16, C-33
NG
Repair
OK
Check trouble symptoms.
NG
Check the harness between each wheel speed sensor and ABS-ECU, and repair if necessary.
OK
Check wheel speed sensor output voltage.
NG
Check wheel speed sensor.
NG
Replace wheel speed sensor.
OK
Check the following connector. E-12
NG
Repair
Check rotor.
NG
Replace rotor.
OK
Check wheel bearing.
OK
Check trouble symptoms.
NG
Replace ABS-ECU.

MT4029600251000X

Fig. 179 Codes 11, 12, 13 & 14: Wheel Speed Sensor System Open Circuit. 1996 3000GT

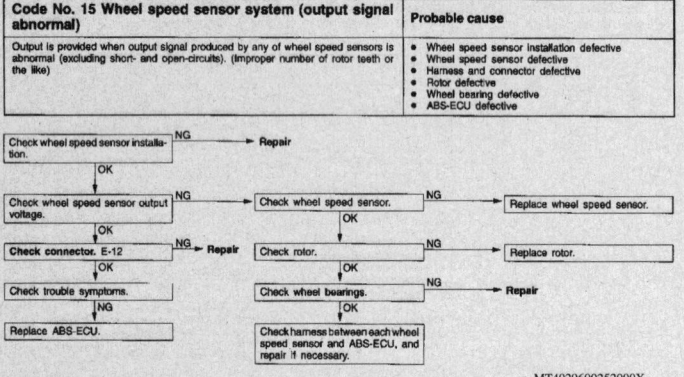

Code No. 15 Wheel speed sensor system (output signal abnormal)	Probable cause
Output is provided when output signal produced by any of wheel speed sensors is abnormal (excluding short- and open-circuits). (Improper number of rotor teeth or the like)	• Wheel speed sensor installation defective • Wheel speed sensor defective • Harness and connector defective • Rotor defective • Wheel bearing defective • ABS-ECU defective

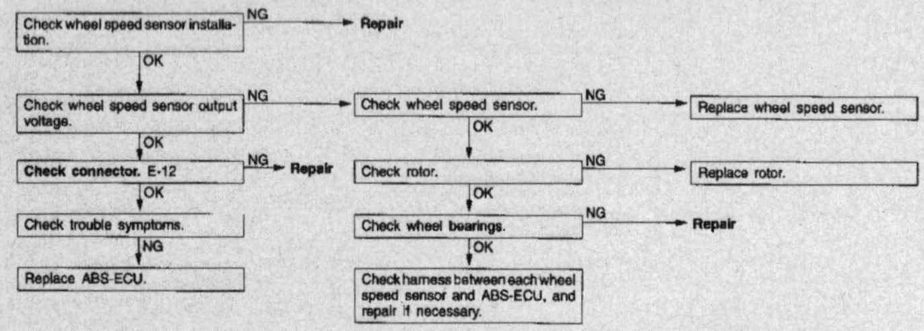
Check wheel speed sensor installation.
NG
Repair
OK
Check wheel speed sensor output voltage.
NG
Check wheel speed sensor.
NG
Replace wheel speed sensor.
OK
Check connector. E-12
NG
Repair
Check rotor.
NG
Replace rotor.
OK
Check trouble symptoms.
NG
Replace ABS-ECU.
Check wheel bearings.
NG
Repair
OK
Check harness between each wheel speed sensor and ABS-ECU, and repair if necessary.

MT4029600252000X

Fig. 180 Code 15: Wheel Speed Sensor System Output Signal Abnormal. 1996 3000GT

Code No. 16 ABS-ECU power supply system (voltage abnormally low or high)	Probable cause
Output is provided when ABS-ECU power supply voltage drops below or rises above the normal value. Output is not provided if power supply voltage returns to normal voltage.	• Harness and connector defective • ABS-ECU defective

Caution
If battery voltage drops or rises while making this check, this code is output as an existing trouble making it impossible to perform correct trouble diagnosis. Before carrying out the following check be sure to check the battery for conditions and charge it if necessary.

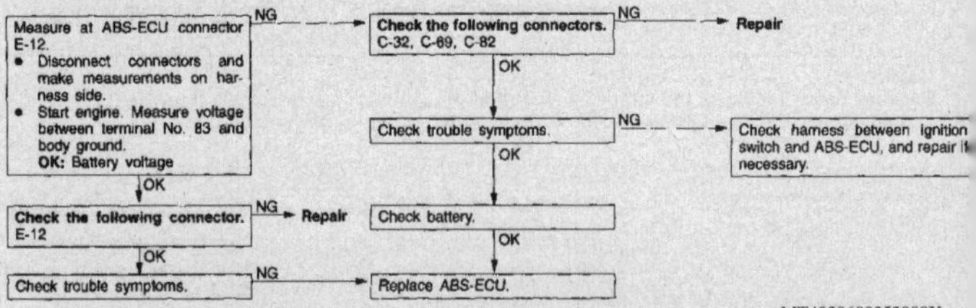
Measure at ABS-ECU connector E-12.
• Disconnect connectors and make measurements on harness side.
• Start engine. Measure voltage between terminal No. 83 and body ground.
OK: Battery voltage
NG
Check the following connectors. C-32, C-69, C-82
NG
Repair
OK
Check trouble symptoms.
NG
Check harness between ignition switch and ABS-ECU, and repair if necessary.
OK
Check battery.
OK
Check the following connector. E-12
NG
Repair
OK
Check trouble symptoms.
NG
Replace ABS-ECU.

MT4029600253000X

Fig. 181 Code 16: ABS ECU Power Supply System Voltage Abnormally Low Or High. 1996 3000GT

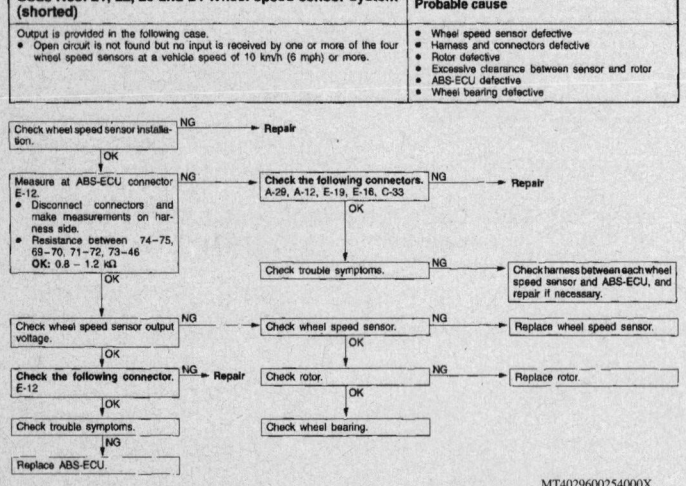

Code Nos. 21, 22, 23 and 24 Wheel speed sensor system (shorted)	Probable cause
Output is provided in the following case. • Open circuit is not found but no input is received by one or more of the four wheel speed sensors at a vehicle speed of 10 km/h (6 mph) or more.	• Wheel speed sensor defective • Harness and connectors defective • Rotor defective • Excessive clearance between sensor and rotor • ABS-ECU defective • Wheel bearing defective

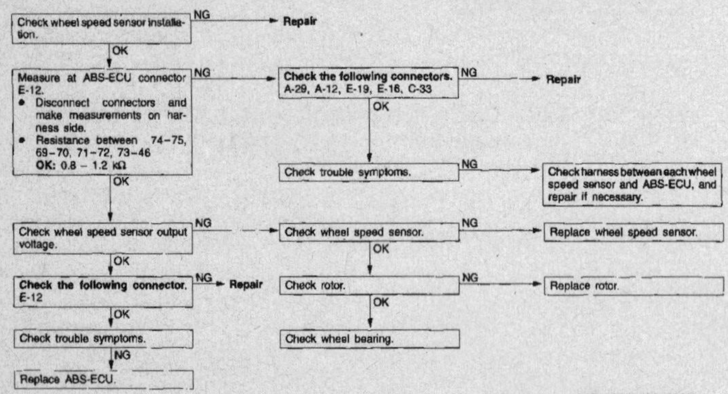
Check wheel speed sensor installation.
NG
Repair
OK
Measure at ABS-ECU connector E-12.
• Disconnect connectors and make measurements on harness side.
• Resistance between 74–75, 69–70, 71–72, 73–46
OK: 0.8 – 1.2 kΩ
NG
Check the following connectors. A-29, A-12, E-19, E-16, C-33
NG
Repair
OK
Check trouble symptoms.
NG
Check harness between each wheel speed sensor and ABS-ECU, and repair if necessary.
OK
Check wheel speed sensor output voltage.
NG
Check wheel speed sensor.
NG
Replace wheel speed sensor.
OK
Check the following connector. E-12
NG
Repair
Check rotor.
NG
Replace rotor.
OK
Check wheel bearing.
OK
Check trouble symptoms.
NG
Replace ABS-ECU.

MT4029600254000X

Fig. 182 Codes 21, 22, 23 & 24: Wheel Speed Sensor System Shorted. 1996 3000GT

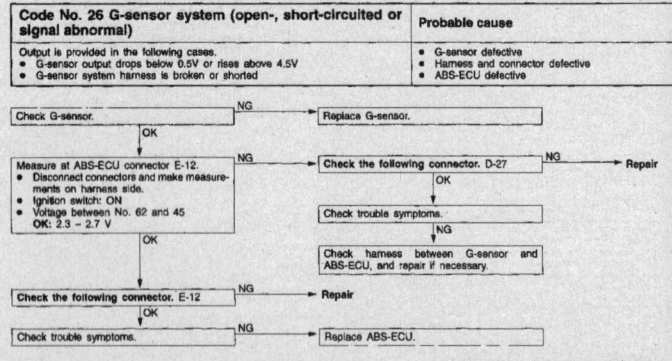

Code No. 26 G-sensor system (open-, short-circuited or signal abnormal)	Probable cause
Output is provided in the following cases. • G-sensor output drops below 0.5V or rises above 4.5V • G-sensor system harness is broken or shorted	• G-sensor defective • Harness and connector defective • ABS-ECU defective

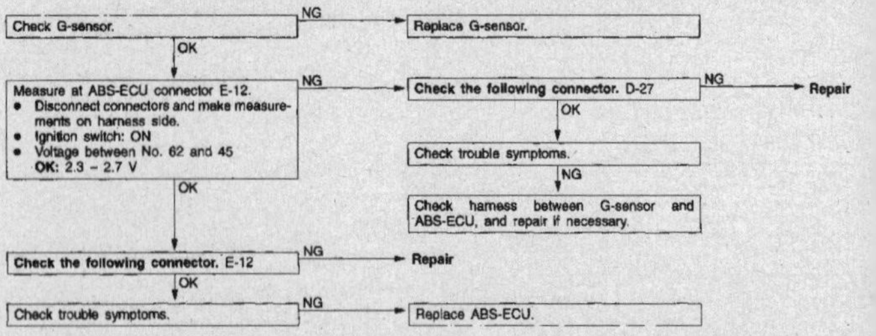
Check G-sensor.
NG
Replace G-sensor.
OK
Measure at ABS-ECU connector E-12.
• Disconnect connectors and make measurements on harness side.
• Ignition switch: ON
• Voltage between No. 62 and 45
OK: 2.3 – 2.7 V
NG
Check the following connector. D-27
NG
Repair
OK
Check trouble symptoms.
NG
Check harness between G-sensor and ABS-ECU, and repair if necessary.
OK
Check the following connector. E-12
NG
Repair
OK
Check trouble symptoms.
NG
Replace ABS-ECU.

MT4029600255000X

Fig. 183 Code 26: G-Sensor System Open, Shorted Or Signal Abnormal. 1996 3000GT

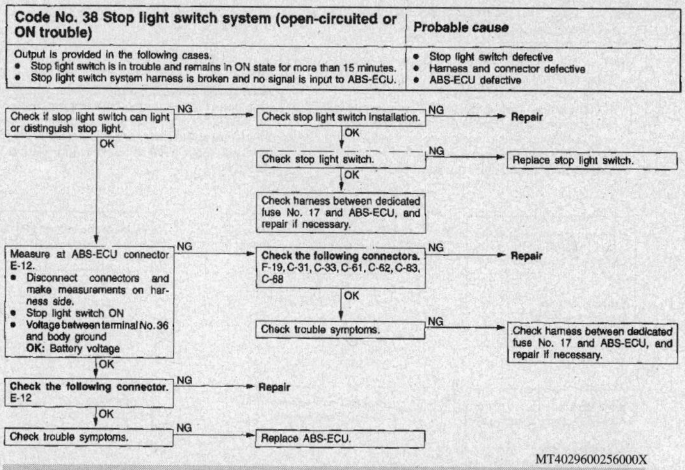
Code No. 38 Stop light switch system (open-circuited or ON trouble)
Probable cause
Output is provided in the following cases.
• Stop light switch is in trouble and remains in ON state for more than 15 minutes.
• Stop light switch system harness is broken and no signal is input to ABS-ECU.
• Stop light switch defective
• Harness and connector defective
• ABS-ECU defective
Check if stop light switch can light or distinguish stop light.
NG
Check stop light switch installation.
NG
Repair
OK
Check stop light switch.
NG
Replace stop light switch.
OK
Check harness between dedicated fuse No. 17 and ABS-ECU, and repair if necessary.
OK
Measure at ABS-ECU connector E-12.
• Disconnect connectors and make measurements on harness side.
• Stop light switch ON
• Voltage between terminal No. 36 and body ground
OK: Battery voltage
NG
Check the following connectors. F-19, C-31, C-33, C-61, C-62, C-83, C-68
NG
Repair
OK
Check trouble symptoms.
NG
Check harness between dedicated fuse No. 17 and ABS-ECU, and repair if necessary.
OK
Check the following connector. E-12
NG
Repair
OK
Check trouble symptoms.
NG
Replace ABS-ECU.
MT4029600256000X

Fig. 184 Code 38: Stop Light Switch System Open Circuit Or ON Trouble. 1996 3000GT

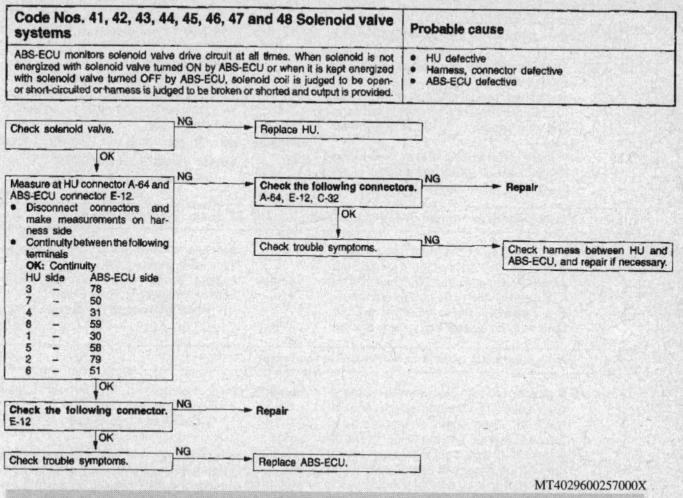
Code Nos. 41, 42, 43, 44, 45, 46, 47 and 48 Solenoid valve systems
Probable cause
ABS-ECU monitors solenoid valve drive circuit at all times. When solenoid is not energized with solenoid valve turned ON by ABS-ECU or when it is kept energized with solenoid valve turned OFF by ABS-ECU, solenoid coil is judged to be open- or short-circuited or harness is judged to be broken or shorted and output is provided.
• HU defective
• Harness, connector defective
• ABS-ECU defective
Check solenoid valve.
NG
Replace HU.
OK
Measure at HU connector A-64 and ABS-ECU connector E-12.
• Disconnect connectors and make measurements on harness side
• Continuity between the following terminals
OK: Continuity
HU side ABS-ECU side
3 – 78
7 – 50
4 – 31
8 – 59
1 – 30
5 – 58
2 – 79
6 – 51
NG
Check the following connectors. A-64, E-12, C-32
NG
Repair
OK
Check trouble symptoms.
NG
Check harness between HU and ABS-ECU, and repair if necessary.
OK
Check the following connector. E-12
NG
Repair
OK
Check trouble symptoms.
NG
Replace ABS-ECU.
MT4029600257000X

Fig. 185 Codes 41, 42, 43, 44, 45, 46, 47 & 48: Solenoid Valve Systems. 1996 3000GT

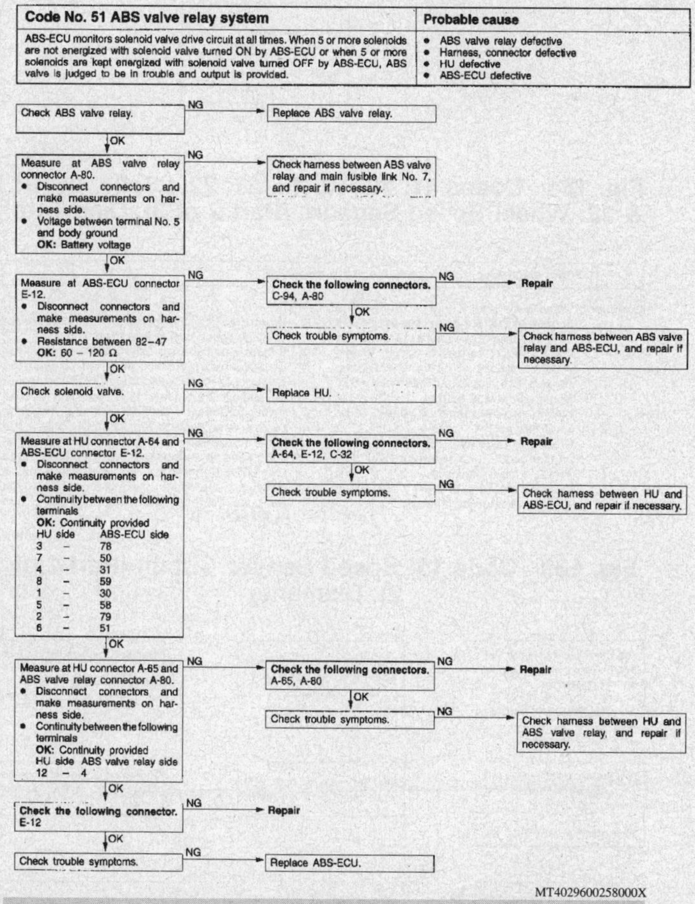
Code No. 51 ABS valve relay system
Probable cause
ABS-ECU monitors solenoid valve drive circuit at all times. When 5 or more solenoids are not energized with solenoid valve turned ON by ABS-ECU or when 5 or more solenoids are kept energized with solenoid valve turned OFF by ABS-ECU, ABS valve is judged to be in trouble and output is provided.
• ABS valve relay defective
• Harness, connector defective
• HU defective
• ABS-ECU defective
Check ABS valve relay.
NG
Replace ABS valve relay.
OK
Measure at ABS valve relay connector A-80.
• Disconnect connectors and make measurements on harness side.
• Voltage between terminal No. 5 and body ground
OK: Battery voltage
NG
Check harness between ABS valve relay and main fusible link No. 7, and repair if necessary.
OK
Measure at ABS-ECU connector E-12.
• Disconnect connectors and make measurements on harness side.
• Resistance between 82–47
OK: 60 – 120 Ω
NG
Check the following connectors. C-94, A-80
NG
Repair
OK
Check trouble symptoms.
NG
Check harness between ABS valve relay and ABS-ECU, and repair if necessary.
OK
Check solenoid valve.
NG
Replace HU.
OK
Measure at HU connector A-64 and ABS-ECU connector E-12.
• Disconnect connectors and make measurements on harness side.
• Continuity between the following terminals
OK: Continuity provided
HU side ABS-ECU side
3 – 78
7 – 50
4 – 31
8 – 59
1 – 30
5 – 58
2 – 79
6 – 51
NG
Check the following connectors. A-64, E-12, C-32
NG
Repair
OK
Check trouble symptoms.
NG
Check harness between HU and ABS-ECU, and repair if necessary.
OK
Measure at HU connector A-65 and ABS valve relay connector A-80.
• Disconnect connectors and make measurements on harness side.
• Continuity between the following terminals
OK: Continuity provided
HU side ABS valve relay side
12 – 4
NG
Check the following connectors. A-65, A-80
NG
Repair
OK
Check trouble symptoms.
NG
Check harness between HU and ABS valve relay, and repair if necessary.
OK
Check the following connector. E-12
NG
Repair
OK
Check trouble symptoms.
NG
Replace ABS-ECU.
MT4029600258000X

Fig. 186 Code 51: ABS Valve Relay System. 1996 3000GT

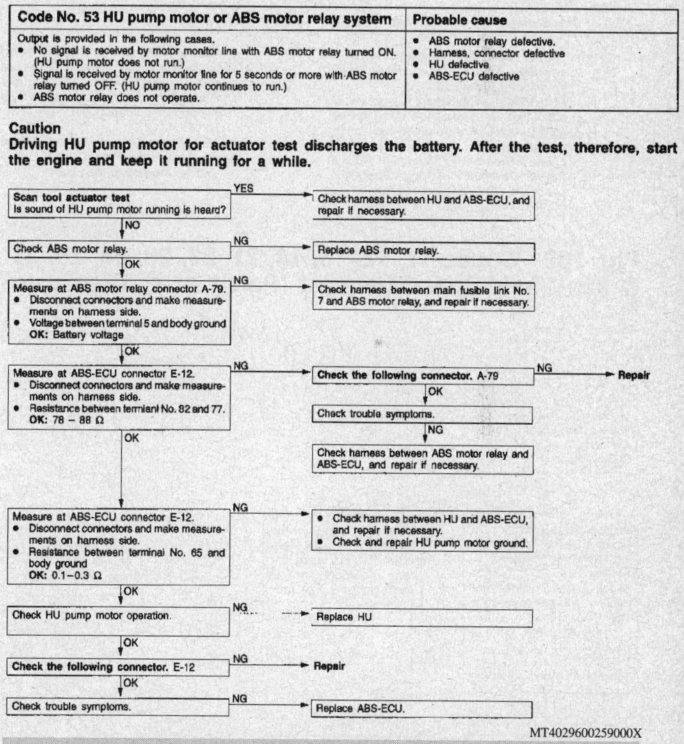
Code No. 53 HU pump motor or ABS motor relay system
Probable cause
Output is provided in the following cases.
• No signal is received by motor monitor line with ABS motor relay turned ON. (HU pump motor does not run.)
• Signal is received by motor monitor line for 5 seconds or more with ABS motor relay turned OFF. (HU pump motor continues to run.)
• ABS motor relay does not operate.
• ABS motor relay defective.
• Harness, connector defective
• HU defective
• ABS-ECU defective
Caution
Driving HU pump motor for actuator test discharges the battery. After the test, therefore, start the engine and keep it running for a while.
Scan tool actuator test
Is sound of HU pump motor running is heard?
YES
Check harness between HU and ABS-ECU, and repair if necessary.
NO
Check ABS motor relay.
NG
Replace ABS motor relay.
OK
Measure at ABS motor relay connector A-79.
• Disconnect connectors and make measurements on harness side.
• Voltage between terminal 5 and body ground
OK: Battery voltage
NG
Check harness between main fusible link No. 7 and ABS motor relay, and repair if necessary.
OK
Measure at ABS-ECU connector E-12.
• Disconnect connectors and make measurements on harness side.
• Resistance between termianl No. 82 and 77.
OK: 78 – 88 Ω
NG
Check the following connector. A-79
NG
Repair
OK
Check trouble symptoms.
NG
Check harness between ABS motor relay and ABS-ECU, and repair if necessary.
OK
Measure at ABS-ECU connector E-12.
• Disconnect connectors and make measurements on harness side.
• Resistance between terminal No. 65 and body ground
OK: 0.1–0.3 Ω
NG
• Check harness between HU and ABS-ECU, and repair if necessary.
• Check and repair HU pump motor ground.
OK
Check HU pump motor operation.
NG
Replace HU
OK
Check the following connector. E-12
NG
Repair
OK
Check trouble symptoms.
NG
Replace ABS-ECU.
MT4029600259000X

Fig. 187 Code 53: HU Pump Motor Or ABS Motor Relay System. 1996 3000GT

E-2	When diagnostic trouble codes No. 11, No. 12, No. 13 or No. 14 are displayed

Comment: These codes are displayed when the sensor with the broken wire can be distinguished, and sensor output drops due to a faulty sensor or a bent rotor, etc., and anti-lock control is continuously operating.

Hint: If there is currently a broken wire in the sensor circuit, when the engine is restarted, the display switches to diagnostic trouble code No. 15. If the same code is displayed even after restarting the engine, the problem is not a broken circuit wire, but something such as an excessive sensor gap.

Remedy: Inspect according to "Wheel Speed Sensor Inspection Flow Chart " while referring to the above.

E-3	When diagnostic trouble codes No. 21, No. 22, No. 23 or No. 24 are displayed

Comment: These problem codes are displayed when a broken wire cannot be verified, but when the vehicle speed reaches 10 km/h (6 mph) or more, no pulses are input.

Hint: The cause is likely to be either a short between the sensor harnesses, a short in the sensor + wire with the body, or an excessive sensor gap.

Remedy: Inspect according to "Wheel Speed Sensor Inspection Flow Chart " while referring to the above.

E-4	When diagnostic trouble code No. 25 is displayed

Comment: A problem in both rear wheel sensors is diagnosed when the signal from either of the front wheel speed sensors is diagnosed as normal, and the wheel speed of both rear wheels is 0 km/h (0 mph) for a continuous 20 second period, even if the wheel speed of the front wheels is 11 km/h (7 mph) or more.

Hint: This code is displayed when there is a short in the sensor harnesses of both rear wheels, or if there is low output from both rear wheel sensors.

Remedy: Inspect according to "Wheel Speed Sensor Inspection Flow Chart " while referring to the above.

NOTE
If the vehicle is raised up, or if the wheels are stuck and only the front wheels are moving, after approximately 20 seconds the ABS warning light will illuminate, and the system will be isolated.
Thus, this code can be output even when the system is normal, so it is only output during a current problem, and is not kept in memory from a previous problem. Accordingly, before turning the ignition switch to OFF, the problem code should be read and written down.

E-5	When diagnostic trouble code No. 31 or No. 32 is displayed

Comment: These codes are displayed when a chipped rotor tooth or a jammed rotor (one tooth) is detected.
Also, they show that there is a request of brake fluid pressure control with the stop light switch OFF from when the vehicle is stationary until the vehicle speed exceeds approximately 15 km/h (9 mph). If the vehicle repeats start and stop and the condition above is detected five times, the ABS warning light will illuminate.

Hint: There is a strong chance that the wheel speed sensor output is low due to a bent rotor tooth or excessive sensor gap. Low sensor output could also be caused by a rare short in the sensor coil.

Remedy: Inspect according to "Wheel Speed Sensor Inspection Flow Chart " while referring to the above.

MT4029100104010X

Fig. 188 Codes 11, 12, 13, 14, 21, 22, 23, 24, 25, 31 & 32: Wheel Speed Sensors (Part 1 of 3). Diamante

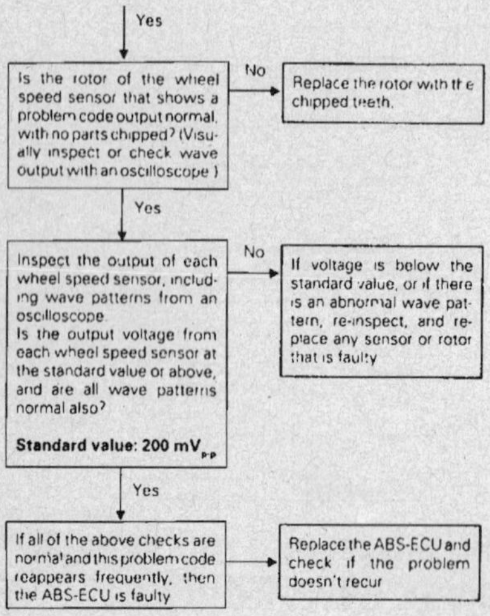

Yes
Is the rotor of the wheel speed sensor that shows a problem code output normal, with no parts chipped? (Visually inspect or check wave output with an oscilloscope.)
No
Replace the rotor with the chipped teeth.
Yes
Inspect the output of each wheel speed sensor, including wave patterns from an oscilloscope.
Is the output voltage from each wheel speed sensor at the standard value or above, and are all wave patterns normal also?
Standard value: 200 mVp-p
No
If voltage is below the standard value, or if there is an abnormal wave pattern, re-inspect, and replace any sensor or rotor that is faulty.
Yes
If all of the above checks are normal and this problem code reappears frequently, then the ABS-ECU is faulty
Replace the ABS-ECU and check if the problem doesn't recur

MT4029100104030X

Fig. 188 Codes 11, 12, 13, 14, 21, 22, 23, 24, 25, 31 & 32: Wheel Speed Sensors (Part 3 of 3). Diamante

Wheel Speed Sensor Inspection Flow Chart

NOTE
1. When there is a faulty contact, inspect the sensor cable by lightly flexing and stretching it.
2. If there is no current problem, a normal value will result even if a problem is detected, so when the malfunction in the sensor circuit indicated cannot be discovered, momentarily turn the ignition switch to OFF, and carry out another driving test. At this time, replace the ABS-ECU only if th same problem code is output. After this, if th code does not reappear, there is a problem wit the ABS-ECU interface. (For a problem that i difficult to reproduce, there is a possibility that th code will recur even when the ABS-ECU is re placed.)

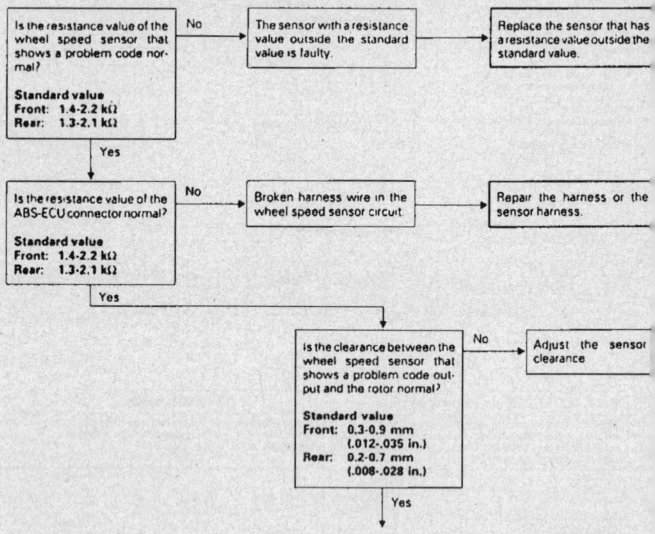

Is the resistance value of the wheel speed sensor that shows a problem code normal?
Standard value
Front: 1.4-2.2 kΩ
Rear: 1.3-2.1 kΩ
No
The sensor with a resistance value outside the standard value is faulty.
Replace the sensor that has a resistance value outside the standard value.
Yes
Is the resistance value of the ABS-ECU connector normal?
Standard value
Front: 1.4-2.2 kΩ
Rear: 1.3-2.1 kΩ
No
Broken harness wire in the wheel speed sensor circuit.
Repair the harness or the sensor harness.
Yes
Is the clearance between the wheel speed sensor that shows a problem code output and the rotor normal?
Standard value
Front: 0.3-0.9 mm (.012-.035 in.)
Rear: 0.2-0.7 mm (.008-.028 in.)
No
Adjust the sensor clearance
Yes

MT4029100104020X

Fig. 188 Codes 11, 12, 13, 14, 21, 22, 23, 24, 25, 31 & 32: Wheel Speed Sensors (Part 2 of 3). Diamante

E-1	When diagnostic trouble code No. 15 is displayed

Comment: There is a broken + wire or – wire in one or more of the four wheel speed sensors detected by a broken wire inspection by the ABS-ECU hardware circuit. In this instance, inspect all of the wheel speed sensors, as it cannot be determined which single wheel is abnormal.

Hint: When using the scan tool, up to 4 codes are displayed.
When this code (No. 15) appears, and a problem code for a specific wheel (nos. 11-14) is also displayed, it is likely that there is a broken wire in the wheel speed sensor indicated by these codes.

NOTE
1. When there is a faulty contact, inspect the sensor cable by lightly flexing and stretching it.
2. If there is no current problem, a normal value will result even if a problem is detected, so when the malfunction in the sensor circuit indicated cannot be discovered, momentarily turn the ignition switch to OFF, and carry out another driving test. At this time, replace the ABS-ECU only if the same problem code is output. After this, if the code does not reappear, there is a problem with the ABS-ECU interface. (For a problem that is difficult to reproduce, there is a possibility that the code will recur even when the ABS-ECU is replaced.)

MT4029100103010X

Fig. 189 Code 15: Speed Sensor Circuit (Part 1 of 2). Diamante

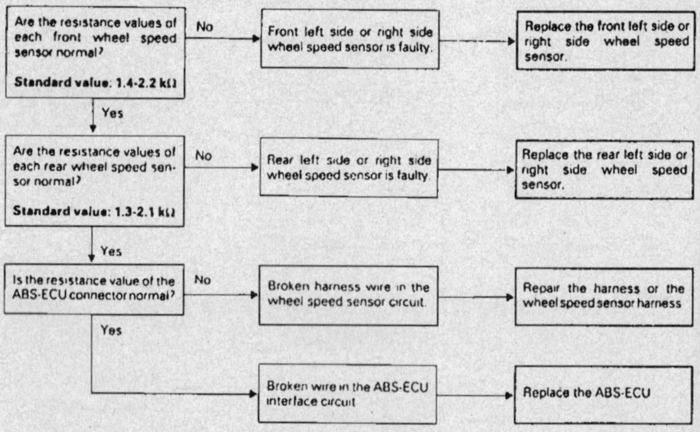

Are the resistance values of each front wheel speed sensor normal?
Standard value: 1.4-2.2 kΩ
No
Front left side or right side wheel speed sensor is faulty.
Replace the front left side or right side wheel speed sensor.
Yes
Are the resistance values of each rear wheel speed sensor normal?
Standard value: 1.3-2.1 kΩ
No
Rear left side or right side wheel speed sensor is faulty.
Replace the rear left side or right side wheel speed sensor.
Yes
Is the resistance value of the ABS-ECU connector normal?
No
Broken harness wire in the wheel speed sensor circuit.
Repair the harness or the wheel speed sensor harness
Yes
Broken wire in the ABS-ECU interface circuit
Replace the ABS-ECU

MT4029100103020X

Fig. 189 Code 15: Speed Sensor Circuit (Part 2 of 2). Diamante

E-6	When diagnostic trouble code No. 16 is displayed

Comment: This indicates that the ABS-ECU power voltage is lower than the standard value. If the voltage returns to standard voltage or above, this problem code will not be output.

Caution
If the battery voltage drops during inspection, this code will be output as a current problem, and correct diagnosis of the problem cannot be made. Before carrying out the following inspection, check the battery level, and refill it if necessary.

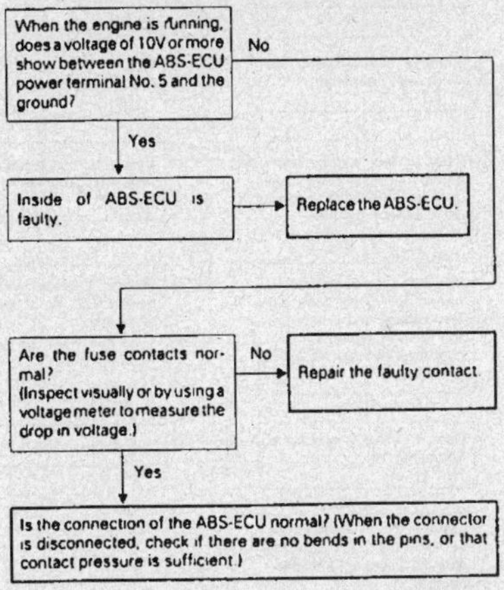
When the engine is running, does a voltage of 10V or more show between the ABS-ECU power terminal No. 5 and the ground?
No
Yes
Inside of ABS-ECU is faulty.
Replace the ABS-ECU.
Are the fuse contacts normal? (Inspect visually or by using a voltage meter to measure the drop in voltage.)
No
Repair the faulty contact.
Yes
Is the connection of the ABS-ECU normal? (When the connector is disconnected, check if there are no bends in the pins, or that contact pressure is sufficient.)

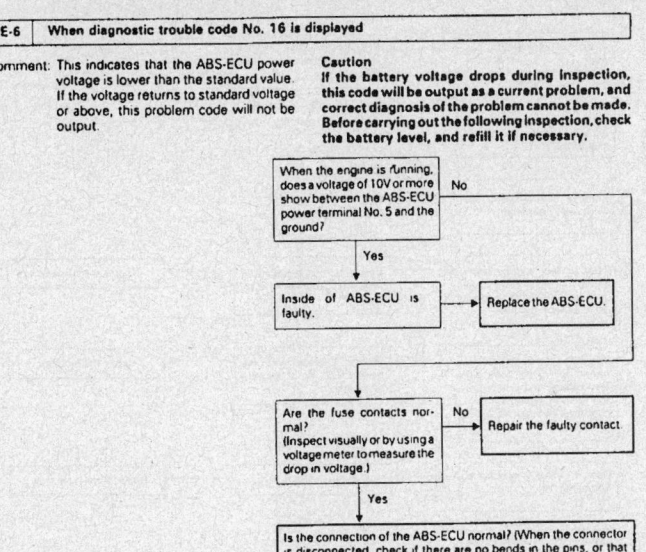

MT4029100105000X

Fig. 190 Code 16: Power Supply Voltage. Diamante

E-7	When diagnostic trouble code No. 35 is displayed

Comment: This indicates that the output voltage of the generator L terminal is low when the ignition key is turned to "ON" and the engine is stopped, or when the engine is running.
If the voltage returns to standard voltage or above, this problem code will not be output.

Hint: When the output voltage of the generator L terminal is low, the charge warning light will illuminate. This code also appears when there is a short in the generator L terminal monitor circuit, but not if there is a broken wire in that circuit.
If the scan tool service data displays No. 35, this problem code is output.

NOTE
If the engine is stopped, this code will be output, even if the situation is normal, so the following inspection should only be carried out if the code is output while the engine is running.

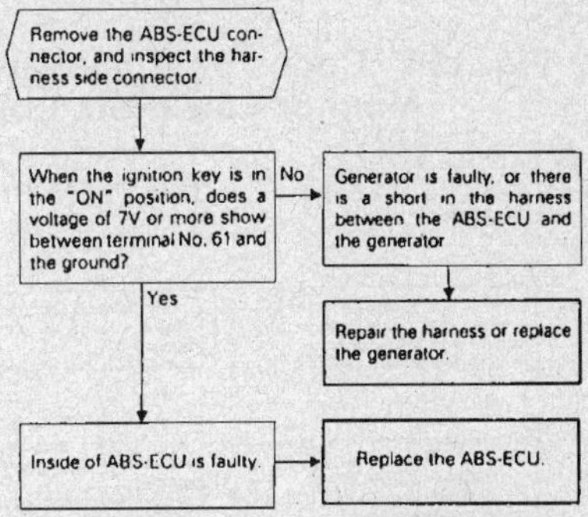
Remove the ABS-ECU connector, and inspect the harness side connector.
When the ignition key is in the "ON" position, does a voltage of 7V or more show between terminal No. 61 and the ground?
No
Generator is faulty, or there is a short in the harness between the ABS-ECU and the generator
Yes
Repair the harness or replace the generator.
Inside of ABS-ECU is faulty.
Replace the ABS-ECU.

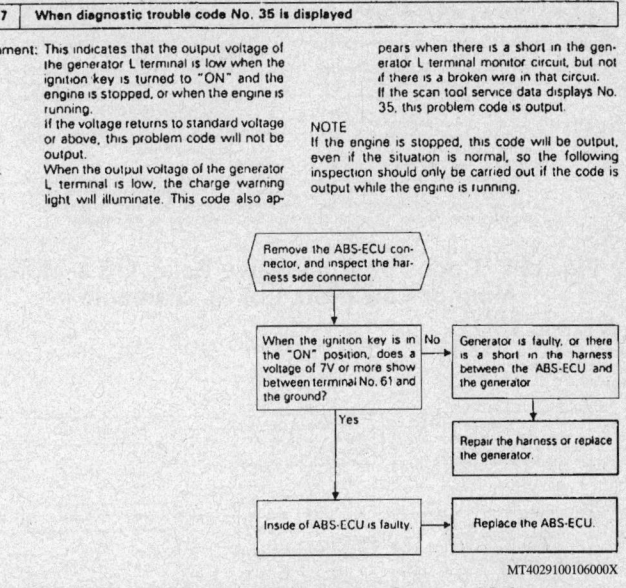

MT4029100106000X

Fig. 190 Code 35: Generator Output Voltage. Diamante

E-8	When diagnostic trouble code No. 37 is displayed

Comment: This indicates that the power source pressure for the hydraulic unit is low. If the pressure returns to standard valve or above, this problem code will not be output.

Remedy: While the engine is idling, wait for the pressure to return (motor and pump drive). If the problem continues after approximately 35 seconds or more have passed, the problem code will change over to No. 61. (Inspect according to Inspection chart D-12.)

Hint: This problem code will be output even if there is a broken wire in the LPWS input harness. (ON problem [short] is not detected.)
LPWS: Low pressure warning switch

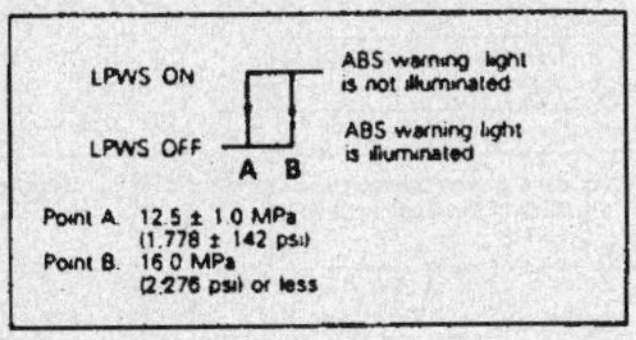
LPWS ON
LPWS OFF
ABS warning light is not illuminated
ABS warning light is illuminated
A B
Point A. 12.5 ± 1.0 MPa (1,778 ± 142 psi)
Point B. 16.0 MPa (2,276 psi) or less

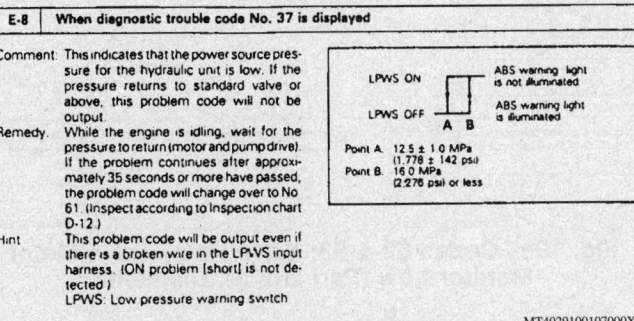

MT4029100107000X

Fig. 191 Code 37: Power Source Pressure For Hydraulic Unit Low. Diamante

E-9	When diagnostic trouble codes No. 41, No. 42, No. 43, No. 44, No. 45 or No. 46 are displayed

Comment: The ABS-ECU normally monitors the solenoid valve drive circuit. If there is no current flowing to the solenoid even when the solenoid is ON, or the current continues to flow to the solenoid even when the solenoid is OFF, the ABS-ECU diagnoses a broken wire or short in the solenoid coil or a broken wire or short in the harness, and this problem code is output.

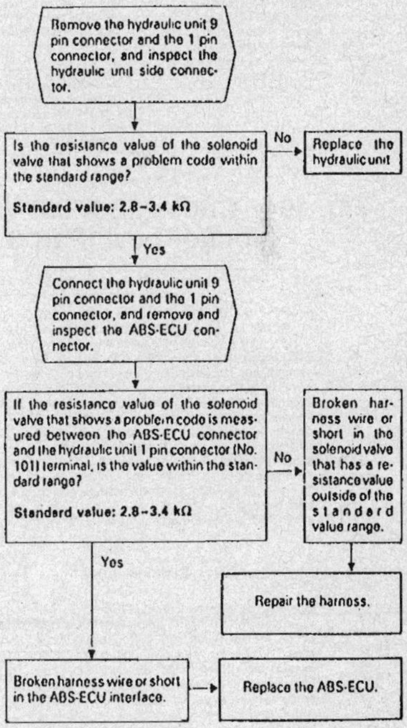
Remove the hydraulic unit 9 pin connector and the 1 pin connector, and inspect the hydraulic unit side connector.
Is the resistance value of the solenoid valve that shows a problem code within the standard range?
Standard value: 2.8–3.4 kΩ
No
Replace the hydraulic unit
Yes
Connect the hydraulic unit 9 pin connector and the 1 pin connector, and remove and inspect the ABS-ECU connector.
If the resistance value of the solenoid valve that shows a problem code is measured between the ABS-ECU connector and the hydraulic unit 1 pin connector (No. 101) terminal, is the value within the standard range?
Standard value: 2.8–3.4 kΩ
No
Broken harness wire or short in the solenoid valve that has a resistance value outside of the standard value range.
Repair the harness.
Yes
Broken harness wire or short in the ABS-ECU interface.
Replace the ABS-ECU.

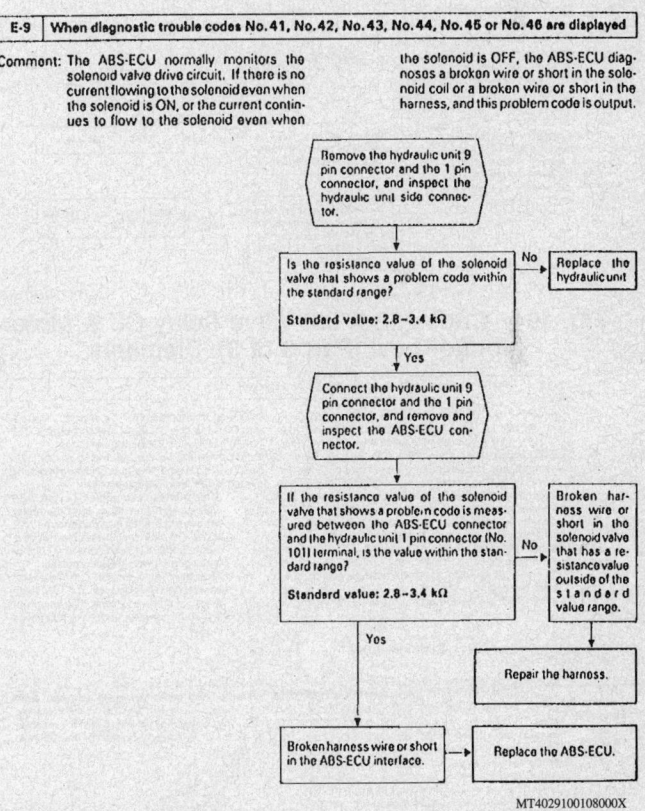

MT4029100108000X

Fig. 192 Codes 41, 42, 43, 44, 45 & 46: Solenoid Valve Drive Circuit. Diamante

E-10	When diagnostic trouble code No. 51 is displayed

Comment: During the initial check when the ignition switch is turned to "ON", if power is being supplied to the solenoid when the valve relay is OFF, the ABS-ECU diagnoses a melted relay contact or a short in the valve relay drive circuit, and the problem code No. 51 is output.

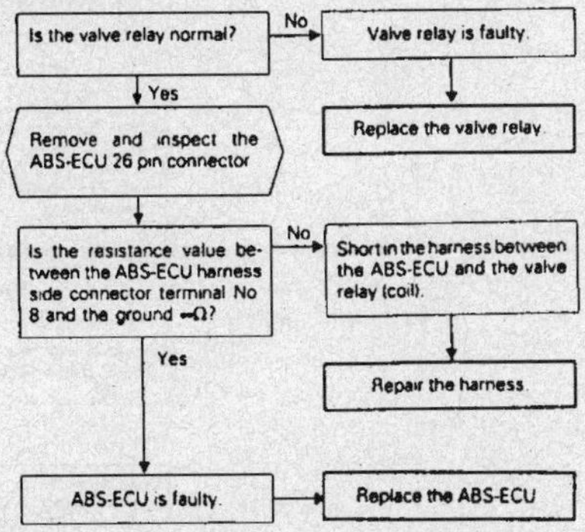
Is the valve relay normal?
No
Valve relay is faulty.
Yes
Replace the valve relay.
Remove and inspect the ABS-ECU 26 pin connector
Is the resistance value between the ABS-ECU harness side connector terminal No. 8 and the ground ∞Ω?
No
Short in the harness between the ABS-ECU and the valve relay (coil).
Yes
Repair the harness.
ABS-ECU is faulty.
Replace the ABS-ECU

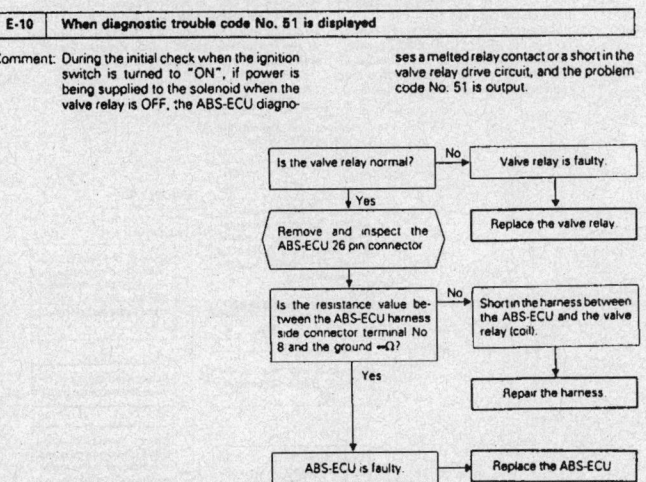

MT4029100109000X

Fig. 193 Code 51: Valve Relay Drive Circuit. Diamante

E-11	When diagnostic trouble code No. 52 or No. 53 is displayed

Comment: During the initial check when the ignition switch is turned to "ON", if power is not being supplied to the solenoid when the valve relay is ON, the ABS-ECU diagnoses an OFF problem in the valve relay (not turned ON), and outputs the problem code No. 52. Also, when the motor pump receives a signal to turn ON and voltage at the motor monitor is LOW, the ABS-ECU outputs the problem code No. 53.

Hint: Because the same circuit is used as the power supply circuit for the valve relay and the motor relay, inspection of the circuit between the ABS fusible link (6) and the valve relay is necessary for both code Nos. 52 and 53.
However, if the ABS system stops functioning after the sound of the motor is heard, or if it stops functioning when the motor relay is force-driven by the scan tool actuator test (No. 08), the power supply and the valve relay system can be considered normal.

Caution
As there is a problem that the accumulator pressure could become higher than necessary, resulting in a bad effect on the system, it is best not to carry out actuator test No. 8 if possible.

MT4029100110010X

Fig. 194 Codes 52 & 53: Valve Relay Off & Motor Monitor Low (Part 1 of 3). Diamante

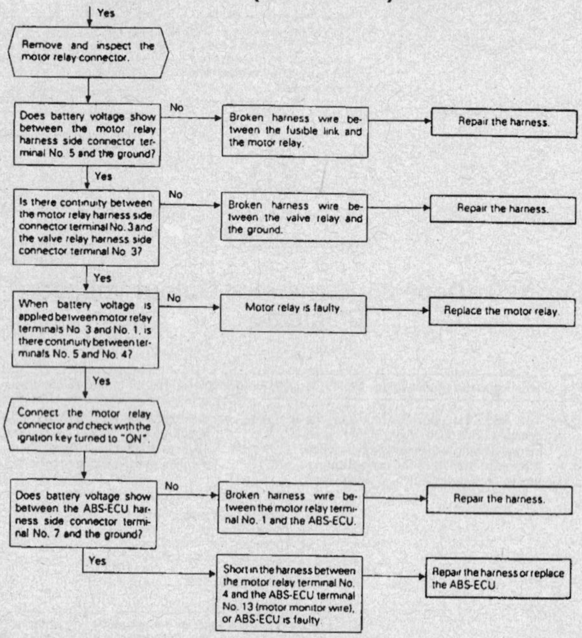

Yes
Remove and inspect the motor relay connector.
Does battery voltage show between the motor relay harness side connector terminal No. 5 and the ground?
No
Broken harness wire between the fusible link and the motor relay.
Repair the harness.
Yes
Is there continuity between the motor relay harness side connector terminal No. 3 and the valve relay harness side connector terminal No. 3?
No
Broken harness wire between the valve relay and the ground.
Repair the harness.
Yes
When battery voltage is applied between motor relay terminals No. 3 and No. 1, is there continuity between terminals No. 5 and No. 4?
No
Motor relay is faulty.
Replace the motor relay.
Yes
Connect the motor relay connector and check with the ignition key turned to "ON".
Does battery voltage show between the ABS-ECU harness side connector terminal No. 7 and the ground?
No
Broken harness wire between the motor relay terminal No. 1 and the ABS-ECU.
Repair the harness.
Yes
Short in the harness between the motor relay terminal No. 4 and the ABS-ECU terminal No. 13 (motor monitor wire), or ABS-ECU is faulty.
Repair the harness or replace the ABS-ECU.

MT4029100110030X

Fig. 194 Codes 52 & 53: Valve Relay Off & Motor Monitor Low (Part 3 of 3). Diamante

E-13	When diagnostic trouble code No. 61 is displayed

Comment: The ABS-ECU outputs this problem code No. 61 in the following cases if there is a fault inside the hydraulic unit.

(1) Even when the pump motor operates for 34 seconds due to demand of the pressure control switch, and then alternately switches OFF for 8.5 seconds and ON for 8.5 seconds, repeating this intermittent operation 4 times (total approx. 1 minute 40 seconds), the accumulator does not recover pressure equal to the pressure control switch standard amount or higher.

(2) When the low pressure warning switch outputs OFF (low pressure) for approximately 35 seconds after the engine is started.

(3) When low pressure warning switch ON (high pressure) is detected after the engine is started, and then the low pressure switch outputs OFF (low pressure) for 10 seconds or longer.

(4) When the pressure control switch is ON (high pressure side) and the low pressure warning switch is OFF (low pressure side).

Hint: After starting the engine, if the ABS warning light illuminates after the motor has been operating intermittently as in (1) above, it is clear that this problem code is output under the conditions in (1) due to faulty pump pressure accumulation.
After starting the engine, if the scan tool service data displays No. 37 (ON [high pressure side]), it is clear that this problem code is output under the conditions in (1).

REMEDY FOR FAULTY PUMP PRESSURE ACCUMULATION

1. Operation to expel N_2 (nitrogen) gas
For a vehicle that hasn't been used for a long period, the high pressure N_2 (nitrogen) gas that is stored inside the hydraulic unit accumulator passes through the rubber diaphragm and collects around the hydraulic unit pump, and this prevents oil pressure from building up even if the hydraulic unit pump is turning, so the following procedure should be carried out to expel the N_2 (nitrogen) that has collected around the pump.

(1) When Using The Scan Tool
With the brake pedal depressed, carry out scan tool actuator tests No. 04–06 in the following way. (The collected gas is leaked into the reservoir by means of the forced actuation of the solenoid valve.)

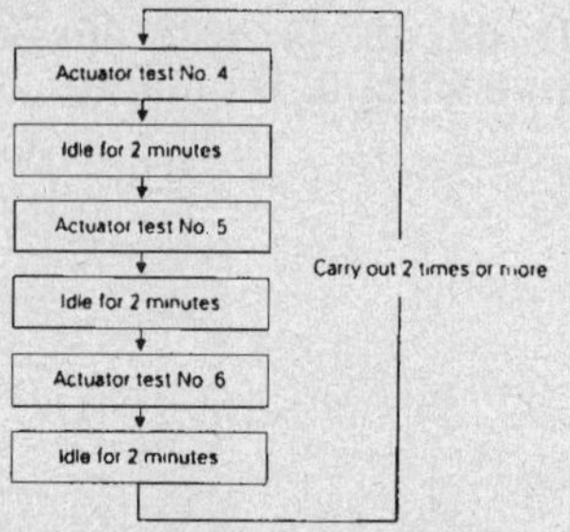

Actuator test No. 4
Idle for 2 minutes
Actuator test No. 5
Carry out 2 times or more
Idle for 2 minutes
Actuator test No. 6
Idle for 2 minutes

MT4029100112010X

Fig. 196 Code 61: Hydraulic Unit (Part 1 of 2). Diamante

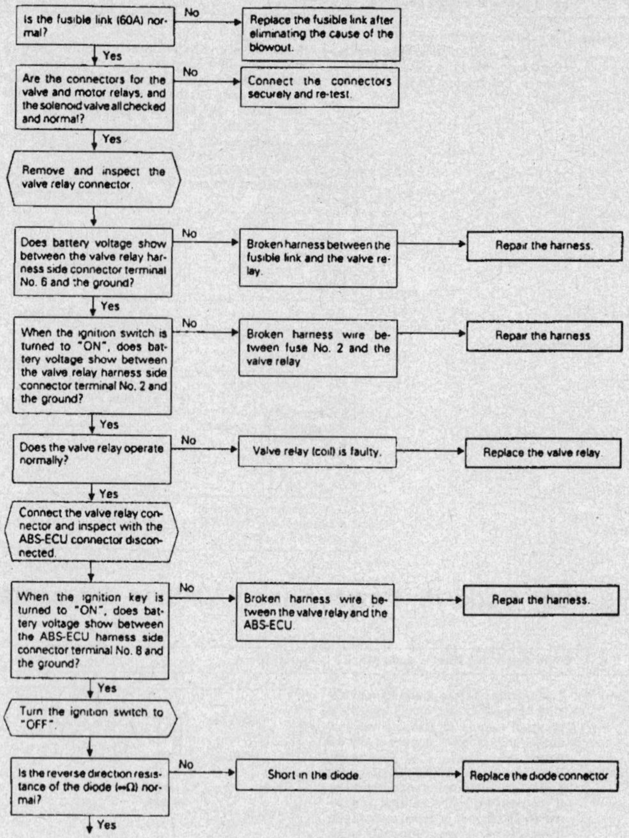

Is the fusible link (60A) normal?
No
Replace the fusible link after eliminating the cause of the blowout.
Yes
Are the connectors for the valve and motor relays, and the solenoid valve all checked and normal?
No
Connect the connectors securely and re-test.
Yes
Remove and inspect the valve relay connector.
Does battery voltage show between the valve relay harness side connector terminal No. 6 and the ground?
No
Broken harness between the fusible link and the valve relay.
Repair the harness.
Yes
When the ignition switch is turned to "ON", does battery voltage show between the valve relay harness side connector terminal No. 2 and the ground?
No
Broken harness wire between fuse No. 2 and the valve relay.
Repair the harness
Yes
Does the valve relay operate normally?
No
Valve relay (coil) is faulty.
Replace the valve relay.
Yes
Connect the valve relay connector and inspect with the ABS-ECU connector disconnected.
When the ignition key is turned to "ON", does battery voltage show between the ABS-ECU harness side connector terminal No. 8 and the ground?
No
Broken harness wire between the valve relay and the ABS-ECU.
Repair the harness.
Yes
Turn the ignition switch to "OFF".
Is the reverse direction resistance of the diode (∞Ω) normal?
No
Short in the diode.
Replace the diode connector
Yes

MT4029100110020X

Fig. 194 Codes 52 & 53: Valve Relay Off & Motor Monitor Low (Part 2 of 3). Diamante

E-12	When diagnostic trouble code No. 54 is displayed

Comment: When the pump motor receives a signal to turn OFF and the motor monitor is ON, if a melted contact, etc. is diagnosed in the motor relay, the ABS-ECU outputs the problem code No. 54.

Hint: Because the motor monitor wire is pulled up into the ABS-ECU by the IG power, this problem code is output if there is a broken wire in the harness, even if the motor relay and the motor are normal.

Caution
If there is a melted contact in the motor relay, the motor will keep turning, even if the ignition witch is turned to OFF. In such a case, immediately remove the fusible link (60A) or disconnect the hydraulic unit 2 pin connector. Excessive running of the motor will cause a reduction in the efficiency of the hydraulic unit solenoid valve.

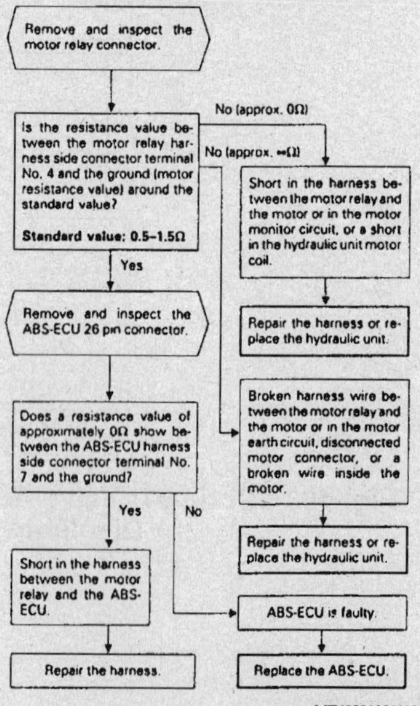

Remove and inspect the motor relay connector.
No (approx. 0Ω)
Is the resistance value between the motor relay harness side connector terminal No. 4 and the ground (motor resistance value) around the standard value?
Standard value: 0.5–1.5Ω
No (approx. ∞Ω)
Short in the harness between the motor relay and the motor or in the motor monitor circuit, or a short in the hydraulic unit motor coil.
Repair the harness or replace the hydraulic unit.
Yes
Remove and inspect the ABS-ECU 26 pin connector.
Does a resistance value of approximately 0Ω show between the ABS-ECU harness side connector terminal No. 7 and the ground?
Broken harness wire between the motor relay and the motor or in the motor earth circuit, disconnected motor connector, or a broken wire inside the motor.
Repair the harness or replace the hydraulic unit.
Yes
No
Short in the harness between the motor relay and the ABS-ECU.
ABS-ECU is faulty.
Repair the harness.
Replace the ABS-ECU.

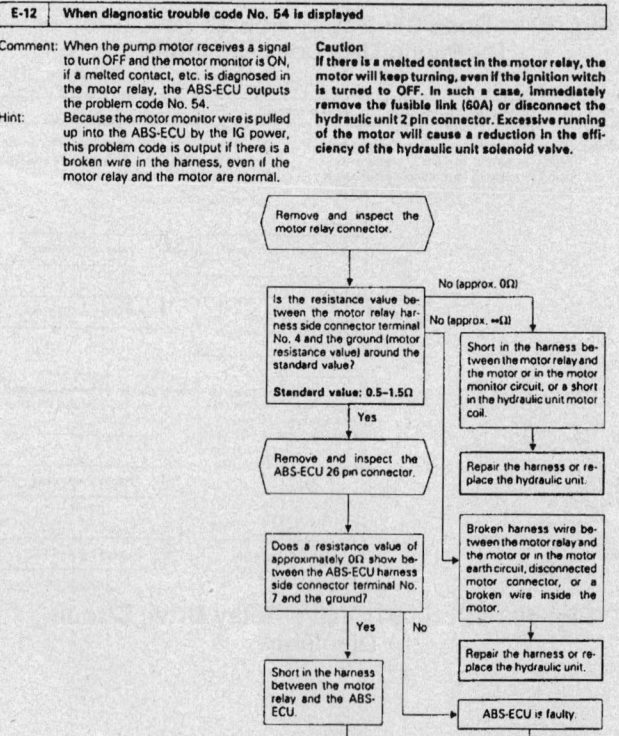

MT4029100111000X

Fig. 195 Code 54: Motor Relay. Diamante

(2) When Not Using The Scan Tool
Start the engine, leave it idling for 2 minutes, and then stop the engine.
Repeat this 10 times or more.
(The collected gas is leaked into the reservoir in the same way as when using the scan tool, by the repeated short-term operation of the solenoid valve during the initial check.)

2. After carrying out the above, if it is normal [No abnormality is detected in the above cases (1) to (3)], carry out a normal bleeding of the brake lines.
3. After carrying out the above, if the motor operates intermittently and this problem code is output, the motor or pump operation is faulty, so replace the hydraulic unit.

INSPECTION OF PRESSURE SWITCHES (WHEN THE MOTOR DOES NOT OPERATE AFTER THE ENGINE HAS BEEN TURNED ON)

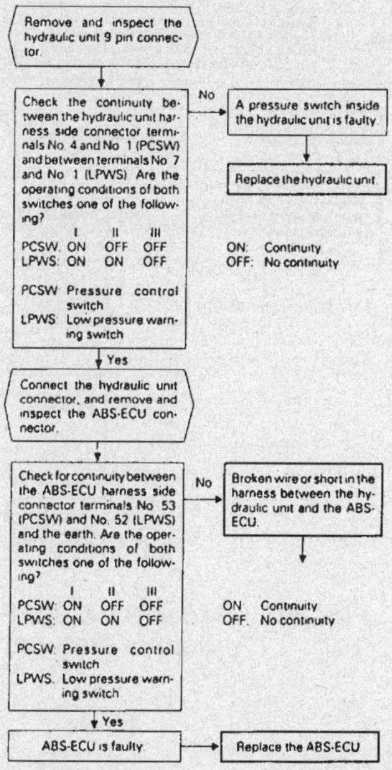

Remove and inspect the hydraulic unit 9 pin connector.
Check the continuity between the hydraulic unit harness side connector terminals No. 4 and No. 1 (PCSW) and between terminals No. 7 and No. 1 (LPWS). Are the operating conditions of both switches one of the following?
I II III
PCSW: ON OFF OFF
LPWS: ON ON OFF
ON: Continuity
OFF: No continuity
PCSW: Pressure control switch
LPWS: Low pressure warning switch
No
A pressure switch inside the hydraulic unit is faulty.
Replace the hydraulic unit.
Yes
Connect the hydraulic unit connector, and remove and inspect the ABS-ECU connector.
Check for continuity between the ABS-ECU harness side connector terminals No. 53 (PCSW) and No. 52 (LPWS) and the earth. Are the operating conditions of both switches one of the following?
I II III
PCSW: ON OFF OFF
LPWS: ON ON OFF
ON: Continuity
OFF: No continuity
PCSW: Pressure control switch
LPWS: Low pressure warning switch
No
Broken wire or short in the harness between the hydraulic unit and the ABS-ECU.
Yes
ABS-ECU is faulty.
Replace the ABS-ECU

MT4029100112020X

Fig. 196 Code 61: Hydraulic Unit (Part 2 of 2). Diamante

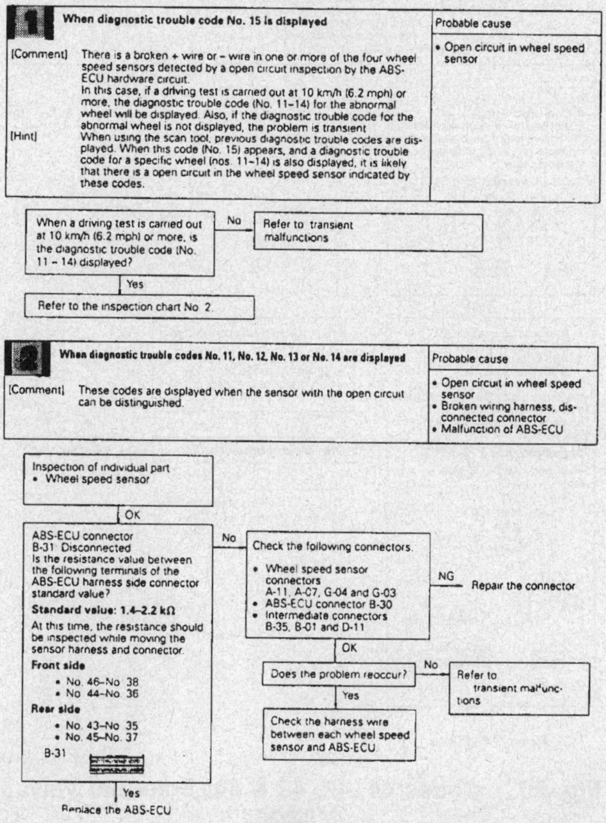

1 When diagnostic trouble code No. 15 is displayed
Probable cause
• Open circuit in wheel speed sensor
[Comment] There is a broken + wire or – wire in one or more of the four wheel speed sensors detected by a open circuit inspection by the ABS-ECU hardware circuit.
In this case, if a driving test is carried out at 10 km/h (6.2 mph) or more, the diagnostic trouble code (No. 11–14) for the abnormal wheel will be displayed. Also, if the diagnostic trouble code for the abnormal wheel is not displayed, the problem is transient.
[Hint] When using the scan tool, previous diagnostic trouble codes are displayed. When this code (No. 15) appears, and a diagnostic trouble code for a specific wheel (nos. 11–14) is also displayed, it is likely that there is a open circuit in the wheel speed sensor indicated by these codes.
When a driving test is carried out at 10 km/h (6.2 mph) or more, is the diagnostic trouble code (No. 11 – 14) displayed?
No
Refer to transient malfunctions
Yes
Refer to the inspection chart No. 2.
2 When diagnostic trouble codes No. 11, No. 12, No. 13 or No. 14 are displayed
Probable cause
• Open circuit in wheel speed sensor
• Broken wiring harness, disconnected connector
• Malfunction of ABS-ECU
[Comment] These codes are displayed when the sensor with the open circuit can be distinguished.
Inspection of individual part
• Wheel speed sensor
OK
ABS-ECU connector B-31 Disconnected
Is the resistance value between the following terminals of the ABS-ECU harness side connector standard value?
Standard value: 1.4–2.2 kΩ
At this time, the resistance should be inspected while moving the sensor harness and connector.
Front side
• No. 46–No. 38
• No. 44–No. 36
Rear side
• No. 43–No. 35
• No. 45–No. 37
B-31
No
Check the following connectors.
• Wheel speed sensor connectors A-11, A-07, G-04 and G-03
• ABS-ECU connector B-30
• Intermediate connectors B-35, B-01 and D-11
NG
Repair the connector
OK
Does the problem reoccur?
No
Refer to transient malfunctions
Yes
Check the harness wire between each wheel speed sensor and ABS-ECU.
Yes
Replace the ABS-ECU

MT4029100124000X

Fig. 198 Codes 11, 12, 13, 14 & 15: Speed Sensors (Open Circuit). Mirage

E-14	When diagnostic trouble code No. 62 is displayed

Comment: Diagnostic trouble code No. 62 is a problem code that is output when the ABS is unable to operate for a long period of time. However, it is possible that the problem could be caused not only by a faulty hydraulic unit, but also by a malfunctioning wheel speed sensor.

Caution
The problem code No. 62 is detected in the following cases, even if the ABS system is normal.
- **If the parking brake is not fully released, or if the brakes are dragging while driving on snow or ice.**
- **When driving with left and right tyres of different sizes (difference in tyre diameter or uneven wear).**
- **When driving for a long period of time on roads with low friction coefficients, such as ice-covered roads.**

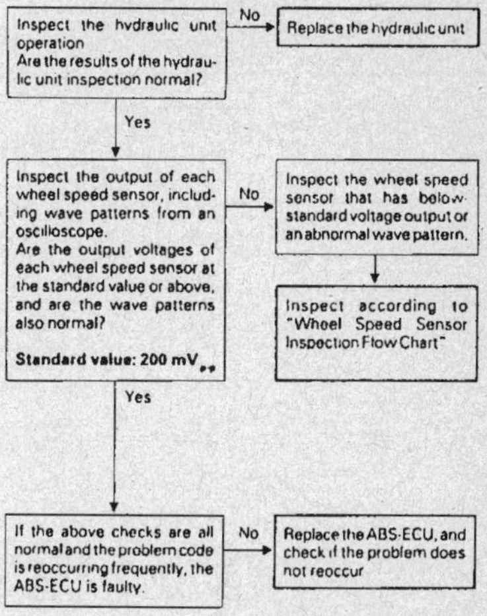

Inspect the hydraulic unit operation
Are the results of the hydraulic unit inspection normal?
No
Replace the hydraulic unit
Yes
Inspect the output of each wheel speed sensor, including wave patterns from an oscilloscope.
Are the output voltages of each wheel speed sensor at the standard value or above, and are the wave patterns also normal?
Standard value: 200 mV
No
Inspect the wheel speed sensor that has below-standard voltage output or an abnormal wave pattern.
Inspect according to "Wheel Speed Sensor Inspection Flow Chart"
Yes
If the above checks are all normal and the problem code is reoccurring frequently, the ABS-ECU is faulty.
No
Replace the ABS-ECU, and check if the problem does not reoccur

MT4029100113000X

Fig. 197 Code 62: Hydraulic Unit Or Wheel Speed Sensor. Diamante

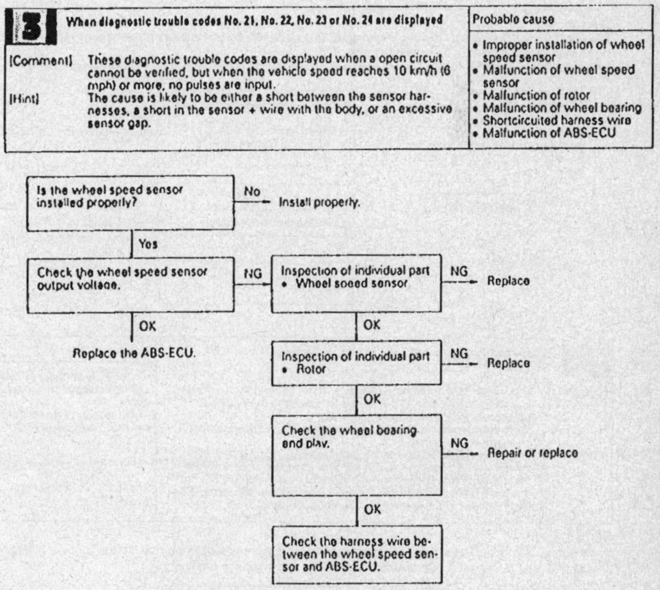

3 When diagnostic trouble codes No. 21, No. 22, No. 23 or No. 24 are displayed
Probable cause
• Improper installation of wheel speed sensor
• Malfunction of wheel speed sensor
• Malfunction of rotor
• Malfunction of wheel bearing
• Shortcircuited harness wire
• Malfunction of ABS-ECU
[Comment] These diagnostic trouble codes are displayed when a open circuit cannot be verified, but when the vehicle speed reaches 10 km/h (6 mph) or more, no pulses are input.
[Hint] The cause is likely to be either a short between the sensor harnesses, a short in the sensor + wire with the body, or an excessive sensor gap.
Is the wheel speed sensor installed properly?
No
Install properly.
Yes
Check the wheel speed sensor output voltage.
NG
Inspection of individual part
• Wheel speed sensor
NG
Replace
OK
Replace the ABS-ECU.
OK
Inspection of individual part
• Rotor
NG
Replace
OK
Check the wheel bearing end play.
NG
Repair or replace
OK
Check the harness wire between the wheel speed sensor and ABS-ECU.

MT4029100125000X

Fig. 199 Codes 21, 22, 23 & 24: Speed Sensors (Short Circuit). Mirage

When diagnostic trouble code No. 25 is displayed	Probable cause
[Comment] A problem in both rear wheel sensors is diagnosed when the signal from either of the front wheel speed sensors is diagnosed as normal, and the wheel speed of both rear wheels is 0 km/h (0 mph) for a continuous 20 second period, even if the wheel speed of the front wheels is 11 km/h (7 mph) or more. [Hint] This code is displayed when there is a short in the sensor harnesses of both rear wheels, or if there is low output from both rear wheel sensors. NOTE If the vehicle is raised up, or if the wheels are stuck and only the front wheels are moving, after approximately 20 seconds the ABS warning light will illuminate, and the system will be isolated. Thus, this code can be output even when the system is normal, so it is only output during a current problem, and is not kept in memory from a previous problem. Accordingly, before turning the ignition switch to OFF, the diagnostic trouble code should be read and written down.	• Improper installation of rear wheel speed sensor • Malfunction of rear wheel speed sensor • Malfunction of rotor • Malfunction of wheel bearing • Shortcircuited harness wire • Malfunction of ABS-ECU

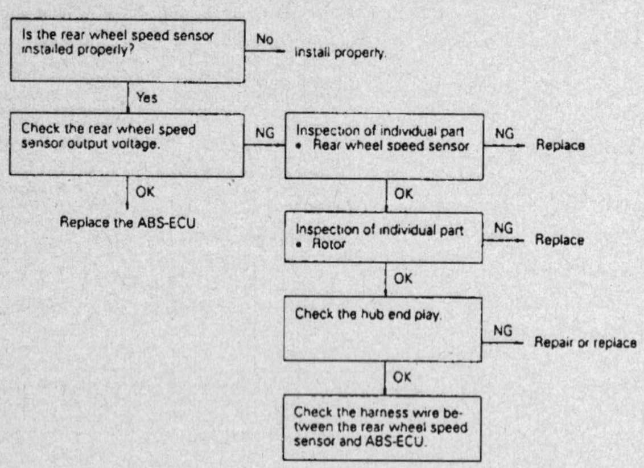

Is the rear wheel speed sensor installed properly?
No
Install properly.
Yes
Check the rear wheel speed sensor output voltage.
NG
Inspection of individual part
• Rear wheel speed sensor
NG
Replace
OK
Replace the ABS-ECU
OK
Inspection of individual part
• Rotor
NG
Replace
OK
Check the hub end play.
NG
Repair or replace
OK
Check the harness wire between the rear wheel speed sensor and ABS-ECU.

MT4029100126000X

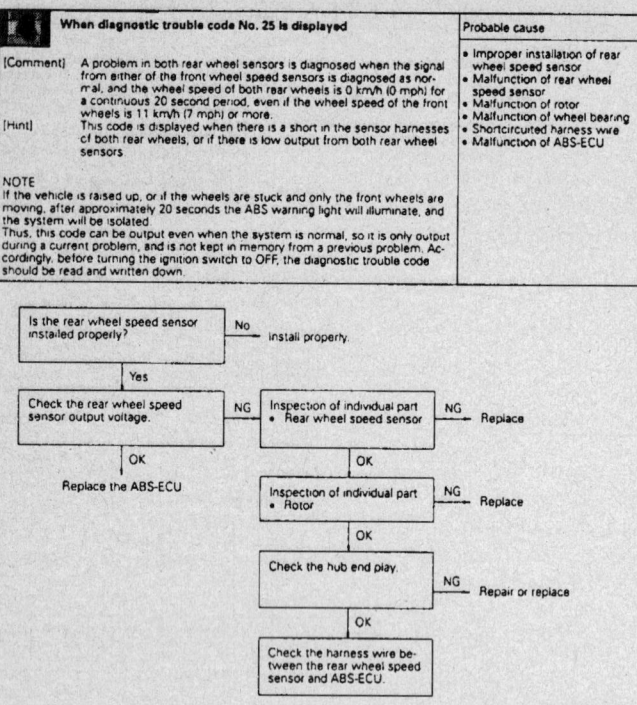

Fig. 200 Code 25: Open Circuit In Both Rear Wheel Speed Sensors. Mirage

When diagnostic trouble codes No. 31 or No. 32 are displayed	Probable cause
[Comment] These codes are displayed when a chipped rotor tooth or a jammed rotor (one tooth) is detected, or if sensor output is low due to a defective sensor and warped rotor and continuous anti-lock braking occurs. Also, they show that there is a request of brake fluid pressure control with the stop light switch OFF from when the vehicle is stationary until the vehicle speed exceeds approximately 15 km/h (9.3 mph). If the vehicle repeats start and stop and the condition above is detected five times, the ABS warning light will illuminate. [Hint] There is a strong chance that the wheel speed sensor output is low due to a bent rotor tooth or excessive sensor gap. Low sensor output could also be caused by a rare short in the sensor coil.	• Improper installation of wheel speed sensor • Malfunction of wheel speed sensor • Malfunction of rotor • Malfunction of wheel bearing • Shortcircuited harness wire • Malfunction of ABS-ECU

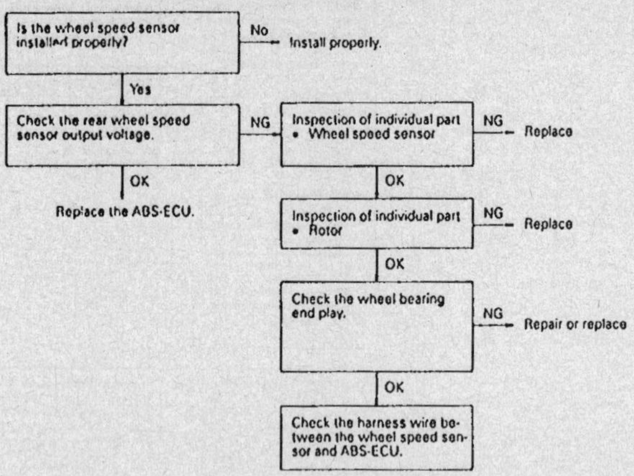

Is the wheel speed sensor installed properly?
No
Install properly.
Yes
Check the rear wheel speed sensor output voltage.
NG
Inspection of individual part
• Wheel speed sensor
NG
Replace
OK
Replace the ABS-ECU.
OK
Inspection of individual part
• Rotor
NG
Replace
OK
Check the wheel bearing end play.
NG
Repair or replace
OK
Check the harness wire between the wheel speed sensor and ABS-ECU.

MT4029100127000X

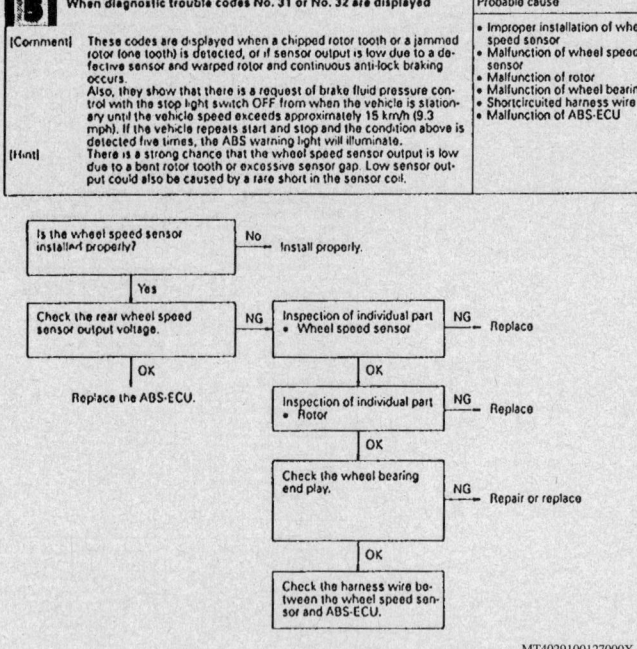

Fig. 201 Codes 31 & 32: Front Wheel Speed Sensor Rotors. Mirage

When diagnostic trouble code No. 16 is displayed	Probable cause
[Comment] This indicates that the ABS-ECU power voltage is lower than the standard value. If the voltage returns to standard voltage or above, this diagnostic trouble code will not be output.	• Disconnected connector. • Malfunction of battery or generator • Malfunction of ABS-ECU

Caution
If the battery voltage drops during inspection, this code will be output as a current problem, and correct diagnosis of the problem cannot be made.
Before carrying out the following inspection, check the battery level, and refill it if necessary.

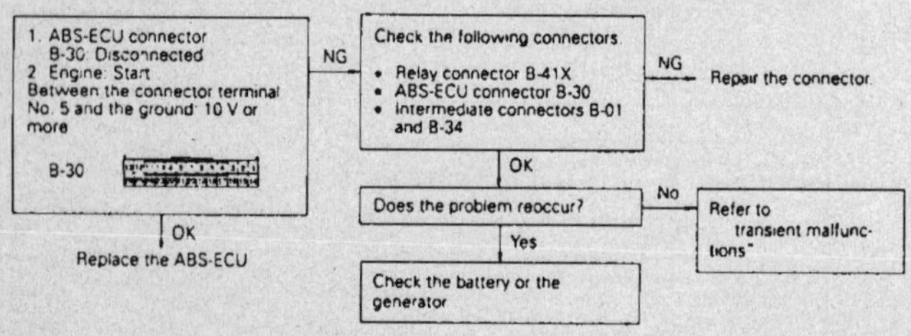

1. ABS-ECU connector B-30: Disconnected
2. Engine: Start
Between the connector terminal No. 5 and the ground: 10 V or more
B-30
NG
Check the following connectors.
• Relay connector B-41X
• ABS-ECU connector B-30
• Intermediate connectors B-01 and B-34
NG
Repair the connector.
OK
Replace the ABS-ECU
OK
Does the problem reoccur?
No
Refer to transient malfunctions"
Yes
Check the battery or the generator

When diagnostic trouble code No. 35 is displayed	Probable cause
[Comment] This indicates that the output voltage of the generator L terminal is low when the ignition key is turned to "ON" and the engine is stopped, or when the engine is running. If the voltage returns to standard voltage or above, this problem code will not be output. [Hint] When the output voltage of the generator L terminal is low, the charge warning light will illuminate. This code also appears when there is a short in the generator L terminal monitor circuit, but not if there is a open circuit in that circuit. If the scan tool service data displays No 35, this diagnostic trouble code is output.	• Incorrectly connected connector, shortcircuited harness wire. • Malfunction of generator • Malfunction of ABS-ECU

NOTE
If the engine is stopped, this code will be output, even if the situation is normal, so the following inspection should only be carried out if the code is output while the engine is running.

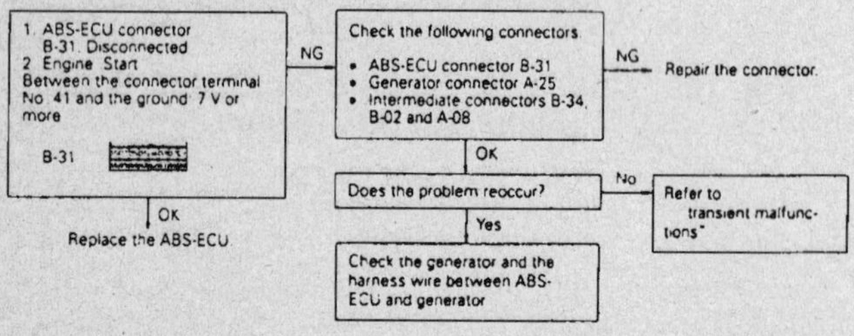

1. ABS-ECU connector B-31: Disconnected
2. Engine: Start
Between the connector terminal No. 41 and the ground: 7 V or more
B-31
NG
Check the following connectors.
• ABS-ECU connector B-31
• Generator connector A-25
• Intermediate connectors B-34, B-02 and A-08
NG
Repair the connector.
OK
Replace the ABS-ECU.
OK
Does the problem reoccur?
No
Refer to transient malfunctions"
Yes
Check the generator and the harness wire between ABS-ECU and generator

MT4029100128000X

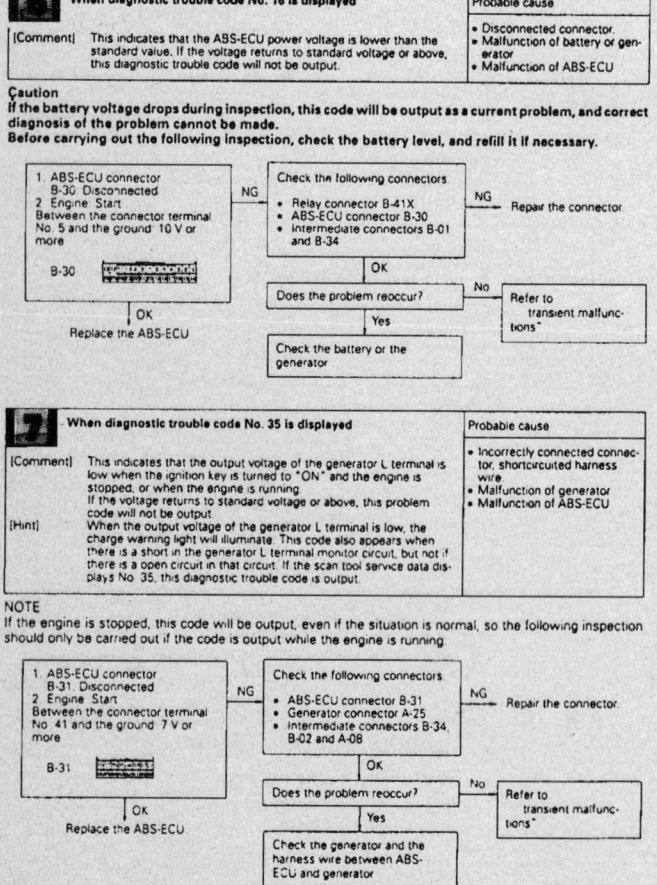

Fig. 202 Codes 16 & 35: Drop Of Battery Voltage & Drop Of Generator Output Voltage. Mirage

When diagnostic trouble codes No. 41, No. 42, No. 43 or No. 44 are displayed	Probable cause
[Comment] The ABS-ECU normally monitors the solenoid valve drive circuit. If there is no current flowing to the solenoid even when the solenoid is ON, or the current continues to flow to the solenoid even when the solenoid is OFF, the ABS-ECU diagnoses a open circuit or short in the solenoid coil or a open circuit or short in the harness, and this diagnostic trouble code is output.	• Malfunction of hydraulic unit • Broken wire, disconnected connector • Shortcircuited harness wire • Malfunction of ABS-ECU

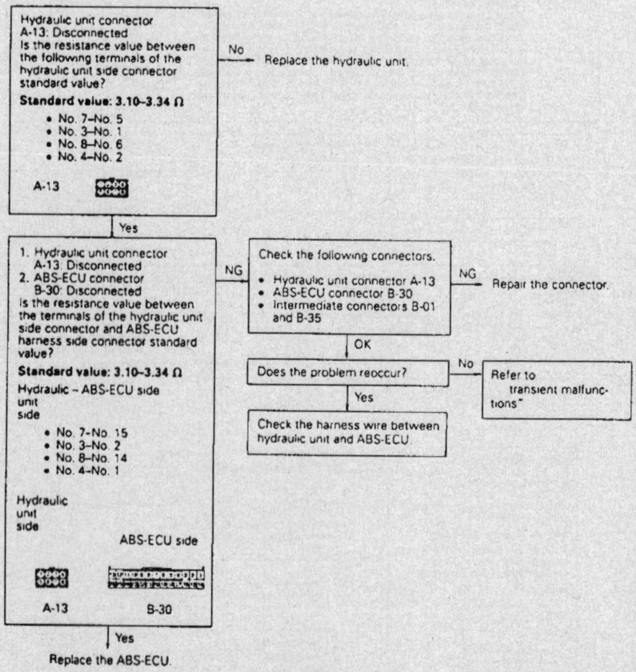

Hydraulic unit connector A-13: Disconnected
Is the resistance value between the following terminals of the hydraulic unit side connector standard value?
Standard value: 3.10–3.34 Ω
• No. 7–No. 5
• No. 3–No. 1
• No. 8–No. 6
• No. 4–No. 2
A-13
No
Replace the hydraulic unit.
Yes
1. Hydraulic unit connector A-13: Disconnected
2. ABS-ECU connector B-30: Disconnected
Is the resistance value between the terminals of the hydraulic unit side connector and ABS-ECU harness side connector standard value?
Standard value: 3.10–3.34 Ω
Hydraulic unit side – ABS-ECU side
• No. 7-No. 15
• No. 3–No. 2
• No. 8–No. 14
• No. 4–No. 1
Hydraulic unit side
ABS-ECU side
A-13
B-30
NG
Check the following connectors.
• Hydraulic unit connector A-13
• ABS-ECU connector B-30
• Intermediate connectors B-01 and B-35
NG
Repair the connector.
OK
Does the problem reoccur?
No
Refer to transient malfunctions"
Yes
Check the harness wire between hydraulic unit and ABS-ECU.
Yes
Replace the ABS-ECU.

MT4029100129000X

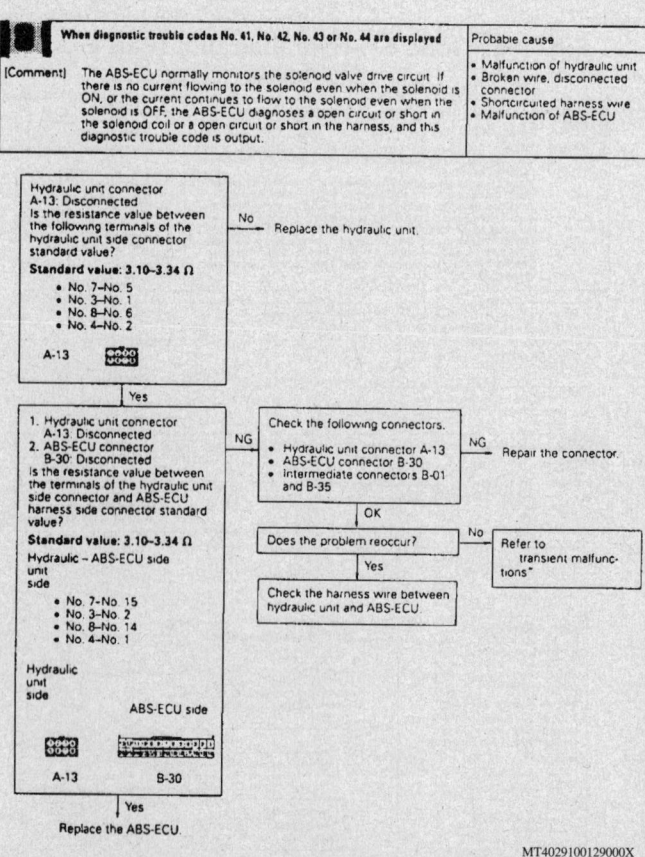

Fig. 203 Codes 41, 42, 43 & 44: Solenoid Valves. Mirage

9 When diagnostic trouble code No. 51 is displayed

	Probable cause
[Comment] During the initial check when the ignition switch is turned to "ON", if power is being supplied to the solenoid when the valve relay is OFF, the ABS-ECU diagnoses a melted relay contact or a short in the valve relay drive circuit, and this diagnostic trouble code is output.	• Malfunction of ABS valve relay • Shortcircuited harness wire • Malfunction of ABS-ECU

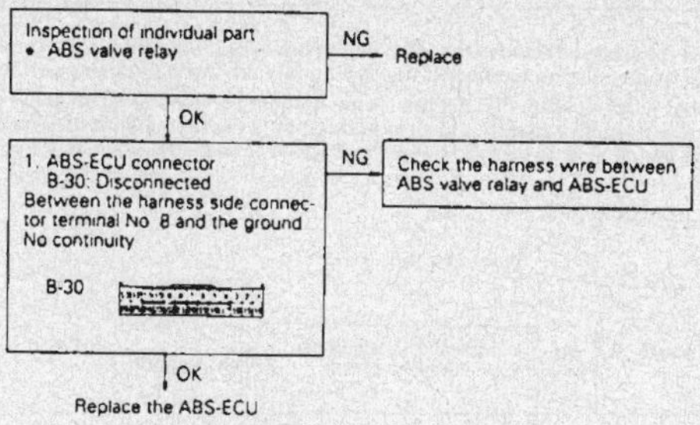
Inspection of individual part
• ABS valve relay
NG
Replace
OK
1. ABS-ECU connector B-30: Disconnected
Between the harness side connector terminal No. 8 and the ground
No continuity
B-30
NG
Check the harness wire between ABS valve relay and ABS-ECU
OK
Replace the ABS-ECU

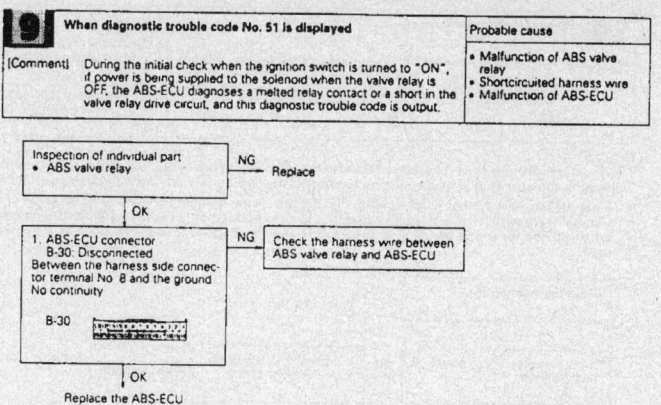

MT4029100130000X

Fig. 204 Code 51: Valve Relay No. 1. Mirage

10 When diagnostic trouble code No. 52 is displayed

	Probable cause
[Comment] During the initial check when the ignition switch is turned to "ON", if power is not being supplied to the solenoid when the valve relay is ON, the ABS-ECU diagnoses an OFF problem in the valve relay (not turned ON), and outputs this diagnostic trouble code.	• Malfunction of ABS valve relay • Broken wire, disconnected connector • Malfunction of ABS-ECU

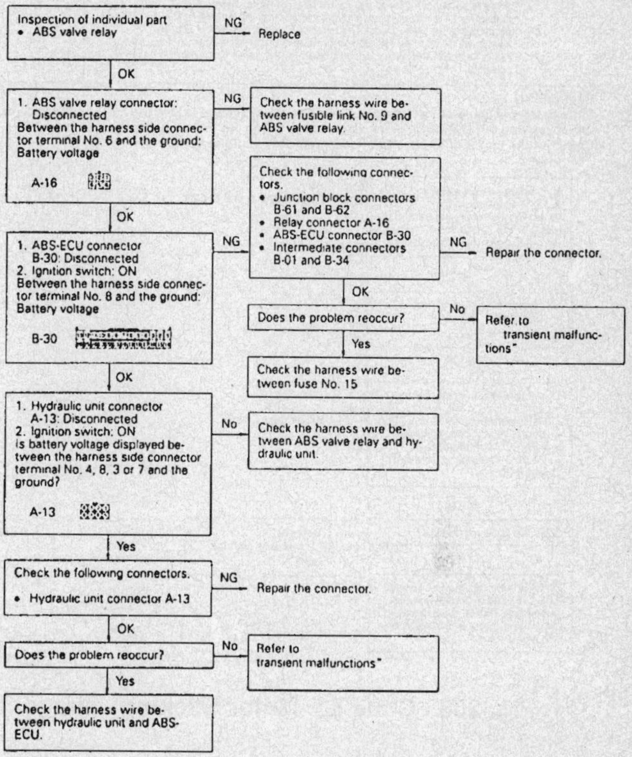
Inspection of individual part
• ABS valve relay
NG
Replace
OK
1. ABS valve relay connector: Disconnected
Between the harness side connector terminal No. 6 and the ground: Battery voltage
A-16
NG
Check the harness wire between fusible link No. 9 and ABS valve relay.
OK
1. ABS-ECU connector B-30: Disconnected
2. Ignition switch: ON
Between the harness side connector terminal No. 8 and the ground: Battery voltage
B-30
NG
Check the following connectors.
• Junction block connectors B-61 and B-62
• Relay connector A-16
• ABS-ECU connector B-30
• Intermediate connectors B-01 and B-34
NG
Repair the connector.
OK
Does the problem reoccur?
No
Refer to transient malfunctions"
Yes
Check the harness wire between fuse No. 15
OK
1. Hydraulic unit connector A-13: Disconnected
2. Ignition switch: ON
Is battery voltage displayed between the harness side connector terminal No. 4, 8, 3 or 7 and the ground?
A-13
No
Check the harness wire between ABS valve relay and hydraulic unit.
Yes
Check the following connectors.
• Hydraulic unit connector A-13
NG
Repair the connector.
OK
Does the problem reoccur?
No
Refer to transient malfunctions"
Yes
Check the harness wire between hydraulic unit and ABS-ECU.

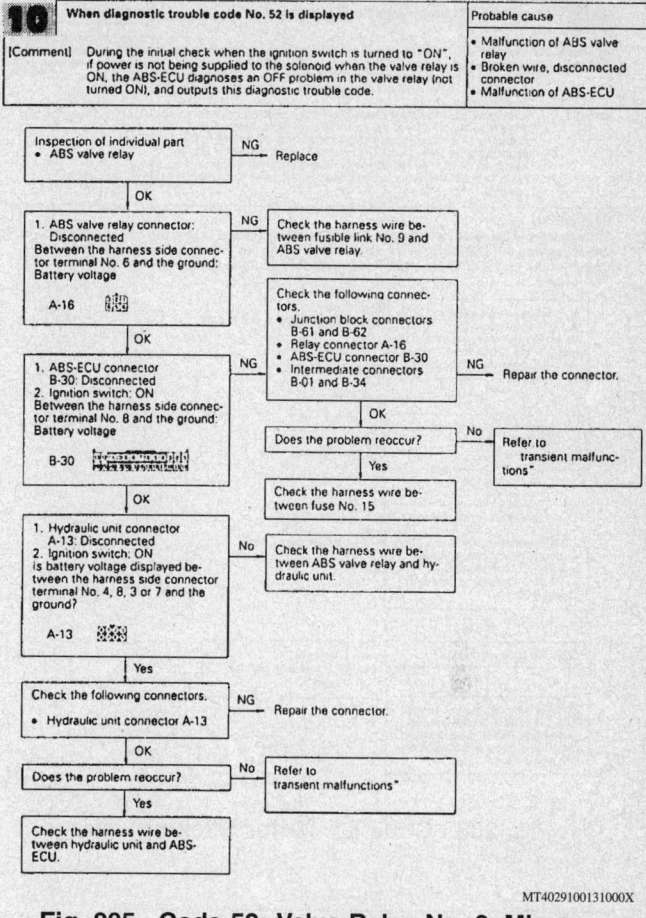

MT4029100131000X

Fig. 205 Code 52: Valve Relay No. 2. Mirage

11 When diagnostic trouble code No. 53 is displayed

	Probable cause
[Comment] When the motor pump receives a signal to turn ON and voltage at the motor monitor is LOW, the ABS-ECU outputs this diagnostic trouble code. [Hint] If the sound of the motor relay operation can be heard when the No. 6 motor relay is driven by a scan tool actuator test, there is probably a short in the motor monitor wire.	• Malfunction of ABS motor relay • Defective harness wire, disconnected connector • Malfunction of ABS-ECU

Caution
In the case of actuator test No. 06, the engine should be started left running for a while after the test is completed to prevent the battery from being drained.

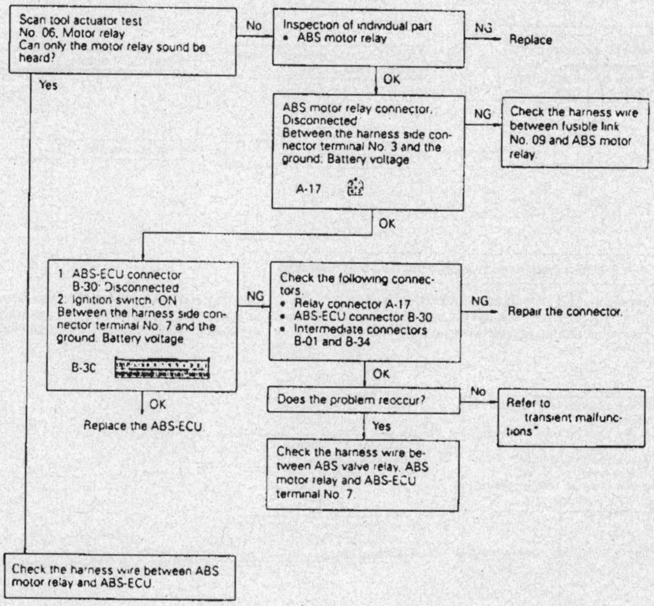
Scan tool actuator test No. 06, Motor relay
Can only the motor relay sound be heard?
No
Inspection of individual part
• ABS motor relay
NG
Replace
OK
ABS motor relay connector, Disconnected
Between the harness side connector terminal No. 3 and the ground: Battery voltage
A-17
NG
Check the harness wire between fusible link No. 09 and ABS motor relay.
OK
1. ABS-ECU connector B-30: Disconnected
2. Ignition switch: ON
Between the harness side connector terminal No. 7 and the ground. Battery voltage
B-30
NG
Check the following connectors.
• Relay connector A-17
• ABS-ECU connector B-30
• Intermediate connectors B-01 and B-34
NG
Repair the connector.
OK
Does the problem reoccur?
No
Refer to transient malfunctions"
Yes
Check the harness wire between ABS valve relay, ABS motor relay and ABS-ECU terminal No. 7.
OK
Replace the ABS-ECU
Yes
Check the harness wire between ABS motor relay and ABS-ECU.

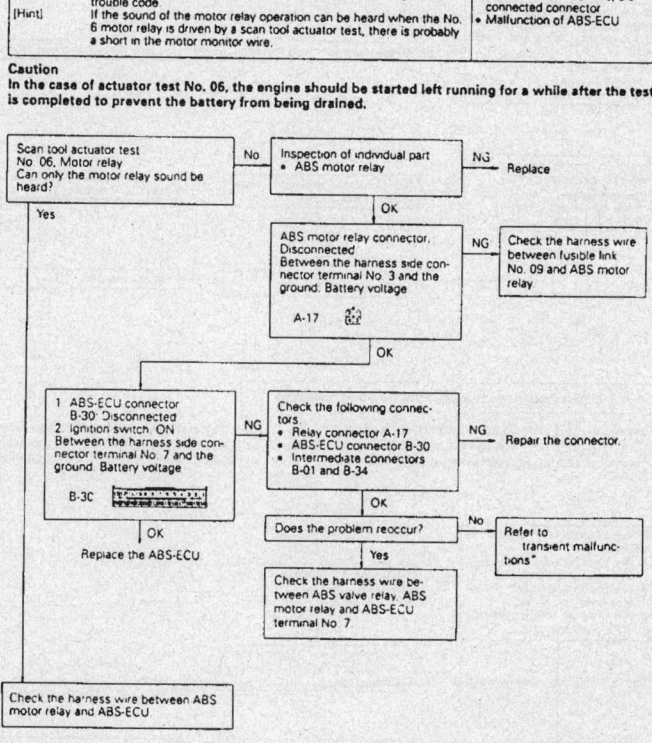

MT4029100132000X

Fig. 206 Code 53: Motor Relay No. 1. Mirage

12 When diagnostic trouble code No. 54 is displayed

	Probable cause
[Comment] When the pump motor receives a signal to turn OFF and the motor monitor is ON, if a melted contact, etc. is diagnosed in the motor relay, the ABS-ECU outputs this diagnostic trouble code. [Hint] Because the motor monitor wire is pulled up into the ABS-ECU by the IG power, this diagnostic trouble code is output if there is a open circuit in the harness, even if the motor relay and the motor are normal.	• Malfunction of ABS motor relay • Malfunction of hydraulic unit • Broken wire, disconnected connector • Malfunction of ABS-ECU

Caution
If there is a melted contact in the motor relay, the motor will keep turning, even if the ignition switch is turned to OFF. In such a case, immediately remove the fusible link (60 A) or disconnect the hydraulic unit A-12 connector. Excessive running of the motor will consume a battery.

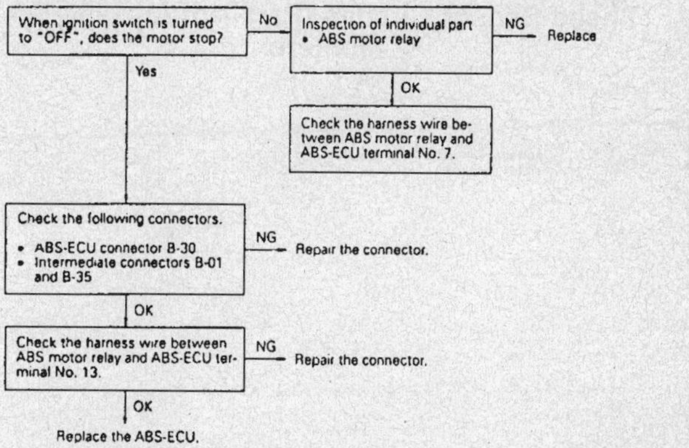
When ignition switch is turned to "OFF", does the motor stop?
No
Inspection of individual part
• ABS motor relay
NG
Replace
OK
Check the harness wire between ABS motor relay and ABS-ECU terminal No. 7.
Yes
Check the following connectors.
• ABS-ECU connector B-30
• Intermediate connectors B-01 and B-35
NG
Repair the connector.
OK
Check the harness wire between ABS motor relay and ABS-ECU terminal No. 13.
NG
Repair the connector.
OK
Replace the ABS-ECU.

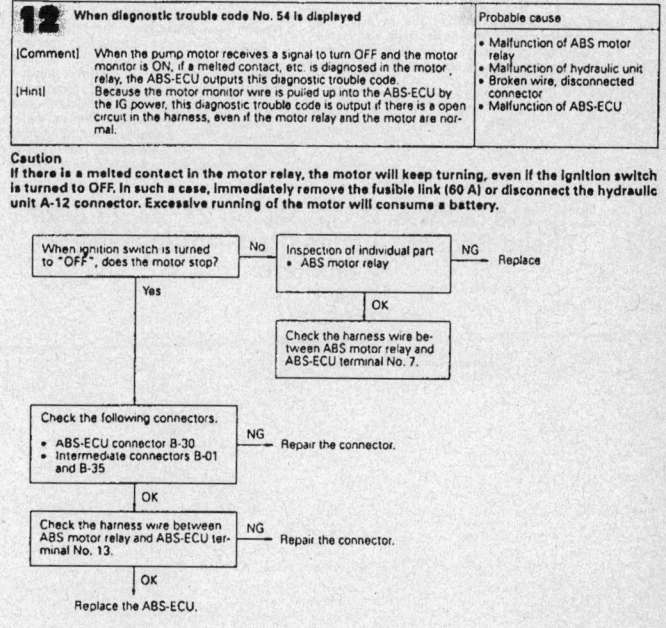

MT4029100133000X

Fig. 207 Code 54: Motor Relay No. 2. Mirage

13 When diagnostic trouble code No. 55 is displayed	Probable cause
[Comment] The ABS-ECU drives the motor after the initial check, and if the motor is diagnosed as not running normally, the motor is driven again when the vehicle speed is 10 km/h (6.2 mph). If the motor operation is diagnosed as not normal at this time also, this diagnostic trouble code is output. [Hint] It is possible for this diagnostic trouble code to be output when there is an abnormality in the motor relay or motor harnesses. If the noise from the motor is not heard after starting the engine without depressing the brake pedal, the rotating shaft of the motor is probably stuck. When the No. 06 motor relay is driven by a scan tool actuator test and the motor doesn't operate, the same judgement is possible.	• Malfunction of hydraulic unit • Bad contact of connector • Defective harness wire

Caution
If the battery is depleted or if the generator L terminal voltage is low, the motor will not be driven, so when carrying out the motor drive check, check to be sure that these things are normal.
Carry out the motor drive check while the vehicle is stationary.

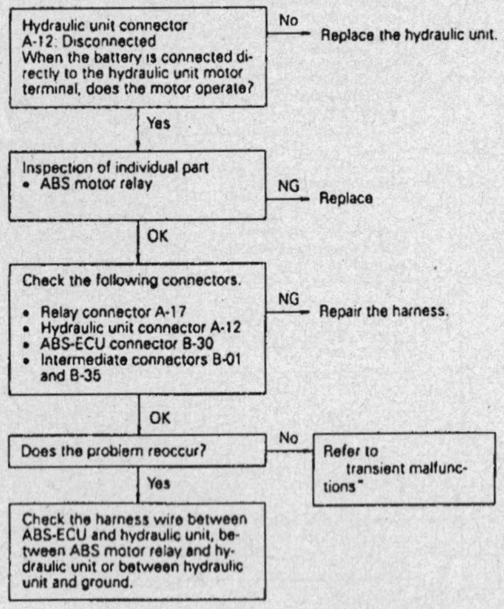

Hydraulic unit connector A-12: Disconnected When the battery is connected directly to the hydraulic unit motor terminal, does the motor operate?
No
Replace the hydraulic unit.
Yes
Inspection of individual part • ABS motor relay
NG
Replace
OK
Check the following connectors.
• Relay connector A-17
• Hydraulic unit connector A-12
• ABS-ECU connector B-30
• Intermediate connectors B-01 and B-35
NG
Repair the harness.
OK
Does the problem reoccur?
No
Refer to transient malfunctions"
Yes
Check the harness wire between ABS-ECU and hydraulic unit, between ABS motor relay and hydraulic unit or between hydraulic unit and ground.

MT4029100134000X

Fig. 208 Code 55: Motor Sticking. Mirage

14 When diagnostic trouble code No. 62 is displayed	Probable cause
[Comment] Diagnostic trouble code No. 62 is a diagnostic trouble code that is output when the ABS is unable to operate for a long period of time. However, it is possible that the problem could be caused not only by a faulty hydraulic unit, but also by a malfunctioning wheel speed sensor.	• Malfunction of hydraulic unit • Malfunction of wheel speed sensor • Malfunction of rotor • Foreign material adhered to wheel speed sensor • Malfunction of wheel bearing

Caution
The diagnostic trouble code No. 62 is detected in the following cases, even if the ABS system is normal. To be sure, the user should be questioned to check if the appropriate driving is not being carried out.

- **If the parking brake is not fully released, of if the brakes are dragging while driving on snow or ice.**
- **When driving with left and right tires of different sizes (difference in tire diameter or uneven wear).**
- **When driving for a long period of time on roads with low friction coefficients, such as ice-covered roads.**

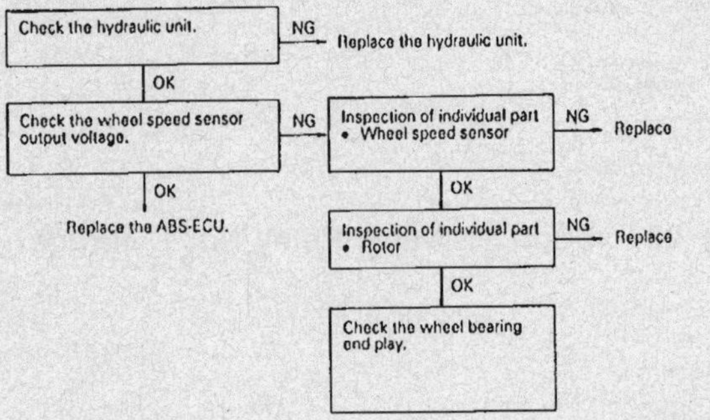

Check the hydraulic unit.
NG
Replace the hydraulic unit.
OK
Check the wheel speed sensor output voltage.
NG
Inspection of individual part • Wheel speed sensor
NG
Replace
OK
Replace the ABS-ECU.
OK
Inspection of individual part • Rotor
NG
Replace
OK
Check the wheel bearing end play.

MT4029100135000X

Fig. 209 Code 62: Hydraulic Unit. Mirage

E-1	When diagnostic trouble code no.11, 12, 13, or 14 are displayed

[Comment] These codes are displayed when there is a broken (+) wire or (-) wire in one of the vehicle speed sensors detected by the ABS-ECU hardware circuit.

(Hint) Apart from a broken wire in a vehicle speed sensor, the cause could also be an intermittent break in a sensor harness or a defective harness connection, so check these also.

NOTE
1. When there is a defective contact, inspect the sensor cable by lightly flexing and stretching it.
2. If there is no current problem, a normal value will result even if a problem is detected, so when the malfunction in the sensor circuit indicated cannot be discovered, momentarily turn the ignition switch to OFF, and carry out another driving test. At this time, replace the ABS-ECU only if the same diagnostic trouble code is output. After this, if the code does not reappear, there is a problem with the ABS-ECU interface. (For a problem that is difficult to reproduce, there is a possibility that the code will recur even when the ABS-ECU is replaced.)

MT4029100145010X

Fig. 210 Codes 11, 12, 13, 14, 21, 22, 23 & 24: Speed Sensor Circuits (Part 1 of 4). 1993–95 Montero

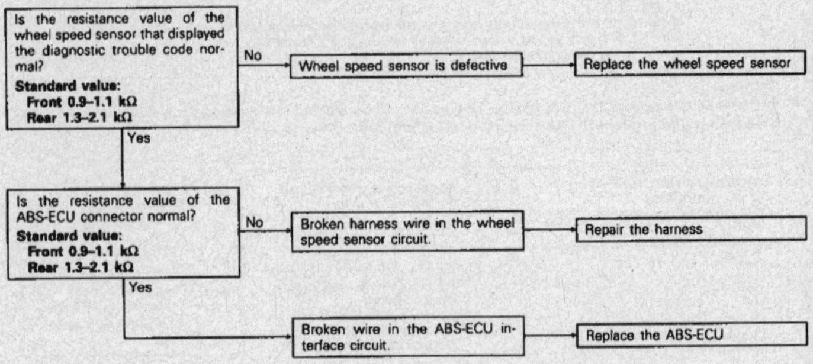

Is the resistance value of the wheel speed sensor that displayed the diagnostic trouble code normal?
Standard value:
Front 0.9–1.1 kΩ
Rear 1.3–2.1 kΩ
No
Wheel speed sensor is defective
Replace the wheel speed sensor
Yes
Is the resistance value of the ABS-ECU connector normal?
Standard value:
Front 0.9–1.1 kΩ
Rear 1.3–2.1 kΩ
No
Broken harness wire in the wheel speed sensor circuit.
Repair the harness
Yes
Broken wire in the ABS-ECU interface circuit.
Replace the ABS-ECU

E-2	When diagnostic trouble code no.15 is displayed

[Comment] This diagnostic trouble code is output when any one of the wheel speed sensor output signals during driving is abnormal.

(Hint) The cause of the abnormal wheel speed sensor output could be noise in the sensor signal from a loose wheel speed sensor.

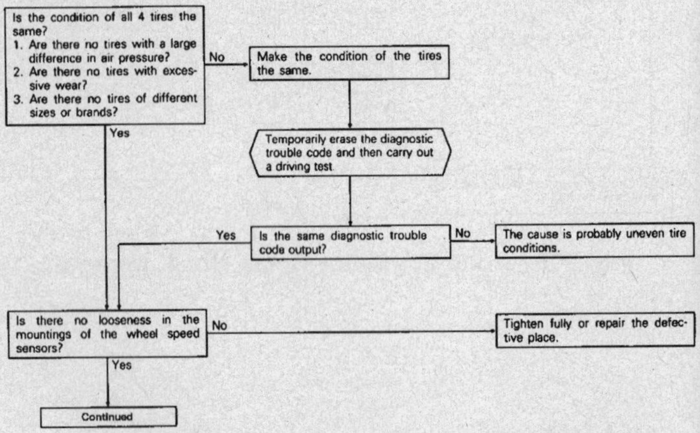

Is the condition of all 4 tires the same?
1. Are there no tires with a large difference in air pressure?
2. Are there no tires with excessive wear?
3. Are there no tires of different sizes or brands?
No
Make the condition of the tires the same.
Yes
Temporarily erase the diagnostic trouble code and then carry out a driving test.
Yes
Is the same diagnostic trouble code output?
No
The cause is probably uneven tire conditions.
Is there no looseness in the mountings of the wheel speed sensors?
No
Tighten fully or repair the defective place.
Yes
Continued

MT4029100145020X

Fig. 210 Codes 11, 12, 13, 14, 21, 22, 23 & 24: Speed Sensor Circuits (Part 2 of 4). 1993–95 Montero

From previous

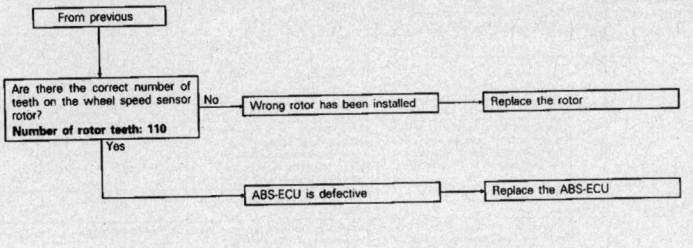

Are there the correct number of teeth on the wheel speed sensor rotor?
Number of rotor teeth: 110

- No → Wrong rotor has been installed → Replace the rotor
- Yes → ABS-ECU is defective → Replace the ABS-ECU

E-3 When diagnostic trouble code no.21, 22, 23 or 24 is displayed

[Comment] These diagnostic trouble codes are displayed when a broken wire cannot be verified, and when the vehicle speed reaches 8 km/h (5 mph) or more, no pulses are input.

(Hint) The cause is likely to be either a short between the sensor harnesses, a short between the sensor (+) wire and the body, or an excessive sensor gap.

NOTE

(1) When there is a defective contact, inspect the sensor cable by lightly flexing and stretching it.

(2) If there is no current problem, a normal value will result even if a problem is detected, so when the malfunction in the sensor circuit indicated cannot be discovered, momentarily erase the diagnostic trouble code and turn the ignition switch to OFF, and carry out another driving test. At this time, replace the ABS-ECU only if the same diagnostic trouble code is output. After this, if the code does not reappear, there is a problem with the ABS-ECU interface. (For a problem that is difficult to reproduce, there is a possibility that the code will recur even when the ABS-ECU is replaced.)

Is the resistance value of the wheel speed sensor that shows a diagnostic trouble code normal?
Standard value:
Front 0.9–1.1 kΩ
Rear 1.3–2.1 kΩ

- No → Wheel speed sensor is defective → Replace the wheel speed sensor
- Yes ↓

Is the resistance value of the ABS-ECU connector normal?
Standard value:
Front 0.9–1.1 kΩ
Rear 1.3–2.1 kΩ

- No → Broken wire in the wheel speed sensor circuit harness → Repair the harness
- Yes ↓

Continued

MT4029100145030X

Fig. 210 Codes 11, 12, 13, 14, 21, 22, 23 & 24: Speed Sensor Circuits (Part 3 of 4). 1993–95 Montero

E-4 When diagnostic trouble code no.16 is displayed

[Comment] This indicates that the ABS-ECU power voltage or the solenoid valve power voltage is lower than the standard value.
If the voltage returns to standard voltage or above, this diagnostic trouble code will not be output.

Caution
If the battery positive voltage drops during inspection, this code will be output as a current problem, and correct diagnostic of the problem cannot be made. Before carrying out the following inspection, check the battery, and charge it if necessary.

When the engine is running, does a voltage of 10V or more show between the ABS-ECU power terminal no. 6 and the ground?

- No → Check that there are no defective contacts in the fusible link or in each connector
- Yes ↓

When the engine is running, does a voltage of 10V or more show between the ABS-ECU solenoid valve voltage monitor terminal no. 62 and the ground?

- No → Check that there are no defective contacts in the fusible link or in each connector
- Yes ↓

Is the ABS-ECU connection normal? (When the connector is disconnected, check if there are no bends in the pins, or that contact pressure is sufficient.)

- No → Repair the ABS-ECU connector
- Yes → ABS-ECU is defective → Replace the ABS-ECU

MT4029100146000X

Fig. 211 Code 16: ECU Power Voltage. 1993–95 Montero

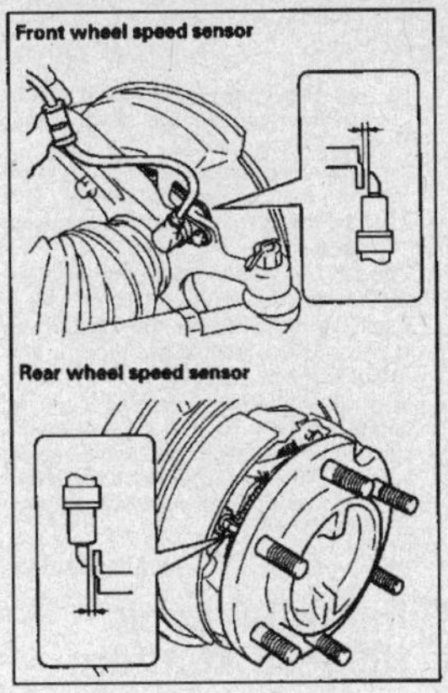

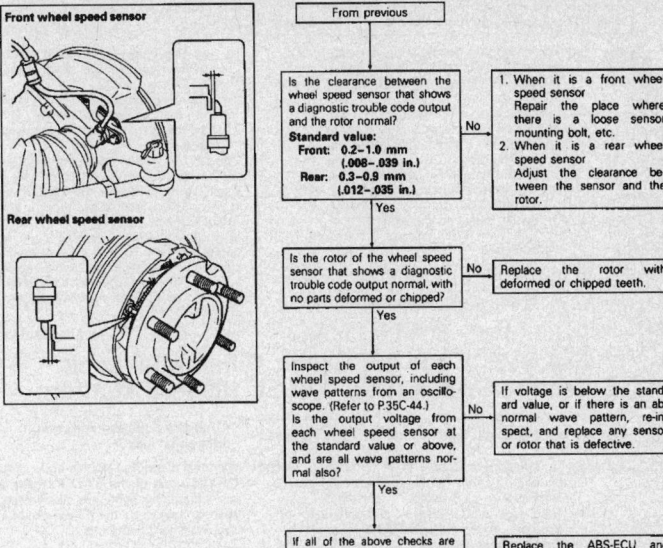

Front wheel speed sensor
Rear wheel speed sensor

From previous

Is the clearance between the wheel speed sensor that shows a diagnostic trouble code output and the rotor normal?
Standard value:
Front: 0.2–1.0 mm (.008–.039 in.)
Rear: 0.3–0.9 mm (.012–.035 in.)

- No → 1. When it is a front wheel speed sensor: Repair the place where there is a loose sensor mounting bolt, etc. 2. When it is a rear wheel speed sensor: Adjust the clearance between the sensor and the rotor.
- Yes ↓

Is the rotor of the wheel speed sensor that shows a diagnostic trouble code output normal, with no parts deformed or chipped?

- No → Replace the rotor with deformed or chipped teeth.
- Yes ↓

Inspect the output of each wheel speed sensor, including wave patterns from an oscilloscope. (Refer to P.35C-44.)
Is the output voltage from each wheel speed sensor at the standard value or above, and are all wave patterns normal also?

- No → If voltage is below the standard value, or if there is an abnormal wave pattern, re-inspect, and replace any sensor or rotor that is defective.
- Yes ↓

If all of the above checks are normal and this diagnostic trouble code reappears frequently, then the ABS-ECU is defective. → Replace the ABS-ECU and check if the problem doesn't recur.

MT4029100145040X

Fig. 210 Codes 11, 12, 13, 14, 21, 22, 23 & 24: Speed Sensor Circuits (Part 4 of 4). 1993–95 Montero

E-5 When diagnostic trouble code no. 25 is displayed

[Comment] This diagnostic trouble code is output by the ABS-ECU when there is a broken harness wire or defective 4WD indicator circuit in the free-wheel engage switch (thick wire in center of circuit diagram).

(Hint) When this diagnostic trouble code is output, and also none of the 4WD indicator lights (excluding the rear differential light) are illuminated, the cause is likely to be the power circuit in the 4WD indicator control unit.

Is the operation of the 4WD indicator light (center differential light) normal?

- No → Broken harness wire (thick wire) between the 4WD indicator control unit and the free-wheel indicator switch, power circuit of the 4WD indicator control unit or 4WD indicator control unit is defective → Repair the harness or replace the 4WD indicator control unit
- Yes ↓

Inspect with the engine running

When the ABS-ECU connector is removed, is the voltage between the harness-side connector terminal no.55 and the ground normal?
For 2WD: battery positive voltage
For 4WD: 0V

- No → Broken harness wire (thick wire) between the ABS-ECU and the free-wheel engage switch → Repair the harness
- Yes → ABS-ECU is defective → Replace the ABS-ECU

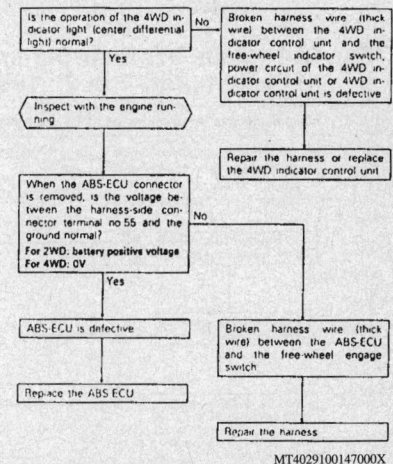

MT4029100147000X

Fig. 212 Code 25: Free Wheel Engage Switch. 1993–95 Montero

E-6	When diagnostic trouble code no. 26 is displayed

(Comment) This diagnostic trouble code is output by the ABS-ECU in the following cases:

- Broken harness wire (thick wire) in the center differential lock detection switch system
- At a vehicle speed of 15 km (9 mph) or higher, the free-wheel engage switch is OFF and the center differential lock switch is ON for a continuous period of 5 seconds or more (Combination switch signal abnormality)
- When the 4WD indicator circuit is defective

(Hint) 1. A combination switch signal abnormality occurs at the following times:

- Broken harness wire (thick wire) in the free-wheel engage switch system or defective switch (stays OFF)
- Short in harness wire (thick wire) in the center differential lock switch system or defective switch (stays ON)

The above malfunctions are also affected by the 4WD indicator, so it might be the case that the malfunction is caused by a trouble symptom in the 4WD indicator.

2. When this diagnostic trouble code is output, and also none of the 4WD indicator lights (excluding the rear differential light) are illuminated, the cause is likely to be the power circuit in the 4WD indicator control unit.

MT4029100148010X

Fig. 213 Code 26: Center Differential Lock Detection Switch (Part 1 of 2). 1993–95 Montero

E-7	When diagnostic trouble code no. 27 is displayed

<Vehicles equipped with rear differential lock>

(Comment) This diagnostic trouble code is output by the ABS-ECU when there is a broken harness wire or a defective rear differential lock circuit (thick wire in circuit diagram) in the rear differential lock detection switch system.

(Hint) When this diagnostic trouble code is output, and also none of the 4WD indicator lights (rear differential light) are illuminated, the cause is likely to be the power circuit in the 4WD indicator control unit.

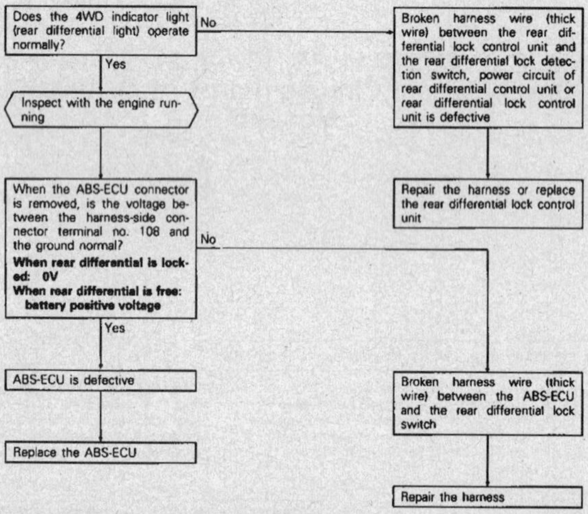

Does the 4WD indicator light (rear differential light) operate normally?
No
Yes
Inspect with the engine running
When the ABS-ECU connector is removed, is the voltage between the harness-side connector terminal no. 108 and the ground normal?
When rear differential is locked: 0V
When rear differential is free: battery positive voltage
No
Yes
ABS-ECU is defective
Replace the ABS-ECU
Broken harness wire (thick wire) between the rear differential lock control unit and the rear differential lock detection switch, power circuit of rear differential control unit or rear differential lock control unit is defective
Repair the harness or replace the rear differential lock control unit
Broken harness wire (thick wire) between the ABS-ECU and the rear differential lock switch
Repair the harness

MT4029100149010X

Fig. 214 Code 27: Rear Differential Lock Detection Switch (Part 1 of 2). 1993–95 Montero

E-8	When diagnostic trouble code no. 31 is displayed

(Comment) This code is displayed when there is an abnormality in the G sensor power voltage (including a short in the G sensor power harness).

(Hint) If there is a short in the G sensor power harness, code no. 32 will be output at the same time as this code.

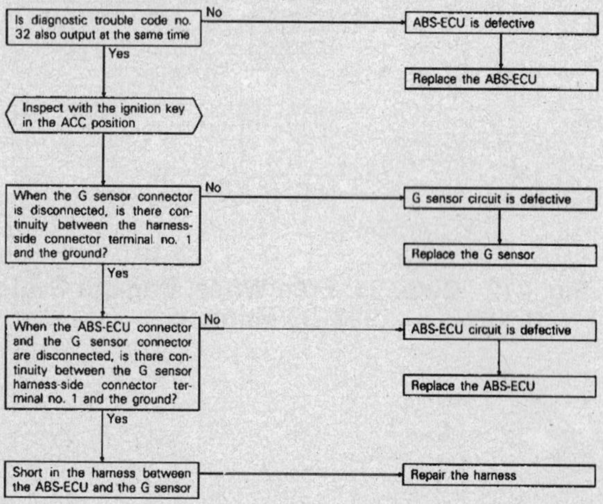

Is diagnostic trouble code no. 32 also output at the same time
No
Yes
ABS-ECU is defective
Replace the ABS-ECU
Inspect with the ignition key in the ACC position
When the G sensor connector is disconnected, is there continuity between the harness-side connector terminal no. 1 and the ground?
No
Yes
G sensor circuit is defective
Replace the G sensor
When the ABS-ECU connector and the G sensor connector are disconnected, is there continuity between the G sensor harness-side connector terminal no. 1 and the ground?
No
Yes
ABS-ECU circuit is defective
Replace the ABS-ECU
Short in the harness between the ABS-ECU and the G sensor
Repair the harness

MT4029100150000X

Fig. 215 Code 31: G Sensor Power Voltage. 1993–95 Montero

Does the 4WD indicator operate normally?

No

Yes

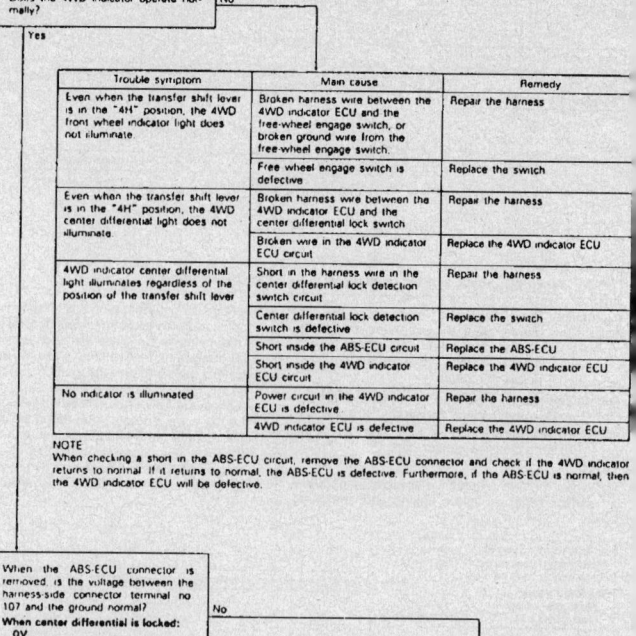

Trouble symptom	Main cause	Remedy
Even when the transfer shift lever is in the "4H" position, the 4WD front wheel indicator light does not illuminate.	Broken harness wire between the 4WD indicator ECU and the free-wheel engage switch, or broken ground wire from the free-wheel engage switch.	Repair the harness
	Free wheel engage switch is defective	Replace the switch
Even when the transfer shift lever is in the "4H" position, the 4WD center differential light does not illuminate.	Broken harness wire between the 4WD indicator ECU and the center differential lock switch	Repair the harness
	Broken wire in the 4WD indicator ECU circuit	Replace the 4WD indicator ECU
4WD indicator center differential light illuminates regardless of the position of the transfer shift lever	Short in the harness wire in the center differential lock detection switch circuit	Repair the harness
	Center differential lock detection switch is defective	Replace the switch
	Short inside the ABS-ECU circuit	Replace the ABS-ECU
	Short inside the 4WD indicator ECU circuit	Replace the 4WD indicator ECU
No indicator is illuminated	Power circuit in the 4WD indicator ECU is defective.	Repair the harness
	4WD indicator ECU is defective	Replace the 4WD indicator ECU

NOTE
When checking a short in the ABS-ECU circuit, remove the ABS-ECU connector and check if the 4WD indicator returns to normal. If it returns to normal, the ABS-ECU is defective. Furthermore, if the ABS-ECU is normal, then the 4WD indicator ECU will be defective.

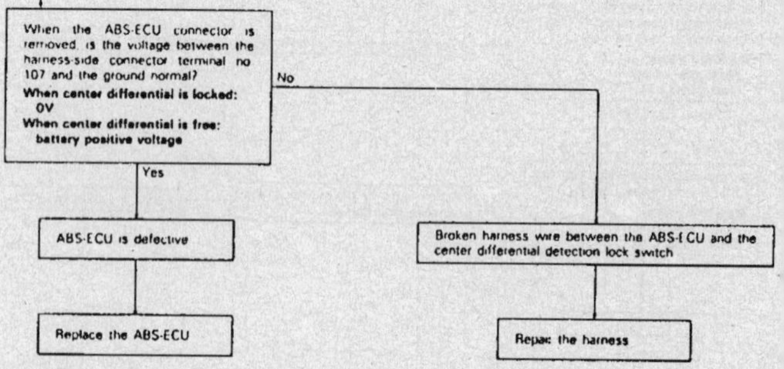

When the ABS-ECU connector is removed, is the voltage between the harness-side connector terminal no 107 and the ground normal?
When center differential is locked: 0V
When center differential is free: battery positive voltage
No
Yes
ABS-ECU is defective
Replace the ABS-ECU
Broken harness wire between the ABS-ECU and the center differential detection lock switch
Repair the harness

MT4029100148020X

Fig. 213 Code 26: Center Differential Lock Detection Switch (Part 2 of 2). 1993–95 Montero

E-7	When diagnostic trouble code no. 27 is displayed

<Vehicles without rear differential lock>

(Comment) For vehicles without rear differential lock, battery positive voltage is applied to the ABS-ECU terminal no. (108). This diagnostic trouble code is output when this line is interrupted.

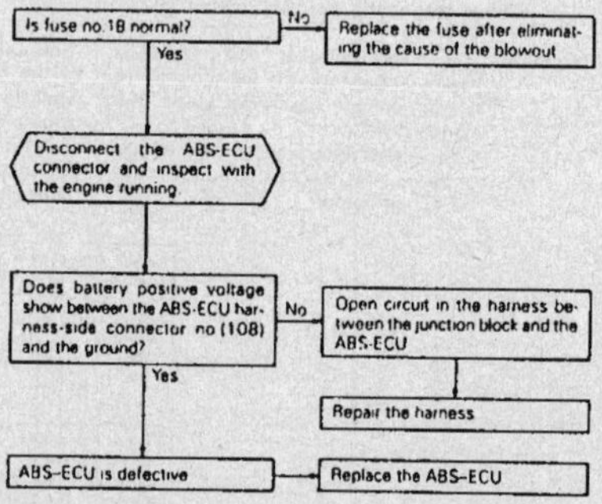

Is fuse no.18 normal?
No
Yes
Replace the fuse after eliminating the cause of the blowout
Disconnect the ABS-ECU connector and inspect with the engine running
Does battery positive voltage show between the ABS-ECU harness-side connector no (108) and the ground?
No
Yes
Open circuit in the harness between the junction block and the ABS-ECU
Repair the harness
ABS-ECU is defective
Replace the ABS-ECU

MT4029100149020X

Fig. 214 Code 27: Rear Differential Lock Detection Switch (Part 2 of 2). 1993–95 Montero

E-9	When diagnostic trouble code no. 32 is displayed

[Comment] This diagnostic trouble code is output when there is an abnormality in the G sensor voltage output. This code is also output when there is a broken wire or short in the G sensor power or signal harness or a broken ground wire.

(Hint) Malfunctions can be distinguished by the G sensor output voltage read by the scan tool service data.

G sensor output voltage (when vehicle is on a horizontal surface)	Main problem location
2.5±0.44V	Normal
0.2V or less	Broken wire or short in the power harness or signal harness
4.8V or more	Broken ground wire
Other than the above	G sensor is defective (including defective installation)

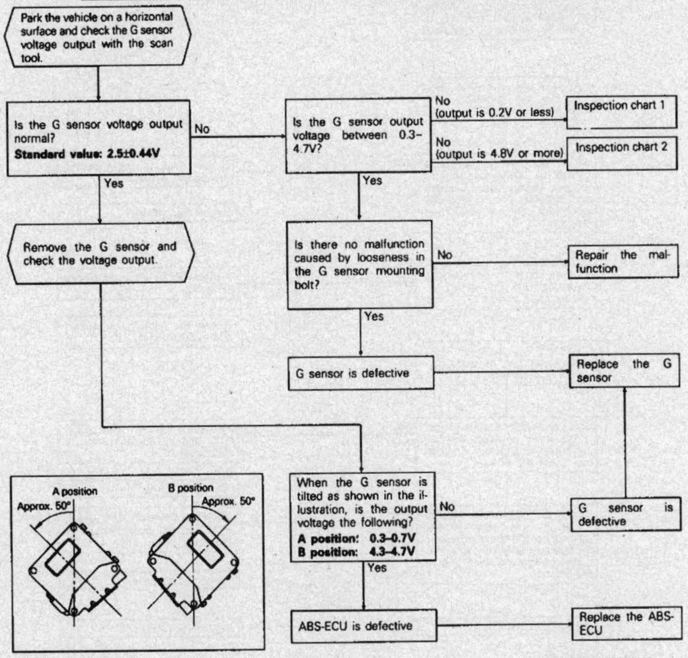

Park the vehicle on a horizontal surface and check the G sensor voltage output with the scan tool.
Is the G sensor voltage output normal? Standard value: 2.5±0.44V
No
Is the G sensor output voltage between 0.3–4.7V?
No (output is 0.2V or less)
Inspection chart 1
No (output is 4.8V or more)
Inspection chart 2
Yes
Yes
Remove the G sensor and check the voltage output.
Is there no malfunction caused by looseness in the G sensor mounting bolt?
No
Repair the malfunction
Yes
G sensor is defective
Replace the G sensor
A position
B position
Approx. 50°
Approx. 50°
When the G sensor is tilted as shown in the illustration, is the output voltage the following? A position: 0.3–0.7V B position: 4.3–4.7V
No
G sensor is defective
Yes
ABS-ECU is defective
Replace the ABS-ECU
MT4029100151010X

Fig. 216 Code 32: G Sensor Output Voltage (Part 1 of 3). 1993–95 Montero

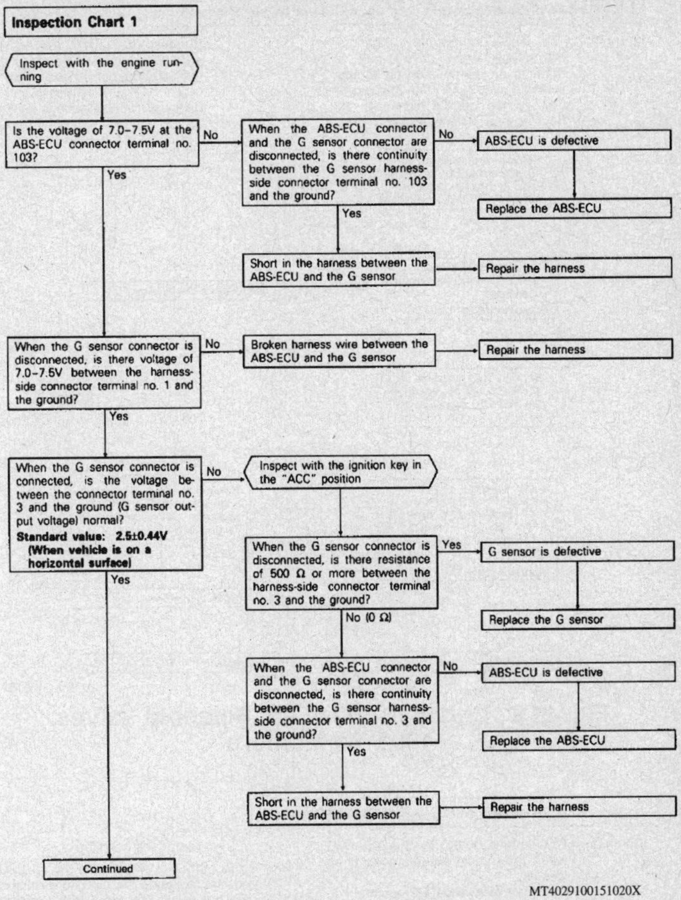

Inspection Chart 1
Inspect with the engine running
Is the voltage of 7.0–7.5V at the ABS-ECU connector terminal no. 103?
No
When the ABS-ECU connector and the G sensor connector are disconnected, is there continuity between the G sensor harness-side connector terminal no. 103 and the ground?
No
ABS-ECU is defective
Replace the ABS-ECU
Yes
Short in the harness between the ABS-ECU and the G sensor
Repair the harness
Yes
When the G sensor connector is disconnected, is there voltage of 7.0–7.5V between the harness-side connector terminal no. 1 and the ground?
No
Broken harness wire between the ABS-ECU and the G sensor
Repair the harness
Yes
When the G sensor connector is connected, is the voltage between the connector terminal no. 3 and the ground (G sensor output voltage) normal? Standard value: 2.5±0.44V (When vehicle is on a horizontal surface)
No
Inspect with the ignition key in the "ACC" position
When the G sensor connector is disconnected, is there resistance of 500 Ω or more between the harness-side connector terminal no. 3 and the ground?
Yes
G sensor is defective
Replace the G sensor
No (0 Ω)
When the ABS-ECU connector and the G sensor connector are disconnected, is there continuity between the G sensor harness-side connector terminal no. 3 and the ground?
No
ABS-ECU is defective
Replace the ABS-ECU
Yes
Short in the harness between the ABS-ECU and the G sensor
Repair the harness
Yes
Continued
MT4029100151020X

Fig. 216 Code 32: G Sensor Output Voltage (Part 2 of 3). 1993–95 Montero

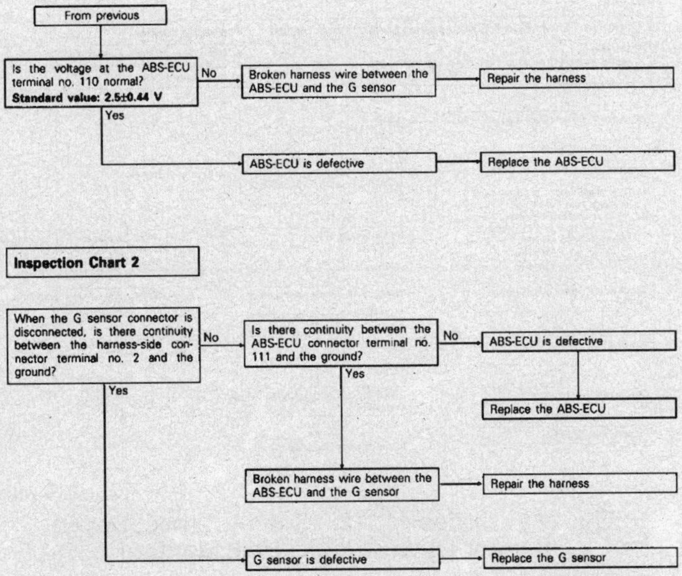

From previous
Is the voltage at the ABS-ECU terminal no. 110 normal? Standard value: 2.5±0.44 V
No
Broken harness wire between the ABS-ECU and the G sensor
Repair the harness
Yes
ABS-ECU is defective
Replace the ABS-ECU
Inspection Chart 2
When the G sensor connector is disconnected, is there continuity between the harness-side connector terminal no. 2 and the ground?
No
Is there continuity between the ABS-ECU connector terminal no. 111 and the ground?
No
ABS-ECU is defective
Replace the ABS-ECU
Yes
Broken harness wire between the ABS-ECU and the G sensor
Repair the harness
Yes
G sensor is defective
Replace the G sensor
MT4029100151030X

Fig. 216 Code 32: G Sensor Output Voltage (Part 3 of 3). 1993–95 Montero

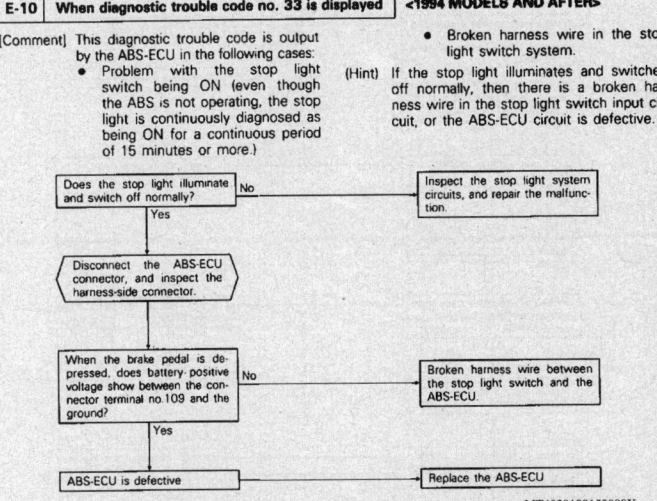

E-10	When diagnostic trouble code no. 33 is displayed

<1994 MODELS AND AFTER>

[Comment] This diagnostic trouble code is output by the ABS-ECU in the following cases:

- Problem with the stop light switch being ON (even though the ABS is not operating, the stop light is continuously diagnosed as being ON for a continuous period of 15 minutes or more.)
- Broken harness wire in the stop light switch system.

(Hint) If the stop light illuminates and switches off normally, then there is a broken harness wire in the stop light switch input circuit, or the ABS-ECU circuit is defective.

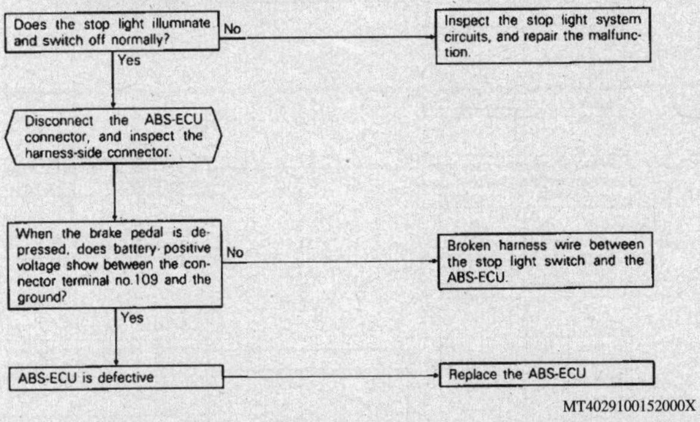

Does the stop light illuminate and switch off normally?
No
Inspect the stop light system circuits, and repair the malfunction.
Yes
Disconnect the ABS-ECU connector, and inspect the harness-side connector.
When the brake pedal is depressed, does battery positive voltage show between the connector terminal no.109 and the ground?
No
Broken harness wire between the stop light switch and the ABS-ECU.
Yes
ABS-ECU is defective
Replace the ABS-ECU
MT4029100152000X

Fig. 217 Code 33: Stop Light Switch. 1993–95 Montero

E-11	When diagnostic trouble code no. 41, 43 or 45 are displayed

[Comment] The ABS-ECU normally monitors the solenoid valve drive circuit. If there is no current flowing to the solenoid even when the solenoid is ON, or the current continues to flow to the solenoid even when the solenoid is OFF, the ABS-ECU diagnoses a broken wire or short in the solenoid coil or a broken wire or short in the harness, and this diagnostic trouble code is output.

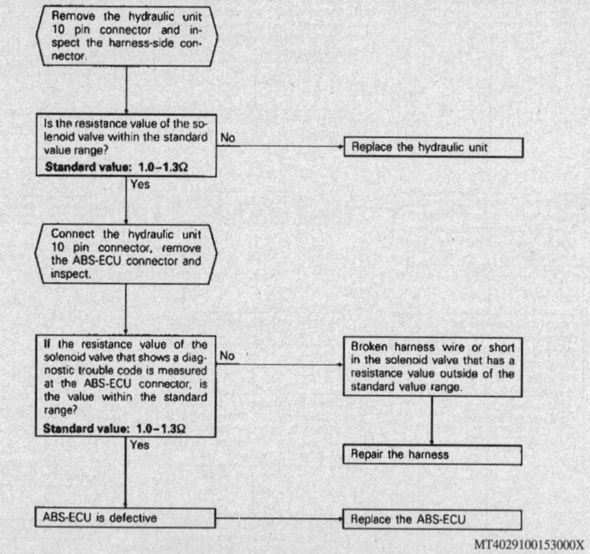

Remove the hydraulic unit 10 pin connector and inspect the harness-side connector.
Is the resistance value of the solenoid valve within the standard value range?
Standard value: 1.0–1.3Ω
No
Replace the hydraulic unit
Yes
Connect the hydraulic unit 10 pin connector, remove the ABS-ECU connector and inspect.
If the resistance value of the solenoid valve that shows a diagnostic trouble code is measured at the ABS-ECU connector, is the value within the standard range?
Standard value: 1.0–1.3Ω
No
Broken harness wire or short in the solenoid valve that has a resistance value outside of the standard value range.
Repair the harness
Yes
ABS-ECU is defective
Replace the ABS-ECU
MT4029100153000X

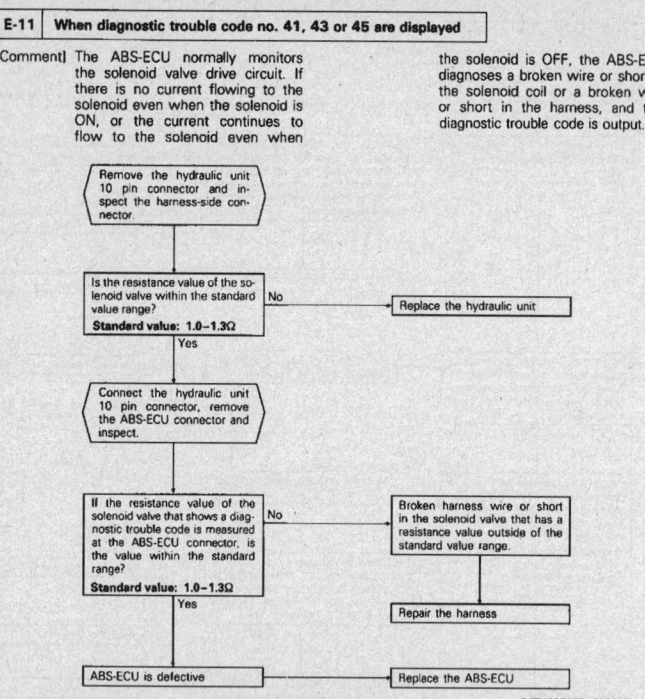

Fig. 218 Codes 41, 43 & 45: Solenoid Valves. 1993–95 Montero

E-12	When diagnostic trouble code no. 51 is displayed

[Comment] When the ignition switch is turned to ON, the valve relay is switched ON and OFF during the initial check, and the ABS-ECU compares the signal to the valve relay and the voltage in the valve power monitor line to check if the valve relay is operating norma Normally, the valve relay is ON, sc power is not being supplied to t valve power monitor line, this diagnos trouble code is output.

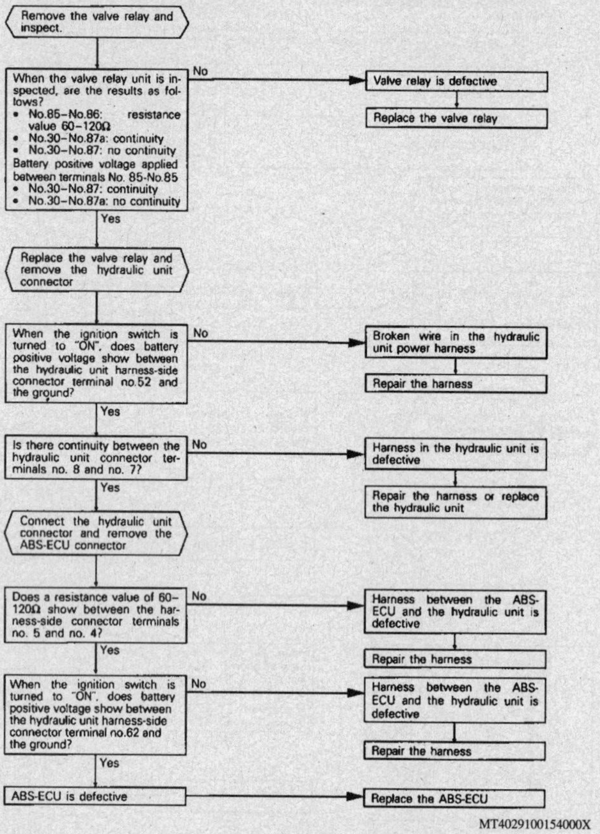

Remove the valve relay and inspect.
When the valve relay unit is inspected, are the results as follows?
• No.85–No.86: resistance value 60–120Ω
• No.30–No.87a: continuity
• No.30–No.87: no continuity
Battery positive voltage applied between terminals No. 85-No.85
• No.30–No.87: continuity
• No.30–No.87a: no continuity
No
Valve relay is defective
Replace the valve relay
Yes
Replace the valve relay and remove the hydraulic unit connector
When the ignition switch is turned to "ON", does battery positive voltage show between the hydraulic unit harness-side connector terminal no.52 and the ground?
No
Broken wire in the hydraulic unit power harness
Repair the harness
Yes
Is there continuity between the hydraulic unit connector terminals no. 8 and no. 7?
No
Harness in the hydraulic unit is defective
Repair the harness or replace the hydraulic unit
Yes
Connect the hydraulic unit connector and remove the ABS-ECU connector
Does a resistance value of 60–120Ω show between the harness-side connector terminals no. 5 and no. 4?
No
Harness between the ABS-ECU and the hydraulic unit is defective
Repair the harness
Yes
When the ignition switch is turned to "ON", does battery positive voltage show between the hydraulic unit harness-side connector terminal no.62 and the ground?
No
Harness between the ABS-ECU and the hydraulic unit is defective
Repair the harness
Yes
ABS-ECU is defective
Replace the ABS-ECU
MT4029100154000X

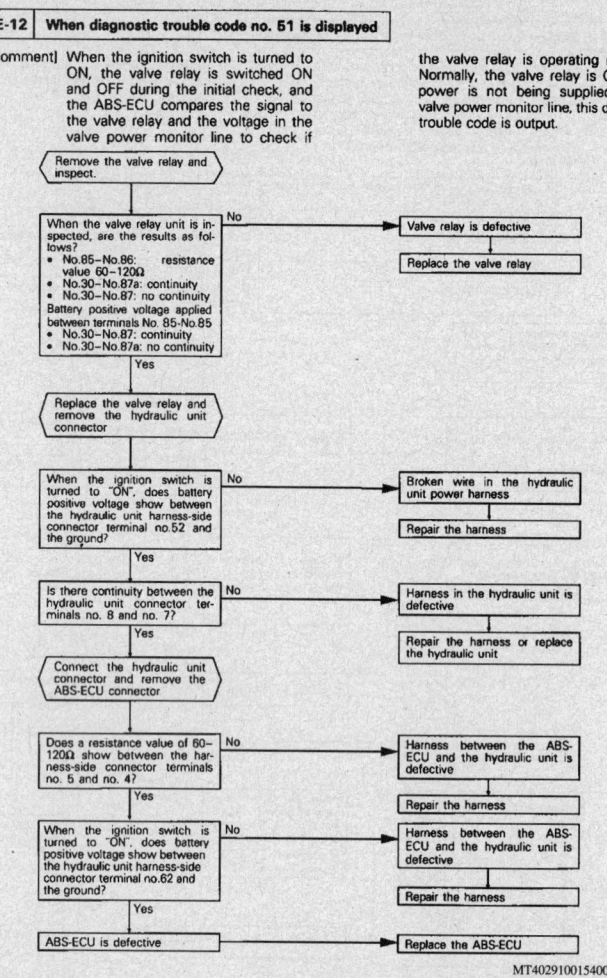

Fig. 219 Code 51: Valve Relay. 1993–95 Montero

E-13	When diagnostic trouble code no. 53 is displayed

[Comment] This code is output by the ABS-ECU when the motor relay or motor is as follows:

- Motor relay does not operate
- Motor will not work due to some problem
- Motor will not work because the ground is insufficient
- Motor will not stop

(Hint) Temporarily turn the ignition switch to OFF and after releasing the fail-safe mechanism, carry out an actuator test with the scan tool. If the sound of the motor working is heard during the scan tool actuator test, there is a broken wire or short in the motor monitor line.

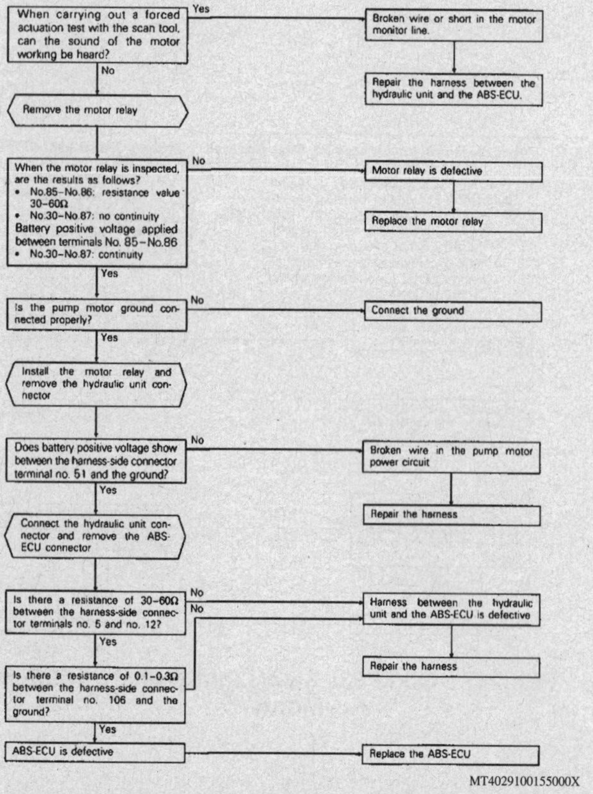

When carrying out a forced actuation test with the scan tool, can the sound of the motor working be heard?
Yes
Broken wire or short in the motor monitor line.
Repair the harness between the hydraulic unit and the ABS-ECU.
No
Remove the motor relay
When the motor relay is inspected, are the results as follows?
• No.85–No.86: resistance value 30–60Ω
• No.30–No.87: no continuity
Battery positive voltage applied between terminals No. 85–No.86
• No.30–No.87: continuity
No
Motor relay is defective
Replace the motor relay
Yes
Is the pump motor ground connected properly?
No
Connect the ground
Yes
Install the motor relay and remove the hydraulic unit connector
Does battery positive voltage show between the harness-side connector terminal no. 51 and the ground?
No
Broken wire in the pump motor power circuit
Repair the harness
Yes
Connect the hydraulic unit connector and remove the ABS-ECU connector
Is there a resistance of 30–60Ω between the harness-side connector terminals no. 5 and no. 12?
No
No
Harness between the hydraulic unit and the ABS-ECU is defective
Repair the harness
Yes
Is there a resistance of 0.1–0.3Ω between the harness-side connector terminal no. 106 and the ground?
Yes
ABS-ECU is defective
Replace the ABS-ECU
MT4029100155000X

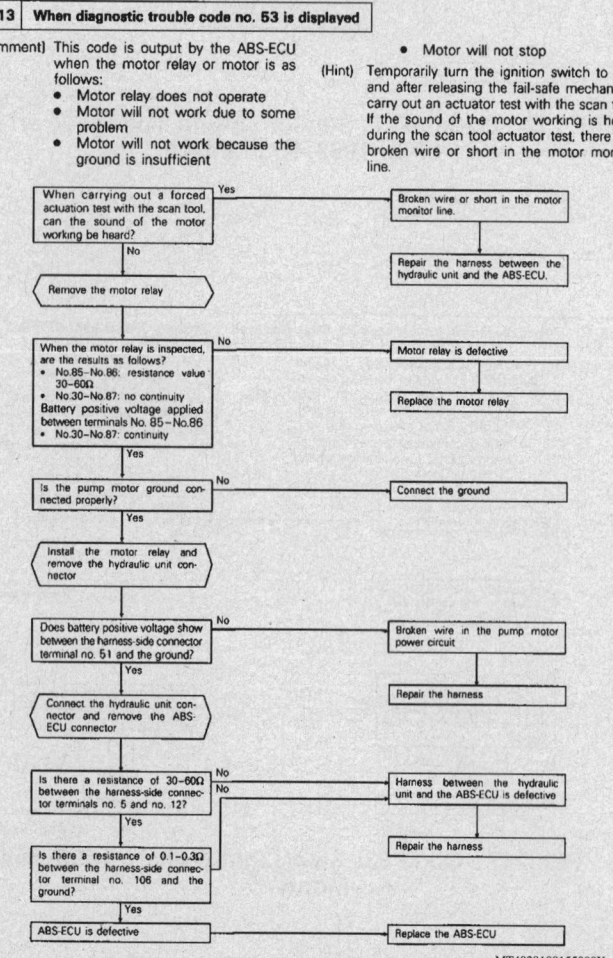

Fig. 220 Code 53: Motor Relay. 1993–95 Montero

Code No.11, 12, 13, 14 Wheel speed sensor open circuit	Probable cause
[Comment] A sensor is open-circuited in the positive or negative line.	• Malfunction of wheel speed sensor • Malfunction of wiring harness or connector • Malfunction of ABS-ECU

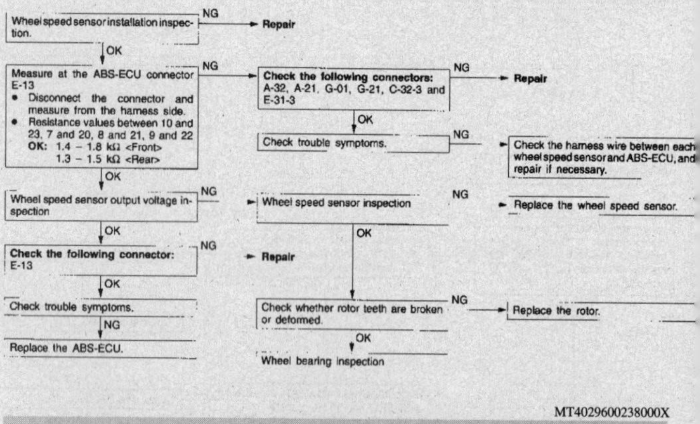

Wheel speed sensor installation inspection.
NG
Repair
OK
Measure at the ABS-ECU connector E-13
• Disconnect the connector and measure from the harness side.
• Resistance values between 10 and 23, 7 and 20, 8 and 21, 9 and 22
OK: 1.4 – 1.8 kΩ <Front>
1.3 – 1.5 kΩ <Rear>
NG
Check the following connectors: A-32, A-21, G-01, G-21, C-32-3 and E-31-3
NG
Repair
OK
Check trouble symptoms.
NG
Check the harness wire between each wheel speed sensor and ABS-ECU, and repair if necessary.
OK
Wheel speed sensor output voltage inspection
NG
Wheel speed sensor inspection
NG
Replace the wheel speed sensor.
OK
OK
Check the following connector: E-13
NG
Repair
OK
Check trouble symptoms.
NG
Replace the ABS-ECU.
Check whether rotor teeth are broken or deformed.
NG
Replace the rotor.
OK
Wheel bearing inspection
MT4029600238000X

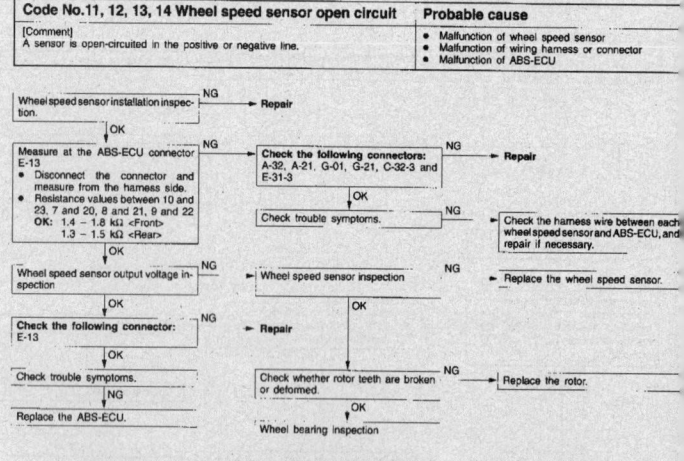

Fig. 221 Codes 11, 12, 13 & 14: Wheel Speed Sensor Open Circuit. 1996 Montero

Code No.15 Wheel speed sensor (Defective output signal)	Probable cause
[Comment] A malfunction (other than an open or short-circuit) is detected in the output signal from a wheel speed sensor while driving.	• Improper installation of wheel speed sensor • Malfunction of wheel speed sensor • Malfunction of rotor • Malfunction of wheel bearing • Malfunction of wiring harness or connector • Malfunction of ABS-ECU

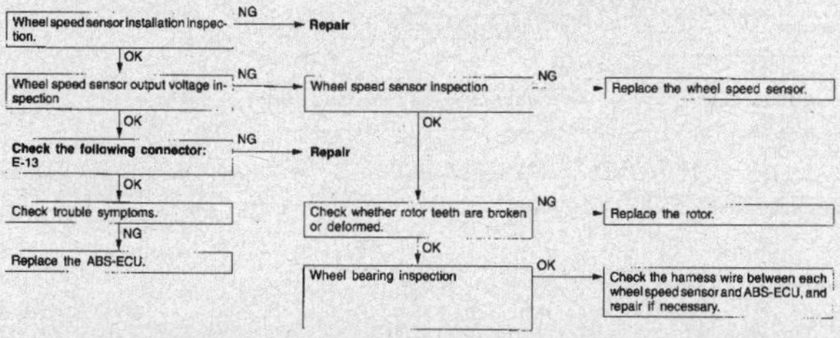
Wheel speed sensor installation inspection.
NG
Repair
OK
Wheel speed sensor output voltage inspection
NG
Wheel speed sensor inspection
NG
Replace the wheel speed sensor.
OK
Check the following connector:
E-13
NG
Repair
OK
Check trouble symptoms.
NG
Replace the ABS-ECU.
Check whether rotor teeth are broken or deformed.
NG
Replace the rotor.
OK
Wheel bearing inspection
OK
Check the harness wire between each wheel speed sensor and ABS-ECU, and repair if necessary.

MT4029600239000X

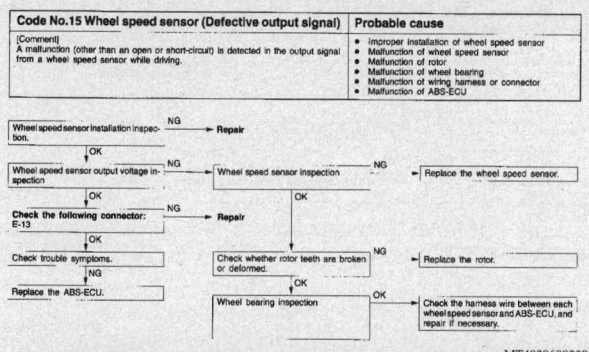

Fig. 222 Code 15: Wheel Speed Sensor Defective Output Signal. 1996 Montero

Code No.21, 22, 23, 24 Wheel speed sensor short circuit	Probable cause
[Comment] The above codes are output in the following cases. • An open circuit cannot be found out, but a wheel speed sensor does not output any signal when driving at 8 km/h or higher. • As the sensor output drops due to a malfunctioning sensor or a warped rotor, anti-lock control is continuously carried out.	• Malfunction of wheel speed sensor • Malfunction of rotor • Malfunction of wheel bearing • Malfunction of wiring harness or connector • Malfunction of ABS-ECU

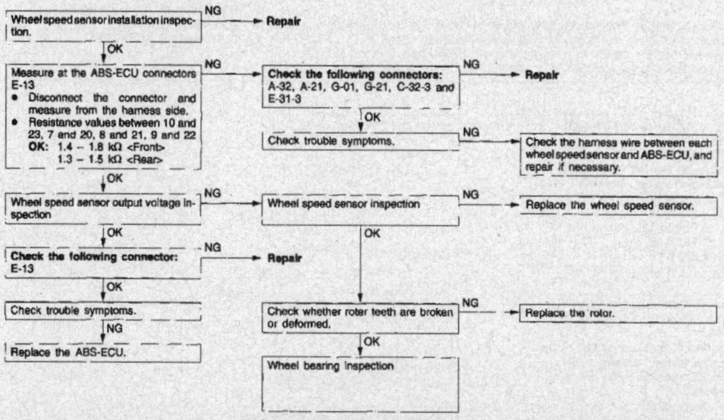
Wheel speed sensor installation inspection.
NG
Repair
OK
Measure at the ABS-ECU connectors E-13
• Disconnect the connector and measure from the harness side.
• Resistance values between 10 and 23, 7 and 20, 8 and 21, 9 and 22
OK: 1.4 – 1.8 kΩ <Front>
1.3 – 1.5 kΩ <Rear>
NG
Check the following connectors:
A-32, A-21, G-01, G-21, C-32-3 and E-31-3
NG
Repair
OK
Check trouble symptoms.
NG
Check the harness wire between each wheel speed sensor and ABS-ECU, and repair if necessary.
OK
Wheel speed sensor output voltage inspection
NG
Wheel speed sensor inspection
NG
Replace the wheel speed sensor.
OK
Check the following connector:
E-13
NG
Repair
OK
Check trouble symptoms.
NG
Replace the ABS-ECU.
Check whether roter teeth are broken or deformed.
NG
Replace the rotor.
OK
Wheel bearing inspection

MT4029600241000X

Fig. 224 Codes 21, 22, 23 & 24: Wheel Speed Sensor Short Circuit. 1996 Montero

Code No.26 Centre differential lock detection switch	Probable cause
[Comment] The above codes are output in the following cases. • There is an open circuit in the center differential lock detection switch system. • The free wheel engage switch remains off and the center differential lock detection switch remains on at a vehicle speed of 15 km/h or more for 5 seconds or more.	• Malfunction of wiring harness or connector • Malfunction of free wheel engage switch • Malfunction of 4WD indicator ECU • Malfunction of center differential lock detection switch • Malfunction of ABS-ECU

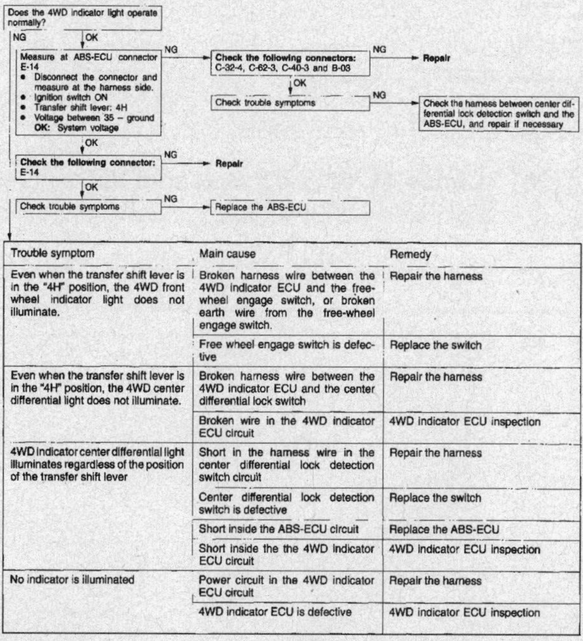
Does the 4WD indicator light operate normally?
NG
OK
Measure at ABS-ECU connector E-14
• Disconnect the connector and measure at the harness side.
• Ignition switch ON
• Transfer shift lever: 4H
• Voltage between 35 – ground
OK: System voltage
NG
Check the following connectors:
C-32-4, C-62-3, C-40-3 and B-03
NG
Repair
OK
Check trouble symptoms
NG
Check the harness between center differential lock detection switch and the ABS-ECU, and repair if necessary
OK
Check the following connector:
E-14
NG
Repair
OK
Check trouble symptoms
NG
Replace the ABS-ECU

Trouble symptom	Main cause	Remedy
Even when the transfer shift lever is in the "4H" position, the 4WD front wheel indicator light does not illuminate.	Broken harness wire between the 4WD indicator ECU and the free-wheel engage switch, or broken earth wire from the free-wheel engage switch.	Repair the harness
	Free wheel engage switch is defective	Replace the switch
Even when the transfer shift lever is in the "4H" position, the 4WD center differential light does not illuminate.	Broken harness wire between the 4WD indicator ECU and the center differential lock switch	Repair the harness
	Broken wire in the 4WD indicator ECU circuit	4WD indicator ECU inspection
4WD indicator center differential light illuminates regardless of the position of the transfer shift lever	Short in the harness wire in the center differential lock detection switch circuit	Repair the harness
	Center differential lock detection switch is defective	Replace the switch
	Short inside the ABS-ECU circuit	Replace the ABS-ECU
	Short inside the the 4WD indicator ECU circuit	4WD indicator ECU inspection
No indicator is illuminated	Power circuit in the 4WD indicator ECU circuit	Repair the harness
	4WD indicator ECU is defective	4WD indicator ECU inspection

NOTE
When checking a short in the ABS-ECU circuit, remove the ABS-ECU connector and check if the 4WD indicator returns to normal. If it returns to normal, the ABS-ECU is defective. Furthermore, if the ABS-ECU is normal, then the 4WD indicator ECU will be defective.

MT4029600243000X

Fig. 226 Code 26: Center Differential Lock Detection Switch. 1996 Montero

Code No.16 Power supply system	Probable cause
[Comment] The ABS-ECU power supply voltage or the solenoid valve power supply voltage is less than the specified value. If the voltage returns to the specified value, this code is no longer output.	• Malfunction of wiring harness or connector. • Malfunction of ABS-ECU

Caution
If the battery voltage drops or rises during inspection, this code will be output as a current problem, and correct diagnosis of the problem cannot be made.
Before carrying out the following inspection, check the battery level, and refill it if necessary.

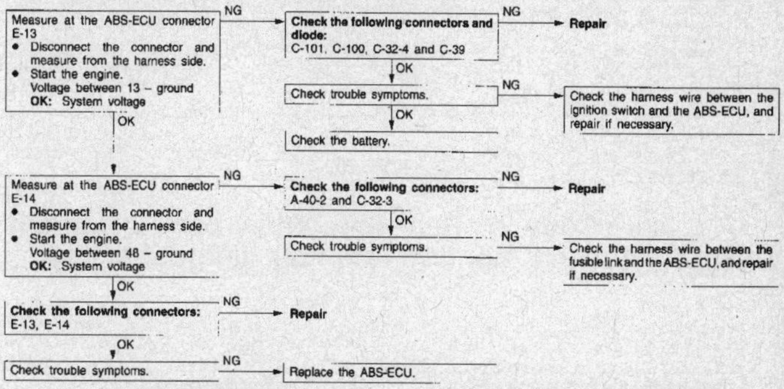
Measure at the ABS-ECU connector E-13
• Disconnect the connector and measure from the harness side.
• Start the engine.
Voltage between 13 – ground
OK: System voltage
NG
Check the following connectors and diode:
C-101, C-100, C-32-4 and C-39
NG
Repair
OK
Check trouble symptoms.
NG
Check the harness wire between the ignition switch and the ABS-ECU, and repair if necessary.
OK
Check the battery.
OK
Measure at the ABS-ECU connector E-14
• Disconnect the connector and measure from the harness side.
• Start the engine.
Voltage between 48 – ground
OK: System voltage
NG
Check the following connectors:
A-40-2 and C-32-3
NG
Repair
OK
Check trouble symptoms.
NG
Check the harness wire between the fusible link and the ABS-ECU, and repair if necessary.
OK
Check the following connectors:
E-13, E-14
NG
Repair
OK
Check trouble symptoms.
NG
Replace the ABS-ECU.

MT4029600240000X

Fig. 223 Code 16: Power Supply System. 1996 Montero

Code No.25 Free wheel engage switch	Probable cause
[Comment] There is an open circuit in the free-wheeling engage switch system.	• Malfunction of wiring harness or connector • Malfunction of 4WD indicator ECU • Malfunction of ABS-ECU

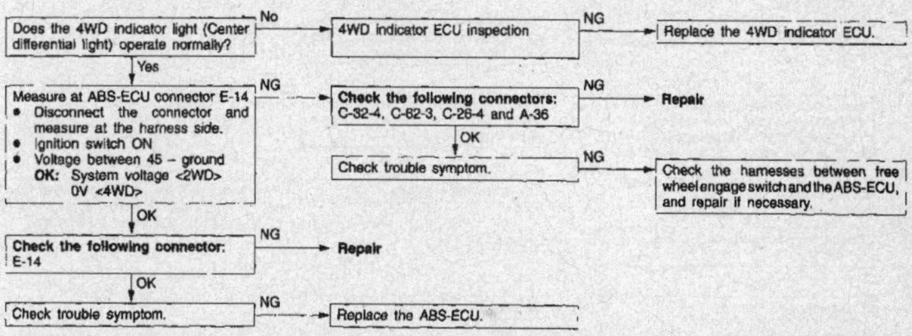
Does the 4WD indicator light (Center differential light) operate normally?
No
4WD indicator ECU inspection
NG
Replace the 4WD indicator ECU.
Yes
Measure at ABS-ECU connector E-14
• Disconnect the connector and measure at the harness side.
• Ignition switch ON
• Voltage between 45 – ground
OK: System voltage <2WD>
0V <4WD>
NG
Check the following connectors:
C-32-4, C-62-3, C-26-4 and A-36
NG
Repair
OK
Check trouble symptom.
NG
Check the harnesses between free wheel engage switch and the ABS-ECU, and repair if necessary.
OK
Check the following connector:
E-14
NG
Repair
OK
Check trouble symptom.
NG
Replace the ABS-ECU.

MT4029600242000X

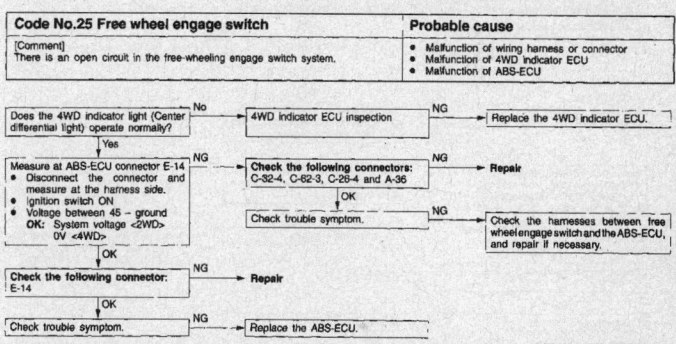

Fig. 225 Code 25: Free Wheel Engage Switch. 1996 Montero

Code No.27 Rear differential lock detection switch <Vehicles with rear differential lock>	Probable cause
[Comment] There is an open circuit in the rear differential lock detection switch system.	• Malfunction of wiring harness or connector • Malfunction of rear differential lock ECU • Malfunction of ABS-ECU

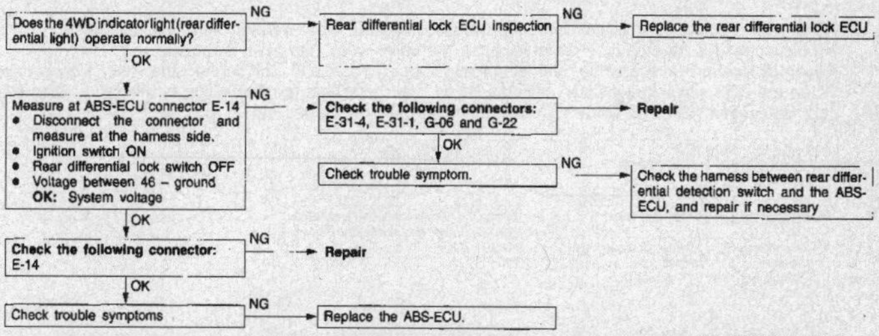
Does the 4WD indicator light (rear differential light) operate normally?
NG
Rear differential lock ECU inspection
NG
Replace the rear differential lock ECU
OK
Measure at ABS-ECU connector E-14
• Disconnect the connector and measure at the harness side.
• Ignition switch ON
• Rear differential lock switch OFF
• Voltage between 46 – ground
OK: System voltage
NG
Check the following connectors:
E-31-4, E-31-1, G-06 and G-22
Repair
OK
Check trouble symptom.
NG
Check the harness between rear differential detection switch and the ABS-ECU, and repair if necessary
OK
Check the following connector:
E-14
NG
Repair
OK
Check trouble symptoms
NG
Replace the ABS-ECU.

MT4029600244000X

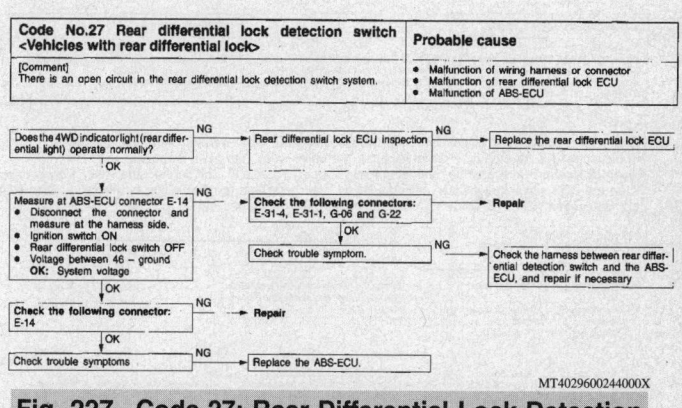

Fig. 227 Code 27: Rear Differential Lock Detection Switch. 1996 Montero w/rear differential lock

Code No.27 Rear differential lock detection switch <Vehicles without rear differential lock>	Probable cause
[Comment] For vehicles without rear differential lock, battery positive voltage is applied to the ABS-ECU terminal no. 46. This diagnostic trouble code is output when this line is interrupted.	• Malfunction of wiring harness or connector • Malfunction of ABS-ECU

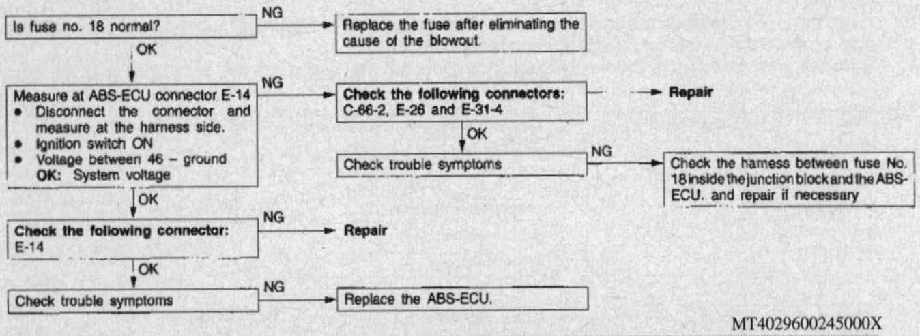

Is fuse no. 18 normal?
NG
Replace the fuse after eliminating the cause of the blowout.
OK
Measure at ABS-ECU connector E-14
• Disconnect the connector and measure at the harness side.
• Ignition switch ON
• Voltage between 46 – ground
OK: System voltage
NG
Check the following connectors: C-66-2, E-26 and E-31-4
Repair
OK
Check trouble symptoms
NG
Check the harness between fuse No. 18 inside the junction block and the ABS-ECU, and repair if necessary
OK
Check the following connector: E-14
NG
Repair
OK
Check trouble symptoms
NG
Replace the ABS-ECU.
MT4029600245000X

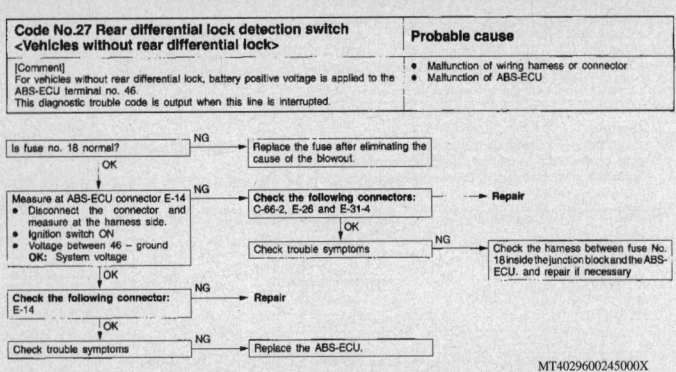

Fig. 228 Code 27: Rear Differential Lock Detection Switch. 1996 Montero less rear differential lock

Code No.32 G-sensor system	Probable cause
[Comment] The above codes are output in the following case. • The G sensor output is less than 0.5 V or more than 4.5 V. • There is an open or short circuit in the G sensor system.	• Malfunction of G-sensor • Malfunction of wiring harness or connector • Malfunction of ABS-ECU

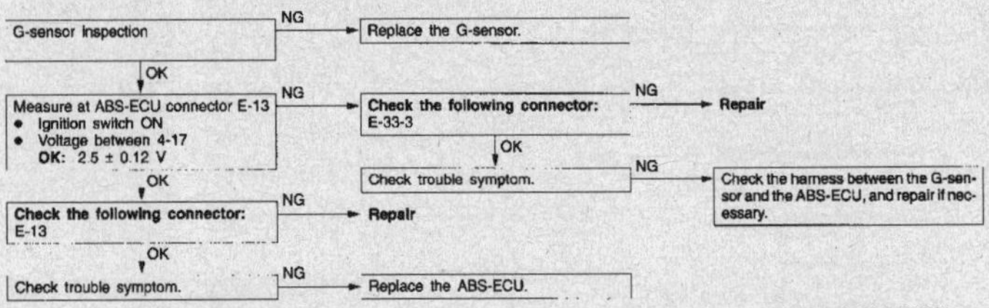

G-sensor inspection
NG
Replace the G-sensor.
OK
Measure at ABS-ECU connector E-13
• Ignition switch ON
• Voltage between 4-17
OK: 2.5 ± 0.12 V
NG
Check the following connector: E-33-3
NG
Repair
OK
Check trouble symptom.
NG
Check the harness between the G-sensor and the ABS-ECU, and repair if necessary.
OK
Check the following connector: E-13
NG
Repair
OK
Check trouble symptom.
NG
Replace the ABS-ECU.
MT4029600246000X

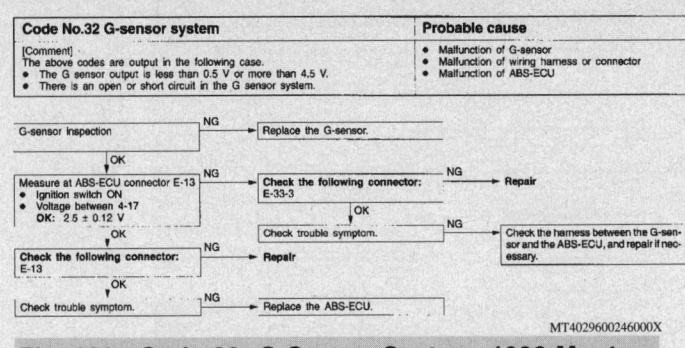

Fig. 229 Code 32: G-Sensor System. 1996 Montero

Code No.33 Stop light switch system	Probable cause
[Comment] The above codes are output in the following cases. • The stop light switch can not be turned off. (the stop light switch stays on for 15 minutes or more even though the ABS is not operating) • There is an open circuit in the stop light switch system.	• Malfunction of stop light switch • Malfunction of harness or connector • Malfunction of ABS-ECU

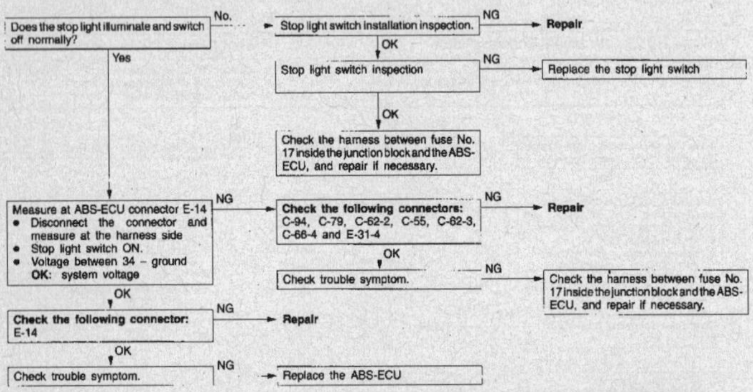

Does the stop light illuminate and switch off normally?
No.
Stop light switch installation inspection.
NG
Repair
OK
Stop light switch inspection
NG
Replace the stop light switch
OK
Check the harness between fuse No. 17 inside the junction block and the ABS-ECU, and repair if necessary.
Yes
Measure at ABS-ECU connector E-14
• Disconnect the connector and measure at the harness side
• Stop light switch ON.
• Voltage between 34 – ground
OK: system voltage
NG
Check the following connectors: C-94, C-79, C-62-2, C-55, C-62-3, C-68-4 and E-31-4
NG
Repair
OK
Check trouble symptom.
NG
Check the harness between fuse No. 17 inside the junction block and the ABS-ECU, and repair if necessary.
OK
Check the following connector: E-14
NG
Repair
OK
Check trouble symptom.
NG
Replace the ABS-ECU
MT4029600247000X

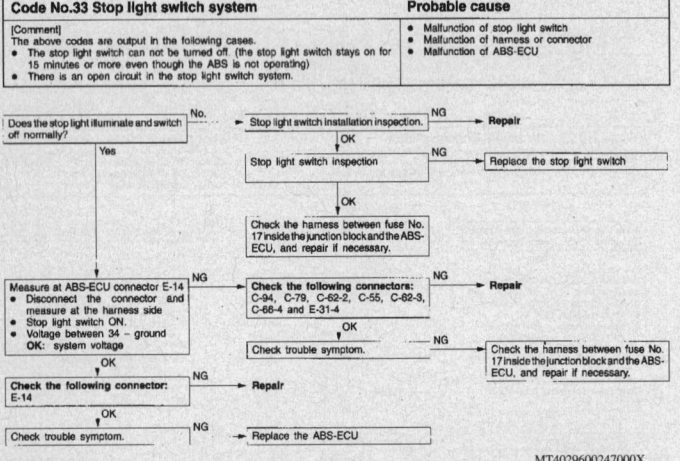

Fig. 230 Code 33: Stop Light Switch System. 1996 Montero

Code No.41, 42, 43 solenoid valve	Probable cause
[Comment] The ABS-ECU always monitors the solenoid drive circuit and judge that there is an open or short circuit in the solenoid coils in the following cases. No current is being supplied to a solenoid even though that solenoid is on. Current continues to be supplied to a solenoid even though that solenoid is off.	• Malfunction of wiring harness • Malfunction of hydraulic unit • Malfunction of ABS-ECU

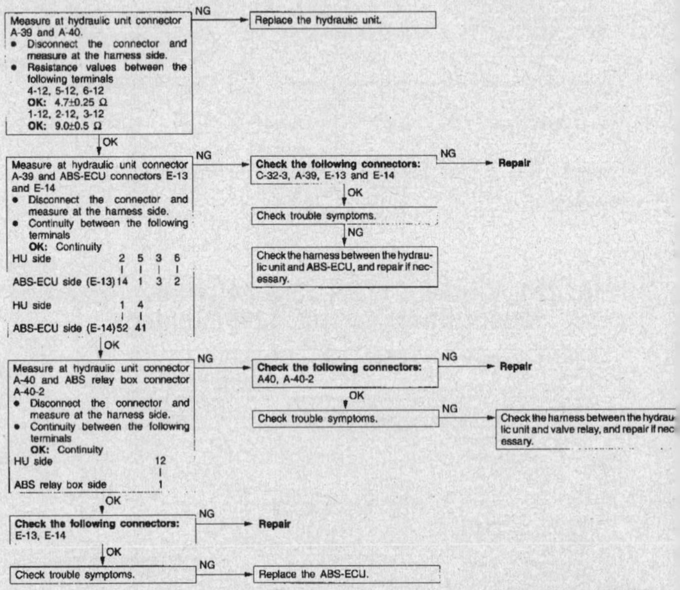

Measure at hydraulic unit connector A-39 and A-40.
• Disconnect the connector and measure at the harness side.
• Resistance values between the following terminals
4-12, 5-12, 6-12
OK: 4.7±0.25 Ω
1-12, 2-12, 3-12
OK: 9.0±0.5 Ω
NG
Replace the hydraulic unit.
OK
Measure at hydraulic unit connector A-39 and ABS-ECU connectors E-13 and E-14
• Disconnect the connector and measure at the harness side.
• Continuity between the following terminals
OK: Continuity
HU side 2 5 3 6
ABS-ECU side (E-13) 14 1 3 2
HU side 1 4
ABS-ECU side (E-14) 52 41
NG
Check the following connectors: C-32-3, A-39, E-13 and E-14
NG
Repair
OK
Check trouble symptoms.
NG
Check the harness between the hydraulic unit and ABS-ECU, and repair if necessary.
OK
Measure at hydraulic unit connector A-40 and ABS relay box connector A-40-2
• Disconnect the connector and measure at the harness side.
• Continuity between the following terminals
OK: Continuity
HU side 12
ABS relay box side 1
NG
Check the following connectors: A40, A-40-2
NG
Repair
OK
Check trouble symptoms.
NG
Check the harness between the hydraulic unit and valve relay, and repair if necessary.
OK
Check the following connectors: E-13, E-14
NG
Repair
OK
Check trouble symptoms.
NG
Replace the ABS-ECU.
MT4029600248000X

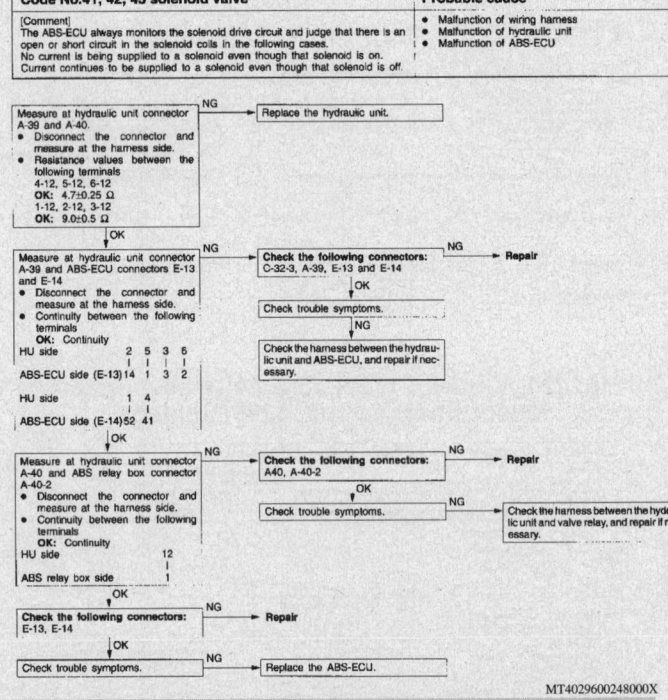

Fig. 231 Codes 41, 42 & 43: Solenoid Valve. 1996 Montero

Code No.51 Valve relay	Probable cause
[Comment] When the ignition switch is turned to ON, the ABS-ECU switches the valve relay off and on to check it as the initial check. The valve relay is normally on. So, if power is not being supplied to the relay, the ABS-ECU will judge that the valve relay is defective.	• Malfunction of valve relay • Malfunction of wiring harness or connector • Malfunction of ABS-ECU • Malfunction of hydraulic unit

NOTE
Whenever reading the diagnostic trouble codes using the ABS warning light, this diagnostic trouble code will be output. That is because the valve relay has been removed.
Repair all locations indicated by other diagnostic trouble codes, and then connect the valve relay connector. When the ABS warning light still indicates No.51 even after that, a malfunction in the valve relay system may be present. So, the following checks should then be carried out.

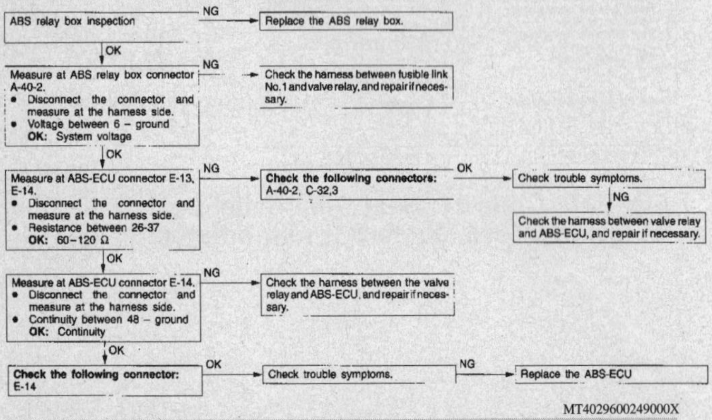

ABS relay box inspection
NG
Replace the ABS relay box.
OK
Measure at ABS relay box connector A-40-2.
• Disconnect the connector and measure at the harness side.
• Voltage between 6 – ground
OK: System voltage
NG
Check the harness between fusible link No.1 and valve relay, and repair if necessary.
OK
Measure at ABS-ECU connector E-13, E-14.
• Disconnect the connector and measure at the harness side.
• Resistance between 26-37
OK: 60 – 120 Ω
NG
Check the following connectors: A-40-2, C-32,3
OK
Check trouble symptoms.
NG
Check the harness between valve relay and ABS-ECU, and repair if necessary.
OK
Measure at ABS-ECU connector E-14.
• Disconnect the connector and measure at the harness side.
• Continuity between 48 – ground
OK: Continuity
NG
Check the harness between the valve relay and ABS-ECU, and repair if necessary.
OK
Check the following connector: E-14
OK
Check trouble symptoms.
NG
Replace the ABS-ECU
MT4029600249000X

Fig. 232 Code 51: Valve Relay. 1996 Montero

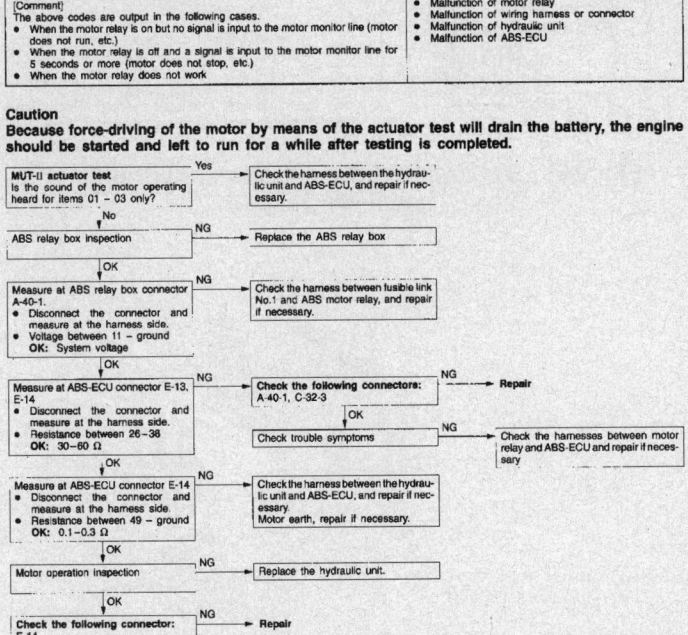

Code No.53 Motor relay, motor	Probable cause
[Comment] The above codes are output in the following cases. • When the motor relay is on but no signal is input to the motor monitor line (motor does not run, etc.) • When the motor relay is off and a signal is input to the motor monitor line for 5 seconds or more (motor does not stop, etc.) • When the motor relay does not work	• Malfunction of motor relay • Malfunction of wiring harness or connector • Malfunction of hydraulic unit • Malfunction of ABS-ECU

Caution
Because force-driving of the motor by means of the actuator test will drain the battery, the engine should be started and left to run for a while after testing is completed.

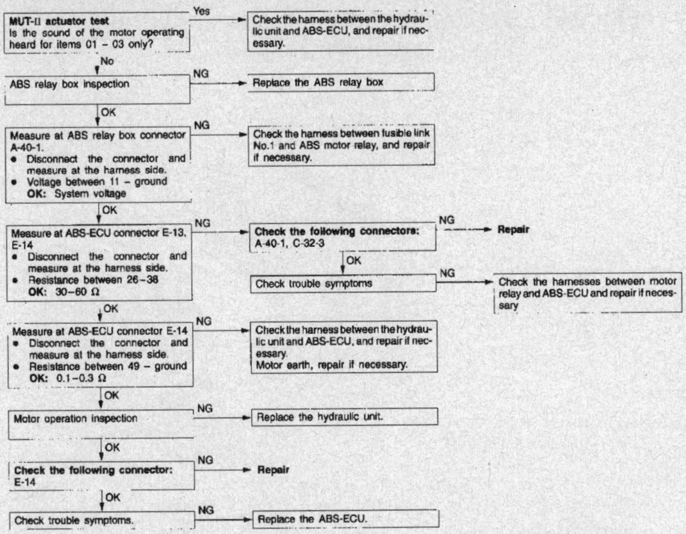

MUT-II actuator test
Is the sound of the motor operating heard for items 01 – 03 only?
Yes
Check the harness between the hydraulic unit and ABS-ECU, and repair if necessary.
No
ABS relay box inspection
NG
Replace the ABS relay box
OK
Measure at ABS relay box connector A-40-1.
• Disconnect the connector and measure at the harness side.
• Voltage between 11 – ground
OK: System voltage
NG
Check the harness between fusible link No.1 and ABS motor relay, and repair if necessary.
OK
Measure at ABS-ECU connector E-13, E-14
• Disconnect the connector and measure at the harness side.
• Resistance between 26–38
OK: 30–60 Ω
NG
Check the following connectors: A-40-1, C-32-3
NG
Repair
OK
Check trouble symptoms
NG
Check the harnesses between motor relay and ABS-ECU and repair if necessary
OK
Measure at ABS-ECU connector E-14
• Disconnect the connector and measure at the harness side.
• Resistance between 49 – ground
OK: 0.1–0.3 Ω
NG
Check the harness between the hydraulic unit and ABS-ECU, and repair if necessary.
Motor earth, repair if necessary.
OK
Motor operation inspection
NG
Replace the hydraulic unit.
OK
Check the following connector: E-14
NG
Repair
OK
Check trouble symptoms.
NG
Replace the ABS-ECU.

MT4029600250000X

Fig. 233 Code 53: Motor Relay & Motor Operation. 1996 Montero

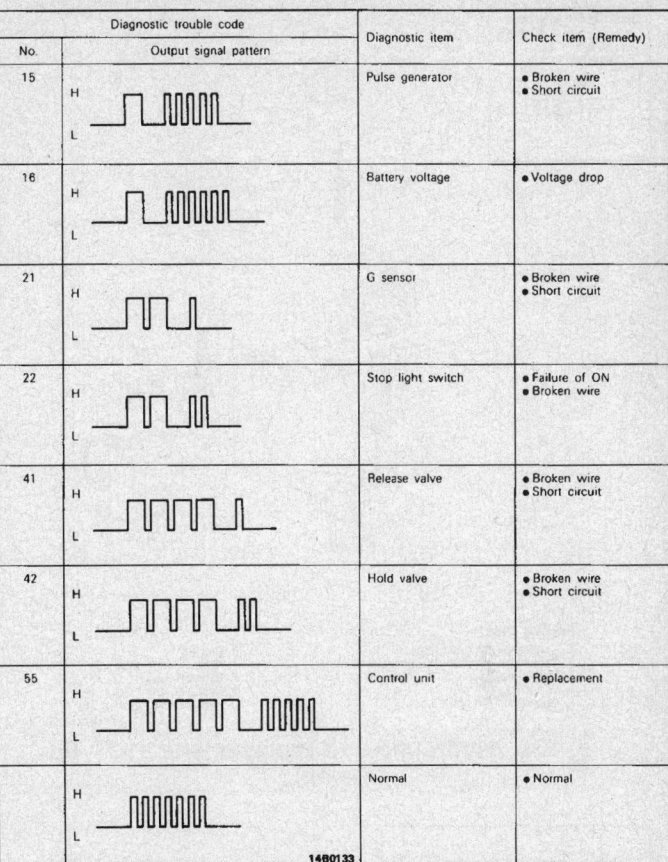

Diagnostic trouble code		Diagnostic item	Check item (Remedy)
No.	Output signal pattern		
15	H / L	Pulse generator	• Broken wire • Short circuit
16	H / L	Battery voltage	• Voltage drop
21	H / L	G sensor	• Broken wire • Short circuit
22	H / L	Stop light switch	• Failure of ON • Broken wire
41	H / L	Release valve	• Broken wire • Short circuit
42	H / L	Hold valve	• Broken wire • Short circuit
55	H / L	Control unit	• Replacement
	H / L	Normal	• Normal

1480133

MT4029100158000X

Fig. 234 Diagnostic Trouble Codes. Pickup

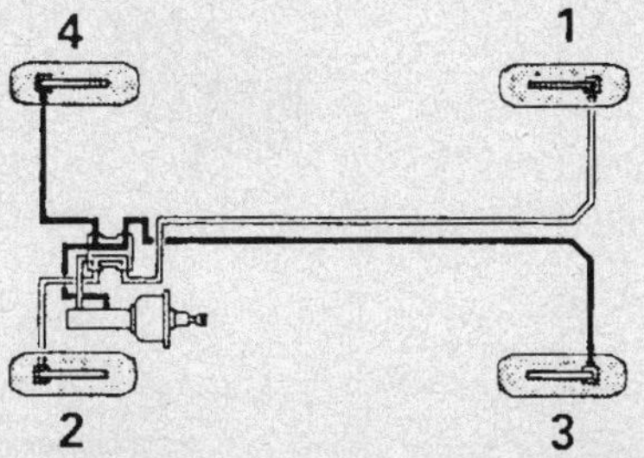

4
1
2
3

MT4029100159000X

Fig. 235 Brake line bleeding sequence. Diamante, Eclipse, Expo, Galant, Mirage & 3000GT

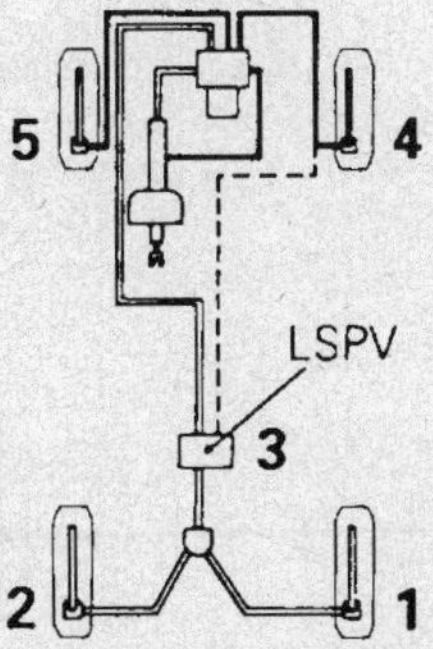

5
4
LSPV
3
2
1

MT4029100160000X

Fig. 236 Brake line bleeding sequence. Montero

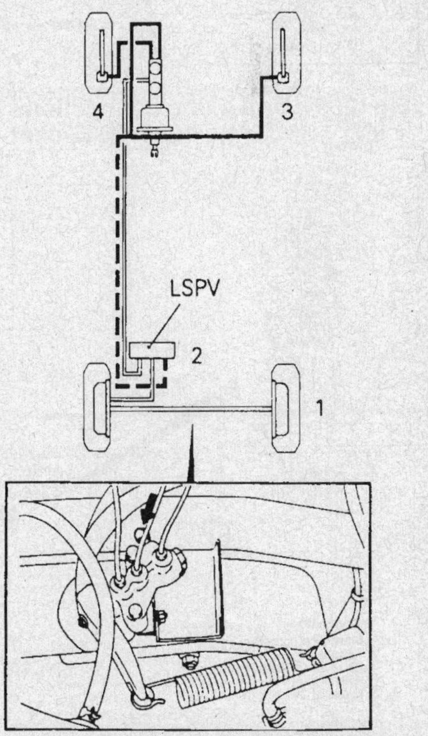

4
3
LSPV
2
1

MT4029100161000X

Fig. 237 Brake line bleeding sequence. Pickup

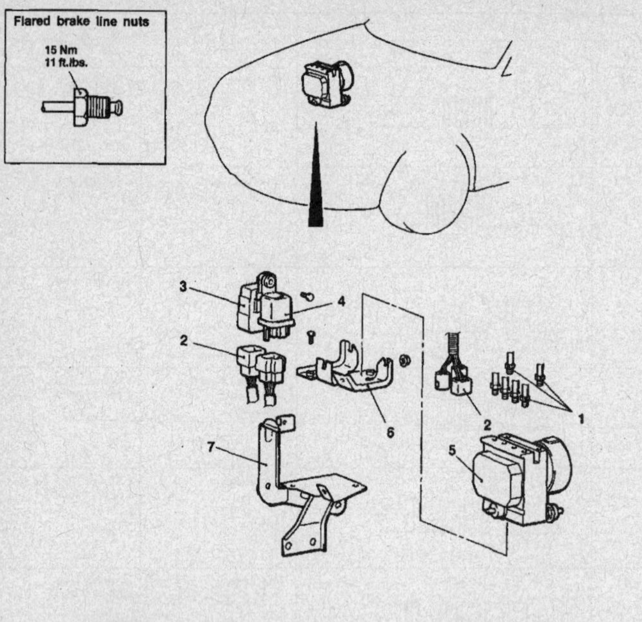
Flared brake line nuts
15 Nm
11 ft.lbs.

Removal steps

1. Connection for brake pipe
2. Connection for harness connector
3. Motor relay
4. Valve relay
5. Connection for brake hose
6. Bracket
7. Hydraulic unit assembly
8. Hydraulic unit
9. Hydraulic unit bracket (A)
10. Hydraulic unit bracket (B)

MT4029400260000X

Fig. 238 Hydraulic unit replacement. 1994–96 Galant

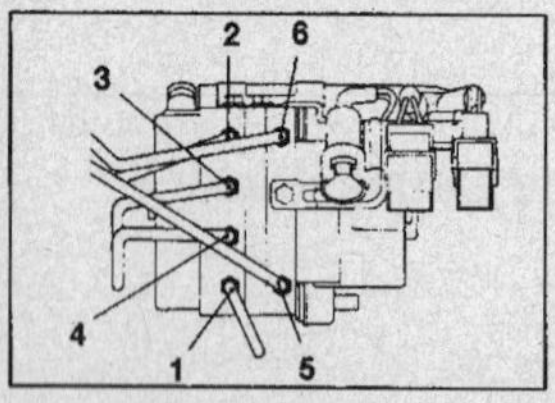

1. Hydraulic unit – Front brake (L.H.)
2. Hydraulic unit – Rear brake (R.H.)
3. Hydraulic unit – Front brake (R.H.)
4. Hydraulic unit – Rear braker (L.H.)
5. Hydraulic unit – Master cylinder (for left front and right rear)
6. Hydraulic unit – Master cylinder (for right front and left rear)

MT4029400261000X

Fig. 239 Brake line connections at hydraulic unit. 1994–96 Galant

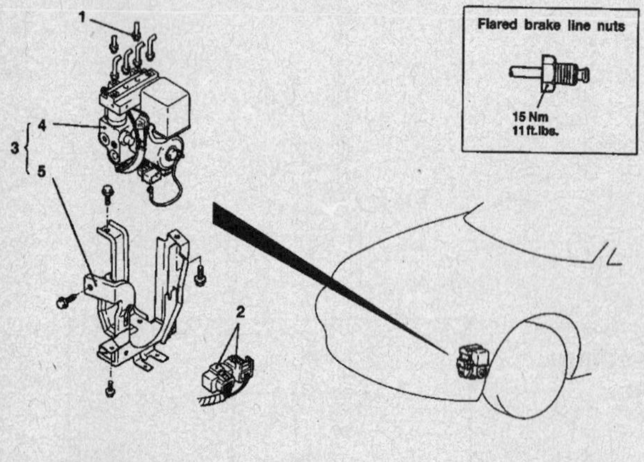
Flared brake line nuts
15 Nm
11 ft.lbs.

Removal steps

1. Brake pipe connection
2. Harness connector
3. Hydraulic unit assembly
4. Hydraulic unit
5. Hydraulic unit bracket

MT4029500262000X

Fig. 240 Hydraulic unit replacement. 1995–96 Eclipse

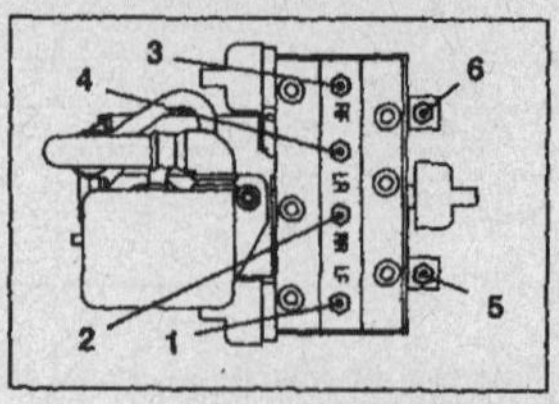

1. Hydraulic unit – Front brake (L.H.)
2. Hydraulic unit – Rear brake (R.H.)
3. Hydraulic unit – Front brake (R.H.)
4. Hydraulic unit – Rear braker (L.H.)
5. Hydraulic unit – Master cylinder (Secondary)
6. Hydraulic unit – Master cylinder (Primary)

MT4029500263000X

Fig. 241 Brake pipe connections at hydraulic unit. 1995–96 Eclipse

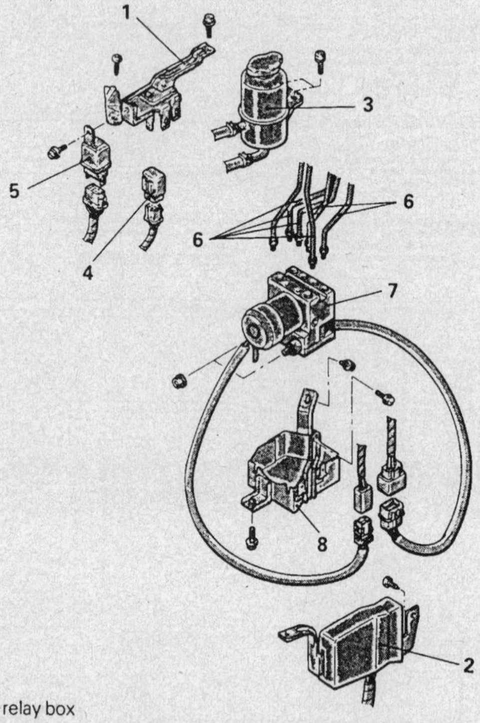

Removal steps

1. Bracket
2. Air conditioning relay box
3. Oil reservoir
4. Motor relay
5. Valve relay
6. Brake pipe
7. Hydraulic unit
8. Hydraulic unit bracket

MT4029100162000X

Fig. 242 Hydraulic unit replacement. Mirage

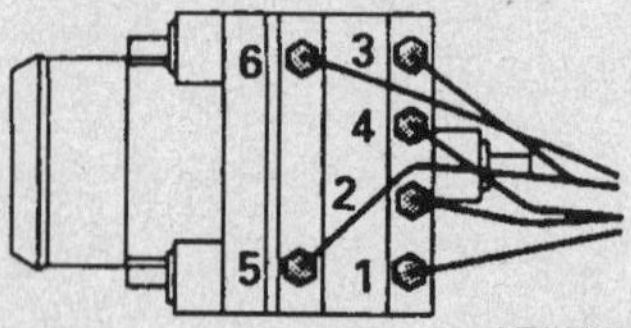

MT4029100163000X

Fig. 243 Brake pipe installation. Mirage

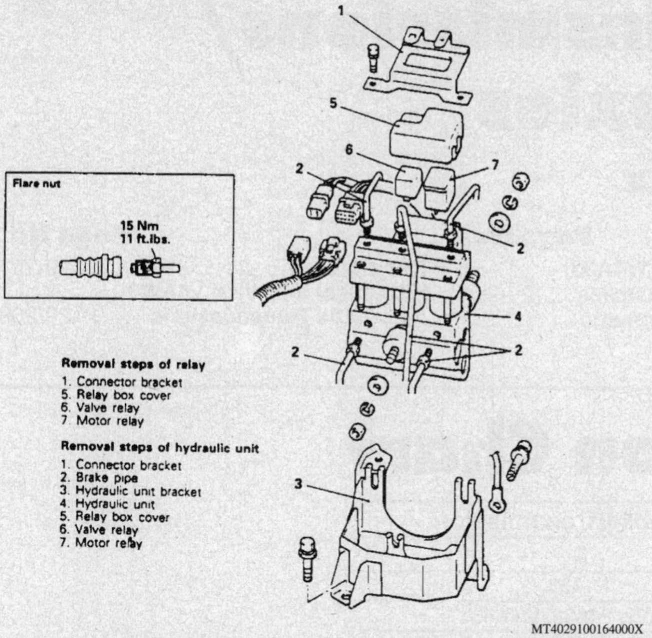
Flare nut
15 Nm
11 ft.lbs.
Removal steps of relay
1. Connector bracket
5. Relay box cover
6. Valve relay
7. Motor relay
Removal steps of hydraulic unit
1. Connector bracket
2. Brake pipe
3. Hydraulic unit bracket
4. Hydraulic unit
5. Relay box cover
6. Valve relay
7. Motor relay
MT4029100164000X

Fig. 244 Hydraulic unit replacement. Montero

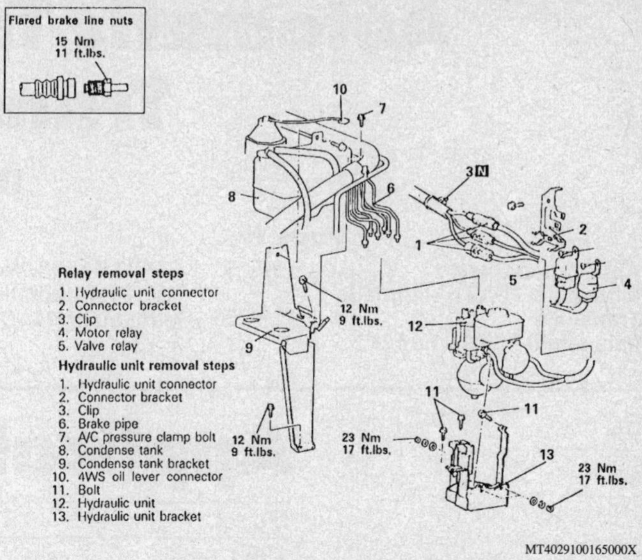
Flared brake line nuts
15 Nm
11 ft.lbs.
Relay removal steps
1. Hydraulic unit connector
2. Connector bracket
3. Clip
4. Motor relay
5. Valve relay
Hydraulic unit removal steps
1. Hydraulic unit connector
2. Connector bracket
3. Clip
6. Brake pipe
7. A/C pressure clamp bolt
8. Condense tank
9. Condense tank bracket
10. 4WS oil lever connector
11. Bolt
12. Hydraulic unit
13. Hydraulic unit bracket
12 Nm
9 ft.lbs.
23 Nm
17 ft.lbs.
MT4029100165000X

Fig. 245 Hydraulic unit replacement. Diamante

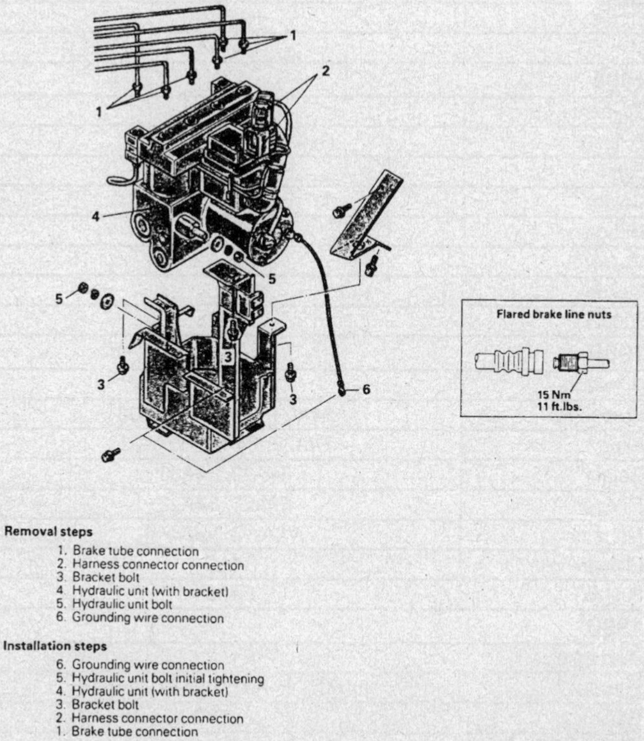
Flared brake line nuts
15 Nm
11 ft.lbs.
Removal steps
1. Brake tube connection
2. Harness connector connection
3. Bracket bolt
4. Hydraulic unit (with bracket)
5. Hydraulic unit bolt
6. Grounding wire connection
Installation steps
6. Grounding wire connection
5. Hydraulic unit bolt initial tightening
4. Hydraulic unit (with bracket)
3. Bracket bolt
2. Harness connector connection
1. Brake tube connection
MT4029100166000X

Fig. 246 Hydraulic unit replacement. 3000GT

Automatic Transmissions/ Transaxles

INDEX

Page No.

Application Chart 29-250
Mitsubishi F3A21 Automatic Transaxle 29-256
Mitsubishi F4AC1, F4A21, F4A23, F4A33, W4A32, W4A33, KM176 Automatic Transaxles 29-261
Mitsubishi R4AC1 Automatic Transmission 29-251
Mitsubishi V4AW2 & V4AW3 Automatic Transmissions 29-282

Application Chart

Model	Transaxle/Transmission
1993	
Diamante	F4A33
Eclipse	F4A22, F4A33, W4A33
Expo	F4A22, F4A23, W4A32
Galant	F4A22
Mirage	F3A21, F4A22
Montero	V4AW2
Pickup	R4AC1
Precis	KM176
3000GT	F4A33
1994	
Diamante	F4A33
Eclipse	F4A22, F4A33, W4A33
Expo	F4A22, F4A23
Galant	F4A23, F4A33
Mirage	F3A21, F4A22
Montero	V4AW2
Pickup	R4AC1
3000GT	F4A33
1995	
Diamante	F4A33
Eclipse	F4AC1, F4A33, W4A33
Expo	F4A22, F4A23, W4A32
Galant	F4A23, F4A33
Mirage	F3A21, F4A22
Montero	V4AW2, V4AW3
Pickup	R4AC1
3000GT	F4A33
1996	
Diamante	F4A33
Eclipse	F4AC1, F4A23, F4A33, W4A33
Galant	F4A23
Mirage	F3A21, F4A22
Montero	V4AW2, V4AW3
Pickup	R4AC1
3000GT	F4A33

Mitsubishi R4AC1 Automatic Transmission

INDEX

	Page No.
Adjustments	29-251
Key Interlock	29-251
Kickdown Band	29-251
Kickdown Cable	29-251
Line Pressure	29-252
Low & Reverse Band	29-252
Shift Lock Cable	29-251
Throttle Pressure	29-253
Description	29-251
Identification	29-251
In-Vehicle Repairs	29-253
Overdrive Housing Yoke Seal Replacement	29-254
Speedometer Pinion Gear Replacement	29-253
Valve Body & Accumulator Piston Replacement	29-254
Maintenance	29-251
Fluid Change	29-251
Fluid Check	29-251
Tightening Specifications	29-255
Transmission, Replace	29-254
Troubleshooting	29-251

IDENTIFICATION

The transmission identification number is located on the vehicle information code plate that is riveted to the firewall in the engine compartment, **Fig. 1**.

DESCRIPTION

This transmission is a four speed fully automatic units. The R4AC1 transmission uses a three element torque converter with a lock-up clutch system.

TROUBLESHOOTING

Refer to **Figs. 2 through 5** when troubleshooting the transmission.

MAINTENANCE

FLUID CHECK

With vehicle on a level surface, start engine and operate at idle. With parking brake applied, place selector lever in Neutral and check fluid level. When checking fluid level, transmission should be at operating temperature (approximately 170°F). Fluid level should be between the Add and Full notches on the dipstick. When adding fluid, use only that labeled Dexron II.

FLUID CHANGE

Under normal operating conditions, automatic transmission fluid change is required at 37,500 miles. Under severe conditions, such as trailer towing, prolonged operation in city traffic or commercial use, fluid and filter should be changed and bands adjusted every 12,000 miles. When refilling transmission, use only Dexron II.

1. Raise and support front of vehicle, then position a drain pan under transmission oil pan.
2. Loosen transmission oil pan attaching bolts, then tap pan at one corner to loosen. Allow fluid to drain and remove pan.
3. Adjust low-reverse band, if necessary.
4. Install replacement transmission filter on bottom of valve body and tighten to specifications.
5. Clean transmission oil pan, then install pan and gasket on transmission. Tighten pan attaching bolts to specifications.
6. Add four quarts of Dexron II type automatic transmission fluid through transmission dipstick tube.
7. Start engine and operate at idle speed for approximately two minutes, then with parking brake applied, move selector lever through all detent positions.
8. Place selector lever in Drive, then check transmission fluid level. Fluid level should be at lower notch on dipstick. Add fluid as necessary.
9. After transmission has reached operating temperature, recheck fluid level. Fluid level should be between the Add and Full notches on the dipstick. Add fluid as necessary.

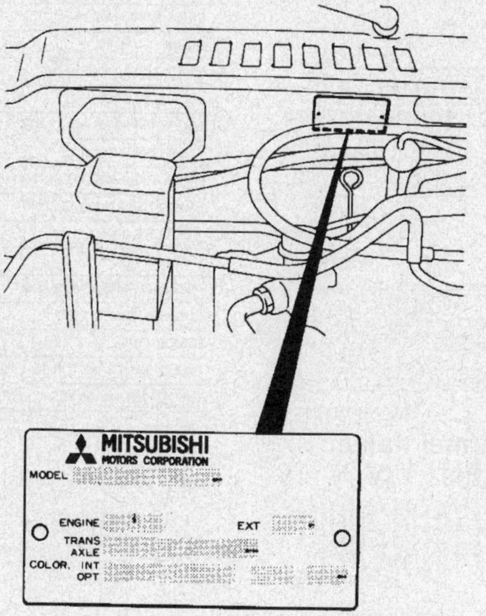

MITSUBISHI
MOTORS CORPORATION
MODEL
ENGINE
EXT
TRANS AXLE
COLOR. INT OPT

MT5029100512000A

Fig. 1 Vehicle information code plate

ADJUSTMENTS

SHIFT LOCK CABLE

1. Place selector lever in Park position and the ignition key in the Lock position.
2. Adjust shift lock cable so amount of protrusion (A) is .02–.18 inch and cable end and clearance (B) between cable end and slider is .02–.06 inch, **Fig. 6.**
3. Ensure proper operation of interlock mechanism.

KEY INTERLOCK

With selector lever in the Park position and the detent pin attached to the wall in the side of R position of detent groove, dimension (D) should be .04–.08 inch, **Fig. 7.**

KICKDOWN CABLE

1. Fix kickdown cable to bell crank lever.
2. Pull inner cable lightly with throttle lever being maintained in idle position.
3. With inner cable being pulled, caulk inner cable stopper so space between stopper and outer cable becomes .031–.059 inch, **Fig. 8.**
4. Pull inner cable and put throttle lever to full open position. Loosen and adjust length of bell crank lever arm so that space between inner cable stopper and cable becomes 1.46–2.50 inch, **Fig. 9.**
5. After adjusting engine to regular idling position, fix inner cable to throttle lever. At this time, fasten outer cable with adjusting nuts so that space between inner cable stopper and outer cable becomes .031–.050 inch, **Fig. 10.**
6. With throttle lever being full open, confirm that space between outer cable and inner cable is 1.30–1.38 inch.

KICKDOWN BAND

The kickdown band adjusting screw is located on the left side of the transmission case, **Fig. 11.**

1. Loosen locknut, then back off adjusting screw approximately five turns.

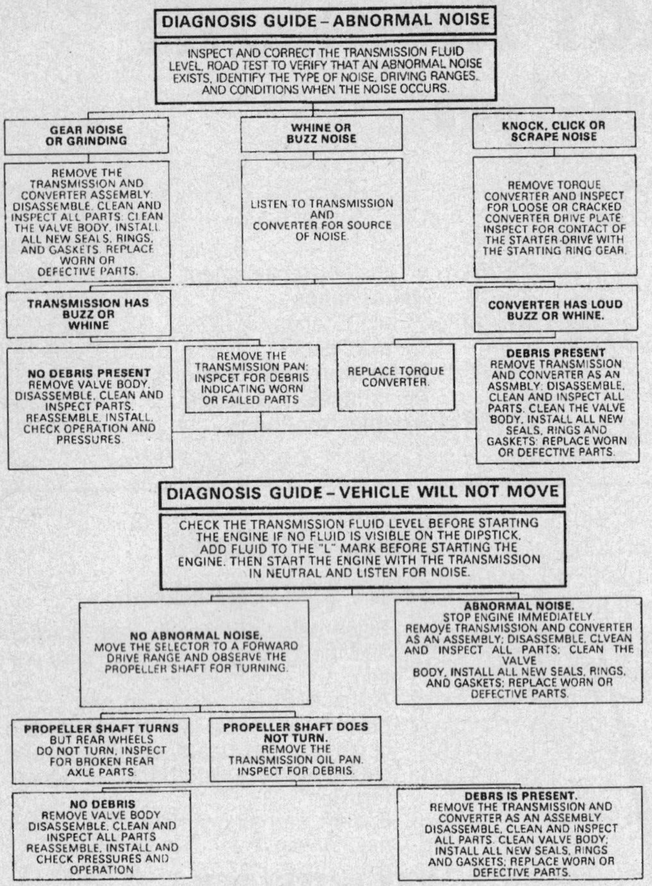
DIAGNOSIS GUIDE – ABNORMAL NOISE
INSPECT AND CORRECT THE TRANSMISSION FLUID LEVEL, ROAD TEST TO VERIFY THAT AN ABNORMAL NOISE EXISTS, IDENTIFY THE TYPE OF NOISE, DRIVING RANGES, AND CONDITIONS WHEN THE NOISE OCCURS.
GEAR NOISE OR GRINDING
WHINE OR BUZZ NOISE
KNOCK, CLICK OR SCRAPE NOISE
REMOVE THE TRANSMISSION AND CONVERTER ASSEMBLY. DISASSEMBLE, CLEAN AND INSPECT ALL PARTS. CLEAN THE VALVE BODY, INSTALL ALL NEW SEALS, RINGS, AND GASKETS. REPLACE WORN OR DEFECTIVE PARTS.
LISTEN TO TRANSMISSION AND CONVERTER FOR SOURCE OF NOISE.
REMOVE TORQUE CONVERTER AND INSPECT FOR LOOSE OR CRACKED CONVERTER DRIVE PLATE. INSPECT FOR CONTACT OF THE STARTER DRIVE WITH THE STARTING RING GEAR.
TRANSMISSION HAS BUZZ OR WHINE.
CONVERTER HAS LOUD BUZZ OR WHINE.
NO DEBRIS PRESENT REMOVE VALVE BODY, DISASSEMBLE, CLEAN AND INSPECT PARTS. REASSEMBLE, INSTALL, CHECK OPERATION AND PRESSURES.
REMOVE THE TRANSMISSION PAN: INSPCET FOR DEBRIS INDICATING WORN OR FAILED PARTS
REPLACE TORQUE CONVERTER.
DEBRIS PRESENT REMOVE TRANSMISSION AND CONVERTER AS AN ASSMBLY. DISASSEMBLE, CLEAN AND INSPECT ALL PARTS. CLEAN THE VALVE BODY. INSTALL ALL NEW SEALS, RINGS AND GASKETS: REPLACE WORN OR DEFECTIVE PARTS.
DIAGNOSIS GUIDE – VEHICLE WILL NOT MOVE
CHECK THE TRANSMISSION FLUID LEVEL BEFORE STARTING THE ENGINE. IF NO FLUID IS VISIBLE ON THE DIPSTICK, ADD FLUID TO THE "L" MARK BEFORE STARTING THE ENGINE. THEN START THE ENGINE WITH THE TRANSMISSION IN NEUTRAL AND LISTEN FOR NOISE.
NO ABNORMAL NOISE, MOVE THE SELECTOR TO A FORWARD DRIVE RANGE AND OBSERVE THE PROPELLER SHAFT FOR TURNING.
ABNORMAL NOISE. STOP ENGINE IMMEDIATELY. REMOVE TRANSMISSION AND CONVERTER AS AN ASSEMBLY; DISASSEMBLE, CLVEAN AND INSPECT ALL PARTS; CLEAN THE VALVE BODY, INSTALL ALL NEW SEALS, RINGS, AND GASKETS; REPLACE WORN OR DEFECTIVE PARTS.
PROPELLER SHAFT TURNS BUT REAR WHEELS DO NOT TURN, INSPECT FOR BROKEN REAR AXLE PARTS.
PROPELLER SHAFT DOES NOT TURN. REMOVE THE TRANSMISSION OIL PAN. INSPECT FOR DEBRIS.
NO DEBRIS REMOVE VALVE BODY DISASSEMBLE, CLEAN AND INSPECT ALL PARTS REASSEMBLE, INSTALL AND CHECK PRESSURES AND OPERATION
DEBRIS IS PRESENT. REMOVE THE TRANSMISSION AND CONVERTER AS AN ASSEMBLY DISASSEMBLE, CLEAN AND INSPECT ALL PARTS. CLEAN VALVE BODY; INSTALL ALL NEW SEALS, RINGS AND GASKETS; REPLACE WORN OR DEFECTIVE PARTS.

MT5029100513010X

Fig. 2 Troubleshooting chart: Abnormal noise, vehicle will not move & fluid leaks (Part 1 of 2)

POSSIBLE CAUSE
Faulty TCC.
Overrunning clutch inner race damaged.
Overrunning clutch worn, broken or seized.
Planetary gearsets broken or seized.
Rear clutch dragging.
Worn or faulty rear clutch.
Insufficient clutch plate clearance.
Faulty cooling system.
Kickdown band adjustment too tight.
Hydraulic pressure too high.
Breather clogged.
High fluid level.
Worn or faulty front clutch.
Kickdown servo band or linkage malfunction.
Worn or broken reaction shaft support seal rings.
Governor malfunction.
Governor support seal rings broken or worn.
Intermediate shaft bearing and/or bushing damaged.
Overrunning clutch not holding.
Kickdown band out of adjustment.
Incorrect throttle linkage adjustment.
Engine idle speed too low.
Aerated fluid.
Worn or broken input shaft seal rings.
Faulty oil pump.
Oil filter clogged.
Incorrect gearshift control linkage adjustment.
Low fluid level.
Low-reverse servo, band or linkage malfunction.
Valve body malfunction or leakage.
Low-reverse band out of adjustment.
Hydraulic pressures too low.
Engine idle speed too high.
Stuck TCC valve.
Stuck switch valve.

CONDITION	1	2	3	4	5	6	7	8	9	10	11	12	13	14	15	16	17	18	19	20	21	22	23	24	25	26	27	28	29	30	31	32	33	34	35
HARSH ENGAGEMENT FROM NEUTAL TO DOR R			×			×																				×				×					×
DELAYED ENGAGEMENT FROM NEUTRAL TO DOR R				×		×	×	×	×	×	×	×	×	×						×			×							×					
RUNAWAY UPSHIFT				×		×		×		×			×		×					×		×	×												
NO UPSHIFT				×		×		×	×						×				×	×	×	×	×											×	
3-2 KICKDOWN RUNAWAY				×		×		×					×		×	×			×			×	×												
NO KICKDOWN OR NORMAL DOWNSHIFT						×									×					×	×	×													
SHIFTS ERRATIC				×		×		×	×	×	×		×		×				×	×	×	×	×												
SLIPS IN FORWARD DRIVE POSITIONS				×		×		×	×	×	×	×	×		×		×													×			×		
SLIPS IN REVERSE ONLY				×	×	×	×	×	×		×		×							×			×												
SLIPS IN ALL POSITIONS				×		×		×		×	×	×	×																						
NO DRIVE IN ANY POSTION				×		×		×		×	×																					×			
NO DRIVE IN FORWARD DRIVE POSTIONS				×		×		×				×					×													×		×	×		
NO DRIVE IN REVERSE				×	×	×	×		×											×			×							×		×			
DRIVES IN NEUTRAL						×			×																				×	×	×				
DRAGS OF LOCKS		×			×						×																×					×	×		
GRATING, SCRAPING GROWLING NOISE					×											×		×														×	×		
BUZZING NOISE						×		×			×		×																					×	
HARD TO FILL, OIL BLOWS OUT FILLER HOLE										×			×											×	×										
TRANSMISSION OVERHEATS	×		×	×				×	×		×																×	×	×						
HARSH UPSHIFT				×											×	×										×									×
DELAYED UPSHIFT															×	×			×	×	×	×	×												
SLIPS IN REVERSE OR MANUAL LOW					×						×																								

MT5029100514000X

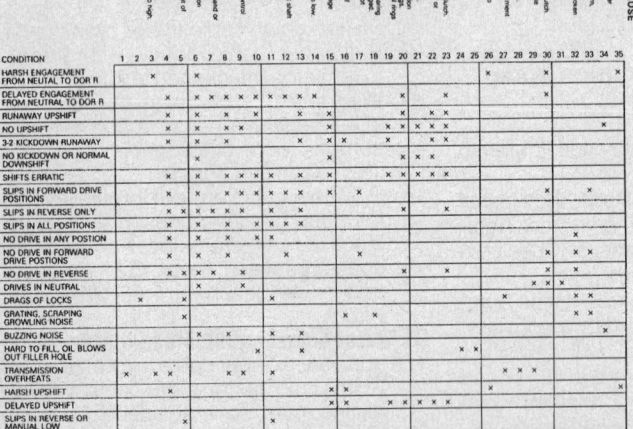

Fig. 3 Troubleshooting chart: General diagnosis

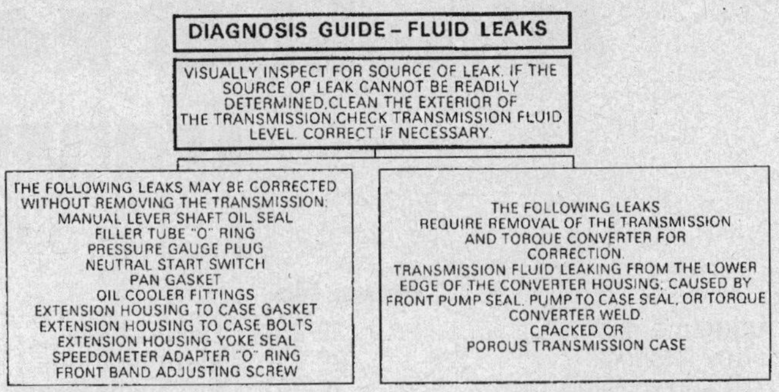
DIAGNOSIS GUIDE – FLUID LEAKS
VISUALLY INSPECT FOR SOURCE OF LEAK. IF THE SOURCE OF LEAK CANNOT BE READILY DETERMINED, CLEAN THE EXTERIOR OF THE TRANSMISSION. CHECK TRANSMISSION FLUID LEVEL. CORRECT IF NECESSARY.
THE FOLLOWING LEAKS MAY BE CORRECTED WITHOUT REMOVING THE TRANSMISSION:
MANUAL LEVER SHAFT OIL SEAL
FILLER TUBE "O" RING
PRESSURE GAUGE PLUG
NEUTRAL START SWITCH
PAN GASKET
OIL COOLER FITTINGS
EXTENSION HOUSING TO CASE GASKET
EXTENSION HOUSING TO CASE BOLTS
EXTENSION HOUSING YOKE SEAL
SPEEDOMETER ADAPTER "O" RING
FRONT BAND ADJUSTING SCREW
THE FOLLOWING LEAKS REQUIRE REMOVAL OF THE TRANSMISSION AND TORQUE CONVERTER FOR CORRECTION.
TRANSMISSION FLUID LEAKING FROM THE LOWER EDGE OF THE CONVERTER HOUSING; CAUSED BY FRONT PUMP SEAL, PUMP TO CASE SEAL, OR TORQUE CONVERTER WELD.
CRACKED OR POROUS TRANSMISSION CASE

MT5029100513020X

Fig. 2 Troubleshooting chart: Abnormal noise, vehicle will not move & fluid leaks (Part 2 of 2)

POSSIBLE CAUSE / CONDITION	NO LOCKUP	WILL NOT UNLOCK	STAYS LOCKED UP TO TOO LOW A SPEED IN DIRECT	LOCKS UP OR DRAGS IN LOW OR SECOND	STALLS OR IS SLUGGISH IN REVERSE	LOUD CHATTER DURING LOCKUP ENGAGEMENT – (COLD)	VIBRATION OR SHUDDER DURING LOCKUP ENGAGEMENT	VIBRATIONS AFTER LOCKUP ENGAGEMENT	VIBRATION WHEN "REVED" IN NEUTRAL	OVERHEATING; OIL BLOWING OUT DIPSTICK OR PUMP SEAL	SHUDDER AFTER LOCKUP ENGAGEMENT
FAULTY OIL PUMP	×			×	×		×				×
STICKING GOVERNOR VALVE	×	×	×								
PLUGGED COOLER, LINES OR FITTINGS					×					×	×
VALVE BODY MALFUNCTION	×	×	×	×	×		×				×
STUCK SWITCH VALVE	×	×	×	×	×					×	
STUCK TCC VALVE	×	×	×								
STUCK TCC TIMING VALVE	×	×	×	×							
STUCK TCC SOLENOID	×		×								
SOLENOID WIRING DISCONNECTED	×										
FAILED TCC SOLENOID	×										
FAILED TRANSMISSION CONTROL UNIT	×		×								
FAULTY TORQUE CONVERTER:	×					×	×	×			×
OUT OF BALANCE									×		
FAILED TCC	×					×					×
LEAKING TURBINE HUB SEAL	×					×					
ALIGN EXHAUST SYSTEM								×			×
TUNE ENGINE							×	×			×
FAULTY INPUT SHAFT OR SEAL RING	×				×						
THROTTLLE LINKAGE MISADJUSTED								×			×

NOTE
TCC Torque Converter Clutch

MT5029100515000X

Fig. 4 Troubleshooting chart: Electronic lockup torque converter

2. Using wrench tool No. C-3380-A and adapter tool No. C3705, or equivalents, **torque** band adjusting screw to 6 ft. lbs.
3. Back off adjusting screw 1⅞ turns, then tighten locknut to specifications while holding adjusting screw.

LOW & REVERSE BAND

1. Raise and support front of vehicle, then drain transmission fluid and remove transmission oil pan.
2. Remove locknut, then **torque** adjusting screw to 30 inch lbs., **Fig. 12.**
3. Back off adjusting screw six turns, then tighten locknut to specifications while holding adjusting screw.
4. Install oil pan and gasket, then tighten bolts to specifications.
5. Fill transmission with Dexron or Dexron II automatic transmission fluid.

LINE PRESSURE

An incorrect throttle pressure setting will cause incorrect line pressure readings even though the pressure adjustment is correct. Always inspect and correct throttle pressure adjustment before adjusting line pressure.

The approximate adjustment is 1⁵⁄₁₆ inch, measured from valve body to inner edge of adjusting nut, **Fig. 13.** However, due to manufacturing tolerances, the adjustment can be varied to obtain specified line pressure.

The adjusting screw may be turned with a suitable hex wrench. One complete turn of adjusting screw changes closed throttle line pressure approximately 1⅔ psi. Turning adjusting screw counterclockwise increases pressure and clockwise turn decreases pressure.

POSSIBLE CAUSE	NO REVERSE OR SLIPS IN REVERSE	NO OVERDRIVE SHIFT	RUNAWAY OVERDRIVE SHIFT	OVERDRIVE SHIFT OCCURS IMMEDIATELY AFTER 2 – 3 SHIFT	EXCESSIVELY DELAYED OVERDRIVE SHIFT	NO 4 – 3 DOWNSHIFT	NO 4 – 3 DOWNSHIFT WITH OVERDRIVE OFF SWITCH	TORQUE CONVERTER LOCKS UP IN 2ND AND 3RD GEARS	HARSH SHIFTS 1 – 2, 2 – 3, AND 3 – 2	LOW GOVERNOR PRESSURE	NOISY
FAILED DIRECT CLUTCH	x										
OVERDRIVE SPRING LOST LOAD	x										
INCORRECT OVERDRIVE PISTON BEARING SPACER	x	x			x						
BLOWN FUSE		x									
FAULTY OVERDRIVE SOLENOID		x		x							
FAULTY WIRING OR CONNECTORS		x		x		x	x				
FAULTY OVERDRIVE OFF SWITCH		x					x				
FAULTY TRANSMISSION CONTROL UNIT		x		x		x	x				
LOW OVERDRIVE PRESSURE		x									
LOWER VALVE BODY MALFUNCTION		x		x		x					
FAILED OVERDRIVE OVERRUNNING CLUTCH			x								x
FAULTY THROTTLE POSITION SENSOR					x						
FAULTY TCC SOLENOID - NOT VENTING						x	x	x	x		
LEAKING GOVERNOR TUBES – BENT										x	
LEAKING GOVERNOR TUBES – LOOSE FIT										x	
GOVERNOR SEAL RINGS BROKEN OR WORN										x	
FAILED OVERDRIVE PISTON BEARING											x
FAILED GEAR TRAIN NEEDLE THRUST BEARINGS											x
FAILED OVERDRIVE PLANETARY GEAR											x

NOTE
TCC Torque Converter Clutch

MT5029100516000X

Fig. 5 Troubleshooting chart: Overdrive unit

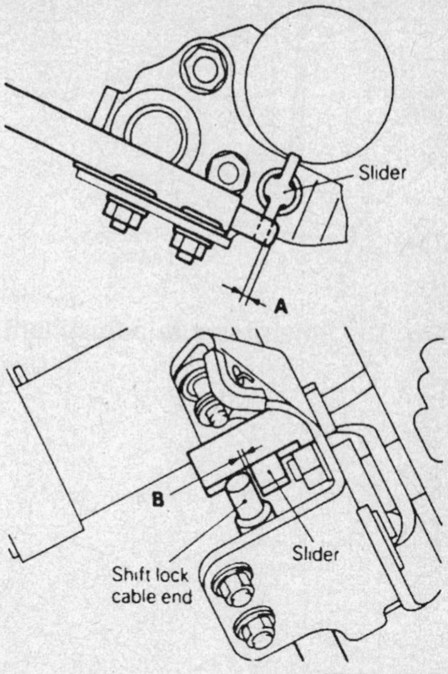
Slider
A
B
Slider
Shift lock
cable end
MT5029100517000X

Fig. 6 Shift lock cable adjustment

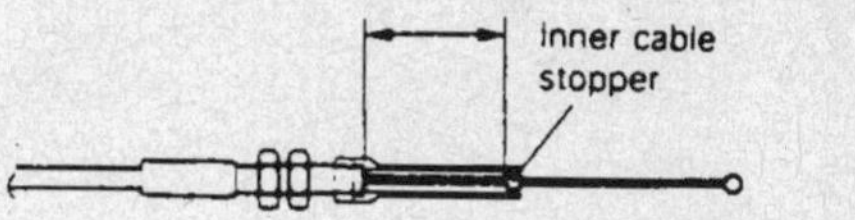
Inner cable
stopper
MT5029100520000X

Fig. 9 Measurement between inner cable stopper and outer cable with throttle lever at full open

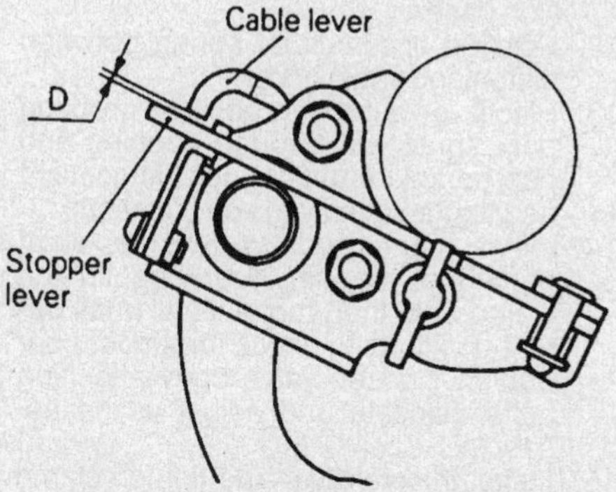
Cable lever
D
Stopper
lever
MT5029100518000X

Fig. 7 Key interlock cable adjustment

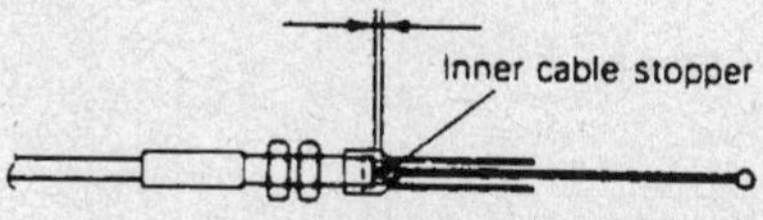
Inner cable stopper
MT5029100519000X

Fig. 8 Measurement between inner cable stopper and outer cable

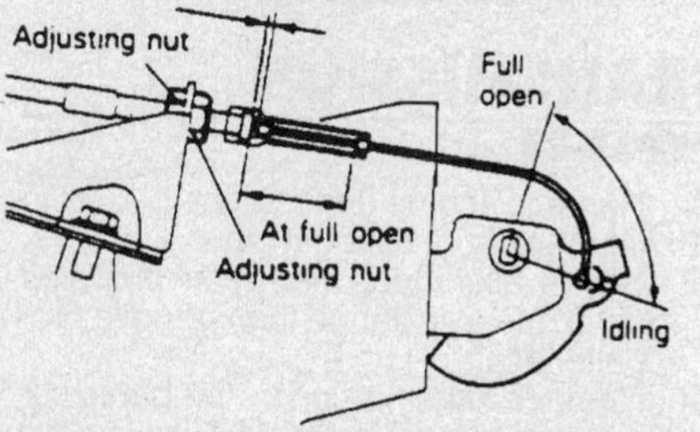
Adjusting nut
Full
open
At full open
Adjusting nut
Idling
MT5029100521000X

Fig. 10 Outer cable adjustment

THROTTLE PRESSURE

Throttle pressure cannot be tested accurately, therefore adjustment should be measured if a malfunction is evident.

1. Insert gauge pin of tool No. C-3763, or equivalent, between throttle lever cam and kickdown lever.
2. By pushing in on tool, compress kickdown valve against its spring so throttle valve is completely bottomed inside the valve body.
3. As force is exerted to compress spring, turn throttle lever stop screw with hex wrench until head of screw touches throttle lever tang with throttle lever cam touching tool and the throttle valve bottomed, **Fig. 14.** Be sure adjustment is made with spring fully compressed and valve bottomed in valve body.

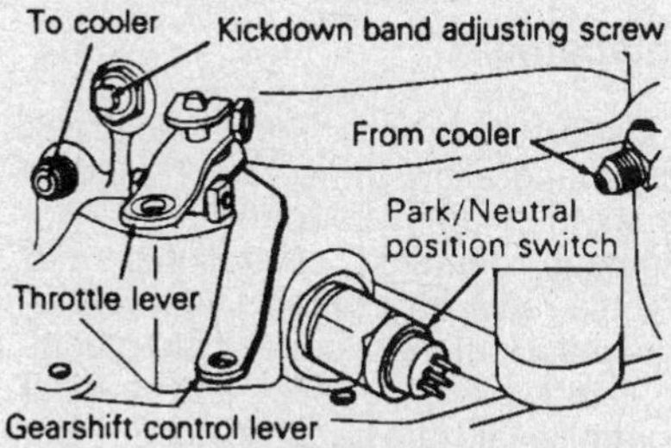
To cooler
Kickdown band adjusting screw
From cooler
Park/Neutral
position switch
Throttle lever
Gearshift control lever
MT5029100522000X

Fig. 11 Kickdown band adjusting screw location

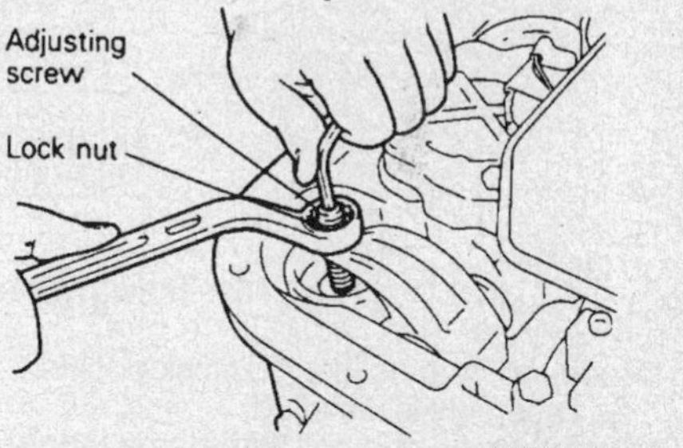
Adjusting
screw
Lock nut
MT5029100523000X

Fig. 12 Low-reverse band adjustment

IN-VEHICLE REPAIRS

SPEEDOMETER PINION GEAR REPLACEMENT

1. Remove bolt and clamp retaining speedometer pinion adapter in extension housing.
2. With cable housing connected, carefully work adapter and pinion out of extension housing.
3. If there is transmission fluid in cable housing, replace seal in adapter, **Fig. 15.**
4. Note number of gear teeth and install speedometer pinion gear into adapter, then fit O-ring over adapter.
5. Rotate speedometer pinion gear and adapter assembly so number on adapter, corresponding to number of

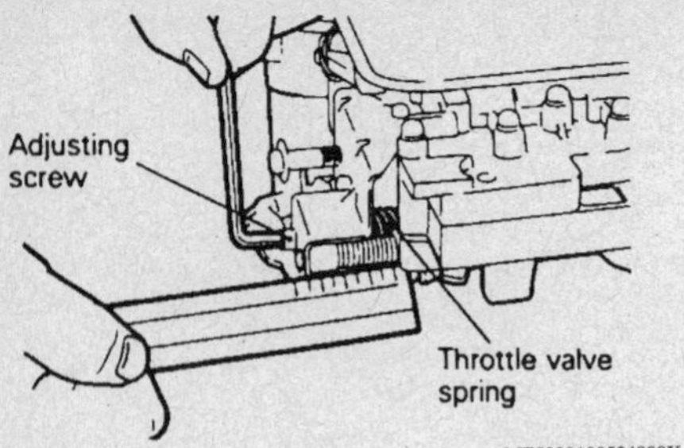
Adjusting screw
Throttle valve spring
MT5029100524000X

Fig. 13 Line pressure adjustment

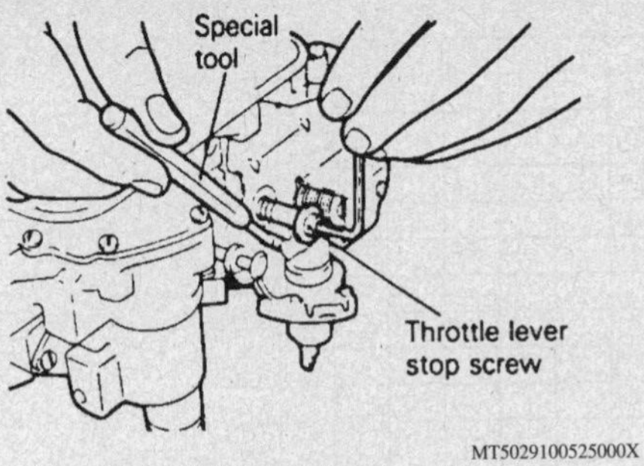
Special tool
Throttle lever stop screw
MT5029100525000X

Fig. 14 Throttle pressure adjustment

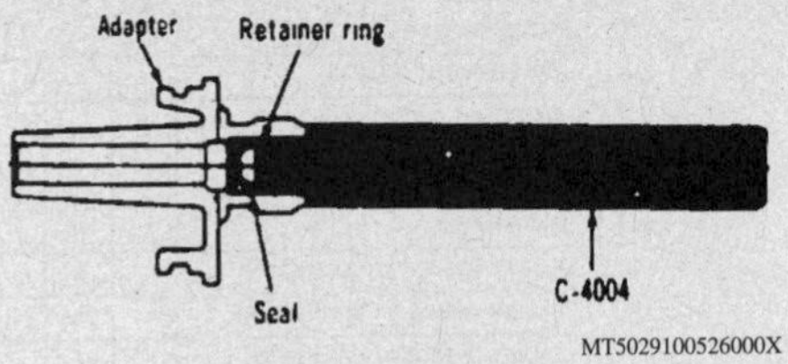
Adapter
Retainer ring
Seal
C-4004
MT5029100526000X

Fig. 15 Speedometer adapter seal installation

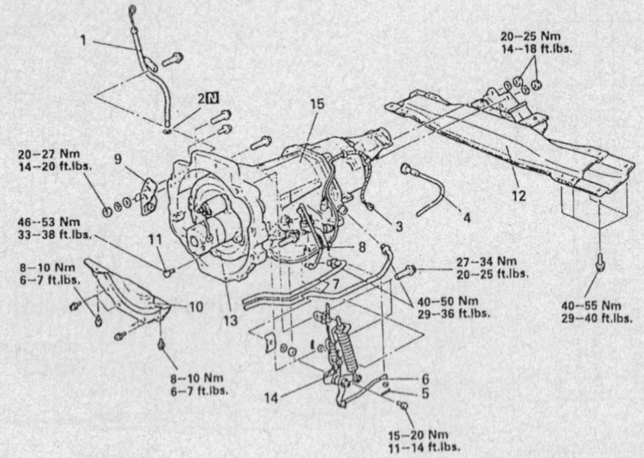
20–25 Nm
14–18 ft.lbs.
20–27 Nm
14–20 ft.lbs.
46–53 Nm
33–38 ft.lbs.
8–10 Nm
6–7 ft.lbs.
27–34 Nm
20–25 ft.lbs.
40–50 Nm
29–36 ft.lbs.
40–55 Nm
29–40 ft.lbs.
8–10 Nm
6–7 ft.lbs.
15–20 Nm
11–14 ft.lbs.

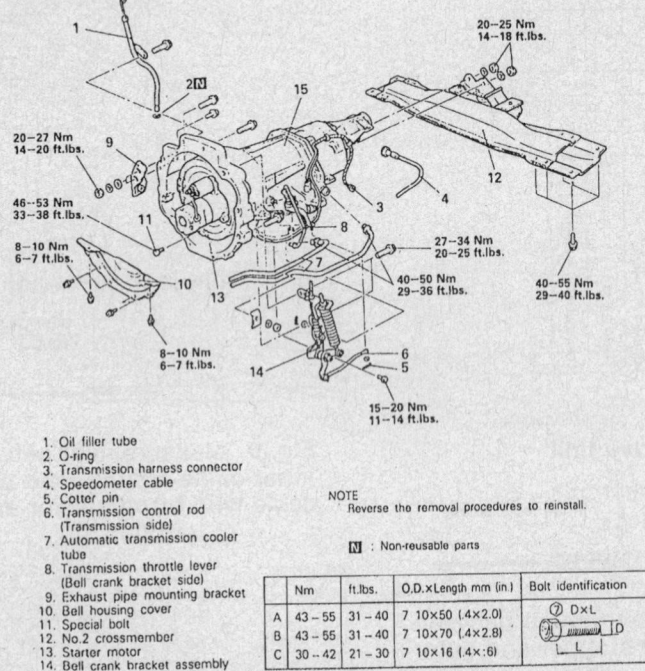

1. Oil filler tube
2. O-ring
3. Transmission harness connector
4. Speedometer cable
5. Cotter pin
6. Transmission control rod (Transmission side)
7. Automatic transmission cooler tube
8. Transmission throttle lever (Bell crank bracket side)
9. Exhaust pipe mounting bracket
10. Bell housing cover
11. Special bolt
12. No.2 crossmember
13. Starter motor
14. Bell crank bracket assembly
15. Transmission assembly

NOTE
Reverse the removal procedures to reinstall.

N : Non-reusable parts

	Nm	ft.lbs.	O.D.×Length mm (in.)	Bolt identification
A	43 – 55	31 – 40	7 10×50 (.4×2.0)	⑦ D×L
B	43 – 55	31 – 40	7 10×70 (.4×2.8)	
C	30 – 42	21 – 30	7 10×16 (.4×:6)	

MT5029100527000X

Fig. 16 Transmission replacement

teeth on gear, is in six o'clock position as assembly is installed.

6. Install clamp and bolt with clamp tangs in adapter positioning slots, then tap adapter firmly into extension housing and tighten sleeve clamp screw to specifications.

OVERDRIVE HOUSING YOKE SEAL REPLACEMENT

1. Mark then remove propeller shaft assembly.
2. Remove overdrive housing yoke seal using seal remover tool No. C-3985, or equivalent.
3. Position new seal in opening of housing and drive it into housing using seal installer tool No. C-3995, or equivalent.
4. Install propeller shaft assembly using marks made during removal.

VALVE BODY & ACCUMULATOR PISTON REPLACEMENT

1. Raise and support vehicle.
2. Loosen oil pan bolts. Tap pan to break loose and allow transmission fluid to drain, then remove oil pan.
3. Remove gearshift control rod and throttle rod A from respective levers of transmission, then loosen clamp bolts to remove throttle lever and manual control lever from transmission.
4. While holding valve body in position, remove valve body to transmission attaching bolts.
5. Lower valve body and pull forward out of case. It may be necessary to rotate propeller shaft to align parking gear and sprag to permit cam on end of parking sprag rod to pass sprag.
6. Remove accumulator piston and spring from transmission case.
7. Inspect piston for nicks, scores or wear, spring for distortion, and rings for freedom in piston grooves and wear or breakage. Replace parts as necessary.
8. If valve body manual lever shaft seal must be replaced, drive it out of case with suitable punch, then drive new

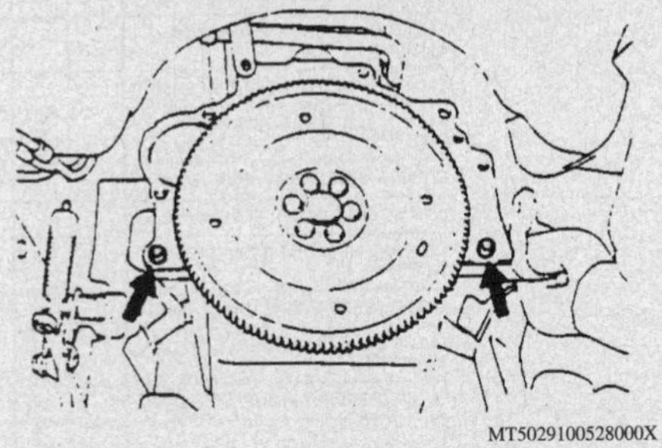
MT5029100528000X

Fig. 17 Transmission alignment pins

seal into case using a 15/16 inch socket and hammer.

9. Place valve body manual lever in low position.
10. Use screwdriver to push park sprag into engagement with parking gear, turning output shaft to verify engagement.
11. Install accumulator piston in transmission case.
12. Position accumulator spring between piston and valve body.
13. Place valve body in position, working park sprag rod through opening and past sprag, then install bolts finger tight and tighten evenly to specifications.
14. Install manual control lever to shaft portion of manual lever and tighten clamp bolt, then move lever to all detent positions to check for smooth operation. Loosen valve body attaching bolts, relocate and adjust as necessary.
15. Install throttle lever and tighten clamp bolt, then connect throttle and control rod and adjust as necessary.
16. Install oil pan and new gasket, then fill transmission fluid to specifications.

TRANSMISSION

REPLACE

1. Remove engine undercover.
2. Remove front exhaust pipe.
3. Scribe alignment marks on propeller shaft and axle flange then remove propeller shaft.
4. Remove transmission in numbered sequence shown in **Fig. 16,** noting the following:
   a. Tilt transmission so rear is lower than front to remove bolt that fastens the starter motor and bell crank bracket.
   b. Pull transmission rearward to disconnect transmission from engine then lower transmission from vehicle. **Ensure torque converter**

does not remain on the engine side, damage to the transmission oil pump could result.

5. Reverse numbered sequence shown in **Fig. 16** to install transmission, noting the following:

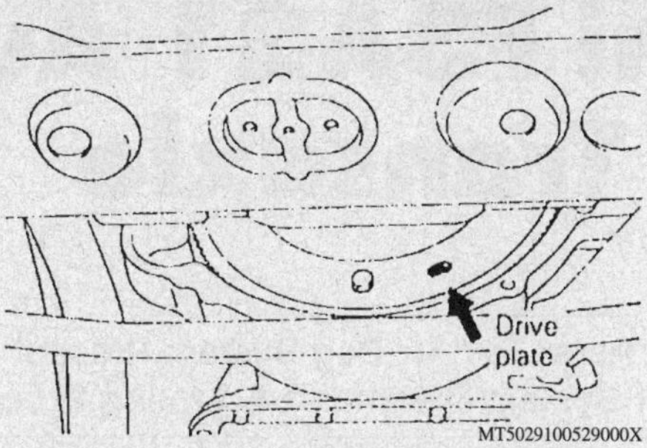
Drive plate
MT5029100529000X

Fig. 18 Transmission driveplate check hole

a. Align centering locations when installing transmission, **Fig. 17.**
b. Install special bolts so that the paint applied to the torque converter can be seen through check hole in driveplate, **Fig. 18.**

TIGHTENING SPECIFICATIONS

Component	Torque/Ft. Lbs.
Bell Crank Bracket	20–25
Bellhousing Cover	6–7
Driveplate To Torque Converter	23
Exhaust Pipe Mounting Bracket	14–20
Kickdown Band Adjusting Screw Locknut	30
Low/Reverse Band Adjusting Screw Locknut	25
No. 2 Crossmember To Frame	29–40
No. 2 Crossmember To Transmission	14–18
Overdrive Unit To Transmission Case	25
Park/Neutral Position Switch	25
Pressure Test Take-Off Plug	10
Selector Lever Rod	7–10
Shift Lock Cable	36–48①
Shift Lock Cable Locknut	7–10
Speedometer Sleeve Clamp Screw	8
Transmission Control Arm	14–20
Transmission Control Cable Locknut	12–19
Transmission Control Rod	11–14
Transmission Filter To Valve Body	35①
Transmission Mounting Bolt (.6 Inch)	21–30
Transmission Mounting Bolt (2.0 & 2.8 Inch)	31–40
Transmission Oil Cooler Eye Bolt	22–25
Transmission Oil Cooler Flare Nut	29–36
Transmission Oil Pan	13
Valve Body Screw	36①
Valve Body To Transmission Case	9

① — Inch lbs.

Mitsubishi F3A21 Automatic Transaxle

NOTE: On Air Bag Equipped Models, Refer To "Air Bag System Precautions" Located In The Front Of This Manual For System Disarming & Arming Procedures.

INDEX

	Page No.
Adjustments	29-256
Line Pressure	29-256
Park/Neutral Position Switch	29-256
Shift Lock Cable	29-256
Throttle Control Cable	29-256
Description	29-256
Identification	29-256
In-Vehicle Repairs	29-257
Control Cable Replacement	29-257
Maintenance	29-256
Fluid Change	29-256
Fluid Check	29-256
Precautions	29-256
Air Bag Systems	29-256
Tightening Specifications	29-260
Transaxle, Replace	29-257
Troubleshooting	29-256
Transaxle	29-256

PRECAUTIONS

AIR BAG SYSTEMS

Refer to "Air Bag System Precautions" in the front of this manual for system disarming and arming procedures.

IDENTIFICATION

The transaxle identification number is located on the vehicle information code plate that is attached on the fender shield in the engine compartment. The plate shows model and body code and engine and transaxle model numbers.

DESCRIPTION

These transaxles are three speed, fully automatic units using an internal damper clutch style torque converter, **Fig. 1.**

TROUBLESHOOTING

TRANSAXLE

Refer to **Figs. 2 and 3** when troubleshooting the transaxle.

MAINTENANCE

FLUID CHECK

The vehicle on level surface, start engine and operate at idle speed. With parking brake applied, place selector lever in Neutral, then remove dipstick and check fluid level. Transaxle should be at operating temperature when checking fluid level (120 to 180°F). Fluid level should be between Add and Full lines on dipstick. If necessary, add Dexron II fluid to bring fluid level within Add and Full lines on dipstick.

FLUID CHANGE

The automatic transaxle fluid should be changed every 30,000 miles on these units. When refilling transaxle, add only Dexron II automatic transaxle fluid.

1. Raise and support front of vehicle, then position drain pan under transaxle and remove drain located at bottom of differential and allow transaxle to drain.
2. Install drain plug, then add 4.2 quarts of the specified automatic transaxle fluid through transaxle dipstick hole.
3. Start engine and check fluid level as described under "Fluid Check" in this section.

ADJUSTMENTS

SHIFT LOCK CABLE

1. Place selector lever in Park position.
2. Fasten the shift lock cable at a position where end of shift lock cable is positioned above the red marking as shown in **Fig. 4.**

THROTTLE CONTROL CABLE

1. Place throttle lever in curb idle position.
2. Raise throttle cable cover B upward, then loosen cable lower mounting bracket bolt, **Fig. 5.**
3. Move cable lower mounting bracket until clearance between nipple and top of cable cover A is .02–.06 inch, then **torque** cable lower mounting bracket bolt to 9–10.5 ft. lbs.
4. With throttle lever in wide open position, pull throttle cable upward to ensure cable has freedom of movement.

LINE PRESSURE

1. Drain transaxle fluid by removing oil pan drain plug.
2. Remove oil pan.
3. Disconnect throttle control cable from throttle cam.
4. Remove oil filter and filter plate.
5. Remove valve body assembly, being careful not to drop manual valve.
6. Adjust line pressure by turning adjusting screw at regulator valve, **Fig. 6,** counterclockwise to increase line pressure or clockwise to decrease line pressure. One complete rotation of adjusting screw will change line pressure approximately 3.7 psi for wide open condition of throttle cable.
7. Ensure O-ring is properly installed in top of valve body, **Fig. 7.**
8. Install valve body assembly, fitting groove of manual valve on manual control shaft detent plate pin.
9. Install valve body attaching bolts in proper positions, **Fig. 8,** and **torque** to 8 ft. lbs. Bolt (A) is .709 inch long, bolt (B) is .984 inch long and bolt (C) is 1.576 inches long.
10. Install filter plate, gasket, and oil filter. **Torque** attaching bolts to 48–60 inch lbs.
11. Connect throttle cable to throttle cam.
12. Install new oil pan gasket, oil pan, washers, and bolts. **Torque** bolts to 7.5–8.5 ft. lbs.
13. Fill transaxle to specifications with Dexron II automatic transaxle fluid.

PARK/NEUTRAL POSITION SWITCH

The following procedure has been revised by a Technical Service Bulletin.

1. Set parking brake and place gear selector lever in Neutral position.
2. Loosen transaxle control cable to manual control lever coupling nut to allow lever to move freely.
3. Place manual control lever in its neutral position, then loosen park/neutral position switch mounting bolts.
4. Rotate switch body until holes in flange and manual control lever are aligned, **Fig. 9,** then **torque** switch mounting bolts to 8 ft. lbs.
5. Pull transaxle control cable gently away from cable housing, then **torque** coupling nut to 8 ft. lbs.
6. Ensure gear selector lever is still in Neutral position, then apply service brakes.
7. Attempt to start engine in all selector lever positions; ensure starting occurs

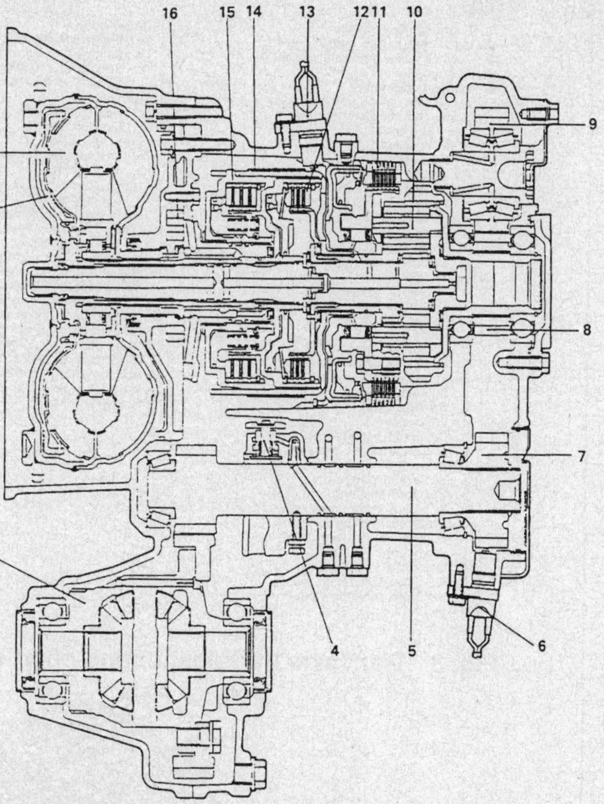
16
15
14
13
12
11
10
9
1
2
8
7
3
4
5
6

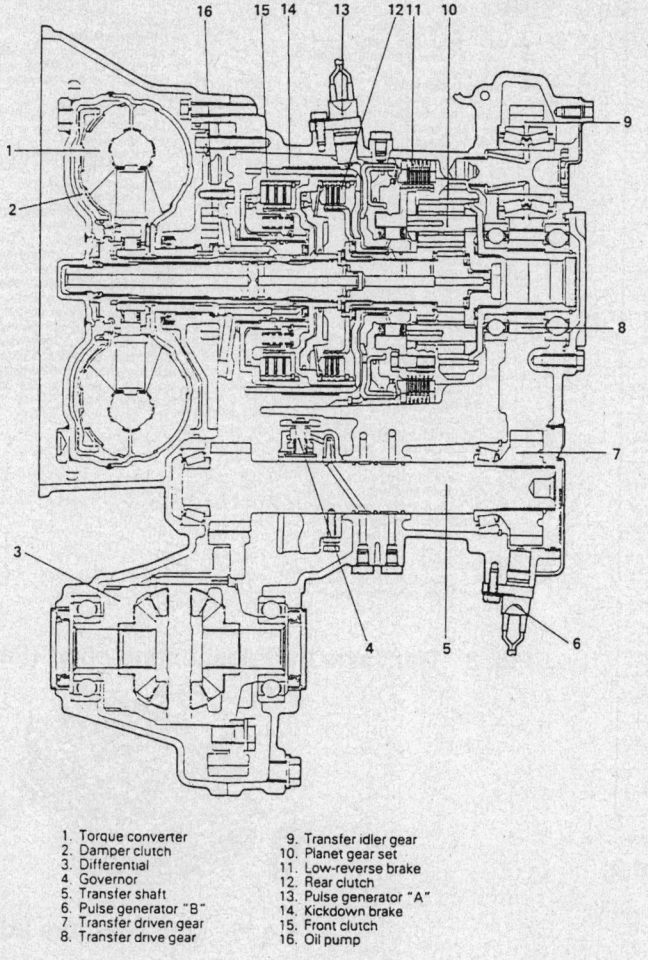

1. Torque converter
2. Damper clutch
3. Differential
4. Governor
5. Transfer shaft
6. Pulse generator "B"
7. Transfer driven gear
8. Transfer drive gear
9. Transfer idler gear
10. Planet gear set
11. Low-reverse brake
12. Rear clutch
13. Pulse generator "A"
14. Kickdown brake
15. Front clutch
16. Oil pump

MT5029100531000X

Fig. 1 Cross sectional view of transaxle

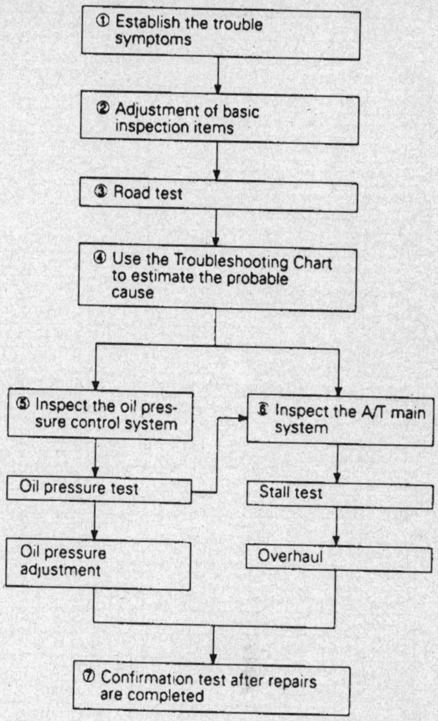
① Establish the trouble symptoms
② Adjustment of basic inspection items
③ Road test
④ Use the Troubleshooting Chart to estimate the probable cause
⑤ Inspect the oil pressure control system
⑥ Inspect the A/T main system
Oil pressure test
Stall test
Oil pressure adjustment
Overhaul
⑦ Confirmation test after repairs are completed

MT5029300534000X

Fig. 2 Troubleshooting flow chart

only in Park or Neutral positions.

IN-VEHICLE REPAIRS

CONTROL CABLE REPLACEMENT

1. Remove air cleaner assembly.
2. Service transaxle controls in numbered sequence shown in **Fig. 10,** as follows:
   a. Place gear selector in Neutral position.
   b. Install adjusting nut loosely on adjuster stud.
   c. Gently pull transaxle control cable in direction shown in **Fig. 11** and tighten nut.

TRANSAXLE

REPLACE

Replace transaxle assembly in numbered sequence shown in **Fig. 12,** noting the following:

1. Remove starter motor assembly leaving electrical harness connected.
2. Raise transaxle enough to remove weight off transaxle mount, then remove transaxle mounting bolts.
3. Support engine assembly using engine support tool No. MZ203827, or equivalent.
4. Remove tie rod end and lower ball joint using ball joint remover tool No. MB991193, or equivalent.
5. Insert a suitable pry bar between the driveshaft and transaxle case and pry driveshaft out of transaxle. Support driveshaft and do not allow to hang from driveshaft boot.
6. Remove three bolts connecting the torque converter to the driveplate.
7. After removing converter bolts push torque converter toward transaxle so that it does not remain on the engine.
8. Support transaxle using a suitable transaxle jack and remove from vehicle by moving assembly to the right and then lowering out of vehicle.
9. After securely inserting torque converter into transaxle, slide it so that value marked A is approximately .472 inch, **Fig. 13,** then install transaxle assembly on to engine.
10. Install driveshaft so that inboard joint of driveshaft is straight and not bent relative to the transaxle.

Problem symptom	Probable cause number
Starter motor does not operate in P and N positions	1
Movement impossible (in D, 2, L and R positions)	3, 4, 11, 14, 15, 21
Movement impossible (in D, 2 and L positions)	8, 23
Movement impossible (in D and 2 positions)	6
Movement impossible (in R position)	7, 9, 11, 17
Engine stalls when shifting from N to R, D	2, 11, 14, 23, 21
Vehicle starts to move in P position	26
High creeping in N position	7, 8
Poor acceleration in 2nd gear	3, 4, 5, 8, 10, 11, 14, 17, 23, 24
Poor acceleration in 3rd gear	3, 4, 5, 11, 17, 18, 23
Shift point displacement when shifting from 1st and 2nd	3, 4, 12, 13, 14, 17, 24
Flare shift 1 → 2	3, 4, 5, 11, 12, 13, 14, 17, 20, 24
Harsh 1 → 2 up shift	11, 12, 13, 14, 17, 20, 24
Shifting up from 1st to 2nd impossible	3, 4, 10, 11, 12, 13, 14, 24
Shift point displacement when shifting from 2nd and 3rd	3, 4, 11, 12, 13, 14, 18
Engine running up when shifting from 2nd to 3rd	3, 4, 5, 11, 14, 17, 18
Harsh 2 → 3 up shift	7, 10, 11, 12, 13, 14
Shifting up from 2nd to 3rd impossible	3, 4, 7, 10, 11, 12, 13, 14
Time lag during kickdown in D range	3, 4, 11, 12, 18, 22
Shock during kickdown in D range	7, 10, 14
No kickdown in D range	12, 13, 18, 22
Large shock felt when shifting from 3rd to 2nd	10, 12, 13, 14, 18, 19
Large shock felt when shifting from 3rd to 1st	12, 13, 14, 24
Large shock felt when shifting from 2nd to 1st	10, 12, 13, 14, 24
Shiting down from 3rd to 2nd impossible	12, 13, 18
Shiting down from 3rd to 1st impossible	12, 13, 18, 19
Shiting down from 2nd to 1st impossible	12, 13, 17
Shifting up to 3rd in 2 range	11, 18, 19, 25
Shifting up in L range	11, 17, 18, 19, 24
Engine braking ineffective in L range	9, 11, 14, 16
Stall rpm too high in R range	3, 4, 7, 9, 11, 14
Stall rpm too high in D range	3, 4, 6, 8, 11, 14
Stall rpm too low	2, 5

MT5029300535010X

Fig. 3 Transaxle troubleshooting chart (Part 1 of 2)

PROBABLE CAUSE

1. Engine starting system
2. Insufficient engine output
3. Poor oil pump discharge pressure
4. Clogged oil filter
5. Torque converter
   a. Malfunction of stator one-way clutch
   b. Burned out stator one-way clutch
6. One-way clutch
   a. Malfunction
   b. Burn out
7. Front clutch
   a. Sticking of piston
   b. Foreign material caught in check valve
   c. Damaged seal ring
   d. Worn disc
   e. Deformed return spring
   f. Excessive clutch clearance
8. Rear clutch
   a. Sticking of piston
   b. Foreign material caught in check valve
   c. Damaged seal ring
   d. Worn disc
   e. Deformed return spring
   f. Excessive clutch clearance
9. Low-reverse brake
   a. Sticking of piston
   b. Damaged seal ring
   c. Worn disc
   d. Deformed return spring
   e. Excessive clutch clearance
10. Kickdown brake
   a. Sticking of piston
   b. Damaged seal ring
   c. Kickdown servo poorly adjusted
   d. Malfunction of anchor rod
   e. Burned out kickdown band
   f. Worn kickdown band
   g. Deformed return spring
   h. Kickdown servo bore worn
   i. Kickdown servo bore check valve malfunction
11. Valve body
   a. Improper installation
   b. Damaged O-ring at installation surfaces
   c. Sticking of check ball
12. Malfunction of throttle valve
13. Governor
   a. Damaged weight
   b. Clogged filter
14. Regulator valve
   a. Improper adjustment
   b. Malfunction
15. Line pressure relief valve
   a. Sticking of ball
   b. Deformed or damaged spring
16. Low-relief valve
   a. Sticking of ball
   b. Deformed or damaged spring
17. Malfunction of 1-2 shift valve
18. Malfunction of 2-3 shift valve
19. Malfunction of 2-3 control valve
20. Malfunction of range control valve
21. Malfunction of torque converter control valve
22. Malfunction of kickdown valve
23. Malfunction of N-D accumulator valve
24. Malfunction of 1-2 accumulator valve
25. Malfunction of 1-2 engine brake valve.
26. Parking mechanism failure

MT5029300535020X

Fig. 3 Transaxle troubleshooting chart (Part 2 of 2)

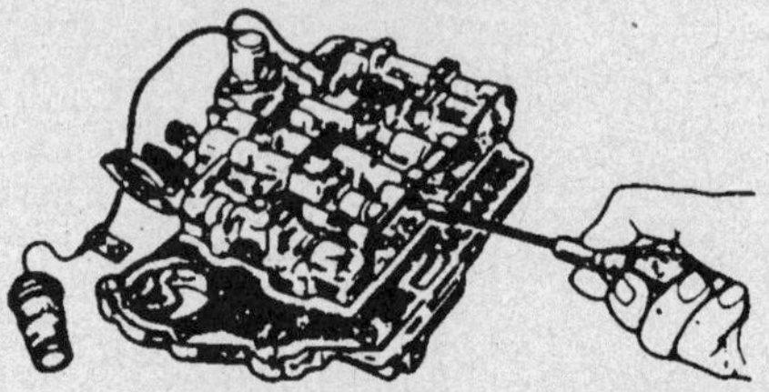

MT5029100540000X

Fig. 6 Line pressure adjustment

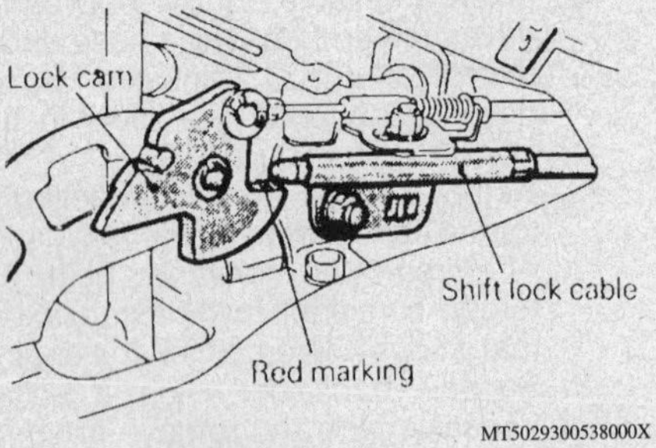
Lock cam
Shift lock cable
Red marking

MT5029300538000X

Fig. 4 Shift lock cable adjustment

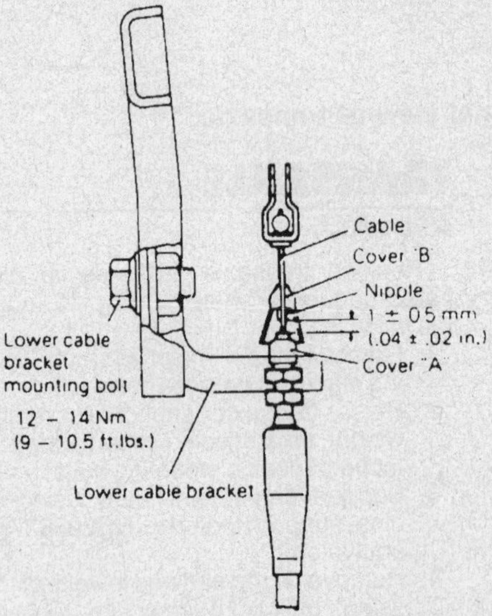
Cable
Cover "B"
Nipple
1 ± 0.5 mm
(.04 ± .02 in.)
Cover "A"
Lower cable bracket mounting bolt
12 – 14 Nm
(9 – 10.5 ft.lbs.)
Lower cable bracket

MT5029100539000X

Fig. 5 Throttle control cable adjustment

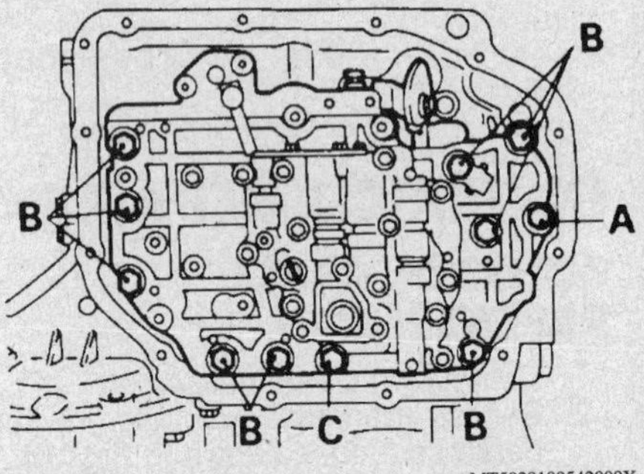
B
B
A
B
C
B

MT5029100542000X

Fig. 8 Valve body attaching bolt locations

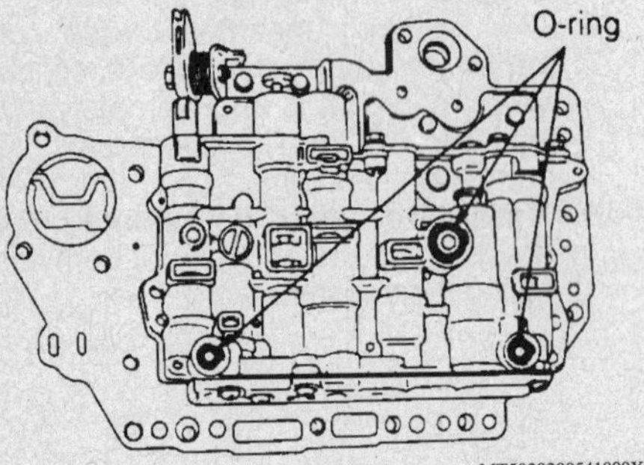
O-ring

MT5029200541000X

Fig. 7 O-ring installation in top of valve body

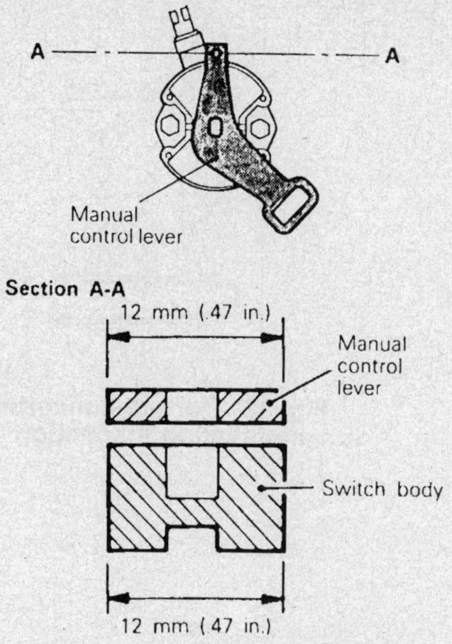
A
A
Manual
control lever
Section A-A
12 mm (.47 in.)
Manual
control
lever
Switch body
12 mm (.47 in.)

MT5029100543000X

Fig. 9 Park/Neutral position switch installation

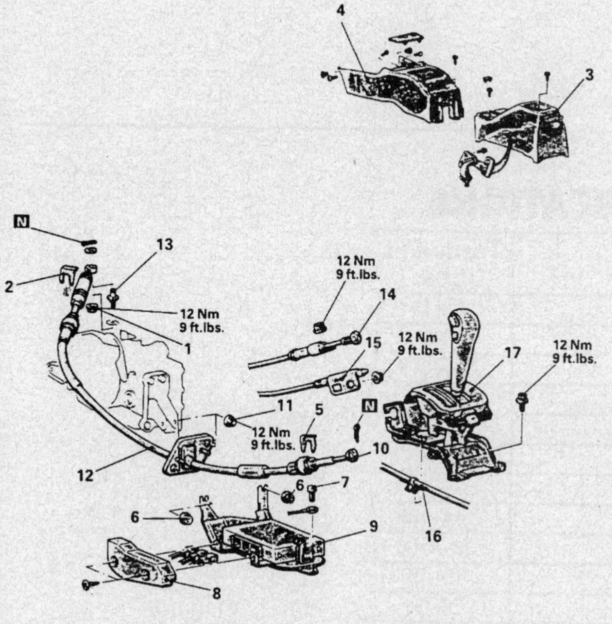
N
13
2
12 Nm
9 ft.lbs.
1
12 Nm
9 ft.lbs.
14
15
12 Nm
9 ft.lbs.
17
12 Nm
9 ft.lbs.
11
5
N
12 Nm
9 ft.lbs.
10
12
6
7
6
9
16
8
4
3

Transaxle control cable assembly removal steps

1. Nut
2. Clip
3. Rear floor console
4. Front floor console
5. Clip
6. Nut
7. Bolt
8. Cover
9. Transaxle control module
10. Connection for the transaxle control cable assembly
11. Nut
12. Transaxle control cable assembly
13. Adjuster

Selector lever assembly removal steps

3. Rear floor console
4. Front floor console
10. Connection for the transaxle control cable assembly
14. Connection of key interlock cable
15. Connection of shift lock cable
16. Clip
17. Selector lever assembly

MT5029300546000X

Fig. 10 Transaxle control cable replacement

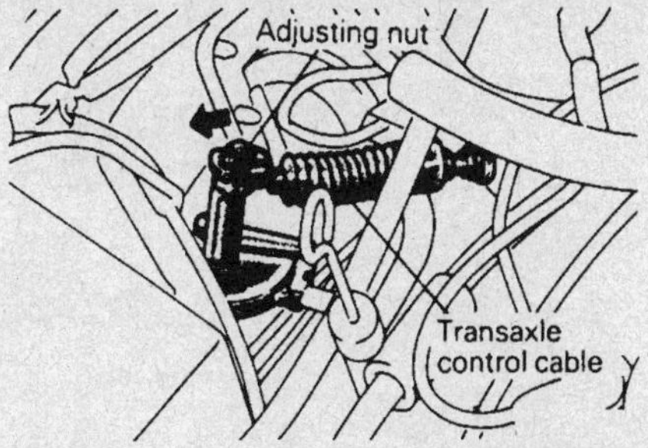
Adjusting nut
Transaxle
control cable

MT5029300547000X

Fig. 11 Control cable adjustment

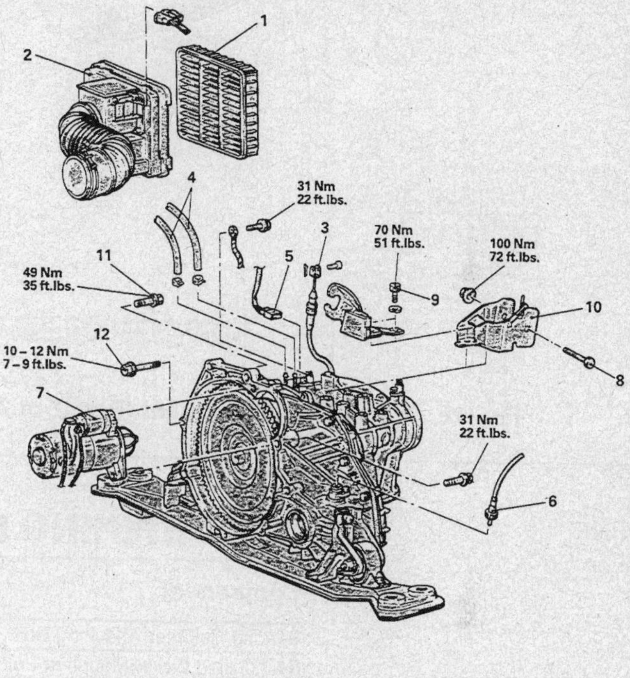
1
2
4
31 Nm
22 ft.lbs.
3
70 Nm
51 ft.lbs.
100 Nm
72 ft.lbs.
11
5
49 Nm
35 ft.lbs.
9
10
12
10 – 12 Nm
7 – 9 ft.lbs.
8
7
31 Nm
22 ft.lbs.
6

Removal steps

1. Air cleaner element
2. Air cleaner cover and hose assembly
3. Manual control lever connection
4. Transaxle oil cooler hoses connection
5. Park/Neutral position switch connector
6. Speedometer cable connection
7. Starter motor
8. Transaxle mount bolt
9. Bolt
10. Transaxle mount bracket
11. Transaxle assembly upper part coupling bolt
12. Bolt
- Support of engine assembly

MT5029300549010X

Fig. 12 Transaxle replacement (Part 1 of 2)

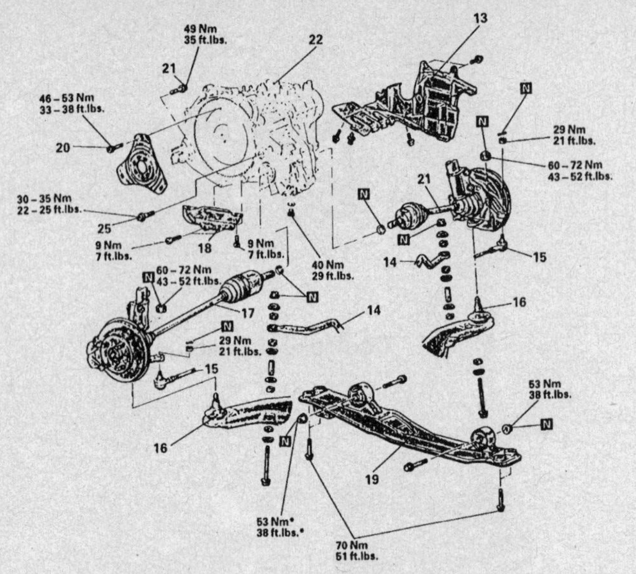
49 Nm
35 ft.lbs.
46 – 53 Nm
33 – 38 ft.lbs.
30 – 35 Nm
22 – 25 ft.lbs.
9 Nm
7 ft.lbs.
60 – 72 Nm
43 – 52 ft.lbs.
40 Nm
29 ft.lbs.
29 Nm
21 ft.lbs.
53 Nm
38 ft.lbs.
53 Nm*
38 ft.lbs.*
70 Nm
51 ft.lbs.

Vehicle lifting up

- Draining of the transaxle fluid
13. Under cover (RH)
14. Connection for stabilizer bar
15. Connection for tie rod end
16. Connection for lower arm ball joint
17. Connection for drive shaft
18. Bell housing cover
19. Center member assembly
20. Drive plate connecting bolt
21. Transaxle assembly lower part coupling bolt
22. Transaxle assembly

NOTE
For tightening locations indicated by the * symbol, first tighten temporarily, and then make the final tightening with the entire weight of the engine applied to the vehicle body.

MT5029300549020X

Fig. 12 Transaxle replacement (Part 2 of 2)

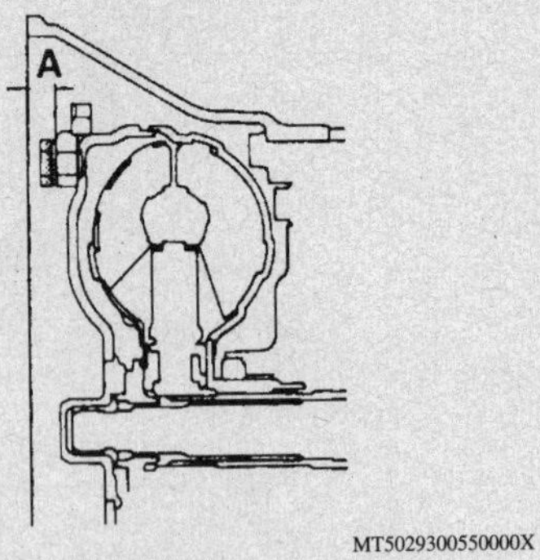
A

MT5029300550000X

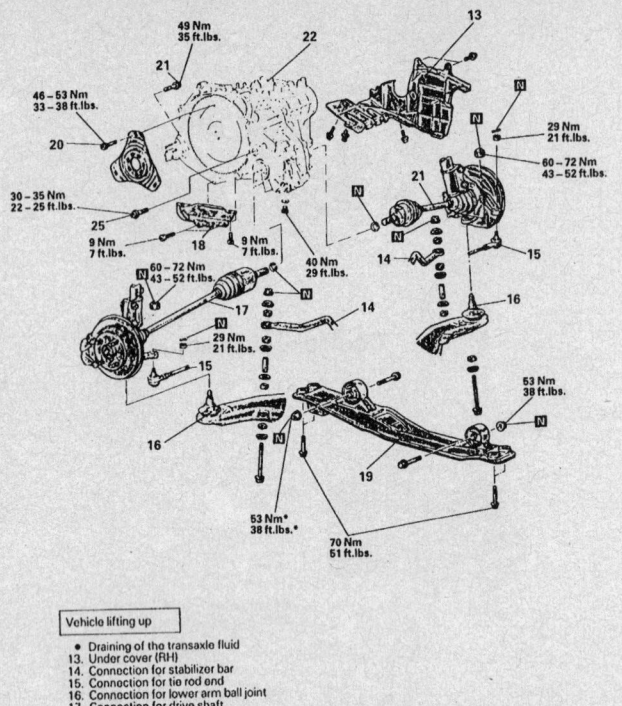

Fig. 13 Torque converter installation inspection

TIGHTENING SPECIFICATIONS

Component	Torque/Ft. Lbs.
Bearing Retainer Attaching Bolt	11–15
Bellhousing Cover Mounting Bolt	7–9
Cable Clip Mounting Bolt	36–48④
Control Cable To Body	7–10
Converter Housing Mounting Bolt	14–16
Differential Drive Gear Bolt	95–101
Driveplate To Torque Converter	34–38
Driveshaft Attaching Nut	144–188
Governor Setscrew	36–48④
Idler Shaft Lock Plate	15–19
Inhibitor Switch Attaching Bolt	8–9
Key Interlock Cable Mounting Nut	36–48④
Lever Assembly To Body	7–10
Lever To Bracket Assembly	10–14
Lower Arm Ball Joint To Knuckle	43–52
Manual Control Lever Attaching Bolt	13–16
Manual Control Lever Setscrew	72–84④
Oil Filter Mounting Bolt	48–60④
Oil Pan Mounting Bolt	96–108④
Oil Pump Housing Bolt	96–108④
Oil Pump Mounting Bolt	18–23
Planetary Carrier Bolt	25–32
Pulse Generator Attaching Bolt	96–108④
Shift Lock Cable Mounting Nuts (Brake Pedal Side)	7–10
Shift Lock Cable Mounting Nuts (Lever Assembly Side)	36–48④

Continued

TIGHTENING SPECIFICATIONS—Continued

Component	Torque/Ft. Lbs.
Sprag Rod Support Bolt	15–19
Starter Motor Mounting Bolt	20–25
Throttle Cam Attaching Bolt	6–7
Tie Rod End To Knuckle	11–25
Transaxle Mounting Bolts ①	31–40
Transaxle Mounting Bolts ②	22–25
Transaxle Mounting Bolts ③	7–8
Transaxle Mounting Bracket To Body	43–58
Transaxle Mounting Bracket To Transaxle	43–58
Valve Body Assembly Bolts	36–48④
Valve Body To Transaxle Case	8

① — .47 inch diameter bolt.
② — .40 inch diameter bolt.
③ — .31 inch diameter bolt.
④ — Inch lbs.

Mitsubishi F4AC1, F4A21, F4A22, F4A23, F4A33, W4A32, W4A33 & KM176 Automatic Transaxles

NOTE: On Air Bag Equipped Models, Refer To "Air Bag System Precautions" Located In The Front Of This Manual For System Disarming & Arming Procedures.

NOTE: Prior To Performing Any Service Operations Listed In This Section, Consult The "Technical Service Bulletins" Section For Related Information.

INDEX

Page No.

Adjustments 29-262
Kickdown Servo 29-262
Line Pressure 29-263
Park/Neutral Position Switch 29-262
Reducing Pressure 29-263
Shift Lock Cable 29-262
Throttle Position Sensor 29-263
Description 29-262
F4A21, F4A22, F4A33 & W4A33 Transaxles 29-262
F4AC1 Transaxle 29-262
W4A32, W4A33 & KM176 Transaxles 29-262
Identification 29-261
In-Vehicle Repairs 29-264
Control Cable Replacement 29-264
Driveshaft Oil Seal Replacement 29-264
Maintenance 29-262
Fluid Change 29-262
Fluid Check 29-262
Precautions 29-261
Air Bag Systems 29-261
Technical Service Bulletins 29-266
Shift Delay Before Warm-Up 29-266
Transaxle Whine 29-266
Tightening Specifications 29-279
Transaxle, Replace 29-264
F4AC1, F4A21, F4A22, F4A23 & F4A33 Transaxles 29-264
KM176 Transaxle 29-266
W4A32 & W4A33 Transaxles 29-265
Troubleshooting 29-262
Shift Lock System 29-262
Transaxle 29-262

PRECAUTIONS

AIR BAG SYSTEMS

Refer to "Air Bag System Precautions" in the front of this manual for system disarming and arming procedures.

IDENTIFICATION

The transaxle identification number is located at the top of the bellhousing as shown in **Figs. 1 and 2.**

DESCRIPTION

F4A21, F4A22, F4A33 & W4A33 TRANSAXLES

The Mitsubishi F4A21, F4A22, F4A33 and W4A33 transaxles, **Figs. 3 through 6,** are four speed, fully automatic transaxles using a three element damper clutch torque converter. Two shift patterns are stored in the control unit of these transaxles. One is the power pattern and the other is the economy pattern. The driver can select and switch to the desired pattern by using the power/economy select switch on the center console.

F4AC1 TRANSAXLE

The F4AC1 automatic transaxle, **Fig. 7,** is a fully adaptive, electronically controlled four speed full automatic transaxle. The F4AC1 transaxle uses a three element type torque converter with torque converter clutch.

The F4AC1 provides four forward speeds with ratios of 2.84:1, 1.57:1, 1.00:1 and .069:1. Reverse ratio is 2.21:1 and the final gear ratio is 4.08:1. It includes damper, underdrive, reverse, 2/4, and low/reverse clutches. It is also equipped with output and input speed sensors.

W4A32, W4A33 & KM176 TRANSAXLES

These four speed transaxles, **Figs. 8 through 10,** are electronically controlled, fully automatic units using a three element damper clutch torque converter.

TROUBLESHOOTING

TRANSAXLE

Refer to **Figs. 11 and 12** when troubleshooting these transaxles.

SHIFT LOCK SYSTEM

Refer to **Fig. 13** when troubleshooting the shift lock system.

MAINTENANCE

FLUID CHECK

Place vehicle on level surface, start engine and operate at idle speed. Shift transaxle through all gear ranges and return to Park. With parking brake applied, place selector lever in Neutral, then remove dipstick and check fluid level. Transaxle should be at operating temperature when checking fluid level (160–180°F). Fluid level should be between ADD and FULL lines on dipstick. If necessary, add Dexron II automatic transaxle fluid to bring fluid level within ADD and FULL lines on dipstick.

FLUID CHANGE

Except F4AC1 Transaxle

The automatic transaxle fluid should be changed every 30,000 miles. When refilling transaxle, add only Dexron II automatic transaxle fluid.

1. Remove drain plug from bottom of differential and drain fluid into a suitable container.
2. Loosen transaxle oil pan attaching bolts, then tap pan at one corner to break loose and drain fluid into a suitable container.
3. Remove oil pan and drain residual fluid.
4. Inspect oil filter for damage or obstructions and replace if necessary.
5. Install drain plug with a new gasket and tighten to specifications.
6. Clean transaxle case and oil pan mating surfaces, then install oil pan with a new gasket and **torque** attaching bolts to 7–9 ft. lbs.
7. Add 4.2 quarts Dexron II automatic transaxle fluid to transaxle through dipstick hole.
8. Run engine at idle for at least two minutes, then shift transaxle through all ranges and recheck fluid level.
9. Add sufficient fluid to bring level to lower mark on dipstick, then run engine until normal operating temperature is reached. Recheck dipstick and ensure fluid level is within Hot range.

F4AC1 Transaxle

The automatic transaxle fluid should be changed every 30,000 miles on these units. When refilling transaxle, add only Mopar ATF Plus (Type 7176), or equivalent.

1. Raise and support front of vehicle, then position drain pan under transaxle.
2. Loosen the transaxle oil pan bolts and tap pan at one corner to break it loose allowing fluid to drain.
3. Install a new filter and O-ring on bottom of valve body and clean oil pan and magnet.
4. Install oil pan and **torque** mounting bolts to 14 ft. lbs.
5. Add 4.0 qts. of transaxle fluid through filler tube.
6. Start engine and check fluid level as outlined under "Fluid Check" in this section.

ADJUSTMENTS

PARK/NEUTRAL POSITION SWITCH

1. Place selector lever in Neutral position.
2. Place manual control lever in Neutral position.
3. Rotate switch body so that manual control lever and switch body holes are aligned, **Fig. 14.**
4. **Torque** park/neutral position switch mounting bolts 7–9 ft. lbs. Do not drop switch body.
5. Loosen transaxle control cable nut and lightly pull end of cable as shown in **Fig. 15.**
6. **Torque** nut to 7–10 ft. lbs.
7. Ensure selector lever is in Neutral position.
8. Ensure selector lever operates on transaxle side in range which corresponds to each position of selector lever.

SHIFT LOCK CABLE

MIRAGE

1. Place selector lever in Park position.
2. Fasten shift lock cable in position at which cable end is above red mark, **Fig. 16.**

DIAMANTE, EXPO & 3000GT

1. With vehicle stopped and engine off, remove floor console and place selector lever in Park position.
2. Place ignition key in Lock position, then loosen key interlock cable nut, **Fig. 17.**
3. While pressing gently upon lock cam in direction of arrow, **Fig. 17,** press on cable to remove slack, then tighten nut.
4. Install console, then inspect key interlock system as follows:
   a. Ensure selector lever cannot be moved out of Park position with ignition key in Lock position or removed and brake pedal depressed.
   b. Ensure selector lever can be moved out of Park position with ignition key in Accessory position, brake pedal depressed and selector lever button pressed.
   c. Ensure ignition key cannot be turned to Lock position with selector lever in any position other than Park.
   d. Ensure ignition key can be smoothly turned to Lock position with selector lever in Park position and lever button released.

GALANT

1993

1. With wheels chocked, parking brake applied and shift lock cable nut loosened, place selector lever in Reverse position, then clamp shift lock cable.
2. Connect shift lock cable to selector lever assembly and tighten nut temporarily, then slide cable until distance between selector lever detent pin and cable is .04–.15 inch.
3. Tighten cable nut completely and ensure cable operates properly.

KICKDOWN SERVO

1. Clean area around kickdown servo switch.
2. Remove snap ring.
3. Remove kickdown servo switch.
4. To prevent rotation of piston, engage pawl of kickdown servo wrench tool No. MD998918, or equivalent, into notch of piston and attach wrench using adapter tool No. MD998916-1-01, or equivalent, **Fig. 18. Do not press in piston with special tool. When mounting adapter on transaxle case, tighten by hand only. Do not over-tighten.**
5. Loosen locknut to before the V groove of adjusting rod and tighten kickdown adjusting inner tool No. MD998916-3-01, or equivalent, until it contacts locknut, **Fig. 19.**
6. Engage kickdown adjusting outer tool No. MD998916-2-01, or equivalent, on

locknut. Rotating outer cylinder counterclockwise and inner cylinder clockwise, lock the locknut and inner tool.

7. Attach torque wrench to inner tool and repeat tightening and returning at a **torque** of 7.2 ft. lbs. two times, then **torque** to 3.6 ft. lbs. Loosen inner tool 2–2¾ turns.
8. Unlock inner tool from locknut by rotating outer cylinder clockwise and the inner cylinder counterclockwise. **When unlocking, apply equal force to both tools.**
9. Tighten locknut by hand until locknut contacts piston. **Torque** locknut to 18–23 ft. lbs.
10. Remove kickdown servo wrench and adapter and install a plug at the low-reverse pressure port.

LINE PRESSURE

1. Drain fluid and remove oil pan and filter assembly.
2. Remove oil temperature sensor.
3. Press solenoid valve harness grommet and connector into transaxle case.
4. Remove valve body assembly. **Use care not to drop manual valve.**
5. **On all models except 1995–96 Eclipse and 1994–96 Galant,** turn regulator valve adjustment screw and adjust so that line pressure is 124–127 psi, **Fig. 20.** When adjustment screw is turned clockwise with the solenoid valves pointed up, the line pressure is lowered; when adjustment screw is turned counterclockwise with the solenoid valves pointed up, the line pressure is raised. **Each 360° turn of adjustment screw adjusts line pressure approximately 5 psi.**
6. **On 1995–96 Eclipse and 1994–96 Galant models,** turn regulator valve adjustment screw and adjust so that line pressure is 126.2–129.1 psi, **Fig. 20.** When adjustment screw is turned clockwise with the solenoid valves pointed up, the line pressure is lowered; when adjustment screw is turned counterclockwise with the solenoid valves pointed up, the line pressure is raised. **Each 360° turn of adjustment screw adjusts line pressure approximately 5.4 psi.**
7. **On all models,** ensure O-ring is installed on upper surface of valve body as shown, **Fig. 21.**
8. Install new solenoid valve harness grommet O-ring.
9. Install harness grommet into case.
10. **On all models except those equipped with F4AC1 transaxle,** install valve body and oil temperature sensor. Tighten valve body bolts to specifications, referring to **Figs. 22 and 23** for correct bolt length position.
    a. Positions marked A use .709 inch long bolts.
    b. Positions marked B use .984 inch long bolts.
    c. Positions marked C use 1.575 inch long bolts.
11. **On models equipped with F4AC1 transaxle,** install valve body and oil temperature sensor.
12. **On all models,** install oil filter, new oil

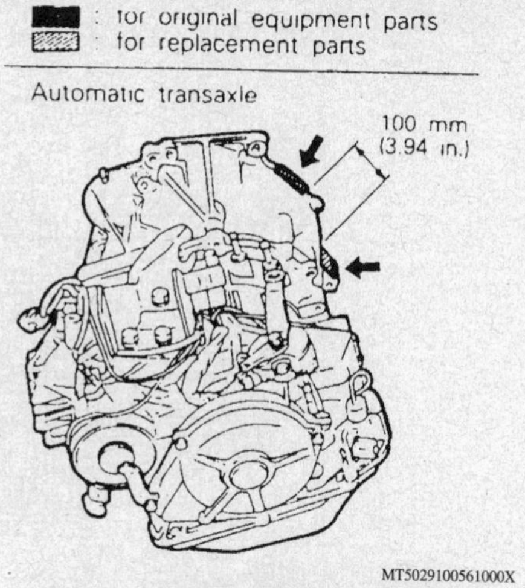

: for original equipment parts
: for replacement parts
Automatic transaxle
100 mm
(3.94 in.)
MT5029100561000X

Fig. 1 F4A21, F4A22, F4A23, F4A33, W4A32, W4A33 & KM176 transaxle identification

pan gasket, oil pan and ATF as outlined under "Fluid Change" in "Maintenance" section.

13. Ensure transaxle oil pressure is correct. Readjust as necessary.

REDUCING PRESSURE

Less Multi-Use Tester

1. Drain transaxle fluid, remove oil pan and filter.
2. Turn adjustment screw of lower valve body and adjust so that reducing pressure is 59–61 psi with a preferred of 60 psi, **Fig. 24.** When adjustment screw is turned clockwise, the reducing pressure becomes lower; when adjustment screw is turned counterclockwise the reducing pressure becomes higher.
3. **On all models except those equipped with KM176 transaxle,** each 360° turn of the adjustment screw adjusts pressure approximately 6.4 psi.
4. **On models equipped with KM176 transaxle,** each 360° turn of adjustment screw adjusts pressure approximately 4.3 psi.
5. **On all models,** install oil filter, new oil pan gasket, oil pan and ATF as outlined under "Fluid Change" in "Maintenance" section.
6. Ensure oil pressure is correct. Readjust as necessary.
7. Install oil filter, new oil pan gasket, oil pan and ATF as outlined under "Fluid Change" in "Maintenance" section.
8. Ensure transaxle oil pressure is correct. Readjust as necessary.

With Multi-Use Tester

1. Adjust screw to obtain the following kickdown brake pressures when pressure control solenoid is activated at 50 percent duty ratio with diagnostic scan tool:
    a. **On Mirage models equipped with F4A21 transaxle,** correct kickdown brake pressure is 38–41 psi.
    b. **On Mirage models equipped with F4A22 transaxle, 1995–96 Eclipse and 1994–96 Galant models,** correct kickdown brake pressure is 35–43 psi.
    c. **On Expo models,** correct kickdown brake pressure is 25–33 psi.
    d. **On Precis, 1993–94 Eclipse and 1993 Galant models,** correct kickdown brake pressure is 38–40 psi.
    e. **On Diamante and 3000GT models,** correct kickdown brake pressure is 39 psi.
2. **On all models except Precis,** ensure reducing pressure is 51–68 psi after adjustment. **This adjustment must be made with oil temperature at 158–176°F. Higher oil temperatures result in lower line pressure at idle, making accurate adjustment difficult.**
3. **On Precis models,** ensure reducing pressure is 53–70 psi after adjustment. **This adjustment must be made with oil temperature at 158–176°F. Higher oil temperatures result in lower line pressure at idle, making accurate adjustment difficult.**

THROTTLE POSITION SENSOR

Less Multi-Use Tester

1. Disconnect throttle position sensor connector.
2. Connect test harness tool No. MB991348, or equivalent, inline.
3. Connect a digital voltmeter between sensor output terminal 2 and sensor ground terminal 4, **Fig. 25.**
4. Turn ignition switch to Run position. **Do not start engine.**
5. Ensure throttle position sensor output voltage is .48–.52 volts.
6. If voltage is not as specified, adjust throttle position sensor as follows:
    a. Loosen throttle position sensor screws and rotate throttle position sensor body clockwise to increase output voltage.
    b. Loosen throttle position sensor screws and rotate throttle position sensor body counterclockwise to decrease output voltage.
7. Tighten throttle position screws and recheck output voltage.

With Multi-Use Tester

1. Connect multi-use tester to diagnosis connector.
2. Select item No. 14 to read throttle position sensor output voltage. Standard voltage is .48–.52 volts.
3. If voltage is not as specified, adjust throttle position sensor as follows:
    a. Loosen throttle position sensor screws and rotate throttle position sensor body clockwise to increase output voltage.
    b. Loosen throttle position sensor screws and rotate throttle position sensor body counterclockwise to decrease output voltage.
4. Tighten throttle position screws and recheck output voltage.

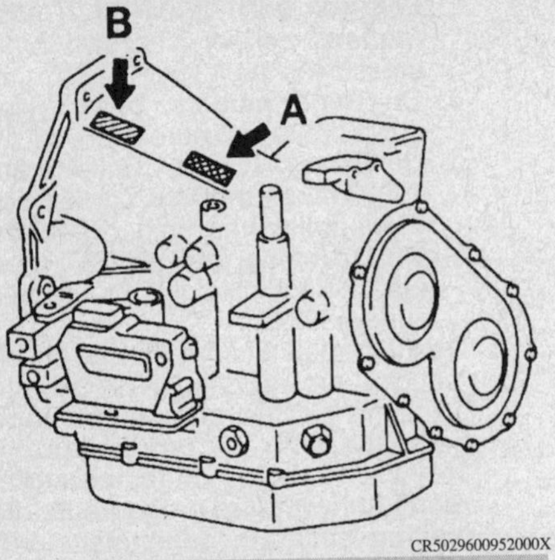
B
A
CR5029600952000X

Fig. 2 F4AC1 transaxle identification

IN-VEHICLE REPAIRS

CONTROL CABLE REPLACEMENT

Refer to **Figs. 26 through 33** when replacing transaxle control cables.

DRIVESHAFT OIL SEAL REPLACEMENT

1993–94 Eclipse & 1993 Galant

1. Remove dust cover, cotter pin and driveshaft nut.
2. Raise and support vehicle.
3. Drain transaxle oil into a suitable container.
4. Disconnect lower arm ball joint from knuckle, then remove stabilizer and strut bars from lower arm.
5. Insert suitable pry bar between transmission case and driveshaft, then pry driveshaft from transmission. **Do not pull on driveshaft and do not insert pry bar deep enough to damage oil seal.**
6. Using tool No. MB990241, or equivalent, remove driveshaft from hub. Remove seal.
7. Reverse procedure to install, noting the following:
   a. Ensure driveshaft washer is correctly installed.
   b. Lower vehicle to ground, then install driveshaft nut and tighten to specifications.
   c. If cotter pin holes do not line up, tighten bolt until holes line up. **Do not exceed maximum tightening specification.**
   d. Install cotter pin. Always use new cotter pins.
   e. Refill transaxle to proper level.

Diamante, Expo, Mirage & 3000GT

1. Raise and support vehicle, then remove front wheels.
2. Remove cotter pin, wheel bearing nut and washer.
3. Disconnect lower control arm ball joint from knuckle using tool No. MB991113, or equivalent.
4. Disconnect tie rod end from knuckle using tool No. MB991113, or equivalent.
5. Disconnect center bearing snap ring if equipped.
6. **On models without center bearing,** proceed as follows:
   a. Insert pry bar between transaxle case and driveshaft, then pry driveshaft from transaxle. **Do not pull on driveshaft, or insert pry bar deep enough to damage oil seal.**
   b. Remove driveshaft from hub using tool No. MB990241-01, or equivalent, then the circlip from driveshaft.
7. **On models with center bearing,** proceed as follows:
   a. Remove driveshaft from transaxle by lightly tapping driveshaft outer race with a plastic hammer. **Do not pull on driveshaft or insert pry bar between transaxle case and driveshaft.**
   b. Remove driveshaft from hub by lightly tapping driveshaft end with plastic hammer.
   c. Remove center bearing bracket attaching bolts, then the center bearing bracket and spacers. Remove seal.
8. **On all models,** reverse procedure to install, noting the following:
   a. **On models with center bearing,** press in driveshaft until center bearing comes in contact with center bearing bracket, then install snap ring into center bearing bracket.
   b. **On all models,** lower vehicle to ground, then attach and adjust driveshaft nut. Tighten nut to specifications.
   c. If cotter pin hole does not line up, tighten bolt until hole lines up. **Do not exceed maximum tightening specification.**

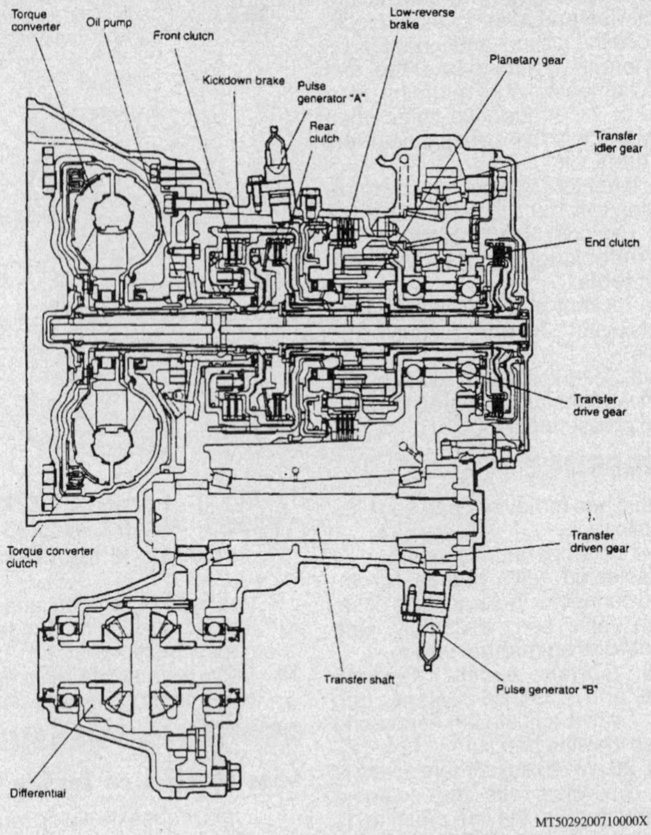
Torque converter
Oil pump
Front clutch
Low-reverse brake
Planetary gear
Kickdown brake
Pulse generator "A"
Rear clutch
Transfer idler gear
End clutch
Transfer drive gear
Transfer driven gear
Torque converter clutch
Transfer shaft
Pulse generator "B"
Differential
MT5029200710000X

Fig. 3 Cross-sectional view of F4A21 automatic transaxle

TRANSAXLE

REPLACE

F4AC1, F4A21, F4A22, F4A23 & F4A33 TRANSAXLES

1. Disconnect battery ground cable.
2. Remove battery and battery tray.
3. Remove air cleaner assembly and, if necessary, engine undercover.
4. Drain transaxle fluid as outlined under "Fluid Change" in "Maintenance" section.
5. Remove transaxle assembly in numbered sequence shown in **Figs. 34 through 40,** noting the following:
   a. **On Expo models equipped with 1.8L engine,** support engine using engine hanger tool No. MB991191, or equivalent.
   b. **On 1995 Eclipse models,** support engine using engine support tool Nos. MZ203827 and MB991453, or equivalents.

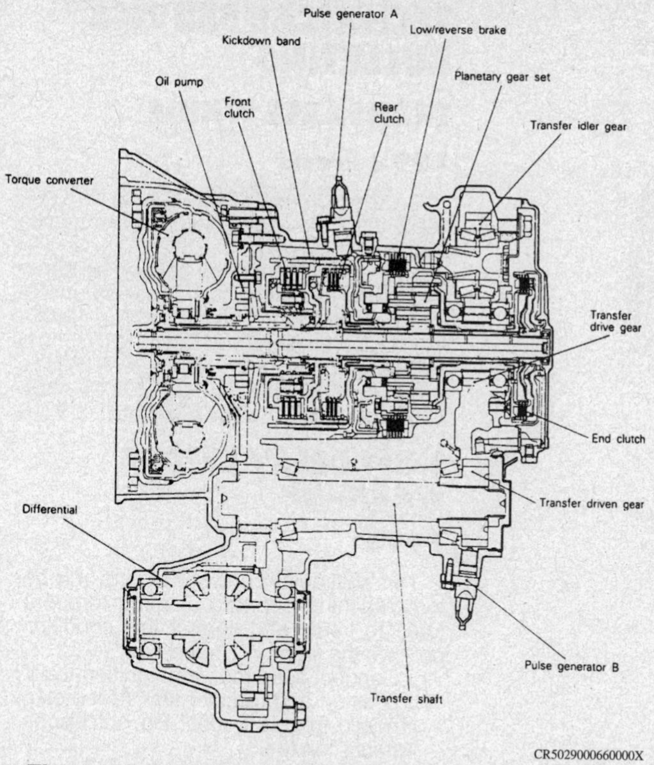
Pulse generator A
Low/reverse brake
Kickdown band
Oil pump
Planetary gear set
Front clutch
Rear clutch
Transfer idler gear
Torque converter
Transfer drive gear
End clutch
Transfer driven gear
Differential
Pulse generator B
Transfer shaft
CR5029000660000X

Fig. 4 Cross-sectional view of F4A22 transaxle

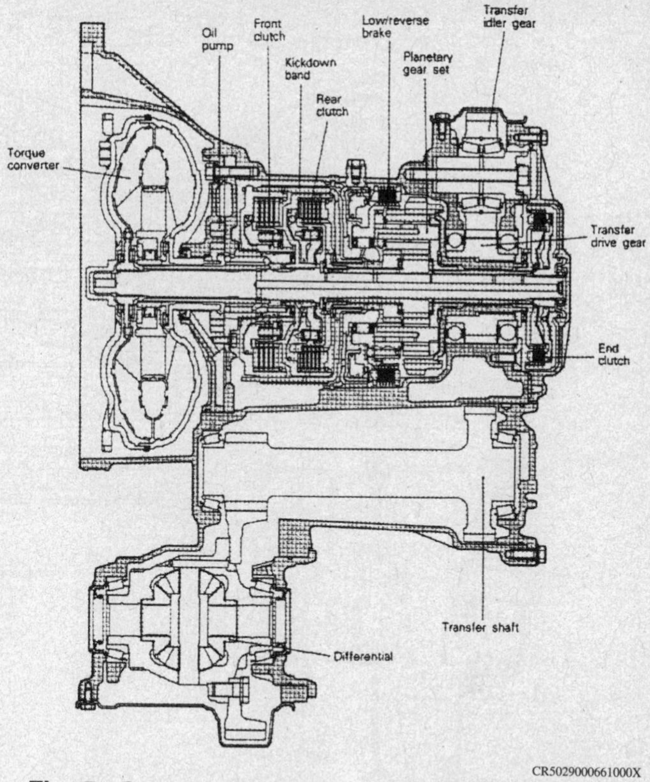
Transfer idler gear
Oil pump
Front clutch
Low/reverse brake
Kickdown band
Planetary gear set
Rear clutch
Torque converter
Transfer drive gear
End clutch
Transfer shaft
Differential
CR5029000661000X

Fig. 5 Cross-sectional view of F4A33 transaxle

c. **On all models except Expo with 1.8L engine and 1995 Eclipse,** support engine using suitable floor jack.
d. **On models equipped with Electronic Controlled Suspension (ECS),** remove ECS compressor leaving hoses attached and secure to body.
e. **On models equipped with Four Wheel Steering (4WS),** remove 4WS oil pump with hoses attached and secure to body.
f. **On all models,** loosen, but do not remove, tie rod end assembly nut using steering linkage puller tool No. MB991113, or equivalent. **Tie cord of special tool to nearby parts to prevent slippage.**
g. Loosen, but do not remove, lower ball joint nut using steering linkage puller tool No. MB991113, or equivalent. **Tie cord of special tool to nearby parts to prevent slippage.**
h. Insert a pry bar between transaxle case and driveshaft and pry driveshaft from transaxle, **Fig. 41.**
i. **On models equipped with F4A33 transaxle,** use puller tool No. MB990241-01, or equivalent, to push out righthand driveshaft from front hub. **Do not pull on driveshaft as damage to the joint will result.**
j. **On all models,** secure driveshaft away from the transaxle case using suitable rope to prevent damage.
k. Remove torque converter driveplate bolts prior to removal of transaxle.
l. After removing torque converter bolts, push torque converter toward transaxle so it does not remain on the engine side.
m. Support transaxle assembly using a suitable jack stand; then, after moving transaxle to the right, lower transaxle from vehicle.

6. Reverse numbered sequence shown in **Figs. 34 through 40** to install transaxle, noting the following:
   a. Ensure all electrical and ground connections are clean and tight.
   b. Refill transaxle with fluid as outlined under “Fluid Change” in “Maintenance” section.
   c. Ensure proper operation of selector and control cables.

W4A32 & W4A33 TRANSAXLES

1. Disconnect battery ground cable.
2. Remove battery and battery tray.
3. Remove air cleaner assembly.
4. Drain transaxle fluid as outlined under “Fluid Change ” in “Maintenance” section.
5. Remove transaxle assembly in numbered sequence shown in **Figs. 42 through 44,** noting the following:
   a. **On Expo models,** support engine using engine hanger tool No. MB991191, or equivalent.
   b. **On all models,** loosen, but do not remove, tie rod end assembly nut using steering linkage puller tool No. MB991113, or equivalent. **Ensure special tool cord is tied to nearby parts to prevent slippage.**
   c. Loosen, but do not remove, lower ball joint nut using steering linkage puller tool No. MB991113, or equivalent. **Tie cord of special tool to nearby parts to prevent slippage.**
   d. Use puller tool No. MB990241-01, or equivalent, to push righthand driveshaft from front hub.
   e. Insert a pry bar between transaxle case and driveshaft and pry driveshafts from transaxle. **Do not pull on driveshaft as damage to the joint will result.**
   f. Remove lefthand driveshaft by lightly tapping driveshaft joint case with a plastic hammer.
   g. Secure driveshaft away from the transaxle case using suitable rope to prevent damage.
   h. Mark location of propeller shaft on rear axle flange, then remove attaching bolts from propeller shaft at rear axle flange.
   i. Disconnect propeller shaft center support bearing and bracket.
   j. Pull propeller shaft from transfer assembly.
   k. Remove transfer assembly attaching bolts then the transfer assembly.
6. Reverse numbered sequence shown in **Figs. 42 through 44** to install transaxle, noting the following:
   a. After installing wheel, lower vehicle to ground and finally tighten wheel bearing nut. If position of cotter pin holes do not match, **torque** nut to 188 ft. lbs. maximum to align holes.
   b. Ensure all electrical connections and ground connections are clean and tight.
   c. Refill transaxle with fluid as outlined under “Fluid Change” in “Maintenance” section.

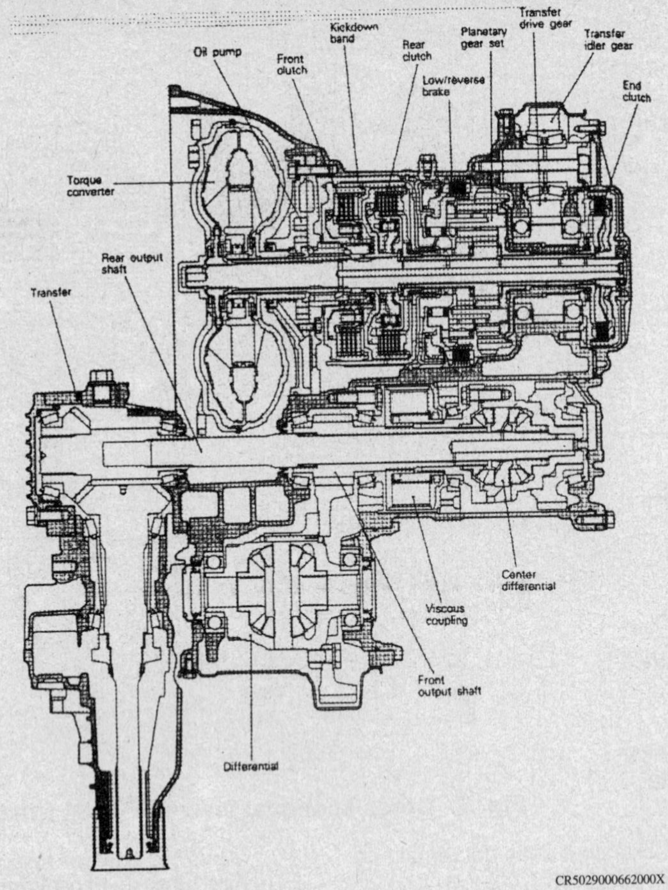

Transfer drive gear
Kickdown band
Planetary gear set
Transfer idler gear
Oil pump
Front clutch
Rear clutch
Low/reverse brake
End clutch
Torque converter
Rear output shaft
Transfer
Center differential
Viscous coupling
Front output shaft
Differential

CR5029000662000X

Fig. 6 Cross-sectional view of W4A33 transaxle

d. Ensure proper operation of selector and control cables. Adjust, if necessary.

KM176 TRANSAXLE

1. Drain transaxle fluid as described under "Fluid Change " in "Maintenance" section.
2. Remove air filter assembly, then disconnect control cable from transaxle.
3. Disconnect speedometer cable and all electrical connectors from transaxle case.
4. Disconnect starter motor wiring and remove starter motor.
5. **On models equipped with electronically controlled suspension,** remove air compressor.
6. **On all models,** raise and support vehicle.
7. Remove stabilizer bar and disconnect tie rod from steering knuckle using puller tool No. MB990635, or equivalent.
8. Disconnect lower ball joint from steering knuckle using puller tool No. MB990635, or equivalent.
9. Remove right and left driveshafts from transaxle and position aside.
10. Remove driveshaft circlips from transaxle case.
11. Remove undercover, then the bellhousing cover.
12. Remove torque converter to driveplate attaching bolts. Rotate crankshaft as necessary to gain access to all three bolts. **After removing attaching bolts, push transaxle into transaxle to avoid leaving torque converter in engine.**
13. Disconnect oil cooler lines from transaxle. **Cap oil cooler lines immediately after disconnecting to prevent contamination.**
14. Support lower part of transaxle using a suitable jack, then remove transaxle to engine attaching bolts.
15. Remove transaxle mount insulator attaching bolts.
16. Slide transaxle to the right, then lower assembly from vehicle.
17. Reverse procedure to install. Install torque converter first into transaxle, then to engine.

TECHNICAL SERVICE BULLETINS

TRANSAXLE WHINE

1993 Precis

On these models built before Nov. 14, 1992, there may be an automatic transaxle whine.

This condition may be caused by transfer gears. To correct this condition, install replacement drive gear kit (part No. 45810-34111), driven gear (part No. 45720-36501) and idler gear (part No. 45735-34111). **Refer to MOTOR'S IMPORTED TRANSMISSION MANUAL for overhaul.**

SHIFT DELAY BEFORE WARM-UP

1993

This shift delay condition occurs only before reaching normal operating temperature. To verify and correct this condition, perform the following procedure:

1. Connect scan tool, turn ignition to ON position and retrieve any stored diagnostic trouble codes. Do not disconnect scan tool.
2. Raise and support vehicle and connect suitable 300 psi oil pressure gauge with adapter to kickdown brake pressure "applied " port. Use part Nos. MT304253 and MD998332-01, or equivalents, for pressure gauge and adapter.
3. With vehicle cold, start engine, apply foot brake and shift transmission between "N" and "D," "N" and "R," "P" and "D," and "P" and "R." If transmission requires more than one second to shift into any of these positions, shift delay may exist.
4. Lower vehicle, start engine and apply parking brake and foot brake. Shift transmission into Drive position while keeping engine at idle.
5. Using scan tool in actuator test mode, activate PCSV for five seconds.
6. If oil pressure gauge reads less than 20 psi, PCSV is not functioning normally and A/T solenoid valve set should be replaced.
7. If oil pressure gauge reads more than 20 psi, PCSV is functioning normally and A/T solenoid valve set does not need to be replaced.
8. Using diagnostic trouble codes retrieved in preceding steps, perform any additional troubleshooting to find the cause of the shift delay. Refer to MOTOR'S IMPORTED TRANSMISSION MANUAL for electronic diagnosis.

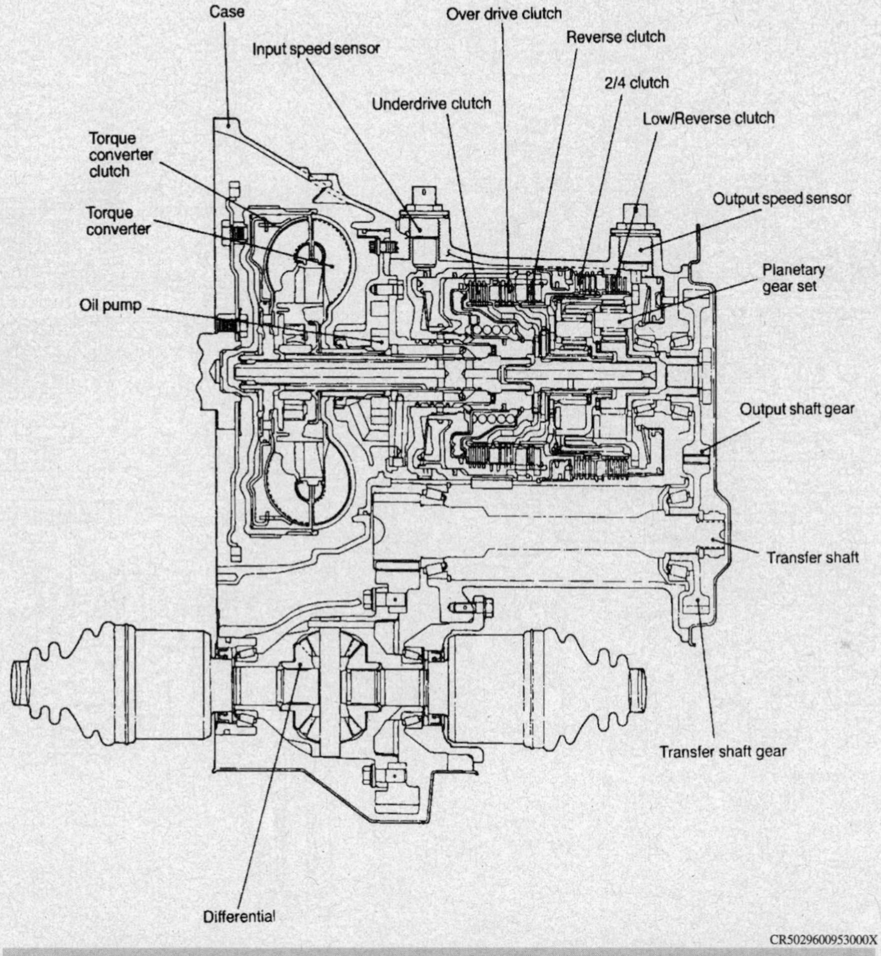
Case
Over drive clutch
Input speed sensor
Reverse clutch
2/4 clutch
Underdrive clutch
Low/Reverse clutch
Torque converter clutch
Torque converter
Output speed sensor
Planetary gear set
Oil pump
Output shaft gear
Transfer shaft
Transfer shaft gear
Differential
CR5029600953000X

Fig. 7 Cross-sectional view of F4AC1 automatic transaxle

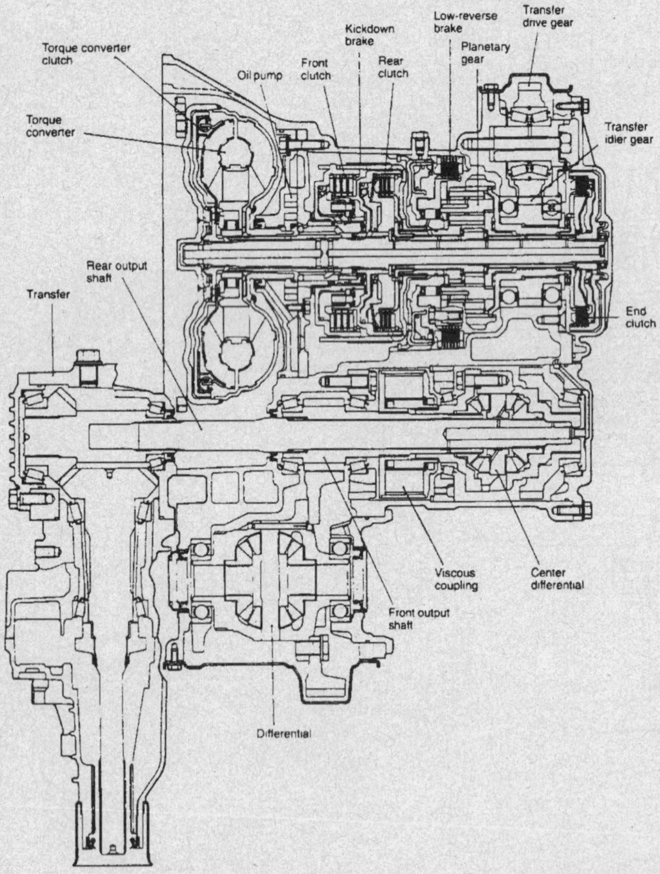
Low-reverse brake
Transfer drive gear
Kickdown brake
Torque converter clutch
Planetary gear
Front clutch
Rear clutch
Oil pump
Torque converter
Transfer idler gear
Rear output shaft
Transfer
End clutch
Viscous coupling
Center differential
Front output shaft
Differential
MT5029200715000X

Fig. 8 W4A32 automatic transaxle

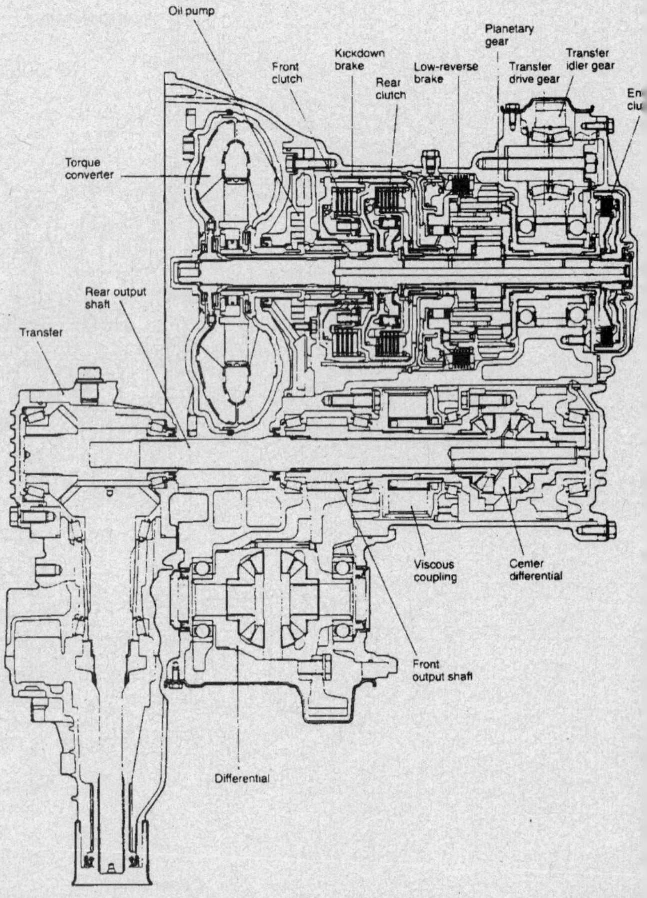
Oil pump
Planetary gear
Kickdown brake
Front clutch
Rear clutch
Low-reverse brake
Transfer drive gear
Transfer idler gear
Torque converter
Rear output shaft
Transfer
Viscous coupling
Center differential
Front output shaft
Differential
MT5029200716000X

Fig. 9 W4A33 automatic transaxle

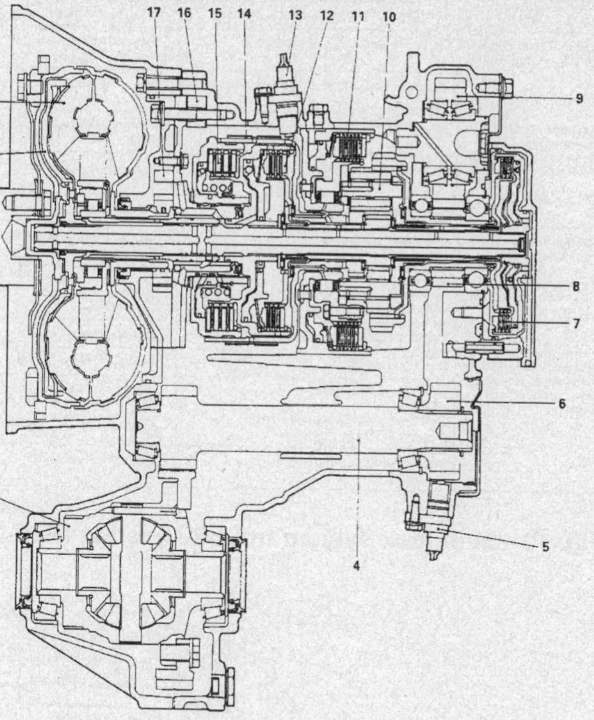

17
16
15
14
13
12
11
10
1
2
9
8
7
6
3
5
4

1. Torque converter
2. Damper clutch
3. Differential
4. Transfer shaft
5. Puls generator B
6. Transfer driven gear
7. End clutch
8. Transfer drive gear
9. Transfer idler gear
10. Planetary gear set
11. Low/reverse brake
12. Rear clutch
13. Pulse generator
14. Kickdown band
15. Front clutch
16. Adaptor
17. Oil pump

MT5028900198000X

Fig. 10 KM176 automatic transaxle

		Presumed cause \ Problem	Driving impossible or abnormal (before start-off)											
			Starter motor won't function	Forward/backward movement impossible	Forward movement impossible	Backward movement impossible	Engine stalls when N → D or R	Clutch slips at D (stall rpm too high)	Clutch slips at R (stall rpm too high)	Stall rpm too low	Vehicle moves at P or N	Engine starts, or vehicle moves, between N R or N-D	Parking doesn't hold	Abnormal vibration-shock when shift to D-2-L-R
Engine	1	Abnormal idling rpm					⊗							×
	2	Performance malfunction					×			×				
Transaxle (power train)	3	Improper adjustment of manual linkage	×	⊗	⊗	⊗		⊗	⊗		⊗	⊗	⊗	⊗
	4	Malfunction of torque convertor		×	×	×				×				
	5	Operation malfunction of oil pump		×	×	×		×	×					
	6	Malfunction of one-way clutch			×			×						
	7	Damaged or worn gear or other rotating part, or improper adjustment of the preload												
	8	Malfunction of parking mechanism									×		×	
	9	Cracked drive plate, or loose bolt		×										
	10	Worn inside diameter of front clutch retainer				×			×					
Oil pressure system (including friction elements)	11	Low fluid level		⊗	⊗	⊗		×	×					
	12	Line pressure too low (seal damaged, leakage, looseness, etc.)		⊗	⊗	⊗		⊗	⊗					
	13	Malfunction of valve body (sticking valve, working cavity, adjustment, etc.)		⊗	⊗	⊗	×	×	×		×	×		×
	14	Malfunction of front clutch or piston				×			×					×
	15	Malfunction of rear clutch or piston			⊗			×						×
	16	Malfunction of kickdown band or piston												
	17	Improper adjustment of kickdown servo												
	18	Malfunction of low-reverse brake or piston		×		×			×					×
	19	O-ring of low-reverse brake circuit between valve body and case not installed				×			×					
	20	Malfunction of end clutch or piston (check ball hole, other)												
Electronic control system	21	Malfunction of inhibitors switch, damaged or disconnected wiring, or improper adjustment	×								×	×		×
	22	Malfunction of TPS, or improper adjustment												×
	23	Pulse generator (A) damaged or disconnected wiring, or short-circuit												
	24	Pulse generator (B) damaged or disconnected wiring, or short-circuit				×								
	25	Malfunction of kickdown servo switch												
	26	SCSV-A or B damaged or disconnected wiring or short-circuit or sticking (valve open)												
	27	Malfunction of ignition signal system												
	28	Incorrectly grounded ground strap												
	29	PCSV damaged or disconnected wiring, or short-circuit												
	30	PCSV damaged or disconnected wiring (valve open)		⊗	⊗	⊗		×	×					
	31	DCCSV damaged or disconnecting wiring (valve closed)												
	32	DCCSV short-circuit or sticking (valve open)					⊗							
	33	Malfunction of overdrive control switch												
	34	Malfunction of accelerator switch, or improper adjustment												×
	35	Malfunction of oil-temperature sensor												
	36	Malfunction of lead switch												
	37	Poor contact of ignition switch												
	38	Malfunction of transaxle control unit												×

NOTE: ⊗ indicates items of high priority during inspection.
Abbreviations: TPS = Throttle position sensor SCSV = Shift control solenoid valve

CR5019000166010X

Fig. 11 Transaxle troubleshooting (Part 1 of 2). Except F4AC1 transaxle

	Transaxle malfunction of shift-shock (after start-off)																Abnormal noise, other			
	Won't shift from 2nd to 3rd	Won't shift to 4th	Overdrive control switch doesn't function	Doesn't shift according to shift pattern (shifting is possible)	Improper start-off (starts off from 2nd, etc.)	Excessive creeping or idling vibration	Excessive vibration-shock when shift 1-2 or 3-4	Excessive vibration-shock when shift 2-3 or 4-3	Excessive vibration-shock during upshift	Excessive vibration-shock during D-2 downshift	Sudden engine rpm increase during upshift	Sudden engine rpm increase during 3-2 shift, excessive vibration	Excessive vibration-shock only when cold	Excessive vibration-shock (other than already described)	Damper clutch won't function	Abnormal vibration in high-load region in low gear (approx. 1 Hz)	Abnormal noise from convertor housing together with engine rpm	Mechanical noise (clatter noise) from convertor housing	Abnormal noise inside transaxle case	3rd gear is held
1						×														
2					×		×	×	×	×			×	×		×				
3		×			×															×
4					×										×	×				
5												×					×			
6																				
7																			×	
8																				
9																		×		
10	×	×									×	×								×
11												×								×
12											⊗	⊗		×						×
13	×			×	×		×	×	×	×	×	×	×	×	×	×				×
14	×							×	×		×									×
15																				×
16							×				×	×								×
17							×				×	×		×						
18										×										×
19																				×
20		⊗					×				×									×
21		×			×															×
22				⊗			×	×	⊗	×	⊗	×		×	×	×				
23							×	×	×	×	×	×		×	×	×				×
24				×											×	×				×
25							×					×								×
26																				×
27							×	×	×	×	×	×		×	×					
28																				×
29																				×
30	×	×									×	×								×
31															×					
32																×				×
33		×	×																	
34					×	×									×					
35														×	×	×				
36																				×
37				×																×
38	×	×	×	×	×	×	×	×	×	×	×	×	×	×	×	×	×			×

PSCV = Pressure control solenoid valve
DCCSV = Damper clutch control solenoid valve

CR5019000166020X

Fig. 11 Transaxle troubleshooting (Part 2 of 2). Except F4AC1 transaxle

Probable cause \ Trouble symptom		Harsh engagement from Neutral(N) to Drive(D)	Harsh engagement from Neutral(N) to Reverse(R)	Delayed engagement from Neutral(N) to Drive(D)	Delayed engagement from Neutral(N) to Reverse(R)	Poor shift quality	Shifts erratically	Dives in Neutral(N)	Drags or locks	Grating, scraping, growling noise	Knocking noise	Buzzing noise during shifts only	Hard to fill oil blows out filler tube	Transaxle overheats	Harsh upshift	No upshift into overdrive	No torque converter control	Harsh downshifts	High shift efforts	Harsh torque converter control shift
Engine performance				×			×								×				×	×
Worn or faulty clutch(es)	Underdrive clutch			×									×	×	×			×		×
	Overdrive clutch					×	×						×	×	×					
	Reverse clutch												×	×			×		×	
	2-4 clutch			×			×						×		×					
	Low/Reverse clutch			×									×		×				×	×
Clutch(es) dragging														×						
Insufficient clutch plate clearance								×						×						
Damaged clutch seal				×													×	×		
Worn or damaged accumulator sealing (s)				×													×	×	×	×
Faulty cooling system								×												
Engine coolant temperature too low					×	×														
Incorrect gear shift control linkage adjustment								×						×	×		×	×		
Shift linkage damaged			×																	
Chipped or damaged gear teeth												×	×							
Planetary gear sets broken or seized												×	×							
Bearings worn or damaged												×	×							
Driveshaft(s) bushing(s) worn or damaged												×								
Worn or broken reaction shaft support sealing				×											×	×	×	×		
Worn or damaged input shaft sealing					×												×	×		
Valve body malfunction or leakage			×	×	×						×			×	×	×	×	×	×	×
Hydraulic pressures too low					×		×	×							×	×	×	×		
Hydraulic pressures too high				×			×												×	×
Faulty oil pump					×			×							×		×	×		
Oil filter clogged									×						×	×	×	×		
Low fluid level				×	×			×			×				×	×	×	×		
High fluid level								×	×											
Aerated fluid				×	×			×	×		×				×	×	×	×		
Engine idle too low																	×	×		
Engine idle too high				×				×											×	×
Normal solenoid operation										×										
Solenoid sound cover loose										×										
Sticking lockup piston		×																		
Torque converter failure					×			×												×

CR5029500782000X

Fig. 12 Inspection matrix for trouble symptoms. F4AC1 transaxle

Symptom	Probable cause	Remedy
Selector lever can be selected into R from P without depressing brake pedal with ignition key in a position other than LOCK.	Damaged lock cam B	Check and replace lock cam B.
	Improperly adjusted shift lock cable, broken inner cable, loose or off connections	Check, adjust or replace the shift lock cable.
	Broken or sagging outer cable (shift lock cable) return spring	Check and replace shift lock cable.
Selector lever cannot be selected into R from P by depressing brake pedal with ignition key in position other than LOCK.	Defective selector lever assembly	Check and replace selector lever assembly.
	Sticking shift lock cable, key interlock cable, and transaxle control cable	Check and replace shift lock cable, key interlock cable, and transaxle control cable.
	Foreign matter wedged in lock cams A and B	Check and adjust lock cams A and B.
	Improperly adjusted shift lock cable, elongated inner cable	Check, adjust, and replace shift lock cable.
	Sticking slide lever and cam lever inside key cylinder	Check and adjust slide lever and cam lever.
Selector lever can be selected into R from P when brake pedal is depressed even though the ignition key is in the LOCK position.	Damaged lock cam A	Check and replace lock cam A.
	Broken or disconnected key interlock cable	Check and replace key interlock cable.
	Damaged slide lever and cam lever inside key cylinder	Check and replace slide lever and cam lever.
Selector lever operation from P to R is not smooth.	Improperly adjusted key interlock cable	Check and adjust key interlock cable.
	Improperly adjusted shift lock cable, elongated inner cable	Check, adjust, and replace shift lock cable.
	Binding lock cams A and B (in rotation)	Check rotating parts of lock cams A and B.
	Defective selector lever assembly	Check and replace selector lever assembly.
	Binding slide lever inside key cylinder	Check slide lever and cam lever.

CR5019000167010X

Fig. 13 Shift lock system troubleshooting (Part 1 of 2)

Symptom	Probable cause	Remedy
Selector lever cannot be shifted from R to P.	Defective selector lever assembly	Check and replace selector lever assembly.
	Improperly adjusted transaxle control cable	Adjust transaxle control cable.
Ignition key cannot be turned to LOCK position with selector lever in P.	Foreign matter wedged in lock cams A and B	Check and replace lock cams A and B.
	Improperly adjusted key interlock cable, sticking inner cable	Check, adjust, and replace key interlock cable.
	Binding slide lever inside key cylinder	Check slide lever.
Ignition key can be turned to LOCK position even with selector lever in position other than P.	Damaged lock cam A	Check and replace lock cam A.
	Loose key cylinder cover	Check and retighten cover.
	Broken key interlock cable, loose connections, elongated inner cable	Check and replace key interlock cable.
	Damaged cam lever inside key cylinder	Check and replace cam lever.
Buzzer does not sound even when selector lever is placed in R position.	Defective buzzer	Check and replace buzzer.
	Open-circuited buzzer circuit harness	Check or correct harness.
	Defective inhibitor switch	Check and replace inhibitor switch.
	Improperly adjusted transaxle control cable	Adjust transaxle control cable.

CR5019000167020X

Fig. 13 Shift lock system troubleshooting (Part 2 of 2)

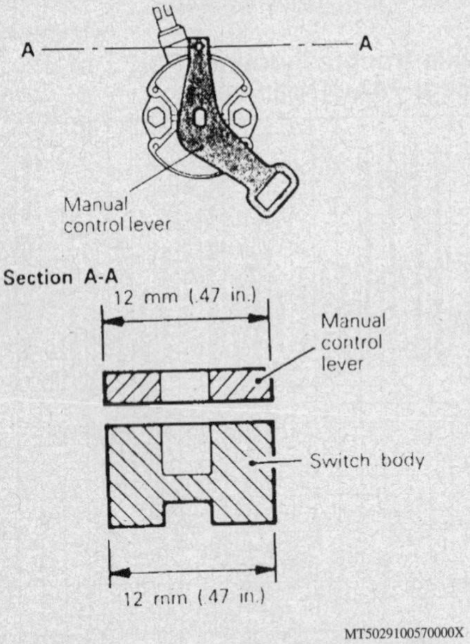
A
A
Manual control lever
Section A-A
12 mm (.47 in.)
Manual control lever
Switch body
12 mm (.47 in.)
MT5029100570000X

Fig. 14 Lever & switch hole alignment

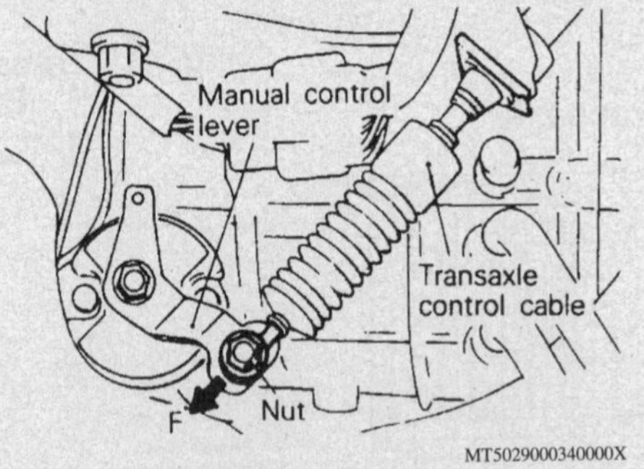
Manual control lever
Transaxle control cable
F
Nut
MT5029000340000X

Fig. 15 Control cable adjustment

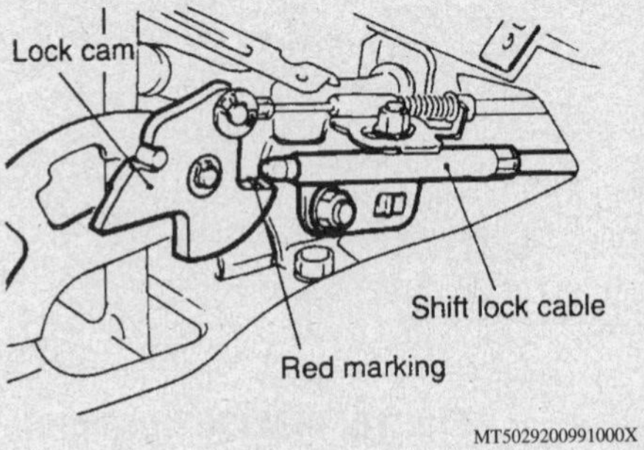
Lock cam
Shift lock cable
Red marking
MT5029200991000X

Fig. 16 Shift lock cable adjustment. Mirage

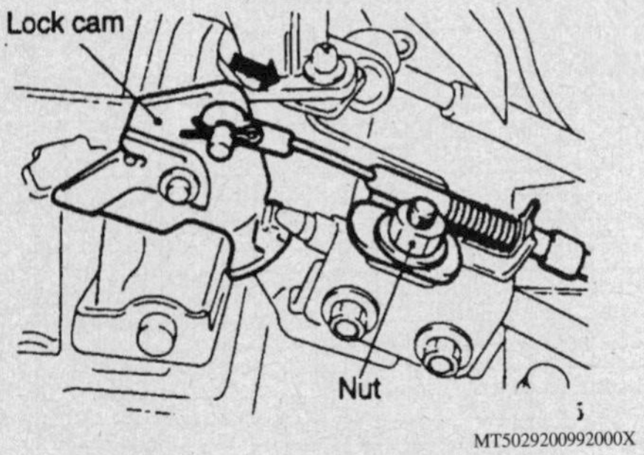
Lock cam
Nut
MT5029200992000X

Fig. 17 Shift lock cable adjustment. Diamante, Expo & 3000GT

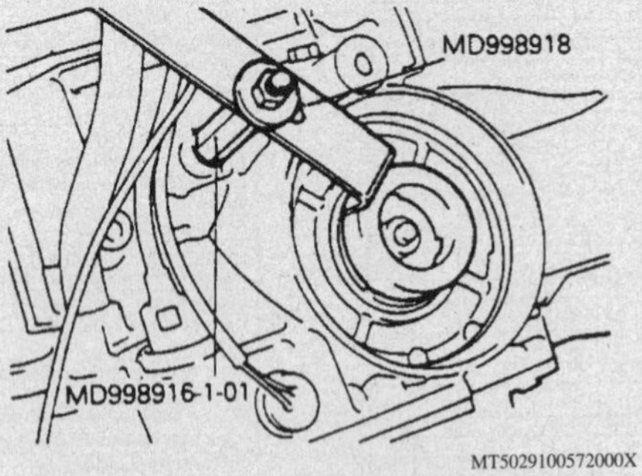
MD998918
MD998916-1-01
MT5029100572000X

Fig. 18 Kickdown servo tool

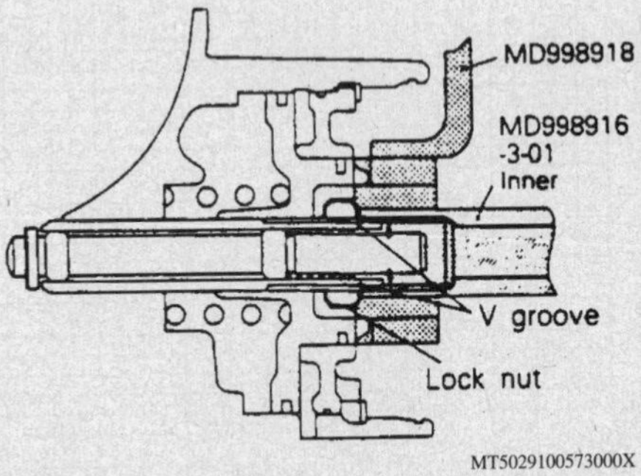
MD998918
MD998916
-3-01
Inner
V groove
Lock nut
MT5029100573000X

Fig. 19 Inner & outer adjusting tool installation

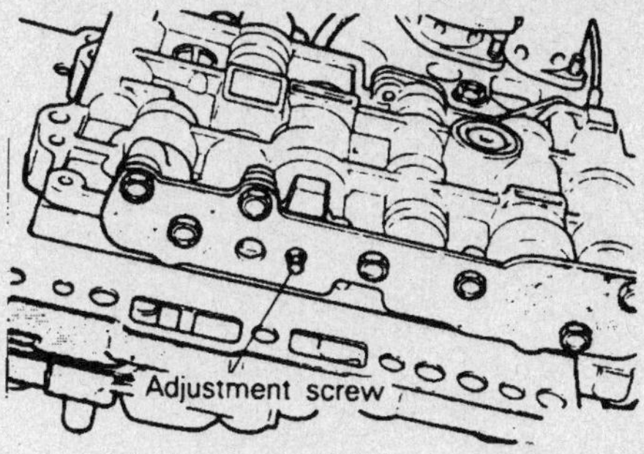
Adjustment screw
MT5029000343000X

Fig. 20 Regulator valve adjustment screw

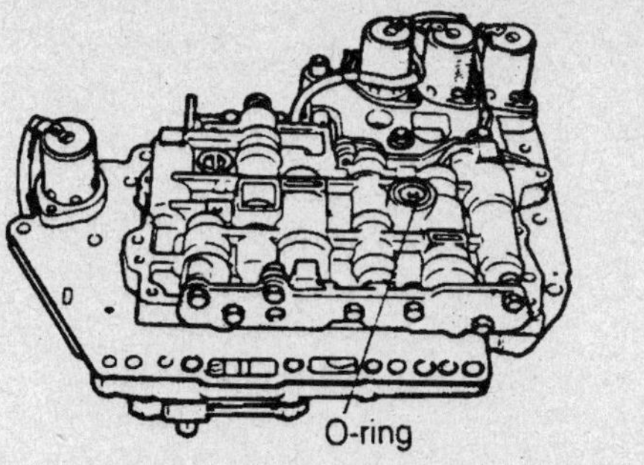
O-ring
MT5029000344000X

Fig. 21 Valve body O-ring position

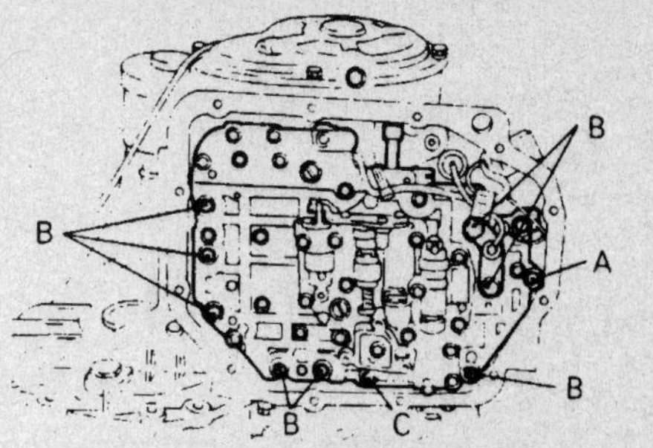
B
B
A
B
B
C
MT5029000345000X

Fig. 22 Valve body bolt location. F4A21, F4A22 & F4A23 transaxles

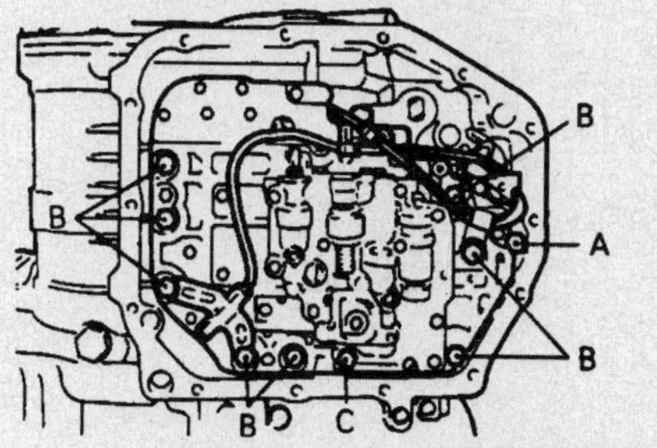
B
B
A
B
B
C
MT5029000346000X

Fig. 23 Valve body bolt location. F4A33, W4A32 & W4A33 transaxles

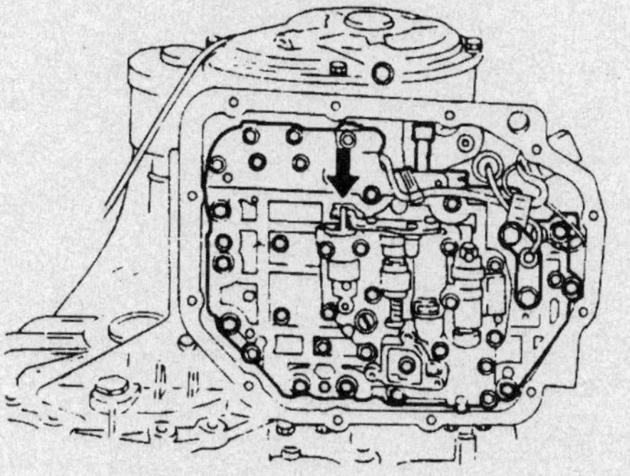
MT5029000347000X

Fig. 24 Reducing pressure adjustment screw

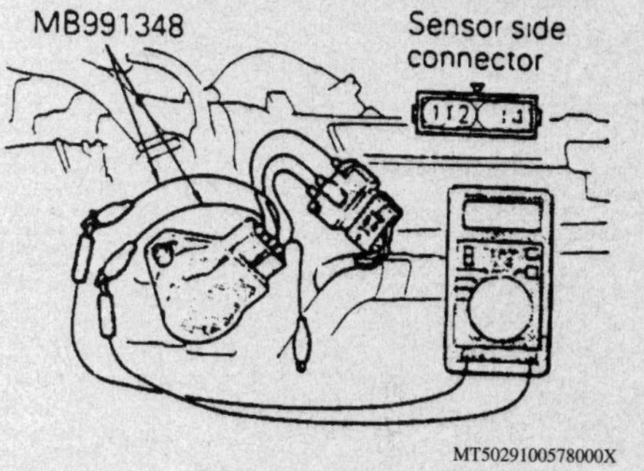
MB991348
Sensor side connector
MT5029100578000X

Fig. 25 Throttle position sensor adjustment

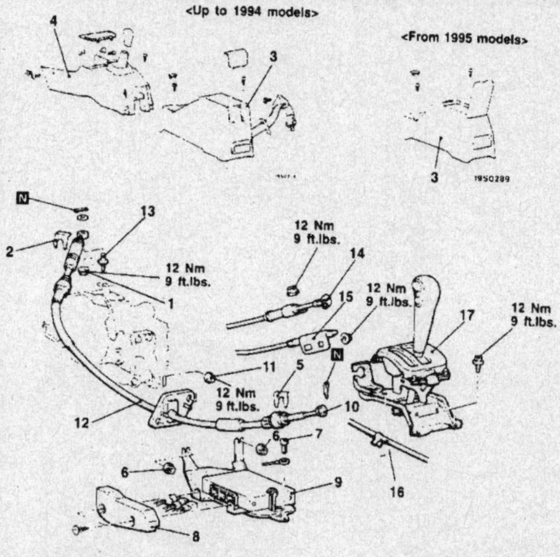
<Up to 1994 models>
<From 1995 models>
12 Nm 9 ft.lbs.
12 Nm 9 ft.lbs.
12 Nm 9 ft.lbs.
12 Nm 9 ft.lbs.
12 Nm 9 ft.lbs.

Transaxle control cable assembly removal steps

1. Nut
2. Clip
3. Rear floor console
4. Front floor console
5. Clip
6. Nut
7. Bolt
8. Cover
9. Transaxle control module
10. Connection for the transaxle control cable assembly
11. Nut
12. Transaxle control cable assembly
13. Adjuster

Selector lever assembly removal steps

3. Rear floor console
4. Front floor console
10. Connection for the transaxle control cable assembly
14. Key interlock cable connection
15. Shift lock cable connection
16. Clip
17. Selector lever assembly

MT5029300994000X

Fig. 26 Control cable replacement. Mirage

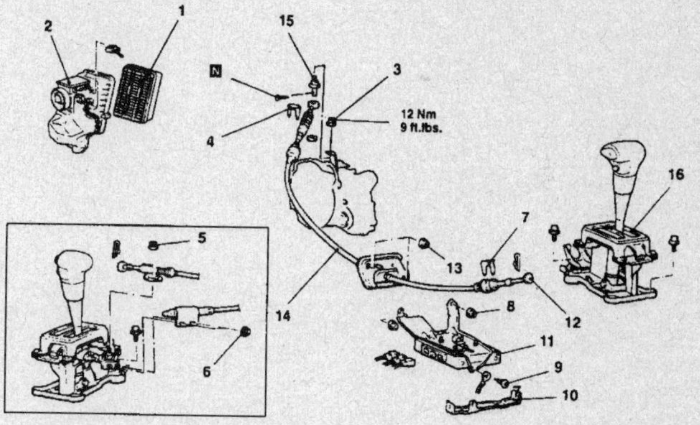
12 Nm 9 ft.lbs.

Transaxle control cable assembly removal steps

1. Air cleaner element
2. Air cleaner cover
3. Nut
4. Clip
5. Connection for the key interlock cable
6. Connection for the shift lock cable
7. Clip
8. Nuts
9. Screw
10. Bracket
11. Transaxle control module (TCM)
12. Connection for the transaxle control cable assembly (selector lever assembly side)
13. Nut
14. Transaxle control cable assembly
15. Adjuster

Selector lever assembly removal steps

5. Connection for the key interlock cable
6. Connection for the shift lock cable
12. Connection for the transaxle control cable assembly (selector lever assembly side)
16. Selector lever assembly

MT5029200995000X

Fig. 27 Control cable replacement. Expo

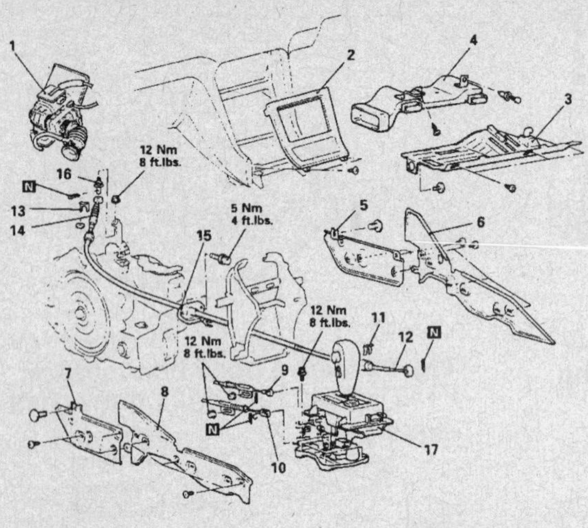

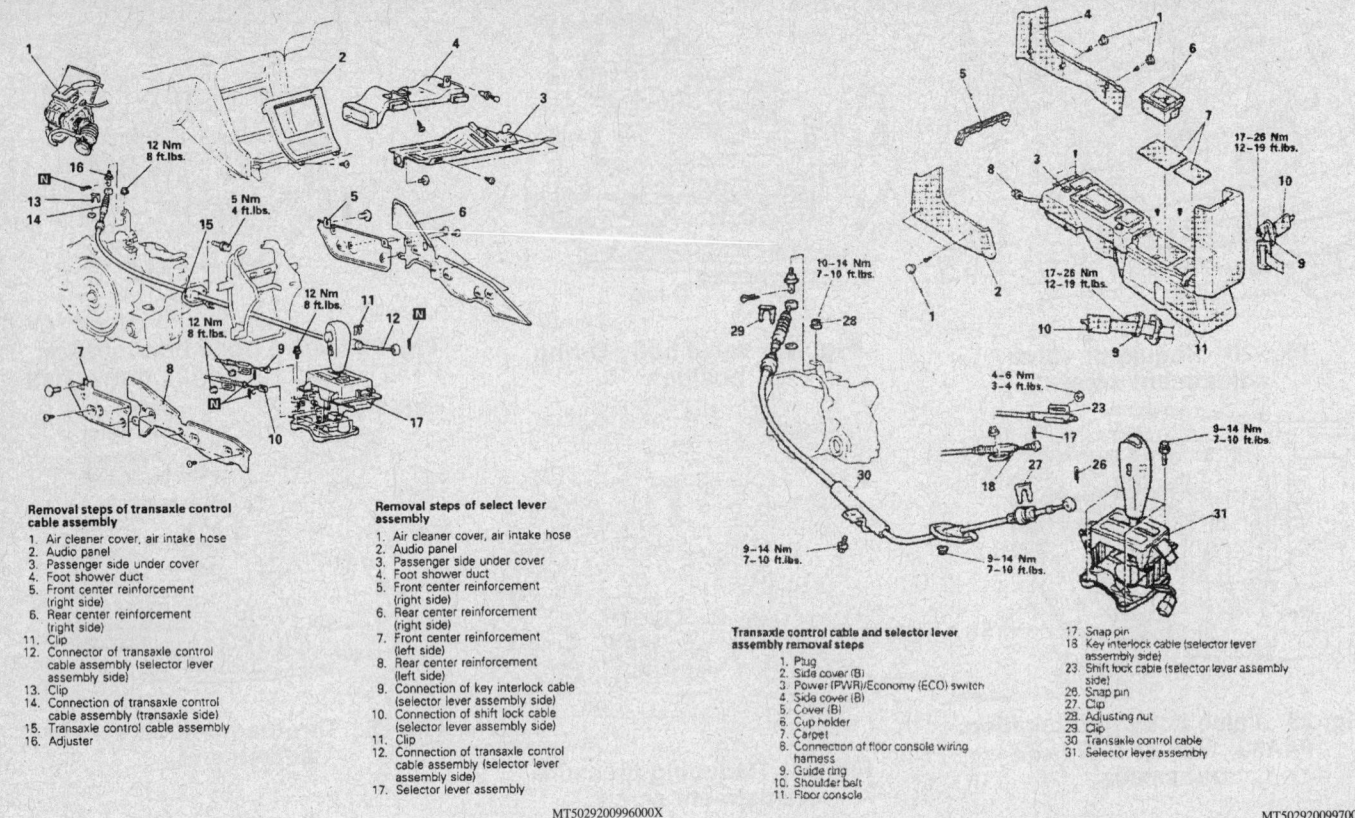

Removal steps of transaxle control cable assembly

1. Air cleaner cover, air intake hose
2. Audio panel
3. Passenger side under cover
4. Foot shower duct
5. Front center reinforcement (right side)
6. Rear center reinforcement (right side)
11. Clip
12. Connector of transaxle control cable assembly (selector lever assembly side)
13. Clip
14. Connection of transaxle control cable assembly (transaxle side)
15. Transaxle control cable assembly
16. Adjuster

Removal steps of select lever assembly

1. Air cleaner cover, air intake hose
2. Audio panel
3. Passenger side under cover
4. Foot shower duct
5. Front center reinforcement (right side)
6. Rear center reinforcement (right side)
7. Front center reinforcement (left side)
8. Rear center reinforcement (left side)
9. Connection of key interlock cable (selector lever assembly side)
10. Connection of shift lock cable (selector lever assembly side)
11. Clip
12. Connection of transaxle control cable assembly (selector lever assembly side)
17. Selector lever assembly

MT5029200996000X

Fig. 28 Control cable replacement. Diamante

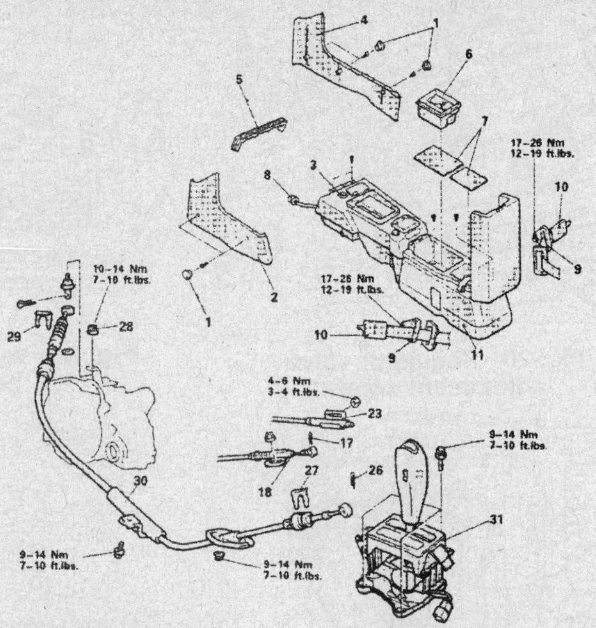

Transaxle control cable and selector lever assembly removal steps

1. Plug
2. Side cover (B)
3. Power (PWR)/Economy (ECO) switch
4. Side cover (B)
5. Cover (B)
6. Cup holder
7. Carpet
8. Connection of floor console wiring harness
9. Guide ring
10. Shoulder belt
11. Floor console
17. Snap pin
18. Key interlock cable (selector lever assembly side)
23. Shift lock cable (selector lever assembly side)
26. Snap pin
27. Clip
28. Adjusting nut
29. Clip
30. Transaxle control cable
31. Selector lever assembly

MT5029200997000X

Fig. 29 Control cable replacement. 1993–94 Eclipse

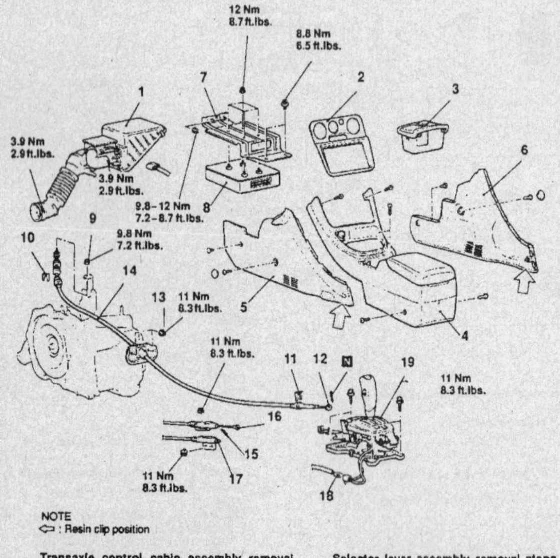

NOTE
⇦ : Resin clip position

Transaxle control cable assembly removal steps

1. Air cleaner and air intake hose assembly
2. Center panel
3. Cup holder assembly
4. Floor console assembly
5. Console side cover LH
6. Console side cover RH
7. TCM bracket
8. Transaxle control module (TCM)
9. Nut
10. Clip
11. Clip
12. Transaxle control cable connection
13. Nut
14. Transaxle control cable assembly

Selector lever assembly removal steps

2. Center panel
3. Cup holder assembly
4. Floor console assembly
5. Console side cover LH
6. Console side cover RH
11. Clip
12. Transaxle control cable connection
15. Snap pin
16. Key interlock cable connection
17. Shift lock cable connection
18. Overdrive switch/position indicator light connector
19. Selector lever assembly

MT5029500998000X

Fig. 30 Control cable replacement. 1995–96 Eclipse

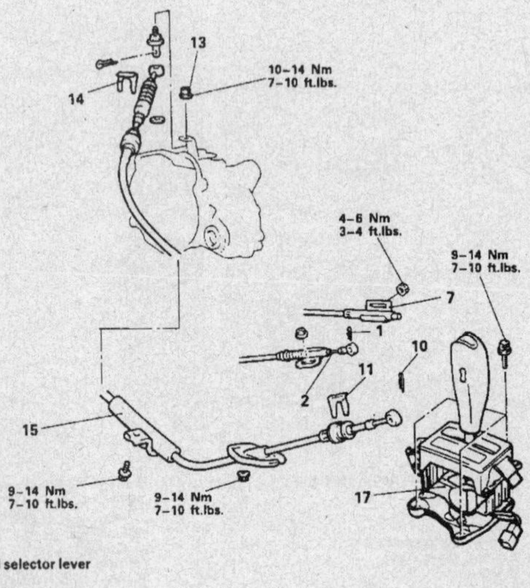

Transaxle control cable and selector lever assmebly removal steps

1. Snap pin
2. Key-interlock cable (selector lever assembly side)
7. Shift-lock cable (selector lever assembly side)
10. Snap pin
11. Clip
12. Snap pin
13. Adjusting nut
14. Clip
15. Transaxle control cable
16. Bushing
17. Selector lever assembly

MT5029200999000X

Fig. 31 Control cable replacement. 1993 Galant

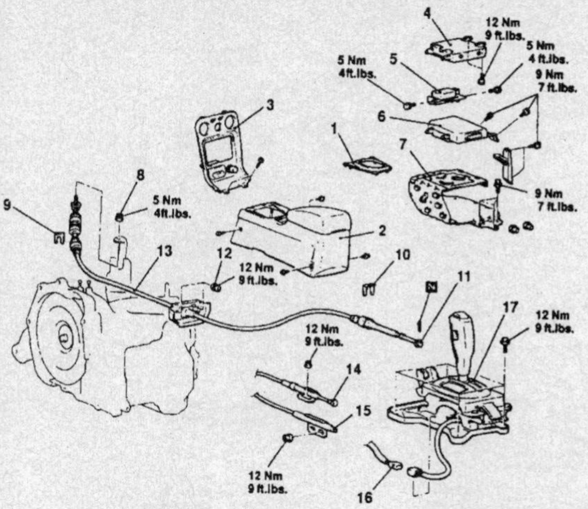
12 Nm
9 ft.lbs.
5 Nm
4 ft.lbs.
9 Nm
7 ft.lbs.
5 Nm
4ft.lbs.
5 Nm
4ft.lbs.
9 Nm
7 ft.lbs.
12 Nm
9 ft.lbs.
12 Nm
9 ft.lbs.
12 Nm
9 ft.lbs.
12 Nm
9 ft.lbs.

Transaxle control cable assembly removal steps

1. Selector lever panel
2. Floor console box
3. Center console panel
4. Engine control module
5. Fuel pump relay module (From 1995 models for California)
6. Transaxle control module (TCM)
7. TCM bracket
8. Nut
9. Clip (engine compartment side)
10. Clip (passenger compartment side)
11. Transaxle control cable connection (selector lever side)
12. Nut
13. Transaxle control cable assembly

Selector lever assembly removal steps

1. Selector lever panel
2. Floor console box
3. Center console panel
10. Clip (passenger compartment side)
11. Transaxle control cable connection (selector lever side)
14. Key interlock cable connection
15. Shift lock cable connection
16. Overdrive switch / position indicator light connector
17. Selector lever assembly

MT5029401000000X

Fig. 32 Control cable replacement. 1994–96 Galant

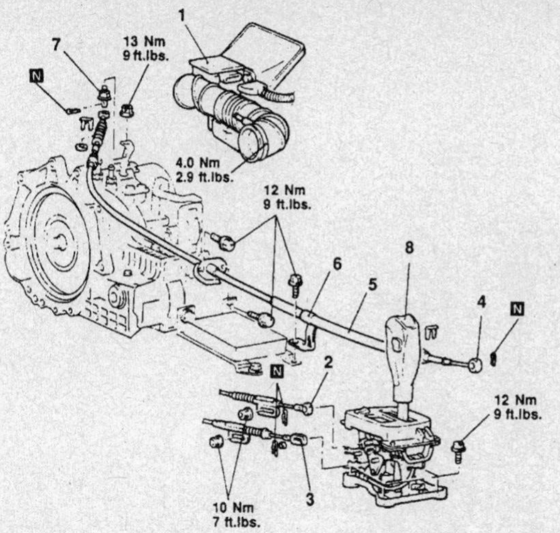
13 Nm
9 ft.lbs.
4.0 Nm
2.9 ft.lbs.
12 Nm
9 ft.lbs.
12 Nm
9 ft.lbs.
10 Nm
7 ft.lbs.

Transaxle control cable removal steps

1. Air cleaner cover, Air intake hose
4. Transaxle control cable assembly connection (Select lever assembly side)
5. Transaxle control cable assembly
6. Clamp
7. Adjuster

Selector lever assembly removal steps

1. Air cleaner cover, Air intake hose
2. Key-interlock cable connection (Selector lever assembly side)
3. Shift-lock cable connection (Selector lever assembly side)
4. Transaxle control cable connection (Selector lever assembly side)
8. Selector lever assembly

MT5029201001000X

Fig. 33 Control cable replacement. 3000GT

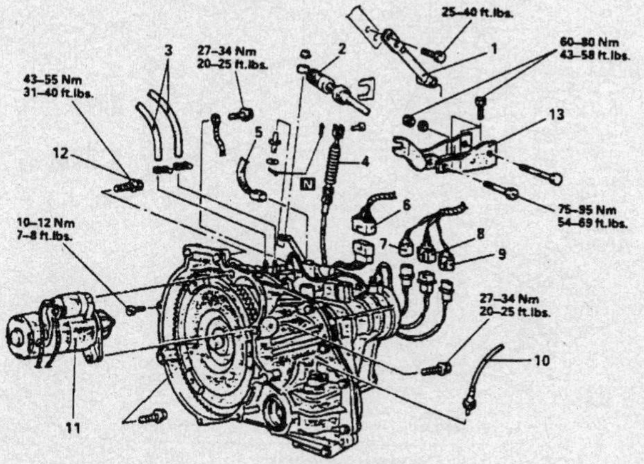
25–40 ft.lbs.
27–34 Nm
20–25 ft.lbs.
60–80 Nm
43–58 ft.lbs.
43–55 Nm
31–40 ft.lbs.
75–95 Nm
54–69 ft.lbs.
10–12 Nm
7–8 ft.lbs.
27–34 Nm
20–25 ft.lbs.

Removal steps

1. Tension rod <DOHC>
2. Transaxle control cable connection
3. Transaxle fluid cooler hose connection
4. Throttle control cable connection <3 A/T>
5. Solenoid valve connector connection
6. Inhibitor switch connector connection
7. Kickdown servo switch connector connection <4 A/T>
8. Pulse generator connector connection <4 A/T>
9. Oil temperature sensor connector connection <4 A/T>
10. Speedometer cable connection
11. Starter
12. Transaxle assembly upper connecting bolt
13. Transaxle mounting bracket

MT5029000349010X

Fig. 34 Transaxle replacement (Part 1 of 2). Mirage, 1993–94 Eclipse w/F4A22 & F4A33 transaxles & 1993 Galant

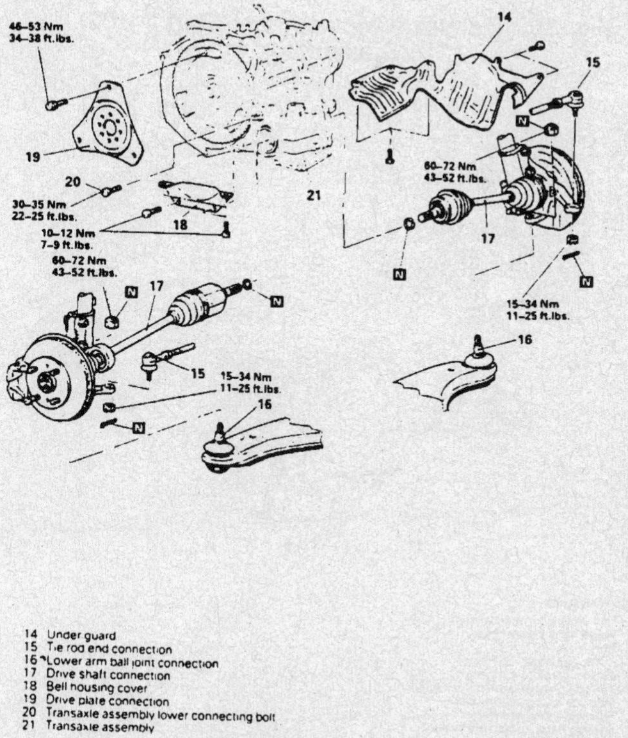
46–53 Nm
34–38 ft.lbs.
60–72 Nm
43–52 ft.lbs.
30–35 Nm
22–25 ft.lbs.
10–12 Nm
7–9 ft.lbs.
60–72 Nm
43–52 ft.lbs.
15–34 Nm
11–25 ft.lbs.
15–34 Nm
11–25 ft.lbs.

14. Under guard
15. Tie rod end connection
16. Lower arm ball joint connection
17. Drive shaft connection
18. Bell housing cover
19. Drive plate connection
20. Transaxle assembly lower connecting bolt
21. Transaxle assembly

MT5029000349020X

Fig. 34 Transaxle replacement (Part 2 of 2). Mirage, 1993–94 Eclipse w/F4A22 & F4A33 transaxles & 1993 Galant

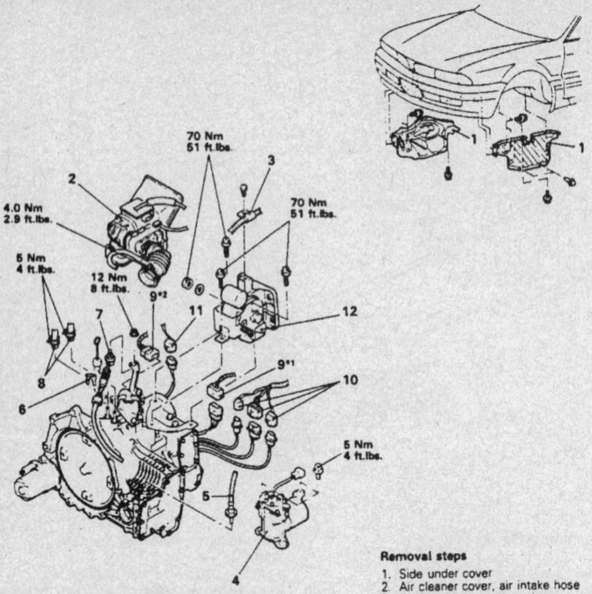
70 Nm
51 ft.lbs.
4.0 Nm
2.9 ft.lbs.
70 Nm
51 ft.lbs.
5 Nm
4 ft.lbs.
12 Nm
8 ft.lbs.
5 Nm
4 ft.lbs.

Removal steps

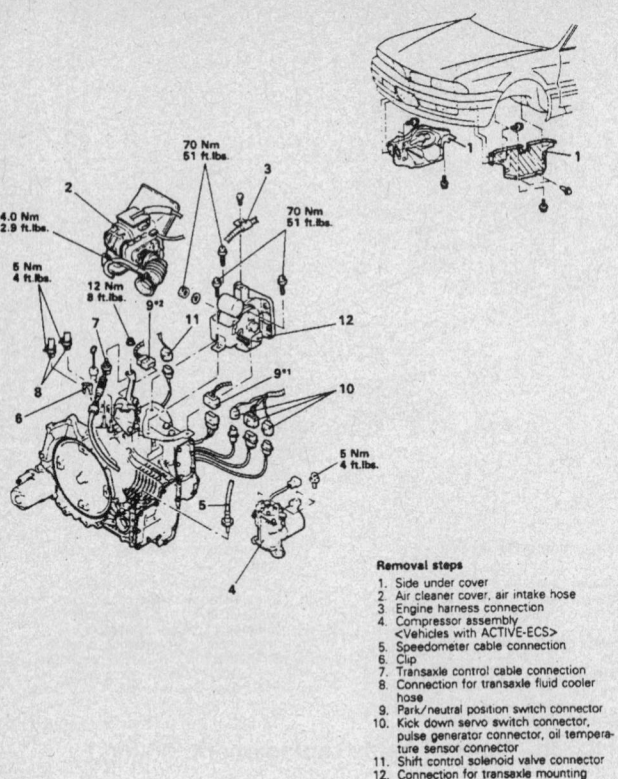

1. Side under cover
2. Air cleaner cover, air intake hose
3. Engine harness connection
4. Compressor assembly <Vehicles with ACTIVE-ECS>
5. Speedometer cable connection
6. Clip
7. Transaxle control cable connection
8. Connection for transaxle fluid cooler hose
9. Park/neutral position switch connector
10. Kick down servo switch connector, pulse generator connector, oil temperature sensor connector
11. Shift control solenoid valve connector
12. Connection for transaxle mounting bracket

NOTE
*1 : <1992 models>
*2 : <From 1993 models>

MT5029200350010X

Fig. 35 Transaxle replacement (Part 1 of 2). Diamante

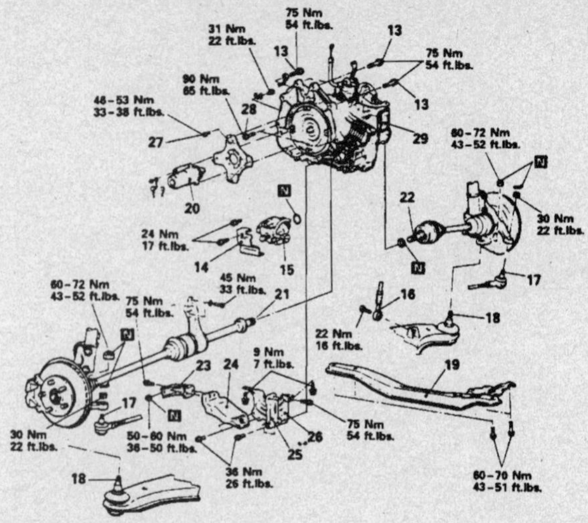
75 Nm
54 ft.lbs.
31 Nm
22 ft.lbs.
75 Nm
54 ft.lbs.
90 Nm
65 ft.lbs.
46-53 Nm
33-38 ft.lbs.
60-72 Nm
43-52 ft.lbs.
24 Nm
17 ft.lbs.
30 Nm
22 ft.lbs.
45 Nm
33 ft.lbs.
60-72 Nm
43-52 ft.lbs.
75 Nm
54 ft.lbs.
22 Nm
16 ft.lbs.
9 Nm
7 ft.lbs.
30 Nm
22 ft.lbs.
50-60 Nm
36-50 ft.lbs.
75 Nm
54 ft.lbs.
36 Nm
26 ft.lbs.
60-70 Nm
43-51 ft.lbs.

13. Transaxle assembly upper connection bolt
14. Heat protector <Vehicles with 4WS>
15. Oil pump assembly <Vehicles with 4WS>
16. Front height sensor rod <Vehicles with ACTIVE-ECS>
17. Connection for tie rod end and knuckle
18. Connection for lower arm ball joint and knuckle
19. Right member
20. Starter
21. Drive shaft (left side), inner shaft assembly
22. Drive shaft (right side)
23. Roll stopper stay A
24. Transaxle stay (Front bank side)
25. Transaxle stay (Rear bank side)
26. Bell housing cover
27. Torque converter connection bolt
28. Transaxle assembly lower connection bolt
29. Transaxle assembly

MT5029200350020X

Fig. 35 Transaxle replacement (Part 2 of 2). Diamante

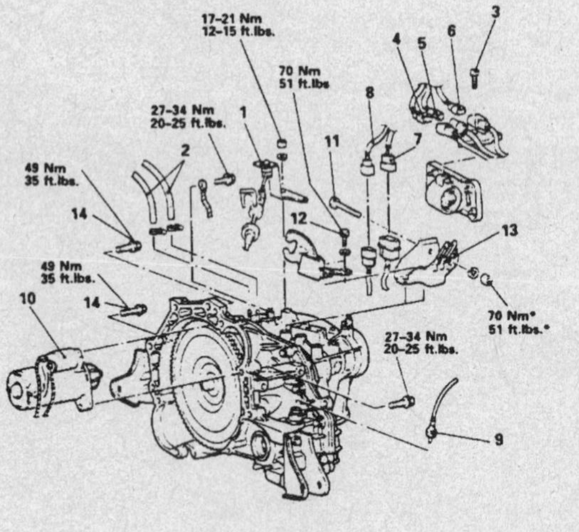
17-21 Nm
12-15 ft.lbs.
70 Nm
51 ft.lbs
27-34 Nm
20-25 ft.lbs.
49 Nm
35 ft.lbs.
49 Nm
35 ft.lbs.
70 Nm*
51 ft.lbs.*
27-34 Nm
20-25 ft.lbs.

Removal steps

1. Connection for manual control lever
2. Transaxle oil cooler hoses
3. Bolt
4. Pulse generator connector
5. Oil temperature connector
6. Kickdown servo switch connector
7. Inhibitor switch connector
8. Solenoid valve connector
9. Speedometer cable connection
10. Starter motor
11. Transaxle mount bolt
12. Bolt
13. Transaxle mount bracket
14. Transaxle assembly upper part coupling bolts

NOTE
For tightening locations indicated by the * symbol, first tighten temporarily, and then make the final tightening with the entire weight of the engine applied to the vehicle body.

MT5029200351010X

Fig. 36 Transaxle replacement (Part 1 of 2). Expo w/F4A22 & F4A23 transaxles

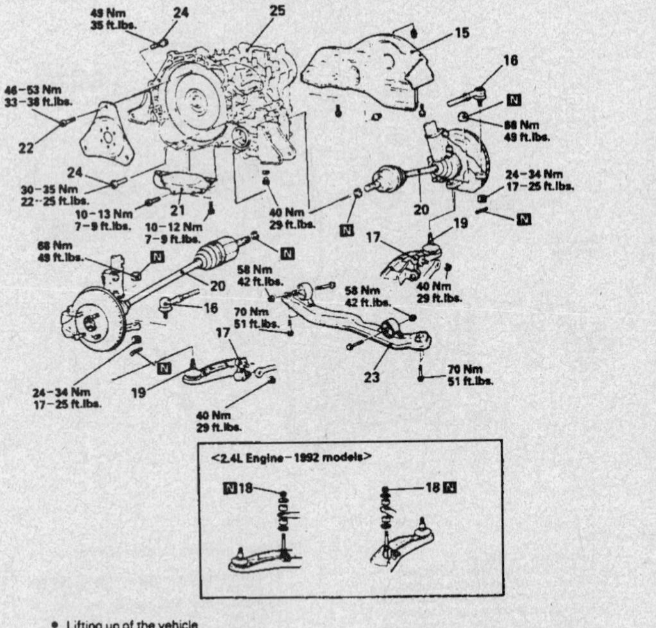
49 Nm
35 ft.lbs.
46-53 Nm
33-38 ft.lbs.
88 Nm
49 ft.lbs.
24-34 Nm
17-25 ft.lbs.
30-35 Nm
22-25 ft.lbs.
10-13 Nm
7-9 ft.lbs.
10-12 Nm
7-9 ft.lbs.
40 Nm
29 ft.lbs.
68 Nm
49 ft.lbs.
58 Nm
42 ft.lbs.
58 Nm
42 ft.lbs.
40 Nm
29 ft.lbs.
70 Nm
51 ft.lbs.
70 Nm
51 ft.lbs.
24-34 Nm
17-25 ft.lbs.
40 Nm
29 ft.lbs.
<2.4L Engine-1992 models>

- Lifting up of the vehicle
15. Under cover (R.H.)
16. Connection for tie rod end
17. Connection for stabilizer bar <except 2.4L Engine-1992 models>
18. Self locking nut <2.4L Engine-1992 models>
19. Connection for lower arm ball joint
- Draining of the transaxle fluid
20. Connection for the drive shaft
21. Bell housing cover
22. Drive plate connecting bolts
23. Center member <except 2.4L Engine-1992 models>
24. Transaxle assembly lower part coupling bolts
25. Transaxle assembly

MT5029200351020X

Fig. 36 Transaxle replacement (Part 2 of 2). Expo w/F4A22 & F4A23 transaxles

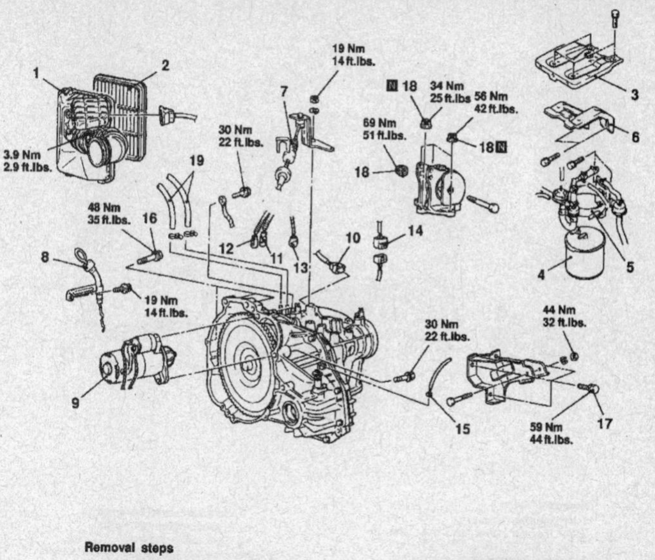

19 Nm
14 ft.lbs.
34 Nm
25 ft.lbs
56 Nm
42 ft.lbs.
69 Nm
51 ft.lbs.
30 Nm
22 ft.lbs.
3.9 Nm
2.9 ft.lbs.
48 Nm
35 ft.lbs.
19 Nm
14 ft.lbs.
30 Nm
22 ft.lbs.
44 Nm
32 ft.lbs.
59 Nm
44 ft.lbs.

Removal steps

1. Air cleaner cover and air intake hose assembly
2. Air cleaner element
3. Battery tray
4. Evaporative emission canister
5. Evaporative emission canister holder
6. Battery tray stay
7. Transaxle control cable connection
8. Oil dipstick and guide assembly
9. Starter motor
10. Park/Neutral position switch connector
11. Oil temperature sensor connector
12. Kick down servo switch connector
13. Solenoid valve connector
14. Pulse generator connector
15. Speedometer connector
16. Transaxle assembly mounting bolts
17. Rear roll stopper bracket mounting bolts
18. Transaxle mounting bracket mounting nuts
19. Transaxle oil cooler hoses connection
- Supporting engine assembly

MT5029501083010X

Fig. 37 Transaxle replacement (Part 1 of 2). Eclipse FWD w/2.4L engine

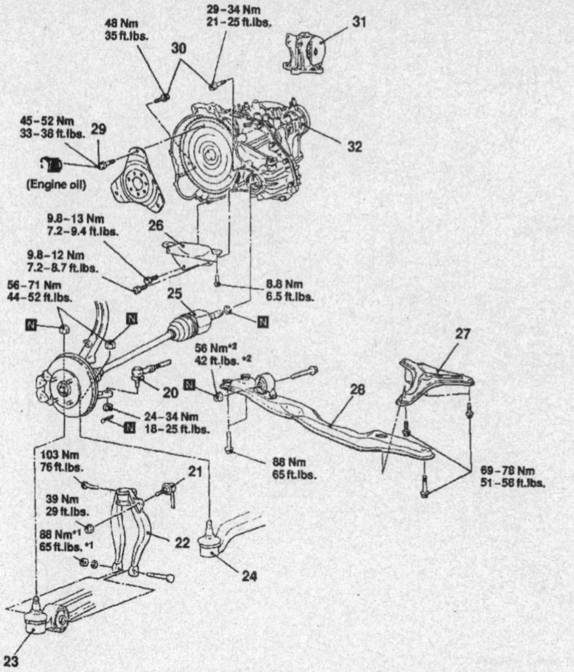

29-34 Nm
21-25 ft.lbs.
48 Nm
35 ft.lbs.
45-52 Nm
33-38 ft.lbs.
(Engine oil)
9.8-13 Nm
7.2-9.4 ft.lbs.
9.8-12 Nm
7.2-8.7 ft.lbs.
56-71 Nm
44-52 ft.lbs.
8.8 Nm
6.5 ft.lbs.
56 Nm*2
42 ft.lbs. *2
24-34 Nm
18-25 ft.lbs.
103 Nm
76 ft.lbs.
88 Nm
65 ft.lbs.
69-78 Nm
51-58 ft.lbs.
39 Nm
29 ft.lbs.
88 Nm*1
65 ft.lbs. *1

From under vehicles

20. Tie rod end ball joint and knuckle connection
21. Stabilizer link connection
22. Damper fork
23. Lateral lower arm ball joint and knuckle connection
24. Compression lower arm ball joint and knuckle connection
25. Drive shaft connection
26. Bell housing cover
27. Stay (R.H.)
28. Centermember assembly
29. Drive plate connecting bolts
30. Transaxle assembly mounting bolts
31. Transaxle mounting bracket
32. Transaxle assembly

Caution

*1: The fasteners marked * should be temporally tightened before they are finally tightened once the total weight of the engine has been placed on the vehicle body.

*2: For tightening locations indicated by the symbol, first tighten temporarily, and then make the final tightening with the entire weight of the engine applied to the vehicle body.

MT5029501083020X

Fig. 37 Transaxle replacement (Part 2 of 2). Eclipse FWD w/2.4L engine

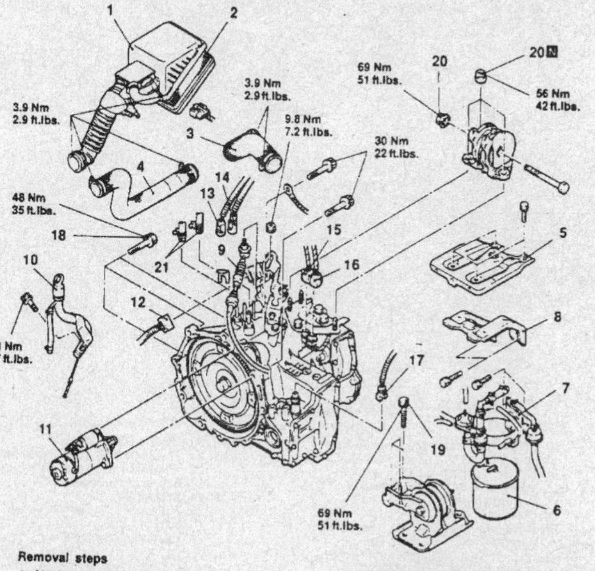

3.9 Nm
2.9 ft.lbs.
3.9 Nm
2.9 ft.lbs.
9.8 Nm
7.2 ft.lbs.
69 Nm
51 ft.lbs.
56 Nm
42 ft.lbs.
30 Nm
22 ft.lbs.
48 Nm
35 ft.lbs.
23 Nm
17 ft.lbs.
69 Nm
51 ft.lbs.

Removal steps

1. Air cleaner cover and air intake hose assembly
2. Air cleaner element
3. Air hose C
4. Air hose A
5. Battery tray
6. Evaporative emission canister
7. Evaporative emission canister holder
8. Battery tray stay
9. Transaxle control cable connection
10. Oil level gauge and guide assembly
11. Starter motor
12. Park/Neutral position switch connector
13. Oil temperature sensor connector
14. Kick down servo switch connector
15. Solenoid valve connector
16. Pulse generator connector
17. Speedometer connector
18. Transaxle assembly mounting bolts
19. Rear roll stopper bracket mounting bolts
20. Transaxle mounting bracket mounting nuts
21. Transaxle oil cooler hoses connection
- Engine assembly supporting

MT5029501002010X

Fig. 38 Transaxle replacement (Part 1 of 2). 1995–96 Eclipse FWD w/2.0L turbocharged engine

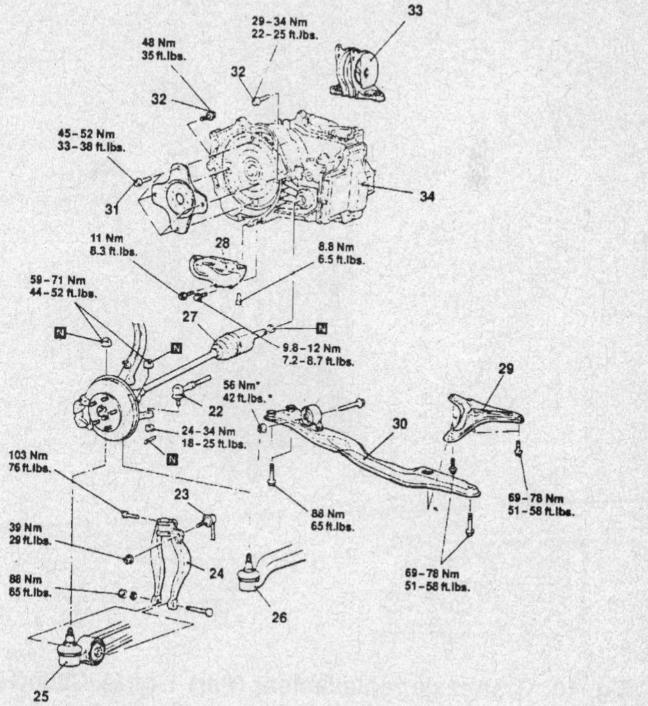

29-34 Nm
22-25 ft.lbs.
48 Nm
35 ft.lbs.
45-52 Nm
33-38 ft.lbs.
11 Nm
8.3 ft.lbs.
8.8 Nm
6.5 ft.lbs.
59-71 Nm
44-52 ft.lbs.
9.8-12 Nm
7.2-8.7 ft.lbs.
56 Nm*
42 ft.lbs.*
24-34 Nm
18-25 ft.lbs.
103 Nm
76 ft.lbs.
88 Nm
65 ft.lbs.
69-78 Nm
51-58 ft.lbs.
39 Nm
29 ft.lbs.
88 Nm
65 ft.lbs.
69-78 Nm
51-58 ft.lbs.

From under vehicles

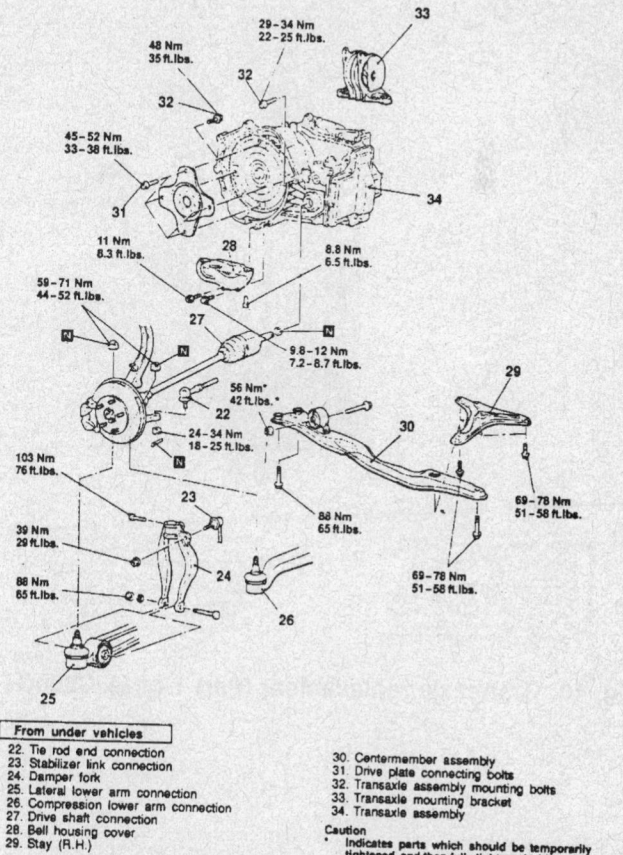

22. Tie rod end connection
23. Stabilizer link connection
24. Damper fork
25. Lateral lower arm connection
26. Compression lower arm connection
27. Drive shaft connection
28. Bell housing cover
29. Stay (R.H.)
30. Centermember assembly
31. Drive plate connecting bolts
32. Transaxle assembly mounting bolts
33. Transaxle mounting bracket
34. Transaxle assembly

Caution

* Indicates parts which should be temporarily tightened, and then fully tightened with the vehicle on the ground in the unladen condition.

MT5029501002020X

Fig. 38 Transaxle replacement (Part 2 of 2). 1995–96 Eclipse FWD w/2.0L turbocharged engine

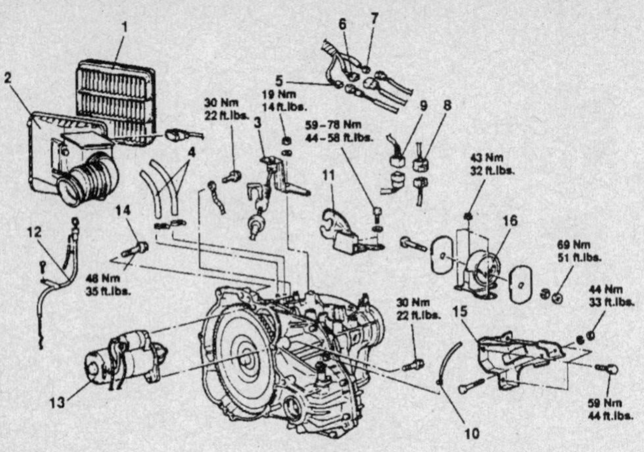
30 Nm
22 ft.lbs.
19 Nm
14 ft.lbs.
59–78 Nm
44–58 ft.lbs.
43 Nm
32 ft.lbs.
69 Nm
51 ft.lbs.
44 Nm
33 ft.lbs.
48 Nm
35 ft.lbs.
30 Nm
22 ft.lbs.
59 Nm
44 ft.lbs.

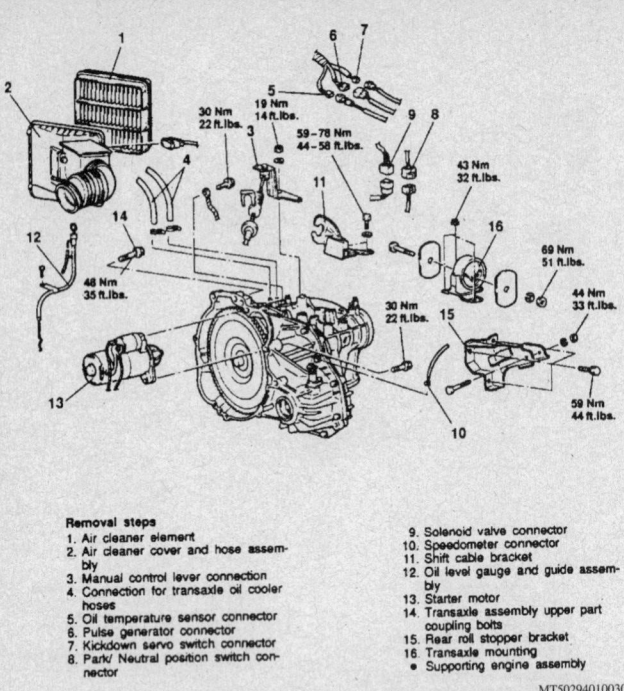

Removal steps
1. Air cleaner element
2. Air cleaner cover and hose assembly
3. Manual control lever connection
4. Connection for transaxle oil cooler hoses
5. Oil temperature sensor connector
6. Pulse generator connector
7. Kickdown servo switch connector
8. Park/ Neutral position switch connector
9. Solenoid valve connector
10. Speedometer connector
11. Shift cable bracket
12. Oil level gauge and guide assembly
13. Starter motor
14. Transaxle assembly upper part coupling bolts
15. Rear roll stopper bracket
16. Transaxle mounting
- Supporting engine assembly

MT5029401003010X

Fig. 39 Transaxle replacement (Part 1 of 2). 1994–96 Galant

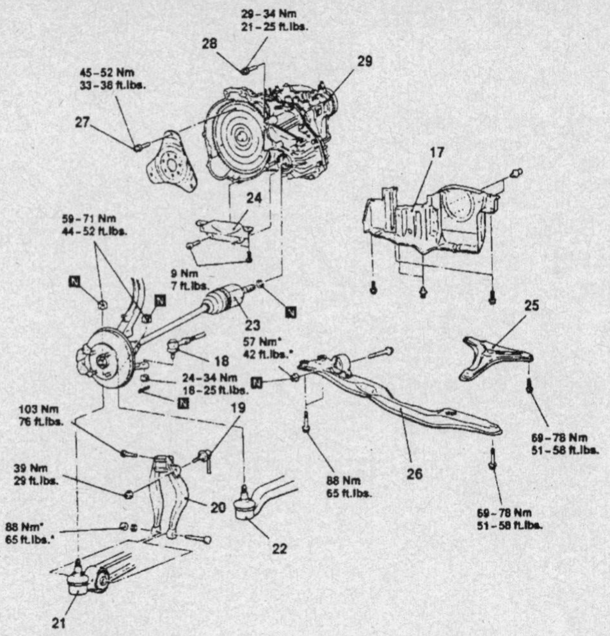
29–34 Nm
21–25 ft.lbs.
45–52 Nm
33–38 ft.lbs.
59–71 Nm
44–52 ft.lbs.
9 Nm
7 ft.lbs.
57 Nm*
42 ft.lbs.*
24–34 Nm
18–25 ft.lbs.
103 Nm
76 ft.lbs.
39 Nm
29 ft.lbs.
88 Nm*
65 ft.lbs.*
88 Nm
65 ft.lbs.
69–78 Nm
51–58 ft.lbs.
69–78 Nm
51–58 ft.lbs.

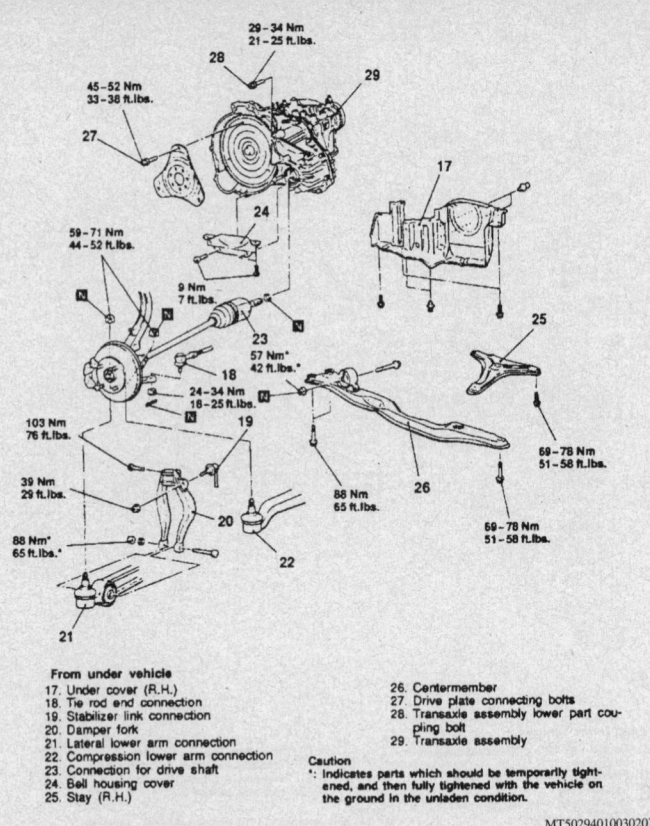

From under vehicle
17. Under cover (R.H.)
18. Tie rod end connection
19. Stabilizer link connection
20. Damper fork
21. Lateral lower arm connection
22. Compression lower arm connection
23. Connection for drive shaft
24. Bell housing cover
25. Stay (R.H.)
26. Centermember
27. Drive plate connecting bolts
28. Transaxle assembly lower part coupling bolt
29. Transaxle assembly

Caution
*: Indicates parts which should be temporarily tightened, and then fully tightened with the vehicle on the ground in the unladen condition.

MT5029401003020X

Fig. 39 Transaxle replacement (Part 2 of 2). 1994–96 Galant

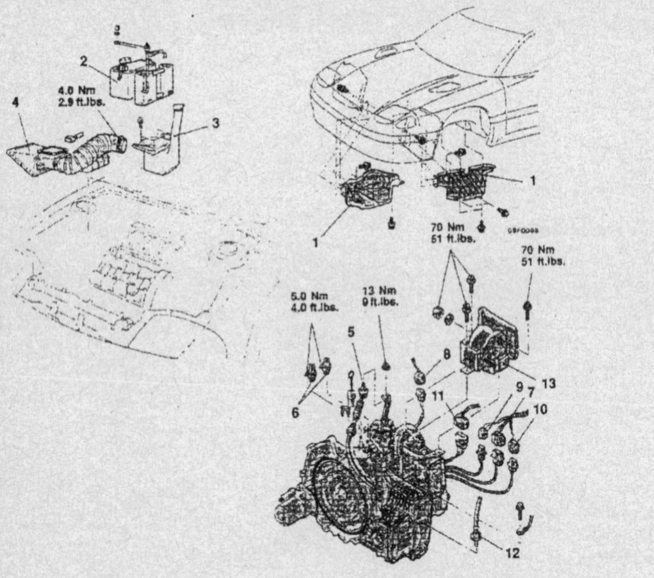
4.0 Nm
2.9 ft.lbs.
70 Nm
51 ft.lbs.
70 Nm
51 ft.lbs.
5.0 Nm
4.0 ft.lbs.
13 Nm
9 ft.lbs.

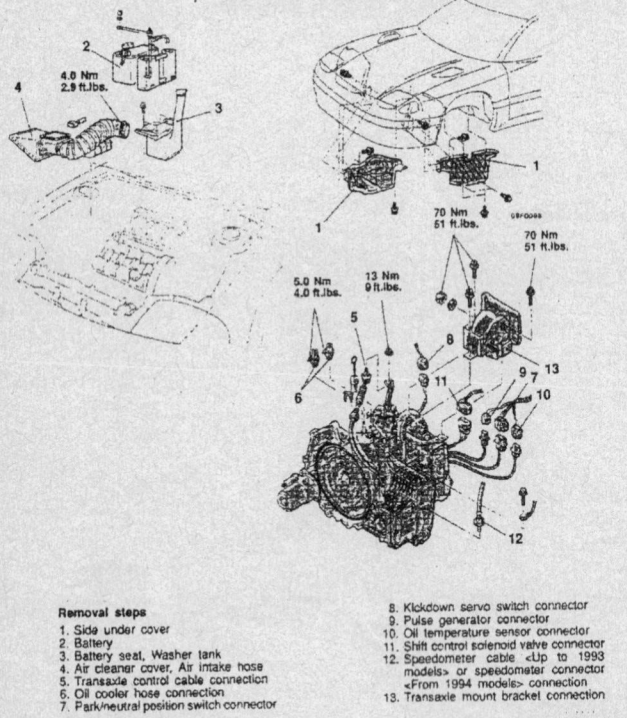

Removal steps
1. Side under cover
2. Battery
3. Battery seat, Washer tank
4. Air cleaner cover, Air intake hose
5. Transaxle control cable connection
6. Oil cooler hose connection
7. Park/neutral position switch connector
8. Kickdown servo switch connector
9. Pulse generator connector
10. Oil temperature sensor connector
11. Shift control solenoid valve connector
12. Speedometer cable <Up to 1993 models> or speedometer connector <From 1994 models> connection
13. Transaxle mount bracket connection

MT5029201004010X

Fig. 40 Transaxle replacement (Part 1 of 2). 3000GT

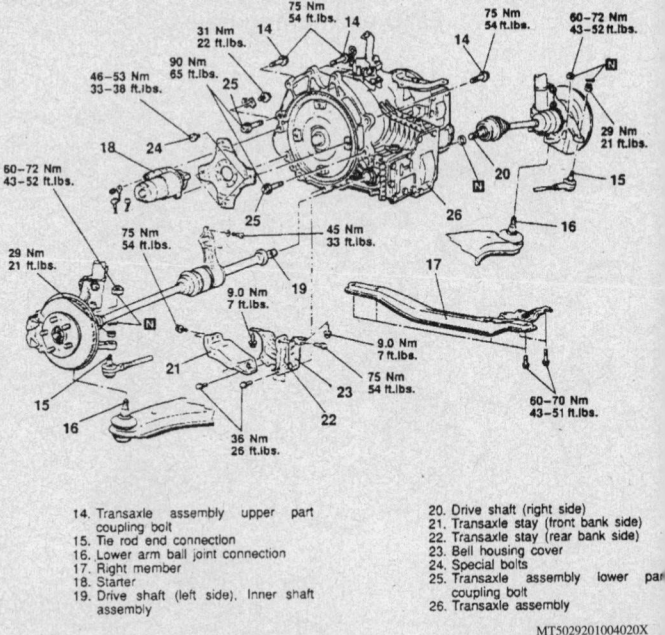

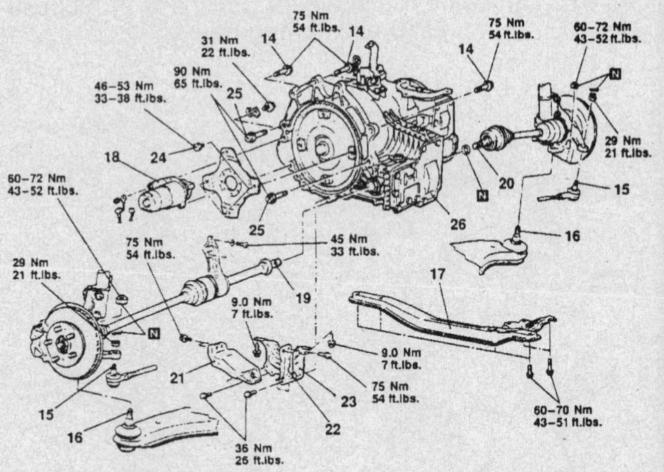
75 Nm
54 ft.lbs.
31 Nm
22 ft.lbs.
90 Nm
65 ft.lbs.
46–53 Nm
33–38 ft.lbs.
75 Nm
54 ft.lbs.
60–72 Nm
43–52 ft.lbs.
29 Nm
21 ft.lbs.
60–72 Nm
43–52 ft.lbs.
75 Nm
54 ft.lbs.
45 Nm
33 ft.lbs.
29 Nm
21 ft.lbs.
9.0 Nm
7 ft.lbs.
9.0 Nm
7 ft.lbs.
75 Nm
54 ft.lbs.
60–70 Nm
43–51 ft.lbs.
36 Nm
26 ft.lbs.

14. Transaxle assembly upper part coupling bolt
15. Tie rod end connection
16. Lower arm ball joint connection
17. Right member
18. Starter
19. Drive shaft (left side), Inner shaft assembly
20. Drive shaft (right side)
21. Transaxle stay (front bank side)
22. Transaxle stay (rear bank side)
23. Bell housing cover
24. Special bolts
25. Transaxle assembly lower part coupling bolt
26. Transaxle assembly

MT5029201004020X

Fig. 40 Transaxle replacement (Part 2 of 2). 3000GT

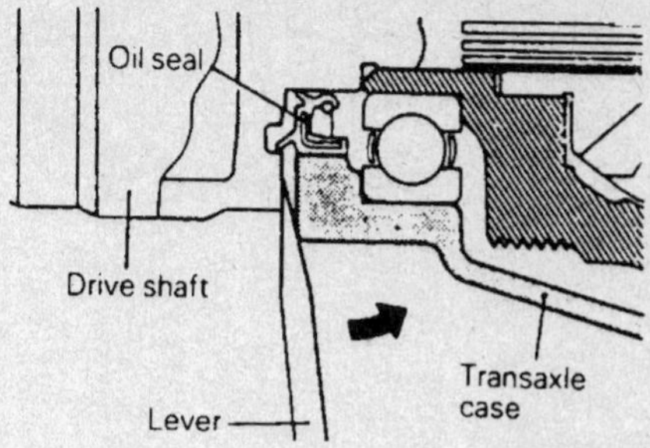
Oil seal
Drive shaft
Transaxle case
Lever

MT5029000352000X

Fig. 41 Driveshaft removal

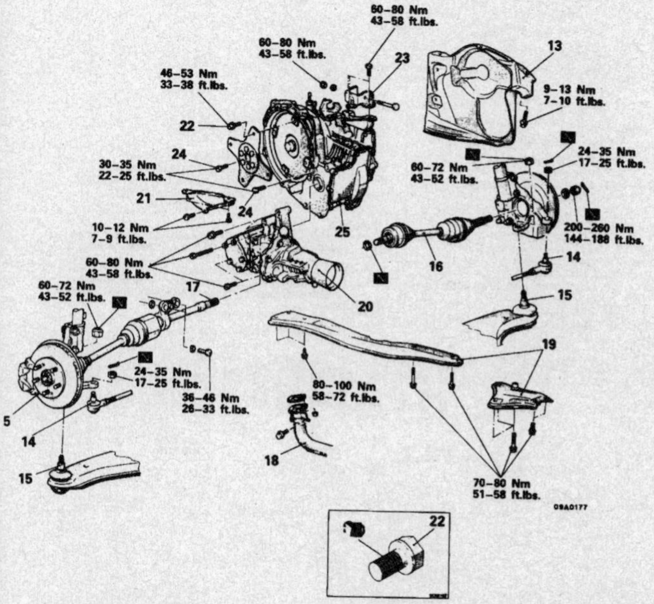
60-80 Nm
43-58 ft.lbs.
60-80 Nm
43-58 ft.lbs.
46-53 Nm
33-38 ft.lbs.
9-13 Nm
7-10 ft.lbs.
30-35 Nm
22-25 ft.lbs.
60-72 Nm
43-52 ft.lbs.
24-35 Nm
17-25 ft.lbs.
10-12 Nm
7-9 ft.lbs.
200-260 Nm
144-188 ft.lbs.
60-80 Nm
43-58 ft.lbs.
60-72 Nm
43-52 ft.lbs.
24-35 Nm
17-25 ft.lbs.
36-46 Nm
26-33 ft.lbs.
80-100 Nm
58-72 ft.lbs.
70-80 Nm
51-58 ft.lbs.

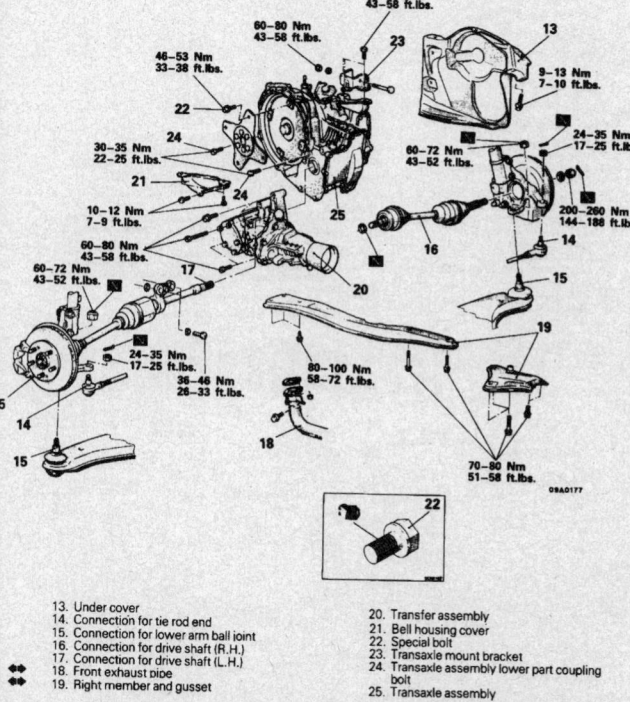

13. Under cover
14. Connection for tie rod end
15. Connection for lower arm ball joint
16. Connection for drive shaft (R.H.)
17. Connection for drive shaft (L.H.)
18. Front exhaust pipe
19. Right member and gusset
20. Transfer assembly
21. Bell housing cover
22. Special bolt
23. Transaxle mount bracket
24. Transaxle assembly lower part coupling bolt
25. Transaxle assembly

MT5029100584020X

Fig. 42 Transaxle replacement (Part 2 of 3). 1993–94 Eclipse w/W4A33 transaxle

Pre-removal and Post-installation Operation
- Removal and Installation of the Battery
- Draining and Supplying of the Transaxle Fluid (Refer to GROUP 00–Maintenance Service.)
- Removal and Installation of the Air Cleaner, Charge Air Cooler and Air Hose A (Refer to GROUP 15–Charge Air Cooler.)

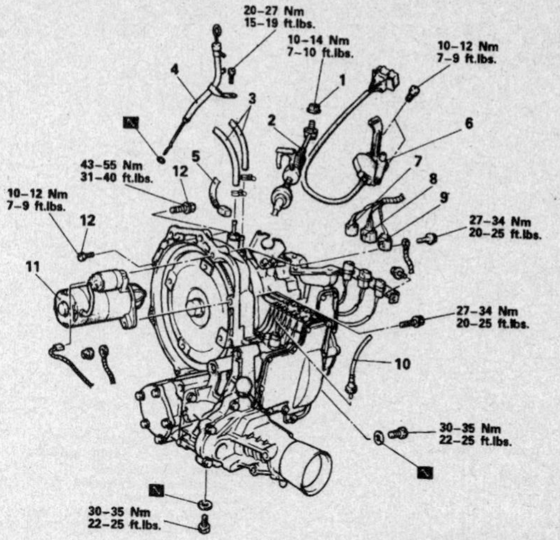
20-27 Nm
15-19 ft.lbs.
10-14 Nm
7-10 ft.lbs.
10-12 Nm
7-9 ft.lbs.
43-55 Nm
31-40 ft.lbs.
10-12 Nm
7-9 ft.lbs.
27-34 Nm
20-25 ft.lbs.
27-34 Nm
20-25 ft.lbs.
30-35 Nm
22-25 ft.lbs.
30-35 Nm
22-25 ft.lbs.

Removal steps

1. Adjusting nut
2. Connection for transaxle control cable
3. Connection for oil cooler hose
4. Transaxle fluid level gauge
5. Connection for solenoid connector
6. Park/Neutral position switch
7. Connection for pulse generator connector
8. Connection for kickdown servo switch connector
9. Connection for oil temperature sensor connector
10. Connection for speedometer cable
11. Starter motor
12. Upper coupling bolt for transaxle assembly and engine assembly

MT5029100584010X

Fig. 42 Transaxle replacement (Part 1 of 3). 1993–94 Eclipse w/W4A33 transaxle

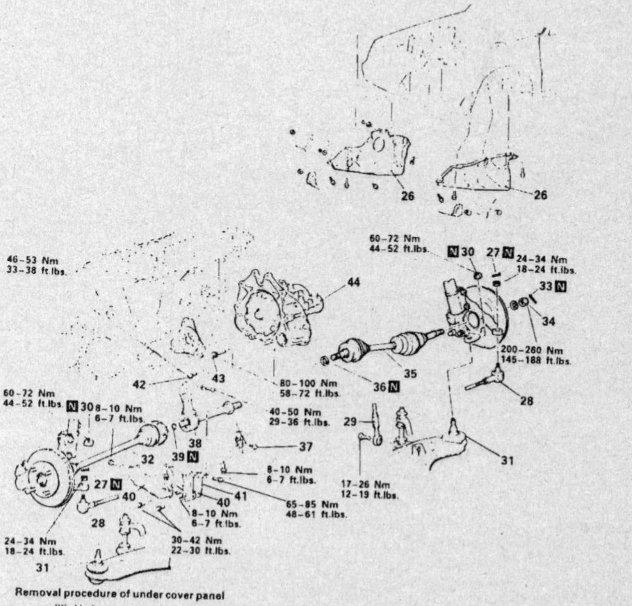
60-72 Nm
44-52 ft.lbs.
46-53 Nm
33-38 ft.lbs.
24-34 Nm
18-24 ft.lbs.
200-260 Nm
145-188 ft.lbs.
80-100 Nm
58-72 ft.lbs.
60-72 Nm
44-52 ft.lbs.
8-10 Nm
6-7 ft.lbs.
40-50 Nm
29-36 ft.lbs.
8-10 Nm
6-7 ft.lbs.
17-26 Nm
12-19 ft.lbs.
65-85 Nm
48-61 ft.lbs.
8-10 Nm
6-7 ft.lbs.
24-34 Nm
18-24 ft.lbs.
30-42 Nm
22-30 ft.lbs.

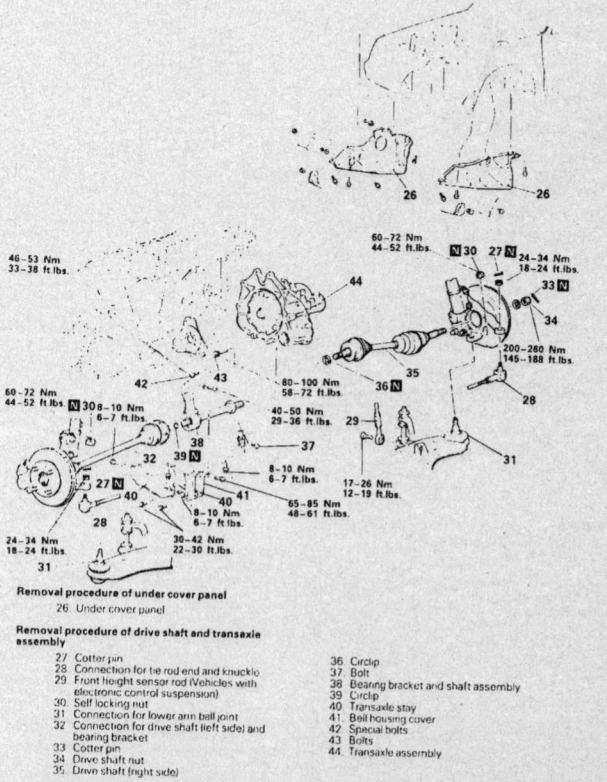

Removal procedure of under cover panel

26. Under cover panel

Removal procedure of drive shaft and transaxle assembly

27. Cotter pin
28. Connection for tie rod end and knuckle
29. Front height sensor rod (Vehicles with electronic control suspension)
30. Self locking nut
31. Connection for lower arm ball joint
32. Connection for drive shaft (left side) and bearing bracket
33. Cotter pin
34. Drive shaft nut
35. Drive shaft (right side)
36. Circlip
37. Bolt
38. Bearing bracket and shaft assembly
39. Circlip
40. Transaxle stay
41. Bell housing cover
42. Special bolts
43. Bolts
44. Transaxle assembly

MT5029100584030X

Fig. 42 Transaxle replacement (Part 3 of 3). 1993–94 Eclipse w/W4A33 transaxle

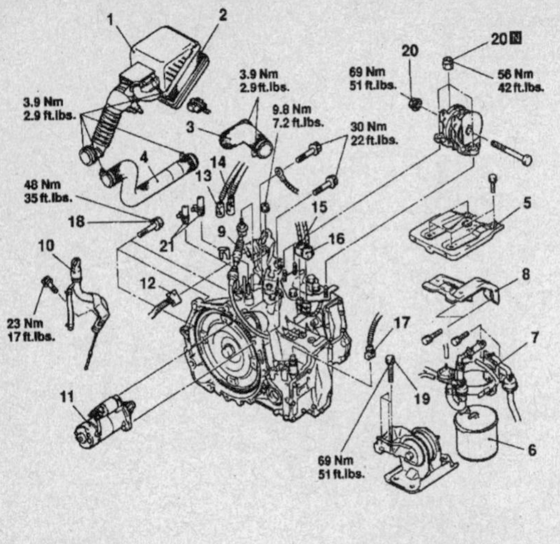
3.9 Nm
2.9 ft.lbs.
3.9 Nm
2.9 ft.lbs.
9.8 Nm
7.2 ft.lbs.
69 Nm
51 ft.lbs.
58 Nm
42 ft.lbs.
30 Nm
22 ft.lbs.
48 Nm
35 ft.lbs.
23 Nm
17 ft.lbs.
69 Nm
51 ft.lbs.

Removal steps

1. Air cleaner cover and air intake hose assembly
2. Air cleaner element
3. Air hose C
4. Air hose A
5. Battery tray
6. Evaporative emission canister
7. Evaporative emission canister holder
8. Battery tray stay
9. Transaxle control cable connection
10. Oil dipstick and guide assembly
11. Starter motor
12. Park/Neutral position switch connector
13. Oil temperature sensor connector
14. Kick down servo switch connector
15. Solenoid valve connector
16. Pulse generator connector
17. Speedometer connector
18. Transaxle assembly mounting bolts
19. Rear roll stopper bracket mounting bolts
20. Transaxle mounting bracket mounting nuts
21. Transaxle oil cooler hoses connection

• Supporting engine assembly

MT5029501084010X

Fig. 43 Transaxle replacement (Part 1 of 2). 1995–96 Eclipse AWD

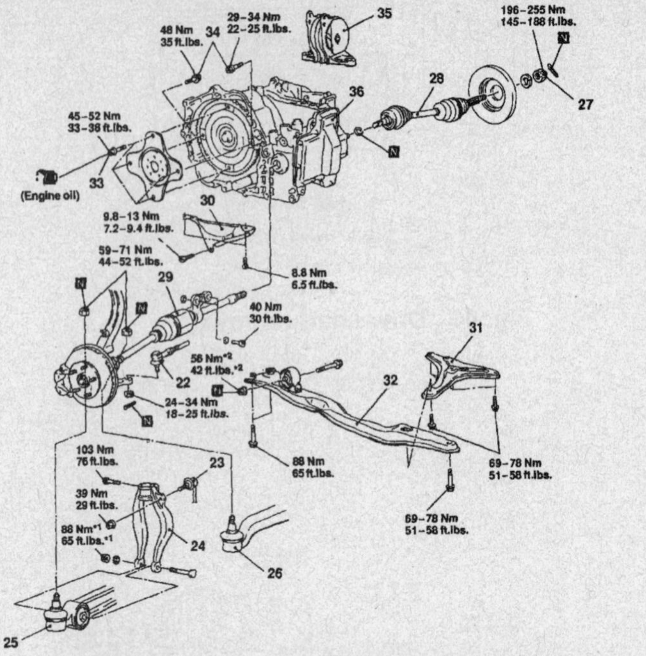
48 Nm
35 ft.lbs.
29–34 Nm
22–25 ft.lbs.
196–255 Nm
145–188 ft.lbs.
45–52 Nm
33–38 ft.lbs.
(Engine oil)
9.8–13 Nm
7.2–9.4 ft.lbs.
59–71 Nm
44–52 ft.lbs.
8.8 Nm
6.5 ft.lbs.
40 Nm
30 ft.lbs.
56 Nm*2
42 ft.lbs.*2
24–34 Nm
18–25 ft.lbs.
103 Nm
76 ft.lbs.
39 Nm
29 ft.lbs.
88 Nm*1
65 ft.lbs.*1
88 Nm
65 ft.lbs.
69–78 Nm
51–58 ft.lbs.
69–78 Nm
51–58 ft.lbs.

From under vehicles

22. Tie rod end ball joint and knuckle connection
23. Stabilizer link connection
24. Damper fork
25. Lateral lower arm ball joint and knuckle connection
26. Compression lower arm ball joint and knuckle connection
27. Drive shaft nut
28. Drive shaft
29. Drive shaft with inner shaft connection
30. Bell housing cover
31. Stay (R.H.)
32. Centermember assembly
33. Drive plate connecting bolts
34. Transaxle assembly mounting bolts
35. Transaxle mounting bracket
36. Transaxle assembly

Caution
*1: Indicates parts which should be temporarily tightened, and then fully tightened with the vehicle on the ground in the unladen condition.
*2: For tightening locations indicated by the symbol, first tighten temporarily, and then make the final tightening with the entire weight of the engine applied to the vehicle body.

MT5029501084020X

Fig. 43 Transaxle replacement (Part 2 of 2). 1995–96 Eclipse AWD

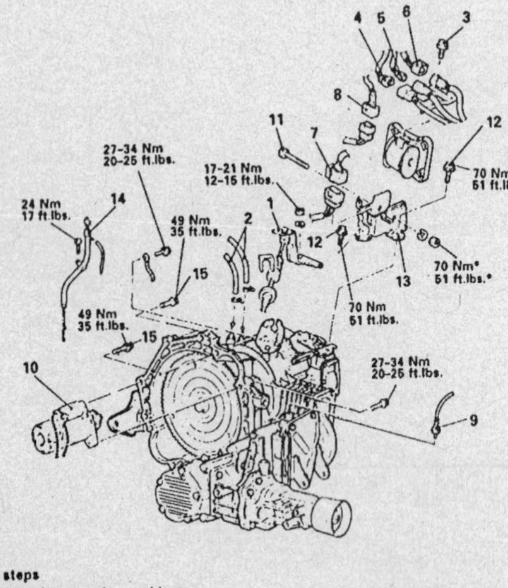
27-34 Nm
20-25 ft.lbs.
17-21 Nm
12-15 ft.lbs.
70 Nm
51 ft.lbs.
24 Nm
17 ft.lbs.
49 Nm
35 ft.lbs.
70 Nm*
51 ft.lbs.*
49 Nm
35 ft.lbs.
70 Nm
51 ft.lbs.
27-34 Nm
20-25 ft.lbs.

Removal steps

1. Connection for manual control lever
2. Transaxle oil cooler hoses
3. Bolt
4. Pulse generator connector
5. Oil temperature connector
6. Kickdown servo switch connector
7. Inhibitor switch connector
8. Solenoid valve connector
9. Speedometer cable connection
10. Starter motor
11. Transaxle mount bolt
12. Bolt
13. Transaxle mount bracket
14. Oil level gauge
15. Transaxle assembly upper part coupling bolts

NOTE
For tightening locations indicated by the * symbol, first tighten temporarily, and then make the final tightening with the entire weight of the engine applied to the vehicle body.

MT5029100585010X

Fig. 44 Transaxle replacement (Part 1 of 2). Expo w/W4A32 transaxle

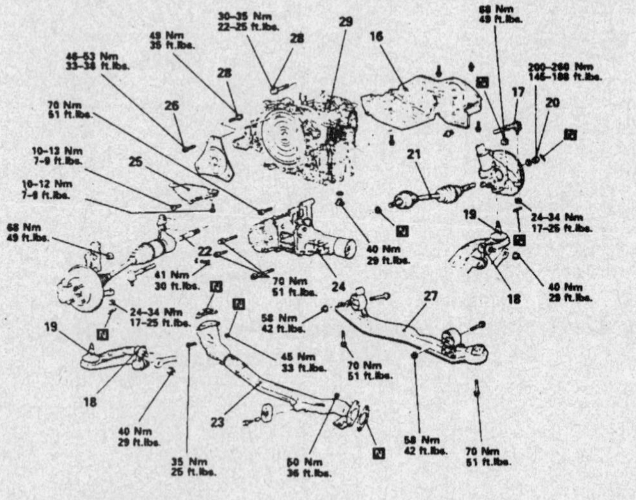
30–35 Nm
22–25 ft.lbs.
49 Nm
35 ft.lbs.
46–53 Nm
33–38 ft.lbs.
68 Nm
49 ft.lbs.
200–260 Nm
146–188 ft.lbs.
70 Nm
51 ft.lbs.
24–34 Nm
17–25 ft.lbs.
40 Nm
29 ft.lbs.
40 Nm
29 ft.lbs.
41 Nm
30 ft.lbs.
70 Nm
51 ft.lbs.
58 Nm
42 ft.lbs.
45 Nm
33 ft.lbs.
70 Nm
51 ft.lbs.
40 Nm
29 ft.lbs.
35 Nm
25 ft.lbs.
50 Nm
36 ft.lbs.
58 Nm
42 ft.lbs.
70 Nm
51 ft.lbs.

• Lifting up of the vehicle
16. Under cover (R.H.)
17. Connection for tie rod end
18. Connection for stabilizer bar
19. Connection for lower arm ball joint
• Draining of the transaxle fluid
20. Drive shaft nut (R.H.)
21. Drive shaft (R.H.)
22. Connection for drive shaft and inner shaft
23. Front exhaust pipe
24. Transfer assembly
25. Bell housing cover
26. Drive plate connecting bolts
27. Center member
28. Transaxle assembly lower part coupling bolts
29. Transaxle assembly

Transfer assembly removal steps

23. Front exhaust pipe
24. Transfer assembly

MT5029100585020X

Fig. 44 Transaxle replacement (Part 2 of 2). Expo w/W4A32 transaxle

TIGHTENING SPECIFICATIONS

Component	Torque/Ft. Lbs.
F4AC1 TRANSAXLE	
Differential Cover	14
Differential Ring Gear	70
Differential Retainer	20
Extension Housing	20
Oil Dipstick & Guide Assembly	9
Oil Pan	14
Output Gear	200
Pump	16
Rear Cover	14
Rear Roll Stopper Bracket	54
Starter To Bellhousing	40
Transaxle Control Cable To Bell Crank	7
Transaxle Mounting Bracket Flange	42
Transaxle Mounting Bracket Through Bolt	51
Transaxle To Engine	70
Transfer Shaft Gear	200
Valve Body	43①
F4A21 TRANSAXLE	
Axle Nut	144–188
Bearing Retainer Attaching Bolt	13–15
Bellhousing Cover	7–9
Cable Clip	36–48①
Control Cable To Body	7–10
Converter Housing	14–16
Differential Drive Gear	95–101
Drain Plug	24
Driveplate To Torque Converter	34–38
Driveshaft Nut	144–188
End Clutch Cover Mounting Bolt	48–60①
Hub Nut	144–188
Idler Shaft Lock Plate	35–43
Inhibitor Switch Attaching Bolt	8–9
Key Interlock Cable Mounting Nut	36–48①
Kickdown Servo Locknut	18–23
Lever Assembly To Body	7–10
Lever To Bracket Assembly	10–14
Lower Arm Ball Joint To Knuckle	43–52
Manual Control Lever	13–16
Manual Control Lever Setscrew	6–7
Oil Filter	48–60①
Oil Pan	96–108①
Oil Pump	18–23
Oil Pump Housing	8–9
Planetary Carrier Bolt	25–32
Pulse Generator Attaching Bolt	8–9
Shift Lock Cable Mounting Nuts (Brake Pedal Side)	7–10
Shift Lock Cable Mounting Nuts (Lever Assembly Side)	36–48①
Sprag Rod Support Bolt	15–19
Starter Motor Mounting Bolt	20–25
Tie Rod End To Knuckle	11–25
Transaxle Mounting Bolts④	31–40
Transaxle Mounting Bolts②	22–25
Transaxle Mounting Bolts③	7–8
Transaxle Mounting Bracket To Body	43–58

Continued

TIGHTENING SPECIFICATIONS—Continued

Component	Torque/Ft. Lbs.
F4A21 TRANSAXLE	
Transaxle Mounting Bracket To Transaxle	43–58
Transfer Shaft Locknut	145–166
Valve Body Assembly Bolts	36–48①
Valve Body Mounting Bolts	8–9
F4A22, F4A23, F4A33, W4A32 & W4A33 TRANSAXLES	
Air Cleaner Mounting Bolt	6
Axle Nut	144–188
Bearing Bracket To Engine	29–36
Bearing Retainer Screw	12–15
Bellhousing Cover To Engine	6
Center Support Bolt	18–25
Control Cable Adjusting Nut	7–10
Converter Housing Bolt	7.5–8.5
Differential Drive Gear Bolt	94–101
Drain Plug	24
Driveplate To Converter	34–38
Driveshaft Nut	144–188
Hub Nut	144–188
Inhibitor Switch	7.5–8.5
Kickdown Servo Piston Plate Screw	5
Lock Plate	35–43
Lower Arm Ball Joint To Knuckle	43–52
Manual Control Lever	13–15
Manual Control Shaft Setscrew	6
Oil Cooler Connector	11–15
Oil Filter	52①
Oil Pan	5–6
Oil Pump Assembly	11–15
One-Way Clutch Outer Race Bolt	18–25
Pressure Check Plug	6
Pulse Generator	8
Pump Housing To Reaction Shaft Support	8
Selector Lever	10–14
Speedometer Sleeve Locking Plate Bolt	36
Sprag Rod Support Bolt	15–19
Starter Motor Mounting Bolt	20–24
Tie Rod End To Knuckle	17–25
Torque Converter To Driveplate	53–55
Transaxle Flange Mounting Bolt	58–72
Transaxle Mounting Bolt & Washer Assembly	47–61
Transaxle Mounting Bracket To Body	29–36
Transaxle Mounting Bracket To Transaxle	43–57
Transaxle Stay To Engine	47–61
Transaxle Stay To Transaxle	22–30
Valve Body Assembly Mounting Bolt	7.5–8.5
Valve Body Bolt	40①
KM176 TRANSAXLE	
Bearing Retainer Screw	12–15
Bellhousing Cover To Engine	7–9
Control Cable To Body	7–10
Converter Housing Bolt	14–16
Cover To Selector Knob	17–24①
Differential Drive Gear Bolt	94–101
Drain Plug	22–25

Continued

TIGHTENING SPECIFICATIONS—Continued

Component	Torque/Ft. Lbs.
KM176 TRANSAXLE	
Driveplate To Converter	34–38
End Clutch Cover	5–6
Hose Bracket	24–48①
Indicator Panel	13–24①
Inhibitor Switch	7–9
Kickdown Locknut	13–23
Lever Assembly To Bracket Assembly	10–14
Lock Plate	35–43
Lower Arm Ball Joint To Knuckle	43–52
Manual Control Lever	36–84①
Manual Control Shaft Setscrew	36–84①
Oil Cooler Hose Clamp	33–48①
Oil Filter	48–60①
Oil Pan Bolt	7–9
Oil Pump Assembly Mounting Bolt	11–15
One-Way Clutch Outer Race Bolt	18–25
Pressure Check Plug	36–48①
Pulse Generator Mounting Bolt	7–9
Pump Housing To Reaction Shaft Support Bolt	7–9
Selector Knob To Lever Assembly	17–24①
Selector Lever Assembly Mounting Bolts	7–10
Special Bolts	33–38
Speedometer Sleeve Locking Plate Bolt	24–48①
Sprag Rod Support Bolt	15–19
Starter Motor Mounting Bolt	20–25
Tie Rod End To Knuckle	17–25
Torque Converter To Driveplate	53–55
Transaxle Mounting Bolt (.47 Inch Bolt & Washer Assembly)	58–72
Transaxle Mounting Bolt (.47 Inch Flange Bolt)	58–72
Transaxle Mounting Bracket To Body	29–36
Transaxle Mounting Bracket To Transaxle	43–57
Transaxle Stay To Engine	47–61
Transaxle Stay To Transaxle	22–30
Valve Body Assembly Mounting Bolt	8–9
Valve Body Bolt	36–48①

① — Inch lbs.

② — .40 inch diameter bolt.

③ — .31 inch diameter bolt.

④ — .47 inch diameter bolt.

Mitsubishi V4AW2 & V4AW3 Automatic Transmissions

NOTE: On Air Bag Equipped Models, Refer To "Air Bag System Precautions" Located In The Front Of This Manual For System Disarming & Arming Procedures.

INDEX

	Page No.
Adjustments	29-282
Park/Neutral Position Switch	29-283
Shift Interlock	29-283
Throttle Control Cable	29-282
Description	29-282
Identification	29-282
Maintenance	29-282
Fluid Change	29-282
Fluid Check	29-282
Precautions	29-282
Air Bag Systems	29-282
Tightening Specifications	29-285
Transmission, Replace	29-283

PRECAUTIONS

AIR BAG SYSTEMS

Refer to "Air Bag System Precautions" in the front of this manual for system disarming and arming procedures.

IDENTIFICATION

The vehicle information code plate is riveted to the bulkhead or to the front end upper bar in the engine compartment. The information code plate displays model, engine, transmission and body color code.

DESCRIPTION

These transmissions, **Figs. 1 and 2,** are both fully automatic four-speed units with a three element type torque converter. The V4AW3, however, is controlled electronically and has on-board diagnostic capabilities.

MAINTENANCE

FLUID CHECK

With vehicle on a level surface, start engine and operate at idle speed until normal operating temperature is reached. With parking brake applied, shift transmission through all ranges, then return to Neutral. Remove dipstick and check fluid level. Fluid level should be within the "HOT" range on dipstick. If necessary, add Dexron II fluid to raise fluid level as specified.

FLUID CHANGE

On four-wheel drive models and models operated under severe conditions, the transmission fluid should be changed every 30,000 miles. When refilling transmission, add only Dexron II automatic transmission fluid.

1. Remove drain plug and drain differential into a suitable container.
2. Install drain plug using a new gasket.
3. Refill automatic transmission fluid through oil level tube until it reaches "COLD" lower limit on dipstick.
4. Run engine at least two minutes, then shift transmission through all ranges and recheck fluid level.
5. Ensure fluid level is between the "HOT" upper and lower limits with transmission fluid at normal operating temperature. Add or remove fluid as necessary.

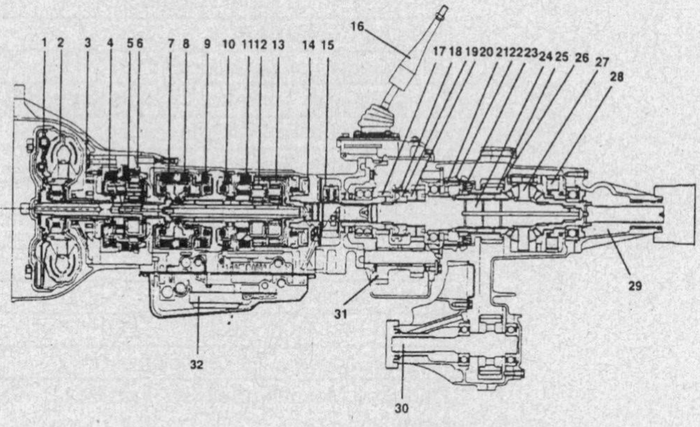

1. Lockup clutch
2. Torque converter
3. Oil pump
4. Overdrive clutch
5. Overdrive brake
6. Overdrive planetary gear
7. Forward clutch
8. Direct clutch
9. Brake No. 1
10. Brake No. 2
11. Brake No. 3
12. Front planetary gear
13. Rear planetary gear
14. Brake No. 3 piston
15. Governor
16. Transfer control lever
17. Input gear
18. High-low sleeve
19. High-low hub
20. Low speed gear
21. Differential lock hub
22. 2WD-4WD synchronizer sleeve
23. 2WD-4WD hub
24. Transfer drive shaft
25. Drive sprocket
26. Chain
27. Center differential
28. Viscous coupling
29. Rear output shaft
30. Front output shaft
31. Counter gear
32. Valve body

MT5029200596000X

Fig. 1 V4AW2 automatic transmission

ADJUSTMENTS

THROTTLE CONTROL CABLE

3.5L & 1993-94 3.0L Engines

1. Check engine idle speed and adjust as necessary.
2. Ensure throttle lever and throttle cable bracket are not bent or deformed.
3. Measure distance between inner cable

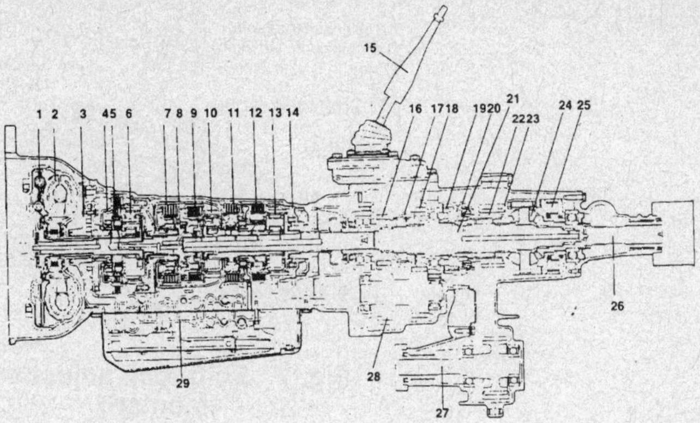

1. Torque converter clutch
2. Torque converter
3. Oil pump
4. Overdrive clutch
5. Overdrive brake
6. Overdrive planetary gear
7. Direct clutch
8. Second coast brake
9. Forward clutch
10. Front planetary gear
11. Second brake
12. First & reverse brake
13. Rear planetary gear
14. First & reverse brake piston
15. Transfer control lever
16. Input gear
17. High-low clutch
18. Low speed gear
19. Differential lock hub
20. 2-4WD synchronizer sleeve
21. Transfer drive shaft
22. Drive sprocket
23. Chain
24. Center differential
25. Viscous coupling
26. Rear output shaft
27. Front output shaft
28. Counter gear
29. Valve body

MT5029400597000X

Fig. 2 V4AW3 automatic transmission

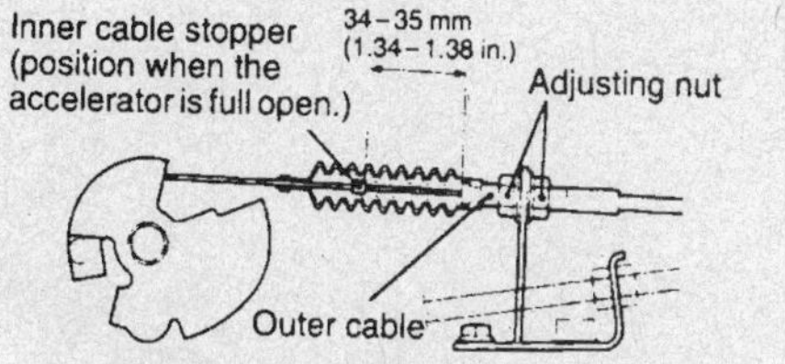
Inner cable stopper
(position when the
accelerator is full open.)
34–35 mm
(1.34–1.38 in.)
Adjusting nut
Outer cable

MT5029500630000X

Fig. 4 Throttle control cable measurement. 1995–96 3.0L engine

stopper and cover end, **Fig. 3,** with accelerator pedal fully depressed. Distance should be .4 inches or less.

4. If distance is not as specified, adjust nut until specification is reached.

1995–96 3.0L Engine

1. Ensure throttle lever and bracket are in good condition, then remove outer cable boot to access inner cable stopper.
2. With throttle lever fully opened, measure distance between inner and outer cable stoppers, **Fig. 4.** Distance should be 1.34–1.38 inches.
3. If distance is not as specified, adjust nut until specification is reached.

PARK/NEUTRAL POSITION SWITCH

1. Place selector lever in Neutral position, then loosen control cable adjusting nut and park/neutral position switch mounting bolt.
2. Rotate park/neutral position switch until Neutral position bosses on switch and adjustment lever are aligned, then tighten switch bolt.
3. Pull transmission control cable gently in direction of arrow, **Fig. 5,** then tighten adjusting nut.
4. Ensure selector lever is in Neutral position and corresponding with transmission lever.

SHIFT INTERLOCK

1. Remove floor console as shown in **Fig. 6.**
2. Ensure selector lever is in "P."
3. Loosen nut clamping shift lock cable, adjust shift lock cable so that end of cable with red mark comes between lobe of lock cam, **Fig. 7,** then tighten nut.
4. Reinstall floor console.

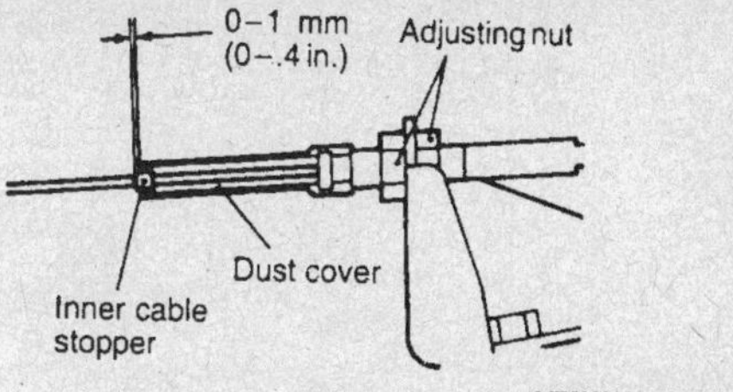
0–1 mm
(0–.4 in.)
Adjusting nut
Dust cover
Inner cable
stopper

MT5029200629000X

Fig. 3 Throttle control cable measurement. 3.5L & 1993–94 3.0L engines

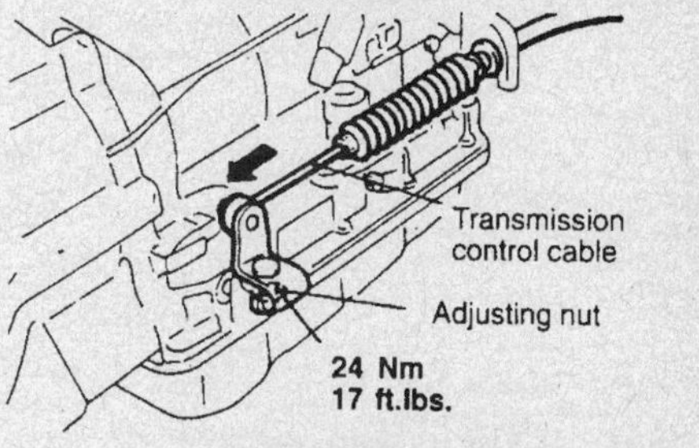
Transmission
control cable
Adjusting nut
24 Nm
17 ft.lbs.

MT5029200631000X

Fig. 5 Transmission control cable adjustment

TRANSMISSION

REPLACE

1. Remove transfer control lever assembly, transfer case protector and front exhaust pipe.
2. Drain transmission and transfer case fluid into a suitable container, then remove front and rear driveshafts.
3. Remove transmission in numbered sequences shown, **Figs. 8 and 9,** noting the following:
   a. Before removing transmission roll stopper, transmission and transfer case assembly must be supported with a suitable jack.
   b. Move transmission away from engine carefully. When transmission and engine have been separated slightly, push torque converter assembly onto transmission side so that it can be removed with transmission.
   c. Note control housing bolt lengths and positions for installation reference.
4. Reverse procedure to install, noting the following:
   a. Remove all old adhesive from control housing and bolts, then apply 3M Stud Locking Compound No. 4170, or equivalent, to bolt threads.
   b. Refer to **Figs. 8 and 9** for transmission to engine bolt tightening specifications. **Specifications vary according to bolt size and location.**
   c. Adjust control cables as necessary when installation is complete.

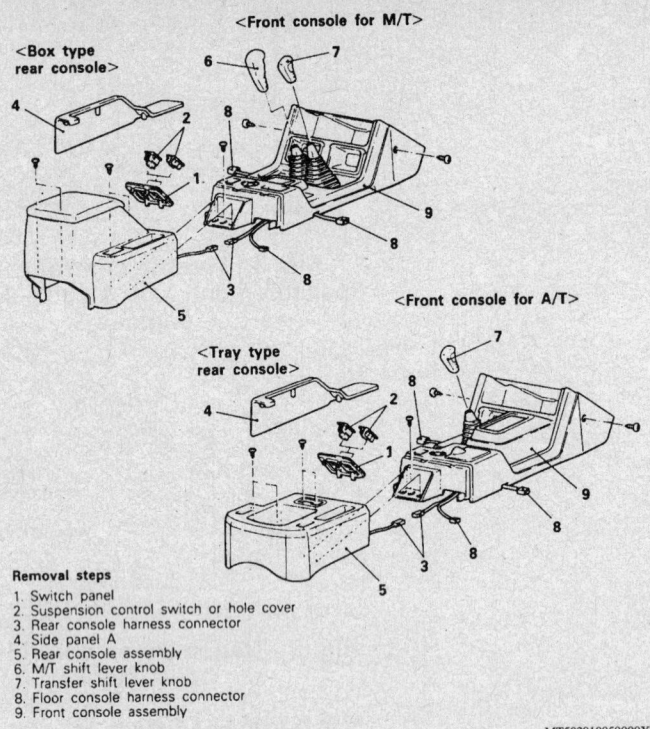

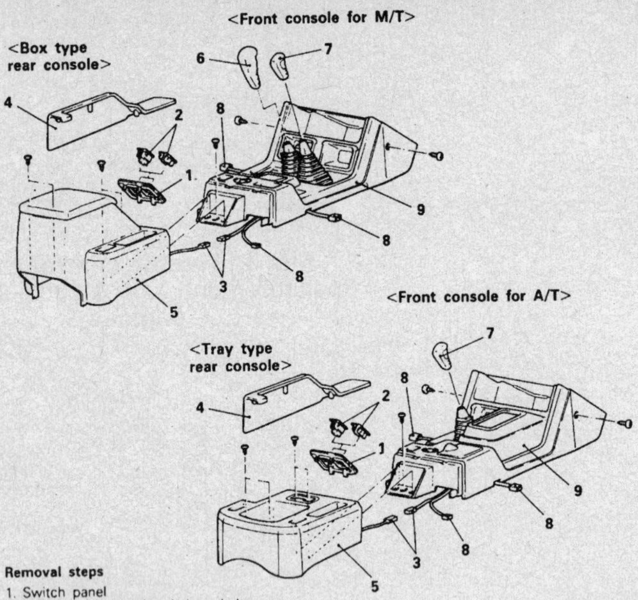
<Front console for M/T>
<Box type
rear console>
<Front console for A/T>
<Tray type
rear console>

Removal steps

1. Switch panel
2. Suspension control switch or hole cover
3. Rear console harness connector
4. Side panel A
5. Rear console assembly
6. M/T shift lever knob
7. Transfer shift lever knob
8. Floor console harness connector
9. Front console assembly

MT502910059000X

Fig. 6 Floor console replacement. Montero

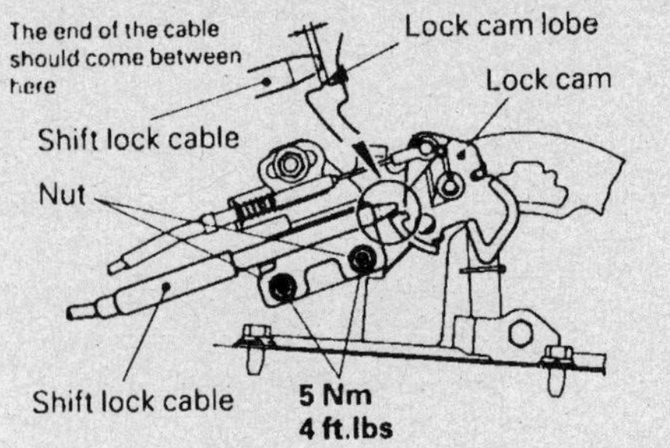
The end of the cable
should come between
here
Lock cam lobe
Lock cam
Shift lock cable
Nut
Shift lock cable
5 Nm
4 ft.lbs

MT5029100591000X

Fig. 7 Shift lock adjustment. Montero

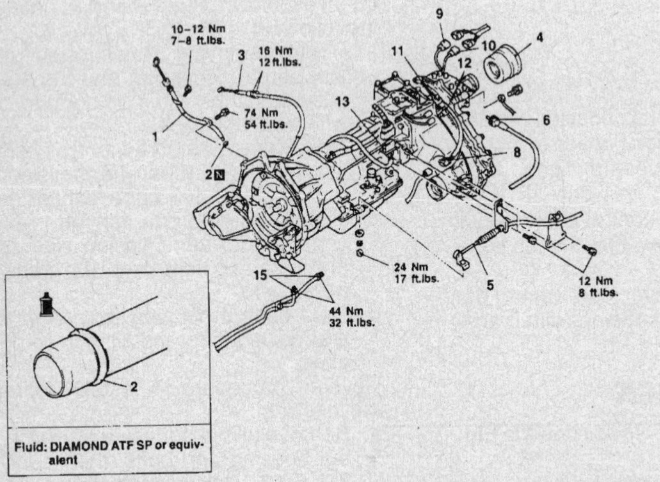
10–12 Nm
7–8 ft.lbs.
16 Nm
12 ft.lbs.
74 Nm
54 ft.lbs.
24 Nm
17 ft.lbs.
12 Nm
8 ft.lbs.
44 Nm
32 ft.lbs.
Fluid: DIAMOND ATF SP or equivalent

Removal steps

1. Fluid filler pipe
2. O-ring
3. Connection for throttle control cable
4. Dust seal guard
5. Connection for transmission control cable
6. Connection for speedometer cable
8. HI/LO detection switch connector
9. 4WD operation detection switch connector
10. Center differential lock operation detection switch connector
11. Center differential lock detection switch connector
12. 2WD/4WD detection switch connector
13. Park/Neutral position switch connector
15. Connection for fluid cooler pipe

MT5029200632010X

Fig. 8 Transmission replacement (Part 1 of 2). 3.0L 12 valve engine

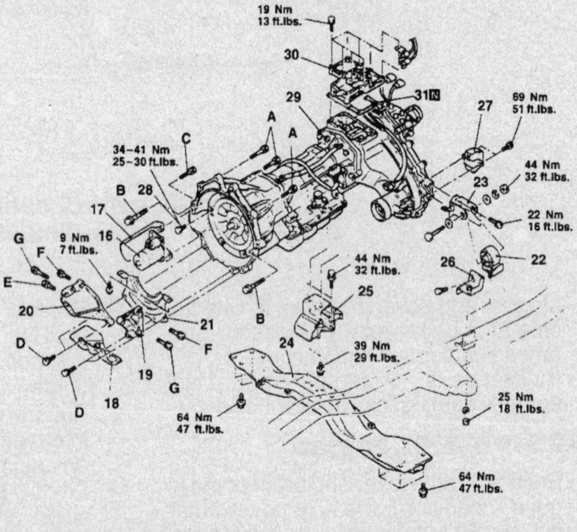
19 Nm
13 ft.lbs.
69 Nm
51 ft.lbs.
34–41 Nm
25–30 ft.lbs.
44 Nm
32 ft.lbs.
22 Nm
16 ft.lbs.
9 Nm
7 ft.lbs.
44 Nm
32 ft.lbs.
39 Nm
29 ft.lbs.
64 Nm
47 ft.lbs.
25 Nm
18 ft.lbs.
64 Nm
47 ft.lbs.

	Nm	ft.lbs.	O.D.×Length mm (in.)	Bolt identification
A	74	54	"7" 12×40 (.5×1.6)	"7" D X L
B	88	65	"7" 12×55 (.5×2.2)	
C	30	22	"7" 10×55 (.4×2.2)	
D	35	26	"7" 10×40 (.4×1.6)	
E	74	54	"7" 12×35 (.5×1.4)	
F	41	31	"7" 10×30 (.4×1.2)	
G	74	54	"7" 12×30 (.5×2.0)	

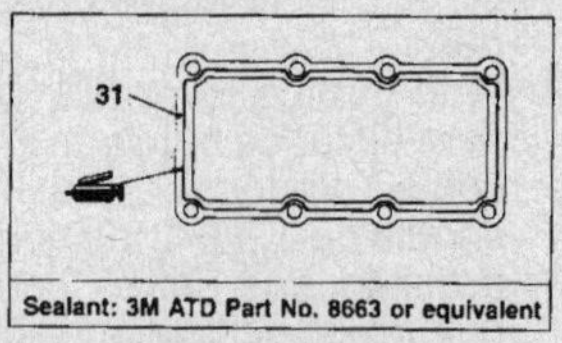
Sealant: 3M ATD Part No. 8663 or equivalent

16. Starter motor
17. Starter cover
18. Heat protector
19. Transmission stay (L.H.)
20. Transmission stay (R.H.)
21. Bell housing cover
22. Transfer roll stopper
23. Transfer mounting bracket
24. No. 2 crossmember
25. Engine mount rear insulator
26. Transfer case protector bracket
27. Mass damper
28. Torque converter connecting bolt
29. Transmission and transfer assembly
31. Gasket
31. Gasket

MT5029200632020X

Fig. 8 Transmission replacement (Part 2 of 2). 3.0L 12 valve engine

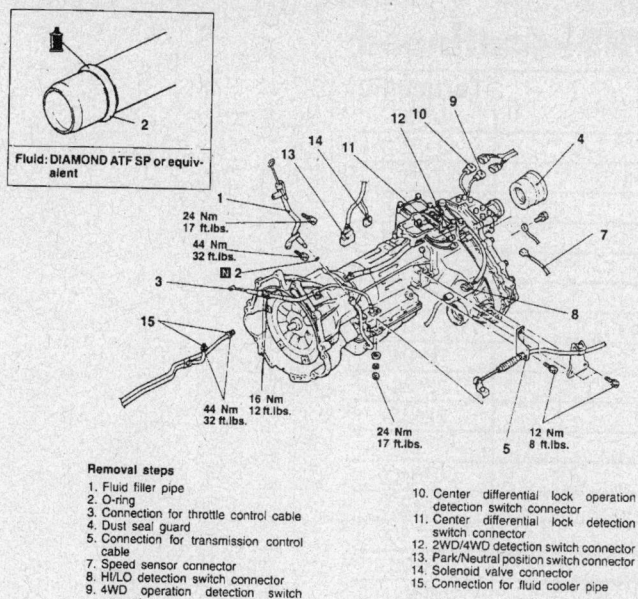

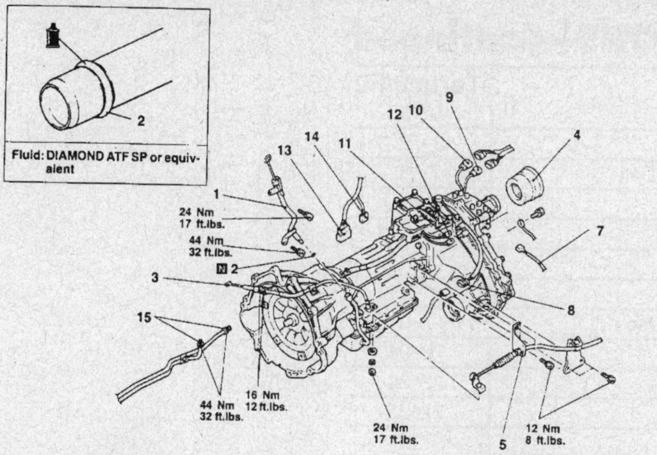
Fluid: DIAMOND ATF SP or equivalent
24 Nm
17 ft.lbs.
44 Nm
32 ft.lbs.
16 Nm
12 ft.lbs.
44 Nm
32 ft.lbs.
24 Nm
17 ft.lbs.
12 Nm
8 ft.lbs.

Removal steps

1. Fluid filler pipe
2. O-ring
3. Connection for throttle control cable
4. Dust seal guard
5. Connection for transmission control cable
7. Speed sensor connector
8. HI/LO detection switch connector
9. 4WD operation detection switch connector
10. Center differential lock operation detection switch connector
11. Center differential lock detection switch connector
12. 2WD/4WD detection switch connector
13. Park/Neutral position switch connector
14. Solenoid valve connector
15. Connection for fluid cooler pipe

MT5029200633010X

Fig. 9 Transmission replacement (Part 1 of 2). 3.0L 24-valve & 3.5L engines

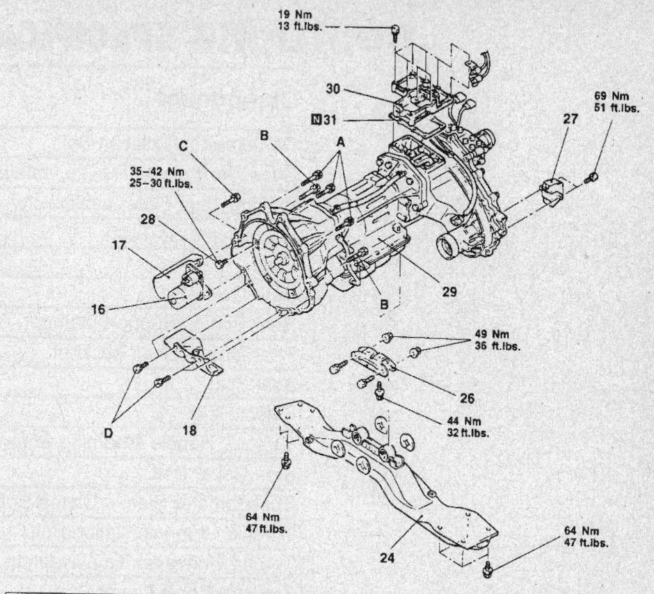
19 Nm
13 ft.lbs.
69 Nm
51 ft.lbs.
35–42 Nm
25–30 ft.lbs.
49 Nm
36 ft.lbs.
44 Nm
32 ft.lbs.
64 Nm
47 ft.lbs.
64 Nm
47 ft.lbs.

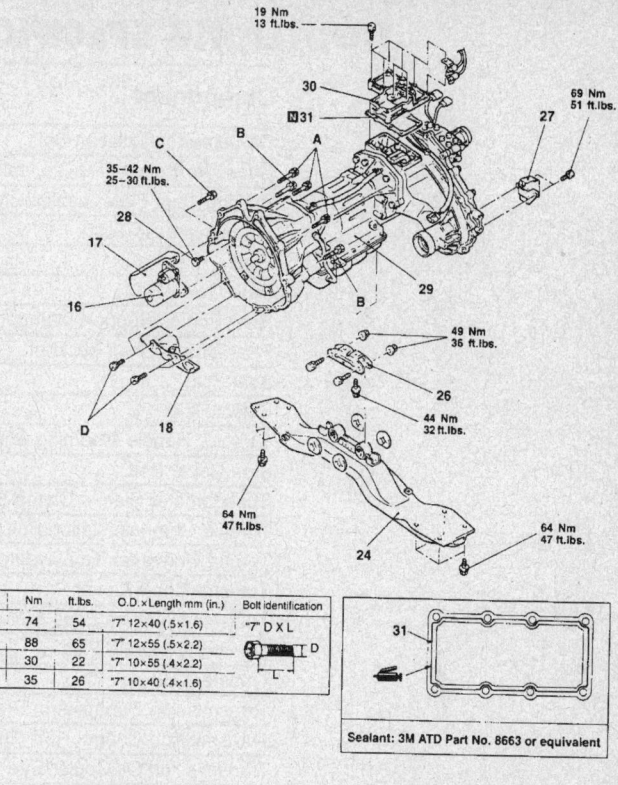

	Nm	ft.lbs.	O.D.×Length mm (in.)	Bolt identification
A	74	54	"7" 12×40 (.5×1.6)	"7" D X L
B	88	65	"7" 12×55 (.5×2.2)	
C	30	22	"7" 10×55 (.4×2.2)	
D	35	26	"7" 10×40 (.4×1.6)	

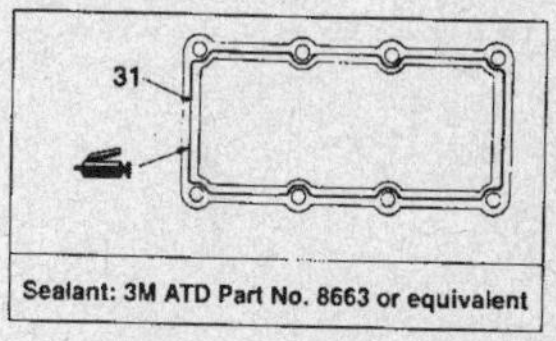
31
Sealant: 3M ATD Part No. 8663 or equivalent

16. Starter motor
17. Starter cover
18. Heat protector
24. No. 2 crossmember
26. Engine rear mount bracket
27. Mass damper
28. Torque converter connecting bolt
29. Transmission and transfer assembly
30. Control housing
31. Gasket

MT5029200633020X

Fig. 9 Transmission replacement (Part 2 of 2). 3.0L 24-valve & 3.5L engines

TIGHTENING SPECIFICATIONS

Component	Torque/Ft. Lbs.
Adapter	25
Center Support	19
Control Housing Bolt	11–15
Control Lever Assembly To Control Housing	60–84③
Control Shaft Setscrew	60–84③
Converter Housing Installation Bolt ①	20–30
Converter Housing Installation Bolt ②	20–30
Cover Bolt	11–15
Cover Plate Installation Screw	43–52③
Cross Shaft Bracket (A) To Body	84–108③
Elbow Connector	48–84③
Inhibitor Switch Attaching Bolt	33–48③
Locking Plate Bolt	11–15
Manual Lever Installation Nut	10–13
No. 2 Crossmember To Frame	40–54
No. 2 Crossmember To Transmission	13–18
Oil Filler Plug	22–25
Oil Filler Tube To Transmission	84–108③
Oil Pan Drain Plug	13–17
Oil Pan Installation Bolt	14–21
Oil Pump Assembly Installation Bolt	13–18
Oil Pump Body & Cover-Tightening Bolt	48–84③

Continued

TIGHTENING SPECIFICATIONS—Continued

Component	Torque/Ft. Lbs.
Oil Screen Installation Bolt	43–52③
Overdrive Solenoid Valve Installation Bolt	7–12
Parking Cam Plate Installation	48–84③
Plug (Hydraulic Test)	7–12
Plug	7–12
Rear Cover Bolt	11–15
Rear Engine Support Member To Frame	7–9
Rear Output Shaft Locknut	72–94
Seal Plug	22–30
Select Plug	22–25
Selector Handle Mounting Screw	.4
Side Cover Bolt	60–84③
Speedometer Sleeve Clamp Bolt	13–19③
Throttle Cam Installation Bolt	52–78③
Torque Converter To Driveplate	25–30
Transfer Chain Cover	26
Transfer Mounting Bolts & Nuts	26
Transfer Oil Drain Plug	24
Transfer Oil Filler Plug	24
Transmission Control Arm Bracket	13–17
Transmission Control Rod (B) To Pin	108③
Transmission Oil Cooler Eye Bolts	22–25
Transmission Oil Cooler Tube Flare Nut	29–36
Transmission To Engine	④
Transmission To Starter	20–25
Union	14–21
Valve Body Assembly Bolts	48③
Valve Body Mounting Bolts	7
4WD Switch	22–30

①— .39 inch diameter bolt.

②— .47 inch diameter bolt.

③— Inch lbs.

④— Refer to “Transmission, Replace” in this section for tightening specifications.

Front Wheel Drive Axles

NOTE: Prior To Performing Any Service Operations Listed In This Section, Consult The "Technical Service Bulletins" Section For Related Information.

INDEX

Page No.

Driveshaft, Replace 29-287
Diamante, Expo, Precis, 3000GT, 1993 Galant & 1993–94 Eclipse 29-287
Mirage 29-287
Montero 29-288
Pickup 29-288
1994–96 Galant & 1995–96 Eclipse 29-287
Driveshaft Service 29-288
AWD Models 29-289
FWD Models 29-288
4WD Models 29-290
Technical Service Bulletins 29-292
CV & Tripot Service Information 29-292
Troubleshooting 29-287

TROUBLESHOOTING

When troubleshooting front wheel drive vehicles, refer to **Fig. 1.**

Symptom	Probable cause	Remedy
Vehicle pulls to one side	Seizure of drive shaft ball joint	Replace
	Abnormal wear, play or seizure of wheel bearing	Replace
	Malfunction of front suspension or steering	Adjust or replace
Vibration	Bend, damage or abnormal wear of drive shaft	Replace
	Play in drive shaft and hub serration	Replace
	Abnormal wear, play or seizure of wheel bearing	Replace
Shimmy	Improper wheel alignment	Adjust or replace
	Malfunction of front suspension or steering	Adjust or replace
Excessive noise	Broken boot, grease leakage	Replace, repack grease
	Bend, damage or abnormal wear of drive shaft	Replace
	Play of drive shaft and hub serration	Replace
	Abnormal wear, play or seizure of center bearing	Replace
	Abnormal wear, play or seizure of wheel bearing	Replace
	Loose wheel nut	Retighten
	Malfunction of front suspension and steering	Adjust or replace

MT3039100009000X

Fig. 1 Front wheel drive troubleshooting chart

DRIVESHAFT

REPLACE

Consult the "Technical Service Bulletins" section for related information.

DIAMANTE, EXPO, PRECIS, 3000GT, 1993 GALANT & 1993-94 ECLIPSE

1. Raise and support vehicle, then remove front wheel.
2. Remove dust cover, cotter pin and driveshaft nut.
3. Drain transmission oil.
4. Disconnect lower arm ball joint from knuckle, then remove stabilizer and strut bars from lower arm.
5. **On models with driveshaft center bearing,** remove bearing bracket attaching bolts.
6. **On all models,** insert suitable pry bar between transmission case and driveshaft, then pry driveshaft from transmission. **Do not pull on driveshaft and do not insert pry bar deep enough to damage oil seal.**
7. Using tool No. MB990767, or equivalent, remove driveshaft from hub.
8. Reverse procedure to install, noting the following:
   a. Ensure driveshaft washer is correctly installed.
   b. Lower vehicle to ground, then attach and adjust driveshaft nut. **Torque** to 144–188 ft. lbs.
   c. If cotter pin holes do not line up, tighten bolt, without exceeding **torque** of 188 ft. lbs., until holes line up.
   d. Install new cotter pin.
   e. Refill transaxle to proper level.

1994-96 GALANT & 1995-96 ECLIPSE

1. Raise and support vehicle, then remove front wheel.
2. Remove cotter pin and driveshaft nut, noting the following:
   a. **Do not allow vehicle weight to rest upon wheel bearing unless absolutely necessary. If weight must be applied to bearing during removal, secure with tool No. MB990998, or equivalent.**
   b. Tool No. MB990767, or equivalent, can be used to prevent hub from rotating while nut is being removed.
3. Loosen, but do not remove, nut securing tie rod end to steering knuckle.
4. Using ball joint separator tool No. MB991113, or equivalent, separate tie rod end ball joint from steering knuckle. Support tool with a suitable cord to keep it in place during ball joint separation.
5. Separate damper fork from stabilizer link ball joint, then remove fork.
6. Using ball joint separator tool No. MB991113, or equivalent, separate lateral and compression lower arm ball joints from steering knuckle. Support tool with a suitable cord to keep it in place during ball joint separation.
7. **On Galant models,** use tool Nos. MB990241 and MB990767, or equivalents, to press driveshaft out of hub assembly.
8. **On all models,** use a suitable pry bar to separate driveshaft from transaxle case. **Do not insert pry bar farther than necessary to remove shaft, as oil seal may be damaged.**
9. Insert cover tool No. MB991461, or equivalent, into transaxle case driveshaft hole to prevent entry of foreign matter.
10. Reverse procedure to install, noting the following:
    a. Install driveshaft washer with convex portion facing outward.
    b. Use tool No. MB990767, or equivalent, to secure hub and **torque** driveshaft nut to 144–188 ft. lbs.
    c. If cotter pin holes do not align, turn driveshaft nut until pin can be inserted. **Do not exceed maximum torque of 188 ft. lbs.**

MIRAGE

1. Raise and support vehicle, then remove front wheels.
2. Remove cotter pin, wheel bearing nut and washer.

3. Disconnect lower control arm ball joint from knuckle using tool No. MB991113, or equivalent.
4. Disconnect tie rod end from knuckle using tool No. MB991113, or equivalent.
5. Disconnect center bearing snap ring if equipped.
6. **On models without center bearing,** proceed as follows:
   a. Insert pry bar between transaxle case and driveshaft, then pry driveshaft from transaxle. **Do not pull on driveshaft, or insert pry bar deep enough to damage oil seal.**
   b. Remove driveshaft from hub using tool No. MB990241-01, or equivalent, then the circlip from driveshaft.
7. **On models with center bearing,** proceed as follows:
   a. Remove driveshaft from transaxle by lightly tapping driveshaft outer race with a plastic hammer. **Do not pull on driveshaft or insert pry bar between transaxle case and driveshaft.**
   b. Remove driveshaft from hub by lightly tapping driveshaft end with plastic hammer.
   c. Remove center bearing bracket attaching bolts, then the center bearing bracket and spacers.
8. **On all models,** reverse procedure to install, noting the following:
   a. **On models with center bearing,** press in driveshaft until center bearing comes in contact with center bearing bracket, then install snap ring into center bearing bracket.
   b. **On all models,** lower vehicle to ground, then attach and adjust driveshaft nut. **Torque** nut to 144–188 ft. lbs.
   c. If cotter pin hole does not line up, tighten bolt without exceeding **torque** of 188 ft. lbs., until hole lines up.

MONTERO

1. Raise and support vehicle, then remove wheel.
2. Remove ABS wheel speed sensor.
3. Remove caliper assembly without disconnecting brake hose. Support caliper out of way. Do not strain brake hose.
4. Remove freewheeling hub cover assembly, then the snap ring from driveshaft.
5. Remove knuckle and front hub assembly as an assembly.
6. Pull left driveshaft out of differential carrier assembly, without damaging oil seal.
7. Remove right driveshaft to differential carrier inner shaft attaching bolts, then pull driveshaft from differential assembly.
8. Reverse procedure to install, noting the following:
   a. Install left driveshaft into front differential carrier using a plastic hammer.
   b. **Torque** right driveshaft to inner shaft attaching bolts to 36–43 ft. lbs.

PICKUP

1. Raise and support vehicle, then remove wheel.
2. Remove caliper assembly without disconnecting brake hose. Support caliper out of way. Do not strain brake hose.
3. Remove freewheeling hub cover assembly and remove snap ring from driveshaft.
4. Remove knuckle and front hub assembly.
5. Pull left driveshaft out of differential carrier assembly without damaging oil seal.
6. Using suitable jack, raise the lower arm.
7. Remove upper mounting nuts from right shock absorber, then the shock absorber from arm post of side frame. **Do not lower jack while disconnecting shock absorber or while it is disconnected. Do not remove jack until upper part of shock absorber has been reconnected to arm post of side frame.**
8. Detach right driveshaft from inner shaft assembly, then remove right driveshaft.
9. Using tool Nos. MB990211 and MB990906, or equivalents, pull inner shaft out of differential carrier without damaging oil seal.
10. Using screwdriver, remove dust seal from housing tube assembly.
11. Reverse procedure to install, noting the following:
    a. **Torque** upper knuckle to ball joint bolts to 44–65 ft. lbs., lower knuckle at ball joints to 87–130 ft. lbs. and freewheeling hub assembly bolts to 8–10 ft. lbs.
    b. Apply multi-purpose grease to lip of dust seal; then, using tool Nos. MB990938 and MB990985, or equivalents, drive dust seal into housing tube end.
    c. Using tool Nos. MB990211 and MB990906, or equivalents, drive inner shaft assembly into differential carrier assembly. Do not damage oil seal.
    d. Replace circlip which is attached to Birfield Joint (BJ) side spline with new one.
    e. Install right driveshaft to inner shaft assembly, then **torque** bolts to 37–43 ft. lbs.
    f. Attach shock absorber to arm post of side frame by installing double nuts. Install first nut so that distance between base of nut and end of strut is .81 inch, then **torque** second nut to 9–13 ft. lbs.
    g. Using plastic mallet, drive left driveshaft into differential carrier assembly. Do not damage oil seal.
    h. Install new circlip on BJ side spline.
    i. Mount knuckle and front hub assembly, then adjust driveshaft axial play as necessary.

DRIVESHAFT SERVICE

FWD MODELS

ECLIPSE, EXPO, GALANT & MIRAGE

Refer to **Figs. 2 through 6** when disassembling the front driveshafts, noting the following:

1. Wrap masking tape on splined end of driveshaft prior to removing joint boot.
2. **On models equipped with a Double Offset Joint (DOJ),** proceed as follows:
   a. Make alignment marks on DOJ inner race and cage.
   b. Remove DOJ cage from inner race by turning cage in a clockwise direction looking at end of driveshaft.
   c. Using a suitable brass drift, tap DOJ inner race off driveshaft.
3. **On all models,** reverse procedure to assemble, noting the following:
   a. Align mating marks made during disassembly.
   b. When installing joint boots, ensure distance between clamps is as shown in **Fig. 7.**
   c. Install dynamic damper, if equipped at distance from outer joint shown in **Fig. 8.**

DIAMANTE & 3000GT

Refer to **Fig. 9** when disassembling the front driveshafts, noting the following:

1. Press off inner shaft using suitable press and bearing remover tool Nos. MB991248 or MD998801, or equivalent.
2. Remove center bearing using bearing remover tool Nos. MB990938 & MB990930, or equivalent.
3. Wrap masking tape on splined end of driveshaft prior to removing joint boot.
4. Reverse procedure to assemble, noting the following:
   a. Install center bearing using bearing installation tool Nos. MB990938 and MB990932, or equivalent.
   b. Apply grease to rear surface of all dust seals.
   c. Install oil seals using oil seal installer tool No. MB990890, or equivalent.
   d. Install inner shaft using bearing installation tool No. MB991172, or equivalent.
   e. Assemble TJ case and inner shaft using shaft installation tool Nos. MB991248 or MD998801, or equivalent.
   f. When installing joint boots ensure distance between clamps is as shown in **Fig. 7.**

PRECIS

Disassemble

1. Remove Double Offset Joint (DOJ) boot band, **Fig. 10.**
2. Remove DOJ boot from DOJ outer race.
3. Using screwdriver, remove circlip.
4. Remove DOJ outer race, then wipe off grease.
5. Remove snap ring, remove DOJ inner

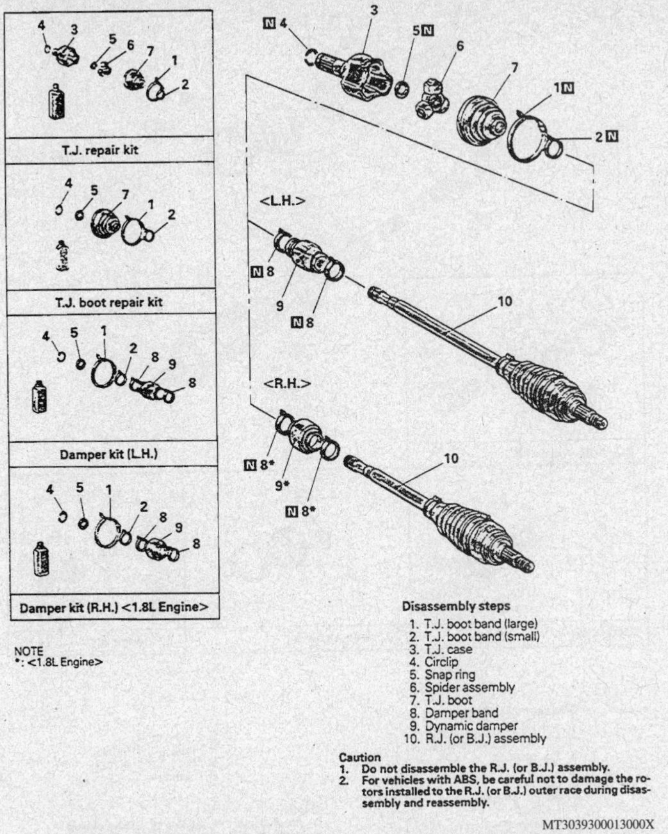
T.J. repair kit
T.J. boot repair kit
Damper kit (L.H.)
Damper kit (R.H.) <1.8L Engine>
<L.H.>
<R.H.>
NOTE
*: <1.8L Engine>
Disassembly steps
1. T.J. boot band (large)
2. T.J. boot band (small)
3. T.J. case
4. Circlip
5. Snap ring
6. Spider assembly
7. T.J. boot
8. Damper band
9. Dynamic damper
10. R.J. (or B.J.) assembly
Caution
1. Do not disassemble the R.J. (or B.J.) assembly.
2. For vehicles with ABS, be careful not to damage the rotors installed to the R.J. (or B.J.) outer race during disassembly and reassembly.
MT3039300013000X

Fig. 2 Exploded view of driveshaft. Mirage

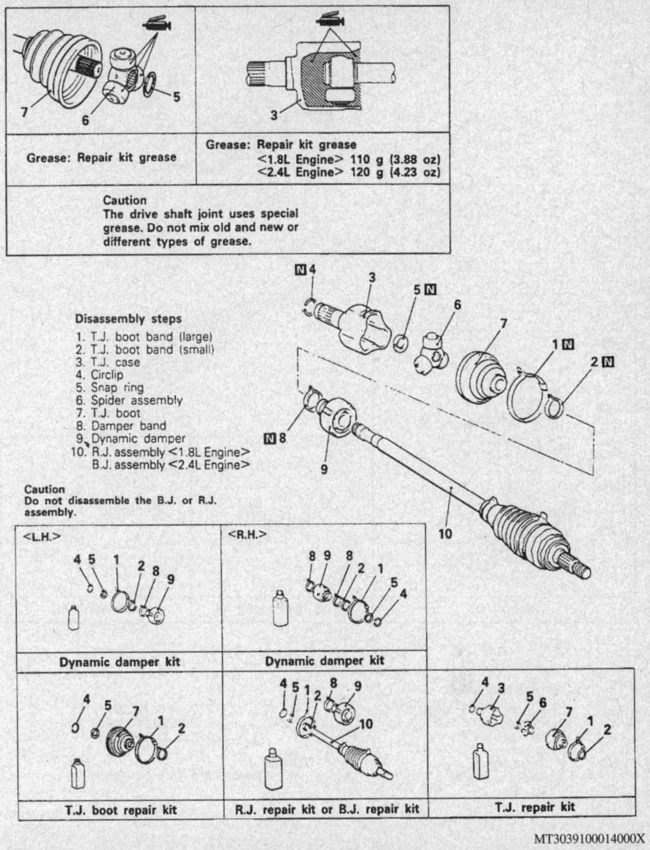
Grease: Repair kit grease
Grease: Repair kit grease
<1.8L Engine> 110 g (3.88 oz)
<2.4L Engine> 120 g (4.23 oz)
Caution
The drive shaft joint uses special grease. Do not mix old and new or different types of grease.
Disassembly steps
1. T.J. boot band (large)
2. T.J. boot band (small)
3. T.J. case
4. Circlip
5. Snap ring
6. Spider assembly
7. T.J. boot
8. Damper band
9. Dynamic damper
10. R.J. assembly <1.8L Engine>
B.J. assembly <2.4L Engine>
Caution
Do not disassemble the B.J. or R.J. assembly.
<L.H.>
<R.H.>
Dynamic damper kit
Dynamic damper kit
T.J. boot repair kit
R.J. repair kit or B.J. repair kit
T.J. repair kit
MT3039100014000X

Fig. 3 Exploded view of driveshaft. Eclipse, Expo & 1993 Galant FWD

race, cage, then the balls as an assembly. Clean assembly. If balls drop out of cage, reinstall with inner race.
6. Wipe grease off spline portion.
7. Remove Birfield Joint (BJ) boot band.
8. Remove DOJ and BJ boots. If boots can be reused, wrap vinyl tape around driveshaft spline so that boots are not damaged as they are removed.
9. Wipe grease off BJ. Do not disassemble.
10. Inspect all components and replace as necessary.

Assemble

1. Wrap vinyl tape around driveshaft spline, then install Birfield Joint (BJ) and Double Offset Joint (DOJ) boots in this order.
2. Fill inside of BJ and BJ boot with specified grease.
3. Place BJ boot over joint, then use new BJ boot bands to secure boot.
4. Using grease supplied with repair kit, lubricate DOJ cage, balls and inner race.
5. Install DOJ cage, balls and inner race onto driveshaft, then fit snap ring securely into groove on driveshaft.
6. Using grease supplied with repair kit, lubricate DOJ outer race, fit driveshaft into DOJ outer race, then apply more grease to DOJ outer race.
7. Install new circlip on driveshaft.
8. When installing new boot bands, ensure distance between center of bands is 3.42–3.66 inch for LH shafts, and 3.23–3.47 inch for RH shafts on turbocharged models, and 3.23–3.47 inch for LH shafts, and 3.42–3.66 inch for RH shafts on non turbocharged models.
9. Wipe excess grease from lips of DOJ and BJ boots.
10. Install new circlip onto DOJ outer race.

AWD MODELS

ECLIPSE & GALANT

Refer to **Fig. 11** when disassembling the front driveshafts, noting the following:

1. Remove inner driveshaft using bearing remover tool Nos. MB991248 and MD998801, or equivalents.
2. Remove center bearing using bearing remover tool No. MB990938-01, or equivalent.
3. Reverse procedure to assemble, noting the following:
   a. Install center bearing using bearing installation tool No. MB990938-01, or equivalent.
   b. Apply grease to all dust seals.
   c. Install dust seals using seal installation tool No. MB990938-01, or equivalent.
   d. Assemble TJ case and inner shaft using shaft installation tool No. MB991248, or equivalent.
   e. When installing joint boots, ensure distance between clamps is 3.35 inches.

EXPO

1.8L Engine

Refer to **Fig. 12** when disassembling the front driveshafts, noting the following:

1. Remove inner shaft and seal plate using bearing removal tool No. MB991248, or equivalent.
2. Remove inner shaft from the center bracket using puller remover tool Nos. MB990197 and MB990930, or equivalents.
3. Remove bearing from center bracket using bearing remover tool Nos. MB990938 and MB990930, or equivalents.
4. Remove Double Offset Joint (DOJ) cage as follows:
   a. Make mating marks on driveshaft and DOJ inner race and DOJ cage.
   b. Remove balls from cage.
   c. Remove DOJ cage from inner race by turning cage in a clockwise direction looking at end of driveshaft.
   d. Using a suitable brass drift, tap DOJ inner race off driveshaft.
5. Reverse procedure to assemble, noting the following:
   a. Align mating marks made during disassembly.
   b. Install center bearing using bearing installation tool Nos. MB990938 and MB990932, or equivalents.
   c. Apply grease to all dust seals.
   d. Install dust seals using seal installation tool Nos. MB990938,

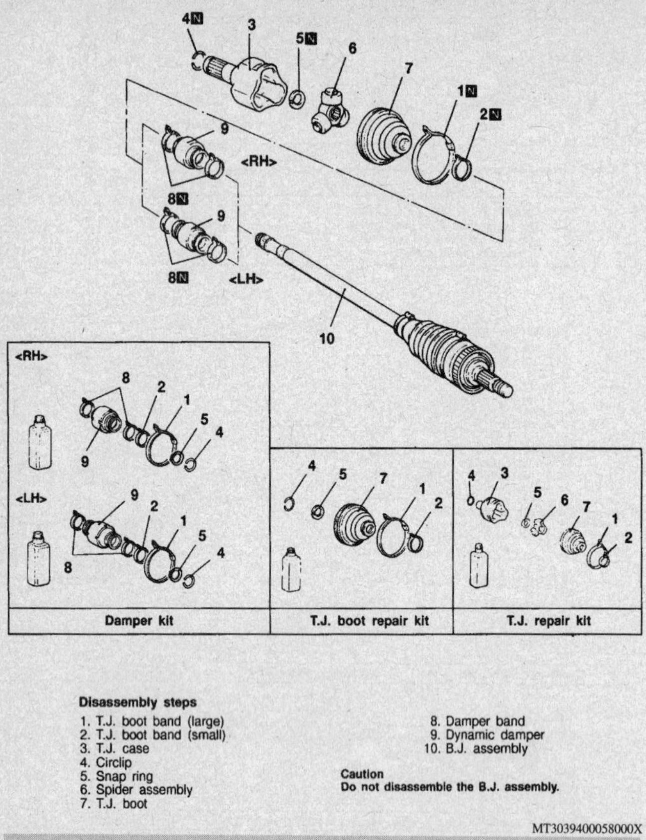

<RH>
<LH>
Damper kit
T.J. boot repair kit
T.J. repair kit
Disassembly steps
1. T.J. boot band (large)
2. T.J. boot band (small)
3. T.J. case
4. Circlip
5. Snap ring
6. Spider assembly
7. T.J. boot
8. Damper band
9. Dynamic damper
10. B.J. assembly
Caution
Do not disassemble the B.J. assembly.
MT3039400058000X

Fig. 4 Exploded view of driveshaft. 1994–96 Galant

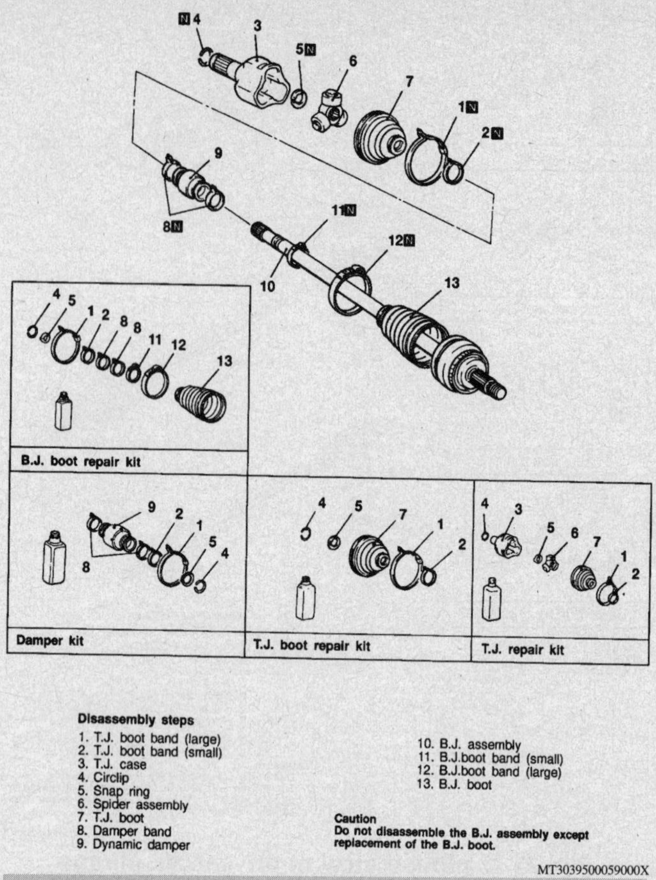

B.J. boot repair kit
Damper kit
T.J. boot repair kit
T.J. repair kit
Disassembly steps
1. T.J. boot band (large)
2. T.J. boot band (small)
3. T.J. case
4. Circlip
5. Snap ring
6. Spider assembly
7. T.J. boot
8. Damper band
9. Dynamic damper
10. B.J. assembly
11. B.J.boot band (small)
12. B.J.boot band (large)
13. B.J. boot
Caution
Do not disassemble the B.J. assembly except replacement of the B.J. boot.
MT3039500059000X

Fig. 5 Exploded view of driveshaft. 1995–96 Eclipse FWD

MB990933 and MB990931, or equivalents.

e. Install inner shaft into inner race using holder tool No. MB991172, or equivalent.
f. Install seal plate and DOJ outer race using installation tool No. MB991248, or equivalent.
g. When installing joint boots, ensure distance between clamps is 3.54 inches.

2.4L Engine

Refer to **Fig. 13** when disassembling the front driveshafts, noting the following:

1. Remove inner shaft and seal plate using bearing removal tool No. MB991248, or equivalent.
2. Remove inner shaft from the center bracket using puller remover tool Nos. MB990197 and MB990930, or equivalents.
3. Remove bearing from center bracket using bearing remover tool Nos. MB990938 and MB990930, or equivalents.
4. Reverse procedure to assemble, noting the following:
   a. Install dynamic damper on driveshaft 7.87 inches away from the outboard joint.
   b. Install center bearing using bearing installation tool Nos. MB990938 and MB990932, or equivalents.
   c. Install inner shaft into inner race using holder tool No. MB991172, or equivalent.
   d. Install seal plate into TJ case using installation tool Nos. MB991248, MB990927 and MB990938, or equivalents.
   e. When installing joint boots, ensure distance between clamps is 3.35 inches.

3000GT

Refer to the "FWD Models" section when servicing the front driveshaft on these models.

4WD MODELS

DISASSEMBLE

Driveshaft

1. Using a suitable screwdriver, remove boot bands, **Fig. 14.**
2. Use screwdriver to remove circlip from Double Offset Joint (DOJ) outer race.
3. Remove driveshaft from DOJ outer race, then wipe away grease.
4. Using screwdriver, remove balls from DOJ cage.
5. Remove DOJ cage from DOJ inner race in direction of Birfield Joint (BJ) by turning DOJ cage 30° from position at which balls were removed.
6. Using pliers, remove snap ring from driveshaft, then the DOJ inner race from driveshaft.
7. Remove circlip from driveshaft.
8. Remove DOJ and BJ boots from driveshaft. Wrap vinyl tape around spline on DOJ side of driveshaft so that boots are not damaged when removed.
9. Using a screwdriver, remove dust cover.
10. Inspect all parts and replace as necessary. **Do not disassemble BJ.**

Inner Shaft

1. Using a suitable hammer, bend down outer circumference of dust cover.
2. Install tool No. MB990560, or equivalent, then press bearing from shaft.
3. Using a suitable screwdriver, remove dust cover.
4. Inspect all parts and replace as necessary.

ASSEMBLE

Inner Shaft

1. Using a suitable pipe with an outside diameter of 2.95 inches and metal thickness of .16 inch, press dust cover onto inner shaft.
2. Using tool No. MB990560, equivalent, press bearing onto shaft.

Driveshaft

1. Using a suitable pipe with an outside diameter of 2.71 inches and metal thickness of .09 inch, press dust cover onto Birfield Joint (BJ) side.
2. Using a suitable pipe with an outside

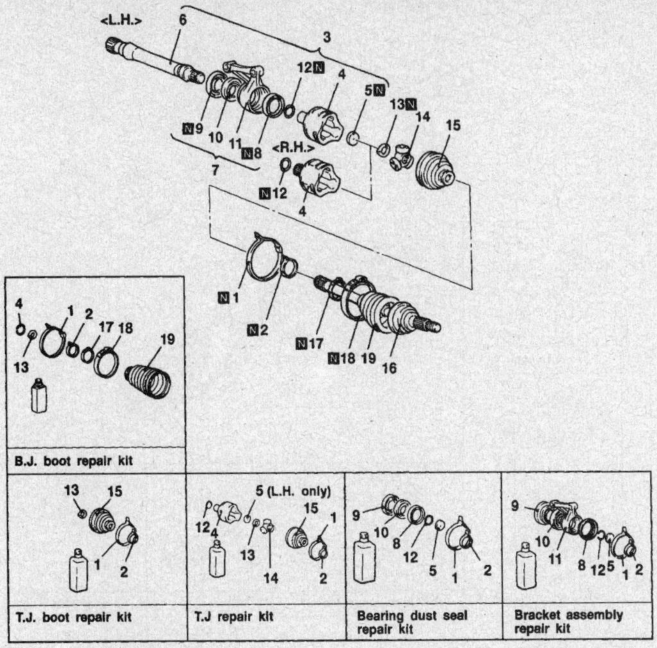
<L.H.>
<R.H.>
B.J. boot repair kit
T.J. boot repair kit
5 (L.H. only)
T.J repair kit
Bearing dust seal repair kit
Bracket assembly repair kit

Disassembly steps
1. T.J. boot band (large)
2. T.J. boot band(small)
3. T.J.case and inner shaft assembly
4. T.J. case
5. Seal plate
6. Inner shaft
7. Bracket assembly
8. Dust seal (outer)
9. Dust seal (inner)
10. Center bearing
11. Center bearing bracket
12. Circlip
13. Snap ring
14. Spider assembly
15. T.J. boot
16. B.J. assembly
17. B.J. boot band (small)
18. B.J. boot band (large)
19. B.J. boot

Caution
Do not disassemble the B.J. assembly except replacement of the B.J. boot.

MT3039500060000X

Fig. 6 Exploded view of driveshaft. 1995–96 Eclipse AWD

Engine	Drive Joint Type	Distance, Inch	
		LH Driveshaft	RH Driveshaft
DIAMANTE			
All	All	3.35	3.35
ECLIPSE			
1.8L	TJ & BJ	2.95	3.35
2.0L & 2.4L	TJ & BJ	3.15	3.15
EXPO			
1.8L	All	3.23	3.23
2.4L	All	3.15	3.15
GALANT			
All	TJ & RJ	3.23	3.35
All	TJ & BJ	3.15	3.15
MIRAGE			
All	All	3.35	3.35
3000GT			
All	All	2.95	2.95

TJ: Tripod Joint RJ: Rzeppa Joint BJ: Birfield Joint

Fig. 7 Boot clamp installation dimension chart

Model	Year	Engine	Dimension	
			LH Driveshaft	RH Driveshaft
Eclipse	1995–96	2.0L Non-Turbo①	—	14.72
		2.0L Non-Turbo②	7.64	14.72
		2.0L Turbo	14.72	—
		2.4L	14.37	8.70
Galant	1994–96	2.4L	14.37	8.70
Mirage	1993–96	1.5L	13.82	13.82
		1.8L	14.37	7.89
Expo	1993–95	1.8L	17.01	7.84
		2.4L	14.37	14.37

① — Automatic transaxle. ② — Manual transaxle.

Fig. 8 Dynamic damper installation dimension

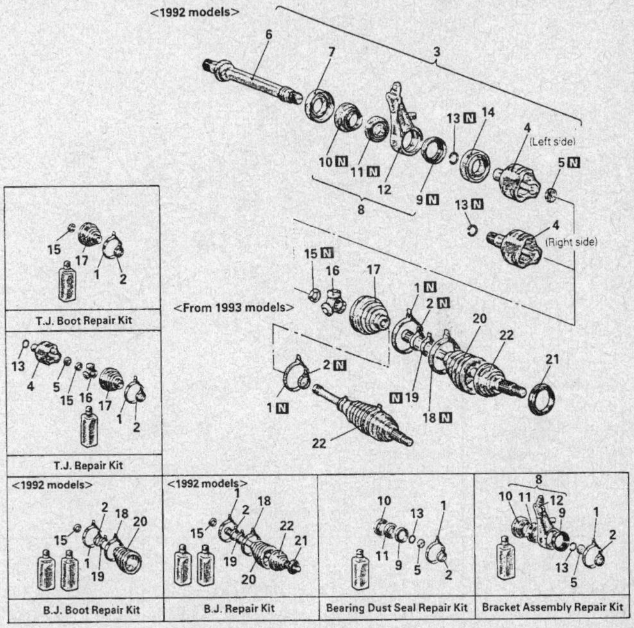
<1992 models>
(Left side)
(Right side)
<From 1993 models>
T.J. Boot Repair Kit
T.J. Repair Kit
<1992 models>
B.J. Boot Repair Kit
B.J. Repair Kit
Bearing Dust Seal Repair Kit
Bracket Assembly Repair Kit

Disassembly steps
1. T.J. boot band (large)
2. T.J. boot band (small)
3. T.J. case and inner shaft assembly
4. T.J. case
5. Seal plate
6. Inner shaft
7. Dust shield
8. Bracket assembly
9. Dust seal outer
10. Dust seal inner
11. Center bearing
12. Center bearing bracket
13. Circlip
14. Dust shield
15. Snap ring
16. Spider assembly
17. T.J. boot
18. B.J. boot band (large)
19. B.J. boot band (small)
20. B.J. boot
21. Dust shield
22. B.J. assembly

(18–21: <1992 models>)

Caution
In the case of AWD-vehicles with ABS, take care not to damage the rotor installed to the B.J. outer race.

MT3039100015000X

Fig. 9 Exploded view of front driveshaft assembly. Diamante & 3000GT FWD

diameter of 2.24 inches and metal thickness of .24 inch, press dust cover onto Double Offset Joint (DOJ) side.
3. Wrap vinyl tape around driveshaft splines to prevent damage to boots.
4. Using grease supplied with repair kit, lubricate driveshaft.
5. Install BJ boot, new boot bands, DOJ boot on driveshaft, then BJ in that order. **BJ and DOJ boots are of different size and shape and must be installed correctly.**
6. Install DOJ cage, small diameter side first, onto driveshaft, then install circlip on driveshaft.
7. Install DOJ inner race onto driveshaft and secure with snap ring.
8. Using grease supplied with repair kit, lubricate DOJ inner race and DOJ cage, then fit balls into cage.
9. Using grease supplied with repair kit, apply 1.8–2.8 ounces to DOJ outer race, then install on driveshaft.
10. Apply an additional 1.8–2.5 ounces of grease to DOJ outer race and install circlip.
11. Using grease supplied with repair kit, lubricate BJ side, then install BJ boot.

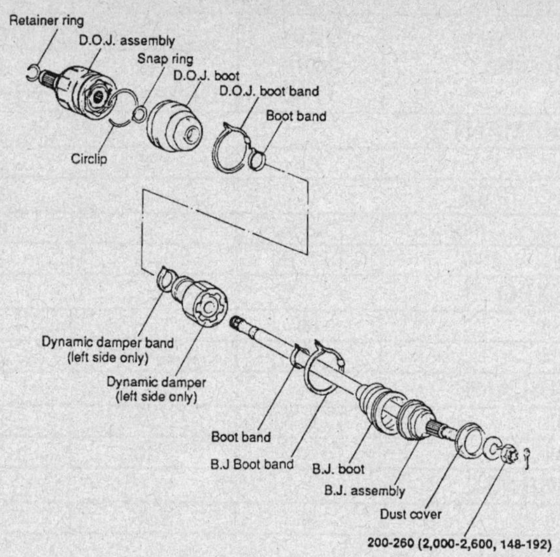
Retainer ring
D.O.J. assembly
Snap ring
D.O.J. boot
D.O.J. boot band
Boot band
Circlip
Dynamic damper band (left side only)
Dynamic damper (left side only)
Boot band
B.J Boot band
B.J. boot
B.J. assembly
Dust cover
200-260 (2,000-2,600, 148-192)

TORQUE: Nm (kg.cm, lb.ft)

MT3039100016000X

Fig. 10 Exploded view of front driveshaft. Precis

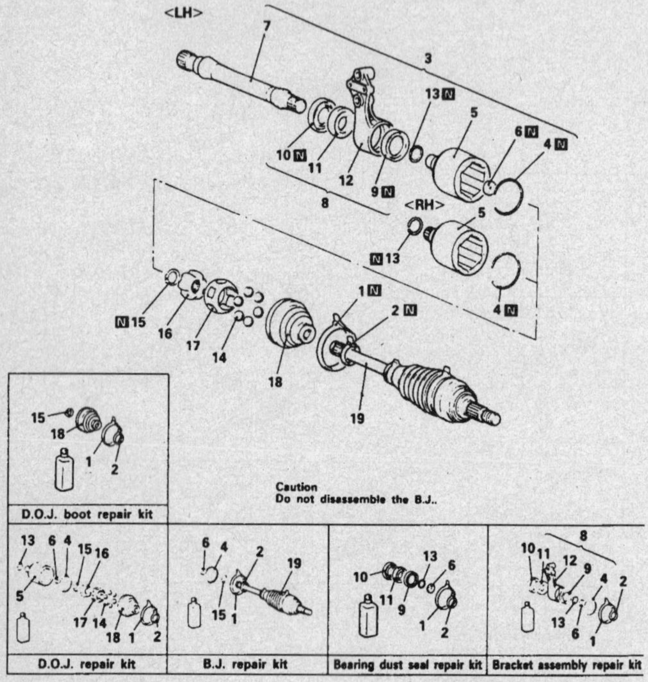
<LH>
<RH>
D.O.J. boot repair kit
Caution
Do not disassemble the B.J..
D.O.J. repair kit
B.J. repair kit
Bearing dust seal repair kit
Bracket assembly repair kit

Disassembly steps
1. D.O.J. boot band (large)
2. D.O.J. boot band (small)
3. D.O.J. outer race and inner shaft assembly
4. Circlip
5. D.O.J. outer race
6. Seal plate
7. Inner shaft
8. Bracket assembly
9. Outer dust seal
10. Inner dust seal
11. Bearing
12. Bracket
13. Circlip
14. Balls
15. Snap ring
16. D.O.J. inner race
17. D.O.J. cage
18. D.O.J. boot
19. B.J. assembly

MT3039100018000X

Fig. 12 Exploded view of front driveshaft. Expo w/1.8L engine

12. Ensure distance of 3.1 inches exists between boot bands, then tighten bands securely.

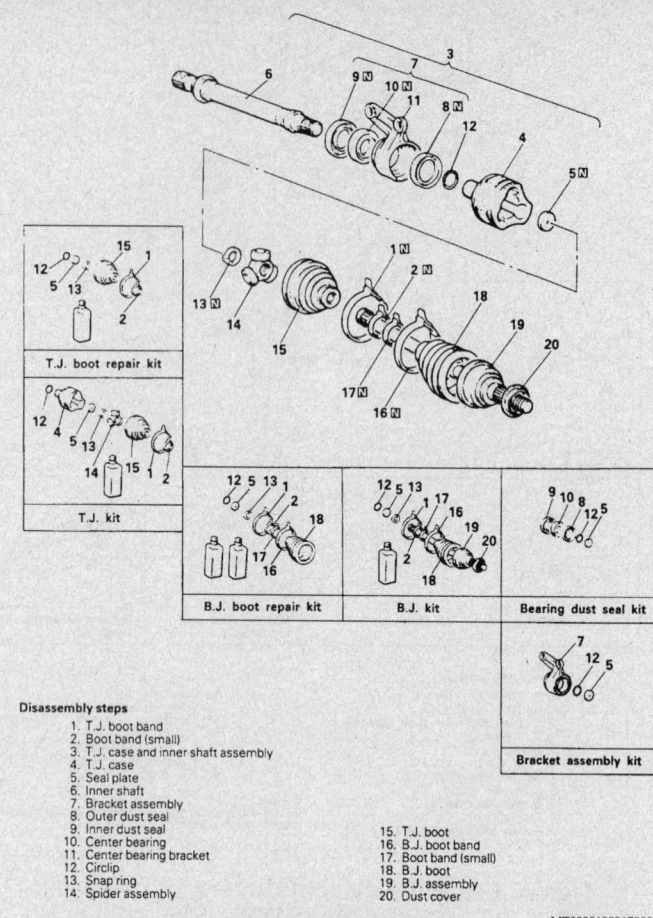

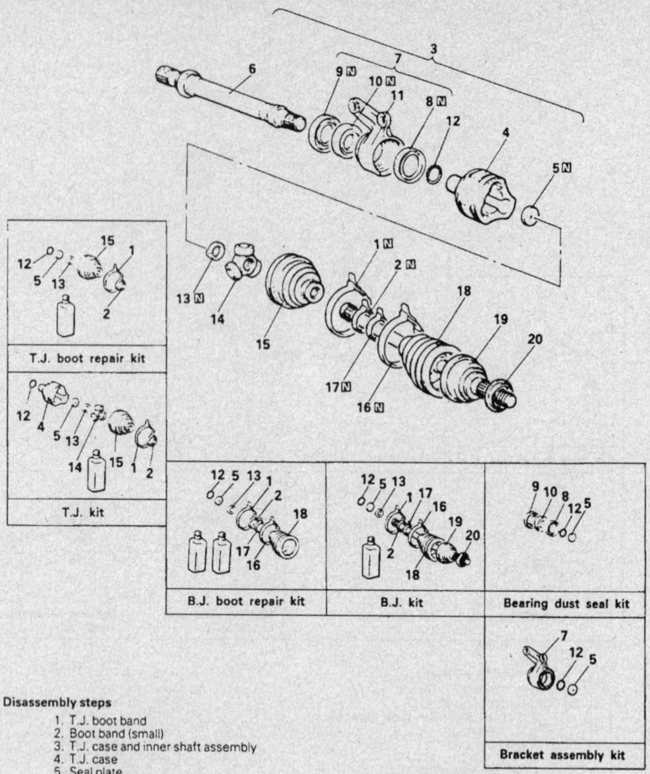
T.J. boot repair kit
T.J. kit
B.J. boot repair kit
B.J. kit
Bearing dust seal kit
Bracket assembly kit

Disassembly steps
1. T.J. boot band
2. Boot band (small)
3. T.J. case and inner shaft assembly
4. T.J. case
5. Seal plate
6. Inner shaft
7. Bracket assembly
8. Outer dust seal
9. Inner dust seal
10. Center bearing
11. Center bearing bracket
12. Circlip
13. Snap ring
14. Spider assembly
15. T.J. boot
16. B.J. boot band
17. Boot band (small)
18. B.J. boot
19. B.J. assembly
20. Dust cover

MT3039100017000X

Fig. 11 Exploded view of front driveshaft. Eclipse & Galant AWD

TECHNICAL SERVICE BULLETINS

CV & TRIPOT SERVICE INFORMATION

1993 Diamante, Expo, Mirage, Montero & 3000GT & 1994 Galant

On these models, should Tripot Joint (TJ) and/or inner driveshaft boot require service, components may be replaced separately. However, if Birfield Joint (BJ) and/or outer driveshaft boot are replaced, complete side of that driveshaft must be replaced as a unit.

Righthand and lefthand side driveshafts on these models are not interchangeable with previous year models.

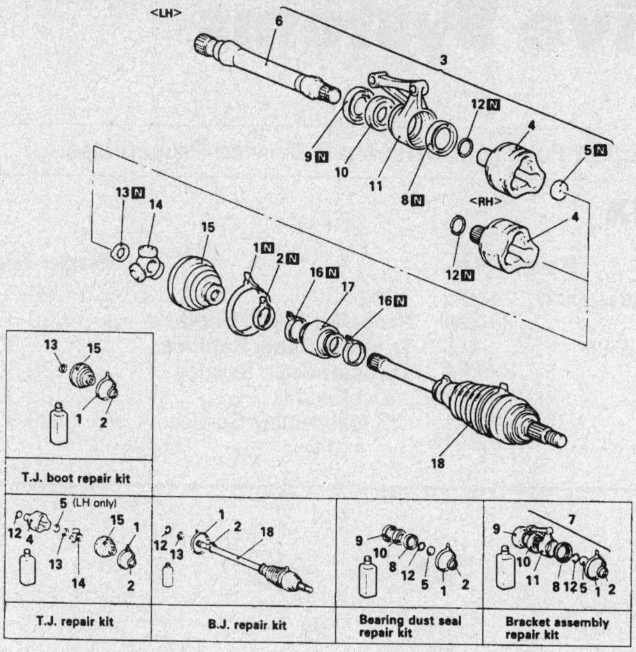
<LH>
<RH>
T.J. boot repair kit
5 (LH only)
T.J. repair kit
B.J. repair kit
Bearing dust seal repair kit
Bracket assembly repair kit

Disassembly steps

1. T.J. boot band
2. Boot band (small)
3. T.J. case and inner shaft assembly
4. T.J. case
5. Seal plate
6. Inner shaft
7. Bracket assembly
8. Outer dust seal
9. Inner dust seal
10. Bearing
11. Center bearing bracket
12. Circlip
13. Snap ring
14. Spider assembly
15. T.J. boot
16. Damper band
17. Dynamic damper
18. B.J. assembly

Caution
Do not disassembly the B.J.

MT3039100019000X

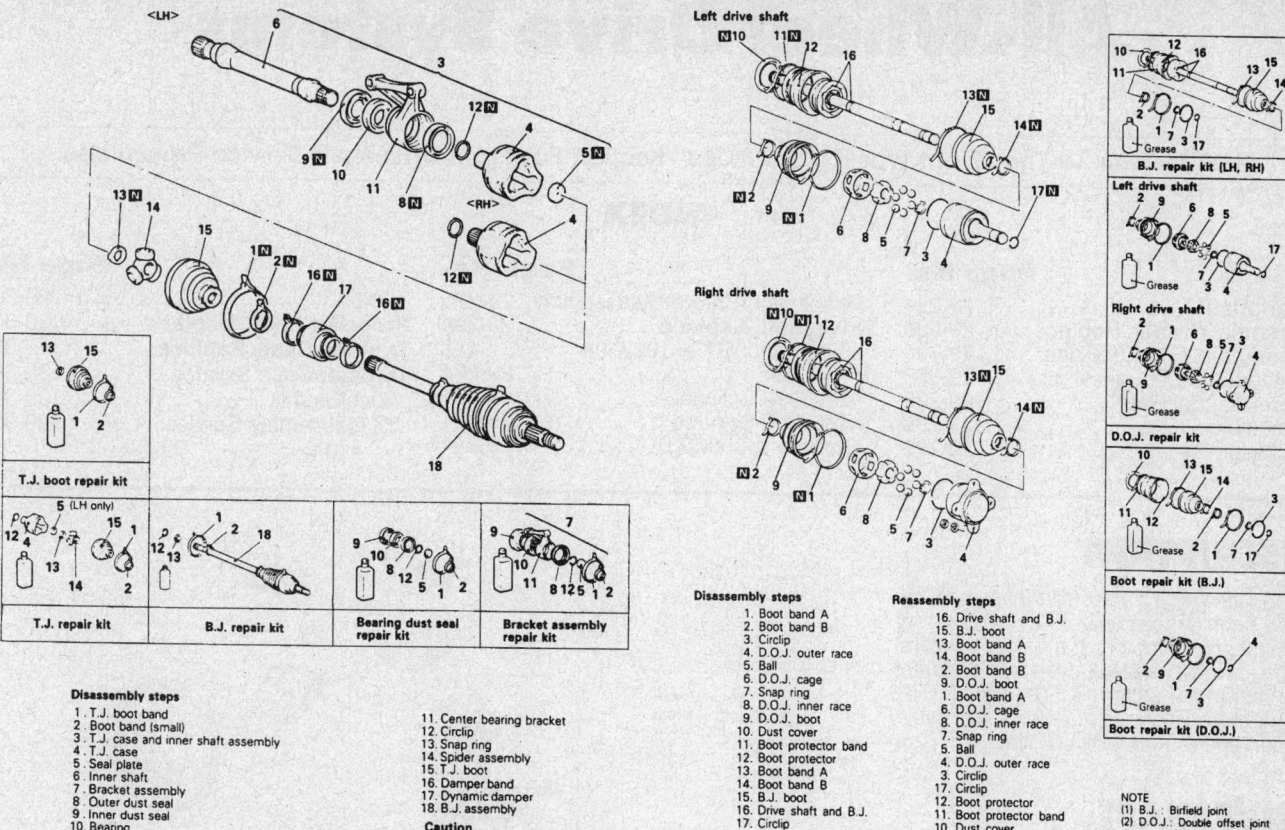

Fig. 13 Exploded view of front driveshaft. Expo w/2.4L engine

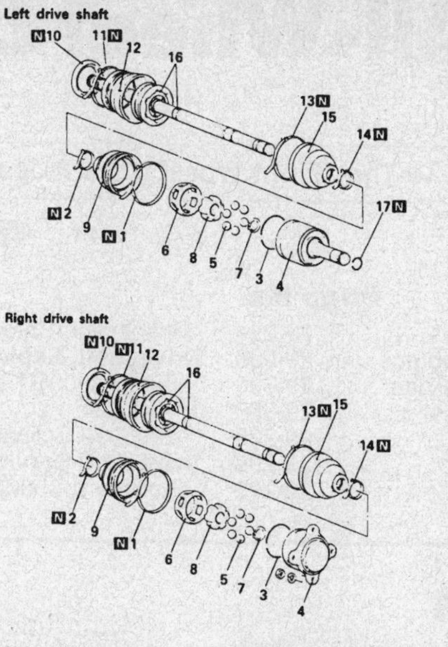
Left drive shaft
Right drive shaft

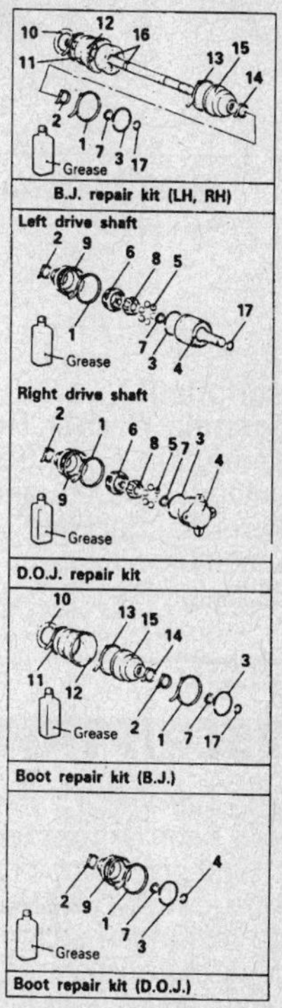
Grease
B.J. repair kit (LH, RH)
Left drive shaft
Right drive shaft
D.O.J. repair kit
Boot repair kit (B.J.)
Boot repair kit (D.O.J.)

Disassembly steps

1. Boot band A
2. Boot band B
3. Circlip
4. D.O.J. outer race
5. Ball
6. D.O.J. cage
7. Snap ring
8. D.O.J. inner race
9. D.O.J. boot
10. Dust cover
11. Boot protector band
12. Boot protector
13. Boot band A
14. Boot band B
15. B.J. boot
16. Drive shaft and B.J.
17. Circlip

Reassembly steps

16. Drive shaft and B.J.
15. B.J. boot
13. Boot band A
14. Boot band B
2. Boot band B
9. D.O.J. boot
1. Boot band A
6. D.O.J. cage
8. D.O.J. inner race
7. Snap ring
5. Ball
4. D.O.J. outer race
3. Circlip
17. Circlip
12. Boot protector
11. Boot protector band
10. Dust cover

NOTE
(1) B.J. : Birfield joint
(2) D.O.J.: Double offset joint

MT3039100020000X

Fig. 14 Exploded view of front driveshaft. Montero & Pickup

All-Wheel Drive Systems

NOTE: Refer To The "Front Wheel Drive Axles" Section For Front Driveshaft Service Procedures.

INDEX

	Page No.
Description	29-294
Differential Carrier, Replace	29-299
Differential Carrier Service	29-300
Limited Slip Differential	29-300
Differential Service	29-295
Assemble	29-296
Disassemble	29-296
Inspection Before Disassembly	29-295
Driveshaft, Replace	29-294
Expo, 3000GT & 1993–94 Eclipse	29-294
1995–96 Eclipse	29-294
Driveshaft Service	29-294
Eclipse & 3000GT	29-294
Expo	29-295
Propeller Shaft, Replace	29-300
Transfer Case, Replace	29-301
Transfer Case Service	29-301
Overhaul	29-301
Subassembly Service	29-302

DESCRIPTION

The All-Wheel Drive (AWD) system is based upon a front wheel drive design. A transversely mounted transaxle delivers torque to front driveshafts, as well as to an integral transfer assembly. The transfer, in turn, operates the rear wheels via a propeller shaft and rear axle differential.

DRIVESHAFT

REPLACE

EXPO, 3000GT & 1993-94 ECLIPSE

Replace driveshaft in numbered sequence shown in **Figs. 1 and 2,** noting the following:

1. **On Eclipse and 3000GT models,** proceed as follows:
   a. Using a suitable pry bar, remove driveshaft from differential carrier, **Fig. 3.**
   b. Install driveshaft oil seal using oil seal installer tool Nos. MB990938-01 and MB991115, or equivalents.
   c. When installing driveshaft, ensure splines of driveshaft do not damage oil seal lip.
2. **On Expo models,** proceed as follows:
   a. Using end yoke retainer tool No. MB990767-01, or equivalent, remove driveshaft nut.
   b. Using a suitable shaft puller tool, press driveshaft out of rear hub, **Fig. 4.**

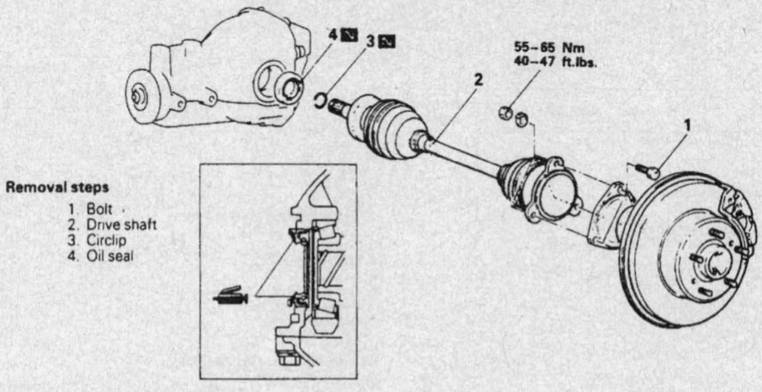

4
3
55-65 Nm
40-47 ft.lbs.
2
1
Removal steps
1. Bolt
2. Drive shaft
3. Circlip
4. Oil seal
MT3039100021000X

Fig. 1 Driveshaft replacement. 3000GT & 1993–94 Eclipse

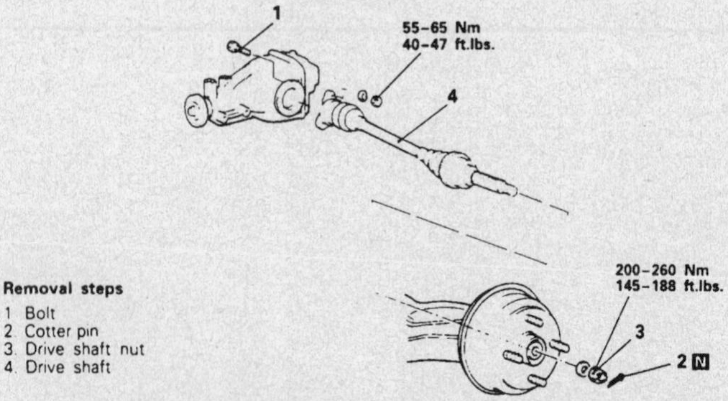

1
55-65 Nm
40-47 ft.lbs.
4
Removal steps
1. Bolt
2. Cotter pin
3. Drive shaft nut
4. Drive shaft
200-260 Nm
145-188 ft.lbs.
3
2
MT3039100022000X

Fig. 2 Driveshaft replacement. Expo

1995-96 ECLIPSE

1. Raise and support vehicle, then remove rear wheel.
2. Remove driveshaft in numbered sequence shown, **Fig. 5,** noting the following:
   a. Use tool No. MB990767, or equivalent, to prevent hub from turning while removing driveshaft nut.
   b. Remove shaft from vehicle by pushing lower portion of knuckle outward while prying shaft away from differential carrier with a suitable pry bar.
   c. Insert tool No. MB991460, or equivalent, into carrier to prevent entry of foreign matter while driveshaft is removed.
   d. If both shafts are to be removed, distinguish lefthand from righthand side for installation reference.
3. Reverse numbered sequence to install, noting the following:
   a. Do not allow driveshaft splines to damage differential carrier oil seal during installation.
   b. Tighten driveshaft nut using tool No. MB990767, or equivalent. If cotter pin holes do not align, tighten nut until pin can be inserted. **Do not exceed torque of 188 ft. lbs.**
   c. Bleed brake system as outlined in "Hydraulic Brake Systems" section.
   d. Adjust parking brake as outlined in "Disc Brakes" or "Drum Brakes" section.

DRIVESHAFT SERVICE

ECLIPSE & 3000GT

Disassemble driveshaft in numbered sequence shown in **Fig. 6,** noting the following:

1. Remove snap ring from driveshaft.
2. Remove spider assembly from driveshaft. **Do not disassemble spider assembly. If Tripod Joint (TJ) of driveshaft assembly is bent, joint may be damaged.**

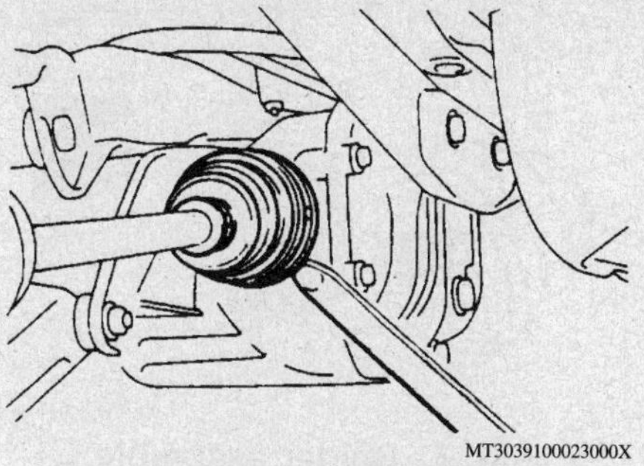
MT3039100023000X

Fig. 3 Driveshaft separation

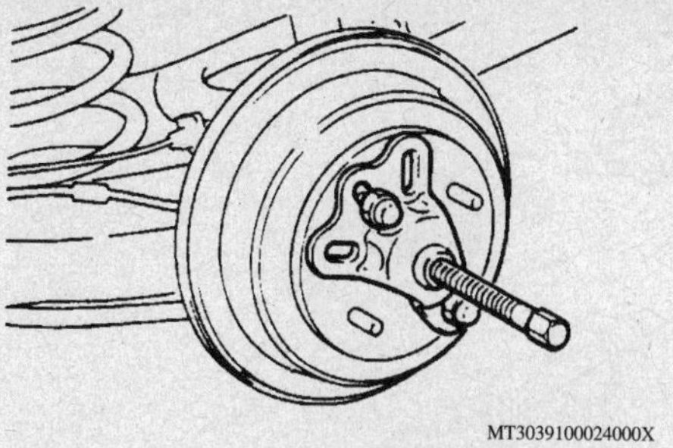
MT3039100024000X

Fig. 4 Driveshaft removal. Expo

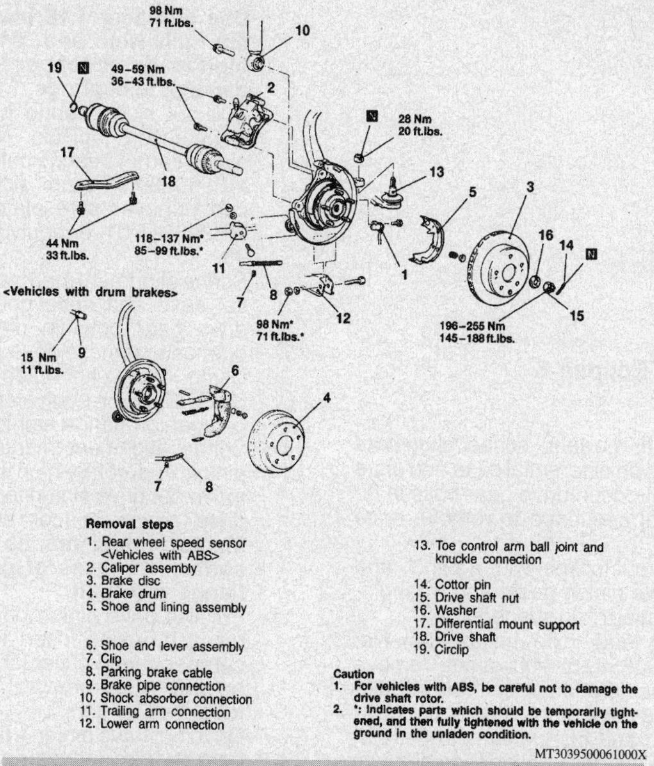
98 Nm
71 ft.lbs.
10
19
49–59 Nm
36–43 ft.lbs.
2
28 Nm
20 ft.lbs.
17
18
13
5
3
44 Nm
33 ft.lbs.
118–137 Nm*
85–99 ft.lbs.*
11
16
14
1
<Vehicles with drum brakes>
7
8
98 Nm*
71 ft.lbs.*
12
196–255 Nm
145–188 ft.lbs.
15
15 Nm
11 ft.lbs.
9
6
4
7
8
Removal steps
1. Rear wheel speed sensor <Vehicles with ABS>
2. Caliper assembly
3. Brake disc
4. Brake drum
5. Shoe and lining assembly
6. Shoe and lever assembly
7. Clip
8. Parking brake cable
9. Brake pipe connection
10. Shock absorber connection
11. Trailing arm connection
12. Lower arm connection
13. Toe control arm ball joint and knuckle connection
14. Cotter pin
15. Drive shaft nut
16. Washer
17. Differential mount support
18. Drive shaft
19. Circlip
Caution
1. For vehicles with ABS, be careful not to damage the drive shaft rotor.
2. *: Indicates parts which should be temporarily tightened, and then fully tightened with the vehicle on the ground in the unladen condition.
MT3039500061000X

Fig. 5 Driveshaft replacement. 1995–96 Eclipse

3. Clean spider assembly.
4. Wrap tape around splines of driveshaft so boot are not damaged when removed.
5. Remove TJ and Birfield Joint (BJ) boots off driveshaft.
6. Wipe grease off BJ. **Do not disassemble.**
7. Reverse numbered sequence to assemble, noting the following:
   a. Wrap tape around splines of driveshaft.
   b. Install BJ boot, bands, TJ boot and bands in that sequence.
   c. Fill inside of BJ and BJ boot with special grease.
   d. Secure BJ boot bands ensuring that driveshaft is at 0° angle to the BJ.
   e. Apply special grease to the spider assembly.
   f. Install spider assembly with chamfered spline end first, **Fig. 7.**
   g. Set TJ boot bands 3.23–3.47 inches apart in order to adjust amount of air inside TJ boot then tighten TJ boot band securely.

EXPO

Disassemble driveshaft in numbered sequence shown in **Fig. 8,** noting the following:

1. Remove Double Offset Joint (DOJ) outer race, and clean cage and balls.
2. Place mating marks on driveshaft, DOJ inner race and DOJ cage, **Fig. 9,** then remove balls.
3. Remove DOJ cage from inner race by sliding it toward opposite end of driveshaft.
4. Remove snap ring off end of driveshaft, then DOJ inner race and cage. **A brass bar and a hammer may be needed to remove inner race.**
5. Wipe grease off spline portion of driveshaft.
6. Wrap tape around splines to protect boots.
7. Remove DOJ and Birfield Joint (BJ) boots. **Do not disassemble BJ.**
8. **On models equipped with Anti-Lock Brake System (ABS),** remove rear speed sensor rotor.
9. **On all models,** reverse numbered sequence in **Fig. 8** to assemble, noting the following:
   a. Wrap tape around spline portion of driveshaft.
   b. **On models equipped with ABS,** press on rear speed sensor rotor.
   c. **On all models,** insert driveshaft in BJ boot, boot band A, C, C and B in that order, **Fig. 10.**
   d. Fill inside of BJ and BJ boot with special grease.
   e. Secure BJ boot bands A and C to shaft and BJ. **Ensure BJ is at a 0° angle with driveshaft to ensure boot contains the specified amount of air.**
   f. Apply special grease to the DOJ cage, ball and DOJ inner race.
   g. Install cage, balls and inner race on driveshaft then install snap ring.
   h. Fill DOJ outer race with special grease. Install driveshaft into DOJ outer race then fill more grease in the DOJ outer race.
   i. Install circlip on DOJ outer race.
   j. Attach the DOJ boot on the DOJ outer race then secure boot with boot band C.
   k. Place boot band B on DOJ. **Do not secure boot band.**
   l. Set DOJ boot bands 2.72–3.18 inches apart, **Fig. 11,** to adjust amount of air inside DOJ boot then tighten DOJ boot band C securely.
   m. Release a part of the DOJ boot from the DOJ outer race to allow pressure to escape from boot.
   n. Tighten boot band B and secure the DOJ boot.

DIFFERENTIAL SERVICE

INSPECTION BEFORE DISASSEMBLY

With differential carrier assembly properly supported, perform the following inspections:

1. Measure final drive gear backlash as follows:
   a. With drive pinion locked into place, measure final drive gear backlash using a suitable dial indicator, **Fig. 12.**
   b. Measure at four points or more in the circumference on the drive gear and ensure backlash is .004–.006 inch.
2. Measure gear runout as follows:
   a. Measure drive gear runout at the shoulder on reverse side of drive gear, **Fig. 13.**
   b. Ensure runout is a maximum of .002 inch.
3. Measure differential gear backlash as follows:
   a. While locking side gear with wedge, measure differential gear backlash with a suitable dial indicator on pinion gear, **Fig. 14.**
   b. Ensure backlash is within the 0–.003 inch limit.

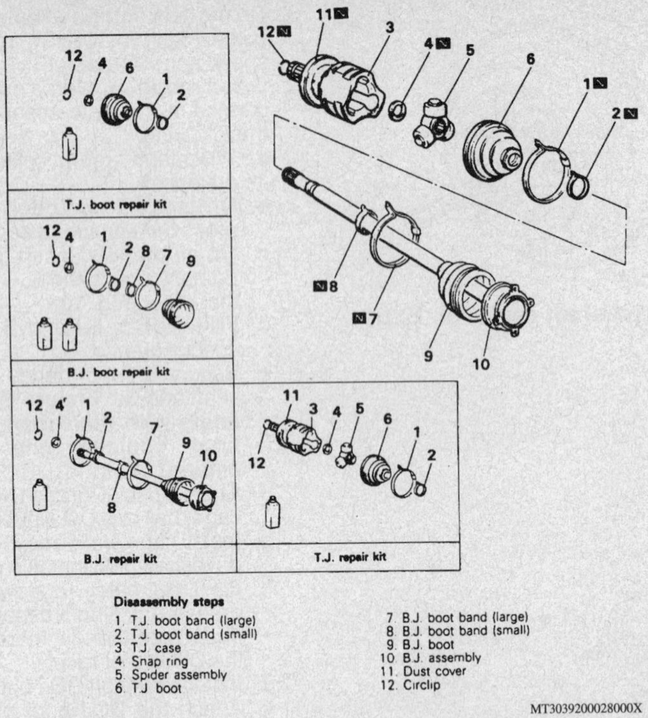
T.J. boot repair kit
B.J. boot repair kit
B.J. repair kit
T.J. repair kit
Disassembly steps
1. T.J. boot band (large)
2. T.J. boot band (small)
3. T.J. case
4. Snap ring
5. Spider assembly
6. T.J. boot
7. B.J. boot band (large)
8. B.J. boot band (small)
9. B.J. boot
10. B.J. assembly
11. Dust cover
12. Circlip
MT3039200028000X

Fig. 6 Driveshaft assembly service. Eclipse & 3000GT

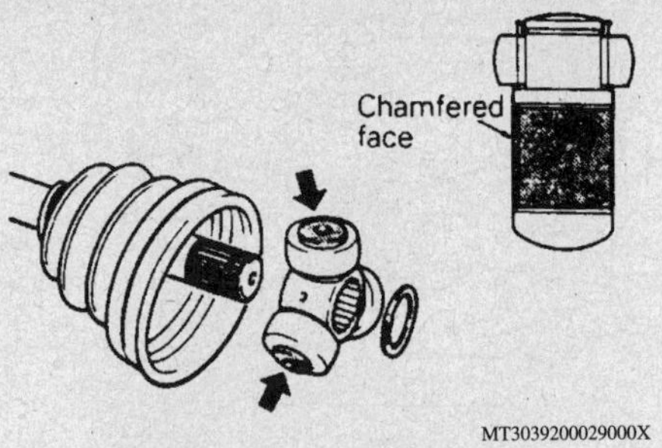
Chamfered face
MT3039200029000X

Fig. 7 Spider assembly installation. Eclipse & 3000GT

4. Inspect final drive gear tooth contact as follows:
   a. Apply a thin, uniform coat of machine blue to both surfaces of the drive gear teeth.
   b. Insert a brass rod between differential carrier and differential case, then rotate companion flange by hand once in each direction while applying a load to the drive gear, so that revolution **torque** of approximately 28–32 inch lbs. is applied to drive pinion, **Fig. 15.**
   c. Check tooth contact condition of drive gear and pinion, **Fig. 16.**

DISASSEMBLE

Disassemble differential assembly in numbered sequence shown in **Figs. 17 and 18,** noting the following:

1. **On Eclipse and Expo models,** proceed as follows:
   a. Slowly and carefully pry out differential case assembly using hammer handles, **Fig. 19. When removing differential case assembly, ensure side bearing outer race is not dropped. Keep right and left side bearing separate.**
   b. **On Expo and 1993–94 Eclipse models,** pull out side bearing inner races by using insert tool No. MT303173, pinion carrier bearing puller tool No. MB990339-01 and side bearing cup remover step plate tool No. MB990811-01, or equivalents, **Fig. 20.**
   c. **On 1995–96 Eclipse models,** place nut on top of differential case, then use removal tool, **Fig. 21,** to remove side bearing inner race.
   d. **On all models,** scribe alignment marks on differential case and drive gear. Loosen drive gear bolts in diagonal sequence to remove drive gear.
   e. Drive out lockpin with a punch and remove pinion gears and washers, side gears and spacers.
   f. Using end yoke holder tool No. MB990850, or equivalent, remove companion flange self-locking nut.
   g. Scribe alignment marks on drive pinion and companion flange. Remove out drive pinion together with drive pinion spacer and shims. **Marks should not be made on contact surfaces of companion flange and shaft.**
   h. Pull out drive pinion bearing inner races by using insert tool, pinion carrier bearing puller tool, and side bearing cup remover step plate tool, or equivalent.
   i. Drive out drive pinion front and rear bearing from gear carrier.
2. **On 3000GT models,** proceed as follows:
   a. Using spanner wrench tool No. MB991367 and pin tool No. MB991385, or equivalents, remove side bearing nut.
   b. Using a suitable press, push differential case until it is pressed against the carrier.
   c. Remove differential case from press. Insert two spacers in diagonally opposite positions between side bearing outer race to be removed and inner race. Using a press, remove outer race. **Do not allow side bearing to drop. Keep right and left bearings separate. Use a spacer 1.18 inches long, .39 inch wide and .04–.08 inch high made of copper to prevent damage to bearings.**
   d. Pull out side bearing inner races using insert tool No. MT303173, pinion carrier bearing puller tool No. MB990339-01 and side bearing cup remover step plate tool No. MB990811-01, or equivalents, **Fig. 20.**
   e. Scribe alignment marks on differential case and drive gear. Loosen drive gear bolts in diagonal sequence to remove drive gear.
   f. Using end yoke holder tool No. MB990850, or equivalent, remove companion flange self-locking nut.
   g. Scribe alignment marks on drive pinion and companion flange. Remove out drive pinion together with drive pinion spacer and shims. **Marks should not be made on contact surfaces of companion flange and shaft.**
   h. Pull out drive pinion bearing inner races by using insert tool, pinion carrier bearing puller tool, and side bearing cup remover step plate tool, or equivalent.
   i. Drive out drive pinion front and rear bearing from gear carrier.

ASSEMBLE

Assemble differential carrier in numbered sequence shown in **Figs. 22 and 23,** noting the following:

1. **On Eclipse and Expo models,** apply grease to oil seal lip; then, using oil seal installer tool No. MB991115 and handle tool No. MB990938-01, or equivalents, press fit oil seal until it is flush with end of gear carrier.
2. **On 3000GT models with Four Wheel Steering (4WS),** tap spring pin into differential case to position shown in **Fig. 24,** before press fitting rear wheel oil pump drive gear. Notch on spring should be in position shown.
3. **On 3000GT models,** with beveled part of rear wheel oil pump drive gear at inner side, press in drive gear, using rear suspension bushing base tool No. MB990890-01, or equivalent, until drive gear contacts end surface of differential case. Ensure drive gear and spring pin are flush.
4. **On Expo, 3000GT and 1993–94 Eclipse models,** press fit drive pinion rear and front bearing outer races onto

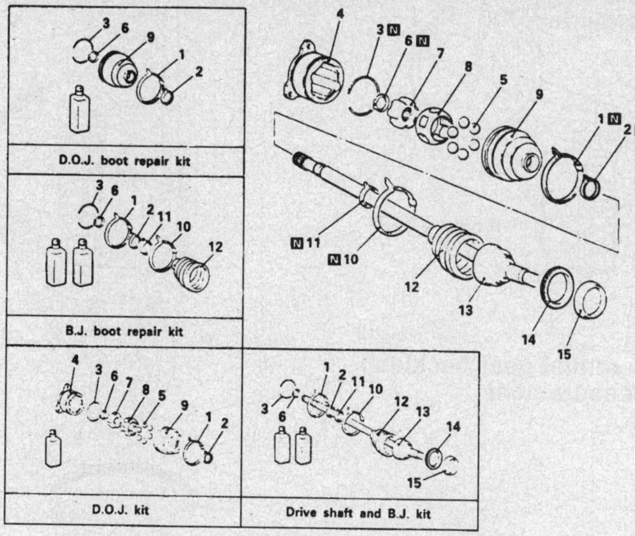
D.O.J. boot repair kit
B.J. boot repair kit
D.O.J. kit
Drive shaft and B.J. kit

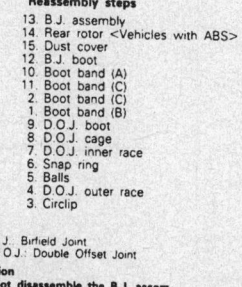

Disassembly steps
1. Boot band (B)
2. Boot band (C)
3. Circlip
4. D.O.J. outer race
5. Balls
6. Snap ring
7. D.O.J. inner race
8. D.O.J. cage
9. D.O.J. boot
10. Boot band (A)
11. Boot band (C)
12. B.J. boot
13. B.J. assembly
14. Rear rotor <Vehicles with ABS>
15. Dust cover

Reassembly steps

13. B.J. assembly
14. Rear rotor <Vehicles with ABS>
15. Dust cover
12. B.J. boot
10. Boot band (A)
11. Boot band (C)
2. Boot band (C)
1. Boot band (B)
9. D.O.J. boot
8. D.O.J. cage
7. D.O.J. inner race
6. Snap ring
5. Balls
4. D.O.J. outer race
3. Circlip

NOTE
(1) B.J.: Birfield Joint
(2) D.O.J.: Double Offset Joint

Caution
Do not disassemble the B.J. assembly.

MT3039100030000X

Fig. 8 Driveshaft assembly service. Expo

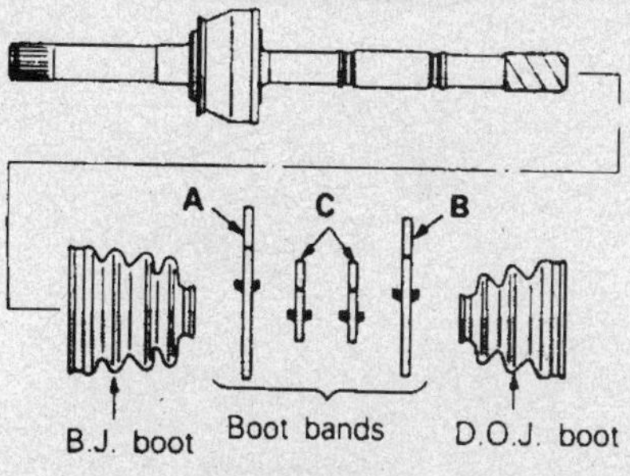
A
C
B
B.J. boot
Boot bands
D.O.J. boot

MT3039100026000X

Fig. 10 Boot & band installation order

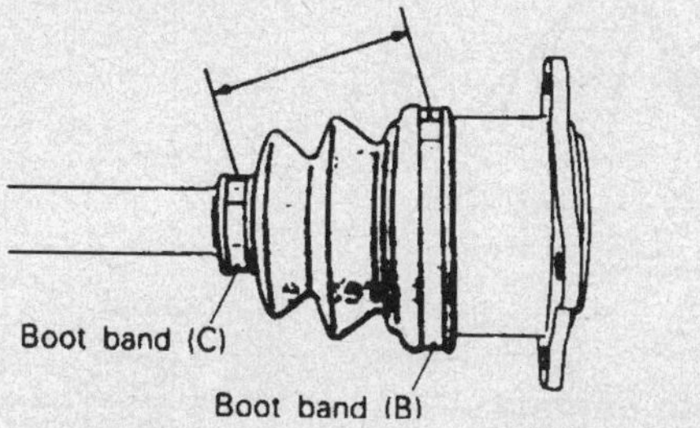
Boot band (C)
Boot band (B)

MT3039100027000X

Fig. 11 DOJ boot clamps installation

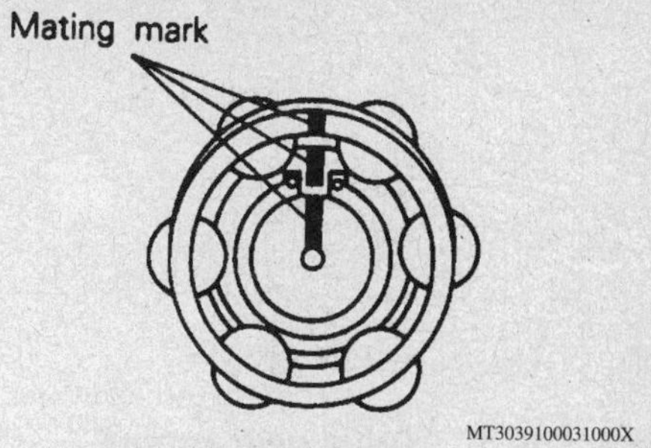
Mating mark

MT3039100031000X

Fig. 9 Mating marks. Expo

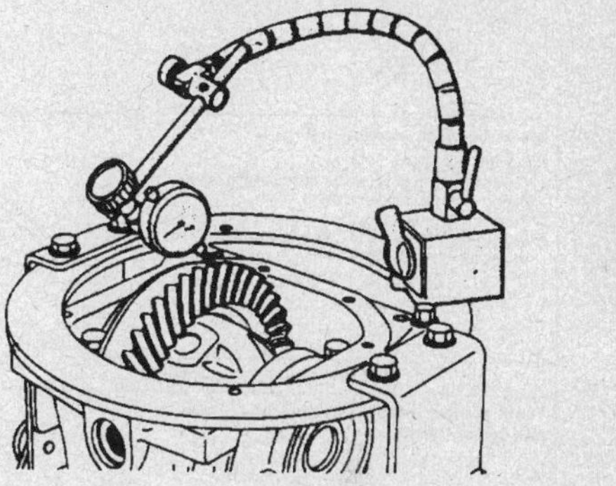

MT3019100006000X

Fig. 12 Final drive gear backlash measurement

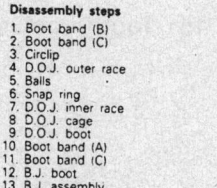

gear carrier using handle tool and bearing and oil seal installer set tool No. MB990925, or equivalent. **Use care not to press in outer race at an angle.**

5. **On 1995–96 Eclipse models,** press fit drive pinion front bearing outer race using tool Nos. MB990932 and MB990938, or equivalents, and rear bearing outer race using tool Nos. MB990935 and MB990938, or equivalents.
6. **On Expo, 3000GT and 1993–94 Eclipse models,** adjust pinion height as follows:
   a. Install special tools as shown in **Figs. 25 and 26.**
   b. Tighten handle of tool until the standard drive pinion turning torque value shown in **Figs. 27 and 28** is obtained.
   c. Measure drive pinion turning torque without oil seal installed.
   d. Position gauge tube tool No. MB990392-01, or equivalent, in side bearing seat of gear carrier, then select a drive pinion rear shim of thickness which corresponds to gap between special tools.
   e. Install selected shim on drive pinion and press fit rear bearing inner race using bearing installer tool No. MT215013, or equivalent.
7. **On 1995–96 Eclipse models,** adjust pinion height as follows:
   a. Apply a thin film of suitable multipurpose grease to mating face of tool washer, **Fig. 29,** then install tools and drive pinion front and rear bearing inner races on gear carrier.
   b. Gradually tighten nut on tool until standard drive pinion turning torque value shown in **Fig. 27** is obtained.
   c. Thoroughly clean side bearing seat, then install tools, **Fig. 30,** and bearing cap. **Ensure tool cutout sections are positioned as shown in Fig. 30** and tool contacts side bearing seat.
   d. Use a suitable feeler gauge to measure clearance (dimension A) between tools, **Fig. 30,** then remove tools.
   e. Use a suitable micrometer to measure tool dimensions B and C, **Fig. 31.**
   f. Install bearing cap, then use a suitable cylinder gauge and micrometer to measure inside diameter of bearing bore (dimension D), **Fig. 32.**
   g. Calculate drive pinion rear shim thickness. Thickness is equal to dimension A + B + C - ½D - 3.39 inches.
   h. Select a shim that is as close to calculated thickness as possible, then fit shim on drive pinion and press fit rear bearing inner race using tool No. MB990728, or equivalent.
8. **On all models,** adjust drive pinion preload as follows:
   a. Install drive pinion front shim(s) between pinion spacer and pinion front bearing inner race.
   b. **On Expo and 3000GT models, torque** companion flange to 135 ft. lbs., using end yoke holder tool to prevent yoke rotation. Do not install oil seal.
   c. **On 1993–94 Eclipse models,**

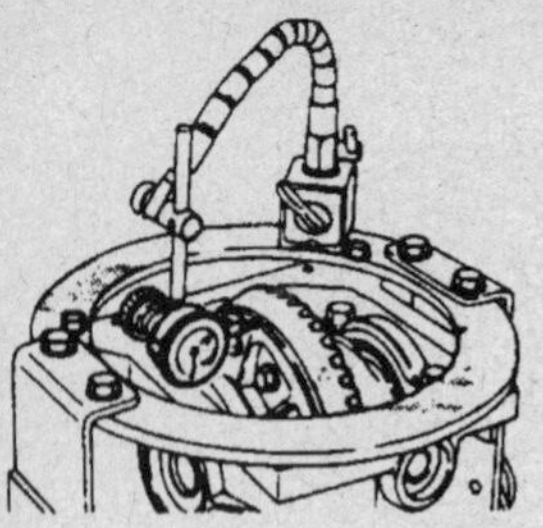
MT3019100007000X

Fig. 13 Drive gear runout measurement

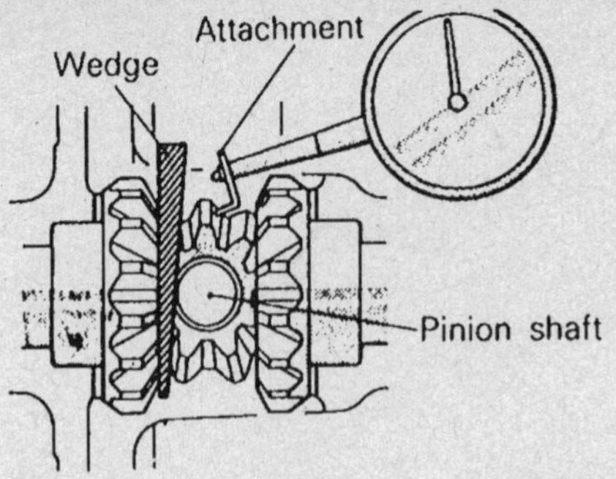
Attachment
Wedge
Pinion shaft
MT3019100008000X

Fig. 14 Differential gear backlash measurement

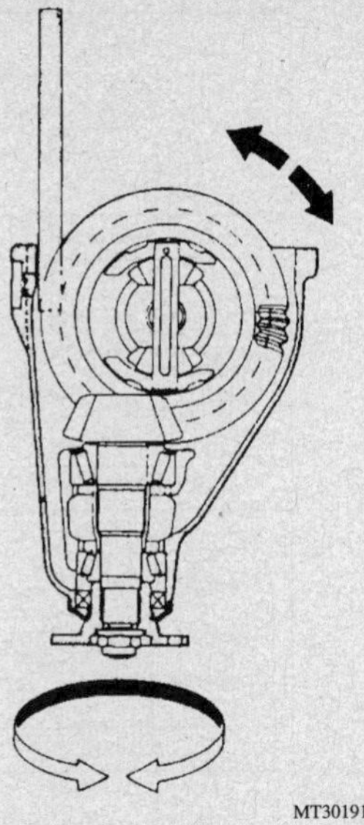
MT3019100009000X

Fig. 15 Tooth contact inspection

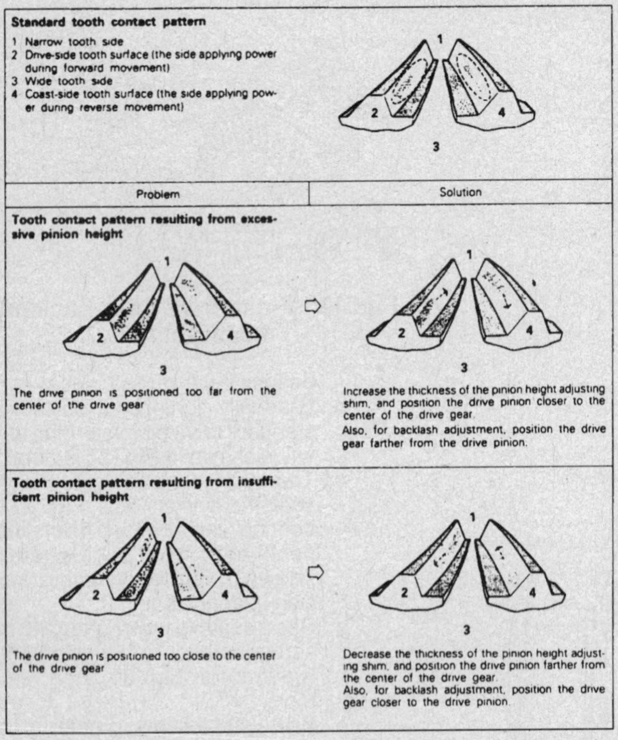
Standard tooth contact pattern
1 Narrow tooth side
2 Drive-side tooth surface (the side applying power during forward movement)
3 Wide tooth side
4 Coast-side tooth surface (the side applying power during reverse movement)
Problem
Solution
Tooth contact pattern resulting from excessive pinion height
The drive pinion is positioned too far from the center of the drive gear
Increase the thickness of the pinion height adjusting shim, and position the drive pinion closer to the center of the drive gear.
Also, for backlash adjustment, position the drive gear farther from the drive pinion.
Tooth contact pattern resulting from insufficient pinion height
The drive pinion is positioned too close to the center of the drive gear
Decrease the thickness of the pinion height adjusting shim, and position the drive pinion farther from the center of the drive gear.
Also, for backlash adjustment, position the drive gear closer to the drive pinion.
MT3019100010000X

Fig. 16 Differential carrier tooth contact

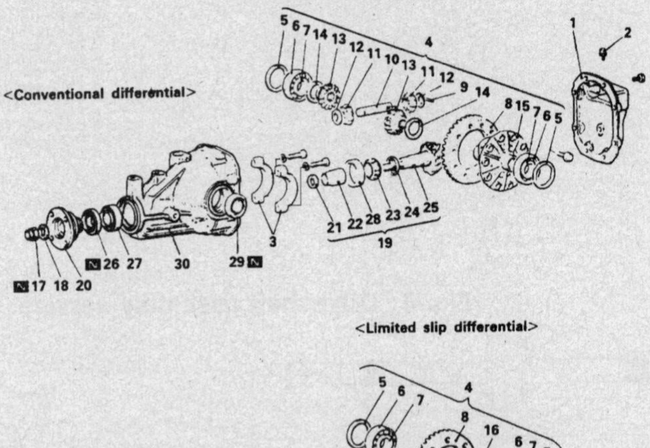
<Conventional differential>
<Limited slip differential>
Disassembly steps
1. Differential cover
2. Vent plug
3. Bearing caps
4. Differential case assembly
5. Side bearing spacers
6. Side bearing outer race
7. Side bearing inner race
8. Drive gear
9. Lock pin
10. Pinion shaft
11. Pinion gears
12. Pinion washers
13. Side gears
14. Side gear spacers
15. Differential case
16. Limited slip differential case assembly
17. Self-locking nut
18. Washer
19. Drive pinion assembly
20. Companion flange
21. Drive pinion front shim (for preload adjustment)
22. Drive pinion spacer
23. Drive pinion rear bearing inner race
24. Drive pinion rear shim (for pinion height adjustment)
25. Drive pinion
26. Oil seal
27. Drive pinion front bearing
28. Drive pinion rear bearing outer race
29. Oil seal
30. Gear carrier
MT3019100011000X

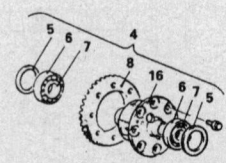

Fig. 17 Rear differential disassembly. Eclipse & Expo

torque companion flange to 116–159 ft. lbs., using end yoke holder tool to prevent yoke rotation. Do not install oil seal.

d. **On 1995–96 Eclipse models, torque** companion flange to 137 ft. lbs., using end yoke holder tool to prevent yoke rotation. Do not install oil seal.
e. **On all models,** ensure drive pinion turning torque is as shown in **Figs. 27 and 28.**
f. If drive pinion turning torque is not within specified range, adjust by replacing drive pinion front shims(s) or drive pinion spacer.
g. Remove companion flange and drive pinion.
h. Install oil seal using suitable oil seal installation tool.
i. Install drive pinion and companion flange aligning marks made during disassembly then tighten companion flange self-locking nut to specification.
j. Measure pinion turning torque with oil seal installed and ensure turning torque is no more than one inch lb. greater than what is shown in **Figs. 27 and 28.**

9. **On models with conventional differential,** adjust differential gear backlash as follows:
   a. Assemble side gears and spacers, pinion gears and washers into differential case.
   b. Temporarily install pinion shaft.
   c. While locking side gear with wedge, measure differential gear backlash with a dial indicator on pinion gear. **The measurement should be made for both pinion gears individually.**
   d. If differential gear backlash exceeds .008 inch, adjust backlash by installing thicker side gear spacers.
   e. Measure differential gear backlash again and confirm it is within the specification.

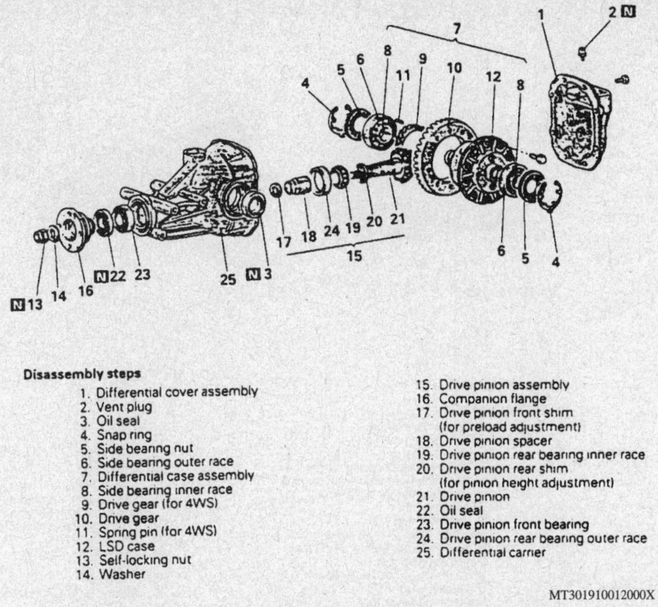
Disassembly steps
1. Differential cover assembly
2. Vent plug
3. Oil seal
4. Snap ring
5. Side bearing nut
6. Side bearing outer race
7. Differential case assembly
8. Side bearing inner race
9. Drive gear (for 4WS)
10. Drive gear
11. Spring pin (for 4WS)
12. LSD case
13. Self-locking nut
14. Washer
15. Drive pinion assembly
16. Companion flange
17. Drive pinion front shim (for preload adjustment)
18. Drive pinion spacer
19. Drive pinion rear bearing inner race
20. Drive pinion rear shim (for pinion height adjustment)
21. Drive pinion
22. Oil seal
23. Drive pinion front bearing
24. Drive pinion rear bearing outer race
25. Differential carrier
MT301910012000X

Fig. 18 Rear differential disassembly. 3000GT

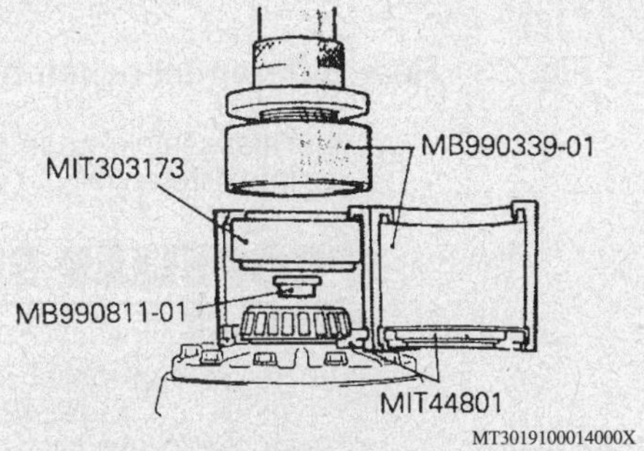
MIT303173
MB990339-01
MB990811-01
MIT44801
MT3019100014000X

Fig. 20 Side bearing inner race removal. Expo, 3000GT & 1993–94 Eclipse

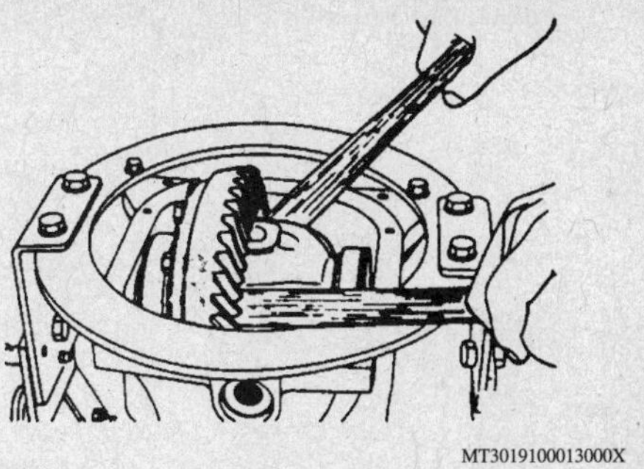
MT3019100013000X

Fig. 19 Differential case replacement

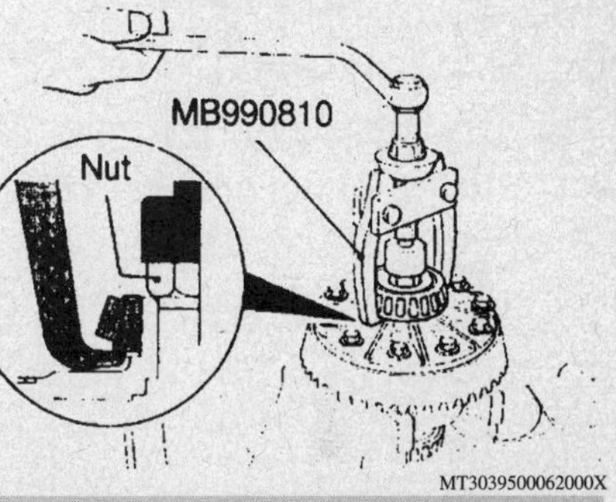
MB990810
Nut
MT3039500062000X

Fig. 21 Side bearing inner race removal. 1995–96 Eclipse

f. After adjustment, ensure backlash is less than limit and differential gear rotates smoothly.
g. When adjustment is impossible, replace side gear pinion gears as a set.
h. Align pinion shaft lockpin hole with differential case and install lockpin.
i. Stake lockpin at two points.

10. **On all models,** clean drive gear attaching bolts.
11. Use a 10mm x 1.25 tap to remove adhesive from threaded holes of drive gear.
12. Install drive gear onto differential case aligning marks made during disassembly. Tighten bolts in a diagonal sequence.
13. Press side bearing inner races onto differential case.
14. **On Eclipse and Expo models,** adjust final drive gear backlash as follows:
    a. Install side bearing spacers, which are thinner than those removed, and mount the differential case assembly into the gear carrier.
    b. Push differential case to one side and measure clearance between gear carrier and side bearing.
    c. Measure thickness of side bearing spacers on one side, select two pairs of spacers which correspond to thickness plus one half of clearance plus .002 inch. Install one pair each to drive pinion side and drive gear side.
    d. Install side bearing spacers and differential case assembly into gear carrier.
    e. Tap side bearing spacers with a suitable brass bar to fit them to side bearing outer race.
    f. Align marks made during disassembling then tighten bearing cap.
    g. With drive pinion locked in place, measure final drive gear backlash.
    h. If backlash is not .004–.006 inch, change bearing spacers as shown in **Fig. 33** to obtain correct backlash.
    i. Check tooth contact as outlined under "Inspection Before Disassembly."
    j. Measure drive gear runout at shoulder on reverse side of drive gear.
    k. If runout exceeds .002 inch, reinstall by changing phase of drive gear and differential case and measure again.
15. **On 3000GT models,** adjust final drive gear backlash as follows:
    a. Using spanner wrench tool No. MB991367 and pin tool No. MB991385, or equivalents, temporarily tighten side bearing nut until just before preloading.
    b. Measure final drive gear backlash at four or more points on drive gear.
    c. Using spanner wrench and pin tools, adjust backlash until a .004–.006 inch value is reached by turning side bearing nut as shown, **Fig. 34.**
    d. Using the spanner wrench to apply preload, turn down both right and left side bearing nuts on half the distance between centers of two neighboring holes, **Fig. 35.**
    e. Install snap ring at either position shown to lock side bearing nut, **Fig. 36.**
    f. Check drive gear and pinion tooth contact as outlined under "Inspection Before Disassembly."
    g. Measure drive gear runout at shoulder on reverse side of drive gear.
    h. If runout exceeds .002 inch, reinstall by changing phase of drive gear and differential case and measure again.
    i. Using suitable oil seal installer, install oil seal flush with gear carrier end face.

DIFFERENTIAL CARRIER

REPLACE

Refer to appropriate chassis section under "Rear Axle & Suspension" for differential carrier replacement procedure.

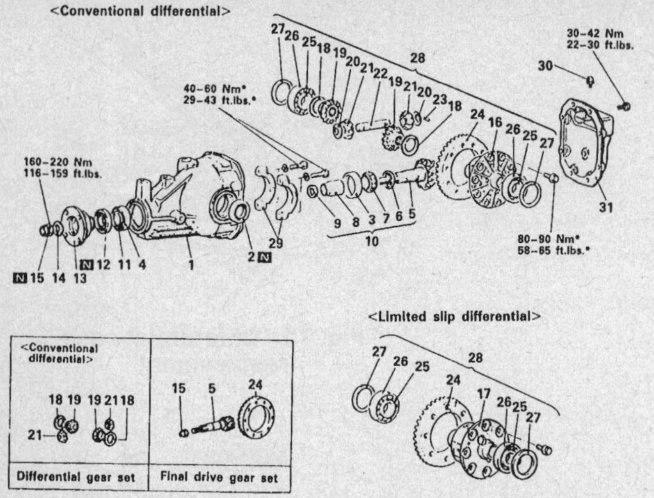
<Conventional differential>
30–42 Nm
22–30 ft.lbs.
40–60 Nm*
29–43 ft.lbs.*
160–220 Nm
116–159 ft.lbs.
80–90 Nm*
58–65 ft.lbs.*
<Limited slip differential>
<Conventional differential>
Differential gear set
Final drive gear set

Reassembly steps

1. Gear carrier
. Oil seal
3. Drive pinion rear bearing outer race
4. Drive pinion front bearing outer race
Adjustment of pinion height
5. Drive pinion
6. Drive pinion rear shim
(for pinion height adjustment)
7. Drive pinion rear bearing inner race
8. Drive pinion spacer
Adjustment of drive pinion preload
9. Drive pinion front shim
(for preload adjustment)
10. Drive pinion assembly
11. Drive pinion front bearing inner race
12. Oil seal
13. Companion flange
14. Washer
15. Self-locking nut
16. Differential case
17. Limited slip (viscous coupling) differential case
Adjustment of differential gear backlash
18. Side gear spacers
19. Side gears
20. Pinion washers
21. Pinion gears
22. Pinion shaft
23. Lock pin
24. Drive gear
25. Side bearing inner race
26. Side bearing outer race
Adjustment of final drive gear backlash
27. Side bearing spacers
28. Differential case assembly
29. Bearing caps
30. Vent plug
31. Differential cover

NOTE
* : Tightening torque with oil applied.

MT3019100015000X

Fig. 22 Rear differential assembly. Eclipse & Expo

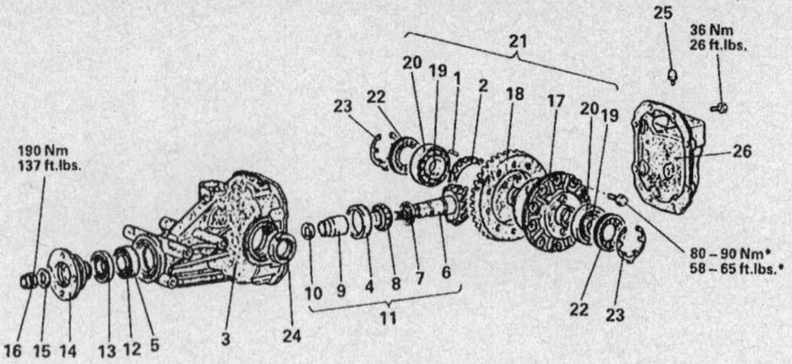
36 Nm
26 ft.lbs.
190 Nm
137 ft.lbs.
80–90 Nm*
58–65 ft.lbs.*

Reassembly steps

1. Spring pin (for 4WS)
2. Drive gear (for 4WS)
3. Differential carrier
4. Drive pinion rear bearing outer race
5. Drive pinion front bearing outer race
Drive pinion height adjustment
6. Drive pinion
7. Drive pinion rear shim
(for drive pinion height adjustment)
8. Drive pinion rear bearing inner race
9. Drive pinion spacer
Drive pinion preload adjustment
10. Drive pinion front shim
11. Drive pinion assembly
12. Drive pinion front bearing inner race
13. Oil seal
14. Companion flange
15. Washer
16. Self-locking nut
17. LSD case
18. Drive gear
19. Side bearing inner race
20. Side bearing outer race
Final drive gear backlash adjustment
21. Differential case assembly
22. Side bearing nut
23. Snap ring
24. Oil seal
25. Vent plug
26. Differential cover assembly

NOTE
*: Tightening torque with oil applied.

MT3019100016000X

Fig. 23 Rear differential assembly. 3000GT

DIFFERENTIAL CARRIER SERVICE

LIMITED SLIP DIFFERENTIAL

Inspection Before Disassembly

1. Secure differential case assembly in a vise so that differential right side gear is facing upward. **When securing in vise, ensure not to hold differential case assembly to tightly.**
2. Insert a .0012 inch feeler gauge at two places between differential case B and right thrust washer, **Fig. 37. Do not insert a feeler gauge in oil groove of differential case B.**
3. Insert tool A of tool kit No. MB990988, or equivalent, at spline part of differential right side gear and ensure right side gear rotates, **Fig. 38.**
4. Replace on of the .0012 inch feeler gauge with a .0035 inch feeler gauge.
5. Insert tool A of tool kit No. MB990988, or equivalent, at spline part of differential right side gear and ensure right side gear does not rotate, **Fig. 38.**
6. If clearance in thrust direction of side gear is within .0012–.0035 inch, backlash of differential gear is normal.
7. If clearance in thrust direction of side gear is not .0012–.0035 inch, remove differential case A and make adjustment by adjusting thickness of left thrust washer.

Disassemble

Disassemble limited slip differential carrier in numbered sequence shown in **Fig. 39.** Right and left thrust washers are of different thickness, and should be identified in some way for reference during assembly.

Assemble

Assemble limited slip differential carrier in reverse numbered sequence shown in **Fig. 39,** noting the following:

1. Align mating marks of differential case A and B when assembling.
2. With pinion mate washers in position, install to differential pinion shaft, then to differential case B, **Fig. 40.**
3. If differential side gear and pinion mate gear have been replaced, select left thrust washer as follows:
   a. Wash differential gear and pinion mate gears in unleaded gasoline.
   b. Install old thrust washer together with gears, viscous unit, pinion mate washer and pinion shaft into differential cases A and B then temporarily tighten screws.
   c. Perform "Inspection Before Disassembly" procedure.
   d. If clearance in thrust direction of side gear is not within .0012–.0035 inch, remove differential case A and make adjustment by changing thickness of left thrust washer. Select one left thrust washer from 11 types in thrust washer kit tool No. MB569243, or equivalent, **Fig. 41.**
4. Reassemble case halves and install into differential.

PROPELLER SHAFT

REPLACE

1. Remove propeller shaft in numbered sequence, **Figs. 42 through 44,** noting the following:
   a. Place mating marks on companion flange and flange yoke for installation reference.
   b. Number of spacers used may vary between models. Note number of spacers for installation reference.
2. Reverse numbered sequence in **Figs. 42 through 44** to install, noting the following:
   a. Do not damage transfer case oil seal lip during installation.
   b. Using a suitable dial indicator, inspect shaft runout after installation; runout should not exceed .024 inch at any point.

TRANSFER CASE

REPLACE

1. Drain transfer oil into a suitable container.
2. Remove transfer case assembly as shown, **Fig. 45,** noting the following:
   a. It may be necessary to disconnect front exhaust pipe to gain working clearance.
   b. Move the transfer case to the left and lower the front side, then remove it from the propeller shaft.
   c. Suspend the propeller shaft so that it can not be sharply bent.
   d. Cover the transfer opening with tool No. MB991193, or equivalent, to prevent transaxle oil discharge and the entry of foreign objects.

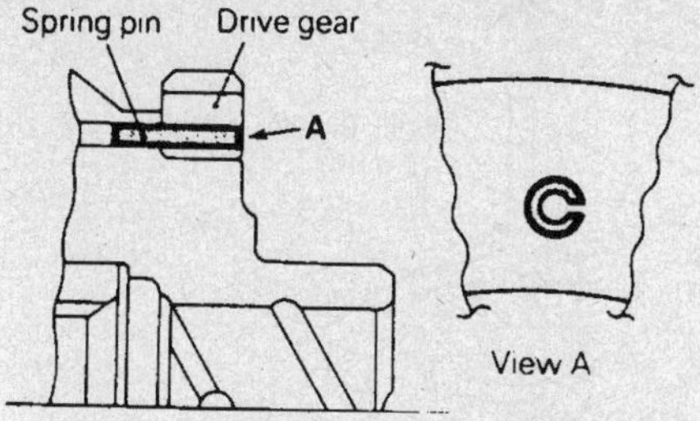
Spring pin
Drive gear
A
View A

MT3019100017000X

Fig. 24 Spring pin installation. 3000GT w/4WS

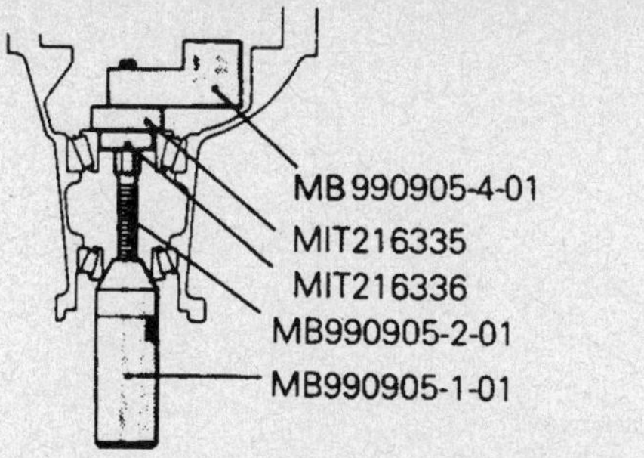
MB990905-4-01
MIT216335
MIT216336
MB990905-2-01
MB990905-1-01

MT3019100018000X

Fig. 25 Pinion height adjustment. Expo & 1993–94 Eclipse

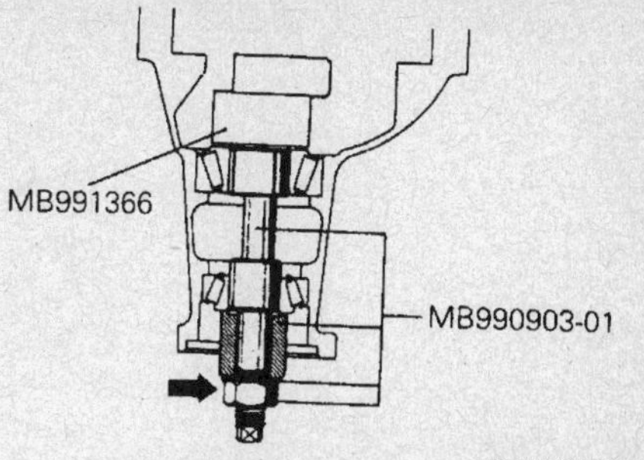
MB991366
MB990903-01

MT3019100019000X

Fig. 26 Pinion height adjustment. 3000GT

Bearing classification	Bearing lubrication	Rotation torque (starting friction torque) Nm (in.lbs.)
New	None (with rust-prevention oil)	0.9–1.2 (8–10)
New/reused	Oil application	0.4–0.5 (3–4)

NOTE
(1) Gradually tighten the handle of the special tool while checking the drive pinion turning torque.
(2) Because the special tool cannot be turned one turn, turn it several times within the range that it can be turned; then, after fitting to the bearing, measure the rotation torque.

MT3019100020000X

Fig. 27 Pinion turning torque. Eclipse & Expo

Bearing classification	Bearing lubrication	Rotation torque Nm (in.lbs.)
New	None (with rust-prevention oil)	0.3 – 0.5 (3 – 4)
New/reused	Gear oil application	0.15 – 0.25 (1 – 2)

NOTE
(1) Gradually tighten the nut of the special tool while checking the drive pinion rotation torque.
(2) Because the special tool cannot be turned one turn, turn it several times within the range that it can be turned; then, after fitting to the bearing, measure the rotation torque.

MT3019100021000X

Fig. 28 Pinion turning torque. 3000GT

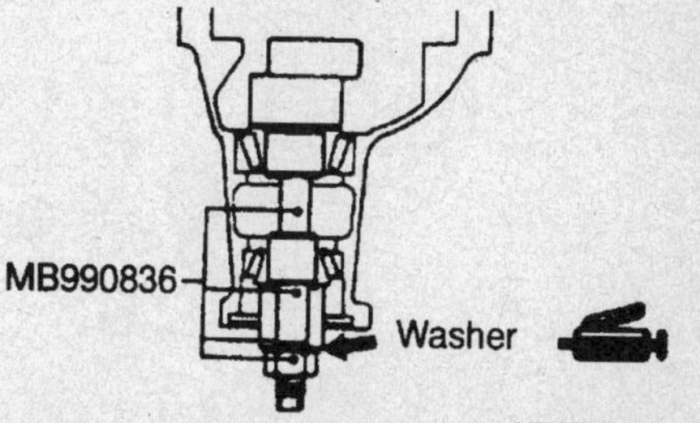
MB990836
Washer

MT3039500063000X

Fig. 29 Drive pinion front & rear bearing inner race installation. 1995–96 Eclipse

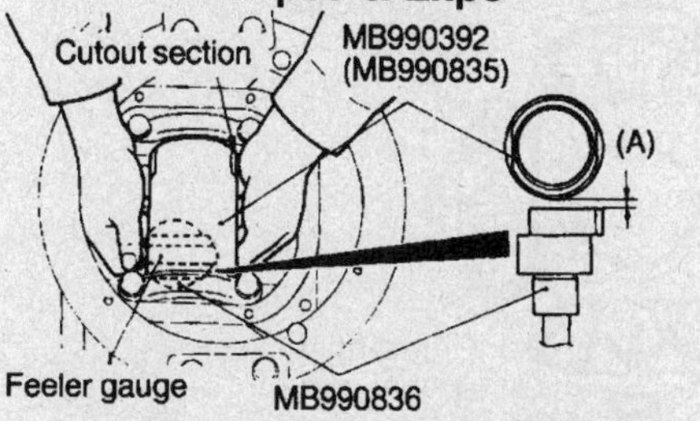
Cutout section
MB990392
(MB990835)
(A)
Feeler gauge
MB990836

MT3039500064000X

Fig. 30 Side bearing tool orientation. 1995–96 Eclipse

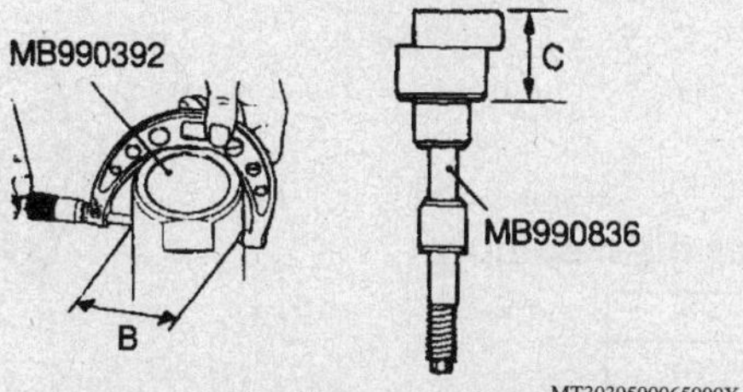
MB990392
C
MB990836
B

MT3039500065000X

Fig. 31 Side bearing clearance measurements. 1995–96 Eclipse

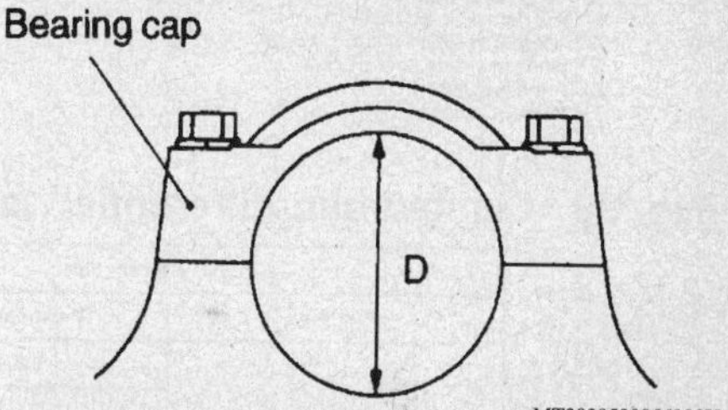
Bearing cap
D

MT3039500066000X

Fig. 32 Bearing cap clearance measurement. 1995–96 Eclipse

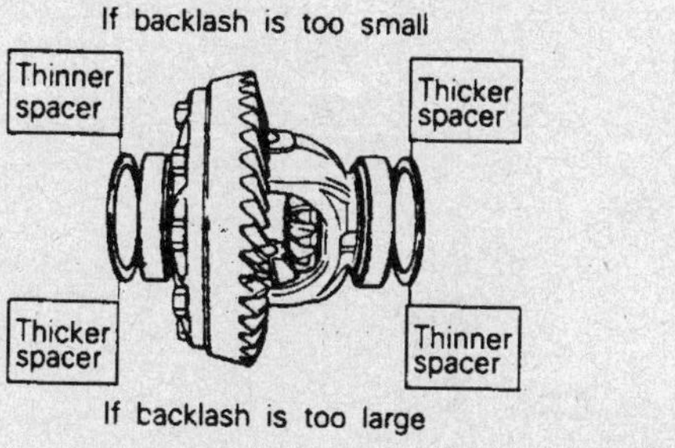
If backlash is too small
Thinner spacer
Thicker spacer
Thicker spacer
Thinner spacer
If backlash is too large

MT3019100022000X

Fig. 33 Gear backlash adjustment. Eclipse & Expo

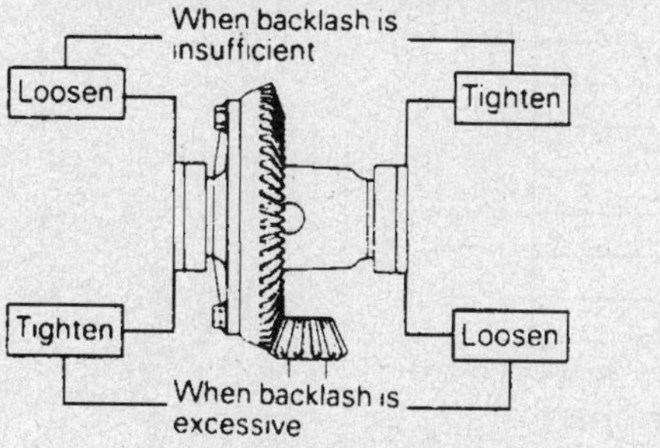
When backlash is insufficient
Loosen
Tighten
Tighten
Loosen
When backlash is excessive

MT3019100023000X

Fig. 34 Gear backlash adjustment. 3000GT

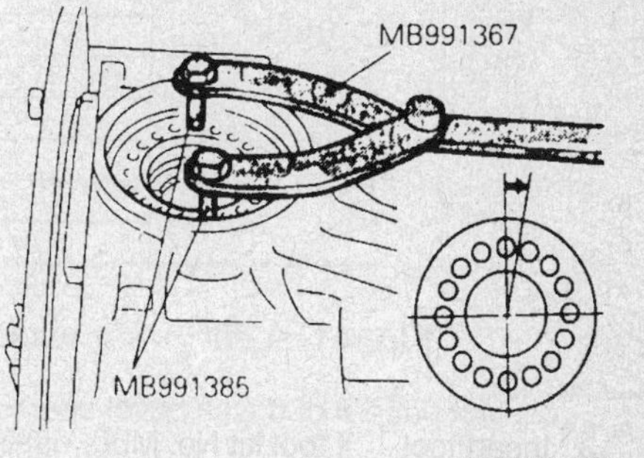
MB991367
MB991385

MT3019100024000X

Fig. 35 Side bearing adjustment. 3000GT

3. Reverse procedure to install. Refill transfer oil.

TRANSFER CASE SERVICE

OVERHAUL

Disassemble transfer assembly in numbered sequence, **Fig. 46.** Reverse procedure to assemble, noting the following:

1. Using a suitable brush, apply a thin,

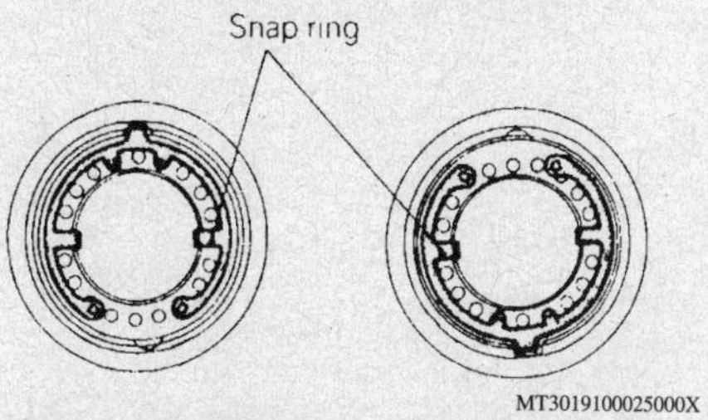
Snap ring

MT3019100025000X

Fig. 36 Bearing nut snap ring installation. 3000GT

even coat of machine blue, **Fig. 47,** to both tooth surfaces of the driven bevel gear.
2. Install the old spacer.
3. Tighten transfer case adapter subassembly on transfer case subassembly.
4. Using tool No. MB99088, or equivalent, turn the drive bevel gear shaft, **Fig. 48,** one turn in the direction of normal and reverse rotation, ensuring

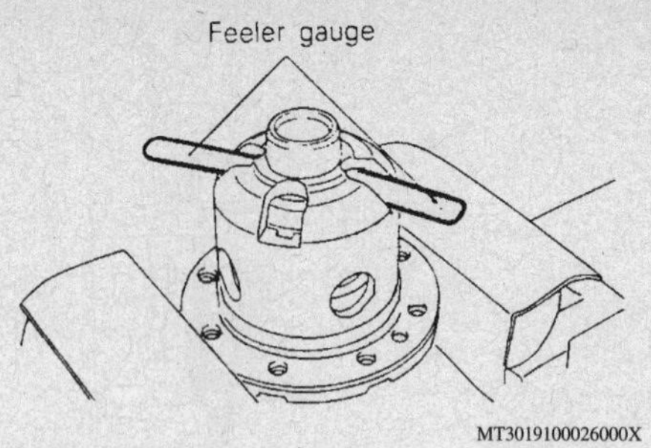
Feeler gauge
MT3019100026000X

Fig. 37 Feeler gauge insertion

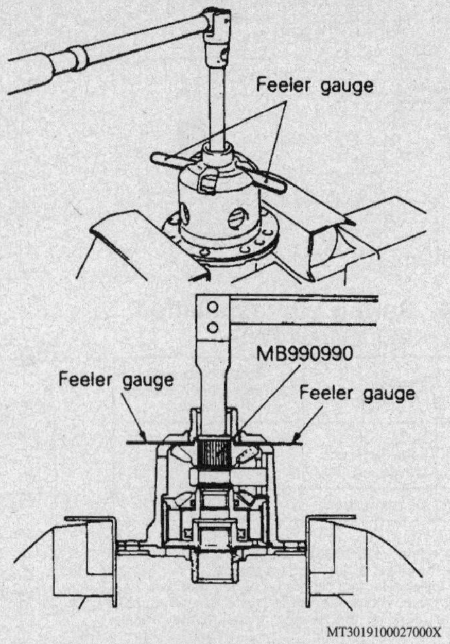
Feeler gauge
MB990990
Feeler gauge
Feeler gauge
MT3019100027000X

Fig. 38 Right side gear inspection

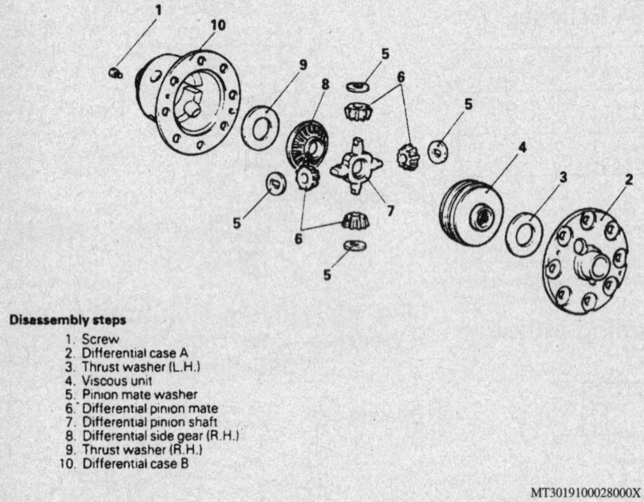
Disassembly steps
1. Screw
2. Differential case A
3. Thrust washer (L.H.)
4. Viscous unit
5. Pinion mate washer
6. Differential pinion mate
7. Differential pinion shaft
8. Differential side gear (R.H.)
9. Thrust washer (R.H.)
10. Differential case B
MT3019100028000X

Fig. 39 Limited slip differential carrier disassembly

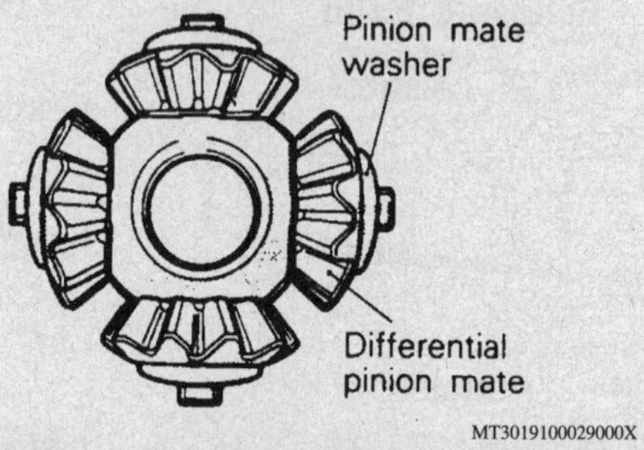
Pinion mate washer
Differential pinion mate
MT3019100029000X

Fig. 40 Differential pinion mate installation

Thrust washer (left)	
Part No.	Thickness mm (in.)
MB569243	0.8 (.031)
	0.9 (.035)
	1.0 (.039)
	1.1 (.043)
	1.15 (.045)
	1.2 (.047)
	1.25 (.049)
	1.3 (.051)
	1.35 (.053)
	1.4 (.055)
	1.5 (.059)

MT3019100030000X

Fig. 41 Left thrust washer chart

contact pattern of driven bevel gear is correct.

5. Ensure backlash between the drive and driven bevel gears is .0031–.0050 inch.

SUBASSEMBLY SERVICE

Transfer Case

Disassemble transfer case subassembly in numbered sequence, **Fig. 49.** Reverse procedure to assemble, noting the following:

1. Using tool No. MD998323-01, or equivalent, install the oil seal.

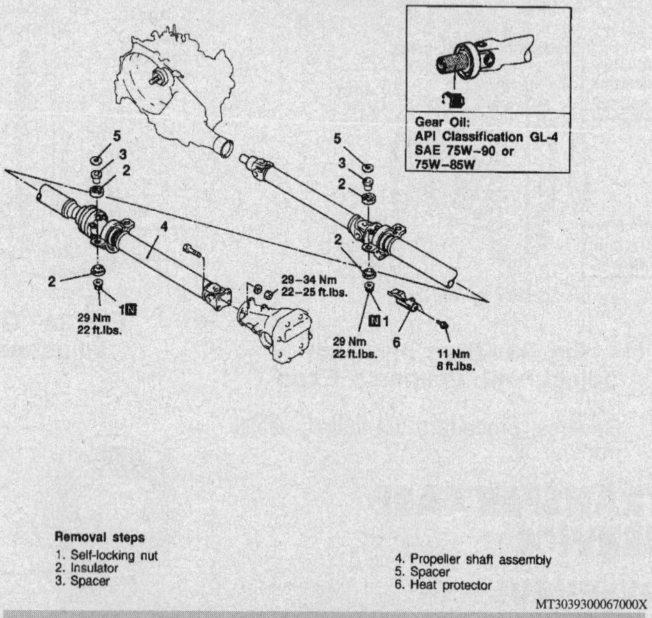
Gear Oil:
API Classification GL-4
SAE 75W-90 or
75W-85W
29–34 Nm
22–25 ft.lbs.
29 Nm
22 ft.lbs.
29 Nm
22 ft.lbs.
11 Nm
8 ft.lbs.
Removal steps
1. Self-locking nut
2. Insulator
3. Spacer
4. Propeller shaft assembly
5. Spacer
6. Heat protector
MT3039300067000X

Fig. 42 Propeller shaft replacement. Eclipse

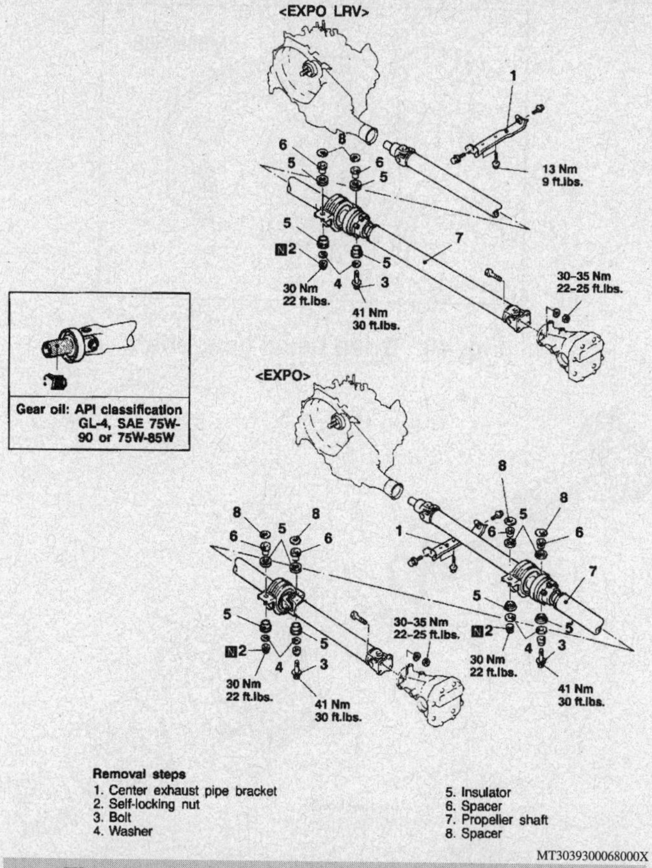
<EXPO LRV>
13 Nm
9 ft.lbs.
30–35 Nm
22–25 ft.lbs.
30 Nm
22 ft.lbs.
41 Nm
30 ft.lbs.
Gear oil: API classification GL-4, SAE 75W-90 or 75W-85W
<EXPO>
Removal steps
1. Center exhaust pipe bracket
2. Self-locking nut
3. Bolt
4. Washer
5. Insulator
6. Spacer
7. Propeller shaft
8. Spacer
MT3039300068000X

Fig. 43 Propeller shaft replacement. Expo

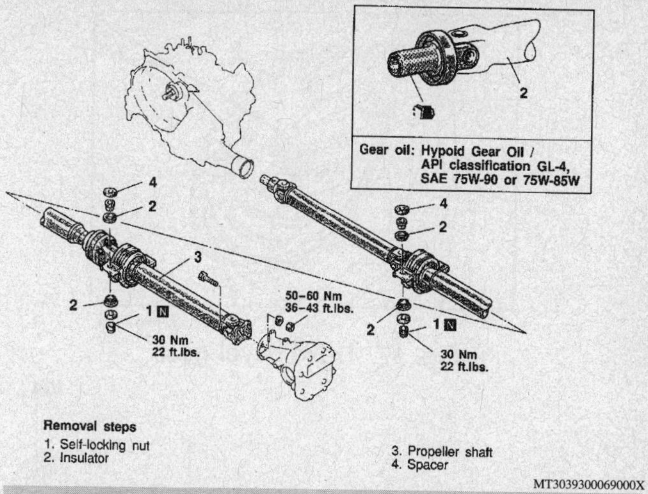
Gear oil: Hypoid Gear Oil / API classification GL-4, SAE 75W-90 or 75W-85W
50–60 Nm
36–43 ft.lbs.
30 Nm
22 ft.lbs.
Removal steps
1. Self-locking nut
2. Insulator
3. Propeller shaft
4. Spacer
MT3039300069000X

Fig. 44 Propeller shaft replacement. 3000GT

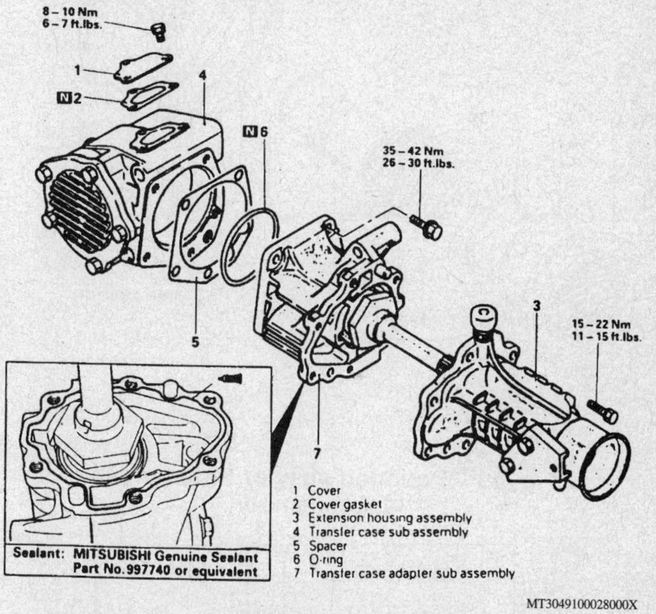
8 – 10 Nm
6 – 7 ft.lbs.
35 – 42 Nm
26 – 30 ft.lbs.
15 – 22 Nm
11 – 15 ft.lbs.
Sealant: MITSUBISHI Genuine Sealant Part No. 997740 or equivalent
1 Cover
2 Cover gasket
3 Extension housing assembly
4 Transfer case sub assembly
5 Spacer
6 O-ring
7 Transfer case adapter sub assembly
MT3049100028000X

Fig. 46 Exploded view of transfer assembly

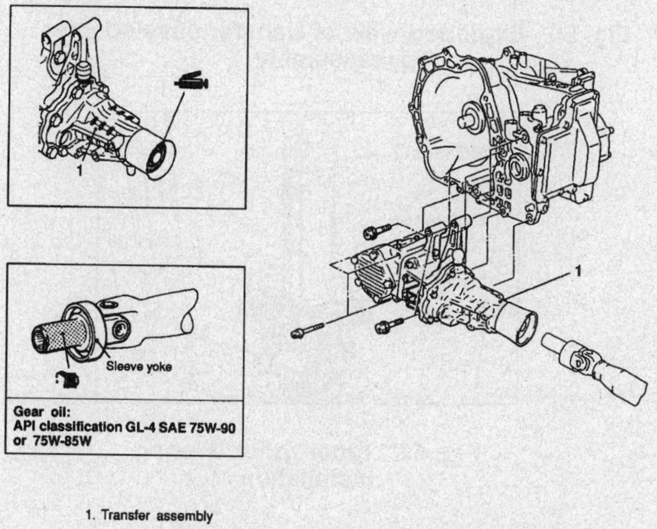
Sleeve yoke
Gear oil: API classification GL-4 SAE 75W-90 or 75W-85W
1. Transfer assembly
MT3049100027000A

Fig. 45 Transfer case assembly replacement

2. Install old spacers which were used previously.
3. Inspect drive bevel gear assembly using tool Nos. MB990988 and MB990326, or equivalents. Drive bevel gear **torque** should be 1.23–1.81 ft. lbs.

Transfer Case Adapter

Disassemble transfer case adapter sub-assembly in numbered sequence, **Fig. 50,** noting the following:

1. Unstake locknut before removal.
2. Remove the locknut using tool No. MIT 307098, or equivalent, **Fig. 51.**
3. Using a press, remove driven bevel gear assembly.
4. Using a screwdriver, remove spacer.
5. Reverse procedure to assemble, noting the following:
   a. Install spacer that was used previously.
   b. Using special tools, **Fig. 52,** install tapered roller bearing.
   c. Tighten driven bevel gear locknut, then stake locknut at two places to lock.

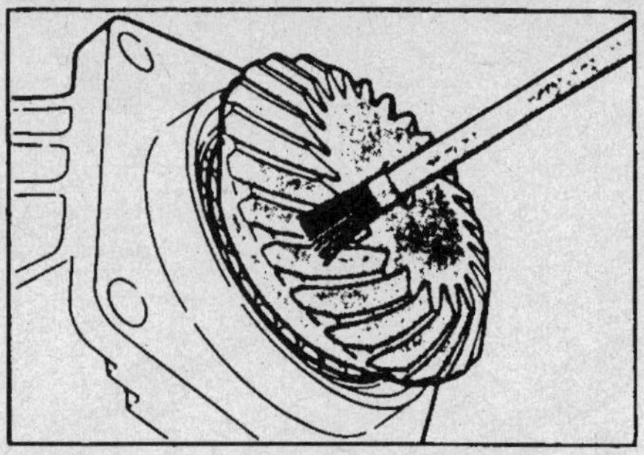

MT3049100029000X

Fig. 47 Drive bevel gear

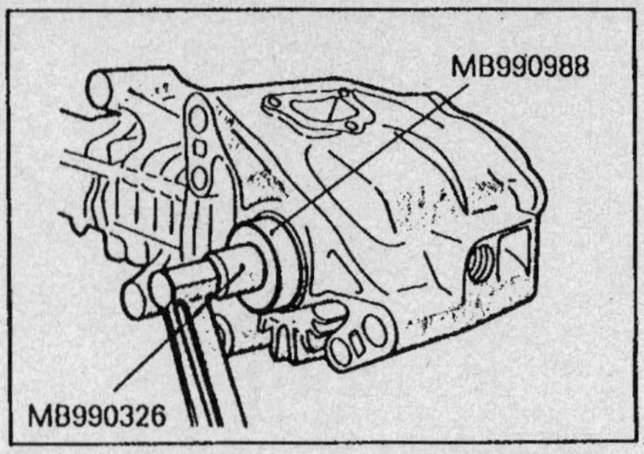
MB990988
MB990326

MT3049100030000X

Fig. 48 Drive bevel gear shaft

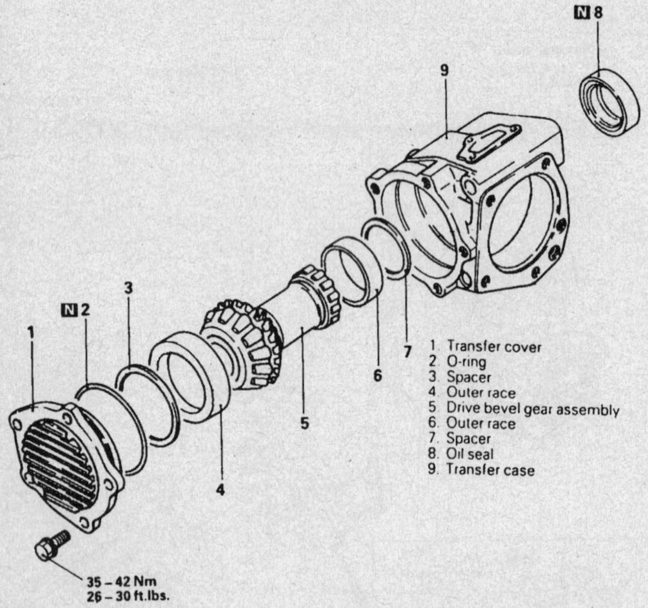
N 8
9
3
N 2
1
7
6
5
4
1. Transfer cover
2. O-ring
3. Spacer
4. Outer race
5. Drive bevel gear assembly
6. Outer race
7. Spacer
8. Oil seal
9. Transfer case
35 – 42 Nm
26 – 30 ft.lbs.

MT3049100031000X

Fig. 49 Exploded view of transfer case subassembly

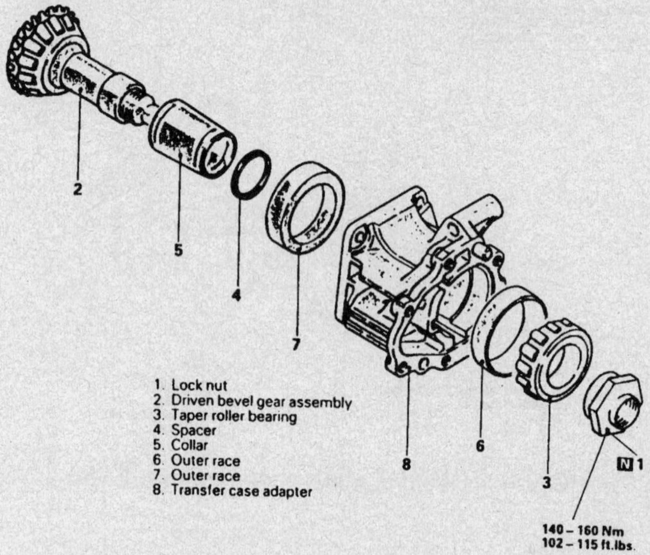
2
5
4
7
8
6
3
N 1
1. Lock nut
2. Driven bevel gear assembly
3. Taper roller bearing
4. Spacer
5. Collar
6. Outer race
7. Outer race
8. Transfer case adapter
140 – 160 Nm
102 – 115 ft.lbs.

MT3049100032000X

Fig. 50 Exploded view of transfer case adapter subassembly

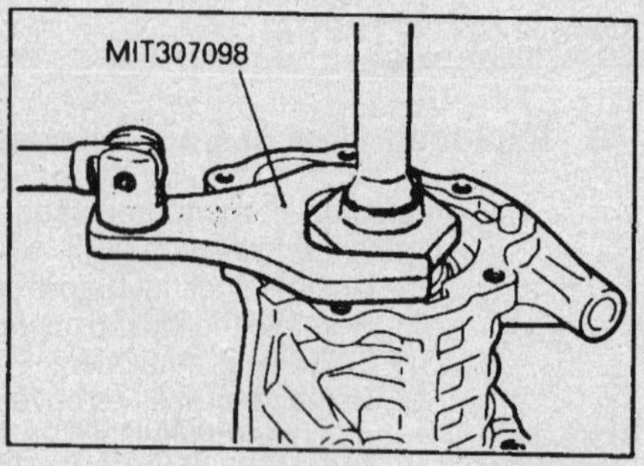
MIT307098

MT3049100033000X

Fig. 51 Driven gear locknut removal

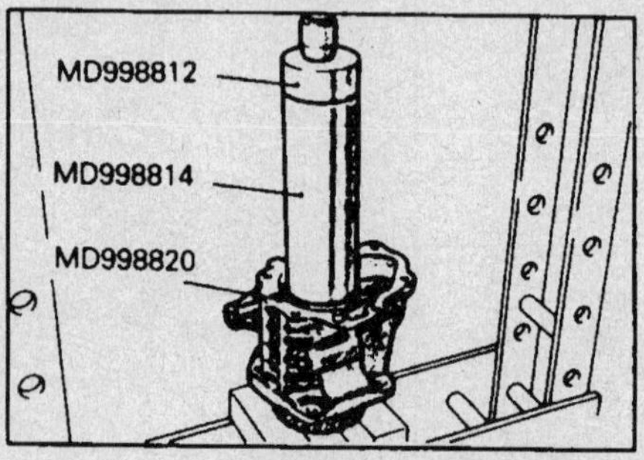
MD998812
MD998814
MD998820

MT3049100034000X

Fig. 52 Taper roller bearing installation

Drive Axles

INDEX

Page No.

Assemble 29-306
Differential Case Assembly 29-306
Drive Pinion 29-307
Side Bearing & Drive Gear 29-308

Page No.

Cleaning & Inspection 29-305
Disassemble 29-305
Differential Case Assembly 29-305

Page No.

Drive Pinion 29-305
Drive Axle Specifications 29-310
Identification 29-305

IDENTIFICATION

Refer to **Fig. 1** to identify drive axles by ratio or number of ring gear teeth.

Year	Model	No. Of Ring Gear Teeth	Gear Ratio
REAR			
1993–95	Pickup	①	②
	Montero	—	③
1996	Pickup	①	②
	Montero④	—	③
	Montero⑤	—	4.636
FRONT			
1993–95	Pickup	38	4.222
	Montero	—	4.625
1996	Pickup	38	4.222
	Montero④	—	③
	Montero⑤	—	4.636

① — Except light duty 2WD models, 38 teeth; light duty 2WD models, 43 teeth.
② — Except light duty 2WD models, 4.222; light duty 2WD models, 3.909.
③ — Models less wide fenders, 4.625; models w/wide fenders, 4.875.
④ — 3.0L 12 valve engine.
⑤ — 3.0L 24 valve & 3.5L engines.

Fig. 1 Drive axle identification

DISASSEMBLE

DIFFERENTIAL CASE ASSEMBLY

Except Limited Slip & Rear Differential Lock

1. If rear differential is being serviced, remove lock plate and side bearing nuts using tool No. MB990201, or equivalent.
2. Remove the carrier cap (bearing cap), **Figs. 2 and 3.**
3. Remove differential case assembly using the wooden handles of two hammers to avoid damaging the gears.
4. Using puller tool No. MB990810 and adapter tool No. MB9990811, or equivalents, remove side bearings. Keep side bearings, nuts and adjusting spacers together for assembly reference.
5. Scribe alignment mark on differential case and drive gear, then remove drive gear attaching bolts and drive gear. Loosen bolts alternately in a diagonal pattern.
6. Remove lockpin with a punch, then remove pinion shaft, pinion gears, side gears and side gear thrust spacers. Keep left and right side components separate for identification during reassembly.

Limited Slip & Rear Differential Lock

1. Remove case from gear carrier, **Fig. 4,** as described under conventional differential.
2. Remove side bearing using tool Nos. MB990339-01, MIT303173 and MB990811-01, or equivalents, **Fig. 5.** Keep adjusting spacers separate to facilitate reassembly.
3. Mark relative position between differential case and drive gear, then loosen and remove drive gear mounting bolts in a diagonal sequence.
4. Evenly loosen differential case attaching bolts A and B, separate the two halves, then remove components from case B. **Separate right and left thrust washers, spring plates, spring discs, friction plates and friction discs to facilitate assembly.**

DRIVE PINION

1. Hold end yoke with tool No. MB990850, or equivalent, on rear differentials, or No. MB990767, or equivalent, on front differentials. Remove mounting nut and end yoke.
2. Scribe alignment mark on end yoke and drive pinion, then tap or push out drive pinion with height adjusting shim, rear bearing inner race, spacer and preload adjusting shim still installed on shaft.
3. Using tool Nos. MB990339 and MB990648, or equivalents, remove drive pinion rear bearing inner race and height adjusting shim from shaft.
4. Remove front and rear pinion bearing outer races. **When removing front outer race, remove and discard oil seal, then remove front bearing inner race.**

CLEANING & INSPECTION

1. Check differential gear tooth contact and replace any gear that is worn or damaged.
2. Check bearings and races and replace if worn, damaged or discolored.
3. Install side gear (with circlip on front differentials), onto splined end of axle shaft. Install assembly in vise, **Fig. 6.** Freeplay should not exceed .020 inch on rear differential or .024 inch on front differential.
4. Inspect differential pinion and pinion shaft; replace if worn or seized.
5. **On models equipped with limited slip differential,** proceed as follows:
   a. Clean all components in solvent.
   b. Inspect sliding and mating surfaces of clutch plate and pressure ring for pitting or damage.
   c. Inspect contact surfaces of friction plates, friction discs, spring plates and spring discs. If any signs of seizure, severe friction or discoloration from heat damage are present, replace damaged components. **Worn area around circumference of friction surfaces is due to spring plate and spring disc; wear is normal.**
   d. Check the six projections on the inner circumference of the friction disc for nicks and dents. Repair using an oil stone, or replace as necessary.
   e. Check the four projections on the outer circumference of friction disc for nicks and dents, then repair using an oil stone, or replace as necessary.

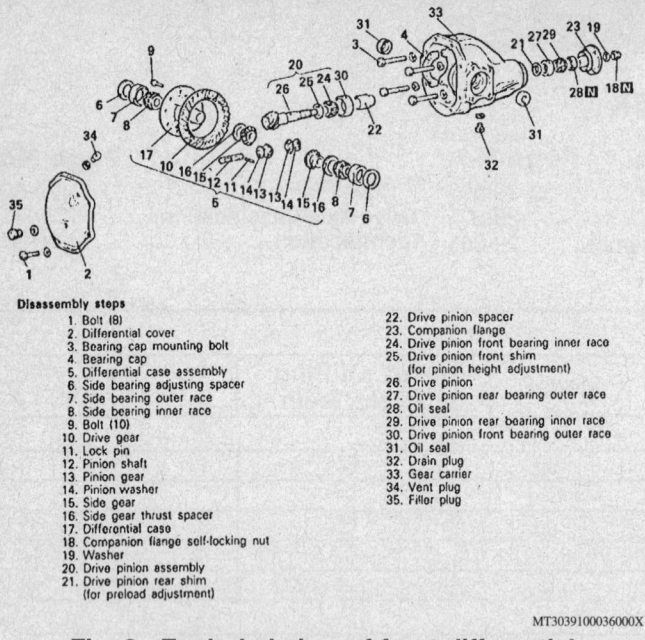

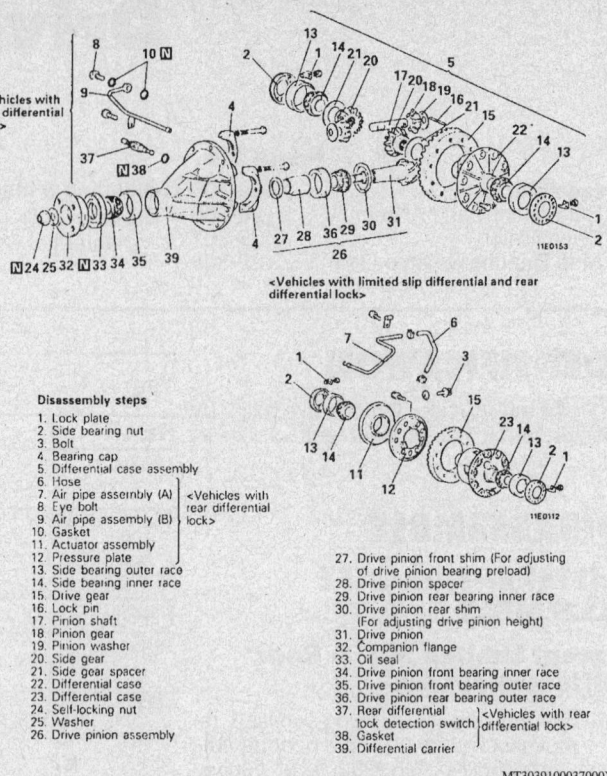

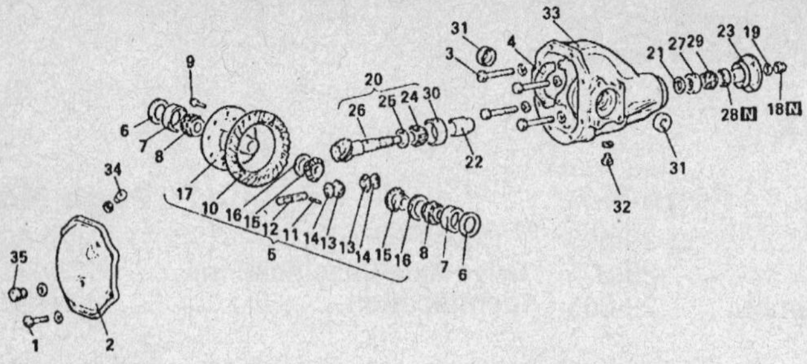

Disassembly steps

1. Bolt (8)
2. Differential cover
3. Bearing cap mounting bolt
4. Bearing cap
5. Differential case assembly
6. Side bearing adjusting spacer
7. Side bearing outer race
8. Side bearing inner race
9. Bolt (10)
10. Drive gear
11. Lock pin
12. Pinion shaft
13. Pinion gear
14. Pinion washer
15. Side gear
16. Side gear thrust spacer
17. Differential case
18. Companion flange self-locking nut
19. Washer
20. Drive pinion assembly
21. Drive pinion rear shim (for preload adjustment)
22. Drive pinion spacer
23. Companion flange
24. Drive pinion front bearing inner race
25. Drive pinion front shim (for pinion height adjustment)
26. Drive pinion
27. Drive pinion rear bearing outer race
28. Oil seal
29. Drive pinion rear bearing inner race
30. Drive pinion front bearing outer race
31. Oil seal
32. Drain plug
33. Gear carrier
34. Vent plug
35. Filler plug

MT3039100036000X

Fig. 2 Exploded view of front differential

<Vehicles with limited slip differential>

Gear oil:
MITSUBISHI Genuine Gear Oil Part No. 8149630EX or equivalent

Caution
Apply the specified gear oil to each component especially careful to coat contact surfaces and sliding surfaces.

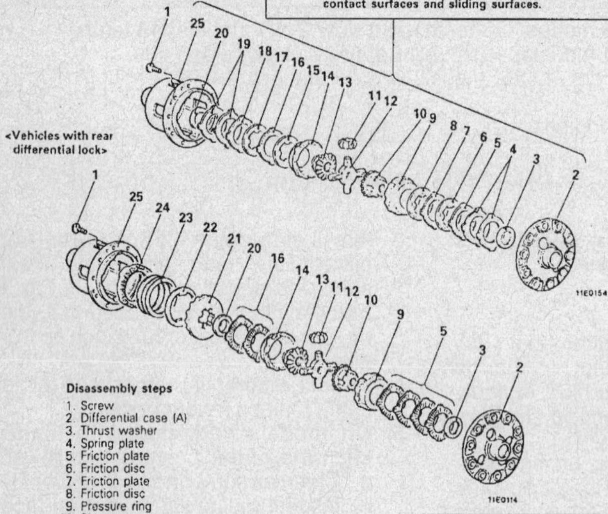
<Vehicles with rear differential lock>

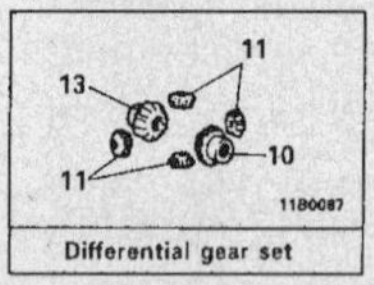

Differential gear set

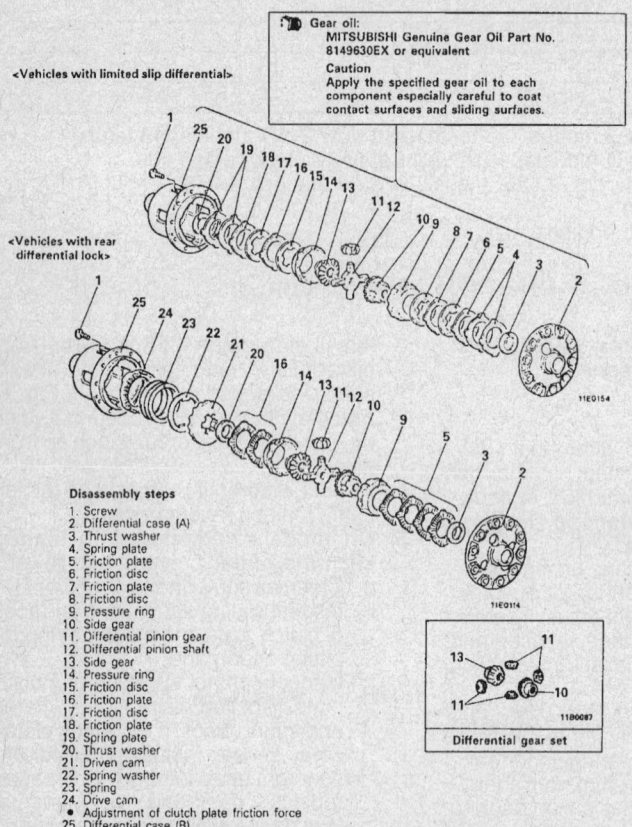

Disassembly steps

1. Screw
2. Differential case (A)
3. Thrust washer
4. Spring plate
5. Friction plate
6. Friction disc
7. Friction plate
8. Friction disc
9. Pressure ring
10. Side gear
11. Differential pinion gear
12. Differential pinion shaft
13. Side gear
14. Pressure ring
15. Friction disc
16. Friction plate
17. Friction disc
18. Friction plate
19. Spring plate
20. Thrust washer
21. Driven cam
22. Spring washer
23. Spring
24. Drive cam
- Adjustment of clutch plate friction force
25. Differential case (B)

MT3039100038000X

Fig. 4 Exploded view of limited slip differential or rear differential lock assembly

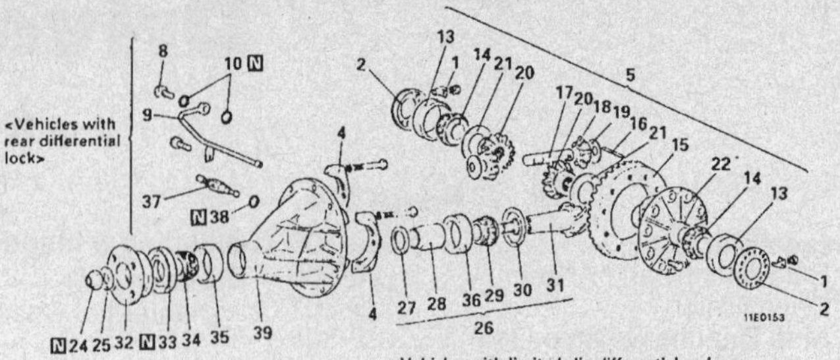
<Vehicles with rear differential lock>

<Vehicles with limited slip differential and rear differential lock>

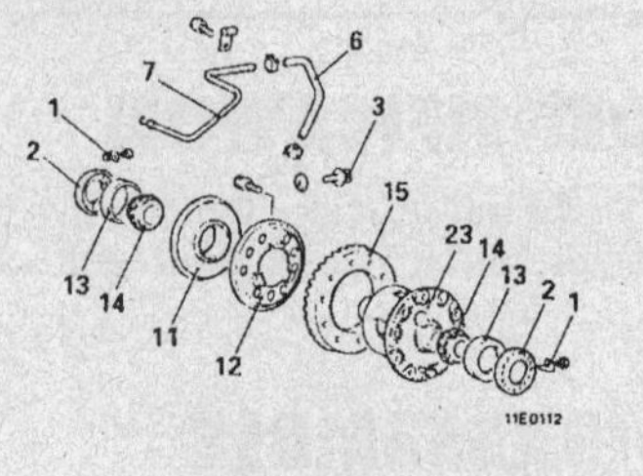

Disassembly steps

1. Lock plate
2. Side bearing nut
3. Bolt
4. Bearing cap
5. Differential case assembly
6. Hose <Vehicles with rear differential lock>
7. Air pipe assembly (A) <Vehicles with rear differential lock>
8. Eye bolt <Vehicles with rear differential lock>
9. Air pipe assembly (B) <Vehicles with rear differential lock>
10. Gasket <Vehicles with rear differential lock>
11. Actuator assembly <Vehicles with rear differential lock>
12. Pressure plate <Vehicles with rear differential lock>
13. Side bearing outer race
14. Side bearing inner race
15. Drive gear
16. Lock pin
17. Pinion shaft
18. Pinion gear
19. Pinion washer
20. Side gear
21. Side gear spacer
22. Differential case
23. Differential case
24. Self-locking nut
25. Washer
26. Drive pinion assembly
27. Drive pinion front shim (For adjusting of drive pinion bearing preload)
28. Drive pinion spacer
29. Drive pinion rear bearing inner race
30. Drive pinion rear shim (For adjusting drive pinion height)
31. Drive pinion
32. Companion flange
33. Oil seal
34. Drive pinion front bearing inner race
35. Drive pinion front bearing outer race
36. Drive pinion rear bearing outer race
37. Rear differential lock detection switch <Vehicles with rear differential lock>
38. Gasket <Vehicles with rear differential lock>
39. Differential carrier <Vehicles with rear differential lock>

MT3039100037000X

Fig. 3 Exploded view of rear differential

f. Inspect the sliding surfaces of the thrust washers and differential case, spring contacting surfaces of differential case, contacting surfaces of pressure rings, sliding surface of thrust washers and sliding surface of hole in side gears and repair as necessary using an oil stone.

g. Check spherical surface of pinion gears and I.D. of pressure rings, then the V-shaped groove in the pressure rings and pinion shaft. Check O.D. of pinion shaft and hole in pinion gear, then the outer and inner circumference of differential case. Inspect sliding surface of thrust block. If any damage is found on these components, repair using an oil stone, or replace as necessary.

h. Inspect friction plates, friction discs, spring discs and spring plates for flatness using a dial indicator. If found to be worn more than .003 inch on friction plate, or .004 inch on clutch plate, replace worn components.

ASSEMBLE

DIFFERENTIAL CASE ASSEMBLY

Except Limited Slip & Rear Differential Lock

1. Install side gear thrust washers and side gears into differential case.
2. Install pinion gears with washers into case. Rotate pinion gears to mesh with side gears.
3. Install pinion shaft. Do not install lockpin at this time.
4. Insert a wedge between side gear and pinion shaft to prevent side gear from turning, then install dial indicator to gear and measure gear backlash. Backlash must not exceed .005 inch on rear differentials, or .006 inch on front differentials. If backlash is not within specifications, replace side gear thrust spacers as needed, then recheck backlash.
5. Align pinion shaft lockpin hole with differential case lockpin hole, then drive

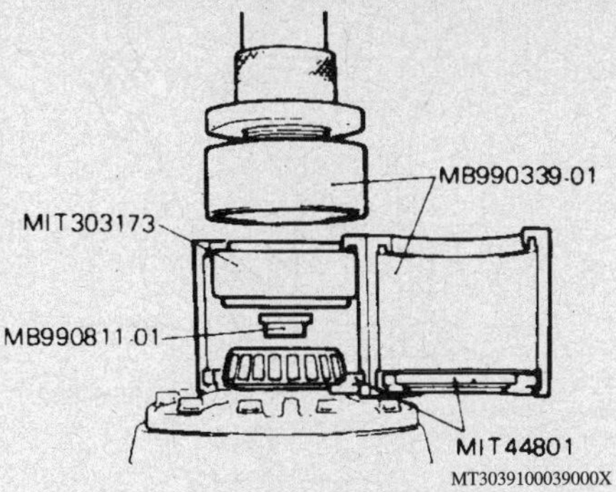
MB990339-01
MIT303173
MB990811-01
MIT44801
MT3039100039000X
Fig. 5 Differential side bearing removal

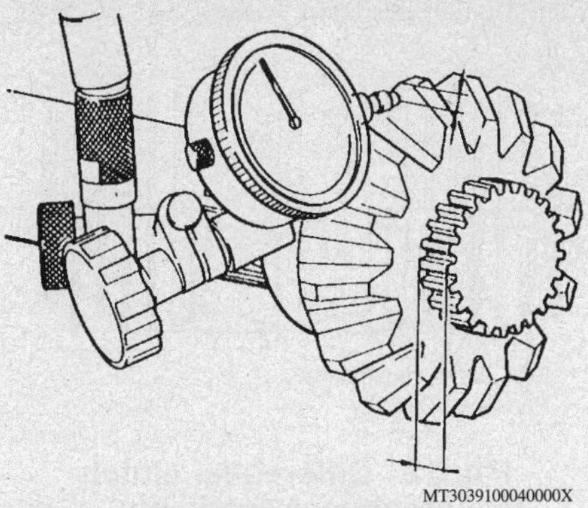
MT3039100040000X
Fig. 6 Driveshaft spline freeplay measurement

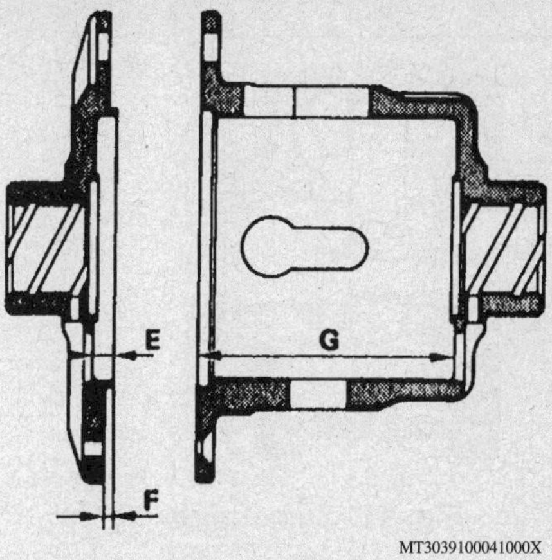
E
G
F
MT3039100041000X
Fig. 7 Differential case depth measurement

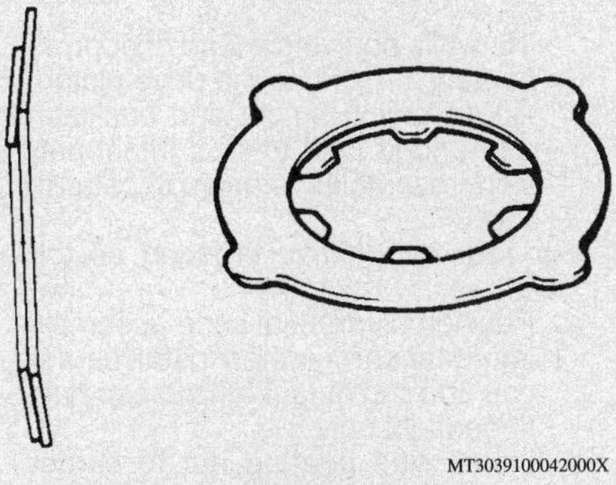
MT3039100042000X
Fig. 8 Plate thickness measurement

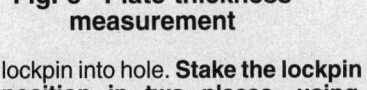

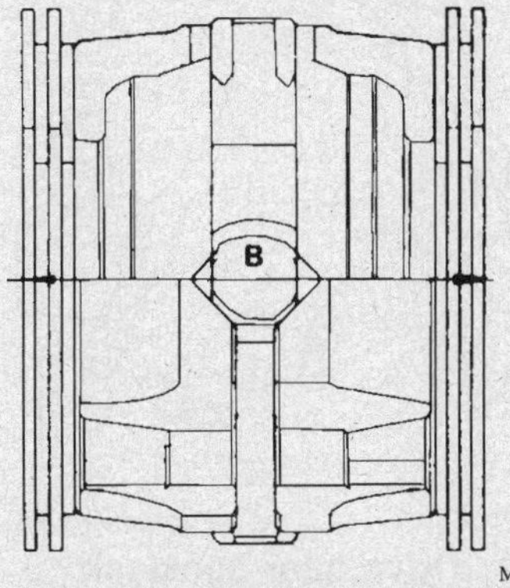
B
MT3039100043000X
Fig. 9 Total width measurement

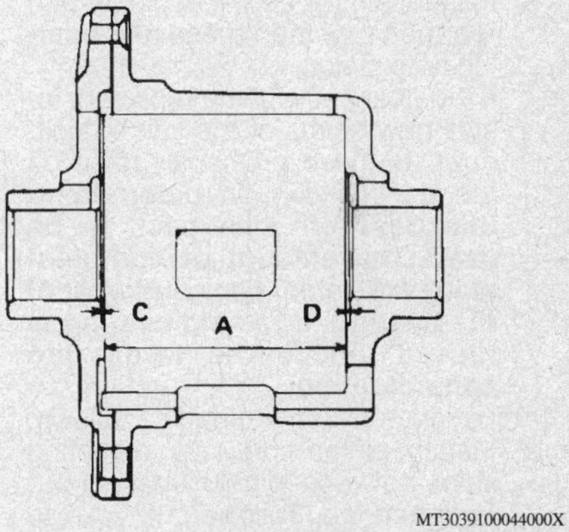
C
A
D
MT3039100044000X
Fig. 10 Thrust washer thickness measurement

lockpin into hole. **Stake the lockpin in position in two places, using a punch.**

6. Remove adhesive tape from drive gear attaching bolts and the internal threads in gear.
7. Apply Loctite No. 271, or equivalent, to drive gear threaded holes, then install gear onto case with reference marks aligned. **Torque** attaching bolts alternately, in a diagonal pattern, to 58–65 ft. lbs.

Limited Slip & Rear Differential Lock

1. Measure differential case depth (A), **Fig. 7,** using formula A = E – F + G.
2. Measure spring disc and plate thickness with both extended in the same direction and one placed over the other as shown, **Fig. 8.** Arrange them so that the difference between left and right is minimized, then measure thicknesses of friction plates and discs in the same manner. **Right side (Lr) and left side (Ll).**
3. Measure thickness of left and right clutch plate assemblies, then find the difference of the two. Difference should not exceed .002 inch. **Clutch plate assembly thickness is thickness of spring, disc, spring plate, friction disc and friction plate.**
4. Assemble right and left friction plates, friction discs, pinion shafts and pressure rings, then measure total width (B), **Fig. 9. Measure distance between clutch plates on a line with V-shaped groove in the pressure ring while pressing from both sides, ensuring groove is secured against pinion shaft. All parts should be dry.**
5. Measure clearance between clutch plate and differential (S), then use the following formula: A(B+Lr+Ll).
6. If the difference (S) between the depth (A) of differential case and the overall width (B) obtained previously, plus the spring plate and spring disc assembly thickness, is not .002–.008 inch, replace friction discs to adjust.
7. Measure distance (A), **Fig. 10,** then the depths of thrust washer contact surfaces, dimensions (C) and (D), in differential cases A and B.
8. Assemble pressure rings, pinion gears, side gears, pinion shafts and thrust washers.
9. Measure distance from back of left pressure ring to edge of thrust washer and ensure difference between the two does not exceed .002 inch. **Measure distance between clutch plates on a line with V-shaped groove in the pressure ring while pressing from both sides, ensuring groove is secured against pinion shaft. All parts should be dry.**
10. Measure overall width shown in **Fig. 11,** as dimension "R."
11. Using width of assembled differential unit and depth of differential case, measure clearance of side gear in axial direction. If clearance is not .002–.007 inch, replace thrust washers to adjust. **Find clearance of side gear in axial direction using formula: A + C + DR.**
12. Before assembly, apply lubricant to all contacting surfaces.
13. Assemble differential clutch and pinion assembly as shown, **Fig. 12.**
14. After assembly, measure rotating torque of assembly using tool No. MB990988, or equivalent. Turning **torque** should be 25–72 ft. lbs. for used clutch plates or 47–72 ft. lbs. for new clutch plates.
15. Remove old adhesive from drive gear attaching bolts, then apply sealer to bolts.
16. Install and finger tighten bolts, then alternately **torque** to 58–65 ft. lbs.

DRIVE PINION

1. Press drive front and rear bearing outer races into gear carrier using tool Nos. MB990934, MB990936 and MB990938, or equivalents.
2. Adjust drive pinion height as follows:
   a. Install tool No. MB990819, or equivalent, and the drive pinion bearings into gear carrier. Apply a thin coat of grease to washer on tool.
   b. Gradually tighten nut on tool until drive pinion preload is 3.5–4.3 inch lbs.
   c. Position cylinder of tool No. MB990552, or equivalent, in side bearing seat of gear carrier, **Fig. 13.**
   d. Using a feeler gauge, measure clearance between the two tools,

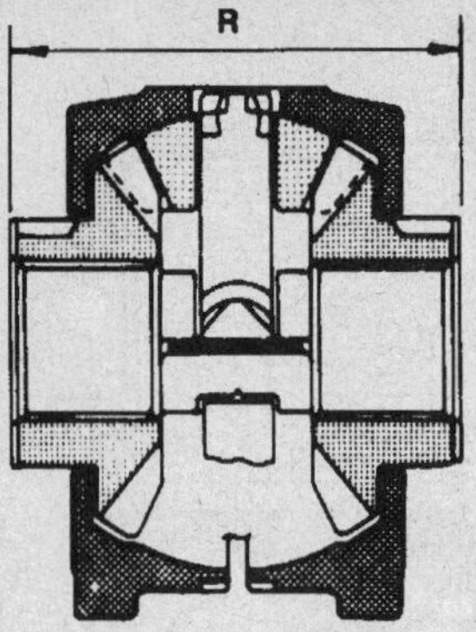
R
MT3039100045000X

Fig. 11 Dimension "R"

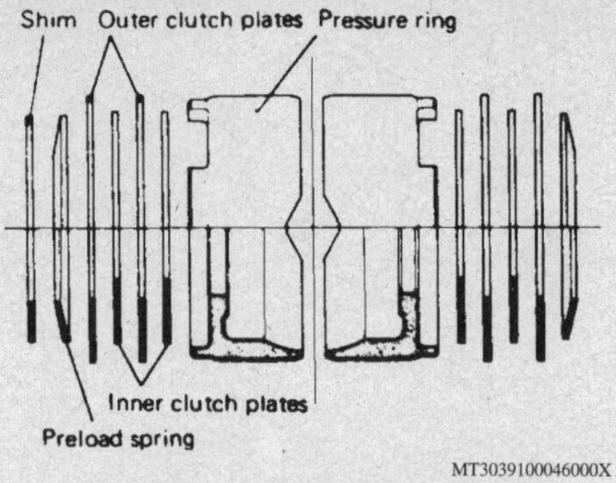
Shim
Outer clutch plates
Pressure ring
Inner clutch plates
Preload spring
MT3039100046000X

Fig. 12 Differential clutch component assembly

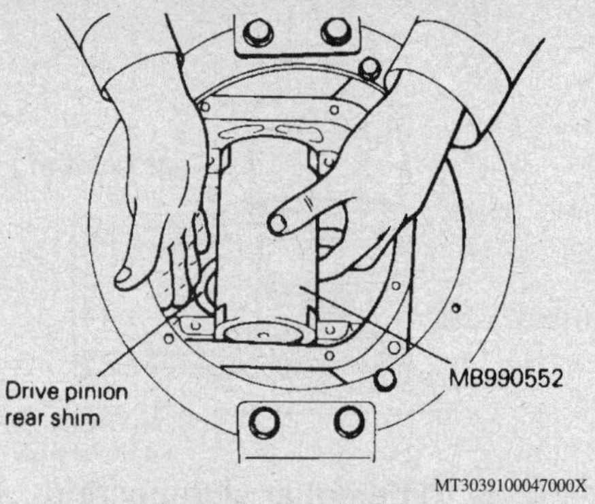
Drive pinion rear shim
MB990552
MT3039100047000X

Fig. 13 Drive pinion height measurement

then select drive pinion rear adjusting shim(s) corresponding to this measurement.

e. Install shim(s) between pinion and rear bearing, then press rear bearing onto pinion.
f. If the gear set is being replaced, install new shims of the same thickness as those previously used on the drive pinion. **In determining thickness of shim pack to be used, the amount of compression of the shim pack and wear of the bearing, if the old bearing is reused, should be taken into consideration.**

3. Adjust drive pinion preload as follows:
   a. Install pinion preload adjusting shim between pinion spacer and front bearing. **Torque** end yoke to 138–180 ft. lbs. on rear differential or 116–159 ft. lbs. on front differential.
   b. Measure drive pinion preload. Preload should measure 3.5–4.3 inch lbs. without oil seal installed.
   c. Adjust preload as necessary by replacing adjusting shims or drive pinion spacers.
4. Remove end yoke, then apply a thin coat of grease to lip of oil seal. Drive seal into gear carrier using tool No. MB990031, or equivalent.
5. Apply grease to end yoke mating surface of seal, then install the end yoke. **Torque** attaching nut to 138–180 ft. lbs. on rear differential or 116–159 ft. lbs. on front differential.

SIDE BEARING & DRIVE GEAR

1. Install side bearing inner race into differential case using tool No. MB990802, or equivalent.
2. **For front differentials,** adjust drive gear backlash as follows:
   a. Install side bearing adjusting spacers, thinner than those removed, to the side gear bearings, then install differential case assembly into gear carrier. **Select adjusting spacers of the same thickness for both the drive pinion side and the drive gear side.**
   b. Push differential case to one side, then measure clearance between

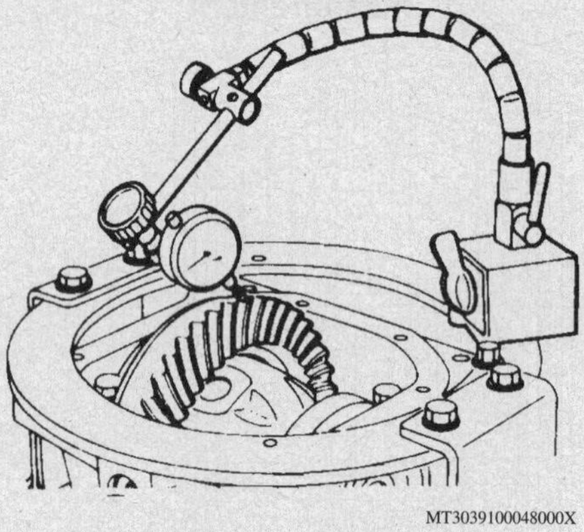
MT3039100048000X

Fig. 14 Drive gear backlash measurement

gear carrier and side bearing adjusting space using two feeler gauges.
   c. Remove, then measure the thickness of side bearing adjusting spacers from one side.
   d. To determine proper thickness spacer to be used, add .002 inch to thickness measured in preceding step and ½ the clearance measured between gear carrier and side bearing adjusting space.
   e. Install one pair of the correct spacers each to the drive pinion side and drive gear side.
   f. Install differential case assembly, with side bearing adjusting spacers, into gear carrier. Gently tap spacers with a brass drift to seat them on bearing outer race.
   g. Install bearing cap with reference marks aligned. **Torque** cap bolts to 40–47 ft. lbs.
   h. With drive pinion locked in place, measure drive gear backlash, **Fig. 14,** at four different points on the drive gear. Backlash should measure .005–.007 inch. If not, replace spacers as necessary to bring within specifications, **Fig. 15.**
   i. Check drive gear and drive pinion for proper tooth contact by applying marking compound to both surfaces of drive gear teeth. Insert a brass rod between carrier and case and rotate spline coupling by hand one revolution in each direction, **Fig. 16,** while applying a load of approximately 2 ft. lbs. to the drive pinion. Adjust pinion height and backlash as needed until tooth contact pattern resembles standard pattern, **Fig. 17.**
3. For rear differential, proceed as follows:
   a. Position differential case assembly into gear carrier, then install carrier cap and cap nuts. **Tighten** cap nuts finger tight only.
   b. Install side bearing nut to carrier cap, then **torque** to 40–47 ft. lbs.
   c. Install side bearing nut on each side of drive gear using tool No. MB990201, or equivalent, then **torque** to 11 ft. lbs. Turn bearing nuts in and out several times until they operate smoothly before final tightening.
   d. Measure drive gear backlash, **Fig. 18.** Backlash should measure .005–.007 inch. If backlash is less than .005 inch, loosen side bearing nut on back side of drive gear and tighten nut on front side of gear by the same amount.
   e. When backlash has been adjusted within specifications, tighten both side bearing nuts by a half pitch to preload side bearings. **One pitch equals the space between two adjacent holes on the side of the side bearing nuts.**
   f. Install lock plate, then **torque** attaching nut to 11–15 ft. lbs.
4. On all differentials, check drive gear and drive pinion for proper tooth contact by applying marking compound to both surfaces of drive gear teeth. Insert a brass rod between carrier and case and rotate yoke end by hand one revolution in each direction, **Fig. 16,** while applying a load of approximately 2 ft. lbs., to the drive pinion. Adjust pinion height and backlash as needed until tooth contact pattern resembles standard pattern, **Fig. 17.**
5. Measure drive gear runout using dial indicator, **Fig. 19.** If runout exceeds .002 inch, change position of drive gear in differential and recheck. If runout still exceeds specification, replace drive gear or differential case as needed.

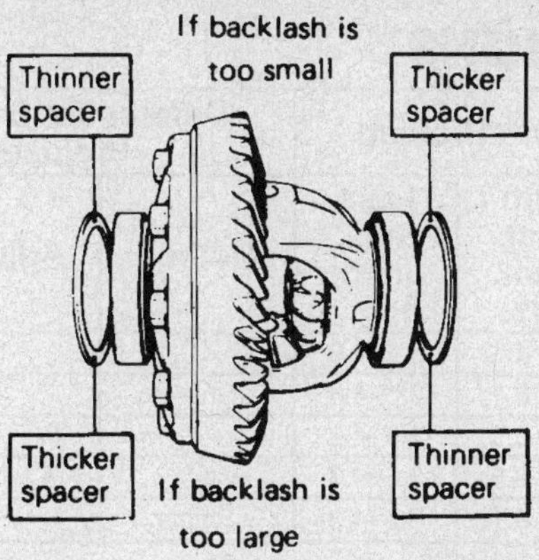
If backlash is
too small
Thinner
spacer
Thicker
spacer
Thicker
spacer
If backlash is
too large
Thinner
spacer

MT3039100049000X

Fig. 15 Drive gear backlash adjustment

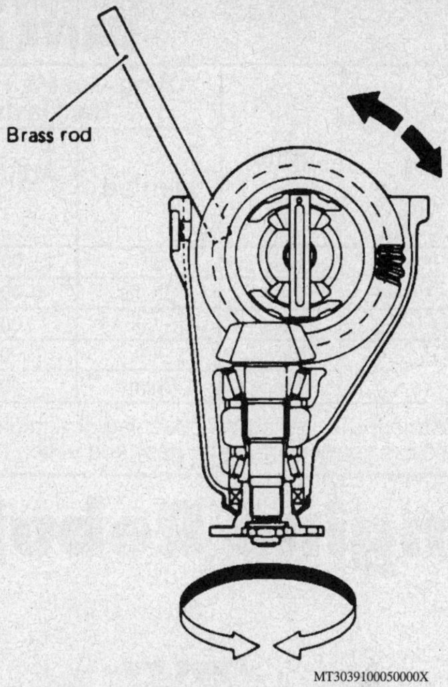
Brass rod

MT3039100050000X

Fig. 16 Gear tooth contact inspection

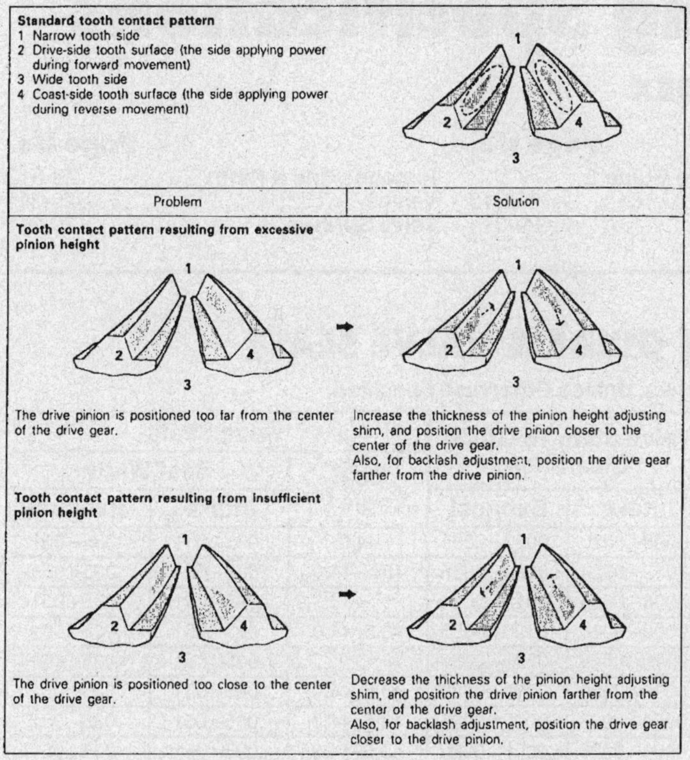
Standard tooth contact pattern
1 Narrow tooth side
2 Drive-side tooth surface (the side applying power during forward movement)
3 Wide tooth side
4 Coast-side tooth surface (the side applying power during reverse movement)
Problem
Solution
Tooth contact pattern resulting from excessive pinion height
The drive pinion is positioned too far from the center of the drive gear.
Increase the thickness of the pinion height adjusting shim, and position the drive pinion closer to the center of the drive gear.
Also, for backlash adjustment, position the drive gear farther from the drive pinion.
Tooth contact pattern resulting from insufficient pinion height
The drive pinion is positioned too close to the center of the drive gear.
Decrease the thickness of the pinion height adjusting shim, and position the drive pinion farther from the center of the drive gear.
Also, for backlash adjustment, position the drive gear closer to the drive pinion.

MT3039100051000X

Fig. 17 Gear tooth contact pattern chart

MT3039100052000X

Fig. 18 Rear differential drive gear backlash measurement

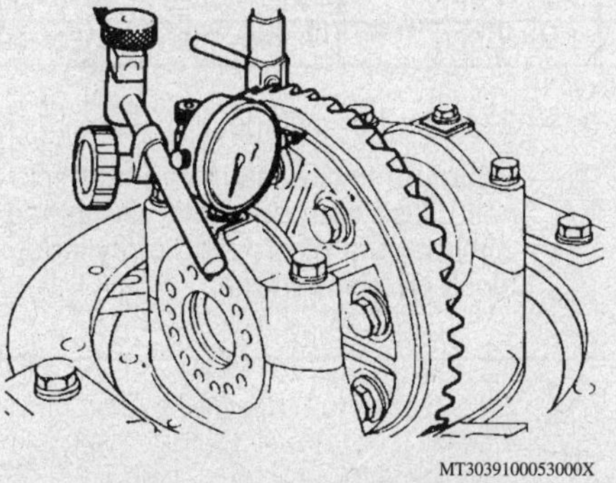

MT3039100053000X

Fig. 19 Drive gear runout measurement

DRIVE AXLE SPECIFICATIONS

Model	Axle	Ring Gear & Pinion Backlash		Pinion Bearing Preload			Differential Bearing Preload	
		Method	Adjustment, inch	Method	With Seal, Inch Lbs.	Less Seal, Inch Lbs.	Method	Adjustment
Montero	Rear	①	.005–.007	Shims	7.4–10.0	5.2–7.8	①	②
	Front	Shims	.004–.006	Shims	4.3–6.1	2.6–4.3	Shims	②
Pickup 2WD	Rear	①	.004–.006	Shims	5.6–6.5	3.5–4.3	①	②
Pickup 4WD	Rear	①	.005–.007	Shims	5.6–6.5	3.5–4.3	①	②
	Front	Shims	.004–.006	Shims	5.2–6.1	3.5–4.3	Shims	②

① — Adjustment is obtained by loosening or tightening differential side bearing adjusting nut.
② — Preload is correct when ring gear and pinion backlash is properly adjusted.

Engine Rebuilding Specifications

INDEX

	Page No.
Camshaft	29-312
Crankshaft, Bearings & Rods	29-312
Cylinder Block	29-313
Cylinder Head, Valve Guide & Valve Seats	29-310
Oil Pump	29-314
Pistons, Pins & Rings	29-313
Valves	29-311
Valve Springs	29-311

CYLINDER HEAD, VALVE GUIDE & VALVE SEATS

All Measurements Given In Inches, Unless Otherwise Specified.

Engine	Year	Cylinder Head Warpage Limit	Cylinder Head Overall Thickness⑤	Valve Stem To Guide Clearance		Valve Seats		
				Intake	Exhaust	Seat Angle (°)	Seat Width Intake	Seat Width Exhaust
1.5L	1993–96	.008	4.209–4.217	.0008–.0020	.0020–.0035	44.0	.035–.051	.035–.051
1.8L	1993–94④	.008	3.480–3.488	.0012–.0024	.0020–.0035	43.5–44.0	.035–.051	.035–.051
	1993–96①	.008	4.720–4.728	.0008–.0016	.0012–.0024	—	.035–.051	.035–.051
2.0L DOHC	1993–96⑥	.008	5.193–5.201	.0008–.0020	.0020–.0035	43.5–44.0	.035–.051	.035–.051
	1995–96⑦	.004	—	.0019–.0026	.0029–.0037	45.0	.035–.051	.035–.051
2.0L SOHC	1993	.008	4.720–4.728	.0008–.0020	.0008–.0028	43.5–44.0	.035–.051	.035–.051
2.4L DOHC	1994–95	.008	5.193–5.201	.0008–.0020	.0020–.0035	43.5–44.0	.035–.051	.035–.051
2.4L SOHC	1993–96①	.008	4.720–4.728	.0008–.0020	.0008–.0028	43.5–44.0	.035–.051	.035–.051
	1993–96④	.008	3.539–3.547	.0008–.0024	.0020–.0035	43.5–44.0	.035–.051	.035–.051
3.0L DOHC	1993–96	.008	5.200	.0008–.0020	.0020–.0035	30.0	.035–.051	.035–.051
3.0L SOHC	1993–96②	.008	3.310	.0012–.0024	.0020–.0035	30.0	.035–.051	.035–.051
	1993–96③	.008	4.720	.0008–.0020	.0016–.0028	30.0	.035–.051	.035–.051
3.5L	1994–96	.008	5.200	.0008–.0020	.0020–.0035	30.0	.035–.051	.035–.051

DOHC: Dual Overhead Cam
SOHC: Single Overhead Cam
① — 4 valves per cylinder.
② — Montero w/12 valve engine, Diamante & Pickup.
③ — Montero w/24 valve engine.
④ — 2 valves per cylinder.
⑤ — Minimum thickness is overall thickness, less warpage limit, combined with amount of grinding of cylinder block gasket surface.
⑥ — Except 1995–96 Eclipse w/non-turbocharged engine.
⑦ — Eclipse w/non-turbocharged engine.

VALVE SPRINGS

All Measurements Given In Inches, Unless Otherwise Specified.

Engine	Year	Free Length		Installed Height	Seated Pressure, Lbs.		Out Of Square Limit (°)
		Intake	Exhaust		Intake	Exhaust	
1.5L	1993–96	1.820	1.840	1.570	51.0	64.0	4
1.8L	1993–94③	1.940	1.940	1.470	68.0	68.0	4
	1993–96①	2.000	2.000	1.740	49.0	49.0	4
2.0L DOHC	1993–94	1.900	1.900	1.570	66.0	66.0	4
	1995–96②	1.850	1.850	1.570	54.0	54.0	4
	1995–96④	1.811	1.811	1.496	55.0–60.0	55.0–60.0	—
2.0L SOHC	1993	2.010	2.010	1.740	60.0	60.0	4
2.4L DOHC	1994–95	1.850	1.850	1.570	54.0	54.0	4
2.4L SOHC	1993–96③	1.960	1.960	1.590	73.0	73.0	4
	1993–96①	2.010	2.010	1.740	60.0	60.0	4
3.0L DOHC	1993–96	1.830	1.830	1.492	52.9	52.9	4
3.0L SOHC	1993–96⑤	1.960	1.960	1.591	72.5	72.5	4
	1993–96⑥	2.010	2.010	1.740	60.0	60.0	4
3.5L	1994–96	1.830	1.830	1.492	52.9	52.9	4

DOHC: Dual Overhead Cam
SOHC: Single Overhead Cam
① — 4 valves per cylinder.
② — Except 1995–96 Eclipse w/non-turbocharged engine.
③ — 2 valves per cylinder.
④ — Eclipse w/non-turbocharged engine.
⑤ — Montero w/12 valve engine, Diamante & Pickup.
⑥ — Montero w/24 valve engine.

VALVES

All Measurements Given In Inches, Unless Otherwise Specified.

Engine	Year	Stem Diameter		Face Angle (°)	Margin		Clearance③	
		Intake	Exhaust		Intake	Exhaust	Intake	Exhaust
1.5L	1993–96	.260	.256	45.0–45.5	.039	.059	.004	.007
1.8L	1993–94⑥	.315	.315	45.0–45.5	.047	.059	⑧	⑧
	1993–96①	.236	.236	45.0–45.5	.039	.051	.004	.008
2.0L DOHC	1993–96②	.315	.311	45.0–45.5	.039	.059	⑧	⑧
	1995–96④	.233–.234	.233	44.5–45.0	.050–.063	.038–.050	⑧	⑧
2.0L SOHC	1993	.260	.256	45.0–45.5	.039	.047	⑧	⑧
2.4L DOHC	1994–95	.315	.311	45.0–45.5	.039	.059	⑧	⑧
2.4L SOHC	1993–96⑥	.236	.232	45.0–45.5	.047	.079	⑧	⑧
	1993–96①	.260	.256	45.0–45.5	.039	.047	⑧	⑧
3.0L DOHC	1993–96	.260	.256	45.0–45.5	.039	.059	⑧	⑧
3.0L SOHC	1993–96⑤	.315	.311	45.0–45.5	.047	.079	⑧	⑧
	1993–96⑦	.236	.236	45.0–45.5	.039	.047	⑧	⑧
3.5L	1994–96	.260	.256	45.0–45.5	.039	.059	⑧	⑧

DOHC: Dual Overhead Cam
SOHC: Single Overhead Cam
① — 4 valves per cylinder.
② — Except 1995–96 Eclipse w/non-turbocharged engine.
③ — Cold engine.
④ — 1995–96 Eclipse w/non-turbocharged engine.
⑤ — Montero w/12 valve engine, Diamante & Pickup.
⑥ — 2 valves per cylinder.
⑦ — Montero w/24 valve engine.
⑧ — Equipped w/hydraulic lash adjusters. No provision for adjustment.

CAMSHAFT

All Measurements Given In Inches, Unless Otherwise Specified.

Engine	Year	Camshaft Endplay	Bearing Bore Diameter	Bearing Clearance	Cam Height		Journal Diameter
					Intake	Exhaust	
1.5L	1993–96	—	—	—	1.53	1.54	1.8100
1.8L	1993–94④	—	—	—	1.41	1.41	1.3400
	1993–95①②	—	—	—	1.49	1.77	1.7700
	1993–96①③	—	—	—	1.48	1.77	1.7700
2.0L DOHC	1993–96⑤	—	—	—	⑦	⑧	1.0200
	1995–96⑥	.006	1.024–1.025	.0027–.0028	—	—	1.0217–1.0224
2.0L SOHC	1993	—	—	—	1.47	1.48	1.7700
2.4L DOHC	1994–95	—	—	—	⑦	⑧	1.0200
2.4L SOHC	1993–96④	—	—	—	1.67	1.67	1.3400
	1993–96①	—	—	—	1.47	1.48	1.7700
3.0L DOHC	1993–96	—	—	—	1.37	1.37	1.0200
3.0L SOHC	1993–96⑨	—	—	—	1.62	1.60	1.3400
	1993–96⑩	—	—	—	1.48	1.45	1.7700
3.5L	1994–96	—	—	—	1.37	1.39	1.0200

DOHC: Dual Overhead Cam
SOHC: Single Overhead Cam
① — 4 valves per cylinder.
② — 1993 Expo w/Federal emissions & Mirage.
③ — 1993 Expo w/California emissions, 1994–95 Expo & 1994–96 Mirage.
④ — 2 valves per cylinder.
⑤ — Except 1995–96 Eclipse w/2.0L non-turbocharged engine.
⑥ — Eclipse w/2.0L non-turbocharged engine.
⑦ — Identification marks A & D, 1.40 inch; marks B, E & K, 1.39 inch; mark J, 1.37 inch.
⑧ — Identification mark A, 1.39 inch; mark C, 1.40 inch; marks H & J, 1.37 inch.
⑨ — Montero w/12 valve engine, Diamante & Pickup.
⑩ — Montero w/24 valve engine.

CRANKSHAFT, BEARINGS & RODS

All Measurements Given In Inches, Unless Otherwise Specified.

Engine	Year	Crankshaft				Bearing Clearance		Connecting Rod Side Clearance
		Standard Journal Diameter		Out of Round (All)	Taper (All)	Main Bearing	Connecting Rod Bearings	
		Main Bearing	Crank Pin					
1.5L	1993–96	1.8900	1.6500	.0002	.0002	.0008–.0020	.0008–.0020	.0039–.0098
1.8L	1993–94①	2.2400	1.7700	.0004	.0004	.0008–.0020	.0008–.0020	.0039–.0098
	1993–96④	1.9700	1.7700	.0002	.0002	.0008–.0016	.0008–.0020	.0039–.0098
2.0L	1993–96②	2.2400	1.7700	.0004	.0004	.0008–.0020	.0008–.0020	.0039–.0098
	1995–96③	2.0469–2.0475	1.8894–1.8900	.0001	.0001	.0008–.0024	.0010–.0023	.0051–.0150
2.4L	1993–96	2.2400	1.7700	.0004	.0004	.0008–.0020	.0008–.0020	.0039–.0098
3.0L DOHC	1993–96	2.3600	1.9700	.0001	.0001	.0008–.0020	.0008–.0020	.0039–.0098
3.0L SOHC	1993–96	2.3600	1.9700	.0002	.0002	.0008–.0020	.0008–.0020	.0039–.0098
3.5L	1994–96	2.5200	2.1700	.0001	.0001	.0008–.0020	.0012–.0020	.0039–.0098

DOHC: Dual Overhead Cam
SOHC: Single Overhead Cam
① — 2 valves per cylinder.
② — Except 1995–96 Eclipse w/2.0L non-turbocharged engine.
③ — Eclipse w/2.0L non-turbocharged engine.
④ — 4 valves per cylinder.

PISTONS, PINS & RINGS

All Measurements Given In Inches, Unless Otherwise Specified.

Engine	Year	Piston Diameter (Std.)	Piston Clearance	Piston Ring End Gap			Compression Ring Side Clearance	
				Compression		Oil		
				No. 1	No. 2		No. 1	No. 2
1.5L	1993–96	2.9700	.0008–.0016	.0079–.0157	.0079–.0138	.0079–.0276	.0012–.0028	.0008–.0024
1.8L	1993–94②	3.1700	.0004–.0012	.0118–.0177	.0079–.0138	.0079–.0276	.0020–.0035	.0008–.0024
	1993–96④	3.1900	.0008–.0016	.0098–.0157	.0157–.0217	.0079–.0236	.0012–.0028	.0008–.0024
2.0L DOHC	1993–96①⑤	3.3500	.0008–.0016	.0098–.0157	.0177–.0236	.0051–.0150	.0008–.0024	.0008–.0024
	1993–94⑥	3.3500	.0012–.0020	.0098–.0157	.0177–.0236	.0051–.0150	.0012–.0028	.0008–.0024
	1995–96⑥	3.3500	.0012–.0020	.0098–.0138	.0157–.0217	.0039–.0157	.0016–.0031	.0008–.0024
	1995–96①③	3.4434–3.4441	.0005–.0017	.0090–.0200	.0190–.0310	.0090–.0260	.0010–.0026	.0010–.0026
2.0L SOHC	1993	3.3500	.0004–.0012	.0098–.0138	.0157–.0236	.0079–.0236	.0008–.0024	.0008–.0024
2.4L DOHC	1994–95	3.4100	—	.0098–.0138	.0177–.0217	.0039–.0157	.0012–.0028	.0012–.0028
2.4L SOHC	1993–96②	3.4100	.0008–.0016	.0098–.0157	.0157–.0236	.0079–.0236	.0012–.0028	.0012–.0028
	1993–96④	3.4100	.0008–.0016	.0098–.0138	.0157–.0236	.0079–.0236	.0012–.0028	.0012–.0028
3.0L	1993–96	3.5800	.0008–.0020	.0118–.0177	.0177–.0236	.0079–.0236	.0012–.0028	.0008–.0024
3.5L	1994–96	3.6600	.0012–.0020	.0118–.0177	.0177–.0236	.0039–.0137	.0012–.0028	.0008–.0024

DOHC: Dual Overhead Cam
SOHC: Single Overhead Cam
① — Non-turbocharged.
② — 2 valves per cylinder.
③ — Eclipse.
④ — 4 valves per cylinder.
⑤ — Except 1995–96 Eclipse.
⑥ — Turbocharged.

CYLINDER BLOCK

All Measurements Given In Inches, Unless Otherwise Specified.

Engine	Year	Cylinder Bore Diameter (Std.)	Cylinder Bore Taper (Max.)	Cylinder Bore Out of Round (Max.)
1.5L	1993–96	2.9700	.0004	.0004
1.8L	1993–94①	3.1730–3.1740	.0004	.0004
	1993–96④	3.1900	.0004	.0004
2.0L	1993–96②	3.3500	.0004	.0004
	1995–96③	3.4450	.0020	.0020
2.4L	1993–96	3.4100	.0004	.0004
3.0L	1993–96	3.5900	.0004	.0004
3.5L	1994–96	3.6600	.0004	.0004

DOHC: Dual Overhead Cam
SOHC: Single Overhead Cam
① — 2 valves per cylinder.
② — Except 1995–96 Eclipse w/non-turbocharged engine.
③ — Eclipse w/non-turbocharged engine.
④ — 4 valves per cylinder.
⑤ — Turbocharged.

OIL PUMP

All Measurements Given In Inches, Unless Otherwise Specified.

Engine	Year	Tip Clearance	Side Clearance		Body Clearance
			Drive Gear	Driven Gear	
1.5L	1993–96	.0024–.0071	.0016–.0039	.0016–.0039	.0039–.0071
1.8L	1993–94④	—	.0031–.0055	.0024–.0047	—
	1993–96⑤	.0024–.0071	.0016–.0039	.0016–.0039	.0039–.0071
2.0L	1993–96①	—	.0031–.0055	.0024–.0047	
	1995–96②	.0008③	—	—	—
2.4L	1993–96	—	.0031–.0055	.0024–.0047	—
3.0L	1993–96	.0024–.0071	.0016–.0039	.0016–.0039	.0039–.0071
3.5L	1994–96	.0024–.0071	.0016–.0039	.0016–.0039	.0039–.0071

① — Except 1995–96 Eclipse w/non-turbocharged engine.
② — Eclipse w/non-turbocharged engine.
③ — Limit.
④ — 2 valves per cylinder.
⑤ — 4 valves per cylinder.

Page No.

NISSAN:

VEHICLE SERVICE:

NX 1600/2000, Sentra & 200SX . . . 30-1

Maxima & 300ZX 31-1

Altima & Stanza 32-1

240SX 33-1

Quest 34-1

Pathfinder & Pickup 35-1

UNIT REPAIR 36-1

PORSCHE 37-1

SAAB 38-1

SUBARU 39-1

GENERAL INFORMATION

Manual Information Locator, Inside Rear Cover

Vehicle Identification 0-1

Air Bag System Precautions 0-8

Service Reminder & Warning Lamp Reset Procedures 0-10

Vehicle Lift Points 0-34

Vehicle Maintenance Schedules 0-69

Electrical Symbol & Wire Color Code Identification 0-139

Page No.

NISSAN:

VEHICLE SERVICE:

NX 1600/2000, Sentra & 200SX . . . 30-1

Maxima & 300ZX 31-1

Altima & Stanza 32-1

240SX 33-1

Quest 34-1

Pathfinder & Pickup 35-1

UNIT REPAIR 36-1

PORSCHE 37-1

SAAB 38-1

SUBARU 39-1

GENERAL INFORMATION

Manual Information Locator, Inside Rear Cover

Vehicle Identification 0-1

Air Bag System Precautions 0-8

Service Reminder & Warning Lamp Reset Procedures 0-10

Vehicle Lift Points 0-34

Vehicle Maintenance Schedules 0-69

Electrical Symbol & Wire Color Code Identification 0-139

NISSAN NX 1600, NX 2000, SENTRA & 200SX

INDEX OF SERVICE OPERATIONS

Page No.

AIR BAG SYSTEM PRECAUTIONS 0-8
AUTOMATIC TRANSMISSIONS/ TRANSAXLES 36-1
BRAKES
- Anti-Lock Brakes 36-1
- Disc Brakes 36-1
- Drum Brakes 36-1
- Hydraulic Brake Systems 36-1
- Power Brake Units 36-1

CLUTCH & MANUAL TRANSAXLE
- Adjustments 30-28
- Clutch, Replace 30-28
- Clutch Pedal Adjustment Specifications 30-29
- Tightening Specifications 30-29
- Transaxle, Replace 30-28

ELECTRICAL
- Air Bags 36-1
- Air Conditioning 36-1
- Alternators 36-1
- Blower Motor, Replace 30-6
- Combination Switch, Replace . 30-5
- Cooling Fans 36-1
- Cruise Control 36-1
- Dash Gauges 36-1
- Dash Panels 36-1
- Distributor, Replace 30-4
- Evaporator Core, Replace 30-6
- Fuel Pump Relay Location 30-4
- Fuse Panel & Flasher Location 30-4
- Headlamp Switch, Replace ... 30-5
- Heater Core, Replace 30-6
- Ignition Lock, Replace 30-4
- Ignition Switch, Replace 30-4
- Instrument Cluster, Replace ... 30-6
- Neutral Safety Switch, Replace 30-5
- Passive Restraints 36-1
- Precautions 30-4
- Radio, Replace 30-6
- Relay Center Location 30-4
- Speed Controls 36-1
- Starter Motors 36-1
- Starter, Replace 30-4
- Steering Columns 36-1
- Steering Wheel, Replace 30-5
- Stop Light Switch, Replace ... 30-5
- Turn Signal Switch, Replace .. 30-5
- Wiper Motor, Replace 30-6
- Wiper Switch, Replace 30-6
- Wiper Systems 36-1

ELECTRICAL SYMBOL IDENTIFICATION 0-139

Page No.

FRONT SUSPENSION & STEERING
- Ball Joint Inspection 30-32
- Coil Spring, Replace 30-32
- Driveshaft, Replace 30-32
- Manual Steering Gears 36-1
- Manual Steering Gear, Replace 30-33
- Power Steering 36-1
- Power Steering Gear, Replace 30-32
- Power Steering Pump, Replace 30-33
- Stabilizer Bar, Replace 30-32
- Strut, Replace 30-32
- Tightening Specifications 30-35
- Transverse Link, Replace 30-32
- Wheel Bearing Inspection 30-32
- Wheel Hub & Steering Knuckle, Replace 30-32

FRONT WHEEL DRIVE AXLES 36-1

GA16DE ENGINE
- Belt Tension Data 30-13
- Component Service 30-9
- Compression Pressure 30-8
- Cooling System Bleed 30-13
- Crankshaft Rear Oil Seal, Replace 30-13
- Cylinder Head, Replace 30-8
- Engine Assemble 30-9
- Engine Disassemble 30-8
- Engine Mount, Replace 30-8
- Engine Rebuilding Specifications 36-1
- Engine, Replace 30-8
- Exhaust Manifold, Replace 30-8
- Front Cover Seal, Replace 30-11
- Fuel Filter, Replace 30-14
- Fuel Pump, Replace 30-13
- Intake Manifold, Replace 30-8
- Oil Pan, Replace 30-13
- Precautions 30-7
- Radiator, Replace 30-13
- Thermostat, Replace 30-13
- Tightening Specifications 30-15
- Timing Chain, Replace 30-11
- Valve Adjustment 30-10
- Valve Clearance Specifications 30-10
- Water Pump, Replace 30-13

REAR AXLE & SUSPENSION
- Coil Spring, Replace 30-30
- Hub & Bearing, Replace 30-30
- Precautions 30-30
- Rear Axle, Replace 30-30
- Stabilizer Bar, Replace 30-30
- Strut, Replace 30-30

Page No.

- Tightening Specifications 30-31
- Wheel Bearing Inspection 30-30

SERVICE REMINDER & WARNING LAMP RESET PROCEDURES 0-10

SPECIFICATIONS
- Fluid Capacities & Cooling System Data 30-3
- Front Wheel Alignment Specifications 30-2
- General Engine Specifications 30-2
- Lubricant Data 30-3
- Rear Wheel Alignment Specifications 30-3
- Tune Up Specifications 30-2

SR20DE ENGINE
- Accel-Drum Unit, Adjust 30-21
- Belt Tension Data 30-21
- Component Service 30-17
- Compression Pressure 30-16
- Cooling System Bleed 30-21
- Crankshaft Rear Oil Seal, Replace 30-20
- Cylinder Head, Replace 30-16
- Engine Assemble 30-17
- Engine Disassemble 30-16
- Engine Mount, Replace 30-16
- Engine Rebuilding Specifications 36-1
- Engine, Replace 30-16
- Exhaust Manifold, Replace 30-16
- Front Cover Seal, Replace 30-19
- Fuel Filter, Replace 30-22
- Fuel Pump, Replace 30-22
- Intake Manifold, Replace 30-16
- Oil Pan, Replace 30-20
- Oil Pump, Replace 30-21
- Precautions 30-16
- Radiator, Replace 30-22
- Thermostat, Replace 30-22
- Tightening Specifications 30-26
- Timing Chain, Replace 30-19
- Valve Adjustment 30-19
- Valve Clearance Specifications 30-19
- Water Pump, Replace 30-22

VEHICLE IDENTIFICATION. 0-1
VEHICLE LIFT POINTS 0-34
VEHICLE MAINTENANCE SCHEDULES 0-69
WHEEL ALIGNMENT 30-35
- Front Wheel Alignment 30-35
- Preliminary Inspection 30-35
- Rear Wheel Alignment 30-36
- Vehicle Ride Height 30-36
- Wheel Alignment Specifications 30-2

WIRE COLOR CODE IDENTIFICATION 0-144

Specifications

GENERAL ENGINE SPECIFICATIONS

Year	Engine Model	Fuel System	Displacement, Liters	Bore x Stroke, Inches (mm)	Compression Ratio	Maximum H.P. @ RPM	Maximum Torque @ RPM	Normal Oil Pressure, psi
1993	GA16DE	TBI	1.6L	2.99 x 3.47 (76 x 88)	9.5	110 @ 6000	108 @ 4000	②
	SR20DE	TBI	2.0L	3.39 x 3.39 (86 x 86)	9.5	140 @ 6400	132 @ 4800	①
1994	GA16DE	MFI	1.6L	2.99 x 3.47 (76 x 88)	9.5	110 @ 6000	108 @ 4000	②
	SR20DE	MFI	2.0L	3.39 x 3.39 (86 x 86)	9.5	140 @ 6400	132 @ 4800	①
1995–96	GA16DE	MFI	1.6L	2.99 x 3.47 (76 x 88)	9.9	115 @ 6000	108 @ 4000	②
	SR20DE	MFI	2.0L	3.39 x 3.39 (86 x 86)	9.5	140 @ 6400	132 @ 4800	①

① — 46–57 psi at 3200 RPM.
② — 50–64 psi at 3000 RPM.

TUNE UP SPECIFICATIONS

Year	Engine Model	Spark Plug Gap, Inch	Ignition Timing		Curb Idle Speed		Fuel Pump Pressure, psi	Valve Lash
			Firing Order	Timing, °BTDC	Man. Trans.	Auto. Trans.①		
1993–94	GA16DE	.041	1-3-4-2	10	650	800N	36	②
	SR20DE	.033	1-3-4-2	15	800	800N	36	②
1995–96	GA16DE	.041	1-3-4-2	8	675	800N	36	②
	SR20DE	.033	1-3-4-2	15	800	800N	36	②

BTDC — Before Top Dead Center
D — Drive.
N — Neutral.

① — When adjusting idle speed, set parking brake & chock drive wheels.

② — Refer to "Valve Adjustment" under specific engine section for valve lash adjustment procedure.

FRONT WHEEL ALIGNMENT SPECIFICATIONS

Year	Model	Caster Angle, Deg.		Camber Angle, Deg.		Kingpin Inclination, Deg.	Toe-In, Inch①	Toe-Out On Turns, Deg.②		Ball Joint
		Limits	Desired	Limits	Desired			Inner Wheel	Outer Wheel	
1993	NX 1600/ 2000	$+1\frac{1}{12}$ to $+2\frac{7}{12}$	$+1\frac{5}{6}$	-1 to $+\frac{1}{2}$	$-\frac{1}{4}$	$+13\frac{1}{4}$ to $+14\frac{3}{4}$	+.04 to +.12	④	⑤	⑧
	Sentra Coupe	$+1\frac{1}{12}$ to $+2\frac{7}{12}$	$+1\frac{5}{6}$	-1 to $+\frac{1}{2}$	$-\frac{1}{4}$	$+13\frac{1}{4}$ to $+14\frac{3}{4}$	+.04 to +.12	④	⑤	⑧
	Sentra Sedan	$+\frac{2}{3}$ to $+2\frac{1}{6}$	$+1\frac{5}{12}$	-1 to $+\frac{1}{2}$	$-\frac{1}{4}$	$+13\frac{1}{4}$ to $+14\frac{3}{4}$	+.04 to +.12	④	③	⑧
1994–95	Sentra	$+\frac{2}{3}$ to $+2\frac{1}{6}$	$+1\frac{5}{12}$	-1 to $+\frac{1}{2}$	$-\frac{1}{4}$	$+13\frac{1}{4}$ to $+14\frac{3}{4}$	+.04 to +.12	④	③	⑧
1995	200SX	$+\frac{2}{3}$ to $+2\frac{1}{6}$	$+1\frac{5}{12}$	-1 to $+\frac{1}{2}$	$-\frac{1}{4}$	$+13\frac{1}{4}$ to $+14\frac{3}{4}$	+.04 to +.12	④	③	⑧
1996	Sentra & 200SX	$+\frac{2}{3}$ to $+2\frac{1}{6}$	$+1\frac{5}{12}$	$-1\frac{1}{3}$ to $+\frac{1}{6}$	$-\frac{7}{12}$	+14 to $+15\frac{1}{2}$	0 to +.16	⑥	⑦	⑧

① — Toe-in (+); toe-out (-).

② — Measure w/wheels @ full lefthand & righthand turn positions.

③ — Models w/GA16DE engine, +34; models w/SR20DE engine, +30.

④ — Models w/GA16DE engine, +39 to +43; models w/SR20DE engine, +33 to +37.

⑤ — Models w/GA16DE engine, +33; models w/SR20DE engine, +30.

⑥ — Models w/manual steering, +38 to +42; models w/power steering, +34 to +38.

⑦ — Models w/manual steering, +34; models w/power steering, +31.

⑧ — Refer to "Front Suspension & Steering" under "Ball Joint Inspection" for inspection procedure.

REAR WHEEL ALIGNMENT SPECIFICATIONS

Year	Model	Camber Angle, Deg.		Toe, Inch①
		Limits	Desired	
1993	NX 1600/2000	–1 11/12 to –5/12	–1 1/6	–.04 to +.12
	Sentra Coupe	–1 11/12 to –5/12	–1 1/6	–.04 to +.12
	Sentra Sedan	–1 2/3 to –1/6	–11/12	–.04 to +.12
1994–95	Sentra	–1 2/3 to –1/6	–11/12	–.04 to +.12
1995	200SX	-1 3/4 to -1/4	-1	-.04 to +.12
1996	Sentra & 200SX	-1 3/4 to -1/4	-1	-.12 to +.20
				-.15 to +.25

① — Toe-in (+); toe-out (-).

FLUID CAPACITIES & COOLING SYSTEM DATA

Year	Model	Coolant Capacity, Qts.	Radiator Cap Relief Pressure, Lbs.	Thermo. Opening Temp., °F	Fuel Tank, Gals.	Engine Oil Refill, Qts.①	Transmission Oil		Differential Oil, Pts.
							Man. Trans., Pts.	Auto. Trans., Qts.②	
1993	Sentra/NX 1600 GA16DE	③	11–14	170	13 1/4	3 3/8	6 1/8	7 3/8	—
	Sentra/NX 2000 SR20DE	④	11–14	170	13 1/4	3 5/8	7 5/8	7 3/8	—
1994	Sentra GA16DE	③	11–14	170	13 1/4	3 3/8	6 1/8	7 3/8	—
	Sentra SR20DE	④	11–14	170	13 1/4	3 5/8	7 5/8	7 3/8	—
1995–96	Sentra &200SX w/GA16DE	⑤	11-14	170	14	3 3/8	6 3/8	7 3/8	—
	Sentra &200SX w/SR20DE	⑥	11-14	170	14	3 5/8	8	7 3/8	—

① — Includes filter.

② — Approximate, make final check w/dipstick.

③ — Man. trans., 5 3/8 qts., auto. trans., 5 5/8 qts.

④ — Man. trans., 5 7/8 qts., auto. trans., 6 1/8 qts.

⑤ — Man. trans., 6 1/4 qts.; auto. trans., 5 5/8 qts.

⑥ — Man. trans., 6 1/2 qts.; auto. trans., 7 qts.

LUBRICANT DATA

Year	Model	Lubricant Type					
		Transaxle		Transfer Case	Rear Axle	Power Steering	Brake System
		Manual	Automatic				
1993–96	All	80W-90 API GL-4	Nissan Matic D ①	—	—	Dexron II/IIE/III	DOT 3

① — Dexron III/Mercon or equivalent automatic transmission fluid may also be used.

Electrical

NOTE: On Air Bag Equipped Models, Refer To "Air Bag System Precautions" Located In The Front Of This Manual For System Disarming & Arming Procedures.

INDEX

	Page No.
Air Bags	36-1
Air Conditioning	36-1
Alternators	36-1
Blower Motor, Replace	30-6
1993–94	30-6
1995–96	30-6
Combination Switch, Replace	30-5
Cooling Fans	36-1
Cruise Control	36-1
Dash Gauges	36-1
Dash Panels	36-1
Distributor, Replace	30-4
Evaporator Core, Replace	30-6
1993–94	30-6
1995–96	30-6
Fuel Pump Relay Location	30-4
Fuse Panel & Flasher Location	30-4
Headlamp Switch, Replace	30-5
Heater Core, Replace	30-6
1993–94	30-6
1995–96	30-6
Ignition Lock, Replace	30-4
Ignition Switch, Replace	30-4
Instrument Cluster, Replace	30-6
Neutral Safety Switch, Replace	30-5
Passive Restraints	36-1
Precautions	30-4
Air Bag Systems	30-4
Radio, Replace	30-6
Relay Center Location	30-4
Speed Controls	36-1
Starter Motors	36-1
Starter, Replace	30-4
Steering Columns	36-1
Steering Wheel, Replace	30-5
Models Less Air Bag	30-6
Models w/Air Bag	30-5
Stop Light Switch, Replace	30-5
Turn Signal Switch, Replace	30-5
Wiper Motor, Replace	30-6
Front	30-6
Rear	30-6
Wiper Switch, Replace	30-6
Front	30-6
Rear	30-6
Wiper System	36-1

PRECAUTIONS

AIR BAG SYSTEMS

Refer to "Air Bag System Precautions" in the front of this manual for system disarming and arming procedures.

FUSE PANEL & FLASHER LOCATION

The fuse panel is located under the lefthand side of the instrument panel, to the left of the steering column.

The combination flasher unit is located behind the center of the instrument panel, to the left of the radio.

FUEL PUMP RELAY LOCATION

The fuel pump relay is located behind the lefthand side of the instrument panel, to the left of the steering column.

RELAY CENTER LOCATION

The primary engine compartment relay box is located on the righthand side of the engine compartment, near the washer fluid reservoir. Two secondary relay boxes are located in the front lefthand side of the engine compartment, on either side of the battery.

STARTER

REPLACE

1. Disconnect battery ground cable.
2. Remove air intake duct.

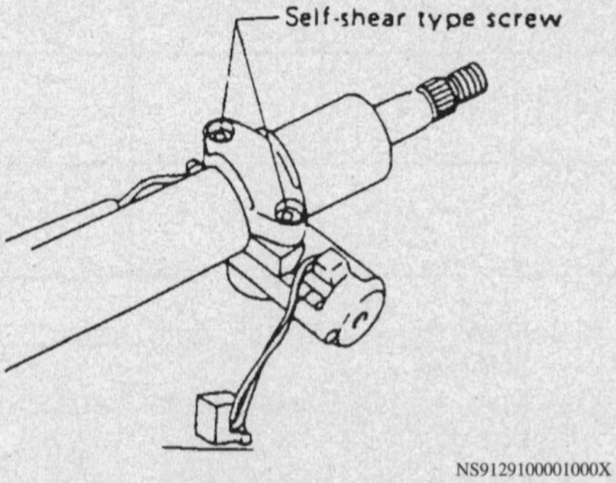
Self-shear type screw
NS9129100001000X

Fig. 1 Ignition lock replacement

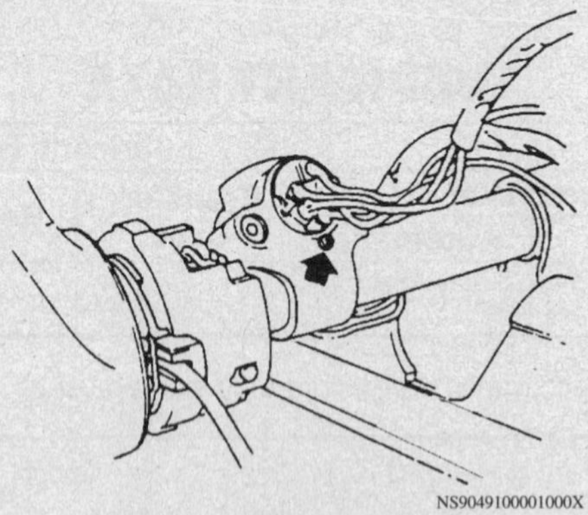
NS9049100001000X

Fig. 2 Ignition switch replacement

3. Disconnect starter wiring from starter.
4. Remove starter retaining bolts, then the starter as follows:
   a. **On GA16DE engine with automatic transaxle,** remove starter from engine side.
   b. **On GA16DE engine with manual transaxle,** remove starter from transaxle side.
   c. **On SR20DE engine,** raise and support vehicle and remove starter from under the vehicle.
5. **On all models,** reverse procedure to install. **Torque** starter motor mounting bolts to 23–31 ft. lbs.

DISTRIBUTOR

REPLACE

1. Disconnect battery ground cable.
2. Position engine No. 1 cylinder at TDC.
3. Remove distributor cap and cables, then position aside.
4. Disconnect distributor electrical connections.
5. Remove distributor flange retaining nuts.
6. Remove distributor.
7. Reverse procedure to install. Ensure distributor rotor is pointing toward No. 1 cylinder spark position.

IGNITION LOCK

REPLACE

1. Tighten ignition lock shear type retaining screws until the screw heads break off, **Fig. 1.**
2. Remove ignition lock.
3. Drill out remaining part of screws.
4. Reverse procedure to install, using shear type screws.

IGNITION SWITCH

REPLACE

1. Remove four upper and lower shell cover retaining screws, then the shell covers.

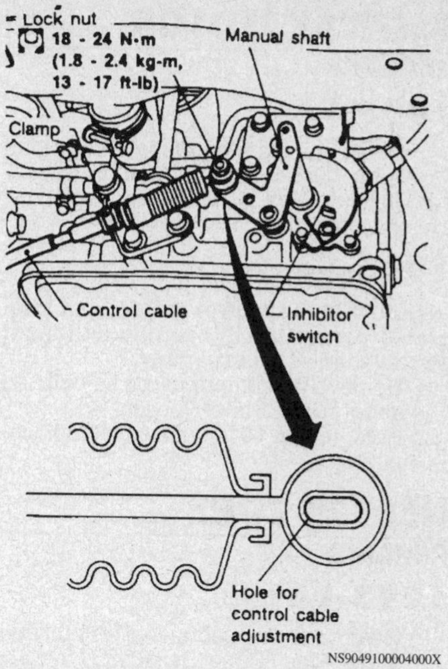
Lock nut
18 - 24 N·m
(1.8 - 2.4 kg-m,
13 - 17 ft-lb)
Manual shaft
Clamp
Control cable
Inhibitor
switch
Hole for
control cable
adjustment
NS9049100004000X

Fig. 3 Control cable adjustment

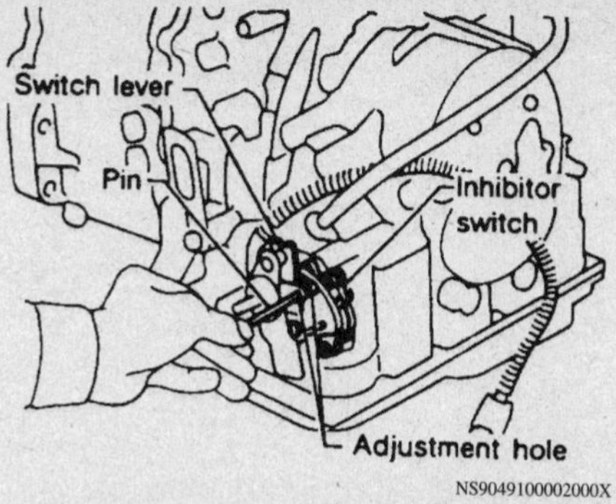
Switch lever
Pin
Inhibitor
switch
Adjustment hole
NS9049100002000X

Fig. 4 Inhibitor switch adjustment

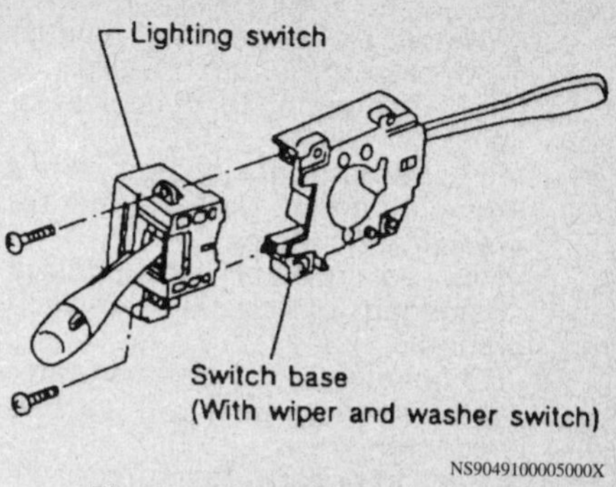
Lighting switch
Switch base
(With wiper and washer switch)
NS9049100005000X

Fig. 5 Headlamp switch replacement

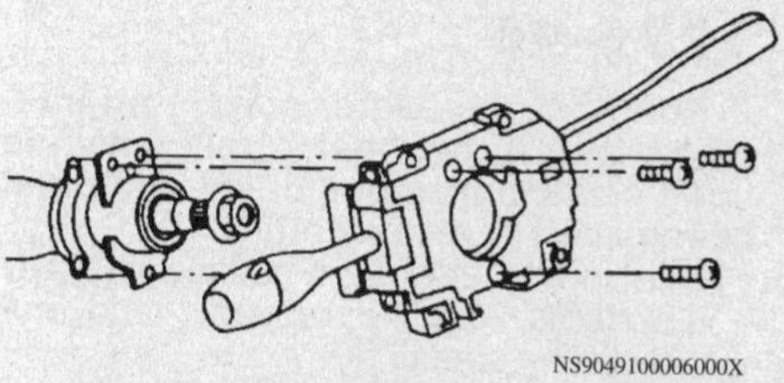
NS9049100006000X

Fig. 6 Combination switch replacement

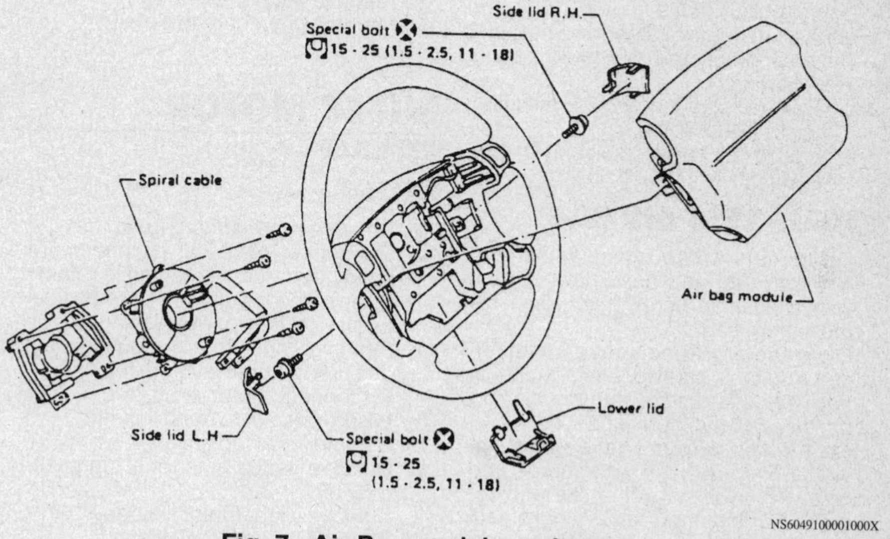
Side lid R.H.
Special bolt
15 - 25 (1.5 - 2.5, 11 - 18)
Spiral cable
Air bag module
Lower lid
Side lid L.H
Special bolt
15 - 25
(1.5 - 2.5, 11 - 18)
NS6049100001000X

Fig. 7 Air Bag module replacement

2. Disconnect electrical connectors from switch.
3. Remove switch retaining screw from steering lock, **Fig. 2.**
4. Remove switch.
5. Reverse procedure to install.

NEUTRAL SAFETY SWITCH

REPLACE

1. Remove control cable end from manual shaft, **Fig. 3.**
2. Set manual shaft in "N" range, then loosen inhibitor switch fixing bolts.
3. Insert a .157 inch (3.9 mm) pin into adjustment hole in both inhibitor switch and manual shaft as vertically as possible, **Fig. 4.**
4. **On all transaxles,** tighten inhibitor switch fixing bolts.
5. Remove pin from adjustment hole, then adjust control cable as follows:
   a. Place selector in "P" position.
   b. Loosen control cable locknut, then place manual shaft in "P" position.
   c. Adjust using long hole in control cable at transaxle end, **Fig. 3.**
   d. **Torque** locknut to 13–17 ft. lbs.
   e. Move selector lever from "P" range to "1" range, ensuring selector lever moves smoothly.
   f. Apply a suitable grease to contacting areas of selector lever and control cable.

HEADLAMP SWITCH

REPLACE

1. Remove steering column covers.
2. Disconnect headlamp switch electrical connector, then remove switch retaining screws and switch, **Fig. 5.** It is not necessary to remove combination switch base to replace headlamp switch.

STOP LIGHT SWITCH

REPLACE

The stop lamp switch is located on the brake pedal support.

1. Disconnect the switch electrical connectors.
2. Loosen switch retaining locknut and remove switch.
3. Reverse procedure to install.

COMBINATION SWITCH

REPLACE

1. Disconnect battery ground cable.
2. Remove horn cover and steering wheel as outlined under "Steering Wheel, Replace."
3. Remove steering column shell covers.
4. Disconnect switch electrical connectors.
5. Remove retaining screws, then the switch, **Fig. 6.**
6. Reverse procedure to install.

TURN SIGNAL SWITCH

REPLACE

1. Remove steering column covers.
2. Disconnect turn signal switch electrical connections, then remove switch retaining screws and turn signal switch, **Fig. 5.** It is not necessary to remove combination switch base to replace turn signal switch.

STEERING WHEEL

REPLACE

MODELS w/AIR BAG

1. Place steering wheel in Neutral position.
2. Remove lower lid from steering wheel, then disconnect air bag module electrical connector, **Fig. 7.**
3. Remove side lids.
4. Using a T50H Torx bit, remove left and right special securing bolts.
5. Remove air bag module and observe the following precautions:

a. **Always place air bag module with pad side facing upward.**
b. **Do not attempt to disassemble air bag module.**
c. **Special bolts are coated with a bonding agent. Discard after removal and replace.**
d. **If any portion of air bag module is damaged or cracked, replace module.**
e. **Do not allow oil, grease or water to come in contact with air bag module.**

6. Set steering wheel to Neutral position, then disconnect horn electrical connector and remove steering wheel attaching nut.
7. Using puller tool No. J25726-A, or equivalent, remove steering wheel.
8. Reverse procedure to install, noting the following:
   a. **Torque** steering wheel retaining nut to 22–29 ft. lbs.
   b. Position air bag module and **torque** new bolts to 11–18 ft. lbs.

MODELS LESS AIR BAG

1. **On models w/two spoke wheel,** pry out horn pad and push pawl clamps with a suitable screwdriver, then remove horn pad.
2. **On models w/three spoke wheel,** insert a suitable screwdriver into hole on back of lower spoke and pry clamps up, then remove horn pad.
3. **On models w/four spoke wheel,** insert a Phillips head screwdriver into hole on lower side of spoke and remove clamps, then remove horn pad.
4. **On all models,** remove steering wheel using puller tool No. J25726-A, or equivalent.
5. Reverse procedure to install. Prior to installation, apply suitable grease to entire surface of turn signal cancel pin and horn contact slip ring.

INSTRUMENT CLUSTER

REPLACE

1. Remove steering column cover and steering wheel if necessary.
2. Remove instrument panel cover if necessary.
3. Remove cluster lid retaining screws, then the cluster lid.
4. Disconnect speedometer cable, cluster retaining nuts and electrical connectors as necessary. The cluster may have to be pulled slightly forward after removing retaining screws to allow access to electrical connectors in rear.
5. Reverse procedure to install.

RADIO

REPLACE

1. Remove cluster lid or instrument panel cover as necessary to gain access to brackets.
2. Remove radio bracket to instrument panel attaching screw, then disconnect electrical leads from radio.

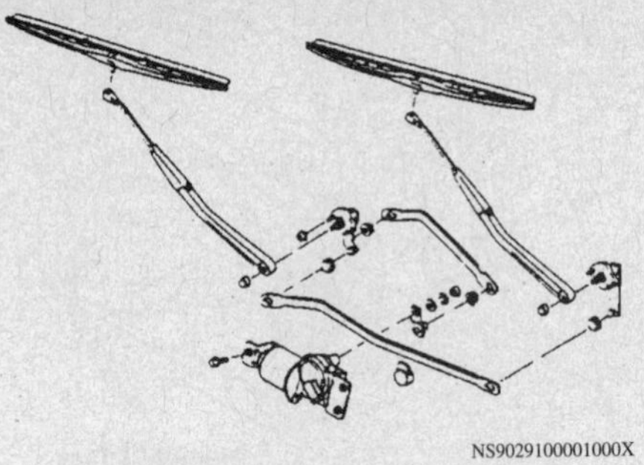
NS9029100001000X

Fig. 8 Exploded view of windshield wiper system

3. Remove radio from vehicle.
4. Reverse procedure to install.

WIPER MOTOR

REPLACE

FRONT

1. Remove wiper arms, **Fig. 8.**
2. Disconnect electrical connector from motor, then remove top grille retaining screws and top grille, where possible, to gain access to wiper linkage.
3. Remove wiper motor mounting bolts and pull motor away from firewall.
4. Disconnect motor shaft from linkage, taking care not to bend linkage.
5. Remove cowl top grille.
6. Remove flange nuts retaining pivot to cowl top.
7. Remove wiper motor linkage.
8. Reverse procedure to install.

REAR

1. Disconnect battery ground cable.
2. Raise rear wiper arm off glass, then remove retaining nut and wiper arm.
3. Remove tailgate inner trim panel, if necessary, and disconnect electrical connection at motor.
4. Remove wiper motor retaining bolts, then the wiper motor.
5. Reverse procedure to install.

WIPER SWITCH

REPLACE

FRONT

The wiper switch is an integrated part of the combination switch and must be replaced as a unit. Refer to "Combination Switch, Replace."

REAR

1. Disconnect battery ground cable.
2. Disconnect electrical connector from switch.
3. Remove switch knob by depressing and/or twisting as necessary.
4. Remove any switch retaining nuts or clips, then remove the switch.
5. Reverse procedure to install.

BLOWER MOTOR

REPLACE

1993–94

1. Remove instrument panel as outlined under "Dash Panel Service."
2. Refer to **Fig. 9** for blower motor replacement.

1995–96

Note that the blower motor is an integrated part of the intake unit and must be replaced as an assembly.

1. Remove instrument panel as outlined under "Dash Panel Service."
2. Refer to **Fig. 10** for intake unit replacement.

HEATER CORE

REPLACE

1993–94

1. Remove instrument panel as outlined under "Dash Panel Service."
2. Refer to **Fig. 9** for heater core replacement.

1995–96

Note that the heater core is an integrated part of the heater unit, which is not a serviceable component and must be replaced as an assembly.

1. Drain and discharge cooling and A/C systems into approved recovery/recycling containers.
2. Remove instrument panel as outlined under "Dash Panel Service."
3. Remove instrument panel reinforcement.
4. Remove cooling unit, **Fig. 10.**
5. Remove heater unit.
6. Reverse procedure to install.

EVAPORATOR CORE

REPLACE

1993–94

1. Disconnect battery ground cable and discharge A/C system into an approved recovery/recycling container.
2. Remove passenger side instrument lower cover and glove compartment.
3. Disconnect wiring harness connectors to evaporator.
4. Separate cooling unit case halves and remove evaporator, **Fig. 9.**
5. Reverse procedure to install.

1995–96

Note that the evaporator core is an integrated part of the cooling unit, which is not a serviceable component and must be replaced as an assembly.

1. Discharge A/C system into an approved recovery/recycling container.
2. Remove instrument panel as outlined under "Dash Panel Service."
3. Remove cooling unit, **Fig. 10.**
4. Reverse procedure to install.

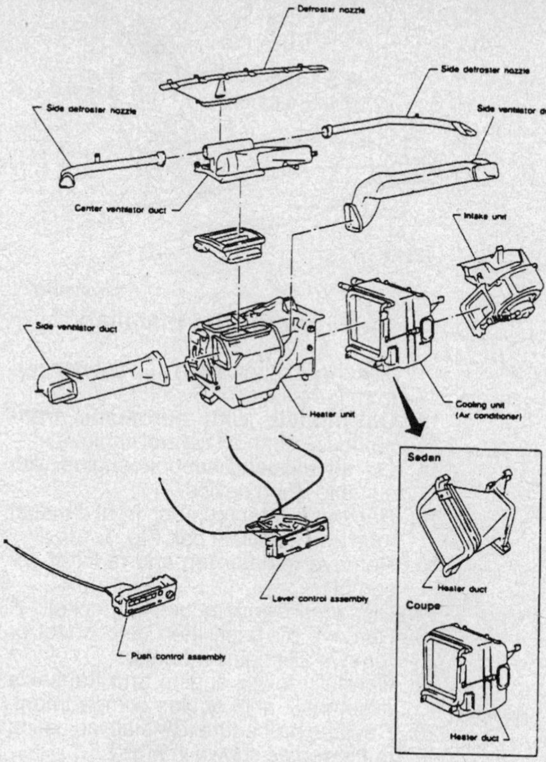
Defroster nozzle
Side defroster nozzle
Side defroster nozzle
Side ventilator duct
Center ventilator duct
Intake unit
Side ventilator duct
Heater unit
Cooling unit (Air conditioner)
Sedan
Heater duct
Coupe
Heater duct
Lever control assembly
Push control assembly

NS7029100045000X

Fig. 9 Exploded view of HVAC system. Sentra & 1993 NX 1600 & NX 2000

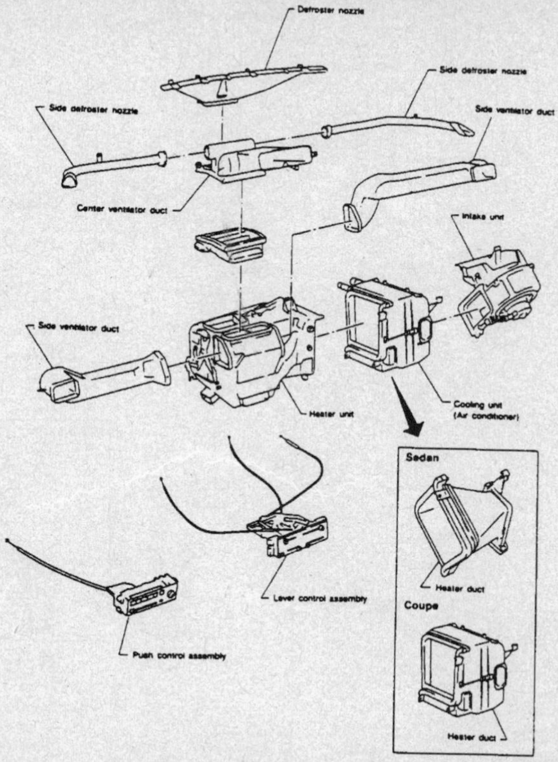
Defroster nozzle
Side defroster nozzle
Side defroster nozzle
Side ventilator duct
Center ventilator duct
Intake unit
Side ventilator duct
Heater unit
Cooling unit (Air conditioner)
Sedan
Heater duct
Coupe
Heater duct
Lever control assembly
Push control assembly

NS7029100045000X

Fig. 10 Exploded view of HVAC system. 1995–96 Sentra & 200SX

GA16DE Engine

NOTE: On Air Bag Equipped Models, Refer To "Air Bag System Precautions" Located In The Front Of This Manual For System Disarming & Arming Procedures.

INDEX

	Page No.
Belt Tension Data	30-13
Component Service	30-9
Valve Oil Seal	30-9
Compression Pressure	30-8
Cooling System Bleed	30-13
Crankshaft Rear Oil Seal, Replace	30-12
Cylinder Head, Replace	30-8
Engine Assemble	30-9
Cylinder Head	30-9
Piston, Rod & Crankshaft	30-10
Engine Disassemble	30-8
Cylinder Head	30-8
Piston, Rod & Crankshaft	30-9
Engine Mount, Replace	30-8
Engine Rebuilding Specifications	36-1
Engine, Replace	30-8
Exhaust Manifold, Replace	30-8
Front Cover Seal, Replace	30-11
Fuel Filter, Replace	30-13
Fuel Pump, Replace	30-13
Intake Manifold, Replace	30-8
Oil Pan, Replace	30-13
Precautions	30-7
Air Bag Systems	30-7
Fuel System Pressure Release	30-7
Radiator, Replace	30-13
Thermostat, Replace	30-13
Tightening Specifications	30-15
Timing Chain, Replace	30-11
Installation	30-11
Removal	30-11
Valve Adjustment	30-10
Valve Clearance Specifications	30-10
Water Pump, Replace	30-13

PRECAUTIONS

AIR BAG SYSTEMS

Refer to "Air Bag System Precautions" in the front of this manual for system disarming and arming procedures.

FUEL SYSTEM PRESSURE RELEASE

1. Remove fuel pump fuse from fuse panel.
2. Start engine.
3. After engine stalls, crank engine two or three times to ensure pressure is released.
4. Turn ignition switch to off position.
5. After fuel system operations are complete, replace fuel pump fuse.

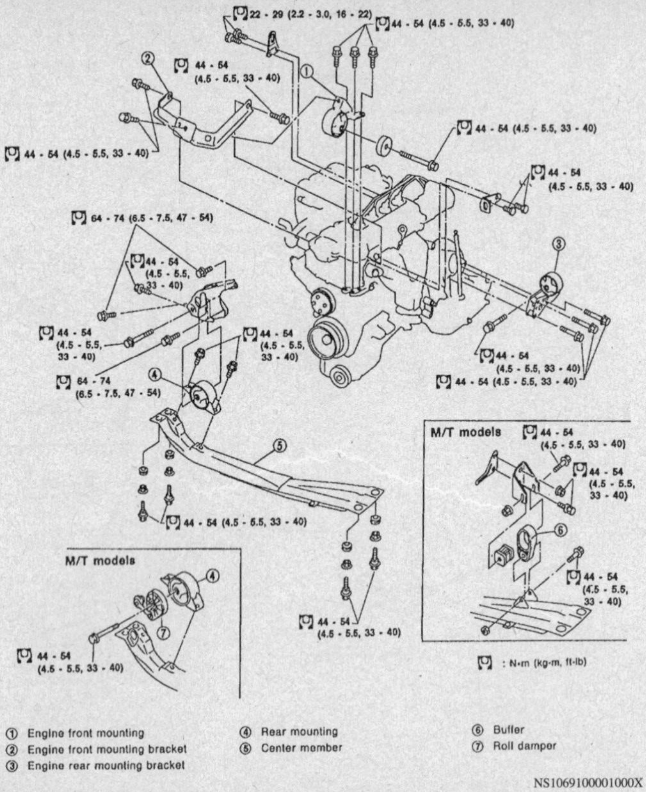
22 - 29 (2.2 - 3.0, 16 - 22)
44 - 54 (4.5 - 5.5, 33 - 40)
64 - 74 (6.5 - 7.5, 47 - 54)
M/T models
M/T models
: N·m (kg-m, ft-lb)
① Engine front mounting
② Engine front mounting bracket
③ Engine rear mounting bracket
④ Rear mounting
⑤ Center member
⑥ Buffer
⑦ Roll damper
NS1069100001000X

Fig. 1 Exploded view of engine mounting brackets

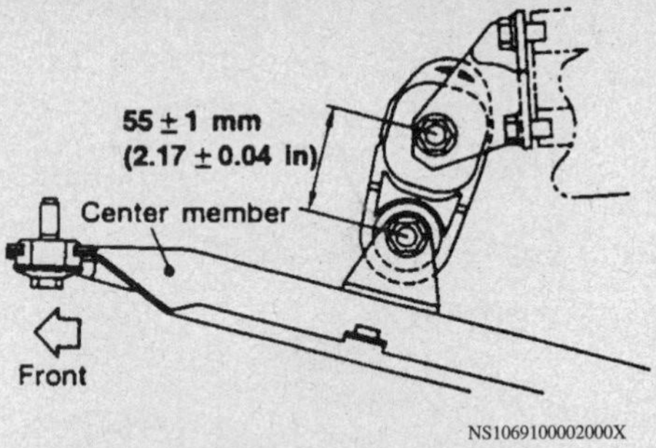
55 ± 1 mm
(2.17 ± 0.04 in)
Center member
Front
NS1069100002000X

Fig. 2 Buffer rod installation

COMPRESSION PRESSURE

1. Start engine and run until engine reaches operating temperature.
2. Turn ignition switch off.
3. Release fuel pressure. Refer to "Precautions"for fuel system pressure release procedure.
4. Remove all spark plugs.
5. Disconnect distributor coil connector.
6. Attach a compression tester to cylinder No. 1.
7. Depress accelerator pedal fully to keep throttle valve wide open.
8. Crank engine and record highest gauge indication.
9. Repeat measurement on each cylinder.
10. Standard compression is 178 psi, minimum pressure is 149 psi and compression difference limit between cylinders is 14 psi.
11. If compression in one or more cylinders is low, pour a small amount of engine oil into cylinders through spark plug holes, then retest compression.
12. If adding oil helps compression, then piston rings may be at fault. If adding oil does not help compression, then valves may be at fault.
13. If compression stays low in two cylinders that are next to each other, then cylinder head gasket may be leaking or both cylinders may have valve component damage.
14. Repair as necessary.

ENGINE MOUNT

REPLACE

Refer to **Fig. 1** for engine mount replacement.

ENGINE

REPLACE

1. Release fuel system pressure as outlined under "Precautions."
2. Disconnect battery ground cable and drain cooling system.
3. Mark hood for installation reference, then remove hood.
4. Remove battery, then the engine coolant reservoir tank and brackets.
5. Remove drive belts.
6. Remove alternator, compressor and power steering pump from engine. Position components out of the way without disconnecting hoses.
7. Disconnect fuel lines, vacuum hoses, wire harness and connectors as necessary.
8. Remove front tire and wheel assemblies.
9. Remove engine undercover and splash shields.
10. Remove brake caliper assembly without disconnecting hydraulic lines, then support caliper from frame using suitable wire.
11. Disconnect tie rod ball joint from knuckle.
12. **On models with manual transaxle,** disconnect control rod and support rod from transaxle.
13. **On models with automatic transaxle,** disconnect control cable.
14. **On all models,** support engine with suitable lifting device.
15. Remove center member, front exhaust tube and stabilizer bar, **Fig. 1.**
16. Remove radiator fan and radiator assembly.
17. Disconnect front mounting bracket.
18. Remove air duct, then disconnect or remove all engine mounts.
19. Carefully lower engine and transaxle assembly out of engine compartment.
20. Reverse procedure to install, adjusting buffer rod as shown in **Fig. 2.**

INTAKE MANIFOLD

REPLACE

For intake manifold replacement procedure, refer to **Figs. 3 through 5** and the cylinder head section of "Engine, Disassemble. "

EXHAUST MANIFOLD

REPLACE

For exhaust manifold replacement procedure, refer to **Fig. 6** and the cylinder head section of the "Engine, Disassemble."

CYLINDER HEAD

REPLACE

Refer to "Timing Chain, Replace" for cylinder head replacement procedure.

ENGINE DISASSEMBLE

CYLINDER HEAD

Refer to **Fig. 7** when performing the following procedure.

1. Remove intake and exhaust manifolds from cylinder head. Refer to "Intake Manifold, Replace" and "Exhaust Manifold, Replace" for removal procedure.
2. Remove valve components using valve spring compression and attachment tool Nos. KV10116200 (J26339-A) and KV10115900 (J26336-20), or equivalents.
3. Remove valve oil seals using seal puller tool No. KV10107902 (J38959), or equivalent.

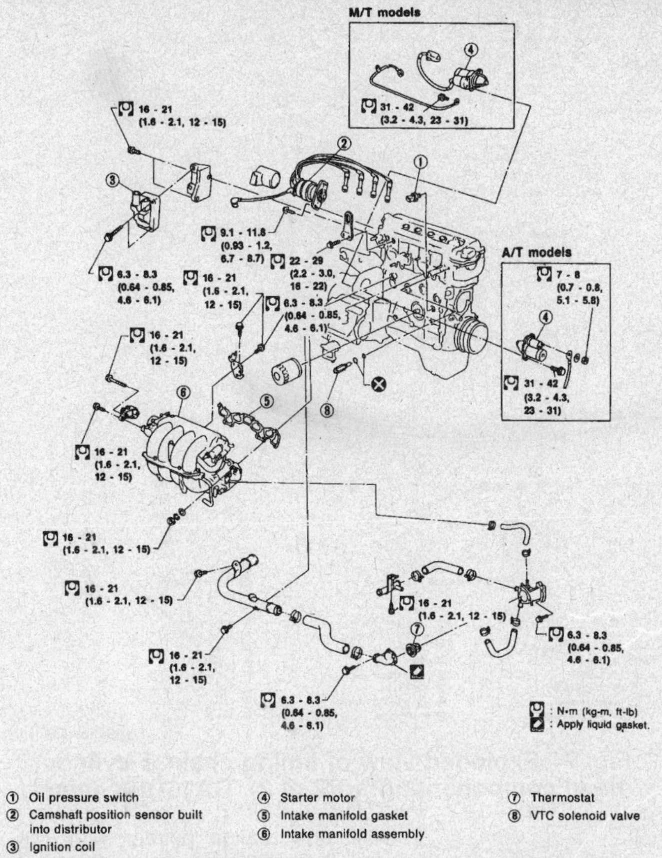
M/T models
A/T models
: N·m (kg-m, ft-lb)
: Apply liquid gasket.
① Oil pressure switch
② Camshaft position sensor built into distributor
③ Ignition coil
④ Starter motor
⑤ Intake manifold gasket
⑥ Intake manifold assembly
⑦ Thermostat
⑧ VTC solenoid valve
NS1069200176000X

Fig. 3 Exploded view of intake manifold

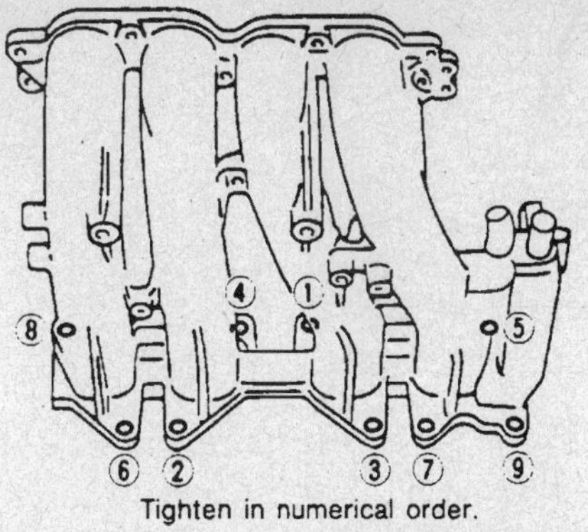
Tighten in numerical order.
NS1069200177000X

Fig. 4 Intake manifold bolt tightening sequence

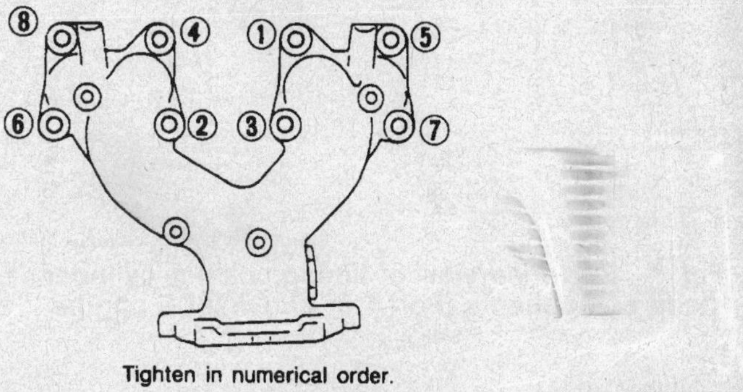
Tighten in numerical order.
NS1069200179000X

Fig. 6 Exhaust manifold bolt tightening sequence

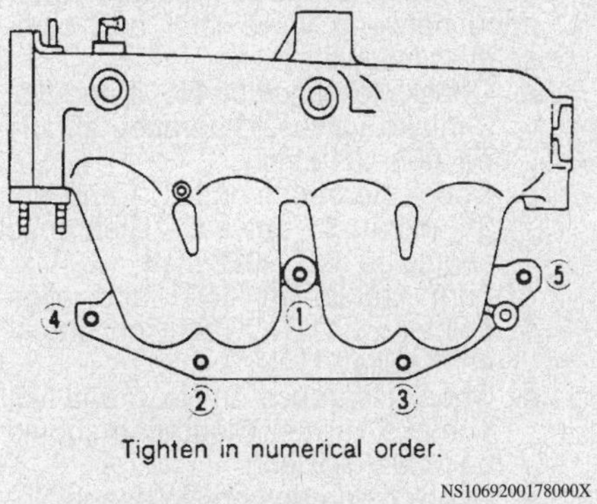
Tighten in numerical order.
NS1069200178000X

Fig. 5 Intake manifold cover bolt tightening sequence

PISTON, ROD & CRANKSHAFT

Refer to **Fig. 8** when performing the following procedure.

1. Place engine on a suitable work stand.
2. Drain coolant and oil, then remove timing chain and cylinder head.
3. Remove oil pan and pump.
4. Remove piston, then the snap rings from the piston assembly.
5. Heat piston and rod assemblies to 140–158°F and push out piston pin. If heat method is not used, piston pins can be pressed out using a suitable press at room temperature.
6. Measure crankshaft endplay using a dial indicator. Endplay should be .0024–.0071 inch.
7. Using sequence shown in **Fig. 9,** remove main bearing caps by loosening bolts in two or three steps.
8. Remove crankshaft.

COMPONENT SERVICE

VALVE OIL SEAL

When removing valve oil seals, ensure piston under valve set being serviced is at TDC. This will prevent valves from falling into cylinder.

1. Remove rocker cover, camshaft, valve spring and valve oil seal.
2. Coat new oil seal with clean engine oil and install.

ENGINE ASSEMBLE

CYLINDER HEAD

Refer to **Fig. 7** when performing the following procedure.

1. Install valve oil seals using seal drift tool No. KV10115600 (J38958), or equivalent.
2. Install valve components using valve spring compression and attachment tool Nos. KV10116200 (J26339-A) and KV10115900 (J26336-20), or equivalents. When installing valve springs, ensure narrow pitch of spring is pointed toward cylinder head.
3. Install intake and exhaust manifolds to cylinder head. Refer to "Intake Manifold, Replace" and "Exhaust Manifold, Replace."

PISTON, ROD & CRANKSHAFT

When performing the following piston, rod and crankshaft repair procedures, refer to **Fig. 8.**

1. Install crankshaft main bearings and caps, then tighten bolts to specifications using sequence shown in **Fig. 10.**
2. If crankshaft endplay was not within specification, replace thrust bearing.
3. Install snap ring on one side of piston pin hole.
4. Heat piston to 140–158°F, then assemble piston, piston pin, connecting rod and new snap ring.
5. **On 1993–94 models,** install piston rings, **Figs. 11 and 12.**
6. **On 1995–96 models,** install piston rings. **Note that 1995 models have only one compression ring and one oil ring, Figs. 13 and 14.**
7. **On all models,** install connecting rod bearings with oil holes aligned, **Fig. 15.**
8. Install piston and rod assemblies into proper cylinder, then **torque** rod bolts to 10–12 ft. lbs. plus an additional 35–40° or 17–21 ft. lbs.
9. **On 1993–94 models,** piston skirt diameter (A) should be 2.9911–2.9915 inches standard piston and dimension (a) .374 inch, **Fig. 16.**
10. **On 1995–96 models,** piston skirt diameter (A) should be 2.9911–2.9915

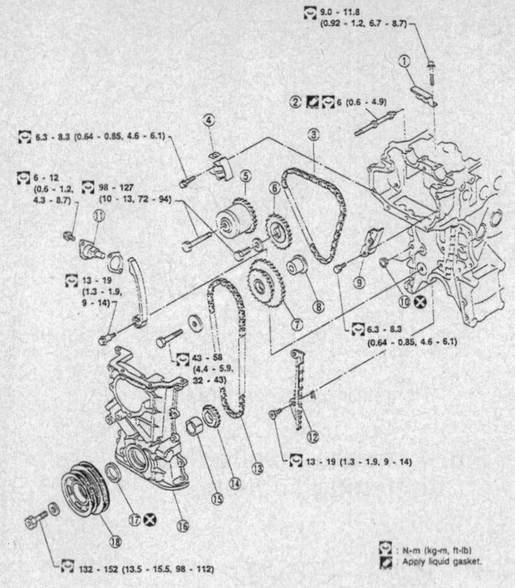

① Chain guide
② Cam sprocket cover gusset
③ Upper timing chain
④ Chain tensioner
⑤ V.T.C. camshaft sprocket (Intake)
⑥ Camshaft sprocket (Exhaust)
⑦ Idler sprocket
⑧ Idler shaft
⑨ Chain guide
⑩ O-ring
⑪ Chain tensioner
⑫ Chain guide
⑬ Lower timing chain
⑭ Crankshaft sprocket
⑮ Oil pump drive spacer
⑯ Front cover
⑰ Oil seal
⑱ Crankshaft pulley

NS1069100005010X

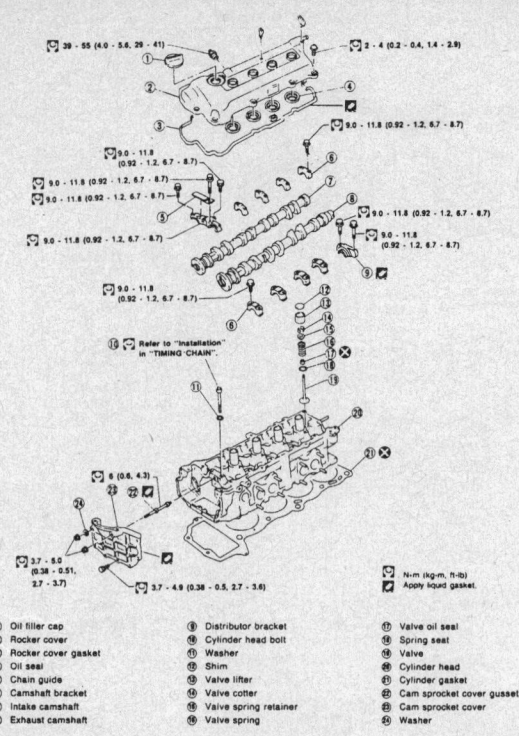

Fig. 7 Exploded view of timing chain & cylinder head components (Part 1 of 2). GA16DE engine

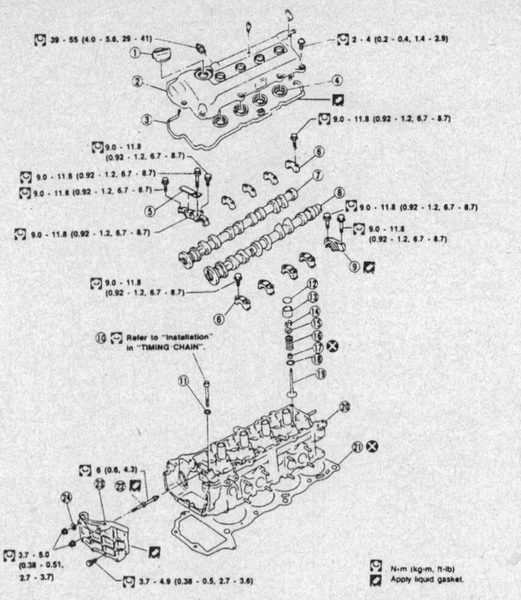

① Oil filler cap
② Rocker cover
③ Rocker cover gasket
④ Oil seal
⑤ Chain guide
⑥ Camshaft bracket
⑦ Intake camshaft
⑧ Exhaust camshaft
⑨ Distributor bracket
⑩ Cylinder head bolt
⑪ Washer
⑫ Shim
⑬ Valve lifter
⑭ Valve cotter
⑮ Valve spring retainer
⑯ Valve spring
⑰ Valve oil seal
⑱ Spring seat
⑲ Valve
⑳ Cylinder head
㉑ Cylinder gasket
㉒ Cam sprocket cover gusset
㉓ Cam sprocket cover
㉔ Washer

NS1069100005020X

Fig. 7 Exploded view of timing chain & cylinder head components (Part 2 of 2). GA16DE engine

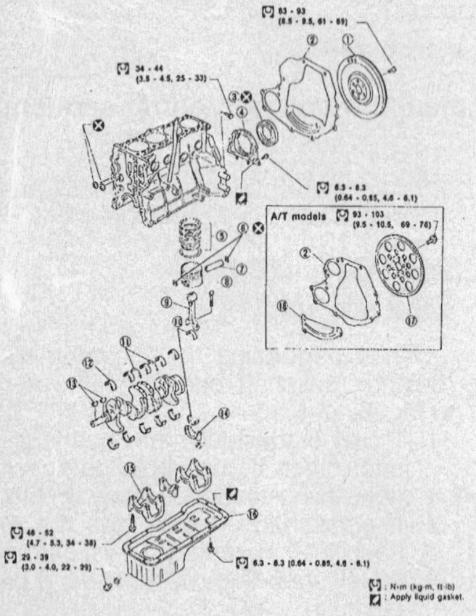

① Flywheel
② Rear plate
③ Rear oil seal
④ Rear oil seal retainer
⑤ Piston ring
⑥ Snap ring
⑦ Piston pin
⑧ Piston
⑨ Connecting rod
⑩ Connecting bearing
⑪ Thrust bearing
⑫ Main bearing
⑬ Key
⑭ Connecting rod cap
⑮ Bearing beam cap
⑯ Oil pan
⑰ Drive plate
⑱ Dust cover

NS1069100003000X

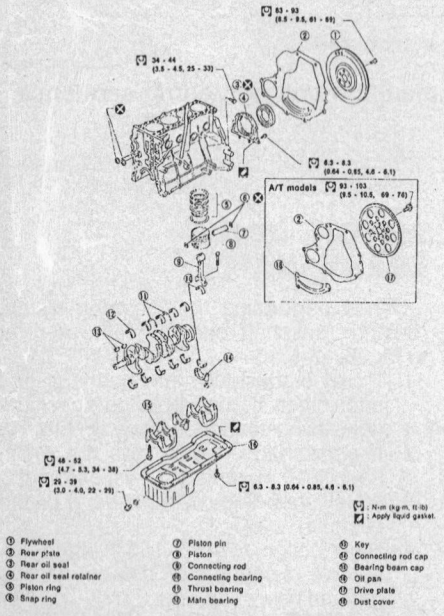

Fig. 8 Exploded view of cylinder block. GA16DE engine

inches standard piston and dimension (a) .390 inch, **Fig. 17.**

11. Connecting rod side clearance should be .0079–.0185 inch. If not, replace connecting rod or crankshaft.

VALVE CLEARANCE SPECIFICATIONS

Refer to "Valve Adjustment" for valve clearance specifications

VALVE ADJUSTMENT

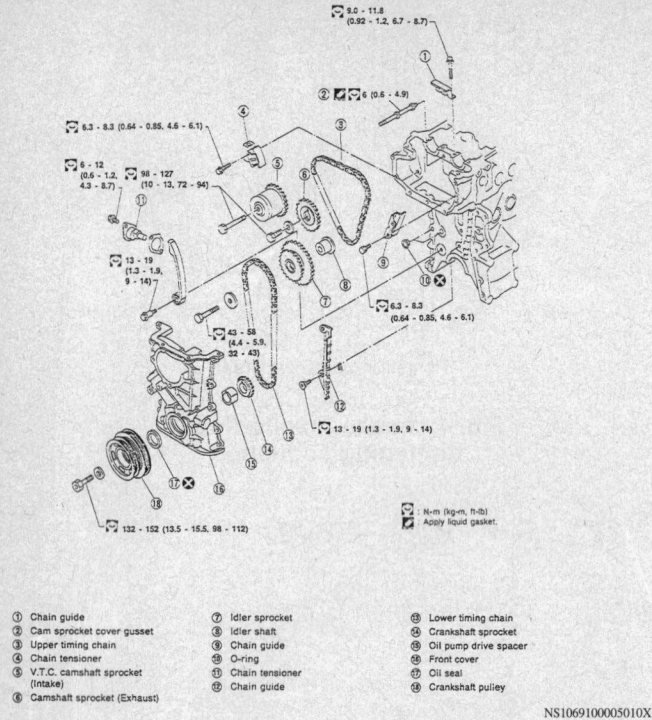

1. Remove rocker cover and all spark plugs.
2. Set No. 1 cylinder at TDC on its compression stroke.
3. Align pointer with TDC mark on crankshaft pulley.
4. Valve lifters on No. 1 cylinder should be loose and valve lifters on No. 4 cylinder should be tight. If lifters are as specified, proceed to step 5. If lifters are not as specified, turn crankshaft 360° and realign pointer with TDC mark on crankshaft pulley, then proceed to step 5.
5. With engine at operating temperature, use a feeler gauge to measure clearance between valve lifter and camshaft as follows:
   a. Check clearance on No. 1 and No. 2 intake valves. Clearance should be .008–.019 inch.
   b. Check clearance on No. 1 and No. 3 exhaust valves. Clearance should be .012–.023 inch.
   c. Turn crankshaft 360° and align pointer with TDC mark on crankshaft pulley.
   d. Check clearance on No. 3 and No. 4 intake valves. Clearance should be .008–.019 inch.
   e. Check clearance on No. 2 and No. 4 exhaust valves. Clearance should be .012–.023 inch.
6. Adjust valves while engine is cold using cam turning tool (A) No. KV10115110 and valve lifter holding tool (B) No. KV10115120, or equivalents, **Fig. 18.**
7. Turn crankshaft to position cam lobe on camshaft of valve to be adjusted upward.
8. Install tool (A) around camshaft, **Fig. 19.**
9. Rotate tool (A) so that lifter is pushed down.
10. Place tool (B) between camshaft and edge of valve filter to retain lifter.
11. Remove tool (A).
12. Remove adjusting shim using a screwdriver and a magnet.
13. Determine replacement adjusting shim size for intake valves using the

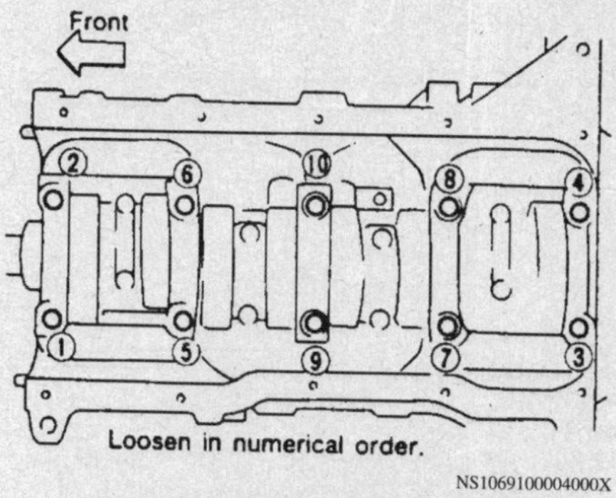
Front
Loosen in numerical order.
NS1069100004000X

Fig. 9 Crankshaft bearing cap bolt removal sequence

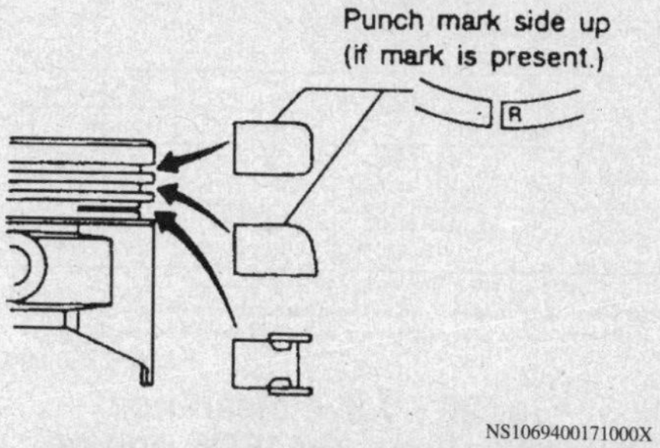
Punch mark side up
(if mark is present.)
NS1069400171000X

Fig. 12 Piston ring installation position

following formula:

a. Use a micrometer to determine thickness of removed shim.

b. Calculate thickness of new shim so valve clearance becomes .010–.013 inch by subtracting .0146 inch from measured valve clearance (M). Then add value of thickness of removed shim (R) to give thickness of new shim (N). N = R + (M - .0146 inch).

14. Determine replacement adjusting shim size for exhaust valves using the following formula:
    a. Use a micrometer to determine thickness of removed shim.
    b. Calculate thickness of new shim so valve clearance becomes .013–.016 inch by subtracting .0157 inch from measured valve clearance (M). Then add value of thickness of removed shim (R) to give thickness of new shim (N). N = R + (M - .0157 inch).
15. Select new shim with thickness as close as possible to calculated value.
16. Install selected shim and check valve clearance, **Fig. 20.**

FRONT COVER SEAL

REPLACE

1. Remove front cover as outlined under "Timing Chain, Replace."
2. Remove front oil seal from front cover.
3. Apply clean engine oil to new front oil seal.
4. Install oil seal into front cover.
5. Install front cover as outlined under "Timing Chain, Replace."

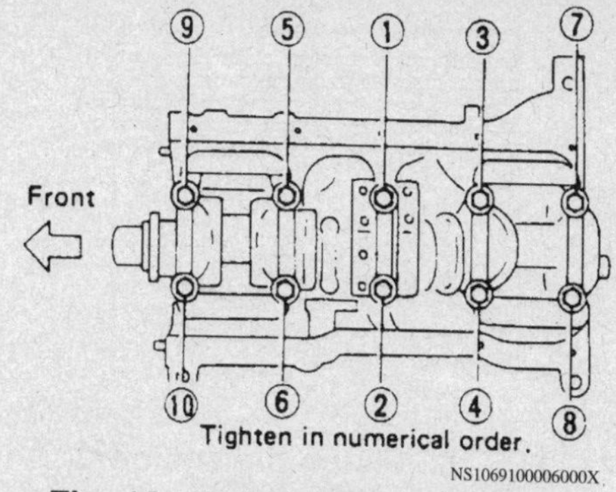
Front
Tighten in numerical order.
NS1069100006000X

Fig. 10 Main bearing cap bolt tightening sequence

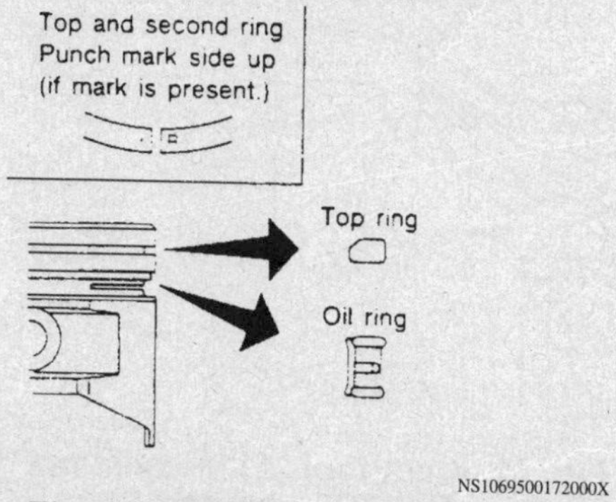
Top and second ring
Punch mark side up
(if mark is present.)
Top ring
Oil ring
NS1069500172000X

Fig. 13 Piston ring punch mark identification. 1995–96

TIMING CHAIN

REPLACE

After removing timing chain, do not turn crankshaft and camshaft separately, or damage to the valves may occur.

Refer to **Fig. 7** when servicing the timing chain.

REMOVAL

1. Drain coolant from radiator and block.
2. Release fuel system pressure as outlined under "Precautions."
3. Remove power steering pump, alternator and A/C drive belts.
4. Remove power steering pump bracket.
5. Remove air duct to intake manifold collector.
6. Remove wheels and splash shields.
7. Remove engine undercover, then the front exhaust pipe.
8. Support engine with a suitable jack or lifting device, then remove engine mount bracket.
9. Remove valve cover, distributor cap, ignition wires and spark plugs.
10. Remove intake manifold support.
11. Set No. 1 piston at TDC on its compression stroke.
12. Remove distributor assembly.
13. Remove camshaft sprocket cover and gusset.
14. Remove water pump pulley, then the thermostat housing.
15. Remove timing chain tensioners and chain guide.
16. Loosen idler sprocket bolt.
17. Remove camshaft sprocket bolts, then

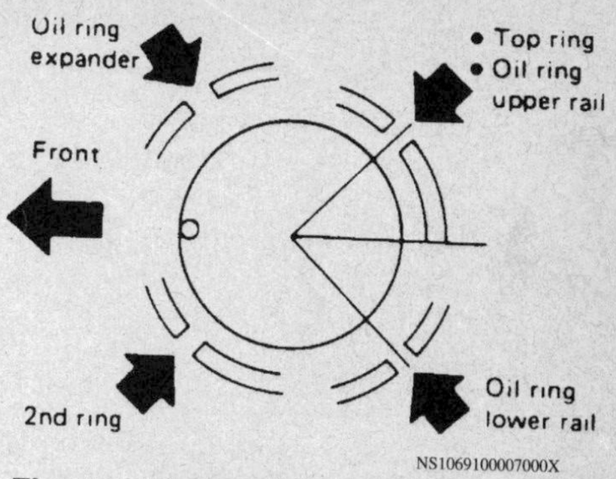
Oil ring
expander
Front
2nd ring
• Top ring
• Oil ring
upper rail
Oil ring
lower rail
NS1069100007000X

Fig. 11 Piston ring gap spacing. 1993–94

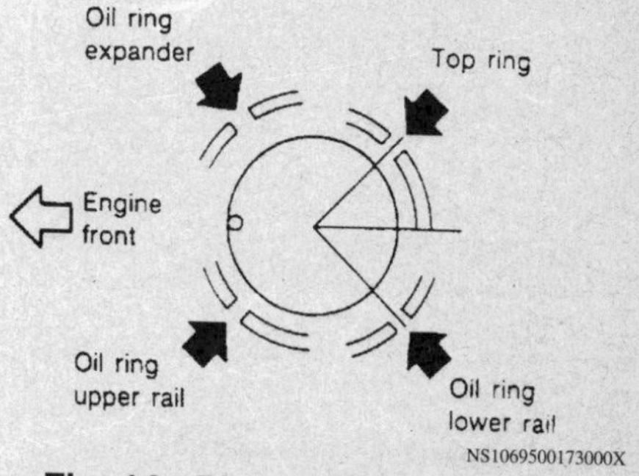
Oil ring
expander
Top ring
Engine
front
Oil ring
upper rail
Oil ring
lower rail
NS1069500173000X

Fig. 14 Piston ring alignment

the sprockets.

18. Using sequence shown in **Fig. 21,** loosen camshaft bracket bolts in two or three steps.
19. Remove camshaft brackets, distributor bracket and camshafts. **Note position of these parts prior to removal. Parts should be reassembled in their original positions.**
20. Remove idler sprocket bolt.
21. Using sequence shown in **Fig. 22,** remove cylinder head bolts in two or three steps.
22. Remove cylinder head and gasket with manifolds attached.
23. Remove idler sprocket shaft from rear side of engine.
24. Remove upper timing chain, then raise and support vehicle.
25. Remove center member, then the oil pan as outlined under "Oil Pan, Replace."
26. Remove oil strainer, then the crankshaft pulley.
27. Support engine using a suitable jack or lifting device, then remove engine front mounting bracket.
28. Remove front cover bolts and front cover.
29. Remove idler sprocket, lower timing chain, oil pump drive spacer, chain guide and crankshaft sprocket.

INSTALLATION

1. Confirm No. 1 cylinder is at TDC on its compression stroke.
2. Install chain guide and crankshaft sprocket.
3. Install lower timing chain as shown in **Fig. 23.**
4. Apply liquid gasket to front cover.
5. Check alignment of mating marks on

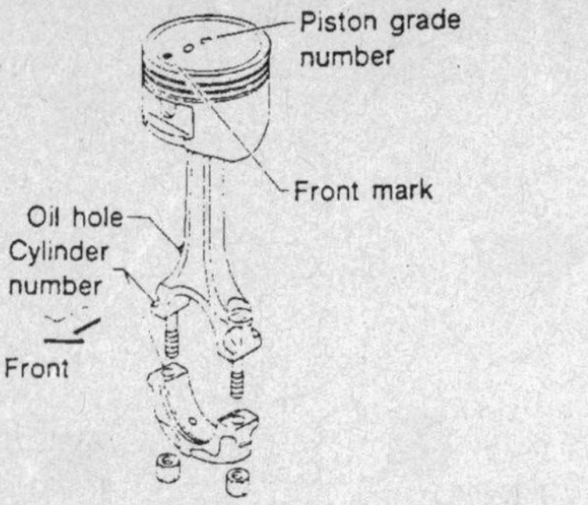
Piston grade
number
Front mark
Oil hole
Cylinder
number
Front

NS1069200174000X

Fig. 15 Connecting rod oil hole alignment

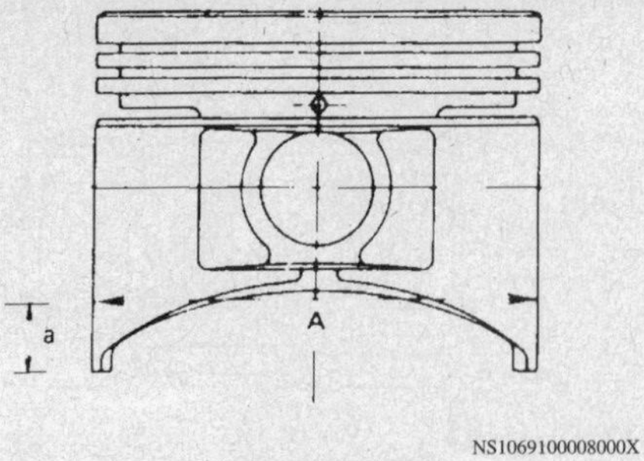
a
A

NS1069100008000X

Fig. 16 Piston dimensions. 1993–94

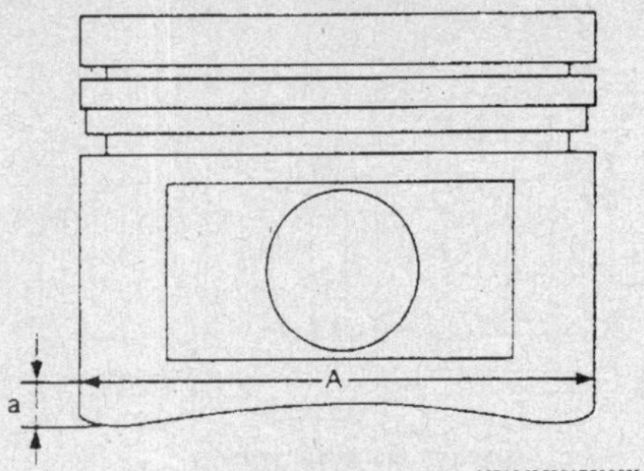
a
A

NS1069500175000X

Fig. 17 Piston dimensions. 1995–96

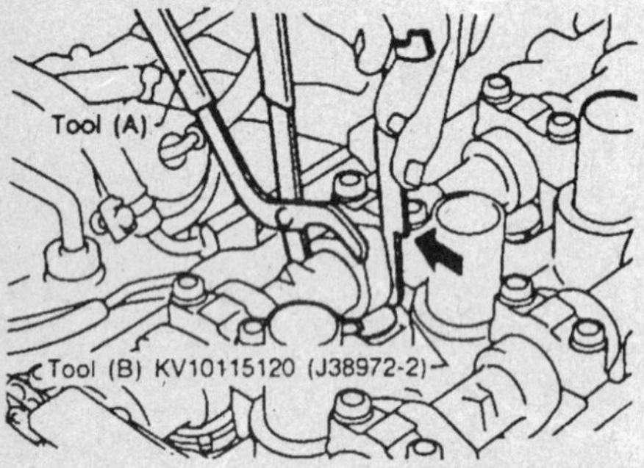
Tool (A)
Tool (B) KV10115120 (J38972-2)

NS1069100009000X

Fig. 18 Valve adjusting tools. GA16DE engine

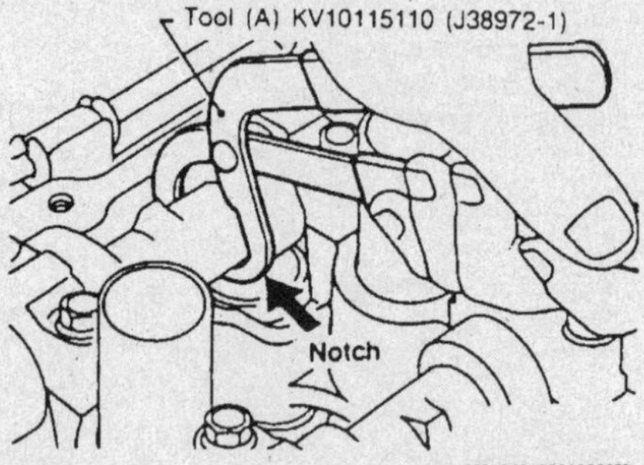
Tool (A) KV10115110 (J38972-1)
Notch

NS1069100010000X

Fig. 19 Cam tool (A) installation. GA16DE engine

Valve clearance:

Unit: mm (in)

	For adjusting		For checking
	Hot	Cold*	Hot
Intake	0.32 - 0.40 (0.013 - 0.016)	0.25 - 0.33 (0.010 - 0.013)	0.21 - 0.49 (0.008 - 0.019)
Exhaust	0.37 - 0.45 (0.015 - 0.018)	0.32 - 0.40 (0.013 - 0.016)	0.30 - 0.58 (0.012 - 0.023)

* At a temperature of approximately 20°C (68°F)

Whenever valve clearance are adjusted to cold specifications, check that the clearances satisfy hot specifications and adjust again if necessary.

NS1069100011000X

Fig. 20 Valve clearance specifications. GA16DE engine

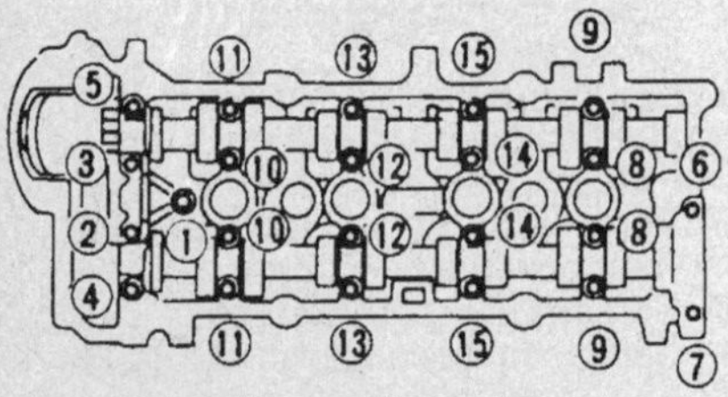
Loosen in numerical order.

NS1069100012000X

Fig. 21 Camshaft bracket bolt removal sequence. GA16DE engine

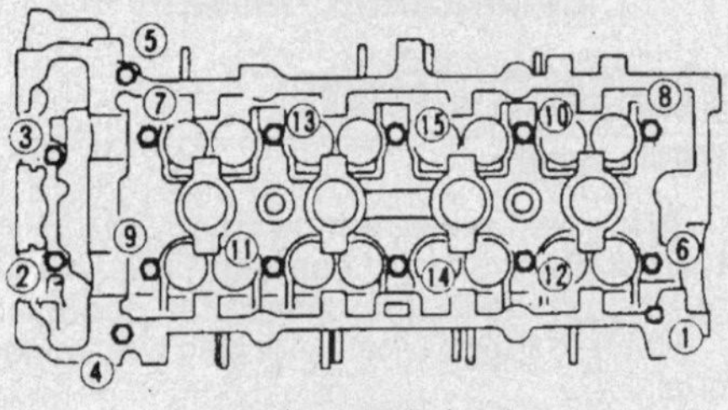
Loosen in numerical order.

NS1069100013000X

Fig. 22 Cylinder head bolt removal sequence. GA16DE engine

chain and crankshaft sprocket.

6. Align oil drive spacer with oil pump.
7. Ensure two O-rings are present in rear of front cover.
8. Put chain to side of chain guide so chain does not make contact with water seal area of front cover. **Be careful not to damage oil seal when installing front cover.**
9. Install engine front mounting bracket.
10. Install oil strainer and pan assembly as outlined under “Oil Pan, Replace.”
11. Install crankshaft pulley.
12. Install center member, then lower vehicle.
13. Install idler sprocket by aligning mating mark on larger sprocket with silver mating mark on lower timing chain, **Fig. 24.**
14. Install upper timing chain by aligning mating mark on smaller sprocket with silver mating mark on upper timing chain. **Ensure sprocket's mating mark faces front of engine.**
15. Install idler sprocket shaft from rear side of engine.
16. Install cylinder head with new gasket. **Ensure head bolt washers are installed with beveled edge pointed away from head. Do not rotate crankshaft and camshaft separately, or valves will strike piston heads.**
17. Using sequence shown in **Fig. 25,** tighten cylinder head bolts 1 through 10 as follows:
    a. **Torque** bolts to 22 ft. lbs.
    b. **Torque** bolts to 43 ft. lbs.
    c. Loosen bolts completely.
    d. **Torque** bolts to 22 ft. lbs.
    e. **Torque** bolts to 43.4 ft. lbs.
18. Using sequence shown in **Fig. 25, torque** cylinder head bolts 11 through 15 to 4.6–6.1 ft. lbs.
19. Install idler sprocket bolt.
20. Install and align camshafts shown in **Fig. 26. Intake and exhaust identification marks are present in the center of the camshaft.**
21. Install and align camshaft and distributor brackets as shown in **Fig. 27.**
22. Apply liquid gasket to distributor bracket, then tighten bolts in two or three steps as shown in **Fig. 28.**
23. If any part of valve assembly or camshaft has been replaced, check and adjust valve clearance as outlined under “Valve, Adjust.”
24. Assemble camshaft sprocket with chain and align mating marks as shown in **Fig. 29.**
25. Install camshaft sprocket bolts.
26. Install upper chain tensioner and chain guide. **Ensure hook used to retain chain tensioner is released.**
27. Install lower chain tensioner, then rotate engine and ensure no problems occur.
28. Ensure No. 1 piston is set at TDC on its compression stroke.
29. Apply liquid gasket to thermostat housing, then install thermostat housing.
30. Install water pump pulley.
31. Install distributor and ensure distributor rotor is pointing toward No. 1 cylinder spark position.
32. Apply liquid gasket to cam sprocket cover gusset and cam sprocket cover.
33. Install cam sprocket gusset and cam sprocket cover.
34. Apply liquid gasket to valve cover and cylinder head mating surfaces.
35. Install valve cover, then tighten valve cover retaining bolts using sequence shown in **Fig. 30.**
36. Install spark plugs, then raise and support vehicle.
37. Install front exhaust pipe, engine undercover, splash shields and wheels.
38. Lower vehicle, then install air cleaner and power steering pump bracket.
39. Install alternator, power steering pump and A/C compressor drive belts.

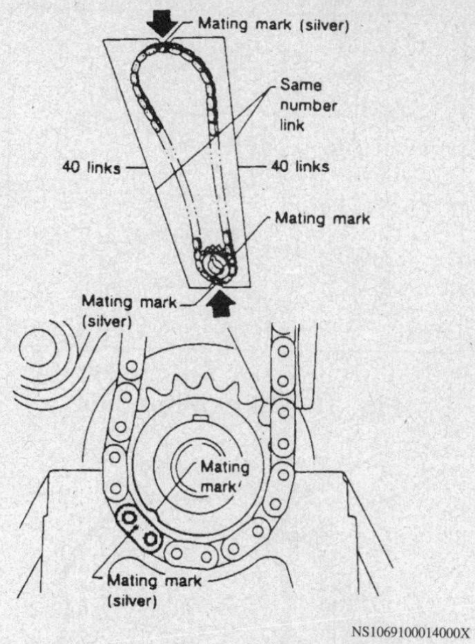
Mating mark (silver)
Same number link
40 links
40 links
Mating mark
Mating mark (silver)
Mating mark
Mating mark (silver)
NS1069100014000X

Fig. 23 Lower timing chain installation. GA16DE engine

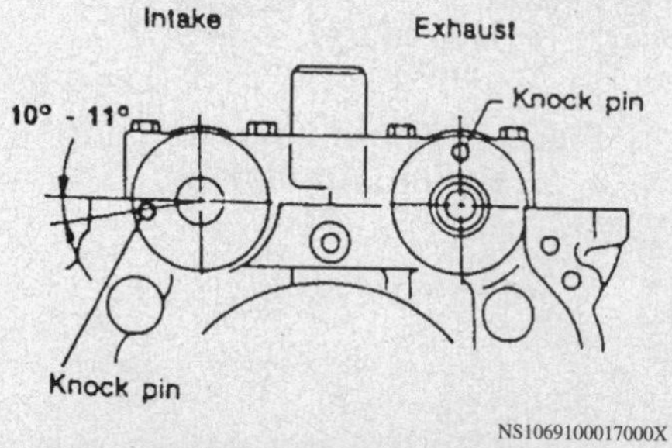
Intake
Exhaust
10° - 11°
Knock pin
Knock pin
NS1069100017000X

Fig. 26 Camshafts installation. GA16DE engine

CRANKSHAFT REAR OIL SEAL

REPLACE

1. Remove flywheel or driveplate, then the rear oil seal retainer.
2. Remove rear oil seal from retainer.
3. Clean mating surfaces, coat new oil seal with clean engine oil and install into retainer.
4. Apply liquid gasket to retainer and install.

OIL PAN

REPLACE

1. Raise and support vehicle, then remove engine undercovers.
2. Drain oil, then remove center member and front exhaust tube.
3. Using pan removal tool No. KV10111100, or equivalent, and a hammer, carefully remove oil pan as shown in **Fig. 31.**
4. Clean any remaining liquid gasket from oil pan and cylinder block mating surfaces.
5. Apply a continuous bead of liquid gasket to pan mating surface, then install oil pan within five minutes of gasket application.

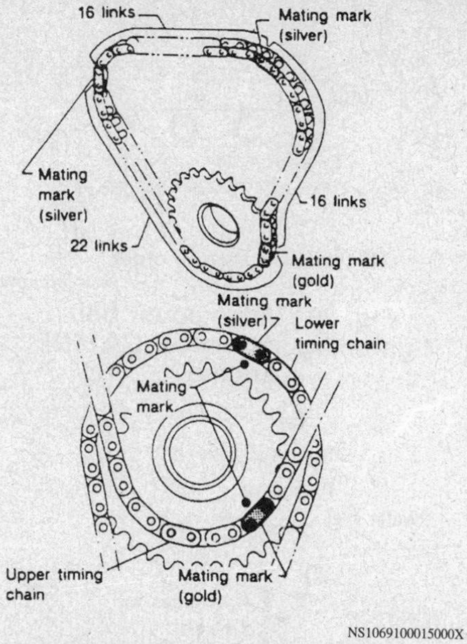
16 links
Mating mark (silver)
Mating mark (silver)
16 links
22 links
Mating mark (gold)
Mating mark (silver)
Lower timing chain
Mating mark
Upper timing chain
Mating mark (gold)
NS1069100015000X

Fig. 24 Timing chains on idler sprocket installation. GA16DE engine

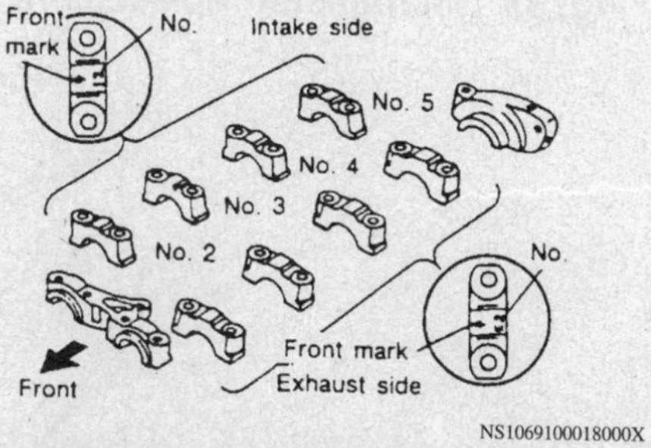
Front mark
No.
Intake side
No. 5
No. 4
No. 3
No. 2
No.
Front mark
Front
Exhaust side
NS1069100018000X

Fig. 27 Camshaft bracket installation. GA16DE engine

6. Install front exhaust tube, center member, and engine undercovers, then lower vehicle.
7. Allow liquid gasket to set at least 30 minutes before refilling engine oil.

BELT TENSION DATA

Refer to **Fig. 32** for belt deflection specifications.

COOLING SYSTEM BLEED

Refer to "Cooling System Bleed" in "SR20DE Engine" section.

THERMOSTAT

REPLACE

1. Disconnect battery ground cable.
2. Disconnect thermoswitch electrical connector, then remove thermoswitch from water inlet, **Fig. 33.**
3. Remove water inlet to thermostat housing attaching bolts.
4. Remove thermostat from thermostat housing.
5. Reverse procedure to install, applying

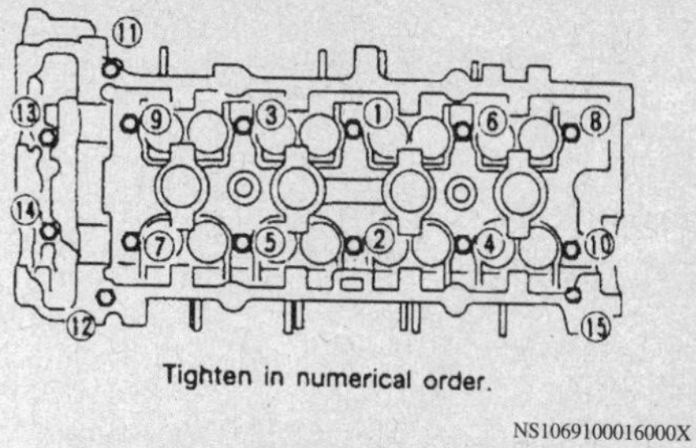
Tighten in numerical order.
NS1069100016000X

Fig. 25 Cylinder head bolt tightening sequence. GA16DE engine

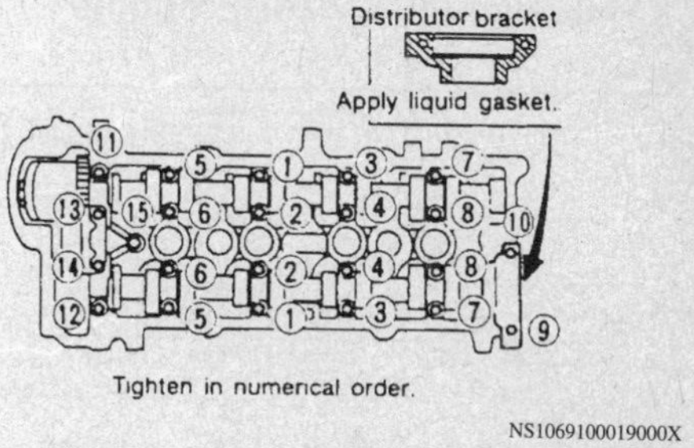
Distributor bracket
Apply liquid gasket.
Tighten in numerical order.
NS1069100019000X

Fig. 28 Camshaft bracket bolt tightening sequence. GA16DE engine

a suitable liquid gasket to water inlet as shown in **Fig. 34.**

WATER PUMP

REPLACE

1. Disconnect battery ground cable and drain cooling system.
2. Remove drive belts from compressor, power steering and alternator.
3. Remove water pump pulley, then the water pump, **Fig. 35.**
4. Clean any traces of liquid gasket from water pump and cylinder block mating surfaces.
5. Reverse procedure to install, applying liquid gasket to mating surface of pump housing.

RADIATOR

REPLACE

1. When performing radiator replacement, refer to **Fig. 36.**
2. Refer to "Cooling System Bleed" in "SR20DE Engine" section.

FUEL PUMP

REPLACE

1. Remove rear seat assembly.
2. Remove fuel pump inspection cover.
3. Disconnect fuel outlet, return tube and electrical connectors.
4. Remove fuel pump screws.
5. Remove fuel gauge assembly and disconnect tubes and connectors, **Fig. 37.**
6. Remove fuel pump assembly.
7. Reverse procedure to install.

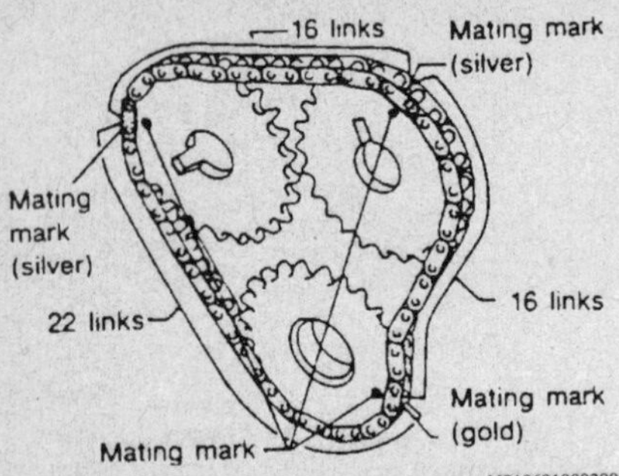

16 links
Mating mark
(silver)
Mating
mark
(silver)
22 links
16 links
Mating mark
(gold)
Mating mark

NS1069100020000X

Fig. 29 Upper timing chain installation. GA16DE engine

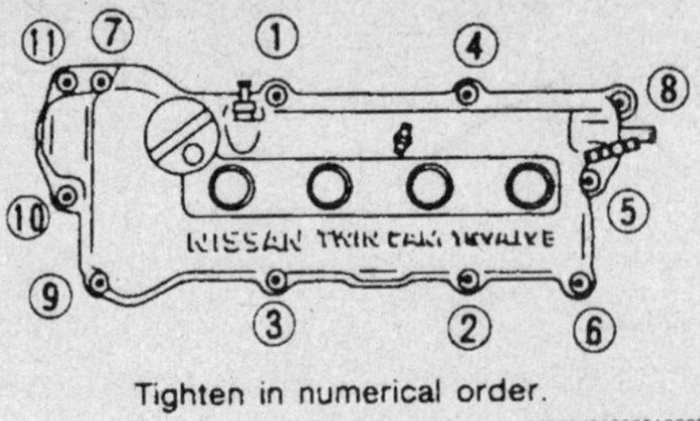

Tighten in numerical order.

NS1069100021000X

Fig. 30 Valve cover bolt tightening sequence. GA16DE engine

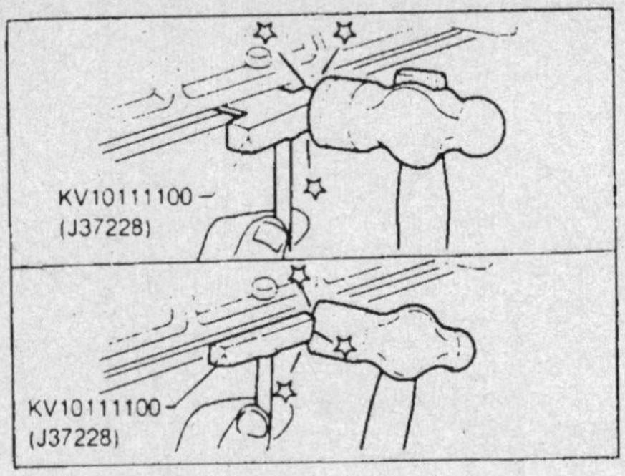

KV10111100
(J37228)
KV10111100
(J37228)

NS1069100022000X

Fig. 31 Oil pan removal

Unit: mm (in)

	Used belt deflection		Deflection of new belt
	Limit	Deflection after adjustment	
Alternator			
With air conditioner compressor	11.5 - 12.5 (0.453 - 0.492)	7 - 8 (0.28 - 0.31)	6.5 - 7.5 (0.256 - 0.295)
Without air conditioner compressor	12 - 13 (0.47 - 0.51)	8 - 9 (0.31 - 0.35)	7 - 8 (0.28 - 0.31)
Power steering oil pump	6 - 7 (0.24 - 0.28)	4 - 5 (0.16 - 0.20)	3.5 - 4.5 (0.138 - 0.177)
Applied pushing force	98 N (10 kg, 22 lb)		

Inspect drive belt deflections when engine is cold.

NS1069100023000X

Fig. 32 Drive belt deflection specifications

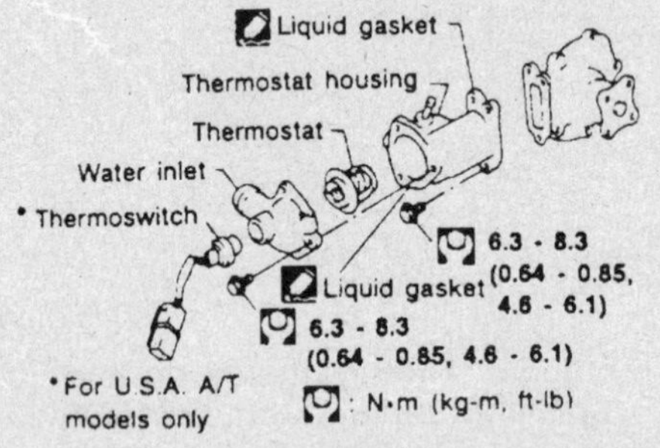

Liquid gasket
Thermostat housing
Thermostat
Water inlet
* Thermoswitch
6.3 - 8.3
(0.64 - 0.85,
4.6 - 6.1)
Liquid gasket
6.3 - 8.3
(0.64 - 0.85, 4.6 - 6.1)
* For U.S.A. A/T
models only
: N·m (kg-m, ft-lb)

NS1089100001000X

Fig. 33 Thermostat replacement

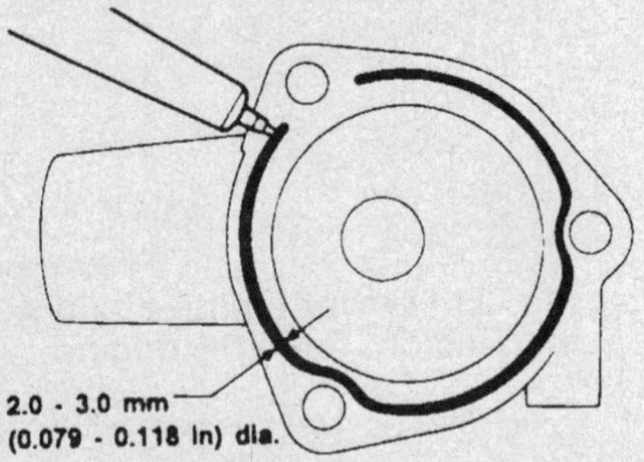

2.0 - 3.0 mm
(0.079 - 0.118 in) dia.

NS1089100002000X

Fig. 34 Thermostat housing sealant application

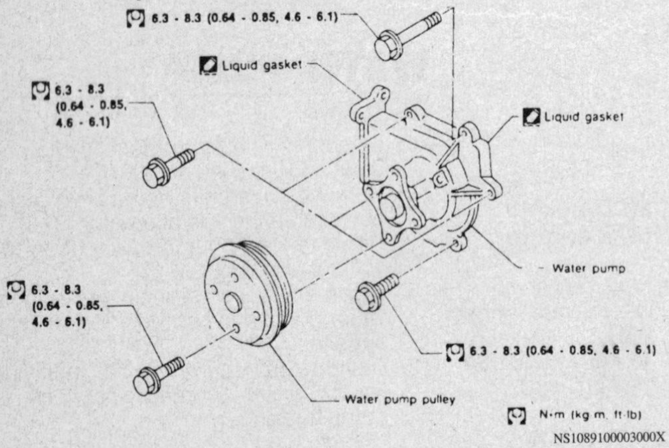

6.3 - 8.3 (0.64 - 0.85, 4.6 - 6.1)
Liquid gasket
6.3 - 8.3
(0.64 - 0.85,
4.6 - 6.1)
Liquid gasket
Water pump
6.3 - 8.3
(0.64 - 0.85,
4.6 - 6.1)
6.3 - 8.3 (0.64 - 0.85, 4.6 - 6.1)
Water pump pulley
N·m (kg-m, ft-lb)

NS1089100003000X

Fig. 35 Water pump replacement

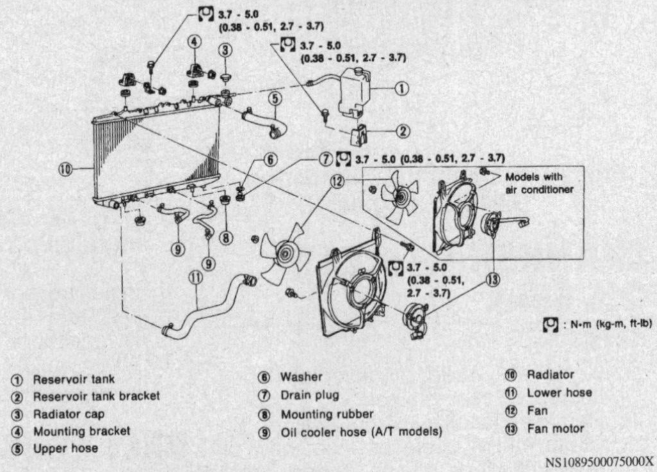

3.7 - 5.0
(0.38 - 0.51, 2.7 - 3.7)
3.7 - 5.0
(0.38 - 0.51, 2.7 - 3.7)
3.7 - 5.0 (0.38 - 0.51, 2.7 - 3.7)
Models with
air conditioner
3.7 - 5.0
(0.38 - 0.51,
2.7 - 3.7)
: N·m (kg-m, ft-lb)
① Reservoir tank
② Reservoir tank bracket
③ Radiator cap
④ Mounting bracket
⑤ Upper hose
⑥ Washer
⑦ Drain plug
⑧ Mounting rubber
⑨ Oil cooler hose (A/T models)
⑩ Radiator
⑪ Lower hose
⑫ Fan
⑬ Fan motor

NS1089500075000X

Fig. 36 Radiator replacement. GA16DE engine

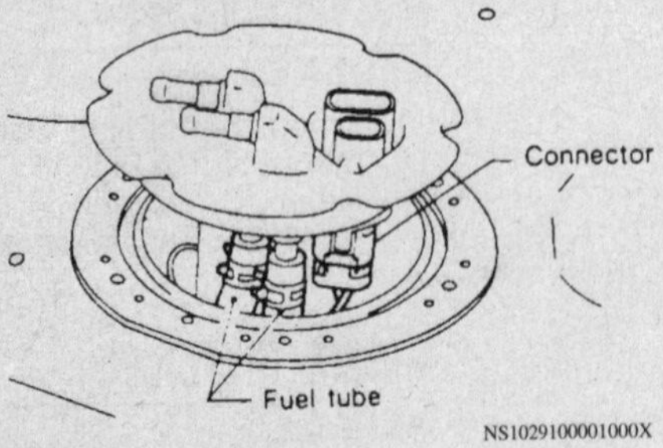

Connector
Fuel tube

NS1029100001000X

Fig. 37 Fuel pump removal

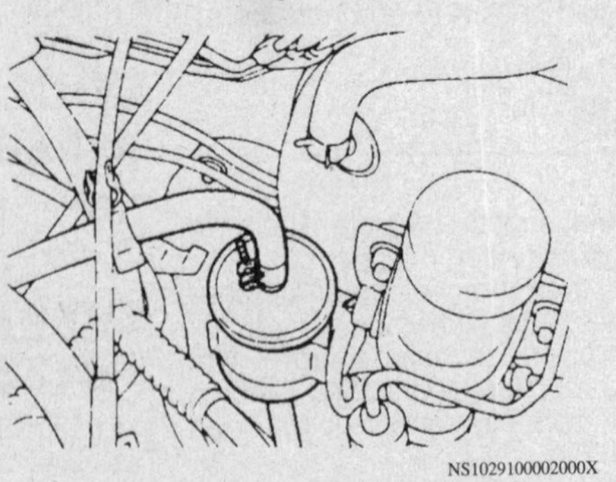

NS1029100002000X

Fig. 38 Fuel filter replacement

FUEL FILTER

REPLACE

1. Relieve fuel system pressure as outlined under "Precautions."
2. Loosen fuel filter hose clamps, **Fig. 38.**
3. Remove fuel filter. **Be careful not to spill fuel over engine compartment.**
4. Reverse procedure to install.

TIGHTENING SPECIFICATIONS

Year	Component	Torque/Ft. Lbs.
1993–96	Air Regulator	12–15
	Alternator Adjusting Bracket	12–15
	Alternator Mounting Bracket	29–33
	BPT Valve Nut	3–4
	Buffer Mounting Bolt	33–40
	Camshaft Brackets	7–9
	Camshaft Sprocket (Exhaust)	72–94
	Cam Sprocket Cover Bolt	3–4
	Cam Sprocket Cover Gusset	4
	Cam Sprocket Cover Nut	3–4
	Center Member	33–40
	Compressor Bracket	27–37
	Connecting Rod Caps	①
	Crank Angle Sensor/Distributor	7–9
	Crankshaft Pulley	98–112
	Cylinder Head	①
	Distributor Bracket	7–9
	Driveplate To Crankshaft Bolt	69–76
	EGR & Canister Control Solenoid Valve	3–4
	EGR Control Valve Securing Nut	12–15
	Engine Front Mounting	33–40
	Engine Front Mounting Bracket	33–40
	Engine Rear Mounting Bracket	33–40
	Engine Temperature Sensor	14–22
	Exhaust Gas Sensor	30–37
	Exhaust Manifold To Exhaust Pipe Nuts	21–25
	Exhaust Manifold	12–15
	Flywheel To Crankshaft Bolts	61–69
	Fuel Gallery Assembly	12–15
	Fuel Pressure Regulator	2–3
	Gusset	12–15
	Idle Air Adjusting Unit	5–6
	Idler Sprocket	32–43
	Ignition Coil	5–6
	Intake Manifold Collector	12–15
	Intake Manifold Mounting Nut	12–15
	Lower Timing Chain Guide	9–14
	Main Bearing Cap	34–38
	Oil Pan	5–6
	Oil Pan Drain Plug	22–29
	Oil Pressure Switch	23–31
	Rear Mounting	33–40
	Rear Oil Seal Retainer	5–6
	Rocker Cover Securing Bolt	2–3
	Roll Damper Bolt	33–40
	Starter Motor Mounting Bolt	23–31
	Thermostat Housing Securing Bolt	5–6
	Throttle Chamber	13–16
	Timing Chain Tensioner	5–6
	Upper Timing Chain Guide	7–9
	VTC Camshaft Sprocket (Intake)	72–94
	Water Inlet	5–6
	Water Outlet Bolt	5–6

① — Refer to "Timing Chain, Replace."

SR20DE Engine

NOTE: On Air Bag Equipped Models, Refer To "Air Bag System Precautions" Located In The Front Of This Manual For System Disarming & Arming Procedures.

INDEX

	Page No.
Accel-Drum Unit, Adjust	30-21
Belt Tension Data	30-21
Component Service	30-17
Valve Oil Seal, Replace	30-17
Compression Pressure	30-16
Cooling System Bleed	30-21
Crankshaft Rear Oil Seal, Replace	30-20
Cylinder Head, Replace	30-16
Engine Assemble	30-17
Cylinder Head	30-17
Piston, Rod & Crankshaft	30-19
Engine Disassemble	30-16
Cylinder Head	30-16
Piston, Rod & Crankshaft	30-17
Engine Mount, Replace	30-16
Engine Rebuilding Specifications	36-1
Engine, Replace	30-16
Exhaust Manifold, Replace	30-16
Front Cover Seal, Replace	30-19
Fuel Filter, Replace	30-22
Fuel Pump, Replace	30-22
Intake Manifold, Replace	30-16
Oil Pan, Replace	30-20
Installation	30-21
Removal	30-21
Oil Pump, Replace	30-21
Precautions	30-16
Air Bag Systems	30-16
Fuel System Pressure Release	30-16
Radiator, Replace	30-22
Thermostat, Replace	30-22
Tightening Specifications	30-26
Timing Chain, Replace	30-19
Installation	30-19
Removal	30-19
Valve Adjustment	30-19
Valve Clearance Specifications	30-19
Water Pump, Replace	30-22

PRECAUTIONS

AIR BAG SYSTEMS

Refer to "Air Bag System Precautions" in the front of this manual for system disarming and arming procedures.

FUEL SYSTEM PRESSURE RELEASE

1. Remove fuel pump fuse from fuse panel.
2. Start engine.
3. After engine stalls, crank engine two or three times to ensure pressure is released.
4. Turn ignition switch to off position.
5. After fuel system operations are complete, replace fuel pump fuse.

COMPRESSION PRESSURE

1. Start engine and run until engine reaches operating temperature.
2. Turn ignition switch off.
3. Release fuel pressure. Refer to "Precautions"for fuel system pressure release procedure.
4. Remove all spark plugs.
5. Disconnect distributor coil connector.
6. Attach a compression tester to cylinder No. 1.
7. Depress accelerator pedal fully to keep throttle valve wide open.
8. Crank engine and record highest gauge indication.
9. Repeat measurement on each cylinder.
10. Standard compression is 199 psi, minimum pressure is 171 psi and compression difference limit between cylinders is 14 psi.
11. If compression in one or more cylinders is low, pour a small amount of engine oil into cylinders through spark plug holes, then retest compression.
12. If adding oil helps compression, then piston rings may be at fault. If adding oil does not help compression, then valves may be at fault.
13. If compression stays low in two cylinders that are next to each other, then cylinder head gasket may be leaking or both cylinders may have valve component damage.
14. Repair as necessary.

ENGINE MOUNT

REPLACE

Refer to **Fig. 1**when replacing the engine mounts.

ENGINE

REPLACE

Refer to **Figs. 1 and 2** when removing the engine.

1. Place vehicle on level ground and block wheels.
2. Release fuel system pressure as outlined under "Precautions."
3. Remove engine undercover.
4. Mark hood for installation reference, then remove hood.
5. Drain cooling system and engine oil.
6. Disconnect fuel and vacuum hoses, wire harness and connectors as necessary. **Label hoses and connectors for installation reference.**
7. Remove front exhaust tube, ball joints and driveshafts.
8. Remove radiator fan and radiator assembly.
9. Remove drive belts.
10. Remove alternator, compressor and power steering pump from engine. Position component out of the way without disconnecting hoses.
11. Support engine with a suitable lifting device or jack, then remove center member.
12. Carefully lower engine and transaxle out of engine compartment.
13. Reverse procedure to install, noting the following:
    a. Install engine mount insulators as shown in **Fig. 3.**
    b. **On models with manual transaxle,** adjust height of engine mounting as shown in **Fig. 4.**

INTAKE MANIFOLD

REPLACE

Refer to "Cylinder Head" section under "Engine Disassemble" to remove the intake manifold and " Engine Assemble" to install the intake manifold.

EXHAUST MANIFOLD

REPLACE

Refer to "Cylinder Head" section under "Engine Disassemble" to remove the exhaust manifold and " Engine Assemble" to install the exhaust manifold.

CYLINDER HEAD

REPLACE

Refer to "Timing Chain, Replace" for cylinder head replacement procedure.

ENGINE DISASSEMBLE

Refer to **Figs. 5 and 6** when disassembling engine.

CYLINDER HEAD

1. Disconnect battery ground cable.

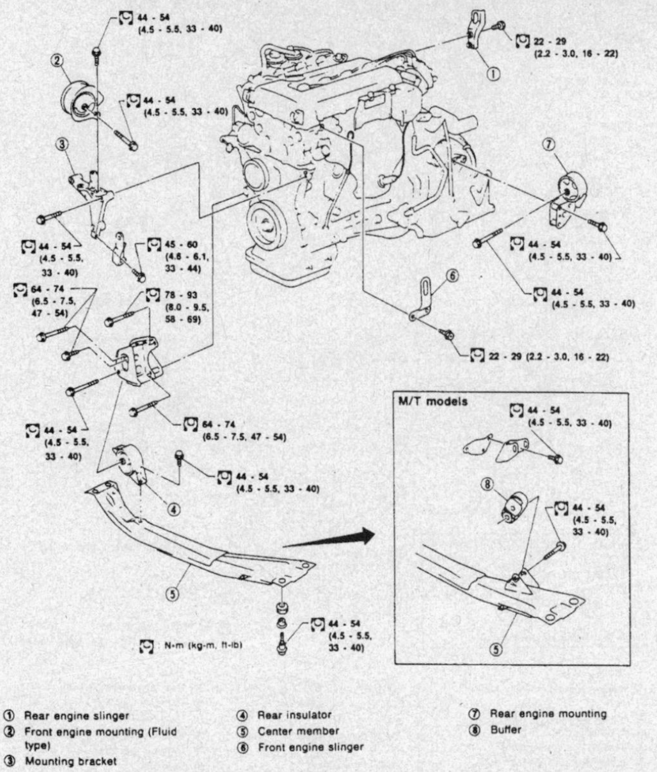
M/T models
N·m (kg-m, ft-lb)
① Rear engine slinger
② Front engine mounting (Fluid type)
③ Mounting bracket
④ Rear insulator
⑤ Center member
⑥ Front engine slinger
⑦ Rear engine mounting
⑧ Buffer
NS1069100024000X

Fig. 1 Engine mount replacement

2. Remove rocker cover, rocker arms, shim rocker arm guides and hydraulic lash adjusters. **Keep components in the order in which they were removed.**
3. Remove throttle chamber with accel-drum unit.
4. Remove EGR tube.
5. Remove exhaust manifold cover, then the exhaust manifold. Remove bolts in sequence shown in **Fig. 7.**
6. Remove fuel tube assembly as follows:
   a. Release fuel system pressure as outlined under "Fuel System Pressure Release."
   b. Disconnect injector harness connectors.
   c. Disconnect vacuum hose from pressure regulator.
   d. Disconnect fuel hoses from fuel tube assembly.
   e. Remove injectors with fuel tube assembly.
7. Remove intake manifold bolts and manifold in sequence shown, **Fig. 8.**
8. Remove intake manifold collector from intake manifold in sequence shown, **Fig. 9.**
9. Remove water outlet.
10. Remove water connector.
11. Remove thermostat housing with water pipe.
12. Remove valve components using valve spring compression and attachment tool Nos. KV10116200 (J26339-A) and KV10115900 (J26336-20), or equivalents.
13. Remove valve oil seals using seal puller tool No. KV10107902 (J38959), or equivalent.

PISTON, ROD & CRANKSHAFT

1. Remove engine as outlined under "Engine, Replace."
2. Remove cylinder head and timing chain as outlined under "Timing Chain, Replace."
3. Remove oil pan as outlined under "Oil Pan, Replace."
4. Remove pistons with connecting rods attached.
5. Remove rear oil seal retainer.
6. Using sequence shown in **Fig. 10,** remove bearing beam bolts in two or three steps.

COMPONENT SERVICE

VALVE OIL SEAL, REPLACE

1. Remove accelerator cable.
2. Remove valve cover and oil separator.
3. Remove camshafts and sprockets as outlined under "Timing Chain, Replace."
4. Remove spark plugs and cables.
5. Install air hose adapter into spark plug hole and apply pressure of 71 psi to hold valves in place.
6. Remove rocker arm, rocker arm guide and shim.
7. Remove valve spring using suitable valve spring compression tool.
8. Remove valve oil seal.
9. Reverse procedure to install, applying engine oil to new seal before installing.

ENGINE ASSEMBLE

CYLINDER HEAD

1. Apply a bead of liquid gasket to water connector mating surface.
2. Using bolt tightening sequence shown in **Fig. 11,** install thermostat housing with water pipe as follows:
   a. **Torque** thermostat housing bolt A to 1.4–3.6 ft. lbs.
   b. **Torque** water pipe bolt C to 12–15 ft. lbs.
   c. **Torque** thermostat housing bolt A to 12–15 ft. lbs.
   d. **Torque** thermostat housing bolt B to 12–15 ft. lbs.
   e. Repeat steps b through d after installing cylinder head.
3. Apply a bead of liquid gasket to mating surface of water outlet, then install water outlet.
4. Install intake manifold collector bolts to intake manifold in reverse sequence shown in **Fig. 9.**
5. Install intake manifold bolts in reverse sequence shown in **Fig. 8.**
6. Install injector tube assembly in reverse order of removal.
7. Install exhaust manifold bolts in reverse sequence shown in **Fig. 6.**
8. Install exhaust manifold cover.
9. Install EGR tube.
10. Install throttle chamber with accel-drum unit. Adjust accel-drum unit as outlined under "Accel-Drum Unit Adjust."
11. Install valve oil seals using seal drift tool No. KV10115600 (J38958), or equivalent.
12. Install valve components in order of removal (except shim), using valve spring compression and attachment tool Nos. KV10116200 (J26339-A) and KV10115900 (J26336-20), or equivalents. When installing valve springs, ensure narrow pitch of spring is pointed toward cylinder head.
13. When replacing valve, cylinder head, shim, rocker arm guide and/or valve seat, select a new valve adjustment shim as follows:
   a. Install dial gauge stand tool No. KV10115700, or equivalent and a suitable dial indicator onto cylinder head.
   b. Measure distance between sliding surface of rocker arm guide and valve stem end. **When measuring, pull lightly on dial gauge stand tool to eliminate any play in tool.**
   c. Shims are available in 17 different thicknesses ranging from .1102 inch to .1260 inch. Select a suitable shim to obtain a zero clearance ± .0010 inch between valve shim and rocker arm guide.
14. Check hydraulic lash as follows:
   a. Push on rocker arm assembly, **Fig. 12.**
   b. If rocker arm can be moved .04 inch, air is trapped in the high pressure chamber.
   c. Remove hydraulic lash adjuster

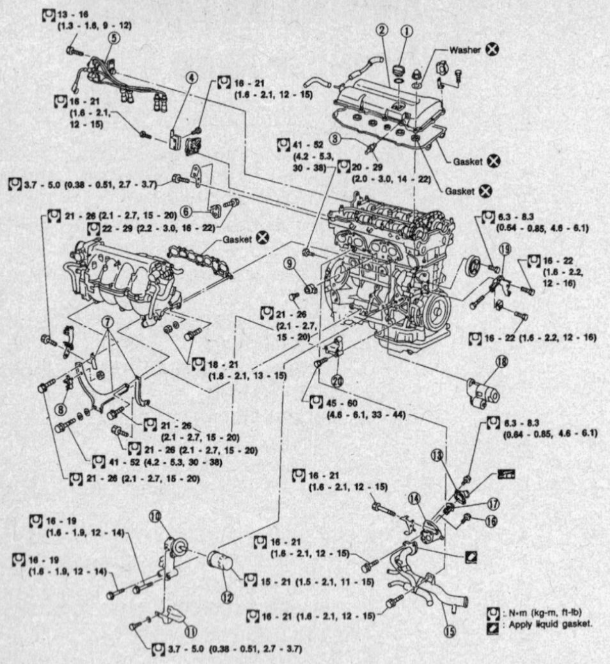
: N·m (kg-m, ft-lb)
: Apply liquid gasket.

1. Oil filler cap
2. Rocker cover
3. PCV valve
4. Ignition coil
5. Camshaft position sensor built into distributor
6. Power transistor
7. Intake manifold supports
8. EGR & canister control solenoid valve
9. Knock sensor
10. Oil filter bracket
11. Oil catcher
12. Oil filter
13. Water inlet
14. Thermostat housing
15. Water pipe assembly
16. Air relief plug
17. Thermostat
18. Starter motor
19. Power steering oil pump adjusting bar
20. Power steering oil pump bracket

NS1069100025010X

Fig. 2 Exploded view of engine outer component (Part 1 of 3)

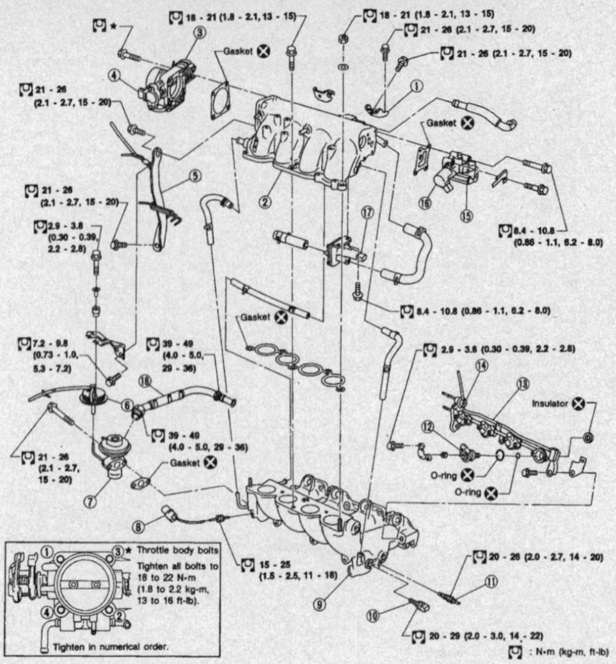
★ Throttle body bolts
Tighten all bolts to 18 to 22 N·m (1.8 to 2.2 kg-m, 13 to 16 ft-lb).
Tighten in numerical order.
: N·m (kg-m, ft-lb)

1. Intake manifold collector support
2. Intake manifold collector
3. Throttle body
4. Throttle position sensor
5. Intake manifold collector support
6. EGRC-BPT valve
7. EGR valve
8. EGR temperature sensor
9. Intake manifold
10. Engine coolant temperature sensor
11. Thermal transmitter
12. Injector
13. Fuel tube assembly
14. Pressure regulator
15. IACV-FICD valve
16. IACV-AAC valve
17. IACV-air regulator
18. EGR tube

NS1069100025020X

Fig. 2 Exploded view of engine outer component (Part 2 of 3)

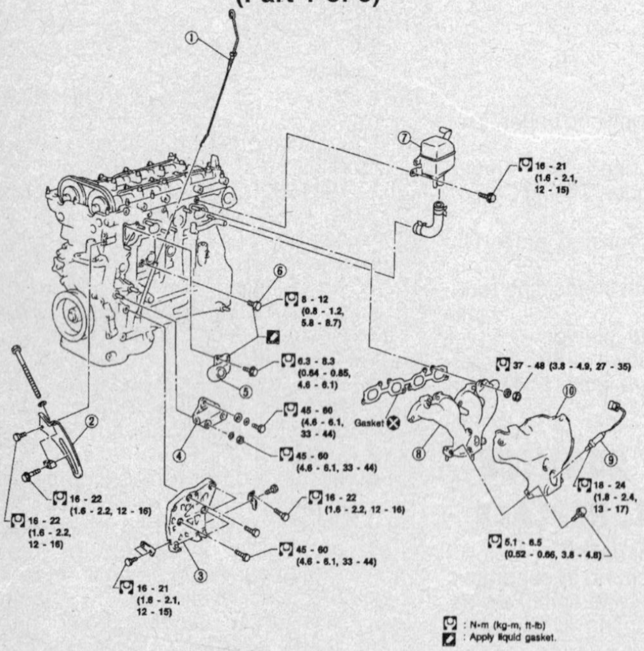
: N·m (kg-m, ft-lb)
: Apply liquid gasket.

1. Oil level gauge
2. Alternator adjusting bar
3. Compressor bracket
4. Alternator bracket
5. Water outlet
6. Drain plug
7. Oil separator
8. Exhaust manifold
9. Heated oxygen sensor
10. Exhaust manifold cover

NS1069100025030X

Fig. 2 Exploded view of engine outer component (Part 3 of 3)

and dip in a container of clean engine oil.

d. While pushing plunger, lightly push check ball using a thin rod. Air is completely bled when plunger no longer moves, **Fig. 13.**

15. Install hydraulic lash adjusters, rocker arm guides, rocker arms, shims and rocker cover.

PISTON, ROD & CRANKSHAFT

1. Install piston on rod as shown in **Fig. 14.**
2. Install piston rings on piston as shown, **Fig. 15.**
3. Install main bearing in proper position on cylinder block and main bearing caps.
4. Install crankshaft, main bearing caps and beam.
5. Using the reverse of sequence shown in **Fig. 10,** tighten bolts as follows:
   a. **Torque** bolts to 24–28 ft. lbs.
   b. **Torque** bolts to 54–61 ft. lbs.
6. Ensure crankshaft endplay is within .0039–.0102 inch.
7. Install connecting rod bearing in connection rods and caps, aligning oil hole.
8. Install pistons with connecting rods into cylinder block with front mark toward front of engine, **Fig. 14.**
9. Install connecting rod caps and **torque** in two steps to 28–33 ft. lbs.
10. Install rear oil seal retainer.

VALVE CLEARANCE SPECIFICATIONS

Valve clearance should be zero ± .0010

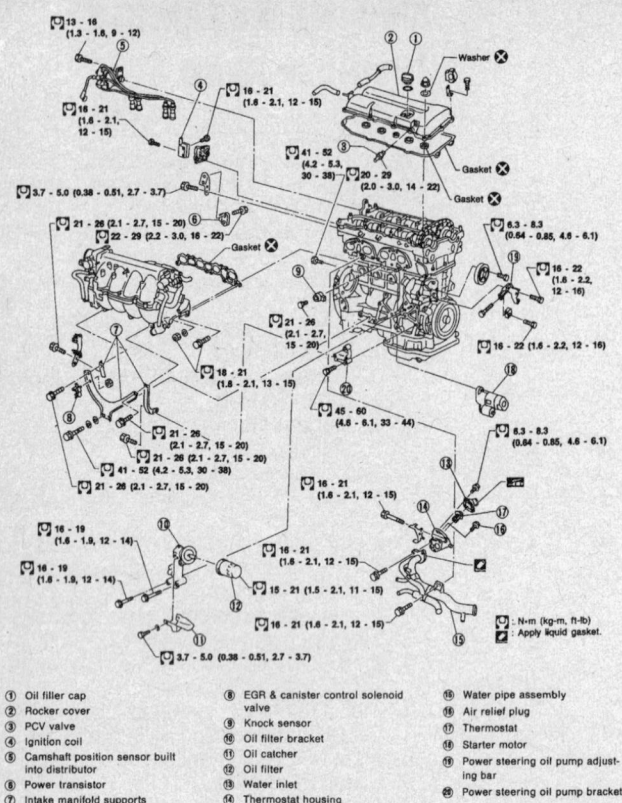

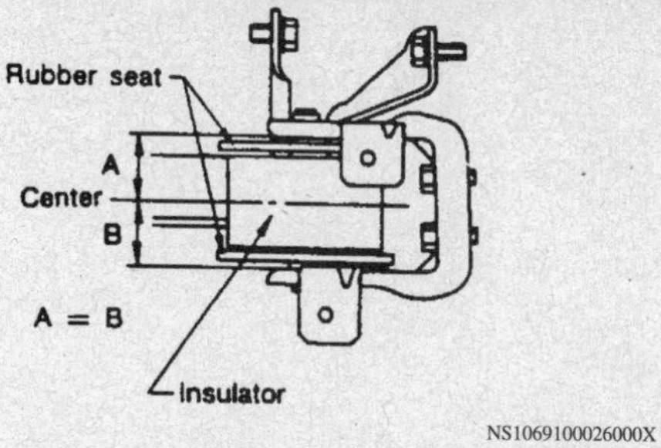
Rubber seat
Center
A
B
A = B
Insulator
NS1069100026000X

Fig. 3 Engine mount insulators installation

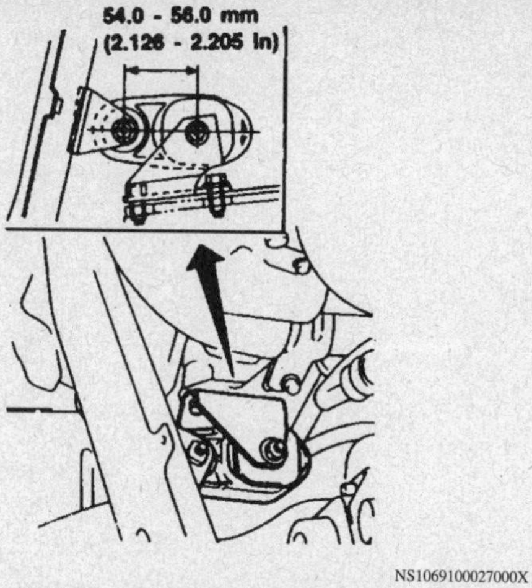
54.0 - 56.0 mm
(2.126 - 2.205 in)
NS1069100027000X

Fig. 4 Engine height adjustment. Models w/manual transaxle

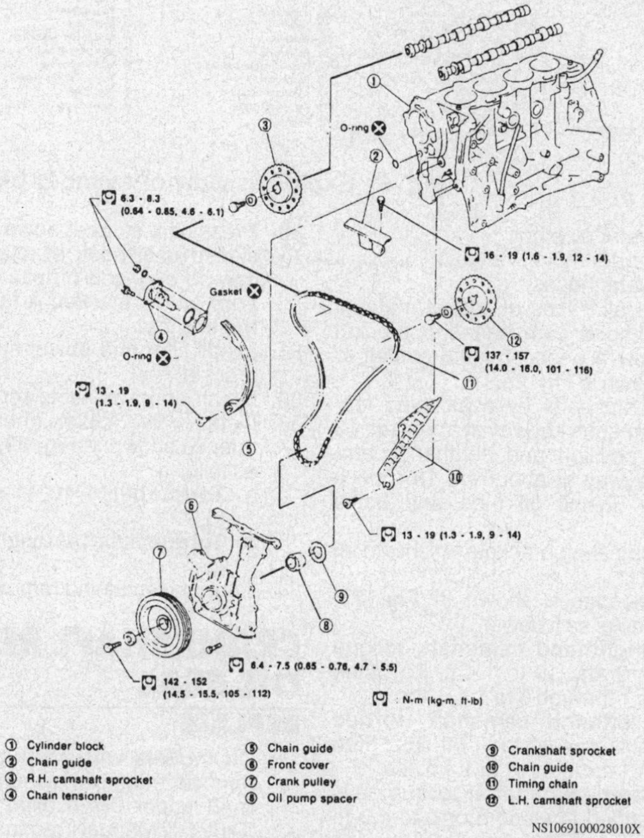
O-ring
6.3 - 8.3
(0.64 - 0.85, 4.6 - 6.1)
Gasket
O-ring
13 - 19
(1.3 - 1.9, 9 - 14)
16 - 19 (1.6 - 1.9, 12 - 14)
137 - 157
(14.0 - 16.0, 101 - 116)
13 - 19 (1.3 - 1.9, 9 - 14)
6.4 - 7.5 (0.65 - 0.76, 4.7 - 5.5)
142 - 152
(14.5 - 15.5, 105 - 112)
: N·m (kg-m, ft-lb)
① Cylinder block
② Chain guide
③ R.H. camshaft sprocket
④ Chain tensioner
⑤ Chain guide
⑥ Front cover
⑦ Crank pulley
⑧ Oil pump spacer
⑨ Crankshaft sprocket
⑩ Chain guide
⑪ Timing chain
⑫ L.H. camshaft sprocket
NS1069100028010X

Fig. 5 Timing chain replacement (Part 1 of 2)

inch. Hydraulic lash adjuster guide inner diameter should be .6693–.6701 inch. Standard clearance between hydraulic lash adjuster and adjuster guides is .0003–.0016 inch.

VALVE ADJUSTMENT

This engine uses hydraulic lash adjusters to maintain a valve clearance of zero ± .0010 inch. If clearance between rocker arm guide and valve shim is greater than .0010 inch, select and install a new shim.

Refer to "Cylinder Head" in "Engine Assembly" for procedure.

FRONT COVER SEAL

REPLACE

1. Remove engine undercover.
2. Remove righthand wheel and engine side cover.
3. Remove drive belts, then the crankshaft pulley.
4. Remove front oil seal.
5. Reverse procedure to install, applying engine oil to seal prior to installation.

TIMING CHAIN

REPLACE

Refer to **Fig. 5** when replacing the timing chain.

REMOVAL

1. Release fuel system pressure as outlined under "Precautions."
2. Remove engine undercover.
3. Remove righthand wheel and engine side cover.
4. Drain engine coolant and oil.
5. Remove radiator and shroud assembly.
6. Remove air duct to intake manifold.
7. Remove drive belts.
8. Remove water pump pulley, alternator and power steering pump.
9. Remove necessary vacuum, fuel and electrical connections. **Label hoses and connectors for installation reference.**
10. Remove spark plugs and cables.
11. Remove valve cover and oil separator, **Fig. 16.**
12. Remove intake manifold supports.
13. Remove oil filter and power steering pump brackets.
14. Set No. 1 cylinder at TDC on its compression stroke, then rotate crankshaft until mating marks on camshaft sprockets are aligned as shown in **Fig. 17.**
15. Remove chain tensioner.
16. Remove distributor, then the timing chain guide.
17. Remove camshaft sprockets.
18. Using sequence shown in **Fig. 18,** remove camshaft brackets.
19. Remove camshafts, oil tube and baffle plate.
20. Remove water hose for cylinder block and hose from heater.
21. Remove starter motor, then the water pipe bolt.
22. Disconnect knock sensor harness connector.
23. Remove EGR tube.
24. Remove cylinder head outside bolts, **Fig. 19.**
25. Using sequence shown in **Fig. 20,** remove cylinder head bolts in two or three steps.
26. Remove cylinder head with manifolds attached.
27. Remove oil pan as outlined under "Oil Pan, Replace."
28. Remove oil pan strainer and baffle plate.
29. Remove crankshaft pulley.
30. Set a suitable transmission jack under main bearing beam.
31. Remove righthand engine mounting.
32. Remove front cover and oil pump drive spacer.
33. Remove timing chain guides and timing chain.

INSTALLATION

1. Install crankshaft sprocket on crankshaft.
2. Position crankshaft so that No. 1 cylinder is at TDC.
3. Align gold mating mark on timing chain

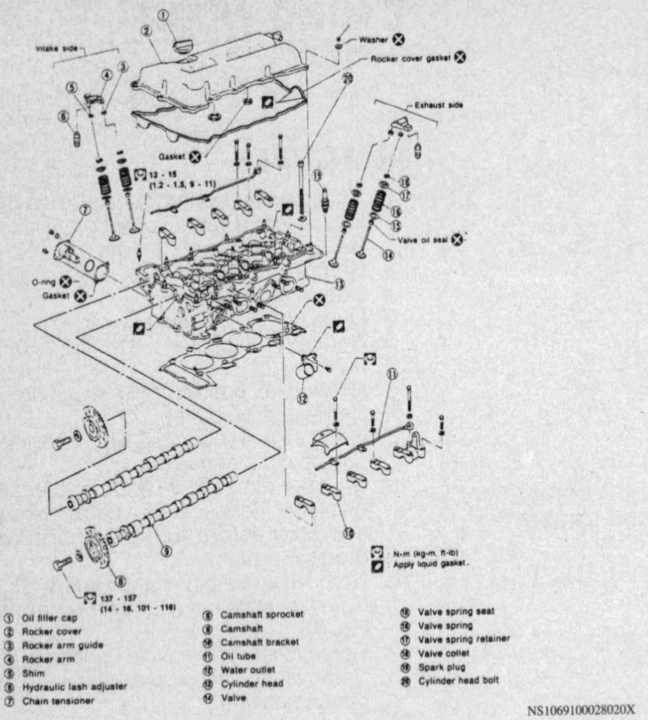
Intake side
Exhaust side
Washer
Rocker cover gasket
Gasket
Valve oil seal
O-ring
137 - 157 (14 - 16, 101 - 116)
: N·m (kg-m, ft-lb)
: Apply liquid gasket.
① Oil filler cap
② Rocker cover
③ Rocker arm guide
④ Rocker arm
⑤ Shim
⑥ Hydraulic lash adjuster
⑦ Chain tensioner
⑧ Camshaft sprocket
⑨ Camshaft
⑩ Camshaft bracket
⑪ Oil tube
⑫ Water outlet
⑬ Cylinder head
⑭ Valve
⑮ Valve spring seat
⑯ Valve spring
⑰ Valve spring retainer
⑱ Valve collet
⑲ Spark plug
⑳ Cylinder head bolt
NS1069100028020X

Fig. 5 Timing chain replacement (Part 2 of 2)

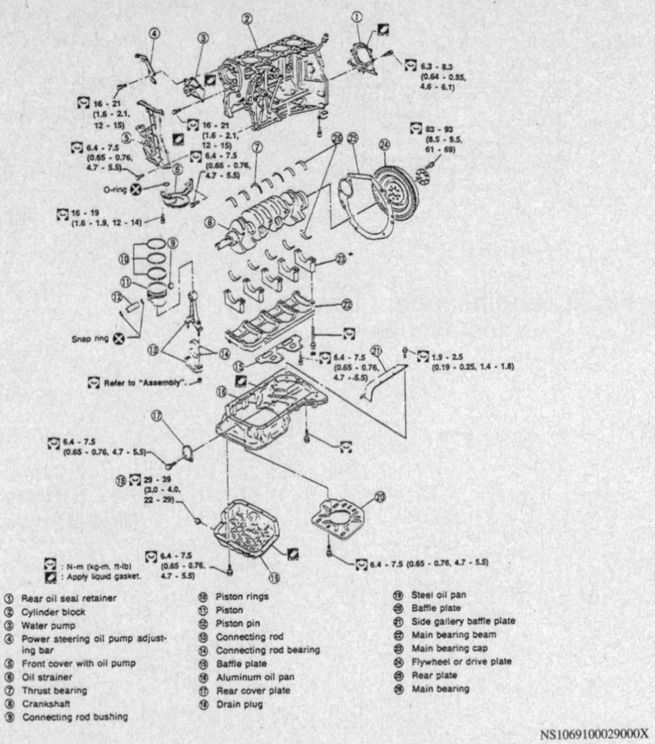
O-ring
Snap ring
Refer to "Assembly".
: N·m (kg-m, ft-lb)
: Apply liquid gasket.
6.4 - 7.5 (0.65 - 0.76, 4.7 - 5.5)
① Rear oil seal retainer
② Cylinder block
③ Water pump
④ Power steering oil pump adjusting bar
⑤ Front cover with oil pump
⑥ Oil strainer
⑦ Thrust bearing
⑧ Crankshaft
⑨ Connecting rod bushing
⑩ Piston rings
⑪ Piston
⑫ Piston pin
⑬ Connecting rod
⑭ Connecting rod bearing
⑮ Baffle plate
⑯ Aluminum oil pan
⑰ Rear cover plate
⑱ Drain plug
⑲ Steel oil pan
⑳ Baffle plate
㉑ Side gallery baffle plate
㉒ Main bearing beam
㉓ Main bearing cap
㉔ Flywheel or drive plate
㉕ Rear plate
㉖ Main bearing
NS1069100029000X

Fig. 6 Exploded view of cylinder block

to crankshaft sprocket, then install timing chain on crankshaft sprocket, **Fig. 21.**

4. Install timing chain guides.
5. Before installing front cover, remove all traces of gasket material on all mounting surfaces.
6. Apply a bead of liquid gasket to mounting surface of front cover, **Fig. 22.**
7. Install oil pump drive spacer and front cover. **Ensure mating marks on timing chain and crankshaft sprocket align.**
8. Remove excess liquid gasket.
9. Install front engine mounting bracket.
10. Install crankshaft pulley and set No. 1 cylinder at TDC on its compression stroke.
11. Install oil strainer and oil pan baffle plate.
12. Install oil pan as outlined under "Oil Pan, Replace."
13. Remove all traces of gasket material from mating surfaces of cylinder head and cylinder block.
14. Prior to installing cylinder head bolts, ensure dimension "A" shown in **Fig. 23**is less than 6.23 inches.
15. Install cylinder head bolts, then using sequence shown in **Fig. 24,** tighten as follows:
    a. **Torque** bolts to 29 ft. lbs.
    b. **Torque** bolts to 58 ft. lbs.
    c. Loosen bolts completely.
    d. **Torque** bolts to 25–33 ft. lbs.
    e. Turn bolts 90–100° clockwise.
    f. Turn bolts an additional 90–100° clockwise.
16. Install cylinder head outside bolts, **Fig. 19.**
17. Install EGR tube.
18. Connect knock sensor harness connector.
19. Install water pipe bolt.
20. Install starter motor.
21. Install water hoses.
22. Remove all traces of gasket material from lefthand camshaft end bracket and apply a bead of liquid gasket to area shown in **Fig. 25.**
23. Install camshafts by positioning lefthand camshaft keyway at about the 12 o'clock position and righthand camshaft keyway at about the 10 o'clock position. Install oil tube and baffle plate.
24. Install camshaft brackets as shown in, **Fig. 26.**
25. Using sequence shown in **Fig. 27,** tighten bolts as follows:
    a. **On righthand camshaft, torque** bolts 9 and 10 to 1.4 ft. lbs., then bolts 1 through 8 to 1.4 ft. lbs.
    b. **On lefthand camshaft, torque** bolts 11 and 12 to 1.4 ft. lbs., then bolts 1 through 10 to 1.4 ft. lbs.
    c. **On both camshafts, torque** bolts described in steps a or b to 4.3 ft. lbs.
    d. **Torque,** bolts marked A, B and C to 8.7 ft. lbs.
    e. **Torque** bolts marked D to 13–19 ft. lbs.
26. Align silver mating mark on timing chain with marks on camshaft sprockets, then install camshaft sprockets.
27. Lock camshaft using a suitable wrench on flats of camshaft and **torque** camshaft bolts in two steps to 101–116 ft. lbs.
28. Install timing chain guide.
29. Install distributor. **Ensure after installing distributor, distributor rotor is positioned at No. 1 cylinder spark position.**
30. Press cam stopper down and press in sleeve until hook of chain tensioner can be engaged on pin, **Fig. 28. Ensure arrow marked A faces front of the engine.**
31. Install filter and power steering pump bracket.
32. Install intake manifold supports.
33. Install valve cover, then using sequence shown in **Fig. 29,** tighten nuts as follows:
    a. **Torque** nuts 1, 10, 11 and 8 to 2.9 ft. lbs.
    b. **Torque** nuts 1 through 13 to 7.2 ft. lbs.
34. Reverse remaining removal steps.

CRANKSHAFT REAR OIL SEAL

REPLACE

1. **On models with manual transaxle,** remove transaxle assembly as outlined under "Transaxle, Replace" in "Clutch & Manual Transmission."
2. **On models with automatic transaxles,** remove transaxle assembly as outlined in "Automatic Transmissions/Transaxles."
3. **On all models,** remove flywheel or driveplate.
4. Remove rear oil seal.
5. Reverse procedure to install, applying engine oil to new seal before installation.

OIL PAN

REPLACE

Refer to **Fig. 30** when replacing the oil pan assembly.

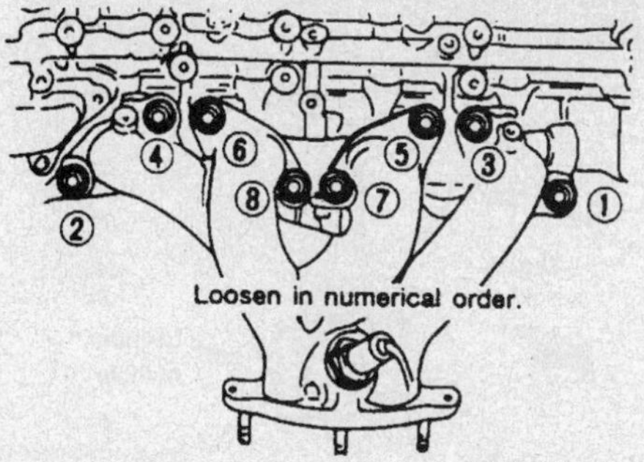
Loosen in numerical order.

NS1079100001000X

Fig. 7 Exhaust manifold bolt removal sequence

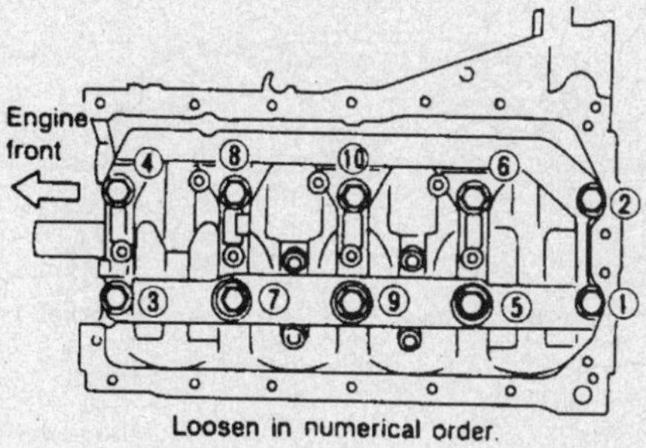
Engine front
Loosen in numerical order.

NS1069100030000X

Fig. 10 Crankshaft bearing beam bolt removal sequence

REMOVAL

1. Remove engine undercover.
2. Drain engine oil into a suitable container.
3. Using sequence shown in **Fig. 31,** remove steel oil pan bolts.
4. Insert oil pan remover tool KV10111100, or equivalent, between steel oil pan and aluminum oil pan, then using a hammer, remove steel oil pan. **Use care not to damage aluminum oil pan when inserting oil pan remover tool.**
5. Remove oil baffle plate.
6. Remove front exhaust tube.
7. Support engine with a suitable lifting device or jack, then remove center member.
8. **On models with automatic transaxles,** remove shift control cable.
9. **On all models,** remove compressor gussets, **Fig. 32.**
10. Remove oil pan rear cover plate.
11. Using sequence shown in **Fig. 33,** remove aluminum oil pan bolts.
12. Remove two engine to transaxle bolts and install them into vacant holes, **Fig. 34.**
13. Tighten bolts to release aluminum oil pan from cylinder block.
14. Insert oil pan remover tool No. KV10111100, or equivalent, between aluminum oil pan and cylinder block, then using a hammer, remove aluminum oil pan. **Use care not to damage aluminum oil pan when inserting oil pan remover tool.**
15. Remove two engine to transaxle bolts, used to remove aluminum oil pan.

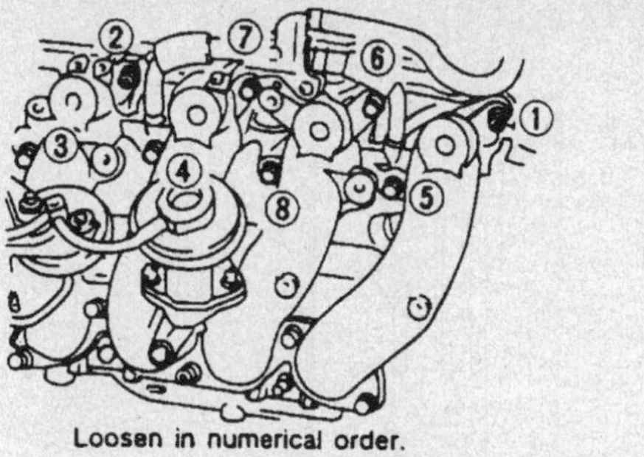
Loosen in numerical order.

NS1059100001000X

Fig. 8 Intake manifold bolt removal sequence

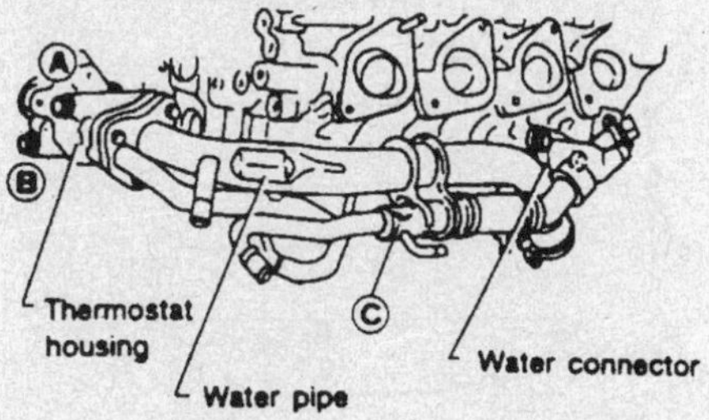
A
B
C
Thermostat housing
Water pipe
Water connector

NS1069100031000X

Fig. 11 Thermostat housing & water pipe bolt tightening sequence

INSTALLATION

1. Remove all traces of gasket material from mating surfaces of oil pans and cylinder block.
2. Apply a bead of liquid gasket to cylinder block mating surface as shown, **Fig. 35. On areas marked with a star, apply gasket to outer side of bolt hole.**
3. Install aluminum oil pan and oil pan bolts, then using sequence shown in **Fig. 36, torque** bolts 1 through 16 to 12–14 ft. lbs. and bolts 17 and 18 to 4.7–5.5 ft. lbs.
4. Install two engine to transaxle bolts.
5. Install rear cover plate.
6. Install compressor gussets.
7. **On models with automatic transaxles,** install shift control cable.
8. **On all models,** install center member.
9. Install front exhaust tube.
10. Install oil pan baffle plate.
11. Apply a bead of liquid gasket to steel oil pan.
12. Install steel oil pan and oil pan bolts, then using sequence shown in **Fig. 37,** tighten bolts to specifications.
13. Wait at least 60 minutes before refilling engine with oil.

OIL PUMP

REPLACE

1. Remove drive belts.
2. Remove cylinder head as outlined under "Cylinder Head, Replace."
3. Remove oil pans as outlined under "Oil Pan, Replace."
4. Remove oil strainer and baffle plate.
5. Remove front cover assembly, **Fig. 38.**

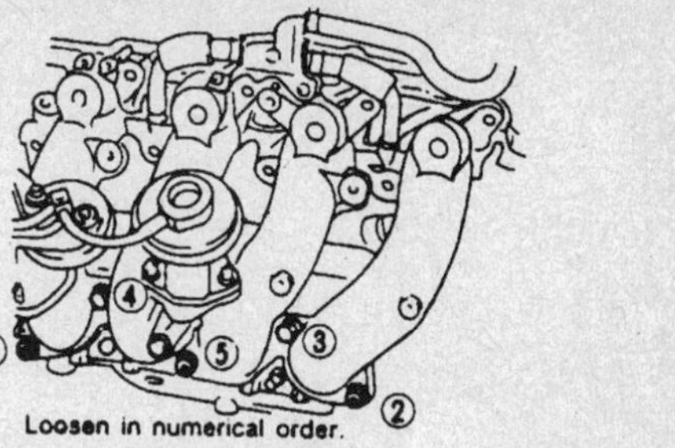
Loosen in numerical order.

NS1059100002000X

Fig. 9 Intake manifold collector bolt removal sequence

6. Reverse procedure to install, noting the following:
   a. Prior to installation, remove all traces of gasket material from mating surfaces.
   b. Apply a bead of liquid gasket to mating surface of front cover assembly.

ACCEL-DRUM UNIT

ADJUST

Adjust accel-drum unit whenever the accel-drum unit, throttle chamber and/or accel-drum unit rod are installed or reinstalled.

1. Install accel-drum unit and throttle chamber.
2. Apply grease all over inside of rod coupling, **Fig. 39.**
3. Insert each coupling to ball links of throttle chamber and accel-drum unit.
4. Loosen adjusting screw locknut.
5. Loosen adjusting screw.
6. Manually turn accel-drum until throttle valve is fully open. **Ensure stopper lever is not touching adjusting screw.**
7. Turn adjusting screw until it touches stopper lever.
8. Back off accel-drum unit.
9. Turn adjusting screw three rotations clockwise.
10. Tighten locknut.

BELT TENSION DATA

Refer to **Fig. 40** for drive belt deflection specifications.

COOLING SYSTEM BLEED

1. Set heater temperature control lever to Max Hot position.
2. Remove radiator fill cap, air relief plug and bleeder cap, **Fig. 41.**
3. Fill radiator and reservoir tank with coolant. Air relief plug should be installed once coolant spills from hole during filling.
4. Reinstall air bleeder cap.
5. Install a suitable steel wire under radiator fill cap to allow coolant to pass into reservoir tank regardless of system pressure.
6. Start engine and raise engine temperature to normal operating temperature.

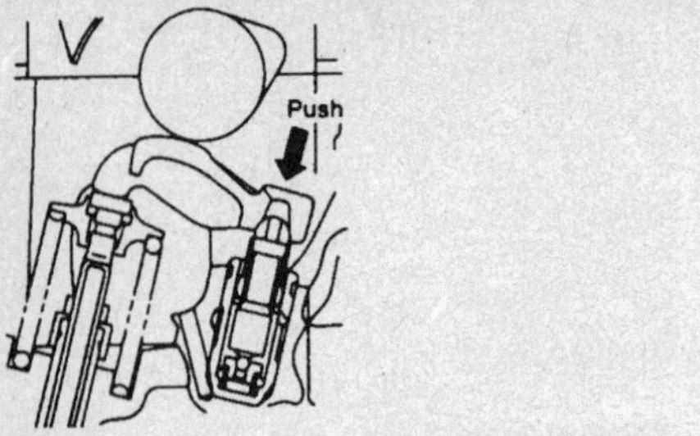
Push

NS1069100032000X

Fig. 12 Hydraulic lash adjuster inspection

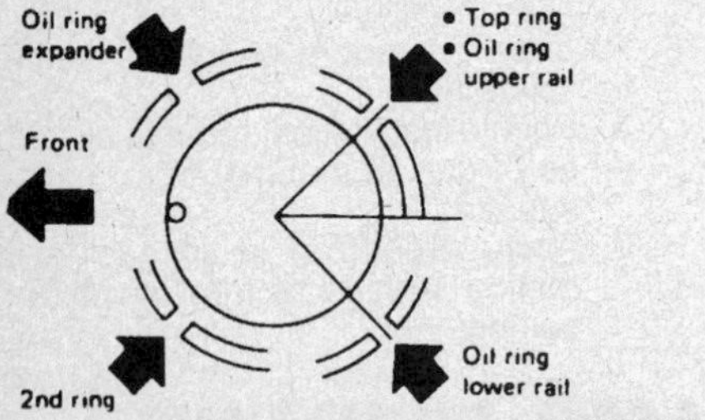
Oil ring expander
• Top ring
• Oil ring upper rail
Front
Oil ring lower rail
2nd ring

NS1069100035000X

Fig. 15 Piston rings installation

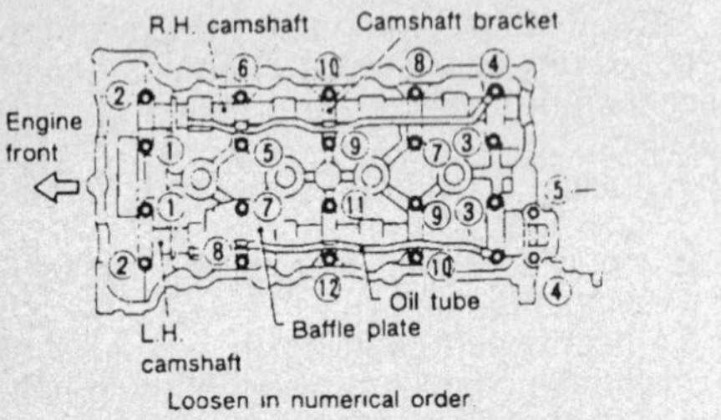
R.H. camshaft
Camshaft bracket
Engine front
Oil tube
Baffle plate
L.H. camshaft
Loosen in numerical order

NS1069100038000X

Fig. 18 Camshaft bracket bolt removal sequence

7. Run engine at 2500 RPM for ten seconds and return to idle. Repeat two or three times. **Watch engine coolant temperature gauge so engine does not overheat.**
8. Stop engine and allow to cool.
9. Fill radiator and reservoir as necessary.
10. Repeat steps 7 through 9 two or three times.
11. Remove steel wire and reinstall filler cap.
12. Raise engine temperature to normal and check for sounds of coolant flow while running engine from idle to 4000 RPM.
13. If sound is heard, bleed air from system as follows:
    a. Allow engine to cool.
    b. Remove air bleeder cap on heater inlet hose.
    c. Attach a suitable transparent hose at air bleeder pipe and place other end into coolant reservoir tank.
    d. Start engine and check for bubbles in reservoir tank.
    e. Set heater temperature control lever to Max Cool position.
    f. Run engine at 2300 RPM until bubbles disappear. **Do not run engine over 2300 RPM because engine damage may occur due to reduced coolant flow.**
    g. Set heater temperature control lever to Max Hot position and check for coolant flow sounds.
    h. If sounds are present, repeat steps e through g.
    i. If sounds are not present, allow engine to cool, remove steel wire and hose attached to air bleeder, then install air bleeder cap.

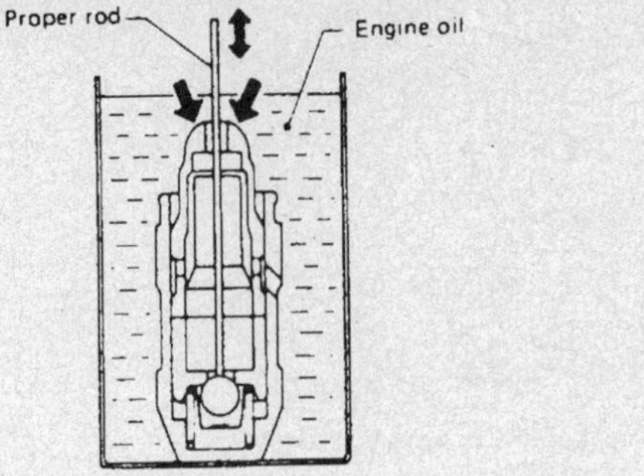
Proper rod
Engine oil

NS1069100033000X

Fig. 13 Bleeding hydraulic lash adjuster

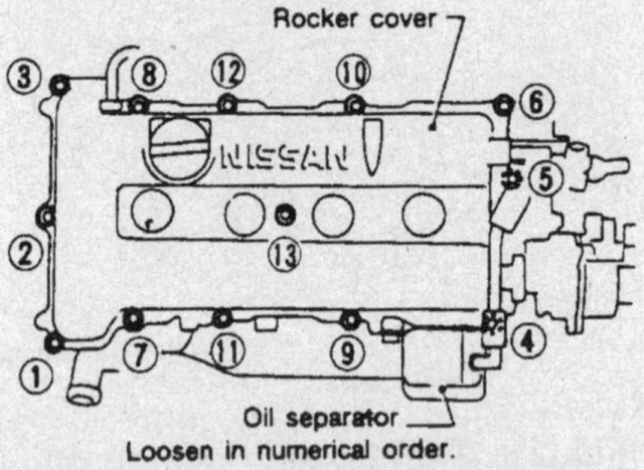
Rocker cover
NISSAN
Oil separator
Loosen in numerical order.

NS1069100036000X

Fig. 16 Valve cover bolt removal sequence

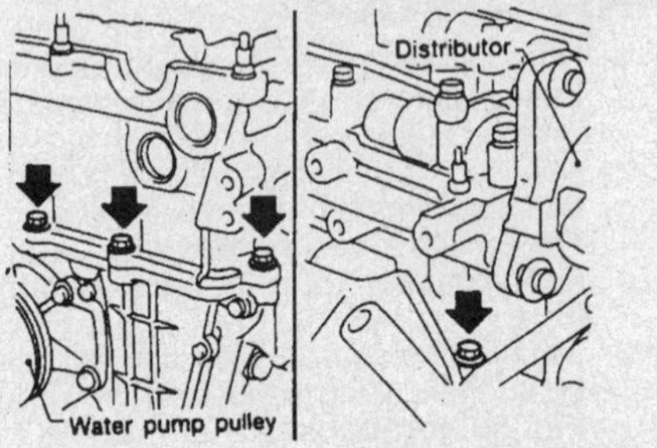
Distributor
Water pump pulley

NS1069100039000X

Fig. 19 Cylinder head outer bolts removal

THERMOSTAT

REPLACE

1. Disconnect battery ground cable, then drain engine coolant.
2. Remove water inlet attaching bolts, then the water inlet, **Fig. 42.**
3. Remove thermostat from thermostat housing.
4. Reverse procedure to install, applying suitable liquid sealant to water inlet.

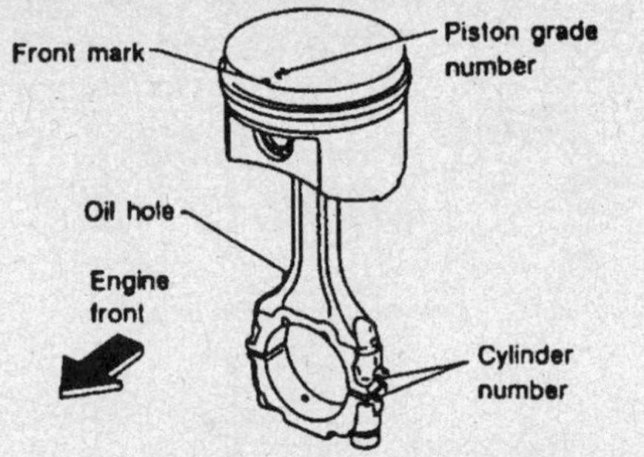
Front mark
Piston grade number
Oil hole
Engine front
Cylinder number

NS1069100034000X

Fig. 14 Piston & connecting rod front mark location

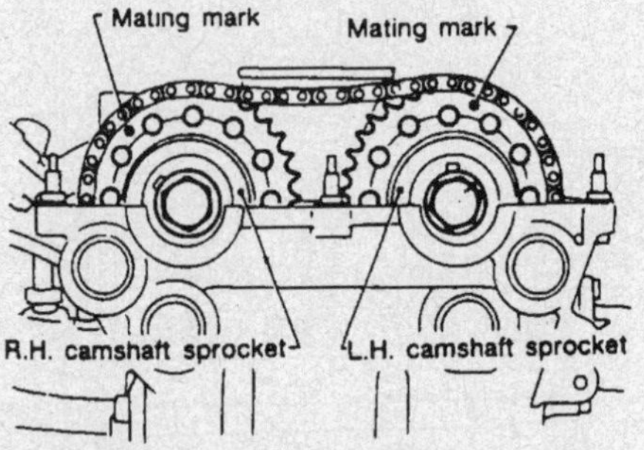
Mating mark
Mating mark
R.H. camshaft sprocket
L.H. camshaft sprocket

NS1069100037000X

Fig. 17 Camshaft timing mark alignment

WATER PUMP

REPLACE

1. Drain cooling system into a suitable container.
2. Remove drive belts.
3. Remove water pump, **Fig. 43.**
4. Reverse procedure to install.

RADIATOR

REPLACE

1. When performing radiator replacement, refer to **Fig. 44.**
2. Refer to "Cooling System Bleed."

FUEL PUMP

REPLACE

1. Remove rear seat assembly.
2. Remove fuel pump inspection cover.
3. Disconnect fuel outlet, return tube and electrical connectors.
4. Remove fuel pump screws.
5. Remove fuel gauge assembly, then disconnect tubes and connectors, **Fig. 45.**
6. Remove fuel pump assembly.
7. Reverse procedure to install.

FUEL FILTER

REPLACE

1. Relieve fuel system pressure as outlined under "Precautions."

2. Loosen fuel filter hose clamps, **Fig. 46.**
3. Remove fuel filter. **Be careful not to spill fuel over engine compartment.**
4. Reverse procedure to install.

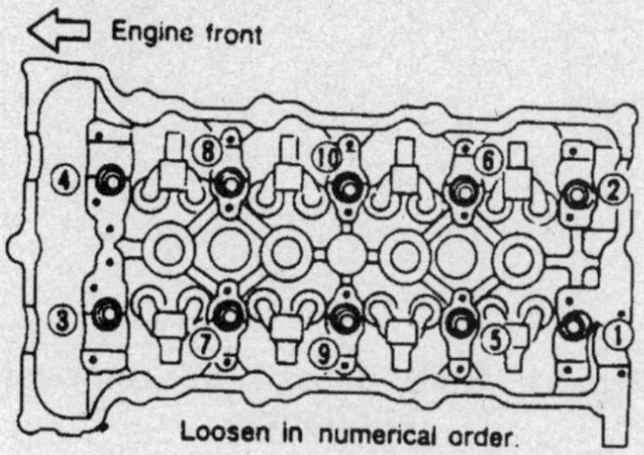
Engine front
Loosen in numerical order.
NS1069100040000X

Fig. 20 Cylinder head bolt removal sequence

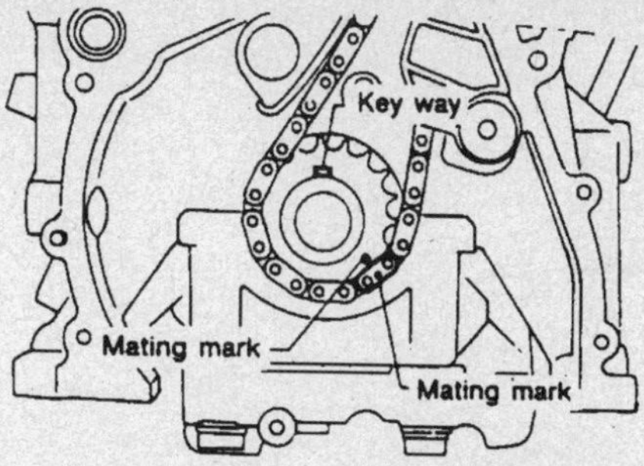
Key way
Mating mark
Mating mark
NS1069100041000X

Fig. 21 Crankshaft timing mark alignment

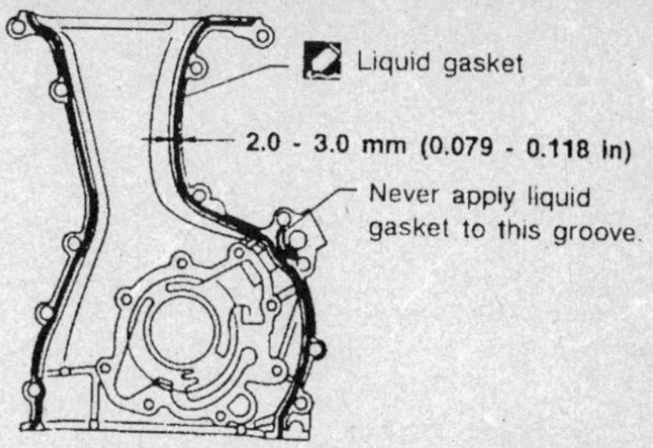
Liquid gasket
2.0 - 3.0 mm (0.079 - 0.118 in)
Never apply liquid gasket to this groove.
NS1069100042000X

Fig. 22 Front cover liquid gasket application

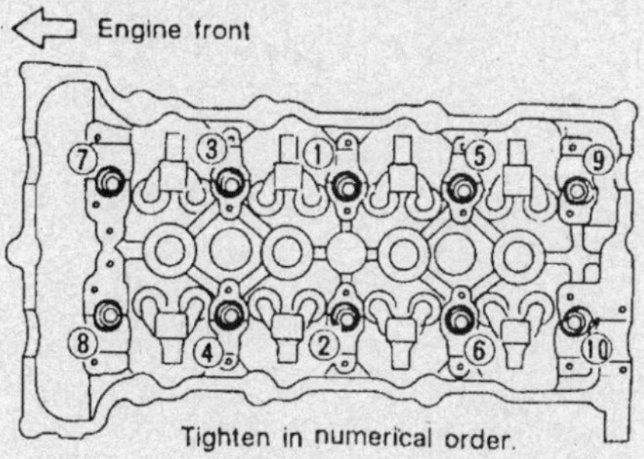
Engine front
Tighten in numerical order.
NS1069100043000X

Fig. 23 Cylinder head bolt measurement

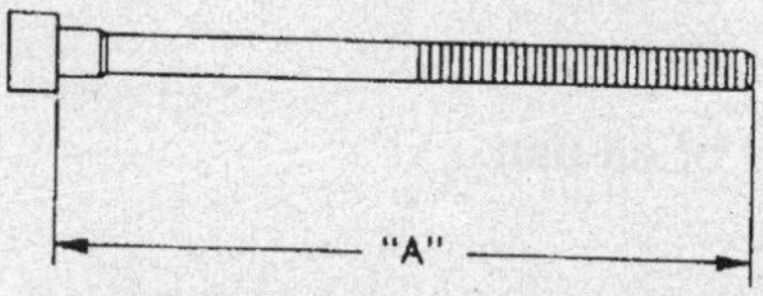
"A"
NS1069100044000X

Fig. 24 Cylinder head bolt tightening sequence

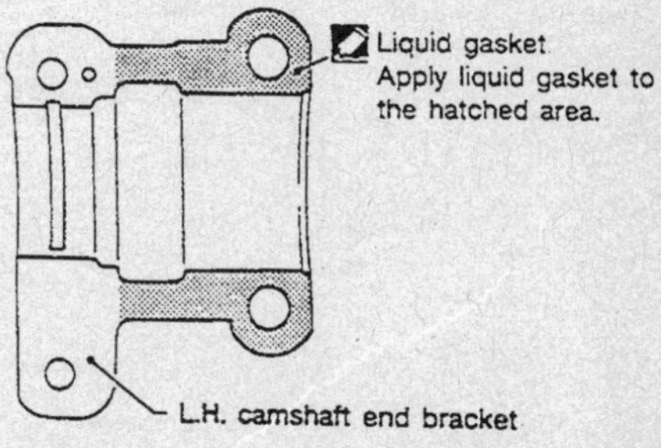
Liquid gasket
Apply liquid gasket to the hatched area.
L.H. camshaft end bracket
NS1069100045000X

Fig. 25 Lefthand camshaft end bracket liquid gasket application

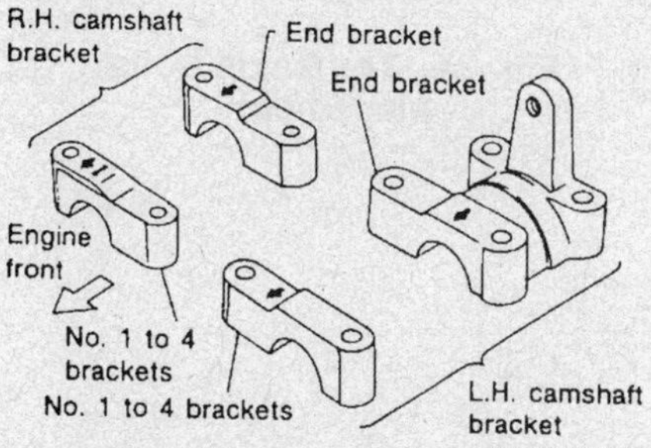
R.H. camshaft bracket
End bracket
End bracket
Engine front
No. 1 to 4 brackets
No. 1 to 4 brackets
L.H. camshaft bracket
NS1069100046000X

Fig. 26 Camshaft bracket installation direction

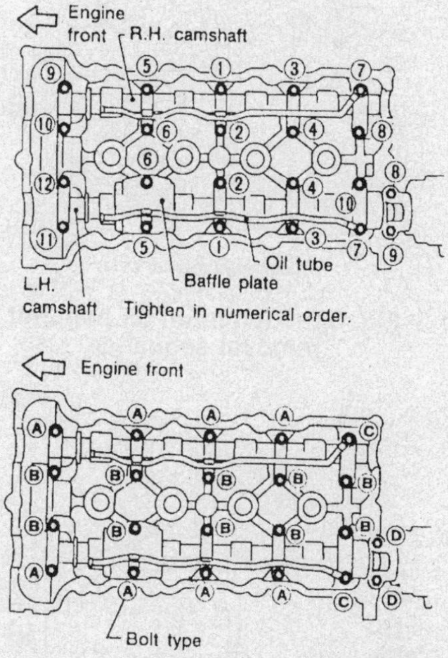
Engine front
R.H. camshaft
Oil tube
Baffle plate
L.H. camshaft
Tighten in numerical order.
Engine front
Bolt type
NS1069100047000X

Fig. 27 Camshaft bracket bolt tightening sequence

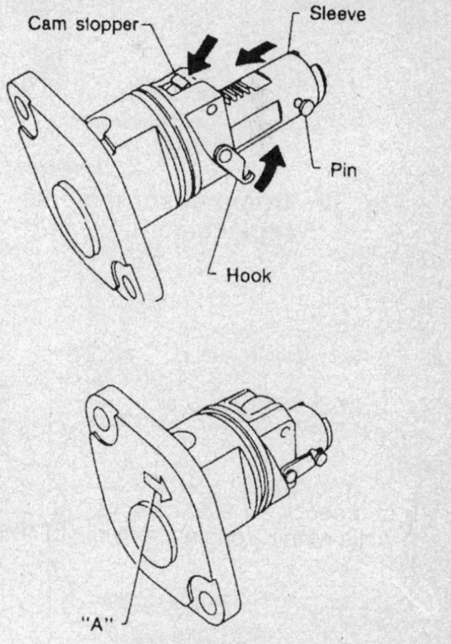
Cam stopper
Sleeve
Pin
Hook
"A"
NS1069100048000X

Fig. 28 Chain tensioner installation

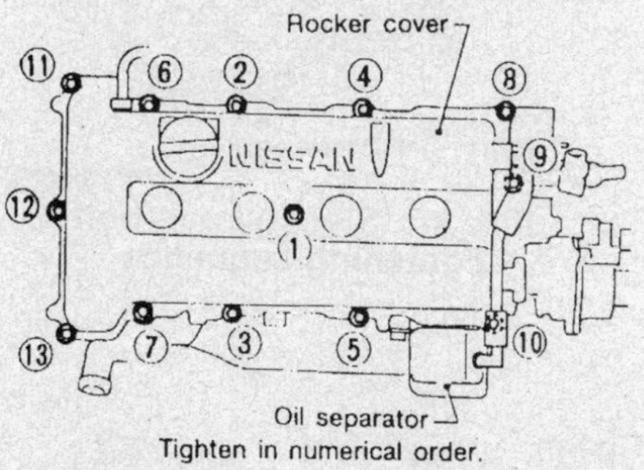
Rocker cover
NISSAN
Oil separator
Tighten in numerical order.
NS1069100049000X

Fig. 29 Valve cover bolt tightening sequence

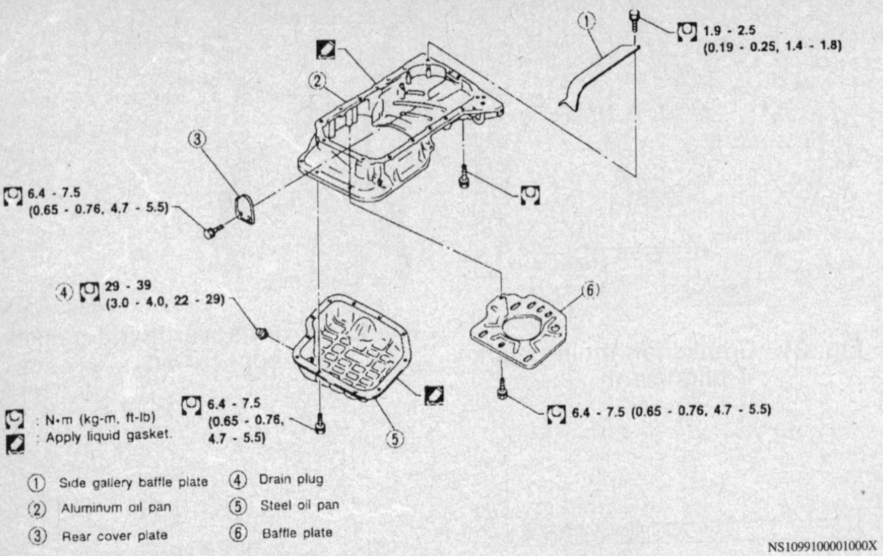
1.9 - 2.5
(0.19 - 0.25, 1.4 - 1.8)
6.4 - 7.5
(0.65 - 0.76, 4.7 - 5.5)
29 - 39
(3.0 - 4.0, 22 - 29)
6.4 - 7.5
(0.65 - 0.76,
4.7 - 5.5)
6.4 - 7.5 (0.65 - 0.76, 4.7 - 5.5)
: N•m (kg-m, ft-lb)
: Apply liquid gasket.
① Side gallery baffle plate
② Aluminum oil pan
③ Rear cover plate
④ Drain plug
⑤ Steel oil pan
⑥ Baffle plate
NS1099100001000X

Fig. 30 Exploded view of oil pan

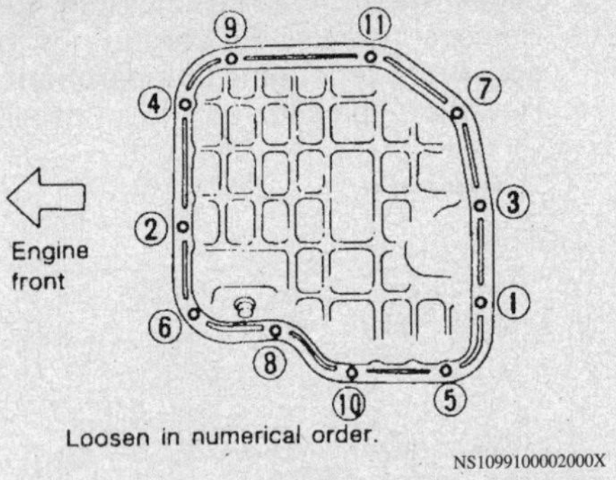
Engine
front
Loosen in numerical order.
NS1099100002000X

Fig. 31 Steel oil pan bolt removal sequence

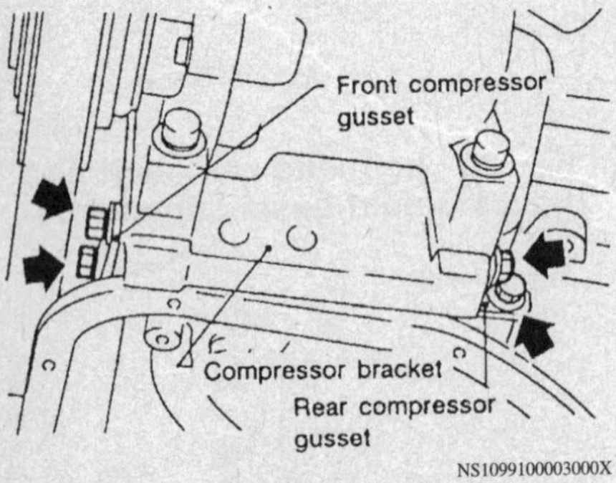
Front compressor
gusset
Compressor bracket
Rear compressor
gusset
NS1099100003000X

Fig. 32 Compressor gussets replacement

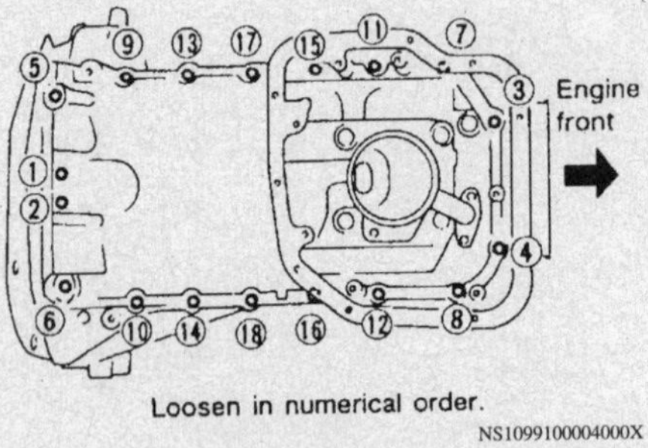
Engine
front
Loosen in numerical order.
NS1099100004000X

Fig. 33 Aluminum oil pan bolt removal sequence

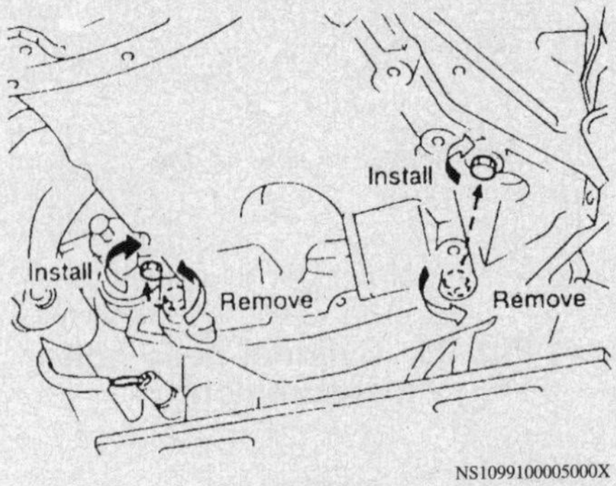
Install
Install
Remove
Remove
NS1099100005000X

Fig. 34 Transaxle bolts placement

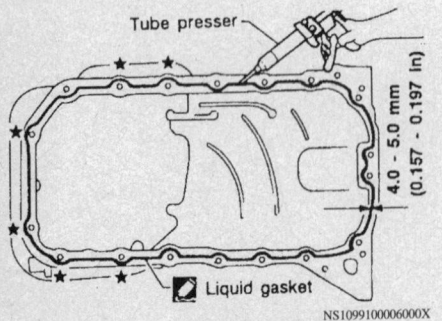

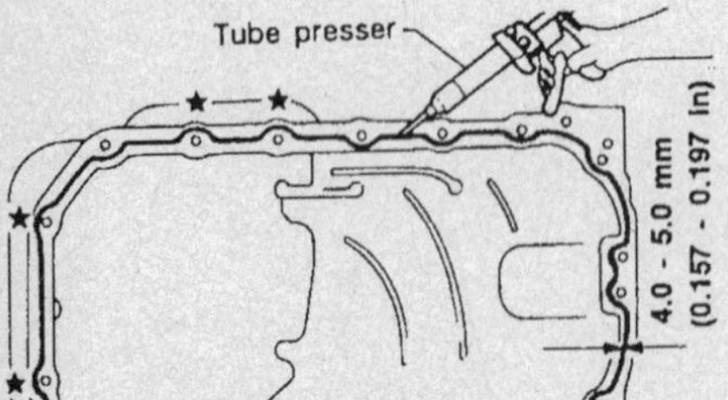
Tube presser
4.0 - 5.0 mm
(0.157 - 0.197 in)
Liquid gasket
NS1099100006000X

Fig. 35 Oil pan liquid gasket application

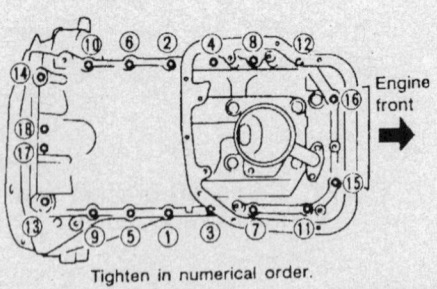

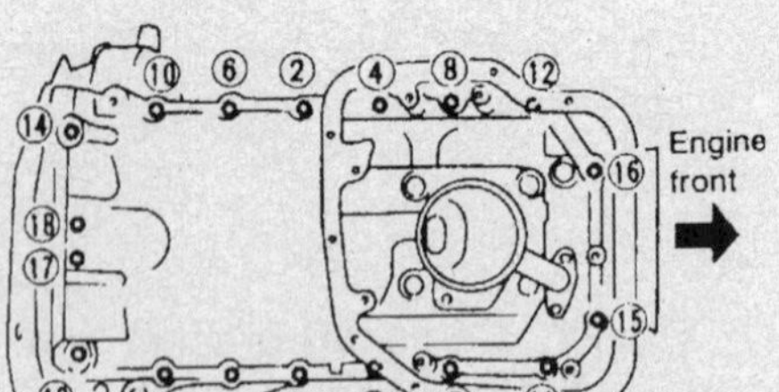
Engine
front
Tighten in numerical order.
NS1099100007000X

Fig. 36 Aluminum oil pan bolt tightening sequence

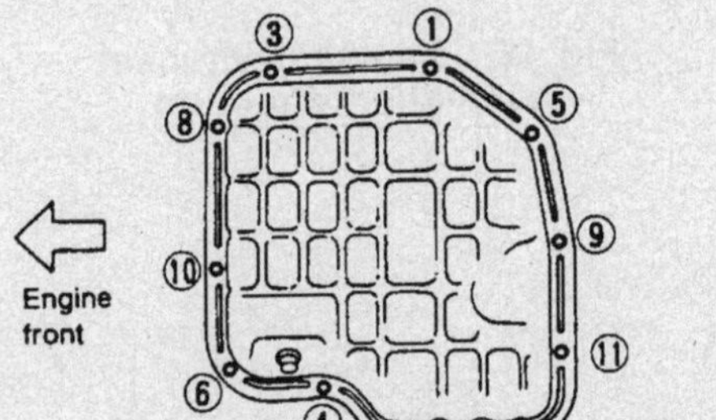
Engine
front
Tighten in numerical order.
NS1099100008000X

Fig. 37 Steel oil pan bolt tightening sequence

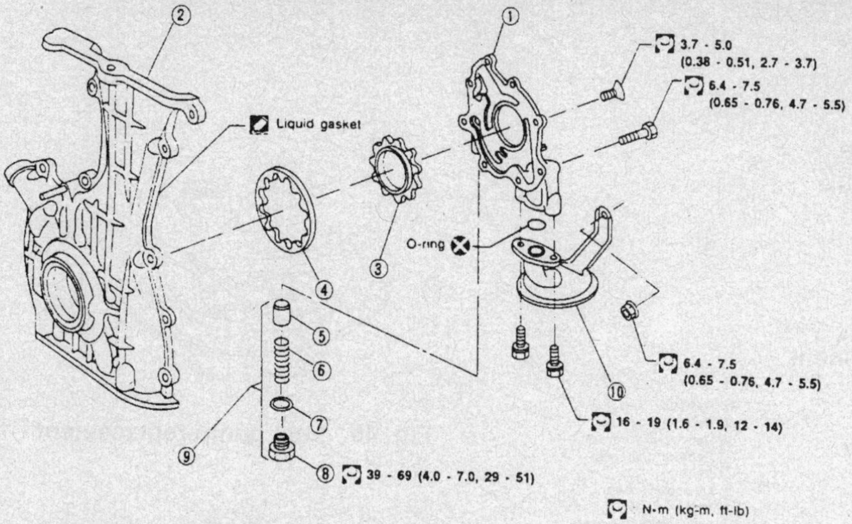

Liquid gasket
3.7 - 5.0
(0.38 - 0.51, 2.7 - 3.7)
6.4 - 7.5
(0.65 - 0.76, 4.7 - 5.5)
O-ring
6.4 - 7.5
(0.65 - 0.76, 4.7 - 5.5)
16 - 19 (1.6 - 1.9, 12 - 14)
39 - 69 (4.0 - 7.0, 29 - 51)
N·m (kg-m, ft-lb)

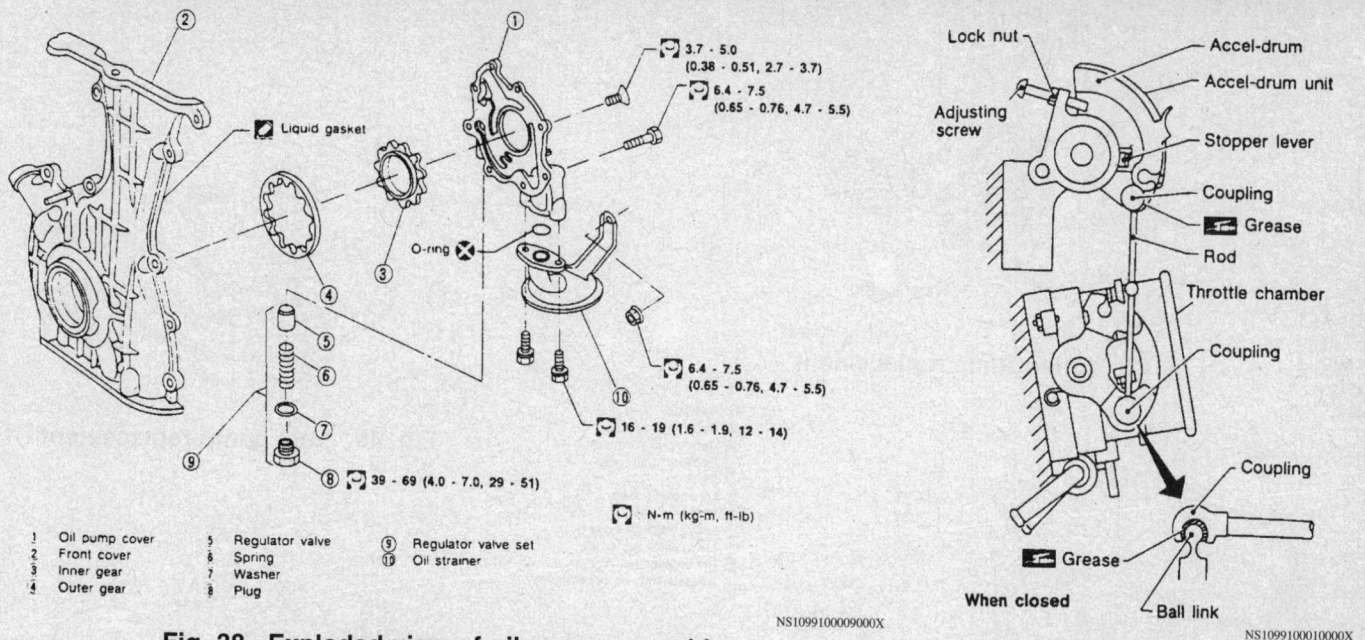

1 Oil pump cover
2 Front cover
3 Inner gear
4 Outer gear
5 Regulator valve
6 Spring
7 Washer
8 Plug
9 Regulator valve set
10 Oil strainer

NS1099100009000X

Fig. 38 Exploded view of oil pump assembly

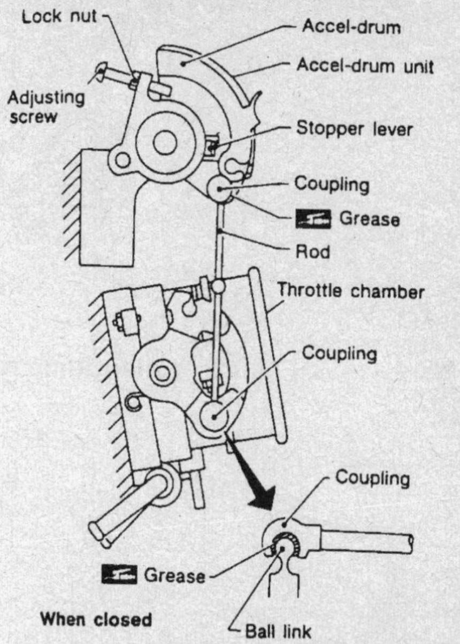

Lock nut
Accel-drum
Accel-drum unit
Adjusting screw
Stopper lever
Coupling
Grease
Rod
Throttle chamber
Coupling
Coupling
Grease
When closed
Ball link

NS1099100010000X

Fig. 39 Accel-drum unit adjustment

Belt deflection:

Unit: mm (in)

	Used belt deflection		Deflection of new belt
	Limit	Deflection after adjustment	
Alternator			
With air conditioner compressor	11.5 - 12.5 (0.453 - 0.492)	7 - 8 (0.28 - 0.31)	6.5 - 7.5 (0.256 - 0.295)
Without air conditioner compressor	12 - 13 (0.47 - 0.51)	8 - 9 (0.31 - 0.35)	7 - 8 (0.28 - 0.31)
Power steering oil pump	6 - 7 (0.24 - 0.28)	4 - 5 (0.16 - 0.20)	3.5 - 4.5 (0.138 - 0.177)
Applied pushing force	98 N (10 kg, 22 lb)		

Inspect drive belt deflections when engine is cold.

NS1069100050000X

Fig. 40 Drive belt deflection specifications

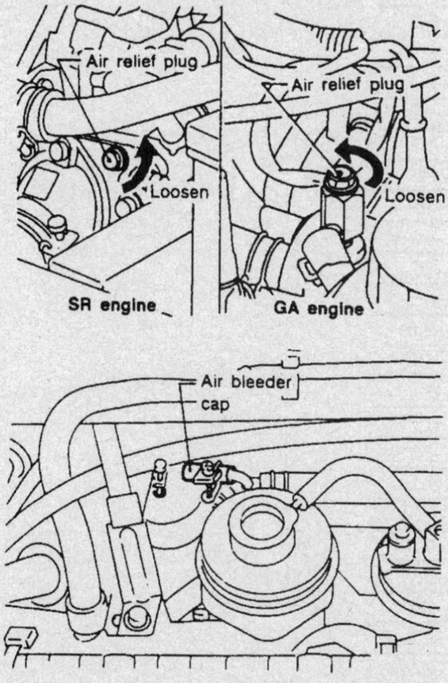

Air relief plug
Loosen
SR engine
Air relief plug
Loosen
GA engine
Air bleeder cap

NS1089100004000X

Fig. 41 Bleeding cooling system

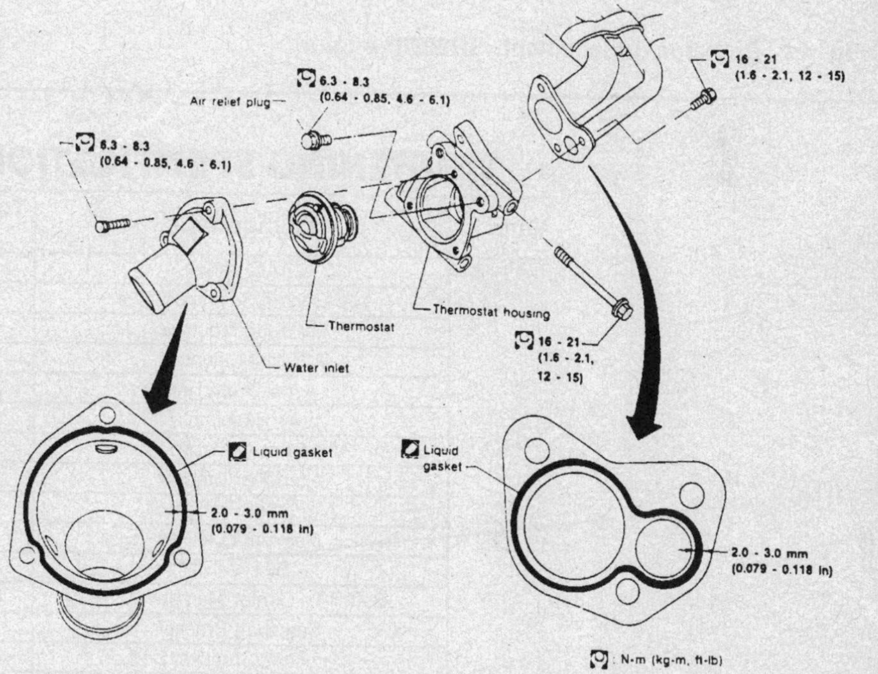

6.3 - 8.3
(0.64 - 0.85, 4.6 - 6.1)
Air relief plug
6.3 - 8.3
(0.64 - 0.85, 4.6 - 6.1)
16 - 21
(1.6 - 2.1, 12 - 15)
Thermostat housing
Thermostat
Water inlet
16 - 21
(1.6 - 2.1,
12 - 15)
Liquid gasket
2.0 - 3.0 mm
(0.079 - 0.118 in)
Liquid gasket
2.0 - 3.0 mm
(0.079 - 0.118 in)
N·m (kg-m, ft-lb)

NS1089100005000X

Fig. 42 Thermostat replacement

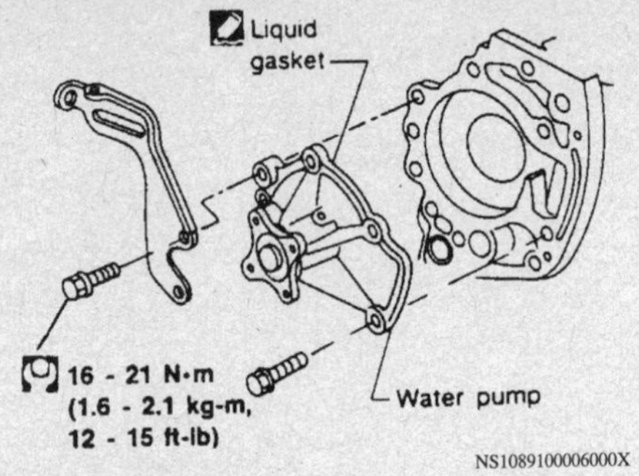
Liquid gasket
16 - 21 N·m
(1.6 - 2.1 kg-m,
12 - 15 ft-lb)
Water pump
NS1089100006000X

Fig. 43 Water pump replacement

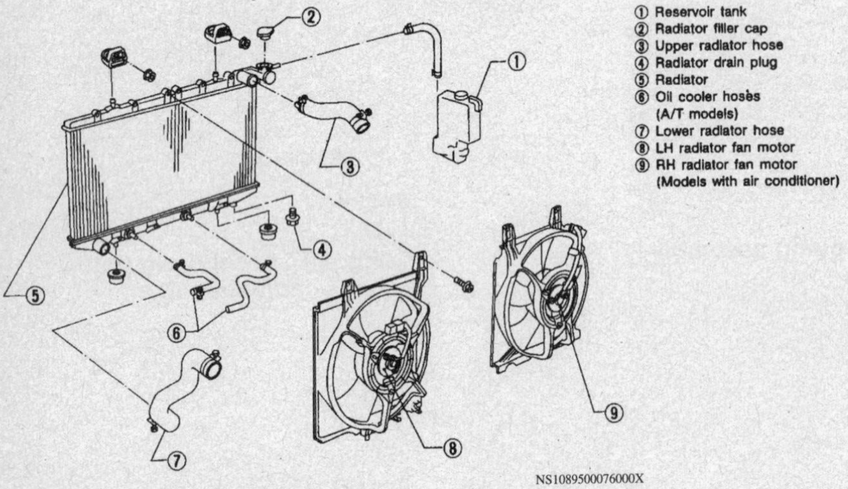
① Reservoir tank
② Radiator filler cap
③ Upper radiator hose
④ Radiator drain plug
⑤ Radiator
⑥ Oil cooler hoses
(A/T models)
⑦ Lower radiator hose
⑧ LH radiator fan motor
⑨ RH radiator fan motor
(Models with air conditioner)
NS1089500076000X

Fig. 44 Radiator replacement. SR20DE engine

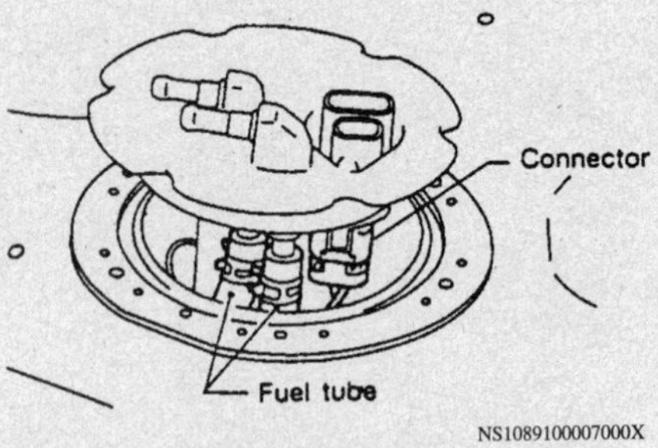
Connector
Fuel tube
NS1089100007000X

Fig. 45 Fuel pump replacement

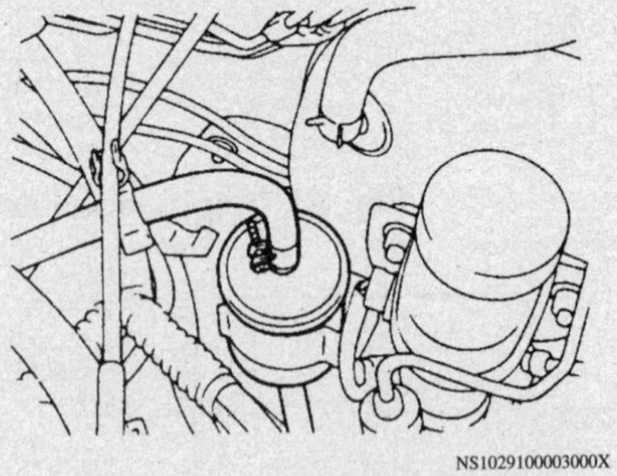
NS1029100003000X

Fig. 46 Fuel filter

TIGHTENING SPECIFICATIONS

Year	Component	Torque/Ft. Lbs.
1993–96	AAC Valve	1.1–6.2
	AIV Control Solenoid Valve	2.2–2.8
	AIV Tube Mounting	4.6–6.1
	AIV Unit Mounting	12–15
	Accel-Drum Unit	13–16
	Air Regulator	6.2–8
	Alternator Adjusting Bar	12–16
	Alternator Bracket	33–44
	Alternator Fixing Bolt	12–16
	Aluminum Oil Pan	②
	BPT Valve	2.2–2.8
	Buffer To Center Member (M/T)	33–40
	Camshaft Bracket	①
	Camshaft Sprocket Bolt	101–116
	Compressor Bracket	33–44
	Connecting Rod Bearing Cap Nut	③
	Crank Angle Sensor/Distributor	9–12
	Crankshaft Pulley	105–112
	Cylinder Block Drain Plug	5.5–8.7
	Detonation Sensor	15–20
	EGR Control Mounting Bracket	15–20
	EGR Control Valve	6.7–8.7
	EGR Tube Mounting	13–15

Continued

TIGHTENING SPECIFICATIONS—Continued

Year	Component	Torque/Ft. Lbs.
1993–96	Engine Temperature Sensor	14–22
	Exhaust Gas Sensor	13–17
	Exhaust Gas Temperature Sensor	11–18
	Exhaust Manifold Cover	3.8–4.8
	Exhaust Manifold Nuts	27–35
	Flywheel To Crankshaft	61–69
	Front Cover	12–15
	Front Engine Mounting (Fluid Type)	33–40
	Front Engine Mounting To Mounting Bracket	33–40
	Front Engine Slinger	16–22
	Ignition Coil	12–15
	Injector Mounting Bracket	2.2–2.8
	Intake Manifold Collector To Intake Manifold	13–15
	Intake Manifold Nuts	13–15
	Intake Manifold Supports	12–15
	Lefthand Camshaft Sprocket	101–116
	Lower Crankcase Oil Pan Drain Plug	4.7–5.5
	Main Bearing Cap	③
	Mounting Bracket To Buffer	33–40
	Mounting Bracket	33–40
	Oil Catcher	2.7–3.7
	Oil Filter Bracket	12–14
	Oil Pan Baffle Plate	4.7–5.5
	Oil Pan Drain Plug	22–29
	Oil Separator Mounting	12–15
	Oil Strainer To Crankcase	4.7–5.5
	Oil Strainer To Front Cover	4.7–5.5
	Power Steering Pump Adjusting Bar	12–15
	Power Steering Pump Bracket	33–44
	Power Transistor	2.7–3.7
	Rear Engine Mounting	33–40
	Rear Engine Slinger	16–22
	Rear Insulator To Center Member	33–40
	Rear Insulator To Mounting Bracket	47–54
	Rear Oil Seal Retainer	4.6–6.1
	Resonator Mounting Bolt	12–15
	Righthand Camshaft Sprocket	4.6–6.1
	Rocker Cover	①
	Side Gallery Baffle Plate	1.4–1.8
	Steel Oil Pan	4.7–5.5
	Thermal Transmitter	4.6–6
	Thermostat Housing	12–15
	Throttle Chamber	④
	Timing Chain Guide	9–14
	Timing Chain Guide	12–14
	Timing Chain Tensioner	①
	Timing Chain	①
	Water Inlet	4.6–6
	Water Outlet	4.6–6.1

①— Refer to "Timing Chain, Replace."
②— Refer to "Oil Pan, Replace."
③— Refer to "Piston, Rod & Crankshaft" under "Engine Assembly."
④— Tighten throttle chamber in two steps; torque all bolts to 6.5–8.0 ft. lbs., then torque all bolts to 13–16 ft. lbs.

Clutch & Manual Transaxle

INDEX

	Page No.
Adjustments	30-28
Clutch Pedal	30-28
Clutch, Replace	30-28
Clutch Pedal Adjustment Specifications	30-29
Tightening Specifications	30-29
Transaxle, Replace	30-28

ADJUSTMENTS

CLUTCH PEDAL

1993-94

1. Adjust clutch pedal height, dimension "H" in **Fig. 1,** to 5.91–6.30 inches using pedal stop or clutch switch.
2. Adjust withdrawal lever play, dimension "B," **Fig. 2,** with the adjuster or locknuts, to .098–.138 inch.
3. Adjust dimension "C," **Fig. 3,** to .004–.039 inch with clutch pedal fully depressed.
4. Measure clutch pedal freeplay as shown in **Fig. 1,** dimension "A."Clutch pedal freeplay should be .425–.594 inch. Clutch pedal freeplay is the sum of play between the clevis pin and clevis pin hole.
5. After above adjustments have been completed, cycle clutch pedal several times to ensure clutch linkage operates smoothly without binding.

1995-96

1. Adjust clutch pedal height, dimension "H" in **Fig. 1,** to 6.02–6.42 inches using pedal stop or clutch switch.
2. Adjust withdrawal lever play, dimension "B," **Fig. 2,** with the adjuster or locknuts, to .098–.138 inch.
3. Adjust dimension "C," **Fig. 3,** to .012–.039 inch with clutch pedal fully depressed.
4. Measure clutch pedal freeplay as shown in **Fig. 1,** dimension "A."Clutch pedal freeplay should be .425–.594 inch. Clutch pedal freeplay is the sum of play between the clevis pin and clevis pin hole.
5. After the above adjustments have been completed, cycle clutch pedal several times to ensure clutch linkage operates smoothly without binding.

CLUTCH

REPLACE

1. Remove transaxle as outlined under "Transaxle, Replace" found in this section.
2. Insert a dummy shaft into the clutch disc hub.

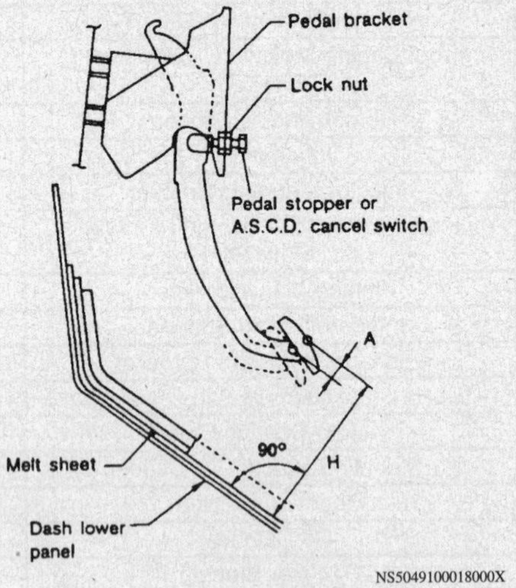

Pedal bracket
Lock nut
Pedal stopper or
A.S.C.D. cancel switch
A
90°
H
Melt sheet
Dash lower
panel
NS5049100018000X

Fig. 1 Clutch pedal free travel & height adjustment

3. Loosen clutch cover attaching bolts alternately.
4. Remove clutch disc and cover assembly.
5. Remove release bearing.
6. Reverse procedure to install.

TRANSAXLE

REPLACE

1. Disconnect battery cables, then remove battery and battery support bracket from vehicle, as necessary.
2. Remove air cleaner assembly and air flow meter, as necessary.
3. Raise and support vehicle.
4. Remove both front propeller shafts. **When disconnecting driveshafts, use care not to damage oil seals. After disconnecting driveshafts, insert a suitable bar so side gears will not rotate and fall into the differential case.**
5. Disconnect control and support rods from transaxle, as necessary.
6. Remove front exhaust pipe attaching bolts.
7. Disconnect all cables and electrical connectors from transaxle.
8. Using a suitable jack, support engine

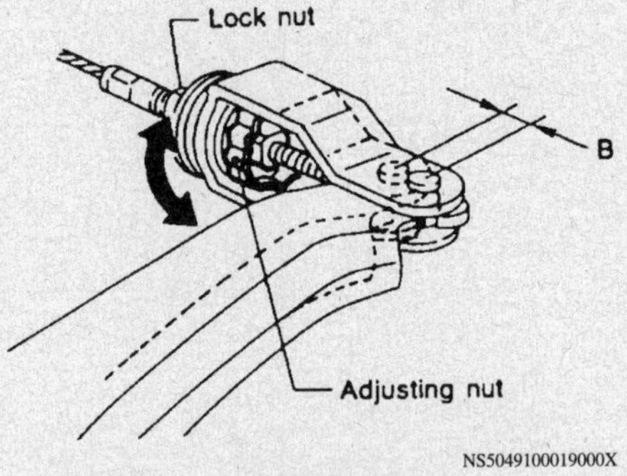

Lock nut
B
Adjusting nut
NS5049100019000X

Fig. 2 Withdrawal lever adjustment

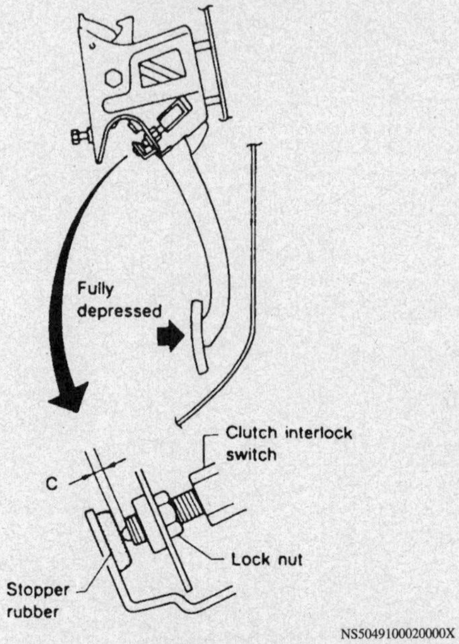

Fully
depressed
Clutch interlock
switch
C
Lock nut
Stopper
rubber
NS5049100020000X

Fig. 3 Clutch interlock switch adjustment

with a wooden block placed between oil pan and jack.
9. Remove starter motor, as necessary.
10. Remove engine mount attaching bolts.
11. Remove engine to transaxle attaching bolts, then separate engine from transaxle and lower transaxle assembly from vehicle.
12. Reverse procedure to install.

CLUTCH PEDAL ADJUSTMENT SPECIFICATIONS

Pedal Height, Inch (mm)	Withdrawal Lever Play, Inch (mm)	Pedal Freeplay, Inch (mm)
5.91–6.30 (150–160)	.098–.138 (2.5–3.5)	.425–.594 (10.8–15.1)

TIGHTENING SPECIFICATIONS

Year	Component	Torque/Ft. Lbs.
1993–96	Bleeder Screw	4–7
	Clutch Cable Locknut	2–3
	Clutch Cover Securing Bolt	16–22
	Clutch Cover To Flywheel	16–22
	Clutch Hose Clamp To Body	6–10
	Clutch Hose To Operating Cylinder Or Clutch Tube	12–14
	Clutch Interlock Switch Locknut	9–11
	Clutch Master Cylinder To Dash Panel	6–8
	Clutch Operating Cylinder	22–30
	Clutch Pedal Bracket Securing Nut	6–8
	Clutch Switch Locknut	9–11
	Clutch Tube Flare Nut	11–13
	Control Lever Socket To Support Rod	6–8
	Control Lever To Control Rod	12–15
	Control Rod To Transaxle	12–16
	Engine Gusset To Engine	22–30
	Engine Mounting Bracket	15–20
	Engine Rear Gusset To Engine	12–15
	Flywheel To Crankshaft	61–69
	Fulcrum Pin Securing Nut	12–16
	Holder Bracket Fixing Bolt	6–8
	Holder Bracket To Support Rod	14–19
	Interlock Switch Locknut	9–11
	Master Cylinder Securing Nut	6–8
	Operating Cylinder Securing Nut	22–30
	Pedal Stopper Locknut	12–16
	Reservoir Band	2–3
	Support Rod Bracket To Transaxle	20–27
	Support Rod To Bracket	23–30
	Support Rod To Engine Mount Bracket	23–30
	Valve Stopper	1–2

Rear Axle & Suspension

INDEX

	Page No.
Coil Spring, Replace	30-30
Hub & Bearing, Replace	30-30
Precautions	30-30
Rear Axle, Replace	30-30
Multi-Link Beam	30-30
Strut Type	30-30
Stabilizer Bar, Replace	30-30
Strut, Replace	30-30
Tightening Specifications	30-31
Wheel Bearing Inspection	30-30

PRECAUTIONS

Prior to removal of rear suspension assembly, disconnect ABS wheel sensor wiring from sensors. Failure to do so may result in damage to sensor wiring causing sensors to become inoperative.

REAR AXLE

REPLACE

STRUT TYPE

Refer to **Fig. 1** when replacing the rear suspension assembly, noting the following:

1. Remove brake caliper assembly and rotor.
2. Remove parallel link, radius rod, stabilizer rod and stabilizer connecting rod attaching bolts.
3. Remove rear seat and trim panel to gain access to upper strut mounting bolts.
4. Remove strut upper mounting bolts.

MULTI-LINK BEAM

Refer to "Rear Axle & Suspension" section found in "Maxima" chapter.

HUB & BEARING

REPLACE

1. Raise and support vehicle.
2. Remove wheel bearing locknut, **Fig. 2.**
3. Remove brake caliper and rotor, then position aside.
4. Remove hub assembly.
5. Reverse procedure to install, adjusting wheel bearing as outlined under "Wheel Bearing Adjust."

WHEEL BEARING INSPECTION

1. Check wheel bearing torque. Torque should measure 137–188 ft. lbs. on 2WD models or 174–231 ft. lbs. on 4WD models.
2. Ensure wheel bearing operates smoothly.
3. Ensure axial play is .0020 inch or less.
4. If axial endplay is more than specified or bearing does not operate smoothly, replace wheel bearing assembly.

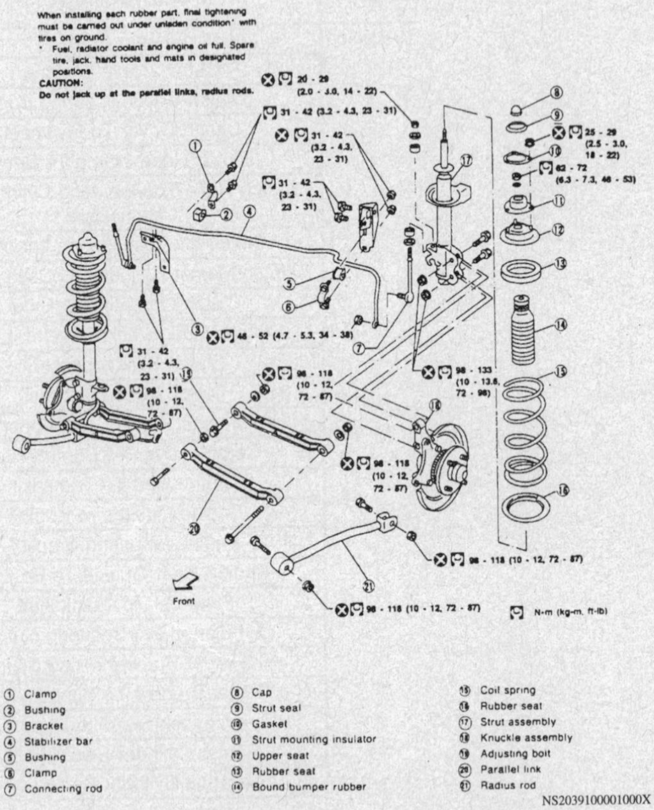

When installing each rubber part, final tightening must be carried out under unladen condition* with tires on ground.
* Fuel, radiator coolant and engine oil full. Spare tire, jack, hand tools and mats in designated positions.
CAUTION:
Do not jack up at the parallel links, radius rods.
Front
N·m (kg-m, ft-lb)
① Clamp
② Bushing
③ Bracket
④ Stabilizer bar
⑤ Bushing
⑥ Clamp
⑦ Connecting rod
⑧ Cap
⑨ Strut seal
⑩ Gasket
⑪ Strut mounting insulator
⑫ Upper seat
⑬ Rubber seat
⑭ Bound bumper rubber
⑮ Coil spring
⑯ Rubber seat
⑰ Strut assembly
⑱ Knuckle assembly
⑲ Adjusting bolt
⑳ Parallel link
㉑ Radius rod
NS2039100001000X

Fig. 1 Exploded view of rear suspension

STRUT

REPLACE

Refer to "Coil Spring, Replace."

COIL SPRING

REPLACE

1. Raise and support vehicle.
2. Remove upper and lower strut attaching nuts and/or bolts, **Fig. 1** then the strut assembly.
3. Place strut assembly in a suitable vise, then loosen piston rod locknut. **Loosen but do not remove.**
4. Compress coil spring using a suitable coil spring compression tool.
5. Remove piston rod locknut.
6. Remove spring components from strut.
7. Reverse procedure to install, noting the following:
   a. Install coil spring in correct direction, **Fig. 3.**
   b. Position coil spring in lower spring seat as shown, **Figs. 3 and 4.**
   c. Install upper spring seat as shown, **Fig. 5.**

STABILIZER BAR

REPLACE

1. Raise and support vehicle.
2. Remove exhaust assembly as necessary.
3. Disconnect stabilizer bar from bushing brackets and locating bolts, then remove stabilizer bar.
4. Reverse procedure to install, aligning stabilizer bar ball joint as shown in **Fig. 6.**

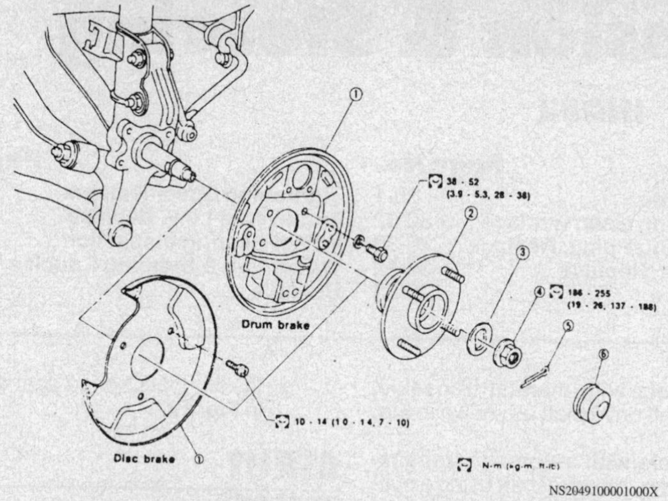
Drum brake
Disc brake
38 - 52 (3.9 - 5.3, 28 - 38)
186 - 255 (19 - 26, 137 - 188)
10 - 14 (1.0 - 1.4, 7 - 10)
N·m (kg-m, ft-lb)
NS2049100001000X

Fig. 2 Exploded view of wheel hub assembly

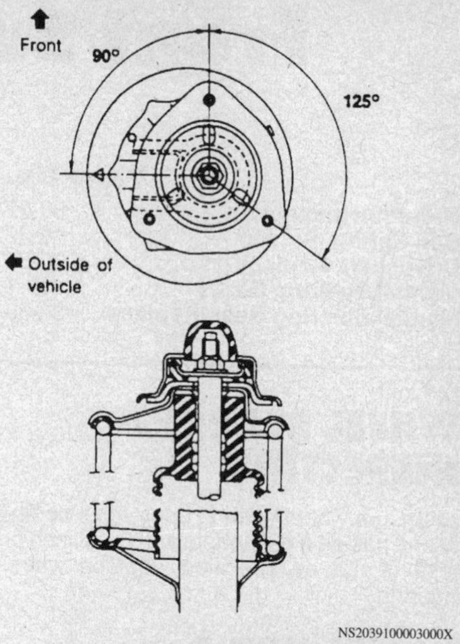
Front
90°
125°
Outside of vehicle
NS2039100003000X

Fig. 5 Upper spring seat installation direction

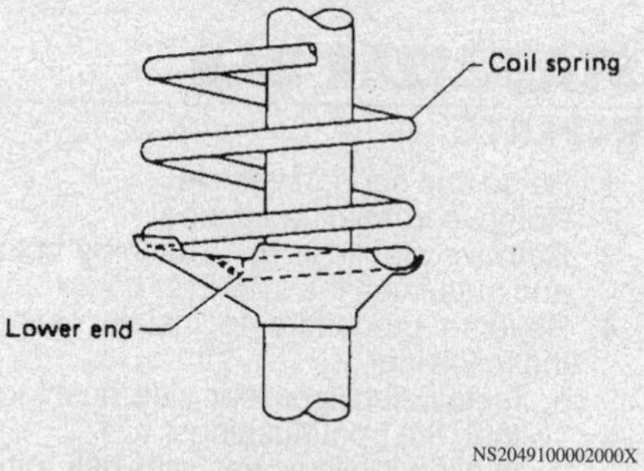
Coil spring
Lower end
NS2049100002000X

Fig. 3 Spring installation direction

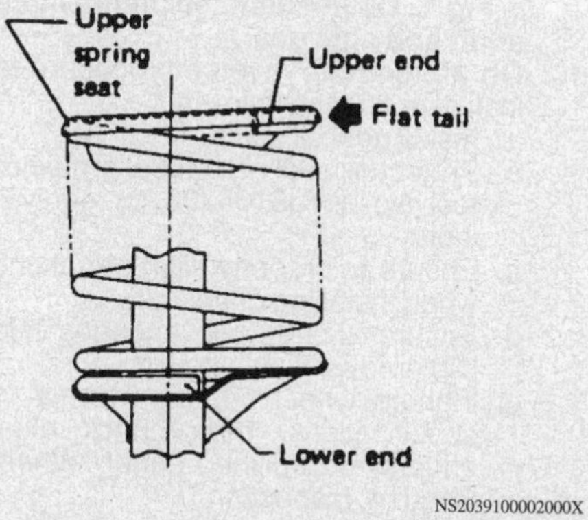
Upper spring seat
Upper end
Flat tail
Lower end
NS2039100002000X

Fig. 4 Coil spring installation

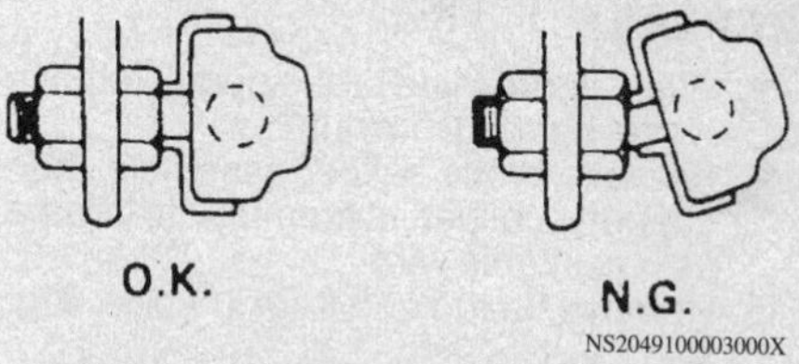
O.K.
N.G.
NS2049100003000X

Fig. 6 Stabilizer bar ball joint socket installation

TIGHTENING SPECIFICATIONS

Year	Component	Torque/ Ft. Lbs.
1993–96	Axle Nut	133-188
	Baffle Plate (Disc Brake) To Knuckle	7–10
	Backing Plate (Drum Brake)	28–38
	Connecting Rod To Strut	14–22
	Driveshaft Nut	133–188
	Hub Nut	133–188
	Parallel Link To Knuckle	72–87
	Parallel Link To Crossmember	72–87
	Radius Rod To Bracket	72–87
	Radius Rod To Knuckle	72–87
	Stabilizer Bar Bracket To Body	23–31
	Stabilizer Bar Clamp	23–31
	Stabilizer Bar To Connecting Rod	34–38
	Strut Mounting Insulator To Body	18–22
	Strut Piston Self-Locking Nut	46–53
	Wheel Bearing Self-Locking Nut	137–188
	Wheel Lug Nuts	72–87

Front Suspension & Steering

INDEX

	Page No.
Ball Joint Inspection	30-32
Coil Spring, Replace	30-32
Driveshaft, Replace	30-32
Manual Steering Gears	36-1
Manual Steering Gear, Replace	30-33
Power Steering	36-1
Power Steering Gear, Replace	30-32
Power Steering Pump, Replace	30-33
Stabilizer Bar, Replace	30-32
Strut, Replace	30-32
Tightening Specifications	30-35
Transverse Link, Replace	30-32
Wheel Bearing Inspection	30-32
Wheel Hub & Steering Knuckle, Replace	30-32

WHEEL BEARING INSPECTION

Ensure wheel bearing operates smoothly and has an axial endplay of .0020 inch or less. If not as specified, replace wheel bearing.

WHEEL HUB & STEERING KNUCKLE

REPLACE

1. While depressing brake pedal, remove wheel bearing locknut.
2. Remove brake caliper assembly, then support caliper assembly to frame using suitable wire.
3. Remove tie rod end from knuckle, **Fig. 1.**
4. Separate driveshaft from knuckle by slightly tapping on end. **Cover boots with a cloth to prevent damage.**
5. Remove strut lower mounting bolts, **Fig. 2.**
6. Loosen lower ball joint nut, then separate lower ball joint from knuckle.
7. Using a suitable tool, drive out hub with inner race from knuckle.
8. Remove wheel bearing inner race, inner and outer grease seals, then the outer bearing race.
9. Reverse procedure to install, checking wheel bearing axial play as outlined under "Wheel Bearing, Inspection."

DRIVESHAFT

REPLACE

1. While depressing brake pedal, remove wheel bearing locknut.
2. Remove brake caliper assembly and support to frame using suitable wire. **Brake hose does not need to be disconnected. Ensure there is no tension on brake hose.**
3. Remove tie rod end from knuckle, **Fig. 1.**
4. Separate driveshaft from knuckle by slightly tapping on end. **Cover boots with a cloth to prevent damage. Be careful not to damage threads on end of driveshaft.**
5. Remove strut lower mounting bolts, **Fig. 2.**
6. Loosen lower ball joint nut, then separate lower ball joint from knuckle.
7. Remove right driveshaft as shown in **Figs. 3 and 4.**
8. **On models with manual transaxle,** remove left driveshaft as shown in **Fig. 5.**
9. **On models with automatic transaxles,** remove left driveshaft using a suitable tool placed on driveshaft end through differential housing, as shown in **Fig. 6. Do not damage pinion mate shaft and side gear.**
10. **On all models,** reverse procedure to install, noting the following:
    a. Install new oil seals.
    b. Protect oil seal using seal protector tool No. KV38106700, or equivalent.
    c. Ensure to properly align serrations when installing driveshaft.
    d. Ensure circular clip engages into clip groove of side gear.
    e. Tighten wheel bearing locknut to specifications, then check axial endplay as outlined under "Wheel Bearing, Inspection."

BALL JOINT INSPECTION

Check ball joint for play. If ball stud is worn, there is excessive play in axial direction or joint is hard to swing, replace lower ball joint.

COIL SPRING

REPLACE

1. Raise and support front of vehicle and remove wheel.
2. Disconnect brake line from strut.
3. Place alignment marks on strut lower bracket and camber adjusting pin.
4. Remove strut to steering knuckle attaching bolts, then separate strut from knuckle, **Fig. 7.**
5. Remove strut to strut tower attaching nuts, then strut assembly from vehicle.
6. Install strut assembly in a vise, then loosen strut rod locknut. **Loosen but do not remove.**
7. Compress coil spring using a suitable coil spring compression tool.
8. Remove piston rod locknut.
9. Remove spring components from strut.
10. Reverse procedure to install, noting the following:
    a. Install coil spring in correct direction, **Fig. 8.**
    b. Position coil spring in lower spring seat as shown in **Fig. 9.**
    c. Install upper spring seat as shown in **Fig. 10.**

STRUT

REPLACE

Refer to "Coil Spring, Replace."

STABILIZER BAR

REPLACE

1. Raise and support vehicle.
2. Remove front exhaust tube.
3. Remove stabilizer bar attaching bolts and nuts, then the stabilizer bar.
4. Reverse procedure to install, noting the following:
    a. Install stabilizer rear side bushing, then the front bushings.
    b. Install stabilizer bar with ball joint socket, as shown in **Fig. 11.**

TRANSVERSE LINK

REPLACE

1. Raise and support vehicle.
2. Remove tie rod ball joint.
3. Remove wheel bearing locknut.
4. Separate driveshaft from knuckle by tapping driveshaft end with a suitable hammer. **Cover boots with a cloth to prevent damage. Be careful not to damage threads on end of driveshaft.**
5. Remove stabilizer bar attaching bolt from transverse link.
6. Separate lower ball joint stud from knuckle using ball joint separating tool No. HT72520000, or equivalent.
7. Remove transverse link bracket attaching bolts, then the transverse link bracket.
8. Remove remaining transverse link assembly attaching bolt, then the transverse link and ball joint assembly.
9. Reverse procedure to install.

POWER STEERING GEAR

REPLACE

1. Raise and support front of vehicle and remove wheels.
2. Disconnect power steering hose clamp, then the hose at steering gear and drain fluid into a suitable container.
3. Disconnect tie rod studs from steering knuckles.

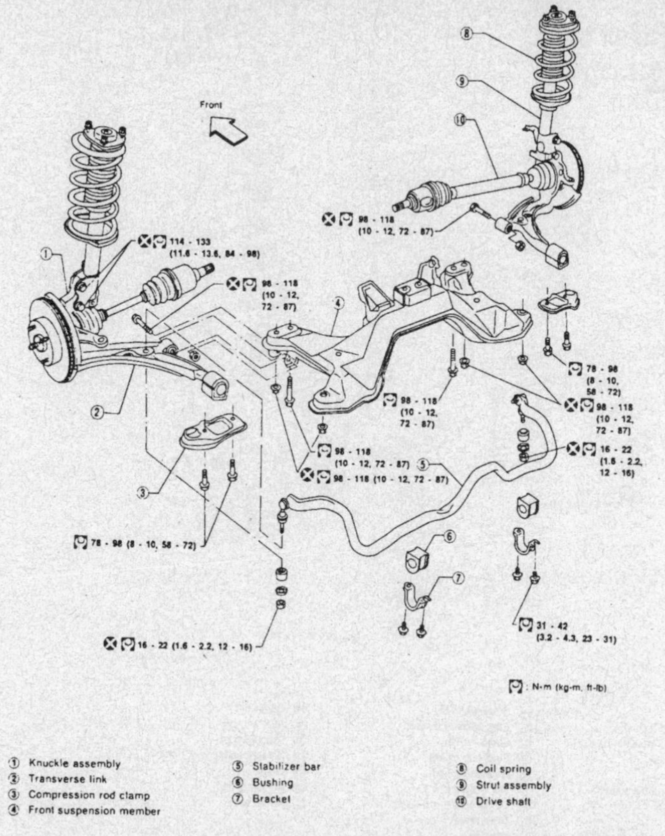
Front
① Knuckle assembly
② Transverse link
③ Compression rod clamp
④ Front suspension member
⑤ Stabilizer bar
⑥ Bushing
⑦ Bracket
⑧ Coil spring
⑨ Strut assembly
⑩ Drive shaft
: N·m (kg-m, ft-lb)

NS3039100001000X

Fig. 1 Exploded view of front axle & suspension

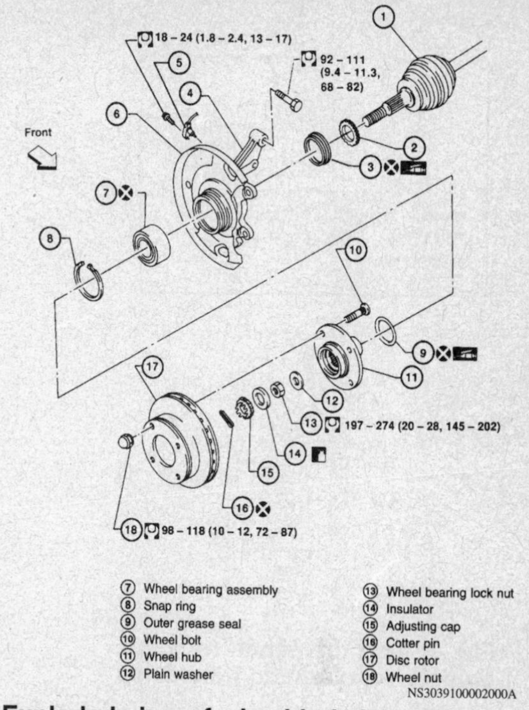
Front
18 – 24 (1.8 – 2.4, 13 – 17)
92 – 111 (9.4 – 11.3, 68 – 82)
197 – 274 (20 – 28, 145 – 202)
98 – 118 (10 – 12, 72 – 87)
: N·m (kg-m, ft-lb)
① Drive shaft
② ABS sensor rotor
③ Inner grease seal
④ Knuckle
⑤ ABS sensor
⑥ Baffle plate
⑦ Wheel bearing assembly
⑧ Snap ring
⑨ Outer grease seal
⑩ Wheel bolt
⑪ Wheel hub
⑫ Plain washer
⑬ Wheel bearing lock nut
⑭ Insulator
⑮ Adjusting cap
⑯ Cotter pin
⑰ Disc rotor
⑱ Wheel nut

NS3039100002000A

Fig. 2 Exploded view of wheel hub & knuckle

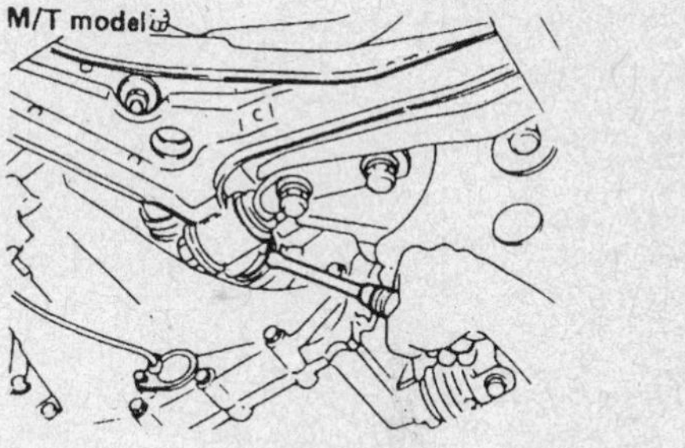
M/T model

NS3039100005000X

Fig. 5 Left driveshaft removal. Models w/manual transaxles

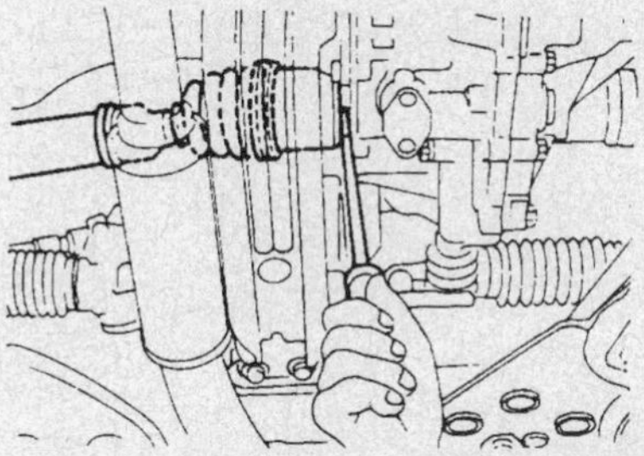

NS3039100003000X

Fig. 3 Right driveshaft removal. Models less support bearing

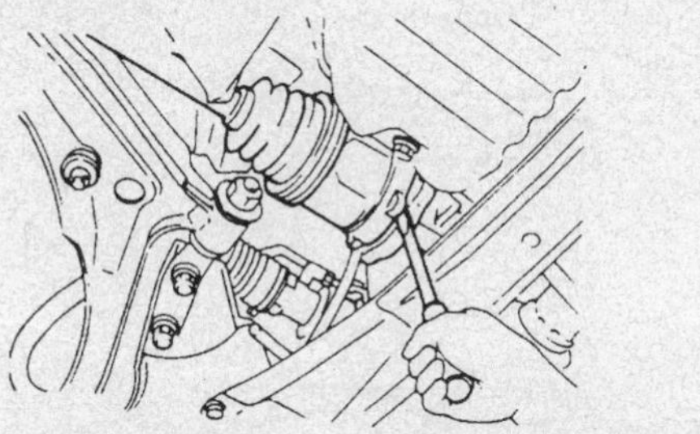

NS3039100004000X

Fig. 4 Right driveshaft removal. Models w/support bearing

4. **On Sentra models,** support transaxle with a suitable jack, then remove exhaust pipe and rear engine mounts, if necessary.
5. **On all models,** remove bolt securing lower joint to steering gear pinion and remove lower joint from pinion.
6. Remove steering gear attaching bolts.
7. Remove steering gear and linkage assembly from vehicle.
8. Reverse procedure to install.

POWER STEERING PUMP

REPLACE

1. Remove A/C compressor drive belt.
2. Loosen idler pulley locknut, then turn adjusting nut counterclockwise and remove power steering pump drive belt.
3. Loosen power steering hoses at pump and remove bolts securing power steering pump to brackets.
4. Raise pump and disconnect power steering hoses. Catch fluid in a suitable container, plug hose ends and ports in power steering pump, and remove pump from vehicle.
5. Reverse procedure to install, then bleed system as follows:
   a. Raise and support front of vehicle.
   b. Run engine for three to five seconds, stop engine, then check and fill power steering pump reservoir as necessary.
   c. Quickly turn steering wheel all the way to the right and to the left ten times.
   d. Start engine and idle for three to five seconds. Stop engine, then check and fill power steering pump reservoir as necessary.
   e. With steering wheel all the way to the right, open bleeder screw to expel air, then tighten bleeder screw.
   f. Repeat procedure until all air has been bled from system.
   g. If air cannot be bled completely after repeated attempts, repeat step "e" with engine running.

MANUAL STEERING GEAR

REPLACE

1. Raise and support front of vehicle and remove wheels.
2. Disconnect tie rod from steering knuckle.
3. Loosen steering gear attaching bolts, then remove bolt securing lower joint to steering gear pinion and remove lower joint from pinion.
4. Remove steering gear housing to body attaching bolts, then the steering gear and linkage assembly from vehicle.
5. Reverse procedure to install.

A/T model

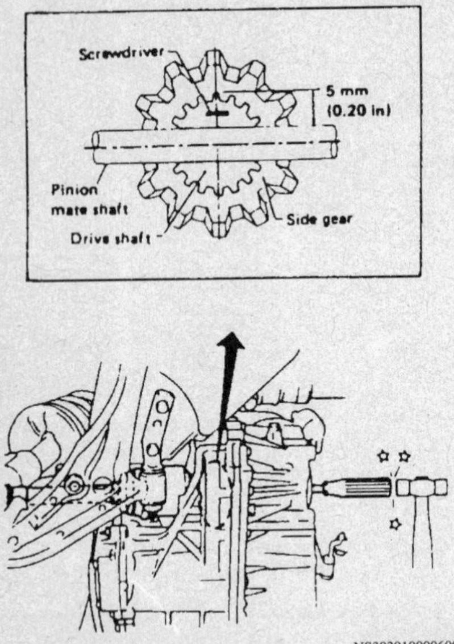
Screwdriver
5 mm
(0.20 in)
Pinion
mate shaft
Side gear
Drive shaft

NS3039100006000X

Fig. 6 Left driveshaft removal. Models w/automatic transaxles

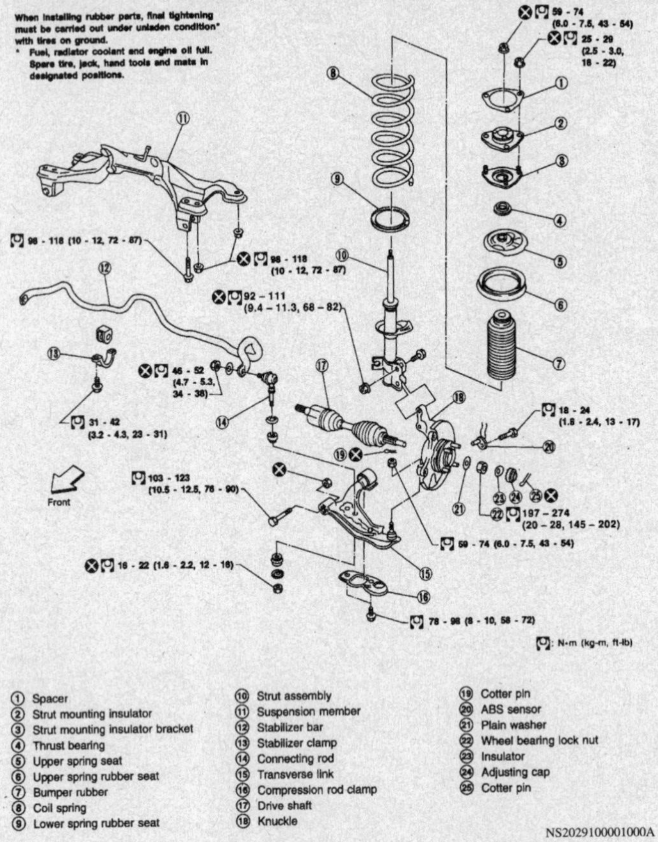
When installing rubber parts, final tightening must be carried out under unladen condition* with tires on ground.
* Fuel, radiator coolant and engine oil full. Spare tire, jack, hand tools and mats in designated positions.
59 - 74 (6.0 - 7.5, 43 - 54)
25 - 29 (2.5 - 3.0, 18 - 22)
98 - 118 (10 - 12, 72 - 87)
98 - 118 (10 - 12, 72 - 87)
92 - 111 (9.4 - 11.3, 68 - 82)
46 - 52 (4.7 - 5.3, 34 - 38)
31 - 42 (3.2 - 4.3, 23 - 31)
18 - 24 (1.8 - 2.4, 13 - 17)
103 - 123 (10.5 - 12.5, 76 - 90)
Front
197 - 274 (20 - 28, 145 - 202)
59 - 74 (6.0 - 7.5, 43 - 54)
16 - 22 (1.6 - 2.2, 12 - 16)
78 - 98 (8 - 10, 58 - 72)
N·m (kg-m, ft-lb)
① Spacer
② Strut mounting insulator
③ Strut mounting insulator bracket
④ Thrust bearing
⑤ Upper spring seat
⑥ Upper spring rubber seat
⑦ Bumper rubber
⑧ Coil spring
⑨ Lower spring rubber seat
⑩ Strut assembly
⑪ Suspension member
⑫ Stabilizer bar
⑬ Stabilizer clamp
⑭ Connecting rod
⑮ Transverse link
⑯ Compression rod clamp
⑰ Drive shaft
⑱ Knuckle
⑲ Cotter pin
⑳ ABS sensor
㉑ Plain washer
㉒ Wheel bearing lock nut
㉓ Insulator
㉔ Adjusting cap
㉕ Cotter pin

NS2029100001000A

Fig. 7 Exploded view of front suspension

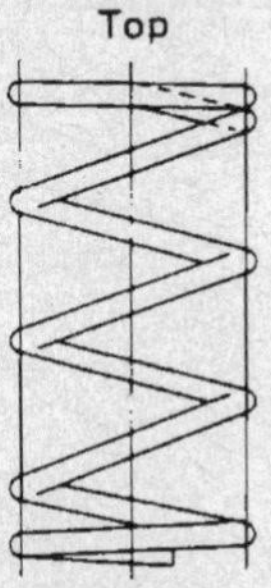
Top
Bottom

NS2029100002000X

Fig. 8 Spring installation direction

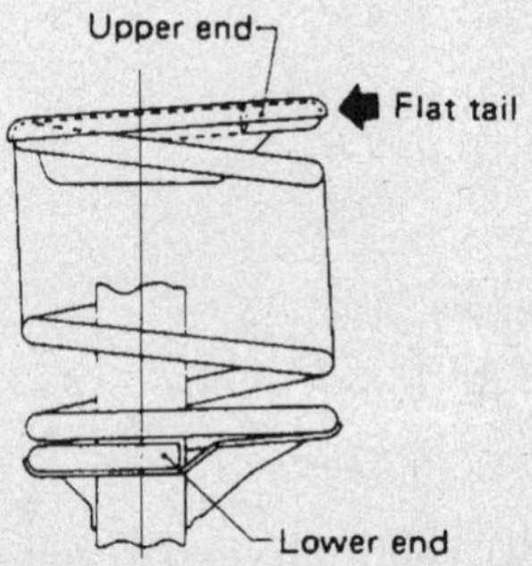
Upper end
Flat tail
Lower end

NS2029100003000X

Fig. 9 Coil spring installation

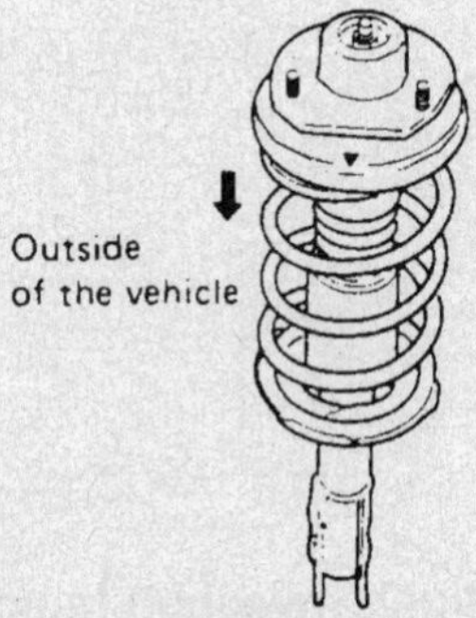
Outside
of the vehicle

NS2029100004000X

Fig. 10 Upper spring seat installation direction

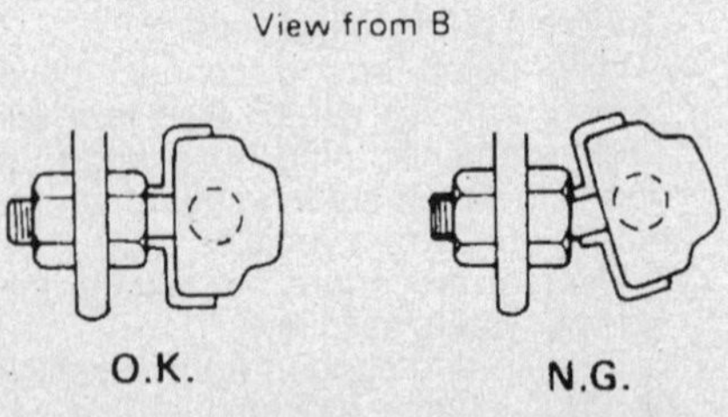
View from B
O.K.
N.G.

NS2029100005000X

Fig. 11 Stabilizer bar ball joint socket Installation

TIGHTENING SPECIFICATIONS

Year	Component	Torque/ Ft. Lbs.
1993–96	ABS Speed Sensor Bolt	13–17
	Axle Nut	145–203
	Axle To Caliper	40–47
	Connecting Rod To Transverse Link	12–16
	Driveshaft Nut	145–203
	Hub Nut	145–203
	Lower Ball Joint Stud Nut	43–54
	Stabilizer Bar Clamp To Body	12–15
	Stabilizer Bar To Ball Joint	25–33
	Strut Assembly Piston Rod Self-Locking Nut	46–53
	Strut Assembly To Body	18–22
	Strut Assembly To Knuckle	84–98
	Tie Rod Locknut	27–34
	Tie Rod Stud Nut	22–29
	Transverse Link Securing Bolt	58–72
	Transverse Securing Nut	72–87
	Wheel Bearing Locknut	145–203
	Wheel Lug Nut	72–87

Wheel Alignment

INDEX

	Page No.
Front Wheel Alignment	30-35
Camber	30-35
Caster & Kingpin Inclination	30-35
Steering Angle	30-36
Toe Setting	30-35
Preliminary Inspection	30-35
Rear Wheel Alignment	30-36
Camber	30-36
Toe-In	30-36
Vehicle Ride Height	30-36
Wheel Alignment Specifications	30-2
Front	30-2
Rear	30-3

PRELIMINARY INSPECTION

Prior to checking and adjusting wheel alignment angles, perform the following checks:

1. Check tire pressure and adjust as necessary.
2. Ensure tires are properly sized and matched.
3. Ensure wheel bearings (front and rear) are properly adjusted.
4. Check steering gear adjustment and ensure steering gear is properly secured to frame.
5. Inspect steering linkage and suspension components for damage and wear. Repair or replace components as necessary.
6. Measure vehicle ride height with vehicle unloaded, and ensure springs are not collapsed.
7. Place vehicle on suitable alignment rack following manufacturer's instructions, then bounce vehicle several times to settle suspension.
8. Check and correct rear wheel camber and toe first, then check and correct front suspension angles in the following order: caster and kingpin inclination, camber, toe setting and turning angle (toe-out on turns).

FRONT WHEEL ALIGNMENT

Correct front wheel alignment is necessary to provide proper handling and to prevent uneven tire wear. To ensure correct alignment, angles should be checked, and if necessary corrected, in the following sequence: caster and kingpin inclination, camber, toe-setting, and the turning angle and toe-out on turns. Front wheel alignment should only be checked after the rear wheels are properly aligned in relation to the vehicle centerline, as most equipment uses the rear wheels as reference for correct front wheel alignment. Front wheel alignment should be checked with the vehicle at normal ride height, and following equipment manufacturer's instructions.

CASTER & KINGPIN INCLINATION

If caster or kingpin angles are not within specifications, check suspension components and sheet metal for damage, distortion and excessive wear. Repair or replace components as necessary.

CAMBER

Camber cannot be adjusted. If camber is not within specifications, inspect suspension and sheet metal for damage, distortion and excessive wear, and repair or replace components as necessary.

TOE SETTING

The toe setting is the measurement of the wheels in relation to the vehicle centerline, **Fig. 1.** The leading edge of each wheel should toe-in or toe-out slightly in relation to the vehicle centerline to ensure proper vehicle tracking. Toe should be inspected using suitable alignment gauges, following manufacturer's instructions. When checking or adjusting toe, always ensure the setting of the left and right wheels is as equal as possible.

Toe is adjusted by loosening the tie rod locknuts or adjusting sleeve bolts and equally altering the length of the tie rods. After toe has been adjusted to specifications, the lengths of the left and right tie rods, **Fig. 2,** should be nearly equal. If tie

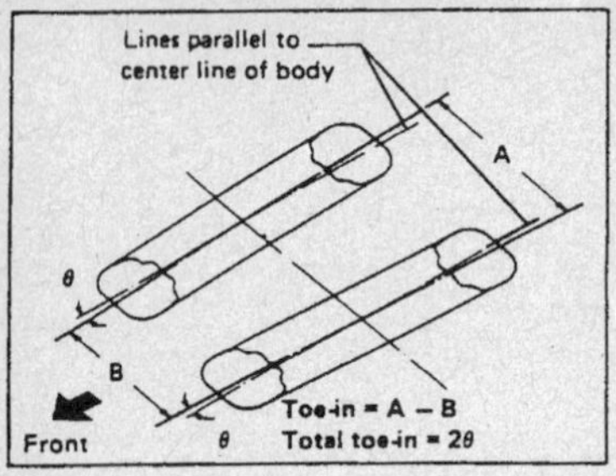
Lines parallel to center line of body
A
θ
B
Front
θ
Toe-in = A − B
Total toe-in = 2θ

NS2049100004000X

Fig. 1 Toe-in measurement

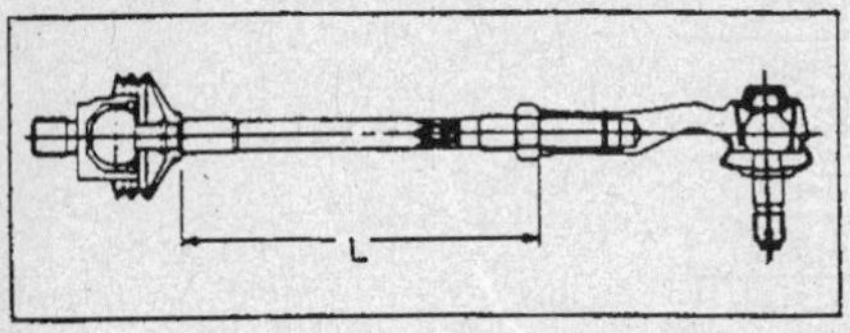
L

NS2049100005000X

Fig. 2 Tie rod length measurement

Year	Model	Front Wheel Turning Angle, Degree	
		Inside	Outside
1993	NX Coupe①	39–43	33
	NX Coupe②	33–37	30
	NX 1600	39–43	33
	NX 2000	33–37	30
	Sentra①	39–43	34
	Sentra②	33–37	30
1994	Sentra①	39–43	34
	Sentra②	33–37	30
1995–96	Sentra①	38–42③	34③
	Sentra①	34–38④	31④
	200SX①	38–42③	34③
	200SX①	34–38④	31④

①–Models w/GA16DE engines.
②–Models w/SR20DE engines.
③–Manual steering.
④–Power steering.

Fig. 3 Turning angle specifications

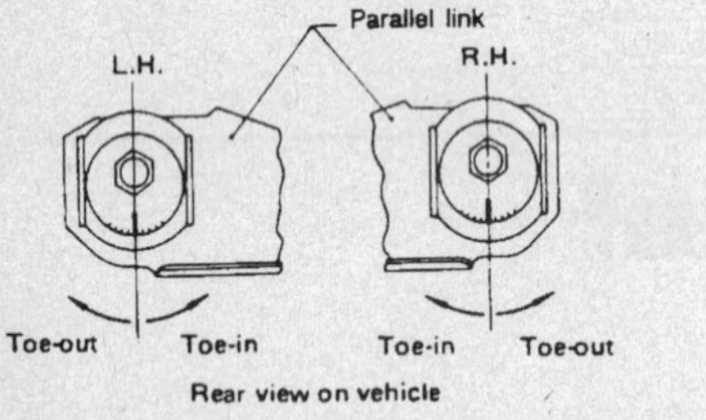
Parallel link
L.H.
R.H.
Toe-out
Toe-in
Toe-in
Toe-out
Rear view on vehicle

NS2049100006000X

Fig. 4 Rear toe-in adjustment

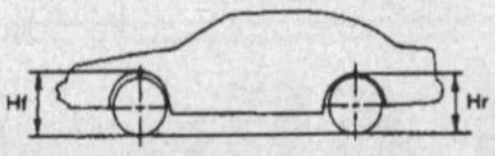
Hf
Hr

Applied model	Sedan			Coupe	
	155SR13	175/70R13	185/60R14	175/70R13	185/60R14 195/55R14
Front (Hf) mm (in)	649 (25.55)		647 (25.47)	641 (25.24)	639 (25.16)
Rear (Hr) mm (in)	636 (25.04)	639 (25.16)	633 (24.92)	637 (25.08)	633 (24.92)

*: Fuel, radiator coolant and engine oil full. Spare tire, jack, hand tools and mats in designated positions.

NS2049100007000X

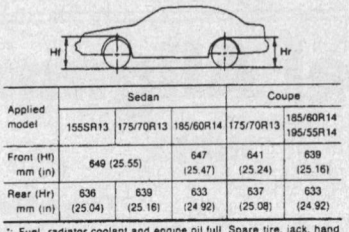

Fig. 5 Vehicle ride height measurement. 1993–94

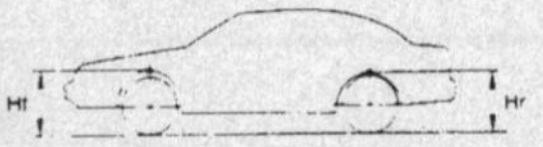
Hf
Hr

Applied model	155SR13	175/70R13	175/65/R14	195/55R15
Front (Hf) mm (in)	659 (25.94)		666 (26.22)	669 (26.34)
Rear (Hr) mm (in)	640 (25.20)	642 (25.28)	648 (25.51)	650 (25.59)

*: Fuel, radiator coolant and engine oil full. Spare tire, jack, hand tools and mats in designated positions.

NS2049500035000X

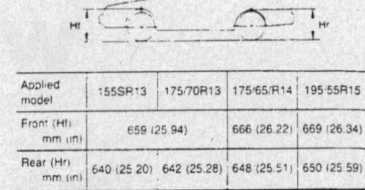

Fig. 6 Vehicle ride height measurement. 1995–96

rod lengths are incorrect, tie rods should be disassembled and adjusted to equal lengths, and the toe setting should be readjusted before checking steering angles. Incorrect tie rod length will adversely affect steering angles and toe-out on turns.

STEERING ANGLE

When a vehicle negotiates a turn, the inner wheel must turn at a sharper angle than the outer wheel, and the outer wheel must travel farther than the inner wheel. Vehicle steering geometry is calculated to allow for these variations, causing the outer wheel to toe-out by a calibrated amount. This toe-out on turns is also referred to as steering angle and on these models, is generally checked at two positions. The first position is at a reference point on the inner wheel travel, while the second position of measurement is at full steering lock. To check steering angles, proceed as follows:

1. Place vehicle on suitable alignment rack and ensure kingpin angle, caster, camber and toe settings are within specifications.
2. Turn steering to full lock and measure inner and outer wheel turning angles.
3. If "turning angles" at full lock are not within specifications, **Fig. 3,** check for damaged steering linkage or improperly adjusted tie rods.
4. If steering linkage and tie rods are satisfactory, check for improper rack or rack piston stroke. Repair steering gear as necessary.

REAR WHEEL ALIGNMENT

The proper alignment of the rear suspension and wheels is essential for proper handling and to providing a reference for front wheel alignment. Always ensure rear wheel alignment is within specifications prior to checking and adjusting front wheel alignment.

CAMBER

The rear wheel camber must be within specifications for proper vehicle handling and to prevent uneven tire wear. Rear camber cannot be adjusted. If rear camber is not within specifications, check for damaged or worn suspension components and deformed sheet metal. Repair as necessary.

TOE-IN

Rear toe is the measurement of the rear wheels in relation to the vehicle centerline, **Fig. 1.**The leading edge of each rear wheel should toe-in slightly toward the vehicle centerline to ensure proper vehicle tracking. Rear toe should be inspected using suitable alignment gauges, following manufacturer's instructions. When checking or adjusting rear toe, always ensure the amount that the left and right wheels toe-in is as equal as possible.

Rear toe-in is adjusted by rotating the cam bolts that secure the transverse link to the axle carrier, **Fig. 4.**

1. Measure total toe-in and toe-in for each wheel following equipment manufacturer's instructions.
2. Scribe matching mark between cam and control arm, then loosen nut securing cam bolt.
3. Rotate cam bolt as needed, **Fig. 4,** to bring toe-in within specifications. Ensure total toe-in is within specifications and divided equally between left and right wheels.
4. Hold position of cam and **torque** nut to 72–87 ft. lbs.
5. Ensure toe-in is still within specifications.

VEHICLE RIDE HEIGHT

When checking ride height, vehicle must be parked on a level surface and tires inflated to proper air pressure. Ensure all fluid levels are to specified level, spare tire and jack are in proper locations.

Bounce vehicle up and down several times, then measure vehicle height from top of wheelwell to ground, **Figs. 5 and 6.** Vehicle height is not adjustable. If vehicle height is not as specified, check for worn springs or suspension parts.

NISSAN MAXIMA & 300ZX

INDEX OF SERVICE OPERATIONS

Page No.

ACTIVE SUSPENSION SYSTEMS 36-1
AIR BAG SYSTEM PRECAUTIONS 0-8
AUTOMATIC TRANSMISSIONS/ TRANSAXLES 36-1
BRAKES
Anti-Lock Brakes 36-1
Disc Brakes 36-1
Drum Brakes 36-1
Hydraulic Brake Systems 36-1
Power Brake Units 36-1
CLUTCH & MANUAL TRANSMISSION
Adjustments 31-36
Clutch, Replace 31-36
Hydraulic System Service 31-36
Tightening Specifications 31-39
Transmission, Replace 31-36
ELECTRICAL
Air Bags 36-1
Air Conditioning 36-1
Alternators 36-1
Blower Motor, Replace 31-7
Coil Pack, Replace 31-4
Combination Switch, Replace 31-5
Cooling Fans 36-1
Cruise Control 36-1
Dash Gauges 36-1
Dash Panels 36-1
Distributor, Replace 31-4
Evaporator Core, Replace 31-7
Fuel Pump Relay Location 31-4
Fuse Panel & Flasher Location 31-4
Headlamp Switch, Replace 31-5
Heater Core, Replace 31-7
Ignition Lock, Replace 31-4
Ignition Switch, Replace 31-4
Instrument Cluster, Replace 31-6
Neutral Safety Switch, Replace 31-5
Passive Restraints 36-1
Precautions 31-4
Radio, Replace 31-6
Relay Center Location 31-4
Speed Controls 36-1
Starter Motors 36-1
Starter, Replace 31-4
Steering Columns 36-1
Steering Wheel, Replace 31-6
Stop Light Switch, Replace 31-5
Turn Signal Switch, Replace 31-6
Wiper Motor, Replace 31-6
Wiper Switch, Replace 31-6
Wiper Systems 36-1
ELECTRICAL SYMBOL IDENTIFICATION 0-139
FRONT SUSPENSION & STEERING
Ball Joint, Replace 31-43
Ball Joint Inspection 31-43
Hub & Bearing, Replace 31-43
Manual Steering Gears 36-1
Power Steering 36-1
Power Steering Gear, Replace 31-44
Power Steering Pump, Replace 31-44
Stabilizer Bar, Replace 31-44
Strut, Replace 31-43
Tightening Specifications 31-46
Transverse Link, Replace 31-44
Wheel Bearing, Adjust 31-43
Wheel Hub & Steering Knuckle, Replace 31-43
FRONT WHEEL DRIVE AXLES 36-1
REAR AXLE & SUSPENSION
Hub & Bearing, Replace 31-39
Knuckle, Replace 31-41
Rear Axle, Replace 31-39
Rear Halfshaft, Replace 31-39
Rear Suspension, Replace 31-39
Stabilizer Bar, Replace 31-41
Strut Service 31-40
Strut, Replace 31-40
Tightening Specifications 31-42
SERVICE REMINDER & WARNING LAMP RESET PROCEDURES 0-10
SPECIFICATIONS
Fluid Capacities & Cooling System Data 31-3
Front Wheel Alignment Specifications 31-3
General Engine Specifications 31-2
Lubricant Data 31-3
Rear Wheel Alignment Specifications 31-3
Tune Up Specifications 31-2
VEHICLE IDENTIFICATION 0-1
VEHICLE LIFT POINTS 0-34
VEHICLE MAINTENANCE SCHEDULES 0-69
VE30DE ENGINE
Belt Tension Data 31-12
Compression Pressure 31-8
Cooling System Bleed 31-12
Crankshaft Rear Oil Seal, Replace 31-11
Crankshaft Seal, Replace 31-11
Cylinder Head, Replace 31-8
Engine Assemble 31-10
Engine Disassemble 31-9
Engine Mount, Replace 31-8
Engine Rebuilding Specifications 36-1
Engine, Replace 31-8
Fuel Filter, Replace 31-13
Fuel Pump, Replace 31-12
Intake Manifold, Replace 31-8
Oil Pan, Replace 31-11
Oil Pump, Replace 31-11
Piston & Rod Assembly 31-10
Precautions 31-8
Radiator, Replace 31-12
Thermostat, Replace 31-12
Tightening Specifications 31-17
Timing Chain, Replace 31-10
Valve Adjustment 31-10
Valve Clearance Specifications 31-10
Water Pump, Replace 31-12
VG30DE & VG30DETT ENGINES
Belt Tension Data 31-27
Compression Pressure 31-24
Cooling System Bleed 31-27
Crankshaft Rear Oil Seal, Replace 31-26
Crankshaft Seal, Replace 31-26
Cylinder Head, Replace 31-25
Engine Assemble 31-25
Engine Disassemble 31-25
Engine Mount, Replace 31-24
Engine Rebuilding Specifications 36-1
Engine, Replace 31-24
Fuel Filter, Replace 31-27
Fuel Pump, Replace 31-27
Intake Manifold, Replace 31-24
Oil Pan, Replace 31-26
Oil Pump, Replace 31-27
Piston & Rod Assembly 31-26
Precautions 31-24
Radiator, Replace 31-27
Technical Service Bulletins 31-28
Thermostat, Replace 31-27
Tightening Specifications 31-30
Timing Belt, Replace 31-25
Turbocharger, Replace 31-27
Valve Adjustment 31-25
Valve Clearance Specifications 31-25
Water Pump, Replace 31-27
VG30E ENGINE
Belt Tension Data 31-22
Compression Pressure 31-18
Cooling System Bleed 31-22
Crankshaft Rear Oil Seal, Replace 31-21
Crankshaft Seal, Replace 31-21
Cylinder Head, Replace 31-18
Engine Assemble 31-19
Engine Disassemble 31-19
Engine Mount, Replace 31-18
Engine Rebuilding Specifications 36-1
Engine, Replace 31-18
Fuel Filter, Replace 31-22
Fuel Pump, Replace 31-22
Intake Manifold, Replace 31-18
Oil Pan, Replace 31-21
Oil Pump, Replace 31-21
Piston & Rod Assembly 31-21
Precautions 31-18
Radiator, Replace 31-22
Thermostat, Replace 31-22
Tightening Specifications 31-23
Timing Belt, Replace 31-20
Valve Adjustment 31-20
Valve Clearance Specifications 31-19
Water Pump, Replace 31-22
VQ30DE ENGINE
Belt Tension Data 31-34
Compression Pressure 31-30
Cooling System Bleed 31-34
Crankshaft Rear Oil Seal, Replace 31-33
Crankshaft Seal, Replace 31-33
Cylinder Head, Replace 31-31
Engine Assemble 31-32
Engine Disassemble 31-31

Page No.

Engine Mount, Replace 31-31
Engine Rebuilding Specifications 36-1
Engine, Replace 31-31
Fuel Filter, Replace 31-35
Fuel Pump, Replace 31-35
Intake Manifold, Replace...... 31-31
Oil Pan, Replace.............. 31-33
Oil Pump, Replace............ 31-34
Piston & Rod Assembly....... 31-33

Page No.

Precautions.................... 31-30
Radiator, Replace............. 31-35
Technical Service Bulletins.... 31-35
Thermostat, Replace.......... 31-34
Tightening Specifications...... 31-36
Timing Chain, Replace........ 31-32
Valve Adjustment 31-32
Valve Clearance Specifications................. 31-32
Water Pump, Replace 31-34

Page No.

WHEEL ALIGNMENT

Front Wheel Alignment........ 31-47
Preliminary Inspection 31-47
Rear Wheel Alignment........ 31-47
Vehicle Ride Height........... 31-48
Wheel Alignment Specifications................. 31-3

WIRE COLOR CODE IDENTIFICATION 0-144

Specifications

GENERAL ENGINE SPECIFICATIONS

Year	Engine Model	Fuel System	Displacement Liters	Bore X Stroke, Inches	Compression Ratio	Maximum HP @ RPM	Maximum Torque @ RPM	Normal Oil Pressure, psi①
1993–94	VE30DE	Fuel Inj.	3.0L	3.43 x 3.27	10.0	190 @ 5600	190 @ 4000	51–65
	VG30E	Fuel Inj.	3.0L	3.43 x 3.27	9.0	160 @ 5200	182 @ 2800	60–74
	VG30DE	Fuel Inj.	3.0L	3.43 x 3.27	10.5	222 @ 6400	198 @ 4800	51–65
	VG30DETT	Fuel Inj.	3.0L	3.43 x 3.27	8.5	②	283 @ 3600	51–65
1995–96	VG30DE	Fuel Inj.	3.0L	3.43 x 3.27	10.5	222 @ 6400	198 @ 4800	51–65
	VG30DETT	Fuel Inj.	3.0L	3.43 x 3.27	8.5	②	283 @ 3600	51–65
	VQ30DE	Fuel Inj.	3.0L	3.66 x 2.89	10.0	190 @ 5600	205 @ 4000	63—80

①— @ 3000 rpm.
②— Manual transmission, 300 HP @ 6400 RPM; Automatic transmission, 280 HP @ 6400 RPM.

TUNE UP SPECIFICATIONS

Year	Engine Model	Spark Plug Gap, Inch	Ignition		Curb Idle Speed		Fuel Pump Pressure, psi	Valve Lash
			Firing Order	Timing ° BTDC	Man. Trans.	Auto. Trans.		
1993–94	VE30DE	.041	1-2-3-4-5-6	15	700–800	700–800N	36	①
	VG30E	.041	1-2-3-4-5-6	15	700–800	700–800N	36	①
	VG30DE	.041	1-2-3-4-5-6	15	650–750	720–820N	43	①
	VG30DETT	.041	1-2-3-4-5-6	15	650–750	700–800N	43	①
1995–96	VQ30DE	.041	1-2-3-4-5-6	15	600–700	650–750N	36	①
	VG30DE	.041	1-2-3-4-5-6	15	650–750	650–750N	43	①
	VG30DETT	.041	1-2-3-4-5-6	15	720–820	700–800N	43	①

BTDC — Before Top Dead Center.
N — Neutral
①— Refer to "Valve Adjustment" under specific engine section.

FRONT WHEEL ALIGNMENT SPECIFICATIONS

Year	Model	Caster Angle, Deg.		Camber Angle, Deg.		Kingpin Inclination, Deg.	Toe-In, Inch①	Toe-Out On Turns, Deg.②		Ball Joint Wear
		Limits	Desired	Limits	Desired			Inner Wheel	Outer Wheel	
1993–94	Maxima	+½ to +2	+1 ¼	−1 to +½	−¼	13 7/12 to 15 1/12	+.04 to +.12	35 to 39	28 to 32	③
1995–96	Maxima	+2 to +3 ½	+2 ¾	−1 to +½	−¼	13 ½ to 15	+.04 to +.12	37 to 41	28 7/10 to 32 7/10	③
1993–96	300ZX	+8 11/12 to +10 5/12	+9 ⅔	−1 7/12 to −1/12	−⅚	12 ⅙ to 13 ⅔	0 to +.08	32 ½ to 36 ½	26 ½ to 30 ½	③

① — Toe-in (+); toe-out (-).
② — Measure w/wheels at full left & righthand turn positions.
③ — Refer to "Ball joint Inspection" in "Front Suspension & Steering" section.

REAR WHEEL ALIGNMENT SPECIFICATIONS

Year	Model	Camber Angle, Deg.		Toe, Inch①
		Limits	Desired	
1993–94	Maxima	−1 ⅓ to +⅙	−5/12	−.12 to −.04
	300ZX	−1 ⅗ to −⅗	−1 1/10	+.016 to +.173
1995–96	Maxima	−1 ¾ to −¼	−1	−.12 to +.20
	300ZX	−1 ½ to −½	−1	+.016 to +.173

① — Toe-in (+); toe-out (-).

FLUID CAPACITIES & COOLING SYSTEM DATA

Model	Coolant Capacity Qts.	Radiator, Cap Relief Pressure Lbs.	Thermo. Opening Temp. °F	Fuel Tank Gals.	Engine Oil Refill Qts.①	Transmission Oil		Differential Oil Pts.
						Man. Trans. Pts.	Auto. Trans. Qts.②	
1993–94								
Maxima VG30E	9 ⅜	11–14	180	18 ½	4 ⅛	10	7 ⅞	—
Maxima VE30DE	11 ¼	11–14	180	18 ½	4	10	9	—
300ZX Non Turbo	9 ½	11–14	170	19	3 ⅝	5 ⅞	8 ¾	③
300ZX Turbo	9 ½	11–14	170	19	3 ⅝	5 ⅞	8 ⅝	3 ⅞
1995–96								
Maxima	11 ¼	11–14	180	18 ½	4 ½	④	10 ⅛	—
300ZX Non Turbo	9 ½	16–18	170	19	3 ⅝	5 ⅞	8 ¾	2 ¾
300ZX Turbo	9 ½	16–18	170	19	3 ⅝	5 ⅞	8 ⅝	3 ⅞

① — Includes filter.
② — Approximate, make final check with dipstick.
③ — 1993, 3 1/2; 1994, 2 3/4.
④ — RS5F50A, 8 pts.; RS5F50V, 7 ⅝ pts.

LUBRICANT DATA

Year	Model	Lubricant Type				
		Transmission		Rear Axle	Power Steering	Brake System
		Manual	Automatic			
1993–96	Maxima	80W-90 GL-4	Nissan Matic D ①	—	Dexron II/IIE/III	DOT 3
	300ZX	75W-90 GL-4	Nissan Matic D ①	80W-90 GL-5	Dexron II/IIE/III	DOT 3

① — Dexron III/Mercon or equivalent automatic transmission fluid may also be used.

Electrical

NOTE: On Air Bag Equipped Models, Refer To "Air Bag System Precautions" Located In Front Of This Manual For System Disarming & Arming Procedures.

INDEX

	Page No.
Air Bags	36-1
Air Conditioning	36-1
Alternators	36-1
Blower Motor, Replace	31-7
Coil Pack, Replace	31-4
Combination Switch, Replace	31-5
Cooling Fans	36-1
Cruise Control	36-1
Dash Gauges	36-1
Dash Panels	36-1
Distributor, Replace	31-4
Evaporator Core, Replace	31-7
Fuel Pump Relay Location	31-4
Fuse Panel & Flasher Location	31-4
Maxima	31-4
300ZX	31-4
Headlamp Switch, Replace	31-5
Maxima	31-5
300ZX	31-5
Heater Core, Replace	31-7
Ignition Lock, Replace	31-4
Ignition Switch, Replace	31-4
Instrument Cluster, Replace	31-6
Neutral Safety Switch, Replace	31-5
Maxima	31-5
300ZX	31-5
Passive Restraints	36-1
Precautions	31-4
Air Bag Systems	31-4
Radio, Replace	31-6
Relay Center Location	31-4
Speed Controls	36-1
Starter, Replace	31-4
Starter Motors	36-1
Steering Columns	36-1
Steering Wheel, Replace	31-6
Less Air Bag	31-6
With Air Bag	31-6
Stop Light Switch, Replace	31-5
Turn Signal Switch, Replace	31-6
Wiper Motor, Replace	31-6
Front	31-6
Rear	31-6
Wiper Switch, Replace	31-6
Front	31-6
Rear	31-6
Wiper Systems	36-1

PRECAUTIONS

AIR BAG SYSTEMS

Refer to "Air Bag System Precautions" in front of this manual for system disarming and arming procedures.

FUSE PANEL & FLASHER LOCATION

300ZX

The fuse panel is located behind left-hand side kick panel. Combination flasher unit is located under center of instrument panel.

MAXIMA

The fuse panel is located behind left-hand side of instrument panel, left of steering column. Combination flasher unit is located behind center of instrument panel.

FUEL PUMP RELAY LOCATION

The fuel pump relay is located behind the lefthand side kick panel.

RELAY CENTER LOCATION

The relay center is located in front left-hand corner of the engine compartment.

STARTER

REPLACE

1. Disconnect battery ground cable.
2. Remove air intake duct, if required.

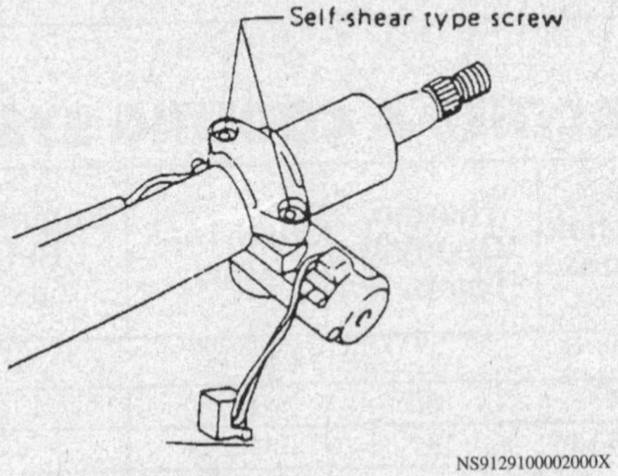
Self-shear type screw
NS9129100002000X

Fig. 1 Ignition lock replacement

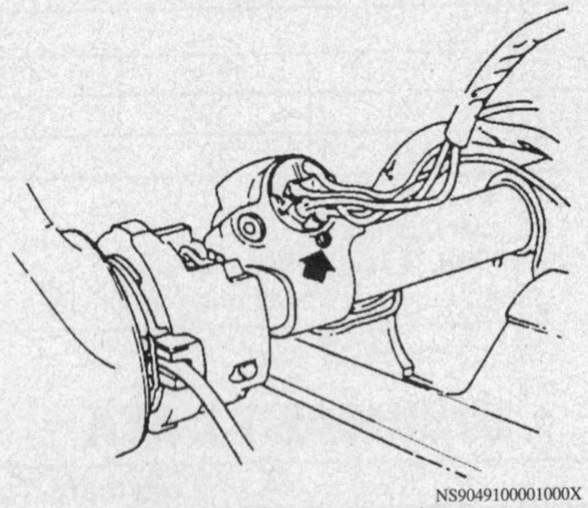
NS9049100001000X

Fig. 2 Ignition switch replacement

3. Disconnect starter wiring from starter.
4. Remove starter motor mounting bolts, then the starter.
5. Reverse procedure to install.

DISTRIBUTOR

REPLACE

1. Disconnect battery ground cable.
2. Position No. 1 cylinder at TDC of its compression stroke.
3. Remove distributor attaching bolt, then the distributor.
4. Reverse procedure to install.

COIL PACK, REPLACE

1. Disconnect battery ground cable.
2. Remove ornament covers.
3. Disconnect coil electrical connectors from each coil.
4. Remove individual coil attaching bolts.
5. Disconnect coils from spark plugs.
6. Reverse procedure to install.

IGNITION LOCK

REPLACE

1. Disconnect battery ground cable.
2. Drill out two shear type retaining screws, **Fig. 1.**
3. Remove ignition lock from steering tube.
4. Reverse procedure to install, ensure shear type screws are used.

IGNITION SWITCH

REPLACE

1. Disconnect battery ground cable.
2. Remove four upper and lower shell cover retaining screws, then the shell covers.

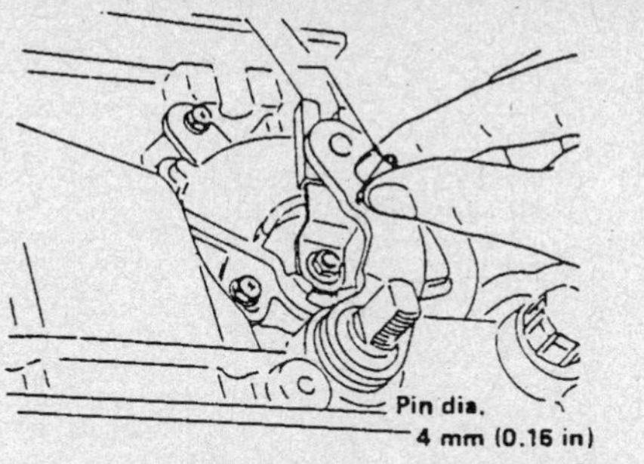
Pin dia.
4 mm (0.16 in)
NS9049100008000X

Fig. 3 Inhibitor switch adjustment. 300ZX

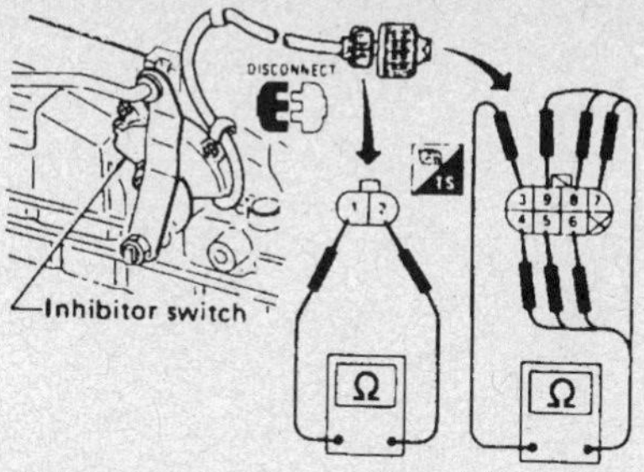
DISCONNECT
Inhibitor switch
Ω
Ω
NS9049100009000X

Fig. 4 Inhibitor switch continuity inspection. 300ZX

Terminal No / Lever position	①	②	③	④	⑤	⑥	⑦	⑧	⑨
P	○	○	○	○					
R			○	—	○				
N	○	○	○	—	—	○			
D			○	—	—	—	○		
2			○	—	—	—	—	○	
1			○	—	—	—	—	—	○

NS9049100010000X

Fig. 5 Inhibitor switch continuity specifications. Maxima w/RE4F04V transaxle & 300ZX

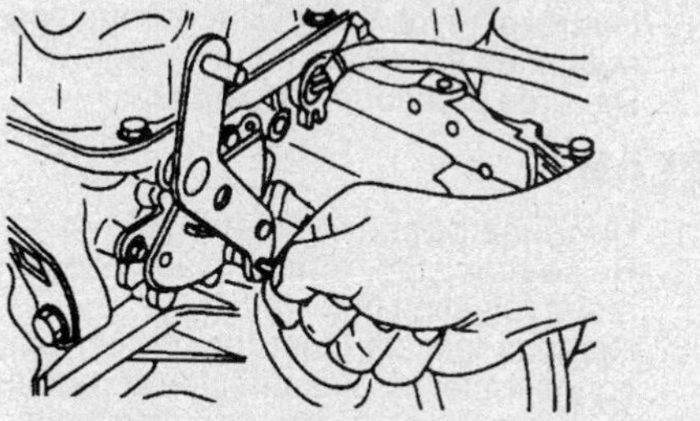
NS9049100011000X

Fig. 6 Inhibitor switch adjustment. Maxima w/VG30E engine

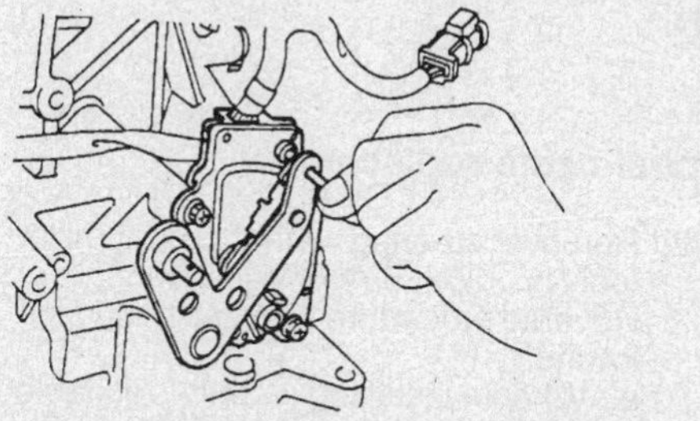
NS9049200012000X

Fig. 7 Inhibitor switch adjustment. Maxima w/VE30DE & VQ30DE engines

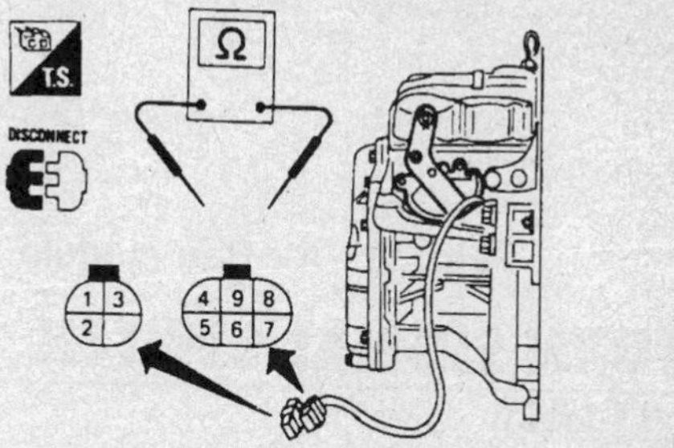
Ω
DISCONNECT
T.S.
1 3
2
4 9 8
5 6 7
NS9049100013000X

Fig. 8 Inhibitor switch continuity inspection. Maxima w/RE4F02A transaxle

Terminal No. / Lever position	①	②	③	④	⑤	⑥	⑦	⑧	⑨
P	○	—	○	○	—	○			
R				○	—	—	○		
N	○	—	○						
		○	—	○					
D				○	○				
2				○	—	—	—	○	
1				○	—	—	—	—	○

NS9049100015000X

Fig. 10 Inhibitor switch continuity specifications. Maxima w/RE4F02A transaxle

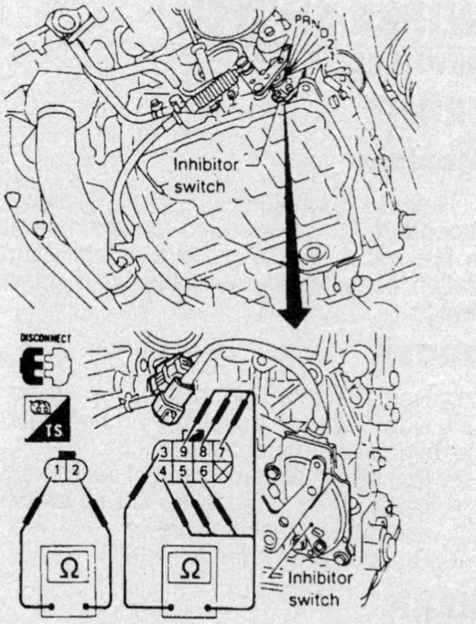
PRND
2
1
Inhibitor switch
DISCONNECT
TS
1 2
3 9 8 7
4 5 6
Ω
Ω
Inhibitor switch
NS9049100014000X

Fig. 9 Inhibitor switch continuity inspection. Maxima w/RE4F04V & RE4F04V transaxles

3. Disconnect electrical connectors from switch.
4. Remove switch retaining screw from steering lock, **Fig. 2.**
5. Reverse procedure to install.

NEUTRAL SAFETY SWITCH

REPLACE

300ZX

1. Place manual valve in Neutral (vertical position).
2. Remove adjustment cover screw.
3. Loosen switch attaching screws.
4. Using suitable alignment pin, move switch until pin falls into hole in rotor, **Fig. 3.**
5. Tighten attaching bolts, then while moving selector lever through all gear ranges, check switch for continuity as shown in **Fig. 4.**
6. Compare results with **Fig. 5.**
7. If switch does not operate as specified, replace switch.

MAXIMA

1. Remove control cable from manual lever, then set selector lever manual lever to Neutral position.
2. Loosen inhibitor switch attaching screws.
3. Insert suitable pin into adjustment holes in both inhibitor switch and switch lever as near vertical as possible, **Figs. 6 and 7.**
4. Tighten attaching bolts, then while moving selector lever through all gear ranges, check switch for continuity as shown in **Figs. 8 and 9.**
5. Compare results with **Figs. 5 and 10.**
6. If switch does not operate as specified, replace switch.

HEADLAMP SWITCH

REPLACE

MAXIMA

Refer to "Combination Switch, Replace." It is not necessary to remove combination switch base to replace light switch.

300ZX

1. Remove retaining screw from lower side of switch assembly on lefthand side of instrument cluster.
2. Pull switch assembly out of instrument panel, then remove switch to switch assembly attaching screws.
3. Reverse procedure to install.

STOP LIGHT SWITCH

REPLACE

Stop light switch is located on brake pedal support.

1. Disconnect switch electrical connectors.
2. Loosen switch retaining locknut and remove switch.
3. Reverse procedure to install.

COMBINATION SWITCH

REPLACE

1. Disconnect battery ground cable.
2. Remove steering wheel as outlined under "Steering Wheel Replace."
3. Remove steering column shell covers.
4. Remove switch retaining screws.
5. Disconnect switch electrical connectors from switch base, then remove switch.
6. Remove switch base, if necessary.
7. Reverse procedure to install.

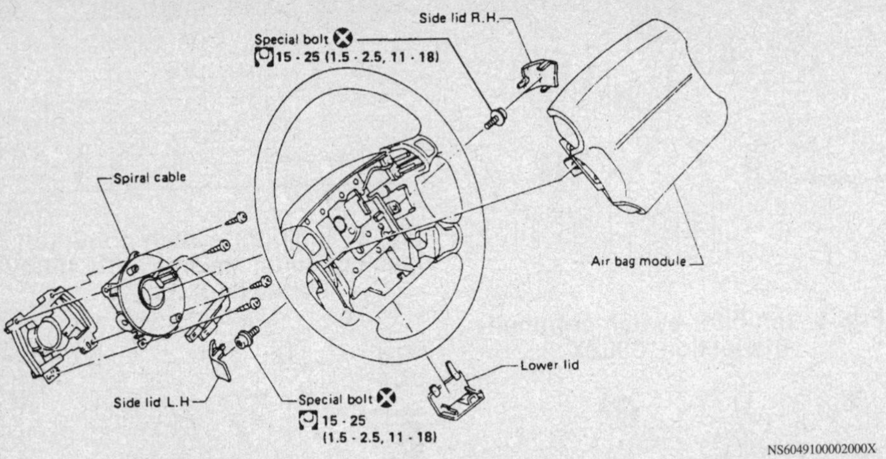
Side lid R.H.
Special bolt
15 - 25 (1.5 - 2.5, 11 - 18)
Spiral cable
Air bag module
Lower lid
Side lid L.H
Special bolt
15 - 25
(1.5 - 2.5, 11 - 18)

NS6049100002000X

Fig. 11 Air Bag module & spiral cable replacement

TURN SIGNAL SWITCH

REPLACE

Refer to "Combination Switch, Replace."

STEERING WHEEL

REPLACE

WITH AIR BAG

1. Disconnect battery ground cable.
2. Place steering wheel In neutral position.
3. Remove left and right side lids, **Fig. 11.**
4. Using special Torx bit T50H or equivalent, remove left and right special bolts.
5. Remove air bag module from steering wheel. **Always place air bag module with pad side facing upward. Do not attempt to disassemble air bag module. Special bolts are coated with a bonding agent, discard after removal and replace. If any portion of air bag module is damaged or cracked, replace module. Do not allow oil, grease or water to come in contact with air bag module.**
6. Ensure steering wheel is in neutral position, then disconnect horn electrical connector and remove steering wheel attaching nut.
7. Remove steering wheel using puller tool No. J25726-A, or equivalent.
8. Reverse procedure to install, noting following:
   a. Install steering wheel aligning spiral cable pin guides, and pull spiral cable connector through steering wheel, **Fig. 12.**
   b. Connect horn connector and secure spiral cable harness with pawls in steering wheel.
   c. **Torque** steering wheel retaining nut to 22–29 ft. lbs.
   d. Position air bag module and install new special bolts, **torque** bolts to 11–18 ft. lbs.

LESS AIR BAG

1. Remove two attaching screws from rear of steering wheel, then the horn pad.
2. Remove steering wheel using puller tool No. J25726-A, or equivalent.
3. Reverse procedure to install noting following:
   a. When installing apply suitable grease to entire surface of turn signal cancel pin and horn contact slip ring.
   b. **Torque** steering wheel attaching nut to 22–29 ft. lbs.

INSTRUMENT CLUSTER

REPLACE

1. Disconnect battery ground cable.
2. Remove steering column cover, steering wheel and combination switch, if necessary.
3. Remove instrument panel cover, if necessary.
4. Remove cluster lid retaining screws, then the cluster lid.
5. Remove cluster retaining screws and nuts.
6. Disconnect speedometer cable and electrical connectors.
7. Reverse procedure to install.

RADIO

REPLACE

1. Disconnect battery ground cable.
2. Remove cluster lid or instrument panel facia.
3. Remove radio bracket to instrument panel attaching screws.
4. Disconnect radio electrical connectors, then remove radio from vehicle.
5. Reverse procedure to install.

WIPER MOTOR

REPLACE

FRONT

1. Disconnect battery ground cable.
2. Remove wiper arms, then disconnect electrical connector from motor, **Fig. 13.**
3. Remove top grille retaining screws and top grille.
4. Remove wiper motor mounting bolts and pull motor away from firewall.

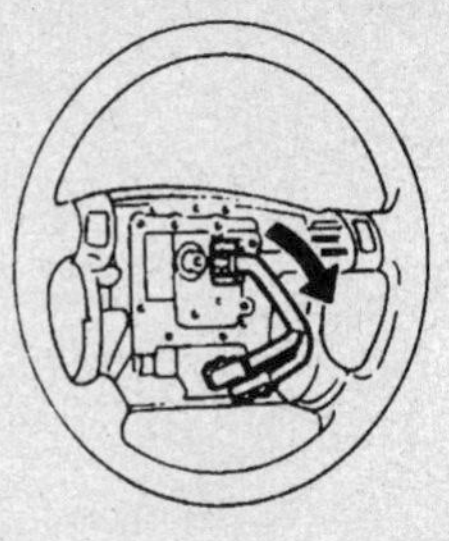

NS6049100003000X

Fig. 12 Spiral cable alignment

5. Disconnect motor shaft from linkage, taking care not to bend linkage.
6. Remove pivot to cowl top retaining nuts, then the wiper motor linkage.
7. Reverse procedure to install.

REAR

1. Disconnect battery ground cable.
2. Raise rear wiper arm off glass and remove retaining nut.
3. Remove tailgate inner trim panel, disconnect electrical connector at motor.
4. Remove wiper motor retaining bolts, then the motor.
5. Reverse procedure to install.

WIPER SWITCH

REPLACE

FRONT

Maxima

Refer to "Combination Switch, Replace" procedure for wiper switch replacement. It is not necessary to remove combination switch base to remove windshield wiper switch.

300ZX

1. Remove retaining screw from lower side of switch assembly on righthand side of instrument cluster.
2. Pull switch assembly out of instrument panel, then remove switch to switch assembly attaching screws.
3. Reverse procedure to install.

REAR

Maxima

1. Disconnect battery ground cable.
2. Disconnect electrical connector from switch.
3. Remove switch knob by depressing and/or twisting as necessary.
4. Remove any switch retaining nuts or clips, then the switch.
5. Reverse procedure to install.

300ZX

1. Disconnect battery ground cable.
2. Remove retaining screw from lower side of switch assembly on righthand side of instrument cluster.
3. Pull switch assembly out of instrument panel, then remove switch to switch assembly attaching screws.
4. Reverse procedure to install.

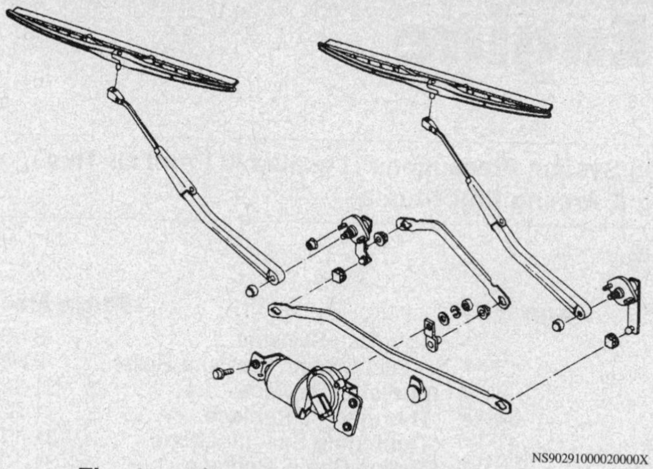
NS90291000020000X

Fig. 13 Exploded view of wiper system

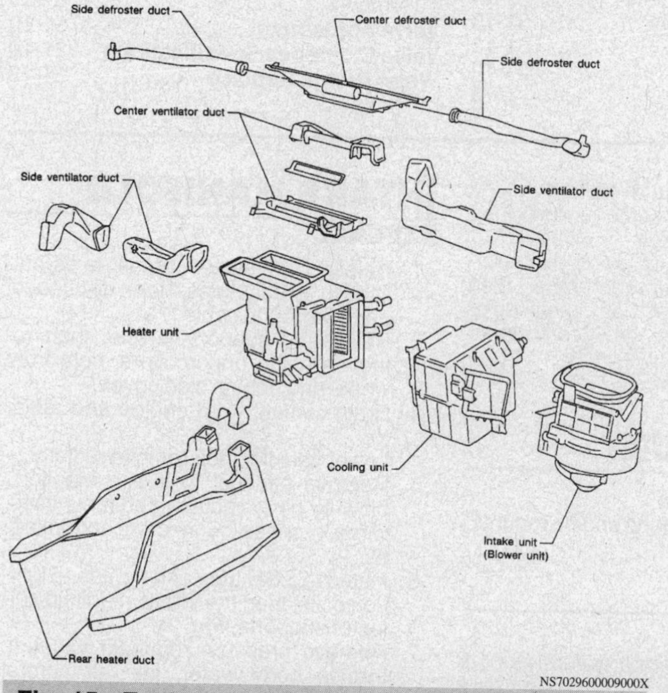
Side defroster duct
Center defroster duct
Side defroster duct
Center ventilator duct
Side ventilator duct
Side ventilator duct
Heater unit
Cooling unit
Intake unit
(Blower unit)
Rear heater duct
NS7029600009000X

Fig. 15 Exploded view of heater system. 1995–96 Maxima

BLOWER MOTOR

REPLACE

Refer to **Figs. 14 through 16** for replacement.

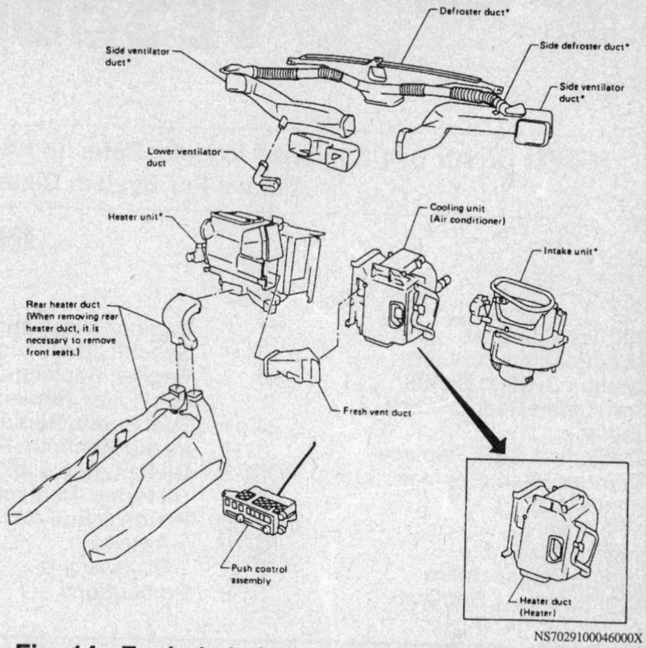
Defroster duct*
Side ventilator duct*
Side defroster duct*
Side ventilator duct*
Lower ventilator duct
Heater unit*
Cooling unit
(Air conditioner)
Intake unit*
Rear heater duct
(When removing rear heater duct, it is necessary to remove front seats.)
Fresh vent duct
Push control assembly
Heater duct
(Heater)
NS7029100046000X

Fig. 14 Exploded view of heater system. 1993–94 Maxima

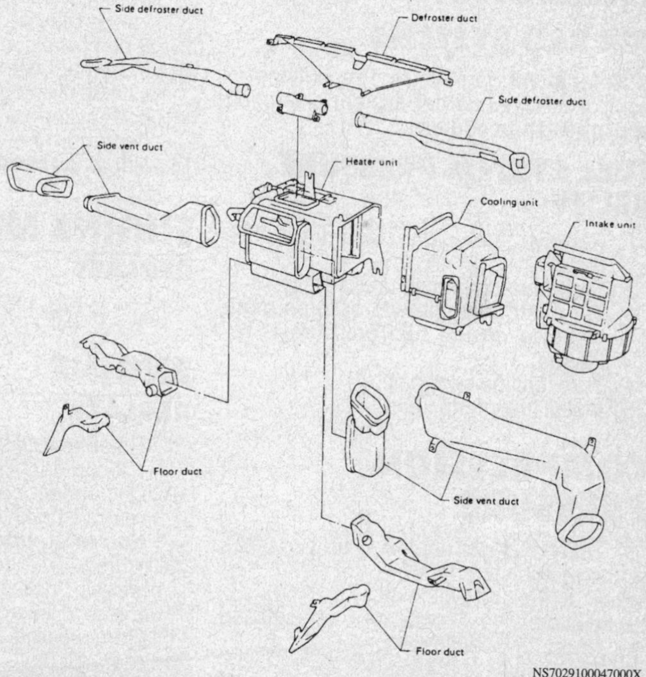
Side defroster duct
Defroster duct
Side defroster duct
Side vent duct
Heater unit
Cooling unit
Intake unit
Floor duct
Side vent duct
Floor duct
NS7029100047000X

Fig. 16 Exploded view of heater system. 300ZX

HEATER CORE

REPLACE

1. Remove instrument panel as outlined under "Dash Panel Service."
2. Refer to **Figs. 14 through 16** for heater core replacement.

EVAPORATOR CORE

REPLACE

1. Discharge A/C system.
2. Remove passenger side instrument lower cover and glove compartment.
3. Disconnect wiring harness connectors to evaporator.
4. Separate cooling unit case halves and remove evaporator, **Figs. 14 through 16.**
5. Reverse procedure to install.

VE30DE Engine

NOTE: On Air Bag Equipped Models, Refer To "Air Bag System Precautions" Located In Front Of This Manual For System Disarming & Arming Procedures.

INDEX

	Page No.
Belt Tension Data	31-12
Compression Pressure	31-8
Cooling System Bleed	31-12
Crankshaft Rear Oil Seal, Replace	31-11
Crankshaft Seal, Replace	31-11
Cylinder Head, Replace	31-8
Installation	31-9
Removal	31-8
Engine Assemble	31-10
Engine Disassemble	31-9
Engine Mount, Replace	31-8
Engine Rebuilding Specifications	36-1
Engine, Replace	31-8
Fuel Filter, Replace	31-13
Fuel Pump, Replace	31-12
Intake Manifold, Replace	31-8
Oil Pan, Replace	31-11
Oil Pump, Replace	31-11
Piston & Rod Assembly	31-10
Assemble	31-10
Disassemble	31-10
Precautions	31-8
Air Bag Systems	31-8
Fuel System Pressure Relief	31-8
Radiator, Replace	31-12
Thermostat, Replace	31-12
Tightening Specifications	31-17
Timing Chain, Replace	31-10
Installation	31-10
Removal	31-10
Valve Adjustment	31-10
Valve Clearance Specifications	31-10
Water Pump, Replace	31-12

PRECAUTIONS

AIR BAG SYSTEMS

Refer to "Air Bag System Precautions" in front of this manual for system disarming and arming procedures.

FUEL SYSTEM PRESSURE RELIEF

1. Remove fuel pump fuse from fuse panel.
2. Start and run engine until it stalls.
3. Try to start engine two or three more times to ensure fuel pressure is released.
4. Turn ignition switch off.
5. Install fuel pump fuse.

COMPRESSION PRESSURE

1. Start and run engine until it reaches operating temperature.
2. Turn ignition switch off.
3. Release fuel pressure as outlined under "Precautions."
4. Remove all spark plugs.
5. Disconnect distributor center cable.
6. Attach a compression tester to cylinder No.1.
7. Depress accelerator pedal fully to keep throttle valve wide open.
8. Crank engine and record highest gauge indication.
9. Repeat measurement on each cylinder.
10. Standard compression is 173 psi at 300 RPM, minimum pressure is 128 psi at 300 RPM and maximum difference between cylinders is 14 psi.
11. If compression in one or more cylinders is low, pour a small amount of engine oil into cylinders through spark plug holes, then retest compression.
12. If adding oil helps compression, then piston rings may be at fault. If adding oil does not help compression, then valves may be at fault.
13. If compression stays low in two cylinders that are next to each other, then cylinder head gasket may be leaking or both cylinders have valve component damage.
14. Repair as necessary.

ENGINE MOUNT

REPLACE

Refer to **Fig. 1** to replace engine mounts.

ENGINE

REPLACE

1. Release fuel system pressure as outlined under "Precautions."
2. Disconnect battery ground cable and remove hood. **Mark hood for installation reference.**
3. Remove vacuum and fuel hoses, wires, harnesses, electrical connectors and linkages.
4. Remove radiator, fans and coupling, then the drive belts.
5. Remove alternator, air conditioning compressor and power steering pump.
6. Raise and support vehicle, then remove engine undercover.
7. Drain engine coolant from cylinder block and radiator.
8. Drain engine oil, then remove front exhaust pipes.
9. Remove drive shafts and ball joints.
10. Attach suitable lifting equipment to engine and support transaxle with a suitable jack.
11. Remove left and right rear engine mounts.
12. Remove center member, then slowly lower transaxle jack and remove engine and transaxle from under vehicle.
13. Reverse procedure to install.

INTAKE MANIFOLD

REPLACE

1. Release fuel system pressure as outlined in "Precautions," then disconnect battery ground cable.
2. Raise and support vehicle, then remove engine undercovers, right front wheel and engine side cover.
3. Drain coolant from engine and radiator.
4. Lower vehicle, then remove radiator.
5. Remove air duct to intake manifold, blow-by pipe, vacuum and fuel hoses, wires, harness, connectors and linkages.
6. Remove EGR tube and righthand ignition coils, then the intake manifold collector supports, **Fig. 2.**
7. Remove pressure regulator vacuum, throttle body water, idle air control valve/auxiliary air control valve, canister purge and blow-by hoses.
8. Remove intake collector retaining bolts in reverse order of collector tightening sequence, **Fig. 3.**
9. Remove lefthand ignition coils and all spark plugs.
10. Remove idle air adjusting (IAA) unit and heater pipe.
11. Remove injector tube assembly, then the righthand vacuum timing control (VTC) solenoid valve.
12. Remove intake manifold retaining bolts in reverse order of manifold tightening sequence, **Fig. 4.**
13. Reverse procedure to install, tightening all bolts to specifications.

CYLINDER HEAD

REPLACE

REMOVAL

1. Remove intake manifold as outlined in "Intake Manifold, Replace."
2. Remove drive belts.

3. Remove A/C compressor without disconnecting A/C pressure lines, position compressor aside.
4. Remove alternator and idler pulley brackets.
5. Remove oil level gauge support and left exhaust manifold retaining bolts in reverse order of tightening, **Fig. 5.**
6. Remove power steering pump and bracket.
7. Remove right exhaust manifold retaining bolts in reverse order of manifold tightening, **Fig. 6.**
8. Remove both rocker covers, then the upper chain guides.
9. Remove upper front covers, then set No. 1 piston at TDC of compression stroke by rotating crankshaft, **Fig. 7.**
10. Rotate crankshaft until mating marks on camshaft sprockets are set at position, **Fig. 8.**
11. Remove crank angle sensor, then the chain tensioners.
12. Remove camshaft sprockets and VTC assemblies.
13. Remove right side exhaust camshaft, camshaft brackets and rocker arms in order, **Fig. 9.**
14. Remove left side exhaust camshaft, camshaft brackets and rocker arms in order, **Fig. 10.**
15. Remove cylinder head outside bolts.
16. Using sequence shown in **Figs. 11 and 12,** loosen cylinder head bolts in two or three steps.
17. Remove cylinder head.

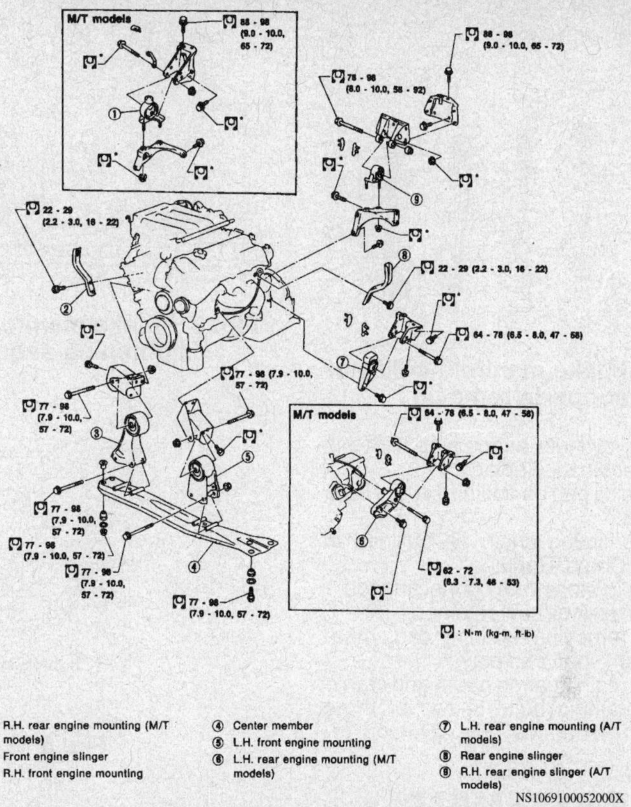
M/T models
M/T models
: N·m (kg-m, ft-lb)
① R.H. rear engine mounting (M/T models)
② Front engine slinger
③ R.H. front engine mounting
④ Center member
⑤ L.H. front engine mounting
⑥ L.H. rear engine mounting (M/T models)
⑦ L.H. rear engine mounting (A/T models)
⑧ Rear engine slinger
⑨ R.H. rear engine slinger (A/T models)
NS1069100052000X

Fig. 1 Engine mounts

INSTALLATION

1. Turn crankshaft until No. 1 piston is at approximately 120° before TDC on compression stroke to prevent any interference of valve and pistons.
2. Apply a continuous bead of liquid gasket to cylinder head mating surface of cylinder block.
3. Install cylinder heads with new gaskets.
4. Using sequence shown in **Figs. 13 and 14,** tighten cylinder head bolts as follows:
   a. **Torque** all bolts to 29 ft. lbs.
   b. Using suitable angle wrench, turn all bolts marked "CRA" 65–70° clockwise.
   c. Using suitable angle wrench, turn all bolts marked "CRB" 70–75° clockwise.
   d. If angle wrench is not available, **torque** all bolts to 90 ft. lbs.
   e. Loosen all bolts completely.
   f. **Torque** all bolts to 25–33 ft. lbs.
   g. Using suitable angle wrench, turn all bolts marked ① 65–70° clockwise.
   h. Using suitable angle wrench, turn all bolts marked ② 70–75° clockwise.
   i. If angle wrench is not available, **torque** all bolts to 87–94 ft. lbs.
   j. Install cylinder head outside bolts.
5. Install exhaust camshafts as follows:
   a. Left and right camshafts have identification marks, (96E RE) indicates righthand camshaft and (96E LE) indicates lefthand camshaft.
   b. Position righthand camshaft key at approximately 10 o'clock, **Fig. 15.**
   c. Position lefthand camshaft key at approximately 12 o'clock, **Fig. 15.**
   d. Install camshaft brackets in their original position.
   e. Prior to installing lefthand exhaust camshaft end bracket, remove all remaining liquid gasket from mating surface of bracket and cylinder head, and completely clean any oil stains.
   f. Apply a continuous bead of liquid gasket to mating surface of lefthand exhaust camshaft bracket as shown in **Fig. 16,** then install bracket.
   g. Using sequence shown in **Figs. 17 and 18,** tighten brackets to specification.
6. Install righthand VTC assembly, then the righthand camshaft sprocket.
7. Line up mating marks on righthand upper timing chain with mating marks on righthand VTC assembly and righthand camshaft sprocket, **Fig. 19.**
8. Before installing righthand upper chain tensioner, press-in sleeve until hook can be engaged on pin. Make sure that hook used to retain chain tensioner is released, **Fig. 20.**
9. Install righthand chain tensioner, refer to **Fig. 21** to ensure correct tensioner is installed.
10. Turn crankshaft clockwise to set No. 1 piston at TDC of compression stroke.
11. Install lefthand VTC assembly, then the lefthand camshaft sprocket.
12. Line up mating marks on lefthand upper timing chain with mating marks on lefthand VTC assembly and lefthand camshaft sprocket, **Fig. 22.**
13. Install lefthand chain tensioner, then ensure upper timing chains are in correct position as shown in **Fig. 23.**
14. Install crank angle sensor, ensure position of camshaft and rotor position of crank angle sensor are as shown in **Fig. 24.**
15. Remove all traces of liquid gasket from mating surfaces and grooves of both upper timing chain covers.
16. Remove any remaining liquid gasket from mating surface of cylinder head.
17. Apply a continuous bead of liquid gasket to mating surface of both upper covers as shown in **Fig. 16,** then install both covers.
18. Install both upper chain guides.
19. Remove all traces of liquid gasket from rocker cover and cylinder head mating surfaces.
20. Apply a continuous bead of liquid gasket to mating surface of rocker cover gaskets and cylinder heads as shown in **Fig. 16.**
21. Using sequence shown in **Figs. 25 and 26,** tighten rocker cover bolts as follows:
   a. **Torque** nuts 1, 2, 12, 11, 9, 14 in that order to 35 inch lbs.
   b. **Torque** nuts 1–14 in sequence to 7 ft. lbs.
22. Install remaining parts in reverse order of removal.

ENGINE DISASSEMBLE

1. Place engine on a work stand, then ensure coolant and oil have drained.

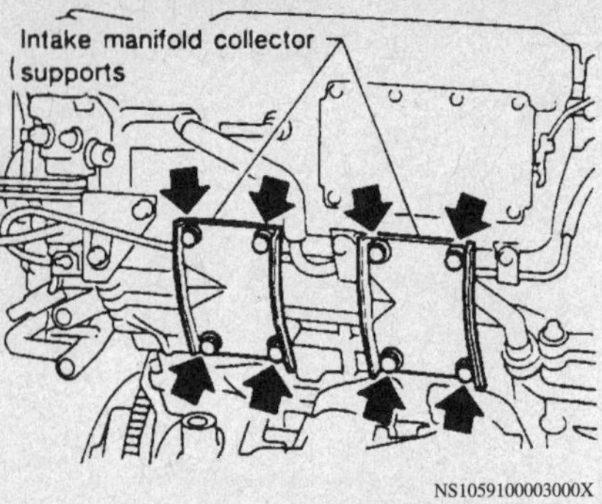
Intake manifold collector supports
NS1059100003000X

Fig. 2 Intake manifold collector supports removal

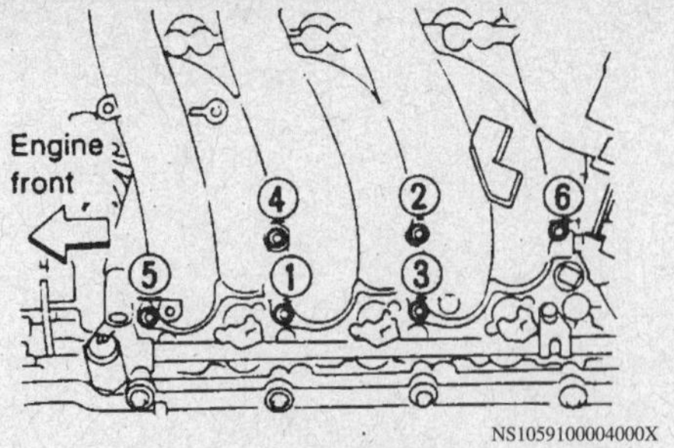
Engine front
NS1059100004000X

Fig. 3 Intake manifold collector tightening sequence

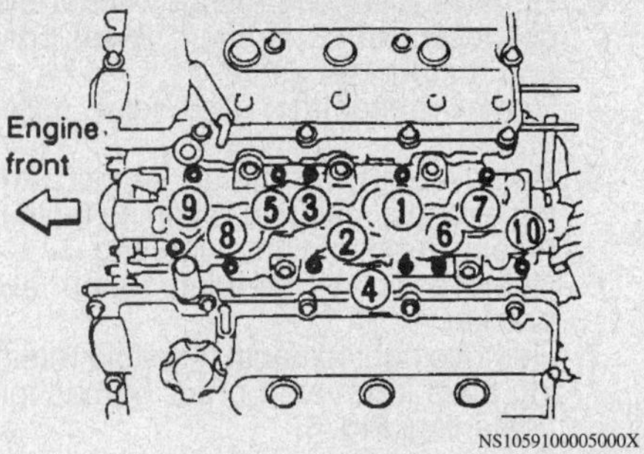
Engine front
NS1059100005000X

Fig. 4 Intake manifold tightening sequence

2. Remove cylinder heads as outlined in "Cylinder Head, Replace."
3. Remove oil pan as outlined in "Oil Pan, Replace."
4. Remove timing chain as outlined in "Timing Chain, Replace."
5. Remove pistons with connecting rod.
6. Remove rear oil seal retainer.
7. Before removing bearing cap, measure crankshaft end play.
8. Loosen main bearing beam and crankshaft retaining bolts in two or three steps in sequence, **Fig. 27,** and remove.

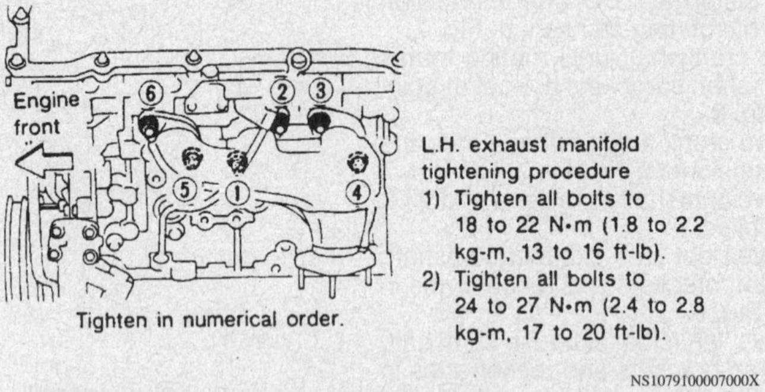
Engine front
Tighten in numerical order.
L.H. exhaust manifold tightening procedure
1) Tighten all bolts to 18 to 22 N•m (1.8 to 2.2 kg-m, 13 to 16 ft-lb).
2) Tighten all bolts to 24 to 27 N•m (2.4 to 2.8 kg-m, 17 to 20 ft-lb).
NS1079100007000X

Fig. 5 Lefthand exhaust manifold tightening sequence

ENGINE ASSEMBLE

1. Install main bearings, **Fig. 28,** crankshaft and bearing cap. Tighten attaching bolts to specifications in sequence, **Fig. 29** in two or three steps.
2. Install piston assemblies with rings properly positioned, **Fig. 30.**
3. Reverse "Engine Disassemble" procedure to complete assembly, noting following:
   a. Tighten cylinder head attaching bolts to specifications using sequence shown in **Figs. 13 and 14,**
   b. Tighten intake manifold attaching bolts in sequence, **Fig. 4** to specifications in two or three steps.

VALVE CLEARANCE SPECIFICATIONS

Engine	Stem-To-Guide Clearance, Inch①	
	Intake	Exhaust
VE30DE	.0008–.0017	.0016–.0025

① — Cold engine.

VALVE ADJUSTMENT

These engines are equipped with hydraulic lash adjusters. No adjustments are required.

TIMING CHAIN

REPLACE

REMOVAL

1. Remove intake manifold as outlined in "Intake Manifold, Replace," **Fig. 31.**
2. Remove cylinder heads as outlined in "Cylinder Head, Replace."
3. Remove water pipe, water pump pulley and water pump, **Fig. 32.**
4. Remove oil pan as outlined in "Oil Pan, Replace."
5. Remove crankshaft pulley, oil strainer and oil filter bracket.
6. Remove front cover, alternator adjusting bar and upper timing chains.
7. Remove chain tensioner, chain guides, idler sprockets and lower timing chain.

INSTALLATION

1. Install crankshaft sprocket on crankshaft, then position crankshaft so that No. 1 piston is set at TDC on compression stroke.
2. Install righthand idler sprocket and chain guides.
3. Position lower timing chain on righthand idler sprocket by aligning mating mark on righthand idler sprocket with silver mating mark on lower timing chain, **Fig. 33.**
4. Install lefthand idler sprocket with lower timing chain.
5. Line up mating marks on lower timing chain with mating marks on lefthand idler sprocket and crankshaft sprocket, **Fig. 34.**
6. Position upper timing chains on idler sprockets by aligning mating marks on idler sprockets with gold mating marks on upper timing chains, **Fig. 35.**
7. Install oil pump drive spacer.
8. Remove all traces of liquid gasket from grooves and mating surface of front cover and cylinder block.
9. Apply a continuous bead of liquid gasket to mating surface of front cover, **Fig. 16.**
10. Install front cover and alternator adjuster bracket.
11. Install oil filter bracket, oil strainer and crankshaft pulley.
12. Set No. 1 piston at TDC of compression stroke.
13. Install oil pan as outlined in "Oil Pan, Replace."
14. Remove all traces of liquid gasket from mating surface and groove of water pump, front cover and water pipe.
15. Apply a continuous bead of liquid gasket to mating surface of water pump, **Fig. 16.**
16. Install water pump and water pump pulley.
17. Install water pipe and tighten bolts to specifications in order, **Fig. 36.**
18. Install cylinder head as outlined in "Cylinder Head, Replace."
19. Install intake manifold as outlined in "Intake Manifold, Replace."

PISTON & ROD ASSEMBLY

DISASSEMBLE

1. Remove piston rings with a ring remover.
2. Remove snap ring, then press out piston pin using piston pin press or heat piston to 140–150°F and remove piston pin. **Keep disassembled parts in order.**

ASSEMBLE

1. Assemble pistons, piston pins and

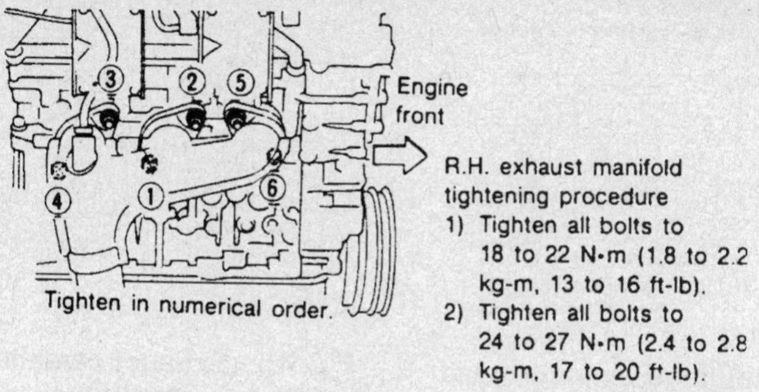
Engine front
Tighten in numerical order.
R.H. exhaust manifold tightening procedure
1) Tighten all bolts to 18 to 22 N•m (1.8 to 2.2 kg-m, 13 to 16 ft-lb).
2) Tighten all bolts to 24 to 27 N•m (2.4 to 2.8 kg-m, 17 to 20 ft-lb).

NS1079100008000X

Fig. 6 Righthand exhaust manifold tightening sequence

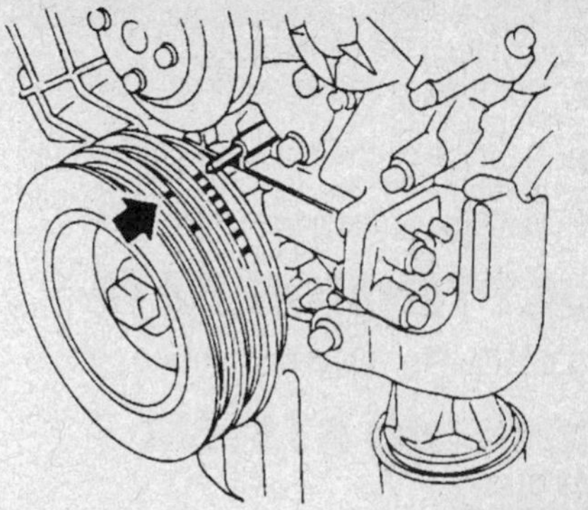

NS1069100069000X

Fig. 7 No. 1 piston at TDC

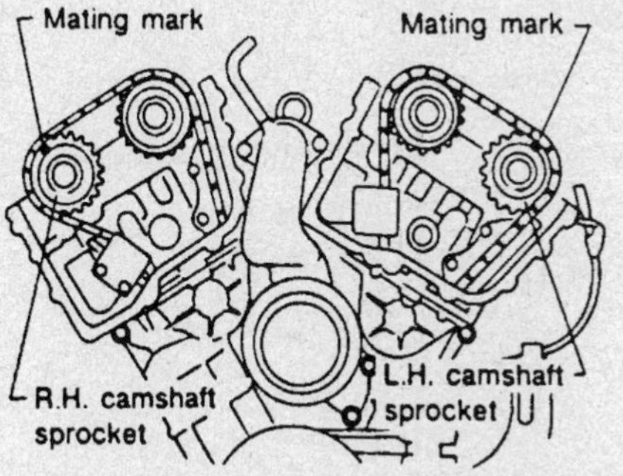
Mating mark
Mating mark
R.H. camshaft sprocket
L.H. camshaft sprocket

NS1069100070000X

Fig. 8 Camshaft sprocket mating marks

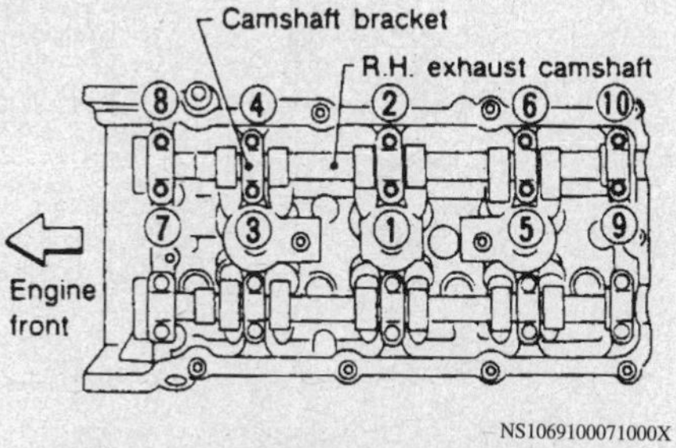
Camshaft bracket
R.H. exhaust camshaft
Engine front

NS1069100071000X

Fig. 9 Righthand exhaust camshaft loosening sequence

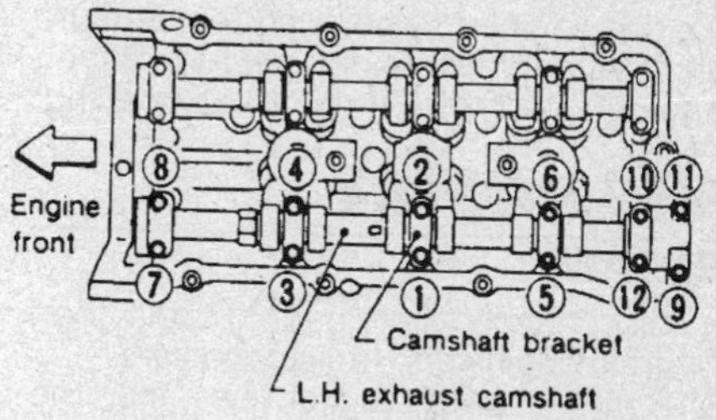
Engine front
Camshaft bracket
L.H. exhaust camshaft

NS1069100072000X

Fig. 10 Lefthand exhaust camshaft loosening sequence

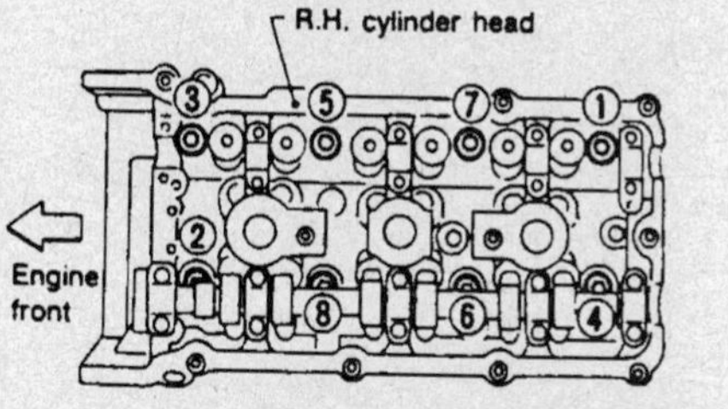
R.H. cylinder head
Engine front

NS1069100073000X

Fig. 11 Righthand cylinder head loosening sequence

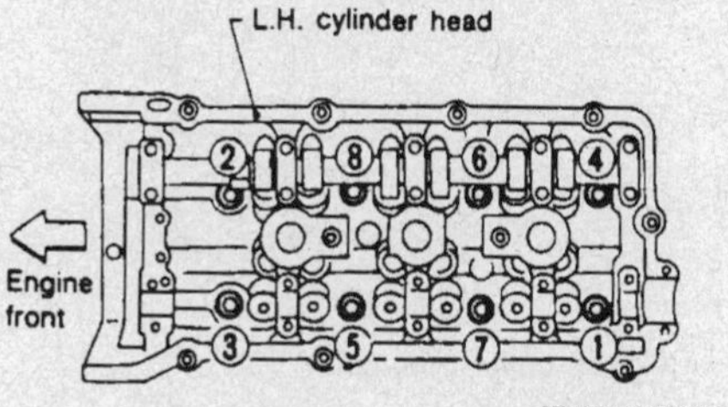
L.H. cylinder head
Engine front

NS1069100074000X

Fig. 12 Lefthand cylinder head loosening sequence

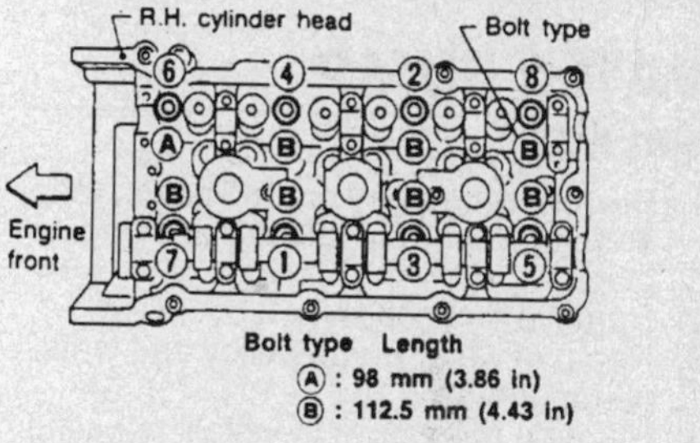
R.H. cylinder head
Bolt type
Engine front
Bolt type Length
Ⓐ : 98 mm (3.86 in)
Ⓑ : 112.5 mm (4.43 in)

NS1069100079000X

Fig. 13 Righthand cylinder head bolt tightening sequence

connecting rods of designated cylinders.
2. Install new snap ring on one side of piston pin.
3. Align piston and connecting rod direction.
4. Ensure stamped numbers on connecting rod and cap correspond to each cylinder.
5. Heat piston to 140–150°F and assemble piston, piston pin, connecting rod and new snap ring.
6. Install piston rings.

CRANKSHAFT SEAL

REPLACE

1. Raise and support vehicle, then remove engine undercover.
2. Remove righthand front wheel and engine side cover.
3. Remove drive belts.
4. Remove crankshaft pulley.
5. Remove front oil seal using suitable oil seal removal tool and being careful not to scratch front cover.
6. Apply engine oil to new oil seal and install using suitable oil seal installation tool.

CRANKSHAFT REAR OIL SEAL

REPLACE

1. Remove flywheel or driveplate.
2. Remove rear oil seal using suitable seal removal tool.
3. Apply engine oil to new seal and install with suitable seal installation tool.

OIL PAN

REPLACE

1. Raise and support vehicle, then drain engine oil.
2. Remove engine lower covers, then the front exhaust tube from support.
3. Support engine at righthand slinger with suitable hoist.
4. Remove engine mounting insulator attaching bolts and nuts, then the center member assembly.
5. Remove oil pan attaching bolts in order, **Fig. 37.**
6. Insert a suitable tool between cylinder block and oil pan, then tap tool side with hammer and remove oil pan. **Do not use a screwdriver, oil pan flange will be deformed. Be careful not to damage aluminum mating surface of cylinder block.**
7. Reverse procedure to install, noting following:
   a. Remove all liquid gasket from oil pan and cylinder block mating surfaces.
   b. Remove dip stick before install oil pan.
   c. Apply sealant to front cover gasket and rear oil seal retainer gasket.
   d. Apply a continuous bead of liquid gasket to mating surface of oil pan.
   e. Tighten bolts and nuts to specifications in reverse order, **Fig. 37.**
   f. Wait at least 30 minutes before refilling engine oil.

OIL PUMP

REPLACE

1. Drain engine oil and remove drive belts.

2. Remove cylinder heads as outlined in "Cylinder Head, Replace."
3. Remove oil pan as outlined in "Oil Pan, Replace."
4. Remove oil strainer and front cover assembly, **Fig. 38.**
5. Reverse procedure to install.

BELT TENSION DATA

Refer to **Fig. 39** for belt tension data.

COOLING SYSTEM BLEED

These engines do not require a specified bleed procedure. After filling cooling system, run engine to operating temperature with radiator/pressure cap off. Air will then be automatically bled through cap opening.

THERMOSTAT

REPLACE

1. Disconnect battery ground cable, then drain engine and radiator coolant.
2. Remove lower radiator hose, then the water inlet, **Fig. 40.**
3. Remove thermostat from thermostat housing.
4. Reverse procedure to install.

WATER PUMP

REPLACE

1. Disconnect battery ground cable, then drain coolant from radiator and engine block.
2. Remove drive belts.
3. Remove water pump pulley and water pump, **Fig. 41.**
4. Reverse procedure to install, applying liquid gasket to mating surfaces of water pump.

RADIATOR

REPLACE

1. Remove undercover, then drain coolant.
2. Disconnect upper and lower radiator hoses, **Fig. 42.**
3. **On models with automatic transaxle,** remove ATF cooler hoses.
4. **On all models,** disconnect reservoir tank hose.
5. Remove radiator attaching bolts and radiator.
6. Reverse procedure to install.

FUEL PUMP

REPLACE

1. Release fuel pump pressure as outlined in "Precautions."
2. Disconnect battery ground cable, then drain fuel into suitable container.
3. Disconnect necessary fuel lines and electrical connectors.
4. Disconnect fuel tank attaching bolts, then lower tank.
5. Remove fuel pump attaching bolts, then the fuel pump.
6. Reverse procedure to install.

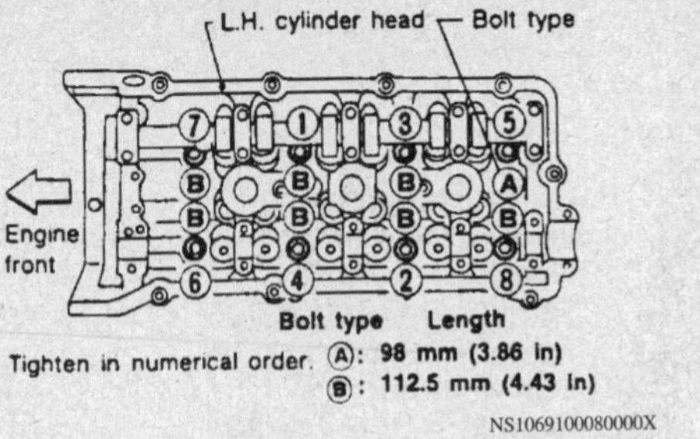
L.H. cylinder head
Bolt type
Engine front
Bolt type Length
Tighten in numerical order.
Ⓐ: 98 mm (3.86 in)
Ⓑ: 112.5 mm (4.43 in)
NS1069100080000X

Fig. 14 Lefthand cylinder head bolt tightening sequence

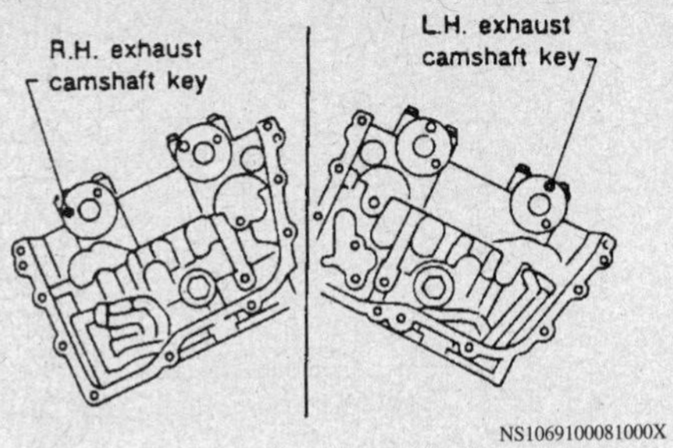
R.H. exhaust camshaft key
L.H. exhaust camshaft key
NS1069100081000X

Fig. 15 Exhaust camshaft keys position

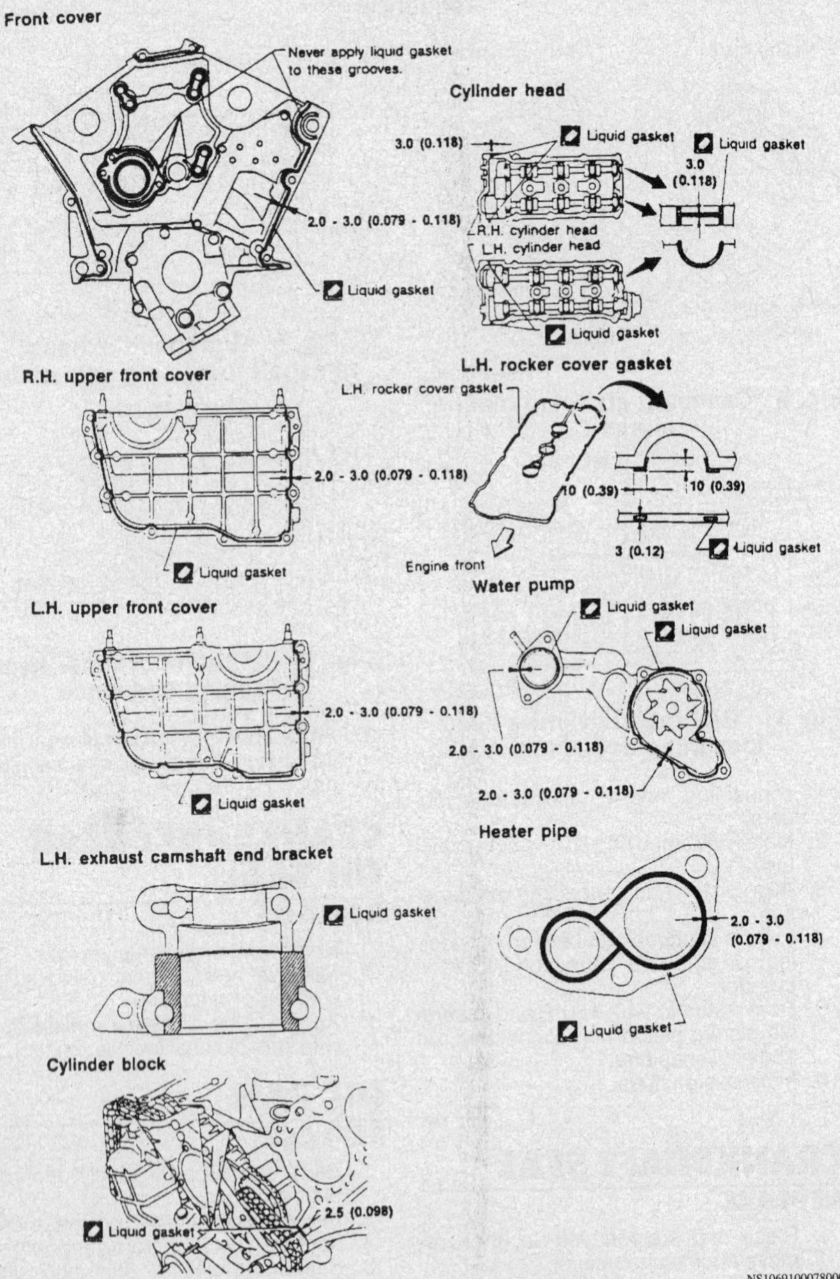
Front cover
Never apply liquid gasket to these grooves.
2.0 - 3.0 (0.079 - 0.118)
Liquid gasket
Cylinder head
3.0 (0.118)
Liquid gasket
Liquid gasket
3.0 (0.118)
R.H. cylinder head
L.H. cylinder head
Liquid gasket
R.H. upper front cover
2.0 - 3.0 (0.079 - 0.118)
Liquid gasket
L.H. rocker cover gasket
L.H. rocker cover gasket
10 (0.39)
10 (0.39)
3 (0.12)
Liquid gasket
Engine front
L.H. upper front cover
2.0 - 3.0 (0.079 - 0.118)
Liquid gasket
Water pump
Liquid gasket
Liquid gasket
2.0 - 3.0 (0.079 - 0.118)
2.0 - 3.0 (0.079 - 0.118)
L.H. exhaust camshaft end bracket
Liquid gasket
Heater pipe
2.0 - 3.0 (0.079 - 0.118)
Liquid gasket
Cylinder block
2.5 (0.098)
Liquid gasket
NS1069100078000X

Fig. 16 Liquid gasket application

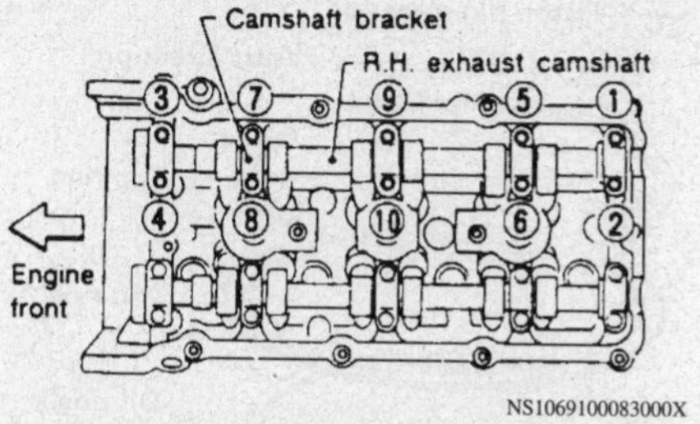
Camshaft bracket
R.H. exhaust camshaft
3 7 9 5 1
4 8 10 6 2
Engine front
NS1069100083000X

Fig. 17 Righthand exhaust camshaft bolt tightening sequence

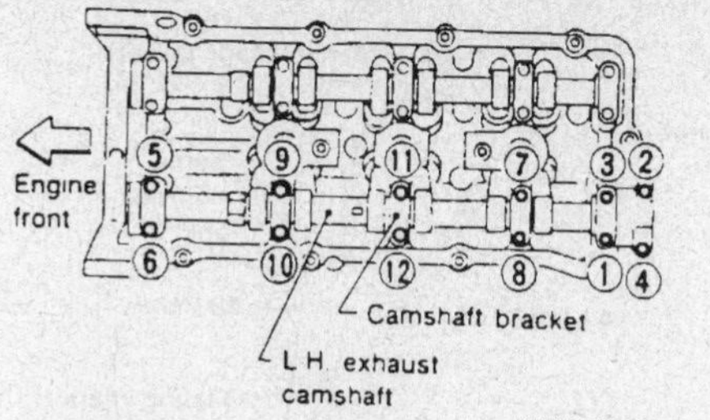
Engine front
5 9 11 7 3 2
6 10 12 8 1 4
Camshaft bracket
L.H. exhaust camshaft
NS1069100084000X

Fig. 18 Lefthand exhaust camshaft bolt tightening sequence

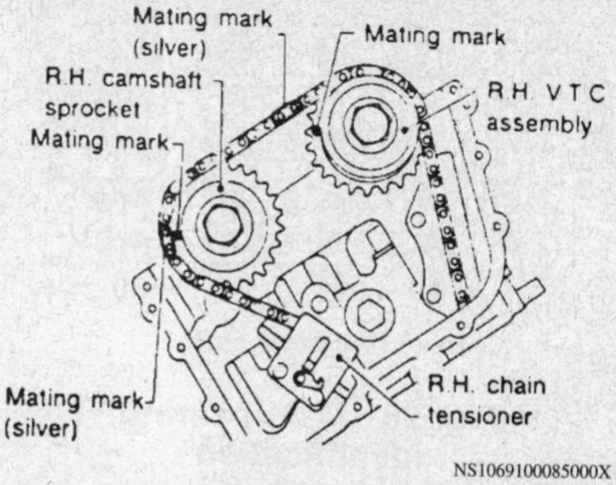
Mating mark (silver)
Mating mark
R.H. camshaft sprocket
Mating mark
R.H. VTC assembly
Mating mark (silver)
R.H. chain tensioner
NS1069100085000X

Fig. 19 Righthand upper timing chain, VTC assembly & camshaft sprocket alignment

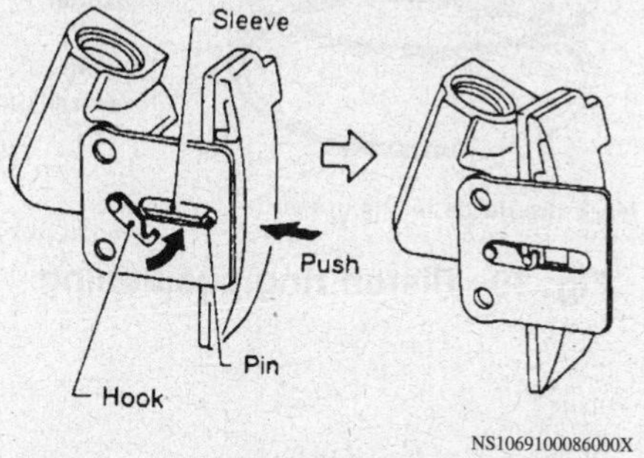
Sleeve
Push
Pin
Hook
NS1069100086000X

Fig. 20 Chain tensioner hook setting

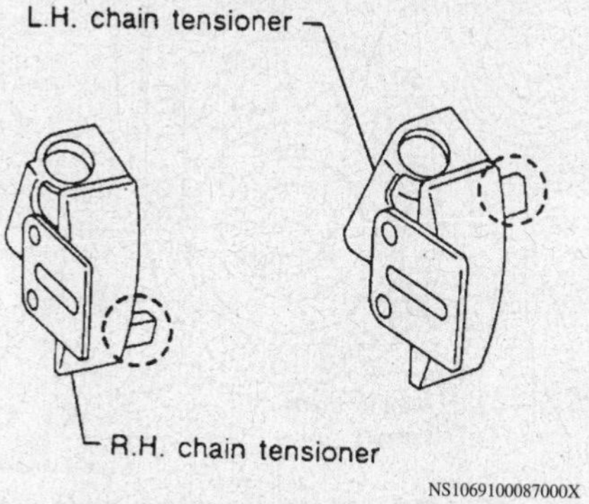
L.H. chain tensioner
R.H. chain tensioner
NS1069100087000X

Fig. 21 Chain tensioner identification

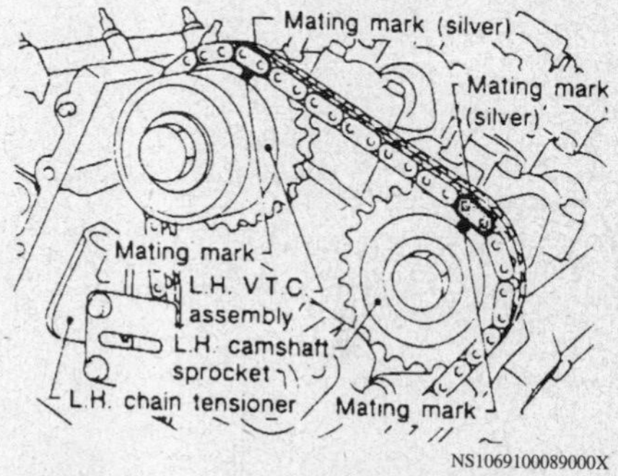
Mating mark (silver)
Mating mark (silver)
Mating mark
L.H. VTC assembly
L.H. camshaft sprocket
L.H. chain tensioner
Mating mark
NS1069100089000X

Fig. 22 Lefthand upper timing chain, VTC assembly & camshaft sprocket alignment

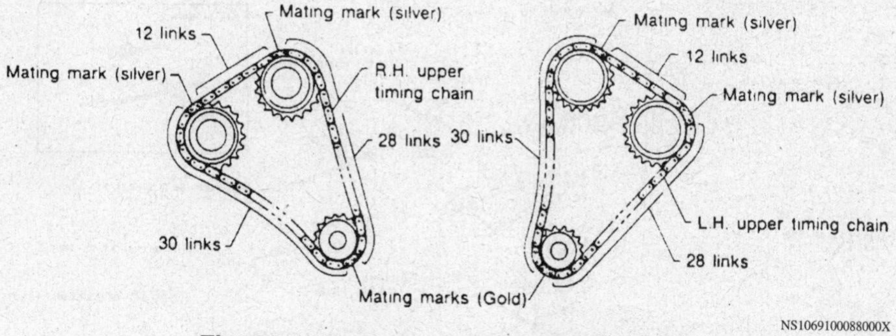
Mating mark (silver)
12 links
Mating mark (silver)
R.H. upper timing chain
28 links
30 links
30 links
Mating marks (Gold)
Mating mark (silver)
12 links
Mating mark (silver)
L.H. upper timing chain
28 links
NS1069100088000X

Fig. 23 Upper timing chains alignment

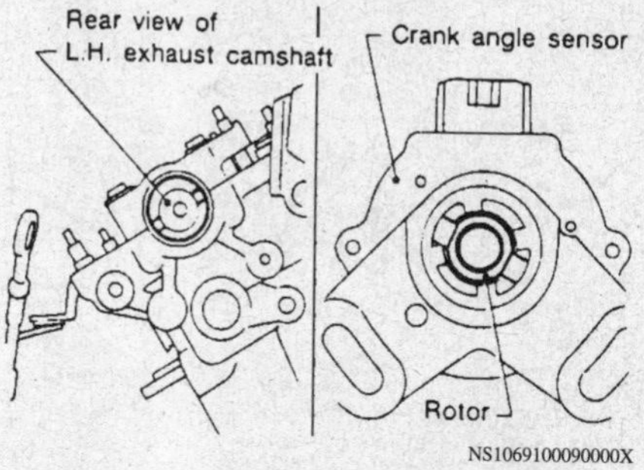
Rear view of L.H. exhaust camshaft
Crank angle sensor
Rotor
NS1069100090000X

Fig. 24 Crank angle sensor positioning Maxima w/VE30DE engine

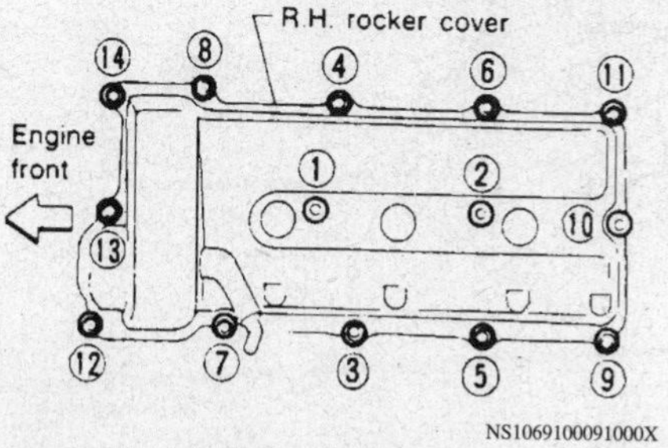
R.H. rocker cover
14 8 4 6 11
Engine front
1 2
13 10
12 7 3 5 9
NS1069100091000X

Fig. 25 Righthand rocker cover tightening sequence

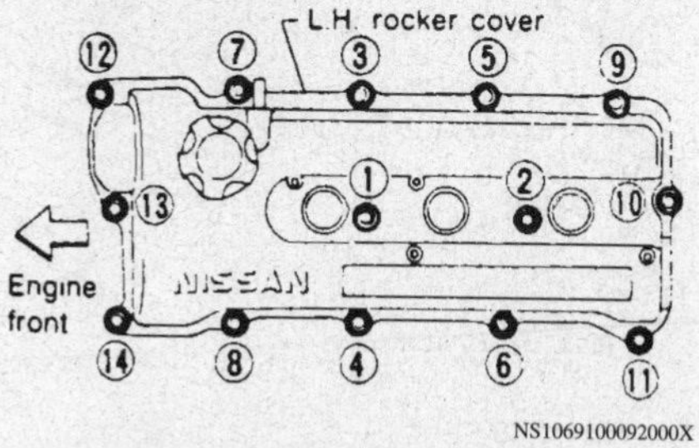
L.H. rocker cover
12 7 3 5 9
1 2
13 10
NISSAN
Engine front
14 8 4 6 11
NS1069100092000X

Fig. 26 Lefthand rocker cover tightening sequence

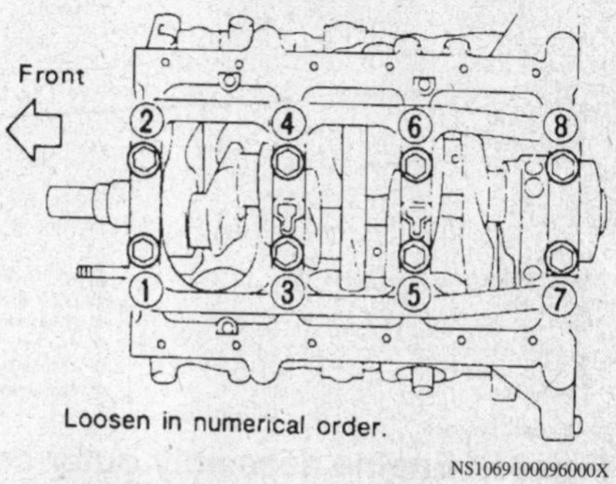
Front
2 4 6 8
1 3 5 7
Loosen in numerical order.
NS1069100096000X

Fig. 27 Main bearing cap bolt loosening sequence

FUEL FILTER

REPLACE

1. Relieve fuel system pressure as outlined in "Precautions."
2. Loosen two fuel filter hose clamps, **Fig. 43.**
3. Disconnect fuel hoses from fuel filter. **Do not allow gasoline to spill over engine compartment.**
4. Reverse procedure to install.

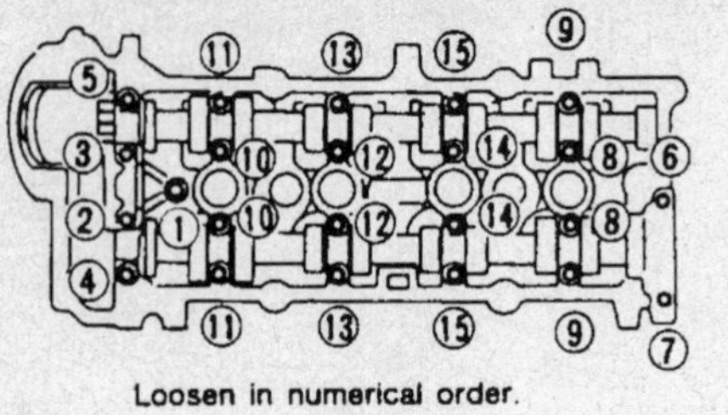
Loosen in numerical order.
NS1069100012000X

Fig. 28 Main bearing identification

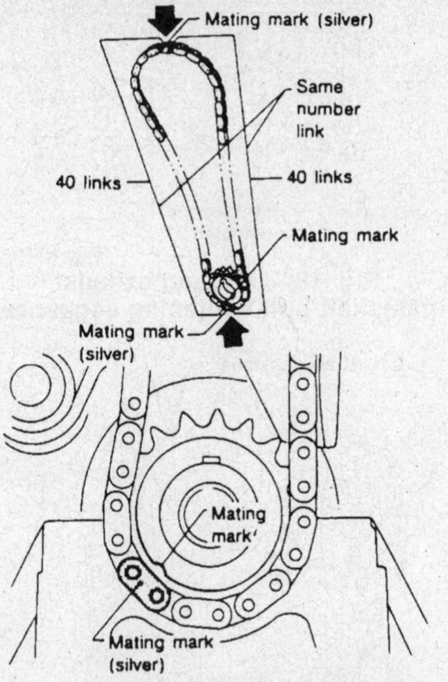
Mating mark (silver)
Same number link
40 links
40 links
Mating mark
Mating mark (silver)
Mating mark'
Mating mark (silver)
NS1069100014000X

Fig. 29 Main bearing bolt tightening sequence

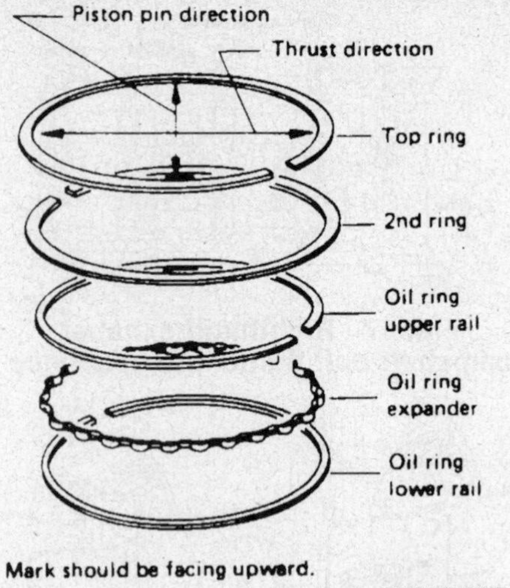
Piston pin direction
Thrust direction
Top ring
2nd ring
Oil ring upper rail
Oil ring expander
Oil ring lower rail
Mark should be facing upward.
NS1069100115000X

Fig. 30 Piston ring positioning

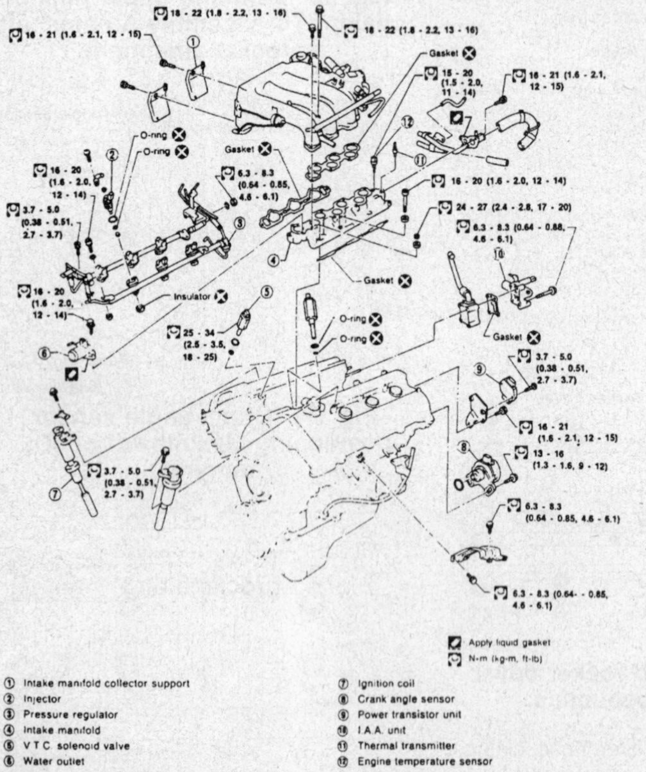
Apply liquid gasket
N·m (kg-m, ft-lb)
① Intake manifold collector support
② Injector
③ Pressure regulator
④ Intake manifold
⑤ V.T.C. solenoid valve
⑥ Water outlet
⑦ Ignition coil
⑧ Crank angle sensor
⑨ Power transistor unit
⑩ I.A.A. unit
⑪ Thermal transmitter
⑫ Engine temperature sensor
NS1069100067010X

Fig. 31 Engine assembly outer components (Part 1 of 3)

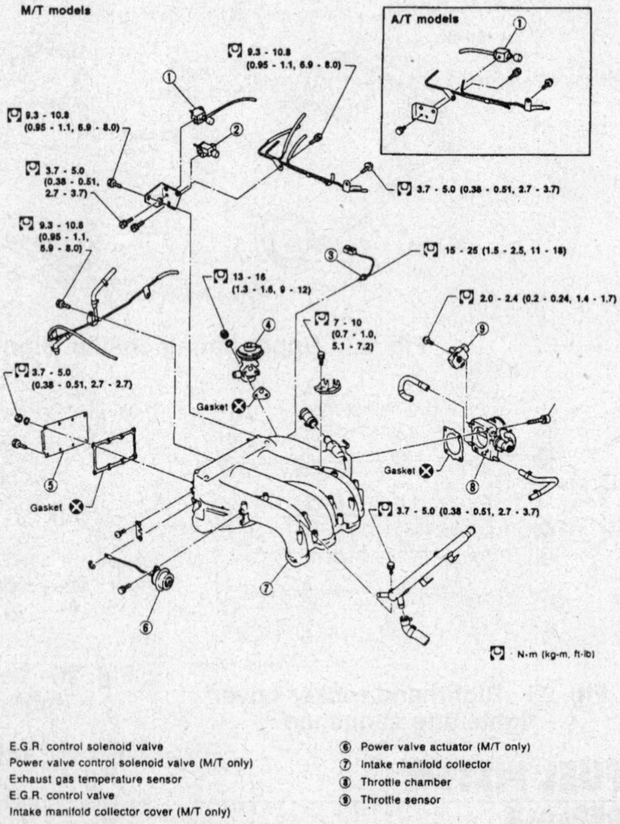
M/T models
A/T models
N·m (kg-m, ft-lb)
① E.G.R. control solenoid valve
② Power valve control solenoid valve (M/T only)
③ Exhaust gas temperature sensor
④ E.G.R. control valve
⑤ Intake manifold collector cover (M/T only)
⑥ Power valve actuator (M/T only)
⑦ Intake manifold collector
⑧ Throttle chamber
⑨ Throttle sensor
NS1069100067020X

Fig. 31 Engine assembly outer components (Part 2 of 3)

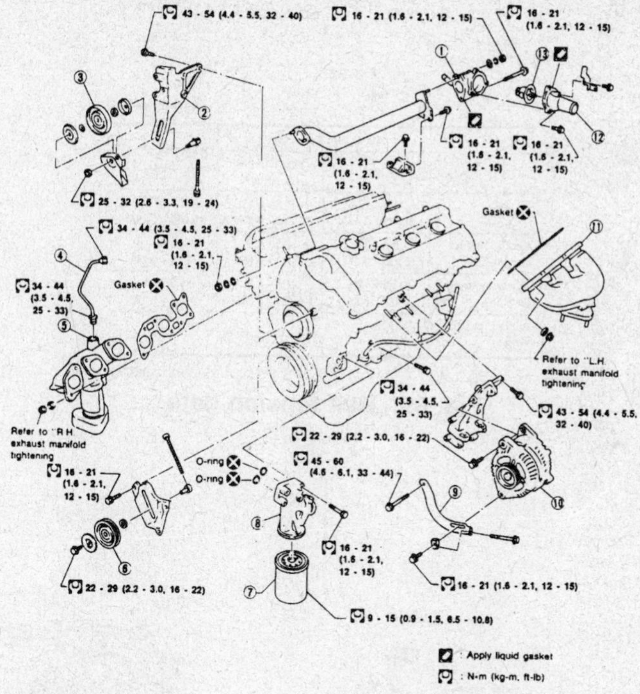

① Thermostat housing
② Power steering oil pump bracket
③ Idler pulley
④ E.G.R. tube
⑤ R.H. exhaust manifold
⑥ Idler pulley
⑦ Oil filter
⑧ Oil filter bracket
⑨ Alternator adjusting bar
⑩ Alternator
⑪ L.H. exhaust manifold
⑫ Water inlet
⑬ Thermostat

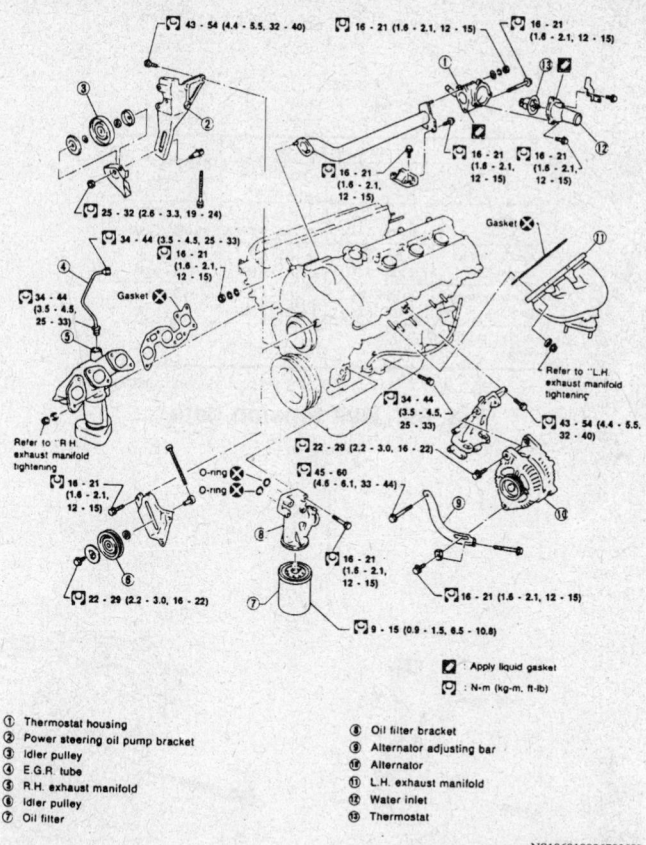

NS1069100067030X

Fig. 31 Engine assembly outer components (Part 3 of 3)

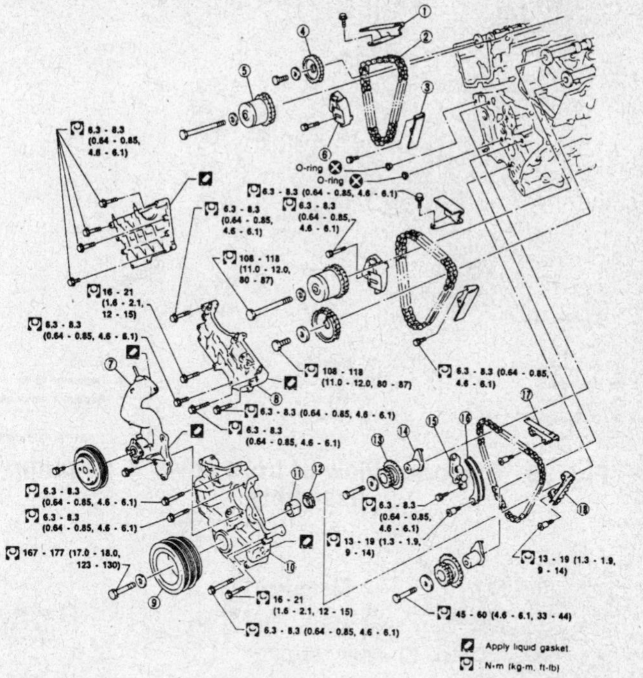

① Chain guide
② Upper timing chain
③ Chain guide (Tension side)
④ Camshaft sprocket
⑤ V.T.C. assembly
⑥ Chain tensioner
⑦ Water pump
⑧ Upper front cover
⑨ Crank pulley
⑩ Front cover
⑪ Oil pump spacer
⑫ Crankshaft sprocket
⑬ Idler sprocket
⑭ Idler shaft
⑮ Chain tensioner
⑯ Chain guide (Slack side)
⑰ Chain guide
⑱ Chain guide (Tension side)

NS1069100068000X

Fig. 32 Exploded view of timing chain & front cover assembly

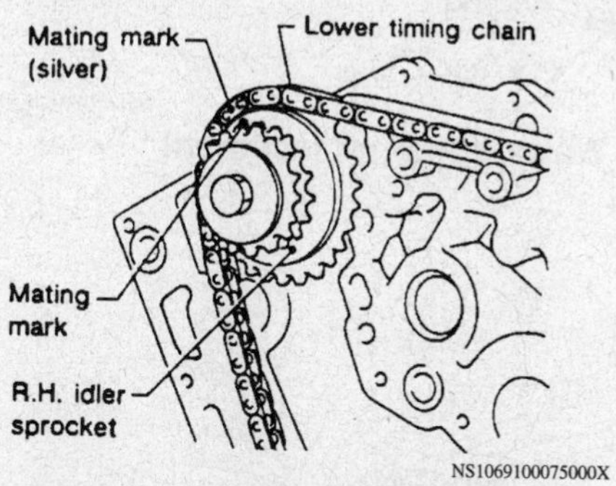
Mating mark (silver)
Lower timing chain
Mating mark
R.H. idler sprocket

NS1069100075000X

Fig. 33 Lower timing chain & righthand idler sprocket mating marks alignment

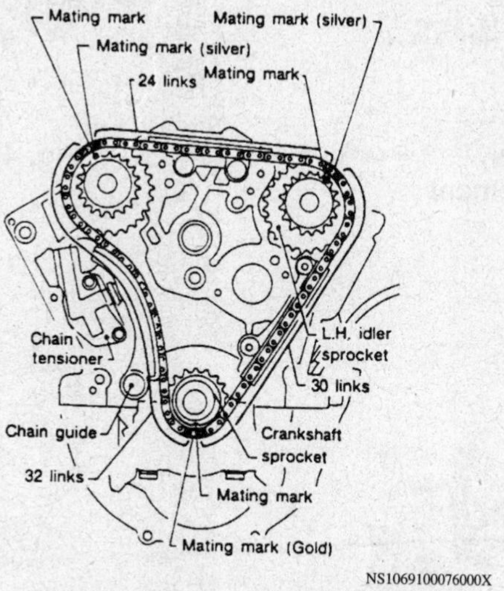
Mating mark
Mating mark (silver)
Mating mark (silver)
24 links
Mating mark
Chain tensioner
L.H. idler sprocket
30 links
Chain guide
Crankshaft sprocket
32 links
Mating mark
Mating mark (Gold)

NS1069100076000X

Fig. 34 Lower timing chain & lefthand idler sprocket mating marks alignment

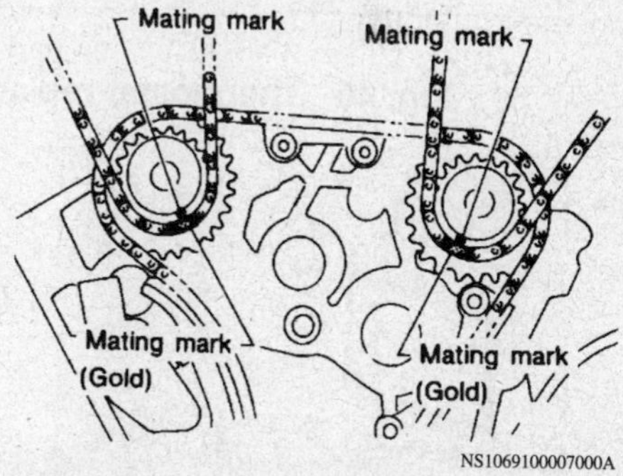
Mating mark
Mating mark
Mating mark (Gold)
Mating mark (Gold)

NS1069100007000A

Fig. 35 Upper timing chains & idler sprockets alignment

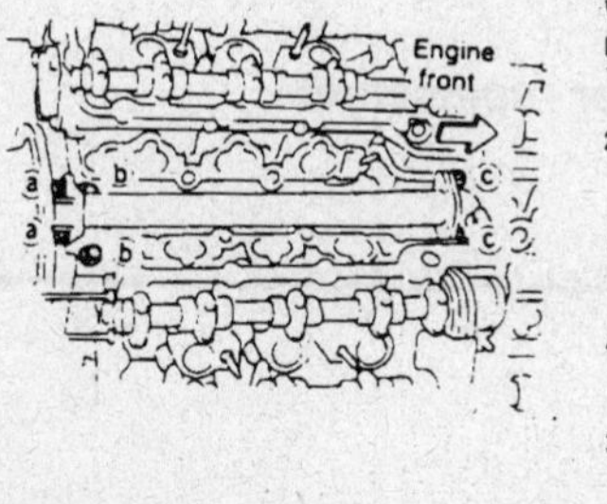
Engine front

Water pipe bolts tightening procedure

1) Tighten ⓐ and ⓑ bolts to finger tight
2) Tighten ⓒ bolts to 16 to 21 N•m (1.6 to 2.1 kg-m, 12 to 15 ft-lb).
3) Tighten ⓐ bolts to 3 to 9 N•m (0.3 to 0.9 kg-m, 2.2 to 6.5 ft-lb).
4) Tighten b bolts to 16 to 21 N•m (1.6 to 2.1 kg-m, 12 to 15 ft-lb).
3) Tighten a bolts to 16 to 21 N•m (1.6 to 2.1 kg-m, 12 to 15 ft-lb).

NS1069100082000X

Fig. 36 Water pipe tightening sequence

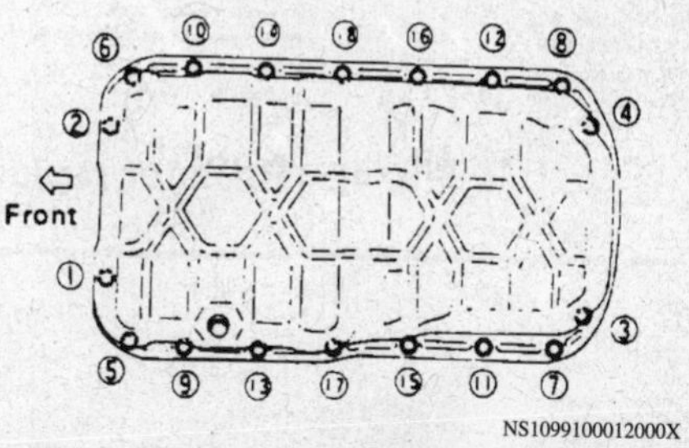
Front

NS1099100012000X

Fig. 37 Oil pan bolt loosening sequence

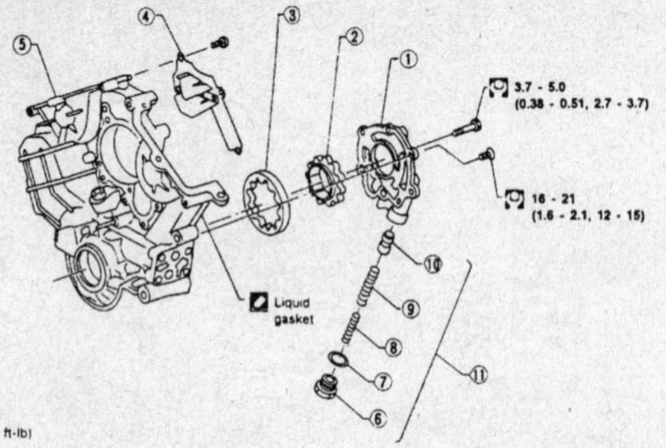
3.7 - 5.0
(0.38 - 0.51, 2.7 - 3.7)
16 - 21
(1.6 - 2.1, 12 - 15)
Liquid gasket
N·m (kg-m, ft-lb)

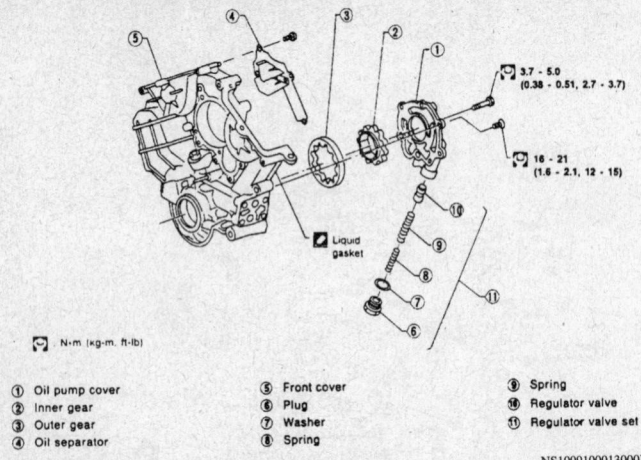

① Oil pump cover
② Inner gear
③ Outer gear
④ Oil separator
⑤ Front cover
⑥ Plug
⑦ Washer
⑧ Spring
⑨ Spring
⑩ Regulator valve
⑪ Regulator valve set

NS1099100013000X

Fig. 38 Exploded view of front cover & oil pump assembly

Unit: mm (in)

	Used belt deflection		Deflection of new belt
	Limit	Deflection after adjustment	
Alternator	11.5 - 12.5 (0.453 - 0.492)	7.5 - 8.5 (0.295 - 0.335)	6.5 - 7.5 (0.256 - 0.295)
Air conditioner compressor	8.5 - 9.5 (0.335 - 0.374)	5.5 - 6.5 (0.217 - 0.256)	5 - 6 (0.20 - 0.24)
Power steering oil pump	11.5 - 12.5 (0.453 - 0.492)	7.5 - 8.5 (0.295 - 0.335)	6.5 - 7.5 (0.256 - 0.295)
Applied pushing force	98 N (10 kg, 22 lb)		

NS1069100120000X

Fig. 39 Belt tension data

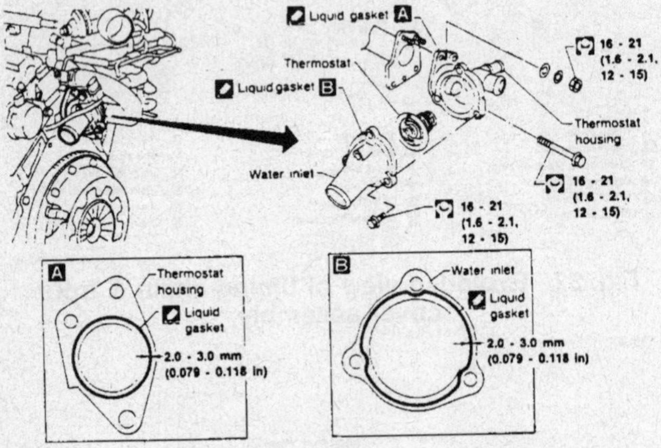
Liquid gasket A
Thermostat
Liquid gasket B
16 - 21
(1.6 - 2.1,
12 - 15)
Thermostat housing
Water inlet
A
Thermostat housing
Liquid gasket
2.0 - 3.0 mm
(0.079 - 0.118 in)
B
Water inlet
Liquid gasket
2.0 - 3.0 mm
(0.079 - 0.118 in)

NS1089100013000X

Fig. 40 Thermostat replacement

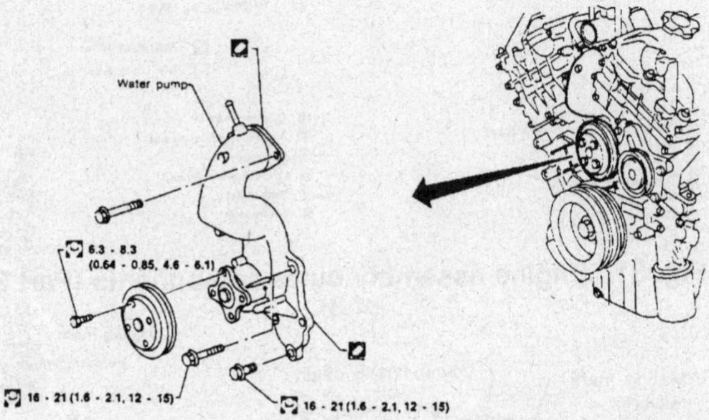
Water pump
6.3 - 8.3
(0.64 - 0.85, 4.6 - 6.1)
16 - 21 (1.6 - 2.1, 12 - 15)
16 - 21 (1.6 - 2.1, 12 - 15)

NS1089100010000X

Fig. 41 Water pump replacement

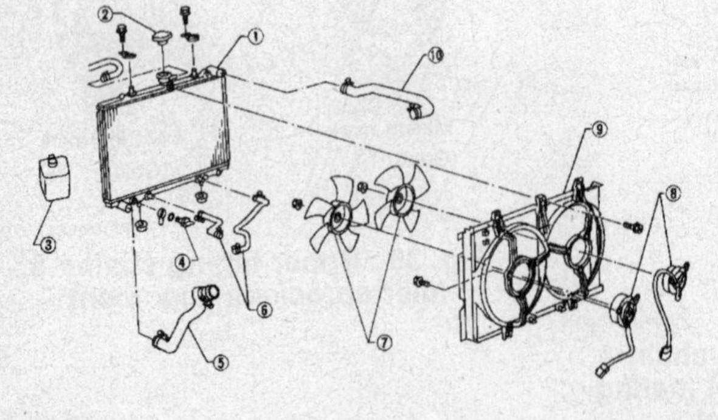

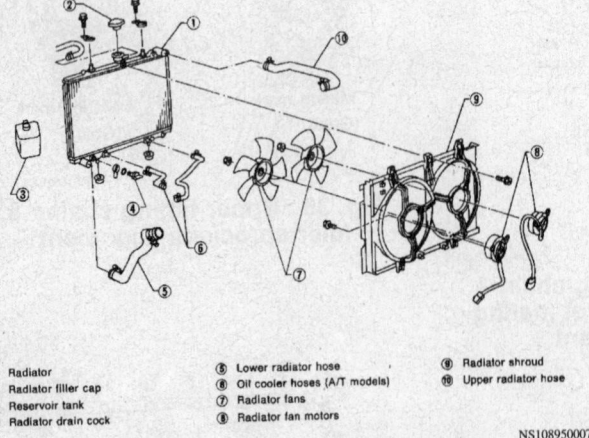

① Radiator
② Radiator filler cap
③ Reservoir tank
④ Radiator drain cock
⑤ Lower radiator hose
⑥ Oil cooler hoses (A/T models)
⑦ Radiator fans
⑧ Radiator fan motors
⑨ Radiator shroud
⑩ Upper radiator hose

NS1089500071000X

Fig. 42 Radiator replacement

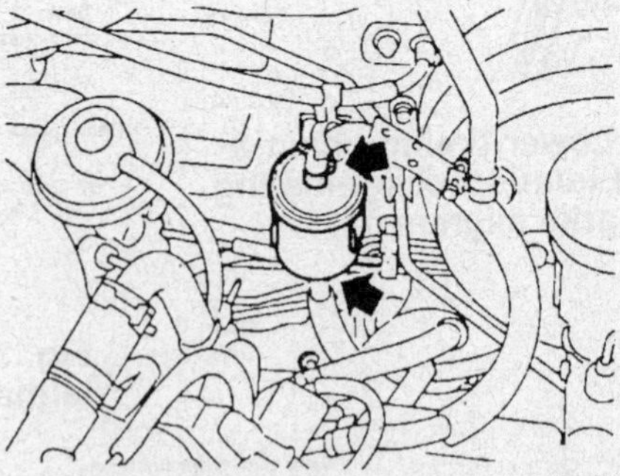

NS1029100004000X

Fig. 43 Fuel filter replacement

TIGHTENING SPECIFICATIONS

Year	Component	Torque/Ft. Lbs.
1993–94	Alternator Adjusting Bolt	12–15
	Alternator Adjustment Bar	33–44
	Alternator Mounting Bolt	16–22
	Camshaft Bracket Bolts	7–9
	Camshaft Sprocket	80–87
	Chain Guide (Tension Side)	9–14
	Crank Pulley	123–130
	Cylinder Head	①
	EGR Tube	25–33
	Exhaust Manifold	③
	Front Cover	②
	Idler Pulley	16–22
	Idler Sprocket	33–44
	Intake Manifold	④
	Intake Manifold Collector	④
	Oil Filter Bracket	12–15
	Power Steering Oil Pump Bracket	32–40
	Thermostat Housing	12–15
	Throttle Sensor	2–3
	Upper Front Cover	②
	Upper Timing Chain Tensioner	5–6
	VTC Assembly	33–44
	VTC Solenoid Valve	18–25
	Water Inlet	12–15
	Water Pipe	12–15
	Water Pump	12–15
	Water Pump Pulley	5–6

①— Refer to "Cylinder Head, Replace" in this section.

②— Shorter bolts, 12–15 ft. lbs.; longer bolts, 5–6 ft. lbs.

③— Refer to "Exhaust Manifold, Replace" in this section.

④— Refer to "Intake Manifold, Replace" in this section.

VG30E Engine

INDEX

	Page No.
Belt Tension Data	31-22
Compression Pressure	31-18
Cooling System Bleed	31-22
Crankshaft Rear Oil Seal, Replace	31-21
Crankshaft Seal, Replace	31-21
Cylinder Head, Replace	31-18
Installation	31-18
Removal	31-18
Engine Assemble	31-19
Engine Disassemble	31-19
Engine Mount, Replace	31-18
Engine Rebuilding Specifications	36-1
Engine, Replace	31-18
Fuel Filter, Replace	31-22
Fuel Pump, Replace	31-22
Intake Manifold, Replace	31-18
Oil Pan, Replace	31-21
Oil Pump, Replace	31-21
Piston & Rod Assembly	31-21
Assemble	31-21
Disassemble	31-21
Precautions	31-18
Air Bag Systems	31-18
Fuel System Pressure Relief	31-18
Radiator, Replace	31-22
Thermostat, Replace	31-22
Tightening Specifications	31-23
Timing Belt, Replace	31-20
Installation	31-20
Removal	31-20
Valve Adjustment	31-20
Valve Clearance Specifications	31-19
Water Pump, Replace	31-22

PRECAUTIONS

AIR BAG SYSTEMS

Refer to "Air Bag System Precautions" in front of this manual for system disarming and arming procedures.

FUEL SYSTEM PRESSURE RELIEF

1. Remove fuel pump fuse from fuse panel.
2. Start and run engine until it stalls.
3. Try to start engine two or three more times to ensure fuel pressure is released.
4. Turn ignition switch off.
5. Install fuel pump fuse.

COMPRESSION PRESSURE

1. Start and run engine until it reaches operating temperature.
2. Turn ignition switch off.
3. Release fuel pressure as outlined under "Precautions."
4. Remove all spark plugs.
5. Disconnect distributor center cable.
6. Attach a compression tester to cylinder No.1.
7. Depress accelerator pedal fully to keep throttle valve wide open.
8. Crank engine and record highest gauge indication.
9. Repeat measurement on each cylinder.
10. At 300 RPM standard compression is 173 psi and minimum pressure is 128 psi. Maximum difference limit between cylinders is 14 psi.
11. If compression in one or more cylinders is low, pour a small amount of engine oil into cylinders through spark plug holes, then retest compression.
12. If adding oil helps compression, then piston rings may be at fault. If adding oil does not help compression, then valves may be at fault.
13. If compression stays low in two cylinders that are next to each other, then cylinder head gasket may be leaking or both cylinders have valve component damage.
14. Repair as necessary.

ENGINE MOUNT

REPLACE

Refer to **Fig. 1** to replace engine mounts.

ENGINE

REPLACE

1. Release fuel system pressure as outlined under "Precautions."
2. Remove hood and disconnect battery ground cable.
3. Disconnect vacuum and fuel hoses, wires, harnesses, electrical connectors and linkages. **Mark hoses and electrical connectors for installation reference.**
4. Drain engine coolant from cylinder block and radiator.
5. Remove radiator, fans and coupling, then the drive belts.
6. Remove alternator, air conditioning compressor and power steering pump.
7. Raise and support, then drain engine oil.
8. Remove exhaust pipes and drive shafts, if necessary.
9. Remove ball joints.
10. Attach suitable lifting equipment to engine and support transaxle with a suitable jack.
11. Remove left and right rear engine mounts.
12. Remove center member, then slowly lower transaxle jack and remove engine and transaxle from under vehicle.
13. Reverse procedure to install.

INTAKE MANIFOLD

REPLACE

1. Release fuel system pressure as outlined in "Precautions," then disconnect battery ground cable.
2. Remove timing belt as outlined in "Timing Belt, Replace."
3. Drain engine coolant, then remove distributor and ignition wires.
4. Separate control wires from intake manifold collector, then remove idle air control valve/auxiliary air control valve, throttle position sensor and closed throttle position switch connectors.
5. Remove air cut valve water, PCV, vacuum gallery, swirl control valve, master cylinder and EGR valve vacuum hoses, then the EGR flare tube.
6. Remove upper intake manifold collector, loosening bolts in reverse tightening order, **Fig. 2.**
7. Remove lower intake manifold collector, **Fig. 3.**
8. Disconnect injector, coolant temperature switch, coolant temperature sensor, power valve control solenoid valve, EGRC solenoid valve and EGR temperature sensor harness connectors.
9. Disconnect vacuum gallery, then the pressure regulator valve and all hoses connected with vacuum gallery.
10. Disconnect heater hose from rear of engine, fuel feed and return hoses, and injector fuel tube assembly.
11. Remove intake manifold bolts in reverse order of tightening, **Fig. 4,** then intake manifold.
12. Reverse procedure to install, tightening bolts to specifications.

CYLINDER HEAD

REPLACE

REMOVAL

1. Remove intake manifold as outlined in "Intake Manifold, Replace."
2. Remove camshaft sprockets and rear timing belt cover
3. Remove exhaust manifold front exhaust tube, then the rocker covers.
4. Remove air conditioning compressor and alternator, then the brackets.
5. Remove cylinder head bolts in order, **Fig. 5,** then cylinder head with exhaust manifold.

INSTALLATION

1. Set No. 1 piston at TDC on compression stroke as follows by aligning

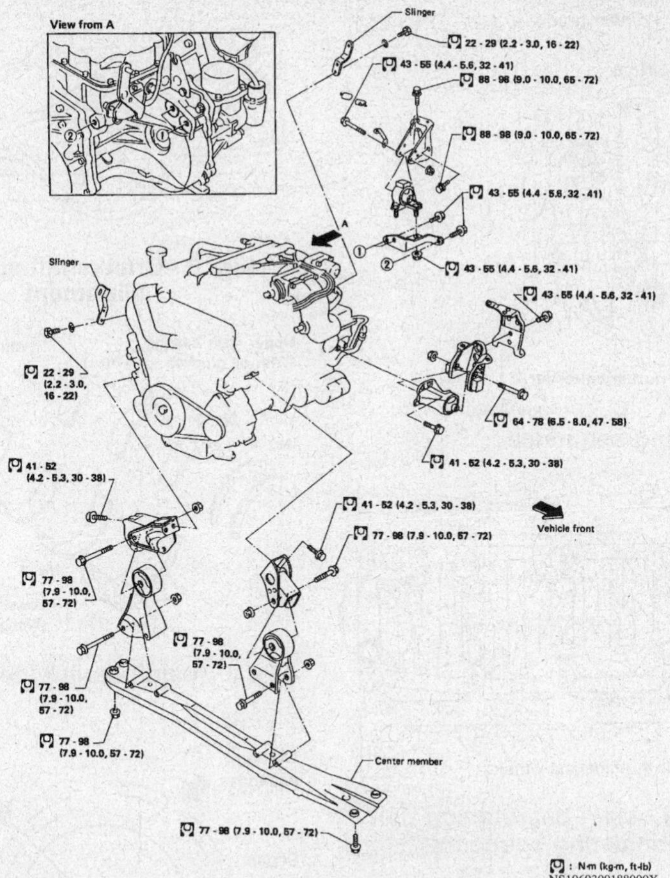
View from A
Slinger
Slinger
Center member
Vehicle front
: N·m (kg-m, ft-lb)
NS1069300188000X

Fig. 1 Engine mounts

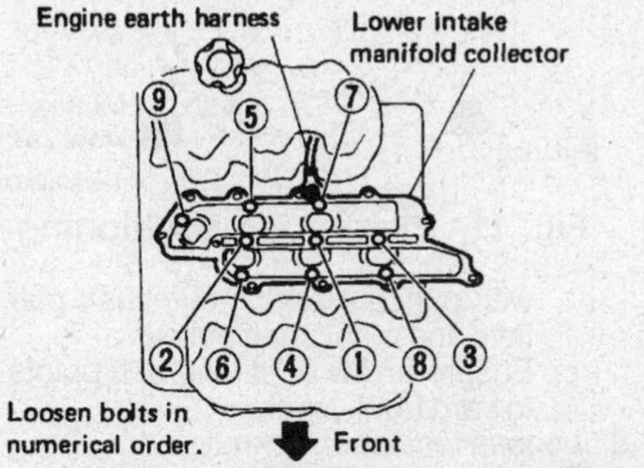
Engine earth harness
Lower intake manifold collector
Loosen bolts in numerical order.
Front
NS1059100016000X

Fig. 3 Lower intake manifold collector bolt loosening sequence

crankshaft sprocket alignment mark with oil pump body mark, **Fig. 6,** and confirm knock pin on camshaft is set at top.

2. Apply sealant to threads and install drain plugs in each side of cylinder block.
3. Install cylinder head with new gasket and washers between bolts and heads. **Do not rotate crankshaft and camshaft separately or valves will hit pistons.**
4. Install cylinder heads bolts in order, **Fig. 7,** and tighten as follows:
   a. Bolts 4, 5, 12 and 13 are 5 inches long, other bolts are 4.17 inches.
   b. **Torque** bolts to 22 ft. lbs.
   c. **Torque** bolts to 43 ft. lbs.
   d. Loosen bolts completely.
   e. **Torque** bolts to 22 ft. lbs.
   f. Use angle wrench and turn bolts clockwise 60–65°.
   g. If angle wrench is not available, **torque bolts to 40–47 ft. lbs.**
5. Install exhaust manifold front tube.
6. Install rear belt cover and camshaft sprockets. **Camshaft sprocket market R3** is for righthand; sprocket **L3** is for lefthand.
7. Install timing belt as outlined in "Timing Belt, Replace."

ENGINE DISASSEMBLE

1. Place engine on a work stand, then ensure coolant and oil have drained.
2. Remove timing belt as outlined in "Timing Belt, Replace."
3. Remove water pump as outlined in "Water Pump, Replace."
4. Remove oil pan as outlined in "Oil Pan, Replace."
5. Remove oil pump as outlined in "Oil Pump, Replace."
6. Remove rear oil seal retainer.
7. Remove intake manifold as outlined in "Intake Manifold, Replace."
8. Remove cylinder heads as outlined in "Cylinder Head, Replace."

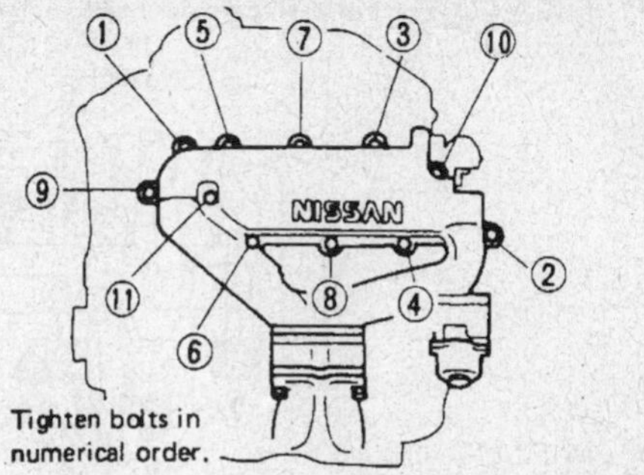
NISSAN
Tighten bolts in numerical order.
NS1059100006000X

Fig. 2 Upper intake manifold collector bolt tightening sequence

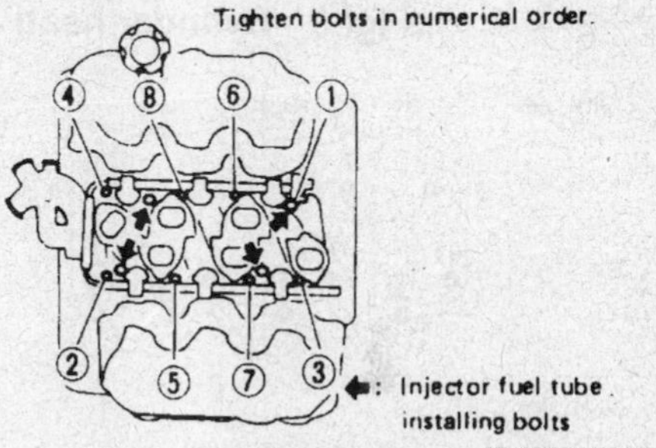
Tighten bolts in numerical order.
Injector fuel tube installing bolts
NS1059100009000X

Fig. 4 Intake manifold bolt tightening sequence

9. Remove pistons with connecting rod.
10. Before removing bearing cap, measure crankshaft end play.
11. Loosen main bearing beam and crankshaft retaining bolts in two or three steps in sequence, **Fig. 8,** and remove.

ENGINE ASSEMBLE

1. Install main bearings, **Fig. 9,** crankshaft and bearing caps. Tighten bearing cap attaching bolts to specifications in sequence, **Fig. 10** in two or three steps.
2. Install piston assemblies with rings properly positioned, **Fig. 11.**
3. Reverse remainder of "Engine Disassemble" procedure to complete assembly, noting following:
   a. Tighten cylinder head attaching bolts to specifications using sequence shown in **Fig. 7.**
   b. Tighten intake manifold attaching bolts in sequence, **Fig. 4** to specifications in two or three steps.

VALVE CLEARANCE SPECIFICATIONS

Engine	Stem-To-Guide Clearance, Inch①	
	Intake	Exhaust
VG30E	.0008–.0021	.0016–.0029

① — Cold.

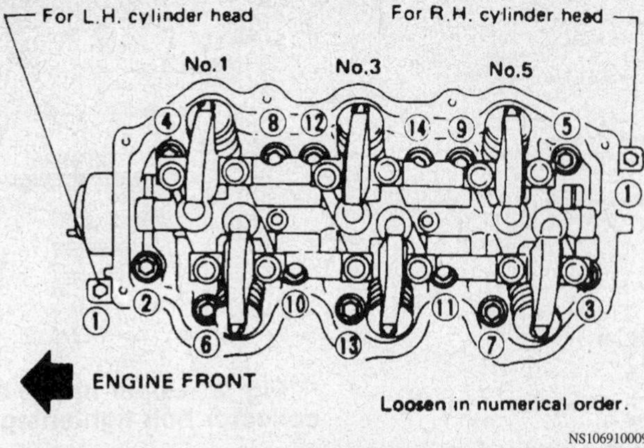
For L.H. cylinder head
For R.H. cylinder head
No.1
No.3
No.5
ENGINE FRONT
Loosen in numerical order.
NS1069100094000X

Fig. 5 Cylinder head bolt loosening sequence

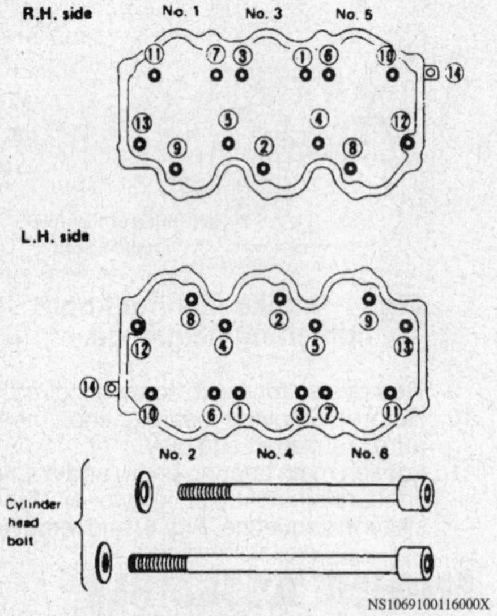
R.H. side
No. 1
No. 3
No. 5
L.H. side
No. 2
No. 4
No. 6
Cylinder head bolt
NS1069100116000X

Fig. 7 Cylinder head bolt tightening sequence

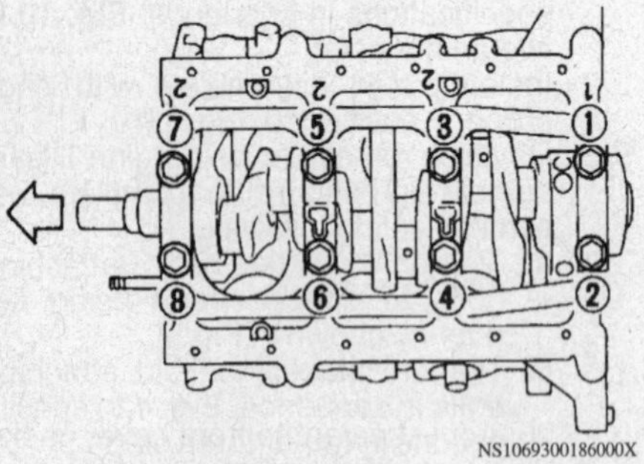
NS1069300186000X

Fig. 10 Main bearing cap bolt tightening sequence

VALVE ADJUSTMENT

These engines are equipped with hydraulic lash adjusters. No adjustments are required.

TIMING BELT

REPLACE

REMOVAL

1. Raise and support vehicle, then remove engine undercovers and drain cooling system.

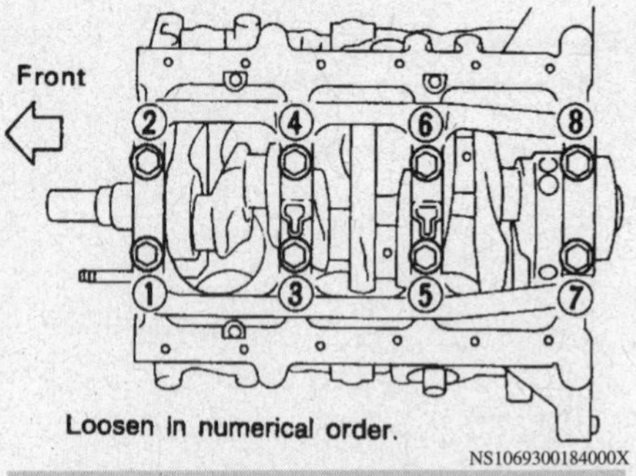
Front
Loosen in numerical order.
NS1069300184000X

Fig. 8 Main bearing cap bolt loosening sequence

2. Remove right front wheel and engine side cover, then the alternator, power steering and air conditioning compressor drive belts.
3. Loosen crankshaft pulley bolt and remove pulley with suitable puller.
4. Remove upper radiator and water inlet hoses.
5. Remove compressor drive belt idler bracket, then the water pump pulley.
6. Remove front upper and lower timing belt covers.
7. Set No. 1 cylinder at TDC of compression stroke by rotating crankshaft.
8. Align punch mark on lefthand camshaft sprocket with punch mark on timing belt upper rear cover, **Fig. 12.**
9. Align punch mark on crankshaft sprocket with notch on oil pump housing.
10. Temporarily install crank pulley bolt on crankshaft so that crankshaft can be rotated.
11. Loosen timing belt tensioner nut, turn tensioner and remove timing belt.

INSTALLATION

1. Ensure No. 1 cylinder is at TDC of compression stroke, **Fig. 13.**
2. Install tensioner and return spring.
3. Using hexagon wrench, turn tensioner clockwise and temporarily tighten tension locknut.
4. Install timing belt, noting following:
   a. Ensure belt is clean and dry.
   b. Align white reference line on belt with punch mark on camshaft pulleys and crankshaft pulley.
   c. Ensure arrow on timing belt points toward front covers.
5. Loosen tensioner locknut.
6. Turn tensioner 70–80° clockwise, then temporarily tighten locknut.
7. Rotate crankshaft at least two times, then slowly position No. 1 cylinder at TDC of compression stroke.
8. Apply a force of 22 lbs. to center of timing belt between righthand camshaft sprocket and tensioner pulley, then loosen tension locknut while preventing tensioner from turning.
9. Position .0138 inch feeler gauge against tensioner pulley, **Fig. 14.** Turn crankshaft clockwise to position gauge at center of tensioner, then tighten tension locknut.
10. Turn crankshaft in either direction and remove feeler gauge.
11. Rotate crankshaft at least two times, then slowly position No. 1 cylinder at TDC of compression stroke.
12. Check timing belt deflection between center of camshaft sprockets. Deflection should be .51–.59 inch with 22 lbs. force applied.

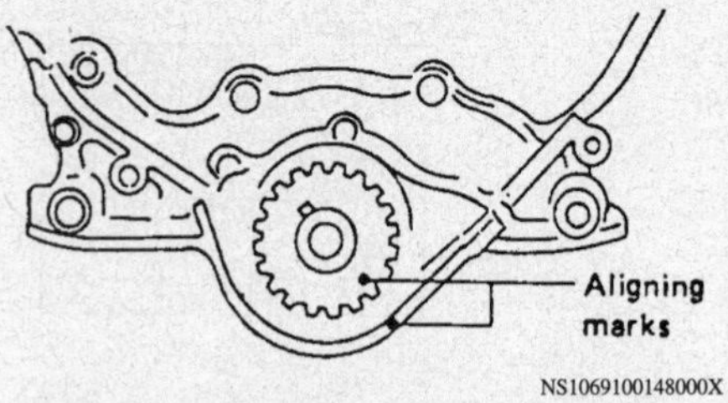
Aligning marks
NS1069100148000X

Fig. 6 Crankshaft sprocket alignment

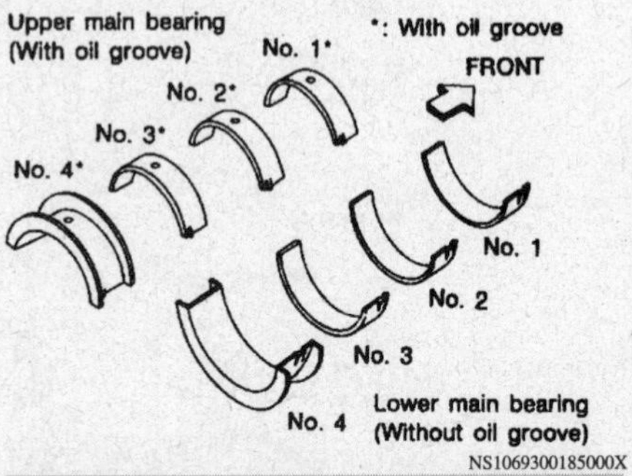
Upper main bearing (With oil groove)
*: With oil groove
FRONT
No. 1*
No. 2*
No. 3*
No. 4*
No. 1
No. 2
No. 3
No. 4
Lower main bearing (Without oil groove)
NS1069300185000X

Fig. 9 Main bearing identification

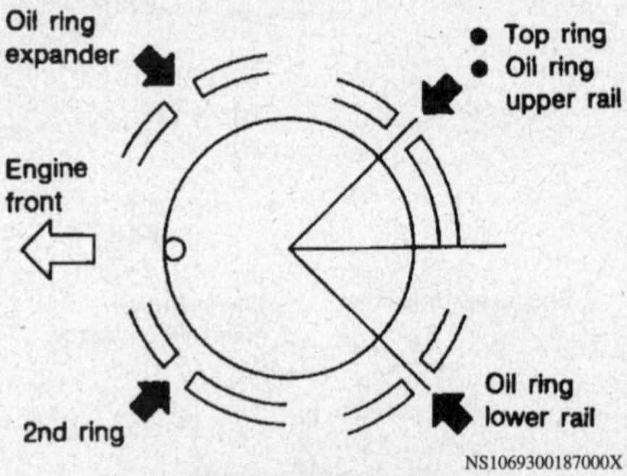
Oil ring expander
Top ring
Oil ring upper rail
Engine front
Oil ring lower rail
2nd ring
NS1069300187000X

Fig. 11 Piston ring positioning

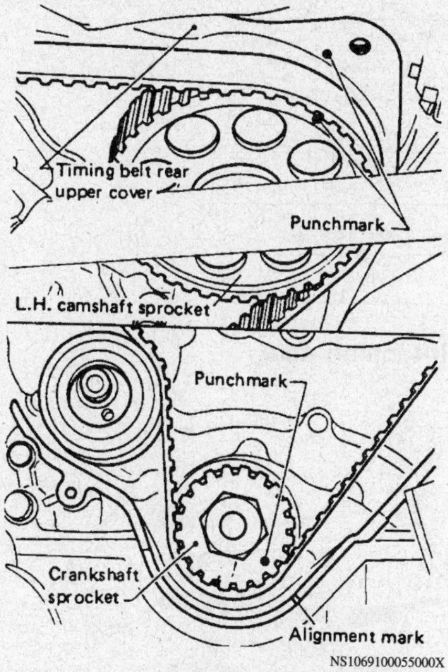
Timing belt rear upper cover
Punchmark
L.H. camshaft sprocket
Punchmark
Crankshaft sprocket
Alignment mark
NS1069100055000X

Fig. 12 Camshaft & crankshaft sprocket alignment

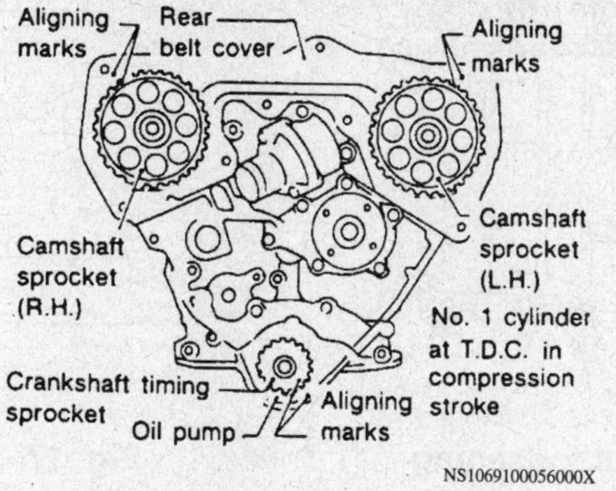
Aligning marks
Rear belt cover
Aligning marks
Camshaft sprocket (R.H.)
Camshaft sprocket (L.H.)
No. 1 cylinder at T.D.C. in compression stroke
Crankshaft timing sprocket
Aligning marks
Oil pump
NS1069100056000X

Fig. 13 Timing marks

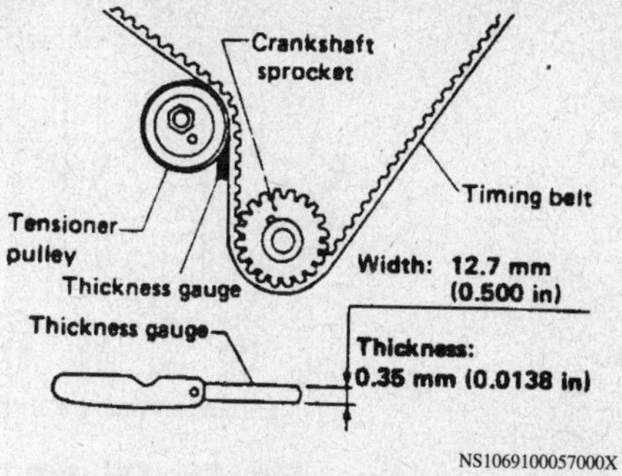
Crankshaft sprocket
Timing belt
Tensioner pulley
Thickness gauge
Width: 12.7 mm (0.500 in)
Thickness gauge
Thickness: 0.35 mm (0.0138 in)
NS1069100057000X

Fig. 14 Timing belt adjustment

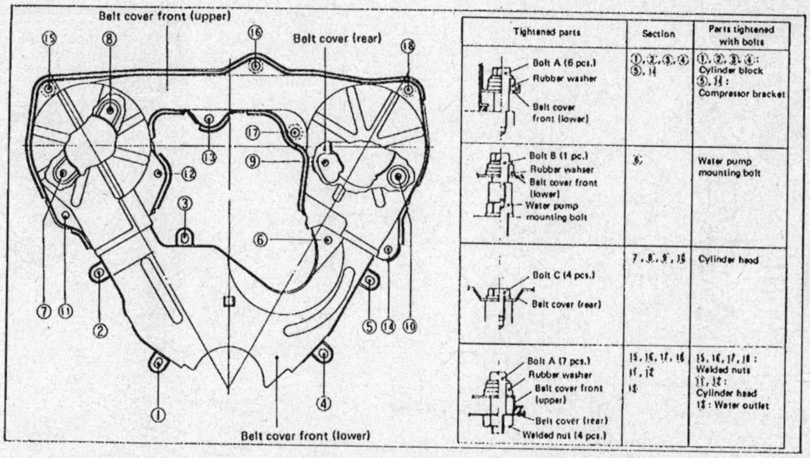
Belt cover front (upper)
Belt cover (rear)
Belt cover front (lower)
Tightened parts
Section
Parts tightened with bolts
NS1069100058000X

Fig. 15 Timing belt cover installation

13. Install lower and upper timing belt covers, **Fig. 15.**
14. Install rocker covers, intake collector and intake manifold if previously removed.
15. Connect hoses, connectors and wires.
16. Install compressor if removed.
17. Install crankshaft pulley and idler bracket of compressor drive belt, tighten pulley bolt to specifications.
18. Install radiator hoses, drive belts and spark plugs.
19. Fill cooling system, run engine and check for leaks.

PISTON & ROD ASSEMBLY

DISASSEMBLE

1. Remove piston rings with a ring remover.
2. Remove snap ring, then press out piston pin using piston pin press or heat piston to 140–150°F and remove piston pin. **Keep disassembled parts in order.**

ASSEMBLE

1. Assemble pistons, piston pins and connecting rods of designated cylinders.
2. Install new snap ring on one side of piston pin.
3. Align piston and connecting rod direction.
4. Ensure stamped numbers on connecting rod and cap correspond to each cylinder.
5. Heat piston to 140–150°F and assemble piston, piston pin, connecting rod and new snap ring.
6. Install piston rings.

CRANKSHAFT SEAL

REPLACE

1. Remove timing belt as outlined in "Timing Belt, Replace."
2. Remove crankshaft sprocket.
3. Remove oil pump assembly as outlined in "Oil Pump, Replace."
4. Remove front oil seal being careful not to scratch front cover.
5. Remove front oil seal from oil pump body.
6. Apply engine oil to new oil seal and install using suitable oil seal installation tool.

CRANKSHAFT REAR OIL SEAL

REPLACE

1. Remove flywheel or driveplate.
2. Remove rear oil seal retainer.
3. Remove rear oil seal.
4. Apply engine oil to new seal and install with suitable seal installation tool.

OIL PAN

REPLACE

1. Raise and support vehicle, then drain engine oil.
2. Remove engine lower covers, then the front exhaust tube from support.
3. Support engine at righthand slinger with suitable hoist.
4. Remove engine mounting insulator attaching bolts and nuts, then the center member assembly.
5. Remove oil pan attaching bolts in order, **Fig. 16.**
6. Insert a suitable tool between cylinder block and oil pan, then tap tool side with hammer and remove oil pan. **Do not use a screwdriver, oil pan flange will be deformed. Be careful not to damage aluminum mating surface of cylinder block.**
7. Reverse procedure to install, noting following:
   a. Remove all liquid gasket from oil pan and cylinder block mating surfaces.
   b. Remove dip stick before install oil pan.
   c. Apply sealant to front cover gasket and rear oil seal retainer gasket.
   d. Apply a continuous bead of liquid gasket to mating surface of oil pan.
   e. Tighten bolts and nuts to specifications in reverse order, **Fig. 16.**
   f. Wait at least 30 minutes before refilling engine oil.

OIL PUMP

REPLACE

1. Drain oil.
2. Remove oil pan as outlined in, "Oil Pan, Replace."
3. Remove oil pump assembly.
4. Reverse procedure to install.

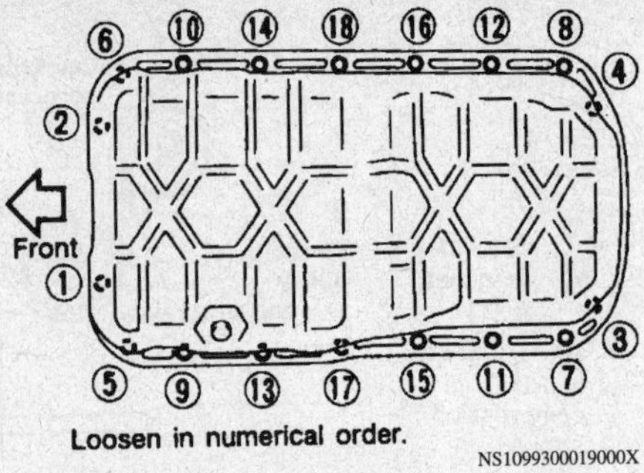

⑥ ⑩ ⑭ ⑱ ⑯ ⑫ ⑧
④
②
Front
①
③
⑤ ⑨ ⑬ ⑰ ⑮ ⑪ ⑦
Loosen in numerical order.
NS1099300019000X

Fig. 16 Oil pan bolt loosening sequence

Unit: mm (in)

	Used belt deflection		Set deflection of new belt
	Limit	Adjusted deflection	
Alternator	12 (0.47)	7 - 9 (0.28 - 0.35)	6 - 8 (0.24 - 0.31)
Air conditioner compressor	9 (0.35)	5 - 7 (0.20 - 0.28)	4 - 6 (0.16 - 0.24)
Power steering oil pump	16 (0.63)	10 - 12 (0.39 - 0.47)	8 - 10 (0.31 - 0.39)
Applied pushing force	98 N (10 kg, 22 lb)		

NS1069100118000X

Fig. 17 Belt tension data

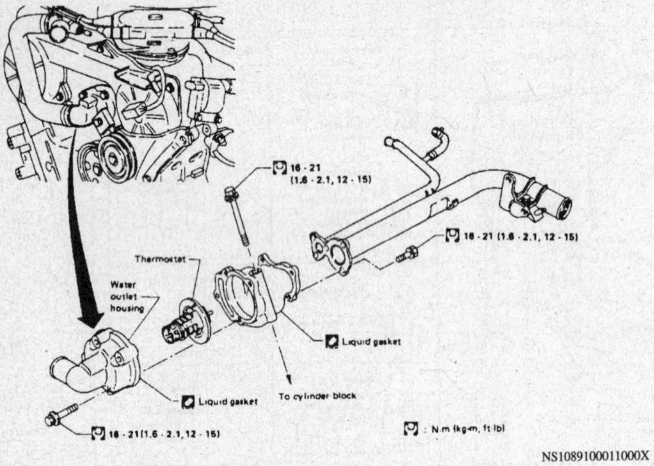

16 - 21 (1.6 - 2.1, 12 - 15)
16 - 21 (1.6 - 2.1, 12 - 15)
Thermostat
Water outlet housing
Liquid gasket
Liquid gasket
To cylinder block
16 - 21 (1.6 - 2.1, 12 - 15)
: N·m (kg-m, ft-lb)
NS1089100011000X

Fig. 18 Thermostat replacement

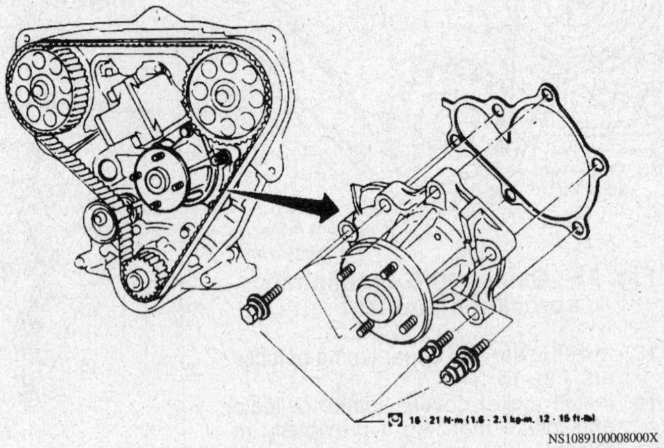

16 - 21 N·m (1.6 - 2.1 kg-m, 12 - 15 ft-lb)
NS1089100008000X

Fig. 19 Water pump replacement

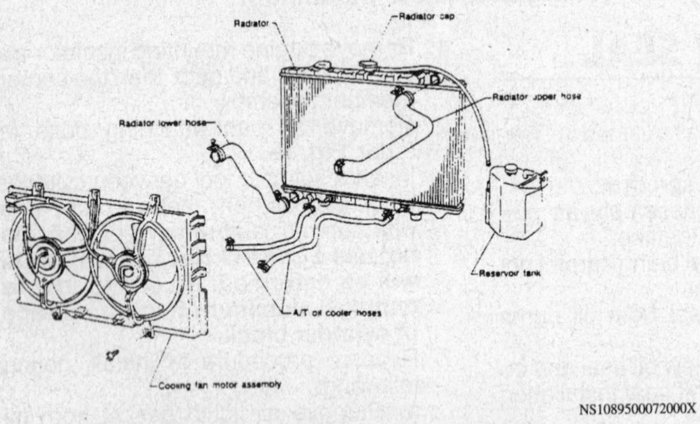

Radiator
Radiator cap
Radiator upper hose
Radiator lower hose
Reservoir tank
A/T oil cooler hoses
Cooling fan motor assembly
NS1089500072000X

Fig. 20 Radiator replacement

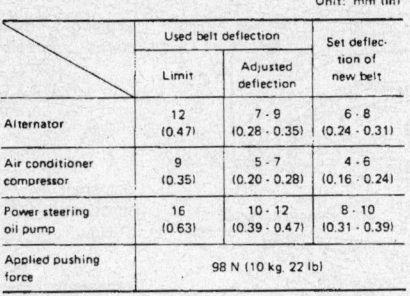

BELT TENSION DATA

Refer to **Fig. 17** for belt tension data.

COOLING SYSTEM BLEED

These engines do not require a specified bleed procedure. After filling cooling system, run engine to operating temperature with radiator/pressure cap off. Air will then be automatically bled through cap opening.

THERMOSTAT

REPLACE

Refer to **Fig. 18** for thermostat removal and installation.

WATER PUMP

REPLACE

1. Disconnect battery ground cable, then drain engine and radiator coolant.
2. Refer to **Fig. 19** to complete water pump replacement procedure.

RADIATOR

REPLACE

1. Remove undercover, then drain coolant.
2. Disconnect upper and lower radiator hoses, **Fig. 20.**
3. **On models with automatic transaxle,** remove ATF cooler hoses.
4. **On all models,** remove radiator attaching bolts and radiator.
5. Reverse procedure to install.

FUEL PUMP

REPLACE

1. Release fuel pump pressure as outlined in "Precautions."
2. Disconnect battery ground cable, then drain fuel into suitable container.
3. Disconnect necessary fuel lines and electrical connectors.
4. Disconnect fuel tank attaching bolts, then lower tank.
5. Remove fuel pump attaching bolts, then the fuel pump.
6. Reverse procedure to install.

FUEL FILTER

REPLACE

1. Relieve fuel system pressure as outlined in "Precautions."
2. Loosen two fuel filter hose clamps, **Fig. 21.**
3. Disconnect fuel hoses from fuel filter. **Do not allow gasoline to spill over engine compartment.**
4. Reverse procedure to install.

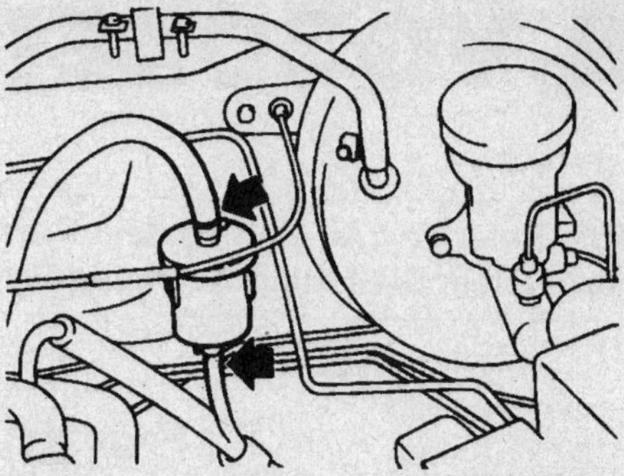
NS1029300025000X

Fig. 21 Fuel filter replacement

TIGHTENING SPECIFICATIONS

Year	Component	Torque/Ft. Lbs.
1993–94	Camshaft Sprocket Bolt	58–65
	Connecting Rod Bearing Caps	②
	Crankshaft Pulley	90–98
	Cylinder Head	①
	Exhaust Manifold	13–17
	Flywheel	61–69
	Intake Manifold	12–17
	Main Bearing Cap	67–74
	Oil Pan Bolts	48–60③
	Rocker Shaft	13–16
	Starter Motor	22–27
	Timing Belt Tensioner	32–43
	Water Pump	12–15

① — Refer to "Cylinder Head, Replace" in this section.

② — Tighten in two steps, first to 12 ft. lbs., then to 28–33 ft. lbs.

③ — Inch lbs.

VG30DE & VG30DETT Engines

NOTE: On Air Bag Equipped Models, Refer To "Air Bag System Precautions" Located In Front Of This Manual For System Disarming & Arming Procedures.

INDEX

	Page No.
Belt Tension Data	31-27
Compression Pressure	31-24
Cooling System Bleed	31-27
Crankshaft Rear Oil Seal, Replace	31-26
Crankshaft Seal, Replace	31-26
Cylinder Head, Replace	31-25
Installation	31-25
Removal	31-25
Engine Assemble	31-25
Engine Disassemble	31-25
Engine Mount, Replace	31-24
Engine Rebuilding Specifications	36-1
Engine, Replace	31-24
Fuel Filter, Replace	31-27
Fuel Pump, Replace	31-27
Intake Manifold, Replace	31-24
Oil Pan, Replace	31-26
Oil Pump, Replace	31-27
Piston & Rod Assembly	31-26
Assemble	31-26
Disassemble	31-26
Precautions	31-24
Air Bag Systems	31-24
Fuel System Pressure Relief	31-24
Radiator, Replace	31-27
Technical Service Bulletins	31-28
Turbocharger Noise	31-28
Thermostat, Replace	31-27
Tightening Specifications	31-30
Timing Belt, Replace	31-25
Installation	31-26
Removal	31-25
Turbocharger, Replace	31-27
Left Side	31-28
Right Side	31-27
Valve Adjustment	31-25
Valve Clearance Specifications	31-25
Water Pump, Replace	31-27

PRECAUTIONS

AIR BAG SYSTEMS

Refer to "Air Bag System Precautions" in front of this manual for system disarming and arming procedures.

FUEL SYSTEM PRESSURE RELIEF

1. Disconnect fuel pump relay, which is located behind lefthand side kick panel.
2. Start and run engine until it stalls.
3. Try to start engine two or three more times to ensure fuel pressure is released.
4. Turn ignition switch off.
5. Reconnect fuel pump relay.

COMPRESSION PRESSURE

1. Start and run engine until it reaches operating temperature.
2. Turn ignition switch off.
3. Release fuel pressure as outlined under "Precautions."
4. Remove all spark plugs.
5. Disconnect camshaft position sensor electrical connector.
6. Attach a compression tester to cylinder No.1.
7. Depress accelerator pedal fully to keep throttle valve wide open.
8. Crank engine and record highest gauge indication.
9. Repeat measurement on each cylinder.
10. **On VG30DE engine,** at 300 RPM, standard compression is 186 psi and minimum pressure is 142 psi, maximum difference between cylinders is 14 psi.
11. **On VG30DETT engine,** at 300 RPM, standard compression is 171 psi and minimum pressure is 128 psi, maximum difference between cylinders is 14 psi.
12. **On all engines,** if compression in one or more cylinders is low, pour a small amount of engine oil into cylinders through spark plug holes, then retest compression.
13. If adding oil helps compression, then piston rings may be at fault. If adding oil does not help compression, then valves may be at fault.
14. If compression stays low in two cylinders that are next to each other, then cylinder head gasket may be leaking or both cylinders have valve component damage.
15. Repair as necessary.

ENGINE MOUNT

REPLACE

Refer to **Fig. 1** to replace engine mounts.

ENGINE

REPLACE

1. Release fuel system pressure as outlined under "Precautions."
2. Remove hood and disconnect battery ground cable.
3. Drain engine coolant from cylinder block and radiator.
4. Disconnect vacuum and fuel hoses, wires, harnesses, electrical connectors and linkages. **Mark hoses and electrical connectors for installation reference.**
5. Remove radiator, fans and coupling, then the drive belts.
6. Remove alternator, then the air conditioning compressor and power steering pump without disconnecting pressure hoses. Position compressor and pump aside.
7. Raise and support vehicle, remove engine undercover and drain engine oil.
8. Remove exhaust pipes and drive shafts, as necessary.
9. **On models with manual transmission,** proceed as follows:
   a. Remove starter motor and clutch cylinder, then disconnect air conditioning tube clamps.
   b. Disconnect steering column lower joint, then remove tension rod fixing bolts.
   c. Loosen transverse link bolts.
   d. Attach suitable lifting equipment to engine and support suspension member with suitable jack.
   e. Remove suspension member and engine mounting bolts.
   f. Slowly lower jack and remove engine with transmission from vehicle.
10. **On models with automatic transmission,** proceed as follows:
    a. Remove starter motor.
    b. Remove transmission.
    c. Attach suitable lifting equipment to engine.
    d. Remove engine mounting bolts.
    e. Lift engine from vehicle.
11. **On all models,** reverse procedure to install.

INTAKE MANIFOLD

REPLACE

1. Release fuel system pressure as outlined in "Precautions," then disconnect battery ground cable.
2. Remove intake manifold collector, then the injector pipe assembly.
3. Remove valve covers.
4. Remove timing belt as outlined in "Timing Belt, Replace."

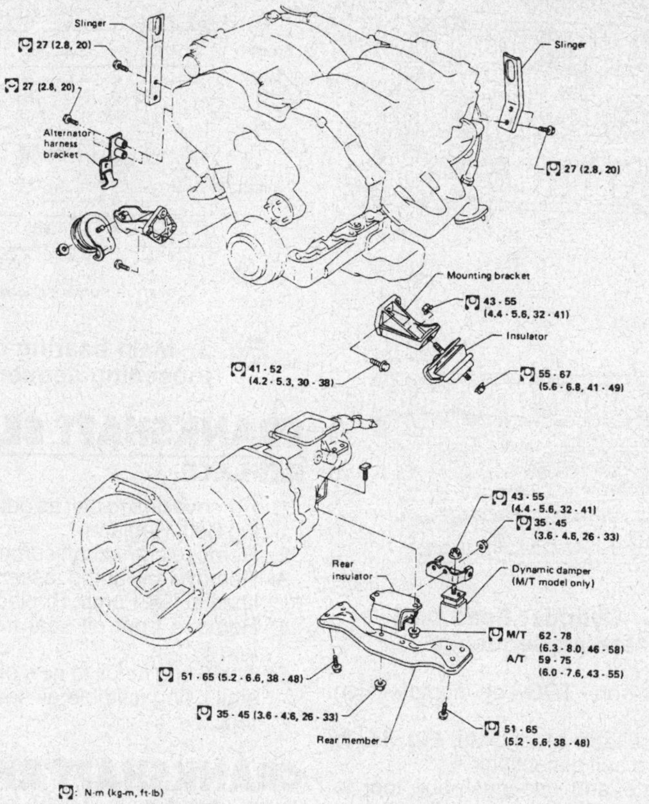
Slinger
27 (2.8, 20)
27 (2.8, 20)
Alternator harness bracket
Slinger
27 (2.8, 20)
Mounting bracket
43 - 55 (4.4 - 5.6, 32 - 41)
Insulator
41 - 52 (4.2 - 5.3, 30 - 38)
55 - 67 (5.6 - 6.8, 41 - 49)
43 - 55 (4.4 - 5.6, 32 - 41)
35 - 45 (3.6 - 4.6, 26 - 33)
Rear insulator
Dynamic damper (M/T model only)
M/T 62 - 78 (6.3 - 8.0, 46 - 58)
A/T 59 - 75 (6.0 - 7.6, 43 - 55)
51 - 65 (5.2 - 6.6, 38 - 48)
35 - 45 (3.6 - 4.6, 26 - 33)
51 - 65 (5.2 - 6.6, 38 - 48)
Rear member
: N·m (kg-m, ft-lb)

NS1069100053000X

Fig. 1 Engine mounts

5. Remove idler pulley and stud bolt.
6. Remove intake manifold.
7. Reverse procedure to install, tightening bolts to specifications.

CYLINDER HEAD

REPLACE

REMOVAL

1. Removal intake manifold as outlined in "Intake Manifold, Replace."
2. Disconnect exhaust manifold front tube.
3. Remove cylinder head bolts in two or three steps, then the cylinder head.

INSTALLATION

1. Set No. 1 piston at TDC on compression stroke by aligning crankshaft sprocket alignment mark with oil pump body mark, **Fig. 2.**
2. Align camshaft sprocket alignment mark with timing belt rear cover mark, **Fig. 3.**
3. Install cylinder head with new gaskets and washers between bolts and head.
4. Tighten cylinder head bolts in order, **Fig. 4,** as follows:
   a. Install shorter bolts in positions 1 and 6.
   b. **Torque** bolts to 29 ft. lbs.
   c. **Torque** bolts to 90 ft. lbs.
   d. Loosen bolts completely.
   e. **Torque** bolts to 25–33 ft. lbs.
   f. Use angle wrench and turn long bolts 70–75° clockwise and short bolts 65–70°.
   g. If angle wrench is not available, **torque** bolts to 90 ft. lbs.
   h. **Torque** outside cylinder head bolts to 7–9 ft. lbs.
5. Install exhaust manifold front tube.
6. Install intake manifold as outlined in "Intake Manifold, Replace."

ENGINE DISASSEMBLE

1. Place engine on a work stand, then ensure coolant and oil have drained.
2. Remove timing belt as outlined in "Timing Belt, Replace."
3. Remove water pump as outlined in "Water Pump, Replace."
4. Remove oil pan as outlined in "Oil Pan, Replace."
5. Remove oil pump as outlined in "Oil Pump, Replace."
6. Remove rear oil seal retainer.
7. Remove intake manifold as outlined in "Intake Manifold, Replace."
8. Remove cylinder heads as outlined in "Cylinder Head, Replace."
9. Remove pistons with connecting rod.
10. Before removing bearing cap, measure crankshaft end play.
11. Loosen main bearing beam and crankshaft retaining bolts in two or three steps in sequence, **Fig. 5,** and remove.

ENGINE ASSEMBLE

1. Install main bearings, **Fig. 6,** crankshaft and bearing cap. Tighten bearing cap attaching bolts to specifications in sequence, **Fig. 7** in two or three steps.

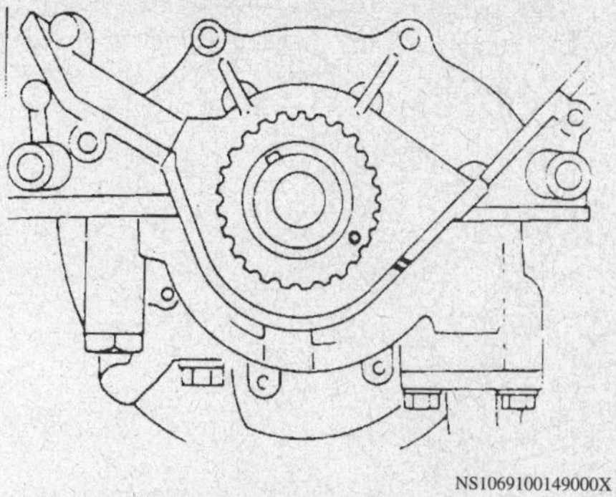

NS1069100149000X

Fig. 2 Crankshaft sprocket & oil pump alignment marks

2. Install piston assemblies with rings properly positioned, **Fig. 8.**
3. Reverse remainder of "Engine Disassemble" procedure to complete assembly, noting following:
   a. Tighten cylinder head attaching bolts to specifications using sequence shown in **Figs. 4 and 7.**
   b. Tighten intake manifold attaching bolts in sequence, **Fig. 9** to specifications in two or three steps.

VALVE CLEARANCE SPECIFICATIONS

Engine	Stem-To-Guide Clearance, Inch①	
	Intake	Exhaust
VG30DE & VG30DETT	.0008–.0021	.0016–.0029

① — Cold.

VALVE ADJUSTMENT

These engines are equipped with hydraulic lash adjusters. No adjustments are required.

TIMING BELT

REPLACE

REMOVAL

1. Raise and support vehicle.
2. Disconnect battery ground cable, then remove engine undercover.
3. Drain engine coolant, then remove radiator.
4. Remove drive belts, cooling fan and coupling.
5. Remove starter motor, then use screwdriver or other suitable tool to keep crankshaft from turning and remove crankshaft pulley bolt, **Fig. 10.**
6. Remove crankshaft pulley with suitable puller.
7. Remove water inlet and outlet, then the front timing belt covers.
8. Install suitable stopper bolt into tensioner arm of auto tensioner, **Fig. 11.**
9. Place No. 1 cylinder at TDC of compression stroke, then remove auto tensioner and timing belt.

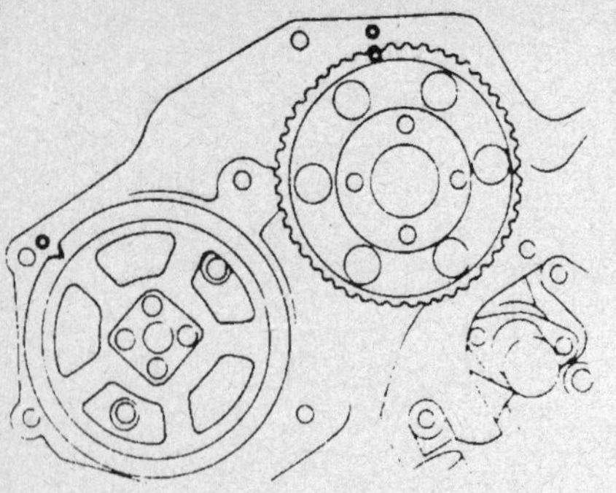

NS1069100150000X

Fig. 3 Camshaft sprocket & timing belt rear cover alignment marks

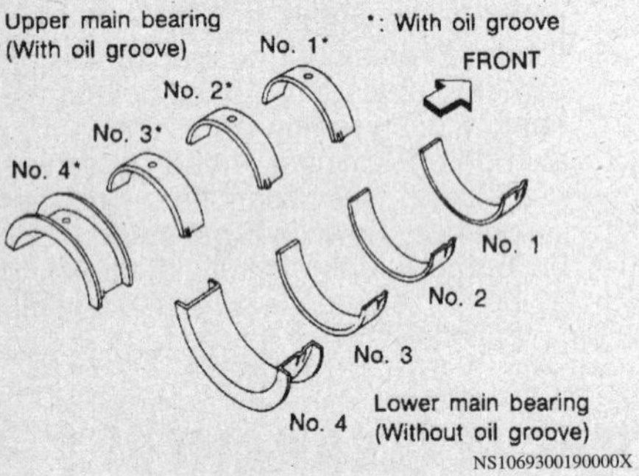
Upper main bearing
(With oil groove)
*: With oil groove
FRONT
No. 1*
No. 2*
No. 3*
No. 4*
No. 1
No. 2
No. 3
No. 4
Lower main bearing
(Without oil groove)

NS1069300190000X

Fig. 6 Main bearing identification

INSTALLATION

1. Ensure No. 1 cylinder at TDC of compression stroke.
2. Align mark on camshaft and crankshaft sprocket with aligning marks on rear belt cover and oil pump housing, **Fig. 12,** then remove spark plugs.
3. Install timing belt aligning white marks on timing belt with matching marks on crankshaft and camshaft sprockets, with arrow on timing belt facing forward, **Fig. 13.**
4. With auto tensioner in suitable vise, adjust arm to .16 inch clearance with pusher, then install stopper bolt into tensioner arm, **Fig. 14. Do not push tensioner bolt arm with stopper bolt installed, possible damage to threaded portion could result.**
5. Install auto tensioner, tighten nut 1 and bolts 2 and 3, **Fig. 15,** slightly by hand.
6. Push tensioner toward timing belt until slight tension on belt is felt, then turn crankshaft clockwise 10° and **torque nut** 1 and bolts 2 and 3, **Fig. 15,** to 12–15 ft. lbs.
7. Turn crankshaft 120° counterclockwise, then loosen nut 1 and bolts 2 and 3 ½ turns to set tensioner body back as far as it will go.
8. Turn crankshaft clockwise and set No. 1 cylinder at TDC of compression stroke.
9. Attach special push-pull gauge tool No. EG14860000, or equivalent, and push pusher end with approximately 13.2 lbs. pressure, then **torque** nut 1 and bolts 2 and 3 to 12–15 ft. lbs.
10. Turn crankshaft 120° clockwise, then 120° counterclockwise and set No. 1

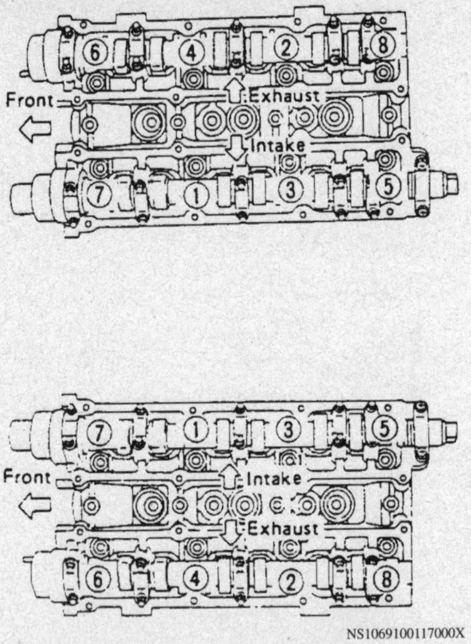
Front
Exhaust
Intake
6
4
2
8
7
1
3
5
Front
Intake
Exhaust
7
1
3
5
6
4
2
8

NS1069100117000X

Fig. 4 Cylinder head bolt tightening sequence

cylinder on TDC of compression stroke.

11. Use a suitable steel plate, **Fig. 16,** to measure belt deflection.
12. Set plate and use push-pull tool to push with 11 lbs. pressure at four points, **Fig. 17,** measuring deflection at each point. Add measurements together, then divide by four, this should equal an average deflection of .24–.28 inch.
13. If not within specification adjust auto tensioner.
14. Remove auto tensioner stopper bolt, after five minutes ensure rod projection between tensioner arm and pusher stays between .138 and .205 inch.
15. Install timing belt cover.

PISTON & ROD ASSEMBLY

DISASSEMBLE

1. Remove piston rings with a ring remover.
2. Remove snap ring, then press out piston pin using piston pin press or heat piston to 140–150°F and remove piston pin. **Keep disassembled parts in order.**

ASSEMBLE

1. Assemble pistons, piston pins and connecting rods of designated cylinders.
2. Install new snap ring on one side of piston pin.
3. Align piston and connecting rod direction.
4. Ensure stamped numbers on connecting rod and cap correspond to each cylinder.
5. Heat piston to 140–150°F and assemble piston, piston pin, connecting rod and new snap ring.
6. Install piston rings.

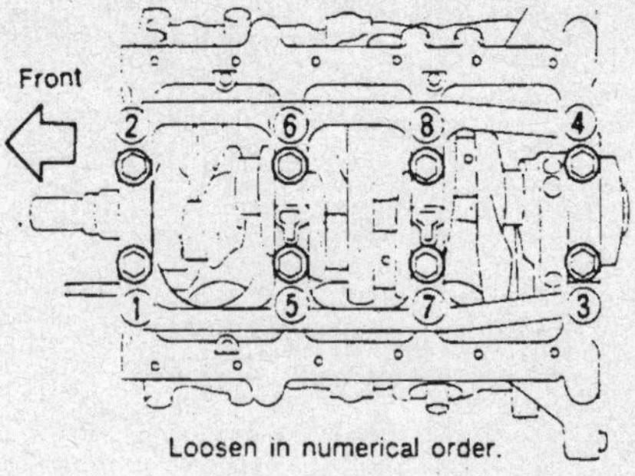
Front
2
6
8
4
1
5
7
3
Loosen in numerical order.

NS1069100155000X

Fig. 5 Main bearing cap bolt loosening sequence

CRANKSHAFT SEAL

REPLACE

1. Remove timing belt as outlined in "Timing Belt, Replace."
2. Remove crankshaft sprocket.
3. Remove oil pump assembly as outlined in "Oil Pump, Replace."
4. Remove front oil seal from oil pump body.
5. Apply engine oil to new oil seal and install using suitable oil seal installation tool.

CRANKSHAFT REAR OIL SEAL

REPLACE

1. Remove flywheel or driveplate.
2. Remove rear oil seal retainer.
3. Remove rear oil seal.
4. Apply engine oil to new seal and install with suitable seal installation tool.

OIL PAN

REPLACE

1. Raise and support vehicle, then drain engine oil and remove engine undercover.
2. Remove oil filter and bracket, then the engine rear gussets.
3. Disconnect A/C tube clamps, then the steering column lower joint.
4. Remove tension rod attaching bolts, then the transverse link bolts.
5. Place a suitable transmission jack under suspension member, then hoist engine with slingers.
6. Remove suspension member attaching bolts, engine mounting bolts, then slowly lower transmission jack.
7. Remove oil pan bolts, then the oil pan.
8. Reverse procedure to install, noting following:
   a. Remove all liquid gasket from oil pan and cylinder block mating surfaces.
   b. Apply sealant to front cover gasket and rear oil seal retainer gasket.
   c. Apply a continuous bead of liquid gasket to mating surface of oil pan.
   d. **Torque** bolts 1–12 to 12–15 ft. lbs. and bolts 13–18 to 55–77 inch lbs. in order, **Fig. 18.**
   e. Wait at least 30 minutes before refilling engine oil.

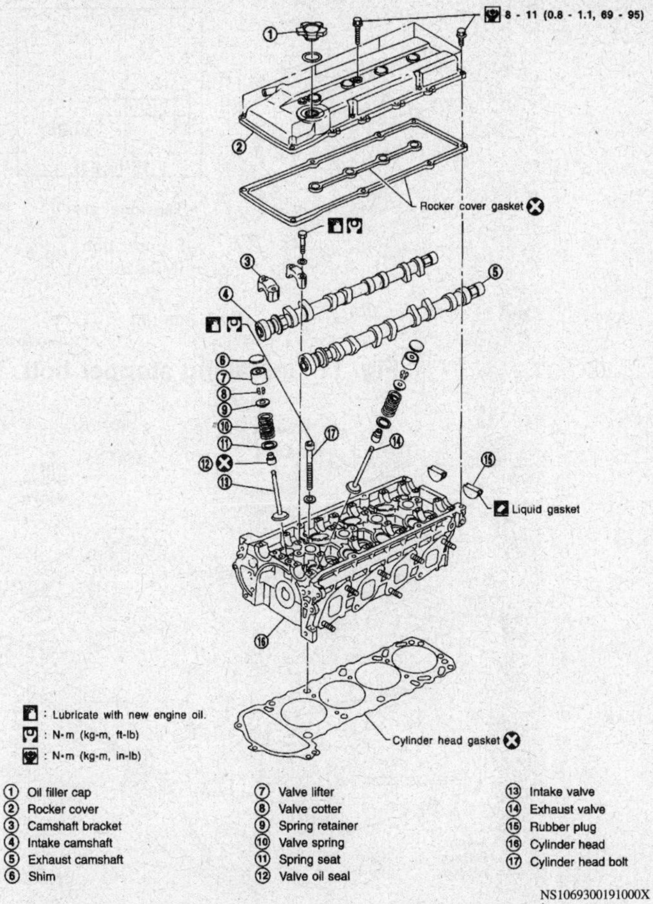
8 - 11 (0.8 - 1.1, 69 - 95)
Rocker cover gasket
Liquid gasket
Cylinder head gasket
: Lubricate with new engine oil.
: N·m (kg-m, ft-lb)
: N·m (kg-m, in-lb)
1 Oil filler cap
2 Rocker cover
3 Camshaft bracket
4 Intake camshaft
5 Exhaust camshaft
6 Shim
7 Valve lifter
8 Valve cotter
9 Spring retainer
10 Valve spring
11 Spring seat
12 Valve oil seal
13 Intake valve
14 Exhaust valve
15 Rubber plug
16 Cylinder head
17 Cylinder head bolt
NS1069300191000X

Fig. 7 Main bearing cap bolt tightening sequence

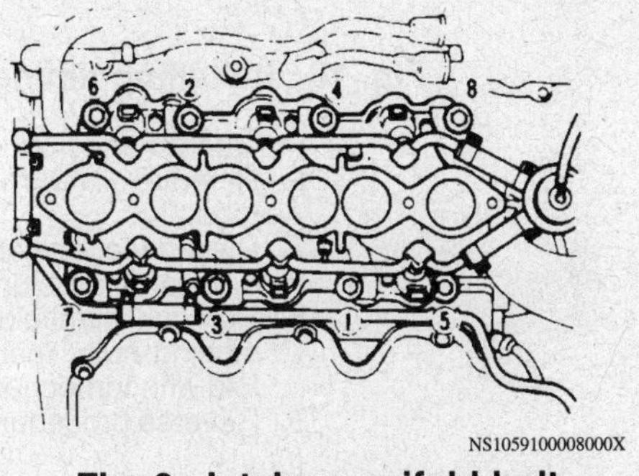
6
2
4
8
7
3
1
5
NS1059100008000X

Fig. 9 Intake manifold bolt tightening sequence

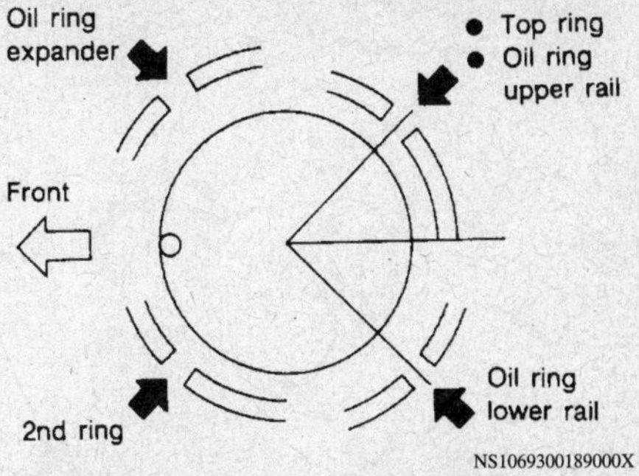
Oil ring expander
Top ring
Oil ring upper rail
Front
Oil ring lower rail
2nd ring
NS1069300189000X

Fig. 8 Piston ring positioning

OIL PUMP

REPLACE

1. Drain oil.
2. Remove oil pan as outlined in, "Oil Pan, Replace."
3. Remove oil pump assembly.
4. Reverse procedure to install.

BELT TENSION DATA

Refer to **Figs. 19** for belt tension data.

COOLING SYSTEM BLEED

These engines do not require a specified bleed procedure. After filling cooling system, run engine to operating temperature with radiator/pressure cap off. Air will then be automatically bled through cap opening.

THERMOSTAT

REPLACE

1. Disconnect battery ground cable, then drain engine and radiator coolant.
2. Remove engine undercover and radiator upper hose.
3. Remove radiator shroud, fan belt, cooling fan and coupling.
4. Remove water inlet, then the thermostat, **Fig. 20.**
5. Reverse procedure to install.

WATER PUMP

REPLACE

1. Disconnect battery ground cable, then drain engine and radiator coolant.
2. Remove undercover, radiator, drive belts, cooling fan and coupling, water inlet and outlet, crank pulley and timing belt cover.
3. Remove water pump, **Fig. 21.**
4. Reverse procedure to install.

RADIATOR

REPLACE

1. Remove undercover, then drain coolant.
2. Disconnect upper and lower radiator hoses, **Fig. 22.**
3. **On models with automatic transaxle,** remove ATF cooler hoses.
4. **On all models,** remove lower shroud.
5. Remove radiator.
6. Reverse procedure to install.

FUEL PUMP

REPLACE

1. Release fuel pump pressure as outlined in "Precautions."
2. Disconnect battery ground cable, then drain fuel into suitable container.
3. Disconnect necessary fuel lines and electrical connectors.
4. Disconnect fuel tank attaching bolts, then lower tank.
5. Remove fuel pump attaching bolts, then the fuel pump.
6. Reverse procedure to install.

FUEL FILTER

REPLACE

1. Relieve fuel system pressure as outlined in "Precautions. "
2. Loosen two fuel filter hose clamps, **Fig. 23.**
3. Disconnect fuel hoses from fuel filter. **Do not allow gasoline to spill over engine compartment.**
4. Reverse procedure to install.

TURBOCHARGER

REPLACE

RIGHT SIDE

1. Disconnect battery ground cable, then remove battery.

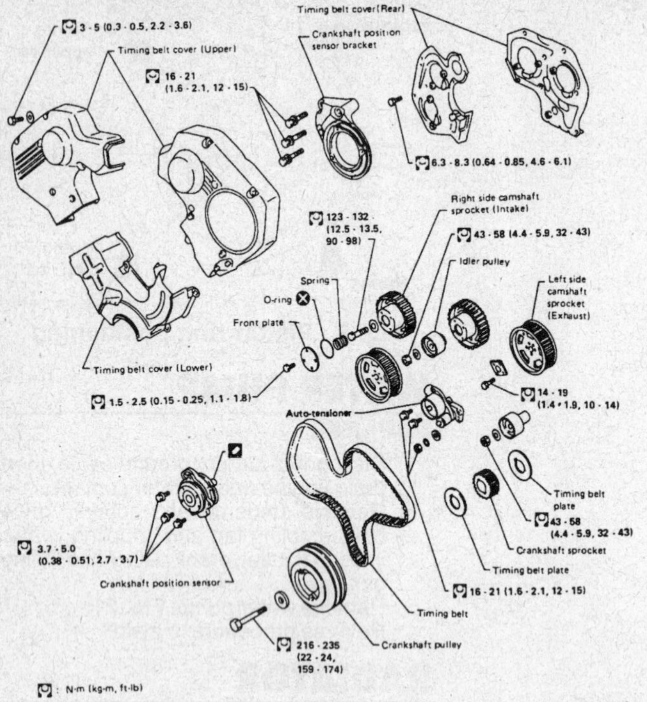
Timing belt cover (Rear)
3 - 5 (0.3 - 0.5, 2.2 - 3.6)
Crankshaft position sensor bracket
Timing belt cover (Upper)
16 - 21 (1.6 - 2.1, 12 - 15)
6.3 - 8.3 (0.64 - 0.85, 4.6 - 6.1)
Right side camshaft sprocket (Intake)
123 - 132 (12.5 - 13.5, 90 - 98)
43 - 58 (4.4 - 5.9, 32 - 43)
Idler pulley
Spring
O-ring
Left side camshaft sprocket (Exhaust)
Front plate
Timing belt cover (Lower)
1.5 - 2.5 (0.15 - 0.25, 1.1 - 1.8)
14 - 19 (1.4 - 1.9, 10 - 14)
Auto-tensioner
Timing belt plate
43 - 58 (4.4 - 5.9, 32 - 43)
3.7 - 5.0 (0.38 - 0.51, 2.7 - 3.7)
Crankshaft sprocket
Timing belt plate
Crankshaft position sensor
16 - 21 (1.6 - 2.1, 12 - 15)
Timing belt
216 - 235 (22 - 24, 159 - 174)
Crankshaft pulley
: N·m (kg-m, ft-lb)

NS1069100059000X

Fig. 10 Timing belt replacement

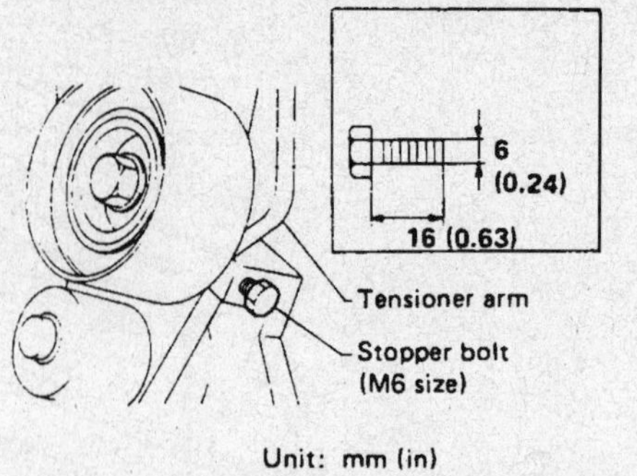
6 (0.24)
16 (0.63)
Tensioner arm
Stopper bolt (M6 size)
Unit: mm (in)

NS1069100060000X

Fig. 11 Installing stopper bolt

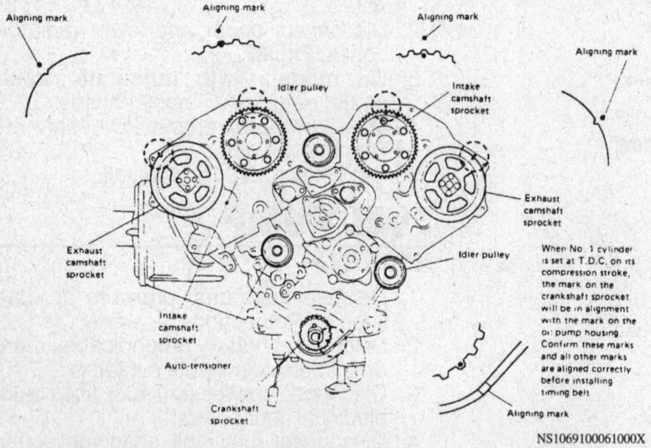
Aligning mark
Aligning mark
Aligning mark
Aligning mark
Idler pulley
Intake camshaft sprocket
Exhaust camshaft sprocket
Exhaust camshaft sprocket
Idler pulley
When No. 1 cylinder is set at T.D.C. on its compression stroke, the mark on the crankshaft sprocket will be in alignment with the mark on the oil pump housing. Confirm these marks and all other marks are aligned correctly before installing timing belt.
Intake camshaft sprocket
Auto-tensioner
Crankshaft sprocket
Aligning mark

NS1069100061000X

Fig. 12 Alignment of camshaft & crankshaft sprockets

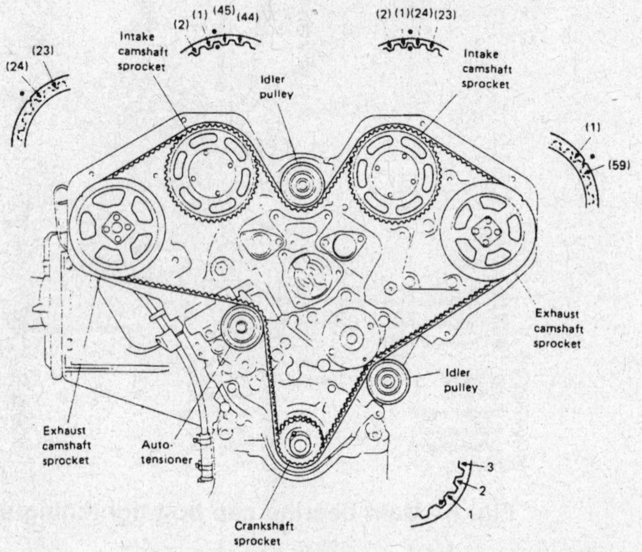
(2) (1) (45) (44)
(2) (1) (24) (23)
(23)
(24)
Intake camshaft sprocket
Intake camshaft sprocket
Idler pulley
(1)
(59)
Exhaust camshaft sprocket
Idler pulley
Exhaust camshaft sprocket
Auto-tensioner
3
2
1
Crankshaft sprocket

NS1069100062000X

Fig. 13 Installing timing belt

2. Remove right part of cowl top, then the air inlet hose and pipe.
3. Disconnect lower exhaust pipe from turbo unit, then remove wiper motor bracket.
4. Disconnect exhaust gas sensor, remove turbochargers water hoses, then the oil inlet tube.
5. Remove pre-catalyst attaching bolts, then the pre-catalyst.
6. Remove front exhaust tube, oil return tube, oil filter, then the oil pressure switch.
7. Remove rod pin from wastegate valve actuator, then the oil filter bracket.
8. Remove turbocharger attaching nuts, then the turbocharger.
9. Reverse procedure to install.

LEFT SIDE

1. Disconnect battery ground cable.
2. Remove brake master cylinder, then the brake booster.
3. Disconnect exhaust gas sensor, then remove air inlet hose and pipe.
4. Disconnect lower exhaust pipe from turbo unit.
5. Disconnect water tubes, then remove pre-catalyst attaching bolts, pre-catalyst and front exhaust pipe.
6. Remove oil return tube, then the water tube.
7. Disconnect actuator bracket and EGR tube form turbo unit.
8. Remove manifold cover, manifold attaching nuts, then the exhaust manifold with turbocharger.
9. Reverse procedure to install.

TECHNICAL SERVICE BULLETINS

TURBOCHARGER NOISE

1993-94

Unusual turbocharger noise may occur during driving because of reduced oil supply to righthand turbocharger.

Oil supply problem may be caused by turbocharger oil inlet clogging. New oil inlet tube is available for installation. New oil inlet tube has been installed on vehicles after VIN JN1CZ24DRX545041.

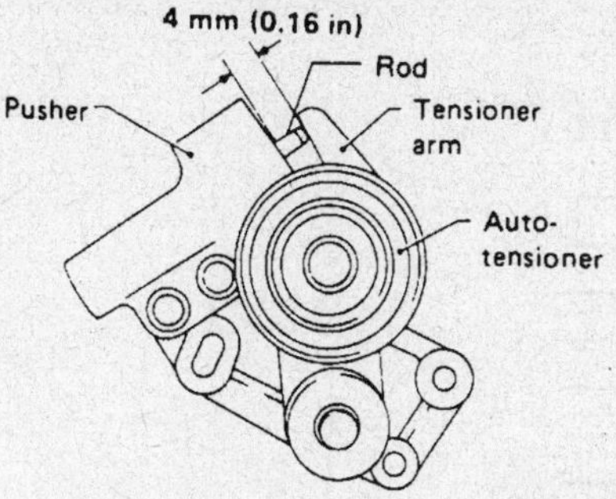
4 mm (0.16 in)
Rod
Pusher
Tensioner
arm
Auto-
tensioner

NS1069100063000X

Fig. 14 Adjusting auto tensioner

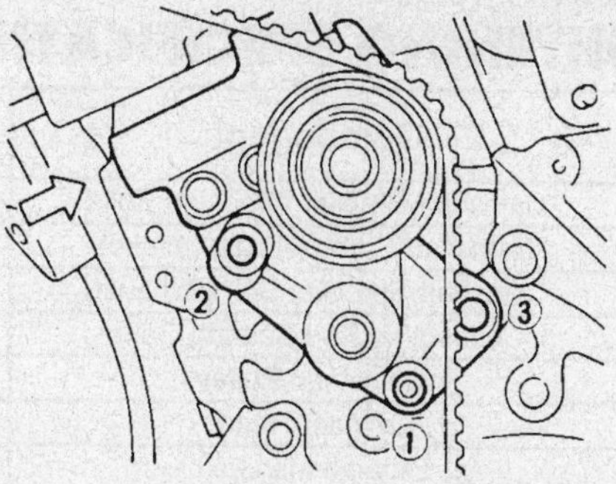

NS1069100064000X

Fig. 15 Auto tensioner attaching nut & bolts

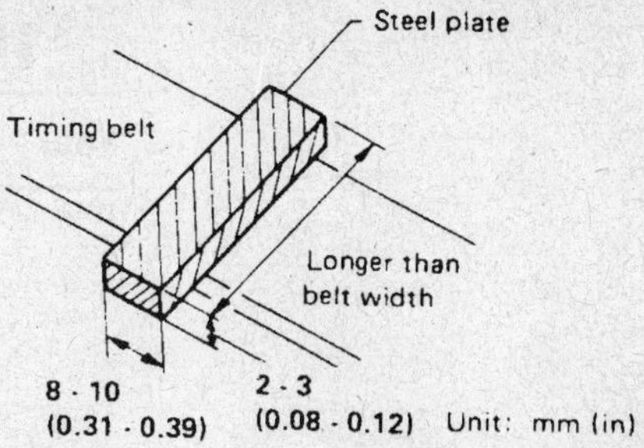
Steel plate
Timing belt
Longer than
belt width
8 - 10
(0.31 - 0.39)
2 - 3
(0.08 - 0.12)
Unit: mm (in)

NS1069100065000X

Fig. 16 Steel plate for checking belt deflection

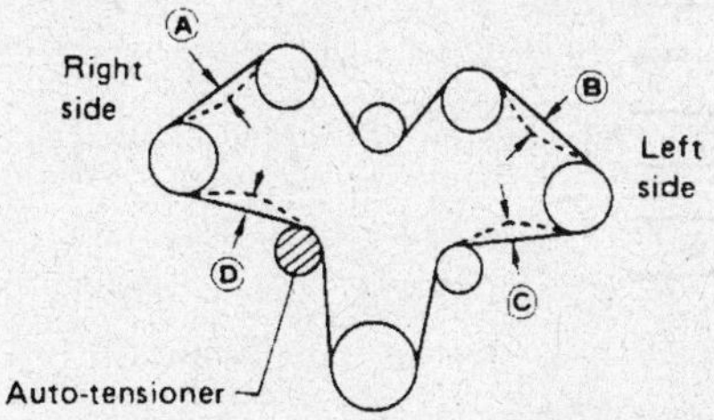
Right
side
Left
side
Auto-tensioner

NS1069100066000X

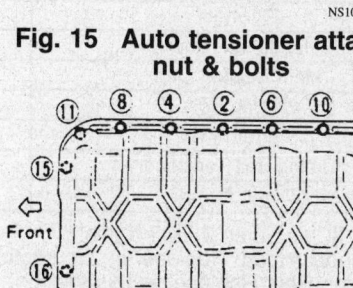

Fig. 17 Checking belt deflection

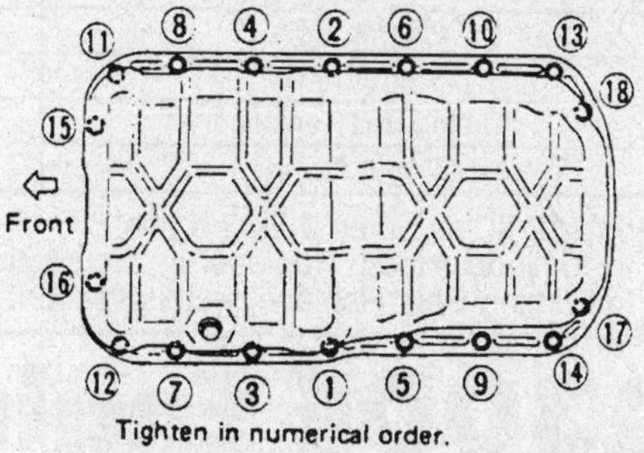
Front
Tighten in numerical order.

NS1099100016000X

Fig. 18 Oil pan bolt tightening sequence

Unit: mm (in)

		Used belt deflection		Deflection of new belt
		Limit	Deflection after adjustment	
Alternator		11.5 (0.453)	7 - 8 (0.28 - 0.31)	6.5 - 7.5 (0.256 - 0.295)
Air conditioner compressor		12.5 (0.492)	8 - 9 (0.31 - 0.35)	7 - 8 (0.28 - 0.31)
Power steering oil pump	Non-Turbo	19 (0.75)	12 - 13.5 (0.472 - 0.531)	10.5 - 11.5 (0.413 - 0.453)
	Turbo	16 (0.63)	10 - 11 (0.39 - 0.43)	9 - 10 (0.35 - 0.39)
Applied pushing force		98 N (10 kg, 22 lb)		

NS1069100119000X

Fig. 19 Belt tension data

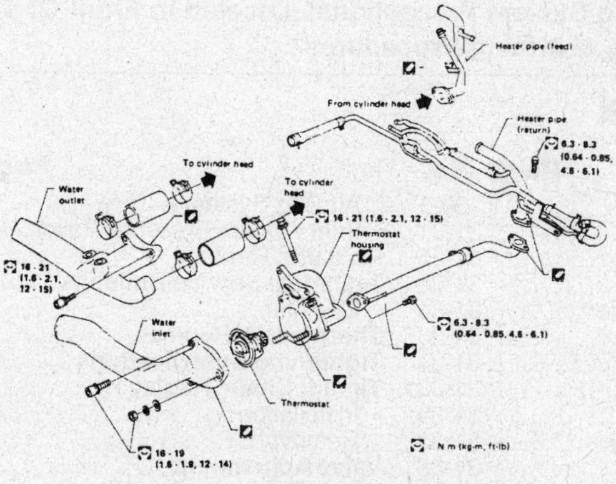
Heater pipe (feed)
From cylinder head
Heater pipe
(return)
6.3 - 8.3
(0.64 - 0.85,
4.6 - 6.1)
To cylinder head
To cylinder
head
Water
outlet
16 - 21 (1.6 - 2.1, 12 - 15)
Thermostat
housing
16 - 21
(1.6 - 2.1,
12 - 15)
Water
inlet
6.3 - 8.3
(0.64 - 0.85, 4.6 - 6.1)
Thermostat
16 - 19
(1.6 - 1.9, 12 - 14)
: N m (kg-m, ft-lb)

NS1089100012000X

Fig. 20 Thermostat replacement

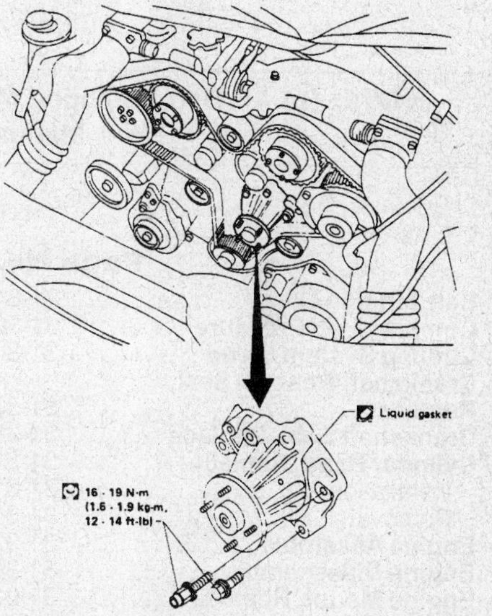
Liquid gasket
16 - 19 N-m
(1.6 - 1.9 kg-m,
12 - 14 ft-lb)

NS1089100009000X

Fig. 21 Water pump replacement

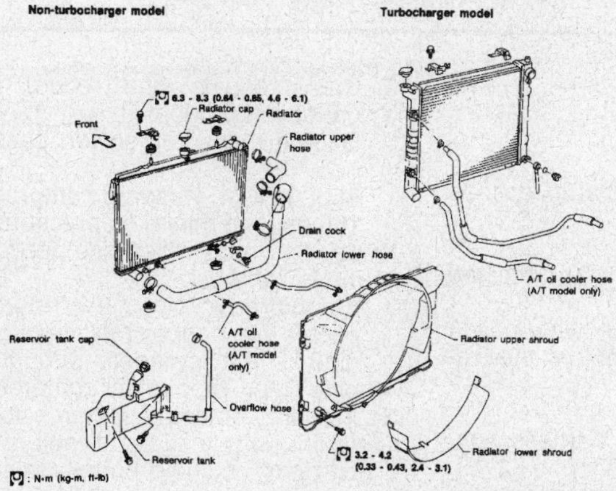
Non-turbocharger model
Turbocharger model
6.3 - 8.3 (0.64 - 0.85, 4.6 - 6.1)
Radiator cap
Radiator
Front
Radiator upper
hose
Drain cock
Radiator lower hose
A/T oil cooler hose
(A/T model only)
Reservoir tank cap
A/T oil
cooler hose
(A/T model
only)
Radiator upper shroud
Overflow hose
Reservoir tank
3.2 - 4.2
(0.33 - 0.43, 2.4 - 3.1)
Radiator lower shroud
: N•m (kg-m, ft-lb)

NS1089500073000X

Fig. 22 Radiator replacement

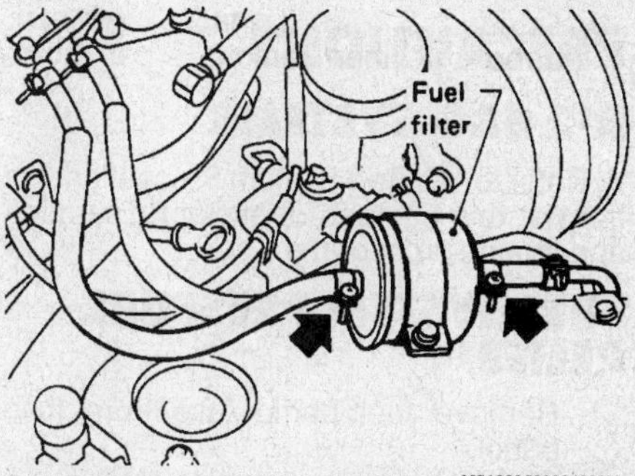
Fuel
filter

NS1029500024000X

Fig. 23 Fuel filter replacement

TIGHTENING SPECIFICATIONS

Year	Component	Torque/Ft. Lbs.
1993–96	Camshaft Bracket Attaching Bolts	7–9
	Camshaft Sprocket Bolt (Intake)	90–98
	Camshaft Sprocket Bolt (Exhaust)	10–14
	Connecting Rod Bearing Caps	①
	Crankshaft Pulley	159–174
	Cylinder Head	②
	Exhaust Manifold	13–17
	Flywheel	61–69
	Intake Manifold	12–17
	Main Bearing Cap	67–74
	Oil Pan Bolts	3.6–5.1
	Starter Motor	22–27
	Timing Belt Tensioner	③
	Water Pump	12–15

① — Tighten to 12 ft. lbs.; then 28–33 ft. lbs.
② — Refer to "Cylinder Head, Replace" in this section.
③ — Refer to "Timing Belt, Replace" in this section.

VQ30DE Engine

NOTE: On Air Bag Equipped Models, Refer To "Air Bag System Precautions" Located In Front Of This Manual For System Disarming & Arming Procedures.

INDEX

	Page No.
Belt Tension Data	31-34
Compression Pressure	31-30
Cooling System Bleed	31-34
Crankshaft Rear Oil Seal, Replace	31-33
Crankshaft Seal, Replace	31-33
Cylinder Head, Replace	31-31
Installation	31-31
Removal	31-31
Engine Assemble	31-32
Engine Disassemble	31-31
Engine Mount, Replace	31-31
Engine Rebuilding	
Specifications	36-1
Engine, Replace	31-31
Fuel Filter, Replace	31-35
Fuel Pump, Replace	31-35
Intake Manifold, Replace	31-31
Oil Pan, Replace	31-33
Installation	31-34
Removal	31-33
Oil Pump, Replace	31-34
Piston & Rod Assembly	31-33
Assemble	31-33
Disassemble	31-33
Precautions	31-30
Air Bag Systems	31-30
Fuel System Pressure Relief	31-30
Radiator, Replace	31-35
Technical Service Bulletins	31-35
Oil Filter	31-35
Thermostat, Replace	31-34
Tightening Specifications	31-36
Timing Chain, Replace	31-32
Installation	31-33
Removal	31-32
Valve Adjustment	31-32
Valve Clearance Specifications	31-32
Water Pump, Replace	31-34

PRECAUTIONS

AIR BAG SYSTEMS

Refer to "Air Bag System Precautions" in front of this manual for system disarming and arming procedures.

FUEL SYSTEM PRESSURE RELIEF

1. Remove fuel pump fuse from fuse panel.
2. Start and run engine until it stalls.
3. Try to start engine two or three more times to ensure fuel pressure is released.
4. Turn ignition switch off.
5. Install fuel pump fuse.

COMPRESSION PRESSURE

1. Start and run engine until it reaches operating temperature.
2. Turn ignition switch off.
3. Release fuel pressure as outlined under "Precautions."
4. Disconnect ignition coil with power transistor harness connectors, then remove ignition coils.
5. Remove all spark plugs.
6. Disconnect all injector harness connectors.
7. Attach a compression tester to cylinder No.1.
8. Depress accelerator pedal fully to keep throttle valve wide open.
9. Crank engine and record highest gauge indication.
10. Repeat measurement on each cylinder.
11. At 300 RPM, standard compression is 185 psi and minimum pressure is 142 psi, maximum difference between cylinders is 14 psi.
12. If compression in one or more cylinders is low, pour a small amount of engine oil into cylinders through spark plug holes, then retest compression.
13. If adding oil helps compression, then piston rings may be at fault. If adding oil does not help compression, then valves may be at fault.
14. If compression stays low in two cylinders that are next to each other, then

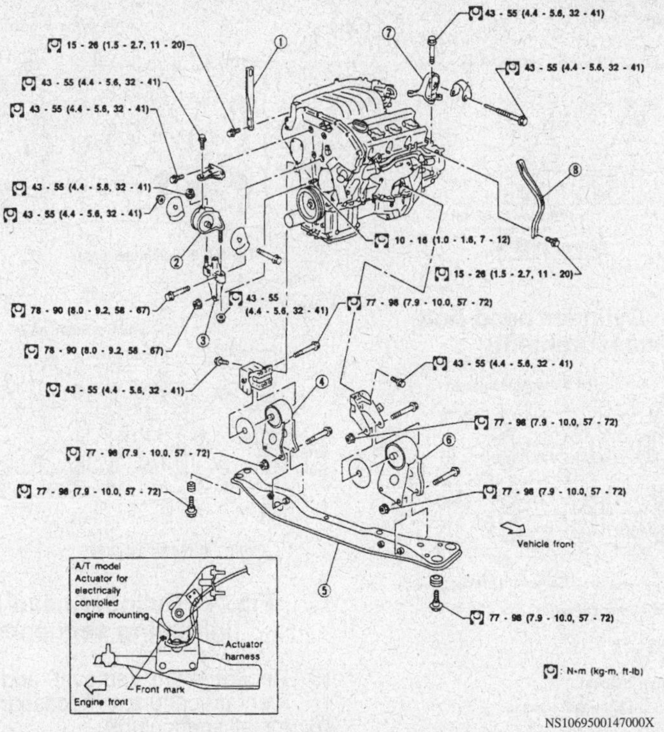
15 - 26 (1.5 - 2.7, 11 - 20)
43 - 55 (4.4 - 5.6, 32 - 41)
10 - 16 (1.0 - 1.6, 7 - 12)
78 - 90 (8.0 - 9.2, 58 - 67)
77 - 98 (7.9 - 10.0, 57 - 72)
Vehicle front
A/T model
Actuator for electrically controlled engine mounting
Actuator harness
Front mark
Engine front
N·m (kg-m, ft-lb)
NS1069500147000X

Fig. 1 Engine mounts

cylinder head gasket may be leaking or both cylinders have valve component damage.

15. Repair as necessary.

ENGINE MOUNT

REPLACE

Refer to **Fig. 1** to replace engine mounts.

ENGINE

REPLACE

1. Disconnect battery ground cable.
2. Release fuel system pressure as outlined under "Precautions."
3. Drain engine coolant from cylinder block and radiator, then drain engine oil.
4. Recover air conditioning coolant.
5. Remove engine undercover and hood.
6. Disconnect vacuum hoses, fuel hoses, electrical wires, harnesses and connectors. **Mark hoses and connectors for installation reference.**
7. Remove front exhaust pipe at manifold.
8. Disconnect ball joints and drive shafts.
9. Remove radiator and electric cooling fans.
10. Remove drive belts.
11. Remove alternator, A/C compressor and power steering pump from engine.
12. Raise and support vehicle and set a suitable transmission jack under transaxle.
13. Lift engine with engine hoist enough to take pressure off of engine mounts.
14. Remove rear engine mounting.
15. **On models with manual transaxle,** disconnect control rod and support rod from transaxle.
16. **On models with automatic transaxle,** disconnect control cable from transaxle.
17. **On all models,** remove front engine mounting.
18. Remove center member, then slowly lower transmission jack.
19. Remove engine with transaxle from under vehicle with transmission jack.
20. Reverse procedure to install.

INTAKE MANIFOLD

REPLACE

1. Release fuel system pressure as outlined in "Precautions," then disconnect battery ground cable.
2. Drain engine and radiator coolant, then remove lefthand rocker cover ornament.
3. Remove intake manifold air duct, collector, fuel hoses, wires, harness and connectors.
4. Remove vacuum, water, canister purge and blow-by hoses.
5. Remove ignition coils and EGR guide tube.
6. Remove righthand cylinder head intake manifold collector supports and intake manifold collector.
7. Remove fuel tube assembly.
8. Remove intake manifold bolts in reverse order of installation, **Fig. 2,** and intake manifold.
9. Reverse procedure to install, **torque** intake manifold bolts and nuts in order to 4–7 ft. lbs., then **torque** bolts to 14–18 ft. lbs. and nuts to 16–20 ft. lbs.

CYLINDER HEAD

REPLACE

REMOVAL

1. Remove intake manifold as outlined in "Intake Manifold, Replace."
2. Remove timing chain as outlined in "Timing Chain, Replace."
3. Remove cylinder heads.

INSTALLATION

Before installing rear timing chain case or cam bracket, removal all traces of liquid gasket. Remove all traces of liquid gasket from cylinder block mating surfaces and remove O-rings.

1. Turn crankshaft until No. 1 piston is set 240° before TDC on compression stroke.
2. Install cylinder heads with new gaskets. **Do not rotate crankshaft and camshaft separately or valves will strike pistons.**
3. Cylinder head bolts are tightened by plastic zone tightening. Measure all bolts, **Fig. 3.** If diameter "d1" minus "d2" exceeds .0043 inch, replace bolt.
4. Tighten cylinder head bolts in order, **Fig. 4,** as follows:
   a. **Torque** bolts to 72 ft. lbs.
   b. Completely loosen bolts.
   c. **Torque** bolts to 25–33 ft. lbs.
   d. Turn bolts 90–95° clockwise.
   e. Turn bolts 90–95° clockwise, again.
5. Install cylinder head outside bolts, **torque** to 7 ft. lbs., loosen completely, and **torque** to 7 ft. lbs. in three steps.
6. Install cam tensioners and apply sealant to No.1 journal head mating surface.
7. Install exhaust and intake camshafts.
8. Install camshaft brackets in original positions and tighten bolts in three steps as follows:
   a. First **torque** bolts in order of 7 to 10, then 1 to 6, to 17 inch lbs., **Fig. 5.**
   b. Second **torque** bolts in numerical order to 52 inch lbs.
   c. Finally **torque** bolts in numerical order to 7–9 ft. lbs.
9. If any part of valve or camshaft assembly has been replaced, check valve clearance as outlined in "Valve Adjustment."
10. Install cylinder block O-rings and apply sealant to hatched portions of rear timing chain case.
11. Align rear timing chain case with dowel pins, then install on cylinder head and block.
12. Tighten bolts to specifications in order, **Fig. 6.**

ENGINE DISASSEMBLE

Prior To Performing Any Service Operations Listed In This Section, Consult "Technical Service Bulletins" Section For Related Information.

1. Place engine on a work stand, then ensure coolant and oil have drained.
2. Remove cylinder heads as outlined in "Cylinder Head, Replace."

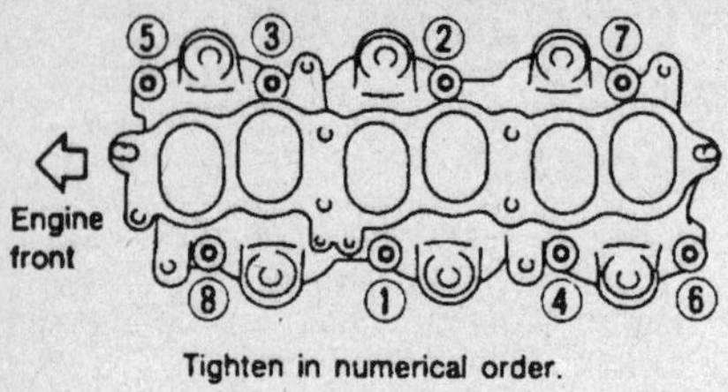
Engine
front
Tighten in numerical order.
NS1059500017000X

Fig. 2 Intake manifold tightening sequence

3. Remove oil pan as outlined in "Oil Pan, Replace."
4. Remove timing chain as outlined in "Timing Chain, Replace."
5. Remove pistons with connecting rod.
6. Remove rear oil seal retainer.
7. Before removing bearing cap, measure crankshaft end play.
8. Loosen main bearing beam and crankshaft retaining bolts in two or three steps in sequence, **Fig. 7,** and remove.

ENGINE ASSEMBLE

1. Install main bearings, **Fig. 8,** crankshaft and bearing cap. Using sequence shown in **Fig. 9, torque** attaching bolts to 24–28 ft. lbs., in two or three steps.
2. Install piston assemblies with rings properly positioned, **Fig. 10.**
3. Reverse remainder of "Engine Disassemble" procedure to complete assembly, noting following:
   a. Tighten cylinder head attaching bolts to specifications using sequence shown in **Fig. 4.**
   b. Tighten intake manifold attaching bolts in sequence, **Fig. 2** to specifications in two or three steps.

VALVE CLEARANCE SPECIFICATIONS

Engine	Stem-To-Guide Clearance, Inch①	
	Intake	Exhaust
VQ30DE	.0100–.0130	.0110–.0150

① — Cold.

VALVE ADJUSTMENT

1. Remove intake manifold collector and rocker cover ornaments, then the rocker covers.
2. Remove spark plugs and set No. 1 piston to TDC on compression stroke.
3. Use feeler gauge to measure and record clearance between valve lifter and camshaft on No. 1 and No. 6 intake valves, and No. 2 and 3 exhaust valves.
4. Turn crankshaft 240° and set No. 3 piston to TDC on compression stroke.
5. Use feeler gauge to measure and record clearance between valve lifter and camshaft on No. 2 and No. 3 intake valves, and No. 4 and 5 exhaust valves.

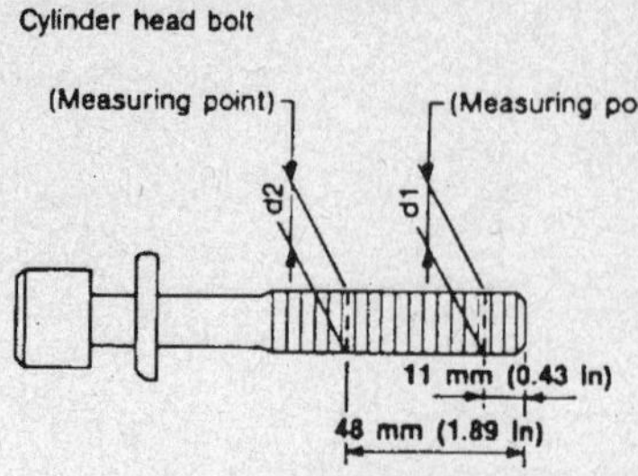
Cylinder head bolt
(Measuring point)
(Measuring point)
d2
d1
11 mm (0.43 In)
48 mm (1.89 In)
NS1069500151000X

Fig. 3 Cylinder head bolt measurement

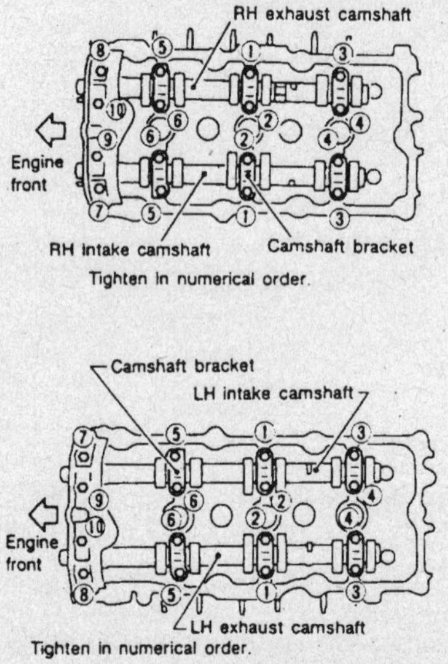
RH exhaust camshaft
Engine
front
RH intake camshaft
Camshaft bracket
Tighten in numerical order.
Camshaft bracket
LH intake camshaft
Engine
front
LH exhaust camshaft
Tighten in numerical order.
NS1069500153000X

Fig. 5 Camshaft bracket tightening sequence

6. Turn crankshaft 240° and set No. 5 piston to TDC on compression stroke.
7. Use feeler gauge to measure and record clearance between valve lifter and camshaft on No. 4 and No. 5 intake valves, and No. 1 and 6 exhaust valves.
8. Turn crankshaft to position cam lobe on valve to be adjusted.
9. Place suitable camshaft pliers around camshaft and rotate so lifter is pushed down.
10. Place suitable lifter stopper between camshaft and edge of lifter and remove pliers.
11. Blow air into hole to separate adjusting shim from valve lifter, then remove shim with small screwdriver and magnetic finger.
12. Measure removed shim and calculate thickness of new shim necessary to obtain specified clearance. New intake shim size equals removed shim size plus measured clearance minus .0118 inch. New exhaust shim size equals removed shim size plus measured clearance minus .0130 inch. Shims are available from .0913 inch to .1161 inch, in .0004 inch steps.
13. Install new shim, attach pliers, rotate, then remove stopper and pliers.
14. Recheck valve clearance.

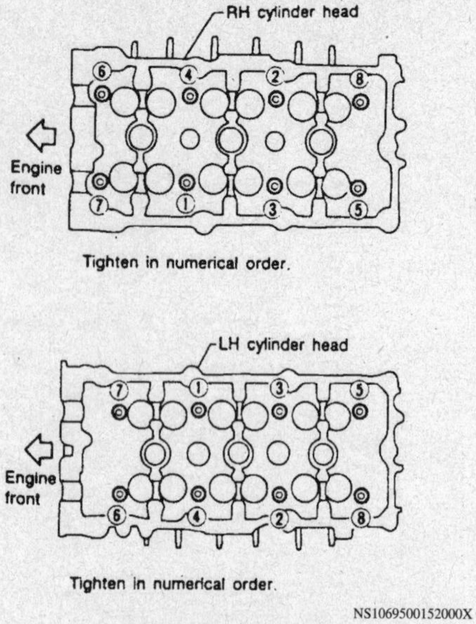
RH cylinder head
Engine
front
Tighten in numerical order.
LH cylinder head
Engine
front
Tighten in numerical order.
NS1069500152000X

Fig. 4 Cylinder head bolt tightening sequence

15. Repeat shim removal and replacement procedure as necessary.
16. Install spark plugs.
17. Install intake rocker covers, rocker cover ornaments and manifold collector.

TIMING CHAIN

REPLACE

REMOVAL

1. Remove intake manifold as outlined in "Intake Manifold, Replace."
2. Remove rocker covers, then raise and support vehicle.
3. Remove engine undercover, righthand front wheel and engine side cover.
4. Remove drive belts, idler pulley bracket and power steering pump.
5. Remove camshaft and crankshaft position sensors, then set No. 1 piston at TDC of compression stroke.
6. Loosen crankshaft pulley bolt, then remove oil pan rear cover plate and set screwdriver or other suitable tool in ring gear to stop crankshaft rotation.
7. Remove crankshaft pulley with suitable puller, then the air conditioning compressor and bracket.
8. Remove front exhaust tube and support.
9. Support right and left sides of engine with suitable hoist, and remove righthand engine mounting, bracket and nuts.
10. Remove center member, then the upper and lower oil pans as outlined in "Oil Pan, Replace."
11. Remove water pump cover, then the front timing chain case bolts and case.
12. Remove internal timing and upper chain guides, then the timing chain tensioner and slack side chain guide.
13. Remove first chain camshaft sprocket bolts, then the first chain camshaft sprockets, crankshaft sprocket and timing chain.

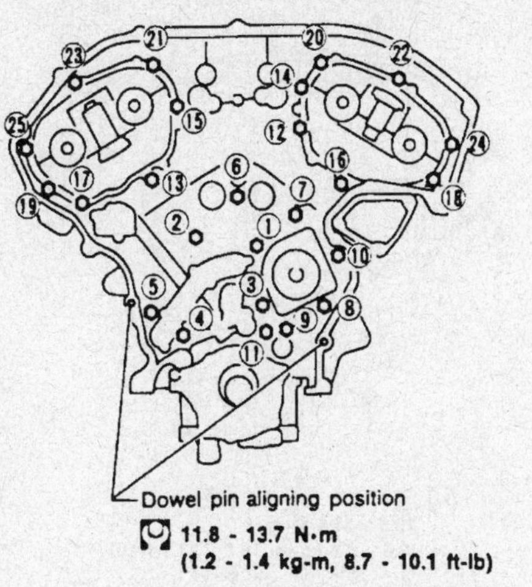
Dowel pin aligning position
11.8 - 13.7 N·m
(1.2 - 1.4 kg-m, 8.7 - 10.1 ft-lb)
NS1069500154000X

Fig. 6 Rear timing chain case tightening sequence

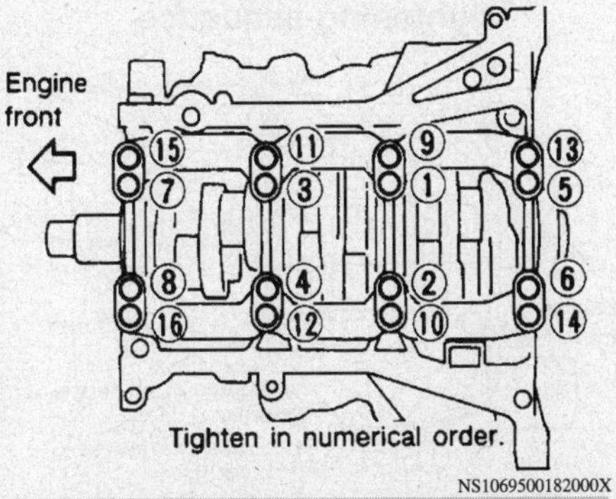
Engine
front
Tighten in numerical order.
NS1069500182000X

Fig. 9 Main bearing bolt tightening sequence

14. Insert suitable stopper pin into camshaft tensioners, then remove second chain exhaust camshaft sprocket bolts and exhaust sprockets.
15. Remove second chain intake camshaft sprocket bolts and intake sprockets.
16. Remove lower chain guide, then scrape all traces of liquid gasket from timing chain case and water pump cover.

INSTALLATION

1. Install crankshaft sprocket, then set No. 1 piston to TDC on compression stroke.
2. Install lower chain guide on dowel pin with front mark on guide facing upside.
3. Align marks on second chain intake and exhaust camshaft sprockets, and second camshaft chain, **Fig. 11.**
4. Install intake and exhaust camshaft sprockets. **Exhaust sprocket is thicker than intake.**
5. Remove camshaft tensioner stopper pins.
6. Align crankshaft sprocket mating mark with chain gold matchmark, **Fig. 12.**
7. Attach lower timing chain on water pump sprocket.
8. Install first chain camshaft sprockets onto timing chain by matching sprocket dowel grooves with camshaft and tighten bolts to specifications.

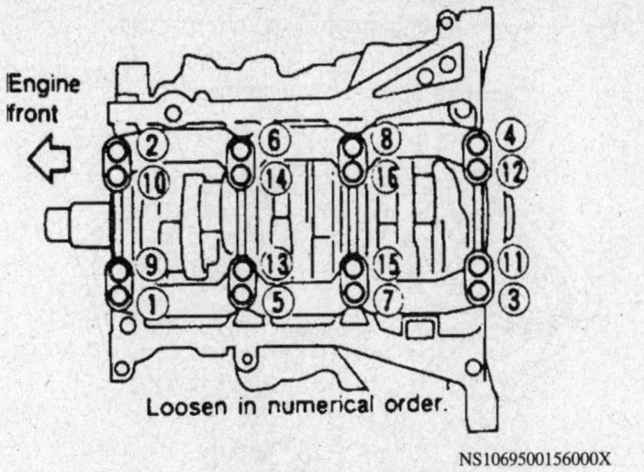
Engine
front
Loosen in numerical order.
NS1069500156000X

Fig. 7 Main bearing cap bolt loosening sequence

9. Install timing chain, ensuring mating marks and matchmarks are aligned.
10. Install internal and upper chain guides, then the tensioner and slack side guide.
11. Apply liquid gasket to front timing chain case and install rear case pin into dowel pin hole of front timing case.
12. **Torque** bolts 1 and 2 to 18.8–23.1 ft. lbs., and bolts 3–20 to 8.7–10.1 ft. lbs. in order, **Fig. 13.**
13. Apply liquid gasket to water pump cover and install.
14. Apply liquid gasket to rocker covers and install.
15. **Torque** rocker cover bolts to 0.7–2.2 ft. lbs. in order, then final **torque** bolts to 4.3–5.8 ft. lbs., **Figs. 14 and 15.**

PISTON & ROD ASSEMBLY

DISASSEMBLE

1. Remove piston rings with a ring remover.
2. Remove snap ring, then press out piston pin using piston pin press or heat piston to 140–150°F and remove piston pin. **Keep disassembled parts in order.**

ASSEMBLE

1. Assemble pistons, piston pins and connecting rods of designated cylinders.
2. Install new snap ring on one side of piston pin.
3. Align piston and connecting rod direction.
4. Ensure stamped numbers on connecting rod and cap correspond to each cylinder.
5. Heat piston to 140–150°F and assemble piston, piston pin, connecting rod and new snap ring.
6. Install piston rings.

CRANKSHAFT SEAL

REPLACE

1. Raise and support vehicle, then remove engine undercover.
2. Remove righthand front wheel and engine side cover.

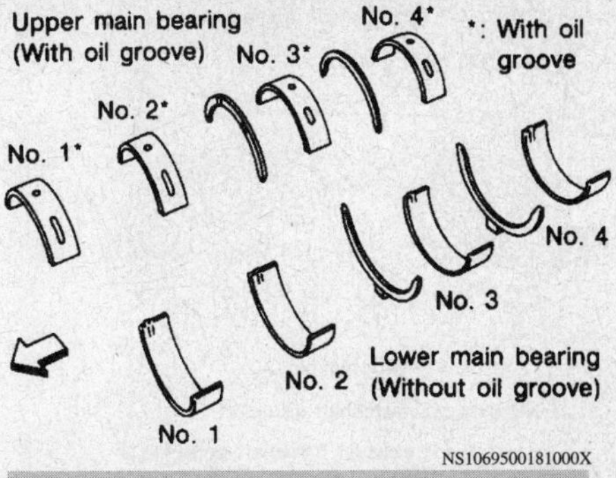
Upper main bearing
(With oil groove)
No. 4*
*: With oil groove
No. 3*
No. 2*
No. 1*
No. 4
No. 3
Lower main bearing
(Without oil groove)
No. 2
No. 1
NS1069500181000X

Fig. 8 Main bearing identification

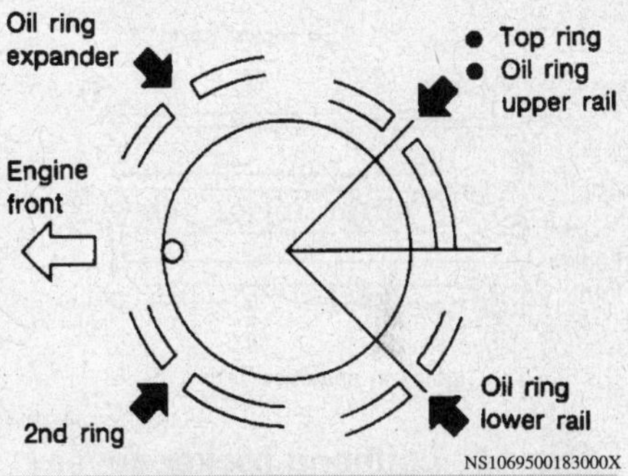
Oil ring
expander
Top ring
Oil ring
upper rail
Engine
front
Oil ring
lower rail
2nd ring
NS1069500183000X

Fig. 10 Piston ring positioning

3. Remove drive belts.
4. Remove crankshaft position sensor.
5. Remove crankshaft pulley.
6. Remove front oil seal being careful not to scratch front cover.
7. Apply engine oil to new oil seal and install using suitable oil seal installation tool.

CRANKSHAFT REAR OIL SEAL

REPLACE

1. Remove flywheel or driveplate.
2. Remove oil pan as outlined in "Oil Pan, Replace."
3. Remove rear oil seal retainer.
4. Remove rear oil seal.
5. Apply engine oil to new seal and install with suitable seal installation tool.

OIL PAN

REPLACE

REMOVAL

1. Remove engine undercover and drain engine oil.
2. Remove steel oil pan bolts in reverse order, **Fig. 16.**
3. Insert suitable tool between steel and aluminum oil pans, then slide tool by tapping slide with hammer and remove steel oil pan. **Do not use screwdriver and be careful not to damage aluminum mating surface.**
4. Remove oil strainer, then the front exhaust tube and support.

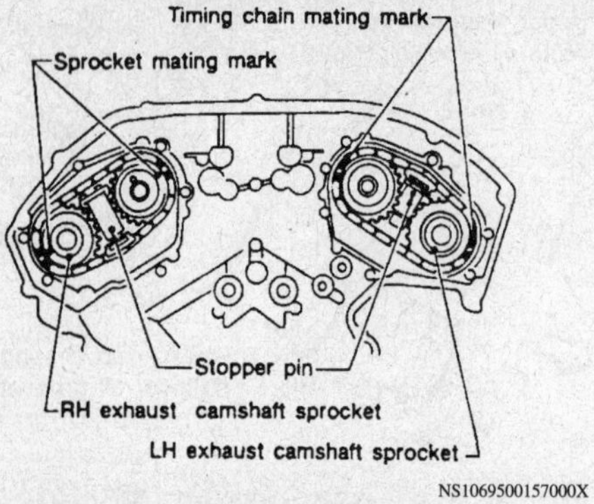
Timing chain mating mark
Sprocket mating mark
Stopper pin
RH exhaust camshaft sprocket
LH exhaust camshaft sprocket
NS1069500157000X

Fig. 11 Second timing chain alignment

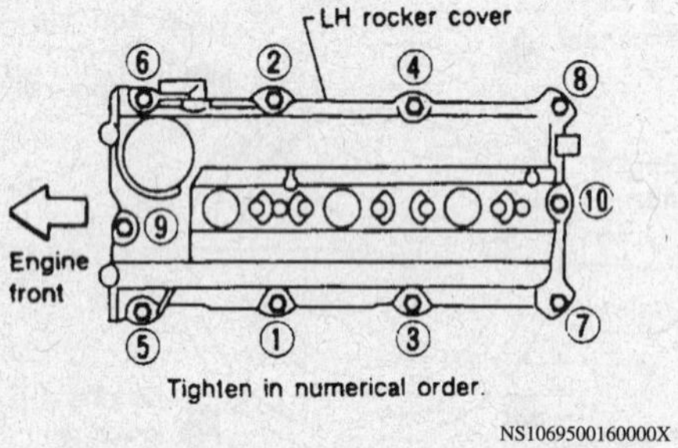
LH rocker cover
Engine front
Tighten in numerical order.
NS1069500160000X

Fig. 14 Lefthand rocker cover bolt tightening sequence

5. Place suitable transmission jack under transaxle and lift engine with slinger.
6. Remove crankshaft position sensors.
7. Remove front and rear engine mounting nuts and bolts, then the center member.
8. Remove drive belts, then the A/C compressor and bracket.
9. Remove rear cover plate.
10. Remove aluminum oil pan bolts in reverse order, **Fig. 17.**
11. Remove transaxle bolts.
12. Insert suitable tool between cylinder block and aluminum oil pans, then slide tool by tapping slide with hammer and remove aluminum oil pan. **Do not use screwdriver and be careful not to damage aluminum mating surface.**
13. Remove baffle plate and cylinder block O-rings.

INSTALLATION

1. Remove all traces of liquid gasket on oil pans and cylinder block mating surfaces.
2. Install baffle plate, then apply sealant to front cover and rear oil seal gaskets.
3. Apply continuous liquid gasket bead to aluminum oil pan mating surface and inner sealing surface.
4. Install O-rings and install aluminum oil pan, tightening bolts in order to specifications, **Fig. 17.**
5. Install transaxle bolts, rear cover plate, A/C compressor and bracket, drive belts, center member, front and rear engine mounting insulator nuts and bolts, crankshaft position sensors, front exhaust tube and support, and oil strainer.
6. Apply continuous liquid gasket bead to

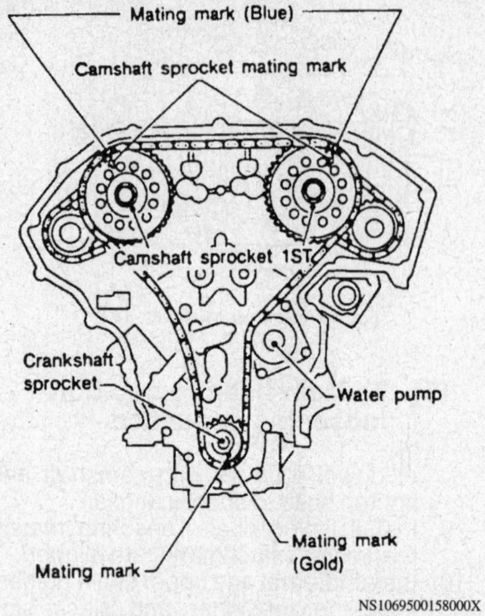
Mating mark (Blue)
Camshaft sprocket mating mark
Camshaft sprocket 1ST
Crankshaft sprocket
Water pump
Mating mark (Gold)
Mating mark
NS1069500158000X

Fig. 12 Timing chain matchmark align

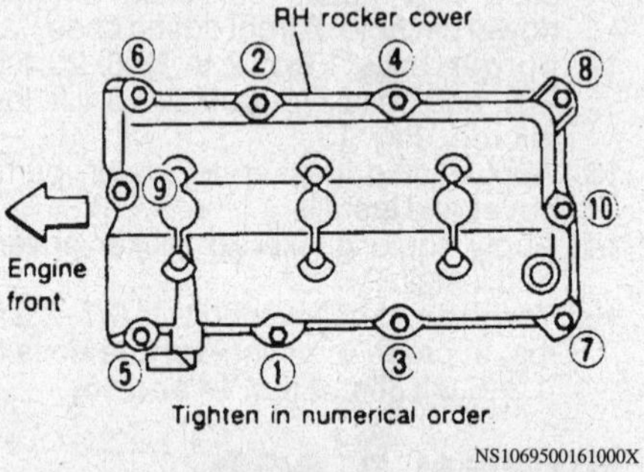
RH rocker cover
Engine front
Tighten in numerical order
NS1069500161000X

Fig. 15 Righthand rocker cover bolt tightening sequence

steel oil pan mating surface and install steel oil pan.

7. Tighten bolts in order to specifications, **Fig. 16.**
8. Wait at least 30 minutes before filling with engine oil.

OIL PUMP

REPLACE

1. Drain engine oil and remove drive belts.
2. Remove oil pan as outlined in "Oil Pan, Replace."
3. Remove water pump and front covers.
4. Remove timing chain as outlined in "Timing Chain, Replace."
5. Remove oil pump assembly.
6. Reverse procedure to install.

BELT TENSION DATA

Refer to **Fig. 18** for belt tension data.

COOLING SYSTEM BLEED

These engines do not require a specified bleed procedure. After filling cooling system, run engine to operating temperature with radiator/pressure cap off. Air will then be automatically bled through cap opening.

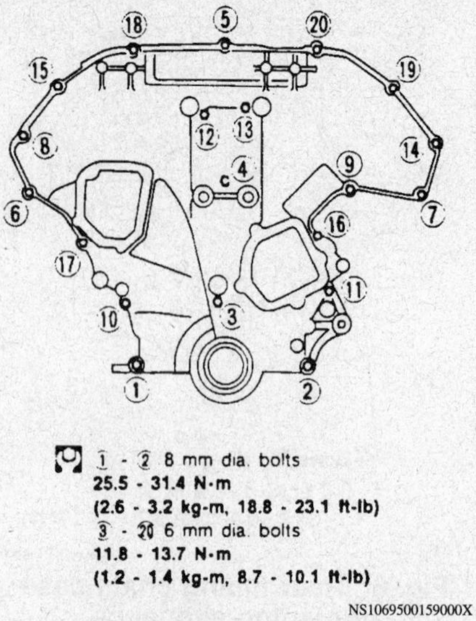
1 - 2 8 mm dia. bolts
25.5 - 31.4 N·m
(2.6 - 3.2 kg-m, 18.8 - 23.1 ft-lb)
3 - 20 6 mm dia. bolts
11.8 - 13.7 N·m
(1.2 - 1.4 kg-m, 8.7 - 10.1 ft-lb)
NS1069500159000X

Fig. 13 Timing chain case bolt tightening sequence

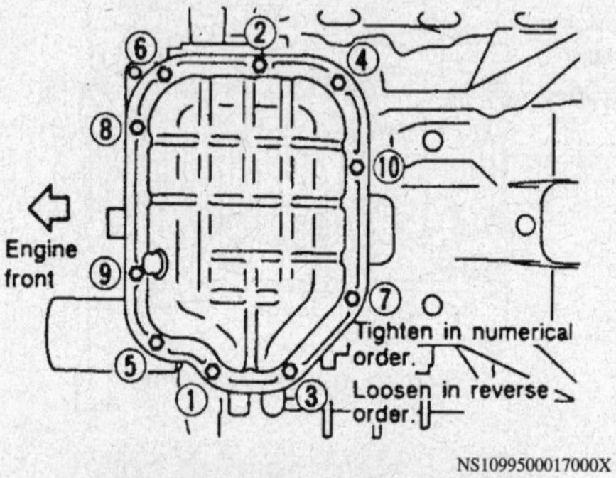
Engine front
Tighten in numerical order.
Loosen in reverse order.
NS1099500017000X

Fig. 16 Steel oil pan bolt tightening sequence

THERMOSTAT

REPLACE

1. Disconnect battery ground cable, then drain engine and radiator coolant.
2. Remove lower radiator hose, then the water inlet, **Fig. 19.**
3. Remove thermostat from thermostat housing.
4. Reverse procedure to install.

WATER PUMP

REPLACE

1. Disconnect battery ground cable, then drain engine and radiator coolant.
2. Remove cylinder block drain plug, then the right engine mounting, mounting bracket and nuts.
3. Remove drive belts and idler pulley bracket.
4. Remove chain tensioner cover and water pump cover, **Fig. 20.**
5. Push timing chain tensioner sleeve, install stopper pin and remove chain tensioner assembly.
6. Remove three water pump attaching bolts, then turn crankshaft 20° counterclockwise to create gap between water pump gear and timing chain.
7. Put two M8 bolts in opposing water pump mounting holes, then alternately

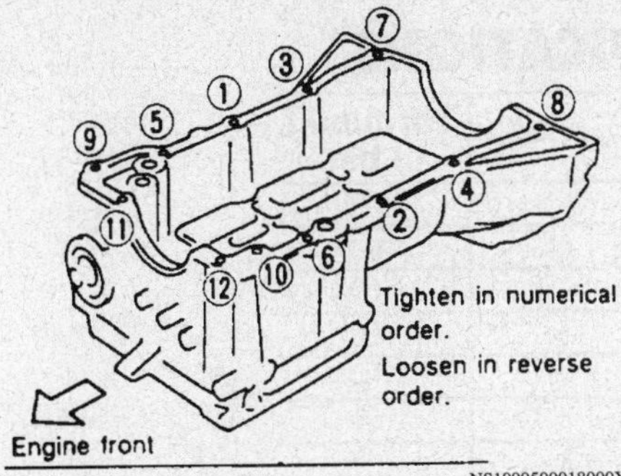
Tighten in numerical order.
Loosen in reverse order.
Engine front

NS1099500018000X

Fig. 17 Aluminum oil pan bolt tightening sequence

Unit: mm (in)

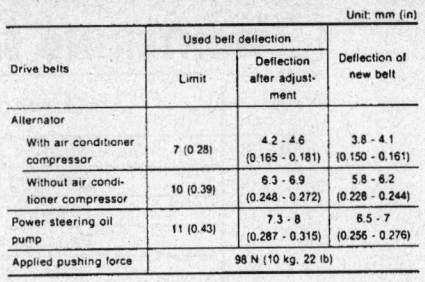

Drive belts	Used belt deflection: Limit	Used belt deflection: Deflection after adjustment	Deflection of new belt
Alternator			
With air conditioner compressor	7 (0.28)	4.2 - 4.6 (0.165 - 0.181)	3.8 - 4.1 (0.150 - 0.161)
Without air conditioner compressor	10 (0.39)	6.3 - 6.9 (0.248 - 0.272)	5.8 - 6.2 (0.228 - 0.244)
Power steering oil pump	11 (0.43)	7.3 - 8 (0.287 - 0.315)	6.5 - 7 (0.256 - 0.276)
Applied pushing force	98 N (10 kg, 22 lb)		

NS1069500162000X

Fig. 18 Belt tension data

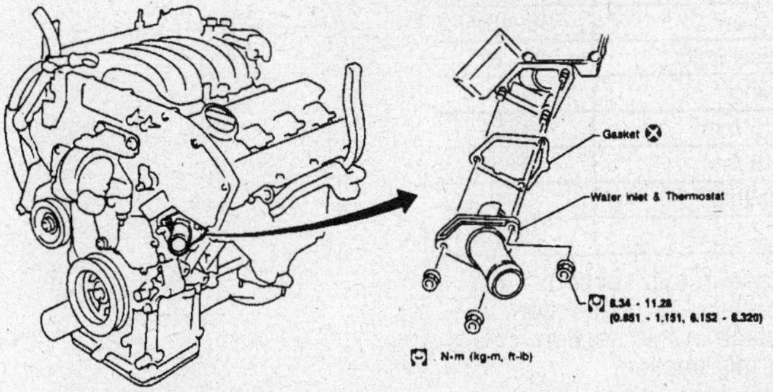
Gasket
Water inlet & Thermostat
N·m (kg-m, ft-lb)

NS1089500069000X

Fig. 19 Thermostat replacement

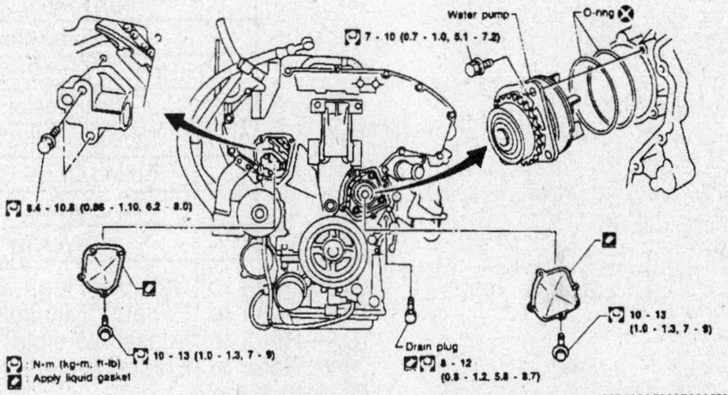
Water pump
O-ring
Drain plug
N·m (kg-m, ft-lb)
Apply liquid gasket

NS1089500070000X

Fig. 20 Water pump replacement

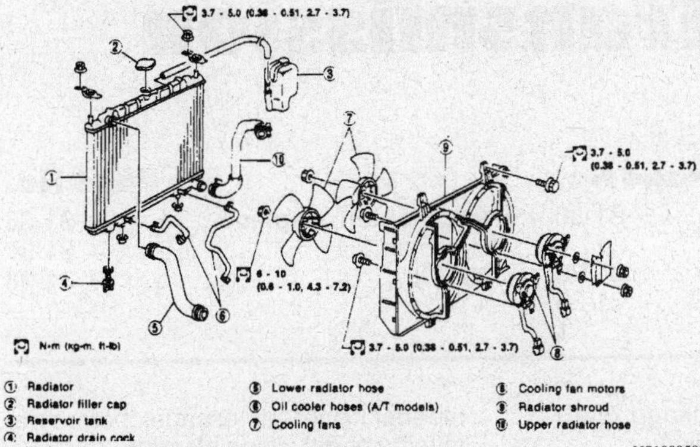
N·m (kg-m, ft-lb)
① Radiator
② Radiator filler cap
③ Reservoir tank
④ Radiator drain cock
⑤ Lower radiator hose
⑥ Oil cooler hoses (A/T models)
⑦ Cooling fans
⑧ Cooling fan motors
⑨ Radiator shroud
⑩ Upper radiator hose

NS1089500074000X

Fig. 21 Radiator replacement

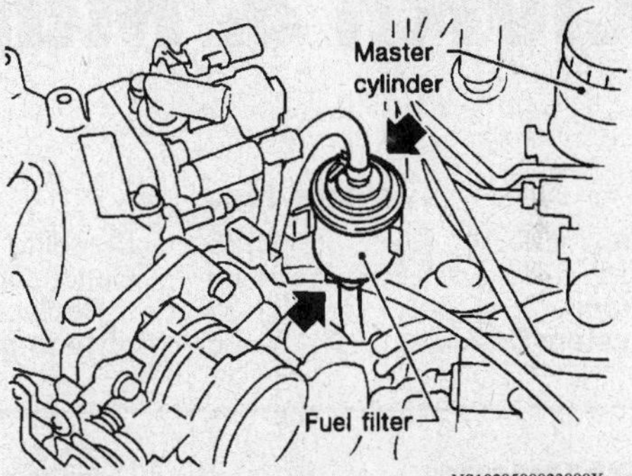
Master cylinder
Fuel filter

NS1029500023000X

Fig. 22 Fuel filter replacement

turn bolts ½ turn until they reach timing chain rear case.
8. Lifting up, remove water pump without hitting timing chain.
9. Reverse procedure to install.

RADIATOR

REPLACE

1. Remove undercover, then drain coolant.
2. Disconnect upper and lower radiator hoses, **Fig. 21.**
3. Remove shroud.
4. **On models with automatic transaxle,** remove ATF cooler hoses.
5. **On all models,** disconnect reservoir tank hose.
6. Remove radiator mounting bracket attaching bolts.
7. Remove radiator.
8. Reverse procedure to install.

FUEL PUMP

REPLACE

1. Release fuel pump pressure as outlined in "Precautions."
2. Disconnect battery ground cable, then drain fuel into suitable container.
3. Disconnect necessary fuel lines and electrical connectors.
4. Disconnect fuel tank attaching bolts, then lower tank.
5. Remove fuel pump attaching bolts, then the fuel pump.
6. Reverse procedure to install.

FUEL FILTER

REPLACE

1. Relieve fuel system pressure as outlined in "Precautions."
2. Loosen two fuel filter hose clamps, **Fig. 22.**
3. Disconnect fuel hoses from fuel filter. **Do not allow gasoline to spill over engine compartment.**
4. Reverse procedure to install.

TECHNICAL SERVICE BULLETINS

OIL FILTER

The oil filter used on this engine is different than filters used on previous engines. It is smaller, has metric threads and internal relief valve. This filter is not interchangeable with previous engines. Use correct filter for application.

TIGHTENING SPECIFICATIONS

Year	Component	Torque/Ft. Lbs.
1995–96	Camshaft Sprocket	88–95
	Connecting Rod Nuts	14–15
	Cylinder Head	①
	Exhaust Manifold	②
	Intake Manifold	③
	Intake Manifold Collector	③
	Main Bearing Cap Bolts	④
	Oil Pan Bolts (Aluminum)	12–14
	Oil Pan Bolts (Steel)	5–6
	Oil Pump Cover Bolt	5
	Oil Pump Cover Screw	36–48⑤
	Rear Timing Chain Case Bolts	9–10
	Thermostat Housing	6–8
	Timing Chain Case (6 mm)	9–10
	Timing Chain Case (8 mm)	19–23
	Timing Chain Sprockets	7–9
	Water Pump	5–7

①— Refer to "Cylinder Head, Replace"in this section.
②— Refer to "Exhaust Manifold, Replace"in this section.
③— Refer to "Intake Manifold, Replace"in this section.
④— Refer to "Engine Assemble" in this section.
⑤— Inch lbs.

Clutch & Manual Transmission

INDEX

	Page No.
Adjustments	31-36
Clutch Pedal	31-36
Clutch, Replace	31-36
Hydraulic System Service	31-36
Bleeding Procedure	31-36
Clutch Operating Cylinder, Replace	31-36
Tightening Specifications	31-39
Transmission, Replace	31-36
Maxima	31-37
300ZX	31-36

ADJUSTMENTS

CLUTCH PEDAL

The clutch hydraulic system must be bled whenever a clutch line has been disconnected or when air has entered system. bleed valve is located on clutch operating cylinder.

1. Adjust clutch pedal height, dimension "H" in **Figs. 1 and 2** to specifications shown in **Fig. 3**.
2. Measure clutch pedal freeplay as shown in **Figs. 1 and 4** dimension "A." Adjust clutch pedal freeplay by rotating clutch master cylinder pushrod inward or outward until specified freeplay is obtained. After completing freeplay adjustment, tighten locknut. Clutch pedal freeplay is sum of play between piston and piston rod.
3. Adjust dimension "C" **Fig. 5** to specifications, with clutch pedal fully depressed.
4. After above adjustments have been completed, cycle clutch pedal several times to ensure clutch linkage operates smoothly without binding.

HYDRAULIC SYSTEM SERVICE

CLUTCH OPERATING CYLINDER, REPLACE

1. Disconnect brake line from operating cylinder. **Do not bend brake line.**
2. Remove cylinder attaching bolts, **Figs. 6 through 8.**
3. Remove operating cylinder.
4. Reverse procedure to install, bleed clutch hydraulic system as outlined under "Clutch Bleeding Procedure."

BLEEDING PROCEDURE

1. Ensure master cylinder reservoir is filled with recommended brake fluid.
2. Connect clear tube to bleeder screw, then depress clutch pedal several times.
3. With pressure on clutch pedal, open bleeder to let air escape, before releasing pedal, close bleeder.
4. Repeat until all air is bled from system.

CLUTCH

REPLACE

1. Remove transmission as outlined under "Manual Transmission Replace," in this section.
2. Insert a dummy shaft into clutch disc hub.
3. Loosen clutch cover attaching bolts alternately.
4. Remove clutch disc and cover assembly.
5. Remove release bearing.
6. Reverse procedure to install.

TRANSMISSION

REPLACE

300ZX

1. Disconnect battery ground cable.

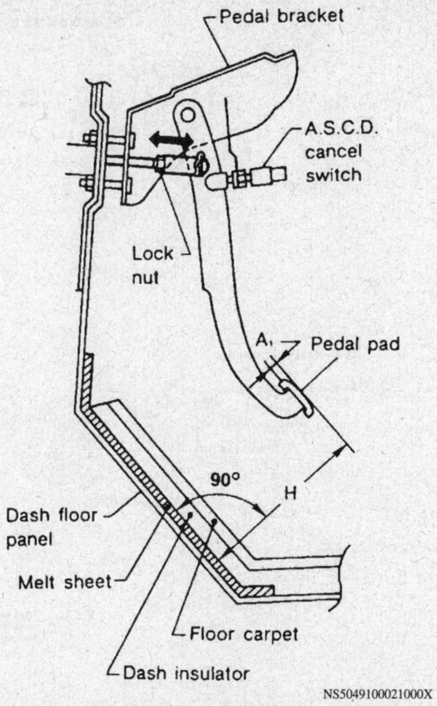
Pedal bracket
A.S.C.D. cancel switch
Lock nut
A
Pedal pad
90°
H
Dash floor panel
Melt sheet
Floor carpet
Dash insulator
NS5049100021000X

Fig. 1 Clutch pedal free travel & height adjustment. Maxima

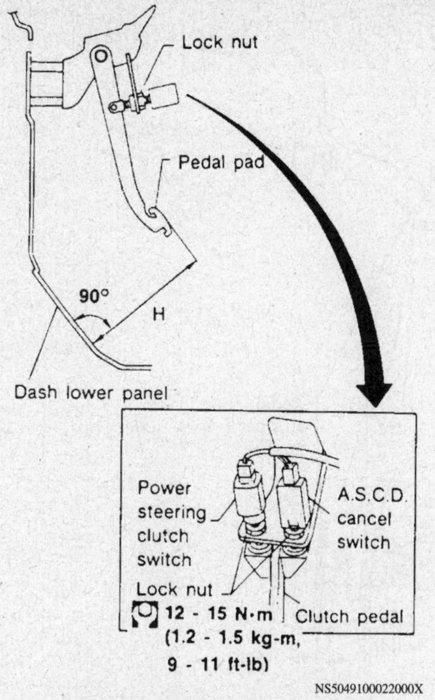
Lock nut
Pedal pad
90°
H
Dash lower panel
Power steering clutch switch
A.S.C.D. cancel switch
Lock nut
12 - 15 N·m (1.2 - 1.5 kg-m, 9 - 11 ft-lb)
Clutch pedal
NS5049100022000X

Fig. 2 Clutch pedal height adjustment. 300ZX

Year	Model	Pedal Height Inch	Pedal Freeplay Inch	Pedal Stop Clearance Inch
1993–94	Maxima	6.50–6.89	.039–.118	.004–.039
	300ZX Less Turbo	7.76–8.15	.039–.118	.039–.079
	300ZX With Turbo	7.20–7.60	.039–.118	.039–.079
1995–96	Maxima	6.61–6.89	.039–.118	.012–.039
	300ZX Less Trubo	7.76–8.15	.039–.118	.039–.079
	300 ZX With Turbo	7.20–7.60	.039–.118	.039–.079

Fig. 3 Clutch pedal height & freeplay specifications

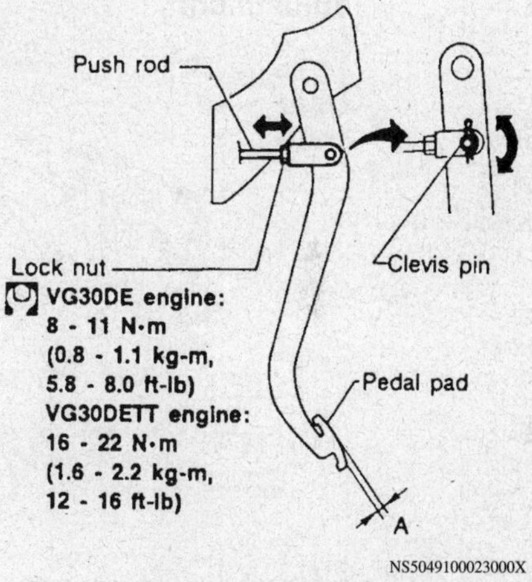
Push rod
Lock nut
VG30DE engine:
8 - 11 N·m
(0.8 - 1.1 kg-m,
5.8 - 8.0 ft-lb)
VG30DETT engine:
16 - 22 N·m
(1.6 - 2.2 kg-m,
12 - 16 ft-lb)
Clevis pin
Pedal pad
A
NS5049100023000X

Fig. 4 Clutch pedal free travel adjustment. 300ZX

2. Remove accelerator linkage.
3. Raise and support vehicle.
4. Remove front exhaust pipe, catalytic converter and exhaust manifold connecting tube.
5. Remove control rod from shift lever.
6. Disconnect all cables and electrical connectors from transmission case.
7. Remove propeller shaft. **Install a plug in extension housing rear opening to prevent fluid spillage.**
8. Remove clutch operating cylinder from clutch housing.
9. Using a suitable jack support engine with a wooden block placed between oil pan and jack. **Do not place jack under oil pan drain plug.**
10. Place transmission control lever in Neutral, then remove E-ring and control lever.
11. Remove rear engine mount and crossmember attaching bolts.
12. Remove starting motor.
13. Remove bolts attaching transmission to engine, then move transmission rearward and lower from vehicle.
14. Reverse procedure to install.

MAXIMA

1. Disconnect battery cables, then remove battery and battery support bracket from vehicle as necessary.
2. Remove air cleaner assembly and air flow meter, as necessary.
3. Raise and support vehicle.
4. Remove both front propeller shafts. **When disconnecting driveshafts, use care not to damage oil seals. After disconnecting driveshafts, insert a suitable bar so that side gears will not rotate and fall into differential case.**
5. Disconnect control and support rods from transmission as necessary.
6. Remove front exhaust pipe attaching bolts.
7. Disconnect all cables and electrical connectors from transaxle.
8. Using a suitable jack, support engine with a wooden block placed between oil pan and jack.
9. Remove starter motor, as necessary.
10. Remove engine mount attaching bolts.
11. Remove engine-to-transaxle attaching bolts, then separate engine from transaxle and lower transaxle assembly from vehicle.
12. Reverse procedure to install.

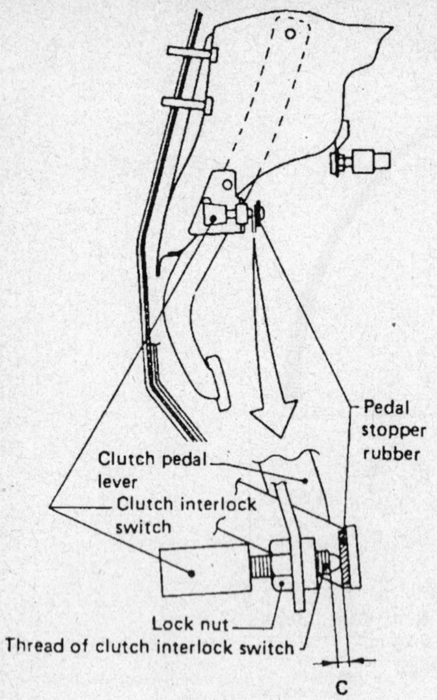
Pedal stopper rubber
Clutch pedal lever
Clutch interlock switch
Lock nut
Thread of clutch interlock switch
C

NS5049100024000X

Fig. 5 Clutch interlock switch adjustment

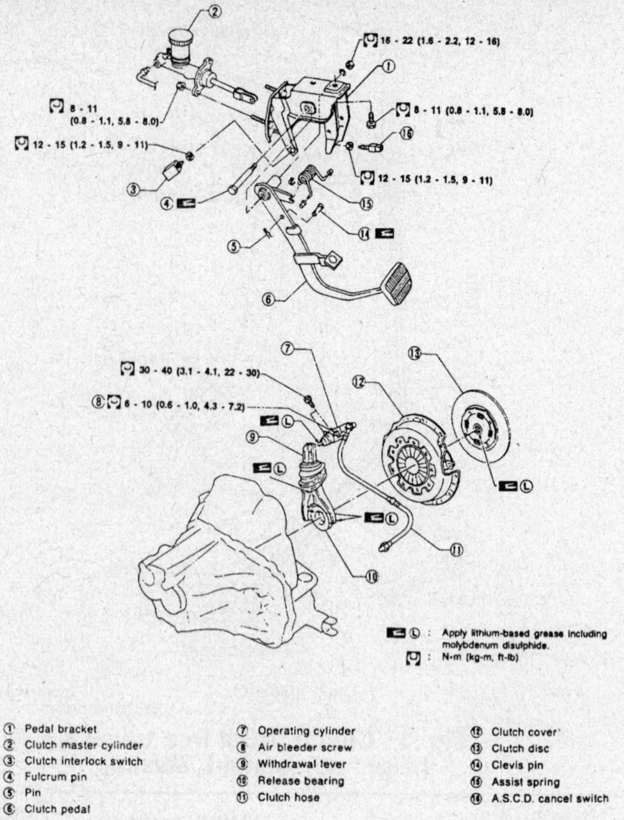
16 - 22 (1.6 - 2.2, 12 - 16)
8 - 11 (0.8 - 1.1, 5.8 - 8.0)
8 - 11 (0.8 - 1.1, 5.8 - 8.0)
12 - 15 (1.2 - 1.5, 9 - 11)
12 - 15 (1.2 - 1.5, 9 - 11)
30 - 40 (3.1 - 4.1, 22 - 30)
6 - 10 (0.6 - 1.0, 4.3 - 7.2)
Apply lithium-based grease including molybdenum disulphide.
N·m (kg-m, ft-lb)
① Pedal bracket
② Clutch master cylinder
③ Clutch interlock switch
④ Fulcrum pin
⑤ Pin
⑥ Clutch pedal
⑦ Operating cylinder
⑧ Air bleeder screw
⑨ Withdrawal lever
⑩ Release bearing
⑪ Clutch hose
⑫ Clutch cover
⑬ Clutch disc
⑭ Clevis pin
⑮ Assist spring
⑯ A.S.C.D. cancel switch

NS5049100025000X

Fig. 6 Exploded view of clutch assembly. Maxima

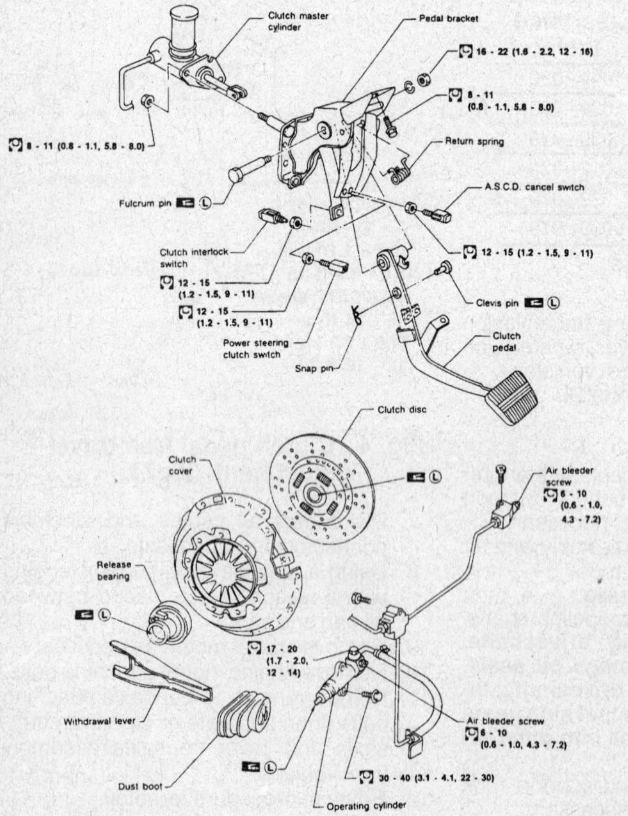
Clutch master cylinder
Pedal bracket
16 - 22 (1.6 - 2.2, 12 - 16)
8 - 11 (0.8 - 1.1, 5.8 - 8.0)
8 - 11 (0.8 - 1.1, 5.8 - 8.0)
Return spring
A.S.C.D. cancel switch
Fulcrum pin
Clutch interlock switch
12 - 15 (1.2 - 1.5, 9 - 11)
12 - 15 (1.2 - 1.5, 9 - 11)
12 - 15 (1.2 - 1.5, 9 - 11)
Power steering clutch switch
Snap pin
Clevis pin
Clutch pedal
Clutch disc
Clutch cover
Air bleeder screw
6 - 10 (0.6 - 1.0, 4.3 - 7.2)
Release bearing
17 - 20 (1.7 - 2.0, 12 - 14)
Withdrawal lever
Air bleeder screw
6 - 10 (0.6 - 1.0, 4.3 - 7.2)
Dust boot
30 - 40 (3.1 - 4.1, 22 - 30)
Operating cylinder
N·m (kg-m, ft-lb)
Apply lithium-based grease including molybdenum disulphide

NS5049100026000X

Fig. 7 Exploded view of clutch assembly. 300ZX w/VG30DE engine

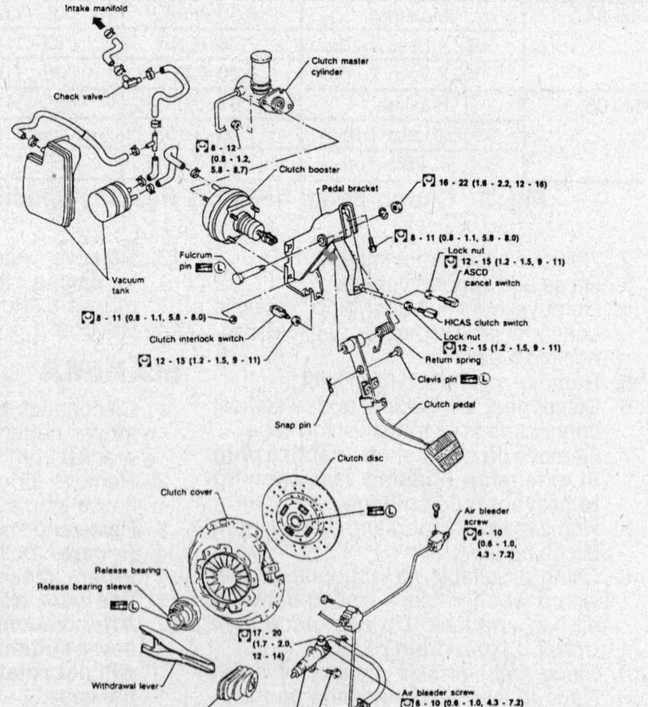
Intake manifold
Check valve
Clutch master cylinder
8 - 12 (0.8 - 1.2, 5.8 - 8.7)
Clutch booster
Pedal bracket
16 - 22 (1.6 - 2.2, 12 - 16)
8 - 11 (0.8 - 1.1, 5.8 - 8.0)
Lock nut
12 - 15 (1.2 - 1.5, 9 - 11)
ASCD cancel switch
Fulcrum pin
Vacuum tank
8 - 11 (0.8 - 1.1, 5.8 - 8.0)
Clutch interlock switch
12 - 15 (1.2 - 1.5, 9 - 11)
HICAS clutch switch
Lock nut
12 - 15 (1.2 - 1.5, 9 - 11)
Return spring
Clevis pin
Clutch pedal
Snap pin
Clutch disc
Clutch cover
Air bleeder screw
6 - 10 (0.6 - 1.0, 4.3 - 7.2)
Release bearing
Release bearing sleeve
17 - 20 (1.7 - 2.0, 12 - 14)
Withdrawal lever
Air bleeder screw
6 - 10 (0.6 - 1.0, 4.3 - 7.2)
Dust boot
30 - 40 (3.1 - 4.1, 22 - 30)
Operating cylinder
N·m (kg-m, ft-lb)
Apply lithium-based grease including molybdenum disulphide.

NS5049100027000X

Fig. 8 Exploded view of clutch assembly. 300ZX w/VG30DETT engine

TIGHTENING SPECIFICATIONS

Year	Component	Torque/Ft. Lbs.
1993–96	Air Bleeder Screw	4–7
	Clutch Cover Assembly Attaching Bolts	①
	Clutch Interlock Switch Locknut	9–11
	Clutch Switch	9–11
	Clutch Tube Flare Nuts	11–13
	Flywheel Bolts	61–69
	Master Cylinder Attaching Nuts	6–8
	Master Cylinder Pushrod Locknut	6–8
	Pedal Stopper Locknut	12–16
	Slave Cylinder Attaching Bolts	22–30
	Supply Valve Stopper	12–24②

①— 300ZX, 25–33 ft. lbs.; Maxima, 16–22 ft. lbs.
②— Inch lbs.

Rear Axle & Suspension

INDEX

	Page No.
Hub & Bearing, Replace	31-39
Maxima	31-39
Knuckle, Replace	31-41
300ZX	31-41
Rear Axle, Replace	31-39
Maxima	31-39
300ZX	31-39
Rear Halfshaft, Replace	31-39
300ZX	31-39
Rear Suspension, Replace	31-39
300ZX	31-39
Stabilizer Bar, Replace	31-41
Strut Service	31-40
Strut, Replace	31-40
Maxima	31-40
300ZX	31-40
Tightening Specifications	31-47

REAR AXLE

REPLACE

MAXIMA

1993-94

1. Raise and support vehicle. **Do not raise vehicle at parallel links or radius rods.**
2. Disconnect brake hydraulic line and parking brake cable at equalizer.
3. Remove parallel link fixing bolt and radius rod fixing bolt, **Fig. 1.**
4. Remove stabilizer fixing bolt, stabilizer connecting rod brackets and parking brake cable fixing bolts.
5. Remove rear shelf and seat.
6. Remove strut securing nuts, then the strut assembly.
7. Reverse procedure to install.

1995-96

Removal

1. Raise and support vehicle, then disconnect ABS wheel sensor, **Fig. 2.**
2. Remove brake caliper assemblies and suspend with wire, then the rotors.
3. Support torsion beam with suitable transmission jack, then raise slightly and remove suspension attaching nuts and bolts.
4. Remove luggage compartment trim, then upper strut mounting nuts and strut assembly.

Installation

1. Temporarily attach torsion beam to vehicle.
2. Place lateral link and control rod horizontally against torsion beam, then tighten lateral link bolts to specifications.
3. Attach shock absorber to vehicle, then tighten lower shock absorber nut to specifications.
4. Tighten torsion beam to specifications with suspension in full rebound position.

300ZX

Refer to **Figs. 3 and 4** for replacement, noting following:

1. Disconnect parking brake cable, then remove brake caliper assembly.
2. Remove rear exhaust pipe.
3. Remove upper strut attaching bolts.
4. Disconnect propeller shaft.
5. Remove suspension attaching nuts, then the rear suspension assembly.
6. Reverse procedure to install.

REAR HALFSHAFT

REPLACE

300ZX

1. Raise and support vehicle, then remove rear wheels.
2. Remove wheel bearing attaching nut, then the side flange attaching nuts and bolts.
3. Remove driveshafts by lightly tapping inward on shafts with a copper hammer.

HUB & BEARING

REPLACE

MAXIMA

1. Raise and support vehicle, then remove rear wheel.
2. Remove rear caliper assembly and support with wire.
3. Remove rear wheel bearing locknut, **Fig. 5.**
4. Remove rear wheel hub bearing.
5. Reverse procedure to install, ensure wheel bearing axial endplay is .0020 inch or less.

REAR SUSPENSION

REPLACE

300ZX

1. Before removal of lower arm mark adjusting pin for reference when installing.
2. Refer to "Rear Axle, Replace" for removal of lower arm.
3. Check ball joint for swing force, turning torque, then vertical endplay as shown in **Fig. 6.**
4. If any of ball joint checks are not within specifications, replace lower arm and ball joint as an assembly.

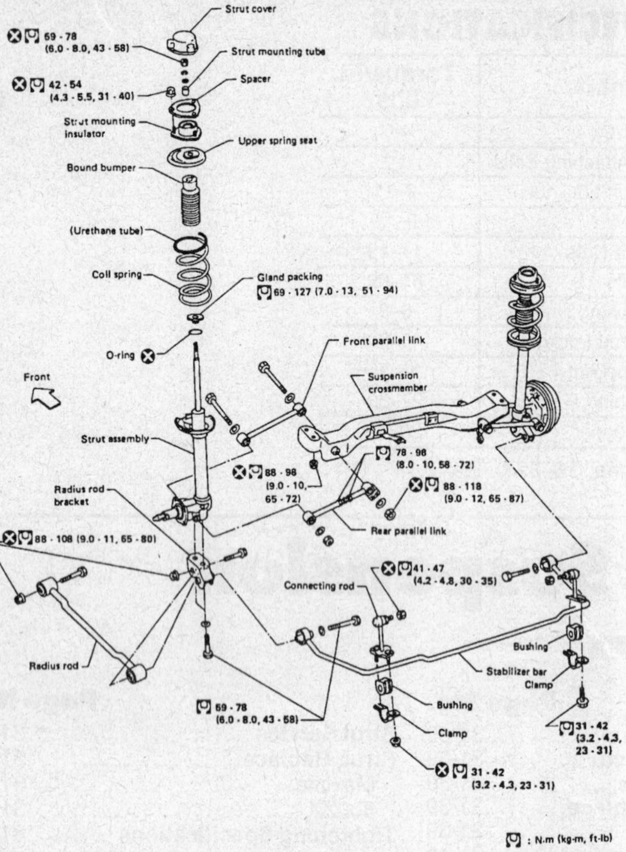
Strut cover
69 - 78 (6.0 - 8.0, 43 - 58)
Strut mounting tube
Spacer
42 - 54 (4.3 - 5.5, 31 - 40)
Strut mounting insulator
Upper spring seat
Bound bumper
(Urethane tube)
Coil spring
Gland packing
69 - 127 (7.0 - 13, 51 - 94)
O-ring
Front
Front parallel link
Suspension crossmember
Strut assembly
78 - 96 (8.0 - 10, 58 - 72)
88 - 98 (9.0 - 10, 65 - 72)
88 - 118 (9.0 - 12, 65 - 87)
Radius rod bracket
Rear parallel link
88 - 108 (9.0 - 11, 65 - 80)
41 - 47 (4.2 - 4.8, 30 - 35)
Connecting rod
Bushing
Radius rod
Stabilizer bar
Clamp
Bushing
69 - 78 (6.0 - 8.0, 43 - 58)
Clamp
31 - 42 (3.2 - 4.3, 23 - 31)
31 - 42 (3.2 - 4.3, 23 - 31)
: N·m (kg-m, ft-lb)
NS2039100004000X

Fig. 1 Exploded view of rear suspension. 1993–94 Maxima

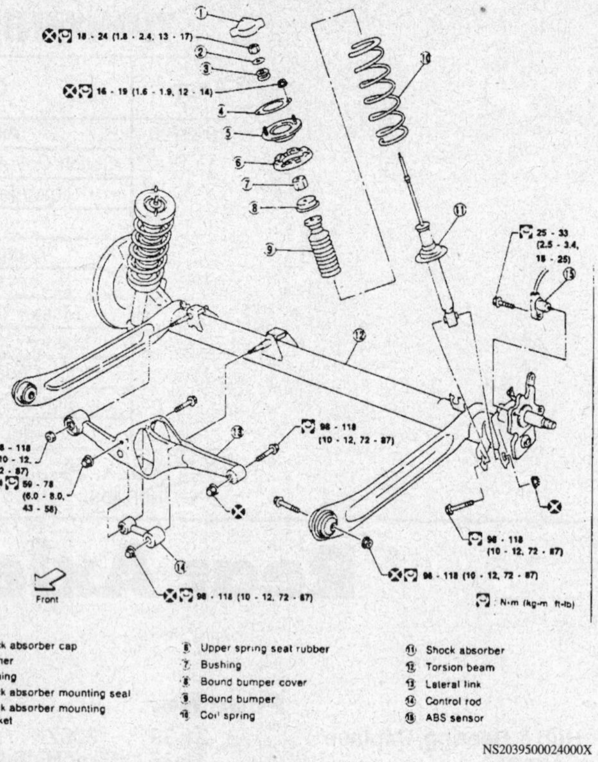
18 - 24 (1.8 - 2.4, 13 - 17)
16 - 19 (1.6 - 1.9, 12 - 14)
25 - 33 (2.5 - 3.4, 18 - 25)
98 - 118 (10 - 12, 72 - 87)
98 - 118 (10 - 12, 72 - 87)
59 - 78 (6.0 - 8.0, 43 - 58)
98 - 118 (10 - 12, 72 - 87)
98 - 118 (10 - 12, 72 - 87)
98 - 118 (10 - 12, 72 - 87)
Front
: N·m (kg-m, ft-lb)
① Shock absorber cap
② Washer
③ Bushing
④ Shock absorber mounting seal
⑤ Shock absorber mounting bracket
⑥ Upper spring seat rubber
⑦ Bushing
⑧ Bound bumper cover
⑨ Bound bumper
⑩ Coil spring
⑪ Shock absorber
⑫ Torsion beam
⑬ Lateral link
⑭ Control rod
⑮ ABS sensor
NS2039500024000X

Fig. 2 Exploded view of rear suspension. 1995–96 Maxima

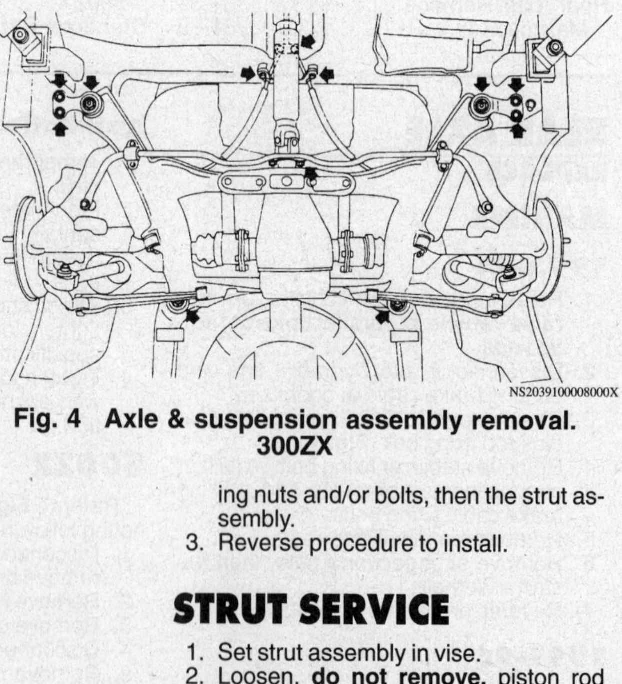
NS2039100008000X

Fig. 4 Axle & suspension assembly removal. 300ZX

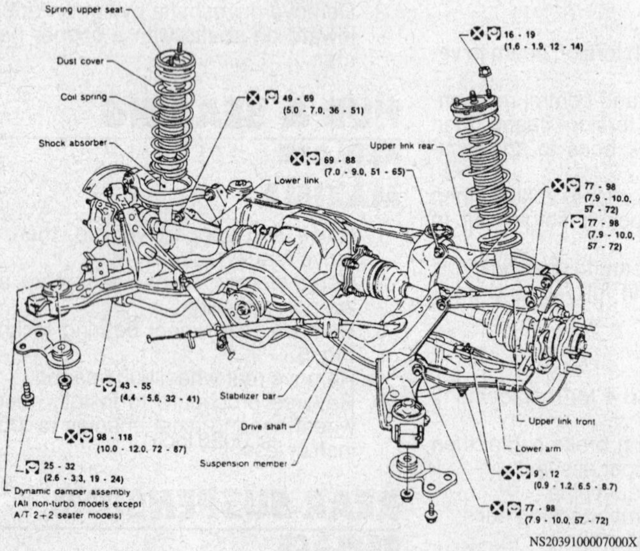
Spring upper seat
Dust cover
Coil spring
Shock absorber
16 - 19 (1.6 - 1.9, 12 - 14)
49 - 69 (5.0 - 7.0, 36 - 51)
Upper link rear
69 - 88 (7.0 - 9.0, 51 - 65)
Lower link
77 - 98 (7.9 - 10.0, 57 - 72)
77 - 98 (7.9 - 10.0, 57 - 72)
43 - 55 (4.4 - 5.6, 32 - 41)
Stabilizer bar
Drive shaft
98 - 118 (10.0 - 12.0, 72 - 87)
25 - 32 (2.6 - 3.3, 19 - 24)
Suspension member
Upper link front
Lower arm
9 - 12 (0.9 - 1.2, 6.5 - 8.7)
77 - 98 (7.9 - 10.0, 57 - 72)
Dynamic damper assembly (All non-turbo models except A/T 2+2 seater models)
NS2039100007000X

Fig. 3 Rear suspension. 300ZX

STRUT

REPLACE

MAXIMA

1. Remove rear axle as outlined in "Rear Axle, Replace."
2. Remove strut from rear axle.
3. Reverse procedure to install.

300ZX

1. Raise and support vehicle.
2. Remove upper and lower strut attaching nuts and/or bolts, then the strut assembly.
3. Reverse procedure to install.

STRUT SERVICE

1. Set strut assembly in vise.
2. Loosen, **do not remove,** piston rod locknut.
3. Compress spring using suitable spring compressor tool until strut upper spring seat can be turned by hand.
4. Remove piston locknut.
5. Remove strut assembly components.
6. Reverse procedure to assemble, noting following:

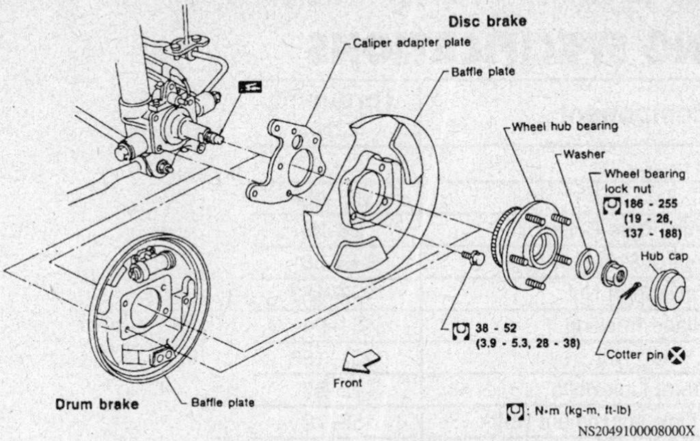
Disc brake
Caliper adapter plate
Baffle plate
Wheel hub bearing
Washer
Wheel bearing lock nut
186 - 255 (19 - 26, 137 - 188)
Hub cap
38 - 52 (3.9 - 5.3, 28 - 38)
Cotter pin
Front
Drum brake
Baffle plate
: N·m (kg-m, ft-lb)
NS2049100008000X

Fig. 5 Wheel hub assembly. Maxima

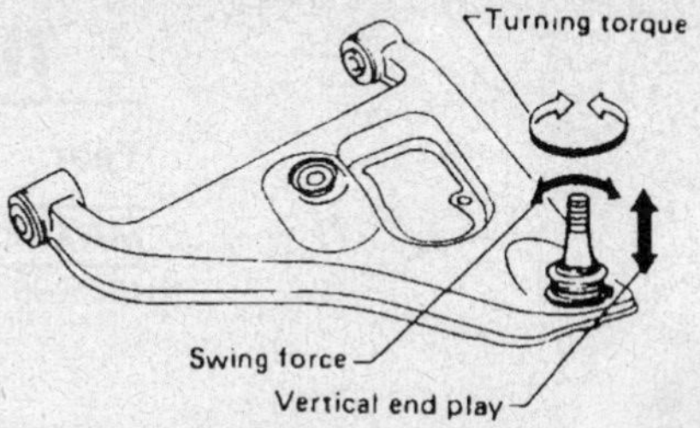
Turning torque
Swing force
Vertical end play

Ball joint specifications	Swing force	7.8 - 54.9 N (0.8 - 5.6 kg, 1.8 - 12.3 lb)
	Turning torque	0.5 - 3.4 N·m (5 - 35 kg-cm, 4.3 - 30.4 in-lb)
	Vertical end play	0 mm (0 in)

NS2049100015000X

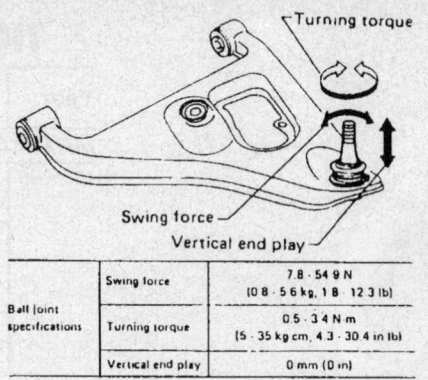

Fig. 6 Lower ball joint inspection. 300ZX

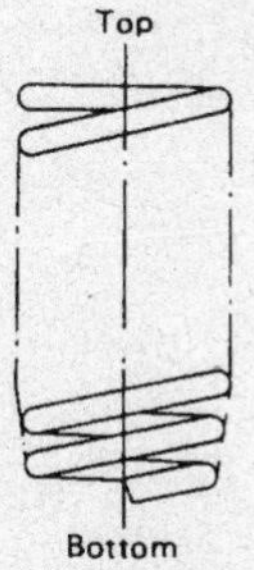
Top
Bottom
NS2049100013000X

Fig. 7 Top & bottom spring position identification

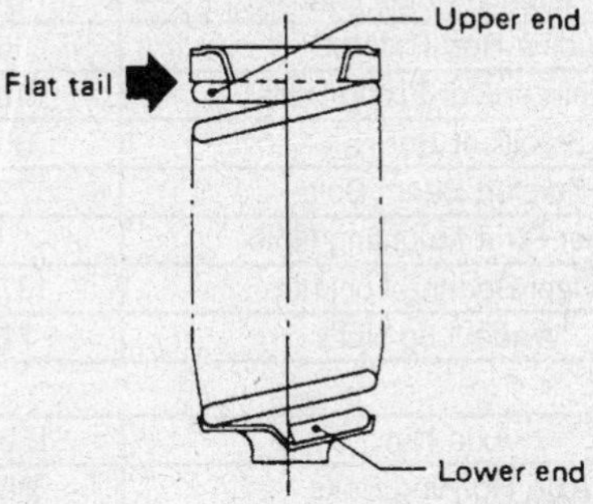
Upper end
Flat tail
Lower end
NS2049100014000X

Fig. 8 Spring installation position

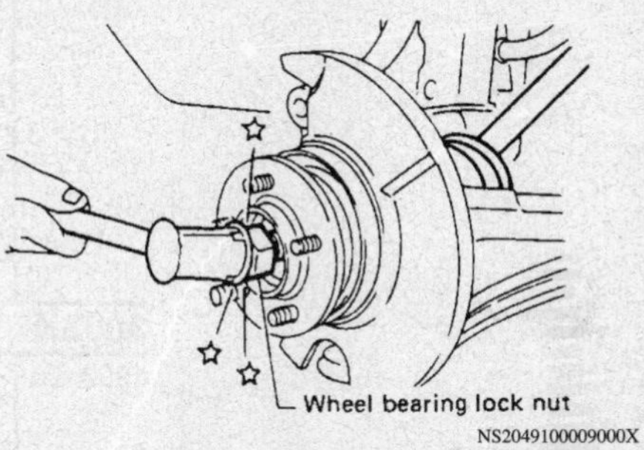
Wheel bearing lock nut
NS2049100009000X

Fig. 9 Driveshaft removal. 300ZX

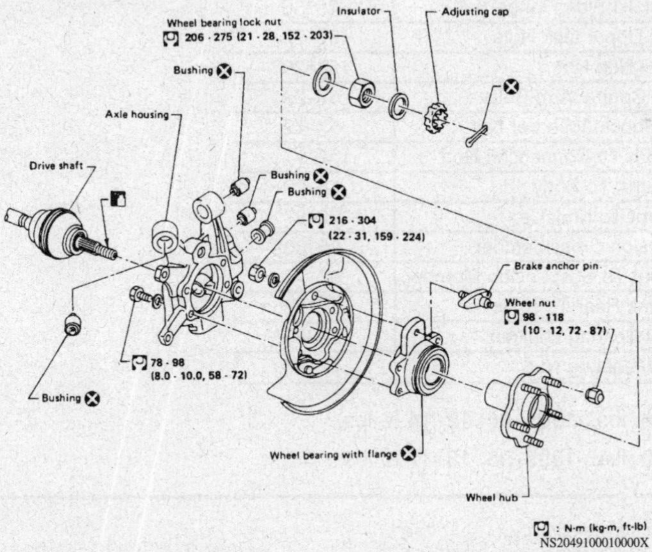
Insulator
Adjusting cap
Wheel bearing lock nut
206 - 275 (21 - 28, 152 - 203)
Bushing
Axle housing
Drive shaft
Bushing
Bushing
216 - 304 (22 - 31, 159 - 224)
Brake anchor pin
Wheel nut
98 - 118 (10 - 12, 72 - 87)
78 - 98 (8.0 - 10.0, 58 - 72)
Bushing
Wheel bearing with flange
Wheel hub
: N·m (kg-m, ft-lb)
NS2049100010000X

Fig. 10 Exploded view of wheel hub & axle housing assembly. 300ZX

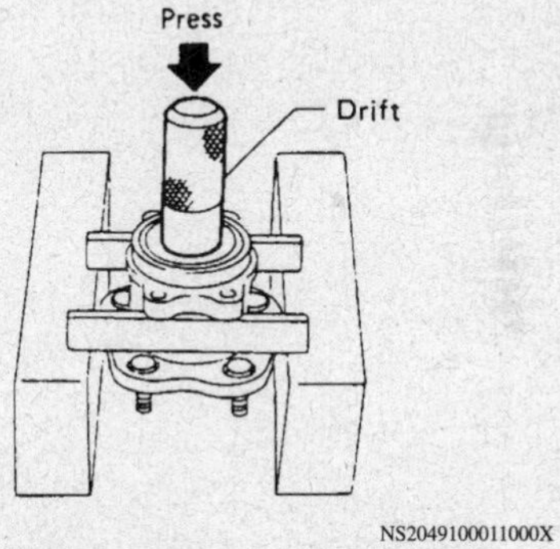
Press
Drift
NS2049100011000X

Fig. 11 Wheel bearing installation. 300ZX

8. Reverse procedure to install, noting following:
   a. Install wheel bearing as shown in **Fig. 11.**
   b. Ensure wheel bearing axial end-play is .0020 inch or less.

a. When installing coil spring, use care not to reverse top and bottom direction, **Fig. 7.**
b. When installing spring on strut, position as shown in **Fig. 8.**

KNUCKLE

REPLACE

300ZX

1. Raise and support vehicle.
2. Remove wheel bearing locknut.
3. Remove brake caliper assembly and support by frame using suitable wire.
4. Separate driveshaft from axle housing (knuckle) by slightly tapping with a suitable soft face hammer, **Fig. 9.**
5. Remove axle housing attaching bolts then axle housing, **Fig. 10.**
6. Remove wheel bearing with flange and wheel hub from axle housing.
7. Using a suitable press, press off wheel bearing from wheel hub.

STABILIZER BAR

REPLACE

1. Raise and support vehicle.
2. Remove exhaust assembly as necessary.
3. Disconnect stabilizer bar from bushing brackets and locating bolts, then remove stabilizer bar.
4. Reverse procedure to install.

TIGHTENING SPECIFICATIONS

Year	Component	Torque/Ft. Lbs.
MAXIMA		
1993–96	Axle Nut	137–188
	Baffle Plate Bolts	28–38
	Control Rod Bolt	43–58
	Driveshaft Nut	137–188
	Gland Packing	51–94
	Hub Nut	137–188
	Lateral Link Bolts	72–87
	Parallel Link Adjustment Nut	58–72
	Parallel Link Fixing Bolt	65–87
	Piston Rod Locknut	②
	Radius Rod Fixing Bolt	65–80
	Stabilizer Bar Fixing Bolts	43–58
	Stabilizer Bar Nuts	30–35
	Torsion Beam Bolt	72–87
	Upper Strut Mounting Nuts	①
	Wheel Bearing Locknut	137–188
	Wheel Lug Nut	72–87
300ZX		
1993–96	Axle Nut	152–203
	Axle Housing Bolts	58–72
	Brake Anchor Pin Nut	159–224
	Driveshaft Nut	152–203
	Driveshaft To Side Flange Bolt	25–33
	Front Upper Link Nuts	57–72
	Hub Nut	152–203
	Lower Control Arm Bolts	57–72
	Lower Shock Absorber Nut	57–72
	Stabilizer Bar To Connecting Rod	7–9
	Strut To Body	18–22
	Strut To Knuckle	72–87
	Suspension Crossmember	65–80
	Upper Link Front To Suspension Member	57–72
	Upper Link Rear To Knuckle	57–72
	Wheel Bearing Locknut	152–203
	Wheel Lug Nut	72–87

① — 1993–94, 31–40 ft. lbs.; 1995–96, 12–14 ft. lbs.

② — 1993–94, 43–58 ft. lbs.; 1995–96, 13–17 ft. lbs.

Front Suspension & Steering

INDEX

	Page No.
Ball Joint, Replace	31-43
Maxima	31-43
Ball Joint Inspection	31-43
Hub & Bearing, Replace	31-43
300ZX	31-43
Manual Steering Gears	36-1
Power Steering	36-1
Power Steering Gear, Replace	31-44
Maxima	31-44
300ZX	31-44
Power Steering Pump, Replace	31-44
Stabilizer Bar, Replace	31-44
Strut, Replace	31-43
Maxima	31-43
300ZX	31-44
Tightening Specifications	31-47
Transverse Link, Replace	31-44
Maxima	31-44
300ZX	31-44
Wheel Bearing, Adjust	31-43
300ZX	31-43
Wheel Hub & Steering Knuckle, Replace	31-43
Maxima	31-43

WHEEL BEARING

ADJUST

300ZX

1. Raise and support vehicle.
2. Remove brake pads.
3. Ensure wheel bearing is tightened to correct specification.
4. Ensure wheel bearing operates smoothly.
5. Using a dial indicator, check axial endplay.
6. If axial endplay is more than .0020 inch, replace wheel bearing.

HUB & BEARING

REPLACE

300ZX

1. Raise and support vehicle, remove wheels.
2. Remove caliper without disconnecting brake line.
3. Using ball joint remover tool No. HT72750000, or equivalent, remove tie-rod ball joint and lower ball joint from steering knuckle.
4. Remove kingpin lower attaching nut, then the steering knuckle assembly.
5. Reverse procedure to install.

WHEEL HUB & STEERING KNUCKLE

REPLACE

MAXIMA

1. Raise and support vehicle, then remove wheels.
2. Remove wheel bearing locknut, **Figs. 1 and 2.**
3. Remove brake caliper. **Do not disconnect brake lines.**
4. Separate tie-rod from knuckle using suitable tool.
5. Remove nuts and bolts as shown in **Fig. 3,** then knuckle assembly.
6. Reverse procedure to install, noting following:
   a. Tighten wheel bearing to specifications.
   b. Ensure wheel bearing axial endplay is not more than .0020 inches.

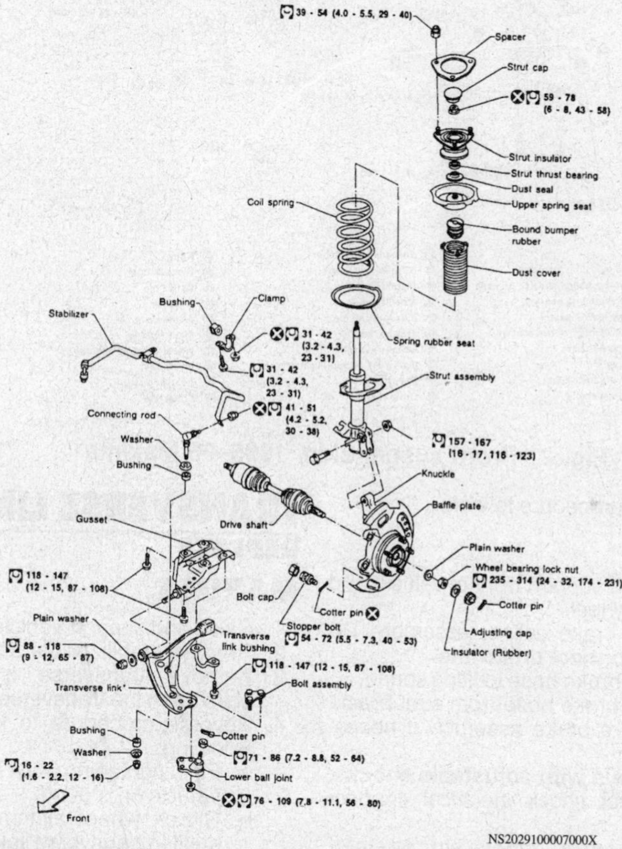

39 - 54 (4.0 - 5.5, 29 - 40)
Spacer
Strut cap
59 - 78
(6 - 8, 43 - 58)
Strut insulator
Strut thrust bearing
Dust seal
Upper spring seat
Bound bumper rubber
Dust cover
Coil spring
Bushing
Clamp
Stabilizer
31 - 42
(3.2 - 4.3,
23 - 31)
Spring rubber seat
31 - 42
(3.2 - 4.3,
23 - 31)
Strut assembly
41 - 51
(4.2 - 5.2,
30 - 38)
Connecting rod
Washer
Bushing
157 - 167
(16 - 17, 116 - 123)
Knuckle
Baffle plate
Gusset
Drive shaft
Plain washer
Wheel bearing lock nut
235 - 314 (24 - 32, 174 - 231)
118 - 147
(12 - 15, 87 - 108)
Bolt cap
Cotter pin
Cotter pin
Plain washer
Stopper bolt
54 - 72 (5.5 - 7.3, 40 - 53)
Adjusting cap
Transverse link bushing
88 - 118
(9 - 12, 65 - 87)
Insulator (Rubber)
118 - 147 (12 - 15, 87 - 108)
Bolt assembly
Transverse link*
Bushing
Cotter pin
Washer
71 - 86 (7.2 - 8.8, 52 - 64)
16 - 22
(1.6 - 2.2, 12 - 16)
Lower ball joint
76 - 109 (7.8 - 11.1, 56 - 80)
Front
NS2029100007000X

Fig. 1 Front suspension. 1993–94 Maxima

BALL JOINT INSPECTION

Check ball joint for play. If ball stud is worn, play in axial direction (C) is more than zero inches, ball joint swing force (A) is not 1.8–12.3 lbs. or ball joint turning torque (B) is not 4.3–30.4 inch lbs., replace ball joint, **Fig. 4.** Before checking, turn ball joint at least 10 revolutions.

BALL JOINT

REPLACE

MAXIMA

1. Remove driveshaft as outlined under "Driveshaft Replace" in "Front Wheel Drive" section, as necessary.
2. Remove ball joint attaching nuts/bolts and ball joint.
3. Reverse procedure to install.

STRUT

REPLACE

MAXIMA

1. Raise and support front of vehicle and remove wheel.
2. Disconnect brake line from strut.
3. Remove strut to steering knuckle attaching bolts, then separate strut from knuckle.
4. Remove strut to strut tower attaching nuts, then the strut assembly from vehicle.

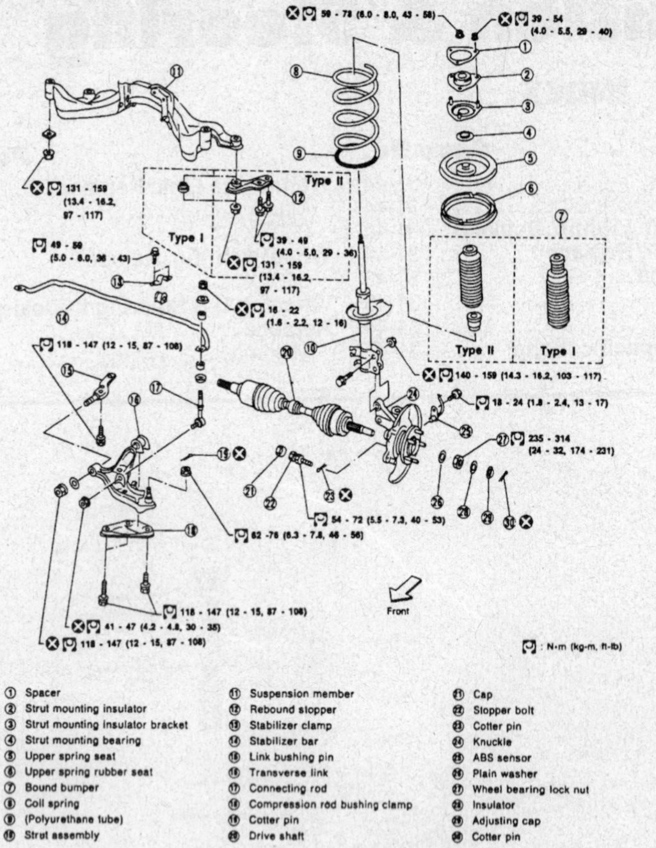
Type I
Type II
Front
: N·m (kg-m, ft-lb)
① Spacer
② Strut mounting insulator
③ Strut mounting insulator bracket
④ Strut mounting bearing
⑤ Upper spring seat
⑥ Upper spring rubber seat
⑦ Bound bumper
⑧ Coil spring
⑨ (Polyurethane tube)
⑩ Strut assembly
⑪ Suspension member
⑫ Rebound stopper
⑬ Stabilizer clamp
⑭ Stabilizer bar
⑮ Link bushing pin
⑯ Transverse link
⑰ Connecting rod
⑱ Compression rod bushing clamp
⑲ Cotter pin
⑳ Drive shaft
㉑ Cap
㉒ Stopper bolt
㉓ Cotter pin
㉔ Knuckle
㉕ ABS sensor
㉖ Plain washer
㉗ Wheel bearing lock nut
㉘ Insulator
㉙ Adjusting cap
㉚ Cotter pin

NS2029500031000X

Fig. 2 Front suspension. 1995–96 Maxima

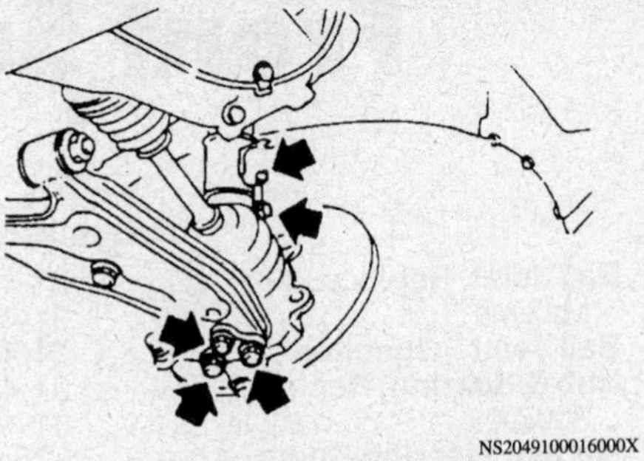

NS2049100016000X

Fig. 3 Knuckle assembly removal. Maxima

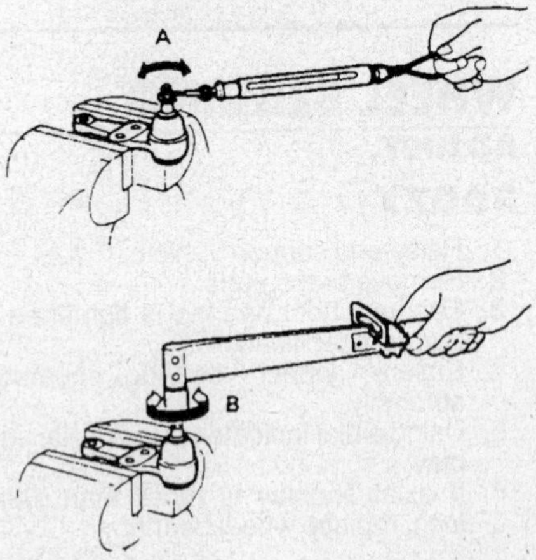
A
B

NS2029100012000X

Fig. 4 Ball joint inspection

5. Reverse procedure to install.

300ZX

1. Raise and support front of vehicle and remove wheel.
2. Remove brake caliper assembly. **Do not disconnect brake line.**
3. Remove brake hose locking spring.
4. Remove brake hose from strut bracket, remove brake assembly if necessary.
5. **On models with adjustable shocks,** disconnect shock electrical connectors.
6. **On all models,** remove strut to steering knuckle attaching bolts, **Fig. 5.**
7. Disconnect knuckle arm from bottom of strut.
8. Remove strut to strut tower attaching nuts, then the strut.
9. Reverse procedure to install.

STABILIZER BAR

REPLACE

1. Raise and support vehicle.
2. Remove stabilizer bar attaching bolts, **Figs. 6 through 8,** then stabilizer bar.
3. Reverse procedure to install, noting following:
   a. When installing bar make sure paint mark and clamp face is in their correct position, **Fig. 9.**
   b. **On Maxima models,** install stabilizer bar with ball joint sockets positioned as shown in **Fig. 10.**

TRANSVERSE LINK

REPLACE

MAXIMA

1. Raise and support vehicle.
2. Remove stabilizer bar attaching bolts.
3. Remove transverse link attaching bolts, then the transverse link.
4. Reverse procedure to install, noting following:
   a. Final tightening must be made with vehicle on ground.
   b. Check wheel alignment after installing transverse link.

300ZX

1. Raise and support vehicle and remove wheels.
2. Remove tension rod and stabilizer bar, **Fig. 5.**
3. Remove ball joint and transverse link mounting nut/bolts, then separate link from crossmember.
4. Reverse procedure to install.

POWER STEERING GEAR

REPLACE

MAXIMA

Refer to **Fig. 11** for power steering gear replacement procedure, noting following:

1. Detach tie rod ball studs from steering knuckle arms using suitable tool.
2. Remove exhaust pipe attaching nut.
3. Remove manual transaxle control linkage or automatic transaxle control cable as necessary.

300ZX

Refer to **Fig. 12** for power steering gear replacement procedure, noting following.

1. When removing power steering hoses plug ports and lines.
2. Set wheels straight ahead before removing lower joint.
3. After removing lower joint put matching mark on pinion shaft and pinion housing.

POWER STEERING PUMP

REPLACE

1. Loosen idler pulley locknut, turn adjusting nut counterclockwise, and remove power steering pump drive belt. **On some air conditioned models, remove air conditioning compressor drive belt.**
2. Loosen power steering hoses at pump and remove bolts securing power steering pump to brackets.
3. Raise pump and disconnect power steering hoses. Catch fluid in a suitable container, plug hose ends and ports in power steering pump, and remove pump from vehicle.

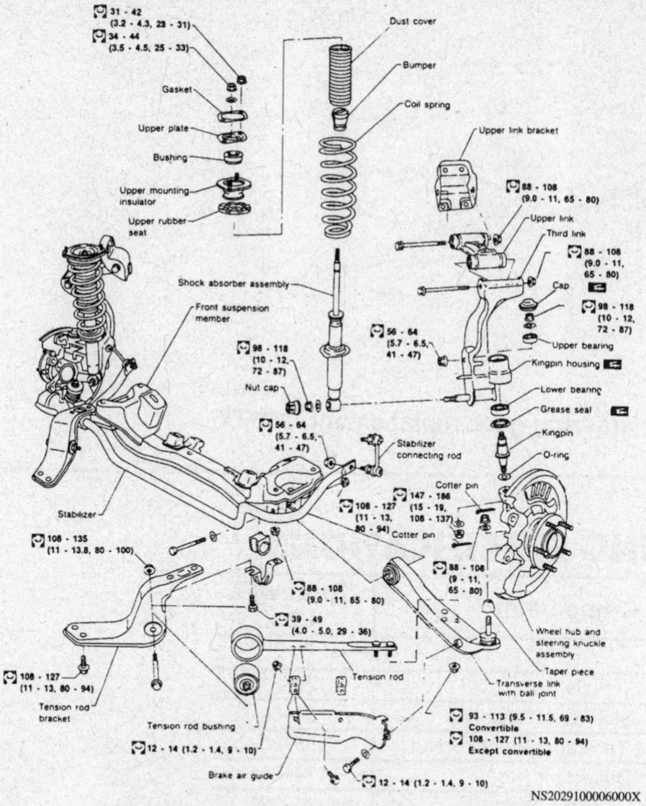
31 - 42 (3.2 - 4.3, 23 - 31)
34 - 44 (3.5 - 4.5, 25 - 33)
Gasket
Upper plate
Bushing
Upper mounting insulator
Upper rubber seat
Dust cover
Bumper
Coil spring
Upper link bracket
88 - 108 (9.0 - 11, 65 - 80)
Upper link
Third link
88 - 108 (9.0 - 11, 65 - 80)
Cap
98 - 118 (10 - 12, 72 - 87)
Upper bearing
Kingpin housing
Lower bearing
Grease seal
Kingpin
O-ring
Shock absorber assembly
Front suspension member
56 - 64 (5.7 - 6.5, 41 - 47)
98 - 118 (10 - 12, 72 - 87)
Nut cap
56 - 64 (5.7 - 6.5, 41 - 47)
Stabilizer connecting rod
Cotter pin
147 - 186 (15 - 19, 108 - 137)
108 - 127 (11 - 13, 80 - 94)
Cotter pin
Stabilizer
108 - 135 (11 - 13.8, 80 - 100)
88 - 108 (9 - 11, 65 - 80)
88 - 108 (9.0 - 11, 65 - 80)
39 - 49 (4.0 - 5.0, 29 - 36)
Wheel hub and steering knuckle assembly
Taper piece
Transverse link with ball joint
Tension rod
108 - 127 (11 - 13, 80 - 94)
Tension rod bracket
Tension rod bushing
12 - 14 (1.2 - 1.4, 9 - 10)
93 - 113 (9.5 - 11.5, 69 - 83) Convertible
108 - 127 (11 - 13, 80 - 94) Except convertible
Brake air guide
12 - 14 (1.2 - 1.4, 9 - 10)
NS2029100006000X

Fig. 5 Front suspension. 300ZX

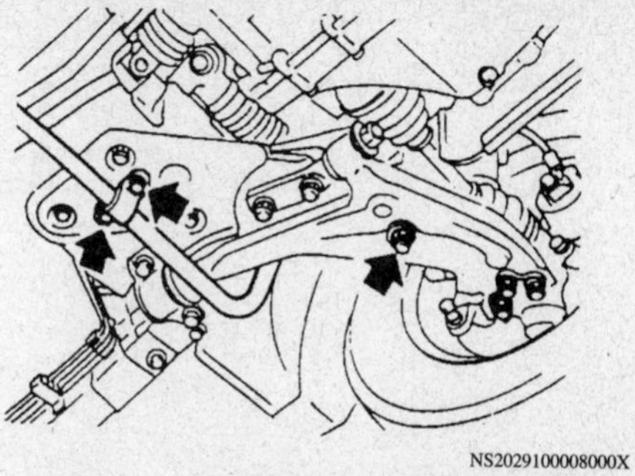
NS2029100008000X

Fig. 6 Stabilizer bar removal. 1993–94 Maxima

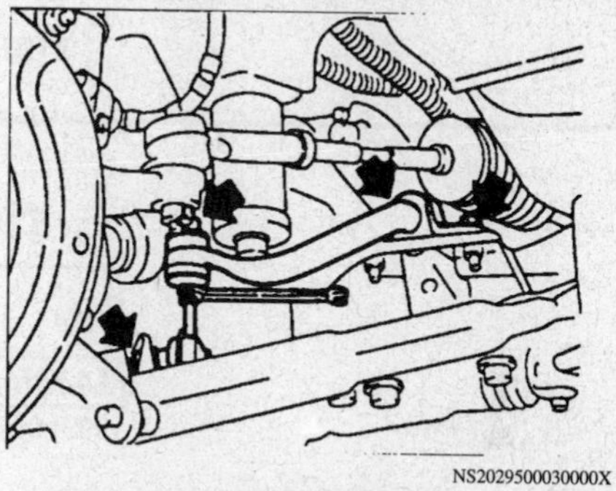
NS2029500030000X

Fig. 7 Stabilizer bar removal. 1995–96 Maxima

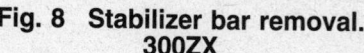

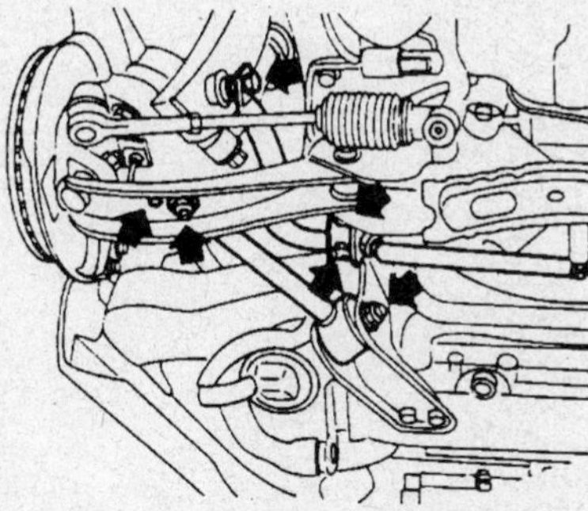
NS2029100009000X

Fig. 8 Stabilizer bar removal. 300ZX

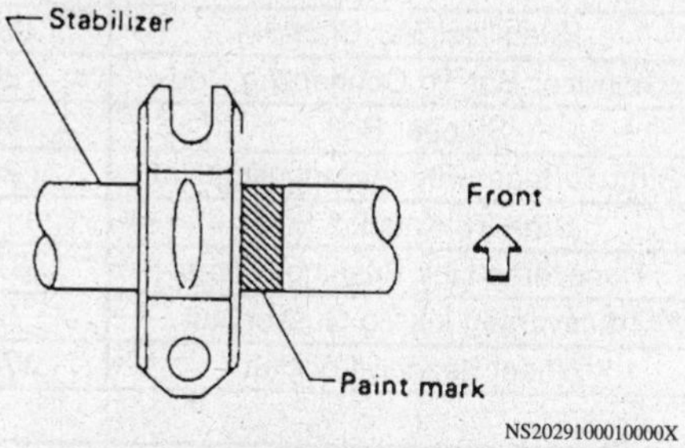
Stabilizer
Front
Paint mark
NS2029100010000X

Fig. 9 Stabilizer & bushing installation

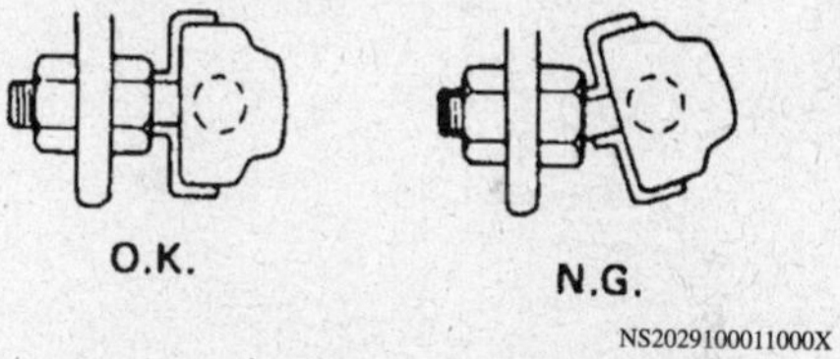
O.K.
N.G.
NS2029100011000X

Fig. 10 Ball joint positioning. Maxima

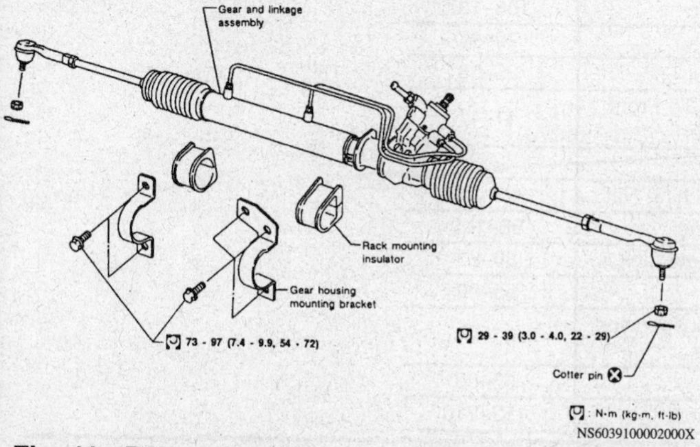
Gear and linkage assembly
Rack mounting insulator
Gear housing mounting bracket
73 - 97 (7.4 - 9.9, 54 - 72)
29 - 39 (3.0 - 4.0, 22 - 29)
Cotter pin
: N·m (kg-m, ft-lb)
NS6039100002000X

Fig. 11 Power steering gear replacement. Maxima

4. Reinstall power steering pump by reversing procedure and bleed system as follows:
   a. Raise and support front of vehicle.
   b. Run engine for 3–5 seconds, stop engine, check and fill power steering pump reservoir as needed.
   c. Quickly turn steering wheel all way to right and left 10 times.
   d. Start engine and idle for 3–5 seconds. Stop engine, check and fill power steering pump reservoir as needed.
   e. With steering wheel all way to right, open bleeder screw, to expel air and tighten bleeder screw.
   f. Repeat procedure until all air has been bled from system.
   g. If air cannot be bled completely after repeated attempts, repeat step e with engine running.

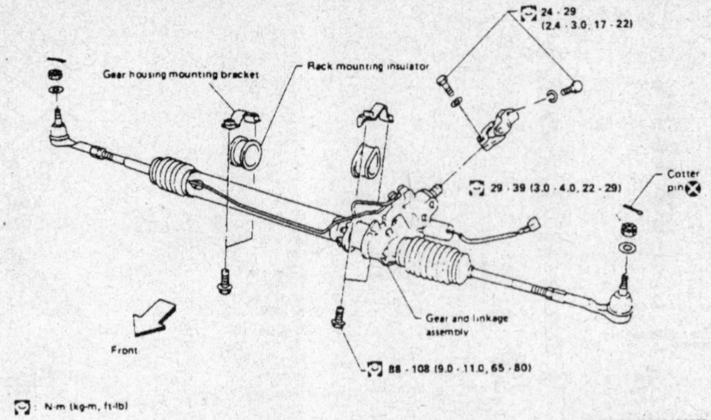
24 - 29
(2.4 - 3.0, 17 - 22)
Gear housing mounting bracket
Rack mounting insulator
29 - 39 (3.0 - 4.0, 22 - 29)
Cotter pin
Gear and linkage assembly
Front
88 - 108 (9.0 - 11.0, 65 - 80)
N·m (kg-m, ft-lb)

NS6039100001000X

Fig. 12 Power steering gear replacement. 300ZX

TIGHTENING SPECIFICATIONS

Year	Component	Torque/Ft. Lbs.
MAXIMA		
1993–96	Axle Nut	174–231
	Ball Joint To Knuckle Nut	52–64
	Ball Joint To Transverse Link Nut	56–80
	Driveshaft Nut	174–231
	Hub Nut	174–231
	Piston Rod Locknut	43–58
	Stabilizer Bar Clamp	23–31
	Stabilizer Bar To Connecting Rod	30–38
	Stopper Bolt	40–53
	Strut To Inner Fender Mounting Nut	29–40
	Strut To Knuckle Bolt	116–123
	Transverse Link Bushing Clamp	87–108
	Transverse Link To Gusset Nut	65–87
	Wheel Bearing Locknut	174–231
300ZX		
1993–96	Axle Nut	152–210
	Ball Joint To Knuckle	65–80
	Driveshaft Nut	152–210
	Hub Nut	152–210
	Kingpin Lower Nut	108–137
	Kingpin Upper Nut	72–87
	Piston Rod Locknut	25–33
	Stabilizer Connecting Rod To Front Suspension Member	41–47
	Strut Lower Nut	72–87
	Strut To Inner Fender Attaching Nut	23–31
	Tension Rod Bushing	80–100
	Tension Rod To Transverse Link	80–83
	Third Link Bolt	65–80
	Transverse Link To Front Suspension Member	80–94
	Upper Link Bolt	65–80
	Wheel Bearing Locknut	152–210

Wheel Alignment

INDEX

	Page No.
Front Wheel Alignment	31-47
Camber	31-47
Caster & Kingpin Inclination	31-47
Steering Angle	31-47
Toe Setting	31-47
Preliminary Inspection	31-47
Rear Wheel Alignment	31-47
Camber	31-47
Toe-In	31-48
Vehicle Ride Height	31-48
Wheel Alignment Specifications	31-3

PRELIMINARY INSPECTION

Prior to checking and adjusting wheel alignment angles, perform following checks:

1. Check tire pressures and adjust as needed.
2. Ensure tires are of proper size and are properly matched.
3. Ensure wheel bearings (front and rear) are properly adjusted.
4. Check steering gear for correct adjustment and that it is properly secured to frame.
5. Inspect steering linkage and suspension components for damage and wear, repair or replace components as needed.
6. Measure vehicle ride height with vehicle unloaded.
7. Place vehicle on suitable alignment rack following manufacturer's instructions, then jounce vehicle several times to settle suspension.
8. Check and correct rear wheel camber and toe first, if applicable, then check and correct front suspension angles in following order: caster and kingpin inclination, camber, toe setting and turning angle (toe-out on turns).

FRONT WHEEL ALIGNMENT

To ensure correct alignment, angles should be checked, and if necessary corrected, in following sequence: caster and kingpin inclination, camber, toe-setting, and turning angle and toe-out on turns. Front wheel alignment should only be checked after ensuring that rear wheels are properly aligned in relation to vehicle centerline, as most equipment uses rear wheels as reference for correct front wheel alignment. Front wheel alignment should be checked with vehicle at normal ride height, and following equipment manufacturer's instructions.

CASTER & KINGPIN INCLINATION

If caster or kingpin angle are not within specifications, check suspension components and sheet metal for damage, distortion and excessive wear, repair or replace components as necessary.

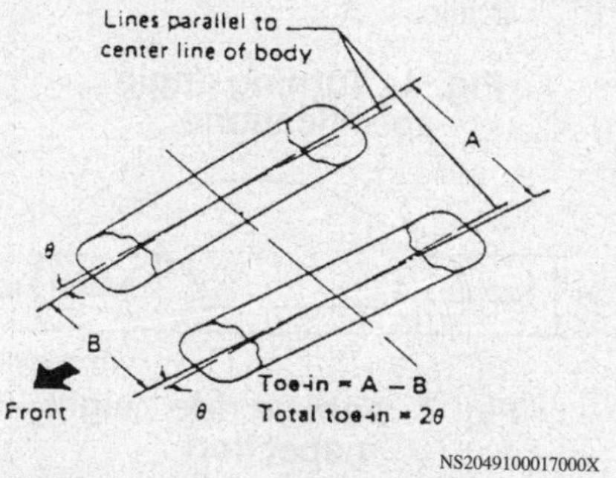

Lines parallel to center line of body
A
B
θ
Front
Toe-in = A – B
Total toe-in = 2θ
NS2049100017000X

Fig. 1 Toe-in measurement

CAMBER

Camber cannot be adjusted. If camber is not within specifications, inspect suspension and sheet metal for damage, distortion and excessive wear, repair or replace components as necessary.

TOE SETTING

Toe setting is measurement of wheels in relation to vehicle centerline, **Fig. 1.** Leading edge of each wheel should toe-in or toe-out slightly in relation to vehicle centerline to ensure proper vehicle tracking. Toe should be inspected using suitable alignment gauges, following manufacturer's instructions. When checking or adjusting toe, always ensure setting of left and right wheels is as equal as possible.

Toe is adjusted by loosening tie rod locknuts or adjusting sleeve bolts and equally altering length of tie rods. After toe has been adjusted to specifications, lengths of left and right tie rods, **Figs. 2 and 3,** should be nearly equal and close to length specified. Incorrect tie rod length will adversely affect steering angles and toe-out on turns.

STEERING ANGLE

When a vehicle negotiates a turn, inner wheel must turn at a sharper angle than outer wheel, and outer wheel must travel farther than inner wheel. Vehicle steering geometry is calculated to allow for these variations, causing outer wheel to toe-out by a calibrated amount. This toe-out on turns is also referred to as steering angle and on these models, is generally checked at two positions. first position is at a reference point on inner wheel travel while second position of measurement is at full steering lock. To check steering angles, proceed as follows:

1. Turn steering to full lock and measure inner and outer wheel turning angles.

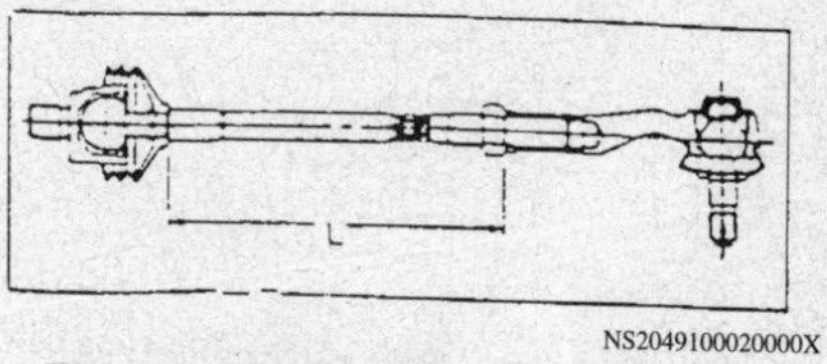

L
NS2049100020000X

Fig. 2 Typical tie rod length measurement

2. If "Turning Angles" at full lock are not within specifications, **Fig. 4,** check for damaged steering linkage or improperly adjusted tie rods.
3. If steering linkage and tie rods are satisfactory, check for improper rack or rack piston stroke and repair steering gear as needed.

REAR WHEEL ALIGNMENT

CAMBER

Rear camber cannot be adjusted. If rear camber is not within specifications, check for damaged or worn suspension components and deformed sheet metal, repair as necessary.

TOE-IN

On models with independent rear suspension, rear toe is measurement of rear wheels in relation to vehicle centerline, **Fig. 1.** leading edge of each rear wheel should toe-in slightly toward vehicle centerline to ensure proper vehicle tracking. Rear toe should be inspected using suitable alignment gauges, following manufacturer's instructions. When checking or adjusting rear toe, always ensure amount that left and right wheels toe-in is as equal as possible.

MAXIMA

1993–94

1. Measure total toe-in for each wheel following equipment manufacturer's instructions.
2. Loosen locknuts and adjust parallel link length to obtain specified toe-in, noting following:
   a. Adjust left and right rear parallel links to same length, **Fig. 5.**
   b. Standard length is 1.97–2.17 inches. If toe-in cannot be properly adjusted with links at equal lengths,

Year	Model	Standard Tie Rod Length Inch
1993	Maxima	7.05
	300ZX	6.10
1994	Maxima	6.81
	300ZX	6.10
1995–96	Maxima	7.98
	300ZX	6.10

Fig. 3 Tie rod length specifications

Year	Model	Turning Angle°①	
		Inner Wheel	Outer Wheel
1993–94	Maxima	35–39②	28–32②
	300ZX	32–36	26.5–30.5
1995–96	Maxima	27–41	28.7–32.7
	300ZX	32–36	26.5–30.5

① — At full lock.
② — On models with power steering with a turning force of 22–33 lbs. applied to rim of steering wheel @ idle.

Fig. 4 Turning angle specifications

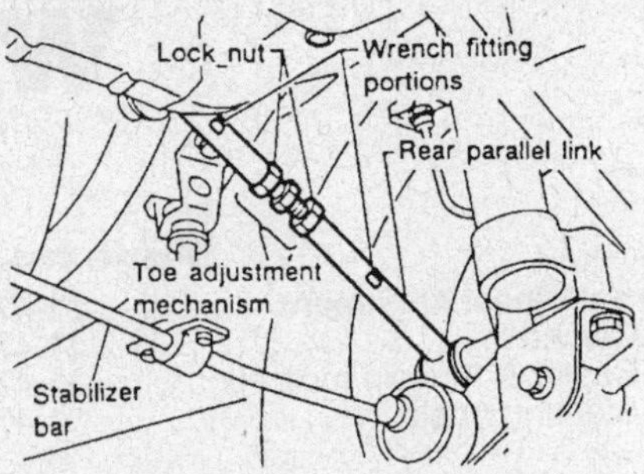
Lock nut
Wrench fitting portions
Rear parallel link
Toe adjustment mechanism
Stabilizer bar

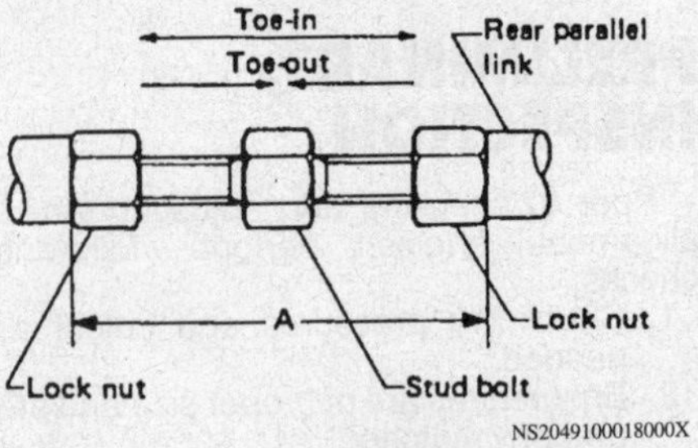
Toe-in
Toe-out
Rear parallel link
A
Lock nut
Lock nut
Stud bolt
NS2049100018000X

Fig. 5 Rear toe-in adjustment. Maxima

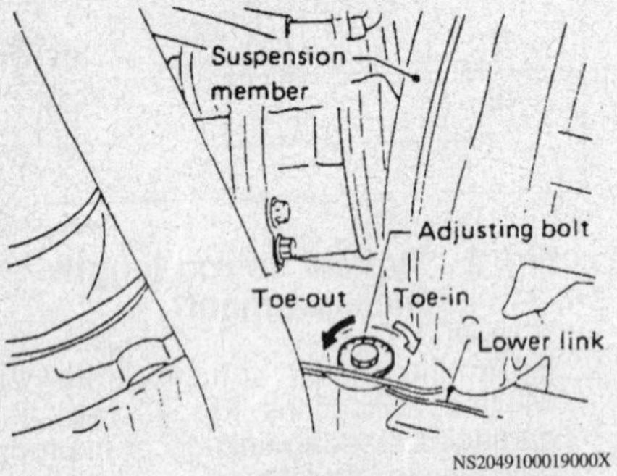
Suspension member
Adjusting bolt
Toe-out
Toe-in
Lower link
NS2049100019000X

Fig. 6 Rear toe-in adjustment. 300ZX

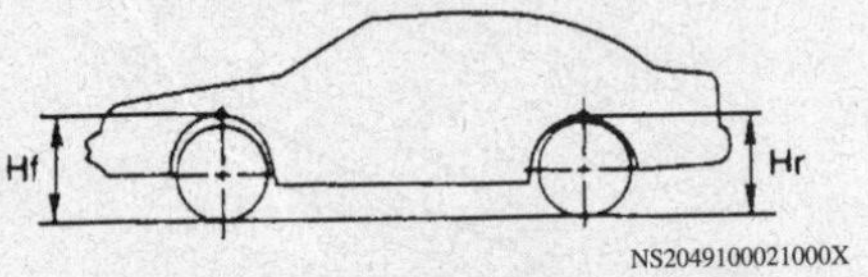
Hf
Hr
NS2049100021000X

Fig. 7 Vehicle ride height inspection

Year	Model/Engine	Vehicle Ride Height Inch, Unladen①	
		Front	Rear
MAXIMA			
1993–94	VE30DE Engine	27.60	27.01
	VG30E Engine	27.72	27.13
1995–96	GXE & GLE	28.07	28.15
	SE	28.07	28.07
300ZX			
1993–96	Two-Seater Less Turbo	26.57	26.61
	Two-Seater w/Turbo	26.57	26.57
	2+2	26.65	26.57

① — Measured @ top of wheel arch.

Fig. 8 Vehicle ride height

check rear suspension for damage or wear, and repair as needed.
3. After adjustment, hold link with suitable wrench to prevent bushing from twisting, then **torque** locknuts to 58–72 ft. lbs.

1995-96

Toe-in is preset and cannot be adjusted. If out of specification, inspect and replace damaged or worn rear suspension parts.

300ZX

Less Four Wheel Steering

1. Measure toe-in following equipment manufacturer's instructions.
2. Adjust toe-in by turning adjusting pin. Each graduation of adjusting pin equals .059 inch, **Fig. 6.**
3. **Torque** adjusting bolt to 51–65 ft. lbs.

With Four Wheel Steering

Rear toe-in can be adjusted by adjusting power cylinder lower links.

1. Measure toe-in for each wheel following equipment manufacturer's instructions.
2. Adjust toe in by adjusting lengths of power cylinder lower links.
3. After adjustment is complete, ensure both lower links are same length.

VEHICLE RIDE HEIGHT

When checking ride height vehicle must be parked on a level surface and tires inflated to proper air pressure. Ensure all fluid levels are to specified level, spare tire and jack are in proper locations.

Bounce vehicle up and down several times, then measure vehicle height from top of wheelwell to ground, **Fig. 7.** Vehicle height is not adjustable. If vehicle height is not as specified, check for worn springs or suspension parts. Vehicle ride heights are shown in **Fig. 8.**

NISSAN ALTIMA

INDEX OF SERVICE OPERATIONS

Page No.

AIR BAG SYSTEM PRECAUTIONS 0-8
AUTOMATIC TRANSMISSIONS/ TRANSAXLES 36-1
BRAKES
Anti-Lock Brakes 36-1
Disc Brakes 36-1
Drum Brakes 36-1
Hydraulic Brake System 36-1
Power Brake Units 36-1
CLUTCH & MANUAL TRANSAXLE
Adjustments 32-8
Clutch, Replace 32-8
Hydraulic System Service 32-8
Tightening Specifications 32-10
Transaxle, Replace 32-8
ELECTRICAL
Air Bags 36-1
Air Conditioning 36-1
Alternators 36-1
Blower Motor, Replace 32-4
Combination Switch, Replace 32-4
Cooling Fans 36-1
Cruise Control 36-1
Dash Gauges 36-1
Dash Panels 36-1
Distributor, Replace 32-3
Evaporator Core, Replace 32-5
Fuel Pump Relay Location 32-3
Fuse Panel & Flasher Location 32-3
Headlamp Switch, Replace 32-3
Heater Core, Replace 32-5
Ignition Lock, Replace 32-3
Ignition Switch, Replace 32-3
Instrument Cluster, Replace 32-4
Neutral Start Switch, Adjust 32-3
Passive Restraints 36-1
Precautions 32-3
Radio, Replace 32-4
Relay Center Location 32-3
Speed Controls 36-1
Starter Motors 36-1
Starter, Replace 32-3
Steering Columns 36-1
Steering Wheel, Replace 32-4
Stop Light Switch, Replace 32-3
Turn Signal Switch, Replace 32-4
Wiper Motor, Replace 32-4
Wiper Switch, Replace 32-4
Wiper Systems 36-1
ELECTRICAL SYMBOL IDENTIFICATION 0-39
FRONT SUSPENSION & STEERING
Ball Joint, Replace 32-12
Ball Joint Inspection 32-12
Knuckle, Replace 32-12
Manual Steering Gears 36-1
Power Steering 36-1
Power Steering Gear, Replace 32-13
Power Steering Pump, Replace 32-13
Strut, Replace 32-12
Tightening Specifications 32-15
Wheel Bearing Inspection 32-12
Wheel Hub & Steering
KA24DE ENGINE
Belt Tension Data 32-7
Compression Pressure 32-6
Engine Mount, Replace 32-6
Engine Rebuilding Specifications
Engine, Replace 32-6
Fuel Filter, Replace 32-7
Fuel Pump, Replace 32-7
Precautions 32-6
Radiator, Replace 32-7
Tightening Specifications 32-8
Valve Adjustment 32-6
Valve Clearance Specifications 32-6
REAR AXLE & SUSPENSION
Coil Spring, Replace 32-11
Parallel & Radius Link, Replace 32-11
Rear Axle, Replace 32-10
Stabilizer Bar, Replace 32-11
Strut, Replace 32-10
Strut Service 32-10
Tightening Specifications 32-12
SERVICE REMINDER & WARNING LAMP RESET PROCEDURES 0-10
SPECIFICATIONS
Fluid Capacities & Cooling System Data 32-2
Front Wheel Alignment Specifications 32-2
General Engine Specifications 32-1
Lubricant Data 32-2
Rear Wheel Alignment Specifications 32-2
Tune Up Specifications 32-2
VEHICLE IDENTIFICATION 0-1
VEHICLE LIFT POINTS 0-34
VEHICLE MAINTENANCE SCHEDULES 0-69
WHEEL ALIGNMENT
Front Wheel Alignment 32-15
Preliminary Inspection 32-15
Rear Wheel Alignment 32-16
Vehicle Ride Height 32-16
Wheel Alignment Specifications 32-1
WIRE COLOR CODE IDENTIFICATION 0-144

Specifications

GENERAL ENGINE SPECIFICATIONS

Year	Engine Model	Fuel System	Displacement Liters	Bore x Stroke, Inches	Compression Ratio	Maximum H.P. @ RPM	Maximum Torque, Ft. Lbs. @ RPM	Normal Oil Pressure, psi①
1993–96	KA24DE	Fuel Inj.	2.4L	3.50 x 3.78	9.2	150 @ 5600	154 @ 4400	60–70

① — At 3000 RPM.

TUNE UP SPECIFICATIONS

Year & Engine	Spark Plug Gap, Inch	Ignition Timing			Curb Idle Speed①		Fast Idle Speed		Fuel Pump Pressure, psi	Valve Lash
		Firing Order②	Timing, °BTDC③	Timing Mark	Man. Trans.	Auto. Trans.	Man. Trans.	Auto. Trans.		
1993–96										
KA24DE	.041	③	20	④	700	700N	⑤	⑤	43	⑥

BTDC — Before Top Dead Center.
N — Neutral.
① — When adjusting idle speed, set parking brake & chock drive wheels.
② — Before disconnecting spark plug wires from distributor cap, determine location of No. 1 wire in cap, as distributor position may have been altered.
③ — No. 1 located front of engine. Firing order 1-3-4-2.
④ — Mark located on pulley.
⑤ — Controlled by ECCS.
⑥ — Refer to "Valve Clearance Specifications."

FRONT WHEEL ALIGNMENT SPECIFICATIONS

Year	Caster Angle, Deg.		Camber Angle, Deg.		King Pin Inclination, Deg.	Toe-In, Inch①	Toe-Out On Turns, Deg.②		Ball Joint Wear
	Limits	Desired	Limits	Desired			Inner Wheel	Outer Wheel	
1993–96	$+1\frac{11}{12}$ to $+3\frac{5}{12}$	$+2\frac{7}{12}$	$-\frac{5}{6}$ to $+\frac{2}{3}$	$-\frac{1}{12}$	$13\frac{1}{3}$ to $14\frac{5}{6}$	0 to +.08	$31\frac{1}{2}$ to $35\frac{1}{3}$	$25\frac{3}{5}$ to $29\frac{3}{5}$	③

① — Toe-in (+); toe-out (-).
② — Measure w/wheels at full lock positions.
③ — Refer to "Ball Joint Inspection" section under "Front Suspension & Steering."

REAR WHEEL ALIGNMENT SPECIFICATIONS

Year	Camber Angle, Deg.		Toe, Inch①
	Limits	Desired	
1993–96	-2 to $-\frac{1}{2}$	$-1\frac{1}{4}$	+.04 to +.12

① — Toe-in (+); toe-out (-).

FLUID CAPACITIES & COOLING SYSTEM DATA

Year	Cooling Capacity, Qts.	Radiator Cap Relief Pressure, Lbs.	Thermo. Opening Temp., °F	Fuel Tank, Gals.	Engine Oil Refill, Qts.①	Transmission Oil		Differential Oil, Pts.
						Man. Trans., Pts.	Auto. Trans., Qts.②	
1993–96	$8\frac{1}{4}$	11–14	170	$15\frac{7}{8}$	$4\frac{1}{8}$	10	10	—

① — Includes filter.
② — Approximate, make final check w/dipstick.

LUBRICANT DATA

Year	Lubricant Type					
	Transmission		Transfer Case	Rear Axle	Power Steering	Brake System
	Manual	Automatic				
1993–96	80W-90 GL-4	Nissan Matic D ①	—	—	Dexron IIE/III	DOT 3

① — Dexron III/Mercon, or equivalent, automatic transmission fluid may also be used.

Electrical

NOTE: On Air Bag Equipped Models, Refer To "Air Bag System Precautions" Located In The Front Of This Manual For System Disarming & Arming Procedures.

INDEX

	Page No.
Air Bags	36-1
Air Conditioning	36-1
Alternators	36-1
Blower Motor, Replace	32-4
Combination Switch, Replace	32-4
Cooling Fans	36-1
Cruise Control	36-1
Dash Gauges	36-1
Dash Panels	36-1
Distributor, Replace	32-3
Evaporator Core, Replace	32-5
Fuel Pump Relay Location	32-3
Fuse Panel & Flasher Location	32-3
Headlamp Switch, Replace	32-3
Heater Core, Replace	32-5
Ignition Lock, Replace	32-3
Ignition Switch, Replace	32-3
Instrument Cluster, Replace	32-4
Neutral Start Switch, Adjust	32-3
Passive Restraints	36-1
Precautions	32-3
Air Bag Systems	32-3
Radio, Replace	32-4
Relay Center Location	32-3
Speed Controls	36-1
Starter Motors	36-1
Starter, Replace	32-3
Steering Columns	36-1
Steering Wheel, Replace	32-4
Stop Light Switch, Replace	32-3
Turn Signal Switch, Replace	32-4
Wiper Motor, Replace	32-4
Front	32-4
Rear	32-4
Wiper Switch, Replace	32-4
Front	32-4
Rear	32-4
Wiper System	36-1

PRECAUTIONS

AIR BAG SYSTEMS

Refer to "Air Bag System Precautions" in the front of this manual for system disarming and arming procedures.

FUSE PANEL & FLASHER LOCATION

The fuse panel is located behind the lower lefthand side of the instrument panel, left of the steering column.

The combination flasher unit is located behind the center of the instrument panel, near the time control module.

FUEL PUMP RELAY LOCATION

The fuel pump relay is located in a relay box No. 2 near the battery in the engine compartment.

RELAY CENTER LOCATION

Relay box No. 1 is located in the righthand side of the engine compartment. Relay box No. 2 is located in the front righthand side of the engine compartment, near the battery.

STARTER

REPLACE

1. Disconnect battery ground cable.
2. Disconnect starter wiring from starter.
3. Remove starter retaining bolts, then the starter.
4. Reverse procedure to install.

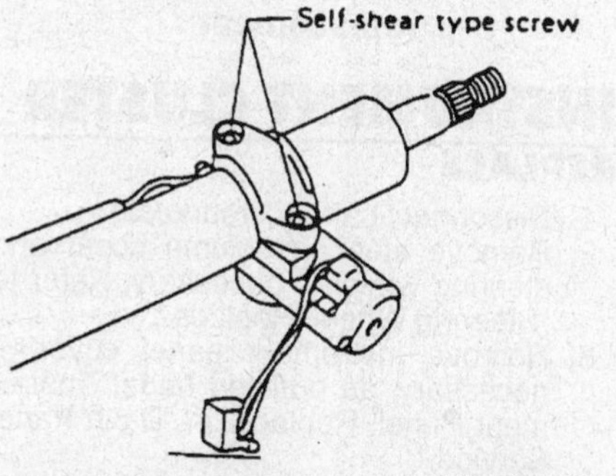
Self-shear type screw
NS9129100003000X

Fig. 1 Ignition lock replacement

DISTRIBUTOR

REPLACE

1. Disconnect battery ground cable.
2. Remove distributor cap and spark plug cables as an assembly.
3. Disconnect distributor electrical connections.
4. Remove distributor retaining bolt.
5. Remove distributor assembly.
6. Reverse procedure to install.

IGNITION LOCK

REPLACE

1. Remove steering wheel as outlined under "Steering Wheel, Replace."
2. Drill out two shear type ignition lock retaining screws, **Fig. 1.**
3. Remove ignition lock from steering column.
4. Reverse procedure to install, using shear type screws.

IGNITION SWITCH

REPLACE

1. Remove four upper and lower shell cover retaining screws, then the shell covers.
2. Disconnect electrical connectors from switch.
3. Remove switch retaining screw from steering lock, **Fig. 2.**
4. Remove switch.
5. Reverse procedure to install.

NEUTRAL START SWITCH

ADJUST

1. Remove control cable from manual shaft.
2. Loosen inhibitor switch attaching screws.
3. Set selector lever manual shaft at Neutral position.
4. Insert suitable pin into adjustment holes in both inhibitor switch and switch lever as near vertical as possible, **Fig. 3.**
5. Tighten inhibitor switch screws.
6. Connect control cable, the check switch for continuity.

HEADLAMP SWITCH

REPLACE

1. Remove steering column covers.
2. Disconnect light switch electrical connections.
3. Remove switch retaining screws, then the light switch, **Fig. 4.** It is not necessary to remove combination switch base when replacing light switch.

STOP LIGHT SWITCH

REPLACE

The stop lamp switch is located on the brake pedal support.

1. Disconnect switch electrical connectors.

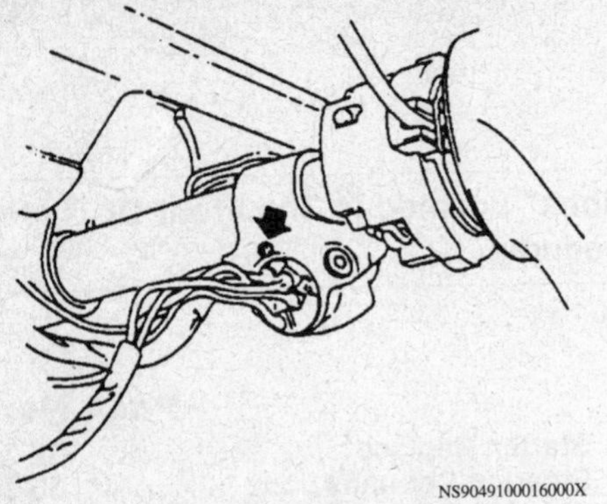
NS9049100016000X

Fig. 2 Ignition switch replacement

2. Loosen switch retaining locknut and remove switch.
3. Reverse procedure to install.

COMBINATION SWITCH

REPLACE

1. Disconnect battery ground cable.
2. Remove horn cover and steering wheel as outlined under "Steering Wheel, Replace."
3. Remove steering column shell covers.
4. Disconnect switch electrical connections.
5. Remove switch base retaining screws and switch, **Fig. 5.**
6. Reverse procedure to install.

TURN SIGNAL SWITCH

REPLACE

Refer to "Headlamp Switch, Replace" for replacement procedure.

STEERING WHEEL

REPLACE

1. Remove air bag module as follows:
   a. Remove left and right air bag module retaining bolts. **Discard bolts.**
   b. Remove air bag module from steering wheel.
   c. **Always place air bag module with pad side facing upward.**
   d. **Do not attempt to disassemble air bag module.**
   e. **Do not drop or impact air bag module. If any portion is deformed or cracked, replace module.**
   f. **Do not allow oil, grease or water to come in contact with the air bag module.**
2. Remove steering wheel using puller tool No. J25726-A, or equivalent.
3. Reverse procedure to install, noting the following:
   a. Apply suitable grease to entire surface of turn signal cancel pin and horn contact slip ring.
   b. Air bag module retaining bolts are coated with a special bonding agent. Always discard old bolts and replace with new ones.

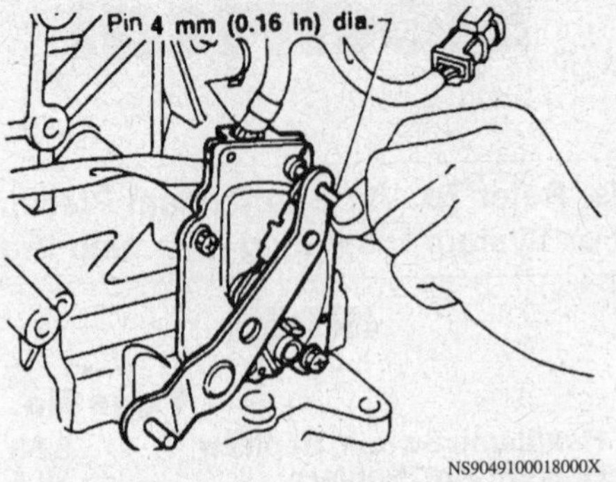
Pin 4 mm (0.16 in) dia.
NS9049100018000X

Fig. 3 Inhibitor switch adjustment

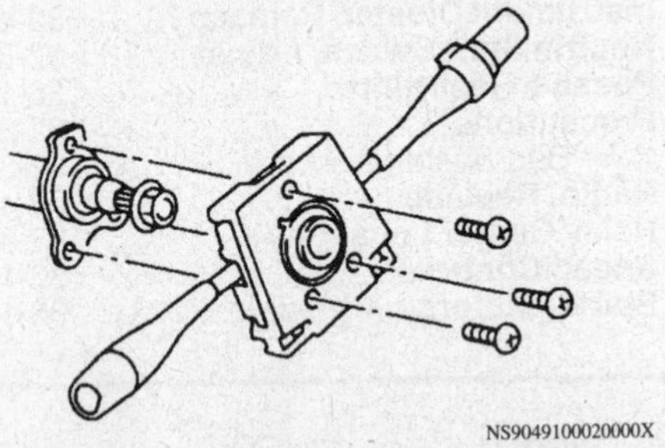
NS9049100020000X

Fig. 5 Combination switch replacement

INSTRUMENT CLUSTER

REPLACE

1. Disconnect battery ground cable.
2. Remove steering column cover and steering wheel, if necessary. Refer to "Steering Wheel, Replace."
3. Remove instrument panel cover, if necessary, as outlined under "Instrument Panel, Replace" in "Dash Panel Service."
4. Remove cluster lid retaining screws, then the cluster lid.
5. Disconnect speedometer cable, cluster retaining nuts and electrical connectors as necessary. The cluster may have to be pulled slightly forward after removing the retaining screws to allow access to the electrical connectors.
6. Reverse procedure to install.

RADIO

REPLACE

1. Disconnect battery ground cable.
2. Remove cluster lid or instrument panel fascia as necessary to gain access to brackets. Refer to "Instrument Panel, Replace"in "Dash Panel Service."
3. Remove radio bracket to instrument panel attaching screw.
4. Disconnect electrical leads from radio.
5. Remove radio from vehicle.
6. Reverse procedure to install.

WIPER MOTOR

REPLACE

FRONT

Refer to **Fig. 6** for wiper system exploded view.

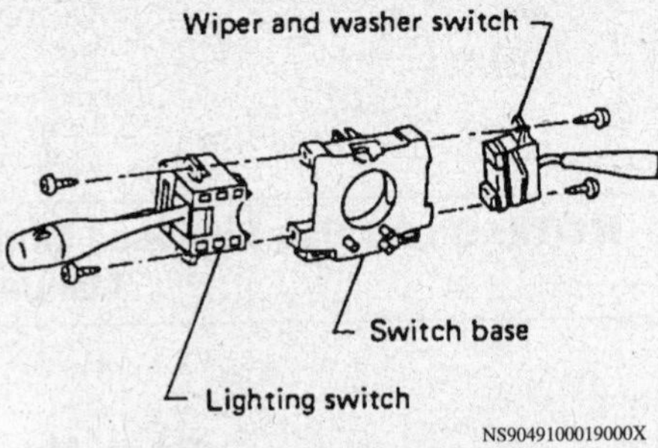
Wiper and washer switch
Switch base
Lighting switch
NS9049100019000X

Fig. 4 Headlamp, turn signal & wiper switch removal

1. Remove wiper arms.
2. Disconnect electrical connector from motor, then remove top grille retaining screws and top grille, where possible, to gain access to wiper linkage.
3. Remove wiper motor mounting bolts and pull motor away from firewall if necessary to gain access. Disconnect motor shaft from linkage taking care not to bend linkage.
4. Remove cowl top grille.
5. Remove flange nuts retaining pivot to cowl top, then the wiper motor linkage.
6. Reverse procedure to install.

REAR

1. Disconnect battery ground cable.
2. Raise rear wiper arm off glass and remove retaining nut.
3. Remove tailgate inner trim panel and disconnect electrical connection at motor.
4. Remove wiper motor retaining bolts, then the wiper motor.
5. Reverse procedure to install.

WIPER SWITCH

REPLACE

FRONT

1. Remove steering column covers.
2. Disconnect wiper switch electrical connections.
3. Remove switch retaining screws, then the light switch, **Fig. 4.** It is not necessary to remove combination switch base when replacing wiper switch.

REAR

1. Disconnect battery ground cable.
2. Disconnect electrical connector from switch.
3. Remove switch knob by depressing and/or twisting as necessary.
4. Remove any switch retaining nuts or clips, then remove the switch.
5. Reverse procedure to install.

BLOWER MOTOR

REPLACE

1. Disconnect battery ground cable and discharge A/C system.
2. Remove passenger side instrument lower cover and glove compartment.
3. Disconnect wiring harness connectors to intake unit, **Fig. 7.**
4. Remove intake unit.

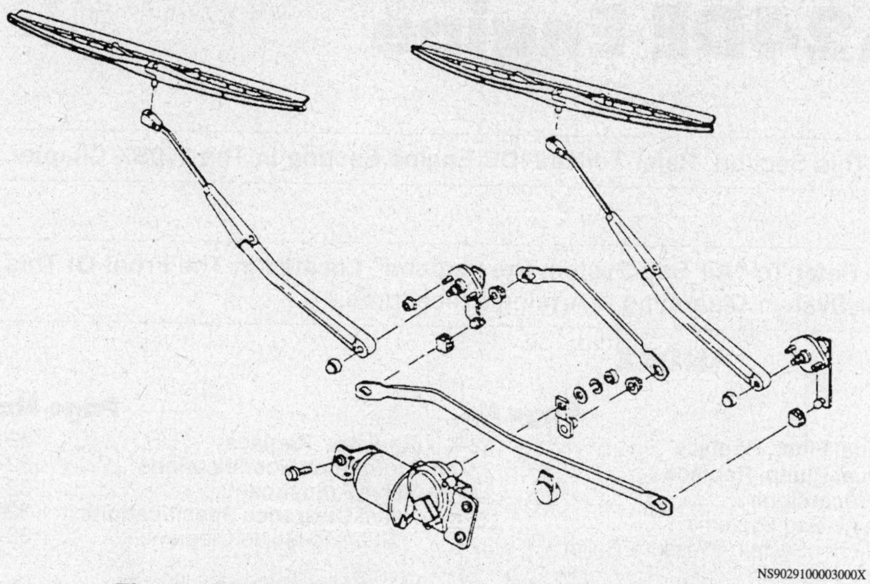
NS9029100003000X

Fig. 6 Exploded view of windshield wiper system

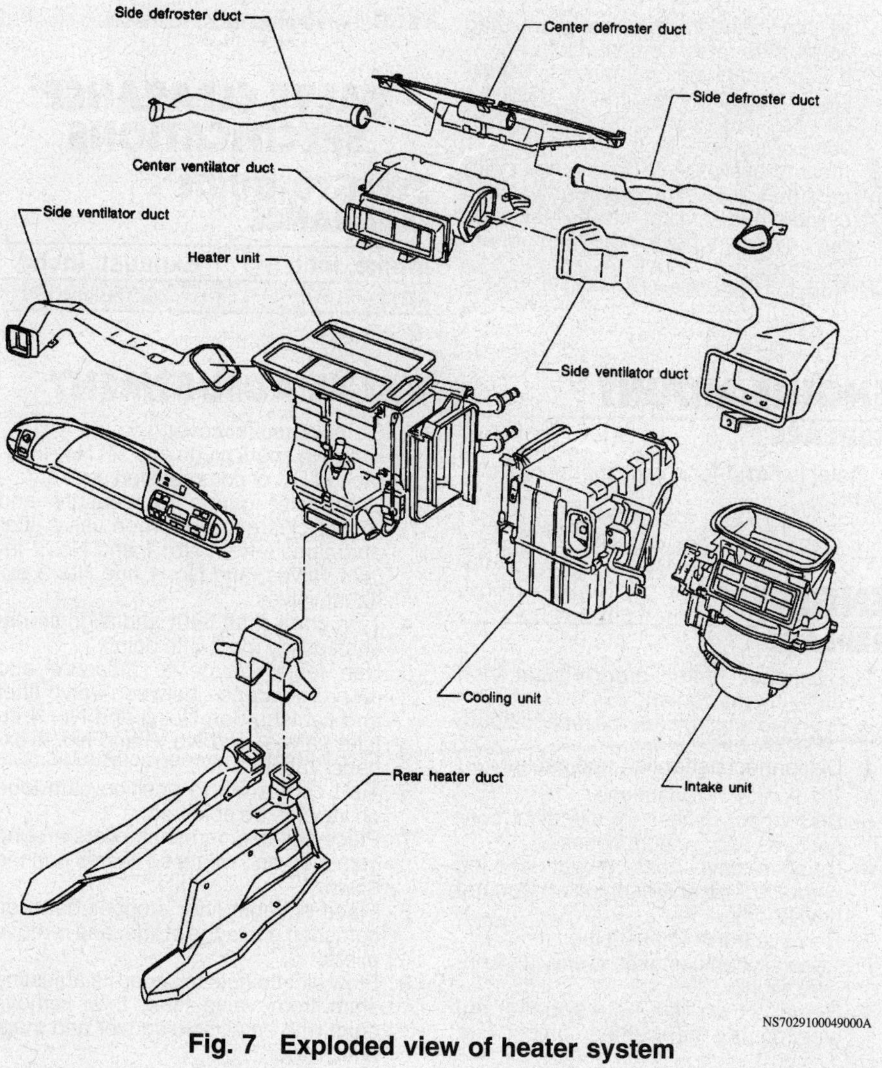
Side defroster duct
Center defroster duct
Side defroster duct
Center ventilator duct
Side ventilator duct
Heater unit
Side ventilator duct
Cooling unit
Rear heater duct
Intake unit
NS7029100049000A

Fig. 7 Exploded view of heater system

5. Remove blower motor from intake unit.
6. Reverse procedure to install.

HEATER CORE

REPLACE

1. Disconnect battery ground cable and drain cooling system.
2. Disconnect heater inlet and outlet coolant pipes from heater unit.
3. Remove instrument panel as outlined in "Dash Panel Service."
4. Disconnect heater ducts, **Fig. 7.**
5. Disconnect wiring harness connectors to heater unit.
6. Remove heater unit.
7. Separate heater unit case halves and remove heater core, **Fig. 7.**
8. Reverse procedure to install.

EVAPORATOR CORE

REPLACE

1. Disconnect battery ground cable and discharge A/C system.
2. Remove passenger side instrument lower cover and glove compartment.
3. Disconnect wiring harness connectors to intake unit.
4. Remove intake unit.
5. Disconnect wiring harness connectors to evaporator.
6. Remove cooling unit.
7. Separate cooling unit case halves and remove evaporator, **Fig. 7.**
8. Reverse procedure to install.

KA24DE Engine

NOTE: For Procedures Not Found In This Section, Refer To KA24DE Engine Section In The 240SX Chapter.

NOTE: On Air Bag Equipped Models, Refer To "Air Bag System Precautions" Located In The Front Of This Manual For System Disarming & Arming Procedures.

INDEX

	Page No.
Belt Tension Data	32-7
Compression Pressure	32-6
Engine Mount, Replace	32-6
Engine Rebuildiing Specifications	36-1
Engine, Replace	32-6
Fuel Filter, Replace	32-7
Fuel Pump, Replace	32-7
Precautions	32-6
Air Bag Systems	32-6
Fuel System Pressure Relief	32-6
Radiator, Replace	32-7
Tightening Specifications	32-8
Valve Adjustment	32-6
Valve Clearance Specifications	32-6
Stem-To-Guide Clearance	32-6

PRECAUTIONS

AIR BAG SYSTEMS

Refer to "Air Bag System Precautions" in the front of this manual for system disarming and arming procedures.

FUEL SYSTEM PRESSURE RELIEF

1. Remove fuel pump fuse from fuse panel.
2. Start engine.
3. Run engine until it stalls.
4. After engine stalls, crank engine two or three times to ensure fuel pressure is released.
5. Turn ignition switch off and install fuse for fuel pump.

COMPRESSION PRESSURE

1. Start engine and run until engine reaches operating temperature.
2. Turn ignition switch off.
3. Release fuel pressure. Refer to "Precautions"for fuel system pressure release procedure.
4. Remove all spark plugs.
5. Disconnect distributor center cable.
6. Attach a compression tester to cylinder No. 1.
7. Depress accelerator pedal fully to keep throttle valve wide open.
8. Crank engine and record highest gauge indication.
9. Repeat measurement on each cylinder.
10. Standard compression is 178 psi at 300 RPM, minimum pressure is 149 psi at 300 RPM and compression difference limit between cylinders is 14 psi.
11. If compression in one or more cylinders is low, pour a small amount of engine oil into cylinders through spark plug holes, then retest compression.
12. If adding oil helps compression, then piston rings may be at fault. If adding oil does not help compression, then valves may be at fault.
13. If compression stays low in two cylinders that are next to each other, then cylinder head gasket may be leaking or both cylinders have valve component damage.
14. Repair as necessary.

ENGINE MOUNT

REPLACE

Refer to **Fig. 1** for engine mount replacement.

ENGINE

REPLACE

1. Disconnect battery ground cable, then drain engine coolant.
2. Remove engine undercover and hood.
3. Drain engine coolant.
4. Release fuel system pressure as outlined under "Precautions."
5. Disconnect necessary electrical connections and vacuum hoses.
6. Remove drive belts, power steering pump, A/C compressor, alternator and driveshafts.
7. Remove front exhaust pipe.
8. Attach suitable engine lift and raise engine slightly.
9. Remove right, left, front and rear engine mounts, then center member, **Fig. 1.**
10. Place suitable jack under transaxle and engine, then lower engine and transaxle assembly.
11. Remove engine to transaxle attaching bolts, then remove engine.
12. Reverse procedure to install.

VALVE CLEARANCE SPECIFICATIONS

STEM-TO-GUIDE CLEARANCE

Intake, Inch①	Exhaust, Inch①
.0012–.0015	.0013–.0016

① — Hot.

VALVE ADJUSTMENT

1. Remove rocker cover.
2. Remove spark plugs and set No. 1 piston to TDC of compression stroke.
3. Use feeler gauge to measure and record clearance between valve lifter and camshaft on No. 1 and No. 2 intake valves, and No. 1 and No. 3 exhaust valves.
4. Turn crankshaft 360° and align crankshaft pulley mark with point.
5. Use feeler gauge to measure and record clearance between valve lifter and camshaft on No. 3 and No. 4 intake valves, and No. 2 and No. 4 exhaust valves.
6. Turn crankshaft to position cam lobe on valve to be adjusted.
7. Place suitable camshaft pliers around camshaft and rotate so lifter is pushed down.
8. Place suitable lifter stopper between camshaft and edge of lifter and remove pliers.
9. Blow air into hole to separate adjusting shim from valve lifter, then remove shim with small screwdriver and magnetic finger.
10. Measure removed shim and calculate thickness of new shim necessary to obtain specified clearance. New intake shim size equals removed shim size plus measured clearance minus

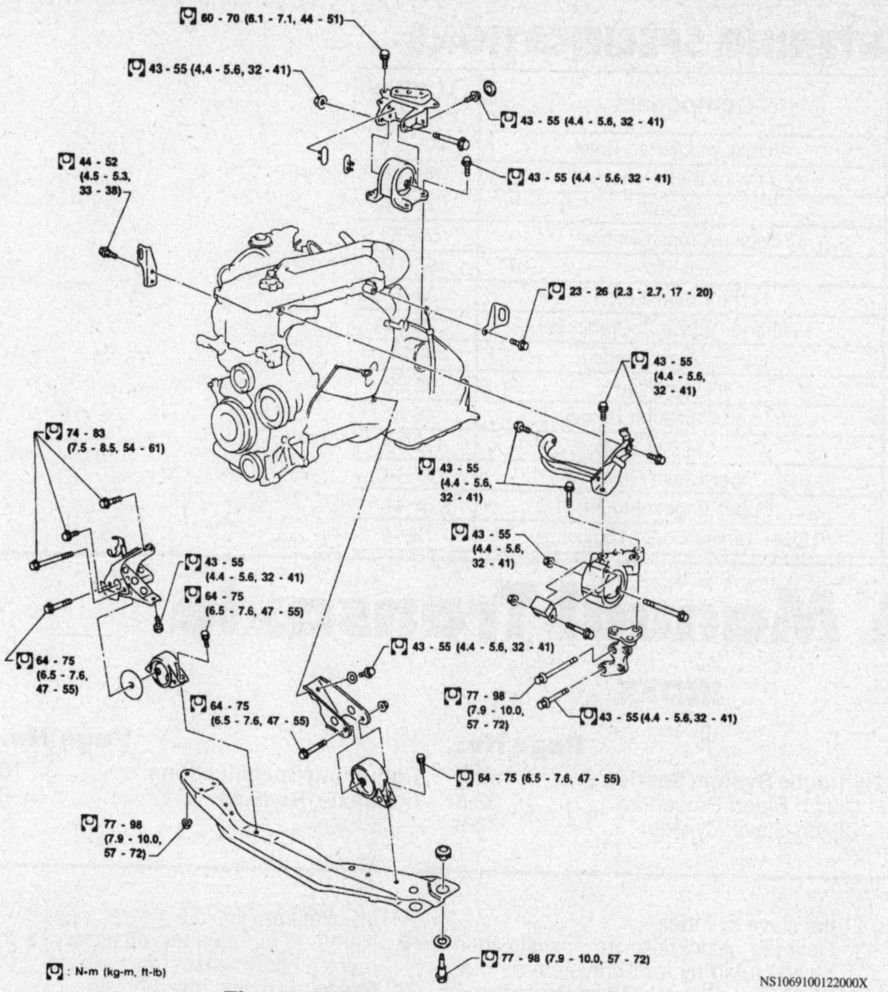
60 - 70 (6.1 - 7.1, 44 - 51)
43 - 55 (4.4 - 5.6, 32 - 41)
43 - 55 (4.4 - 5.6, 32 - 41)
43 - 55 (4.4 - 5.6, 32 - 41)
44 - 52 (4.5 - 5.3, 33 - 38)
23 - 26 (2.3 - 2.7, 17 - 20)
43 - 55 (4.4 - 5.6, 32 - 41)
74 - 83 (7.5 - 8.5, 54 - 61)
43 - 55 (4.4 - 5.6, 32 - 41)
43 - 55 (4.4 - 5.6, 32 - 41)
43 - 55 (4.4 - 5.6, 32 - 41)
64 - 75 (6.5 - 7.6, 47 - 55)
64 - 75 (6.5 - 7.6, 47 - 55)
43 - 55 (4.4 - 5.6, 32 - 41)
64 - 75 (6.5 - 7.6, 47 - 55)
77 - 98 (7.9 - 10.0, 57 - 72)
43 - 55 (4.4 - 5.6, 32 - 41)
64 - 75 (6.5 - 7.6, 47 - 55)
77 - 98 (7.9 - 10.0, 57 - 72)
77 - 98 (7.9 - 10.0, 57 - 72)
: N·m (kg-m, ft-lb)

NS1069100122000X

Fig. 1 Engine mount replacement

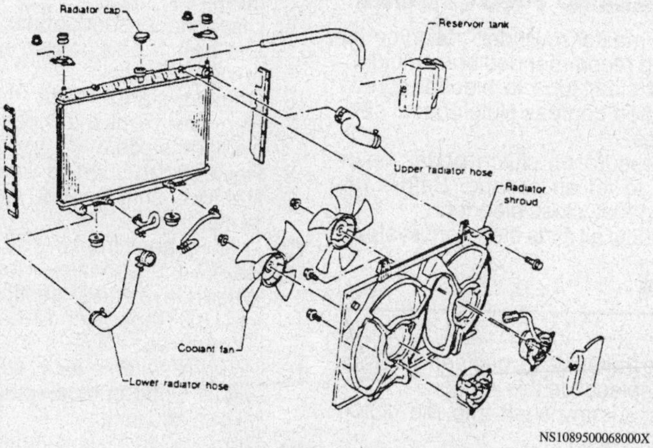
Radiator cap
Reservoir tank
Upper radiator hose
Radiator shroud
Coolant fan
Lower radiator hose

NS1089500068000X

Fig. 3 Radiator replacement

(.0138 inch on 1993–94 engines or .0146 inch on 1995–96 engines). New exhaust shim size equals removed shim size plus measured clearance minus (.0146 inch on 1993–94 engines or .0146 inch on 1995–96 engines). Shims are available from .0772 inch to .1055 inch, in .0008 inch steps.

11. Install new shim, attach pliers, rotate, then remove stopper and pliers.
12. Recheck valve clearance.
13. Repeat shim removal and replacement procedure as necessary.
14. Reverse procedure to install.

BELT TENSION DATA

Refer to **Fig. 2** for belt deflection specifications.

Unit: mm (in)

	Used belt deflection: Limit	Used belt deflection: Deflection after adjustment	Deflection of new belt
Generator & Power steering oil pump	8 (0.31)	6 - 7 (0.24 - 0.28)	5 - 6 (0.20 - 0.24)
Air conditioning compressor	10 (0.39)	7 - 8 (0.28 - 0.31)	6 - 7 (0.24 - 0.28)
Applied pushing force	98 N (10 kg, 22 lb)		

NS1069100124000X

Fig. 2 Belt deflection specifications

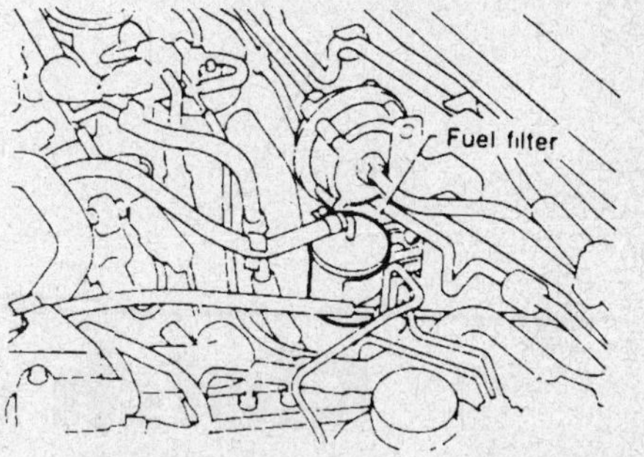
Fuel filter

NS1029100006000X

Fig. 4 Fuel filter location

RADIATOR

REPLACE

1. Disconnect battery ground cable and drain coolant.
2. Disconnect radiator upper and lower hoses, **Fig. 3.**
3. **On models with automatic transmission,** remove automatic transmission oil cooler lines.
4. **On all models,** remove radiator shroud.
5. Disconnect reservoir tank hose.
6. Lift radiator out of vehicle carefully to avoid damage.
7. Reverse procedure to install.

FUEL PUMP

REPLACE

1. Release fuel pump pressure as outlined under "Precautions."
2. Disconnect battery ground cable, then drain fuel into suitable container.
3. Disconnect necessary fuel lines and electrical connectors.
4. Remove fuel tank attaching bolts, then the lower tank.
5. Remove fuel pump attaching bolts, then the fuel pump.
6. Reverse procedure to install.

FUEL FILTER

REPLACE

1. Release fuel system pressure as outlined under "Precautions."
2. Loosen two fuel filter hose clamps, **Fig. 4.**
3. Remove fuel filter. **Wrap filter with a rag to prevent fuel spillage.**
4. Reverse procedure to install.

TIGHTENING SPECIFICATIONS

Year	Component	Torque/ Ft. Lbs.
1993–96	Aluminum Oil Pan Bolts	4.7–5.5
	Crankshaft Pulley	105–112
	Driveplate	105–112
	Engine Crossmember	57–72
	Flywheel	105-112
	Front Exhaust Pipe	22-27
	Lefthand Camshaft Sprocket	123-130
	Lower Chain Guide	9-14
	Oil Drain Plug	22-29
	Righthand Camshaft Sprocket	48-61
	Steel Oil Pan Bolts	12-14
	Upper Chain Guide	12-14
	Upper Engine Mount	32-41
	Upper Timing Chain Tensioner	12-14

Clutch & Manual Transaxle

INDEX

	Page No.
Adjustments	32-8
Clutch Pedal	32-8
Clutch, Replace	32-8
Hydraulic System Service	32-8
Clutch Bleed Procedure	32-8
Clutch Slave Cylinder	32-8
Tightening Specifications	32-10
Transaxle, Replace	32-8

ADJUSTMENTS

CLUTCH PEDAL

The clutch hydraulic system must be bled whenever a clutch line has been disconnected or when air has entered the system. The bleed valve is located on the clutch operating cylinder.

1. Adjust clutch pedal height, dimension "H" in **Fig. 1,** to 6.50–6.89 inches using pedal stopper or ASCD cancel switch.
2. Adjust pedal freeplay, dimension "A" in **Fig. 2,** to .039–.118 inch by rotating the master cylinder pushrod inward or outward. After adjustment has been completed, tighten locknut.
3. While fully depressing clutch pedal, adjust clearance between stopper rubber and threaded end of clutch interlock switch, **Fig. 3.** After adjustment is completed, tighten locknut.
4. After the above adjustments have been completed, cycle clutch pedal several times to ensure clutch linkage operates smoothly without binding.

HYDRAULIC SYSTEM SERVICE

CLUTCH SLAVE CYLINDER

1. Disconnect brake line from slave cylinder. **Do not bend brake line.**
2. Remove cylinder attaching bolts, then the slave cylinder.
3. Reverse procedure to install, then bleed clutch hydraulic system as outlined under "Clutch Bleed Procedure."

CLUTCH BLEED PROCEDURE

1. Ensure master cylinder reservoir is filled with recommended brake fluid.
2. Connect clear tube to bleeder screw, **Fig. 4,** then depress clutch pedal several times.
3. With pressure on clutch pedal, open bleeder to let air escape. Before releasing pedal, close bleeder.
4. Repeat until all air is bled from system.

CLUTCH

REPLACE

1. Remove transaxle as outlined in "Transaxle Replace" in this section.
2. Insert a dummy shaft into the clutch disc hub.
3. Loosen clutch cover attaching bolts alternately.
4. Remove clutch disc and cover assembly.
5. Remove release bearing.
6. Reverse procedure to install.

TRANSAXLE

REPLACE

1. Disconnect battery cables, then remove battery and battery support bracket from vehicle.
2. Remove air cleaner assembly with mass air flow sensor from vehicle.
3. Remove air duct from vehicle.
4. Remove clutch operating cylinder from transaxle.
5. Disconnect speedometer pinion, position switch and ground harness connectors.
6. Remove starter motor from transaxle.
7. Remove crankshaft position sensor from transaxle.
8. Raise and support vehicle.
9. Remove shift control rod from transaxle.
10. Drain gear oil from transaxle.
11. Remove driveshafts. Refer to "Front Wheel Drive Axles" section under "Nissan Unit Repair" for driveshaft removal procedures.
12. Using a suitable jack, support engine with a wooden block placed between oil pan and jack.
13. Remove rear and lefthand engine mounts from vehicle.
14. Raise jack for access to lower housing bolts. Remove bolts, then lower jack.
15. Remove transaxle to engine mounting bolts.
16. Lower transaxle while supporting it with a jack.
17. Reverse procedure to install, tightening engine to transaxle bolts as shown in **Fig. 5.**

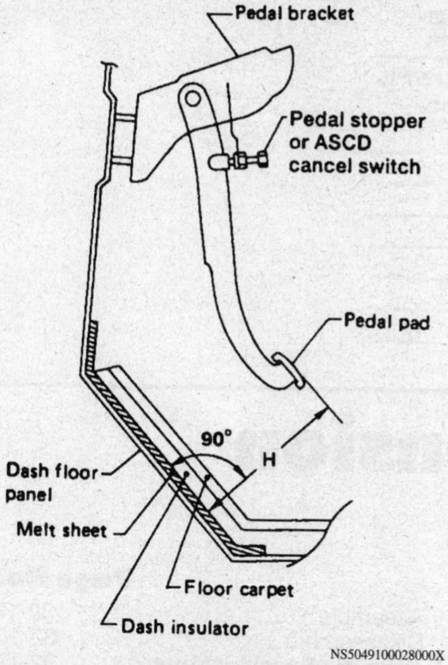
Pedal bracket
Pedal stopper
or ASCD
cancel switch
Pedal pad
90°
H
Dash floor
panel
Melt sheet
Floor carpet
Dash insulator
NS5049100028000X

Fig. 1 Clutch pedal free travel & height adjustment

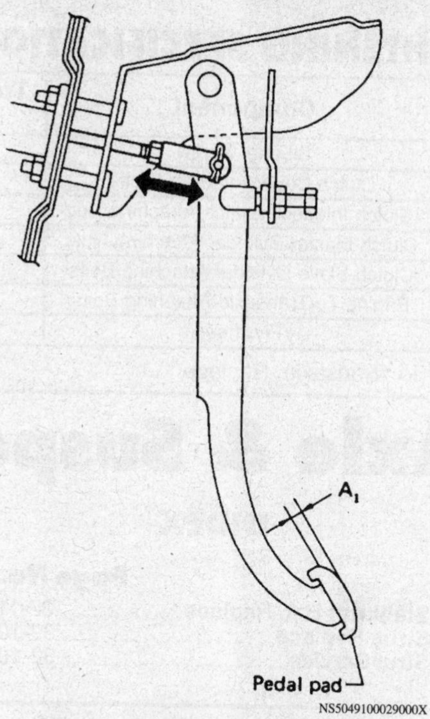
A1
Pedal pad
NS5049100029000X

Fig. 2 Clutch pedal freeplay adjustment

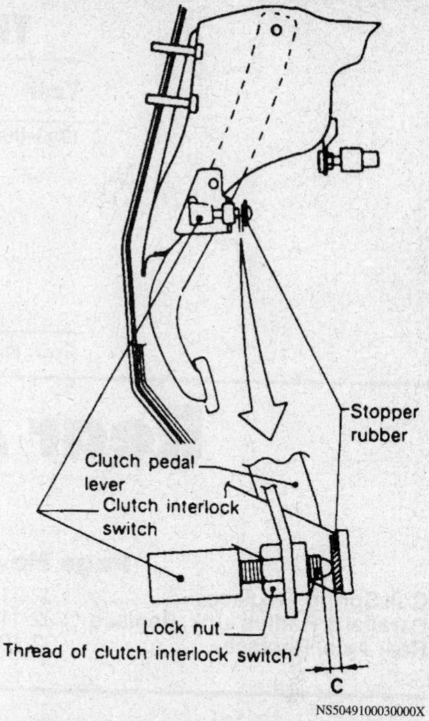
Stopper
rubber
Clutch pedal
lever
Clutch interlock
switch
Lock nut
Thread of clutch interlock switch
C
NS5049100030000X

Fig. 3 Clutch interlock switch adjustment

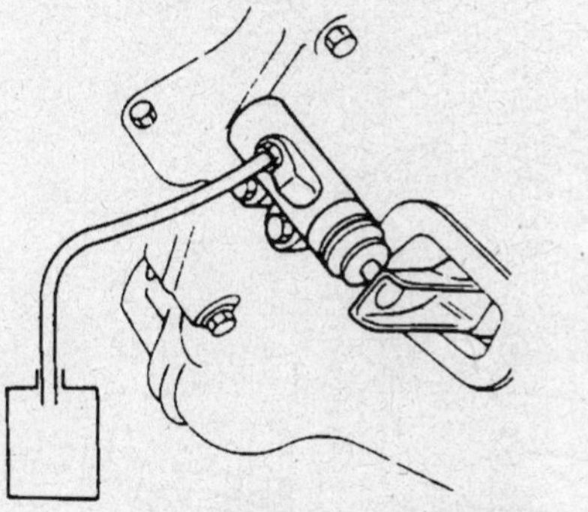
NS5049100031000X

Fig. 4 Clutch bleed procedure

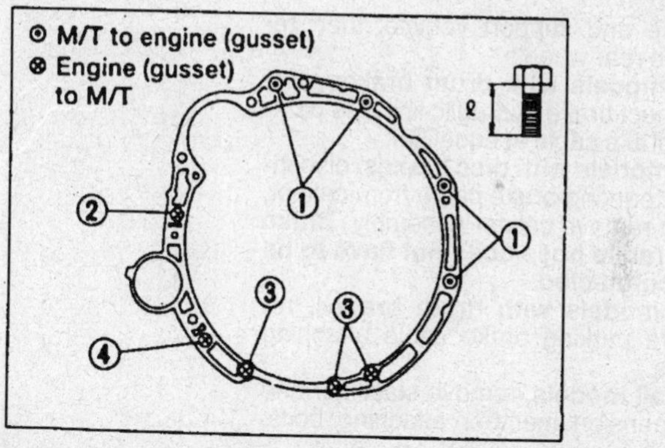
M/T to engine (gusset)
Engine (gusset) to M/T
ℓ
1
2
3
4

Bolt No.	Tightening torque N·m (kg-m, ft-lb)	mm (in)
1	39 - 49 (4.0 - 5.0, 29 - 36)	45 (1.77)
2	39 - 49 (4.0 - 5.0, 29 - 36)	48 (1.89)
3	30 - 40 (3.1 - 4.1, 22 - 30)	30 (1.18)
4	30 - 40 (3.1 - 4.1, 22 - 30)	40 (1.57)

NS5039100068000X

Fig. 5 Transmission to engine tightening specifications

TIGHTENING SPECIFICATIONS

Year	Component	Torque/Ft. Lbs.
1993–96	Bleeder Screw	4–7
	Clutch Cover Attaching Bolts	16–22
	Clutch Interlock Switch Attaching Nut	9–11
	Clutch Master Cylinder Attaching Nuts	5.8–8.0
	Clutch Slave Cylinder Attaching Bolts	22–30
	Engine To Transaxle Attaching Bolts	①
	Flywheel	105–112

①— Refer to "Transaxle, Replace."

Rear Axle & Suspension

INDEX

	Page No.		Page No.		Page No.
Coil Spring, Replace	32-11	Stabilizer Bar, Replace	32-11	Assemble	32-11
Parallel & Radius Link, Replace	32-11	Strut, Replace	32-10	Disassemble	32-10
Rear Axle, Replace	32-10	Strut Service	32-10	Tightening Specifications	32-12

REAR AXLE

REPLACE

1. Raise and support vehicle, then remove rear wheels.
2. **On models with drum brakes,** disconnect brake hydraulic line and parking brake cable at equalizer.
3. **On models with disc brakes,** disconnect parking brake cable from caliper, then remove caliper assembly. **Brake hydraulic hose does not have to be disconnected.**
4. **On models with drum brakes,** remove parking brake cable attaching bolts.
5. **On all models,** remove stabilizer and suspension member attaching bolts, **Fig. 1.**
6. Lower vehicle, then remove rear seat and parcel shelf.
7. Remove upper strut retaining nuts.
8. Reverse procedure to install.

STRUT

REPLACE

Refer to "Axle, Replace" procedure for strut replacement.

STRUT SERVICE

DISASSEMBLE

1. Position strut assembly into a suitable vise, then loosen piston rod locknut. **Do not remove piston rod locknut at this time.**
2. Using spring compressor tool No. HT71780000, or equivalent, compress coil spring until the strut mounting insulator can be turned by hand.
3. Remove piston rod locknut.
4. Using gland packing removal tool No. ST35490000, or equivalent, remove gland packing.
5. Retract piston rod by pushing it down until it bottoms, then slowly withdraw piston rod from cylinder together with piston guide.

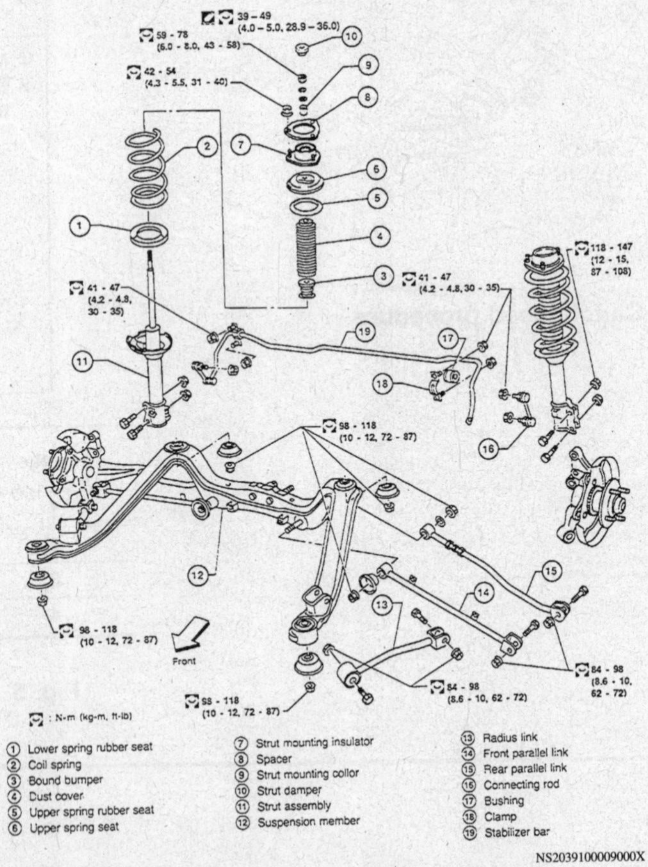

39 – 49 (4.0 – 5.0, 28.9 – 36.0)
59 - 78 (6.0 - 8.0, 43 - 58)
42 - 54 (4.3 - 5.5, 31 - 40)
41 - 47 (4.2 - 4.8, 30 - 35)
41 - 47 (4.2 - 4.8, 30 - 35)
118 - 147 (12 - 15, 87 - 108)
98 - 118 (10 - 12, 72 - 87)
98 - 118 (10 - 12, 72 - 87)
Front
98 - 118 (10 - 12, 72 - 87)
84 - 98 (8.6 - 10, 62 - 72)
84 - 98 (8.6 - 10, 62 - 72)
: N·m (kg-m, ft-lb)
① Lower spring rubber seat
② Coil spring
③ Bound bumper
④ Dust cover
⑤ Upper spring rubber seat
⑥ Upper spring seat
⑦ Strut mounting insulator
⑧ Spacer
⑨ Strut mounting collor
⑩ Strut damper
⑪ Strut assembly
⑫ Suspension member
⑬ Radius link
⑭ Front parallel link
⑮ Rear parallel link
⑯ Connecting rod
⑰ Bushing
⑱ Clamp
⑲ Stabilizer bar
NS2039100009000X

Fig. 1 Exploded view of rear suspension

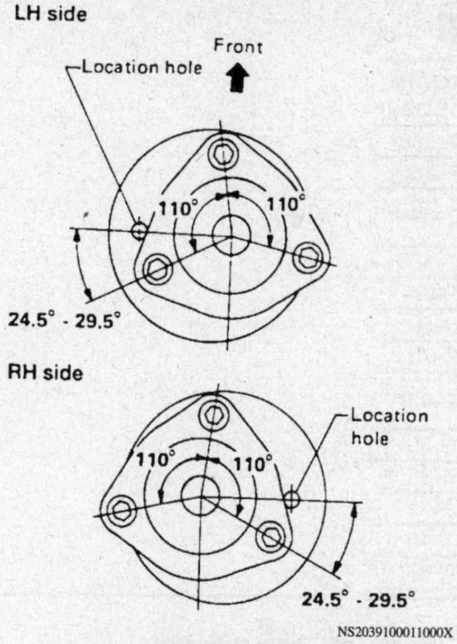
LH side
Front
Location hole
110°
110°
24.5° - 29.5°
RH side
Location hole
110°
110°
24.5° - 29.5°
NS2039100011000X

Fig. 2 Upper spring seat positioning

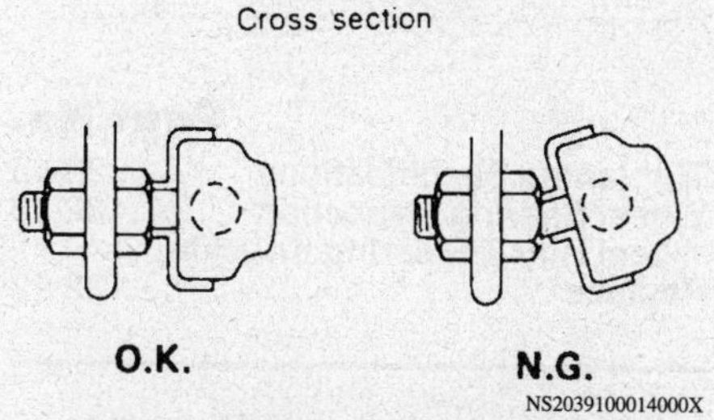
Cross section
O.K.
N.G.
NS2039100014000X

Fig. 5 Stabilizer bar ball joint socket position

ASSEMBLE

1. Install gland packing.
2. Place spring on strut assembly, then install dust cover and upper spring rubber seat.
3. Install upper spring seat, **Fig. 2.**
4. Install strut mounting insulator, spacer and strut mounting collar.
5. Install piston rod locknut.
6. After placing coil spring in position on lower spring seat, release spring compressor gradually.

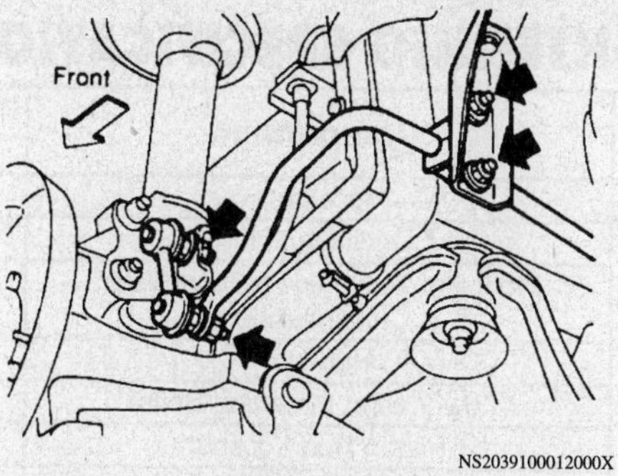
Front
NS2039100012000X

Fig. 3 Stabilizer bar removal

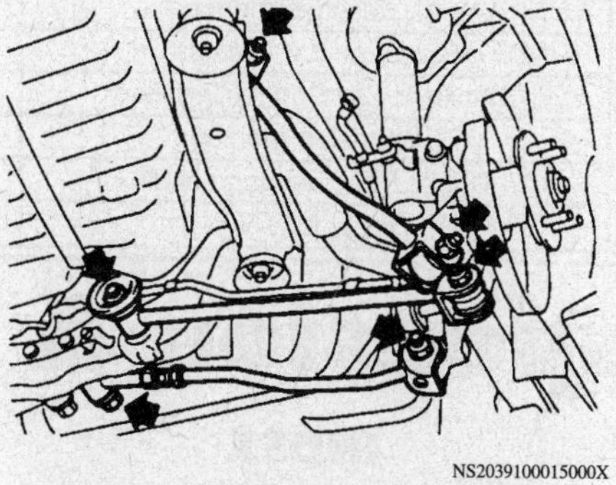
NS2039100015000X

Fig. 6 Parallel & radius link removal

7. Tighten piston rod locknut to specifications.

COIL SPRING

REPLACE

Refer to "Strut, Replace" for procedure.

STABILIZER BAR

REPLACE

1. Raise and support vehicle.
2. Remove stabilizer bar, **Fig. 3.**
3. Reverse procedure to install, noting the following:
   a. Ensure paint marks are positioned as shown in **Fig. 4.**
   b. Ensure stabilizer ball joint socket is properly placed, **Fig. 5.**

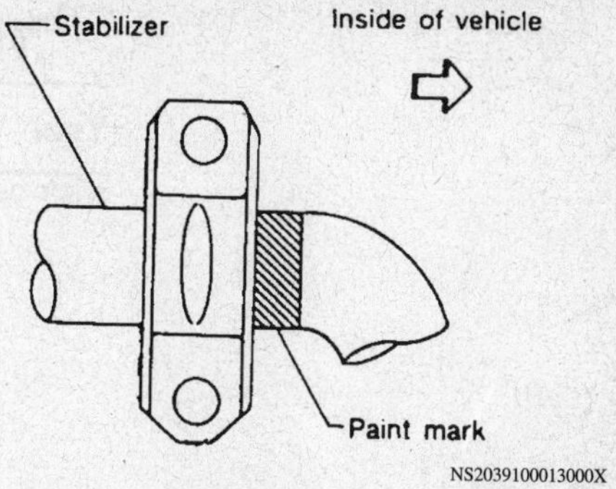
Stabilizer
Inside of vehicle
Paint mark
NS2039100013000X

Fig. 4 Stabilizer bar installation

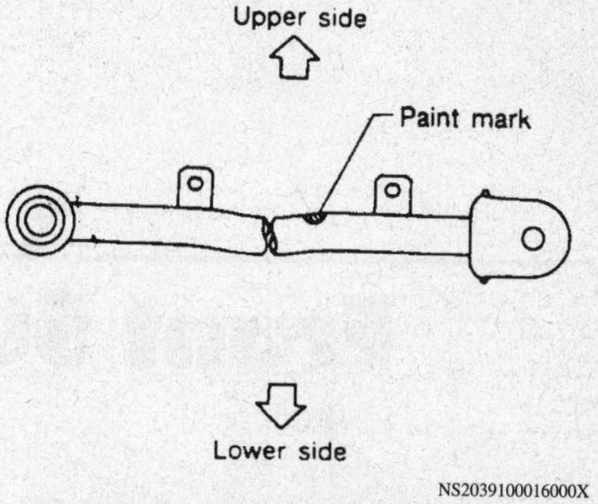
Upper side
Paint mark
Lower side
NS2039100016000X

Fig. 7 Front parallel link installation

PARALLEL & RADIUS LINK

REPLACE

1. Raise and support vehicle.
2. Remove parallel and radius link, **Fig. 6.**
3. Reverse procedure to install, noting the following:
   a. When installing front parallel link, ensure paint mark faces in the correct direction, **Fig. 7.**
   b. Final tightening of the parallel and radius link must be done with tires on ground.
   c. Check rear wheel alignment.

TIGHTENING SPECIFICATIONS

Year	Component	Torque/ Ft. Lbs.
1993–96	Axle Nut	137–188
	Driveshaft Nut	137–188
	Front Parallel Link To Suspension Crossmember	72–87
	Hub Nut	137–188
	Lower Strut Mounting Bolts	87–108
	Piston Rod Locknut	43–58
	Radius Link To Suspension Crossmember	62–72
	Rear Parallel Link To Suspension Crossmember	72–87
	Stabilizer Bar Clamps	30–35
	Stabilizer Bar Connecting Rod	30–35
	Suspension Member	62–72
	Upper Strut Securing Nuts	31–40
	Wheel Lug Nut	72–87

Front Suspension & Steering

INDEX

	Page No.
Ball Joint, Replace	32-12
Lower	32-12
Ball Joint Inspection	32-12
Manual Steering Gears	36-1
Power Steering	36-1
Power Steering Gear, Replace	32-13
Power Steering Pump, Replace	32-13
Strut, Replace	32-12
Tightening Specifications	32-15
Wheel Bearing Inspection	32-12
Wheel Hub & Steering Knuckle, Replace	32-12

WHEEL BEARING INSPECTION

1. Raise and support vehicle.
2. Remove brake pads.
3. Ensure wheel bearing is tightened to the correct specification.
4. Ensure wheel bearing operates smoothly.
5. Check axial endplay.
6. If axial endplay is not .0020 inch or less, replace wheel bearing.

WHEEL HUB & STEERING KNUCKLE

REPLACE

1. Raise and support vehicle, then remove wheel.
2. Remove wheel bearing locknut, **Fig. 1,** then the brake caliper. **Brake hose need not be disconnected from brake caliper. Do not depress brake pedal with caliper removed.**
3. Separate tie rod from knuckle using a suitable tool.
4. Separate driveshafts from knuckle by lightly tapping end of driveshaft.
5. Remove knuckle attaching bolts as shown in **Fig. 2,** then the knuckle.
6. To remove wheel bearing assembly from knuckle, proceed as follows:
   a. Drive hub with inner race from knuckle using suitable tool.
   b. Remove bearing inner race, then the grease seal.
   c. Using a screwdriver, remove inner grease seal from knuckle.
   d. Remove inner and outer snap rings.
   e. Using a suitable tool, press out bearing outer race.
7. To install wheel bearing assembly into knuckle, proceed as follows:
   a. Install inner snap ring into groove of knuckle.
   b. Using a suitable press, press new wheel bearing assembly into knuckle. **Do not press inner race of wheel bearing assembly. Do not apply oil or grease to mating surfaces of wheel bearing outer race and knuckle.**
   c. Install outer snap ring into groove of knuckle.
   d. Pack grease seal lip with multi-purpose grease, then install outer grease seal.
   e. Install inner grease seal, then press hub into knuckle.
8. Reverse steps 1 through 5 to install wheel hub and steering knuckle assembly.

BALL JOINT INSPECTION

Check ball joint for play. If ball stud is worn, play in axial direction (C) is more than zero inches, ball joint swing force (A) is not 1.8–12.3 lbs. or ball joint turning torque (B) is not 4.3–30.4 inch lbs., replace ball joint, **Fig. 3.** Before checking, turn ball joint at least ten revolutions.

BALL JOINT

REPLACE

LOWER

1. Raise and support vehicle, then remove wheel.
2. Remove stabilizer connecting rod from transverse link.
3. Remove cotter pin and locknut securing lower ball joint to knuckle.
4. Strike knuckle with a hammer to separate lower ball joint from knuckle.
5. Remove bolts and nuts shown in **Fig. 4.**
6. Remove transverse link and lower ball joint.
7. Reverse procedure to install, noting the following:
   a. Final tightening of bolts and nuts must be done with vehicle at curb height and tires on the ground.
   b. Check wheel alignment.

STRUT

REPLACE

1. Raise and support front of vehicle, then remove wheels.
2. Disconnect brake line from strut if necessary.

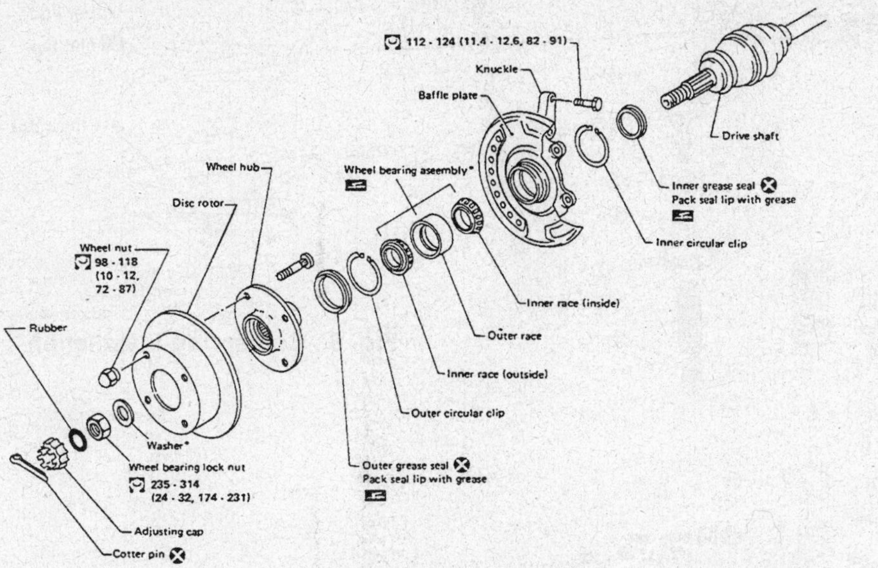
112 - 124 (11.4 - 12.6, 82 - 91)
Knuckle
Baffle plate
Drive shaft
Wheel hub
Wheel bearing assembly*
Disc rotor
Inner grease seal
Pack seal lip with grease
Inner circular clip
Wheel nut
98 - 118
(10 - 12,
72 - 87)
Inner race (inside)
Rubber
Outer race
Inner race (outside)
Outer circular clip
Washer*
Wheel bearing lock nut
235 - 314
(24 - 32, 174 - 231)
Outer grease seal
Pack seal lip with grease
Adjusting cap
Cotter pin
NS2049100022000X

Fig. 1 Exploded view of wheel hub & steering knuckle

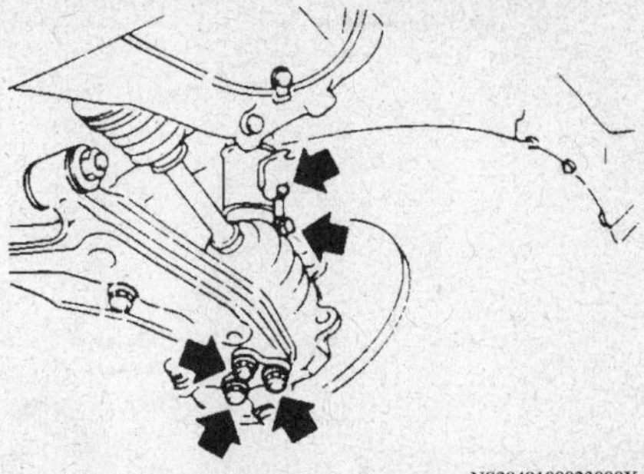
NS2049100023000X

Fig. 2 Knuckle & hub assembly removal

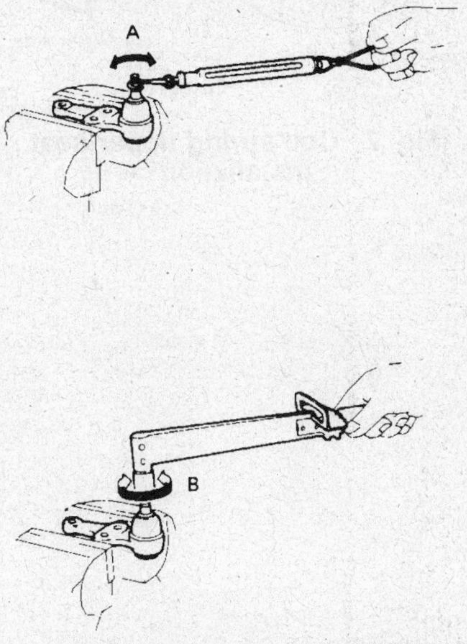
A
B
NS2029100013000X

Fig. 3 Ball joint inspection

3. Remove strut to steering knuckle attaching nuts and bolts, **Fig. 5.**
4. Remove strut to strut tower attaching nuts, then the strut assembly from the vehicle.
5. To disassemble strut assembly, proceed as follows:
   a. Secure strut assembly in a vise.
   b. Loosen piston rod locknut. **Do not remove piston rod locknut at this time.**
   c. Using spring compressor tool No. HT71780000, or equivalent, compress coil spring until strut mounting insulator can be turned by hand.
   d. Remove piston rod locknut.
   e. Remove remaining parts from strut assembly.

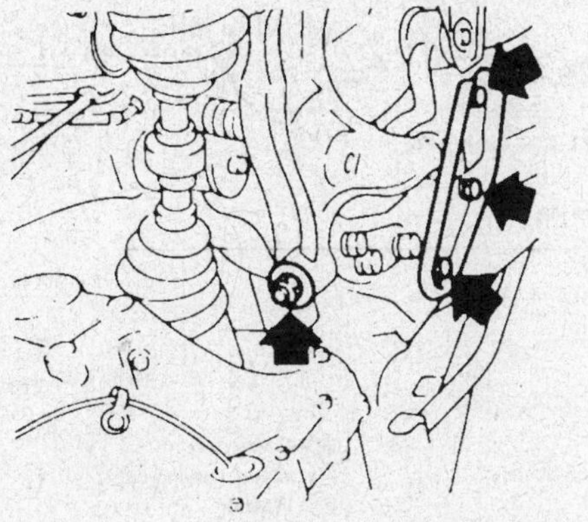
NS2029100019000X

Fig. 4 Transverse link & lower ball joint removal

6. To assemble strut assembly, proceed as follows:
   a. Install bound bumper and dust cover.
   b. Install spring, position spring as shown in **Figs. 6.**
   c. Install upper spring seat, ensure it is positioned as shown in **Fig. 7.**
   d. Install strut lock washer, then the strut mounting insulator.
   e. Install piston rod locknut and tighten to specifications.
   f. Install cap and spacer.
7. Reverse steps 1 through 4 to install strut assembly.

POWER STEERING GEAR

REPLACE

1. Raise and support front of vehicle, then remove wheels.
2. Disconnect power steering hose clamp, then the hose at steering gear and drain fluid into a suitable container.
3. Disconnect tie rod studs from steering knuckles.
4. Remove bolt securing lower joint to steering gear pinion and remove lower joint from pinion. Refer to **Fig. 8,** when replacing power steering gear.
5. Remove steering gear attaching bolts.
6. Remove steering gear and linkage assembly from vehicle.
7. Reverse procedure to install.

POWER STEERING PUMP

REPLACE

1. Remove air conditioning compressor drive belt.
2. Loosen idler pulley locknut.
3. Turn adjusting nut counterclockwise and remove power steering pump drive belt.
4. Loosen power steering hoses at pump and remove bolts securing power steering pump to brackets.
5. Raise pump and disconnect power steering hoses. Catch fluid in a suitable container, plug hose ends and ports in power steering pump, and remove pump from vehicle.
6. Reverse procedure to install, then bleed system as follows:
   a. Raise and support front of vehicle.
   b. Run engine for three to five seconds, stop engine, check and fill power steering pump reservoir as needed.
   c. Quickly turn steering wheel all the way to right and left ten times.
   d. Start engine and idle for three to five seconds. Stop engine, check and fill power steering pump reservoir as needed.
   e. With steering wheel all the way to the right, open bleeder screw, to expel air and tighten bleeder screw.
   f. Repeat procedure until all air has been bled from system.
   g. If air cannot be bled completely after repeated attempts, repeat step e with engine running.

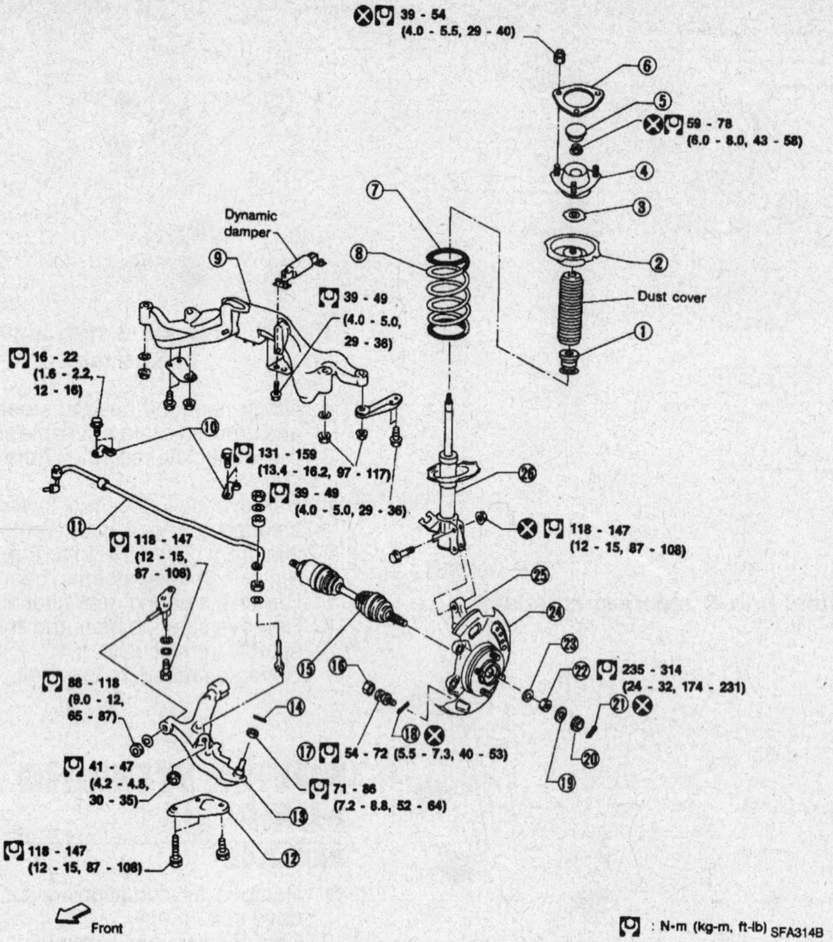
39 - 54
(4.0 - 5.5, 29 - 40)
59 - 78
(6.0 - 8.0, 43 - 58)
Dynamic damper
Dust cover
39 - 49
(4.0 - 5.0,
29 - 36)
16 - 22
(1.6 - 2.2,
12 - 16)
131 - 159
(13.4 - 16.2, 97 - 117)
39 - 49
(4.0 - 5.0, 29 - 36)
118 - 147
(12 - 15,
87 - 108)
118 - 147
(12 - 15, 87 - 108)
88 - 118
(9.0 - 12,
65 - 87)
235 - 314
(24 - 32, 174 - 231)
54 - 72 (5.5 - 7.3, 40 - 53)
41 - 47
(4.2 - 4.8,
30 - 35)
71 - 86
(7.2 - 8.8, 52 - 64)
118 - 147
(12 - 15, 87 - 108)
Front
: N·m (kg-m, ft-lb) SFA314B

1. Bound bumper assembly
2. Upper spring seat
3. Strut mounting insulator
4. Plain washer
5. Cap
6. Spacer
7. (Polyuretane tube)
8. Coil spring
9. Front suspension member
10. Stabilizer clamp
11. Stabilizer
12. Compression rod bushing
13. Transverse link
14. Cotter pin
15. Drive shaft
16. Cap
17. Stopper bolt
18. Cotter pin
19. Insulator (Rubber)
20. Adjusting cap
21. Cotter pin
22. Wheel bearing cap
23. Washer
24. Baffle plate
25. Knuckle
26. Strut assembly
27. Dynamic damper assembly

NS2029100015000X

Fig. 5 Exploded view of front suspension

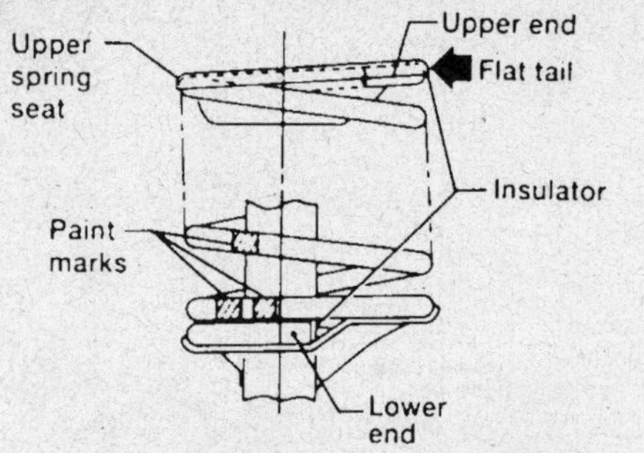
Upper spring seat
Upper end
Flat tail
Insulator
Paint marks
Lower end

NS2029100016000X

Fig. 6 Coil spring installation

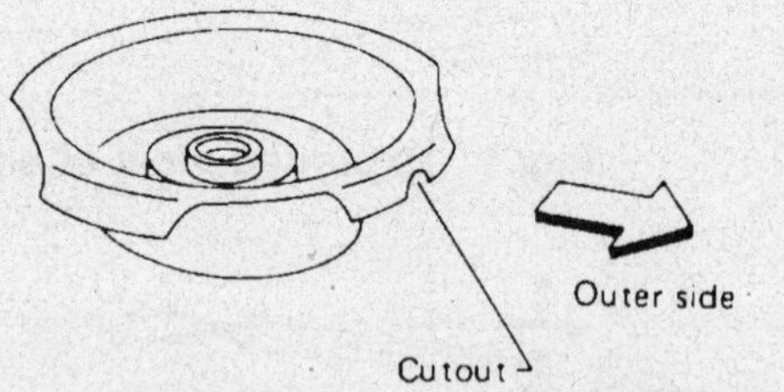
Outer side
Cutout

NS2029100018000X

Fig. 7 Coil spring upper seat installation

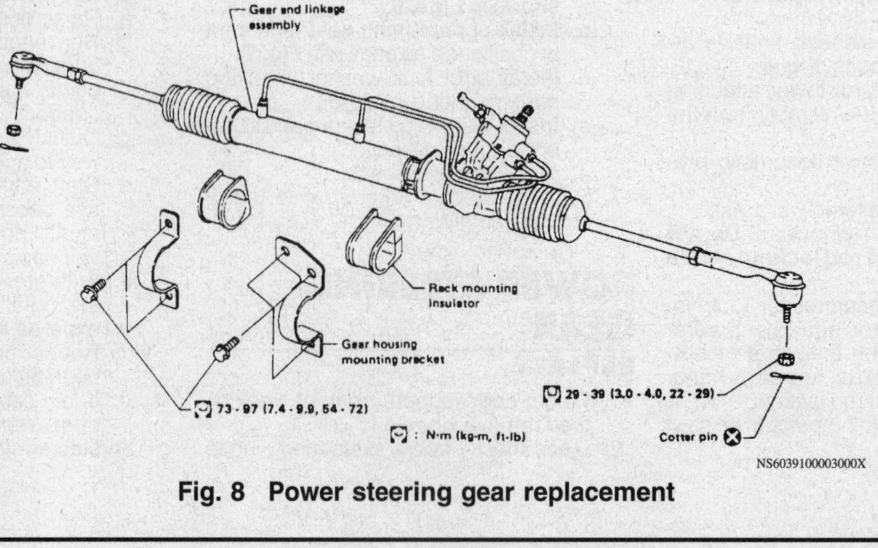
Gear and linkage assembly
Rack mounting insulator
Gear housing mounting bracket
73 - 97 (7.4 - 9.9, 54 - 72)
29 - 39 (3.0 - 4.0, 22 - 29)
: N·m (kg-m, ft-lb)
Cotter pin

NS6039100003000X

Fig. 8 Power steering gear replacement

TIGHTENING SPECIFICATIONS

Year	Component	Torque/Ft. Lbs.
1993–96	Axle Nut	174–231
	Ball Joint Attaching Nut	56–80
	Driveshaft Nut	174–231
	Hub Nut	174–231
	Piston Rod Locknut	43–58
	Steering Gear Attaching Bolts	54–72
	Steering Knuckle Upper Attaching Bolt	82–91
	Strut To Lower Knuckle Arm Attaching Bolts	82–91
	Tie Rod Attaching Nut	22–29
	Transverse Link Attaching Nuts	65–87
	Transverse Link Bracket Attaching Nuts	87–108
	Upper Strut Attaching Bolts	43–53
	Wheel Bearing Locknut	174–231
	Wheel Lug Nut	72–87

Wheel Alignment

INDEX

	Page No.
Front Wheel Alignment	32-15
Camber	32-15
Caster & Kingpin Inclination	32-15
Steering Angle	32-16
Toe Setting	32-15
Preliminary Inspection	32-15
Rear Wheel Alignment	32-16
Camber	32-16
Toe-In	32-16
Vehicle Ride Height	32-16
Wheel Alignment Specifications	32-2

PRELIMINARY INSPECTION

Prior to checking and adjusting wheel alignment angles, perform the following inspections:

1. Check tire pressures and adjust as needed.
2. Ensure tires are of the proper size and are properly matched.
3. Ensure wheel bearings are properly adjusted.
4. Check steering gear adjustment and ensure steering gear is properly secured to frame.
5. Inspect steering linkage and suspension components for damage and wear, and repair or replace components as needed.
6. Measure vehicle ride height with vehicle unloaded and ensure springs are not collapsed.
7. Place vehicle on suitable alignment rack following manufacturer's instructions, then jounce vehicle several times to settle suspension.
8. Check and correct rear wheel camber and toe first, if applicable, then check and correct front suspension angles in the following order: caster and kingpin inclination, camber, toe setting and turning angle (toe-out on turns).

FRONT WHEEL ALIGNMENT

Correct front wheel alignment is necessary to provide proper handling and to prevent uneven tire wear. To ensure correct alignment, angles should be checked, and if necessary corrected, in the following sequence: caster and kingpin inclination, camber, toe-setting, and the turning angle and toe-out on turns. Front wheel alignment should only be checked after ensuring the rear wheels are properly aligned in relation to the vehicle centerline, as most equipment uses the rear wheels as reference for correct front wheel alignment. Front wheel alignment should be checked with the vehicle at normal ride height, and following equipment manufacturer's instructions.

CASTER & KINGPIN INCLINATION

Kingpin inclination is a function of the steering knuckle design and cannot be adjusted. Caster, the alignment angle which provides the self-centering steering effect, is not adjustable. If caster or kingpin angle are not within specifications, check suspension components and sheet metal for damage, distortion and excessive wear, repair or replace as necessary.

CAMBER

Camber cannot be adjusted. If camber is not within specifications, inspect suspension and sheet metal for damage, distortion and excessive wear, and repair or replace components as needed.

TOE SETTING

The toe setting is the measurement of the wheels in relation to the vehicle centerline, **Fig. 1.** The leading edge of each wheel should toe-in or toe-out slightly in relation to the vehicle centerline to ensure proper vehicle tracking. Toe should be inspected using suitable alignment gauges, following manufacturer's instructions. When checking or adjusting toe, always ensure the setting of the left and right wheels is as equal as possible.

Toe is adjusted by loosening the tie rod locknuts or adjusting sleeve bolts and equally altering the length of the tie rods. After toe has been adjusted to specifications, the lengths of the left and right tie rods, **Fig. 2,** should be nearly equal. If tie rod lengths are incorrect, tie rods should be disassembled and adjusted to equal

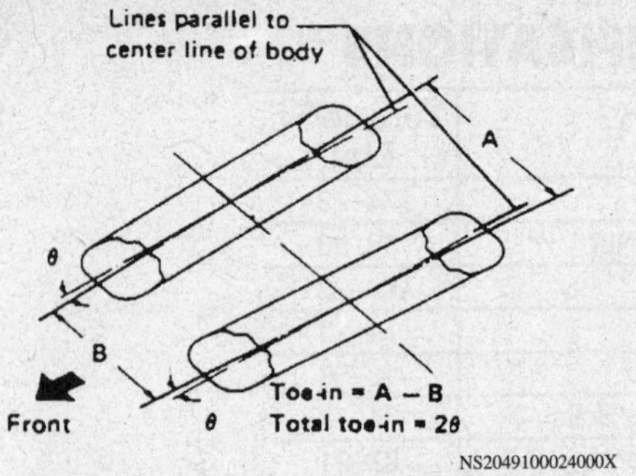
Lines parallel to
center line of body
A
B
Front
Toe-in = A – B
Total toe-in = 2θ
NS2049100024000X

Fig. 1 Toe-in measurement

Year	Model	Turning Angle①	
		Inner Wheel	Outer Wheel
1993–96	Altima	32–35°	26–29°

① — At full lock.

Fig. 3 Turning angle specifications

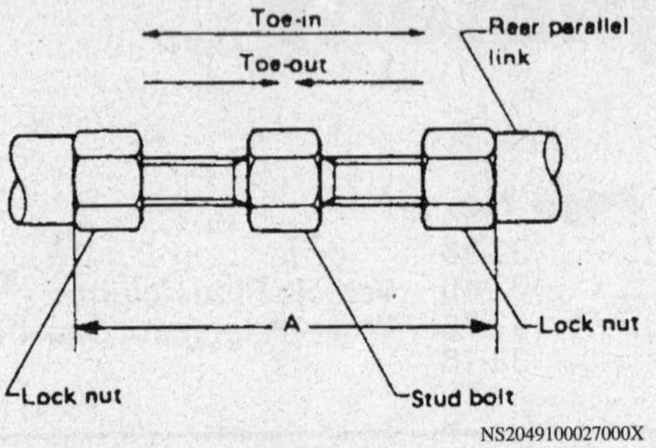
Toe-in
Toe-out
Rear parallel
link
A
Lock nut
Lock nut
Stud bolt
NS2049100027000X

Fig. 5 Parallel link length measurement

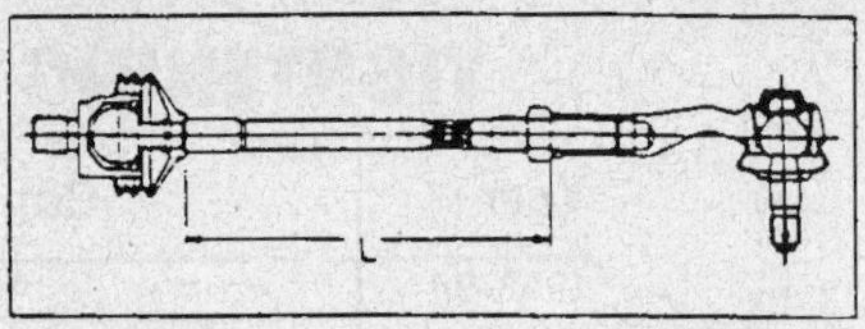
L
NS2049100025000X

Fig. 2 Tie rod length measurement

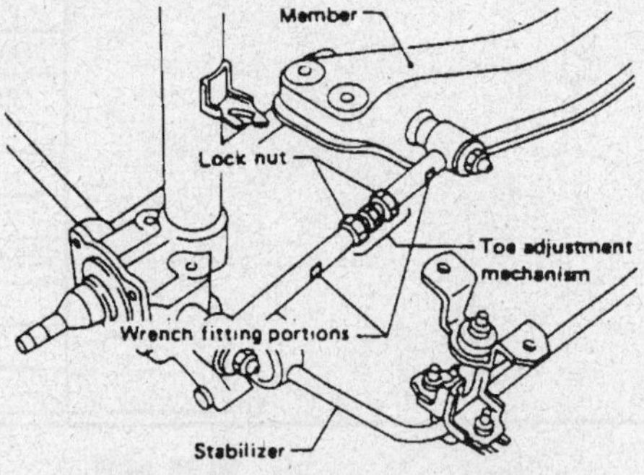
Member
Lock nut
Toe adjustment
mechanism
Wrench fitting portions
Stabilizer
NS2049100026000X

Fig. 4 Rear toe-in adjustment

lengths, and the toe setting should be readjusted before checking steering angles. Incorrect tie rod length will adversely affect steering angles and toe-out on turns.

STEERING ANGLE

1. Set wheel in a straight ahead position.
2. Position front wheel on turning radius gauge.
3. Rotate fully steering wheel to right and left.
4. Ensure turning angle is as specified in **Fig. 3.**

REAR WHEEL ALIGNMENT

The proper alignment of the rear suspension and wheels is essential for proper handling and to providing a reference for front wheel alignment. Always ensure rear wheel alignment is within specifications prior to checking and adjusting front wheel alignment.

CAMBER

Rear camber cannot be adjusted. If rear camber is not within specifications, check for damaged or worn suspension components and deformed sheet metal, and repair as needed.

TOE-IN

On models with independent rear suspension, rear toe is the measurement of the rear wheels in relation to the vehicle centerline, **Fig. 1.** The leading edge of each rear wheel should toe-in slightly toward the vehicle centerline to ensure proper vehicle tracking. Rear toe should be inspected using suitable alignment gauges, following manufacturer's instructions. When checking or adjusting rear toe, always ensure the amount that the left and right wheels toe-in is as equal as possible.

Rear toe-in is adjusted by varying the length of the rear parallel links, **Fig. 4.**

1. Measure total toe-in and toe-in for each wheel following equipment manufacturer's instructions.
2. Loosen locknuts and adjust parallel link length to obtain specified toe-in, noting the following:
   a. Adjust left and right rear parallel links to the same length A, **Fig. 5.**
   b. Standard length is 1.97–2.17 inches. If toe-in cannot be properly adjusted with links at equal length, and at or near specified standard length, check rear suspension for damage and wear, and repair as needed.
3. After adjustment, hold link with suitable wrench to prevent bushing from twisting, then **torque** locknuts to 58–72 ft. lbs.

VEHICLE RIDE HEIGHT

When checking ride height vehicle must be parked on a level surface and tires inflated to proper air pressure. Ensure all fluid levels are to specified level, spare tire and jack are in proper locations.

Bounce vehicle up and down several times, then measure vehicle height from top of wheelwell to ground. Vehicle height is not adjustable. If vehicle height is not as specified, check for worn springs or suspension parts. Vehicle ride heights are as follows:

1. **On SE models,** vehicle ride height should be 27.17 inches in the front of vehicle and 26.69 inches in the rear of vehicle.
2. **On XE/GLE/GXE models,** vehicle ride height should be 27.20 inches in the front of vehicle and 26.77 inches in the rear of vehicle.

NISSAN 240SX

INDEX OF SERVICE OPERATIONS

Page No.

AIR BAG SYSTEM PRECAUTIONS 0-8
AUTOMATIC TRANSMISSIONS/ TRANSAXLES 36-1
BRAKES
- Anti-Lock Brakes 36-1
- Disc Brakes 36-1
- Drum Brakes 36-1
- Hydraulic Brake Systems 36-1
- Power Brake Units 36-1

CLUTCH & MANUAL TRANSMISSION
- Adjustments 33-13
- Clutch, Replace 33-13
- Hydraulic System Service 33-13
- Tightening Specifications 33-14
- Transmission, Replace 33-13

ELECTRICAL
- Air Bags 36-1
- Air Conditioning 36-1
- Alternators 36-1
- Blower Motor, Replace 33-5
- Combination Switch, Replace 33-4
- Cooling Fans 36-1
- Cruise Control 36-1
- Dash Gauges 36-1
- Dash Panels 36-1
- Distributor, Replace 33-3
- Evaporator Core, Replace 33-5
- Fuel Pump Relay Location 33-3
- Fuse Panel & Flasher Location 33-3
- Headlamp Switch, Replace 33-4
- Heater Core, Replace 33-5
- Ignition Lock, Replace 33-3
- Ignition Switch, Replace 33-3
- Instrument Cluster, Replace 33-4
- Neutral Safety Switch, Replace 33-4
- Passive Restraints 36-1
- Precautions 33-3
- Radio, Replace 33-4
- Relay Center Location 33-3
- Speed Controls 36-1
- Starter Motors 36-1
- Starter, Replace 33-3
- Steering Columns 36-1
- Steering Wheel, Replace 33-4
- Stop Light Switch, Replace 33-4
- Turn Signal Switch, Replace 33-4
- Wiper Motor, Replace 33-4
- Wiper Switch, Replace 33-4
- Wiper Systems 36-1
- Wiper Transmission, Replace 33-5

ELECTRICAL SYMBOL IDENTIFICATION 0-139
FRONT SUSPENSION & STEERING
- Ball Joint, Replace 33-18
- Ball Joint Inspection 33-17
- Manual Steering Gears 36-1
- Power Steering 36-1
- Power Steering Gear, Replace 33-19
- Power Steering Pump, Replace 33-19
- Strut, Replace 33-18
- Tension Strut, Replace 33-18
- Tightening Specifications 33-19
- Transverse Link, Replace 33-18
- Wheel Bearing, Adjust 33-17
- Wheel Hub & Steering Knuckle, Replace 33-17

FRONT WHEEL DRIVE AXLES 36-1
KA24DE ENGINE
- Belt Tension Data 33-11
- Compression Pressure 33-6
- Cooling System Bleed 33-11
- Crankshaft Rear Oil Seal, Replace 33-11
- Crankshaft Seal, Replace 33-11
- Cylinder Head, Replace 33-7
- Engine Assemble 33-9
- Engine Disassemble 33-8
- Engine Mount, Replace 33-7
- Engine Rebuilding Specifications 36-1
- Engine, Replace 33-7
- Exhaust Manifold, Replace 33-7
- Fuel Filter, Replace 33-11
- Fuel Pump, Replace 33-11
- Intake Manifold, Replace 33-7
- Oil Pan, Replace 33-11
- Oil Pump, Replace 33-11
- Precautions 33-6
- Radiator, Replace 33-11
- Technical Service Bulletins 33-12
- Thermostat, Replace 33-11
- Tightening Specifications 33-12
- Timing Chain, Replace 33-10
- Valve Adjustment 33-9
- Valve Clearance Specifications 33-9
- Water Pump, Replace 33-11

REAR AXLE & SUSPENSION
- Hub & Bearing, Replace 33-15
- Rear Suspension, Replace 33-15
- Stabilizer Bar, Replace 33-15
- Strut, Replace 33-15
- Strut Service 33-15
- Tightening Specifications 33-17

SERVICE REMINDER & WARNING LAMP RESET PROCEDURES 0-10
SPECIFICATIONS
- Fluid Capacities & Cooling System Data 33-2
- Front Wheel Alignment Specifications 33-2
- General Engine Specifications 33-2
- Lubricant Data 33-3
- Rear Wheel Alignment Specifications 33-2
- Tune Up Specifications 33-2

VEHICLE IDENTIFICATION 0-1
VEHICLE LIFT POINTS 0-34
VEHICLE MAINTENANCE SCHEDULES 0-69
WHEEL ALIGNMENT
- Front Wheel Alignment 33-20
- Preliminary Inspection 33-20
- Rear Wheel Alignment 33-20
- Vehicle Ride Height 33-20
- Wheel Alignment Specifications 33-2

WIRE COLOR CODE IDENTIFICATION 0-144

Specifications

GENERAL ENGINE SPECIFICATIONS

Year	Engine Model	Fuel System	Displacement Liters	Bore X Stroke Inches	Compression Ratio	Maximum HP @ RPM	Maximum Torque @ RPM	Normal Oil Pressure psi
1993–96	KA24DE	Fuel Inj.	2.4L	3.50 X 3.78	9.5	155 @ 5600	160 @ 4400	60–70

TUNE UP SPECIFICATIONS

Year	Engine Model	Spark Plug Gap Inch	Ignition Timing		Curb Idle Speed①		Fast Idle Speed		Fuel Pump Pressure psi	Valve Lash
			Firing Order	Timing °BTDC	Man. Trans.	Auto. Trans.	Man. Trans.	Auto. Trans.		
1993–96	KA24DE	.041	1-3-4-2	20	700	700N	—	—	34	②

BTDC: Before Top Dead Center.
N: Neutral.
① — When adjusting idle speed, set parking brake & chock drive wheels.
② — Refer to "Valve Adjustment" under "KA24E Engine."

FRONT WHEEL ALIGNMENT SPECIFICATIONS

Year	Caster Angle, Deg.		Camber Angle, Deg.		King Pin Inclination, Deg.	Toe-in Inch①	Toe-Out On Turns, Deg.②		Ball Joint Wear
	Limits	Desired	Limits	Desired			Inner Wheel	Outer Wheel	
1993–96	+6 to +7 ½	+6 ¾	—1 ½ to 0	–¾	12 ½ to 14	+.012 to +.091	39 to 43	33	③

① — Toe-in (+); toe-out (-).
② — Measure w/wheels at full left & righthand turn positions.
③ — Refer to "Ball Joint Inspection" under "Front Suspension & Steering."

REAR WHEEL ALIGNMENT SPECIFICATIONS

Year	Camber Angle, Deg.		Toe, Inch①
	Limits	Desired	
1993–94	–1 ⅗ to –⅗	–1 ⅒	+.20 to +.177
1995–96	–1 ⅔ to –⅔	–1 ⅙	0 to +.197

① — Toe-in (+); toe-out (–).

FLUID CAPACITIES & COOLING SYSTEM DATA

Year	Coolant Capacity Qts.	Radiator, Cap Relief Pressure Lbs.	Thermo. Opening Temp. °F	Fuel Tank Gals.	Engine Oil Refill Qts.①	Transmission Oil		Differential Oil Pts.
						Man. Trans. Pts.	Auto. Trans. Qts.②	
1993–94	7 ⅛	11–14	170	15 ⅞	3 ¾	5 ⅛	8 ¾	③
1995–96	7 ¼	11-14	170	17 ⅛	4	5 ⅛	8 ¾	2 ¾

① — Includes filter.
② — Approximate, make final check w/dipstick.
③ — R200, 2 3/4 pts.; R200V, 3 1/8 pts.

LUBRICANT DATA

Year	Lubricant Type					
	Transmission		Transfer Case	Rear Axle	Power Steering	Brake System
	Manual	Automatic				
1993–96	75W-90 GL-4	Nissan Matic D ①	—	80W-90 GL-5	Dexron II/IIE/III	DOT 3

① — Dexron III/Mercon or equivalent automatic transmission fluid may also be used.

Electrical

NOTE: On Air Bag Equipped Models, Refer To "Air Bag System Precautions" Located In Front Of This Manual For System Disarming & Arming Procedures.

INDEX

	Page No.
Air Bags	36-1
Air Conditioning	36-1
Alternators	36-1
Blower Motor, Replace	33-5
Combination Switch, Replace	33-4
Cooling Fans	36-1
Cruise Control	36-1
Dash Gauges	36-1
Dash Panels	36-1
Distributor, Replace	33-3
Evaporator Core, Replace	33-5
Fuel Pump Relay Location	33-3
Fuse Panel & Flasher Location	33-3
Headlamp Switch, Replace	33-4
Heater Core, Replace	33-5
Ignition Lock, Replace	33-3
Ignition Switch, Replace	33-3
Instrument Cluster, Replace	33-4
Neutral Safety Switch, Replace	33-4
Passive Restraints	36-1
Precautions	33-3
Air Bag Systems	33-3
Radio, Replace	33-4
Relay Center Location	33-3
Speed Controls	36-1
Starter Motors	36-1
Starter, Replace	33-3
Steering Columns	36-1
Steering Wheel, Replace	33-4
Stop Light Switch, Replace	33-4
Turn Signal Switch, Replace	33-4
Wiper Motor, Replace	33-4
Front	33-4
Rear	33-4
Wiper Switch, Replace	33-4
Front	33-4
Rear	33-4
Wiper Systems	36-1
Wiper Transmission, Replace	33-5

PRECAUTIONS

AIR BAG SYSTEMS

Refer to "Air Bag System Precautions" in front of this manual for system disarming and arming procedures.

FUSE PANEL & FLASHER LOCATION

The fuse panel is located under lefthand side of the instrument panel, left of the steering column.

The combination flasher unit is located behind the lefthand side of the instrument panel, near the steering column.

FUEL PUMP RELAY LOCATION

The fuel pump relay is located behind the driver's side kick panel near the fuse panel.

RELAY CENTER LOCATION

Relay center No. 1 is located at the front lefthand side of the engine compartment. Relay center No. 2 is located on the righthand side of the engine compartment, rear of the battery.

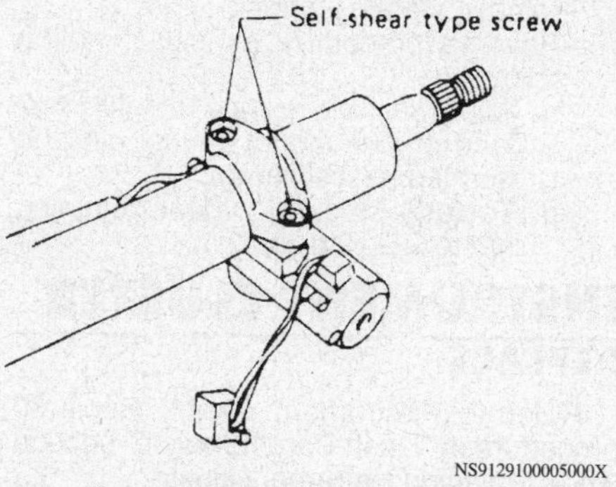

Self-shear type screw
NS9129100005000X

Fig. 1 Ignition lock replacement

STARTER

REPLACE

1. Disconnect battery ground cable.
2. **On models with automatic transmission,** proceed as follows:
   a. Support transmission with suitable jack.
   b. Remove four rear mounting bracket bolts.
   c. Slightly lower transmission.
   d. Remove ATF level gauge pipe.
3. **On all models,** disconnect starter wiring from starter.
4. Remove starter retaining bolts and starter.
5. Reverse procedure to install.

DISTRIBUTOR

REPLACE

1. Disconnect battery ground cable.
2. Remove distributor cap and spark plug cables as an assembly.
3. Disconnect distributor electrical connections.
4. Remove distributor retaining bolt.
5. Remove distributor assembly.
6. Reverse procedure to install, **torque** distributor retaining bolt to 12–14 ft. lbs.

IGNITION LOCK

REPLACE

Ignition lock is retained by two shear type screws, **Fig. 1.** It is necessary to drill out these screws to remove ignition lock from steering tube. When installing, ensure shear type screws are used.

IGNITION SWITCH

REPLACE

1. Remove four upper and lower shell cover retaining screws, then shell covers.
2. Disconnect electrical connectors from switch.
3. Remove switch retaining screw from steering lock, **Fig. 2.**
4. Remove switch.

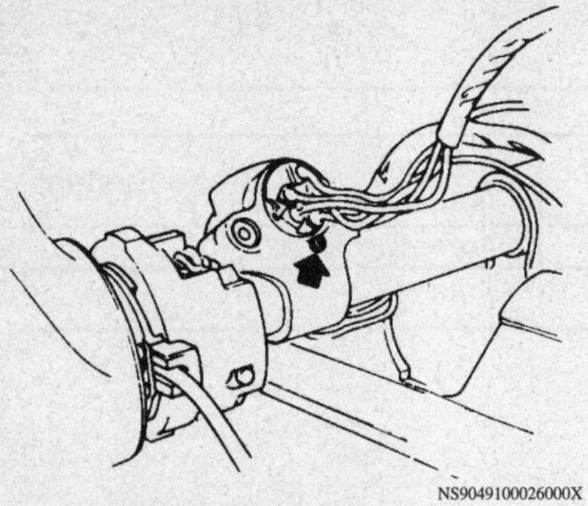
NS9049100026000X

Fig. 2 Ignition switch replacement

5. Reverse procedure to install.

NEUTRAL SAFETY SWITCH

REPLACE

1. Loosen inhibitor switch attaching screws, **Fig. 3.**
2. Set selector lever manual shaft at Neutral position.
3. Insert suitable pin into adjustment holes in both inhibitor switch and switch lever as near vertical as possible, then tighten screws.
4. Check switch for continuity, replace as necessary.

HEADLAMP SWITCH

REPLACE

1. Remove steering column covers.
2. Disconnect light switch electrical connectors.
3. Remove switch retaining screws and light switch. It is not necessary to remove combination switch base to replace light switch.
4. Reverse procedure to install.

STOP LIGHT SWITCH

REPLACE

Stop light switch is located on brake pedal support.

1. Disconnect switch electrical connectors.
2. Loosen switch retaining locknut and remove switch.
3. Reverse procedure to install.

COMBINATION SWITCH

REPLACE

1. Remove horn cover and steering wheel as outlined in "Steering Wheel, Replace."
2. Remove steering column shell covers.
3. Disconnect switch electrical connections.
4. Remove retaining screws.
5. Push switch toward instrument panel, then turn switch clockwise and remove combination switch base assembly.
6. Reverse procedure to install.

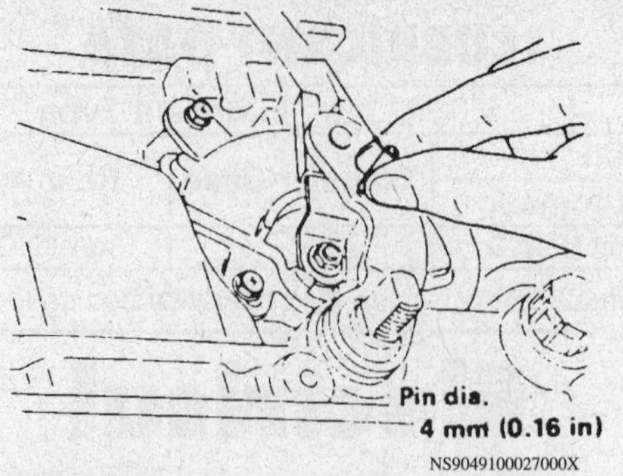
Pin dia.
4 mm (0.16 in)
NS9049100027000X

Fig. 3 Adjusting inhibitor switch

TURN SIGNAL SWITCH

REPLACE

1. Remove steering column covers.
2. Disconnect turn signal switch electrical connections.
3. Remove switch retaining screws, then turn signal switch. It is not necessary to remove combination switch base to replace turn signal switch.
4. Reverse procedure to install.

STEERING WHEEL

REPLACE

1. Disconnect battery ground cable.
2. **On 1993–94 models,** remove horn pad.
3. **On 1995–96 models,** remove drivers side air bag as outlined in "Passive Restraints."
4. **On all models,** remove steering wheel retaining nut.
5. Use suitable steering wheel puller and remove steering wheel.
6. Reverse procedure to install, noting following:
   a. Apply suitable grease to entire surface of turn signal cancel pin and horn contact slip ring.
   b. **Torque** steering wheel retaining nut to 22–29 ft. lbs.

INSTRUMENT CLUSTER

REPLACE

Refer to "Instrument Panel, Replace" procedure in "Dash Panel Service" section when replacing instrument cluster.

1. Remove steering column cover and steering wheel.
2. Remove gear shift boot.
3. Remove instrument panel cover.
4. Remove cluster lid retaining screws, then the cluster lid.
5. Disconnect speedometer cable, cluster retaining nuts and electrical connectors. Cluster may have to be pulled slightly forward after removing retaining screws to allow access to electrical connectors.
6. Reverse procedure to install.

RADIO

REPLACE

Refer to "Instrument Panel, Replace" procedure in "Dash Panel Service" section when replacing radio.

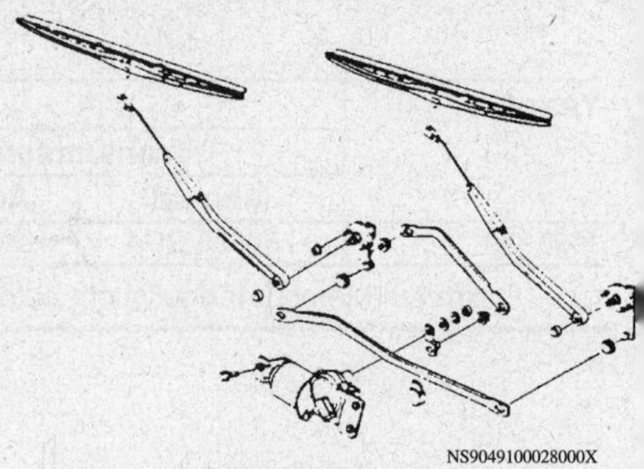
NS9049100028000X

Fig. 4 Windshield wiper system

1. Disconnect battery ground cable.
2. Remove cluster lid or instrument panel fascia to gain access to brackets.
3. Remove radio bracket to instrument panel attaching screw.
4. Disconnect electrical leads from radio.
5. Remove radio from vehicle.
6. Reverse procedure to install.

WIPER MOTOR

REPLACE

FRONT

Refer to **Fig. 4** for typical wiper system exploded view.

1. Remove wiper arms.
2. Disconnect electrical connector from motor, then remove top grille retaining screws and top grille.
3. Remove wiper motor mounting bolts and pull motor away from firewall.
4. Disconnect motor shaft from linkage taking care not to bend linkage.
5. Remove cowl top grille.
6. Remove flange nuts retaining pivot to cowl top.
7. Remove wiper motor linkage.
8. Reverse procedure to install.

REAR

1. Disconnect battery ground cable.
2. Raise rear wiper arm off glass and remove retaining nut.
3. Remove tailgate inner trim panel and disconnect electrical connection at motor.
4. Remove wiper motor retaining bolts, then the wiper motor.
5. Reverse procedure to install.

WIPER SWITCH

REPLACE

FRONT

1. Remove steering column covers.
2. Disconnect wiper switch electrical connections.
3. Remove switch retaining screws, then the switch. It is not necessary to remove combination switch base to replace wiper switch.
4. Reverse procedure to install.

REAR

1. Disconnect electrical connector from switch.

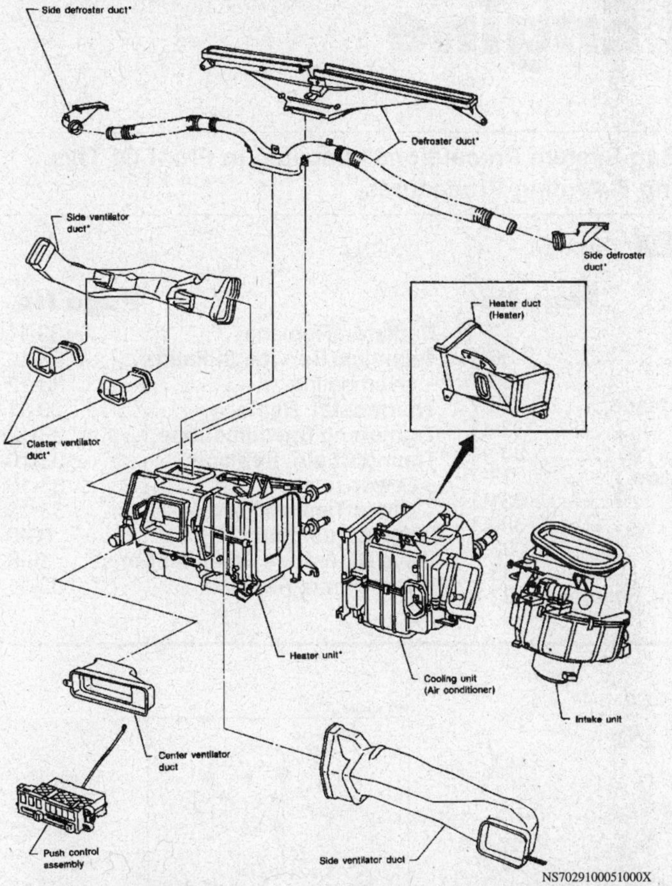
Side defroster duct*
Defroster duct*
Side ventilator duct*
Side defroster duct*
Heater duct (Heater)
Claster ventilator duct*
Heater unit*
Cooling unit (Air conditioner)
Intake unit
Center ventilator duct
Push control assembly
Side ventilator duct

NS7029100051000X

Fig. 5 Exploded view of heater system. 1993–94

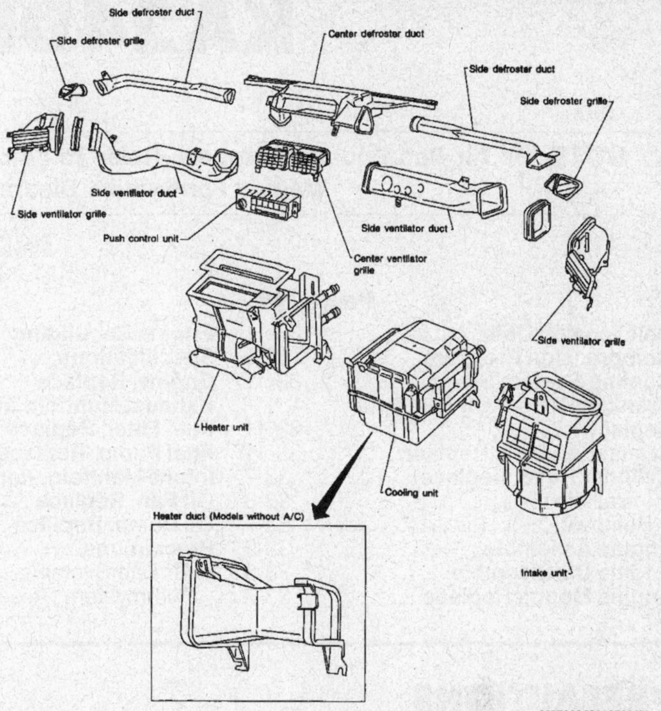
Side defroster duct
Side defroster grille
Center defroster duct
Side defroster duct
Side defroster grille
Side ventilator duct
Side ventilator grille
Push control unit
Side ventilator duct
Center ventilator grille
Side ventilator grille
Heater unit
Cooling unit
Heater duct (Models without A/C)
Intake unit

NS7029500107000X

Fig. 6 Exploded view of heater system. 1995–96

2. Remove switch knob by depressing and/or twisting as necessary.
3. Remove any switch retaining nuts or clips, then switch.
4. Reverse procedure to install.

WIPER TRANSMISSION

REPLACE

Refer to "Wiper Motor, Replace" for wiper transmission replacement.

BLOWER MOTOR

REPLACE

1. Disconnect battery ground cable and discharge A/C system.
2. Remove passenger side instrument lower cover and glove compartment.
3. Disconnect wiring harness connectors from intake unit, **Figs. 5 and 6.**
4. Remove intake unit.
5. Remove blower motor from intake unit.
6. Reverse procedure to install.

HEATER CORE

REPLACE

1. Disconnect battery ground cable and drain cooling system.
2. Disconnect heater inlet and outlet coolant pipes from heater unit.
3. Remove instrument panel as outlined in "Dash Panel Service."
4. Disconnect heater ducts, **Figs. 5 and 6.**
5. Disconnect wiring harness connectors from heater unit.
6. Remove heater unit.
7. Separate heater unit case halves and remove heater core.
8. Reverse procedure to install.

EVAPORATOR CORE

REPLACE

1. Disconnect battery ground cable, then discharge and recover A/C refrigerant.
2. Remove passenger side instrument lower cover and glove compartment.
3. Disconnect wiring harness connectors from intake unit.
4. Remove intake unit.
5. Disconnect wiring harness connectors from evaporator.
6. Remove cooling unit.
7. Separate cooling unit case halves and remove evaporator, **Figs. 5 and 6.**
8. Reverse procedure to install.

KA24DE Engine

NOTE: On Air Bag Equipped Models, Refer To "Air Bag System Precautions" Located In Front Of This Manual For System Disarming & Arming Procedures.

INDEX

	Page No.
Belt Tension Data	33-11
Compression Pressure	33-6
Cooling System Bleed	33-11
Crankshaft Rear Oil Seal, Replace	33-11
Crankshaft Seal, Replace	33-11
Cylinder Head, Replace	33-7
Installation	33-8
Removal	33-7
Engine Assemble	33-9
Engine Disassemble	33-8
Engine Mount, Replace	33-7
Engine Rebuilding Specifications	36-1
Engine, Replace	33-7
Exhaust Manifold, Replace	33-7
Fuel Filter, Replace	33-11
Fuel Pump, Replace	33-11
Intake Manifold, Replace	33-7
Oil Pan, Replace	33-11
Oil Pump, Replace	33-11
Precautions	33-6
Air Bag Systems	33-6
Fuel System Pressure Release	33-6
Radiator, Replace	33-11
Technical Service Bulletins	33-12
Overheating	33-12
Thermostat, Replace	33-11
Tightening Specifications	33-12
Timing Chain, Replace	33-10
Lower Timing Chain	33-10
Upper Timing Chain	33-10
Valve Adjustment	33-9
Valve Clearance Specifications	33-9
Water Pump, Replace	33-11

PRECAUTIONS

AIR BAG SYSTEMS

Refer to "Air Bag System Precautions" in front of this manual for system disarming and arming procedures.

FUEL SYSTEM PRESSURE RELEASE

1. Remove fuel pump fuse from fuse panel.
2. Start engine.
3. After engine stops, crank engine two or three times to release all fuel pressure.
4. Turn ignition switch to the Off position.
5. After fuel system service is complete, replace fuel pump fuse.

COMPRESSION PRESSURE

1. Start engine and run until engine reaches operating temperature.
2. Turn ignition switch off.
3. Release fuel pressure as outlined under "Precautions."
4. Remove all spark plugs.
5. Disconnect distributor center cable.
6. Attach a compression tester to cylinder No.1.
7. Depress accelerator pedal fully to keep throttle valve wide open.
8. Crank engine and record highest gauge indication.
9. Repeat measurement on each cylinder.
10. Standard compression pressure is 179 psi, minimum pressure is 151 psi. Difference between cylinders should not exceed 14 psi.
11. If compression in one or more cylinders is low, pour a small amount of engine oil into cylinders through spark plug holes, then retest compression.
12. If adding oil helps compression, then piston rings may be at fault. If adding oil does not help compression, then the valves may be at fault.
13. If compression stays low in two cylinders that are next to each other, then cylinder head gasket may be leaking or both cylinders have valve component damage.
14. Repair as necessary.

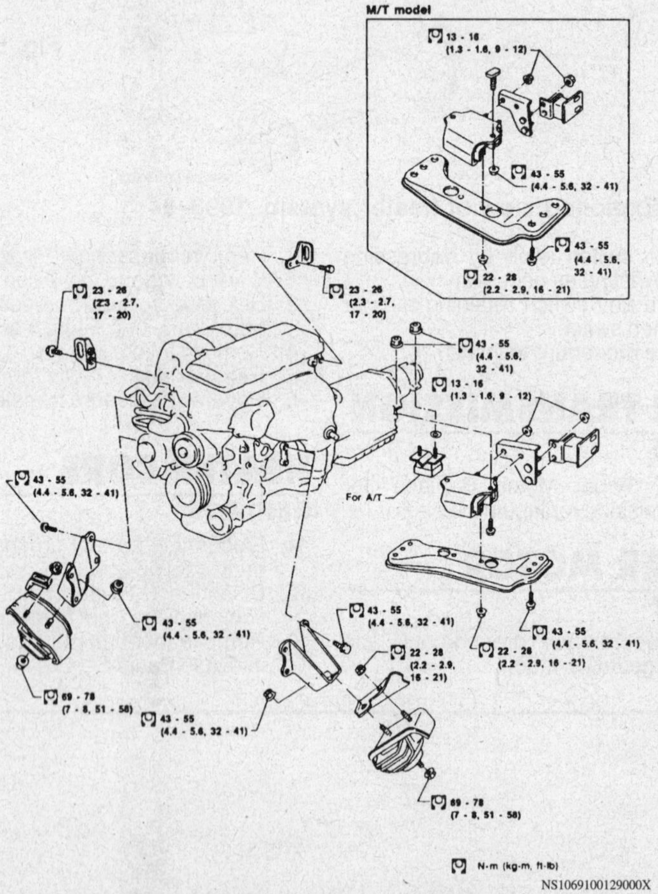

M/T model
13 - 16
(1.3 - 1.6, 9 - 12)
43 - 55
(4.4 - 5.6, 32 - 41)
43 - 55
(4.4 - 5.6, 32 - 41)
22 - 28
(2.2 - 2.9, 16 - 21)
23 - 26
(2.3 - 2.7, 17 - 20)
23 - 26
(2.3 - 2.7, 17 - 20)
43 - 55
(4.4 - 5.6, 32 - 41)
13 - 16
(1.3 - 1.6, 9 - 12)
For A/T
43 - 55
(4.4 - 5.6, 32 - 41)
43 - 55
(4.4 - 5.6, 32 - 41)
43 - 55
(4.4 - 5.6, 32 - 41)
22 - 28
(2.2 - 2.9, 16 - 21)
22 - 28
(2.2 - 2.9, 16 - 21)
43 - 55
(4.4 - 5.6, 32 - 41)
69 - 78
(7 - 8, 51 - 58)
43 - 55
(4.4 - 5.6, 32 - 41)
69 - 78
(7 - 8, 51 - 58)
N·m (kg-m, ft-lb)
NS1069100129000X

Fig. 1 Engine mounting brackets

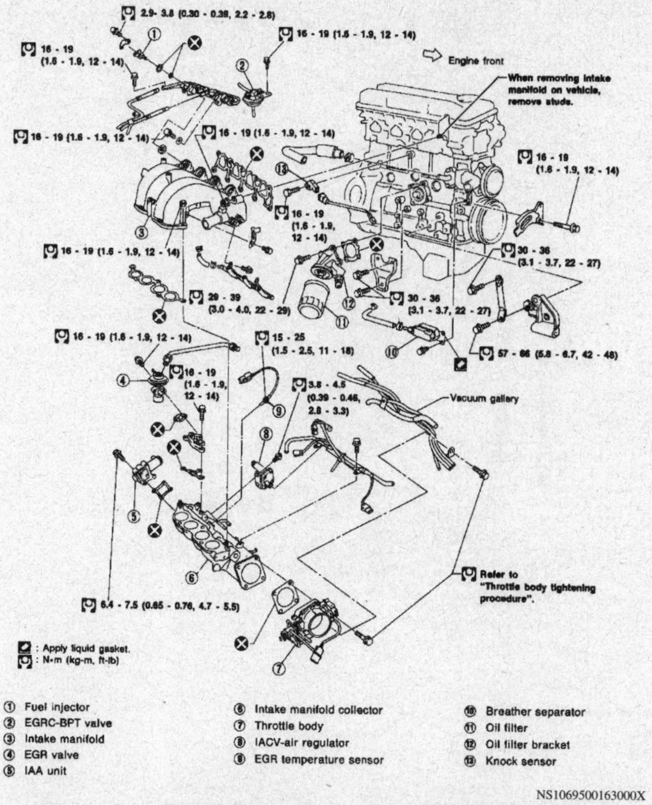
Engine front
When removing intake manifold on vehicle, remove studs.
Vacuum gallery
Refer to "Throttle body tightening procedure".
: Apply liquid gasket.
: N·m (kg-m, ft-lb)
① Fuel injector
② EGRC-BPT valve
③ Intake manifold
④ EGR valve
⑤ IAA unit
⑥ Intake manifold collector
⑦ Throttle body
⑧ IACV-air regulator
⑨ EGR temperature sensor
⑩ Breather separator
⑪ Oil filter
⑫ Oil filter bracket
⑬ Knock sensor
NS1069500163000X

Fig. 2 Exploded view of engine lefthand outer components

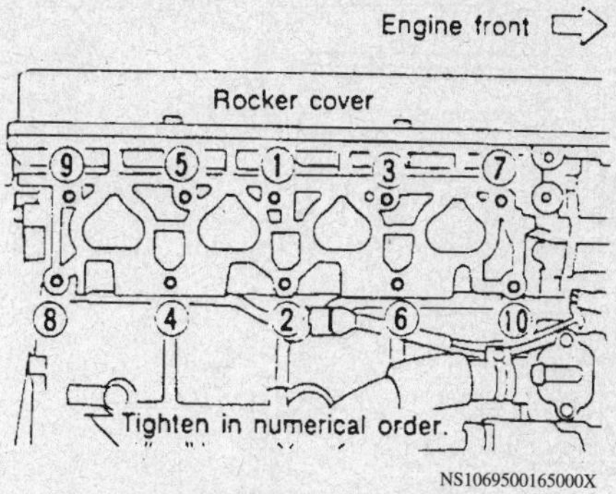
Engine front
Rocker cover
Tighten in numerical order.
NS1069500165000X

Fig. 3 Intake manifold bolt tightening sequence

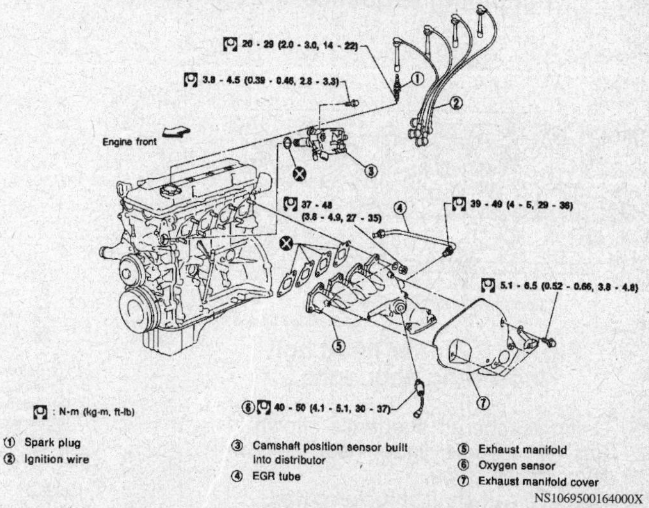
Engine front
: N·m (kg-m, ft-lb)
① Spark plug
② Ignition wire
③ Camshaft position sensor built into distributor
④ EGR tube
⑤ Exhaust manifold
⑥ Oxygen sensor
⑦ Exhaust manifold cover
NS1069500164000X

Fig. 5 Exploded view of engine righthand outer components

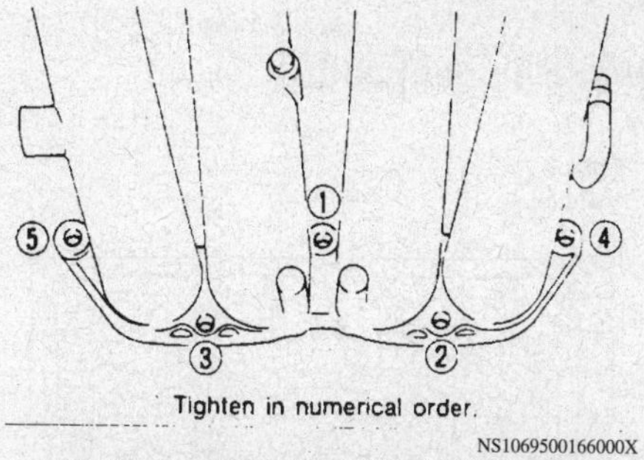
Tighten in numerical order.
NS1069500166000X

Fig. 4 Intake manifold collector bolt tightening sequence

ENGINE MOUNT

REPLACE

Refer to **Fig. 1** for engine mount replacement.

ENGINE

REPLACE

1. Place vehicle on level ground and block wheels.
2. Release fuel pressure as outlined in "Precautions."
3. **On models with automatic transmission,** remove transmission as outlined in "Transmission, Replace"in "RE4R01A, RE4R03A & RL4R01A Automatic Transmissions " section.
4. **On models with manual transmission,** remove transmission as outlined in "Transmission, Replace"in "Clutch & Manual Transmission" section.
5. **On all models,** remove engine undercover and hood.
6. Drain coolant from engine and radiator.
7. Drain engine oil.
8. Remove vacuum hoses, fuel tubes, wires, harnesses and connectors. **Mark vacuum hoses, wires and connectors for installation reference.**
9. Remove front exhaust pipes from exhaust manifolds.
10. Remove radiator and shroud, then drive belts.
11. Remove A/C pump and power steering pump from engine.
12. Install a suitable engine lifting device to cylinder head.
13. Remove engine mounting bolts from both sides, then slowly raise engine.
14. Reverse procedure to install.

INTAKE MANIFOLD

REPLACE

Refer to **Figs. 2 through 4** for intake manifold service.

EXHAUST MANIFOLD

REPLACE

Refer to **Figs. 5 and 6** for exhaust manifold service.

CYLINDER HEAD

REPLACE

REMOVAL

1. Release fuel system pressure as outlined in "Precautions."
2. Drain engine oil and coolant.
3. Remove vacuum hoses, fuel tubes, wires, harness and electrical connectors from cylinder head and front covers. **Mark vacuum hoses, wires and electrical connectors for installation reference.**
4. Remove exhaust manifold cover and front exhaust pipe
5. Remove air duct, cooling fan with coupling and radiator shroud.
6. Disconnect injector harness connector, then remove injector tube assembly with injectors.
7. Remove spark plugs and cables.
8. Turn crankshaft and set No. 1 piston at TDC on compression stroke.
9. Remove rocker cover and gasket, **Fig. 7.**
10. Remove distributor.
11. Hold camshaft with a suitable wrench and remove camshaft sprockets.
12. Remove camshaft brackets and camshaft. **Place brackets and camshaft aside in order of removal. These components must be installed in original position.**

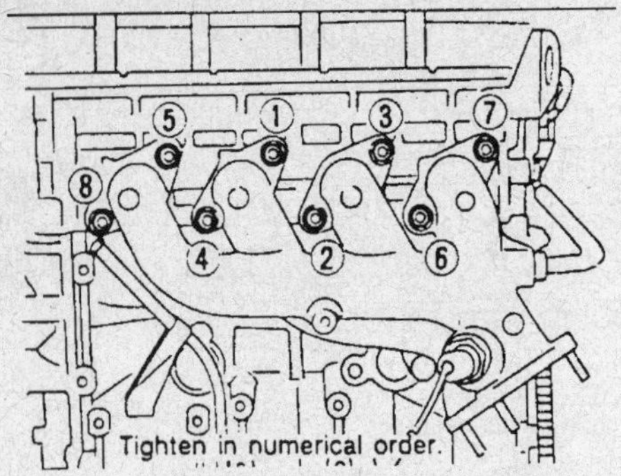
Tighten in numerical order.
NS1069500167000X

Fig. 6 Exhaust manifold nut tightening sequence

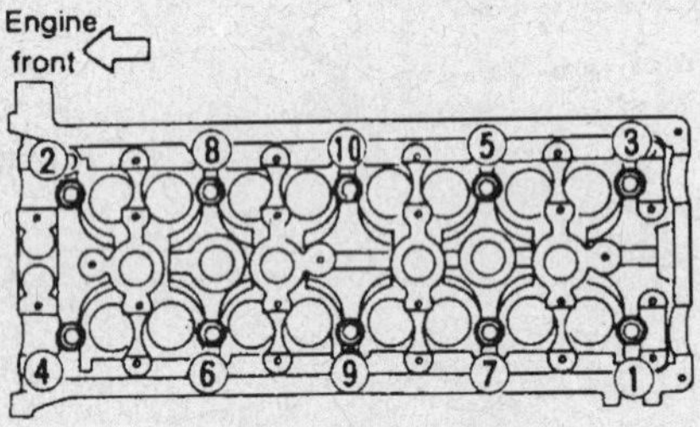
Engine front
Loosen in numerical order.
NS1069100135000X

Fig. 8 Cylinder head bolt loosening sequence

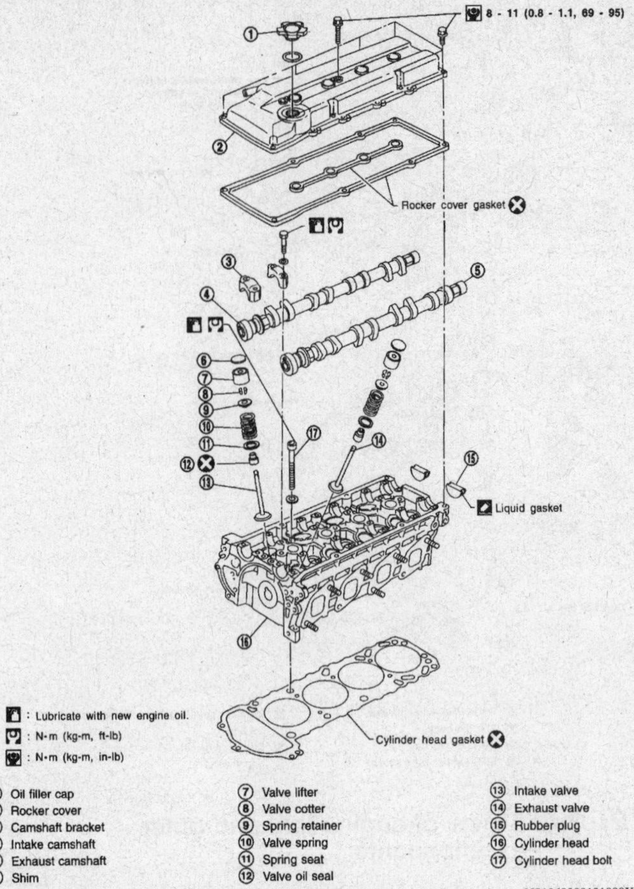
8 - 11 (0.8 - 1.1, 69 - 95)
Rocker cover gasket
Liquid gasket
Cylinder head gasket
: Lubricate with new engine oil.
: N·m (kg-m, ft-lb)
: N·m (kg-m, in-lb)
1 Oil filler cap
2 Rocker cover
3 Camshaft bracket
4 Intake camshaft
5 Exhaust camshaft
6 Shim
7 Valve lifter
8 Valve cotter
9 Spring retainer
10 Valve spring
11 Spring seat
12 Valve oil seal
13 Intake valve
14 Exhaust valve
15 Rubber plug
16 Cylinder head
17 Cylinder head bolt
NS1069300191000X

Fig. 7 Exploded view of cylinder head

13. Using numbered sequence shown in **Fig. 8,** loosen cylinder head bolts in two or three steps.
14. Remove camshaft sprocket cover.
15. Push upper chain tensioner piston and insert suitable pin into pin hole, then remove tensioner, upper chain guides and upper timing chain.
16. Remove idler sprocket bolt.
17. Remove cylinder head with intake and exhaust manifolds as an assembly.
18. Remove cylinder head gasket.

INSTALLATION

1. Install idler shaft, cylinder head gasket and cylinder head.
2. Temporarily finger tighten cylinder head bolts.
3. Align gold marking on upper timing chain with mark on idler sprocket, **Fig. 9,** then install upper timing chain, chain tensioner and chain guide. **Remove pin to release tensioner piston.**
4. Apply a bead of liquid gasket to mating surfaces of front cover.
5. Ensure mating marks on timing chain and idler sprocket are aligned, then install camshaft sprocket cover.
6. Using sequence shown in **Fig. 10,** tighten cylinder head bolts as follows:
   a. **Torque** bolts to 22 ft. lbs.
   b. **Torque** bolts to 59 ft. lbs.
   c. Loosen all bolts completely.
   d. **Torque** bolts 18–25 ft. lbs.
   e. If using a angle wrench, turn head bolts 86–91° clockwise.
   f. If using torque wrench, **torque** head bolts to 55–62 ft. lbs.
7. Install camshaft and camshaft brackets, then using sequence shown in **Fig. 11,** tighten bolts as follows:

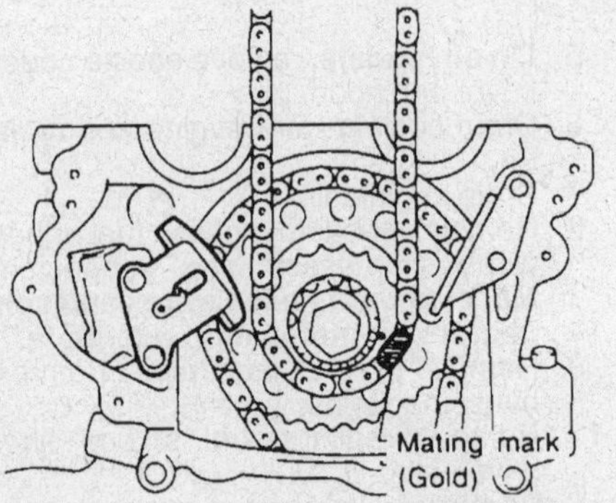
Mating mark (Gold)
NS1069100136000X

Fig. 9 Aligning upper timing chain on idler pulley

   a. **Torque** bolts to 16.8 inch lbs.
   b. **Torque** bolts to 7–9 ft. lbs.
8. Align gold marking on chain with mark on camshaft sprockets, then install sprocket on camshaft, **Fig. 12.**
9. Install chain guide between both camshaft sprockets.
10. Apply liquid gasket to rubber plugs and install rubber plugs, then move them by hand to evenly spread liquid gasket and install plugs flush with cylinder head surface.
11. Ensure No. 1 cylinder is at TDC, and distributor rotor is set at No. 1 cylinder spark position, then install distributor. **Ensure distributor shaft marks align**

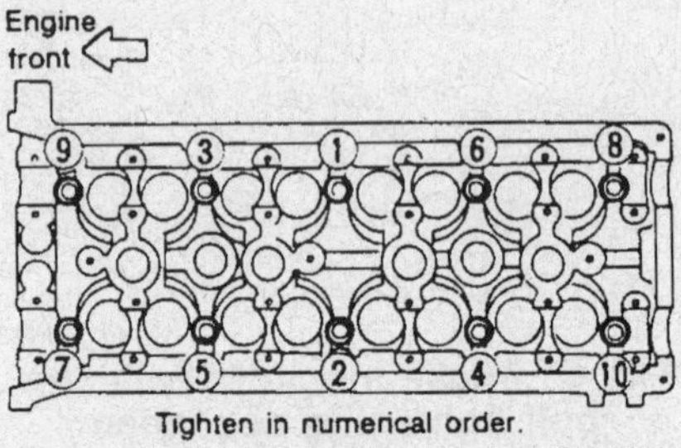
Engine front
Tighten in numerical order.
NS1069100137000X

Fig. 10 Cylinder head bolt tightening sequence

with housing indent mark.

12. Install rocker cover using tightening sequence shown in **Fig. 13**.
13. Install spark plugs and wires.
14. Connect injector harness, then install injector tube assembly and injectors.
15. Install radiator shroud, cooling fan with coupling and air duct.
16. Install vacuum hoses, fuel tubes, wires and harness connectors.

ENGINE DISASSEMBLE

1. Place engine on work stand.
2. Remove timing chain as outlined in "Timing Chain, Replace."
3. Remove pistons with connecting rods.
4. Remove main bearing beam and crankshaft, loosening bolts in two or three steps in order shown, **Fig. 14.**

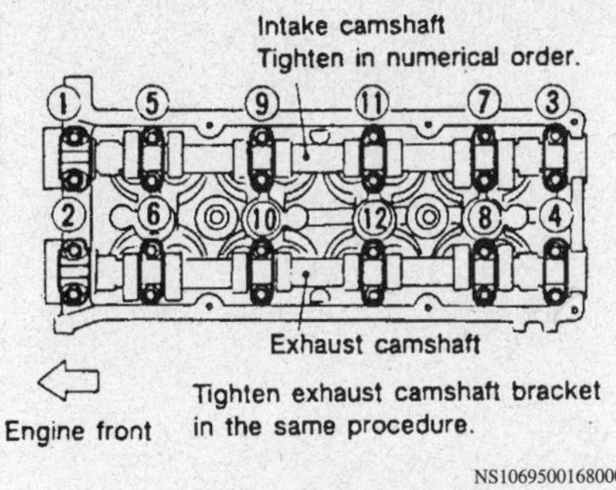
Intake camshaft
Tighten in numerical order.
Exhaust camshaft
Engine front
Tighten exhaust camshaft bracket in the same procedure.
NS1069500168000X

Fig. 11 Camshaft tightening sequence

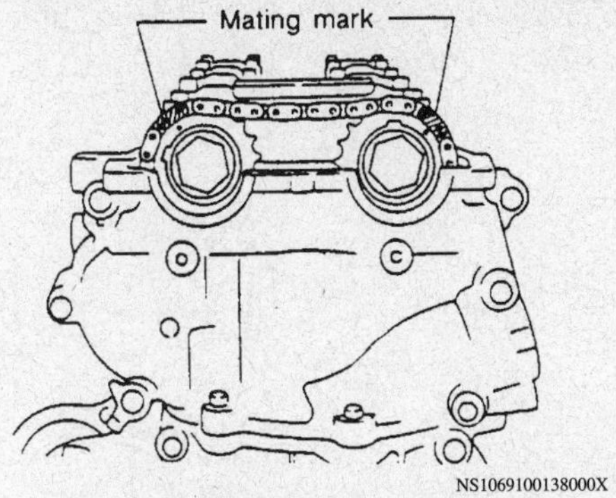
Mating mark
NS1069100138000X

Fig. 12 Aligning upper timing chain on camshafts

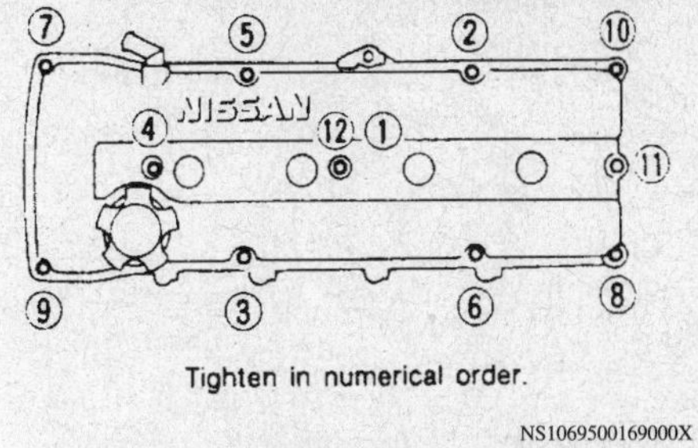
NISSAN
Tighten in numerical order.
NS1069500169000X

Fig. 13 Rocker cover tightening sequence

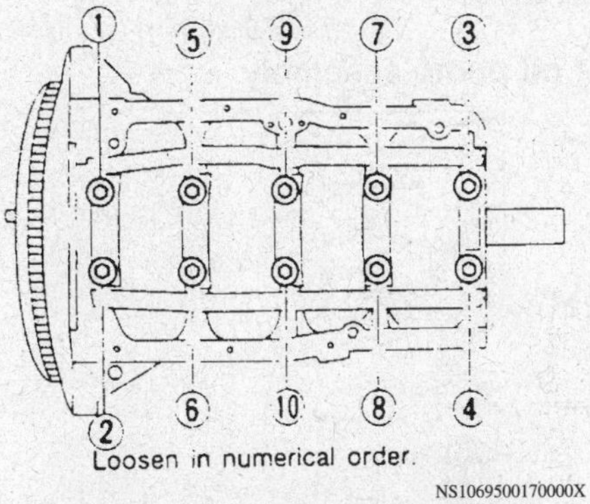
Loosen in numerical order.
NS1069500170000X

Fig. 14 Main bearing cap bolt loosening sequence

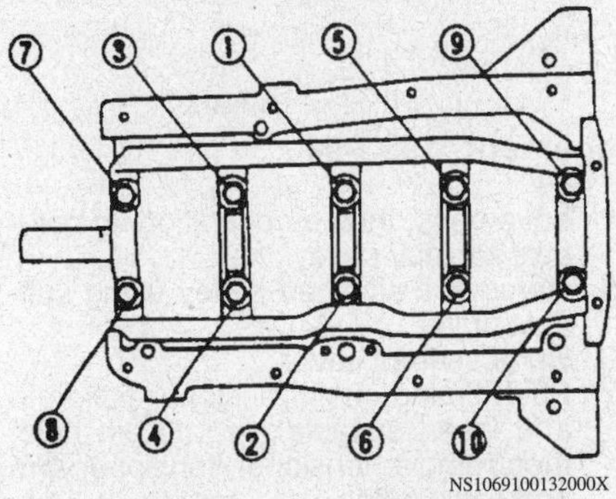
NS1069100132000X

Fig. 15 Main bearing cap bolt tightening sequence

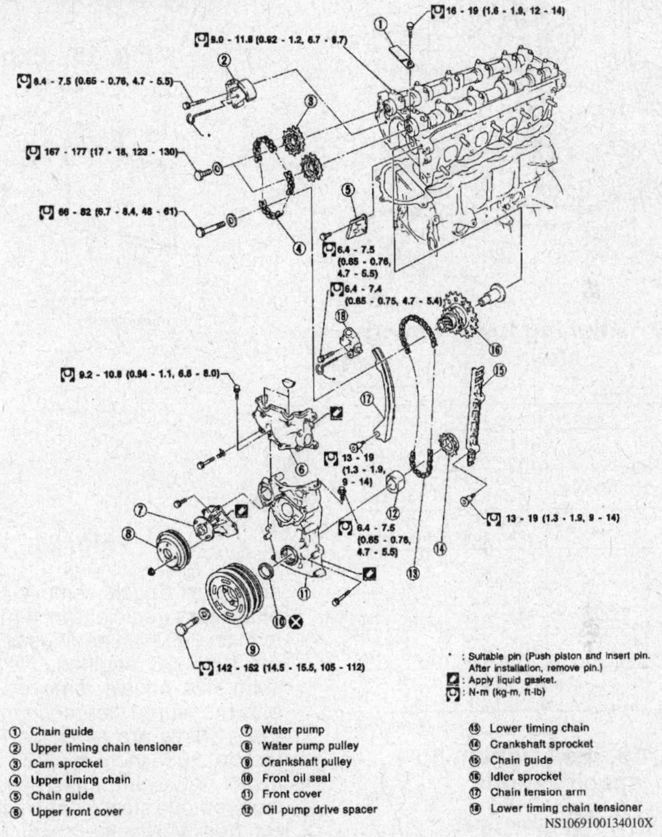
142 - 152 (14.5 - 15.5, 105 - 112)
* : Suitable pin (Push piston and insert pin. After installation, remove pin.)
: Apply liquid gasket.
: N•m (kg-m, ft-lb)
① Chain guide
② Upper timing chain tensioner
③ Cam sprocket
④ Upper timing chain
⑤ Chain guide
⑥ Upper front cover
⑦ Water pump
⑧ Water pump pulley
⑨ Crankshaft pulley
⑩ Front oil seal
⑪ Front cover
⑫ Oil pump drive spacer
⑬ Lower timing chain
⑭ Crankshaft sprocket
⑮ Chain guide
⑯ Idler sprocket
⑰ Chain tension arm
⑱ Lower timing chain tensioner
NS1069100134010X

Fig. 16 Exploded view of timing chain components

ENGINE ASSEMBLE

1. Install new snap ring on one side of piston pin hole, heat piston to 140–158°F and assemble piston, pin, connecting rod and snap ring.
2. Install piston rings with punch mark side of compression rings facing up.
3. Install main bearings and bearing beam. **Torque** bolts in two or three steps to specifications in order shown, **Fig. 15.**
4. Install connecting rod bearings on connecting rods. Ensure oil hole in rod and bearing match.
5. Install piston and rod assemblies, ensure mark on piston faces front.
6. Install connecting rod bearing caps. **Torque** nuts to 10–12 ft. lbs. noting the following:
   a. If using an angle wrench, turn an additional 60–65° clockwise.
   b. If angle wrench is not available, **torque** to 28–33 ft. lbs.

VALVE CLEARANCE SPECIFICATIONS

Stem-To-Guide Clearance, Inch①	
Intake	Exhaust
1993–94	
.0012–.0015	.0013–.0016
1995–96	
.0013–.0016	.0013–.0016

① — Hot.

VALVE ADJUSTMENT

1. Remove rocker cover.
2. Remove spark plugs and set No. 1 piston to TDC on compression stroke.
3. Use feeler gauge to measure and record clearance between valve lifter and camshaft on No. 1 and No. 2 intake valves, and No. 1 and 3 exhaust valves.
4. Turn crankshaft 360° and align crankshaft pulley mark with point.
5. Use feeler gauge to measure and record clearance between valve lifter and camshaft on No. 3 and No. 4 intake valves, and No. 2 and 4 exhaust valves.
6. Turn crankshaft to position cam lobe on valve to be adjusted.
7. Place suitable camshaft pliers around camshaft and rotate so lifter is pushed down.
8. Place suitable lifter stopper between

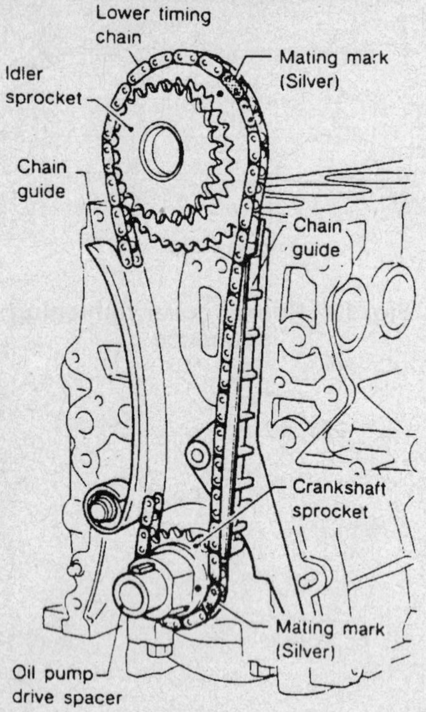
Lower timing chain
Idler sprocket
Mating mark (Silver)
Chain guide
Chain guide
Crankshaft sprocket
Mating mark (Silver)
Oil pump drive spacer

NS1069100139000X

Fig. 17 Aligning lower timing chain

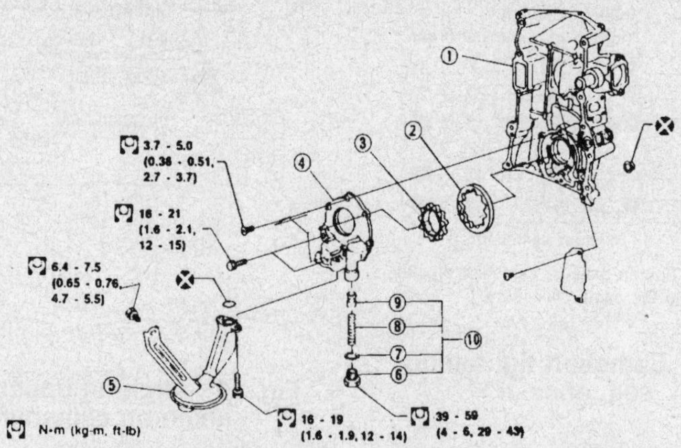
3.7 - 5.0 (0.38 - 0.51, 2.7 - 3.7)
16 - 21 (1.6 - 2.1, 12 - 15)
6.4 - 7.5 (0.65 - 0.76, 4.7 - 5.5)
16 - 19 (1.6 - 1.9, 12 - 14)
39 - 59 (4 - 6, 29 - 43)
N·m (kg-m, ft-lb)

NS1099100015000X

Fig. 18 Exploded view of oil pump assembly

Unit: mm (in)

	Used belt deflection: Limit	Used belt deflection: Deflection after adjustment	Deflection of new belt
Alternator	11 (0.43)	7 - 8 (0.28 - 0.31)	6 - 7 (0.24 - 0.28)
Air conditioner compressor	12 (0.47)	7.5 - 8.5 (0.295 - 0.335)	6.5 - 7.5 (0.256 - 0.295)
Power steering oil pump			
Without SUPER HICAS	13 (0.51)	7.5 - 8.5 (0.295 - 0.335)	6.5 - 7.5 (0.256 - 0.295)
With SUPER HICAS	9 (0.35)	6.5 - 7.5 (0.256 - 0.295)	5.5 - 6.5 (0.217 - 0.256)
Applied pushing force	98 N (10 kg, 22 lb)		

NS1069100141000X

Fig. 19 Belt tightening specifications

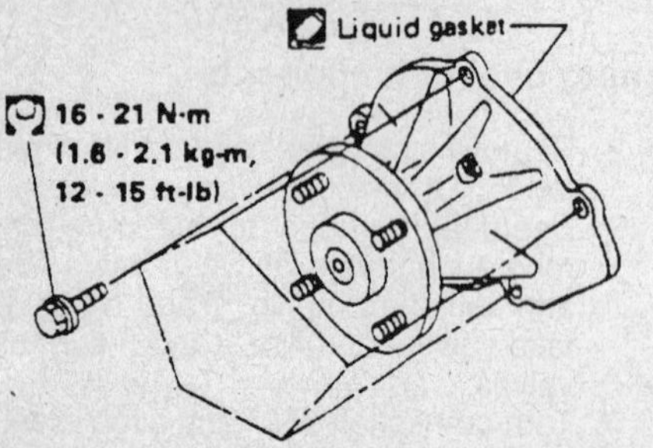
Liquid gasket
16 - 21 N·m
(1.6 - 2.1 kg-m,
12 - 15 ft-lb)

NS1089100015000X

Fig. 20 Water pump replacement

camshaft and edge of lifter and remove pliers.

9. Blow air into hole to separate adjusting shim from valve lifter, then remove shim with small screwdriver and magnetic finger.
10. Measure removed shim and calculate thickness of new shim necessary to obtain specified clearance. New intake shim size equals removed shim size plus measured clearance minus .0138 inch on 1993–94 engines or .0146 inch on 1995–96 engines. New exhaust shim size equals removed shim size plus measured clearance minus .0146 inch. Shims are available from .0772 inch to .1055 inch, in .0008 inch steps.
11. Install new shim, attach pliers, rotate, then remove stopper and pliers.
12. Recheck valve clearance.
13. Repeat shim removal and replacement procedure as necessary.
14. Reverse procedure to install.

TIMING CHAIN

REPLACE

UPPER TIMING CHAIN

For upper timing chain service refer to "Cylinder Head, Replace," **Fig. 16.**

LOWER TIMING CHAIN

Removal

1. Remove cylinder head as outlined in "Cylinder Head, Replace."
2. Remove oil pan as outlined in "Oil Pan, Replace."
3. Remove oil strainer.
4. Remove power steering pump, alternator and air conditioning compressor drive belts, then air conditioning compressor idler pulley.
5. Remove crankshaft pulley using suitable puller.
6. Remove front cover.
7. Push timing chain tensioner piston in and insert suitable pin into pin hole, then remove tensioner, tensioner arm and chain guide.
8. Remove lower timing chain and idler sprocket.

Installation

1. Install crankshaft sprocket. **Ensure mating marks on crankshaft sprocket face toward front of engine.**
2. Position No. 1 cylinder at TDC on compression stroke.
3. Align silver mark on timing chain with mark on crankshaft and idler sprockets then install idler sprocket and lower timing chain, **Fig. 17.**
4. Install chain tensioner arm and chain guide.
5. Install lower timing chain tensioner and remove pin to release piston.
6. Apply continuous liquid gasket bead to front cover and install.
7. Install crankshaft pulley, oil strainer and oil pan.
8. Install component parts below engine.
9. Install air compressor idler pulley.
10. Install new cylinder head as outlined in

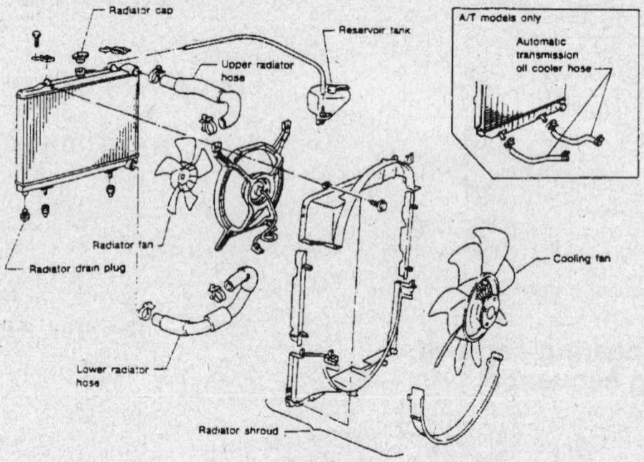
Radiator cap
Reservoir tank
Upper radiator hose
A/T models only
Automatic transmission oil cooler hose
Radiator fan
Radiator drain plug
Cooling fan
Lower radiator hose
Radiator shroud

NS1089100076000X

Fig. 21 Radiator replacement. 1993-94

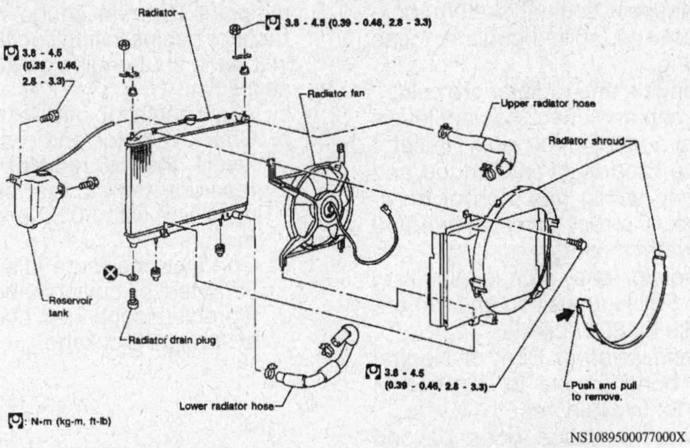
Radiator
3.8 - 4.5 (0.39 - 0.46, 2.8 - 3.3)
3.8 - 4.5 (0.39 - 0.46, 2.8 - 3.3)
Radiator fan
Upper radiator hose
Radiator shroud
Reservoir tank
Radiator drain plug
3.8 - 4.5 (0.39 - 0.46, 2.8 - 3.3)
Lower radiator hose
Push and pull to remove.
N·m (kg-m, ft-lb)
NS1089500077000X

Fig. 22 Radiator replacement. 1995–96

"Cylinder Head, Replace."

CRANKSHAFT SEAL

REPLACE

1. Remove radiator shroud attaching screws and shroud.
2. Remove crankshaft pulley attaching bolt and pulley, then remove front oil seal using screw driver or equivalent to pry out seal.
3. Apply engine oil to new seal and use suitable oil seal tool to install.

CRANKSHAFT REAR OIL SEAL

REPLACE

1. **On models with manual transmission,** remove transmission as outlined in "Clutch & Manual Transmission."
2. **On models with automatic transmission,** remove transmission as outlined in "Automatic Transmission/ Transaxles."
3. **On all models,** remove flywheel or driveplate, then the rear oil seal retainer.
4. Using a suitable scraper, remove all traces of liquid gasket from matting surface.
5. Remove rear oil seal from rear oil seal retainer.
6. Coat new seal with engine oil and use suitable seal tool to install into retainer.
7. Apply liquid gasket or equivalent to retainer and install.

OIL PAN

REPLACE

1. Raise and support vehicle, then drain engine oil.
2. Remove power steering tube, then front stabilizer bar mounting bolts.
3. Use suitable hoist to hold engine with slingers attached to cylinder head.
4. Remove tension rod bolts at transverse links, then front stabilizer bar mounting bolts and nuts from side member.
5. Remove left and right side engine mounting bolts.
6. Remove gussets, then disconnect steering shaft lower joint.
7. Remove power steering tube bracket mounting bolts at left tension rod bracket.
8. Support front suspension member with suitable jack and lower approximately 2 ½ inches, then remove pan bolts.
9. Insert a suitable tool between cylinder block and oil pan, then tap tool side with hammer and remove oil pan. **Do not use a screwdriver, oil pan flange will be deformed. Be careful not to damage aluminum mating surface of cylinder block.**
10. Pull pan from front while lowering front suspension member. Use care when separating pan from block.
11. Reverse procedure to install, noting following:
    a. Remove all remaining liquid gasket from pan and cylinder block mating surfaces.
    b. Apply a continuous bead of liquid gasket to oil pan mating surface.
    c. Install pan within five minutes of applying gasket.
    d. Wait at least 30 minutes before refilling engine with oil.

OIL PUMP

REPLACE

1. Remove front cover as outlined in "Timing Chain, Replace."
2. Turn front cover over and remove oil pump cover, **Fig. 18.**
3. Reverse procedure to install.

BELT TENSION DATA

Refer to **Fig. 19** for drive belt deflection specifications. Measure drive belt deflection when engine is cold.

COOLING SYSTEM BLEED

Prior To Performing Any Service Operations Listed In This Section, Consult "Technical Service Bulletins"Section For Related Information.

This engines does not require a specified bleed procedure. After filling cooling system, run engine to operating temperature with radiator/pressure cap off. Air will then be automatically bled through cap opening.

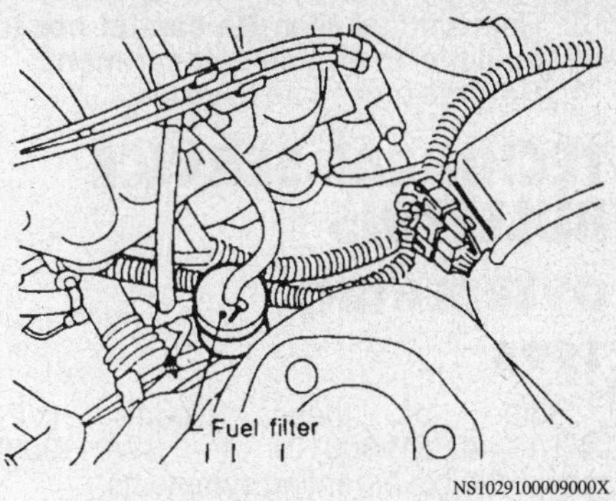
Fuel filter
NS1029100009000X

Fig. 23 Fuel filter

THERMOSTAT

REPLACE

1. Drain cooling system, then disconnect radiator hose from thermostat housing.
2. Remove thermostat housing attaching bolts, then housing.
3. Remove thermostat from housing.
4. Reverse procedure to install.

WATER PUMP

REPLACE

1. Disconnect battery ground cable and drain cooling system.
2. Remove fan coupling with fan, then power steering, alternator and air conditioning compressor drive belts.
3. Remove water pump and gasket, **Fig. 20.**
4. Reverse procedure to install, using new gasket.

RADIATOR

REPLACE

To service radiator, refer to **Figs. 21 and 22.**

FUEL PUMP

REPLACE

1. Release fuel system pressure as outlined in "Precautions."
2. Raise and support vehicle.
3. Drain fuel tank into a suitable container.
4. Support fuel tank using a suitable transmission stand.
5. Lower fuel tank to gain access to fuel pump.
6. Disconnect fuel pump hoses and electrical connections.
7. Remove fuel pump from vehicle.
8. Reverse procedure to install.

FUEL FILTER

REPLACE

1. Release fuel system pressure as outlined in "Precautions."
2. Loosen fuel filter hose clamps, **Fig. 23.**

3. Remove fuel filter. **Be careful not to spill fuel in engine compartment.**
4. Reverse procedure to install.

TECHNICAL SERVICE BULLETINS

OVERHEATING

1995

Some of these models (VIN JN1AS44D*SW000101 to SW011903) may exhibit overheating symptoms.

This problem may be caused by air in the cooling system due to insufficient coolant system bleeding. To correct this problem, proceed as follows:

1. Visually inspect coolant system looking for leakage, spilled coolant, loose clamps, etc.
2. Ensure engine and radiator are cold.
3. Remove cap and check coolant levels in radiator and reservoir tank. Radiator should be filled to overflow tube and reservoir to within one inch of maximum line. Correct level with 50/50 coolant/water mixture.
4. Install radiator cap, start engine, set heater to Full Hot position and run engine at idle for 30 seconds.
5. With transmission in Park or Neutral position, bring engine to 3000 RPM and hold for five minutes.
6. If temperature gauge goes beyond midpoint (Normal gauge reading) or radiator begins losing coolant to reservoir tank, shut engine off and proceed as follows:
   a. Allow engine to cool for one hour.
   b. Check radiator and reservoir tank levels, then fill radiator to top and reservoir tank to just below maximum line with 50/50 coolant/water mixture.
   c. Conduct one more idle then 3000 RPM test as outlined above.
   d. If problem continues, check cooling system for blockage.

TIGHTENING SPECIFICATIONS

Year	Component	Torque/Ft. Lbs.
1993–96	Camshaft Sprocket Bolt	123-130
	Connecting Rod Bearing Caps	34-41
	Crankshaft Pulley	105-112
	Cylinder Head	①
	Exhaust Manifold	27-35
	Flywheel	105-112
	Main Bearing	34-38
	Oil Pan Bolts	56-66②
	Oil Pan Drain Plug	22-29
	Water Pump	12-14

① — Refer to Cylinder Head, Replace.

② — Inch lbs.

Clutch & Manual Transmission

INDEX

	Page No.
Adjustments	33-13
Clutch Pedal	33-13
Clutch, Replace	33-13
Hydraulic System Service	33-13
Clutch Bleed Procedure	33-13
Clutch Slave Cylinder, Replace	33-13
Tightening Specifications	33-14
Transmission, Replace	33-13

ADJUSTMENTS

CLUTCH PEDAL

Clutch hydraulic system must be bled whenever a clutch line has been disconnected or when air has entered system. Bleed valve is located on clutch operating cylinder.

1. Adjust clutch pedal height dimension "H ," **Fig. 1,** to specifications, **Fig. 2,** using pedal stop or clutch switch.
2. Adjust dimension "C," **Fig. 3,** to specifications, **Fig. 2,** with clutch pedal fully depressed.
3. Adjust clutch pedal freeplay dimension "A," **Fig. 1,** to specification, **Fig. 2.** Adjust clutch pedal freeplay by rotating clutch master cylinder pushrod inward or outward until specified freeplay is obtained. After completing freeplay adjustment, tighten locknut. Clutch pedal freeplay is sum of play between piston and piston rod.
4. After above adjustments have been completed, cycle clutch pedal several times to ensure clutch linkage operates smoothly without binding.

HYDRAULIC SYSTEM SERVICE

CLUTCH SLAVE CYLINDER, REPLACE

1. Drain fluid from clutch system into a suitable container.
2. Disconnect clutch hose from clutch tube.
3. Remove clutch slave cylinder mounting bolt, then the clutch slave cylinder.
4. Reverse procedure to install. Bleed hydraulic system as outlined under "Bleed Procedure."

CLUTCH BLEED PROCEDURE

1. Fill reservoir to full level with brake fluid.
2. Connect a transparent vinyl tube to air bleeder valve, **Fig. 4.**
3. Fully depress clutch pedal several times.

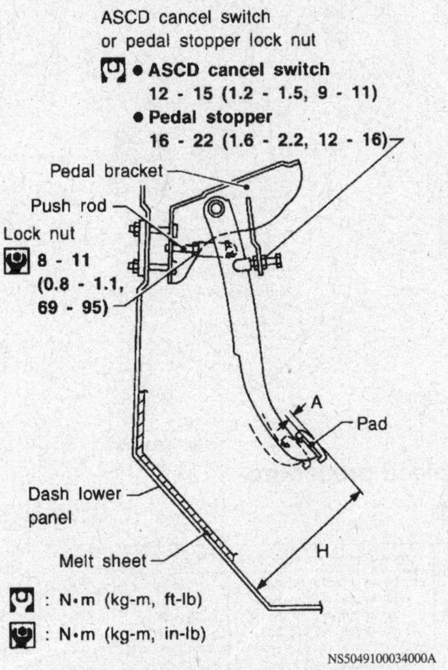

ASCD cancel switch
or pedal stopper lock nut
• ASCD cancel switch
12 - 15 (1.2 - 1.5, 9 - 11)
• Pedal stopper
16 - 22 (1.6 - 2.2, 12 - 16)
Pedal bracket
Push rod
Lock nut
8 - 11
(0.8 - 1.1,
69 - 95)
A
Pad
Dash lower
panel
Melt sheet
H
: N•m (kg-m, ft-lb)
: N•m (kg-m, in-lb)
NS5049100034000A

Fig. 1 Clutch pedal free travel & height adjustment

4. With clutch fully depressed, open bleeder valve to release air.
5. Close bleeder valve when pedal reaches floor.
6. Repeat steps 3 through 5 until all air is bleed from clutch system.
7. Bleed air from clutch piping connector according to steps 3 through 6.
8. Repeat procedure several times to ensure all air is removed from clutch system.
9. If clutch is still not fully operational (offers very little resistance), proceed as follows:
   a. Raise and support front of vehicle two feet.
   b. Continue pumping fluid through both air bleeder valves in an alternating fashion one valve at a time.
   c. Ensure transparent tubes are submerged in container fluid.
   d. Frequently check reservoir fluid level.
   e. If air pockets continue to prevent full clutch operation, flush entire system and refill reservoir with approximately 20 oz. of fluid.

CLUTCH

REPLACE

1. Remove transmission as outlined in "Transmission, Replace."
2. Insert a dummy shaft into clutch disc hub.
3. Loosen clutch cover attaching bolts alternately.
4. Remove clutch disc and cover assembly.
5. Remove release bearing.
6. Reverse procedure to install.

TRANSMISSION

REPLACE

1. Disconnect battery ground cable, then raise and support vehicle.
2. Remove shift lever with control housing, then remove crankshaft position sensor from upper side of transmission.
3. Remove clutch operating cylinder from clutch housing.
4. Disconnect speed sensor, OD position switch, reverse lamp switch, rear heated oxygen sensor and neutral position switch harness connectors.
5. Remove starter motor, then propeller shaft. **Install a plug in extension housing rear opening to prevent fluid spillage.**
6. Remove gussets and exhaust pipe mounting bracket.
7. Support transmission with suitable jack, then remove rear mounting bracket.
8. Lower transmission as much as possible and remove mounting bolts, then remove transmission from engine and vehicle.
9. Reverse procedure to install, tightening transmission to engine bolts to specifications, **Fig. 5.**

Year	Clutch Pedal Adjustment Specifications, Inches		
	Height	Freeplay	Stop Clearance
1993–94	7.32-7.72	.039-.118	.039-.079
1995–96	7.56-7.95	.039-.118	.012-.039

Fig. 2 Clutch pedal specifications

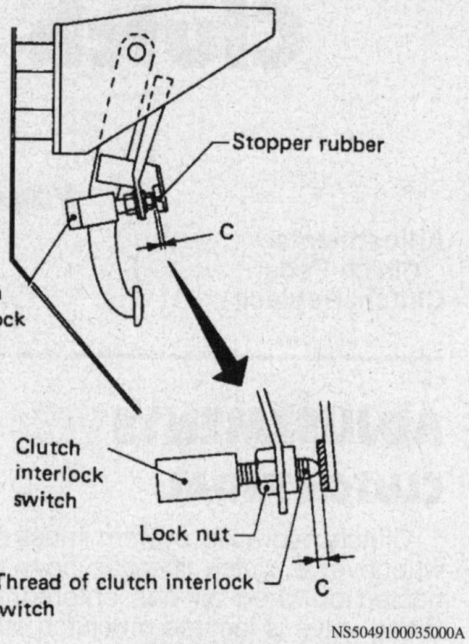
Stopper rubber
C
Clutch
interlock
switch
Clutch
interlock
switch
Lock nut
Thread of clutch interlock
switch
C
NS5049100035000A

Fig. 3 Clutch interlock switch adjustment

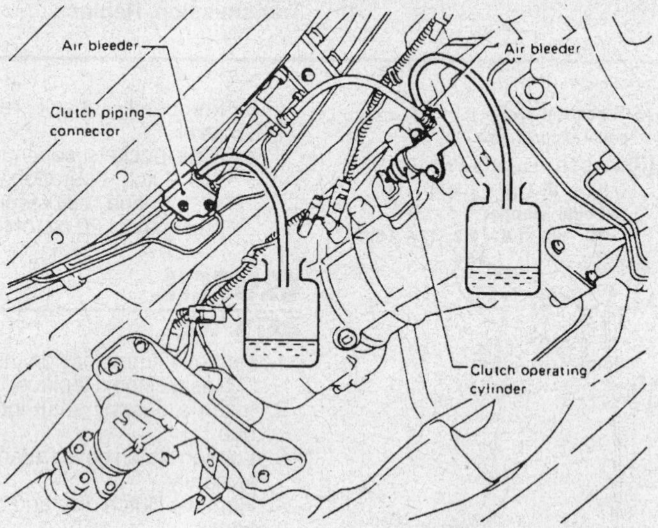
Air bleeder
Clutch piping
connector
Air bleeder
Clutch operating
cylinder
NS5049100036000X

Fig. 4 Clutch bleed procedure

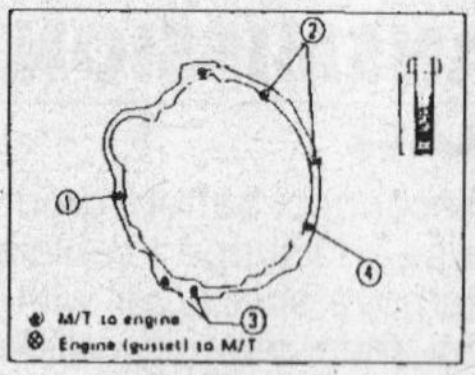
②
①
④
③
M/T to engine
Engine (gusset) to M/T

Bolt No.	Tightening torque N·m (kg·m, ft·lb)	ℓ mm (in)
1	39 - 49 (4.0 - 5.0, 29 - 36)	70 (2.76)
2	39 - 49 (4.0 - 5.0, 29 - 36)	60 (2.36)
3	29 - 39 (3.0 - 4.0, 22 - 29)	30 (1.18)
4	39 - 49 (4.0 - 5.0, 29 - 36)	25 (0.98)
Gusset to engine	29 - 39 (3.0 - 4.0, 22 - 29)	

NS5039100069000X

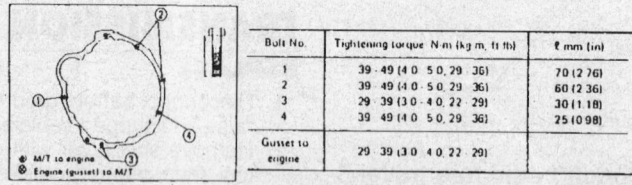

Fig. 5 Transmission to engine tightening specification

TIGHTENING SPECIFICATIONS

Year	Component	Torque/Ft. Lbs.
1993–96	Air Bleeder Screw	48-84②
	Clutch Cover Cylinder	16-22
	Clutch Master Cylinder	5-8
	Flywheel	105-112
	Slave Cylinder Mounting Bolt	22-30
	Transmission To Engine	①

① — Refer to "Transmission, Replace."

② — Inch lbs.

Rear Axle & Suspension

INDEX

	Page No.
Hub & Bearing, Replace	33-15
Rear Suspension, Replace	33-15
Stabilizer Bar, Replace	33-15
Strut, Replace	33-15
Strut Service	33-15
Tightening Specifications	33-17

HUB & BEARING

REPLACE

1. Raise and support vehicle.
2. Remove wheel bearing locknut.
3. Remove brake caliper assembly and support by frame using suitable wire.
4. Separate driveshaft from axle housing by slightly tapping with a suitable soft face hammer, **Fig. 1.**
5. Remove axle housing attaching bolts then axle housing, **Fig. 2.**
6. Remove wheel bearing with flange and wheel hub from axle housing.
7. Using a suitable press, press off wheel bearing from wheel hub.
8. Reverse procedure to install, noting following:
   a. Install wheel bearing as shown in **Fig. 3.**
   b. Check and ensure wheel bearing axial endplay is .0020 inch or less.

REAR SUSPENSION

REPLACE

1. Disconnect ABS sensor and move away from rear suspension assembly, then remove exhaust pipe, propeller shaft rear end and disconnect parking brake cable.
2. Remove brake caliper assembly and suspend on wire.
3. Remove rear parcel shelf, then remove upper shock absorber nuts. **Do not remove piston rod lock nut.**
4. Remove suspension member mounting nuts, **Figs. 4 and 5.**
5. Draw out rear axle and suspension assembly.
6. Before removing any suspension component, put matchmarks on adjusting pin.
7. Reverse procedure to install, noting following:
   a. Final tightening must be done with curb weight on wheels, on ground.
   b. After installation, check wheel alignment.

STRUT

REPLACE

1. Raise and support vehicle.
2. Remove upper and lower strut attaching nuts and bolts, **Figs. 6 and 7.**
3. Remove coil spring and strut assembly.

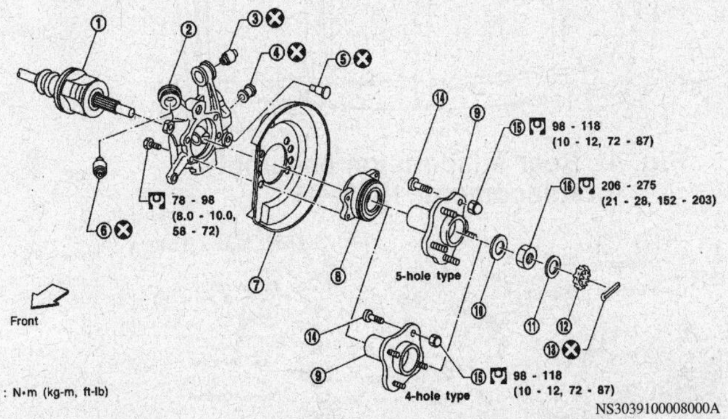

98 - 118
(10 - 12, 72 - 87)
206 - 275
(21 - 28, 152 - 203)
78 - 98
(8.0 - 10.0,
58 - 72)
5-hole type
4-hole type
Front
: N·m (kg-m, ft-lb)
NS3039100008000A

Fig. 1 Wheel hub & axle housing

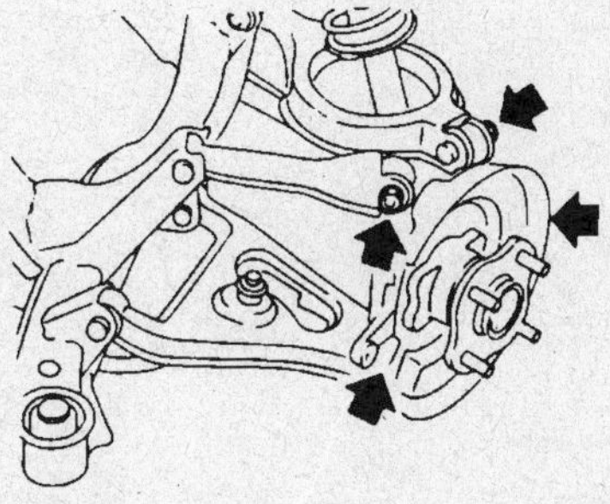

NS3039100009000X

Fig. 2 Axle housing removal

4. Reverse procedure to install.

STRUT SERVICE

1. Set strut assembly in vise using suitable holding tool.
2. Compress spring using suitable spring compressor until strut upper spring seat can be turned by hand.
3. Loosen, **do not remove,** piston rod locknut.
4. Remove piston locknut.
5. Remove strut assembly components.
6. Reverse procedure to assemble, noting following:
   a. When installing coil spring, use care not to reverse top and bottom direction, **Fig. 8.**
   b. When installing spring on strut, position as shown in **Fig. 8.**
   c. When installing upper spring seat, position as shown in **Fig. 9.**

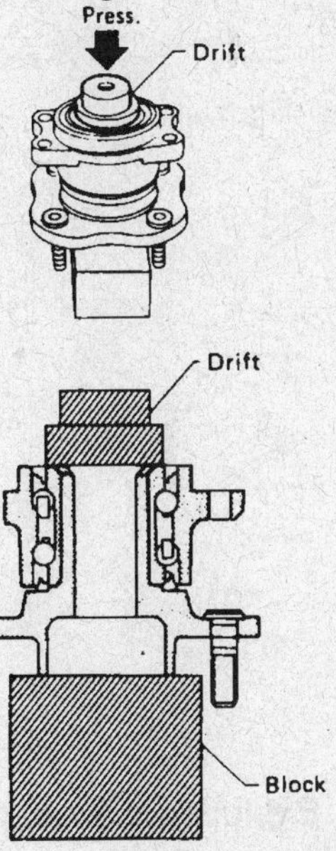

Press.
Drift
Drift
Block
NS3039100010000X

Fig. 3 Wheel hub bearing installation

STABILIZER BAR

REPLACE

1. Raise and support vehicle.
2. Remove exhaust assembly as necessary.
3. Disconnect stabilizer bar from bushing brackets and locating bolts, then remove stabilizer bar.
4. Reverse procedure to install.

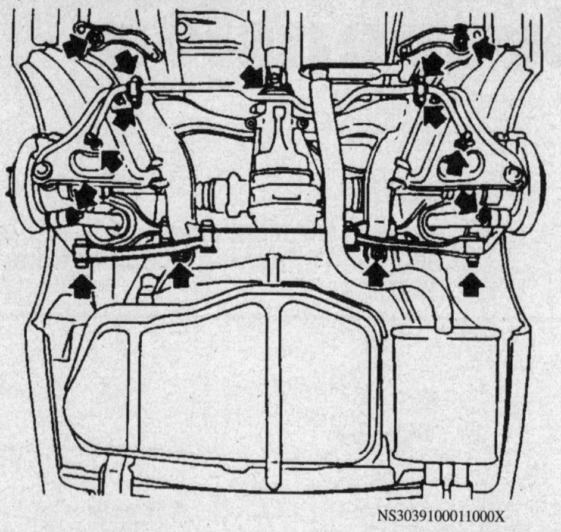
NS3039100011000X

Fig. 4 Rear suspension assembly replacement. 1993–94

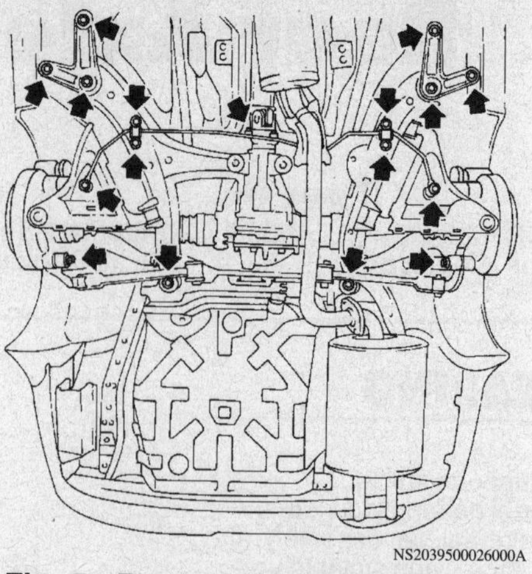
NS2039500026000A

Fig. 5 Rear suspension assembly replacement. 1995–96

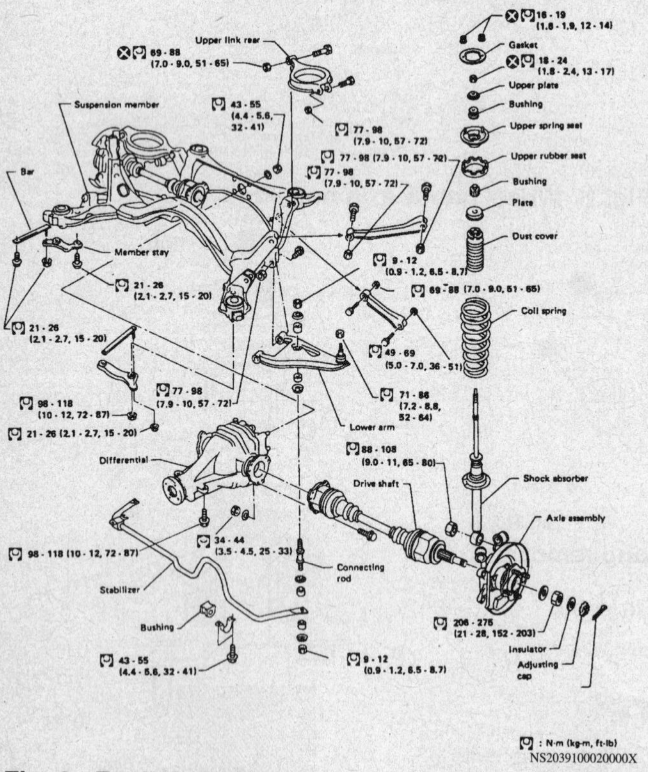
16 - 19 (1.6 - 1.9, 12 - 14)
Gasket
18 - 24 (1.8 - 2.4, 13 - 17)
Upper plate
Bushing
Upper spring seat
Upper rubber seat
Bushing
Plate
Dust cover
Coil spring
Upper link rear
69 - 88 (7.0 - 9.0, 51 - 65)
Suspension member
43 - 55 (4.4 - 5.6, 32 - 41)
77 - 98 (7.9 - 10, 57 - 72)
Bar
Member stay
21 - 26 (2.1 - 2.7, 15 - 20)
9 - 12 (0.9 - 1.2, 6.5 - 8.7)
49 - 69 (5.0 - 7.0, 36 - 51)
71 - 86 (7.2 - 8.8, 52 - 64)
98 - 118 (10 - 12, 72 - 87)
Lower arm
Differential
88 - 108 (9.0 - 11, 65 - 80)
Drive shaft
Shock absorber
Axle assembly
34 - 44 (3.5 - 4.5, 25 - 33)
Connecting rod
Stabilizer
Bushing
206 - 275 (21 - 28, 152 - 203)
Insulator
Adjusting cap
: N·m (kg-m, ft-lb)
NS2039100020000X

Fig. 6 Exploded view of rear suspension. 1993–94

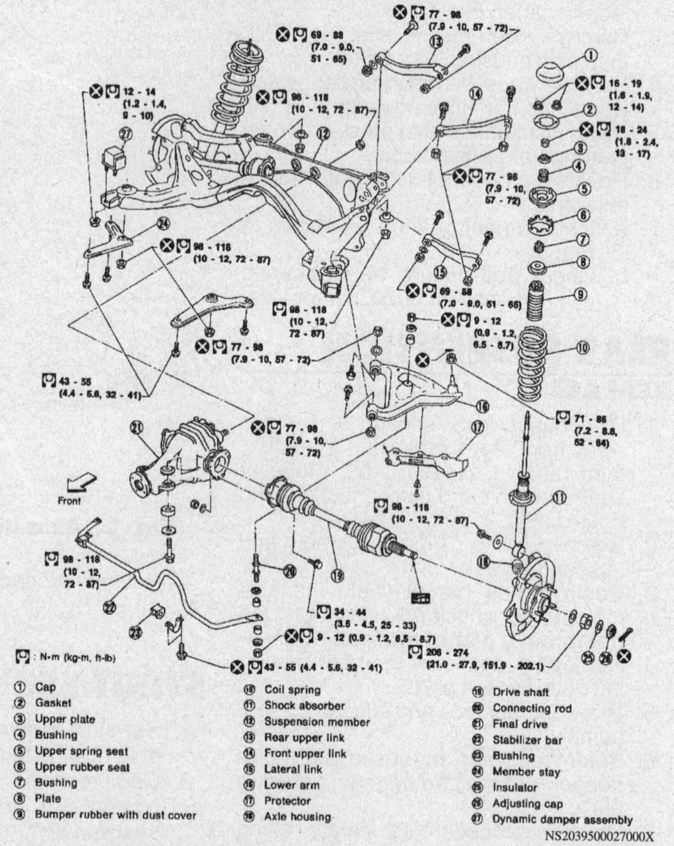
Front
: N·m (kg-m, ft-lb)
① Cap
② Gasket
③ Upper plate
④ Bushing
⑤ Upper spring seat
⑥ Upper rubber seat
⑦ Bushing
⑧ Plate
⑨ Bumper rubber with dust cover
⑩ Coil spring
⑪ Shock absorber
⑫ Suspension member
⑬ Rear upper link
⑭ Front upper link
⑮ Lateral link
⑯ Lower arm
⑰ Protector
⑱ Axle housing
⑲ Drive shaft
⑳ Connecting rod
㉑ Final drive
㉒ Stabilizer bar
㉓ Bushing
㉔ Member stay
㉕ Insulator
㉖ Adjusting cap
㉗ Dynamic damper assembly
NS2039500027000X

Fig. 7 Exploded view of rear suspension. 1995–96

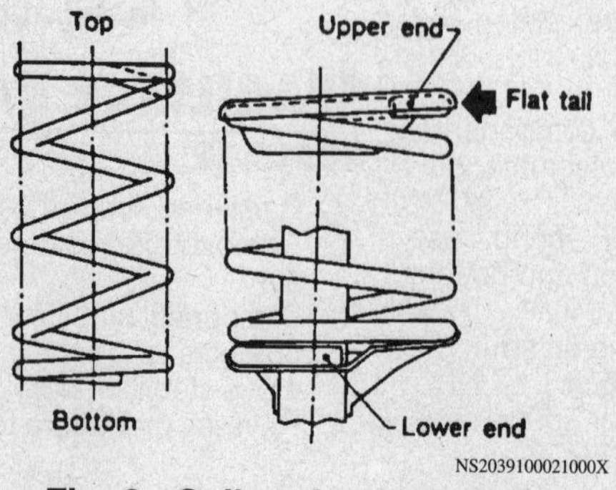
Top
Upper end
Flat tail
Bottom
Lower end
NS2039100021000X

Fig. 8 Coil spring installation

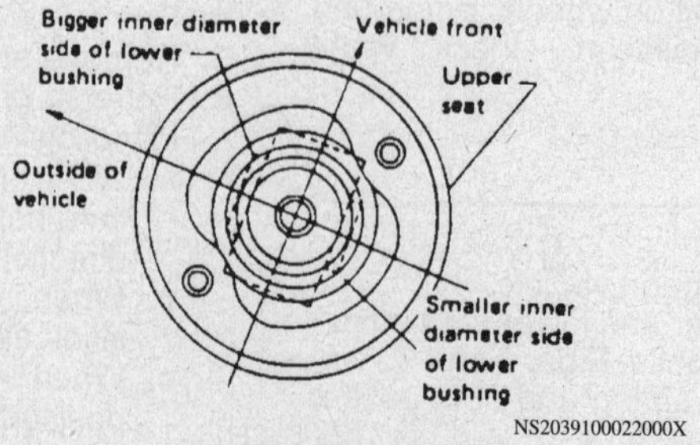
Bigger inner diameter side of lower bushing
Vehicle front
Upper seat
Outside of vehicle
Smaller inner diameter side of lower bushing
NS2039100022000X

Fig. 9 Upper spring seat installation

TIGHTENING SPECIFICATIONS

Year	Component	Torque/Ft. Lbs.
1993–96	Axle Nut	152-203
	Driveshaft Nut	152-203
	Hub Nut	152-203
	Parallel Link To Strut	65-87
	Parallel Link To Suspension Member	65-87
	Parking Brake Adjuster Locknut	28-38①
	Parking Brake Control Lever To Body	5.8-8.0
	Radius Rod Bracket To Strut	43-58
	Radius Rod To Body	65-80
	Radius Rod To Knuckle	47-61
	Strut To Body	18-22
	Strut To Knuckle	72-87
	Suspension Crossmember	65-80
	Wheel Bearing Locknut	18-25
	Wheel Lug Nut	72-87

① — Inch lbs.

Front Suspension & Steering

INDEX

	Page No.
Ball Joint, Replace	33-18
Ball Joint Inspection	33-17
Manual Steering Gears	36-1
Power Steering	36-1
Power Steering Gear, Replace	33-19
Power Steering Pump, Replace	33-19
Strut, Replace	33-18
Tension Strut, Replace	33-18
Tightening Specifications	33-19
Transverse Link, Replace	33-18
Wheel Bearing, Adjust	33-17
Wheel Hub & Steering Knuckle, Replace	33-17

WHEEL BEARING

ADJUST

1. Raise and support vehicle.
2. Remove brake pads.
3. Ensure wheel bearing is tightened to specification.
4. Ensure wheel bearing operates smoothly.
5. Check axial endplay.
6. **On 1993–94 models,** if axial endplay is more than .0012 inch, replace wheel bearing.
7. **On 1995–96 models,** if axial endplay is more than .0020 inch, replace wheel bearing.

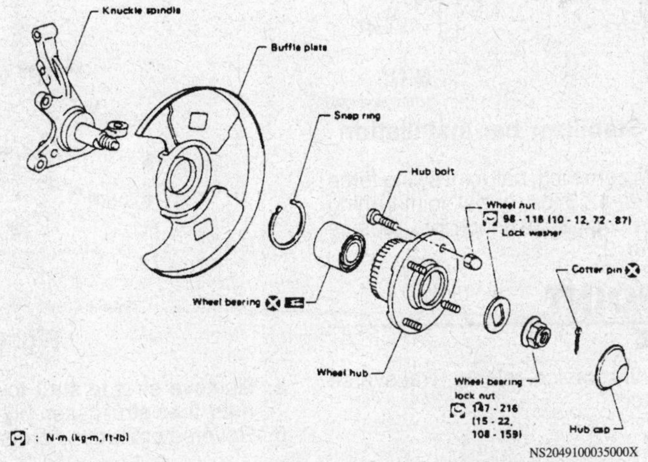

Knuckle spindle
Buffle plate
Snap ring
Hub bolt
Wheel nut
98 - 118 (10 - 12, 72 - 87)
Lock washer
Cotter pin
Wheel bearing
Wheel hub
Wheel bearing lock nut
147 - 216 (15 - 22, 108 - 159)
Hub cap
: N·m (kg-m, ft-lb)
NS2049100035000X

Fig. 1 Exploded view of wheel hub assembly

WHEEL HUB & STEERING KNUCKLE

REPLACE

1. Raise and support vehicle, then remove wheel.
2. Remove brake caliper assembly and support from frame using suitable wire.
3. Remove brake rotor.
4. Remove wheel bearing locknut, **Fig. 1.**
5. Remove wheel hub from spindle.
6. Separate tie rod ball joint and lower ball joint from knuckle.
7. Remove strut to knuckle attaching bolts.
8. Remove knuckle assembly from vehicle.
9. Reverse procedure to install, checking bearing axial endplay as outlined in "Wheel Bearing, Adjust."

BALL JOINT INSPECTION

Before checking, turn ball joint at lease ten revolutions. Check ball joint for play. If ball stud is worn, play in axial direction (C)

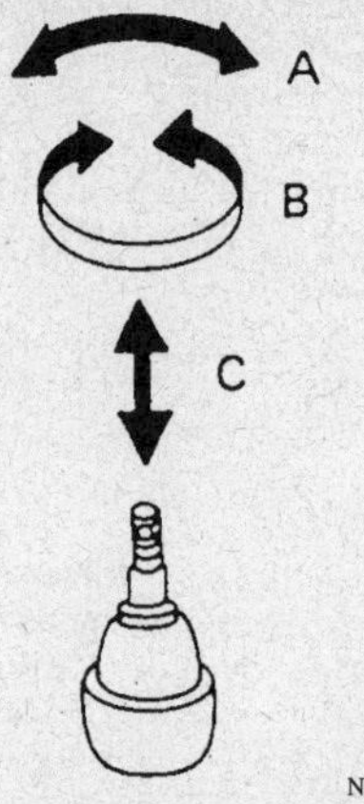
A
B
C

NS2029100025000X

Fig. 2 Ball joint inspection

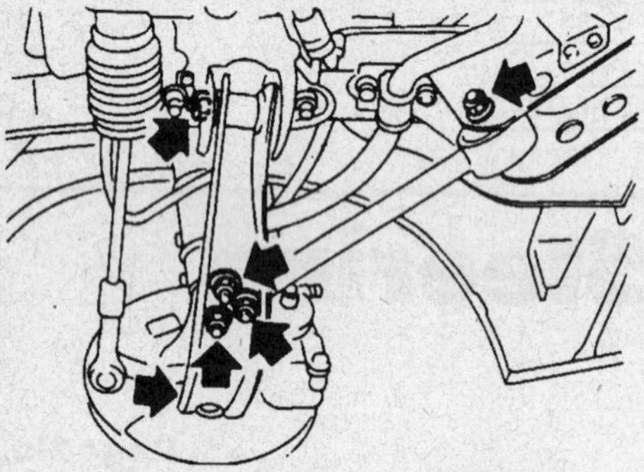

NS2029100023000X

Fig. 4 Tension rod & stabilizer bar removal

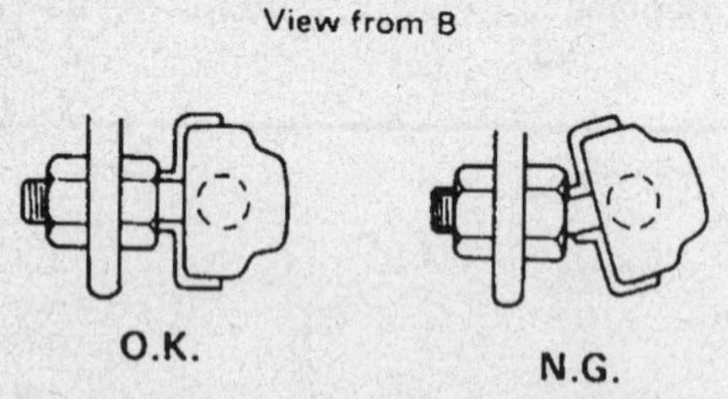
View from B
O.K.
N.G.

NS2029100024000X

Fig. 5 Stabilizer bar installation

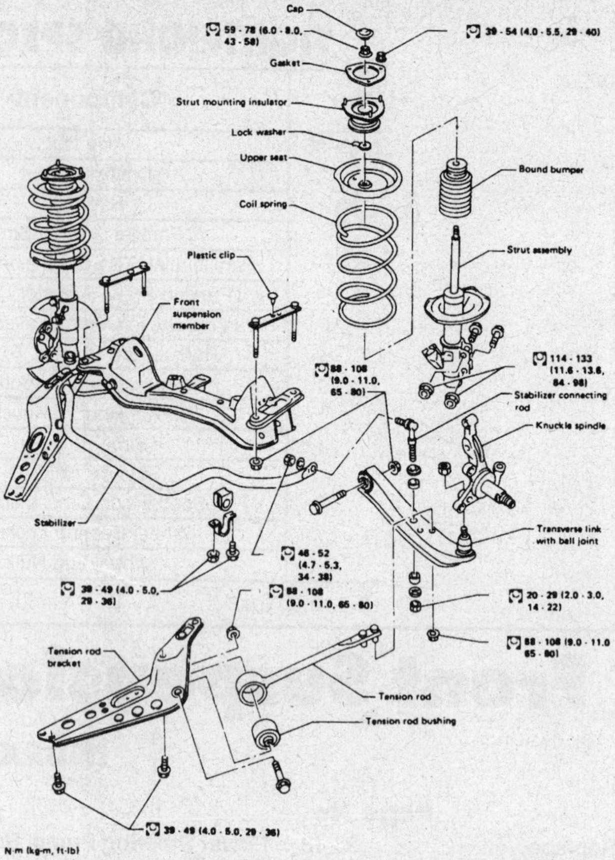
Cap
59 - 78 (6.0 - 8.0, 43 - 58)
39 - 54 (4.0 - 5.5, 29 - 40)
Gasket
Strut mounting insulator
Lock washer
Upper seat
Bound bumper
Coil spring
Strut assembly
Plastic clip
Front suspension member
88 - 108 (9.0 - 11.0, 65 - 80)
114 - 133 (11.6 - 13.6, 84 - 98)
Stabilizer connecting rod
Knuckle spindle
Stabilizer
Transverse link with ball joint
46 - 52 (4.7 - 5.3, 34 - 38)
39 - 49 (4.0 - 5.0, 29 - 36)
88 - 108 (9.0 - 11.0, 65 - 80)
20 - 29 (2.0 - 3.0, 14 - 22)
88 - 108 (9.0 - 11.0 65 - 80)
Tension rod bracket
Tension rod
Tension rod bushing
39 - 49 (4.0 - 5.0, 29 - 36)
: N·m (kg-m, ft-lb)

NS2029100022000X

Fig. 3 Exploded view of front suspension

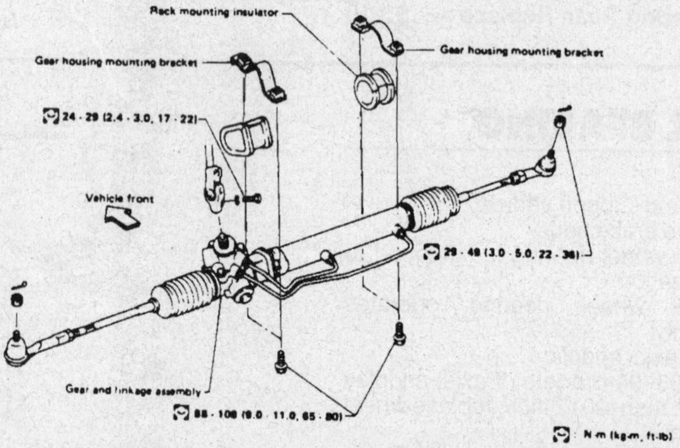
Rack mounting insulator
Gear housing mounting bracket
Gear housing mounting bracket
24 - 29 (2.4 - 3.0, 17 - 22)
Vehicle front
29 - 49 (3.0 - 5.0, 22 - 36)
Gear and linkage assembly
88 - 108 (9.0 - 11.0, 65 - 80)
: N·m (kg-m, ft-lb)

NS6039100006000X

Fig. 6 Steering gear replacement

is more than zero inch, ball joint swing force (A) is not 1.8–12.3 lbs. or ball joint turning torque (B) is not 4.3–30.4 inch lbs., replace ball joint, **Fig. 2.**

BALL JOINT

REPLACE

For ball joint service, refer to "Transverse Link, Replace."

STRUT

REPLACE

1. Raise and support front of vehicle, then remove wheel.
2. Disconnect brake line from strut.
3. Place alignment marks on strut lower bracket and camber adjusting pin.
4. Remove strut to steering knuckle attaching bolts, then separate strut from knuckle, **Fig. 3.**
5. Remove strut to strut tower attaching nuts, then strut assembly from vehicle.
6. Reverse procedure to install.

TRANSVERSE LINK

REPLACE

1. Raise and support vehicle and remove wheels.
2. Remove tension rod and stabilizer bar, **Fig. 3.**
3. Remove ball joint and transverse link mounting nut/bolts, then separate link from crossmember.
4. Reverse procedure to install.

TENSION STRUT

REPLACE

1. Raise and support vehicle.
2. Remove tension rod and stabilizer bar attaching bolts, **Fig. 4.**
3. Remove tension rod and stabilizer bar from vehicle.
4. Reverse procedure to install, ensure

stabilizer bar is installed with ball joint socket properly placed, **Fig. 5.**

POWER STEERING GEAR

REPLACE

Refer to **Fig. 6** for power steering gear replacement procedure, noting the following.

1. When removing power steering hoses plug ports and lines.
2. Set wheels in a straight-ahead position before removing lower joint.
3. After removing lower joint, put matching mark on pinion shaft and pinion housing.

POWER STEERING PUMP

REPLACE

1. **On models with air conditioning,** remove air conditioning compressor drive belt.
2. **On all models,** loosen idler pulley locknut, turn adjusting nut counterclockwise and remove power steering pump drive belt.
3. Loosen power steering hoses at pump and remove bolts securing power steering pump to brackets.
4. Raise pump and disconnect power steering hoses, catch fluid in a suitable container.
5. Plug hose ends and ports in power steering pump, then remove pump from vehicle.
6. Reverse procedure to install, then bleed system as follows:
   a. Raise and support front of vehicle.
   b. Run engine for 3–5 seconds, stop engine, check and fill power steering pump reservoir as needed.
   c. Quickly turn steering wheel all way to right and left 10 times.
   d. Start engine and idle for 3–5 seconds. Stop engine, check and fill power steering pump reservoir as needed.
   e. With steering wheel all way to right, open bleeder screw, expel air, then tighten bleeder screw.
   f. Repeat procedure until all air has been bled from system.
   g. If air cannot be bled completely after repeated attempts, repeat step e with engine running.

TIGHTENING SPECIFICATIONS

Year	Component	Torque/Ft. Lbs.
1993–96	Axle Nut	152-210
	Brake Caliper	53-72
	Driveshaft Nut	152-210
	Front Suspension Member To Body	65-80
	Hub Nut	152-210
	Stabilizer Bar To Body	29-36
	Stabilizer Bar To Link	34-38
	Stabilizer Link To Transverse Link	14-22
	Steering Column Coupling To Gear	17-22
	Steering Gear Mounting Bracket	65-80
	Steering Pump To Bracket	23-31
	Strut Piston Nut	43-58
	Strut To Body	29-40
	Strut To Knuckle	84-89
	Tension Rod Bracket Bolts	29-36
	Tension Rod To Tension Bracket	65-80
	Tension Rod To Transverse Link	65-80
	Tie Rod End To Knuckle	22-36
	Transverse Link To Front Suspension Member	65-80
	Wheel Bearing Locknut	108-159
	Wheel Lug Nut	72-87

Wheel Alignment

INDEX

	Page No.
Front Wheel Alignment	33-20
Camber	33-20
Caster & Kingpin Inclination	33-20
Steering Angle	33-20
Toe-In	33-20
Preliminary Inspection	33-20
Rear Wheel Alignment	33-20
Camber	33-20
Toe-In	33-20
Vehicle Ride Height	33-20
Wheel Alignment Specifications	33-2

PRELIMINARY INSPECTION

Before checking and adjusting wheel alignment angles, perform following checks:

1. Check tire pressures and adjust as needed.
2. Ensure tires are of proper size and that tires are properly matched.
3. Ensure wheel bearings (front and rear) are properly adjusted.
4. Check steering gear adjustment and ensure steering gear is properly secured to frame.
5. Inspect steering linkage and suspension components for damage and wear, and repair or replace components as needed.
6. Measure vehicle ride height with vehicle unloaded, ensure springs are not collapsed.
7. Place vehicle on suitable alignment rack following manufacturer's instructions, then jounce vehicle several times to settle suspension.
8. Check and correct rear wheel camber and toe first, if applicable, then check and correct front suspension angles in following order: caster and kingpin inclination, camber, toe setting and turning angle (toe-out on turns).

FRONT WHEEL ALIGNMENT

Front wheel alignment should only be checked after rear wheels are properly aligned in relation to vehicle centerline, as most equipment uses rear wheels as reference for correct front wheel alignment. Front wheel alignment should be checked with vehicle at normal ride height and following equipment manufacturer's instructions.

CASTER & KINGPIN INCLINATION

Caster and kingpin inclination cannot be adjusted. If caster or kingpin angle are not within specifications, check suspension components and sheet metal for damage, distortion and excessive wear, repair or replace as necessary.

CAMBER

Camber cannot be adjusted. If camber is not within specifications, inspect suspension and sheet metal for damage, distortion and excessive wear. Repair or replace components as necessary.

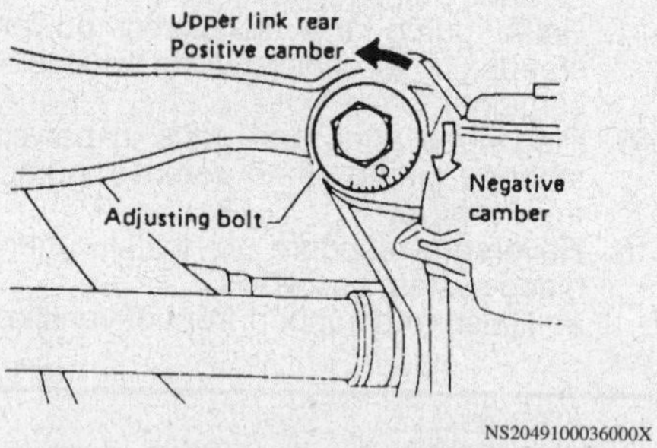

Upper link rear
Positive camber
Negative camber
Adjusting bolt
NS2049100036000X

Fig. 1 Rear camber adjustment

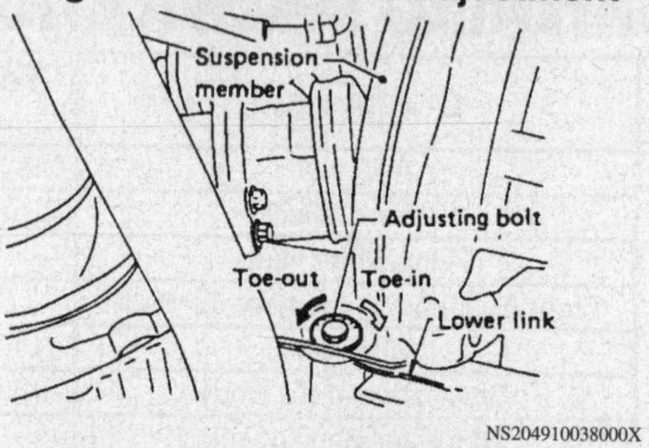

Suspension member
Adjusting bolt
Toe-out
Toe-in
Lower link
NS204910038000X

Fig. 2 Rear toe-in adjustment

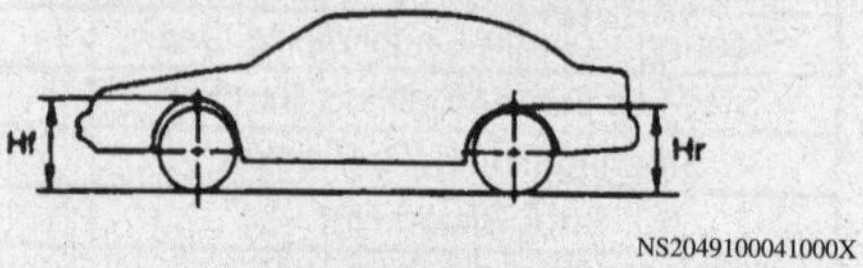

Hf
Hr
NS2049100041000X

Fig. 3 Measuring vehicle ride height

TOE-IN

1. Joust front end several times to eliminate friction, then set steering wheel in straight ahead position.
2. Ensure tie rods are same length.
3. Loosen lock nuts, then adjust toe-in by turning tie rods.
4. Tighten lock nuts to specifications.

STEERING ANGLE

1. Set wheels in a straight ahead position.
2. Position front wheels on turning radius gauge.
3. Rotate steering wheel fully to right and left.
4. Ensure inner turning angle is within specifications.

REAR WHEEL ALIGNMENT

CAMBER

1. Measure camber for each wheel following equipment manufacturer's instructions.
2. Scribe matching mark between cam and upper rear link, then loosen nut securing link bushing bolt.
3. Rotate cam bolt, **Fig. 1,** to bring camber within specifications. Each graduation represents 4° camber change.
4. When camber is within specifications, hold position of cam bolt and **torque** nut to 51–65 ft. lbs.
5. Ensure camber is still within specifications.

TOE-IN

1. Draw a base line across tire tread.
2. Measure toe-in for each wheel following equipment manufacturer's instructions.
3. Rotate bolt, **Fig. 2,** to bring toe-in within specifications. Each graduation of bolt will change toe-in on one side approximately .059 inch on 1993–94 models, or .051 inch on 1995–96 models.
4. When toe-in is within specifications, hold position of bolt and **torque** nut to 51–65 ft. lbs.
5. Ensure toe-in is still within specifications.

VEHICLE RIDE HEIGHT

1. Parked on a level surface and tires inflated to proper air pressure.
2. Ensure all fluid levels are to specified level, spare tire and jack are in proper locations.
3. Bounce vehicle up and down several times, then measure vehicle height from top of wheelwell to ground, **Fig. 3.**
4. Vehicle ride height is not adjustable. If vehicle height is not within specifications, check for worn springs or suspension parts.
5. **On models with 205/55R16 tires,** front wheel arch height should be 27.32 inches and rear 26.38 inches.
6. **On 1995–96 models with 195/60R15 tires,**front wheel arch height should be 27.05 inches and rear 26.10 inches.

NISSAN QUEST

INDEX OF SERVICE OPERATIONS

	Page No.
AIR BAG SYSTEM PRECAUTIONS	0-8
AUTOMATIC TRANSMISSIONS/ TRANSAXLES	36-1
BRAKES	
Anti-Lock Brakes	36-1
Disc Brakes	36-1
Drum Brakes	36-1
Hydraulic Brake Systems	36-1
Power Brake Units	36-1
ELECTRICAL	
Air Bags	36-1
Air Conditioning	36-1
Alternators	36-1
Alternator, Replace	34-3
Blower Motor, Replace	34-5
Combination Switch, Replace	34-4
Cooling Fans	36-1
Cruise Control	36-1
Dash Gauges	36-1
Dash Panels	36-1
Distributor, Replace	34-3
Evaporator Core, Replace	34-6
Fuel Pump Relay Location	34-3
Fuse Panel & Flasher Location	34-3
Headlamp Switch, Replace	34-4
Heater Core, Replace	34-6
Ignition Lock, Replace	34-3
Ignition Switch, Replace	34-4
Instrument Cluster, Replace	34-4
Neutral Safety Switch, Replace	34-4
Passive Restraints	36-1
Precautions	34-3
Radio, Replace	34-4
Relay Center Location	34-3
Speed Controls	36-1
Starter Motors	36-1
Starter, Replace	34-3
Steering Columns	36-1
Steering Wheel, Replace	34-4
Stop Light Switch, Replace	34-4
Wiper Motor, Replace	34-5
Wiper Systems	36-1
Wiper Transmission, Replace	34-5
ELECTRICAL SYMBOL IDENTIFICATION	0-139
FRONT SUSPENSION & STEERING	
Ball Joint, Replace	34-12
Ball Joint Inspection	34-12
Coil Spring & Strut Service	34-13
Coil Spring, Replace	34-12
Control Arm, Replace	34-13
Control Arm Bushing, Replace	34-13
Description	34-12
Hub & Bearing Service	34-12
Manual Steering Gears	36-1
Power Steering	36-1
Power Steering Gear, Replace	34-14
Power Steering Pump, Replace	34-14
Stabilizer Bar, Replace	34-13
Strut, Replace	34-12
Tightening Specifications	34-15
Transverse Link, Replace	34-13
Wheel Bearing, Adjust	34-12
Wheel Hub & Steering Knuckle, Replace	34-12
FRONT WHEEL DRIVE AXLES	36-1
REAR AXLE & SUSPENSION	
Hub & Bearing, Replace	34-10
Hub & Bearing Service	34-10
Leaf Spring, Replace	34-11
Rear Axle, Replace	34-10
Rear Wheel Spindle, Replace	34-11
Shock Absorber, Replace	34-11
Stabilizer Bar, Replace	34-11
Tightening Specifications	34-11
SERVICE REMINDER & WARNING LAMP RESET PROCEDURES	0-10
SPECIFICATIONS	
Fluid Capacities & Cooling System Data	34-2
Front Wheel Alignment Specifications	34-2
General Engine Specifications	34-1
Lubricant Data	34-3
Rear Wheel Alignment Specifications	34-2
Tune Up Specifications	34-2
VEHICLE IDENTIFICATION	0-1
VEHICLE LIFT POINTS	0-34
VEHICLE MAINTENANCE SCHEDULES	0-69
VG30E ENGINE	
Belt Tension Data	34-8
Compression Pressure	34-6
Cooling System Bleed	34-8
Crankshaft Rear Oil Seal, Replace	34-7
Engine Mount, Replace	34-7
Engine Rebuilding Specifications	36-1
Engine, Replace	34-7
Fuel Filter, Replace	34-9
Fuel Pump, Replace	34-8
Precautions	34-6
Radiator, Replace	34-8
Tightening Specifications	34-9
Valve Adjustment	34-7
Valve Clearance Specifications	34-7
WHEEL ALIGNMENT	
Front Wheel Alignment	34-15
Kingpin, Adjust	34-16
Preliminary Inspection	34-15
Rear Wheel Alignment	34-15
Vehicle Ride Height	34-16
Wheel Alignment Specifications	34-2
WIRE COLOR CODE IDENTIFICATION	0-144

Specifications

GENERAL ENGINE SPECIFICATIONS

Year	Engine Model	Engine	Fuel System	Bore & Stroke	Comp. Ratio	Horsepower @ RPM	Torque Ft. Lbs. @ RPM	Normal Oil Pressure, psi
1993–96	VG30E	3.0L	MFI	3.43 x 3.27	9.0	151 @ 4800	174 @ 4400	57–70①

① — At 3200 RPM.

TUNE UP SPECIFICATIONS

Year	Engine Model	Liter	Spark Plug Gap	Ignition Timing, °BTDC			Curb Idle Speed, RPM	Fast Idle Speed, RPM	Fuel Pump Pressure, psi	Valve Lash
				Firing Order	Auto. Trans.	Mark Location, Fig.				
1993–96	VG30E	3.0	.033	1-2-3-4-5-6	15	A	750N	①	36–38②	③

BTDC: Before Top Dead Center.
① — Controlled by idle control system.
② — With engine running.
③ — Refer to "Valve Adjustment" section under "VG30E Engine."

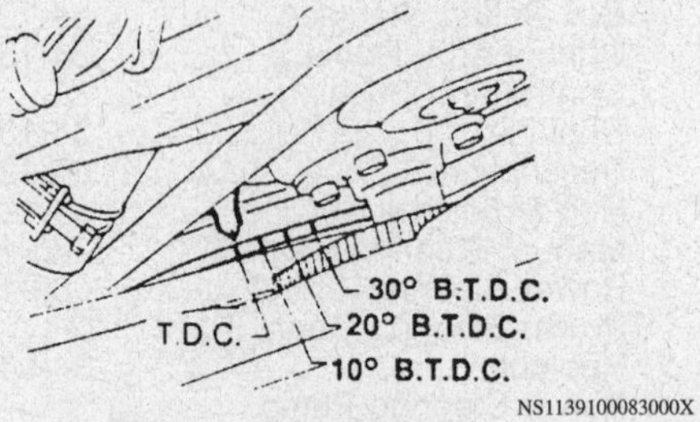
30° B.T.D.C.
20° B.T.D.C.
10° B.T.D.C.
T.D.C.
NS1139100083000X

Fig. A

FRONT WHEEL ALIGNMENT SPECIFICATIONS

Year	Caster Angle, Degree		Camber Angle, Degree		Front Turning Angle, Degree		Kingpin Inclination, Degrees	Ball Joint
	Limits	Desired	Limits	Desired	Inside	Outside		
1993	+1/20 to +1 7/12	+3/4	−1/2 to +1	+1/4	36–40	28–32	12 5/6 to 14 1/3	①
1994–96	+1/20 to +1 11/20	+4/5	+9/20 to +1 1/20	+3/4	36–40	28–32	12 5/6 to 14 1/3	①

① — Refer to "Ball Joint Inspection" section under "Front Suspension & Steering."

REAR WHEEL ALIGNMENT SPECIFICATIONS

Year	Camber Angle, Degree		Toe-In, Degree
	Limits	Desired	
1993	−1/4 to +1/4	0	−.06 to +.06
1994–96	−1/4 to +1/4	0	−.16 to +.16

FLUID CAPACITIES & COOLING SYSTEM DATA

Year	Engine, Liter	Coolant Capacity, Qts.		Radiator Cap Relief Pressure, psi	Thermo Opening, Temp. °F	Fuel Tank, Gals.	Engine Oil Refill, Qts.①	Transaxle Oil, Qts.
		Less A/C	With A/C					
1993–96	3.0L	②	②	12–16	180	20	4.2③	10

① — Approximate, make final check w/dipstick.
② — With trailer package, less rear heater, 11.6 qts., w/rear heater, 13 qts.; less trailer package, less rear heater, 10.7 qts., w/rear heater, 12.1 qts.
③ — Includes filter.

LUBRICANT DATA

Year	Model	Lubricant Type				
		Transaxle	Transfer Case	Rear Axle	Power Steering	Brake System
1993–96	All	Nissan Matic D ①	—	—	Ford Premium Power Steering Fluid	DOT 3

① — Dexron III/Mercon or equivalent automatic transmission fluid may also be used.

Electrical

NOTE: On Air Bag Equipped Models, Refer To "Air Bag System Precautions" Located In Front Of This Manual For System Disarming & Arming Procedures.

INDEX

	Page No.
Air Bags	36-1
Air Conditioning	36-1
Alternator, Replace	34-3
Alternators	36-1
Blower Motor, Replace	34-5
Front	34-5
Rear	34-6
Combination Switch, Replace	34-4
Cooling Fans	36-1
Cruise Control	36-1
Dash Gauges	36-1
Dash Panels	36-1
Distributor, Replace	34-3
Evaporator Core, Replace	34-6
Front	34-6
Rear	34-6
Fuel Pump Relay Location	34-3
Fuse Panel & Flasher Location	34-3
Headlamp Switch, Replace	34-4
Heater Core, Replace	34-6
Front	34-6
Rear	34-6
Ignition Lock, Replace	34-3
Ignition Switch, Replace	34-4
Instrument Cluster, Replace	34-4
Neutral Safety Switch, Replace	34-4
Passive Restraints	36-1
Precautions	34-3
Air Bag Systems	34-3
Radio, Replace	34-4
Relay Center Location	34-3
Speed Controls	36-1
Starter Motors	36-1
Starter, Replace	34-3
Steering Columns	36-1
Steering Wheel, Replace	34-4
Models Less Air Bag	34-4
Models w/Air Bag	34-4
Stop Light Switch, Replace	34-4
Wiper Motor, Replace	34-5
Front	34-5
Rear	34-5
Wiper Systems	36-1
Wiper Transmission, Replace	34-5

PRECAUTIONS

AIR BAG SYSTEMS

Refer to "Air Bag System Precautions" in front of this manual for system disarming and arming procedures.

FUSE PANEL & FLASHER LOCATION

Fuse panel is located on lefthand side of instrument panel above hood release lever behind fuse panel cover. Flasher module is located behind lefthand side of instrument panel, on righthand side of steering column.

FUEL PUMP RELAY LOCATION

The fuel pump relay is located in the lefthand engine compartment relay box.

RELAY CENTER LOCATION

The lefthand relay box is located in front lefthand corner of engine compartment, in front of battery. The righthand relay box is located on the front righthand side of engine compartment, along inner fender.

STARTER

REPLACE

1. Disconnect battery ground cable and remove air intake system.
2. Disconnect battery cable from starter motor.
3. Disconnect brush cable from magnetic switch assembly.
4. Disconnect harness connector from starter motor harness.
5. Remove starter motor attaching bolts, then starter.
6. Reverse procedure to install.

ALTERNATOR

REPLACE

1. Disconnect battery ground cable and loosen idler pulley adjusting bolt, then remove A/C compressor belt.
2. Remove engine undercover.
3. Disconnect alternator harness and remove harness bracket.
4. Loosen alternator mounting bolt, then remove drive belt.
5. Remove alternator from vehicle.
6. Reverse procedure to install.

DISTRIBUTOR

REPLACE

1. Disconnect battery ground cable remove distributor cover.
2. Loosen three distributor cap attaching screws, then position cap and spark plug wires aside.
3. Disconnect distributor ground connector from housing.
4. Disconnect electrical connector from distributor.
5. Remove distributor electrical connector from bracket.
6. Rotate engine until No. 1 piston is at TDC of compression stroke, ensure crankshaft pulley yellow timing mark and lower timing belt cover timing pointer are aligned.
7. Mark installation alignment between rotor and engine.
8. Remove distributor attaching bolt, then distributor.
9. Reverse procedure to install.

IGNITION LOCK

REPLACE

1. Disconnect battery ground cable and remove three lower steering column cover attaching screws, then cover.
2. Turn ignition to On position.

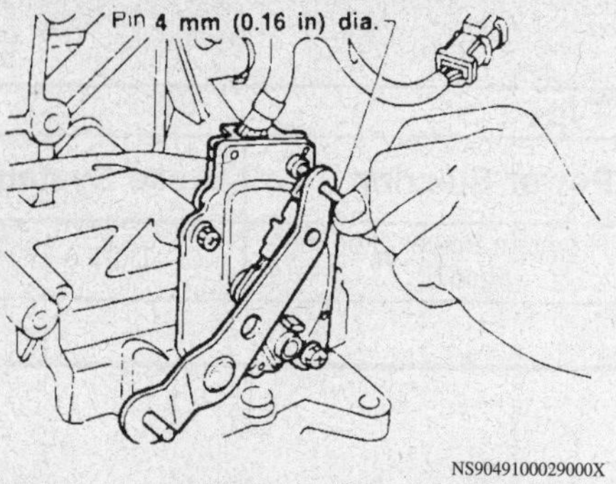
Pin 4 mm (0.16 in) dia.
NS9049100029000X

Fig. 1 Adjusting inhibitor switch

3. Place suitable ⅛ inch wire pin or small drift punch in ignition lock cylinder access hole, then depress retaining pin while pulling lock cylinder rearward to remove.
4. Reverse procedure to install. Lock cylinder is fully seated in housing when pin snaps into access hole.

IGNITION SWITCH

REPLACE

1. Disconnect battery ground cable remove lower dash panel attaching screw, then pull panel rearward to disengage.
2. Remove four lefthand knee reinforcement plate attaching bolts, then plate.
3. Remove ignition switch harness attaching bolts, then disconnect harness from switch.
4. Remove two ignition switch attaching screws, then switch assembly.
5. Reverse procedure to install.

NEUTRAL SAFETY SWITCH

REPLACE

1. Remove control cable from manual shaft.
2. Set manual shaft to "N " position, then loosen inhibitor switch fixing bolts.
3. Insert pin into adjustment holes in both inhibitor switch and manual shaft as near vertical as possible, **Fig. 1.**
4. Tighten inhibitor switch fixing bolts and remove pin from adjustment holes.
5. Attach control cable to manual shaft.

HEADLAMP SWITCH

REPLACE

1. Disconnect battery ground cable pull headlamp switch, autolamp, I/P dimmer switch from instrument cluster bezel.
2. Disconnect headlamp switch electrical connector, then autolamp, I/P dimmer switch assembly electrical connector.
3. Remove two headlamp switch attaching screws, then remove switch.
4. Reverse procedure to install.

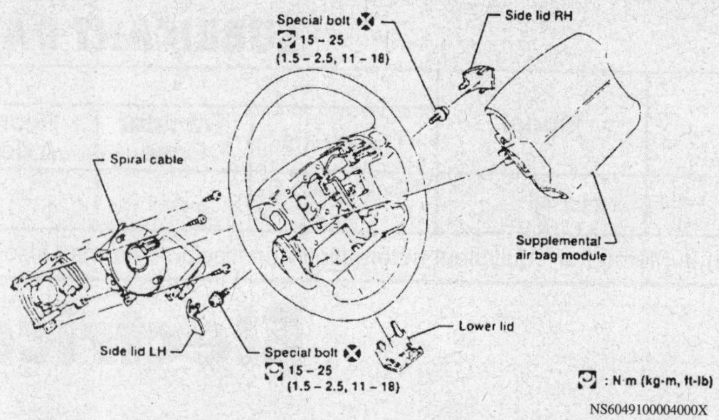
Special bolt
15 - 25
(1.5 - 2.5, 11 - 18)
Side lid RH
Spiral cable
Supplemental air bag module
Lower lid
Side lid LH
Special bolt
15 - 25
(1.5 - 2.5, 11 - 18)
: N·m (kg-m, ft-lb)
NS6049100004000X

Fig. 2 Steering wheel replacement. Models w/air bag

STOP LIGHT SWITCH

REPLACE

1. Disconnect battery ground cable.
2. Depress switch electrical connector tabs, then disconnect electrical connector.
3. Loosen switch locknut, then remove switch.
4. Reverse procedure to install, Adjust switch height as follows:
   a. Measure distance between brake pedal stopper and threaded end of switch, .012–.039 inch should be indicated.
   b. If not as indicated, loosen switch locknut and adjust switch until height is within specification.
   c. **Torque** switch locknut to 9–11 ft. lbs.

COMBINATION SWITCH

REPLACE

1. Disconnect battery ground cable remove ignition lock cylinder as described under "Ignition Lock, Replace."
2. Remove upper steering column cover.
3. Remove two combination switch attaching screws.
4. Disconnect two switch electrical connectors, then remove switch.
5. Reverse procedure to install.

STEERING WHEEL

REPLACE

MODELS LESS AIR BAG

1. Disconnect battery ground cable.
2. Remove horn pad attaching screw, located behind steering wheel.
3. Disconnect horn electrical connector, then remove horn pad assembly.
4. Remove steering wheel attaching bolt.
5. Remove mass damper attaching screws, then damper.
6. Scribe aligning marks on steering wheel hub and steering column shaft.
7. Using steering wheel puller tool No. ST27180001, or equivalent, remove steering wheel.
8. Reverse procedure to install. **Torque** steering wheel attaching bolt to 22–31 ft. lbs.

MODELS w/AIR BAG

1. Remove LH and RH steering wheel side lids to expose special bolts, **Fig 2.**
2. Using a T50H Torx bit, remove and discard LH and RH special bolts, then remove air bag module. **Always place air bag module with pad facing upward.**
3. Set steering wheel in neutral position.
4. Remove steering wheel bolt, then disconnect horn connector.
5. Using steering wheel puller, remove steering wheel.
6. Reverse procedure to install, using new special bolts to secure air bag module.

INSTRUMENT CLUSTER

REPLACE

1. Disconnect battery ground cable remove lower console center cover, then lower instrument cover.
2. Disconnect lamp harness connector.
3. Remove instrument pocket, then lefthand side lower instrument panel.
4. Remove lefthand side knee reinforcement plate.
5. Remove steering column to instrument panel mounting nuts, then lower steering column.
6. Remove instrument cluster lid.
7. Remove instrument cluster to instrument panel attaching screws.
8. Pull cluster rearward and disconnect cluster harness connectors.
9. Remove cluster from vehicle.
10. Reverse procedure to install.

RADIO

REPLACE

1. Disconnect battery ground cable pull ashtray assembly rearward to remove.
2. Remove control console bezel attaching screw, then remove bezel.
3. Remove climate control panel attaching screws, then control panel.
4. Disconnect climate control panel from rear of radio and tape chassis.
5. Remove four radio attaching screws.
6. Pull radio assembly rearward, then disconnect radio electrical connectors and antenna cables.

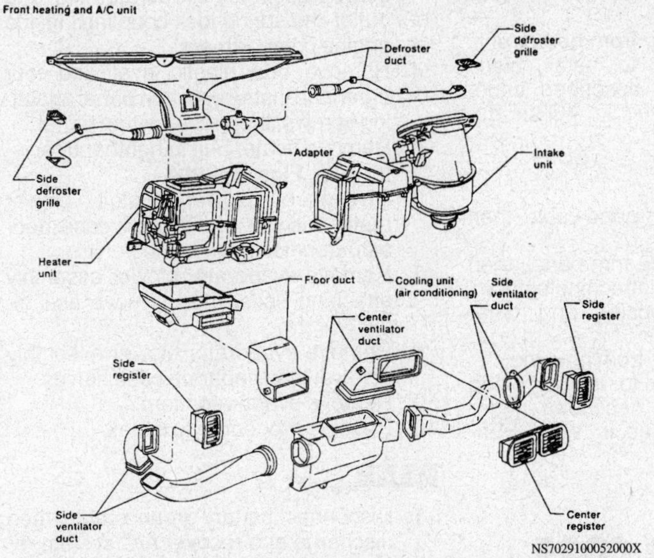
Front heating and A/C unit
Side defroster grille
Defroster duct
Adapter
Intake unit
Side defroster grille
Heater unit
Floor duct
Cooling unit (air conditioning)
Side ventilator duct
Side register
Center ventilator duct
Side register
Side ventilator duct
Center register
NS7029100052000X

Fig. 3 Exploded view of front A/C & heater unit. 1993–95

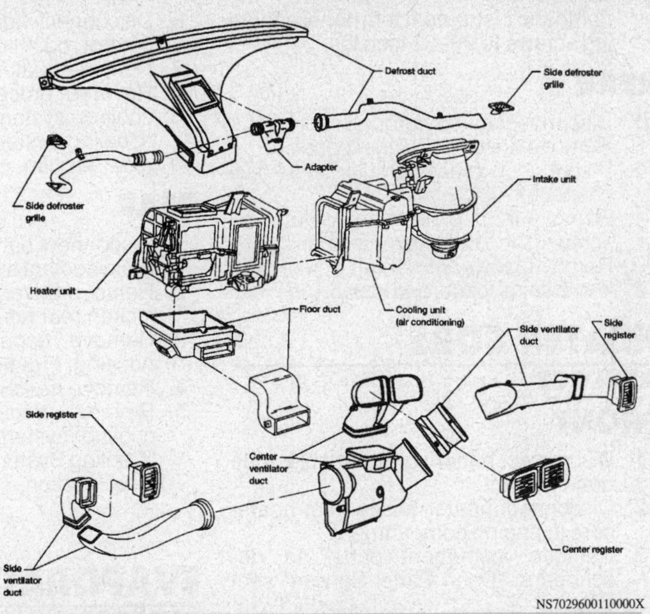
Defrost duct
Side defroster grille
Adapter
Intake unit
Side defroster grille
Heater unit
Floor duct
Cooling unit (air conditioning)
Side ventilator duct
Side register
Side register
Center ventilator duct
Side ventilator duct
Center register
NS7029600110000X

Fig. 4 Exploded view of front A/C & heater unit. 1996

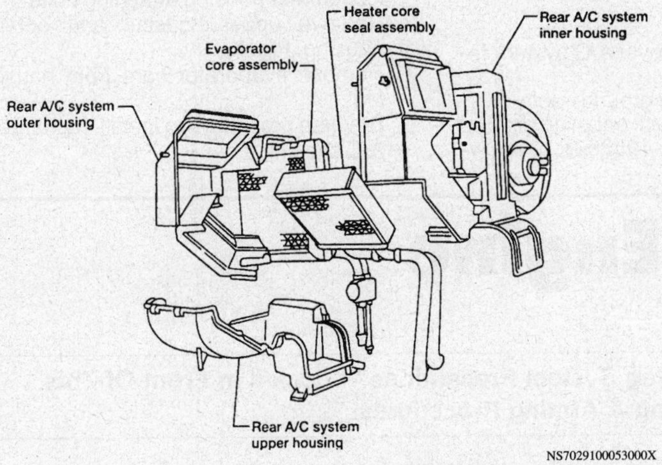
Heater core seal assembly
Rear A/C system inner housing
Evaporator core assembly
Rear A/C system outer housing
Rear A/C system upper housing
NS7029100053000X

Fig. 5 Exploded view of rear A/C & heater unit

7. Remove radio to bracket attaching screws, then remove radio from bracket.
8. Reverse procedure to install.

WIPER MOTOR

REPLACE

FRONT

1. Disconnect battery ground cable.
2. Remove wiper arm and blade assembly.
3. Remove ten lower windshield molding attaching plastic screws.
4. Remove five windshield side trim attaching screws from each side.
5. Disconnect washer hose from lower windshield molding Y connector.
6. Remove windshield molding.
7. Disconnect wiper motor electrical connector.
8. Remove wiper motor assembly attaching bolts, then motor assembly.
9. Remove four bracket to motor attaching locknuts and bolts, then separate motor from bracket.
10. Reverse procedure to install. **Torque** wiper motor attaching bolts to 52–68 inch lbs.

REAR

1. Disconnect battery ground cable.
2. Remove rear wiper arm and blade assembly.
3. Remove rear wiper motor shaft nut cover, then attaching nut.
4. Remove outer collar and seal from liftgate.
5. Remove liftgate trim panel.
6. **On models equipped with opening liftgate glass,** remove liftgate glass latch cover.
7. **On all models,** remove rear courtesy lamps.
8. Carefully remove plastic weather barrier at adhesive areas.
9. Disconnect rear wiper electrical connector.
10. Remove three wiper motor attaching bracket bolts.
11. Remove wiper motor shaft inner collar, then two wiper motor to bracket attaching bolts.
12. Slide wiper motor connector from bracket, then remove motor.
13. Reverse procedure to install, noting following:
    a. **Torque** wiper motor shaft to 53–71 inch. lbs.
    b. **Torque** wiper motor bracket bolts to 52–68 inch. lbs.
    c. **Torque** wiper motor to bracket bolts to 45 inch. lbs.

WIPER TRANSMISSION

REPLACE

1. Mark installation alignment on end of wiper linkage. Remove front wiper motor as outlined under "Wiper Motor, Replace."
2. Using suitable screwdrivers, remove each end of wiper linkage.
3. Remove two dust covers.
4. Remove motor pivot shaft attaching nut.
5. Using suitable screwdrivers, remove pivot arm and dust cover.
6. Reverse procedure to install.

BLOWER MOTOR

REPLACE

FRONT

1. Disconnect battery ground cable.
2. Remove one plastic rivet and four righthand instrument trim panel attaching screws, then remove trim panel.
3. Disconnect blower motor electrical connector.
4. Remove blower motor air vent tubes.
5. Remove three blower motor attaching screws, then remove blower motor.
6. Remove blower motor fan from motor as required.
7. Reverse procedure to install. **Torque**

righthand instrument trim panel attaching screws to 23–32 inch lbs.

REAR

1. Disconnect battery ground cable.
2. Remove driver's side trim panel.
3. Disconnect blower motor electrical connector.
4. Remove three blower motor attaching screws, then the blower motor.
5. Remove blower motor fan from motor.
6. Reverse procedure to install.

HEATER CORE

REPLACE

FRONT

1. Disconnect battery ground cable, then drain coolant.
2. Disconnect heater hoses from heater core in engine compartment.
3. Remove instrument panel as described in "Dash Panel Service" section.
4. Disconnect heater unit ducts, **Figs. 3 and 4.**
5. Remove two heater unit attaching bolts, then disconnect door motor electrical connectors.
6. Remove heater unit from vehicle.
7. Remove heater pipe plate, then heater core retainer.
8. Disconnect heater core shutoff valve control rod.
9. Remove heater core from heater unit.
10. Reverse procedure to install, bleed cooling system as described under "Cooling System Bleed" in "VG30E Engine" section.

REAR

1. Disconnect battery ground cable, then drain coolant system.
2. Remove driver's side trim panel, then loosen rear housing attaching bolts.
3. Remove upper housing and outer housing, **Fig. 5.**
4. Remove heater core from housing.
5. Reverse procedure to install, bleed cooling system as described under "Cooling System Bleed" in "VG30E Engine" section.

EVAPORATOR CORE

REPLACE

FRONT

1. Discharge and recover A/C system refrigerant.
2. Disconnect battery ground cable.
3. Using A/C spring lock coupling disconnect tool No. T84L-19623-B, or equivalent, disconnect evaporator inlet and outlet line spring lock couplings inside engine compartment.
4. Remove one plastic rivet and four righthand instrument trim panel attaching screws, then remove trim panel.
5. Remove heater unit to righthand register duct, **Figs. 3 and 4.**
6. Disconnect blower motor, blower motor resistor and blower case door actuator electrical connectors.
7. Remove evaporator blower assembly attaching bolts, then remove assembly.
8. Remove evaporator blower assembly screws, then separate case halves.
9. Remove evaporator core.
10. Reverse procedure to install.

REAR

1. Disconnect battery ground cable, then discharge and recover A/C system refrigerant.
2. Remove driver's side trim panel, then loosen rear housing attaching bolts.
3. Remove upper housing and outer housing, **Fig. 5.**
4. Remove evaporator core from housing.
5. Reverse procedure to install, recharge A/C system.

VG30E Engine

NOTE: On Air Bag Equipped Models, Refer To "Air Bag System Precautions" Located In Front Of This Manual For System Disarming & Arming Procedures.

NOTE: For Procedures Not Found In This Section, Refer To VG30E Engine Section In Nissan Maxima & 300ZX Chapter.

INDEX

	Page No.
Belt Tension Data	34-8
Compression Pressure	34-6
Cooling System Bleed	34-8
Crankshaft Rear Oil Seal, Replace	34-7
Engine Mount, Replace	34-7
Engine Rebuilding Specifications	36-1
Engine, Replace	34-7
Fuel Filter, Replace	34-9
Fuel Pump, Replace	34-8
Precautions	34-6
Air Bag Systems	34-6
Fuel System Pressure Relief	34-6
Radiator, Replace	34-8
Tightening Specifications	34-9
Valve Adjustment	34-7
Valve Clearance Specifications	34-7

PRECAUTIONS

AIR BAG SYSTEMS

Refer to "Air Bag System Precautions" in front of this manual for system disarming and arming procedures.

FUEL SYSTEM PRESSURE RELIEF

1. Remove fuel pump fuse from fuse panel, then start engine.
2. After engine stalls, crank engine over two more times to ensure all pressure has been relieved, then turn ignition switch Off and install fuel pump fuse.

COMPRESSION PRESSURE

1. Start engine and run until engine reaches operating temperature.
2. Turn ignition switch off.
3. Release fuel pressure as outlined under "Precautions."
4. Remove all spark plugs.
5. Disconnect distributor center cable.
6. Attach a compression tester to cylinder No.1.
7. Depress accelerator pedal fully to keep throttle valve wide open.
8. Crank engine and record highest gauge indication.

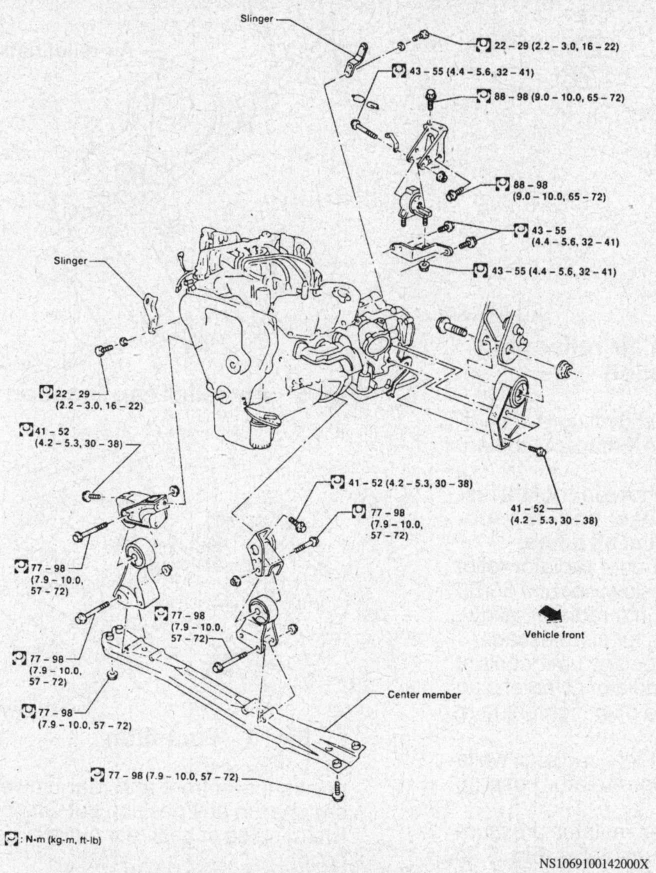
Slinger
22 – 29 (2.2 – 3.0, 16 – 22)
43 – 55 (4.4 – 5.6, 32 – 41)
88 – 98 (9.0 – 10.0, 65 – 72)
41 – 52 (4.2 – 5.3, 30 – 38)
77 – 98 (7.9 – 10.0, 57 – 72)
Center member
Vehicle front
: N·m (kg-m, ft-lb)
NS1069100142000X

Fig. 1 Engine & transaxle mounts. 1993–95

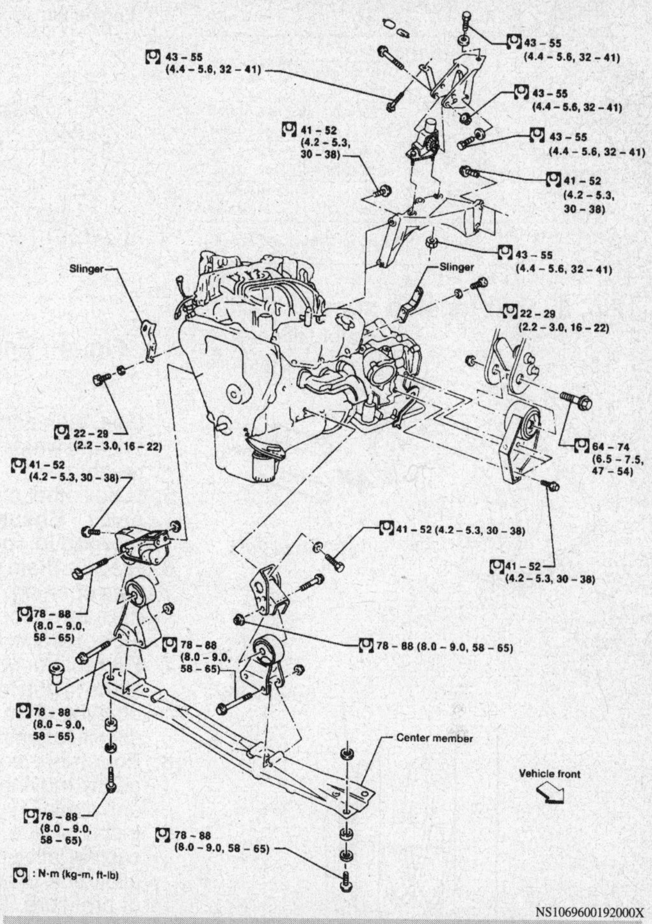
Slinger
43 – 55 (4.4 – 5.6, 32 – 41)
41 – 52 (4.2 – 5.3, 30 – 38)
22 – 29 (2.2 – 3.0, 16 – 22)
64 – 74 (6.5 – 7.5, 47 – 54)
78 – 88 (8.0 – 9.0, 58 – 65)
Center member
Vehicle front
: N·m (kg-m, ft-lb)
NS1069600192000X

Fig. 2 Engine & transaxle mounts. 1996

9. Repeat measurement on each cylinder.
10. Standard compression is 173 psi at 300 RPM, minimum pressure is 128 psi at 300 RPM and compression difference limit between cylinders is 14 psi.
11. If compression in one or more cylinders is low, pour a small amount of engine oil into cylinders through spark plug holes, then retest compression.
12. If adding oil helps compression, then piston rings may be at fault. If adding oil does not help compression, then valves may be at fault.
13. If compression stays low in two cylinders that are next to each other, then cylinder head gasket may be leaking or both cylinders have valve component damage.
14. Repair as necessary.

ENGINE MOUNT

REPLACE

Refer to **Figs. 1 and 2** when replacing engine mounts.

ENGINE

REPLACE

1. Relieve fuel system pressure as described under "Precautions," then drain cooling system.
2. Disconnect battery ground cable raise and support vehicle.
3. Remove front wheels, engine undercovers and side cover.
4. Remove vacuum hoses, fuel hoses, wires, harnesses and connectors. **Mark vacuum hoses, wires and connectors, for installation reference.**
5. Remove front exhaust pipes, ball joints and driveshafts.
6. Lower vehicle and remove drive belts, alternator, A/C compressor and power steering oil pump from engine.
7. Raise and support vehicle, and position a suitable engine lifting device under engine and transaxle.
8. Remove lefthand side rear engine mounting bolts, **Fig. 1.**
9. Remove righthand side rear engine mounting.
10. Remove center member mounting bolts, **Fig. 1.**
11. Slowly lower engine and transaxle from vehicle.
12. Remove upper transaxle to engine bolts, then exhaust bracket.
13. Remove front and rear transaxle to engine brace bolts, then lower transaxle to engine bolt.
14. Remove torque converter to flex plate bolts, then separate transaxle from engine assembly.
15. Reverse procedure to install. Tighten fasteners to specifications.

VALVE CLEARANCE SPECIFICATIONS

Engine	Stem-To-Guide Clearance, Inch①	
	Intake	Exhaust
VE30DE	.0008–.0017	.0016–.0025

① — Cold.

VALVE ADJUSTMENT

These engines are equipped with hydraulic lash adjusters. No adjustments are required.

CRANKSHAFT REAR OIL SEAL

REPLACE

1. Disconnect battery ground cable, then remove transaxle assembly as described under "Transaxle, Replace" in "Automatic Transmissions" section.
2. Remove flex plate, then use seal remover T92C-6700-CH to remove rear main seal from housing.
3. Apply a small amount of clean engine oil to lip of new seal, then use rear

Unit: mm (in)

	Used belt deflection		Deflection of new belt
	Limit	Deflection after adjustment	
Generator	12 (0.47)	7.5 - 8.5 (0.295 - 0.335)	6.5 - 7.5 (0.256 - 0.295)
Air conditioning compressor	10 (0.39)	5 - 7 (0.20 - 0.28)	4 - 6 (0.16 - 0.24)
Power steering oil pump	16 (0.63)	10 - 12 (0.39 - 0.47)	8 - 10 (0.31 - 0.39)
Applied pushing force	98 N (10 kg, 22 lb)		

NS1069100146000X

Fig. 3 Belt tension specifications

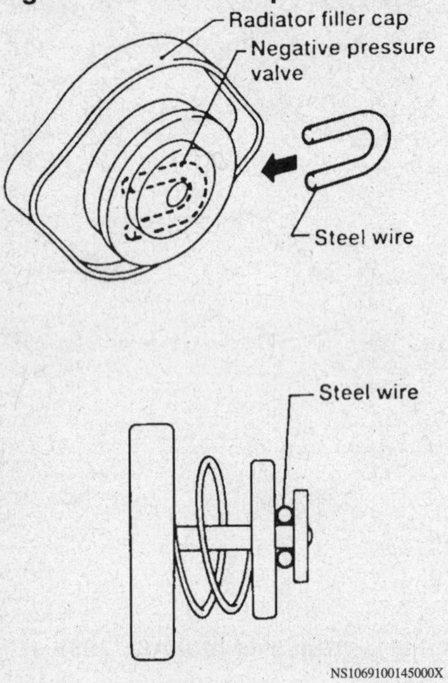
Radiator filler cap
Negative pressure valve
Steel wire
Steel wire

NS1069100145000X

Fig. 6 Installing wire on radiator pressure cap

crankshaft seal replacer T92P-6701-AH to install rear main seal until it is flush with edge of rear main seal housing.

4. Install flex plate, then transaxle assembly as described under "Transaxle, Replace" in "Automatic Transmissions" section.
5. Connect battery ground cable.

BELT TENSION DATA

Refer to **Fig. 3** for drive belt tension specifications.

COOLING SYSTEM BLEED

1. Turn ignition switch On and set front temperature control knob to full warm position. **On vehicles with rear heater, ensure rear blower switch is in any position except Off.**
2. Loosen engine air relief plug, **Fig. 4,** then radiator air relief plug three turns. **Do not remove radiator air relief plug.**
3. Remove air duct, then loosen heater pipe air relief clamp and remove cap, **Fig. 5.**
4. Install a hose to heater pipe air relief

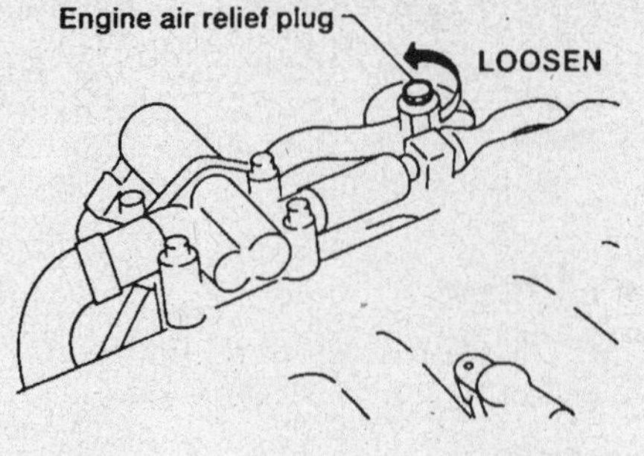
Engine air relief plug
LOOSEN

NS1069100143000X

Fig. 4 Engine air relief plug location

tube, then add a 50/50 mixture of coolant and water to MAX mark on coolant reservoir.

5. Install other end of hose in coolant reservoir. **Ensure hose end is submerged in coolant at all times.**
6. Place a drain pan under radiator relief plug opening, then slowly pour a 50/50 mixture of coolant into radiator, allowing several minutes for air to escape.
7. Fill radiator with coolant until coolant starts to drip from radiator air relief plug opening, then close plug, tightening to specifications.
8. Pour more coolant into radiator while gently moving upper radiator hose up and down.
9. Install a wire under radiator pressure cap negative pressure valve, **Fig. 6,** to allow flow of air and coolant regardless of pressure. Do not install cap at this time.
10. With engine air relief plug open, radiator filler cap off, and selector lever in P position, start and run engine at 2000 RPM until lower radiator hose becomes hot, indicating thermostat has opened. **If coolant comes out of engine air relief plug, close it. If coolant level in radiator filler neck lowers, add coolant, If coolant overflows from radiator filler neck, install radiator pressure cap (with wire installed).**
11. Close engine air relief plug if it is not already closed, then stop engine and allow to cool down completely.
12. Refill radiator and coolant reservoir as necessary, then install radiator pressure cap (with wire installed) and again warm engine to normal operating temperature.
13. Observe temperature gauge closely. If gauge begins to rise above normal, stop engine and allow to cool down completely, then refill radiator and coolant reservoir as necessary.
14. **On models less rear heater,** run engine at 3000 RPM with temperature control knob in full warm position for five minutes or until outlet air is hot. **Keep coolant reservoir at MAX level. Repeat procedure three times to ensure no air is trapped in system.**
15. **On models with rear heater,** proceed as follows
    a. Run engine at 3000 RPM with front temperature control knob in full cool

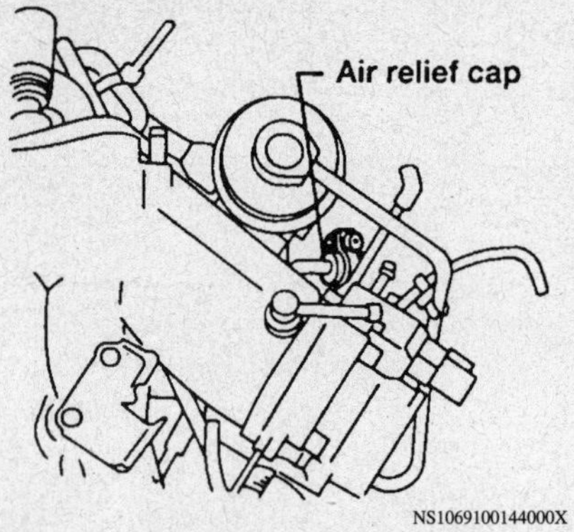
Air relief cap

NS1069100144000X

Fig. 5 Air relief cap location

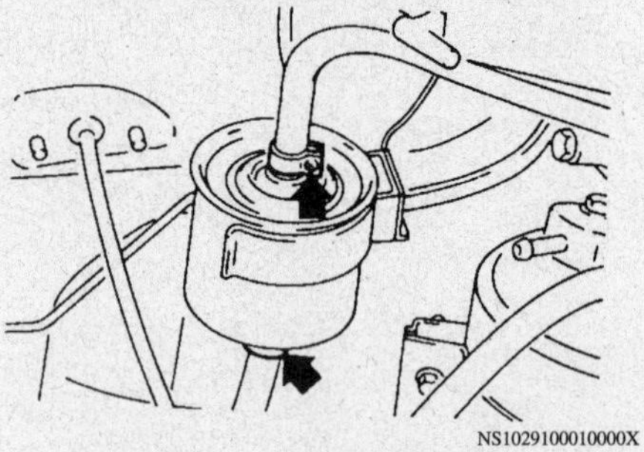

NS1029100010000X

Fig. 7 Fuel filter

position, and front and rear blower switches in any position but Off, for five minutes or until rear outlet air is hot.
    b. Repeat procedure three times to ensure no air is trapped in system.
    c. Turn rear blower switch to Off position, front temperature control knob to full warm position until front outlet air is hot.
16. **On all models,** stop engine, then pour coolant mixture into coolant reservoir to MAX level.
17. Allow engine to cool down, then remove radiator pressure cap.
18. Remove wire and reinstall radiator pressure cap, then remove hose from heater pipe air relief tube and quickly reinstall cap and clamp.
19. Install air duct.

RADIATOR

REPLACE

1. Remove under cover and drain coolant.
2. Disconnect upper and lower radiator hoses, then remove ATF cooler hoses.
3. Disconnect reservoir tank hose, then remove right hand bolt from fuse box and place fuse box aside.
4. Disconnect cooling fan harness connects and remove radiator.
5. Reverse procedure to install.

FUEL PUMP

REPLACE

1. Relieve fuel pressure as described under "Precautions, " then remove fuel tank.
2. Clean area of fuel tank around fuel pump, then remove fuel pump bolts.

3. Lift fuel pump from fuel tank. Remove and discard O-ring.
4. Reverse procedure to install, noting following:
   a. Install new O-ring.
   b. Tighten fuel pump bolts to specifications.

FUEL FILTER

REPLACE

1. Relieve fuel pressure as described under "Precautions," then loosen fuel filter hose clamps, **Fig. 7.**
2. Disconnect and plug fuel filter hoses from filter, then remove filter from bracket.
3. Reverse procedure to install.

TIGHTENING SPECIFICATIONS

Year	Component	Torque/Ft. Lbs.
1993–95	A/C Compressor Drive Belt Tensioner	15
	A/C Compressor To Accessory Bracket	33–44
	Alternator Bracket To Oil Pump	15
	Alternator Lock Bolt	12–15
	Alternator To Accessory Bracket	17–19
	Converter Inlet Pipe To Exhaust Bracket	32
	Converter Inlet To Three-Way Catalytic Converter	32–40
	Distributor Hold-Down	10–12
	Engine Mount Bracket	30–38
	Engine Mount Through Bolt	57–72
	Exhaust Bracket To Transaxle	22–30
	Exhaust Manifold To Converter Inlet	32–40
	Flex Plate	61–69
	Front Exhaust Manifold Flange Cover	48–59①
	Front LH Transaxle Mount	30–38
	Front Transaxle To Engine	22–30
	Oil Drain Plug	22–29
	Oil Filter Adapter	12–15
	Power Steering Pump To Bracket	11–15
	Power Transistor Bracket To Cylinder Head Bolt	18
	Pressure Regulator Cap	29–51
	Radiator/Heater Pipe Bracket	15
	Rear Main Seal Housing	6
	Rear RH Transaxle Mount	32–41
	Rear Transaxle To Engine	22–30
	Thermostat Housing	12–15
	Torque Converter To Flex Plate	33–43
	Transaxle To Engine Brace	22–30
	Transverse Member	57–72
	Upper Radiator Hose Bracket	34–48
	Upper Radiator Hose Clamps	14–17
	Upper Transaxle To Engine	29–36
	Wheel Lug Nut	72–87

① — Inch lbs.

Rear Axle & Suspension

INDEX

	Page No.
Hub & Bearing, Replace	34-10
Hub & Bearing Service	34-10
Leaf Spring, Replace	34-11
Rear Axle, Replace	34-10
Rear Wheel Spindle, Replace	34-11
Shock Absorber, Replace	34-11
Stabilizer Bar, Replace	34-11
Tightening Specifications	34-11

REAR AXLE

REPLACE

Refer to **Fig. 1**during replacement procedures.

1. Raise and support vehicle.
2. Support axle with jack stands or hoist.
3. Remove rear wheel and tire assemblies.
4. If equipped, remove stabilizer bar as described under "Stabilizer Bar, Replace."
5. Remove hub/bearing assemblies as described in "Hub & Bearing, Replace."
6. Remove wheel speed sensor bolts, sensor and sensor cable to axle bracket bolt.
7. Remove brake lines from axle.
8. Remove backing plate, then wire backing plate aside.
9. Remove spindle as described under "Rear Wheel Spindle, Replace."
10. Remove dual-load spring valve.
11. Remove shock absorber nuts and washers, then shock absorber.
12. Remove U-bolt nuts and washers, then U-bolts.
13. Remove alignment bolt cover plates and U-bolt alignment plates.
14. Remove axle from vehicle.
15. Reverse procedure to install. Tighten bolts to specifications.

HUB & BEARING

REPLACE

1. Raise and support vehicle.
2. Remove wheel and tire assembly.
3. Remove brake drum, grease cap and cotter pin, **Fig. 2.** Discard and replace cotter pin.
4. Remove hub/bearing assembly nut and washer, then hub/bearing assembly.
5. Reverse procedure to install. Tighten bolts to specifications.

HUB & BEARING SERVICE

Refer to **Fig. 2** during service procedures.

1. Remove hub/bearing assembly as described under "Hub & Bearing, Replace."
2. Remove snap ring, then using press and suitable bearing cup removal tool, press bearing from hub.

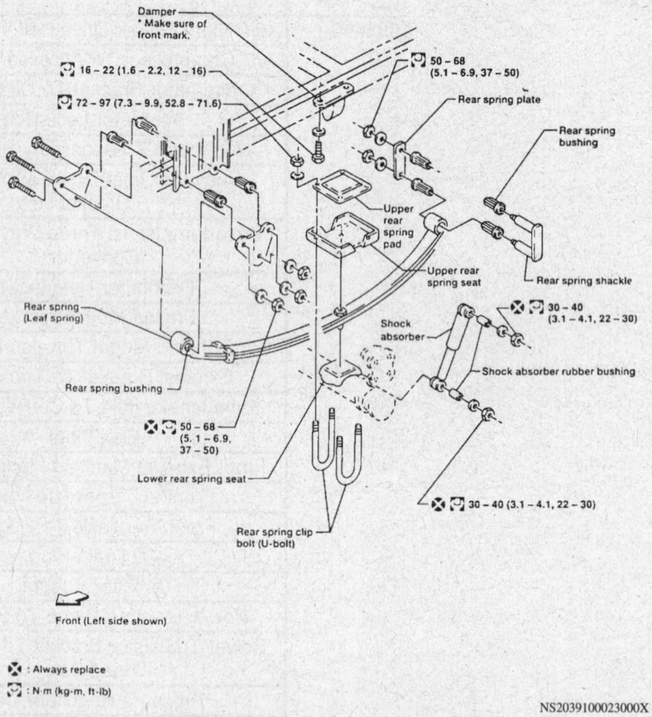

Damper
* Make sure of front mark.
16 – 22 (1.6 – 2.2, 12 – 16)
72 – 97 (7.3 – 9.9, 52.8 – 71.6)
50 – 68 (5.1 – 6.9, 37 – 50)
Rear spring plate
Rear spring bushing
Upper rear spring pad
Upper rear spring seat
Rear spring shackle
Rear spring (Leaf spring)
30 – 40 (3.1 – 4.1, 22 – 30)
Shock absorber
Shock absorber rubber bushing
Rear spring bushing
50 – 68 (5. 1 – 6.9, 37 – 50)
Lower rear spring seat
30 – 40 (3.1 – 4.1, 22 – 30)
Rear spring clip bolt (U-bolt)
Front (Left side shown)
: Always replace
: N·m (kg-m, ft-lb)
NS2039100023000X

Fig. 1 Rear suspension

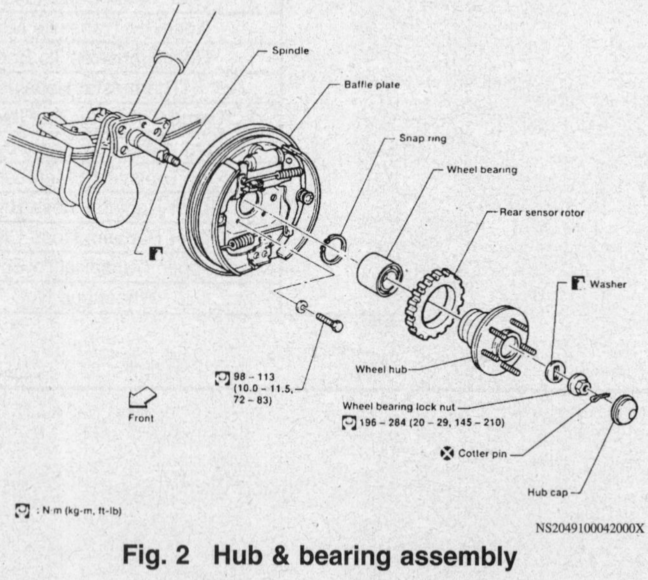

Spindle
Baffle plate
Snap ring
Wheel bearing
Rear sensor rotor
Washer
Wheel hub
98 – 113 (10.0 – 11.5, 72 – 83)
Front
Wheel bearing lock nut
196 – 284 (20 – 29, 145 – 210)
Cotter pin
Hub cap
: N·m (kg-m, ft-lb)
NS2049100042000X

Fig. 2 Hub & bearing assembly

3. Using a press and suitable pinion bearing pressing tool, press bearing into hub.
4. Install snap ring and hub/bearing assembly. Tighten bolts to specifications.

REAR WHEEL SPINDLE

REPLACE

1. Remove backing plate.
2. Remove spindle.
3. Reverse procedure to install. Tighten bolts to specifications.

SHOCK ABSORBER

REPLACE

1. Raise and support vehicle.
2. Remove upper and lower shock absorber nuts and washers, then shock absorber.
3. Reverse procedure to install. Tighten bolts to specifications.

LEAF SPRING

REPLACE

Refer to **Fig. 1** during replacement procedures.

1. Raise and support vehicle.
2. Support axle with a floor jack or hoist.
3. Remove U-bolt nuts, washers, U-bolts, alignment bolt cover plate and U-bolt alignment cover plate.
4. Remove shackle nuts, shackle end plate and shackle.
5. Remove leaf spring front nut and bolt. Raise vehicle until weight is off axle enough to easily remove leaf spring.
6. Reverse procedure to install noting following:
   a. When installing left leaf spring, ensure leaf spring front bolt is installed with head of bolt on front mounting plate marked INNER and threaded end of bolt on front mounting plate marked OUTER.
   b. When installing right leaf spring, ensure leaf spring front bolt is installed with head of bolt on front mounting plate marked OUTER and threaded end of bolt on front mounting plate marked INNER.

STABILIZER BAR

REPLACE

1. Raise and support vehicle.
2. Hold stabilizer bar link studs with a wrench and remove stabilizer bar to link nuts.
3. Disconnect stabilizer bar from link studs.
4. Loosen, but do not remove, upper stabilizer bar to axle bolts.
5. Remove lower stabilizer bar to axle bolts.
6. Slide stabilizer bar down until stabilizer bar mounting brackets clear loosened bolts, then remove bar from rear axle.
7. Reverse procedure to install. Tighten bolts to specifications.

TIGHTENING SPECIFICATIONS

Year	Component	Torque/ Ft.Lbs.
1993–96	Axle Nut	145–210
	Axle Bumper Stop	12–16
	Driveshaft Nut	145–210
	Front Mounting Plate	37–50
	Hub Nut	145–210
	Leaf Spring	37–50
	Shackle Nuts	37–50
	Shock Absorber	22–30
	Stabilizer Bar To Axle	23–31
	Stabilizer Bar To Link	29–33
	Stabilizer Link To Chassis	12–16
	U-Bolt Nuts	53–72
	Wheel Lug Nuts	72–87
	Wheel Speed Sensor	16–21①
	Wheel Speed Sensor Cable Bracket To Axle	35–44①

① — Inch lbs.

Front Suspension & Steering

NOTE: On Air Bag Equipped Models, Refer To "Air Bag System Precautions" Located In The Front Of This Manual For System Disarming & Arming Procedures.

INDEX

	Page No.
Ball Joint, Replace	34-12
Ball Joint Inspection	34-12
Coil Spring, Replace	34-12
Coil Spring & Strut Service	34-13
Control Arm, Replace	34-13
Control Arm Bushing, Replace	34-13
Description	34-12
Hub & Bearing Service	34-12
Manual Steering Gears	36-1
Power Steering	36-1
Power Steering Gear, Replace	34-14
Power Steering Pump, Replace	34-14
Stabilizer Bar, Replace	34-13
Strut, Replace	34-12
Tightening Specifications	34-15
Transverse Link, Replace	34-13
Wheel Bearing, Adjust	34-12
Wheel Hub & Steering Knuckle, Replace	34-12

DESCRIPTION

The independent front suspension consists of MacPherson struts riding in a heavy rubber spring seat. A forged steering knuckle bolts to bottom end of strut and also locates ball joint. A stabilizer bar connected to both control arms via stabilizer bar links controls vehicle's body lean while cornering. Each control arm attaches to a control arm gusset which is attached directly to chassis.

WHEEL BEARING

ADJUST

Bearing is not adjustable. If Abnormal noise is indicated, bearing may require replacement. Noise will occur if bearing is dirty, worn or dry. bearings are sealed and can not be cleaned or greased.

WHEEL HUB & STEERING KNUCKLE

REPLACE

Refer to **Fig. 1** during replacement procedures.

1. Raise and support vehicle.
2. Remove wheel and tire assembly.
3. Remove wheel bearing locknut.
4. Remove front brake caliper and wire aside. It is not necessary to disconnect brake line. **Do not touch brake pedal, or piston may pop out.**
5. Remove brake rotor.
6. Using ball joint remover tool No. J25730-A, or equivalent, separate tie rod ball joint from knuckle.
7. Remove strut to steering knuckle/wheel hub assembly nuts and bolts.
8. Remove ball joint cotter pin from ball joint shaft. Loosen ball joint nut until it contacts outer CV joint.
9. Strike steering knuckle with a hammer while pulling down on control arm until ball joint breaks free from steering knuckle.
10. Remove ball joint nut. Separate ball joint from steering knuckle/wheel hub assembly.
11. Remove wheel speed sensor bolt.
12. Separate driveshaft from knuckle by lightly tapping it. If it is hard to remove, use a puller.
13. Remove steering knuckle/wheel hub assembly from vehicle.
14. Reverse procedure to install, noting following:
    a. Before tightening wheel bearing locknut, apply oil to threaded portion of driveshaft and to both sides of plain washer.
    b. Ensure wheel bearing operates smoothly.
    c. Check wheel bearing axial endplay.

HUB & BEARING SERVICE

Refer to **Fig. 2** during service procedures.

1. Remove steering knuckle/wheel hub assembly as described under "Steering Knuckle & Hub Assembly, Replace."
2. Using a hammer, drive wheel hub from knuckle.
3. Remove snap ring.
4. Using a suitable pressing tool, press wheel bearing from steering knuckle.
5. Reverse procedure to install noting following:
    a. **Do not press inner race of wheel bearing, press only on outer race.**
    b. **Do not apply oil or grease to mating surfaces of wheel bearing outer race and knuckle.**
    c. When pressing wheel hub into knuckle, wheel bearing inner race must be held as shown in **Fig. 3.**
    d. Ensure wheel bearing operates smoothly.
    e. Check wheel bearing axial endplay.

BALL JOINT INSPECTION

Raise and support vehicle. Grasp tire and rock wheel up and down, inspect ball joint in control arm at bottom of steering knuckle. If movement is indicated, replace ball joint.

BALL JOINT

REPLACE

Refer to **Fig. 1** during replacement procedures.

1. Raise and support vehicle.
2. Remove wheel and tire assembly.
3. Remove and discard cotter pin from ball joint shaft. Cotter pin must be replaced.
4. Loosen ball joint nut until it contacts outer CV joint.
5. Strike steering knuckle with a hammer while pulling down on control arm until ball joint breaks free from steering knuckle.
6. Remove ball joint nut, then ball joint to control arm nuts.
7. Remove ball joint and three-stud shackle from control arm.
8. Reverse procedure to install. Tighten bolts to specifications.

COIL SPRING

REPLACE

Refer to **Fig. 1** during replacement procedures.

1. Use a grease pencil or suitable marking device and put an alignment mark on inside of strut mounting block and chassis strut tower.
2. Raise and support vehicle.
3. Remove wheel and tire assembly.
4. Remove wheel speed sensor cable bracket bolts and position cable aside.
5. Remove brake hose U-clip and position aside.
6. Remove strut to steering knuckle/wheel hub assembly nuts and bolts.
7. Separate strut from steering knuckle.
8. Remove mounting locknuts.
9. Remove coil spring/strut assembly from vehicle.
10. Reverse procedure to install. Tighten bolts to specifications.

STRUT

REPLACE

Refer to "Coil Spring, Replace" for procedure.

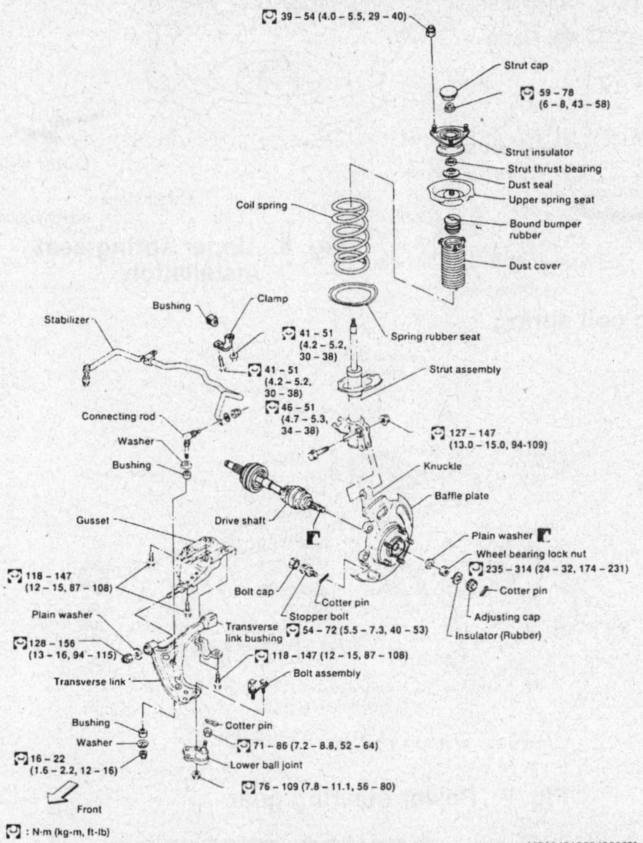
39 – 54 (4.0 – 5.5, 29 – 40)
Strut cap
59 – 78 (6 – 8, 43 – 58)
Strut insulator
Strut thrust bearing
Dust seal
Upper spring seat
Coil spring
Bound bumper rubber
Dust cover
Clamp
Bushing
Stabilizer
41 – 51 (4.2 – 5.2, 30 – 38)
Spring rubber seat
41 – 51 (4.2 – 5.2, 30 – 38)
Strut assembly
46 – 51 (4.7 – 5.3, 34 – 38)
Connecting rod
Washer
Bushing
127 – 147 (13.0 – 15.0, 94-109)
Knuckle
Baffle plate
Gusset
Drive shaft
Plain washer
Wheel bearing lock nut
235 – 314 (24 – 32, 174 – 231)
118 – 147 (12 – 15, 87 – 108)
Bolt cap
Cotter pin
Cotter pin
Plain washer
Stopper bolt
Adjusting cap
Transverse link bushing
54 – 72 (5.5 – 7.3, 40 – 53)
Insulator (Rubber)
128 – 156 (13 – 16, 94 – 115)
118 – 147 (12 – 15, 87 – 108)
Bolt assembly
Transverse link
Bushing
Cotter pin
Washer
71 – 86 (7.2 – 8.8, 52 – 64)
16 – 22 (1.6 – 2.2, 12 – 16)
Lower ball joint
76 – 109 (7.8 – 11.1, 56 – 80)
Front
: N·m (kg-m, ft-lb)

NS2049100043000X

Fig. 1 Exploded view of front suspension

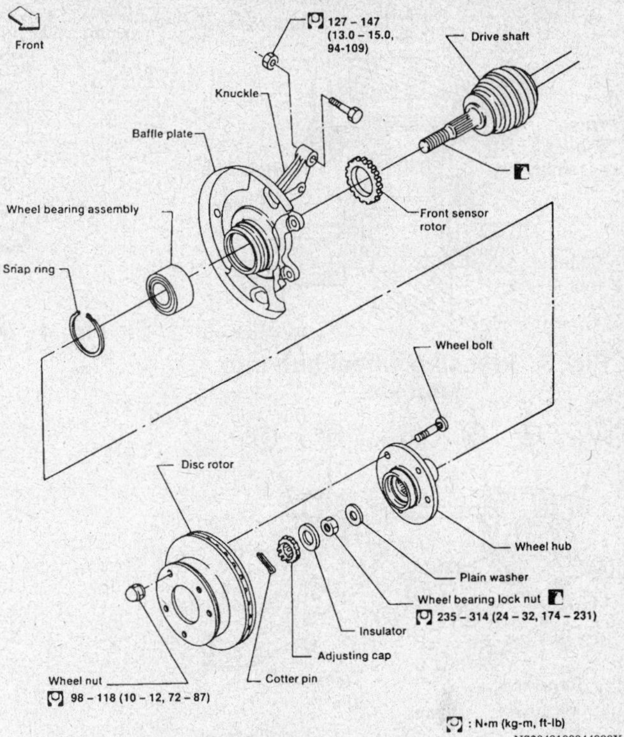
Front
127 – 147 (13.0 – 15.0, 94-109)
Drive shaft
Knuckle
Baffle plate
Wheel bearing assembly
Front sensor rotor
Snap ring
Wheel bolt
Disc rotor
Wheel hub
Plain washer
Wheel bearing lock nut
235 – 314 (24 – 32, 174 – 231)
Insulator
Adjusting cap
Cotter pin
Wheel nut
98 – 118 (10 – 12, 72 – 87)
: N·m (kg-m, ft-lb)

NS2049100044000X

Fig. 2 Exploded view of hub & wheel bearing assembly

COIL SPRING & STRUT SERVICE

Refer to **Fig. 1** during service procedures.

1. Remove coil spring/strut assembly as described under "Coil Spring, Replace."
2. Place assembly in suitable vise and remove strut nut cover.
3. Loosen, but do not remove, piston rod locknut.
4. Use spring compressor tool No. HT1780000, or equivalent to compress coil spring.
5. Remove piston rod locknut and rubber mounting block.
6. Remove strut insulator, strut thrust bearing, dust seal, upper spring seat, bound bumper rubber and coil spring.
7. Slowly release tension from strut compressor.
8. Reverse procedure to install, noting following:
   a. Position coil spring on strut assembly as shown in **Fig. 4.**
   b. When installing upper spring seat, ensure its cutout portion is facing outer side of vehicle, inline with strut to knuckle attachment point, **Fig. 5.**
   c. Tighten bolts to specifications.

CONTROL ARM

REPLACE

Refer to **Fig. 1** during replacement procedures.

1. Raise and support vehicle.
2. Remove wheel and tire assembly.
3. Remove ball joint as described under "Ball Joint, Replace."
4. Remove stabilizer link to control arm nut.
5. Remove stabilizer link shaft from control arm.
6. Remove rear control arm bolts and mounting bracket.
7. Remove control arm, then pull rear of control arm down and gently pry control arm forward and off gusset.
8. Reverse procedure to install. Tighten bolts to specifications.

CONTROL ARM BUSHING

REPLACE

1. Remove control arm as described under "Control Arm, Replace."
2. Using a suitable pressing tool, press bushing out of control arm.
3. Reverse procedure to install. Tighten bolts to specifications.

STABILIZER BAR

REPLACE

Refer to **Fig. 1** during replacement procedures.

1. Raise and support vehicle.
2. Remove stabilizer bar to stabilizer link nuts.
3. Remove stabilizer bar to control arm gusset nuts and bolts.
4. Remove stabilizer bar mounting brackets.
5. Gently pry stabilizer bar ends off stabilizer links and remove bar.
6. Reverse procedure to install. Tighten bolts to specifications.

TRANSVERSE LINK

REPLACE

1. Remove stabilizer bar as described under "Stabilizer Bar, Replace."
2. Remove transverse link and transverse link gusset attaching bolts.
3. Remove transverse link and transverse link gusset.
4. Reverse procedure to install, noting following:
   a. Install attaching bolts in order shown in **Fig. 6.**
   b. Final tightening of bolts must be done with vehicle at curb weight and tires on ground.
   c. Check wheel alignment.

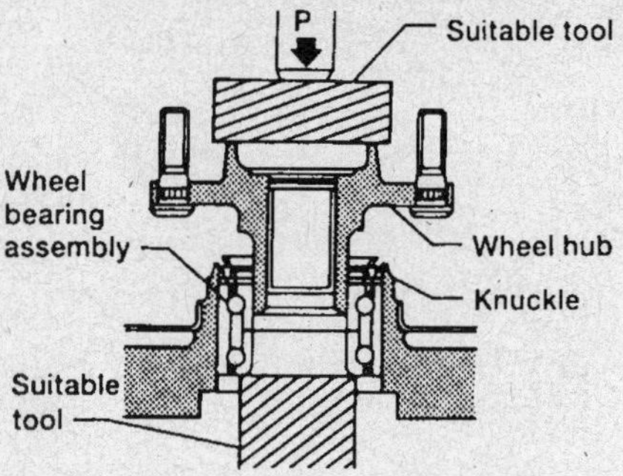
P
Suitable tool
Wheel bearing assembly
Wheel hub
Knuckle
Suitable tool
NS2049100045000X

Fig. 3 Pressing wheel hub into knuckle

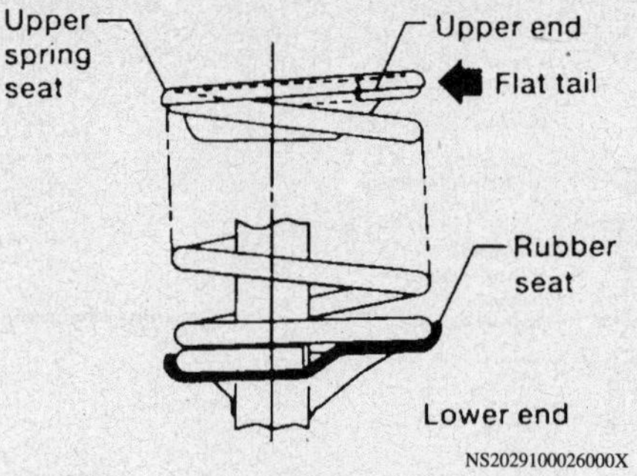
Upper spring seat
Upper end
Flat tail
Rubber seat
Lower end
NS2029100026000X

Fig. 4 Installing coil spring

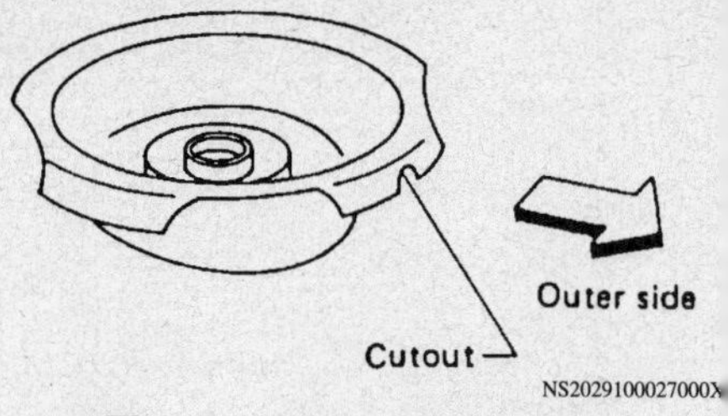
Outer side
Cutout
NS2029100027000X

Fig. 5 Upper spring seat installation

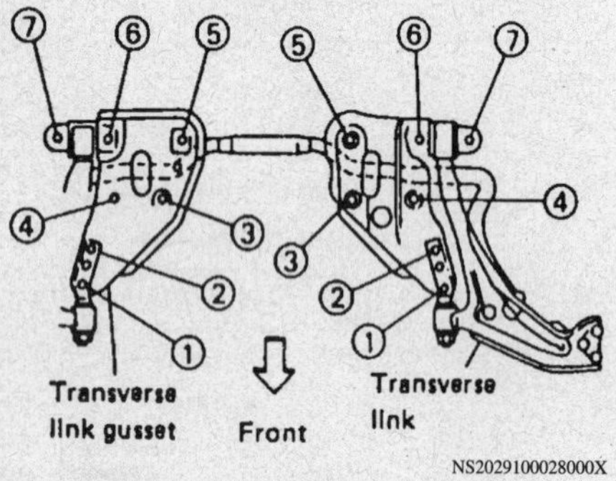
Transverse link gusset
Front
Transverse link
NS2029100028000X

Fig. 6 Transverse link & transverse link gusset bolt installation sequence

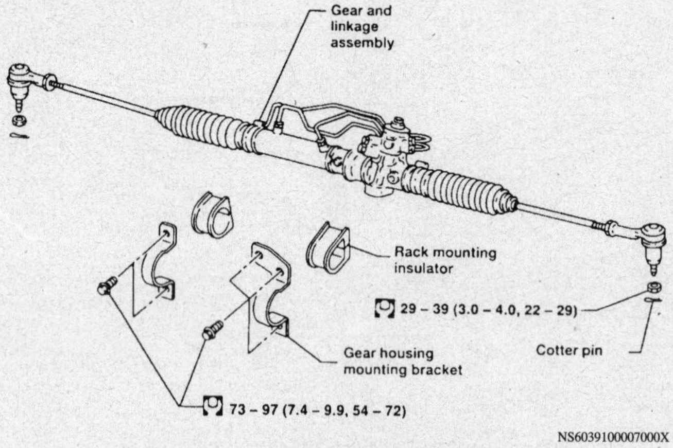
Gear and linkage assembly
Rack mounting insulator
29 – 39 (3.0 – 4.0, 22 – 29)
Gear housing mounting bracket
Cotter pin
73 – 97 (7.4 – 9.9, 54 – 72)
NS6039100007000X

Fig. 7 Power steering gear

POWER STEERING GEAR

REPLACE

1. Place drain pan under steering gear.
2. Remove brake fluid reservoir screws, then position reservoir aside and suspend with wire.
3. Remove junction block high-pressure line from steering gear and position line aside.
4. Raise and support vehicle.
5. Remove front tire and wheel assemblies.
6. Remove stabilizer bar as described under "Stabilizer Bar, Replace."
7. Separate tie rod ends from steering knuckles, **Fig. 7.**
8. Pull steering gear dust boot back and have an assistant turn steering column shaft until clamp bolt is accessible, then lock steering column.
9. Remove clamp bolt from intermediate shaft lower universal joint.
10. Loosen low-pressure hose clamp and disconnect hose from steering gear. Position line out of way.
11. Remove five steering gear mounting bolts.
12. Remove mounting brackets.
13. Carefully slide steering gear to left and remove from vehicle.
14. Reverse procedure to install, noting following:
    a. Slide steering gear in from left and position pinion shaft just below intermediate shaft lower universal joint.
    b. Raise gear so plastic aligning tab on pinion shaft enters clamp bolt gap on intermediate shaft universal joint.
    c. Mounting brackets are marked UP with arrows pointing to one end of bracket. Ensure brackets are installed correctly.
    d. Tighten bolts to specifications.

POWER STEERING PUMP

REPLACE

1. Disconnect battery ground cable.
2. Raise and support vehicle.
3. Remove power steering pump pulley as follows:
    a. Remove water pump and power steering pump drive belt.
    b. Use Strap Wrench D85L-6000-A or equivalent and hold pulley while removing pulley nut.
4. Place drain pan under pump.
5. Remove hose connection bolt from pump, position high-pressure hose and connection out of way.
6. Remove pump inlet hose bolts and position hose out of way.
7. Remove front bolts, then rear bolt.
8. Remove pump from vehicle.
9. Reverse procedure to install. Tighten bolts to specifications.

TIGHTENING SPECIFICATIONS

Year	Component	Torque/ Ft.Lbs.
1993–96	Axle Nut	174–231
	Clamp Bolt	17–22
	Driveshaft Nut	174–231
	Front Steering Pump Bolt	11–15
	Hub Nut	174–231
	Junction Block Bolt	18–26①
	Junction Block/High-Pressure Line	11–18
	Power Steering Pump Inlet Hose Bolts	10–13
	Power Steering Pump Pulley Nut	40–50
	Rear Housing Bolts	23–31
	Rear Steering Pump Bolt	11–15
	Steering Gear Bolts	54–72
	Upper High-Pressure Hose Bolt	36–51
	Upper Right Cooling Line Bolt	18–26①

① — Inch lbs.

Wheel Alignment

INDEX

Page No.

Front Wheel Alignment 34-15
Caster & Camber 34-15
Toe-In 34-15
Kingpin, Adjust 34-16
Preliminary Inspection 34-15
Rear Wheel Alignment 34-15
Vehicle Ride Height 34-16
Wheel Alignment Specifications . 34-2

PRELIMINARY INSPECTION

Inspect following components, then adjust, repair or replace as required prior to performing front wheel alignment.

1. Inflate tires to cold specifications.
2. Ensure tires are of same size, ply rating and load rating.
3. Inspect for excessive wheel bearing endplay.
4. Inspect for worn or damaged ball joints.
5. Inspect steering gear mounting bolts for proper torque.
6. Inspect control arm for bent or damaged condition.
7. Inspect control arm to frame bushings for looseness or wear.
8. Inspect suspension components for wear or damage.
9. Inspect vehicle ride height as outlined under "Vehicle Ride Height."

FRONT WHEEL ALIGNMENT

CASTER & CAMBER

Caster and camber are preset at factory and are not adjustable. If caster or camber angles are not within specifications, replace suspension components responsible for incorrect angles.

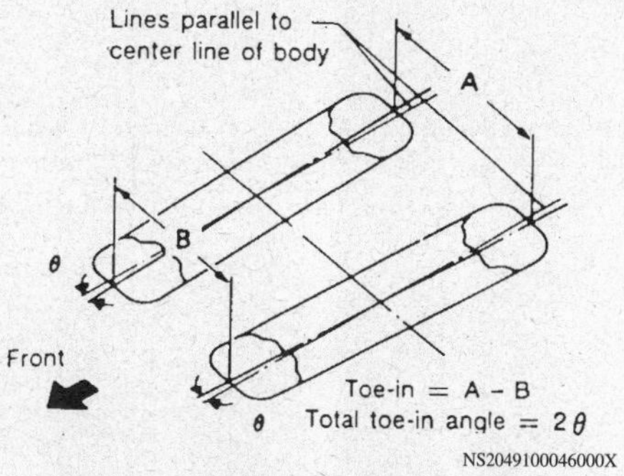
Lines parallel to center line of body
A
B
θ
Front
Toe-in = A − B
Total toe-in angle = 2θ
NS2049100046000X

Fig. 1 Toe-in measurement

TOE-IN

1. Loosen jam nuts at tie rod ends and release clips at small ends of steering gear boots. **Ensure boots are free on tie rods to prevent twisting.**
2. Adjust toe-in to specification by turning tie rod ends in or out an equal amount on each side to keep steering wheel centered, **Fig. 1.**
3. Check front tracking. **Follow equipment manufacturers instructions.**

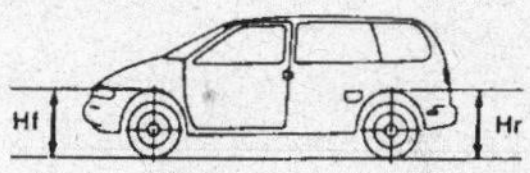
Hf
Hr

Applied model	All
Front (Hf) mm (in)	
Standard/Optional suspension	772 ± 10 (30.39 ± 0.39)
Rear (Hr) mm (in)	
Standard suspension	793 ± 10 (31.22 ± 0.39)
Optional suspension	793 ± 10 (31.22 ± 0.39)

: Fuel, radiator coolant and engine oil full. Spare tire, jack, hand tools and mats in designated positions.

NS2049100047000X

Fig. 2 Vehicle ride height measurement locations & specifications

4. **Torque** tie rod end jam nuts to 58–72 ft. lbs. and install clips.

REAR WHEEL ALIGNMENT

Rear camber and toe-in are preset at factory and are not adjustable. If camber or toe-in angles are not within specifications, replace suspension components responsible for incorrect angles.

KINGPIN

ADJUST

Kingpin inclination is preset at factory and is not adjustable. If kingpin inclination is not within specifications, replace suspension components responsible for incorrect angles.

VEHICLE RIDE HEIGHT

Refer to **Fig. 2** for vehicle ride height measurement locations and specifications.

NISSAN PATHFINDER & PICKUP

INDEX OF SERVICE OPERATIONS

	Page No.
AIR BAG SYSTEM PRECAUTIONS	0-8
AUTOMATIC TRANSMISSIONS/ TRANSAXLES	36-1
BRAKES	
Anti-Lock Brakes	36-1
Disc Brakes	36-1
Drum Brakes	36-1
Hydraulic Brake Systems	36-1
Power Brake Units	36-1
CLUTCH & MANUAL TRANSMISSION	
Adjustments	35-21
Clutch, Replace	35-21
Hydraulic System Service	35-21
Tightening Specifications	35-22
Transmission, Replace	35-21
ELECTRICAL	
Air Bags	36-1
Air Conditioning	36-1
Alternator, Replace	35-5
Alternators	36-1
Blower Motor, Replace	35-7
Combination Switch, Replace	35-6
Cooling Fans	36-1
Cruise Control	36-1
Dash Gauges	36-1
Dash Panels	36-1
Distributor, Replace	35-5
Evaporator Core, Replace	35-7
Fuel Pump Relay Location	35-5
Fuse Panel & Flasher Location	35-5
Headlamp Switch, Replace	35-5
Heater Core, Replace	35-7
Ignition Lock, Replace	35-5
Ignition Switch, Replace	35-5
Instrument Cluster, Replace	35-6
Neutral Safety Switch, Adjust	35-5
Passive Restraints	36-1
Precautions	35-5
Radio, Replace	35-6
Relay Center Location	35-5
Speed Controls	36-1
Starter Motors	36-1
Starter, Replace	35-5
Steering Columns	36-1
Steering Wheel, Replace	35-6
Stop Light Switch, Replace	35-5
Turn Signal Switch, Replace	35-6
Wiper Motor, Replace	35-6
Wiper Switch, Replace	35-7
Wiper Systems	36-1
ELECTRICAL SYMBOL IDENTIFICATION	0-139
FRONT SUSPENSION & STEERING	
Ball Joint, Replace	35-28
Ball Joint Inspection	35-28
Hub & Bearing, Replace	35-27
Locking Hub Service	35-27
Manual Steering Gear, Replace	35-31
Manual Steering Gears	36-1
Power Steering	36-1
Power Steering Gear, Replace	35-30
Power Steering Pump, Replace	35-30
Power Steering Transfer Gear, Replace	35-30
Shock Absorber, Replace	35-29
Stabilizer Bar, Replace	35-30
Strut Damper, Replace	35-30
Tightening Specifications	35-32
Torsion Bar, Replace	35-29
Wheel Bearing, Adjust	35-27
FRONT WHEEL DRIVE AXLES	36-1
KA24E ENGINE	
Belt Tension Data	35-11
Camshaft, Replace	35-10
Compression Pressure	35-8
Cooling System Bleed	35-11
Crankshaft Rear Oil Seal, Replace	35-10
Crankshaft Seal, Replace	35-10
Cylinder Head, Replace	35-8
Engine Disassemble	35-9
Engine Mount, Replace	35-8
Engine Rebuilding Specifications	36-1
Engine, Replace	35-8
Exhaust Manifold, Replace	35-8
Fuel Filter, Replace	35-11
Fuel Pump, Replace	35-11
Intake Manifold, Replace	35-8
Main & Rod Bearings	35-10
Oil Pan, Replace	35-11
Oil Pump, Replace	35-11
Piston & Rod Assembly	35-10
Pistons, Pins & Rings	35-10
Precautions	35-8
Radiator, Replace	35-11
Thermostat, Replace	35-11
Tightening Specifications	35-12
Timing Chain, Replace	35-9
Timing Chain Tensioner, Replace	35-10
Valve Adjustment	35-9
Valve Clearance Specifications	35-9
Water Pump, Replace	35-11
REAR AXLE & SUSPENSION	
Coil Spring, Replace	35-23
Leaf Spring, Replace	35-23
Rear Axle, Replace	35-22
Rear Axle Shaft, Replace	35-22
Shock Absorber, Replace	35-23
Stabilizer Bar, Replace	35-23
Tightening Specifications	35-26
SERVICE REMINDER & WARNING LAMP RESET PROCEDURES	0-10
SPECIFICATIONS	
Fluid Capacities & Cooling System Data	35-3
Front Wheel Alignment Specifications	35-3
General Engine Specifications	35-2
Lubricant Data	35-4
Tune Up Specifications	35-2
TRANSFER CASE	
Tightening Specifications	35-27
Transfer Case, Replace	35-26
VEHICLE IDENTIFICATION	0-1
VEHICLE LIFT POINTS	0-34
VEHICLE MAINTENANCE SCHEDULES	0-69
VG30E & VG33E ENGINES	
Belt Tension Data	35-15
Compression Pressure	35-13
Cylinder Head, Replace	35-14
Engine Mount, Replace	35-14
Engine Rebuilding Specifications	36-1
Engine, Replace	35-14
Exhaust Manifold, Replace	35-14
Fuel Filter, Replace	35-16
Fuel Pump, Replace	35-15
Intake Manifold, Replace	35-14
Oil Pan, Replace	35-15
Oil Pump, Replace	35-15
Precautions	35-13
Radiator, Replace	35-15
Tightening Specifications	35-20
Valve Adjustment	35-15
Valve Clearance Specifications	35-15
Water Pump, Replace	35-15
WHEEL ALIGNMENT	
Front Wheel Alignment	35-33
Preliminary Inspection	35-33
Vehicle Ride Height	35-34
Wheel Alignment Specifications	35-3
WIRE COLOR CODE IDENTIFICATION	0-144

Specifications

GENERAL ENGINE SPECIFICATIONS

Year	Engine	Fuel System	Displacement, Liters	Bore x Stroke, Inches (mm)	Compression Ratio	Maximum H.P. @ RPM	Maximum Torque @ RPM	Normal Oil Pressure, psi
1993–95	KA24E	Fuel Inj.	2.4L	3.50 x 3.78 (89 x 96)	8.6	140 @ 5600	152 @ 4400	60–70①
	VG30E	Fuel Inj.	3.0L	3.43 x 3.27 (87 x 83)	9.0	—	—	53–65①
1996	KA24E	Fuel Inj.	2.4L	3.50 x 3.78 (89 x 96)	8.6	140 @ 5600	152 @ 4400	60–70①
	VG33E	Fuel Inj.	3.3L	3.60 x 3.27 (92 x 83)	8.9	168 @ 4800	196 @ 2800	60–65①

① — 3000 RPM.

TUNE UP SPECIFICATIONS

Year, Model & Engine	Spark Plug Gap, Inch	Ignition Timing			Curb Idle Speed②		Fast Idle Speed		Fuel Pressure, psi	Valve Lash
		Firing Order Fig.①	Timing, °BTDC	Timing Mark Fig.	Man. Trans.	Auto. Trans.	Man. Trans.	Auto. Trans.		
1993										
Pathfinder KA24E	.041	⑥	10	A	800	800N	③	③	43	④
Pathfinder VG30E	.033	⑤	15	B	750	750N	③	③	43	④
Pickup KA24E	.041	⑥	10	A	800	800N	③	③	43	④
Pickup VG30E	.033	⑤	15	B	750	750N	③	③	43	④
1994–95										
Pathfinder KA24E	.041	⑥	10	A	800	800N	③	③	43	④
Pathfinder VG30E	.033	⑤	15	B	750	750N	③	③	43	④
Pickup KA24E	.041	⑥	10	A	800	800N	③	③	43	④
Pickup VG30E	.033	⑤	15	B	750	750N	③	③	43	④
1996										
Pathfinder VG33E	.033	⑤	15	C	750	750N	③	③	43	④
Pickup KA24E	.041	⑥	10	A	800	800N	③	③	43	④

BTDC — Before Top Dead Center.

N — Neutral.

D — Drive.

① — Before disconnecting spark plug wires from distributor cap, determine location of No. 1 wire in cap, as distributor position may have been altered from that shown.

② — When adjusting idle speed, set parking brake & chock drive wheels.

③ — Controlled by ECCS.

④ — Refer to "Valve Adjustment" in specific engine section.

⑤ — Cylinder number from front of engine to rear; right bank 1, 3, 5; left bank 2, 4, 6. Firing order, 1-2-3-4-5-6.

⑥ — No. 1 located front of engine. Firing order, 1-3-4-2.

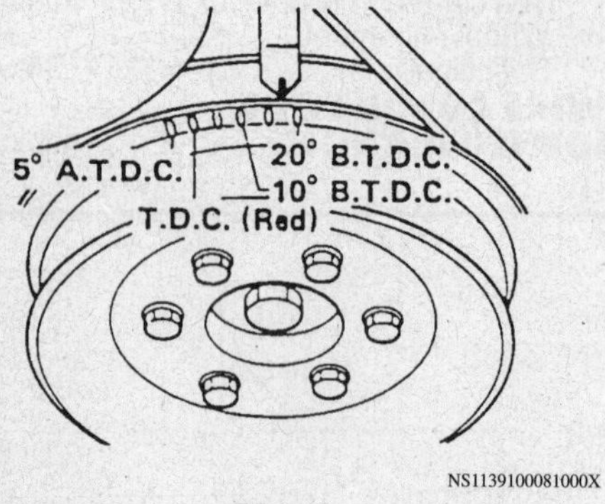
5° A.T.D.C.
20° B.T.D.C.
10° B.T.D.C.
T.D.C. (Red)

NS1139100081000X

Fig. A

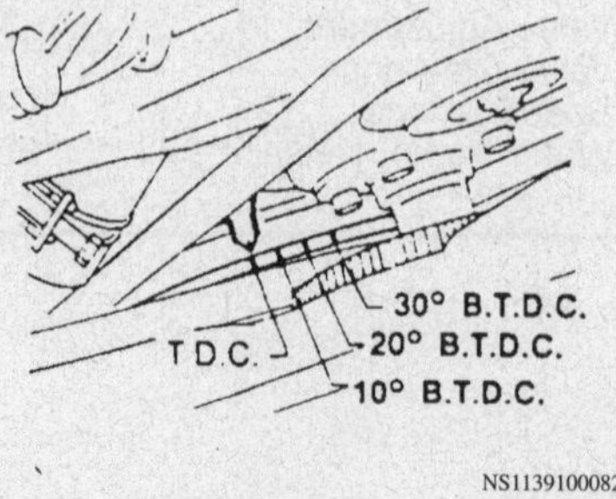
30° B.T.D.C.
T.D.C.
20° B.T.D.C.
10° B.T.D.C.

NS1139100082000X

Fig. B

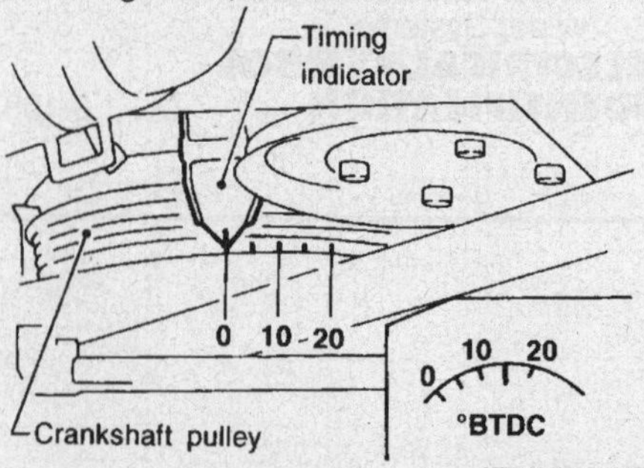
Timing indicator
0 10 - 20
10 20
0
°BTDC
Crankshaft pulley

NS1139600160000X

Fig. C

FRONT WHEEL ALIGNMENT SPECIFICATIONS

Year	Model	Caster Angle, Deg.		Camber Angle, Deg.		Kingpin Inclination, Deg.	Toe-In, Inch①	Toe-Out On Turns, Deg.②		Ball Joint Wear
		Limits	Desired	Limits	Desired			Inner Wheel	Outer Wheel	
1993	Pathfinder	+11/20 to +1 7/60	+1 7/15	−1/12 to +1 5/12	+2/3	7 1/3 to 8 5/6	+.08 to +.24	③	④	⑤
	Pickup 2WD	−2/5 to +1 1/10	+11/30	−1/3 to +1 1/6	+5/12	8 1/3 to 9 5/6	+.04 to +.02	36 to 38	33 to 35	⑤
	Pickup 4WD	+11/20 to +1 7/60	+1 7/15	−1/12 to +1 5/12	+2/3	7 1/3 to 8 5/6	+.08 to +.24	③	④	⑤
1994–95	Pathfinder	+4/5 to +1 4/5	+1 7/15	−1/6 to +1 1/6	+2/3	7 3/5 to 8 3/5	+.12 to +.20	③	④	⑤
	Pickup 2WD	−2/15 to +13/15	+11/30	−1/12 to +11/12	+5/12	8 7/12 to 9 7/12	+.08 to +.16	36 to 38	33 to 35	⑤
	Pickup 4WD	+4/5 to +1 4/5	+1 7/15	−1/6 to +1 1/6	+2/3	7 3/5 to 8 3/5	+.12 to +.20	③	④	⑤
1996	Pathfinder	+2 1/4 to +3 3/4	+3	−7/12 to + 11/12	+1/16	13 7/12 to 15 1/12	+.04 to +.12	30 to 34	28 to 31	⑤
	Pickup 2WD	−23/60 to +1 7/60	+11/30	−1/3 to +1 1/6	+5/12	8 7/12 to 9 7/12	+.08 to +.16	36 to 38	33 to 35	⑤
	Pickup 4WD	+11/20 to +2 1/20	+1 3/10	−1/12 to +1 5/12	+2/3	7 3/5 to 8 3/5	+.12 to +.20	33 to 35	31 to 33	⑤

2WD — Two Wheel Drive.
4WD — Four Wheel Drive.
① — Toe-in (+); toe-out (-).
② — Measure w/wheels @ full lefthand & righthand turn positions.
③ — Models less 31 x 10.5R15 tires, 33 to 35 deg.; models w/31 x 10.5R15 tires, 27 to 29 deg.
④ — Models less 31 x 10.5R15 tires, 31 to 33 deg.; models w/31 x 10.5R15 tires, 25 to 27 deg.
⑤ — Refer to "Ball Joint Inspection" section under "Front Suspension & Steering."

FLUID CAPACITIES & COOLING SYSTEM DATA

Year	Model	Coolant Capacity, Qts.	Radiator Cap Relief Pressure, Lbs.	Thermo. Opening Temp., °F	Fuel Tank, Gals.	Engine Oil Refill, Qts.①	Transmission Oil		Transfer Case Oil, Pts.	Differential Oil, Pts.	
							Man. Trans., Pts.	Auto. Trans., Qts.②		Front	Rear
1993–94	Pathfinder 2WD	11 3/8	11–14	170	21 1/8	4 1/4	5 1/8	8 3/8	—	—	5 7/8
	Pathfinder 4WD	12 3/8	11–14	170	21 1/8	4 1/8	7 5/8	9	4 3/4	3 1/8	5 7/8
	Pickup KA24E 2WD	8 5/8	11–14	170	③	4 1/8	4 1/4	8 3/8	—	—	3 1/8
	Pickup KA24E 4WD	9 1/2	11–14	170	③	3 1/2	8 1/2	9	4 3/4	2 3/4	2 3/4
	Pickup VG30E 2WD	11 3/8	11–14	170	③	4 1/4	5 1/8	8 3/8	—	—	5 7/8
	Pickup VG30E 4WD	12 3/8	11–14	170	③	3 5/8	7 5/8	9	4 3/4	3 1/8	5 7/8
1995	Pathfinder 2WD	11 3/8	11–14	170	21 1/8	4 1/4	5 1/8	8 3/8	—	—	5 7/8
	Pathfinder 4WD	12 3/8	11–14	170	21 1/8	4 1/8	4 1/8	9	4 3/4	3 1/8	5 7/8
	Pickup KA24E 2WD	8 5/8	11–14	170	③	4 1/8	4 1/4	8 3/8	—	—	3 1/8
	Pickup KA24E 4WD	9 1/2	11–14	170	③	3 1/2	8 1/2	9	4 3/4	2 3/4	2 3/4

Continued

FLUID CAPACITIES & COOLING SYSTEM DATA—Continued

Year	Model	Coolant Capacity, Qts.	Radiator Cap Relief Pressure, Lbs.	Thermo. Opening Temp., °F	Fuel Tank, Gals.	Engine Oil Refill, Qts.①	Transmission Oil		Transfer Case Oil, Pts.	Differential Oil, Pts.	
							Man. Trans., Pts.	Auto. Trans., Qts.②		Front	Rear
1995	Pickup VG30E 2WD	11⅜	11–14	170	③	4¼	5⅛	8⅜	—	—	5⅞
	Pickup VG30E 4WD	12⅜	11–14	170	③	3⅝	7⅝	9	4¾	3⅛	5⅞
1996	Pathfinder 2WD	11⅜	11–14	170	21⅛	4¼	5⅛	8⅜	—	—	5⅞
	Pathfinder 4WD	12⅜	11–14	170	21⅛	4⅛	4⅛	9	4¾	4⅜	5⅞
	Pickup 2WD	8⅝	11–14	170	15⅞	4⅛	4¼	8⅜	—	—	3⅛
	Pickup 4WD	9½	11–14	170	15⅞	4⅜	10⅜	8⅜	4¾	2¾	5⅞

2WD — Two wheel drive.
4WD — Four wheel drive.
① — Includes filter.
② — Approximate, make final check w/dipstick.
③ — 4-cylinder & 2WD Pickup SE models w/V6, 15⅞ gals.; V6 models except Pickup SE, 21⅛ gals.

LUBRICANT DATA

Year	Model	Lubricant Type					
		Transmission		Transfer Case	Rear Axle	Power Steering	Brake System
		Manual	Automatic				
1993–96	Pathfinder & Pickup	75W-90 GL-4	Nissan Matic D①	Dexron IIE	80W-90 GL-5②	Dexron II/IIE/III	DOT 3

① — Dexron III/Mercon automatic transmission fluid, or equivalent, may also be used.
② — With limited slip differential, use gear oil approved for Nissan LSD.

Electrical

NOTE: On Air Bag Equipped Models, Refer To "Air Bag System Precautions" Located In The Front Of This Manual For System Disarming & Arming Procedures.

INDEX

	Page No.
Air Bags	36-1
Air Conditioning	36-1
Alternator, Replace	35-5
Alternators	36-1
Blower Motor, Replace	35-7
Combination Switch, Replace	35-6
Cooling Fans	36-1
Cruise Control	36-1
Dash Gauges	36-1
Dash Panels	36-1
Distributor, Replace	35-5
Evaporator Core, Replace	35-7
Fuel Pump Relay Location	35-5
Fuse Panel & Flasher Location	35-5
Headlamp Switch, Replace	35-5
Heater Core, Replace	35-7
Ignition Lock, Replace	35-5
Ignition Switch, Replace	35-5
Instrument Cluster, Replace	35-6
Neutral Safety Switch, Adjust	35-5
Passive Restraints	36-1
Precautions	35-5
Air Bag Systems	35-5
Radio, Replace	35-6
Relay Center Location	35-5
Speed Controls	36-1
Starter Motors	36-1
Starter, Replace	35-5
Steering Columns	36-1
Steering Wheel, Replace	35-6
Stop Light Switch, Replace	35-5
Turn Signal Switch, Replace	35-6
Wiper Motor, Replace	35-6
Front	35-6
Rear	35-6
Wiper Switch, Replace	35-7
Front	35-7
Rear	35-7
Wiper Systems	36-1

PRECAUTIONS

AIR BAG SYSTEMS

Refer to "Air Bag System Precautions" in the front of this manual for system disarming and arming procedures.

FUSE PANEL & FLASHER LOCATION

The fuse panel is located under the lefthand side of the instrument panel.

The combination flasher unit is located behind the lefthand side of the instrument panel, near the top of the clutch pedal.

FUEL PUMP RELAY LOCATION

The fuel pump relay is located in the engine compartment relay block on the lefthand side of the engine compartment, behind the battery.

RELAY CENTER LOCATION

The relay center is located in the rear righthand side of the engine compartment.

STARTER

REPLACE

1. Disconnect battery ground cable.
2. Disconnect starter wiring from starter.
3. Remove starter retaining bolts, then the starter.
4. Reverse procedure to install.

ALTERNATOR

REPLACE

1. Disconnect battery ground cable.
2. Loosen alternator adjusting bolt.
3. Remove alternator drive belt.
4. Remove two alternator retaining bolts, then disconnect alternator electrical connector.
5. Remove alternator from the vehicle.
6. Reverse procedure to install.

DISTRIBUTOR

REPLACE

1. Disconnect battery ground cable.
2. Rotate engine to TDC.
3. Disconnect spark plug wires and all electrical connectors.
4. Remove distributor mounting bolt and distributor.
5. Reverse procedure to install.

IGNITION LOCK

REPLACE

The ignition lock is retained by two shear type screws, **Fig. 1.** It is necessary to drill out these screws to remove ignition lock from steering tube. When installing, ensure the shear type screws are used.

IGNITION SWITCH

REPLACE

1. Remove the four upper and lower shell cover retaining screws, then the shell covers.
2. Disconnect electrical connectors from switch.
3. Remove switch retaining screw from steering lock, **Fig. 2.**
4. Remove switch.
5. Reverse procedure to install.

NEUTRAL SAFETY SWITCH

ADJUST

1. Loosen inhibitor switch attaching screws, **Fig. 3.**
2. Set selector lever manual shaft at Neutral position.
3. Insert suitable pin into adjustment holes in both inhibitor switch and switch lever as near vertical as possible, then tighten screws.
4. Check switch for continuity, **Fig. 4.** If continuity is not as specified, replace switch.

HEADLAMP SWITCH

REPLACE

1. Disconnect battery ground cable.
2. Remove steering wheel as outlined under "Steering Wheel, Replace."
3. Remove steering column shell covers.
4. Disconnect switch electrical connections.
5. Remove headlamp switch attaching screw and the switch from combination switch base, **Fig 5.**
6. Reverse procedure to install.

STOP LIGHT SWITCH

REPLACE

The stop lamp switch is located on the brake pedal support.

1. Disconnect battery ground cable.
2. Disconnect switch electrical connectors.
3. Loosen switch retaining locknut and remove switch.
4. Reverse procedure to install.

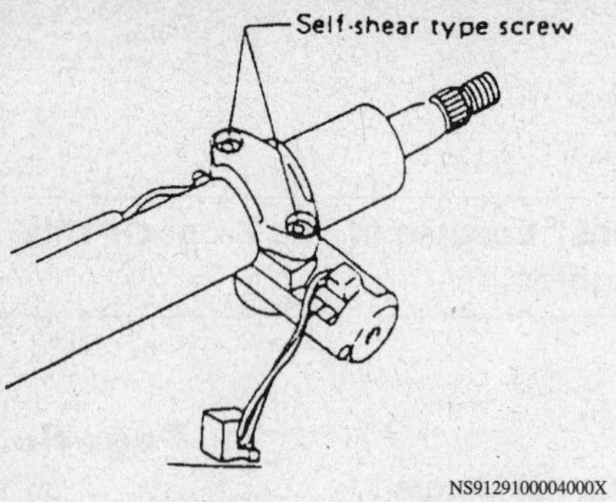
Self-shear type screw
NS9129100004000X

Fig. 1 Ignition lock replacement

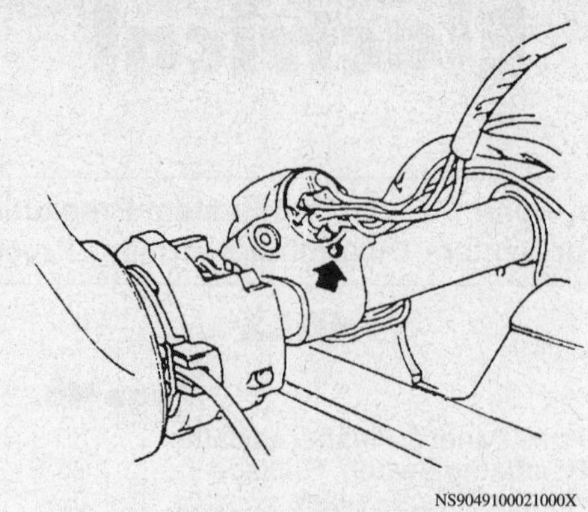
NS9049100021000X

Fig. 2 Ignition switch replacement

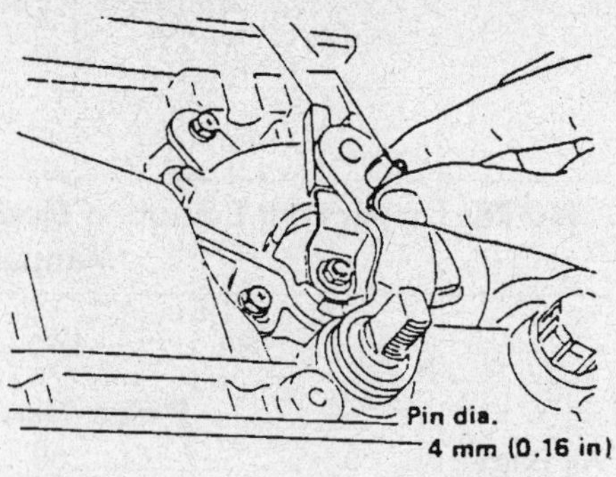
Pin dia.
4 mm (0.16 in)
NS9049100022000X

Fig. 3 Inhibitor switch adjustment

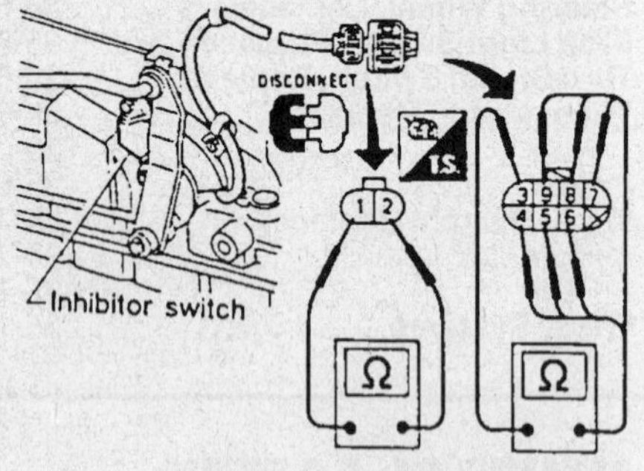
DISCONNECT
Inhibitor switch
1 2
3 9 8 7
4 5 6
Ω
Ω

Lever position	Terminal No.								
	①	②	③	④	⑤	⑥	⑦	⑧	⑨
P	○	○	○	○					
R			○	—	○				
N	○	○	○	—	—	○			
D			○	—	—	—	○		
2			○	—	—	—	—	○	
1			○	—	—	—	—	—	○

NS9049100023000X

Fig. 4 Inhibitor switch continuity check

COMBINATION SWITCH

REPLACE

1. Disconnect battery ground cable.
2. Remove steering wheel as outlined under "Steering Wheel, Replace."
3. Remove steering column shell covers.
4. Disconnect switch electrical connections.
5. Remove combination switch base attaching screw and turn after pushing on it, **Fig 6.**
6. Reverse procedure to install.

TURN SIGNAL SWITCH

REPLACE

1. Disconnect battery ground cable.
2. Remove steering wheel as outlined under "Steering Wheel, Replace."
3. Remove steering column shell covers.
4. Disconnect switch electrical connections.
5. Remove turn signal switch attaching screw and the switch from combination switch base, **Fig 5.**
6. Reverse procedure to install.

STEERING WHEEL

REPLACE

1. Remove horn pad.
2. Remove two attaching screws from rear of steering wheel.
3. Remove steering wheel using puller tool No. J25726-A, or equivalent.
4. Reverse procedure to install. Apply suitable grease to entire surface of turn signal cancel pin and horn contact slip ring.

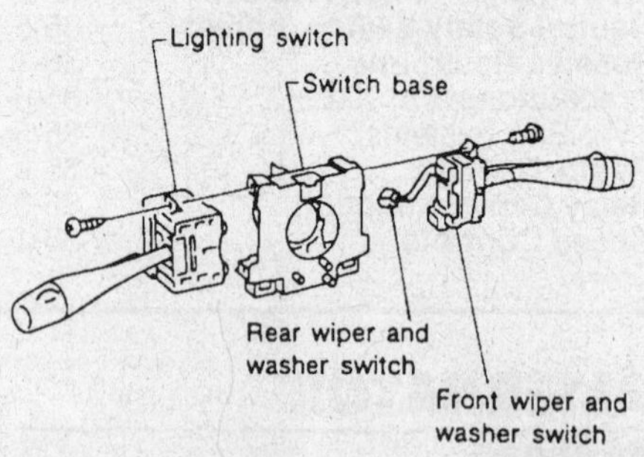
Lighting switch
Switch base
Rear wiper and washer switch
Front wiper and washer switch
NS9049100024000X

Fig. 5 Headlamp & turn signal switch replacement

INSTRUMENT CLUSTER

REPLACE

1. Disconnect battery ground cable.
2. Remove instrument panel as outlined under "Instrument Panel, Replace " in the "Dash Panel Service"section.
3. Remove steering column cover and steering wheel as necessary.
4. Remove instrument panel cover.
5. Remove cluster lid retaining screws and remove cluster lid.
6. Disconnect speedometer cable, cluster retaining nuts and electrical connectors as necessary. The cluster may have to be pulled slightly forward after removing the retaining screws to allow access to the electrical connectors in the rear.
7. Reverse procedure to install.

RADIO

REPLACE

1. Remove instrument panel as outlined under "Instrument Panel Replace " in the "Dash Panel Service"section.
2. Disconnect battery ground cable.
3. Remove cluster lid or instrument panel fascia as necessary to gain access to brackets.

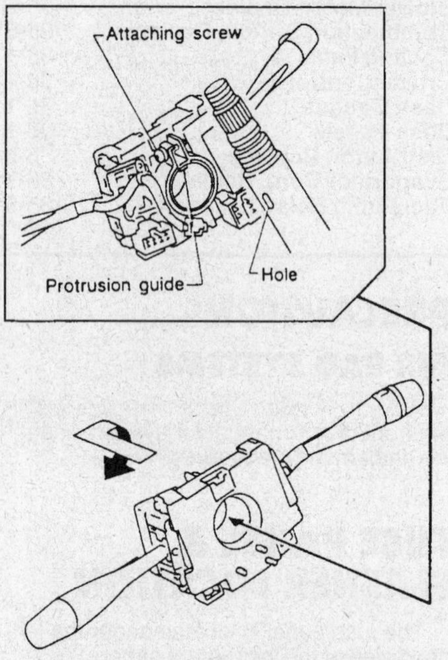
Attaching screw
Protrusion guide
Hole
NS9049100025000X

Fig. 6 Combination switch replacement

4. Remove radio bracket to instrument panel attaching screw.
5. Disconnect electrical leads from radio.
6. Remove radio from vehicle.
7. Reverse procedure to install.

WIPER MOTOR

REPLACE

FRONT

1. Disconnect battery ground cable.
2. Remove wiper arms, **Fig. 7.**
3. Remove cowl top grille.
4. Remove stop ring connecting wiper motor arm to connecting rod, then disconnect wiper motor electrical connector from beneath instrument panel.
5. Remove wiper motor retaining bolts and the wiper motor.
6. Remove flange nuts retaining pivot to cowl top, then remove wiper motor linkage.
7. Reverse procedure to install.

REAR

1. Disconnect battery ground cable.

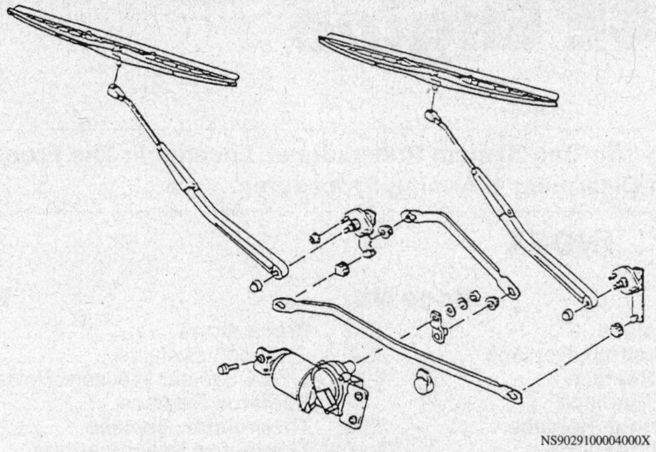
NS9029100004000X

Fig. 7 Exploded view of windshield wiper system

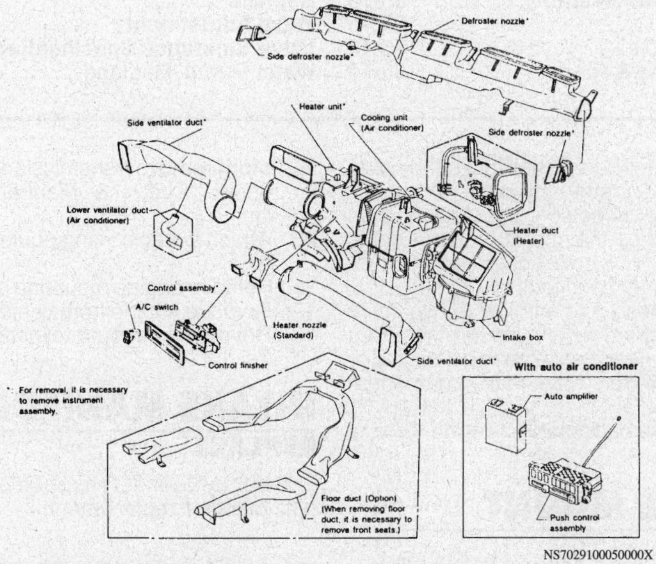
Defroster nozzle*
Side defroster nozzle*
Heater unit*
Cooling unit (Air conditioner)
Side ventilator duct*
Side defroster nozzle*
Lower ventilator duct (Air conditioner)
Heater duct (Heater)
Control assembly*
A/C switch
Heater nozzle (Standard)
Intake box
Control finisher
Side ventilator duct*
With auto air conditioner
Auto amplifier
*: For removal, it is necessary to remove instrument assembly.
Floor duct (Option) (When removing floor duct, it is necessary to remove front seats.)
Push control assembly
NS7029100050000X

Fig. 8 Exploded view of A/C & heater system

2. Raise rear wiper arm off glass and remove retaining nut.
3. Remove rear wiper arm.
4. Remove tailgate inner trim panel and disconnect electrical connector at motor.
5. Remove wiper motor retaining bolts, then the wiper motor.
6. Reverse procedure to install.

WIPER SWITCH

REPLACE

FRONT

Refer to the "Combination Switch, Replace" procedure for wiper switch replacement. It is not necessary to remove combination switch base to remove windshield wiper switch.

REAR

1. Disconnect battery ground cable.
2. Disconnect electrical connector from switch.
3. Remove switch knob by depressing and/or twisting as necessary.
4. Remove any switch retaining nuts or clips, then remove the switch.
5. Reverse procedure to install.

BLOWER MOTOR

REPLACE

Refer to **Fig. 8** for blower motor replacement.

HEATER CORE

REPLACE

Refer to **Fig. 8** for heater core replacement.

EVAPORATOR CORE

REPLACE

1. Disconnect battery ground cable and discharge A/C system. **Discharge only into the proper recycling equipment. Do not release refrigerant into the air.**
2. Remove passenger side instrument lower cover and glove compartment.
3. Disconnect wiring harness connectors to evaporator.
4. Separate cooling unit case halves and remove evaporator, **Fig. 8.**
5. Reverse procedure to install.

KA24E Engine

NOTE: On Air Bag Equipped Models, Refer To "Air Bag System Precautions" Located In The Front Of This Manual For System Disarming & Arming Procedures.

INDEX

	Page No.
Belt Tension Data	35-11
Camshaft, Replace	35-10
Compression Pressure	35-8
Cooling System Bleed	35-11
Crankshaft Rear Oil Seal, Replace	35-10
Crankshaft Seal, Replace	35-10
Cylinder Head, Replace	35-8
Engine Disassemble	35-9
Engine Mount, Replace	35-8
Engine Rebuilding Specifications	36-1
Engine, Replace	35-8
Exhaust Manifold, Replace	35-8
Fuel Filter, Replace	35-11
Fuel Pump, Replace	35-11
Intake Manifold, Replace	35-8
Main & Rod Bearings	35-10
Oil Pan, Replace	35-11
Oil Pump, Replace	35-11
Piston & Rod Assembly	35-10
Assemble	35-10
Disassemble	35-10
Pistons, Pins & Rings	35-10
Precautions	35-8
Air Bag Systems	35-8
Fuel System Pressure Release	35-8
Radiator, Replace	35-11
Thermostat, Replace	35-11
Tightening Specifications	35-12
Timing Chain, Replace	35-9
Timing Chain Tensioner, Replace	35-10
Valve Adjustment	35-9
Valve Clearance Specifications	35-9
Water Pump, Replace	35-11

PRECAUTIONS

AIR BAG SYSTEMS

Refer to "Air Bag System Precautions" in the front of this manual for system disarming and arming procedures.

FUEL SYSTEM PRESSURE RELEASE

1. Remove fuel pump fuse from fuse panel.
2. Start engine.
3. Run engine until it stalls.
4. After engine stalls, crank engine two or three times to ensure fuel pressure is released.
5. Turn ignition switch off and install fuse for fuel pump.

COMPRESSION PRESSURE

1. Start engine and run until engine reaches operating temperature.
2. Turn ignition switch off.
3. Release fuel pressure. Refer to "Precautions"for fuel system pressure release procedure.
4. Remove all spark plugs.
5. Disconnect distributor coil cable.
6. Attach a compression tester to cylinder No. 1.
7. Depress accelerator pedal fully to keep throttle valve wide open.
8. Crank engine and record highest gauge indication.
9. Repeat measurement on each cylinder.
10. Standard compression is 192 psi, minimum pressure is 142 psi and compression difference limit between cylinders is 14 psi.
11. If compression in one or more cylinders is low, pour a small amount of engine oil into cylinders through spark plug holes, then retest compression.
12. If adding oil helps compression, then piston rings may be at fault. If adding oil does not help compression, then valves may be at fault.
13. If compression stays low in two cylinders that are next to each other, then cylinder head gasket may be leaking or both cylinders have valve component damage.
14. Repair as necessary.

ENGINE MOUNT

REPLACE

Refer to **Fig. 1** when replacing engine mounts.

ENGINE

REPLACE

1. Disconnect battery ground cable.
2. Release fuel system pressure as outlined under "Precautions."
3. Drain engine coolant from cylinder block and radiator.
4. Disconnect or remove all hoses, linkages, electrical connectors and accessories necessary for engine removal. **Mark hoses and connectors for installation reference.**
5. Remove radiator with shroud and cooling fan.
6. Remove drive belts, then the power steering pump and A/C compressor. **Do not disconnect power steering hydraulic lines or A/C compressor refrigerant lines.**
7. Remove front exhaust tube.
8. **On models with automatic transmission,** remove transmission as outlined under "Automatic Transmission/ Transaxle " in "Nissan Unit Repair."
9. **On models with manual transmission,** remove transmission as outlined under "Clutch & Manual Transmission."
10. Attach suitable lifting equipment to engine.
11. Remove engine mounting bolts, **Fig. 1.**
12. Remove engine from vehicle.
13. Reverse procedure to install.

INTAKE MANIFOLD

REPLACE

Refer to "Cylinder Head, Replace" for intake manifold replacement.

EXHAUST MANIFOLD

REPLACE

Refer to "Cylinder Head, Replace" for exhaust manifold replacement.

CYLINDER HEAD

REPLACE

With the timing belt removed, avoid turning the camshaft or crankshaft. If movement is required, exercise extreme caution to avoid valve damage caused by piston contact.

1. Disconnect battery ground cable.
2. Release fuel system pressure as outlined under "Precautions."
3. Drain engine coolant from cylinder block and radiator.
4. Remove power steering drive belt, pump, idler pulley and brackets.
5. Disconnect vacuum hoses for swirl control valve and pressure control solenoid valve.
6. Remove accelerator wire bracket.
7. Disconnect EGR tube from exhaust manifold.
8. Remove bolts which hold intake manifold collector to intake manifold.

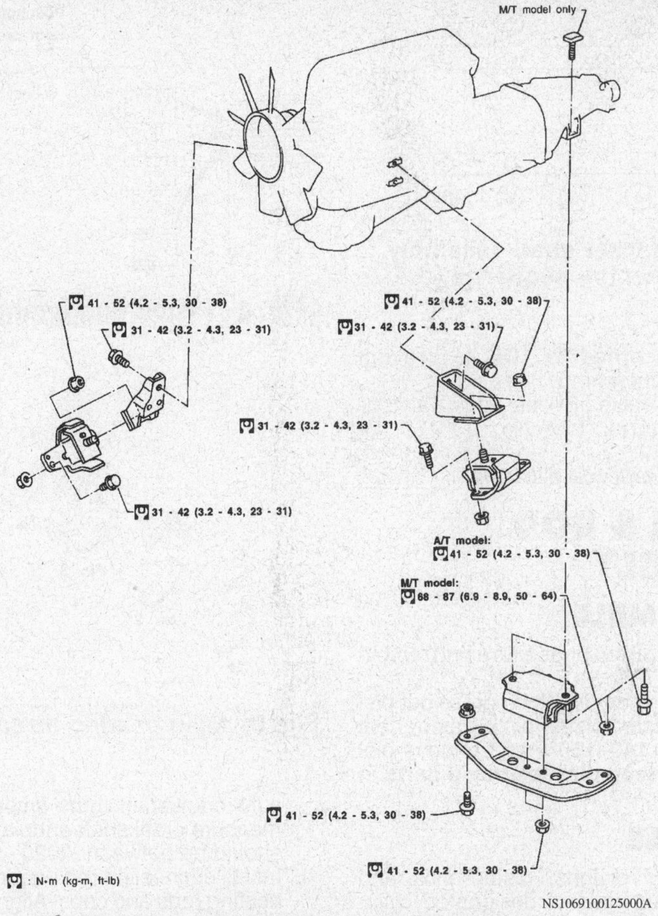
M/T model only
41 - 52 (4.2 - 5.3, 30 - 38)
31 - 42 (3.2 - 4.3, 23 - 31)
41 - 52 (4.2 - 5.3, 30 - 38)
31 - 42 (3.2 - 4.3, 23 - 31)
31 - 42 (3.2 - 4.3, 23 - 31)
31 - 42 (3.2 - 4.3, 23 - 31)
A/T model:
41 - 52 (4.2 - 5.3, 30 - 38)
M/T model:
68 - 87 (6.9 - 8.9, 50 - 64)
41 - 52 (4.2 - 5.3, 30 - 38)
41 - 52 (4.2 - 5.3, 30 - 38)
: N·m (kg-m, ft-lb)
NS1069100125000A

Fig. 1 Engine mount replacement

9. Remove bolts which hold intake manifold to cylinder head while raising collector upwards.
10. Remove exhaust manifold attaching bolts and manifold.
11. Remove rocker cover.
12. Set No. 1 piston at TDC on its compression stroke. Check position by looking at distributor rotor position.
13. Loosen camshaft sprocket bolt and support timing chain by using chain stopper tool No. KV10105800, or equivalent.
14. Remove camshaft sprocket.
15. Remove front timing cover to cylinder head bolts.
16. Remove cylinder head attaching bolts in numerical order in two or three steps, **Fig. 2.**
17. Reverse procedure to install, noting the following:
    a. Install cylinder head with new gasket and tighten cylinder head bolts to specifications in numerical order, **Fig. 3.**
    b. **Torque** all cylinder head bolts to 22 ft. lbs., then to 58 ft. lbs.
    c. Loosen all bolts completely.
    d. **Torque** all cylinder head bolts to 22 ft. lbs.
    e. Using an angle wrench, or equivalent, turn all cylinder head bolts 80–85 degrees clockwise. If an angle wrench is not available, **torque** all bolts to 54–61 ft. lbs.

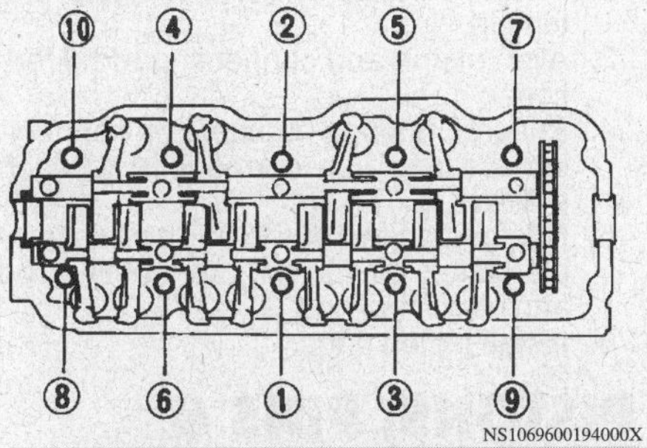
⑩ ④ ② ⑤ ⑦
⑧ ⑥ ① ③ ⑨
NS1069600194000X

Fig. 3 Cylinder head bolt tightening sequence

    f. Tighten all remaining fasteners to specifications.

ENGINE DISASSEMBLE

1. Place engine on work stand.
2. Drain oil and remaining coolant.
3. Remove oil pan as outlined under "Oil Pan, Replace."
4. Remove timing chain as outlined under "Timing Chain, Replace."
5. Remove water pump as outlined under "Water Pump, Replace."
6. Remove cylinder head as outlined under "Cylinder Head, Replace."
7. Remove pistons with connecting rod.
8. Remove bearing caps and crankshaft.

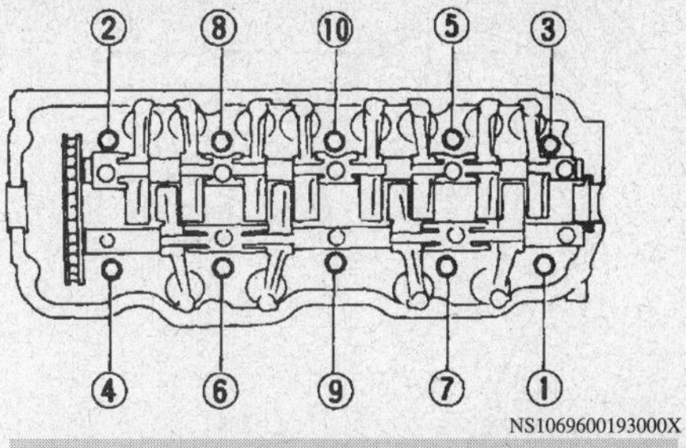
② ⑧ ⑩ ⑤ ③
④ ⑥ ⑨ ⑦ ①
NS1069600193000X

Fig. 2 Cylinder head loosening sequence

Bearing cap bolts should be loosened in two or three steps.

9. Reverse procedure to install, noting to tighten to specifications.

VALVE CLEARANCE SPECIFICATIONS

Engine	Stem-To-Guide Clearance, Inch①	
	Intake	Exhaust
KA24E	.0008–.0021	.0016–.0028

① — Cold.

VALVE ADJUSTMENT

These engines are equipped with hydraulic lash adjusters. No adjustments are required.

TIMING CHAIN

REPLACE

1. Disconnect battery ground cable.
2. Drain engine coolant from radiator.
3. Remove radiator shroud and cooling fan.
4. Remove power steering, compressor and generator drive belts.
5. Remove all spark plugs.
6. Set No. 1 piston at TDC on its compression stroke.
7. Remove power steering pump, idler pulley and power steering pump brackets.
8. Remove compressor idler pulley.
9. Remove crankshaft pulley with a suitable puller.
10. Remove oil pump with pump drive spindle. Refer to "Oil Pump, Replace."
11. Remove rocker cover.
12. Remove oil pan. Refer to "Oil Pan, Replace."
13. Remove front cover.
14. Remove chain tensioner and guides.
15. Remove timing chain and camshaft sprocket.
16. Remove oil thrower, oil pump drive gear and crankshaft sprocket.
17. Reverse procedure to install, noting the following:
    a. Refer to **Fig. 4** for timing chain and sprocket alignment marks.
    b. Using suitable scraper, clean mating surface of front cover, then

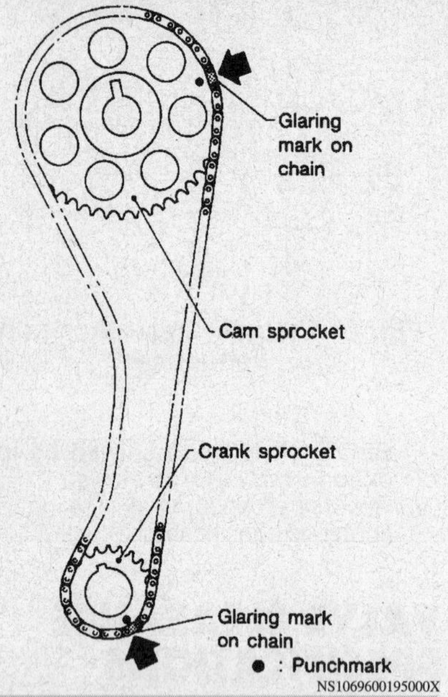
Glaring mark on chain
Cam sprocket
Crank sprocket
Glaring mark on chain
● : Punchmark
NS1069600195000X

Fig. 4 Timing chain alignment

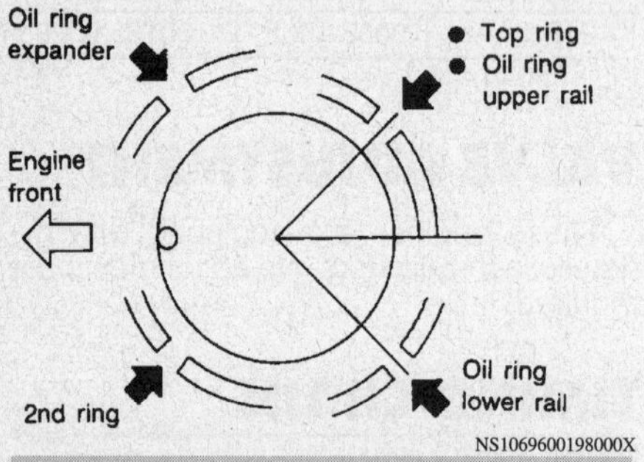
Oil ring expander
● Top ring
● Oil ring upper rail
Engine front
Oil ring lower rail
2nd ring
NS1069600198000X

Fig. 7 Piston ring alignment

apply ⅛ inch bead of liquid gasket, or equivalent, around inside of bolt holes.

c. Tighten to specifications.

TIMING CHAIN TENSIONER

REPLACE

Refer to "Timing Chain, Replace" for timing chain tensioner replacement.

CAMSHAFT

REPLACE

1. Disconnect battery ground cable.
2. Remove valve cover.
3. Remove rocker shaft assembly in sequence, **Fig. 5,** in two or three steps.
4. Measure camshaft endplay. Endplay should be between .0028–.0059 inch.
5. Remove and support camshaft sprocket.
6. Remove camshaft.
7. Remove valve components using valve spring compressor tool No. KV10109210, or equivalent. **Set piston concerned to TDC to prevent valve from falling.**
8. Remove valve oil seals using valve oil seal removal tool No. J36467, or equivalent.
9. Reverse procedure to install.

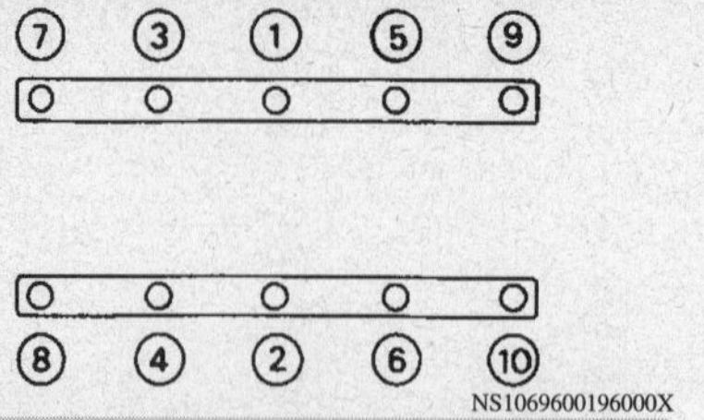
7 3 1 5 9
8 4 2 6 10
NS1069600196000X

Fig. 5 Rocker shaft assembly loosening sequence

PISTON & ROD ASSEMBLY

DISASSEMBLE

1. Remove piston rings with a ring remover.
2. Remove snap ring, then press out piston pin using piston pin press or heat piston to 140–150°F and remove piston pin. **Keep disassembled parts in order.**

ASSEMBLE

1. Assemble pistons, piston pins and connecting rods of designated cylinders.
2. Install new snap ring on one side of piston pin.
3. Align piston and connecting rod direction.
4. Ensure stamped numbers on connecting rod and cap correspond to each cylinder.
5. Heat piston to 140–150°F and assemble piston, piston pin, connecting rod and new snap ring.
6. Install piston rings.

PISTONS, PINS & RINGS

1. Heat piston to 140–158°F and assemble piston, piston pin and connecting rod using piston pin press stand assembly tool No. KV10110300, or equivalent. **After assembly, ensure connecting rod swings smoothly.**
2. Set piston rings as shown, **Fig. 6.**
3. Align piston rings so end gaps are positioned properly, **Fig. 7.**

MAIN & ROD BEARINGS

1. Set main bearings in their proper positions on cylinder block and main bearing beam, **Fig. 8,** then apply engine oil to bearing surfaces.
2. Install crankshaft and main bearing beam and tighten to specifications in two or three steps in sequence, **Fig. 9.**
3. After installing bearing cap bolts, make sure crankshaft turns smoothly, then measure crankshaft endplay. Endplay should be between .0020–.0071 inch.
4. Install connecting rod bearings in connecting rods and caps. Align oil hole in rod and bearing, then apply engine oil to bearing surface, bolt threads and seating surfaces.
5. Install piston and connecting rod assemblies with mark on piston head facing toward front of engine, using piston installation tool No. EM03470000 (J8037), or equivalent.
6. Install connecting rod bearing caps by first tightening to a **torque** of 10–12 ft. lbs., then tighten bolts an additional 60–65° clockwise with suitable angle wrench.

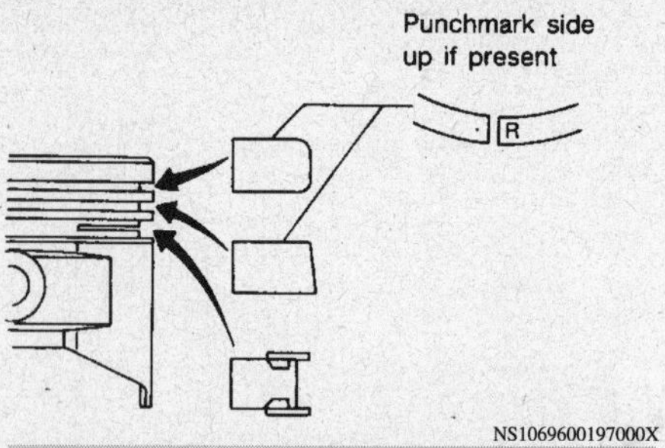
Punchmark side up if present
R
NS1069600197000X

Fig. 6 Piston ring arrangement

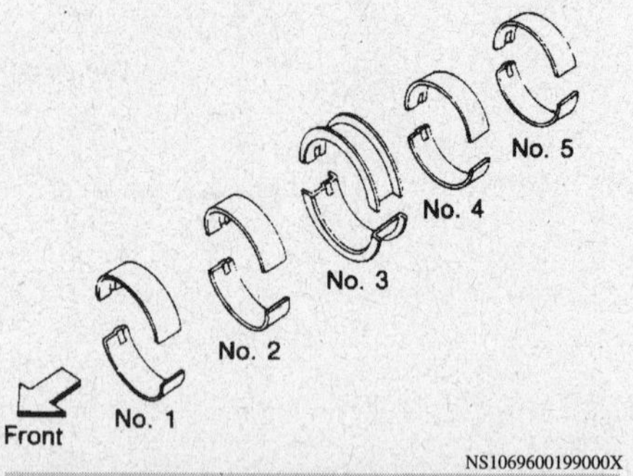
No. 5
No. 4
No. 3
No. 2
No. 1
Front
NS1069600199000X

Fig. 8 Main bearing arrangement

CRANKSHAFT SEAL

REPLACE

1. Disconnect battery ground cable.
2. Remove radiator shroud.
3. Remove drive belts.
4. Remove crankshaft pulley with suitable puller.
5. Remove front oil seal using screw driver, or equivalent. While prying out seal, be careful not to scratch front cover.
6. Apply engine oil to new seal and install in correct direction using suitable tool, **Fig. 10.**

CRANKSHAFT REAR OIL SEAL

REPLACE

1. Remove flywheel or driveplate.
2. Remove rear oil seal retainer.
3. Remove rear oil seal from retainer using suitable seal removal tool.

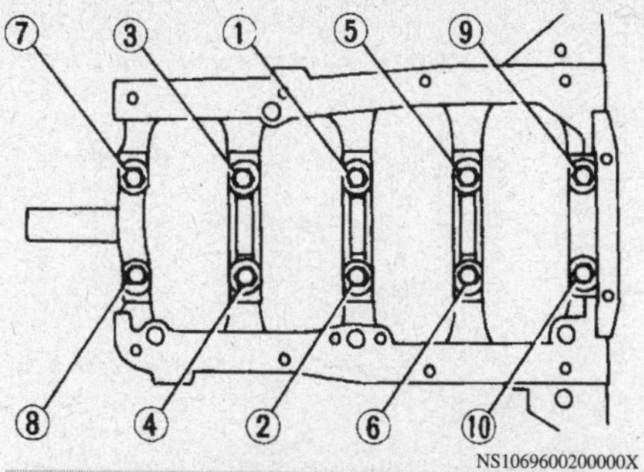
7
3
1
5
9
8
4
2
6
10
NS1069600200000X

Fig. 9 Bearing cap tightening sequence.

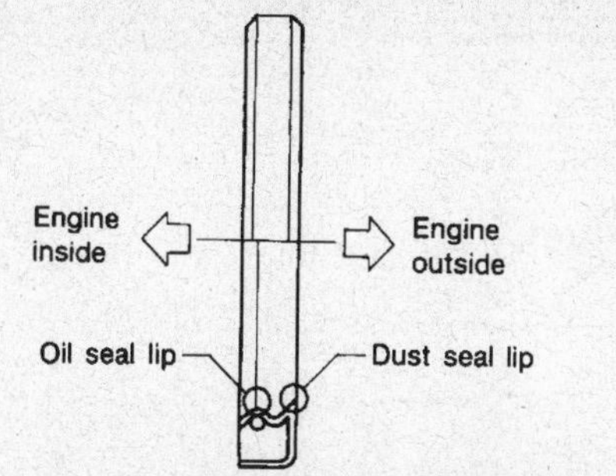
Engine inside
Engine outside
Oil seal lip
Dust seal lip
NS1099600021000X

Fig. 10 Oil seal installation direction

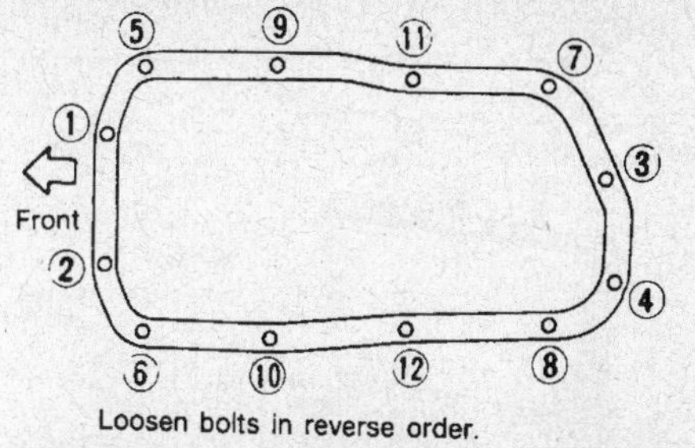
5
9
11
7
1
3
Front
2
4
6
10
12
8
Loosen bolts in reverse order.
NS1099600020000X

Fig. 11 Oil pan bolt loosening sequence

4. Apply engine oil to new seal and install in correct direction using suitable installation tool, **Fig. 10.**
5. Clean mating surface of seal retainer using scraper or equivalent.
6. Apply ⅛ inch bead of liquid gasket or equivalent around inner side of bolt holes on seal retainer.
7. Install seal retainer.

OIL PAN

REPLACE

1. Raise and support vehicle.
2. Drain engine oil.
3. Remove front stabilizer bar attaching bolts and nuts from bottom side member.
4. Using suitable equipment, lift engine.
5. Remove oil pan bolts in order, **Fig. 11.**
6. Insert seal cutter tool No. KV10111100 (J37228), or equivalent, between cylinder block and oil pan. **Do not insert screwdriver, or oil pan flange will be damaged.**
7. Slide tool by tapping on side of tool with a suitable hammer.
8. Pull out oil pan from front side.
9. Reverse procedure to install, noting the following:
   a. Clean oil pan mating surface with a suitable scraper tool.
   b. Apply ⅛ inch bead of liquid gasket or equivalent to mating surface of oil pan.
   c. Tighten oil pan mounting bolts to specifications in reverse order of loosening sequence, **Fig. 11.**

OIL PUMP

REPLACE

1. Raise and support vehicle.
2. Drain engine oil.
3. Turn crankshaft so that No. 1 cylinder is at TDC on its compression stroke.
4. Remove oil pump attaching bolts.
5. Remove oil pump, oil seal and gasket.
6. Reverse procedure to install, noting the following:
   a. Apply engine oil to gears, then align punch mark on drive spindle and oil hole on oil pump.
   b. Install new oil seal and gasket.
   c. Install oil pump and tighten attaching bolts to specifications.

Unit: mm (in)

	Used belt deflection		Deflection of new belt
	Limit	Deflection after adjustment	
Generator	17 (0.67)	10 - 12 (0.39 - 0.47)	8 - 10 (0.31 - 0.39)
Air conditioner compressor	16 (0.63)	10 - 12 (0.39 - 0.47)	8 - 10 (0.31 - 0.39)
Power steering oil pump	15 (0.59)	9 - 11 (0.35 - 0.43)	7 - 9 (0.28 - 0.35)
Applied pushing force	98 N (10 kg, 22 lb)		

NS1139600161000X

Fig. 12 Belt deflection

BELT TENSION DATA

Refer to **Fig. 12** for belt tension data.

COOLING SYSTEM BLEED

1. Open radiator cap and air relief plug.
2. Fill radiator with coolant to specified level.
3. Close air relief plug.
4. Run engine and bring to operating temperature.
5. Race engine two or three times under no-load.
6. Stop engine and let cool, then add coolant as necessary.

THERMOSTAT

REPLACE

1. Disconnect battery ground cable, then drain engine and radiator coolant.
2. Remove air cleaner and air duct assembly.
3. Remove radiator hose, then the water inlet housing.
4. Remove thermostat from thermostat housing.
5. Reverse procedure to install. Clean mating surface of water inlet and apply ⅛ inch bead of liquid gasket, or equivalent, to mating surface of water inlet.

WATER PUMP

REPLACE

1. Drain engine coolant from engine.
2. Remove fan coupling with fan.
3. Remove power steering, generator and A/C compressor drive belts.
4. Remove water pump attaching bolts and pump.
5. Reverse procedure to install, noting to clean mating surface of water pump and apply ⅛ inch bead of liquid gasket, or equivalent, to mating surface of water pump.

RADIATOR

REPLACE

1. Disconnect battery ground cable.
2. Remove undercover panel and drain coolant.
3. Disconnect radiator upper and lower hoses, **Fig. 13.**
4. **On models with automatic transmission,** remove automatic transmission oil cooler lines.
5. **On all models,** remove radiator lower shroud.
6. Disconnect reservoir tank hose.
7. Lift radiator out of vehicle, using care to avoid damage.
8. Reverse procedure to install.

FUEL PUMP

REPLACE

1. Release fuel system pressure as outlined under "Precautions."
2. Disconnect battery ground cable.
3. Remove fuel filler tube attaching bolts, **Fig. 14.**
4. Remove fuel tank protector.
5. Support fuel tank with a suitable jack, then remove fuel tank to frame attaching bolts.
6. Lower tank to gain access to fuel lines, then disconnect fuel lines and electrical connector at fuel pump.
7. Lower tank and remove fuel pump from fuel tank.
8. Reverse procedure to install.

FUEL FILTER

REPLACE

1. Release fuel system pressure as outlined under "Precautions."
2. Loosen fuel filter hose clamps, **Fig. 15.**
3. Remove fuel filter from vehicle. **Be careful not to spill fuel over engine compartment.**
4. Reverse procedure to install.

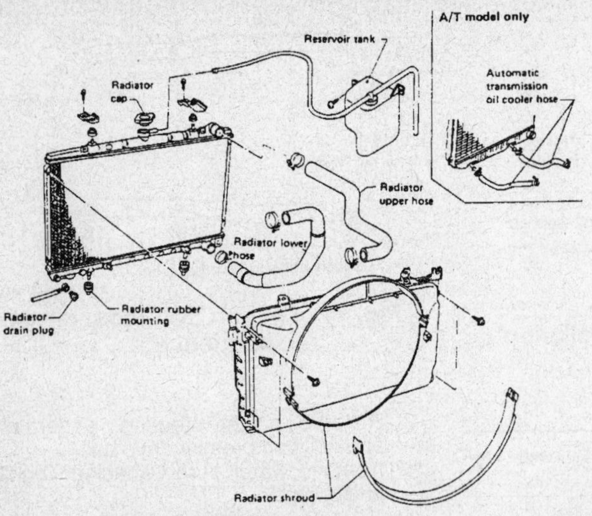
A/T model only
Reservoir tank
Radiator cap
Automatic transmission oil cooler hose
Radiator upper hose
Radiator lower hose
Radiator drain plug
Radiator rubber mounting
Radiator shroud

NS1089500047000X

Fig. 13 Radiator removal

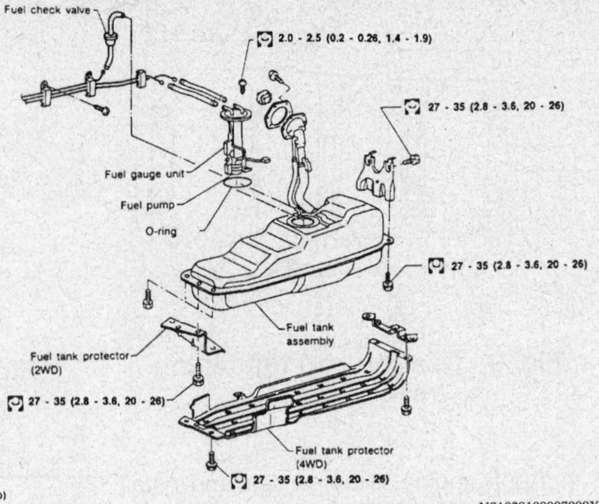
Fuel check valve
2.0 - 2.5 (0.2 - 0.26, 1.4 - 1.9)
27 - 35 (2.8 - 3.6, 20 - 26)
Fuel gauge unit
Fuel pump
O-ring
27 - 35 (2.8 - 3.6, 20 - 26)
Fuel tank assembly
Fuel tank protector (2WD)
27 - 35 (2.8 - 3.6, 20 - 26)
Fuel tank protector (4WD)
27 - 35 (2.8 - 3.6, 20 - 26)
: N·m (kg-m, ft-lb)

NS1029100007000X

Fig. 14 Fuel pump removal

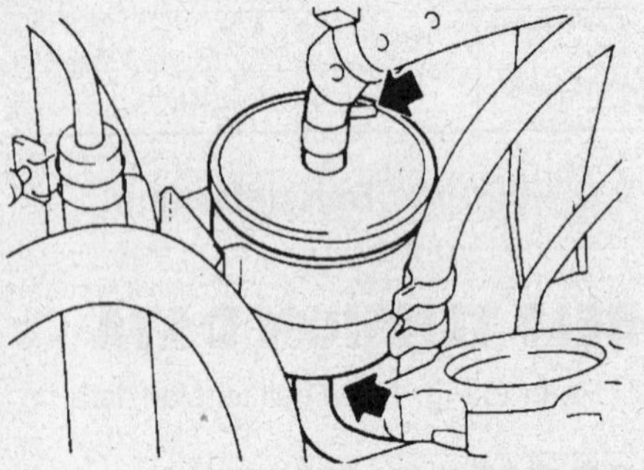

NS1029100008000X

Fig. 15 Fuel filter

TIGHTENING SPECIFICATIONS

Year	Component	Torque/Ft. Lbs.
1993–96	Alternator Adjusting Bar Bolt	12–15
	Alternator Bracket To Engine Bolts	33–43
	Alternator Through Bolt	33–44
	Camshaft Sprocket	87–116
	Connecting Rod Bearing Caps	①
	Crank Pulley Bolts	7–9
	Crank Pulley Dampner Bolt	105–112
	Cylinder Head Bolt	②
	Distributor Mounting Bolt	7–9
	Driveplate Bolt	③
	Exhaust Gas Sensor	30–37
	Exhaust Manifold Bolts	12–15
	Exhaust Manifold Cover Bolts	2.9–3.6
	Front Cover Bolts	5.1–5.8
	Main Bearing Cap Bolts	34–38
	Motor Mount Through Bolt	30–38
	Motor Mount To Engine	23–31
	Motor Mount To Frame	23–31
	Oil Filter	11–15
	Oil Filter Bracket	12–15
	Oil Pan Bolts	5.1–5.8
	Oil Pan Drain Plug	22–29

Continued

TIGHTENING SPECIFICATIONS—Continued

Year	Component	Torque/Ft. Lbs.
1993–96	Oil Pressure Sender	12–15
	Oil Strainer Bolts	12–15
	Radiator Support	2–3
	Rear Oil Seal Retainer	5.1–5.8
	Rocker Shaft Bolt	27–30
	Timing Chain Guide Bolts	9–14
	Timing Chain Tensioner Bolt	5.1–5.8
	Valve Rocker Cover	2.9–5.8
	Water Inlet Bolts	12–15
	Water Pump Bolts	12–15
	Water Pump Pulley Nuts	5.1–5.8

①— Refer to "Main & Rod Bearings."
②— Refer to "Cylinder Head, Replace."
③— Automatic transmission, 69–76 ft. lbs.; manual transmission, 105–112 ft. lbs.

VG30E & VG33E Engines

NOTE: On Air Bag Equipped Models, Refer To "Air Bag System Precautions" Located In The Front Of This Manual For System Disarming & Arming Procedures.

NOTE: For Procedures Not Covered In This Section, Refer To The Maxima & 300ZX Engine Section For VG30E Engine.

INDEX

	Page No.
Belt Tension Data	35-15
Compression Pressure	35-13
Cylinder Head, Replace	35-14
Engine Mount, Replace	35-14
Engine Rebuilding Specifications	36-1
Engine, Replace	35-14
Exhaust Manifold, Replace	35-14
Fuel Filter, Replace	35-16
1993–95	35-16
1996	35-16
Fuel Pump, Replace	35-15
1993–95	35-15
1996	35-16
Intake Manifold, Replace	35-14
Oil Pan, Replace	35-15
Oil Pump, Replace	35-15
Precautions	35-13
Air Bag Systems	35-13
Fuel System Pressure Release	35-13
Radiator, Replace	35-15
Tightening Specifications	35-20
Valve Adjustment	35-15
Valve Clearance Specifications	35-15
Water Pump, Replace	35-15

PRECAUTIONS

AIR BAG SYSTEMS

Refer to "Air Bag System Precautions" in the front of this manual for system disarming and arming procedures.

FUEL SYSTEM PRESSURE RELEASE

1. Remove fuel pump fuse from fuse panel.
2. Start engine.
3. Run engine until it stalls.
4. After engine stalls, crank engine two or three times to ensure fuel pressure is released.
5. Turn ignition switch off and install fuse for fuel pump.

COMPRESSION PRESSURE

1. Start engine and run until engine reaches operating temperature.
2. Turn ignition switch off.
3. Release fuel pressure. Refer to "Precautions" for fuel system pressure release procedure.
4. Remove all spark plugs.
5. Disconnect distributor coil cable.
6. Attach a compression tester to cylinder No. 1.
7. Depress accelerator pedal fully to keep throttle valve wide open.
8. Crank engine and record highest gauge indication.
9. Repeat measurement on each cylinder.
10. Standard compression is 173 psi at 300 RPM, minimum pressure is 128 psi at 300 RPM and compression difference limit between cylinders is 14 psi.
11. If compression in one or more cylinders is low, pour a small amount of engine oil into cylinders through spark plug holes, then retest compression.
12. If adding oil helps compression, then piston rings may be at fault. If adding oil does not help compression, then valves may be at fault.
13. If compression stays low in two cylinders that are next to each other, then cylinder head gasket may be leaking or both cylinders have valve component damage.
14. Repair as necessary.

ENGINE MOUNT

REPLACE

Refer to **Figs. 1 through 3** when replacing engine mounts.

ENGINE

REPLACE

1. Release fuel system pressure as outlined under "Precautions."
2. Disconnect battery ground cable.
3. Remove engine undercover and hood.
4. Drain engine coolant from cylinder block and radiator.
5. Disconnect or remove all hoses, linkages, electrical connectors and accessories necessary for engine removal. **Mark hoses and connectors for installation reference.**
6. Remove radiator with shroud and cooling fan.
7. Remove drive belts, then the power steering pump and A/C compressor. **Do not disconnect power steering hydraulic lines or A/C compressor refrigerant lines.**
8. Remove front exhaust tube.
9. **On models with automatic transmission,** remove transmission as outlined under "Automatic Transmission/ Transaxle" in "Nissan Unit Repair."
10. **On models with manual transmission,** remove transmission as outlined under "Clutch & Manual Transmission."
11. Attach suitable lifting equipment to engine.
12. **On VG30E engine,** remove engine mounting bolts, **Fig. 1. Do not loosen front engine mounting insulator cover securing nuts. When cover is removed, damper oil flows out and mounting insulator will not function.**
13. **On VG33E engine,** remove engine mounting bolts, **Fig. 2.**
14. **On all models,** remove engine from vehicle.
15. Reverse procedure to install.

INTAKE MANIFOLD

REPLACE

1. Release fuel system pressure as outlined under "Precautions."
2. Remove timing belt as outlined under "Timing Belt, Replace" in "VG30E Engine" section of "Nissan Maxima & 300ZX" chapter.
3. Drain coolant from engine and radiator.
4. Separate automatic speed control and accelerator control cable from intake manifold collector, **Figs. 4 and 5.**
5. Remove the following from the intake manifold collector:
   a. Harness connectors for IACV-AAC valve.
   b. Throttle position sensor and throttle position switch.
   c. Ignition coil and power transistor.
   d. EGRC-solenoid valve and IACV-air regulator.
   e. **On California models,** EGR temperature sensor.
   f. **On all models,** water and heater hoses.
   g. PCV hose and righthand rocker cover.
   h. Vacuum hoses for canister, brake master cylinder and pressure regulator.
   i. EGR tube, ground harness and air duct hose.
   j. **Mark all vacuum hoses and electrical connectors for installation reference.**
6. Remove fuel feed and fuel return hoses from injector tube assembly.
7. Disconnect all injector harness connectors.
8. Remove injector fuel tube assembly.
9. Disconnect coolant temperature switch and thermal switch harness connectors.
10. Remove water hose from thermostat housing.
11. Using loosening sequence, **Fig. 6,** remove intake manifold.
12. Reverse procedure to install. Using sequence shown in **Fig. 7,** tighten intake manifold bolts as follows:
    a. **Torque** all bolts to 2.2–3.6 ft. lbs.
    b. **Torque** all nuts to 2.2–3.6 ft. lbs.
    c. **Torque** all bolts an additional 12–14 ft. lbs.
    d. **Torque** all nuts an additional 17–20 ft. lbs.
    e. **Torque** all bolts an additional 12–14 ft. lbs.
    f. **Torque** all nuts an additional 17–20 ft. lbs.

EXHAUST MANIFOLD

REPLACE

1. Disconnect battery ground cable.
2. Remove exhaust pipe to exhaust manifold attaching nuts.
3. Disconnect any vacuum hoses or electrical connectors that interfere with manifold removal, **Figs. 4 and 5.** Mark hoses and connectors for installation reference.
4. Remove A/C compressor from its bracket and position aside. **Do not disconnect refrigerant lines.**
5. Remove alternator from its bracket and position aside.
6. Remove compressor and alternator brackets.
7. Using sequence shown in **Figs. 8 and 9,** remove exhaust manifold attaching bolts.
8. Remove manifolds from engine.
9. Reverse procedure to install. Tighten manifold attaching bolts to specifications using sequence shown in **Figs. 10 and 11.**

CYLINDER HEAD

REPLACE

1. Disconnect battery ground cable.
2. Release fuel system pressure as outlined under "Precautions."
3. Remove timing belt as outlined under "Timing Belt, Replace."
4. Drain engine coolant from cylinder block and radiator.
5. Separate ASCD and accelerator control wire from intake manifold collector.
6. Remove intake manifold collector from engine as follows:
   a. Disconnect connectors for IACV-AAC valve, throttle position sensor, throttle position switch, ignition coil, power transistor, EGRC solenoid valve and EGR temperature sensor.
   b. Disconnect water hoses from collector.
   c. Disconnect heater hoses.
   d. Disconnect PCV hose from righthand rocker cover.
   e. Disconnect vacuum hoses for EVAP canister, master brake cylinder and pressure regulator.
   f. Disconnect purge hose from EVAP canister
   g. Disconnect EGR tube.
   h. Disconnect ground harnesses.
   i. Disconnect air duct hose.
   j. Remove intake manifold collector.
7. Remove fuel feed and fuel return hoses from injector fuel tube assembly.
8. Disconnect all injector harness connectors.
9. Remove injector fuel tube assembly.
10. Remove intake manifold from engine as follows:
    a. Disconnect engine coolant temperature switch harness connector.
    b. Disconnect thermal transmitter harness connector.
    c. Disconnect water hose from thermostat housing.
    d. Remove intake manifold.
11. Remove both camshaft sprockets.
12. Remove rear timing belt cover.
13. Remove distributor and ignition wires.
14. Remove harness clamp from righthand rocker cover.
15. Remove front exhaust tube from exhaust manifold.
16. Remove compressor and power steering pump.
17. Remove alternator.
18. Remove compressor and alternator bracket.
19. Remove valve cover bolts in sequence, **Fig. 12,** then remove both valve covers.
20. Remove cylinder head bolts in sequence, **Fig. 13,** then the cylinder head with exhaust manifold.
21. Remove exhaust manifold from cylinder head. Refer to "Exhaust Manifold, Replace."
22. Reverse procedure to install. Using sequence shown in **Fig. 14,** tighten cylinder head bolts as follows:
    a. **Torque** all bolts to 22 ft. lbs.
    b. **Torque** all bolts to 43 ft. lbs.
    c. Loosen all bolts completely.
    d. **Torque** all bolts to 22 ft. lbs.
    e. Turn all bolts an additional 60–65° clockwise. If an angle wrench is not

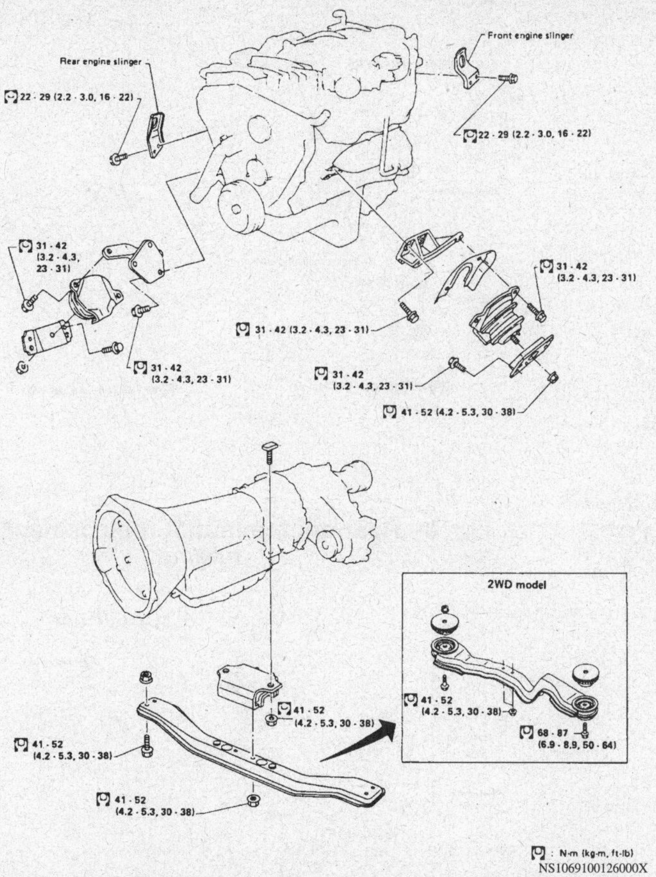

Rear engine slinger
22 - 29 (2.2 - 3.0, 16 - 22)
Front engine slinger
22 - 29 (2.2 - 3.0, 16 - 22)
31 - 42 (3.2 - 4.3, 23 - 31)
31 - 42 (3.2 - 4.3, 23 - 31)
31 - 42 (3.2 - 4.3, 23 - 31)
31 - 42 (3.2 - 4.3, 23 - 31)
31 - 42 (3.2 - 4.3, 23 - 31)
41 - 52 (4.2 - 5.3, 30 - 38)
2WD model
41 - 52 (4.2 - 5.3, 30 - 38)
68 - 87 (6.9 - 8.9, 50 - 64)
41 - 52 (4.2 - 5.3, 30 - 38)
41 - 52 (4.2 - 5.3, 30 - 38)
41 - 52 (4.2 - 5.3, 30 - 38)
: N·m (kg-m, ft-lb)
NS1069100126000X

Fig. 1 Engine mount replacement. VG30E engine

available, **torque** all bolts to 40–47 ft. lbs.

VALVE CLEARANCE SPECIFICATIONS

Engine	Stem-To-Guide Clearance, Inch①	
	Intake	Exhaust
VG30E	.0008–.0021	.0016–.0029
VG33E	.0008–.0021	.0016–.0019

① — Cold.

VALVE ADJUSTMENT

These engines are equipped with hydraulic lash adjusters. No adjustments are required.

OIL PAN

REPLACE

1. Remove undercover, then drain engine oil.
2. **On 2WD models,** remove stabilizer bracket bolts.
3. **On 4WD models,** proceed as follows:
   a. Disconnect front propeller shaft from differential carrier.
   b. Remove front driveshaft attaching bolts.
   c. Remove front differential carrier member bolts.
   d. Support front differential carrier with suitable jack and remove attaching fixing bolts.
   e. Remove front differential carrier bleeder hose.
4. **On 2WD models,** remove front suspension crossmember.
5. **On 4WD models,** proceed as follows:
   a. Remove differential front mounting bolts.
   b. Remove front differential carrier.
   c. Remove front differential carrier mounting bracket.
6. **On all models,** remove idler arm.
7. Remove starter motor.
8. **On 4WD models,** proceed as follows:
   a. Remove transmission to rear engine mounting bracket attaching nuts.
   b. Remove engine mounting bolts or nuts.
9. **On all models,** remove engine gussets.
10. **On 4WD models,** raise engine if necessary and disconnect exhaust tube.
11. **On all models,** loosen oil pan attaching bolts using sequence shown in **Figs. 15 and 16.**
12. Remove oil pump assembly.
13. Remove dipstick. **If dipstick is left in engine, the end of it may be caught between main bearing beam and windage tray of oil pan during oil pan installation.**
14. Reverse procedure to install, noting the following:
    a. Apply a continuous bead of suitable sealant .138–.177 inch wide to oil pan mating surface.
    b. Tighten bolts in reverse order of removal.

OIL PUMP

REPLACE

1. Disconnect battery ground cable.
2. Drain oil from engine and coolant from radiator.
3. Remove air duct from engine compartment.
4. Remove cooling fan.
5. Disconnect upper and lower radiator hoses.
6. Remove fan shroud.
7. Remove drive belts.
8. Remove crankshaft pulley and front and lower belt covers.
9. Remove oil pan.
10. Remove oil strainer, **Figs. 17 and 18.**
11. Remove oil pump assembly.
12. Reverse procedure to install, noting the following:
    a. Install new oil seal and gasket.
    b. Apply engine oil to inner and outer gears of pump.
    c. Tighten to specifications.

BELT TENSION DATA

Refer to **Figs. 19 and 20** for belt deflection specifications. Check drive belt tension when engine is cold.

WATER PUMP

REPLACE

1. Drain coolant from drain cocks on both sides of cylinder block and radiator.
2. Remove drive belts.
3. Remove water pump attaching bolts, **Fig. 21.**
4. Remove water pump from engine. **Do not spill coolant on timing belt.**
5. Reverse procedure to install.

RADIATOR

REPLACE

1. Disconnect battery ground cable.
2. Remove undercover panel and drain coolant.
3. Remove air duct.
4. Disconnect radiator upper and lower hoses, **Figs. 22 and 23.**
5. **On models with automatic transmission,** remove automatic transmission oil cooler lines.
6. **On all models,** remove radiator lower shroud.
7. Disconnect reservoir tank hose.
8. Carefully lift radiator out of vehicle to avoid damage.
9. Reverse procedure to install.

FUEL PUMP

REPLACE

1993–95

Refer to "Fuel Pump, Replace" under "KA24E Engine."

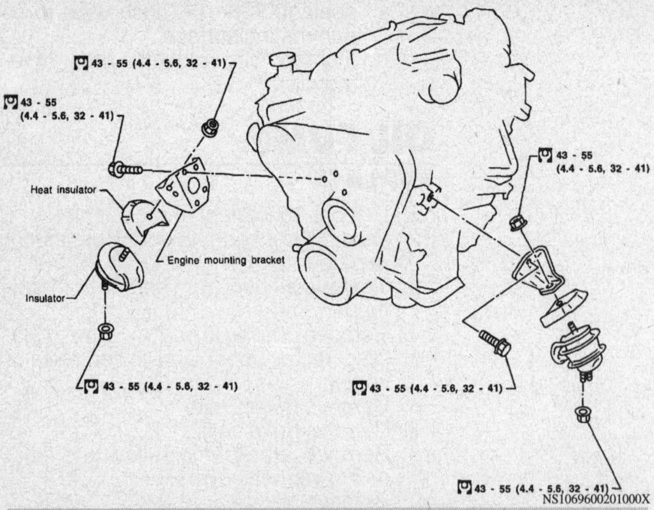
43 - 55 (4.4 - 5.6, 32 - 41)
43 - 55
(4.4 - 5.6, 32 - 41)
Heat insulator
Engine mounting bracket
Insulator
43 - 55
(4.4 - 5.6, 32 - 41)
43 - 55 (4.4 - 5.6, 32 - 41)
43 - 55 (4.4 - 5.6, 32 - 41)
43 - 55 (4.4 - 5.6, 32 - 41)
NS1069600201000X

Fig. 2 Front engine mount replacement. VG33E engine

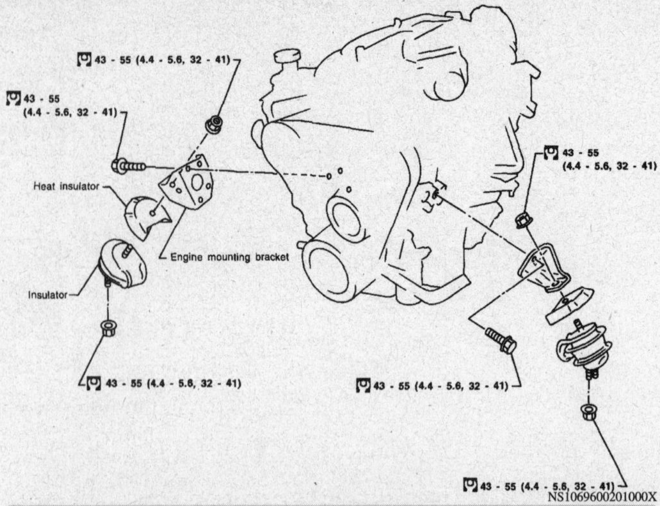
43 - 55 (4.4 - 5.6, 32 - 41)
43 - 55
(4.4 - 5.6, 32 - 41)
Heat insulator
Engine mounting bracket
Insulator
43 - 55
(4.4 - 5.6, 32 - 41)
43 - 55 (4.4 - 5.6, 32 - 41)
43 - 55 (4.4 - 5.6, 32 - 41)
43 - 55 (4.4 - 5.6, 32 - 41)
NS1069600201000X

Fig. 3 Rear engine mount replacement. VG33E engine

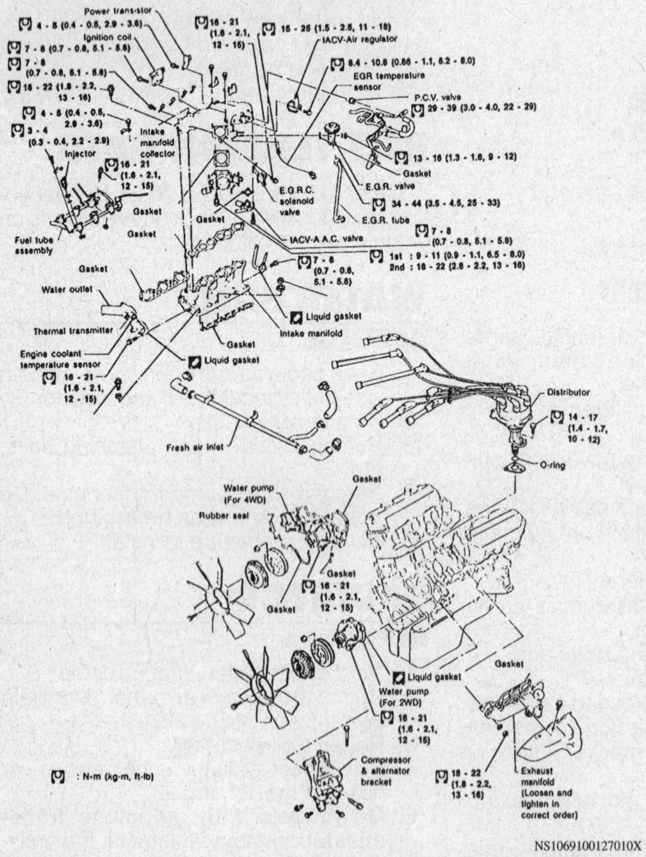
Power transistor
Ignition coil
IACV-Air regulator
EGR temperature sensor
P.C.V. valve
Intake manifold collector
Injector
E.G.R.C. solenoid valve
E.G.R. valve
E.G.R. tube
Gasket
Fuel tube assembly
IACV-A A.C. valve
Water outlet
Thermal transmitter
Engine coolant temperature sensor
Liquid gasket
Intake manifold
Distributor
O-ring
Fresh air inlet
Water pump (For 4WD)
Rubber seal
Water pump (For 2WD)
Compressor & alternator bracket
Exhaust manifold (Loosen and tighten in correct order)
: N·m (kg-m, ft-lb)
NS1069100127010X

Fig. 4 Outer components (Part 1 of 2). VG30E engine

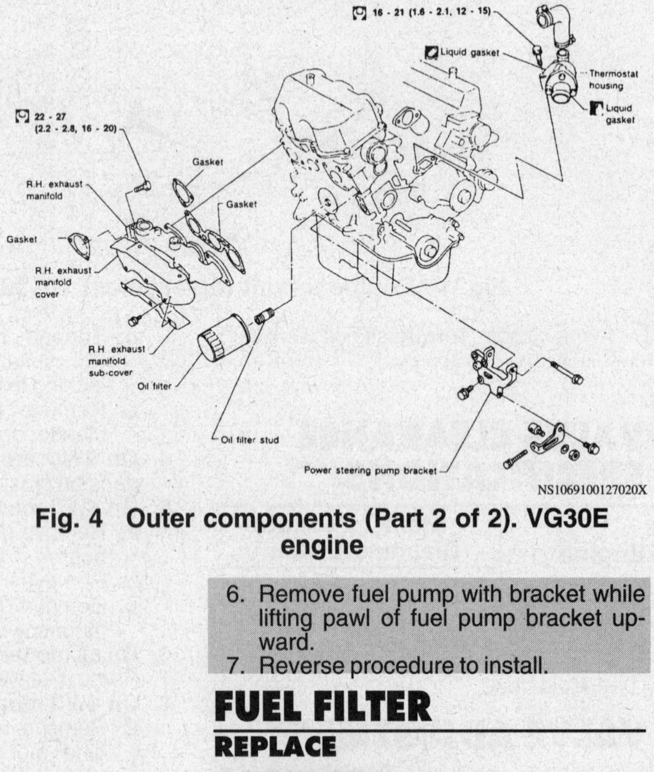
16 - 21 (1.6 - 2.1, 12 - 15)
Liquid gasket
Thermostat housing
Liquid gasket
22 - 27
(2.2 - 2.8, 16 - 20)
Gasket
R.H. exhaust manifold
Gasket
Gasket
R.H. exhaust manifold cover
R.H. exhaust manifold sub-cover
Oil filter
Oil filter stud
Power steering pump bracket
NS1069100127020X

Fig. 4 Outer components (Part 2 of 2). VG30E engine

1996

1. Disconnect battery ground cable.
2. Release fuel system pressure as outlined under "Precautions."
3. Remove inspection hole cover located behind rear seat, **Fig. 24.**
4. Disconnect harness connectors and fuel tubes from upper plate of fuel gauge. **Put mating marks on tubes for correct installation.**
5. Remove fuel gauge retainer and fuel gauge.
6. Remove fuel pump with bracket while lifting pawl of fuel pump bracket upward.
7. Reverse procedure to install.

FUEL FILTER

REPLACE

1993-95

Refer to "Fuel Filter, Replace" under "KA24E Engine."

1996

1. Release fuel system pressure as outlined under "Precautions."
2. Loosen fuel filter hose clamps, **Fig. 25.**
3. Remove fuel filter from vehicle. **Be careful not to spill fuel over engine compartment.**
4. Reverse procedure to install.

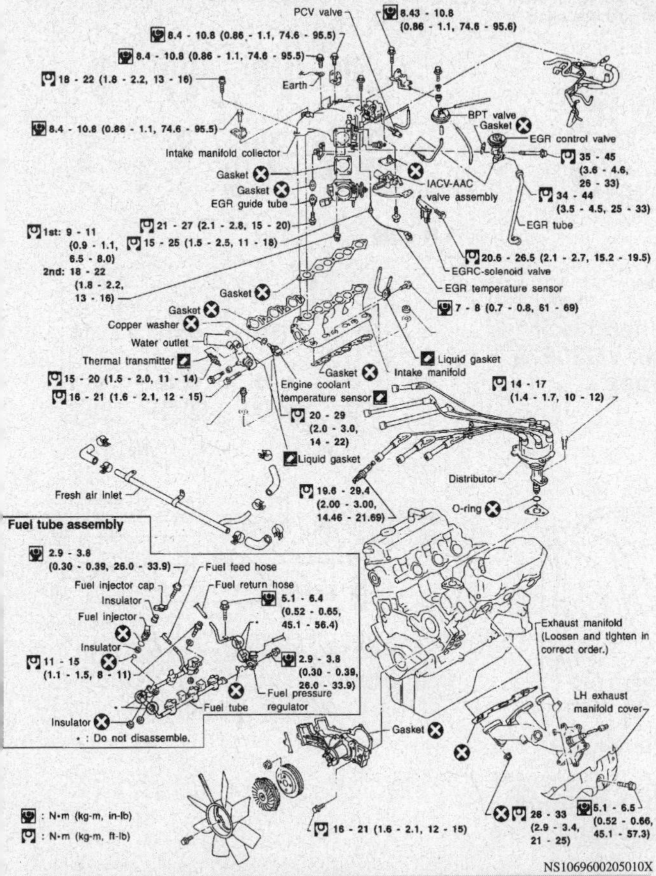
PCV valve
8.43 - 10.8 (0.86 - 1.1, 74.6 - 95.6)
8.4 - 10.8 (0.86 - 1.1, 74.6 - 95.5)
8.4 - 10.8 (0.86 - 1.1, 74.6 - 95.5)
18 - 22 (1.8 - 2.2, 13 - 16)
Earth
8.4 - 10.8 (0.86 - 1.1, 74.6 - 95.5)
BPT valve
Gasket
EGR control valve
Intake manifold collector
35 - 45 (3.6 - 4.6, 26 - 33)
Gasket
Gasket
EGR guide tube
IACV-AAC valve assembly
34 - 44 (3.5 - 4.5, 25 - 33)
EGR tube
1st: 9 - 11 (0.9 - 1.1, 6.5 - 8.0)
2nd: 18 - 22 (1.8 - 2.2, 13 - 16)
21 - 27 (2.1 - 2.8, 15 - 20)
15 - 25 (1.5 - 2.5, 11 - 18)
20.6 - 26.5 (2.1 - 2.7, 15.2 - 19.5)
EGRC-solenoid valve
EGR temperature sensor
Gasket
Gasket
7 - 8 (0.7 - 0.8, 61 - 69)
Copper washer
Water outlet
Thermal transmitter
Liquid gasket
Gasket
Intake manifold
15 - 20 (1.5 - 2.0, 11 - 14)
16 - 21 (1.6 - 2.1, 12 - 15)
Engine coolant temperature sensor
14 - 17 (1.4 - 1.7, 10 - 12)
20 - 29 (2.0 - 3.0, 14 - 22)
Liquid gasket
Distributor
Fresh air inlet
19.6 - 29.4 (2.00 - 3.00, 14.46 - 21.69)
O-ring
Fuel tube assembly
2.9 - 3.8 (0.30 - 0.39, 26.0 - 33.9)
Fuel feed hose
Fuel injector cap
Fuel return hose
Insulator
5.1 - 6.4 (0.52 - 0.65, 45.1 - 56.4)
Fuel injector
Insulator
11 - 15 (1.1 - 1.5, 8 - 11)
2.9 - 3.8 (0.30 - 0.39, 26.0 - 33.9)
Fuel pressure regulator
Fuel tube
Insulator
• : Do not disassemble.
Exhaust manifold (Loosen and tighten in correct order.)
LH exhaust manifold cover
Gasket
: N•m (kg-m, in-lb)
: N•m (kg-m, ft-lb)
16 - 21 (1.6 - 2.1, 12 - 15)
28 - 33 (2.9 - 3.4, 21 - 25)
5.1 - 6.5 (0.52 - 0.66, 45.1 - 57.3)
NS1069600205010X

Fig. 5 Outer components (Part 1 of 2). VG33E engine

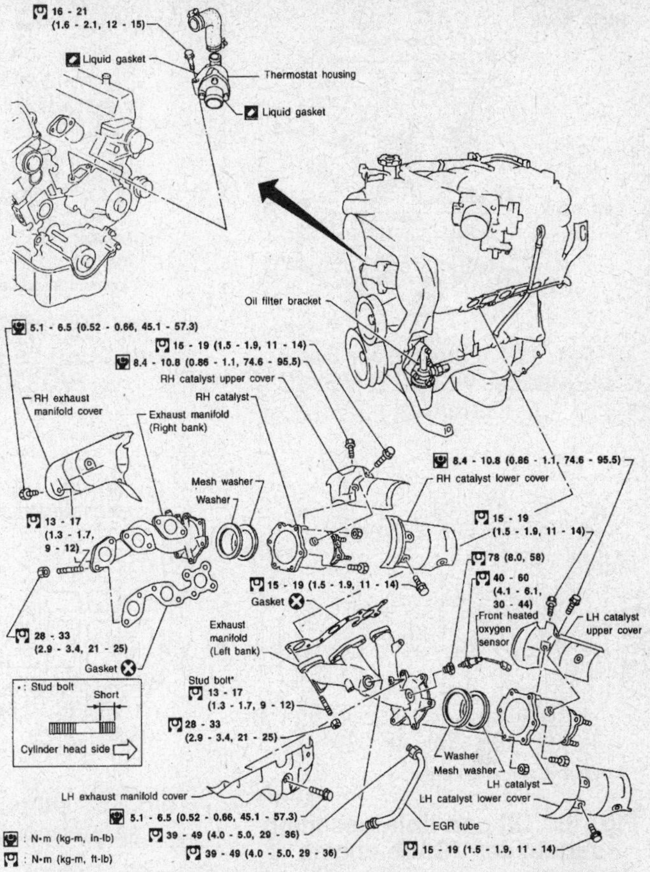
16 - 21 (1.6 - 2.1, 12 - 15)
Liquid gasket
Thermostat housing
Liquid gasket
Oil filter bracket
5.1 - 6.5 (0.52 - 0.66, 45.1 - 57.3)
15 - 19 (1.5 - 1.9, 11 - 14)
8.4 - 10.8 (0.86 - 1.1, 74.6 - 95.5)
RH catalyst upper cover
RH exhaust manifold cover
RH catalyst
Exhaust manifold (Right bank)
8.4 - 10.8 (0.86 - 1.1, 74.6 - 95.5)
RH catalyst lower cover
Mesh washer
Washer
13 - 17 (1.3 - 1.7, 9 - 12)
15 - 19 (1.5 - 1.9, 11 - 14)
78 (8.0, 58)
15 - 19 (1.5 - 1.9, 11 - 14)
40 - 60 (4.1 - 6.1, 30 - 44)
Gasket
Front heated oxygen sensor
LH catalyst upper cover
Exhaust manifold (Left bank)
28 - 33 (2.9 - 3.4, 21 - 25)
Gasket
•: Stud bolt
Short
Cylinder head side
Stud bolt*
13 - 17 (1.3 - 1.7, 9 - 12)
28 - 33 (2.9 - 3.4, 21 - 25)
Washer
Mesh washer
LH catalyst
LH catalyst lower cover
LH exhaust manifold cover
5.1 - 6.5 (0.52 - 0.66, 45.1 - 57.3)
EGR tube
39 - 49 (4.0 - 5.0, 29 - 36)
39 - 49 (4.0 - 5.0, 29 - 36)
15 - 19 (1.5 - 1.9, 11 - 14)
: N•m (kg-m, in-lb)
: N•m (kg-m, ft-lb)
NS1069600205020X

Fig. 5 Outer components (Part 2 of 2). VG33E engine

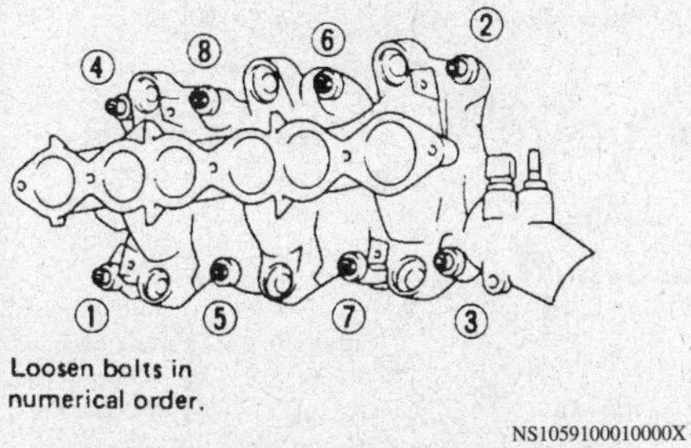
Loosen bolts in numerical order.
NS1059100010000X

Fig. 6 Intake manifold bolt loosening sequence. VG30E & VG33E engines

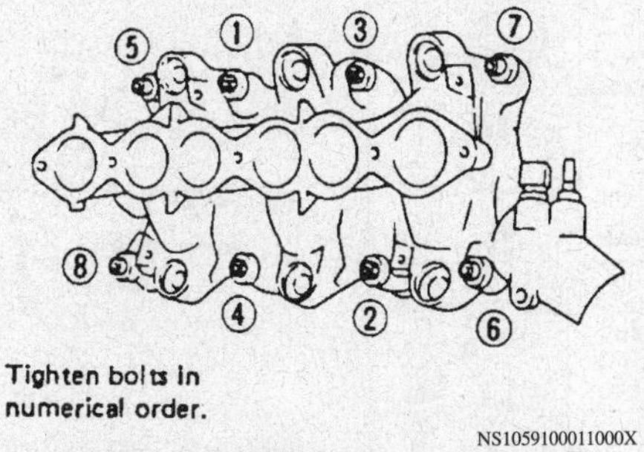
Tighten bolts in numerical order.
NS1059100011000X

Fig. 7 Intake manifold bolt tightening sequence. VG30E & VG33E engines

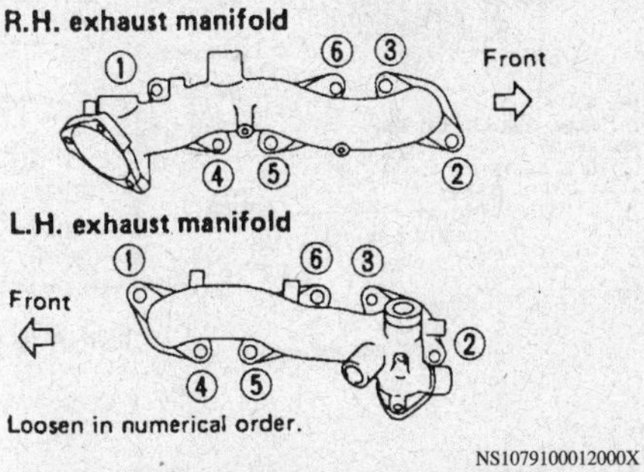
R.H. exhaust manifold
Front
L.H. exhaust manifold
Front
Loosen in numerical order.
NS1079100012000X

Fig. 8 Exhaust manifold bolt loosening sequence. VG30E engine

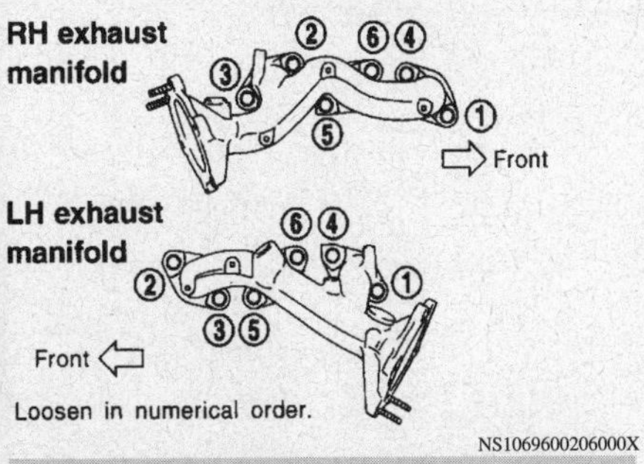
RH exhaust manifold
Front
LH exhaust manifold
Front
Loosen in numerical order.
NS1069600206000X

Fig. 9 Exhaust manifold bolt loosening sequence. VG33E engine

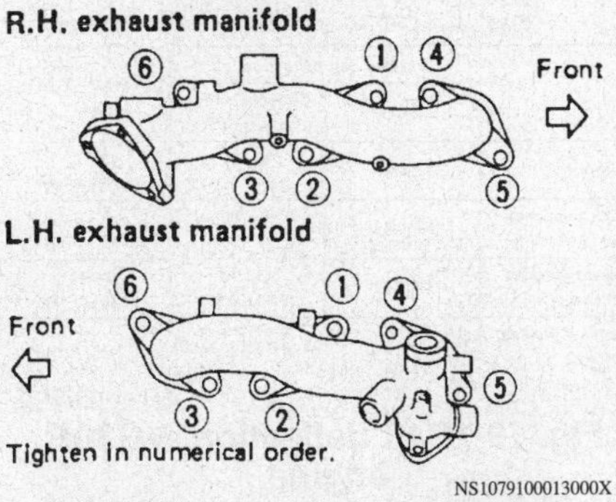
R.H. exhaust manifold
Front
L.H. exhaust manifold
Front
Tighten in numerical order.
NS1079100013000X

Fig. 10 Exhaust manifold bolt tightening sequence. VG30E engine

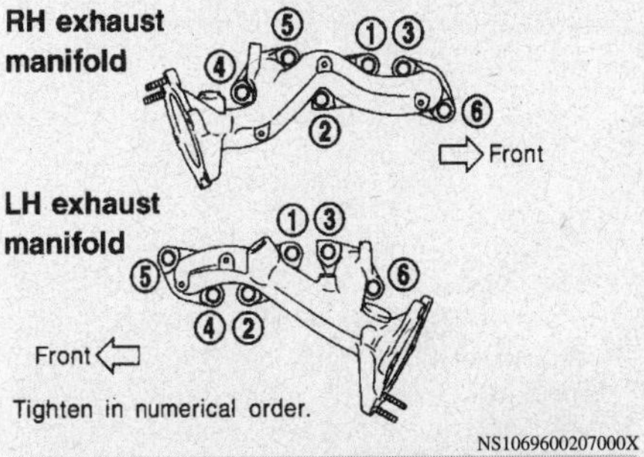
RH exhaust manifold
Front
LH exhaust manifold
Front
Tighten in numerical order.
NS1069600207000X

Fig. 11 Exhaust manifold bolt tightening sequence. VG33E engine

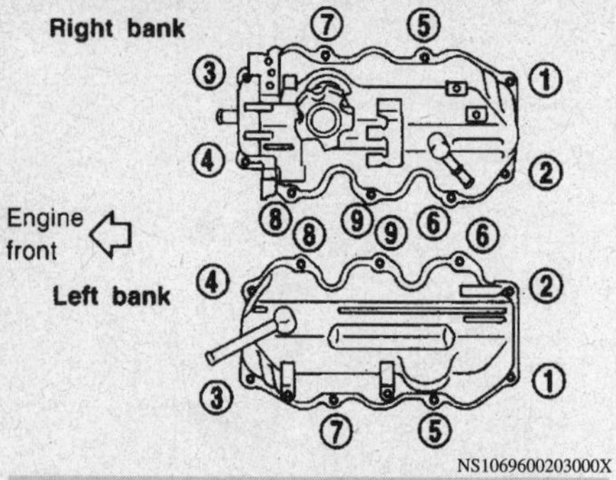
Right bank
Engine front
Left bank

NS1069600203000X

Fig. 12 Valve cover bolt sequence. VG30E & VG33E engines

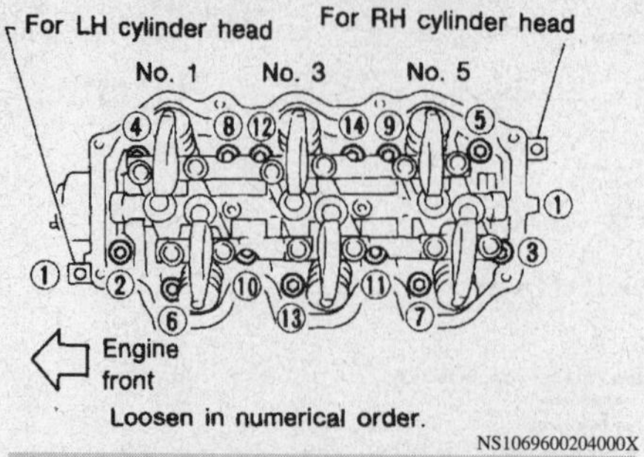
For LH cylinder head
For RH cylinder head
No. 1
No. 3
No. 5
Engine front
Loosen in numerical order.

NS1069600204000X

Fig. 13 Cylinder head bolt loosening sequence. VG30E & VG33E engines

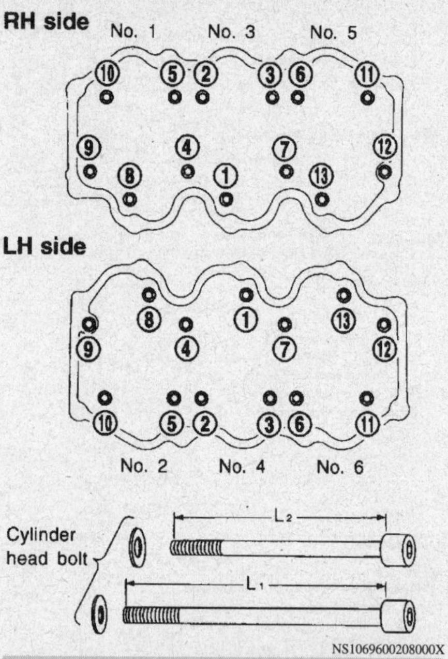
RH side
No. 1
No. 3
No. 5
LH side
No. 2
No. 4
No. 6
Cylinder head bolt
L₂
L₁

NS1069600208000X

Fig. 14 Cylinder head bolt tightening sequence. VG30E & VG33E engines

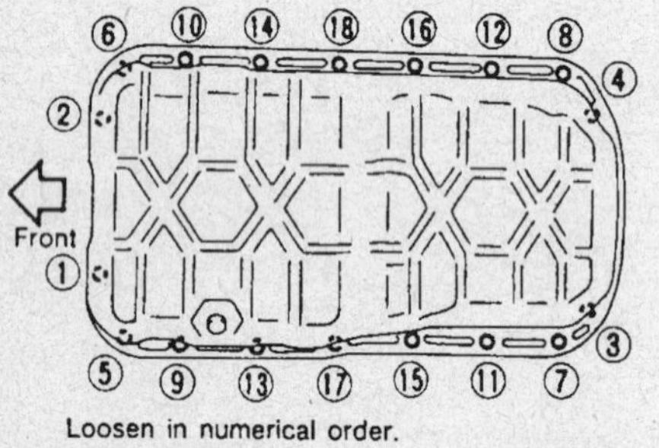
Front
Loosen in numerical order.

NS1099100014000X

Fig. 15 Oil pan bolt loosening sequence. VG30E engine

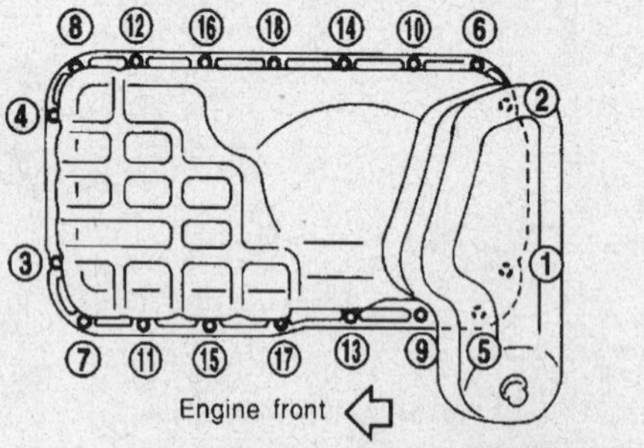
Engine front

NS1099600022000X

Fig. 16 Oil pan bolt loosening sequence. VG33E engine

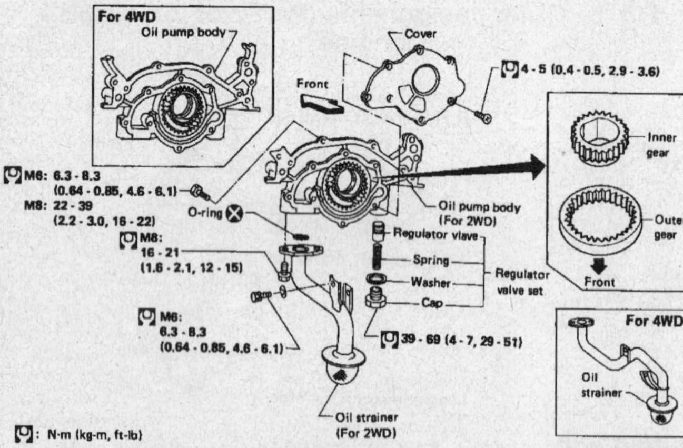
For 4WD
Oil pump body
Front
Cover
4 - 5 (0.4 - 0.5, 2.9 - 3.6)
M6: 6.3 - 8.3 (0.64 - 0.85, 4.6 - 6.1)
M8: 22 - 39 (2.2 - 3.0, 16 - 22)
O-ring
M8: 16 - 21 (1.6 - 2.1, 12 - 15)
Oil pump body (For 2WD)
Regulator viave
Spring
Washer
Cap
Regulator valve set
Inner gear
Outer gear
Front
M6: 6.3 - 8.3 (0.64 - 0.85, 4.6 - 6.1)
39 - 69 (4 - 7, 29 - 51)
For 4WD
Oil strainer
Oil strainer (For 2WD)
: N·m (kg-m, ft-lb)

NS1099300023000X

Fig. 17 Exploded view of oil pump. VG30E engine

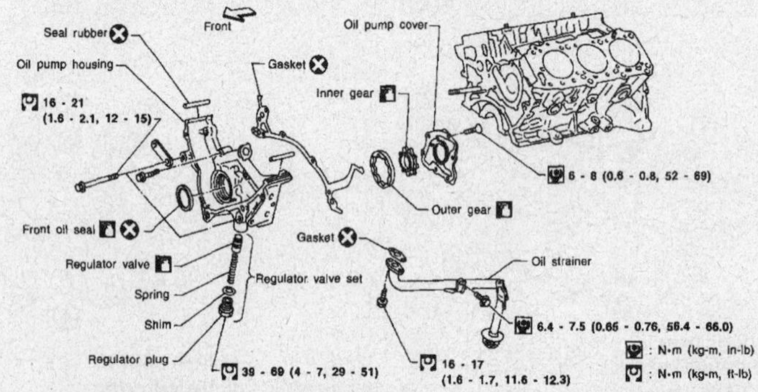
Seal rubber
Front
Oil pump cover
Oil pump housing
Gasket
Inner gear
16 - 21 (1.6 - 2.1, 12 - 15)
6 - 8 (0.6 - 0.8, 52 - 69)
Outer gear
Front oil seal
Gasket
Regulator valve
Regulator valve set
Oil strainer
Spring
Shim
6.4 - 7.5 (0.65 - 0.76, 56.4 - 66.0)
Regulator plug
39 - 69 (4 - 7, 29 - 51)
16 - 17 (1.6 - 1.7, 11.6 - 12.3)
: N·m (kg-m, in-lb)
: N·m (kg-m, ft-lb)

NS1099600024000X

Fig. 18 Exploded view of oil pump. VG33E engine

Unit: mm (in)

	Used belt deflection		Deflection of new belt
	Limit	Deflection after adjustment	
Alternator	12 (0.47)	6 - 8 (0.24 - 0.31)	5 - 7 (0.20 - 0.28)
Air conditioner compressor	16 (0.63)	9 - 11 (0.35 - 0.43)	7 - 9 (0.28 - 0.35)
Power steering oil pump	17 (0.67)	11 - 13 (0.43 - 0.51)	9 - 11 (0.35 - 0.43)
Applied pushing force	98 N (10 kg, 22 lb)		

NS1069100128000X

Fig. 19 Belt deflection. VG30E engine

Unit: mm (in)

	Used belt deflection		Deflection of new belt
	Limit	Deflection after adjustment	
Alternator	10.5 (0.413)	6 - 7 (0.24 - 0.28)	5.5 - 6.5 (0.217 - 0.256)
Air conditioner compressor	16.5 (0.650)	9 - 11 (0.35 - 0.43)	9 - 10 (0.35 - 0.39)
Power steering oil pump	18 (0.71)	9 - 10 (0.35 - 0.39)	9 - 11 (0.35 - 0.43)
Applied pushing force	98 N (10 kg, 22 lb)		

NS1069600209000X

Fig. 20 Belt deflection. VG33E engine

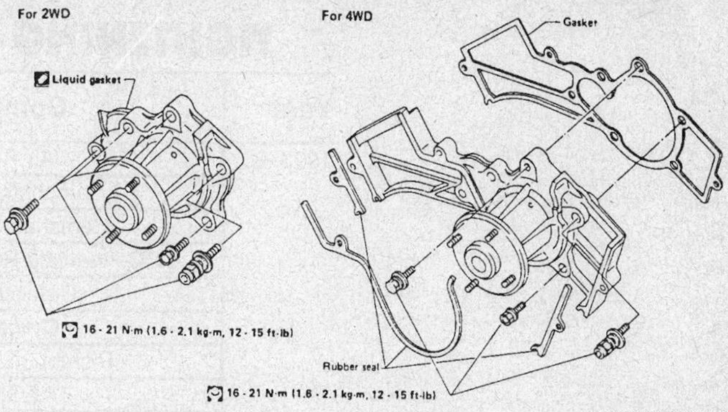
For 2WD
For 4WD
Gasket
Liquid gasket
16 - 21 N·m (1.6 - 2.1 kg-m, 12 - 15 ft-lb)
Rubber seal
16 - 21 N·m (1.6 - 2.1 kg-m, 12 - 15 ft-lb)

NS1089100014000X

Fig. 21 Water pump. VG30E & VG33E engines

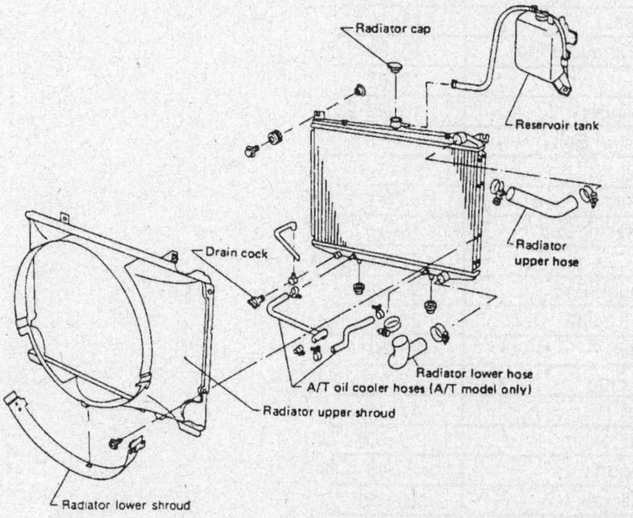
Radiator cap
Reservoir tank
Drain cock
Radiator upper hose
Radiator lower hose
A/T oil cooler hoses (A/T model only)
Radiator upper shroud
Radiator lower shroud

NS1089500048000X

Fig. 22 Radiator removal. VG30E engine

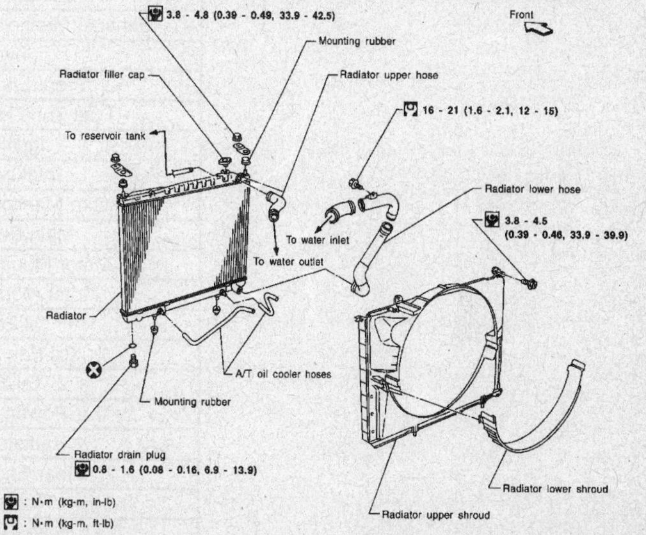
3.8 - 4.8 (0.39 - 0.49, 33.9 - 42.5)
Front
Mounting rubber
Radiator filler cap
Radiator upper hose
16 - 21 (1.6 - 2.1, 12 - 15)
To reservoir tank
Radiator lower hose
To water inlet
3.8 - 4.5 (0.39 - 0.46, 33.9 - 39.9)
To water outlet
Radiator
A/T oil cooler hoses
Mounting rubber
Radiator drain plug
0.8 - 1.6 (0.08 - 0.16, 6.9 - 13.9)
: N·m (kg-m, in-lb)
: N·m (kg-m, ft-lb)
Radiator lower shroud
Radiator upper shroud

NS1089600078000X

Fig. 23 Radiator removal. VG33E engine

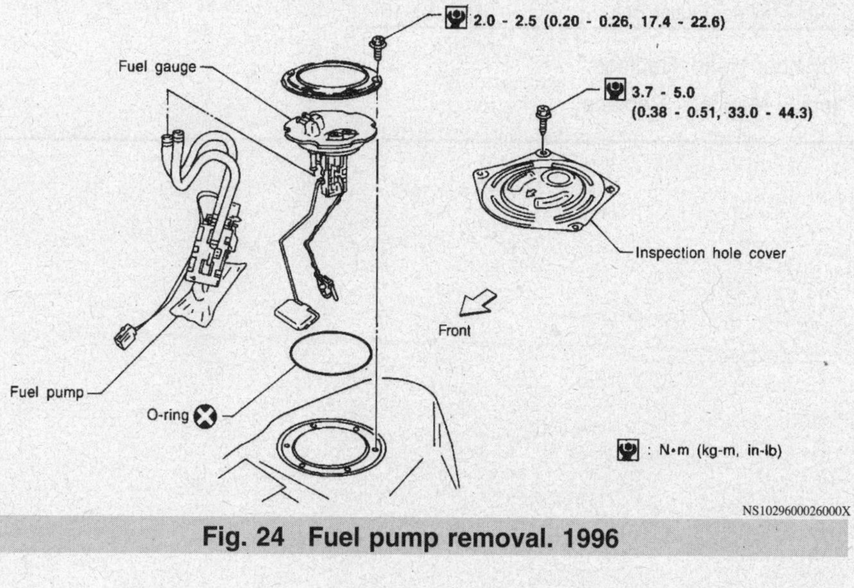
2.0 - 2.5 (0.20 - 0.26, 17.4 - 22.6)
Fuel gauge
3.7 - 5.0
(0.38 - 0.51, 33.0 - 44.3)
Inspection hole cover
Front
Fuel pump
O-ring
: N•m (kg-m, in-lb)

NS1029600026000X

Fig. 24 Fuel pump removal. 1996

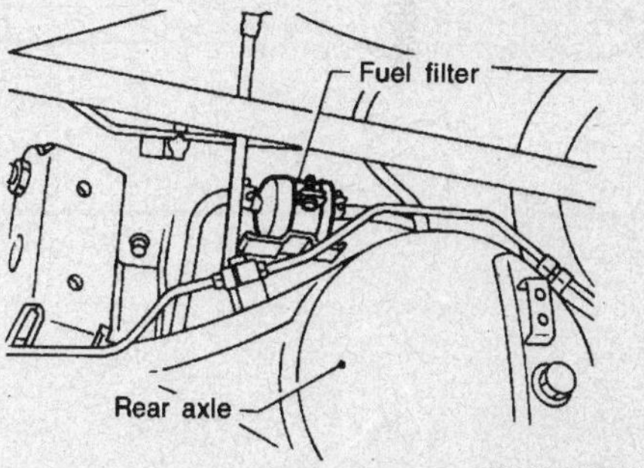
Fuel filter
Rear axle

NS1029600027000X

Fig. 25 Fuel filter. 1996

TIGHTENING SPECIFICATIONS

Year	Component	Torque/ Ft. Lbs.
1993–96	Air Regulator	6.2–8
	Camshaft Locate Plate	58–65
	Camshaft Sprocket Bolt	58–65
	Connecting Rod Bearing Caps	33–40
	Crankshaft Pulley	90–98
	Cylinder Head	①
	Distributor Mounting Bolt	10–12
	EGR Tube	25–33
	EGR Valve	9–12
	Exhaust Manifold	13–16
	Exhaust Manifold To Exhaust Pipe	16–20
	Flywheel	72–80
	Front Engine Slinger	16–22
	Fuel Tube Hold-Down Bolt	12–15
	Ignition Coil	5.1–5.8
	Intake Manifold	②
	Intake Manifold Collector Bolt	13–16
	Main Bearing Cap	67–74
	Motor Mount Through Bolt	30–38
	Motor Mount To Engine	23–31
	Oil Pan Bolts	3.6–5.1
	Oil Pan Drain Plug	22–29
	Oil Strainer	12–15
	Power Transistor	2.9–3.6
	Radiator Support	2.5–3
	Rear Engine Slinger	16–22
	Rocker Cover	.7–2.2
	Rocker Shaft	13–16
	Thermostat Housing	12–15
	Timing Belt Covers	2.2–3.6
	Timing Belt Tensioner	32–43
	Water Outlet Bolt	12–15

① — Refer to "Cylinder Head, Replace."

② — Refer to "Intake Manifold, Replace."

Clutch & Manual Transmission

INDEX

	Page No.
Adjustments	35-21
Clutch Pedal	35-21
Clutch, Replace	35-21
Hydraulic System Service	35-21
Clutch Master Cylinder, Replace	35-21
Clutch Operating Cylinder, Replace	35-21
Clutch System Bleed	35-21
Tightening Specifications	35-22
Transmission, Replace	35-21

ADJUSTMENTS

CLUTCH PEDAL

1. Adjust clutch pedal height, dimension "H" in **Fig. 1,** as follows:
   a. **On models with KA24E engines,** 9.29–9.69 inches.
   b. **On models with VG30E engines,** 8.94–9.33 inches.
   c. **On models with VG33E engines,** 7.13–7.52 inches.
2. **On all models,** adjust clearance between pedal stopper bracket and threaded end of clutch interlock switch with clutch pedal fully depressed. Clearance should be .012–.039 inch.
3. Measure clutch pedal freeplay as shown in **Fig. 1,** dimension "A."Clutch pedal freeplay is the sum of play between piston and piston rod. Clutch pedal freeplay should be as follows:
   a. On models with KA24E and VG30E engines, .039–.059 inch.
   b. On models with VG33E engines, .350–.630 inch.
4. **On all models,** adjust clutch pedal freeplay by rotating the clutch master cylinder pushrod inward or outward until the specified freeplay is obtained. After completing freeplay adjustment, tighten locknut.
5. After the above adjustments have been completed, cycle clutch pedal several times to ensure clutch linkage operates smoothly without binding.

HYDRAULIC SYSTEM SERVICE

CLUTCH MASTER CYLINDER, REPLACE

The clutch hydraulic system must be bled whenever a clutch line has been disconnected or when air has entered the system.

1. Disconnect clutch master cylinder pushrod from clutch pedal.
2. Disconnect clutch hydraulic line from clutch master cylinder.
3. Remove master cylinder mounting nuts and master cylinder.
4. Reverse procedure to install.

CLUTCH OPERATING CYLINDER, REPLACE

The clutch hydraulic system must be bled whenever a clutch line has been disconnected or when air has entered the system.

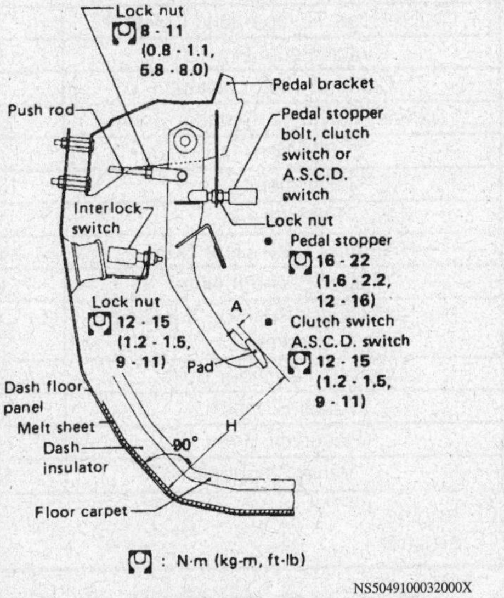

Lock nut
8 - 11
(0.8 - 1.1,
5.8 - 8.0)
Pedal bracket
Push rod
Pedal stopper bolt, clutch switch or A.S.C.D. switch
Interlock switch
Lock nut
● Pedal stopper
16 - 22
(1.6 - 2.2,
12 - 16)
Lock nut
12 - 15
(1.2 - 1.5,
9 - 11)
A
● Clutch switch
A.S.C.D. switch
12 - 15
(1.2 - 1.5,
9 - 11)
Pad
Dash floor panel
Melt sheet
Dash insulator
H
90°
Floor carpet
: N·m (kg-m, ft-lb)
NS5049100032000X

Fig. 1 Clutch pedal free travel & height adjustment

1. Disconnect hydraulic hose from clutch operating cylinder.
2. Remove mounting bolts and clutch operating cylinder.
3. Reverse procedure to install.

CLUTCH SYSTEM BLEED

Carefully monitor fluid level at master cylinder during bleeding operation.

1. Fill reservoir with recommended brake fluid.
2. Connect transparent vinyl tube to air bleeder valve, **Fig. 2.**
3. Fully depress clutch pedal several times.
4. With clutch pedal fully depressed, open bleeder valve to release air.
5. Close bleeder valve.
6. Repeat steps three through five until clear brake fluid comes out of bleeder valve.

CLUTCH

REPLACE

1. Remove transmission as outlined under "Transmission, Replace."
2. Insert a dummy shaft into the clutch disc hub.
3. Loosen clutch cover attaching bolts alternately.
4. Remove clutch disc and cover assembly.
5. Remove release bearing.

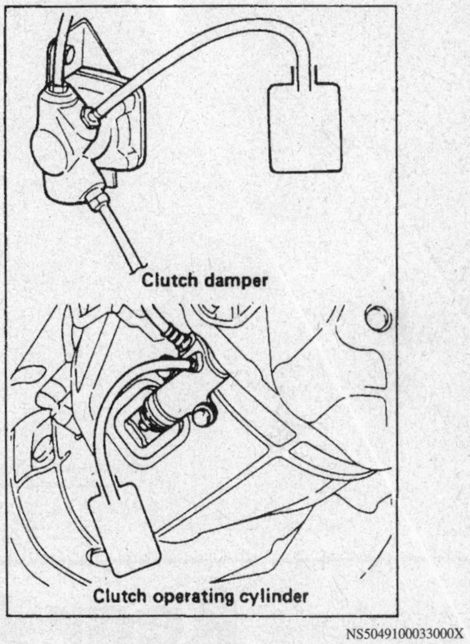

Clutch damper
Clutch operating cylinder
NS5049100033000X

Fig. 2 Clutch damper & operating cylinder bleed

6. Reverse procedure to install.

TRANSMISSION

REPLACE

1. Disconnect battery ground cable.
2. Raise and support vehicle.
3. Disconnect parking brake cable.
4. **On 2WD models,** remove propeller shaft.
5. **On 4WD models,** remove front and rear propeller shafts, torsion bar springs, then front differential carrier crossmember.
6. **On all models,** disconnect front exhaust pipe.
7. Disconnect electrical connectors as necessary.
8. **On 2WD models,** disconnect speedometer cable.
9. **On all models,** remove clutch operating cylinder.
10. Remove starter motor.
11. Support transmission with suitable jack.
12. Remove console box.
13. Place selector lever in Neutral position, then remove F-ring and selector lever.
14. Remove rear engine mount attaching nuts, then remove crossmember.

15. Remove transmission to engine attaching bolts.
16. Slide transmission rearward and lower from vehicle.
17. Reverse procedure to install.

TIGHTENING SPECIFICATIONS

Year	Component	Torque/Ft. Lbs.
1993–96	Air Bleeder	5.1–6.5
	Clutch Cover Bolt	16–22
	Clutch Hose Eye Bolt	12–14
	Clutch Hose Mounting Bracket	5.8–8
	Clutch Hose To Operating Cylinder	12–14
	Clutch Pedal Bracket	5.8–8
	Clutch Switch Locknut	9–11
	Damper Cover To Cylinder Body	2.7–3.7
	Flywheel①	72–80
	Flywheel②	105–112
	Fulcrum Pin	12–16
	Hydraulic Tube Flare Nuts	11–13
	Master Cylinder Nuts	5.8–8
	Master Cylinder Pushrod Adjusting Locknut	5.8–8.7
	Operating Cylinder Bolts	22–30
	Pedal Stopper	12–16
	Reservoir Band	1.8–2.9
	Valve Stopper	1.1–2.2

① — VG30E engine.
② — KA24E engine.

Rear Axle & Suspension

INDEX

	Page No.
Coil Spring, Replace	35-23
Leaf Spring, Replace	35-23
Rear Axle, Replace	35-22
Pathfinder	35-22
Pickup	35-22
Rear Axle Shaft, Replace	35-22
Disc Brakes	35-23
Drum Brakes	35-22
Shock Absorber, Replace	35-23
Stabilizer Bar, Replace	35-23
Tightening Specifications	35-26

REAR AXLE

REPLACE

PATHFINDER

1. Raise and support vehicle.
2. Disconnect brake hydraulic line and parking brake cable.
3. Support axle with suitable jack.
4. Disconnect stabilizer rod, upper and lower links and the panhard rod from body, **Figs. 1 and 2.**
5. Disconnect propeller shaft.
6. Remove upper shock absorber attaching nuts.
7. Lower jack slowly until coil spring are extended fully.
8. Reverse procedure to install. When tightening rubber parts, vehicle should be in unloaded condition with tires on ground.

PICKUP

1. Raise and support vehicle.
2. Disconnect brake hydraulic line and parking brake cable.
3. Support axle with suitable jack.
4. Disconnect propeller shaft.
5. Remove upper shock absorber attaching nuts.
6. Remove front and rear leaf spring attaching bolts and nuts.
7. Lower axle assembly with jack.
8. Reverse procedure to install. When tightening rubber parts, vehicle should be in unloaded condition with tires on ground.

REAR AXLE SHAFT

REPLACE

DRUM BRAKES

1. Raise and support rear of vehicle and remove rear wheel.
2. Disconnect parking brake cable and brake hydraulic line. Plug end of hydraulic line to prevent fluid loss and entrance of dirt.
3. Remove wheel bearing cage to baffle plate attaching nuts, **Figs. 3 through 5.**
4. Using axle shaft puller tool No. KV40101000 and slide hammer tool No. ST36230000, or equivalents, remove axle shaft assembly from rear axle case, **Fig. 6.**
5. Replace oil seal in axle case.
6. Support axle assembly in a vise, and unbend lock washer away from bearing locknut.
7. Remove bearing locknut as shown in **Fig. 7.**
8. Remove wheel bearing, bearing cage and baffle plate from axle shaft using bearing puller tool No. HT72480000

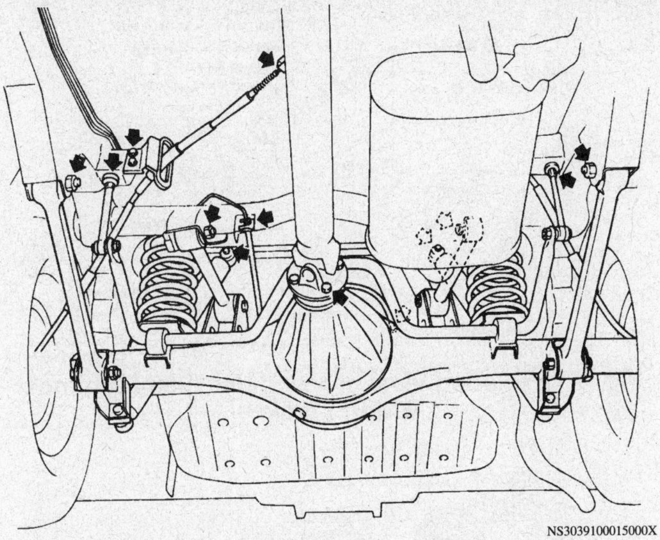
NS3039100015000X

Fig. 1 Rear axle replacement. 1993–95 Pathfinder

(J25852–B), or equivalent, **Fig. 8.**

9. Remove grease seal in bearing cage with screwdriver or equivalent.
10. Remove wheel bearing assembly with a brass drift or equivalent.
11. Reverse procedure to install, noting the following:
    a. When installing new oil seal, coat sealing lip with multi-purpose grease.
    b. Apply gear oil to spline of axle shaft and multi-purpose grease to seal surface of axle shaft.
    c. Adjust axle endplay to specification in "Drive Axle" section.

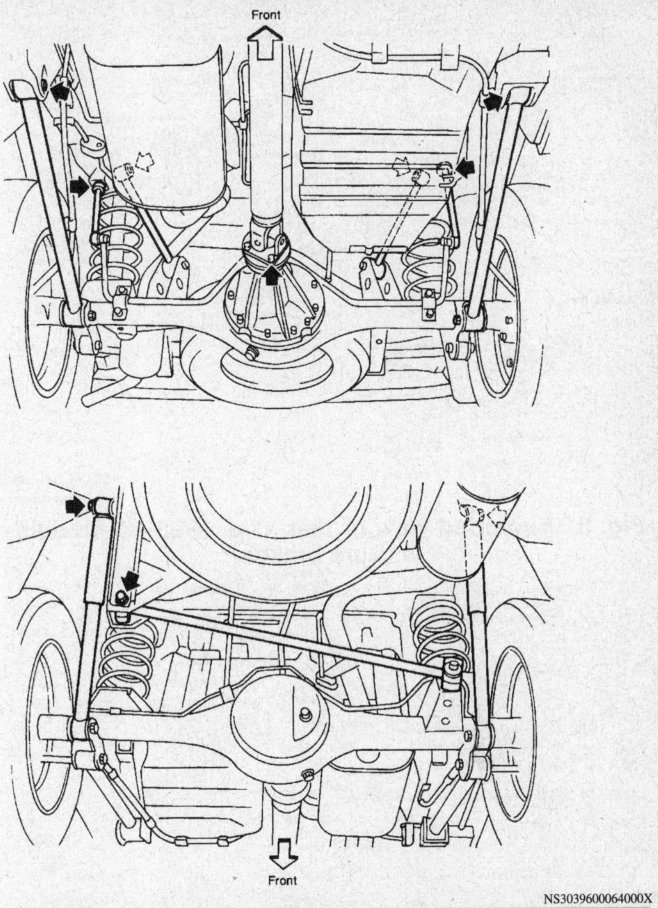
Front
Front
NS3039600064000X

Fig. 2 Rear axle replacement. 1996 Pathfinder

DISC BRAKES

1. Raise and support rear of vehicle and remove rear wheels.
2. Remove brake caliper assembly and rotor.
3. Disconnect parking brake cable and brake tube.
4. Remove nuts securing bearing housing to baffle plate, **Fig. 9.**
5. Using sliding hammer tool No. ST36230000 and axle stand tool No. KV40101000, or equivalents, pull out axle shaft, **Fig. 10.**
6. Remove oil seal from axle housing.
7. Mount axle shaft in a suitable vise, then using a screwdriver, unbend lock washer. **Do not reuse lock washer.**
8. Remove bearing locknut, **Fig. 7.**
9. Remove wheel bearing, bearing housing and baffle plate from axle shaft.
10. Remove bearing outer side inner race from axle shaft.
11. Remove bearing outer race with suitable tool, **Fig. 11.**
12. Reverse procedure to install.

SHOCK ABSORBER

REPLACE

1. Raise and support rear of vehicle.
2. Disconnect shock absorber at upper and lower mountings, **Figs. 12 through 14.**
3. Remove shock absorber from vehicle.
4. Reverse procedure to install.

COIL SPRING

REPLACE

1. Raise vehicle and support underbody member on both sides.
2. Support rear axle with floor jack and remove both lower shock absorber mounting bolts. Remove rear wheels if necessary.
3. Slowly lower rear axle assembly and remove coil springs after they are fully extended.
4. Reverse procedure to install.

LEAF SPRING

REPLACE

1. Raise and support rear of vehicle at chassis. Support rear axle to relieve tension from spring.
2. Disconnect shock absorber at lower mounting and remove U-bolts and spring plates.
3. **On 4WD models,** remove one or two parking brake rear cable clamps on side of leaf springs.
4. **On 2WD models,** raise jack under differential. On 4WD pickup models, lower jack.
5. **On all models,** disconnect spring from rear shackle, **Figs. 12 and 13.**
6. Disconnect spring from front body attachment.
7. Remove spring from vehicle.
8. Reverse procedure to install.

STABILIZER BAR

REPLACE

1. Raise and support vehicle.
2. Remove exhaust assembly as necessary.
3. Disconnect stabilizer bar from bushing and locating bolts, then remove stabilizer bar.
4. Reverse procedure to install.

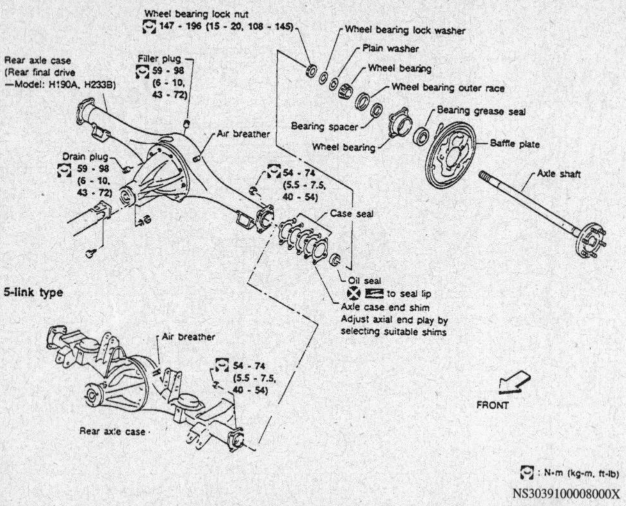
Wheel bearing lock nut
147 - 196 (15 - 20, 108 - 145)
Wheel bearing lock washer
Plain washer
Wheel bearing
Wheel bearing outer race
Bearing grease seal
Baffle plate
Axle shaft
Rear axle case
(Rear final drive
—Model: H190A, H233B)
Filler plug
59 - 98
(6 - 10,
43 - 72)
Air breather
Bearing spacer
Wheel bearing
Drain plug
59 - 98
(6 - 10,
43 - 72)
54 - 74
(5.5 - 7.5,
40 - 54)
Case seal
Oil seal
to seal lip
Axle case end shim
Adjust axial end play by
selecting suitable shims
5-link type
Air breather
54 - 74
(5.5 - 7.5,
40 - 54)
Rear axle case
FRONT
: N·m (kg-m, ft-lb)
NS3039100008000X

Fig. 3 Exploded view of rear axle. 1993–95 Models w/drum brakes

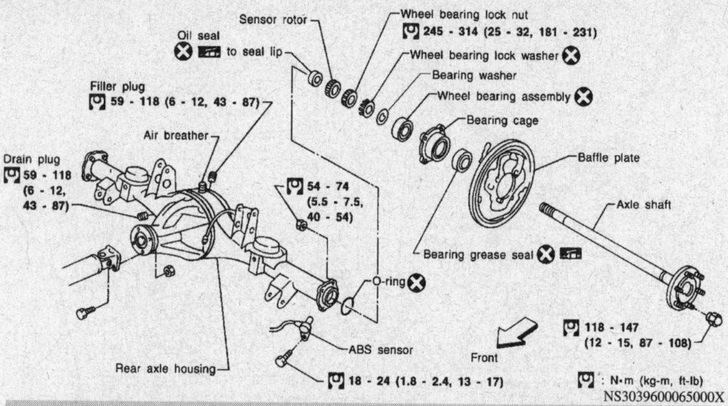
Sensor rotor
Oil seal
to seal lip
Wheel bearing lock nut
245 - 314 (25 - 32, 181 - 231)
Wheel bearing lock washer
Bearing washer
Wheel bearing assembly
Bearing cage
Filler plug
59 - 118 (6 - 12, 43 - 87)
Air breather
Drain plug
59 - 118
(6 - 12,
43 - 87)
54 - 74
(5.5 - 7.5,
40 - 54)
Baffle plate
Axle shaft
Bearing grease seal
O-ring
ABS sensor
Front
118 - 147
(12 - 15, 87 - 108)
Rear axle housing
18 - 24 (1.8 - 2.4, 13 - 17)
: N·m (kg-m, ft-lb)
NS3039600065000X

Fig. 4 Exploded view of rear axle. 1996 Pathfinder w/drum brakes

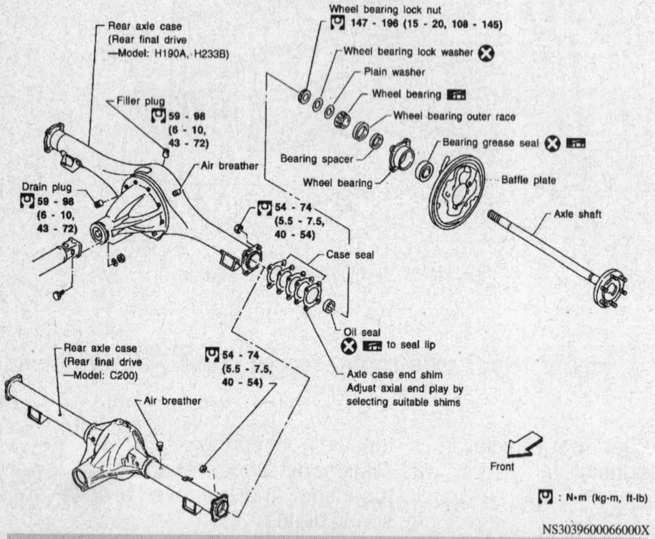
Rear axle case
(Rear final drive
—Model: H190A, H233B)
Wheel bearing lock nut
147 - 196 (15 - 20, 108 - 145)
Wheel bearing lock washer
Plain washer
Wheel bearing
Wheel bearing outer race
Filler plug
59 - 98
(6 - 10,
43 - 72)
Bearing grease seal
Bearing spacer
Air breather
Wheel bearing
Baffle plate
Drain plug
59 - 98
(6 - 10,
43 - 72)
54 - 74
(5.5 - 7.5,
40 - 54)
Axle shaft
Case seal
Oil seal
to seal lip
Rear axle case
(Rear final drive
—Model: C200)
54 - 74
(5.5 - 7.5,
40 - 54)
Air breather
Axle case end shim
Adjust axial end play by
selecting suitable shims
Front
: N·m (kg-m, ft-lb)
NS3039600066000X

Fig. 5 Exploded view of rear axle. 1996 Pickup w/drum brakes

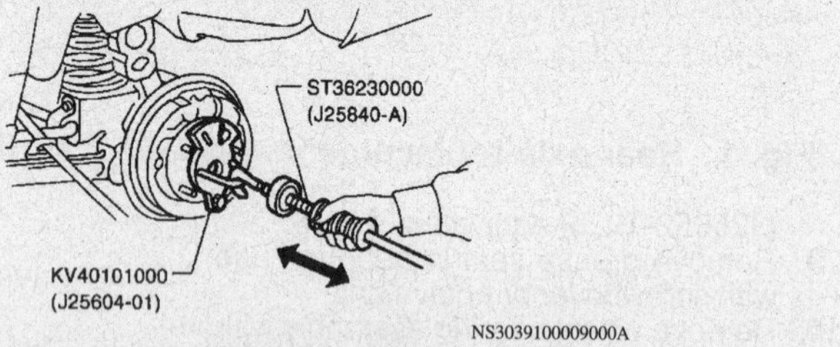
ST36230000
(J25840-A)
KV40101000
(J25604-01)
NS3039100009000A

Fig. 6 Axle shaft removal. Models w/drum brakes

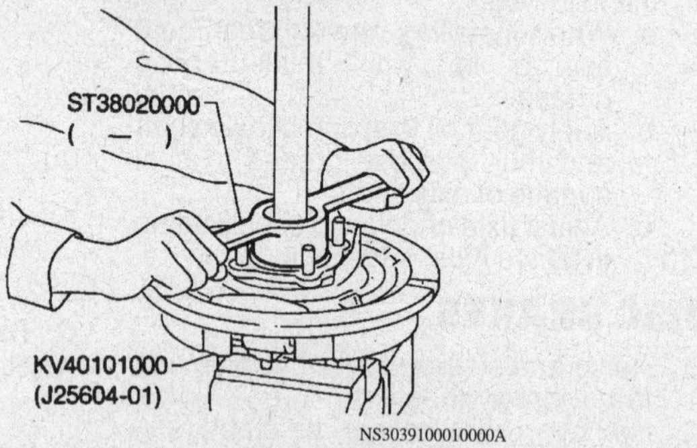
ST38020000
(—)
KV40101000
(J25604-01)
NS3039100010000A

Fig. 7 Rear axle bearing locknut removal

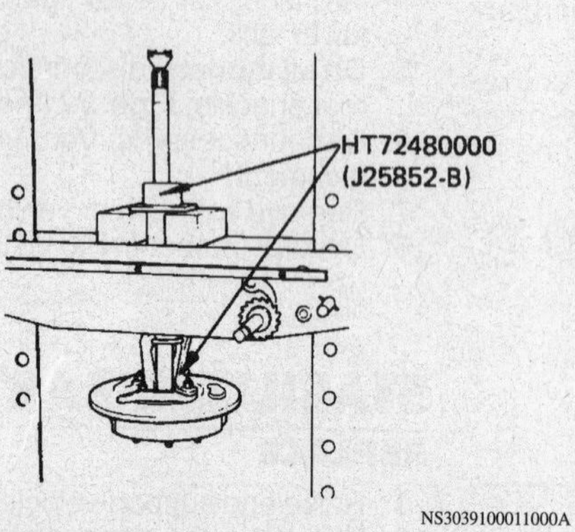
HT72480000
(J25852-B)
NS3039100011000A

Fig. 8 Wheel bearing removal. Models w/drum brakes

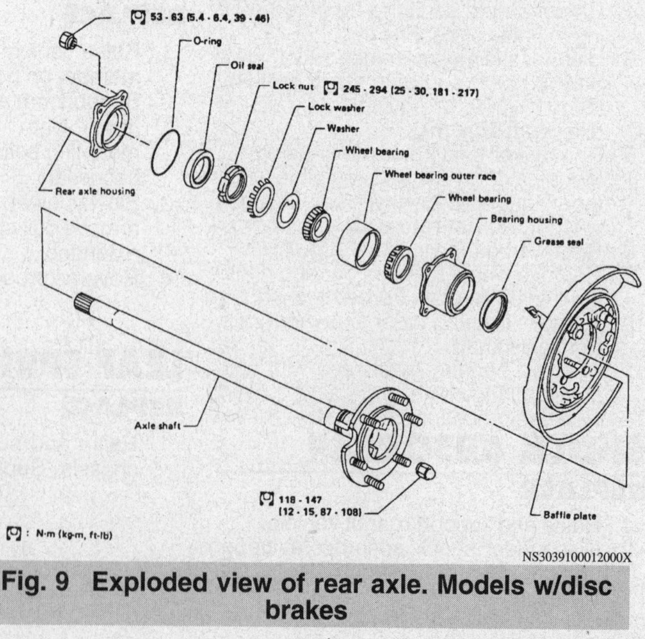
53 - 63 (5.4 - 6.4, 39 - 46)
O-ring
Oil seal
Lock nut
245 - 294 (25 - 30, 181 - 217)
Lock washer
Washer
Wheel bearing
Wheel bearing outer race
Wheel bearing
Bearing housing
Grease seal
Rear axle housing
Axle shaft
118 - 147
(12 - 15, 87 - 108)
Baffle plate
: N·m (kg-m, ft-lb)
NS3039100012000X

Fig. 9 Exploded view of rear axle. Models w/disc brakes

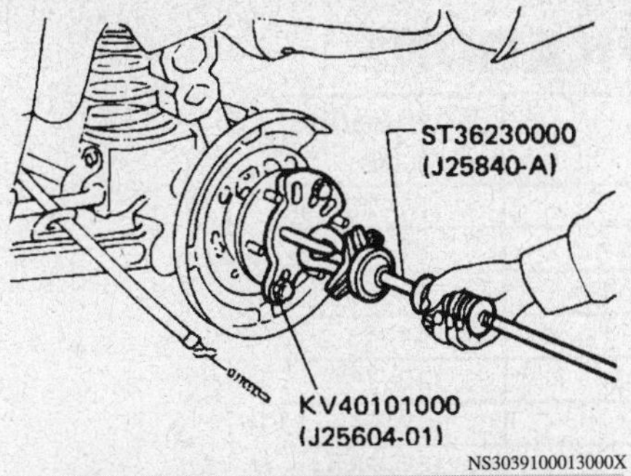
ST36230000
(J25840-A)
KV40101000
(J25604-01)
NS3039100013000X

Fig. 10 Axle shaft removal. Models w/disc brakes

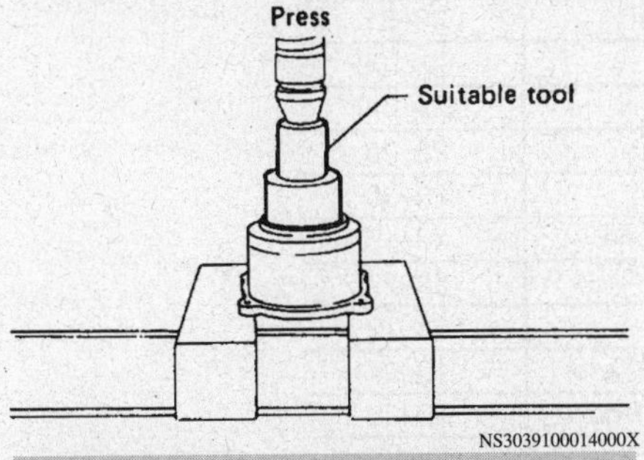
Press
Suitable tool
NS3039100014000X

Fig. 11 Outer race removal. Models w/disc brakes

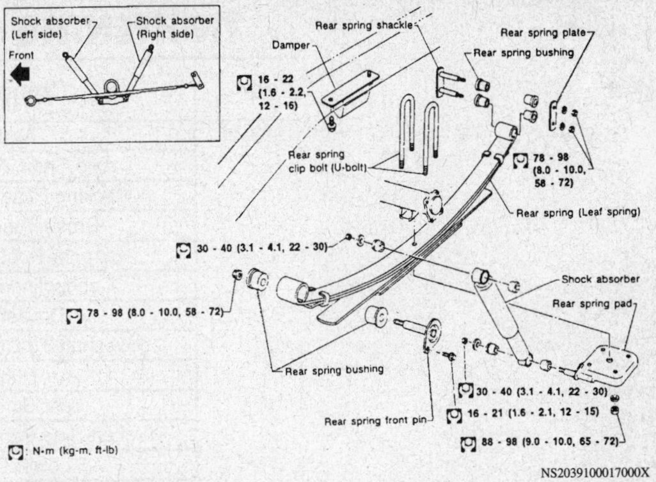
Shock absorber (Left side)
Shock absorber (Right side)
Front
Rear spring shackle
Damper
Rear spring plate
Rear spring bushing
16 - 22 (1.6 - 2.2, 12 - 16)
Rear spring clip bolt (U-bolt)
78 - 98 (8.0 - 10.0, 58 - 72)
Rear spring (Leaf spring)
30 - 40 (3.1 - 4.1, 22 - 30)
Shock absorber
Rear spring pad
78 - 98 (8.0 - 10.0, 58 - 72)
Rear spring bushing
30 - 40 (3.1 - 4.1, 22 - 30)
16 - 21 (1.6 - 2.1, 12 - 15)
Rear spring front pin
88 - 98 (9.0 - 10.0, 65 - 72)
: N·m (kg-m, ft-lb)
NS2039100017000X

Fig. 12 Leaf spring rear suspension. 2WD models

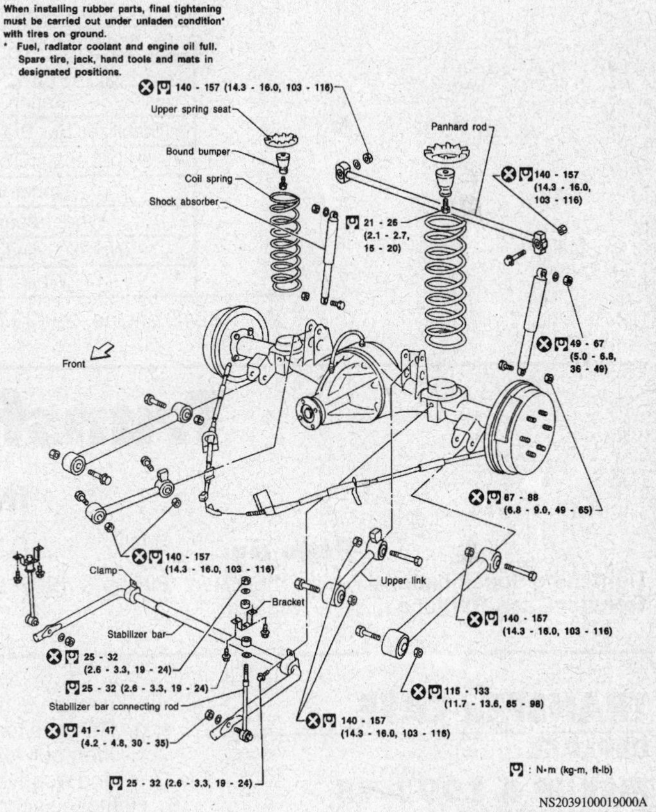
When installing rubber parts, final tightening must be carried out under unladen condition* with tires on ground.
* Fuel, radiator coolant and engine oil full. Spare tire, jack, hand tools and mats in designated positions.
140 - 157 (14.3 - 16.0, 103 - 116)
Upper spring seat
Panhard rod
Bound bumper
Coil spring
140 - 157 (14.3 - 16.0, 103 - 116)
Shock absorber
21 - 26 (2.1 - 2.7, 15 - 20)
49 - 67 (5.0 - 6.8, 36 - 49)
Front
67 - 88 (6.8 - 9.0, 49 - 65)
140 - 157 (14.3 - 16.0, 103 - 116)
Clamp
Upper link
Bracket
140 - 157 (14.3 - 16.0, 103 - 116)
Stabilizer bar
25 - 32 (2.6 - 3.3, 19 - 24)
25 - 32 (2.6 - 3.3, 19 - 24)
115 - 133 (11.7 - 13.6, 85 - 98)
Stabilizer bar connecting rod
41 - 47 (4.2 - 4.8, 30 - 35)
140 - 157 (14.3 - 16.0, 103 - 116)
: N·m (kg-m, ft-lb)
25 - 32 (2.6 - 3.3, 19 - 24)
NS2039100019000A

Fig. 14 Coil spring rear suspension

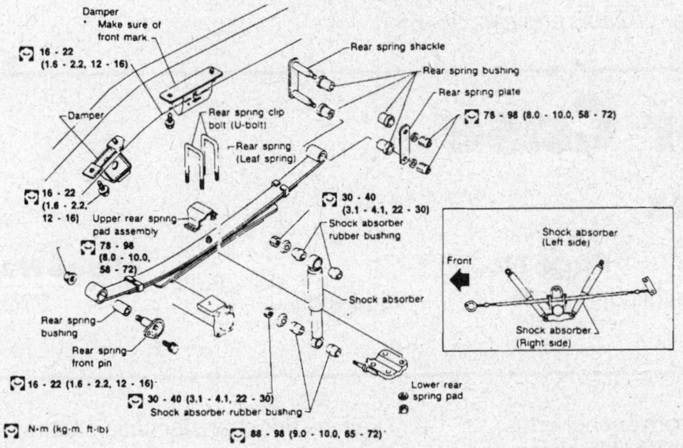
Damper
* Make sure of front mark.
16 - 22 (1.6 - 2.2, 12 - 16)
Rear spring shackle
Rear spring bushing
Rear spring plate
Damper
Rear spring clip bolt (U-bolt)
78 - 98 (8.0 - 10.0, 58 - 72)
Rear spring (Leaf spring)
16 - 22 (1.6 - 2.2, 12 - 16)
Upper rear spring pad assembly
78 - 98 (8.0 - 10.0, 58 - 72)
30 - 40 (3.1 - 4.1, 22 - 30)
Shock absorber rubber bushing
Shock absorber (Left side)
Front
Shock absorber
Shock absorber (Right side)
Rear spring bushing
Rear spring front pin
16 - 22 (1.6 - 2.2, 12 - 16)
30 - 40 (3.1 - 4.1, 22 - 30)
Shock absorber rubber bushing
Lower rear spring pad
N·m (kg-m, ft-lb)
88 - 98 (9.0 - 10.0, 65 - 72)
NS2039100018000X

Fig. 13 Leaf spring rear suspension. 4WD models

TIGHTENING SPECIFICATIONS

Year	Component	Torque/Ft. Lbs.
1993–96	Axle Nut	181–231
	Axle Shaft To Wheel Hub	42–55
	Backing Plate Mounting Bolt	39–46
	Brake Tube Flare Nut	11–13
	Bumper Rubber Fixing Bolt	12–15
	Connecting Rod To Body	19–24
	Driveshaft Nut	181–231
	Driveshaft To Companion Flange	①
	Hub Nut	181–231
	Leaf Spring U-bolt	65–72
	Left Side Panhard Rod Nut	36–51
	Lower Link Bolt	80–108
	Right Side Panhard Rod Bolt	80–108
	Shock Absorber Lower Nut	22–30
	Shock Absorber Upper Nut	22–30
	Spring Front Pin Bolt To Frame	12–15
	Spring Front Pin Nut	58–72
	Spring Shackle	58–72
	Stabilizer Bar Bracket To Axle Case	19–24
	Stabilizer Bar To Connecting Rod	30–35
	Upper Link Bolt	80–108
	Wheel Bearing Locknut	181–231
	Wheel Cylinder Air Breather	5.1–6.5
	Wheel Lug Nut	87–108

①— KA24E engine, 29–33 ft. lbs.; VG30E engines, 58–65 ft. lbs.

Transfer Case

INDEX

Page No.		Page No.		Page No.	
Tightening Specifications	35-27	Pickup & 1993–95 Pathfinder ...	35-26	1996 Pathfinder.................	35-26
Transfer Case, Replace	35-26				

TRANSFER CASE

REPLACE

PICKUP & 1993–95 PATHFINDER

1. Raise and support vehicle.
2. Drain oil from transfer case and transmission.
3. Put match marks on flanges and separate propeller shaft from final drive.
4. Pull propeller shaft from transmission, then plug rear oil seal.
5. Remove torsion bar spring as follows:
   a. Remove wheel.
   b. Remove anchor arm bolt.
   c. Remove dust cover, then disconnect snap ring from anchor arm.
   d. Remove torque arm attaching nuts, then pull torsion bar spring forward and remove with torque arm.
6. Remove second crossmember.
7. Remove transfer control lever from transfer outer shift lever.
8. Carefully remove transfer case from transmission.
9. Reverse procedure to install. Apply suitable sealant to mating surfaces and tighten transfer case mounting bolts to specifications.

1996 PATHFINDER

1. Raise and support vehicle.
2. Drain oil from transfer case and transmission.
3. Remove exhaust front and rear tubes.
4. Remove front and rear propeller shaft.
5. Insert plug into rear oil seal.
6. Disconnect neutral safety position and 4WD switch harness connectors.
7. Remove transfer control lever from transfer outer shift lever.
8. Carefully remove transfer case from transmission.
9. Reverse procedure to install. Apply Nissan sealant part No. KP610-00250, or equivalent, to mating surfaces and tighten transfer case mounting bolts to specifications.

TIGHTENING SPECIFICATIONS

Year	Component	Torque/Ft. Lbs.
1993–96	Anchor Bolt Locknut	22–30
	Drain Plug	18–25
	Front Propeller Shaft Flange Nut	29–33
	Rear Propeller Shaft Locknut	181–217
	Transfer Case Mounting Bolts	23–30
	Transfer Control Lever Bracket Screws	12–15

Front Suspension & Steering

INDEX

	Page No.
Ball Joint, Replace	35-28
Pickup & 1993–95 Pathfinder	35-28
1996 Pathfinder	35-29
Ball Joint Inspection	35-28
Pickup & 1993–95 Pathfinder	35-28
1996 Pathfinder	35-28
Hub & Bearing, Replace	35-27
2WD	35-28
4WD	35-27
Locking Hub Service	35-27
Manual Steering Gear, Replace	35-31
Manual Steering Gears	36-1
Power Steering	36-1
Power Steering Gear, Replace	35-30
Pickup & 1993–95 Pathfinder	35-30
1996 Pathfinder	35-30
Power Steering Pump, Replace	35-30
Power Steering Transfer Gear, Replace	35-30
1996 Pathfinder	35-30
Shock Absorber, Replace	35-29
Pickup & 1993–95 Pathfinder	35-29
Stabilizer Bar, Replace	35-30
Strut Damper, Replace	35-30
1996 Pathfinder	35-30
Tightening Specifications	35-32
Torsion Bar, Replace	35-29
Pickup & 1993–95 Pathfinder	35-29
Wheel Bearing, Adjust	35-27

WHEEL BEARING

ADJUST

Prior to adjusting wheel bearing preload, ensure bearings are in satisfactory condition and properly lubricated. Apply suitable grease to threaded portion of spindle and the contact surface of the outer bearing to ensure proper adjustment.

1. Raise and support front of vehicle, then remove wheel and locking hub assembly.
2. Remove caliper retaining bolts and secure caliper aside. **Do not allow caliper to hang from brake hose.**
3. Tighten wheel bearing locknut to specification, then rotate hub several revolutions in both directions to seat bearings.
4. Loosen wheel bearing nut until torque on nut is zero and bearing axial play is zero.
5. **Torque** bearing locknut to .4–1.1 ft. lbs., then rotate hub several revolutions to seat bearings, then **torque** locknut an additional .4–1.1 ft. lbs.
6. Connect spring scale to wheel stud, measure hub starting torque through 90° of rotation and record measurement as "A."
7. Install lock washer and retaining screw, if equipped, tightening bearing locknut up to an additional 30° to align washer and nut.
8. Rotate hub several turns in each direction to seat bearings, then connect spring scale to wheel stud, measure hub starting torque through 90° of rotation and record measurement as "B."
9. Calculate wheel bearing preload by subtracting measurement A from measurement B. If remainder is not 1.59–4.72 lbs., repeat steps 3–8 until correct preload is obtained.
10. If bearings do not operate smoothly, or if preload cannot be properly adjusted as outlined, remove hub and inspect bearings.

LOCKING HUB SERVICE

1. Place locking hub in free position, raise and support front of vehicle, and remove wheel.
2. Remove bolts securing locking hub housing.
3. With brake pedal depressed, remove housing assembly, **Figs. 1 and 2.**
4. **On models with manual locking hub,** remove snap ring from drive axle, then withdraw drive clutch from hub.
5. **On models with automatic locking hub,** proceed as follows:
   a. Remove snap ring from drive axle, then withdraw washer A, washer B and brake B from hub, **Fig. 3.**
   b. Remove brake A from housing, assemble brakes A and B together as shown in **Fig. 3,** then measure thickness of assembly. If assembly thickness is less than .606 inch (15.4 mm), brakes should be replaced.
   c. Reassemble housing using new O-ring.
6. **On all models,** reverse procedure to install, using new snap rings and tighten locking hub mounting bolts to specification.

HUB & BEARING

REPLACE

4WD

1. Remove locking hub as outlined.
2. Remove brake caliper retaining bolts and secure caliper aside. **Do not allow caliper to hang from brake hose.**
3. Remove retaining screw and lock washer, then remove bearing locknut using suitable puller.
4. Remove hub assembly from steering knuckle, taking care not to drop outer bearing.
5. Remove outer bearing, pry seal from rear of hub, then remove inner bearing.
6. Scribe matching marks between hub and rotor, then separate rotor from hub.
7. Clean hub and bearings with suitable solvent and blow dry with compressed air.
8. Inspect bearings for damage scoring and wear, and replace as needed.
9. If bearings are to be replaced, replace bearing outer races as follows:
   a. Drive outer races from hub using suitable drift.
   b. Install new outer races using suitable driver. Ensure races are fully seated in hub. Replace hub if bearing outer races are loose in hub.
10. Pack bearings with suitable grease,

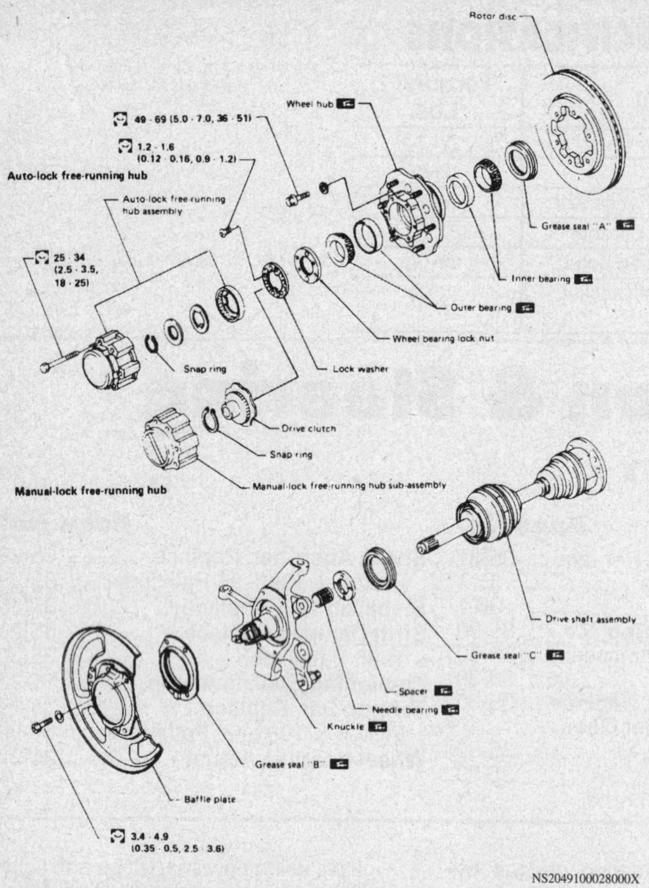
Rotor disc
Wheel hub
49 - 69 (5.0 - 7.0, 36 - 51)
1.2 - 1.6 (0.12 - 0.16, 0.9 - 1.2)
Auto-lock free-running hub
Auto-lock free-running hub assembly
25 - 34 (2.5 - 3.5, 18 - 25)
Grease seal "A"
Inner bearing
Outer bearing
Wheel bearing lock nut
Snap ring
Lock washer
Drive clutch
Snap ring
Manual-lock free-running hub
Manual-lock free-running hub sub-assembly
Drive shaft assembly
Grease seal "C"
Spacer
Needle bearing
Knuckle
Grease seal "B"
Baffle plate
3.4 - 4.9 (0.35 - 0.5, 2.5 - 3.6)
NS2049100028000X

Fig. 1 Exploded view of front axle. 4WD Pickup

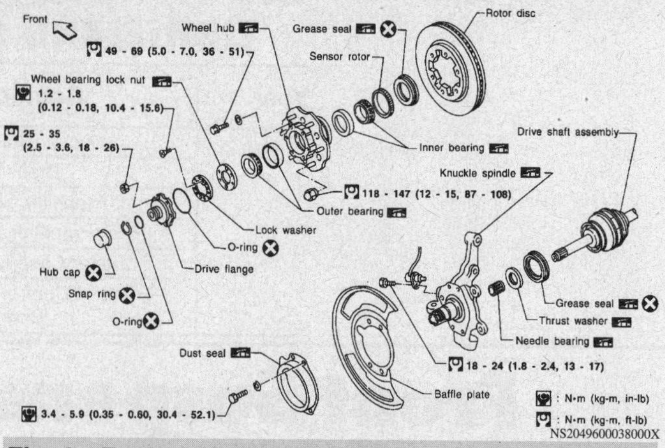
Front
Wheel hub
Grease seal
Rotor disc
49 - 69 (5.0 - 7.0, 36 - 51)
Sensor rotor
Wheel bearing lock nut
1.2 - 1.8 (0.12 - 0.18, 10.4 - 15.6)
25 - 35 (2.5 - 3.6, 18 - 26)
Drive shaft assembly
Inner bearing
Knuckle spindle
118 - 147 (12 - 15, 87 - 108)
Outer bearing
Lock washer
O-ring
Drive flange
Hub cap
Snap ring
O-ring
Grease seal
Thrust washer
Needle bearing
Dust seal
18 - 24 (1.8 - 2.4, 13 - 17)
Baffle plate
3.4 - 5.9 (0.35 - 0.60, 30.4 - 52.1)
: N·m (kg-m, in-lb)
: N·m (kg-m, ft-lb)
NS2049600038000X

Fig. 2 Exploded view of front axle. 4WD Pathfinder

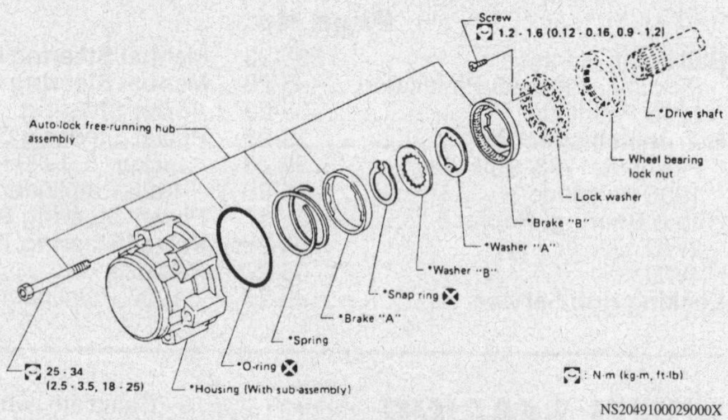
Screw
1.2 - 1.6 (0.12 - 0.16, 0.9 - 1.2)
*Drive shaft
Auto-lock free-running hub assembly
Wheel bearing lock nut
Lock washer
*Brake "B"
*Washer "A"
*Washer "B"
*Snap ring
*Brake "A"
*Spring
*O-ring
25 - 34 (2.5 - 3.5, 18 - 25)
*Housing (With sub-assembly)
: N·m (kg-m, ft-lb)
NS2049100029000X

Fig. 3 Exploded view of automatic locking hub assembly

working grease through rollers from wide end of bearing with palm of hand. Keep bearings covered until installation.

11. Mount rotor on hub with matching marks aligned and tighten bolts to specification.
12. Pack center of hub with suitable grease, then install inner bearing in hub.
13. Coat seal lip with grease, then install seal in rear of hub using suitable driver.
14. Install hub assembly and adjust wheel bearing preload as outlined under "Wheel Bearing, Adjust."
15. Reverse remaining procedure to complete installation. When installing locking hub, select snap ring that will provide .004–.012 endplay at drive axle.

2WD

1. Raise and support vehicle, remove wheels.
2. Remove caliper without disconnecting brake line.
3. Remove wheel hub cap, cotter pin, wheel bearing locknut.
4. Remove wheel hub, rotor and wheel bearings from spindle, **Fig. 4 and 5.**
5. Remove rotor and bearings from hub. **Inspect components for wear and/ or damage, replace as necessary.**
6. Using a suitable tool, remove bearing races, if necessary, from hub assembly.
7. Reverse procedure to install.

BALL JOINT INSPECTION

PICKUP & 1993–95 PATHFINDER

Upper

1. Raise and support front of vehicle.
2. Clamp dial indicator onto transverse link and place indicator tip on lower edge of brake caliper.
3. Ensure front wheels are straight and brake pedal is depressed.
4. Place a pry bar between transverse link and inner rim of wheel.
5. While pushing and releasing pry bar, observe maximum dial indicator value.
6. Movement should not exceed .063 inch. If ball joint movement is beyond specifications, replace ball joint as necessary.

Lower

1. Raise and support front of vehicle.
2. Remove tire and wheel assembly.
3. Clamp dial indicator onto upper link and place indicator tip on knuckle near ball joint.
4. Jack up lower link approximately .79 inch.
5. Place a pry bar between upper link and upper link spindle.
6. While pushing and releasing pry bar, observe maximum dial indicator value. Movement should not exceed .063 inch for 2WD models and .020 for 4WD models. If ball joint movement is beyond specifications, replace ball joint as necessary.

1996 PATHFINDER

Transverse Link & Lower

1. Raise and support front of vehicle.
2. Remove tire and wheel assembly.
3. Check transverse link for damage, cracks or deformation.
4. Check transverse link rubber bushing for damage.
5. Check ball joint for excessive play.
6. Replace lower ball joint assembly if any of the following exists:
   a. Ball stud is worn.
   b. Joint is hard to swing.
   c. Play in axial direction is excessive.
   d. Any vertical endplay.
7. Check dust cover for damage.

BALL JOINT REPLACE

PICKUP & 1993–95 PATHFINDER

Upper

1. Raise and support front of vehicle and

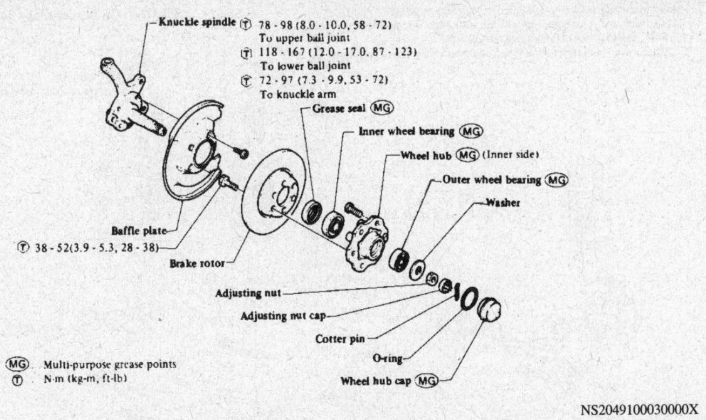
Knuckle spindle
78 - 98 (8.0 - 10.0, 58 - 72)
To upper ball joint
118 - 167 (12.0 - 17.0, 87 - 123)
To lower ball joint
72 - 97 (7.3 - 9.9, 53 - 72)
To knuckle arm
Grease seal MG
Inner wheel bearing MG
Wheel hub MG (Inner side)
Outer wheel bearing MG
Washer
Baffle plate
38 - 52 (3.9 - 5.3, 28 - 38)
Brake rotor
Adjusting nut
Adjusting nut cap
Cotter pin
O-ring
Wheel hub cap MG
MG : Multi-purpose grease points
N·m (kg-m, ft-lb)
NS2049100030000X

Fig. 4 Exploded view of wheel hub assembly. 2WD Pickup

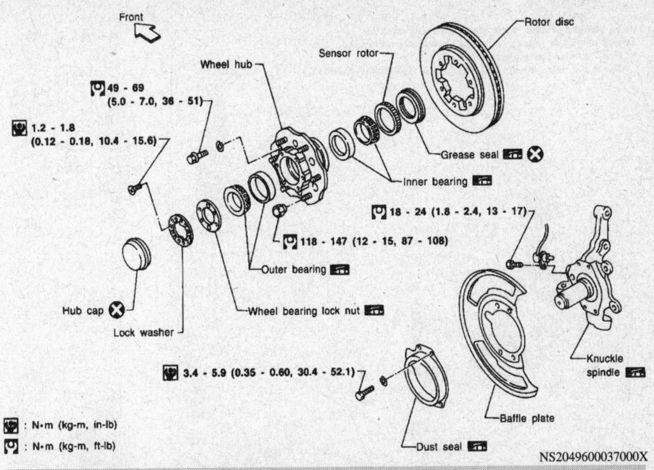
Front
Rotor disc
Sensor rotor
Wheel hub
49 - 69
(5.0 - 7.0, 36 - 51)
1.2 - 1.8
(0.12 - 0.18, 10.4 - 15.6)
Grease seal
Inner bearing
18 - 24 (1.8 - 2.4, 13 - 17)
118 - 147 (12 - 15, 87 - 108)
Outer bearing
Hub cap
Wheel bearing lock nut
Lock washer
Knuckle spindle
3.4 - 5.9 (0.35 - 0.60, 30.4 - 52.1)
Baffle plate
: N·m (kg-m, in-lb)
: N·m (kg-m, ft-lb)
Dust seal
NS2049600037000X

Fig. 5 Exploded view of wheel hub assembly. 2WD Pathfinder

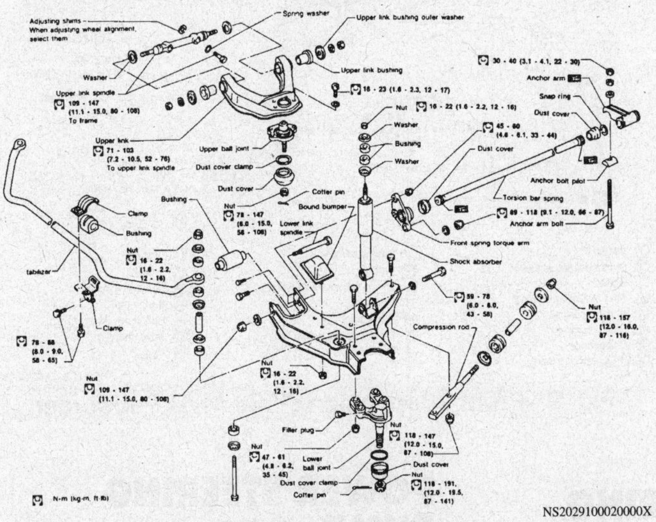
NS2029100020000X

Fig. 6 Front suspension. 4WD Pickup & 1993–95 Pathfinder

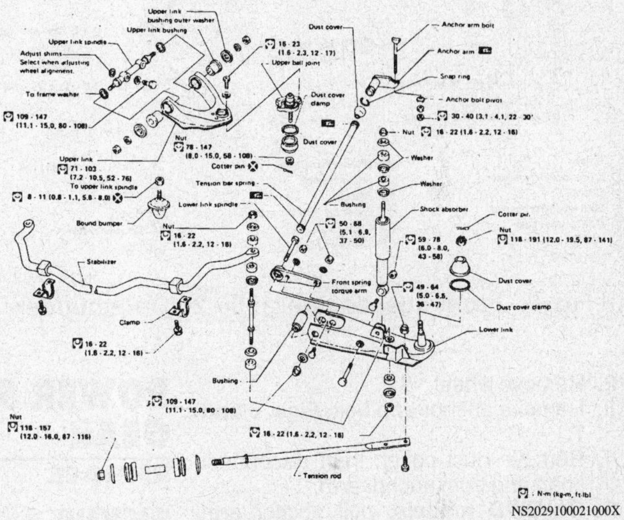
NS2029100021000X

Fig. 7 Front suspension. 2WD Pickup & 1993–95 Pathfinder

remove wheel. **Do not raise on lower link assembly.**
2. Remove shock absorber upper attaching bolt, if necessary.
3. Using suitable jack, raise lower link and remove upper ball joint tightening nut, then press ball joint out of knuckle.
4. Remove the upper link spindle attaching bolts and upper link. **Adjusting shims are behind spindle.**
5. Remove ball joint attaching nuts, then the ball joint, **Figs. 6 and 7.**
6. Remove nuts and washers from both ends of upper link spindle, then press spindle and bushings out of link.
7. Reverse procedure to install.

Lower

1. Raise and support front of vehicle and remove wheel.
2. Remove torsion bar, refer to "Torsion Bar Spring, Replace."
3. Remove lower shock absorber attaching bolt, **Figs. 6 and 7.**
4. Disconnect stabilizer connecting rod and tension or compression rod from lower link.
5. Remove ball joint tightening nut, then press ball joint from knuckle spindle.
6. Remove the lower link spindle and lower link assembly.
7. Remove ball joint attaching nuts, then the ball joint.
8. Remove nuts and washers from both ends of lower link spindle, then press spindle and bushings out of link.
9. Reverse procedure to install.

1996 PATHFINDER

Transverse Link & Lower

1. Raise and support front of vehicle and remove wheel.
2. **On 4WD models,** separate drive shaft from knuckle.
3. **On all models,** separate lower ball joint stud from knuckle, **Figs. 8 and 9.**
4. Remove lower ball joint assembly from transverse link.
5. Remove transverse link.
6. Reverse procedure to install, noting that final tightening must be carried out at curb weight with tires on ground.

SHOCK ABSORBER

REPLACE

PICKUP & 1993-95 PATHFINDER

1. Raise and support vehicle.
2. Remove wheel.
3. Disconnect shock absorber from upper mounting, **Figs. 6 and 7.**
4. Disconnect shock absorber from lower mounting.
5. Remove shock absorber from vehicle.
6. Reverse procedure to install.

TORSION BAR

REPLACE

PICKUP & 1993-95 PATHFINDER

1. Raise and support vehicle.

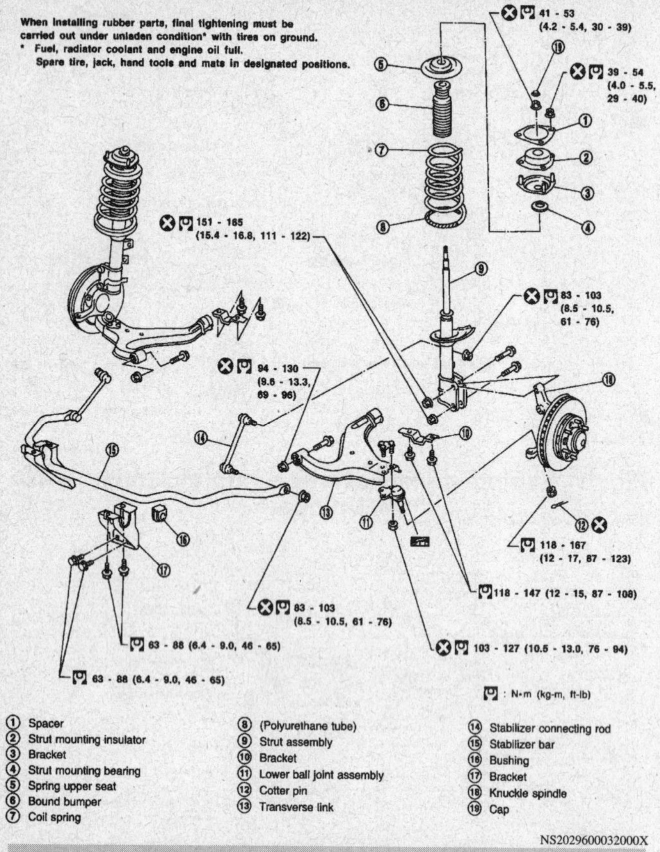
When installing rubber parts, final tightening must be carried out under unladen condition* with tires on ground.
* Fuel, radiator coolant and engine oil full.
Spare tire, jack, hand tools and mats in designated positions.
41 - 53 (4.2 - 5.4, 30 - 39)
39 - 54 (4.0 - 5.5, 29 - 40)
151 - 165 (15.4 - 16.8, 111 - 122)
83 - 103 (8.5 - 10.5, 61 - 76)
94 - 130 (9.6 - 13.3, 69 - 96)
118 - 167 (12 - 17, 87 - 123)
118 - 147 (12 - 15, 87 - 108)
83 - 103 (8.5 - 10.5, 61 - 76)
63 - 88 (6.4 - 9.0, 46 - 65)
103 - 127 (10.5 - 13.0, 76 - 94)
63 - 88 (6.4 - 9.0, 46 - 65)
: N·m (kg-m, ft-lb)
1 Spacer
2 Strut mounting insulator
3 Bracket
4 Strut mounting bearing
5 Spring upper seat
6 Bound bumper
7 Coil spring
8 (Polyurethane tube)
9 Strut assembly
10 Bracket
11 Lower ball joint assembly
12 Cotter pin
13 Transverse link
14 Stabilizer connecting rod
15 Stabilizer bar
16 Bushing
17 Bracket
18 Knuckle spindle
19 Cap
NS2029600032000X

Fig. 8 Front suspension. 1996 2WD Pathfinder

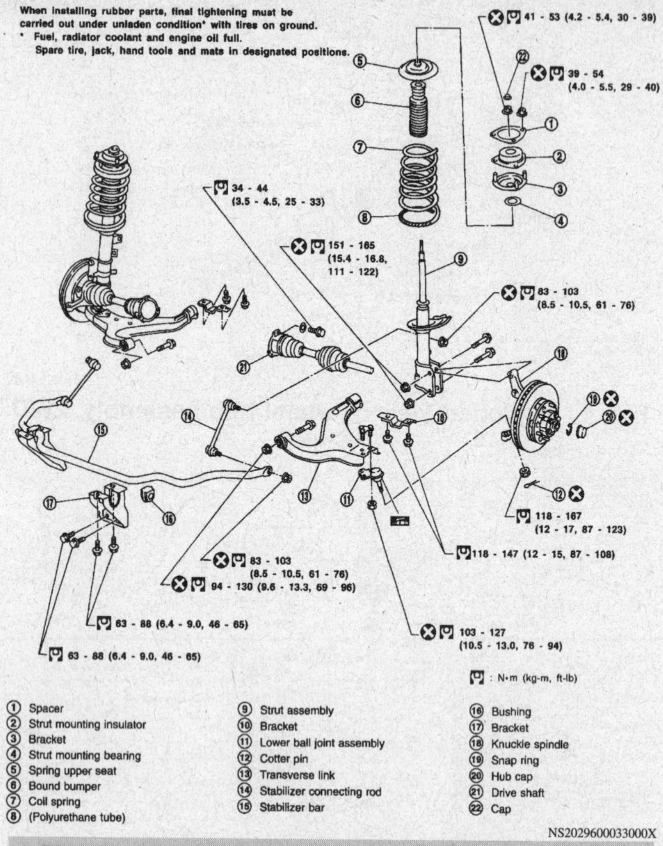
When installing rubber parts, final tightening must be carried out under unladen condition* with tires on ground.
* Fuel, radiator coolant and engine oil full.
Spare tire, jack, hand tools and mats in designated positions.
41 - 53 (4.2 - 5.4, 30 - 39)
39 - 54 (4.0 - 5.5, 29 - 40)
34 - 44 (3.5 - 4.5, 25 - 33)
151 - 165 (15.4 - 16.8, 111 - 122)
83 - 103 (8.5 - 10.5, 61 - 76)
118 - 167 (12 - 17, 87 - 123)
118 - 147 (12 - 15, 87 - 108)
83 - 103 (8.5 - 10.5, 61 - 76)
94 - 130 (9.6 - 13.3, 69 - 96)
63 - 88 (6.4 - 9.0, 46 - 65)
103 - 127 (10.5 - 13.0, 76 - 94)
63 - 88 (6.4 - 9.0, 46 - 65)
: N·m (kg-m, ft-lb)
1 Spacer
2 Strut mounting insulator
3 Bracket
4 Strut mounting bearing
5 Spring upper seat
6 Bound bumper
7 Coil spring
8 (Polyurethane tube)
9 Strut assembly
10 Bracket
11 Lower ball joint assembly
12 Cotter pin
13 Transverse link
14 Stabilizer connecting rod
15 Stabilizer bar
16 Bushing
17 Bracket
18 Knuckle spindle
19 Snap ring
20 Hub cap
21 Drive shaft
22 Cap
NS2029600033000X

Fig. 9 Front suspension. 1996 4WD Pathfinder

2. Remove wheel.
3. Remove anchor arm bolt, **Figs. 6 and 7.**
4. Remove dust cover, then disconnect snap ring from anchor arm.
5. **On 2WD models,** pull anchor arm rearward, then remove torsion bar spring rearward. Remove torque arm.
6. **On 4WD models,** remove torque arm attaching nuts, then pull torsion bar spring forward and remove with torque arm.
7. **On all models,** reverse procedure to install.

STABILIZER BAR

REPLACE

Refer to **Figs. 6 through 9** for stabilizer bar replacement.

STRUT DAMPER

REPLACE

1996 PATHFINDER

On these models, refer to **Fig. 10** for strut damper replacement.

POWER STEERING GEAR

REPLACE

PICKUP & 1993-95 PATHFINDER

On these models, refer to **Fig. 11** for power steering gear replacement.

1996 PATHFINDER

On these models, refer to **Fig. 12** for power steering gear replacement.

POWER STEERING TRANSFER GEAR

REPLACE

1996 PATHFINDER

1. Set wheels in straight forward position. Straight forward position is indicated by a protrusion on surface of power steering gear rear cover cap and matching mark on rear housing.
2. Remove steering column upper and lower joint from transfer gear, **Fig. 13.**
3. Remove transfer gear assembly.
4. Reverse procedure to install.

POWER STEERING PUMP

REPLACE

1. Loosen idler pulley locknut, turn adjusting nut counterclockwise, and remove power steering pump drive belt.
2. **On models with A/C,** remove air conditioning compressor drive belt.
3. **On all models,** loosen power steering hoses at pump and remove bolts securing power steering pump to brackets.
4. Raise pump and disconnect power steering hoses. Catch fluid in a suitable container, plug hose ends and ports in power steering pump, and remove pump from vehicle.
5. Reinstall power steering pump by reversing procedure and bleed system as follows:
   a. Raise and support front of vehicle.
   b. Run engine for three to five seconds, stop engine, check and fill power steering pump reservoir as needed.
   c. Quickly turn steering wheel all the way to right and left 10 times.
   d. Start engine and idle for three to five seconds. Stop engine, check and fill power steering pump reservoir as needed.
   e. With steering wheel all the way to the right, open bleeder screw, to expel air and tighten bleeder screw.

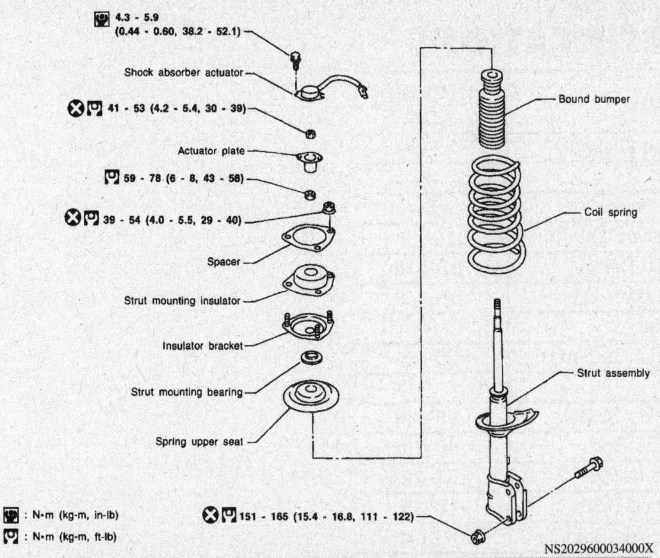
4.3 - 5.9
(0.44 - 0.60, 38.2 - 52.1)
Shock absorber actuator
41 - 53 (4.2 - 5.4, 30 - 39)
Actuator plate
59 - 78 (6 - 8, 43 - 58)
39 - 54 (4.0 - 5.5, 29 - 40)
Spacer
Strut mounting insulator
Insulator bracket
Strut mounting bearing
Spring upper seat
Bound bumper
Coil spring
Strut assembly
151 - 165 (15.4 - 16.8, 111 - 122)
: N•m (kg-m, in-lb)
: N•m (kg-m, ft-lb)
NS2029600034000X

Fig. 10 Exploded view of strut damper. 1996 Pathfinder

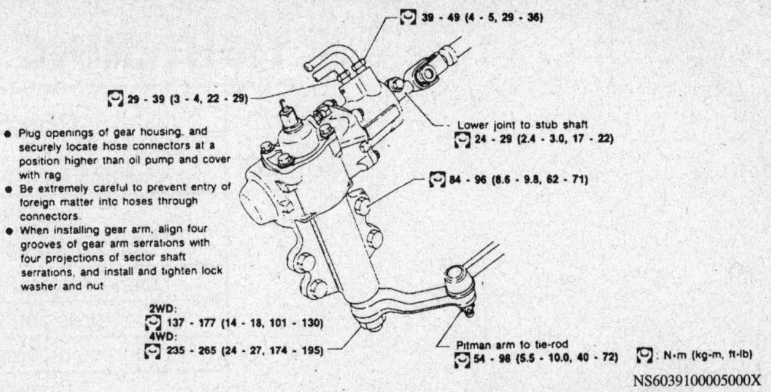
39 - 49 (4 - 5, 29 - 36)
29 - 39 (3 - 4, 22 - 29)
• Plug openings of gear housing, and securely locate hose connectors at a position higher than oil pump and cover with rag
• Be extremely careful to prevent entry of foreign matter into hoses through connectors.
• When installing gear arm, align four grooves of gear arm serrations with four projections of sector shaft serrations, and install and tighten lock washer and nut
Lower joint to stub shaft
24 - 29 (2.4 - 3.0, 17 - 22)
84 - 96 (8.6 - 9.8, 62 - 71)
2WD:
137 - 177 (14 - 18, 101 - 130)
4WD:
235 - 265 (24 - 27, 174 - 195)
Pitman arm to tie-rod
54 - 98 (5.5 - 10.0, 40 - 72)
: N•m (kg-m, ft-lb)
NS6039100005000X

Fig. 11 Power steering gear replacement. Pickup & 1993–95 Pathfinder w/PB48S type steering gear (PB56S type steering gear similar)

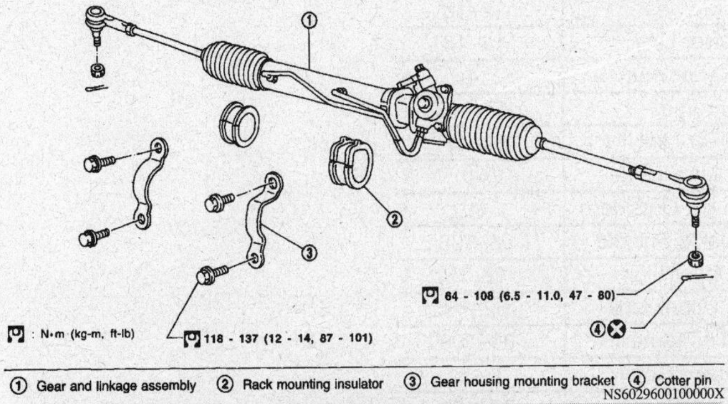
①
②
③
84 - 108 (6.5 - 11.0, 47 - 80)
④⊗
: N•m (kg-m, ft-lb)
118 - 137 (12 - 14, 87 - 101)
① Gear and linkage assembly ② Rack mounting insulator ③ Gear housing mounting bracket ④ Cotter pin
NS6029600100000X

Fig. 12 Power steering gear replacement. 1996 Pathfinder

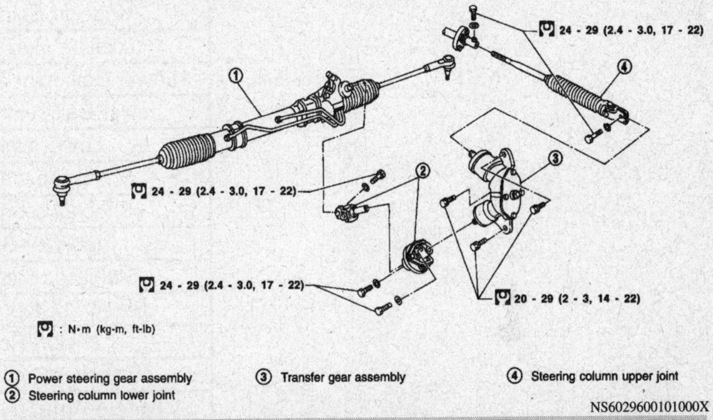
24 - 29 (2.4 - 3.0, 17 - 22)
24 - 29 (2.4 - 3.0, 17 - 22)
24 - 29 (2.4 - 3.0, 17 - 22)
20 - 29 (2 - 3, 14 - 22)
: N•m (kg-m, ft-lb)
① Power steering gear assembly
② Steering column lower joint
③ Transfer gear assembly
④ Steering column upper joint
NS6029600101000X

Fig. 13 Power steering transfer gear replacement. 1996 Pathfinder

f. Repeat procedure until all air has been bled from system.
g. If air cannot be bled completely after repeated attempts, repeat step e with engine running.

MANUAL STEERING GEAR

REPLACE

On these models, refer to **Fig. 14** for manual steering gear replacement procedure.

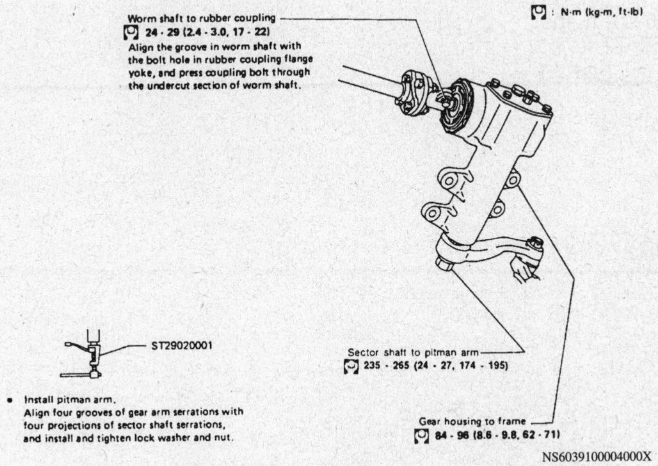
Worm shaft to rubber coupling
24 - 29 (2.4 - 3.0, 17 - 22)
Align the groove in worm shaft with the bolt hole in rubber coupling flange yoke, and press coupling bolt through the undercut section of worm shaft.
: N·m (kg-m, ft-lb)
ST29020001
• Install pitman arm.
Align four grooves of gear arm serrations with four projections of sector shaft serrations, and install and tighten lock washer and nut.
Sector shaft to pitman arm
235 - 265 (24 - 27, 174 - 195)
Gear housing to frame
84 - 98 (8.6 - 9.8, 62 - 71)
NS6039100004000X

Fig. 14 Manual steering gear replacement

TIGHTENING SPECIFICATIONS

Year	Component	Torque/Ft. Lbs.
1993–96	Anchor Adjusting Bolt Locknut	22–30
	Axle Nut	⑥
	Bound Bumper To Frame④	5.8–8
	Bound Bumper To Lower Link①	12–16
	Compression Rod To Body①	87–116
	Compression Rod To Lower Link①	87–108
	Driveshaft Nut	⑥
	Driveshaft To Differential Carrier①	25–33
	Hub Nut	⑥
	Knuckle Arm To Knuckle Spindle	53–72
	Knuckle Arm To Tie Rod	40–72
	Knuckle Spindle To Caliper	53–72
	Locking Hub Mounting Bolts	18–25
	Lower Ball Joint To Knuckle Spindle	87–141
	Lower Ball Joint To Lower Link①	35–45
	Lower Link To Frame	80–108
	Shock Absorber Lower Bolt	43–58
	Shock Absorber Upper Bolt	12–16
	Stabilizer Bar To Frame	12–16
	Stabilizer Bar To Lower Link	12–16
	Steering Stopper Bolt Locknut	⑤
	Tension Rod To Frame	87–116
	Tension Rod To Lower Link	36–47
	Torque Arm To Lower Link Inside	②
	Torque Arm To Lower Link Outside	③
	Upper Ball Joint To Knuckle Spindle	58–108
	Upper Ball Joint To Upper Link	12–15
	Upper Link Spindle To Upper Link	52–76
	Upper Link Spindle To Frame	80–108
1993–96	Wheel Hub To Disc Brake Rotor	36–51
	Wheel Lug Nut	87–108

① — 4WD.
② — 2WD, 37–50 ft. lbs.; 4WD, 33–44 ft. lbs.
③ — 2WD, 37–50 ft. lbs.; 4WD, 66–87 ft. lbs.
④ — 2WD.
⑤ — 2WD, 20-27 ft. lbs.; 4WD, 56–72 ft. lbs.
⑥ — 2WD, 25–29 ft. lbs.; 4WD, 58–72 ft. lbs.

Wheel Alignment

INDEX

	Page No.		Page No.		Page No.
Front Wheel Alignment	35-33	Steering Angle	35-34	**Vehicle Ride Height**	35-34
Camber	35-33	Toe Setting	35-33	**Wheel Alignment Specifications**	35-3
Caster & Kingpin Inclination	35-33	**Preliminary Inspection**	35-33		

PRELIMINARY INSPECTION

Prior to checking and adjusting wheel alignment angles, perform the following checks:

1. Check tire pressures and adjust as needed.
2. Ensure tires are of the proper size and tires are properly matched.
3. Ensure wheel bearings (front and rear) are properly adjusted.
4. Check steering gear adjustment and ensure steering gear is properly secured to frame.
5. Inspect steering linkage and suspension components for damage and wear, and repair or replace components as needed.
6. Measure vehicle ride height with vehicle unloaded, and ensure springs are not collapsed.
7. Place vehicle on suitable alignment rack following manufacturer's instructions, then jounce vehicle several times to settle suspension.
8. Check and correct rear wheel camber and toe first, if applicable, then check and correct front suspension angles in the following order: caster and kingpin inclination, camber, toe setting and turning angle (toe-out on turns).

FRONT WHEEL ALIGNMENT

Correct front wheel alignment is necessary to provide proper handling and to prevent uneven tire wear. To ensure correct alignment, angles should be checked, and if necessary corrected, in the following sequence: caster and kingpin inclination, camber, toe-setting, and the turning angle and toe-out on turns. Front wheel alignment should only be checked after ensuring rear wheels are properly aligned in relation to the vehicle centerline, as most equipment uses the rear wheels as reference for correct front wheel alignment. Front wheel alignment should be checked with the vehicle at normal ride height, and following equipment manufacturer's instructions.

CASTER & KINGPIN INCLINATION

Kingpin inclination is a function of the steering knuckle design and cannot be adjusted. Caster is the alignment angle which provides the self-centering steering effect. For caster adjustment, refer to camber adjustment, as the caster and camber are both adjusted by inserting shims between the upper control arm spindle and the crossmember.

CAMBER

Caster and camber are adjusted together by varying the thickness of shims between the upper control arm shaft and crossmember. To check and adjust caster and camber, proceed as follows:

1. Prior to checking and adjusting caster and camber, ensure front suspension height is within specifications as follows:
   a. Measure suspension height of suspension arm pivot (A) and height of tension rod attaching bolt or steering stopper bracket (B), **Figs. 1 and 2.**
   b. Subtract measurement (B) from measurement (A) to determine suspension height (H). 2WD Models should measure 4.37–4.53 inches and 4WD models should measure 1.73–1.89 inches.
   c. If vehicle height is not within specifications, jounce vehicle several times to settle suspension. If height is still not within specifications, check suspension and repair or replace component as needed before continuing with alignment procedure.
2. Check caster and camber and refer to wheel alignment specifications.
3. If caster and or camber are not within specifications, place suitable jack under lower control arm, raise arm to remove tension from upper control arm and loosen nuts securing upper control arm to crossmember.
4. Replace shims between upper control arm shaft and crossmember, noting the following:
   a. Do not use more than three shims at any one position, and ensure shim thickness does not exceed .315 inch (8 mm).
   b. When installing shims with a right angle tab at the top, ensure tab faces control arm shaft, insert shim from bracket side and only use one shim of this type at any one position.
   c. To adjust caster, vary thickness of shims between front and rear positions. When thickness of front shim is increased, caster decreases. When increasing shim thickness at the rear position, caster increases.

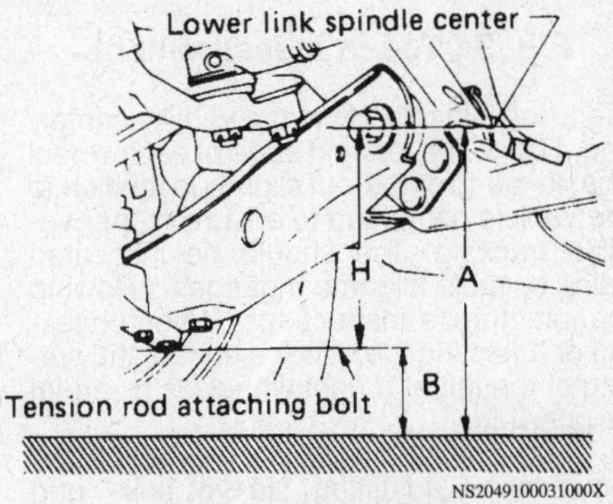
Lower link spindle center
H
A
B
Tension rod attaching bolt
NS2049100031000X

Fig. 1 Front suspension height measurement. 2WD

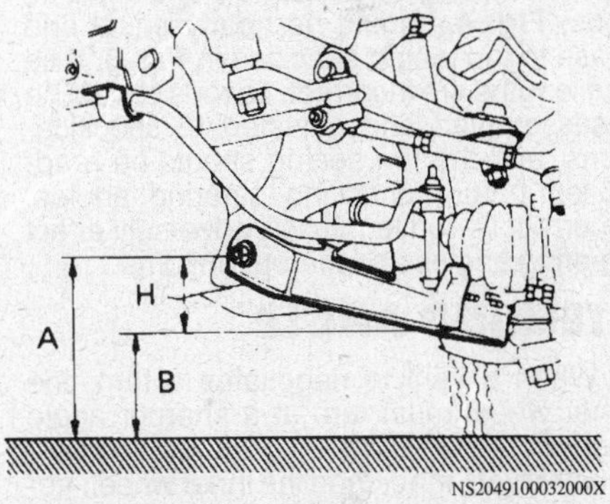
H
A
B
NS2049100032000X

Fig. 2 Front suspension height measurement. 4WD

When performing adjustment, ensure difference in shim thickness between front and rear positions does not exceed .079 inch (2 mm). **Camber angle is affected by varying shim thickness to perform caster adjustment. Always adjust caster angle first, then reduce or increase shim thickness equally at front and rear positions to adjust camber.**

   d. To adjust camber, add shims of equal thickness to both front and rear positions to move camber toward a more positive value, or decrease shim thickness equally at front and rear positions to move camber toward a more negative value.
5. Tighten upper control arm nuts and ensure caster and camber are still within specifications.

TOE SETTING

The toe setting is the measurement of

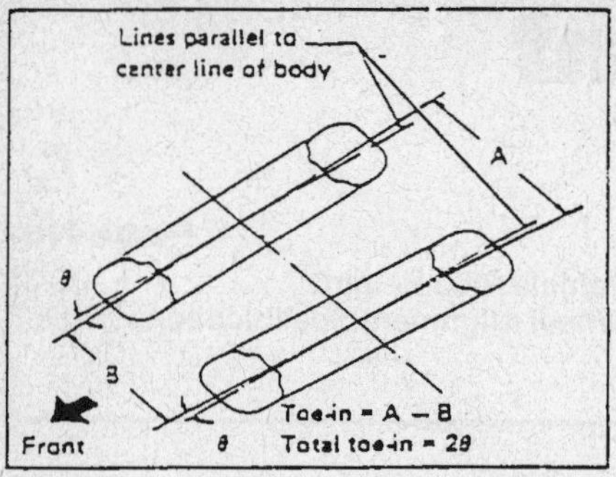
Lines parallel to
center line of body
A
θ
B
Toe-in = A − B
Front
θ
Total toe-in = 2θ

NS2049100033000X

Fig. 3 Toe-in measurement

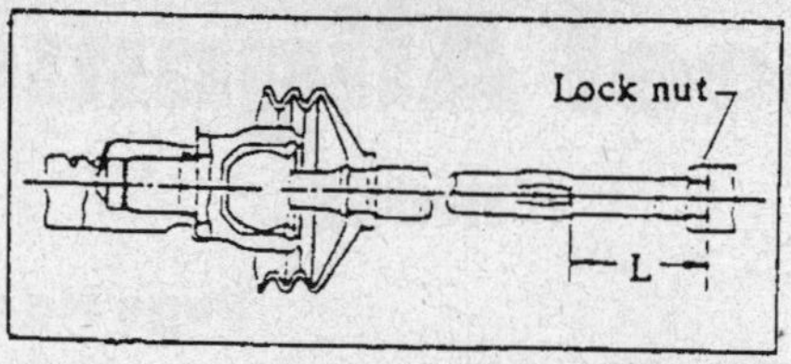
Lock nut
L

NS2049100034000X

Fig. 4 Tie rod length measurement

Model	Manual Steering	Power Steering
Pathfinder	11.06	11.06
Pickup 2WD	13.54	13.54
Pickup 4WD	11.06	11.06

Fig. 5 Tie rod length specifications

Year	Model	Toe-Out On Turns		Turning Angle①	
		Inner Wheel	Outer Wheel	Inner Wheel	Outer Wheel
1993–95	Pathfinder	22°	20°	27–29°	25–27°
	Pickup 2WD	22°	20°	36–38°	33–35°
	Pickup 4WD	22°	20°	②	②
1996	Pathfinder	22°	20°	32–36°	30–33°
	Pickup 2WD	22°	20°	36–38°	33–35°
	Pickup 4WD	22°	20°	②	②

2WD — 2 Wheel Drive. 4WD — 4 Wheel Drive.
① — At full lock.
② — Except 31 X 10.5 R15 tires: inner wheel, 33–35°; outer wheel, 31–33°. 31 X 10.5 R15 tires: inner wheel, 27–29°; outer wheel 25–27°.

Fig. 6 Turning angle specifications

the wheels in relation to the vehicle centerline, **Fig. 3.**The leading edge of each wheel should toe-in or toe-out slightly in relation to the vehicle centerline to ensure proper vehicle tracking. Toe should be inspected using suitable alignment gauges, following manufacturer's instructions. When checking or adjusting toe, always ensure the setting of the left and right wheels is as equal as possible.

Toe is adjusted by loosening the tie rod locknuts or adjusting sleeve bolts and equally altering the length of the tie rods. After toe has been adjusted to specifications, the lengths of the left and right tie rods, **Fig. 4,** should be nearly equal and close to the length specified in **Fig. 5.** If tie rod lengths are incorrect, tie rods should be disassembled and adjusted to specifications, and the toe setting should be readjusted before checking steering angles. Incorrect tie rod length will adversely affect steering angles and toe-out on turns.

STEERING ANGLE

When a vehicle negotiates a turn, the inner wheel must turn at a sharper angle than the outer wheel, and the outer wheel must travel farther than the inner wheel. Vehicle steering geometry is calculated to allow for these variations, causing the outer wheel to toe-out by a calibrated amount. This toe-out on turns is also referred to as steering angle and on these models, is generally checked at two positions. The first position is at a reference point on the inner wheel travel while the second position of measurement is at full steering lock. To check steering angles, proceed as follows:

1. Place vehicle on suitable alignment rack and ensure kingpin angle, caster, camber and toe settings are within specifications.
2. Turn wheels from straight-ahead position until the inner wheel is at the position specified for "Toe-Out On Turns" shown in **Fig. 6.** If the outer wheel reference angle is incorrect, check for damaged or improperly adjusted tie rods. Perform check in both left and right directions.
3. **On models less rack and pinion steering,** proceed as follows:
   a. Rotate steering to full lock in each direction.
   b. Adjust inner wheel "Turning Angle" to value specified in **Fig. 6,** by adjusting position of steering stop.
   c. With inner wheel adjusted to specifications, outer wheel turning angle should be as specified in **Fig. 6.** If outer wheel turning angle is incorrect, repair or replace steering linkage as needed.
4. **On models with rack and pinion steering,** proceed as follows:
   a. Turn steering to full lock and measure inner and outer wheel turning angles.
   b. If "Turning Angles" at full lock are not within specifications, **Fig. 6,** check for damaged steering linkage or improperly adjusted tie rods.
   c. If steering linkage and tie rods are satisfactory, check for improper rack or rack piston stroke and repair steering gear as needed.

VEHICLE RIDE HEIGHT

When checking ride height vehicle must be parked on a level surface and tires inflated to proper air pressure. Ensure all fluid levels are to specified level, spare tire and jack are in proper locations.

Bounce vehicle up and down several times, then measure vehicle height as outlined in "Camber" under "Front Wheel Alignment." If vehicle height is not as specified, Readjust vehicle posture using anchor arm adjusting nut.

NISSAN UNIT REPAIR

TABLE OF CONTENTS

	Page No.
ACTIVE SUSPENSION SYSTEM	36-260
AIR BAG SYSTEM	36-87
AIR CONDITIONING	36-1
ALL WHEEL DRIVE SYSTEMS	36-248
ALTERNATORS	36-45
ANTI-LOCK BRAKES	36-145
AUTOMATIC TRANSMISSION/TRANSAXLE	36-218
COOLING FANS	36-9
DASH GAUGES	36-30
DASH PANEL SERVICE	36-99
DISC BRAKES	36-122
DRIVE AXLES	36-249
DRUM BRAKES	36-131
ENGINE REBUILDING SPECIFICATIONS	36-264
FOUR WHEEL STEERING	36-119
FRONT WHEEL DRIVE AXLES	36-244
HYDRAULIC BRAKE SYSTEMS	36-138
MANUAL STEERING GEARS	36-107
POWER BRAKE UNITS	36-144
POWER STEERING	36-109
SPEED CONTROL SYSTEMS	36-48
STARTER MOTORS	36-39
STEERING COLUMNS	36-104
WIPER SYSTEM	36-82

Air Conditioning

INDEX

	Page No.
A/C Specifications	36-8
Belt Tension Data	36-2
Altima	36-2
Maxima	36-2
Pathfinder & Pickup	36-2
Quest	36-2
1993 NX 1600, NX 2000 & Sentra	36-2
1994 Sentra	36-2
1995–96 Sentra & 200SX	36-2
240SX	36-2
300ZX	36-3
Oil Charge	36-2
Altima, Maxima, Pathfinder, Pickup, 1994–96 Sentra, 200SX, 240SX & 300ZX	36-2
Quest	36-2
1993 NX 1600, NX 2000, Sentra & 240SX	36-2
1993 300ZX	36-2
Performance Test	36-1
Precautions	36-1
R12 Refrigerant	36-1
R134a Refrigerant	36-1
Refrigerant Recovery	36-3

PRECAUTIONS

R134A REFRIGERANT

1. R-12 and R-134a refrigerant must never be mixed. If refrigerants are mixed, compressor failure will probably occur.
2. When filling system with oil, use specified A/C System lubricant. If specified oil is not used, compressor failure will probably occur.
3. Nissan A/C System Type R Part No. KLH00-PAGRO or equivalent refrigerant oil absorbs moisture from the atmosphere at a rapid rate, the following precautions must be followed when using this lubricant:
   a. When removing components from the vehicle, immediately cap component to minimize the entry of moisture from the atmosphere.
   b. When installing components on a vehicle, do not remove cap until just before connecting components. Complete connection of all refrigerant loop components as quickly as possible to minimize entry of moisture into system.
   c. Use specified lubrication oil from a sealed container only. Containers must be sealed immediately after dispensing lubrication oil. Lubrication oil in containers which are not properly sealed will become moisture saturated.
   d. **Avoid breathing A/C refrigerant and lubricant vapor or mist. Exposure may irritate eyes, nose and throat.**
   e. When removing refrigerant from the system, always use service equipment certified by the requirements of SAE J2210 (R-134a recycling equipment) or J2209 (R-134a recovery equipment). If accidental system discharge does occur, ventilate work area before resuming system service.
   f. Do not allow lubrication oil to come in contact with styrofoam parts. Damage may result.

R12 REFRIGERANT

1. Do not release refrigerant into the air. Use approved recovery/recycling equipment to capture refrigerant every time the A/C system is discharged.
2. Always wear eye and hand protection when working with any A/C system.
3. Do not store or heat refrigerant containers above 125°F (52°C).
4. Do not heat refrigerant with an open flame, if container needs warming, place bottom of container in a warm pail of water.
5. Keep refrigerant away from open flames, a poisonous gas will be produced if refrigerant burns.
6. Refrigerant will displace oxygen, be certain to work in a well ventilated area.
7. Do not introduce compressed air to any refrigerant container or component.

PERFORMANCE TEST

1. Vehicle should be located in a shaded,

Recirculating-to-discharge air temperature table

Inside air (Recirculating air) at blower assembly inlet		Discharge air temperature at center ventilator °C (°F)
Relative humidity %	Air temperature °C (°F)	
50 - 60	20 (68)	4.0 - 5.4 (39 - 42)
	25 (77)	4.2 - 5.6 (40 - 42)
	30 (86)	8.5 - 11.1 (47 - 52)
	35 (95)	13.5 - 16.7 (56 - 62)
	40 (104)	18.5 - 22.3 (65 - 72)
60 - 70	20 (68)	5.4 - 6.8 (42 - 44)
	25 (77)	5.6 - 8.0 (42 - 46)
	30 (86)	11.1 - 14.1 (52 - 57)
	35 (95)	16.7 - 20.3 (62 - 69)
	40 (104)	22.3 - 26.5 (72 - 80)

Ambient air temperature-to-compressor pressure table

Ambient air		High-pressure (Discharge side) kPa (kg/cm², psi)	Low-pressure (Suction side) kPa (kg/cm², psi)
Relative humidity %	Air temperature °C (°F)		
50 - 70	20 (68)	834 - 1,098 (8.5 - 11.2, 121 - 159)	122.6 - 161.8 (1.25 - 1.65, 17.8 - 23.5)
	25 (77)	1,049 - 1,363 (10.7 - 13.9, 152 - 198)	137.3 - 181.4 (1.4 - 1.85, 19.9 - 26.3)
	30 (86)	1,226 - 1,618 (12.5 - 16.5, 178 - 235)	152.0 - 201.0 (1.55 - 2.05, 22.0 - 29.2)
	35 (95)	1,255 - 1,716 (12.8 - 17.5, 182 - 249)	166.7 - 230.5 (1.7 - 2.35, 24.2 - 33.4)
	40 (104)	1,540 - 2,030 (15.7 - 20.7, 223 - 294)	201.0 - 289.3 (2.05 - 2.95, 29.2 - 41.9)

NS7029100054000X

Fig. 1 Air conditioning performance test chart. Altima

Recirculating-to-discharge air temperature table

Inside air (Recirculating air) at blower assembly inlet		Discharge air temperature at center ventilator °C (°F)
Relative humidity %	Air temperature °C (°F)	
50 - 60	20 (68)	1.6 - 3.4 (35 - 38)
	25 (77)	5.6 - 7.9 (42 - 46)
	30 (86)	9.6 - 12.4 (49 - 54)
	35 (95)	13.5 - 16.7 (56 - 62)
	40 (104)	17.4 - 21.2 (63 - 70)
60 - 70	20 (68)	3.4 - 5.0 (38 - 41)
	25 (77)	7.9 - 10.1 (46 - 59)
	30 (86)	12.4 - 15.1 (54 - 59)
	35 (95)	16.7 - 20.1 (62 - 68)
	40 (104)	21.2 - 25.2 (70 - 79)

Ambient air temperature-to-compressor pressure table

Ambient air		High-pressure (Discharge side) kPa (kg/cm², psi)	Low-pressure (Suction side) kPa (kg/cm², psi)
Relative humidity %	Air temperature °C (°F)		
50 - 70	20 (68)	754 - 1,128 (7.6 - 11.5, 108 - 164)	73.6 - 147.1 (0.75 - 1.5, 10.7 - 21.3)
	25 (77)	1,040 - 1,471 (10.6 - 15.0, 151 - 213)	108 - 186 (1.1 - 1.9, 16 - 27)
	30 (86)	1,334 - 1,804 (13.6 - 18.4, 193 - 262)	142.2 - 230.5 (1.45 - 2.35, 20.6 - 33.4)
	35 (95)	1,628 - 2,138 (16.6 - 21.8, 236 - 310)	176.5 - 269.7 (1.8 - 2.75, 25.6 - 39.1)
	40 (104)	1,922 - 2,471 (19.6 - 25.2, 279 - 358)	206 - 314 (2.1 - 3.2, 30 - 46)

NS7029100055000X

Fig. 2 Air conditioning performance test chart. 1993 Maxima

well ventilated area.

2. Close all doors and leave drivers window open.
3. Open vehicle hood and connect gauge set to A/C system.
4. Insert a thermometer in the vent outlet, then determine relative humidity and ambient air temperature.
5. **On manually operated models,** position temperature lever to "Cold," mode door to "Vent," intake door to "Recirc" and fan speed to "Max."
6. **On automatically operated models,** set up ACTIVE-TEST with CONSULT and set each component as follows:
   a. Set mode door to "VENT."
   b. Set intake door to "REC."
   c. Set air mix door to "FULL-COLD."
   d. Set compressor to "ON."
   e. Set blower motor to "12V."
   f. Set up self diagnosis step 2 and set code No. "66."
7. **On all models,** start engine and run at 1500 RPM for at least 10 minutes.
8. Compare discharge air temperature, high pressure reading and low pressure reading with the charts in **Figs. 1 through 16.**
9. Any results found outside of specifications may indicate a need for further inspection and/or repair.

OIL CHARGE

Refer to "Precautions" before adding oil to refrigerant systems.

1993 300ZX

Adjust oil quantity according to the chart in **Fig. 17.**

1993 NX 1600, NX 2000, SENTRA & 240SX

Adjust oil quantity according to the charts in **Fig. 18.**

ALTIMA, MAXIMA, PATHFINDER, PICKUP, 1994-96 SENTRA, 200SX, 240SX & 300ZX

Refer to "R-134a Refrigerant" under "Precautions" before adjusting oil level. Adjust oil quantity according to the charts in Figs. 19 and 20.

QUEST

A replacement FX-15 compressor contains seven fluid ounces of oil. Before installing the replacement compressor, drain oil from old compressor into a measured container. Drain refrigerant oil from the new compressor into a measured container. If the amount of oil that was removed from the old compressor is greater than five ounces, pour five ounces of clean refrigerant oil into the new compressor discharge port. If old compressor has between three and five ounces of oil, pour the same amount of clean oil into the compressor.

When replacing any other A/C system component, refer to **Figs. 21 and 22** for amount of oil that needs to be added.

BELT TENSION DATA

ALTIMA

Using 22 lbs. of force, belt deflection should be .24–.28 inch for a new belt and .28–.31 inch for a used belt.

MAXIMA

1993

Using 22 ft. lbs. of force, belt deflection should be .16–.24 inch for a new belt and .20–.28 inch for a used belt.

1994

Using 22 ft. lbs. of force, belt deflection should be .20–.24 inch for a new belt and .217–.256 inch for a used belt.

1995-96

Alternator drive belt deflection on models with A/C is .165–.181 inch for a used belt and .15–.16 inch for a new belt.

PATHFINDER & PICKUP

Using 22 ft. lbs. of force, belt deflection should be .28–.35 inch for a new belt and .35–.43 inch for a used belt.

1993 NX 1600, NX 2000 & SENTRA

Using 22 ft. lbs. of force, belt deflection should be .26–.30 inch for a new belt and .28–.31 inch for a used belt.

1994 SENTRA

Using 22 ft. lbs. of force, belt deflection should be .20–.28 inch for a new belt and .24–.31 inch for a used belt.

1995-96 SENTRA & 200SX

Alternator drive belt deflection on models with A/C is .28–.31 inch for a used belt and .256–.295 inch for a new belt.

QUEST

Using 22 ft. lbs. of force, belt deflection should be .16–.24 inch for a new belt and .20–.28 inch for a used belt.

240SX

Using 22 ft. lbs. of force, belt deflection

Recirculating-to-discharge air temperature table

...e air (Re... ulating air) ...lower a...nbly inlet		Discharge air temperature at center ventilator °C (°F)
Relative hu... ty %	Air tem... °C	
50 - 60	20 (68)	3 0 - 3.7 (37 - 39)
	25 (77)	5.4 - 6.8 (42 - 44)
	30 (86)	8.5 - 10 6 (47 - 51)
	35 (95)	14 2 - 17.8 (58 - 64)
60 - 70	(68)	3.7 - 4.6 (39 - 40)
	25 (77)	6.8 - 8 0 (44 - 46)
	30 (86)	10.6 - 12.8 (51 - 55)
	35 (95)	17.8 - 21.4 (64 - 71)

Ambient air temperature-to-compressor pressure table

Ambient air		High-pressure (Discharge side) kPa (kg/cm², psi)	Low-pressure (Suction side) kPa (kg/cm², psi)
Relative humidity %	Air temperature °C (°F)		
50 - 70	20 (68)	1.079 - 1,334 (11.0 - 13 6, 156 - 193)	108 - 137 (1.1 - 1.4, 16 - 20)
	25 (77)	1,295 - 1.589 (13 2 - 16 2, 188 - 230)	127 - 157 (1.3 - 1.6, 18 - 23)
	30 (86)	1,491 - 1,844 (15.2 - 18 8, 216 - 267)	147 - 177 (1.5 - 1.8, 21 - 26)
	35 (95)	1,706 - 2,099 (17.4 - 21.4, 247 - 304)	177 - 216 (1.8 - 2 2, 26 - 31)
	40 (104)	1,903 - 2.354 (19.4 - 24 0, 276 - 341)	216 - 265 (2.2 - 2.7, 31 - 38)

NS7029400056000X

Fig. 3 Air conditioning performance test chart. 1994 Maxima

Recirculating-to-discharge air temperature table

Inside air(Recirculating air) at blower assembly inlet		Discharge air temperature at center ventilator °C (°F)
Relative humidity %	Air temperature °C (°F)	
50 - 60	20 (68)	5.9 - 7.8 (43 - 46)
	25 (77)	8.0 - 10.7 (46 - 51)
	30 (86)	11.0 - 14.4 (52 - 58)
	35 (95)	14.8 - 19.4 (59 - 67)
60 - 70	20 (68)	7.8 - 9.9 (46 - 50)
	25 (77)	10.7 - 13 6 (51 - 56)
	30 (86)	14.4 - 18.2 (58 - 65)
	35 (95)	19.4 - 24.8 (67 - 77)

Ambient air temperature-to-compressor pressure table

Ambient air		High-pressure (Discharge side) kPa (kg/cm², psi)	Low-pressure (Suction side) kPa (kg/cm², psi)
Relative humidity %	Air temperature °C (°F)		
50 - 70	20 (68)	608 - 912 (6 2 - 9.3, 88 - 132)	177 - 245 (1.8 - 2 5, 26 - 36)
	25 (77)	814 - 1.147 (8 3 - 11 7, 118 - 166)	186 - 255 (1 9 - 2 6, 27 - 37)
	30 (86)	1,020 - 1.402 (10 4 - 14 3, 148 - 203)	196 - 265 (2.0 - 2.7, 28 - 38)
	35 (95)	1.236 - 1.638 (12 6 - 16.7, 179 - 237)	226 - 314 (2 3 - 3.2, 33 - 46)

NS7029100057000X

Fig. 5 Air conditioning performance test chart. 1993 NX 1600, NX 2000 & Sentra

Recirculating-to-discharge air temperature table

Inside air (Recirculating air) at blower assembly inlet		Discharge air temperature at center ventilator °C (°F)
Relative humidity %	Air temperature °C (°F)	
50 - 60	20 (68)	4 4 - 7.0 (40 - 45)
	25 (77)	7.9 - 11.1 (46 - 52)
	30 (86)	11.6 - 15.8 (53 - 60)
	35 (95)	15.4 - 20 4 (60 - 69)
	40 (104)	19.6 - 26.0 (67 - 79)
60 - 70	20 (68)	7 0 - 9.3 (45 - 49)
	25 (77)	11.1 - 14.5 (52 - 58)
	30 (86)	15.8 - 20.2 (60 - 68)
	35 (95)	20.4 - 26.2 (69 - 79)
	40 (104)	26.0 - 33 6 (79 - 92)

Ambient air temperature-to-operating pressure table

Ambient air		High-pressure (Discharge side) kPa (kg/cm², psi)	Low-pressure (Suction side) kPa (kg/cm², psi)
Relative humidity %	Air temperature °C (°F)		
50 - 70	20 (68)	1.010 - 1,314 (10.3 - 13.4, 146 - 191)	108 - 206 (1.1 - 2 1, 16 - 30)
	25 (77)	1.236 - 1.599 (12.6 - 16.3, 179 - 232)	118 - 226 (1.2 - 2 3, 17 - 33)
	30 (86)	1.471 - 1.883 (15.0 - 19.2, 213 - 273)	137 - 265 (1.4 - 2.7, 20 - 38)
	35 (95)	1.893 - 2,167 (19.3 - 22.1, 274 - 314)	157 - 324 (1.6 - 3.3, 23 - 47)
	40 (104)	1,922 - 2.452 (19.6 - 25.0, 279 - 356)	196 - 392 (2.0 - 4.0, 28 - 57)

NS7029500103000X

Fig. 7 Air conditioning performance test chart. 1995–96 Sentra & 200SX

Recirculating-to-discharge air temperature table

Inside air (Recirculating air) at blower assembly inlet		Discharge air temperature at center ventilator °C (°F)
Relative humidity %	Air temperature °C (°F)	
50 - 60	20 (68)	1.5 - 2.6 (35 - 37)
	25 (77)	3.7 - 5.7 (39 - 42)
	30 (86)	7.6 - 10.0 (46 - 50)
	35 (95)	12.4 - 15.2 (54 - 59)
60 - 70	20 (68)	2.6 - 3.6 (37 - 38)
	25 (77)	5.7 - 7.6 (42 - 46)
	30 (86)	10.0 - 12.4 (50 - 54)
	35 (95)	15.2 - 18.0 (59 - 64)

Ambient air temperature-to-compressor pressure table

Ambient air		High-pressure (Discharge side) kPa (kg/cm², psi)	Low-pressure (Suction side) kPa (kg/cm², psi)
Relative humidity %	Air temperature °C (°F)		
50 - 70	20 (68)	785 - 1.040 (8.0 - 10 6, 114 - 151)	137 - 167 (1.4 - 1.7, 20 - 24)
	25 (77)	981 - 1,304 (10 0 - 13 3, 142 - 189)	137 - 167 (1 4 - 1.7, 20 - 24)
	30 (86)	1,167 - 1.550 (11.9 - 15 8, 169 - 225)	147 - 177 (1.5 - 1.8, 21 - 26)
	35 (95)	1,373 - 1,804 (14 0 - 18 4, 199 - 262)	157 - 186 (1.6 - 1.9, 23 - 27)
	40 (104)	1,550 - 2,059 (15.8 - 21 0, 225 - 299)	167 - 206 (1.7 - 2 1, 24 - 30)

NS7029500102000X

Fig. 4 Air conditioning performance test chart. 1995–96 Maxima

Recirculating-to-discharge air temperature table

Inside air(Recirculating air) at blower assembly inlet		Discharge air temperature at center ventilator °C (°F)
Relative humidity %	Air temperature °C (°F)	
50 - 60	25 (77)	8.8 - 11.3 (48 - 52)
	30 (86)	12.3 - 15 2 (54 - 59)
	35 (95)	15 6 - 19 3 (60 - 67)
60 - 70	25 (77)	11.3 - 14 0 (52 - 57)
	30 (86)	15 2 - 18 6 (59 - 65)
	35 (95)	19 3 - 23 5 (67 - 74)

Ambient air temperature-to-compressor pressure table

Ambient air		High-pressure (Discharge side) kPa (kg/cm², psi)	Low-pressure (Suction side) kPa (kg/cm², psi)
Relative humidity %	Air temperature °C (°F)		
50 - 70	25 (77)	892 - 1,255 (9.1 - 12 8, 129 - 182)	167 - 275 (1.7 - 2 8, 24 - 40)
	30 (86)	1,118 - 1,334 (11.4 - 13 6, 162 - 193)	177 - 294 (1.8 - 3.0, 26 - 43)
	35 (95)	1,344 - 1,804 (13.7 - 18.4, 195 - 262)	186 - 314 (1.9 - 3 2, 27 - 46)

NS7029400058000X

Fig. 6 Air conditioning performance test chart. 1994 Sentra

should be .26–.30 inch for a new belt and .30–.34 inch for a used belt.

300ZX

Using 22 ft. lbs. of force, belt deflection should be .28–.31 inch for a new belt and .31–.35 inch for a used belt.

REFRIGERANT RECOVERY

Connect and operate refrigerant recovery system according to the manufacturers instructions.

Recirculating-to-discharge air temperature table

Inside air (Recirculating air) at blower assembly inlet		Discharge air temperature at center ventilator °C (°F)
Relative humidity %	Air temperature °C (°F)	
50 - 60	20 (68)	6.6 - 8.3 (44 - 47)
	25 (77)	10.4 - 12.4 (51 - 54)
	30 (86)	14.2 - 16.7 (58 - 62)
	35 (95)	18.2 - 21.0 (65 - 70)
	40 (104)	22.0 - 25.2 (72 - 77)
60 - 70	20 (68)	8.3 - 9.8 (47 - 50)
	25 (77)	12.4 - 14.4 (54 - 58)
	30 (86)	16.7 - 18.9 (62 - 66)
	35 (95)	21.0 - 23.6 (70 - 74)
	40 (104)	25.2 - 28.1 (77 - 83)

Ambient air temperature-to-compressor pressure table

Ambient air		High-pressure (Discharge side) kPa (kg/cm², psi)	Low-pressure (Suction side) kPa (kg/cm², psi)
Relative humidity %	Air temperature °C (°F)		
50 - 70	20 (68)	961 - 1,187 (9.8 - 12.1, 139 - 172)	108 - 157 (1.1 - 1.6, 16 - 23)
	25 (77)	1,295 - 1,599 (13.2 - 16.3, 188 - 232)	161.8 - 215.8 (1.65 - 2.2, 23.5 - 31.3)
	30 (86)	1,285 - 1,569 (13.1 - 16, 186 - 228)	167 - 216 (1.7 - 2.2, 24 - 31)
	35 (95)	1,520 - 1,863 (15.5 - 19, 220 - 270)	235 - 284 (2.4 - 2.9, 34 - 41)
	40 (104)	1,765 - 2,158 (18 - 22, 256 - 313)	289.3 - 353.1 (2.95 - 3.6, 41.9 - 51.2)

NS7029300061000X

Fig. 8 Air conditioning performance test chart. Pickup & 1993–95 Pathfinder

Recirculating-to-discharge air temperature table

Inside air (Recirculating air) at blower assembly inlet		Discharge air temperature at center ventilator °C (°F)
Relative humidity %	Air temperature °C (°F)	
50 - 60	25 (77)	6.0 - 9.0 (43 - 48)
	30 (86)	10.0 - 13.6 (50 - 56)
	35 (95)	15.2 - 19.5 (59 - 67)
	40 (104)	22.5 - 27.1 (73 - 81)
60 - 70	25 (77)	9.0 - 12.2 (48 - 54)
	30 (86)	13.6 - 17.2 (56 - 63)
	35 (95)	19.5 - 23.7 (67 - 75)
	40 (104)	27.1 - 32.3 (81 - 90)

Ambient air temperature-to-operating pressure table

Ambient air		High-pressure (Discharge side) kPa (kg/cm², psi)	Low-pressure (Suction side) kPa (kg/cm², psi)
Relative humidity %	Air temperature °C (°F)		
50 - 70	25 (77)	1,226 - 1,638 (12.5 - 16.7, 178 - 237)	172 - 250 (1.75 - 2.55, 25 - 36)
	30 (86)	1,422 - 1,883 (14.5 - 19.2, 206 - 273)	196 - 275 (2.0 - 2.8, 28 - 40)
	35 (95)	1,657 - 2,187 (16.9 - 22.3, 240 - 317)	231 - 309 (2.35 - 3.15, 33 - 45)
	40 (104)	1,922 - 2,501 (19.6 - 25.5, 279 - 363)	280 - 373 (2.85 - 3.8, 41 - 54)

NS7029600111000X

Fig. 9 Air conditioning performance test chart. 1996 Pathfinder

Recirculating-to-discharge air temperature table

Inside air (Recirculating air) at blower assembly inlet		Discharge air temperature at center ventilator °C (°F)
Relative humidity %	Air temperature °C (°F)	
50 - 60	20 (68)	2.2 - 7.8 (36 - 46)
	25 (77)	2.2 - 7.8 (36 - 46)
	30 (86)	2.2 - 7.8 (36 - 46)
	35 (95)	4.5 - 10.0 (40 - 50)
	40 (104)	7.2 - 12.8 (45 - 55)
60 - 70	20 (68)	3.3 - 8.9 (38 - 48)
	25 (77)	3.3 - 8.9 (38 - 48)
	30 (86)	3.3 - 8.9 (38 - 48)
	35 (95)	5.6 - 11.1 (42 - 52)
	40 (104)	8.3 - 13.9 (47 - 57)

Ambient air temperature-to-compressor pressure table

Ambient air		High-pressure (Discharge side) kPa (kg/cm², psi)	Low-pressure (Suction side) kPa (kg/cm², psi)
Relative humidity %	Air temperature °C (°F)		
50 - 70	20 (68)	686 - 1,344 (7.0 - 13.7, 100 - 195)	152 - 314 (1.5 - 3.2, 22 - 46)
	25 (77)	824 - 1,520 (8.4 - 15.5, 119 - 220)	152 - 314 (1.5 - 3.2, 22 - 46)
	30 (86)	1,000 - 1,687 (10.2 - 17.2, 145 - 245)	152 - 314 (1.5 - 3.2, 22 - 46)
	35 (95)	1,108 - 1,932 (11.3 - 19.7, 161 - 280)	152 - 314 (1.5 - 3.2, 22 - 46)
	40 (104)	1,481 - 2,344 (15.1 - 23.9, 215 - 340)	152 - 314 (1.5 - 3.2, 22 - 46)

NS7029100062000X

Fig. 10 Air conditioning performance test chart. 1993 Quest less rear A/C

Recirculating-to-discharge air temperature table

Inside air (Recirculating air) at blower assembly inlet		Discharge air temperature at center ventilator °C (°F)
Relative humidity %	Air temperature °C (°F)	
50 - 60	20 (68)	2.2 - 7.8 (36 - 46)
	25 (77)	2.2 - 7.8 (36 - 46)
	30 (86)	2.2 - 7.8 (36 - 46)
	35 (95)	4.5 - 10.0 (40 - 50)
	40 (104)	7.2 - 12.8 (45 - 55)
60 - 70	20 (68)	3.3 - 8.9 (38 - 48)
	25 (77)	3.3 - 8.9 (38 - 48)
	30 (86)	3.3 - 8.9 (38 - 48)
	35 (95)	5.6 - 11.1 (42 - 52)
	40 (104)	8.3 - 13.9 (47 - 57)

Ambient air temperature-to-compressor pressure table

Ambient air		High-pressure (Discharge side) kPa (kg/cm², psi)	Low-pressure (Suction side) kPa (kg/cm², psi)
Relative humidity %	Air temperature °C (°F)		
50 - 70	20 (68)	686 - 1,344 (7.0 - 13.7, 100 - 195)	152 - 314 (1.5 - 3.2, 22 - 46)
	25 (77)	824 - 1,520 (8.4 - 15.5, 119 - 220)	152 - 314 (1.5 - 3.2, 22 - 46)
	30 (86)	1,000 - 1,687 (10.2 - 17.2, 145 - 245)	152 - 314 (1.5 - 3.2, 22 - 46)
	35 (95)	1,108 - 1,932 (11.3 - 19.7, 161 - 280)	152 - 314 (1.5 - 3.2, 22 - 46)
	40 (104)	1,481 - 2,344 (15.1 - 23.9, 215 - 340)	152 - 314 (1.5 - 3.2, 22 - 46)

NS7029100063000X

Fig. 11 Air conditioning performance test chart. 1993 Quest w/rear A/C

NORMAL FIXED ORIFICE TUBE REFRIGERANT SYSTEM PRESSURE/TEMPERATURE RELATIONSHIPS

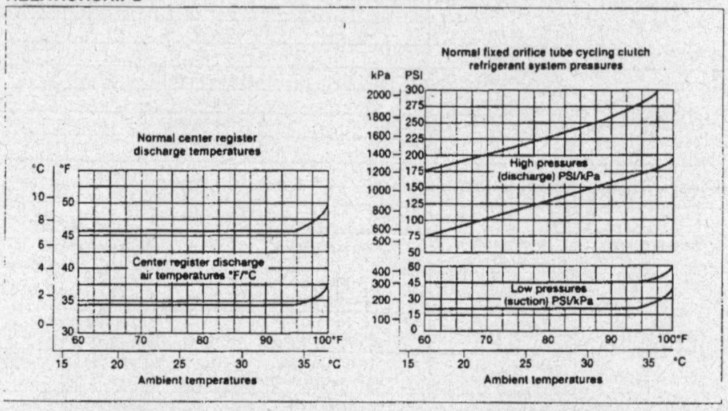
Normal center register discharge temperatures
Center register discharge air temperatures °F/°C
Ambient temperatures
Normal fixed orifice tube cycling clutch refrigerant system pressures
High pressures (discharge) PSI/kPa
Low pressures (suction) PSI/kPa
Ambient temperatures

NORMAL FIXED ORIFICE TUBE REFRIGERANT SYSTEM CLUTCH CYCLE TIMING RATES

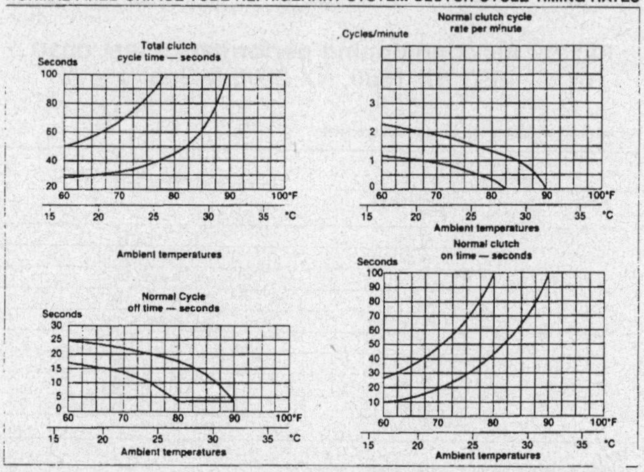
Total clutch cycle time — seconds
Normal clutch cycle rate per minute
Cycles/minute
Ambient temperatures
Normal Cycle off time — seconds
Normal clutch on time — seconds
Ambient temperatures

NS7029500105000X

Fig. 12 Air conditioning performance test chart. 1994–96 Quest

Recirculating-to-discharge air temperature table

Inside air (Recirculating air) at blower assembly inlet		Discharge air temperature at center ventilator °C (°F)
Relative humidity %	Air temperature °C (°F)	
50 - 60	25 (77)	6.5 - 8.7 (44 - 48)
	30 (86)	10 0 - 12.4 (50 - 54)
	35 (95)	13 4 - 16.1 (56 - 61)
	40 (104)	17.7 - 20.7 (64 - 69)
60 - 70	25 (77)	8 7 - 11.0 (48 - 52)
	30 (86)	12.4 - 14 8 (54 - 59)
	35 (95)	16.1 - 18.7 (61 - 66)
	40 (104)	20.7 - 23.4 (69 - 74)

Ambient air temperature-to-compressor pressure table

Ambient air		High-pressure (Discharge side) kPa (kg/cm², psi)	Low-pressure (Suction side) kPa (kg/cm², psi)
Relative humidity %	Air temperature °C (°F)		
50 - 70	25 (77)	745 - 912 (7 6 - 9 3, 108 - 132)	177 - 216 (1 8 - 2.2, 26 - 31)
	30 (86)	883 - 1,089 (9 0 - 11.1, 128 - 158)	157 - 196 (1.6 - 2.0, 23 - 28)
	35 (95)	1,040 - 1,275 (10.6 - 13.0, 151 - 185)	167 - 216 (1.7 - 2.2, 24 - 31)
	40 (104)	1,196 - 1,451 (12.2 - 14.8, 173 - 210)	177 - 255 (1.8 - 2.6, 26 - 37)

NS7029100065000X

Fig. 13 Air conditioning performance test chart. 1993 240SX

Recirculating-to-discharge air temperature table

Inside air at blower assembly inlet for RECIRC*		Discharge air temperature at center ventilator °C (°F)
Relative humidity %	Air temperature °C (°F)	
50 - 60	20 (68)	3 7 - 6 3 (39 - 43)
	25 (77)	8.3 - 11.5 (47 - 53)
	30 (86)	13.0 - 16.6 (55 - 62)
	35 (95)	17 6 - 21.8 (64 - 71)
	40 (104)	22.2 - 27.0 (72 - 81)
60 - 70	20 (68)	6 3 - 9.2 (43 - 49)
	25 (77)	11.5 - 14.9 (53 - 59)
	30 (86)	16.6 - 20.5 (62 - 69)
	35 (95)	21.8 - 26.1 (71 - 79)
	40 (104)	27.0 - 31.8 (81 - 89)

* Thermometer should be placed at intake unit under RH side of instrument panel.

Ambient air temperature-to-operating pressure table

Ambient air		High-pressure (Discharge side) kPa (kg/cm², psi)	Low-pressure (Suction side) kPa (kg/cm², psi)
Relative humidity %	Air temperature °C (°F)		
50 - 70	20 (68)	736 - 892 (7.5 - 9.1, 107 - 129)	147 - 226 (1.5 - 2 3, 21 - 33)
	25 (77)	922 - 1,118 (9.4 - 11 4, 134 - 162)	147 - 226 (1.5 - 2 3, 21 - 33)
	30 (86)	1,157 - 1,393 (11.8 - 14.2, 168 - 202)	147 - 226 (1.5 - 2.3, 21 - 33)
	35 (95)	1,393 - 1,687 (14.2 - 17 2, 202 - 245)	157 - 265 (1.6 - 2.7, 23 - 38)
	40 (104)	1,638 - 2,001 (16.7 - 20 4, 237 - 290)	196 - 324 (2.0 - 3.3, 28 - 47)

NS7029500104000X

Fig. 14 Air conditioning performance test chart. 1994–96 240SX

Recirculating-to-discharge air temperature table

Inside air(Recirculating air) at blower assembly inlet		Discharge air temperature at center ventilator °C (°F)
Relative humidity %	Air temperature °C (°F)	
50 - 60	20 (68)	5.9 - 7.8 (43 - 46)
	25 (77)	8.0 - 10.7 (46 - 51)
	30 (86)	11.0 - 14 4 (52 - 58)
	35 (95)	14.8 - 19.4 (59 - 67)
60 - 70	20 (68)	7.8 - 9.9 (46 - 50)
	25 (77)	10.7 - 13.6 (51 - 56)
	30 (86)	14 4 - 18.2 (58 - 65)
	35 (95)	19.4 - 24.8 (67 - 77)

Ambient air temperature-to-compressor pressure table

Ambient air		High-pressure (Discharge side) kPa (kg/cm², psi)	Low-pressure (Suction side) kPa (kg/cm², psi)
Relative humidity %	Air temperature °C (°F)		
50 - 70	20 (68)	608 - 912 (6.2 - 9.3, 88 - 132)	177 - 245 (1.8 - 2.5, 26 - 36)
	25 (77)	814 - 1,147 (8.3 - 11.7, 118 - 166)	186 - 255 (1.9 - 2.6, 27 - 37)
	30 (86)	1,020 - 1,402 (10.4 - 14.3, 148 - 203)	196 - 265 (2.0 - 2.7, 28 - 38)
	35 (95)	1,236 - 1,638 (12.6 - 16.7, 179 - 237)	226 - 314 (2.3 - 3.2, 33 - 46)

NS7029100066000X

Fig. 15 Air conditioning performance test chart. 1993 300ZX

Recirculating-to-discharge air temperature table

Inside air(Recirculating air) at blower assembly inlet		Discharge air temperature at center ventilator °C (°F)
Relative humidity %	Air temperature °C (°F)	
50 - 60	20 (68)	5.8 - 7.5 (42 - 46)
	25 (77)	9.3 - 11.0 (49 - 52)
	30 (86)	13.9 - 15.8 (57 - 60)
	35 (95)	18.8 - 20.9 (66 - 70)
	40 (104)	23.3 - 25.5 (74 - 78)
60 - 70	20 (68)	7.5 - 9.0 (46 - 48)
	25 (77)	11.0 - 13.0 (52 - 55)
	30 (86)	15.8 - 17.0 (60 - 63)
	35 (95)	20.9 - 22.6 (70 - 73)
	40 (104)	22.5 - 27.3 (73 - 81)

Ambient air temperature-to-operating pressure table

Ambient air		High-pressure (Discharge side) kPa (kg/cm², psi)	Low-pressure (Suction side) kPa (kg/cm², psi)
Relative humidity %	Air temperature °C (°F)		
50 - 70	20 (68)	1,030 - 1,245 (10.5 - 12.7, 149 - 181)	181.4 - 221.6 (1.85 - 2.26, 26.3 - 32.1)
	25 (77)	1,118 - 1,373 (11.4 - 14.0, 162 - 199)	185.4 - 226.5 (1.89 - 2.31, 26.9 - 32.8)
	30 (86)	1,344 - 1,638 (13.7 - 16.7, 195 - 237)	220.7 - 269.7 (2.25 - 2.75, 32.0 - 39.1)
	35 (95)	1,569 - 1,922 (16.0 - 19.6, 228 - 279)	269.7 - 328.5 (2.75 - 3.35, 39.1 - 47.6)
	40 (104)	1,814 - 2,207 (18.5 - 22.5, 263 - 320)	314 - 382 (3.2 - 3.9, 46 - 55)

NS7029500106000X

Fig. 16 Air conditioning performance test chart. 1994–96 300ZX

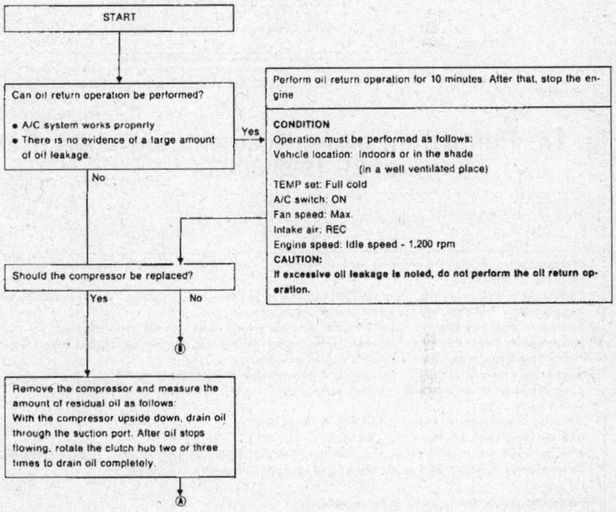
START
Can oil return operation be performed?
• A/C system works properly
• There is no evidence of a large amount of oil leakage.
Yes
No
Perform oil return operation for 10 minutes. After that, stop the engine
CONDITION
Operation must be performed as follows:
Vehicle location: Indoors or in the shade (in a well ventilated place)
TEMP set: Full cold
A/C switch: ON
Fan speed: Max.
Intake air: REC
Engine speed: Idle speed - 1,200 rpm
CAUTION:
If excessive oil leakage is noted, do not perform the oil return operation.
Should the compressor be replaced?
Yes
No
Remove the compressor and measure the amount of residual oil as follows:
With the compressor upside down, drain oil through the suction port. After oil stops flowing, rotate the clutch hub two or three times to drain oil completely.
A

NS7029100069010X

Fig. 17 Refrigerant oil replacement flow chart (Part 1 of 2). 1993 300ZX

Ⓐ

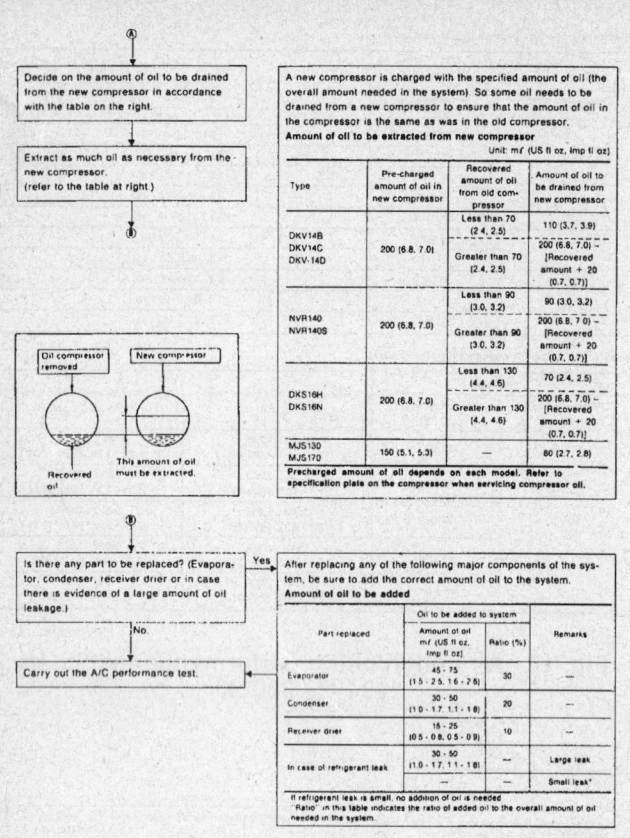

Decide on the amount of oil to be drained from the new compressor in accordance with the table on the right.

Extract as much oil as necessary from the new compressor. (refer to the table at right.)

Ⓑ

A new compressor is charged with the specified amount of oil (the overall amount needed in the system). So some oil needs to be drained from a new compressor to ensure that the amount of oil in the compressor is the same as was in the old compressor.

Amount of oil to be extracted from new compressor

Unit: mℓ (US fl oz, Imp fl oz)

Type	Pre-charged amount of oil in new compressor	Recovered amount of oil from old compressor	Amount of oil to be drained from new compressor
DKV14B DKV14C DKV-14D	200 (6.8, 7.0)	Less than 70 (2.4, 2.5)	110 (3.7, 3.9)
		Greater than 70 (2.4, 2.5)	200 (6.8, 7.0) – [Recovered amount + 20 (0.7, 0.7)]
NVR140 NVR140S	200 (6.8, 7.0)	Less than 90 (3.0, 3.2)	90 (3.0, 3.2)
		Greater than 90 (3.0, 3.2)	200 (6.8, 7.0) – [Recovered amount + 20 (0.7, 0.7)]
DKS16H DKS16N	200 (6.8, 7.0)	Less than 130 (4.4, 4.6)	70 (2.4, 2.5)
		Greater than 130 (4.4, 4.6)	200 (6.8, 7.0) – [Recovered amount + 20 (0.7, 0.7)]
MJS130 MJS170	150 (5.1, 5.3)	—	80 (2.7, 2.8)

Precharged amount of oil depends on each model. Refer to specification plate on the compressor when servicing compressor oil.

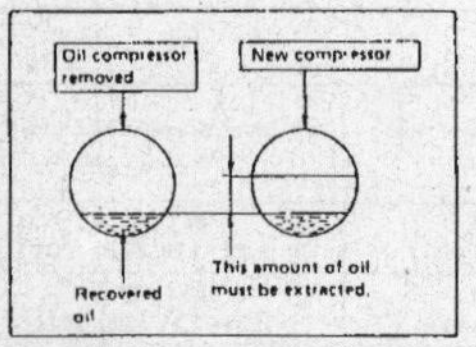

Oil compressor removed
New compressor
Recovered oil
This amount of oil must be extracted.

Ⓑ

Is there any part to be replaced? (Evaporator, condenser, receiver drier or in case there is evidence of a large amount of oil leakage.)

Yes → After replacing any of the following major components of the system, be sure to add the correct amount of oil to the system.

Amount of oil to be added

Part replaced	Oil to be added to system: Amount of oil mℓ (US fl oz, Imp fl oz)	Oil to be added to system: Ratio (%)	Remarks
Evaporator	45 - 75 (1.5 - 2.5, 1.6 - 2.6)	30	—
Condenser	30 - 50 (1.0 - 1.7, 1.1 - 1.8)	20	—
Receiver drier	15 - 25 (0.5 - 0.8, 0.5 - 0.9)	10	—
In case of refrigerant leak	30 - 50 (1.0 - 1.7, 1.1 - 1.8)	—	Large leak
	—	—	Small leak*

If refrigerant leak is small, no addition of oil is needed
"Ratio" in this table indicates the ratio of added oil to the overall amount of oil needed in the system.

No → Carry out the A/C performance test.

NS7029100069020X

Fig. 17 Refrigerant oil replacement flow chart (Part 2 of 2). 1993 300ZX

Ⓐ

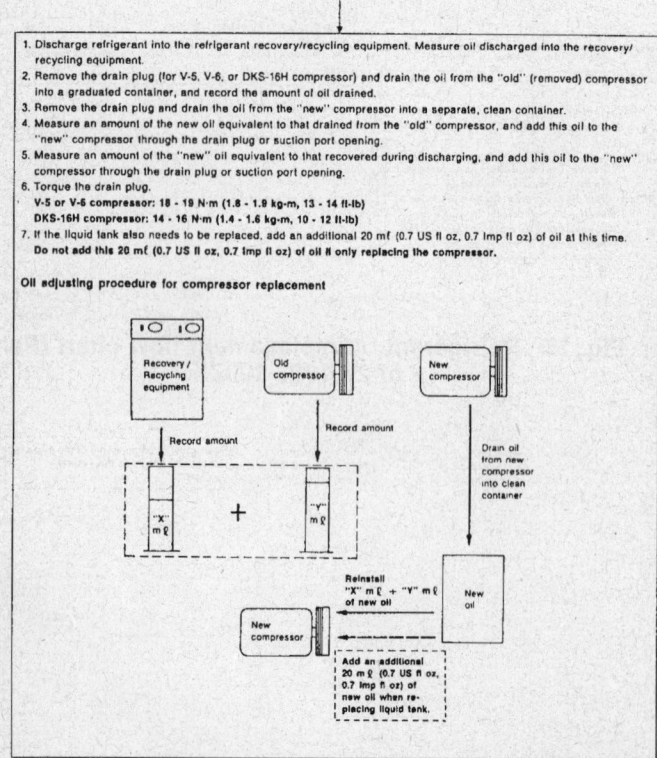

1. Discharge refrigerant into the refrigerant recovery/recycling equipment. Measure oil discharged into the recovery/recycling equipment.
2. Remove the drain plug (for V-5, V-6, or DKS-16H compressor) and drain the oil from the "old" (removed) compressor into a graduated container, and record the amount of oil drained.
3. Remove the drain plug and drain the oil from the "new" compressor into a separate, clean container.
4. Measure an amount of the new oil equivalent to that drained from the "old" compressor, and add this oil to the "new" compressor through the drain plug or suction port opening.
5. Measure an amount of the "new" oil equivalent to that recovered during discharging, and add this oil to the "new" compressor through the drain plug or suction port opening.
6. Torque the drain plug.
   V-5 or V-6 compressor: 18 - 19 N·m (1.8 - 1.9 kg-m, 13 - 14 ft-lb)
   DKS-16H compressor: 14 - 16 N·m (1.4 - 1.6 kg-m, 10 - 12 ft-lb)
7. If the liquid tank also needs to be replaced, add an additional 20 mℓ (0.7 US fl oz, 0.7 Imp fl oz) of oil at this time.
   Do not add this 20 mℓ (0.7 US fl oz, 0.7 Imp fl oz) of oil if only replacing the compressor.

Oil adjusting procedure for compressor replacement

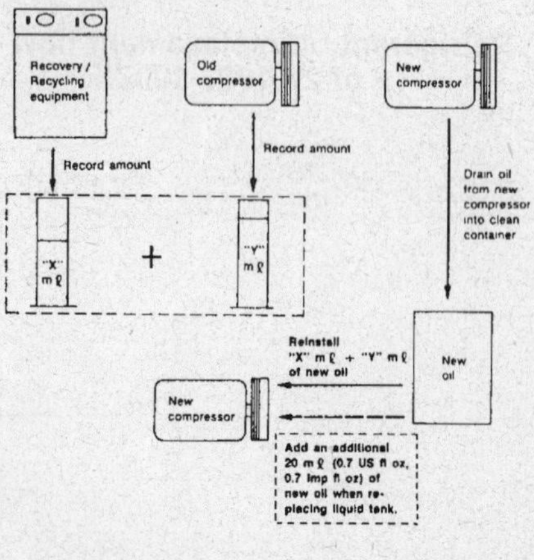

Recovery / Recycling equipment
Old compressor
New compressor
Record amount
Record amount
Drain oil from new compressor into clean container
"X" mℓ
+
"Y" mℓ
Reinstall "X" mℓ + "Y" mℓ of new oil
New oil
New compressor
Add an additional 20 mℓ (0.7 US fl oz, 0.7 Imp fl oz) of new oil when replacing liquid tank.

NS7029300072020X

Fig. 18 Refrigerant oil replacement flow chart (Part 2 of 2). 1993 NX 1600, NX 2000, Sentra & 240SX

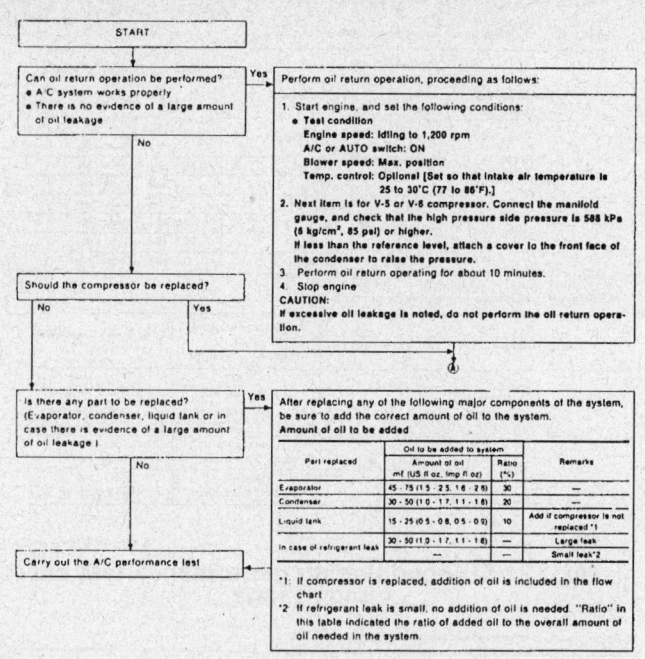

START

Can oil return operation be performed?
- A/C system works properly
- There is no evidence of a large amount of oil leakage

Yes → Perform oil return operation, proceeding as follows:

1. Start engine, and set the following conditions:
   - **Test condition**
     Engine speed: Idling to 1,200 rpm
     A/C or AUTO switch: ON
     Blower speed: Max. position
     Temp. control: Optional [Set so that intake air temperature is 25 to 30°C (77 to 86°F).]
2. **Next item is for V-5 or V-6 compressor. Connect the manifold gauge, and check that the high pressure side pressure is 588 kPa (6 kg/cm², 85 psi) or higher.**
   If less than the reference level, attach a cover to the front face of the condenser to raise the pressure.
3. Perform oil return operating for about 10 minutes.
4. Stop engine

CAUTION:
If excessive oil leakage is noted, do not perform the oil return operation.

No → Should the compressor be replaced?

Yes → Ⓐ

No → Is there any part to be replaced? (Evaporator, condenser, liquid tank or in case there is evidence of a large amount of oil leakage.)

Yes → After replacing any of the following major components of the system, be sure to add the correct amount of oil to the system.

Amount of oil to be added

Part replaced	Oil to be added to system: Amount of oil mℓ (US fl oz, Imp fl oz)	Oil to be added to system: Ratio (%)	Remarks
Evaporator	45 - 75 (1.5 - 2.5, 1.6 - 2.6)	30	—
Condenser	30 - 50 (1.0 - 1.7, 1.1 - 1.8)	20	—
Liquid tank	15 - 25 (0.5 - 0.8, 0.5 - 0.9)	10	Add if compressor is not replaced *1
In case of refrigerant leak	30 - 50 (1.0 - 1.7, 1.1 - 1.8)	—	Large leak
	—	—	Small leak*2

*1: If compressor is replaced, addition of oil is included in the flow chart
*2: If refrigerant leak is small, no addition of oil is needed. "Ratio" in this table indicated the ratio of added oil to the overall amount of oil needed in the system.

No → Carry out the A/C performance test

NS7029300072010X

Fig. 18 Refrigerant oil replacement flow chart (Part 1 of 2). 1993 NX 1600, NX 2000, Sentra & 240SX

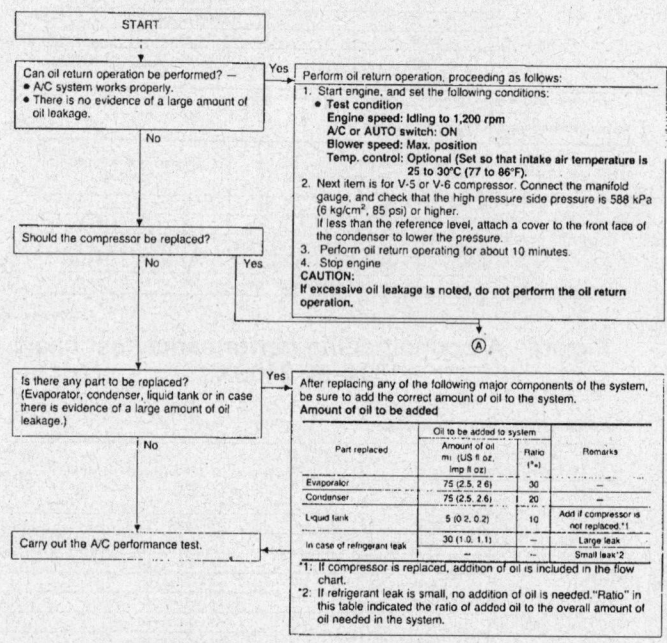

START

Can oil return operation be performed? —
- A/C system works properly.
- There is no evidence of a large amount of oil leakage.

Yes → Perform oil return operation, proceeding as follows:

1. Start engine, and set the following conditions:
   - **Test condition**
     Engine speed: Idling to 1,200 rpm
     A/C or AUTO switch: ON
     Blower speed: Max. position
     Temp. control: Optional (Set so that intake air temperature is 25 to 30°C (77 to 86°F).
2. Next item is for V-5 or V-6 compressor. Connect the manifold gauge, and check that the high pressure side pressure is 588 kPa (6 kg/cm², 85 psi) or higher.
   If less than the reference level, attach a cover to the front face of the condensor to lower the pressure.
3. Perform oil return operating for about 10 minutes.
4. Stop engine

CAUTION:
If excessive oil leakage is noted, do not perform the oil return operation.

No → Should the compressor be replaced?

Yes → Ⓐ

No → Is there any part to be replaced? (Evaporator, condenser, liquid tank or in case there is evidence of a large amount of oil leakage.)

Yes → After replacing any of the following major components of the system, be sure to add the correct amount of oil to the system.

Amount of oil to be added

Part replaced	Oil to be added to system: Amount of oil ml (US fl oz, Imp fl oz)	Oil to be added to system: Ratio (%)	Remarks
Evaporator	75 (2.5, 2.6)	30	–
Condenser	75 (2.5, 2.6)	20	–
Liquid tank	5 (0.2, 0.2)	10	Add if compressor is not replaced.*1
In case of refrigerant leak	30 (1.0, 1.1)	–	Large leak
	–	–	Small leak*2

*1: If compressor is replaced, addition of oil is included in the flow chart.
*2: If refrigerant leak is small, no addition of oil is needed."Ratio" in this table indicated the ratio of added oil to the overall amount of oil needed in the system.

No → Carry out the A/C performance test.

NS7029300070010X

Fig. 19 Refrigerant oil replacement flow chart (Part 1 of 2). Maxima, Pathfinder/Pickup, 1993 Altima, 1994–96 Sentra, 200SX & 300ZX

Ⓐ

1. Discharge refrigerant into refrigerant recovery/recycling equipment. Measure oil discharged into the recovery/recycling equipment.
2. Remove the drain plug (for V-5 or V-6, and DKS-16H compressor) and drain the oil from the "old" (removed) compressor into a graduated container, and record the amount of oil drained.
3. Remove the drain plug and drain the oil from the "new" compressor into a separate, clean container.
4. Measure an amount of the new oil equivalent to that drained from the "old" compressor, and add this oil to the "new" compressor through the drain plug or suction port opening.
5. Measure an amount of the "new" oil equivalent to that recovered during discharging, and add this oil to the "new" compressor through the drain plug or suction port opening.
6. Torque the drain plug.
   V-5 or V-6 compressor: 18 - 19 N·m (1.8 - 1.9 kg-m, 13 - 14 ft-lb)
   DKS-16H compressor: 14 - 16 N·m (1.4 - 1.6 kg-m, 10 - 12 ft-lb)
7. If the liquid tank also needs to be replaced, add an additional 5 mℓ (0.2 US fl oz, 0.2 Imp fl oz) of oil at this time.
   Do not add this 5 mℓ (0.2 US fl oz, 0.2 Imp fl oz) of oil if only replacing the compressor.

Oil adjusting procedure for compressor replacement

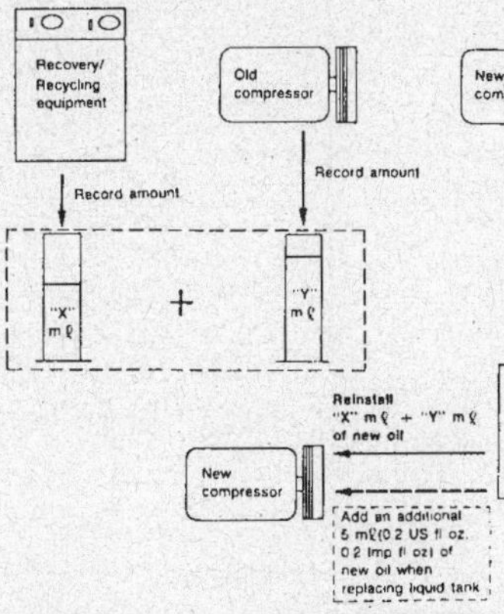

Recovery/ Recycling equipment
Old compressor
New compressor
Record amount
Record amount
Drain oil from new compressor into clean container
"X" mℓ
+
"Y" mℓ
Reinstall "X" mℓ + "Y" mℓ of new oil
New oil
New compressor
Add an additional 5 mℓ(0.2 US fl oz, 0.2 Imp fl oz) of new oil when replacing liquid tank

NS7029300070020X

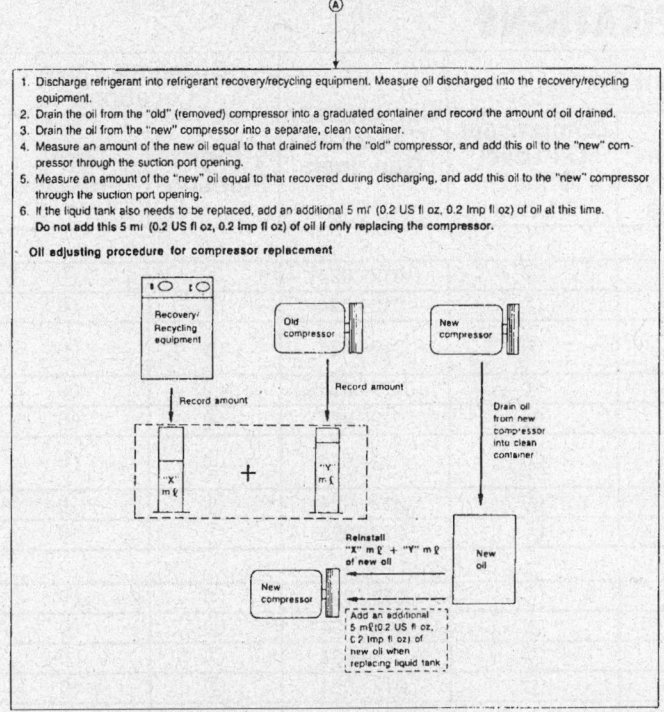

Fig. 19 Refrigerant oil replacement flow chart (Part 2 of 2). Maxima, Pathfinder/Pickup, 1993 Altima, 1994–96 Sentra, 200SX & 300ZX

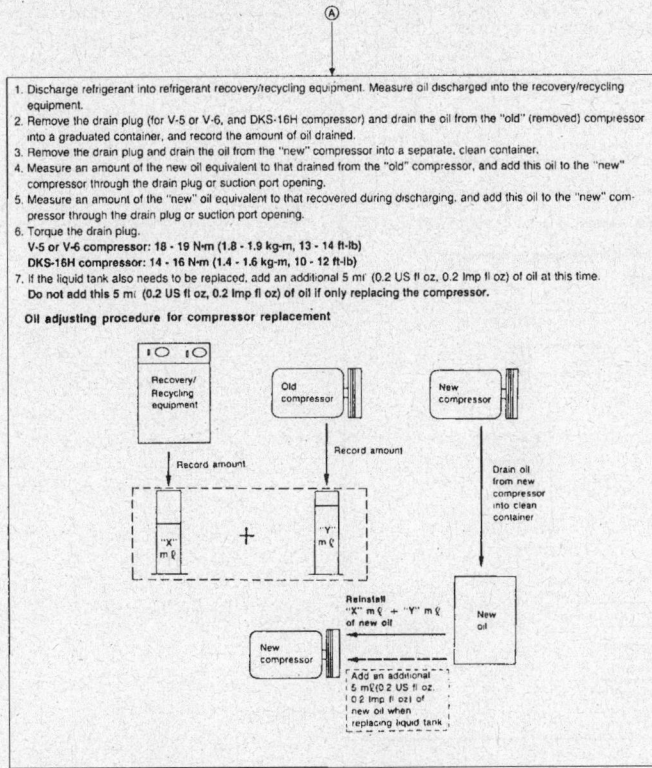

Ⓐ

1. Discharge refrigerant into refrigerant recovery/recycling equipment. Measure oil discharged into the recovery/recycling equipment.
2. Drain the oil from the "old" (removed) compressor into a graduated container and record the amount of oil drained.
3. Drain the oil from the "new" compressor into a separate, clean container.
4. Measure an amount of the new oil equal to that drained from the "old" compressor, and add this oil to the "new" compressor through the suction port opening.
5. Measure an amount of the "new" oil equal to that recovered during discharging, and add this oil to the "new" compressor through the suction port opening.
6. If the liquid tank also needs to be replaced, add an additional 5 mℓ (0.2 US fl oz, 0.2 Imp fl oz) of oil at this time.
   Do not add this 5 mℓ (0.2 US fl oz, 0.2 Imp fl oz) of oil if only replacing the compressor.

Oil adjusting procedure for compressor replacement

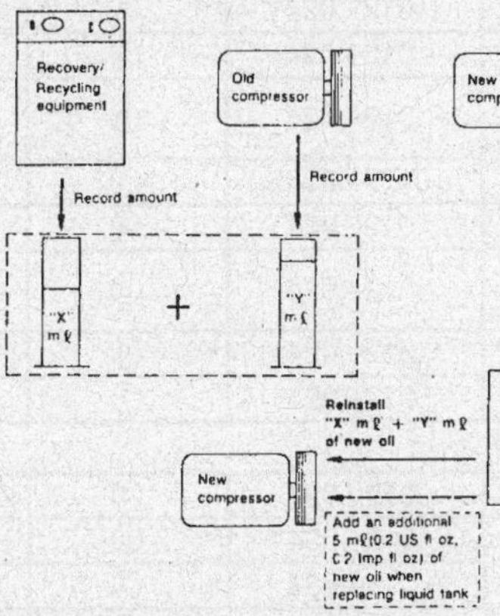

Recovery/ Recycling equipment
Old compressor
New compressor
Record amount
Record amount
Drain oil from new compressor into clean container
"X" mℓ
+
"Y" mℓ
Reinstall "X" mℓ + "Y" mℓ of new oil
New oil
New compressor
Add an additional 5 mℓ(0.2 US fl oz, 0.2 Imp fl oz) of new oil when replacing liquid tank

NS7029400071020X

Fig. 20 Refrigerant oil replacement flow chart (Part 2 of 2). 1994–96 Altima & 240SX

START

Can oil return operation be performed? —
- A/C system works properly.
- There is no evidence of a large amount of oil leakage.

Yes → Perform oil return operation, proceeding as follows:
1. Start engine, and set the following conditions:
   - **Test condition**
     Engine speed: Idling to 1,200 rpm
     A/C or AUTO switch: ON
     RECIRC switch: OFF
     Fan speed: Max. position
     Temp. control: Optional (Set so that intake air temperature is 25 to 30°C (77 to 86°F).
2. **Perform oil return operation for 10 minutes.**
3. **Stop engine**

CAUTION:
If excessive oil leakage is noted, do not perform the oil return operation.

No ↓

Should the compressor be replaced?

No / Yes → Ⓐ (Go to next page)

Is there any part to be replaced? (Evaporator, condenser, liquid tank or in case there is evidence of a large amount of oil leakage.)

Yes → After replacing any of the following major components of the system, be sure to add the correct amount of oil to the system.
Amount of oil to be added

Part replaced	Oil to be added to system: Amount of oil mℓ (US fl oz, Imp fl oz)	Ratio (%)	Remarks
Evaporator	75 (2.5, 2.6)	30	—
Condenser	75 (2.5, 2.6)	20	—
Liquid tank	5 (0.2, 0.2)	10	Add if compressor is not replaced.*1
In case of refrigerant leak	30 (1.0, 1.1)	—	Large leak
	—	—	Small leak*2

*1: If compressor is replaced, addition of oil is included in the flow chart.
*2: If refrigerant leak is small, no addition of oil is needed.
"Ratio" in this table indicated the ratio of added oil to the overall amount of oil needed in the system.

No ↓

Carry out the A/C performance test.

NS7029400071010X

Fig. 20 Refrigerant oil replacement flow chart (Part 1 of 2). 1994–96 Altima & 240SX

Major unit	Amount of oil to be added mℓ (US fl oz, Imp fl oz)	Remarks
Cooling unit, evaporator	90 (3.0, 3.2)	Add compressor oil little by little from the low pressure side of the system cycle.
Condenser	30 (1.0, 1.1)	
Accumulator drier	60 (2.0, 2.1)	Add if compressor is not replaced.
In case of refrigerant leak	30 - 50 (1.0 - 1.7, 1.1 - 1.8)	Add if large of oil leak is indicated.
	—	Addition of oil is not required if no oil leak is indicated.

NS7029300073000X

Fig. 21 Refrigerant oil replacement chart. 1993 Quest

START

Can lubricant return operation be performed? —
- A/C system works properly.
- There is no evidence of a large amount of lubricant leakage.

Yes → Perform lubricant return operation, proceeding as follows:
1. Start engine, and set the following conditions:
   - **Test condition**
     Engine speed: Idling to 1,200 rpm
     A/C or AUTO switch: ON
     RECIRC switch: OFF
     Fan speed: Max. position
     Temp. control: Optional (Set so that intake air temperature is 25 to 30°C (77 to 86°F).
2. **Perform lubricant return operation for 10 minutes.**
3. **Stop engine**

CAUTION:
If excessive lubricant leakage is noted, do not perform the lubricant return operation.

No ↓

Should the compressor be replaced?

No / Yes → Ⓐ (Go to next page)

Is there any part to be replaced? (Evaporator, condenser, accumulator or in case there is evidence of a large amount of lubricant leakage.)

Yes → After replacing any of the following major components of the system, be sure to add the correct amount of lubricant to the system.
Amount of lubricant to be added

Part replaced	Lubricant to be added to system: Amount of lubricant mℓ (US fl oz, Imp fl oz)	Ratio (%)	Remarks
Evaporator	90 (3.0, 3.2)	30	Add compressor lubricant little by little from the low pressure side of the system cycle.
Condenser	30 (1.0, 1.1)	20	
Accumulator	60 (2.0, 2.1)	10	Add if compressor is not replaced.*1
In case of refrigerant leak	30 - 50 (1.0 - 1.7, 1.1 - 1.8)	—	Add if large lubricant leak is indicated.
	—	—	Addition of lubricant is not required if no leak is indicated

*1: If compressor is replaced, addition of lubricant is included in the flow chart.
*2: If refrigerant leak is small, no addition of lubricant is needed.
"Ratio" in this table indicated the ratio of added lubricant to the overall amount of lubricant needed in the system.

No ↓

Carry out the A/C performance test.

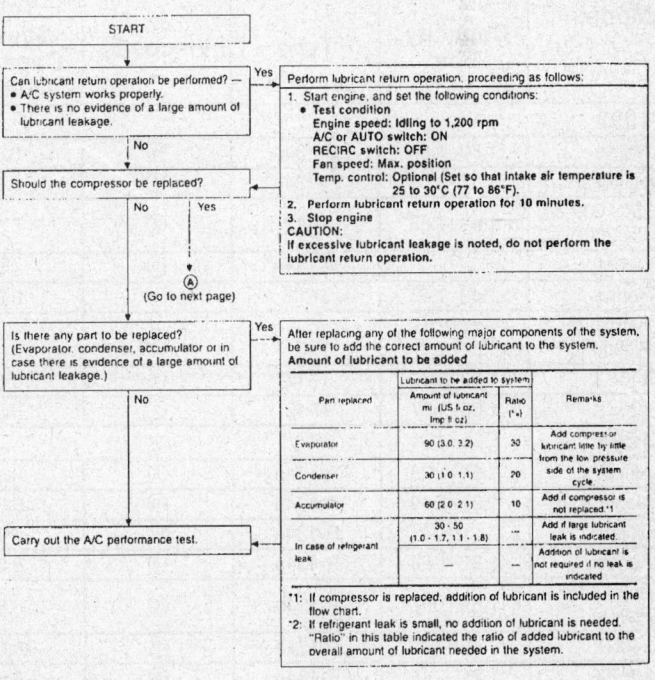

NS7029400074010X

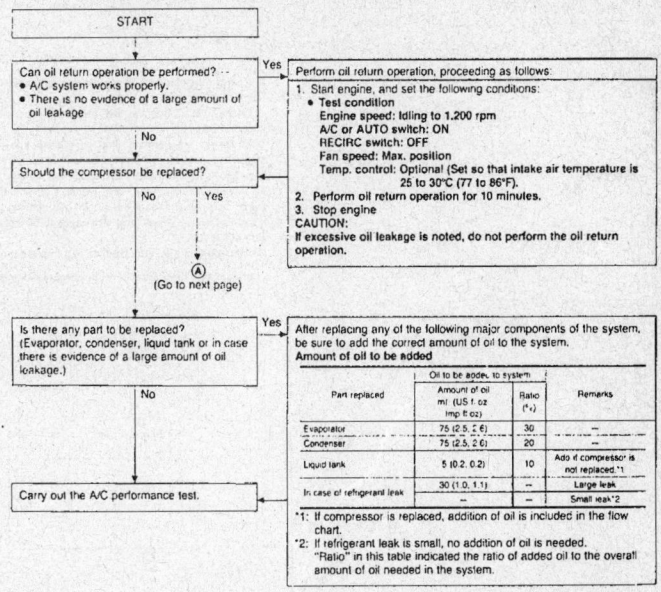

Fig. 22 Refrigerant oil replacement chart (Part 1 of 2). 1994–96 Quest

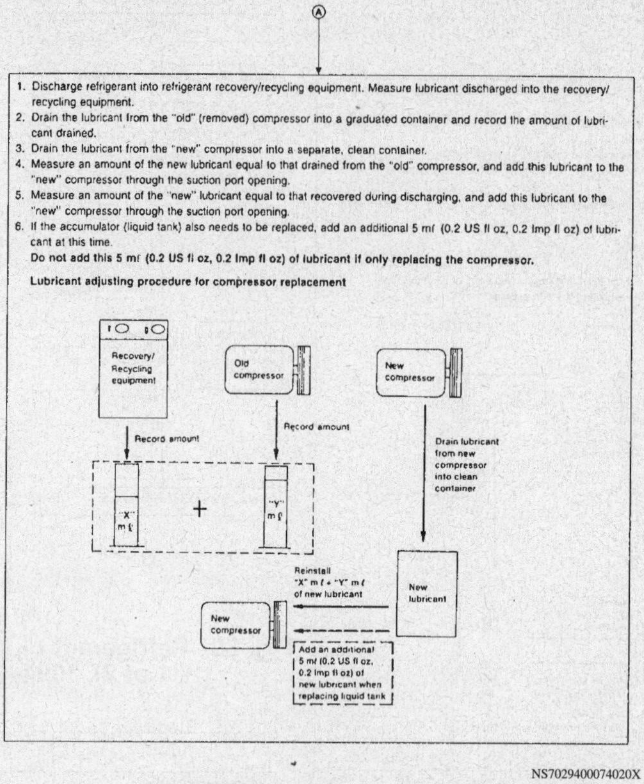
A
1. Discharge refrigerant into refrigerant recovery/recycling equipment. Measure lubricant discharged into the recovery/recycling equipment.
2. Drain the lubricant from the "old" (removed) compressor into a graduated container and record the amount of lubricant drained.
3. Drain the lubricant from the "new" compressor into a separate, clean container.
4. Measure an amount of the new lubricant equal to that drained from the "old" compressor, and add this lubricant to the "new" compressor through the suction port opening.
5. Measure an amount of the "new" lubricant equal to that recovered during discharging, and add this lubricant to the "new" compressor through the suction port opening.
6. If the accumulator (liquid tank) also needs to be replaced, add an additional 5 mℓ (0.2 US fl oz, 0.2 Imp fl oz) of lubricant at this time.
Do not add this 5 mℓ (0.2 US fl oz, 0.2 Imp fl oz) of lubricant if only replacing the compressor.
Lubricant adjusting procedure for compressor replacement
Recovery/Recycling equipment
Old compressor
New compressor
Record amount
Record amount
Drain lubricant from new compressor into clean container
"X" mℓ
+
"Y" mℓ
Reinstall "X" mℓ + "Y" mℓ of new lubricant
New lubricant
New compressor
Add an additional 5 mℓ (0.2 US fl oz, 0.2 Imp fl oz) of new lubricant when replacing liquid tank
NS7029400074020X

Fig. 22 Refrigerant oil replacement chart (Part 2 of 2). 1994–96 Quest

A/C SPECIFICATIONS

Model	Refrigerant		Refrigerant Oil			Compressor Clutch Air Gap, Inch	Charging Valve Locations	
	Capacity, Lbs.	Type	Viscosity	Total System Capacity, Ounces	Compressor Oil Level Check, Inches		High Pressure	Low Pressure
1993								
Altima	1.50–1.80	R-134a	⑥	6.8	②	.012–.024	③	④
Maxima	1.87–2.09	R-134a	⑥	6.8	②	.012–.024	③	④
NX 1600 & NX 2000	1.43–1.65	R-12	①	6.8	②	.012–.024	③	④
Quest	⑦	R-134a	⑧	⑤	②	.0177–.0335	③	④
Sentra	1.43–1.65	R-12	①	6.8	②	.012–.024	③	④
Pathfinder & Pickup	1.65–1.87	R-134a	⑥	6.8	②	.012–.024	③	④
240SX	1.80–2.00	R-12	①	8.5	②	.012–.024	③	④
300ZX	1.65–1.87	R-12	①	6.8	②	.012–.024	③	④
1994								
Altima	1.54–1.76	R-134a	⑥	6.8	②	.012–.024	③	④
Maxima	1.87–2.09	R-134a	⑨	6.8	②	.012–.024	③	④
Quest	⑪	R-134a	⑩	⑤	②	.018–.034	③	④
Sentra	1.32–1.54	R-134a	⑥	6.8	②	.012–.024	③	④
Pathfinder & Pickup	1.65–1.87	R-134a	⑥	6.8	②	.012–.024	③	④
240SX	1.54	R-134a	⑨	8.5	②	.012–.024	③	④
300ZX	1.21–1.43	R-134a	⑨	6.8	②	.012–.024	③	④
1995–96								
Altima	1.54–1.76	R-134a	⑥	6.8	②	.012–.024	③	④

Continued

A/C SPECIFICATIONS—Continued

Model	Refrigerant		Refrigerant Oil			Compressor Clutch Air Gap, Inch	Charging Valve Locations	
	Capacity, Lbs.	Type	Viscosity	Total System Capacity, Ounces	Compressor Oil Level Check, Inches		High Pressure	Low Pressure
1995–96								
Maxima	1.71–1.82	R-134a	⑨	8.5	②	.012–.024	③	④
Quest	⑪	R-134a	⑩	⑤	②	.018–.034	③	④
Sentra & 200SX	1.32–1.54	R-134a	⑥	6.8	②	.012–.024	③	④
Pathfinder & Pickup	1.65–1.87	R-134a	⑥	7.0	②	.012–.024	③	④
240SX	1.32–1.54	R-134a	⑨	8.5	②	.012–.024	③	④
300ZX	1.21–1.43	R-134a	⑨	6.8	②	.012–.024	③	④

① — Suniso 5GS or equivalent.
② — Oil level inches cannot be checked.
③ — On high pressure line.
④ — On low pressure line.
⑤ — Less rear A/C, 7 ounces; with rear A/C, 10 ounces.
⑥ — Nissan A/C System Oil Type R, part No. KLH00-RAGR0, or equivalent.
⑦ — Less rear A/C, 2.25 lbs.; with rear A/C, 3.5 lbs.
⑧ — Motorcraft YN-9 or equivalent.
⑨ — Nissan A/C System Oil Type S, part No. KLH00-PAGS0, or equivalent.
⑩ — Nissan A/C System Oil Type F or equivalent.
⑪ — Less rear A/C, 2.0 lbs.; with rear A/C, 3.25 lbs.

Cooling Fans

NOTE: Electrical Symbol & Wire Color Code Identification Located In The Front Of This Manual May Be Used As An Aid When Using Wiring Circuits Found In This Section.

INDEX

	Page No.
Component Diagnosis & Testing	36-11
Radiator Fan Motors	36-11
Radiator Fan Relays	36-11
Thermo Switch/Sensor	36-11
Component Replacement	36-11
Cooling Fan Motor	36-11
Thermo Switch/Sensor	36-11
Description	36-9
Altima	36-9
Maxima	36-10
NX 1600, NX 2000, Sentra & 200SX	36-10
Quest	36-10
240SX	36-10
300ZX	36-10
System Diagnosis & Testing	36-11
Maxima	36-11
NX 1600, NX 2000, Sentra & 200SX	36-11
Quest	36-11
240SX	36-11
300ZX	36-11

DESCRIPTION

ALTIMA

These models use an engine coolant temperature sensor, vehicle speed sensor, A/C "ON" signal and A/C pressure signal to input signals to the ECM. The module uses these input signals to open and close the two coolant fan relays.

With vehicle speed below 12 mph, A/C switch off, A/C triple-pressure switch off and engine coolant temperature below 203°F, both relays will remain open and cooling fans should be off. With engine temperature between 203°F and 221°F, relay No. 1 should close and low speed coolant fan should come on. With engine temperature 221°F or more, both relays should close and both cooling fans should come on.

With vehicle speed below 12 mph, A/C switch on, A/C triple-pressure off and engine coolant temperature below 221°F, the low coolant fan relay should close and low speed coolant fan should be on. With engine coolant temperature above 221°F, both coolant fan relays should close and both coolant fans should be on.

With vehicle speed below 12 mph, A/C switch on and A/C triple-pressure on, both coolant fan relays should close and both fans should be on regardless of engine temperature.

With vehicle speed between 12 and 50 mph, A/C switch off, A/C triple-pressure off and engine coolant temperature below 203°F, both relays will remain open and coolant fans should be off. With engine coolant temperature between 203°F and 212°F, the low coolant fan relay should close and low speed coolant fan should be on. With engine coolant temperature above 212°F, both coolant fan relays should close and both coolant fans should be on.

With vehicle speed between 12 and 50 mph, A/C switch on, A/C triple-pressure switch on or off and engine coolant temperature below 212°F, the low speed coolant fan relay should close and low speed coolant fan should be on. With engine coolant temperature over 212°F, both relays should close and both fans should be on.

With vehicle speed over 50 mph, A/C switch on or off, A/C triple-pressure switch on or off and engine coolant temperature below 203°F, both relays will remain open and both fans should be off, With engine coolant temperature between 203°F and 212°F, the low speed coolant fan relay should close and low speed coolant fan should be on. With engine coolant temperature over 212°F, both relays should close and both fans should be on.

MAXIMA

These models use one thermo sensor and three relays to control cooling fan operation.

With A/C off and engine coolant temperature below 205°F, the cooling fans will not operate. When coolant temperature exceeds 207°F, relay No. 1 closes and cooling fan operates at low speed. When coolant temperature exceeds 225°F, relays No. 2 and 3 close and cooling fan operates at high speed.

With A/C switch on and engine coolant below 201°F, relay No. 1 closes and cooling fan operates at low speed. When coolant temperature exceeds 203°F, relays No. 2 and 3 close and cooling fan operates at high speed.

NX 1600, NX 2000, SENTRA & 200SX

Manual Transaxle

These models use an engine temperature sensor, vehicle speed sensor and A/C "ON" signal to input signals to the ECM. The control unit uses these input signals to open and close the coolant fan relay.

With A/C off and engine coolant temperature below 201°F, the cooling fan relay should remain open and cooling fans should not operate.

With A/C off and coolant temperature is between 203°F and 210°F and vehicle speed is below 12 mph, the cooling fan relay should remain open and cooling fans should not operate.

With A/C off and coolant temperature is between 203°F and 210°F and vehicle speed is above 12 mph, the cooling fan relay should close and activate both cooling fans.

With A/C off and coolant temperature is over 212°F, the cooling fan relay should close and activate both cooling fans.

With A/C on, engine coolant temperature below 201°F and vehicle speed is over 50 mph, the cooling fan relay should remain open and cooling fans should not operate.

With A/C on, engine coolant temperature is below 201°F and vehicle speed is below 49 mph, the cooling fan relay should close and activate both cooling fans.

With A/C on and engine coolant temperature is over 202°F, the cooling fan relay should close and activate both cooling fans.

Automatic Transaxle

These models use an engine temperature sensor, vehicle speed sensor and A/C "ON" signal to input signals to the ECM. The control unit uses these input signals to open and close the three coolant fan relays.

With A/C off and engine coolant temperature below 202°F, the coolant fan relays will remain open and coolant fans should not operate.

With A/C off and engine coolant is between 203°F and 210°F, the coolant fan relays should activate the low speed coolant fan.

With A/C off, engine coolant temperature is between 211°F and 219°F and vehicle speed is 12 mph or less, the coolant fan relays should activate the low speed coolant fan.

With A/C off, engine coolant temperature is between 211°F and 219°F and vehicle speed is more than 12 mph, the coolant fan relays should activate both the low and high speed coolant fans.

With A/C off and engine coolant temperature is 221°F or more, the coolant fan relays should activate both the low and high speed coolant fans.

With A/C on, engine coolant temperature below 202°F and vehicle speed is 50 mph or more, the coolant fan relays should remain open and coolant fans should not operate.

With A/C on, engine coolant temperature below 202°F and vehicle speed is 49 mph or less, the coolant fan relays should activate the low speed coolant fan.

With A/C on and engine coolant is between 203°F and 210°F, the coolant fan relays should activate the low speed coolant fan.

With A/C on, engine coolant temperature is between 211°F and 219°F and vehicle speed is 12 mph or less, the coolant fan relays should activate the low speed coolant fan.

With A/C on, engine coolant temperature is between 211°F and 219°F and vehicle speed is more than 12 mph, the coolant fan relays should activate both the low and high speed coolant fans.

With A/C on and engine coolant temperature is 221°F or more, the coolant fan relays should activate both the low and high speed coolant fans.

QUEST

These models use an engine coolant temperature sensor, vehicle speed sensor and A/C switch to input signals to the ECM. The module uses these input signals to open and close the coolant fan relays.

With engine coolant temperature below 201°F and A/C switch off, the coolant fan relays should be open and coolant fan should not be on. With engine coolant temperature between 203°F and 210°F and A/C switch off, the low speed coolant fan relay should close and coolant fan should be running at low speed. With engine coolant temperature between 212°F and 219°F, A/C switch off and vehicle speed is less than 12 mph, the low speed coolant fan relay should close and coolant fan should be running at low speed. With engine coolant temperature between 212°F and 219°F, A/C switch off and vehicle speed is more than 12 mph, the high speed coolant fan relay should close and coolant fan should be running at high speed. With engine coolant temperature over 221°F and A/C switch off, the high speed coolant fan relay should close and coolant fan should be running at high speed.

With engine coolant temperature 201°F or less, A/C switch on and vehicle speed is 68 mph or more, the coolant fan relays should be open and the coolant fan should be off. With engine coolant temperature 201°F or less, A/C switch on and vehicle speed is less than 68 mph, the low speed coolant fan relay should close and the coolant fan should run at low speed. With engine coolant temperature between 203°F and 219°F, A/C switch on and vehicle speed is 12 mph or less, the low speed coolant fan relay should be closed and coolant fan should be running at low speed. With engine coolant temperature between 203°F and 219°F, A/C switch on and vehicle speed is more than 12 mph, the high speed coolant fan relay should be closed and coolant fan should be running at high speed. With engine coolant temperature more than 221°F and A/C switch on, the high speed coolant fan relay should be closed and coolant fan should be running, regardless of vehicle speed.

240SX

These models use an engine coolant temperature sensor, vehicle speed sensor, A/C On signal and A/C pressure signal to input signals to the ECM. The module uses these input signals to open and close the two coolant fan relays.

With vehicle speed below 12 mph, A/C switch off and engine coolant temperature below 203°F, both relays will remain open and cooling fans should be off. With engine temperature between 203°F and 212°F, relay No. 1 should close and low speed coolant fan should come on. With engine temperature 212°F or more, both relays should close and both cooling fans should be on.

With vehicle speed below 12 mph, A/C switch on, A/C triple-pressure off and engine coolant temperature below 212°F, the low coolant fan relay should close and the low speed coolant fan should be on. With engine coolant temperature above 212°F, both coolant fan relays should close and both coolant fans should be on.

With vehicle speed below 12 mph, A/C switch on and A/C triple-pressure on, both coolant fan relays should close and both fans should be on regardless of engine temperature.

300ZX

These models use an engine temperature sensor, vehicle speed sensor and A/C "ON" signal to input signals to the ECM. The control unit uses these input signals to open and close the two coolant fan relays.

With A/C switch off and engine coolant temperature 219°F or below, cooling fan relay will be open and coolant fan should not come on. With engine coolant temperature 221°F or over, cooling fan relays will be closed and cooling fan should come on.

On non-turbo models, A/C switch on, engine coolant temperature below 201°F and vehicle speed less than 24 mph, cooling fan relay should be open and coolant fan should not be on. With engine coolant temperature 203°F or more and vehicle speed less than 24 mph, cooling fan relays should be closed and cooling fan should operate at high speed. With engine coolant temperature below 219°F and vehicle speed more than 25 mph, cooling fan relays should be open and cooling fan should not come on. With engine coolant temperature 221°F or more and vehicle speed more than 25 mph, cooling fan relays should be closed and cooling fan should operate at high speed.

On turbo models, A/C switch on, engine coolant temperature below 192°F and vehicle speed less than 24 mph, cooling fan relay should be open and coolant fan should not be on. With engine coolant temperature between 194°F and 210°F and vehicle speed less than 24 mph, low speed cooling fan relay should be closed and cooling fan should operate at low speed. With engine coolant temperature below 219°F and vehicle speed more than 25 mph, cooling fan relays should be open and cooling fan should not come on. With engine coolant temperature 221°F or more and vehicle speed more than 25 mph, cooling fan relays should be closed and cooling fan should operate at high speed.

SYSTEM DIAGNOSIS & TESTING

MAXIMA

Refer to diagnosis charts, **Figs. 1 through 3** to diagnose the cooling fan system.

NX 1600, NX 2000, SENTRA & 200SX

1993-94

Refer to diagnosis charts, **Figs. 4 through 6** to diagnose the cooling fan system.

1995-96

Refer to diagnosis charts, **Figs. 7 and 8** to diagnose cooling fan system.

QUEST

Refer to diagnosis chart in **Fig. 9,** to diagnose the cooling fan system.

240SX

Refer to diagnosis chart in **Fig. 10** to diagnose the cooling fan system.

300ZX

Refer to diagnosis chart in **Figs. 11 and 12** to diagnose the cooling fan system.

COMPONENT DIAGNOSIS & TESTING

RADIATOR FAN RELAYS

ALTIMA & MAXIMA

Refer to **Figs. 13 and 14** for fan relay testing, if test results are not as specified, replace relay.

QUEST

Refer to **Fig. 15** for fan relay testing, if test results are not as specified, replace relay.

NX 1600, NX 2000, SENTRA & 200SX

Refer to **Figs. 15 and 13** for fan relay testing, if test results are not as specified, replace relay.

300ZX

Refer to **Fig. 15** for fan relay testing, if test results are not as specified, replace relay.

RADIATOR FAN MOTORS

ALTIMA & MAXIMA

Refer to **Fig. 16** for fan motor testing, if test results are not as specified, replace motor.

QUEST

Refer to **Fig. 17** for fan motor testing, if test results are not as specified, replace motor.

NX 1600, NX 2000, SENTRA & 200SX

1993-94 w/Automatic Transaxle

Refer to **Fig. 16** for fan motor testing, if test results are not as specified, replace motor.

1993-94 w/Manual Transaxle

1. Disconnect fan motor harness connectors.
2. Supply battery voltage to fan harness connectors as shown in **Fig. 18.**
3. If fan motors do not come on when battery voltage is applied, replace fan motor.

1995-96

Refer to **Fig. 19** for fan motor testing, if test results are not as specified, replace motor.

240SX

Refer to **Fig. 20** for fan motor testing, if test results are not as specified, replace motor.

THERMO SWITCH/SENSOR

300ZX

1. Remove thermo switch/sensor as outlined under "Thermo Switch/Sensor, Replace."
2. Connect suitable ohmmeter across switch terminals, then immerse lower part of switch in water. Ohmmeter should indicate an open circuit.
3. Heat water until temperature reaches approximately 212°F. Switch contacts should close and the ohmmeter should indicate continuity.
4. If switch does not operate properly, replace it.

COMPONENT REPLACEMENT

THERMO SWITCH/SENSOR

300ZX

The thermo switch is located on left side of engine.

1. Disconnect battery ground cable.
2. Drain cooling system into suitable container.
3. Disconnect thermo switch wiring, then remove switch.
4. Reverse procedure to install.

COOLING FAN MOTOR

ALTIMA

Refer to **Fig. 21,** for cooling fan motor replacement.

MAXIMA

Refer to **Figs. 22 through 24** for cooling fan motor replacement.

NX 1600, NX 2000, SENTRA & 200SX

Refer to **Figs. 25 and 26** for cooling fan motor replacement.

QUEST

Refer to **Fig. 27** for cooling fan motor replacement.

240SX

Refer to **Fig. 28** for cooling fan motor replacement.

300ZX

1. Disconnect battery ground cable.
2. Disconnect fan motor electrical connector.
3. Remove fan motor assembly attaching bolts, then the fan motor assembly.
4. Reverse procedure to install.

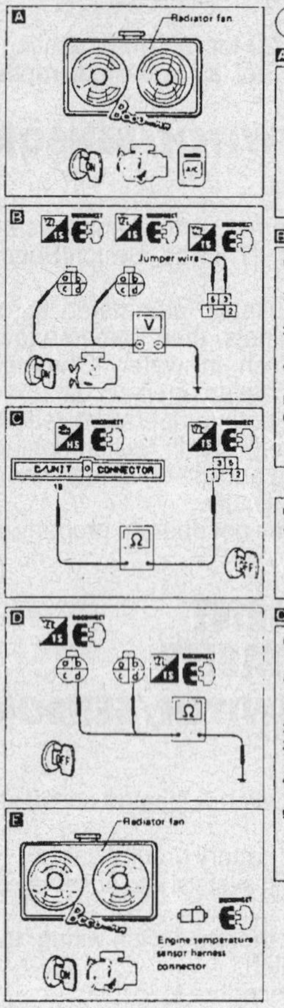

INSPECTION START

A CHECK RADIATOR FAN LOW SPEED CIRCUIT.
1) Start engine.
2) Turn air conditioner switch "ON".
3) Make sure that both radiator fan motors operate at low speed.

O.K. → ⊕⊕
N.G. ↓

B CHECK POWER SUPPLY.
1) Stop engine.
2) Disconnect radiator fan relay-1.
3) Connect jumper wire between terminals ③ and ⑤.
4) Disconnect both radiator fan motor harness connectors.
5) Turn ignition switch "ON".
6) Check voltage between terminal ⓐ and ground.
Voltage: Battery voltage

N.G. → Check the following items.
1) "GY" fusible link
2) "R" fusible link
3) Joint connector (E51)
O.K. → Repair harness or connectors.

O.K. ↓

CHECK COMPONENT (Radiator fan relay-1).

O.K. ↓

C CHECK HARNESS CONTINUITY BETWEEN E.C.U. AND RADIATOR FAN RELAY-1.
1) Turn ignition switch "OFF".
2) Disconnect jumper wire.
3) Reconnect both radiator fan harness connectors.
4) Disconnect E.C.U. S.M.J. harness connector.
5) Check harness continuity between E.C.U. terminal ⑲ and terminal ①.
Continuity should exist.

N.G. → Repair harness or connectors.

O.K. ↓ ⊕

NS1089100025010X

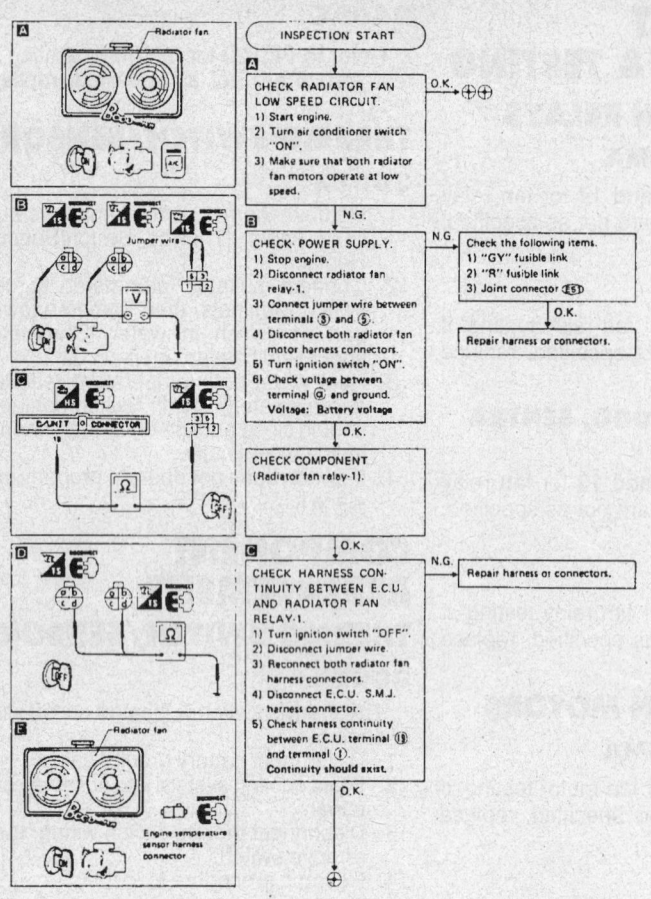

Fig. 1 Cooling fan diagnosis (Part 1 of 3). Maxima w/VG30E engine

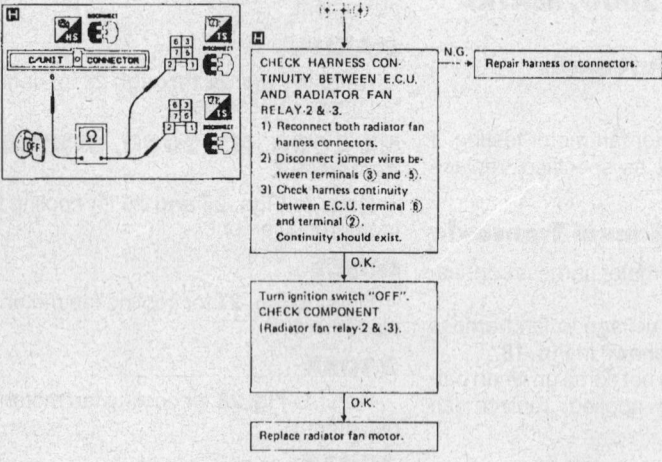

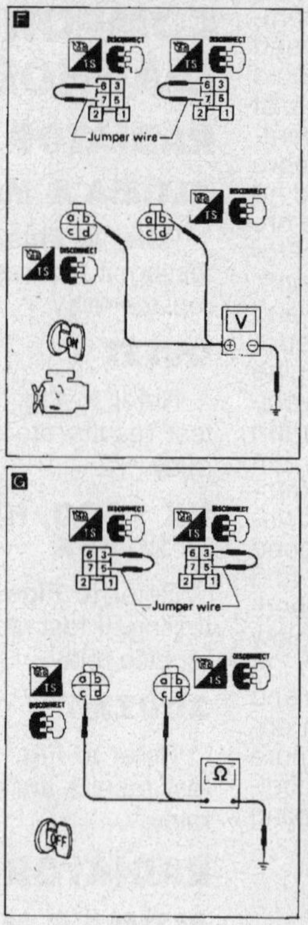

⊕

D CHECK GROUND CIRCUIT.
1) Disconnect both radiator fan harness connectors.
2) Check harness continuity between terminal ⓓ and ground.
Continuity should exist.

N.G. → Repair harness or connectors.

O.K. ↓

Replace radiator fan.

E CHECK RADIATOR FAN HIGH-SPEED CIRCUIT. ← ⊕⊕
1) Start engine.
2) Disconnect engine temperature sensor harness connector.
3) Make sure that both radiator fans operate at high speed.

O.K. → INSPECTION END

N.G. ↓

F CHECK POWER SUPPLY.
1) Stop engine.
2) Disconnect radiator fan relay-2 & -3.
3) Connect jumper wire between terminals ⑥ and ⑦.
4) Disconnect both radiator fan harness connectors.
5) Turn ignition switch "ON".
6) Check voltage between terminal ⓑ and ground.
Voltage: Battery voltage

N.G. → Check the following items.
1) "GY" fusible link
2) "R" fusible link
3) Joint connector (E51)
O.K. → Repair harness or connectors.

O.K. ↓

G CHECK GROUND CIRCUIT.
1) Turn ignition switch "OFF".
2) Disconnect jumper wire between terminals ⑥ and ⑦.
3) Connect jumper wire between terminals ⑤ and ⑨.
4) Check harness continuity between terminal ⓒ and ground.
Continuity should exist.

N.G. → Repair harness or connectors.

O.K. ↓ ⊕⊕⊕

NS1089100025020X

Fig. 1 Cooling fan diagnosis (Part 2 of 3). Maxima w/VG30E engine

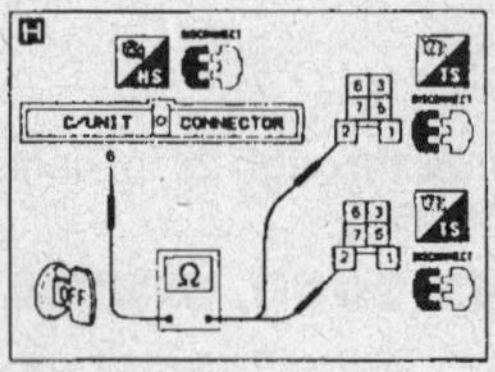

⊕⊕⊕

H CHECK HARNESS CONTINUITY BETWEEN E.C.U. AND RADIATOR FAN RELAY-2 & -3.
1) Reconnect both radiator fan harness connectors.
2) Disconnect jumper wires between terminals ③ and ⑤.
3) Check harness continuity between E.C.U. terminal ⑧ and terminal ②.
Continuity should exist.

N.G. → Repair harness or connectors.

O.K. ↓

Turn ignition switch "OFF".
CHECK COMPONENT (Radiator fan relay-2 & -3).

O.K. ↓

Replace radiator fan motor.

NS1089100025030X

Fig. 1 Cooling fan diagnosis (Part 3 of 3). Maxima w/VG30E engine

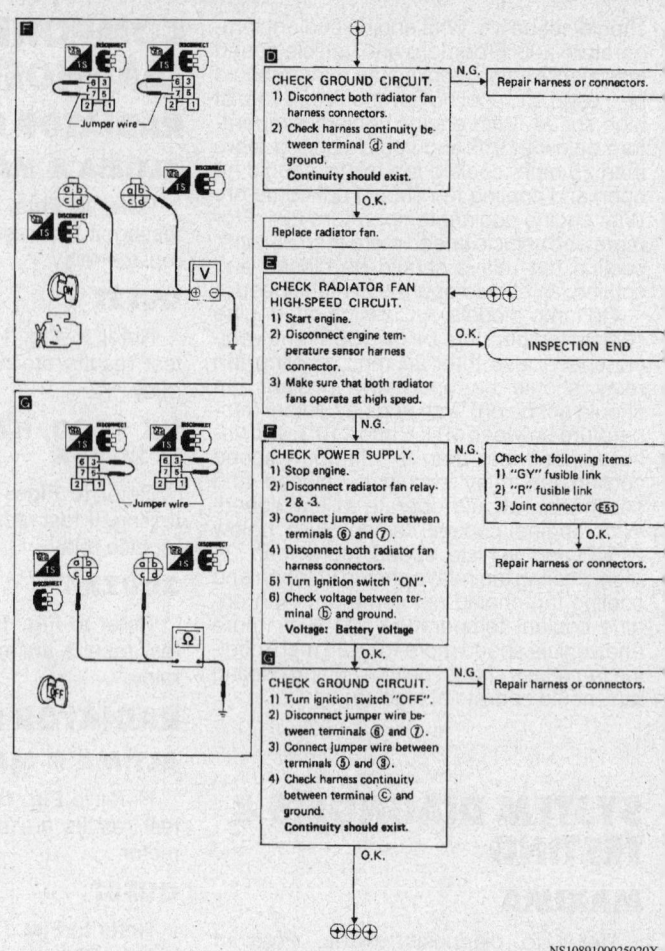

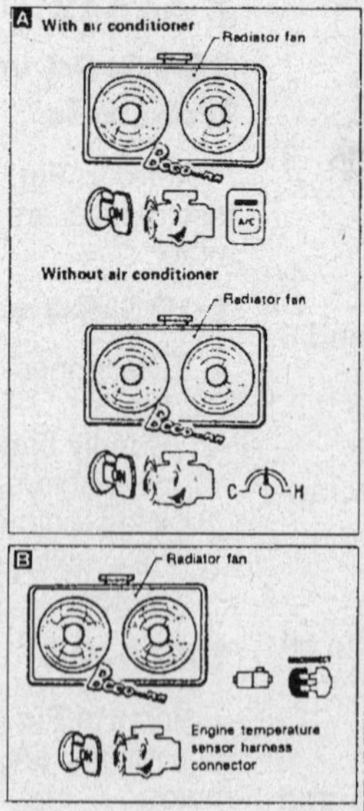

INSPECTION START

A CHECK RADIATOR FAN LOW SPEED OPERATION.
With air conditioner
1) Start engine.
2) Set temperature lever at full cold position.
3) Turn air conditioner switch "ON".
4) Turn blower fan switch "ON".
5) Run engine at idle for a few minutes with air conditioner operating.
6) Make sure that radiator fan operates at low speed.
Without air conditioner
1) Start engine.
2) Keep engine speed at about 2,000 rpm until engine is warmed up sufficiently.
3) Make sure that radiator fan begins to operate at low speed during warm-up.

N.G. → Check radiator fan low speed control circuit. (Go to PROCEDURE A.)

O.K. ↓

B CHECK RADIATOR FAN HIGH SPEED OPERATION.
1) Turn air conditioner switch "OFF".
2) Turn blower fan switch "OFF".
(Steps 1) and 2) are only performed for models with air conditioner.)
3) Stop engine.
4) Disconnect engine temperature sensor harness connector.
5) Restart engine and make sure that radiator fan operates at high speed

N.G. → Check radiator fan high speed control circuit. (Go to PROCEDURE B.)

O.K. ↓

INSPECTION END

NS1089100026010X

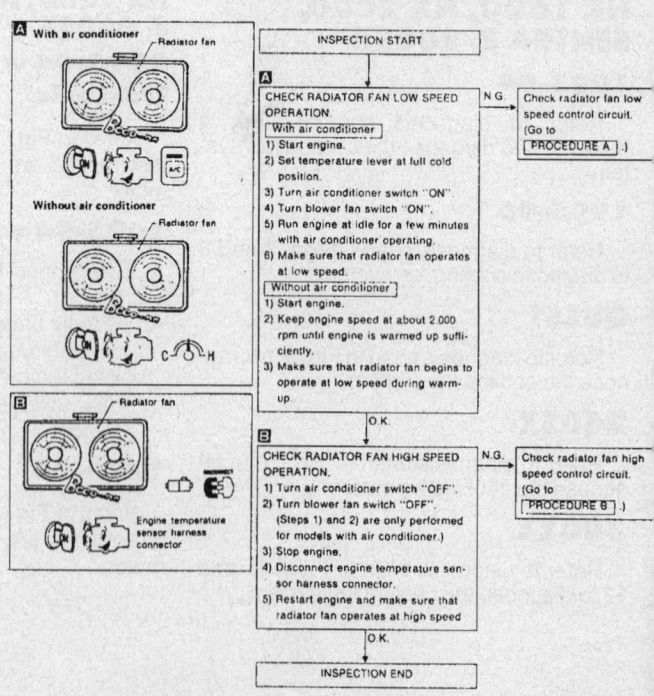

Fig. 2 Cooling fan diagnosis (Part 1 of 5). Maxima w/VE30DE engine

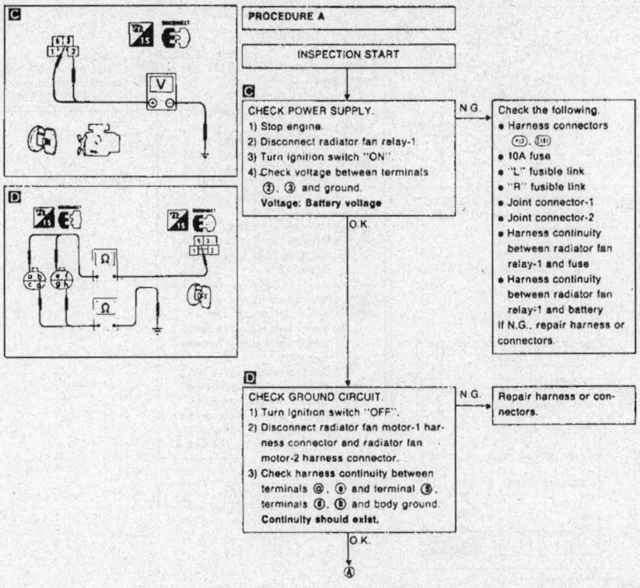
PROCEDURE A
INSPECTION START
C
CHECK POWER SUPPLY.
1) Stop engine.
2) Disconnect radiator fan relay-1.
3) Turn ignition switch "ON".
4) Check voltage between terminals ②, ③ and ground.
Voltage: Battery voltage
N.G.
Check the following.
• Harness connectors
• 10A fuse
• "L" fusible link
• "R" fusible link
• Joint connector-1
• Joint connector-2
• Harness continuity between radiator fan relay-1 and fuse
• Harness continuity between radiator fan relay-1 and battery
If N.G., repair harness or connectors.
O.K.
D
CHECK GROUND CIRCUIT.
1) Turn ignition switch "OFF".
2) Disconnect radiator fan motor-1 harness connector and radiator fan motor-2 harness connector.
3) Check harness continuity between terminals ©, ⓓ and terminal ⑤, terminals ⓓ, ⓑ and body ground.
Continuity should exist.
N.G.
Repair harness or connectors.
O.K.
Ⓐ

NS1089100026020X

Fig. 2 Cooling fan diagnosis (Part 2 of 5). Maxima w/VE30DE engine

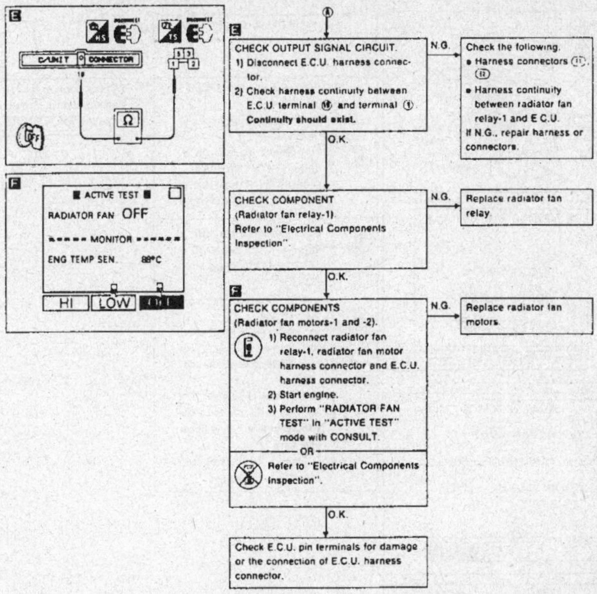
Ⓐ
E
C/UNIT
CONNECTOR
CHECK OUTPUT SIGNAL CIRCUIT.
1) Disconnect E.C.U. harness connector.
2) Check harness continuity between E.C.U. terminal ⑯ and terminal ①.
Continuity should exist.
N.G.
Check the following.
• Harness connectors
• Harness continuity between radiator fan relay-1 and E.C.U.
If N.G., repair harness or connectors.
O.K.
F
ACTIVE TEST
RADIATOR FAN OFF
MONITOR
ENG TEMP SEN. 88°C
HI
LOW
CHECK COMPONENT
(Radiator fan relay-1)
Refer to "Electrical Components Inspection".
N.G.
Replace radiator fan relay.
O.K.
CHECK COMPONENTS
(Radiator fan motors-1 and -2).
1) Reconnect radiator fan relay-1, radiator fan motor harness connector and E.C.U. harness connector.
2) Start engine.
3) Perform "RADIATOR FAN TEST" in "ACTIVE TEST" mode with CONSULT.
OR
Refer to "Electrical Components Inspection".
N.G.
Replace radiator fan motors.
O.K.
Check E.C.U. pin terminals for damage or the connection of E.C.U. harness connector.

NS1089100026030X

Fig. 2 Cooling fan diagnosis (Part 3 of 5). Maxima w/VE30DE engine

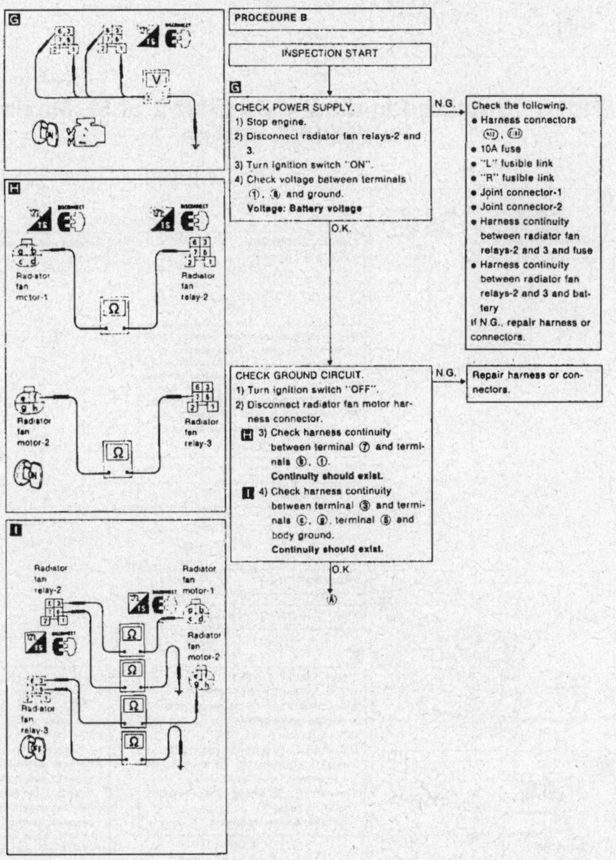
PROCEDURE B
INSPECTION START
G
CHECK POWER SUPPLY.
1) Stop engine.
2) Disconnect radiator fan relays-2 and 3.
3) Turn ignition switch "ON".
4) Check voltage between terminals ①, ⑧ and ground.
Voltage: Battery voltage
N.G.
Check the following.
• Harness connectors
• 10A fuse
• "L" fusible link
• "R" fusible link
• Joint connector-1
• Joint connector-2
• Harness continuity between radiator fan relays-2 and 3 and fuse
• Harness continuity between radiator fan relays-2 and 3 and battery
If N.G., repair harness or connectors.
O.K.
CHECK GROUND CIRCUIT.
1) Turn ignition switch "OFF".
2) Disconnect radiator fan motor harness connector.
H 3) Check harness continuity between terminal ⑦ and terminals ⑤, ①.
Continuity should exist.
I 4) Check harness continuity between terminal ③ and terminals ©, ⓓ, terminal ⑤ and body ground.
Continuity should exist.
N.G.
Repair harness or connectors.
O.K.
Ⓐ
Radiator fan motor-1
Radiator fan relay-2
Radiator fan motor-2
Radiator fan relay-3

NS1089100026040X

Fig. 2 Cooling fan diagnosis (Part 4 of 5). Maxima w/VE30DE engine

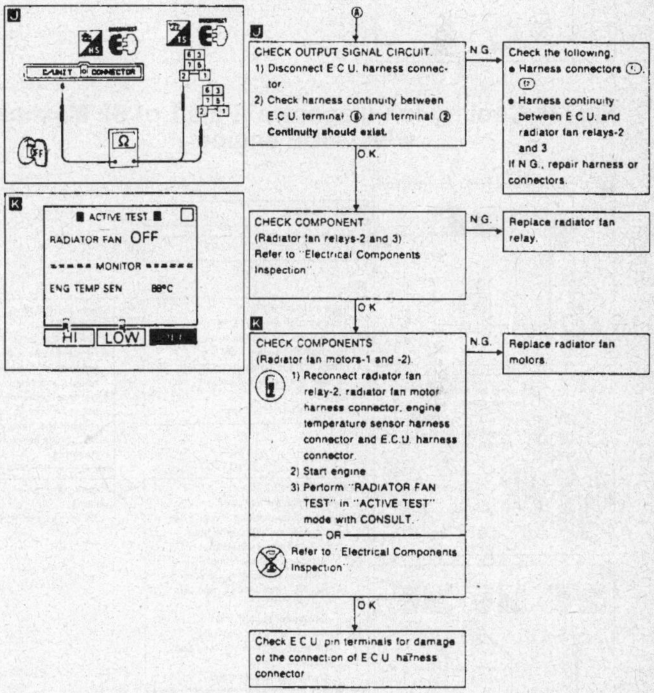
Ⓐ
J
C/UNIT
CONNECTOR
CHECK OUTPUT SIGNAL CIRCUIT.
1) Disconnect E.C.U. harness connector.
2) Check harness continuity between E.C.U. terminal ⑥ and terminal ②.
Continuity should exist.
N.G.
Check the following.
• Harness connectors
• Harness continuity between E.C.U. and radiator fan relays-2 and 3
If N.G., repair harness or connectors.
O.K.
K
ACTIVE TEST
RADIATOR FAN OFF
MONITOR
ENG TEMP SEN 88°C
HI
LOW
CHECK COMPONENT
(Radiator fan relays-2 and 3)
Refer to "Electrical Components Inspection".
N.G.
Replace radiator fan relay.
O.K.
CHECK COMPONENTS
(Radiator fan motors-1 and -2).
1) Reconnect radiator fan relay-2, radiator fan motor harness connector, engine temperature sensor harness connector and E.C.U. harness connector.
2) Start engine
3) Perform "RADIATOR FAN TEST" in "ACTIVE TEST" mode with CONSULT.
OR
Refer to "Electrical Components Inspection".
N.G.
Replace radiator fan motors.
O.K.
Check E.C.U. pin terminals for damage or the connection of E.C.U. harness connector

NS1089100026050X

Fig. 2 Cooling fan diagnosis (Part 5 of 5). Maxima w/VE30DE engine

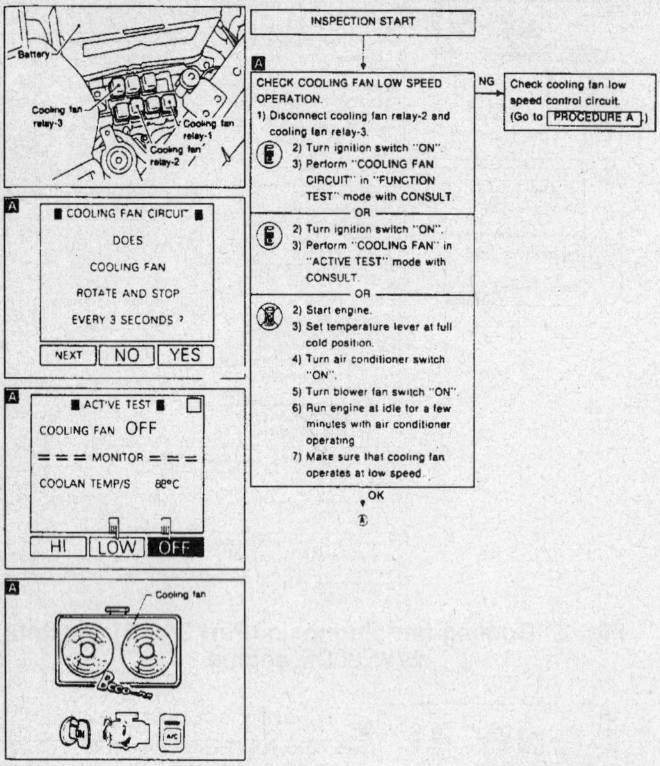
Battery
Cooling fan relay-3
Cooling fan relay-1
Cooling fan relay-2
COOLING FAN CIRCUIT
DOES COOLING FAN ROTATE AND STOP EVERY 3 SECONDS ?
NEXT NO YES
ACTIVE TEST
COOLING FAN OFF
MONITOR
COOLAN TEMP/S 88°C
HI LOW OFF
Cooling fan
INSPECTION START
CHECK COOLING FAN LOW SPEED OPERATION.
1) Disconnect cooling fan relay-2 and cooling fan relay-3.
2) Turn ignition switch "ON".
3) Perform "COOLING FAN CIRCUIT" in "FUNCTION TEST" mode with CONSULT.
OR
2) Turn ignition switch "ON".
3) Perform "COOLING FAN" in "ACTIVE TEST" mode with CONSULT.
OR
2) Start engine.
3) Set temperature lever at full cold position.
4) Turn air conditioner switch "ON".
5) Turn blower fan switch "ON".
6) Run engine at idle for a few minutes with air conditioner operating.
7) Make sure that cooling fan operates at low speed.
NG
Check cooling fan low speed control circuit. (Go to PROCEDURE A.)
OK

NS1089500056010X

Fig. 3 Cooling fan diagnosis (Part 1 of 5). Maxima w/VQ30DE engine

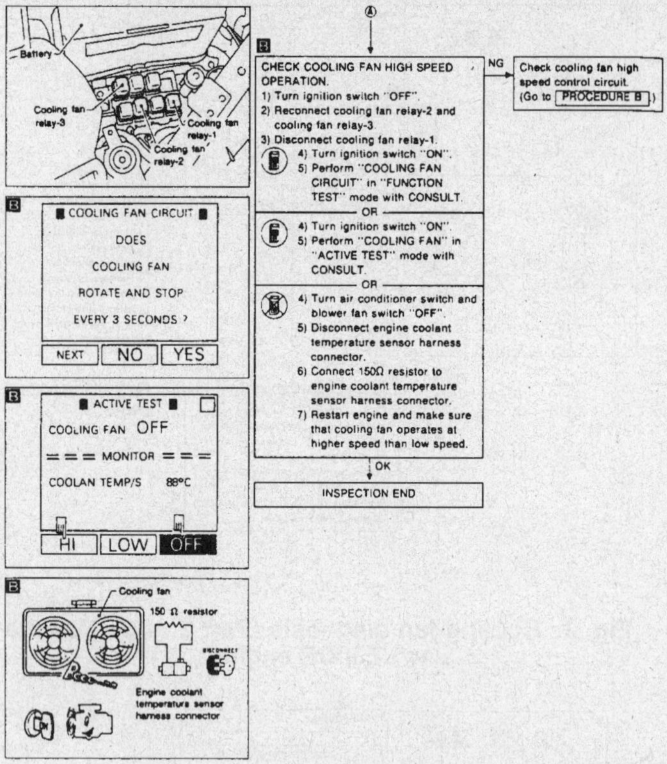
Battery
Cooling fan relay-3
Cooling fan relay-1
Cooling fan relay-2
COOLING FAN CIRCUIT
DOES COOLING FAN ROTATE AND STOP EVERY 3 SECONDS ?
NEXT NO YES
ACTIVE TEST
COOLING FAN OFF
MONITOR
COOLAN TEMP/S 88°C
HI LOW OFF
Cooling fan
150 Ω resistor
Engine coolant temperature sensor harness connector
CHECK COOLING FAN HIGH SPEED OPERATION.
1) Turn ignition switch "OFF".
2) Reconnect cooling fan relay-2 and cooling fan relay-3.
3) Disconnect cooling fan relay-1.
4) Turn ignition switch "ON".
5) Perform "COOLING FAN CIRCUIT" in "FUNCTION TEST" mode with CONSULT.
OR
4) Turn ignition switch "ON".
5) Perform "COOLING FAN" in "ACTIVE TEST" mode with CONSULT.
OR
4) Turn air conditioner switch and blower fan switch "OFF".
5) Disconnect engine coolant temperature sensor harness connector.
6) Connect 150Ω resistor to engine coolant temperature sensor harness connector.
7) Restart engine and make sure that cooling fan operates at higher speed than low speed.
NG
Check cooling fan high speed control circuit. (Go to PROCEDURE B.)
OK
INSPECTION END

NS1089500056020X

Fig. 3 Cooling fan diagnosis (Part 2 of 5). Maxima w/VQ30DE engine

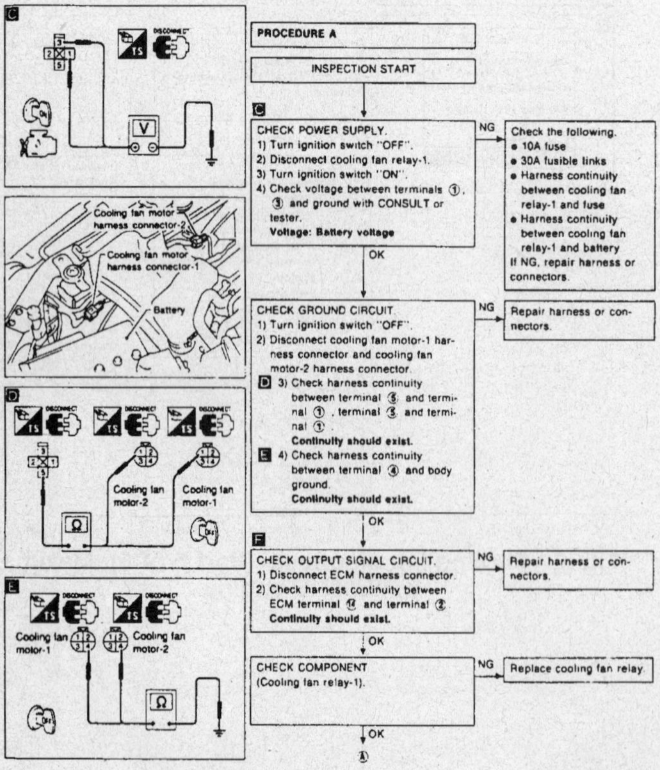
Cooling fan motor harness connector-2
Cooling fan motor harness connector-1
Battery
Cooling fan motor-2
Cooling fan motor-1
PROCEDURE A
INSPECTION START
CHECK POWER SUPPLY.
1) Turn ignition switch "OFF".
2) Disconnect cooling fan relay-1.
3) Turn ignition switch "ON".
4) Check voltage between terminals ①, ③ and ground with CONSULT or tester.
Voltage: Battery voltage
NG
Check the following.
• 10A fuse
• 30A fusible links
• Harness continuity between cooling fan relay-1 and fuse
• Harness continuity between cooling fan relay-1 and battery
If NG, repair harness or connectors.
OK
CHECK GROUND CIRCUIT.
1) Turn ignition switch "OFF".
2) Disconnect cooling fan motor-1 harness connector and cooling fan motor-2 harness connector.
3) Check harness continuity between terminal ⑤ and terminal ①, terminal ③ and terminal ①.
Continuity should exist.
4) Check harness continuity between terminal ④ and body ground.
Continuity should exist.
NG
Repair harness or connectors.
OK
CHECK OUTPUT SIGNAL CIRCUIT.
1) Disconnect ECM harness connector.
2) Check harness continuity between ECM terminal ⑭ and terminal ②.
Continuity should exist.
NG
Repair harness or connectors.
OK
CHECK COMPONENT (Cooling fan relay-1).
NG
Replace cooling fan relay.
OK

NS1089500056030X

Fig. 3 Cooling fan diagnosis (Part 3 of 5). Maxima w/VQ30DE engine

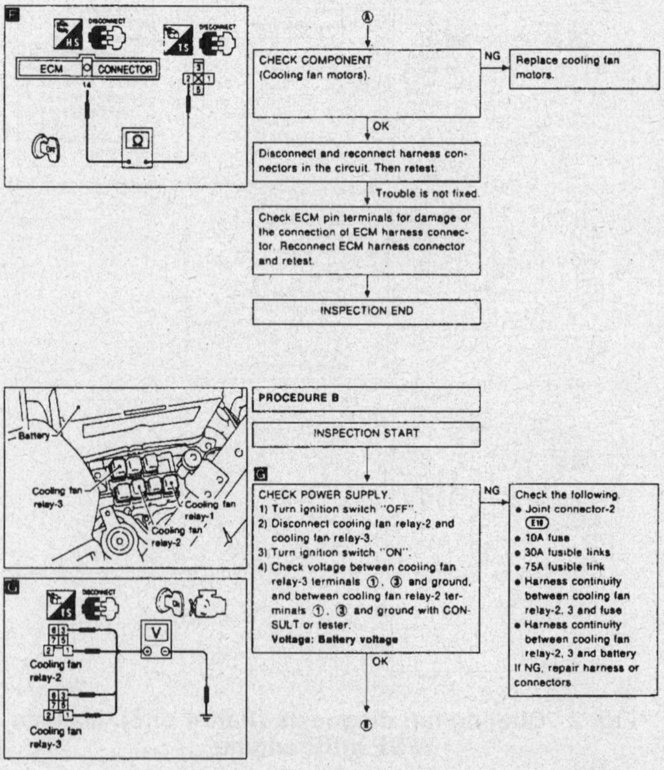
ECM
CONNECTOR
CHECK COMPONENT (Cooling fan motors).
NG
Replace cooling fan motors.
OK
Disconnect and reconnect harness connectors in the circuit. Then retest.
Trouble is not fixed.
Check ECM pin terminals for damage or the connection of ECM harness connector. Reconnect ECM harness connector and retest.
INSPECTION END
Battery
Cooling fan relay-3
Cooling fan relay-1
Cooling fan relay-2
PROCEDURE B
INSPECTION START
CHECK POWER SUPPLY.
1) Turn ignition switch "OFF".
2) Disconnect cooling fan relay-2 and cooling fan relay-3.
3) Turn ignition switch "ON".
4) Check voltage between cooling fan relay-3 terminals ①, ③ and ground, and between cooling fan relay-2 terminals ①, ③ and ground with CONSULT or tester.
Voltage: Battery voltage
NG
Check the following.
• Joint connector-2 (E19)
• 10A fuse
• 30A fusible links
• 75A fusible link
• Harness continuity between cooling fan relay-2, 3 and fuse
• Harness continuity between cooling fan relay-2, 3 and battery
If NG, repair harness or connectors.
OK

NS1089500056040X

Fig. 3 Cooling fan diagnosis (Part 4 of 5). Maxima w/VQ30DE engine

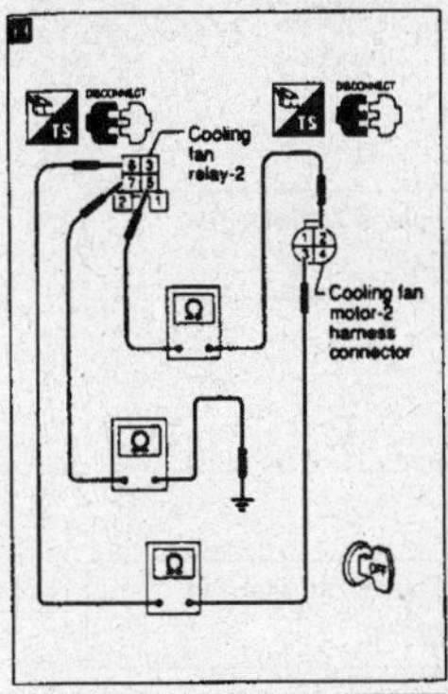
H
DISCONNECT
Cooling fan relay-2
Cooling fan motor-2 harness connector

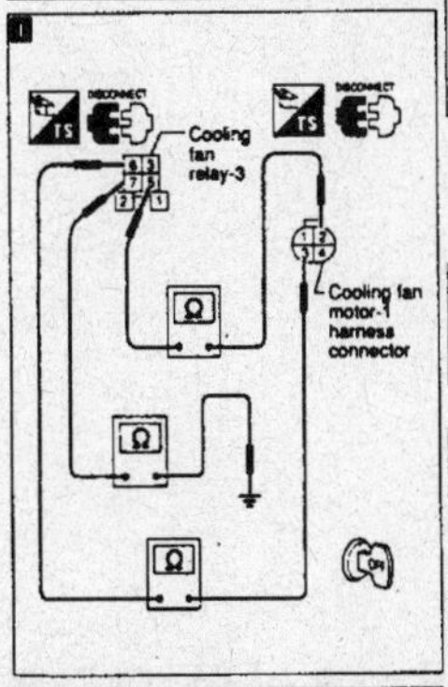
I
DISCONNECT
Cooling fan relay-3
Cooling fan motor-1 harness connector

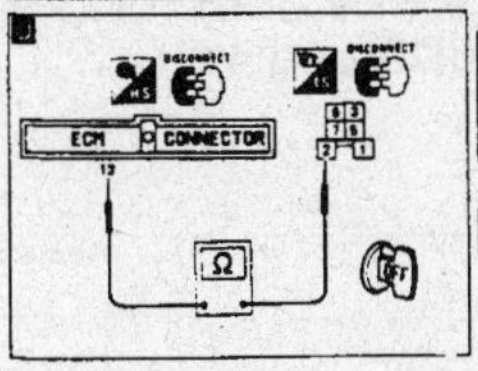
J
DISCONNECT
ECM CONNECTOR

Ⓑ

H CHECK GROUND CIRCUIT.
1) Turn ignition switch "OFF".
2) Disconnect cooling fan motor-1 harness connector and cooling fan motor-2 harness connector.
H 3) Check harness continuity between terminal ⑤ and terminal ②, terminal ⑥ and terminal ③, terminal ⑦ and body ground.
Continuity should exist.
I 4) Check harness continuity between terminal ⑤ and terminal ②, terminal ⑥ and terminal ③, terminal ⑦ and body ground.
Continuity should exist.

NG → Repair harness or connectors.

OK ↓

J CHECK OUTPUT SIGNAL CIRCUIT.
1) Disconnect ECM harness connector.
2) Check harness continuity between ECM terminal ⑬ and terminal ②.
Continuity should exist.

NG → Check the following.
- Harness connectors F26, E13
- Joint connector-3 E11
- Harness continuity between cooling fan relay-2 and ECM

If NG, repair harness or connectors.

OK ↓

CHECK COMPONENT (Cooling fan relay-2, 3).

NG → Replace cooling fan relays.

OK ↓

CHECK COMPONENTS (Cooling fan motors).

NG → Replace cooling fan motors.

OK ↓

Disconnect and reconnect harness connectors in the circuit. Then retest.

↓ Trouble is not fixed.

Check ECM pin terminals for damage or the connection of ECM harness connector. Reconnect ECM harness connector and retest.

↓

INSPECTION END

NS1089500056050X

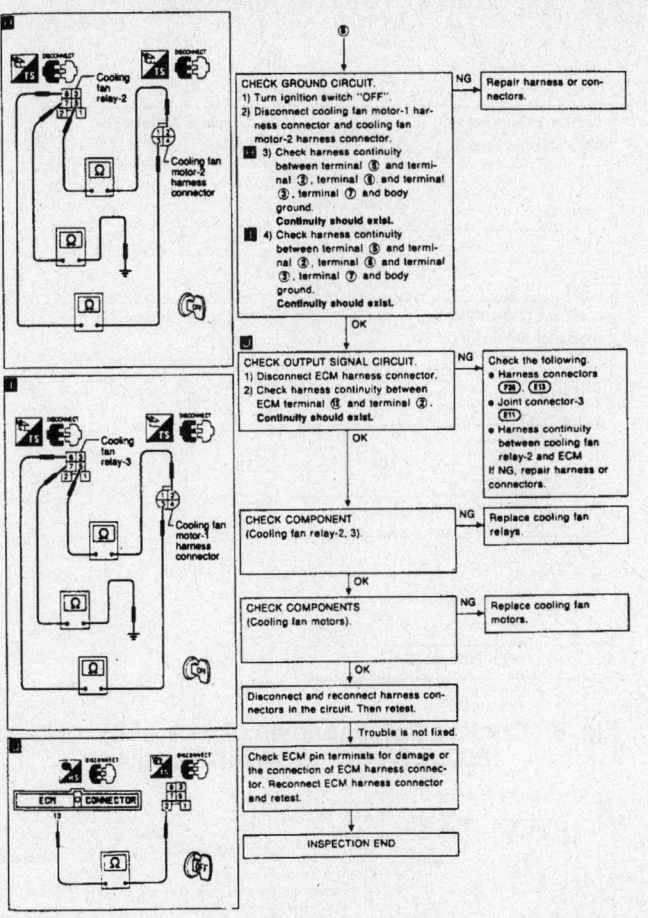

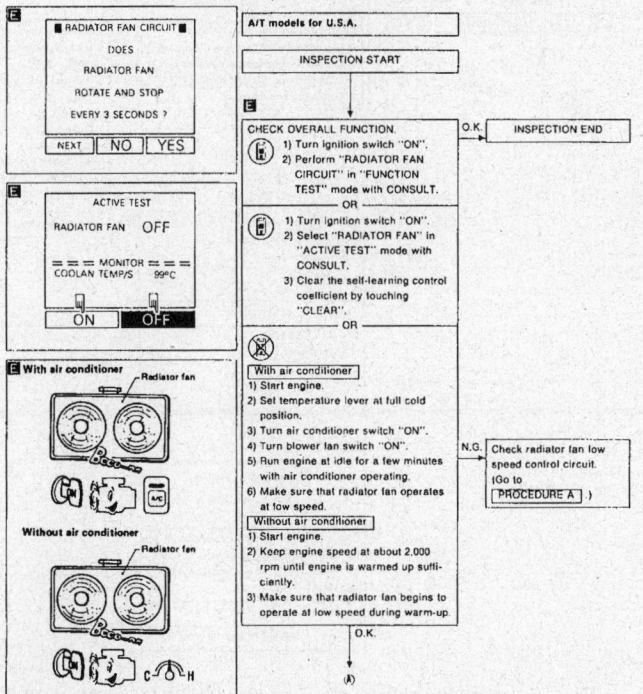

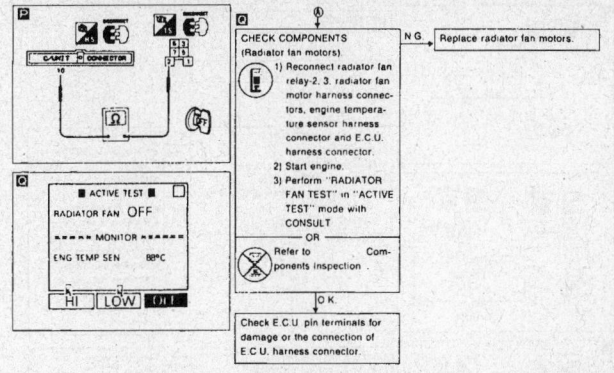

Fig. 3 Cooling fan diagnosis (Part 5 of 5). Maxima w/VQ30DE engine

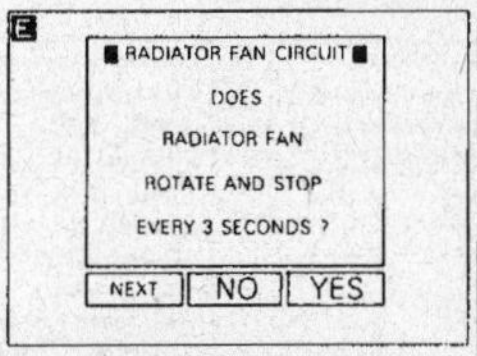
E
RADIATOR FAN CIRCUIT
DOES
RADIATOR FAN
ROTATE AND STOP
EVERY 3 SECONDS ?
NEXT
NO
YES

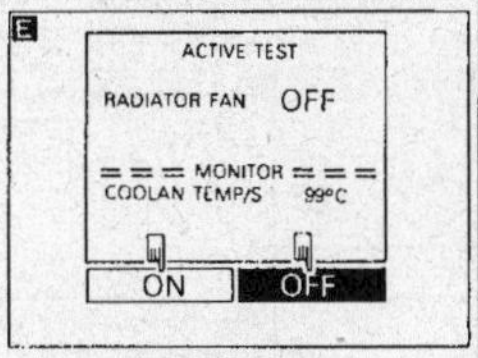
E
ACTIVE TEST
RADIATOR FAN OFF
MONITOR
COOLAN TEMP/S 99°C
ON
OFF

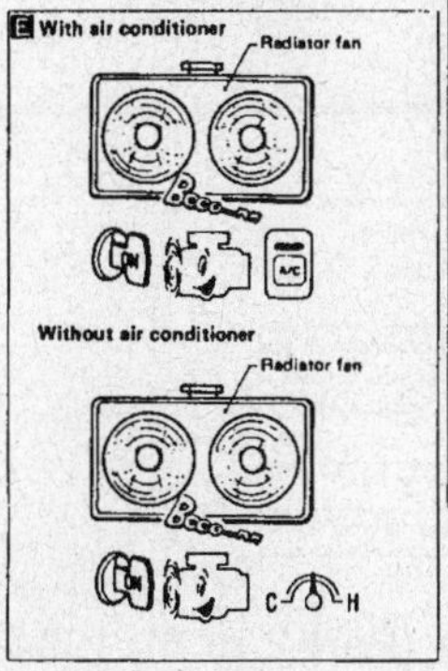
E With air conditioner
Radiator fan
Without air conditioner
Radiator fan
C
H

A/T models for U.S.A.

INSPECTION START

↓

E CHECK OVERALL FUNCTION.
1) Turn ignition switch "ON".
2) Perform "RADIATOR FAN CIRCUIT" in "FUNCTION TEST" mode with CONSULT.

— OR —

1) Turn ignition switch "ON".
2) Select "RADIATOR FAN" in "ACTIVE TEST" mode with CONSULT.
3) Clear the self-learning control coefficient by touching "CLEAR".

— OR —

With air conditioner
1) Start engine.
2) Set temperature lever at full cold position.
3) Turn air conditioner switch "ON".
4) Turn blower fan switch "ON".
5) Run engine at idle for a few minutes with air conditioner operating.
6) Make sure that radiator fan operates at low speed.

Without air conditioner
1) Start engine.
2) Keep engine speed at about 2,000 rpm until engine is warmed up sufficiently.
3) Make sure that radiator fan begins to operate at low speed during warm-up.

O.K. → INSPECTION END

N.G. → Check radiator fan low speed control circuit. (Go to PROCEDURE A.)

O.K. ↓

Ⓐ

NS1089200027020X

Fig. 4 Cooling fan diagnosis (Part 2 of 6). 1993 NX 1600 & Sentra w/GA16DE engine

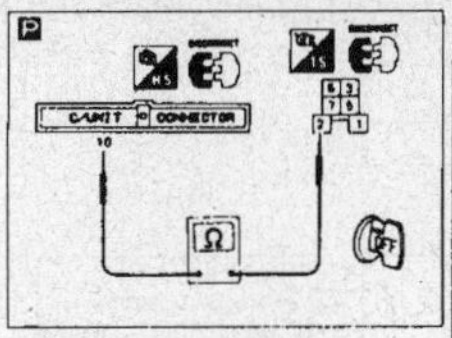
P
CAMIT CONNECTOR

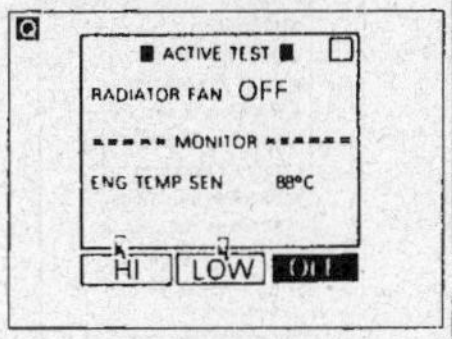
Q
ACTIVE TEST
RADIATOR FAN OFF
MONITOR
ENG TEMP SEN 88°C
HI
LOW
OFF

Ⓐ

Q CHECK COMPONENTS (Radiator fan motors).
1) Reconnect radiator fan relay-2, 3, radiator fan motor harness connectors, engine temperature sensor harness connector and E.C.U. harness connector.
2) Start engine.
3) Perform "RADIATOR FAN TEST" in "ACTIVE TEST" mode with CONSULT.

— OR —

Refer to Components inspection.

N.G. → Replace radiator fan motors.

O.K. ↓

Check E.C.U. pin terminals for damage or the connection of E.C.U. harness connector.

NS1089200027010X

Fig. 4 Cooling fan diagnosis (Part 1 of 6). 1993 NX 1600 & Sentra w/GA16DE engine

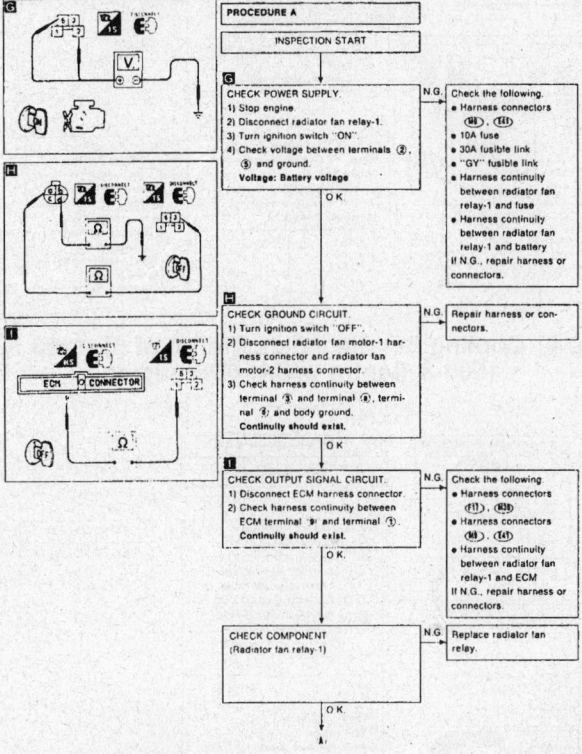

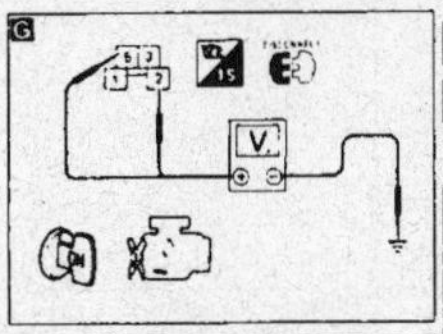
G

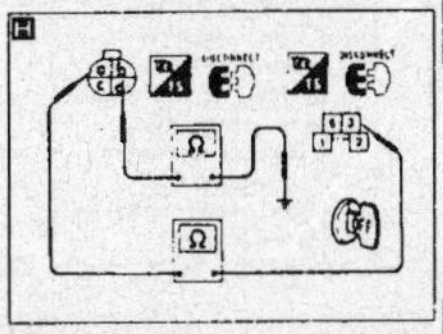
H

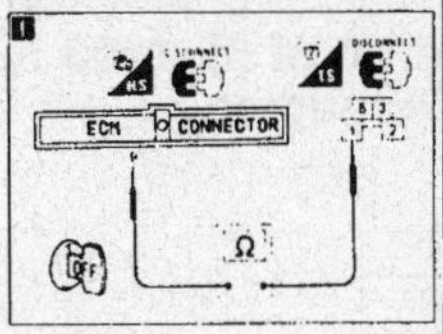
I
ECM CONNECTOR

PROCEDURE A

INSPECTION START

↓

G CHECK POWER SUPPLY.
1) Stop engine.
2) Disconnect radiator fan relay-1.
3) Turn ignition switch "ON".
4) Check voltage between terminals ②, ⑤ and ground.
Voltage: Battery voltage

N.G. → Check the following.
- Harness connectors M8, E41
- 10A fuse
- 30A fusible link
- "GY" fusible link
- Harness continuity between radiator fan relay-1 and fuse
- Harness continuity between radiator fan relay-1 and battery

If N.G., repair harness or connectors.

O.K. ↓

H CHECK GROUND CIRCUIT.
1) Turn ignition switch "OFF".
2) Disconnect radiator fan motor-1 harness connector and radiator fan motor-2 harness connector.
3) Check harness continuity between terminal ③ and terminal ⑥, terminal ⑦ and body ground.
Continuity should exist.

N.G. → Repair harness or connectors.

O.K. ↓

I CHECK OUTPUT SIGNAL CIRCUIT.
1) Disconnect ECM harness connector.
2) Check harness continuity between ECM terminal ⑨ and terminal ③.
Continuity should exist.

N.G. → Check the following.
- Harness connectors F11, M38
- Harness connectors M8, E41
- Harness continuity between radiator fan relay-1 and ECM

If N.G., repair harness or connectors.

O.K. ↓

CHECK COMPONENT (Radiator fan relay-1)

N.G. → Replace radiator fan relay.

O.K. ↓

Ⓐ

NS1089200027030X

Fig. 4 Cooling fan diagnosis (Part 3 of 6). 1993 NX 1600 & Sentra w/GA16DE engine

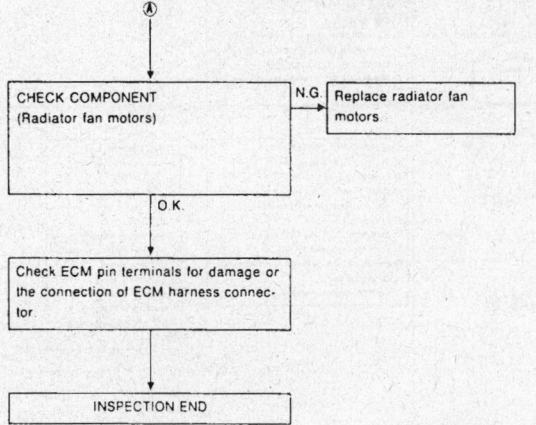

Ⓐ

↓

CHECK COMPONENT (Radiator fan motors)

N.G. → Replace radiator fan motors

O.K. ↓

Check ECM pin terminals for damage or the connection of ECM harness connector.

↓

INSPECTION END

NS1089200027040X

Fig. 4 Cooling fan diagnosis (Part 4 of 6). 1993 NX 1600 & Sentra w/GA16DE engine

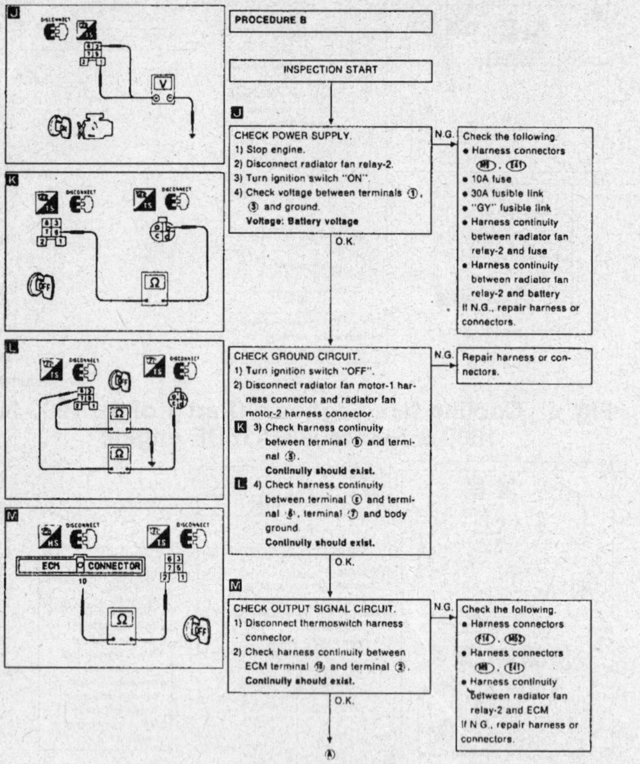
PROCEDURE B
INSPECTION START
J CHECK POWER SUPPLY.
1) Stop engine.
2) Disconnect radiator fan relay-2.
3) Turn ignition switch "ON".
4) Check voltage between terminals ①, ③ and ground.
Voltage: Battery voltage
N.G. Check the following.
• Harness connectors
• 10A fuse
• 30A fusible link
• "GY" fusible link
• Harness continuity between radiator fan relay-2 and fuse
• Harness continuity between radiator fan relay-2 and battery
If N.G., repair harness or connectors.
O.K.
CHECK GROUND CIRCUIT.
1) Turn ignition switch "OFF".
2) Disconnect radiator fan motor-1 harness connector and radiator fan motor-2 harness connector.
K 3) Check harness continuity between terminal ⑤ and terminal ③.
Continuity should exist.
L 4) Check harness continuity between terminal ⑥ and terminal ⑥, terminal ⑦ and body ground.
Continuity should exist.
N.G. Repair harness or connectors.
O.K.
M CHECK OUTPUT SIGNAL CIRCUIT.
1) Disconnect thermoswitch harness connector.
2) Check harness continuity between ECM terminal ⑩ and terminal ②.
Continuity should exist.
N.G. Check the following.
• Harness connectors
• Harness connectors
• Harness continuity between radiator fan relay-2 and ECM
If N.G., repair harness or connectors.
O.K.
Ⓐ
DISCONNECT
V
Ω
ECM CONNECTOR
10

NS1089200027050X

Fig. 4 Cooling fan diagnosis (Part 5 of 6). 1993 NX 1600 & Sentra w/GA16DE engine

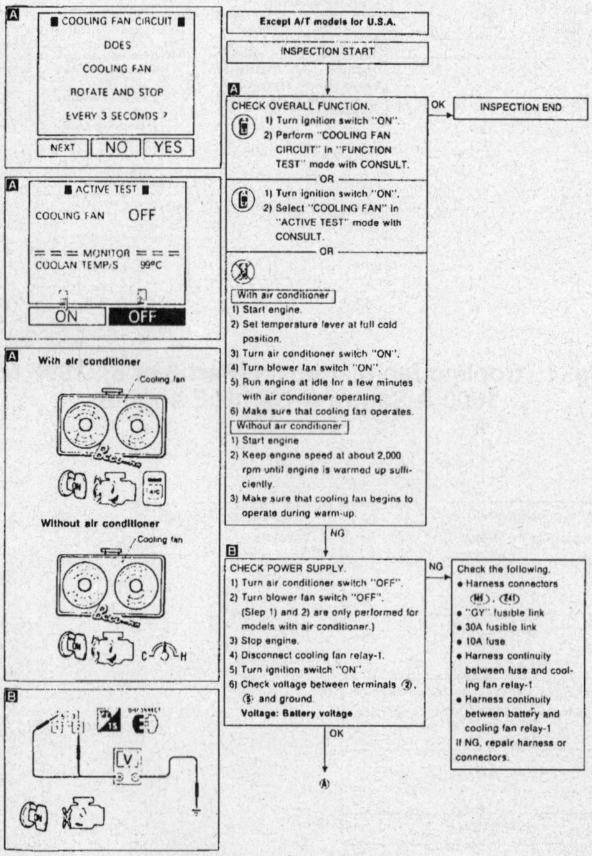
■ COOLING FAN CIRCUIT ■
DOES
COOLING FAN
ROTATE AND STOP
EVERY 3 SECONDS ?
NEXT NO YES
■ ACTIVE TEST ■
COOLING FAN OFF
=== MONITOR ===
COOLAN TEMP/S 99°C
ON OFF
With air conditioner
Cooling fan
Without air conditioner
Cooling fan
Except A/T models for U.S.A.
INSPECTION START
A CHECK OVERALL FUNCTION.
1) Turn ignition switch "ON".
2) Perform "COOLING FAN CIRCUIT" in "FUNCTION TEST" mode with CONSULT.
— OR —
1) Turn ignition switch "ON".
2) Select "COOLING FAN" in "ACTIVE TEST" mode with CONSULT.
— OR —
With air conditioner
1) Start engine.
2) Set temperature lever at full cold position.
3) Turn air conditioner switch "ON".
4) Turn blower fan switch "ON".
5) Run engine at idle for a few minutes with air conditioner operating.
6) Make sure that cooling fan operates.
Without air conditioner
1) Start engine
2) Keep engine speed at about 2,000 rpm until engine is warmed up sufficiently.
3) Make sure that cooling fan begins to operate during warm-up.
OK INSPECTION END
NG
B CHECK POWER SUPPLY.
1) Turn air conditioner switch "OFF".
2) Turn blower fan switch "OFF".
(Step 1) and 2) are only performed for models with air conditioner.)
3) Stop engine.
4) Disconnect cooling fan relay-1.
5) Turn ignition switch "ON".
6) Check voltage between terminals ②, ⑤ and ground.
Voltage: Battery voltage
NG Check the following.
• Harness connectors
• "GY" fusible link
• 30A fusible link
• 10A fuse
• Harness continuity between fuse and cooling fan relay-1
• Harness continuity between battery and cooling fan relay-1
If NG, repair harness or connectors.
OK
Ⓐ

NS1089400028010X

Fig. 5 Cooling fan diagnosis (Part 1 of 6). 1994 Sentra w/GA16DE engine

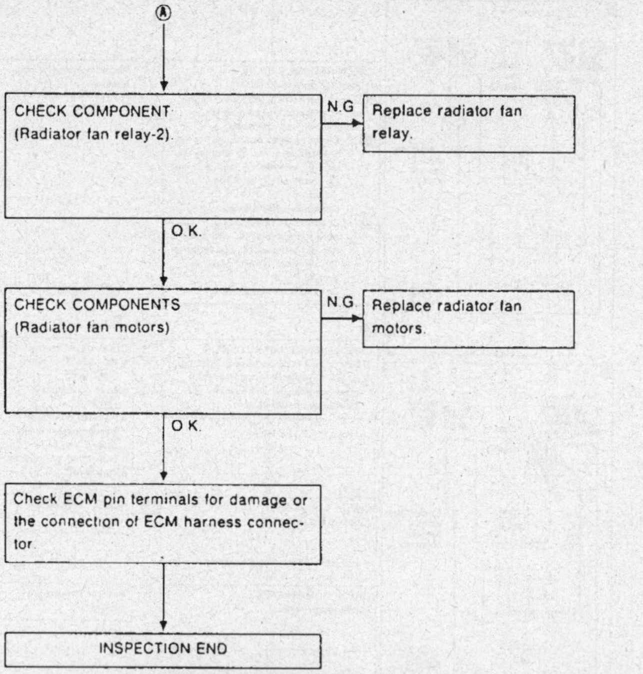
Ⓐ
CHECK COMPONENT
(Radiator fan relay-2).
N.G Replace radiator fan relay.
O.K.
CHECK COMPONENTS
(Radiator fan motors)
N.G. Replace radiator fan motors.
O.K.
Check ECM pin terminals for damage or the connection of ECM harness connector.
INSPECTION END

NS1089200027060X

Fig. 4 Cooling fan diagnosis (Part 6 of 6). 1993 NX 1600 & Sentra w/GA16DE engine

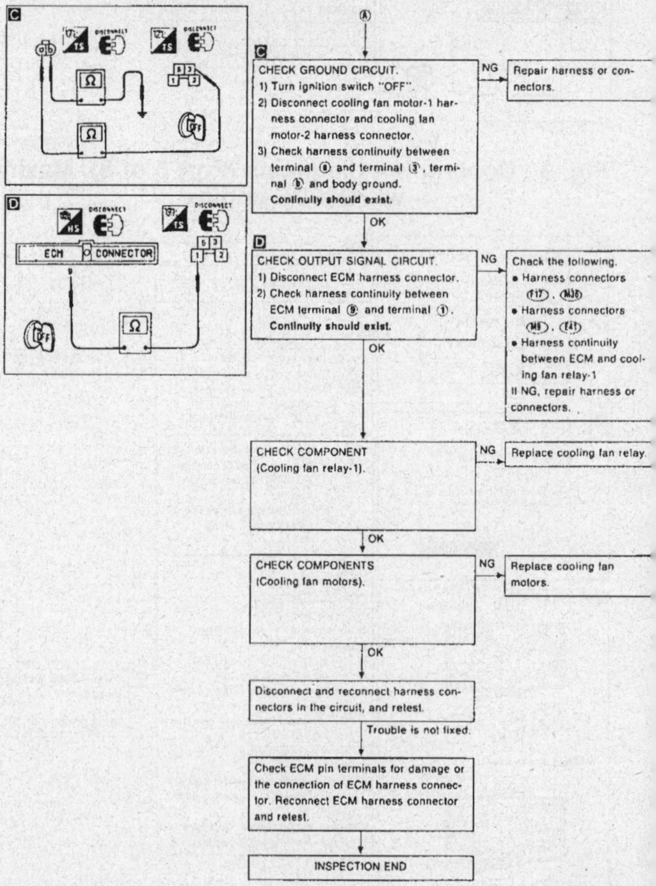
Ⓐ
C CHECK GROUND CIRCUIT.
1) Turn ignition switch "OFF".
2) Disconnect cooling fan motor-1 harness connector and cooling fan motor-2 harness connector.
3) Check harness continuity between terminal ⑥ and terminal ③, terminal ⑤ and body ground.
Continuity should exist.
NG Repair harness or connectors.
OK
D CHECK OUTPUT SIGNAL CIRCUIT.
1) Disconnect ECM harness connector.
2) Check harness continuity between ECM terminal ⑨ and terminal ①.
Continuity should exist.
NG Check the following.
• Harness connectors
• Harness connectors
• Harness continuity between ECM and cooling fan relay-1
If NG, repair harness or connectors.
OK
CHECK COMPONENT
(Cooling fan relay-1).
NG Replace cooling fan relay.
OK
CHECK COMPONENTS
(Cooling fan motors).
NG Replace cooling fan motors.
OK
Disconnect and reconnect harness connectors in the circuit, and retest.
Trouble is not fixed.
Check ECM pin terminals for damage or the connection of ECM harness connector. Reconnect ECM harness connector and retest.
INSPECTION END
ECM CONNECTOR
Ω

NS1089400028020X

Fig. 5 Cooling fan diagnosis (Part 2 of 6). 1994 Sentra w/GA16DE engine

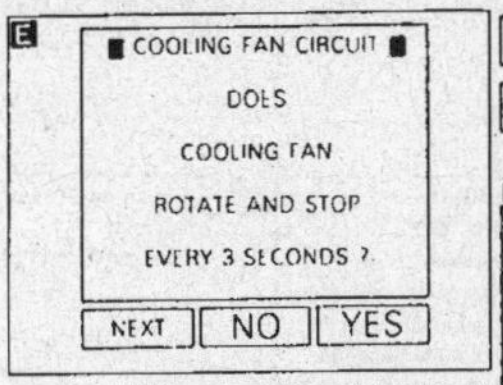
E
■ COOLING FAN CIRCUIT ■
DOES
COOLING FAN
ROTATE AND STOP
EVERY 3 SECONDS ?
NEXT
NO
YES

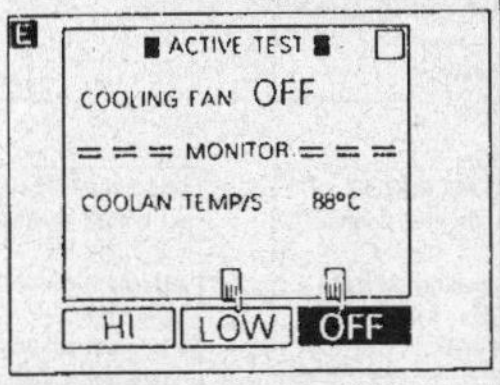
E
■ ACTIVE TEST ■
COOLING FAN OFF
= = = MONITOR = = =
COOLAN TEMP/S 88°C
HI
LOW
OFF

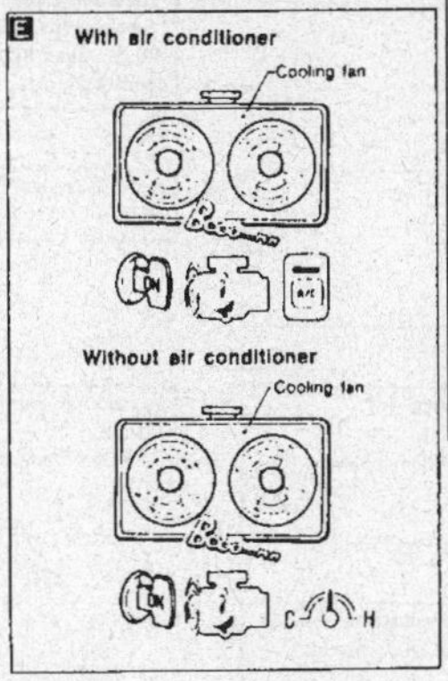
E
With air conditioner
Cooling fan
Without air conditioner
Cooling fan

A/T models for U.S.A.

INSPECTION START

E
CHECK COOLING FAN LOW SPEED OPERATION.
1) Disconnect cooling fan relay-2.
2) Turn ignition switch "ON".
3) Perform "COOLING FAN CIRCUIT" in "FUNCTION TEST" mode with CONSULT.
— OR —
2) Turn ignition switch "ON".
3) Perform "COOLING FAN" in "ACTIVE TEST" mode with CONSULT.
— OR —
With air conditioner
1) Start engine.
2) Set temperature lever at full cold position.
3) Turn air conditioner switch "ON".
4) Turn blower fan switch "ON".
5) Run engine at idle for a few minutes with air conditioner operating.
6) Make sure that cooling fan operates at low speed.
Without air conditioner
1) Start engine.
2) Keep engine speed at about 2,000 rpm until engine is warmed up sufficiently.
3) Make sure that cooling fan begins to operate at low speed during warm-up.

NG → Check cooling fan low speed control circuit. (Go to PROCEDURE A)

OK → Ⓐ

NS1089400028030X

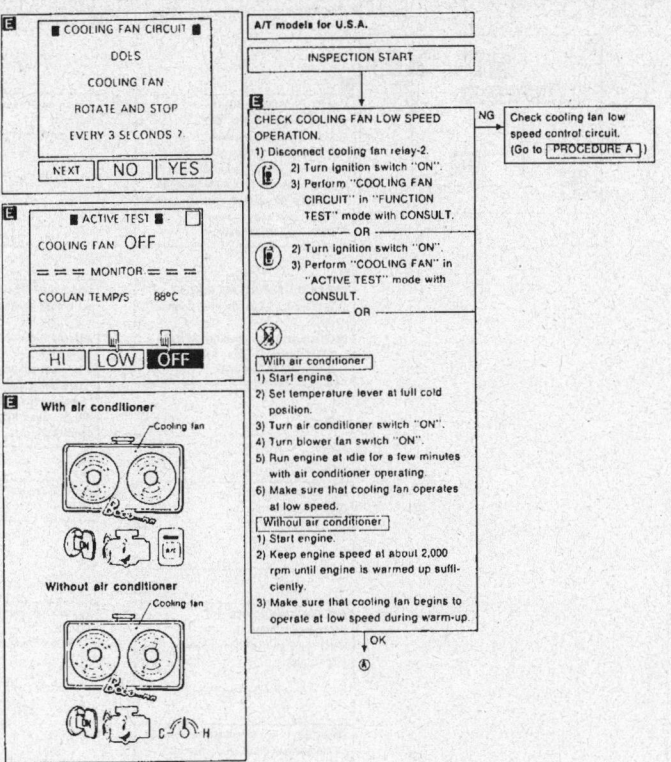

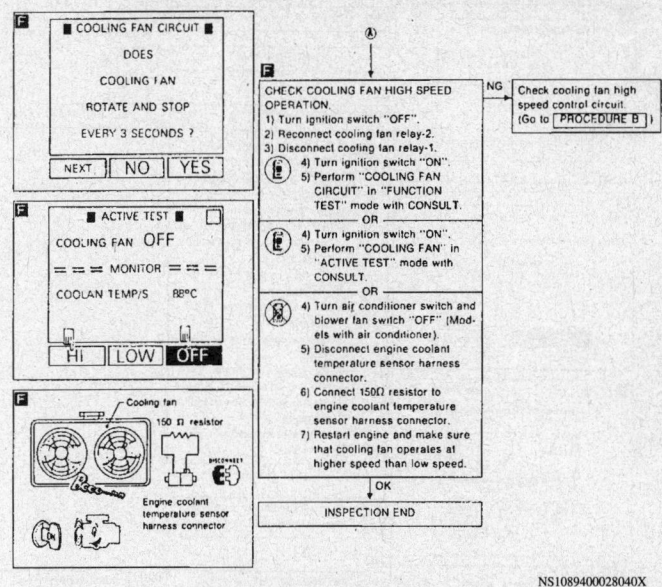

Fig. 5 Cooling fan diagnosis (Part 3 of 6). 1994 Sentra w/GA16DE engine

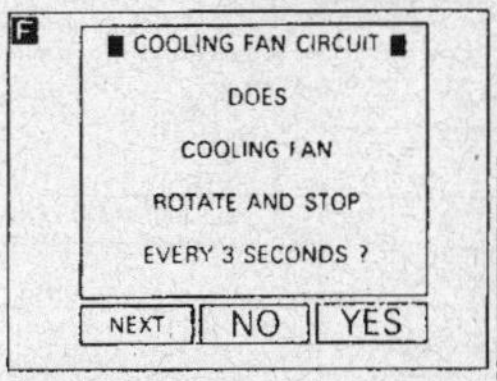
F
■ COOLING FAN CIRCUIT ■
DOES
COOLING FAN
ROTATE AND STOP
EVERY 3 SECONDS ?
NEXT
NO
YES

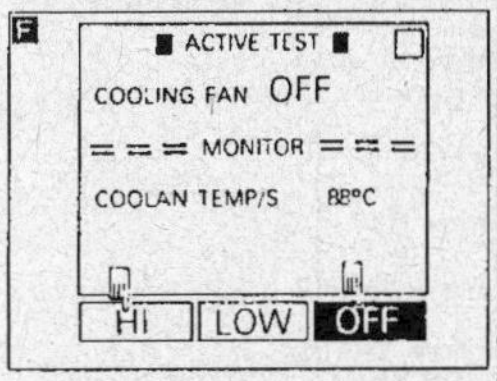
F
■ ACTIVE TEST ■
COOLING FAN OFF
= = = MONITOR = = =
COOLAN TEMP/S 88°C
HI
LOW
OFF

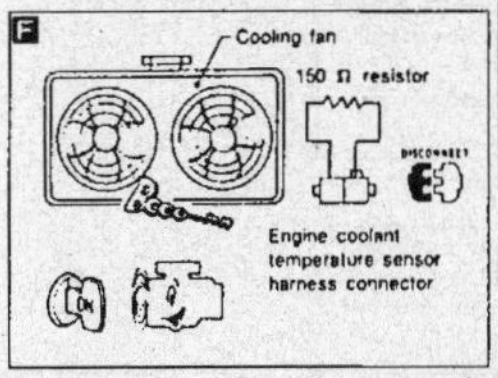
F
Cooling fan
150 Ω resistor
DISCONNECT
Engine coolant temperature sensor harness connector

Ⓐ

F
CHECK COOLING FAN HIGH SPEED OPERATION.
1) Turn ignition switch "OFF".
2) Reconnect cooling fan relay-2.
3) Disconnect cooling fan relay-1.
4) Turn ignition switch "ON".
5) Perform "COOLING FAN CIRCUIT" in "FUNCTION TEST" mode with CONSULT.
— OR —
4) Turn ignition switch "ON".
5) Perform "COOLING FAN" in "ACTIVE TEST" mode with CONSULT.
— OR —
4) Turn air conditioner switch and blower fan switch "OFF" (Models with air conditioner).
5) Disconnect engine coolant temperature sensor harness connector.
6) Connect 150Ω resistor to engine coolant temperature sensor harness connector.
7) Restart engine and make sure that cooling fan operates at higher speed than low speed.

NG → Check cooling fan high speed control circuit. (Go to PROCEDURE B)

OK → INSPECTION END

NS1089400028040X

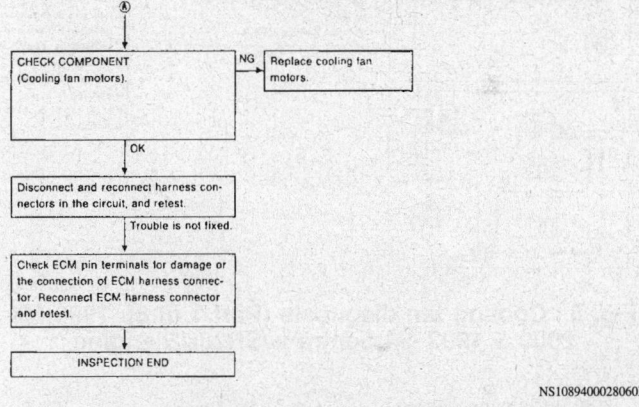

Fig. 5 Cooling fan diagnosis (Part 4 of 6). 1994 Sentra w/GA16DE engine

Ⓐ

CHECK COMPONENT (Cooling fan motors).

NG → Replace cooling fan motors.

OK ↓

Disconnect and reconnect harness connectors in the circuit, and retest.

Trouble is not fixed. ↓

Check ECM pin terminals for damage or the connection of ECM harness connector. Reconnect ECM harness connector and retest.

INSPECTION END

NS1089400028060X

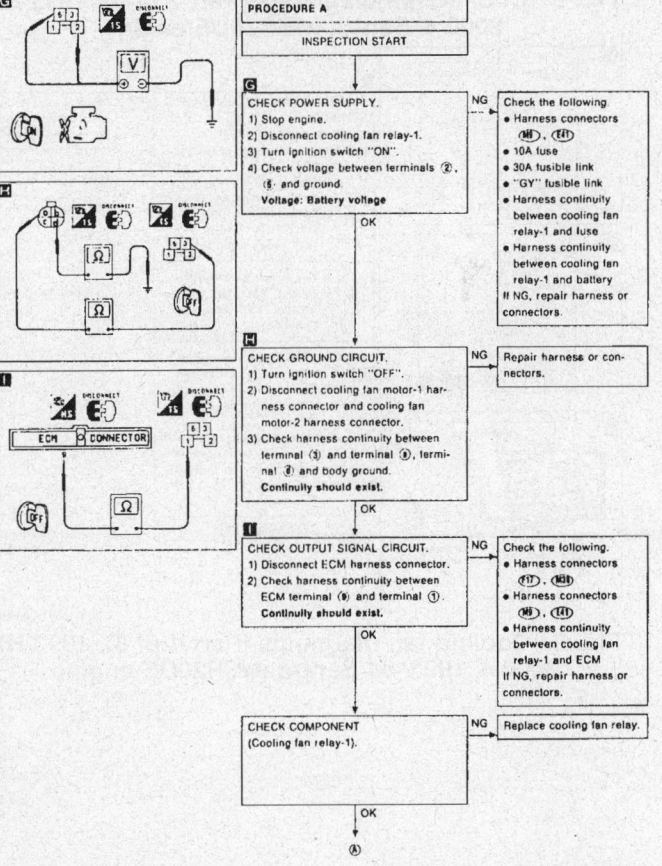

Fig. 5 Cooling fan diagnosis (Part 6 of 6). 1994 Sentra w/GA16DE engine

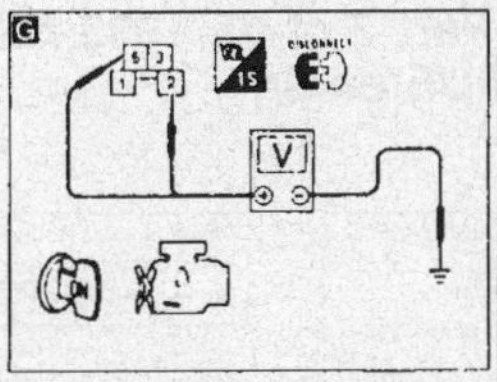
G
DISCONNECT
V

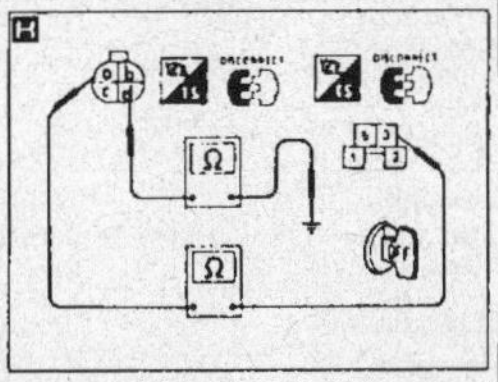
H
DISCONNECT
DISCONNECT
Ω
Ω

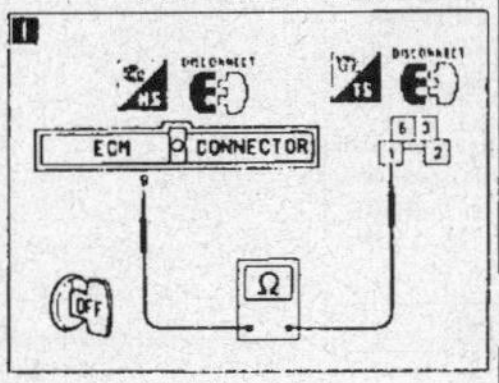
I
DISCONNECT
DISCONNECT
ECM
CONNECTOR
Ω

PROCEDURE A

INSPECTION START

G
CHECK POWER SUPPLY.
1) Stop engine.
2) Disconnect cooling fan relay-1.
3) Turn ignition switch "ON".
4) Check voltage between terminals ②, ⑤ and ground.
Voltage: Battery voltage

NG → Check the following.
- Harness connectors (M8), (E41)
- 10A fuse
- 30A fusible link
- "GY" fusible link
- Harness continuity between cooling fan relay-1 and fuse
- Harness continuity between cooling fan relay-1 and battery

If NG, repair harness or connectors.

OK ↓

H
CHECK GROUND CIRCUIT.
1) Turn ignition switch "OFF".
2) Disconnect cooling fan motor-1 harness connector and cooling fan motor-2 harness connector.
3) Check harness continuity between terminal ③ and terminal ⑤, terminal ⑧ and body ground.
Continuity should exist.

NG → Repair harness or connectors.

OK ↓

I
CHECK OUTPUT SIGNAL CIRCUIT.
1) Disconnect ECM harness connector.
2) Check harness continuity between ECM terminal ⑨ and terminal ①.
Continuity should exist.

NG → Check the following.
- Harness connectors (F17), (M38)
- Harness connectors (M8), (E41)
- Harness continuity between cooling fan relay-1 and ECM

If NG, repair harness or connectors.

OK ↓

CHECK COMPONENT (Cooling fan relay-1).

NG → Replace cooling fan relay.

OK → Ⓐ

NS1089400028050X

Fig. 5 Cooling fan diagnosis (Part 5 of 6). 1994 Sentra w/GA16DE engine

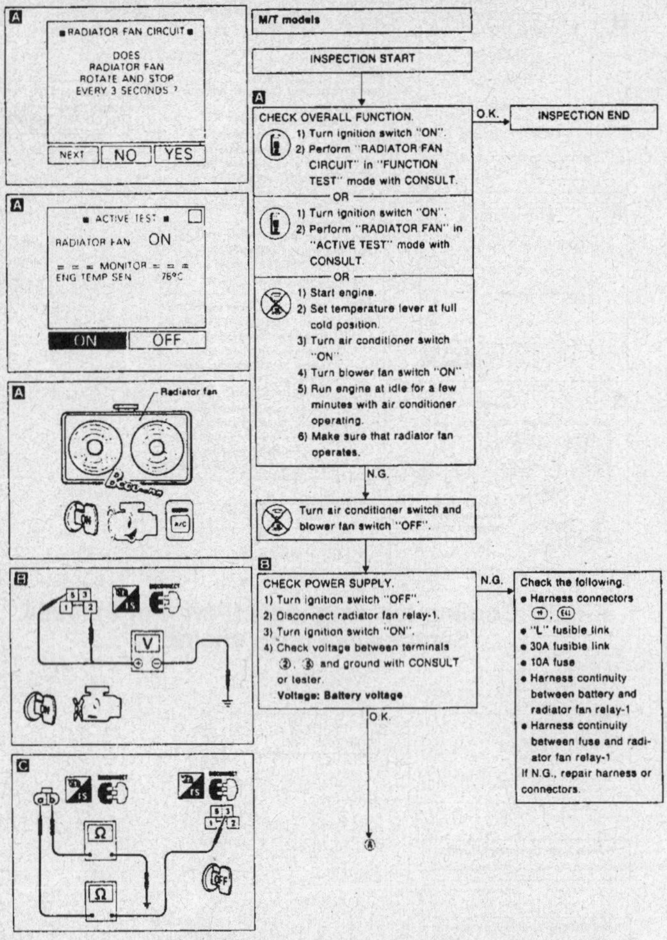
RADIATOR FAN CIRCUIT
DOES RADIATOR FAN ROTATE AND STOP EVERY 3 SECONDS ?
NEXT NO YES
ACTIVE TEST
RADIATOR FAN ON
MONITOR
ENG TEMP SEN 76°C
ON OFF
Radiator fan
M/T models
INSPECTION START
CHECK OVERALL FUNCTION.
1) Turn ignition switch "ON".
2) Perform "RADIATOR FAN CIRCUIT" in "FUNCTION TEST" mode with CONSULT.
OR
1) Turn ignition switch "ON".
2) Perform "RADIATOR FAN" in "ACTIVE TEST" mode with CONSULT.
OR
1) Start engine.
2) Set temperature lever at full cold position.
3) Turn air conditioner switch "ON".
4) Turn blower fan switch "ON".
5) Run engine at idle for a few minutes with air conditioner operating.
6) Make sure that radiator fan operates.
O.K.
INSPECTION END
N.G.
Turn air conditioner switch and blower fan switch "OFF".
CHECK POWER SUPPLY.
1) Turn ignition switch "OFF".
2) Disconnect radiator fan relay-1.
3) Turn ignition switch "ON".
4) Check voltage between terminals ③, ⑤ and ground with CONSULT or tester.
Voltage: Battery voltage
N.G.
Check the following.
• Harness connectors
• "L" fusible link
• 30A fusible link
• 10A fuse
• Harness continuity between battery and radiator fan relay-1
• Harness continuity between fuse and radiator fan relay-1
If N.G., repair harness or connectors.
O.K.

NS1089200029010X

Fig. 6 Cooling fan diagnosis (Part 1 of 8). 1993 NX 2000 & 1993–94 Sentra w/SR20DE engine

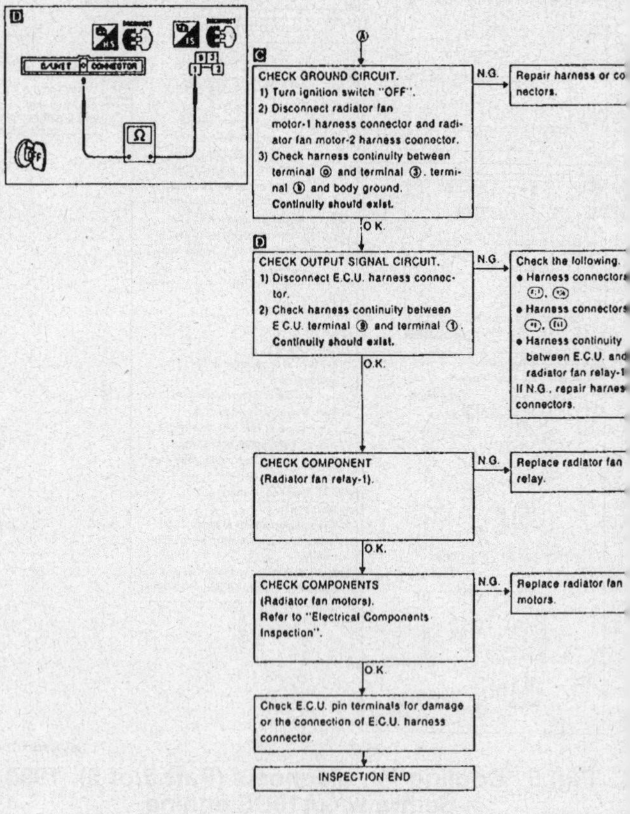
E/UNIT CONNECTOR
CHECK GROUND CIRCUIT.
1) Turn ignition switch "OFF".
2) Disconnect radiator fan motor-1 harness connector and radiator fan motor-2 harness connector.
3) Check harness continuity between terminal ⑥ and terminal ③, terminal ⑤ and body ground.
Continuity should exist.
N.G.
Repair harness or connectors.
O.K.
CHECK OUTPUT SIGNAL CIRCUIT.
1) Disconnect E.C.U. harness connector.
2) Check harness continuity between E.C.U. terminal ⑧ and terminal ①.
Continuity should exist.
N.G.
Check the following.
• Harness connectors
• Harness connectors
• Harness continuity between E.C.U. and radiator fan relay-1
If N.G., repair harness or connectors.
O.K.
CHECK COMPONENT (Radiator fan relay-1).
N.G.
Replace radiator fan relay.
O.K.
CHECK COMPONENTS (Radiator fan motors).
Refer to "Electrical Components Inspection".
N.G.
Replace radiator fan motors.
O.K.
Check E.C.U. pin terminals for damage or the connection of E.C.U. harness connector.
INSPECTION END

NS1089200029020X

Fig. 6 Cooling fan diagnosis (Part 2 of 8). 1993 NX 2000 & Sentra w/SR20DE engine

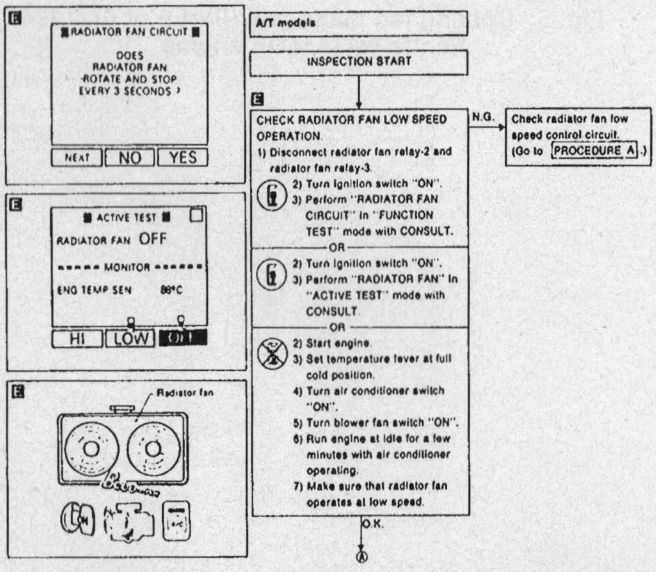
RADIATOR FAN CIRCUIT
DOES RADIATOR FAN ROTATE AND STOP EVERY 3 SECONDS ?
NEXT NO YES
A/T models
INSPECTION START
CHECK RADIATOR FAN LOW SPEED OPERATION.
1) Disconnect radiator fan relay-2 and radiator fan relay-3.
2) Turn ignition switch "ON".
3) Perform "RADIATOR FAN CIRCUIT" in "FUNCTION TEST" mode with CONSULT.
OR
2) Turn ignition switch "ON".
3) Perform "RADIATOR FAN" in "ACTIVE TEST" mode with CONSULT.
OR
2) Start engine.
3) Set temperature lever at full cold position.
4) Turn air conditioner switch "ON".
5) Turn blower fan switch "ON".
6) Run engine at idle for a few minutes with air conditioner operating.
7) Make sure that radiator fan operates at low speed.
N.G.
Check radiator fan low speed control circuit.
(Go to PROCEDURE A.)
O.K.
ACTIVE TEST
RADIATOR FAN OFF
MONITOR
ENG TEMP SEN 88°C
HI LOW OFF
Radiator fan

NS1089200029030X

Fig. 6 Cooling fan diagnosis (Part 3 of 8). 1993 NX 2000 & 1993–94 Sentra w/SR20DE engine

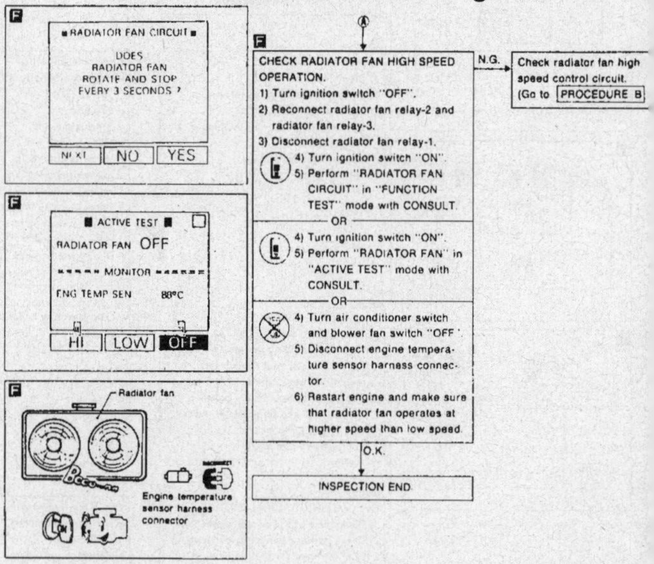
RADIATOR FAN CIRCUIT
DOES RADIATOR FAN ROTATE AND STOP EVERY 3 SECONDS ?
NEXT NO YES
ACTIVE TEST
RADIATOR FAN OFF
MONITOR
ENG TEMP SEN 88°C
HI LOW OFF
Radiator fan
Engine temperature sensor harness connector
CHECK RADIATOR FAN HIGH SPEED OPERATION.
1) Turn ignition switch "OFF".
2) Reconnect radiator fan relay-2 and radiator fan relay-3.
3) Disconnect radiator fan relay-1.
4) Turn ignition switch "ON".
5) Perform "RADIATOR FAN CIRCUIT" in "FUNCTION TEST" mode with CONSULT.
OR
4) Turn ignition switch "ON".
5) Perform "RADIATOR FAN" in "ACTIVE TEST" mode with CONSULT.
OR
4) Turn air conditioner switch and blower fan switch "OFF".
5) Disconnect engine temperature sensor harness connector.
6) Restart engine and make sure that radiator fan operates at higher speed than low speed.
N.G.
Check radiator fan high speed control circuit.
(Go to PROCEDURE B)
O.K.
INSPECTION END

NS1089200029040X

Fig. 6 Cooling fan diagnosis (Part 4 of 8). 1993 NX 2000 & 1993–94 Sentra w/SR20DE engine

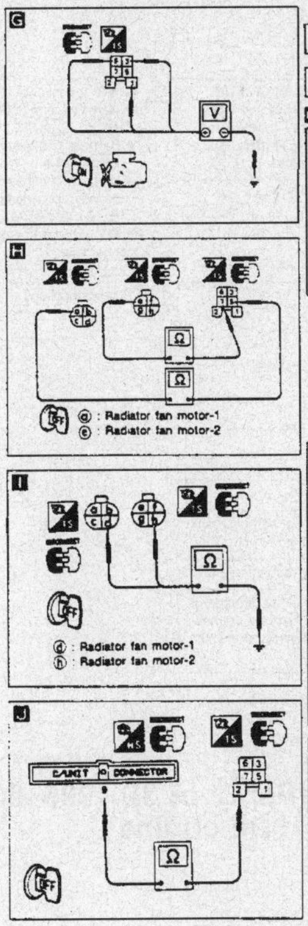
G
H
ⓐ : Radiator fan motor-1
ⓑ : Radiator fan motor-2
I
ⓒ : Radiator fan motor-1
ⓓ : Radiator fan motor-2
J
E.C.U. CONNECTOR

PROCEDURE A

INSPECTION START

G

CHECK POWER SUPPLY.
1) Turn ignition switch "OFF".
2) Disconnect radiator fan relay-1.
3) Turn ignition switch "ON".
4) Check voltage between terminals ①, ③ ⑥ and ground with CONSULT or tester.
Voltage: Battery voltage

N.G. → Check the following.
- Harness connectors [illegible], [illegible]
- 10A fuse
- 30A fusible link
- "L" fusible link
- Harness continuity between radiator fan relay-1 and fuse
- Harness continuity between radiator fan relay-1 and battery

If N.G., repair harness or connectors.

O.K. ↓

CHECK GROUND CIRCUIT.
1) Turn ignition switch "OFF".
2) Disconnect radiator fan motor-1 harness connector and radiator fan motor-2 harness connector.
H 3) Check harness continuity between terminal ⑤ and terminal ⓒ, terminal ⑦ and terminal ⓔ.
Continuity should exist.
I 4) Check harness continuity between terminals ⓓ, ⓗ and body ground.
Continuity should exist.

N.G. → Repair harness or connectors.

O.K. ↓

J

CHECK OUTPUT SIGNAL CIRCUIT.
1) Disconnect E.C.U. harness connector.
2) Check harness continuity between E.C.U. terminal ⑨ and terminal ②.
Continuity should exist.

N.G. → Check the following.
- Harness connectors [illegible], [illegible]
- Harness connectors [illegible], [illegible]
- Harness continuity between radiator fan relay-1 and E.C.U.

If N.G., repair harness or connectors.

O.K. ↓

CHECK COMPONENT
(Radiator fan relay-1).

N.G. → Replace radiator fan relay.

O.K. ↓

Ⓐ

NS1089200029050X

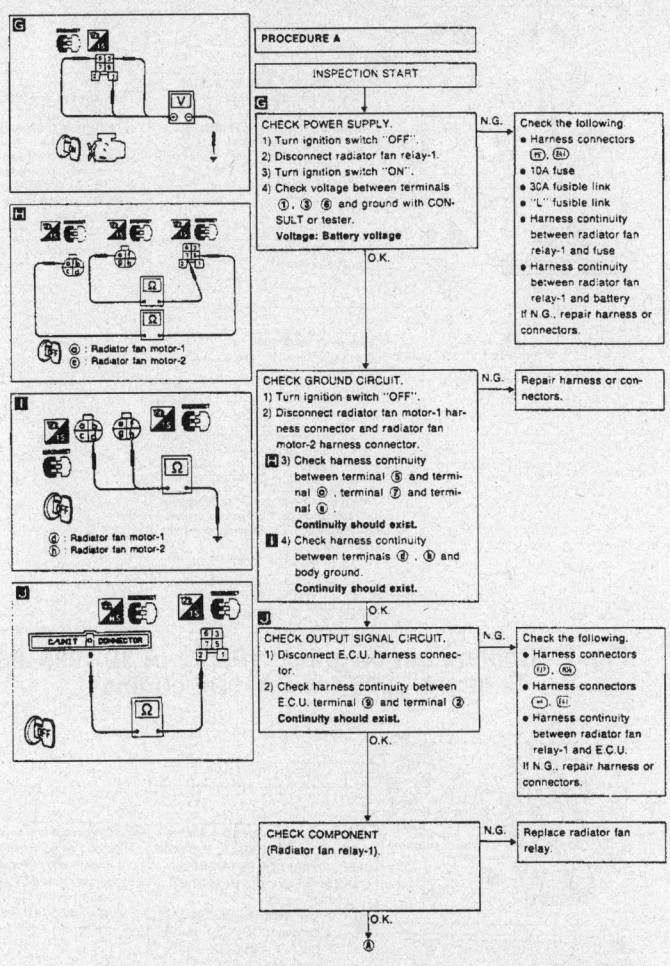

Fig. 6 Cooling fan diagnosis (Part 5 of 8). 1993 NX 2000 & 1993–94 Sentra w/SR20DE engine

Ⓐ

CHECK COMPONENT
(Radiator fan motors).

N.G. → Replace radiator fan motors.

O.K. ↓

Check E.C.U. pin terminals for damage or the connection of E.C.U. harness connector.

↓

INSPECTION END

NS1089200029070X

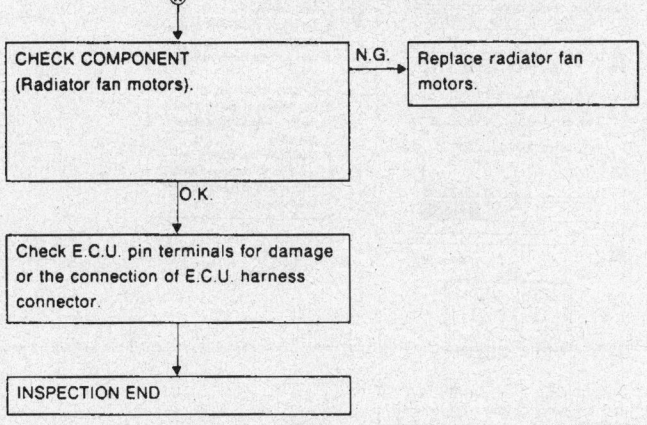

Fig. 6 Cooling fan diagnosis (Part 7 of 8). 1993 NX 2000 & 1993–94 Sentra w/SR20DE engine

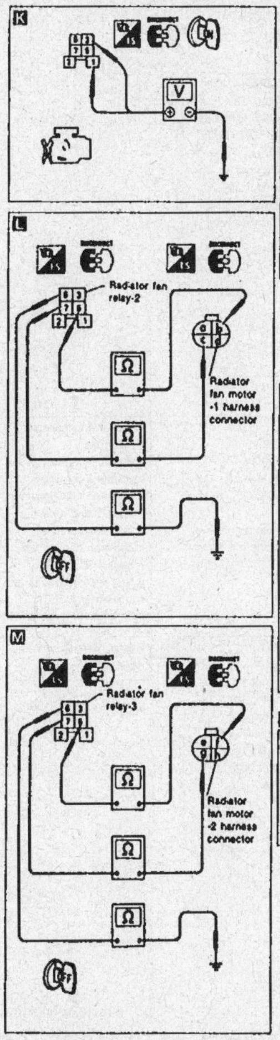
K
L
Radiator fan relay-2
Radiator fan motor -1 harness connector
M
Radiator fan relay-3
Radiator fan motor -2 harness connector

PROCEDURE B

INSPECTION START

K

CHECK POWER SUPPLY.
1) Turn ignition switch "OFF".
2) Disconnect radiator fan relay-2 and radiator fan relay-3.
3) Turn ignition switch "ON".
4) Check voltage between terminals ①, ③ and ground with CONSULT or tester.
Voltage: Battery voltage

N.G. → Check the following.
- Harness connectors [illegible], [illegible]
- 10A fuse
- 30A fusible link
- "L" fusible link
- Harness continuity between radiator fan relay-2, 3 and fuse
- Harness continuity between radiator fan relay-2, 3 and battery

If N.G., repair harness or connectors.

O.K. ↓

CHECK GROUND CIRCUIT.
1) Turn ignition switch "OFF".
2) Disconnect radiator fan motor-1 harness connector and radiator fan motor-2 harness connector.
L 3) Check harness continuity between terminal ⑤ and terminal ⓑ, terminal ⑦ and terminal ⓔ, terminal ⑥ and body ground.
Continuity should exist.
M 4) Check harness continuity between terminal ⑤ and terminal ⓕ, terminal ⑦ and terminal ⓖ, terminal ⑥ and body ground.
Continuity should exist.

N.G. → Repair harness or connectors.

O.K. ↓

N

CHECK OUTPUT SIGNAL CIRCUIT.
1) Disconnect E.C.U. harness connector.
2) Check harness continuity between E.C.U. terminal ⑩ and terminal ②.
Continuity should exist.

N.G. → Check the following.
- Harness connectors [illegible], [illegible]
- Harness connectors [illegible], [illegible]
- Harness continuity between radiator fan relay-2, 3 and E.C.U.

If N.G., repair harness or connectors.

O.K. ↓

Ⓐ

NS1089200029060X

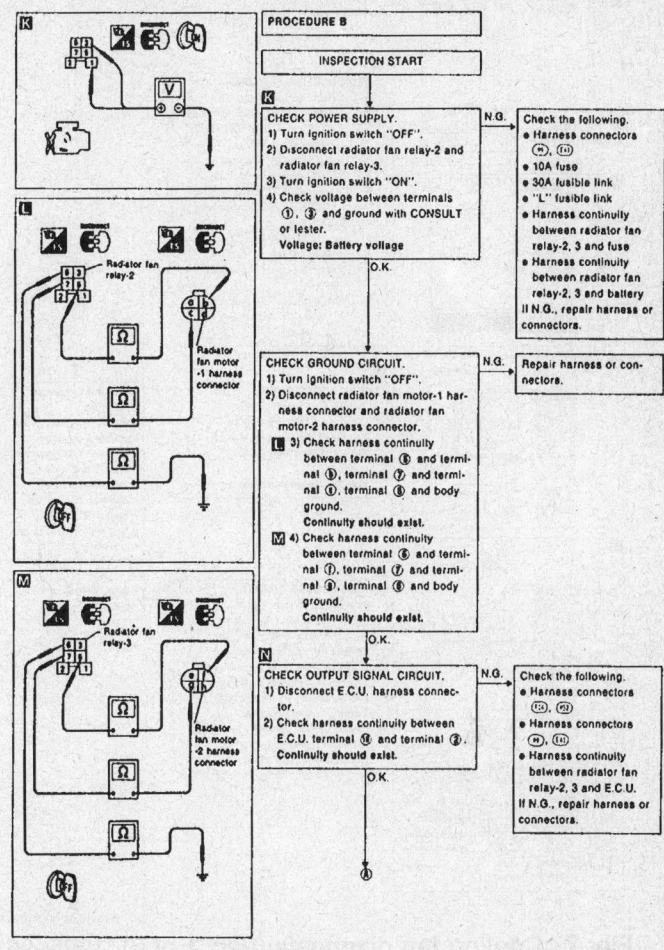

Fig. 6 Cooling fan diagnosis (Part 6 of 8). 1993 NX 2000 & 1993–94 Sentra w/SR20DE engine

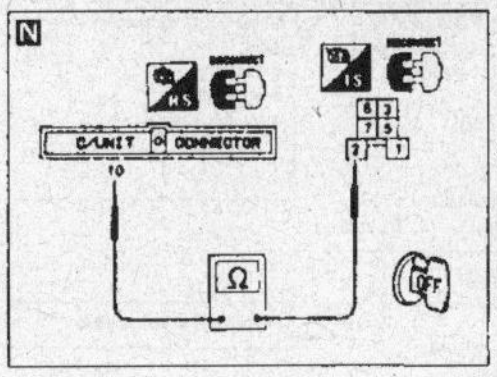
N
E.C.U. CONNECTOR

Ⓐ

CHECK COMPONENT
(Radiator fan relay-2, 3).

N.G. → Replace radiator fan relays.

O.K. ↓

CHECK COMPONENTS
(Radiator fan motors).

N.G. → Replace radiator fan motors.

O.K. ↓

Check E.C.U. pin terminals for damage or the connection of E.C.U. harness connector.

↓

INSPECTION END

NS1089200029080X

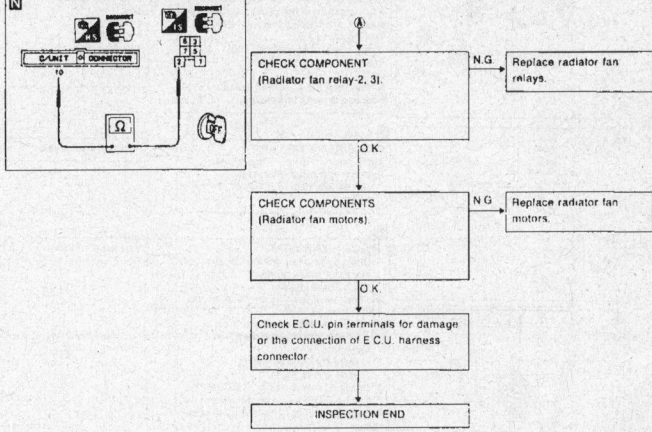

Fig. 6 Cooling fan diagnosis (Part 8 of 8). 1993 NX 2000 & 1993–94 Sentra w/SR20DE engine

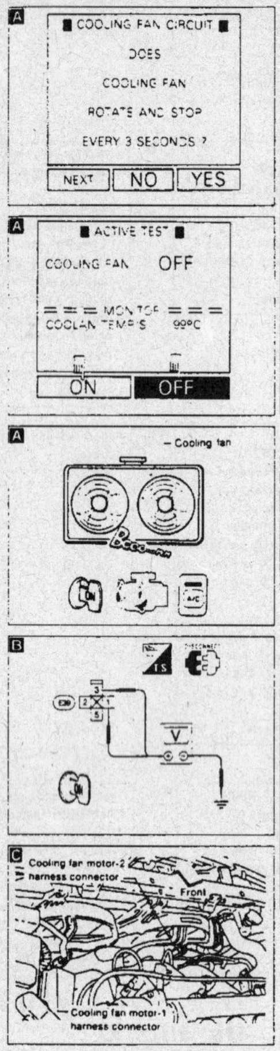
COOLING FAN CIRCUIT
DOES
COOLING FAN
ROTATE AND STOP
EVERY 3 SECONDS ?
NEXT NO YES
ACTIVE TEST
COOLING FAN OFF
MONITOR
COOLAN TEMP/S 99°C
ON OFF
Cooling fan
Cooling fan motor-2 harness connector
Front
Cooling fan motor-1 harness connector

INSPECTION START

A CHECK COOLING FAN OPERATION. — OK → Ⓑ
1. Turn ignition switch "ON".
2. Perform "COOLING FAN CIRCUIT" in "FUNCTION TEST" mode with CONSULT.

OR

1. Turn ignition switch "ON".
2. Perform "COOLING FAN" in "ACTIVE TEST" mode with CONSULT.

OR

1. Start engine.
2. Turn air conditioner switch "ON".
3. Turn blower fan switch "ON".
4. Make sure that cooling fan operates.

↓ NG

B CHECK POWER SUPPLY.
1. Turn ignition switch "ON".
2. Disconnect cooling fan relay-1.
3. Check voltage between terminals ① , ③ and ground with CONSULT or tester.
Voltage: Battery voltage

NG → Check the following.
- 10A fuse
- 30A fusible link
- Harness continuity between cooling fan relay-1 and fuse
- Harness continuity between cooling fan relay-1 and battery

If NG, repair harness or connectors.

↓ OK

C CHECK GROUND CIRCUIT.
1. Turn ignition switch "ON".
2. Disconnect cooling fan motor-1 harness connector and cooling fan motor-2 harness connector.
3. Check harness continuity between cooling fan motor terminals ① and cooling fan relay-1 terminal ⑤ .
Continuity should exist.
4. Check harness continuity between terminal ② and body ground.
Continuity should exist.

NG → Repair harness or connectors.

↓ OK

Ⓐ

NS1089500057010X

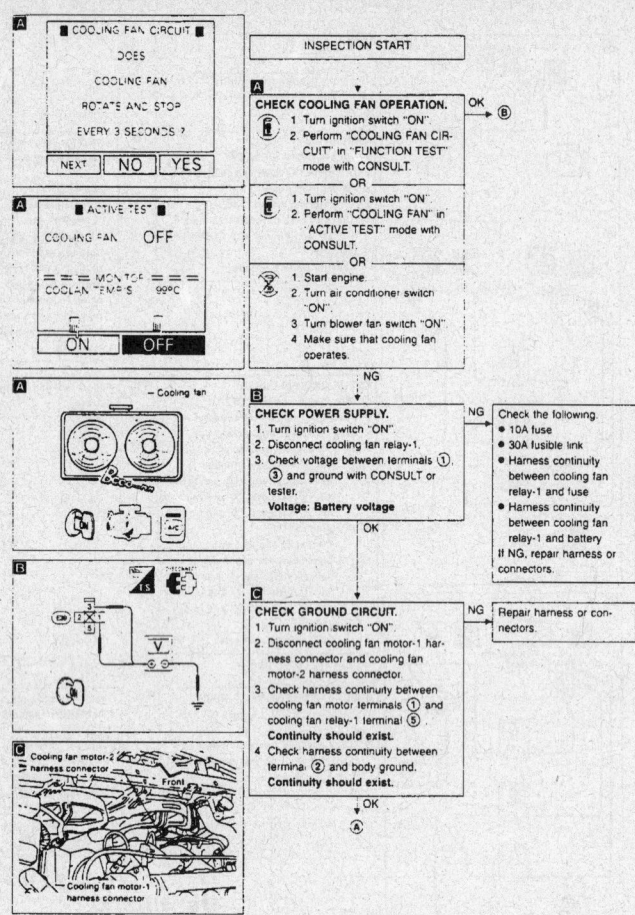

Fig. 7 Cooling fan diagnosis (Part 1 of 3). 1995–96 Sentra & 200SX w/GA16DE engine

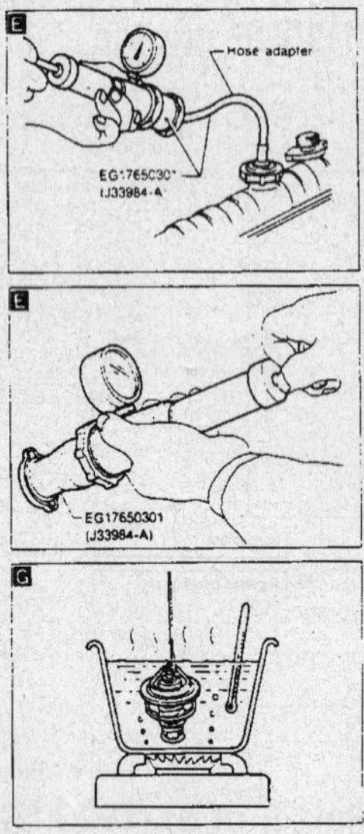
Hose adapter
EG17650301
(J33984-A)

Ⓑ

E CHECK COOLING SYSTEM FOR LEAK.
Apply pressure to the cooling system with a tester, and check if the pressure drops.
Testing pressure:
157 kPa (1.6 kg/cm², 23 psi)
Pressure should not drop.
CAUTION:
Higher than the specified pressure may cause radiator damage.

NG → Check the following for leak.
- Hose
- Radiator
- Water pump

↓ OK

E CHECK RADIATOR CAP.
Apply pressure to cap with a tester.
Radiator cap relief pressure:
59 - 98 kPa (0.6 - 1.0 kg/cm², 9 - 14 psi)

NG → Replace radiator cap.

↓ OK

G CHECK THERMOSTAT.
1. Check valve seating condition at normal room temperatures.
It should seat tightly.
2. Check valve opening temperature and maximum valve lift.
Valve opening temperature:
76.5°C (170°F) [standard]
Valve lift:
More than 8.0 mm/90°C (0.31 in/194°F)
3. Check if valve is closed at 5°C (9°F) below valve opening temperature.
For details, refer to "Thermostat" in LC section.

NG → Replace thermostat

↓ OK

Check engine coolant temperature sensor.

NG → Replace engine coolant temperature sensor.

↓

If the cause can not be isolated, go to "MAIN 12 CAUSES OF OVERHEATING"

↓

INSPECTION END

NS1089500057030X

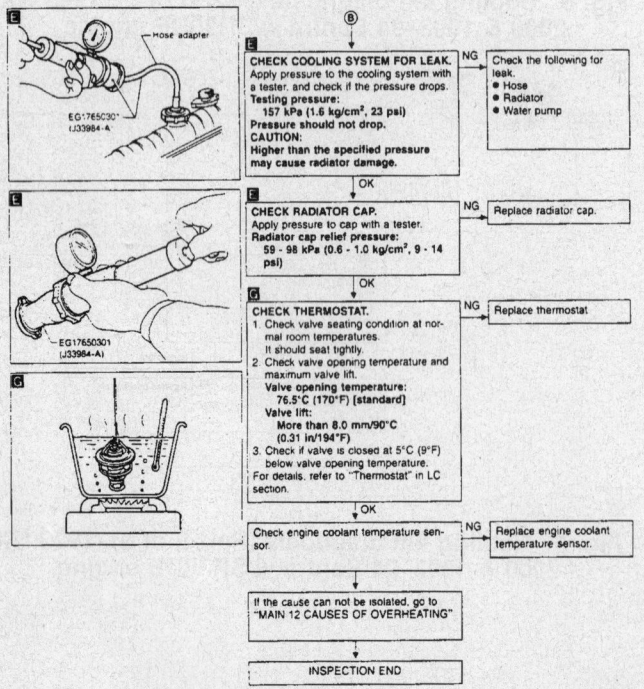

Fig. 7 Cooling fan diagnosis (Part 3 of 3). 1995–96 Sentra & 200SX w/GA16DE engine

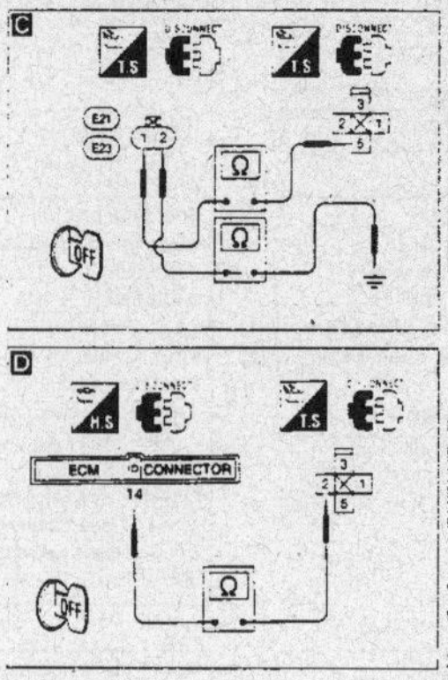
ECM
CONNECTOR
14

Ⓐ

D CHECK OUTPUT SIGNAL CIRCUIT.
1. Disconnect ECM harness connector.
2. Check harness continuity between ECM terminal ⑭ and terminal ② .
Continuity should exist.

NG → Check the following.
- Harness connectors M16 , E101
- Harness connectors F27 , M33
- Harness continuity between cooling fan relay-1 and ECM

If NG, repair harness or connectors.

↓ OK

CHECK COMPONENT (Cooling fan relay-1).

NG → Replace cooling fan relay

↓ OK

CHECK COMPONENT (Cooling fan motors-1 and -2).

NG → Replace cooling fan motors.

↓ OK

Disconnect and reconnect harness connectors in the circuit. Then retest.

↓ Trouble is not fixed.

Check ECM pin terminals for damage or the connection of ECM harness connector. Reconnect ECM harness connector and retest.

↓

INSPECTION END

NS1089500057020X

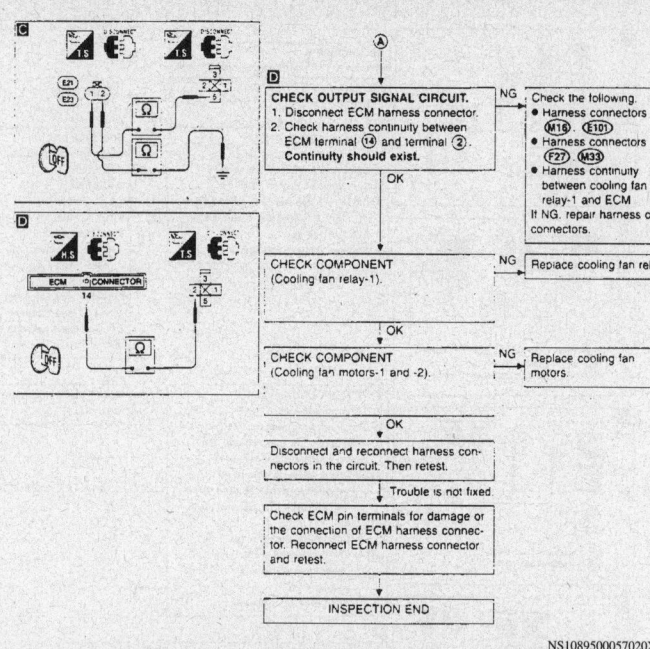

Fig. 7 Cooling fan diagnosis (Part 2 of 3). 1995–96 Sentra & 200SX w/GA16DE engine

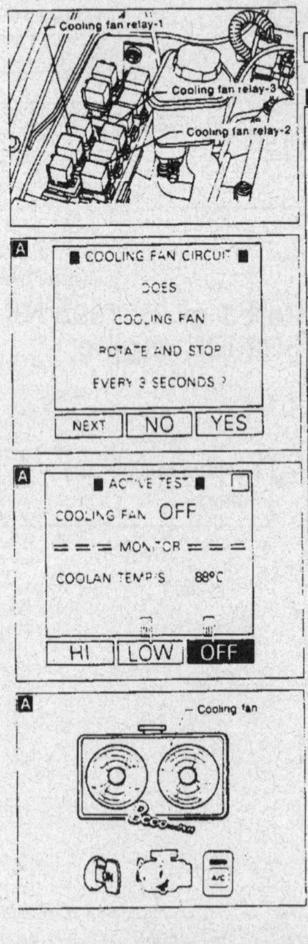
Cooling fan relay-1
Cooling fan relay-3
Cooling fan relay-2
COOLING FAN CIRCUIT
DOES
COOLING FAN
ROTATE AND STOP
EVERY 3 SECONDS ?
NEXT NO YES
ACTIVE TEST
COOLING FAN OFF
MONITOR
COOLAN TEMP/S 88°C
HI LOW OFF
Cooling fan

INSPECTION START

A CHECK COOLING FAN LOW SPEED OPERATION (A/T MODELS) AND HIGH SPEED OPERATION (M/T MODELS).
1. Disconnect cooling fan relays-2 and -3 for A/T models.
2. Turn ignition switch "ON".
3. Perform "COOLING FAN CIRCUIT" in "FUNCTION TEST" mode with CONSULT.

OR

2. Turn ignition switch "ON".
3. Perform "COOLING FAN" in "ACTIVE TEST" mode with CONSULT.

OR

2. Start engine.
3. Set temperature lever at full cold position.
4. Turn air conditioner switch "ON".
5. Turn blower fan switch "ON".
6. Run engine at idle for a few minutes with air conditioner operating.
7. Make sure that cooling fan operates at low speed for A/T models and at high speed for M/T models.

NG → Check cooling fan low speed control circuit (A/T models) and high speed control circuit (M/T models). (Go to PROCEDURE A.)

↓ OK

Ⓐ

NS1089500058010X

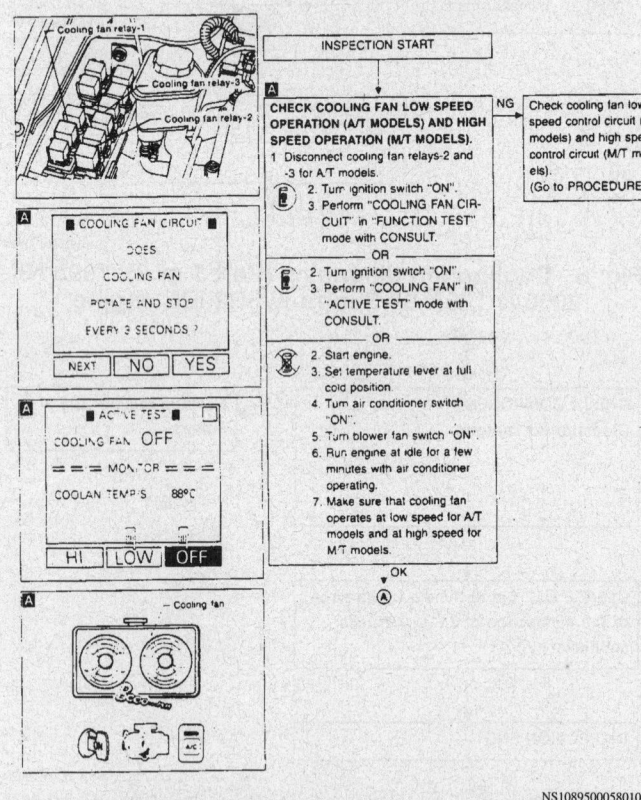

Fig. 8 Cooling fan diagnosis (Part 1 of 6). 1995–96 Sentra & 200SX w/SR20DE engine

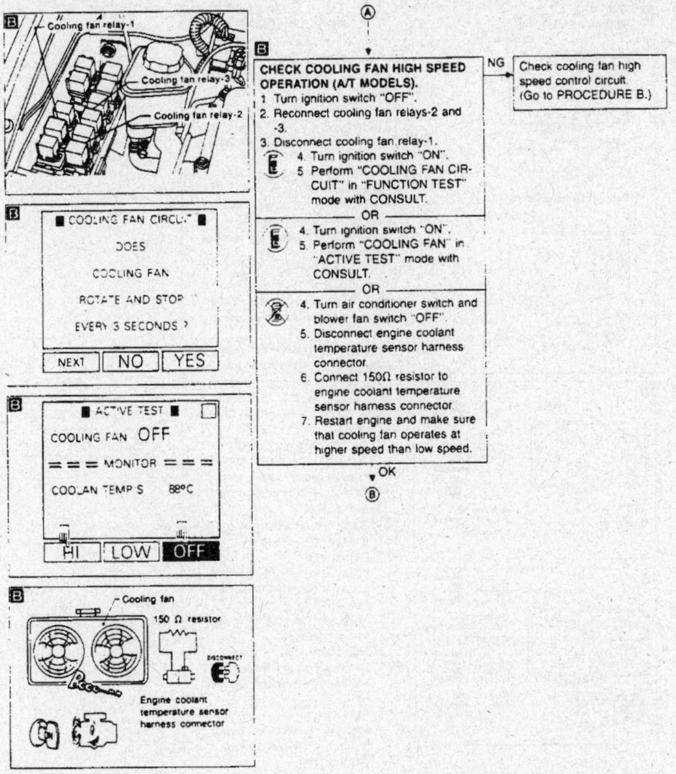
Cooling fan relay-1
Cooling fan relay-3
Cooling fan relay-2
COOLING FAN CIRCUIT
DOES
COOLING FAN
ROTATE AND STOP
EVERY 3 SECONDS ?
NEXT NO YES
ACTIVE TEST
COOLING FAN OFF
=== MONITOR ===
COOLAN TEMP/S 88°C
HI LOW OFF
Cooling fan
150 Ω resistor
Engine coolant temperature sensor harness connector
Ⓐ
CHECK COOLING FAN HIGH SPEED OPERATION (A/T MODELS).
1. Turn ignition switch "OFF".
2. Reconnect cooling fan relays-2 and -3.
3. Disconnect cooling fan relay-1.
4. Turn ignition switch "ON".
5. Perform "COOLING FAN CIRCUIT" in "FUNCTION TEST" mode with CONSULT.
OR
4. Turn ignition switch "ON".
5. Perform "COOLING FAN" in "ACTIVE TEST" mode with CONSULT.
OR
4. Turn air conditioner switch and blower fan switch "OFF".
5. Disconnect engine coolant temperature sensor harness connector.
6. Connect 150Ω resistor to engine coolant temperature sensor harness connector.
7. Restart engine and make sure that cooling fan operates at higher speed than low speed.
NG
Check cooling fan high speed control circuit. (Go to PROCEDURE B.)
OK
Ⓑ

NS1089500058020X

Fig. 8 Cooling fan diagnosis (Part 2 of 6). 1995–96 Sentra & 200SX w/SR20DE engine

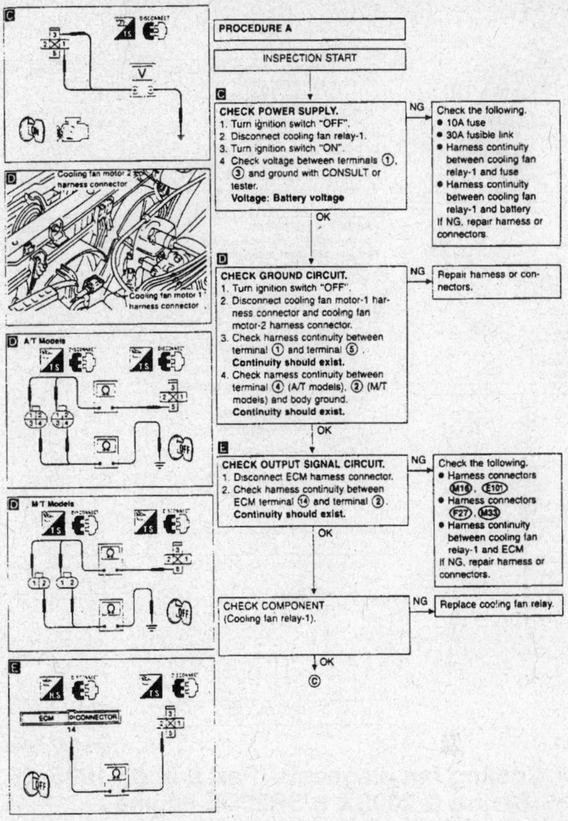
PROCEDURE A
INSPECTION START
CHECK POWER SUPPLY.
1. Turn ignition switch "OFF".
2. Disconnect cooling fan relay-1.
3. Turn ignition switch "ON".
4. Check voltage between terminals ①, ③ and ground with CONSULT or tester.
Voltage: Battery voltage
NG
Check the following.
• 10A fuse
• 30A fusible link
• Harness continuity between cooling fan relay-1 and fuse
• Harness continuity between cooling fan relay-1 and battery
If NG, repair harness or connectors.
OK
CHECK GROUND CIRCUIT.
1. Turn ignition switch "OFF".
2. Disconnect cooling fan motor-1 harness connector and cooling fan motor-2 harness connector.
3. Check harness continuity between terminal ① and terminal ⑤.
Continuity should exist.
4. Check harness continuity between terminal ④ (A/T models), ② (M/T models) and body ground.
Continuity should exist.
NG
Repair harness or connectors.
OK
CHECK OUTPUT SIGNAL CIRCUIT.
1. Disconnect ECM harness connector.
2. Check harness continuity between ECM terminal ⑭ and terminal ②.
Continuity should exist.
NG
Check the following.
• Harness connectors M16, E101
• Harness connectors F27, M33
• Harness continuity between cooling fan relay-1 and ECM
If NG, repair harness or connectors.
OK
CHECK COMPONENT
(Cooling fan relay-1).
NG
Replace cooling fan relay.
OK
Ⓒ
Cooling fan motor-2 harness connector
Cooling fan motor-1 harness connector
A/T Models
M/T Models
ECM
CONNECTOR
14

NS1089500058030

Fig. 8 Cooling fan diagnosis (Part 3 of 6). 1995–96 Sentra & 200SX w/SR20DE engine

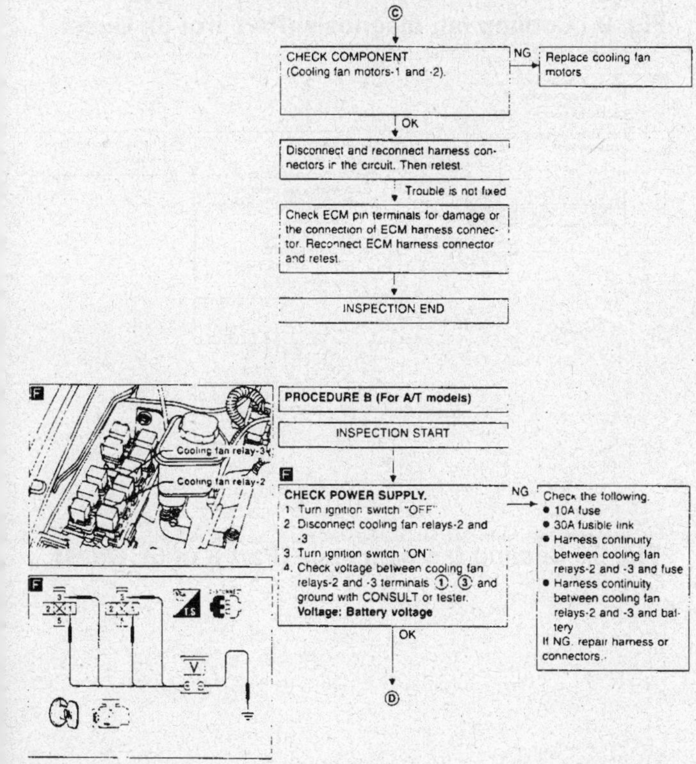
Ⓒ
CHECK COMPONENT
(Cooling fan motors-1 and -2).
NG
Replace cooling fan motors
OK
Disconnect and reconnect harness connectors in the circuit. Then retest.
Trouble is not fixed
Check ECM pin terminals for damage or the connection of ECM harness connector. Reconnect ECM harness connector and retest.
INSPECTION END
Cooling fan relay-3
Cooling fan relay-2
PROCEDURE B (For A/T models)
INSPECTION START
CHECK POWER SUPPLY.
1. Turn ignition switch "OFF".
2. Disconnect cooling fan relays-2 and -3
3. Turn ignition switch "ON".
4. Check voltage between cooling fan relays-2 and -3 terminals ①, ③ and ground with CONSULT or tester.
Voltage: Battery voltage
NG
Check the following.
• 10A fuse
• 30A fusible link
• Harness continuity between cooling fan relays-2 and -3 and fuse
• Harness continuity between cooling fan relays-2 and -3 and battery
If NG, repair harness or connectors.
OK
Ⓓ

NS1089500058040X

Fig. 8 Cooling fan diagnosis (Part 4 of 6). 1995–96 Sentra & 200SX w/SR20DE engine

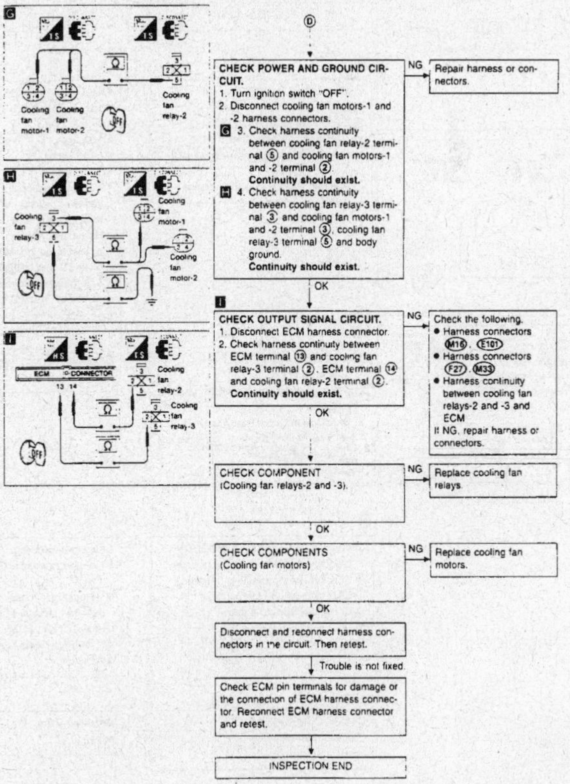
Ⓓ
CHECK POWER AND GROUND CIRCUIT.
1. Turn ignition switch "OFF".
2. Disconnect cooling fan motors-1 and -2 harness connectors.
3. Check harness continuity between cooling fan relay-2 terminal ⑤ and cooling fan motors-1 and -2 terminal ②.
Continuity should exist.
4. Check harness continuity between cooling fan relay-3 terminal ③ and cooling fan motors-1 and -2 terminal ③, cooling fan relay-3 terminal ⑤ and body ground.
Continuity should exist.
NG
Repair harness or connectors.
OK
CHECK OUTPUT SIGNAL CIRCUIT.
1. Disconnect ECM harness connector.
2. Check harness continuity between ECM terminal ⑬ and cooling fan relay-3 terminal ②, ECM terminal ⑭ and cooling fan relay-2 terminal ②.
Continuity should exist.
NG
Check the following.
• Harness connectors M16, E101
• Harness connectors F27, M33
• Harness continuity between cooling fan relays-2 and -3 and ECM
If NG, repair harness or connectors.
OK
CHECK COMPONENT
(Cooling fan relays-2 and -3).
NG
Replace cooling fan relays.
OK
CHECK COMPONENTS
(Cooling fan motors)
NG
Replace cooling fan motors.
OK
Disconnect and reconnect harness connectors in the circuit. Then retest.
Trouble is not fixed
Check ECM pin terminals for damage or the connection of ECM harness connector. Reconnect ECM harness connector and retest.
INSPECTION END
Cooling fan motor-1
Cooling fan motor-2
Cooling fan relay-2
Cooling fan relay-3
ECM
CONNECTOR
13 14

NS1089500058050X

Fig. 8 Cooling fan diagnosis (Part 5 of 6). 1995–96 Sentra & 200SX w/SR20DE engine

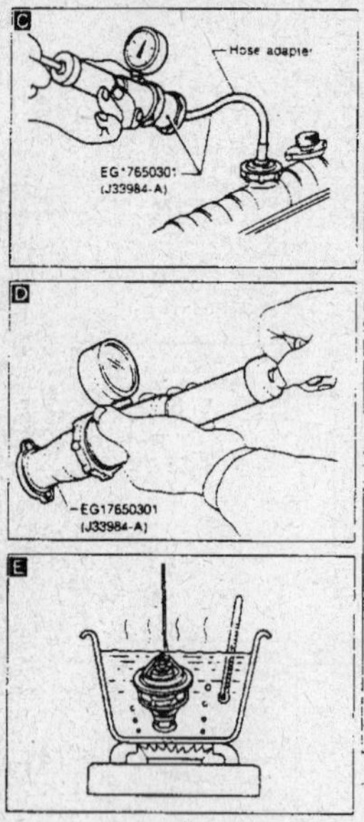
C
Hose adapter
EG17650301
(J33984-A)
D
EG17650301
(J33984-A)
E

Ⓑ

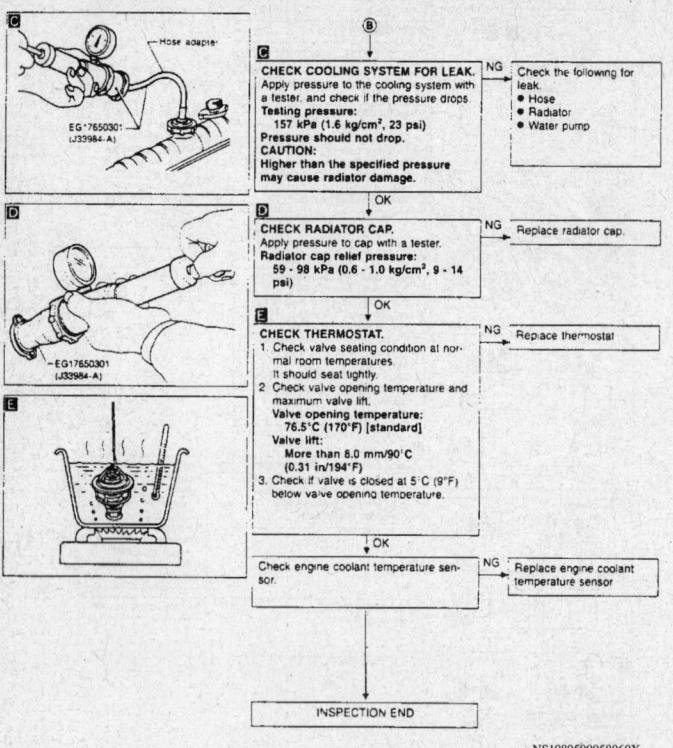

C **CHECK COOLING SYSTEM FOR LEAK.**
Apply pressure to the cooling system with a tester, and check if the pressure drops.
Testing pressure:
157 kPa (1.6 kg/cm², 23 psi)
Pressure should not drop.
CAUTION:
Higher than the specified pressure may cause radiator damage.

NG → Check the following for leak.
- Hose
- Radiator
- Water pump

OK

D **CHECK RADIATOR CAP.**
Apply pressure to cap with a tester.
Radiator cap relief pressure:
59 - 98 kPa (0.6 - 1.0 kg/cm², 9 - 14 psi)

NG → Replace radiator cap.

OK

E **CHECK THERMOSTAT.**
1. Check valve seating condition at normal room temperatures.
It should seat tightly.
2. Check valve opening temperature and maximum valve lift.
Valve opening temperature:
76.5°C (170°F) [standard]
Valve lift:
More than 8.0 mm/90°C (0.31 in/194°F)
3. Check if valve is closed at 5°C (9°F) below valve opening temperature.

NG → Replace thermostat

OK

Check engine coolant temperature sensor.

NG → Replace engine coolant temperature sensor

INSPECTION END

NS1089500058060X

Fig. 8 Cooling fan diagnosis (Part 6 of 6). 1995–96 Sentra & 200SX w/SR20DE engine

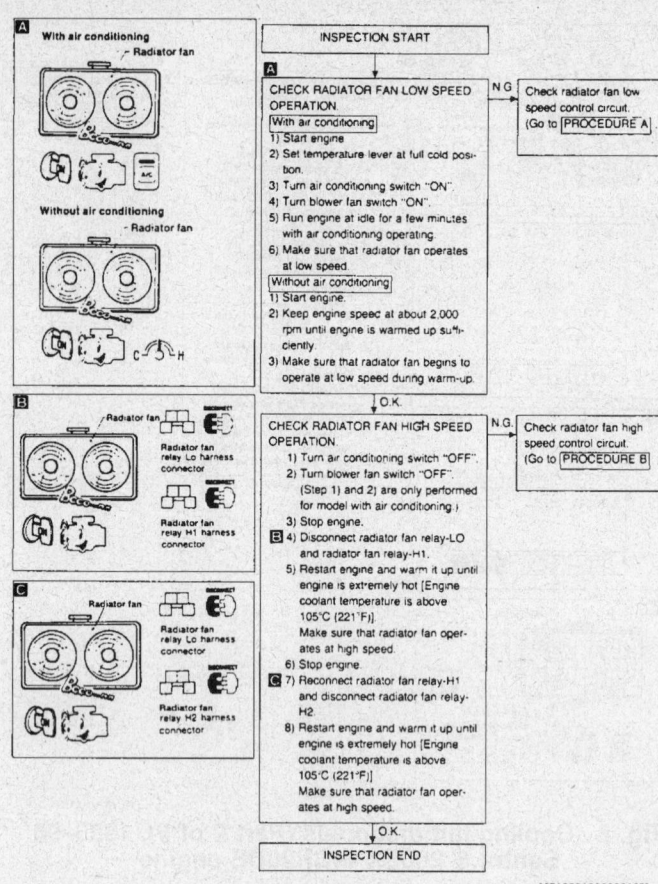

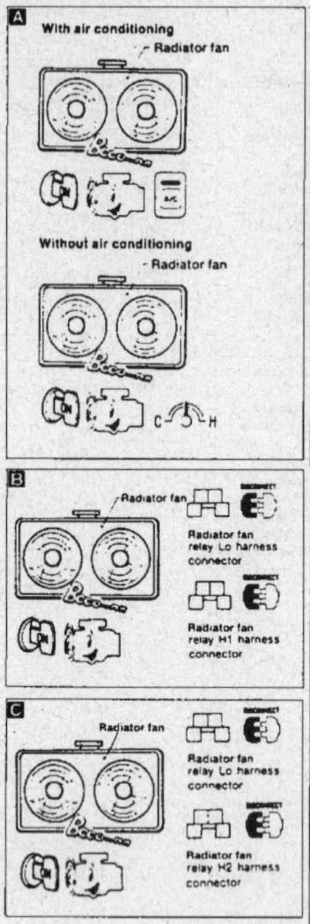
A
With air conditioning
Radiator fan
Without air conditioning
Radiator fan
B
Radiator fan
Radiator fan relay Lo harness connector
Radiator fan relay H1 harness connector
C
Radiator fan
Radiator fan relay Lo harness connector
Radiator fan relay H2 harness connector

INSPECTION START

A CHECK RADIATOR FAN LOW SPEED OPERATION.
With air conditioning
1) Start engine.
2) Set temperature lever at full cold position.
3) Turn air conditioning switch "ON".
4) Turn blower fan switch "ON".
5) Run engine at idle for a few minutes with air conditioning operating.
6) Make sure that radiator fan operates at low speed.
Without air conditioning
1) Start engine.
2) Keep engine speed at about 2,000 rpm until engine is warmed up sufficiently.
3) Make sure that radiator fan begins to operate at low speed during warm-up.

N.G. → Check radiator fan low speed control circuit. (Go to PROCEDURE A.)

O.K.

CHECK RADIATOR FAN HIGH SPEED OPERATION.
1) Turn air conditioning switch "OFF".
2) Turn blower fan switch "OFF".
(Step 1) and 2) are only performed for model with air conditioning.)
3) Stop engine.
B 4) Disconnect radiator fan relay-LO and radiator fan relay-H1.
5) Restart engine and warm it up until engine is extremely hot [Engine coolant temperature is above 105°C (221°F)].
Make sure that radiator fan operates at high speed.
6) Stop engine.
C 7) Reconnect radiator fan relay-H1 and disconnect radiator fan relay-H2.
8) Restart engine and warm it up until engine is extremely hot [Engine coolant temperature is above 105°C (221°F)].
Make sure that radiator fan operates at high speed.

N.G. → Check radiator fan high speed control circuit. (Go to PROCEDURE B.)

O.K.

INSPECTION END

NS1089100030010X

Fig. 9 Cooling fan diagnosis (Part 1 of 6). Quest

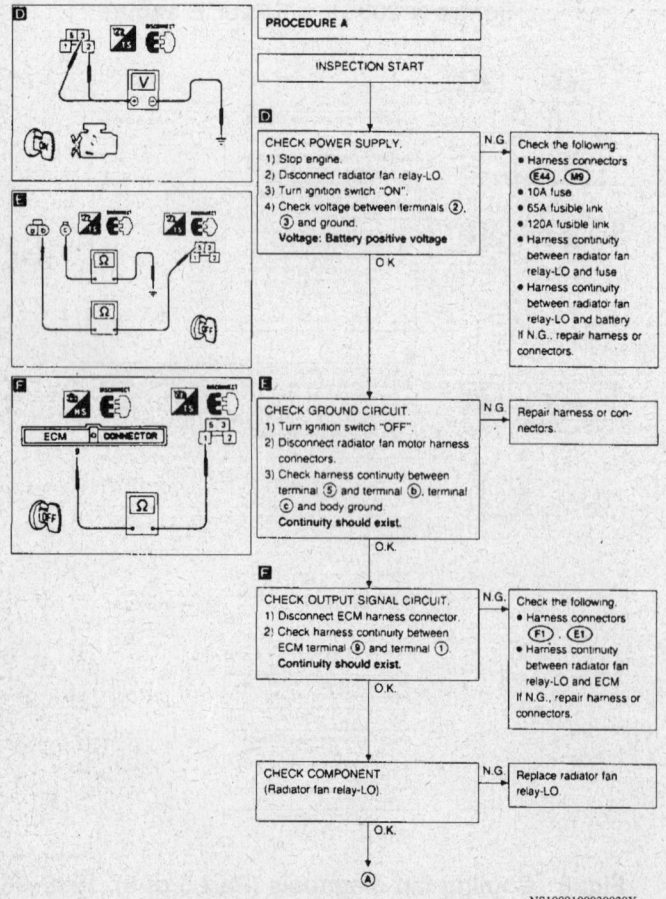

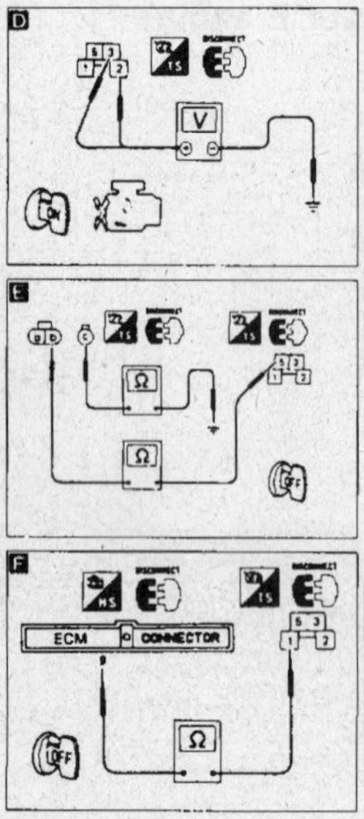
D
V
E
Ω
Ω
F
ECM
CONNECTOR
Ω

PROCEDURE A

INSPECTION START

D CHECK POWER SUPPLY.
1) Stop engine.
2) Disconnect radiator fan relay-LO.
3) Turn ignition switch "ON".
4) Check voltage between terminals ②, ③ and ground.
Voltage: Battery positive voltage

N.G. → Check the following.
- Harness connectors (E44), (M9)
- 10A fuse
- 65A fusible link
- 120A fusible link
- Harness continuity between radiator fan relay-LO and fuse
- Harness continuity between radiator fan relay-LO and battery
If N.G., repair harness or connectors.

OK

E CHECK GROUND CIRCUIT.
1) Turn ignition switch "OFF".
2) Disconnect radiator fan motor harness connectors.
3) Check harness continuity between terminal ⓢ and terminal ⓑ, terminal ⓒ and body ground.
Continuity should exist.

N.G. → Repair harness or connectors.

O.K.

F CHECK OUTPUT SIGNAL CIRCUIT.
1) Disconnect ECM harness connector.
2) Check harness continuity between ECM terminal ⑨ and terminal ①.
Continuity should exist.

N.G. → Check the following.
- Harness connectors (F1), (E1)
- Harness continuity between radiator fan relay-LO and ECM
If N.G., repair harness or connectors.

O.K.

CHECK COMPONENT (Radiator fan relay-LO).

N.G. → Replace radiator fan relay-LO.

O.K.

Ⓐ

NS1089100030020X

Fig. 9 Cooling fan diagnosis (Part 2 of 6). Quest

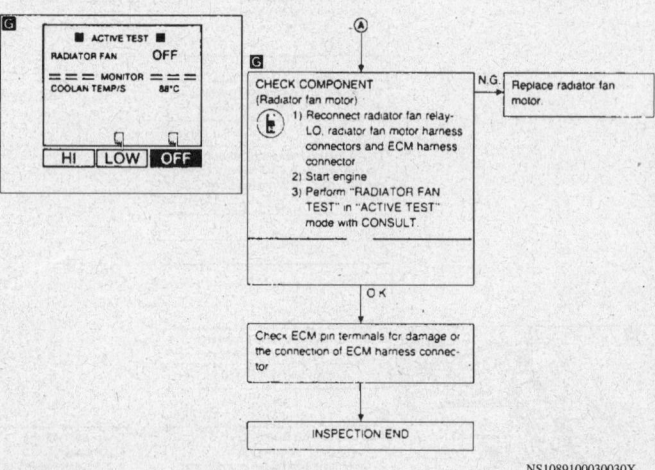

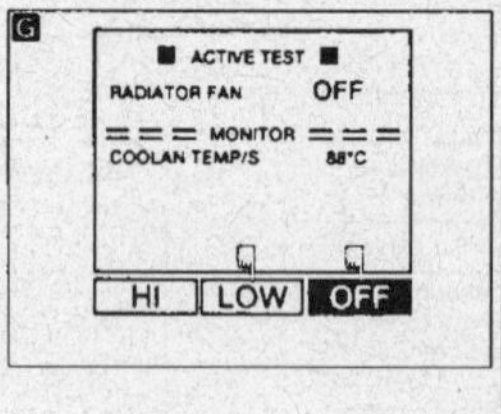
G
ACTIVE TEST
RADIATOR FAN OFF
MONITOR
COOLAN TEMP/S 88°C
HI
LOW
OFF

Ⓐ

G CHECK COMPONENT (Radiator fan motor).
1) Reconnect radiator fan relay-LO, radiator fan motor harness connectors and ECM harness connector.
2) Start engine.
3) Perform "RADIATOR FAN TEST" in "ACTIVE TEST" mode with CONSULT.

N.G. → Replace radiator fan motor.

OK

Check ECM pin terminals for damage or the connection of ECM harness connector.

INSPECTION END

NS1089100030030X

Fig. 9 Cooling fan diagnosis (Part 3 of 6). Quest

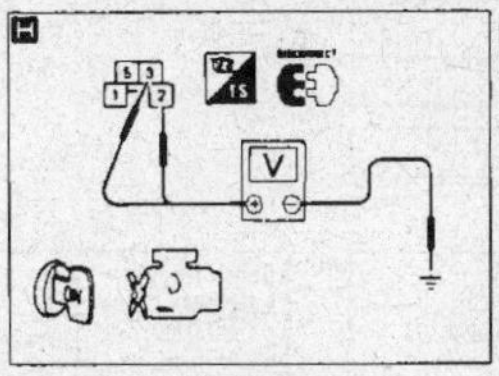
H

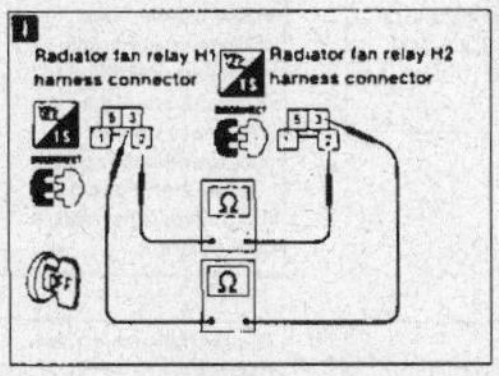
I
Radiator fan relay H1 harness connector
Radiator fan relay H2 harness connector

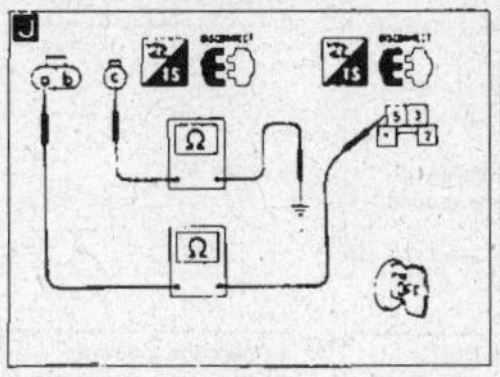
J

PROCEDURE B

INSPECTION START

H

CHECK POWER SUPPLY 1.
1) Stop engine.
2) Disconnect radiator fan relay-H1.
3) Turn ignition switch "ON".
4) Check voltage between terminals ②, ③ and ground.
Voltage: Battery positive voltage

N.G. → Check the following.
- Harness connectors (E44), (M9)
- 10A fuse
- 65A fusible link
- 120A fusible link
- Harness continuity between radiator fan relay-H1 and fuse
- Harness continuity between radiator fan relay-H1 and battery

If N.G., repair harness or connectors.

O.K.

I

CHECK POWER SUPPLY 2
1) Turn ignition switch "OFF".
2) Disconnect radiator fan relay-H2.
4) Check harness continuity between terminals ② and terminal ②, terminal ③ and terminal ③.
Continuity should exist.

N.G. → Repair harness or connectors.

O.K.

J

CHECK GROUND CIRCUIT 1
1) Disconnect radiator fan motor harness connectors.
2) Check harness continuity between terminal ⓐ and radiator fan relay-H1 terminal ⑤, terminal ⓒ and body ground.
Continuity should exist.

N.G. → Repair harness or connectors.

O.K.

Ⓐ

NS1089100030040X

Fig. 9 Cooling fan diagnosis (Part 4 of 6). Quest

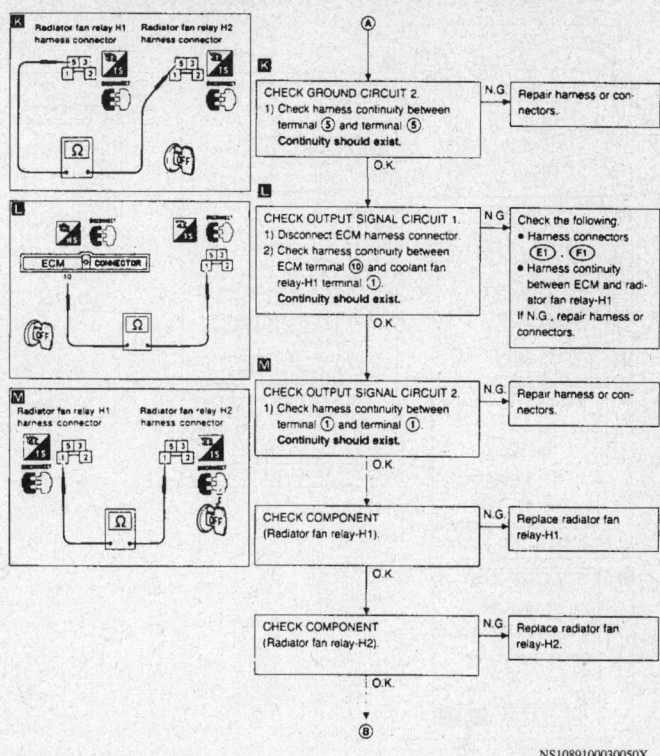

K
Radiator fan relay H1 harness connector
Radiator fan relay H2 harness connector

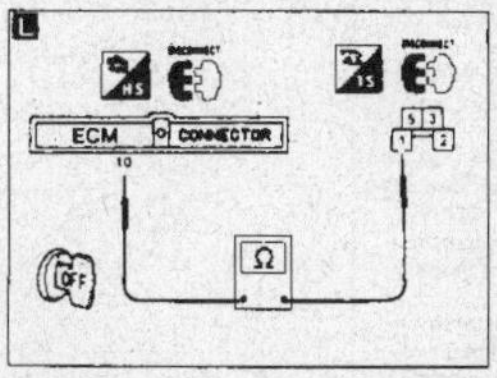
L
ECM
CONNECTOR
10

M
Radiator fan relay H1 harness connector
Radiator fan relay H2 harness connector

Ⓐ

K

CHECK GROUND CIRCUIT 2.
1) Check harness continuity between terminal ⑤ and terminal ⑤.
Continuity should exist.

N.G. → Repair harness or connectors.

O.K.

L

CHECK OUTPUT SIGNAL CIRCUIT 1.
1) Disconnect ECM harness connector.
2) Check harness continuity between ECM terminal ⑩ and coolant fan relay-H1 terminal ①.
Continuity should exist.

N.G. → Check the following.
- Harness connectors (E1), (F1)
- Harness continuity between ECM and radiator fan relay-H1

If N.G., repair harness or connectors.

O.K.

M

CHECK OUTPUT SIGNAL CIRCUIT 2.
1) Check harness continuity between terminal ① and terminal ①.
Continuity should exist.

N.G. → Repair harness or connectors.

O.K.

CHECK COMPONENT
(Radiator fan relay-H1).

N.G. → Replace radiator fan relay-H1.

O.K.

CHECK COMPONENT
(Radiator fan relay-H2).

N.G. → Replace radiator fan relay-H2.

O.K.

Ⓑ

NS1089100030050X

Fig. 9 Cooling fan diagnosis (Part 5 of 6). Quest

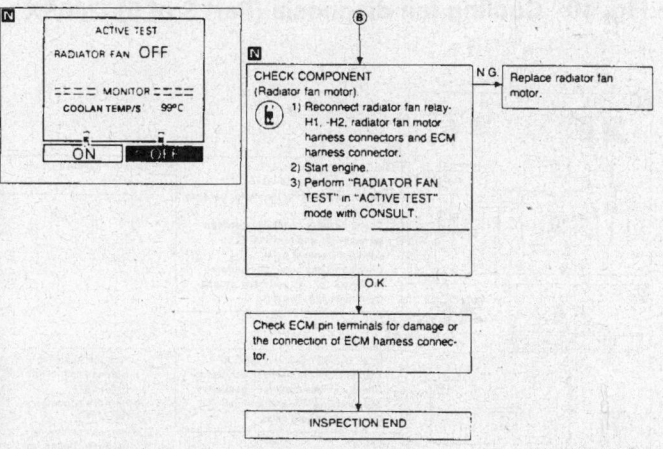

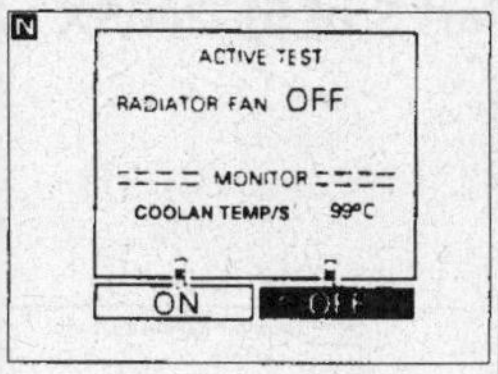
N
ACTIVE TEST
RADIATOR FAN OFF
MONITOR
COOLAN TEMP/S 99°C
ON
OFF

Ⓑ

N

CHECK COMPONENT
(Radiator fan motor).
1) Reconnect radiator fan relay-H1, -H2, radiator fan motor harness connectors and ECM harness connector.
2) Start engine.
3) Perform "RADIATOR FAN TEST" in "ACTIVE TEST" mode with CONSULT.

N.G. → Replace radiator fan motor.

O.K.

Check ECM pin terminals for damage or the connection of ECM harness connector.

INSPECTION END

NS1089100030060X

Fig. 9 Cooling fan diagnosis (Part 6 of 6). Quest

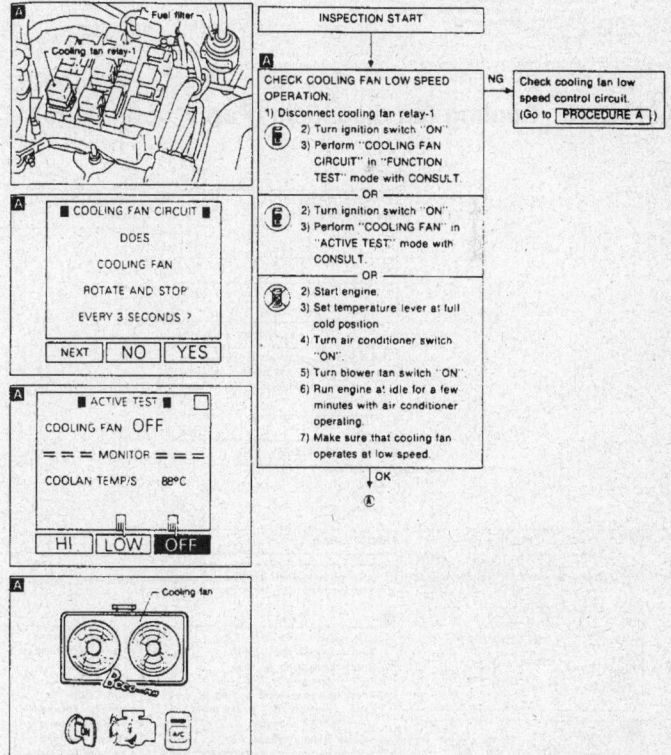

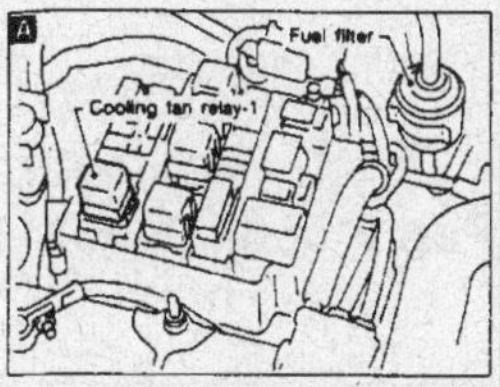
A
Fuel filter
Cooling fan relay-1

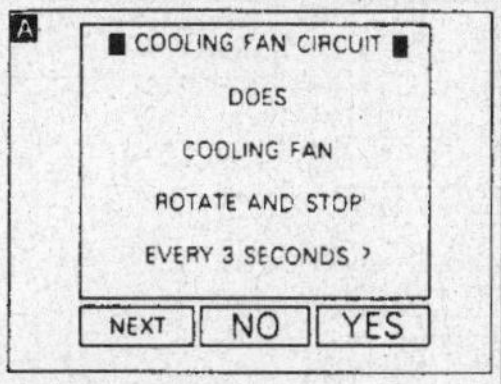
A
COOLING FAN CIRCUIT
DOES
COOLING FAN
ROTATE AND STOP
EVERY 3 SECONDS ?
NEXT
NO
YES

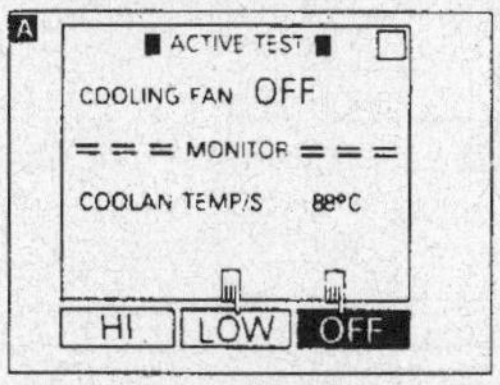
A
ACTIVE TEST
COOLING FAN OFF
MONITOR
COOLAN TEMP/S 88°C
HI
LOW
OFF

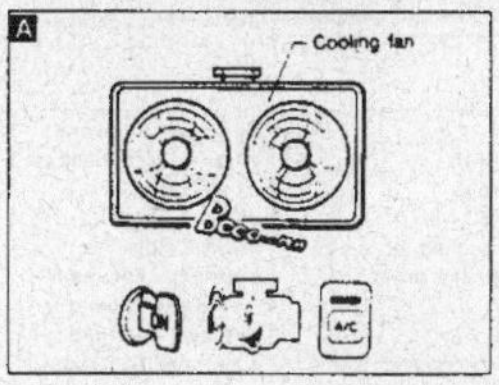
A
Cooling fan

INSPECTION START

A

CHECK COOLING FAN LOW SPEED OPERATION.
1) Disconnect cooling fan relay-1
2) Turn ignition switch "ON".
3) Perform "COOLING FAN CIRCUIT" in "FUNCTION TEST" mode with CONSULT.

— OR —

2) Turn ignition switch "ON".
3) Perform "COOLING FAN" in "ACTIVE TEST" mode with CONSULT.

— OR —

2) Start engine.
3) Set temperature lever at full cold position.
4) Turn air conditioner switch "ON".
5) Turn blower fan switch "ON".
6) Run engine at idle for a few minutes with air conditioner operating.
7) Make sure that cooling fan operates at low speed.

NG → Check cooling fan low speed control circuit. (Go to PROCEDURE A.)

OK

Ⓒ

NS1089500059010X

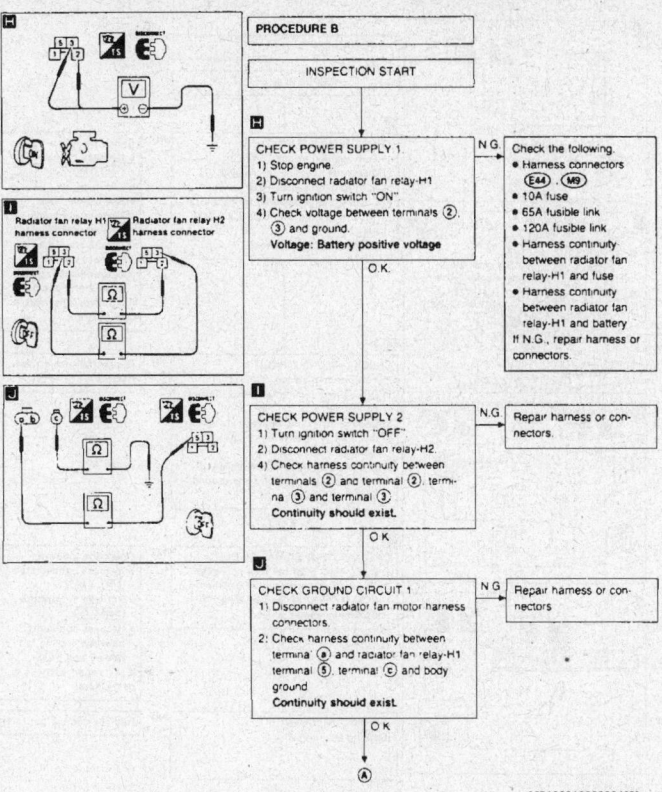

Fig. 10 Cooling fan diagnosis (Part 1 of 5). 240SX

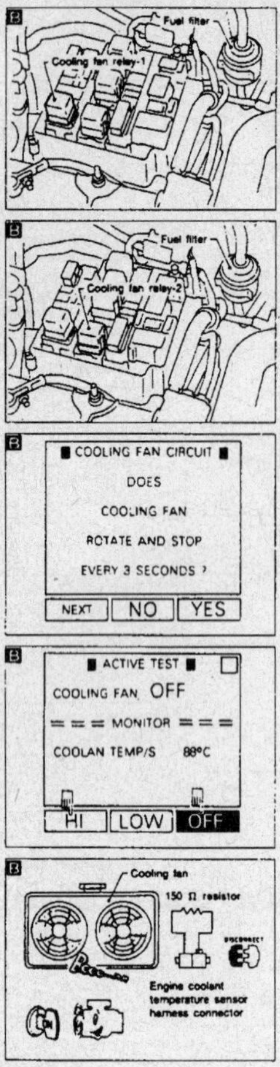
Fuel filter
Cooling fan relay-1
Fuel filter
Cooling fan relay-2
COOLING FAN CIRCUIT
DOES
COOLING FAN
ROTATE AND STOP
EVERY 3 SECONDS ?
NEXT
NO
YES
ACTIVE TEST
COOLING FAN OFF
MONITOR
COOLAN TEMP/S 88°C
HI
LOW
OFF
Cooling fan
150 Ω resistor
DISCONNECT
Engine coolant temperature sensor harness connector

Ⓐ

B CHECK COOLING FAN HIGH SPEED OPERATION.
1) Turn ignition switch "OFF".
2) Reconnect cooling fan relay-1.
3) Disconnect cooling fan relay-2.
4) Turn ignition switch "ON".
5) Perform "COOLING FAN CIRCUIT" in "FUNCTION TEST" mode with CONSULT.
— OR —
4) Turn ignition switch "ON".
5) Perform "COOLING FAN" in "ACTIVE TEST" mode with CONSULT.
— OR —
4) Turn air conditioner switch and blower fan switch "OFF".
5) Disconnect engine coolant temperature sensor harness connector.
6) Connect 150Ω resistor to engine coolant temperature sensor harness connector.
7) Restart engine and make sure that cooling fan operates at higher speed than low speed.

NG → Check cooling fan high speed control circuit. (Go to PROCEDURE B.)

OK ↓

INSPECTION END

NS1089500059020X

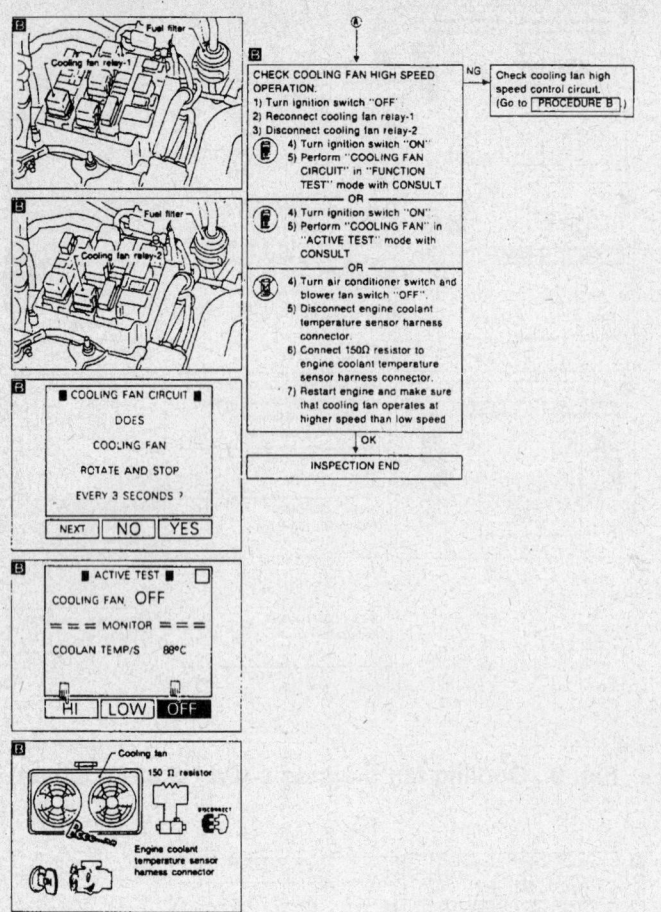

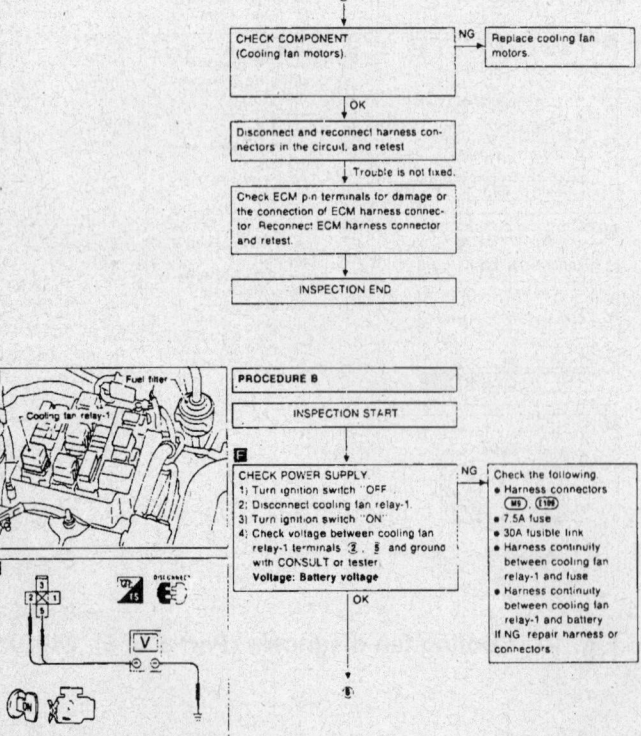

Fig. 10 Cooling fan diagnosis (Part 2 of 5). 240SX

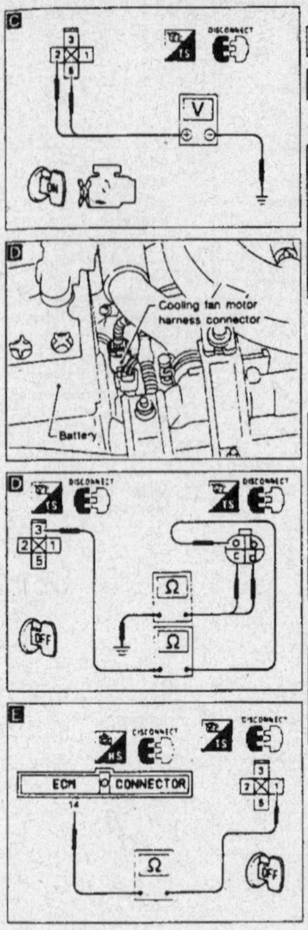
DISCONNECT
V
Cooling fan motor harness connector
Battery
DISCONNECT
Ω
Ω
DISCONNECT
ECM
CONNECTOR
14
Ω

PROCEDURE A

INSPECTION START

C CHECK POWER SUPPLY.
1) Turn ignition switch "OFF".
2) Disconnect cooling fan relay-2.
3) Turn ignition switch "ON".
4) Check voltage between terminals ②, ③ and ground with CONSULT or tester.
Voltage: Battery voltage

NG → Check the following.
- Harness connectors M9, E100
- 7.5A fuse
- 30A fusible links
- Harness continuity between cooling fan relay-2 and fuse
- Harness continuity between cooling fan relay-2 and battery

If NG, repair harness or connectors.

OK ↓

D CHECK GROUND CIRCUIT.
1) Turn ignition switch "OFF".
2) Disconnect cooling fan motor harness connector.
3) Check harness continuity between terminal ③ and terminal ⓐ.
Continuity should exist.
4) Check harness continuity between terminals ⓒ, ⓓ and body ground.
Continuity should exist.

NG → Repair harness or connectors.

OK ↓

E CHECK OUTPUT SIGNAL CIRCUIT.
1) Disconnect ECM harness connector.
2) Check harness continuity between ECM terminal ⑭ and terminal ①.
Continuity should exist.

NG → Check the following.
- Harness connectors E100, M9
- Harness connectors M63, F3
- Harness continuity between cooling fan relay-2 and ECM

If NG, repair harness or connectors.

OK ↓

CHECK COMPONENT (Cooling fan relay-2).

NG → Replace cooling fan relay.

OK ↓

Ⓐ

NS1089500059030X

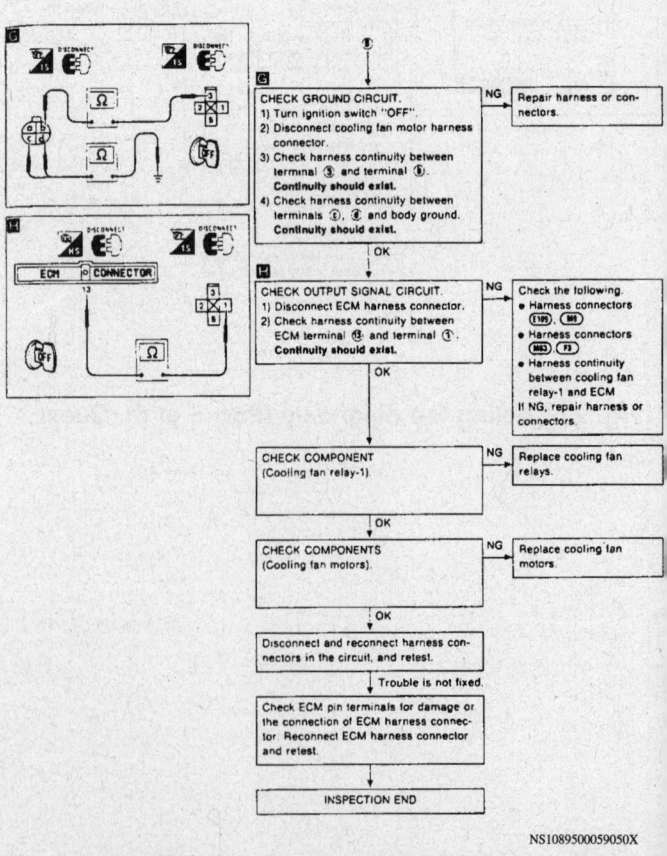

Fig. 10 Cooling fan diagnosis (Part 3 of 5). 240SX

Ⓐ

CHECK COMPONENT (Cooling fan motors).

NG → Replace cooling fan motors.

OK ↓

Disconnect and reconnect harness connectors in the circuit, and retest.

↓ Trouble is not fixed.

Check ECM pin terminals for damage or the connection of ECM harness connector. Reconnect ECM harness connector and retest.

↓

INSPECTION END

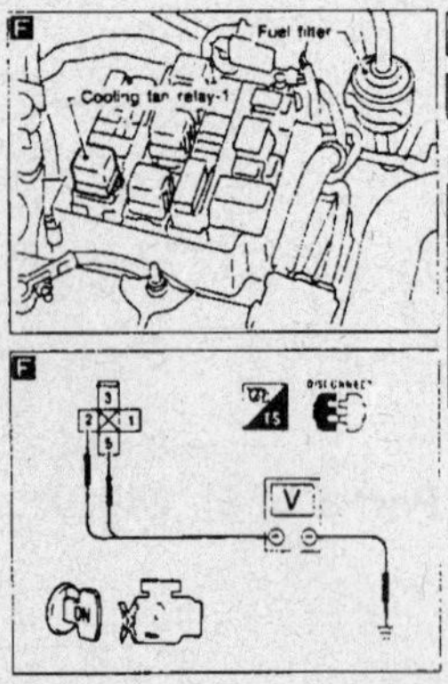
Fuel filter
Cooling fan relay-1
DISCONNECT
V

PROCEDURE B

INSPECTION START

F CHECK POWER SUPPLY.
1) Turn ignition switch "OFF".
2) Disconnect cooling fan relay-1.
3) Turn ignition switch "ON".
4) Check voltage between cooling fan relay-1 terminals ②, ⑤ and ground with CONSULT or tester.
Voltage: Battery voltage

NG → Check the following.
- Harness connectors M9, E100
- 7.5A fuse
- 30A fusible link
- Harness continuity between cooling fan relay-1 and fuse
- Harness continuity between cooling fan relay-1 and battery

If NG, repair harness or connectors.

OK ↓

Ⓑ

NS1089500059040X

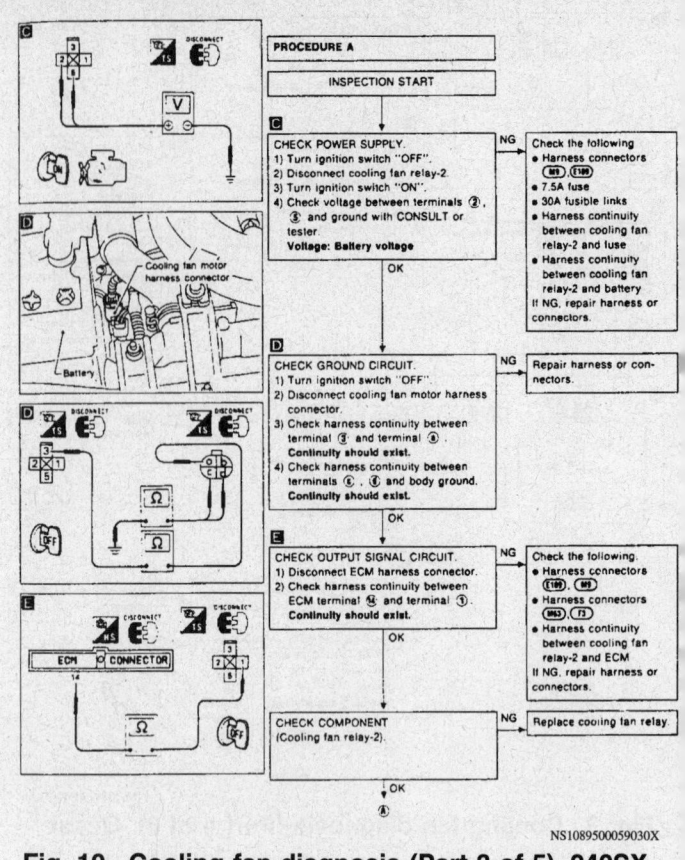

Fig. 10 Cooling fan diagnosis (Part 4 of 5). 240SX

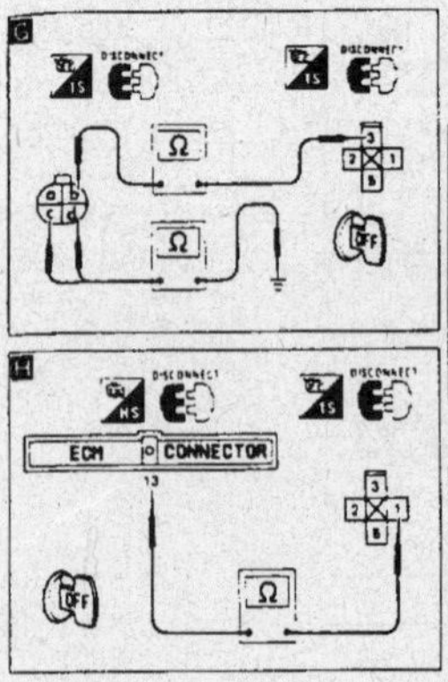
DISCONNECT
Ω
Ω
DISCONNECT
ECM
CONNECTOR
13
Ω

Ⓑ

G CHECK GROUND CIRCUIT.
1) Turn ignition switch "OFF".
2) Disconnect cooling fan motor harness connector.
3) Check harness continuity between terminal ③ and terminal ⓑ.
Continuity should exist.
4) Check harness continuity between terminals ⓒ, ⓓ and body ground.
Continuity should exist.

NG → Repair harness or connectors.

OK ↓

H CHECK OUTPUT SIGNAL CIRCUIT.
1) Disconnect ECM harness connector.
2) Check harness continuity between ECM terminal ⑬ and terminal ①.
Continuity should exist.

NG → Check the following.
- Harness connectors E100, M9
- Harness connectors M63, F3
- Harness continuity between cooling fan relay-1 and ECM

If NG, repair harness or connectors.

OK ↓

CHECK COMPONENT (Cooling fan relay-1).

NG → Replace cooling fan relays.

OK ↓

CHECK COMPONENTS (Cooling fan motors).

NG → Replace cooling fan motors.

OK ↓

Disconnect and reconnect harness connectors in the circuit, and retest.

↓ Trouble is not fixed.

Check ECM pin terminals for damage or the connection of ECM harness connector. Reconnect ECM harness connector and retest.

↓

INSPECTION END

NS1089500059050X

Fig. 10 Cooling fan diagnosis (Part 5 of 5). 240SX

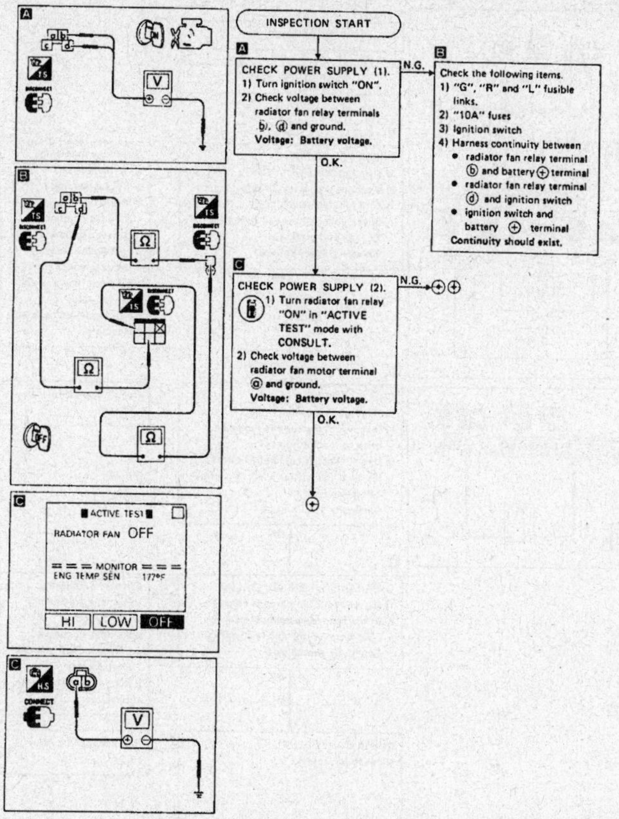
INSPECTION START
A
CHECK POWER SUPPLY (1).
1) Turn ignition switch "ON".
2) Check voltage between radiator fan relay terminals ⓑ, ⓓ and ground.
Voltage: Battery voltage.
N.G.
B
Check the following items.
1) "G", "R" and "L" fusible links.
2) "10A" fuses
3) Ignition switch
4) Harness continuity between
• radiator fan relay terminal ⓑ and battery ⊕ terminal
• radiator fan relay terminal ⓓ and ignition switch
• ignition switch and battery ⊕ terminal
Continuity should exist.
O.K.
C
CHECK POWER SUPPLY (2).
1) Turn radiator fan relay "ON" in "ACTIVE TEST" mode with CONSULT.
2) Check voltage between radiator fan motor terminal ⓐ and ground.
Voltage: Battery voltage.
N.G.
O.K.
ACTIVE TEST
RADIATOR FAN OFF
MONITOR
ENG TEMP SEN 177°F
HI
LOW
OFF
V
Ω

NS1089100032010X

Fig. 11 Cooling fan diagnosis (Part 1 of 2). 1993 300ZX

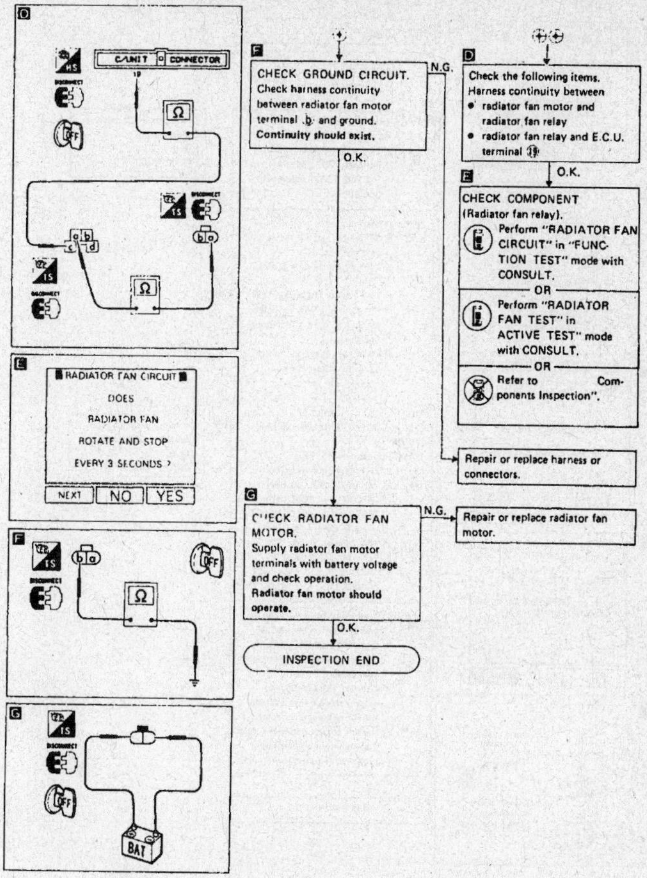
C/UNIT CONNECTOR
F
CHECK GROUND CIRCUIT.
Check harness continuity between radiator fan motor terminal ⓑ and ground.
Continuity should exist.
N.G.
D
Check the following items.
Harness continuity between
• radiator fan motor and radiator fan relay
• radiator fan relay and E.C.U. terminal
O.K.
E
CHECK COMPONENT (Radiator fan relay).
Perform "RADIATOR FAN CIRCUIT" in "FUNCTION TEST" mode with CONSULT.
OR
Perform "RADIATOR FAN TEST" in ACTIVE TEST" mode with CONSULT.
OR
Refer to Components Inspection".
Repair or replace harness or connectors.
RADIATOR FAN CIRCUIT
DOES RADIATOR FAN ROTATE AND STOP EVERY 3 SECONDS ?
NEXT
NO
YES
G
CHECK RADIATOR FAN MOTOR.
Supply radiator fan motor terminals with battery voltage and check operation.
Radiator fan motor should operate.
N.G.
Repair or replace radiator fan motor.
O.K.
INSPECTION END
BAT
Ω

NS1089100032020X

Fig. 11 Cooling fan diagnosis (Part 2 of 2). 1993 300ZX

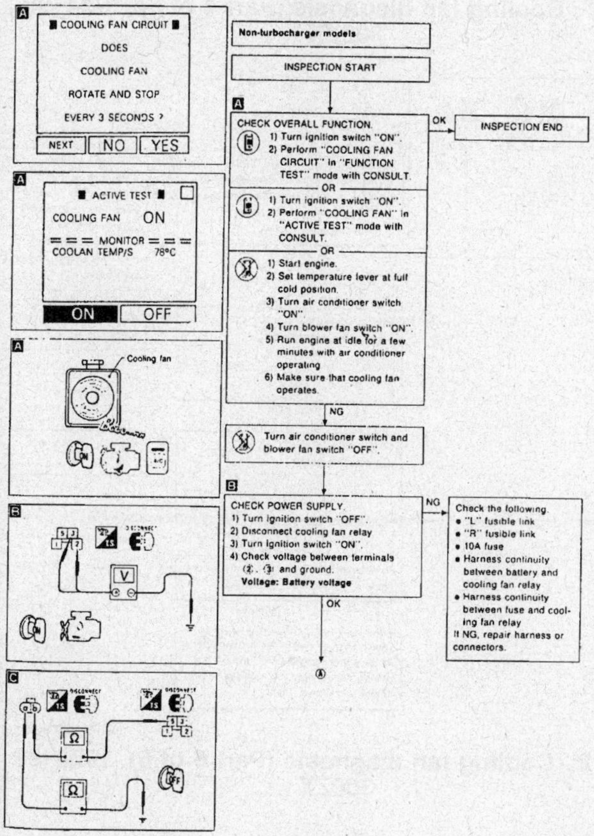
COOLING FAN CIRCUIT
DOES COOLING FAN ROTATE AND STOP EVERY 3 SECONDS ?
NEXT
NO
YES
ACTIVE TEST
COOLING FAN ON
MONITOR
COOLAN TEMP/S 78°C
ON
OFF
Cooling fan
Non-turbocharger models
INSPECTION START
A
CHECK OVERALL FUNCTION.
1) Turn ignition switch "ON".
2) Perform "COOLING FAN CIRCUIT" in "FUNCTION TEST" mode with CONSULT.
OR
1) Turn ignition switch "ON".
2) Perform "COOLING FAN" in "ACTIVE TEST" mode with CONSULT.
OR
1) Start engine.
2) Set temperature lever at full cold position.
3) Turn air conditioner switch "ON".
4) Turn blower fan switch "ON".
5) Run engine at idle for a few minutes with air conditioner operating.
6) Make sure that cooling fan operates.
OK
INSPECTION END
NG
Turn air conditioner switch and blower fan switch "OFF".
B
CHECK POWER SUPPLY.
1) Turn ignition switch "OFF".
2) Disconnect cooling fan relay
3) Turn ignition switch "ON".
4) Check voltage between terminals ②, ③ and ground.
Voltage: Battery voltage
NG
Check the following.
• "L" fusible link
• "R" fusible link
• 10A fuse
• Harness continuity between battery and cooling fan relay
• Harness continuity between fuse and cooling fan relay
If NG, repair harness or connectors.
OK
Ⓐ
V
Ω

NS1089400033010X

Fig. 12 Cooling fan diagnosis (Part 1 of 6). 1994–96 300ZX

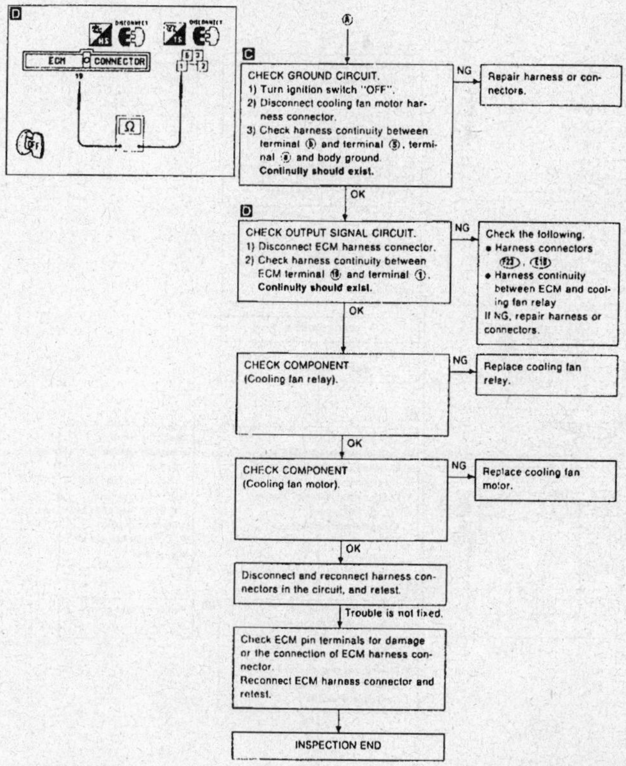
ECM CONNECTOR
Ω
Ⓐ
C
CHECK GROUND CIRCUIT.
1) Turn ignition switch "OFF".
2) Disconnect cooling fan motor harness connector.
3) Check harness continuity between terminal ⓑ and terminal ⑤, terminal ⓐ and body ground.
Continuity should exist.
NG
Repair harness or connectors.
OK
D
CHECK OUTPUT SIGNAL CIRCUIT.
1) Disconnect ECM harness connector.
2) Check harness continuity between ECM terminal ⑲ and terminal ①.
Continuity should exist.
NG
Check the following.
• Harness connectors
• Harness continuity between ECM and cooling fan relay
If NG, repair harness or connectors.
OK
CHECK COMPONENT (Cooling fan relay).
NG
Replace cooling fan relay.
OK
CHECK COMPONENT (Cooling fan motor).
NG
Replace cooling fan motor.
OK
Disconnect and reconnect harness connectors in the circuit, and retest.
Trouble is not fixed.
Check ECM pin terminals for damage or the connection of ECM harness connector.
Reconnect ECM harness connector and retest.
INSPECTION END

NS1089400033020X

Fig. 12 Cooling fan diagnosis (Part 2 of 6). 1994–96 300ZX

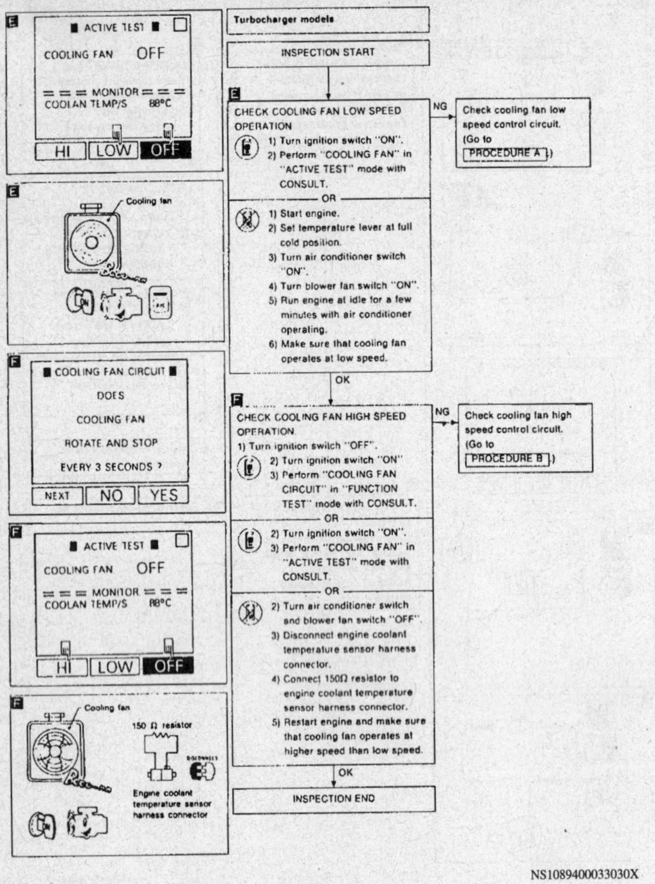
ACTIVE TEST
COOLING FAN OFF
MONITOR
COOLAN TEMP/S 88°C
HI LOW OFF
Cooling fan
COOLING FAN CIRCUIT
DOES COOLING FAN ROTATE AND STOP EVERY 3 SECONDS ?
NEXT NO YES
ACTIVE TEST
COOLING FAN OFF
MONITOR
COOLAN TEMP/S 88°C
HI LOW OFF
Cooling fan
150 Ω resistor
Engine coolant temperature sensor harness connector
Turbocharger models
INSPECTION START
CHECK COOLING FAN LOW SPEED OPERATION
1) Turn ignition switch "ON".
2) Perform "COOLING FAN" in "ACTIVE TEST" mode with CONSULT.
OR
1) Start engine.
2) Set temperature lever at full cold position.
3) Turn air conditioner switch "ON".
4) Turn blower fan switch "ON".
5) Run engine at idle for a few minutes with air conditioner operating.
6) Make sure that cooling fan operates at low speed.
NG
Check cooling fan low speed control circuit. (Go to PROCEDURE A.)
OK
CHECK COOLING FAN HIGH SPEED OPERATION
1) Turn ignition switch "OFF".
2) Turn ignition switch "ON".
3) Perform "COOLING FAN CIRCUIT" in "FUNCTION TEST" mode with CONSULT.
OR
2) Turn ignition switch "ON".
3) Perform "COOLING FAN" in "ACTIVE TEST" mode with CONSULT.
OR
2) Turn air conditioner switch and blower fan switch "OFF".
3) Disconnect engine coolant temperature sensor harness connector.
4) Connect 150Ω resistor to engine coolant temperature sensor harness connector.
5) Restart engine and make sure that cooling fan operates at higher speed than low speed.
NG
Check cooling fan high speed control circuit. (Go to PROCEDURE B.)
OK
INSPECTION END
NS1089400033030X

Fig. 12 Cooling fan diagnosis (Part 3 of 6). 1994–96 300ZX

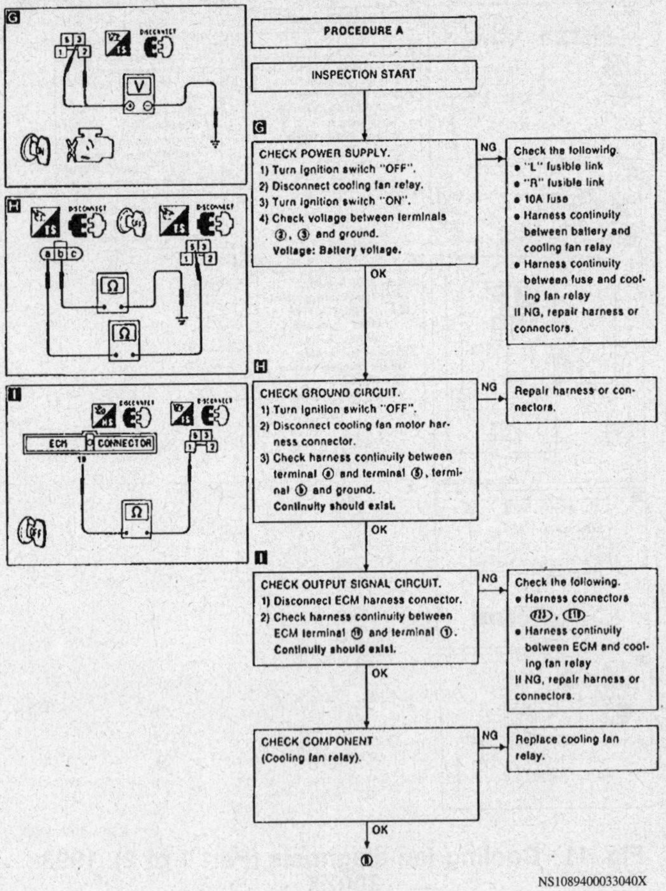
PROCEDURE A
INSPECTION START
CHECK POWER SUPPLY.
1) Turn ignition switch "OFF".
2) Disconnect cooling fan relay.
3) Turn ignition switch "ON".
4) Check voltage between terminals ②, ③ and ground.
Voltage: Battery voltage.
NG
Check the following.
• "L" fusible link
• "R" fusible link
• 10A fuse
• Harness continuity between battery and cooling fan relay
• Harness continuity between fuse and cooling fan relay
If NG, repair harness or connectors.
OK
CHECK GROUND CIRCUIT.
1) Turn ignition switch "OFF".
2) Disconnect cooling fan motor harness connector.
3) Check harness continuity between terminal ⓐ and terminal ⑤, terminal ⓑ and ground.
Continuity should exist.
NG
Repair harness or connectors.
OK
CHECK OUTPUT SIGNAL CIRCUIT.
1) Disconnect ECM harness connector.
2) Check harness continuity between ECM terminal ⑲ and terminal ①.
Continuity should exist.
NG
Check the following.
• Harness connectors (F23), (E19)
• Harness continuity between ECM and cooling fan relay
If NG, repair harness or connectors.
OK
CHECK COMPONENT (Cooling fan relay).
NG
Replace cooling fan relay.
OK
ECM CONNECTOR
NS1089400033040X

Fig. 12 Cooling fan diagnosis (Part 4 of 6). 1994–96 300ZX

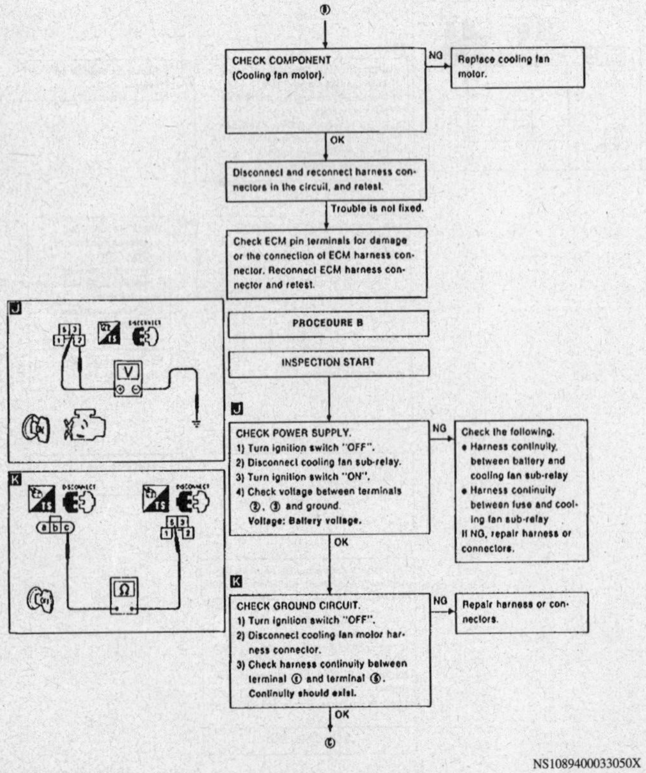
CHECK COMPONENT (Cooling fan motor).
NG
Replace cooling fan motor.
OK
Disconnect and reconnect harness connectors in the circuit, and retest.
Trouble is not fixed.
Check ECM pin terminals for damage or the connection of ECM harness connector. Reconnect ECM harness connector and retest.
PROCEDURE B
INSPECTION START
CHECK POWER SUPPLY.
1) Turn ignition switch "OFF".
2) Disconnect cooling fan sub-relay.
3) Turn ignition switch "ON".
4) Check voltage between terminals ②, ③ and ground.
Voltage: Battery voltage.
NG
Check the following.
• Harness continuity between battery and cooling fan sub-relay
• Harness continuity between fuse and cooling fan sub-relay
If NG, repair harness or connectors.
OK
CHECK GROUND CIRCUIT.
1) Turn ignition switch "OFF".
2) Disconnect cooling fan motor harness connector.
3) Check harness continuity between terminal ⓒ and terminal ⑤.
Continuity should exist.
NG
Repair harness or connectors.
OK
NS1089400033050X

Fig. 12 Cooling fan diagnosis (Part 5 of 6). 1994–96 300ZX

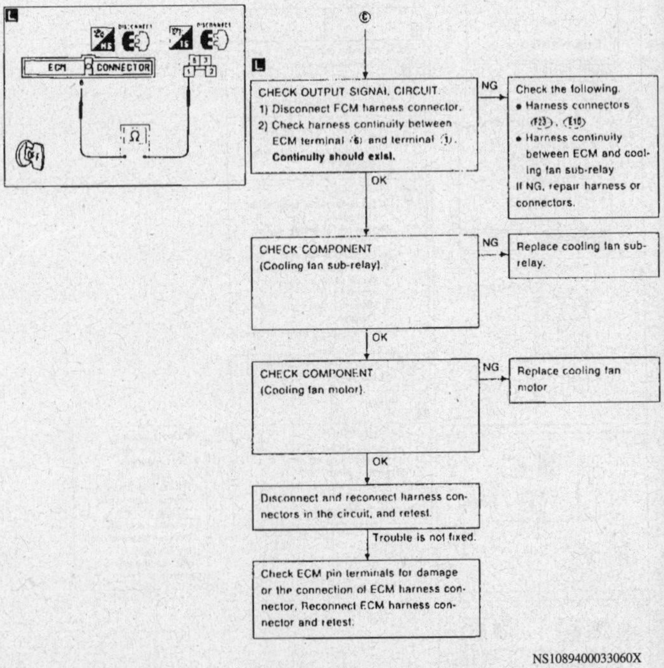
ECM CONNECTOR
CHECK OUTPUT SIGNAL CIRCUIT.
1) Disconnect ECM harness connector.
2) Check harness continuity between ECM terminal ⑥ and terminal ①.
Continuity should exist.
NG
Check the following.
• Harness connectors (F23), (E19)
• Harness continuity between ECM and cooling fan sub-relay
If NG, repair harness or connectors.
OK
CHECK COMPONENT (Cooling fan sub-relay).
NG
Replace cooling fan sub-relay.
OK
CHECK COMPONENT (Cooling fan motor).
NG
Replace cooling fan motor.
OK
Disconnect and reconnect harness connectors in the circuit, and retest.
Trouble is not fixed.
Check ECM pin terminals for damage or the connection of ECM harness connector. Reconnect ECM harness connector and retest.
NS1089400033060X

Fig. 12 Cooling fan diagnosis (Part 6 of 6). 1994–96 300ZX

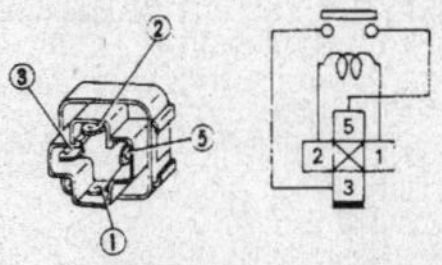

②
③
⑤
①
5
2
1
3

Check continuity between terminals ③ and ⑤.

Conditions	Continuity
12V direct current supply between terminals ① and ②	Yes
No current supply	No

NS1089500060000X

Fig. 13 Cooling fan relay inspection. Altima, Maxima, 240SX & 1995–96 Sentra & 200SX

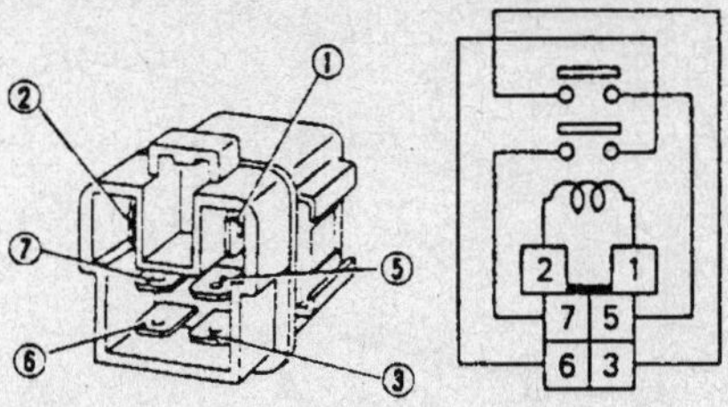

①
②
⑦
⑤
⑥
③
2
1
7
5
6
3

Check continuity between terminals ③ and ⑤, ⑥ and ⑦.

Conditions	Continuity
12V direct current supply between terminals ① and ②	Yes
No current supply	No

NS1089100035000X

Fig. 14 Cooling fan relay inspection. Altima & Maxima

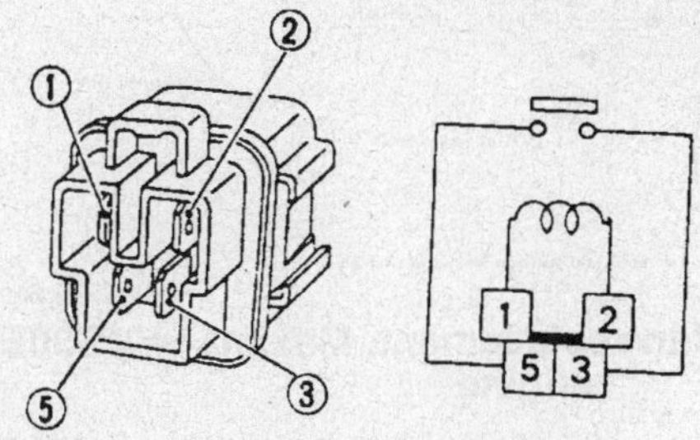

①
②
⑤
③
1
2
5
3

Check continuity between terminals ③ and ⑤.

Conditions	Continuity
12V direct current supply between terminals ① and ②	Yes
No current supply	No

NS1089100034000X

Fig. 15 Cooling fan relay inspection. Quest, 300ZX & 1993–94 NX1600, NX2000 & Sentra w/manual transaxle

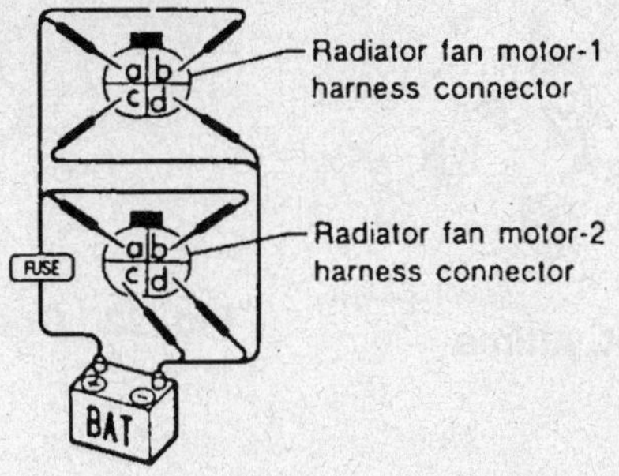

Radiator fan motor-1 harness connector
Radiator fan motor-2 harness connector
FUSE
BAT

	Speed	Terminals	
		(+)	(−)
Radiator fan motor-1	Low	ⓑ	ⓒ
	High	ⓐ, ⓑ	ⓒ, ⓓ
Radiator fan motor-2	Low	ⓑ	ⓒ
	High	ⓐ, ⓑ	ⓒ, ⓓ

NS1089100037000X

Fig. 16 Cooling fan motor inspection. Altima, Maxima, 1993–94 NX1600, NX2000 & Sentra w/automatic transaxle

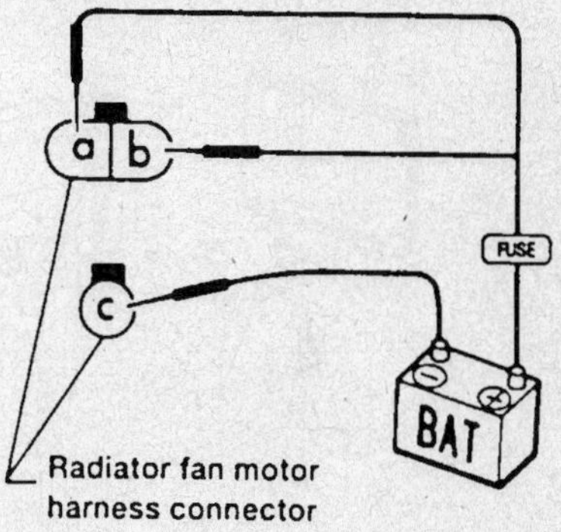

a
b
c
FUSE
BAT
Radiator fan motor harness connector

	Speed	Terminals	
		(+)	(−)
Radiator fan motor	Low	ⓐ	ⓒ
	High	ⓑ	ⓒ

NS1089100038000X

Fig. 17 Cooling fan motor inspection. Quest

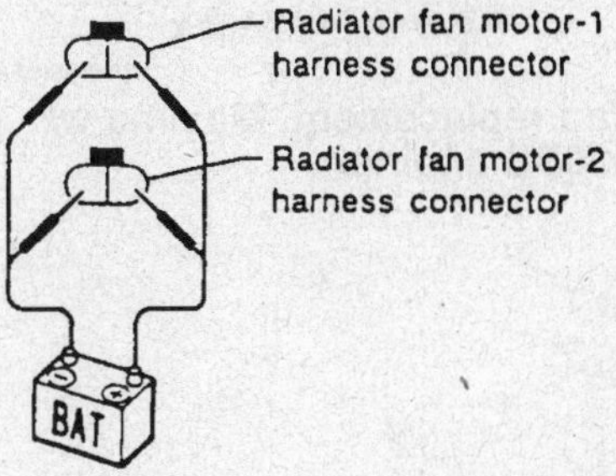

Radiator fan motor-1 harness connector
Radiator fan motor-2 harness connector
BAT

NS1089100039000X

Fig. 18 Cooling fan motor inspection. 1993–94 NX1600, NX2000, Sentra w/manual transaxle

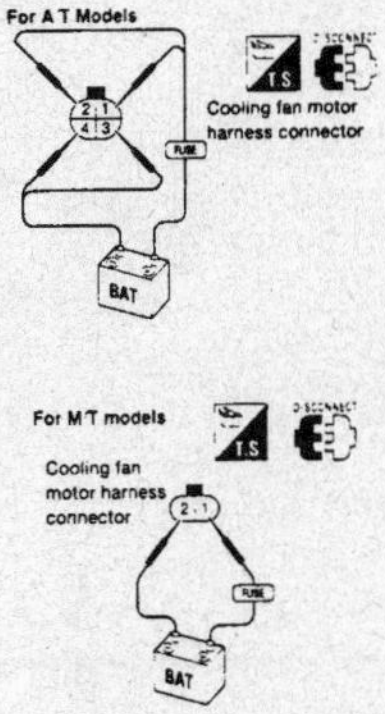

For A/T Models
Cooling fan motor harness connector
BAT
For M/T models
Cooling fan motor harness connector
BAT

1. Disconnect cooling fan motor harness connectors.
2. Supply cooling fan motor terminals with battery voltage and check operation.

	Speed	Terminals	
		(⊕)	(⊖)
Cooling fan motor	Low (A/T models)	①	④
	High (A/T models)	②	③
	High (M/T models)	①	②

Cooling fan motor should operate.
If NG, replace cooling fan motor.

NS1089500061000X

Fig. 19 Cooling fan motors inspection. 1995–96 Sentra & 200SX

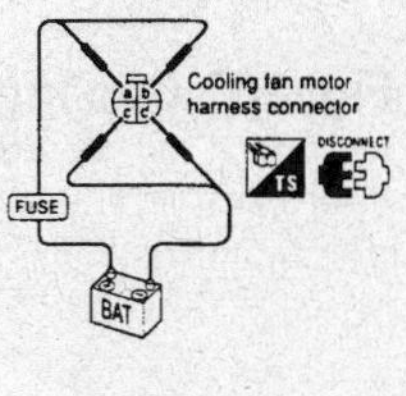

Cooling fan motor harness connector
DISCONNECT
FUSE
BAT

1. Disconnect cooling fan motor harness connectors.
2. Supply cooling fan motor terminals with battery voltage and check operation.

	Speed	Terminals	
		(⊕)	(⊖)
Cooling fan motor	Low	ⓐ	ⓓ
	High	ⓐ, ⓑ	ⓒ, ⓓ

Cooling fan motor should operate.
If NG, replace cooling fan motor.

NS1089500062000X

Fig. 20 Cooling fan motor inspection. 240SX

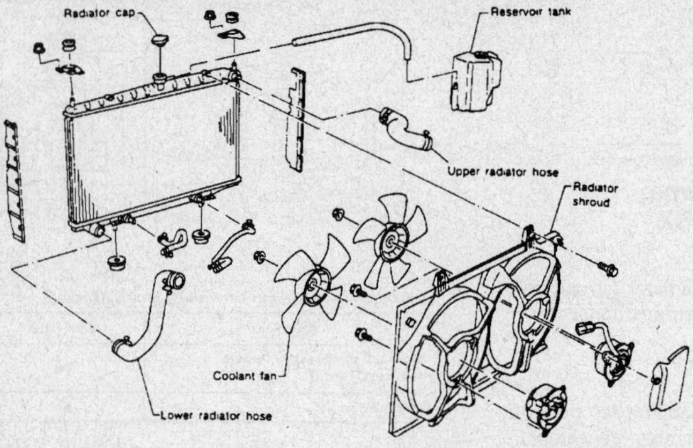
Radiator cap
Reservoir tank
Upper radiator hose
Radiator shroud
Coolant fan
Lower radiator hose

NS1089100040000X

Fig. 21 Cooling fan replacement. Altima

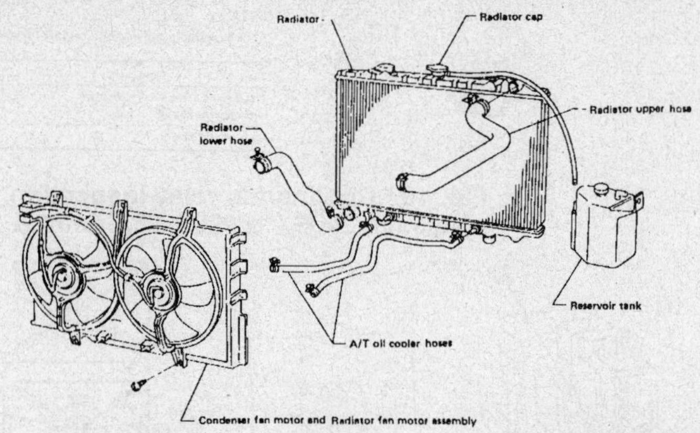
Radiator
Radiator cap
Radiator upper hose
Radiator lower hose
Reservoir tank
A/T oil cooler hoses
Condenser fan motor and Radiator fan motor assembly

NS1089100042000X

Fig. 22 Cooling fan replacement. Maxima w/VG30E engine

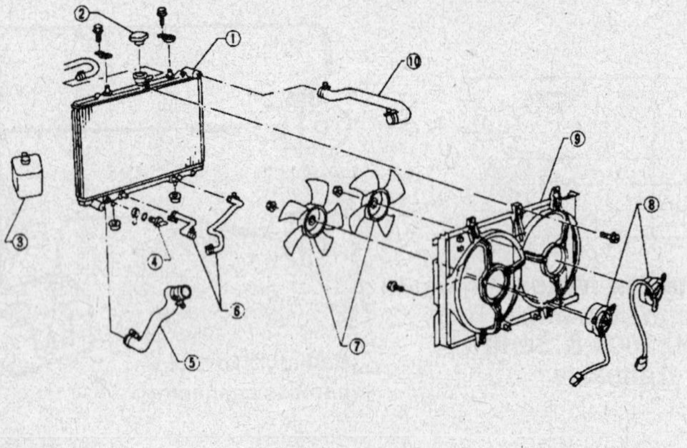

① Radiator
② Radiator filler cap
③ Reservoir tank
④ Radiator drain cock
⑤ Lower radiator hose
⑥ Oil cooler hoses (A/T models)
⑦ Radiator fans
⑧ Radiator fan motors
⑨ Radiator shroud
⑩ Upper radiator hose

NS1089100043000X

Fig. 23 Cooling fan replacement. Maxima w/ VE30DE engine

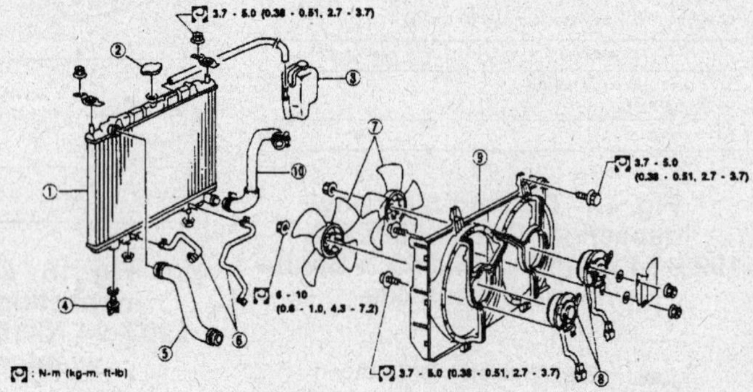
3.7 - 5.0 (0.38 - 0.51, 2.7 - 3.7)
3.7 - 5.0 (0.38 - 0.51, 2.7 - 3.7)
6 - 10 (0.6 - 1.0, 4.3 - 7.2)
3.7 - 5.0 (0.38 - 0.51, 2.7 - 3.7)
: N-m (kg-m, ft-lb)

NS1089500063000X

Fig. 24 Cooling fan replacement. Maxima w/ VQ30DE engine

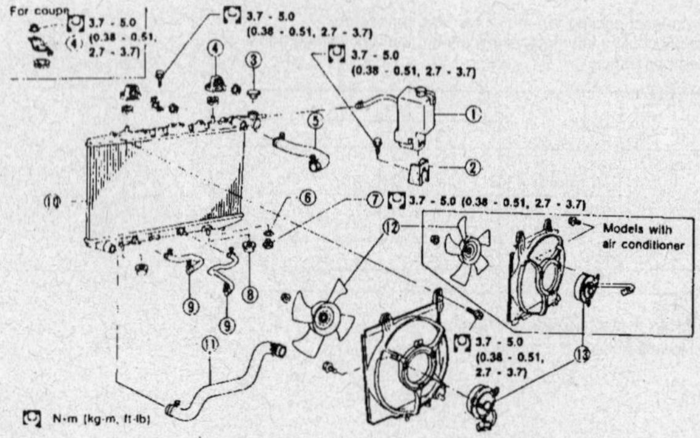
For coupe
3.7 - 5.0 (0.38 - 0.51, 2.7 - 3.7)
3.7 - 5.0 (0.38 - 0.51, 2.7 - 3.7)
3.7 - 5.0 (0.38 - 0.51, 2.7 - 3.7)
3.7 - 5.0 (0.38 - 0.51, 2.7 - 3.7)
Models with air conditioner
3.7 - 5.0 (0.38 - 0.51, 2.7 - 3.7)
N-m (kg-m, ft-lb)

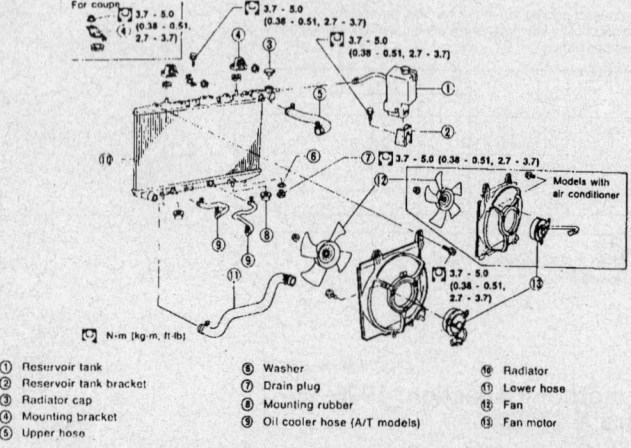

① Reservoir tank
② Reservoir tank bracket
③ Radiator cap
④ Mounting bracket
⑤ Upper hose
⑥ Washer
⑦ Drain plug
⑧ Mounting rubber
⑨ Oil cooler hose (A/T models)
⑩ Radiator
⑪ Lower hose
⑫ Fan
⑬ Fan motor

NS1089100044000X

Fig. 25 Cooling fan replacement. NX 1600, Sentra & 200SX w/GA16DE engine

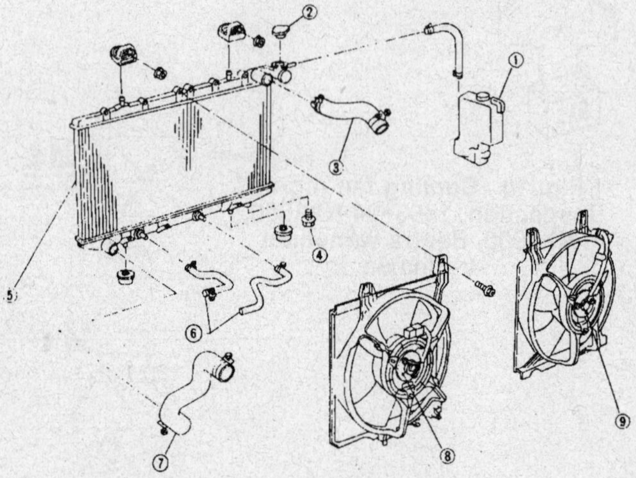

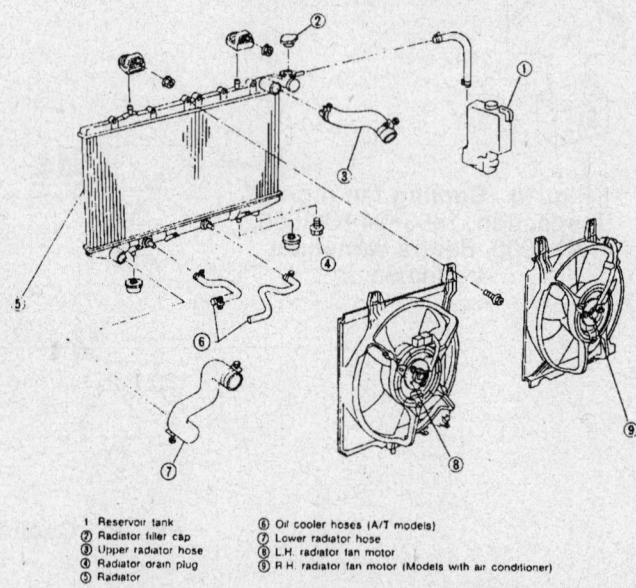

1 Reservoir tank
② Radiator filler cap
③ Upper radiator hose
④ Radiator drain plug
⑤ Radiator
⑥ Oil cooler hoses (A/T models)
⑦ Lower radiator hose
⑧ L.H. radiator fan motor
⑨ R.H. radiator fan motor (Models with air conditioner)

NS1089100045000X

Fig. 26 Cooling fan replacement. NX 2000, Sentra & 200SX w/SR20DE engine

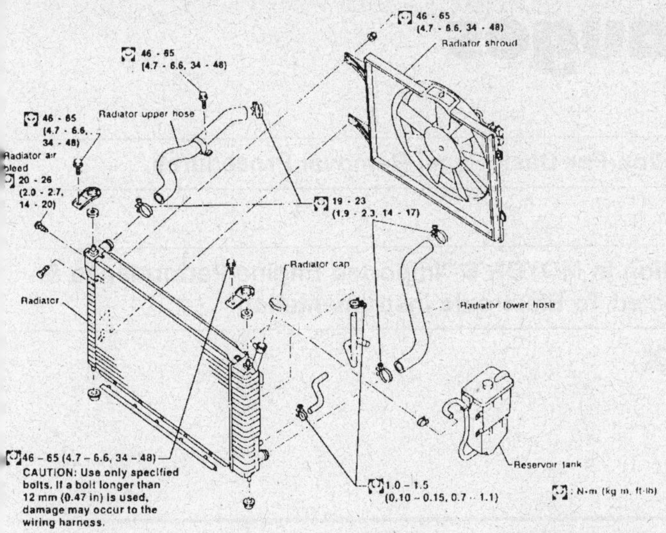
46 - 65 (4.7 - 6.6, 34 - 48)
Radiator shroud
46 - 65 (4.7 - 6.6, 34 - 48)
46 - 65 (4.7 - 6.6, 34 - 48)
Radiator upper hose
Radiator air bleed
20 - 26 (2.0 - 2.7, 14 - 20)
19 - 23 (1.9 - 2.3, 14 - 17)
Radiator cap
Radiator
Radiator lower hose
Reservoir tank
46 – 65 (4.7 – 6.6, 34 – 48)
CAUTION: Use only specified bolts. If a bolt longer than 12 mm (0.47 in) is used, damage may occur to the wiring harness.
1.0 – 1.5 (0.10 – 0.15, 0.7 – 1.1)
: N·m (kg-m, ft-lb)

NS1089100046000X

Fig. 27 Cooling fan replacement. Quest

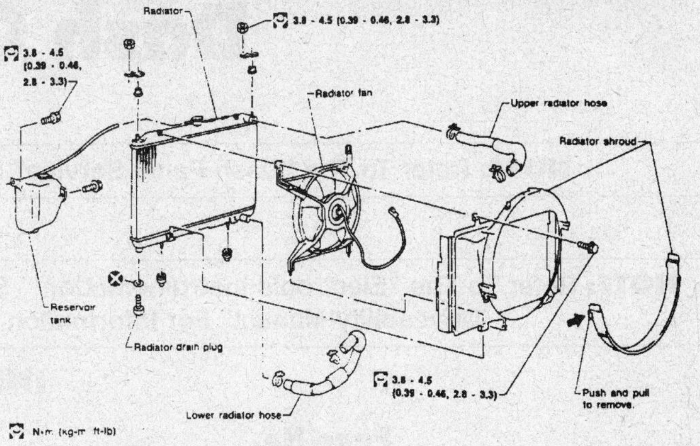
Radiator
3.8 - 4.5 (0.39 - 0.46, 2.8 - 3.3)
3.8 - 4.5 (0.39 - 0.46, 2.8 - 3.3)
Radiator fan
Upper radiator hose
Radiator shroud
Reservoir tank
Radiator drain plug
Lower radiator hose
3.8 - 4.5 (0.39 - 0.46, 2.8 - 3.3)
Push and pull to remove.
N·m (kg-m ft-lb)

NS1089500064000X

Fig. 28 Cooling fan replacement. 240SX

Dash Gauges

NOTE: Refer To The "Dash Panel Service" Section For Dash Panel Removal Procedures.

NOTE: Refer To The "Electronic Instrumentation " Section In MOTOR'S "Imported Engine Performance & Driveability Manual" For Information Related To Electronic Instrumentation.

INDEX

	Page No.
Gauges	36-30
Inspection	36-30

GAUGES

INSPECTION

Fuel Gauge & Water Temperature Gauge

Refer to **Figs. 1 through 18** for fuel and water temperature gauge diagnosis.

Fuel Tank Gauge Unit

Remove fuel tank gauge unit from the fuel tank, then connect an ohmmeter between terminals of the gauge unit connector as shown in **Figs. 19 through 30.** Compare results with specifications in **Figs. 31 through 44.** Repair or replace as necessary.

Thermal Transmitter

Connect an ohmmeter to the thermal transmitter as shown in **Figs. 45 and 46.** With water temperature at 140°F, resistance should be approximately 70–90 ohms. With water temperature at 212°F, resistance should be approximately 21–24 ohms.

Oil Pressure Switch

Connect an ohmmeter as shown in **Figs. 47 and 48,** then compare results with **Figs. 49 and 50.**

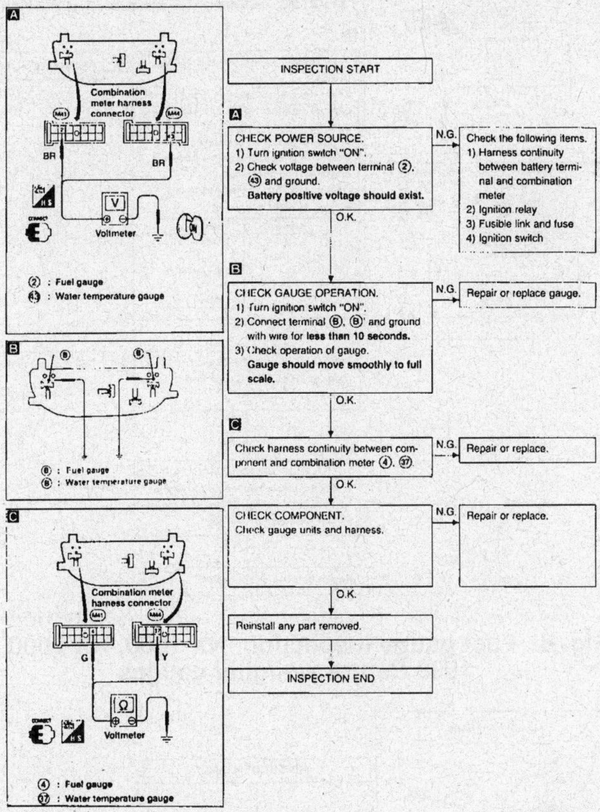
A
Combination meter harness connector
BR
BR
Voltmeter
② : Fuel gauge
㊸ : Water temperature gauge
B
Ⓑ : Fuel gauge
Ⓑ' : Water temperature gauge
C
Combination meter harness connector
G
Y
Voltmeter
④ : Fuel gauge
㊲ : Water temperature gauge
INSPECTION START
A
CHECK POWER SOURCE.
1) Turn ignition switch "ON".
2) Check voltage between terminal ②, ㊸ and ground.
Battery positive voltage should exist.
N.G.
Check the following items.
1) Harness continuity between battery terminal and combination meter
2) Ignition relay
3) Fusible link and fuse
4) Ignition switch
O.K.
B
CHECK GAUGE OPERATION.
1) Turn ignition switch "ON".
2) Connect terminal Ⓑ, Ⓑ' and ground with wire for less than 10 seconds.
3) Check operation of gauge.
Gauge should move smoothly to full scale.
N.G.
Repair or replace gauge.
O.K.
C
Check harness continuity between component and combination meter ④, ㊲.
N.G.
Repair or replace.
O.K.
CHECK COMPONENT.
Check gauge units and harness.
N.G.
Repair or replace.
O.K.
Reinstall any part removed.
INSPECTION END
NS9099100002000X

Fig. 1 Fuel gauge & water temperature gauge inspection. Altima

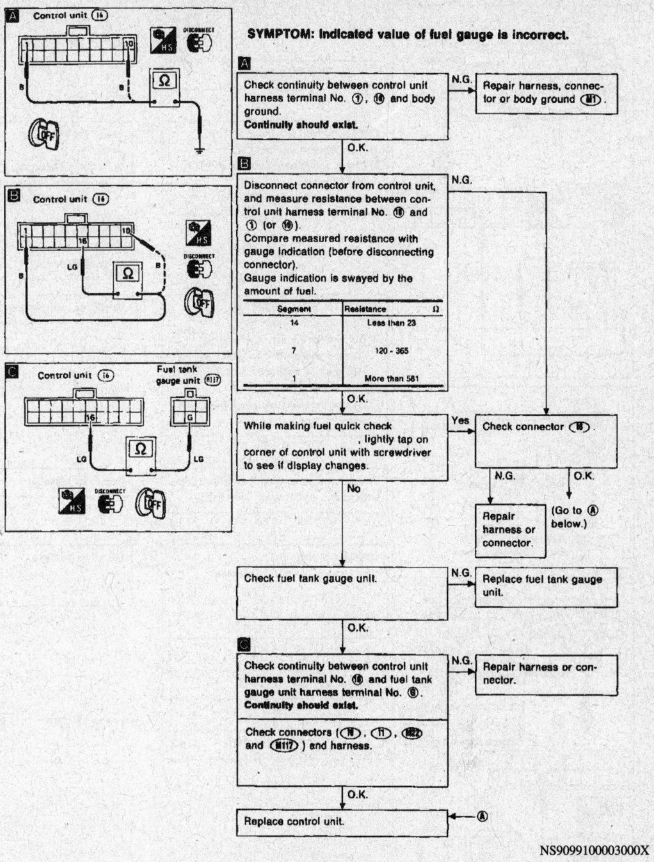
A
Control unit
B
Control unit
LG
C
Control unit
Fuel tank gauge unit
LG
LG
SYMPTOM: Indicated value of fuel gauge is incorrect.
A
Check continuity between control unit harness terminal No. ①, ⑩ and body ground.
Continuity should exist.
N.G.
Repair harness, connector or body ground.
O.K.
B
Disconnect connector from control unit, and measure resistance between control unit harness terminal No. ⑯ and ① (or ⑩).
Compare measured resistance with gauge indication (before disconnecting connector).
Gauge indication is swayed by the amount of fuel.
Segment
Resistance Ω
14
Less than 23
7
120 - 365
1
More than 581
N.G.
O.K.
While making fuel quick check, lightly tap on corner of control unit with screwdriver to see if display changes.
Yes
Check connector.
N.G.
O.K.
Repair harness or connector.
(Go to Ⓐ below.)
No
Check fuel tank gauge unit.
N.G.
Replace fuel tank gauge unit.
O.K.
C
Check continuity between control unit harness terminal No. ⑯ and fuel tank gauge unit harness terminal No. Ⓖ.
Continuity should exist.
N.G.
Repair harness or connector.
Check connectors and harness.
O.K.
Replace control unit.
Ⓐ
NS9099100003000X

Fig. 2 Fuel gauge inspection. Maxima w/digital gauges

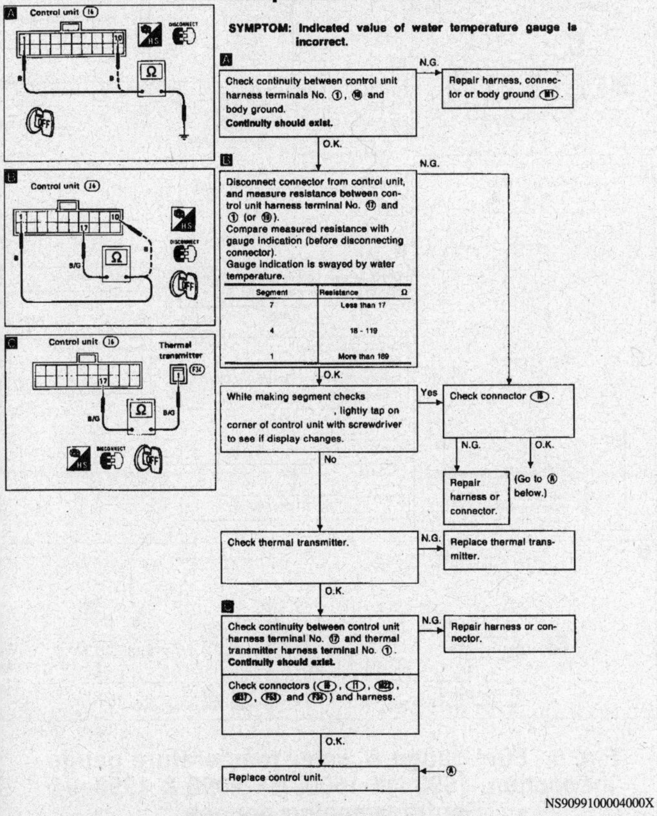
A
Control unit
B
Control unit
B/G
C
Control unit
Thermal transmitter
B/G
B/G
SYMPTOM: Indicated value of water temperature gauge is incorrect.
A
Check continuity between control unit harness terminals No. ①, ⑩ and body ground.
Continuity should exist.
N.G.
Repair harness, connector or body ground.
O.K.
B
Disconnect connector from control unit, and measure resistance between control unit harness terminal No. ⑰ and ① (or ⑩).
Compare measured resistance with gauge indication (before disconnecting connector).
Gauge indication is swayed by water temperature.
Segment
Resistance Ω
7
Less than 17
4
18 - 119
1
More than 189
N.G.
O.K.
While making segment checks, lightly tap on corner of control unit with screwdriver to see if display changes.
Yes
Check connector.
N.G.
O.K.
Repair harness or connector.
(Go to Ⓐ below.)
No
Check thermal transmitter.
N.G.
Replace thermal transmitter.
O.K.
C
Check continuity between control unit harness terminal No. ⑰ and thermal transmitter harness terminal No. ①.
Continuity should exist.
N.G.
Repair harness or connector.
Check connectors and harness.
O.K.
Replace control unit.
Ⓐ
NS9099100004000X

Fig. 3 Water temperature gauge inspection. Maxima w/digital gauges

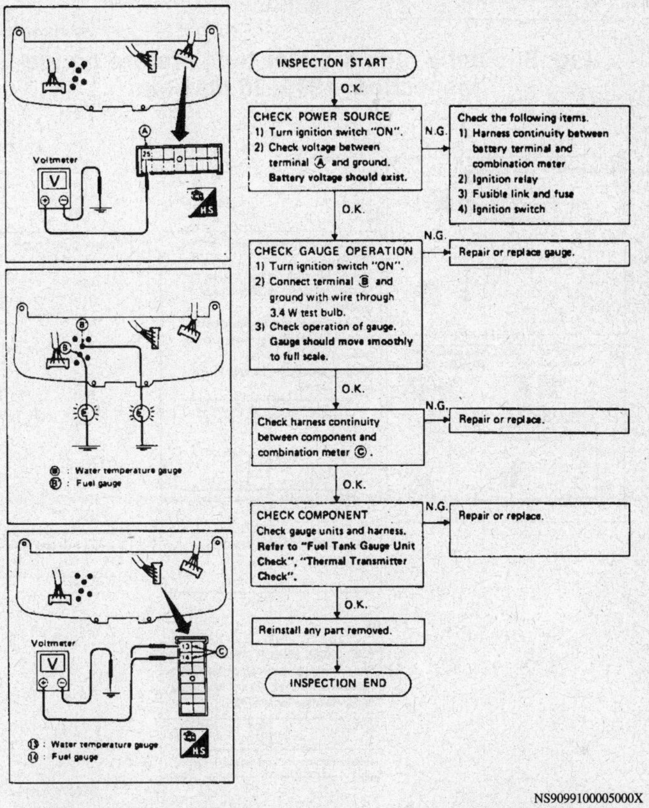
Voltmeter
Ⓐ
25
Ⓑ
Ⓑ : Water temperature gauge
Ⓑ : Fuel gauge
Voltmeter
13
14
Ⓒ
⑬ : Water temperature gauge
⑭ : Fuel gauge
INSPECTION START
O.K.
CHECK POWER SOURCE
1) Turn ignition switch "ON".
2) Check voltage between terminal Ⓐ and ground.
Battery voltage should exist.
N.G.
Check the following items.
1) Harness continuity between battery terminal and combination meter
2) Ignition relay
3) Fusible link and fuse
4) Ignition switch
O.K.
CHECK GAUGE OPERATION
1) Turn ignition switch "ON".
2) Connect terminal Ⓑ and ground with wire through 3.4 W test bulb.
3) Check operation of gauge.
Gauge should move smoothly to full scale.
N.G.
Repair or replace gauge.
O.K.
Check harness continuity between component and combination meter Ⓒ.
N.G.
Repair or replace.
O.K.
CHECK COMPONENT
Check gauge units and harness.
Refer to "Fuel Tank Gauge Unit Check", "Thermal Transmitter Check".
N.G.
Repair or replace.
O.K.
Reinstall any part removed.
INSPECTION END
NS9099100005000X

Fig. 4 Fuel gauge & water temperature gauge inspection. 1993–94 Maxima w/analog gauges

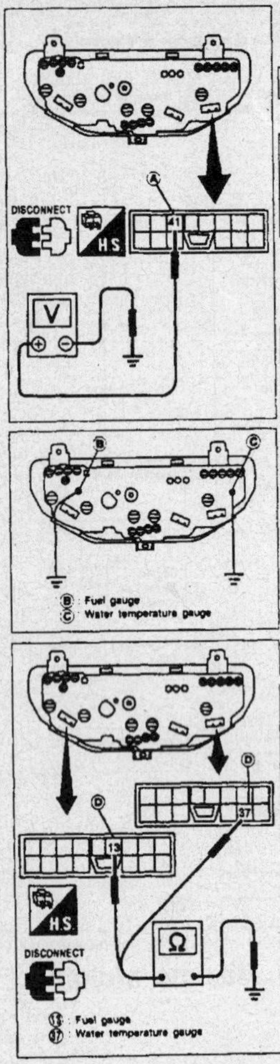
DISCONNECT
41
Ⓐ
H.S.
Ⓑ
Ⓒ
Ⓑ : Fuel gauge
Ⓒ : Water temperature gauge
Ⓓ
13
37
DISCONNECT
⑬ : Fuel gauge
㊲ : Water temperature gauge

INSPECTION START

↓

CHECK POWER SOURCE.
1) Turn ignition switch "ON".
2) Check voltage between terminal Ⓐ and ground.
Battery voltage should exist.

NG → Check the following items.
1) Harness continuity between battery terminal and combination meter
2) Ignition relay
3) Fusible link and fuse
4) Ignition switch

OK ↓

CHECK GAUGE OPERATION.
1) Turn ignition switch "ON".
2) Connect terminals Ⓑ (Fuel), Ⓒ (Temp.) and ground with wire for **less than 10 seconds.**
3) Check operation of gauge.
Gauge should move smoothly to full scale.

NG → Repair or replace gauge.

OK ↓

Check harness continuity between component and combination meter Ⓓ.

NG → Repair or replace.

OK ↓

CHECK COMPONENT.
Check gauge units and harness.

NG → Repair or replace.

OK ↓

Reinstall any part removed.

↓

INSPECTION END

NS9099500069000X

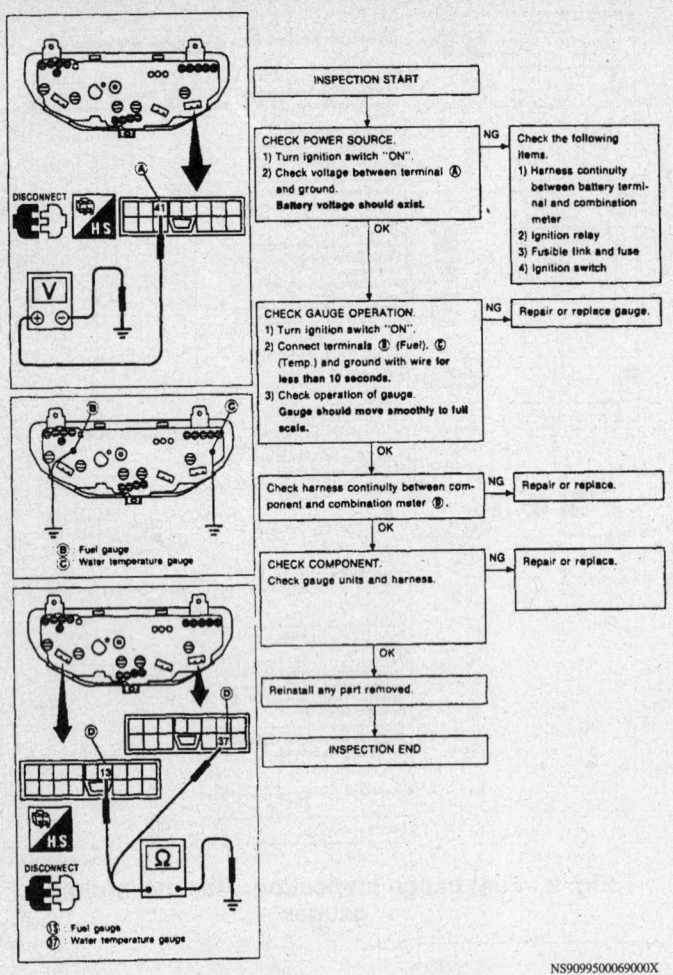

Fig. 5 Fuel gauge & water temperature gauge inspection. 1995–96 Maxima

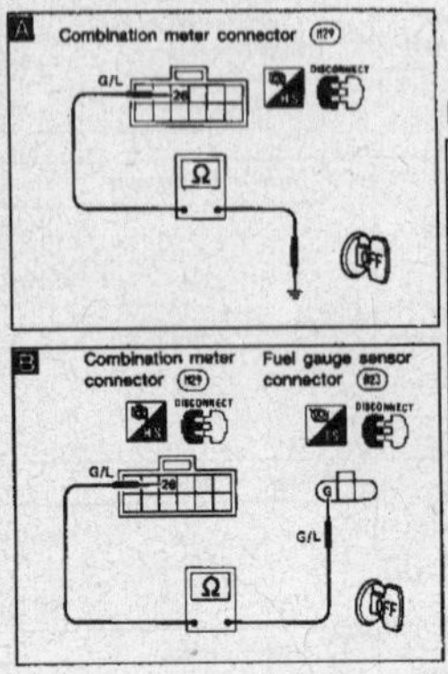
A Combination meter connector
G/L
26
B Combination meter connector
Fuel gauge sensor connector
G/L
26
G/L

A

FUEL GAUGE SENSOR INPUT SIGNAL CHECK
Check resistance between digital meter harness terminal No. 26 and body ground.
Compare measured resistance with indication of gauge segment (before disconnecting connector).
Gauge indication is changed by the amount of fuel.

Segment	Resistance (Ω)
14	Approx. 12
≀	≀
8	Approx. 33
≀	≀
1	Approx. 76

N.G. → Replace digital meter.

O.K. ↓

FUEL GAUGE SENSOR CHECK

N.G. → Replace fuel tank gauge unit.

O.K. ↓

B

FUEL GAUGE SENSOR CIRCUIT CHECK
Check continuity between digital meter harness terminal No. 26 and fuel gauge sensor harness terminal Ⓖ.

N.G. ↓

Repair harness or connector.

NS9099200010000X

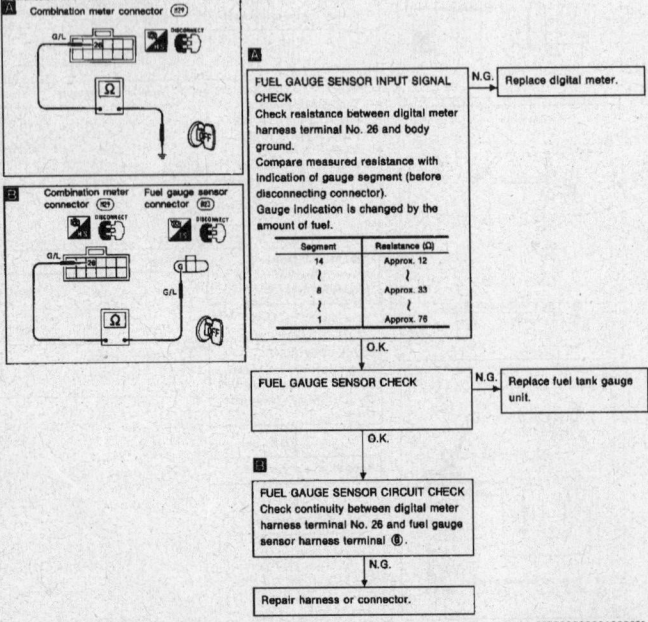

Fig. 7 Water temperature gauge inspection. 1993 NX 1600, NX 2000 & Sentra w/digital gauges

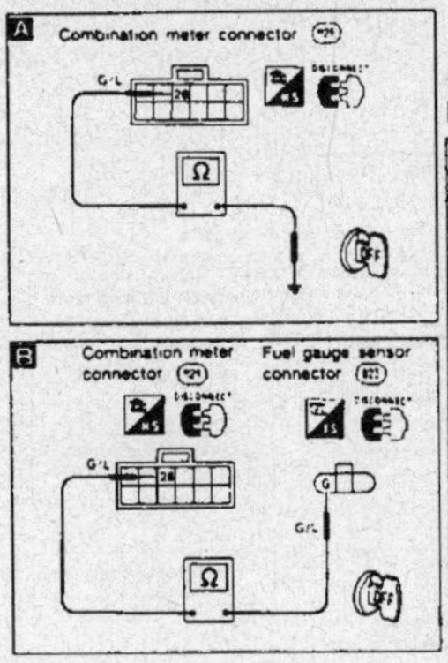
A Combination meter connector
G/L
26
B Combination meter connector
Fuel gauge sensor connector
G/L
26
G/L

SYMPTOM: Indicated value of fuel gauge is incorrect.

A

FUEL GAUGE SENSOR INPUT SIGNAL CHECK
Check resistance between digital meter harness terminal No. 26 and body ground
Compare measured resistance with indication of gauge segment (before disconnecting connector).
Gauge indication is changed by the amount of fuel.

Segment	Resistance (Ω)
14	Approx. 12
≀	≀
8	Approx. 33
≀	≀
1	Approx. 76

N.G. → Replace digital meter.

O.K. ↓

FUEL GAUGE SENSOR CHECK
Refer to "Fuel Tank Gauge Unit Check".

N.G. → Replace fuel tank gauge unit.

O.K. ↓

B

FUEL GAUGE SENSOR CIRCUIT CHECK
Check continuity between digital meter harness terminal No. 26 and fuel gauge sensor harness terminal Ⓖ.

N.G. ↓

Repair harness or connector.

NS9099200009000X

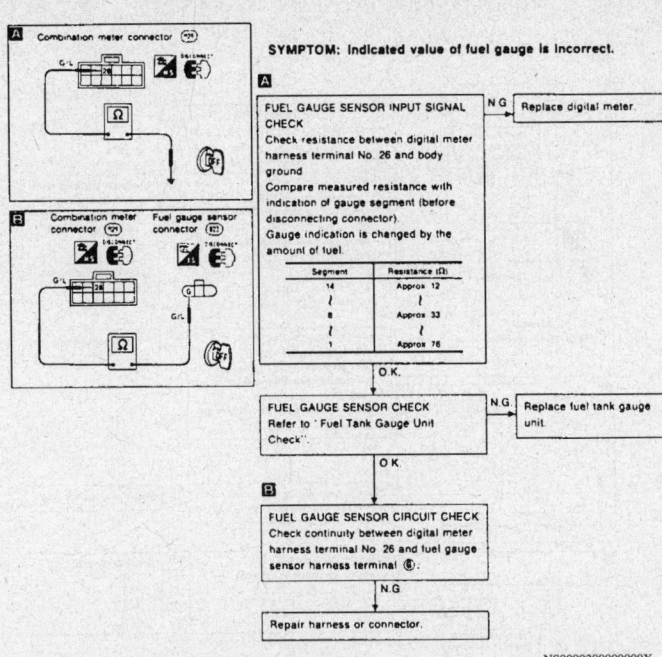

Fig. 6 Fuel gauge inspection. NX 1600, NX 2000 & 1993 Sentra w/digital gauges

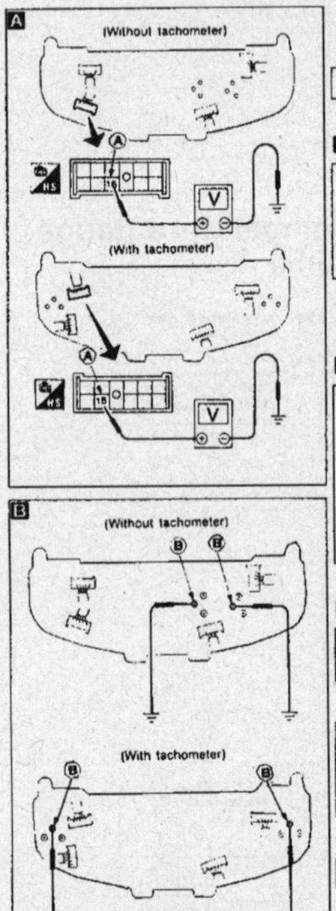
A
(Without tachometer)
(With tachometer)
Ⓐ
B
(Without tachometer)
(With tachometer)
Ⓑ : Fuel gauge
Ⓑ' : Water temperature gauge

INSPECTION START

↓

A

CHECK POWER SOURCE.
1) Turn ignition switch "ON".
2) Check voltage between terminal Ⓐ and ground.
Battery voltage should exist.

N.G. → Check the following items.
1) Harness continuity between battery terminal and combination meter
2) Ignition relay
3) Fusible link and fuse
4) Ignition switch

O.K. ↓

B

CHECK GAUGE OPERATION.
1) Turn ignition switch "ON".
2) Connect terminals Ⓑ (Fuel), Ⓑ' (Temp.) and ground with wire for **less than 10 seconds.**
3) Check operation of gauge.
Gauge should move smoothly to full scale.

N.G. → Repair or replace gauge.

O.K. ↓

C

Check harness continuity between component and combination meter Ⓒ.

N.G. → Repair or replace.

O.K. ↓

CHECK COMPONENT.
Check gauge units and harness.
Refer to "Fuel Tank Gauge Unit Check", "Thermal Transmitter Check".

N.G. → Repair or replace.

O.K. ↓

Reinstall any part removed.

↓

INSPECTION END

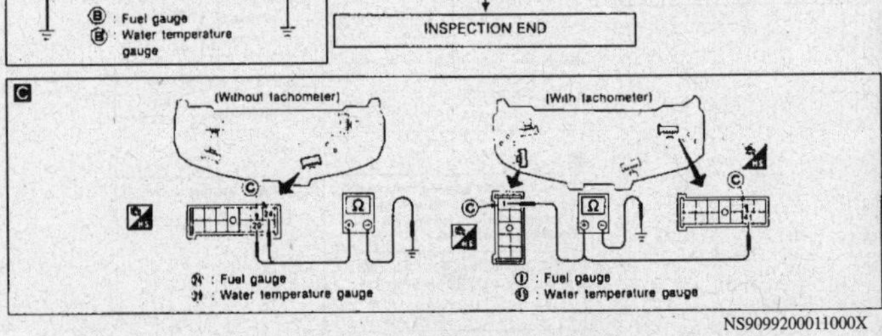
C
(Without tachometer)
(With tachometer)
Ⓒ
: Fuel gauge
: Water temperature gauge
: Fuel gauge
: Water temperature gauge

NS9099200011000X

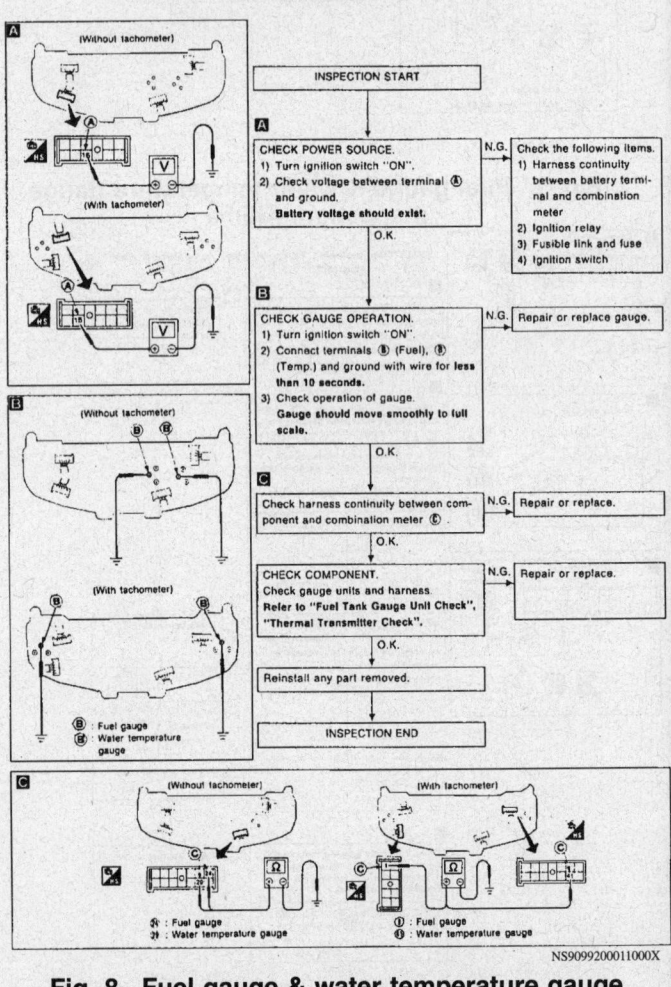

Fig. 8 Fuel gauge & water temperature gauge inspection. 1993 NX 1600, NX 2000 & 1993–94 Sentra w/analog gauges

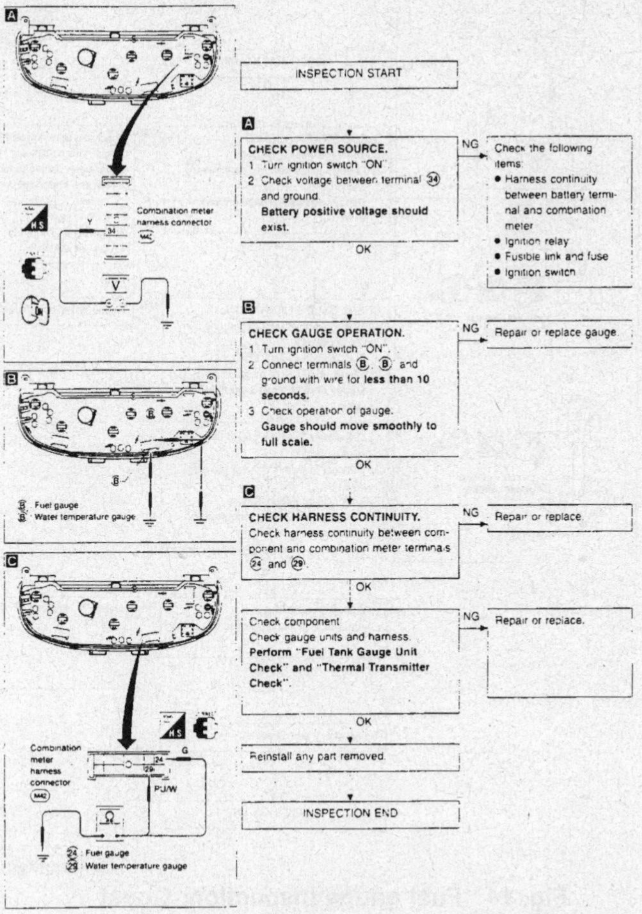
INSPECTION START
A
CHECK POWER SOURCE.
1. Turn ignition switch "ON".
2. Check voltage between terminal 34 and ground.
Battery positive voltage should exist.
NG
Check the following items:
• Harness continuity between battery terminal and combination meter
• Ignition relay
• Fusible link and fuse
• Ignition switch
OK
B
CHECK GAUGE OPERATION.
1. Turn ignition switch "ON".
2. Connect terminals B, B' and ground with wire for less than 10 seconds.
3. Check operation of gauge.
Gauge should move smoothly to full scale.
NG
Repair or replace gauge.
OK
C
CHECK HARNESS CONTINUITY.
Check harness continuity between component and combination meter terminals 24 and 29.
NG
Repair or replace.
OK
Check component.
Check gauge units and harness.
Perform "Fuel Tank Gauge Unit Check" and "Thermal Transmitter Check".
NG
Repair or replace.
OK
Reinstall any part removed.
INSPECTION END
Combination meter harness connector
Fuel gauge
Water temperature gauge

NS9099500070000X

Fig. 9 Fuel gauge & water temperature gauge inspection. 1995–96 Sentra & 200SX less tachometer

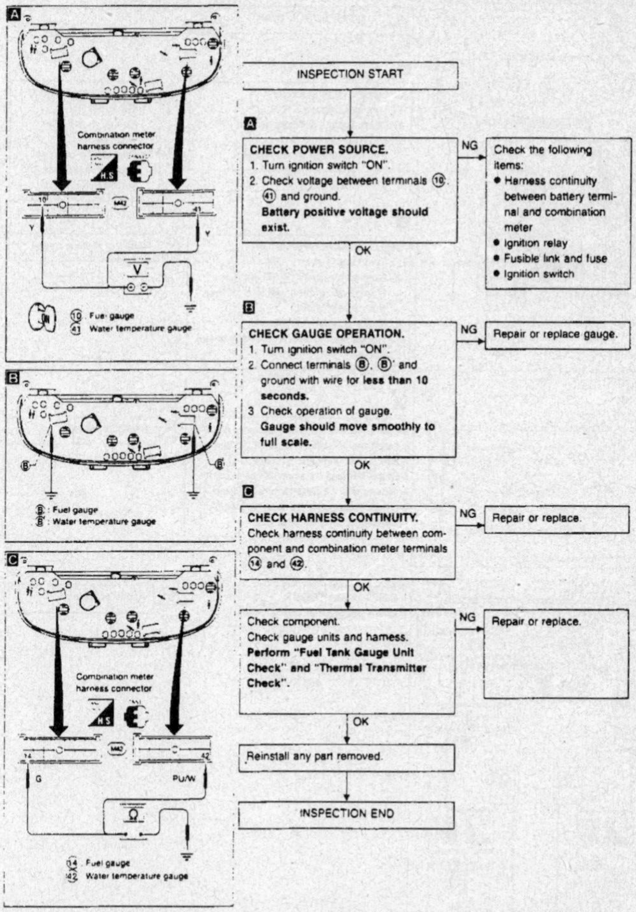
INSPECTION START
A
CHECK POWER SOURCE.
1. Turn ignition switch "ON".
2. Check voltage between terminals 10, 41 and ground.
Battery positive voltage should exist.
NG
Check the following items:
• Harness continuity between battery terminal and combination meter
• Ignition relay
• Fusible link and fuse
• Ignition switch
OK
B
CHECK GAUGE OPERATION.
1. Turn ignition switch "ON".
2. Connect terminals B, B' and ground with wire for less than 10 seconds.
3. Check operation of gauge.
Gauge should move smoothly to full scale.
NG
Repair or replace gauge.
OK
C
CHECK HARNESS CONTINUITY.
Check harness continuity between component and combination meter terminals 14 and 42.
NG
Repair or replace.
OK
Check component.
Check gauge units and harness.
Perform "Fuel Tank Gauge Unit Check" and "Thermal Transmitter Check".
NG
Repair or replace.
OK
Reinstall any part removed.
INSPECTION END
Combination meter harness connector
Fuel gauge
Water temperature gauge

NS9099500071000X

Fig. 10 Fuel gauge & water temperature gauge inspection. 1995–96 Sentra & 200SX w/tachometer

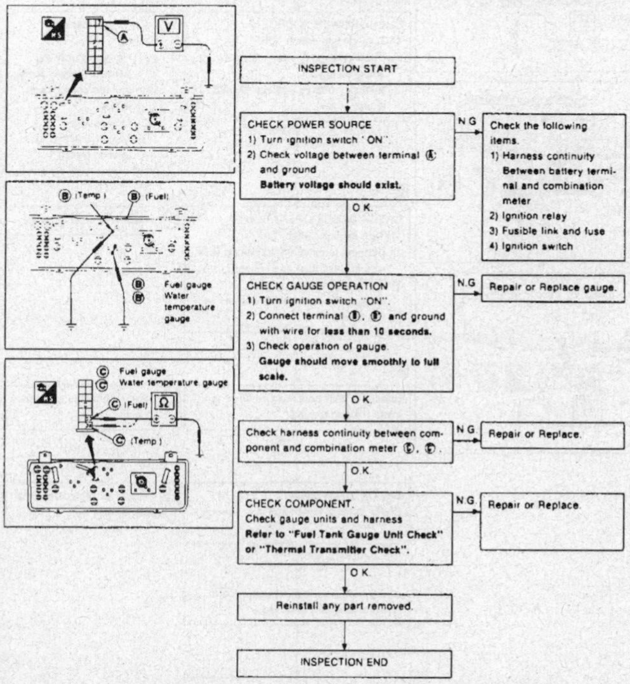
INSPECTION START
CHECK POWER SOURCE
1) Turn ignition switch "ON".
2) Check voltage between terminal A and ground
Battery voltage should exist.
N.G
Check the following items.
1) Harness continuity Between battery terminal and combination meter
2) Ignition relay
3) Fusible link and fuse
4) Ignition switch
O.K.
CHECK GAUGE OPERATION
1) Turn ignition switch "ON".
2) Connect terminal B, B and ground with wire for less than 10 seconds.
3) Check operation of gauge.
Gauge should move smoothly to full scale.
N.G
Repair or Replace gauge.
O.K.
Check harness continuity between component and combination meter C, C.
N.G
Repair or Replace.
O.K.
CHECK COMPONENT.
Check gauge units and harness
Refer to "Fuel Tank Gauge Unit Check" or "Thermal Transmitter Check".
N.G.
Repair or Replace.
O.K.
Reinstall any part removed.
INSPECTION END
Fuel gauge
Water temperature gauge

NS9099200012000X

Fig. 11 Fuel gauge & water temperature gauge inspection. 1993 Pathfinder & Pickup

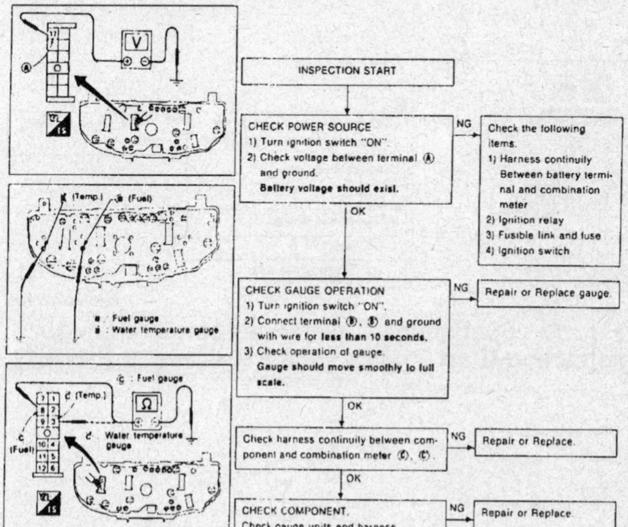
INSPECTION START
CHECK POWER SOURCE
1) Turn ignition switch "ON".
2) Check voltage between terminal A and ground.
Battery voltage should exist.
NG
Check the following items.
1) Harness continuity Between battery terminal and combination meter
2) Ignition relay
3) Fusible link and fuse
4) Ignition switch
OK
CHECK GAUGE OPERATION
1) Turn ignition switch "ON".
2) Connect terminal B, B and ground with wire for less than 10 seconds.
3) Check operation of gauge.
Gauge should move smoothly to full scale.
NG
Repair or Replace gauge.
OK
Check harness continuity between component and combination meter C, C.
NG
Repair or Replace.
OK
CHECK COMPONENT.
Check gauge units and harness
NG
Repair or Replace.
OK
Reinstall any part removed.
INSPECTION END
Fuel gauge
Water temperature gauge

NS9099400013000X

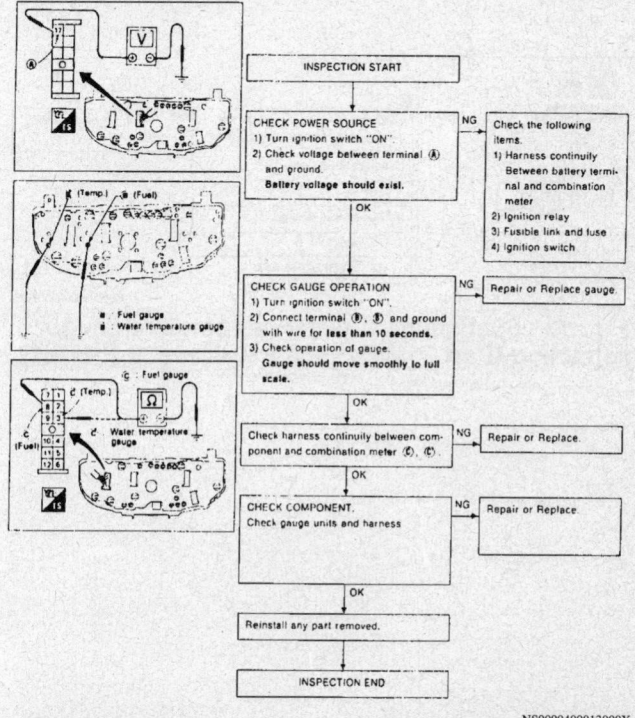

Fig. 12 Fuel gauge & water temperature gauge inspection. 1994–95 Pathfinder & Pickup

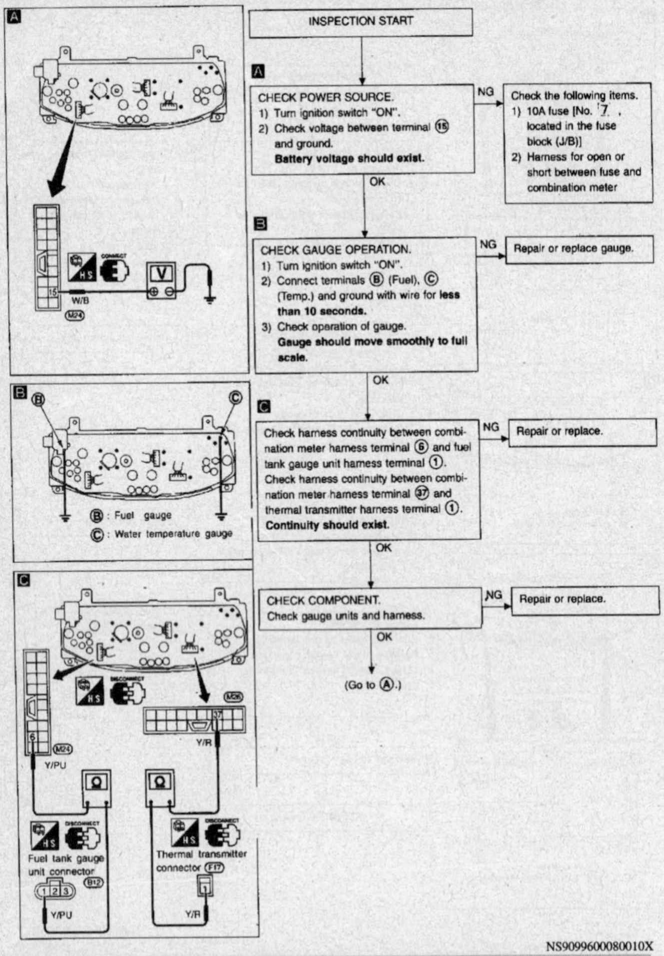

A
INSPECTION START
A
CHECK POWER SOURCE.
1) Turn ignition switch "ON".
2) Check voltage between terminal ⑮ and ground.
Battery voltage should exist.
NG
Check the following items.
1) 10A fuse [No. 7, located in the fuse block (J/B)]
2) Harness for open or short between fuse and combination meter
OK
B
CHECK GAUGE OPERATION.
1) Turn ignition switch "ON".
2) Connect terminals Ⓑ (Fuel), Ⓒ (Temp.) and ground with wire for less than 10 seconds.
3) Check operation of gauge.
Gauge should move smoothly to full scale.
NG
Repair or replace gauge.
OK
C
Check harness continuity between combination meter harness terminal ⑥ and fuel tank gauge unit harness terminal ①.
Check harness continuity between combination meter harness terminal ㊲ and thermal transmitter harness terminal ①.
Continuity should exist.
NG
Repair or replace.
OK
CHECK COMPONENT.
Check gauge units and harness.
NG
Repair or replace.
OK
(Go to Ⓐ.)
W/B
M24
B
Ⓑ : Fuel gauge
Ⓒ : Water temperature gauge
C
M26
Y/R
Y/PU
Fuel tank gauge unit connector B12
Thermal transmitter connector F17

NS9099600080010X

Fig. 13 Fuel gauge & water temperature gauge inspection (Part 1 of 2). 1996 Pathfinder & Pickup

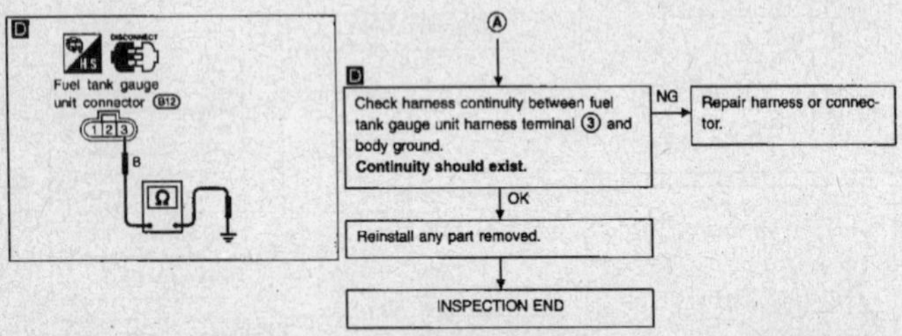

D
Fuel tank gauge unit connector B12
B
Ⓐ
D
Check harness continuity between fuel tank gauge unit harness terminal ③ and body ground.
Continuity should exist.
NG
Repair harness or connector.
OK
Reinstall any part removed.
INSPECTION END

NS9099600080020X

Fig. 13 Fuel gauge & water temperature gauge inspection (Part 2 of 2). 1996 Pathfinder & Pickup

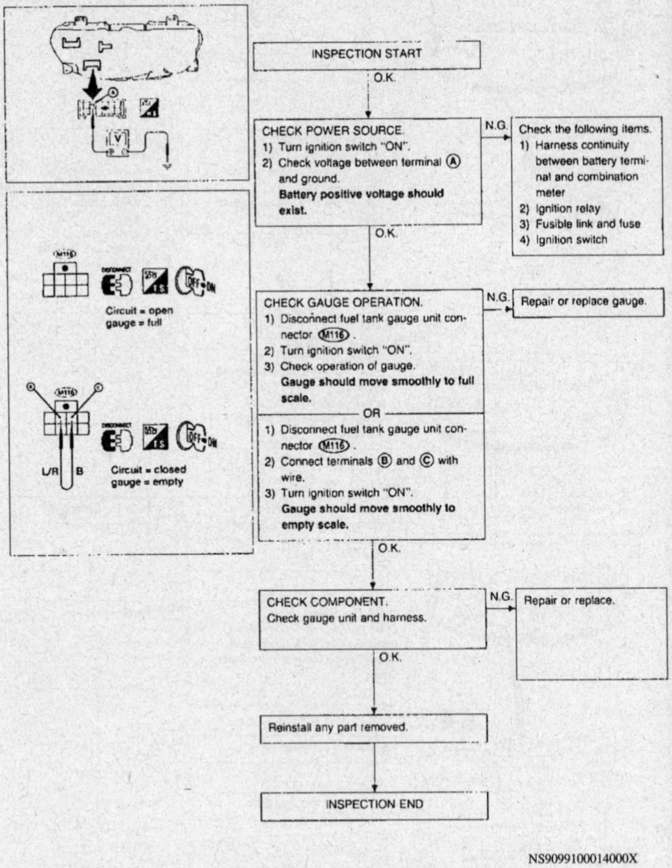

INSPECTION START
O.K.
CHECK POWER SOURCE.
1) Turn ignition switch "ON".
2) Check voltage between terminal Ⓐ and ground.
Battery positive voltage should exist.
N.G.
Check the following items.
1) Harness continuity between battery terminal and combination meter
2) Ignition relay
3) Fusible link and fuse
4) Ignition switch
O.K.
CHECK GAUGE OPERATION.
1) Disconnect fuel tank gauge unit connector M116.
2) Turn ignition switch "ON".
3) Check operation of gauge.
Gauge should move smoothly to full scale.
OR
1) Disconnect fuel tank gauge unit connector M116.
2) Connect terminals Ⓑ and Ⓒ with wire.
3) Turn ignition switch "ON".
Gauge should move smoothly to empty scale.
N.G.
Repair or replace gauge.
O.K.
CHECK COMPONENT.
Check gauge unit and harness.
N.G.
Repair or replace.
O.K.
Reinstall any part removed.
INSPECTION END
Circuit = open
gauge = full
L/R
B
Circuit = closed
gauge = empty

NS9099100014000X

Fig. 14 Fuel gauge inspection. Quest

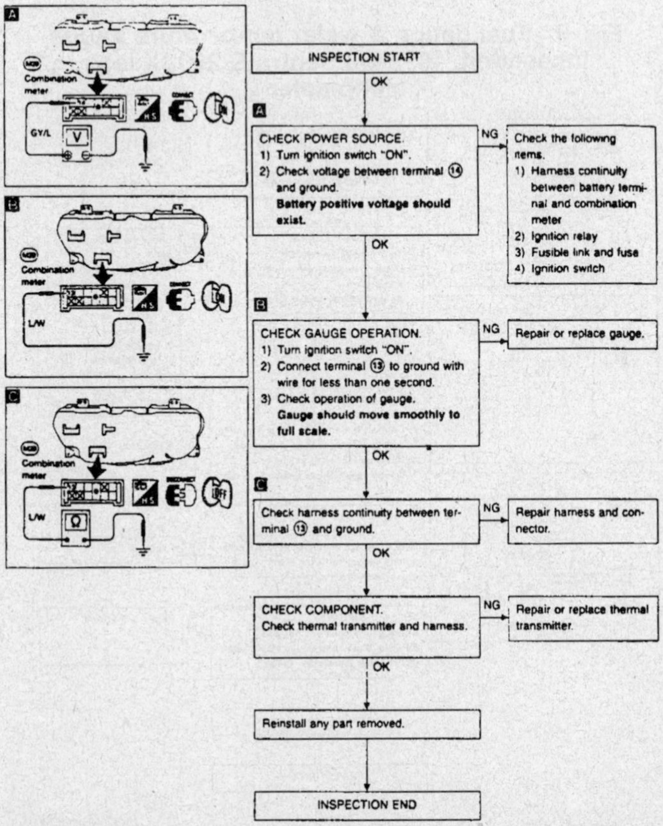

A
Combination meter
GY/L
B
L/W
C
INSPECTION START
OK
A
CHECK POWER SOURCE.
1) Turn ignition switch "ON".
2) Check voltage between terminal ⑭ and ground.
Battery positive voltage should exist.
NG
Check the following items.
1) Harness continuity between battery terminal and combination meter
2) Ignition relay
3) Fusible link and fuse
4) Ignition switch
OK
B
CHECK GAUGE OPERATION.
1) Turn ignition switch "ON".
2) Connect terminal ⑬ to ground with wire for less than one second.
3) Check operation of gauge.
Gauge should move smoothly to full scale.
NG
Repair or replace gauge.
OK
C
Check harness continuity between terminal ⑬ and ground.
NG
Repair harness and connector.
OK
CHECK COMPONENT.
Check thermal transmitter and harness.
NG
Repair or replace thermal transmitter.
OK
Reinstall any part removed.
INSPECTION END

NS9099100015000X

Fig. 15 Water temperature gauge inspection. Quest

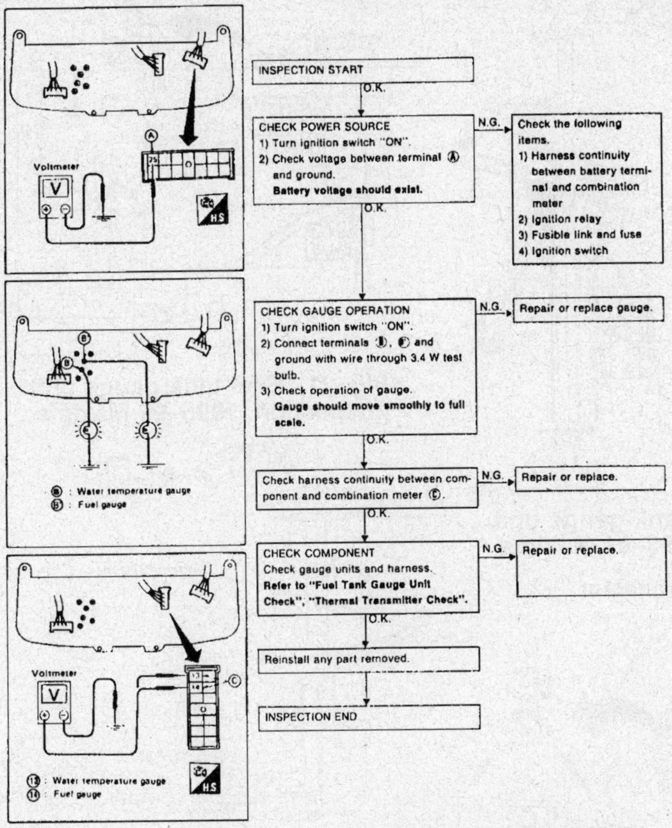
Voltmeter
V
HS
INSPECTION START
O.K.
CHECK POWER SOURCE
1) Turn ignition switch "ON".
2) Check voltage between terminal (A) and ground.
Battery voltage should exist.
N.G.
Check the following items.
1) Harness continuity between battery terminal and combination meter
2) Ignition relay
3) Fusible link and fuse
4) Ignition switch
O.K.
CHECK GAUGE OPERATION
1) Turn ignition switch "ON".
2) Connect terminals (B), (F) and ground with wire through 3.4 W test bulb.
3) Check operation of gauge.
Gauge should move smoothly to full scale.
N.G.
Repair or replace gauge.
O.K.
Check harness continuity between component and combination meter (C).
N.G.
Repair or replace.
O.K.
CHECK COMPONENT
Check gauge units and harness.
Refer to "Fuel Tank Gauge Unit Check", "Thermal Transmitter Check".
N.G.
Repair or replace.
O.K.
Reinstall any part removed.
INSPECTION END
(B) : Water temperature gauge
(F) : Fuel gauge
Voltmeter
(13) : Water temperature gauge
(14) : Fuel gauge

NS9099100017000X

Fig. 16 Fuel gauge & water temperature gauge inspection. 1993 240SX

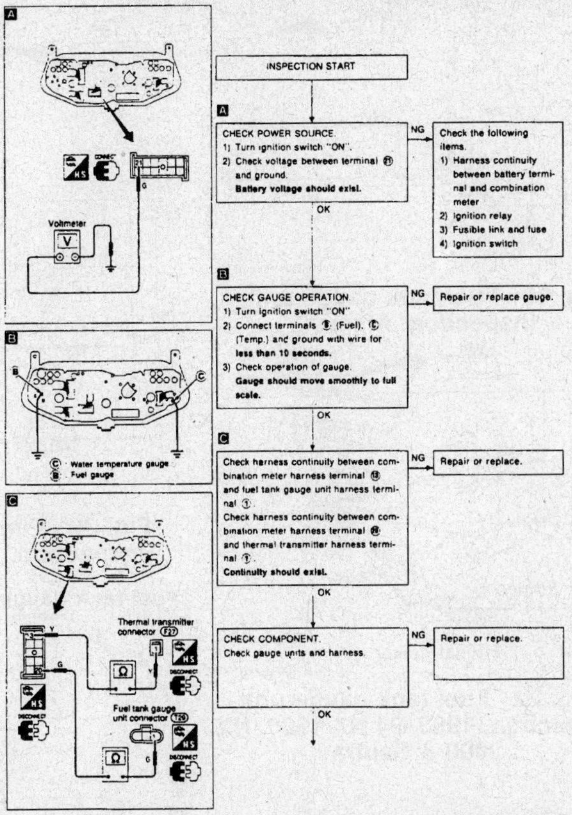
A
INSPECTION START
A
CHECK POWER SOURCE.
1) Turn ignition switch "ON".
2) Check voltage between terminal (21) and ground.
Battery voltage should exist.
NG
Check the following items.
1) Harness continuity between battery terminal and combination meter
2) Ignition relay
3) Fusible link and fuse
4) Ignition switch
OK
Voltmeter
B
CHECK GAUGE OPERATION.
1) Turn ignition switch "ON"
2) Connect terminals (B) (Fuel), (C) (Temp.) and ground with wire for less than 10 seconds.
3) Check operation of gauge.
Gauge should move smoothly to full scale.
NG
Repair or replace gauge.
OK
(C) : Water temperature gauge
(B) : Fuel gauge
C
Check harness continuity between combination meter harness terminal (13) and fuel tank gauge unit harness terminal (1).
Check harness continuity between combination meter harness terminal (8) and thermal transmitter harness terminal (1).
Continuity should exist.
NG
Repair or replace.
OK
Thermal transmitter connector (F27)
Fuel tank gauge unit connector (T29)
CHECK COMPONENT.
Check gauge units and harness.
NG
Repair or replace.
OK

NS9099500072010X

Fig. 17 Fuel gauge & water temperature gauge inspection (Part 1 of 2). 1994–96 240SX

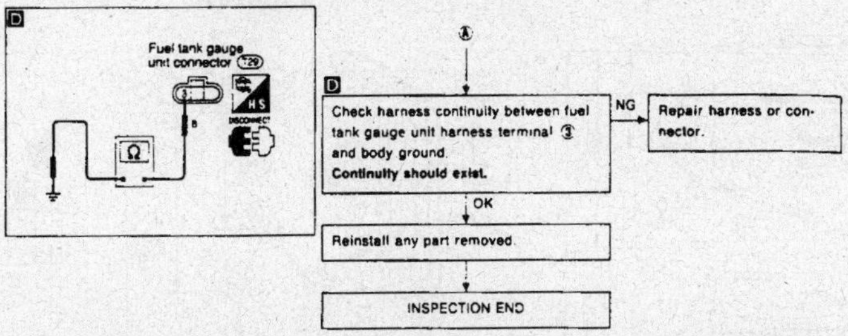
D
Fuel tank gauge unit connector (T29)
(A)
D
Check harness continuity between fuel tank gauge unit harness terminal (3) and body ground.
Continuity should exist.
NG
Repair harness or connector.
OK
Reinstall any part removed.
INSPECTION END

NS9099500072020X

Fig. 17 Fuel gauge & water temperature gauge inspection (Part 2 of 2). 1994–96 240SX

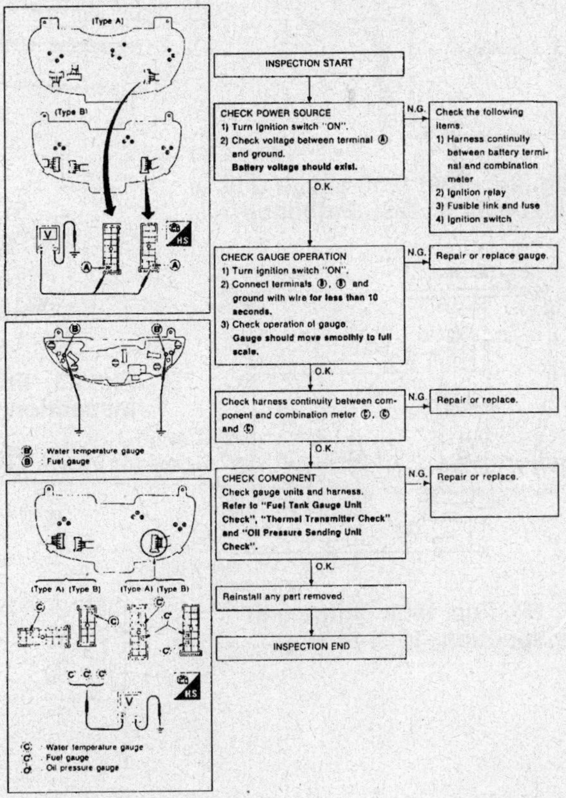
(Type A)
(Type B)
INSPECTION START
CHECK POWER SOURCE
1) Turn ignition switch "ON".
2) Check voltage between terminal (A) and ground.
Battery voltage should exist.
N.G.
Check the following items.
1) Harness continuity between battery terminal and combination meter
2) Ignition relay
3) Fusible link and fuse
4) Ignition switch
O.K.
CHECK GAUGE OPERATION
1) Turn ignition switch "ON".
2) Connect terminals (B), (B) and ground with wire for less than 10 seconds.
3) Check operation of gauge.
Gauge should move smoothly to full scale.
N.G.
Repair or replace gauge.
O.K.
Check harness continuity between component and combination meter (C), (C) and (C)
N.G.
Repair or replace.
O.K.
CHECK COMPONENT
Check gauge units and harness.
Refer to "Fuel Tank Gauge Unit Check", "Thermal Transmitter Check" and "Oil Pressure Sending Unit Check".
N.G.
Repair or replace.
O.K.
Reinstall any part removed.
INSPECTION END
(B) : Water temperature gauge
(B) : Fuel gauge
(Type A) (Type B) (Type A) (Type B)
(C) : Water temperature gauge
(C) : Fuel gauge
(C) : Oil pressure gauge

NS9099100018000X

Fig. 18 Fuel gauge & water temperature gauge inspection. 300ZX

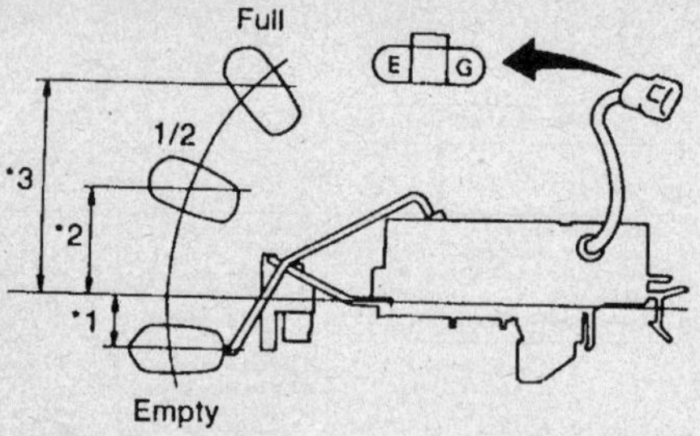
Full
1/2
*3
*2
*1
Empty
E G

NS9099100019000X

Fig. 19 Fuel tank gauge unit inspection. Altima

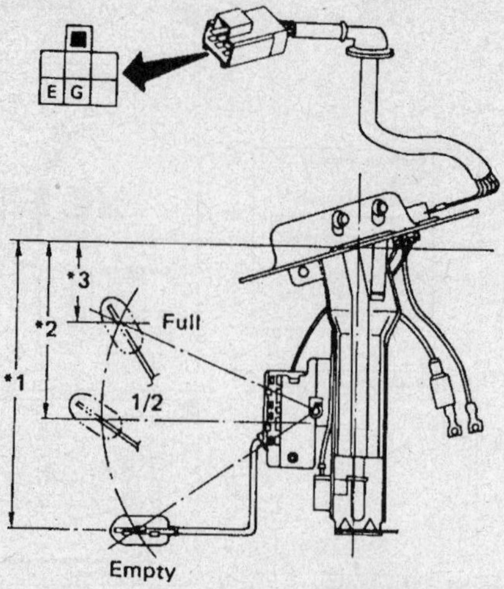
E G
*3
*2
*1
Full
1/2
Empty

NS9099100020000X

Fig. 20 Fuel tank gauge unit inspection. 1993–94 Maxima

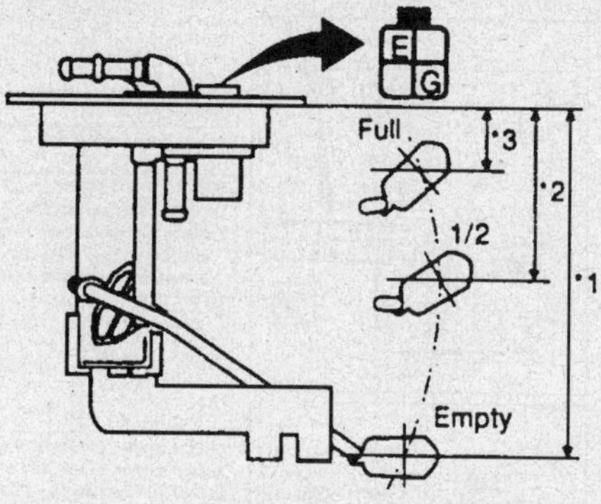
E
G
Full
*3
*2
*1
1/2
Empty

NS9099500073000X

Fig. 21 Fuel tank gauge unit inspection. 1995–96 Maxima

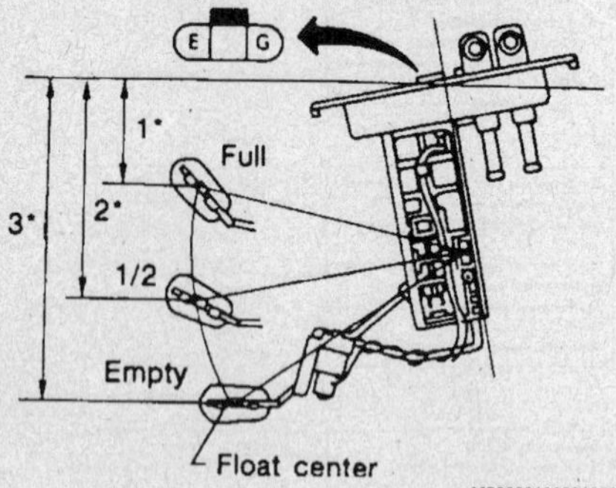
E G
1*
Full
3*
2*
1/2
Empty
Float center

NS9099100021000X

Fig. 22 Fuel tank gauge unit inspection. 1993–94 NX 1600, NX 2000 & Sentra

Fuel tank gauge connector

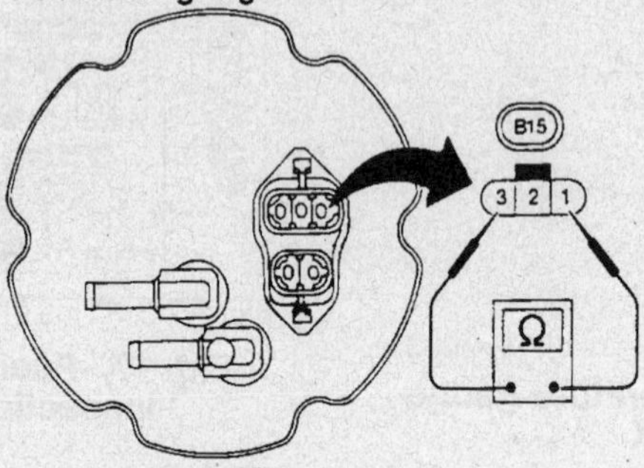
B15
3 2 1
Ω

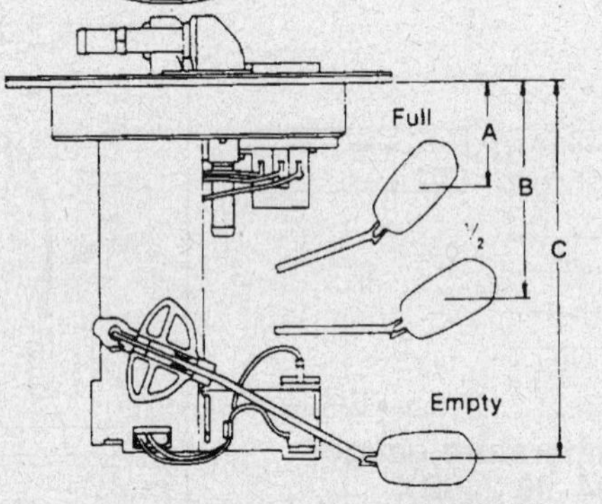
Full
A
B
½
C
Empty

NS9099500074000X

Fig. 23 Fuel tank gauge unit inspection. 1995–96 Sentra & 200SX

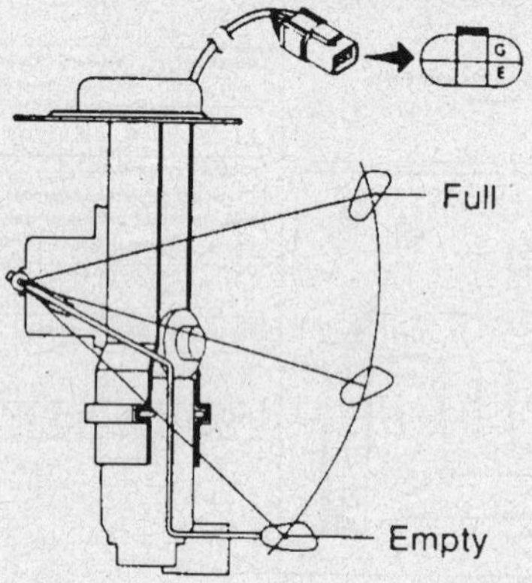
G
E
Full
Empty

NS9099100022000X

Fig. 24 Fuel tank gauge unit inspection. 1993–95 Pathfinder & Pickup

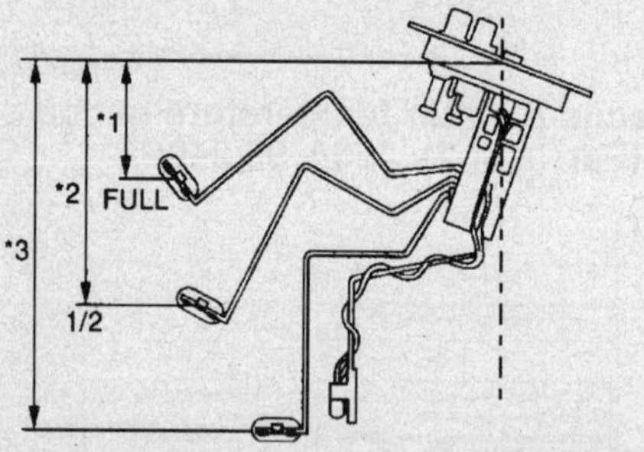
*1
*2
FULL
*3
1/2

NS9099600081000X

Fig. 25 Fuel tank gauge unit inspection. 1996 Pathfinder

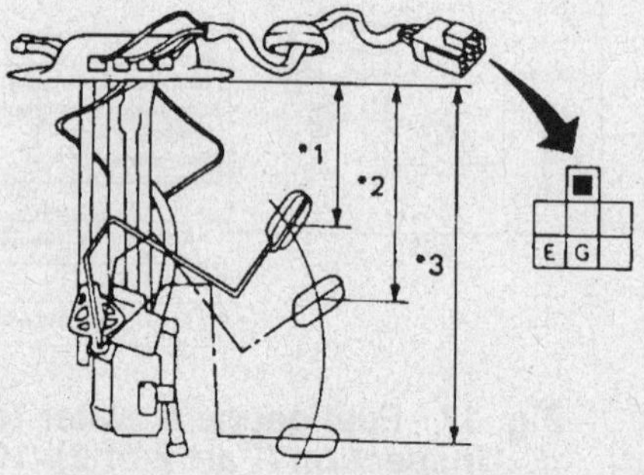
*1
*2
*3
E G

NS9099100025000X

Fig. 28 Fuel tank gauge unit inspection. 1993–94 240SX

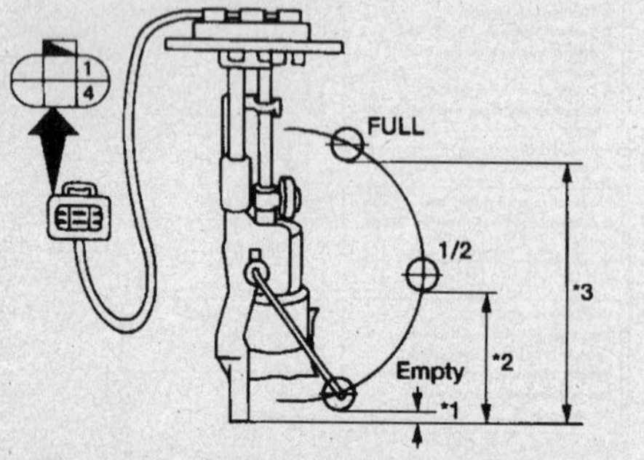
1
4
FULL
1/2
*3
Empty
*2
*1

NS9099600082000X

Fig. 26 Fuel tank gauge unit inspection. 1996 Pickup

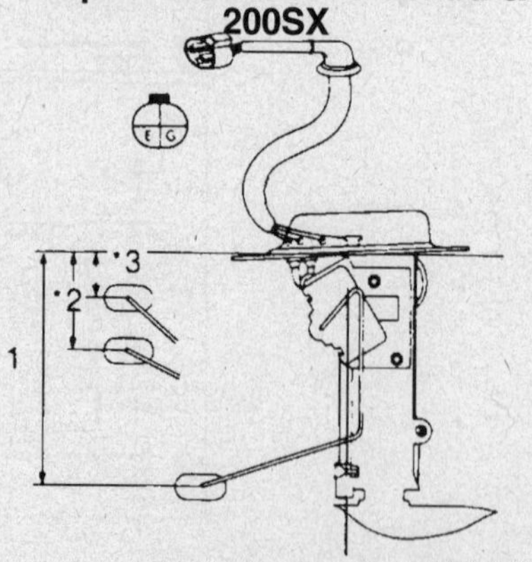
E G
*3
*2
1

NS9099100023000X

Fig. 27 Fuel tank gauge unit inspection. Quest

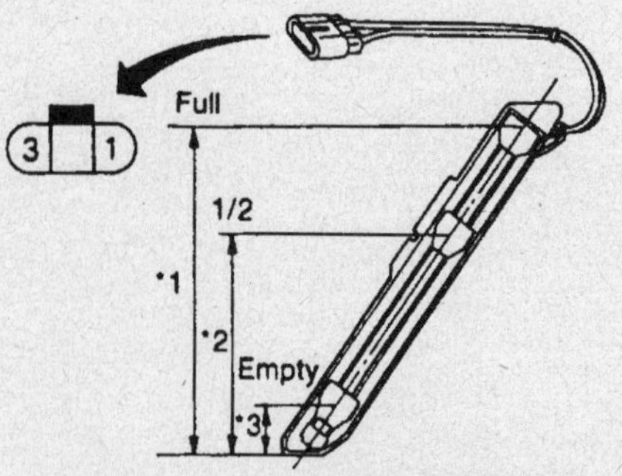
3
1
Full
1/2
*1
*2
Empty
*3

NS9099500075000X

Fig. 29 Fuel tank gauge unit inspection. 1995–96 240SX

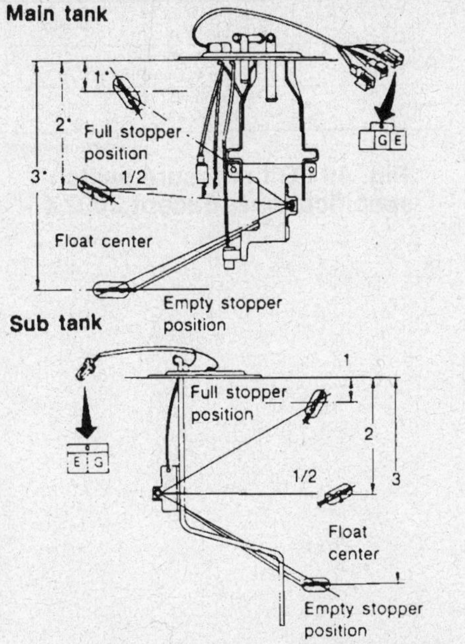
Main tank
1*
2*
Full stopper position
1/2
3*
Float center
G E
Empty stopper position
Sub tank
E G
Full stopper position
1
2
1/2
3
Float center
Empty stopper position

NS9099100026000X

Fig. 30 Fuel tank gauge unit inspection. 300ZX

Ohmmeter (+)	Ohmmeter (−)	Float position mm (in)			Resistance value (Ω)
G	E	*1	Full	58 (2 28)	Approx 4 - 6
		*2	1/2	108 (4 25)	Approx 27 - 35
		*3	Empty	164 (6 46)	Approx 73 - 85

NS9099100030000X

Fig. 35 Fuel tank gauge unit resistance specifications. NX 1600, NX 2000 & 1993–94 Sentra

Ohmmeter (+)	Ohmmeter (−)	Float position mm (in)			Resistance value (Ω)
①	③	*1	Full	96 (3.78)	Approx. 4 - 6
		*2	1/2	188 (7.40)	30 - 34
		*3	Empty	257 (10.12)	80 - 83

*1 and *3: When float rod is in contact with stopper.

NS9099600083000X

Fig. 38 Fuel tank gauge unit resistance specifications. 1996 Pathfinder

Ohmmeter (+)	Ohmmeter (−)	Float position mm (in)			Resistance Ω	Fuel value ℓ (US gal, Imp gal)
G	E	*1	Full	Approx 92 (3.62)	4 3 - 5 8	57 6 (15-1/4, 12-5/8)
		*2	1/2	Approx 154 (6 06)	27 7 - 34.3	32 9 (8-3/4, 7-1/4)
		*3	Empty	Approx 226 (8 90)	78.3 - 84 8	6 6 (1-3/4, 1-1/2)

NS9099100034000X

Fig. 41 Fuel tank gauge unit resistance specifications. 1993–94 240SX

Ohmmeter (+)	Ohmmeter (−)	Float position mm (in)			Resistance value (Ω)
G	E	1*	Full	21.0 (0.827)	4.3 - 5 8
		2*	1/2	115 0 (4.53)	27 7 - 34.3
		3*	Empty	207 0 (8.15)	78 3 - 84 8

1* and 3*. When float rod is in contact with stopper

NS9099100036000X

Fig. 44 Fuel tank gauge unit resistance specifications. 300ZX 4 seater

Ohmmeter (+)	Ohmmeter (−)	Float position mm (in)			Resistance value (Ω)
G	E	*3	Full	80 5 (3 169)	Approx. 4 5 - 6
		*2	1 2	29 4 (1 157)	Approx 31 5 - 33 5
		*1	Empty	19 0 (0 748)	Approx 80 - 83

NS9099100027000X

Fig. 31 Fuel tank gauge unit resistance specifications. Altima

Ohmmeter (+)	Ohmmeter (−)	Float position mm (in)			Resistance value (Ω)
G	E	*3	Full	48 (1 89)	Approx. 4 - 6
		*2	1/2	112 (4.41)	27 - 34
		*1	Empty	172 (6.77)	78 - 85

*1 and *3: When float rod is in contact with stopper.

NS9099100029000X

Fig. 33 Fuel tank gauge unit resistance specifications. 1993–94 Maxima w/analog gauge

Ohmmeter (+)	Ohmmeter (−)	Float position mm (in)			Resistance value (Ω)
①	③	A	Full	35.8 (1 409)	Approx. 4.5 - 6
		B	1/2	85.9 (3.382)	Approx. 31.5 - 33.5
		C	Empty	128.8 (5.071)	Approx. 80 - 83

NS9099500077000X

Fig. 36 Fuel tank gauge unit resistance specifications. 1995–96 Sentra & 200SX

Ohmmeter (+)	Ohmmeter (−)	Float position mm (in)			Resistance value (Ω)
①	④	*3	Full	245.0 (9.646)	Approx. 4 - 7
		*2	1/2	119.0 (4.685)	Approx. 31 - 34
		*1	Empty	12.0 (0.472)	Approx. 79 - 84

NS9099600084000X

Fig. 39 Fuel tank gauge unit resistance specifications. 1996 Pickup

Ohmmeter (+)	Ohmmeter (−)	Float position mm (in)			Resistance value (Ω)
①	③	*1	Full	356 (14.02)	Approx. 4 - 6
		*2	1/2	245 (9.65)	30 - 35
		*3	Empty	50 (1.97)	80 - 84

*1 and *3: When float rod is in contact with stopper.

NS9099500078000X

Fig. 42 Fuel tank gauge unit resistance specifications. 1995–96 240SX

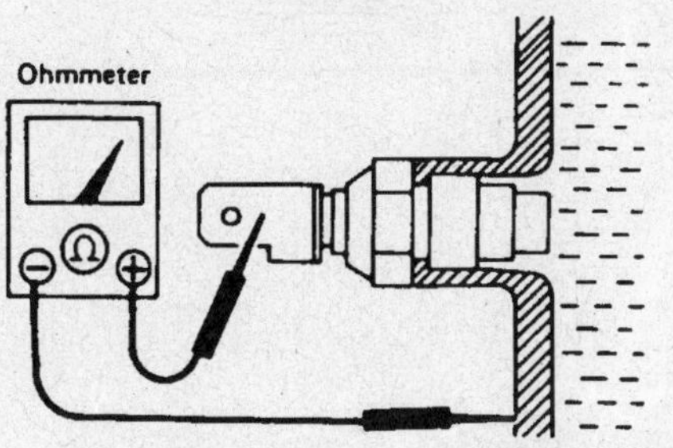
Ohmmeter

NS9099100037000X

Fig. 45 Thermal transmitter inspection. Except 1993–94 Pathfinder & Pickup

Ohmmeter (+)	Ohmmeter (−)	Float position mm (in)			Resistance value Ω
G	E	*3	Full	47 (1 85)	15 18
		*2	1 2	121 (4.76)	178 - 195
		*1	Empty	172 (6.77)	929 - 1,009

NS9099100028000X

Fig. 32 Fuel tank gauge unit resistance specifications. 1993–94 Maxima w/digital gauge

Ohmmeter (+)	Ohmmeter (−)	Float position mm (in)			Resistance value (Ω)
G	E	*3	Full	33 (1.30)	Approx. 5 - 8
		*2	1/2	91 (3.58)	32 - 35
		*1	Empty	159 (6.26)	80 - 83

*1 and *3: When float rod is in contact with stopper.

NS9099500076000X

Fig. 34 Fuel tank gauge unit resistance specifications. 1995–96 Maxima

Ohmmeter (+)	Ohmmeter (−)	Model	Float position	Resistance value
⑥	⑥	Truck	Full	Approx. 3 8 - 8.5Ω
			Empty	Approx 83 6 - 93.6Ω

NS9099200031000X

Fig. 37 Fuel tank gauge unit resistance specifications. 1993–95 Pathfinder & Pickup

Ohmmeter (+)	Ohmmeter (−)	Float position mm (in)			Resistance value (Ω)
G	E	*3	Full	23 (0 91)	Approx 160
		*2	1/2	93 (3 66)	78
		*1	Empty	151 (5 94)	15

NS9099100032000X

Fig. 40 Fuel tank gauge unit resistance specifications. Quest

Ohmmeter (+)	Ohmmeter (−)	Float position mm (in)				Resistance value (Ω)
G	E	1*	Full	Main	41.0 (1.614)	8.5 - 11.6
				Sub	40 0 (1.575)	
		2*	1/2	Main	137.0 (5 39)	55.4 - 68.6
				Sub	139 5 (5 49)	
		3*	Empty	Main	232 0 (9 13)	157 6 - 170 6
				Sub	261.0 (10 28)	

1* and 3*. When float rod is in contact with stopper.

NS9099100035000X

Fig. 43 Fuel tank gauge unit resistance specifications. 300ZX 2 seater

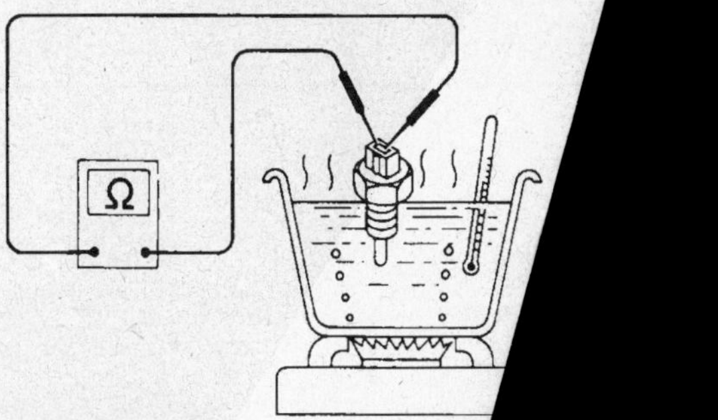
Ω

NS90991

Fig. 46 Thermal transmitt inspection. 1993–94 Pathfin Pickup

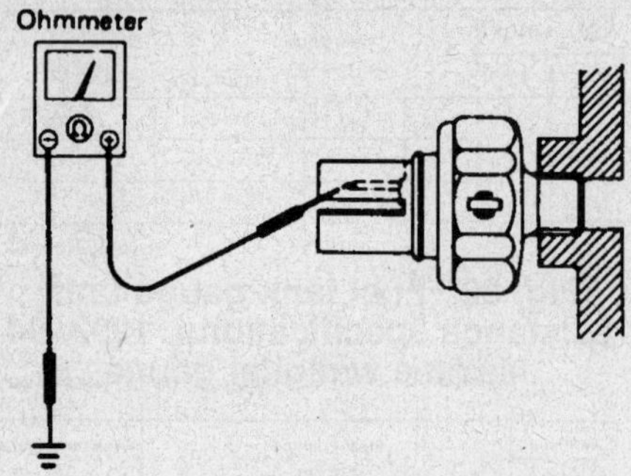
Ohmmeter

NS9099100039000X

Fig. 47 Oil pressure switch inspection. Except 300ZX, 1993–94 Pathfinder & Pickup

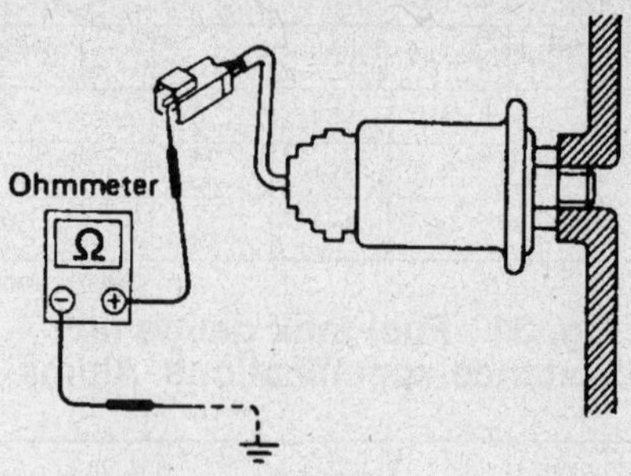
Ohmmeter
Ω

NS9099100040000X

Fig. 48 Oil pressure switch inspection. 300ZX, 1993–94 Pathfinder & Pickup

	Oil pressure kPa (kg cm², psi)	Continuity
Engine start	More than 10 - 20 (0.1 - 0.2, 1.4 - 2.8)	NO
Engine stop	Less than 10 - 20 (0.1 - 0.2 1.4 - 2.8)	YES

NS9099100041000X

Fig. 49 Oil pressure switch specifications. Except 300ZX

Oil pressure kPa (kg/cm² psi)	Resistance (Ω)
0 (0, 0) (Engine is stopped)	More than 83
392 (4, 57)	Approx. 26 - 37
588 (6, 85)	Approx. 18 - 26

NS9099100042000X

Fig. 50 Oil pressure switch specifications. 300ZX

Starter Motors

INDEX

	Page No.
Application Chart	36-39
Description	36-41
Diagnosis & Testing	36-41
Starter Solenoid Test	36-41
Starter Test	36-41
Specification Chart	36-43

APPLICATION CHART

Year	Model	Engine	Starter Number
1993	Altima	KA24DE	M1T73881ZC
	Altima	KA24DE	S114-754
	Maxima	VG30E	S114-461A
	Maxima	VE30DE①	S114-461A
	Maxima	VE30DE②	S114-756
	Pathfinder & Pickup	KA24E	M1T60281
	Pathfinder & Pickup	KA24E	M3T38482
	Pathfinder & Pickup	KA24E	S114-527A
	Pathfinder & Pickup	KA24E	S114-607B
	Pathfinder & Pickup	KA24E	S114-703A
	Pathfinder & Pickup	VG30E	S114-528
	Quest	VG30E	S114-757
	Sentra/NX 1600 & NX 2000	GA16DE①③	M1T77281
	Sentra/NX 1600 & NX 2000	GA16DE①③	S114-769
	Sentra/NX 1600 & NX 2000	GA16DE①④	M3T37783
1993	Sentra/NX 1600 & NX 2000	GA16DE①④	S114-630
	Sentra/NX 1600 & NX 2000	GA16DE②	S114-767
	Sentra/NX 1600 & NX 2000	SR20DE	M1T72985A
	Sentra/NX 1600 & NX 2000	SR20DE	S114-701B
	240SX	KA24DE	M1T72781A
	300ZX	VG30DE, VG30DETT	M2T25281
1994	Altima	KA24DE	M1T73881ZC
	Altima	KA24DE	S114-754A
	Maxima	VG30E	S114-461A
	Maxima	VE30DE①	S114-461A
	Maxima	VE30DE②	S114-756
	Pathfinder & Pickup	KA24E	M1T60281
	Pathfinder & Pickup	KA24E	M3T38482
	Pathfinder & Pickup	KA24E	S114-527A
	Pathfinder & Pickup	KA24E	S114-607B
	Pathfinder & Pickup	KA24E	S114-703A

Continued

APPLICATION CHART—Continued

Year	Model	Engine	Starter Number
1994	Pathfinder & Pickup	VG30E	S114-528
	Quest	VG30E	M1T64285
	Sentra	GA16DE①③	M1T77281
	Sentra	GA16DE①③	S114-769
	Sentra	GA16DE①④	M3T37783
	Sentra	GA16DE①④	S114-630
	Sentra	GA16DE②	S114-767
	Sentra	SR20DE	M1T72985A
	Sentra	SR20DE	S114-701B
	240SX	KA24DE	M1T72781A
	300ZX	VG30DE,VG30DETT	M2T25281
1995	Altima	KA24DE	M1T73881ZC
	Altima	KA24DE	S114-754A
	Maxima	VQ30DE	S114-801A
	Pathfinder & Pickup	KA24E	M1T60281
	Pathfinder & Pickup	KA24E	M3T38482
	Pathfinder & Pickup	KA24E	S114-527A
	Pathfinder & Pickup	KA24E	S114-607B
	Pathfinder & Pickup	KA24E	S114-703A
	Pathfinder & Pickup	VG30E	S114-528
	Pathfinder	VG33E	
	Quest	VG30E	M001T64285
	Sentra & 200SX	GA16DE	M0T80281ZC
	Sentra & 200SX	GA16DE	M2T42983ZC
	Sentra & 200SX	GA16DE	S114-802A
	Sentra & 200SX	SR20DE	S114-701C
1995	Sentra & 200SX	SR20DE	M1T72985A
	240SX	KA24DE	M1T72781A
	300ZX	VG30DE,VG30DETT	M2T25281
1996	Altima	KA24DE	M1T73881ZC
	Altima	KA24DE	S114-754A
	Maxima	VQ30DE	S114-801A
	Pathfinder	VG33E	MOT60181
	Pickup	KA24E	M000T60081ZC③
	Pickup	KA24E	M003T70381④
	Quest	VG30E	M001T64285
	Sentra & 200SX	GA16DE	M0T80281ZC
	Sentra & 200SX	GA16DE	M2T42983ZC
	Sentra & 200SX	GA16DE	S114-802A
	Sentra & 200SX	SR20DE	S114-701C
	Sentra & 200SX	SR20DE	M1T72985A
	240SX	KA24DE	M1T72781B
	300ZX	VG30DE,VG30DETT	M2T25282

① — Manual transaxle.
② — Automatic transaxle.
③ — Except California.
④ — California.

DESCRIPTION

Nissan starters are of two types, direct drive and gear reduction. The direct drive starter **Fig. 1,** is equipped with an overrunning clutch type starter drive. A solenoid switch is mounted on the starter motor.

Gear reduction starters, **Figs. 2 and 3,** may use a planetary gear train or a idler gear train to transmit armature rotation to the pinion shaft. A solenoid switch is mounted on the starter motor.

DIAGNOSIS & TESTING

STARTER TEST

Refer to **Fig. 4** for starter in-vehicle testing.

STARTER SOLENOID TEST

1. Disconnect battery ground cable.
2. Disconnect "M" terminal of starter motor, **Fig. 5.**
3. Using a suitable ohmmeter, check continuity between "S" terminal of starter motor and switch body. Continuity should exist. If continuity does not exist, starter solenoid is defective. Replace as necessary.
4. Check for continuity between "S" and "M" terminals of starter motor. Continuity should exist. If continuity does not exist, starter solenoid is defective. Replace as necessary.

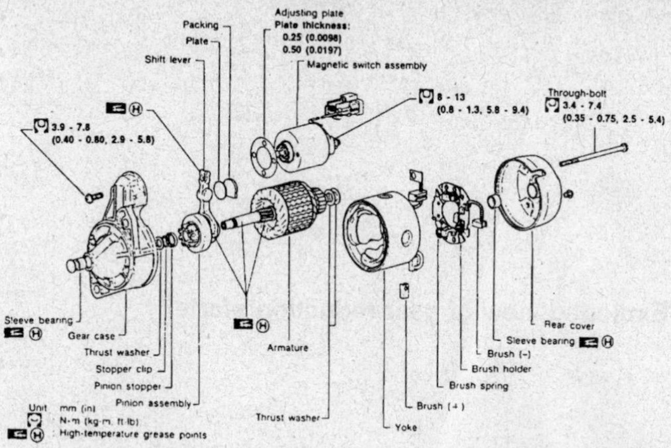

Adjusting plate
Plate thickness:
0.25 (0.0098)
0.50 (0.0197)
Packing
Plate
Shift lever
Magnetic switch assembly
3.9 - 7.8
(0.40 - 0.80, 2.9 - 5.8)
8 - 13
(0.8 - 1.3, 5.8 - 9.4)
Through-bolt
3.4 - 7.4
(0.35 - 0.75, 2.5 - 5.4)
Sleeve bearing
Gear case
Thrust washer
Stopper clip
Pinion stopper
Pinion assembly
Armature
Thrust washer
Yoke
Brush (+)
Brush spring
Brush holder
Brush (-)
Sleeve bearing
Rear cover
Unit mm (in)
N·m (kg-m, ft-lb)
High-temperature grease points

NS1129100001000X

Fig. 1 Exploded view of direct drive starter

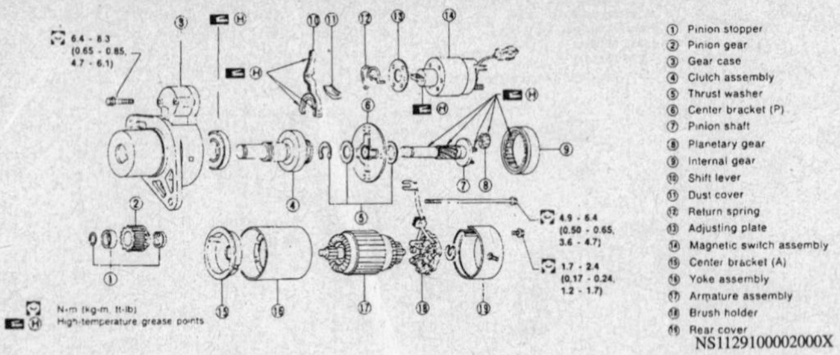

6.4 - 8.3 (0.65 - 0.85, 4.7 - 6.1)
4.9 - 6.4 (0.50 - 0.65, 3.6 - 4.7)
1.7 - 2.4 (0.17 - 0.24, 1.2 - 1.7)
N·m (kg-m, ft-lb)
High-temperature grease points
① Pinion stopper
② Pinion gear
③ Gear case
④ Clutch assembly
⑤ Thrust washer
⑥ Center bracket (P)
⑦ Pinion shaft
⑧ Planetary gear
⑨ Internal gear
⑩ Shift lever
⑪ Dust cover
⑫ Return spring
⑬ Adjusting plate
⑭ Magnetic switch assembly
⑮ Center bracket (A)
⑯ Yoke assembly
⑰ Armature assembly
⑱ Brush holder
⑲ Rear cover
NS1129100002000X

Fig. 2 Exploded view of gear reduction starter

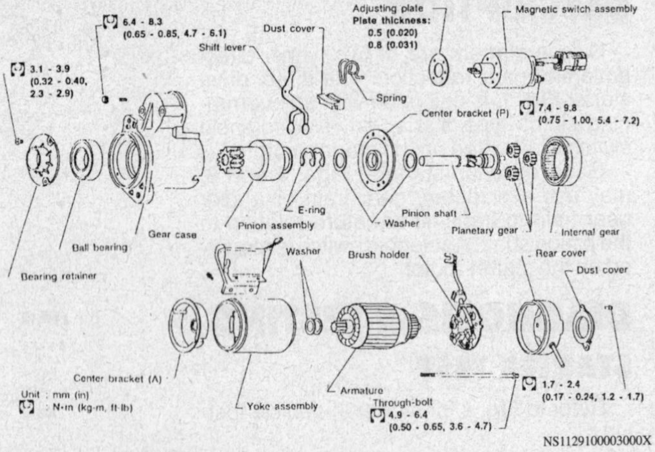

6.4 - 8.3 (0.65 - 0.85, 4.7 - 6.1)
3.1 - 3.9 (0.32 - 0.40, 2.3 - 2.9)
Dust cover
Shift lever
Adjusting plate
Plate thickness:
0.5 (0.020)
0.8 (0.031)
Magnetic switch assembly
Spring
Center bracket (P)
7.4 - 9.8 (0.75 - 1.00, 5.4 - 7.2)
E-ring
Pinion shaft
Pinion assembly
Washer
Planetary gear
Internal gear
Gear case
Ball bearing
Bearing retainer
Washer
Brush holder
Rear cover
Dust cover
Center bracket (A)
Unit : mm (in)
: N·m (kg-m, ft-lb)
Yoke assembly
Armature
Through-bolt
4.9 - 6.4 (0.50 - 0.65, 3.6 - 4.7)
1.7 - 2.4 (0.17 - 0.24, 1.2 - 1.7)
NS1129100003000X

Fig. 3 Exploded view of planetary gear reduction starter

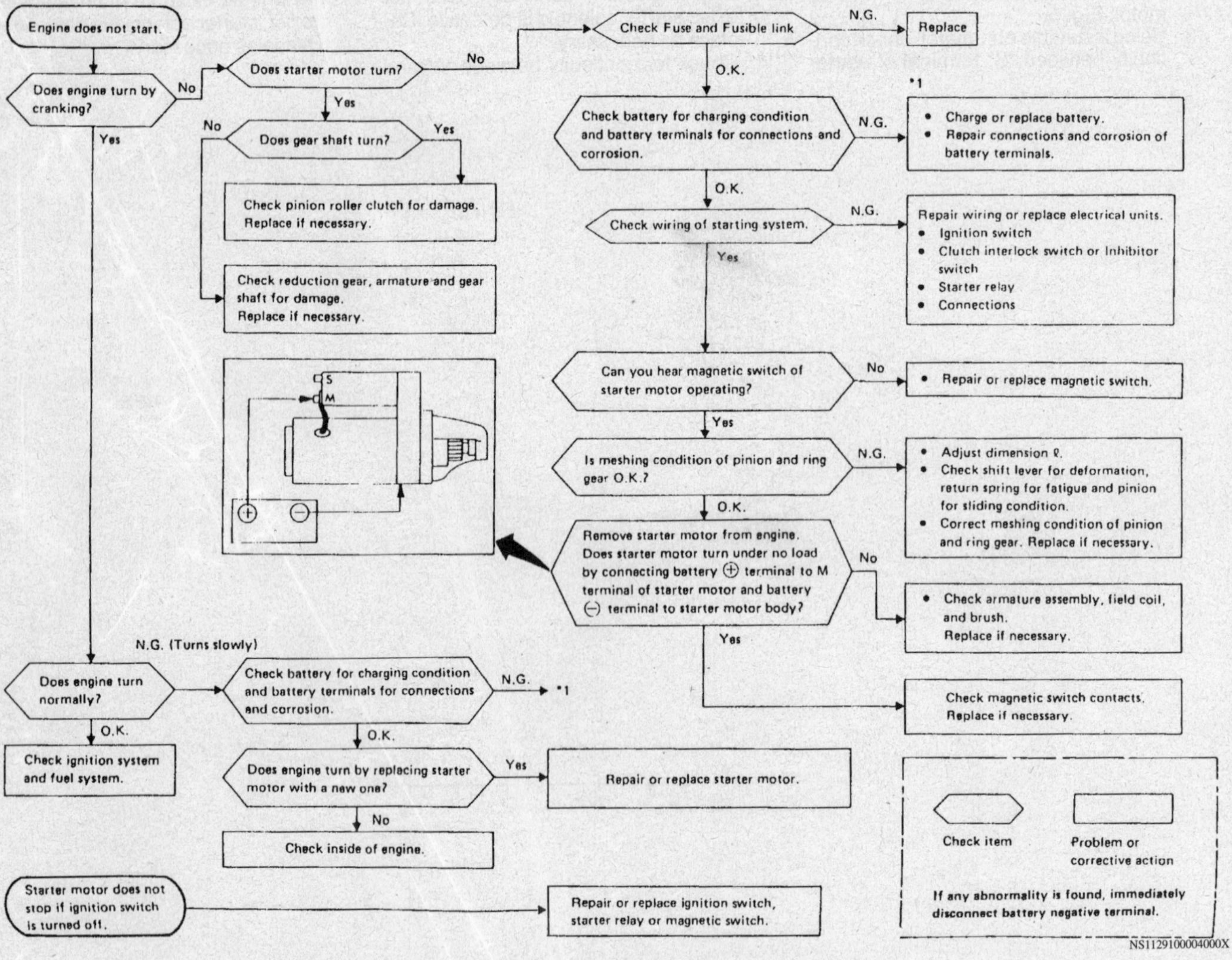

Engine does not start.
Does engine turn by cranking?
No
Does starter motor turn?
No
Check Fuse and Fusible link
N.G.
Replace
O.K.
*1
Check battery for charging condition and battery terminals for connections and corrosion.
N.G.
• Charge or replace battery.
• Repair connections and corrosion of battery terminals.
O.K.
Check wiring of starting system.
N.G.
Repair wiring or replace electrical units.
• Ignition switch
• Clutch interlock switch or Inhibitor switch
• Starter relay
• Connections
Yes
Can you hear magnetic switch of starter motor operating?
No
• Repair or replace magnetic switch.
Yes
Is meshing condition of pinion and ring gear O.K.?
N.G.
• Adjust dimension ℓ.
• Check shift lever for deformation, return spring for fatigue and pinion for sliding condition.
• Correct meshing condition of pinion and ring gear. Replace if necessary.
O.K.
Remove starter motor from engine. Does starter motor turn under no load by connecting battery ⊕ terminal to M terminal of starter motor and battery ⊖ terminal to starter motor body?
No
• Check armature assembly, field coil, and brush. Replace if necessary.
Yes
Check magnetic switch contacts. Replace if necessary.
Yes
No
Does gear shaft turn?
Yes
Check pinion roller clutch for damage. Replace if necessary.
Check reduction gear, armature and gear shaft for damage. Replace if necessary.
S
M
Yes
N.G. (Turns slowly)
Does engine turn normally?
Check battery for charging condition and battery terminals for connections and corrosion.
N.G.
*1
O.K.
Check ignition system and fuel system.
O.K.
Does engine turn by replacing starter motor with a new one?
Yes
Repair or replace starter motor.
No
Check inside of engine.
Starter motor does not stop if ignition switch is turned off.
Repair or replace ignition switch, starter relay or magnetic switch.
Check item
Problem or corrective action
If any abnormality is found, immediately disconnect battery negative terminal.
NS1129100004000X

Fig. 4 Starter test

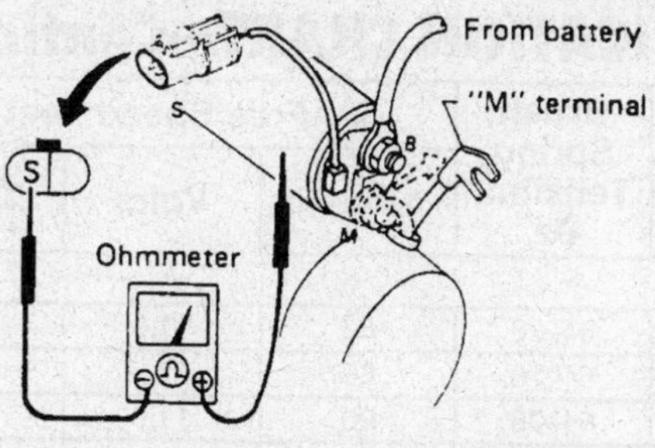
From battery
"M" terminal
S
B
M
Ohmmeter
NS1129100005000X

Fig. 5 Starter solenoid test

SPECIFICATION CHART

Starter Number	Brush Spring Tension, Oz.	Free Speed Test		
		Amps①	Volts	Starter RPM②
1993				
M1T60281	48–96	50–75	11.0	3000
M1T72088	48–96	75	11.0	4000
M1T72281A	70	75	12.0	3000
M1T72781A	49–91	50	11.0	4000
M1T72985	48–96	75	11.0	4000
M1T72985A	50–96	50	11.0	4000
M1T73881ZC	50–91	88	11.0	3000
M2T25281	49–91	70	11.0	2000
M2T53883	48–96	100	11.0	2000
M3T37783	48–96	60	11.5	6500
M3T38482	48–96	60	11.5	6500
S114-461A	64–78	100	11.5	3000
S114-486	48–64	100	11.0	3900
S114-525	70	90	12.0	2950
S114-527A	64	90	11.0	2950
S114-528	64	90	11.0	2650
S114-534	64–80	90	11.0	2950
S114-607B	64–78	60	11.5	7000
S114-630	64–78	60	11.5	7000
S114-701B	64	90	11.0	2950
S114-703A	64	90	11.0	2950
S114-754	53–64	85	11.0	2950
S114-756	64–78	90	11.0	2950
S114-757	64–78	90	11.0	2900
S114-767	53–64	90	11.0	2950
S114-769	53–64	85	11.0	2950
1994				
M1T60281	50–91	50–75	11.0	3000
M177281	50–91	75	11.0	3000
M1T64285	64–78	90	11.0	2900
M1T72781A	49–91	50	11.0	4000
M1T72985A	50–91	75	11.0	4000
M1T73881ZC	50–91	88	11.0	3000
M2T25281	49–91	70	11.0	2000
M3T37783	50–91	60	11.5	6500
M3T38482	50–91	60	11.5	6500
S114-461A	64–78	100	11.0	3000
S114-527A	64–78	90	11.0	2950
S114-528	64–78	90	11.0	2650

Continued

SPECIFICATION CHART—Continued

Starter Number	Brush Spring Tension, Oz.	Free Speed Test		
		Amps①	Volts	Starter RPM②
1994				
S114-607B	64–78	60	11.5	7000
S114-630	64–78	60	11.5	7000
S114-701B	64–78	90	11.0	2950
S114-703A	64–78	90	11.0	2950
S114-754A	53–64	85	11.0	2950
S114-756	64–78	90	11.0	2950
S114-767	53–64	90	11.0	2950
S114-769	53–64	85	11	2950
1995				
M001T64285	64-78	90	11	2900
M0T80281ZC	43–85	90	11.0	2750
M1T60281	50–91	50–75	11.0	3000
M1T72781A	49–91	50	11.0	4000
M1T72985A	50–91	75	11.0	4000
M1T73881ZC	50–91	88	11.0	3000
M2T25281	49–91	70	11.0	2000
M2T42983ZC	50–91	53	11.5	6000
M3T38482	50–91	60	11.5	6500
S114-527A	64–78	90	11.0	2950
S114-528	64–78	90	11.0	2650
S114-607B	64–78	60	11.5	7000
S114-701C	64–78	90	11.0	2950
S114-703A	64–78	90	11.0	2950
S114-754A	53–64	85	11.0	2950
S114-801A	46–64	90	11.0	2900
S114-802A	46–64	90	11.0	2700
1996				
M001T64285	64–78	90	11	2900
M0T80281ZC	43–85	90	11.0	2750
M1T60281	50–91	50–75	11.0	3000
M1T72781B	50–91	50–75	11.0	3000
M1T72985A	50–91	75	11.0	4000
M1T73881ZC	50–91	88	11.0	3000
M2T25282	49–91	70	11.0	2000
M2T42983ZC	50–91	53	11.5	6000
M3T38482	50–91	60	11.5	6500
S114-527A	64–78	90	11.0	2950
S114-528	64–78	90	11.0	2650
S114-607B	64–78	60	11.5	7000
S114-701B	64–78	90	11.0	2950
S114-701C	64–78	90	11.0	2950
S114-703A	64–78	90	11.0	2950
S114-754A	53–64	85	11.0	2950
S114-767	53–64	90	11.0	2950
S114-801A	46–64	90	11.0	2900
S114-802A	46–64	90	11.0	2700

① — Maximum.

② — Minimum.

Alternators

INDEX

	Page No.
Alternator Specifications	36-47
Application Chart	36-45
Description	36-46
Diagnosis & Testing	36-46

APPLICATION CHART

Year	Model	Engine	Alternator Number
1993	Altima	KA24DE	LR180-736B
	Maxima	VG30E	LR190-711②
	Maxima	VE30DE	LR195-701②
	Pathfinder & Pickup	KA24E	LR160-723B
	Pathfinder & Pickup	VG30E	LR170-739
	Quest	VG30E	A4T02591ZC
	Sentra/NX 1600 & NX 2000	GA16DE	A5T04392A②
	Sentra/NX 1600 & NX 2000	GA16DE	LR170-738C①
	Sentra/NX 1600 & NX 2000	SR20DE	A2T13894②
	Sentra/NX 1600 & NX 2000	SR20DE	LR180-725①
	240SX	KA24DE	LR180-729①
	300ZX	VG30DE	LR180-724①
	300ZX	VG30DETT	A3T05192②
1994	Altima	KA24DE	LR180-736B
	Maxima	VG30E	LR190-711②
	Maxima	VE30DE	LR195-701②
	Pathfinder & Pickup	KA24E	LR160-724
	Pathfinder & Pickup	VG30E	LR170-739
	Quest	VG30E	A4T02591ZC
	Sentra	GA16DE	A5T04392A②
	Sentra	GA16DE	LR170-738C①
	Sentra	SR20DE	A2T13894②
	Sentra	SR20DE	LR180-725C①
	240SX	KA24DE	LR180-729①
	300ZX	VG30DE	LR180-724①
	300ZX	VG30DETT	A2T33593A②
1995	Altima	KA24DE	LR180-736B
	Maxima	VQ30DE	LR11250-702①
	Pathfinder & Pickup	KA24E	LR160-724
	Pathfinder & Pickup	VG30E	LR170-739
	Quest	VG30E	A4T02591ZC
	Sentra & 200SX	GA16DE	LR170-748
	Sentra & 200SX	SR20DE	LR180-741H
	240SX	KA24DE	LR180-729①
	300ZX	VG30DE	LR180-724①
	300ZX	VG30DETT	A2T33593A②

Continued

APPLICATION CHART—Continued

Year	Model	Engine	Alternator Number
1996	Altima	KA24DE	LR180-736B
	Maxima	VQ30DE	LR1125-702B①
	Maxima	VQ30DE	LR1110-705①
	Pathfinder	KA24E	LR190-729
	Pickup	VG30E	LR160-727
	Quest	VG30E	A4T02591ZC
	Sentra & 200SX	GA16DE	LR170-748①
	Sentra & 200SX	SR20DE	LR180-741H①
	240SX	KA24DE	LR180-742①
	240SX	KA24DE	LR190-724①
	300ZX	VG30DE	LR180-724C①
	300ZX	VG30DETT	A2T33593A②

① — Hitachi.
② — Mitsubishi.

DESCRIPTION

Alternators are composed of the same functional parts as the conventional D.C. generator but they operate differently. The field is called a rotor and is the turning portion of the unit. A generating part, called a stator, is the stationary member, comparable to the armature in a D.C. generator. The regulator, similar to those used in a D.C. system, regulates the output of the alternator-rectifier system, **Figs. 1 and 2.**

The power source of the system is the alternator. Current is transmitted from the field terminal of the regulator through a slip ring to the field coil and back to ground through another slip ring. The strength of the field regulates the output of the alternating current. This alternating current is then transmitted from the alternator to the rectifier where it is converted to direct current.

DIAGNOSIS & TESTING

1. Turn ignition switch to on position and note charge lamp.
2. If lamp lights proceed to step 7. If lamp does not light proceed to next step.
3. Disconnect two wire connectors labeled S and L, then using a jumper wire connect L terminal to a suitable ground.
4. If charge lamp lights proceed to next step. If lamp does not light the bulb in the instrument cluster is defective. **Steps 5 and 6 do not apply to models equipped with Mitsubishi alternators. On these models, if charge lamp lights, the internal regulator or some other internal component is defective and the alternator must be removed for bench testing.**
5. Reconnect two wire connectors, then insert a short stiff length of wire through the access hole at back of alternator until it contacts outer brush. Ground other end of wire to alternator case which will actually ground the F terminal internally, **Fig. 3.**
6. If charge lamp remains lit, the internal regulator is defective and will require disassembly of the alternator for repair. If lamp goes out, some other internal component is defective therefore alternator must be removed for bench testing.
7. With engine idling if charge lamp is lit, a defective internal component exists in the alternator and requires removal for bench testing. If the charge lamp is not lit, proceed to next step.
8. With engine speed at 1500 RPM and headlights on, if charge lamp is not lit proceed to next step. If lamp is lit dimly, let engine idle and measure voltage across B and L terminals. If voltage is more than .5 volts a defective internal

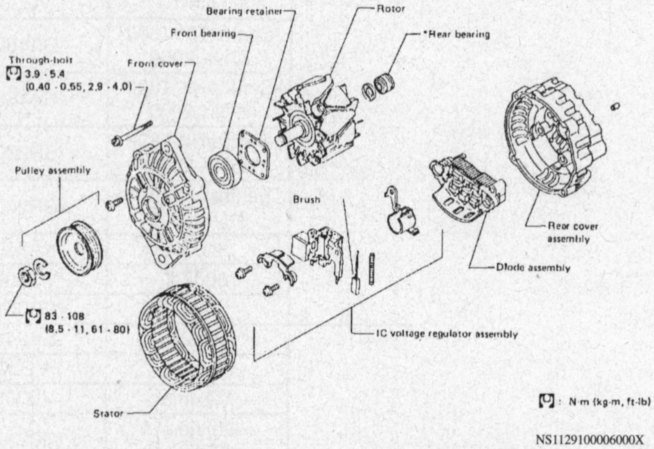
Bearing retainer
Rotor
Front bearing
*Rear bearing
Through-bolt
3.9 - 5.4
(0.40 - 0.55, 2.9 - 4.0)
Front cover
Pulley assembly
Brush
Rear cover assembly
Diode assembly
83 - 108
(8.5 - 11, 61 - 80)
IC voltage regulator assembly
Stator
: N·m (kg-m, ft-lb)
NS1129100006000X

Fig. 1 Exploded view of Hitachi alternator

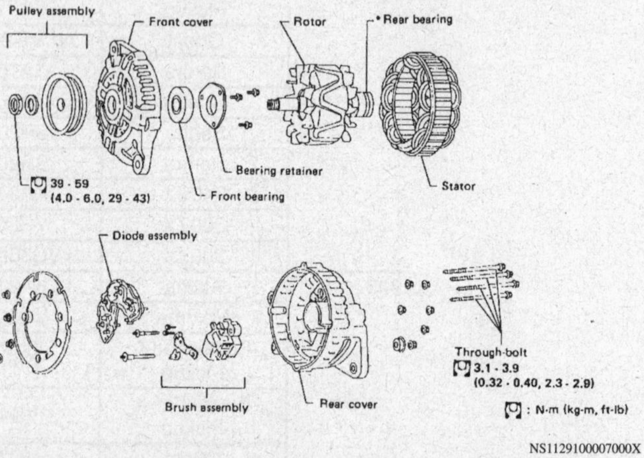
Pulley assembly
Front cover
Rotor
*Rear bearing
39 - 59
(4.0 - 6.0, 29 - 43)
Bearing retainer
Front bearing
Stator
Diode assembly
Through-bolt
3.1 - 3.9
(0.32 - 0.40, 2.3 - 2.9)
Brush assembly
Rear cover
: N·m (kg-m, ft-lb)
NS1129100007000X

Fig. 2 Exploded view of Mitsubishi alternator

component exists in the alternator and requires removal for bench testing. **If voltage is less than .5 volts, alternator if considered to be in satisfactory condition.**

9. With engine at 1500 RPM measure voltage at B terminal, making sure S terminal is properly connected.
10. If voltage reading is above 15.5 volts, the internal regulator is faulty and requires removal of alternator for replacement. If voltage reading is between 13 and 15 volts proceed to next step.

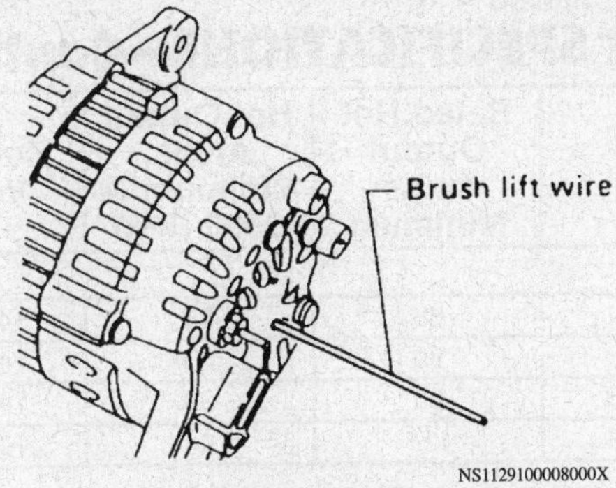
Brush lift wire
NS1129100008000X

Fig. 3 Alternator "F" terminal ground

11. With engine idling and headlights on, if charge lamp is lit a defective internal component exists in the alternator and requires removal for bench testing. If charge lamp is not lit, alternator is considered to be in satisfactory condition.

ALTERNATOR SPECIFICATIONS

Model	Rated Hot Output Amps. Minimum	Hot Output Amps. Minimum @ 2500 RPM	Regulated Voltage
1993			
A2T13894	80	65	14.1–14.7
A2T29892	80	60	14.1–14.7
A3T05192	90	65	14.1–14.7
A4T02591ZC	110	85	14.1–14.7
A5T04392A	70	50	14.1–14.7
LR160-723B	60	48	14.1–14.7
LR170-738C	70	50	14.1–14.7
LR170-739	70	50	14.1–14.7
LR180-724	80	65	14.1–14.7
LR180-725C	80	63	14.1–14.7
LR180-729	80	63	14.1–14.7
LR180-736B	80	63	14.1–14.7
LR190-711	90	63	14.1–14.7
LR195-701	95	80	14.1–14.7
1994			
A2T13894	80	65	14.1–14.7
A2T29892	80	60	14.1–14.7
A2T33593A	90	61	14.1–14.7
A4T02591ZC	110	85	14.1–14.7
A5T04392A	70	50	14.1–14.7
LR160-724	60	48	14.1–14.7
LR170-738C	70	50	14.1–14.7
LR170-739	70	50	14.1–14.7
LR180-724	80	65	14.1–14.7
LR180-725C	80	63	14.1–14.7
LR180-729	80	63	14.1–14.7
LR180-736B	80	63	14.1–14.7
LR190-711	90	63	14.1–14.7
LR195-701	95	80	14.1–14.7
1995			
A2T13894	80	65	14.1–14.7
A2T29892	80	60	14.1–14.7
A2T33593A	90	61	14.1–14.7
A4T02591ZC	110	85	14.1–14.7
LR160-724	60	48	14.1–14.7
LR170-739	70	50	14.1–14.7
LR170-748	70	50	14.1–14.7

Continued

ALTERNATOR SPECIFICATIONS—Continued

Model	Rated Hot Output Amps. Minimum	Hot Output Amps. Minimum @ 2500 RPM	Regulated Voltage
1995			
LR180-724	80	65	14.1–14.7
LR180-729	80	63	14.1–14.7
LR180-736B	80	63	14.1–14.7
LR1125-702	125	94	14.1–14.7
1996			
A2T33593A	90	61	14.1–14.7
A4T02591ZC	110	85	14.1–14.7
LR160-727	57	48	14.1–14.7
LR170-739	70	50	14.1–14.7
LR170-748	70	50	14.1–14.7
LR180-724	80	65	14.1–14.7
LR180-742	77	65	14.1–14.7
LR180-736B	80	63	14.1–14.7
LR190-724	87	65	14.1–14.7
LR190-729	87	65	14.1–14.7
LR1110-705	105	82	14.1–14.7
LR1125-702B	123	94	14.1–14.7

Speed Control Systems

INDEX

	Page No.
Adjustments	36-48
ASCD Wire	36-48
Component Diagnosis & Testing	36-49
Altima, Sentra, 200SX, NX 1600, NX 2000 & 300ZX	36-49
Maxima, Pathfinder, Pickup, Quest & 240SX	36-49
Description	36-48
Diagnostic Chart Index	36-49
System Diagnosis & Testing	36-48
240SX	36-49
300ZX	36-49
Altima	36-48
Maxima & Quest	36-48
NX 1600, NX 2000, Sentra & 200SX	36-48
Pathfinder & Pickup	36-48

DESCRIPTION

The speed control system is composed of On-Off, Set-Accelerate, Coast, Resume (if equipped) switches. The system includes vacuum hoses, servo (throttle actuator) assembly, speed sensor, check valve assembly, and depending on model, a clutch switch and stop light switch.

To operate speed control system, the engine must be running and vehicle speed must exceed 30 mph. When the On-Off switch is actuated, the system is ready to accept a set speed signal. When vehicle speed stabilizes (exceeds 30 mph), and the On switch is engaged, the operator may depress or release the Set-Accelerate button. This speed will be maintained until a new speed has been set, brake pedal has been depressed, or the system is turned off.

ADJUSTMENTS

ASCD WIRE

1. Confirm adjustment of accelerator cable.
2. Loosen adjusting nut on the ASCD wire ½ to 1 turn from full closed position of throttle cable.
3. Tighten adjusting locknut.

SYSTEM DIAGNOSIS & TESTING

ALTIMA

Refer to **Figs. 1 through 8** for diagnostic charts.

MAXIMA & QUEST

1993-95

Refer to **Figs. 9 through 22** for diagnostic charts.

1996

Refer to **Fig. 23** for Fail-Safe system diagnostic check, then refer to "Component Diagnosis & Testing" for component diagnostic charts.

PATHFINDER & PICKUP

1993-95

Refer to **Figs. 24 through 29** for diagnostic charts.

1996

Refer to **Fig. 30** for Fail-Safe system diagnostic check, then refer to "Component Diagnosis & Testing" for component diagnostic charts.

NX 1600, NX 2000, SENTRA & 200SX

1993—94

Refer to **Figs. 31 through 38** for diagnostic charts.

1995—96

Refer to **Figs. 39 through 46** for diagnostic charts.

240SX

1993-94

Refer to **Figs. 47 through 54** for diagnostic charts.

1995

Refer to **Figs. 55 through 62** for diagnostic charts.

1996

Refer to **Fig. 63** for Fail-Safe system diagnostic check, then refer to "Component Diagnosis & Testing" for component diagnostic charts.

300ZX

Refer to **Figs. 64 through 71** for diagnostic charts.

COMPONENT DIAGNOSIS & TESTING

ALTIMA, SENTRA, 200SX, NX 1600, NX 2000 & 300ZX

ELECTRICAL COMPONENT CHECK

Refer to **Figs. 72 through 75** for ASCD electrical component check procedures.

ASCD ACTUATOR CHECK

Refer to **Figs. 76 through 78** for ASCD actuator test procedures.

MAXIMA, PATHFINDER, PICKUP, QUEST & 240SX

1993-95

ASCD Actuator Check

Refer to **Figs. 79 through 81** for ASCD actuator test procedures.

Electrical Component Check

On 1993–94 models, refer to **Fig. 82** for ASCD electrical component check procedure.

On 1995 models, refer to **Fig. 83** for ASCD electrical component check procedure.

1996

Power Supply & Ground Circuit Check

Refer to **Figs. 84 through 87** for diagnostic charts.

ASCD Main Switch Check

Refer to **Figs. 88 through 92** for diagnostic charts.

ASDC Hold Relay Circuit Check

Refer to **Figs. 93 through 97** for diagnostic charts.

ASCD Cancel Switch Check

Refer to **Figs. 98 through 101** for diagnostic charts.

ASCD Steering Switch Check

Refer to **Figs. 102 through 105** for diagnostic charts.

Vehicle Speed Sensor Check

Refer to **Figs. 106 through 110** for diagnostic charts.

ASCD Actuator Check

Refer to **Figs. 111 through 114** for diagnostic charts.

Vacuum Hose & Accel Wire Check

Refer to **Figs. 115 through 118** for diagnostic charts.

DIAGNOSTIC CHART INDEX

Test	Description	Year	Page No.	Fig. No.
ALTIMA				
Test 1	ASCD Control Cannot Be Set	1993–96	36-52	1
Test 2	Engine Hunts	1993–96	36-52	2
Test 3	Large Difference Between Set Vehicle Speed & Actual Speed	1993–96	36-52	3
Test 4	Deceleration Is Greatest Immediately After ASCD Has Been Set	1993–96	36-52	4
Test 5	ACCEL Switch Will Not Operate	1993–96	36-53	5
Test 6	RESUME Switch Will Not Operate	1993–96	36-53	6
Test 7	Set Speed Cannot Be Cancelled	1993–96	36-53	7
Test 8	"CRUISE" Indicator Lamp Blinks	1993–96	36-53	8
—	Actuator Check	1993–96	36-73	76
—	Electrical Component Check	1993–96	36-71	72
MAXIMA				
Test 1	ASCD Control Unit Cannot Be Set Properly	1993–94	36-54	9
Test 2	Resume Switch Will Not Operate	1993–94	36-54	10
Test 3	Cancel Switch Will Not Operate	1993–94	36-54	11
Test 4	Engine Hunts	1993–94	36-54	12
Test 5	Large Difference Between Set Vehicle Speed & Actual Speed	1993–94	36-54	13
Test 6	Set Speed Cannot Be Cancelled	1993–94	36-54	14
Test 1	Speed Control Cannot Be Set	1995	36-55	15
Test 2	Engine Hunts	1995	36-56	16
Test 3	Large Difference Between Set Speed & Actual Speed	1995	36-56	17
Test 4	Deceleration Is Greatest Immediately After ASCD Has Been Set	1995	36-56	18
Test 5	Set Speed Cannot Be Canceled	1995	36-56	19
Test 6	ACCEL Switch Will Not Operate	1995	36-56	20
Test 7	RESUME Switch Will Not Operate	1995	36-57	21
Test 8	Cruise Indicator Lamp Blinks	1995	36-57	22
—	Actuator Check	1993–95	36-74	79

Continued

DIAGNOSTIC CHART INDEX—Continued

Test	Description	Year	Page No.	Fig. No.
MAXIMA				
—	Fail-Safe System Check	1996	36-57	23
Test 1	Power Supply & Ground Circuit Check	1996	36-75	84
Test 2	ASCD Main Switch Check	1996	36-76	88
Test 3	ASCD Hold Relay Circuit Check	1996	36-76	93
Test 4	ASCD Cancel Switch Check	1996	36-78	98
Test 5	ASCD Steering Switch Check	1996	36-79	102
Test 6	Vehicle Speed Sensor Check	1996	36-80	106
Test 7	ASCD Actuator Check	1996	36-80	111
Test 8	Vacuum Hose & Accel Wire Check	1996	36-81	115
PATHFINDER & PICKUP				
Test 1	ASCD Control Unit Cannot Be Set Properly	—	36-58	24
Test 2	RESUME Switch Will Not Operate	1993–95	36-58	25
Test 3	Accelerator Switch Will Not Operate	1993–95	36-58	26
Test 4	Engine Hunts	1993–95	36-58	27
Test 5	Large Difference Between Set Vehicle Speed & Actual Speed	1993–95	36-59	28
Test 6	OD Cancel Circuit Check	1993–95	36-59	29
—	Actuator Check	1993–95	36-74	80
—	Fail-Safe System Check	1996	36-59	30
Test 1	Power Supply & Ground Circuit Check	1996	36-75	85
Test 2	ASCD Main Switch Check	1996	36-76	89
Test 2	ASCD Main Switch Check	1996	36-76	90
Test 3	ASCD Hold Relay Circuit Check	1996	36-77	94
Test 3	ASCD Hold Relay Circuit Check	1996	36-77	95
Test 4	ASCD Cancel Switch Check	1996	36-78	99
Test 5	ASCD Steering Switch Check	1996	36-79	103
Test 6	Vehicle Speed Sensor Check	1996	36-80	107
Test 6	Vehicle Speed Sensor Check	1996	36-80	108
Test 7	ASCD Actuator Check	1996	36-81	112
Test 8	Vacuum Hose & Accel Wire Check	1996	36-81	116
QUEST				
Test 1	ASCD Control Unit Cannot Be Set Properly	1993–95	36-54	9
Test 2	Resume Switch Will Not Operate	1993–95	36-54	10
Test 3	Cancel Switch Will Not Operate	1993–95	36-54	11
Test 4	Engine Hunts	1993–95	36-54	12
Test 5	Large Difference Between Set Vehicle Speed & Actual Speed	1993–95	36-54	13
Test 6	Set Speed Cannot Be Cancelled	1993–95	36-54	14
—	Actuator Check	1993–95	36-74	79
—	Fail-Safe System Check	1996	36-57	23
Test 1	Power Supply & Ground Circuit Check	1996	36-75	86
Test 2	ASCD Main Switch Check	1996	36-76	91
Test 3	ASCD Hold Relay Circuit Check	1996	36-77	96
Test 4	ASCD Cancel Switch Check	1996	36-78	100
Test 5	ASCD Steering Switch Check	1996	36-79	104
Test 6	Vehicle Speed Sensor Check	1996	36-80	109
Test 7	ASCD Actuator Check	1996	36-81	113
Test 8	Vacuum Hose & Accel Wire Check	1996	36-81	117
SENTRA, NX 1600, NX 2000 & 200SX				
Test 1	ASCD Control Cannot Be Set	1993–94	36-59	31
Test 2	Engine Hunts	1993–94	36-60	32
Test 3	Large Difference Between Set Vehicle Speed & Actual Speed	1993–94	36-60	33
Test 4	Deceleration Is Greatest Immediately After ASCD Has Been Set	1993–94	36-60	34
Test 5	ACCEL Switch Will Not Operate	1993–94	36-60	35
Test 6	RESUME Switch Will Not Operate	1993–94	36-61	36
Test 7	Set Speed Cannot Be Cancelled	1993–94	36-61	37
Test 8	CRUISE Indicator Lamp Blinks	1993–94	36-61	38

Continued

DIAGNOSTIC CHART INDEX—Continued

Test	Description	Year	Page No.	Fig. No.
SENTRA, NX 1600, NX 2000 & 200SX				
Test 1	Speed Control Cannot Be Set	1995–96	36-61	39
Test 2	Engine Hunts	1995–96	36-62	40
Test 3	Large Difference Between Set Vehicle Speed & Actual Speed	1995–96	36-62	41
Test 4	Deceleration Is Greatest Immediately After ASCD Has Been Set	1995–96	36-62	42
Test 5	ACCEL Switch Will Not Operate	1995–96	36-62	43
Test 6	RESUME Switch Will Not Operate	1995–96	36-63	44
Test 7	Set Speed Cannot Be Canceled	1995–96	36-63	45
Test 8	CRUISE Indicator Lamp Blinks	1995–96	36-63	46
—	Electrical Component Check	1993–94	36-72	73
—	Electrical Component Check	1995–96	36-72	74
—	Actuator Check	1993–96	36-73	77
240SX				
Test 1	ASCD Control Unit Cannot Be Set	1993–94	36-63	47
Test 2	Engine Hunts	1993–94	36-64	48
Test 3	Large Difference Between Set Vehicle Speed & Actual Speed	1993–94	36-64	49
Test 4	Deceleration Is Greatest Immediately After ASCD Has Been Set	1993–94	36-64	50
Test 5	ACCEL Switch Will Not Operate	1993–94	36-64	51
Test 6	RESUME Switch Will Not Operate	1993–94	36-65	52
Test 7	Set Speed Cannot Be Cancelled	1993–94	36-65	53
Test 8	CRUISE Indicator Lamp Blinks	1993–94	36-65	54
Test 1	Speed Control Cannot Be Set	1995	36-65	55
Test 2	Engine Hunts	1995	36-66	56
Test 3	Large Difference Between Set Vehicle Speed & Actual Speed	1995	36-66	57
Test 4	Deceleration Is Greatest Immediately After ASCD Has Been Set	1995	36-67	58
Test 5	ACCEL Switch Will Not Operate	1995	36-67	59
Test 6	RESUME Switch Will Not Operate	1995	36-67	60
Test 7	Set Speed Cannot Be Canceled	1995	36-67	61
Test 8	CRUISE Indicator Lamp Blinks	1995	36-68	62
—	Actuator Check	1993–95	36-74	81
—	Electrical Component Check	1993–94	36-74	82
—	Electrical Component Check	1995	36-75	83
—	Fail-Safe System Check	1996	36-68	63
Test 1	Power Supply & Ground Circuit Check	1996	36-76	87
Test 2	ASCD Main Switch Check	1996	36-76	92
Test 3	ASCD Hold Relay Circuit Check	1996	36-77	97
Test 4	ASCD Cancel Switch Check	1996	36-78	101
Test 5	ASCD Steering Switch Check	1996	36-79	105
Test 6	Vehicle Speed Sensor Check	1996	36-80	110
Test 7	ASCD Actuator Check	1996	36-81	114
Test 8	Vacuum Hose & Accel Wire Check	1996	36-81	118
300ZX				
Test 1	ASCD Control Unit Cannot Be Set	1993–96	36-68	64
Test 2	Engine Hunts	1993–96	36-69	65
Test 3	Large Difference Between Set Vehicle Speed & Actual Speed	1993–96	36-69	66
Test 4	Deceleration Is Greatest Immediately After ASCD Has Been Set	1993–96	36-69	67
Test 5	ACCEL Switch Will Not Operate	1993–96	36-70	68
Test 6	RESUME Switch Will Not Operate	1993–96	36-70	69
Test 7	Set Speed Cannot Be Cancelled	1993–96	36-70	70
Test 8	CRUISE Indicator Lamp Blinks	1993–96	36-71	71
—	Actuator Check	1993–96	36-73	78
—	Electrical Component Check	1993–96	36-72	75
—	Electrical Component Check	1993–96	36-73	75

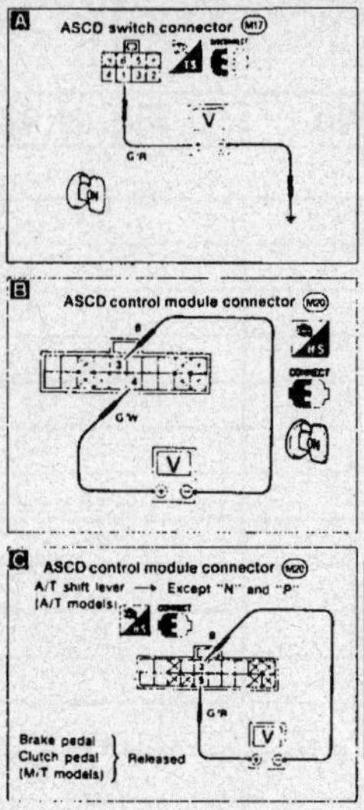
A
ASCD switch connector (M17)
B
ASCD control module connector (M20)
C
ASCD control module connector (M20)
A/T shift lever → Except "N" and "P" (A/T models)
Brake pedal
Clutch pedal (M/T models)
Released

Turn ASCD switch "OFF" and "ON" to make sure indicator illuminates.
- N.G. → **A** CHECK POWER SUPPLY FOR ASCD SWITCH.
  1. Disconnect switch harness connector.
  2. Do approx. 12 volts exist between switch harness terminal ① and body ground?
  - No → Check fuse and harness.
  - Yes → CHECK ASCD SWITCH. CHECK ASCD HOLD RELAY.
- O.K. ↓

B CHECK POWER SUPPLY CIRCUIT FOR ASCD CONTROL MODULE.
1. Turn ASCD switch "ON".
2. Check voltage between control module harness terminals ④ and ③.

Battery positive voltage should exist.
- N.G. → Check continuity between control module harness terminal ④ and ASCD hold relay.
- O.K. ↓

C CHECK CUT-OFF CIRCUIT FOR ASCD CONTROL MODULE.
Check voltage between control module harness terminals ⑤ and ③.
Battery positive voltage should exist.
- N.G. → CHECK ASCD CANCEL SWITCH, ASCD CLUTCH PEDAL POSITION SWITCH (M/T models) AND INHIBITOR SWITCH (A/T models). CHECK INHIBITOR RELAY (A/T models).
- O.K. ↓ Ⓐ

NS1109100001010X

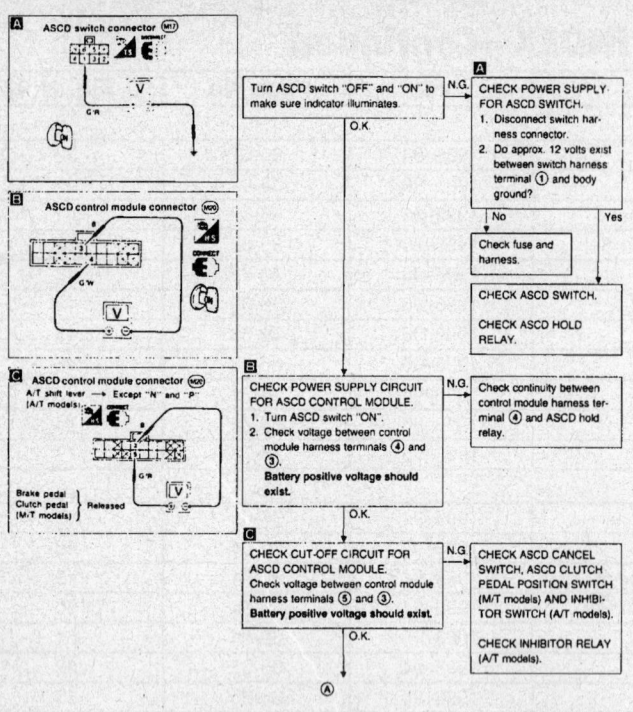

Fig. 1 Test 1: ASCD Control Cannot Be Set (Part 1 of 2). Altima

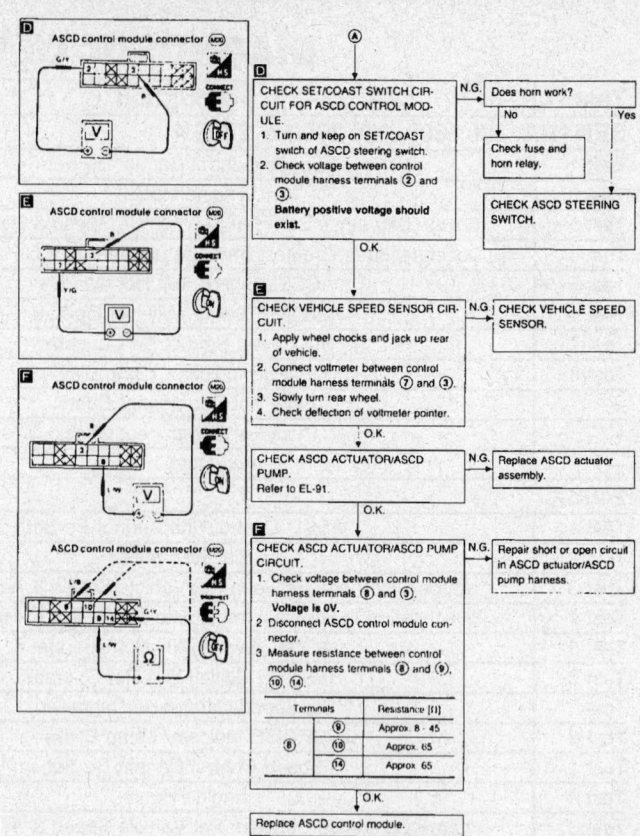

Check vacuum hose for breakage, cracks or fracture.
- N.G. → Repair or replace hose.
- O.K. ↓

Does ASCD wire move smoothly?
- N.G. → Repair or replace wire.
- O.K. ↓

CHECK ASCD ACTUATOR/ASCD PUMP.
- N.G. → Replace ASCD actuator assembly.
- O.K. ↓

Replace ASCD control module.

NS1109100002000X

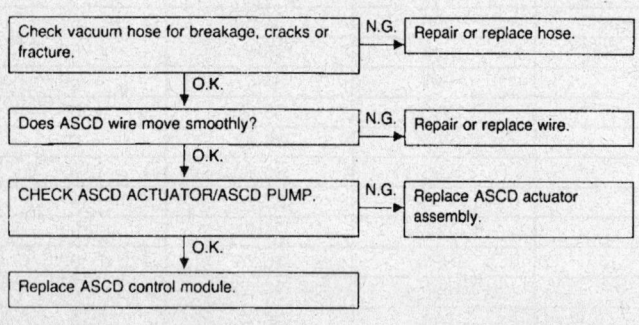

Fig. 2 Test 2: Engine Hunts. Altima

Check tension of ASCD wire and that ASCD wire moves smoothly.
- N.G. → ADJUST OR REPLACE ASCD WIRE.
- O.K. ↓

Check vacuum hose for breakage, cracks or fracture.
- N.G. → Repair or replace hose.
- O.K. ↓

CHECK ASCD ACTUATOR/ASCD PUMP.
- N.G. → Replace ASCD actuator assembly.
- O.K. ↓

Replace ASCD control module.

NS1109100004000X

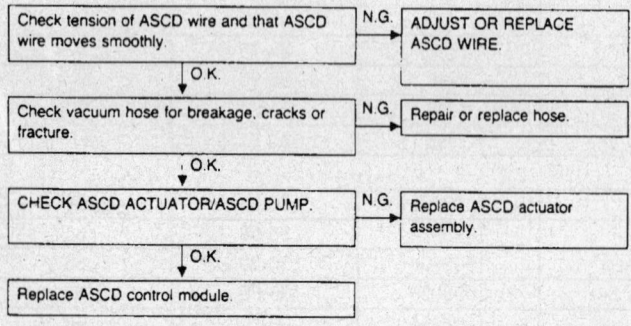

Fig. 4 Test 4: Deceleration Is Greatest Immediately After ASCD Has Been Set. Altima

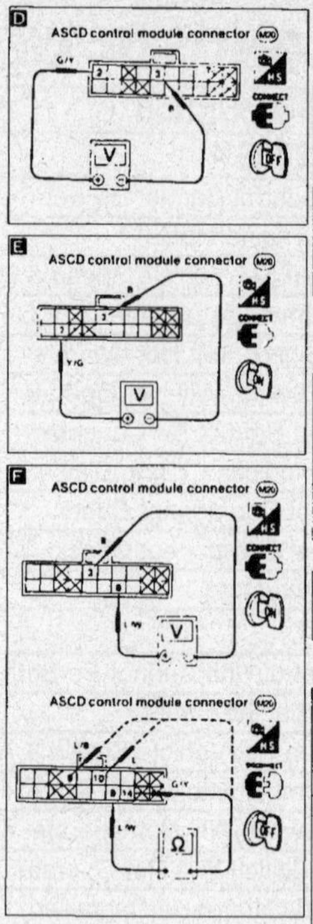
D
ASCD control module connector (M20)
E
ASCD control module connector (M20)
F
ASCD control module connector (M20)
ASCD control module connector (M20)

Ⓐ ↓

D CHECK SET/COAST SWITCH CIRCUIT FOR ASCD CONTROL MODULE.
1. Turn and keep on SET/COAST switch of ASCD steering switch.
2. Check voltage between control module harness terminals ② and ③.

Battery positive voltage should exist.
- N.G. → Does horn work?
  - No → Check fuse and horn relay.
  - Yes → CHECK ASCD STEERING SWITCH.
- O.K. ↓

E CHECK VEHICLE SPEED SENSOR CIRCUIT.
1. Apply wheel chocks and jack up rear of vehicle.
2. Connect voltmeter between control module harness terminals ⑦ and ③.
3. Slowly turn rear wheel.
4. Check deflection of voltmeter pointer.
- N.G. → CHECK VEHICLE SPEED SENSOR.
- O.K. ↓

CHECK ASCD ACTUATOR/ASCD PUMP. Refer to EL-91.
- N.G. → Replace ASCD actuator assembly.
- O.K. ↓

F CHECK ASCD ACTUATOR/ASCD PUMP CIRCUIT.
1. Check voltage between control module harness terminals ⑧ and ③.
   Voltage is 0V.
2. Disconnect ASCD control module connector.
3. Measure resistance between control module harness terminals ⑧ and ⑨, ⑩, ⑭.

Terminals		Resistance [Ω]
⑧	⑨	Approx. 8 - 45
	⑩	Approx. 65
	⑭	Approx. 65

- N.G. → Repair short or open circuit in ASCD actuator/ASCD pump harness.
- O.K. ↓

Replace ASCD control module.

NS1109100001020X

Fig. 1 Test 1: ASCD Control Cannot Be Set (Part 2 of 2). Altima

Check ASCD wire and ASCD actuator move smoothly.
- N.G. → Replace wire or ASCD actuator assembly.
- O.K. ↓

Check vacuum hose for breakage, cracks or fracture.
- N.G. → Repair or replace hose.
- O.K. ↓

CHECK ASCD ACTUATOR/ASCD PUMP.
- N.G. → Replace ASCD actuator assembly.
- O.K. ↓

Replace ASCD control module.

NS1109100003000X

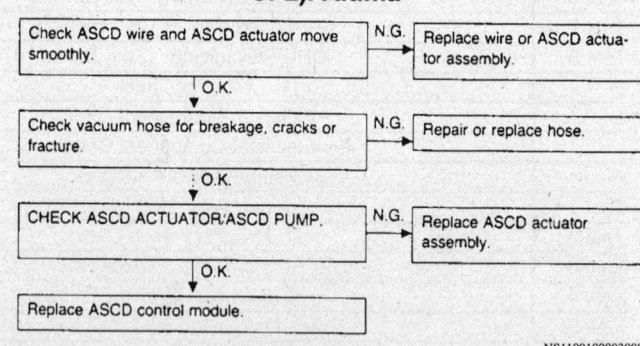

Fig. 3 Test 3: Large Difference Between Set Vehicle Speed & Actual Speed. Altima

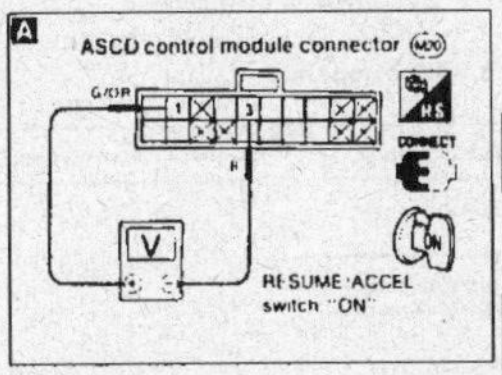
A
ASCD control module connector (M20)
G/OR
RESUME/ACCEL switch "ON"

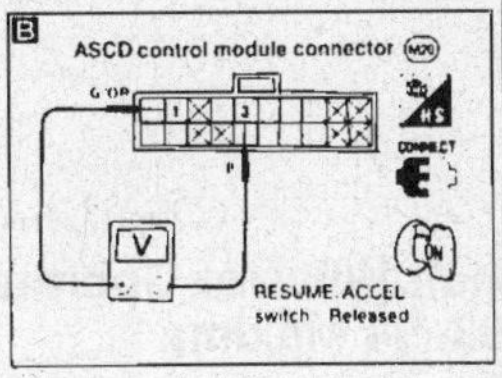
B
ASCD control module connector (M20)
G/OR
RESUME/ACCEL switch Released

- Check constant-speed function for operating using SET/COAST switch.
  - N.G. → Peform "DIAGNOSTIC PROCEDURE 1".
  - O.K. ↓
- **A** Check voltage between control module harness terminals ① and ③ after turning on and holding RESUME/ACCEL switch. **Battery positive voltage should exist.**
  - O.K. → CHECK ASCD STEERING SWITCH.
  - O.K. ↓
- **B** Check voltage between control module harness terminals ① and ③ after releasing RESUME/ACCEL switch. **Voltage is 0V.**
  - N.G. → CHECK ASCD STEERING SWITCH.
  - O.K. ↓
- **C** Does vehicle accelerate when RESUME/ACCEL switch is turned on?
  - No → Replace control module.
  - Yes ↓
- Does vehicle maintain the new (faster) speed when RESUME/ACCEL switch is released?
  - No → Replace control module.
  - Yes ↓
- System is O.K.

NS1109100005000X

Fig. 5 Test 5: ACCEL Switch Will Not Operate. Altima

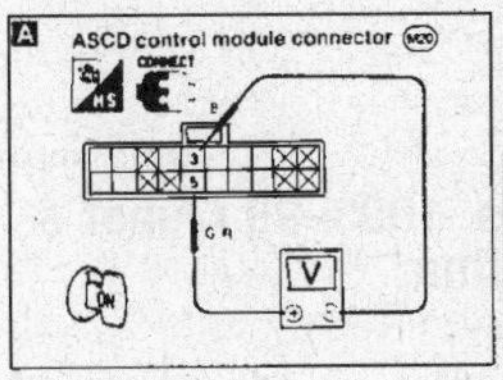
A
ASCD control module connector (M20)
G/R

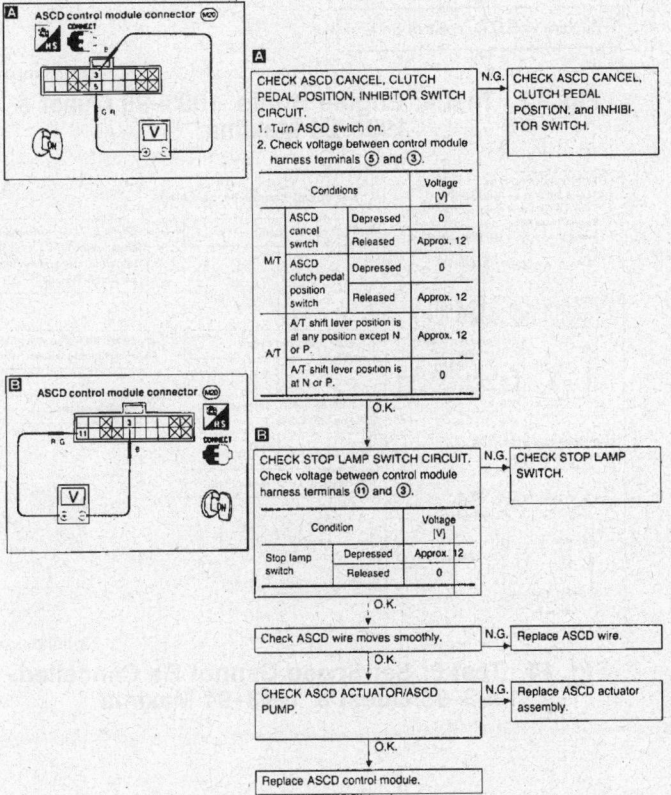

- **A** CHECK ASCD CANCEL, CLUTCH PEDAL POSITION, INHIBITOR SWITCH CIRCUIT.
  1. Turn ASCD switch on.
  2. Check voltage between control module harness terminals ⑤ and ③.

Conditions			Voltage [V]
M/T	ASCD cancel switch	Depressed	0
		Released	Approx. 12
	ASCD clutch pedal position switch	Depressed	0
		Released	Approx. 12
A/T	A/T shift lever position is at any position except N or P.		Approx. 12
	A/T shift lever position is at N or P.		0

  - N.G. → CHECK ASCD CANCEL, CLUTCH PEDAL POSITION, and INHIBITOR SWITCH.
  - O.K. ↓

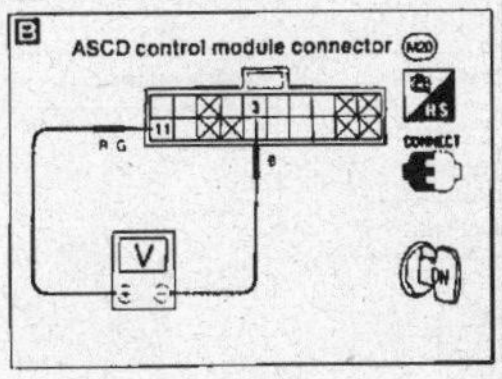
B
ASCD control module connector (M20)
R/G

- **B** CHECK STOP LAMP SWITCH CIRCUIT. Check voltage between control module harness terminals ⑪ and ③.

Condition		Voltage [V]
Stop lamp switch	Depressed	Approx. 12
	Released	0

  - N.G. → CHECK STOP LAMP SWITCH.
  - O.K. ↓
- Check ASCD wire moves smoothly.
  - N.G. → Replace ASCD wire.
  - O.K. ↓
- CHECK ASCD ACTUATOR/ASCD PUMP.
  - N.G. → Replace ASCD actuator assembly.
  - O.K. ↓
- Replace ASCD control module.

NS1109100007000X

Fig. 7 Test 7: Set Speed Cannot Be Cancelled. Altima

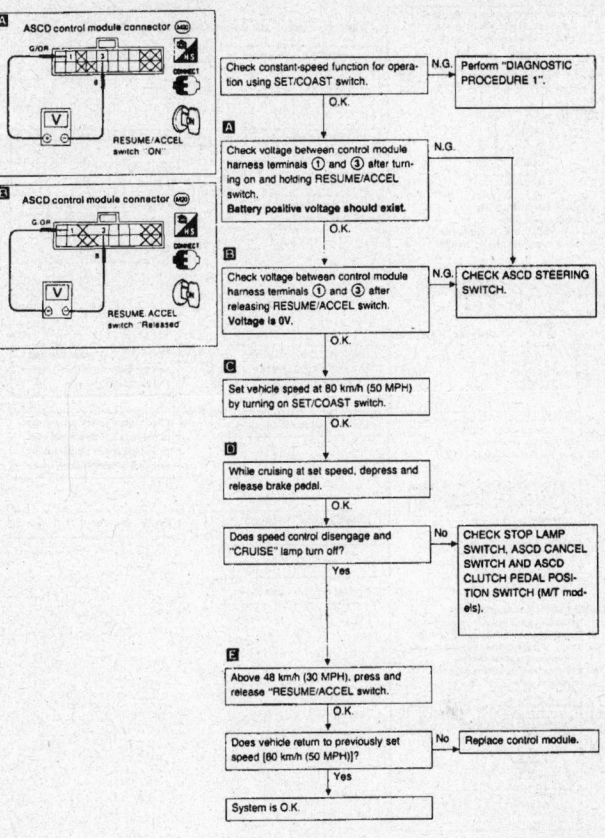

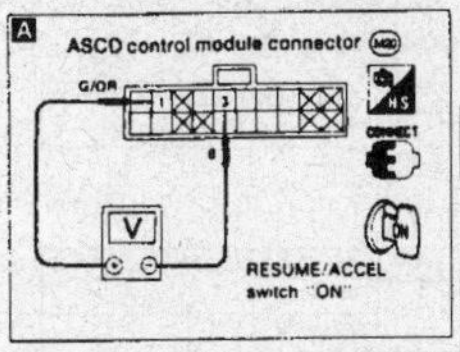
A
ASCD control module connector (M20)
G/OR
RESUME/ACCEL switch "ON"

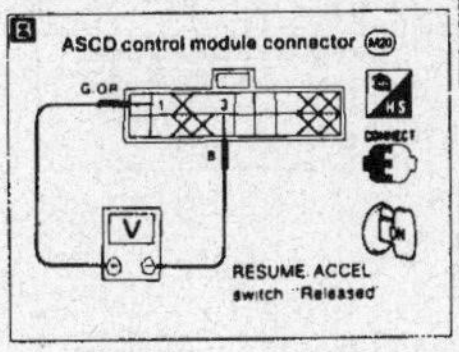
B
ASCD control module connector (M20)
G/OR
RESUME ACCEL switch "Released"

- Check constant-speed function for operation using SET/COAST switch.
  - N.G. → Perform "DIAGNOSTIC PROCEDURE 1".
  - O.K. ↓
- **A** Check voltage between control module harness terminals ① and ③ after turning on and holding RESUME/ACCEL switch. **Battery positive voltage should exist.**
  - N.G. → CHECK ASCD STEERING SWITCH.
  - O.K. ↓
- **B** Check voltage between control module harness terminals ① and ③ after releasing RESUME/ACCEL switch. **Voltage is 0V.**
  - N.G. → CHECK ASCD STEERING SWITCH.
  - O.K. ↓
- **C** Set vehicle speed at 80 km/h (50 MPH) by turning on SET/COAST switch.
  - O.K. ↓
- **D** While cruising at set speed, depress and release brake pedal.
  - O.K. ↓
- Does speed control disengage and "CRUISE" lamp turn off?
  - No → CHECK STOP LAMP SWITCH, ASCD CANCEL SWITCH AND ASCD CLUTCH PEDAL POSITION SWITCH (M/T models).
  - Yes ↓
- **E** Above 48 km/h (30 MPH), press and release "RESUME/ACCEL switch.
  - O.K. ↓
- Does vehicle return to previously set speed [80 km/h (50 MPH)]?
  - No → Replace control module.
  - Yes ↓
- System is O.K.

NS1109100006000X

Fig. 6 Test 6: RESUME Switch Will Not Operate. Altima

- Does indicator lamp blink when ASCD main switch is turned to "ON" again?
  - Yes → Does indicator lamp blink when brake pedal is depressed slowly?
    - Yes → Adjust stop lamp switch and ASCD cancel switch.
    - No → CHECK ASCD STEERING SWITCH.
      - N.G. → Replace ASCD steering switch.
      - O.K. → Replace control module.
  - No ↓
- CHECK ASCD ACTUATOR/ASCD PUMP.
  - N.G. → Replace ASCD actuator assembly.
  - O.K. ↓

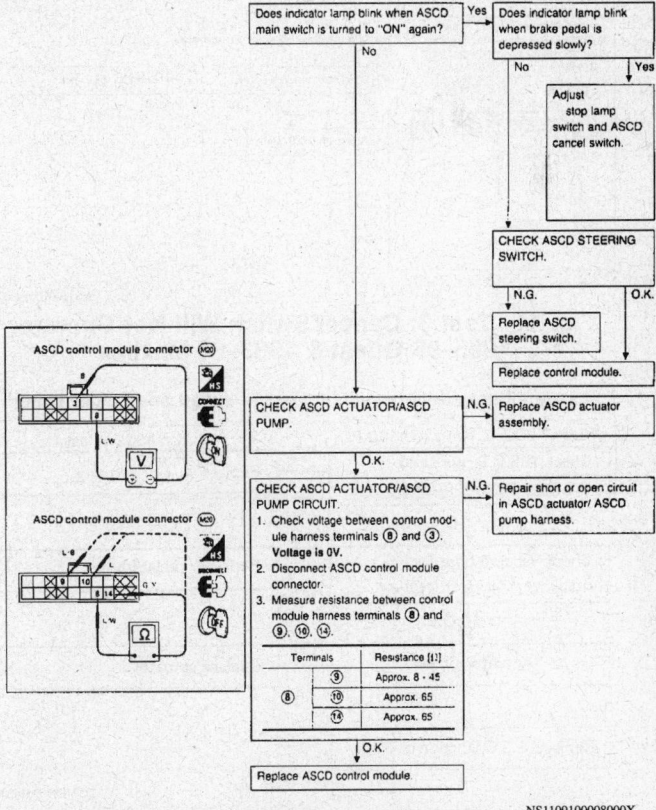

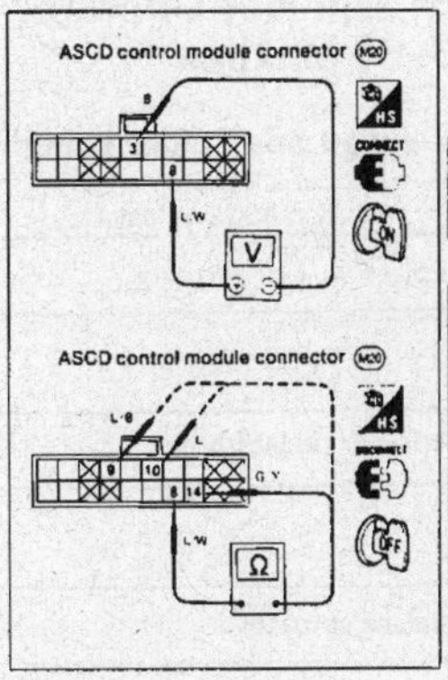
ASCD control module connector (M20)
L/W
ASCD control module connector (M20)
L/B
L
G/Y
L/W

- CHECK ASCD ACTUATOR/ASCD PUMP CIRCUIT.
  1. Check voltage between control module harness terminals ⑧ and ③. **Voltage is 0V.**
  2. Disconnect ASCD control module connector.
  3. Measure resistance between control module harness terminals ⑧ and ⑨, ⑩, ⑭.

Terminals		Resistance [Ω]
⑧	⑨	Approx. 8 - 45
	⑩	Approx. 65
	⑭	Approx. 65

  - N.G. → Repair short or open circuit in ASCD actuator/ ASCD pump harness.
  - O.K. ↓
- Replace ASCD control module.

NS1109100008000X

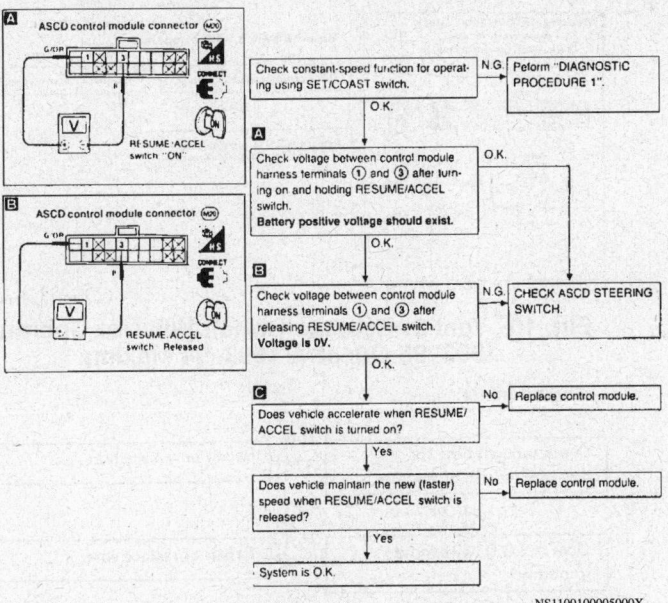

Fig. 8 Test 8: "CRUISE" Indicator Lamp Blinks. Altima

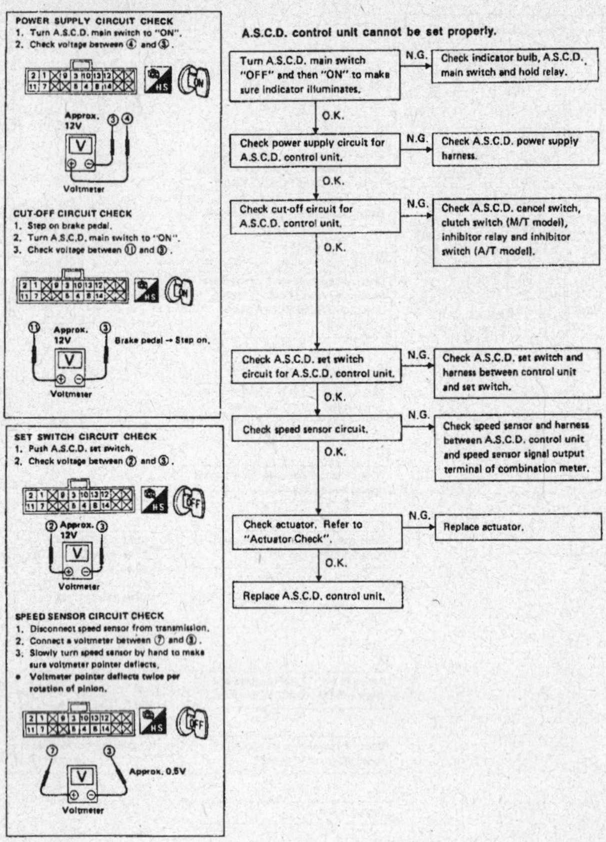
POWER SUPPLY CIRCUIT CHECK
1. Turn A.S.C.D. main switch to "ON".
2. Check voltage between ④ and ⑤.
Approx. 12V
Voltmeter
CUT-OFF CIRCUIT CHECK
1. Step on brake pedal.
2. Turn A.S.C.D. main switch to "ON".
3. Check voltage between ⑪ and ③.
Approx. 12V
Brake pedal → Step on.
Voltmeter
SET SWITCH CIRCUIT CHECK
1. Push A.S.C.D. set switch.
2. Check voltage between ② and ③.
Approx. 12V
Voltmeter
SPEED SENSOR CIRCUIT CHECK
1. Disconnect speed sensor from transmission.
2. Connect a voltmeter between ⑦ and ③.
3. Slowly turn speed sensor by hand to make sure voltmeter pointer deflects.
• Voltmeter pointer deflects twice per rotation of pinion.
Approx. 0.5V
Voltmeter
A.S.C.D. control unit cannot be set properly.
Turn A.S.C.D. main switch "OFF" and then "ON" to make sure indicator illuminates.
N.G.
Check indicator bulb, A.S.C.D. main switch and hold relay.
O.K.
Check power supply circuit for A.S.C.D. control unit.
N.G.
Check A.S.C.D. power supply harness.
O.K.
Check cut-off circuit for A.S.C.D. control unit.
N.G.
Check A.S.C.D. cancel switch, clutch switch (M/T model), inhibitor relay and inhibitor switch (A/T model).
O.K.
Check A.S.C.D. set switch circuit for A.S.C.D. control unit.
N.G.
Check A.S.C.D. set switch and harness between control unit and set switch.
O.K.
Check speed sensor circuit.
N.G.
Check speed sensor and harness between A.S.C.D. control unit and speed sensor signal output terminal of combination meter.
O.K.
Check actuator. Refer to "Actuator Check".
N.G.
Replace actuator.
O.K.
Replace A.S.C.D. control unit.

NS1109100010000X

Fig. 9 Test 1: ASCD Control Unit Cannot Be Set Properly. 1993–95 Quest & 1993–94 Maxima

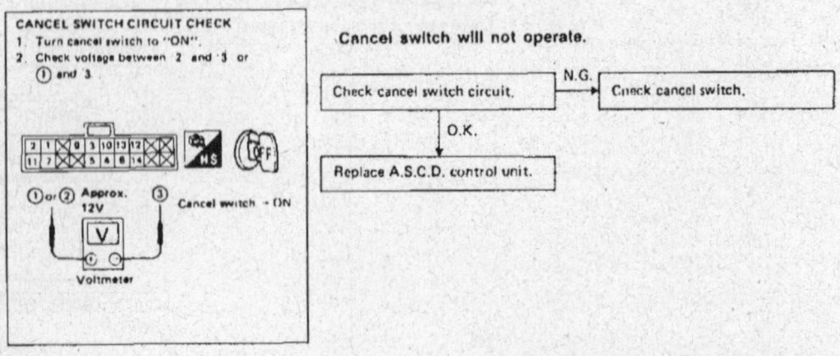
CANCEL SWITCH CIRCUIT CHECK
1. Turn cancel switch to "ON".
2. Check voltage between ② and ③ or ① and ③.
① or ② Approx. 12V ③
Cancel switch → ON
Voltmeter
Cancel switch will not operate.
Check cancel switch circuit.
N.G.
Check cancel switch.
O.K.
Replace A.S.C.D. control unit.

NS1109100012000X

Fig. 11 Test 3: Cancel Switch Will Not Operate. 1993–95 Quest & 1993–94 Maxima

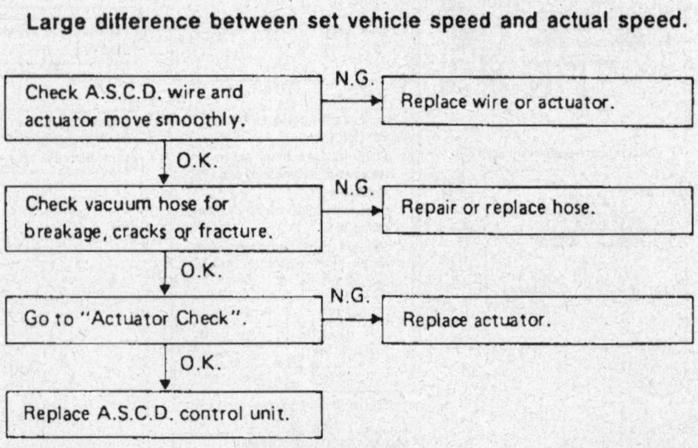
Large difference between set vehicle speed and actual speed.
Check A.S.C.D. wire and actuator move smoothly.
N.G.
Replace wire or actuator.
O.K.
Check vacuum hose for breakage, cracks or fracture.
N.G.
Repair or replace hose.
O.K.
Go to "Actuator Check".
N.G.
Replace actuator.
O.K.
Replace A.S.C.D. control unit.

NS1109100014000X

Fig. 13 Test 5: Large Difference Between Set Vehicle Speed & Actual Speed. 1993–95 Quest & 1993–94 Maxima

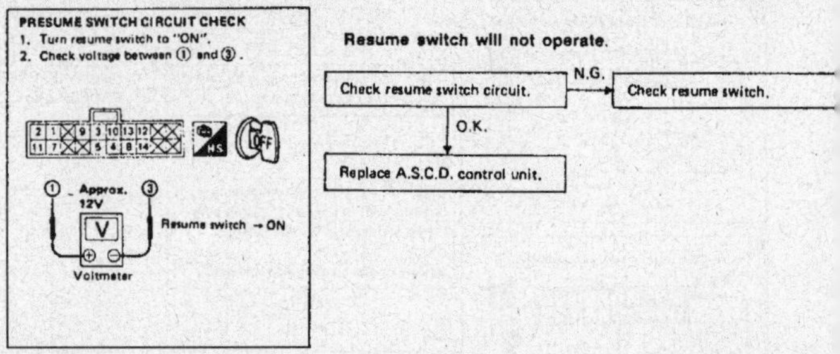
RESUME SWITCH CIRCUIT CHECK
1. Turn resume switch to "ON".
2. Check voltage between ① and ③.
Approx. 12V
Resume switch → ON
Voltmeter
Resume switch will not operate.
Check resume switch circuit.
N.G.
Check resume switch.
O.K.
Replace A.S.C.D. control unit.

NS1109100011000X

Fig. 10 Test 2: Resume Switch Will Not Operate. 1993–95 Quest & 1993–94 Maxima

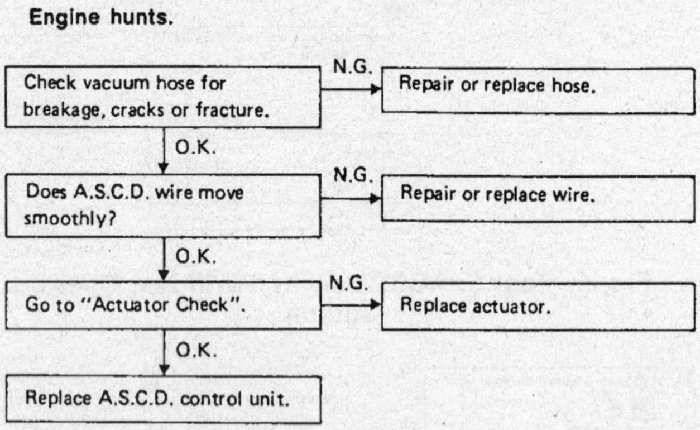
Engine hunts.
Check vacuum hose for breakage, cracks or fracture.
N.G.
Repair or replace hose.
O.K.
Does A.S.C.D. wire move smoothly?
N.G.
Repair or replace wire.
O.K.
Go to "Actuator Check".
N.G.
Replace actuator.
O.K.
Replace A.S.C.D. control unit.

NS1109100013000X

Fig. 12 Test 4: Engine Hunts. 1993–95 Quest & 1993–94 Maxima

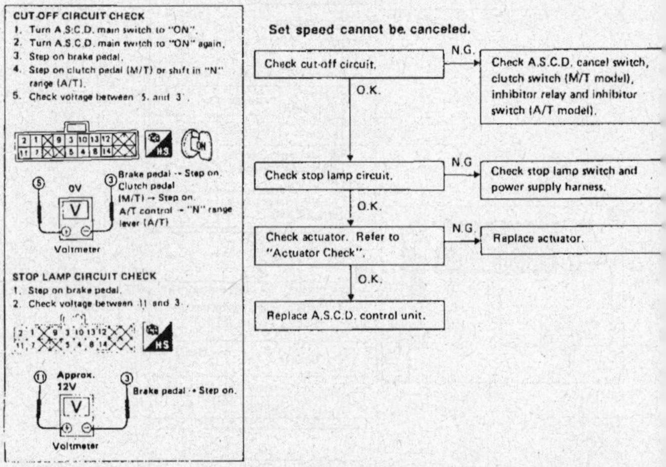
CUT-OFF CIRCUIT CHECK
1. Turn A.S.C.D. main switch to "ON".
2. Turn A.S.C.D. main switch to "ON" again.
3. Step on brake pedal.
4. Step on clutch pedal (M/T) or shift in "N" range (A/T).
5. Check voltage between ⑤ and ③.
0V
Brake pedal → Step on.
Clutch pedal (M/T) → Step on.
A/T control → "N" range lever (A/T)
Voltmeter
STOP LAMP CIRCUIT CHECK
1. Step on brake pedal.
2. Check voltage between ⑪ and ③.
Approx. 12V
Brake pedal → Step on.
Voltmeter
Set speed cannot be canceled.
Check cut-off circuit.
N.G.
Check A.S.C.D. cancel switch, clutch switch (M/T model), inhibitor relay and inhibitor switch (A/T model).
O.K.
Check stop lamp circuit.
N.G.
Check stop lamp switch and power supply harness.
O.K.
Check actuator. Refer to "Actuator Check".
N.G.
Replace actuator.
O.K.
Replace A.S.C.D. control unit.

NS1109100015000X

Fig. 14 Test 6: Set Speed Cannot Be Cancelled. 1993–95 Quest & 1993–94 Maxima

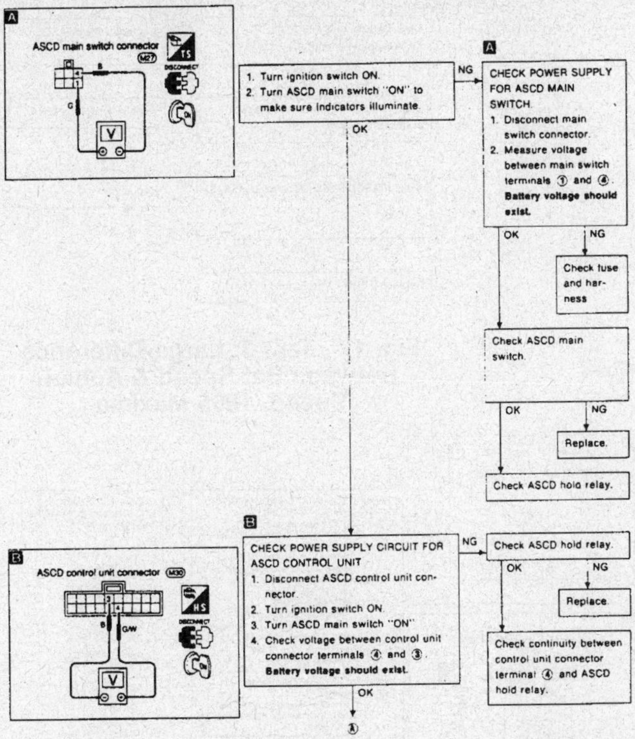
A
ASCD main switch connector (M27)
1. Turn ignition switch ON.
2. Turn ASCD main switch "ON" to make sure indicators illuminate.
NG
OK
A
CHECK POWER SUPPLY FOR ASCD MAIN SWITCH.
1. Disconnect main switch connector.
2. Measure voltage between main switch terminals ① and ④.
Battery voltage should exist.
OK
NG
Check fuse and harness
Check ASCD main switch.
OK
NG
Replace.
Check ASCD hold relay.
B
ASCD control unit connector (M30)
CHECK POWER SUPPLY CIRCUIT FOR ASCD CONTROL UNIT
1. Disconnect ASCD control unit connector.
2. Turn ignition switch ON.
3. Turn ASCD main switch "ON"
4. Check voltage between control unit connector terminals ④ and ③.
Battery voltage should exist.
NG
Check ASCD hold relay.
OK
NG
Replace.
Check continuity between control unit connector terminal ④ and ASCD hold relay.
OK
Ⓐ
NS1109500069010X

Fig. 15 Test 1: Speed Control Cannot Be Set (Part 1 of 4). 1995 Maxima

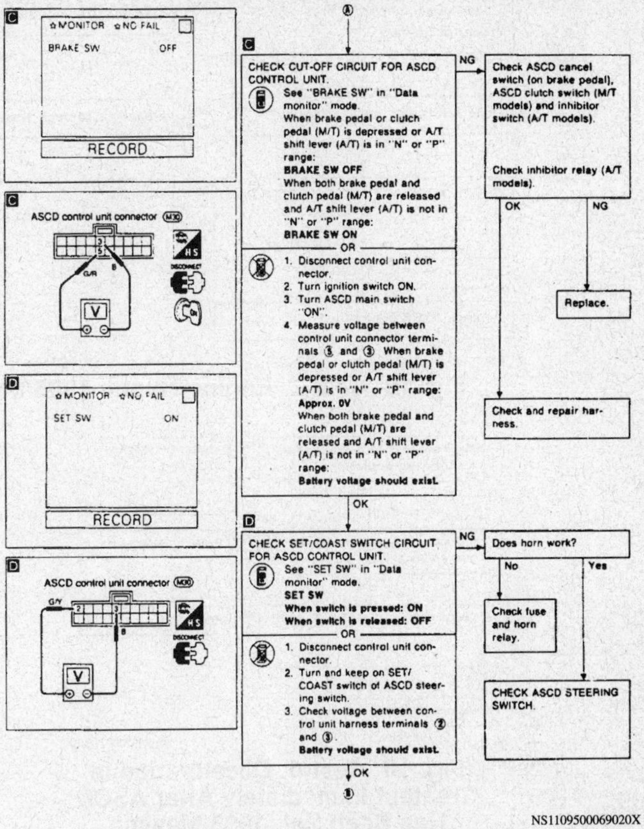
C
MONITOR NO FAIL
BRAKE SW OFF
RECORD
Ⓐ
C
CHECK CUT-OFF CIRCUIT FOR ASCD CONTROL UNIT.
See "BRAKE SW" in "Data monitor" mode.
When brake pedal or clutch pedal (M/T) is depressed or A/T shift lever (A/T) is in "N" or "P" range:
BRAKE SW OFF
When both brake pedal and clutch pedal (M/T) are released and A/T shift lever (A/T) is not in "N" or "P" range:
BRAKE SW ON
OR
1. Disconnect control unit connector.
2. Turn ignition switch ON.
3. Turn ASCD main switch "ON".
4. Measure voltage between control unit connector terminals ⑤ and ③. When brake pedal or clutch pedal (M/T) is depressed or A/T shift lever (A/T) is in "N" or "P" range:
Approx. 0V
When both brake pedal and clutch pedal (M/T) are released and A/T shift lever (A/T) is not in "N" or "P" range:
Battery voltage should exist.
NG
Check ASCD cancel switch (on brake pedal), ASCD clutch switch (M/T models) and inhibitor switch (A/T models).
Check inhibitor relay (A/T models).
OK
NG
Replace.
Check and repair harness.
C
ASCD control unit connector (M30)
D
MONITOR NO FAIL
SET SW ON
RECORD
OK
D
CHECK SET/COAST SWITCH CIRCUIT FOR ASCD CONTROL UNIT.
See "SET SW" in "Data monitor" mode.
SET SW
When switch is pressed: ON
When switch is released: OFF
OR
1. Disconnect control unit connector.
2. Turn and keep on SET/COAST switch of ASCD steering switch.
3. Check voltage between control unit harness terminals ② and ③.
Battery voltage should exist.
NG
Does horn work?
No
Yes
Check fuse and horn relay.
CHECK ASCD STEERING SWITCH.
D
ASCD control unit connector (M30)
OK
Ⓑ
NS1109500069020X

Fig. 15 Test 1: Speed Control Cannot Be Set (Part 2 of 4). 1995 Maxima

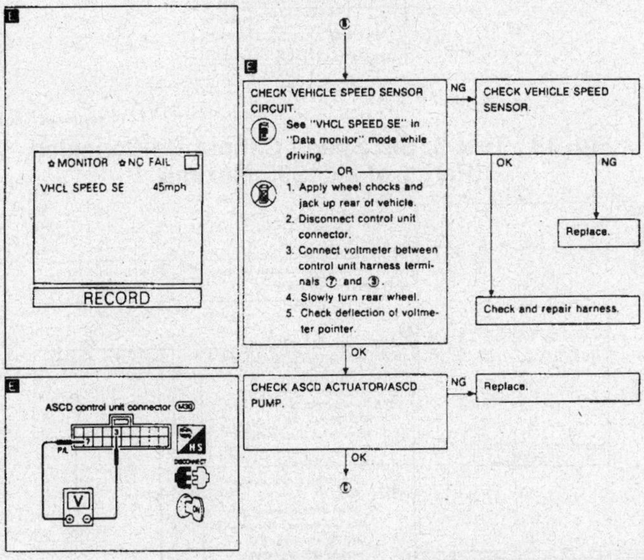
E
MONITOR NO FAIL
VHCL SPEED SE 45mph
RECORD
Ⓑ
E
CHECK VEHICLE SPEED SENSOR CIRCUIT.
See "VHCL SPEED SE" in "Data monitor" mode while driving.
OR
1. Apply wheel chocks and jack up rear of vehicle.
2. Disconnect control unit connector.
3. Connect voltmeter between control unit harness terminals ⑦ and ③.
4. Slowly turn rear wheel.
5. Check deflection of voltmeter pointer.
NG
CHECK VEHICLE SPEED SENSOR.
OK
NG
Replace.
Check and repair harness.
OK
CHECK ASCD ACTUATOR/ASCD PUMP.
NG
Replace.
OK
Ⓒ
E
ASCD control unit connector (M30)
NS1109500069030X

Fig. 15 Test 1: Speed Control Cannot Be Set (Part 3 of 4). 1995 Maxima

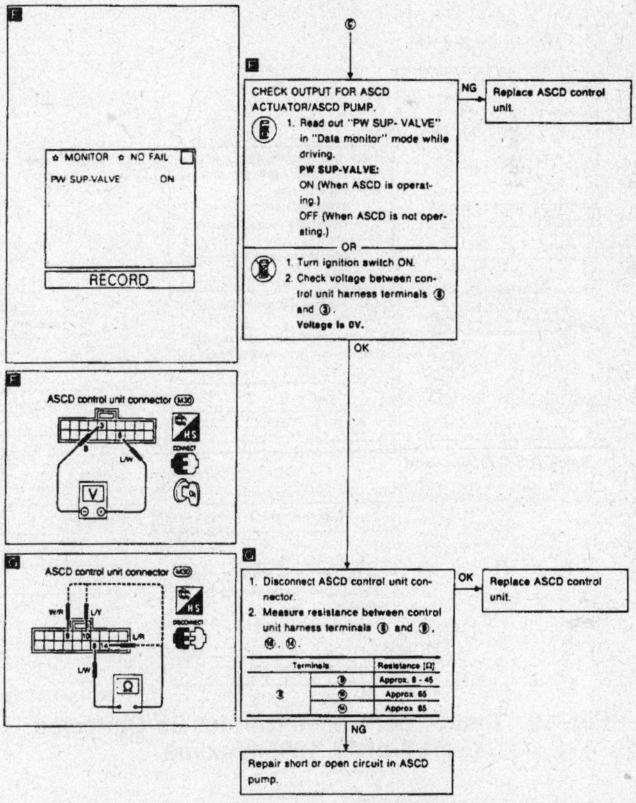
F
MONITOR NO FAIL
PW SUP-VALVE ON
RECORD
Ⓒ
F
CHECK OUTPUT FOR ASCD ACTUATOR/ASCD PUMP.
1. Read out "PW SUP-VALVE" in "Data monitor" mode while driving.
PW SUP-VALVE:
ON (When ASCD is operating.)
OFF (When ASCD is not operating.)
OR
1. Turn ignition switch ON.
2. Check voltage between control unit harness terminals ⑧ and ③.
Voltage is 0V.
NG
Replace ASCD control unit.
OK
F
ASCD control unit connector (M30)
G
ASCD control unit connector (M30)
G
1. Disconnect ASCD control unit connector.
2. Measure resistance between control unit harness terminals ③ and ⑨, ⑩, ⑭.
Terminals
Resistance [Ω]
③ ⑨ Approx. 8 - 45
⑩ Approx. 65
⑭ Approx. 65
OK
Replace ASCD control unit.
NG
Repair short or open circuit in ASCD pump.
NS1109500069040X

Fig. 15 Test 1: Speed Control Cannot Be Set (Part 4 of 4). 1995 Maxima

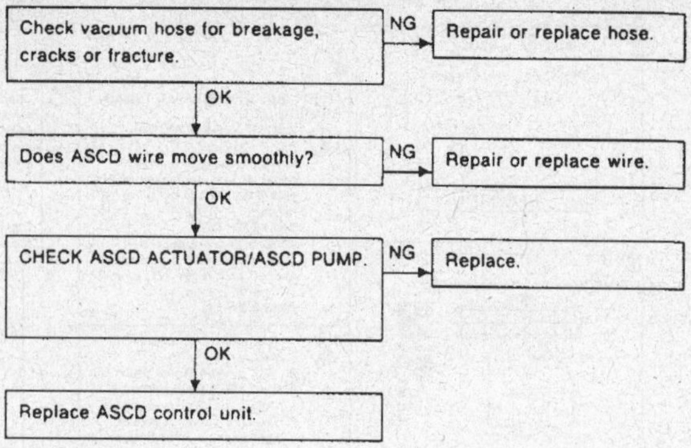

Check vacuum hose for breakage, cracks or fracture.
NG
Repair or replace hose.
OK
Does ASCD wire move smoothly?
NG
Repair or replace wire.
OK
CHECK ASCD ACTUATOR/ASCD PUMP.
NG
Replace.
OK
Replace ASCD control unit.

NS1109500070000X

Fig. 16 Test 2: Engine Hunts. 1995 Maxima

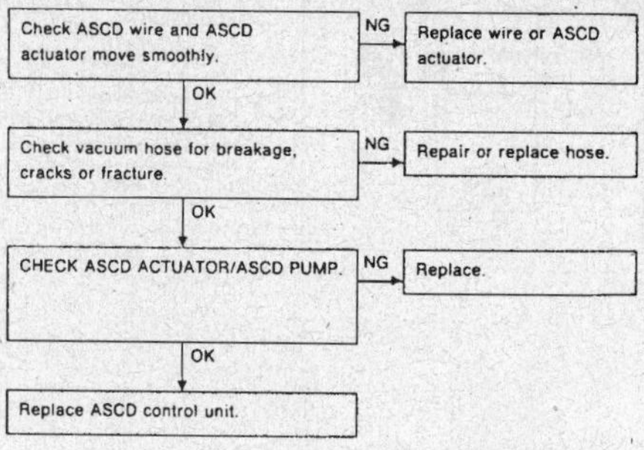

Check ASCD wire and ASCD actuator move smoothly.
NG
Replace wire or ASCD actuator.
OK
Check vacuum hose for breakage, cracks or fracture.
NG
Repair or replace hose.
OK
CHECK ASCD ACTUATOR/ASCD PUMP.
NG
Replace.
OK
Replace ASCD control unit.

NS1109500071000X

Fig. 17 Test 3: Large Difference Between Set Speed & Actual Speed. 1995 Maxima

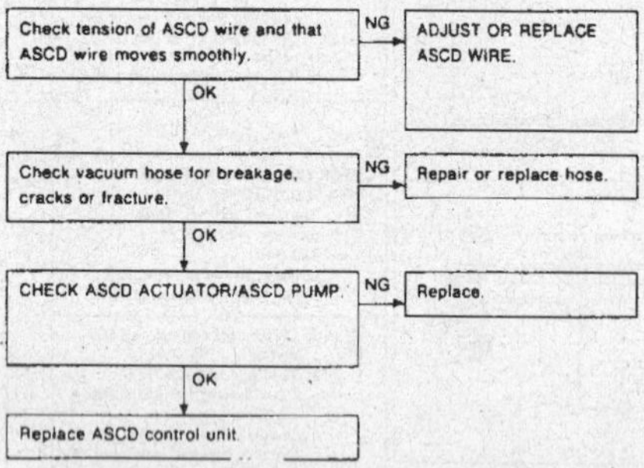

Check tension of ASCD wire and that ASCD wire moves smoothly.
NG
ADJUST OR REPLACE ASCD WIRE.
OK
Check vacuum hose for breakage, cracks or fracture.
NG
Repair or replace hose.
OK
CHECK ASCD ACTUATOR/ASCD PUMP.
NG
Replace.
OK
Replace ASCD control unit.

NS1109500072000X

Fig. 18 Test 4: Deceleration Is Greatest Immediately After ASCD Has Been Set. 1995 Maxima

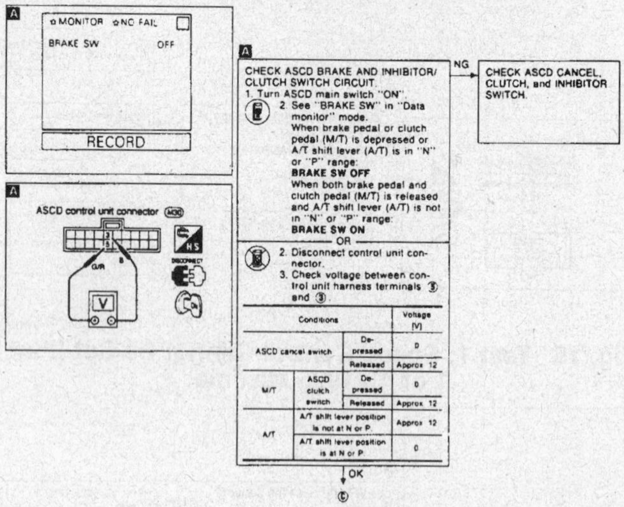

A
MONITOR NO FAIL
BRAKE SW OFF
RECORD
A
ASCD control unit connector
A
CHECK ASCD BRAKE AND INHIBITOR/CLUTCH SWITCH CIRCUIT.
1. Turn ASCD main switch "ON".
2. See "BRAKE SW" in "Data monitor" mode.
When brake pedal or clutch pedal (M/T) is depressed or A/T shift lever (A/T) is in "N" or "P" range:
BRAKE SW OFF
When both brake pedal and clutch pedal (M/T) is released and A/T shift lever (A/T) is not in "N" or "P" range:
BRAKE SW ON
OR
2. Disconnect control unit connector.
3. Check voltage between control unit harness terminals ⑤ and ③.
Conditions
Voltage [V]
ASCD cancel switch
Depressed
0
Released
Approx 12
M/T
ASCD clutch switch
Depressed
0
Released
Approx 12
A/T
A/T shift lever position is not at N or P.
Approx 12
A/T shift lever position is at N or P.
0
NG
CHECK ASCD CANCEL, CLUTCH, and INHIBITOR SWITCH.
OK
C

NS1109500073010X

Fig. 19 Test 5: Set Speed Cannot Be Canceled (Part 1 of 2). 1995 Maxima

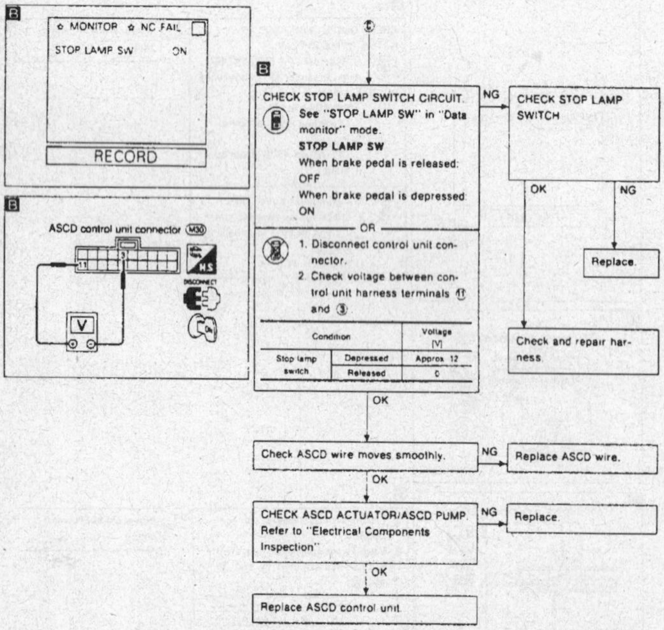

B
MONITOR NO FAIL
STOP LAMP SW ON
RECORD
B
ASCD control unit connector
C
B
CHECK STOP LAMP SWITCH CIRCUIT.
See "STOP LAMP SW" in "Data monitor" mode.
STOP LAMP SW
When brake pedal is released: OFF
When brake pedal is depressed: ON
OR
1. Disconnect control unit connector.
2. Check voltage between control unit harness terminals ⑪ and ③.
Condition
Voltage [V]
Stop lamp switch
Depressed
Approx. 12
Released
0
NG
CHECK STOP LAMP SWITCH
OK
NG
Replace.
Check and repair harness.
OK
Check ASCD wire moves smoothly.
NG
Replace ASCD wire.
OK
CHECK ASCD ACTUATOR/ASCD PUMP.
Refer to "Electrical Components Inspection"
NG
Replace.
OK
Replace ASCD control unit.

NS1109500073020X

Fig. 19 Test 5: Set Speed Cannot Be Canceled (Part 2 of 2). 1995 Maxima

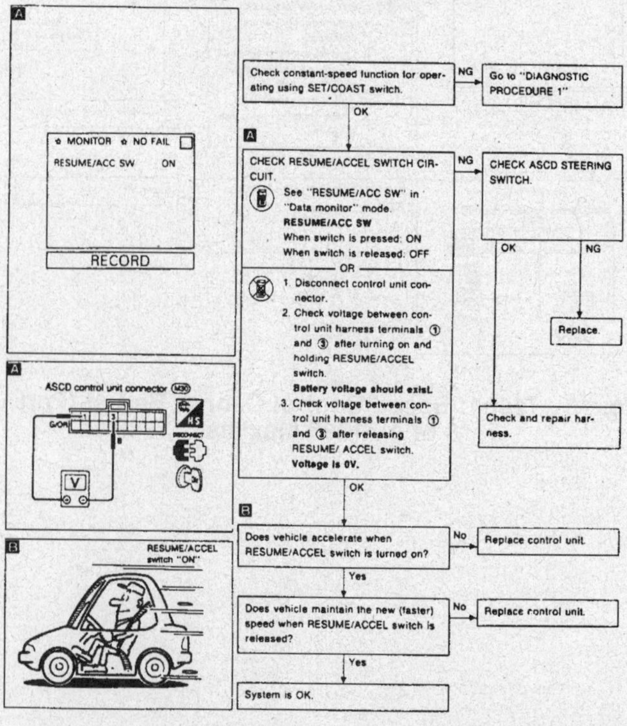

A
MONITOR NO FAIL
RESUME/ACC SW ON
RECORD
A
ASCD control unit connector
B
RESUME/ACCEL switch "ON"
Check constant-speed function for operating using SET/COAST switch.
NG
Go to "DIAGNOSTIC PROCEDURE 1"
OK
A
CHECK RESUME/ACCEL SWITCH CIRCUIT.
See "RESUME/ACC SW" in "Data monitor" mode.
RESUME/ACC SW
When switch is pressed: ON
When switch is released: OFF
OR
1. Disconnect control unit connector.
2. Check voltage between control unit harness terminals ① and ③ after turning on and holding RESUME/ACCEL switch.
Battery voltage should exist.
3. Check voltage between control unit harness terminals ① and ③ after releasing RESUME/ ACCEL switch.
Voltage is 0V.
NG
CHECK ASCD STEERING SWITCH.
OK
NG
Replace.
Check and repair harness.
OK
B
Does vehicle accelerate when RESUME/ACCEL switch is turned on?
No
Replace control unit.
Yes
Does vehicle maintain the new (faster) speed when RESUME/ACCEL switch is released?
No
Replace control unit.
Yes
System is OK.

NS1109500074000X

Fig. 20 Test 6: ACCEL Switch Will Not Operate. 1995 Maxima

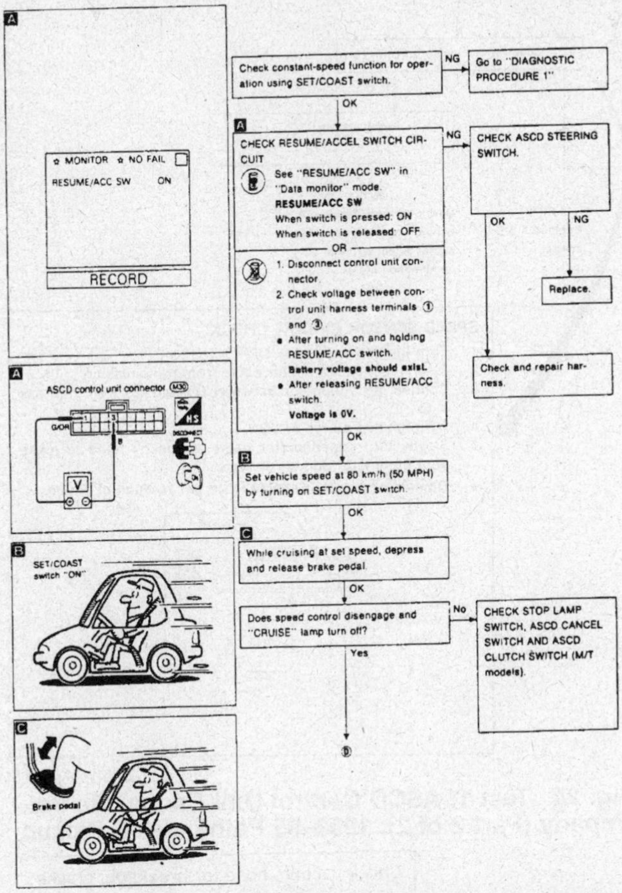

A
☆ MONITOR ☆ NO FAIL
RESUME/ACC SW ON
RECORD
A
ASCD control unit connector M30
G/OR
B
V
DISCONNECT
B
SET/COAST switch "ON"
C
Brake pedal
Check constant-speed function for operation using SET/COAST switch.
NG
Go to "DIAGNOSTIC PROCEDURE 1"
OK
A
CHECK RESUME/ACCEL SWITCH CIRCUIT
See "RESUME/ACC SW" in "Data monitor" mode.
RESUME/ACC SW
When switch is pressed: ON
When switch is released: OFF
OR
1. Disconnect control unit connector.
2. Check voltage between control unit harness terminals ① and ③.
• After turning on and holding RESUME/ACC switch.
Battery voltage should exist.
• After releasing RESUME/ACC switch.
Voltage is 0V.
NG
CHECK ASCD STEERING SWITCH.
OK
NG
Replace.
Check and repair harness.
OK
B
Set vehicle speed at 80 km/h (50 MPH) by turning on SET/COAST switch.
OK
C
While cruising at set speed, depress and release brake pedal.
OK
Does speed control disengage and "CRUISE" lamp turn off?
No
CHECK STOP LAMP SWITCH, ASCD CANCEL SWITCH AND ASCD CLUTCH SWITCH (M/T models).
Yes
D

NS1109500075010X

Fig. 21 Test 7: RESUME Switch Will Not Operate (Part 1 of 2). 1995 Maxima

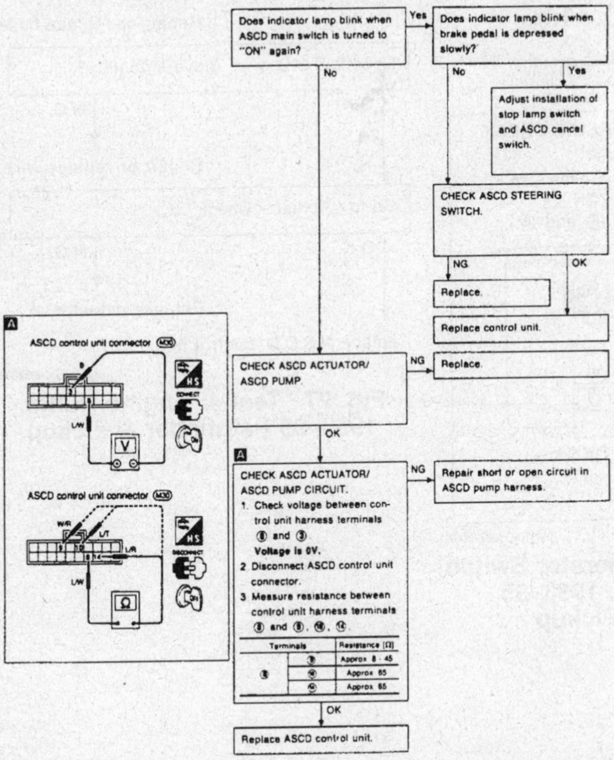

Does indicator lamp blink when ASCD main switch is turned to "ON" again?
Yes
Does indicator lamp blink when brake pedal is depressed slowly?
No
Yes
Adjust installation of stop lamp switch and ASCD cancel switch.
CHECK ASCD STEERING SWITCH.
NG
OK
Replace.
Replace control unit.
No
A
ASCD control unit connector M30
L/W
V
CONNECT
ASCD control unit connector M30
W/R
L/T
L/R
L/W
Ω
DISCONNECT
CHECK ASCD ACTUATOR/ ASCD PUMP.
NG
Replace.
OK
A
CHECK ASCD ACTUATOR/ ASCD PUMP CIRCUIT.
1. Check voltage between control unit harness terminals ⑧ and ③.
Voltage is 0V.
2 Disconnect ASCD control unit connector.
3 Measure resistance between control unit harness terminals ⑧ and ⑨, ⑩, ⑭.
Terminals | Resistance (Ω)
⑧ ⑨ Approx 8 - 45
⑩ Approx 65
⑭ Approx 65
NG
Repair short or open circuit in ASCD pump harness.
OK
Replace ASCD control unit.

NS1109500076000X

Fig. 22 Test 8: Cruise Indicator Lamp Blinks. 1995 Maxima

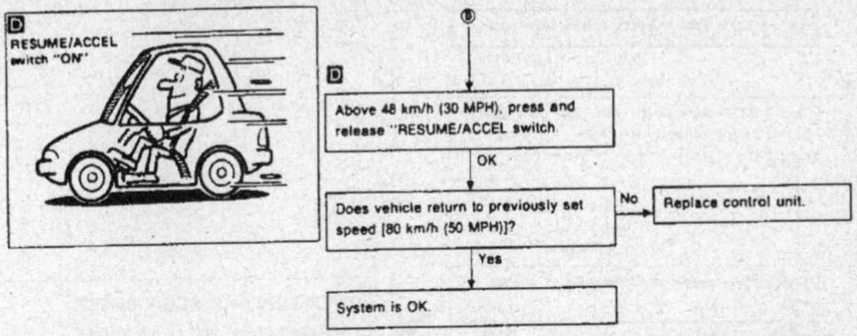

D
RESUME/ACCEL switch "ON"
D
D
Above 48 km/h (30 MPH), press and release "RESUME/ACCEL switch.
OK
Does vehicle return to previously set speed [80 km/h (50 MPH)]?
No
Replace control unit.
Yes
System is OK.

NS1109500075020X

Fig. 21 Test 7: RESUME Switch Will Not Operate (Part 2 of 2). 1995 Maxima

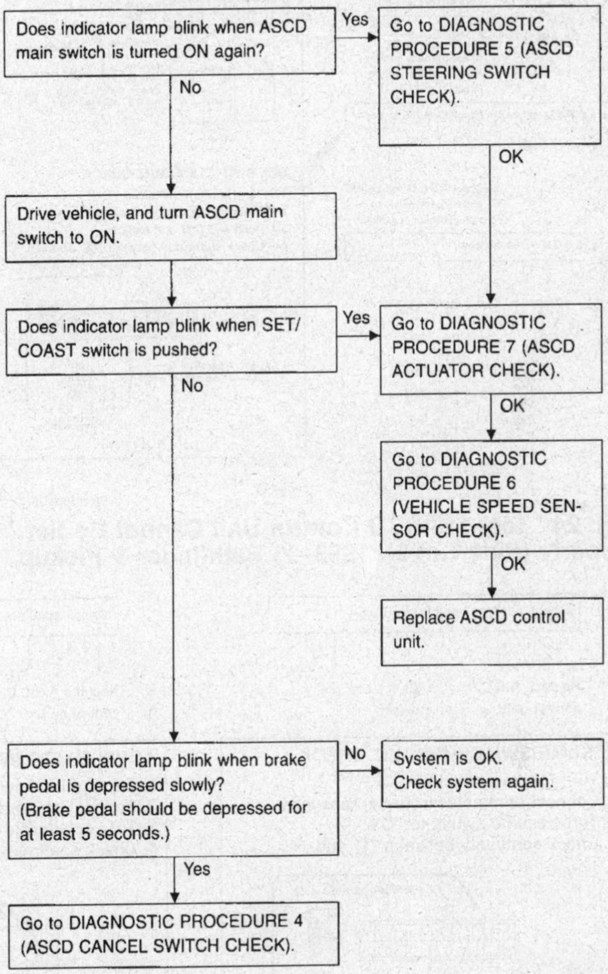

Does indicator lamp blink when ASCD main switch is turned ON again?
Yes
Go to DIAGNOSTIC PROCEDURE 5 (ASCD STEERING SWITCH CHECK).
No
OK
Drive vehicle, and turn ASCD main switch to ON.
Does indicator lamp blink when SET/ COAST switch is pushed?
Yes
Go to DIAGNOSTIC PROCEDURE 7 (ASCD ACTUATOR CHECK).
No
OK
Go to DIAGNOSTIC PROCEDURE 6 (VEHICLE SPEED SENSOR CHECK).
OK
Replace ASCD control unit.
Does indicator lamp blink when brake pedal is depressed slowly? (Brake pedal should be depressed for at least 5 seconds.)
No
System is OK. Check system again.
Yes
Go to DIAGNOSTIC PROCEDURE 4 (ASCD CANCEL SWITCH CHECK).

NS1109600122000X

Fig. 23 Fail-Safe System Check. 1996 Maxima & Quest

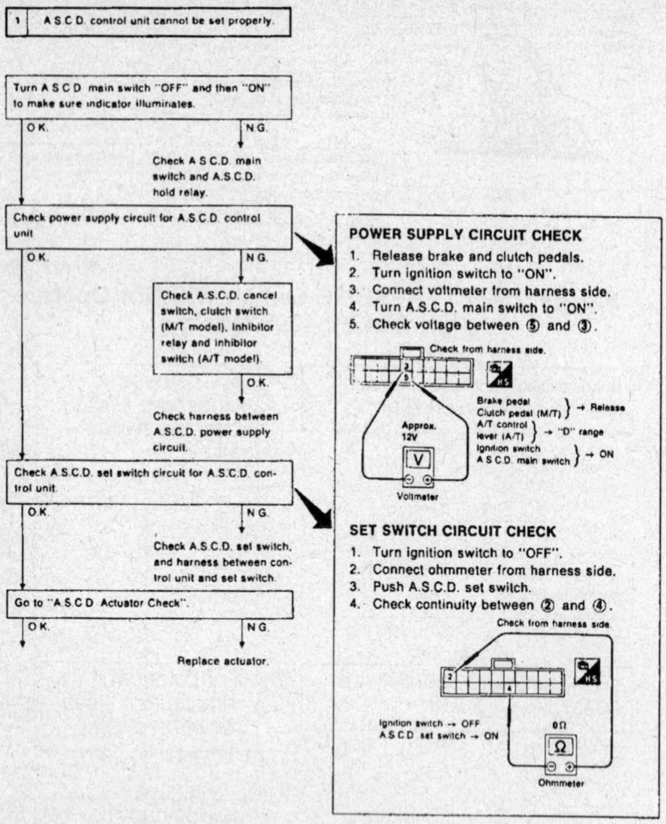
1 A.S.C.D. control unit cannot be set properly.
Turn A.S.C.D. main switch "OFF" and then "ON" to make sure indicator illuminates.
O.K.
N.G.
Check A.S.C.D. main switch and A.S.C.D. hold relay.
Check power supply circuit for A.S.C.D. control unit
O.K.
N.G.
Check A.S.C.D. cancel switch, clutch switch (M/T model), inhibitor relay and inhibitor switch (A/T model).
O.K.
Check harness between A.S.C.D. power supply circuit.
Check A.S.C.D. set switch circuit for A.S.C.D. control unit.
O.K.
N.G.
Check A.S.C.D. set switch, and harness between control unit and set switch.
Go to "A.S.C.D. Actuator Check".
O.K.
N.G.
Replace actuator.
POWER SUPPLY CIRCUIT CHECK
1. Release brake and clutch pedals.
2. Turn ignition switch to "ON".
3. Connect voltmeter from harness side.
4. Turn A.S.C.D. main switch to "ON".
5. Check voltage between ⑤ and ③.
Check from harness side.
HS
Brake pedal
Clutch pedal (M/T) → Release
A/T control lever (A/T) → "D" range
Ignition switch
A.S.C.D. main switch → ON
Approx. 12V
V
Voltmeter
SET SWITCH CIRCUIT CHECK
1. Turn ignition switch to "OFF".
2. Connect ohmmeter from harness side.
3. Push A.S.C.D. set switch.
4. Check continuity between ② and ④.
Check from harness side.
HS
Ignition switch → OFF
A.S.C.D. set switch → ON
0Ω
Ω
Ohmmeter

NS1109300022010X

Fig. 24 Test 1: ASCD Control Unit Cannot Be Set Properly (Part 1 of 2). 1993–95 Pathfinder & Pickup

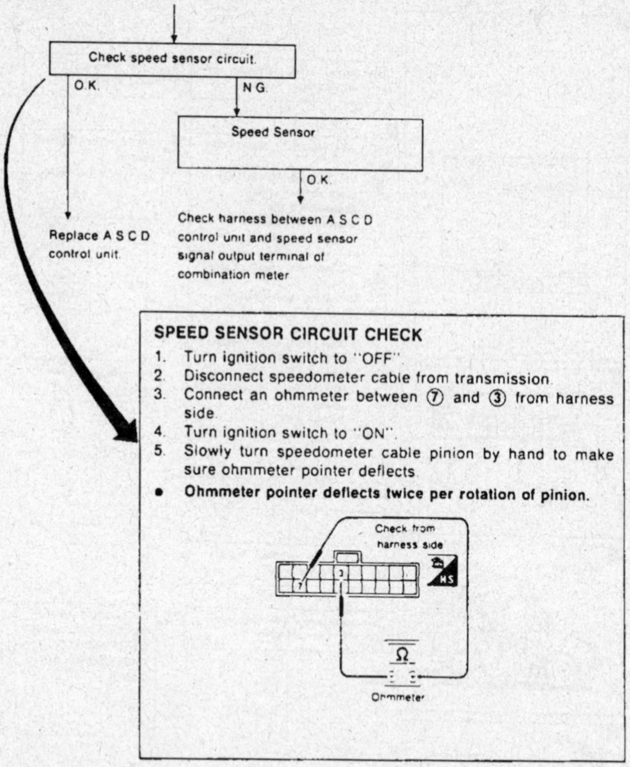
Check speed sensor circuit.
O.K.
N.G.
Speed Sensor
O.K.
Replace A.S.C.D. control unit.
Check harness between A.S.C.D. control unit and speed sensor signal output terminal of combination meter
SPEED SENSOR CIRCUIT CHECK
1. Turn ignition switch to "OFF".
2. Disconnect speedometer cable from transmission.
3. Connect an ohmmeter between ⑦ and ③ from harness side.
4. Turn ignition switch to "ON".
5. Slowly turn speedometer cable pinion by hand to make sure ohmmeter pointer deflects.
• Ohmmeter pointer deflects twice per rotation of pinion.
Check from harness side
HS
Ω
Ohmmeter

NS1109300022020X

Fig. 24 Test 1: ASCD Control Unit Cannot Be Set Properly (Part 2 of 2). 1993–95 Pathfinder & Pickup

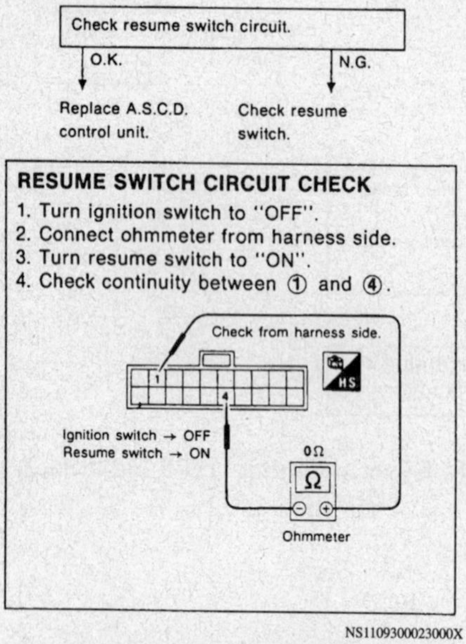
Check resume switch circuit.
O.K.
N.G.
Replace A.S.C.D. control unit.
Check resume switch.
RESUME SWITCH CIRCUIT CHECK
1. Turn ignition switch to "OFF".
2. Connect ohmmeter from harness side.
3. Turn resume switch to "ON".
4. Check continuity between ① and ④.
Check from harness side.
HS
Ignition switch → OFF
Resume switch → ON
0Ω
Ω
Ohmmeter

NS1109300023000X

Fig. 25 Test 2: RESUME Switch Will Not Operate. 1993–95 Pathfinder & Pickup

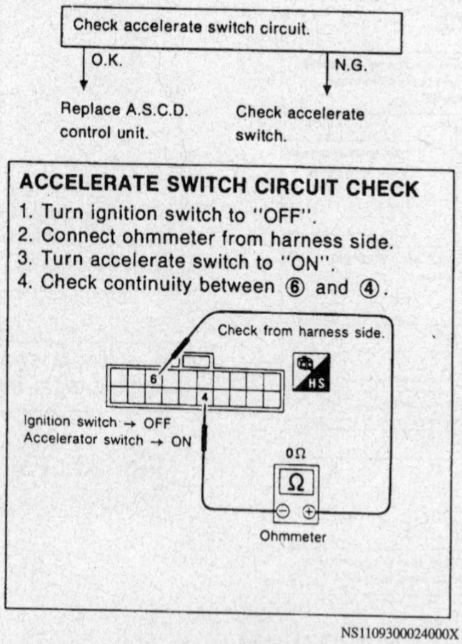
Check accelerate switch circuit.
O.K.
N.G.
Replace A.S.C.D. control unit.
Check accelerate switch.
ACCELERATE SWITCH CIRCUIT CHECK
1. Turn ignition switch to "OFF".
2. Connect ohmmeter from harness side.
3. Turn accelerate switch to "ON".
4. Check continuity between ⑥ and ④.
Check from harness side.
HS
Ignition switch → OFF
Accelerator switch → ON
0Ω
Ω
Ohmmeter

NS1109300024000X

Fig. 26 Test 3: Accelerator Switch Will Not Operate. 1993–95 Pathfinder & Pickup

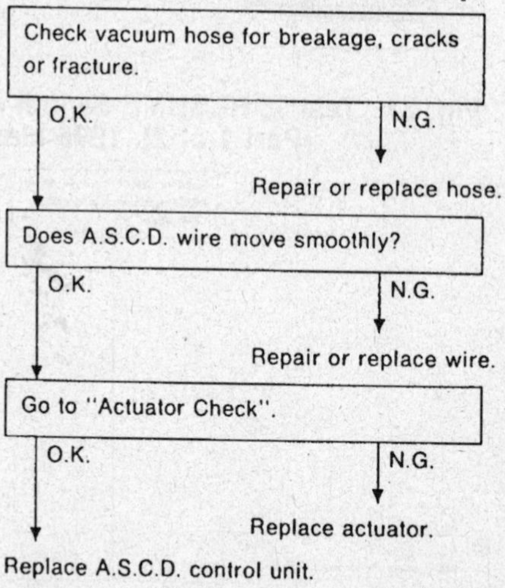
Check vacuum hose for breakage, cracks or fracture.
O.K.
N.G.
Repair or replace hose.
Does A.S.C.D. wire move smoothly?
O.K.
N.G.
Repair or replace wire.
Go to "Actuator Check".
O.K.
N.G.
Replace actuator.
Replace A.S.C.D. control unit.

NS1109300025000X

Fig. 27 Test 4: Engine Hunts. 1993–95 Pathfinder & Pickup

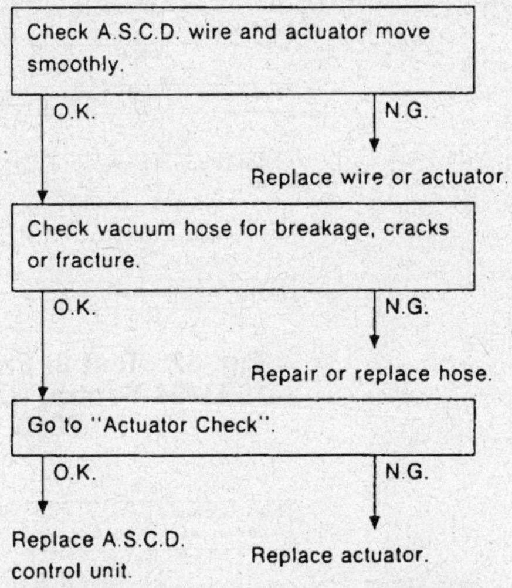

Check A.S.C.D. wire and actuator move smoothly.
O.K.
N.G.
Replace wire or actuator.
Check vacuum hose for breakage, cracks or fracture.
O.K.
N.G.
Repair or replace hose.
Go to "Actuator Check".
O.K.
N.G.
Replace A.S.C.D. control unit.
Replace actuator.

NS1109300026000X

Fig. 28 Test 5: Large Difference Between Set Vehicle Speed & Actual Speed. 1993–95 Pathfinder & Pickup

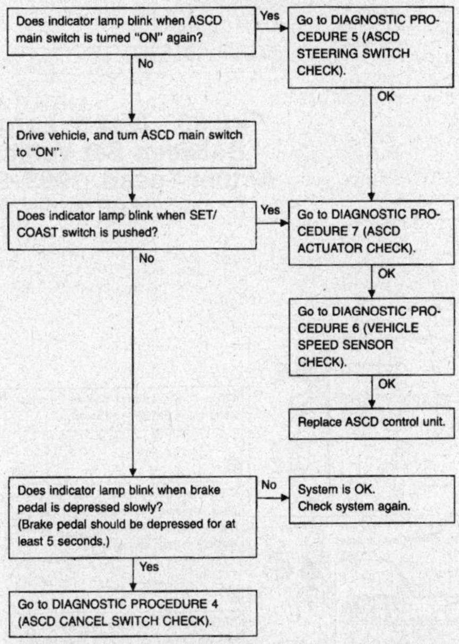

Does indicator lamp blink when ASCD main switch is turned "ON" again?
Yes
Go to DIAGNOSTIC PROCEDURE 5 (ASCD STEERING SWITCH CHECK).
No
OK
Drive vehicle, and turn ASCD main switch to "ON".
Does indicator lamp blink when SET/COAST switch is pushed?
Yes
Go to DIAGNOSTIC PROCEDURE 7 (ASCD ACTUATOR CHECK).
No
OK
Go to DIAGNOSTIC PROCEDURE 6 (VEHICLE SPEED SENSOR CHECK).
OK
Replace ASCD control unit.
Does indicator lamp blink when brake pedal is depressed slowly? (Brake pedal should be depressed for at least 5 seconds.)
No
System is OK. Check system again.
Yes
Go to DIAGNOSTIC PROCEDURE 4 (ASCD CANCEL SWITCH CHECK).

NS1109600123000X

Fig. 30 Fail-Safe System Check. 1996 Pathfinder & Pickup

6	A/T model only	• When A S C D is set while vehicle is operating in "O.D." range, O.D. will be cancelled and shifting to O D cannot be made thereafter • O D will not be cancelled even if actual vehicle speed is 6 km/h (4 MPH) lower than set speed (Set speed cannot be maintained) • O D will not be cancelled even if accelerator switch is turned "ON".

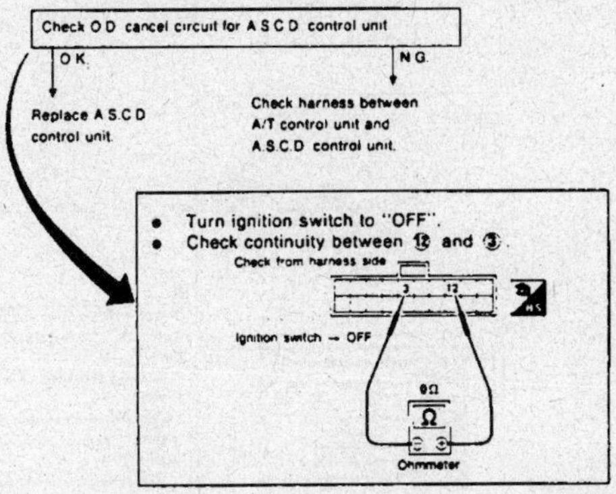

Check O D cancel circuit for A S C D control unit
O K.
N G.
Replace A S.C D control unit.
Check harness between A/T control unit and A.S.C.D control unit.
• Turn ignition switch to "OFF".
• Check continuity between ⑫ and ③.
Check from harness side
Ignition switch → OFF
0Ω
Ohmmeter

NS1109300027000X

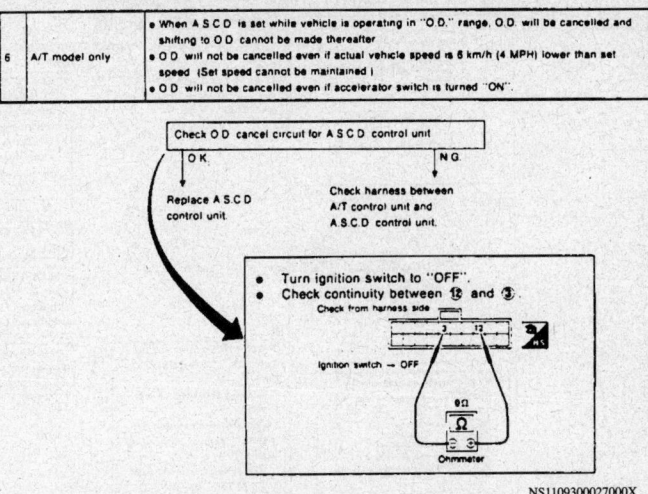

Fig. 29 Test 6: OD Cancel Circuit Check. 1993–95 Pathfinder & Pickup

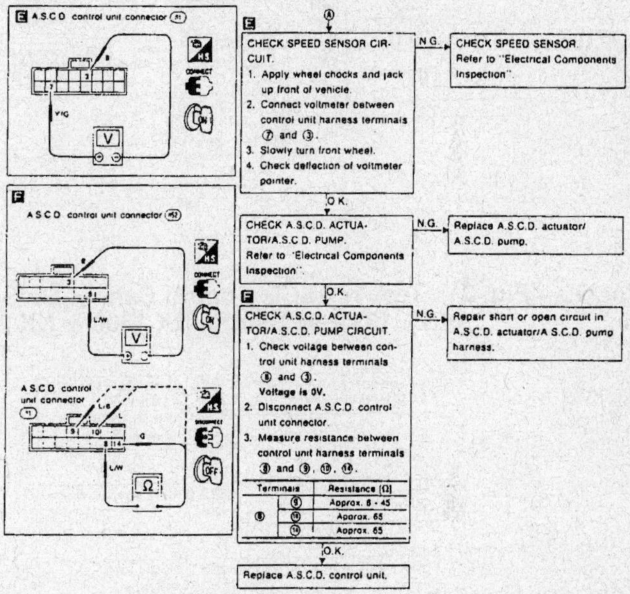

A.S.C.D. control unit connector
CHECK SPEED SENSOR CIRCUIT.
1. Apply wheel chocks and jack up front of vehicle.
2. Connect voltmeter between control unit harness terminals ⑦ and ③.
3. Slowly turn front wheel.
4. Check deflection of voltmeter pointer.
N.G.
CHECK SPEED SENSOR. Refer to "Electrical Components Inspection".
O.K.
CHECK A.S.C.D. ACTUATOR/A.S.C D. PUMP. Refer to "Electrical Components Inspection".
N.G.
Replace A.S.C.D. actuator/A.S.C.D. pump.
O.K.
CHECK A.S.C.D. ACTUATOR/A.S.C.D. PUMP CIRCUIT.
1. Check voltage between control unit harness terminals ⑧ and ③. Voltage is 0V.
2. Disconnect A.S.C.D. control unit connector.
3. Measure resistance between control unit harness terminals ⑧ and ⑨, ⑩, ⑭.
Terminals | Resistance [Ω]
⑧ ⑨ Approx. 8 - 45
⑩ Approx. 65
⑭ Approx. 65
N.G.
Repair short or open circuit in A.S.C.D. actuator/A S.C.D. pump harness.
O.K.
Replace A.S.C.D. control unit.

NS1109100028010X

Fig. 31 Test 1: ASCD Control Cannot Be Set (Part 1 of 2). 1993–94 Sentra, NX 1600 & NX 2000

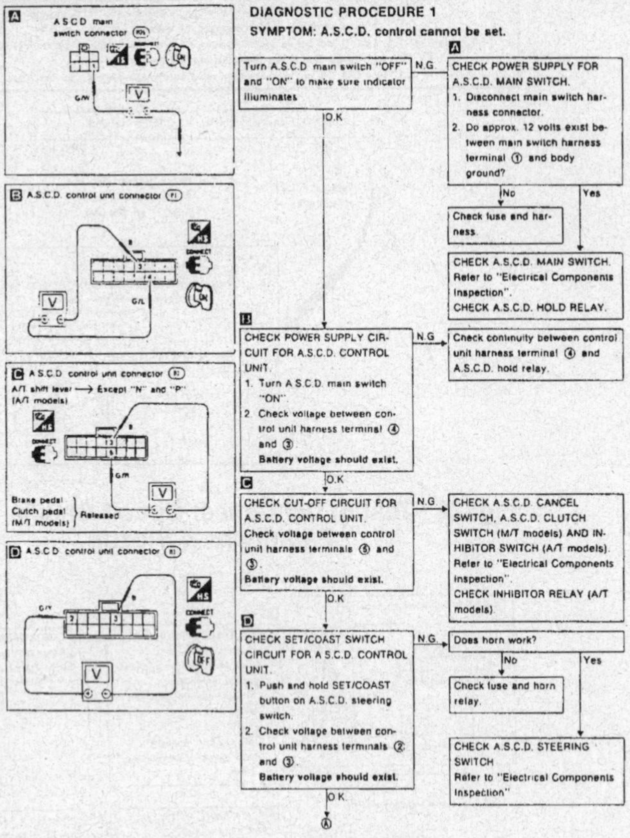
A
A.S.C.D. main switch connector
G/W
B A.S.C.D. control unit connector
G/L
C A.S.C.D. control unit connector
A/T shift lever → Except "N" and "P" (A/T models)
G/M
Brake pedal
Clutch pedal (M/T models)
Released
D A.S.C.D. control unit connector
G/Y
DIAGNOSTIC PROCEDURE 1
SYMPTOM: A.S.C.D. control cannot be set.
Turn A.S.C.D. main switch "OFF" and "ON" to make sure indicator illuminates.
N.G.
CHECK POWER SUPPLY FOR A.S.C.D. MAIN SWITCH.
1. Disconnect main switch harness connector.
2. Do approx. 12 volts exist between main switch harness terminal ① and body ground?
No
Yes
Check fuse and harness.
CHECK A.S.C.D. MAIN SWITCH. Refer to "Electrical Components Inspection".
CHECK A.S.C.D. HOLD RELAY.
O.K.
B
CHECK POWER SUPPLY CIRCUIT FOR A.S.C.D. CONTROL UNIT.
1. Turn A.S.C.D. main switch "ON".
2. Check voltage between control unit harness terminal ④ and ③.
Battery voltage should exist.
N.G.
Check continuity between control unit harness terminal ④ and A.S.C.D. hold relay.
O.K.
C
CHECK CUT-OFF CIRCUIT FOR A.S.C.D. CONTROL UNIT.
Check voltage between control unit harness terminals ⑤ and ③.
Battery voltage should exist.
N.G.
CHECK A.S.C.D. CANCEL SWITCH, A.S.C.D. CLUTCH SWITCH (M/T models) AND INHIBITOR SWITCH (A/T models). Refer to "Electrical Components Inspection".
CHECK INHIBITOR RELAY (A/T models).
O.K.
D
CHECK SET/COAST SWITCH CIRCUIT FOR A.S.C.D. CONTROL UNIT.
1. Push and hold SET/COAST button on A.S.C.D. steering switch.
2. Check voltage between control unit harness terminals ② and ③.
Battery voltage should exist.
N.G.
Does horn work?
No
Yes
Check fuse and horn relay.
CHECK A.S.C.D. STEERING SWITCH
Refer to "Electrical Components Inspection".
O.K.
Ⓐ

NS1109100028020X

Fig. 31 Test 1: ASCD Control Cannot Be Set (Part 2 of 2). 1993–94 Sentra, NX 1600 & NX 2000

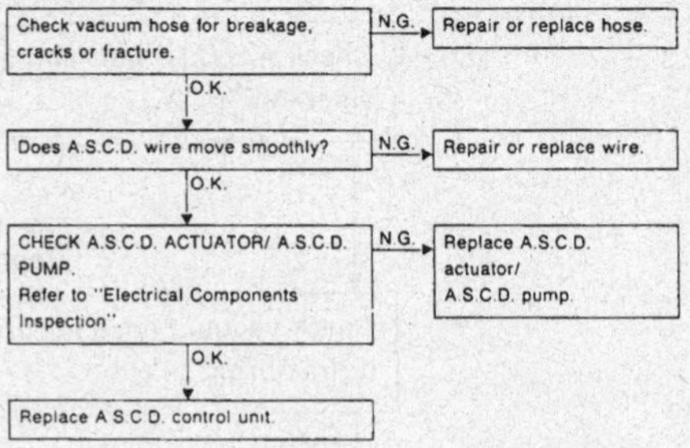
Check vacuum hose for breakage, cracks or fracture.
N.G.
Repair or replace hose.
O.K.
Does A.S.C.D. wire move smoothly?
N.G.
Repair or replace wire.
O.K.
CHECK A.S.C.D. ACTUATOR/ A.S.C.D. PUMP.
Refer to "Electrical Components Inspection".
N.G.
Replace A.S.C.D. actuator/ A.S.C.D. pump.
O.K.
Replace A.S.C.D. control unit.

NS1109100029000X

Fig. 32 Test 2: Engine Hunts. 1993–94 Sentra, NX 1600 & NX 2000

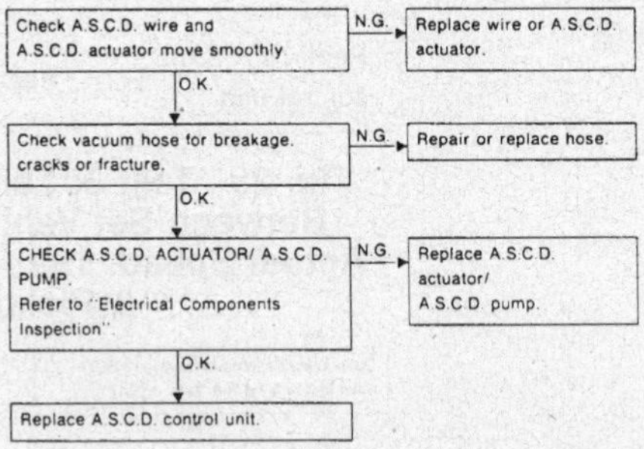
Check A.S.C.D. wire and A.S.C.D. actuator move smoothly.
N.G.
Replace wire or A.S.C.D. actuator.
O.K.
Check vacuum hose for breakage, cracks or fracture.
N.G.
Repair or replace hose.
O.K.
CHECK A.S.C.D. ACTUATOR/ A.S.C.D. PUMP.
Refer to "Electrical Components Inspection".
N.G.
Replace A.S.C.D. actuator/ A.S.C.D. pump.
O.K.
Replace A.S.C.D. control unit.

NS1109100030000X

Fig. 33 Test 3: Large Difference Between Set Vehicle Speed & Actual Speed. 1993–94 Sentra, NX 1600 & NX 2000

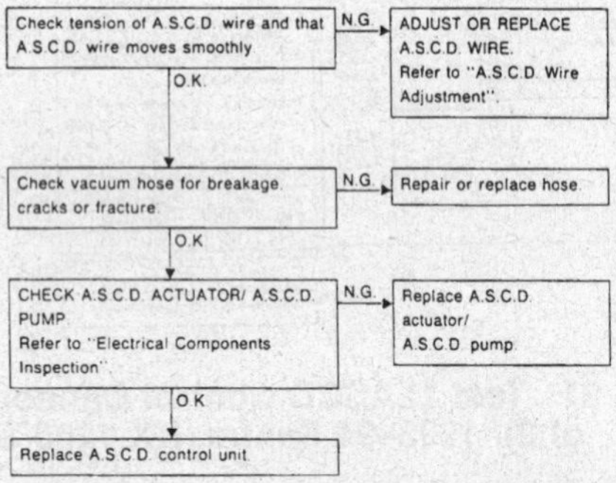
Check tension of A.S.C.D. wire and that A.S.C.D. wire moves smoothly.
N.G.
ADJUST OR REPLACE A.S.C.D. WIRE.
Refer to "A.S.C.D. Wire Adjustment".
O.K.
Check vacuum hose for breakage, cracks or fracture.
N.G.
Repair or replace hose.
O.K.
CHECK A.S.C.D. ACTUATOR/ A.S.C.D. PUMP.
Refer to "Electrical Components Inspection".
N.G.
Replace A.S.C.D. actuator/ A.S.C.D. pump.
O.K.
Replace A.S.C.D. control unit.

NS1109100031000X

Fig. 34 Test 4: Deceleration Is Greatest Immediately After ASCD Has Been Set. 1993–94 Sentra, NX 1600 & NX 2000

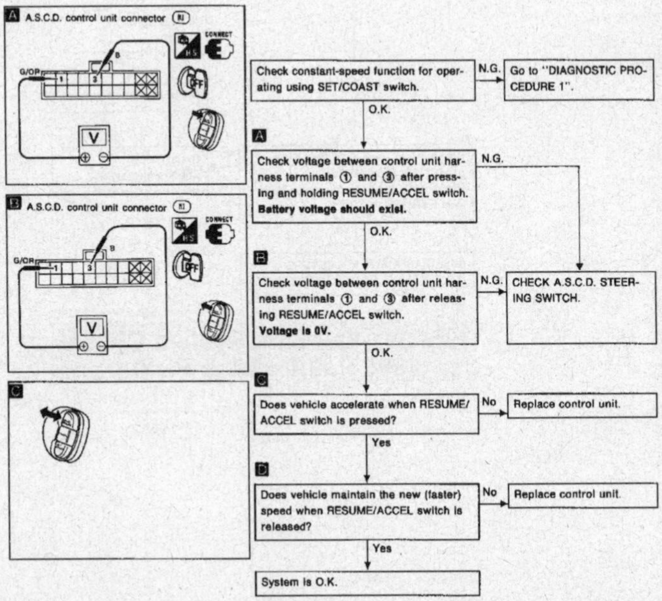
A A.S.C.D. control unit connector
G/OR
B A.S.C.D. control unit connector
G/OR
C
Check constant-speed function for operating using SET/COAST switch.
N.G.
Go to "DIAGNOSTIC PROCEDURE 1".
O.K.
A
Check voltage between control unit harness terminals ① and ③ after pressing and holding RESUME/ACCEL switch.
Battery voltage should exist.
N.G.
O.K.
B
Check voltage between control unit harness terminals ① and ③ after releasing RESUME/ACCEL switch.
Voltage is 0V.
N.G.
CHECK A.S.C.D. STEERING SWITCH.
O.K.
C
Does vehicle accelerate when RESUME/ACCEL switch is pressed?
No
Replace control unit.
Yes
D
Does vehicle maintain the new (faster) speed when RESUME/ACCEL switch is released?
No
Replace control unit.
Yes
System is O.K.

NS1109100032000X

Fig. 35 Test 5: ACCEL Switch Will Not Operate. 1993–94 Sentra, NX 1600 & NX 2000

A A.S.C.D. control unit connector

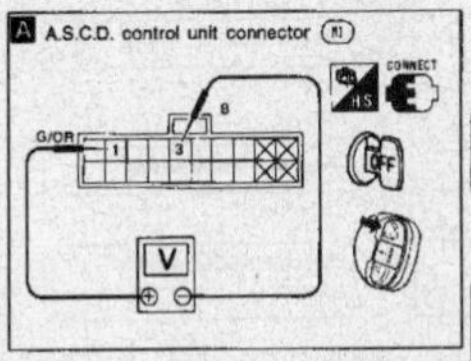

B A.S.C.D. control unit connector

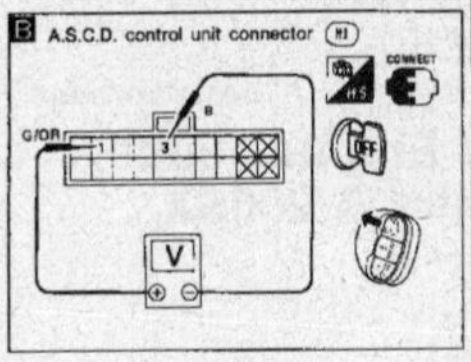

Check constant-speed function for operation using SET/COAST switch. — N.G. → Go to "DIAGNOSTIC PROCEDURE 1".

O.K.

A

Check voltage between control unit harness terminals ① and ③ after pressing and holding RESUME/ACCEL switch. **Battery voltage should exist.** — N.G. → CHECK A.S.C.D. STEERING SWITCH.

O.K.

B

Check voltage between control unit harness terminals ① and ③ after releasing RESUME/ACCEL switch. **Voltage is 0V.** — N.G. → CHECK A.S.C.D. STEERING SWITCH.

O.K.

C

Set vehicle speed at 80 km/h (50 MPH) by pressing SET/COAST switch.

O.K.

D

While cruising at set speed, depress and release brake pedal.

O.K.

Does speed control disengage and "CRUISE" lamp turn off? — No → CHECK STOP LAMP SWITCH, A.S.C.D. CANCEL SWITCH AND A.S.C.D. CLUTCH SWITCH (M/T models).

Yes

E

Above 48 km/h (30 MPH), press and release "RESUME/ACCEL switch.

O.K.

Does vehicle return to previously set speed [80 km/h (50 MPH)]? — No → Replace control unit.

Yes

System is O.K.

NS1109100033000X

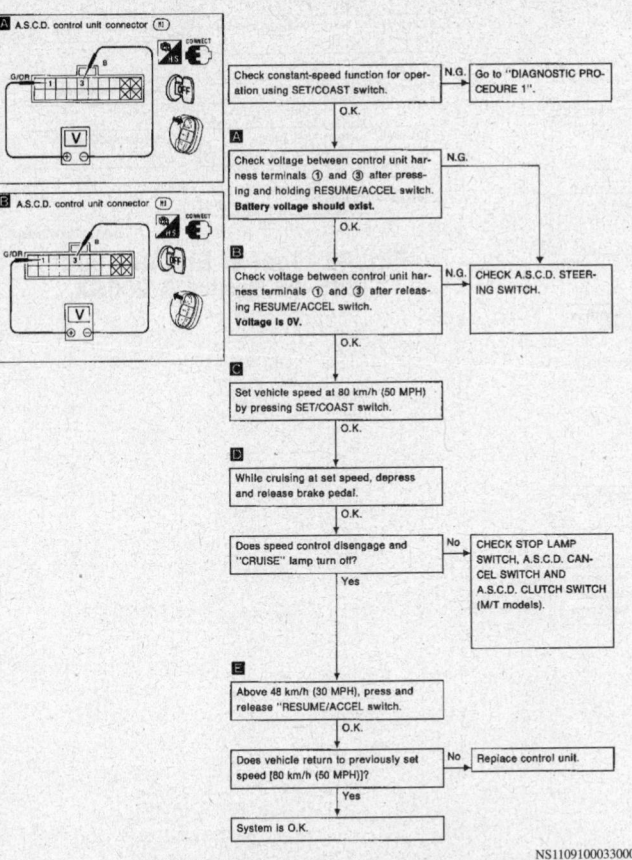

Fig. 36 Test 6: RESUME Switch Will Not Operate. 1993–94 Sentra, NX 1600 & NX 2000

A A.S.C.D. control unit connector

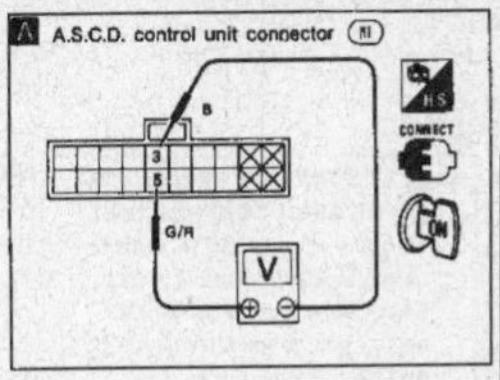

B A.S.C.D. control unit connector

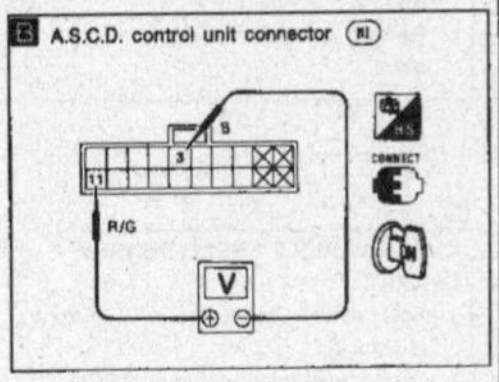

A

CHECK A.S.C.D. CANCEL, CLUTCH, INHIBITOR SWITCH CIRCUIT.
1. Turn A.S.C.D. main switch "ON".
2. Check voltage between control unit harness terminals ⑤ and ③.

Conditions			Voltage [V]
M/T	A.S.C.D. cancel switch	Depressed	0
		Released	Approx. 12
	A.S.C.D. clutch switch	Depressed	0
		Released	Approx. 12
A/T	A/T shift lever position is at any position except N or P.		Approx. 12
	A/T shift lever position is at N or P.		0

N.G. → CHECK A.S.C.D. CANCEL, CLUTCH, and INHIBITOR SWITCH.

O.K.

B

CHECK STOP LAMP SWITCH CIRCUIT. Check voltage between control unit harness terminals ⑪ and ③.

Condition		Voltage [V]
Stop lamp switch	Depressed	Approx. 12
	Released	0

N.G. → CHECK STOP LAMP SWITCH.

O.K.

Check A.S.C.D. wire moves smoothly. — N.G. → Replace A.S.C.D. wire.

O.K.

CHECK A.S.C.D. ACTUATOR/A.S.C.D. PUMP. Refer to "Electrical Components Inspection". — N.G. → Replace A.S.C.D. actuator/A.S.C.D. pump.

O.K.

Replace A.S.C.D. control unit.

NS1109100034000X

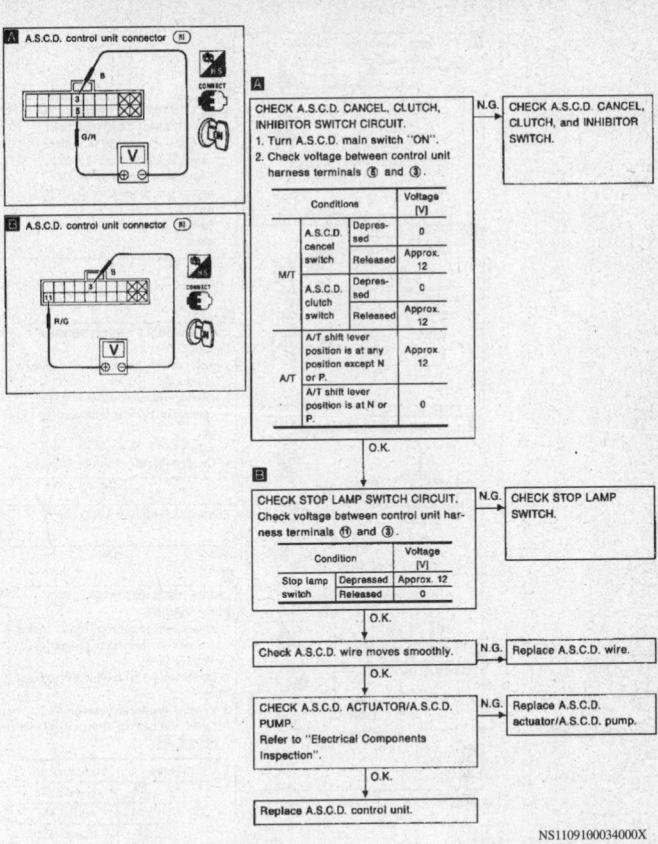

Fig. 37 Test 7: Set Speed Cannot Be Cancelled. 1993–94 Sentra, NX 1600 & NX 2000

DIAGNOSTIC PROCEDURE 8

SYMPTOM: "CRUISE" indicator lamp blinks.

Does indicator lamp blink when A.S.C.D. main switch is turned to "ON" again? — Yes → Does indicator lamp blink when brake pedal is depressed slowly?

- Yes → Adjust installation of stop lamp switch and A.S.C.D. cancel switch. Refer to BR section.
- No → CHECK A.S.C.D. STEERING SWITCH. Refer to "Electrical Components Inspection".
  - N.G. → Replace A.S.C.D. steering switch.
  - O.K. → Replace control unit.

No

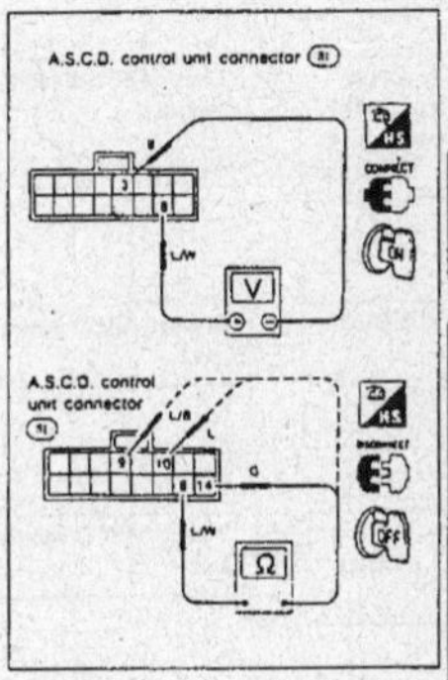

CHECK A.S.C.D. ACTUATOR/A.S.C.D. PUMP. Refer to "Electrical Components Inspection". — N.G. → Replace A.S.C.D. actuator/A.S.C.D. pump

O.K.

CHECK A.S.C.D. ACTUATOR/A.S.C.D. PUMP CIRCUIT.
1. Check voltage between control unit harness terminals ⑧ and ③. **Voltage is 0V.**
2. Disconnect A.S.C.D. control unit connector.
3. Measure resistance between control unit harness terminals ⑧ and ⑨, ⑩, ⑭.

Terminals		Resistance [Ω]
⑧	⑨	Approx. 8 - 45
	⑩	Approx. 65
	⑭	Approx. 65

N.G. → Repair short or open circuit in A.S.C.D. actuator/A.S.C.D. pump harness.

O.K.

Replace A.S.C.D. control unit.

NS1109100035000X

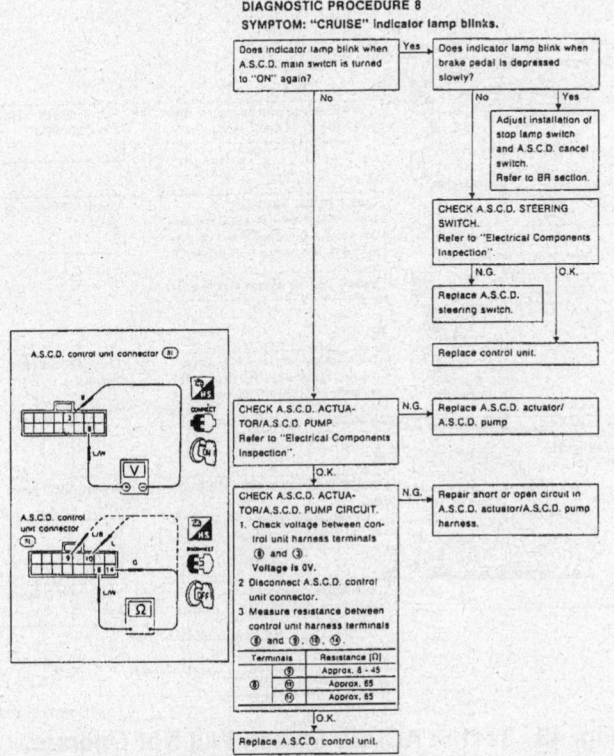

Fig. 38 Test 8: CRUISE Indicator Lamp Blinks. 1993–94 Sentra, NX 1600 & NX 2000

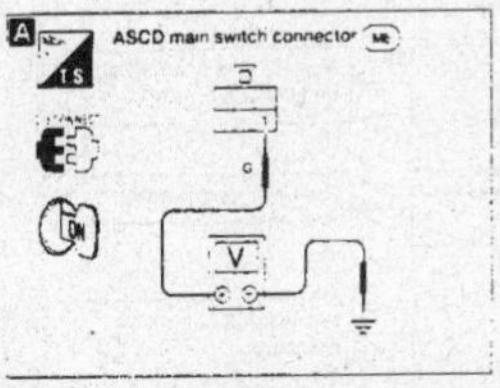

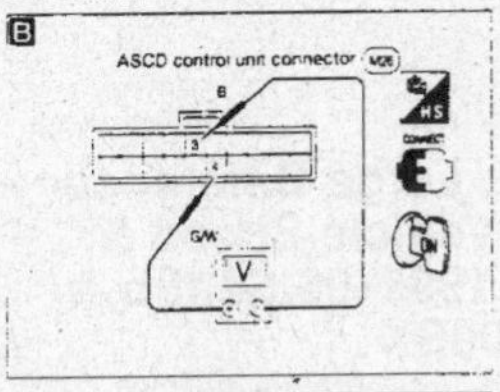

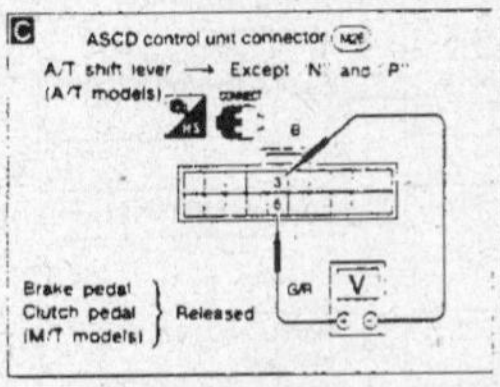

Turn ASCD main switch "OFF" and "ON" to make sure indicator illuminates. — NG → A

A

CHECK POWER SUPPLY FOR ASCD MAIN SWITCH.
1. Disconnect switch harness connector.
2. Does approx. 12 volts exist between switch harness terminal ① and body ground?

- No → Check fuse and harness.
- Yes → Check ASCD main switch. Check ASCD hold relay.

OK

B

CHECK POWER SUPPLY CIRCUIT FOR ASCD CONTROL UNIT.
1. Turn ASCD main switch "ON".
2. Check voltage between ASCD control unit harness terminals ④ and ③. **Battery positive voltage should exist.**

NG → Check continuity between ASCD control unit harness terminal ④ and ASCD hold relay terminal ③.

OK

C

CHECK CUT-OFF CIRCUIT FOR ASCD CONTROL UNIT. Check voltage between ASCD control unit harness terminals ⑤ and ③. **Battery positive voltage should exist.**

NG → Check ASCD cancel switch, ASCD clutch pedal position switch (M/T models) and inhibitor switch (A/T models). Check inhibitor relay (A/T models).

OK

Ⓐ

NS1109500077010X

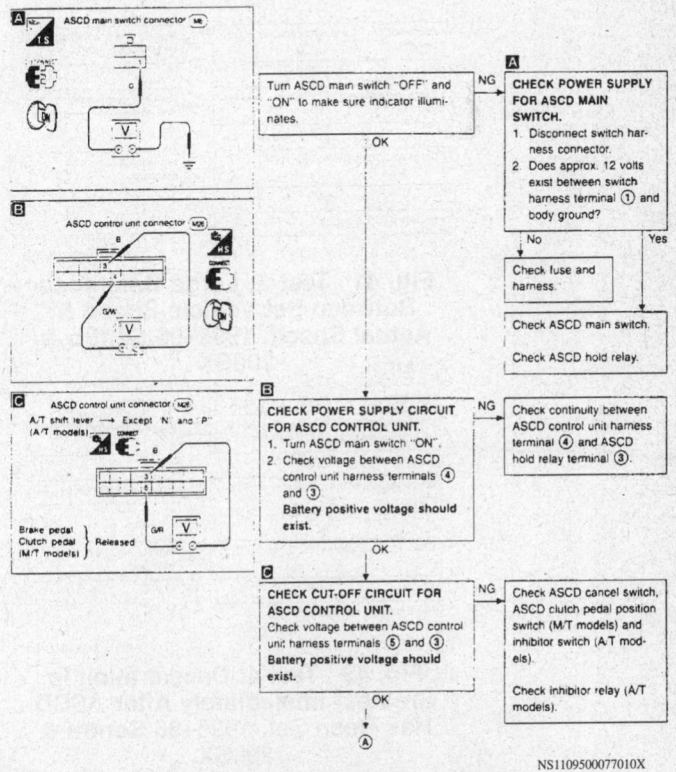

Fig. 39 Test 1: Speed Control Cannot Be Set (Part 1 of 2). 1995–96 Sentra & 200SX

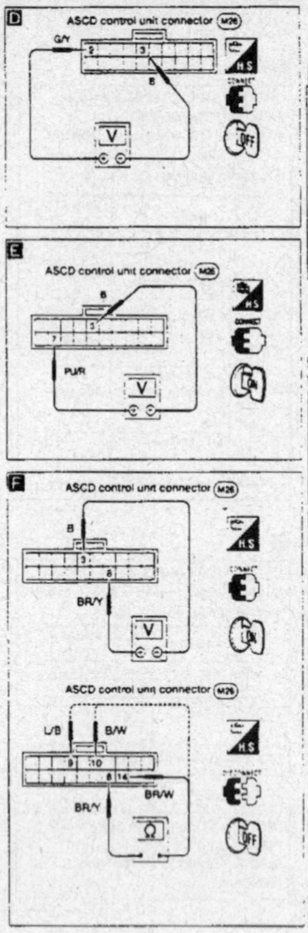
D
ASCD control unit connector (M26)
G/Y
B
E
ASCD control unit connector (M26)
B
PU/R
F
ASCD control unit connector (M26)
B
BR/Y
ASCD control unit connector (M26)
L/B
B/W
BR/W
BR/Y

(A)

D

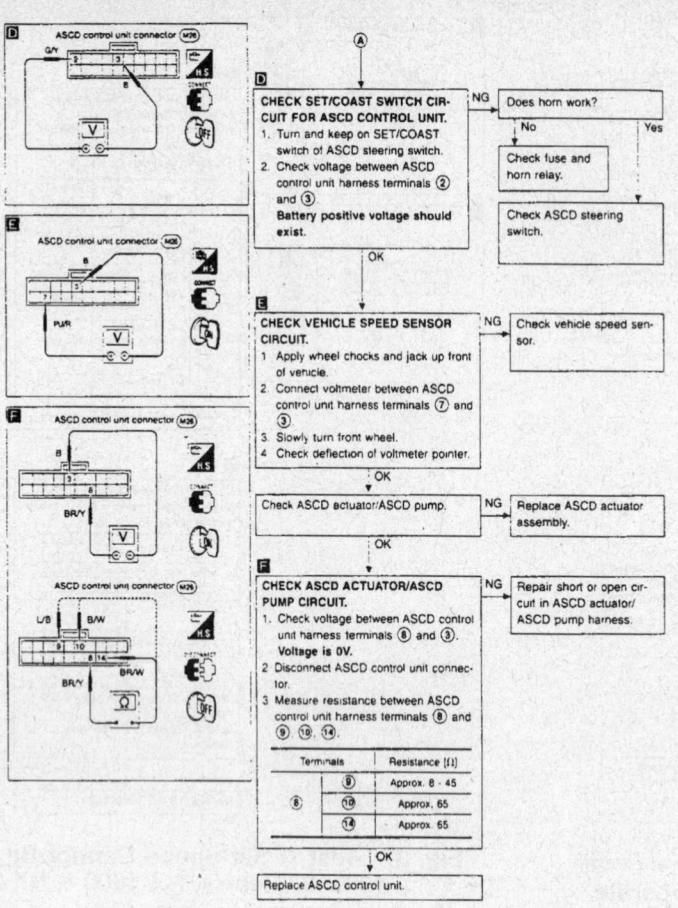

CHECK SET/COAST SWITCH CIRCUIT FOR ASCD CONTROL UNIT.
1. Turn and keep on SET/COAST switch of ASCD steering switch.
2. Check voltage between ASCD control unit harness terminals ② and ③.
Battery positive voltage should exist.

- NG → Does horn work?
  - No → Check fuse and horn relay.
  - Yes → Check ASCD steering switch.
- OK ↓

E

CHECK VEHICLE SPEED SENSOR CIRCUIT.
1. Apply wheel chocks and jack up front of vehicle.
2. Connect voltmeter between ASCD control unit harness terminals ⑦ and ③.
3. Slowly turn front wheel.
4. Check deflection of voltmeter pointer.

- NG → Check vehicle speed sensor.
- OK ↓

Check ASCD actuator/ASCD pump.

- NG → Replace ASCD actuator assembly.
- OK ↓

F

CHECK ASCD ACTUATOR/ASCD PUMP CIRCUIT.
1. Check voltage between ASCD control unit harness terminals ⑧ and ③.
Voltage is 0V.
2. Disconnect ASCD control unit connector.
3. Measure resistance between ASCD control unit harness terminals ⑧ and ⑨, ⑩, ⑭.

Terminals		Resistance (Ω)
⑧	⑨	Approx. 8 - 45
	⑩	Approx. 65
	⑭	Approx. 65

- NG → Repair short or open circuit in ASCD actuator/ASCD pump harness.
- OK ↓

Replace ASCD control unit.

NS1109500077020X

Fig. 39 Test 1: Speed Control Cannot Be Set (Part 2 of 2). 1995–96 Sentra & 200SX

Check vacuum hose for breakage, cracks or fracture.
- NG → Repair or replace hose.
- OK ↓

Does ASCD wire move smoothly?
- NG → Repair or replace wire.
- OK ↓

Check ASCD actuator/ASCD pump.
- NG → Replace ASCD actuator assembly.
- OK ↓

Replace ASCD control unit.

NS1109500078000X

Fig. 40 Test 2: Engine Hunts. 1995–96 Sentra & 200SX

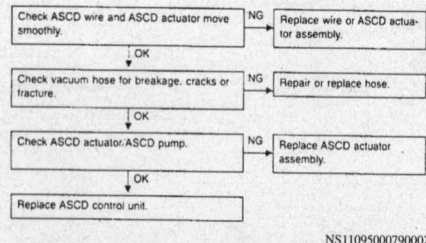

Check ASCD wire and ASCD actuator move smoothly.
- NG → Replace wire or ASCD actuator assembly.
- OK ↓

Check vacuum hose for breakage, cracks or fracture.
- NG → Repair or replace hose.
- OK ↓

Check ASCD actuator/ASCD pump.
- NG → Replace ASCD actuator assembly.
- OK ↓

Replace ASCD control unit.

NS1109500079000X

Fig. 41 Test 3: Large Difference Between Set Vehicle Speed & Actual Speed. 1995–96 Sentra & 200SX

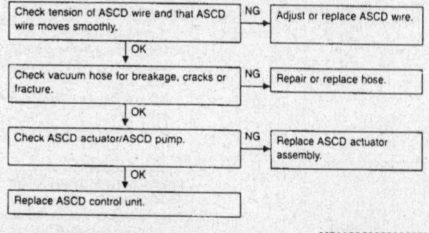

Check tension of ASCD wire and that ASCD wire moves smoothly.
- NG → Adjust or replace ASCD wire.
- OK ↓

Check vacuum hose for breakage, cracks or fracture.
- NG → Repair or replace hose.
- OK ↓

Check ASCD actuator/ASCD pump.
- NG → Replace ASCD actuator assembly.
- OK ↓

Replace ASCD control unit.

NS1109500080000X

Fig. 42 Test 4: Deceleration Is Greatest Immediately After ASCD Has Been Set. 1995–96 Sentra & 200SX

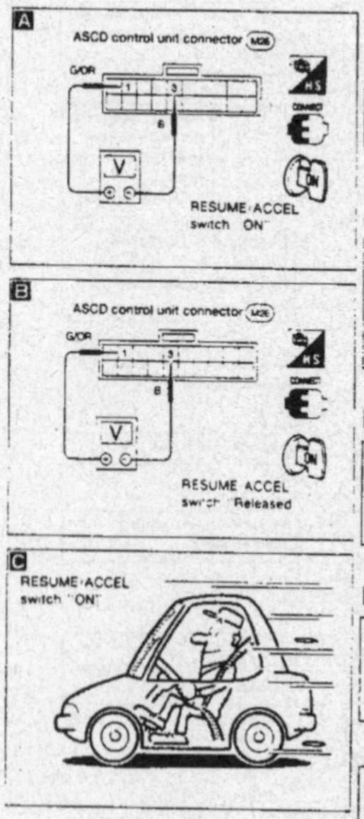
A
ASCD control unit connector (M26)
G/OR
B
RESUME/ACCEL switch "ON"
B
ASCD control unit connector (M26)
G/OR
B
RESUME/ACCEL switch "Released"
C
RESUME/ACCEL switch "ON"

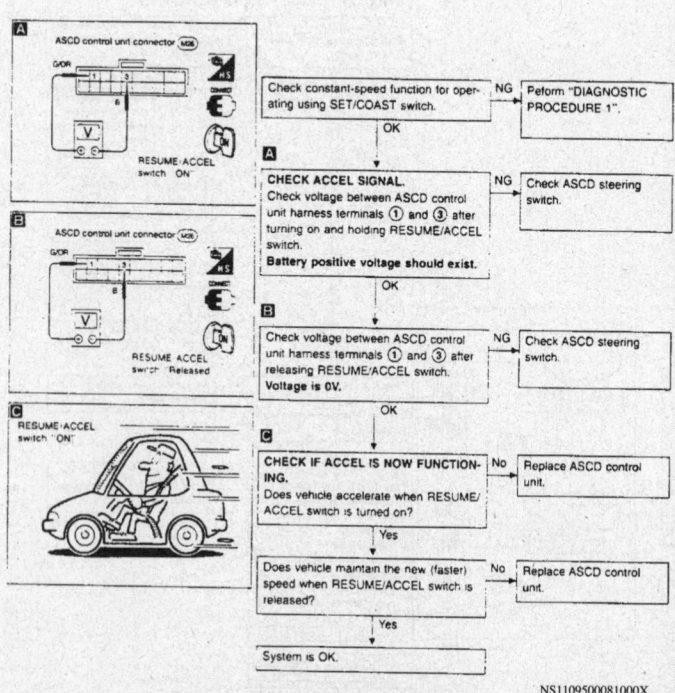

Check constant-speed function for operating using SET/COAST switch.
- NG → Peform "DIAGNOSTIC PROCEDURE 1".
- OK ↓

A

CHECK ACCEL SIGNAL.
Check voltage between ASCD control unit harness terminals ① and ③ after turning on and holding RESUME/ACCEL switch.
Battery positive voltage should exist.

- NG → Check ASCD steering switch.
- OK ↓

B

Check voltage between ASCD control unit harness terminals ① and ③ after releasing RESUME/ACCEL switch.
Voltage is 0V.

- NG → Check ASCD steering switch.
- OK ↓

C

CHECK IF ACCEL IS NOW FUNCTIONING.
Does vehicle accelerate when RESUME/ACCEL switch is turned on?

- No → Replace ASCD control unit.
- Yes ↓

Does vehicle maintain the new (faster) speed when RESUME/ACCEL switch is released?

- No → Replace ASCD control unit.
- Yes ↓

System is OK.

NS1109500081000X

Fig. 43 Test 5: ACCEL Switch Will Not Operate. 1995–96 Sentra & 200SX

A
ASCD control unit connector (M26)
G/OR
RESUME/ACCEL switch "ON"
B
ASCD control unit connector (M26)
G/OR
RESUME/ACCEL switch "Released"
C
SET/COAST switch "ON"
D
Brake pedal
E
RESUME/ACCEL switch "ON"

Check constant-speed function for operation using SET/COAST switch. — NG → Perform "DIAGNOSTIC PROCEDURE 1".

OK

A
CHECK RESUME SIGNAL.
Check voltage between ASCD control unit harness terminals ① and ③ after turning on and holding RESUME/ACCEL switch.
Battery positive voltage should exist. — NG → Check ASCD steering switch.

OK

B
Check voltage between ASCD control unit harness terminals ① and ③ after releasing RESUME/ACCEL switch.
Voltage is 0V. — NG → Check ASCD steering switch.

OK

C
CHECK IF RESUME IS NOW FUNCTIONING.
Set vehicle speed at 80 km/h (50 MPH) by turning on SET/COAST switch.

OK

D
While cruising at set speed, depress and release brake pedal.

OK

Does speed control disengage and "CRUISE" lamp turn off? — No → Check stop lamp switch, ASCD cancel switch and ASCD clutch pedal position switch (M/T models).

Yes

E
Above 48 km/h (30 MPH), press and release RESUME/ACCEL switch.

OK

Does vehicle return to previously set speed [80 km/h (50 MPH)]? — No → Replace ASCD control unit.

Yes

System is OK.

NS1109500082000X

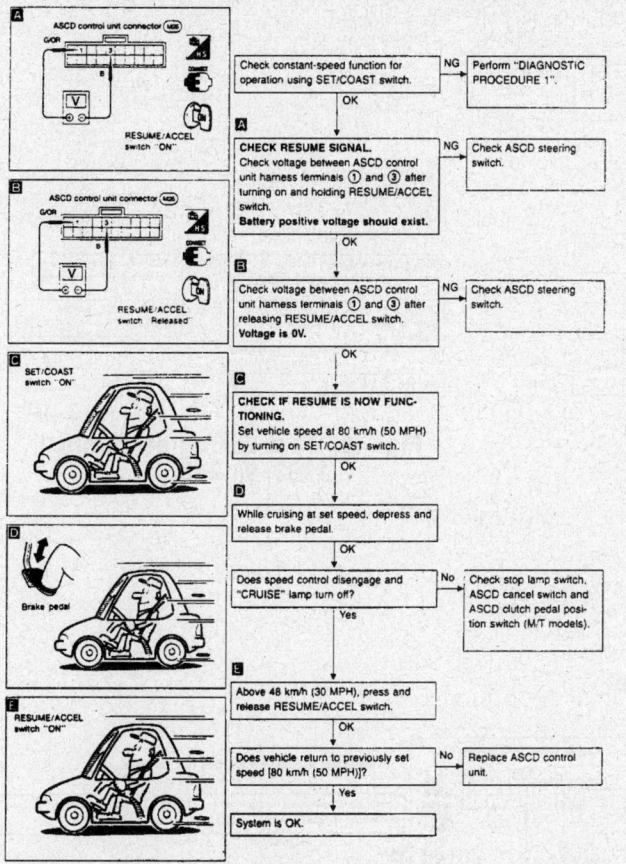

Fig. 44 Test 6: RESUME Switch Will Not Operate. 1995–96 Sentra & 200SX

A
ASCD control unit connector (M26)
G/R
B
ASCD control unit connector (M26)
R/G

A
CHECK ASCD CANCEL, CLUTCH PEDAL POSITION, INHIBITOR SWITCH CIRCUIT.
1. Turn ASCD main switch on.
2. Check voltage between ASCD control unit harness terminals ⑤ and ③.

Conditions			Voltage [V]
M/T	ASCD cancel switch	Depressed	0
		Released	Approx. 12
	ASCD clutch pedal position switch	Depressed	0
		Released	Approx. 12
A/T	A/T shift lever position is at any position except N or P.		Approx. 12
	A/T shift lever position is at N or P.		0

NG → Check ASCD cancel, clutch pedal position, and inhibitor switch.

OK

B
CHECK STOP LAMP SWITCH CIRCUIT.
Check voltage between ASCD control unit harness terminals ⑪ and ③.

Condition		Voltage [V]
Stop lamp switch	Depressed	Approx. 12
	Released	0

NG → Check stop lamp switch.

OK

Check ASCD wire moves smoothly. — NG → Replace ASCD wire.

OK

Check ASCD actuator/ASCD pump. — NG → Replace ASCD actuator assembly.

OK

Replace ASCD control unit.

NS1109500083000X

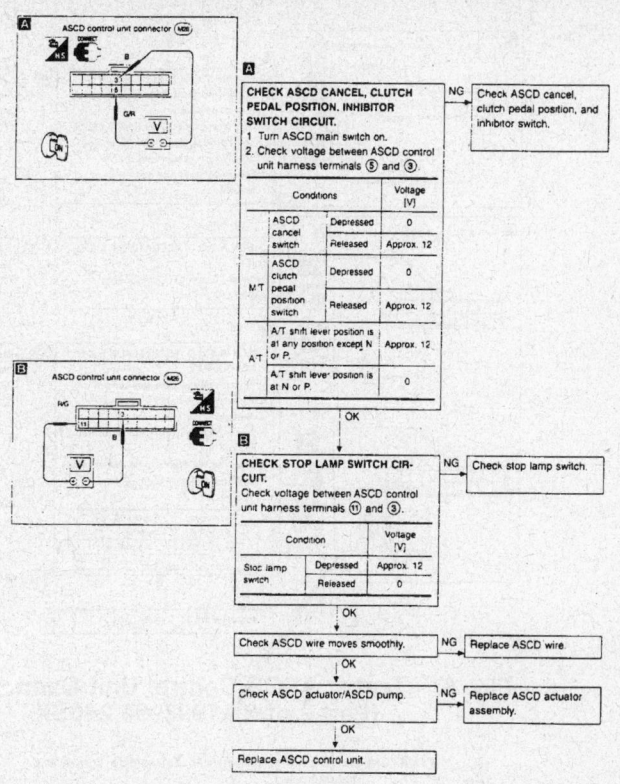

Fig. 45 Test 7: Set Speed Cannot Be Canceled. 1995–96 Sentra & 200SX

Does indicator lamp blink when ASCD main switch is turned to "ON" again? — Yes → Does indicator lamp blink when brake pedal is depressed slowly?
- Yes → Adjust installation of stop lamp switch and ASCD cancel switch.
- No → Check ASCD steering switch.
  - NG → Replace ASCD steering switch.
  - OK → Replace ASCD control unit.

No

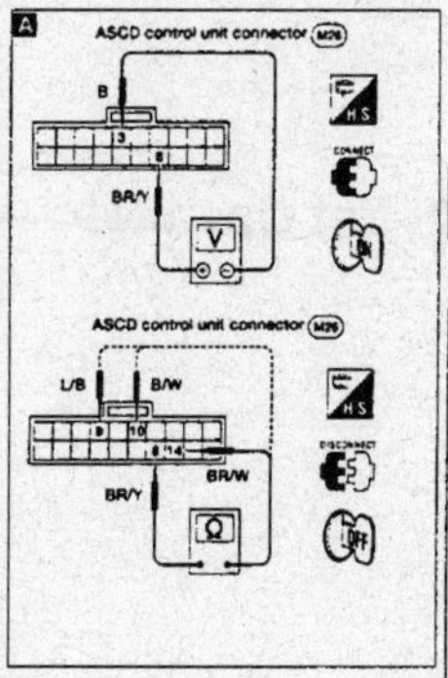
A
ASCD control unit connector (M26)
BR/Y
ASCD control unit connector (M26)
L/B
B/W
BR/Y
BR/W

Check ASCD actuator/ASCD pump. — NG → Replace ASCD actuator assembly.

OK

A
Check ASCD actuator/ASCD pump circuit.
1. Check voltage between ASCD control unit harness terminals ⑧ and ③.
Voltage is 12V.
2. Disconnect ASCD control unit connector.
3. Measure resistance between ASCD control unit harness terminals ⑧ and ⑨, ⑩, ⑭.

Terminals		Resistance [Ω]
⑧	⑨	Approx. 8 - 45
	⑩	Approx. 65
	⑭	Approx. 65

NG → Repair short or open circuit in ASCD actuator/ ASCD pump harness.

OK

Replace ASCD control unit.

NS1109500084000X

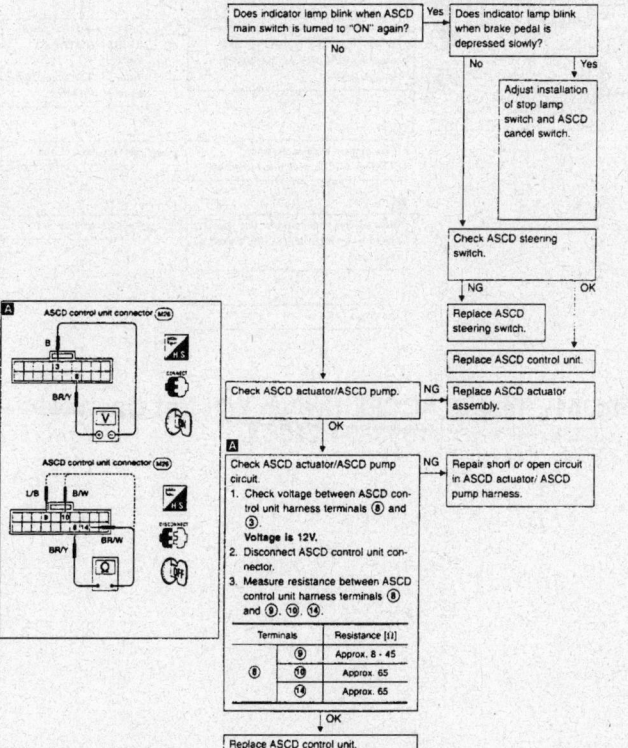

Fig. 46 Test 8: CRUISE Indicator Lamp Blinks. 1995–96 Sentra & 200SX

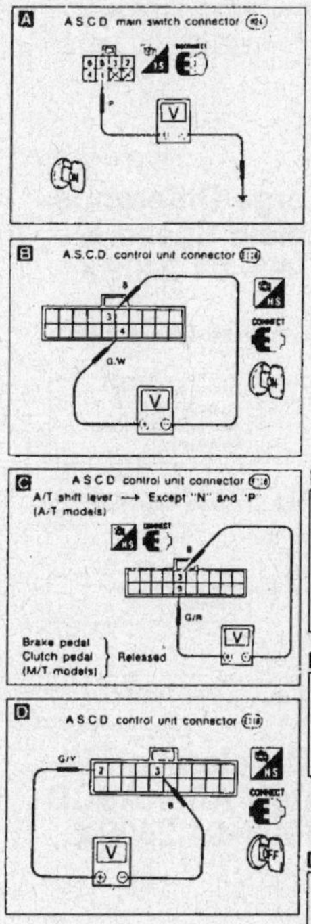
A
A S C D main switch connector (E6)
B
A.S.C.D. control unit connector (E14)
G.W
C
A S C D control unit connector (E14)
A/T shift lever → Except "N" and "P" (A/T models)
G/R
Brake pedal
Clutch pedal (M/T models)
Released
D
A S C D control unit connector (E14)
G/Y

DIAGNOSTIC PROCEDURE 1
SYMPTOM: A.S.C.D. control cannot be set.

Turn A.S.C.D. main switch "OFF" and "ON" to make sure indicator illuminates. — N.G. → A
CHECK POWER SUPPLY FOR A.S.C.D. MAIN SWITCH.
1. Disconnect main switch harness connector.
2. Do approx. 12 volts exist between main switch harness terminal ① and body ground?
- No → Check fuse and harness.
- Yes → CHECK A.S.C.D. MAIN SWITCH. Refer to "Electrical Components Inspection". CHECK A.S.C.D. HOLD RELAY.

O.K.

B
CHECK POWER SUPPLY CIRCUIT FOR A.S.C.D. CONTROL UNIT.
1. Turn A.S.C.D. main switch "ON".
2. Check voltage between control unit harness terminals ④ and ③.
Battery voltage should exist. — N.G. → Check continuity between control unit harness terminal ④ and A.S.C.D. hold relay.

O.K.

C
CHECK CUT-OFF CIRCUIT FOR A.S.C.D. CONTROL UNIT.
Check voltage between control unit harness terminals ⑤ and ③.
Battery voltage should exist. — N.G. → CHECK A.S.C.D. CANCEL SWITCH, A.S.C.D. CLUTCH SWITCH (M/T models) AND INHIBITOR SWITCH (A/T models). Refer to "Electrical Components Inspection". CHECK INHIBITOR RELAY (A/T models).

O.K.

D
CHECK SET/COAST SWITCH CIRCUIT FOR A.S.C.D. CONTROL UNIT.
1. Turn and keep on SET/COAST switch of A.S.C.D. combination (steering) switch.
2. Check voltage between control unit harness terminals ② and ③.
Battery voltage should exist. — N.G. → Does horn work?
- No → Check fuse and horn relay.
- Yes → CHECK A.S.C.D. COMBINATION (STEERING) SWITCH. Refer to "Electrical Components Inspection".

O.K.

Ⓐ

NS1109200044010X

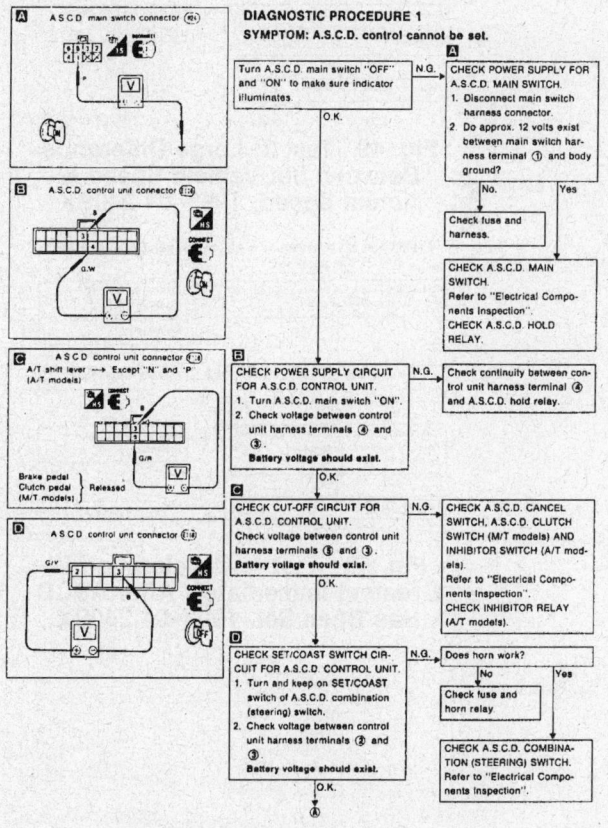

Fig. 47 Test 1: ASCD Control Unit Cannot Be Set (Part 1 of 2). 1993–94 240SX

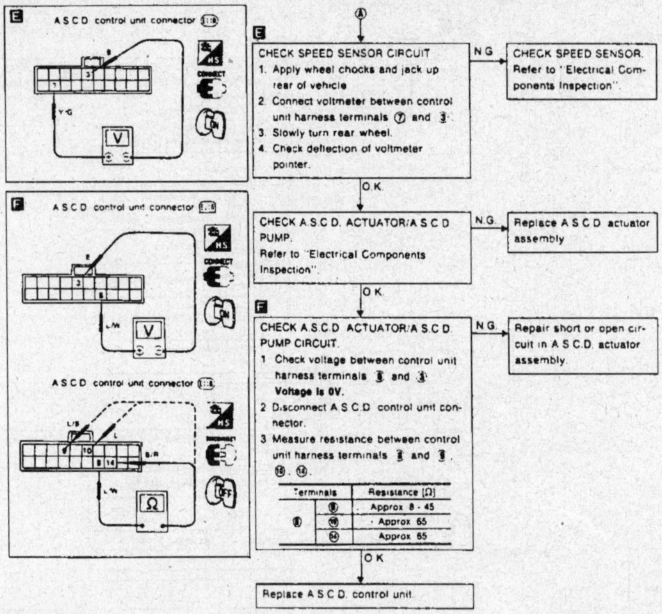
E
A S C D control unit connector
V
F
A S C D control unit connector
V
A S C D control unit connector
Ω
A
E
CHECK SPEED SENSOR CIRCUIT
1. Apply wheel chocks and jack up rear of vehicle
2. Connect voltmeter between control unit harness terminals ⑦ and ③.
3. Slowly turn rear wheel.
4. Check deflection of voltmeter pointer.
N.G.
CHECK SPEED SENSOR. Refer to "Electrical Components Inspection".
O.K.
CHECK A.S.C.D. ACTUATOR/A.S.C.D. PUMP. Refer to "Electrical Components Inspection".
N.G.
Replace A.S.C.D. actuator assembly.
O.K.
F
CHECK A.S.C.D. ACTUATOR/A.S.C.D. PUMP CIRCUIT.
1. Check voltage between control unit harness terminals ⑧ and ③.
Voltage is 0V.
2. Disconnect A.S.C.D. control unit connector.
3. Measure resistance between control unit harness terminals ⑧ and ⑨, ⑯, ⑭.
N.G.
Repair short or open circuit in A.S.C.D. actuator assembly.
Terminals
Resistance [Ω]
⑧ ⑨ Approx 8 - 45
⑯ Approx 65
⑭ Approx 65
O.K.
Replace A.S.C.D. control unit.

NS1109200044020X

Fig. 47 Test 1: ASCD Control Unit Cannot Be Set (Part 2 of 2). 1993–94 240SX

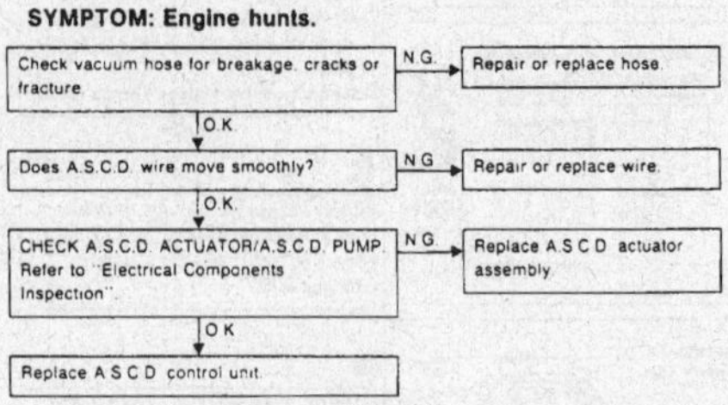
SYMPTOM: Engine hunts.
Check vacuum hose for breakage, cracks or fracture.
N.G.
Repair or replace hose.
O.K.
Does A.S.C.D. wire move smoothly?
N.G.
Repair or replace wire.
O.K.
CHECK A.S.C.D. ACTUATOR/A.S.C.D. PUMP. Refer to "Electrical Components Inspection".
N.G.
Replace A.S.C.D. actuator assembly.
O.K.
Replace A.S.C.D. control unit.

NS1109200045000X

Fig. 48 Test 2: Engine Hunts. 1993–94 240SX

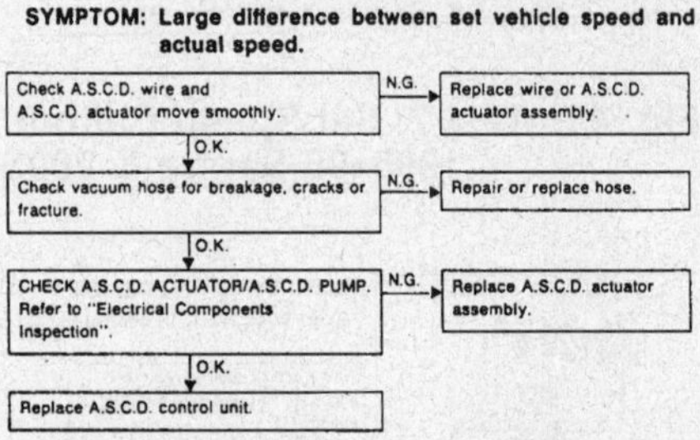
SYMPTOM: Large difference between set vehicle speed and actual speed.
Check A.S.C.D. wire and A.S.C.D. actuator move smoothly.
N.G.
Replace wire or A.S.C.D. actuator assembly.
O.K.
Check vacuum hose for breakage, cracks or fracture.
N.G.
Repair or replace hose.
O.K.
CHECK A.S.C.D. ACTUATOR/A.S.C.D. PUMP. Refer to "Electrical Components Inspection".
N.G.
Replace A.S.C.D. actuator assembly.
O.K.
Replace A.S.C.D. control unit.

NS1109200049000X

Fig. 49 Test 3: Large Difference Between Set Vehicle Speed & Actual Speed. 1993–94 240SX

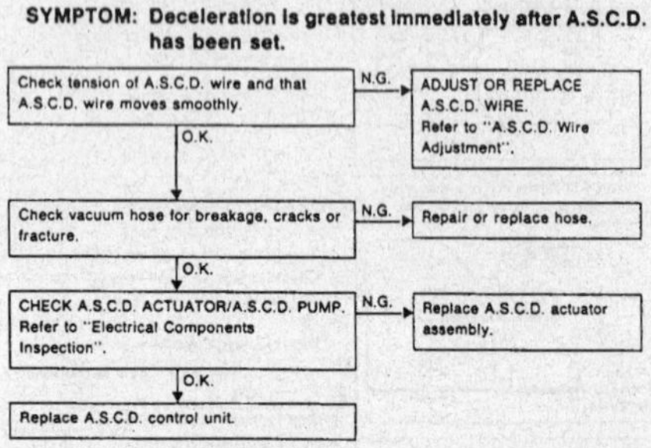
SYMPTOM: Deceleration is greatest immediately after A.S.C.D. has been set.
Check tension of A.S.C.D. wire and that A.S.C.D. wire moves smoothly.
N.G.
ADJUST OR REPLACE A.S.C.D. WIRE. Refer to "A.S.C.D. Wire Adjustment".
O.K.
Check vacuum hose for breakage, cracks or fracture.
N.G.
Repair or replace hose.
O.K.
CHECK A.S.C.D. ACTUATOR/A.S.C.D. PUMP. Refer to "Electrical Components Inspection".
N.G.
Replace A.S.C.D. actuator assembly.
O.K.
Replace A.S.C.D. control unit.

NS1109200050000X

Fig. 50 Test 4: Deceleration Is Greatest Immediately After ASCD Has Been Set. 1993–94 240SX

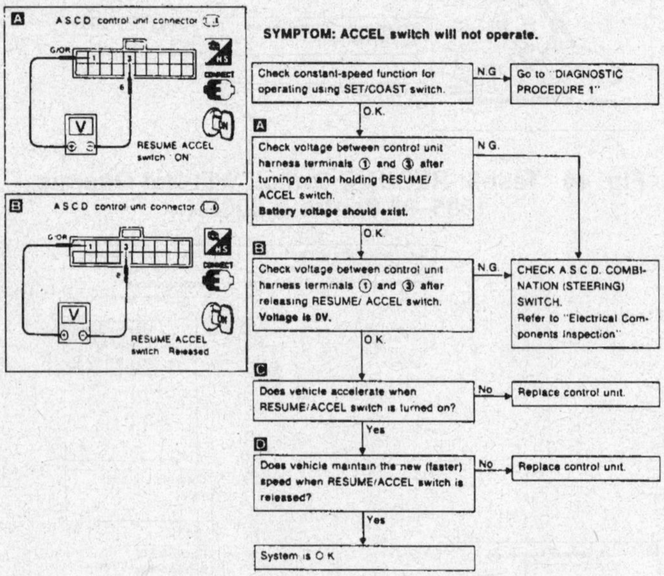
A
A S C D control unit connector
G/OR
V
RESUME ACCEL switch "ON"
B
A S C D control unit connector
G/OR
V
RESUME ACCEL switch Released
SYMPTOM: ACCEL switch will not operate.
Check constant-speed function for operating using SET/COAST switch.
N.G.
Go to "DIAGNOSTIC PROCEDURE 1"
O.K.
A
Check voltage between control unit harness terminals ① and ③ after turning on and holding RESUME/ACCEL switch.
Battery voltage should exist.
N.G.
O.K.
B
Check voltage between control unit harness terminals ① and ③ after releasing RESUME/ ACCEL switch.
Voltage is 0V.
N.G.
CHECK A.S.C.D. COMBINATION (STEERING) SWITCH. Refer to "Electrical Components Inspection"
O.K.
C
Does vehicle accelerate when RESUME/ACCEL switch is turned on?
No
Replace control unit.
Yes
D
Does vehicle maintain the new (faster) speed when RESUME/ACCEL switch is released?
No
Replace control unit.
Yes
System is O.K.

NS1109200051000X

Fig. 51 Test 5: ACCEL Switch Will Not Operate. 1993–94 240SX

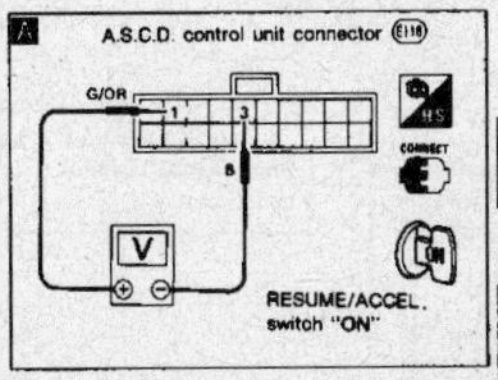
A
A.S.C.D. control unit connector E118
G/OR
1
3
B
V
RESUME/ACCEL switch "ON"

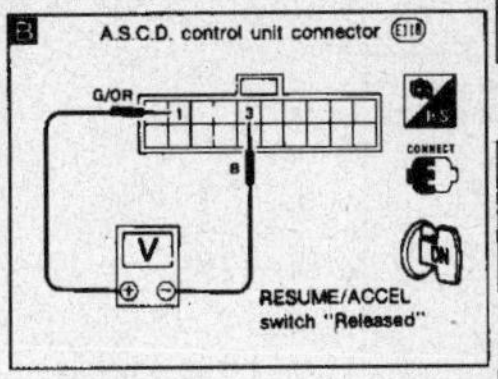
B
A.S.C.D. control unit connector E118
G/OR
1
3
B
V
RESUME/ACCEL switch "Released"

Check constant-speed function for operation using SET/COAST switch. — N.G. → Go to "DIAGNOSTIC PROCEDURE 1".

O.K. ↓

A Check voltage between control unit harness terminals ① and ③ after turning on and holding RESUME/ACCEL switch. **Battery voltage should exist.** — N.G. → CHECK A.S.C.D. COMBINATION (STEERING) SWITCH.

O.K. ↓

B Check voltage between control unit harness terminals ① and ③ after releasing RESUME/ACCEL switch. **Voltage is 0V.** — N.G. → CHECK A.S.C.D. COMBINATION (STEERING) SWITCH.

O.K. ↓

C Set vehicle speed at 80 km/h (50 MPH) by turning on SET/COAST switch.

O.K. ↓

D While cruising at set speed, depress and release brake pedal.

O.K. ↓

Does speed control disengage and "CRUISE" lamp turn off? — No → CHECK STOP LAMP SWITCH, A.S.C.D. CANCEL SWITCH AND A.S.C.D. CLUTCH SWITCH (M/T models).

Yes ↓

E Above 48 km/h (30 MPH), press and release "RESUME/ACCEL" switch.

O.K. ↓

Does vehicle return to previously set speed [80 km/h (50 MPH)]? — No → Replace control unit.

Yes ↓

System is O.K.

NS1109200052000X

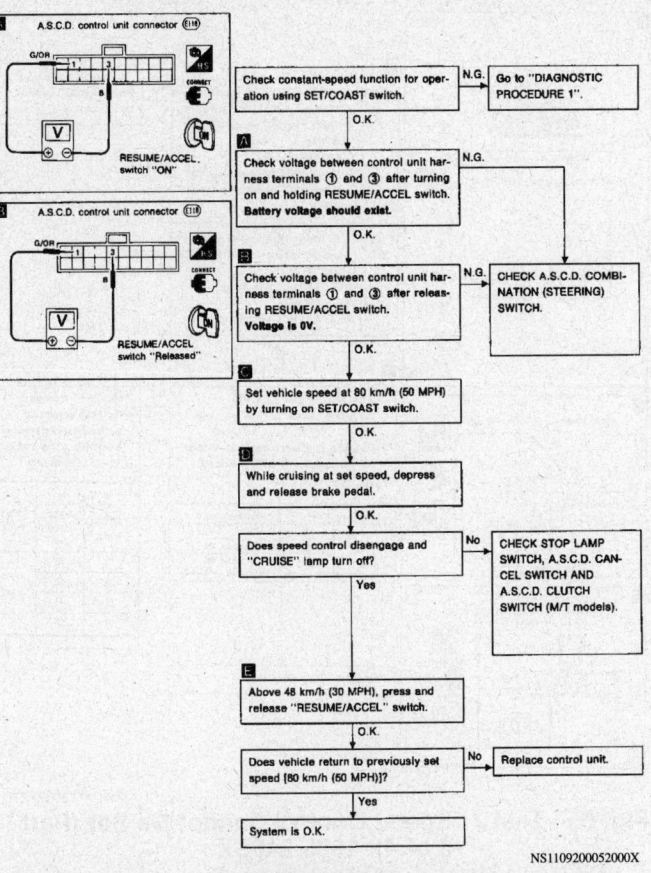

Fig. 52 Test 6: RESUME Switch Will Not Operate. 1993–94 240SX

SYMPTOM: "CRUISE" indicator lamp blinks.

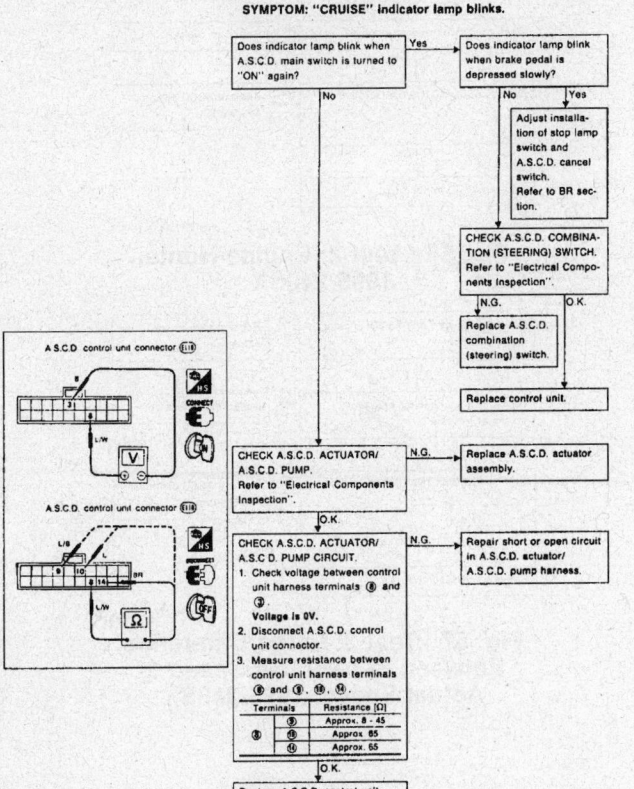

Does indicator lamp blink when A.S.C.D. main switch is turned to "ON" again? — Yes → Does indicator lamp blink when brake pedal is depressed slowly?

- Yes → Adjust installation of stop lamp switch and A.S.C.D. cancel switch. Refer to BR section.
- No → CHECK A.S.C.D. COMBINATION (STEERING) SWITCH. Refer to "Electrical Components Inspection".
  - N.G. → Replace A.S.C.D. combination (steering) switch.
  - O.K. → Replace control unit.

No ↓

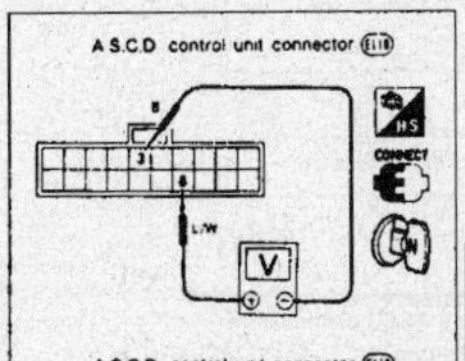
A.S.C.D. control unit connector E118
B
3
8
L/W
V

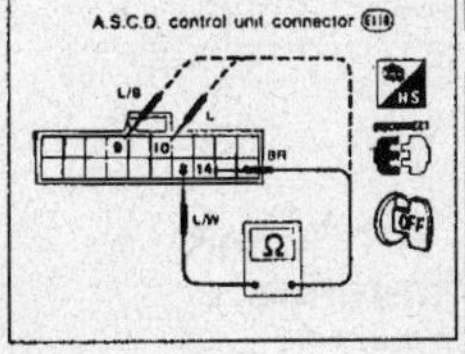
A.S.C.D. control unit connector E118
L/B
L
9
10
8
14
BR
L/W
Ω

CHECK A.S.C.D. ACTUATOR/A.S.C.D. PUMP. Refer to "Electrical Components Inspection". — N.G. → Replace A.S.C.D. actuator assembly.

O.K. ↓

CHECK A.S.C.D. ACTUATOR/A.S.C.D. PUMP CIRCUIT. — N.G. → Repair short or open circuit in A.S.C.D. actuator/A.S.C.D. pump harness.

1. Check voltage between control unit harness terminals ⑧ and ③. **Voltage is 0V.**
2. Disconnect A.S.C.D. control unit connector.
3. Measure resistance between control unit harness terminals ⑧ and ⑨, ⑩, ⑭.

Terminals		Resistance [Ω]
⑧	⑨	Approx. 8 - 45
	⑩	Approx. 65
	⑭	Approx. 65

O.K. ↓

Replace A.S.C.D. control unit.

NS1109200047000X

Fig. 54 Test 8: CRUISE Indicator Lamp Blinks. 1993–94 240SX

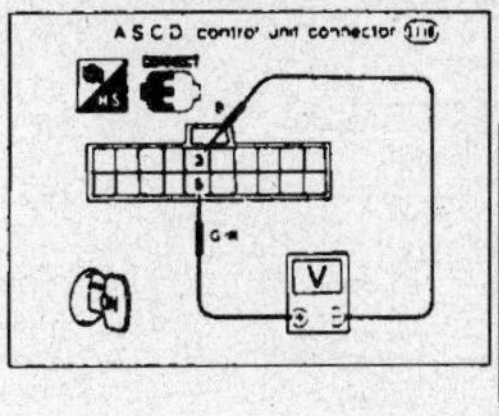
A.S.C.D. control unit connector E118
3
6
G/R
V

SYMPTOM: Set speed cannot be cancelled.

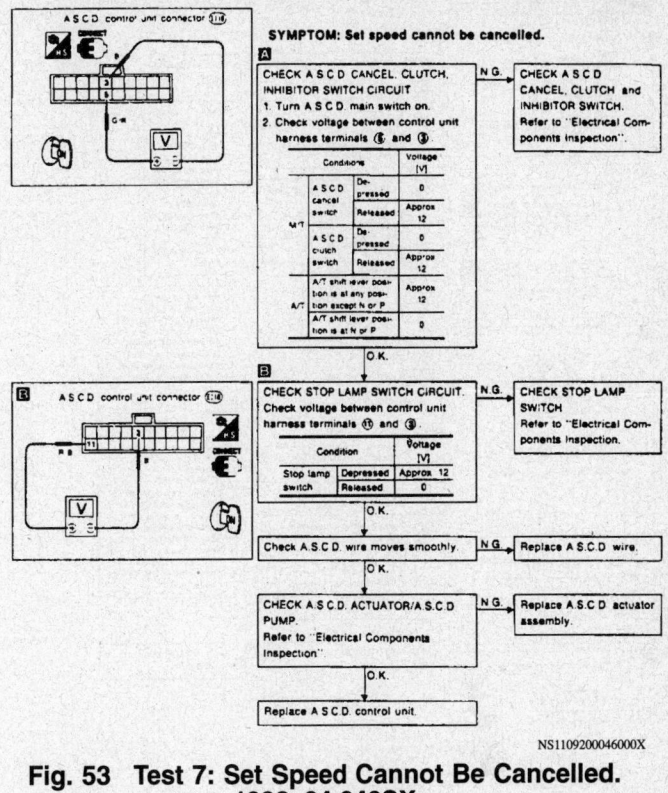

A CHECK A.S.C.D. CANCEL, CLUTCH, INHIBITOR SWITCH CIRCUIT — N.G. → CHECK A.S.C.D. CANCEL, CLUTCH and INHIBITOR SWITCH. Refer to "Electrical Components Inspection".

1. Turn A.S.C.D. main switch on.
2. Check voltage between control unit harness terminals ⑥ and ③.

Conditions			Voltage [V]
M/T	A.S.C.D. cancel switch	Depressed	0
		Released	Approx. 12
	A.S.C.D. clutch switch	Depressed	0
		Released	Approx. 12
A/T	A/T shift lever position is at any position except N or P		Approx. 12
	A/T shift lever position is at N or P		0

O.K. ↓

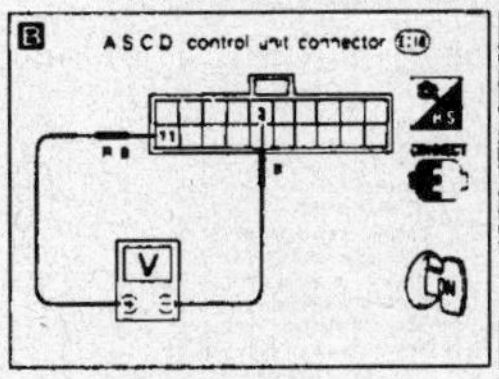
B
A.S.C.D. control unit connector E118
11
3
R/B
B
V

B CHECK STOP LAMP SWITCH CIRCUIT. Check voltage between control unit harness terminals ⑪ and ③. — N.G. → CHECK STOP LAMP SWITCH. Refer to "Electrical Components Inspection".

Condition		Voltage [V]
Stop lamp switch	Depressed	Approx. 12
	Released	0

O.K. ↓

Check A.S.C.D. wire moves smoothly. — N.G. → Replace A.S.C.D. wire.

O.K. ↓

CHECK A.S.C.D. ACTUATOR/A.S.C.D. PUMP. Refer to "Electrical Components Inspection". — N.G. → Replace A.S.C.D. actuator assembly.

O.K. ↓

Replace A.S.C.D. control unit.

NS1109200046000X

Fig. 53 Test 7: Set Speed Cannot Be Cancelled. 1993–94 240SX

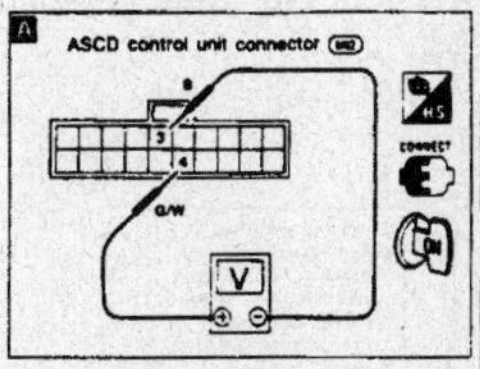
A
ASCD control unit connector M82
3
4
G/W
V

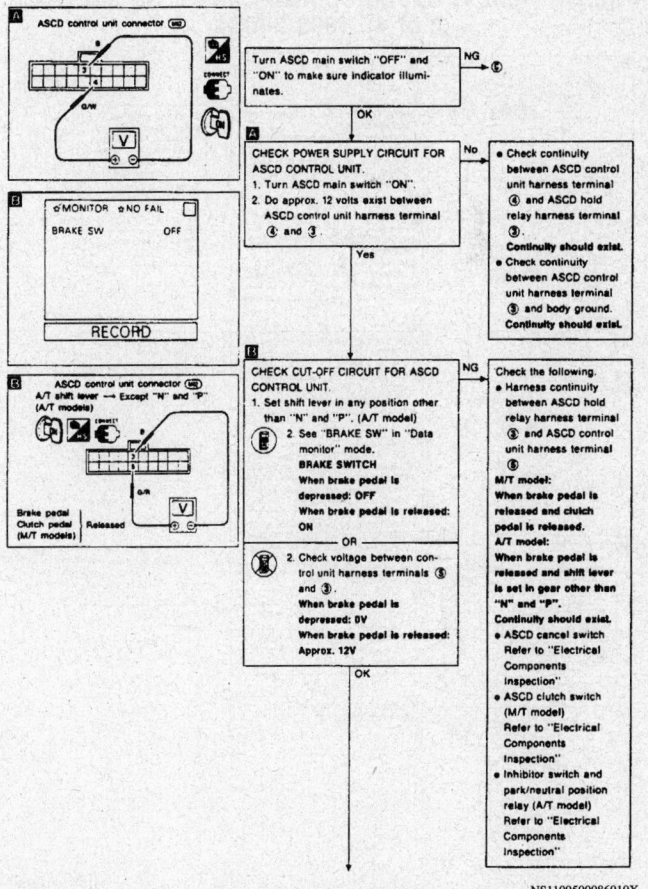

Turn ASCD main switch "OFF" and "ON" to make sure indicator illuminates. — NG → ⓔ

OK ↓

A CHECK POWER SUPPLY CIRCUIT FOR ASCD CONTROL UNIT. — No →
- Check continuity between ASCD control unit harness terminal ④ and ASCD hold relay harness terminal ③. **Continuity should exist.**
- Check continuity between ASCD control unit harness terminal ③ and body ground. **Continuity should exist.**

1. Turn ASCD main switch "ON".
2. Do approx. 12 volts exist between ASCD control unit harness terminal ④ and ③.

Yes ↓

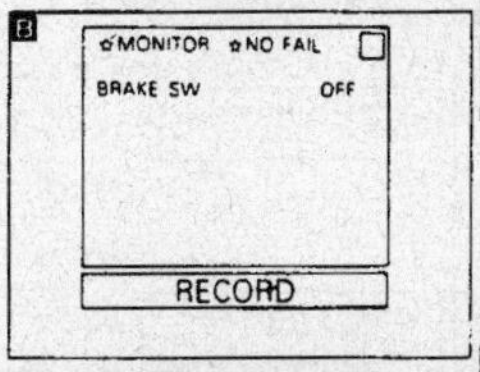
B
MONITOR
NO FAIL
BRAKE SW
OFF
RECORD

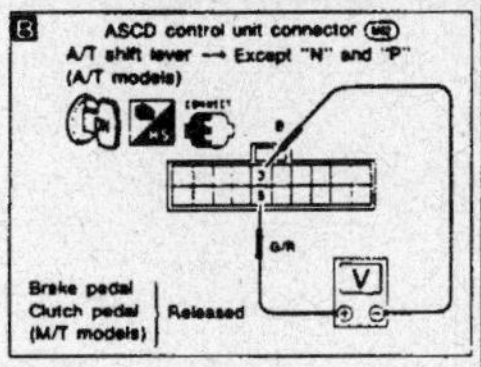
B
ASCD control unit connector M82
A/T shift lever → Except "N" and "P" (A/T models)
G/R
V
Brake pedal
Clutch pedal (M/T models)
Released

B CHECK CUT-OFF CIRCUIT FOR ASCD CONTROL UNIT. — NG → Check the following.
- Harness continuity between ASCD hold relay harness terminal ③ and ASCD control unit harness terminal ⑤ **M/T model: When brake pedal is released and clutch pedal is released. A/T model: When brake pedal is released and shift lever is set in gear other than "N" and "P". Continuity should exist.**
- ASCD cancel switch Refer to "Electrical Components Inspection"
- ASCD clutch switch (M/T model) Refer to "Electrical Components Inspection"
- Inhibitor switch and park/neutral position relay (A/T model) Refer to "Electrical Components Inspection"

1. Set shift lever in any position other than "N" and "P". (A/T model)
   2. See "BRAKE SW" in "Data monitor" mode. **BRAKE SWITCH When brake pedal is depressed: OFF When brake pedal is released: ON**

   — OR —

   2. Check voltage between control unit harness terminals ⑤ and ③. **When brake pedal is depressed: 0V When brake pedal is released: Approx. 12V**

OK ↓

NS1109500086010X

Fig. 55 Test 1: Speed Control Cannot Be Set (Part 1 of 4). 1995 240SX

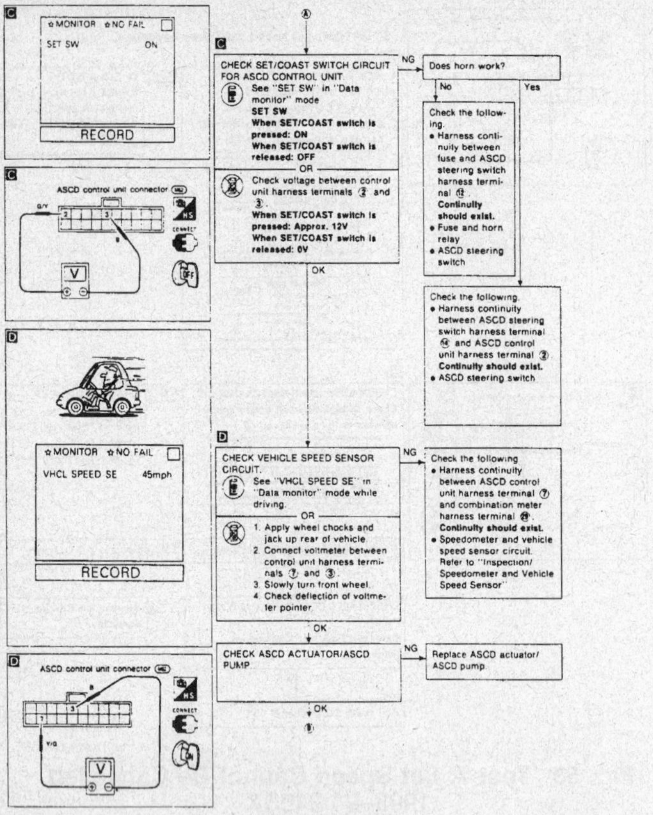
☆MONITOR ☆NO FAIL
SET SW ON
RECORD
ASCD control unit connector
☆MONITOR ☆NO FAIL
VHCL SPEED SE 45mph
RECORD
ASCD control unit connector
Ⓐ
C
CHECK SET/COAST SWITCH CIRCUIT FOR ASCD CONTROL UNIT.
See "SET SW" in "Data monitor" mode
SET SW
When SET/COAST switch is pressed: ON
When SET/COAST switch is released: OFF
OR
Check voltage between control unit harness terminals ② and ③.
When SET/COAST switch is pressed: Approx. 12V
When SET/COAST switch is released: 0V
NG
Does horn work?
No
Yes
Check the following.
• Harness continuity between fuse and ASCD steering switch harness terminal ⑫.
Continuity should exist.
• Fuse and horn relay
• ASCD steering switch
Check the following.
• Harness continuity between ASCD steering switch harness terminal ⑭ and ASCD control unit harness terminal ②.
Continuity should exist.
• ASCD steering switch
OK
D
CHECK VEHICLE SPEED SENSOR CIRCUIT.
See "VHCL SPEED SE" in "Data monitor" mode while driving.
OR
1. Apply wheel chocks and jack up rear of vehicle.
2. Connect voltmeter between control unit harness terminals ⑦ and ③.
3. Slowly turn front wheel.
4. Check deflection of voltmeter pointer.
NG
Check the following
• Harness continuity between ASCD control unit harness terminal ⑦ and combination meter harness terminal ㉙.
Continuity should exist.
• Speedometer and vehicle speed sensor circuit. Refer to "Inspection/Speedometer and Vehicle Speed Sensor"
OK
CHECK ASCD ACTUATOR/ASCD PUMP.
NG
Replace ASCD actuator/ASCD pump.
OK
Ⓑ

NS1109500086020X

Fig. 55 Test 1: Speed Control Cannot Be Set (Part 2 of 4). 1995 240SX

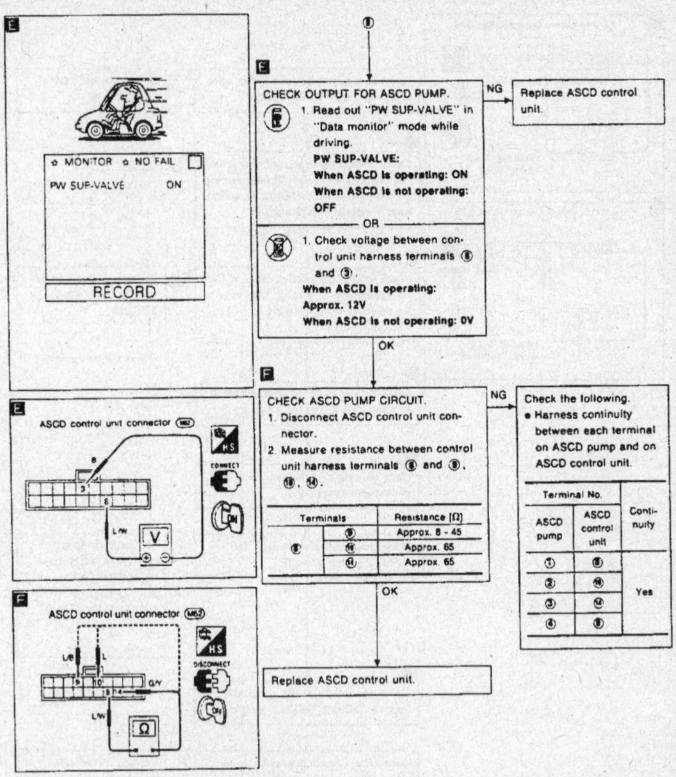
☆MONITOR ☆NO FAIL
PW SUP-VALVE ON
RECORD
ASCD control unit connector
ASCD control unit connector
Ⓑ
E
CHECK OUTPUT FOR ASCD PUMP.
1. Read out "PW SUP-VALVE" in "Data monitor" mode while driving.
PW SUP-VALVE:
When ASCD is operating: ON
When ASCD is not operating: OFF
OR
1. Check voltage between control unit harness terminals ⑧ and ③.
When ASCD is operating: Approx. 12V
When ASCD is not operating: 0V
NG
Replace ASCD control unit.
OK
F
CHECK ASCD PUMP CIRCUIT.
1. Disconnect ASCD control unit connector.
2. Measure resistance between control unit harness terminals ⑧ and ⑨, ⑬, ⑭.
Terminals | Resistance [Ω]
⑧ ⑨ Approx. 8 - 45
⑬ Approx. 65
⑭ Approx. 65
NG
Check the following.
• Harness continuity between each terminal on ASCD pump and on ASCD control unit.
Terminal No.
ASCD pump | ASCD control unit | Continuity
① ⑧
② ⑬ Yes
③ ⑭
④ ⑨
OK
Replace ASCD control unit.

NS1109500086030X

Fig. 55 Test 1: Speed Control Cannot Be Set (Part 3 of 4). 1995 240SX

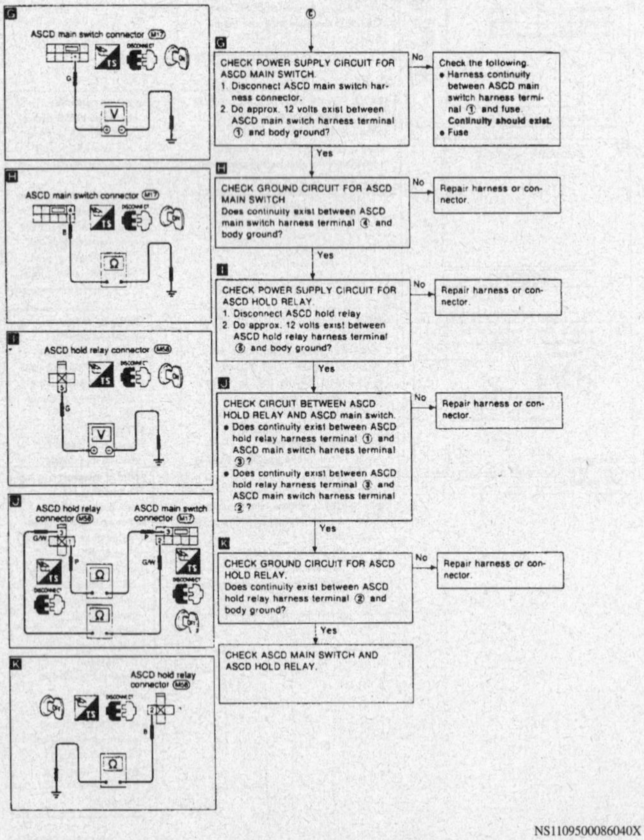
ASCD main switch connector (M17)
ASCD main switch connector (M17)
ASCD hold relay connector (M58)
ASCD hold relay connector (M58)
ASCD main switch connector (M17)
ASCD hold relay connector (M58)
Ⓒ
G
CHECK POWER SUPPLY CIRCUIT FOR ASCD MAIN SWITCH.
1. Disconnect ASCD main switch harness connector.
2. Do approx. 12 volts exist between ASCD main switch harness terminal ① and body ground?
No
Check the following.
• Harness continuity between ASCD main switch harness terminal ① and fuse.
Continuity should exist.
• Fuse
Yes
H
CHECK GROUND CIRCUIT FOR ASCD MAIN SWITCH
Does continuity exist between ASCD main switch harness terminal ④ and body ground?
No
Repair harness or connector.
Yes
I
CHECK POWER SUPPLY CIRCUIT FOR ASCD HOLD RELAY.
1. Disconnect ASCD hold relay
2. Do approx. 12 volts exist between ASCD hold relay harness terminal ⑤ and body ground?
No
Repair harness or connector.
Yes
J
CHECK CIRCUIT BETWEEN ASCD HOLD RELAY AND ASCD main switch.
• Does continuity exist between ASCD hold relay harness terminal ① and ASCD main switch harness terminal ③?
• Does continuity exist between ASCD hold relay harness terminal ③ and ASCD main switch harness terminal ②?
No
Repair harness or connector.
Yes
K
CHECK GROUND CIRCUIT FOR ASCD HOLD RELAY.
Does continuity exist between ASCD hold relay harness terminal ② and body ground?
No
Repair harness or connector.
Yes
CHECK ASCD MAIN SWITCH AND ASCD HOLD RELAY.

NS1109500086040X

Fig. 55 Test 1: Speed Control Cannot Be Set (Part 4 of 4). 1995 240SX

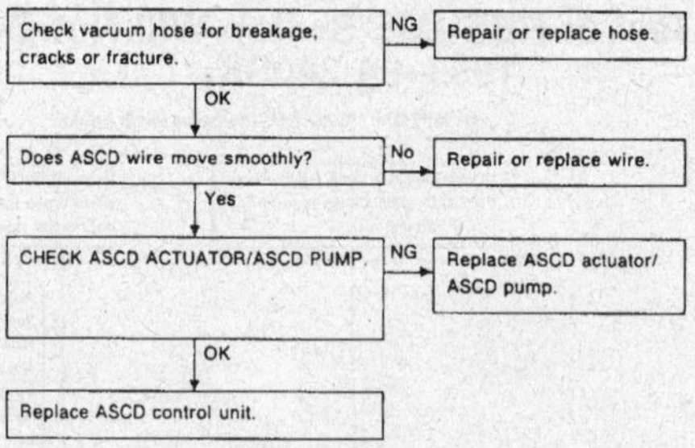
Check vacuum hose for breakage, cracks or fracture.
NG
Repair or replace hose.
OK
Does ASCD wire move smoothly?
No
Repair or replace wire.
Yes
CHECK ASCD ACTUATOR/ASCD PUMP.
NG
Replace ASCD actuator/ASCD pump.
OK
Replace ASCD control unit.

NS1109500087000X

Fig. 56 Test 2: Engine Hunts. 1995 240SX

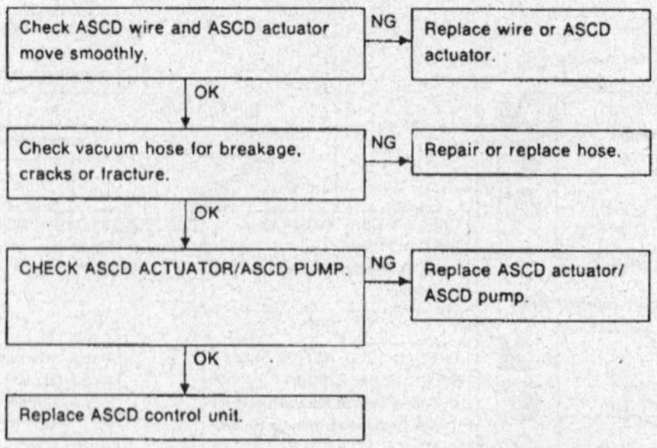
Check ASCD wire and ASCD actuator move smoothly.
NG
Replace wire or ASCD actuator.
OK
Check vacuum hose for breakage, cracks or fracture.
NG
Repair or replace hose.
OK
CHECK ASCD ACTUATOR/ASCD PUMP.
NG
Replace ASCD actuator/ASCD pump.
OK
Replace ASCD control unit.

NS1109500088000X

Fig. 57 Test 3: Large Difference Between Set Vehicle Speed & Actual Speed. 1995 240SX

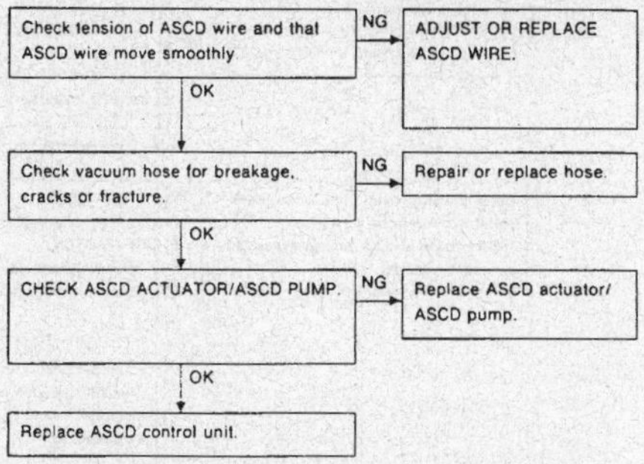
Check tension of ASCD wire and that ASCD wire move smoothly
NG
ADJUST OR REPLACE ASCD WIRE.
OK
Check vacuum hose for breakage, cracks or fracture.
NG
Repair or replace hose.
OK
CHECK ASCD ACTUATOR/ASCD PUMP.
NG
Replace ASCD actuator/ ASCD pump.
OK
Replace ASCD control unit.

NS1109500089000X

Fig. 58 Test 4: Deceleration Is Greatest Immediately After ASCD Has Been Set. 1995 240SX

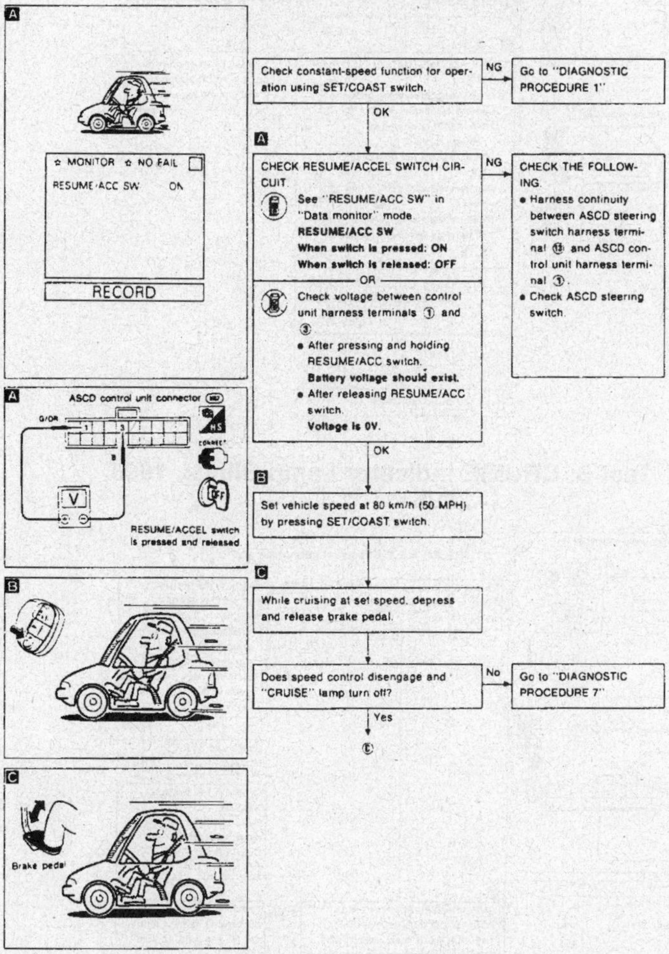
A
☆ MONITOR ☆ NO FAIL
RESUME/ACC SW ON
RECORD
Check constant-speed function for operation using SET/COAST switch.
NG
Go to "DIAGNOSTIC PROCEDURE 1"
OK
A
CHECK RESUME/ACCEL SWITCH CIRCUIT.
See "RESUME/ACC SW" in "Data monitor" mode.
RESUME/ACC SW
When switch is pressed: ON
When switch is released: OFF
OR
Check voltage between control unit harness terminals ⑦ and ③.
• After pressing and holding RESUME/ACC switch.
Battery voltage should exist.
• After releasing RESUME/ACC switch.
Voltage is 0V.
NG
CHECK THE FOLLOWING.
• Harness continuity between ASCD steering switch harness terminal ⑬ and ASCD control unit harness terminal ⑦.
• Check ASCD steering switch.
A
ASCD control unit connector
G/OR
RESUME/ACCEL switch is pressed and released
OK
B
Set vehicle speed at 80 km/h (50 MPH) by pressing SET/COAST switch.
B
C
While cruising at set speed, depress and release brake pedal.
C
Brake pedal
Does speed control disengage and "CRUISE" lamp turn off?
No
Go to "DIAGNOSTIC PROCEDURE 7"
Yes
Ⓒ

NS1109500091010X

Fig. 60 Test 6: RESUME Switch Will Not Operate (Part 1 of 2). 1995 240SX

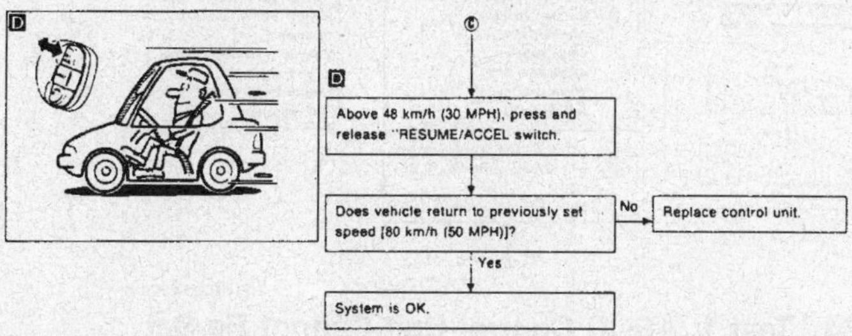
D
Ⓒ
D
Above 48 km/h (30 MPH), press and release "RESUME/ACCEL switch.
Does vehicle return to previously set speed [80 km/h (50 MPH)]?
No
Replace control unit.
Yes
System is OK.

NS1109500091020X

Fig. 60 Test 6: RESUME Switch Will Not Operate (Part 2 of 2). 1995 240SX

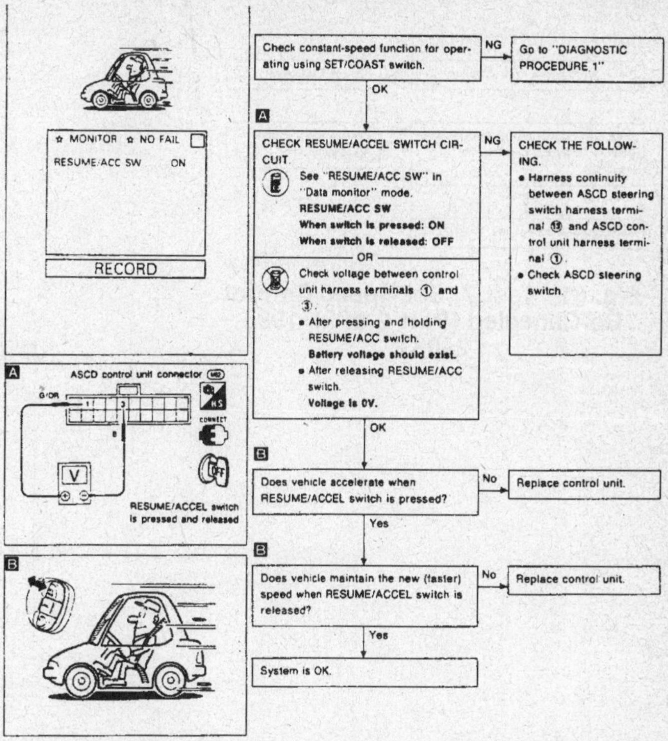
Check constant-speed function for operating using SET/COAST switch.
NG
Go to "DIAGNOSTIC PROCEDURE 1"
OK
A
☆ MONITOR ☆ NO FAIL
RESUME/ACC SW ON
RECORD
CHECK RESUME/ACCEL SWITCH CIRCUIT.
See "RESUME/ACC SW" in "Data monitor" mode.
RESUME/ACC SW
When switch is pressed: ON
When switch is released: OFF
OR
Check voltage between control unit harness terminals ⑦ and ③.
• After pressing and holding RESUME/ACC switch.
Battery voltage should exist.
• After releasing RESUME/ACC switch.
Voltage is 0V.
NG
CHECK THE FOLLOWING.
• Harness continuity between ASCD steering switch harness terminal ⑬ and ASCD control unit harness terminal ⑦.
• Check ASCD steering switch.
A
ASCD control unit connector
G/OR
RESUME/ACCEL switch is pressed and released
OK
B
Does vehicle accelerate when RESUME/ACCEL switch is pressed?
No
Replace control unit.
Yes
B
Does vehicle maintain the new (faster) speed when RESUME/ACCEL switch is released?
No
Replace control unit.
Yes
System is OK.

NS1109500090000X

Fig. 59 Test 5: ACCEL Switch Will Not Operate. 1995 240SX

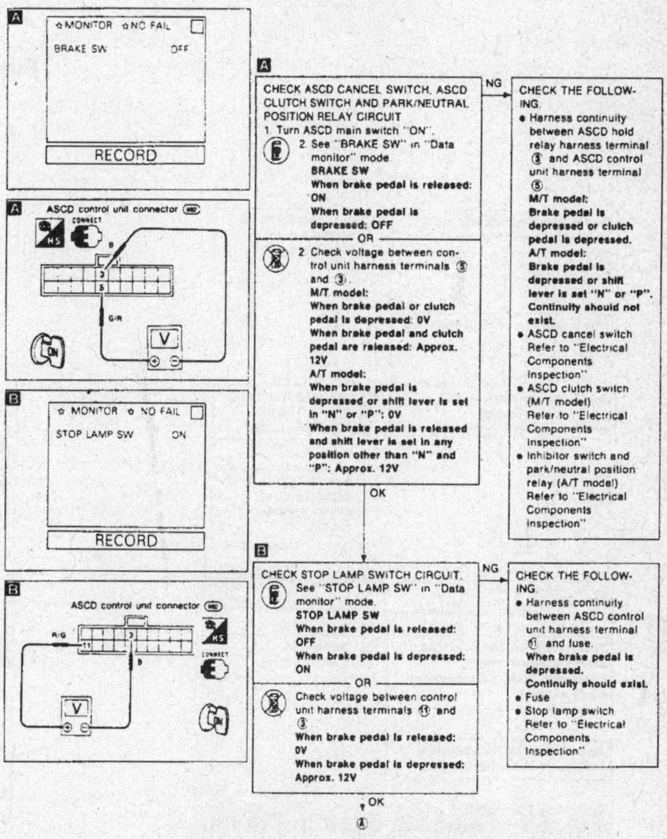
A
☆MONITOR ☆NO FAIL
BRAKE SW OFF
RECORD
A
CHECK ASCD CANCEL SWITCH, ASCD CLUTCH SWITCH AND PARK/NEUTRAL POSITION RELAY CIRCUIT
1. Turn ASCD main switch "ON".
2. See "BRAKE SW" in "Data monitor" mode.
BRAKE SW
When brake pedal is released: ON
When brake pedal is depressed: OFF
OR
2. Check voltage between control unit harness terminals ⑤ and ③.
M/T model:
When brake pedal or clutch pedal is depressed: 0V
When brake pedal and clutch pedal are released: Approx. 12V
A/T model:
When brake pedal is depressed or shift lever is set in "N" or "P": 0V
When brake pedal is released and shift lever is set in any position other than "N" and "P": Approx. 12V
NG
CHECK THE FOLLOWING.
• Harness continuity between ASCD hold relay harness terminal ③ and ASCD control unit harness terminal ⑤.
M/T model:
Brake pedal is depressed or clutch pedal is depressed.
A/T model:
Brake pedal is depressed or shift lever is set "N" or "P".
Continuity should not exist.
• ASCD cancel switch Refer to "Electrical Components Inspection"
• ASCD clutch switch (M/T model) Refer to "Electrical Components Inspection"
• Inhibitor switch and park/neutral position relay (A/T model) Refer to "Electrical Components Inspection"
A
ASCD control unit connector
G/R
OK
B
☆ MONITOR ☆ NO FAIL
STOP LAMP SW ON
RECORD
B
CHECK STOP LAMP SWITCH CIRCUIT.
See "STOP LAMP SW" in "Data monitor" mode.
STOP LAMP SW
When brake pedal is released: OFF
When brake pedal is depressed: ON
OR
Check voltage between control unit harness terminals ⑪ and ③.
When brake pedal is released: 0V
When brake pedal is depressed: Approx. 12V
NG
CHECK THE FOLLOWING.
• Harness continuity between ASCD control unit harness terminal ⑪ and fuse.
When brake pedal is depressed.
Continuity should exist.
• Fuse
• Stop lamp switch Refer to "Electrical Components Inspection"
B
ASCD control unit connector
R/G
OK
Ⓐ

NS1109500092010X

Fig. 61 Test 7: Set Speed Cannot Be Canceled (Part 1 of 2). 1995 240SX

(A)

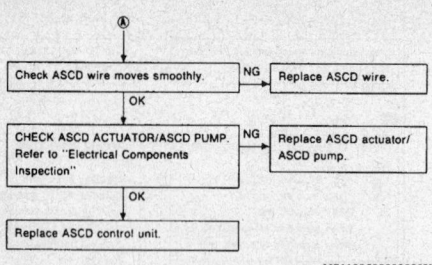

- Check ASCD wire moves smoothly. — NG → Replace ASCD wire.
- OK ↓
- CHECK ASCD ACTUATOR/ASCD PUMP. Refer to "Electrical Components Inspection" — NG → Replace ASCD actuator/ ASCD pump.
- OK ↓
- Replace ASCD control unit.

NS1109500092020X

Fig. 61 Test 7: Set Speed Cannot Be Canceled (Part 2 of 2). 1995 240SX

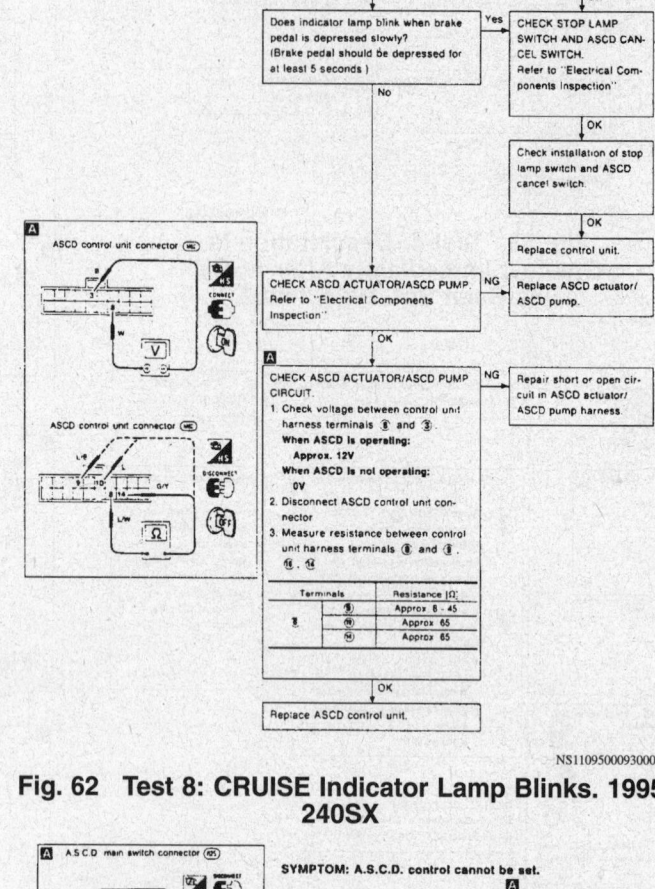

- Does indicator lamp blink when ASCD main switch is turned to "ON" again? — Yes → CHECK ASCD STEERING SWITCH. Refer to "Electrical Components Inspection" — OK ↓
- No ↓
- Does indicator lamp blink when brake pedal is depressed slowly? (Brake pedal should be depressed for at least 5 seconds.) — Yes → CHECK STOP LAMP SWITCH AND ASCD CANCEL SWITCH. Refer to "Electrical Components Inspection" — OK → Check installation of stop lamp switch and ASCD cancel switch. — OK → Replace control unit.
- No ↓
- CHECK ASCD ACTUATOR/ASCD PUMP. Refer to "Electrical Components Inspection" — NG → Replace ASCD actuator/ ASCD pump.
- OK ↓
- [A] CHECK ASCD ACTUATOR/ASCD PUMP CIRCUIT. — NG → Repair short or open circuit in ASCD actuator/ ASCD pump harness.
  1. Check voltage between control unit harness terminals (8) and (3).
     When ASCD is operating:
     Approx. 12V
     When ASCD is not operating:
     0V
  2. Disconnect ASCD control unit connector
  3. Measure resistance between control unit harness terminals (8) and (5), (16), (14)

Terminals		Resistance (Ω)
(8)	(5)	Approx 8 - 45
	(16)	Approx 65
	(14)	Approx 65

- OK ↓
- Replace ASCD control unit.

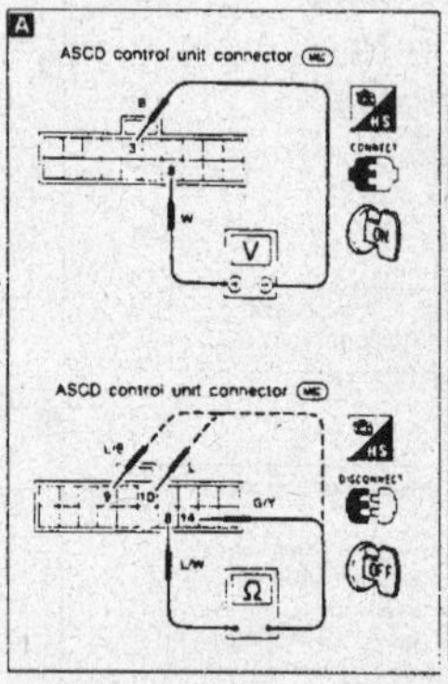
A
ASCD control unit connector
ASCD control unit connector

NS1109500093000X

Fig. 62 Test 8: CRUISE Indicator Lamp Blinks. 1995 240SX

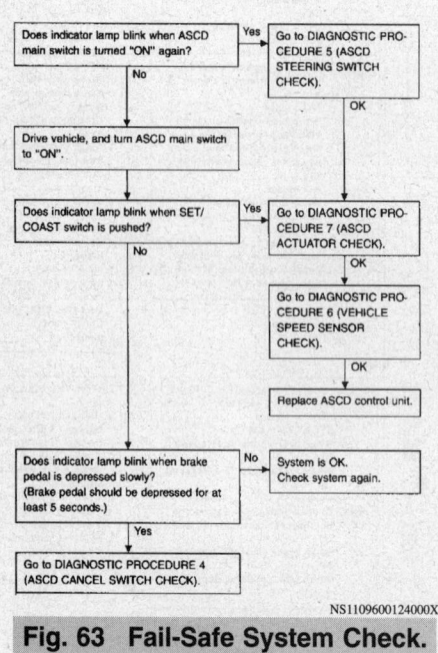

- Does indicator lamp blink when ASCD main switch is turned "ON" again? — Yes → Go to DIAGNOSTIC PROCEDURE 5 (ASCD STEERING SWITCH CHECK). — OK ↓
- No ↓
- Drive vehicle, and turn ASCD main switch to "ON".
- Does indicator lamp blink when SET/ COAST switch is pushed? — Yes → Go to DIAGNOSTIC PROCEDURE 7 (ASCD ACTUATOR CHECK). — OK → Go to DIAGNOSTIC PROCEDURE 6 (VEHICLE SPEED SENSOR CHECK). — OK → Replace ASCD control unit.
- No ↓
- Does indicator lamp blink when brake pedal is depressed slowly? (Brake pedal should be depressed for at least 5 seconds.) — No → System is OK. Check system again.
- Yes ↓
- Go to DIAGNOSTIC PROCEDURE 4 (ASCD CANCEL SWITCH CHECK).

NS1109600124000X

Fig. 63 Fail-Safe System Check. 1996 240SX

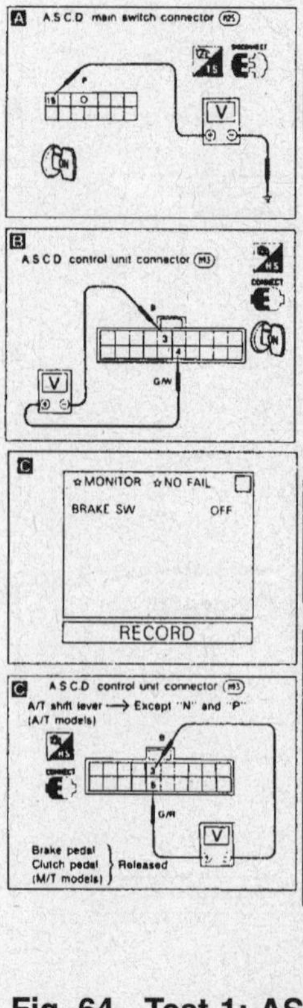
A
B
A.S.C.D. control unit connector
C
MONITOR
NO FAIL
BRAKE SW
OFF
RECORD
C
A.S.C.D. control unit connector
A/T shift lever → Except "N" and "P" (A/T models)
Brake pedal
Clutch pedal (M/T models)
Released

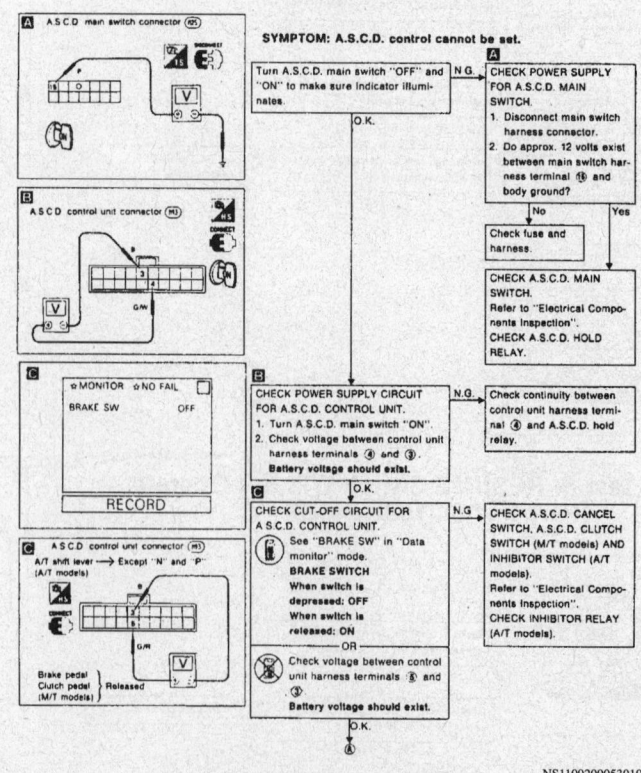

SYMPTOM: A.S.C.D. control cannot be set.

- Turn A.S.C.D. main switch "OFF" and "ON" to make sure indicator illuminates. — N.G. → [A] CHECK POWER SUPPLY FOR A.S.C.D. MAIN SWITCH.
  1. Disconnect main switch harness connector.
  2. Do approx. 12 volts exist between main switch harness terminal (16) and body ground?
  - No → Check fuse and harness.
  - Yes → CHECK A.S.C.D. MAIN SWITCH. Refer to "Electrical Components Inspection". CHECK A.S.C.D. HOLD RELAY.
- O.K. ↓
- [B] CHECK POWER SUPPLY CIRCUIT FOR A.S.C.D. CONTROL UNIT. — N.G. → Check continuity between control unit harness terminal (4) and A.S.C.D. hold relay.
  1. Turn A.S.C.D. main switch "ON".
  2. Check voltage between control unit harness terminals (4) and (3). **Battery voltage should exist.**
- O.K. ↓
- [C] CHECK CUT-OFF CIRCUIT FOR A.S.C.D. CONTROL UNIT. — N.G → CHECK A.S.C.D. CANCEL SWITCH, A.S.C.D. CLUTCH SWITCH (M/T models) AND INHIBITOR SWITCH (A/T models). Refer to "Electrical Components Inspection". CHECK INHIBITOR RELAY (A/T models).
  - See "BRAKE SW" in "Data monitor" mode.
    BRAKE SWITCH
    When switch is depressed: OFF
    When switch is released: ON
  - OR
  - Check voltage between control unit harness terminals (5) and (3). **Battery voltage should exist.**
- O.K. ↓
- (A)

NS1109200053010X

Fig. 64 Test 1: ASCD Control Unit Cannot Be Set (Part 1 of 3). 300ZX

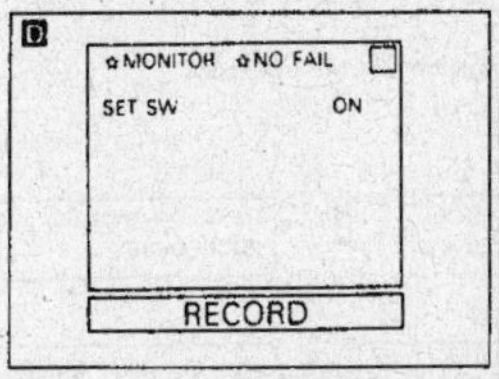
D
☆MONITOR ☆NO FAIL
SET SW ON
RECORD

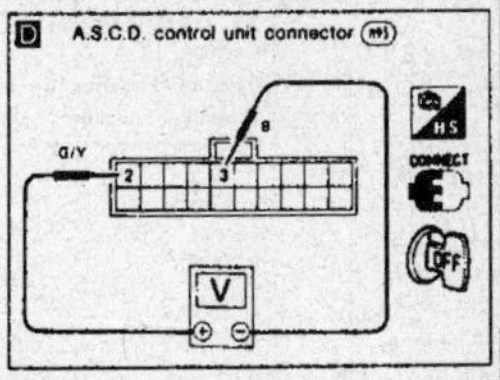
D A.S.C.D. control unit connector
G/Y
2
3
8
V

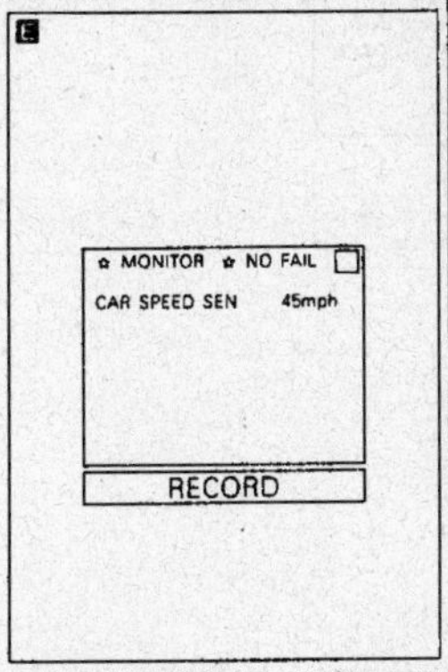
E
☆ MONITOR ☆ NO FAIL
CAR SPEED SEN 45mph
RECORD

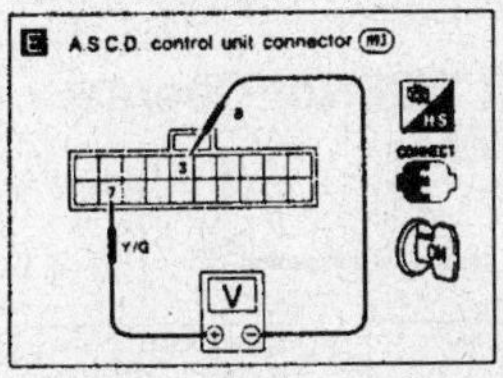
E A.S.C.D. control unit connector
7
3
8
Y/G
V

(A)

D CHECK SET/COAST SWITCH CIRCUIT FOR A.S.C.D. CONTROL UNIT.
See "SET SW" in "Data monitor" mode.
SET SW
When switch is pressed: ON
When switch is released: OFF
— OR —
1. Turn and keep on SET/COAST switch of A.S.C.D. combination (steering) switch.
2. Check voltage between control unit harness terminals ② and ③.
Battery voltage should exist.

N.G. → Does horn work?
- No → Check fuse and horn relay.
- Yes → CHECK A.S.C.D. COMBINATION (STEERING) SWITCH. Refer to "Electrical Components Inspection".

O.K. ↓

E CHECK SPEED SENSOR CIRCUIT.
See "CAR SPEED SEN" in "Data monitor" mode while driving.
— OR —
1. Apply wheel chocks and jack up rear of vehicle.
2. Connect voltmeter between control unit harness terminals ⑦ and ③.
3. Slowly turn rear wheel.
4. Check deflection of voltmeter pointer.

N.G. → CHECK SPEED SENSOR. Refer to "Electrical Components Inspection".

O.K. ↓

CHECK A.S.C.D. ACTUATOR/A.S.C.D. PUMP. Refer to "Electrical Components Inspection".

N.G. → Replace A.S.C.D. actuator assembly.

O.K. ↓

(B)

NS1109200053020X

Fig. 64 Test 1: ASCD Control Unit Cannot Be Set (Part 2 of 3). 300ZX

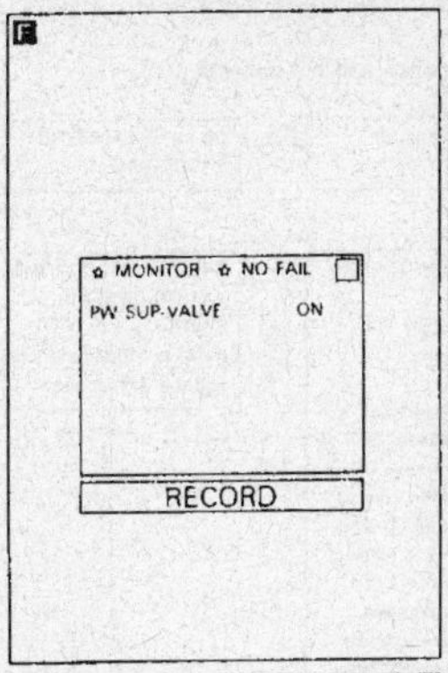
F
☆ MONITOR ☆ NO FAIL
PW SUP-VALVE ON
RECORD

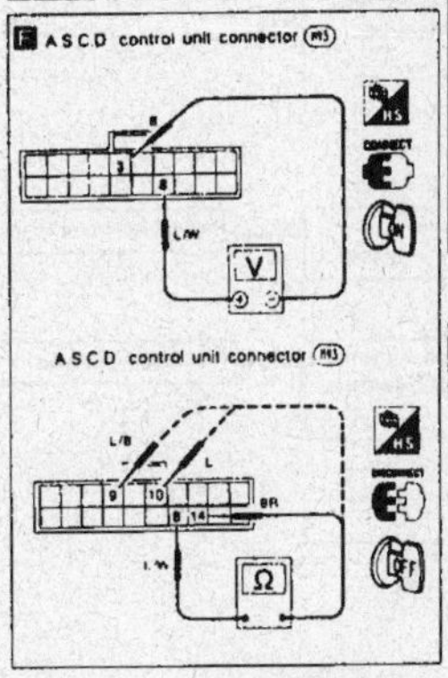
F A.S.C.D. control unit connector
8
3
8
L/W
V
A.S.C.D. control unit connector
L/B
L
9
10
8
14
BR
L/W
Ω

(B)

F CHECK OUTPUT FOR A.S.C.D. ACTUATOR/A.S.C.D. PUMP.
1. Read out "PW SUP- VALVE" in "Data monitor" mode while driving.
PW SUP-VALVE:
ON (When A.S.C.D. is operating.)
OFF (When A.S.C.D. is not operating.)
— OR —
1. Check voltage between control unit harness terminals ⑧ and ③.
Voltage is 8V.

N.G. → Repair A.S.C.D. control unit.

O.K. ↓

1. Disconnect A.S.C.D. control unit connector.
2. Measure resistance between control unit harness terminals ⑧ and ⑨, ⑩, ⑭.

Terminals		Resistance [Ω]
⑧	⑨	Approx. 8 - 45
	⑩	Approx. 65
	⑭	Approx. 65

O.K. → Repair A.S.C.D. control unit.

N.G. ↓

Repair short or open circuit in A.S.C.D. actuator assembly.

NS1109200053030X

Fig. 64 Test 1: ASCD Control Unit Cannot Be Set (Part 3 of 3). 300ZX

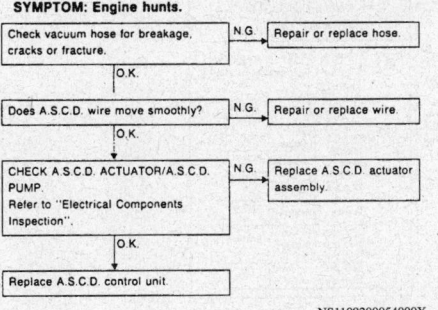

SYMPTOM: Engine hunts.

Check vacuum hose for breakage, cracks or fracture. — N.G. → Repair or replace hose.

O.K. ↓

Does A.S.C.D. wire move smoothly? — N.G. → Repair or replace wire.

O.K. ↓

CHECK A.S.C.D. ACTUATOR/A.S.C.D. PUMP. Refer to "Electrical Components Inspection". — N.G. → Replace A.S.C.D. actuator assembly.

O.K. ↓

Replace A.S.C.D. control unit.

NS1109200054000X

Fig. 65 Test 2: Engine Hunts. 300ZX

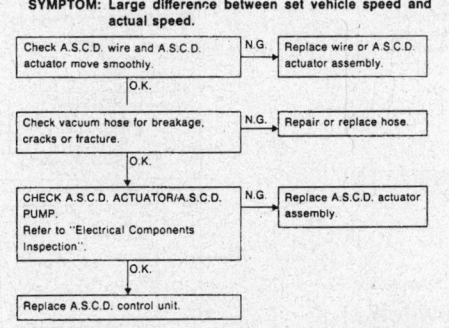

SYMPTOM: Large difference between set vehicle speed and actual speed.

Check A.S.C.D. wire and A.S.C.D. actuator move smoothly. — N.G. → Replace wire or A.S.C.D. actuator assembly.

O.K. ↓

Check vacuum hose for breakage, cracks or fracture. — N.G. → Repair or replace hose.

O.K. ↓

CHECK A.S.C.D. ACTUATOR/A.S.C.D. PUMP. Refer to "Electrical Components Inspection". — N.G. → Replace A.S.C.D. actuator assembly.

O.K. ↓

Replace A.S.C.D. control unit.

NS1109200055000X

Fig. 66 Test 3: Large Difference Between Set Vehicle Speed & Actual Speed. 300ZX

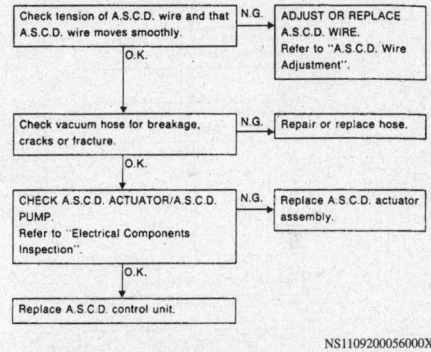

SYMPTOM: Deceleration is greatest immediately after A.S.C.D. has been set.

Check tension of A.S.C.D. wire and that A.S.C.D. wire moves smoothly. — N.G. → ADJUST OR REPLACE A.S.C.D. WIRE. Refer to "A.S.C.D. Wire Adjustment".

O.K. ↓

Check vacuum hose for breakage, cracks or fracture. — N.G. → Repair or replace hose.

O.K. ↓

CHECK A.S.C.D. ACTUATOR/A.S.C.D. PUMP. Refer to "Electrical Components Inspection". — N.G. → Replace A.S.C.D. actuator assembly.

O.K. ↓

Replace A.S.C.D. control unit.

NS1109200056000X

Fig. 67 Test 4: Deceleration Is Greatest Immediately After ASCD Has Been Set. 300ZX

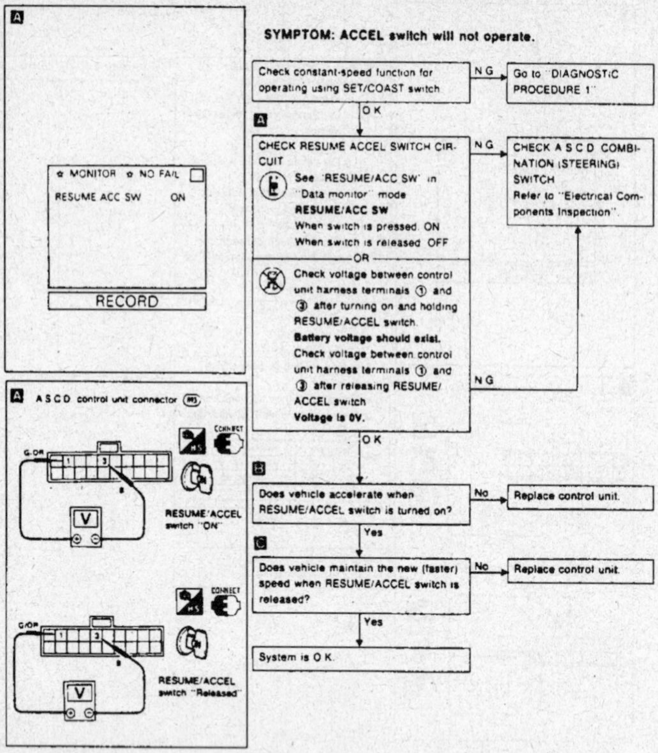
SYMPTOM: ACCEL switch will not operate.
Check constant-speed function for operating using SET/COAST switch
N G
Go to "DIAGNOSTIC PROCEDURE 1"
O K
A
CHECK RESUME ACCEL SWITCH CIRCUIT
See "RESUME/ACC SW" in "Data monitor" mode
RESUME/ACC SW
When switch is pressed: ON
When switch is released: OFF
OR
Check voltage between control unit harness terminals ① and ③ after turning on and holding RESUME/ACCEL switch.
Battery voltage should exist.
Check voltage between control unit harness terminals ① and ③ after releasing RESUME/ACCEL switch
Voltage is 0V.
N G
CHECK A.S.C.D. COMBINATION (STEERING) SWITCH
Refer to "Electrical Components Inspection".
O K
B
Does vehicle accelerate when RESUME/ACCEL switch is turned on?
No
Replace control unit.
Yes
C
Does vehicle maintain the new (faster) speed when RESUME/ACCEL switch is released?
No
Replace control unit.
Yes
System is O.K.
MONITOR NO FAIL
RESUME ACC SW ON
RECORD
A.S.C.D. control unit connector (M3)
G/OR
RESUME/ACCEL switch "ON"
RESUME/ACCEL switch "Released"
CONNECT

NS1109200057000X

Fig. 68 Test 5: ACCEL Switch Will Not Operate. 300ZX

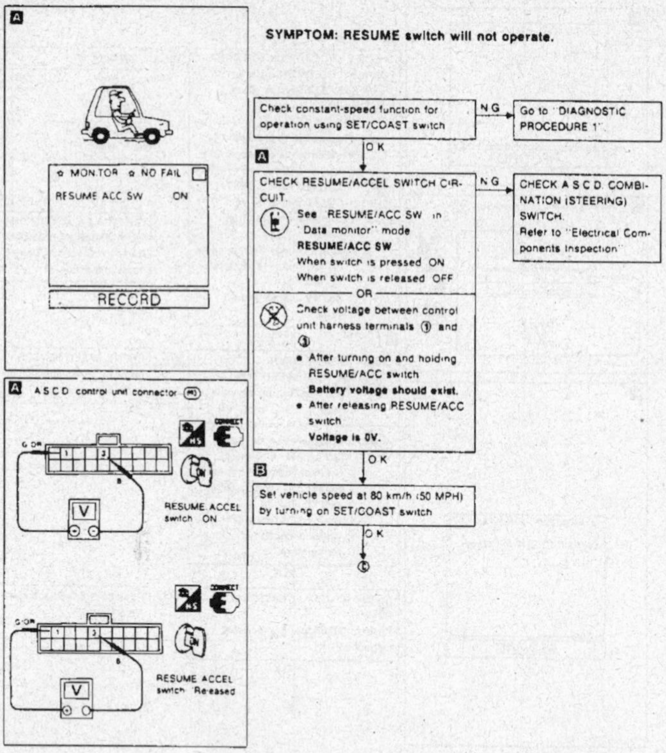
SYMPTOM: RESUME switch will not operate.
Check constant-speed function for operation using SET/COAST switch
N G
Go to "DIAGNOSTIC PROCEDURE 1".
O K
A
CHECK RESUME/ACCEL SWITCH CIRCUIT
See "RESUME/ACC SW" in "Data monitor" mode
RESUME/ACC SW
When switch is pressed: ON
When switch is released: OFF
OR
Check voltage between control unit harness terminals ① and ③.
• After turning on and holding RESUME/ACC switch
Battery voltage should exist.
• After releasing RESUME/ACC switch
Voltage is 0V.
N G
CHECK A.S.C.D. COMBINATION (STEERING) SWITCH.
Refer to "Electrical Components Inspection".
O K
B
Set vehicle speed at 80 km/h (50 MPH) by turning on SET/COAST switch
O K
MONITOR NO FAIL
RESUME ACC SW ON
RECORD
A.S.C.D. control unit connector (M3)
G/OR
RESUME ACCEL switch ON
RESUME ACCEL switch Released
CONNECT

NS1109200058010X

Fig. 69 Test 6: RESUME Switch Will Not Operate (Part 1 of 2). 300ZX

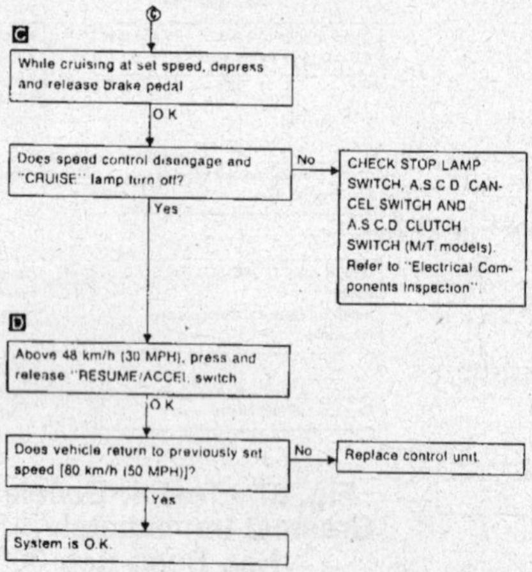
C
While cruising at set speed, depress and release brake pedal
O K
Does speed control disengage and "CRUISE" lamp turn off?
No
CHECK STOP LAMP SWITCH, A.S.C.D. CANCEL SWITCH AND A.S.C.D. CLUTCH SWITCH (M/T models). Refer to "Electrical Components Inspection".
Yes
D
Above 48 km/h (30 MPH), press and release "RESUME/ACCEL switch
O K
Does vehicle return to previously set speed [80 km/h (50 MPH)]?
No
Replace control unit.
Yes
System is O.K.

NS1109200058020X

Fig. 69 Test 6: RESUME Switch Will Not Operate (Part 2 of 2). 300ZX

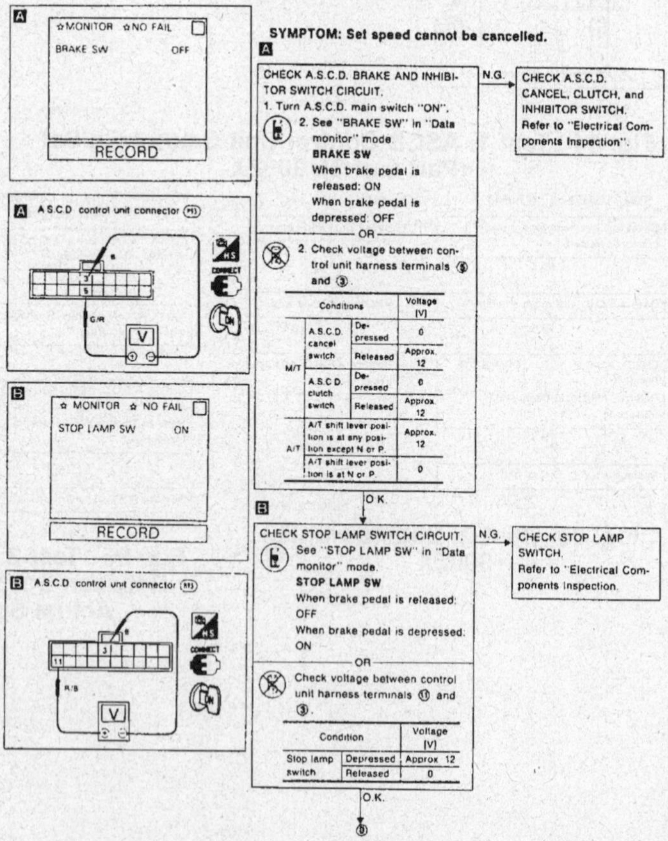
SYMPTOM: Set speed cannot be cancelled.
A
CHECK A.S.C.D. BRAKE AND INHIBITOR SWITCH CIRCUIT.
1. Turn A.S.C.D. main switch "ON".
2. See "BRAKE SW" in "Data monitor" mode
BRAKE SW
When brake pedal is released: ON
When brake pedal is depressed: OFF
OR
2. Check voltage between control unit harness terminals ⑤ and ③.
N.G.
CHECK A.S.C.D. CANCEL, CLUTCH, and INHIBITOR SWITCH. Refer to "Electrical Components Inspection".
O.K.
B
CHECK STOP LAMP SWITCH CIRCUIT.
See "STOP LAMP SW" in "Data monitor" mode.
STOP LAMP SW
When brake pedal is released: OFF
When brake pedal is depressed: ON
OR
Check voltage between control unit harness terminals ⑪ and ③.
N.G.
CHECK STOP LAMP SWITCH. Refer to "Electrical Components Inspection.
O.K.
MONITOR NO FAIL
BRAKE SW OFF
RECORD
A.S.C.D. control unit connector (M3)
G/R
MONITOR NO FAIL
STOP LAMP SW ON
RECORD
B A.S.C.D. control unit connector (M3)
R/B
CONNECT

Conditions			Voltage [V]
M/T	A.S.C.D. cancel switch	Depressed	0
		Released	Approx. 12
	A.S.C.D. clutch switch	Depressed	0
		Released	Approx. 12
A/T	A/T shift lever position is at any position except N or P.		Approx. 12
	A/T shift lever position is at N or P.		0

Condition		Voltage [V]
Stop lamp switch	Depressed	Approx. 12
	Released	0

NS1109200059010X

Fig. 70 Test 7: Set Speed Cannot Be Cancelled (Part 1 of 2). 300ZX

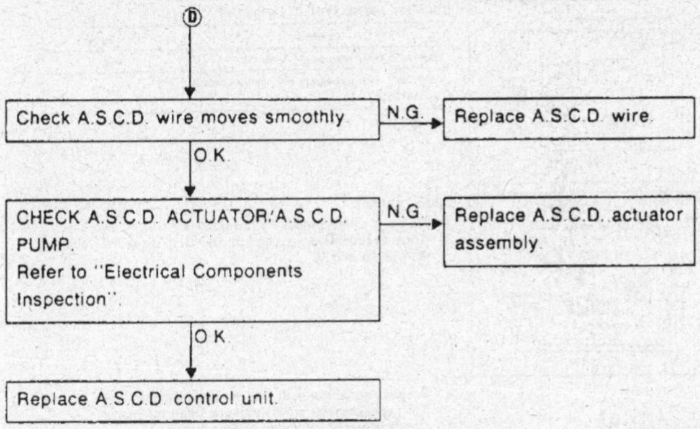
D
Check A.S.C.D. wire moves smoothly.
N.G.
Replace A.S.C.D. wire.
O.K.
CHECK A.S.C.D. ACTUATOR/A.S.C.D. PUMP.
Refer to "Electrical Components Inspection".
N.G.
Replace A.S.C.D. actuator assembly.
O.K.
Replace A.S.C.D. control unit.

NS1109200059020X

Fig. 70 Test 7: Set Speed Cannot Be Cancelled (Part 2 of 2). 300ZX

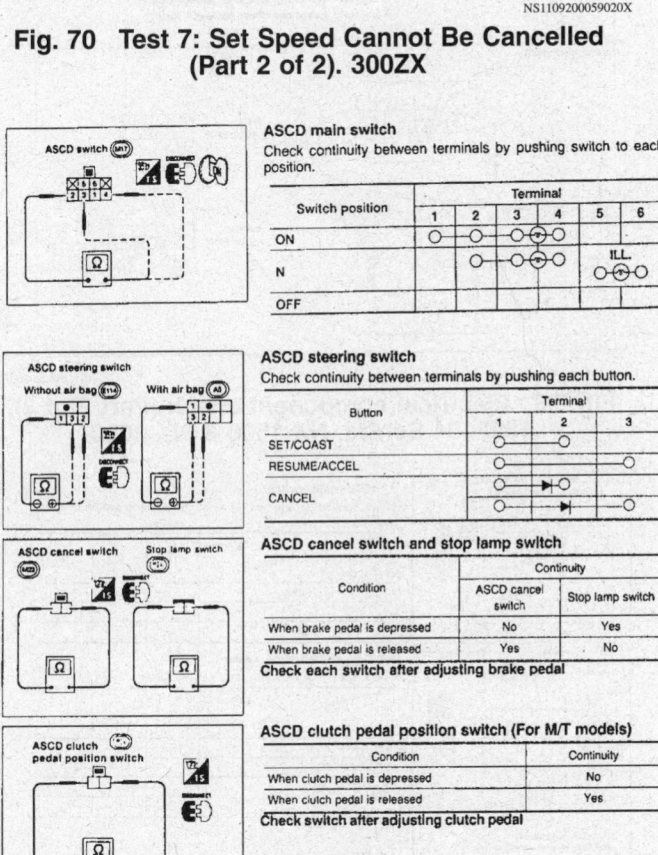

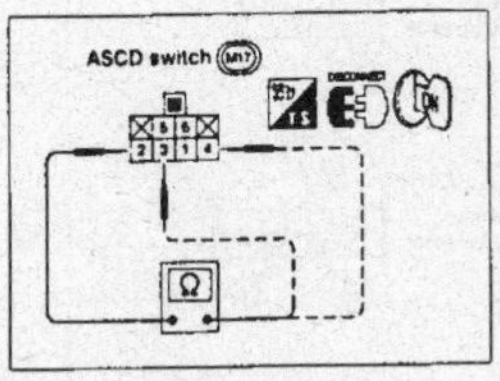
ASCD switch

ASCD main switch

Check continuity between terminals by pushing switch to each position.

Switch position	Terminal 1	2	3	4	5	6
ON	O—	—O—	—O—(lamp)	—O		
N		O—	—O—(lamp)	—O	ILL. O—(lamp)	—O
OFF						

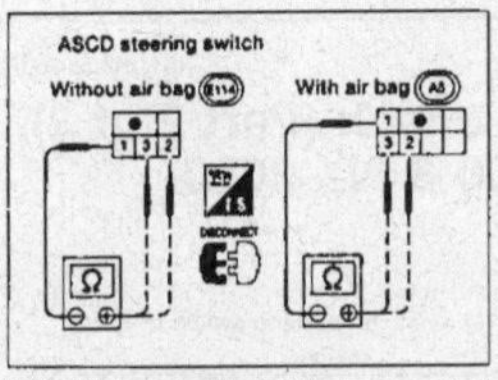
ASCD steering switch
Without air bag
With air bag

ASCD steering switch

Check continuity between terminals by pushing each button.

Button	Terminal 1	2	3
SET/COAST	O—	—O	
RESUME/ACCEL	O—	———	—O
CANCEL	O—	—▶|—O	
	O—	—▶|—	—O

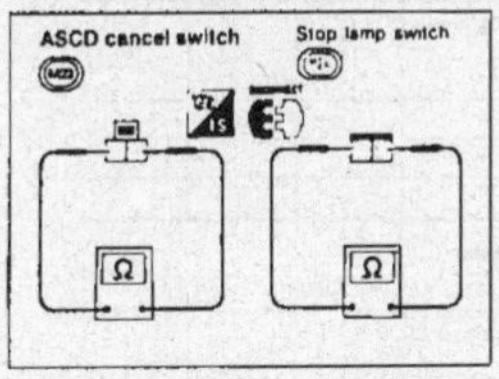
ASCD cancel switch
Stop lamp switch

ASCD cancel switch and stop lamp switch

Condition	Continuity: ASCD cancel switch	Continuity: Stop lamp switch
When brake pedal is depressed	No	Yes
When brake pedal is released	Yes	No

Check each switch after adjusting brake pedal

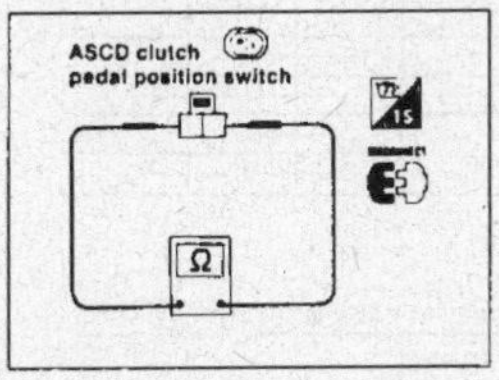
ASCD clutch pedal position switch

ASCD clutch pedal position switch (For M/T models)

Condition	Continuity
When clutch pedal is depressed	No
When clutch pedal is released	Yes

Check switch after adjusting clutch pedal

NS1109100009010X

Fig. 72 Electrical component check (Part 1 of 2). Altima

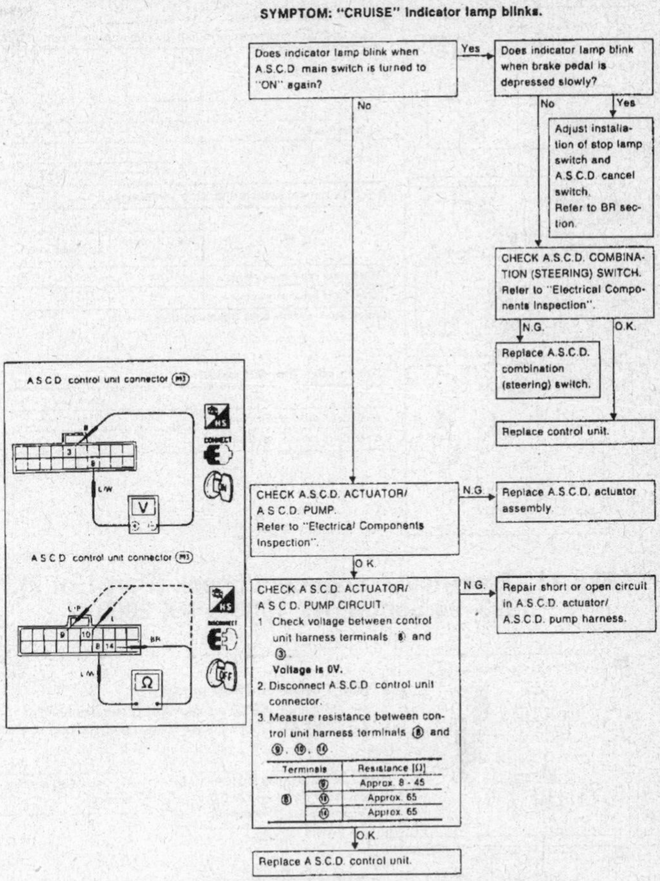
SYMPTOM: "CRUISE" indicator lamp blinks.
Does indicator lamp blink when A.S.C.D. main switch is turned to "ON" again?
Yes
Does indicator lamp blink when brake pedal is depressed slowly?
No
Yes
Adjust installation of stop lamp switch and A.S.C.D. cancel switch. Refer to BR section.
CHECK A.S.C.D. COMBINATION (STEERING) SWITCH. Refer to "Electrical Components Inspection".
N.G.
O.K.
Replace A.S.C.D. combination (steering) switch.
Replace control unit.
A.S.C.D. control unit connector
CHECK A.S.C.D. ACTUATOR/ A.S.C.D. PUMP. Refer to "Electrical Components Inspection".
N.G.
Replace A.S.C.D. actuator assembly.
O.K.
CHECK A.S.C.D. ACTUATOR/ A.S.C.D. PUMP CIRCUIT.
1. Check voltage between control unit harness terminals ⑥ and ③.
Voltage is 0V.
2. Disconnect A.S.C.D. control unit connector.
3. Measure resistance between control unit harness terminals ⑧ and ⑨, ⑩, ⑭.
Terminals
Resistance [Ω]
⑧ ⑨ Approx. 8 - 45
⑩ Approx. 65
⑭ Approx. 65
N.G.
Repair short or open circuit in A.S.C.D. actuator/ A.S.C.D. pump harness.
O.K.
Replace A.S.C.D. control unit.

NS1109200060000X

Fig. 71 Test 8: CRUISE Indicator Lamp Blinks. 300ZX

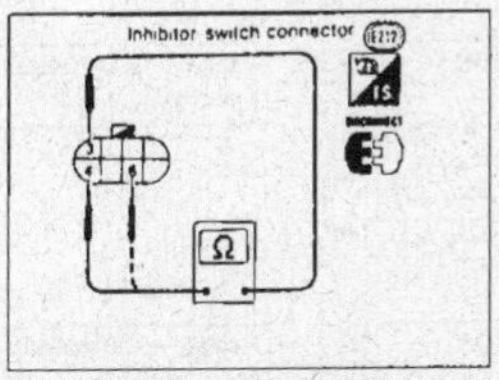
Inhibitor switch connector

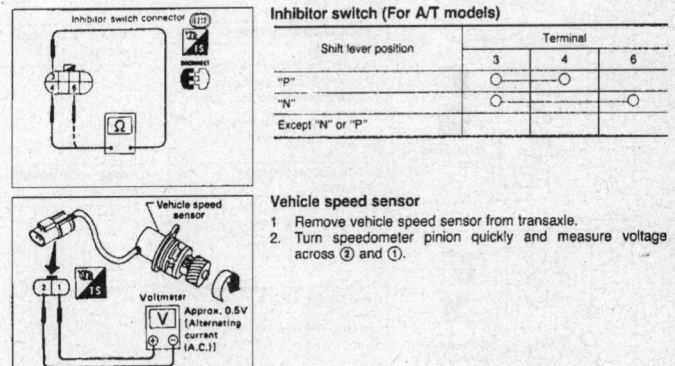

Inhibitor switch (For A/T models)

Shift lever position	Terminal 3	4	6
"P"	O—	—O	
"N"	O—	———	—O
Except "N" or "P"			

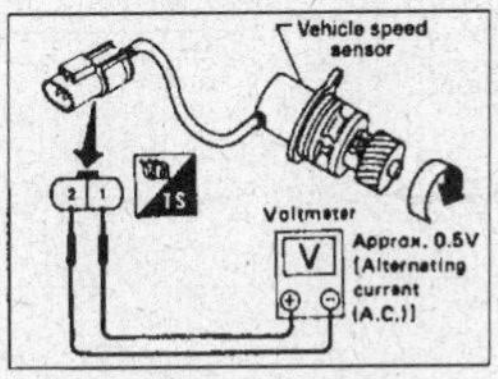
Vehicle speed sensor
Voltmeter
Approx. 0.5V (Alternating current (A.C.))

Vehicle speed sensor

1. Remove vehicle speed sensor from transaxle.
2. Turn speedometer pinion quickly and measure voltage across ② and ①.

NS1109100009020X

Fig. 72 Electrical component check (Part 2 of 2). Altima

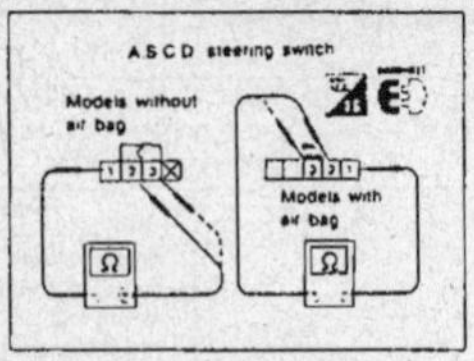
ASCD steering switch
Models without air bag
Models with air bag

A.S.C.D. steering switch

Check continuity between terminals by pushing each button.

Button \ Terminal	1	2	3
SET/COAST	○	○	
RESUME/ACCEL	○		○
CANCEL	○—▶|—	○	
	○—▶|—		○

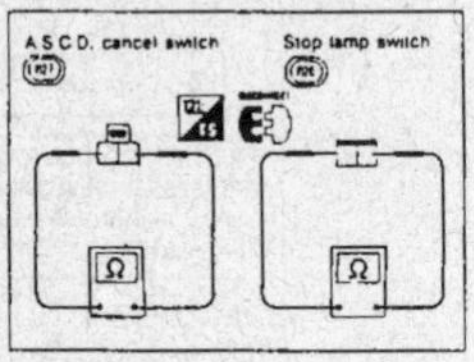
A.S.C.D. cancel switch
Stop lamp switch

A.S.C.D. cancel switch and stop lamp switch

Condition	Continuity	
	A.S.C.D. cancel switch	Stop lamp switch
When brake pedal is depressed	No	Yes
When brake pedal is released	Yes	No

Check each switch after adjusting brake pedal

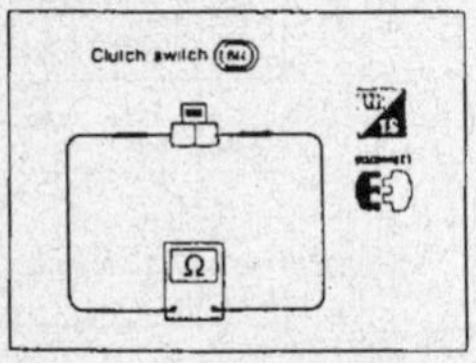
Clutch switch

Clutch switch (For M/T models)

Condition	Continuity
When clutch pedal is depressed	No
When clutch pedal is released	Yes

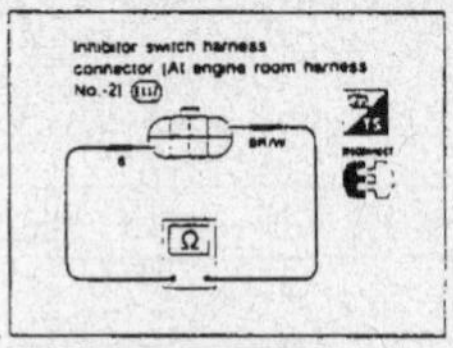
Inhibitor switch harness connector (At engine room harness No.-2)

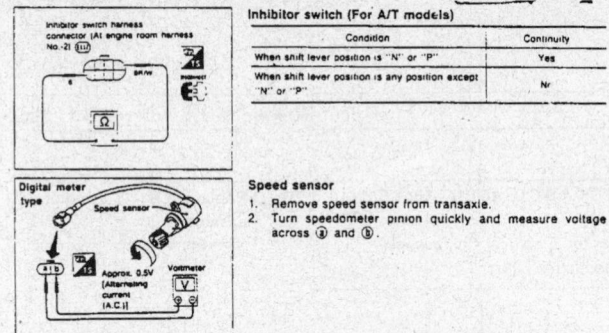

Inhibitor switch (For A/T models)

Condition	Continuity
When shift lever position is "N" or "P"	Yes
When shift lever position is any position except "N" or "P"	No

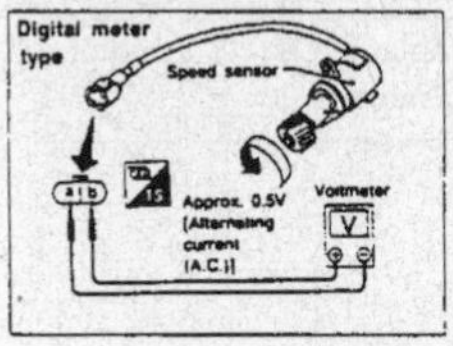
Digital meter type
Speed sensor
Approx. 0.5V (Alternating current (A.C.))
Voltmeter

Speed sensor

1. Remove speed sensor from transaxle.
2. Turn speedometer pinion quickly and measure voltage across ⓐ and ⓑ.

- A speed sensor is built into the speedometer.
1. Turn speedometer slowly using a small screwdriver.
2. Check continuity of speed sensor circuit.

Continuity exists two times for each turn .

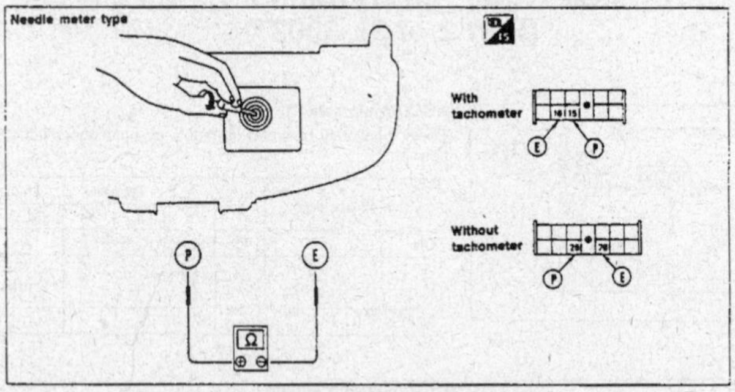
Needle meter type
With tachometer
Without tachometer

NS1109100036010X

Fig. 73 Electrical component check (Part 1 of 2). 1993–94 Sentra, NX 1600 & NX 2000

NS1109100036020X

Fig. 73 Electrical component check (Part 2 of 2). 1993–94 Sentra, NX 1600 & NX 2000

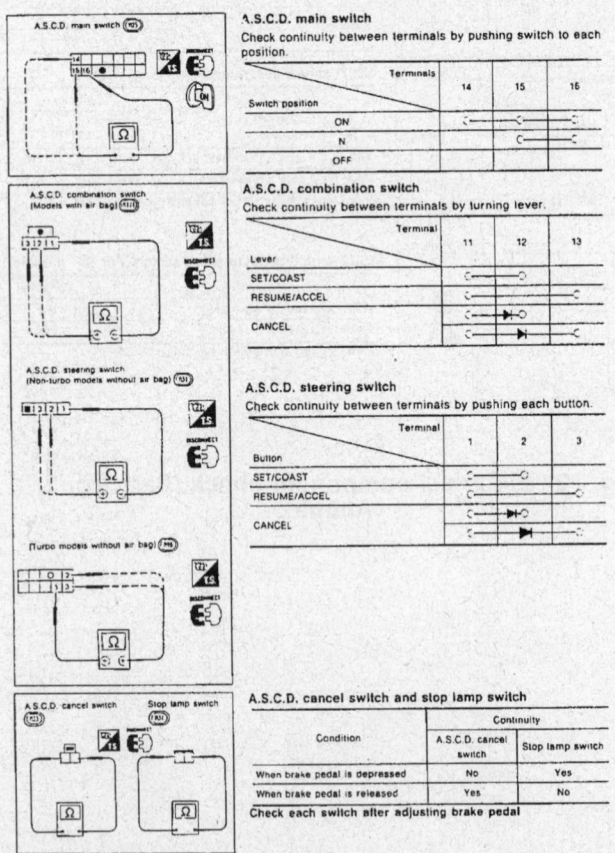

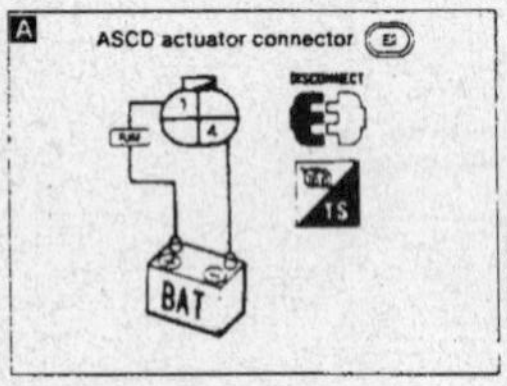
A
ASCD actuator connector
BAT

ASCD actuator/ASCD pump

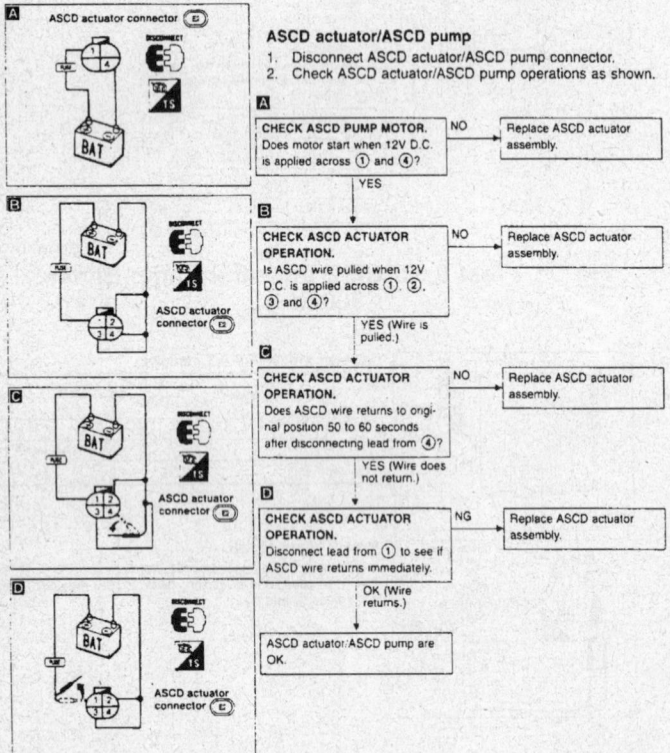

1. Disconnect ASCD actuator/ASCD pump connector.
2. Check ASCD actuator/ASCD pump operations as shown.

A

CHECK ASCD PUMP MOTOR. Does motor start when 12V D.C. is applied across ① and ④? — NO → Replace ASCD actuator assembly.

YES ↓

B

CHECK ASCD ACTUATOR OPERATION. Is ASCD wire pulled when 12V D.C. is applied across ①, ②, ③ and ④? — NO → Replace ASCD actuator assembly.

YES (Wire is pulled.) ↓

C

CHECK ASCD ACTUATOR OPERATION. Does ASCD wire returns to original position 50 to 60 seconds after disconnecting lead from ④? — NO → Replace ASCD actuator assembly.

YES (Wire does not return.) ↓

D

CHECK ASCD ACTUATOR OPERATION. Disconnect lead from ① to see if ASCD wire returns immediately. — NG → Replace ASCD actuator assembly.

OK (Wire returns.) ↓

ASCD actuator/ASCD pump are OK.

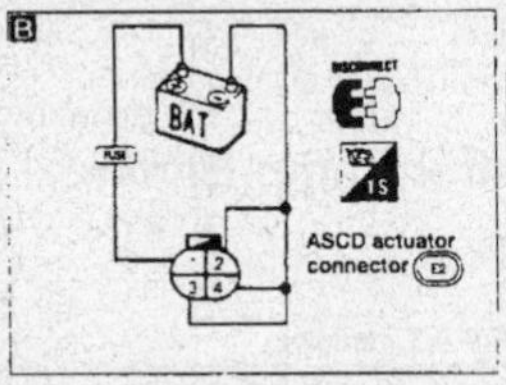
B
BAT
ASCD actuator connector

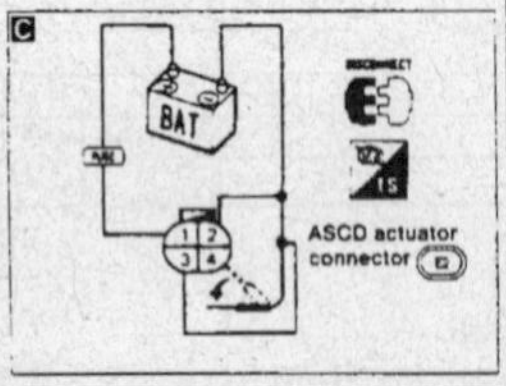
C
BAT
ASCD actuator connector

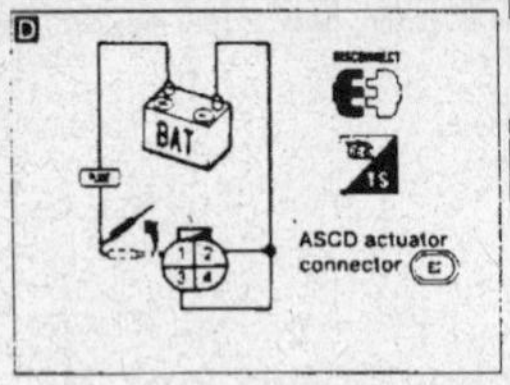
D
BAT
ASCD actuator connector

NS1109500085000X

Fig. 74 Electrical component check. 1995–96 Sentra & 200SX

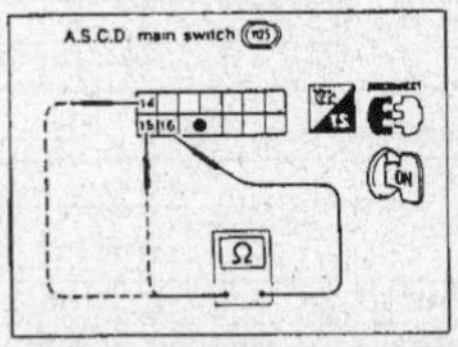
A.S.C.D. main switch

A.S.C.D. main switch

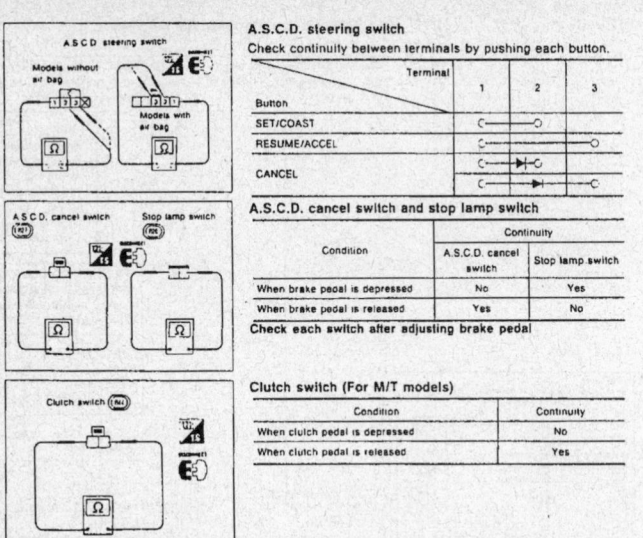

Check continuity between terminals by pushing switch to each position.

Switch position \ Terminals	14	15	16
ON	○	○	○
N		○	○
OFF			

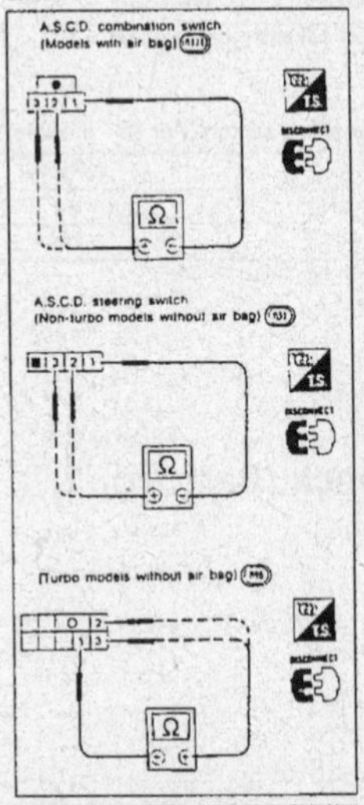
A.S.C.D. combination switch (Models with air bag)
A.S.C.D. steering switch (Non-turbo models without air bag)
(Turbo models without air bag)

A.S.C.D. combination switch

Check continuity between terminals by turning lever.

Lever \ Terminal	11	12	13
SET/COAST	○	○	
RESUME/ACCEL	○		○
CANCEL	○—▶|—	○	
	○—▶|—		○

A.S.C.D. steering switch

Check continuity between terminals by pushing each button.

Button \ Terminal	1	2	3
SET/COAST	○	○	
RESUME/ACCEL	○		○
CANCEL	○—▶|—	○	
	○—▶|—		○

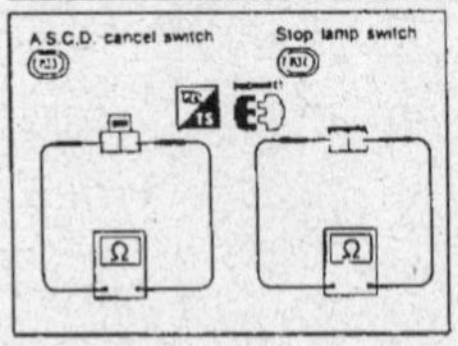
A.S.C.D. cancel switch
Stop lamp switch

A.S.C.D. cancel switch and stop lamp switch

Condition	Continuity	
	A.S.C.D. cancel switch	Stop lamp switch
When brake pedal is depressed	No	Yes
When brake pedal is released	Yes	No

Check each switch after adjusting brake pedal

NS1109200061010X

Fig. 75 Electrical component check (Part 1 of 2). 300ZX

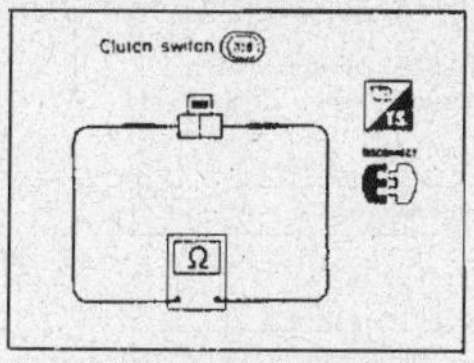
Clutch switch
Ω

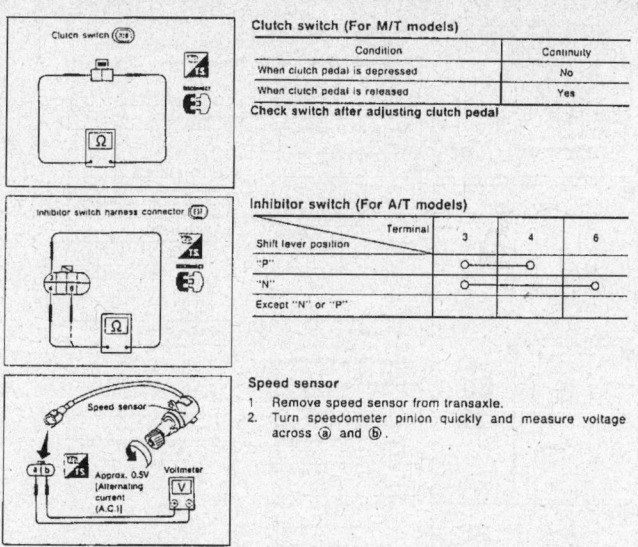

Clutch switch (For M/T models)

Condition	Continuity
When clutch pedal is depressed	No
When clutch pedal is released	Yes

Check switch after adjusting clutch pedal

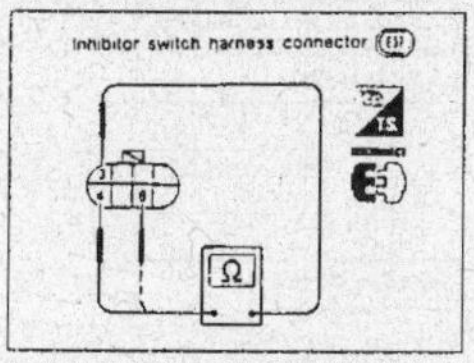
Inhibitor switch harness connector
Ω

Inhibitor switch (For A/T models)

Shift lever position \ Terminal	3	4	6
"P"	o—	—o	
"N"	o—	—	—o
Except "N" or "P"			

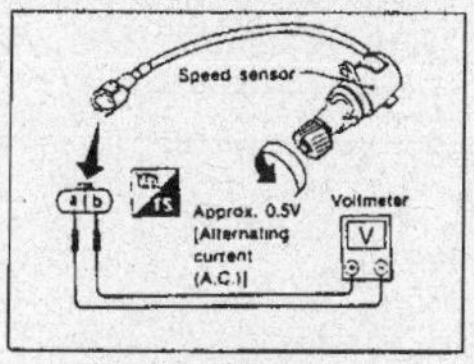
Speed sensor
Approx. 0.5V (Alternating current (A.C.))
Voltmeter
V

Speed sensor

1. Remove speed sensor from transaxle.
2. Turn speedometer pinion quickly and measure voltage across ⓐ and ⓑ.

NS1109200061020X

Fig. 75 Electrical component check (Part 2 of 2). 300ZX

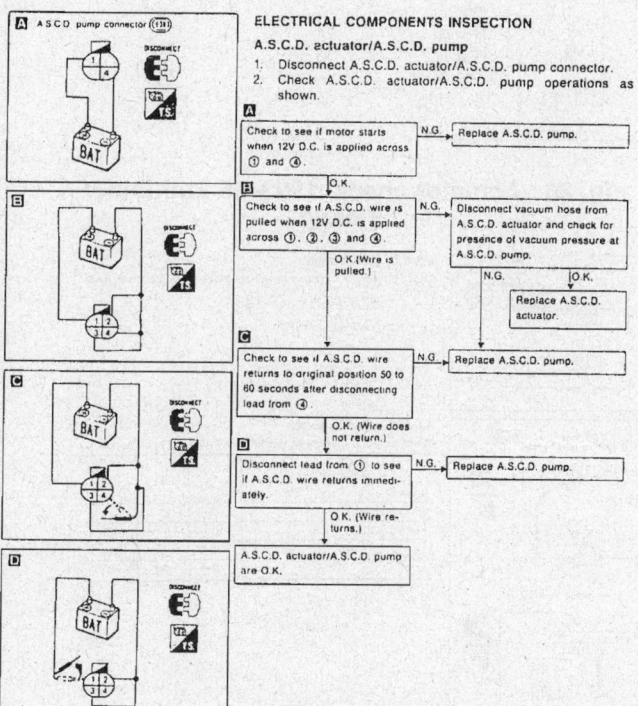

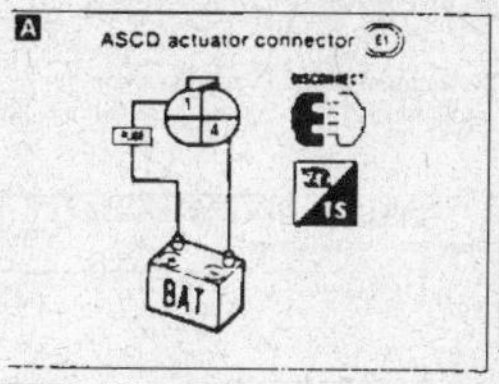
A
ASCD actuator connector
BAT

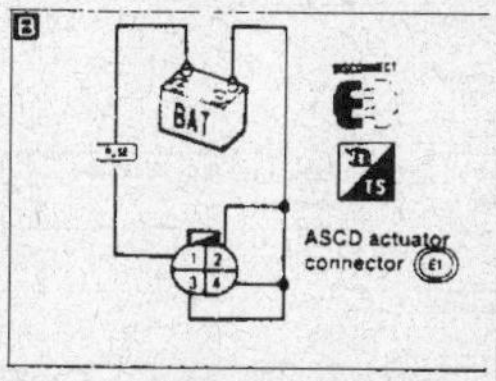
B
BAT
ASCD actuator connector

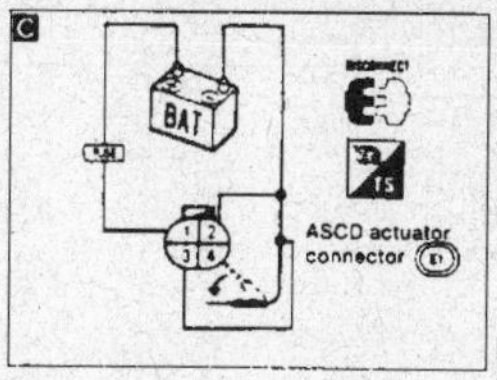
C
BAT
ASCD actuator connector

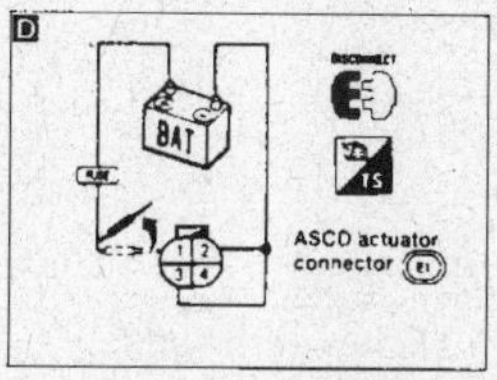
D
BAT
ASCD actuator connector

ASCD actuator/ASCD pump

1. Disconnect ASCD actuator ASCD pump connector.
2. Check ASCD actuator ASCD pump operations as shown.

A Check to see if motor starts when 12V D.C is applied across ① and ④. — N.G → Replace ASCD actuator assembly.
O.K. ↓

B Check to see if ASCD wire is pulled when 12V D.C. is applied across ①, ②, ③ and ④. — N.G → Replace ASCD actuator assembly.
O.K. (Wire is pulled.) ↓

C Check to see if ASCD wire returns to original position 50 to 60 seconds after disconnecting lead from ④. — N.G → Replace ASCD actuator assembly.
O.K. (Wire does not return.) ↓

D Disconnect lead from ① to see if ASCD wire returns immediately. — N.G. → Replace ASCD actuator assembly.
O.K. (Wire returns.) ↓

ASCD actuator/ASCD pump are O.K.

NS1109100062000X

Fig. 76 Actuator check. Altima

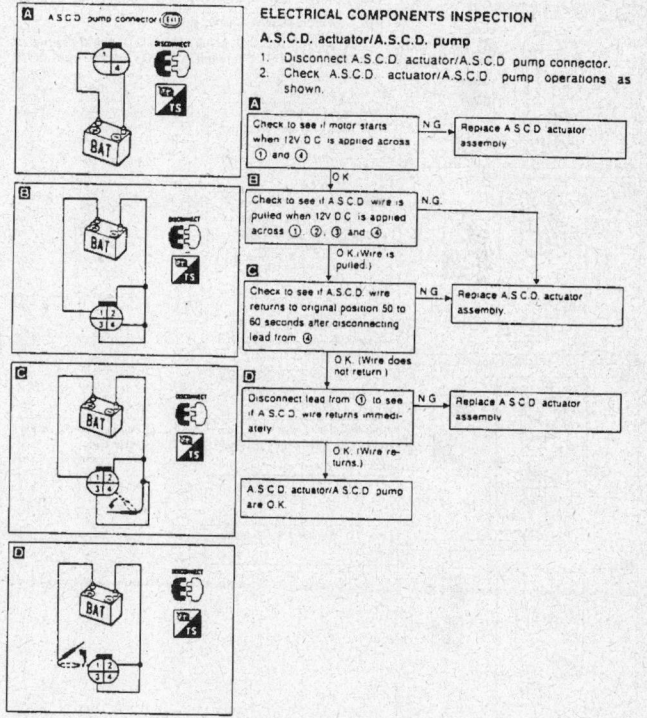

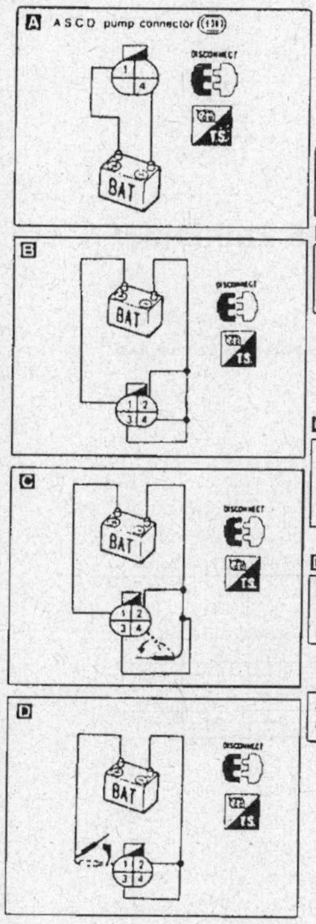
A
A.S.C.D. pump connector
BAT
B
C
D

ELECTRICAL COMPONENTS INSPECTION

A.S.C.D. actuator/A.S.C.D. pump

1. Disconnect A.S.C.D. actuator/A.S.C.D. pump connector.
2. Check A.S.C.D. actuator/A.S.C.D. pump operations as shown.

A Check to see if motor starts when 12V D.C. is applied across ① and ④. — N.G. → Replace A.S.C.D. pump.
O.K. ↓

B Check to see if A.S.C.D. wire is pulled when 12V D.C. is applied across ①, ②, ③ and ④. — N.G. → Disconnect vacuum hose from A.S.C.D. actuator and check for presence of vacuum pressure at A.S.C.D. pump. — O.K. → Replace A.S.C.D. actuator. / N.G. → Replace A.S.C.D. pump.
O.K. (Wire is pulled.) ↓

C Check to see if A.S.C.D. wire returns to original position 50 to 60 seconds after disconnecting lead from ④. — N.G. → Replace A.S.C.D. pump.
O.K. (Wire does not return.) ↓

D Disconnect lead from ① to see if A.S.C.D. wire returns immediately. — N.G. → Replace A.S.C.D. pump.
O.K. (Wire returns.) ↓

A.S.C.D. actuator/A.S.C.D. pump are O.K.

NS1109100065000X

Fig. 77 Actuator check. Sentra, 200SX, NX 1600 & NX 2000

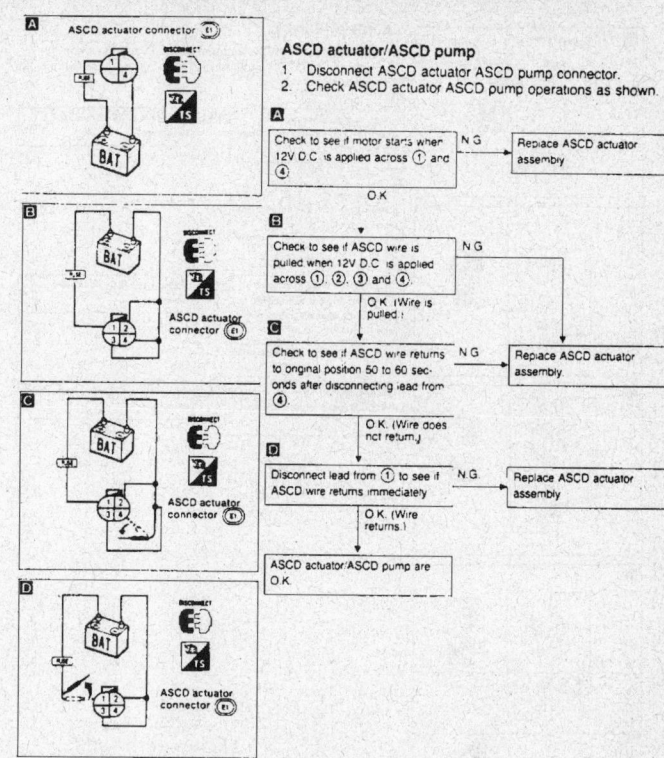

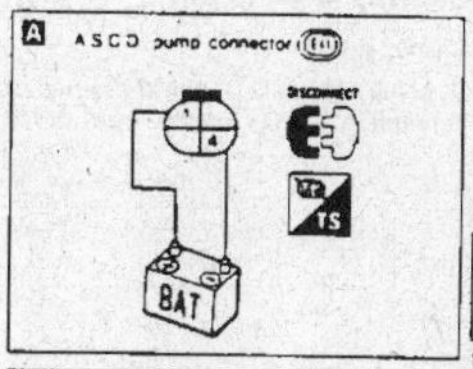
A
A.S.C.D. pump connector
BAT

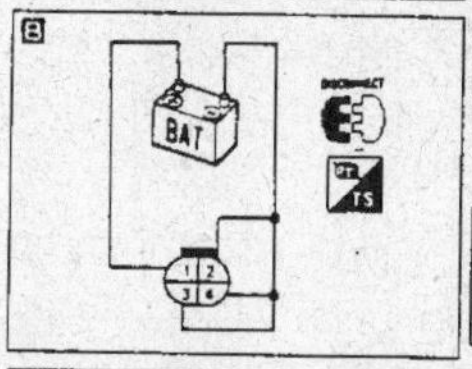
B
BAT

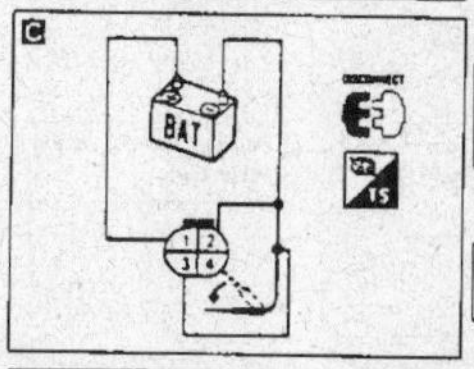
C
BAT

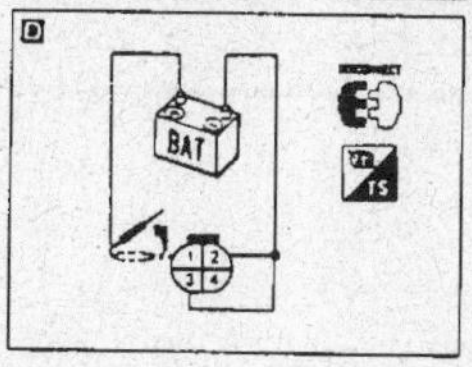
D
BAT

ELECTRICAL COMPONENTS INSPECTION

A.S.C.D. actuator/A.S.C.D. pump

1. Disconnect A.S.C.D. actuator/A.S.C.D. pump connector.
2. Check A.S.C.D. actuator/A.S.C.D. pump operations as shown.

A Check to see if motor starts when 12V D.C. is applied across ① and ④. — N.G. → Replace A.S.C.D. actuator assembly.
O.K. ↓

B Check to see if A.S.C.D. wire is pulled when 12V D.C. is applied across ①, ②, ③ and ④. — N.G. → Replace A.S.C.D. actuator assembly.
O.K. (Wire is pulled.) ↓

C Check to see if A.S.C.D. wire returns to original position 50 to 60 seconds after disconnecting lead from ④. — N.G. → Replace A.S.C.D. actuator assembly.
O.K. (Wire does not return.) ↓

D Disconnect lead from ① to see if A.S.C.D. wire returns immediately. — N.G. → Replace A.S.C.D. actuator assembly.
O.K. (Wire returns.) ↓

A.S.C.D. actuator/A.S.C.D. pump are O.K.

NS1109100068000X

Fig. 78 Actuator check. 300ZX

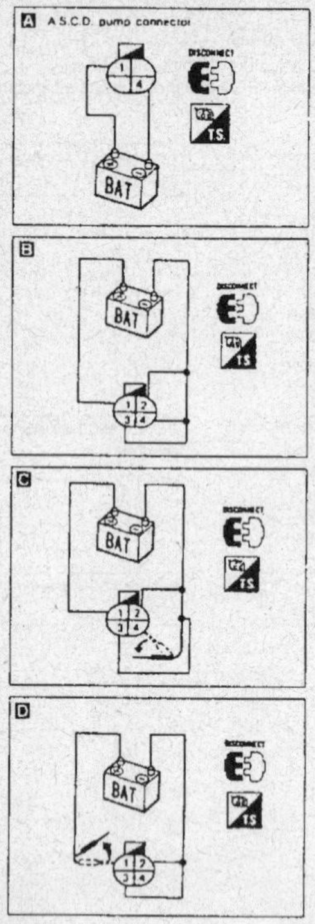
A.S.C.D. pump connector
DISCONNECT
BAT
T.S.

Actuator Check

1. Disconnect A.S.C.D. actuator/A.S.C.D. pump connector.
2. Check A.S.C.D. actuator/A.S.C.D. pump operations as shown.

A Check to see if motor starts when 12V D.C. is applied across ① and ④. — N.G. → Replace A.S.C.D. actuator assembly.
O.K. ↓

B Check to see if A.S.C.D. wire is pulled when 12V D.C. is applied across ①, ②, ③ and ④. — N.G. → Replace A.S.C.D. actuator assembly.
O.K. (Wire is pulled.) ↓

C Check to see if A.S.C.D. wire returns to original position 50 to 60 seconds after disconnecting lead from ④. — N.G. → Replace A.S.C.D. actuator assembly.
O.K. (Wire does not return.) ↓

D Disconnect lead from ① to see if A.S.C.D. wire returns immediately. — N.G. → Replace A.S.C.D. actuator assembly.
O.K. (Wire returns.) ↓

A.S.C.D. actuator/A.S.C.D. pump are O.K.

NS1109100063000X

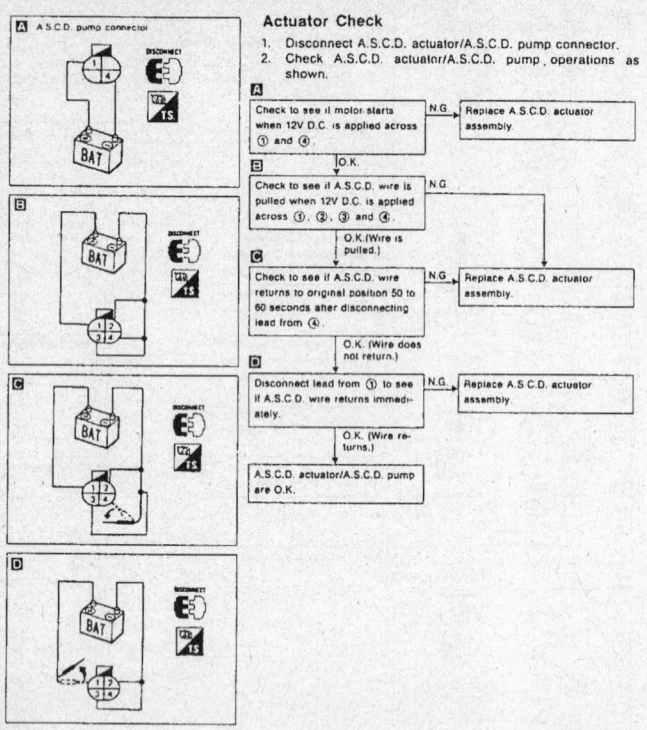

Fig. 79 Actuator check. 1993–95 Maxima & Quest

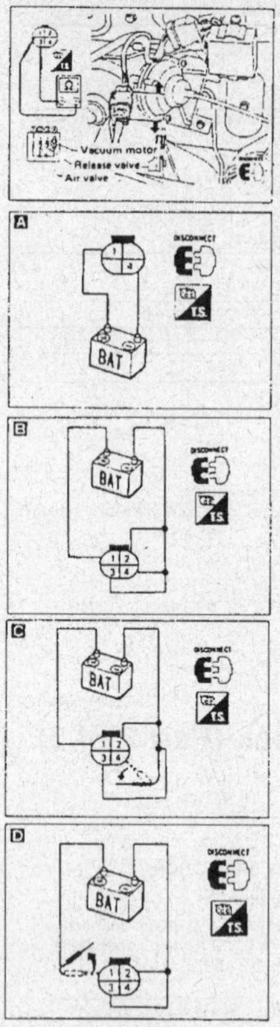
Vacuum motor
Release valve
Air valve
BAT
T.S.

Actuator Check

1. Disconnect A.S.C.D. actuator/A.S.C.D. pump connector.
2. Check A.S.C.D. actuator/A.S.C.D. pump operations as shown.

A Check to see if motor starts when 12V D.C. is applied across ① and ④. — N.G. → Replace A.S.C.D. pump.
O.K. ↓

B Check to see if A.S.C.D. wire is pulled when 12V D.C. is applied across ①, ②, ③ and ④. — N.G. → Disconnect vacuum hose from A.S.C.D. actuator and check for presence of vacuum pressure at A.S.C.D. pump. — N.G. → Replace A.S.C.D. pump. / O.K. → Replace A.S.C.D. actuator.
O.K. (Wire is pulled.) ↓

C Check to see if A.S.C.D. wire returns to original position 50 to 60 seconds after disconnecting lead from ④. — N.G. → Replace A.S.C.D. pump.
O.K. (Wire does not return.) ↓

D Disconnect lead from ① to see if A.S.C.D. wire returns immediately. — N.G. → Replace A.S.C.D. pump.
O.K. (Wire returns.) ↓

A.S.C.D. actuator/A.S.C.D. pump are O.K.

NS1109100064000X

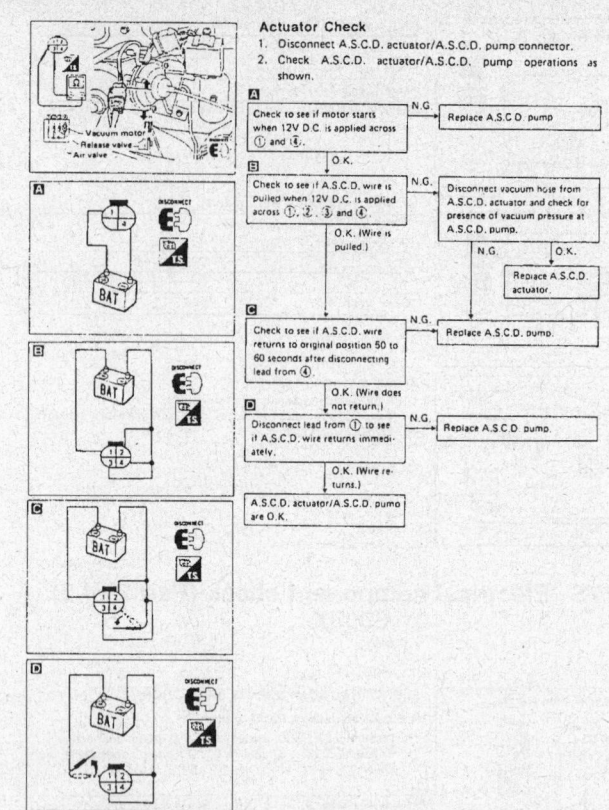

Fig. 80 Actuator check. 1993–95 Pathfinder & Pickup

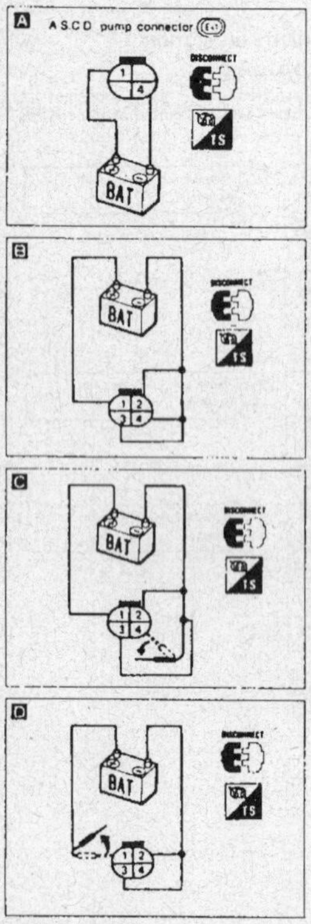
A.S.C.D. pump connector
DISCONNECT
BAT
T.S.

ELECTRICAL COMPONENTS INSPECTION

A.S.C.D. actuator/A.S.C.D. pump

1. Disconnect A.S.C.D. actuator/A.S.C.D. pump connector.
2. Check A.S.C.D. actuator/A.S.C.D. pump operations as shown.

A Check to see if motor starts when 12V D.C. is applied across ① and ④. — N.G. → Replace A.S.C.D. actuator assembly.
O.K. ↓

B Check to see if A.S.C.D. wire is pulled when 12V D.C. is applied across ①, ②, ③ and ④. — N.G. → Replace A.S.C.D. actuator assembly.
O.K. (Wire is pulled.) ↓

C Check to see if A.S.C.D. wire returns to original position 50 to 60 seconds after disconnecting lead from ④. — N.G. → Replace A.S.C.D. actuator assembly.
O.K. (Wire does not return.) ↓

D Disconnect lead from ① to see if A.S.C.D. wire returns immediately. — N.G. → Replace A.S.C.D. actuator assembly.
O.K. (Wire returns.) ↓

A.S.C.D. actuator/A.S.C.D. pump are O.K.

NS1109200067000X

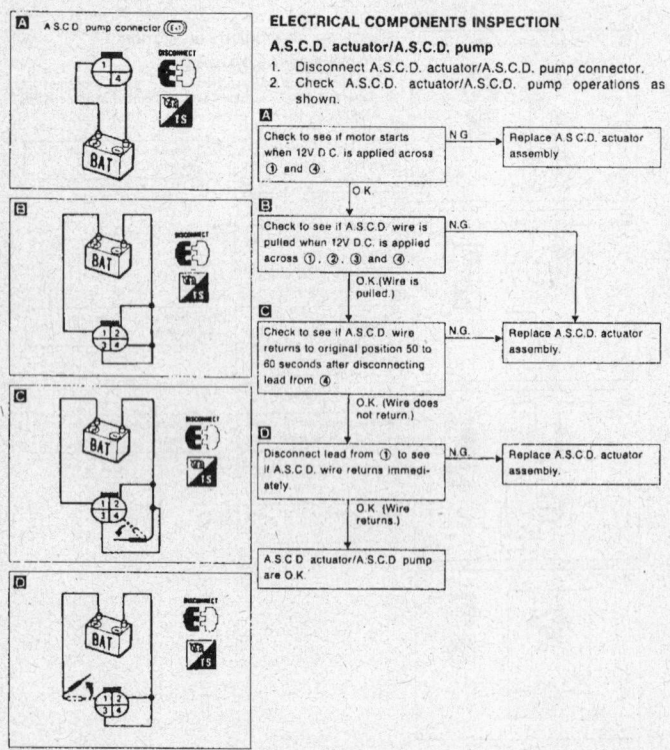

Fig. 81 Actuator check. 1993–95 240SX

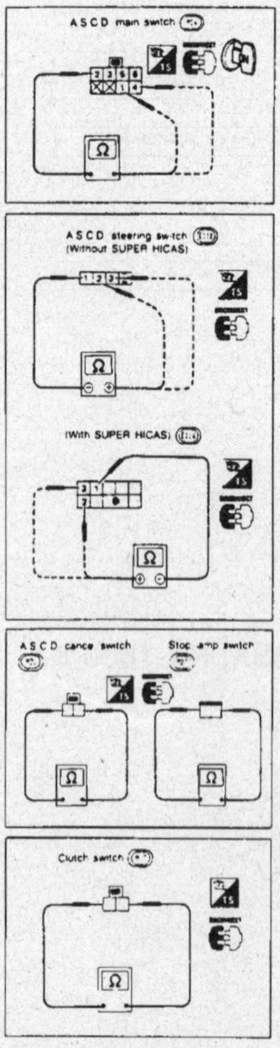
A.S.C.D. main switch
A.S.C.D. steering switch (Without SUPER HICAS)
(With SUPER HICAS)
A.S.C.D. cancel switch
Stop lamp switch
Clutch switch

A.S.C.D. main switch

Check continuity between terminals by pushing switch to each position.

A.S.C.D. steering switch

Check continuity between terminals by pushing each button.

Button \ Terminal	1	2	3
SET/COAST	○──	──○	
RESUME/ACCEL	○──	────	──○
CANCEL	○──	─▶├○	
	○──	──▶├──	──○

A.S.C.D. cancel switch and stop lamp switch

Condition	Continuity	
	A.S.C.D. cancel switch	Stop lamp switch
When brake pedal is depressed	No	Yes
When brake pedal is released	Yes	No

Check each switch after adjusting brake pedal — refer to BR section.

Clutch switch (For M/T models)

Condition	Continuity
When clutch pedal is depressed	No
When clutch pedal is released	Yes

Check switch after adjusting clutch pedal — refer to CL section.

NS1109200048010X

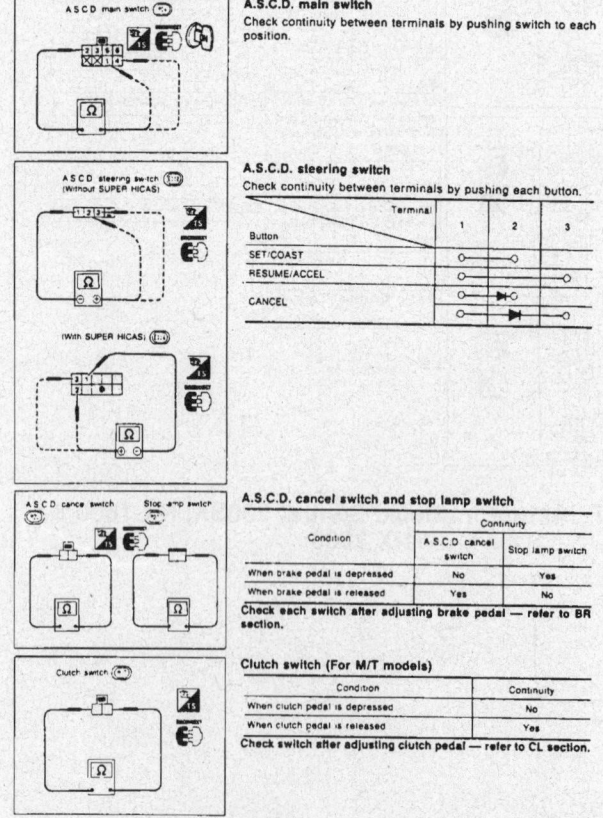

Fig. 82 Electrical component check (Part 1 of 2). 1993–94 240SX

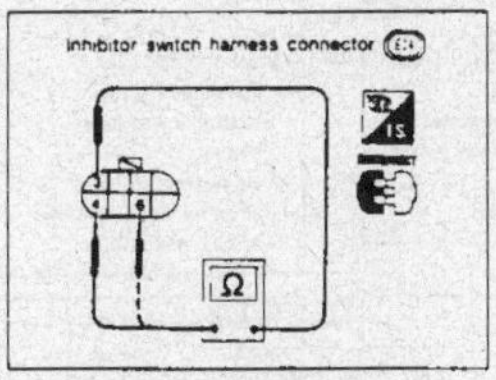
Inhibitor switch harness connector
Ω

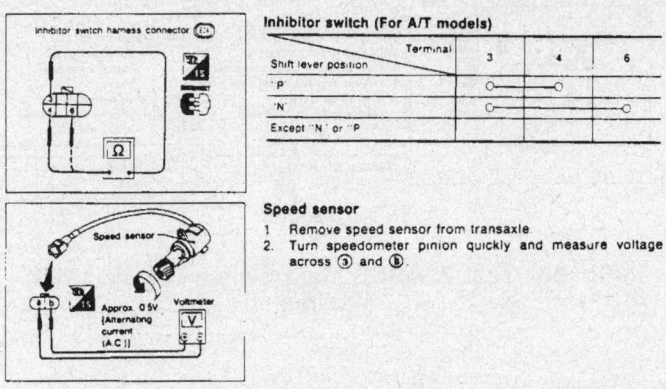

Inhibitor switch (For A/T models)

Shift lever position \ Terminal	3	4	6
"P"	O	O	
"N"	O		O
Except "N" or "P"			

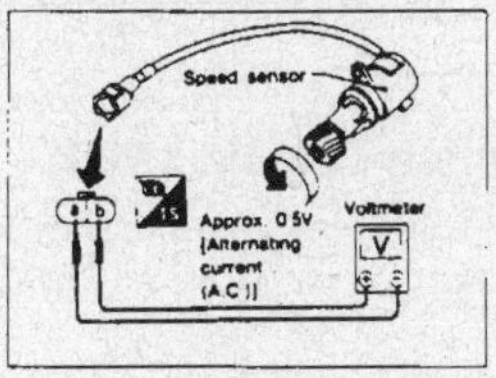
Speed sensor
Approx. 0.5V (Alternating current [A.C.])
Voltmeter
V

Speed sensor

1. Remove speed sensor from transaxle.
2. Turn speedometer pinion quickly and measure voltage across ③ and ⑤.

NS1109200048020X

Fig. 82 Electrical component check (Part 2 of 2). 1993–94 240SX

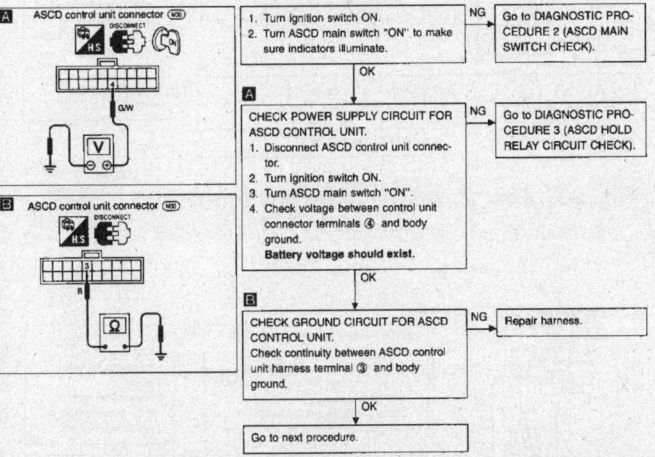

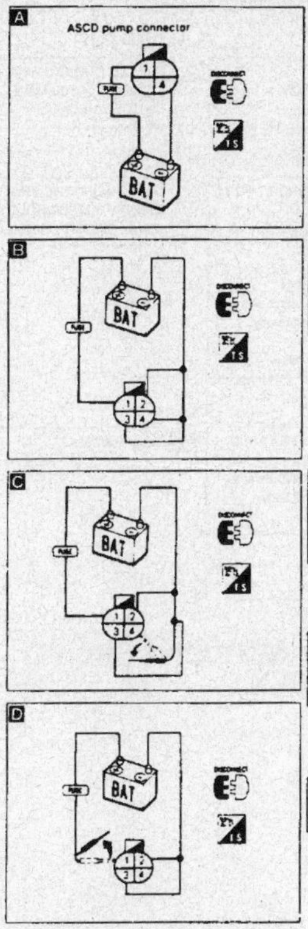
ASCD pump connector
BAT

ASCD actuator/ASCD pump

1. Disconnect ASCD pump connector.
2. Check ASCD actuator/ASCD pump operations as shown.

A — Check to see if motor starts when 12V DC is applied across ① and ④.
- NG → Replace ASCD pump.
- OK ↓

B — Check to see if ASCD wire is pulled when 12V DC is applied across ①, ②, ③ and ④.
- NG → Disconnect vacuum hose from ASCD actuator and check for presence of vacuum pressure at ASCD pump.
  - NG → Replace ASCD pump.
  - OK → Replace ASCD actuator.
- OK (wire is pulled.) ↓

C — Check to see if ASCD wire returns to original position 50 to 60 seconds after disconnecting lead from ④.
- NG → Replace ASCD pump.
- OK (Wire does not return.) ↓

D — Disconnect lead from ① to see if ASCD wire returns immediately.
- NG → Replace ASCD pump.
- OK (Wire returns.) ↓

ASCD actuator/ASCD pump are OK.

NS1109500094000X

Fig. 83 Electrical component check. 1995 240SX

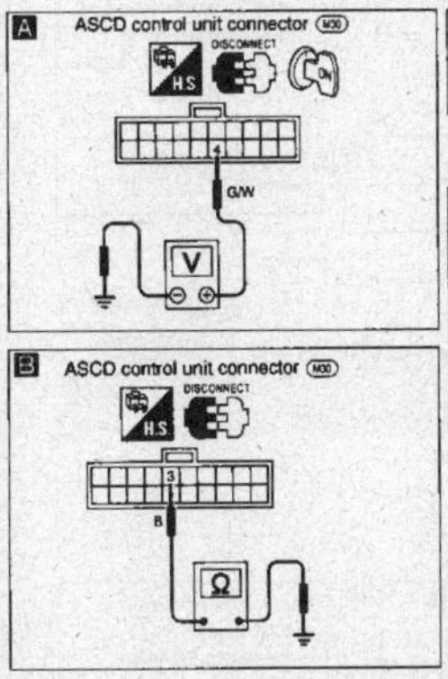
A ASCD control unit connector M30
DISCONNECT
H.S.
G/W
V
B ASCD control unit connector M30
DISCONNECT
H.S.
B
Ω

1. Turn ignition switch ON.
2. Turn ASCD main switch "ON" to make sure indicators illuminate.
- NG → Go to DIAGNOSTIC PROCEDURE 2 (ASCD MAIN SWITCH CHECK).
- OK ↓

A — CHECK POWER SUPPLY CIRCUIT FOR ASCD CONTROL UNIT.
1. Disconnect ASCD control unit connector.
2. Turn ignition switch ON.
3. Turn ASCD main switch "ON".
4. Check voltage between control unit connector terminals ④ and body ground.

Battery voltage should exist.
- NG → Go to DIAGNOSTIC PROCEDURE 3 (ASCD HOLD RELAY CIRCUIT CHECK).
- OK ↓

B — CHECK GROUND CIRCUIT FOR ASCD CONTROL UNIT.
Check continuity between ASCD control unit harness terminal ③ and body ground.
- NG → Repair harness.
- OK ↓

Go to next procedure.

NS1109600106000X

Fig. 84 Test 1: Power Supply & Ground Circuit Check. 1996 Maxima

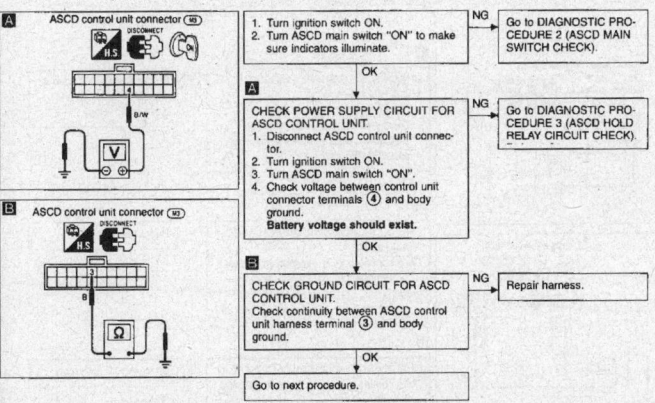

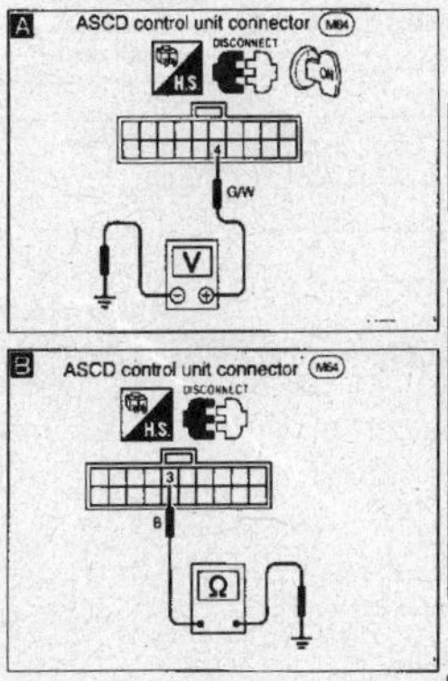
A ASCD control unit connector M64
DISCONNECT
H.S.
G/W
V
B ASCD control unit connector M64
DISCONNECT
H.S.
B
Ω

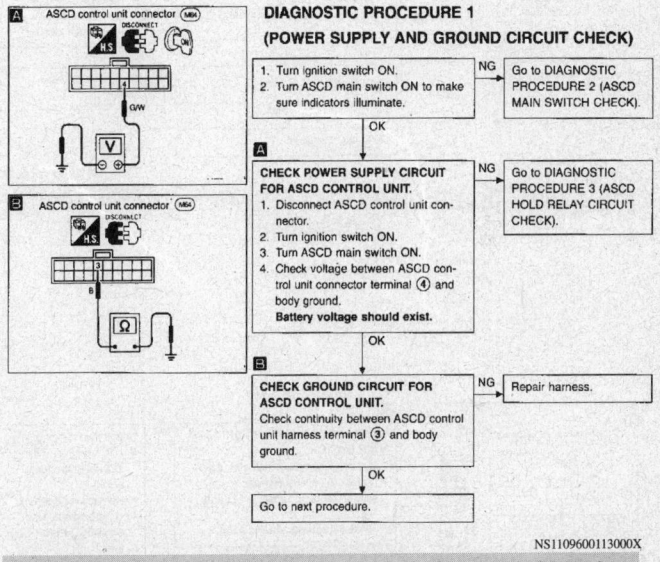

DIAGNOSTIC PROCEDURE 1
(POWER SUPPLY AND GROUND CIRCUIT CHECK)

1. Turn ignition switch ON.
2. Turn ASCD main switch ON to make sure indicators illuminate.
- NG → Go to DIAGNOSTIC PROCEDURE 2 (ASCD MAIN SWITCH CHECK).
- OK ↓

A — **CHECK POWER SUPPLY CIRCUIT FOR ASCD CONTROL UNIT.**
1. Disconnect ASCD control unit connector.
2. Turn ignition switch ON.
3. Turn ASCD main switch ON.
4. Check voltage between ASCD control unit connector terminal ④ and body ground.

Battery voltage should exist.
- NG → Go to DIAGNOSTIC PROCEDURE 3 (ASCD HOLD RELAY CIRCUIT CHECK).
- OK ↓

B — **CHECK GROUND CIRCUIT FOR ASCD CONTROL UNIT.**
Check continuity between ASCD control unit harness terminal ③ and body ground.
- NG → Repair harness.
- OK ↓

Go to next procedure.

NS1109600113000X

Fig. 86 Test 1: Power Supply & Ground Circuit Check. 1996 Quest

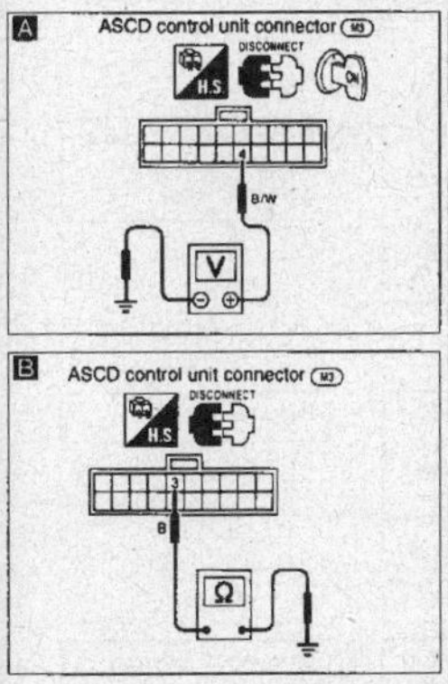
A ASCD control unit connector M3
DISCONNECT
H.S.
B/W
V
B ASCD control unit connector M3
DISCONNECT
H.S.
B
Ω

1. Turn ignition switch ON.
2. Turn ASCD main switch "ON" to make sure indicators illuminate.
- NG → Go to DIAGNOSTIC PROCEDURE 2 (ASCD MAIN SWITCH CHECK).
- OK ↓

A — CHECK POWER SUPPLY CIRCUIT FOR ASCD CONTROL UNIT.
1. Disconnect ASCD control unit connector.
2. Turn ignition switch ON.
3. Turn ASCD main switch "ON".
4. Check voltage between control unit connector terminals ④ and body ground.

Battery voltage should exist.
- NG → Go to DIAGNOSTIC PROCEDURE 3 (ASCD HOLD RELAY CIRCUIT CHECK).
- OK ↓

B — CHECK GROUND CIRCUIT FOR ASCD CONTROL UNIT.
Check continuity between ASCD control unit harness terminal ③ and body ground.
- NG → Repair harness.
- OK ↓

Go to next procedure.

NS1109600095000X

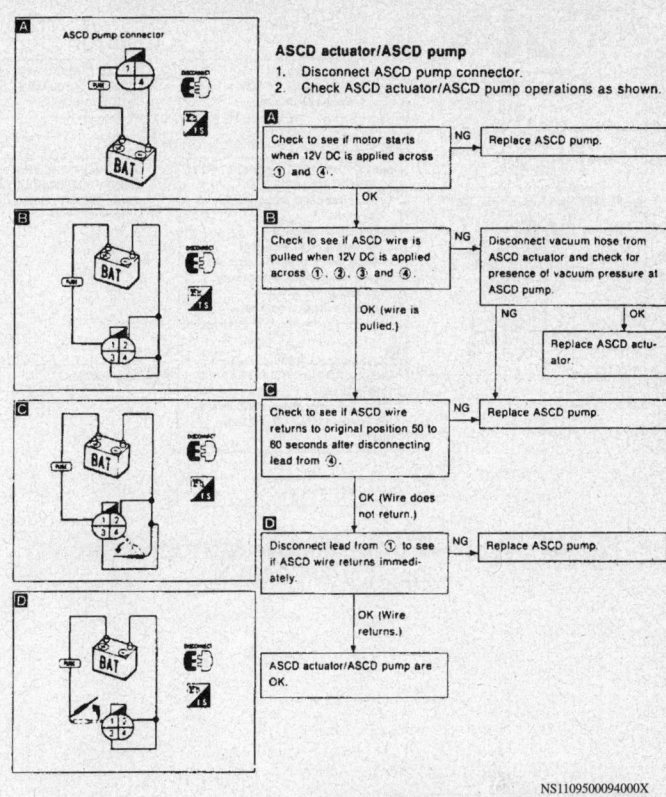

Fig. 85 Test 1: Power Supply & Ground Circuit Check. 1996 Pathfinder & Pickup

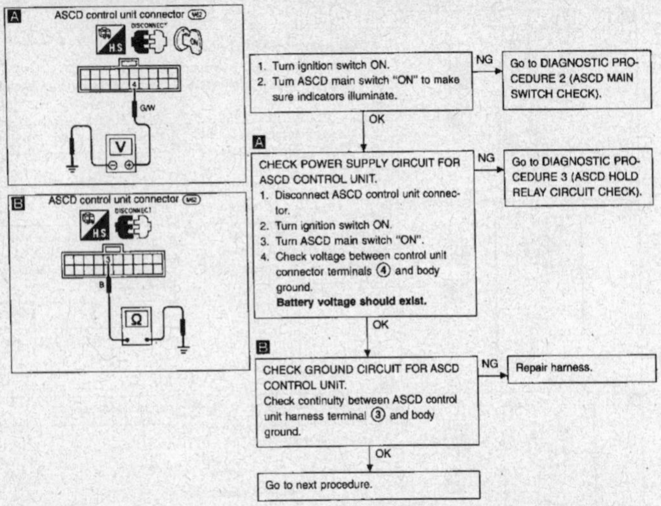
A
ASCD control unit connector (M2)
DISCONNECT
H.S
G/W
V
B
ASCD control unit connector (M2)
DISCONNECT
H.S
B
Ω
1. Turn ignition switch ON.
2. Turn ASCD main switch "ON" to make sure indicators illuminate.
NG
Go to DIAGNOSTIC PROCEDURE 2 (ASCD MAIN SWITCH CHECK).
OK
A
CHECK POWER SUPPLY CIRCUIT FOR ASCD CONTROL UNIT.
1. Disconnect ASCD control unit connector.
2. Turn ignition switch ON.
3. Turn ASCD main switch "ON".
4. Check voltage between control unit connector terminals ④ and body ground.
Battery voltage should exist.
NG
Go to DIAGNOSTIC PROCEDURE 3 (ASCD HOLD RELAY CIRCUIT CHECK).
OK
B
CHECK GROUND CIRCUIT FOR ASCD CONTROL UNIT.
Check continuity between ASCD control unit harness terminal ③ and body ground.
NG
Repair harness.
OK
Go to next procedure.

NS1109600125000X

Fig. 87 Test 1: Power Supply & Ground Circuit Check. 1996 240SX

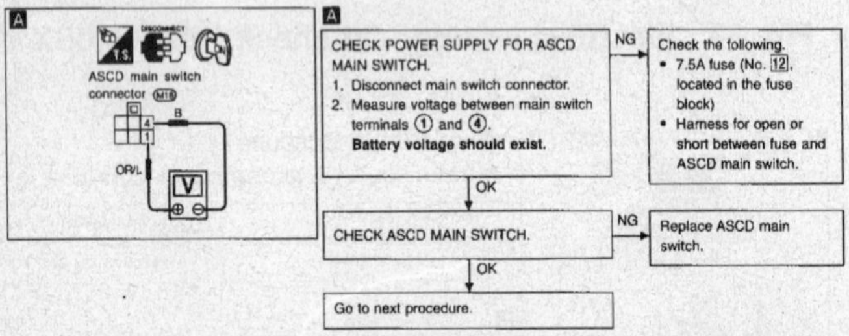
A
DISCONNECT
T.S
ASCD main switch connector (M18)
B
OR/L
V
A
CHECK POWER SUPPLY FOR ASCD MAIN SWITCH.
1. Disconnect main switch connector.
2. Measure voltage between main switch terminals ① and ④.
Battery voltage should exist.
NG
Check the following.
• 7.5A fuse (No. 12, located in the fuse block)
• Harness for open or short between fuse and ASCD main switch.
OK
CHECK ASCD MAIN SWITCH.
NG
Replace ASCD main switch.
OK
Go to next procedure.

NS1109600096000X

Fig. 89 Test 2: ASCD Main Switch Check. 1996 Pathfinder

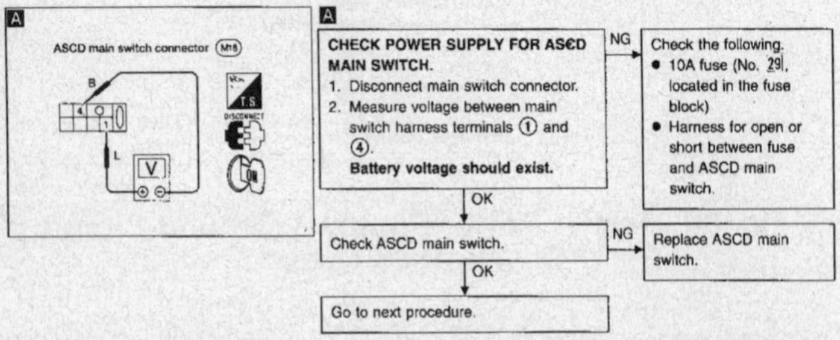
A
ASCD main switch connector (M18)
B
L
V
T.S
DISCONNECT
A
CHECK POWER SUPPLY FOR ASCD MAIN SWITCH.
1. Disconnect main switch connector.
2. Measure voltage between main switch harness terminals ① and ④.
Battery voltage should exist.
NG
Check the following.
• 10A fuse (No. 29, located in the fuse block)
• Harness for open or short between fuse and ASCD main switch.
OK
Check ASCD main switch.
NG
Replace ASCD main switch.
OK
Go to next procedure.

NS1109600121000X

Fig. 91 Test 2: ASCD Main Switch Check. 1996 Quest

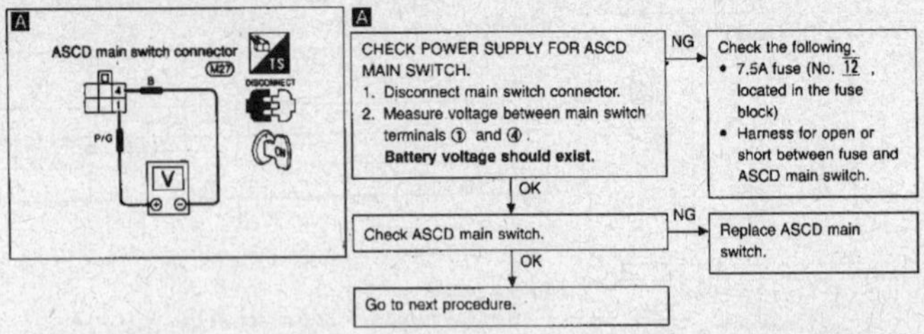
A
ASCD main switch connector (M27)
T.S
DISCONNECT
P/G
V
A
CHECK POWER SUPPLY FOR ASCD MAIN SWITCH.
1. Disconnect main switch connector.
2. Measure voltage between main switch terminals ① and ④.
Battery voltage should exist.
NG
Check the following.
• 7.5A fuse (No. 12, located in the fuse block)
• Harness for open or short between fuse and ASCD main switch.
OK
Check ASCD main switch.
NG
Replace ASCD main switch.
OK
Go to next procedure.

NS1109600120000X

Fig. 88 Test 2: ASCD Main Switch Check. 1996 Maxima

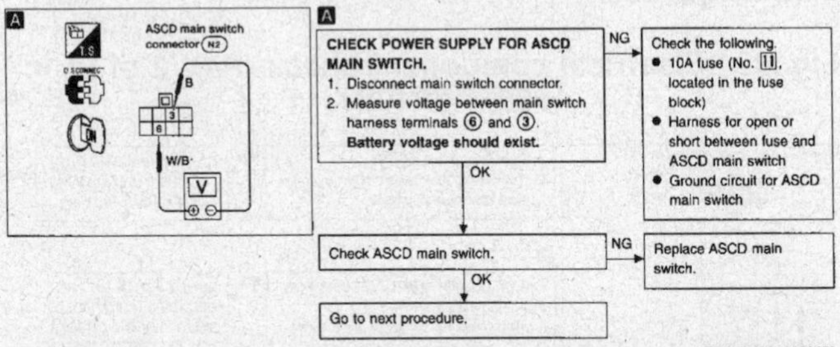
A
T.S
DISCONNECT
ASCD main switch connector (N2)
B
W/B
V
A
CHECK POWER SUPPLY FOR ASCD MAIN SWITCH.
1. Disconnect main switch connector.
2. Measure voltage between main switch harness terminals ⑥ and ③.
Battery voltage should exist.
NG
Check the following.
• 10A fuse (No. 11, located in the fuse block)
• Harness for open or short between fuse and ASCD main switch
• Ground circuit for ASCD main switch
OK
Check ASCD main switch.
NG
Replace ASCD main switch.
OK
Go to next procedure.

NS1109600103000X

Fig. 90 Test 2: ASCD Main Switch Check. 1996 Pickup

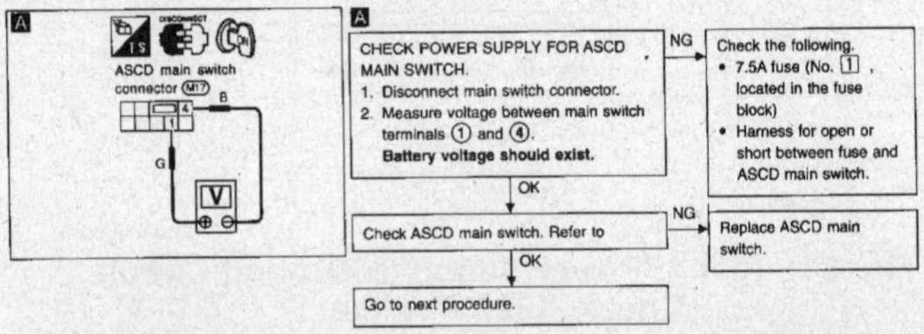
A
T.S
DISCONNECT
ASCD main switch connector (M17)
B
G
V
A
CHECK POWER SUPPLY FOR ASCD MAIN SWITCH.
1. Disconnect main switch connector.
2. Measure voltage between main switch terminals ① and ④.
Battery voltage should exist.
NG
Check the following.
• 7.5A fuse (No. 1, located in the fuse block)
• Harness for open or short between fuse and ASCD main switch.
OK
Check ASCD main switch. Refer to
NG
Replace ASCD main switch.
OK
Go to next procedure.

NS1109600126000X

Fig. 92 Test 2: ASCD Main Switch Check. 1996 240SX

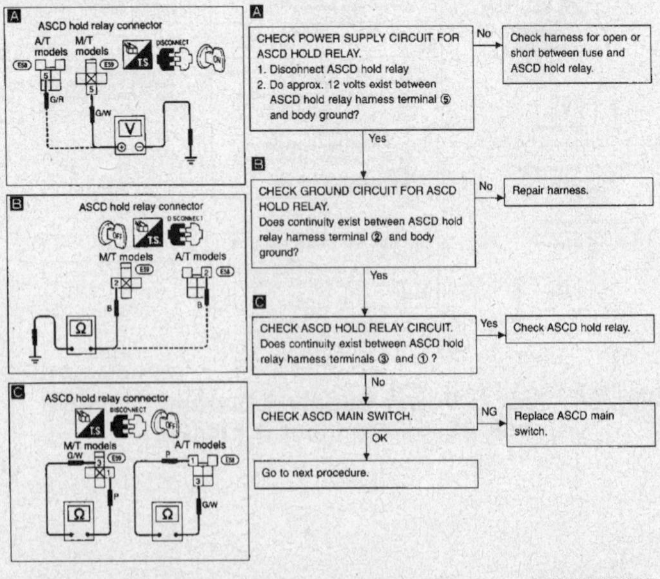
A
ASCD hold relay connector
A/T models
M/T models
DISCONNECT
T.S
G/R
G/W
V
B
ASCD hold relay connector
DISCONNECT
T.S
M/T models
A/T models
B
Ω
C
ASCD hold relay connector
DISCONNECT
T.S
M/T models
A/T models
G/W
P
Ω
A
CHECK POWER SUPPLY CIRCUIT FOR ASCD HOLD RELAY.
1. Disconnect ASCD hold relay
2. Do approx. 12 volts exist between ASCD hold relay harness terminal ⑤ and body ground?
No
Check harness for open or short between fuse and ASCD hold relay.
Yes
B
CHECK GROUND CIRCUIT FOR ASCD HOLD RELAY.
Does continuity exist between ASCD hold relay harness terminal ② and body ground?
No
Repair harness.
Yes
C
CHECK ASCD HOLD RELAY CIRCUIT.
Does continuity exist between ASCD hold relay harness terminals ③ and ① ?
Yes
Check ASCD hold relay.
No
CHECK ASCD MAIN SWITCH.
NG
Replace ASCD main switch.
OK
Go to next procedure.

NS1109600107000X

Fig. 93 Test 3: ASCD Hold Relay Circuit Check. 1996 Maxima

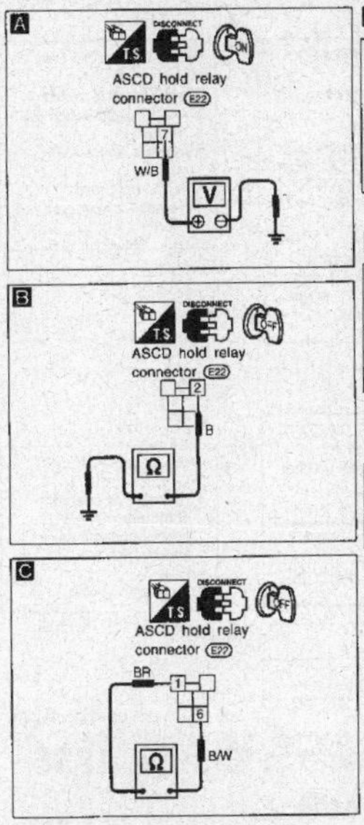
A
DISCONNECT
T.S.
ON
ASCD hold relay connector E22
W/B
V
B
ASCD hold relay connector E22
B
Ω
C
ASCD hold relay connector E27
BR
B/W
Ω

A CHECK POWER SUPPLY CIRCUIT FOR ASCD HOLD RELAY.
1. Disconnect ASCD hold relay.
2. Do approx. 12 volts exist between ASCD hold relay harness terminal ⑦ and body ground?

- No → Check harness for open or short between fuse and ASCD hold relay.
- Yes ↓

B CHECK GROUND CIRCUIT FOR ASCD HOLD RELAY.
Does continuity exist between ASCD hold relay harness terminal ② and body ground?

- No → Repair harness.
- Yes ↓

C CHECK ASCD HOLD RELAY CIRCUIT.
Does continuity exist between ASCD hold relay harness terminals ⑥ and ①?

- Yes → Check ASCD hold relay.
- No ↓

CHECK ASCD MAIN SWITCH.

- NG → Replace ASCD main switch.
- OK ↓

Go to next procedure.

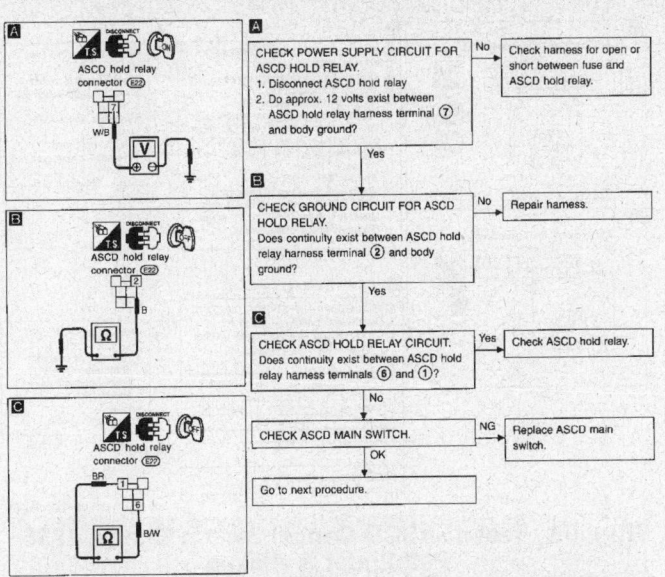

NS1109600097000X

Fig. 94 Test 3: ASCD Hold Relay Circuit Check. 1996 Pathfinder

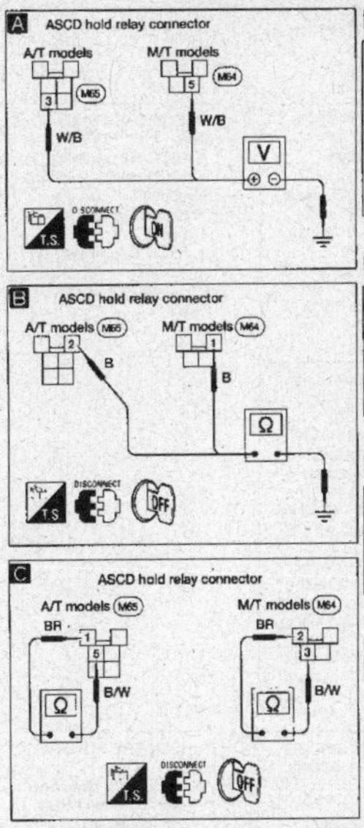
A ASCD hold relay connector
A/T models
M/T models
M65
M64
W/B
V
B ASCD hold relay connector
A/T models M65
M/T models M64
B
Ω
C ASCD hold relay connector
A/T models M65
M/T models M64
BR
B/W
Ω

A CHECK POWER SUPPLY CIRCUIT FOR ASCD HOLD RELAY.
1. Disconnect ASCD hold relay.
2. Do approx. 12 volts exist between ASCD hold relay harness terminal ⑤ (M/T models) or ③ (A/T models) and body ground?

- No → Check harness for open or short between fuse and ASCD hold relay.
- Yes ↓

B CHECK GROUND CIRCUIT FOR ASCD HOLD RELAY.
Does continuity exist between ASCD hold relay harness terminal ① (M/T models) or ② (A/T models) and body ground?

- No → Repair harness.
- Yes ↓

C CHECK ASCD HOLD RELAY CIRCUIT.
Does continuity exist between ASCD hold relay harness terminals ② and ③ (M/T models) or ① and ⑤ (A/T models)?

- Yes → Check ASCD hold relay.
- No ↓

CHECK ASCD MAIN SWITCH.

- NG → Replace ASCD main switch.
- OK ↓

Go to next procedure.

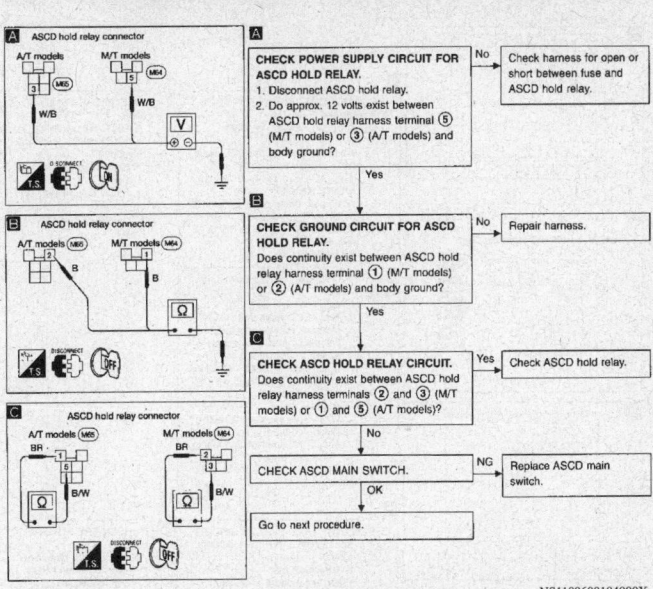

NS1109600104000X

Fig. 95 Test 3: ASCD Hold Relay Circuit Check. 1996 Pickup

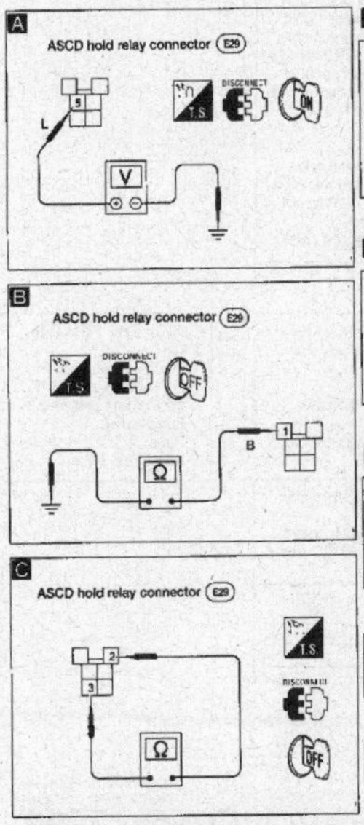
A
ASCD hold relay connector E29
L
V
B
ASCD hold relay connector E29
B
Ω
C
ASCD hold relay connector E29
Ω

A CHECK POWER SUPPLY CIRCUIT FOR ASCD HOLD RELAY.
1. Disconnect ASCD hold relay.
2. Do approx. 12 volts exist between ASCD hold relay harness terminal ⑤ and body ground?

- No → Check harness for open or short between fuse and ASCD hold relay.
- Yes ↓

B CHECK GROUND CIRCUIT FOR ASCD HOLD RELAY.
Does continuity exist between ASCD hold relay harness terminal ① and body ground?

- No → Repair harness.
- Yes ↓

C CHECK ASCD HOLD RELAY CIRCUIT.
Does continuity exist between ASCD hold relay harness terminals ③ and ②?

- Yes → Check ASCD hold relay.
- No ↓

CHECK ASCD MAIN SWITCH.
Refer to EL-219.

- NG → Replace ASCD main switch.
- OK ↓

Go to next procedure.

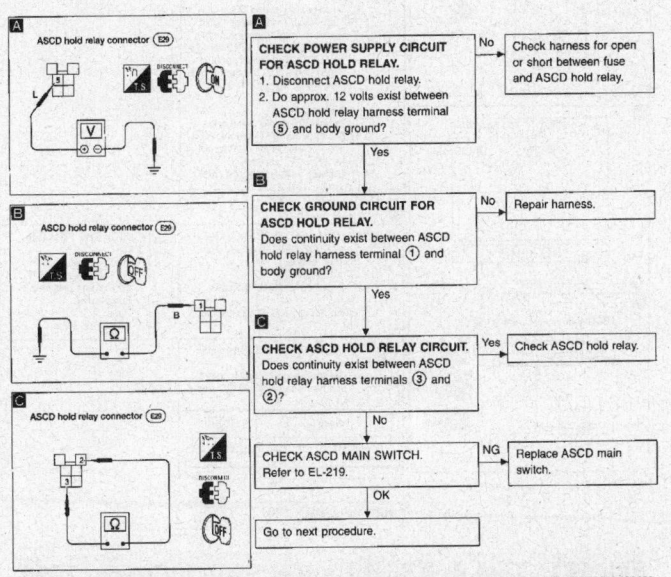

NS1109600114000X

Fig. 96 Test 3: ASCD Hold Relay Circuit Check. 1996 Quest

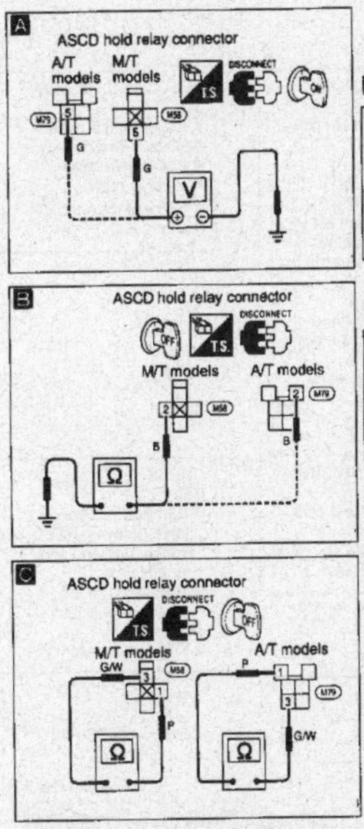
A
ASCD hold relay connector
A/T models
M/T models
G
V
B
ASCD hold relay connector
M/T models
A/T models
Ω
C
ASCD hold relay connector
M/T models
A/T models
G/W
P
Ω

A CHECK POWER SUPPLY CIRCUIT FOR ASCD HOLD RELAY.
1. Disconnect ASCD hold relay
2. Do approx. 12 volts exist between ASCD hold relay harness terminal ⑤ and body ground?

- No → Check harness for open or short between fuse and ASCD hold relay.
- Yes ↓

B CHECK GROUND CIRCUIT FOR ASCD HOLD RELAY.
Does continuity exist between ASCD hold relay harness terminal ② and body ground?

- No → Repair harness.
- Yes ↓

C CHECK ASCD HOLD RELAY CIRCUIT.
Does continuity exist between ASCD hold relay harness terminals ③ and ①?

- Yes → Check ASCD hold relay.
- No ↓

CHECK ASCD MAIN SWITCH.

- NG → Replace ASCD main switch.
- OK ↓

Go to next procedure.

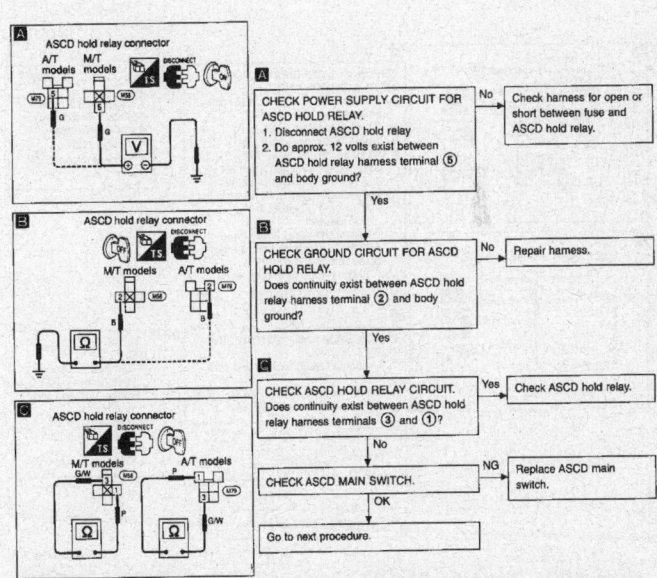

NS1109600127000X

Fig. 97 Test 3: ASCD Hold Relay Circuit Check. 1996 240SX

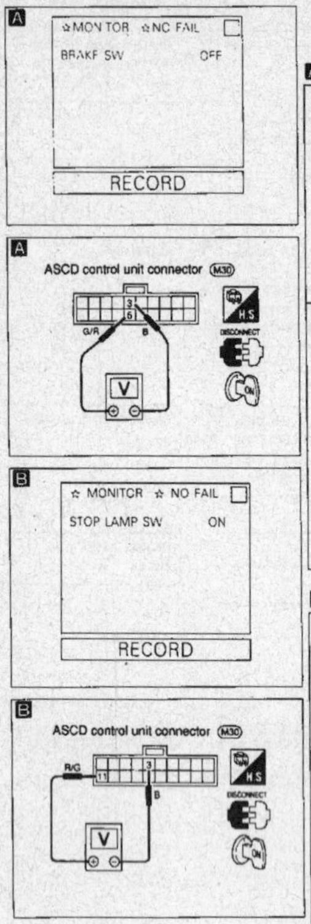
A
☆MONITOR ☆NO FAIL
BRAKE SW OFF
RECORD
A
ASCD control unit connector (M30)
G/R
B
V
DISCONNECT
H.S.
B
☆ MONITOR ☆ NO FAIL
STOP LAMP SW ON
RECORD
B
ASCD control unit connector (M30)
R/G
B
V

A

CHECK CUT-OFF CIRCUIT FOR ASCD CONTROL UNIT.
See "BRAKE SW" in "Data monitor" mode.
When brake pedal or clutch pedal (M/T) is depressed or A/T shift lever (A/T) is in "N" or "P" range:
BRAKE SW OFF
When both brake pedal and clutch pedal (M/T) are released or A/T shift lever (A/T) is not in "N" or "P" range:
BRAKE SW ON

— OR —

1. Disconnect control unit connector.
2. Turn ignition switch ON.
3. Turn ASCD main switch "ON".
4. Measure voltage between control unit connector terminals ⑤ and ③. When brake pedal or clutch pedal (M/T) is depressed or A/T shift lever (A/T) is in "N" or "P" range:
Approx. 0V
When both brake pedal and clutch pedal (M/T) are released or A/T shift lever (A/T) is not in "N" or "P" range:
Battery voltage should exist.

NG → CHECK THE FOLLOWING.
- ASCD cancel switch
- ASCD clutch switch (M/T model)
- Inhibitor switch (A/T model)
- ASCD hold relay (A/T model)
- Harness for open or short

OK ↓

B

CHECK STOP LAMP SWITCH CIRCUIT.
See "STOP LAMP SW" in "Data monitor" mode.
STOP LAMP SW
When brake pedal is released:
OFF
When brake pedal is depressed:
ON

— OR —

1. Disconnect control unit connector.
2. Check voltage between control unit harness terminals ⑪ and ③.

Condition		Voltage [V]
Stop lamp switch	Depressed	Approx. 12
	Released	0

NG → CHECK THE FOLLOWING.
- Harness for open or short between ASCD control unit and stop lamp switch.
- Fuse
- Stop lamp switch

OK ↓

ASCD cancel switch is OK.

NS1109600108000X

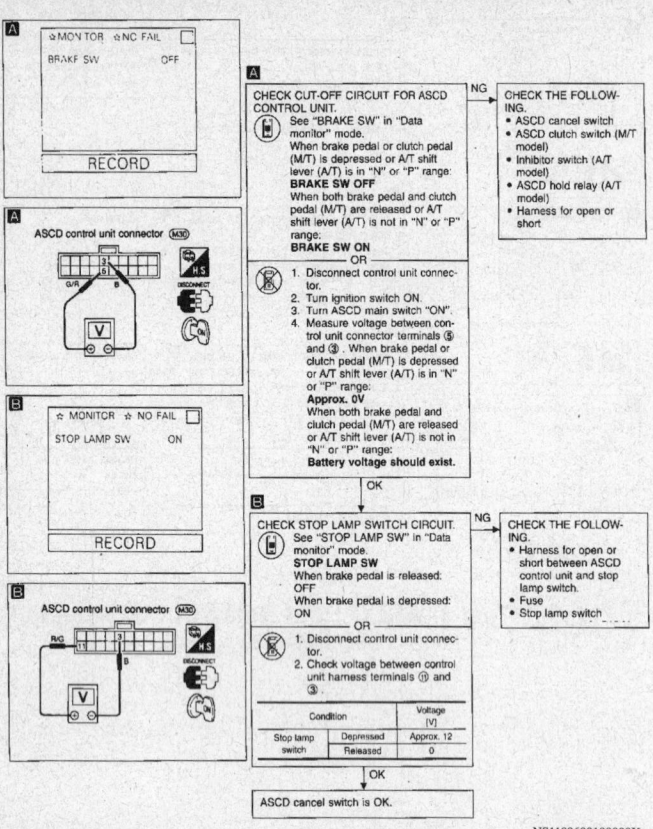

Fig. 98 Test 4: ASCD Cancel Switch Check. 1996 Maxima

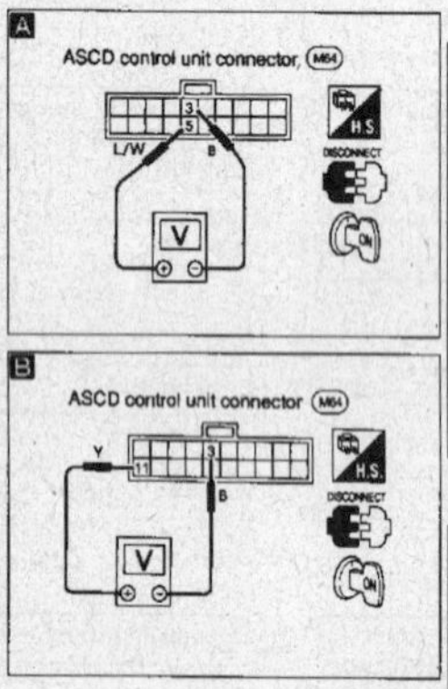
A
ASCD control unit connector (M64)
L/W
B
V
B
ASCD control unit connector (M64)
Y
B
V

A

CHECK CUT-OFF CIRCUIT FOR ASCD CONTROL UNIT.
1. Disconnect ASCD control unit connector.
2. Turn ignition switch ON.
3. Turn ASCD main switch ON.
4. Measure voltage between ASCD control unit connector terminals ⑤ and ③. **When brake pedal is depressed or A/T shift lever is in ("N") or ("P") position:**
Approx. 0V
When brake pedal is released or A/T shift lever is in any positions other than ("N") or ("P"):
Battery voltage should exist.

NG → CHECK THE FOLLOWING.
- ASCD cancel switch
- Inhibitor switch
- ASCD hold relay
- Inhibitor relay
- Harness for open or short

OK ↓

B

CHECK STOP LAMP SWITCH CIRCUIT.
1. Disconnect ASCD control unit connector.
2. Check voltage between ASCD control unit harness terminals ⑪ and ③.

Condition		Voltage [V]
Stop lamp switch	Depressed	Approx. 12
	Released	0

NG → CHECK THE FOLLOWING.
- Harness for open or short between ASCD control unit and stop lamp switch.
- 15A fuse (No. 22, located in the fuse block)
- Stop lamp switch

OK ↓

ASCD cancel switch is OK.

NS1109600115000X

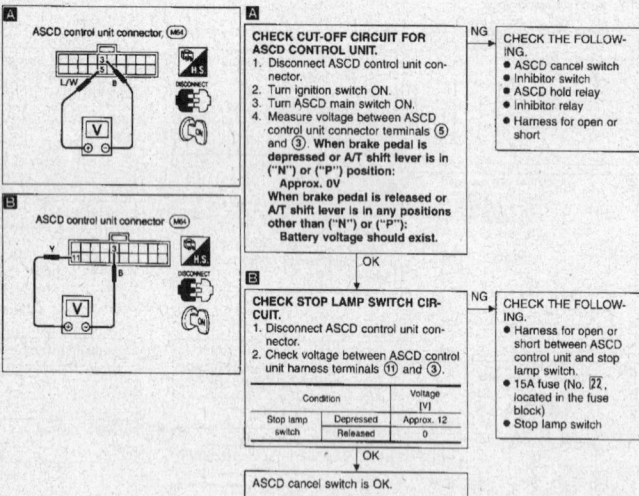

Fig. 100 Test 4: ASCD Cancel Switch Check. 1996 Quest

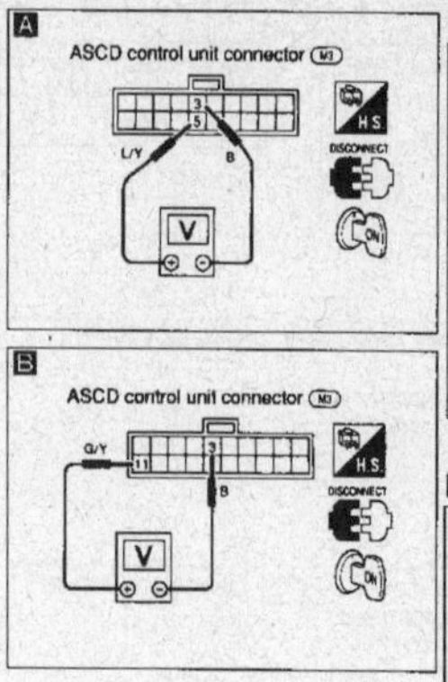
A
ASCD control unit connector (M3)
L/Y
B
V
B
ASCD control unit connector (M3)
G/Y
B
V

A

CHECK CUT-OFF CIRCUIT FOR ASCD CONTROL UNIT.
1. Disconnect control unit connector.
2. Turn ignition switch ON.
3. Turn ASCD main switch "ON".
4. Measure voltage between control unit connector terminals ⑤ and ③. When brake pedal or clutch pedal (M/T) is depressed or A/T shift lever (A/T) is in "N" or "P" range:
Approx. 0V
When both brake pedal and clutch pedal (M/T) are released or A/T shift lever (A/T) is not in "N" or "P" range:
Battery voltage should exist.

NG → CHECK THE FOLLOWING.
- ASCD cancel switch
- ASCD clutch switch (M/T model)
- Inhibitor switch (A/T model)
- ASCD hold relay
- Harness for open or short

OK ↓

B

CHECK STOP LAMP SWITCH CIRCUIT.
1. Disconnect control unit connector.
2. Check voltage between control unit harness terminals ⑪ and ③.

Condition		Voltage [V]
Stop lamp switch	Depressed	Approx. 12
	Released	0

NG → CHECK THE FOLLOWING.
- Harness for open or short between ASCD control unit and stop lamp switch
- Fuse
- Stop lamp switch

OK ↓

ASCD cancel switch is OK.

NS1109600098000X

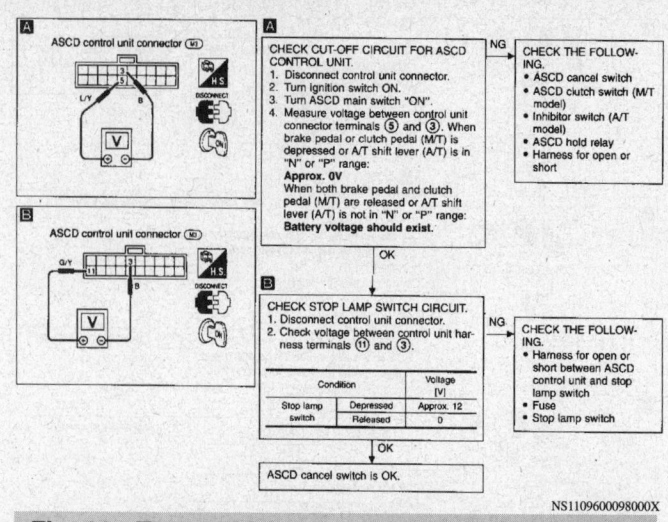

Fig. 99 Test 4: ASCD Cancel Switch Check. 1996 Pathfinder & Pickup

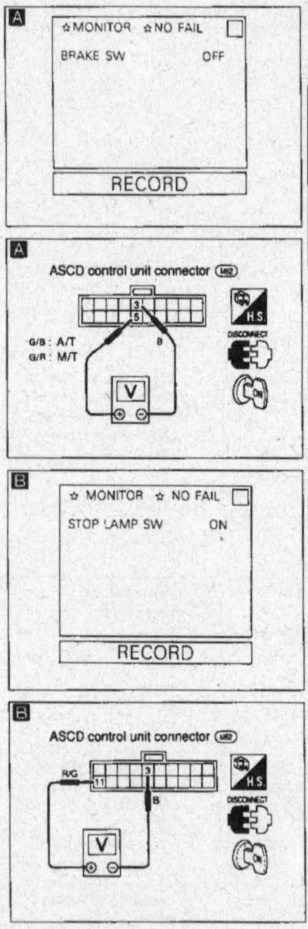
A
☆MONITOR ☆NO FAIL
BRAKE SW OFF
RECORD
A
ASCD control unit connector (M2)
G/B : A/T
G/R : M/T
B
V
B
☆ MONITOR ☆ NO FAIL
STOP LAMP SW ON
RECORD
B
ASCD control unit connector (M2)
R/G
B
V

A

CHECK CUT-OFF CIRCUIT FOR ASCD CONTROL UNIT.
See "BRAKE SW" in "Data monitor" mode.
When brake pedal or clutch pedal (M/T) is depressed or A/T shift lever (A/T) is in "N" or "P" range:
BRAKE SW OFF
When both brake pedal and clutch pedal (M/T) are released and A/T shift lever (A/T) is not in "N" or "P" range:
BRAKE SW ON

— OR —

1. Disconnect control unit connector.
2. Turn ignition switch ON.
3. Turn ASCD main switch "ON".
4. Measure voltage between control unit connector terminals ⑤ and ③. When brake pedal or clutch pedal (M/T) is depressed or A/T shift lever (A/T) is in "N" or "P" range:
Approx. 0V
When both brake pedal and clutch pedal (M/T) are released and A/T shift lever (A/T) is not in "N" or "P" range:
Battery voltage should exist.

NG → CHECK THE FOLLOWING.
- ASCD cancel switch
- ASCD clutch switch (M/T model)
- Inhibitor switch (A/T model)
- ASCD hold relay (A/T model)
- Harness for open or short

OK ↓

B

CHECK STOP LAMP SWITCH CIRCUIT.
See "STOP LAMP SW" in "Data monitor" mode.
STOP LAMP SW
When brake pedal is released:
OFF
When brake pedal is depressed:
ON

— OR —

1. Disconnect control unit connector.
2. Check voltage between control unit harness terminals ⑪ and ③.

Condition		Voltage [V]
Stop lamp switch	Depressed	Approx. 12
	Released	0

NG → CHECK THE FOLLOWING.
- Harness for open or short between ASCD control unit and stop lamp switch.
- Fuse
- Stop lamp switch

OK ↓

ASCD cancel switch is OK.

NS1109600128000X

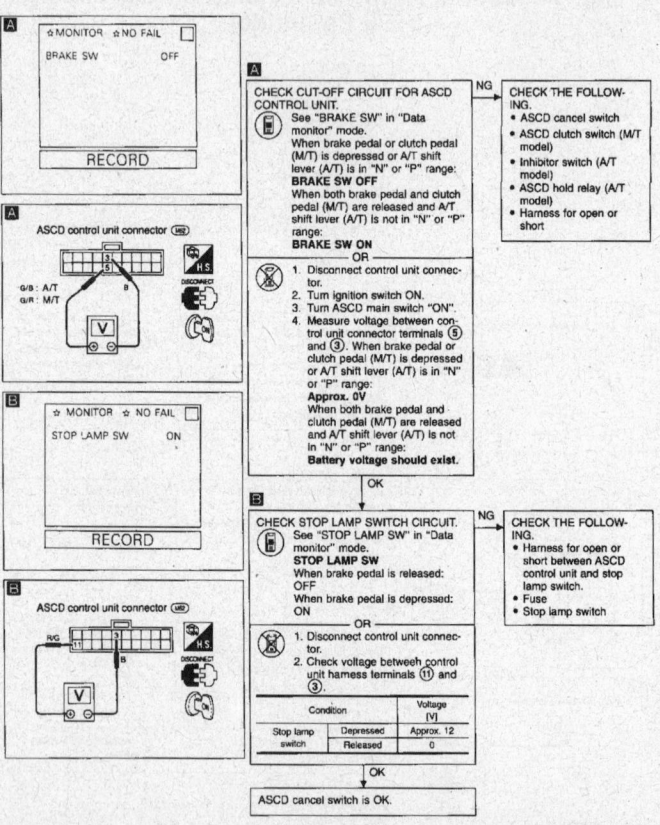

Fig. 101 Test 4: ASCD Cancel Switch Check. 1996 240SX

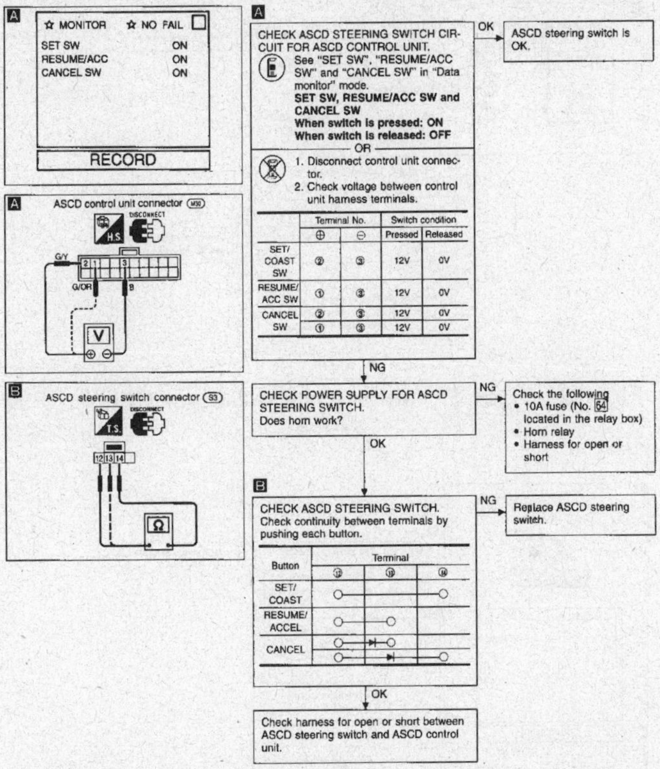
A
MONITOR NO FAIL
SET SW ON
RESUME/ACC ON
CANCEL SW ON
RECORD
A
ASCD control unit connector
DISCONNECT
H.S.
G/Y
G/OR
B
V
B
ASCD steering switch connector
T.S.
12 13 14
Ω
A
CHECK ASCD STEERING SWITCH CIRCUIT FOR ASCD CONTROL UNIT.
See "SET SW", "RESUME/ACC SW" and "CANCEL SW" in "Data monitor" mode.
SET SW, RESUME/ACC SW and CANCEL SW
When switch is pressed: ON
When switch is released: OFF
OR
1. Disconnect control unit connector.
2. Check voltage between control unit harness terminals.
Terminal No. ⊕ ⊖ Switch condition Pressed Released
SET/COAST SW 2 3 12V 0V
RESUME/ACC SW 1 3 12V 0V
CANCEL SW 2 3 12V 0V
1 3 12V 0V
OK
ASCD steering switch is OK.
NG
CHECK POWER SUPPLY FOR ASCD STEERING SWITCH.
Does horn work?
NG
Check the following.
• 10A fuse (No. 64 located in the relay box)
• Horn relay
• Harness for open or short
OK
B
CHECK ASCD STEERING SWITCH.
Check continuity between terminals by pushing each button.
NG
Replace ASCD steering switch.
Button Terminal 12 13 14
SET/COAST
RESUME/ACCEL
CANCEL
OK
Check harness for open or short between ASCD steering switch and ASCD control unit.
NS1109600109000X

Fig. 102 Test 5: ASCD Steering Switch Check. 1996 Maxima

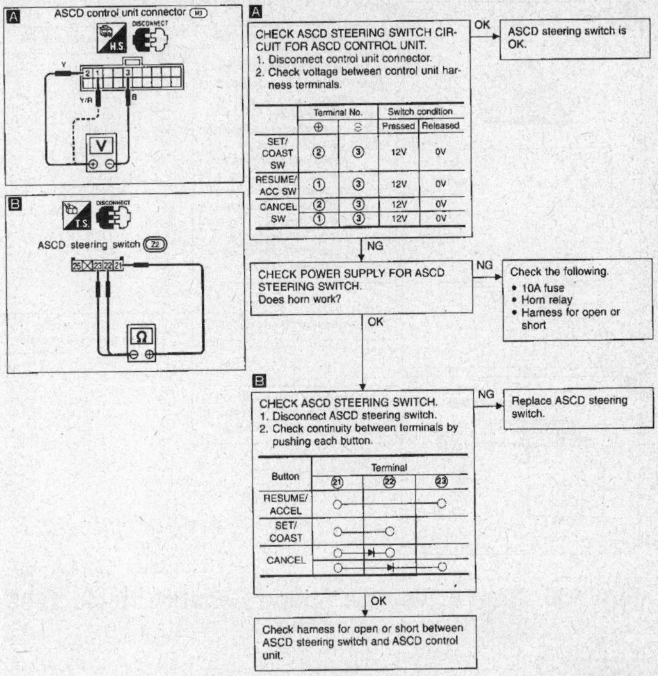
A
ASCD control unit connector
DISCONNECT
H.S.
Y
Y/R
B
V
B
DISCONNECT
T.S.
ASCD steering switch
Ω
A
CHECK ASCD STEERING SWITCH CIRCUIT FOR ASCD CONTROL UNIT.
1. Disconnect control unit connector.
2. Check voltage between control unit harness terminals.
Terminal No. ⊕ ⊖ Switch condition Pressed Released
SET/COAST SW 2 3 12V 0V
RESUME/ACC SW 1 3 12V 0V
CANCEL SW 2 3 12V 0V
1 3 12V 0V
OK
ASCD steering switch is OK.
NG
CHECK POWER SUPPLY FOR ASCD STEERING SWITCH.
Does horn work?
NG
Check the following.
• 10A fuse
• Horn relay
• Harness for open or short
OK
B
CHECK ASCD STEERING SWITCH.
1. Disconnect ASCD steering switch.
2. Check continuity between terminals by pushing each button.
NG
Replace ASCD steering switch.
Button Terminal 21 22 23
RESUME/ACCEL
SET/COAST
CANCEL
OK
Check harness for open or short between ASCD steering switch and ASCD control unit.
NS1109600099000X

Fig. 103 Test 5: ASCD Steering Switch Check. 1996 Pathfinder & Pickup

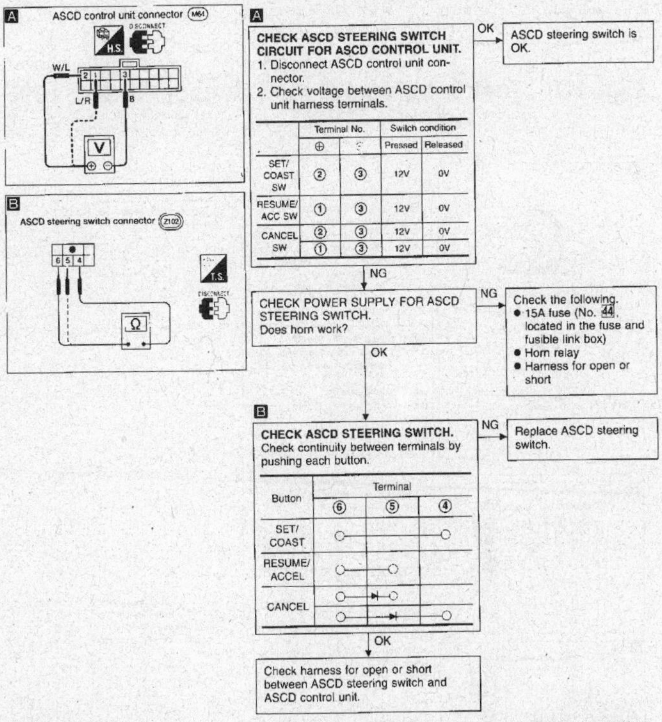
A
ASCD control unit connector
DISCONNECT
H.S.
W/L
L/R
B
V
B
ASCD steering switch connector
6 5 4
Ω
T.S.
DISCONNECT
A
CHECK ASCD STEERING SWITCH CIRCUIT FOR ASCD CONTROL UNIT.
1. Disconnect ASCD control unit connector.
2. Check voltage between ASCD control unit harness terminals.
Terminal No. ⊕ ⊖ Switch condition Pressed Released
SET/COAST SW 2 3 12V 0V
RESUME/ACC SW 1 3 12V 0V
CANCEL SW 2 3 12V 0V
1 3 12V 0V
OK
ASCD steering switch is OK.
NG
CHECK POWER SUPPLY FOR ASCD STEERING SWITCH.
Does horn work?
NG
Check the following.
• 15A fuse (No. 44, located in the fuse and fusible link box)
• Horn relay
• Harness for open or short
OK
B
CHECK ASCD STEERING SWITCH.
Check continuity between terminals by pushing each button.
NG
Replace ASCD steering switch.
Button Terminal 6 5 4
SET/COAST
RESUME/ACCEL
CANCEL
OK
Check harness for open or short between ASCD steering switch and ASCD control unit.
NS1109600116000X

Fig. 104 Test 5: ASCD Steering Switch Check. 1996 Quest

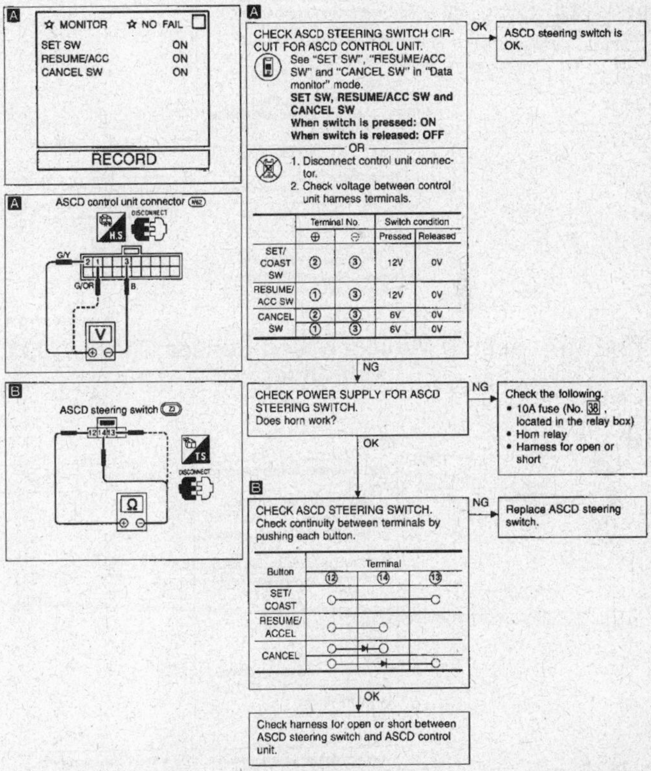
A
MONITOR NO FAIL
SET SW ON
RESUME/ACC ON
CANCEL SW ON
RECORD
A
ASCD control unit connector
DISCONNECT
H.S.
G/Y
G/OR
B
V
B
ASCD steering switch
12 14 13
T.S.
DISCONNECT
Ω
A
CHECK ASCD STEERING SWITCH CIRCUIT FOR ASCD CONTROL UNIT.
See "SET SW", "RESUME/ACC SW" and "CANCEL SW" in "Data monitor" mode.
SET SW, RESUME/ACC SW and CANCEL SW
When switch is pressed: ON
When switch is released: OFF
OR
1. Disconnect control unit connector.
2. Check voltage between control unit harness terminals.
Terminal No. ⊕ ⊖ Switch condition Pressed Released
SET/COAST SW 2 3 12V 0V
RESUME/ACC SW 1 3 12V 0V
CANCEL SW 2 3 6V 0V
1 3 6V 0V
OK
ASCD steering switch is OK.
NG
CHECK POWER SUPPLY FOR ASCD STEERING SWITCH.
Does horn work?
NG
Check the following.
• 10A fuse (No. 38, located in the relay box)
• Horn relay
• Harness for open or short
OK
B
CHECK ASCD STEERING SWITCH.
Check continuity between terminals by pushing each button.
NG
Replace ASCD steering switch.
Button Terminal 12 14 13
SET/COAST
RESUME/ACCEL
CANCEL
OK
Check harness for open or short between ASCD steering switch and ASCD control unit.
NS1109600129000X

Fig. 105 Test 5: ASCD Steering Switch Check. 1996 240SX

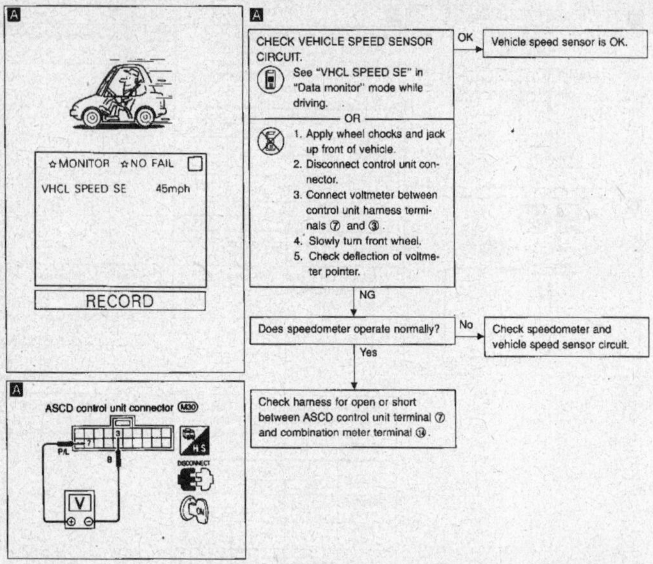
A
☆MONITOR ☆NO FAIL
VHCL SPEED SE 45mph
RECORD
A
CHECK VEHICLE SPEED SENSOR CIRCUIT.
See "VHCL SPEED SE" in "Data monitor" mode while driving.
OR
1. Apply wheel chocks and jack up front of vehicle.
2. Disconnect control unit connector.
3. Connect voltmeter between control unit harness terminals ⑦ and ③.
4. Slowly turn front wheel.
5. Check deflection of voltmeter pointer.
OK
Vehicle speed sensor is OK.
NG
Does speedometer operate normally?
No
Check speedometer and vehicle speed sensor circuit.
Yes
Check harness for open or short between ASCD control unit terminal ⑦ and combination meter terminal ⑭.
A
ASCD control unit connector (M30)
P/L
B
V
H.S
DISCONNECT
NS1109600110000X

Fig. 106 Test 6: Vehicle Speed Sensor Check. 1996 Maxima

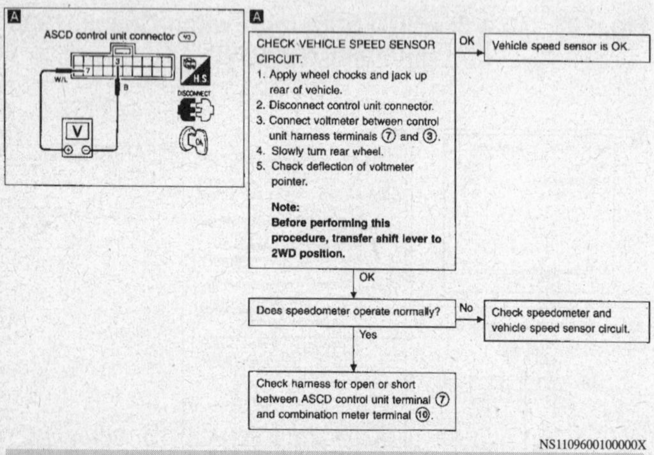
A
ASCD control unit connector
W/L
B
V
H.S
DISCONNECT
A
CHECK VEHICLE SPEED SENSOR CIRCUIT.
1. Apply wheel chocks and jack up rear of vehicle.
2. Disconnect control unit connector.
3. Connect voltmeter between control unit harness terminals ⑦ and ③.
4. Slowly turn rear wheel.
5. Check deflection of voltmeter pointer.
Note:
Before performing this procedure, transfer shift lever to 2WD position.
OK
Vehicle speed sensor is OK.
OK
Does speedometer operate normally?
No
Check speedometer and vehicle speed sensor circuit.
Yes
Check harness for open or short between ASCD control unit terminal ⑦ and combination meter terminal ⑩.
NS1109600100000X

Fig. 107 Test 6: Vehicle Speed Sensor Check. 1996 Pathfinder

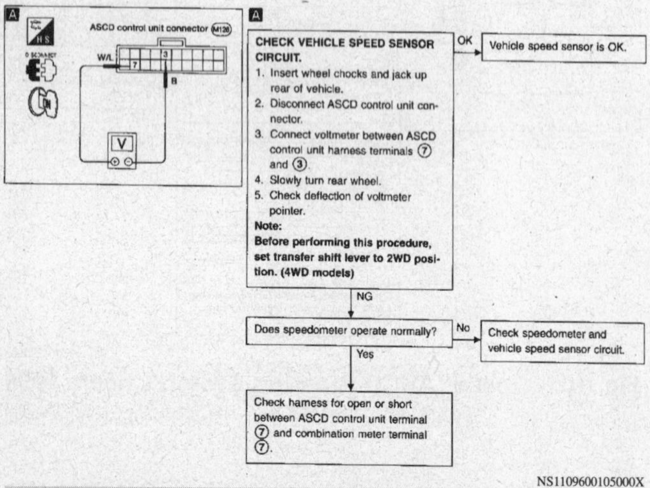
A
H.S
DISCONNECT
ASCD control unit connector (M126)
W/L
B
V
A
CHECK VEHICLE SPEED SENSOR CIRCUIT.
1. Insert wheel chocks and jack up rear of vehicle.
2. Disconnect ASCD control unit connector.
3. Connect voltmeter between ASCD control unit harness terminals ⑦ and ③.
4. Slowly turn rear wheel.
5. Check deflection of voltmeter pointer.
Note:
Before performing this procedure, set transfer shift lever to 2WD position. (4WD models)
OK
Vehicle speed sensor is OK.
NG
Does speedometer operate normally?
No
Check speedometer and vehicle speed sensor circuit.
Yes
Check harness for open or short between ASCD control unit terminal ⑦ and combination meter terminal ⑦.
NS1109600105000X

Fig. 108 Test 6: Vehicle Speed Sensor Check. 1996 Pickup

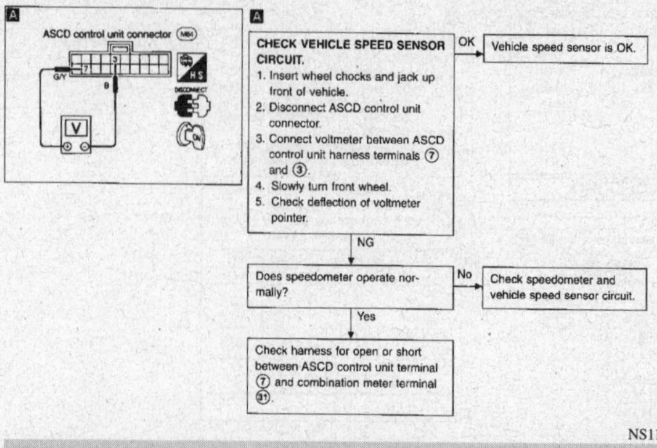
A
ASCD control unit connector (M84)
G/Y
B
V
H.S
DISCONNECT
A
CHECK VEHICLE SPEED SENSOR CIRCUIT.
1. Insert wheel chocks and jack up front of vehicle.
2. Disconnect ASCD control unit connector.
3. Connect voltmeter between ASCD control unit harness terminals ⑦ and ③.
4. Slowly turn front wheel.
5. Check deflection of voltmeter pointer.
OK
Vehicle speed sensor is OK.
NG
Does speedometer operate normally?
No
Check speedometer and vehicle speed sensor circuit.
Yes
Check harness for open or short between ASCD control unit terminal ⑦ and combination meter terminal ㉛.
NS1109600117000X

Fig. 109 Test 6: Vehicle Speed Sensor Check. 1996 Quest

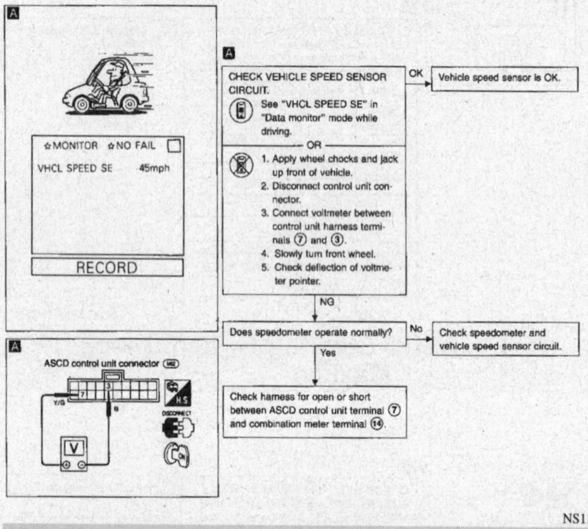
A
☆MONITOR ☆NO FAIL
VHCL SPEED SE 45mph
RECORD
A
CHECK VEHICLE SPEED SENSOR CIRCUIT.
See "VHCL SPEED SE" in "Data monitor" mode while driving.
OR
1. Apply wheel chocks and jack up front of vehicle.
2. Disconnect control unit connector.
3. Connect voltmeter between control unit harness terminals ⑦ and ③.
4. Slowly turn front wheel.
5. Check deflection of voltmeter pointer.
OK
Vehicle speed sensor is OK.
NG
Does speedometer operate normally?
No
Check speedometer and vehicle speed sensor circuit.
Yes
Check harness for open or short between ASCD control unit terminal ⑦ and combination meter terminal ⑭.
A
ASCD control unit connector (M2)
Y/G
B
V
H.S
DISCONNECT
NS1109600130000X

Fig. 110 Test 6: Vehicle Speed Sensor Check. 1996 240SX

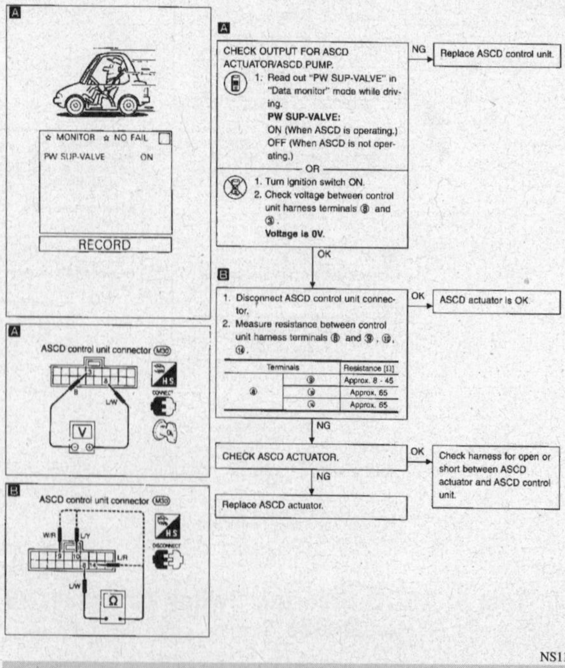
A
☆MONITOR ☆NO FAIL
PW SUP-VALVE ON
RECORD
A
CHECK OUTPUT FOR ASCD ACTUATOR/ASCD PUMP.
1. Read out "PW SUP-VALVE" in "Data monitor" mode while driving.
PW SUP-VALVE:
ON (When ASCD is operating.)
OFF (When ASCD is not operating.)
OR
1. Turn ignition switch ON.
2. Check voltage between control unit harness terminals ⑧ and ③.
Voltage is 0V.
NG
Replace ASCD control unit.
OK
B
1. Disconnect ASCD control unit connector.
2. Measure resistance between control unit harness terminals ⑧ and ⑨, ⑬, ⑭.
Terminals | Resistance [Ω]
⑧ ⑨ Approx. 8 - 45
⑬ Approx. 65
⑭ Approx. 65
OK
ASCD actuator is OK.
NG
CHECK ASCD ACTUATOR.
OK
Check harness for open or short between ASCD actuator and ASCD control unit.
NG
Replace ASCD actuator.
A
ASCD control unit connector (M30)
B
L/W
V
H.S
CONNECT
B
ASCD control unit connector (M30)
W/R
L/Y
L/R
L/W
Ω
H.S
DISCONNECT
NS1109600111000X

Fig. 111 Test 7: ASCD Actuator Check. 1996 Maxima

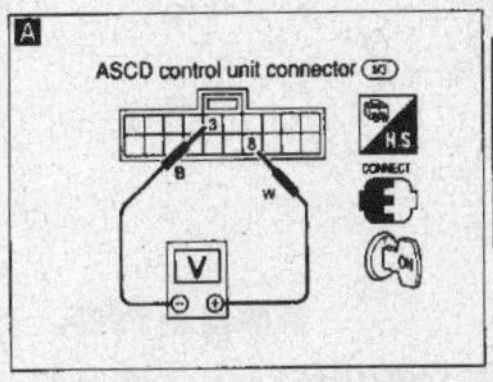
A
ASCD control unit connector
B
W
V
HS
CONNECT

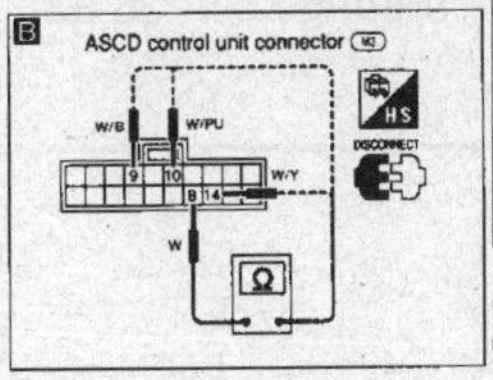
B
ASCD control unit connector
W/B
W/PU
W/Y
W
Ω
HS
DISCONNECT

A

CHECK OUTPUT FOR ASCD ACTUATOR/ASCD PUMP.
1. Turn ignition switch ON.
2. Check voltage between control unit harness terminals ⑧ and ③.
Voltage is 0V.

NG → Replace ASCD control unit.

OK ↓

B

1. Disconnect ASCD control unit connector.
2. Measure resistance between control unit harness terminals ⑧ and ⑨, ⑩, ⑭.

Terminals		Resistance [Ω]
⑧	⑨	Approx. 8 - 45
	⑩	Approx. 65
	⑭	Approx. 65

OK → ASCD actuator is OK.

NG ↓

CHECK ASCD ACTUATOR.

OK → Check and repair harness.

NG ↓

Replace ASCD actuator.

NS1109600101000X

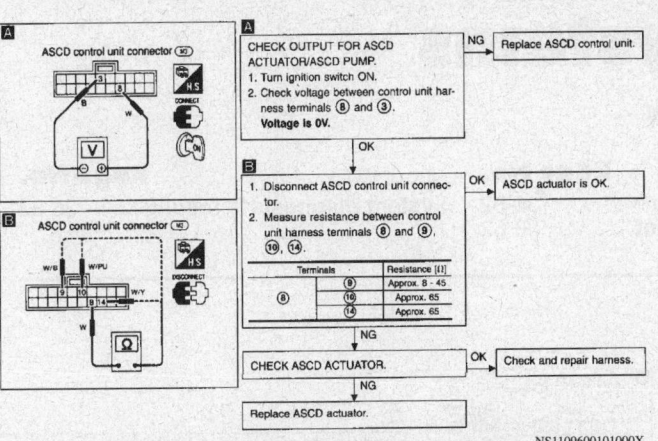

Fig. 112 Test 7: ASCD Actuator Check. 1996 Pathfinder & Pickup

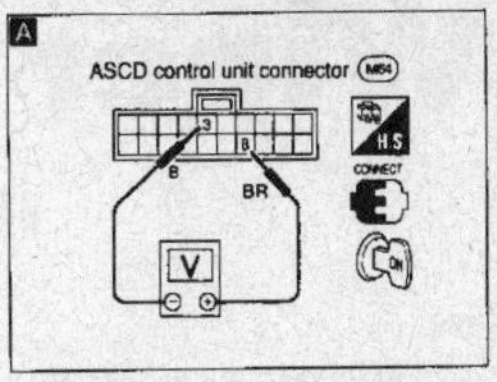
A
ASCD control unit connector
B
BR
V
HS
CONNECT

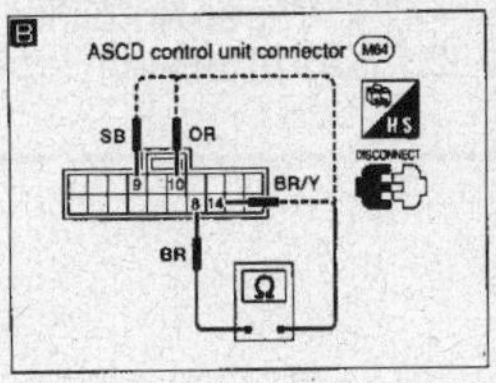
B
ASCD control unit connector
SB
OR
BR/Y
BR
Ω
HS
DISCONNECT

A

CHECK OUTPUT FOR ASCD ACTUATOR/ASCD PUMP.
1. Turn ignition switch ON.
2. Check voltage between ASCD control unit harness terminals ⑧ and ③.
Voltage is 0V.

NG → Replace ASCD control unit.

OK ↓

B

1. Disconnect ASCD control unit connector.
2. Measure resistance between ASCD control unit harness terminals ⑧ and ⑨, ⑩, ⑭.

Terminals		Resistance [Ω]
⑧	⑨	Approx. 8 - 45
	⑩	Approx. 65
	⑭	Approx. 65

OK → ASCD actuator is OK.

NG ↓

Check ASCD actuator. Refer to EL-219.

OK → Check harness for open or short between ASCD actuator and ASCD control unit.

NG ↓

Replace ASCD actuator.

NS1109600118000X

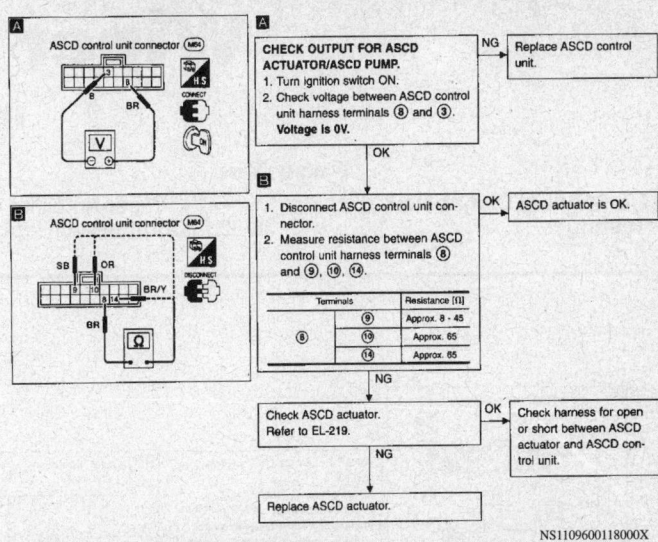

Fig. 113 Test 7: ASCD Actuator Check. 1996 Quest

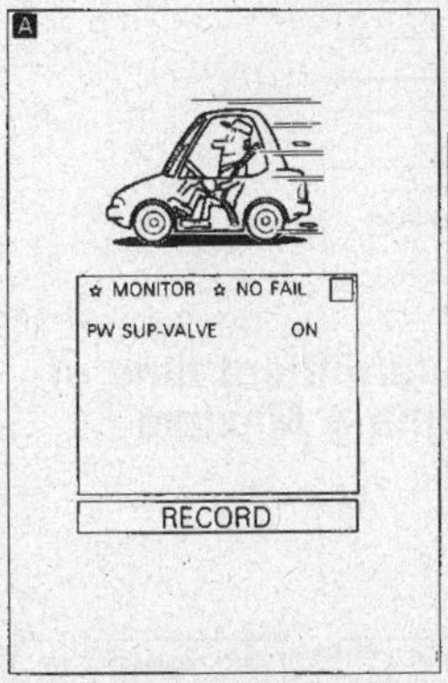
A
☆ MONITOR ☆ NO FAIL
PW SUP-VALVE ON
RECORD

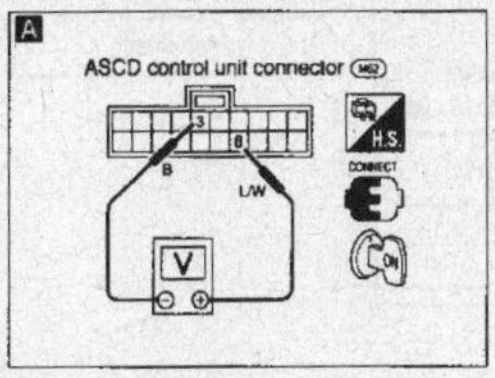
A
ASCD control unit connector
B
L/W
V
HS
CONNECT

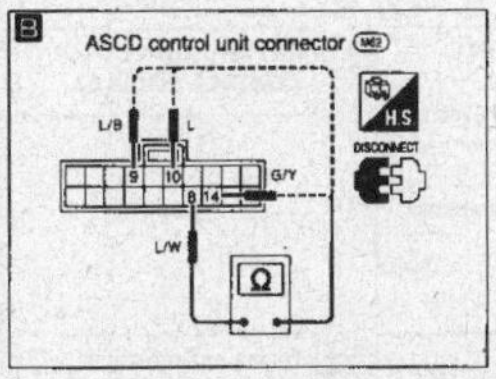
B
ASCD control unit connector
L/B
L
G/Y
L/W
Ω
HS
DISCONNECT

DIAGNOSTIC PROCEDURE 7

(ASCD ACTUATOR CHECK)

A

CHECK OUTPUT FOR ASCD ACTUATOR/ASCD PUMP.
1. Read out "PW SUP-VALVE" in "Data monitor" mode while driving.
PW SUP-VALVE:
ON (When ASCD is operating.)
OFF (When ASCD is not operating.)

— OR —

1. Turn ignition switch ON.
2. Check voltage between control unit harness terminals ⑧ and ③.
Voltage is 0V.

NG → Replace ASCD control unit.

OK ↓

B

1. Disconnect ASCD control unit connector.
2. Measure resistance between control unit harness terminals ⑧ and ⑨, ⑩, ⑭.

Terminals		Resistance [Ω]
⑧	⑨	Approx. 8 - 45
	⑩	Approx. 65
	⑭	Approx. 65

OK → ASCD actuator is OK.

NG ↓

CHECK ASCD ACTUATOR.

OK → Check harness for open or short between ASCD actuator and ASCD control unit.

NG ↓

Replace ASCD actuator.

NS1109600131000X

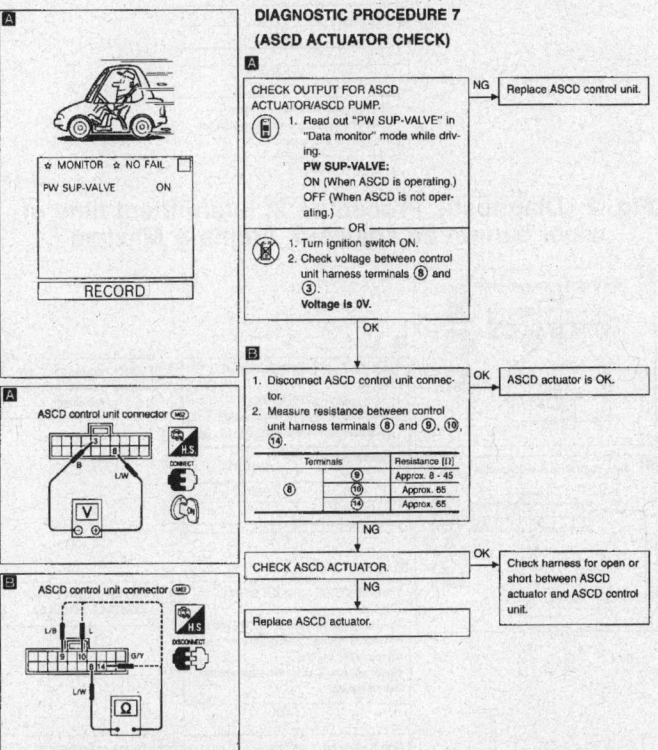

Fig. 114 Test 7: ASCD Actuator Check. 1996 240SX

Check vacuum hose for breakage, cracks or fracture.

NG → Repair or replace hose.

OK ↓

Check ASCD wire smoothly.

NG → Repair or replace wire. Refer to "ASCD WIRE ADJUSTMENT"

OK ↓

Vacuum hose and accelerator wire are OK.

NS1109600112000X

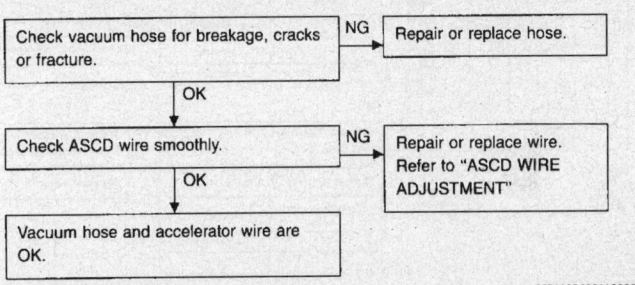

Fig. 115 Test 8: Vacuum Hose & Accel Wire Check. 1996 Maxima

Check vacuum hose for breakage, cracks or fracture.

NG → Repair or replace hose.

OK ↓

Check ASCD wire smoothly.

NG → Repair or replace wire.

OK ↓

Vacuum hose and accelerator wire are OK.

NS1109600102000X

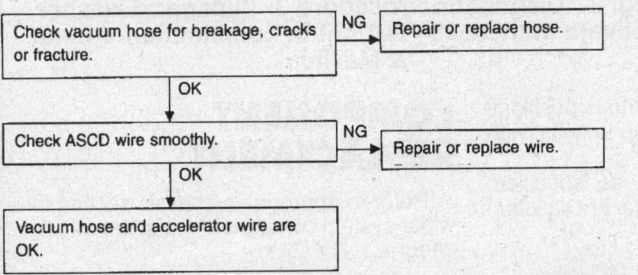

Fig. 116 Test 8: Vacuum Hose & Accel Wire Check. 1996 Pathfinder & Pickup

Check vacuum hose for breakage, cracks or fracture.

NG → Repair or replace hose.

OK ↓

Check ASCD wire operates smoothly.

NG → Repair or replace wire. Refer to "ASCD WIRE ADJUSTMENT".

OK ↓

Vacuum hose and ASCD wire are OK.

NS1109600119000X

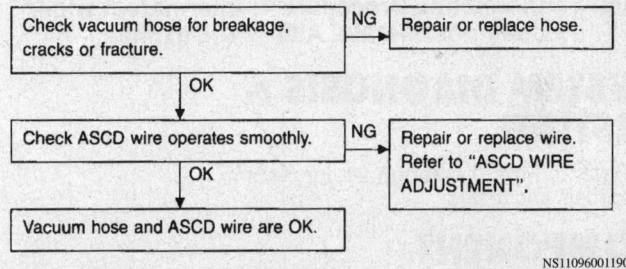

Fig. 117 Test 8: Vacuum Hose & Accel Wire Check. 1996 Quest

Check vacuum hose for breakage, cracks or fracture.

NG → Repair or replace hose.

OK ↓

Check ASCD wire smoothly.

NG → Repair or replace wire.

OK ↓

Vacuum hose and accelerator wire are OK.

NS1109600132000X

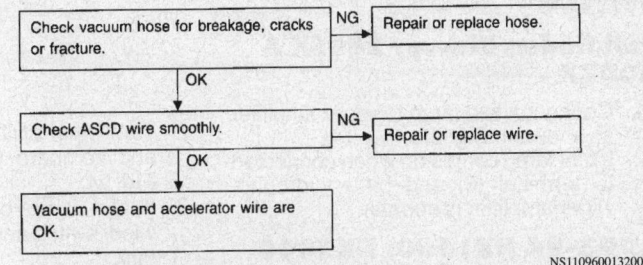

Fig. 118 Test 8: Vacuum Hose & Accel Wire Check. 1996 240SX

Wiper Systems

INDEX

	Page No.
Component Diagnosis & Testing	36-82
Wiper Amplifier & Switch	36-82
Component Replacement	36-82
System Diagnosis & Testing	36-82

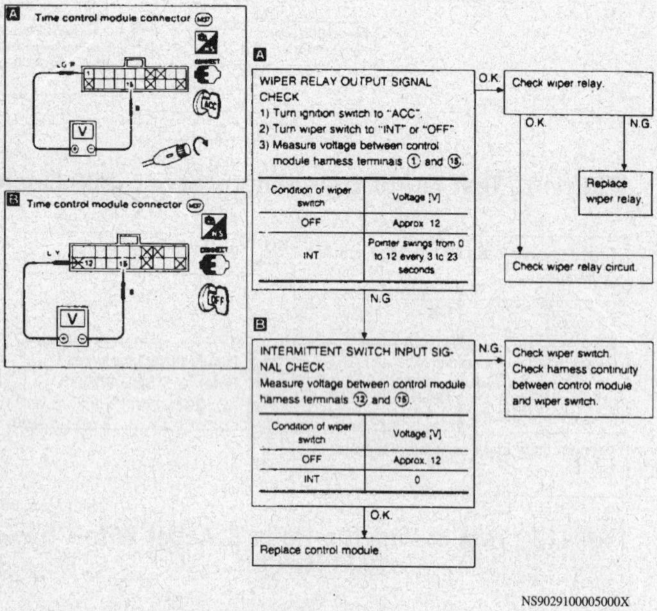

A Time control module connector
B Time control module connector
WIPER RELAY OUTPUT SIGNAL CHECK
1) Turn ignition switch to "ACC".
2) Turn wiper switch to "INT" or "OFF".
3) Measure voltage between control module harness terminals ① and ⑱.
Condition of wiper switch
Voltage [V]
OFF
Approx. 12
INT
Pointer swings from 0 to 12 every 3 to 23 seconds
O.K.
Check wiper relay.
O.K.
N.G.
Replace wiper relay.
Check wiper relay circuit.
N.G.
INTERMITTENT SWITCH INPUT SIGNAL CHECK
Measure voltage between control module harness terminals ⑫ and ⑱.
Condition of wiper switch
Voltage [V]
OFF
Approx. 12
INT
0
N.G.
Check wiper switch.
Check harness continuity between control module and wiper switch.
O.K.
Replace control module.
NS9029100005000X

Fig. 1 Diagnostic Procedure 1: Intermittent wiper does not operate. Altima & Maxima

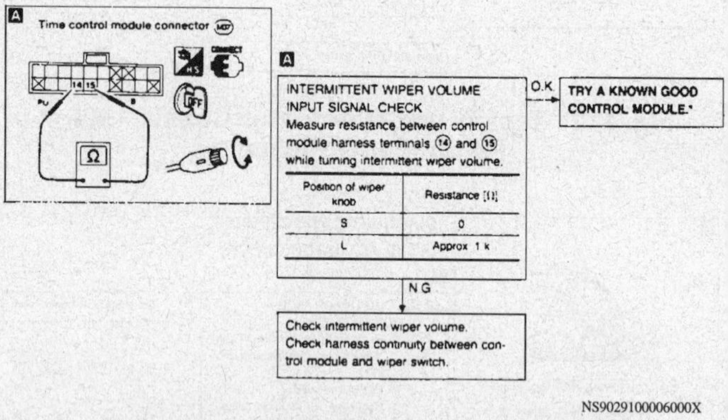

A Time control module connector
INTERMITTENT WIPER VOLUME INPUT SIGNAL CHECK
Measure resistance between control module harness terminals ⑭ and ⑮ while turning intermittent wiper volume.
Position of wiper knob
Resistance [Ω]
S
0
L
Approx. 1 k
O.K.
TRY A KNOWN GOOD CONTROL MODULE.*
N.G.
Check intermittent wiper volume.
Check harness continuity between control module and wiper switch.
NS9029100006000X

Fig. 2 Diagnostic Procedure 2: Intermittent time of wiper cannot be adjusted. Altima & Maxima

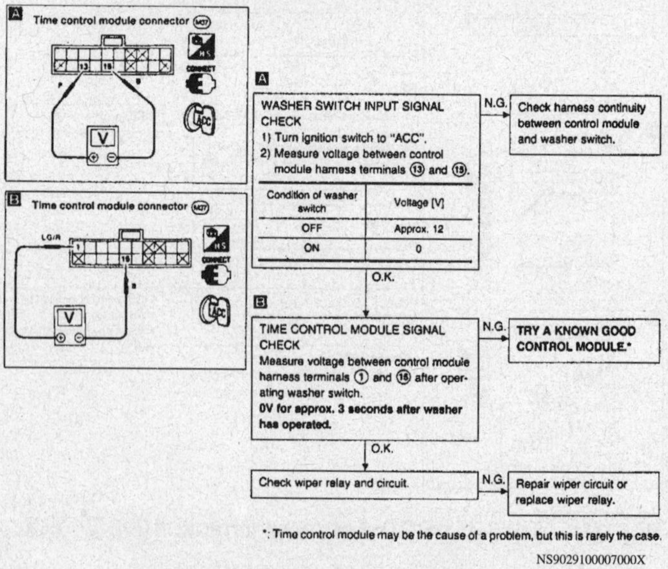

A Time control module connector
B Time control module connector
WASHER SWITCH INPUT SIGNAL CHECK
1) Turn ignition switch to "ACC".
2) Measure voltage between control module harness terminals ⑬ and ⑱.
Condition of washer switch
Voltage [V]
OFF
Approx. 12
ON
0
N.G.
Check harness continuity between control module and washer switch.
O.K.
TIME CONTROL MODULE SIGNAL CHECK
Measure voltage between control module harness terminals ① and ⑱ after operating washer switch.
0V for approx. 3 seconds after washer has operated.
N.G.
TRY A KNOWN GOOD CONTROL MODULE.*
O.K.
Check wiper relay and circuit.
N.G.
Repair wiper circuit or replace wiper relay.
*: Time control module may be the cause of a problem, but this is rarely the case.
NS9029100007000X

Fig. 3 Diagnostic Procedure 3: Wiper and washer activate individually but not in combination. Altima & Maxima

SYSTEM DIAGNOSIS & TESTING

Refer to **Figs. 1 through 21,** for system diagnosis and testing.

COMPONENT DIAGNOSIS & TESTING

WIPER AMPLIFIER & SWITCH

Pathfinder, Pickup, 240SX & 300ZX

1. Connect a test lamp to wiper amplifier as shown in **Fig. 22.**
2. If test lamp comes on when connected to terminal (6) and battery ground, wiper amplifier is normal.

1993-94 NX1600, NX2000 & Sentra

1. Connect a test lamp to wiper amplifier as shown in **Fig. 23.**
2. Turn wiper switch to various positions and compare test lamp results with **Fig. 24.**
3. If test lamp operates as specified, wiper switch and amplifier are satisfactory.

COMPONENT REPLACEMENT

Refer to appropriate chassis section for wiper system component replacement procedures.

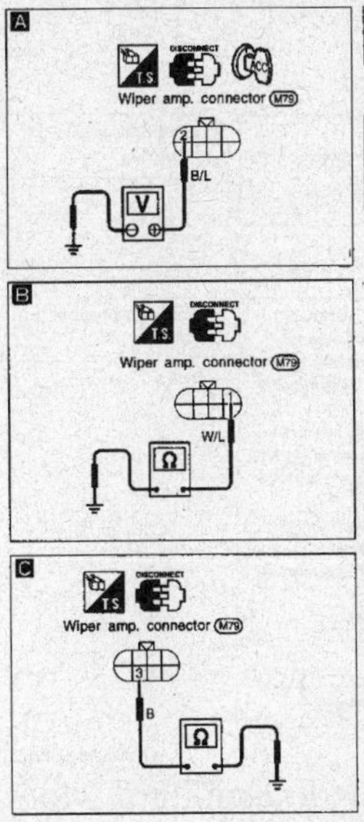
A
DISCONNECT
Wiper amp. connector M79
B/L
V
B
DISCONNECT
Wiper amp. connector M79
W/L
Ω
C
DISCONNECT
Wiper amp. connector M79
3
B
Ω

Check whether wiper operates with the wiper switch at Lo position.
- NG → Check wiper motor and circuit.
- OK ↓

A
1) Disconnect wiper amp. connector.
2) Measure voltage between wiper amp. harness terminal ② and body ground.
Battery voltage should exist.
- NG →
  - Check wiper switch.
  - Check wiper motor.
  - Check harness for open or short between wiper amp. harness terminal ② and wiper switch harness terminal ⑬. **Continuity should exist.**
  - Check harness continuity between wiper switch harness terminal ⑭ and wiper motor harness terminal ②. **Continuity should exist.**
- OK ↓

B
INTERMITTENT SWITCH INPUT SIGNAL CHECK
Check harness continuity between wiper amp. harness terminal ① and body ground.

Condition of wiper switch	Continuity
OFF	No
INT	Yes

- NG →
  - Check wiper switch.
  - Check harness for open or short between wiper amp. harness terminal ① and wiper switch harness terminal ⑮. **Continuity should exist.**
  - Check harness continuity between wiper switch harness terminal ⑰ and body ground. **Continuity should exist.**
- OK ↓

C
WIPER AMP. GROUND CIRCUIT CHECK
Check harness continuity between wiper amp. harness terminal ③ and body ground.
Continuity should exist.
- NG → Repair harness or connector.
- OK ↓

Replace wiper amp.

NS9029600022000X

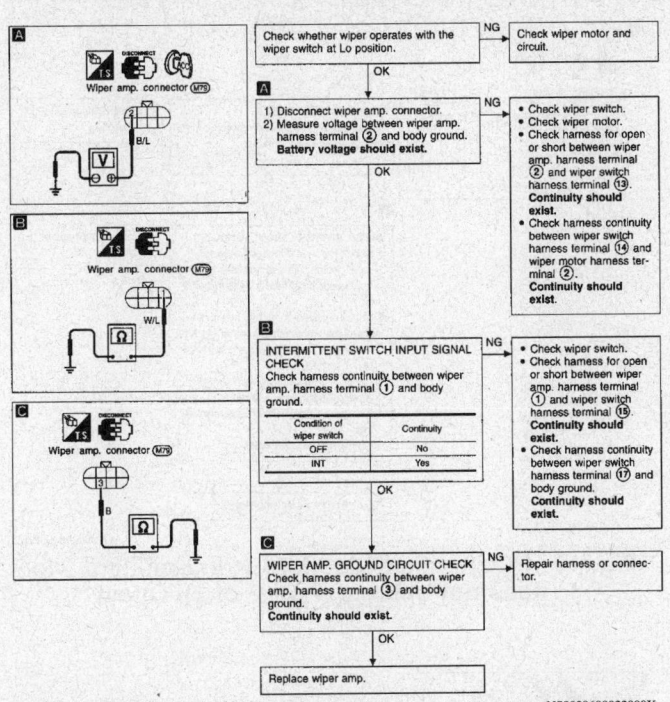

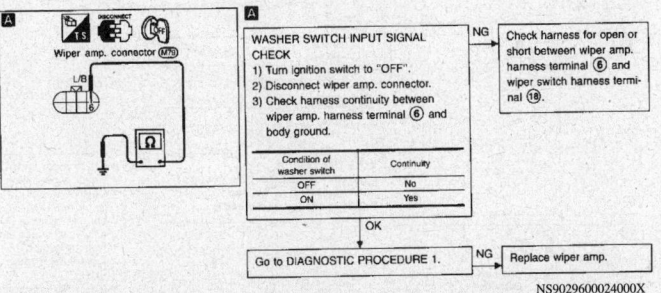

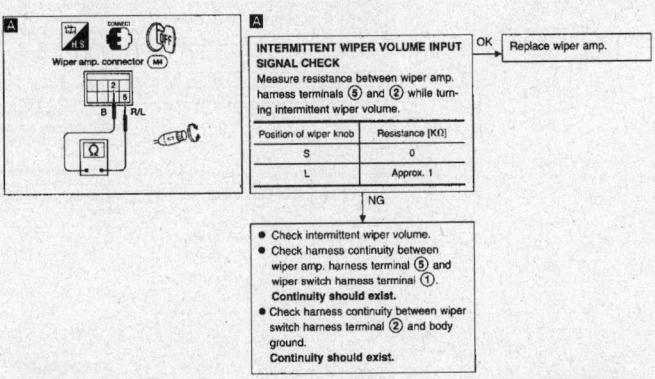

Fig. 4 Diagnostic Procedure 1: Intermittent wiper does not operate. Pathfinder

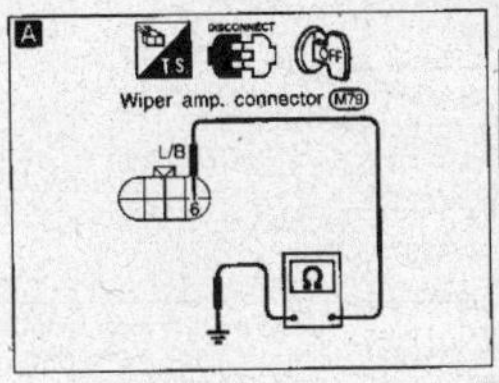
A
DISCONNECT
Wiper amp. connector M79
W/L
1
Ω

A
WASHER SWITCH INPUT SIGNAL CHECK
1) Turn ignition switch to "OFF".
2) Disconnect wiper amp. connector.
3) Check harness continuity between wiper amp. harness terminal ⑥ and body ground.

Condition of washer switch	Continuity
OFF	No
ON	Yes

- NG → Check harness for open or short between wiper amp. harness terminal ⑥ and wiper switch harness terminal ⑱.
- OK ↓

Go to DIAGNOSTIC PROCEDURE 1.
- NG → Replace wiper amp.

NS9029600024000X

Fig. 6 Diagnostic Procedure 3: Wiper and washer activate individually but not in combination. Pathfinder

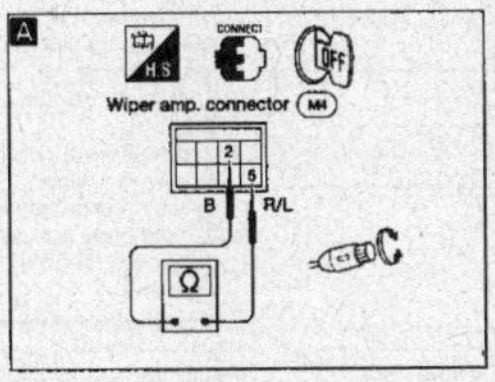
A
CONNECT
Wiper amp. connector M4
2
5
B
R/L
Ω

A
INTERMITTENT WIPER VOLUME INPUT SIGNAL CHECK
Measure resistance between wiper amp. harness terminals ⑤ and ② while turning intermittent wiper volume.

Position of wiper knob	Resistance [KΩ]
S	0
L	Approx. 1

- OK → Replace wiper amp.
- NG ↓
  - Check intermittent wiper volume.
  - Check harness continuity between wiper amp. harness terminal ⑤ and wiper switch harness terminal ①. **Continuity should exist.**
  - Check harness continuity between wiper switch harness terminal ② and body ground. **Continuity should exist.**

NS9029600026000X

Fig. 8 Diagnostic Procedure 2: Intermittent time of wiper cannot be adjusted. Pickup

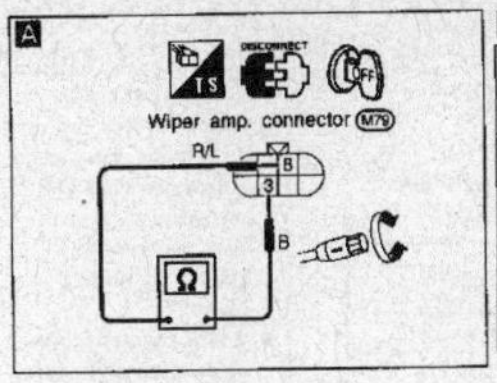
A
DISCONNECT
Wiper amp. connector M79
R/L
8
3
B
Ω

A
INTERMITTENT WIPER VOLUME INPUT SIGNAL CHECK
1) Disconnect wiper amp. connector.
2) Measure resistance between wiper amp. harness terminals ⑧ and ③ while turning intermittent wiper volume.

Position of wiper knob	Resistance [Ω]
S	0
L	Approx. 1 k

- OK → Replace wiper amp.
- NG ↓
  - Check intermittent wiper volume.
  - Check harness continuity between wiper amp. harness terminal ⑧ and wiper switch harness terminal ⑲.

  Check harness continuity between wiper switch harness terminal ⑳ and body ground.

NS9029600023000X

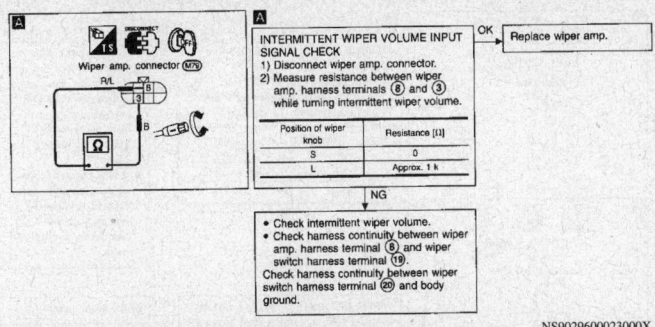

Fig. 5 Diagnostic Procedure 2: Intermittent time of wiper cannot be adjusted. Pathfinder

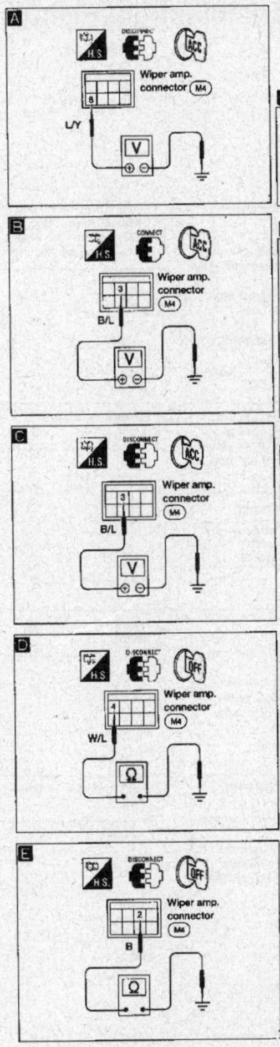
A
H.S.
ACC
Wiper amp. connector M4
8
L/Y
V
B
H.S.
CONNECT
ACC
Wiper amp. connector M4
3
B/L
V
C
H.S.
DISCONNECT
ACC
Wiper amp. connector M4
3
B/L
V
D
H.S.
DISCONNECT
OFF
Wiper amp. connector M4
4
W/L
Ω
E
H.S.
DISCONNECT
OFF
Wiper amp. connector M4
2
B
Ω

A
CHECK POWER SUPPLY FOR WIPER AMPLIFIER.
1. Turn ignition switch to ACC.
2. Measure voltage between wiper amplifier terminal ⑧ and body ground.
Battery voltage should exist.
- NG → Check 20A fuse (No. 7), located in the fuse block), harness and connector.
- OK ↓

B
WIPER AMP. OUTPUT SIGNAL CHECK.
1. Turn ignition switch to ACC.
2. Move wiper switch to INT or OFF.
3. Measure voltage between wiper amp. harness terminal ③ and body ground.

Condition of wiper switch	Voltage [V]
OFF	Approx. 12
INT	Pointer swings from 0 to 12 every 7 seconds

- OK → Check wiper motor and circuit.
- NG ↓

C
VOLTAGE CHECK.
1. Disconnect wiper amp. connector.
2. Turn ignition switch to ACC.
3. Measure voltage between wiper amp. harness terminal ③ and body ground.
Battery voltage should exist.
- NG →
  - Check wiper switch.
  - Check wiper motor.
  - Check harness continuity between wiper amp. harness terminal ③ and wiper switch harness terminal ⑧. **Continuity should exist.**
  - Check harness continuity between wiper switch harness terminal ④ and wiper motor harness terminal ②. **Continuity should exist.**
- OK ↓

D
INTERMITTENT SWITCH INPUT SIGNAL CHECK.
Check harness continuity between wiper amp. harness terminal ④ and body ground.

Condition of wiper switch	Continuity
OFF	No
INT	Yes

- NG →
  - Check wiper switch.
  - Check harness continuity between wiper amp. harness terminal ④ and wiper switch harness terminal ⑦. **Continuity should exist.**
  - Check harness continuity between wiper switch harness terminal ⑤ and body ground. **Continuity should exist.**
- OK ↓

E
WIPER AMP. GROUND CIRCUIT CHECK.
Check harness continuity between wiper amp. harness terminal ② and body ground.
Continuity should exist.
- NG → Repair harness or connector.
- OK ↓

Replace wiper amp.

NS9029600025000X

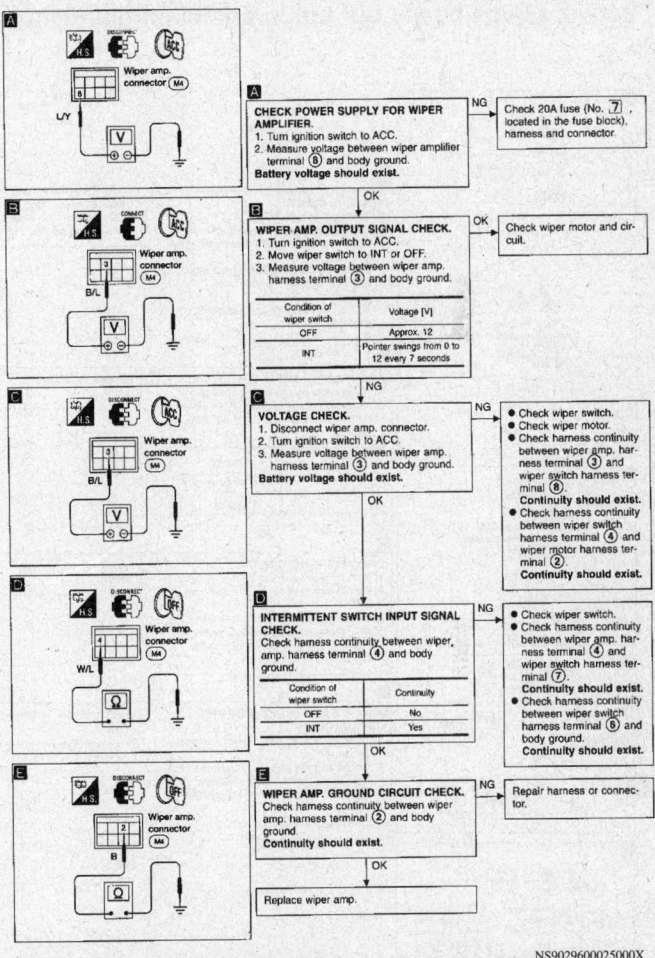

Fig. 7 Diagnostic Procedure 1: Intermittent wiper does not operate. Pickup

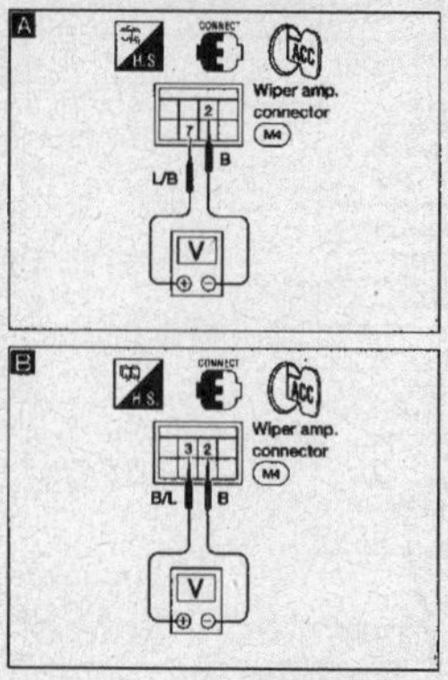

A

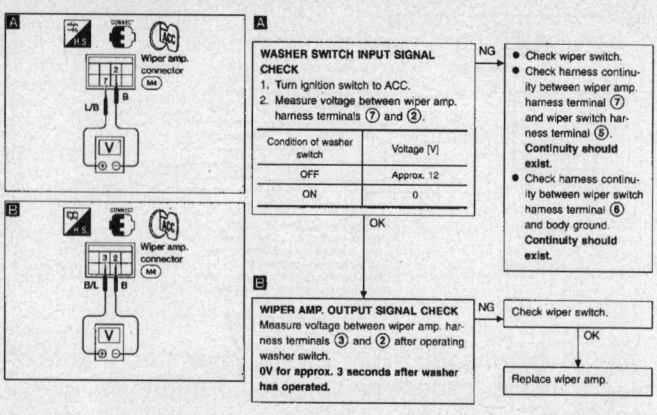

WASHER SWITCH INPUT SIGNAL CHECK
1. Turn ignition switch to ACC.
2. Measure voltage between wiper amp. harness terminals ⑦ and ②.

Condition of washer switch	Voltage [V]
OFF	Approx. 12
ON	0

NG → • Check wiper switch.
• Check harness continuity between wiper amp. harness terminal ⑦ and wiper switch harness terminal ⑤. **Continuity should exist.**
• Check harness continuity between wiper switch harness terminal ⑥ and body ground. **Continuity should exist.**

OK ↓

B

WIPER AMP. OUTPUT SIGNAL CHECK
Measure voltage between wiper amp. harness terminals ③ and ② after operating washer switch.
0V for approx. 3 seconds after washer has operated.

NG → Check wiper switch. → OK → Replace wiper amp.

NS9029600027000X

Fig. 9 Diagnostic Procedure 3: Wiper and washer activate individually but not in combination. Pickup

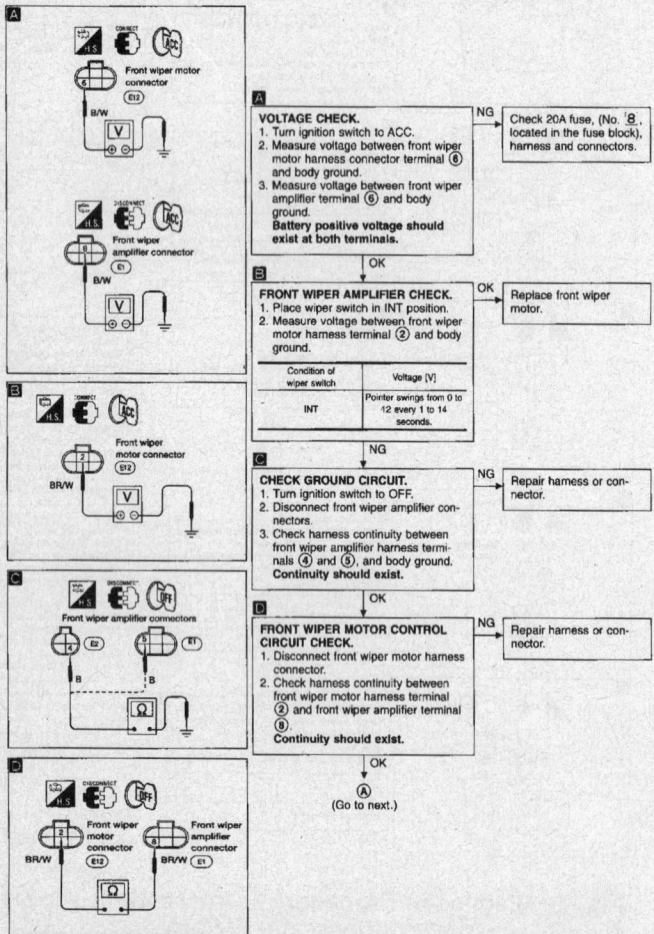

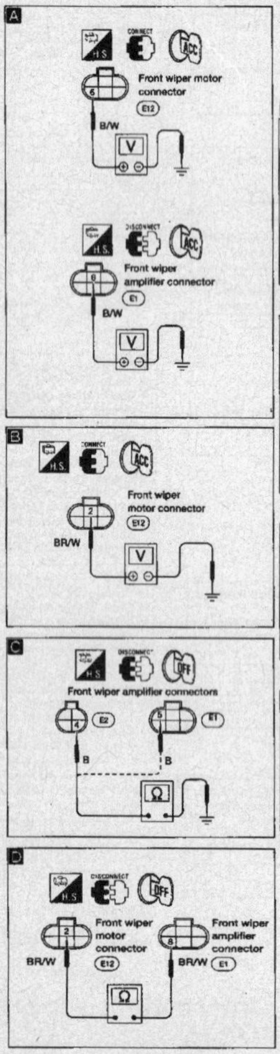

A

VOLTAGE CHECK.
1. Turn ignition switch to ACC.
2. Measure voltage between front wiper motor harness connector terminal ⑥ and body ground.
3. Measure voltage between front wiper amplifier terminal ⑥ and body ground.
Battery positive voltage should exist at both terminals.

NG → Check 20A fuse, (No. 8, located in the fuse block), harness and connectors.

OK ↓

B

FRONT WIPER AMPLIFIER CHECK.
1. Place wiper switch in INT position.
2. Measure voltage between front wiper motor harness terminal ② and body ground.

Condition of wiper switch	Voltage [V]
INT	Pointer swings from 0 to 12 every 1 to 14 seconds.

OK → Replace front wiper motor.

NG ↓

C

CHECK GROUND CIRCUIT.
1. Turn ignition switch to OFF.
2. Disconnect front wiper amplifier connectors.
3. Check harness continuity between front wiper amplifier harness terminals ④ and ⑤, and body ground.
Continuity should exist.

NG → Repair harness or connector.

OK ↓

D

FRONT WIPER MOTOR CONTROL CIRCUIT CHECK.
1. Disconnect front wiper motor harness connector.
2. Check harness continuity between front wiper motor harness terminal ② and front wiper amplifier terminal ⑧.
Continuity should exist.

NG → Repair harness or connector.

OK ↓

Ⓐ (Go to next.)

NS9029600028010X

Fig. 10 Diagnostic Procedure 1: Intermittent wiper does not operate (Part 1 of 2). Quest

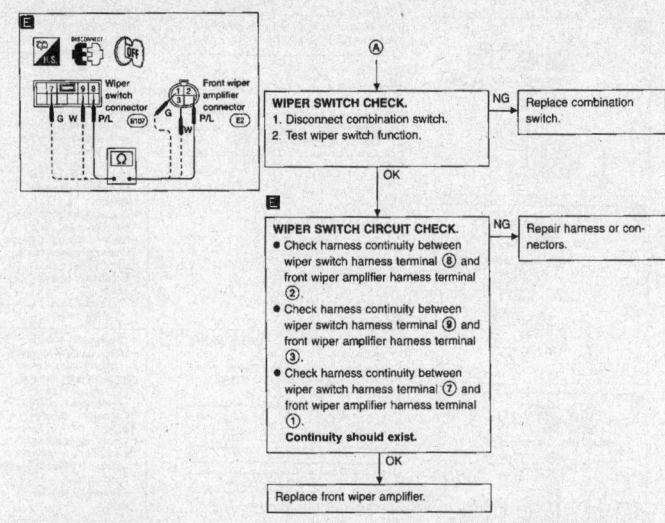

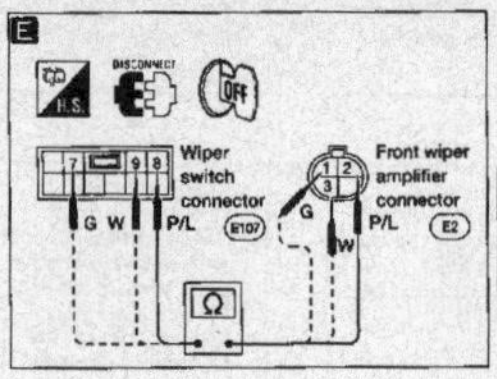

Ⓐ ↓

WIPER SWITCH CHECK.
1. Disconnect combination switch.
2. Test wiper switch function.

NG → Replace combination switch.

OK ↓

E

WIPER SWITCH CIRCUIT CHECK.
• Check harness continuity between wiper switch harness terminal ⑧ and front wiper amplifier harness terminal ②.
• Check harness continuity between wiper switch harness terminal ⑨ and front wiper amplifier harness terminal ③.
• Check harness continuity between wiper switch harness terminal ⑦ and front wiper amplifier harness terminal ①.
Continuity should exist.

NG → Repair harness or connectors.

OK ↓

Replace front wiper amplifier.

NS9029600028020X

Fig. 10 Diagnostic Procedure 1: Intermittent wiper does not operate (Part 2 of 2). Quest

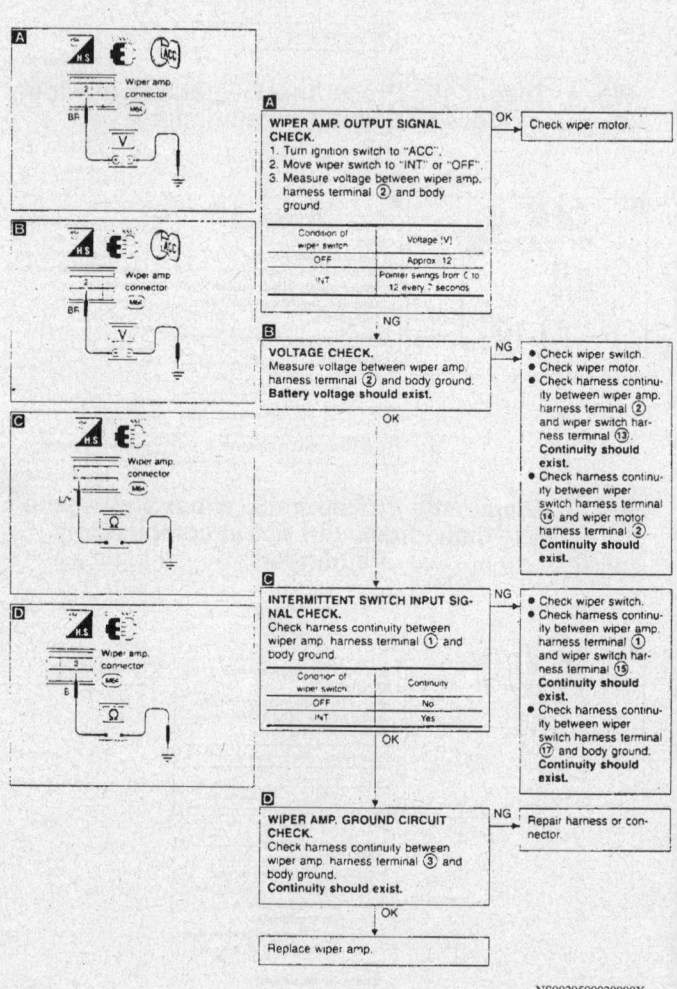

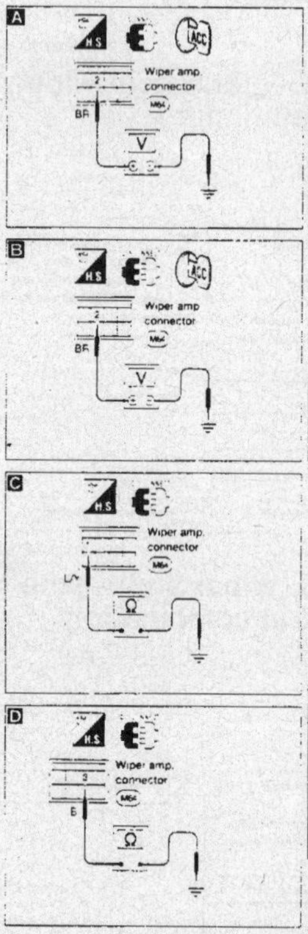

A

WIPER AMP. OUTPUT SIGNAL CHECK.
1. Turn ignition switch to "ACC".
2. Move wiper switch to "INT" or "OFF".
3. Measure voltage between wiper amp. harness terminal ② and body ground.

Condition of wiper switch	Voltage [V]
OFF	Approx. 12
INT	Pointer swings from 0 to 12 every [illegible] seconds

OK → Check wiper motor.

NG ↓

B

VOLTAGE CHECK.
Measure voltage between wiper amp. harness terminal ② and body ground.
Battery voltage should exist.

NG → • Check wiper switch.
• Check wiper motor.
• Check harness continuity between wiper amp. harness terminal ② and wiper switch harness terminal ⑬. **Continuity should exist.**
• Check harness continuity between wiper switch harness terminal ⑭ and wiper motor harness terminal ②. **Continuity should exist.**

OK ↓

C

INTERMITTENT SWITCH INPUT SIGNAL CHECK.
Check harness continuity between wiper amp. harness terminal ① and body ground.

Condition of wiper switch	Continuity
OFF	No
INT	Yes

NG → • Check wiper switch.
• Check harness continuity between wiper amp. harness terminal ① and wiper switch harness terminal ⑮. **Continuity should exist.**
• Check harness continuity between wiper switch harness terminal ⑰ and body ground. **Continuity should exist.**

OK ↓

D

WIPER AMP. GROUND CIRCUIT CHECK.
Check harness continuity between wiper amp. harness terminal ③ and body ground.
Continuity should exist.

NG → Repair harness or connector.

OK ↓

Replace wiper amp.

NS9029500020000X

Fig. 11 Diagnostic Procedure 1: Intermittent wiper does not operate. 1995–96 Sentra & 200SX

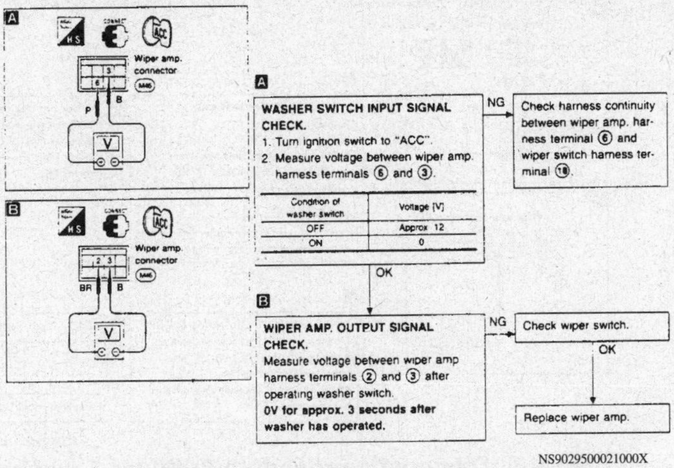
A
Wiper amp. connector
B
Wiper amp. connector
A
WASHER SWITCH INPUT SIGNAL CHECK.
1. Turn ignition switch to "ACC".
2. Measure voltage between wiper amp. harness terminals ⑥ and ③.
Condition of washer switch
Voltage (V)
OFF
Approx. 12
ON
0
NG
Check harness continuity between wiper amp. harness terminal ⑥ and wiper switch harness terminal ⑱.
OK
B
WIPER AMP. OUTPUT SIGNAL CHECK.
Measure voltage between wiper amp harness terminals ② and ③ after operating washer switch.
0V for approx. 3 seconds after washer has operated.
NG
Check wiper switch.
OK
Replace wiper amp.
NS9029500021000X

Fig. 12 Diagnostic Procedure 2: Wiper & washer operate individually but not in combination. 1995–96 Sentra & 200SX

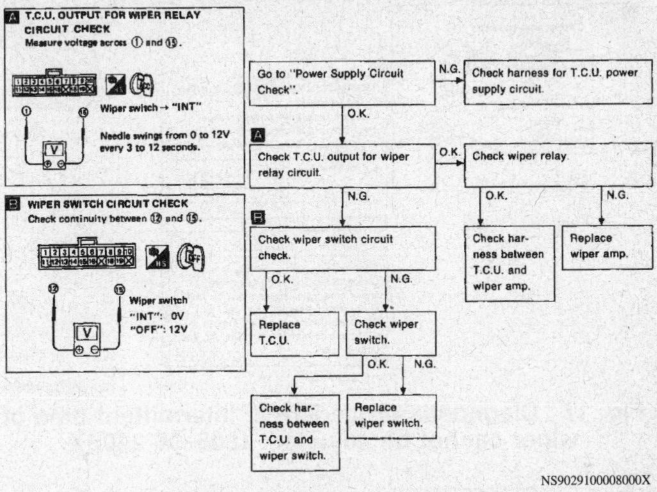
A
T.C.U. OUTPUT FOR WIPER RELAY CIRCUIT CHECK
Measure voltage across ① and ⑮.
Wiper switch → "INT"
Needle swings from 0 to 12V every 3 to 12 seconds.
B
WIPER SWITCH CIRCUIT CHECK
Check continuity between ⑫ and ⑮.
Wiper switch
"INT": 0V
"OFF": 12V
Go to "Power Supply Circuit Check".
N.G.
Check harness for T.C.U. power supply circuit.
O.K.
A
Check T.C.U. output for wiper relay circuit.
O.K.
Check wiper relay.
N.G.
O.K.
N.G.
Check harness between T.C.U. and wiper amp.
Replace wiper amp.
B
Check wiper switch circuit check.
O.K.
N.G.
Replace T.C.U.
Check wiper switch.
O.K.
N.G.
Check harness between T.C.U. and wiper switch.
Replace wiper switch.
NS9029100008000X

Fig. 13 Diagnostic Procedure 1: Intermittent wiper does not operate. 1993 240SX

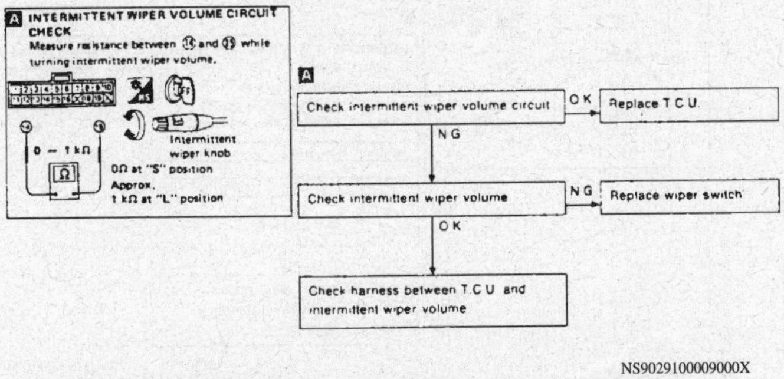
A
INTERMITTENT WIPER VOLUME CIRCUIT CHECK
Measure resistance between ⑭ and ⑮ while turning intermittent wiper volume.
0 – 1 kΩ
Intermittent wiper knob
0Ω at "S" position
Approx. 1 kΩ at "L" position
A
Check intermittent wiper volume circuit
O.K.
Replace T.C.U.
N.G.
Check intermittent wiper volume
N.G.
Replace wiper switch
O.K.
Check harness between T.C.U. and intermittent wiper volume
NS9029100009000X

Fig. 14 Diagnostic Procedure 2: Intermittent time of wiper cannot be adjusted. 1993 240SX

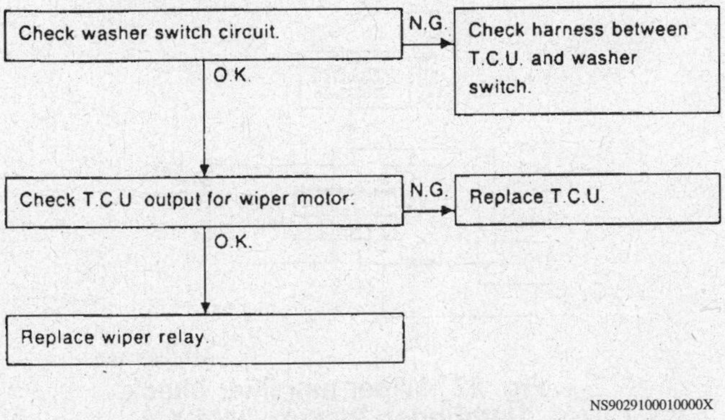
Check washer switch circuit.
N.G.
Check harness between T.C.U. and washer switch.
O.K.
Check T.C.U output for wiper motor.
N.G.
Replace T.C.U.
O.K.
Replace wiper relay.
NS9029100010000X

Fig. 15 Diagnostic Procedure 3: Wiper and washer activate individually but not in combination. 1993 240SX

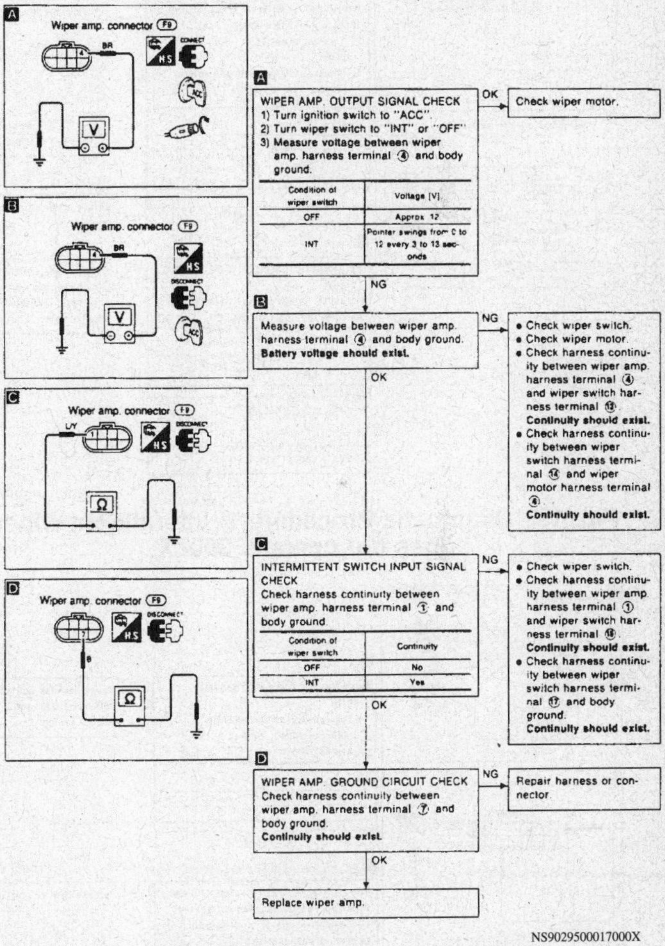
A
Wiper amp. connector
B
Wiper amp. connector
C
Wiper amp. connector
D
Wiper amp. connector
A
WIPER AMP. OUTPUT SIGNAL CHECK
1) Turn ignition switch to "ACC".
2) Turn wiper switch to "INT" or "OFF".
3) Measure voltage between wiper amp. harness terminal ④ and body ground.
Condition of wiper switch
Voltage (V)
OFF
Approx. 12
INT
Pointer swings from 0 to 12 every 3 to 13 seconds
OK
Check wiper motor.
NG
B
Measure voltage between wiper amp. harness terminal ④ and body ground.
Battery voltage should exist.
NG
• Check wiper switch.
• Check wiper motor.
• Check harness continuity between wiper amp. harness terminal ④ and wiper switch harness terminal ⑬.
Continuity should exist.
• Check harness continuity between wiper switch harness terminal ⑭ and wiper motor harness terminal ④.
Continuity should exist.
OK
C
INTERMITTENT SWITCH INPUT SIGNAL CHECK
Check harness continuity between wiper amp. harness terminal ① and body ground.
Condition of wiper switch
Continuity
OFF
No
INT
Yes
NG
• Check wiper switch.
• Check harness continuity between wiper amp harness terminal ① and wiper switch harness terminal ⑱.
Continuity should exist.
• Check harness continuity between wiper switch harness terminal ⑰ and body ground.
Continuity should exist.
OK
D
WIPER AMP. GROUND CIRCUIT CHECK
Check harness continuity between wiper amp. harness terminal ⑦ and body ground.
Continuity should exist.
NG
Repair harness or connector.
OK
Replace wiper amp.
NS9029500017000X

Fig. 16 Diagnostic Procedure 1: Intermittent wiper does not operate. 1995–96 240SX

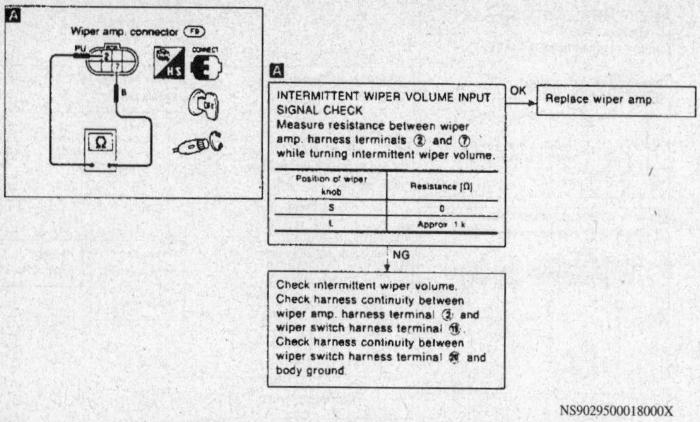
A
Wiper amp. connector F9
A
INTERMITTENT WIPER VOLUME INPUT SIGNAL CHECK
Measure resistance between wiper amp. harness terminals ② and ⑦ while turning intermittent wiper volume.
Position of wiper knob | Resistance [Ω]
S | 0
L | Approx. 1 k
OK
Replace wiper amp.
NG
Check intermittent wiper volume.
Check harness continuity between wiper amp. harness terminal ② and wiper switch harness terminal ⑪.
Check harness continuity between wiper switch harness terminal ⑪ and body ground.
NS9029500018000X

Fig. 17 Diagnostic procedure 2: Intermittent time of wiper cannot be adjusted. 1995–96 240SX

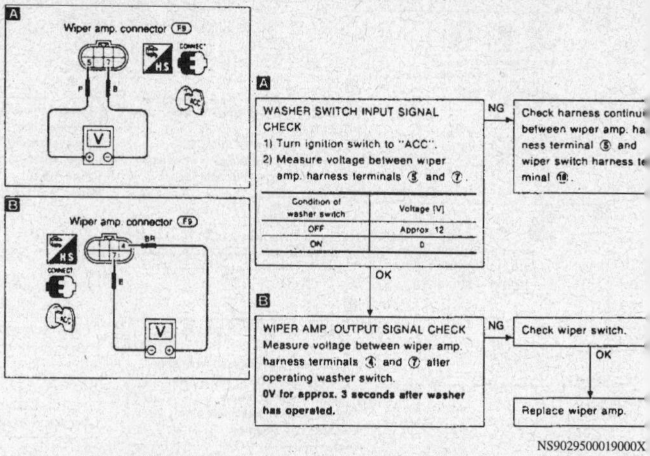
A
Wiper amp. connector F9
B
Wiper amp. connector F9
A
WASHER SWITCH INPUT SIGNAL CHECK
1) Turn ignition switch to "ACC".
2) Measure voltage between wiper amp. harness terminals ⑤ and ⑦.
Condition of washer switch | Voltage [V]
OFF | Approx. 12
ON | 0
NG
Check harness continuity between wiper amp. harness terminal ⑤ and wiper switch harness terminal ⑱.
OK
B
WIPER AMP. OUTPUT SIGNAL CHECK
Measure voltage between wiper amp. harness terminals ④ and ⑦ after operating washer switch.
0V for approx. 3 seconds after washer has operated.
NG
Check wiper switch.
OK
Replace wiper amp.
NS9029500019000X

Fig. 18 Diagnostic procedure 3: Wiper & washer activate individually but not in combination. 1995–96 240SX

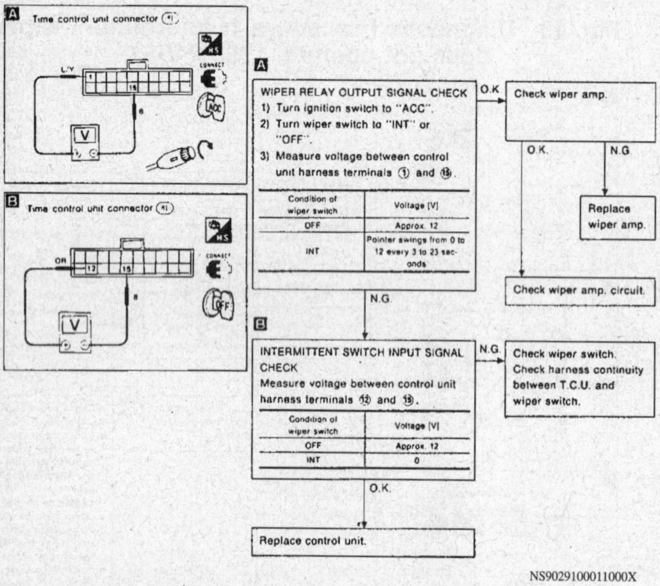
A
Time control unit connector
B
Time control unit connector
A
WIPER RELAY OUTPUT SIGNAL CHECK
1) Turn ignition switch to "ACC".
2) Turn wiper switch to "INT" or "OFF".
3) Measure voltage between control unit harness terminals ① and ⑬.
Condition of wiper switch | Voltage [V]
OFF | Approx. 12
INT | Pointer swings from 0 to 12 every 3 to 23 seconds
O.K.
Check wiper amp.
O.K.
N.G.
Replace wiper amp.
Check wiper amp. circuit.
N.G.
B
INTERMITTENT SWITCH INPUT SIGNAL CHECK
Measure voltage between control unit harness terminals ⑫ and ⑬.
Condition of wiper switch | Voltage [V]
OFF | Approx. 12
INT | 0
N.G.
Check wiper switch.
Check harness continuity between T.C.U. and wiper switch.
O.K.
Replace control unit.
NS9029100011000X

Fig. 19 Diagnostic Procedure 1: Intermittent wiper does not operate. 300ZX

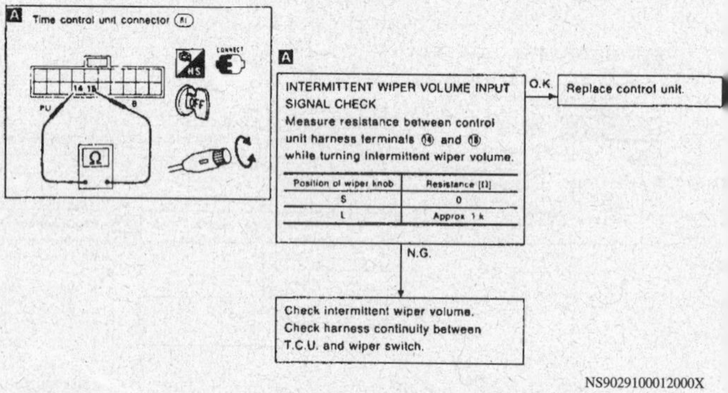
A
Time control unit connector
A
INTERMITTENT WIPER VOLUME INPUT SIGNAL CHECK
Measure resistance between control unit harness terminals ⑭ and ⑱ while turning intermittent wiper volume.
Position of wiper knob | Resistance [Ω]
S | 0
L | Approx. 1 k
O.K.
Replace control unit.
N.G.
Check intermittent wiper volume.
Check harness continuity between T.C.U. and wiper switch.
NS9029100012000X

Fig. 20 Diagnostic Procedure 2: Intermittent time of wiper cannot be adjusted. 300ZX

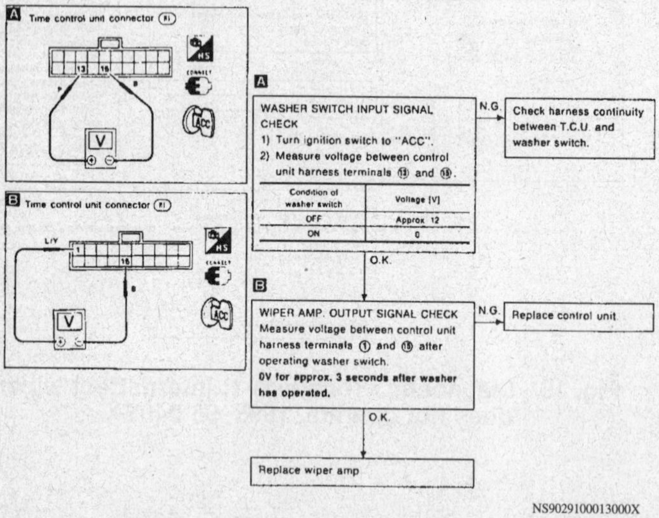
A
Time control unit connector
B
Time control unit connector
A
WASHER SWITCH INPUT SIGNAL CHECK
1) Turn ignition switch to "ACC".
2) Measure voltage between control unit harness terminals ⑬ and ⑯.
Condition of washer switch | Voltage [V]
OFF | Approx. 12
ON | 0
N.G.
Check harness continuity between T.C.U. and washer switch.
O.K.
B
WIPER AMP. OUTPUT SIGNAL CHECK
Measure voltage between control unit harness terminals ① and ⑬ after operating washer switch.
0V for approx. 3 seconds after washer has operated.
N.G.
Replace control unit.
O.K.
Replace wiper amp.
NS9029100013000X

Fig. 21 Diagnostic Procedure 3: Wiper and washer activate individually but not in combination. 300ZX

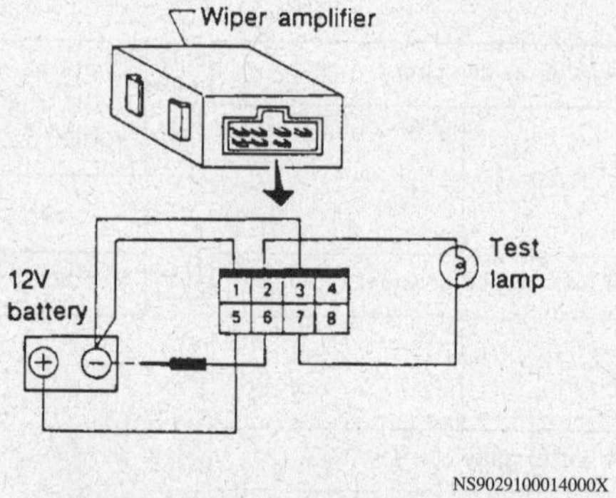
Wiper amplifier
12V battery
Test lamp
1 2 3 4
5 6 7 8
NS9029100014000X

Fig. 22 Wiper amplifier check. Pathfinder, Pickup, 240SX & 300ZX

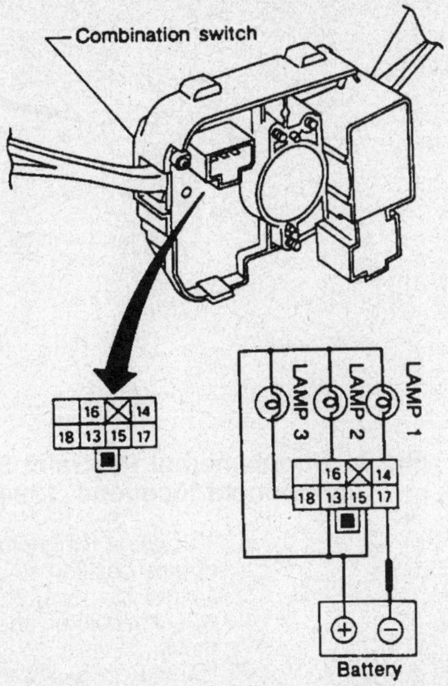
Combination switch
16
14
18
13
15
17
LAMP 1
LAMP 2
LAMP 3
Battery

NS9029100016000X

Fig. 23 Test lamp connection to wiper switch. 1993–94 NX 1600, NX 2000 & Sentra

Wiper switch position	Test lamp		
	1	2	3
OFF	—	—	—
INT or LO	○	—	—
HI	—	○	—
WASH	○	—	○

○: Lamp "ON", —: Lamp "OFF"

NS9029100015000X

Fig. 24 Wiper system test lamp results. 1993–94 NX 1600, NX 2000 & Sentra

Air Bag System

NOTE: Electrical Symbol & Wire Color Code Identification Located In The Front Of This Manual May Be Used As An Aid When Using Wiring Circuits Found In This Section.

INDEX

	Page No.
Air Bag System Disarming & Arming	36-88
Arming	36-88
Disarming	36-88
Collision Inspection	36-89
Component Locations	36-89
Component Service	36-89
Air Bag Module Disposal	36-96
Control/Diagnosis Sensor Unit, Replace	36-91
Driver's Air Bag Module, Replace	36-93
Passenger's Air Bag Module, Replace	36-93
Sensors, Replace	36-89
Spiral Cable, Replace	36-95
Description & Operation	36-88
Diagnosis & Testing	36-89
Precautions	36-88
Scheduled Maintenance	36-88
Technical Service Bulletins	36-97
Unwanted Air Bag Deployment When Replacing Combination Switch	36-97
Tightening Specifications	36-97
Wire Harness & Connector Repair	36-89

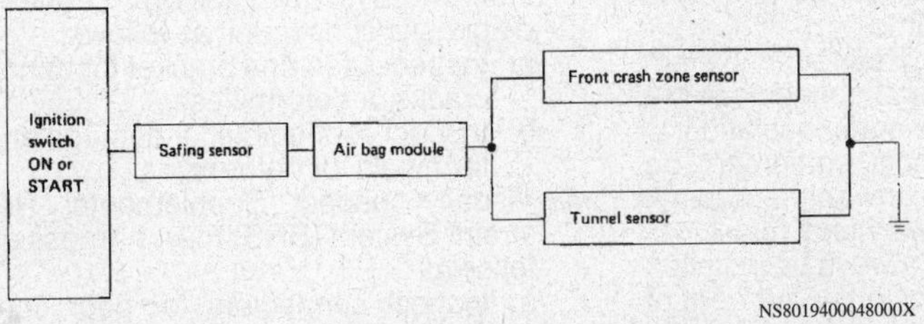
Ignition switch ON or START
Safing sensor
Air bag module
Front crash zone sensor
Tunnel sensor

NS8019400048000X

Fig. 1 Supplemental Restraint System (SRS) operation. 1994–95 Quest & 1994 Altima, Maxima & Sentra

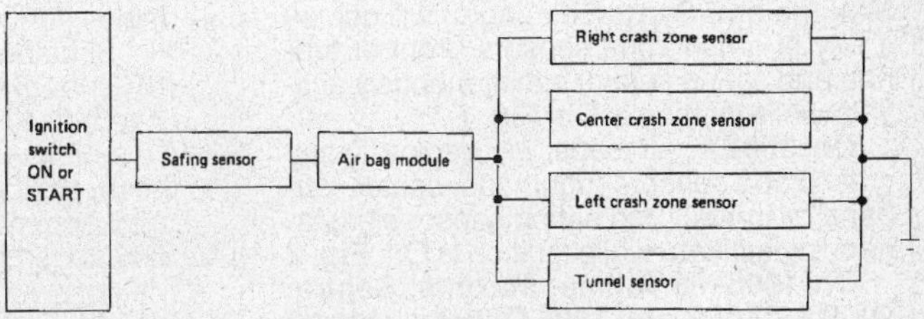
Ignition switch ON or START
Safing sensor
Air bag module
Right crash zone sensor
Center crash zone sensor
Left crash zone sensor
Tunnel sensor

NS8019400049000X

Fig. 2 Supplemental Restraint System (SRS) operation. 300ZX

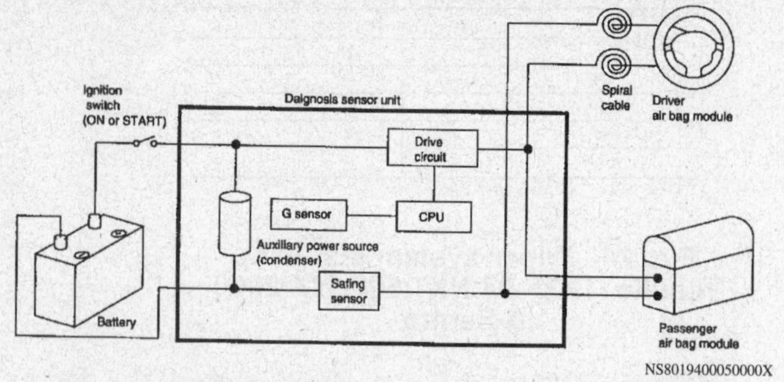
Ignition switch (ON or START)
Diagnosis sensor unit
Drive circuit
G sensor
CPU
Auxiliary power source (condenser)
Safing sensor
Battery
Spiral cable
Driver air bag module
Passenger air bag module
NS8019400050000X

Fig. 3 Supplemental Restraint System (SRS) operation. 1995–96 Altima, Maxima, Sentra, 200SX, 240SX & 1996 Truck 2WD, Quest & Pathfinder

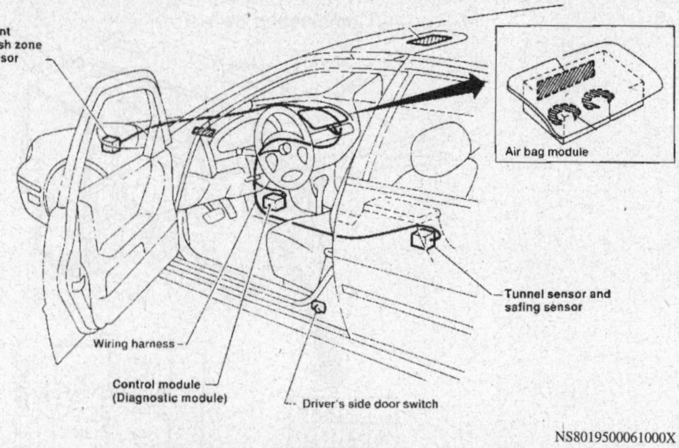
Front crash zone sensor
Air bag module
Tunnel sensor and safing sensor
Wiring harness
Control module (Diagnostic module)
Driver's side door switch
NS8019500061000X

Fig. 4 Supplemental Restraint System (SRS) component locations. 1994 Altima

AIR BAG SYSTEM DISARMING & ARMING

Disarming

1. Turn ignition switch to the OFF position, then disconnect battery ground cable.
2. **Wait a minimum of 10 minutes for air bag system to discharge. The system will retain power for approximately 10 minutes after disconnecting the battery ground cable. It is possible for the air bag to deploy during this time.**
3. Remove steering wheel lower lid and disconnect air bag module electrical connector.

Arming

1. With battery ground cable disconnected, connect air bag module connector.
2. Ensure no one is inside of the vehicle, then connect battery ground cable.
3. Turn ignition switch to the ON position and observe SRS warning light.
4. SRS warning light should illuminate for approximately seven seconds, then turn off and remain off for at least 45 seconds. This indicates SRS is functioning properly.
5. If SRS warning light does not respond as indicated, a malfunction in the SRS is indicated.

DESCRIPTION & OPERATION

On 1994–95 Quest and 1994 Altima, Maxima and Sentra, air bag(s) will deploy if any of crash zone sensors (front or tunnel) and safing sensor simultaneously activate while ignition is On, **Fig. 1**

On 300ZX, air bags will deploy if any crash zone sensors (righthand, center, lefthand or tunnel) and safing sensor simultaneously activate while ignition is On, **Fig. 2**

On 1995–96 Altima, Maxima, Sentra, 200SX, 240SX and 1996 Quest, air bag(s) will deploy if diagnosis sensor unit activates while ignition is in On or Start position, **Fig. 3**

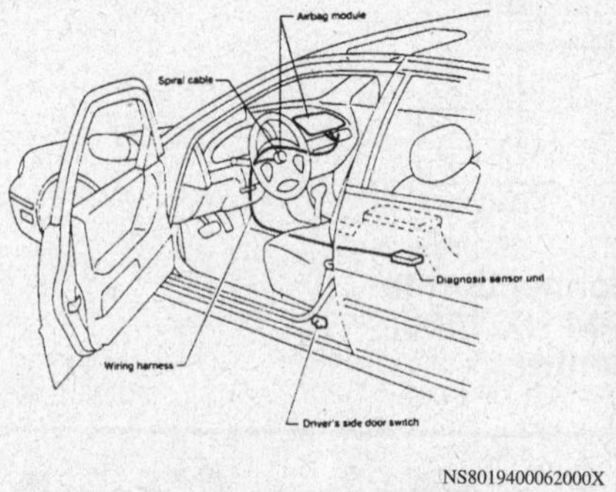
Airbag module
Spiral cable
Diagnosis sensor unit
Wiring harness
Driver's side door switch
NS8019400062000X

Fig. 5 Supplemental Restraint System (SRS) component locations. 1995–96 Altima

On 1996 Truck 2WD and Pathfinder, air bag(s) will deploy if diagnosis sensor unit activates while ignition is in On position, **Fig. 3.**

On 1996 Truck 4WD models, air bag will deploy if G-sensor and/or crash zone sensor activates simultaneously with the safing sensor while the ignition switch is in the On position.

On all models, when ignition is turned to On or Start, the air bag warning lamp should light for about seven seconds, then go off. This indicates the Supplemental Restraint System (SRS) is operating normally. A failure is present if the lamp is illuminated for seven seconds and then flashing every half second, or if lamp does not light.

PRECAUTIONS

1. After disarming system, wait a minimum of 10 minutes for air bag system to discharge. System will retain power for approximately 10 minutes after disconnection. It is possible for air bag to deploy during this time.
2. All Supplemental Restraint System (SRS) harnesses and connectors are covered with yellow outer insulation.
3. Do not use electrical equipment on these circuits, as unwanted deployment or personal injury may result.
4. SRS sensors must always be installed with arrow mark facing toward front of vehicle.
5. Inspect sensors for cracks, deformities or rust before installation and replace as required.
6. The spiral cable must be aligned with neutral position since its rotations are limited. Do not attempt to turn steering wheel or column after steering gear removal.
7. Handle air bag module carefully. Always place air bag with pad side facing upward.
8. After removing any Supplemental Restraint System (SRS) component, discard old retaining bolts and install replacements.
9. Conduct self–diagnosis as described in "Diagnosis and Testing" to ensure proper operation of entire Supplemental Restraint System (SRS).

SCHEDULED MAINTENANCE

The air bag system should be inspected every 10 years from date of manufacture as noted on certification label located on driver's door jam.

1. Ensure air bag warning lamp lights for seven seconds when ignition is turned to On or Start. After approximately seven seconds, the warning lamp should go off.
2. Visually inspect Supplemental Restraint System (SRS) sensors as follows:
   a. Inspect sensors to ensure arrow marks face toward front of vehicle.
   b. Inspect body, sensors and brackets for dents, cracks, deformities and/or rust.
   c. Inspect sensor harness for binds, connectors for damage and terminals for deformities.
3. Visually inspect Supplemental Restraint System (SRS) control/diagnostic/sensor unit as follows:
   a. Inspect case and bracket for dents, cracks or deformities.
   b. Inspect connectors for damage and terminals for deformities.
4. Visually inspect Supplemental Restraint System (SRS) main harness as follows:
   a. Inspect connectors for poor connections.
   b. Inspect harness for binds, connectors for damage and terminals for deformities.

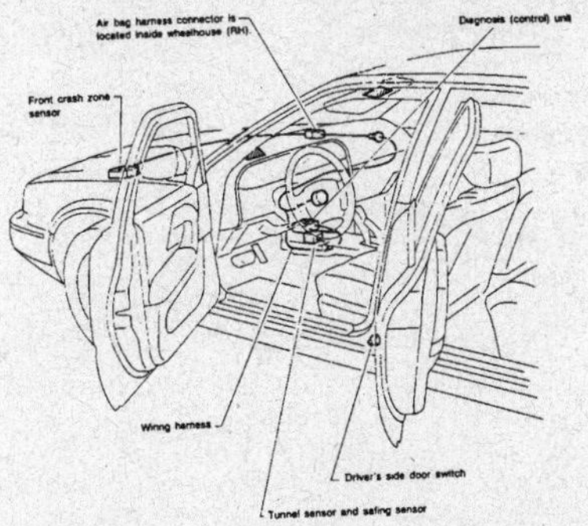
Air bag harness connector is located inside wheelhouse (RH).
Diagnosis (control) unit
Front crash zone sensor
Wiring harness
Driver's side door switch
Tunnel sensor and safing sensor

NS8019500063000X

Fig. 6 Supplemental Restraint System (SRS) component locations. 1994 Maxima

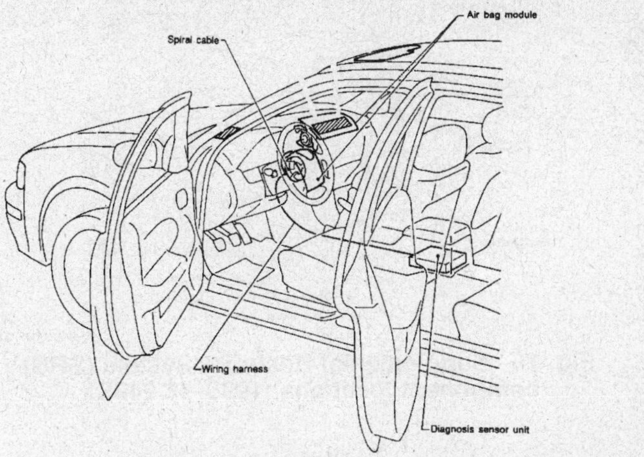
Air bag module
Spiral cable
Wiring harness
Diagnosis sensor unit

NS8019400064000X

Fig. 7 Supplemental Restraint System (SRS) component locations. 1995–96 Maxima

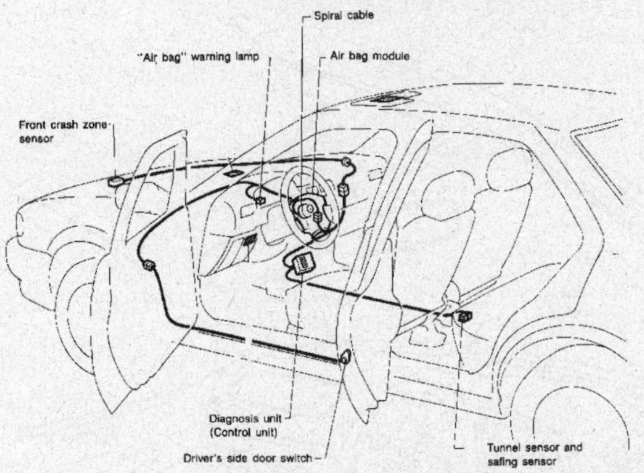
Spiral cable
"Air bag" warning lamp
Air bag module
Front crash zone sensor
Diagnosis unit (Control unit)
Driver's side door switch
Tunnel sensor and safing sensor

NS8019500065000X

Fig. 8 Supplemental Restraint System (SRS) component locations. 1994 Sentra

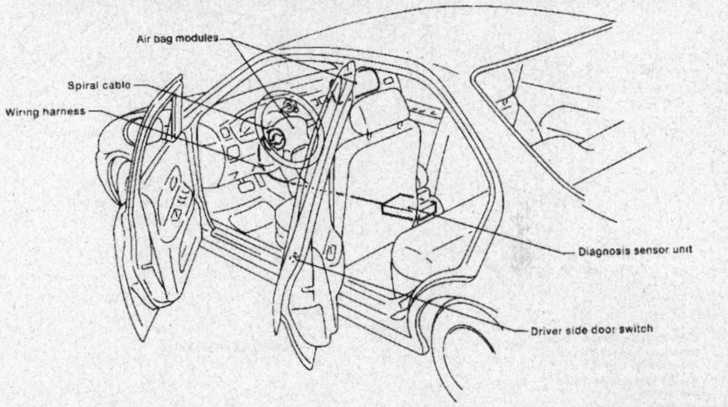
Air bag modules
Spiral cable
Wiring harness
Diagnosis sensor unit
Driver side door switch

NS8019500066000X

Fig. 9 Supplemental Restraint System (SRS) component locations. 1995–96 Sentra

5. Visually inspect Supplemental Restraint System (SRS) spiral cable as follows:
   a. Visually inspect lockpins and combination switch for damage.
   b. Inspect connectors, flat cable and protective tape for damage.
   c. Inspect steering wheel for noise, binds or difficult operation.
6. Visually inspect air bags and steering wheel as follows:
   a. Remove air bag(s) as described under "Component Service "
   b. Inspect harness cover and connectors for damage and terminals for deformities.
   c. Install air bag module to inspect fit or alignment with steering wheel.
   d. Inspect steering wheel for excessive freeplay.
   e. Install passenger air bag to inspect fit or alignment with instrument panel.

WIRE HARNESS & CONNECTOR REPAIR

SRS wiring is covered by yellow protective coating. Supplemental Restraint System (SRS) wiring should not be spliced, soldered or repaired. If wiring or connectors are found to be damaged or worn, SRS wiring harness should be replaced. When replacing SRS wiring harness, ensure harness is properly routed and all electrical connectors are securely installed.

COMPONENT LOCATIONS

Refer to **Figs. 4 through 15** for SRS component locations.

DIAGNOSIS & TESTING

Refer to MOTOR's Air Bag Manual for complete diagnosis & testing information.

COLLISION INSPECTION

On vehicles which have experienced an air bag system deployment, certain SRS components must be replaced. To determine which components require replacement, refer to the "General Information " section located at the front of this manual.

1. Inspect SRS components. Replace any SRS components showing visible damage such as dents, cracks or deformities.
2. Conduct self–diagnosis test as described in "Diagnosis and Testing."

COMPONENT SERVICE

Disarm air bag system as described under "Air Bag System Disarming and Arming."

Special bolts are coated with a bonding agent. Discard them and replace with new bolts. Tighten bolts to specifications.

Ensure all sensors, control units and brackets are free of deformities, dents, cracks and/or rust. Replace parts showing any visible signs of damage.

SENSORS, REPLACE

ALTIMA

1994

Disarm SRS as described under "Air Bag System Disarming and Arming." Refer to **Fig. 16** to replace front crash zone sensor, and **Fig. 17** to replace tunnel and safing sensor.

MAXIMA

1994

Disarm SRS as described under "Air Bag System Disarming and Arming." Refer to **Fig. 18** to replace front crash zone sensor, and **Fig. 19** to replace tunnel and safing sensor.

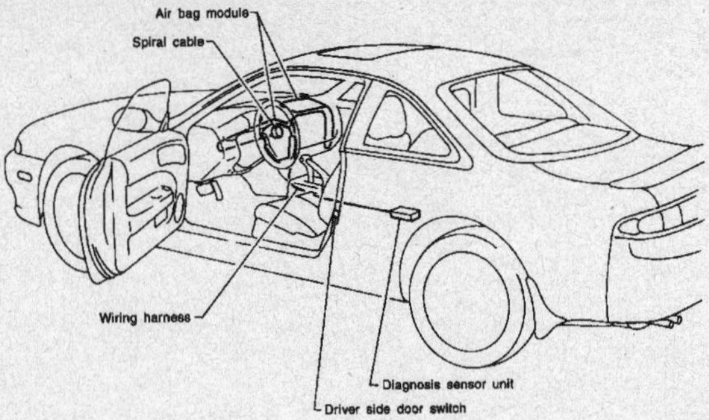
Air bag module
Spiral cable
Wiring harness
Diagnosis sensor unit
Driver side door switch

NS8019500067000A

Fig. 10 Supplemental Restraint System (SRS) component locations. 1995–96 240SX

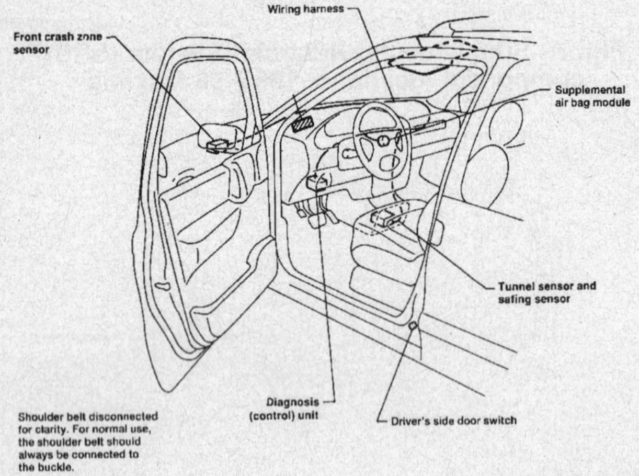
Wiring harness
Front crash zone sensor
Supplemental air bag module
Tunnel sensor and safing sensor
Diagnosis (control) unit
Driver's side door switch
Shoulder belt disconnected for clarity. For normal use, the shoulder belt should always be connected to the buckle.

NS8019400069000X

Fig. 12 Supplemental Restraint System (SRS) component locations. 1994–95 Quest

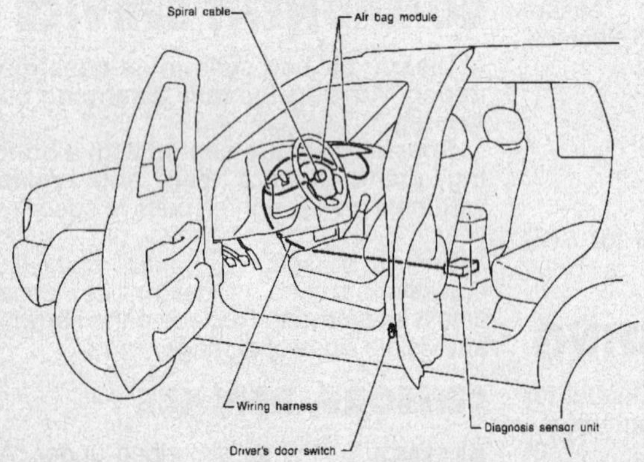
Spiral cable
Air bag module
Wiring harness
Driver's door switch
Diagnosis sensor unit

NS8019600125000X

Fig. 14 Supplemental Restraint System (SRS) component locations. 1996 Pathfinder

SENTRA

1994

Disarm SRS as described under "Air Bag System Disarming and Arming." Refer to **Fig. 20** to replace front crash zone sensor, and **Fig. 21** to replace tunnel and safing sensor.

300ZX

Disarm SRS as described under "Air Bag

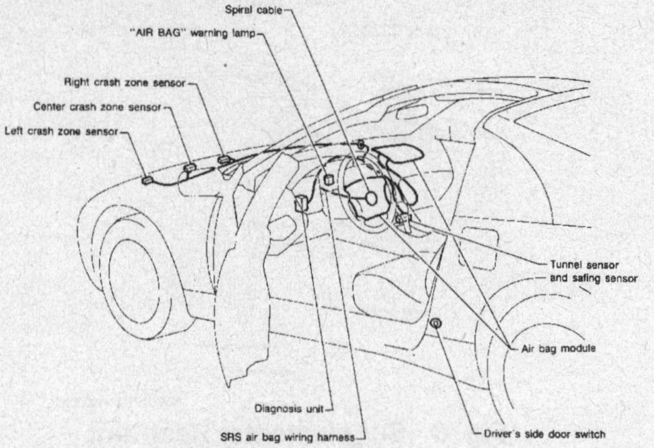
Spiral cable
"AIR BAG" warning lamp
Right crash zone sensor
Center crash zone sensor
Left crash zone sensor
Tunnel sensor and safing sensor
Air bag module
Diagnosis unit
SRS air bag wiring harness
Driver's side door switch

NS8019400068000X

Fig. 11 Supplemental Restraint System (SRS) component locations. 300ZX

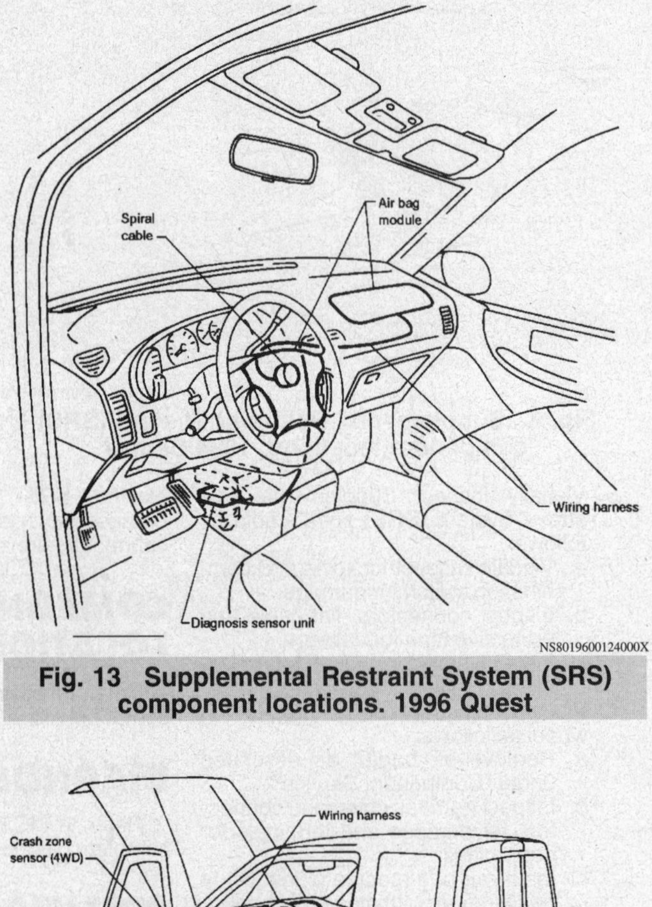
Spiral cable
Air bag module
Wiring harness
Diagnosis sensor unit

NS8019600124000X

Fig. 13 Supplemental Restraint System (SRS) component locations. 1996 Quest

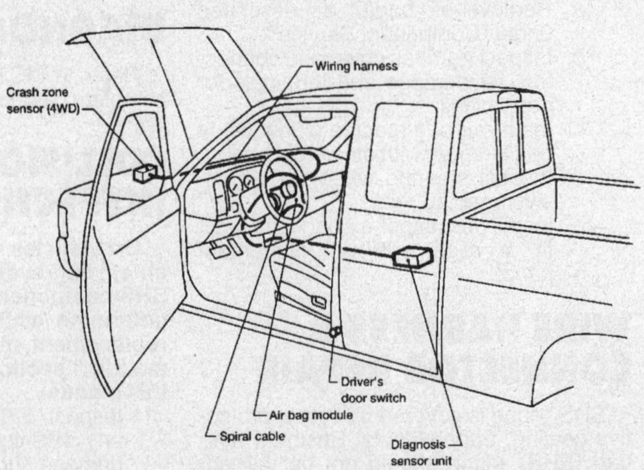
Wiring harness
Crash zone sensor (4WD)
Driver's door switch
Air bag module
Spiral cable
Diagnosis sensor unit

NS8019600126000X

Fig. 15 Supplemental Restraint System (SRS) component locations. Truck

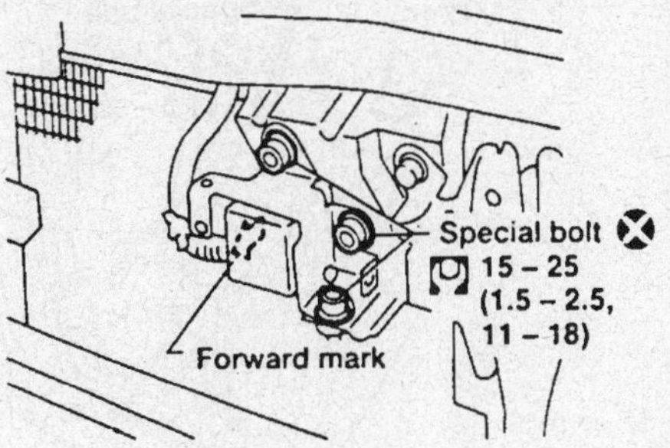
Special bolt
15 – 25
(1.5 – 2.5,
11 – 18)
Forward mark

NS8019400090000X

Fig. 16 Front crash zone sensor replacement. 1994 Altima

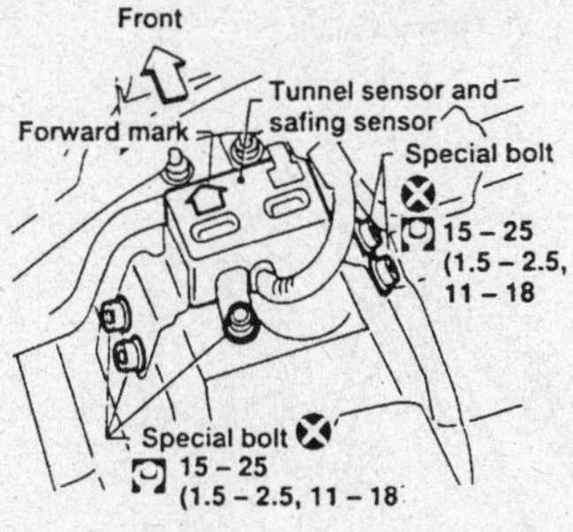
Front
Forward mark
Tunnel sensor and
safing sensor
Special bolt
15 – 25
(1.5 – 2.5,
11 – 18
Special bolt
15 – 25
(1.5 – 2.5, 11 – 18

NS8019400091000X

Fig. 17 Tunnel & safing sensor replacement. 1994 Altima

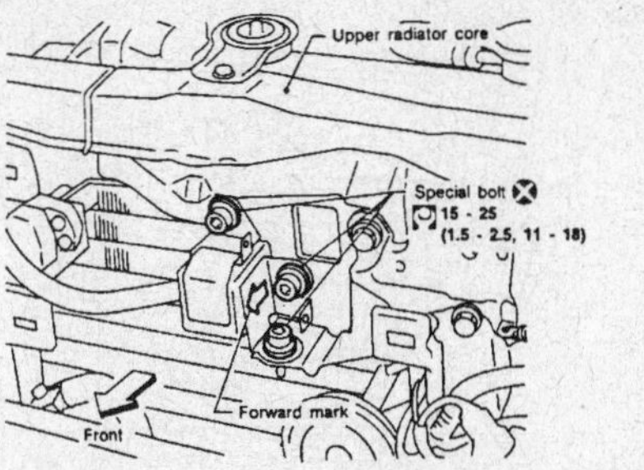
Upper radiator core
Special bolt
15 - 25
(1.5 - 2.5, 11 - 18)
Forward mark
Front

NS8019400092000X

Fig. 18 Front crash zone sensor replacement. 1994 Maxima

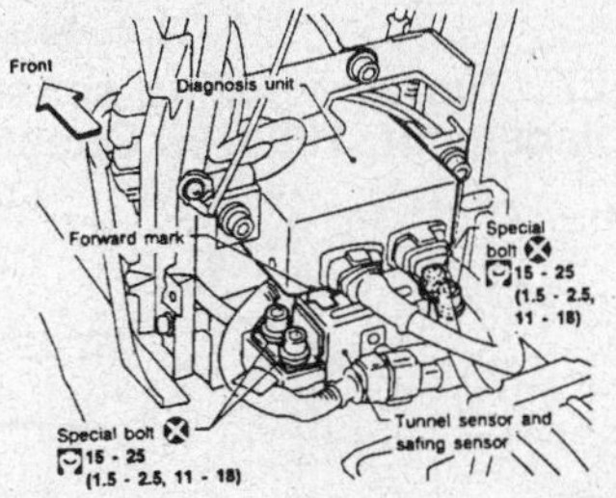
Front
Diagnosis unit
Forward mark
Special bolt
15 - 25
(1.5 - 2.5,
11 - 18)
Special bolt
15 - 25
(1.5 - 2.5, 11 - 18)
Tunnel sensor and
safing sensor

NS8019400093000X

Fig. 19 Control unit & tunnel & safing sensor replacement. 1994 Maxima

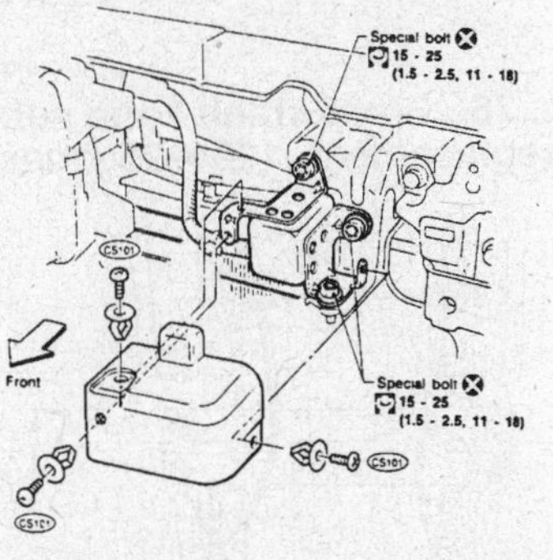
Special bolt
15 - 25
(1.5 - 2.5, 11 - 18)
Front
Special bolt
15 - 25
(1.5 - 2.5, 11 - 18)

NS8019400094000X

Fig. 20 Front crash zone sensor replacement. 1994 Sentra

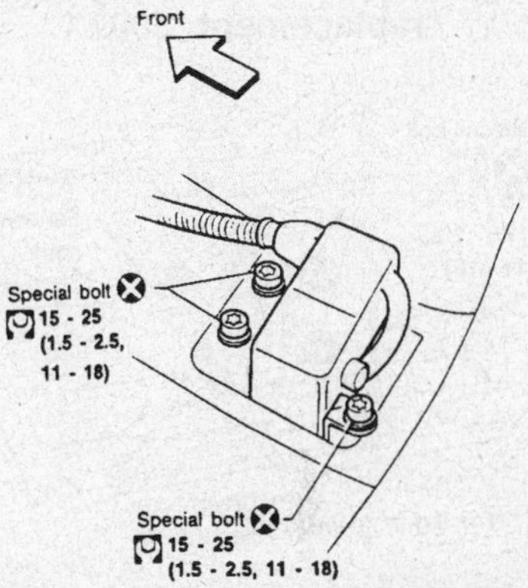
Front
Special bolt
15 - 25
(1.5 - 2.5,
11 - 18)
Special bolt
15 - 25
(1.5 - 2.5, 11 - 18)

NS8019400095000X

Fig. 21 Tunnel & safing sensor replacement. 1994 Sentra

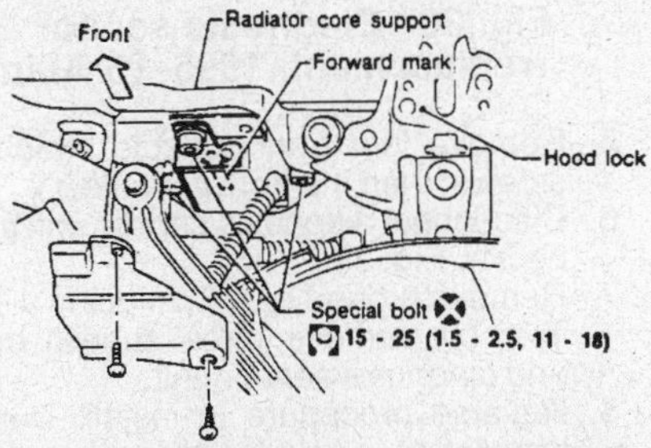
Front
Radiator core support
Forward mark
Hood lock
Special bolt
15 - 25 (1.5 - 2.5, 11 - 18)

NS8019400096000X

Fig. 22 Center crash zone sensor replacement. 300ZX

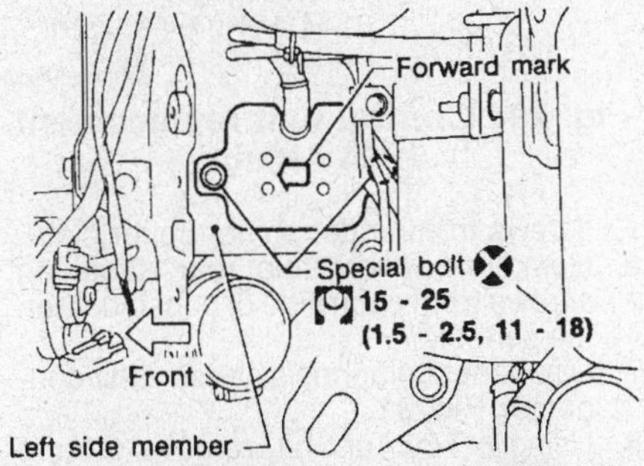
Forward mark
Special bolt
15 - 25
(1.5 - 2.5, 11 - 18)
Front
Left side member

NS8019400097000X

Fig. 23 Lefthand crash zone sensor replacement. 300ZX

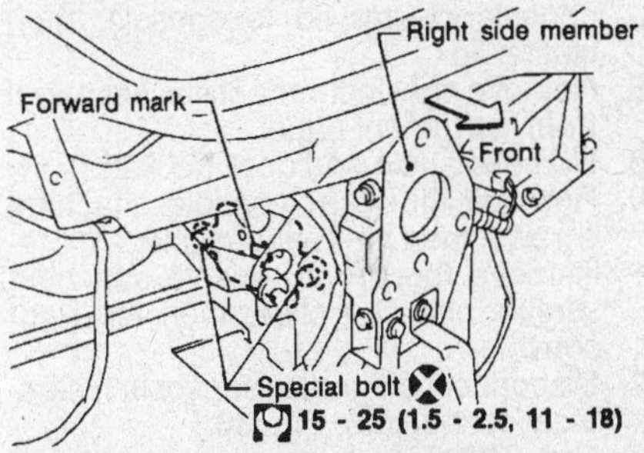
Right side member
Forward mark
Front
Special bolt
15 - 25 (1.5 - 2.5, 11 - 18)

NS8019400098000X

Fig. 24 Righthand crash zone sensor replacement. 300ZX

System Disarming and Arming." Refer to **Figs. 22 through 24** to replace crash zone sensors, and **Fig. 25** to replace tunnel and safing sensor.

1994–95 QUEST

Disarm SRS as described under "Air Bag System Disarming and Arming." Refer to **Fig. 26** to replace front crash zone sensor, and **Fig. 27** to replace tunnel and safing sensor.

1996 TRUCK 4WD

Crash Zone Sensor

1. Disarm SRS as described under "Air Bag System Disarming and Arming."
2. Disconnect driver air bag module connector.
3. Disconnect crash zone connector.
4. Remove crash zone sensor attaching bolts, **Fig. 28,** then the sensor.
5. Reverse procedure to install. During installation, arrow marking on crash zone sensor unit must face toward front of vehicle. Use new coated bolts when installing sensor.

CONTROL/DIAGNOSIS SENSOR UNIT, REPLACE

ALTIMA

1994

Disarm SRS as described under "Air Bag System Disarming and Arming." Refer to **Fig. 29** to replace control unit.

1995–96

1. Disarm SRS as described under "Air Bag System Disarming and Arming."
2. Disconnect driver and passenger air bag module connectors.
3. Remove driver side lower instrument panel cover two attaching screws, then the cover.
4. Remove five instrument cluster trim cover attaching screws, then disconnect electrical connectors and remove cover.
5. Unsnap left instrument finisher panel from instrument panel, then disconnect electrical connectors and remove panel.
6. Remove glove compartment from instrument panel.

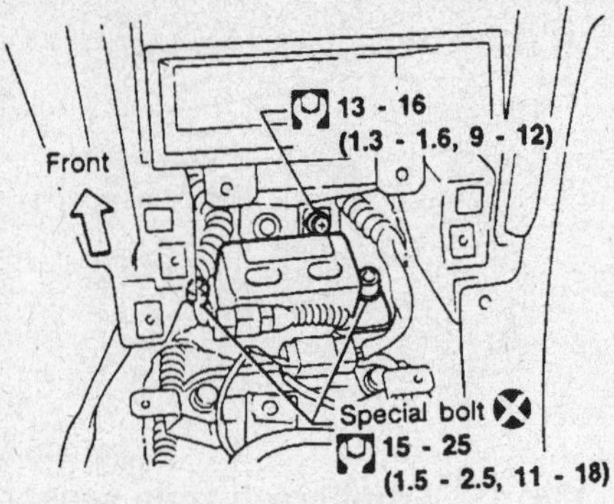
13 - 16
(1.3 - 1.6, 9 - 12)
Front
Special bolt
15 - 25
(1.5 - 2.5, 11 - 18)

NS8019400099000X

Fig. 25 Tunnel & safing sensor replacement. 300ZX

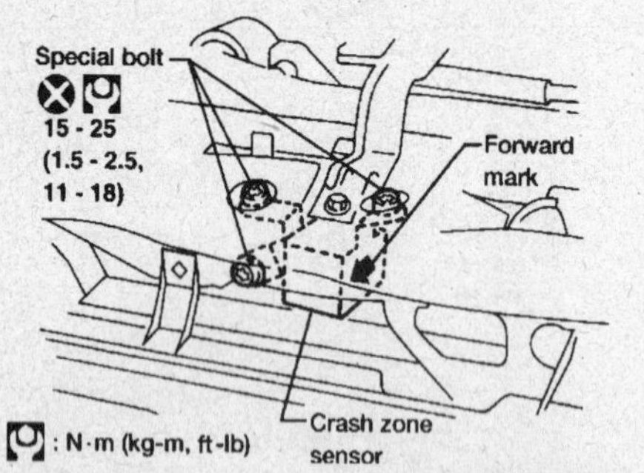
Special bolt
15 - 25
(1.5 - 2.5,
11 - 18)
Forward mark
: N·m (kg-m, ft-lb)
Crash zone sensor

NS8019600148000X

Fig. 28 Crash zone sensor replacement. 1996 Truck 4WD

7. Remove seven screws attaching front console cluster lid to console, then cluster lid.
8. Remove right instrument finisher panel from instrument panel.
9. Remove audio and deck pockets.
10. Remove four rear console attaching screws, then the rear console.
11. Remove four front console attaching screws and two clips, then the front console.
12. Disconnect diagnosis sensor unit electrical connectors, **Fig. 30.**
13. Use T50 Torx bit to remove special bolts, then remove control unit.
14. Reverse procedure to install. During installation, arrow marking on diagnosis sensor unit must face toward front of vehicle. Use new coated bolts when installing diagnosis sensor unit.

MAXIMA

1994

Disarm SRS as described under "Air Bag System Disarming and Arming." Refer to **Fig. 19** to replace control unit.

1995–96

1. Disarm SRS as described under "Air Bag System Disarming and Arming."
2. Disconnect driver and passenger air bag module connectors.
3. Remove transmission shifter cover plate.
4. Remove ash tray.
5. Remove two center console attaching screws from under shifter cover plate.
6. Remove two console rear attaching screws from each side of console, then the console
7. Disconnect diagnosis sensor unit connector, **Fig. 31.**
8. Using a T50 Torx bit, remove ground bolt and three special bolts securing diagnosis sensor unit, then the unit.
9. Reverse procedure to install. During installation, arrow marking on diagnosis sensor unit must face toward front of vehicle. Use new coated bolts when installing diagnosis sensor unit.

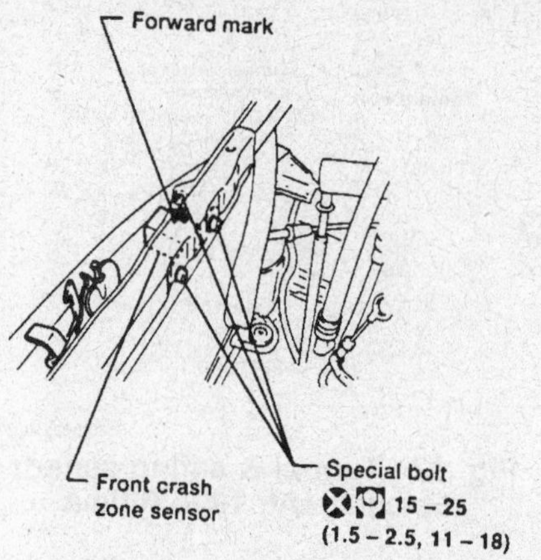
Forward mark
Front crash zone sensor
Special bolt
15 – 25
(1.5 – 2.5, 11 – 18)

NS8019400100000X

Fig. 26 Front crash zone sensor replacement. 1994–95 Quest

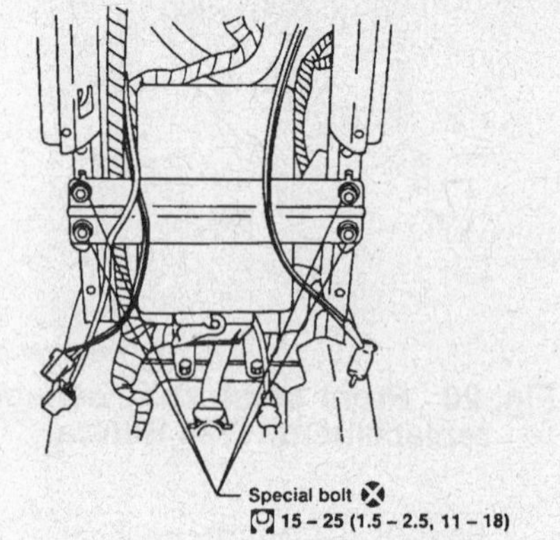
Special bolt
15 – 25 (1.5 – 2.5, 11 – 18)

NS8019400102000X

Fig. 29 Control unit replacement. 1994 Altima

SENTRA & 200SX

1994

Disarm SRS as described under "Air Bag System Disarming and Arming." Refer to **Fig. 32** to replace control unit.

1995–96

1. Disarm SRS as described under "Air Bag System Disarming and Arming."
2. Disconnect driver and passenger air bag module connectors.
3. Remove transmission shifter trim plate from console.
4. Remove four rear console attaching screws, then the rear console.
5. Remove four front console attaching screws, then the front console.
6. Disconnect diagnosis sensor unit connector, **Fig. 33.**
7. Remove ground bolt, then using a T50 Torx bit, remove three special bolts and diagnosis sensor unit.
8. Reverse procedure to install. During installation, arrow marking on diagnosis sensor unit must face toward front of vehicle. Use new coated bolts when installing diagnosis sensor unit.

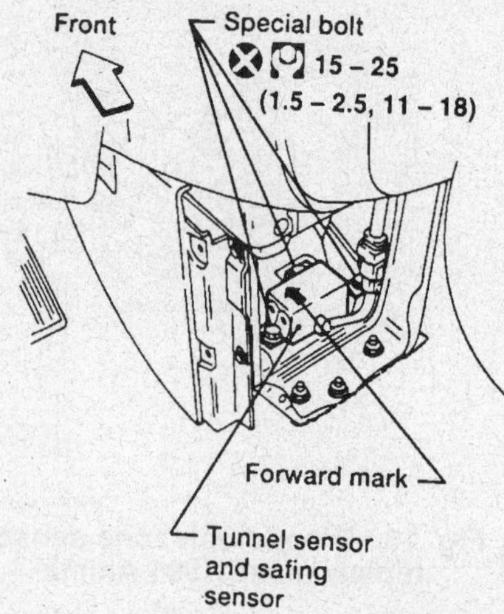
Front
Special bolt
15 – 25
(1.5 – 2.5, 11 – 18)
Forward mark
Tunnel sensor and safing sensor

NS8019400101000X

Fig. 27 Tunnel & safing sensor replacement. 1994–95 Quest

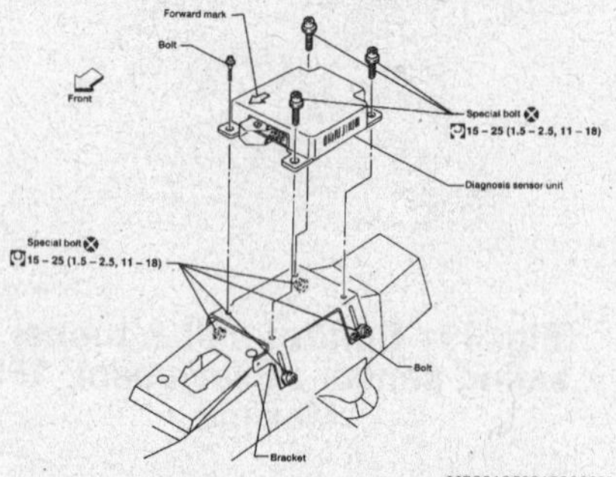
Forward mark
Bolt
Front
Special bolt
Diagnosis sensor unit
Bracket

NS8019500103000X

Fig. 30 Diagnosis sensor unit replacement. 1995–96 Altima

240SX

1. Disarm SRS as described under "Air Bag System Disarming and Arming."
2. Disconnect driver and passenger air bag module connectors.
3. Remove rear seat assembly.
4. Remove diagnosis sensor unit cover.
5. Disconnect diagnosis sensor unit connector, **Fig. 34.**
6. Remove bolt, then use T50 Torx bit to remove special bolts and control unit.
7. Reverse procedure to install. During installation, arrow marking on diagnosis sensor unit must face toward front of vehicle. Use new coated bolts when installing diagnosis sensor unit.

300ZX

Disarm SRS as described under "Air Bag

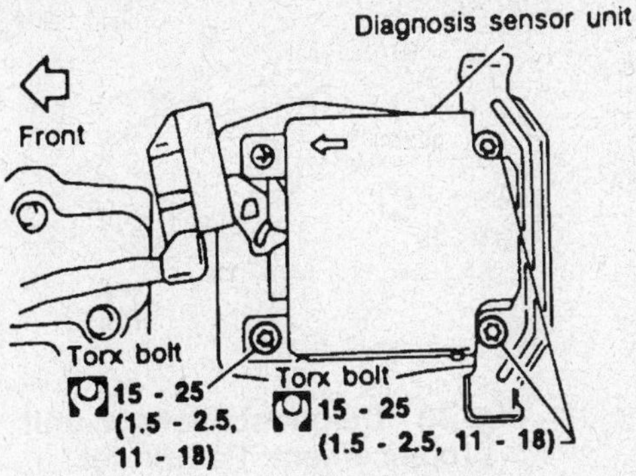
Diagnosis sensor unit
Front
Torx bolt
15 - 25 (1.5 - 2.5, 11 - 18)
Torx bolt
15 - 25 (1.5 - 2.5, 11 - 18)

NS8019500104000X

Fig. 31 Diagnosis sensor unit replacement. 1995–96 Maxima

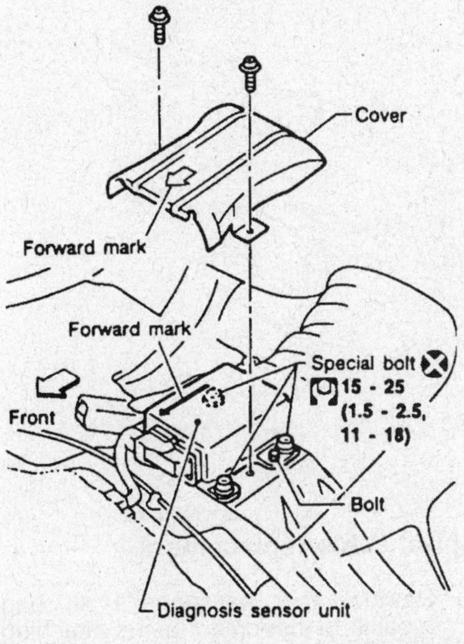
Cover
Forward mark
Forward mark
Special bolt
15 - 25 (1.5 - 2.5, 11 - 18)
Front
Bolt
Diagnosis sensor unit

NS8019500107000X

Fig. 34 Diagnosis sensor unit replacement. 240SX

System Disarming and Arming." Refer to **Fig. 35** to replace control unit. Use new coated bolts when installing diagnosis sensor unit. After completing installation, arm SRS as described under "Air Bag System Disarming and Arming."

QUEST

1994–95

Disarm SRS as described under "Air Bag System Disarming and Arming." Refer to **Fig. 36** to replace control unit. Use new coated bolts when installing diagnosis sensor unit. After completing installation, arm SRS as described under "Air Bag System Disarming and Arming."

1996

1. Disarm SRS as described under "Air Bag System Disarming and Arming."
2. Disconnect driver and passenger air bag module connectors.
3. Remove console box or CD magazine.
4. Disconnect and remove anti-lock brake control unit.

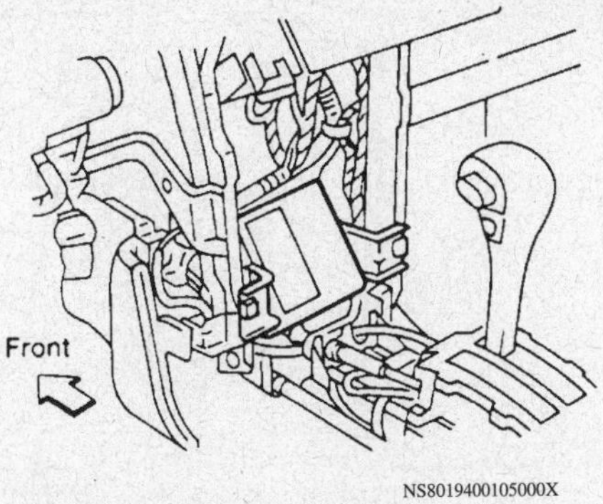
Front

NS8019400105000X

Fig. 32 Control unit replacement. 1994 Sentra

5. Disconnect diagnosis sensor unit connector, **Fig. 37.**
6. Remove ground bolt, then using a T50 Torx bit, remove three special bolts and diagnosis sensor unit.
7. Reverse procedure to install. During installation, arrow marking on diagnosis sensor unit must face toward front of vehicle. Use new coated bolts when installing diagnosis sensor unit.

PATHFINDER

1. Disarm SRS as described under "Air Bag System Disarming and Arming."
2. Disconnect driver and passenger air bag module connectors.
3. Remove ash tray.
4. Remove transmission shift lever cover or boot.
5. Remove console attaching screws, then disconnect electrical connectors and remove console.
6. Disconnect diagnosis sensor unit connector, **Fig. 38.**
7. Remove ground bolt, then using a T50 Torx bit, remove three special bolts and diagnosis sensor unit.
8. Reverse procedure to install. During installation, arrow marking on diagnosis sensor unit must face toward front of vehicle. Use new coated bolts when installing diagnosis sensor unit.

TRUCK

1. Disarm SRS as described under "Air Bag System Disarming and Arming."
2. Disconnect driver's air bag module connectors.
3. Remove console attaching screws, then the console.
4. Disconnect diagnosis sensor unit connector, **Fig. 39.**
5. Remove ground bolt, then using a T50 Torx bit, remove three special bolts and diagnosis sensor unit.
6. Reverse procedure to install. During installation, arrow marking on diagnosis sensor unit must face toward front of vehicle. Use new coated bolts when installing diagnosis sensor unit.

DRIVER'S AIR BAG MODULE, REPLACE

REMOVAL

1. Disarm SRS as described under "Air Bag System Disarming and Arming."

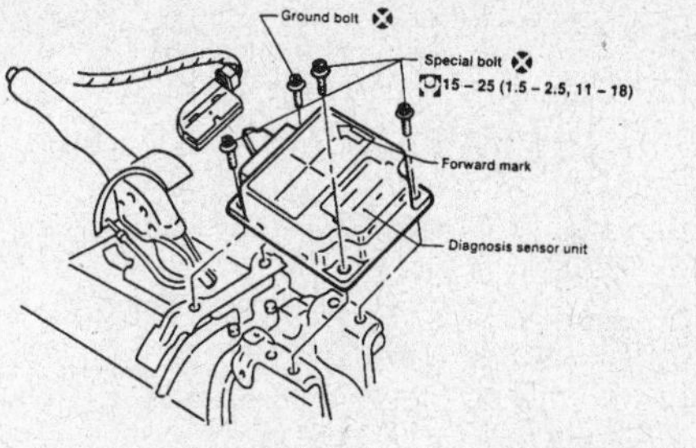
Ground bolt
Special bolt
15 – 25 (1.5 – 2.5, 11 – 18)
Forward mark
Diagnosis sensor unit

NS8019500106000X

Fig. 33 Diagnosis sensor unit replacement. 1995–96 Sentra & 200SX

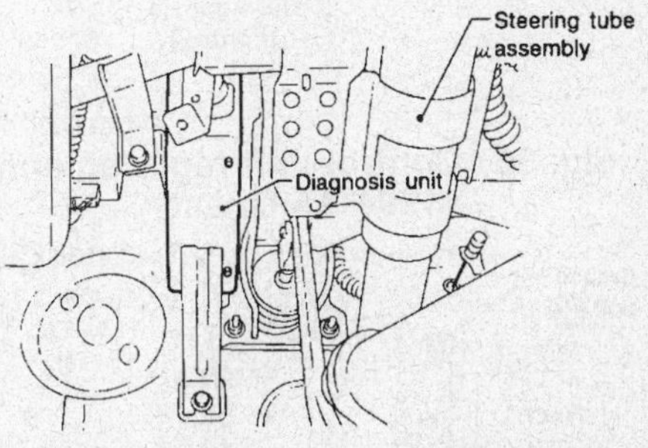
Steering tube assembly
Diagnosis unit

NS8019400108000X

Fig. 35 Control unit replacement. 300ZX

2. Remove lower lid from steering wheel, then disconnect air bag module connector.
3. Set steering wheel in straight–ahead position, then remove side lids, **Fig. 40.**
4. Use Torx bit to remove left and right air bag module attaching bolts.
5. Remove air bag module from steering wheel.

INSTALLATION

1. Install air bag module and secure with new attaching bolts, then tighten to torque listed in "Tightening Specifications."
2. Connect air bag module electrical connector.
3. Install steering column covers and steering wheel lid.
4. Arm SRS as described under "Air Bag System Disarming and Arming."
5. Ensure entire SRS operates properly using Consult tool or warning lamp self–diagnosis. **Air bag warning lamp will light for about seven seconds when ignition is turned to On or Start. If lamp remains on or fails to light, refer to "Diagnosis and Testing."**

PASSENGER'S AIR BAG MODULE, REPLACE

ALTIMA

1994–95

1. Disarm SRS as described under "Air Bag System Disarming and Arming."
2. Remove glove compartment lid and glove compartment.

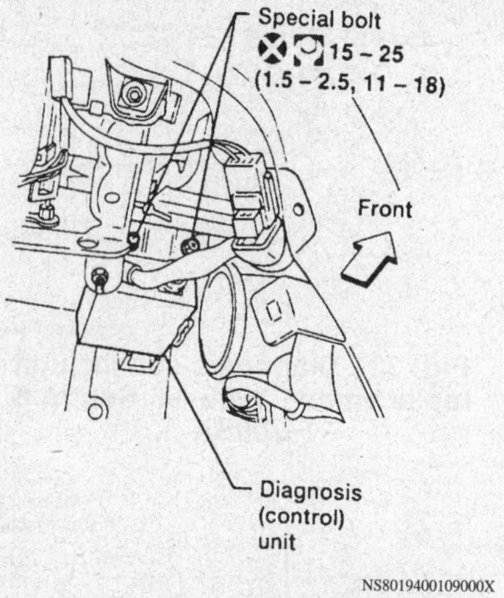
Special bolt
15 - 25
(1.5 - 2.5, 11 - 18)
Front
Diagnosis
(control)
unit
NS8019400109000X

Fig. 36 Control unit replacement. 1994–95 Quest

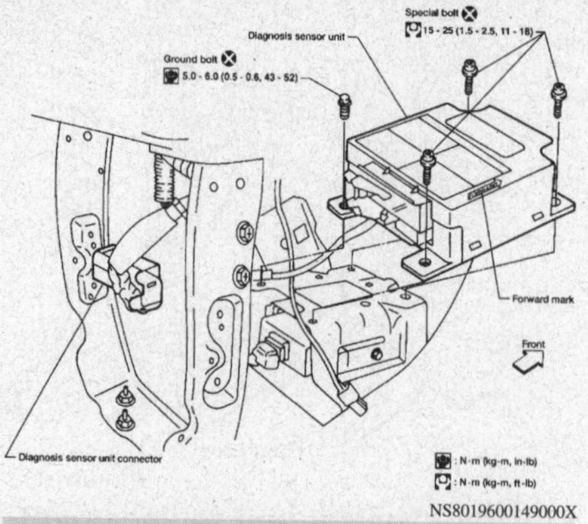
Special bolt
Diagnosis sensor unit
Ground bolt
Forward mark
Front
Diagnosis sensor unit connector
NS8019600149000X

Fig. 37 Diagnosis sensor unit replacement. 1996 Quest

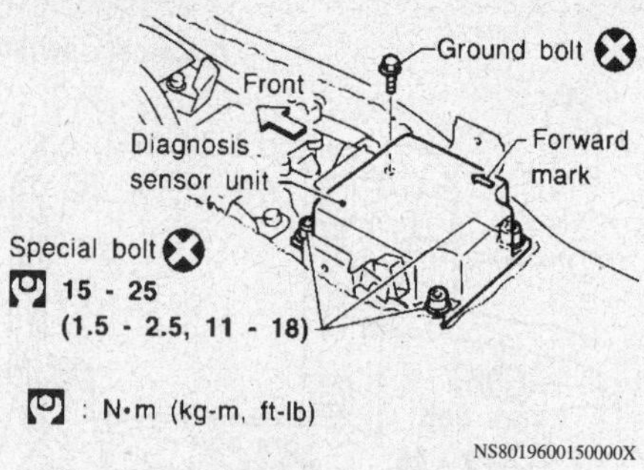
Ground bolt
Front
Diagnosis
sensor unit
Forward
mark
Special bolt
15 - 25
(1.5 - 2.5, 11 - 18)
: N·m (kg-m, ft-lb)
NS8019600150000X

Fig. 38 Diagnosis sensor unit replacement. Pathfinder

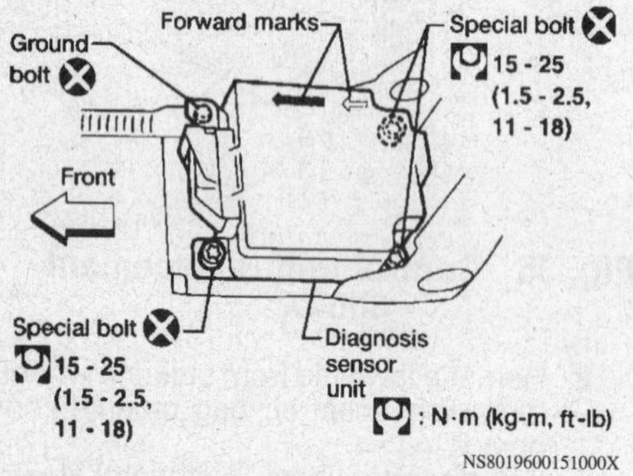
Forward marks
Ground
bolt
Special bolt
15 - 25
(1.5 - 2.5,
11 - 18)
Front
Special bolt
15 - 25
(1.5 - 2.5,
11 - 18)
Diagnosis
sensor
unit
: N·m (kg-m, ft-lb)
NS8019600151000X

Fig. 39 Diagnosis sensor unit replacement. Truck

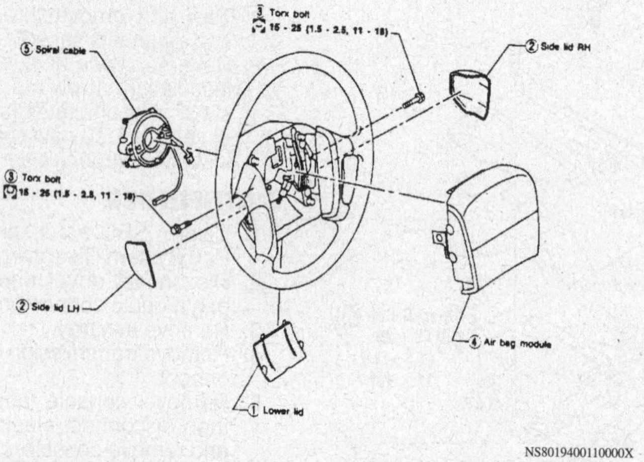
Spiral cable
Torx bolt
Side lid RH
Side lid LH
Air bag module
Lower lid
NS8019400110000X

Fig. 40 Driver air bag & spiral cable replacement

3. Disconnect passengers air bag module connectors.
4. Remove two special bolts from front of passengers air bag module, **Fig. 41.**
5. Remove four screws from left and right sides of passengers air bag module.
6. Remove passenger air bag module by releasing tabs at upper portion of instrument panel.
7. Reverse procedure to install. When installing, ensure module wiring harness is properly routed between air bag module and mounting bracket.

1996

1. Disarm SRS as described under "Air Bag System Disarming and Arming."
2. Remove glove compartment lid and glove compartment.
3. Disconnect passengers air bag module connector.
4. Remove two Torx 50 bolts retaining air bag module to brackets, **Fig. 42.**
5. Loosen screws at left and right side of passengers air bag module.
6. Remove passenger air bag module by releasing tabs at upper portion of instrument panel.
7. Reverse procedure to install. When installing, ensure module wiring harness is properly routed between air bag module and mounting bracket.

MAXIMA

1995–96

1. Disarm SRS as described under "Air Bag System Disarming and Arming."
2. Open glove compartment door, then disconnect passenger inflator connect from body connector, **Fig. 43.**
3. Remove glove compartment lid and glove compartment.
4. Disconnect passenger's air bag module connector.
5. Remove A/C intake unit.
6. Remove passenger's air bag module attaching bolts, **Fig. 44.**
7. Remove passenger's air bag module from instrument panel.
8. Reverse procedure to install. When installing, ensure module wiring harness is properly routed between air bag module and mounting bracket.

SENTRA & 200SX

1. Disarm SRS as described under "Air Bag System Disarming and Arming."
2. Remove glove compartment lid and glove compartment.
3. Disconnect passenger's air bag module connector.
4. Remove two Torx 50 bolts retaining air bag module to brackets, **Fig. 45.**
5. Remove four passenger's air bag module to instrument panel attaching nuts.
6. Remove passenger's air bag module by releasing tabs at upper portion of instrument panel.
7. Reverse procedure to install. When installing, ensure module wiring harness is properly routed between air bag module and mounting bracket.

240SX

1. Disarm SRS as described under "Air Bag System Disarming and Arming."
2. Remove connector bracket from passenger air bag module, then disconnect electrical connector from body harness, **Fig. 46.**
3. Remove instrument panel.
4. Remove passenger's air bag module attaching bolts, **Fig. 47.**
5. Remove passenger's air bag module from instrument panel.
6. Reverse procedure to install. When installing, ensure module wiring harness is properly routed between air bag module and mounting bracket.

300ZX

1. Disarm SRS as described under "Air Bag System Disarming and Arming."

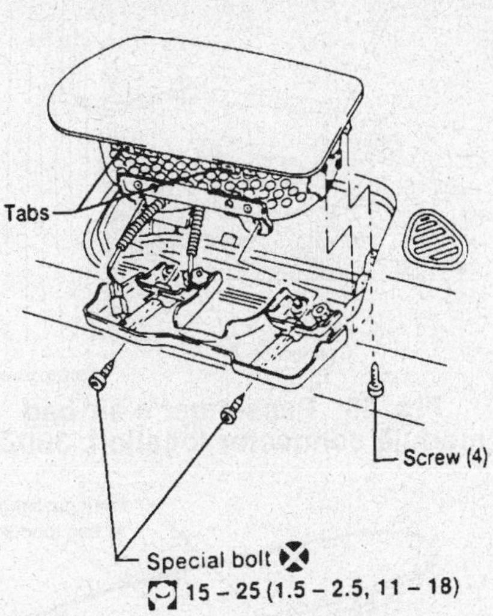
Tabs
Screw (4)
Special bolt
15 – 25 (1.5 – 2.5, 11 – 18)
NS8019400111000X

Fig. 41 Passenger's air bag replacement. 1994–95 Altima

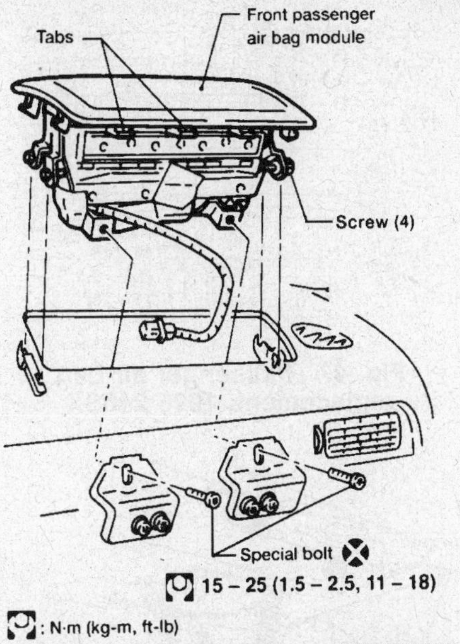
Tabs
Front passenger air bag module
Screw (4)
Special bolt
15 – 25 (1.5 – 2.5, 11 – 18)
: N·m (kg-m, ft-lb)
NS8019600152000X

Fig. 42 Passenger's air bag module replacement. 1996 Altima

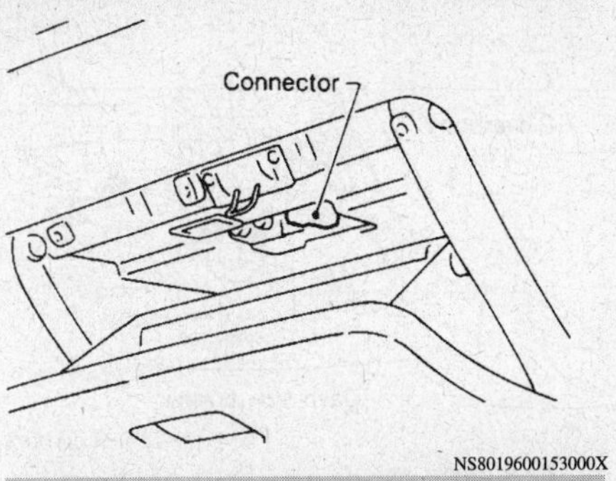
Connector
NS8019600153000X

Fig. 43 Passenger's inflator connector location. 1996 Maxima

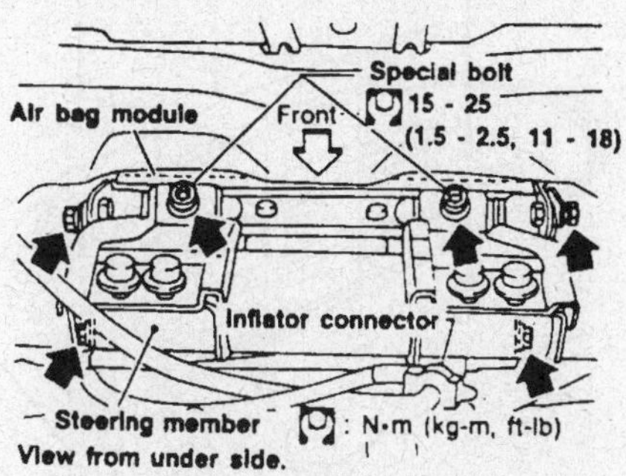
Special bolt
15 - 25
(1.5 - 2.5, 11 - 18)
Air bag module
Front
Inflator connector
Steering member
: N·m (kg-m, ft-lb)
View from under side.
NS8019500112000X

Fig. 44 Passenger air bag replacement. 1995–96 Maxima

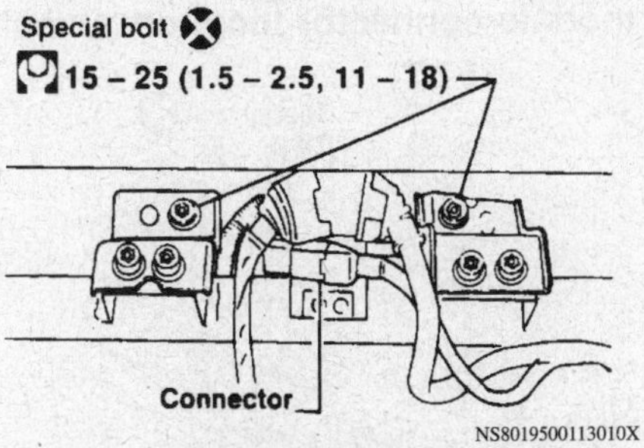
Special bolt
15 – 25 (1.5 – 2.5, 11 – 18)
Connector
NS8019500113010X

Fig. 45 Passenger air bag replacement (Part 1 of 2). 1995–96 Sentra & 200SX

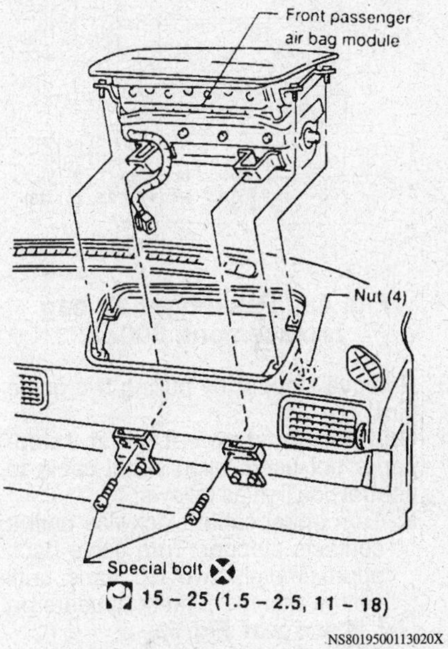
Front passenger air bag module
Nut (4)
Special bolt
15 – 25 (1.5 – 2.5, 11 – 18)
NS8019500113020X

Fig. 45 Passenger air bag replacement (Part 2 of 2). 1995–96 Sentra & 200SX

2. Remove passenger side instrument panel lower cover.
3. Disconnect passenger's air bag module connector, **Fig. 48.**
4. Remove instrument panel.
5. Remove special bolts from left and right side of passenger's air bag module, **Fig. 49.**
6. Remove passenger's air bag module from instrument panel.
7. Reverse procedure to install. When installing, ensure module wiring harness is properly routed between air bag module and mounting bracket.

QUEST

1. Disarm SRS as described under "Air Bag System Disarming and Arming."
2. Remove access panel from behind glove compartment.
3. Disconnect passenger's air bag module connector, **Fig. 50.**
4. Remove glove compartment.
5. Remove four passenger's air bag module attaching nuts, **Fig. 51.**
6. Remove passenger's air bag module from instrument panel.
7. Reverse procedure to install. When installing, ensure module wiring harness is properly routed between air bag module and mounting bracket.

PATHFINDER

1. Disarm SRS as described under "Air Bag System Disarming and Arming."
2. Remove glove compartment.
3. Disconnect passenger's air bag module connector from body harness.
4. Remove panel from lower passenger side of instrument panel.
5. Remove special bolt from front of passenger's air bag module, **Fig. 52.**
6. Remove instrument panel. Refer to "Dash Panel, Replace " section under "Dash Panel Service" for removal procedure.
7. Remove bolts from left and right side of passenger's air bag module.
8. Remove passenger's air bag module from instrument panel.
9. Reverse procedure to install. When installing, ensure module wiring harness is properly routed between air bag module and mounting bracket. Tighten bolts to specifications.

SPIRAL CABLE, REPLACE

REMOVAL

1. Disarm SRS as described under "Air Bag System Disarming and Arming."
2. Ensure steering wheel is in straight–ahead position.
3. Disconnect horn electrical connector, then remove steering wheel retaining nut.
4. Using suitable steering wheel puller, remove steering wheel.
5. Remove steering column upper and lower covers.
6. Attach spiral cable stopper to spiral cable or body with tape.
7. Disconnect electrical connector, then remove four attaching screws and spiral cable.

INSTALLATION

1. Ensure ignition is turned Off.
2. Install spiral cable, tighten attaching screws to specifications, then connect electrical connector.

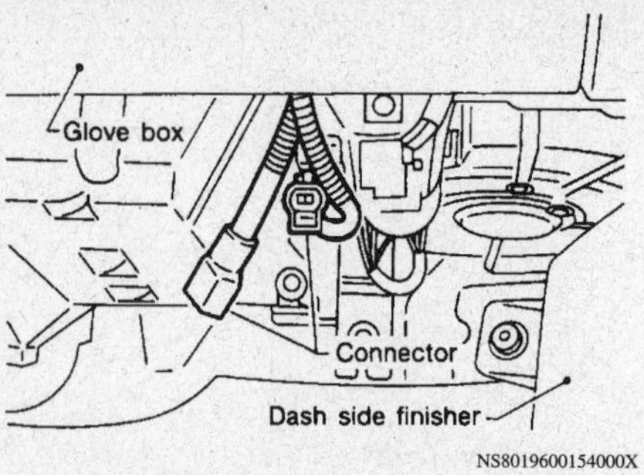
Glove box
Connector
Dash side finisher
NS8019600154000X

Fig. 46 Passenger's air bag module connector location. 240SX

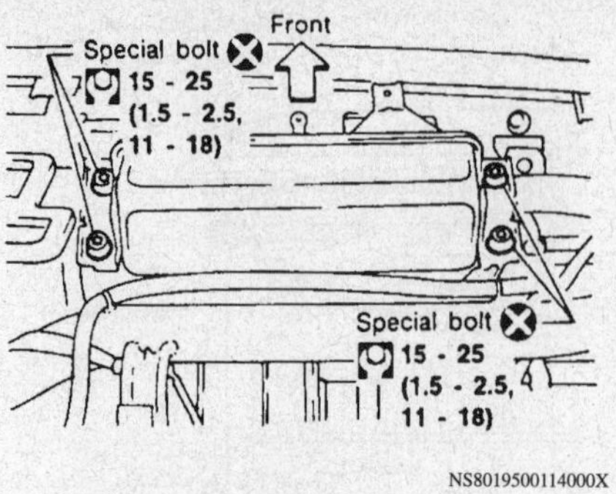
Front
Special bolt
15 - 25
(1.5 - 2.5,
11 - 18)
Special bolt
15 - 25
(1.5 - 2.5,
11 - 18)
NS8019500114000X

Fig. 47 Passenger air bag replacement. 1995 240SX

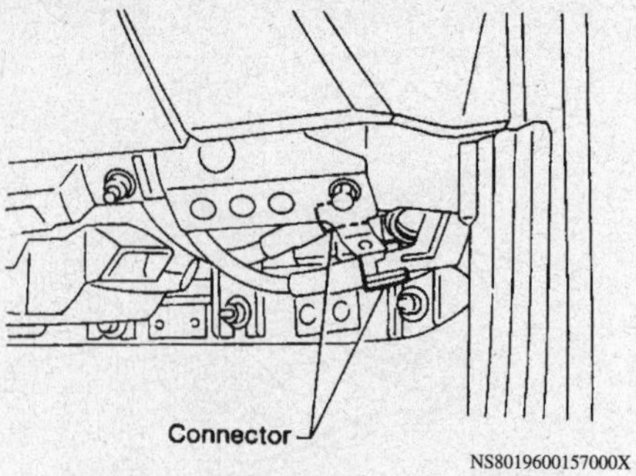
Connector
NS8019600157000X

Fig. 48 Passenger's air bag module connector location. 300ZX

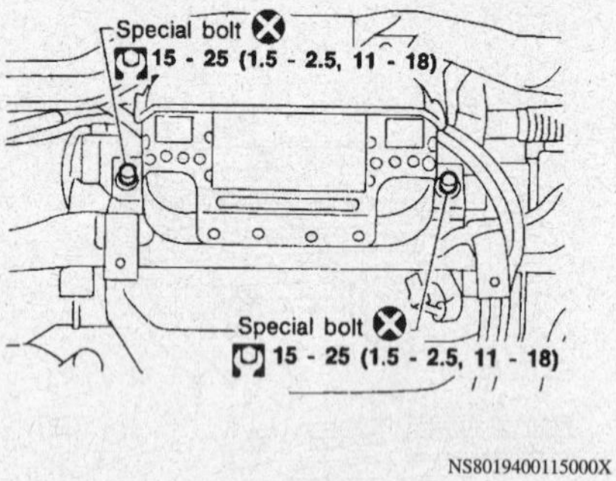
Special bolt
15 - 25 (1.5 - 2.5, 11 - 18)
Special bolt
15 - 25 (1.5 - 2.5, 11 - 18)
NS8019400115000X

Fig. 49 Passenger air bag replacement. 300ZX

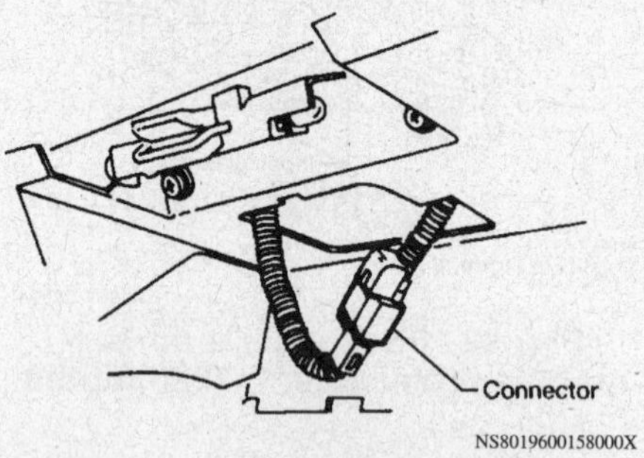
Connector
NS8019600158000X

Fig. 50 Passenger's air bag module connector location. Quest

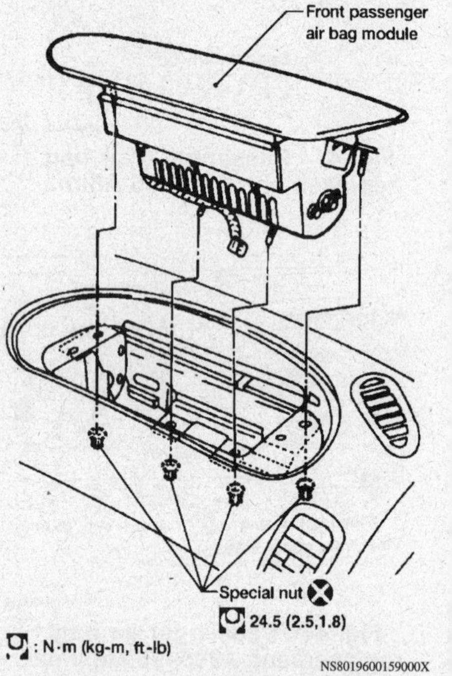
Front passenger air bag module
Special nut
24.5 (2.5,1.8)
: N·m (kg-m, ft-lb)
NS8019600159000X

Fig. 51 Passenger's air bag module replacement. Quest

3. Remove stopper by pulling two guide pins.
4. **On 1994 model except Quest,** if stopper is not used, align spiral cable to neutral position as follows:
   a. Turn spiral cable clockwise until it contacts stopper. Turn cable back approximately two full turns until yellow alignment mark appears on lefthand gear, **Fig. 53.**
   b. Align spiral cable's arrow mark with this yellow mark.
5. **On 1995–96 models except Quest,** if stopper is not used, align spiral cable to neutral position as follows:
   a. Turn spiral cable clockwise until it contacts stopper, then turn cable back 2.5 turns.
   b. Align cable arrow marks, **Fig. 54.**
6. **On Quest models,** if stopper is not used, align spiral cable to neutral position as follows:
   a. Turn spiral cable clockwise until it contacts stopper.
   b. Place alignment marks on inner and outer portions of spiral cable housing, **Fig. 55.**
   c. Rotate spiral cable 3 turns in the clockwise direction and align match marks. Use tape to hold spiral cable in position.
7. Install steering wheel, aligning spiral cable guide pins, then pull spiral cable connector through wheel.
8. Connect horn electrical connector, then secure spiral cable harness with pawls in steering wheel.
9. Tighten steering wheel retaining nut to specifications.

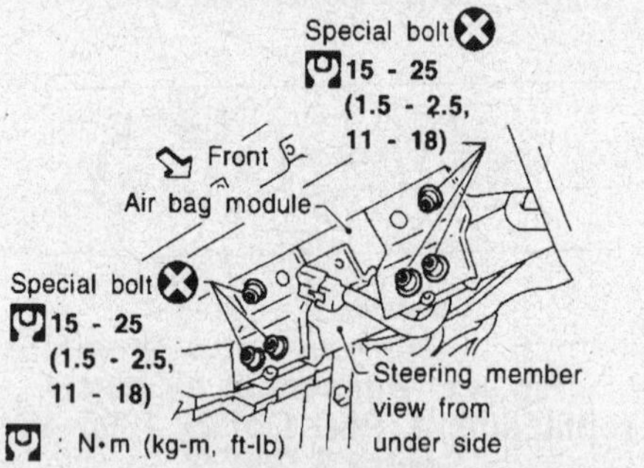
Special bolt
15 - 25
(1.5 - 2.5,
11 - 18)
Front
Air bag module
Special bolt
15 - 25
(1.5 - 2.5,
11 - 18)
: N·m (kg-m, ft-lb)
Steering member
view from
under side
NS8019600160000X

Fig. 52 Passenger's air bag module front attaching bolts. Pathfinder

AIR BAG MODULE DISPOSAL

Before scrapping an air bag module or vehicle equipped with an air bag, the air bag must be deployed.

PRECAUTIONS

1. Vehicle should be placed outdoors with at least 20 feet of open space on all sides.
2. Remove battery from vehicle and position at least 15 feet from vehicle lefthand door.
3. Before deploying air bag, ensure no people, animals or objects are within 20 feet of vehicle.
4. Wear goggles when handling air bag modules.
5. Use care not to inhale gas produced by air bag deployment.
6. Do not handle deployed air bag for 30 minutes after deployment, due to extremely high temperatures. Never apply water to deployed air bag.
7. After disconnecting battery, wait at least 10 to 12 minutes before proceeding with disposal procedure.
8. Never disassemble an air bag. It cannot be used again.
9. Seal deployed air bag assemblies in heavy duty plastic bags, then dispose with other automotive scrap.
10. Wash hands after handling any deployed SRS components.

DEPLOYMENT TOOL INSPECTION

1. Locate fully charged 12 volt battery at least 15 feet away from vehicle.
2. Connect special deployment tool No. J38381, or equivalent, to battery and ensure green lamp marked "Deployment Tool Power"on righthand side lights. If red lamp lights, reverse battery connections.

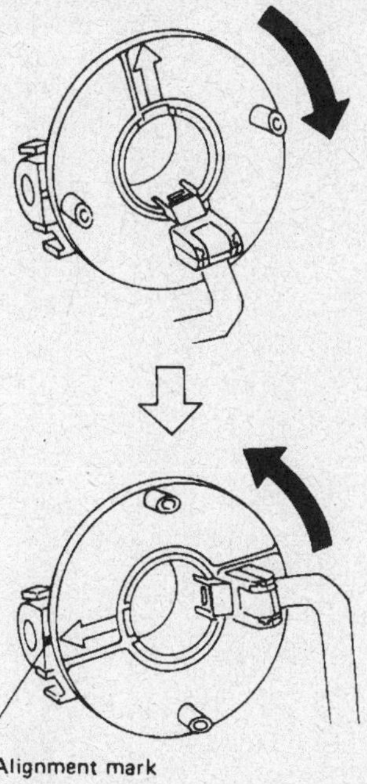
Alignment mark
NS8019400116000X

Fig. 53 Spiral cable alignment. 1994 models except Quest

3. Connect deployment tool male and female check connectors.
4. Push tool switch to On position to ensure lefthand lamp marked "Air Bag Connector Voltage " lights. If lamp does not light, replace deployment tool.

DEPLOYING AIR BAG MODULE

Inside Vehicle

When vehicle is to be scrapped, deploy air bag module(s) while still mounted in vehicle.

1. Vehicle should be placed outdoors with at least 20 feet of open space on all sides.
2. Disarm SRS as described under "Air Bag System Disarming and Arming."
3. Remove battery from vehicle and position at least 15 feet from vehicle lefthand door.
4. **On models equipped with passenger air bag,** attach special deployment tool adapters No. J38382-30.
5. **On all models,** connect deployment tool connector to air bag module(s).

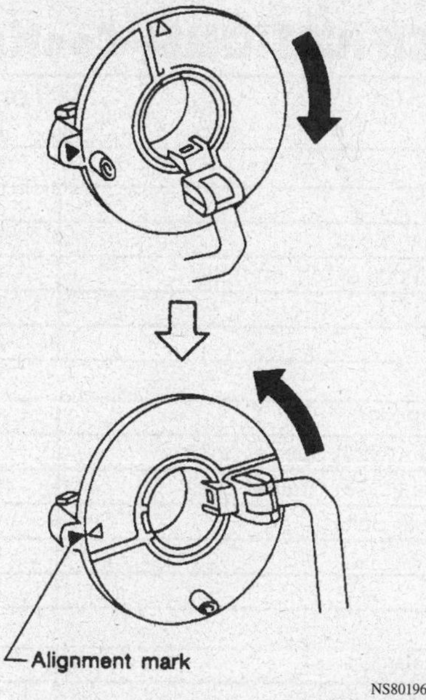
Alignment mark
NS8019600162000X

Fig. 54 Spiral cable alignment. 1995–96 models except Quest

6. Connect deployment tool to battery. Ensure righthand lamp marked "Deployment Tool Power" lights.
7. Before deploying air bag, ensure no people, animals or objects are within 20 feet of vehicle.
8. Press deployment tool switch. Lefthand lamp marked "Air Bag Connector Voltage" will light and air bag will deploy.
9. Dispose of air bag module.

Outside Vehicle

Activate only one air bag at a time.

1. Disarm SRS as described under "Air Bag System Disarming and Arming."
2. Remove air bag assembly from vehicle as described in, "Air Bag Assembly, Replace."
3. Securely anchor air bag module to vise.
4. Connect special deployment tool to air bag module connector.
5. At least 15 feet from air bag assembly, connect deployment tool to battery. Ensure righthand lamp marked "Deployment Tool Power"glows green.
6. Before beginning deployment, ensure no people, animals or objects are within 20 feet of air bag.

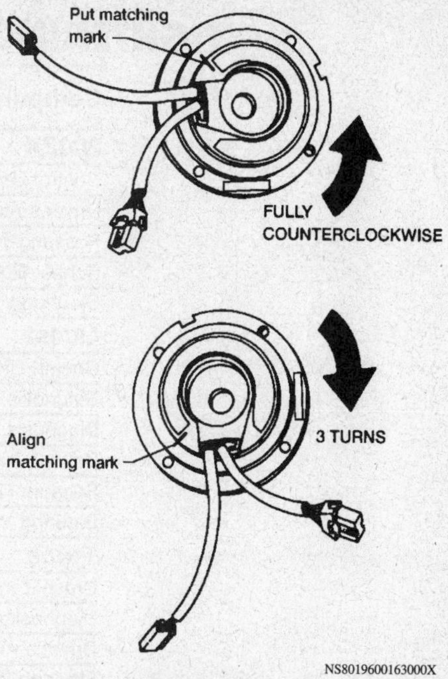
Put matching mark
FULLY COUNTERCLOCKWISE
Align matching mark
3 TURNS
NS8019600163000X

Fig. 55 Spiral cable alignment. Quest

7. Press deployment tool button. Lefthand lamp marked "Air Bag Connector Voltage" will light and module will deploy.

TECHNICAL SERVICE BULLETINS

UNWANTED AIR BAG DEPLOYMENT WHEN REPLACING COMBINATION SWITCH

1993-94 Altima

On these models, unwanted air bag deployment may result from improper combination switch replacement.

This condition may be caused by air bag circuit connector **A5** being connected to the combination switch. To correct this condition, clearly mark connectors during disassembly. Plastic E1 15 turn signal circuit connector is white. **Connector A5 is yellow, but may have a black rubber protector.**

TIGHTENING SPECIFICATIONS

Component	Torque/Ft. Lbs.
Altima, Maxima, Pathfinder, Sentra, 200SX & 240SX	
Control/Diagnosis Sensor Unit Bolts	11–18
Driver's Air Bag Module to Steering Wheel Bolts	11–18
Passenger's Air Bag Module Torx 50 Bolts	11–18
Sensor Bolts (1994)	11–18
Steering Wheel Nut	22–29

Continued

TIGHTENING SPECIFICATIONS—Continued

Component	Torque/Ft. Lbs.
300ZX	
Control Unit Bolts	11–18
Driver's Air Bag Module Bolts	11–18
Passenger's Air Bag Module Torx 50 Bolts	11–18
Sensor Bolts	11–18
Steering Wheel Nut	22–19
Quest	
Control Unit Bolts (1994–95)	11–18
Diagnosis Sensor Unit (1996) Special Bolts	11–18
Diagnosis Sensor Unit (1996) Ground Bolts	43–52①
Driver's Air Bag Module Bolts	11–18
Sensors (1994–95)	11–18
Steering Wheel Nut	22–29
Truck	
Crash Zone Sensor (4WD)	11–18
Diagnosis Sensor Unit	11–18
Driver's Air Bag Module Bolts	11–18
Steering Wheel Nut	22–29

① — Inch lbs.

Dash Panel Service

NOTE: Refer To The "Dash Gauges" Section For Related Information.

NOTE: On Air Bag Equipped Models, Refer To "Air Bag System Precautions" Located In The Front Of This Manual For System Disarming & Arming Procedures.

INDEX

	Page No.
Dash Panel, Replace	36-99
Altima	36-99
Maxima	36-99
Pathfinder & Pickup	36-99
Quest	36-99
Sentra, NX1600, NX2000 & 200SX	36-99
240SX	36-99
300ZX	36-99
Precautions	36-99
Air Bag Systems	36-99

PRECAUTIONS

AIR BAG SYSTEMS

Refer to "Air Bag System Precautions" in the front of this manual for system disarming and arming procedures.

DASH PANEL

REPLACE

ALTIMA

Refer to **Fig. 1,** for instrument panel replacement.

MAXIMA

Refer to **Figs. 2 and 3** when replacing these dash panels.

SENTRA, NX1600, NX2000 & 200SX

Refer to **Figs. 4 and 5** when replacing these dash panels.

PATHFINDER & PICKUP

Refer to **Figs. 6 through 8** when replacing these dash panels.

QUEST

Refer to **Figs. 9 and 10** for instrument panel replacement.

240SX

Refer to **Figs. 11 and 12** when replacing these dash panels.

300ZX

Refer to **Figs. 13 and 14** when replacing these dash panels.

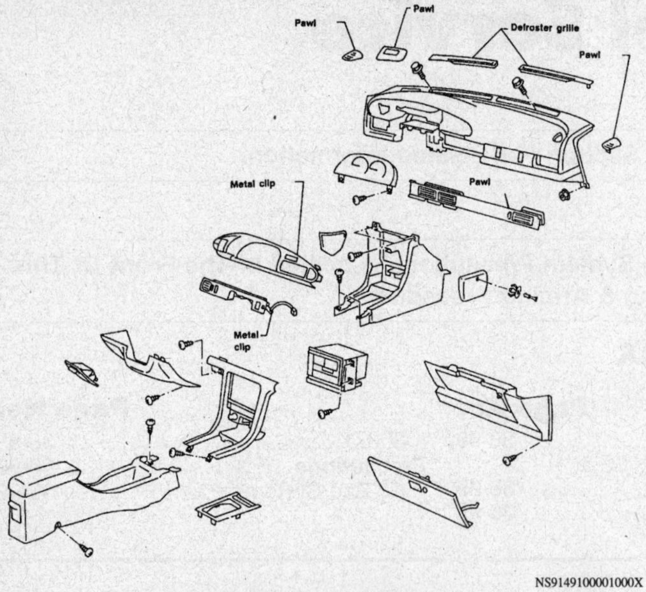
Pawl
Pawl
Defroster grille
Pawl
Metal clip
Pawl
Metal clip
NS9149100001000X

Fig. 1 Exploded view of instrument panel. Altima

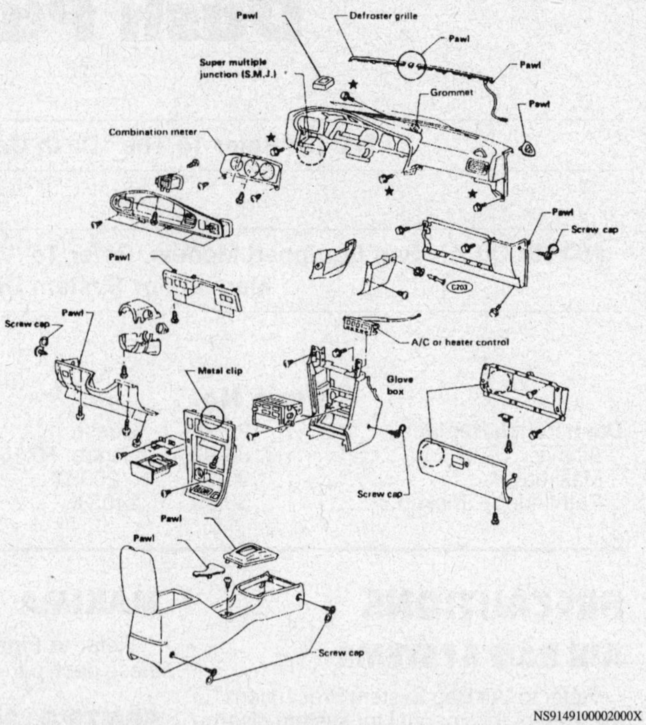
Pawl
Defroster grille
Pawl
Super multiple junction (S.M.J.)
Pawl
Grommet
Pawl
Combination meter
Pawl
Screw cap
Pawl
C203
Screw cap
Pawl
A/C or heater control
Metal clip
Glove box
Screw cap
Pawl
Pawl
Screw cap
NS9149100002000X

Fig. 2 Exploded view of instrument panel. 1993–94 Maxima

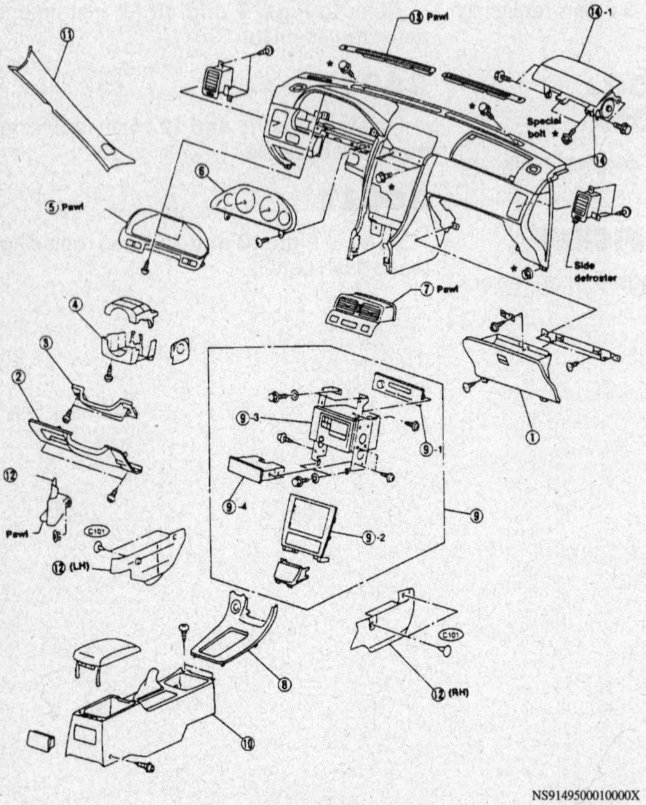
Pawl
Special bolt
Pawl
Side defroster
Pawl
Pawl
C101
(LH)
(RH)
NS9149500010000X

Fig. 3 Exploded view of instrument panel. 1995–96 Maxima

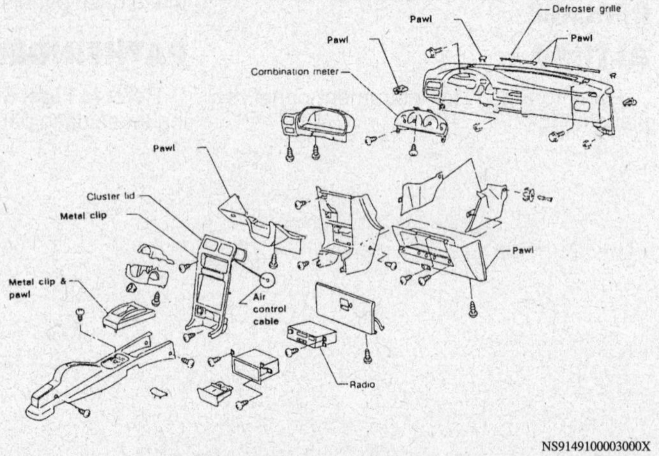
Defroster grille
Pawl
Pawl
Pawl
Combination meter
Pawl
Cluster lid
Metal clip
Pawl
Metal clip & pawl
Air control cable
Radio
NS9149100003000X

Fig. 4 Exploded view of instrument panel. 1993–94 Sentra, 1993 NX1600 & NX2000

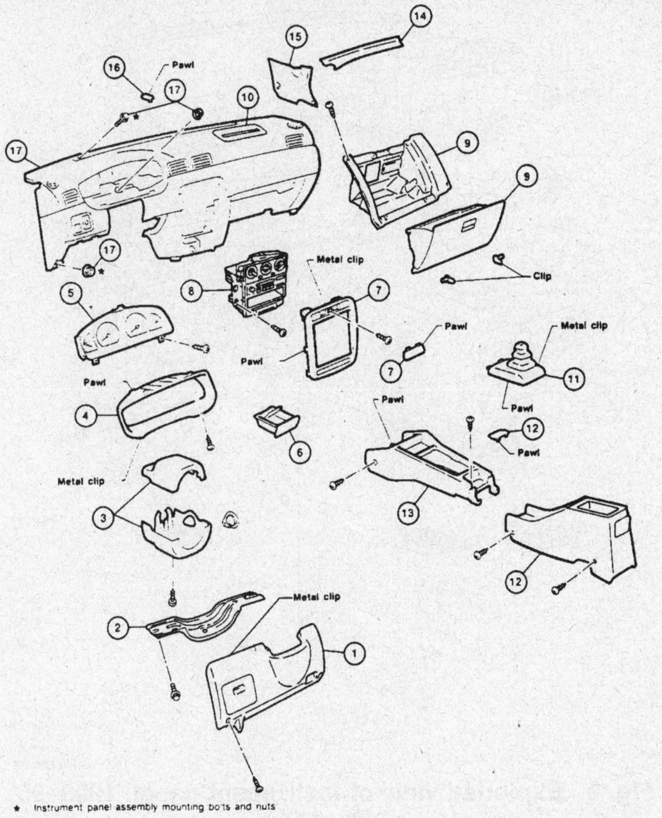
Pawl
Metal clip
Clip
★ Instrument panel assembly mounting bolts and nuts
NS9149500011000X

Fig. 5 Exploded view of instrument panel. 1995–96 Sentra & 200SX

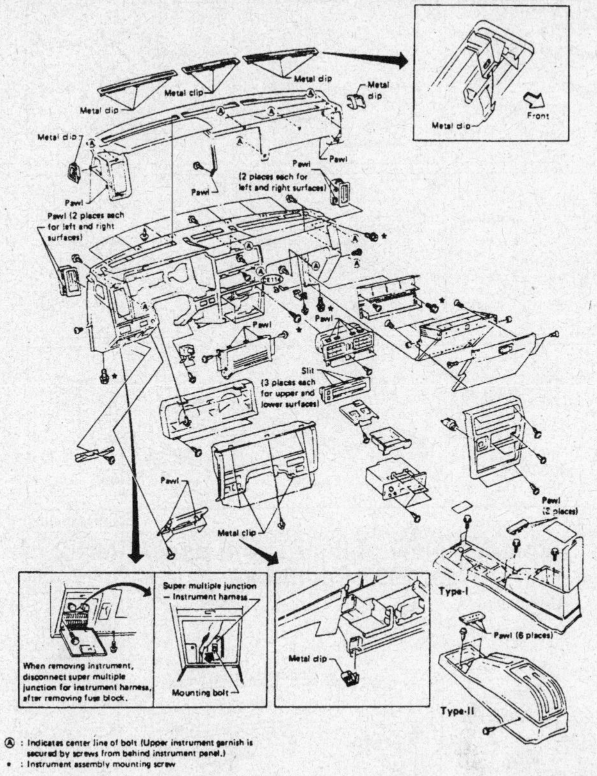
Metal clip
Pawl
Pawl (2 places each for left and right surfaces)
Slit (3 places each for upper and lower surfaces)
Front
Super multiple junction – Instrument harness
When removing instrument, disconnect super multiple junction for instrument harness, after removing fuse block.
Mounting bolt
Type-I
Pawl (6 places)
Type-II
Ⓐ : Indicates center line of bolt (Upper instrument garnish is secured by screws from behind instrument panel.)
★ : Instrument assembly mounting screw
NS9149100005000X

Fig. 6 Exploded view of instrument panel. 1993 Pathfinder & Pickup

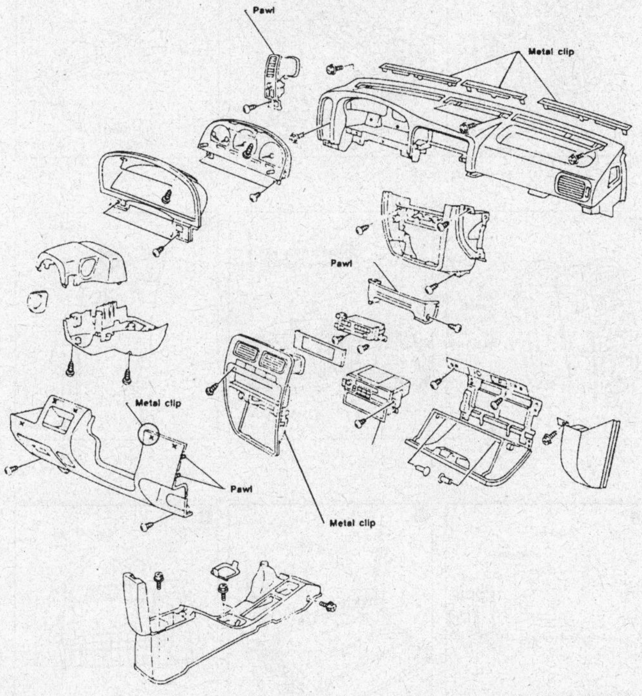
Pawl
Metal clip
NS9149400006000X

Fig. 7 Exploded view of instrument panel. 1994–95 Pathfinder & 1994–96 Pickup

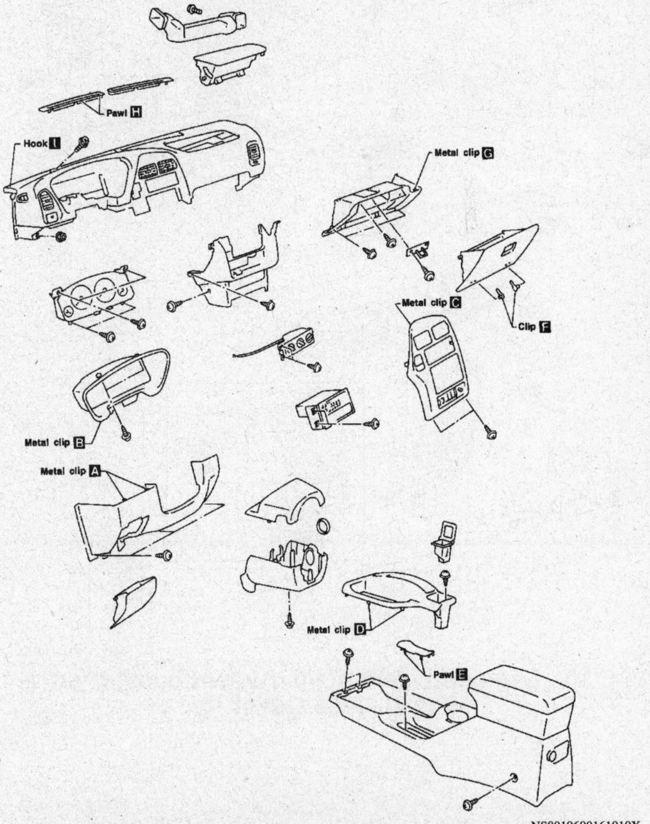
Pawl H
Hook I
Metal clip G
Metal clip C
Clip F
Metal clip B
Metal clip A
Metal clip D
Pawl E
NS8019600161010X

Fig. 8 Exploded view of instrument panel (Part 1 of 2). 1996 Pathfinder

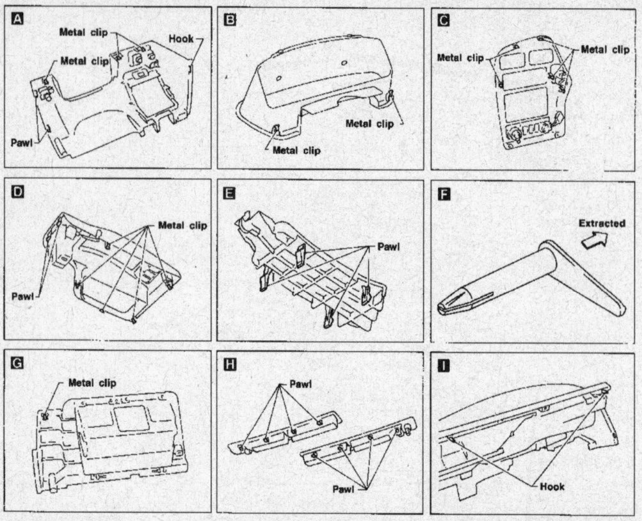
A
Metal clip
Hook
Metal clip
Pawl
B
Metal clip
Metal clip
C
Metal clip
Metal clip
D
Metal clip
Pawl
E
Pawl
F
Extracted
G
Metal clip
H
Pawl
Pawl
I
Hook

NS8019600161020X

Fig. 8 Exploded view of instrument panel (Part 2 of 2). 1996 Pathfinder

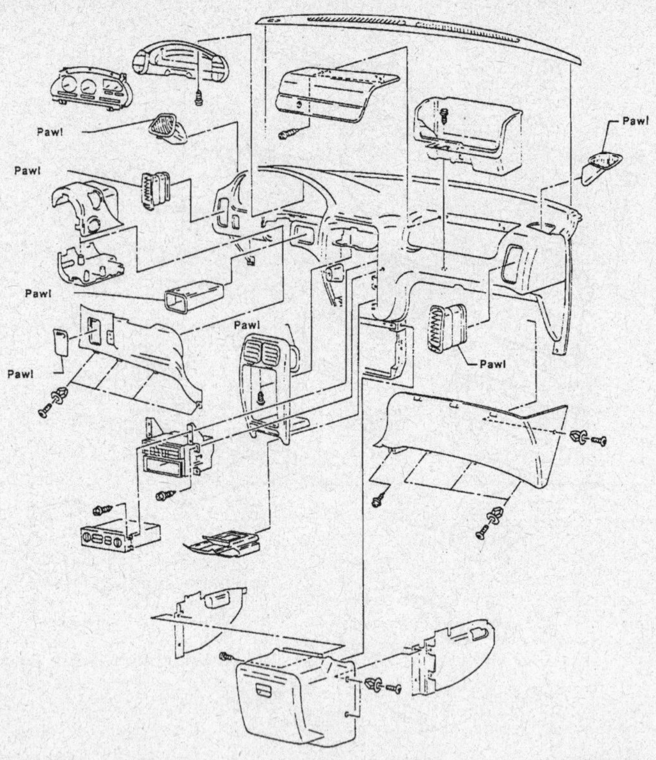
Pawl
Pawl
Pawl
Pawl
Pawl
Pawl
Pawl

NS9149100007000X

Fig. 9 Exploded view of instrument panel. 1993–95 Quest

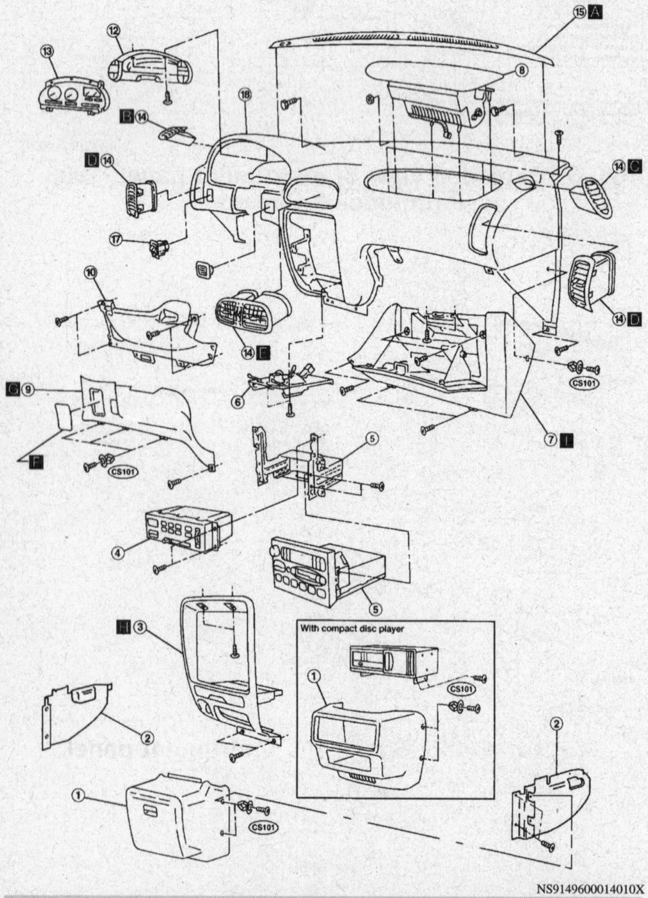
With compact disc player
CS101
CS101
CS101
CS101

NS9149600014010X

Fig. 10 Exploded view of instrument panel (Part 1 of 2). 1996 Quest

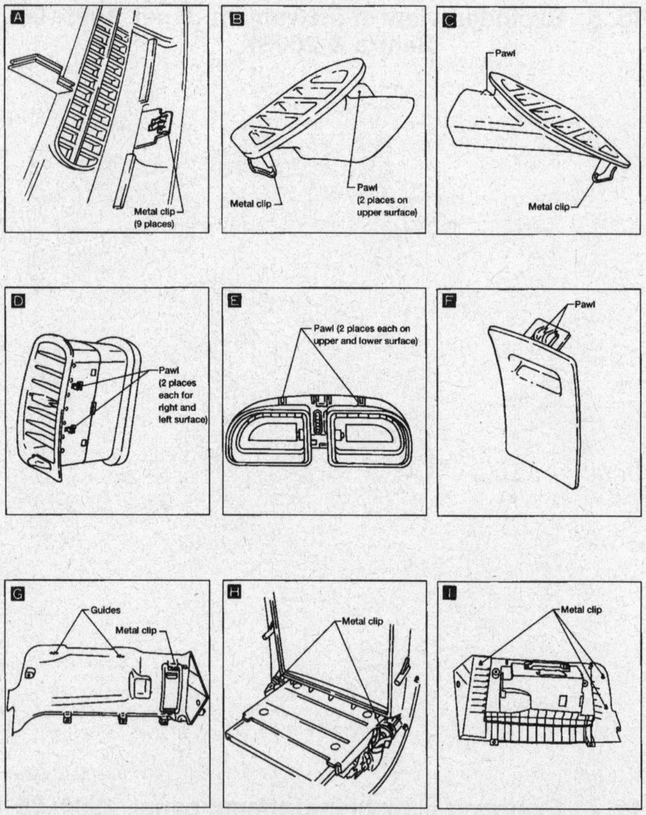
A
Metal clip
(9 places)
B
Metal clip
Pawl
(2 places on upper surface)
C
Pawl
Metal clip
D
Pawl
(2 places each for right and left surface)
E
Pawl (2 places each on upper and lower surface)
F
Pawl
G
Guides
Metal clip
H
Metal clip
I
Metal clip

NS9149600014020X

Fig. 10 Exploded view of instrument panel (Part 2 of 2). 1996 Quest

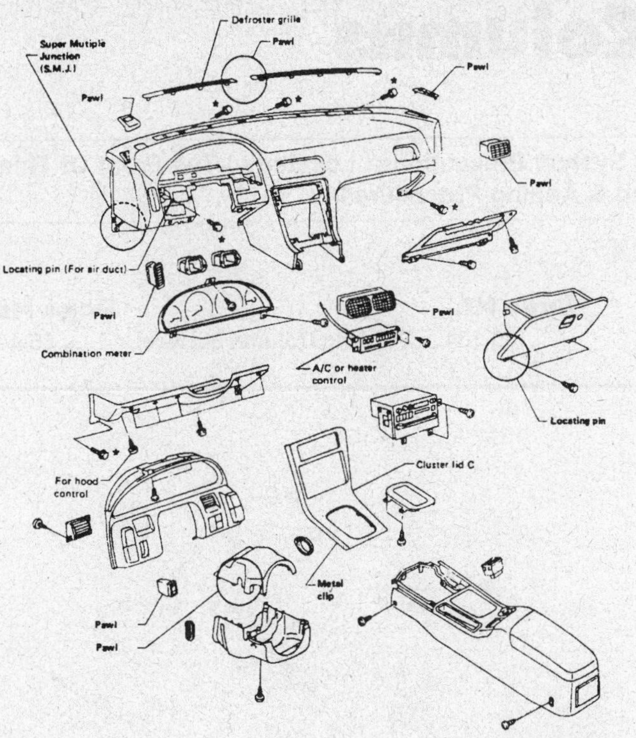

Defroster grille
Super Mutiple Junction (S.M.J.)
Pawl
Locating pin (For air duct)
Combination meter
A/C or heater control
Locating pin
For hood control
Cluster lid C
Metal clip

★ : Instrument panel assembly mounting bo

NS9149100008000X

Fig. 11 Exploded view of instrument panel. 1993 240SX

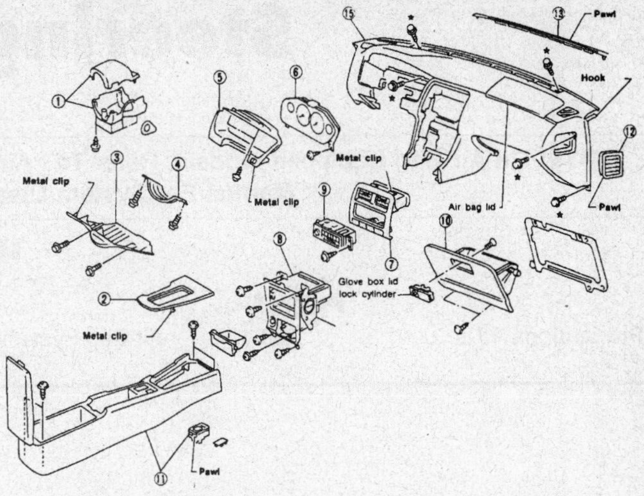

Pawl
Hook
Metal clip
Air bag lid
Glove box lid lock cylinder

★ : Instrument panel assembly mounting bolts and nuts

NS9149500012000X

Fig. 12 Exploded view of instrument panel. 1994–96 240SX

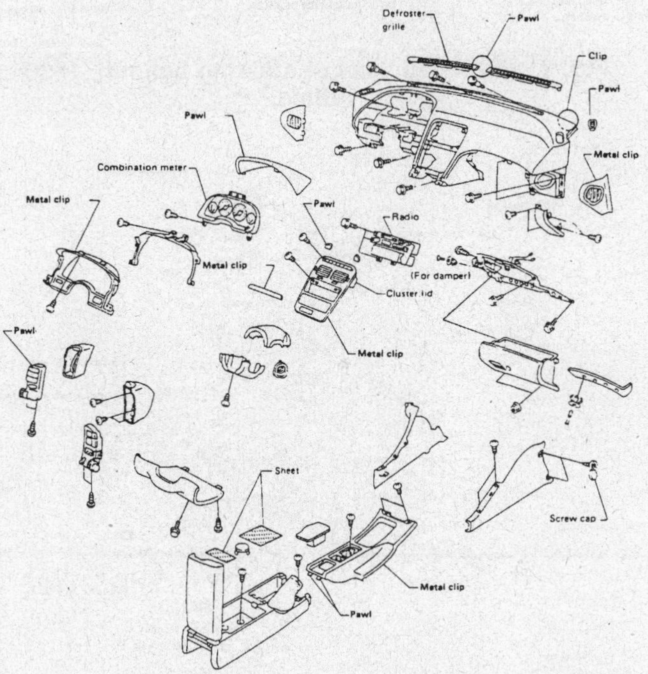

Defroster grille
Pawl
Clip
Metal clip
Combination meter
Radio
(For damper)
Cluster lid
Sheet
Screw cap

NS9149100009000X

Fig. 13 Exploded view of instrument panel. 1993–94 300ZX

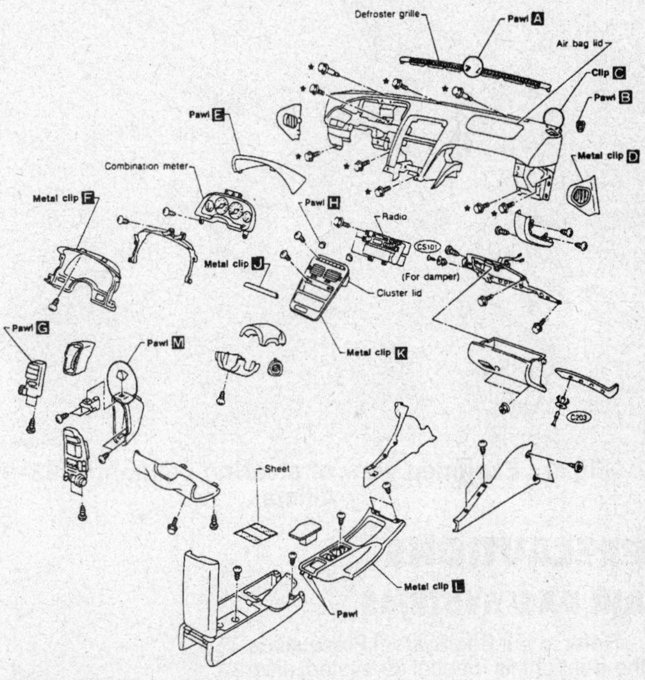

Defroster grille
Pawl A
Air bag lid
Clip C
Pawl B
Pawl E
Metal clip D
Combination meter
Metal clip F
Pawl H
Radio
Metal clip J
(For damper)
Cluster lid
Pawl G
Pawl M
Metal clip K
Sheet
Metal clip L
Pawl

▨ : Double-faced adhesive tape

★ : Instrument panel assembly mounting bolts

NS9149500013000X

Fig. 14 Exploded view of instrument panel. 1995–96 300ZX

Steering Columns

NOTE: On Air Bag Equipped Models, Refer To "Air Bag System Precautions" Located In The Front Of This Manual For System Disarming & Arming Procedures.

INDEX

	Page No.
Precautions	36-104
Air Bag Systems	36-104
Steering Column Service	36-104

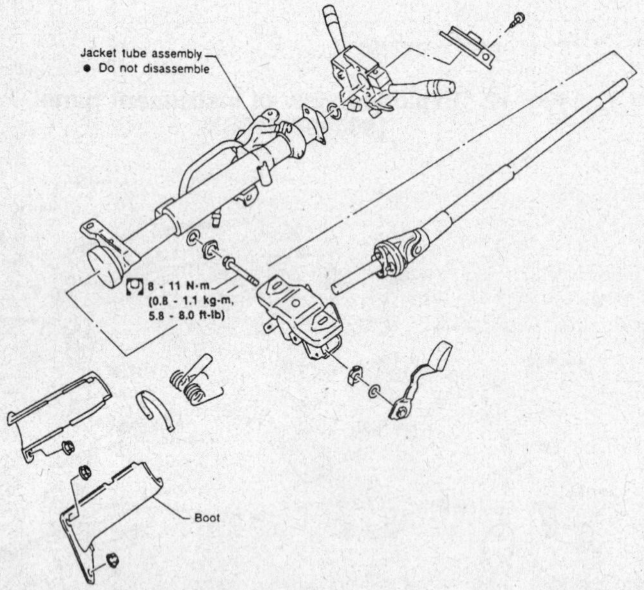

Jacket tube assembly
• Do not disassemble
8 - 11 N·m
(0.8 - 1.1 kg-m,
5.8 - 8.0 ft-lb)
Boot

NS6049100005000X

Fig. 1 Exploded view of steering column. 1993–95 Altima

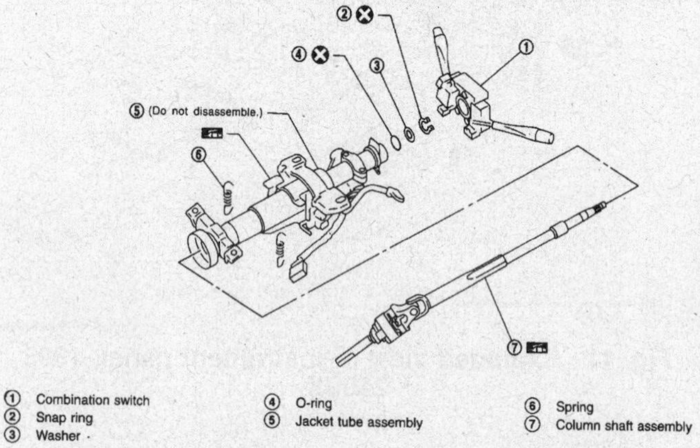

⑤ (Do not disassemble.)
① Combination switch
② Snap ring
③ Washer
④ O-ring
⑤ Jacket tube assembly
⑥ Spring
⑦ Column shaft assembly

NS6049600015000X

Fig. 2 Exploded view of steering column. 1996 Altima

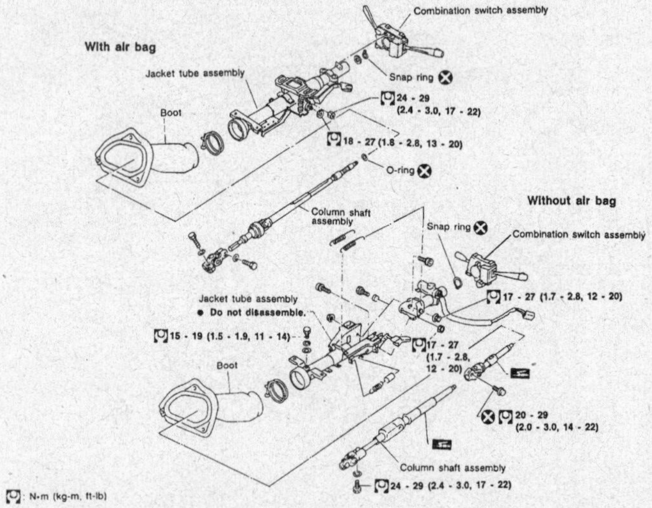

With air bag
Combination switch assembly
Jacket tube assembly
Snap ring
24 - 29 (2.4 - 3.0, 17 - 22)
Boot
18 - 27 (1.8 - 2.8, 13 - 20)
O-ring
Column shaft assembly
Without air bag
Snap ring
Combination switch assembly
17 - 27 (1.7 - 2.8, 12 - 20)
Jacket tube assembly
• Do not disassemble.
15 - 19 (1.5 - 1.9, 11 - 14)
17 - 27 (1.7 - 2.8, 12 - 20)
Boot
20 - 29 (2.0 - 3.0, 14 - 22)
Column shaft assembly
24 - 29 (2.4 - 3.0, 17 - 22)
: N·m (kg-m, ft-lb)

NS6049100006000X

Fig. 3 Exploded view of steering column. 1993–94 Maxima

PRECAUTIONS

AIR BAG SYSTEMS

Refer to "Air Bag System Precautions" in the front of this manual for system disarming and arming procedures.

STEERING COLUMN SERVICE

For steering column service, refer to **Figs. 1 through 13.**

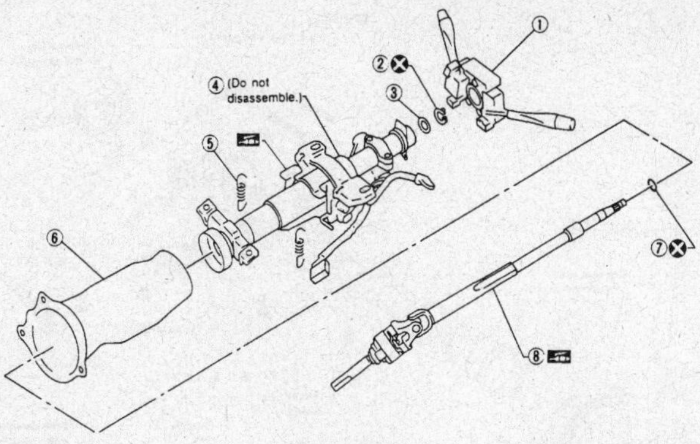
(Do not disassemble.)

1. Combination switch
2. Snap ring
3. Washer
4. Jacket tube assembly
5. Spring
6. Steering column lower cover
7. O-ring
8. Column shaft assembly

NS6049500013000X

Fig. 4 Exploded view of steering column. 1995–96 Maxima

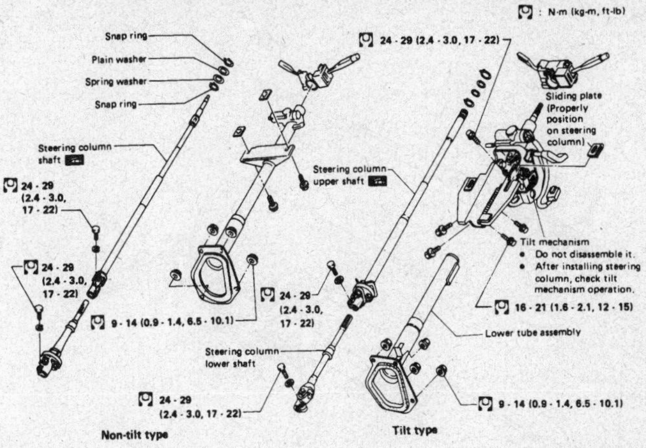
N·m (kg-m, ft-lb)
Snap ring
Plain washer
Spring washer
Snap ring
24 - 29 (2.4 - 3.0, 17 - 22)
Sliding plate (Properly position on steering column)
Steering column shaft
Steering column upper shaft
Tilt mechanism
Do not disassemble it.
After installing steering column, check tilt mechanism operation.
16 - 21 (1.6 - 2.1, 12 - 15)
Lower tube assembly
9 - 14 (0.9 - 1.4, 6.5 - 10.1)
Steering column lower shaft
9 - 14 (0.9 - 1.4, 6.5 - 10.1)
Non-tilt type
Tilt type

NS6049100007000X

Fig. 5 Exploded view of steering column. 1993–95 Pathfinder & Pickup

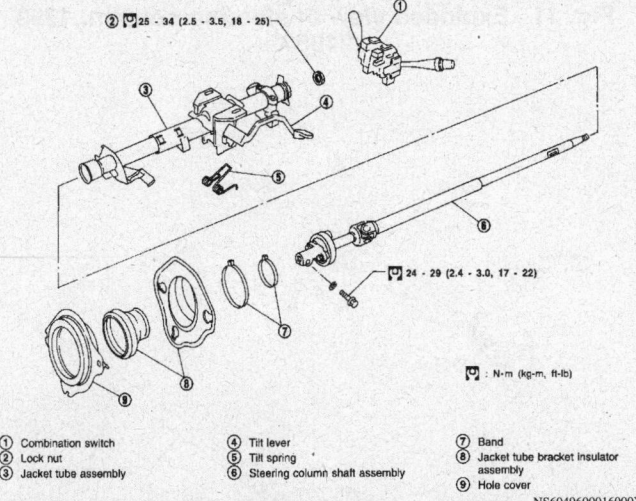

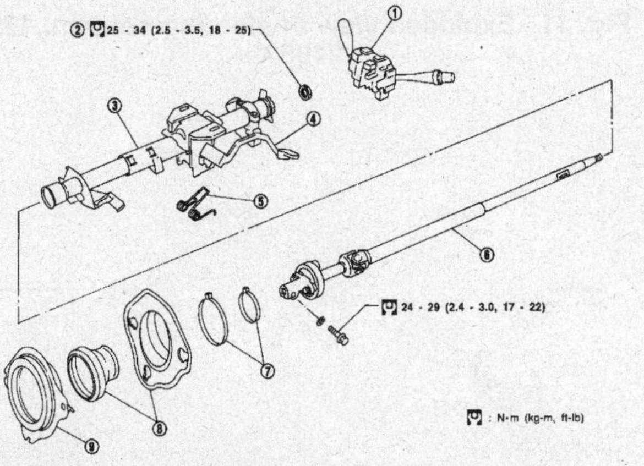
25 - 34 (2.5 - 3.5, 18 - 25)
24 - 29 (2.4 - 3.0, 17 - 22)
N·m (kg-m, ft-lb)

1. Combination switch
2. Lock nut
3. Jacket tube assembly
4. Tilt lever
5. Tilt spring
6. Steering column shaft assembly
7. Band
8. Jacket tube bracket insulator assembly
9. Hole cover

NS6049600016000X

Fig. 6 Exploded view of steering column. 1996 Pathfinder

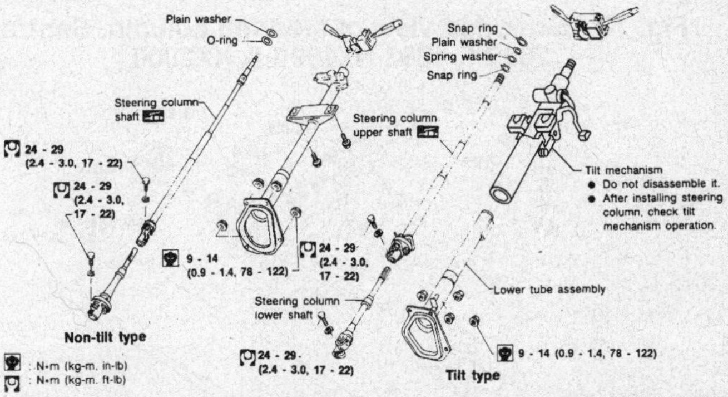
Plain washer
O-ring
Snap ring
Plain washer
Spring washer
Snap ring
Steering column shaft
Steering column upper shaft
24 - 29 (2.4 - 3.0, 17 - 22)
Tilt mechanism
Do not disassemble it.
After installing steering column, check tilt mechanism operation.
9 - 14 (0.9 - 1.4, 78 - 122)
Lower tube assembly
Steering column lower shaft
Non-tilt type
N·m (kg-m, in-lb)
N·m (kg-m, ft-lb)
9 - 14 (0.9 - 1.4, 78 - 122)
Tilt type

NS6049600017000X

Fig. 7 Exploded view of steering column. 1996 Pickup

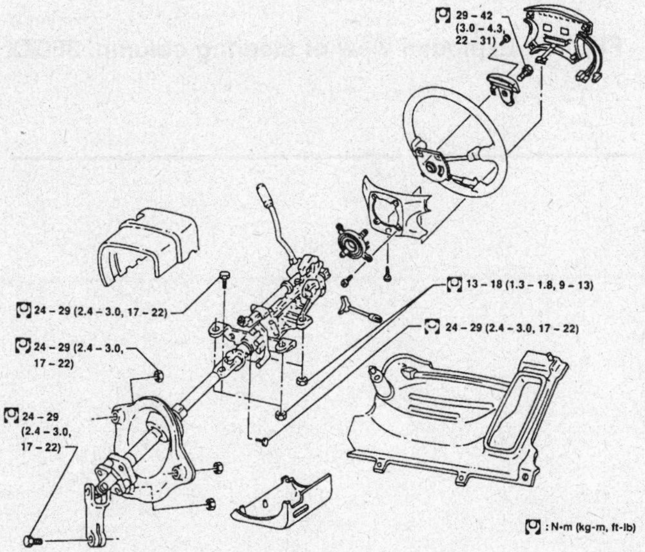
29 – 42 (3.0 – 4.3, 22 – 31)
13 – 18 (1.3 – 1.8, 9 – 13)
24 – 29 (2.4 – 3.0, 17 – 22)
24 – 29 (2.4 – 3.0, 17 – 22)
24 – 29 (2.4 – 3.0, 17 – 22)
24 – 29 (2.4 – 3.0, 17 – 22)
N·m (kg-m, ft-lb)

NS6049100008000X

Fig. 8 Exploded view of steering column. 1993–95 Quest

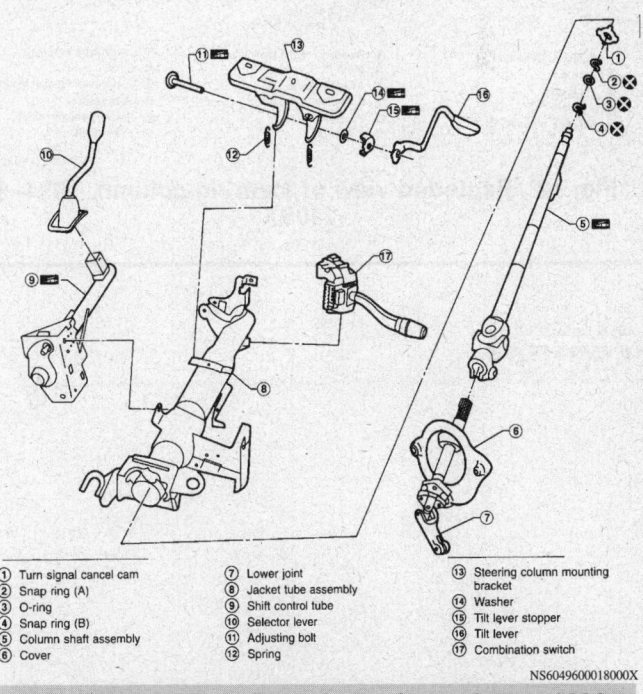

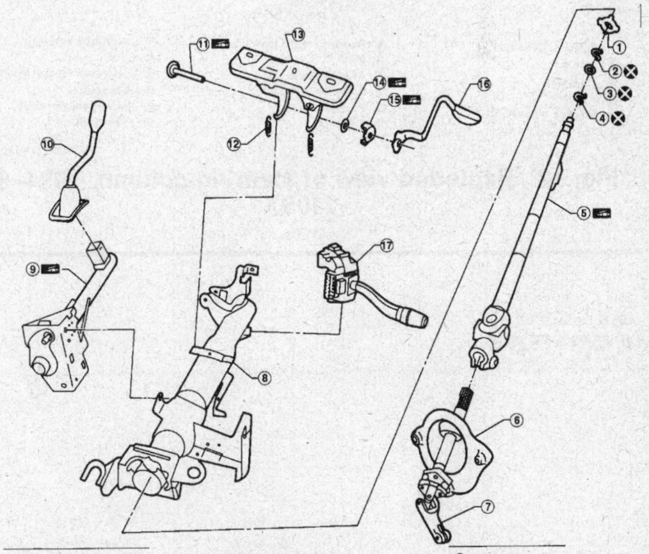

1. Turn signal cancel cam
2. Snap ring (A)
3. O-ring
4. Snap ring (B)
5. Column shaft assembly
6. Cover
7. Lower joint
8. Jacket tube assembly
9. Shift control tube
10. Selector lever
11. Adjusting bolt
12. Spring
13. Steering column mounting bracket
14. Washer
15. Tilt lever stopper
16. Tilt lever
17. Combination switch

NS6049600018000X

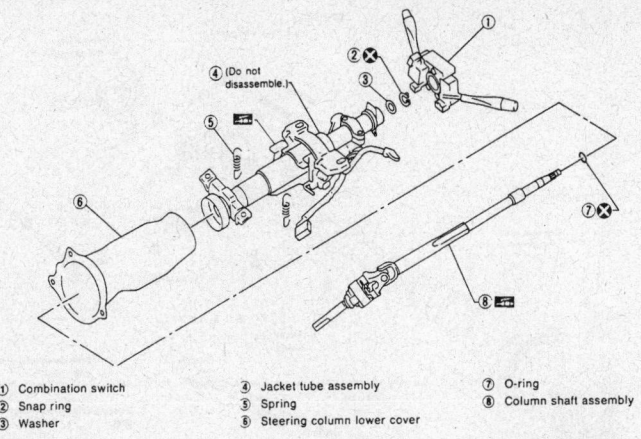

Fig. 9 Exploded view of steering column. 1996 Quest

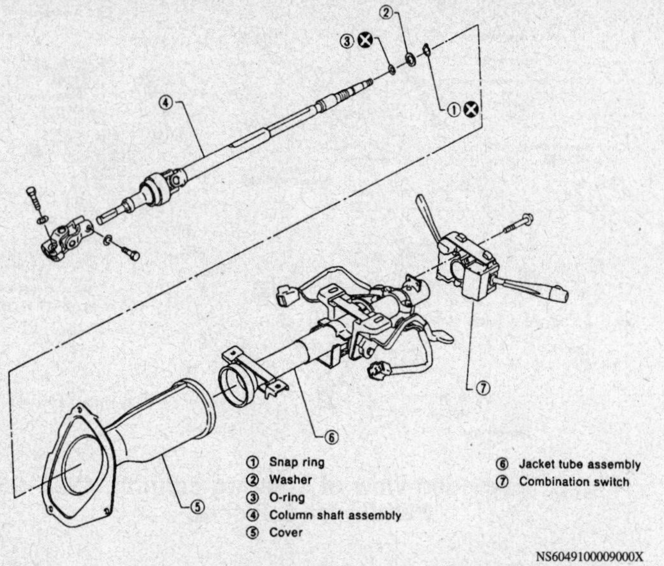
① Snap ring
② Washer
③ O-ring
④ Column shaft assembly
⑤ Cover
⑥ Jacket tube assembly
⑦ Combination switch

NS6049100009000X

Fig. 10 Exploded view of steering column. Sentra, 200SX, 1993 NX1600 & NX2000

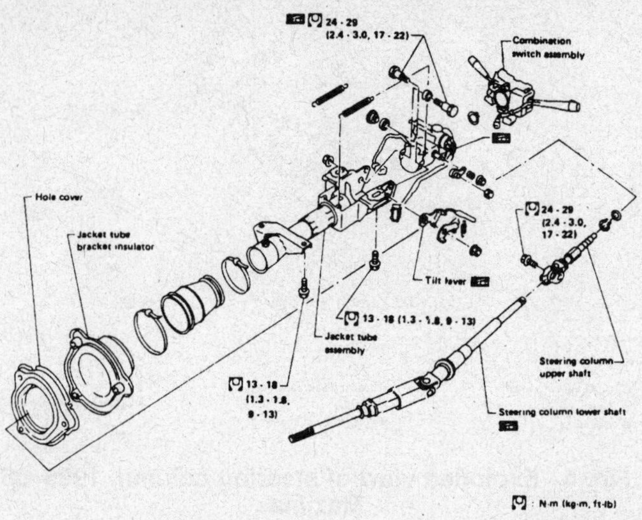
24 - 29
(2.4 - 3.0, 17 - 22)
Combination switch assembly
Hole cover
Jacket tube bracket insulator
24 - 29
(2.4 - 3.0, 17 - 22)
Tilt lever
13 - 18 (1.3 - 1.8, 9 - 13)
Jacket tube assembly
13 - 18
(1.3 - 1.8, 9 - 13)
Steering column upper shaft
Steering column lower shaft
: N·m (kg-m, ft-lb)

NS6049100011000X

Fig. 11 Exploded view of steering column. 1993 240SX

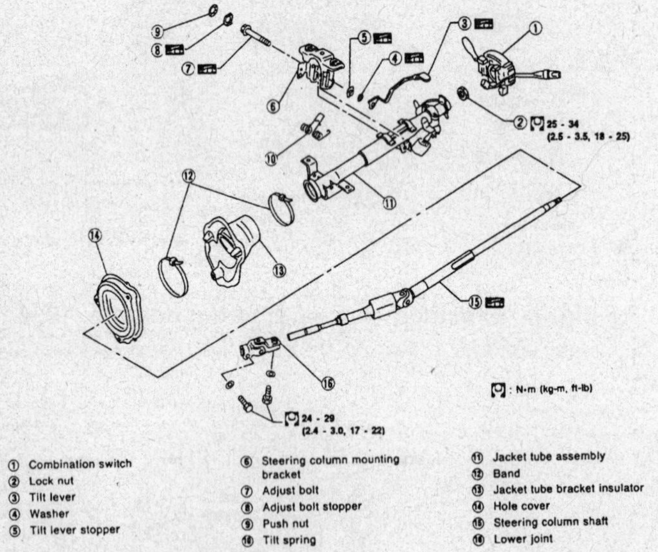
25 - 34
(2.5 - 3.5, 18 - 25)
24 - 29
(2.4 - 3.0, 17 - 22)
: N·m (kg-m, ft-lb)
① Combination switch
② Lock nut
③ Tilt lever
④ Washer
⑤ Tilt lever stopper
⑥ Steering column mounting bracket
⑦ Adjust bolt
⑧ Adjust bolt stopper
⑨ Push nut
⑩ Tilt spring
⑪ Jacket tube assembly
⑫ Band
⑬ Jacket tube bracket insulator
⑭ Hole cover
⑮ Steering column shaft
⑯ Lower joint

NS6049500014000X

Fig. 12 Exploded view of steering column. 1994–96 240SX

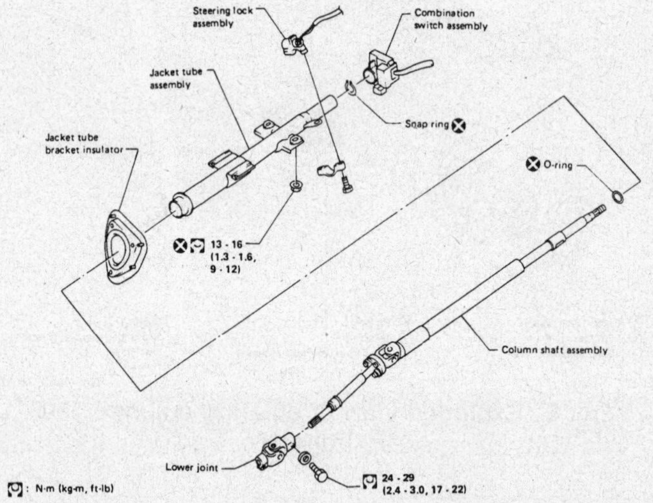
Steering lock assembly
Combination switch assembly
Jacket tube assembly
Snap ring
Jacket tube bracket insulator
O-ring
13 - 16
(1.3 - 1.6, 9 - 12)
Column shaft assembly
Lower joint
24 - 29
(2.4 - 3.0, 17 - 22)
: N·m (kg-m, ft-lb)

NS6049100012000X

Fig. 13 Exploded view of steering column. 300ZX

Manual Steering Gears

NOTE: On Air Bag Equipped Models, Refer To "Air Bag System Precautions" Located In The Front Of This Manual For System Disarming & Arming Procedures.

INDEX

	Page No.
Precautions	36-107
Air Bag Systems	36-107
Rack & Pinion Type	36-108
Assemble	36-108
Disassemble	36-108
Recirculating Ball Type	36-107
Assemble	36-107
Disassemble	36-107
Tightening Specifications	36-108

PRECAUTIONS

AIR BAG SYSTEMS

Refer to "Air Bag System Precautions" in the front of this manual for system disarming and arming procedures.

RECIRCULATING BALL TYPE

DISASSEMBLE

1. Remove filler plug and drain oil.
2. Secure steering gear in vise with suitable holding fixture and set worm gear in straight ahead position.
3. Remove sector shaft cover attaching bolts, **Fig. 1.**
4. Remove sector shaft with sector shaft cover by pushing from opposite end.
5. Remove sector shaft cover from sector shaft.
6. Remove sector shaft oil seal, if necessary.
7. Using tool No. KV48101500, or equivalent, loosen adjusting plug locknut.
8. Remove worm gear with worm bearing.
9. Using suitable tools, remove oil seal from adjusting plug.

ASSEMBLE

Before assembling, lubricate all metal parts with gear oil and apply suitable lubricant in space between sealing lips of new sector shaft and adjusting plug oil seals.

1. Fit worm gear assembly with worm gear bearing in gear housing.
2. Using suitable tool, install adjusting plug.
3. Rotate worm shaft a few turns in both directions to settle worm bearing, then measure worm bearing preload. Preload should be 1.7–5.2 inch lbs.
4. Apply suitable sealant to locknut, install and tighten locknut, then ensure preload is still within specifications.
5. Select and install shaft adjusting screw shim that provides endplay of .0004–.0012 inch between sector shaft and adjusting screw.
6. Coat seal contacting face of oil seal with gear oil, then press oil seal into steering gear housing.

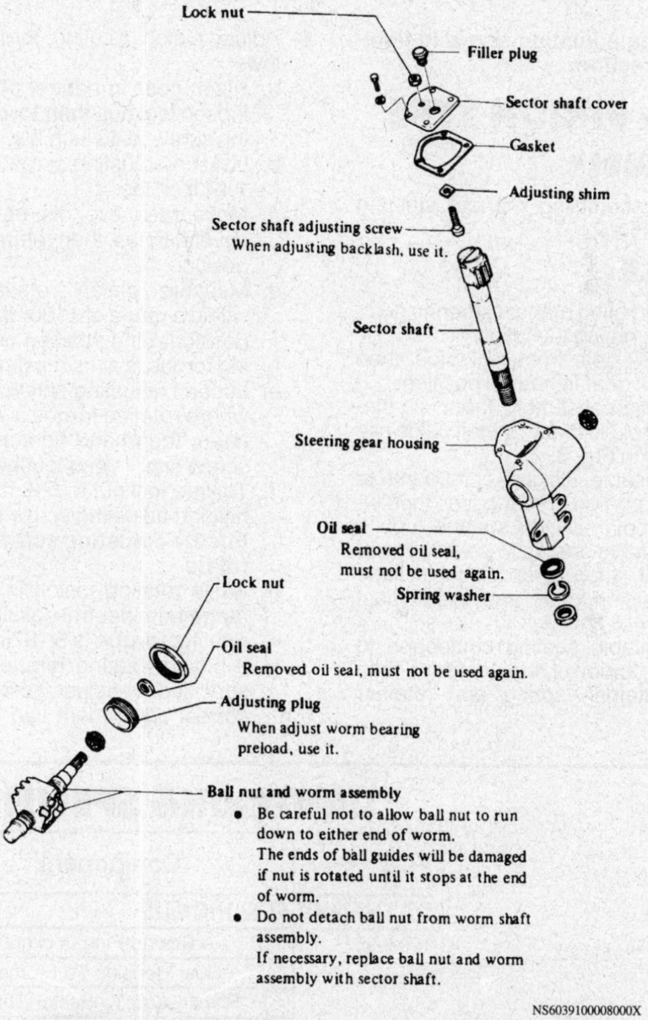

Lock nut
Filler plug
Sector shaft cover
Gasket
Adjusting shim
Sector shaft adjusting screw
When adjusting backlash, use it.
Sector shaft
Steering gear housing
Oil seal
Removed oil seal, must not be used again.
Spring washer
Lock nut
Oil seal
Removed oil seal, must not be used again.
Adjusting plug
When adjust worm bearing preload, use it.
Ball nut and worm assembly
• Be careful not to allow ball nut to run down to either end of worm.
The ends of ball guides will be damaged if nut is rotated until it stops at the end of worm.
• Do not detach ball nut from worm shaft assembly.
If necessary, replace ball nut and worm assembly with sector shaft.
NS6039100008000X

Fig. 1 Recirculating ball type steering gear

7. Install sector cover on adjusting screw with sector shaft.
8. Set worm gear in straight ahead position, then insert sector shaft and sector cover assembly with gasket into gear housing, being careful not to scratch oil seal.
9. **Torque** sector cover attaching bolts to 11–18 ft. lbs.
10. Fill assembly with gear oil and install filler plug.
11. Rotate worm gear a few turns in both directions to settle steering gear, then measure steering gear preload in straight ahead direction. Preload should be 7.4–10.9 inch lbs. **Backlash at gear arm top end should be 0–.004 inch.**
12. If steering gear preload is not within specifications, readjust adjusting screw to obtain correct preload. **Always adjust steering gear preload**

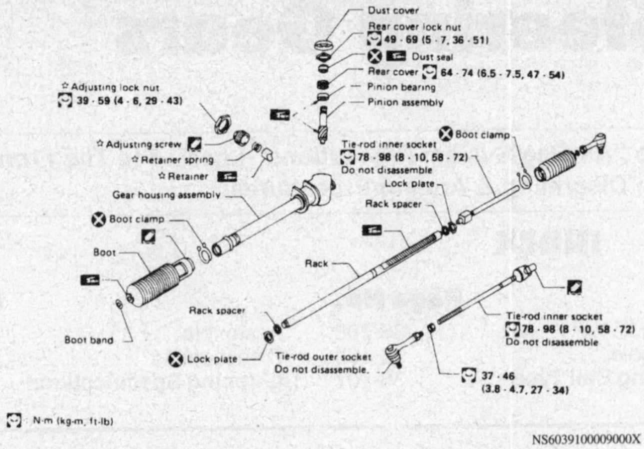
Dust cover
Rear cover lock nut
49 - 69 (5 - 7, 36 - 51)
Dust seal
Rear cover 64 - 74 (6.5 - 7.5, 47 - 54)
Pinion bearing
Pinion assembly
☆ Adjusting lock nut
39 - 59 (4 - 6, 29 - 43)
☆ Adjusting screw
☆ Retainer spring
☆ Retainer
Gear housing assembly
Boot clamp
Boot
Boot band
Tie-rod inner socket
78 - 98 (8 - 10, 58 - 72)
Do not disassemble
Boot clamp
Lock plate
Rack spacer
Rack
Rack spacer
Lock plate
Tie-rod outer socket
Do not disassemble.
Tie-rod inner socket
78 - 98 (8 - 10, 58 - 72)
Do not disassemble
37 - 46
(3.8 - 4.7, 27 - 34)
N·m (kg-m, ft-lb)
NS6039100009000X

Fig. 2 Rack & pinion manual steering gear

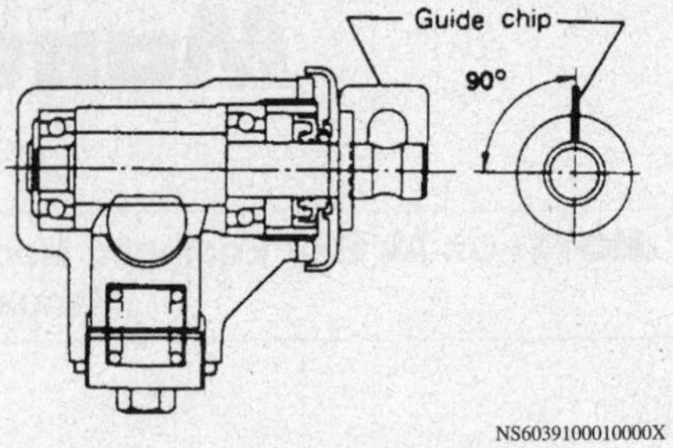
Guide chip
90°
NS6039100010000X

Fig. 3 Pinion guide clip installation

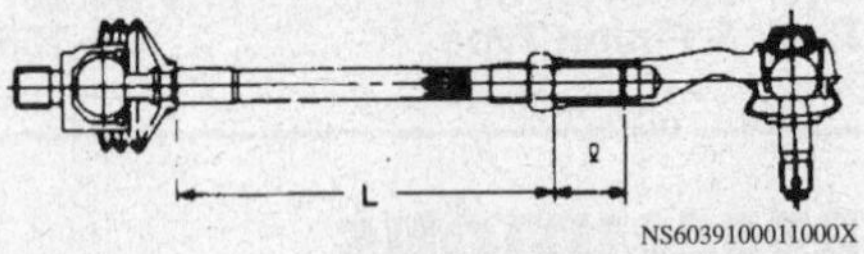
L
ℓ
NS6039100011000X

Fig. 4 Tie rod length adjustment

by turning adjusting screw in tightening direction.

RACK & PINION TYPE

DISASSEMBLE

When disassembling manual steering gear, refer to **Fig. 2**

ASSEMBLE

When assembling manual steering gear, refer to **Fig. 2,** noting the following:

1. Install rack gear from rack side, then place rack gear in neutral position.
2. Install pinion assembly, then with pinion rack held in place, install guide clip as shown in **Fig. 3.**
3. Apply suitable locking compound to threaded portion of rear cover, then install rear cover using a suitable tool.
4. Apply suitable grease to sealing lips of dust seal, then wrap suitable tape around pinion gear and install dust seal.
5. Apply suitable sealing compound to threaded portion of retainer cover, then install retainer, spring and retainer cover.
6. Adjust pinion rotating torque as follows:
   a. Place gear in neutral position and loosen locknut, then **torque** adjusting screw to 43 inch lbs.
   b. Loosen adjusting screw, then re to 1.74 inch lbs.
   c. Move rack over its entire stroke several times, then return to neutral position.
   d. Measure pinion rotating torque within a range of ±180° from neutral position. Find position where rotating torque is at its maximum.
   e. Loosen adjusting screw at position where rotating torque is at its maximum, then hand tighten adjusting screw until its end touches retainer.
   f. **Torque** locknut to 6–8 ft. lbs. while holding adjusting screw in position. **Ensure adjusting screw does not rotate.**
   g. While rotating pinion in the ±100° range from neutral position, ensure rotating **torque** is 6–10 inch lbs.
   h. If pinion rotating torque is not as specified, readjust as required. If correct adjustment can not be obtained, replace retainer spring.
7. Apply suitable locking compound to threaded portion of tie rod inner socket, then install inner socket into rack end together with new lock plate. **Ensure lock plate ratchet enters groove at end portion of rack.**
8. Tighten tie rod inner socket, then bend lock plate at two cutout portions of inner socket. **Remove burrs after bending lock plate to prevent damaging boot.**
9. Tighten outer socket locknut so tie rod length "L" is 6.94 inches and screwed length "l" is .98 inch or more, **Fig. 4.**
10. Measure rack stroke. Ensure stroke is 2.894 inches on both sides.
11. Apply suitable sealing compound to contact surfaces between boot and gear housing, then install boot and boot clamps. **Ensure boot clamps do not interfere with any other parts. Also, use caution not to twist boot.**

TIGHTENING SPECIFICATIONS

Year	Component	Torque/Ft. Lbs.
PATHFINDER & PICKUP		
1993–96	Adjusting Plug Locknut	166–188
	Gear Housing To Frame	62–71
	Pitman Arm To Sector Shaft	174–195
	Sector Shaft Adjusting Locknut	25–40
	Sector Shaft Cover Bolt	33–40
NX 1600, NX 2000, SENTRA & 200SX		
1993–96	Adjusting Screw Locknut	29–43
	Gear Housing Clamp Bolt	54–72
	Rear Cover Locknut	36–51
	Tie Rod Locknut	27–34
	Tie Rod To Gear	58–72
	Tie Rod To Knuckle	22–29

Power Steering

NOTE: On Air Bag Equipped Models, Refer To "Air Bag System Precautions" Located In The Front Of This Manual For System Disarming & Arming Procedures.

INDEX

	Page No.
Application Chart	36-109
Description	36-110
Twin Orifice Power Steering	36-110
Diagnosis & Testing	36-110
Twin Orifice Power Steering	36-110
Power Steering Pressure Specifications	36-109
Power Steering System Service	36-110
Oil Pump Service	36-112
Power Rack & Pinion Type	36-110
Power Recirculating Ball Type	36-110
Precautions	36-110
Air Bag Systems	36-110
Tightening Specifications	36-118

APPLICATION CHART

Model	Year	Rack Id. No.
Altima	1993–96	PR26K
Maxima	1993	PR26SC
	1994–96	PR26AC
Pathfinder	1993	PB56S & PB48S
	1994–95	PB59K & PB48S
	1996	PR32K
Pickup	1993	PB56S & PB48S
	1994–96	PB59K & PB48S
Quest	1993–96	PR28T
Sentra, NX 1600 & NX 2000	1993	PR24SC
	1994	PR24AC
Sentra & 200SX	1995–96	PR24T
240SX	1993–94	PR24SC
	1995–96	PR24AC
300ZX	1993–94	PR26SE
	1995–96	PR26AE

POWER STEERING PRESSURE SPECIFICATIONS

Year	Vehicle	Maximum Pressure At Idle, psi
1993	Altima	1109–1194
	Maxima	1109–1194
	Pickup & Pathfinder	1109–1194
	Quest	1067–1209
	Sentra, Nx 1600 & NX 2000	1109–1194
	240SX	①
	300ZX	②
1994	Altima	1109–1194
	Maxima	1109–1194
	Pickup & Pathfinder	1109–1194
	Quest	1067–1209
	Sentra	1109–1194
	240SX	①
	300ZX	1109–1194

Continued

POWER STEERING PRESSURE SPECIFICATIONS—Continued

Year	Vehicle	Maximum Pressure At Idle, psi
1995	Altima	1109–1194
	Maxima	1180–1126
	Pickup & Pathfinder	1109–1194
	Quest	1067–1209
	Sentra & 200SX	1038–1123
	240SX	1251–1337
	300ZX	1109–1194
1996	Altima	1109–1194
	Maxima	1180–1126
	Pathfinder	1251–1337
	Pickup	1109–1194
	Quest	1067–1209
	Sentra & 200SX	1038–1123
	240SX	1251–1337
	300ZX	1109–1194

①— Main pump, 1038–1123 psi. sub pump for models with 4 wheel steering, 924–995 psi.

②— Main pump, 1109–1194 psi. sub pump for models with 4 wheel steering, 924–995 psi.

PRECAUTIONS

AIR BAG SYSTEMS

Refer to "Air Bag System Precautions" in the front of this manual for system disarming and arming procedures.

DESCRIPTION

TWIN ORIFICE POWER STEERING

The twin orifice power steering system, **Fig. 1,** uses a vehicle speed sensing electronic control design. Valve sensitivity is controlled in response to vehicle speed to achieve maximum steering effort.

When a vehicle speed signal is not entered into the control unit for about 10 seconds during normal operations, a fail safe system activates to maintain a steering effort similar to that of high speed operation. If a foot brake, parking brake or transmission position signal is not entered the steering system is held in a fail safe control state. This symptom is referred to as "Heavy Steering During Stationary Turns."

DIAGNOSIS & TESTING

TWIN ORIFICE POWER STEERING

When diagnosing the twin orifice power steering system refer to **Figs. 2 through 4** for diagnostic procedures.

POWER STEERING SYSTEM SERVICE

POWER RECIRCULATING BALL TYPE

PB48S & PB59K

Only the sealing parts of the gear assembly can be replaced, **Fig. 5.** The internal components of the steering gear must be replaced as an assembly.

Sector Shaft Oil Seal, Replace

1. Remove steering gear and set stub shaft in straight ahead position, which is 2.14 turns from lock position.
2. Remove bolts securing sector shaft cover and free sector shaft and cover by lightly tapping sector shaft with a suitable mallet.
3. Place a roll of plastic film around the end of sector shaft, **Fig. 6,** and remove sector shaft from steering gear.
4. Remove dust cover, snap ring, dust cover special washer, back-up ring and oil seal, as required.
5. Replace O-ring seal on sector shaft cover.
6. Reverse procedure to assemble.

Rear Housing Seal, Replace

1. Remove steering gear from vehicle and mount in a suitable holding fixture.
2. Loosen but do not remove rear housing bolts.
3. Turn sector shaft slightly to raise intermediate cover through piston.
4. Turn stub shaft and place piston (worm gear) in its straight ahead position.
5. Remove sector shaft.
6. Pull out rear housing, intermediate cover, and worm gear as an assembly, **Fig. 7.**
7. To remove rear housing, turn assembly with worm gear facing bench and tap lightly on stub shaft with a suitable mallet.
8. Remove rear housing seal and O-rings from both sides of intermediate cover.
9. To assemble, reverse procedure. Tighten rear housing attaching bolts in a criss-cross pattern.

POWER RACK & PINION TYPE

PR24AC, PR24SC, PR26K, PR26AC, PR26AE, PR26SC, PR26SE & PR32K

Disassemble

When disassembling power steering gears refer to **Figs. 8 through 11,** noting the following:

1. Before disassembling, measure pinion rotating torque and record, then drain fluid.
2. Remove pinion gear, tie rod outer sockets and boots.
3. Loosen tie rod inner socket by prying up staking, then remove retainer and pinion assembly.
4. Drill staked portion of the end cover with a .079–.098 inch drill bit, then remove gear housing end cover and draw rack out of tube.
5. Remove rack seal ring by heating with a heat gun, then replace with a new one by heating and installing by hand.
6. Remove center bushing and rack oil seal with a tape wrapped socket and extension bar.

Pinion Rotating Torque Adjustment

1. With gears at neutral without fluid, coat adjusting screw with locking sealant and install it.
2. Lightly tighten locknut, then **torque** adjusting screw to 43–52 inch lbs. Loosen it, then retorque to .43–1.74 inch lbs.
3. Move rack through entire stroke several times.
4. Measure pinion rotating torque within 180° from neutral and stop at point of greatest resistance.
5. Loosen adjusting screw, then **torque** to 43–52 inch lbs. Loosen adjusting screw 40–60°.
6. If steering gear rack sliding force is not 27.6–37.5 lbs. at neutral point, or 27.6–41.9 lbs. away from neutral point, repeat procedure from step 2. If still not within specifications, replace steering gear.
7. Measure pinion rotating within 100° of neutral point.
8. The maximum value allowable is 3.5 ft. lbs. and the minimum is 16 inch lbs.

Assemble

1. Using seal installation tool No. KV48104400, or equivalent, compress the outside of rack seal ring to position and secure it on rack. **Insert tool on rack from the tooth side.**
2. Use a plastic film to protect rack oil seal from damage from rack teeth and install rack oil seal. Remove plastic film after installation. **Lips of rack oil seal face each other.**
3. Install center bushing and rack oil seal with rack assembly, then tighten cylinder end cover to specifications. Stake housing to secure end cover.
4. Set rack gear in neutral position so that dimension L, **Fig. 12,** is 2.697 inches, then coat pinion oil seal with multi-purpose grease and install into pinion housing. Ensure lip of seal faces up.
5. Install new pinion bearing adjusting shim(s), then install pinion seal ring on pinion gear assembly using a heat gun to heat seal ring before installing.
6. Coat needle bearing roller and oil seal lip with multi-purpose grease and install pinion assembly to housing.
7. Coat rear oil seal lip with multi-purpose grease and install into rear housing, then install rear cover cap as shown in **Fig. 13 and 14.**
8. **On 300ZX models,** install solenoid valve.
9. **On all models,** install diaphragm spring to retainer in the following order; retainer, spring washer, diaphragm spring.
10. Attach lock plate (2), to side rod inner socket (1), then apply locking sealant to inner socket threads and screw inner socket into rack and tighten to specifications. Bend lock plate at two cut out portions.
11. Tighten outer socket nut to specifications, after adjusting dimension L, **Fig. 15,** to 6.96 inches.
12. Measure and adjust rack stroke, then coat rubber boot contact surface with grease and install boot and clamps.

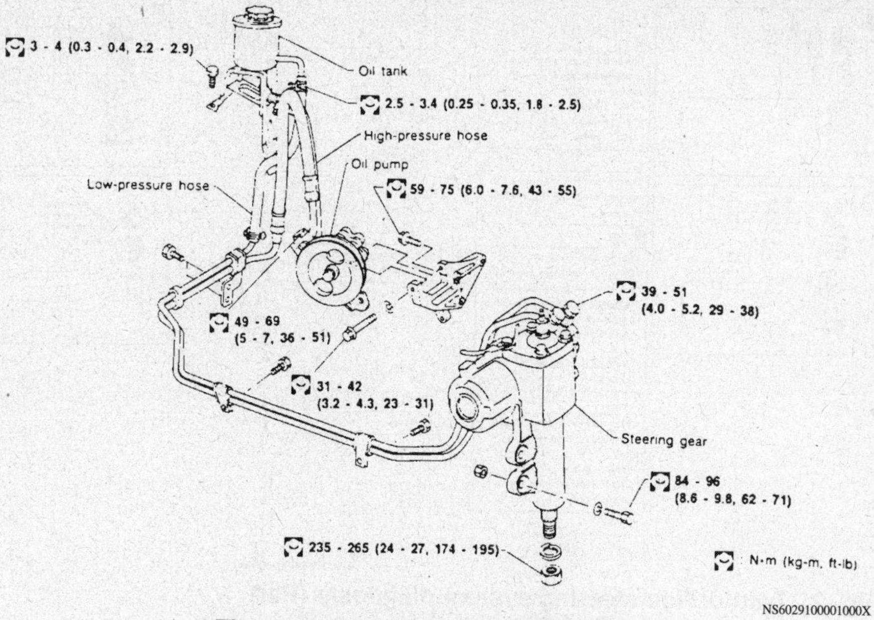
3 - 4 (0.3 - 0.4, 2.2 - 2.9)
Oil tank
2.5 - 3.4 (0.25 - 0.35, 1.8 - 2.5)
High-pressure hose
Oil pump
Low-pressure hose
59 - 75 (6.0 - 7.6, 43 - 55)
39 - 51 (4.0 - 5.2, 29 - 38)
49 - 69 (5 - 7, 36 - 51)
31 - 42 (3.2 - 4.3, 23 - 31)
Steering gear
84 - 96 (8.6 - 9.8, 62 - 71)
235 - 265 (24 - 27, 174 - 195)
N·m (kg-m, ft-lb)
NS6029100001000X

Fig. 1 Twin orifice steering system

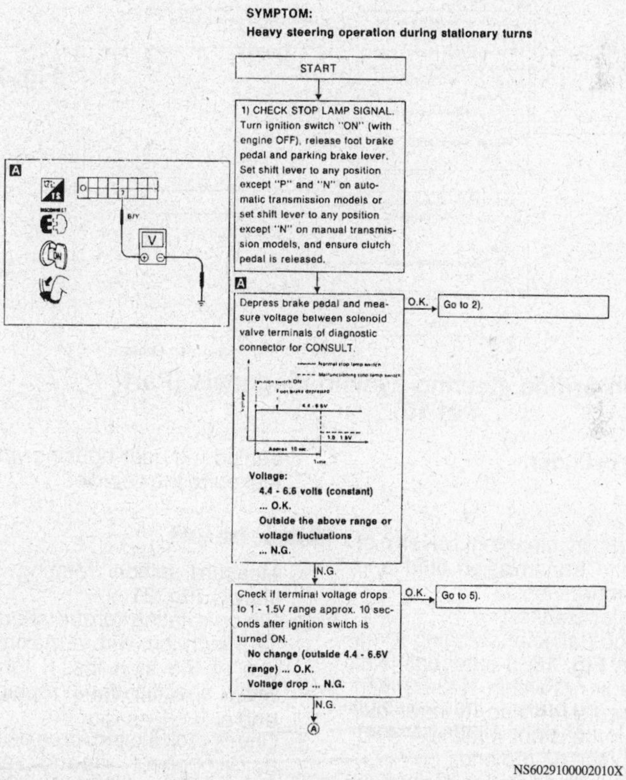
SYMPTOM:
Heavy steering operation during stationary turns
START
1) CHECK STOP LAMP SIGNAL. Turn ignition switch "ON" (with engine OFF), release foot brake pedal and parking brake lever. Set shift lever to any position except "P" and "N" on automatic transmission models or set shift lever to any position except "N" on manual transmission models, and ensure clutch pedal is released.
A
Depress brake pedal and measure voltage between solenoid valve terminals of diagnostic connector for CONSULT.
O.K.
Go to 2).
Voltage:
4.4 - 6.6 volts (constant) ... O.K.
Outside the above range or voltage fluctuations ... N.G.
N.G.
Check if terminal voltage drops to 1 - 1.5V range approx. 10 seconds after ignition switch is turned ON.
No change (outside 4.4 - 6.6V range) ... O.K.
Voltage drop ... N.G.
O.K.
Go to 5).
N.G.
A
NS6029100002010X

Fig. 2 Twin orifice steering system diagnosis (Part 1 of 10)

PR24T & PR28T

When performing repair procedures on this power steering rack, use a vise with soft jaws to hold the steering gear housing. Do not grip the cylinder in a vise.

Disassemble

1. Disconnect gear housing tube and drain fluid, **Fig. 16 and 17.**
2. Measure pinion rotating torque as described under "Adjustment."
3. Remove tie-rod outer sockets and boots.
4. Remove tie-rod inner sockets.
5. **Do not attempt to disassemble gear**

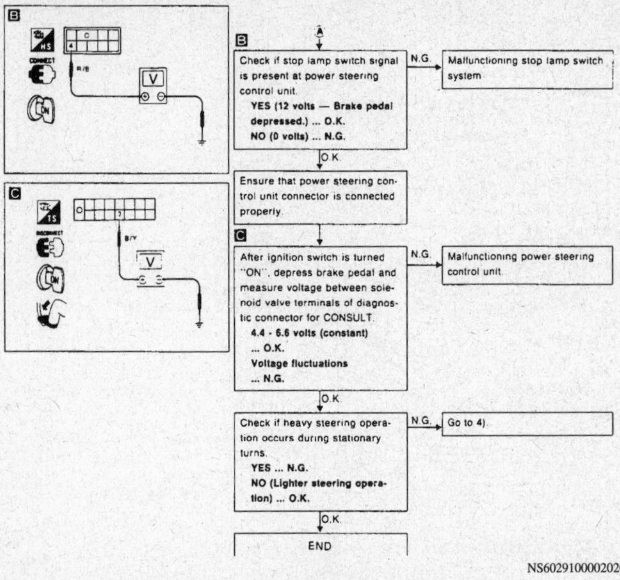
B
Check if stop lamp switch signal is present at power steering control unit.
YES (12 volts — Brake pedal depressed.) ... O.K.
NO (0 volts) ... N.G.
N.G.
Malfunctioning stop lamp switch system
O.K.
Ensure that power steering control unit connector is connected properly.
C
After ignition switch is turned "ON", depress brake pedal and measure voltage between solenoid valve terminals of diagnostic connector for CONSULT.
4.4 - 6.6 volts (constant) ... O.K.
Voltage fluctuations ... N.G.
N.G.
Malfunctioning power steering control unit
O.K.
Check if heavy steering operation occurs during stationary turns.
YES ... N.G.
NO (Lighter steering operation) ... O.K.
N.G.
Go to 4).
O.K.
END
NS6029100002020X

Fig. 2 Twin orifice steering system diagnosis (Part 2 of 10)

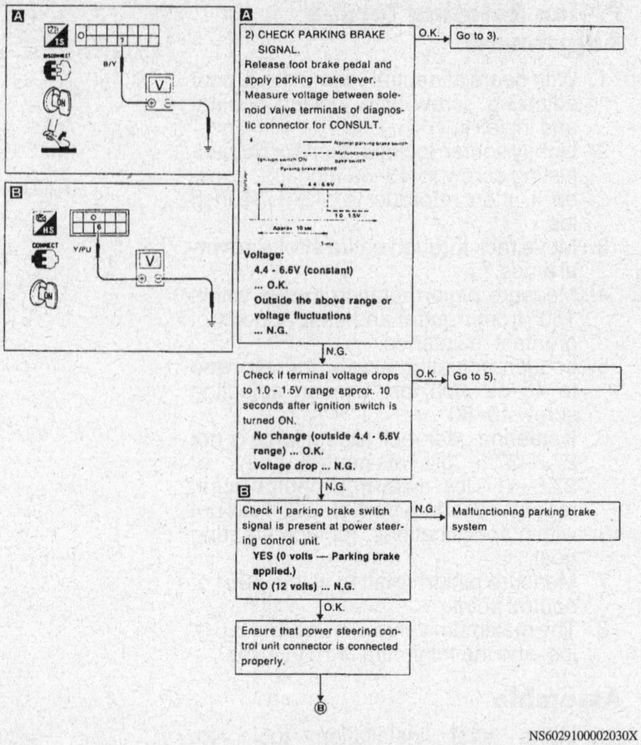
A
2) CHECK PARKING BRAKE SIGNAL.
Release foot brake pedal and apply parking brake lever.
Measure voltage between solenoid valve terminals of diagnostic connector for CONSULT.
O.K.
Go to 3).
Voltage:
4.4 - 6.6V (constant) ... O.K.
Outside the above range or voltage fluctuations ... N.G.
N.G.
Check if terminal voltage drops to 1.0 - 1.5V range approx. 10 seconds after ignition switch is turned ON.
No change (outside 4.4 - 6.6V range) ... O.K.
Voltage drop ... N.G.
O.K.
Go to 5).
N.G.
B
Check if parking brake switch signal is present at power steering control unit.
YES (0 volts — Parking brake applied.)
NO (12 volts) ... N.G.
N.G.
Malfunctioning parking brake system
O.K.
Ensure that power steering control unit connector is connected properly.
NS6029100002030X

Fig. 2 Twin orifice steering system diagnosis (Part 3 of 10)

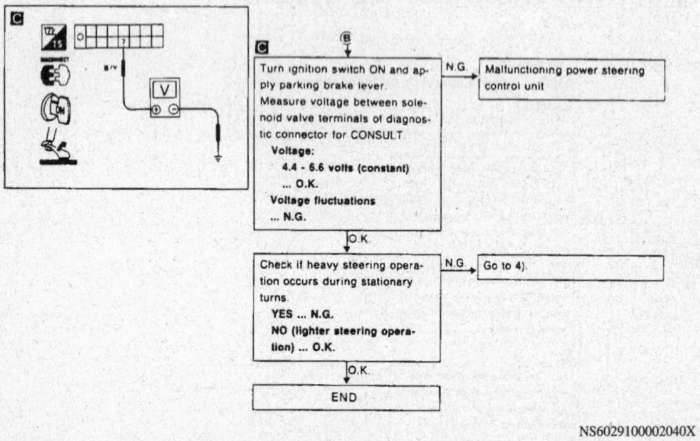
C
Turn ignition switch ON and apply parking brake lever.
Measure voltage between solenoid valve terminals of diagnostic connector for CONSULT.
Voltage:
4.4 - 6.6 volts (constant) ... O.K.
Voltage fluctuations ... N.G.
N.G.
Malfunctioning power steering control unit
O.K.
Check if heavy steering operation occurs during stationary turns.
YES ... N.G.
NO (lighter steering operation) ... O.K.
N.G.
Go to 4).
O.K.
END
NS6029100002040X

Fig. 2 Twin orifice steering system diagnosis (Part 4 of 10)

housing or cylinder.

Inspection

Clean all parts in cleaning solvent or Type F automatic transmission fluid and blow dry with compressed air.

1. Check boot for cracks.
2. Check tie-rod ball joint swinging force as shown in **Fig. 18.** If outer ball joint swing force is not within .4–30.9 inch lbs.; replace tie-rod end. If inner ball joint swing force is not within .04–4.41 inch lbs; replace tie-rod end.
3. Check tie-rod end rotating torque as shown in **Fig. 19.** If rotating torque is not within 1.3–5.5 inch lbs; replace tie-rod end.

Assemble

1. Install tie-rod end inner and outer sockets.
2. Tighten outer socket locknut to specifications.
3. Measure rack stroke as shown in **Fig. 20,** rack stroke should be 2.83 inches. Adjust stroke as necessary.
4. To prevent interference with other parts. Install boot clamps so they are behind the gear housing when it is attached to the vehicle.

Adjustment

1. Measure pinion rotating torque as shown, **Fig. 21.**
2. Pinion rotating torque should be 4.3–12.5 inch lbs. with a maximum deviation of 3.5 inch lbs. If torque is not within specifications, replace steering rack.
3. Check rack sliding force as follows:
   a. Disconnect tie-rod ends from knuckle assembly.
   b. Start engine and bleed air completely.
   c. Disconnect steering column lower joint from gear.
   d. Keep engine at idle speed and make sure steering fluid has reached normal operating temperature.
   e. While pulling tie-rod end slowly in the (±2.56 inch) range from the neutral position, ensure sliding force is less than 60 lbs., **Fig. 22.**
   f. Check rack outside of (±2.56 inch) range, sliding force should not be above 13 lbs.
   g. If sliding force is not within specifications, repeat adjustment procedure.

OIL PUMP SERVICE

When performing this procedure ensure work area is clean. Do not use rags when cleaning parts, use nylon cloths or paper towels. Do not let foreign matter enter or contact parts.

1. Remove snap ring, then draw driveshaft out of pump, **Fig. 23.**
2. Using a screwdriver, remove oil seal.
3. Remove connector, then the control valve from front housing. **Do not drop control valve.**
4. Disassemble remaining parts as shown in **Fig. 23.**
5. Reverse procedure to assemble, noting the following:
   a. Use new seals and O-rings, ensure they are installed properly and in the correct direction.
   b. Cam ring, rotor and vanes must be replaced as a set.
   c. Coat all parts with automatic transmission fluid prior to assembly.
   d. When installing rotor, refer to **Fig. 24,** for correct direction.
   e. When inserting vanes into rotor, rounded surfaces of the vanes must be facing the cam ring side as shown in **Fig. 25.**
   f. **On electronically controlled pumps,** a wave washer is installed instead of the spring.
   g. **On all pumps,** insert pin into groove of front housing, then install the rotor and cam ring as shown in **Fig. 26.**

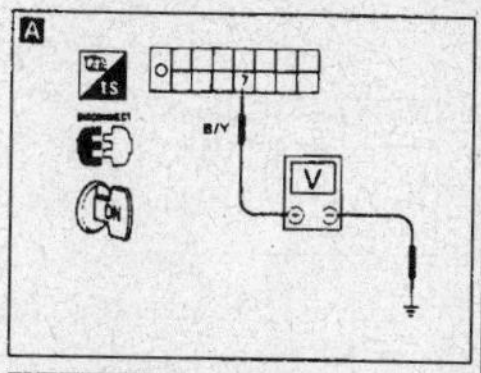
A
B/Y

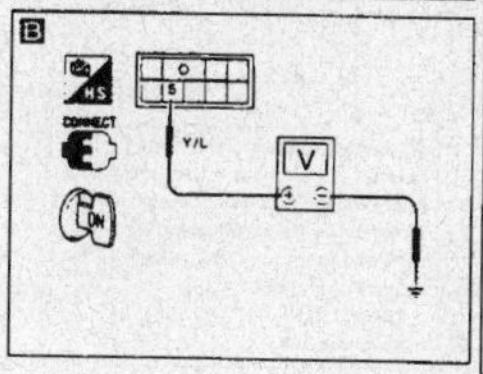
B
Y/L

A

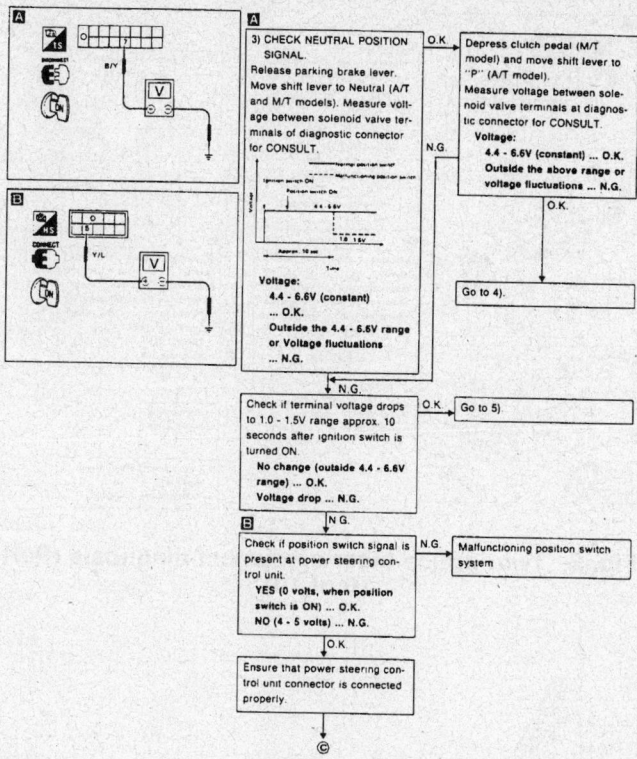

3) CHECK NEUTRAL POSITION SIGNAL.
Release parking brake lever. Move shift lever to Neutral (A/T and M/T models). Measure voltage between solenoid valve terminals of diagnostic connector for CONSULT.

Voltage:
4.4 - 6.6V (constant) ... O.K.
Outside the 4.4 - 6.6V range or Voltage fluctuations ... N.G.

O.K. → Depress clutch pedal (M/T model) and move shift lever to "P" (A/T model).
Measure voltage between solenoid valve terminals at diagnostic connector for CONSULT.
Voltage:
4.4 - 6.6V (constant) ... O.K.
Outside the above range or voltage fluctuations ... N.G.

O.K. → Go to 4).

N.G. ↓

Check if terminal voltage drops to 1.0 - 1.5V range approx. 10 seconds after ignition switch is turned ON.
No change (outside 4.4 - 6.6V range) ... O.K.
Voltage drop ... N.G.

O.K. → Go to 5).

N.G. ↓

B

Check if position switch signal is present at power steering control unit.
YES (0 volts, when position switch is ON) ... O.K.
NO (4 - 5 volts) ... N.G.

N.G. → Malfunctioning position switch system

O.K. ↓

Ensure that power steering control unit connector is connected properly.

↓ ©

NS6029100002050X

Fig. 2 Twin orifice steering system diagnosis (Part 5 of 10)

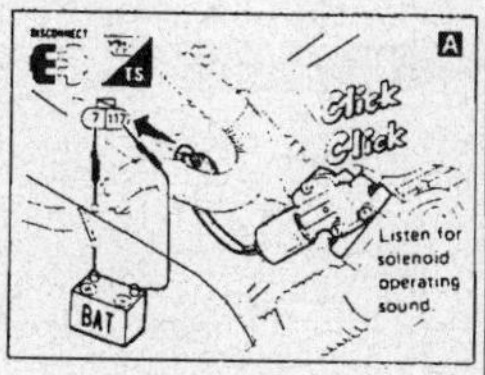
A
Click
Click
Listen for solenoid operating sound.
BAT

A

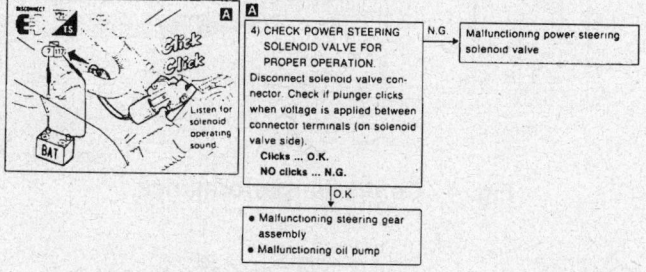

4) CHECK POWER STEERING SOLENOID VALVE FOR PROPER OPERATION.
Disconnect solenoid valve connector. Check if plunger clicks when voltage is applied between connector terminals (on solenoid valve side).
Clicks ... O.K.
NO clicks ... N.G.

N.G. → Malfunctioning power steering solenoid valve

O.K. ↓

- Malfunctioning steering gear assembly
- Malfunctioning oil pump

NS6029100002070X

Fig. 2 Twin orifice steering system diagnosis (Part 7 of 10)

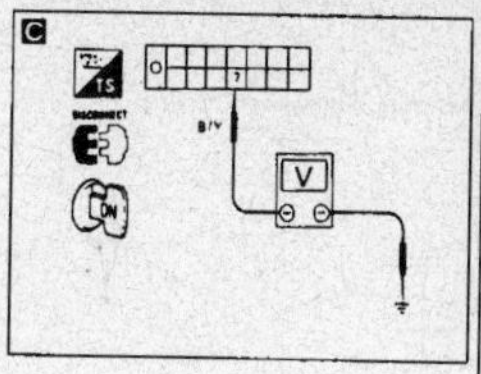
C
B/Y

©

C

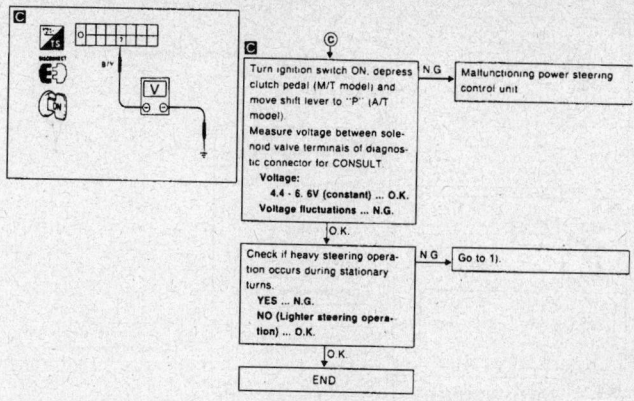

Turn ignition switch ON, depress clutch pedal (M/T model) and move shift lever to "P" (A/T model).
Measure voltage between solenoid valve terminals of diagnostic connector for CONSULT.
Voltage:
4.4 - 6.6V (constant) ... O.K.
Voltage fluctuations ... N.G.

N.G. → Malfunctioning power steering control unit

O.K. ↓

Check if heavy steering operation occurs during stationary turns.
YES ... N.G.
NO (Lighter steering operation) ... O.K.

N.G. → Go to 1).

O.K. ↓

END

NS6029100002060X

Fig. 2 Twin orifice steering system diagnosis (Part 6 of 10)

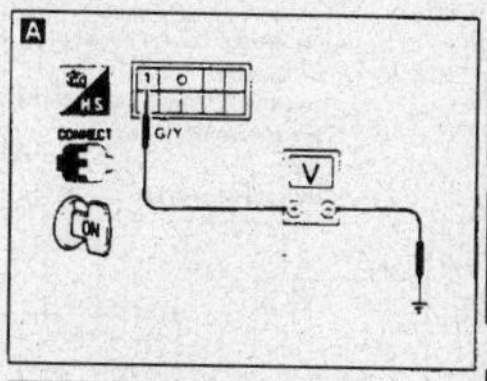
A
G/Y

A

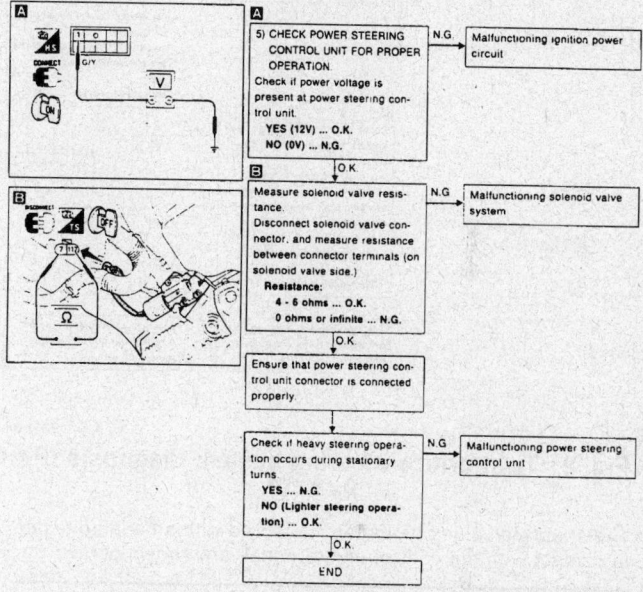

5) CHECK POWER STEERING CONTROL UNIT FOR PROPER OPERATION.
Check if power voltage is present at power steering control unit.
YES (12V) ... O.K.
NO (0V) ... N.G.

N.G. → Malfunctioning ignition power circuit

O.K. ↓

B

Measure solenoid valve resistance.
Disconnect solenoid valve connector, and measure resistance between connector terminals (on solenoid valve side.)
Resistance:
4 - 6 ohms ... O.K.
0 ohms or infinite ... N.G.

N.G. → Malfunctioning solenoid valve system

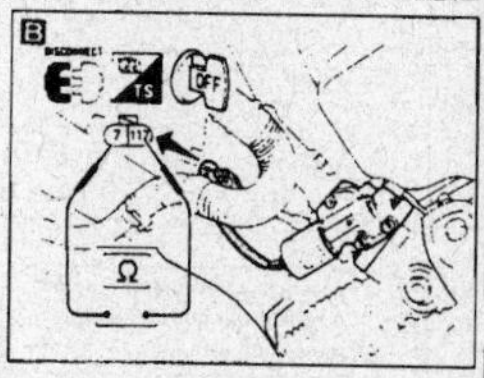
B
OFF
Ω

O.K. ↓

Ensure that power steering control unit connector is connected properly.

↓

Check if heavy steering operation occurs during stationary turns.
YES ... N.G.
NO (Lighter steering operation) ... O.K.

N.G. → Malfunctioning power steering control unit

O.K. ↓

END

NS6029100002080X

Fig. 2 Twin orifice steering system diagnosis (Part 8 of 10)

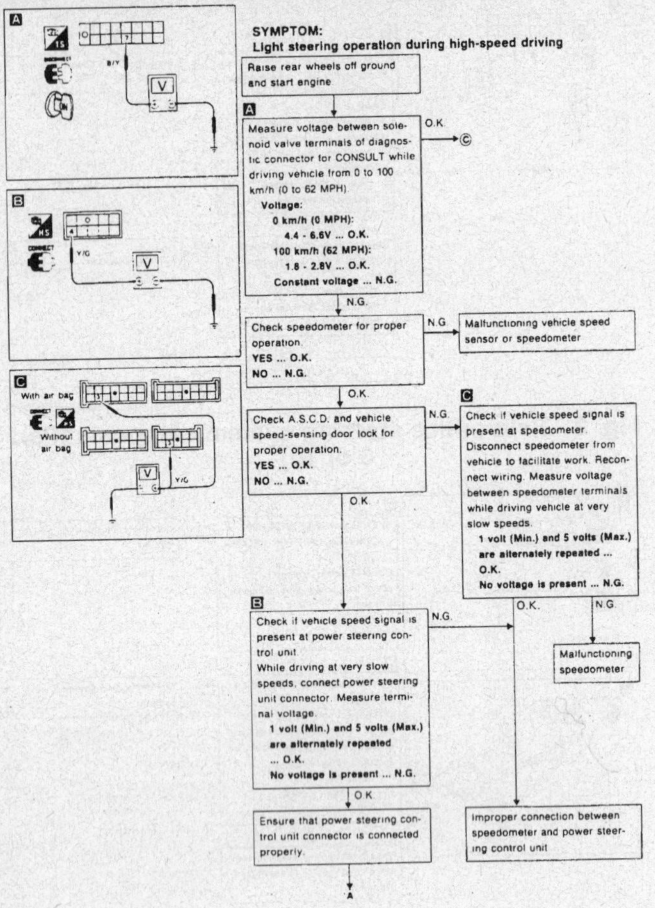
SYMPTOM:
Light steering operation during high-speed driving
Raise rear wheels off ground and start engine.
A
Measure voltage between solenoid valve terminals of diagnostic connector for CONSULT while driving vehicle from 0 to 100 km/h (0 to 62 MPH).
Voltage:
0 km/h (0 MPH):
4.4 - 6.6V ... O.K.
100 km/h (62 MPH):
1.8 - 2.8V ... O.K.
Constant voltage ... N.G.
O.K.
N.G.
Check speedometer for proper operation.
YES ... O.K.
NO ... N.G.
N.G.
Malfunctioning vehicle speed sensor or speedometer
O.K.
Check A.S.C.D. and vehicle speed-sensing door lock for proper operation.
YES ... O.K.
NO ... N.G.
N.G.
C
Check if vehicle speed signal is present at speedometer.
Disconnect speedometer from vehicle to facilitate work. Reconnect wiring. Measure voltage between speedometer terminals while driving vehicle at very slow speeds.
1 volt (Min.) and 5 volts (Max.) are alternately repeated ... O.K.
No voltage is present ... N.G.
O.K.
B
Check if vehicle speed signal is present at power steering control unit.
While driving at very slow speeds, connect power steering unit connector. Measure terminal voltage.
1 volt (Min.) and 5 volts (Max.) are alternately repeated ... O.K.
No voltage is present ... N.G.
N.G.
O.K.
N.G.
Malfunctioning speedometer
O.K.
Ensure that power steering control unit connector is connected properly.
Improper connection between speedometer and power steering control unit
A
With air bag
Without air bag
B/Y
Y/G
V

NS6029100002090X

Fig. 2 Twin orifice steering system diagnosis (Part 9 of 10)

The standard values (voltage), measured with an analog tester in contact with the control unit terminal, are shown below:

Terminal No.	Application	Standard value
1	Power	Approx. 12V
2	Ground	0V
3	Vehicle speed sensor input	1 volt (min.) and 5 volts (max.) are alternately repeated when vehicle is driven at very slow speeds.
4	Stop lamp switch input	Pressed: Approx. 12V Released: 0V
5	Neutral switch input	0V (clutch engaged and shift lever in "N") ... M/T models 0V (selector lever in "N" or "P") ... A/T models 4 - 5V (except for the above)
6	Parking brake switch input	Applied: 0V Released: Approx. 12V
7	Power steering solenoid valve output	0 km/h 4.4 - 6.6V 100 km/h 1.8 - 2.8V Fail-safe 1.0 - 1.5V

NS6029100011000X

Fig. 3 Control unit inspection table

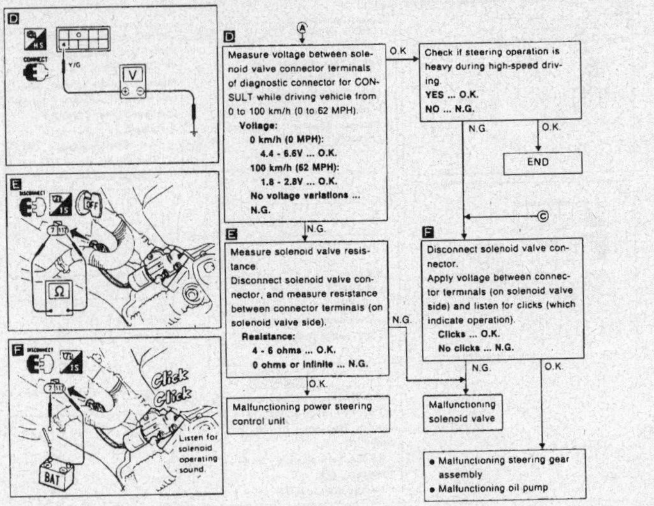
A
D
Measure voltage between solenoid valve connector terminals of diagnostic connector for CONSULT while driving vehicle from 0 to 100 km/h (0 to 62 MPH).
Voltage:
0 km/h (0 MPH):
4.4 - 6.6V ... O.K.
100 km/h (62 MPH):
1.8 - 2.8V ... O.K.
No voltage variations ... N.G.
O.K
Check if steering operation is heavy during high-speed driving.
YES ... O.K.
NO ... N.G.
N.G.
O.K.
END
C
N.G.
E
Measure solenoid valve resistance.
Disconnect solenoid valve connector, and measure resistance between connector terminals (on solenoid valve side).
Resistance:
4 - 6 ohms ... O.K.
0 ohms or infinite ... N.G.
N.G.
O.K.
Malfunctioning power steering control unit
F
Disconnect solenoid valve connector.
Apply voltage between connector terminals (on solenoid valve side) and listen for clicks (which indicate operation).
Clicks ... O.K.
No clicks ... N.G.
N.G.
O.K.
Malfunctioning solenoid valve
• Malfunctioning steering gear assembly
• Malfunctioning oil pump
Click
Click
Listen for solenoid operating sound.
BAT
Y/G
V

NS6029100002100X

Fig. 2 Twin orifice steering system diagnosis (Part 10 of 10)

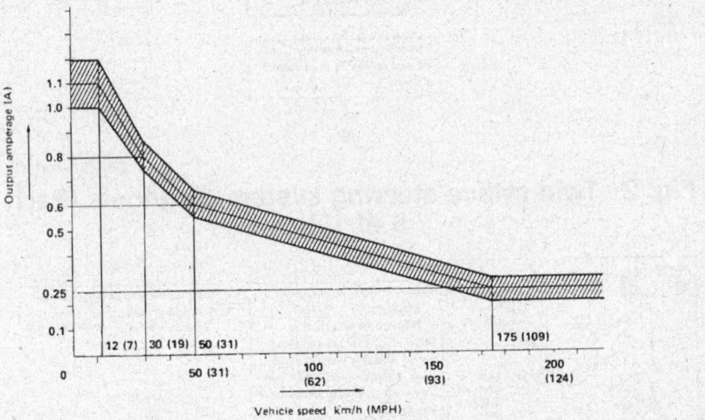
Output amperage (A)
1.1
1.0
0.8
0.6
0.5
0.25
0.1
0
12 (7)
30 (19)
50 (31)
175 (109)
50 (31)
100 (62)
150 (93)
200 (124)
Vehicle speed km/h (MPH)

NS6029100012000X

Fig. 4 Controller performance

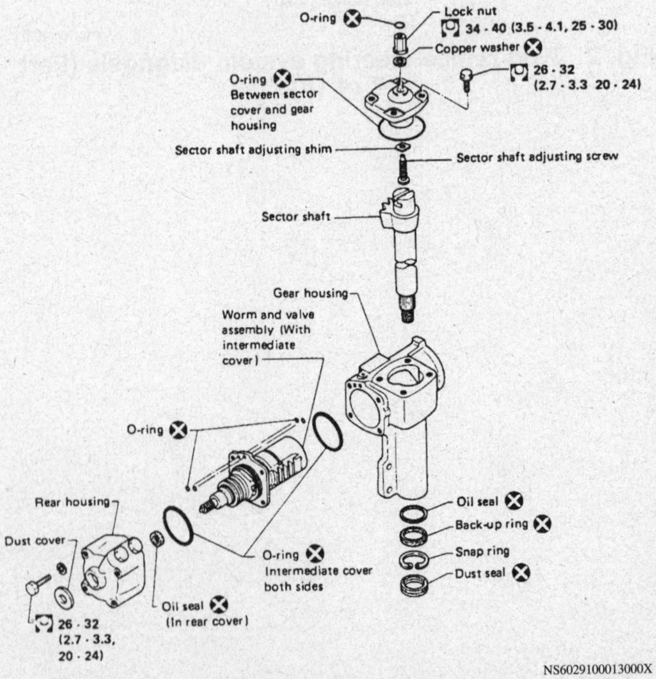
O-ring
Lock nut
34 - 40 (3.5 - 4.1, 25 - 30)
Copper washer
O-ring
Between sector cover and gear housing
26 - 32 (2.7 - 3.3 20 - 24)
Sector shaft adjusting shim
Sector shaft adjusting screw
Sector shaft
Gear housing
Worm and valve assembly (With intermediate cover)
O-ring
Rear housing
Dust cover
Oil seal
Back-up ring
Snap ring
Dust seal
O-ring
Intermediate cover both sides
Oil seal
(In rear cover)
26 - 32
(2.7 - 3.3, 20 - 24)

NS6029100013000X

Fig. 5 Recirculating ball type power steering gear

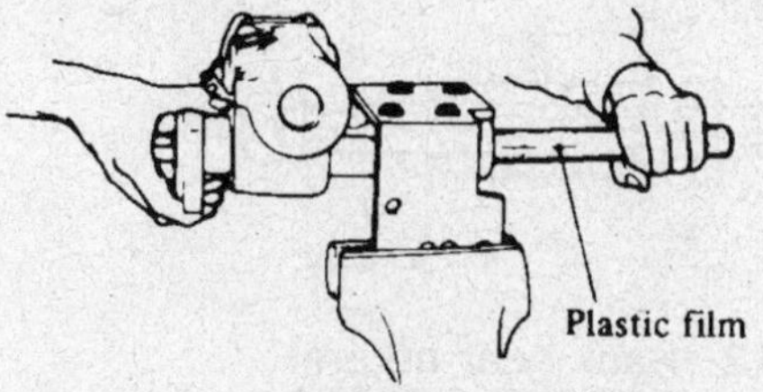
Plastic film

NS6029100014000X

Fig. 6 Sector shaft removal. Recirculating ball type power steering gear

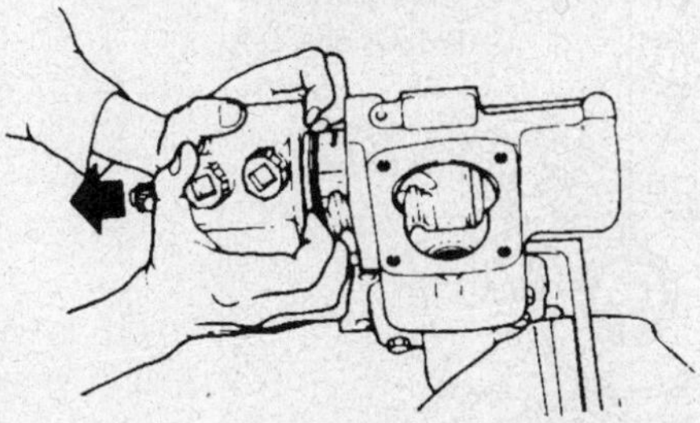

NS6029100015000X

Fig. 7 Rear housing & worm gear removal. Recirculating ball type power steering gear

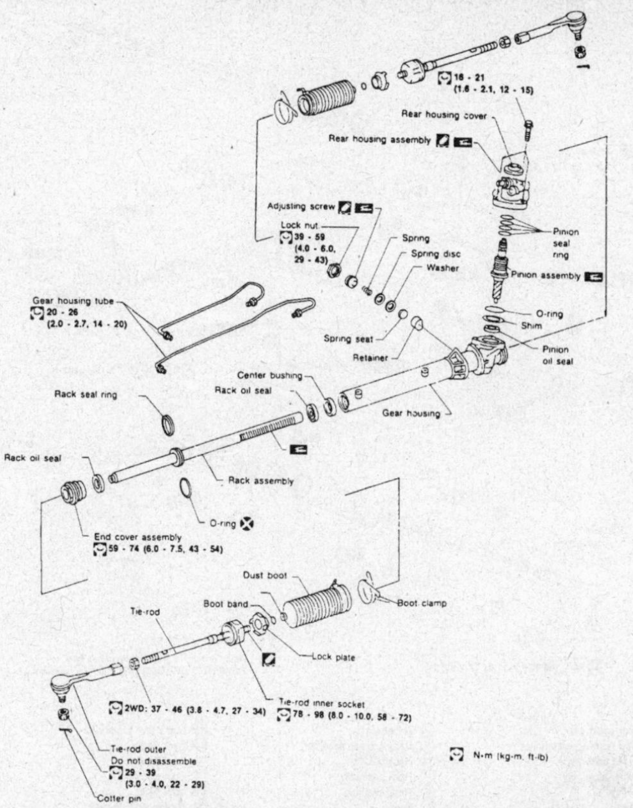
16 - 21
(1.6 - 2.1, 12 - 15)
Rear housing cover
Rear housing assembly
Adjusting screw
Lock nut
39 - 59
(4.0 - 6.0,
29 - 43)
Spring
Spring disc
Washer
Pinion seal ring
Pinion assembly
Gear housing tube
20 - 26
(2.0 - 2.7, 14 - 20)
O-ring
Shim
Spring seat
Retainer
Pinion oil seal
Center bushing
Rack oil seal
Rack seal ring
Gear housing
Rack oil seal
Rack assembly
O-ring
End cover assembly
59 - 74 (6.0 - 7.5, 43 - 54)
Dust boot
Boot band
Boot clamp
Tie-rod
Lock plate
2WD: 37 - 46 (3.8 - 4.7, 27 - 34)
Tie-rod inner socket
78 - 98 (8.0 - 10.0, 58 - 72)
Tie-rod outer
Do not disassemble
29 - 39
(3.0 - 4.0, 22 - 29)
Cotter pin
N·m (kg-m, ft-lb)

NS6029100016000X

Fig. 8 Exploded view of power rack & pinion steering gear. PR24AC, PR24SC, PR26AC & PR26SC

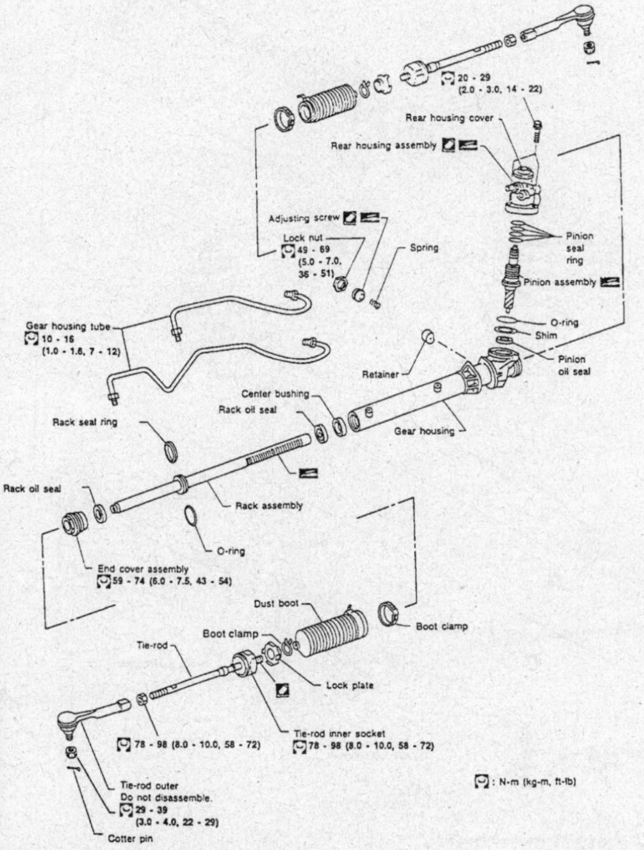
20 - 29
(2.0 - 3.0, 14 - 22)
Rear housing cover
Rear housing assembly
Adjusting screw
Lock nut
49 - 69
(5.0 - 7.0,
36 - 51)
Spring
Pinion seal ring
Pinion assembly
Gear housing tube
10 - 16
(1.0 - 1.6, 7 - 12)
O-ring
Shim
Retainer
Pinion oil seal
Center bushing
Rack oil seal
Gear housing
Rack seal ring
Rack oil seal
Rack assembly
O-ring
End cover assembly
59 - 74 (6.0 - 7.5, 43 - 54)
Dust boot
Boot clamp
Tie-rod
Boot clamp
Lock plate
78 - 98 (8.0 - 10.0, 58 - 72)
Tie-rod inner socket
78 - 98 (8.0 - 10.0, 58 - 72)
Tie-rod outer
Do not disassemble.
29 - 39
(3.0 - 4.0, 22 - 29)
Cotter pin
: N·m (kg-m, ft-lb)

NS6029100017000X

Fig. 9 Exploded view of power rack & pinion steering gear. PR26K

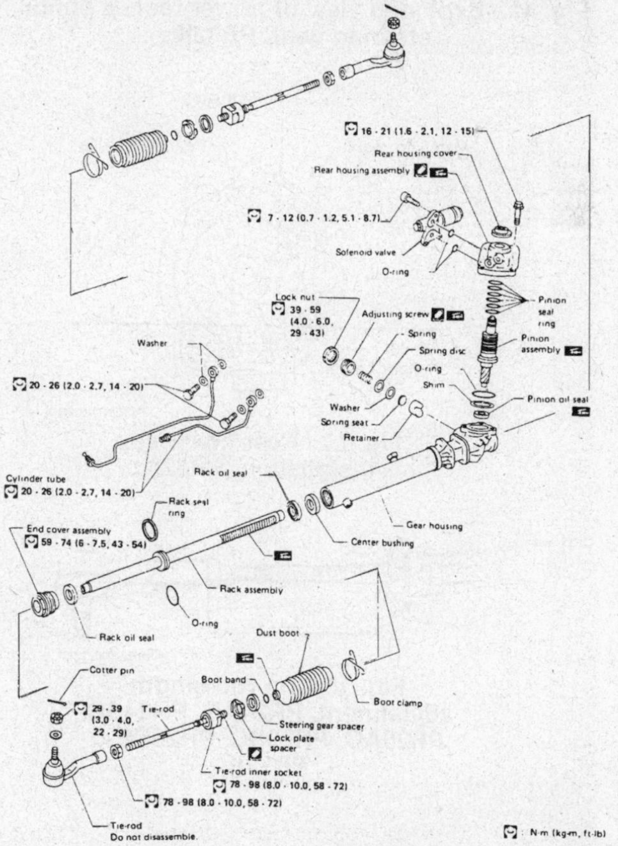
16 - 21 (1.6 - 2.1, 12 - 15)
Rear housing cover
Rear housing assembly
7 - 12 (0.7 - 1.2, 5.1 - 8.7)
Solenoid valve
O-ring
Lock nut
39 - 59
(4.0 - 6.0,
29 - 43)
Adjusting screw
Spring
Spring disc
O-ring
Shim
Pinion seal ring
Pinion assembly
Pinion oil seal
Washer
20 - 26 (2.0 - 2.7, 14 - 20)
Washer
Spring seat
Retainer
Cylinder tube
20 - 26 (2.0 - 2.7, 14 - 20)
Rack oil seal
Rack seal ring
Gear housing
End cover assembly
59 - 74 (6 - 7.5, 43 - 54)
Center bushing
Rack assembly
O-ring
Rack oil seal
Dust boot
Cotter pin
Boot band
Boot clamp
29 - 39
(3.0 - 4.0,
22 - 29)
Tie-rod
Steering gear spacer
Lock plate spacer
Tie-rod inner socket
78 - 98 (8.0 - 10.0, 58 - 72)
78 - 98 (8.0 - 10.0, 58 - 72)
Tie-rod
Do not disassemble.
: N·m (kg-m, ft-lb)

NS6029100018000X

Fig. 10 Exploded view of power rack & pinion steering gear. PR26SE & PR26AE

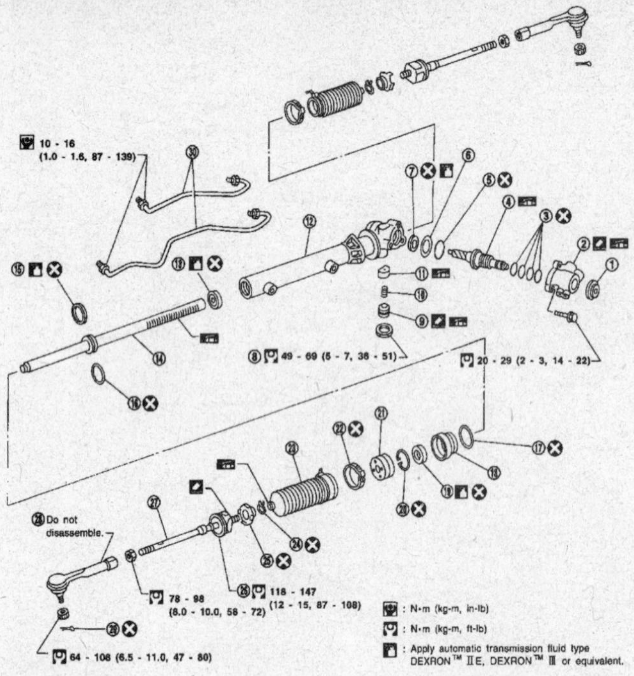
10 - 16
(1.0 - 1.6, 87 - 139)
8 49 - 69 (5 - 7, 36 - 51)
20 - 29 (2 - 3, 14 - 22)
28 Do not disassemble.
78 - 98
(8.0 - 10.0, 58 - 72)
26 118 - 147
(12 - 15, 87 - 108)
64 - 108 (6.5 - 11.0, 47 - 80)
: N•m (kg-m, in-lb)
: N•m (kg-m, ft-lb)
: Apply automatic transmission fluid type DEXRON™ II E, DEXRON™ III or equivalent.

1. Rear cover cap
2. Rear housing assembly
3. Pinion seal ring
4. Pinion assembly
5. O-ring
6. Shim
7. Pinion oil seal
8. Lock nut
9. Adjusting screw
10. Spring
11. Retainer
12. Gear housing assembly
13. Rack oil seal
14. Rack assembly
15. Rack seal ring
16. O-ring
17. O-ring
18. Rack bushing
19. Rack oil seal
20. Snap ring
21. End cover assembly
22. Boot clamp
23. Dust boot
24. Boot clamp
25. Lock plate
26. Tie-rod inner socket
27. Tie-rod
28. Tie-rod outer socket
29. Cotter pin
30. Cylinder tube

NS6029600102000X

Fig. 11 Exploded view of power rack & pinion steering gear. PR32K

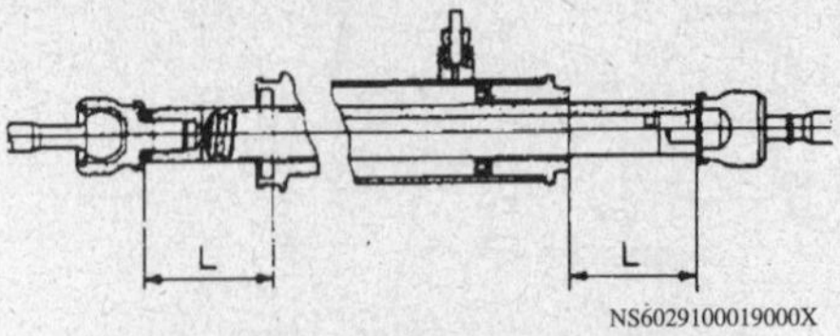
L
L

NS6029100019000X

Fig. 12 Rack gear neutral position. PR24AC, PR24SC, PR26AC, PR26SC, PR26SE & PR32K

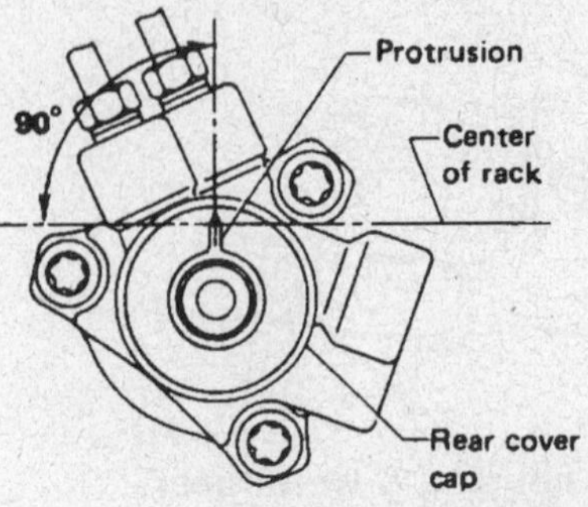
Protrusion
90°
Center of rack
Rear cover cap

NS6029100020000X

Fig. 13 Rear cover cap installation. PR24AC, PR24SC, PR26AC, PR26SC & PR26SE

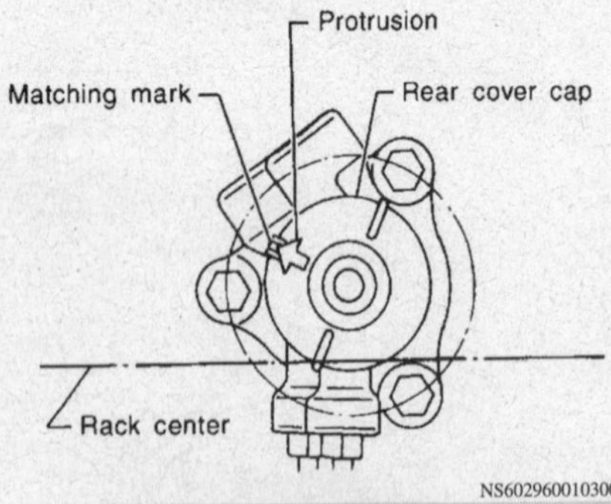
Protrusion
Matching mark
Rear cover cap
Rack center

NS6029600103000X

Fig. 14 Rear cover cap installation. PR32K

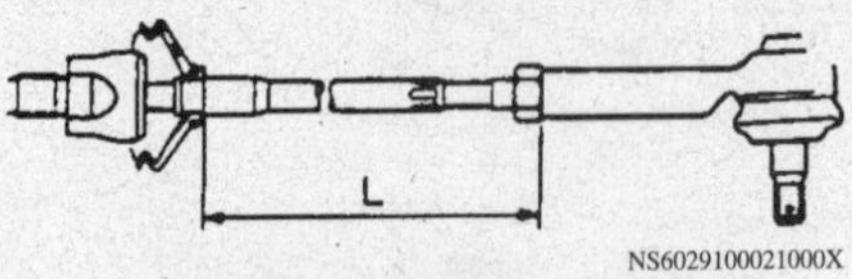
L

NS6029100021000X

Fig. 15 Tie rod length adjustment. PR24AC, PR24SC, PR26AC, PR26SC, PR26SE & PR32K

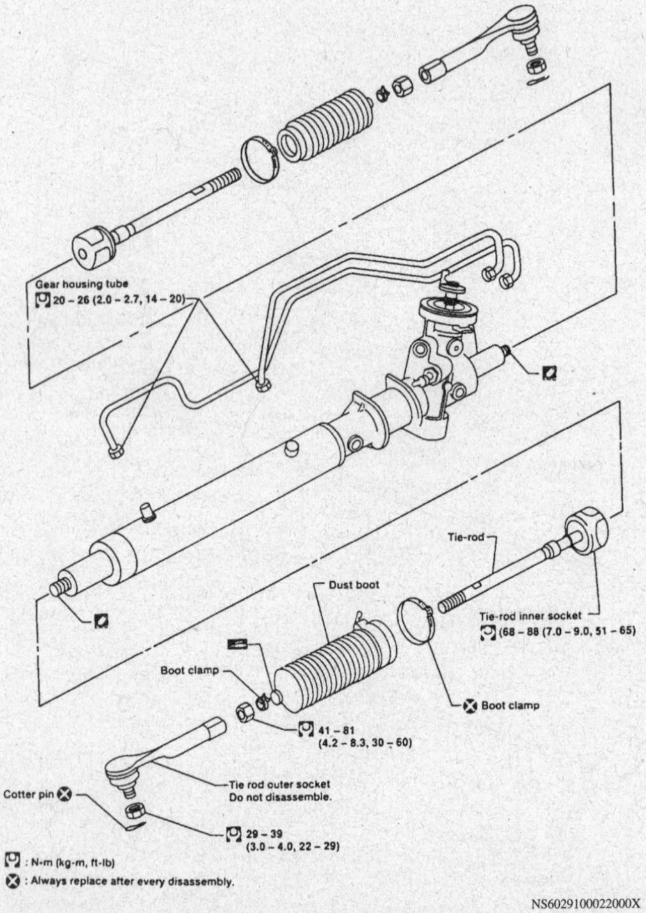
Gear housing tube
20 – 26 (2.0 – 2.7, 14 – 20)
Tie-rod
Dust boot
Tie-rod inner socket
(68 – 88 (7.0 – 9.0, 51 – 65)
Boot clamp
Boot clamp
41 – 81
(4.2 – 8.3, 30 – 60)
Cotter pin
Tie rod outer socket
Do not disassemble.
29 – 39
(3.0 – 4.0, 22 – 29)
: N•m (kg-m, ft-lb)
: Always replace after every disassembly.

NS6029100022000X

Fig. 16 Disassembled view of rack & pinion type power steering gear. PR28T

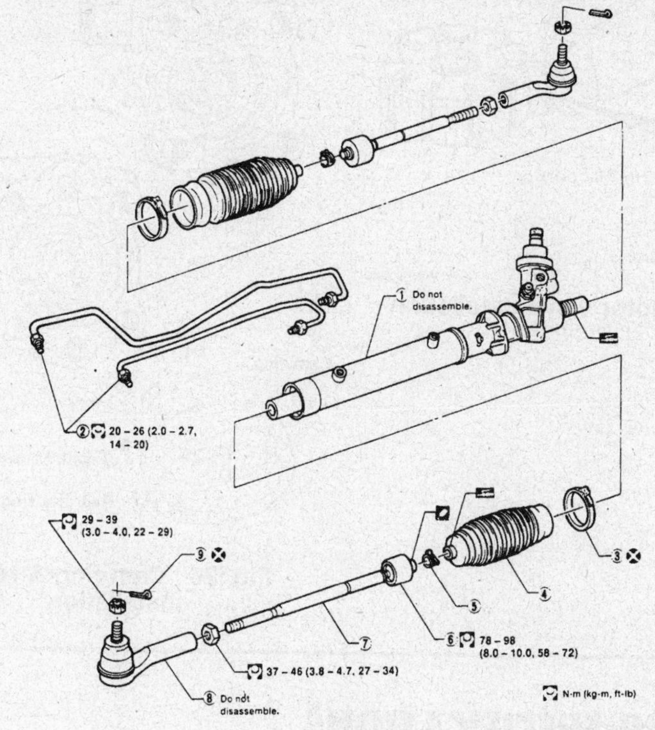
Do not disassemble.
20 - 26 (2.0 - 2.7, 14 - 20)
29 - 39 (3.0 - 4.0, 22 - 29)
78 - 98 (8.0 - 10.0, 58 - 72)
37 - 46 (3.8 - 4.7, 27 - 34)
Do not disassemble.
N·m (kg-m, ft-lb)

① Steering gear
② Gear housing tube
③ Boot clamp
④ Dust boot
⑤ Boot band
⑥ Tie-rod inner socket
⑦ Tie-rod
⑧ Tie-rod outer socket
⑨ Cotter pin

NS6029500099000X

Fig. 17 Disassembled view of rack & pinion type power steering gear. PR24T

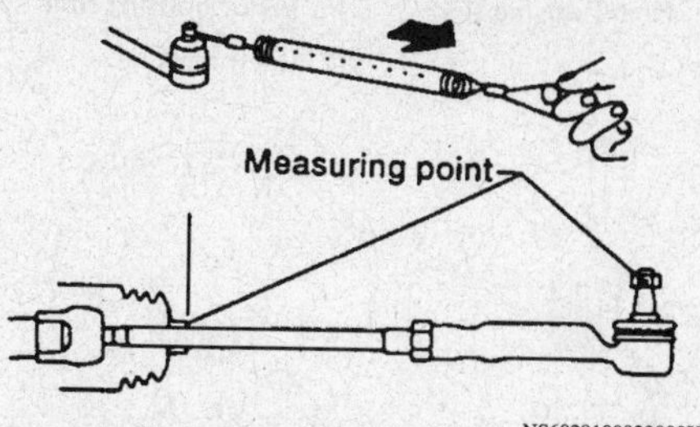
Measuring point

NS6029100023000X

Fig. 18 Tie-rod ball joint swinging force inspection. PR24T & PR28T

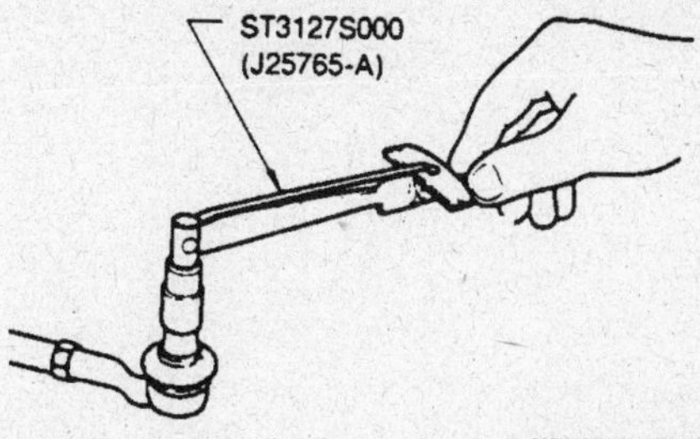
ST3127S000
(J25765-A)

NS6029100024000X

Fig. 19 Tie-rod end rotating torque inspection. PR24T & PR28T

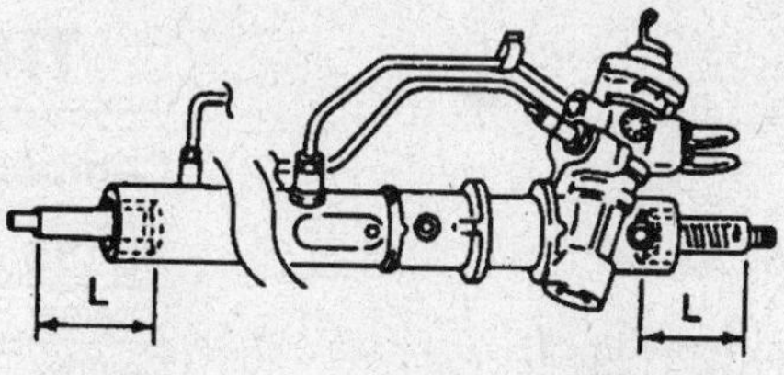
L
L

NS6029100025000X

Fig. 20 Rack stroke measurement. PR28T & PR24T

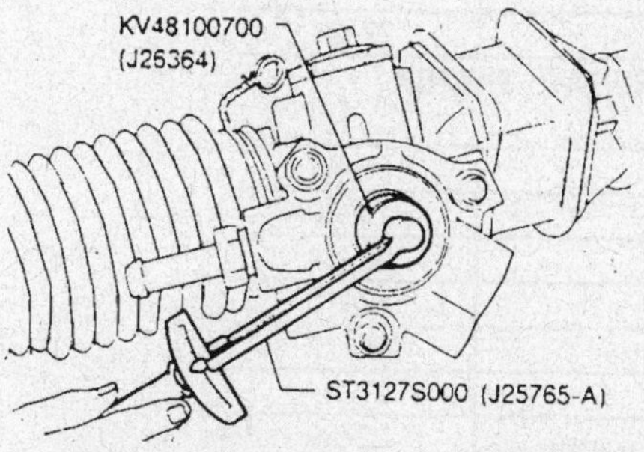
KV48100700
(J26364)
ST3127S000 (J25765-A)

NS6029100026000X

Fig. 21 Pinion rotating torque measurement. PR24T & PR28T

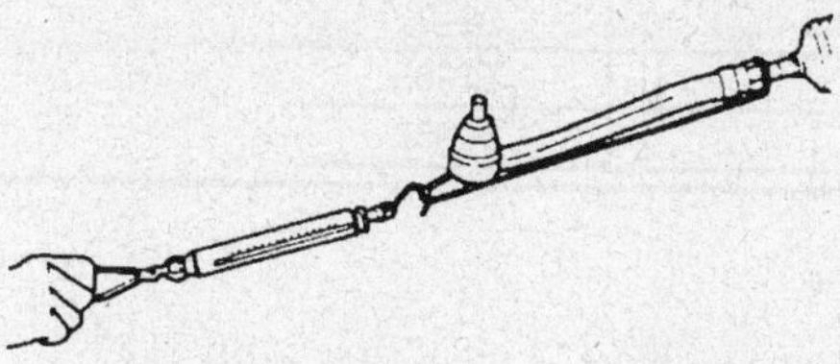

NS6029100027000X

Fig. 22 Rack sliding force measurement. PR24T & PR28T

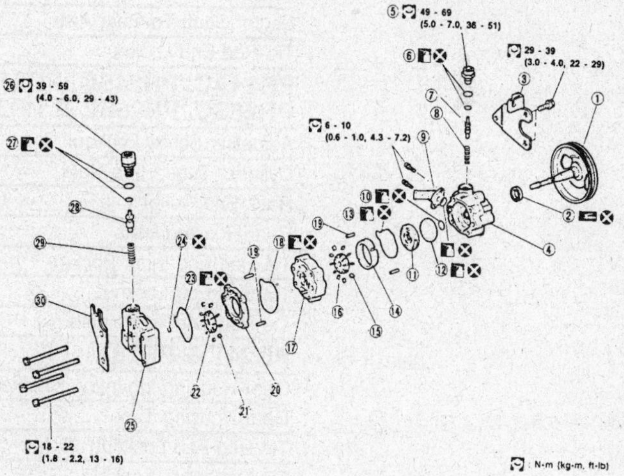
49 - 69 (5.0 - 7.0, 36 - 51)
29 - 39 (3.0 - 4.0, 22 - 29)
39 - 59 (4.0 - 6.0, 29 - 43)
6 - 10 (0.6 - 1.0, 4.3 - 7.2)
18 - 22 (1.8 - 2.2, 13 - 16)
N·m (kg-m, ft-lb)

① Pulley
② Oil seal
③ Bracket
④ Front housing
⑤ Outlet connector
⑥ O-ring
⑦ Flow control valve
⑧ Spring
⑨ Inlet connector
⑩ O-ring
⑪ Side plate
⑫ O-ring
⑬ O-ring
⑭ Cam
⑮ Vane
⑯ Rotor
⑰ Center housing
⑱ O-ring
⑲ Pin
⑳ Cam
㉑ Vane
㉒ Rotor
㉓ O-ring
㉔ Snap ring
㉕ Rear housing
㉖ Outlet connector
㉗ O-ring
㉘ Flow control valve
㉙ Spring
㉚ Bracket

NS6029100028000X

Fig. 23 Exploded view of oil pump assembly

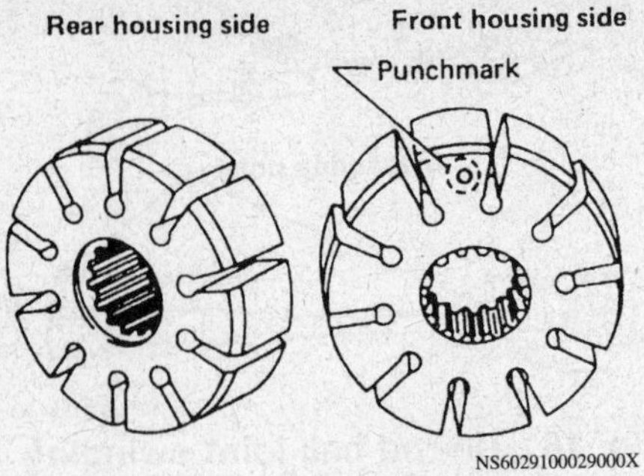
Rear housing side
Front housing side
Punchmark
NS6029100029000X

Fig. 24 Rotor installation

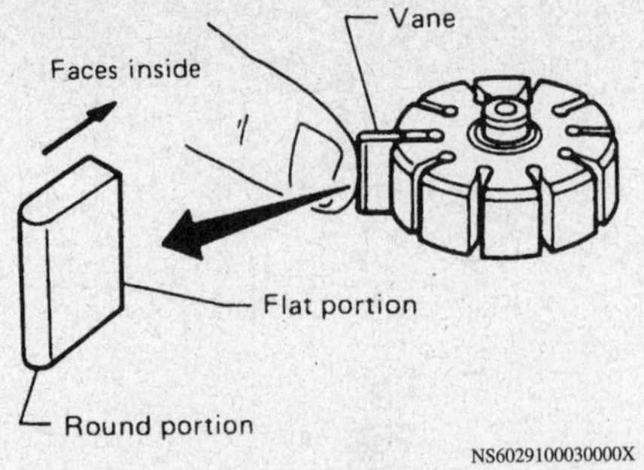
Vane
Faces inside
Flat portion
Round portion
NS6029100030000X

Fig. 25 Rotor vane installation

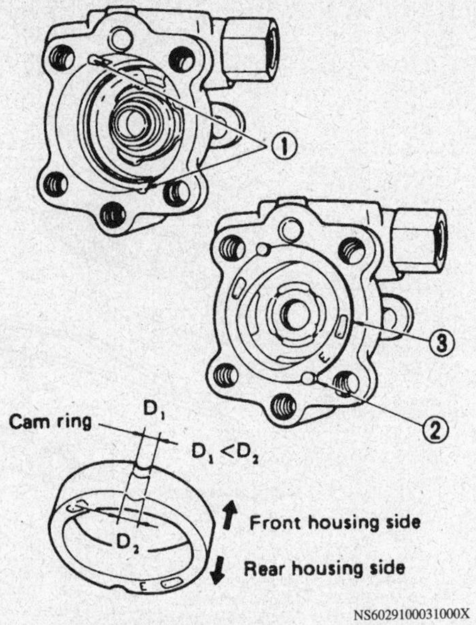
①
③
②
Cam ring
D1
D1 <D2
D2
Front housing side
Rear housing side
NS6029100031000X

Fig. 26 Cam ring & rotor installation

TIGHTENING SPECIFICATIONS

Component	Torque/Ft. Lbs.
PB48S & PB59K	
Breather Screw	5–7
Cylinder Tube Flare Nuts	14–20
Gear Housing Cover Bolts	20–24
Rear Housing Bolts	20–24
Sector Shaft Locknut	21–25
Sector Shaft To Gear Arm	94–108
Tie Rod End Locknut	27–34
PR24AC, PR24SC, PR26AC, PR26AE, PR26K, PR26SC, PR26SE & PR32K	
Adjusting Screw Locknut	29–43
Cylinder Tube Flare Nuts	14–20
Rack End Cover	43–54
Rear Housing Bolts	12–15
Tie Rod End Inner Socket	58–72
Tie Rod End Locknut	27–34
Tie Rod End To Spindle	22–29
PR24T & PR28T	
Gear Housing Mounting Bracket	54–72
Gear Housing Tube	14–20
Tie Rod End Locknut	22–29
Tie Rod Inner Socket	51–65
Tie Rod Outer Socket Nut	30–60

Four Wheel Steering

INDEX

	Page No.
Description	36-119
Diagnosis & Testing	36-119
Inspection	36-119
Fluid Level Inspection	36-119
HICAS System Operation	36-119
Leak Inspection	36-119
System Service	36-119
Hydraulic System Bleed	36-120
Oil Pump Service	36-120
Power Cylinder Service	36-119

DESCRIPTION

The Super HICAS system is comprised of a steering angle sensor, power steering solenoid, control unit and actuator.

INSPECTION

FLUID LEVEL INSPECTION

Maintain fluid level so that the lower surface of the float is maintained between the L and H marks on the gauge rod. The fluid level should be checked when the engine is stopped and the fluid temperature is above 86°F. Recommended fluid is Dexron type automatic transmission fluid. **Never over fill.**

LEAK INSPECTION

Check lines for proper attachment, leaks, cracks, damage, loose connections, chafing and deterioration. Fluid leakage should be checked for when oil temperature in normal with engine idling.

HICAS SYSTEM OPERATION

Ensure shift lever is in the Park position on models with automatic transmission or in Neutral position on models with manual transmissions before checking HICAS system operations.

Consult Tool

1. Have an assistant inside vehicle then raise and support vehicle in such a way to allow all four wheel to spin freely.
2. Connect consult tool to diagnostic connector and start engine.
3. Tough START on consult tool display.
4. Touch HICAS, ACTIVE TEST and SIMULATED DRIVE in that order.
5. Touch START when MAIN SIGNALS displayed is reversed.
6. Touch START. After simulated drive condition has continued for five minutes, it will automatically cancel and Consult tool will then show TEST IS INTERRUPTED TO AVOID OIL TEMP. RISE display. **To cancel this mode during self diagnosis, touch CANCEL.**
7. Operate engine at speeds greater than 2000 RPM and turn steering wheel 180° in one direction from the neutral position.
8. Measure extension value of one power cylinder rod and retraction value of the other, **Fig. 1.**
9. Turn steering wheel 180° in opposite direction from the neutral position and measure extension and retraction of power cylinder rod.
10. Determine strokes of respective power cylinder by adding measured extension and retraction values.
11. **Measure rod strokes in as short a period of time as possible.**
12. Specification for when steering wheel is turned to the right or left is .12 inch, with a total stroke of .24 inch.

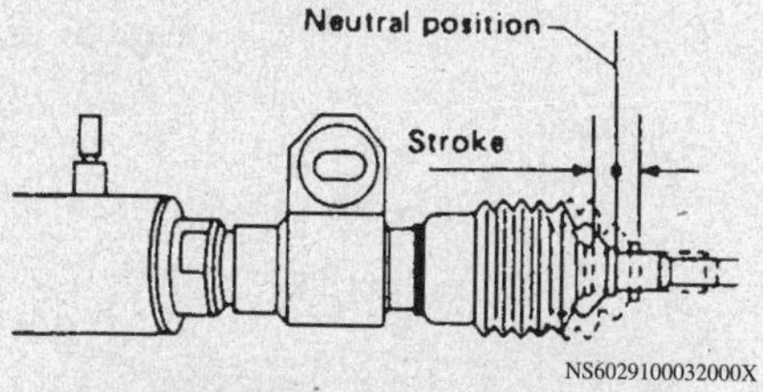
Neutral position
Stroke
NS6029100032000X

Fig. 1 Measuring rod strokes

HICAS Warning Light

1. Have an assistant inside vehicle then raise and support vehicle in such a way to allow all four wheel to spin freely.
2. Set HICAS system in self diagnosis as follows:
   a. Turn ignition switch to Off position.
   b. Position shift lever in Park or Neutral position on models with automatic transmission or Neutral on models with manual transmissions.
   c. Turn ignition switch to On position.
   d. Immediately start engine.
   e. Turn steering wheel from left to right at least 20° from the neutral position five times or more then depress foot brake pedal at least five times within 10 seconds after ignition switch has been turned On. **Do not depress foot brake pedal during operation check, or operation will stop.**
3. Place steering wheel to a point approximately 10° from the neutral position and check to ensure rear wheels turn to the left and right alternately.
4. Operate engine at speeds greater than 2000 RPM and turn steering wheel 180° in one direction from the neutral position.
5. Measure extension value of one power cylinder rod and retraction value of the other, **Fig. 1.**
6. Turn steering wheel 180° in opposite direction from the neutral position and measure extension and retraction of power cylinder rod.
7. Determine strokes of respective power cylinder by adding measured extension and retraction values.
8. **Measure rod strokes in as short a period of time as possible.**
9. Specification for when steering wheel is turned to the right or left is .12 inch, with a total stroke of .24 inch.

DIAGNOSIS & TESTING

SYSTEM SERVICE

POWER CYLINDER SERVICE

Replacement

Detach power cylinder lower links from axle housing sockets using suitable tool, then disconnect oil pipes from power cylinder and remove power cylinders, **Fig. 2.**

Before installing power cylinder on suspension member, wipe power cylinder bracket and mating surface of suspension member. Using the left side of the bracket as a reference point, locate the right side oblong hole and install power cylinder. Install power cylinder and oil pipes. After installation check toe in and bleed hydraulic system.

Overhaul

1. Remove dust boot clamps and move boots toward outer links, **Fig. 3.**
2. Attach wrenches to left and right ball joint sockets and turn in direction shown in **Fig. 4.** Remove one of the loosened lower links.
3. Loosen stroke stopper nut from lower link assembly and remove stroke stopper.
4. While holding width across flats section of rod end from which stroke stopper was removed, remove other lower link assembly.
5. Reverse procedure to assemble, noting the following:
   a. Apply Loctite to inner ball joint threads.
   b. After installing stroke stopper, loosen locknut which secures stroke stopper.
   c. Turn stroke stopper until clearance between inner ball joint and stroke stopper is .12 inch on each side, **Fig. 5.**
   d. **Torque** locknut to 36–51 ft. lbs.
   e. Recheck clearance between inner ball joint and stroke stopper on each side.

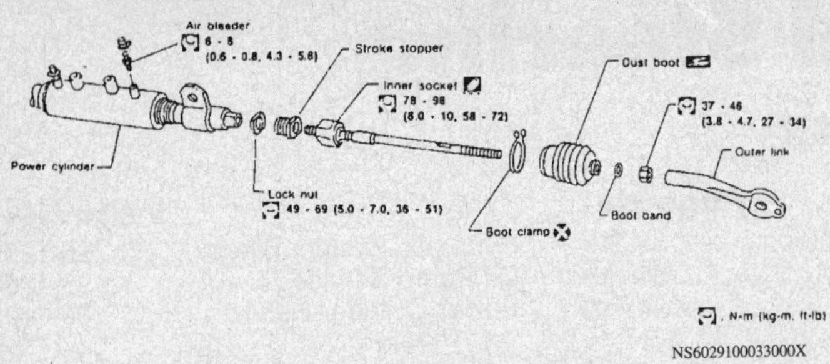
Air bleeder
6 - 8
(0.6 - 0.8, 4.3 - 5.8)
Stroke stopper
Inner socket
78 - 98
(8.0 - 10, 58 - 72)
Dust boot
37 - 46
(3.8 - 4.7, 27 - 34)
Outer link
Power cylinder
Lock nut
49 - 69 (5.0 - 7.0, 36 - 51)
Boot clamp
Boot band
N·m (kg-m, ft-lb)
NS6029100033000X

Fig. 2 Power cylinder removal

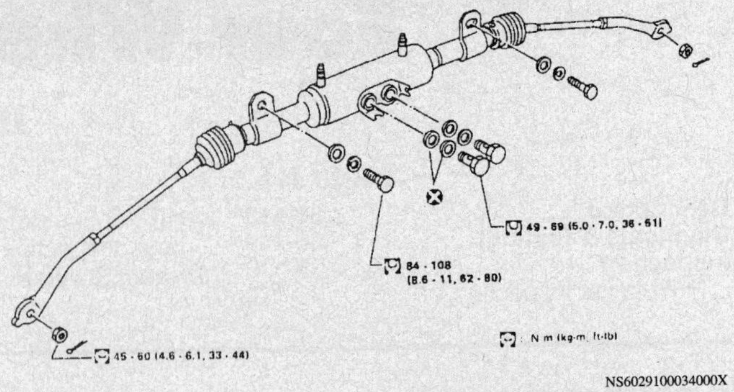
49 - 69 (5.0 - 7.0, 36 - 51)
84 - 108
(8.6 - 11, 62 - 80)
45 - 60 (4.6 - 6.1, 33 - 44)
N·m (kg-m, ft-lb)
NS6029100034000X

Fig. 3 Exploded view of power cylinder

NS6029100035000X

Fig. 4 Lower link removal

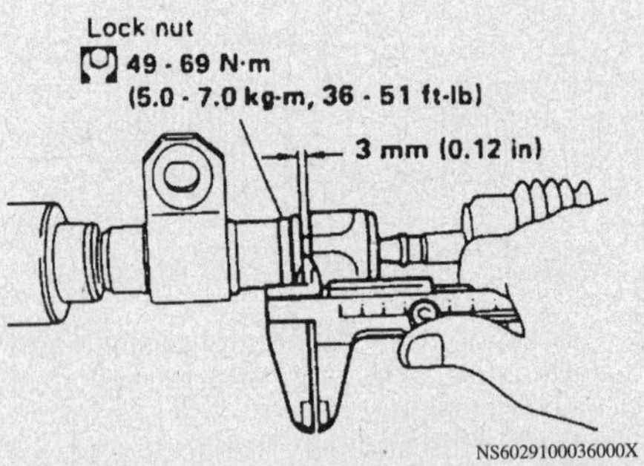
Lock nut
49 - 69 N·m
(5.0 - 7.0 kg-m, 36 - 51 ft-lb)
3 mm (0.12 in)
NS6029100036000X

Fig. 5 Stroke stopper removal

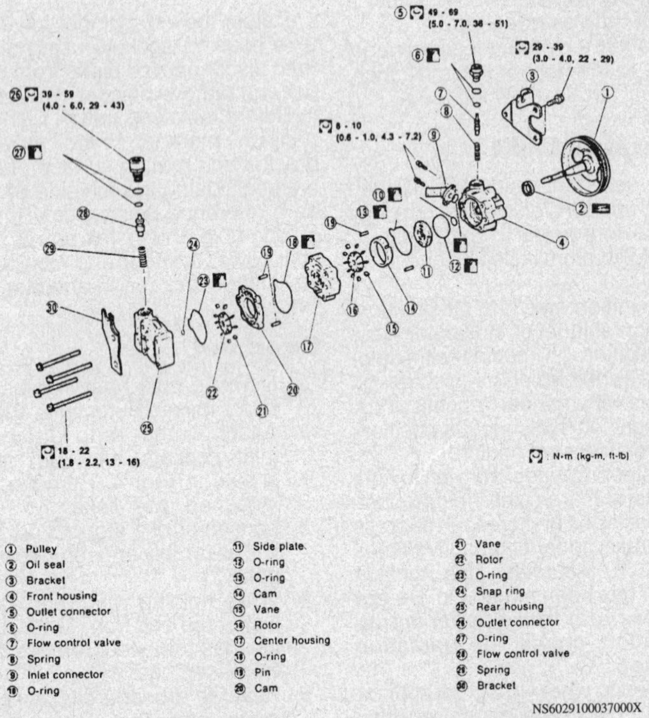
49 - 69
(5.0 - 7.0, 36 - 51)
29 - 39
(3.0 - 4.0, 22 - 29)
39 - 59
(4.0 - 6.0, 29 - 43)
18 - 22
(1.8 - 2.2, 13 - 16)
N·m (kg-m, ft-lb)
1 Pulley
2 Oil seal
3 Bracket
4 Front housing
5 Outlet connector
6 O-ring
7 Flow control valve
8 Spring
9 Inlet connector
10 O-ring
11 Side plate
12 O-ring
13 O-ring
14 Cam
15 Vane
16 Rotor
17 Center housing
18 O-ring
19 Pin
20 Cam
21 Vane
22 Rotor
23 O-ring
24 Snap ring
25 Rear housing
26 Outlet connector
27 O-ring
28 Flow control valve
29 Spring
30 Bracket
NS6029100037000X

Fig. 6 Exploded view of oil pump. 240SX

f. Install dust boot using new boot band.

OIL PUMP SERVICE

Replacement

1. Remove oil pump drive belt.
2. Drain fluid into a suitable container.
3. Disconnect and plug oil pipes.
4. Remove oil pump mounting bolts then the oil pump.
5. Reverse procedure to install, bleeding hydraulic system.

Disassemble

Parts which can be disassembled are strictly limited. Never disassemble parts other than those specified. Refer to **Figs. 6 and 7** to disassemble the oil pump assembly, noting the following:

1. Remove inlet and outlet connectors. **The discharge connector incorporates a flow control valve. Ensure care is taken not to drop connector.**
2. Remove end cover assembly then the driveshaft snap ring and the driveshaft.
3. Remove front cover oil seal.

Assemble

Refer to **Figs. 6 and 7** to assemble the oil pump assembly, noting the following:

1. Ensure O-ring and oil seal are properly installed.
2. Coat each part with ATF when assembling.
3. Cam ring, rotor and vanes must be replaced as a set if necessary.
4. Cam ring shape is different between front and rear, ensure front side cam ring is installed with punch mark set on pulley side and that rear side cam ring is installed with punch mark set on rear housing side, **Figs. 8 and 9.**
5. Ensure rotor is installed in correct direction, **Fig. 10.**
6. When assembling vanes to rotor, rounded surface of vanes must face cam ring side.
7. Tighten rear housing bolts in a diagonal sequence as follows:
   a. **On 240SX models, torque** bolts to 6–8 ft. lbs., then to 13–16 ft. lbs.
   b. **On 300ZX models, torque** bolts to 23–31 ft. lbs.

HYDRAULIC SYSTEM BLEED

Before bleeding air from HICAS system, ensure air is bleed from the power steering system as described in the "Power Steering" section.

Using Consult Tool

1. Place shift lever in Park on models with automatic transmissions or Neutral on models with manual transmissions.
2. Have an assistant inside vehicle then raise and support vehicle in such a way to allow all four wheel to spin freely.
3. Connect consult tool to diagnostic connector and start engine.
4. Tough START on consult tool display.
5. Touch HICAS, ACTIVE TEST and SIMULATED DRIVE in that order.
6. Touch START when MAIN SIGNALS displayed is reversed.
7. Connect a clear hose to the right and left power cylinder bleeder valve and place the other into a container of clean fluid.

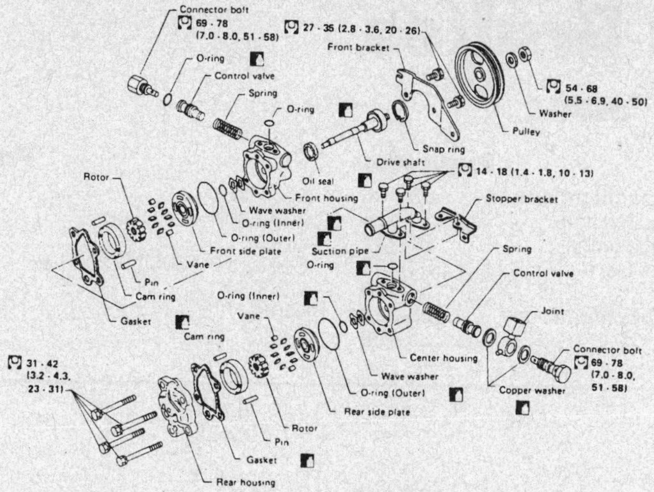
Connector bolt
69 - 78
(7.0 - 8.0, 51 - 58)
27 - 35 (2.8 - 3.6, 20 - 26)
Front bracket
O-ring
Control valve
Spring
O-ring
54 - 68
(5.5 - 6.9, 40 - 50)
Washer
Pulley
Snap ring
Drive shaft
Oil seal
14 - 18 (1.4 - 1.8, 10 - 13)
Rotor
Front housing
Stopper bracket
Wave washer
O-ring (Inner)
O-ring (Outer)
Front side plate
Suction pipe
Spring
Vane
O-ring
Control valve
Pin
Cam ring
O-ring (Inner)
Joint
Gasket
Vane
Cam ring
Center housing
Connector bolt
69 - 78
(7.0 - 8.0,
51 - 58)
31 - 42
(3.2 - 4.3,
23 - 31)
Wave washer
O-ring (Outer)
Copper washer
Rear side plate
Rotor
Pin
Gasket
Rear housing

NS6029100038000X

Fig. 7 Exploded view of oil pump. 300ZX

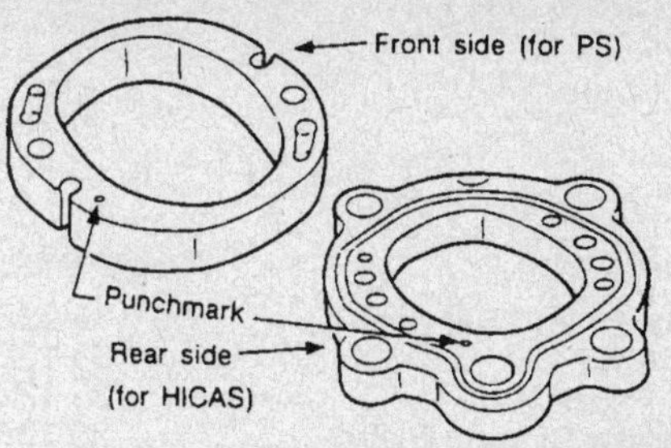
Front side (for PS)
Punchmark
Rear side
(for HICAS)

NS6029100039000X

Fig. 8 Cam ring installation. 240SX

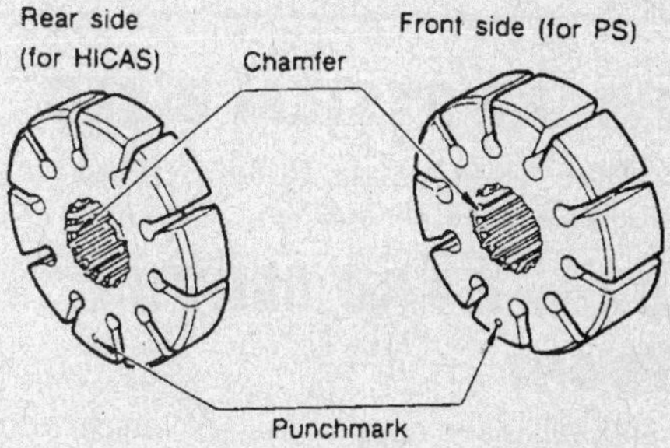
Rear side
(for HICAS)
Chamfer
Front side (for PS)
Punchmark

NS6029100041000X

Fig. 10 Pump rotor installation

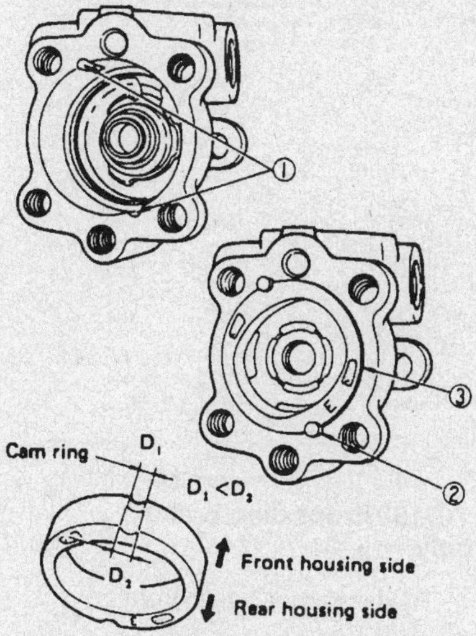
1
3
2
Cam ring
D1
D1 <D2
D2
Front housing side
Rear housing side

NS6029100040000X

Fig. 9 Cam ring installation. 300ZX

8. Touch start.
9. Operate engine at speeds greater than 2000 RPM and turn steering wheel 180° to the right from the neutral position.
10. Loosen right power cylinder bleeder valve to bleed air, then retighten valve.
11. Return steering wheel to neutral position.
12. Repeat steps 9 through 11 turning steering wheel to left.
13. Repeat steps 9 through 12 until there are no air bubbles in fluid. **While bleeding air from power cylinders, never allow fluid level to drop below inlet port of reservoir tank.**
14. Tough CANCEL on Consult tool and turn engine Off.

Using HICAS Warning Light

1. Have an assistant inside vehicle then raise and support vehicle in such a way to allow all four wheel to spin freely.
2. Place HICAS system in self diagnosis as follows:
   a. Turn ignition switch to Off position.
   b. Place shift lever in Park on models with automatic transmissions or Neutral on models with manual transmissions.
   c. Turn ignition switch to On position and immediately start engine.
   d. Turn steering wheel from left to right at least 20° from the neutral position five times or more then depress foot brake pedal at least five times within 10 seconds after ignition switch has been turned On.
3. Connect a clear hose to the right and left power cylinder bleeder valve and the other end into a container of clean fluid.
4. Place steering wheel within 10° from the neutral position and check to ensure rear wheels turn to the left and right alternately.
5. Operate engine at idle speeds and turn steering wheel 180° to right from the neutral position.
6. Loosen right power cylinder bleeder valve to bleed air, then retighten valve.
7. Return steering wheel to neutral position.
8. Repeat steps 4 through 7 turning steering wheel to left.
9. Repeat steps 4 through 8 until there are no air bubbles in fluid. **While bleeding air from power cylinders, never allow fluid level to drop below inlet port of reservoir tank.**
10. Turn ignition switch to Off position to complete self diagnosis operation.

Disc Brakes

INDEX

	Page No.
Brake Pad Service	36-122
Front	36-122
Rear	36-122
Brake System Bleed	36-122
Caliper Service	36-122
Front	36-122
Rear	36-122
Disc Brake Specifications	36-126
Caliper Specifications	36-126
Rotor Specifications	36-127
Parking Brake Service	36-123
Adjustment	36-123
Tightening Specifications	36-128
Altima	36-128
Maxima	36-128
Pathfinder & Pickup	36-129
Quest	36-129
Sentra NX1600/NX2000 & 200SX	36-129
240SX	36-130
300ZX	36-130

BRAKE SYSTEM BLEED

Refer to "Hydraulic Brake Systems" for brake bleed procedure.

BRAKE PAD SERVICE

FRONT

1. Raise and support front of vehicle and remove wheel.
2. Remove brake hose lock spring if necessary and lower pin bolt **Figs. 1 through 12,** then pivot caliper body upwards.
3. Remove pad retainers, inner and outer shims and the pads.
4. Install new inner pad and pivot caliper downward.
5. Compress piston(s) by inserting bar through caliper opening and prying against torque member.
6. Pivot caliper upwards, then install outer pad, inner and outer shims and pad retainers.
7. Position caliper body and install lower pin.

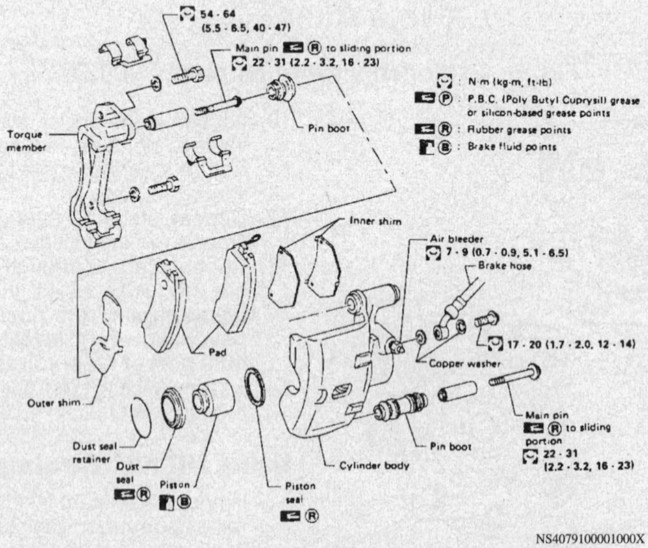
54 - 64
(5.5 - 6.5, 40 - 47)
Main pin Ⓡ to sliding portion
22 - 31 (2.2 - 3.2, 16 - 23)
N·m (kg-m, ft-lb)
Ⓟ : P.B.C. (Poly Butyl Cuprysil) grease or silicon-based grease points
Ⓡ : Rubber grease points
Ⓑ : Brake fluid points
Torque member
Pin boot
Inner shim
Air bleeder
7 - 9 (0.7 - 0.9, 5.1 - 6.5)
Brake hose
Pad
17 - 20 (1.7 - 2.0, 12 - 14)
Copper washer
Outer shim
Main pin
Ⓡ to sliding portion
22 - 31
(2.2 - 3.2, 16 - 23)
Dust seal retainer
Dust seal
Piston
Pin boot
Cylinder body
Piston seal

NS4079100001000X

Fig. 1 Exploded view of AD18V front disc brake assembly

REAR

Except AD14VB, OPZ11V & OPZ11VB

1. Raise and support rear of vehicle and remove wheel.
2. Disconnect parking brake cable and remove spring retainer, if necessary.
   a. **On 240SX models,** disconnect parking cable stay fixing bolt and lock spring.
3. **On all models,** remove pin bolts, **Figs. 13 through 16.**
4. Remove pad springs, pads and pad shims.
5. Reverse procedure to install. Turn piston clockwise to retract it into cylinder body.

AD14VB & OPZ11VB

1. Raise and support rear of vehicle and remove wheels.
2. Remove caliper guide pin, then swing cylinder body upward.
3. Remove pad retainer, then the pads and shims, **Figs. 17 and 18.**
4. To install new pads, bring piston and yoke into position by turning outer piston clockwise until it retracts into caliper body.
5. Move yoke with lever until clearance to install inner and outer pads are equal.
6. Install pads and new shims, making sure tab on back of pad is aligned with groove in piston.
7. Install pad retainers.

OPZ11V

1. Raise and support rear of vehicle and remove wheels.
2. Remove clip from pad pin.
3. Remove pad pin.
4. Remove cross spring.
5. Pull out outer pad.
6. Push back outer piston with suitable tool and install new pad.
7. Install cross spring, pad, pin and clip.

CALIPER SERVICE

FRONT

REPLACEMENT

1. Raise and support front of vehicle and remove wheel.
2. Disconnect brake hose from brake tube.
3. Remove caliper assembly from spindle.
4. Reverse procedure to install.

OVERHAUL

1. Remove pin bolts and separate cylinder body from torque member, **Figs. 1 through 12.**
2. Remove pad retainers, shims and brake pads.
3. Feed compressed air gradually into caliper port and force out piston(s) with dust seals.
4. Remove piston seals, sub pins, main pins and dust seals, **Fig. 1 through 12.**
5. Reverse procedure to assemble.

REAR

REPLACEMENT

Except AD14VB, OPZ11V & OPZ11VB

1. Disconnect parking brake cable and brake hose.
2. Remove caliper attaching bolts, then the caliper from vehicle.
3. Reverse procedure to install.

AD14VB, OPZ11V & OPZ11VB

1. Disconnect brake tube and hand brake

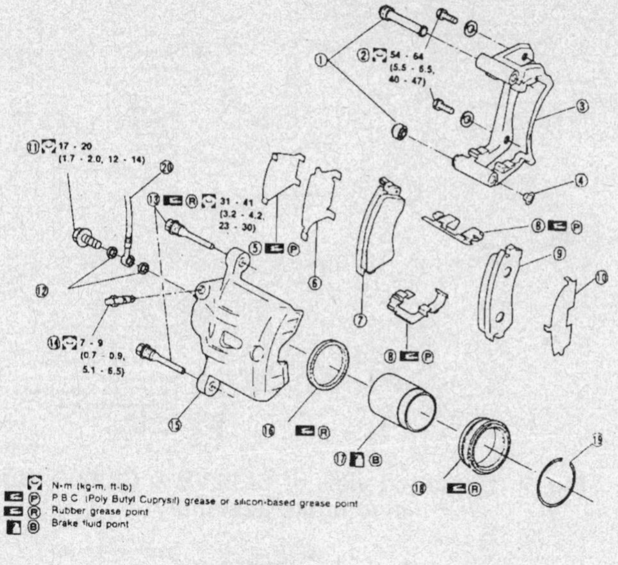
N·m (kg-m, ft-lb)
P.B.C. (Poly Butyl Cuprysil) grease or silicon-based grease point
Rubber grease point
Brake fluid point
① Pin boot
② Torque member fixing bolt
③ Torque member
④ Plug
⑤ Shim cover
⑥ Inner shim
⑦ Inner pad
⑧ Pad retainer
⑨ Outer pad
⑩ Outer shim
⑪ Connecting bolt
⑫ Copper washer
⑬ Sliding pin
⑭ Air bleeder
⑮ Cylinder body
⑯ Piston seal
⑰ Piston
⑱ Piston boot
⑲ Piston boot retainer
⑳ Brake hose

NS4079100002000X

Fig. 2 Exploded view of AD18VE front disc brake assembly

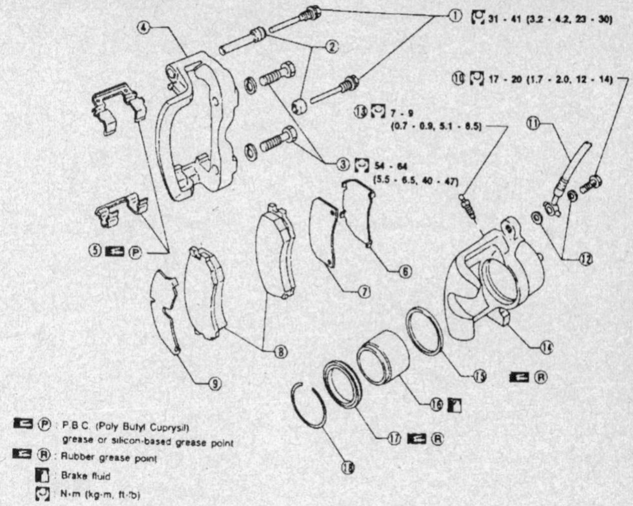
P.B.C. (Poly Butyl Cuprysil) grease or silicon-based grease point
Rubber grease point
Brake fluid
N·m (kg-m, ft-lb)
① Main pin bolt
② Pin boot
③ Torque member fixing bolt
④ Torque member
⑤ Pad retainer
⑥ Shim cover
⑦ Inner shim
⑧ Pad
⑨ Outer shim
⑩ Connecting bolt
⑪ Brake hose
⑫ Copper washer
⑬ Air bleeder
⑭ Cylinder body
⑮ Piston seal
⑯ Piston
⑰ Dust seal
⑱ Piston boot retainer

NS4079100003000X

Fig. 3 Exploded view of AD22VF front disc brake assembly

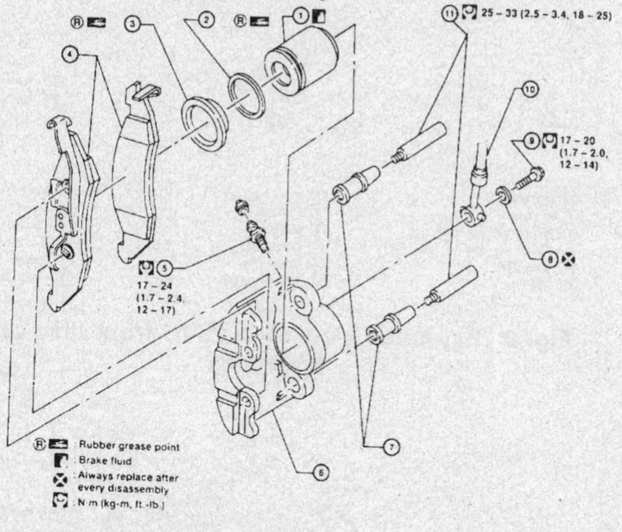
Rubber grease point
Brake fluid
Always replace after every disassembly
N·m (kg-m, ft.-lb.)
① Piston
② Piston seal
③ Dust seal
④ Pad
⑤ Air bleeder
⑥ Cylinder body
⑦ Pin boot
⑧ Copper washer
⑨ Connecting bolt
⑩ Brake hose
⑪ Main pin bolt

NS4079100004000X

Fig. 4 Exploded view of AD28VX front disc brake assembly

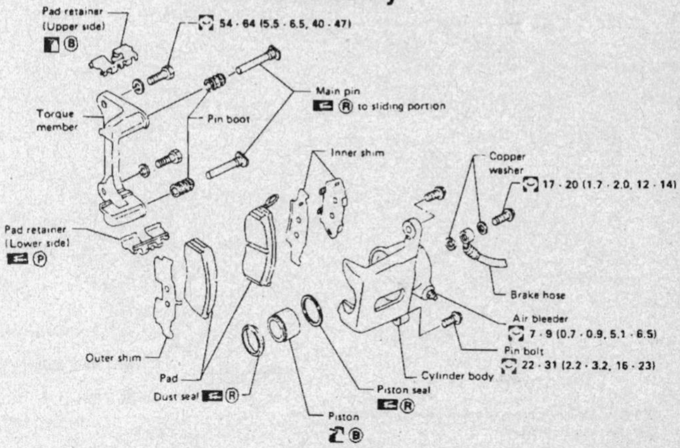
Pad retainer (Upper side)
Torque member
Pin boot
Main pin
Inner shim
Copper washer
Pad retainer (Lower side)
Brake hose
Air bleeder
Pin bolt
Outer shim
Pad
Dust seal
Cylinder body
Piston seal
Piston

NS4079100005000X

Fig. 5 Exploded view of CL18B front disc brake assembly

cable from caliper assembly.
2. Remove caliper mounting bolts and the caliper.
3. To install, reverse procedure.

OVERHAUL

Except AD14VB, OPZ11V & OPZ11VB

1. Remove outer spring retainer, if equipped.
2. Remove pin bolts, then separate cylinder body and torque member.
3. Remove piston by rotating it counterclockwise with pliers.
4. Remove ring, adjusting nut, ball bearing, wave washer, spacers and cup from piston, as required.
5. Pry ring A, **Figs. 13 through 16,** off of cylinder body, then remove spring cover, spring and seat.
6. Pry ring B off of cylinder body, then remove key plate, pushrod and rod.
7. Remove O-ring from pushrod, then pry piston seal out of cylinder body.
8. Remove return spring, nut, spring washer and lever, then adjusting cam and cam boot.
9. Remove pins and pin boots.
10. Reverse procedure to assemble.

AD14VB, OPZ11V & OPZ11VB

Disassemble caliper assembly as shown in **Figs. 17 and 18,** noting the following:

1. Carefully remove piston retainer using a suitable screwdriver.
2. Apply compressed air to back side of piston to remove piston and dust seal.

PARKING BRAKE SERVICE

ADJUSTMENT

Refer to "Drum Brakes" for adjustment procedures.

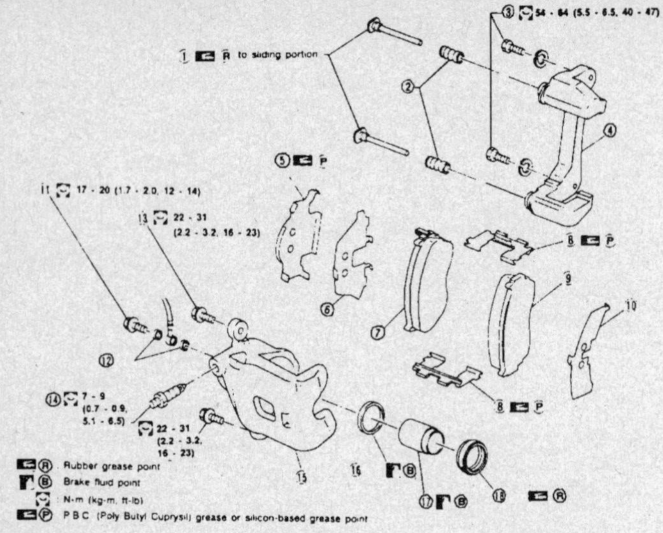
① R to sliding portion
③ 54 - 64 (5.5 - 6.5, 40 - 47)
⑤ P
⑪ 17 - 20 (1.7 - 2.0, 12 - 14)
⑬ 22 - 31 (2.2 - 3.2, 16 - 23)
⑧ P
⑭ 7 - 9 (0.7 - 0.9, 5.1 - 6.5)
22 - 31 (2.2 - 3.2, 16 - 23)
Ⓡ Rubber grease point
Ⓑ Brake fluid point
N·m (kg-m, ft-lb)
Ⓟ P.B.C (Poly Butyl Cuprysil) grease or silicon-based grease point

① Main pin	⑦ Inner pad	⑬ Main pin bolt
② Pin boot	⑧ Pad retainer	⑭ Bleed valve
③ Torque member fixing bolt	⑨ Outer pad	⑮ Cylinder body
④ Torque member	⑩ Outer shim	⑯ Piston seal
⑤ Shim cover	⑪ Connecting bolt	⑰ Piston
⑥ Inner shim	⑫ Copper washer	⑱ Piston boot

NS4079100006000X

Fig. 6 Exploded view of CL18VD, CL18VE, CL22VD & CL22VE front disc brake assembly

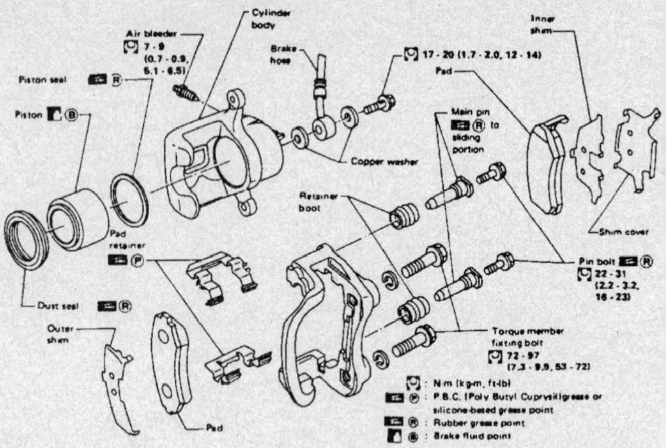
Cylinder body
Air bleeder
7 - 9 (0.7 - 0.9, 5.1 - 6.5)
Brake hose
17 - 20 (1.7 - 2.0, 12 - 14)
Inner shim
Pad
Piston seal Ⓡ
Piston Ⓑ
Main pin Ⓡ to sliding portion
Copper washer
Retainer boot
Pad retainer Ⓟ
Shim cover
Pin bolt Ⓡ
22 - 31 (2.2 - 3.2, 16 - 23)
Dust seal Ⓡ
Outer shim
Torque member fixing bolt
72 - 97 (7.3 - 9.9, 53 - 72)
Pad
N·m (kg-m, ft-lb)
Ⓟ: P.B.C. (Poly Butyl Cuprysil)grease or silicone-based grease point
Ⓡ: Rubber grease point
Ⓑ: Brake fluid point

NS4079100007000X

Fig. 7 Exploded view of CL22VB & CL22VF front disc brake assembly

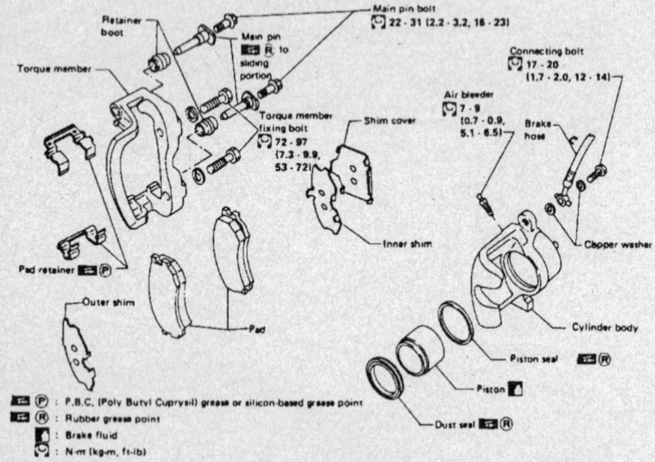
Retainer boot
Main pin bolt
22 - 31 (2.2 - 3.2, 16 - 23)
Main pin Ⓡ to sliding portion
Torque member
Connecting bolt
17 - 20 (1.7 - 2.0, 12 - 14)
Torque member fixing bolt
72 - 97 (7.3 - 9.9, 53 - 72)
Shim cover
Air bleeder
7 - 9 (0.7 - 0.9, 5.1 - 6.5)
Brake hose
Inner shim
Copper washer
Pad retainer Ⓟ
Outer shim
Pad
Cylinder body
Piston seal Ⓡ
Piston
Dust seal Ⓡ
Ⓟ: P.B.C. (Poly Butyl Cuprysil) grease or silicon-based grease point
Ⓡ: Rubber grease point
: Brake fluid
: N·m (kg-m, ft-lb)

NS4079100008000X

Fig. 8 Exploded view of CL25VA front disc brake assembly

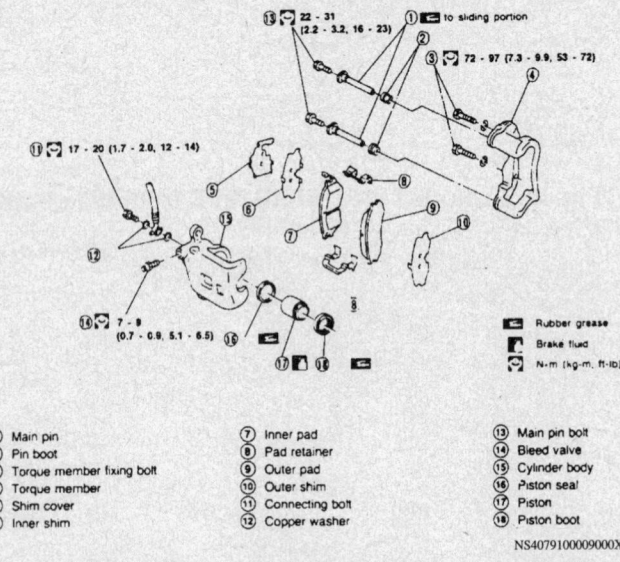

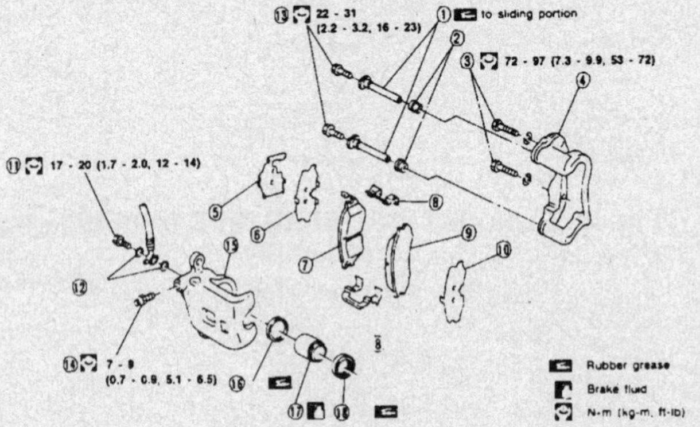
⑬ 22 - 31 (2.2 - 3.2, 16 - 23)
① to sliding portion
③ 72 - 97 (7.3 - 9.9, 53 - 72)
⑪ 17 - 20 (1.7 - 2.0, 12 - 14)
⑭ 7 - 9 (0.7 - 0.9, 5.1 - 6.5)
Rubber grease
Brake fluid
N·m (kg-m, ft-lb)

① Main pin	⑦ Inner pad	⑬ Main pin bolt
② Pin boot	⑧ Pad retainer	⑭ Bleed valve
③ Torque member fixing bolt	⑨ Outer pad	⑮ Cylinder body
④ Torque member	⑩ Outer shim	⑯ Piston seal
⑤ Shim cover	⑪ Connecting bolt	⑰ Piston
⑥ Inner shim	⑫ Copper washer	⑱ Piston boot

NS4079100009000X

Fig. 9 Exploded view of CL25VB front disc brake assembly

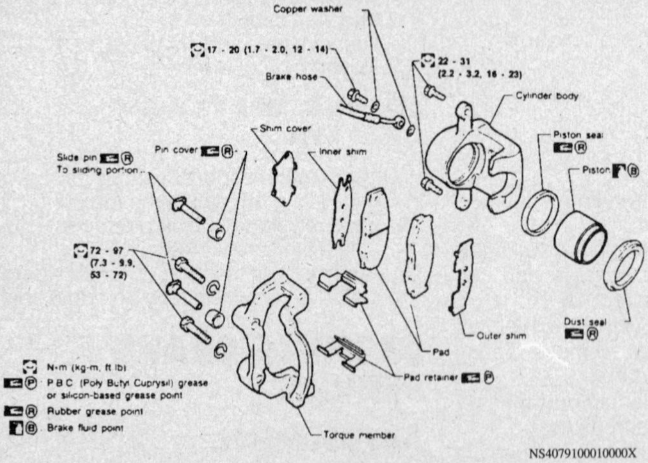
Copper washer
17 - 20 (1.7 - 2.0, 12 - 14)
Brake hose
22 - 31 (2.2 - 3.2, 16 - 23)
Cylinder body
Shim cover
Slide pin Ⓡ To sliding portion
Pin cover Ⓡ
Inner shim
Piston seal Ⓡ
Piston Ⓑ
72 - 97 (7.3 - 9.9, 53 - 72)
Dust seal Ⓡ
Outer shim
Pad
Pad retainer Ⓟ
Torque member
N·m (kg-m, ft-lb)
Ⓟ P.B.C (Poly Butyl Cuprysil) grease or silicon-based grease point
Ⓡ Rubber grease point
Ⓑ Brake fluid point

NS4079100010000X

Fig. 10 Exploded view of CL28VA front disc brake assembly

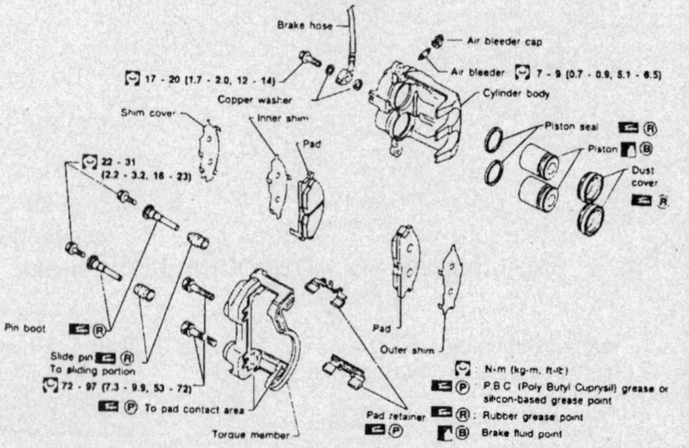
Brake hose
Air bleeder cap
Air bleeder 7 - 9 (0.7 - 0.9, 5.1 - 6.5)
17 - 20 (1.7 - 2.0, 12 - 14)
Copper washer
Cylinder body
Shim cover
Inner shim
Piston seal Ⓡ
Piston Ⓑ
Dust cover Ⓡ
22 - 31 (2.2 - 3.2, 16 - 23)
Pad
Pin boot Ⓡ
Slide pin Ⓡ To sliding portion
72 - 97 (7.3 - 9.9, 53 - 72)
Ⓟ To pad contact area
Outer shim
Pad retainer Ⓟ
Torque member
N·m (kg-m, ft-lb)
Ⓟ P.B.C (Poly Butyl Cuprysil) grease or silicon-based grease point
Ⓡ Rubber grease point
Ⓑ Brake fluid point

NS4079100011000X

Fig. 11 Exploded view of CL28VD front disc brake assembly

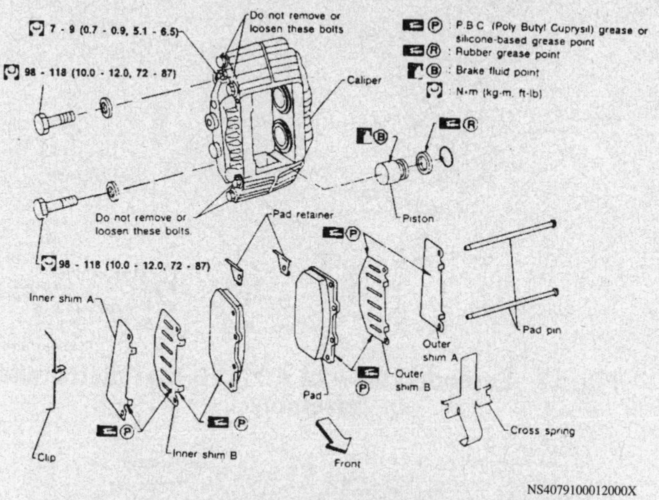
7 - 9 (0.7 - 0.9, 5.1 - 6.5)
Do not remove or loosen these bolts
98 - 118 (10.0 - 12.0, 72 - 87)
Caliper
P.B.C. (Poly Butyl Cuprysil) grease or silicone-based grease point
Rubber grease point
Brake fluid point
N·m (kg-m, ft-lb)
Piston
Do not remove or loosen these bolts.
Pad retainer
98 - 118 (10.0 - 12.0, 72 - 87)
Inner shim A
Pad pin
Outer shim A
Outer shim B
Pad
Cross spring
Clip
Inner shim B
Front
NS4079100012000X

Fig. 12 Exploded view of OPF25V, OPZ25V & OPZ25VA front disc brake assemblies

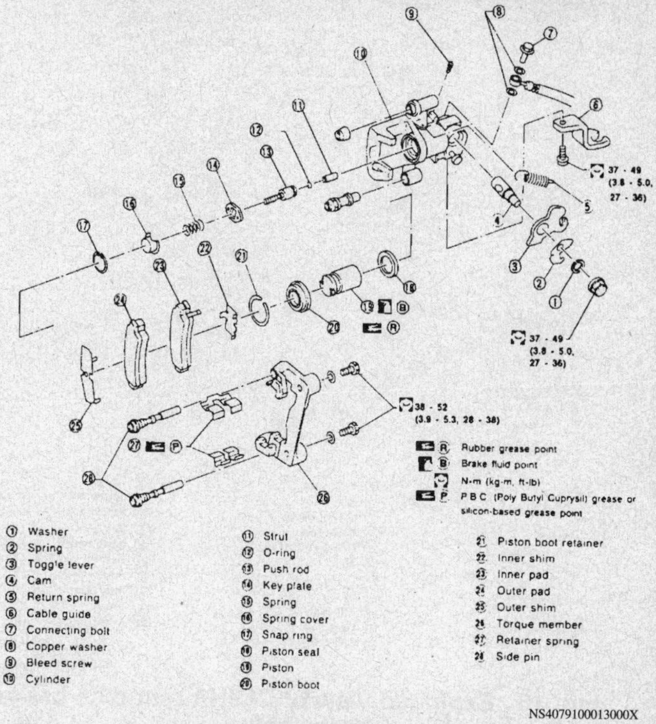
37 - 49 (3.8 - 5.0, 27 - 36)
38 - 52 (3.9 - 5.3, 28 - 38)
Rubber grease point
Brake fluid point
N·m (kg-m, ft-lb)
P.B.C. (Poly Butyl Cuprysil) grease or silicon-based grease point
① Washer
② Spring
③ Toggle lever
④ Cam
⑤ Return spring
⑥ Cable guide
⑦ Connecting bolt
⑧ Copper washer
⑨ Bleed screw
⑩ Cylinder
⑪ Strut
⑫ O-ring
⑬ Push rod
⑭ Key plate
⑮ Spring
⑯ Spring cover
⑰ Snap ring
⑱ Piston seal
⑲ Piston
⑳ Piston boot
㉑ Piston boot retainer
㉒ Inner shim
㉓ Inner pad
㉔ Outer pad
㉕ Outer shim
㉖ Torque member
㉗ Retainer spring
㉘ Side pin
NS4079100013000X

Fig. 13 Exploded view of AD7HA rear disc brake assembly

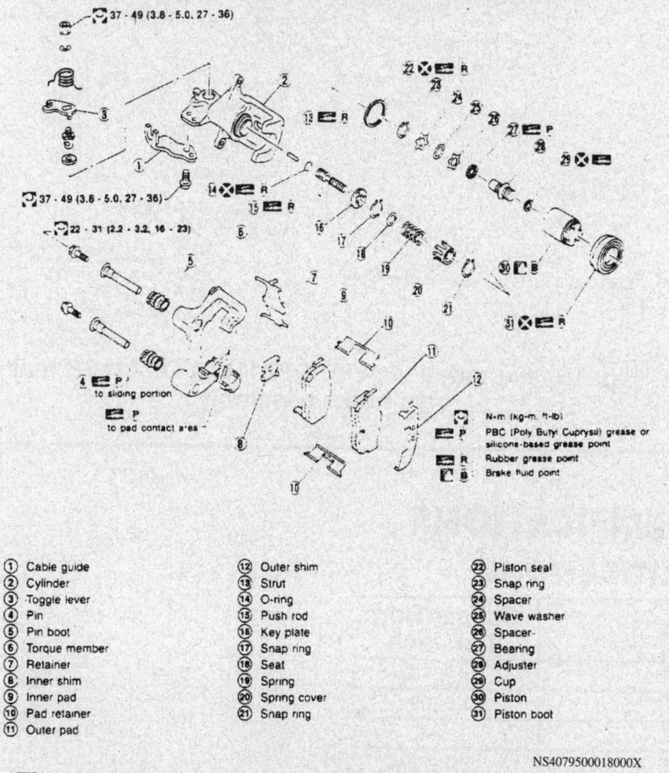
37 - 49 (3.8 - 5.0, 27 - 36)
37 - 49 (3.8 - 5.0, 27 - 36)
22 - 31 (2.2 - 3.2, 16 - 23)
to sliding portion
to pad contact area
N·m (kg-m, ft-lb)
PBC (Poly Butyl Cuprysil) grease or silicone-based grease point
Rubber grease point
Brake fluid point
① Cable guide
② Cylinder
③ Toggle lever
④ Pin
⑤ Pin boot
⑥ Torque member
⑦ Retainer
⑧ Inner shim
⑨ Inner pad
⑩ Pad retainer
⑪ Outer pad
⑫ Outer shim
⑬ Strut
⑭ O-ring
⑮ Push rod
⑯ Key plate
⑰ Snap ring
⑱ Seat
⑲ Spring
⑳ Spring cover
㉑ Snap ring
㉒ Piston seal
㉓ Snap ring
㉔ Spacer
㉕ Wave washer
㉖ Spacer
㉗ Bearing
㉘ Adjuster
㉙ Cup
㉚ Piston
㉛ Piston boot
NS4079500018000X

Fig. 14 Exploded view of CL7HB rear disc brake assembly

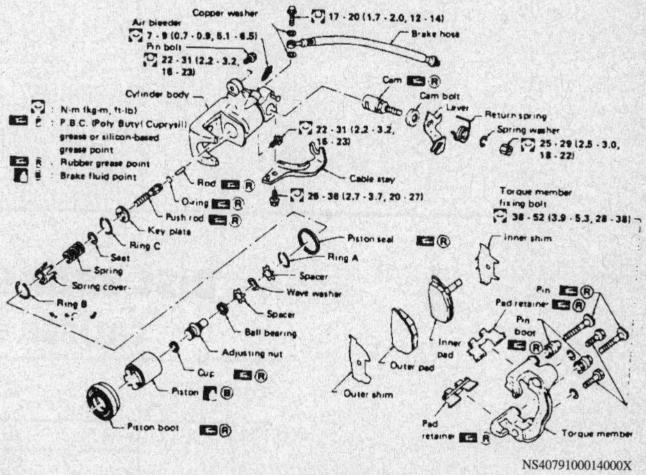
Copper washer
Air bleeder
17 - 20 (1.7 - 2.0, 12 - 14)
7 - 9 (0.7 - 0.9, 5.1 - 6.5)
Pin bolt
22 - 31 (2.2 - 3.2, 16 - 23)
Brake hose
Cylinder body
Cam
Cam bolt
Lever
Return spring
Spring washer
25 - 29 (2.5 - 3.0, 18 - 22)
N·m (kg-m, ft-lb)
P.B.C. (Poly Butyl Cuprysil) grease or silicon-based grease point
Rubber grease point
Brake fluid point
22 - 31 (2.2 - 3.2, 16 - 23)
Cable stay
Rod
O-ring
Push rod
Key plate
Ring C
Seat
Spring
Spring cover
Ring B
26 - 38 (2.7 - 3.7, 20 - 27)
Torque member fixing bolt
38 - 52 (3.9 - 5.3, 28 - 38)
Piston seal
Ring A
Spacer
Wave washer
Spacer
Ball bearing
Adjusting nut
Cup
Piston
Piston boot
Inner shim
Pin
Pad retainer
Pin boot
Inner pad
Outer pad
Outer shim
Pad retainer
Torque member
NS4079100014000X

Fig. 15 Exploded view of CL9H & CL11H rear disc brake assembly

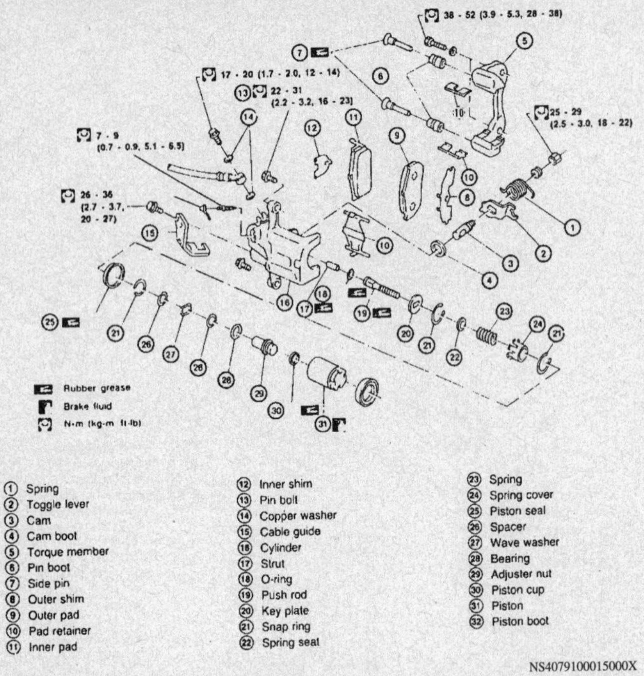
① Spring
② Toggle lever
③ Cam
④ Cam boot
⑤ Torque member
⑥ Pin boot
⑦ Side pin
⑧ Outer shim
⑨ Outer pad
⑩ Pad retainer
⑪ Inner pad
⑫ Inner shim
⑬ Pin bolt
⑭ Copper washer
⑮ Cable guide
⑯ Cylinder
⑰ Strut
⑱ O-ring
⑲ Push rod
⑳ Key plate
㉑ Snap ring
㉒ Spring seat
㉓ Spring
㉔ Spring cover
㉕ Piston seal
㉖ Spacer
㉗ Wave washer
㉘ Bearing
㉙ Adjuster nut
㉚ Piston cup
㉛ Piston
㉜ Piston boot
Rubber grease
Brake fluid
N·m (kg-m, ft-lb)
NS4079100015000X

Fig. 16 Exploded view of CL9HA rear disc brake assembly

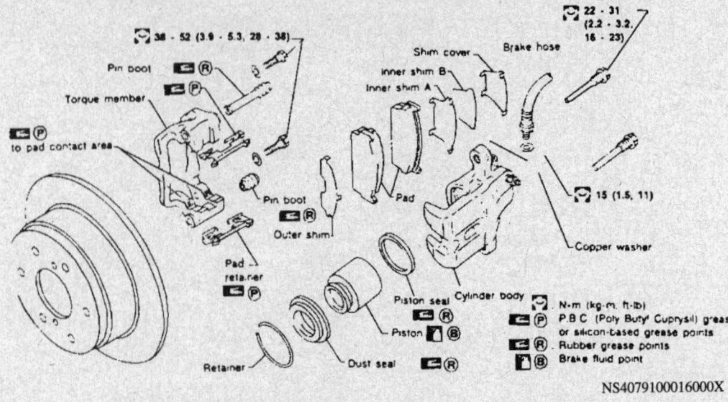
NS4079100016000X

Fig. 17 Exploded view of AD14VB rear disc brake assembly

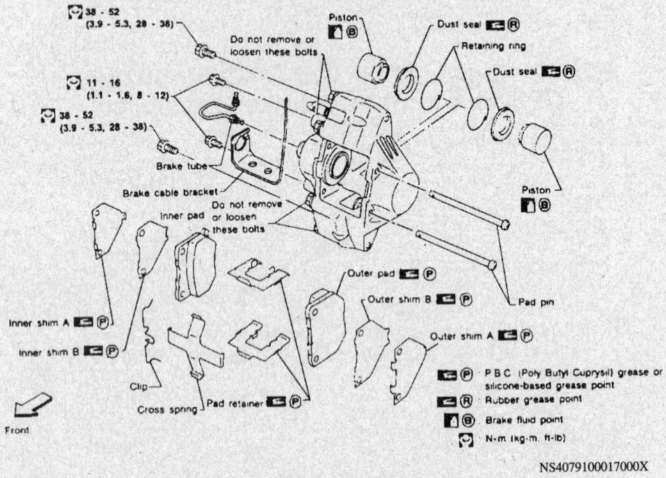
NS4079100017000X

Fig. 18 Exploded view of OPZ11V & OPZ11VB rear disc brake assembly

DISC BRAKE SPECIFICATIONS

CALIPER SPECIFICATIONS

Year	Caliper	Caliper Bore Dia. Inch
1993	AD7HA①	1.1870
	AD14VB①	1.6862
	AD18VE	2.1260
	AD22VF	2.1260
	AD28VX	2.3620
	CL9HA①	1.3370
	CL9H①	1.3370
	CL18VD	1.8940
	CL22VB	2.1260
	CL25VA	2.2520
	CL25VB	2.2520
	CL28VA	2.3860
	CL28VD	1.6850
	OPZ11VB①	1.5000
	OPZ25VA	1.5925

Continued

DISC BRAKE SPECIFICATIONS—Continued

CALIPER SPECIFICATIONS

Year	Caliper	Caliper Bore Dia. Inch
1994	AD7HA①	1.1870
	AD14VB①	1.6862
	AD18VE	2.1260
	AD28VX	2.3620
	CL9HA①	1.3370
	CL9H①	1.3370
	CL18VD	1.8940
	CL22VB	2.1260
	CL25VA	2.2520
	CL25VB	2.2520
	CL28VA	2.3860
	CL28VD	1.6850
	OPZ11V①	1.5000
	OPF25VA	1.5925
1995–96	AD14VB①	1.6862
	AD28VX	2.3620
	CL7HB①	1.2500
	CL9HA①	1.3370
	CL11H①	1.5030
	CL22VB	2.1260
	CL22VD	2.1260
	CL22VE	2.1260
	CL22VF	2.1260
	CL25VA	2.2520
	CL25VB	2.2520
	CL28VA	2.3860
	CL28VD	1.6850
	OPZ11V①	1.5000
	OPF25VA	1.5925

① — Rear disc.

ROTOR SPECIFICATIONS

Year	Model	Minimum Refinish Thickness. Inch	Lateral Runout (T.I.R.)
1993	Altima	②	.0028
	Maxima	⑥	.0028
	NX 1600	⑤	.0028
	NX 2000	⑤	.0028
	Pathfinder	③	.0028
	Pickup	③	.0028
	Quest	.94	.0028
	Sentra	⑤	.0028
	240SX	②	.0028
	300ZX	④	.0028
1994	Altima	②	.0028
	Maxima	⑥	.0028
	Pathfinder	③	.0028
	Pickup	③	.0028
	Quest	.94	.0028
	Sentra	⑤	.0028
	240SX	②	.0028
	300ZX	④	.0028

Continued

ROTOR SPECIFICATIONS—Continued

Year	Model	Minimum Refinish Thickness. Inch	Lateral Runout (T.I.R.)
1995–96	Altima	②	.0028
	Maxima	⑥	.0028
	Pathfinder	③	.0028
	Pickup	③	.0028
	Quest	.94	.0028
	Sentra & 200SX	⑦	.0028
	240SX	①	.0028
	300ZX	④	.0028

① — Front, .709 inch; rear, .310 inch.
② — Front w/out ABS .709; front w/ABS, .787; rear, .315.
③ — 2WD w/KA24E engine, .787 inch; except 2WD w/KA24E engine, .945 inch; rear, .630 inch.
④ — Front: 1.102 inch. Rear, .630 inch.
⑤ — Front w/CL18VD & AD18V style, .630 inch; front w/AD22VF style, .945 inch; rear .236 inch
⑥ — Front, .787 inch; rear, .315 inch.
⑦ — Front, .620 inch; rear, .236 inch.

TIGHTENING SPECIFICATIONS
ALTIMA

Year	Component	Torque/Ft. lbs.
1993–96	Air Bleeder	5–6
	Backing Plate To Axle	28–38
	Brake Pedal Mounting Bracket	6–8
	Brake Fluid Line Connecting Bolt	12–14
	Caliper Pin Bolt	16–23
	Front Caliper Bracket	53–72
	Rear Caliper Bracket	28–38
	Stop Lamp Switch	9–11
	Wheel Cylinder To Backing Plate	5–8

MAXIMA

Year	Component	Torque/Ft. Lbs.
1993–96	Baffle Plate & Adapter Plate Bolts	28–38
	Brake Booster To Body	6–8
	Brake Booster To Master Cylinder	6–8
	Brake Hose Connector	12–14
	Brake Pedal Bracket	6–8
	Brake Tube Connector Mounting Bolt	11–13
	Brake Tube Flare Nut	11–13
	Caliper Bleeder	5–7
	Caliper Pin Bolt	16–23
	Input Rod Locknut	12–16
	Parking Brake Adjuster Locknut	4–5
	Parking Brake Cable Clamp	9–12
	Parking Brake Control Lever To Body	9–12
	Stop Lamp Switch Locknut	9–11
	Torque Member Fixing Bolt	①
	Wheel Cylinder Bleeder	5–7
	Wheel Cylinder To Backing Plate	5–8

① — Front, 53–72 ft. lbs.; rear, 28–38 ft. lbs.

PATHFINDER & PICKUP

Year	Component	Torque/Ft. Lbs.
1993–96	Air Bleeder	5–6
	Backing Plate Fixing Bolts	39–46
	Brake Booster To Body	6–8
	Brake Hose Connector	12–14
	Brake Hose Connector	12–15
	Brake Pedal Bracket To Body	6–8
	Brake Pedal Fulcrum Shaft	12–16
	Brake Tube Flare Nut	11–13
	Four Way Connector Fixing Bolt	45–60①
	Front Caliper Fixing Bolts	16–23
	Front Torque Member Fixing Bolts	53–72
	Load Sensing Valve Air Bleeder	5–6
	Load Sensing Valve Fixing Bolt	12–15
	Master Cylinder To Brake Booster	6–8
	Rear Caliper Fixing Bolts	16–23
	Rear Torque Member Fixing Bolts	28–38
	Stop Lamp Switch	9–11
	Three Way Connector Fixing Bolt	45–60
	Wheel Cylinder Fixing Bolts	5–8

① — Inch lbs.

QUEST

Year	Component	Torque/Ft. lbs.
1993–96	Backing Plate To Axle	26–38
	Front Air Bleeder	12–17
	Front Caliper Main Pin Bolt	18–25
	Front Hydraulic Line Connecting Bolt	12–14
	Rear Air Bleeder	5.1–6.5
	Wheel Cylinder Bolt	4.3–8.0

SENTRA, NX1600/NX2000 & 200SX

Year	Component	Torque/Ft. Lbs.
1993–96	Air Bleeder	5–6
	Backing Plate Fixing Bolt	28–38
	Brake Hose To Caliper Bolt	12–14
	Brake Tube To Connector	11–13
	Cable Guide Fixing Bolt①	27–36
	Caliper Fixing Bolt	②
	Parking Brake Cable To Backing Plate	39–56④
	Torque Member Fixing Bolt	③
	Wheel Cylinder Bolt	4.3–8

① — Models w/AD7HA calipers.
② — Models except CL18VD calipers, 23–30 ft. lbs; models w/CL18VD calipers, 16–23 ft. lbs.
③ — Models except AD7HA calipers, 40–47 ft. lbs; models w/AD7HA calipers, 28–38 ft. lbs.
④ — Inch lbs.

240SX

Year	Component	Torque/Ft. Lbs.
1993–96	Air Bleeder	5–6
	Brake Booster To Body	9–12
	Brake Hose Connecting Bolt	12–14
	Brake Hose Connector Bolt	12–14
	Brake Pedal Bracket To Body	5.8–8
	Brake Pedal Fulcrum Shaft	12–16
	Brake Tube Flare Nut	11–13
	Caliper Fixing Bolt	16–23
	Front Torque Member Fixing Bolt	53–72
	Master Cylinder To Brake Booster	6–8
	Parking Brake Cable Stay	20–27
	Rear Torque Member Fixing Bolt	28–38
	Stop Lamp Switch Locknut	9–11

300ZX

Year	Component	Torque/Ft. Lbs.
1993–96	Brake Booster To Master Cylinder	6–8
	Brake Booster To Pedal Bracket	9–12
	Brake Pedal To Bracket	12–16
	Caliper Pin	5–7
	Front Caliper Mounting Bolts	72–87
	Pedal Bracket To Body	6–8
	Rear Caliper Mounting Bolts	28–38
	Speed Control Cancel Switch	9–11
	Stop Light Switch	9–11

Drum Brakes

INDEX

Page No.

Adjustments 36-132
Parking Brake 36-132
Application Chart 36-131
Brake Service 36-131
Altima 36-131
Maxima 36-131
Pathfinder & Pickup 36-132
Quest 36-132
Sentra, NX 1600, NX 2000 & 200SX 36-131
Drum Brake Specifications 36-135
Tightening Specifications 36-135
Altima 36-135
Maxima 36-136
Pathfinder & Pickup 36-136
Quest 36-136
Sentra, NX1600/NX2000 & 200SX 36-137
300ZX 36-137

APPLICATION CHART

Year	Model	Type
1993	Altima	LT23E
	Maxima	LT23B
	Pathfinder & Pickup	LT26B
	Pathfinder & Pickup	LT30A
	Pathfinder & Pickup	DS19HB①
	Quest	LT25X
	Sentra/NX 1600/NX 2000	LT18C
	300ZX	DS17HD①
1994	Altima	LT23E
	Maxima	LT23B
	Pathfinder & Pickup	LT26B
	Pathfinder & Pickup	LT30A
	Pathfinder & Pickup	DS19HB①
	Quest	LT25X
	Sentra	LT18C
	300ZX	DS17HD①
1995–96	Altima	LT23E
	Pathfinder & Pickup	LT26B
	Pathfinder & Pickup	LT30A
	Pathfinder & Pickup	DS19HB①
	Quest	LT25X
	Sentra & 200SX	LT18C
	300ZX	DS17HD①

① — Parking drum brake.

BRAKE SERVICE

ALTIMA

1. Raise and support rear of vehicle, then remove rear wheel.
2. Fully release parking brake.
3. Remove brake drum, if drum is hard to remove, proceed as follows:
   a. Remove plug from rear side of backing plate.
   b. Using a suitable tool, push stopper towards backing plate to gain clearance between brake shoe and drum as shown in **Fig. 1.**
   c. Install two bolts into outside of brake drum as shown in **Fig. 2,** then gradually tighten the two bolts until drum separates from the brake shoes.
4. Push in shoe hold-down pins from behind backing plate, **Fig. 3.**
5. Pull out brake shoes.
6. Using pliers, remove lower return spring.
7. Separate shoes, one at a time, from wheel cylinder and remove from backing plate with adjuster assembly attached. **Be careful not to damage wheel cylinder boot.**
8. Disconnect parking brake cable from toggle lever, then remove adjuster return spring and shoe return spring.
9. Remove retainer ring, then separate toggle lever and brake shoe.
10. Reverse procedure to install, noting the following:
    a. Measure inside diameter of brake drum, replace if necessary.
    b. Apply grease to brake shoe contact areas shown in **Fig. 3.**
    c. Adjust parking brake and bleed brake hydraulic system.

MAXIMA

1. Fully release parking brake control lever.
2. Raise and support vehicle.
3. Remove hub cap and wheel bearing locknut.
4. Remove brake drum.
5. Refer to **Fig. 4** to remove brake shoes.
6. Reverse procedure to install, noting the following:
   a. Measure inside diameter of brake drum, replace if necessary.
   b. Apply grease to brake shoe contact areas.

SENTRA, NX 1600, NX 2000 & 200SX

1. Raise and support rear of vehicle.
2. Fully release parking brake.
3. Remove brake drum, if drum is difficult to remove, proceed as follows:

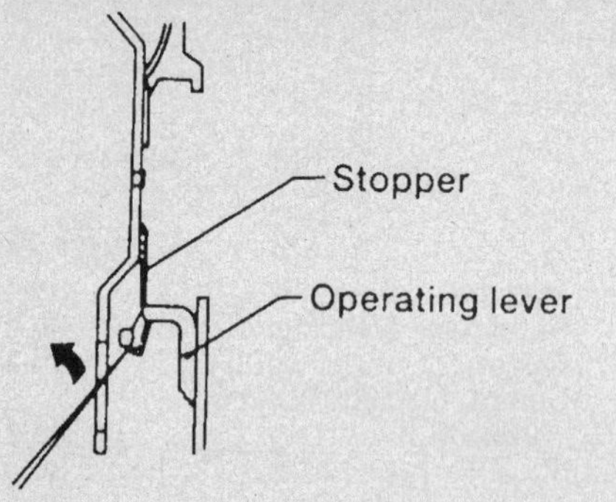
Stopper
Operating lever
NS4089100001000X

Fig. 1 Brake shoe & brake drum clearance adjustment. Altima

a. Remove plug from rear of backing plate.
b. Shorten adjuster to increase clearance between brake shoe and drum.
c. Install two bolt into brake drum as shown in **Fig. 2,** then gradually tighten bolts until drum separates from the brake shoes.

4. Remove brake shoes retainers, **Fig. 5.**
5. Rotate brake shoes forward and remove lower return spring.
6. Disconnect parking brake cable from toggle lever.
7. Remove retainer ring, then separate toggle lever and brake shoe.
8. Reverse procedure to install, noting the following:
   a. Measure inside diameter of brake drum, replace if necessary.
   b. Apply grease to brake shoe contact areas shown in **Fig. 5.**
   c. Adjust parking brake and bleed brake hydraulic system.

PATHFINDER & PICKUP

1. Fully release parking brake control lever.
2. Raise and support vehicle.
3. Remove brake drum.
4. Refer to **Figs. 6 and 7** to remove brake shoes.
5. Reverse procedure to install, noting the following:
   a. Measure inside diameter of brake drum, replace if necessary.
   b. Apply grease to brake shoe contact areas shown in **Figs. 6 and 7.**
   c. Adjust parking brake and bleed brake hydraulic system.

QUEST

1. Raise and support rear of vehicle, then remove rear wheel.
2. Fully release parking brake.
3. Remove brake drum, if drum is hard to remove, proceed as follows:
   a. Remove plug from rear side of backing plate.
   b. Using a suitable tool, loosen adjuster to gain clearance between brake shoe and drum.
   c. Install two bolts into outside of brake drum as shown in **Fig. 2,** then gradually tighten the two bolts until drum separates from the brake shoes.
4. Push in shoe hold-down pins from behind backing plate, **Fig. 8.**
5. Pull out brake shoes.
6. Using pliers, remove lower return spring.
7. Separate shoes, one at a time, from wheel cylinder and remove from backing plate with adjuster assembly attached. **Be careful not to damage wheel cylinder boot.**
8. Disconnect parking brake cable from toggle lever, then remove adjuster return spring and shoe return spring.
9. Remove retainer ring, then separate toggle lever and brake shoe.
10. Reverse procedure to install, noting the following:
    a. Measure inside diameter of brake drum, replace if necessary.
    b. Apply grease to brake shoe contact areas shown in **Fig. 8.**
    c. Adjust parking brake and bleed brake hydraulic system.

ADJUSTMENTS

PARKING BRAKE

Altima

1. Prior to adjustment, check the following:
   a. **On models with rear disc brakes,** ensure toggle lever returns to stopper when parking brake lever is released, **Fig. 9.**
   b. **On all models,** ensure there is no drag when parking brake lever is released.
2. Release parking brake lever and loosen adjusting nut.
3. Start engine and depress brake pedal fully at least 10 times with engine running.
4. Pull parking brake control lever 4–5 notches, then adjust control lever by turning adjusting nut, **Fig. 10.**
5. Pull control lever using approximately 44 lbs. of force, parking brake should be engaged when lever stroke is 7–8 notches.
6. Bend parking brake warning lamp switch plate so that brake warning lamp comes on when parking brake lever is pulled one notch or less.

Maxima

1. Pull parking brake lever with a force of 44 lbs. and ensure lever travels 9–11 notches.

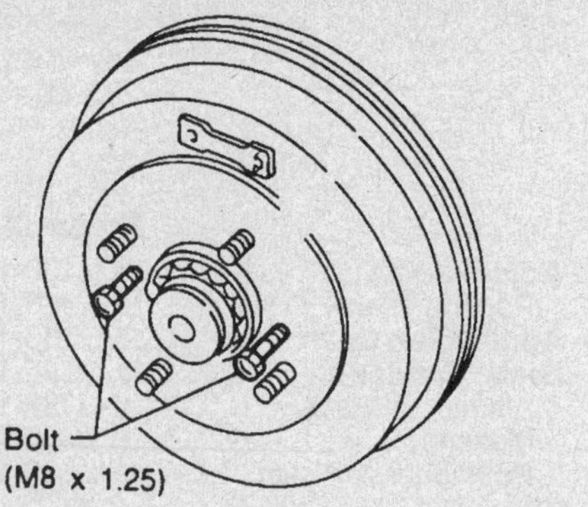
Bolt
(M8 x 1.25)
NS4089100002000X

Fig. 2 Brake drum removal

2. Rotate adjuster, **Fig. 11** until proper stroke is obtained, then tighten locknut.

Sentra, NX 1600, NX 2000, 200SX & 300ZX

1. Pull parking brake lever with a force of 44 lbs. and ensure lever travels is as follows:
   a. **On NX1600, NX2000, Sentra and 200SX** 7–11 notches.
   b. **On 300ZX,** 6–9 notches.
2. Rotate adjuster, **Fig. 11** until proper stroke is obtained, then tighten locknut.

Pathfinder & Pickup

1. Pull parking brake lever with a force of 44 lbs. and ensure lever travel is as follows:
   a. **On 2WD Pickup models,** 10–12 notches.
   b. **On 4WD Pickup models,** 9–11 notches.
   c. **On Pathfinder,** 7–9 notches.
2. Rotate adjuster, **Fig. 12,** until proper stroke is obtained, then tighten locknut.

Quest

1. Depress brake pedal several times until clicking sound from rear brakes stops.
2. Ensure there is no drag when parking brake pedal is released.
3. Loosen locknut, then rotate adjusting nut, **Fig. 13.**
4. Tighten locknut and adjusting nut.
5. Press down on parking brake pedal using approximately 44 lbs. of force, parking brake should be engaged when pedal is stroke is 11–12 notches.

240SX

1. Pull parking brake lever with a force of 44 lbs. and ensure lever travels 6–8 notches.
2. Rotate adjuster, **Fig. 14,** until proper stroke is obtained, then tighten locknut.

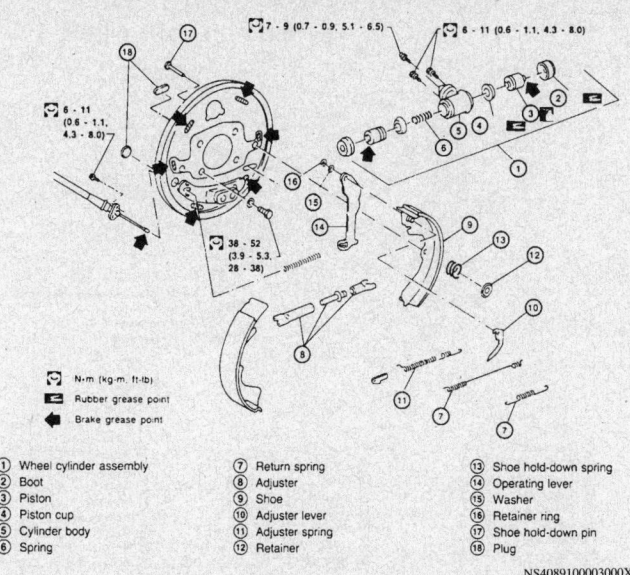

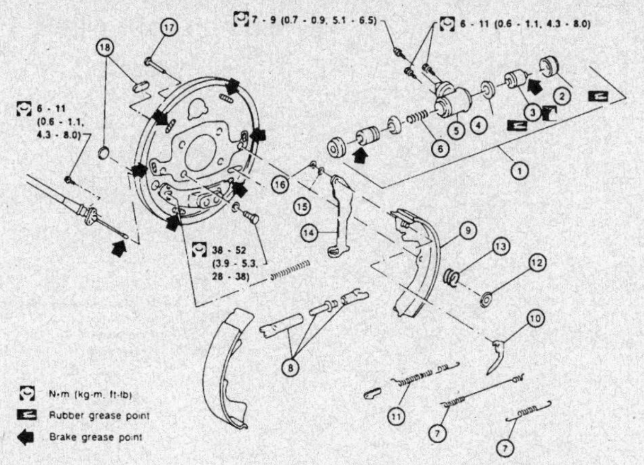
7 - 9 (0.7 - 0.9, 5.1 - 6.5)
6 - 11 (0.6 - 1.1, 4.3 - 8.0)
6 - 11 (0.6 - 1.1, 4.3 - 8.0)
38 - 52 (3.9 - 5.3, 28 - 38)
N·m (kg-m, ft-lb)
Rubber grease point
Brake grease point

① Wheel cylinder assembly
② Boot
③ Piston
④ Piston cup
⑤ Cylinder body
⑥ Spring
⑦ Return spring
⑧ Adjuster
⑨ Shoe
⑩ Adjuster lever
⑪ Adjuster spring
⑫ Retainer
⑬ Shoe hold-down spring
⑭ Operating lever
⑮ Washer
⑯ Retainer ring
⑰ Shoe hold-down pin
⑱ Plug

NS4089100003000X

Fig. 3 Exploded view of drum brakes. Altima

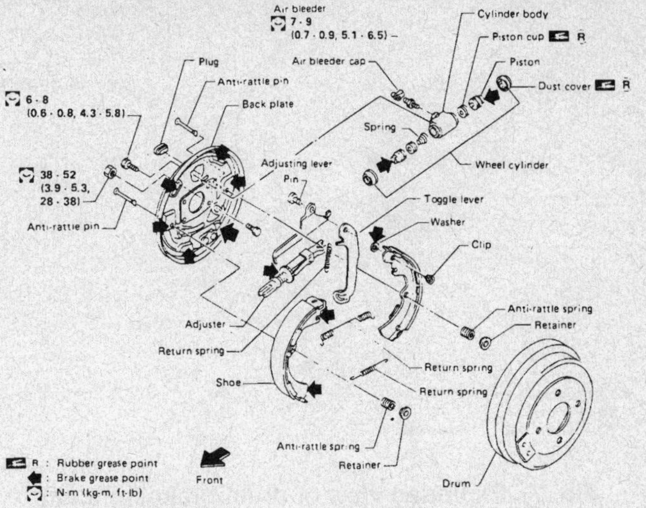
Air bleeder
7 - 9 (0.7 - 0.9, 5.1 - 6.5)
Cylinder body
Piston cup R
Plug
Air bleeder cap
Piston
Anti-rattle pin
Dust cover R
6 - 8 (0.6 - 0.8, 4.3 - 5.8)
Back plate
Spring
Adjusting lever
Wheel cylinder
38 - 52 (3.9 - 5.3, 28 - 38)
Pin
Toggle lever
Anti-rattle pin
Washer
Clip
Anti-rattle spring
Retainer
Adjuster
Return spring
Return spring
Shoe
Return spring
Anti-rattle spring
Retainer
Drum
R : Rubber grease point
: Brake grease point
: N·m (kg-m, ft-lb)
Front

NS4089100004000X

Fig. 4 Exploded view of drum brakes. Maxima

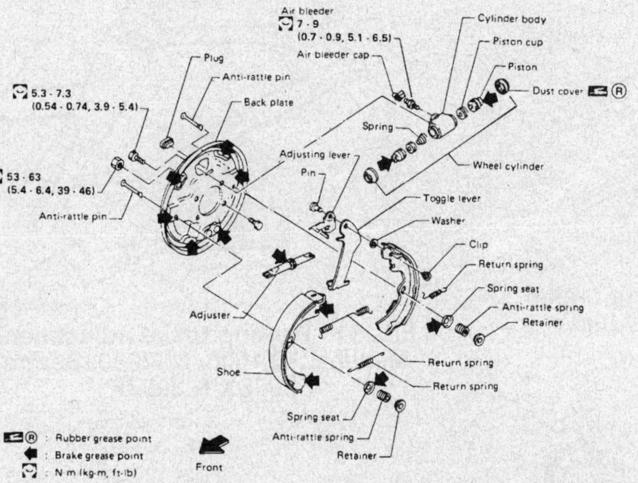
Air bleeder
7 - 9 (0.7 - 0.9, 5.1 - 6.5)
Cylinder body
Piston cup
Air bleeder cap
Plug
Piston
Anti-rattle pin
5.3 - 7.3 (0.54 - 0.74, 3.9 - 5.4)
Dust cover R
Back plate
Spring
Adjusting lever
Wheel cylinder
53 - 63 (5.4 - 6.4, 39 - 46)
Pin
Toggle lever
Anti-rattle pin
Washer
Clip
Return spring
Spring seat
Anti-rattle spring
Retainer
Adjuster
Shoe
Return spring
Return spring
Spring seat
Anti-rattle spring
Retainer
R : Rubber grease point
: Brake grease point
: N·m (kg-m, ft-lb)
Front

NS4089100005000X

Fig. 5 Exploded view of drum brakes. Sentra, NX 1600, NX 2000 & 200SX

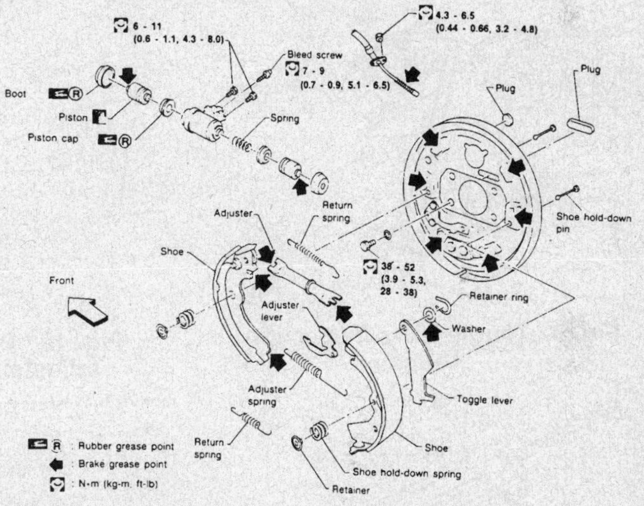
6 - 11 (0.6 - 1.1, 4.3 - 8.0)
4.3 - 6.5 (0.44 - 0.66, 3.2 - 4.8)
Bleed screw
7 - 9 (0.7 - 0.9, 5.1 - 6.5)
Boot R
Piston
Piston cap R
Spring
Plug
Plug
Adjuster
Return spring
Shoe hold-down pin
Shoe
Front
38 - 52 (3.9 - 5.3, 28 - 38)
Retainer ring
Adjuster lever
Washer
Adjuster spring
Toggle lever
Return spring
Shoe
Shoe hold-down spring
Retainer
R : Rubber grease point
: Brake grease point
: N·m (kg-m, ft-lb)

NS4089100006000X

Fig. 6 Exploded view of drum brakes. Pathfinder less SE option & Pickup w/2WD

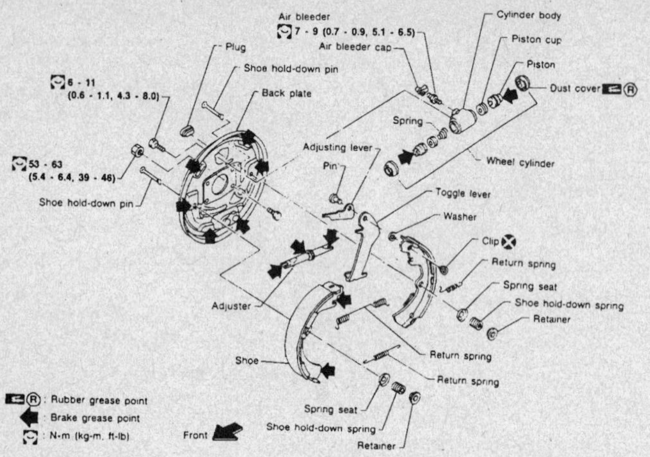
Air bleeder
7 - 9 (0.7 - 0.9, 5.1 - 6.5)
Air bleeder cap
Cylinder body
Piston cup
Piston
Dust cover
Plug
Shoe hold-down pin
6 - 11
(0.6 - 1.1, 4.3 - 8.0)
Back plate
Spring
Adjusting lever
Wheel cylinder
Pin
53 - 63
(5.4 - 6.4, 39 - 46)
Shoe hold-down pin
Toggle lever
Washer
Clip
Return spring
Spring seat
Shoe hold-down spring
Retainer
Adjuster
Return spring
Shoe
Return spring
Spring seat
Shoe hold-down spring
Retainer
: Rubber grease point
: Brake grease point
: N-m (kg-m, ft-lb)
Front

NS4089100007000X

Fig. 7 Exploded view of drum brakes. Pickup w/4WD

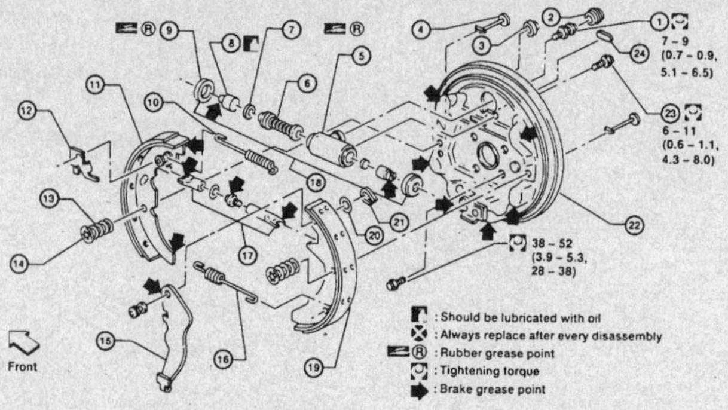
7 - 9
(0.7 - 0.9,
5.1 - 6.5)
6 - 11
(0.6 - 1.1,
4.3 - 8.0)
38 - 52
(3.9 - 5.3,
28 - 38)
Front
: Should be lubricated with oil
: Always replace after every disassembly
: Rubber grease point
: Tightening torque
: Brake grease point

1. Air bleeder
2. Air bleeder cap
3. Shoe inspection hole plug
4. Shoe hold-down pin
5. Cylinder body
6. Spring
7. Piston cap
8. Piston
9. Dust cover
10. Adjuster spring
11. Shoe
12. Adjusting lever
13. Shoe hold-down spring
14. Retainer
15. Toggle lever
16. Return spring
17. Adjuster
18. Wheel cylinder
19. Shoe
20. Washer
21. Retainer ring
22. Back plate
23. Wheel cylinder bolt
24. Adjuster plug

NS4089100008000X

Fig. 8 Exploded view of drum brakes. Quest

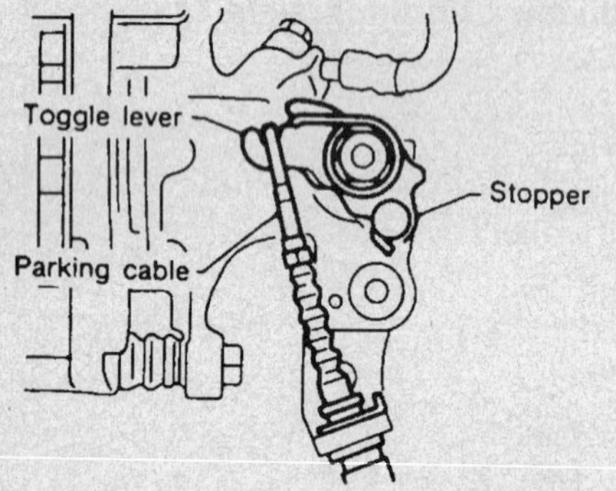
Toggle lever
Stopper
Parking cable

NS4089100010000X

Fig. 9 Toggle lever inspection. Altima

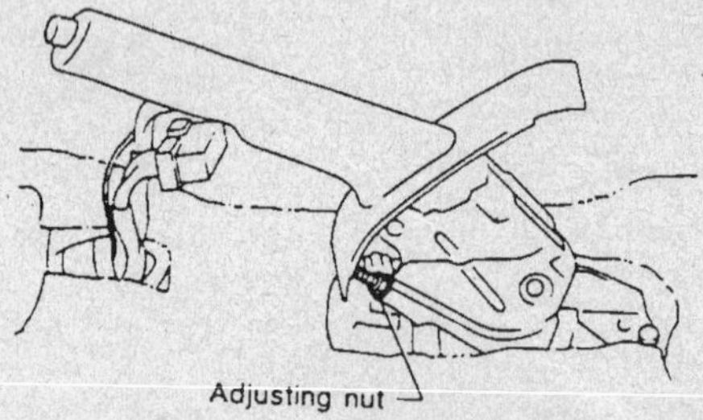
Adjusting nut

NS4089100011000X

Fig. 10 Parking brake adjustment. Altima

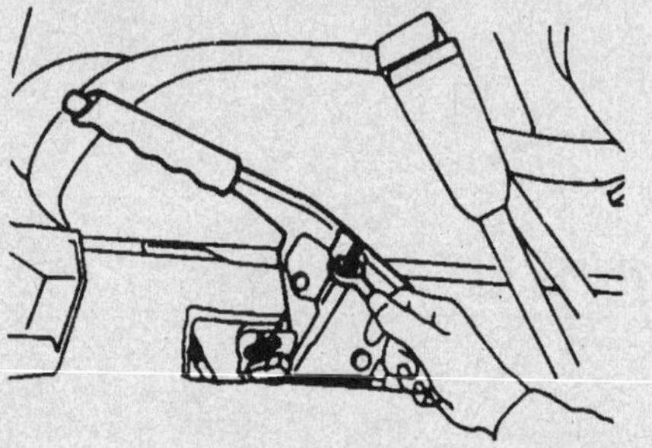

NS4089100012000X

Fig. 11 Parking brake adjustment. Maxima, NX1600, NX2000, Sentra, 200SX & 300ZX

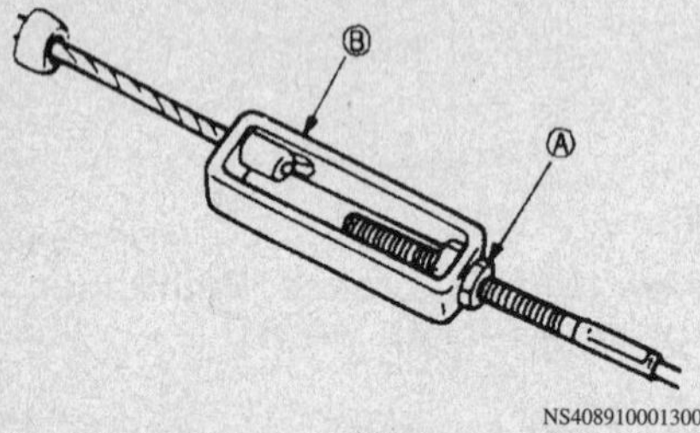
B
A

NS4089100013000X

Fig. 12 Parking brake adjustment. Pathfinder & Pickup

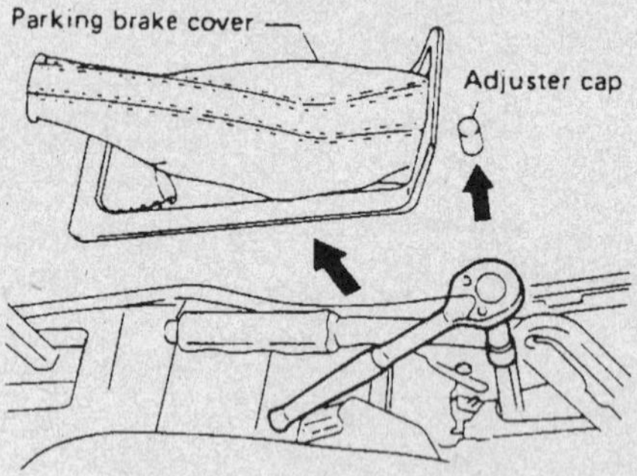
Parking brake cover
Adjuster cap

NS4089100014000X

Fig. 13 Parking brake adjustment. Quest

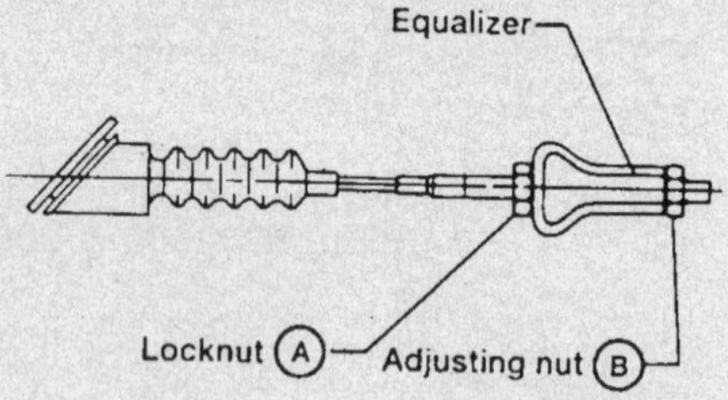
Equalizer
Locknut A
Adjusting nut B

NS4089100015000X

Fig. 14 Parking brake adjustment. 240SX

DRUM BRAKE SPECIFICATIONS

Year	Model	Brake Drum Inside Dia., Inch	Maximum Refinish Dia., Inch
1993	Altima	9.00	9.06
	Maxima	9.00	9.06
	NX 1600	7.09	7.13
	NX 2000	7.09	7.13
	Pathfinder	10.24	10.30
	Pickup①	10.24	10.30
	Pickup②	11.61	11.67
	Quest	9.84	9.90
	Sentra	7.09	7.13
1994	Altima	9.00	9.06
	Maxima	9.00	9.06
	Pathfinder	10.24	10.30
	Pickup①	10.24	10.30
	Pickup②	11.61	11.67
	Quest	9.84	9.90
	Sentra	7.09	7.13
1995–96	Altima	9.00	9.06
	Pathfinder	10.24	10.30
	Pickup①	10.24	10.30
	Pickup②	11.61	11.67
	Quest	9.84	9.90
	Sentra	7.09	7.13

① — 2WD models.
② — 4WD models.

TIGHTENING SPECIFICATIONS

ALTIMA

Year	Component	Torque/Ft. lbs.
1993–96	Air Bleeder	5–6
	Backing Plate To Axle	28–38
	Brake Pedal Mounting Bracket	6–8
	Brake Fluid Line Connecting Bolt	12–14
	Caliper Pin Bolt	16–23
	Front Caliper Bracket	53–72
	Rear Caliper Bracket	28–38
	Stop Lamp Switch	9–11
	Wheel Cylinder To Backing Plate	5–8

MAXIMA

Year	Component	Torque/Ft. Lbs.
1993–94	Baffle Plate & Adapter Plate Bolts	28–38
	Brake Booster To Body	6–8
	Brake Booster To Master Cylinder	6–8
	Brake Hose Connector	12–14
	Brake Pedal Bracket	6–8
	Brake Tube Connector Mounting Bolt	11–13
	Brake Tube Flare Nut	11–13
	Caliper Bleeder	5–7
	Caliper Pin Bolt	16–23
	Input Rod Locknut	12–16
	Parking Brake Adjuster Locknut	4–5
	Parking Brake Cable Clamp	9–12
	Parking Brake Control Lever To Body	9–12
	Stop Lamp Switch Locknut	9–11
	Torque Member Fixing Bolt	①
	Wheel Cylinder Bleeder	5–7
	Wheel Cylinder To Backing Plate	5–8

① — Front, 53–72 ft. lbs.; rear, 28–38 ft. lbs.

PATHFINDER & PICKUP

Year	Component	Torque/Ft. Lbs.
1993–96	Air Bleeder	5–6
	Backing Plate Fixing Bolts	39–46
	Brake Booster To Body	6–8
	Brake Hose Connector	12–14
	Brake Hose Connector	12–15
	Brake Pedal Bracket To Body	6–8
	Brake Pedal Fulcrum Shaft	12–16
	Brake Tube Flare Nut	11–13
	Four Way Connector Fixing Bolt	44–60①
	Front Caliper Fixing Bolts	16–23
	Front Torque Member Fixing Bolts	53–72
	Load Sensing Valve Air Bleeder	5–6
	Load Sensing Valve Fixing Bolt	12–15
	Master Cylinder To Brake Booster	6–8
	Rear Caliper Fixing Bolts	16–23
	Rear Torque Member Fixing Bolts	28–38
	Stop Lamp Switch	9–11
	Three Way Connector Fixing Bolt	44–60①
	Wheel Cylinder Fixing Bolts	5–8

① — Inch lbs.

QUEST

Year	Component	Torque/Ft. lbs.
1993–96	Backing Plate To Axle	26–38
	Front Air Bleeder	12–17
	Front Caliper Main Pin Bolt	18–25
	Front Hydraulic Line Connecting Bolt	12–14
	Rear Air Bleeder	5–6
	Wheel Cylinder Bolt	5–8

SENTRA, NX1600/NX2000 & 200SX

Year	Component	Torque/Ft. Lbs.
1993–96	Air Bleeder	5–6
	Backing Plate Fixing Bolt	28–38
	Brake Hose To Caliper Bolt	12–14
	Brake Tube To Connector	11–13
	Cable Guide Fixing Bolt①	27–36
	Caliper Fixing Bolt	②
	Parking Brake Cable To Backing Plate	39–55④
	Torque Member Fixing Bolt	③
	Wheel Cylinder Bolt	5–8

① — Models w/AD7HA calipers.
② — Models except CL18VD calipers, 23–30 ft. lbs.; models w/CL18VD calipers, 16–23 ft. lbs.
③ — Models except AD7HA calipers, 40–47 ft. lbs.; models w/AD7HA calipers, 28–38 ft. lbs.
④ — Inch lbs.

300ZX

Year	Component	Torque/Ft. Lbs.
1993–96	Brake Booster To Master Cylinder	6–8
	Brake Booster To Pedal Bracket	9–12
	Brake Pedal To Bracket	12–16
	Caliper Pin	5–7
	Front Caliper Mounting Bolts	72–87
	Pedal Bracket To Body	6–8
	Rear Caliper Mounting Bolts	28–38
	Speed Control Cancel Switch	9–11
	Stop Light Switch	9–11

Hydraulic Brake Systems

INDEX

	Page No.
Adjustments	36-138
Brake Booster Output Rod	36-138
Brake Pedal	36-138
Brake System Bleed	36-139
Anti-Lock Brakes	36-139
Less Anti-Lock Brakes	36-139
Component Replacement	36-138
Master Cylinder, Replace	36-138
Component Service	36-138
Master Cylinder Overhaul	36-138
Proportioning Valve	36-138

ADJUSTMENTS

BRAKE BOOSTER OUTPUT ROD

Refer to "Output Rod Adjust" in the "Power Brake Units" section.

BRAKE PEDAL

1. Adjust brake pedal free height dimension "H" in **Fig. 1,** to specifications **Fig. 2,** using brake booster input rod **Fig. 3.** Ensure tip of input rod stays inside clevis pin.
2. With motor running, measure brake pedal depressed height dimension "D"in **Fig. 1,** is within specifications **Fig. 2.** If not within specifications check for leak in brake system, air in system, problem with master cylinder, wheel cylinder or brake caliper. Repair or replace as necessary.
3. Measure clearance dimension "C" **Fig. 1.** Clearance between pedal stopper and threaded end of brake light switch should be .012–0.39 inches. Clearance between pedal stopper and threaded end of ASCD switch if equipped, should be .012–0.39 inches.
4. Measure pedal freeplay dimension "A," **Fig. 1.** Pedal freeplay should be between .04–.12 inches.

COMPONENT REPLACEMENT

MASTER CYLINDER, REPLACE

Do not spill brake fluid on painted areas, it may cause paint damage.

1. Connect a vinyl tube to the bleeder screws.
2. Depress brake pedal, open bleeder valves and drain fluid into suitable container. Repeat until master cylinder is empty.
3. Disconnect brake lines, remove master cylinder attaching nuts, then master cylinder.
4. Reverse procedure to install, bleed brakes as outlined under "Brake Bleeding Procedure."

COMPONENT SERVICE

MASTER CYLINDER OVERHAUL

OVERHAUL

Refer to **Figs. 4 through 13,** for master cylinder overhaul procedures, noting the following:

1. If piston assembly is stuck in cylinder bore, gradually apply air to fluid outlet port.
2. Replace stopper cap if claws are damaged. Bend claw inward when installing new stopper.

CLEANING & INSPECTION

Examine reservoirs for foreign matter and check all passages for restrictions. If there is any indication of contamination or evidence of corrosion, service the hydraulic system as needed.

When disassembled, wash all parts in denatured alcohol or clean brake fluid. Use an air hose to blow out all passages, orifices and valve holes. Air dry and place parts on clean paper or lint-free cloth.

1. Check components for wear, damage, or corrosion. Replace as needed.
2. Check master cylinder bore for scoring, rust, pitting or etching. Replace as necessary.

PROPORTIONING VALVE

SERVICE

On models with external proportioning valves, when replacing proportioning valve refer to **Figs. 14 through 17.**

TESTING

Altima, NX 1600, NX 2000, Sentra & 200SX

1. Check and fill brake fluid as required.
2. Connect pressure checking tool No. KV991V0010, or equivalent to air bleeders of front and rear brakes on either left or right sides, **Fig. 18.**
3. Bleed air from tool.
4. Depress brake pedal and check fluid pressure.
5. Compare pressure readings to specifications in **Figs. 19 and 20.**
6. If output pressure is not within specifications, replace proportioning valve.
7. Bleed brake system as described under "Brake System Bleed."

Maxima

If twin load sensing valve is damaged, replace as an assembly.

1. With one person sitting in drivers seat, set rear axle load to 1323 lbs. by positioning weight in trunk area.
2. Install pressure gauge KV991V0010 as shown in **Fig. 21.** Then bleed air from front and rear brake lines.
3. Apply brakes, bring front brake pressure up to 711 psi. Rear brake pressure should be 555–679 psi.
4. Apply brakes, bring front brake pressure up to 1422 psi. Rear brake pressure should be 739–939 psi.
5. If rear brake pressure is not within specifications, adjust sensor spring length by the adjusting bolt as shown in **Fig. 22.**
6. If pressure after adjusting spring is not within specifications, replace twin load sensing valve.

Pathfinder & Pickup

If load sensing valve is damaged, replace as an assembly.

1. With one person sitting in drivers seat, set rear axle load to 221 lbs. by positioning weight in cargo area.
2. Install pressure gauge KV991V0010 as shown in **Fig. 23.** Then bleed air from front and rear brake lines.
3. Apply brakes, bring front brake pressure to 1422 psi and check rear brake pressure. Refer to **Fig. 24,** for specifications.
4. If brake pressure is not within specifications adjust bracket as follows:
   a. Adjust bracket in the direction of "R" when pressure is below specifications, **Fig. 25.**
   b. Adjust bracket in the direction of "L" when pressure is above specifications, **Fig. 25.**

Quest

1. Check length of dual load sensing valve spring in unladen condition, **Fig. 26.**
2. Spring length should be 5.945–6.063 inch. If spring length is not within specified length, adjust spring length by moving eye bracket while pushing lever toward "A" direction.
3. Connect pressure checking tool No. KV991V0010, or equivalent to air bleeders of front and rear brakes on either left or right sides, **Fig. 18.**
4. Bleed air from tool.
5. Depress brake pedal until front brake

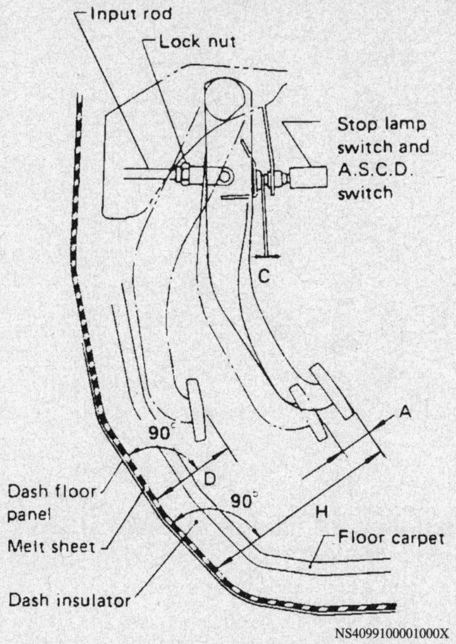
Input rod
Lock nut
Stop lamp switch and A.S.C.D. switch
C
90°
A
D
90°
H
Dash floor panel
Melt sheet
Floor carpet
Dash insulator
NS4099100001000X

Fig. 1 Brake pedal adjustment

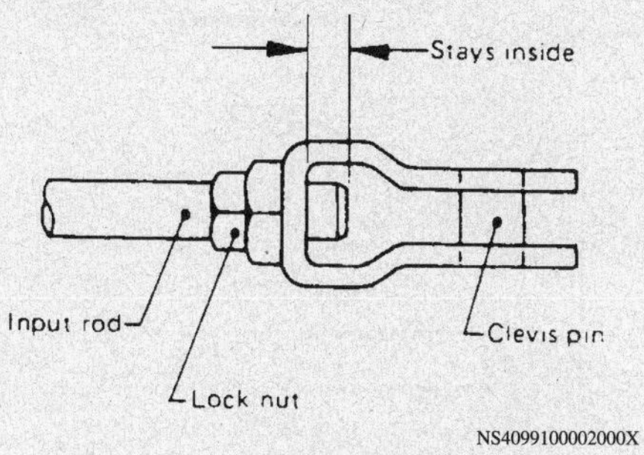
Stays inside
Input rod
Clevis pin
Lock nut
NS4099100002000X

Fig. 3 Input rod adjustment

Year	Model	Free Height Inches		Depressed Height Inches①	
		Man. Trans.	Auto. Trans.	Man. Trans.	Auto. Trans.
1993–96	Altima	6.65–7.05	6.97–7.36	3.54	3.54
	Maxima	6.26–6.65	6.65—7.05	3.54	3.54
	NX 1600, NX 2000, Sentra & 200SX	5.83–6.22	6.18–6.57	②	③
	Pathfinder & Pickup	8.23–8.62	8.35–8.74	4.72	4.72
	Quest	—	7.68–8.07	—	4.53
	240SX	6.97–7.36	7.32–7.72	3.94	3.94
	300ZX	7.32–7.72	7.68–8.07	3.94	4.13

① — Minimum inches.
② — Man. trans. w/GA16DE engine 2.95; w/SR20DE engine 3.15 sedan; 2.95 NX & 200SX models.
③ — Auto. trans. w/GA16DE engine 3.15; w/SR20DE engine 3.35.

Fig. 2 Brake pedal free height & depressed height specifications

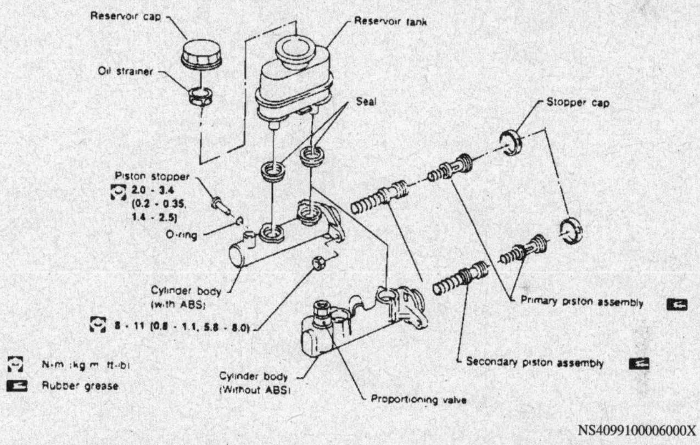
Reservoir cap
Reservoir tank
Oil strainer
Seal
Stopper cap
Piston stopper
2.0 - 3.4 (0.2 - 0.35, 1.4 - 2.5)
O-ring
Cylinder body (with ABS)
8 - 11 (0.8 - 1.1, 5.8 - 8.0)
Primary piston assembly
Secondary piston assembly
Rubber grease
Cylinder body (Without ABS)
Proportioning valve
NS4099100006000X

Fig. 4 Exploded view of master cylinder. Altima

fluid pressure reaches 853 psi. Hold pedal in that position and read rear brake pressure. Pressure should be 475–825 psi.

6. Depress brake pedal until front brake fluid pressure reaches 1706 psi. Hold pedal in that position and read rear brake pressure. Pressure should be 813–1064 psi.
7. If rear brake pressure is not within specifications, replace dual load sensing valve.

BRAKE SYSTEM BLEED

LESS ANTI-LOCK BRAKES

Do not spill brake fluid on painted surfaces, it may cause damage to the paint. If brake fluid is spilled, wash immediately with water.

1. Place container under master cylinder to avoid spillage, then fill master cylinder with brake fluid.
2. Connect hose to bleeder valves, then depress brake pedal several times.
3. With pressure applied to pedal open bleeder valve to release air trapped in system.
4. Close bleeder, then release pedal slowly.
5. Repeat steps 3 and 4 as outlined above until all air is removed from system.
6. Bleed air from system in order as follows:
   a. Left rear wheel.
   b. Right front wheel.
   c. Right rear wheel.
   d. Left front wheel.

ANTI-LOCK BRAKES

Do not spill brake fluid on painted surfaces, it may cause damage to the paint. If brake fluid is spilled, wash immediately with water.

1. Place container under master cylinder to avoid spillage, then fill master cylinder with brake fluid.
2. Connect hose to bleeder valves, then depress brake pedal several times.
3. With pressure applied to pedal open bleeder valve to release air trapped in system.
4. Close bleeder, then release pedal slowly.
5. Repeat steps 3 and 4 as outlined above until all air is removed from system.
6. Bleed air from system in order as follows:
   a. Left rear wheel.
   b. Right rear wheel.
   c. Left front wheel.
   d. Right front wheel.
   e. Front air bleeder on ABS actuator.
   f. Rear air bleeder on ABS actuator.

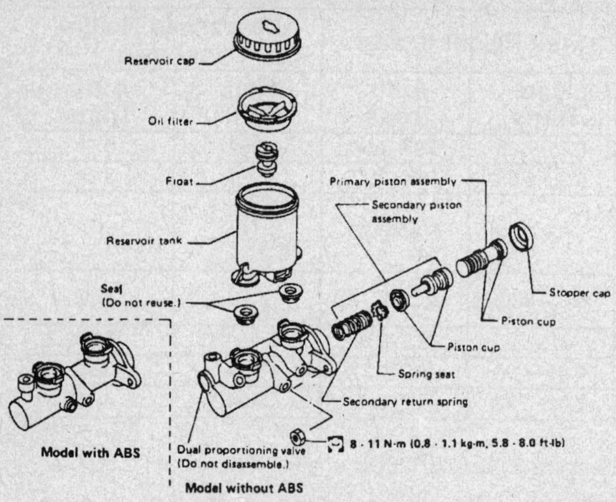
Reservoir cap
Oil filter
Float
Reservoir tank
Seal
(Do not reuse.)
Primary piston assembly
Secondary piston assembly
Stopper cap
Piston cup
Piston cup
Spring seat
Secondary return spring
Model with ABS
Dual proportioning valve
(Do not disassemble.)
Model without ABS
8 - 11 N·m (0.8 - 1.1 kg-m, 5.8 - 8.0 ft-lb)

NS4099100003000X

Fig. 5 Exploded view of master cylinder. 1993–95 Maxima, Pathfinder & Pickup

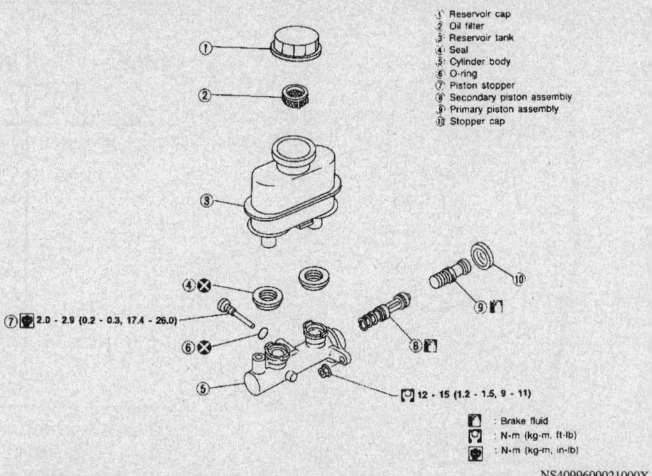
① Reservoir cap
② Oil filter
③ Reservoir tank
④ Seal
⑤ Cylinder body
⑥ O-ring
⑦ Piston stopper
⑧ Secondary piston assembly
⑨ Primary piston assembly
⑩ Stopper cap
⑦ 2.0 - 2.9 (0.2 - 0.3, 17.4 - 26.0)
12 - 15 (1.2 - 1.5, 9 - 11)
: Brake fluid
: N·m (kg-m, ft-lb)
: N·m (kg-m, in-lb)

NS4099600021000X

Fig. 6 Exploded view of master cylinder. 1996 Maxima

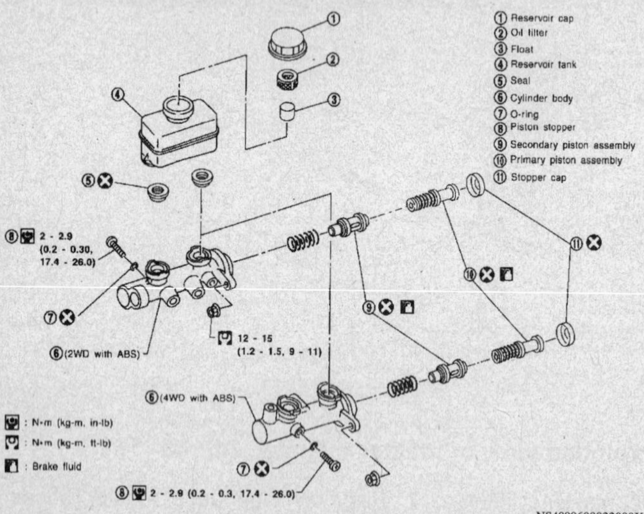
① Reservoir cap
② Oil filter
③ Float
④ Reservoir tank
⑤ Seal
⑥ Cylinder body
⑦ O-ring
⑧ Piston stopper
⑨ Secondary piston assembly
⑩ Primary piston assembly
⑪ Stopper cap
⑧ 2 - 2.9 (0.2 - 0.30, 17.4 - 26.0)
⑥(2WD with ABS)
12 - 15 (1.2 - 1.5, 9 - 11)
⑥(4WD with ABS)
: N·m (kg-m, in-lb)
: N·m (kg-m, ft-lb)
: Brake fluid
⑧ 2 - 2.9 (0.2 - 0.3, 17.4 - 26.0)

NS4099600022000X

Fig. 7 Exploded view of master cylinder. 1996 Pathfinder

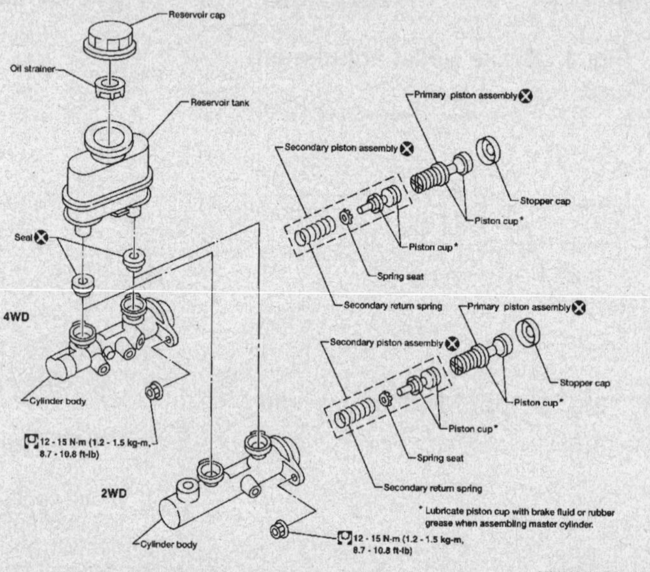
Reservoir cap
Oil strainer
Reservoir tank
Primary piston assembly
Secondary piston assembly
Stopper cap
Piston cup*
Piston cup*
Spring seat
Secondary return spring
Seal
4WD
Cylinder body
12 - 15 N·m (1.2 - 1.5 kg-m, 8.7 - 10.8 ft-lb)
2WD
* Lubricate piston cup with brake fluid or rubber grease when assembling master cylinder.

NS4099600023000X

Fig. 8 Exploded view of master cylinder. 1996 Pickup

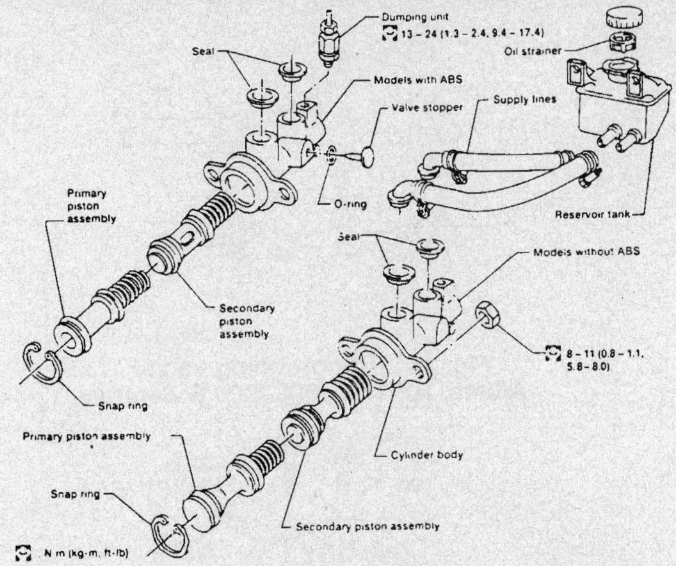

Dumping unit
13 – 24 (1.3 – 2.4, 9.4 – 17.4)
Oil strainer
Seal
Models with ABS
Valve stopper
Supply lines
Primary piston assembly
O-ring
Reservoir tank
Seal
Models without ABS
Secondary piston assembly
8 – 11 (0.8 – 1.1, 5.8 – 8.0)
Snap ring
Primary piston assembly
Cylinder body
Snap ring
Secondary piston assembly
N·m (kg-m, ft-lb)

NS4099100007000X

Fig. 9 Exploded view of master cylinder. Quest

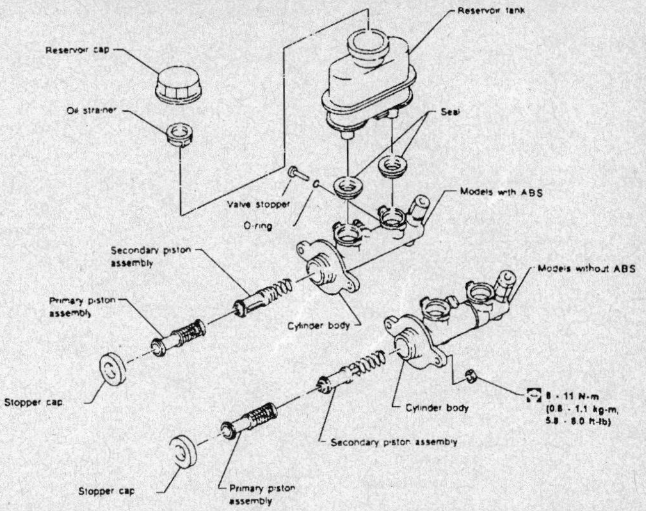

Reservoir tank
Reservoir cap
Oil strainer
Seal
Valve stopper
O-ring
Models with ABS
Secondary piston assembly
Models without ABS
Primary piston assembly
Cylinder body
Stopper cap
8 - 11 N·m (0.8 - 1.1 kg-m, 5.8 - 8.0 ft-lb)
Cylinder body
Secondary piston assembly
Stopper cap
Primary piston assembly

NS4099100004000X

Fig. 10 Exploded view of master cylinder. 1993–95 NX 1600, NX 2000, Sentra & 200SX

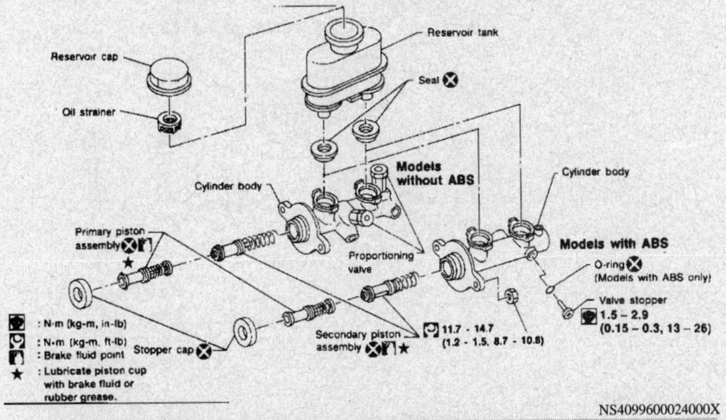

Reservoir tank
Reservoir cap
Seal
Oil strainer
Models without ABS
Cylinder body
Cylinder body
Primary piston assembly
Proportioning valve
Models with ABS
O-ring (Models with ABS only)
Valve stopper
1.5 – 2.9 (0.15 – 0.3, 13 – 26)
: N·m (kg-m, in-lb)
: N·m (kg-m, ft-lb)
: Brake fluid point
: Lubricate piston cup with brake fluid or rubber grease.
Stopper cap
Secondary piston assembly
11.7 - 14.7 (1.2 - 1.5, 8.7 - 10.8)

NS4099600024000X

Fig. 11 Exploded view of master cylinder. 1996 Sentra & 200SX

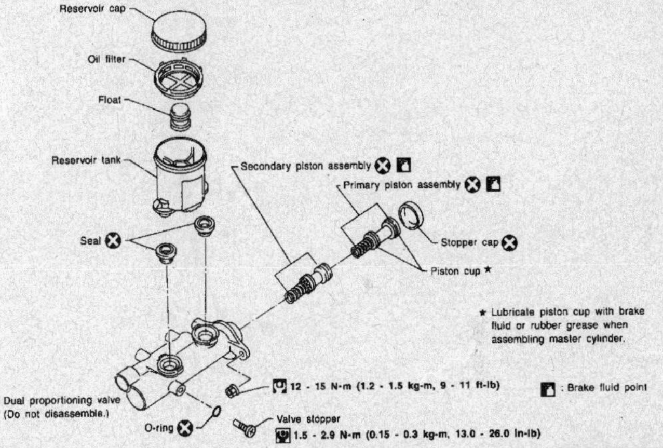

Reservoir cap
Oil filter
Float
Reservoir tank
Secondary piston assembly
Primary piston assembly
Seal
Stopper cap
Piston cup ★
★ Lubricate piston cup with brake fluid or rubber grease when assembling master cylinder.
12 - 15 N·m (1.2 - 1.5 kg-m, 9 - 11 ft-lb)
: Brake fluid point
Dual proportioning valve (Do not disassemble.)
O-ring
Valve stopper
1.5 - 2.9 N·m (0.15 - 0.3 kg-m, 13.0 - 26.0 in-lb)

NS4099100005000A

Fig. 12 Exploded view of master cylinder. 300ZX & 1993–95 240SX

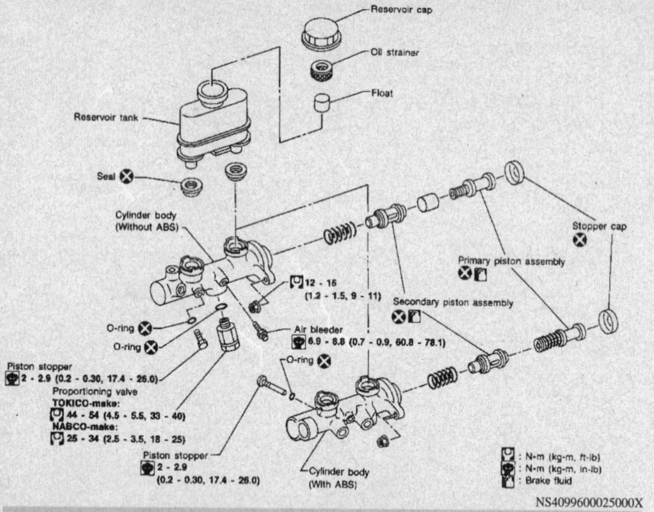
Reservoir cap
Oil strainer
Float
Reservoir tank
Seal
Cylinder body
(Without ABS)
Stopper cap
Primary piston assembly
12 - 16
(1.2 - 1.5, 9 - 11)
Secondary piston assembly
O-ring
O-ring
Air bleeder
6.9 - 8.8 (0.7 - 0.9, 60.8 - 78.1)
O-ring
Piston stopper
2 - 2.9 (0.2 - 0.30, 17.4 - 26.0)
Proportioning valve
TOKICO-make:
44 - 54 (4.5 - 5.5, 33 - 40)
NABCO-make:
25 - 34 (2.5 - 3.5, 18 - 25)
Piston stopper
2 - 2.9
(0.2 - 0.30, 17.4 - 26.0)
Cylinder body
(With ABS)
: N·m (kg-m, ft-lb)
: N·m (kg-m, in-lb)
: Brake fluid

NS4099600025000X

Fig. 13 Exploded view of master cylinder. 1996 240SX

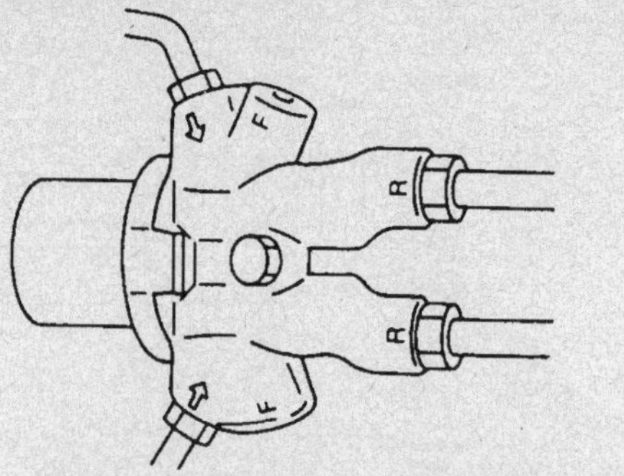

NS4099100008000X

Fig. 14 Proportioning valve. Altima, NX 1600, NX 2000 & Sentra

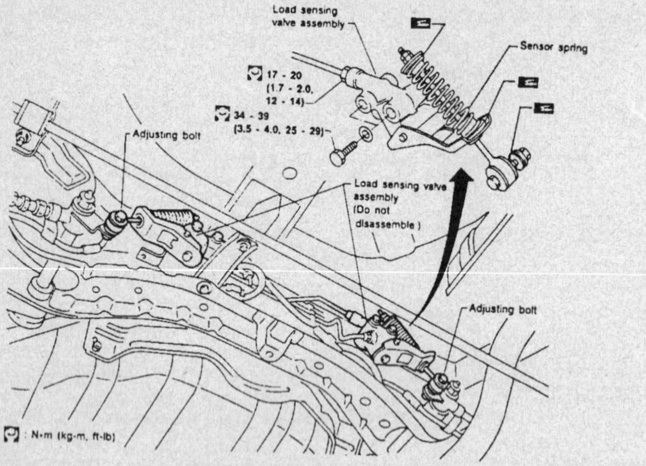
Load sensing
valve assembly
Sensor spring
17 - 20
(1.7 - 2.0,
12 - 14)
34 - 39
(3.5 - 4.0, 25 - 29)
Adjusting bolt
Load sensing valve
assembly
(Do not
disassemble.)
Adjusting bolt
: N·m (kg-m, ft-lb)

NS4099100009000X

Fig. 15 Twin load sensing valve. Maxima

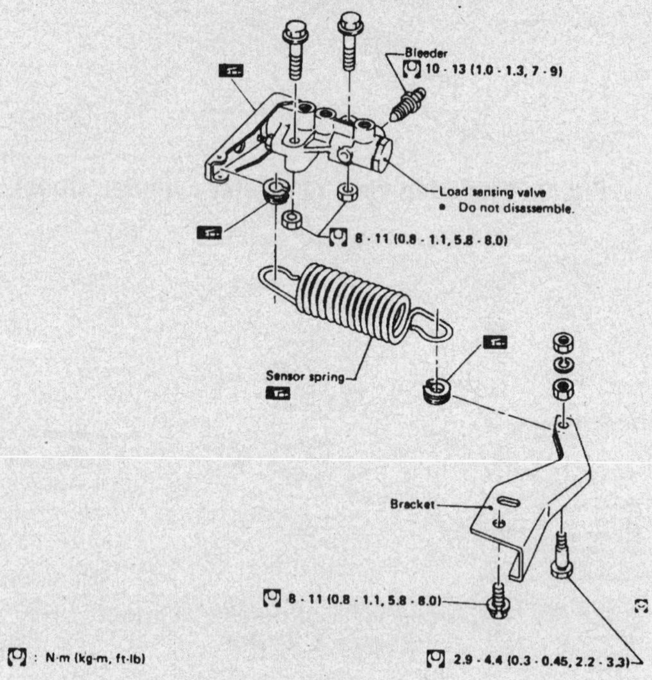
Bleeder
10 - 13 (1.0 - 1.3, 7 - 9)
Load sensing valve
• Do not disassemble.
8 - 11 (0.8 - 1.1, 5.8 - 8.0)
Sensor spring
Bracket
8 - 11 (0.8 - 1.1, 5.8 - 8.0)
: N·m (kg-m, ft-lb)
2.9 - 4.4 (0.3 - 0.45, 2.2 - 3.3)

NS4099100010000X

Fig. 16 Load sensing valve. Pathfinder & Pickup

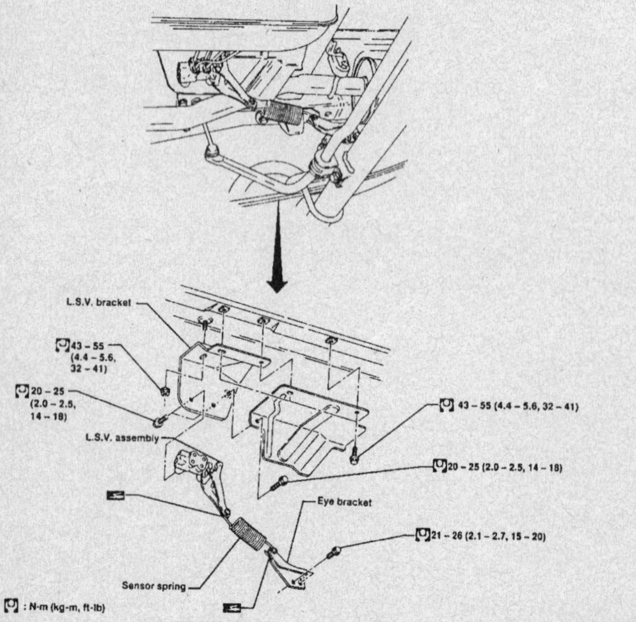
L.S.V. bracket
43 - 55
(4.4 - 5.6,
32 - 41)
20 - 25
(2.0 - 2.5,
14 - 18)
43 - 55 (4.4 - 5.6, 32 - 41)
L.S.V. assembly
20 - 25 (2.0 - 2.5, 14 - 18)
Eye bracket
21 - 26 (2.1 - 2.7, 15 - 20)
Sensor spring
: N·m (kg-m, ft-lb)

NS4099100011000X

Fig. 17 Dual load sensing valve. Quest

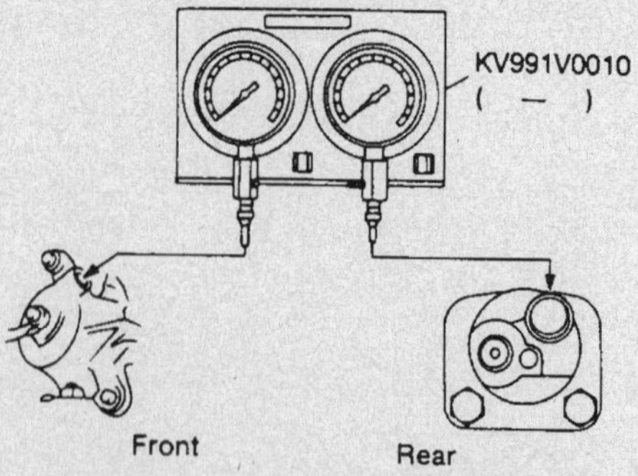
KV991V0010
(—)
Front
Rear

NS4099100012000X

Fig. 18 Pressure gauge installation. Altima, NX 1600, NX 2000, Sentra & 200SX

Unit: kPa (kg/cm², psi)

	Without ABS	With ABS
Applied pressure (Front brake) D_1	5,394 (55, 782)	5,884 (60, 853)
Output pressure (Rear brake) D_2	2,452 - 2,844 (25 - 29, 356 - 412)	3,334 - 3,727 (34 - 38, 483 - 540)

NS4099100013000X

Fig. 19 Pressure specification chart. Altima

Applied model	Without A B S			With A B S	
	GA16DE	SR20DE		Except SE model	SE model
		SR	SE		
Applied pressure (Front brake) kPa (kg/cm² psi)	7.355 (75. 1 067)	5.394 (55. 782)	6.865 (70. 995)	4.904 (50. 711)	6.375 (65. 924)
Output pressure (Rear brake) kPa (kg/cm² psi)	4.413 - 4.805 (45 - 49. 640 - 697)	2.452 - 2.844 (25 -29. 356 - 412)	3.923 - 4.3'5 (40 - 44. 569 - 626)	1.961 - 2.354 (20 - 24. 284 - 341)	3.432 - 3.825 (35 - 39. 498 - 555)

NS4099100014000X

Fig. 20 Pressure specification chart. NX 1600, NX 2000, Sentra & 200SX

NS4099100017000X

Fig. 23 Pressure gauges connection. Pathfinder & Pickup

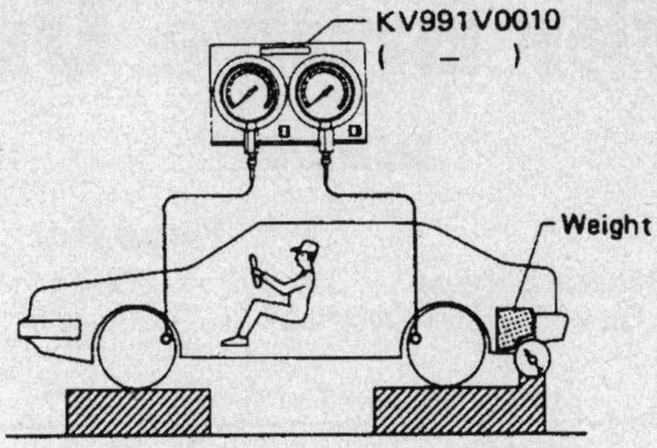
KV991V0010
(—)
Weight

NS4099100015000X

Fig. 21 Pressure gauge installation. Maxima

	KA24E	VG30E	
		Except H.D. *	H.D. *
Without weight	2,942 - 3,727 (30 - 38. 427 - 540)	3,040 - 3.825 (31 - 39. 441 - 555)	3.040 - 3.825 (31 - 39. 441 - 555)
With weight	3,432 - 4.805 (35 - 49. 498 - 697)	4,119 - 5.492 (42 - 56. 597 - 796)	3.923 - 5.296 (40 - 54. 569 - 768)

*H.D.: Heavy duty models.

NS4099200018000X

Fig. 24 Pressure specification chart. Pathfinder & Pickup

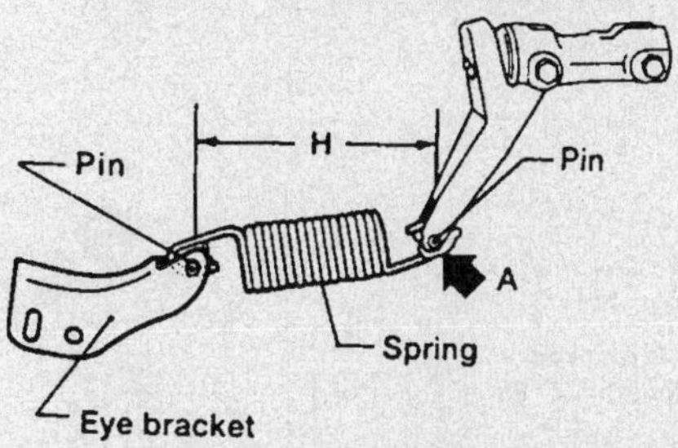
Pin
H
Pin
A
Spring
Eye bracket

NS4099100020000X

Fig. 26 Dual load sensing valve spring adjustment. Quest

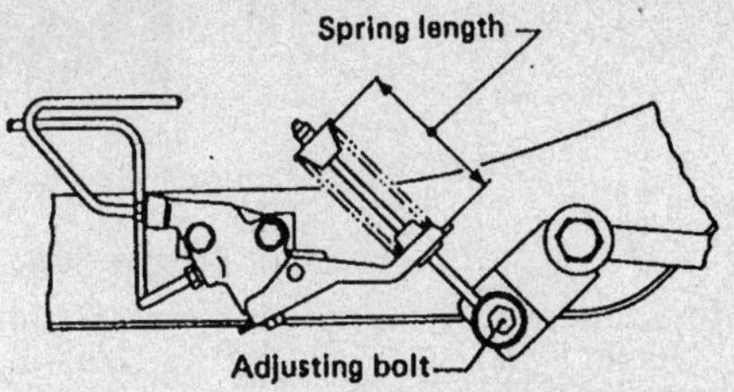
Spring length
Adjusting bolt

NS4099100016000X

Fig. 22 Sensor spring adjustment. Maxima

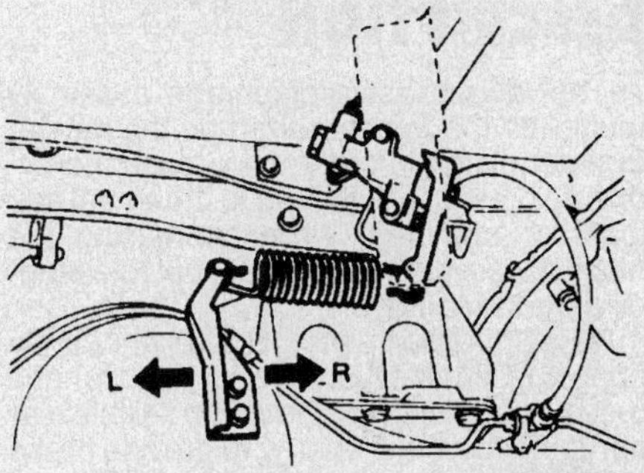
L
R

NS4099100019000X

Fig. 25 Sensor spring adjustment. Pathfinder & Pickup

Power Brake Units

INDEX

	Page No.
Adjustments	36-144
Output Rod	36-144
Description	36-144
General Service	36-144
Brake Booster Overhaul	36-144
Brake Booster, Replace	36-144
Power Brake Unit Service	36-144
Troubleshooting	36-144

DESCRIPTION

The vacuum assist diaphragm assembly multiplies the force exerted on the master cylinder piston in order to increase the hydraulic pressure delivered to the wheel calipers or cylinders, while decreasing the effort necessary to obtain acceptable stopping performance.

Vacuum assist units get their energy by opposing engine vacuum to atmospheric pressure. A piston, cylinder and flexible diaphragm utilize this energy to provide brake assistance. The diaphragm is balanced with engine vacuum until brake pedal is depressed, allowing atmospheric pressure to unbalance the unit and apply force to the brake system.

TROUBLESHOOTING

1. With engine off, depress brake pedal several times. There should be no change in pedal stroke.
2. With brake pedal depressed, start engine. Pedal should go down slightly.
3. Run engine for two minutes, then turn engine off. Depress brake pedal slowly several times.
4. Pedal should go down further the first time and rise gradually the second and third time **Fig. 1.** If this happens the booster is airtight.
5. With engine running and brake pedal depressed, stop engine.
6. If after 30 seconds there is no change in pedal movement, the booster is airtight.

ADJUSTMENTS

OUTPUT ROD

1. Apply 19.96 inch HG of vacuum to brake booster using a suitable vacuum pump, **Fig. 2.**
2. Check output rod length as shown in **Fig. 2.**
3. **On 1993 NX1600, NX2000 and Sentra with M20 brake booster,** adjust output rod length to .1919–.2018 inch.
4. **On models except 1993 NX1600, NX2000 and Sentra with M20 brake booster,** adjust output rod length to .4045–.4144 inch.

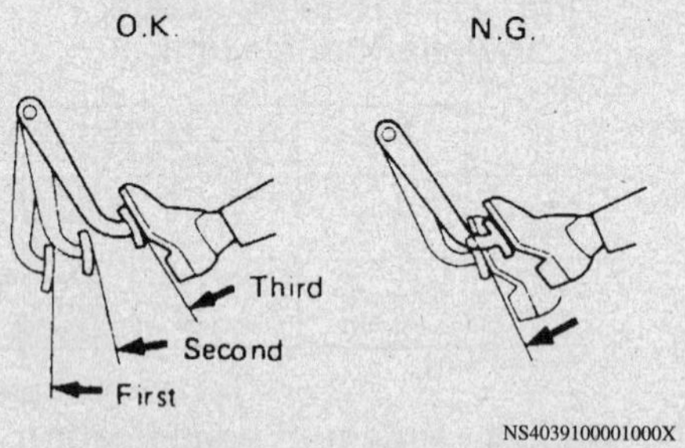
O.K.
N.G.
Third
Second
First
NS4039100001000X

Fig. 1 Brake booster inspection

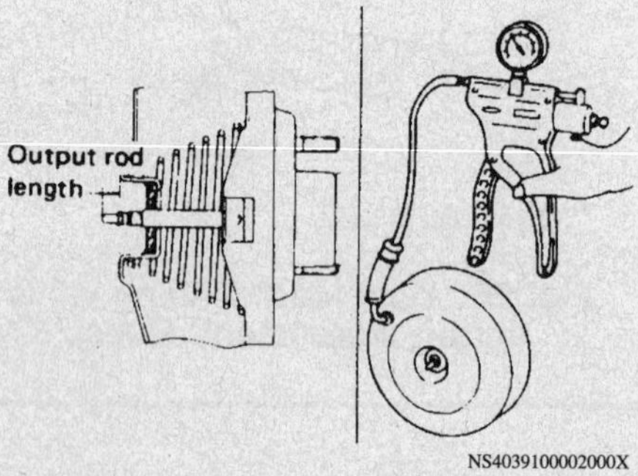
Output rod length
NS4039100002000X

Fig. 2 Output rod adjustment

GENERAL SERVICE

BRAKE BOOSTER, REPLACE

1. Remove master cylinder as outlined in "Master Cylinder Replace" in the "Hydraulic Brake System"section.
2. Disconnect brake booster clevis pin on brake pedal.
3. Disconnect check valve hose at power booster.
4. **On 1993 NX1600, NX2000 and Sentra with GA16DE engine,** remove intake manifold.
5. **On all models,** remove booster attaching nuts, then brake booster.
6. Reverse Procedure to install, noting the following:
   a. Check and adjust output rod as outlined in "Adjustments " in this section.
   b. Bleed system as outlined in "Hydraulic Brake System. "

BRAKE BOOSTER OVERHAUL

POWER BRAKE UNIT SERVICE

These units cannot be overhauled. They must be replaced if malfunctions occur.

Anti-Lock Brakes

NOTE: On Air Bag Equipped Models, Refer To "Air Bag System Precautions" Located In The Front Of This Manual For System Disarming & Arming Procedures.

INDEX

	Page No.
Description	36-145
Diagnosis & Testing	36-145
Accessing Diagnostic Trouble Codes	36-145
Clearing Diagnostic Trouble Codes	36-145
Diagnostic Trouble Code Diagnosis	36-145
Diagnostic Chart Index	36-167
Electrical Components Inspection	36-145
Altima, NX 1600, NX 2000, Sentra & 200SX	36-145
Maxima, 240SX & 300ZX	36-146
Pathfinder & Pickup	36-147
Quest	36-147
Ground Circuit Check	36-147
Actuator Motor Ground	36-147
Relay Box Ground	36-147
Precautions	36-145
Air Bag Systems	36-145
Brake Fluid Safety	36-145
System Service	36-147
Brake System Bleed	36-147
Component Replacement	36-147
Troubleshooting	36-145

PRECAUTIONS

AIR BAG SYSTEMS

Refer to "Air Bag System Precautions" in the front of this manual for system disarming and arming procedures.

BRAKE FLUID SAFETY

Do not allow brake fluid to contact painted areas, never reuse brake fluid and never use mineral oils such as gasoline or kerosine that will ruin rubber parts of hydraulic system.

DESCRIPTION

Both the four wheel and Rear wheel Anti-Lock Brake systems, **Figs. 1 through 10,** use a control unit, hydraulic actuator and wheel speed sensors to control brake fluid pressure and prevent wheel lock during severe braking conditions. With this system, directional stability is improved and steerability maintained even when panic braking on wet, sandy, snowy or icy road conditions.

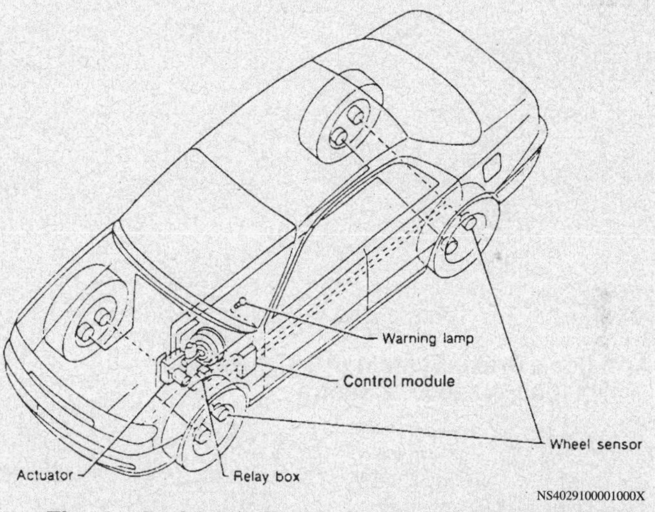
Warning lamp
Control module
Wheel sensor
Actuator
Relay box
NS4029100001000X

Fig. 1 Anti-Lock Brake System (ABS). Altima

TROUBLESHOOTING

The electronic control unit accepts input signals from sensors and drives actuators. It is essential that both input and output signals are stable and accurate. Refer to **Figs. 11 through 22** for preliminary system checks.

DIAGNOSIS & TESTING

ACCESSING DIAGNOSTIC TROUBLE CODES

When a problem occurs in the ABS system, a warning light will flash on the instrument panel. To activate ABS self-diagnosis, ground the self diagnosis (check) terminal located on the data link connector. Refer to **Figs. 23 through 25** for self-diagnostic procedures. The location of the malfunction is indicated by the number ABS warning light flashes. Refer to **Figs. 26 through 33** for warning lamp flash codes.

DIAGNOSTIC TROUBLE CODE DIAGNOSIS

When performing system diagnosis, refer to wiring circuits **Figs. 34 through 50** and diagnosis procedure charts **Figs. 51 through 197.**

CLEARING DIAGNOSTIC TROUBLE CODES

To erase malfunction (trouble) codes from the control module memory, disconnect the check terminal from the ground. Within ten seconds of disconnecting the check terminal from the ground on Quest models or within 12.5 seconds on Altima models, ground the check terminal three times for a period of at least one second. The ABS warning lamp should remain on while erasing the malfunction (trouble) codes, and should go out after the erase mode has been completed. After erasing the malfunction (trouble) codes, rerun the self-diagnostic mode to verify that the malfunction (trouble) codes no longer appear.

ELECTRICAL COMPONENTS INSPECTION

ALTIMA, NX 1600, NX 2000, SENTRA & 200SX

Wheel Sensors

Check resistance between wheel sensor connector terminals, **Fig. 198.** Resistance should be 1.0–1.25 K-ohms.

Actuator Motor Relay

Check continuity between motor relay terminals as shown in **Figs. 199 and 200.**

Solenoid Valve Relay

Check continuity between solenoid valve relay terminals as shown in **Figs. 201 and 202.**

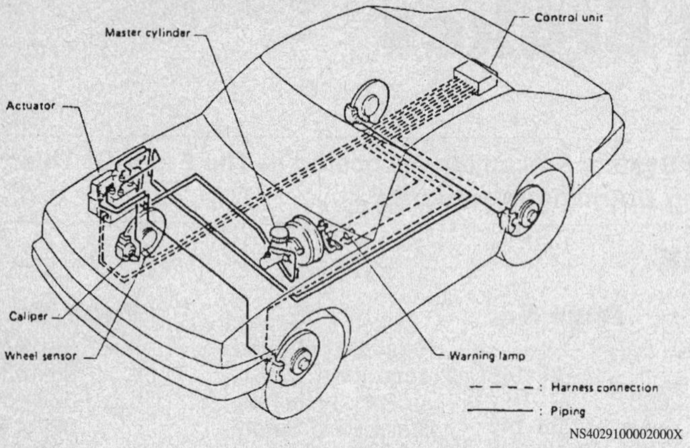
Master cylinder
Control unit
Actuator
Caliper
Wheel sensor
Warning lamp
- - - - : Harness connection
——— : Piping
NS4029100002000X

Fig. 2 Anti-Lock Brake System (ABS). 1993–94 Maxima

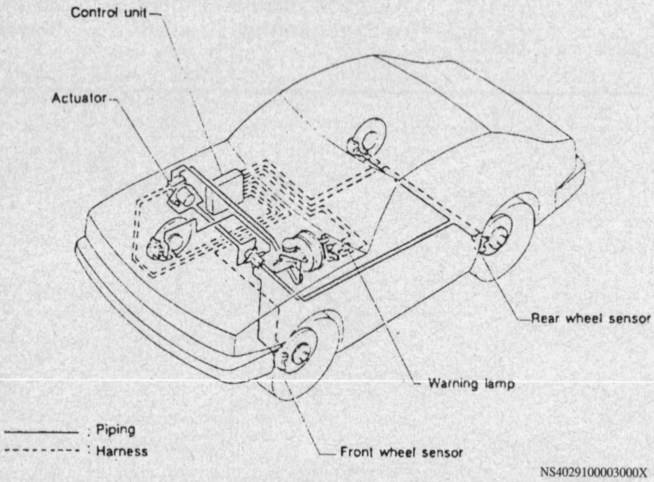
Control unit
Actuator
Rear wheel sensor
Warning lamp
Front wheel sensor
——— : Piping
- - - - : Harness
NS4029100003000X

Fig. 4 Anti-Lock Brake System (ABS). 1993–94 NX1600, NX2000 & Sentra

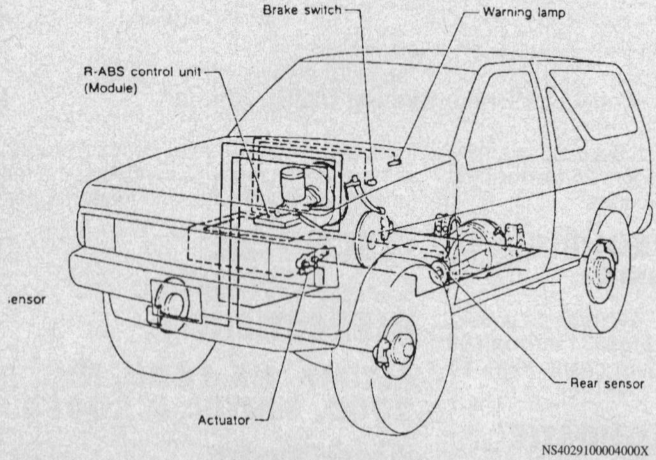
Brake switch
Warning lamp
R-ABS control unit
(Module)
Rear sensor
Actuator
NS4029100004000X

Fig. 6 Anti-Lock Brake System (ABS). Pickup & 1993–95 Pathfinder

MAXIMA, 240SX & 300ZX

Refer to **Fig. 203** for electrical component inspection.

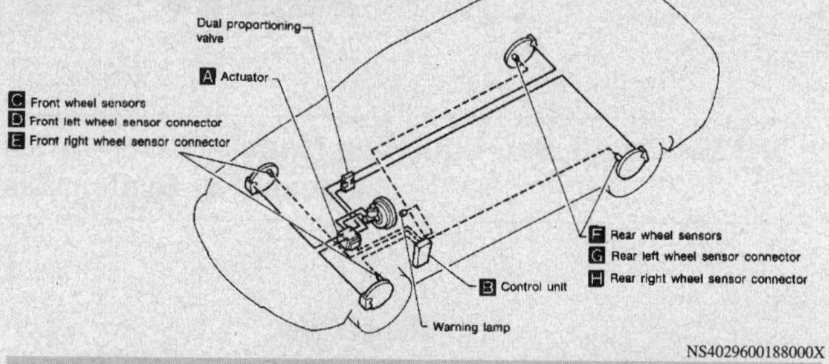
Dual proportioning valve
A Actuator
C Front wheel sensors
D Front left wheel sensor connector
E Front right wheel sensor connector
F Rear wheel sensors
G Rear left wheel sensor connector
H Rear right wheel sensor connector
B Control unit
Warning lamp
NS4029600188000X

Fig. 3 Anti-Lock Brake System (ABS). 1995–96 Maxima

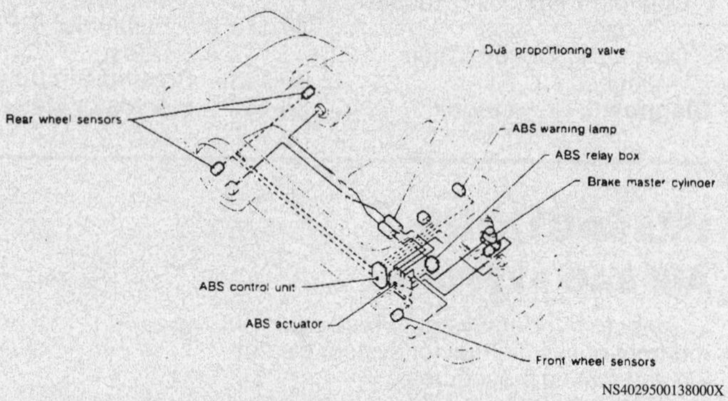
Dual proportioning valve
Rear wheel sensors
ABS warning lamp
ABS relay box
Brake master cylinder
ABS control unit
ABS actuator
Front wheel sensors
NS4029500138000X

Fig. 5 Anti-Lock Brake System (ABS). 1995–96 Sentra & 200SX

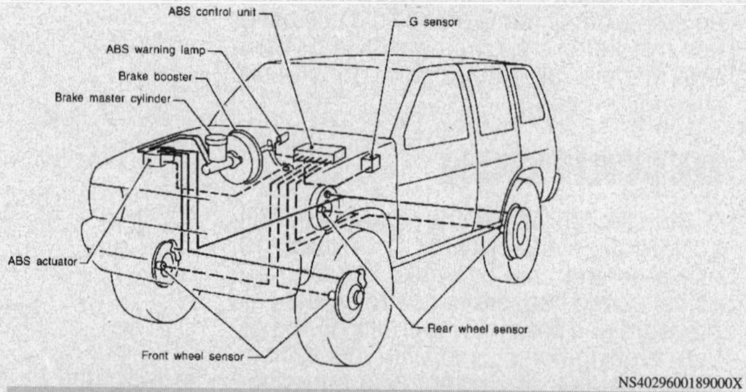
ABS control unit
G sensor
ABS warning lamp
Brake booster
Brake master cylinder
ABS actuator
Rear wheel sensor
Front wheel sensor
NS4029600189000X

Fig. 7 Anti-Lock Brake System (ABS). 1996 Pathfinder

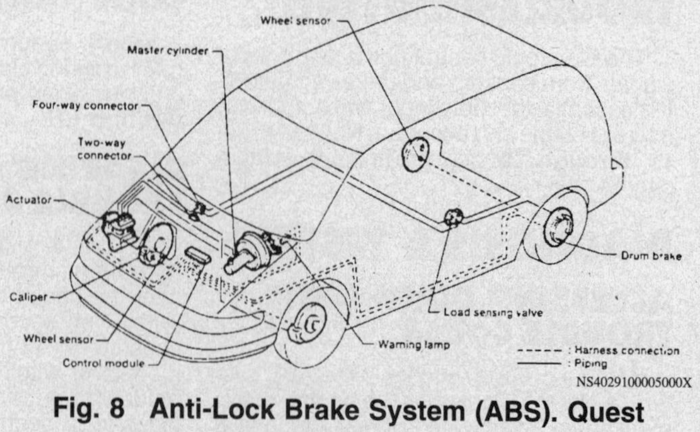
Wheel sensor
Master cylinder
Four-way connector
Two-way connector
Actuator
Drum brake
Caliper
Load sensing valve
Wheel sensor
Warning lamp
Control module
- - - - : Harness connection
——— : Piping
NS4029100005000X

Fig. 8 Anti-Lock Brake System (ABS). Quest

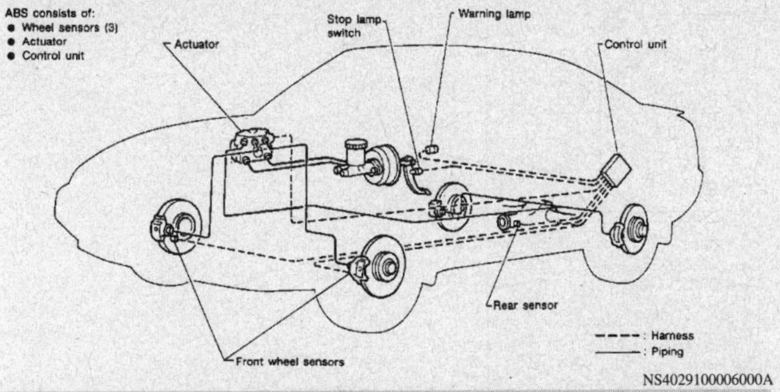
ABS consists of:
• Wheel sensors (3)
• Actuator
• Control unit
Actuator
Stop lamp switch
Warning lamp
Control unit
Rear sensor
Front wheel sensors
----: Harness
——: Piping

NS4029100006000A

Fig. 9 Anti-Lock Brake System (ABS). 240SX

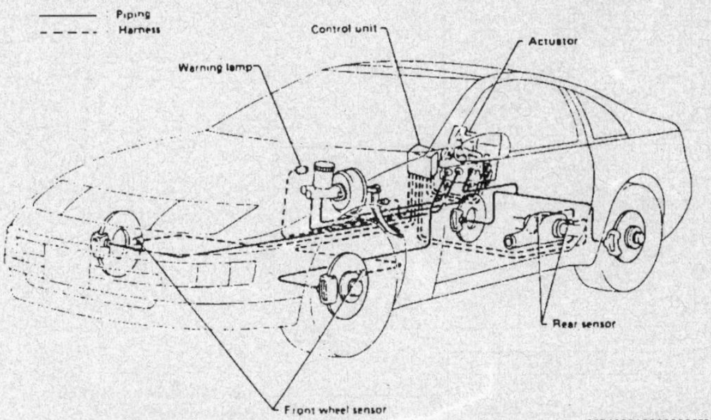
Piping
Harness
Control unit
Warning lamp
Actuator
Rear sensor
Front wheel sensor

NS4029100009000X

Fig. 10 Anti-Lock Brake System (ABS). 300ZX

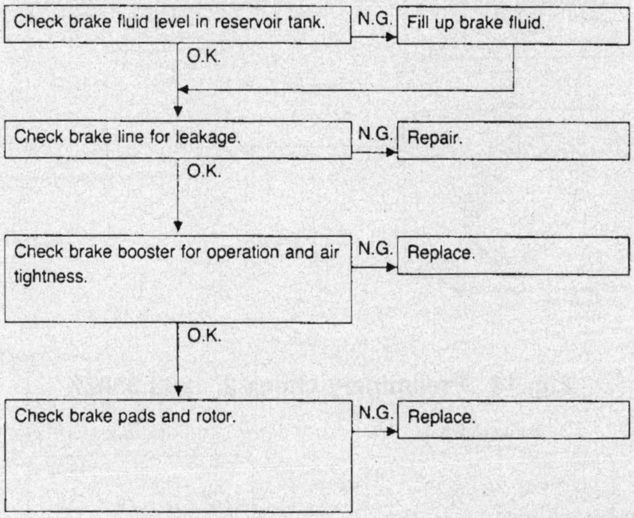
Check brake fluid level in reservoir tank.
N.G.
Fill up brake fluid.
O.K.
Check brake line for leakage.
N.G.
Repair.
O.K.
Check brake booster for operation and air tightness.
N.G.
Replace.
O.K.
Check brake pads and rotor.
N.G.
Replace.

NS4029100011000X

Fig. 11 Preliminary check 1. 1993–94 Except Pathfinder & Pickup

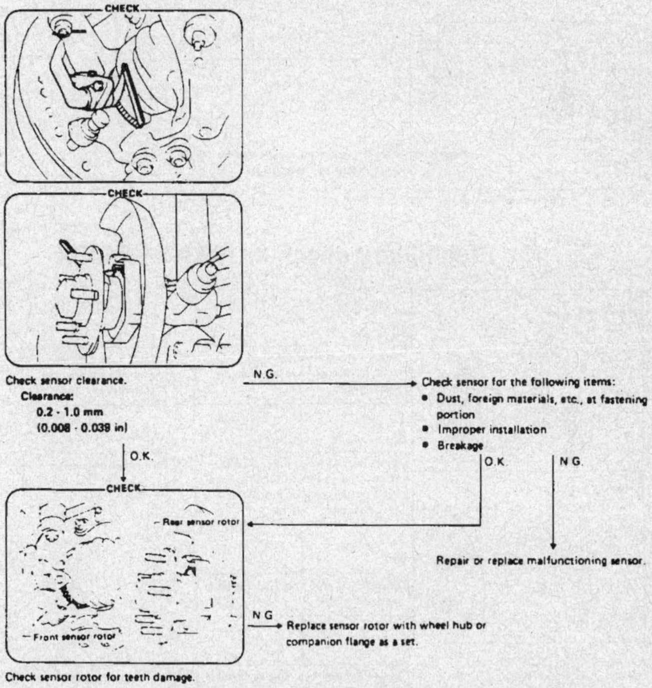
CHECK
CHECK
Check sensor clearance.
Clearance:
0.2 - 1.0 mm
(0.008 - 0.039 in)
N.G.
Check sensor for the following items:
• Dust, foreign materials, etc., at fastening portion
• Improper installation
• Breakage
O.K.
N.G.
O.K.
CHECK
Rear sensor rotor
Repair or replace malfunctioning sensor.
N.G.
Replace sensor rotor with wheel hub or companion flange as a set.
Front sensor rotor
Check sensor rotor for teeth damage.

NS4029100012000X

Fig. 12 Preliminary check 2. 1993–94 Maxima

PATHFINDER & PICKUP

Refer to **Fig. 204** for electrical component inspection.

QUEST

Wheel Sensors

Check resistance between wheel sensor connector terminals, **Fig. 205.** Resistance should be .9–1.1 K-ohms.

Actuator Motor Relay

Check continuity between motor relay terminals as shown in **Figs. 206 and 207.**

Solenoid Valve Relay

Check continuity between solenoid valve relay terminals as shown in **Figs. 208 and 209.**

GROUND CIRCUIT CHECK

ACTUATOR MOTOR GROUND

When performing actuator motor ground circuit check, refer to **Figs. 210 through 213.** Resistance between both terminals should be zero ohms.

RELAY BOX GROUND

Altima

Check resistance between relay box harness connector terminal and ground, **Fig. 214.** Resistance should be zero ohms.

SYSTEM SERVICE

Brake System Bleed

Refer to “Hydraulic Brake Systems” for brake bleeding procedure.

Component Replacement

When replacing components, refer to **Figs. 215 through 225,** for component location.

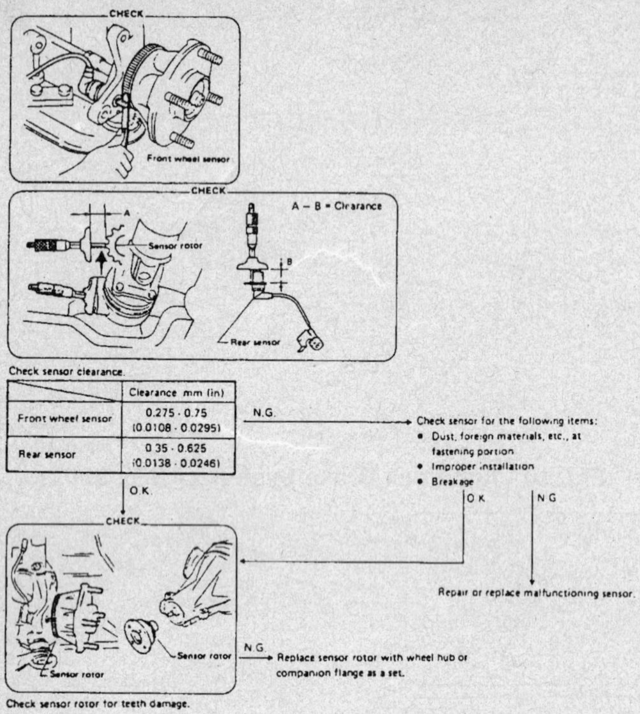
CHECK
Front wheel sensor
CHECK
A − B = Clearance
Sensor rotor
Rear sensor
Check sensor clearance.
Clearance mm (in)
Front wheel sensor 0.275 - 0.75 (0.0108 - 0.0295)
Rear sensor 0.35 - 0.625 (0.0138 - 0.0246)
N.G.
Check sensor for the following items:
• Dust, foreign materials, etc., at fastening portion
• Improper installation
• Breakage
O.K.
N.G.
O.K.
CHECK
Repair or replace malfunctioning sensor.
Sensor rotor
Sensor rotor
N.G.
Replace sensor rotor with wheel hub or companion flange as a set.
Check sensor rotor for teeth damage.

NS4029100013000X

Fig. 13 Preliminary check 2. 1993–94 240SX

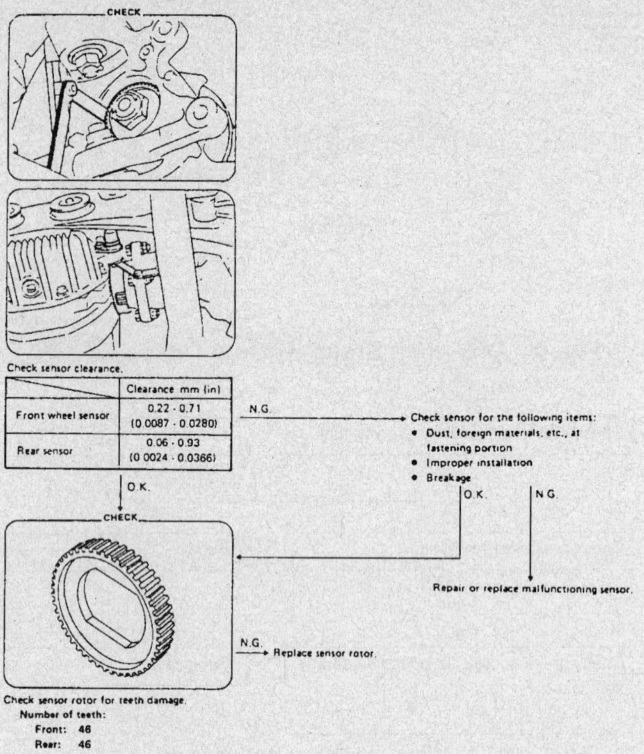
CHECK
Check sensor clearance.
Clearance mm (in)
Front wheel sensor 0.22 - 0.71 (0.0087 - 0.0280)
Rear sensor 0.06 - 0.93 (0.0024 - 0.0366)
N.G.
Check sensor for the following items:
• Dust, foreign materials, etc., at fastening portion
• Improper installation
• Breakage
O.K.
N.G.
O.K.
CHECK
Repair or replace malfunctioning sensor.
N.G.
Replace sensor rotor.
Check sensor rotor for teeth damage.
Number of teeth:
Front: 46
Rear: 46

NS4029100014000X

Fig. 14 Preliminary check 2. 1993 300ZX

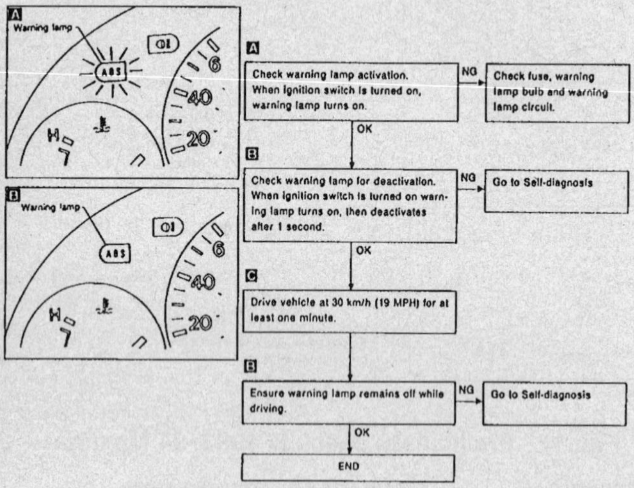
A
Warning lamp
ABS
B
Warning lamp
ABS
A
Check warning lamp activation. When ignition switch is turned on, warning lamp turns on.
NG
Check fuse, warning lamp bulb and warning lamp circuit.
OK
B
Check warning lamp for deactivation. When ignition switch is turned on warning lamp turns on, then deactivates after 1 second.
NG
Go to Self-diagnosis
OK
C
Drive vehicle at 30 km/h (19 MPH) for at least one minute.
D
Ensure warning lamp remains off while driving.
NG
Go to Self-diagnosis
OK
END

NS4029400015000X

Fig. 15 Preliminary check 2. 1994 300ZX

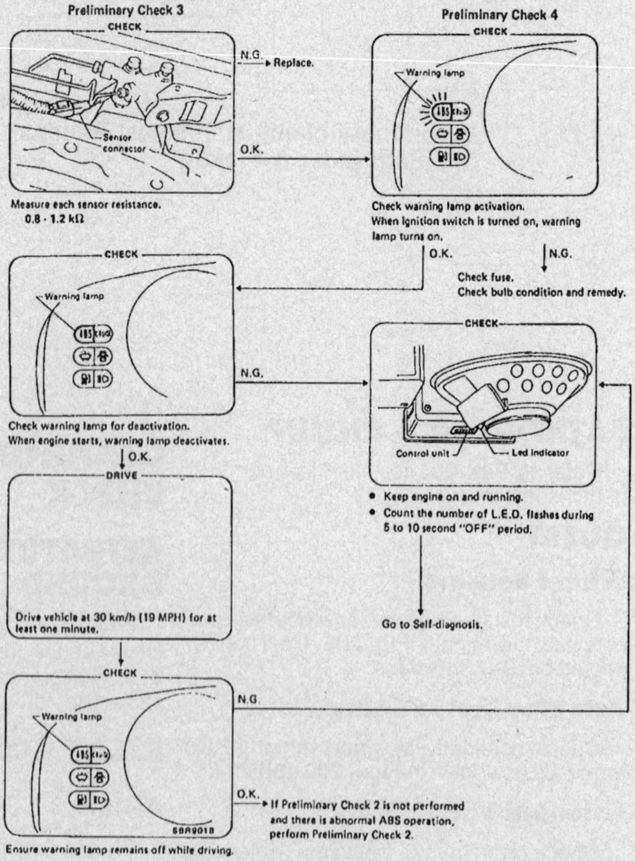
Preliminary Check 3
CHECK
N.G.
Replace.
Sensor connector
Measure each sensor resistance.
0.8 - 1.2 kΩ
O.K.
Preliminary Check 4
CHECK
Warning lamp
Check warning lamp activation.
When ignition switch is turned on, warning lamp turns on.
O.K.
N.G.
Check fuse.
Check bulb condition and remedy.
CHECK
Warning lamp
N.G.
CHECK
Control unit
Led indicator
Check warning lamp for deactivation.
When engine starts, warning lamp deactivates.
O.K.
DRIVE
• Keep engine on and running.
• Count the number of L.E.D. flashes during 5 to 10 second "OFF" period.
Drive vehicle at 30 km/h (19 MPH) for at least one minute.
Go to Self-diagnosis.
CHECK
Warning lamp
N.G.
O.K.
If Preliminary Check 2 is not performed and there is abnormal ABS operation, perform Preliminary Check 2.
SBR901B
Ensure warning lamp remains off while driving.

NS4029100016000X

Fig. 16 Preliminary check 3 & 4. 1993–94 Maxima

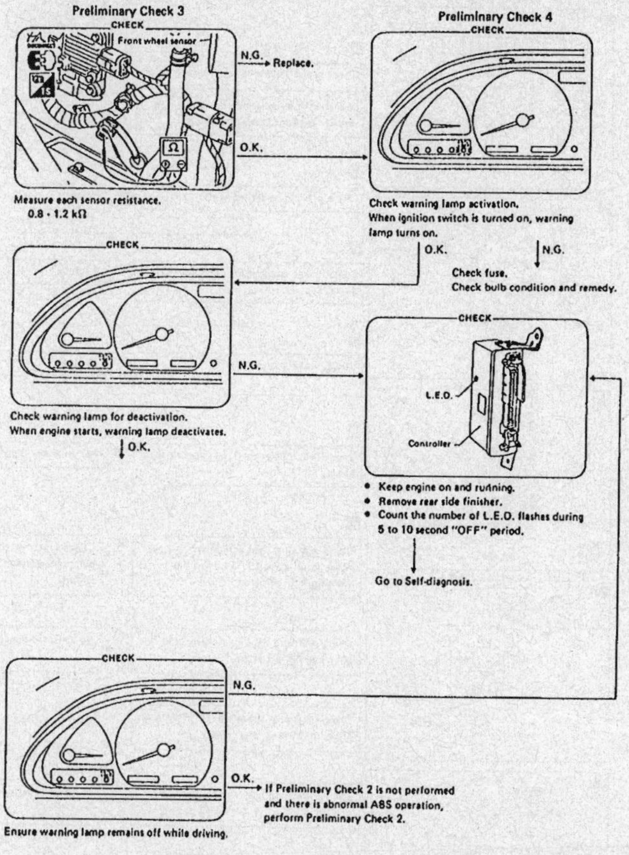

Preliminary Check 3
CHECK
Front wheel sensor
N.G.
Replace.
O.K.
Measure each sensor resistance.
0.8 - 1.2 kΩ
Preliminary Check 4
CHECK
Check warning lamp activation.
When ignition switch is turned on, warning lamp turns on.
O.K.
N.G.
Check fuse.
Check bulb condition and remedy.
CHECK
N.G.
Check warning lamp for deactivation.
When engine starts, warning lamp deactivates.
O.K.
CHECK
L.E.D.
Controller
Keep engine on and running.
Remove rear side finisher.
Count the number of L.E.D. flashes during 5 to 10 second "OFF" period.
Go to Self-diagnosis.
CHECK
N.G.
O.K.
If Preliminary Check 2 is not performed and there is abnormal ABS operation, perform Preliminary Check 2.
Ensure warning lamp remains off while driving.

NS4029100017000X

Fig. 17 Preliminary check 3 & 4. 1993–94 240SX

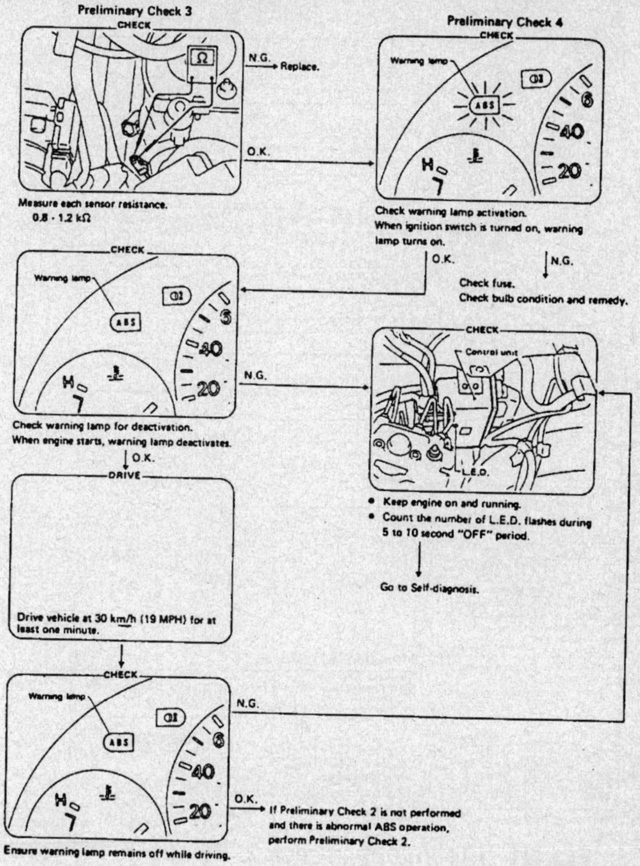

Preliminary Check 3
CHECK
N.G.
Replace.
O.K.
Measure each sensor resistance.
0.8 - 1.2 kΩ
Preliminary Check 4
CHECK
Warning lamp
ABS
Check warning lamp activation.
When ignition switch is turned on, warning lamp turns on.
O.K.
N.G.
Check fuse.
Check bulb condition and remedy.
CHECK
Warning lamp
ABS
N.G.
Check warning lamp for deactivation.
When engine starts, warning lamp deactivates.
O.K.
DRIVE
Drive vehicle at 30 km/h (19 MPH) for at least one minute.
CHECK
Control unit
L.E.D.
Keep engine on and running.
Count the number of L.E.D. flashes during 5 to 10 second "OFF" period.
Go to Self-diagnosis.
CHECK
Warning lamp
ABS
N.G.
O.K.
If Preliminary Check 2 is not performed and there is abnormal ABS operation, perform Preliminary Check 2.
Ensure warning lamp remains off while driving.

NS4029100018000X

Fig. 18 Preliminary check 3 & 4. 1993–94 300ZX

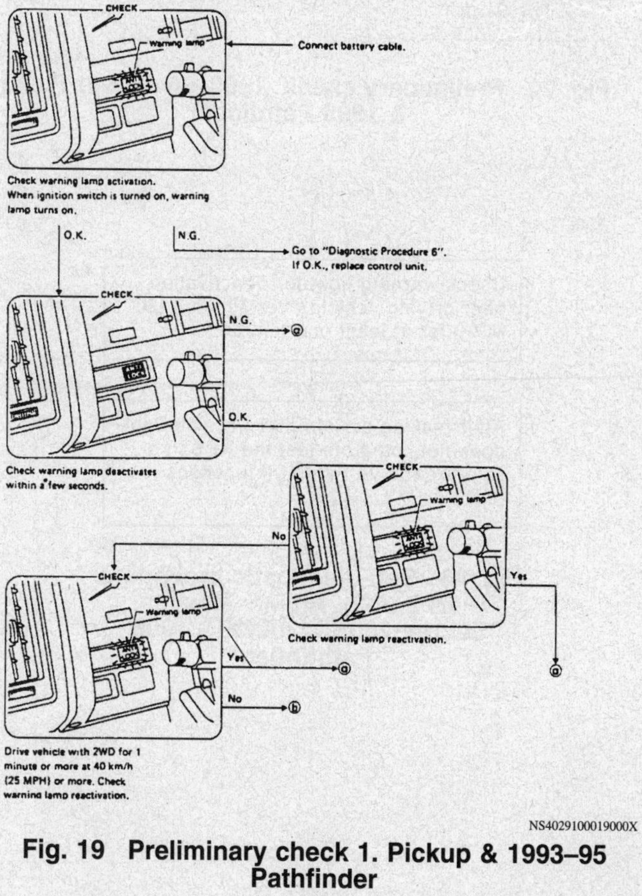

CHECK
Warning lamp
Connect battery cable.
Check warning lamp activation.
When ignition switch is turned on, warning lamp turns on.
O.K.
N.G.
Go to "Diagnostic Procedure 6".
If O.K., replace control unit.
CHECK
N.G.
O.K.
Check warning lamp deactivates within a few seconds.
CHECK
Warning lamp
No
Yes
Check warning lamp reactivation.
CHECK
Warning lamp
Yes
No
Drive vehicle with 2WD for 1 minute or more at 40 km/h (25 MPH) or more. Check warning lamp reactivation.

NS4029100019000X

Fig. 19 Preliminary check 1. Pickup & 1993–95 Pathfinder

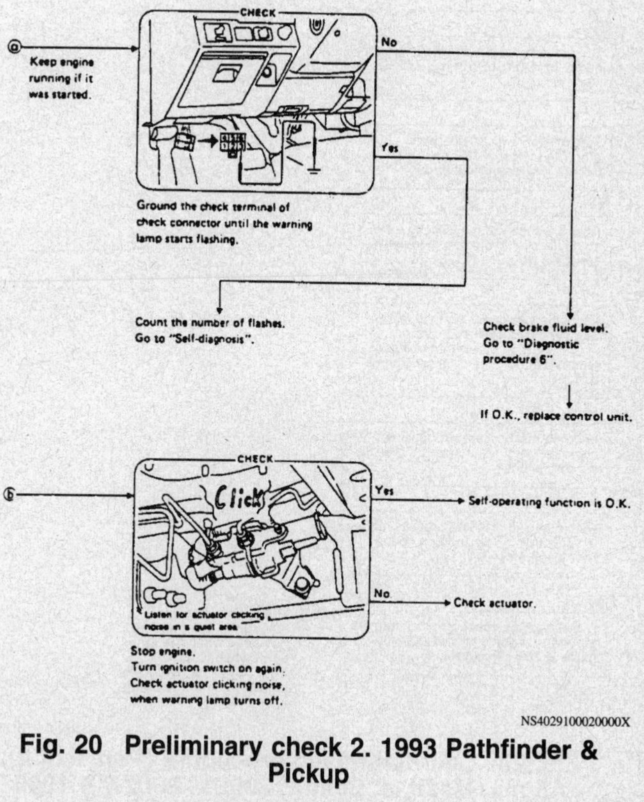

Keep engine running if it was started.
CHECK
No
Yes
Ground the check terminal of check connector until the warning lamp starts flashing.
Count the number of flashes.
Go to "Self-diagnosis".
Check brake fluid level.
Go to "Diagnostic procedure 6".
If O.K., replace control unit.
CHECK
Click
Yes
Self-operating function is O.K.
No
Check actuator.
Listen for actuator clicking noise in a quiet area.
Stop engine.
Turn ignition switch on again.
Check actuator clicking noise, when warning lamp turns off.

NS4029100020000X

Fig. 20 Preliminary check 2. 1993 Pathfinder & Pickup

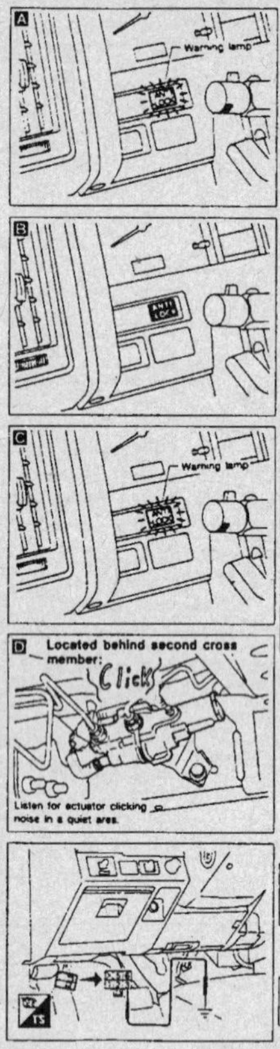
A
Warning lamp
B
C
Warning lamp
D
Located behind second cross member:
Click
Listen for actuator clicking noise in a quiet area.

A

- 1) Turn ignition switch on.
  2) Check warning lamp activation. When ignition switch is turned on, warning lamp should turn on.
  - No → Go to "Diagnostic Procedure 6". If OK, replace control unit.
  - Yes ↓

B

- Check warning lamp deactivates within a few seconds.
  - No → Go to Preliminary Check 2 below.
  - Yes ↓

C

- Check warning lamp reactivation.
  - Yes → Go to Preliminary Check 2 below.
  - No ↓
- 1) Drive vehicle with 2WD for 1 minute or more at 40 km/h (25 MPH) or more.
  2) Check warning lamp reactivation.
  - Yes → Go to Preliminary Check 2 below.
  - No ↓

D

- 1) Stop engine.
  2) Turn ignition switch on again. Check actuator clicking noise, when warning lamp turns off.
  - OK → Self-operating function is OK
  - NG ↓
- Check actuator. Refer to "Electrical Components Inspection".

Preliminary Check 2

- 1) Start engine.
  2) Ground the check terminal of check connector.
  3) Check the warning lamp flashing.
  - No → Check brake fluid level. Go to "Diagnostic Procedure 6". ↓ OK → Replace control unit.
  - Yes ↓
- Count the number of flashes. Go to "Self-diagnosis".

NS4029400021000X

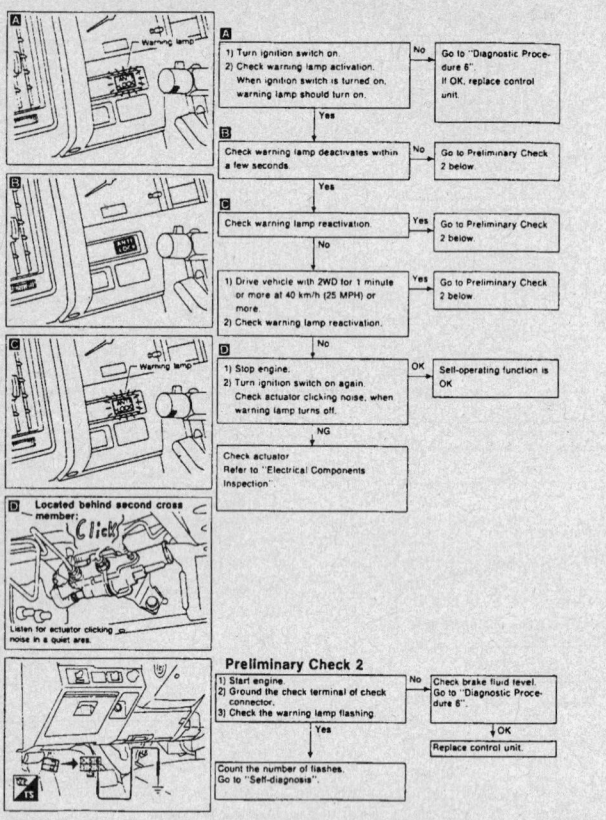

Fig. 21 Preliminary check 2. Pickup & 1994–95 Pathfinder

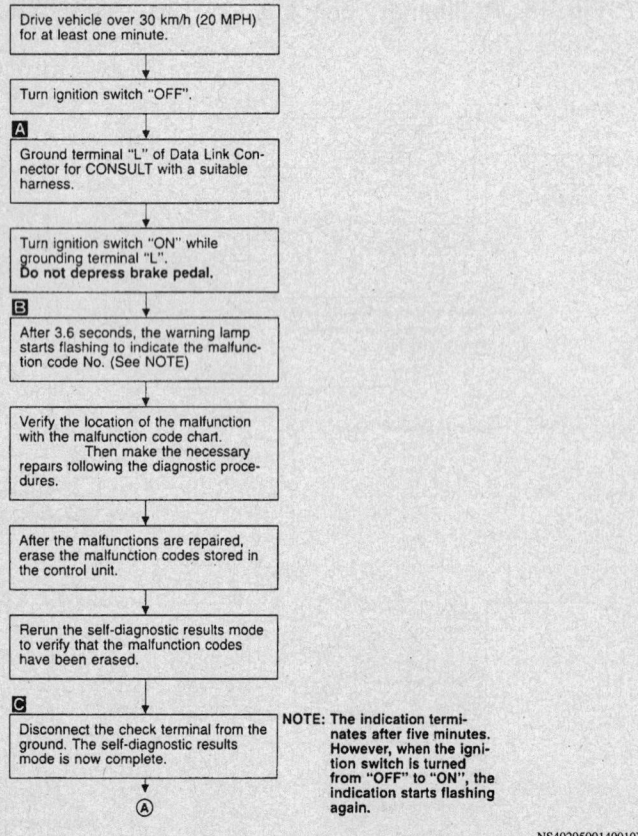

- Drive vehicle over 30 km/h (20 MPH) for at least one minute.
- ↓
- Turn ignition switch "OFF".
- ↓ **A**
- Ground terminal "L" of Data Link Connector for CONSULT with a suitable harness.
- ↓
- Turn ignition switch "ON" while grounding terminal "L". **Do not depress brake pedal.**
- ↓ **B**
- After 3.6 seconds, the warning lamp starts flashing to indicate the malfunction code No. (See NOTE)
- ↓
- Verify the location of the malfunction with the malfunction code chart. Then make the necessary repairs following the diagnostic procedures.
- ↓
- After the malfunctions are repaired, erase the malfunction codes stored in the control unit.
- ↓
- Rerun the self-diagnostic results mode to verify that the malfunction codes have been erased.
- ↓ **C**
- Disconnect the check terminal from the ground. The self-diagnostic results mode is now complete.
- ↓
- Ⓐ

NOTE: The indication terminates after five minutes. However, when the ignition switch is turned from "OFF" to "ON", the indication starts flashing again.

NS4029500140010X

Fig. 23 Self-diagnostic procedure (Part 1 of 2). Altima, Maxima, Sentra, 200SX, 300ZX & 1996 Pathfinder

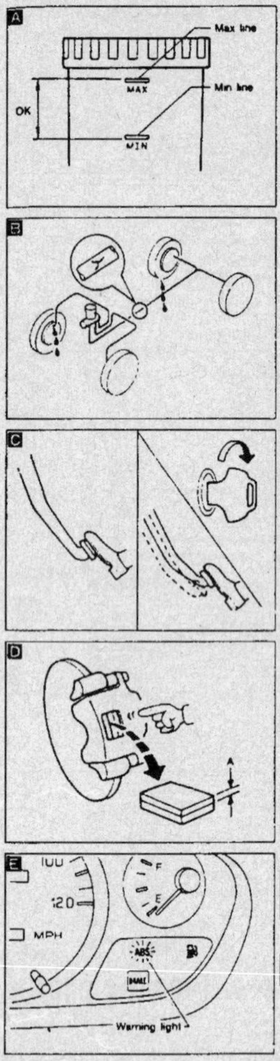
A
Max line
MAX
Min line
OK
MIN
B
C
D
E
Warning light

A

- Check brake fluid level in reservoir tank
- Low fluid level may indicate brake pad wear or leakage from brake line.
- ↓

B

- Check brake line for leakage.
  - NG → Repair.
  - OK ↓

C

- Check brake booster for operation and air tightness.
  - NG → Replace.
  - OK ↓

D

- Check brake pads and rotor.
  - NG → Replace.
  - OK ↓

A

- Check brake fluid level in reservoir tank again.
  - NG → Fill up brake fluid.
  - OK ↓

E

- Check warning light activation. When ignition switch is turned on, warning light turns on
  - NG → Check fuse, warning light bulb and warning light circuit.
  - OK ↓
- Check warning light for deactivation after engine is started.
  - NG → Go to Self-diagnosis
  - OK ↓
- Drive vehicle at speeds over 15 km/h (9 MPH) for at least one minute.
- ↓
- Ensure warning light remains off while driving.
  - NG → Go to Self-diagnosis
  - OK ↓
- END

NS4029500139000X

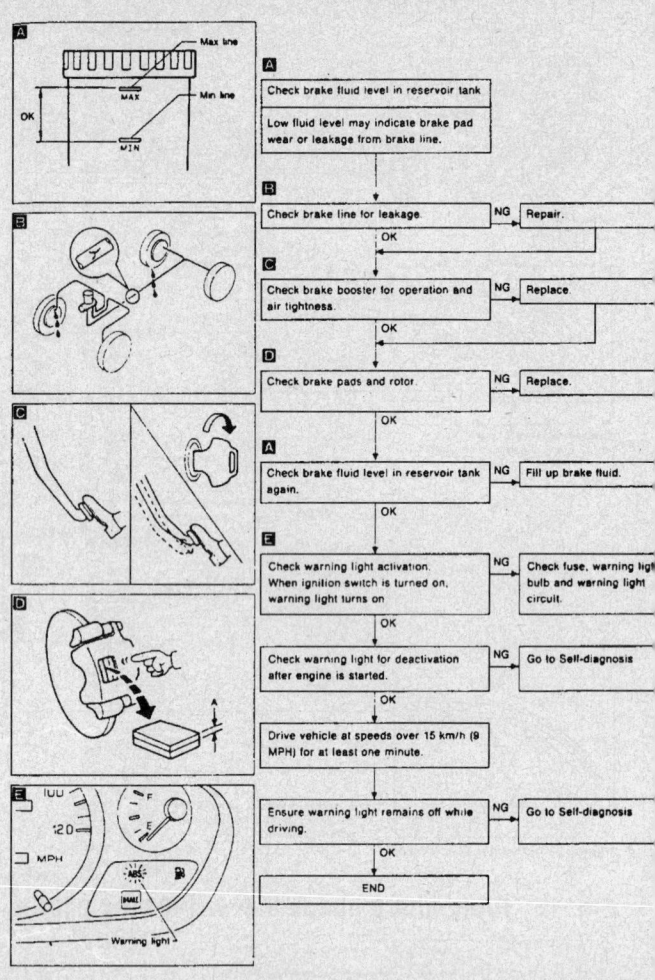

Fig. 22 Preliminary check. 1995–96 except Pickup & 1995 Pathfinder

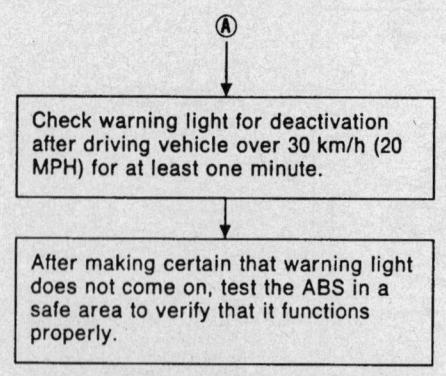

- Ⓐ
- ↓
- Check warning light for deactivation after driving vehicle over 30 km/h (20 MPH) for at least one minute.
- ↓
- After making certain that warning light does not come on, test the ABS in a safe area to verify that it functions properly.

NS4029500140020X

Fig. 23 Self-diagnostic procedure (Part 2 of 2). Altima, Maxima, Sentra, 200SX, 300ZX & 1996 Pathfinder

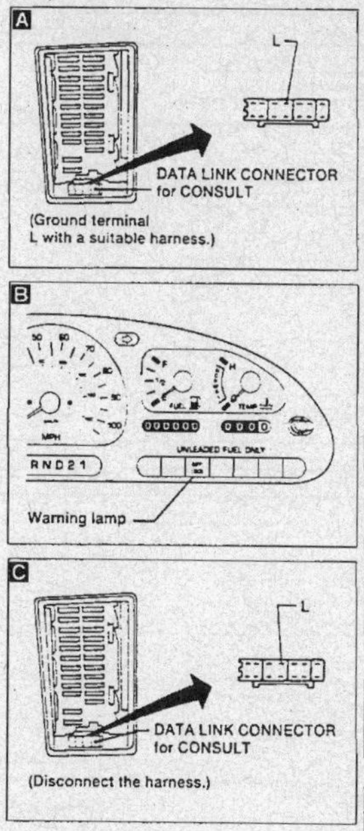
A
L
DATA LINK CONNECTOR for CONSULT
(Ground terminal L with a suitable harness.)
B
Warning lamp
C
L
DATA LINK CONNECTOR for CONSULT
(Disconnect the harness.)

Check fuses before starting Self-diagnosis.

↓

Turn ignition switch "OFF".

↓ A

Ground terminal "L" of "DATA LINK CONNECTOR for CONSULT" with a suitable harness.

↓

Turn ignition switch "ON" while grounding terminal "L".
Do not depress brake pedal.

↓ B

After 3.2 seconds, the warning lamp starts flashing to indicate the malfunction code No.

↓

After verifying the location of the malfunction with the malfunction code chart, make the necessary repairs following the instructions in the diagnostic procedures.

↓

After the malfunctions are repaired, erase the malfunction codes stored in the control module.

↓

Rerun the self-diagnostic results mode to verify that the malfunction codes have been erased.

↓ C

Disconnect the check terminal from the ground. The self-diagnostic results mode is now complete.

↓

(A)

NS4029100089010X

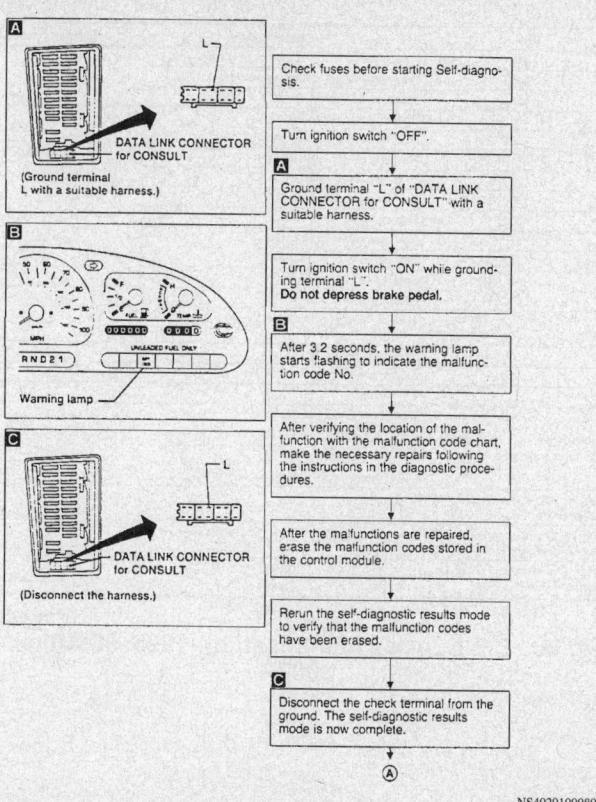

Fig. 24 Self-diagnostic procedure (Part 1 of 2). Quest

(A)

↓

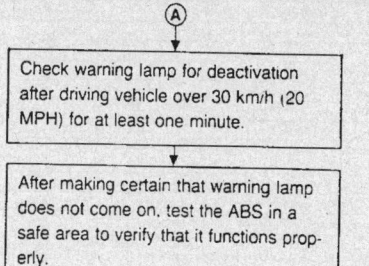

Check warning lamp for deactivation after driving vehicle over 30 km/h (20 MPH) for at least one minute.

↓

After making certain that warning lamp does not come on, test the ABS in a safe area to verify that it functions properly.

NS4029100089020X

Fig. 24 Self-diagnostic procedure (Part 2 of 2). Quest

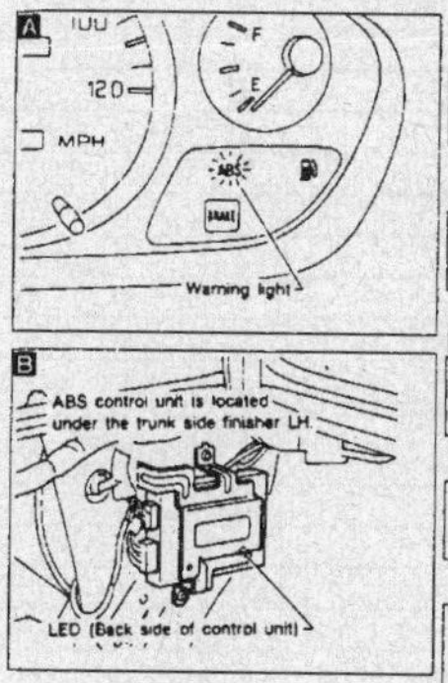
A
MPH
Warning light
B
ABS control unit is located under the trunk side finisher LH.
LED (Back side of control unit)

Start engine.
Drive vehicle over 15 km/h (9 MPH) for at least one minute.

↓ A

Stop vehicle with engine running.
Make sure that the ABS warning light activates.

↓ B

The LED on the ABS control unit flashes to indicate the malfunction code No.

↓

Verify the location of the malfunction with the malfunction code chart.
Then make necessary repairs following the diagnostic procedures.

↓

After the malfunctions are repaired, erase the self-diagnostic results stored in the control unit.
Disconnect connectors for ABS control unit or the battery negative terminal for at least one minute.

↓

Check warning light for deactivation after driving vehicle over 15 km/h (9 MPH) for at least one minute.

↓

Test the ABS in a safe area to verify that it functions properly.

NS4029500141000X

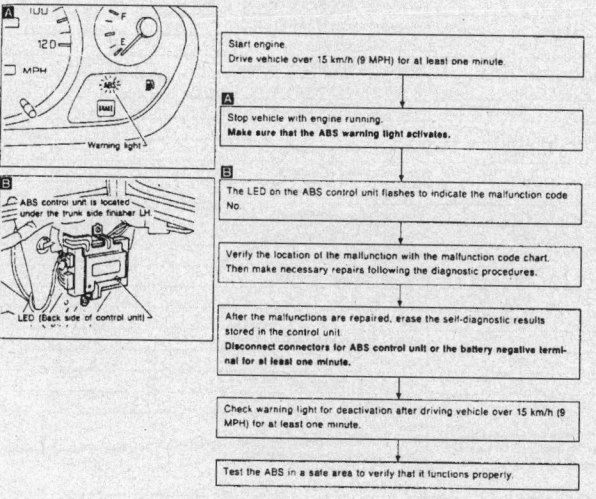

Fig. 25 Self-diagnostic procedure. 240SX

No. of L.E.D. flashes	Malfunctioning part or unit
1	Left front actuator solenoid circuit
2	Right front actuator solenoid circuit
3	Right rear actuator solenoid circuit
4	Left rear actuator solenoid circuit
5	Left front wheel sensor circuit
6	Right front wheel sensor circuit
7	Right rear wheel sensor circuit
8	Left rear wheel sensor circuit
9	Motor and motor relay
10	Solenoid valve relay
16 or continuous	Control unit
Warning activates and L.E.D. "OFF"	Power supply or ground circuit for control unit

NS4029100022000X

Fig. 26 L.E.D. self diagnostic code identification chart. 1993–94 Maxima, 240SX & 300ZX

No. of L.E.D. flashes	Malfunctioning parts or circuit	Diagnostic Procedure
1	Left front actuator solenoid circuit	8
2	Right front actuator solenoid circuit	8
3	Both actuator solenoid circuits	8
5	Left front wheel sensor circuit	9
6	Right front wheel sensor circuit	9
7	Right rear wheel sensor circuit	9
8	Left rear wheel sensor circuit	9
9	Motor and motor relay	10
10	Solenoid valve relay	11
15	Sensor rotor	12
16	Control unit	13
Warning activates and L.E.D. "OFF"	Power supply and ground circuit	14

NS4029100023000X

Fig. 27 L.E.D. code identification. 1993–94 NX 1600, NX 2000 & Sentra

Code No. (No. of LED flashes)	Malfunctioning part	Diagnostic procedure
45	Actuator front left outlet solenoid valve	3
46	Actuator front left inlet solenoid valve	3
41	Actuator front right outlet solenoid valve	3
42	Actuator front right inlet solenoid valve	3
51	Actuator rear right outlet solenoid valve	3
52	Actuator rear right inlet solenoid valve	3
55	Actuator rear left inlet solenoid valve	3
56	Actuator rear left inlet solenoid valve	3
25	Front left sensor (open-circuit)	4
26	Front left sensor (short-circuit)	4
21	Front right sensor (open-circuit)	4
22	Front right sensor (short-circuit)	4
35	Rear left sensor (open-circuit)	4
36	Rear left sensor (short-circuit)	4
31	Rear right sensor (open-circuit)	4
32	Rear right sensor (short-circuit)	4
18	Sensor rotor	4
61	Actuator motor or motor relay	5
63	Solenoid valve relay	6
57	Power supply (Low voltage)	7
71	Control unit	8
Warning lamp stays on when ignition switch is turned on.	Control unit power supply circuit Warning lamp bulb circuit Control unit or control unit connector Solenoid valve relay stuck Power supply for solenoid valve relay coil	2
Warning lamp stays on, during self-diagnosis.	Control unit	—
Warning lamp does not come on when ignition switch is turned on.	Fuse, warning lamp bulb or warning lamp circuit Control unit	1
Warning lamp does not come on during self-diagnosis.	Control unit	—
Pedal vibration and noise	—	9
Long stopping distance	—	10
Unexpected pedal action	—	11
ABS does not work.	—	12
ABS works frequently.	—	13

NS4029500142000X

Fig. 28 L.E.D. code identification. 1995–96 Maxima, Sentra & 200SX

Code No. (No. of LED flashes)	Malfunctioning part and circuit	Diagnostic procedure
01	Front right sensor (open-circuit)	4
02	Front left sensor (open-circuit)	4
03	Rear sensor (open-circuit)	4
05	Front right sensor (short-circuit)	4
06	Front left sensor (short-circuit)	4
07	Rear sensor (short-circuit)	4
11	Actuator front right inlet solenoid valve (open-circuit)	3
12	Actuator front left inlet solenoid valve (open-circuit)	3
13	Actuator rear inlet solenoid valve (open-circuit)	3
15	Actuator front right outlet solenoid valve (open-circuit)	3
16	Actuator front left outlet solenoid valve (open-circuit)	3
17	Actuator rear outlet solenoid valve (open-circuit)	3
21	Actuator front right inlet solenoid valve (short-circuit)	3
22	Actuator front left inlet solenoid valve (short-circuit)	3
23	Actuator rear inlet solenoid valve (short-circuit)	3
25	Actuator front right outlet solenoid valve (short-circuit)	3
26	Actuator front left outlet solenoid valve (short-circuit)	3
27	Actuator rear outlet solenoid valve (short-circuit)	3
41	Solenoid valve relay circuit (unable to turn off)	6
42	Solenoid valve relay circuit (unable to turn on)	6
43	Actuator motor or motor relay (unable to turn off)	5
44	Actuator motor or motor relay (unable to turn on)	5
47	Power supply (High voltage)	7
48	Power supply (Low voltage)	7
45, 46, 77 LED deactivation or continuous activation	Control unit Ground circuit	2
Warning light does not come on when ignition switch is turned on.	Fuse, warning light bulb or warning light circuit Control unit power supply circuit	1
Pedal vibration and noise	—	9
Long stopping distance	—	10
Unexpected pedal action	—	11
ABS does not work.	—	12
ABS works frequently.	—	13

NS4029500143000X

Fig. 29 L.E.D. code identification. 1995–96 240SX

Code No.	Applied Part	Diagnostic Procedure
45*	Front left actuator solenoid	2
41*	Front right actuator solenoid	2
55*	Rear actuator solenoid	2
25	Front left sensor (open-circuit)	3
26	Front left sensor (frequency error)	3
21	Front right sensor (open-circuit)	3
22	Front right sensor (frequency error)	3
35	Rear left sensor (open-circuit)	3
36	Rear left sensor (frequency error)	3
31	Rear right sensor (open-circuit)	3
32	Rear right sensor (frequency error)	3
61	Actuator motor or motor relay	4
63*	Solenoid valve relay	2
71	Control module	5
Warning lamp stays on, does not blink.	Solenoid valve relay stuck or control module power supply circuit	2
Warning lamp does not come on	Warning lamp bulb	1

NS4029100091000A

Fig. 31 L.E.D. code identification. Quest

No. of warning flashes	Detected items	Malfunctioning cause or part		Diagnostic Procedure
2	Actuator	ISO solenoid	Open	Diagnostic Procedure 7
7			Shorted	Diagnostic Procedure 7
4			Blocked	Diagnostic Procedure 8
3		DUMP solenoid	Open	Diagnostic Procedure 9
8			Short circuit	Diagnostic Procedure 9
9	Sensor	Open		Diagnostic Procedure 10
10		Short circuit		Diagnostic Procedure 10
6		Erratic		Diagnostic Procedure 11
13, 14 or 15	Control Unit	–		Diagnostic Procedure 12
5	Other			Diagnostic Procedure 13

NS4029100024000X

Fig. 32 L.E.D. code identification. Pickup & 1993–95 Pathfinder

Code No.	Malfunctioning part	Diagnostic procedure
45	Front left actuator solenoid valve	3
41	Front right actuator solenoid valve	
55	Rear actuator solenoid valve	
25	Front left sensor (open-circuit)	4
26	Front left sensor (short-circuit)	
21	Front right sensor (open-circuit)	
22	Front right sensor (short-circuit)	
35	Rear left sensor (open-circuit)	
36	Rear left sensor (short-circuit)	
31	Rear right sensor (open-circuit)	
32	Rear right sensor (short-circuit)	
18	Sensor rotor	
61	Actuator motor or motor relay	5
63	Solenoid valve relay circuit (except power supply for relay coil)	6
57	Power supply (Low voltage)	7
16	Stop lamp switch circuit	8
71	Control unit	9
Warning lamp stays on when ignition switch is turned on.	Control unit power supply circuit Warning lamp bulb circuit Control unit or control unit connector Solenoid valve relay stuck Power supply for solenoid valve relay coil	2
Warning lamp stays on only during self-diagnosis.	Control unit	—
Warning lamp does not come on when ignition switch is turned on.	Fuse, warning lamp bulb or warning lamp circuit Control unit	1
Warning lamp does not come on only during self-diagnosis.	Control unit	—

NS4029500144000X

Fig. 30 L.E.D. code identification. 1995–96 Altima & 300ZX

Code No. (No. of warning lamp flashes)	Malfunctioning part	Diagnostic procedure
45	Actuator front left outlet solenoid valve	3
46	Actuator front left inlet solenoid valve	3
41	Actuator front right outlet solenoid valve	3
42	Actuator front right inlet solenoid valve	3
55	Actuator rear outlet solenoid valve	3
56	Actuator rear inlet solenoid valve	3
25★2	Front left sensor (open-circuit)	4
26★2	Front left sensor (short-circuit)	4
21★2	Front right sensor (open-circuit)	4
22★2	Front right sensor (short-circuit)	4
31★2	Rear right sensor (open-circuit)	4
32★2	Rear right sensor (short-circuit)	4
35★2	Rear left sensor (open-circuit)	4
36★2	Rear left sensor (short-circuit)	4
18★2	Sensor rotor	4
17★1	G sensor	8
61	Actuator motor or motor relay	5
63	Solenoid valve relay	6
57	Power supply (Low voltage)	7
71	Control unit	9
Warning lamp stays on when ignition switch is turned on	Control unit power supply circuit Warning lamp bulb circuit Control unit or control unit connector Solenoid valve relay stuck Power supply for solenoid valve relay coil	2
Warning lamp does not come on when ignition switch is turned on	Fuse, warning lamp bulb or warning lamp circuit Control unit	1
Pedal vibration and noise	—	10
Long stopping distance	—	11
Unexpected pedal action	—	12
ABS does not work	—	13
ABS works frequently	—	14

★1: 4WD model only.
★2: If a tire slips on rough roads for more than 10 seconds, the ABS warning lamp may come on. In this case, the malfunctioning code regarding the wheel sensors may be memorized. Turn OFF the ignition switch, restart the engine and drive the vehicle at speeds above 30 km/h (20 MPH).

NS4029600190000X

Fig. 33 L.E.D. code identification. 1996 Pathfinder

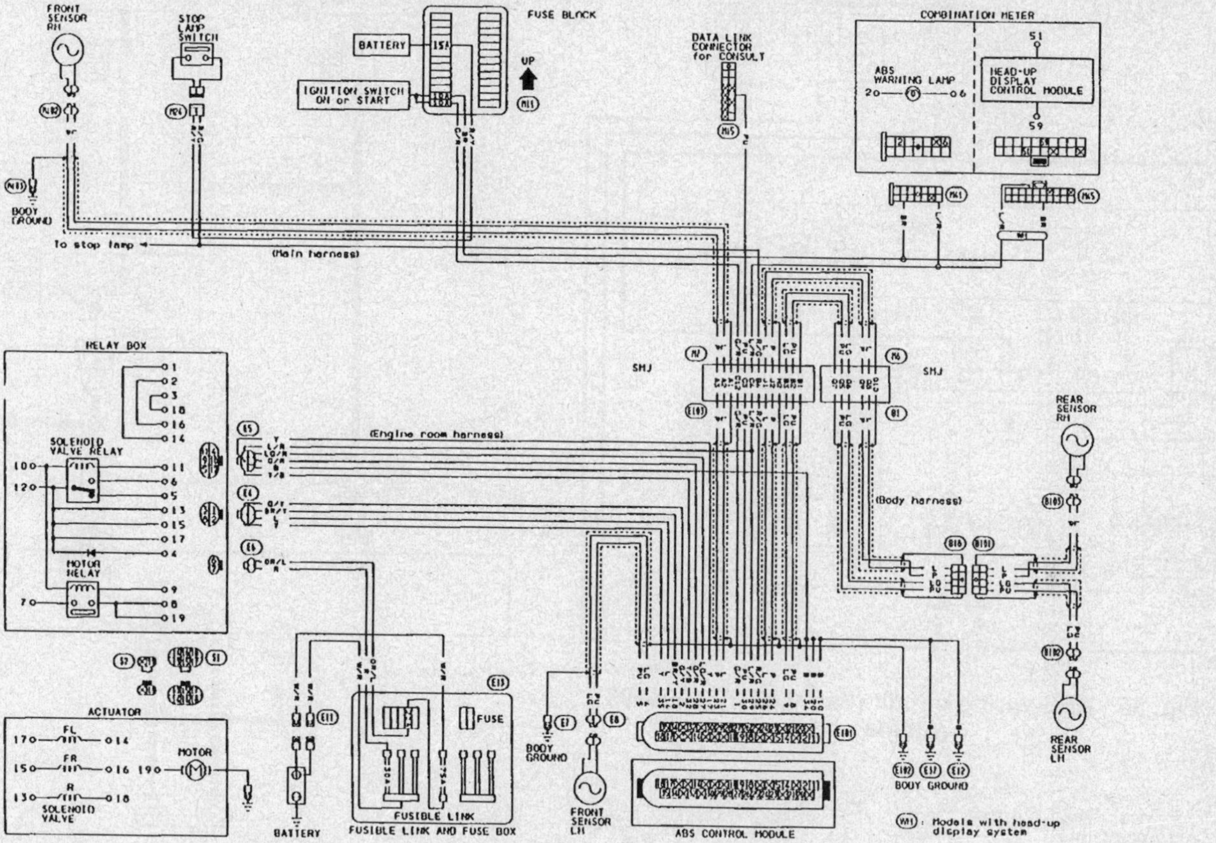
FRONT SENSOR RH
STOP LAMP SWITCH
FUSE BLOCK
BATTERY
IGNITION SWITCH ON or START
UP
DATA LINK CONNECTOR for CONSULT
COMBINATION METER
ABS WARNING LAMP
HEAD-UP DISPLAY CONTROL MODULE
BODY GROUND
To stop lamp
(Main harness)
RELAY BOX
SOLENOID VALVE RELAY
MOTOR RELAY
(Engine room harness)
SMJ
REAR SENSOR RH
(Body harness)
ACTUATOR
MOTOR
SOLENOID VALVE
FUSE
FUSIBLE LINK
BATTERY
FUSIBLE LINK AND FUSE BOX
BODY GROUND
FRONT SENSOR LH
ABS CONTROL MODULE
REAR SENSOR LH
(WH): Models with head-up display system

NS4029300092000X

Fig. 34 ABS wiring circuit. 1993 Altima

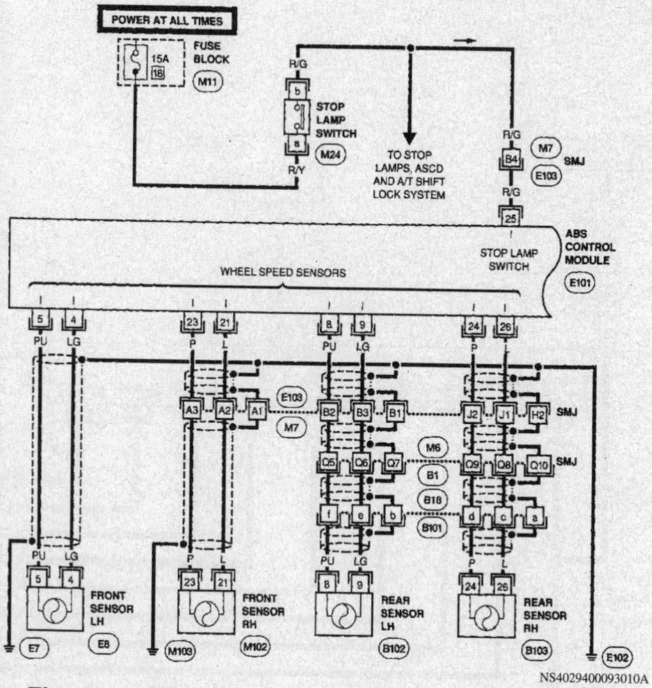
POWER AT ALL TIMES
FUSE BLOCK
STOP LAMP SWITCH
TO STOP LAMPS, ASCD AND A/T SHIFT LOCK SYSTEM
SMJ
ABS CONTROL MODULE
WHEEL SPEED SENSORS
STOP LAMP SWITCH
FRONT SENSOR LH
FRONT SENSOR RH
REAR SENSOR LH
REAR SENSOR RH

NS4029400093010A

Fig. 35 ABS wiring circuit (Part 1 of 3). 1994–95 Altima

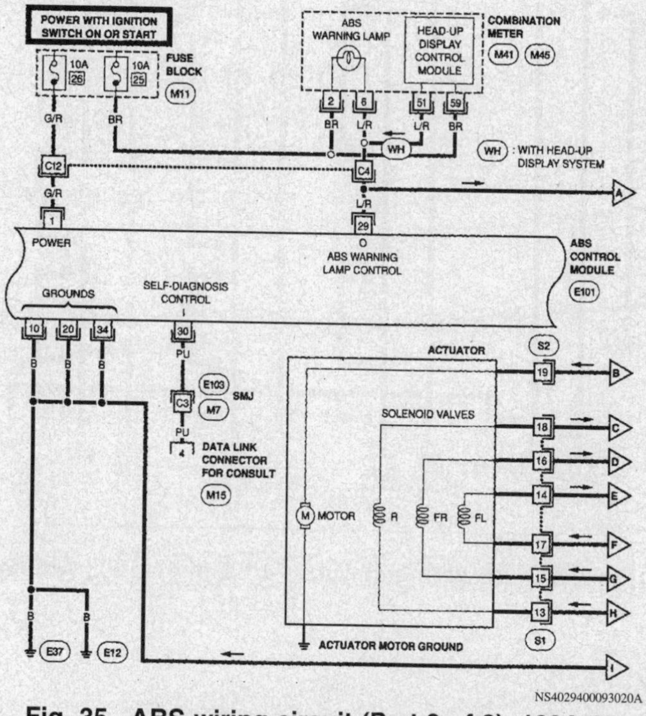
POWER WITH IGNITION SWITCH ON OR START
FUSE BLOCK
ABS WARNING LAMP
HEAD-UP DISPLAY CONTROL MODULE
COMBINATION METER
(WH) : WITH HEAD-UP DISPLAY SYSTEM
POWER
ABS WARNING LAMP CONTROL
ABS CONTROL MODULE
GROUNDS
SELF-DIAGNOSIS CONTROL
SMJ
DATA LINK CONNECTOR FOR CONSULT
ACTUATOR
SOLENOID VALVES
MOTOR
ACTUATOR MOTOR GROUND

NS4029400093020A

Fig. 35 ABS wiring circuit (Part 2 of 3). 1994–95 Altima

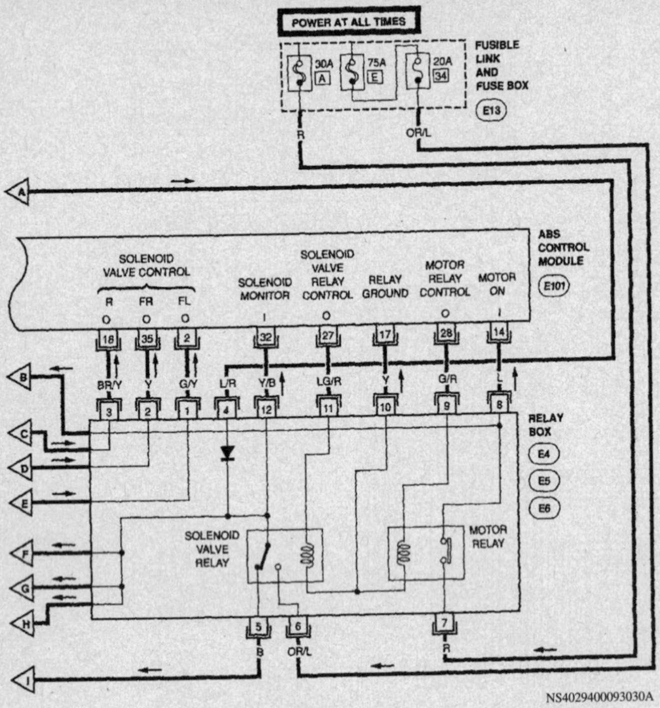
POWER AT ALL TIMES
30A A
75A E
20A 34
FUSIBLE LINK AND FUSE BOX
E13
R
OR/L
ABS CONTROL MODULE
E101
SOLENOID VALVE CONTROL
R FR FL
SOLENOID MONITOR
SOLENOID VALVE RELAY CONTROL
RELAY GROUND
MOTOR RELAY CONTROL
MOTOR ON
BR/Y Y G/Y L/R Y/B LG/R Y G/R L
RELAY BOX
E4
E5
E6
SOLENOID VALVE RELAY
MOTOR RELAY
B OR/L R
NS4029400093030A

Fig. 35 ABS wiring circuit (Part 3 of 3). 1994–95 Altima

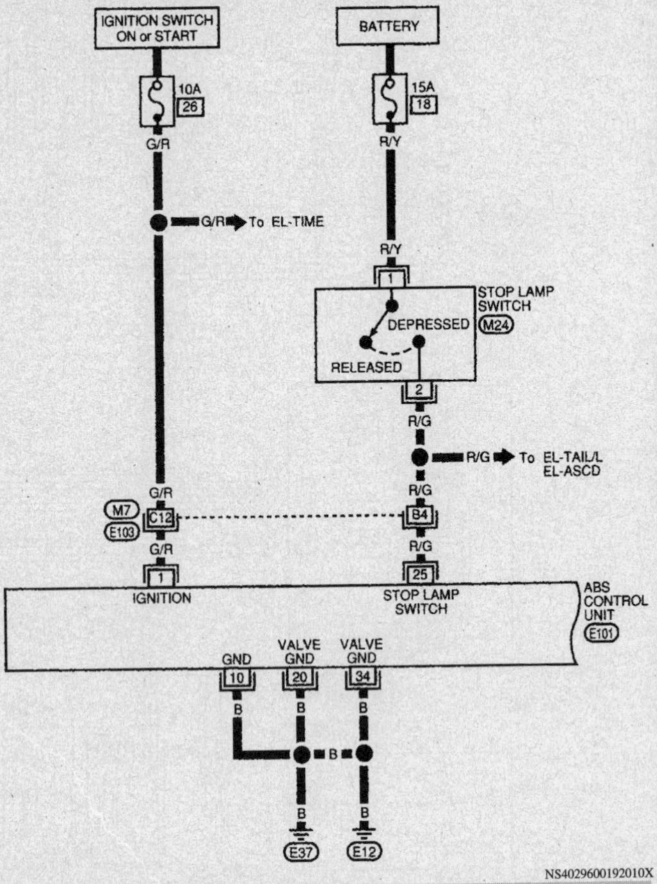
IGNITION SWITCH ON or START
BATTERY
10A 26
15A 18
G/R
R/Y
G/R To EL-TIME
STOP LAMP SWITCH
M24
DEPRESSED
RELEASED
R/G
R/G To EL-TAIL/L EL-ASCD
M7
E103
C12
B4
IGNITION
STOP LAMP SWITCH
ABS CONTROL UNIT
E101
GND
VALVE GND
VALVE GND
B
E37
E12
NS4029600192010X

Fig. 36 ABS wiring circuit (Part 1 of 4). 1996 Altima

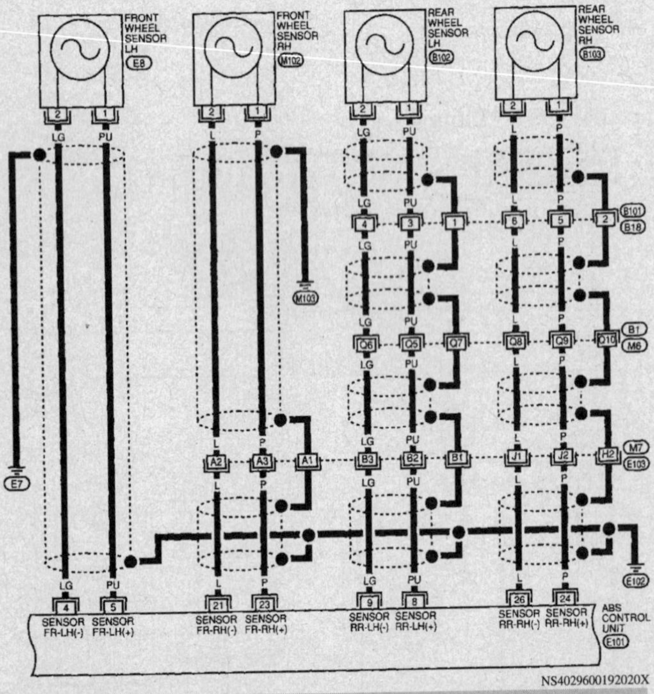
FRONT WHEEL SENSOR LH
E8
FRONT WHEEL SENSOR RH
M102
REAR WHEEL SENSOR LH
B102
REAR WHEEL SENSOR RH
B103
LG PU L P
B101
B18
B1
M6
M7
E103
M103
E7
E102
SENSOR FR-LH(-)
SENSOR FR-LH(+)
SENSOR FR-RH(-)
SENSOR FR-RH(+)
SENSOR RR-LH(-)
SENSOR RR-LH(+)
SENSOR RR-RH(-)
SENSOR RR-RH(+)
ABS CONTROL UNIT
E101
NS4029600192020X

Fig. 36 ABS wiring circuit (Part 2 of 4). 1996 Altima

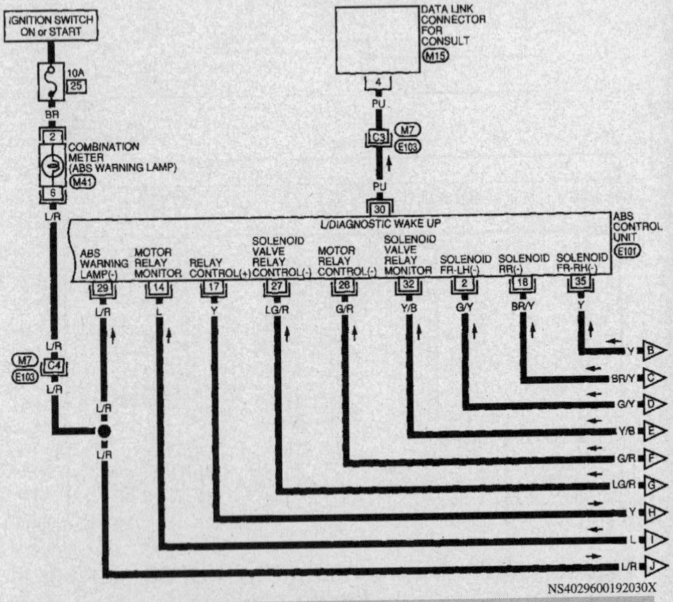
IGNITION SWITCH ON or START
10A 25
BR
COMBINATION METER (ABS WARNING LAMP)
M41
L/R
DATA LINK CONNECTOR FOR CONSULT
M15
PU
M7
E103
L/DIAGNOSTIC WAKE UP
ABS CONTROL UNIT
E101
ABS WARNING LAMP(-)
MOTOR RELAY MONITOR
RELAY CONTROL(+)
SOLENOID VALVE RELAY CONTROL(-)
MOTOR RELAY CONTROL(-)
SOLENOID VALVE RELAY MONITOR
SOLENOID FR-LH(-)
SOLENOID RR(-)
SOLENOID FR-RH(-)
L/R L Y LG/R G/R Y/B G/Y BR/Y Y
NS4029600192030X

Fig. 36 ABS wiring circuit (Part 3 of 4). 1996 Altima

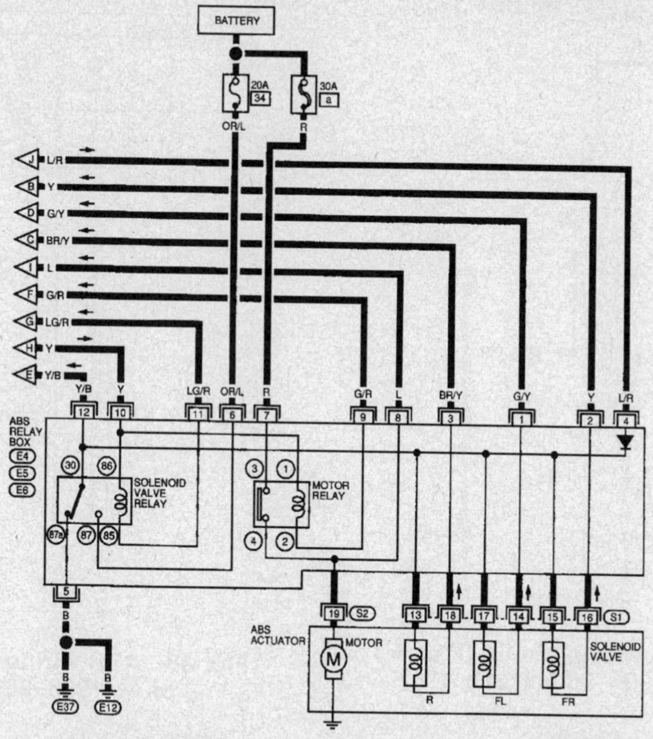

BATTERY
20A
34
30A
a
OR/L
R
L/R
Y
G/Y
BR/Y
L
G/R
LG/R
Y
Y/B
ABS RELAY BOX
E4
E5
E6
SOLENOID VALVE RELAY
MOTOR RELAY
ABS ACTUATOR
MOTOR
SOLENOID VALVE
E37
E12
NS4029600192040X

Fig. 36 ABS wiring circuit (Part 4 of 4). 1996 Altima

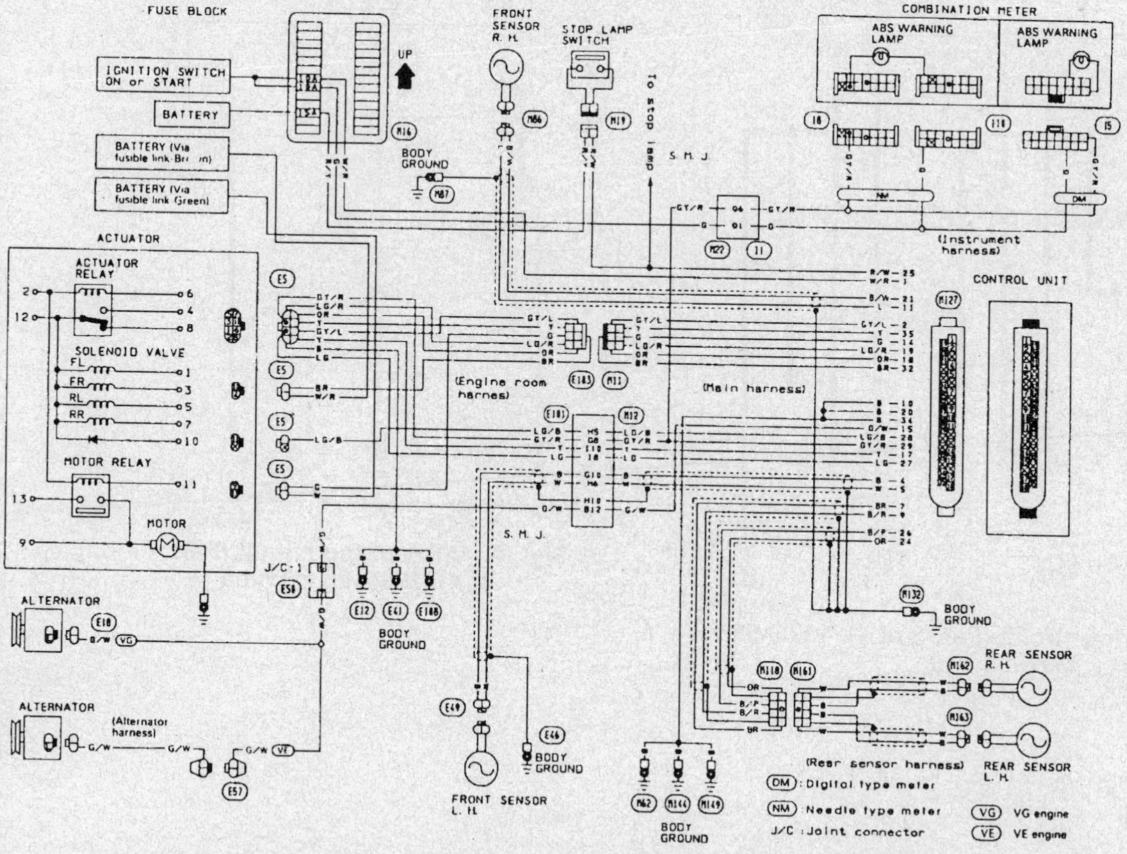

FUSE BLOCK
IGNITION SWITCH ON or START
BATTERY
BATTERY (Via fusible link Green)
UP
FRONT SENSOR R. H.
STOP LAMP SWITCH
to stop lamp
BODY GROUND
COMBINATION METER
ABS WARNING LAMP
ABS WARNING LAMP
(Instrument harness)
CONTROL UNIT
ACTUATOR
ACTUATOR RELAY
SOLENOID VALVE
MOTOR RELAY
MOTOR
(Engine room harness)
(Main harness)
S. M. J.
J/C-1
ALTERNATOR
ALTERNATOR
(Alternator harness)
BODY GROUND
FRONT SENSOR L. H.
REAR SENSOR R. H.
REAR SENSOR L. H.
(Rear sensor harness)
DM: Digital type meter
NM: Needle type meter
J/C: Joint connector
VG: VG engine
VE: VE engine
NS4029100025000X

Fig. 37 ABS wiring circuit. 1993–94

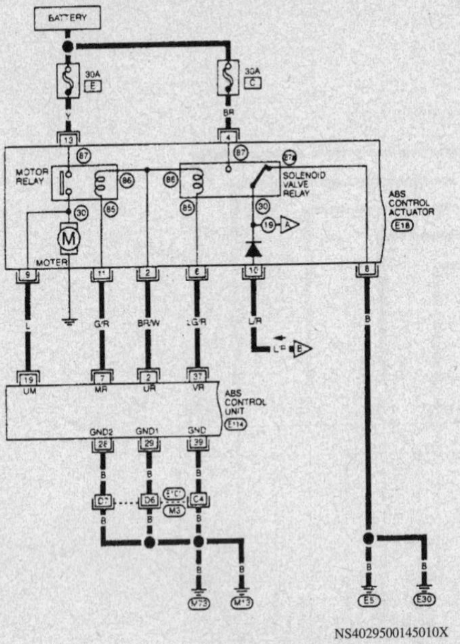

BATTERY
30A
30A
MOTOR RELAY
SOLENOID VALVE RELAY
ABS CONTROL ACTUATOR
MOTER
ABS CONTROL UNIT
GND2
GND1
GND
NS4029500145010X

Fig. 38 ABS wiring circuit (Part 1 of 4). 1995–96 Maxima

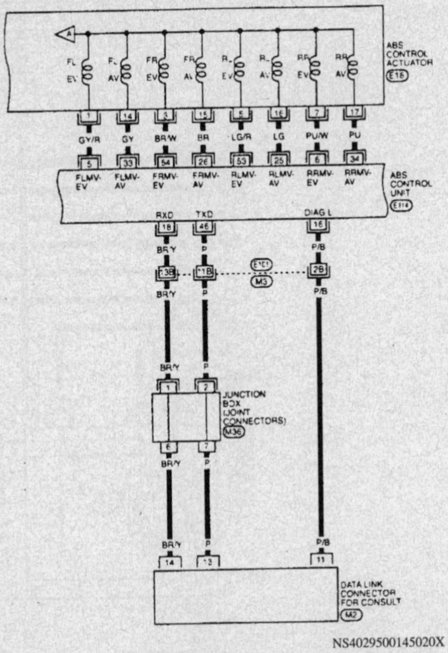

ABS CONTROL ACTUATOR
ABS CONTROL UNIT
RXD
TXD
DIAG L
JUNCTION BOX (JOINT CONNECTORS)
DATA LINK CONNECTOR FOR CONSULT
NS4029500145020X

Fig. 38 ABS wiring circuit (Part 2 of 4). 1995–96 Maxima

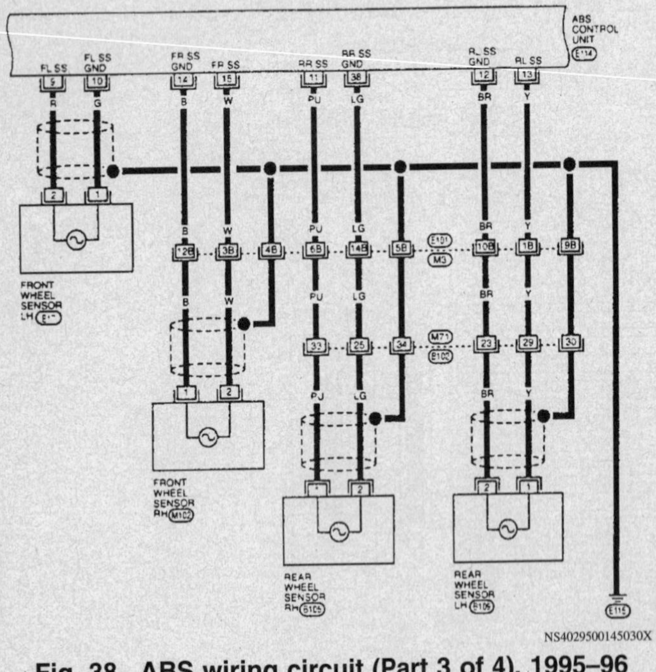

ABS CONTROL UNIT
FL SS
FL SS GND
FR SS GND
FR SS
RR SS
RR SS GND
RL SS GND
RL SS
FRONT WHEEL SENSOR LH
FRONT WHEEL SENSOR RH
REAR WHEEL SENSOR RH
REAR WHEEL SENSOR LH
NS4029500145030X

Fig. 38 ABS wiring circuit (Part 3 of 4). 1995–96 Maxima

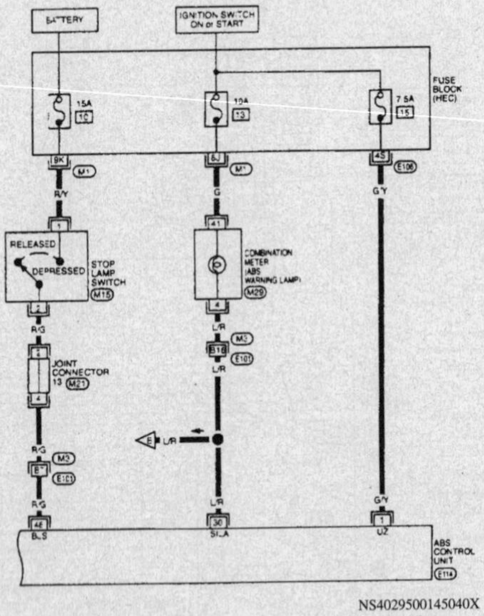

BATTERY
IGNITION SWITCH ON or START
FUSE BLOCK (J/B)
15A
10A
7.5A
RELEASED
DEPRESSED
STOP LAMP SWITCH
COMBINATION METER (ABS WARNING LAMP)
JOINT CONNECTOR 13
ABS CONTROL UNIT
NS4029500145040X

Fig. 38 ABS wiring circuit (Part 4 of 4). 1995–96 Maxima

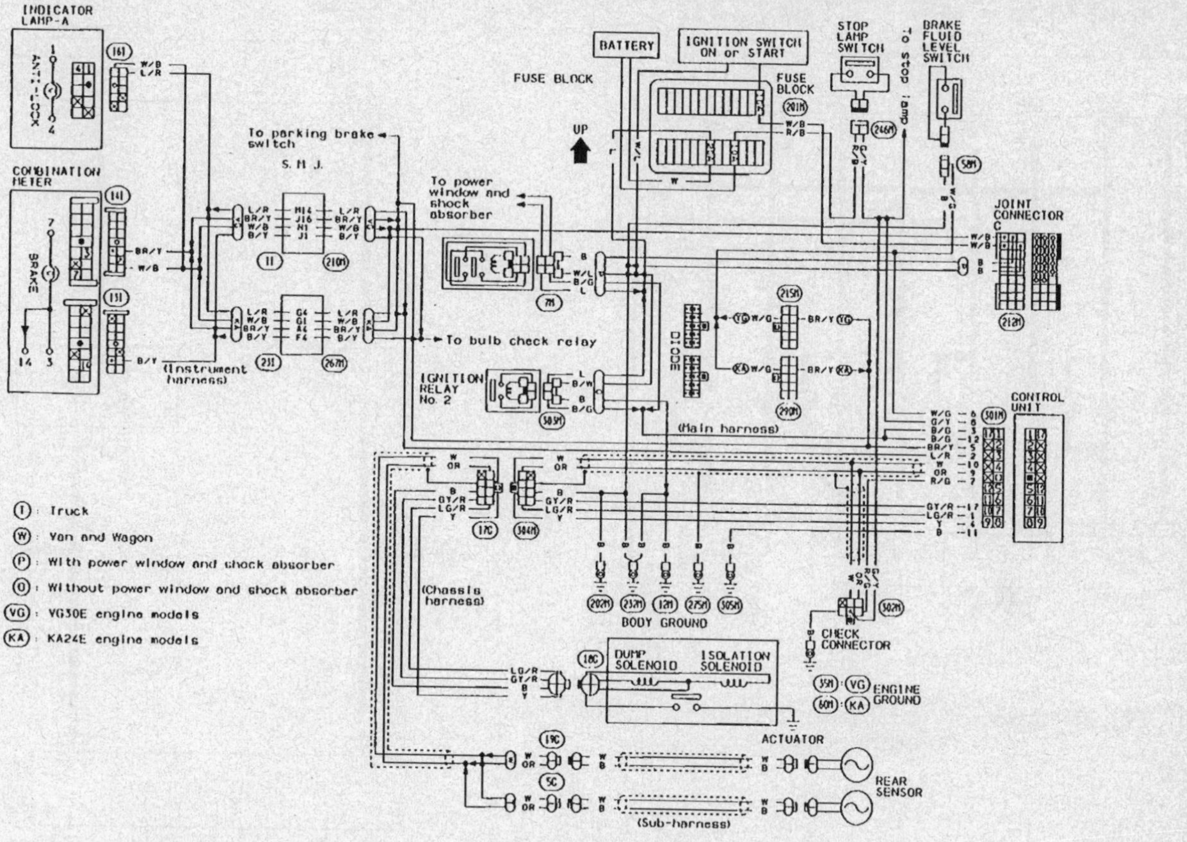
INDICATOR LAMP-A
ANTI-LOCK
COMBINATION METER
BRAKE
To parking brake switch
S.M.J.
To power window and shock absorber
To bulb check relay
(Instrument harness)
BATTERY
IGNITION SWITCH ON or START
FUSE BLOCK
UP
STOP LAMP SWITCH
BRAKE FLUID LEVEL SWITCH
JOINT CONNECTOR C
IGNITION RELAY No. 2
DIODE
(Main harness)
CONTROL UNIT
(T): Truck
(W): Van and Wagon
(P): With power window and shock absorber
(O): Without power window and shock absorber
(VG): VG30E engine models
(KA): KA24E engine models
(Chassis harness)
BODY GROUND
CHECK CONNECTOR
DUMP SOLENOID
ISOLATION SOLENOID
ENGINE GROUND
ACTUATOR
REAR SENSOR
(Sub-harness)
NS4029300032000X

Fig. 39 ABS wiring circuit. 1993–95 Pathfinder & Pickup

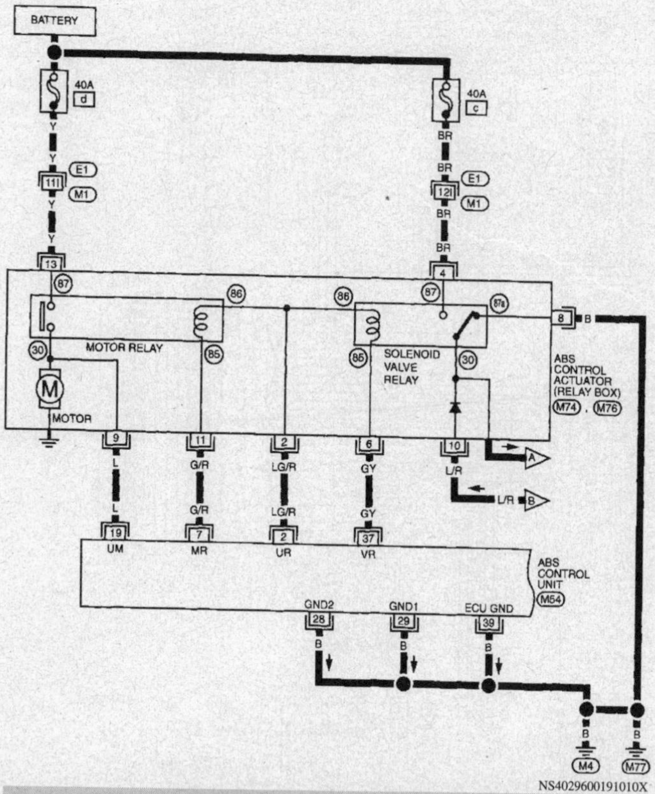
BATTERY
40A
MOTOR RELAY
SOLENOID VALVE RELAY
MOTOR
ABS CONTROL ACTUATOR (RELAY BOX)
ABS CONTROL UNIT
UM
MR
UR
VR
GND2
GND1
ECU GND
NS4029600191010X

Fig. 40 ABS wiring circuit (Part 1 of 4). 1996 Pathfinder

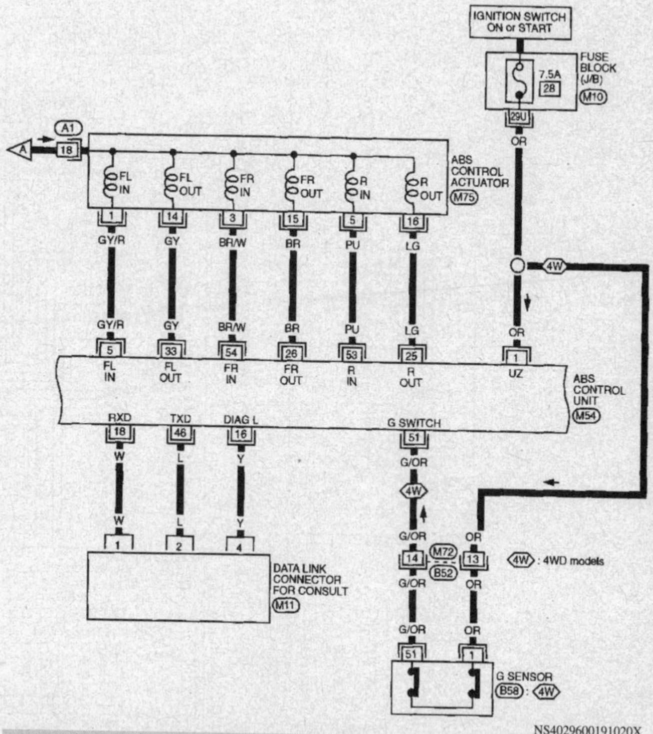
IGNITION SWITCH ON or START
FUSE BLOCK (J/B)
7.5A
FL IN
FL OUT
FR IN
FR OUT
R IN
R OUT
ABS CONTROL ACTUATOR
ABS CONTROL UNIT
UZ
RXD
TXD
DIAG L
G SWITCH
DATA LINK CONNECTOR FOR CONSULT
4W : 4WD models
G SENSOR
NS4029600191020X

Fig. 40 ABS wiring circuit (Part 2 of 4). 1996 Pathfinder

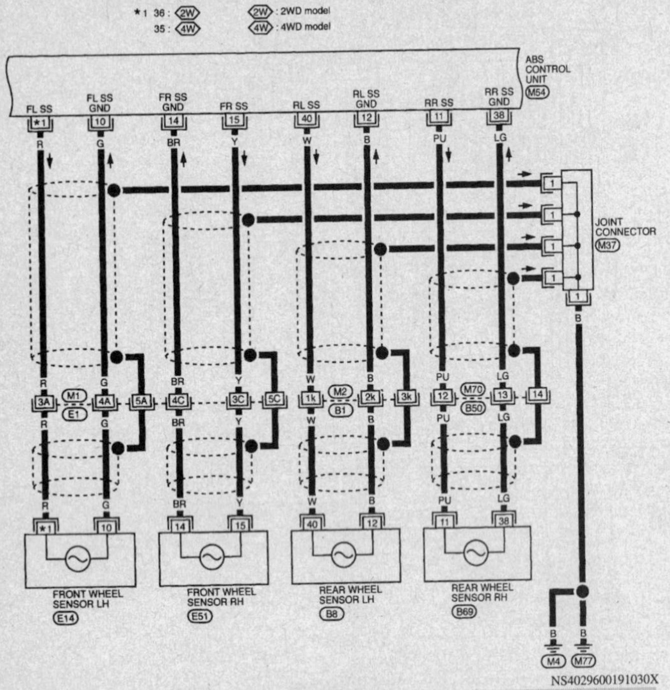
*1 36 : 2W
35 : 4W
2W : 2WD model
4W : 4WD model
ABS CONTROL UNIT
M54
FL SS
FL SS GND
FR SS GND
FR SS
RL SS
RL SS GND
RR SS
RR SS GND
JOINT CONNECTOR
M37
FRONT WHEEL SENSOR LH
E14
FRONT WHEEL SENSOR RH
E51
REAR WHEEL SENSOR LH
B8
REAR WHEEL SENSOR RH
B69
M4
M77
NS4029600191030X

Fig. 40 ABS wiring circuit (Part 3 of 4). 1996 Pathfinder

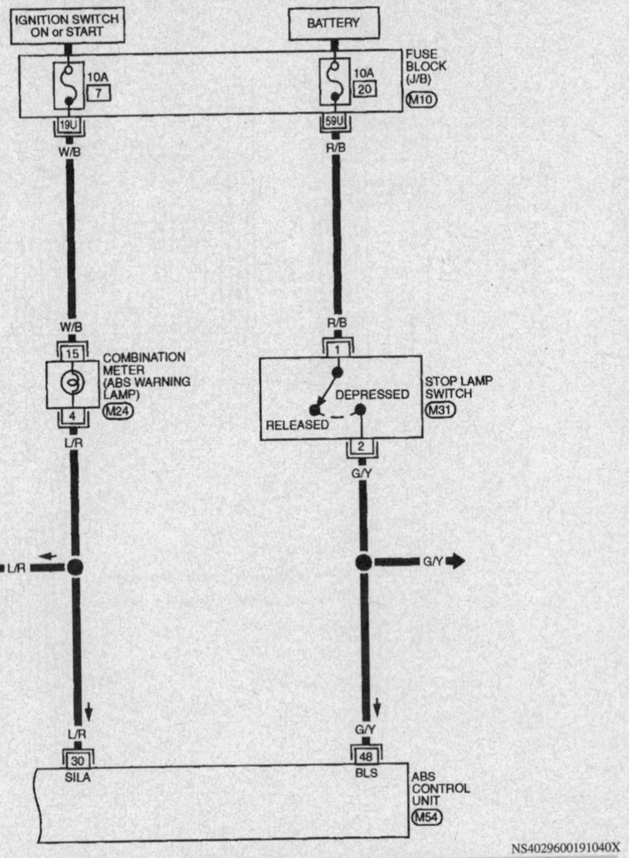
IGNITION SWITCH ON or START
BATTERY
FUSE BLOCK (J/B)
M10
10A
10A
W/B
R/B
COMBINATION METER (ABS WARNING LAMP)
M24
STOP LAMP SWITCH
M31
DEPRESSED
RELEASED
L/R
G/Y
SILA
BLS
ABS CONTROL UNIT
M54
NS4029600191040X

Fig. 40 ABS wiring circuit (Part 4 of 4). 1996 Pathfinder

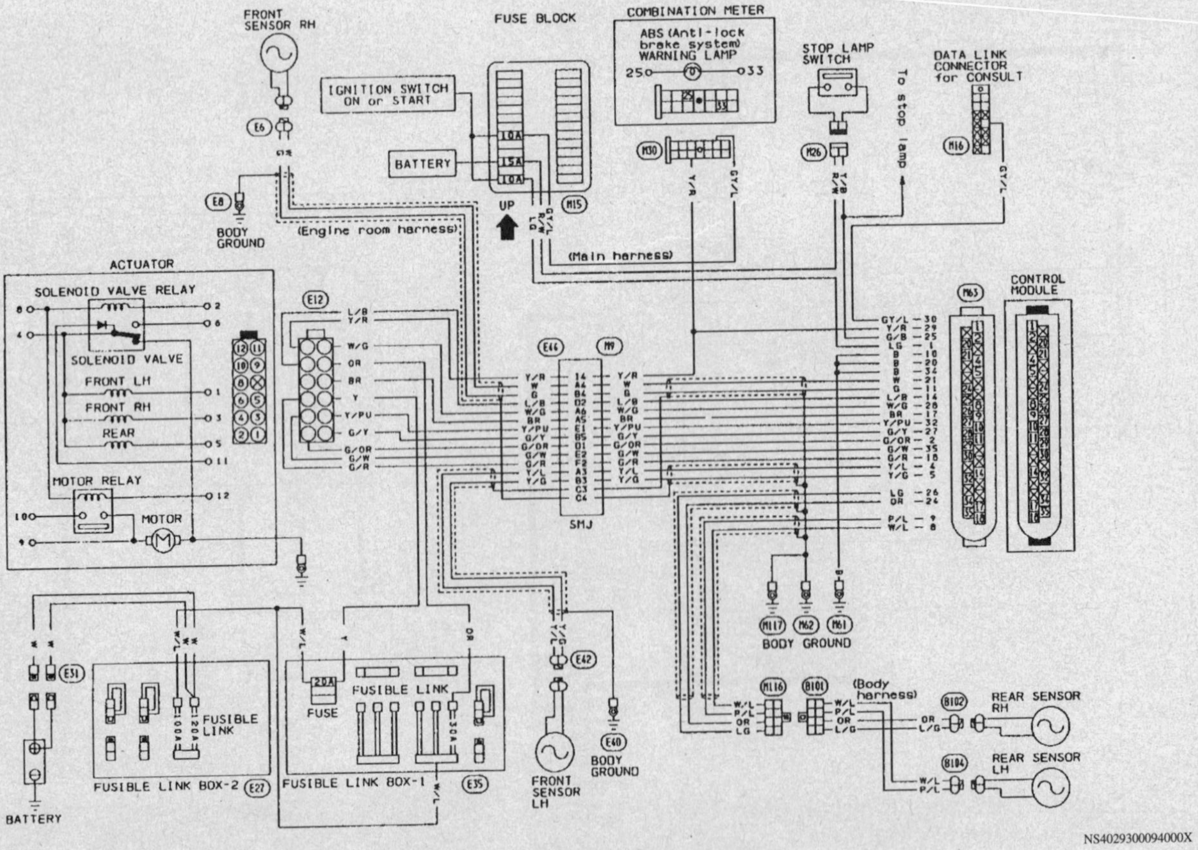
FRONT SENSOR RH
FUSE BLOCK
COMBINATION METER
ABS (Anti-lock brake system) WARNING LAMP
STOP LAMP SWITCH
To stop lamp
DATA LINK CONNECTOR for CONSULT
IGNITION SWITCH ON or START
BATTERY
BODY GROUND
(Engine room harness)
(Main harness)
UP
ACTUATOR
SOLENOID VALVE RELAY
SOLENOID VALVE
FRONT LH
FRONT RH
REAR
MOTOR RELAY
MOTOR
CONTROL MODULE
SMJ
BODY GROUND
FUSE
FUSIBLE LINK
FUSIBLE LINK BOX-2
FUSIBLE LINK BOX-1
BATTERY
FRONT SENSOR LH
BODY GROUND
(Body harness)
REAR SENSOR RH
REAR SENSOR LH
NS4029300094000X

Fig. 41 ABS wiring circuit. 1993 Quest

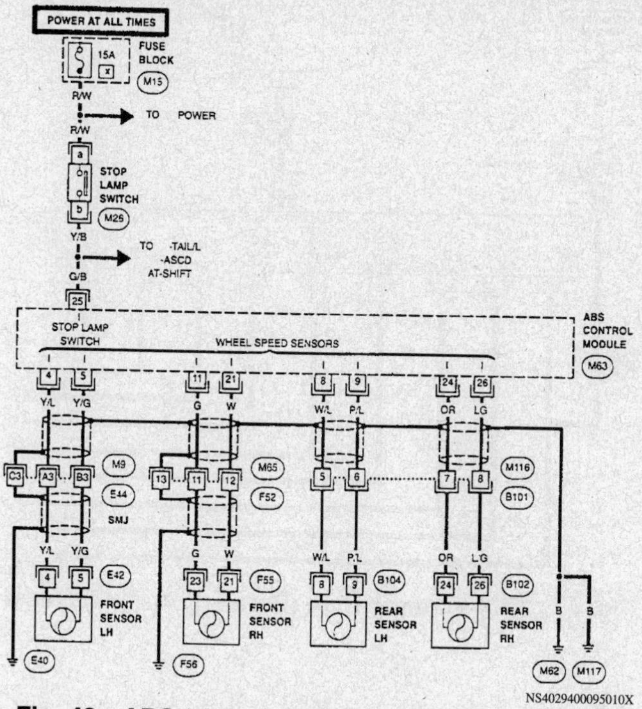
POWER AT ALL TIMES
15A
FUSE BLOCK
M15
R/W
TO POWER
STOP LAMP SWITCH
M25
Y/B
TO -TAIL/L -ASCD AT-SHIFT
G/B
STOP LAMP SWITCH
WHEEL SPEED SENSORS
ABS CONTROL MODULE
M63
Y/L
Y/G
G
W
W/L
P/L
OR
LG
M9
E44
SMJ
M65
F52
M116
B101
E42
FRONT SENSOR LH
F55
FRONT SENSOR RH
B104
REAR SENSOR LH
B102
REAR SENSOR RH
B
E40
F56
M62
M117
NS4029400095010X

Fig. 42 ABS wiring circuit (Part 1 of 3). 1994–95 Quest

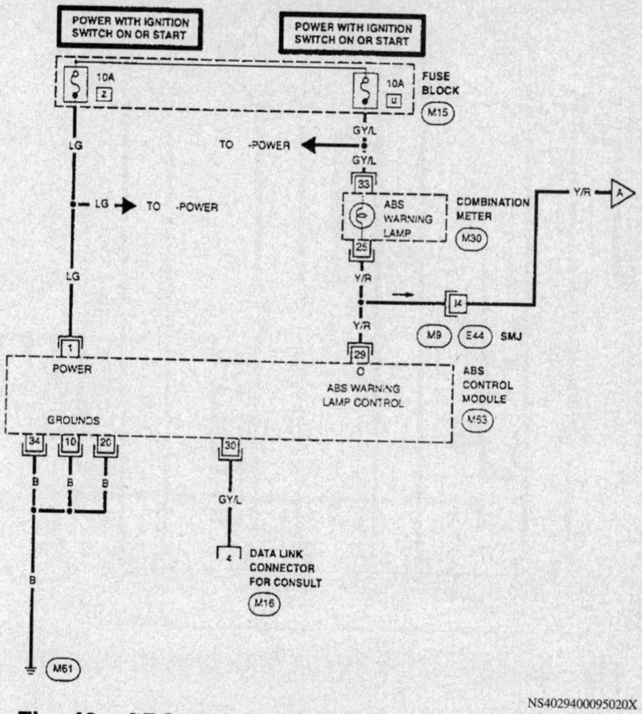
POWER WITH IGNITION SWITCH ON OR START
POWER WITH IGNITION SWITCH ON OR START
10A
10A
FUSE BLOCK
M15
LG
GY/L
TO -POWER
TO -POWER
ABS WARNING LAMP
COMBINATION METER
M30
Y/R
M9
E44
SMJ
POWER
ABS WARNING LAMP CONTROL
GROUNDS
ABS CONTROL MODULE
M63
B
GY/L
DATA LINK CONNECTOR FOR CONSULT
M16
M61
NS4029400095020X

Fig. 42 ABS wiring circuit (Part 2 of 3). 1994–95 Quest

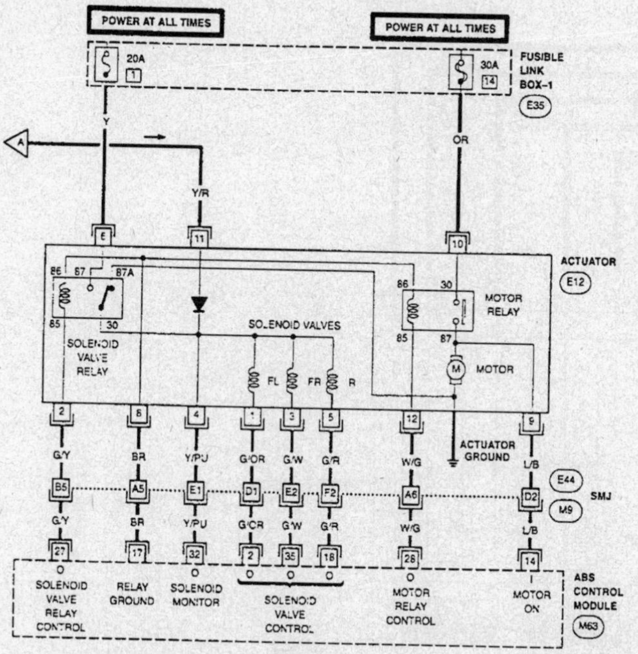
POWER AT ALL TIMES
POWER AT ALL TIMES
20A
30A
FUSIBLE LINK BOX-1
E35
Y
Y/R
OR
ACTUATOR
E12
SOLENOID VALVE RELAY
SOLENOID VALVES
FL
FR
R
MOTOR RELAY
MOTOR
ACTUATOR GROUND
G/Y
BR
Y/PU
G/OR
G/W
G/R
W/G
L/B
E44
SMJ
M9
SOLENOID VALVE RELAY CONTROL
RELAY GROUND
SOLENOID MONITOR
SOLENOID VALVE CONTROL
MOTOR RELAY CONTROL
MOTOR ON
ABS CONTROL MODULE
M63
NS4029400095030X

Fig. 42 ABS wiring circuit (Part 3 of 3). 1994–95 Quest

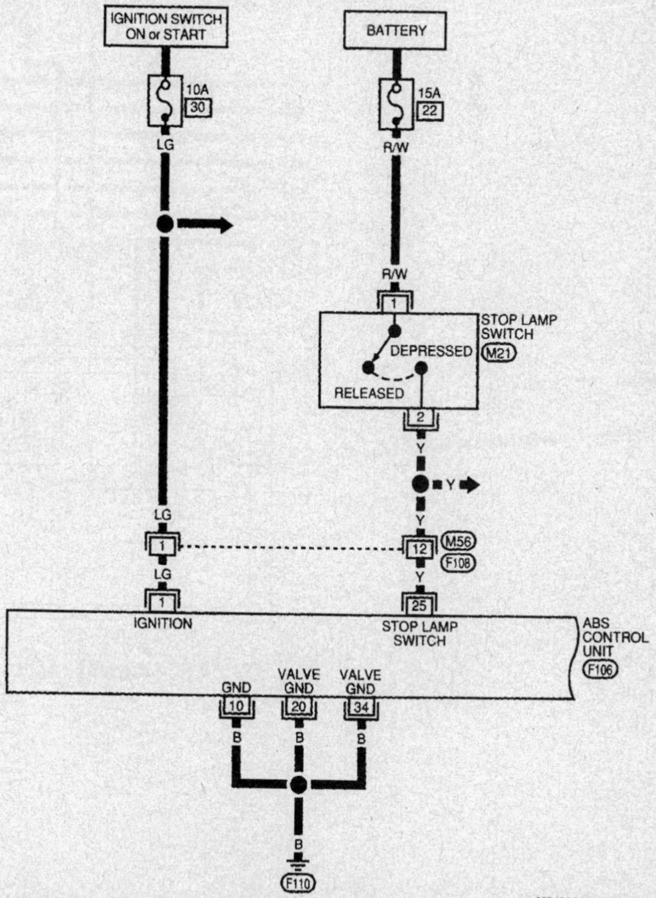
IGNITION SWITCH ON or START
BATTERY
10A
15A
LG
R/W
STOP LAMP SWITCH
DEPRESSED
M21
RELEASED
Y
M56
F108
IGNITION
STOP LAMP SWITCH
ABS CONTROL UNIT
F106
GND
VALVE GND
VALVE GND
B
F110
NS4029600193010X

Fig. 43 ABS wiring circuit (Part 1 of 4). 1996 Quest

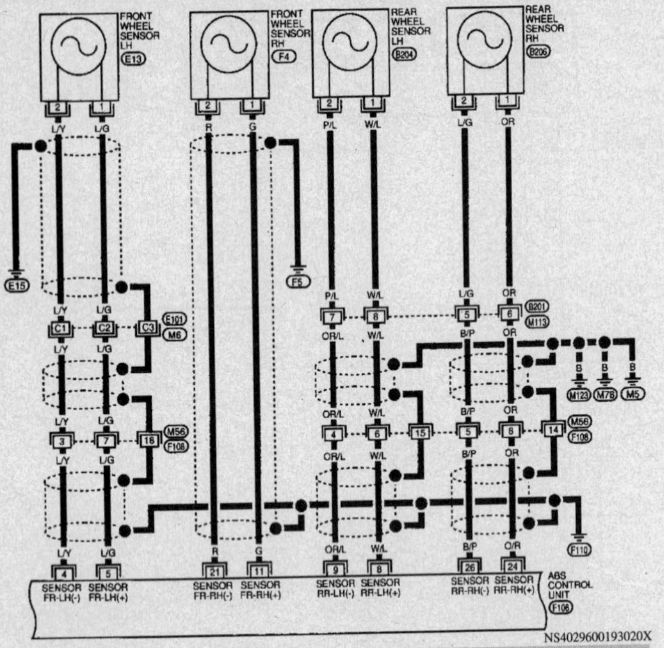
FRONT WHEEL SENSOR LH
E13
FRONT WHEEL SENSOR RH
F4
REAR WHEEL SENSOR LH
B204
REAR WHEEL SENSOR RH
B206
E15
F5
E101
M6
M56
F108
B201
M113
M123
M78
M5
F110
SENSOR FR-LH(-)
SENSOR FR-LH(+)
SENSOR FR-RH(-)
SENSOR FR-RH(+)
SENSOR RR-LH(-)
SENSOR RR-LH(+)
SENSOR RR-RH(-)
SENSOR RR-RH(+)
ABS CONTROL UNIT
F106
NS4029600193020X

Fig. 43 ABS wiring circuit (Part 2 of 4). 1996 Quest

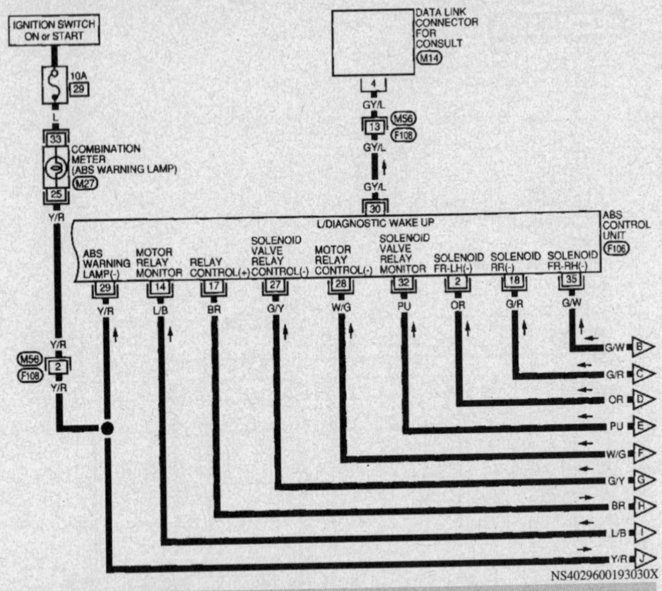
IGNITION SWITCH ON or START
10A
29
COMBINATION METER (ABS WARNING LAMP)
M27
DATA LINK CONNECTOR FOR CONSULT
M14
M56
F108
L/DIAGNOSTIC WAKE UP
ABS CONTROL UNIT
F106
ABS WARNING LAMP(-)
MOTOR RELAY MONITOR
RELAY CONTROL(+)
SOLENOID VALVE RELAY CONTROL(-)
MOTOR RELAY CONTROL(-)
SOLENOID VALVE RELAY MONITOR
SOLENOID FR-LH(-)
SOLENOID RR(-)
SOLENOID FR-RH(-)
NS4029600193030X

Fig. 43 ABS wiring circuit (Part 3 of 4). 1996 Quest

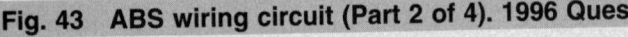

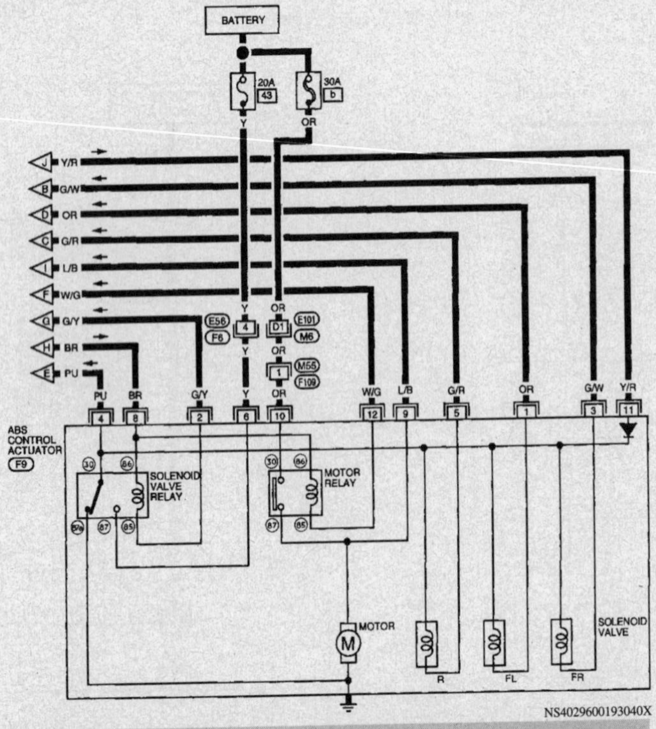
BATTERY
20A
43
30A
b
E56
F6
E101
M6
M56
F109
ABS CONTROL ACTUATOR
F9
SOLENOID VALVE RELAY
MOTOR RELAY
MOTOR
SOLENOID VALVE
R
FL
FR
NS4029600193040X

Fig. 43 ABS wiring circuit (Part 4 of 4). 1996 Quest

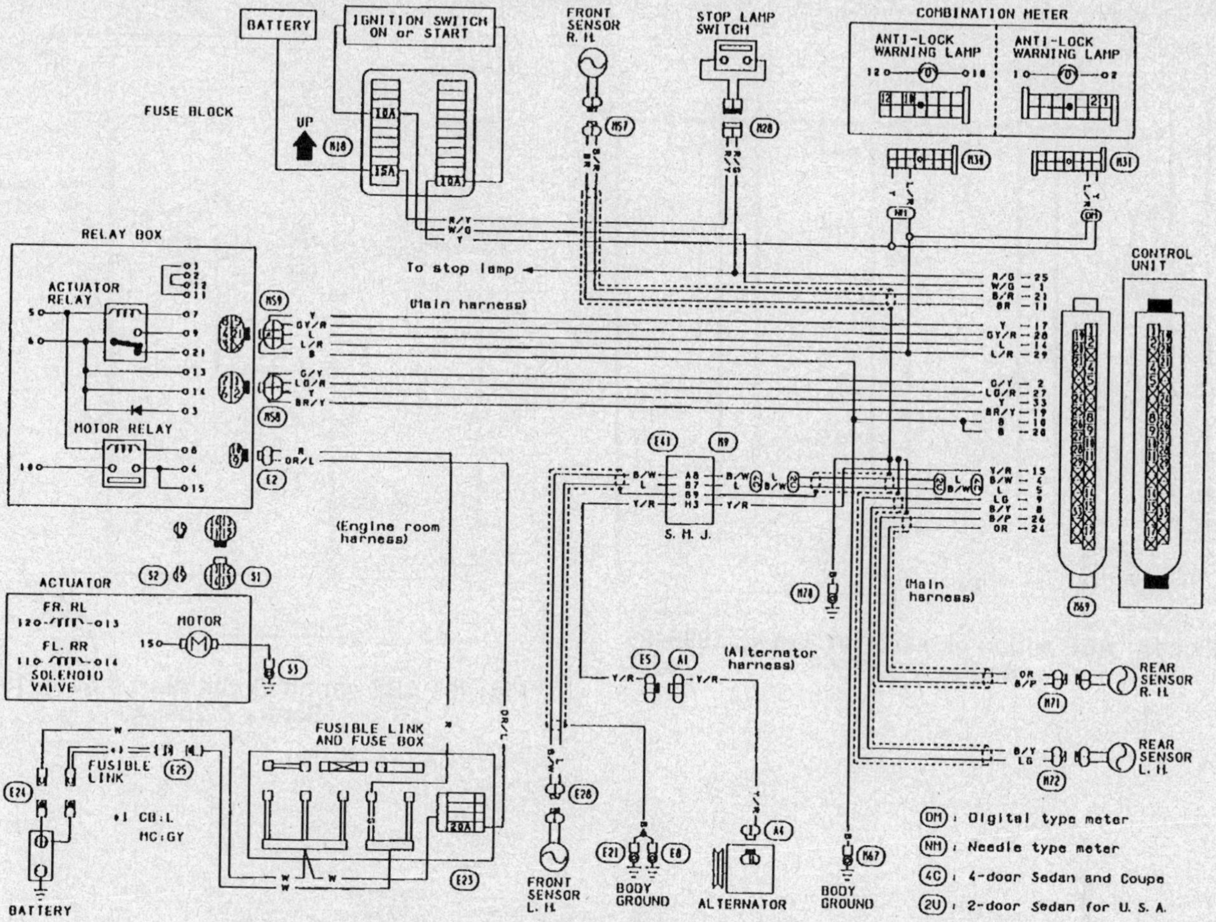

NS4029100026000X

Fig. 44 ABS wiring circuit. 1993–94 NX1600, NX2000 & Sentra

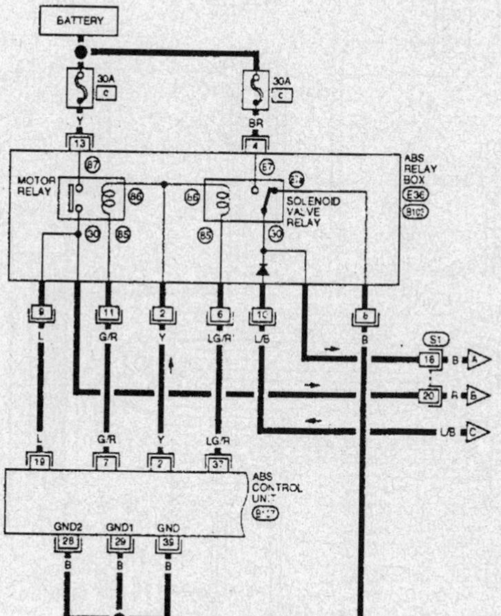

NS4029500146010X

Fig. 45 ABS wiring circuit (Part 1 of 4). 1995–96 Sentra & 200SX

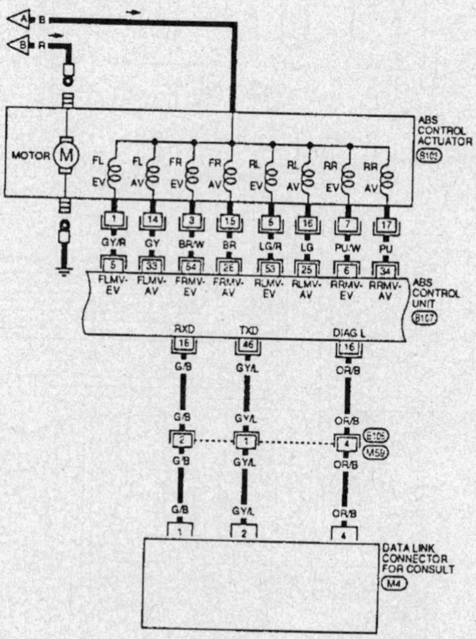

NS4029500146020X

Fig. 45 ABS wiring circuit (Part 2 of 4). 1995–96 Sentra & 200SX

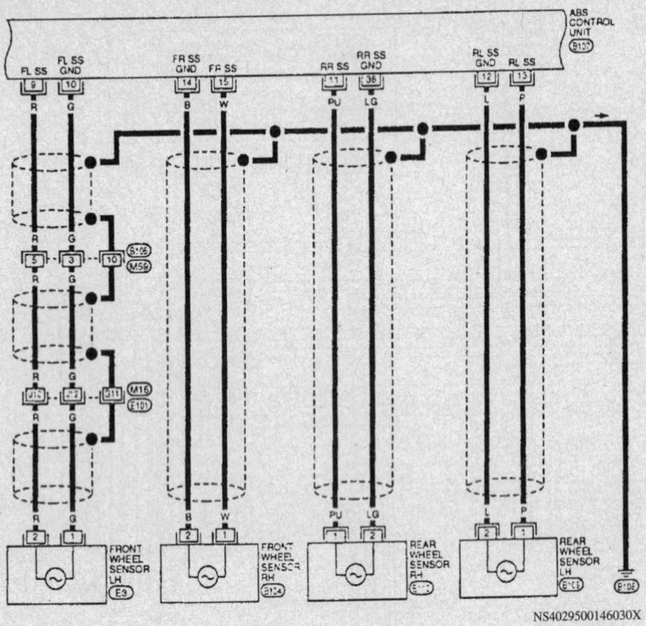
ABS CONTROL UNIT
FL SS
FL SS GND
FR SS GND
FR SS
RR SS
RR SS GND
RL SS GND
RL SS
FRONT WHEEL SENSOR LH
FRONT WHEEL SENSOR RH
REAR WHEEL SENSOR RH
REAR WHEEL SENSOR LH
NS4029500146030X

Fig. 45 ABS wiring circuit (Part 3 of 4). 1995–96 Sentra & 200SX

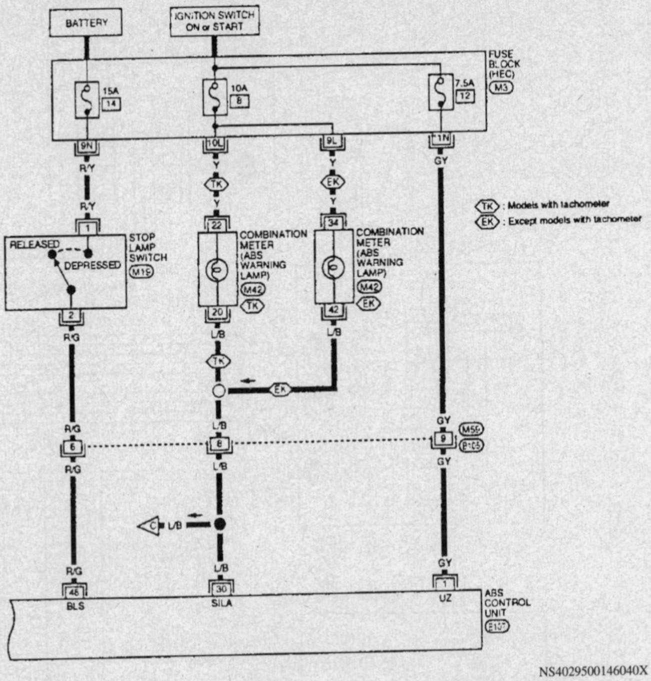
BATTERY
IGNITION SWITCH ON or START
FUSE BLOCK (HEC)
15A
10A
7.5A
STOP LAMP SWITCH
RELEASED
DEPRESSED
COMBINATION METER (ABS WARNING LAMP)
TK : Models with tachometer
EK : Except models with tachometer
BLS
SILA
UZ
ABS CONTROL UNIT
NS4029500146040X

Fig. 45 ABS wiring circuit (Part 4 of 4). 1995–96 Sentra & 200SX

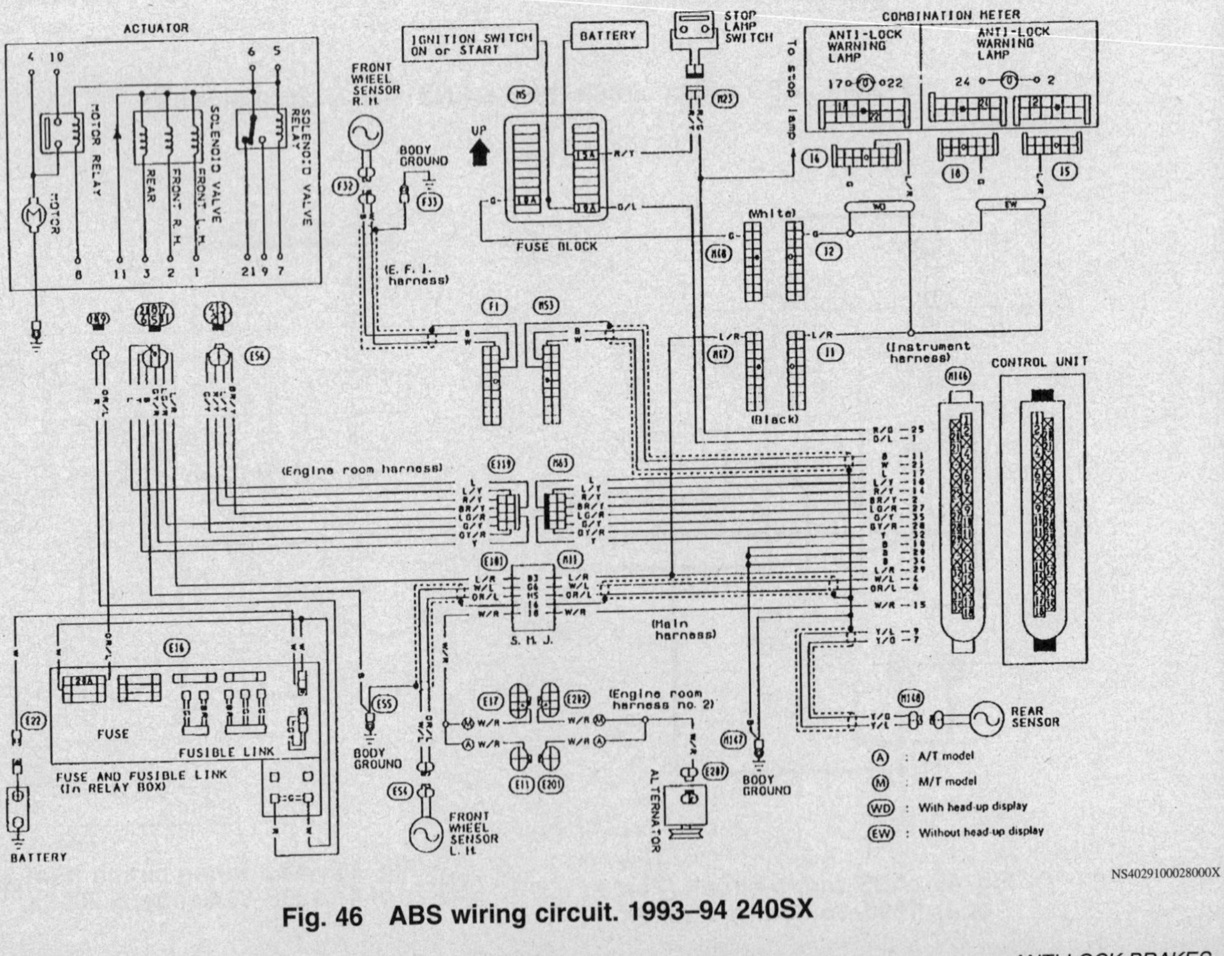

Fig. 46 ABS wiring circuit. 1993–94 240SX

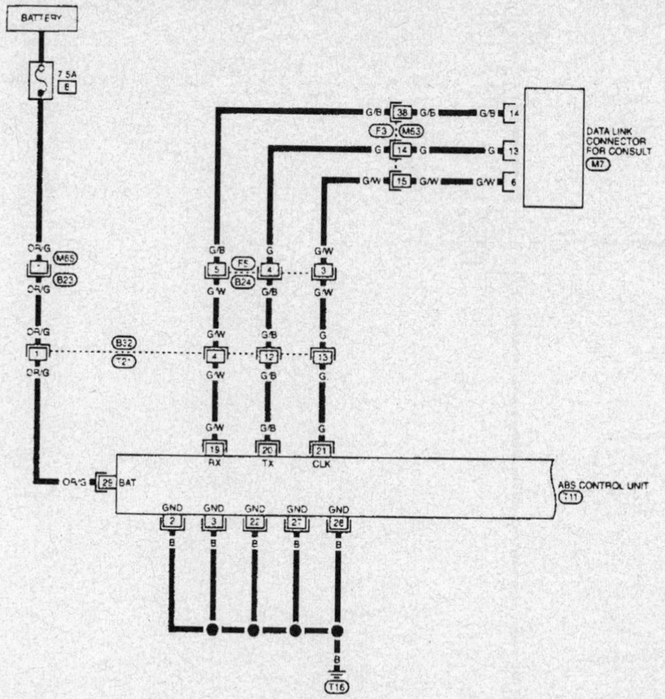
BATTERY
7.5A
DATA LINK CONNECTOR FOR CONSULT
M7
RX
TX
CLK
BAT
ABS CONTROL UNIT
T11
GND
T16
NS4029500147010X

Fig. 47 ABS wiring circuit (Part 1 of 5). 1995–96 240SX

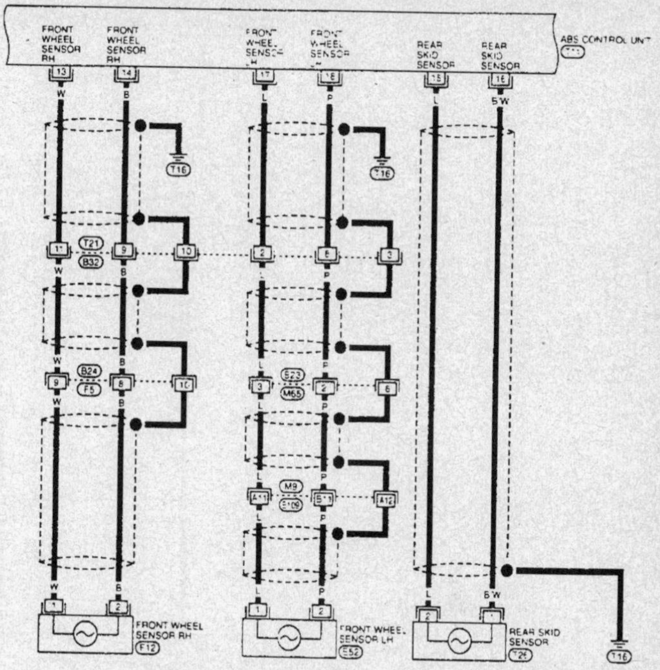
FRONT WHEEL SENSOR RH
FRONT WHEEL SENSOR LH
REAR SKID SENSOR
ABS CONTROL UNIT
T11
T16
FRONT WHEEL SENSOR RH
F12
FRONT WHEEL SENSOR LH
E52
REAR SKID SENSOR
T26
NS4029500147020X

Fig. 47 ABS wiring circuit (Part 2 of 5). 1995–96 240SX

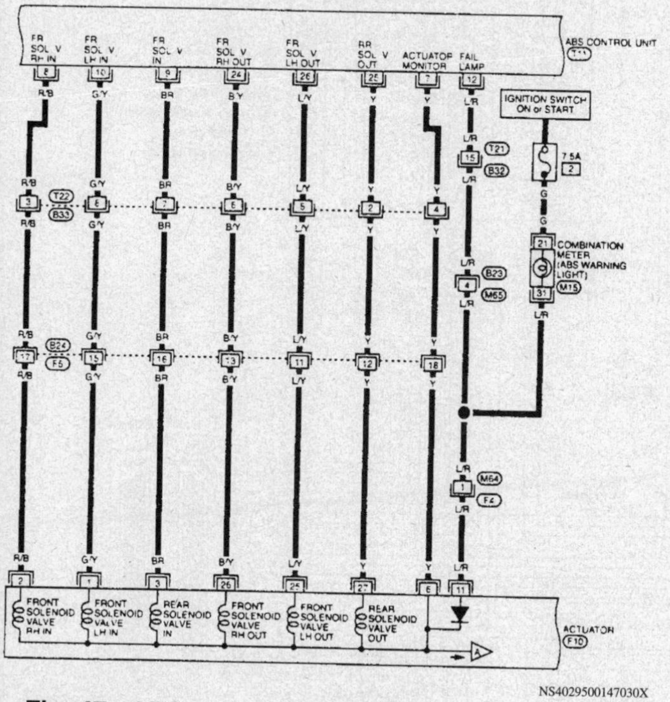
FR SOL V RH IN
FR SOL V LH IN
FR SOL V IN
FR SOL V RH OUT
FR SOL V LH OUT
RR SOL V OUT
ACTUATOR MONITOR
FAIL LAMP
ABS CONTROL UNIT
T11
IGNITION SWITCH ON or START
7.5A
COMBINATION METER (ABS WARNING LIGHT)
M15
FRONT SOLENOID VALVE RH IN
FRONT SOLENOID VALVE LH IN
REAR SOLENOID VALVE IN
FRONT SOLENOID VALVE RH OUT
FRONT SOLENOID VALVE LH OUT
REAR SOLENOID VALVE OUT
ACTUATOR
F10
NS4029500147030X

Fig. 47 ABS wiring circuit (Part 3 of 5). 1995–96 240SX

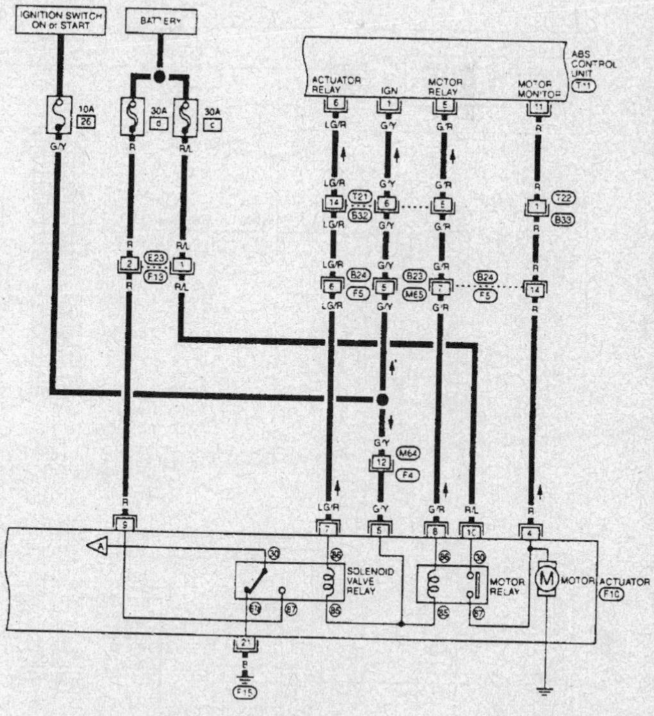
IGNITION SWITCH ON or START
BATTERY
10A
30A
30A
ABS CONTROL UNIT
T11
ACTUATOR RELAY
IGN
MOTOR RELAY
MOTOR MONITOR
SOLENOID VALVE RELAY
MOTOR RELAY
MOTOR
ACTUATOR
F10
F15
NS4029500147040X

Fig. 47 ABS wiring circuit (Part 4 of 5). 1995–96 240SX

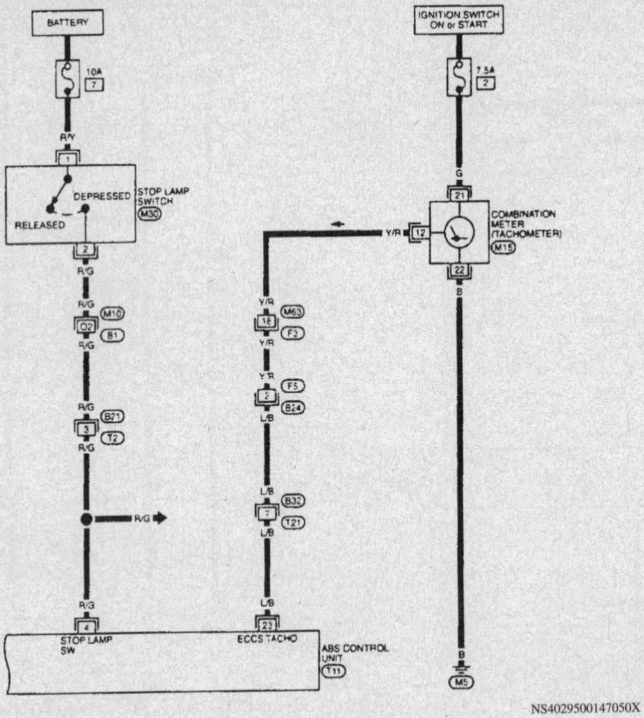

Fig. 47 ABS wiring circuit (Part 5 of 5). 1995–96 240SX

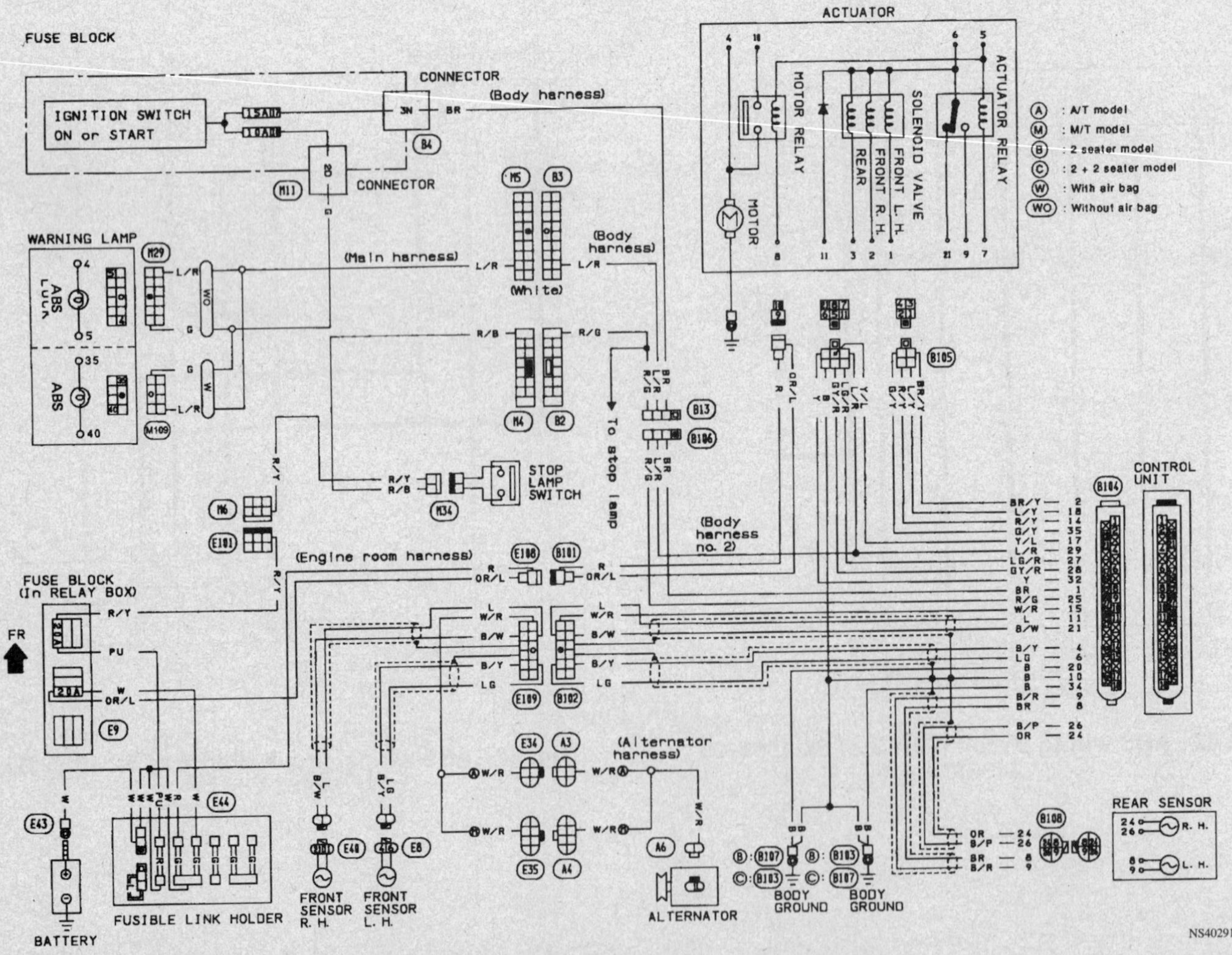

Fig. 48 ABS wiring circuit. 1993 300ZX

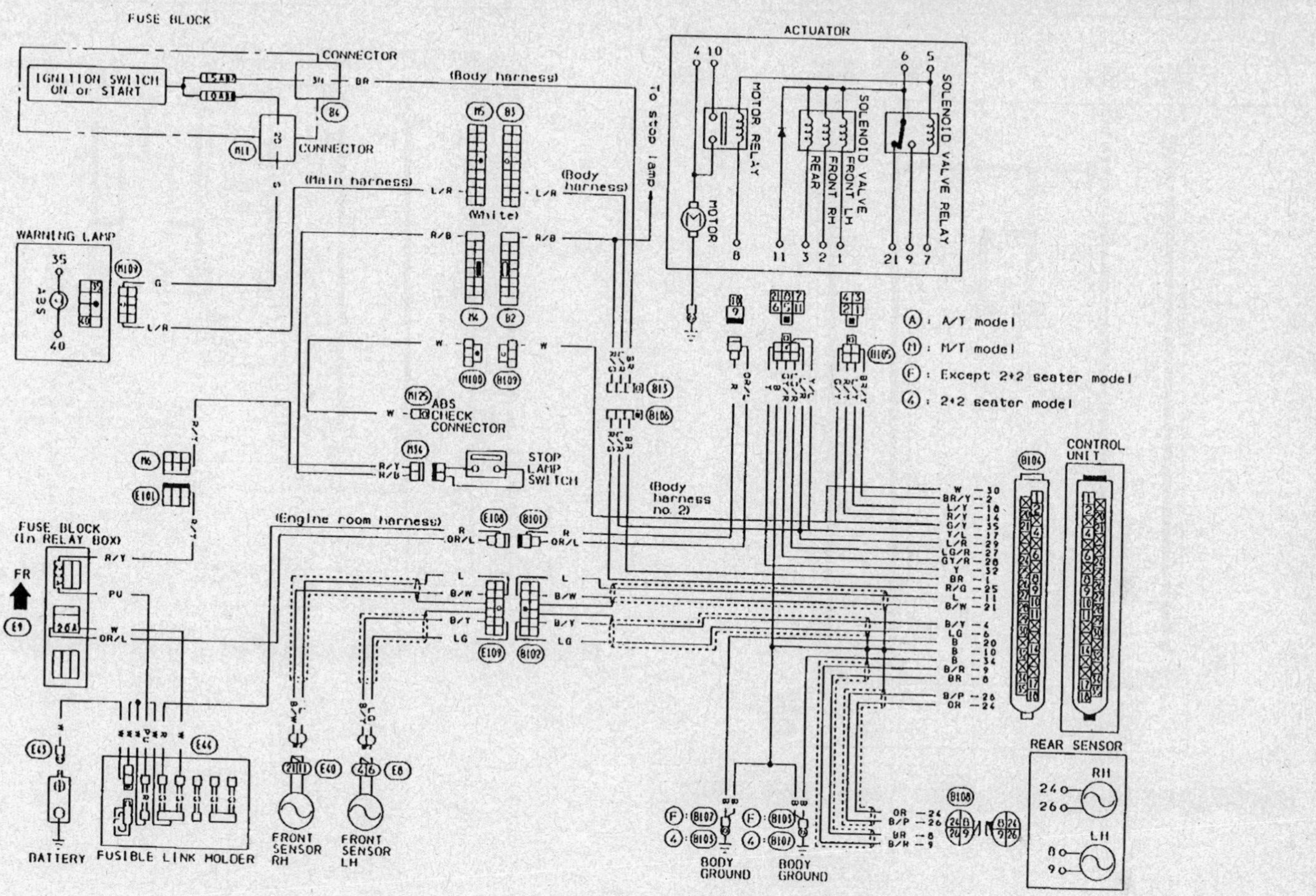
FUSE BLOCK
IGNITION SWITCH ON or START
CONNECTOR
(Body harness)
To stop lamp
ACTUATOR
MOTOR RELAY
SOLENOID VALVE FRONT LH
FRONT RH
REAR
SOLENOID VALVE RELAY
MOTOR
(Main harness)
(Body harness)
(White)
WARNING LAMP
ABS CHECK CONNECTOR
STOP LAMP SWITCH
Ⓐ: A/T model
Ⓜ: M/T model
Ⓕ: Except 2+2 seater model
④: 2+2 seater model
CONTROL UNIT
(Body harness no. 2)
(Engine room harness)
FUSE BLOCK (In RELAY BOX)
FR
REAR SENSOR
RH
LH
BATTERY
FUSIBLE LINK HOLDER
FRONT SENSOR RH
FRONT SENSOR LH
BODY GROUND
BODY GROUND

NS4029400030000X

Fig. 49 ABS wiring circuit. 1994–95 300ZX

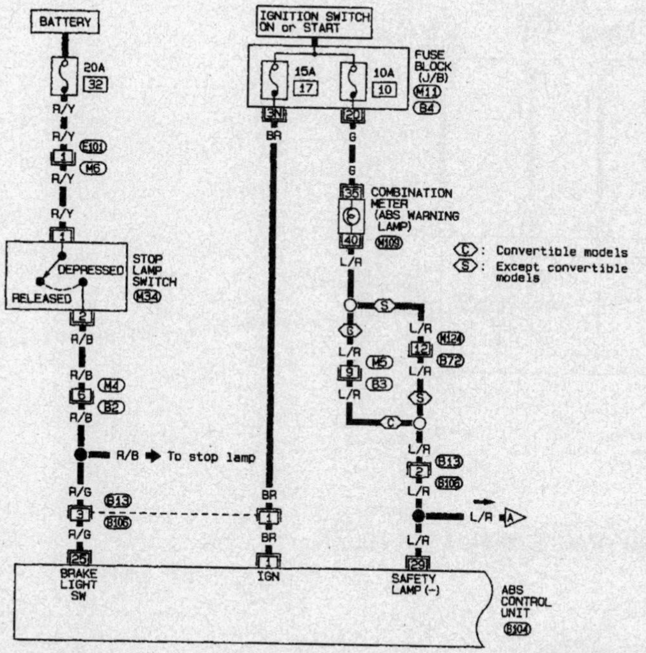
BATTERY
20A
IGNITION SWITCH ON or START
15A
10A
FUSE BLOCK (J/B)
COMBINATION METER (ABS WARNING LAMP)
Ⓒ: Convertible models
Ⓢ: Except convertible models
STOP LAMP SWITCH
DEPRESSED
RELEASED
R/B To stop lamp
BRAKE LIGHT SW
IGN
SAFETY LAMP (–)
ABS CONTROL UNIT

NS4029600194010X

Fig. 50 ABS wiring circuit (Part 1 of 5). 1996 300ZX

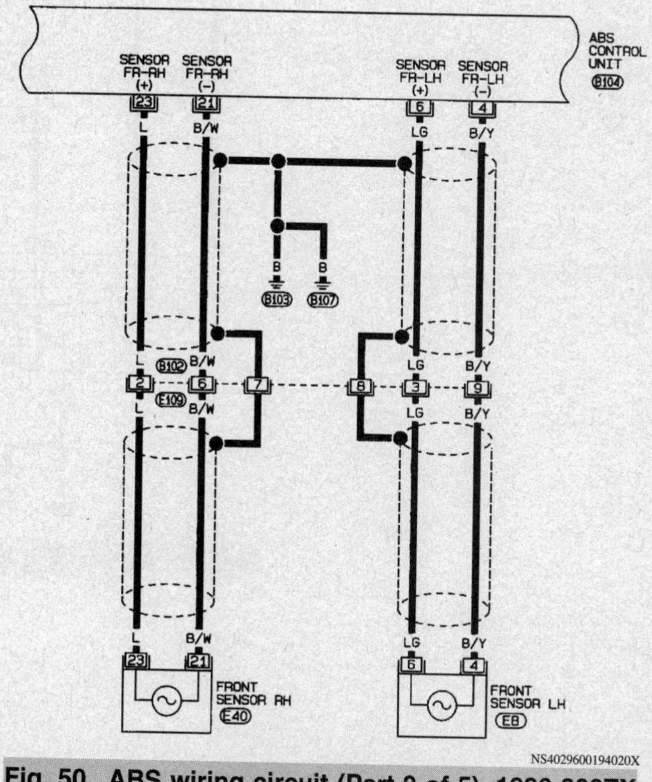
ABS CONTROL UNIT
SENSOR FR-RH (+)
SENSOR FR-RH (–)
SENSOR FR-LH (+)
SENSOR FR-LH (–)
FRONT SENSOR RH
FRONT SENSOR LH

NS4029600194020X

Fig. 50 ABS wiring circuit (Part 2 of 5). 1996 300ZX

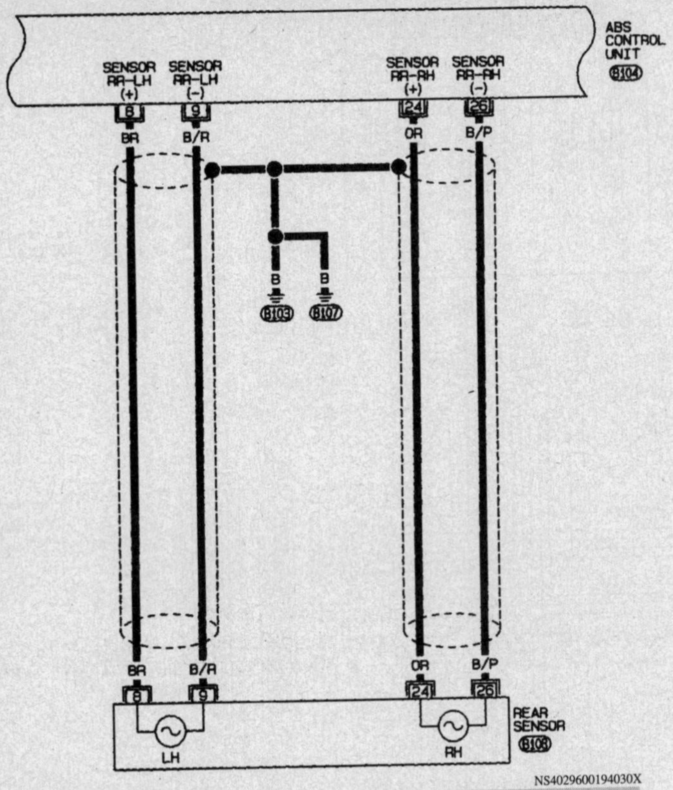
ABS CONTROL UNIT
B104
SENSOR RR-LH (+)
SENSOR RR-LH (-)
SENSOR RR-RH (+)
SENSOR RR-RH (-)
BR
B/R
OR
B/P
B
B103
B107
REAR SENSOR
B108
LH
RH
NS4029600194030X

Fig. 50 ABS wiring circuit (Part 3 of 5). 1996 300ZX

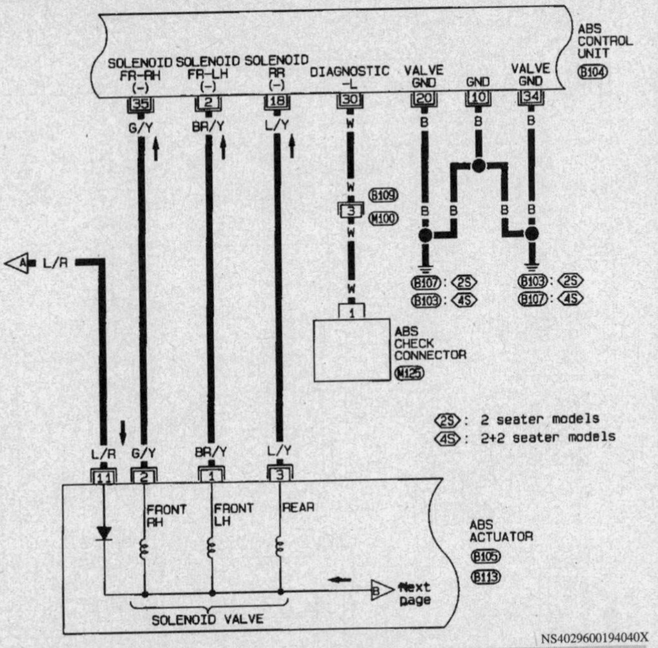
ABS CONTROL UNIT
B104
SOLENOID FR-RH (-)
SOLENOID FR-LH (-)
SOLENOID RR (-)
DIAGNOSTIC -L
VALVE GND
GND
VALVE GND
G/Y
BR/Y
L/Y
W
B
B109
M100
B107 : 2S
B103 : 4S
B103 : 2S
B107 : 4S
ABS CHECK CONNECTOR
M125
2S : 2 seater models
4S : 2+2 seater models
A
L/R
FRONT RH
FRONT LH
REAR
ABS ACTUATOR
B105
B113
Next page
SOLENOID VALVE
NS4029600194040X

Fig. 50 ABS wiring circuit (Part 4 of 5). 1996 300ZX

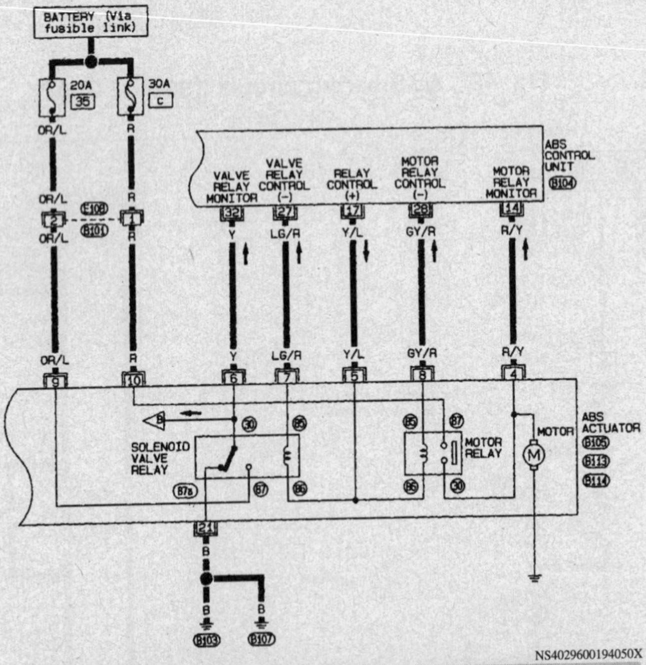
BATTERY (Via fusible link)
20A
30A
OR/L
R
E108
B101
ABS CONTROL UNIT
B104
VALVE RELAY MONITOR
VALVE RELAY CONTROL (-)
RELAY CONTROL (+)
MOTOR RELAY CONTROL (-)
MOTOR RELAY MONITOR
Y
LG/R
Y/L
GY/R
R/Y
SOLENOID VALVE RELAY
MOTOR RELAY
MOTOR
ABS ACTUATOR
B105
B113
B114
B
B103
B107
NS4029600194050X

Fig. 50 ABS wiring circuit (Part 5 of 5). 1996 300ZX

DIAGNOSTIC CHART INDEX

Test	Description	Year	Page No.	Fig. No.
ALTIMA				
Test 1	Warning Lamp Does Not Work Before Engine Starts	1993–95	36-170	51
Test 2	Warning Lamp Does Not Blink But Stays On Continuously	1993–95	36-170	52
Test 3	Actuator Solenoid/Malfunction Codes 45, 41 or 55	1993–95	36-170	53
Test 4	Wheel Sensor Or Rotor	1993–95	36-170	54
Test 5	Motor Relay Or Motor	1993–95	36-171	55
Test 6	Solenoid Valve Relay	1993–95	36-171	56
Test 7	Low Voltage	1993–95	36-172	57
Test 8	Stop Lamp Switch Circuit	1993–95	36-172	58
Test 9	Control Module	1993–95	36-172	59
Test 1	Warning Lamp Does Not Work When Ignition Switch Is On	1996	36-172	60
Test 2	Warning Lamp Stays On When Ignition Switch Is On	1996	36-172	61
Test 3	Actuator Solenoid Valve	1996	36-173	62
Test 4	Wheel Sensor Or Rotor	1996	36-173	63
Test 5	Motor Relay Or Motor	1996	36-174	64
Test 6	Solenoid Valve Relay	1996	36-174	65
Test 7	Power Supply Low Voltage	1996	36-175	66
Test 8	Stop Lamp Switch Circuit	1996	36-175	67
Test 9	Control Unit	1996	36-175	68
Test 10	Pedal Vibration & Noise	1996	36-175	69
Test 11	Long Stopping Distance	1996	36-175	70
Test 12	Unexpected Pedal Action	1996	36-176	71
Test 13	ABS Does Not Work	1996	36-176	72
Test 14	ABS Works Frequently	1996	36-176	73
MAXIMA				
Test 1	Pedal Vibration & Noise	1993–94	36-176	74
Test 2	Long Stopping Distance	1993–94	36-176	75
Test 3	Abnormal Pedal Action	1993–94	36-176	76
Test 4	ABS Doesn't Work	1993–94	36-176	77
Test 5	ABS Works But Warning Activates	1993–94	36-176	78
Test 6	ABS Works Frequently	1993–94	36-177	79
Test 7	Actuator Solenoid	1993–94	36-177	82
Test 8	Wheel Speed Sensor	1993–94	36-178	84
Test 9	Actuator Motor Relay	1993–94	36-178	86
Test 10	Actuator Solenoid Valve Relay	1993–94	36-179	88
Test 11	Control Unit	1993–94	36-179	90
Test 12	Control Unit Or Power Supply & Ground Circuit	1993–94	36-179	91
Test 1	Warning Light Does Not Work Before Engine Starts	1995–96	36-180	92
Test 2	Warning Light Stays On Continuously	1995–96	36-180	93
Test 3	Actuator Solenoid Valve	1995–96	36-181	94
Test 4	Wheel Sensor Rotor	1995–96	36-181	95
Test 5	Motor Relay Or Motor	1995–96	36-182	96
Test 6	Solenoid Valve Relay	1995–96	36-182	97
Test 7	Power Supply Low Voltage	1995–96	36-183	98
Test 8	Control Unit	1995–96	36-183	99
Test 9	Pedal Vibration & Noise	1995–96	36-183	100
Test 10	Long Stopping Distance	1995–96	36-183	101
Test 11	Unexpected Pedal Action	1995–96	36-183	102
Test 12	ABS Does Not Work	1995–96	36-184	103
Test 13	ABS Works Frequently	1995–96	36-184	104
NX 1600, NX 2000 & 1993–94 SENTRA				
Test 1	Pedal Vibration & Noise	1993–94	36-191	127
Test 2	Long Stopping Distance	1993–94	36-191	128
Test 3	Unexpected Pedal Action	1993–94	36-191	129
Test 4	ABS Doesn't Work	1993–94	36-191	130
Test 5	ABS Works But Warning Activates	1993–94	36-191	131
Test 6	ABS Works Frequently	1993–94	36-192	132

Continued

DIAGNOSTIC CHART INDEX—Continued

Test	Description	Year	Page No.	Fig. No.
NX 1600, NX 2000 & 1993–94 SENTRA				
Test 7	Warning Never Activates	1993–94	36-192	133
Test 8	Actuator Solenoid	1993–94	36-192	134
Test 9	Wheel Speed Sensor	1993–94	36-192	135
Test 10	Actuator Motor Relay	1993–94	36-193	136
Test 11	Actuator Solenoid Valve Relay	1993–94	36-193	137
Test 12	Sensor & Sensor Rotor	1993–94	36-193	138
Test 13	Control Unit	1993–94	36-193	139
Test 14	Control Unit Or Power Supply & Ground Circuit	1993–94	36-193	140
200SX & 1995–96 SENTRA				
Test 1	Warning Lamp Does Not Come On When Ignition Switch Is Turned On	1995–96	36-194	141
Test 2	Warning Light Stays On When Ignition Switch Is Turned On	1995–96	36-194	142
Test 3	ABS Actuator Solenoid Valve	1995–96	36-195	143
Test 4	Wheel Sensor Or Rotor	1995–96	36-195	144
Test 5	Motor Relay Or Motor	1995–96	36-196	145
Test 6	Solenoid Valve Relay	1995–96	36-196	146
Test 7	Power Supply Low Voltage	1995–96	36-197	147
Test 8	Control Unit	1995–96	36-197	148
Test 9	Pedal Vibration & Noise	1995–96	36-197	149
Test 10	Long Stopping Distance	1995–96	36-197	150
Test 11	Unexpected Pedal Action	1995–96	36-197	151
Test 12	ABS Does Not Work	1995–96	36-197	152
Test 13	ABS Works Frequently	1995–96	36-198	153
PATHFINDER				
Test 1	Pedal Vibration Or Noise	1993–95	36-198	154
Test 2	Long Stopping Distance	1993–95	36-198	155
Test 3	Brake Pedal Stroke Is Abnormally Large	1993–95	36-198	156
Test 4	R-ABS Doesn't Work	1993–95	36-198	157
Test 5	R-ABS Works Frequently	1993–95	36-198	158
Test 6	Main Power Supply & Ground circuit	1993–95	36-199	159
Test 7	Actuator ISO Solenoid Short Circuit Or Open	1993–95	36-199	160
Test 8	Actuator ISO Solenoid Blocked	1993–95	36-199	161
Test 9	Actuator Dump Solenoid Short Circuit	1993–95	36-199	162
Test 10	Sensor Open Or Short Circuit	1993–95	36-200	163
Test 11	Sensor Signal Erratic	1993–95	36-200	164
Test 12	Control Unit	1993–95	36-200	165
Test 13	Other Problems	1993–95	36-200	166
Test 1	Warning Lamp Does Not Work When Ignition Is On	1996	36-200	167
Test 2	Warning Lamp Stays On When Ignition Switch Is On	1996	36-201	168
Test 3	ABS Control Actuator Solenoid Valve	1996	36-201	169
Test 4	Wheel Sensor Or Rotor	1996	36-202	170
Test 5	Motor Relay Or Motor	1996	36-203	171
Test 6	Solenoid Valve Relay	1996	36-203	172
Test 7	Power Supply Low Voltage	1996	36-204	173
Test 8	G Sensor	1996	36-204	174
Test 9	Control Unit	1996	36-204	175
Test 10	Pedal Vibration & Noise	1996	36-204	176
Test 11	Long Stopping Distance	1996	36-205	177
Test 12	Unexpected Pedal Action	1996	36-205	178
Test 13	ABS Does Not Work	1996	36-205	179
Test 14	ABS Works Frequently	1996	36-205	180
PICKUP				
Test 1	Pedal Vibration Or Noise	1993–96	36-198	154
Test 2	Long Stopping Distance	1993–96	36-198	155
Test 3	Brake Pedal Stroke Is Abnormally Large	1993–96	36-198	156
Test 4	R-ABS Doesn't Work	1993–96	36-198	157

Continued

DIAGNOSTIC CHART INDEX—Continued

Test	Description	Year	Page No.	Fig. No.
PICKUP				
Test 5	R-ABS Works Frequently	1993–96	36-198	158
Test 6	Main Power Supply & Ground circuit	1993–96	36-199	159
Test 7	Actuator ISO Solenoid Short Circuit Or Open	1993–96	36-199	160
Test 8	Actuator ISO Solenoid Blocked	1993–96	36-199	161
Test 9	Actuator Dump Solenoid Short Circuit	1993–96	36-199	162
Test 10	Sensor Open Or Short Circuit	1993–96	36-200	163
Test 11	Sensor Signal Erratic	1993–96	36-200	164
Test 12	Control Unit	1993–96	36-200	165
Test 13	Other Problems	1993–96	36-200	166
QUEST				
Test 1	Warning Lamp Does Not Work Before Engine Starts	1993–95	36-205	181
Test 2	Warning Lamp Does Not Blink But Stays On Continuously	1993–95	36-206	182
Test 3	Wheel Sensor	1993–95	36-206	183
Test 4	Motor Relay Or Motor	1993–95	36-207	184
Test 5	Control Module	1993–95	36-207	185
Test 1	Warning Lamp Does Not Work When Ignition Is On	1996	36-207	186
Test 2	Warning Lamp Stays On When Ignition Switch Is On	1996	36-207	187
Test 3	ABS Control Actuator Solenoid Valve	1996	36-208	188
Test 4	Wheel Sensor Or Rotor	1996	36-208	189
Test 5	Motor Relay Or Motor	1996	36-209	190
Test 6	Solenoid Valve Relay	1996	36-210	191
Test 7	Control Unit	1996	36-210	192
Test 8	Pedal Vibration & Noise	1996	36-210	193
Test 9	Long Stopping Distance	1996	36-210	194
Test 10	Unexpected Pedal Action	1996	36-211	195
Test 11	ABS Does Not Work	1996	36-211	196
Test 12	ABS Works Frequently	1996	36-211	197
240SX				
Test 1	Pedal Vibration & Noise	1993–94	36-176	74
Test 2	Long Stopping Distance	1993–94	36-176	75
Test 3	Abnormal Pedal Action	1993–94	36-176	76
Test 4	ABS Doesn't Work	1993–94	36-176	77
Test 5	ABS Works But Warning Activates	1993–94	36-176	78
Test 6	ABS Works Frequently	1993–94	36-177	80
Test 7	Actuator Solenoid	1993–94	36-177	83
Test 8	Wheel Speed Sensor	1993–94	36-178	85
Test 9	Actuator Motor Relay	1993–94	36-178	87
Test 10	Actuator Solenoid Valve Relay	1993–94	36-179	89
Test 11	Control Unit	1993–94	36-179	90
Test 12	Control Unit Or Power Supply & Ground Circuit	1993–94	36-179	91
Test 1	Warning Lamp Does Not Work When Ignition Is Turned On	1995–96	36-184	105
Test 2	Control Unit Or Ground Circuit	1995–96	36-184	106
Test 3	Actuator Solenoid Valve	1995–96	36-185	107
Test 4	Wheel Sensor Or Rotor	1995–96	36-185	108
Test 5	Motor Relay Or Motor	1995–96	36-186	109
Test 6	Solenoid Valve Relay	1995–96	36-186	110
Test 7	Power Supply	1995–96	36-187	111
Test 8	Memory Volt Stop	1995–96	36-187	112
Test 9	Pedal Vibration & Noise	1995–96	36-187	113
Test 10	Long Stopping Distance	1995–96	36-187	114
Test 11	Unexpected Pedal Action	1995–96	36-188	115
Test 12	ABS Does Not Work	1995–96	36-188	116
Test 13	ABS Works Frequently	1995–96	36-188	117
300ZX				
Test 1	Pedal Vibration & Noise	1993	36-176	74

Continued

DIAGNOSTIC CHART INDEX—Continued

Test	Description	Year	Page No.	Fig. No.
300ZX				
Test 2	Long Stopping Distance	1993	36-176	75
Test 3	Abnormal Pedal Action	1993	36-176	76
Test 4	ABS Doesn't Work	1993	36-176	77
Test 5	ABS Works But Warning Activates	1993	36-176	78
Test 6	ABS Works Frequently	1993	36-177	81
Test 7	Actuator Solenoid	1993	36-177	83
Test 8	Wheel Speed Sensor	1993	36-178	85
Test 9	Actuator Motor Relay	1993	36-178	87
Test 10	Actuator Solenoid Valve Relay	1993	36-179	89
Test 11	Control Unit	1993	36-179	90
Test 12	Control Unit Or Power Supply & Ground Circuit	1993	36-179	91
Test 1	Warning Lamp Does Not Work Before Engine Starts	1994–96	36-188	118
Test 2	Warning Lamp Stays On Continuously	1994–96	36-188	119
Test 3	Actuator Solenoid Valve	1994–96	36-189	120
Test 4	Wheel Sensor Or Rotor	1994–96	36-189	121
Test 5	Motor Relay Or Motor	1994–96	36-189	122
Test 6	Solenoid Valve Relay	1994–96	36-190	123
Test 7	Power Supply Low Voltage	1994–96	36-191	124
Test 8	Stop Lamp Switch Circuit	1994–96	36-191	125
Test 9	Control Unit	1994–96	36-191	126

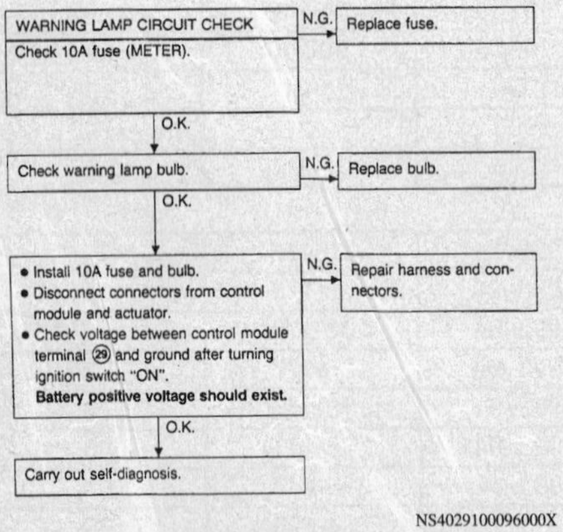
WARNING LAMP CIRCUIT CHECK
Check 10A fuse (METER).
N.G.
Replace fuse.
O.K.
Check warning lamp bulb.
N.G.
Replace bulb.
O.K.
• Install 10A fuse and bulb.
• Disconnect connectors from control module and actuator.
• Check voltage between control module terminal ㉙ and ground after turning ignition switch "ON".
Battery positive voltage should exist.
N.G.
Repair harness and connectors.
O.K.
Carry out self-diagnosis.
NS4029100096000X

Fig. 51 Test 1: Warning Lamp Does Not Work Before Engine Starts. 1993–95 Altima

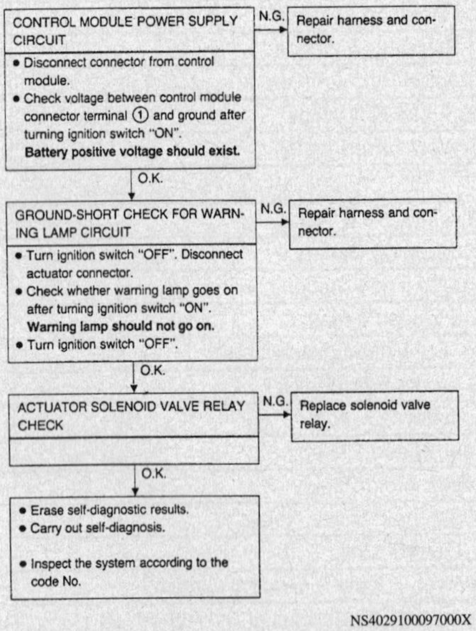
CONTROL MODULE POWER SUPPLY CIRCUIT
• Disconnect connector from control module.
• Check voltage between control module connector terminal ① and ground after turning ignition switch "ON".
Battery positive voltage should exist.
N.G.
Repair harness and connector.
O.K.
GROUND-SHORT CHECK FOR WARNING LAMP CIRCUIT
• Turn ignition switch "OFF". Disconnect actuator connector.
• Check whether warning lamp goes on after turning ignition switch "ON".
Warning lamp should not go on.
• Turn ignition switch "OFF".
N.G.
Repair harness and connector.
O.K.
ACTUATOR SOLENOID VALVE RELAY CHECK
N.G.
Replace solenoid valve relay.
O.K.
• Erase self-diagnostic results.
• Carry out self-diagnosis.
• Inspect the system according to the code No.
NS4029100097000X

Fig. 52 Test 2: Warning Lamp Does Not Blink But Stays On Continuously. 1993–95 Altima

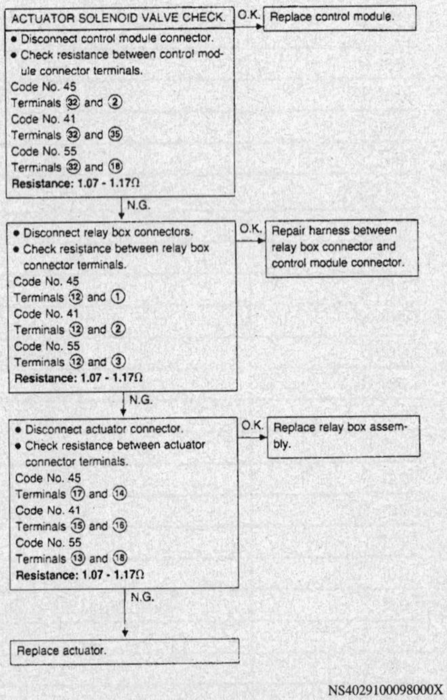
ACTUATOR SOLENOID VALVE CHECK
• Disconnect control module connector.
• Check resistance between control module connector terminals.
Code No. 45
Terminals ㉜ and ②
Code No. 41
Terminals ㉜ and ㉟
Code No. 55
Terminals ㉜ and ⑱
Resistance: 1.07 - 1.17Ω
O.K.
Replace control module.
N.G.
• Disconnect relay box connectors.
• Check resistance between relay box connector terminals.
Code No. 45
Terminals ⑫ and ①
Code No. 41
Terminals ⑫ and ②
Code No. 55
Terminals ⑫ and ③
Resistance: 1.07 - 1.17Ω
O.K.
Repair harness between relay box connector and control module connector.
N.G.
• Disconnect actuator connector.
• Check resistance between actuator connector terminals.
Code No. 45
Terminals ⑰ and ⑭
Code No. 41
Terminals ⑮ and ⑯
Code No. 55
Terminals ⑬ and ⑯
Resistance: 1.07 - 1.17Ω
O.K.
Replace relay box assembly.
N.G.
Replace actuator.
NS4029100098000X

Fig. 53 Test 3: Actuator Solenoid/ Malfunction Codes 45, 41 or 55. 1993–95 Altima

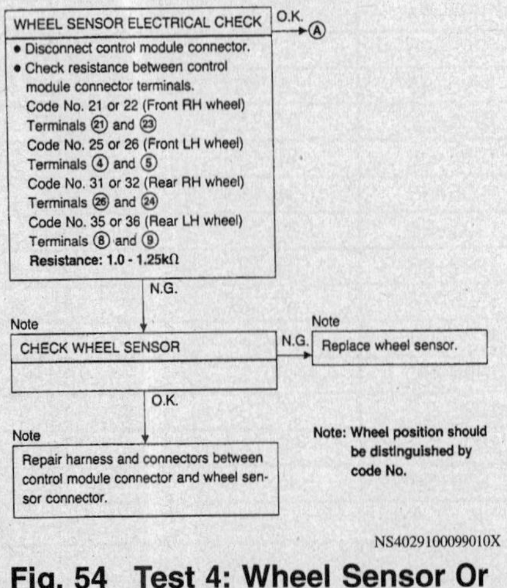
WHEEL SENSOR ELECTRICAL CHECK
• Disconnect control module connector.
• Check resistance between control module connector terminals.
Code No. 21 or 22 (Front RH wheel)
Terminals ㉑ and ㉓
Code No. 25 or 26 (Front LH wheel)
Terminals ④ and ⑤
Code No. 31 or 32 (Rear RH wheel)
Terminals ㉖ and ㉔
Code No. 35 or 36 (Rear LH wheel)
Terminals ⑧ and ⑨
Resistance: 1.0 - 1.25kΩ
O.K.
Ⓐ
N.G.
Note
CHECK WHEEL SENSOR
N.G.
Note
Replace wheel sensor.
O.K.
Note
Repair harness and connectors between control module connector and wheel sensor connector.
Note: Wheel position should be distinguished by code No.
NS4029100099010X

Fig. 54 Test 4: Wheel Sensor Or Rotor (Part 1 of 2). 1993–95 Altima

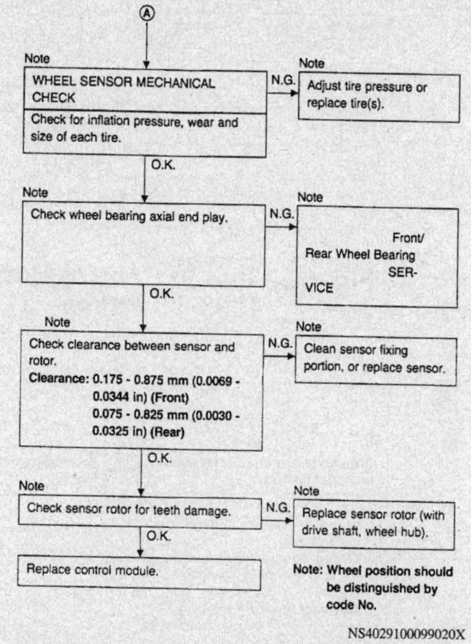
A
Note
WHEEL SENSOR MECHANICAL CHECK
Check for inflation pressure, wear and size of each tire.
N.G.
Note
Adjust tire pressure or replace tire(s).
O.K.
Note
Check wheel bearing axial end play.
N.G.
Note
Front/ Rear Wheel Bearing SER- VICE
O.K.
Note
Check clearance between sensor and rotor.
Clearance: 0.175 - 0.875 mm (0.0069 - 0.0344 in) (Front)
0.075 - 0.825 mm (0.0030 - 0.0325 in) (Rear)
N.G.
Note
Clean sensor fixing portion, or replace sensor.
O.K.
Note
Check sensor rotor for teeth damage.
N.G.
Note
Replace sensor rotor (with drive shaft, wheel hub).
O.K.
Replace control module.
Note: Wheel position should be distinguished by code No.
NS4029100099020X

Fig. 54 Test 4: Wheel Sensor Or Rotor (Part 2 of 2). 1993–95 Altima

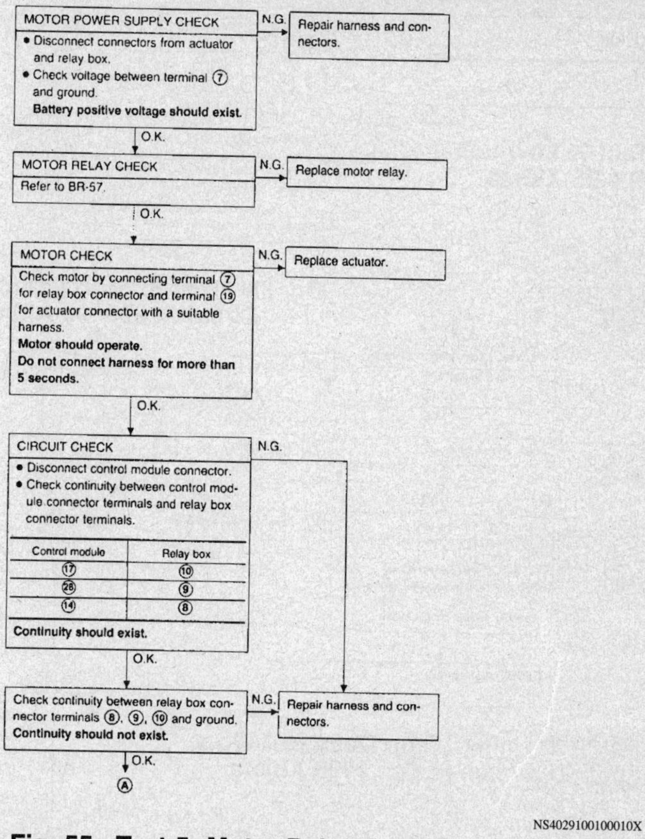
MOTOR POWER SUPPLY CHECK
• Disconnect connectors from actuator and relay box.
• Check voltage between terminal (7) and ground.
Battery positive voltage should exist.
N.G.
Repair harness and connectors.
O.K.
MOTOR RELAY CHECK
Refer to BR-57.
N.G.
Replace motor relay.
O.K.
MOTOR CHECK
Check motor by connecting terminal (7) for relay box connector and terminal (19) for actuator connector with a suitable harness.
Motor should operate.
Do not connect harness for more than 5 seconds.
N.G.
Replace actuator.
O.K.
CIRCUIT CHECK
• Disconnect control module connector.
• Check continuity between control module connector terminals and relay box connector terminals.
Control module | Relay box
(17) | (10)
(28) | (9)
(14) | (8)
Continuity should exist.
N.G.
O.K.
Check continuity between relay box connector terminals (8), (9), (10) and ground.
Continuity should not exist.
N.G.
Repair harness and connectors.
O.K.
A
NS4029100100010X

Fig. 55 Test 5: Motor Relay Or Motor (Part 1 of 2). 1993–95 Altima

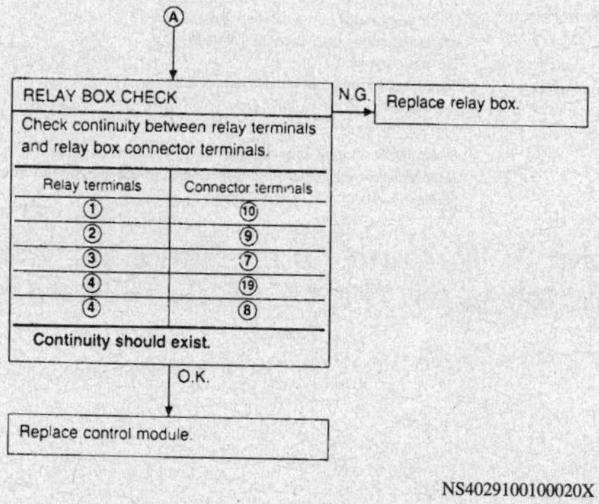
A
RELAY BOX CHECK
Check continuity between relay terminals and relay box connector terminals.
Relay terminals | Connector terminals
(1) | (10)
(2) | (9)
(3) | (7)
(4) | (19)
(4) | (8)
Continuity should exist.
N.G.
Replace relay box.
O.K.
Replace control module.
NS4029100100020X

Fig. 55 Test 5: Motor Relay Or Motor (Part 2 of 2). 1993–95 Altima

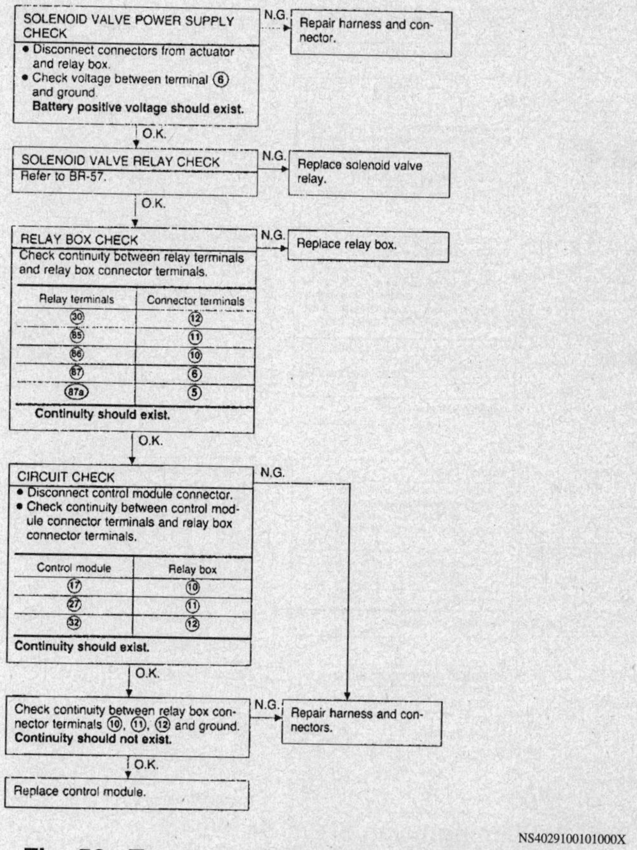
SOLENOID VALVE POWER SUPPLY CHECK
• Disconnect connectors from actuator and relay box.
• Check voltage between terminal (6) and ground.
Battery positive voltage should exist.
N.G.
Repair harness and connector.
O.K.
SOLENOID VALVE RELAY CHECK
Refer to BR-57.
N.G.
Replace solenoid valve relay.
O.K.
RELAY BOX CHECK
Check continuity between relay terminals and relay box connector terminals.
Relay terminals | Connector terminals
(30) | (12)
(85) | (11)
(86) | (10)
(87) | (6)
(87a) | (5)
Continuity should exist.
N.G.
Replace relay box.
O.K.
CIRCUIT CHECK
• Disconnect control module connector.
• Check continuity between control module connector terminals and relay box connector terminals.
Control module | Relay box
(17) | (10)
(27) | (11)
(32) | (12)
Continuity should exist.
N.G.
O.K.
Check continuity between relay box connector terminals (10), (11), (12) and ground.
Continuity should not exist.
N.G.
Repair harness and connectors.
O.K.
Replace control module.
NS4029100101000X

Fig. 56 Test 6: Solenoid Valve Relay. 1993–95 Altima

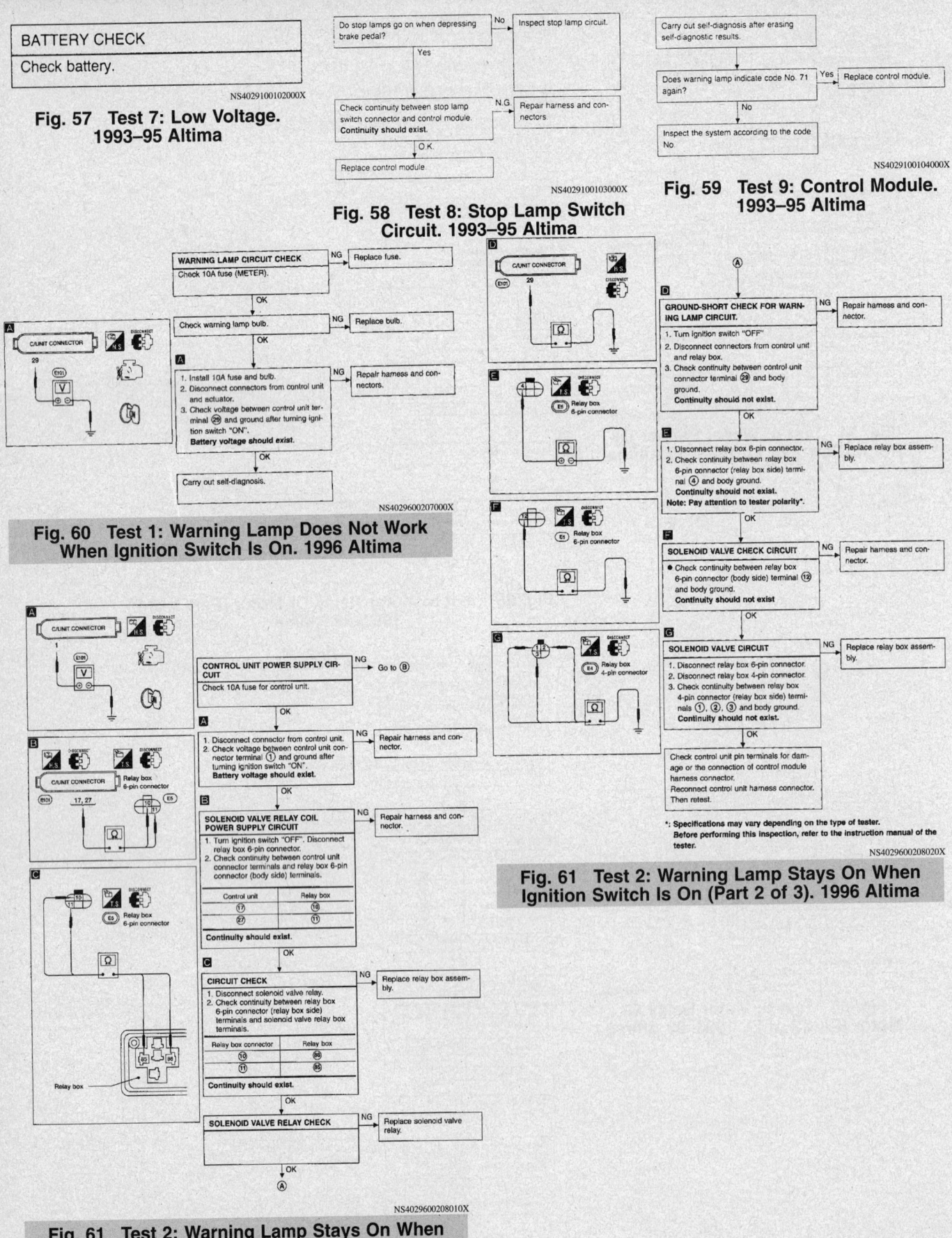

BATTERY CHECK

Check battery.

NS4029100102000X

Fig. 57 Test 7: Low Voltage. 1993–95 Altima

Do stop lamps go on when depressing brake pedal? — No → Inspect stop lamp circuit.

Yes ↓

Check continuity between stop lamp switch connector and control module. **Continuity should exist.** — N.G. → Repair harness and connectors.

O.K. ↓

Replace control module.

NS4029100103000X

Fig. 58 Test 8: Stop Lamp Switch Circuit. 1993–95 Altima

Carry out self-diagnosis after erasing self-diagnostic results.

↓

Does warning lamp indicate code No. 71 again? — Yes → Replace control module.

No ↓

Inspect the system according to the code No.

NS4029100104000X

Fig. 59 Test 9: Control Module. 1993–95 Altima

WARNING LAMP CIRCUIT CHECK
Check 10A fuse (METER). — NG → Replace fuse.

OK ↓

Check warning lamp bulb. — NG → Replace bulb.

OK ↓

A

1. Install 10A fuse and bulb.
2. Disconnect connectors from control unit and actuator.
3. Check voltage between control unit terminal ㉙ and ground after turning ignition switch "ON".

Battery voltage should exist. — NG → Repair harness and connectors.

OK ↓

Carry out self-diagnosis.

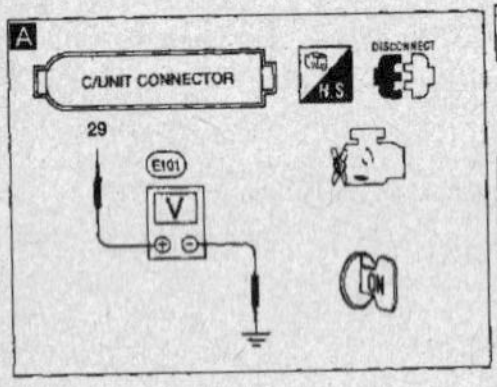
A
C/UNIT CONNECTOR
DISCONNECT
H.S.
29
E101
V

NS4029600207000X

Fig. 60 Test 1: Warning Lamp Does Not Work When Ignition Switch Is On. 1996 Altima

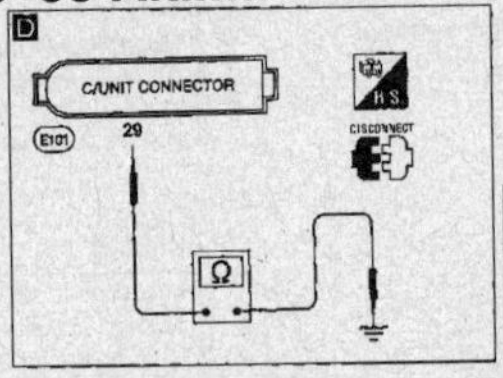
D
C/UNIT CONNECTOR
H.S.
DISCONNECT
E101
29
Ω

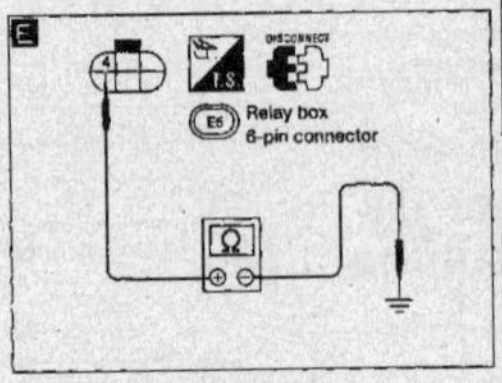
E
DISCONNECT
T.S.
4
E5
Relay box
6-pin connector
Ω

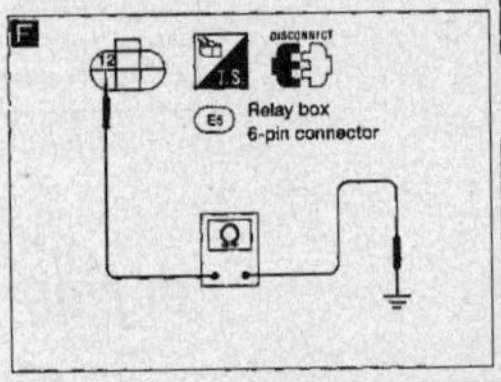
F
DISCONNECT
T.S.
12
E5
Relay box
6-pin connector
Ω

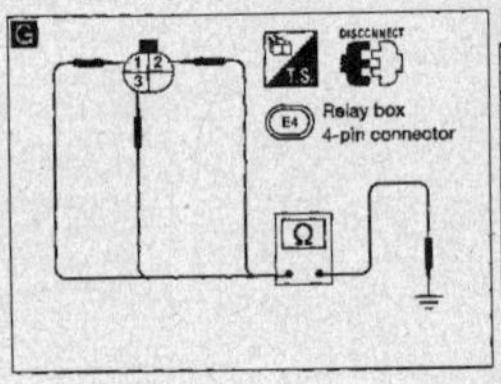
G
DISCONNECT
T.S.
1 2
3
E4
Relay box
4-pin connector
Ω

Ⓐ ↓

D

GROUND-SHORT CHECK FOR WARNING LAMP CIRCUIT.

1. Turn ignition switch "OFF"
2. Disconnect connectors from control unit and relay box.
3. Check continuity between control unit connector terminal ㉙ and body ground.

Continuity should not exist. — NG → Repair harness and connector.

OK ↓

E

1. Disconnect relay box 6-pin connector.
2. Check continuity between relay box 6-pin connector (relay box side) terminal ④ and body ground.

Continuity should not exist.
Note: Pay attention to tester polarity*. — NG → Replace relay box assembly.

OK ↓

F

SOLENOID VALVE CHECK CIRCUIT

- Check continuity between relay box 6-pin connector (body side) terminal ⑫ and body ground.

Continuity should not exist — NG → Repair harness and connector.

OK ↓

G

SOLENOID VALVE CIRCUIT

1. Disconnect relay box 6-pin connector.
2. Disconnect relay box 4-pin connector.
3. Check continuity between relay box 4-pin connector (relay box side) terminals ①, ②, ③ and body ground.

Continuity should not exist. — NG → Replace relay box assembly.

OK ↓

Check control unit pin terminals for damage or the connection of control module harness connector.
Reconnect control unit harness connector.
Then retest.

***: Specifications may vary depending on the type of tester. Before performing this inspection, refer to the instruction manual of the tester.**

NS4029600208020X

Fig. 61 Test 2: Warning Lamp Stays On When Ignition Switch Is On (Part 2 of 3). 1996 Altima

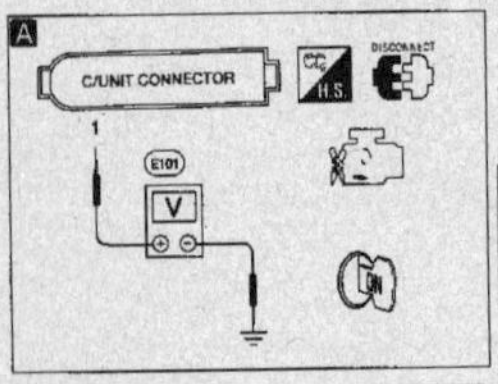
A
C/UNIT CONNECTOR
H.S.
DISCONNECT
1
E101
V

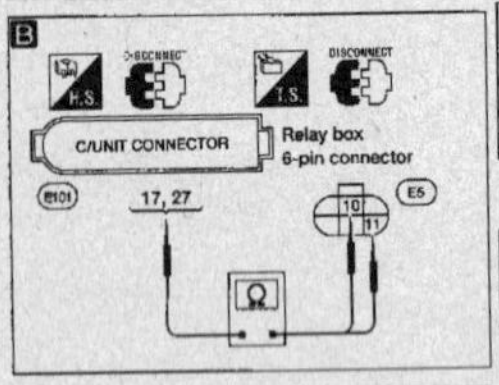
B
H.S.
DISCONNECT
T.S.
DISCONNECT
C/UNIT CONNECTOR
Relay box
6-pin connector
E101
17, 27
10
11
E5
Ω

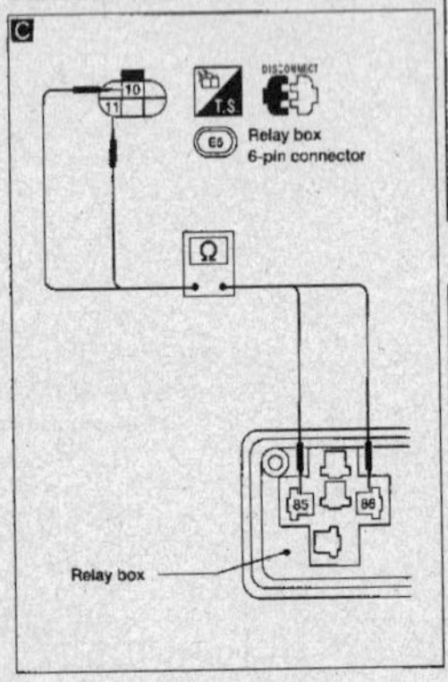
C
10
11
T.S.
DISCONNECT
E5
Relay box
6-pin connector
Ω
85
86
Relay box

CONTROL UNIT POWER SUPPLY CIRCUIT
Check 10A fuse for control unit. — NG → Go to Ⓑ

OK ↓

A

1. Disconnect connector from control unit.
2. Check voltage between control unit connector terminal ① and ground after turning ignition switch "ON".

Battery voltage should exist. — NG → Repair harness and connector.

OK ↓

B

SOLENOID VALVE RELAY COIL POWER SUPPLY CIRCUIT

1. Turn ignition switch "OFF". Disconnect relay box 6-pin connector.
2. Check continuity between control unit connector terminals and relay box 6-pin connector (body side) terminals.

Control unit	Relay box
⑰	⑩
㉗	⑪

Continuity should exist. — NG → Repair harness and connector.

OK ↓

C

CIRCUIT CHECK

1. Disconnect solenoid valve relay.
2. Check continuity between relay box 6-pin connector (relay box side) terminals and solenoid valve relay box terminals.

Relay box connector	Relay box
⑩	86
⑪	85

Continuity should exist. — NG → Replace relay box assembly.

OK ↓

SOLENOID VALVE RELAY CHECK — NG → Replace solenoid valve relay.

OK ↓

Ⓐ

NS4029600208010X

Fig. 61 Test 2: Warning Lamp Stays On When Ignition Switch Is On (Part 1 of 3). 1996 Altima

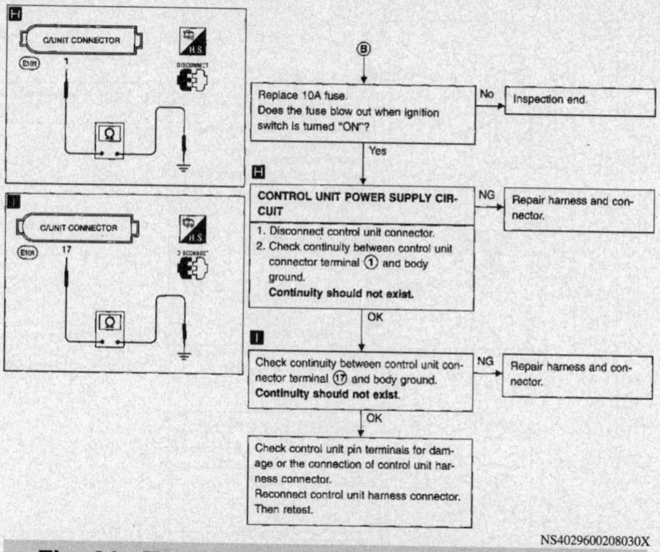
H
C/UNIT CONNECTOR
E101
1
H.S.
DISCONNECT
Ω
B
Replace 10A fuse.
Does the fuse blow out when ignition switch is turned "ON"?
No
Inspection end.
Yes
H
CONTROL UNIT POWER SUPPLY CIRCUIT
1. Disconnect control unit connector.
2. Check continuity between control unit connector terminal ① and body ground.
Continuity should not exist.
NG
Repair harness and connector.
OK
I
C/UNIT CONNECTOR
E101
17
I
Check continuity between control unit connector terminal ⑰ and body ground.
Continuity should not exist.
NG
Repair harness and connector.
OK
Check control unit pin terminals for damage or the connection of control unit harness connector.
Reconnect control unit harness connector.
Then retest.
NS4029600208030X

Fig. 61 Test 2: Warning Lamp Stays On When Ignition Switch Is On (Part 3 of 3). 1996 Altima

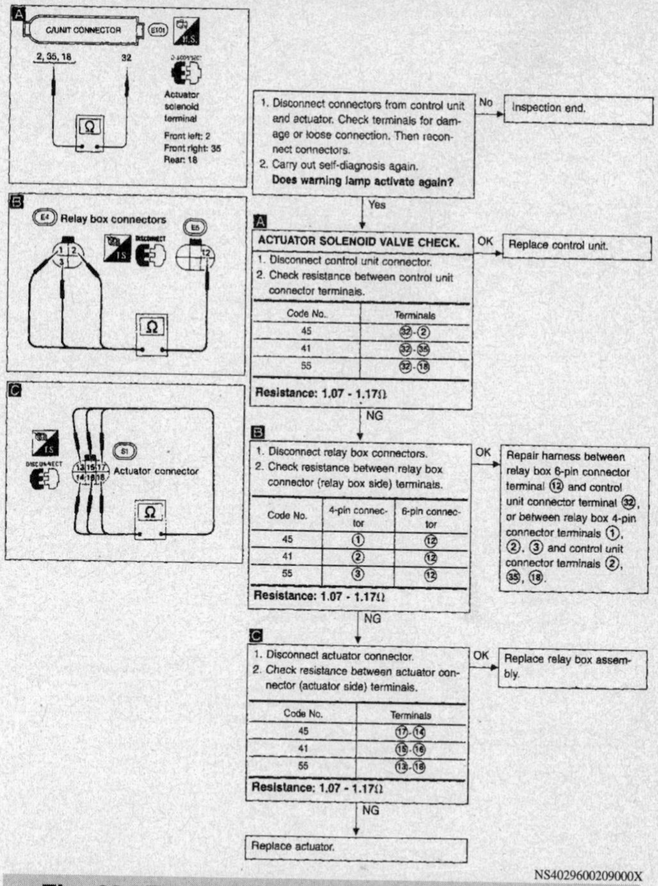
A
C/UNIT CONNECTOR
E101
H.S.
2, 35, 18
32
DISCONNECT
Actuator solenoid terminal
Front left: 2
Front right: 35
Rear: 18
Ω
1. Disconnect connectors from control unit and actuator. Check terminals for damage or loose connection. Then reconnect connectors.
2. Carry out self-diagnosis again.
Does warning lamp activate again?
No
Inspection end.
Yes
A
ACTUATOR SOLENOID VALVE CHECK.
1. Disconnect control unit connector.
2. Check resistance between control unit connector terminals.
Code No. | Terminals
45 | ㉜-②
41 | ㉜-㉟
55 | ㉜-⑱
Resistance: 1.07 - 1.17Ω
OK
Replace control unit.
NG
B
Relay box connectors
E4
E5
I.S.
DISCONNECT
B
1. Disconnect relay box connectors.
2. Check resistance between relay box connector (relay box side) terminals.
Code No. | 4-pin connector | 6-pin connector
45 | ① | ⑫
41 | ② | ⑫
55 | ③ | ⑫
Resistance: 1.07 - 1.17Ω
OK
Repair harness between relay box 6-pin connector terminal ⑫ and control unit connector terminal ㉜, or between relay box 4-pin connector terminals ①, ②, ③ and control unit connector terminals ②, ㉟, ⑱.
NG
C
S1
Actuator connector
DISCONNECT
C
1. Disconnect actuator connector.
2. Check resistance between actuator connector (actuator side) terminals.
Code No. | Terminals
45 | ⑰-⑭
41 | ⑮-⑯
55 | ⑬-⑱
Resistance: 1.07 - 1.17Ω
OK
Replace relay box assembly.
NG
Replace actuator.
NS4029600209000X

Fig. 62 Test 3: Actuator Solenoid Valve. 1996 Altima

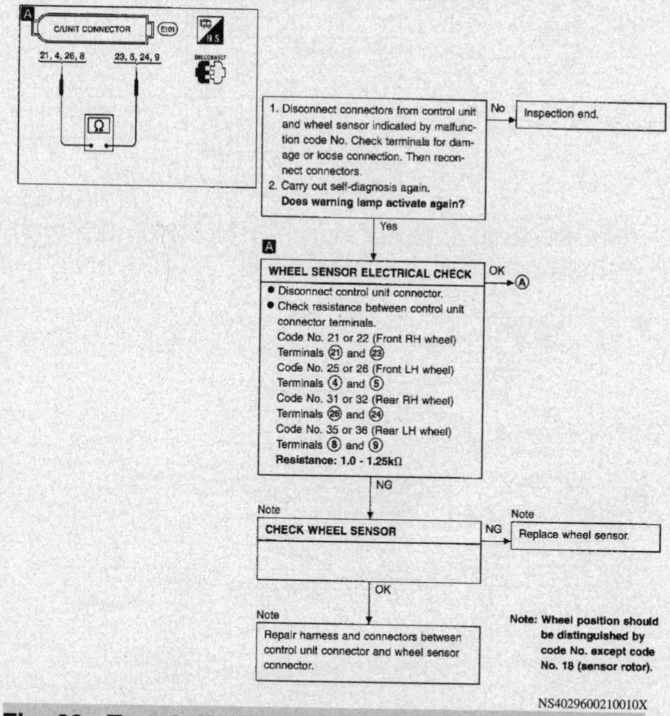
A
C/UNIT CONNECTOR
E101
21, 4, 26, 8
23, 5, 24, 9
H.S.
DISCONNECT
Ω
1. Disconnect connectors from control unit and wheel sensor indicated by malfunction code No. Check terminals for damage or loose connection. Then reconnect connectors.
2. Carry out self-diagnosis again.
Does warning lamp activate again?
No
Inspection end.
Yes
A
WHEEL SENSOR ELECTRICAL CHECK
• Disconnect control unit connector.
• Check resistance between control unit connector terminals.
Code No. 21 or 22 (Front RH wheel)
Terminals ㉑ and ㉓
Code No. 25 or 26 (Front LH wheel)
Terminals ④ and ⑤
Code No. 31 or 32 (Rear RH wheel)
Terminals ㉖ and ㉔
Code No. 35 or 36 (Rear LH wheel)
Terminals ⑧ and ⑨
Resistance: 1.0 - 1.25kΩ
OK
Ⓐ
NG
Note
CHECK WHEEL SENSOR
NG
Note
Replace wheel sensor.
OK
Note
Repair harness and connectors between control unit connector and wheel sensor connector.
Note: Wheel position should be distinguished by code No. except code No. 18 (sensor rotor).
NS4029600210010X

Fig. 63 Test 4: Wheel Sensor Or Rotor (Part 1 of 2). 1996 Altima

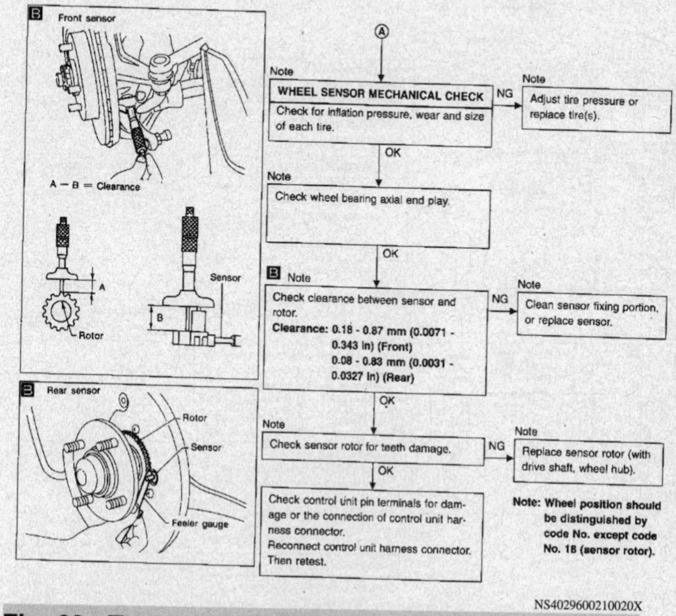
B
Front sensor
A − B = Clearance
A
B
Sensor
Rotor
B
Rear sensor
Rotor
Sensor
Feeler gauge
Ⓐ
Note
WHEEL SENSOR MECHANICAL CHECK
Check for inflation pressure, wear and size of each tire.
NG
Note
Adjust tire pressure or replace tire(s).
OK
Note
Check wheel bearing axial end play.
OK
B
Note
Check clearance between sensor and rotor.
Clearance: 0.18 - 0.87 mm (0.0071 - 0.343 in) (Front)
0.08 - 0.83 mm (0.0031 - 0.0327 in) (Rear)
NG
Note
Clean sensor fixing portion, or replace sensor.
OK
Note
Check sensor rotor for teeth damage.
NG
Note
Replace sensor rotor (with drive shaft, wheel hub).
OK
Check control unit pin terminals for damage or the connection of control unit harness connector.
Reconnect control unit harness connector.
Then retest.
Note: Wheel position should be distinguished by code No. except code No. 18 (sensor rotor).
NS4029600210020X

Fig. 63 Test 4: Wheel Sensor Or Rotor (Part 2 of 2). 1996 Altima

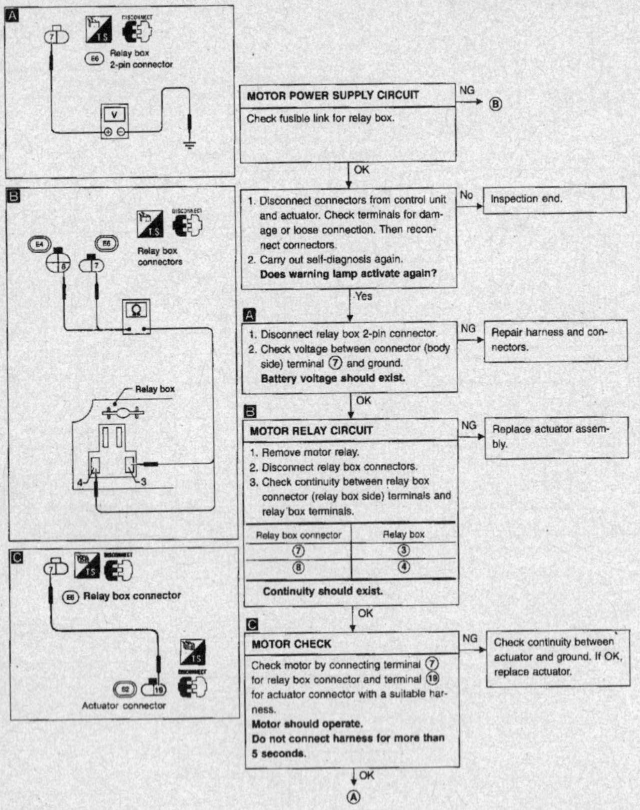
A
Relay box 2-pin connector
MOTOR POWER SUPPLY CIRCUIT
Check fusible link for relay box.
NG
OK
B
Relay box connectors
1. Disconnect connectors from control unit and actuator. Check terminals for damage or loose connection. Then reconnect connectors.
2. Carry out self-diagnosis again.
Does warning lamp activate again?
No
Inspection end.
Yes
A
1. Disconnect relay box 2-pin connector.
2. Check voltage between connector (body side) terminal ⑦ and ground.
Battery voltage should exist.
NG
Repair harness and connectors.
OK
Relay box
B
MOTOR RELAY CIRCUIT
1. Remove motor relay.
2. Disconnect relay box connectors.
3. Check continuity between relay box connector (relay box side) terminals and relay box terminals.
Relay box connector
Relay box
⑦
③
⑧
④
Continuity should exist.
NG
Replace actuator assembly.
OK
C
Relay box connector
Actuator connector
MOTOR CHECK
Check motor by connecting terminal ⑦ for relay box connector and terminal ⑲ for actuator connector with a suitable harness.
Motor should operate.
Do not connect harness for more than 5 seconds.
NG
Check continuity between actuator and ground. If OK, replace actuator.
OK
Ⓐ

NS4029600211010X

Fig. 64 Test 5: Motor Relay Or Motor (Part 1 of 3). 1996 Altima

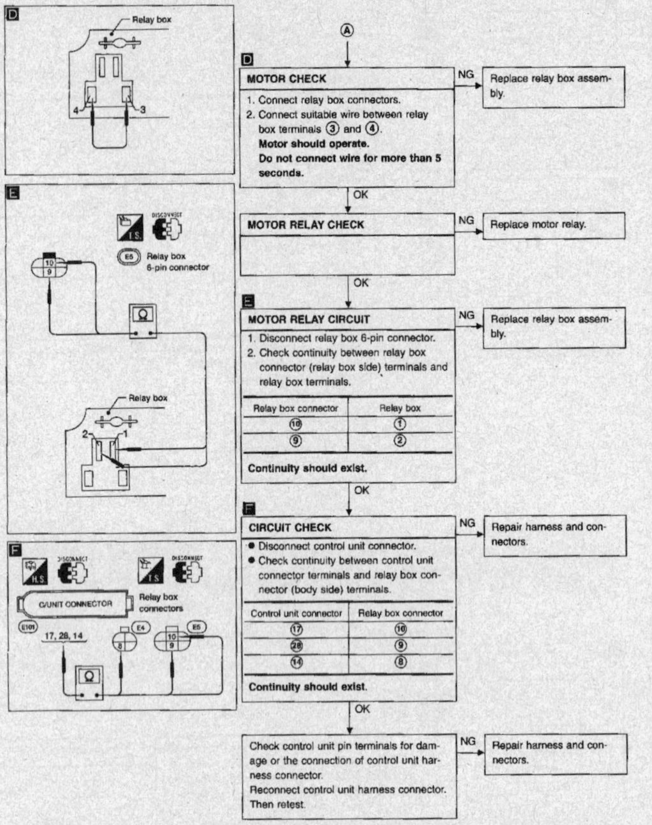
D
Relay box
Ⓐ
MOTOR CHECK
1. Connect relay box connectors.
2. Connect suitable wire between relay box terminals ③ and ④.
Motor should operate.
Do not connect wire for more than 5 seconds.
NG
Replace relay box assembly.
OK
E
Relay box 6-pin connector
MOTOR RELAY CHECK
NG
Replace motor relay.
OK
E
MOTOR RELAY CIRCUIT
1. Disconnect relay box 6-pin connector.
2. Check continuity between relay box connector (relay box side) terminals and relay box terminals.
Relay box connector
Relay box
⑩
①
⑨
②
Continuity should exist.
NG
Replace relay box assembly.
OK
F
C/UNIT CONNECTOR
Relay box connectors
17, 28, 14
CIRCUIT CHECK
• Disconnect control unit connector.
• Check continuity between control unit connector terminals and relay box connector (body side) terminals.
Control unit connector
Relay box connector
⑰
⑩
㉘
⑨
⑭
⑧
Continuity should exist.
NG
Repair harness and connectors.
OK
Check control unit pin terminals for damage or the connection of control unit harness connector.
Reconnect control unit harness connector.
Then retest.
NG
Repair harness and connectors.

NS4029600211020X

Fig. 64 Test 5: Motor Relay Or Motor (Part 2 of 3). 1996 Altima

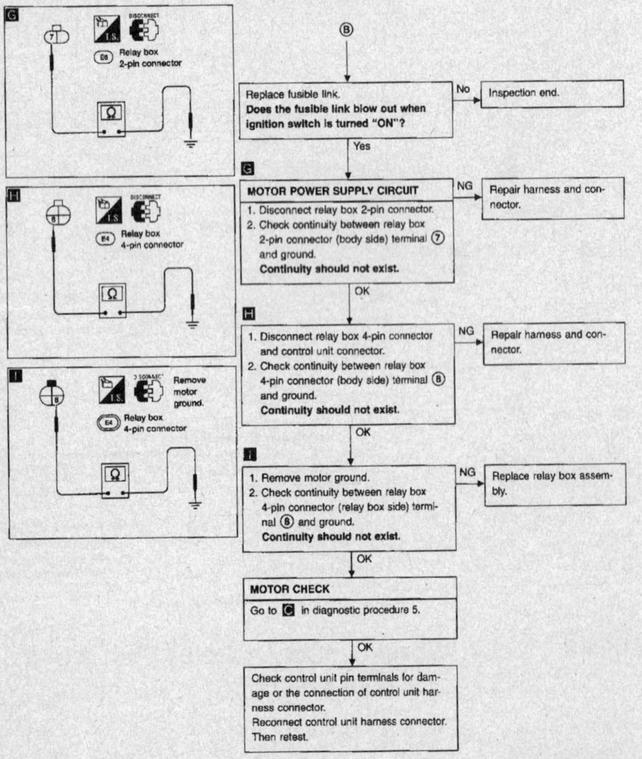
G
Relay box 2-pin connector
Ⓑ
Replace fusible link.
Does the fusible link blow out when ignition switch is turned "ON"?
No
Inspection end.
Yes
G
MOTOR POWER SUPPLY CIRCUIT
1. Disconnect relay box 2-pin connector.
2. Check continuity between relay box 2-pin connector (body side) terminal ⑦ and ground.
Continuity should not exist.
NG
Repair harness and connector.
OK
H
Relay box 4-pin connector
H
1. Disconnect relay box 4-pin connector and control unit connector.
2. Check continuity between relay box 4-pin connector (body side) terminal ⑧ and ground.
Continuity should not exist.
NG
Repair harness and connector.
OK
I
Remove motor ground.
Relay box 4-pin connector
I
1. Remove motor ground.
2. Check continuity between relay box 4-pin connector (relay box side) terminal ⑧ and ground.
Continuity should not exist.
NG
Replace relay box assembly.
OK
MOTOR CHECK
Go to C in diagnostic procedure 5.
OK
Check control unit pin terminals for damage or the connection of control unit harness connector.
Reconnect control unit harness connector.
Then retest.

NS4029600211030X

Fig. 64 Test 5: Motor Relay Or Motor (Part 3 of 3). 1996 Altima

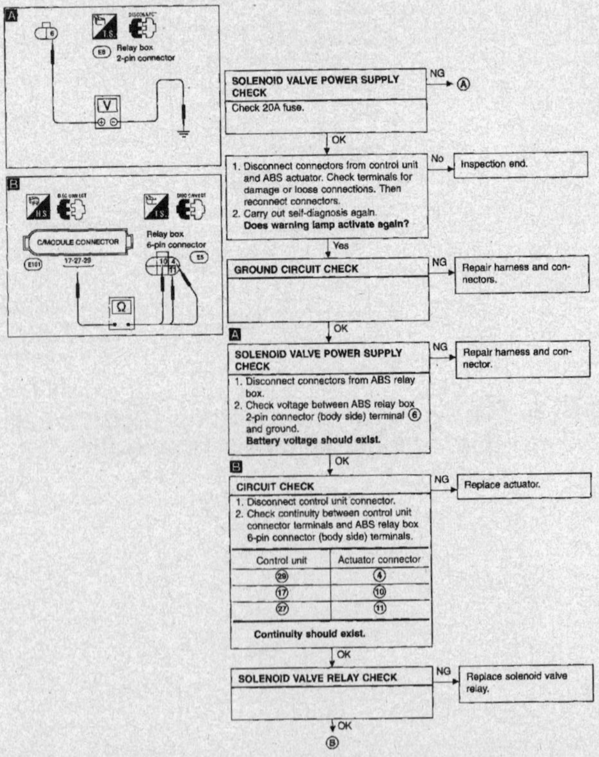
A
Relay box 2-pin connector
SOLENOID VALVE POWER SUPPLY CHECK
Check 20A fuse.
NG
Ⓐ
OK
B
C/MODULE CONNECTOR
17-27-29
Relay box 6-pin connector
1. Disconnect connectors from control unit and ABS actuator. Check terminals for damage or loose connections. Then reconnect connectors.
2. Carry out self-diagnosis again.
Does warning lamp activate again?
No
Inspection end.
Yes
GROUND CIRCUIT CHECK
NG
Repair harness and connectors.
OK
A
SOLENOID VALVE POWER SUPPLY CHECK
1. Disconnect connectors from ABS relay box.
2. Check voltage between ABS relay box 2-pin connector (body side) terminal ⑥ and ground.
Battery voltage should exist.
NG
Repair harness and connector.
OK
B
CIRCUIT CHECK
1. Disconnect control unit connector.
2. Check continuity between control unit connector terminals and ABS relay box 6-pin connector (body side) terminals.
Control unit
Actuator connector
㉙
④
⑰
⑩
㉗
⑪
Continuity should exist.
NG
Replace actuator.
OK
SOLENOID VALVE RELAY CHECK
NG
Replace solenoid valve relay.
OK
Ⓑ

NS4029600212010X

Fig. 65 Test 6: Solenoid Valve Relay (Part 1 of 2). 1996 Altima

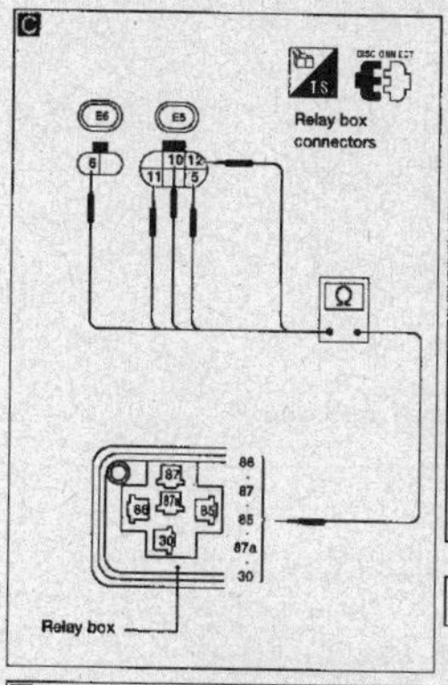
C
DISCONNECT
Relay box connectors
E6
E5
Relay box
86
87
85
87a
30

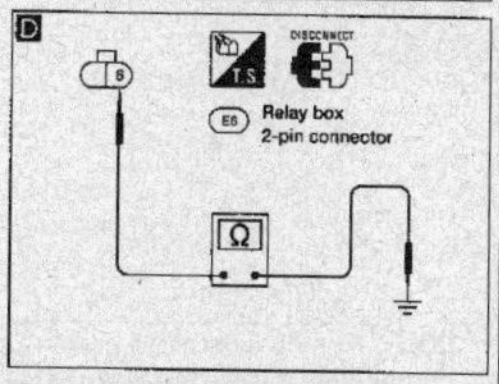
D
DISCONNECT
Relay box 2-pin connector

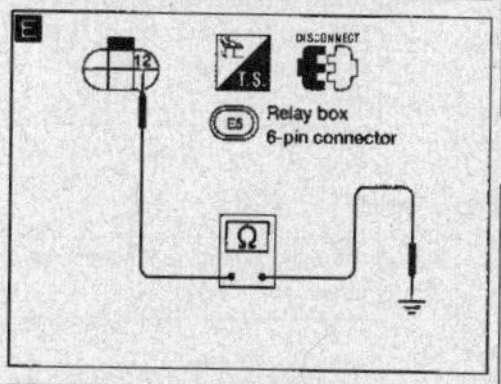
E
DISCONNECT
Relay box 6-pin connector

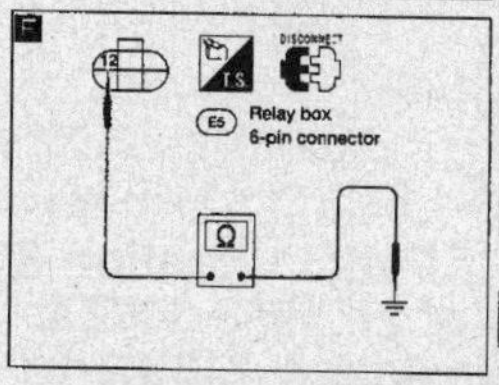
F
DISCONNECT
Relay box 6-pin connector

(B)

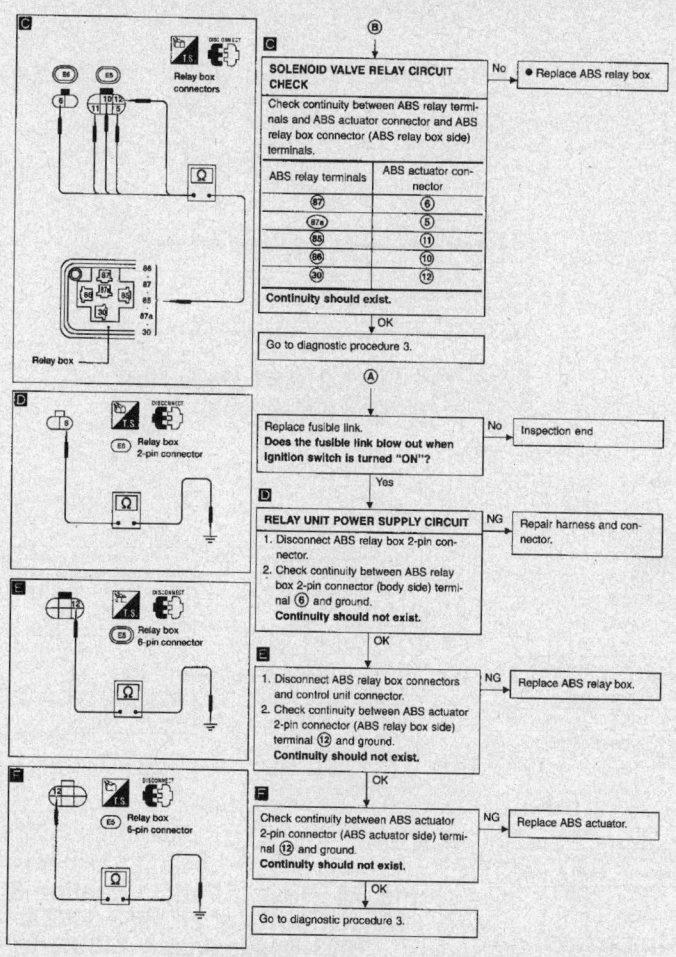

C SOLENOID VALVE RELAY CIRCUIT CHECK

Check continuity between ABS relay terminals and ABS actuator connector and ABS relay box connector (ABS relay box side) terminals.

ABS relay terminals	ABS actuator connector
(87)	(6)
(87a)	(5)
(85)	(11)
(86)	(10)
(30)	(12)

Continuity should exist.

- No → • Replace ABS relay box.
- OK → Go to diagnostic procedure 3.

(A)

Replace fusible link. **Does the fusible link blow out when ignition switch is turned "ON"?**

- No → Inspection end
- Yes ↓

D RELAY UNIT POWER SUPPLY CIRCUIT

1. Disconnect ABS relay box 2-pin connector.
2. Check continuity between ABS relay box 2-pin connector (body side) terminal (6) and ground.

Continuity should not exist.

- NG → Repair harness and connector.
- OK ↓

E

1. Disconnect ABS relay box connectors and control unit connector.
2. Check continuity between ABS actuator 2-pin connector (ABS relay box side) terminal (12) and ground.

Continuity should not exist.

- NG → Replace ABS relay box.
- OK ↓

F

Check continuity between ABS actuator 2-pin connector (ABS actuator side) terminal (12) and ground.

Continuity should not exist.

- NG → Replace ABS actuator.
- OK → Go to diagnostic procedure 3.

NS4029600212020X

Fig. 65 Test 6: Solenoid Valve Relay (Part 2 of 2). 1996 Altima

A
C/UNIT CONNECTOR
E101
1
DISCONNECT
V

- • Disconnect control unit connectors. Check terminals for damage or connection. Then reconnect connectors.
- • Carry out self-diagnosis again.

Does warning lamp activate again?

- No → Inspection end.
- Yes ↓

A CONTROL UNIT POWER SUPPLY CHECK

- • Disconnect control unit connector.
- • Check voltage between control unit connector terminal (1) and ground.

Battery voltage should exist when ignition switch is turned ON.

- NG → (A)
- OK ↓

CONTROL UNIT GROUND CHECK

- NG → Repair harness and connectors.
- OK ↓

Check control unit pin terminals for damage or the connection of control unit harness connector. Reconnect control unit harness connector. Then retest.

(A)

Check 10A fuse.

- NG → Replace fuse.
- OK ↓

Check continuity between battery and control unit connector terminal (1).

- NG → Repair harness and connectors.
- OK ↓

Check battery.

NS4029600213000X

Fig. 66 Test 7: Power Supply Low Voltage. 1996 Altima

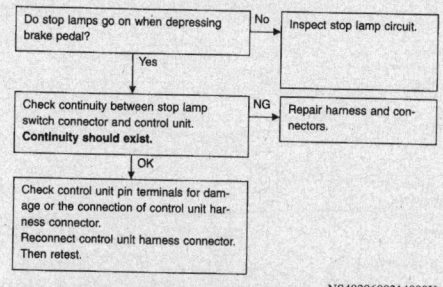

Do stop lamps go on when depressing brake pedal?

- No → Inspect stop lamp circuit.
- Yes ↓

Check continuity between stop lamp switch connector and control unit. **Continuity should exist.**

- NG → Repair harness and connectors.
- OK ↓

Check control unit pin terminals for damage or the connection of control unit harness connector. Reconnect control unit harness connector. Then retest.

NS4029600214000X

Fig. 67 Test 8: Stop Lamp Switch Circuit. 1996 Altima

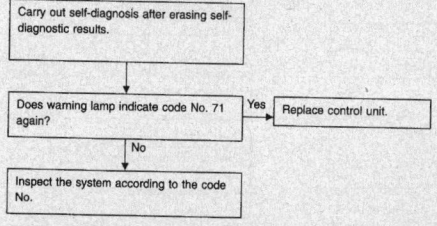

Carry out self-diagnosis after erasing self-diagnostic results.

↓

Does warning lamp indicate code No. 71 again?

- Yes → Replace control unit.
- No ↓

Inspect the system according to the code No.

NS4029600215000X

Fig. 68 Test 9: Control Unit. 1996 Altima

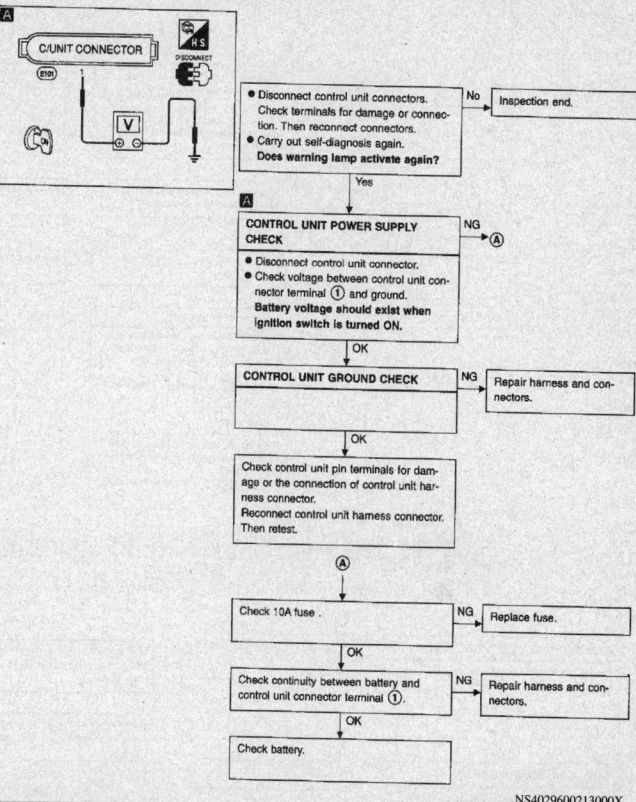

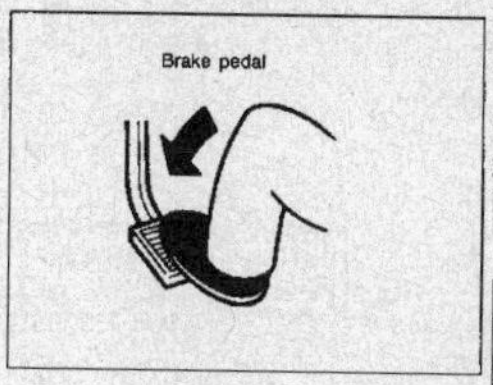
Brake pedal

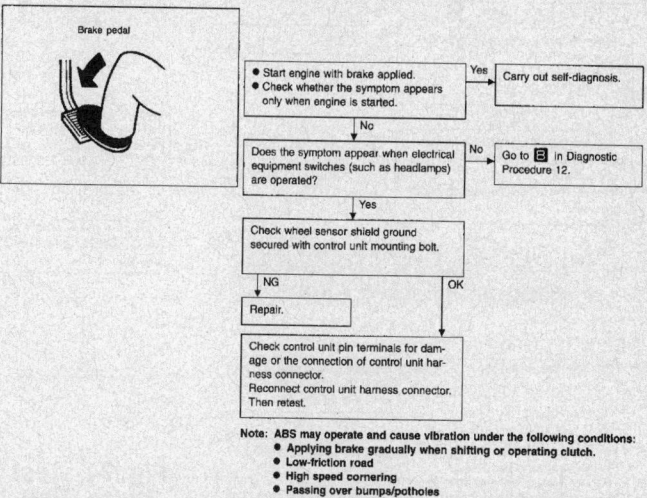

- • Start engine with brake applied.
- • Check whether the symptom appears only when engine is started.

- Yes → Carry out self-diagnosis.
- No ↓

Does the symptom appear when electrical equipment switches (such as headlamps) are operated?

- No → Go to B in Diagnostic Procedure 12.
- Yes ↓

Check wheel sensor shield ground secured with control unit mounting bolt.

- NG → Repair.
- OK → Check control unit pin terminals for damage or the connection of control unit harness connector. Reconnect control unit harness connector. Then retest.

Note: ABS may operate and cause vibration under the following conditions:

- **Applying brake gradually when shifting or operating clutch.**
- **Low-friction road**
- **High speed cornering**
- **Passing over bumps/potholes**
- **Engine speed is over 5,000 rpm with vehicle stopped.**

NS4029600216000X

Fig. 69 Test 10: Pedal Vibration & Noise. 1996 Altima

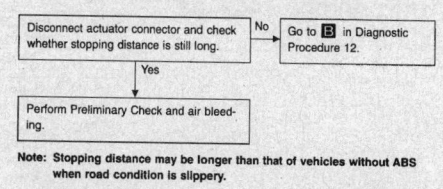

Disconnect actuator connector and check whether stopping distance is still long.

- No → Go to B in Diagnostic Procedure 12.
- Yes ↓

Perform Preliminary Check and air bleeding.

Note: Stopping distance may be longer than that of vehicles without ABS when road condition is slippery.

NS4029600217000X

Fig. 70 Test 11: Long Stopping Distance. 1996 Altima

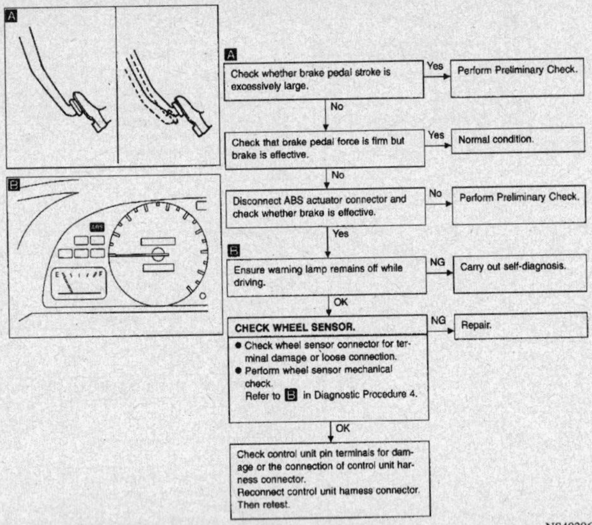
A
Check whether brake pedal stroke is excessively large.
Yes
Perform Preliminary Check.
No
Check that brake pedal force is firm but brake is effective.
Yes
Normal condition.
No
Disconnect ABS actuator connector and check whether brake is effective.
No
Perform Preliminary Check.
Yes
B
Ensure warning lamp remains off while driving.
NG
Carry out self-diagnosis.
OK
CHECK WHEEL SENSOR.
• Check wheel sensor connector for terminal damage or loose connection.
• Perform wheel sensor mechanical check.
Refer to B in Diagnostic Procedure 4.
NG
Repair.
OK
Check control unit pin terminals for damage or the connection of control unit harness connector.
Reconnect control unit harness connector. Then retest.

NS4029600218000X

Fig. 71 Test 12: Unexpected Pedal Action. 1996 Altima

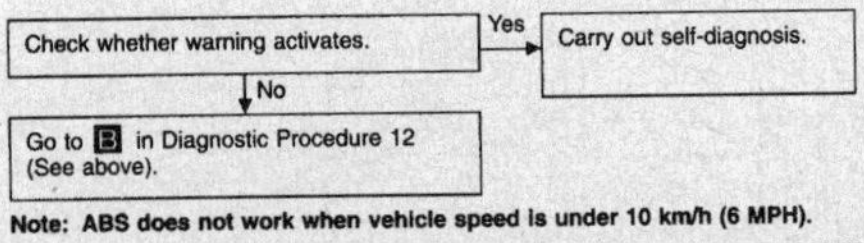
Check whether warning activates.
Yes
Carry out self-diagnosis.
No
Go to B in Diagnostic Procedure 12 (See above).
Note: ABS does not work when vehicle speed is under 10 km/h (6 MPH).

NS4029600219000X

Fig. 72 Test 13: ABS Does Not Work. 1996 Altima

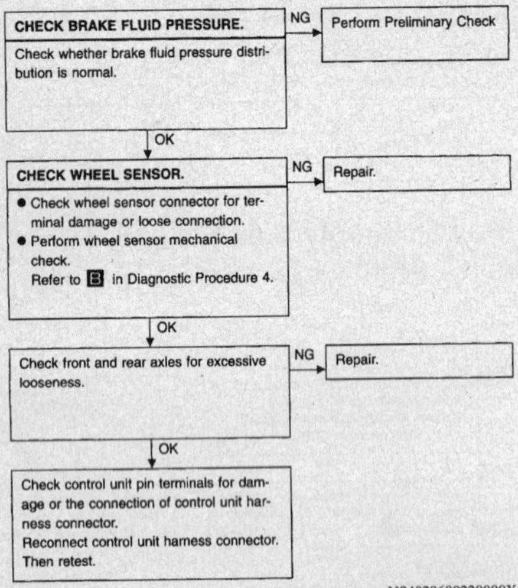
CHECK BRAKE FLUID PRESSURE.
Check whether brake fluid pressure distribution is normal.
NG
Perform Preliminary Check
OK
CHECK WHEEL SENSOR.
• Check wheel sensor connector for terminal damage or loose connection.
• Perform wheel sensor mechanical check.
Refer to B in Diagnostic Procedure 4.
NG
Repair.
OK
Check front and rear axles for excessive looseness.
NG
Repair.
OK
Check control unit pin terminals for damage or the connection of control unit harness connector.
Reconnect control unit harness connector.
Then retest.

NS4029600220000X

Fig. 73 Test 14: ABS Works Frequently. 1996 Altima

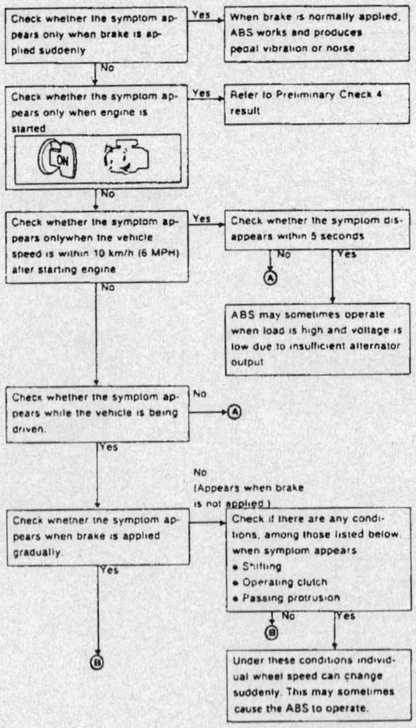
Check whether the symptom appears only when brake is applied suddenly
Yes
When brake is normally applied, ABS works and produces pedal vibration or noise
No
Check whether the symptom appears only when engine is started
Yes
Refer to Preliminary Check 4 result
No
Check whether the symptom appears only when the vehicle speed is within 10 km/h (6 MPH) after starting engine
Yes
Check whether the symptom disappears within 5 seconds
No
A
Yes
ABS may sometimes operate when load is high and voltage is low due to insufficient alternator output
No
Check whether the symptom appears while the vehicle is being driven.
No
A
Yes
Check whether the symptom appears when brake is applied gradually.
No (Appears when brake is not applied.)
Check if there are any conditions, among those listed below, when symptom appears
• Shifting
• Operating clutch
• Passing protrusion
No
B
Yes
Under these conditions individual wheel speed can change suddenly. This may sometimes cause the ABS to operate.
Yes
B

NS4029100033010X

Fig. 74 Test 1: Pedal Vibration & Noise (Part 1 of 2). 1993 300ZX, 1993–94 Maxima & 240SX

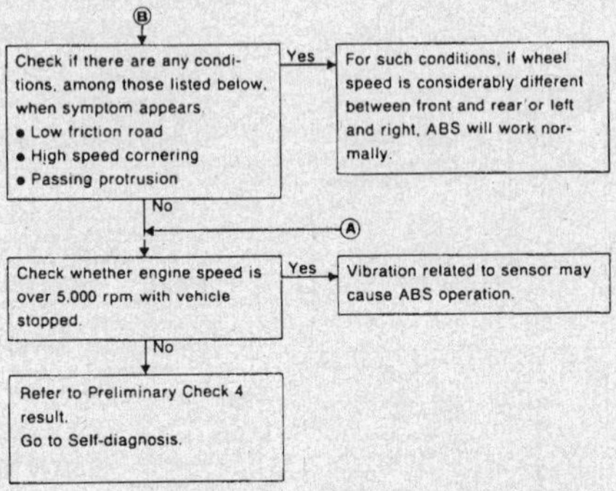
B
Check if there are any conditions, among those listed below, when symptom appears.
• Low friction road
• High speed cornering
• Passing protrusion
Yes
For such conditions, if wheel speed is considerably different between front and rear or left and right, ABS will work normally.
No
A
Check whether engine speed is over 5,000 rpm with vehicle stopped.
Yes
Vibration related to sensor may cause ABS operation.
No
Refer to Preliminary Check 4 result.
Go to Self-diagnosis.

NS4029100033020X

Fig. 74 Test 1: Pedal Vibration & Noise (Part 2 of 2). 1993 300ZX, 1993–94 Maxima & 240SX

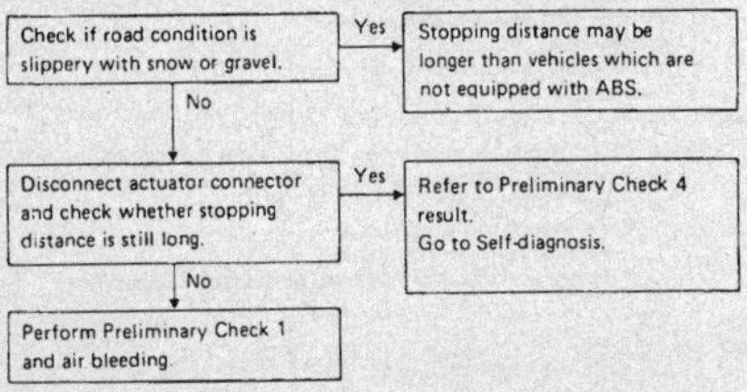
Check if road condition is slippery with snow or gravel.
Yes
Stopping distance may be longer than vehicles which are not equipped with ABS.
No
Disconnect actuator connector and check whether stopping distance is still long.
Yes
Refer to Preliminary Check 4 result.
Go to Self-diagnosis.
No
Perform Preliminary Check 1 and air bleeding.

NS4029100034000X

Fig. 75 Test 2: Long Stopping Distance. 1993 300ZX, 1993–94 Maxima & 240SX

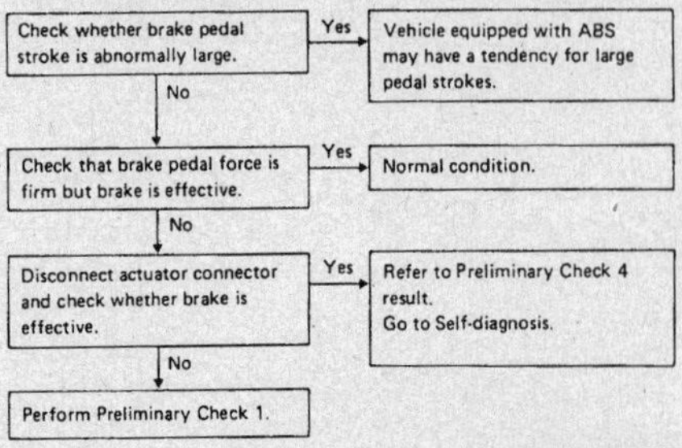
Check whether brake pedal stroke is abnormally large.
Yes
Vehicle equipped with ABS may have a tendency for large pedal strokes.
No
Check that brake pedal force is firm but brake is effective.
Yes
Normal condition.
No
Disconnect actuator connector and check whether brake is effective.
Yes
Refer to Preliminary Check 4 result.
Go to Self-diagnosis.
No
Perform Preliminary Check 1.

NS4029100035000X

Fig. 76 Test 3: Abnormal Pedal Action. 1993 300ZX, 1993–94 Maxima & 240SX

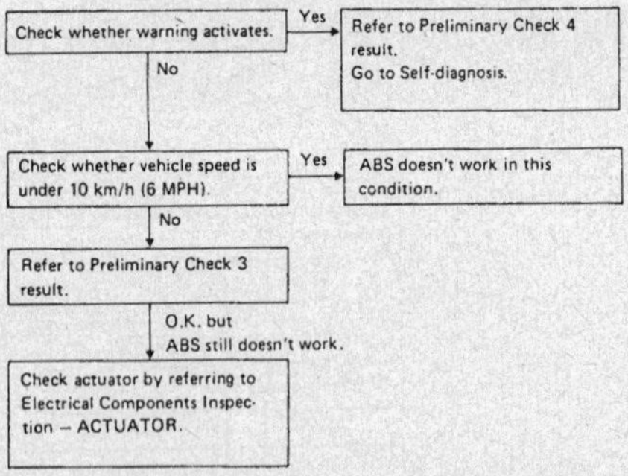
Check whether warning activates.
Yes
Refer to Preliminary Check 4 result.
Go to Self-diagnosis.
No
Check whether vehicle speed is under 10 km/h (6 MPH).
Yes
ABS doesn't work in this condition.
No
Refer to Preliminary Check 3 result.
O.K. but ABS still doesn't work.
Check actuator by referring to Electrical Components Inspection – ACTUATOR.

NS4029100036000X

Fig. 77 Test 4: ABS Doesn't Work. 1993 300ZX, 1993–94 Maxima & 240SX

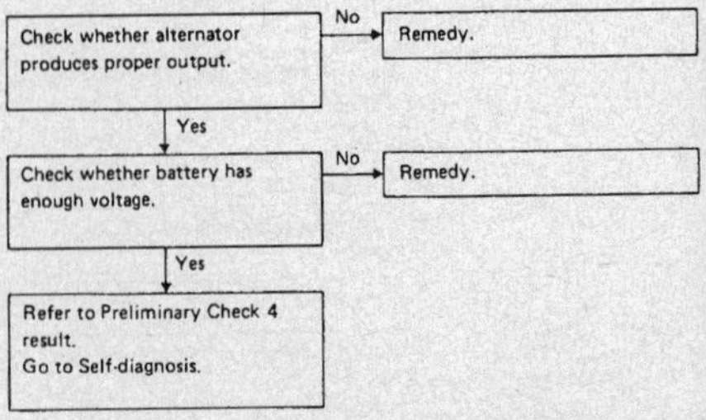
Check whether alternator produces proper output.
No
Remedy.
Yes
Check whether battery has enough voltage.
No
Remedy.
Yes
Refer to Preliminary Check 4 result.
Go to Self-diagnosis.

NS4029100037000X

Fig. 78 Test 5: ABS Works But Warning Activates. 1993 300ZX, 1993–94 Maxima & 240SX

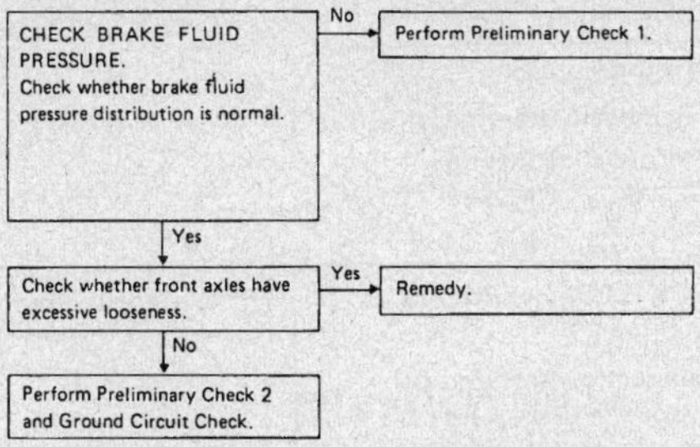
CHECK BRAKE FLUID PRESSURE.
Check whether brake fluid pressure distribution is normal.
No
Perform Preliminary Check 1.
Yes
Check whether front axles have excessive looseness.
Yes
Remedy.
No
Perform Preliminary Check 2 and Ground Circuit Check.

NS4029100038000X

Fig. 79 Test 6: ABS Works Frequently. 1993–94 Maxima

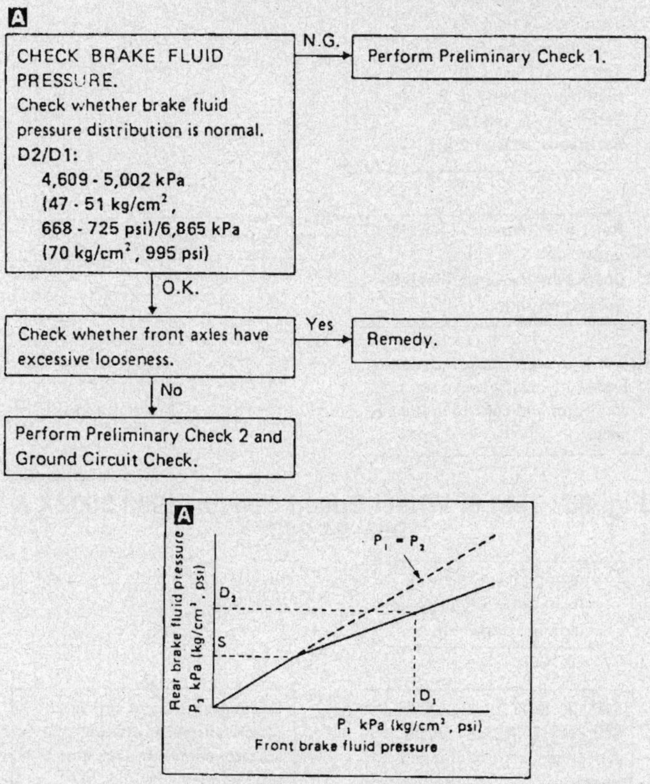
A
CHECK BRAKE FLUID PRESSURE.
Check whether brake fluid pressure distribution is normal.
D2/D1:
4,609 - 5,002 kPa
(47 - 51 kg/cm², 668 - 725 psi)/6,865 kPa
(70 kg/cm², 995 psi)
N.G.
Perform Preliminary Check 1.
O.K.
Check whether front axles have excessive looseness.
Yes
Remedy.
No
Perform Preliminary Check 2 and Ground Circuit Check.
A
P1 = P2
D2
S
D1
Rear brake fluid pressure P2 kPa (kg/cm², psi)
P1 kPa (kg/cm², psi)
Front brake fluid pressure

NS4029100041000X

Fig. 81 Test 6: ABS Works Frequently. 1993 300ZX

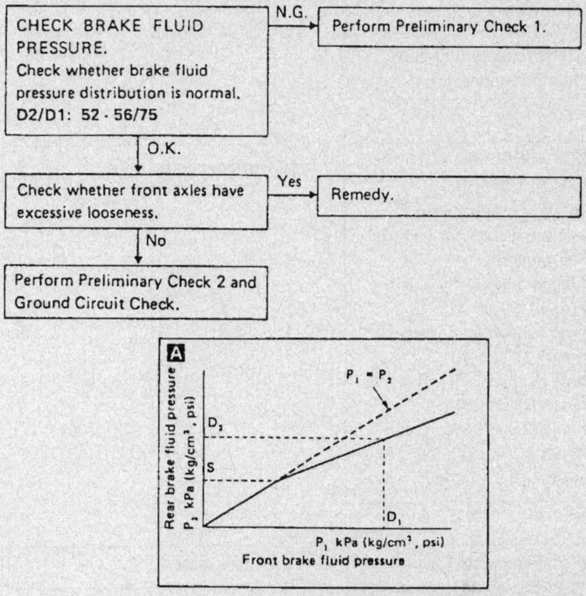
CHECK BRAKE FLUID PRESSURE.
Check whether brake fluid pressure distribution is normal.
D2/D1: 52 - 56/75
N.G.
Perform Preliminary Check 1.
O.K.
Check whether front axles have excessive looseness.
Yes
Remedy.
No
Perform Preliminary Check 2 and Ground Circuit Check.
A
P1 = P2
D2
S
D1
Rear brake fluid pressure P2 kPa (kg/cm², psi)
P1 kPa (kg/cm², psi)
Front brake fluid pressure

NS4029100040000X

Fig. 80 Test 6: ABS Works Frequently. 1993–94 240SX

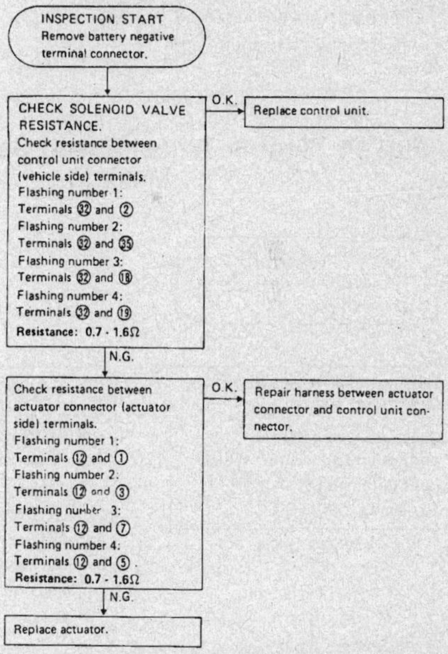
INSPECTION START
Remove battery negative terminal connector.
CHECK SOLENOID VALVE RESISTANCE.
Check resistance between control unit connector (vehicle side) terminals.
Flashing number 1:
Terminals 32 and 2
Flashing number 2:
Terminals 32 and 35
Flashing number 3:
Terminals 32 and 18
Flashing number 4:
Terminals 32 and 19
Resistance: 0.7 - 1.6Ω
O.K.
Replace control unit.
N.G.
Check resistance between actuator connector (actuator side) terminals.
Flashing number 1:
Terminals 12 and 1
Flashing number 2:
Terminals 12 and 3
Flashing number 3:
Terminals 12 and 7
Flashing number 4:
Terminals 12 and 5.
Resistance: 0.7 - 1.6Ω
O.K.
Repair harness between actuator connector and control unit connector.
N.G.
Replace actuator.

NS4029100042000X

Fig. 82 Test 7: Actuator Solenoid. 1993–94 Maxima

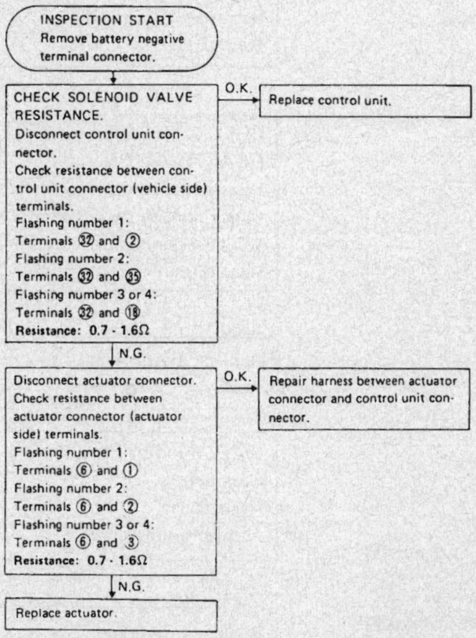
INSPECTION START
Remove battery negative terminal connector.
CHECK SOLENOID VALVE RESISTANCE.
Disconnect control unit connector.
Check resistance between control unit connector (vehicle side) terminals.
Flashing number 1:
Terminals 32 and 2
Flashing number 2:
Terminals 32 and 35
Flashing number 3 or 4:
Terminals 32 and 18
Resistance: 0.7 - 1.6Ω
O.K.
Replace control unit.
N.G.
Disconnect actuator connector.
Check resistance between actuator connector (actuator side) terminals.
Flashing number 1:
Terminals 6 and 1
Flashing number 2:
Terminals 6 and 2
Flashing number 3 or 4:
Terminals 6 and 3
Resistance: 0.7 - 1.6Ω
O.K.
Repair harness between actuator connector and control unit connector.
N.G.
Replace actuator.

NS4029100043000X

Fig. 83 Test 7: Actuator Solenoid. 1993 300ZX & 1993–94 240SX

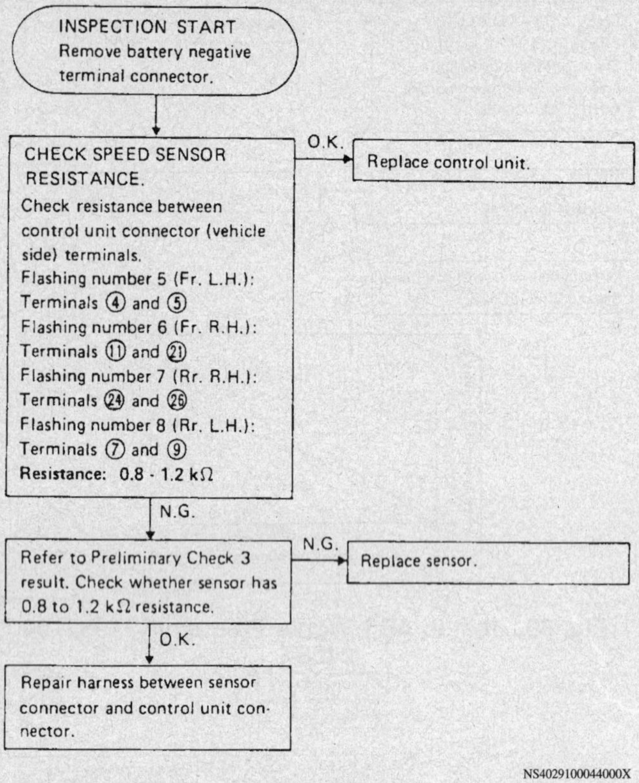
INSPECTION START
Remove battery negative terminal connector.
CHECK SPEED SENSOR RESISTANCE.
Check resistance between control unit connector (vehicle side) terminals.
Flashing number 5 (Fr. L.H.): Terminals (4) and (5)
Flashing number 6 (Fr. R.H.): Terminals (11) and (21)
Flashing number 7 (Rr. R.H.): Terminals (24) and (26)
Flashing number 8 (Rr. L.H.): Terminals (7) and (9)
Resistance: 0.8 - 1.2 kΩ
O.K.
Replace control unit.
N.G.
Refer to Preliminary Check 3 result. Check whether sensor has 0.8 to 1.2 kΩ resistance.
N.G.
Replace sensor.
O.K.
Repair harness between sensor connector and control unit connector.
NS4029100044000X

Fig. 84 Test 8: Wheel Speed Sensor. 1993–94 Maxima

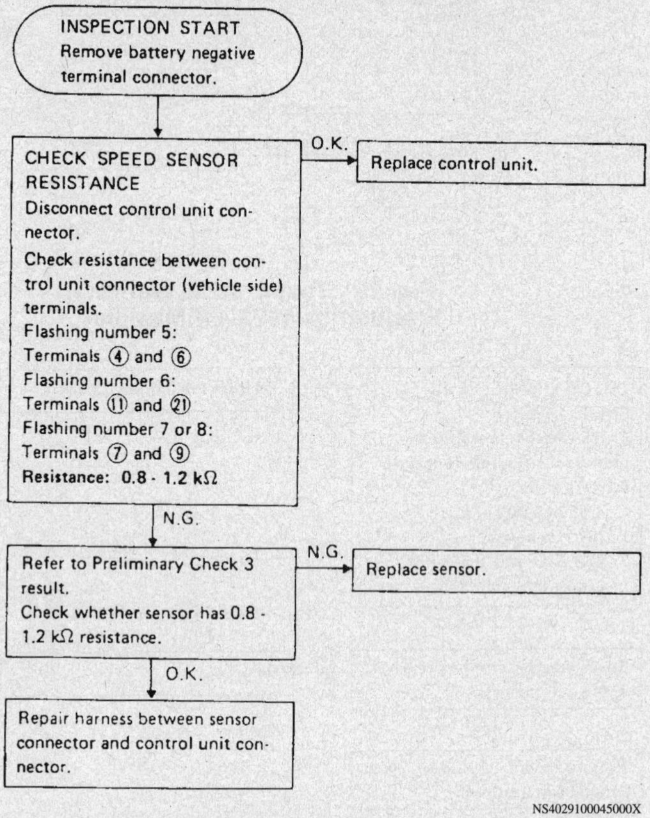
INSPECTION START
Remove battery negative terminal connector.
CHECK SPEED SENSOR RESISTANCE
Disconnect control unit connector.
Check resistance between control unit connector (vehicle side) terminals.
Flashing number 5: Terminals (4) and (6)
Flashing number 6: Terminals (11) and (21)
Flashing number 7 or 8: Terminals (7) and (9)
Resistance: 0.8 - 1.2 kΩ
O.K.
Replace control unit.
N.G.
Refer to Preliminary Check 3 result.
Check whether sensor has 0.8 - 1.2 kΩ resistance.
N.G.
Replace sensor.
O.K.
Repair harness between sensor connector and control unit connector.
NS4029100045000X

Fig. 85 Test 8: Wheel Speed Sensor. 1993 300ZX & 1993–94 240SX

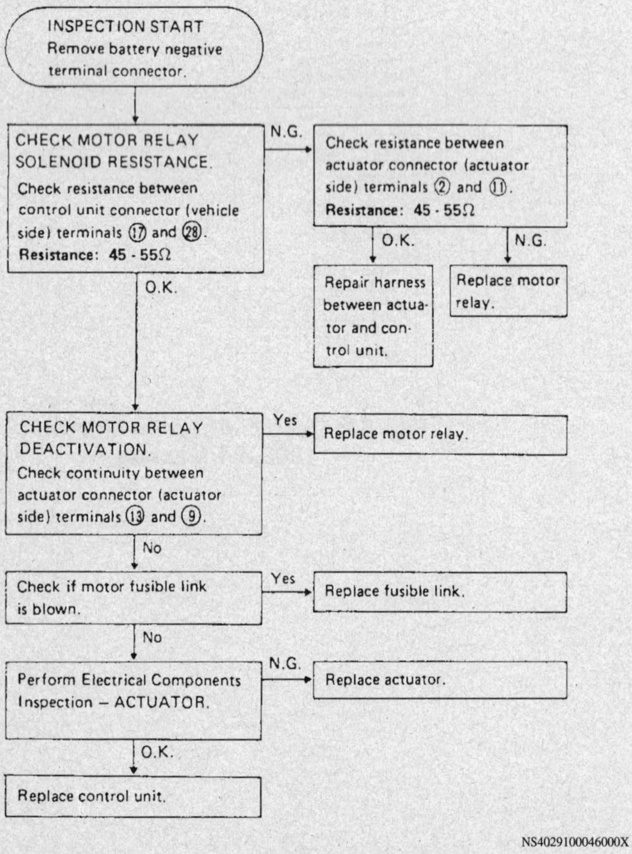
INSPECTION START
Remove battery negative terminal connector.
CHECK MOTOR RELAY SOLENOID RESISTANCE.
Check resistance between control unit connector (vehicle side) terminals (17) and (28).
Resistance: 45 - 55Ω
N.G.
Check resistance between actuator connector (actuator side) terminals (2) and (11).
Resistance: 45 - 55Ω
O.K.
Repair harness between actuator and control unit.
N.G.
Replace motor relay.
O.K.
CHECK MOTOR RELAY DEACTIVATION.
Check continuity between actuator connector (actuator side) terminals (13) and (9).
Yes
Replace motor relay.
No
Check if motor fusible link is blown.
Yes
Replace fusible link.
No
Perform Electrical Components Inspection – ACTUATOR.
N.G.
Replace actuator.
O.K.
Replace control unit.
NS4029100046000X

Fig. 86 Test 9: Actuator Motor Relay. 1993–94 Maxima

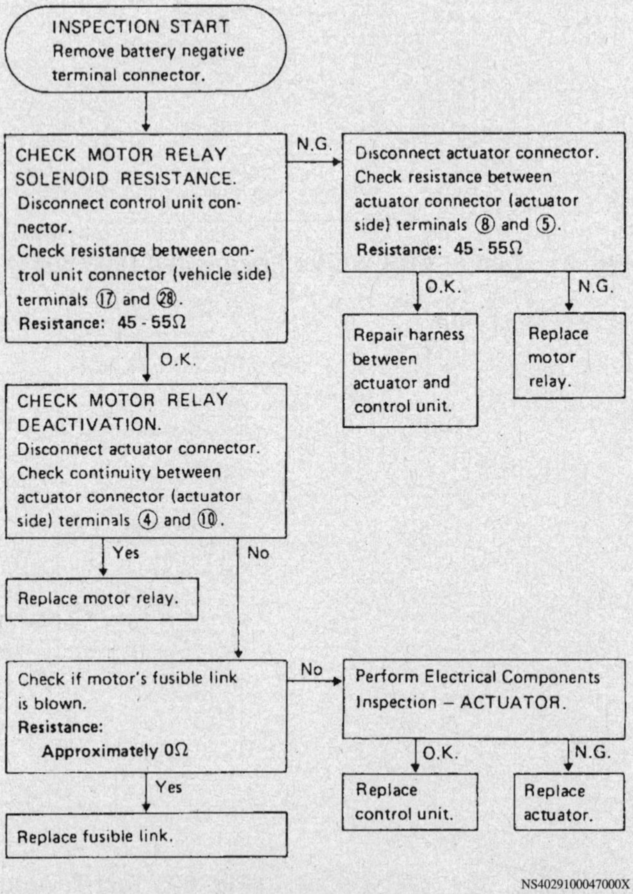
INSPECTION START
Remove battery negative terminal connector.
CHECK MOTOR RELAY SOLENOID RESISTANCE.
Disconnect control unit connector.
Check resistance between control unit connector (vehicle side) terminals (17) and (28).
Resistance: 45 - 55Ω
N.G.
Disconnect actuator connector.
Check resistance between actuator connector (actuator side) terminals (8) and (5).
Resistance: 45 - 55Ω
O.K.
Repair harness between actuator and control unit.
N.G.
Replace motor relay.
O.K.
CHECK MOTOR RELAY DEACTIVATION.
Disconnect actuator connector.
Check continuity between actuator connector (actuator side) terminals (4) and (10).
Yes
Replace motor relay.
No
Check if motor's fusible link is blown.
Resistance:
Approximately 0Ω
Yes
Replace fusible link.
No
Perform Electrical Components Inspection – ACTUATOR.
O.K.
Replace control unit.
N.G.
Replace actuator.
NS4029100047000X

Fig. 87 Test 9: Actuator Motor Relay. 1993 300ZX & 1993–94 240SX

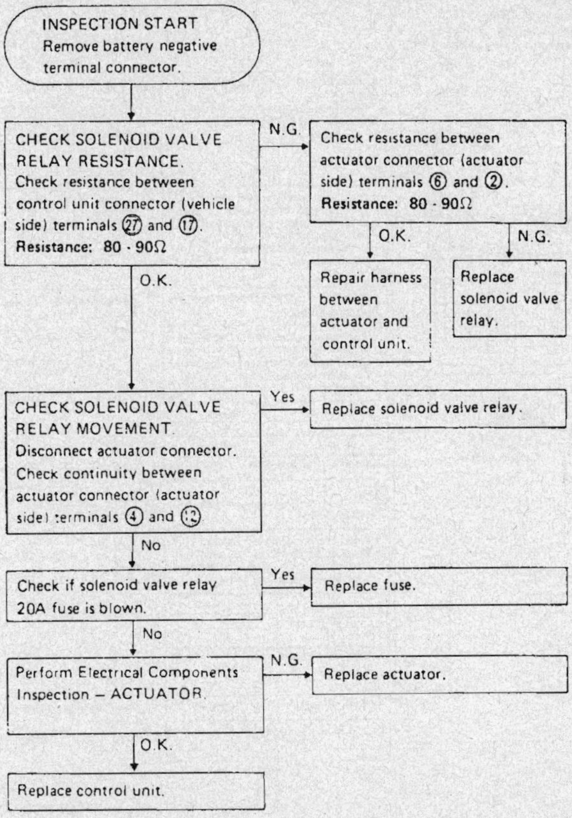
INSPECTION START
Remove battery negative terminal connector.
CHECK SOLENOID VALVE RELAY RESISTANCE.
Check resistance between control unit connector (vehicle side) terminals ㉗ and ⑰.
Resistance: 80 - 90Ω
N.G.
Check resistance between actuator connector (actuator side) terminals ⑥ and ②.
Resistance: 80 - 90Ω
O.K.
N.G.
Repair harness between actuator and control unit.
Replace solenoid valve relay.
O.K.
CHECK SOLENOID VALVE RELAY MOVEMENT.
Disconnect actuator connector.
Check continuity between actuator connector (actuator side) terminals ④ and ⑫
Yes
Replace solenoid valve relay.
No
Check if solenoid valve relay 20A fuse is blown.
Yes
Replace fuse.
No
Perform Electrical Components Inspection – ACTUATOR.
N.G.
Replace actuator.
O.K.
Replace control unit.

NS4029100048000X

Fig. 88 Test 10: Actuator Solenoid Valve Relay. 1993–94 Maxima

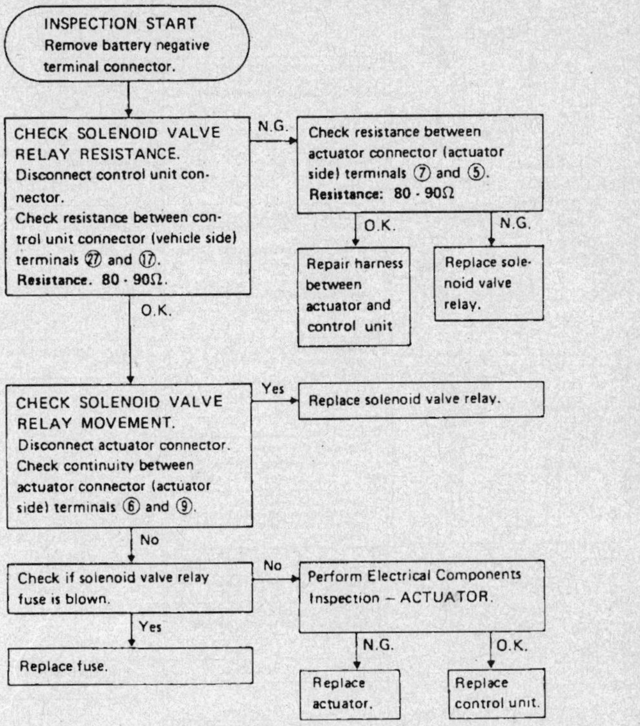
INSPECTION START
Remove battery negative terminal connector.
CHECK SOLENOID VALVE RELAY RESISTANCE.
Disconnect control unit connector.
Check resistance between control unit connector (vehicle side) terminals ㉗ and ⑰.
Resistance. 80 - 90Ω.
N.G.
Check resistance between actuator connector (actuator side) terminals ⑦ and ⑤.
Resistance: 80 - 90Ω
O.K.
N.G.
Repair harness between actuator and control unit
Replace solenoid valve relay.
O.K.
CHECK SOLENOID VALVE RELAY MOVEMENT.
Disconnect actuator connector.
Check continuity between actuator connector (actuator side) terminals ⑥ and ⑨.
Yes
Replace solenoid valve relay.
No
Check if solenoid valve relay fuse is blown.
No
Perform Electrical Components Inspection – ACTUATOR.
N.G.
O.K.
Replace actuator.
Replace control unit.
Yes
Replace fuse.

NS4029100049000X

Fig. 89 Test 10: Actuator Solenoid Valve Relay. 1993 300ZX & 1993–94 240SX

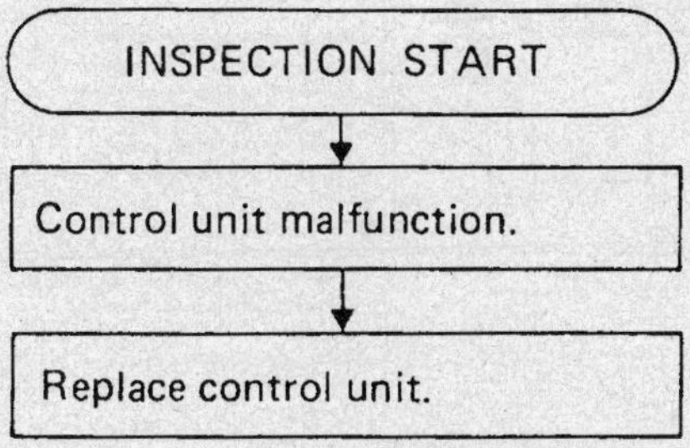
INSPECTION START
Control unit malfunction.
Replace control unit.

NS4029100050000X

Fig. 90 Test 11: Control Unit. 1993 300ZX, 1993–94 Maxima & 240SX

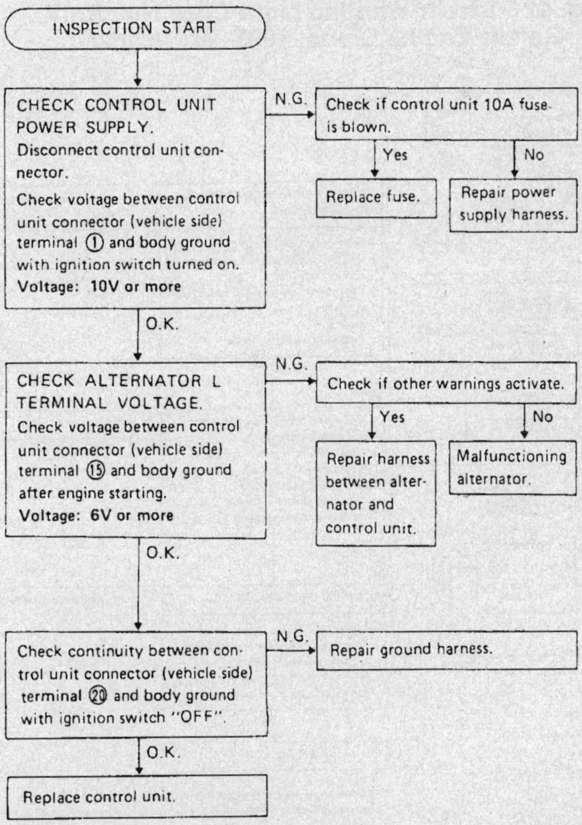
INSPECTION START
CHECK CONTROL UNIT POWER SUPPLY.
Disconnect control unit connector.
Check voltage between control unit connector (vehicle side) terminal ① and body ground with ignition switch turned on.
Voltage: 10V or more
N.G.
Check if control unit 10A fuse is blown.
Yes
No
Replace fuse.
Repair power supply harness.
O.K.
CHECK ALTERNATOR L TERMINAL VOLTAGE.
Check voltage between control unit connector (vehicle side) terminal ⑮ and body ground after engine starting.
Voltage: 6V or more
N.G.
Check if other warnings activate.
Yes
No
Repair harness between alternator and control unit.
Malfunctioning alternator.
O.K.
Check continuity between control unit connector (vehicle side) terminal ⑳ and body ground with ignition switch "OFF".
N.G.
Repair ground harness.
O.K.
Replace control unit.

NS4029100051000X

Fig. 91 Test 12: Control Unit Or Power Supply & Ground Circuit. 1993 300ZX, 1993–94 Maxima & 240SX

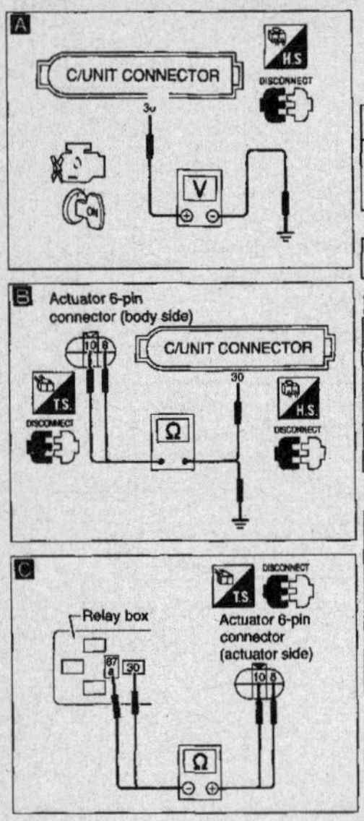

A
C/UNIT CONNECTOR
H.S
DISCONNECT
B
Actuator 6-pin connector (body side)
C/UNIT CONNECTOR
T.S
H.S
DISCONNECT
C
Relay box
T.S
DISCONNECT
Actuator 6-pin connector (actuator side)

WARNING LAMP CIRCUIT CHECK
Check 10A fuse 13 for warning lamp.
NG → Replace fuse.
↓ OK

Check warning lamp bulb.
NG → Replace bulb.
↓ OK

A
- Install 10A fuse and bulb.
- Disconnect connectors from control unit and actuator.
- Check voltage between control unit connector terminal ㉚ and ground after turning ignition switch "ON".

Battery voltage should exist after turning ignition switch "ON".

NG → Repair harness and connectors.
↓ OK

B
- Check continuity between actuator connector (body side) and control unit terminals.

Actuator	Control unit
⑩	㉚
⑧	Ground

Continuity should exist.

NG → Repair harness and connectors.
↓ OK

C
- Remove solenoid valve relay.
- Check continuity between actuator connector (actuator side) and relay box terminals.

Actuator	Relay box
⑩ ⊕	㉚ ⊖
⑧	87a

Continuity should exist.
Note: Pay attention to tester polarity*.

NG → Replace actuator.
↓ OK

SOLENOID VALVE RELAY CHECK
NG → Replace solenoid valve relay.
↓ OK

Go to diagnostic procedure 7.

***: Specifications may vary depending on the type of tester.**
Before performing this inspection, refer to the instruction manual of the tester.

NS4029500148000X

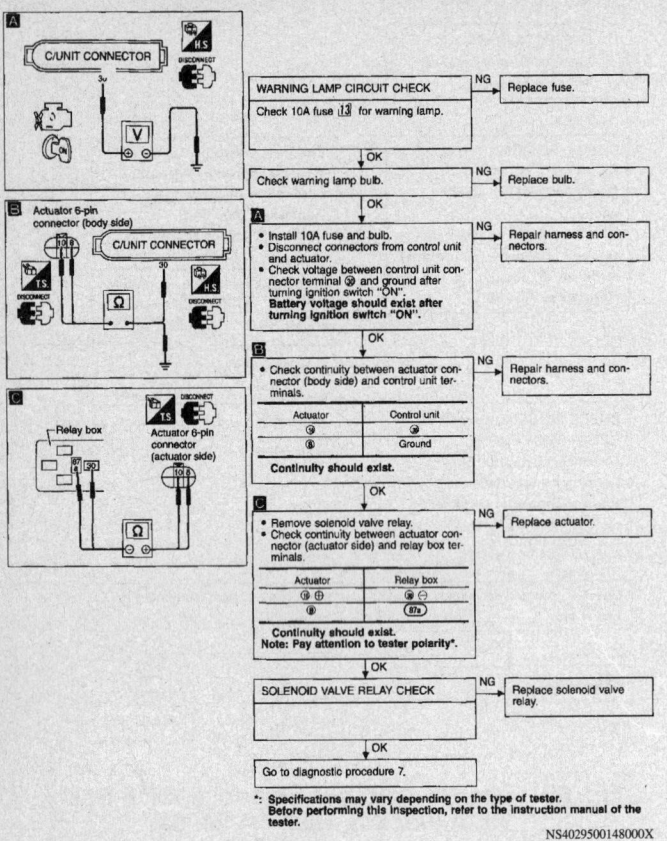

Fig. 92 Test 1: Warning Light Does Not Work Before Engine Starts. 1995–96 Maxima

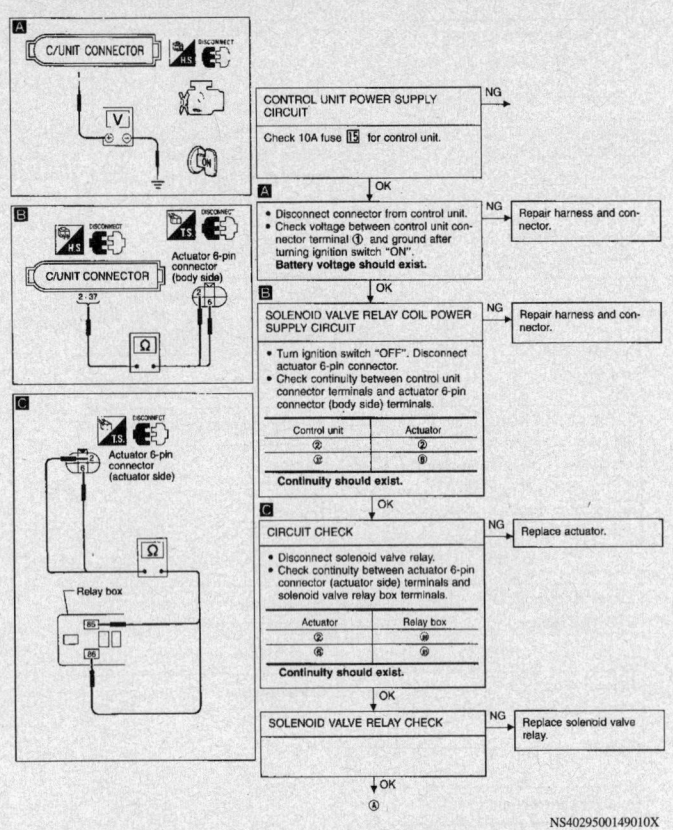

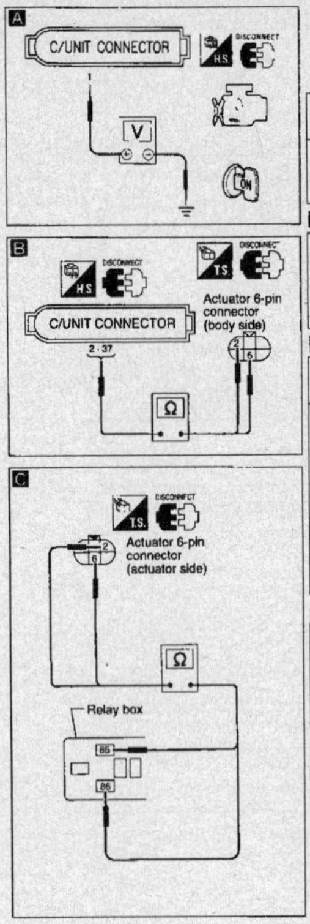

A
C/UNIT CONNECTOR
H.S
DISCONNECT
B
DISCONNECT
H.S
T.S
Actuator 6-pin connector (body side)
C/UNIT CONNECTOR
C
T.S
DISCONNECT
Actuator 6-pin connector (actuator side)
Relay box

CONTROL UNIT POWER SUPPLY CIRCUIT
Check 10A fuse 15 for control unit.
NG →
↓ OK

A
- Disconnect connector from control unit.
- Check voltage between control unit connector terminal ① and ground after turning ignition switch "ON".

Battery voltage should exist.

NG → Repair harness and connector.
↓ OK

B
SOLENOID VALVE RELAY COIL POWER SUPPLY CIRCUIT
- Turn ignition switch "OFF". Disconnect actuator 6-pin connector.
- Check continuity between control unit connector terminals and actuator 6-pin connector (body side) terminals.

Control unit	Actuator
②	②
㊲	⑥

Continuity should exist.

NG → Repair harness and connector.
↓ OK

C
CIRCUIT CHECK
- Disconnect solenoid valve relay.
- Check continuity between actuator 6-pin connector (actuator side) terminals and solenoid valve relay box terminals.

Actuator	Relay box
②	㊱
⑥	㉟

Continuity should exist.

NG → Replace actuator.
↓ OK

SOLENOID VALVE RELAY CHECK
NG → Replace solenoid valve relay.
↓ OK
Ⓐ

NS4029500149010X

Fig. 93 Test 2: Warning Light Stays On Continuously (Part 1 of 3). 1995–96 Maxima

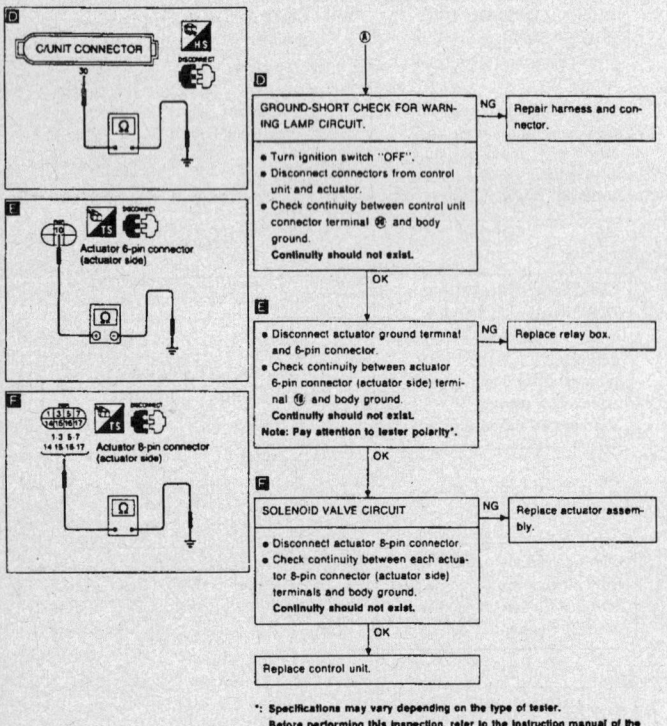

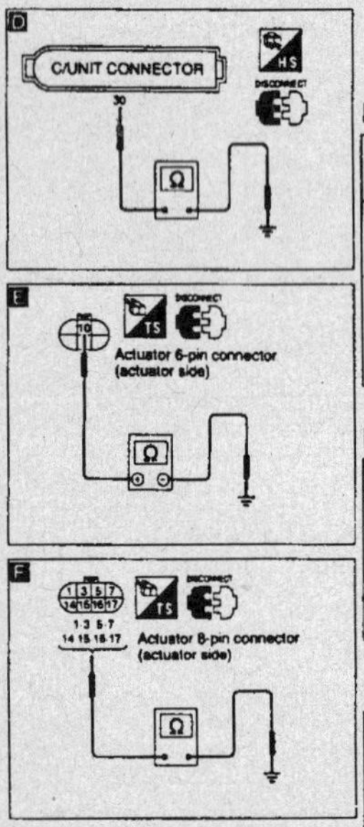

D
C/UNIT CONNECTOR
H.S
DISCONNECT
E
T.S
DISCONNECT
Actuator 6-pin connector (actuator side)
F
T.S
DISCONNECT
Actuator 8-pin connector (actuator side)

Ⓐ

D
GROUND-SHORT CHECK FOR WARNING LAMP CIRCUIT.
- Turn ignition switch "OFF".
- Disconnect connectors from control unit and actuator.
- Check continuity between control unit connector terminal ㉚ and body ground.

Continuity should not exist.

NG → Repair harness and connector.
↓ OK

E
- Disconnect actuator ground terminal and 6-pin connector.
- Check continuity between actuator 6-pin connector (actuator side) terminal ⑩ and body ground.

Continuity should not exist.
Note: Pay attention to tester polarity*.

NG → Replace relay box.
↓ OK

F
SOLENOID VALVE CIRCUIT
- Disconnect actuator 8-pin connector.
- Check continuity between each actuator 8-pin connector (actuator side) terminals and body ground.

Continuity should not exist.

NG → Replace actuator assembly.
↓ OK

Replace control unit.

***: Specifications may vary depending on the type of tester.**
Before performing this inspection, refer to the instruction manual of the tester.

NS4029500149020X

Fig. 93 Test 2: Warning Light Stays On Continuously (Part 2 of 3). 1995–96 Maxima

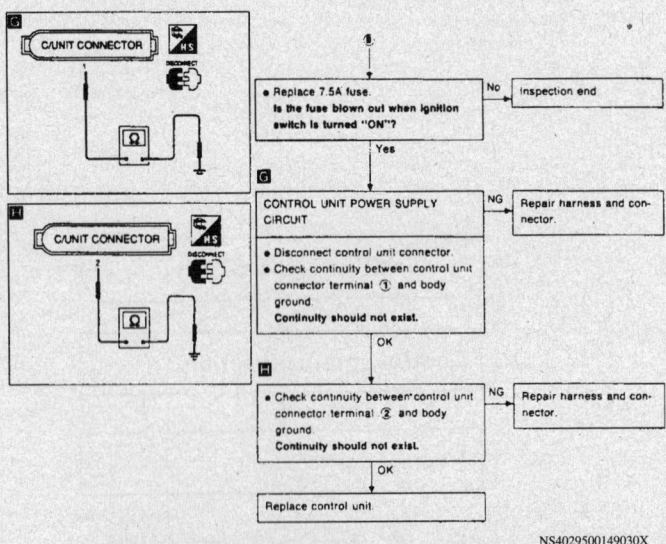

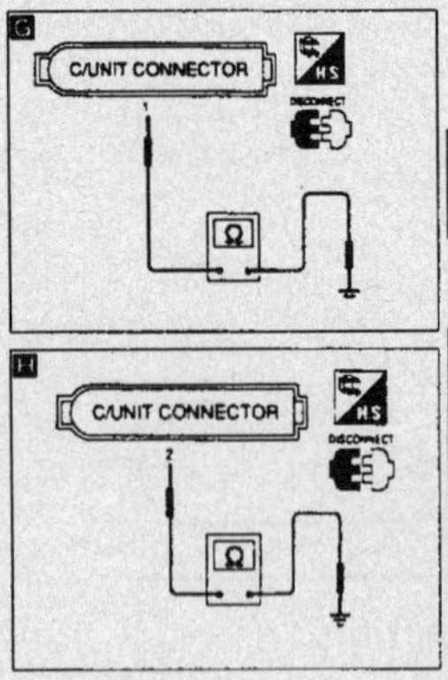

G
C/UNIT CONNECTOR
H.S
DISCONNECT
H
C/UNIT CONNECTOR
H.S
DISCONNECT

Ⓑ

- Replace 7.5A fuse.

Is the fuse blown out when ignition switch is turned "ON"?

No → Inspection end
↓ Yes

G
CONTROL UNIT POWER SUPPLY CIRCUIT
- Disconnect control unit connector.
- Check continuity between control unit connector terminal ① and body ground.

Continuity should not exist.

NG → Repair harness and connector.
↓ OK

H
- Check continuity between control unit connector terminal ② and body ground.

Continuity should not exist.

NG → Repair harness and connector.
↓ OK

Replace control unit.

NS4029500149030X

Fig. 93 Test 2: Warning Light Stays On Continuously (Part 3 of 3). 1995–96 Maxima

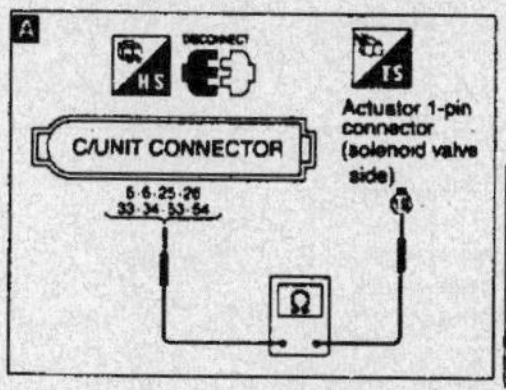
A
C/UNIT CONNECTOR
5 6 25 26
33 34 53 54
Actuator 1-pin connector (solenoid valve side)
19

- Disconnect connectors from control unit and actuator. Check terminals for damage or loose connection. Then reconnect connectors.
- Carry out self-diagnosis again.
Does warning light activate again?

No → Inspection end

Yes ↓

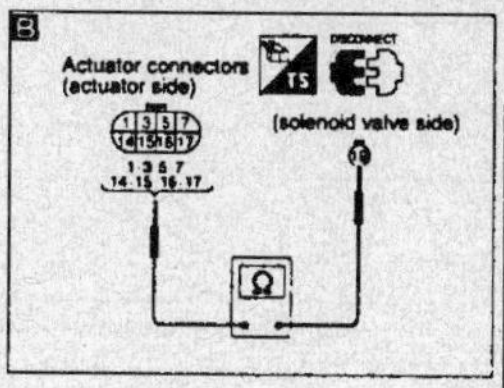
B
Actuator connectors (actuator side)
1 3 5 7
14 15 16 17
(solenoid valve side)
19

A

ACTUATOR SOLENOID VALVE CHECK — OK → Ⓐ

- Disconnect connectors from control unit and actuator.
- Check resistance between control unit connector terminals and actuator 1-pin connector (solenoid valve side) terminal.

Code No.	Control unit	Actuator	Resistance
41	26	19	4.4 - 6.0Ω
45	33	19	
51	34	19	
55	25	19	
42	54	19	8.5 - 9.5Ω
46	5	19	
52	6	19	
56	53	19	

NG ↓

B

- Disconnect actuator 8-pin connector.
- Check resistance between actuator 8-pin connector (actuator side) terminals and 1-pin connector (solenoid valve side) terminal.

Code No.	Actuator	Resistance
41	16 - 19	4.4 - 6.0Ω
45	14 - 19	
51	17 - 19	
55	15 - 19	
42	3 - 19	8.5 - 9.5Ω
46	1 - 19	
52	7 - 19	
56	5 - 19	

OK → Repair harness and connector between control unit connector terminal and actuator 8-pin connector terminal

NG ↓

Replace actuator.

NS4029500150010X

Fig. 94 Test 3: Actuator Solenoid Valve (Part 1 of 2). 1995–96 Maxima

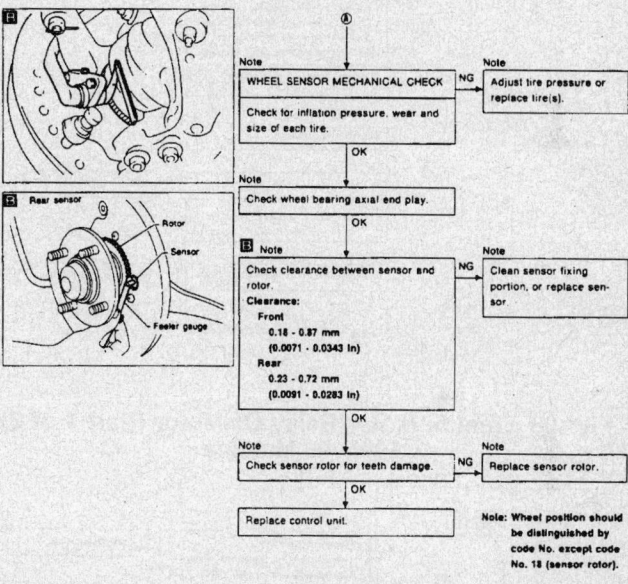

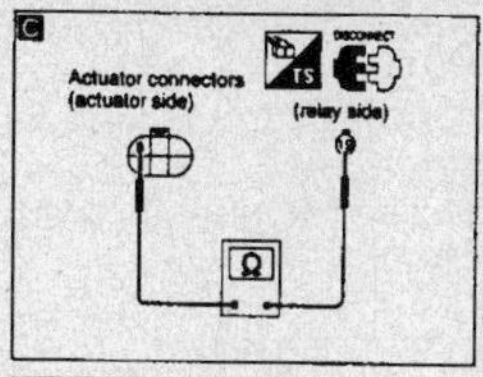
C
Actuator connectors (actuator side)
(relay side)
19

Ⓐ ↓

C

- Check continuity between actuator 1-pin connector (relay side) terminal 19 and 6-pin connector (actuator side) terminal 8.
Continuity should exist.

OK → Go to diagnostic procedure 7

NG ↓

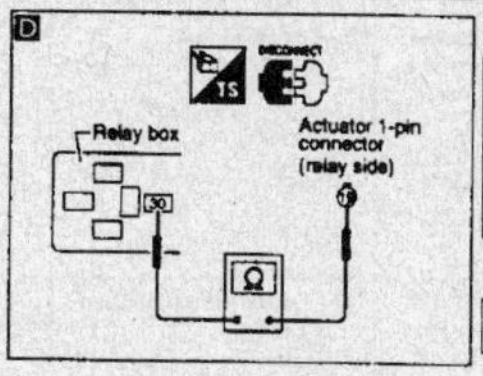
D
Relay box
Actuator 1-pin connector (relay side)
30
19

D

- Remove solenoid valve relay.
- Check continuity between actuator 1-pin connector (relay side) terminal 19 and relay box terminal 30.
Continuity should exist.

NG → Replace actuator.

OK ↓

Go to diagnostic procedure 6

NS4029500150020X

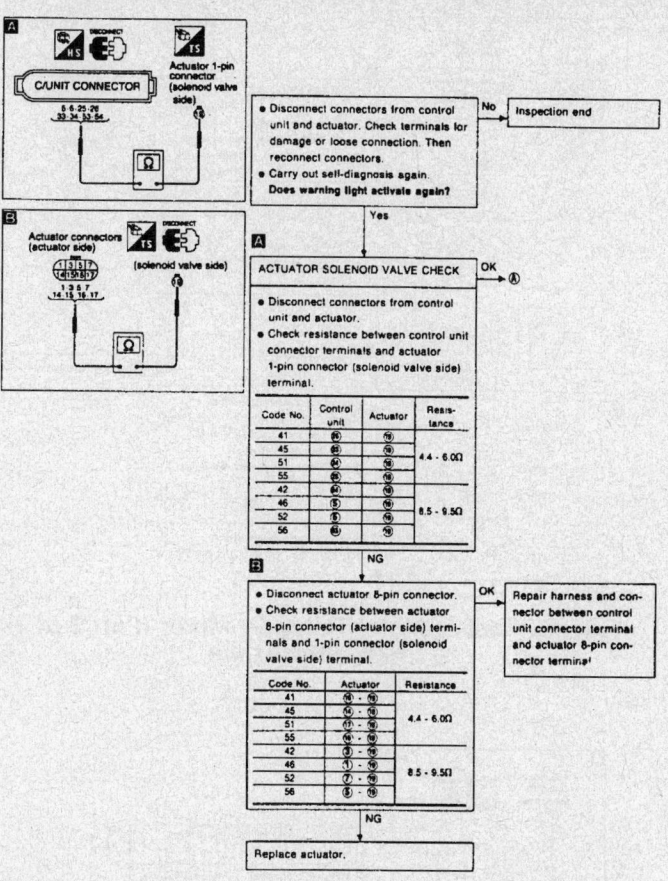

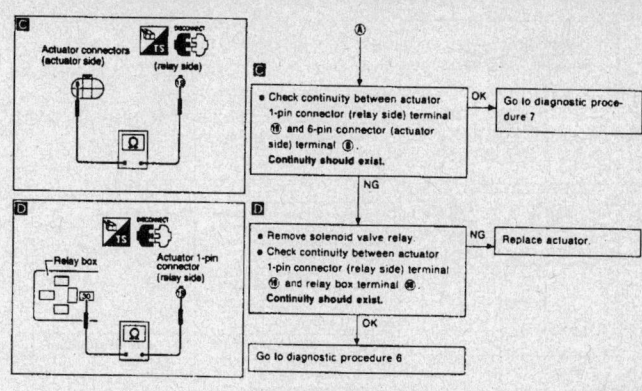

Fig. 94 Test 3: Actuator Solenoid Valve (Part 2 of 2). 1995–96 Maxima

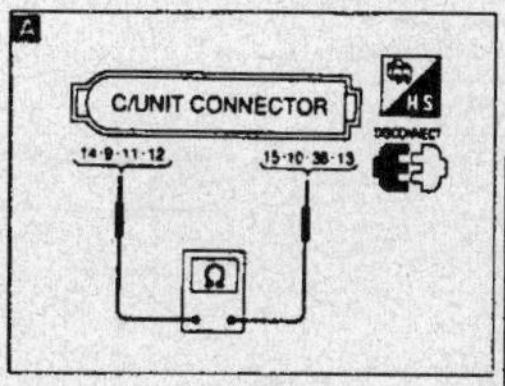
A
C/UNIT CONNECTOR
14 9 11 12
15 10 38 13

- Disconnect connectors from control unit and wheel sensor of malfunction code No. Check terminals for damage or loose connection. Then reconnect connectors.
- Carry out self-diagnosis again.
Does warning light activate again?

No → Inspection end

Yes ↓

A

WHEEL SENSOR ELECTRICAL CHECK — OK → Ⓐ

- Disconnect control unit connector.
- Check resistance between control unit connector terminals.
Code No. 21 or 22 (Front RH wheel)
Terminals 14 and 15
Code No. 25 or 26 (Front LH wheel)
Terminals 9 and 10
Code No. 31 or 32 (Rear RH wheel)
Terminals 11 and 38
Code No. 35 or 36 (Rear LH wheel)
Terminals 12 and 13
Resistance: 0.8 - 1.2 kΩ

NG ↓

Note: **CHECK WHEEL SENSOR.** — NG → Note: Replace wheel sensor.

OK ↓

Note: Repair harness and connectors between control unit connector and wheel sensor connector.

Note: Wheel position should be distinguished by code No. except code No. 18 (sensor rotor).

NS4029500151010X

Fig. 95 Test 4: Wheel Sensor Rotor (Part 1 of 2). 1995–96 Maxima

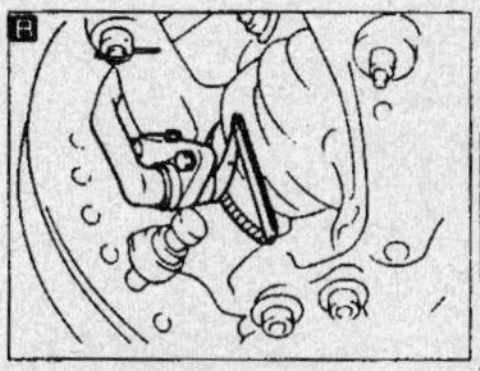
B

Ⓐ ↓

Note: **WHEEL SENSOR MECHANICAL CHECK** — NG → Note: Adjust tire pressure or replace tire(s).

Check for inflation pressure, wear and size of each tire.

OK ↓

Note: Check wheel bearing axial end play.

OK ↓

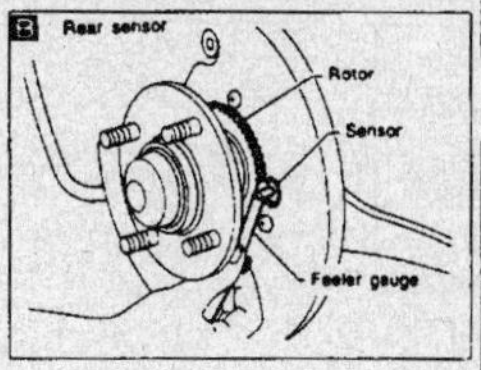
B
Rear sensor
Rotor
Sensor
Feeler gauge

B Note: Check clearance between sensor and rotor.
Clearance:
Front
0.18 - 0.87 mm
(0.0071 - 0.0343 in)
Rear
0.23 - 0.72 mm
(0.0091 - 0.0283 in)

NG → Note: Clean sensor fixing portion, or replace sensor.

OK ↓

Note: Check sensor rotor for teeth damage. — NG → Note: Replace sensor rotor.

OK ↓

Replace control unit.

Note: Wheel position should be distinguished by code No. except code No. 18 (sensor rotor).

NS4029500151020X

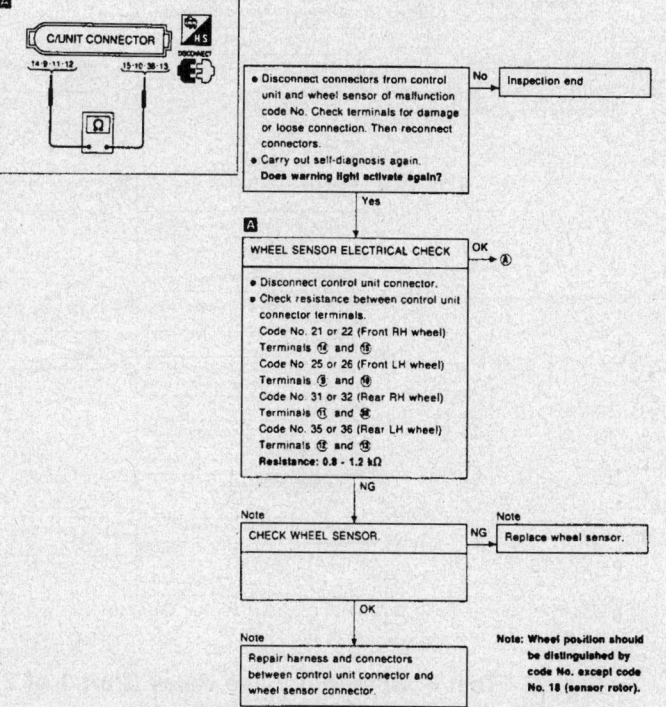

Fig. 95 Test 4: Wheel Sensor Rotor (Part 2 of 2). 1995–96 Maxima

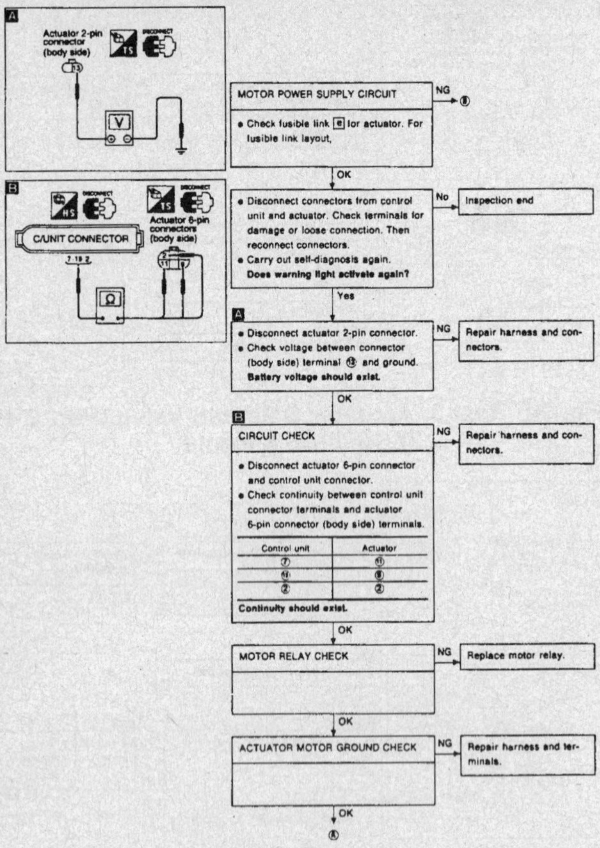
Actuator 2-pin connector (body side)
MOTOR POWER SUPPLY CIRCUIT
• Check fusible link e for actuator. For fusible link layout.
NG
OK
C/UNIT CONNECTOR
Actuator 6-pin connectors (body side)
• Disconnect connectors from control unit and actuator. Check terminals for damage or loose connection. Then reconnect connectors.
• Carry out self-diagnosis again.
Does warning light activate again?
No
Inspection end
Yes
• Disconnect actuator 2-pin connector.
• Check voltage between connector (body side) terminal ⑬ and ground.
Battery voltage should exist.
Repair harness and connectors.
CIRCUIT CHECK
• Disconnect actuator 6-pin connector and control unit connector.
• Check continuity between control unit connector terminals and actuator 6-pin connector (body side) terminals.
Control unit
Actuator
Continuity should exist.
Repair harness and connectors.
MOTOR RELAY CHECK
Replace motor relay.
ACTUATOR MOTOR GROUND CHECK
Repair harness and terminals.

NS4029500152010X

Fig. 96 Test 5: Motor Relay Or Motor (Part 1 of 3). 1995–96 Maxima

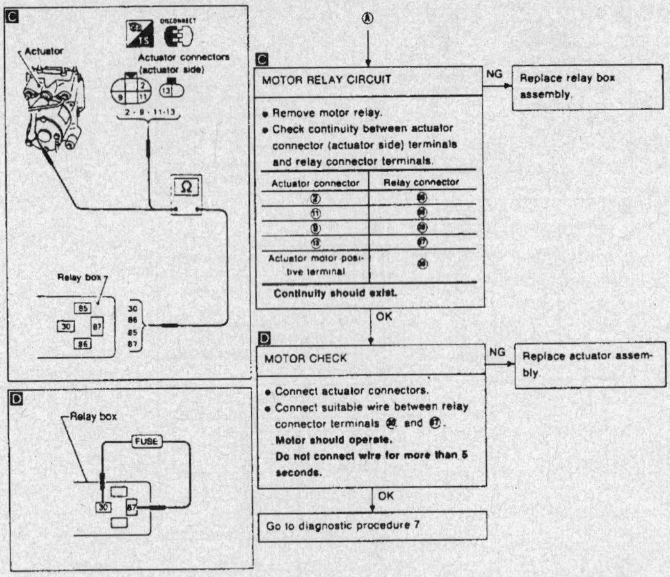
Actuator
Actuator connectors (actuator side)
Relay box
MOTOR RELAY CIRCUIT
• Remove motor relay.
• Check continuity between actuator connector (actuator side) terminals and relay connector terminals.
Actuator connector
Relay connector
Actuator motor positive terminal
Continuity should exist.
NG
Replace relay box assembly.
OK
FUSE
MOTOR CHECK
• Connect actuator connectors.
• Connect suitable wire between relay connector terminals ⑳ and ⑰.
Motor should operate.
Do not connect wire for more than 5 seconds.
Replace actuator assembly.
Go to diagnostic procedure 7

NS4029500152020X

Fig. 96 Test 5: Motor Relay Or Motor (Part 2 of 3). 1995–96 Maxima

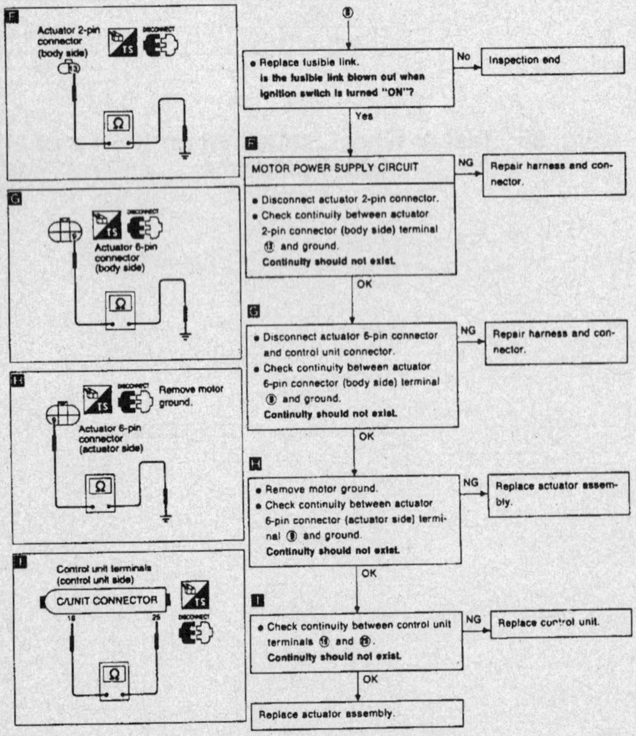
Actuator 2-pin connector (body side)
• Replace fusible link.
Is the fusible link blown out when ignition switch is turned "ON"?
No
Inspection end
Yes
MOTOR POWER SUPPLY CIRCUIT
• Disconnect actuator 2-pin connector.
• Check continuity between actuator 2-pin connector (body side) terminal ⑬ and ground.
Continuity should not exist.
NG
Repair harness and connector.
OK
Actuator 6-pin connector (body side)
• Disconnect actuator 6-pin connector and control unit connector.
• Check continuity between actuator 6-pin connector (body side) terminal ⑧ and ground.
Continuity should not exist.
Repair harness and connector.
Remove motor ground.
Actuator 6-pin connector (actuator side)
• Remove motor ground.
• Check continuity between actuator 6-pin connector (actuator side) terminal ⑧ and ground.
Continuity should not exist.
Replace actuator assembly.
Control unit terminals (control unit side)
C/UNIT CONNECTOR
• Check continuity between control unit terminals ⑱ and ㉕.
Continuity should not exist.
Replace control unit.
Replace actuator assembly.

NS4029500152030X

Fig. 96 Test 5: Motor Relay Or Motor (Part 3 of 3). 1995–96 Maxima

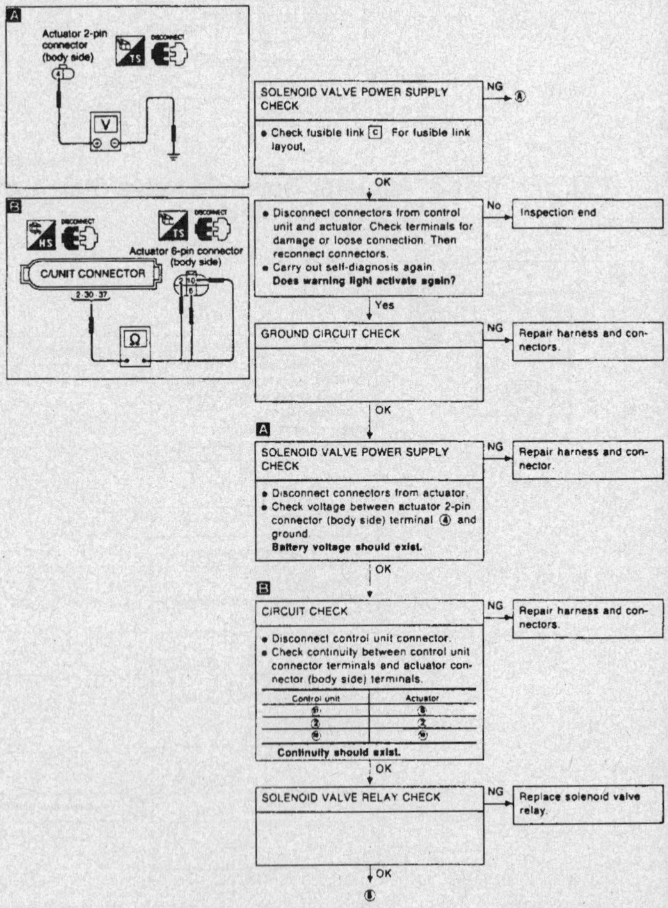
Actuator 2-pin connector (body side)
SOLENOID VALVE POWER SUPPLY CHECK
• Check fusible link C. For fusible link layout.
NG
OK
C/UNIT CONNECTOR
Actuator 6-pin connector (body side)
• Disconnect connectors from control unit and actuator. Check terminals for damage or loose connection. Then reconnect connectors.
• Carry out self-diagnosis again.
Does warning light activate again?
No
Inspection end
Yes
GROUND CIRCUIT CHECK
Repair harness and connectors.
SOLENOID VALVE POWER SUPPLY CHECK
• Disconnect connectors from actuator.
• Check voltage between actuator 2-pin connector (body side) terminal ④ and ground.
Battery voltage should exist.
Repair harness and connector.
CIRCUIT CHECK
• Disconnect control unit connector.
• Check continuity between control unit connector terminals and actuator connector (body side) terminals.
Control unit
Actuator
Continuity should exist.
Repair harness and connectors.
SOLENOID VALVE RELAY CHECK
Replace solenoid valve relay.

NS4029500153010X

Fig. 97 Test 6: Solenoid Valve Relay (Part 1 of 2). 1995–96 Maxima

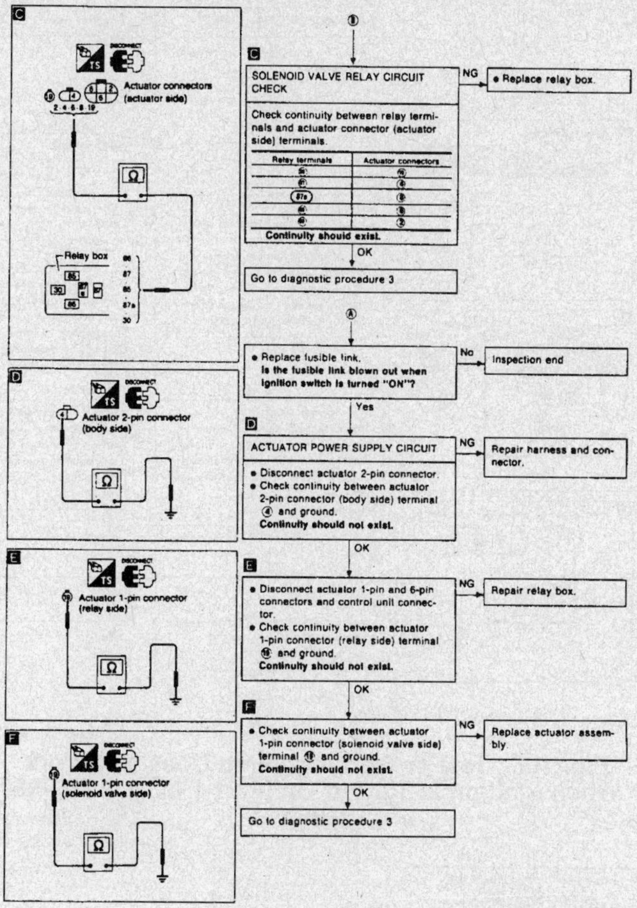
C
Actuator connectors (actuator side)
2·4·6·8·19
Relay box
86
87
85
87a
30
C
SOLENOID VALVE RELAY CIRCUIT CHECK
Check continuity between relay terminals and actuator connector (actuator side) terminals.
Relay terminals
Actuator connectors
Continuity should exist.
NG
• Replace relay box.
OK
Go to diagnostic procedure 3
Ⓐ
• Replace fusible link.
Is the fusible link blown out when ignition switch is turned "ON"?
No
Inspection end
Yes
D
Actuator 2-pin connector (body side)
D
ACTUATOR POWER SUPPLY CIRCUIT
• Disconnect actuator 2-pin connector.
• Check continuity between actuator 2-pin connector (body side) terminal ④ and ground.
Continuity should not exist.
NG
Repair harness and connector.
OK
E
Actuator 1-pin connector (relay side)
E
• Disconnect actuator 1-pin and 6-pin connectors and control unit connector.
• Check continuity between actuator 1-pin connector (relay side) terminal ⑲ and ground.
Continuity should not exist.
NG
Repair relay box.
OK
F
Actuator 1-pin connector (solenoid valve side)
F
• Check continuity between actuator 1-pin connector (solenoid valve side) terminal ⑲ and ground.
Continuity should not exist.
NG
Replace actuator assembly.
OK
Go to diagnostic procedure 3

NS4029500153020X

Fig. 97 Test 6: Solenoid Valve Relay (Part 2 of 2). 1995–96 Maxima

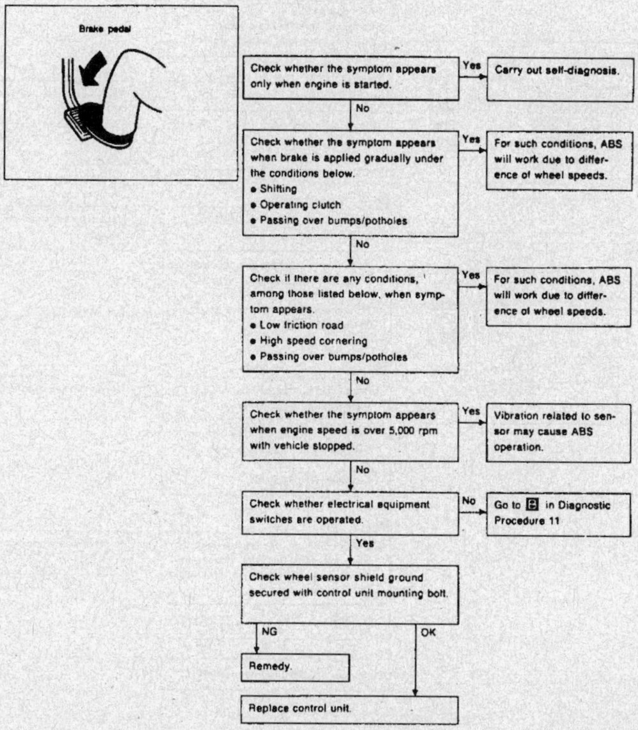
Brake pedal
Check whether the symptom appears only when engine is started.
Yes
Carry out self-diagnosis.
No
Check whether the symptom appears when brake is applied gradually under the conditions below.
• Shifting
• Operating clutch
• Passing over bumps/potholes
Yes
For such conditions, ABS will work due to difference of wheel speeds.
No
Check if there are any conditions, among those listed below, when symptom appears.
• Low friction road
• High speed cornering
• Passing over bumps/potholes
Yes
For such conditions, ABS will work due to difference of wheel speeds.
No
Check whether the symptom appears when engine speed is over 5,000 rpm with vehicle stopped.
Yes
Vibration related to sensor may cause ABS operation.
No
Check whether electrical equipment switches are operated.
No
Go to B in Diagnostic Procedure 11
Yes
Check wheel sensor shield ground secured with control unit mounting bolt.
NG
OK
Remedy.
Replace control unit.

NS4029500156000X

Fig. 100 Test 9: Pedal Vibration & Noise. 1995–96 Maxima

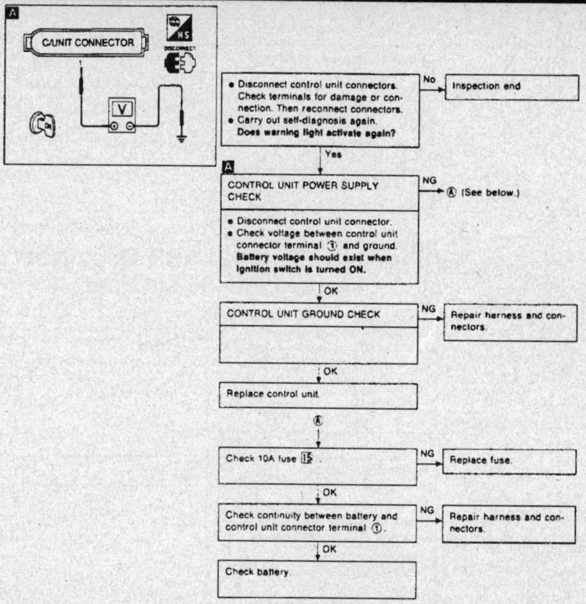
A
C/UNIT CONNECTOR
V
• Disconnect control unit connectors. Check terminals for damage or connection. Then reconnect connectors.
• Carry out self-diagnosis again.
Does warning light activate again?
No
Inspection end
Yes
A
CONTROL UNIT POWER SUPPLY CHECK
• Disconnect control unit connector.
• Check voltage between control unit connector terminal ① and ground.
Battery voltage should exist when ignition switch is turned ON.
NG
Ⓐ (See below.)
OK
CONTROL UNIT GROUND CHECK
NG
Repair harness and connectors.
OK
Replace control unit.
Ⓐ
Check 10A fuse 15.
NG
Replace fuse.
OK
Check continuity between battery and control unit connector terminal ①.
NG
Repair harness and connectors.
OK
Check battery.

NS4029500154000X

Fig. 98 Test 7: Power Supply Low Voltage. 1995–96 Maxima

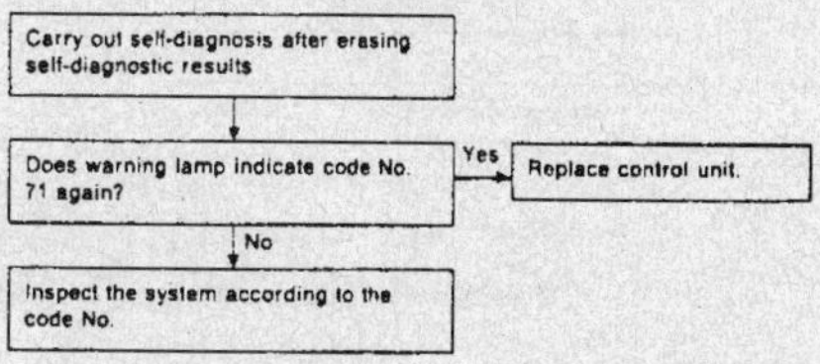
Carry out self-diagnosis after erasing self-diagnostic results
Does warning lamp indicate code No. 71 again?
Yes
Replace control unit.
No
Inspect the system according to the code No.

NS4029500155000X

Fig. 99 Test 8: Control Unit. 1995–96 Maxima

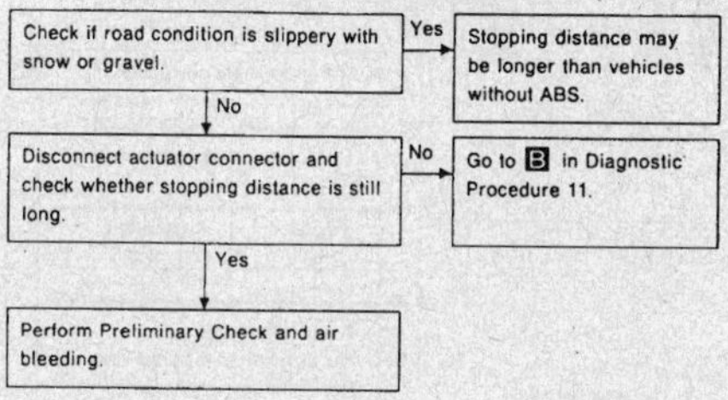
Check if road condition is slippery with snow or gravel.
Yes
Stopping distance may be longer than vehicles without ABS.
No
Disconnect actuator connector and check whether stopping distance is still long.
No
Go to B in Diagnostic Procedure 11.
Yes
Perform Preliminary Check and air bleeding.

NS4029500157000X

Fig. 101 Test 10: Long Stopping Distance. 1995–96 Maxima

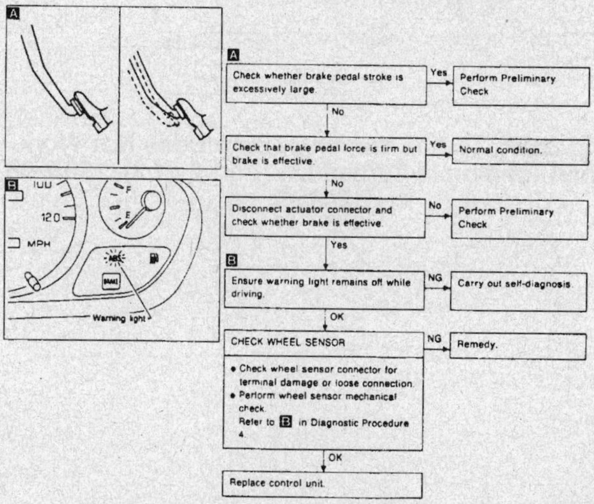
A
B
120
MPH
Warning light
A
Check whether brake pedal stroke is excessively large.
Yes
Perform Preliminary Check
No
Check that brake pedal force is firm but brake is effective.
Yes
Normal condition.
No
Disconnect actuator connector and check whether brake is effective.
No
Perform Preliminary Check
Yes
B
Ensure warning light remains off while driving.
NG
Carry out self-diagnosis.
OK
CHECK WHEEL SENSOR
• Check wheel sensor connector for terminal damage or loose connection.
• Perform wheel sensor mechanical check.
Refer to B in Diagnostic Procedure 4.
NG
Remedy.
OK
Replace control unit.

NS4029500158000X

Fig. 102 Test 11: Unexpected Pedal Action. 1995–96 Maxima

- Check whether warning activates. — Yes → Carry out self-diagnosis.
- No ↓
- Check symptom condition whether vehicle speed is under 10 km/h (6 MPH). — Yes → ABS does not work in this condition.
- No ↓
- Go to B in Diagnostic Procedure 11

NS4029500159000X

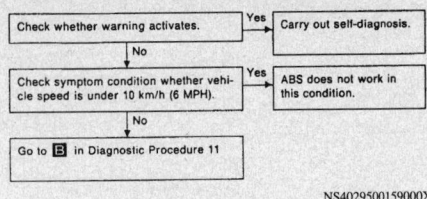

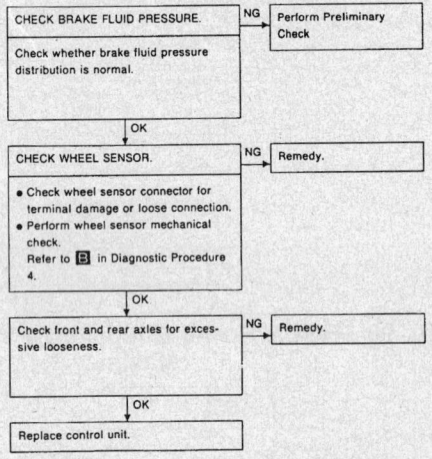

Fig. 103 Test 12: ABS Does Not Work. 1995–96 Maxima

- CHECK BRAKE FLUID PRESSURE. Check whether brake fluid pressure distribution is normal. — NG → Perform Preliminary Check
- OK ↓
- CHECK WHEEL SENSOR.
  - Check wheel sensor connector for terminal damage or loose connection.
  - Perform wheel sensor mechanical check. Refer to B in Diagnostic Procedure 4.
  - — NG → Remedy.
- OK ↓
- Check front and rear axles for excessive looseness. — NG → Remedy.
- OK ↓
- Replace control unit.

NS4029500160000X

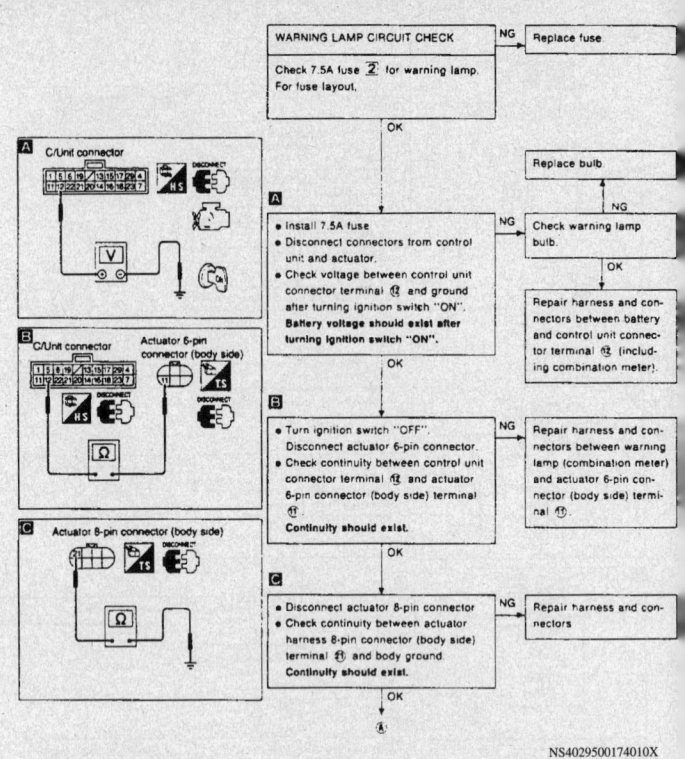

Fig. 104 Test 13: ABS Works Frequently. 1995–96 Maxima

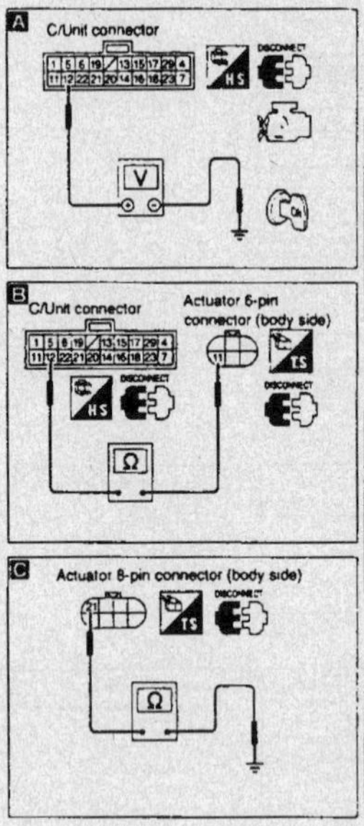

A
C/Unit connector
DISCONNECT
HS
B
C/Unit connector
Actuator 6-pin connector (body side)
DISCONNECT
TS
HS
C
Actuator 8-pin connector (body side)
DISCONNECT
TS

- WARNING LAMP CIRCUIT CHECK. Check 7.5A fuse 2 for warning lamp. For fuse layout. — NG → Replace fuse.
- OK ↓
- A
  - Install 7.5A fuse
  - Disconnect connectors from control unit and actuator.
  - Check voltage between control unit connector terminal 12 and ground after turning ignition switch "ON". **Battery voltage should exist after turning ignition switch "ON".**
  - — NG → Check warning lamp bulb. — NG → Replace bulb; OK → Repair harness and connectors between battery and control unit connector terminal 12 (including combination meter).
- OK ↓
- B
  - Turn ignition switch "OFF". Disconnect actuator 6-pin connector.
  - Check continuity between control unit connector terminal 12 and actuator 6-pin connector (body side) terminal 11. **Continuity should exist.**
  - — NG → Repair harness and connectors between warning lamp (combination meter) and actuator 6-pin connector (body side) terminal 11.
- OK ↓
- C
  - Disconnect actuator 8-pin connector
  - Check continuity between actuator harness 8-pin connector (body side) terminal 11 and body ground. **Continuity should exist.**
  - — NG → Repair harness and connectors
- OK ↓ (A)

NS4029500174010X

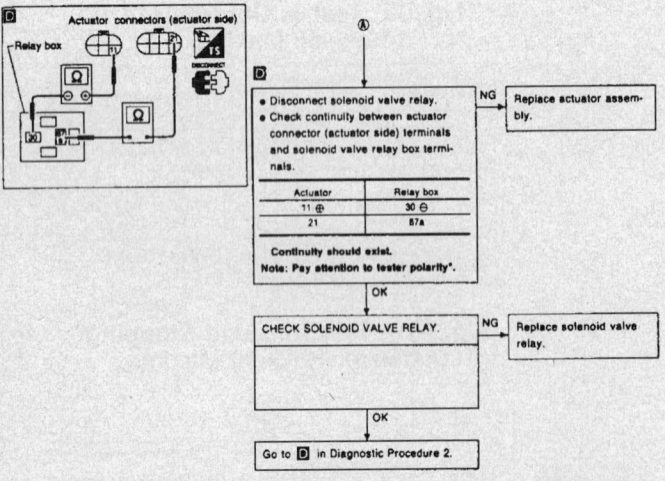

Fig. 105 Test 1: Warning Lamp Does Not Work When Ignition Is Turned On (Part 1 of 2). 1995–96 240SX

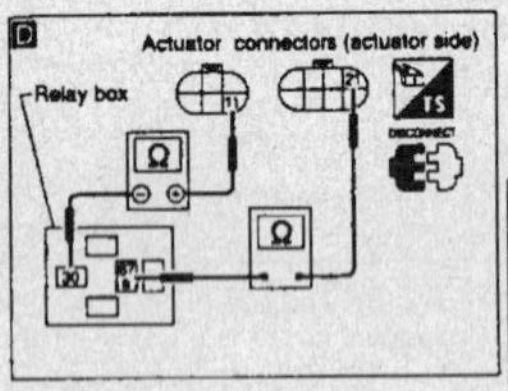

D
Actuator connectors (actuator side)
Relay box
DISCONNECT
TS

(A) ↓

- D
  - **Disconnect solenoid valve relay.**
  - **Check continuity between actuator connector (actuator side) terminals and solenoid valve relay box terminals.**

Actuator	Relay box
11 ⊕	30 ⊖
21	87a

Continuity should exist.
Note: Pay attention to tester polarity*.

- — NG → **Replace actuator assembly.**
- OK ↓
- CHECK SOLENOID VALVE RELAY. — NG → **Replace solenoid valve relay.**
- OK ↓
- Go to D in Diagnostic Procedure 2.

NS4029500174020X

Fig. 105 Test 1: Warning Lamp Does Not Work When Ignition Is Turned On (Part 2 of 2). 1995–96 240SX

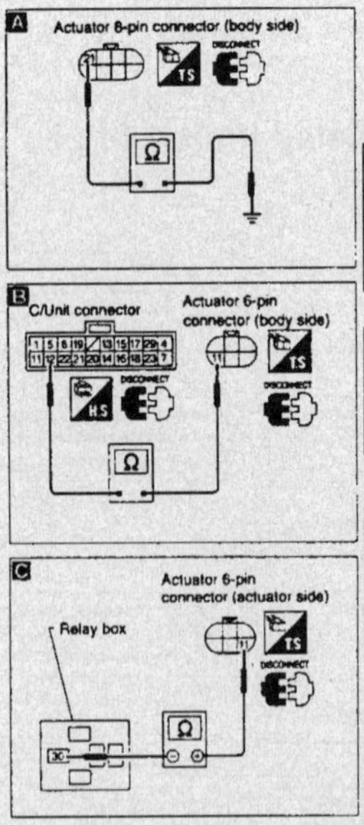

A
Actuator 8-pin connector (body side)
DISCONNECT
TS
B
C/Unit connector
Actuator 6-pin connector (body side)
TS
HS
DISCONNECT
C
Actuator 6-pin connector (actuator side)
Relay box
TS
DISCONNECT

- Disconnect connectors from control unit and actuator. Check terminals for damage or connection. Then reconnect connectors.
- Carry out self-diagnosis again. **Does warning light activate again?**
- — No → Inspection end
- Yes ↓
- SOLENOID VALVE RELAY CHECK — NG → Replace solenoid valve relay.
- OK ↓
- A SOLENOID VALVE RELAY GROUND CIRCUIT
  - Disconnect actuator 8-pin connector.
  - Check continuity between actuator 8-pin connector (body side) terminal 11 and body ground. **Continuity should exist.**
  - — NG → Repair harness and connectors.
- OK ↓
- B
  - Disconnect control unit connectors and actuator 6-pin connector.
  - Check continuity between control unit connector terminal 12 and actuator 6-pin connector (body side) terminal 11. **Continuity should exist.**
  - — NG → Repair harness and connectors.
- OK ↓
- C
  - Check continuity between actuator 6-pin connector (actuator side) terminal 11 and solenoid valve relay box terminal 30.

Actuator	Relay box	Continuity
11 ⊕	30 ⊖	Yes
11 ⊖	30 ⊕	No

Note: Pay attention to tester polarity*.

- — NG → Replace actuator assembly.
- OK ↓ (B)

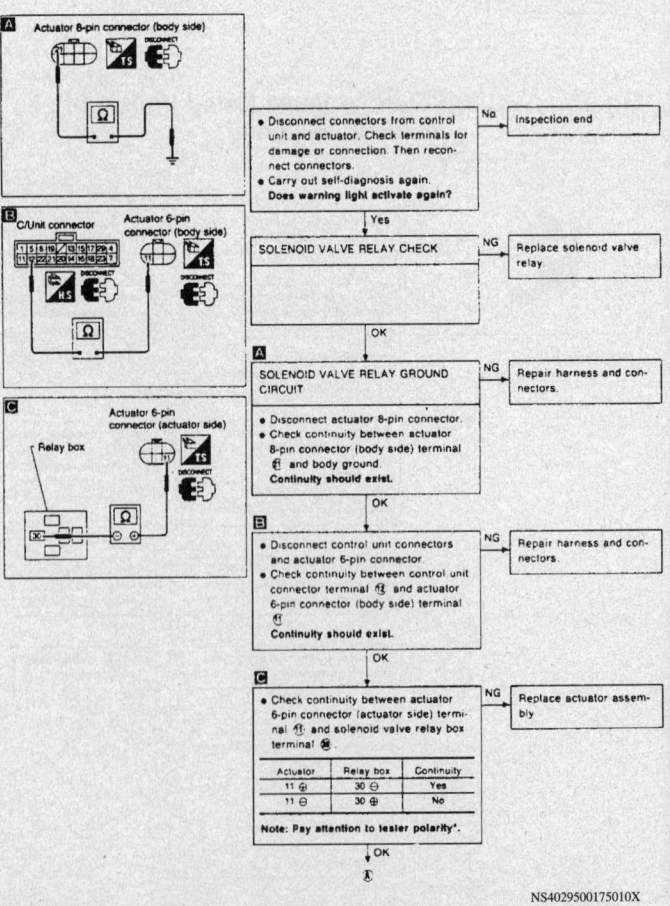

NS4029500175010X

Fig. 106 Test 2: Control Unit Or Ground Circuit (Part 1 of 2). 1995–96 240SX

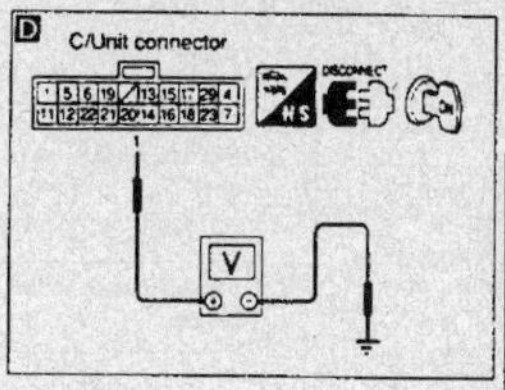
D
C/Unit connector
1
V

Ⓐ

D

CONTROL UNIT POWER SUPPLY CIRCUIT

- Check voltage between control unit connector terminal ① and body ground after turning ignition switch "ON".

Battery voltage should exist after turning ignition switch "ON".

NG → Check 10A fuse 26 for control unit. For fuse layout,
- NG → Replace fuse.
- OK → Repair harness and connectors.

OK ↓

CONTROL UNIT GROUND CIRCUIT

NG → Repair harness and connectors.

OK ↓

Go to Diagnostic Procedure 4

OK ↓

Replace ABS control unit.

NS4029500175020X

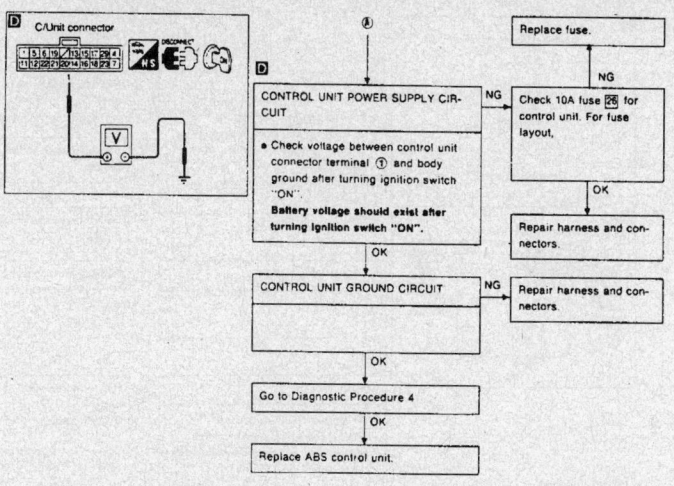

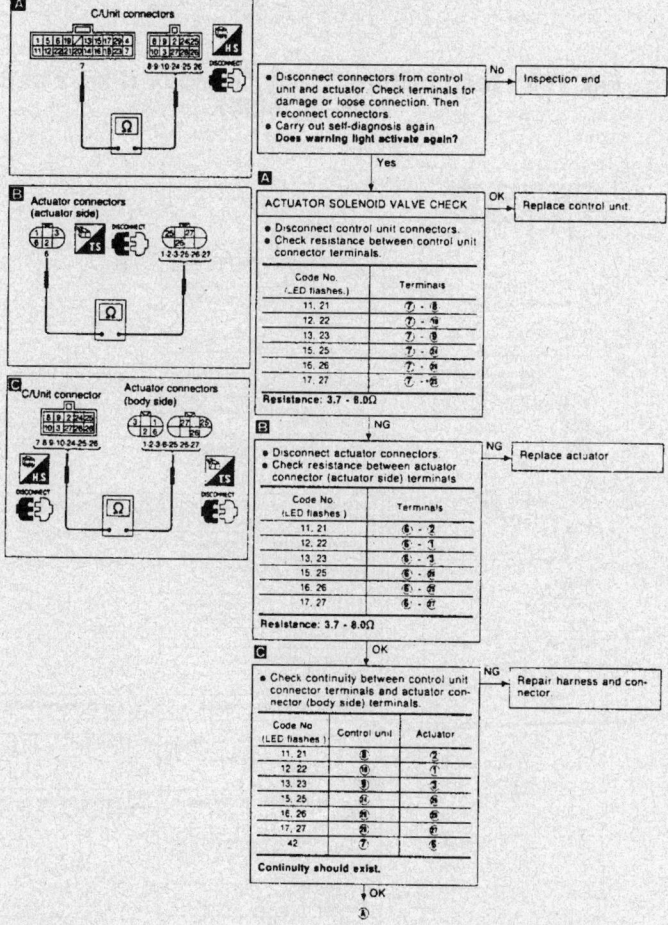

Fig. 106 Test 2: Control Unit Or Ground Circuit (Part 2 of 2). 1995–96 240SX

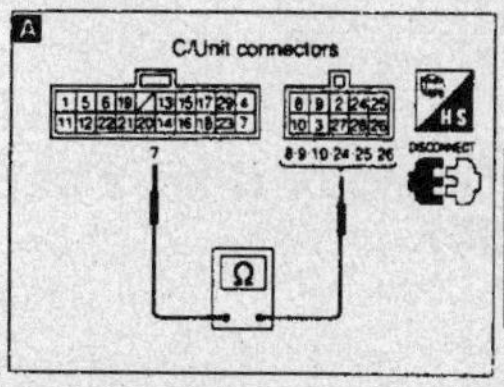
A
C/Unit connectors
7
8 9 10 24 25 26
Ω

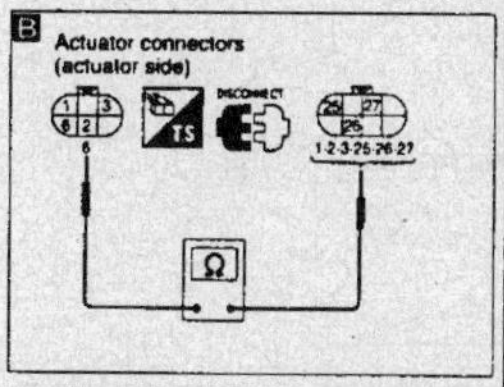
B
Actuator connectors
(actuator side)
6
1 2 3 25 26 27
Ω

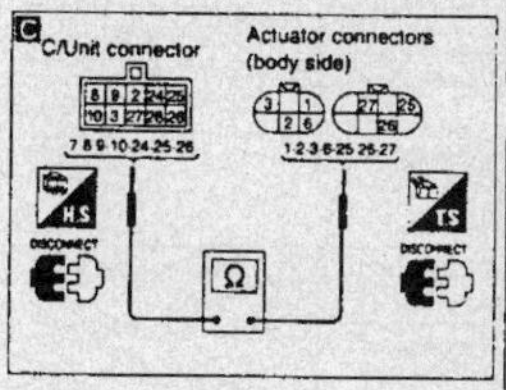
C
C/Unit connector
Actuator connectors
(body side)
7 8 9 10 24 25 26
1 2 3 6 25 26 27
Ω

- Disconnect connectors from control unit and actuator. Check terminals for damage or loose connection. Then reconnect connectors.
- Carry out self-diagnosis again

Does warning light activate again?

No → Inspection end

Yes ↓

A

ACTUATOR SOLENOID VALVE CHECK

OK → Replace control unit.

- Disconnect control unit connectors.
- Check resistance between control unit connector terminals.

Code No. (LED flashes.)	Terminals
11, 21	⑦ - ⑧
12, 22	⑦ - ⑩
13, 23	⑦ - ⑨
15, 25	⑦ - ㉔
16, 26	⑦ - ㉖
17, 27	⑦ - ㉕

Resistance: 3.7 - 8.0Ω

NG ↓

B

- Disconnect actuator connectors.
- Check resistance between actuator connector (actuator side) terminals

NG → Replace actuator

Code No. (LED flashes.)	Terminals
11, 21	⑥ - ②
12, 22	⑥ - ①
13, 23	⑥ - ③
15, 25	⑥ - ㉕
16, 26	⑥ - ㉖
17, 27	⑥ - ㉗

Resistance: 3.7 - 8.0Ω

OK ↓

C

- Check continuity between control unit connector terminals and actuator connector (body side) terminals.

NG → Repair harness and connector.

Code No (LED flashes.)	Control unit	Actuator
11, 21	⑧	②
12, 22	⑩	①
13, 23	⑨	③
15, 25	㉔	㉕
16, 26	㉖	㉖
17, 27	㉕	㉗
42	⑦	⑥

Continuity should exist.

OK ↓

Ⓐ

NS4029500176010X

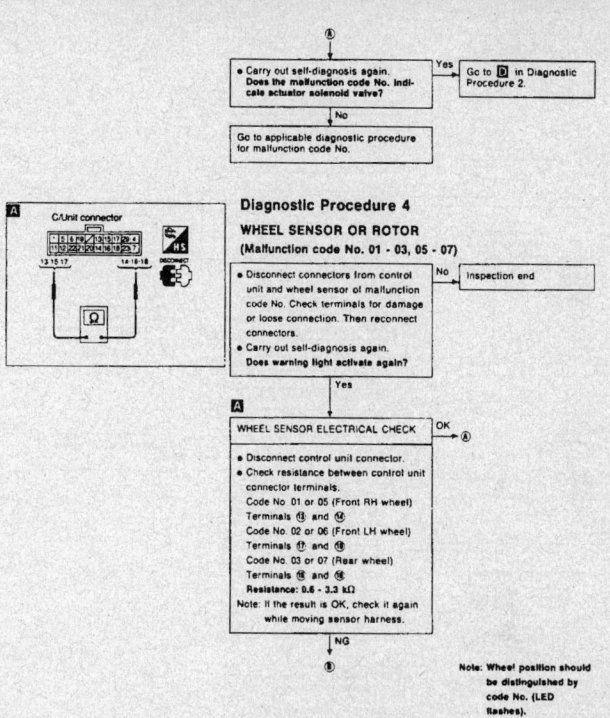

Fig. 107 Test 3: Actuator Solenoid Valve (Part 1 of 2). 1995–96 240SX

Ⓐ

- Carry out self-diagnosis again.

Does the malfunction code No. indicate actuator solenoid valve?

Yes → Go to D in Diagnostic Procedure 2.

No ↓

Go to applicable diagnostic procedure for malfunction code No.

NS4029500176020X

Fig. 107 Test 3: Actuator Solenoid Valve (Part 2 of 2). 1995–96 240SX

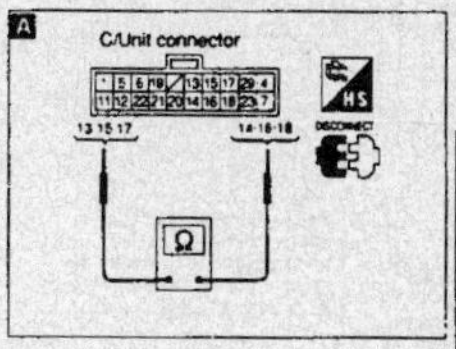
A
C/Unit connector
13 15 17
14 16 18
Ω

Diagnostic Procedure 4

WHEEL SENSOR OR ROTOR

(Malfunction code No. 01 - 03, 05 - 07)

- Disconnect connectors from control unit and wheel sensor of malfunction code No. Check terminals for damage or loose connection. Then reconnect connectors.
- Carry out self-diagnosis again.

Does warning light activate again?

No → Inspection end

Yes ↓

A

WHEEL SENSOR ELECTRICAL CHECK

OK → Ⓑ

- Disconnect control unit connector.
- Check resistance between control unit connector terminals.

Code No. 01 or 05 (Front RH wheel)
Terminals ⑬ and ⑭
Code No. 02 or 06 (Front LH wheel)
Terminals ⑰ and ⑱
Code No. 03 or 07 (Rear wheel)
Terminals ⑮ and ⑯

Resistance: 0.6 - 3.3 kΩ

Note: If the result is OK, check it again while moving sensor harness.

NG ↓

Ⓑ

Note: Wheel position should be distinguished by code No. (LED flashes).

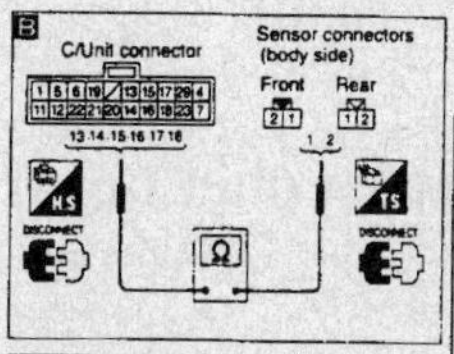
B
C/Unit connector
Sensor connectors
(body side)
Front
Rear
13 14 15 16 17 18
1 2
Ω

Ⓑ

B

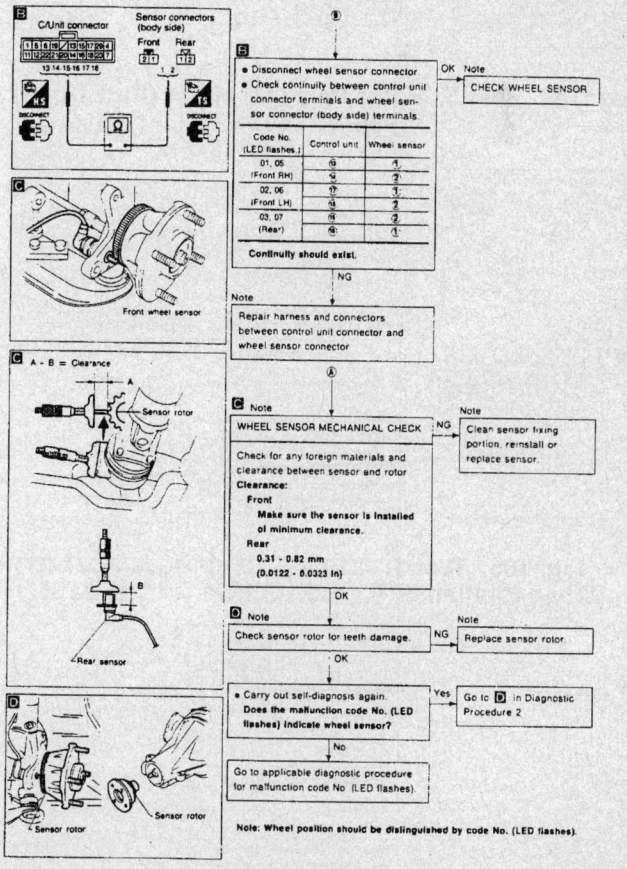

- Disconnect wheel sensor connector.
- Check continuity between control unit connector terminals and wheel sensor connector (body side) terminals.

OK Note → CHECK WHEEL SENSOR

Code No. (LED flashes.)	Control unit	Wheel sensor
01, 05 (Front RH)	⑬	①
	⑭	②
02, 06 (Front LH)	⑰	①
	⑱	②
03, 07 (Rear)	⑮	②
	⑯	①

Continuity should exist.

NG ↓

Note

Repair harness and connectors between control unit connector and wheel sensor connector

Ⓐ

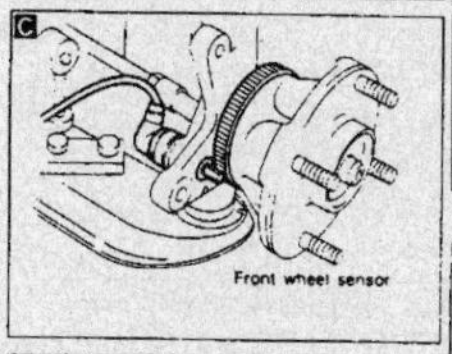
C
Front wheel sensor

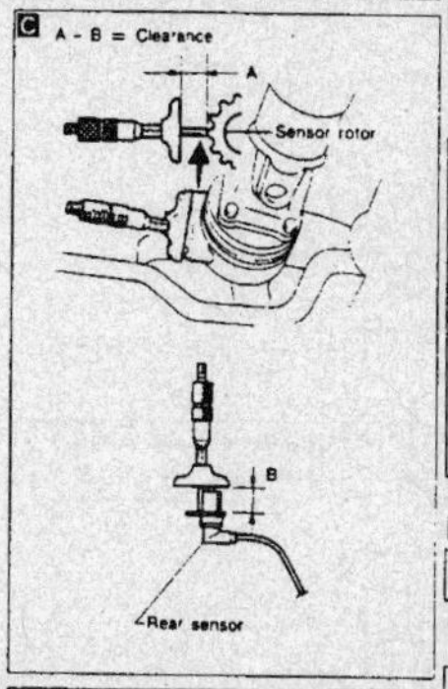
C
A - B = Clearance
A
Sensor rotor
B
Rear sensor

C Note

WHEEL SENSOR MECHANICAL CHECK

NG → Note: Clean sensor fixing portion, reinstall or replace sensor.

Check for any foreign materials and clearance between sensor and rotor

Clearance:

Front

Make sure the sensor is installed at minimum clearance.

Rear

0.31 - 0.82 mm

(0.0122 - 0.0323 in)

OK ↓

D Note

Check sensor rotor for teeth damage.

NG → Note: Replace sensor rotor.

OK ↓

- Carry out self-diagnosis again.

Does the malfunction code No. (LED flashes) indicate wheel sensor?

Yes → Go to D in Diagnostic Procedure 2

No ↓

Go to applicable diagnostic procedure for malfunction code No. (LED flashes).

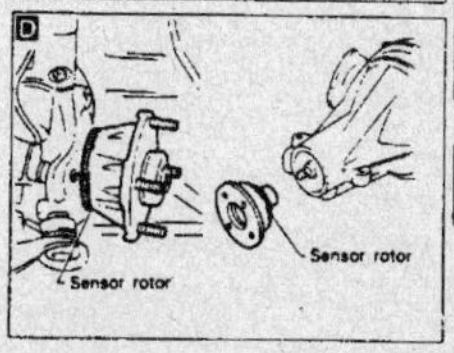
D
Sensor rotor
Sensor rotor

Note: Wheel position should be distinguished by code No. (LED flashes).

NS4029500177000X

Fig. 108 Test 4: Wheel Sensor Or Rotor. 1995–96 240SX

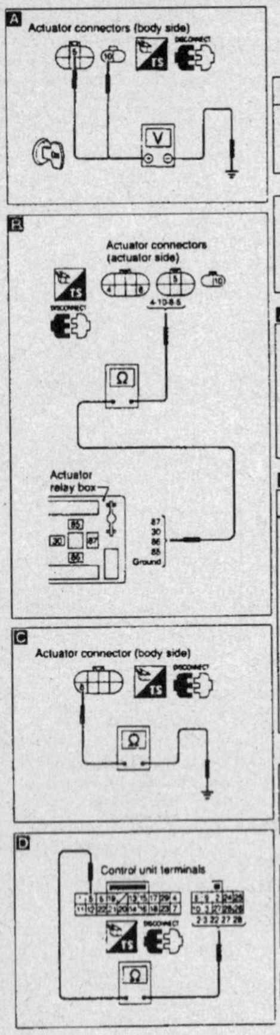
A
Actuator connectors (body side)
B
Actuator connectors (actuator side)
Actuator relay box
87
30
86
85
Ground
C
Actuator connector (body side)
D
Control unit terminals

MOTOR POWER SUPPLY CIRCUIT

- Check 30A fusible link [d] and 10A fuse [26] for actuator. For fusible link and fuse layout.

NG → (B)

OK ↓

- Disconnect connectors from control unit and actuator. Check terminals for damage or loose connection. Then reconnect connectors.
- Carry out self-diagnosis again.
Does warning light activate again?

No → Inspection end

Yes ↓

A

- Disconnect actuator connectors.
- Check voltage between connector (body side) terminals and ground.

Terminals	Ignition switch
(5) - ground	ON position
(11) - ground	—

Battery voltage should exist.

NG → Repair harness and connectors between battery and actuator connector (body side) terminals.

OK ↓

B

MOTOR RELAY CIRCUIT

- Remove motor relay.
- Disconnect actuator connectors.
- Check continuity between actuator connector (actuator side) terminals and relay connector terminals or body ground.

Actuator connector	Relay connector	Continuity
(4)	(87)	Yes
(10)	(30)	Yes
(8)	(86)	Yes
(5)	(85)	Yes
(4)	Ground	No

NG → Replace actuator assembly.

OK ↓

C

- Check continuity between actuator connector (body side) terminal (8) and ground.
Continuity should not exist.

OK → (A)

NG ↓

D

- Disconnect control unit connectors.
- Check continuity between control unit terminals (control unit side) (5) and (2), (3), (22), (27), (28).
Continuity should not exist.

OK → Repair harness and connectors.

NG ↓

Replace control unit.

NS4029500178010X

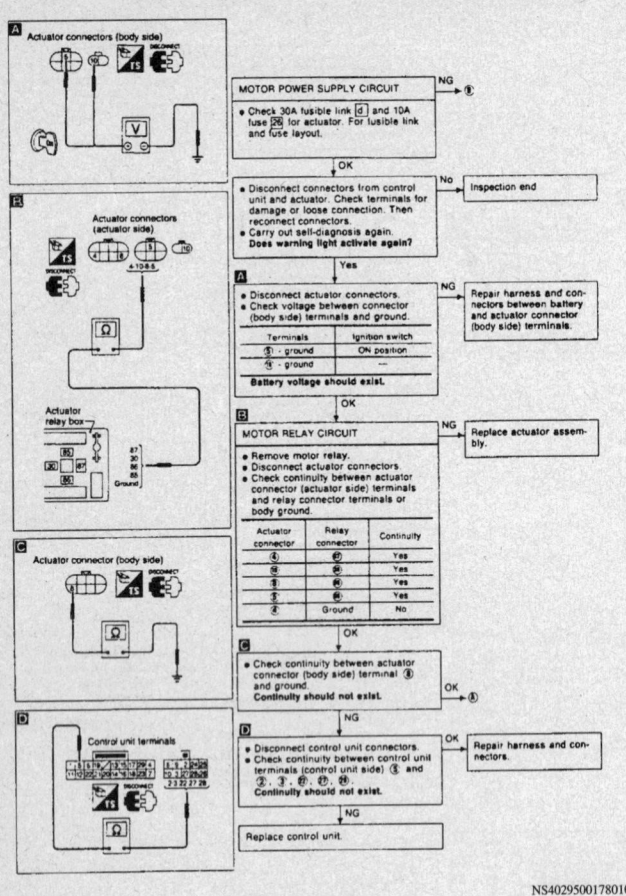

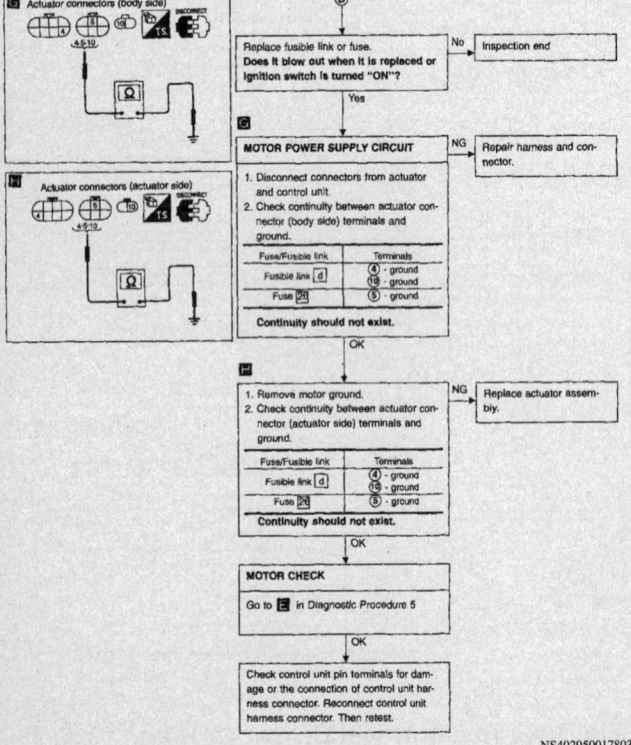

Fig. 109 Test 5: Motor Relay Or Motor (Part 1 of 3). 1995–96 240SX

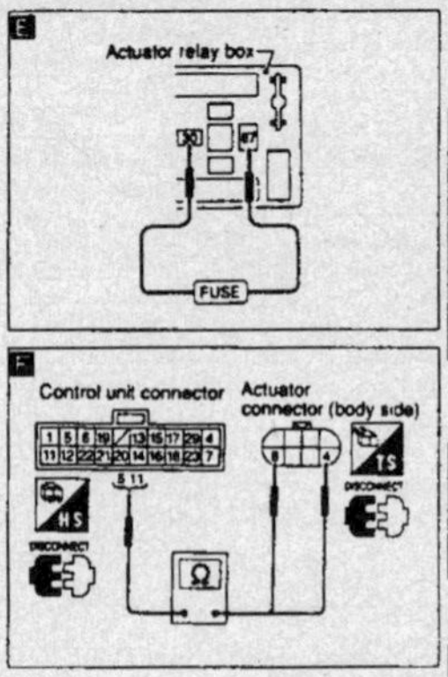
E
Actuator relay box
FUSE
F
Control unit connector
Actuator connector (body side)

(A) ↓

E

MOTOR CHECK

- Connect actuator connectors.
- Connect suitable wire between relay connector terminals (87) and (30).
Motor should operate.
Do not connect wire for more than 5 seconds.

NG → Check actuator motor ground — OK → Replace actuator assembly; NG → Repair harness and terminals

OK ↓

MOTOR RELAY CHECK

NG → Replace motor relay.

OK ↓

F

CIRCUIT CHECK

- Disconnect control unit connector.
- Check continuity between control unit connector terminals and actuator connector (body side) terminals.

Control unit	Actuator
(5)	(8)
(11)	(4)

Continuity should exist.

NG → Repair harness and connectors.

OK ↓

Go to **D** in Diagnostic Procedure 2.

NS4029500178020X

Fig. 109 Test 5: Motor Relay Or Motor (Part 2 of 3). 1995–96 240SX

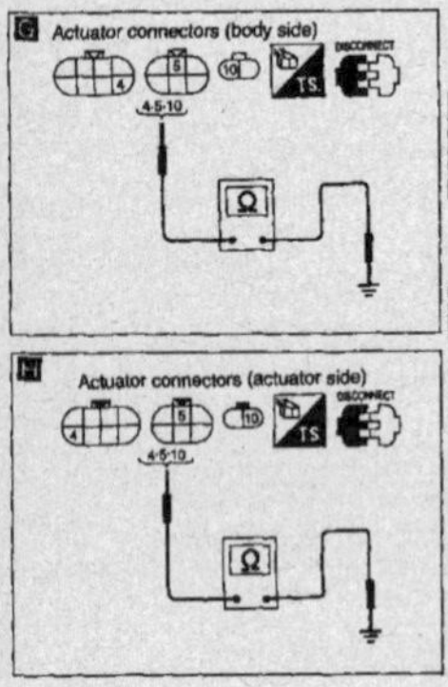
G
Actuator connectors (body side)
4-5-10
H
Actuator connectors (actuator side)
4-5-10

(B) ↓

Replace fusible link or fuse.
Does it blow out when it is replaced or ignition switch is turned "ON"?

No → Inspection end

Yes ↓

G

MOTOR POWER SUPPLY CIRCUIT

1. Disconnect connectors from actuator and control unit.
2. Check continuity between actuator connector (body side) terminals and ground.

Fuse/Fusible link	Terminals
Fusible link [d]	(4) - ground (10) - ground
Fuse [26]	(5) - ground

Continuity should not exist.

NG → Repair harness and connector.

OK ↓

H

1. Remove motor ground.
2. Check continuity between actuator connector (actuator side) terminals and ground.

Fuse/Fusible link	Terminals
Fusible link [d]	(4) - ground (10) - ground
Fuse [26]	(5) - ground

Continuity should not exist.

NG → Replace actuator assembly.

OK ↓

MOTOR CHECK

Go to **E** in Diagnostic Procedure 5

OK ↓

Check control unit pin terminals for damage or the connection of control unit harness connector. Reconnect control unit harness connector. Then retest.

NS4029500178030X

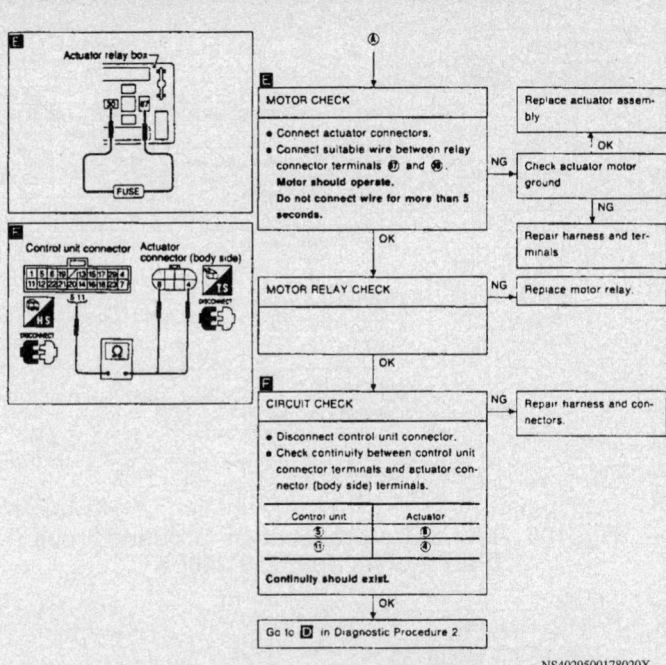

Fig. 109 Test 5: Motor Relay Or Motor (Part 3 of 3). 1995–96 240SX

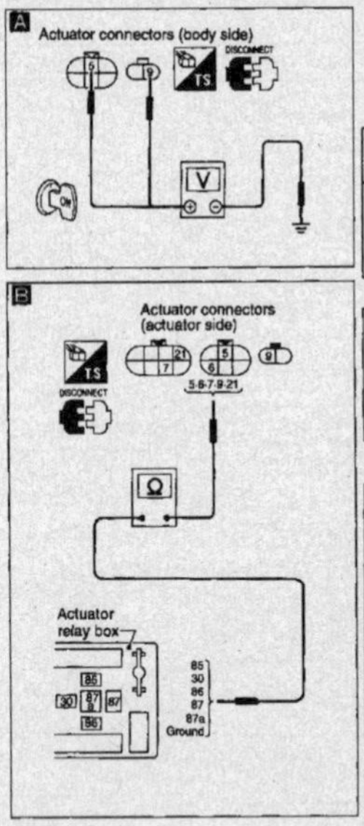
A
Actuator connectors (body side)
B
Actuator connectors (actuator side)
5-6-7-9-21
Actuator relay box
85
30
86
87
87a
Ground

SOLENOID VALVE POWER SUPPLY CHECK

Check 30A fusible link [c] and 10A fuse [28] for actuator.

NG → (B)

OK ↓

1. Disconnect connectors from control unit and actuator. Check terminals for damage or loose connection. Then reconnect connectors.
2. Carry out self-diagnosis again.
Does warning lamp activate again?

No → Inspection end

Yes ↓

A

SOLENOID VALVE POWER SUPPLY CHECK

1. Disconnect connectors from actuator.
2. Check voltage between actuator 2-pin connector (body side) terminals and ground.

Terminals	Ignition switch
(5) - ground	ON position
(9) - ground	—

Battery voltage should exist.

NG → Repair harness and connector.

OK ↓

SOLENOID VALVE RELAY CHECK

NG → Replace solenoid valve relay.

OK ↓

B

SOLENOID VALVE RELAY CIRCUIT CHECK

Check continuity between relay terminals and actuator connector (actuator side) terminals.

Relay terminals	Connector terminals	Continuity
(30)	(6)	Yes
(87)	(9)	Yes
(87a)	(21)	Yes
(86)	(7)	Yes
(85)	(5)	Yes
Ground	(7)	No

NG → Replace actuator.

OK ↓

(A)

NS4029500179010X

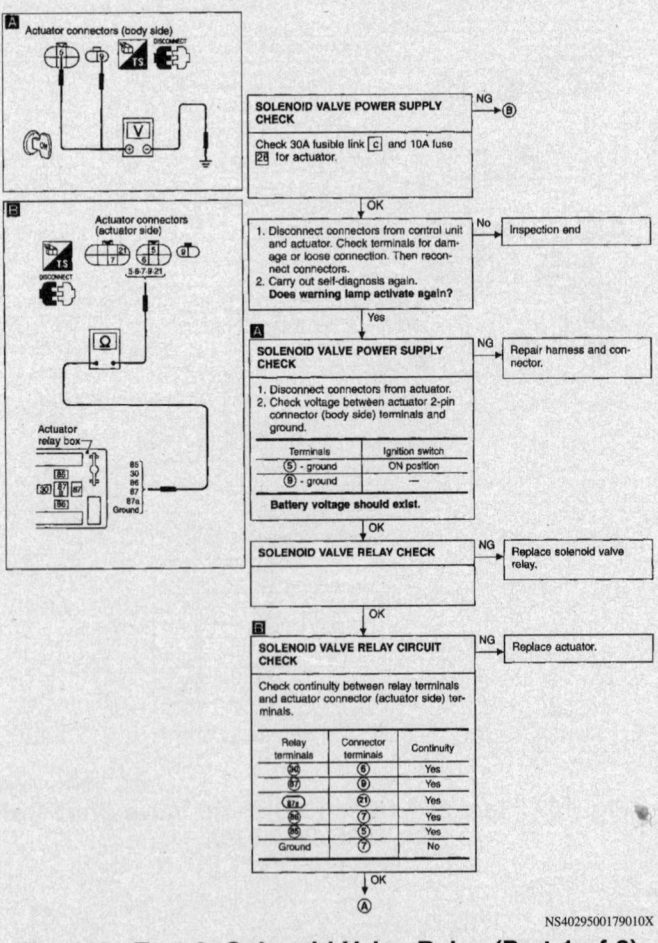

Fig. 110 Test 6: Solenoid Valve Relay (Part 1 of 3). 1995–96 240SX

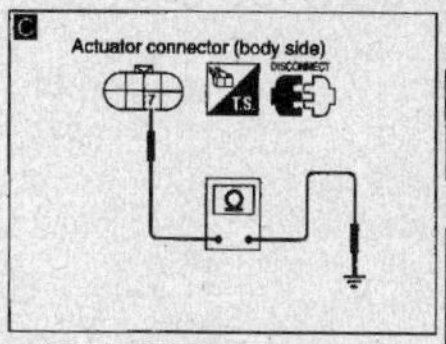
C
Actuator connector (body side)
DISCONNECT
T.S.

Ⓐ

C Check continuity between actuator connector (body side) terminal ⑦ and ground.
Continuity should not exist.
- OK → Ⓒ
- NG ↓

D
1. Disconnect control unit connectors.
2. Check continuity between control unit terminals (control unit side) ⑥ and ②, ③, ㉒, ㉗, ㉘.

Continuity should not exist.
- NG → Check control unit pin terminals for damage or the connection of control unit harness connector. Reconnect control unit harness connector. Then retest.
- OK ↓

Repair harness and connectors.

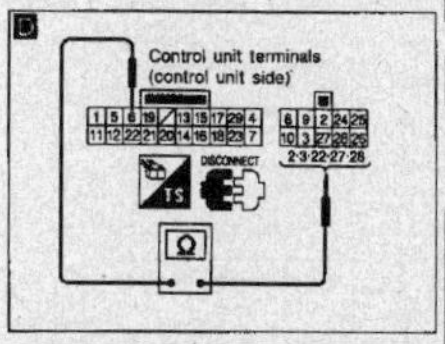
D
Control unit terminals
(control unit side)
DISCONNECT
T.S.
2·3·22·27·28

Ⓒ

E CIRCUIT CHECK
1. Disconnect control unit connector.
2. Check continuity between control unit connector terminals and actuator connector (body side) terminals.

Control unit	Actuator
⑥	⑦
⑦	⑥
Ground	㉑

Continuity should exist.
- NG → Repair harness and connectors.
- OK ↓

Go to **D** in Diagnostic Procedure 2.

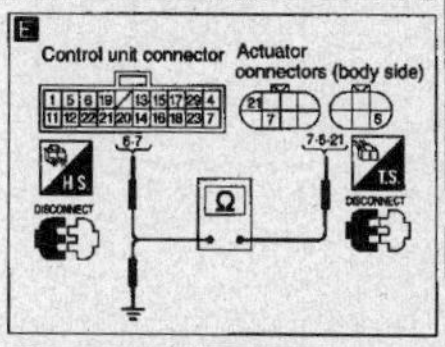
E
Control unit connector
Actuator connectors (body side)
H.S.
DISCONNECT
T.S.
6·7
7·6·21

Ⓑ

Replace fusible link or fuse.
Does it blow out when it is replaced or ignition switch is turned "ON"?
- No → Inspection end
- Yes ↓

F ACTUATOR POWER SUPPLY CIRCUIT
1. Disconnect connectors from actuator and control unit.
2. Check continuity between actuator connector (body side) terminals and ground.

Fuse/Fusible link	Terminals
Fusible link [c]	⑥ - ground ⑨ - ground
Fuse [26]	⑤ - ground

Continuity should not exist.
- NG → Repair harness and connector.
- OK ↓

Ⓓ

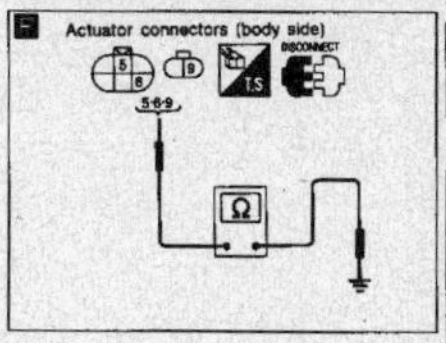
F
Actuator connectors (body side)
DISCONNECT
T.S.
5·6·9

NS4029500179020X

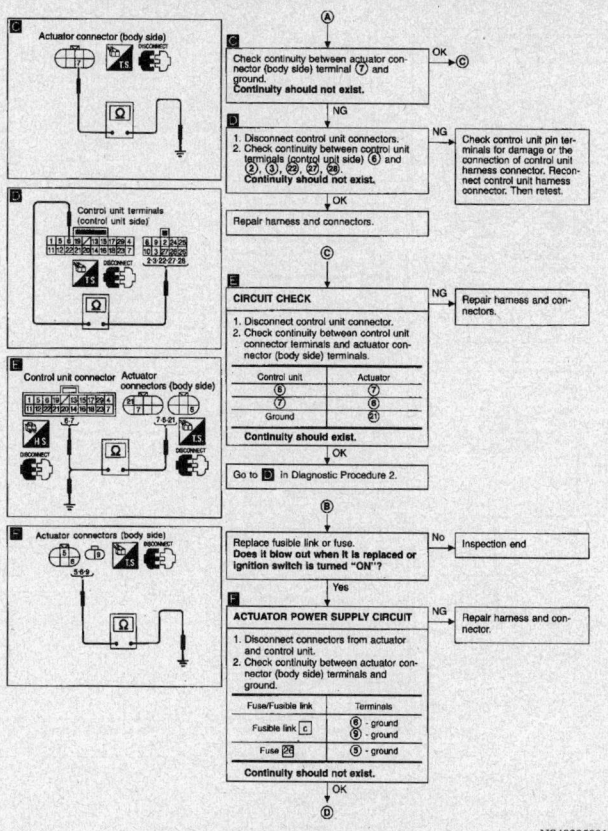

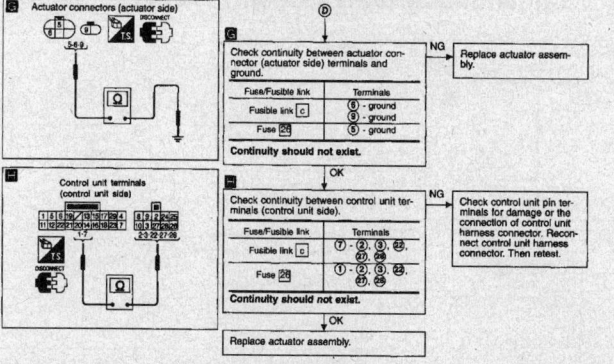

Fig. 110 Test 6: Solenoid Valve Relay (Part 2 of 3). 1995–96 240SX

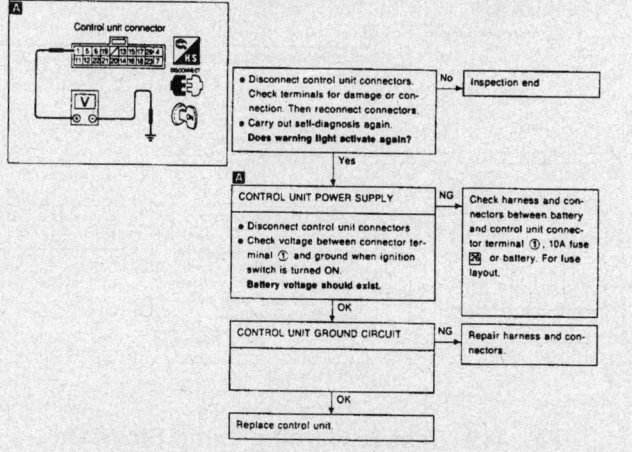

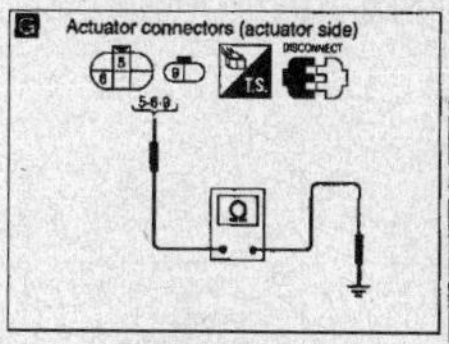
G
Actuator connectors (actuator side)
DISCONNECT
T.S.
5·6·9

Ⓓ

G Check continuity between actuator connector (actuator side) terminals and ground.

Fuse/Fusible link	Terminals
Fusible link [c]	⑥ - ground ⑨ - ground
Fuse [26]	⑤ - ground

Continuity should not exist.
- NG → Replace actuator assembly.
- OK ↓

H Check continuity between control unit terminals (control unit side).

Fuse/Fusible link	Terminals
Fusible link [c]	⑦ - ②, ③, ㉒, ㉗, ㉘
Fuse [26]	① - ②, ③, ㉒, ㉗, ㉘

Continuity should not exist.
- NG → Check control unit pin terminals for damage or the connection of control unit harness connector. Reconnect control unit harness connector. Then retest.
- OK ↓

Replace actuator assembly.

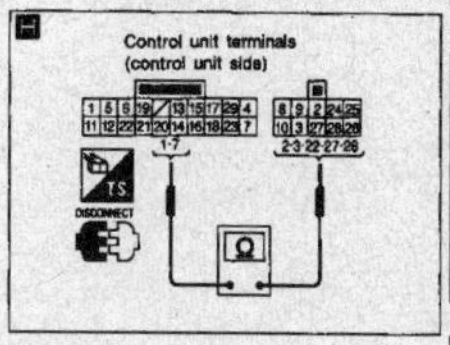
H
Control unit terminals
(control unit side)
T.S.
DISCONNECT
1·7
2·3·22·27·28

NS4029500179030X

Fig. 110 Test 6: Solenoid Valve Relay (Part 3 of 3). 1995–96 240SX

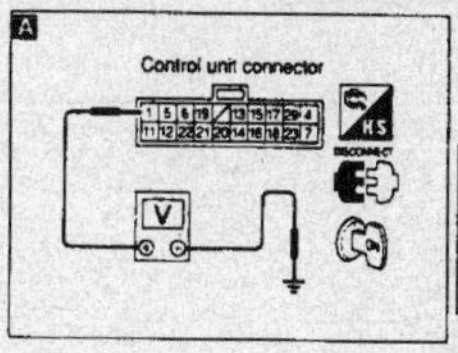
A
Control unit connector
H.S.
DISCONNECT

- Disconnect control unit connectors. Check terminals for damage or connection. Then reconnect connectors.
- Carry out self-diagnosis again.

Does warning light activate again?
- No → Inspection end
- Yes ↓

A CONTROL UNIT POWER SUPPLY
- Disconnect control unit connectors
- Check voltage between connector terminal ① and ground when ignition switch is turned ON.

Battery voltage should exist.
- NG → Check harness and connectors between battery and control unit connector terminal ①, 10A fuse [26] or battery. For fuse layout.
- OK ↓

CONTROL UNIT GROUND CIRCUIT
- NG → Repair harness and connectors.
- OK ↓

Replace control unit.

NS4029500180000X

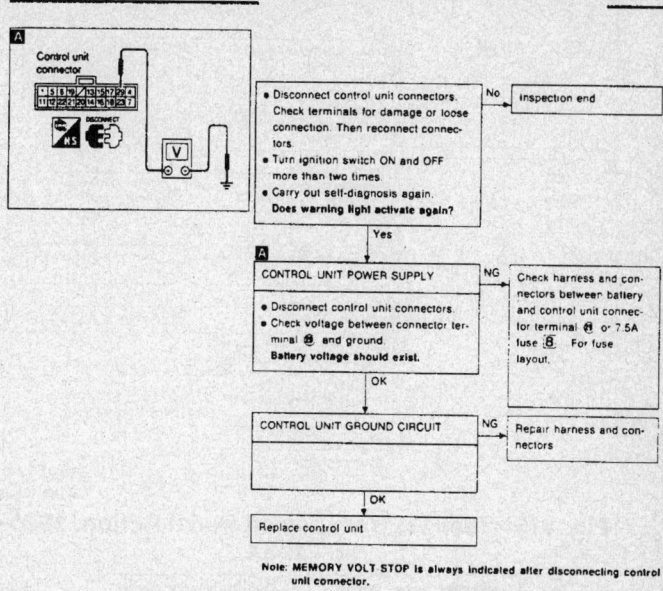

Fig. 111 Test 7: Power Supply. 1995–96 240SX

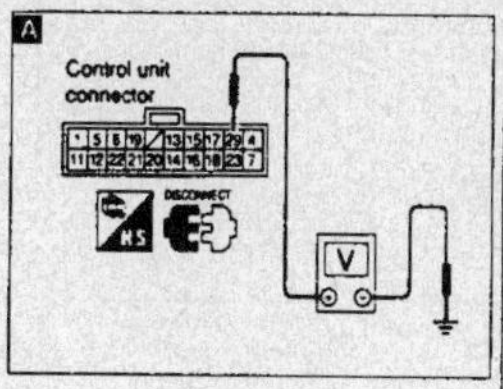
A
Control unit connector
DISCONNECT
H.S.
V

- Disconnect control unit connectors. Check terminals for damage or loose connection. Then reconnect connectors.
- Turn ignition switch ON and OFF more than two times.
- Carry out self-diagnosis again.

Does warning light activate again?
- No → Inspection end
- Yes ↓

A CONTROL UNIT POWER SUPPLY
- Disconnect control unit connectors.
- Check voltage between connector terminal ⑧ and ground.

Battery voltage should exist.
- NG → Check harness and connectors between battery and control unit connector terminal ⑧ or 7.5A fuse [8]. For fuse layout.
- OK ↓

CONTROL UNIT GROUND CIRCUIT
- NG → Repair harness and connectors
- OK ↓

Replace control unit

Note: MEMORY VOLT STOP is always indicated after disconnecting control unit connector.

NS4029500181000X

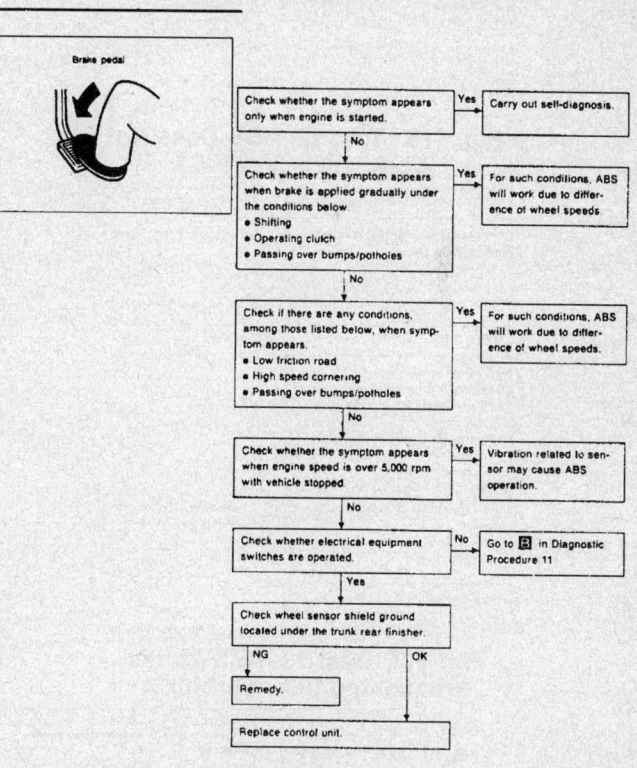

Fig. 112 Test 8: Memory Volt Stop. 1995–96 240SX

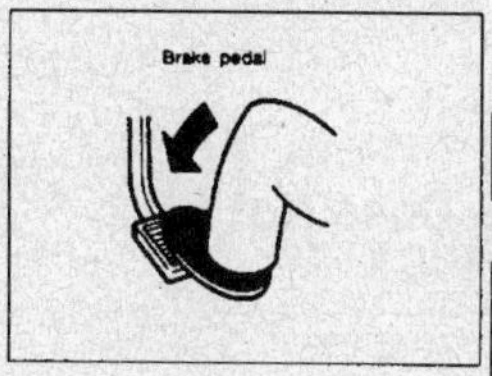
Brake pedal

Check whether the symptom appears only when engine is started.
- Yes → Carry out self-diagnosis.
- No ↓

Check whether the symptom appears when brake is applied gradually under the conditions below.
- Shifting
- Operating clutch
- Passing over bumps/potholes

- Yes → For such conditions, ABS will work due to difference of wheel speeds.
- No ↓

Check if there are any conditions, among those listed below, when symptom appears.
- Low friction road
- High speed cornering
- Passing over bumps/potholes

- Yes → For such conditions, ABS will work due to difference of wheel speeds.
- No ↓

Check whether the symptom appears when engine speed is over 5,000 rpm with vehicle stopped.
- Yes → Vibration related to sensor may cause ABS operation.
- No ↓

Check whether electrical equipment switches are operated.
- No → Go to **B** in Diagnostic Procedure 11
- Yes ↓

Check wheel sensor shield ground located under the trunk rear finisher.
- NG → Remedy.
- OK → Replace control unit.

NS4029500182000X

Fig. 113 Test 9: Pedal Vibration & Noise. 1995–96 240SX

Check if road condition is slippery with snow or gravel.
- Yes → Stopping distance may be longer than vehicles without ABS.
- No ↓

Disconnect actuator connector and check whether stopping distance is still long.
- No → Go to **B** in Diagnostic Procedure 11
- Yes ↓

Perform Preliminary Check and air bleeding.

NS4029500183000X

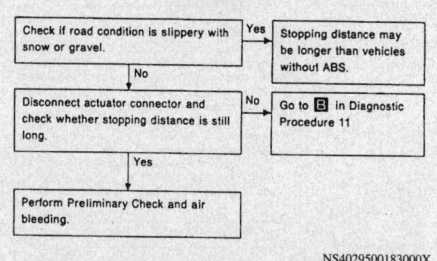

Fig. 114 Test 10: Long Stopping Distance. 1995–96 240SX

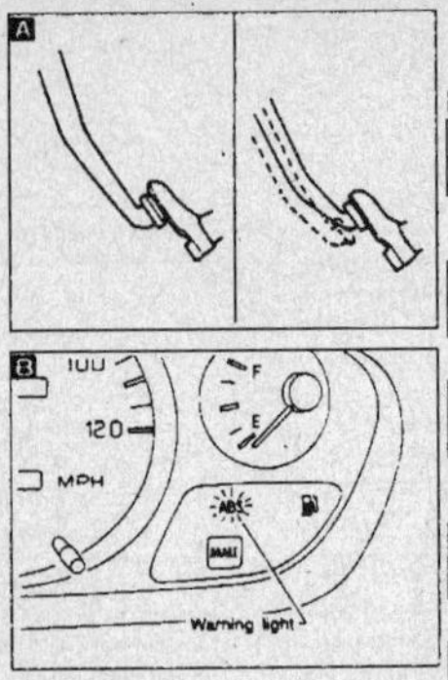
A
B
Warning light

A

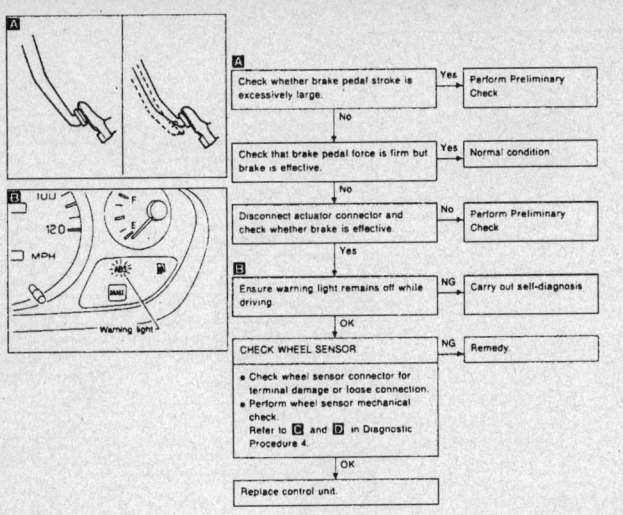

Check whether brake pedal stroke is excessively large. — Yes → Perform Preliminary Check

No ↓

Check that brake pedal force is firm but brake is effective. — Yes → Normal condition.

No ↓

Disconnect actuator connector and check whether brake is effective. — No → Perform Preliminary Check

Yes ↓

B

Ensure warning light remains off while driving. — NG → Carry out self-diagnosis

OK ↓

CHECK WHEEL SENSOR — NG → Remedy.

- Check wheel sensor connector for terminal damage or loose connection.
- Perform wheel sensor mechanical check.
  Refer to C and D in Diagnostic Procedure 4.

OK ↓

Replace control unit.

NS4029500184000X

Fig. 115 Test 11: Unexpected Pedal Action. 1995–96 240SX

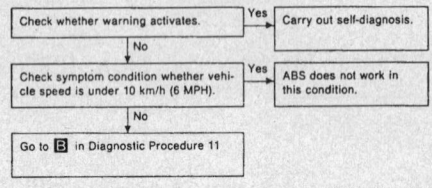

Check whether warning activates. — Yes → Carry out self-diagnosis.

No ↓

Check symptom condition whether vehicle speed is under 10 km/h (6 MPH). — Yes → ABS does not work in this condition.

No ↓

Go to B in Diagnostic Procedure 11

NS4029500185000X

Fig. 116 Test 12: ABS Does Not Work. 1995–96 240SX

CHECK BRAKE FLUID PRESSURE. — NG → Perform Preliminary Check

Check whether brake fluid pressure distribution is normal.

OK ↓

CHECK WHEEL SENSOR. — NG → Remedy.

- Check wheel sensor connector for terminal damage or loose connection.
- Perform wheel sensor mechanical check.
  Refer to C and D in Diagnostic Procedure 4.

OK ↓

Check front axles for excessive looseness. — NG → Remedy.

OK ↓

Replace control unit.

NS4029500186000X

Fig. 117 Test 13: ABS Works Frequently. 1995–96 240SX

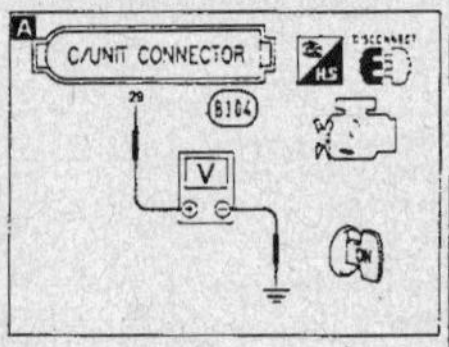
A
C/UNIT CONNECTOR
29
B104
V

WARNING LAMP CIRCUIT CHECK — NG → Replace fuse.

Check 10A fuse for warning lamp. For

OK ↓

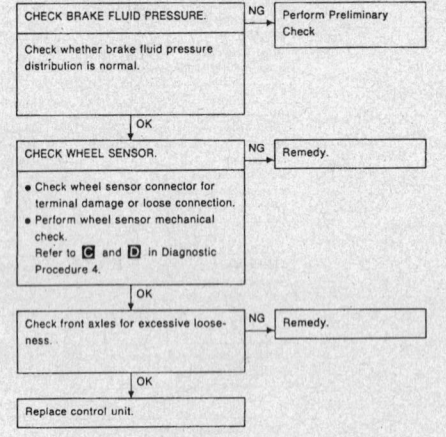

Check warning lamp bulb. — NG → Replace bulb.

OK ↓

A

- Install 10A fuse and bulb.
- Disconnect connectors from control unit and actuator.
- Check voltage between control unit terminal 29 and ground after turning ignition switch "ON".

Battery voltage should exist for one second after turning ignition switch "ON".

— NG → Repair harness and connectors.

OK ↓

Carry out self-diagnosis

NS4029400052000X

Fig. 118 Test 1: Warning Lamp Does Not Work Before Engine Starts. 1994–96 300ZX

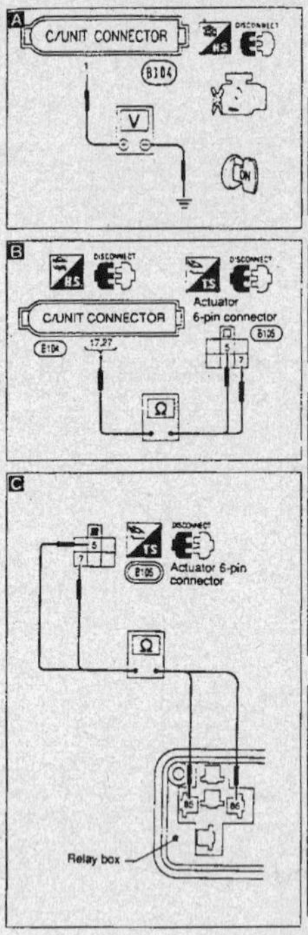
A
C/UNIT CONNECTOR
B104
V
B
C/UNIT CONNECTOR
B104
17,27
Actuator 6-pin connector
B125
C
Actuator 6-pin connector
Relay box

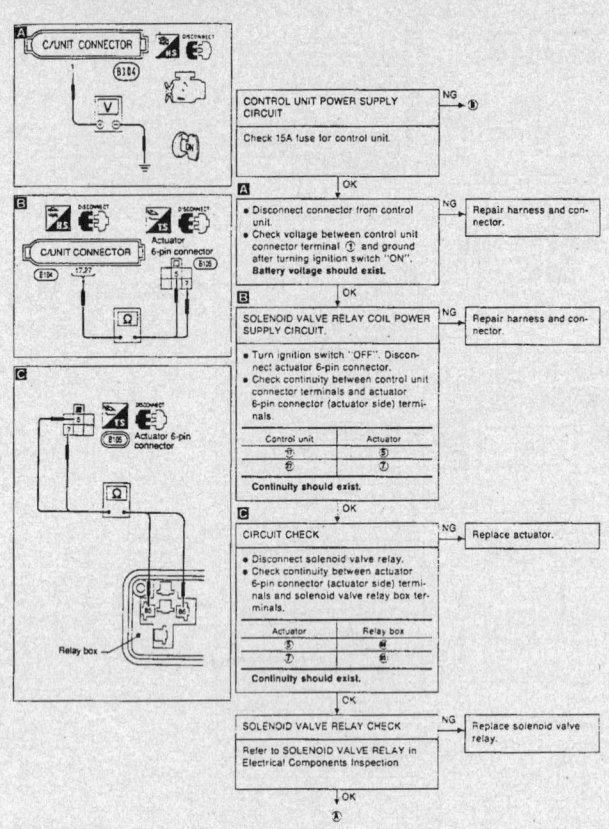

CONTROL UNIT POWER SUPPLY CIRCUIT — NG → B

Check 15A fuse for control unit.

OK ↓

A

- Disconnect connector from control unit.
- Check voltage between control unit connector terminal 1 and ground after turning ignition switch "ON".

Battery voltage should exist.

— NG → Repair harness and connector.

OK ↓

B

SOLENOID VALVE RELAY COIL POWER SUPPLY CIRCUIT. — NG → Repair harness and connector.

- Turn ignition switch "OFF". Disconnect actuator 6-pin connector.
- Check continuity between control unit connector terminals and actuator 6-pin connector (actuator side) terminals.

Control unit	Actuator
17	5
27	7

Continuity should exist.

OK ↓

C

CIRCUIT CHECK — NG → Replace actuator.

- Disconnect solenoid valve relay.
- Check continuity between actuator 6-pin connector (actuator side) terminals and solenoid valve relay box terminals.

Actuator	Relay box
5	86
7	85

Continuity should exist.

OK ↓

SOLENOID VALVE RELAY CHECK — NG → Replace solenoid valve relay.

Refer to SOLENOID VALVE RELAY in Electrical Components Inspection

OK ↓

A

NS4029400053010X

Fig. 119 Test 2: Warning Lamp Stays On Continuously (Part 1 of 3). 1994–96 300ZX

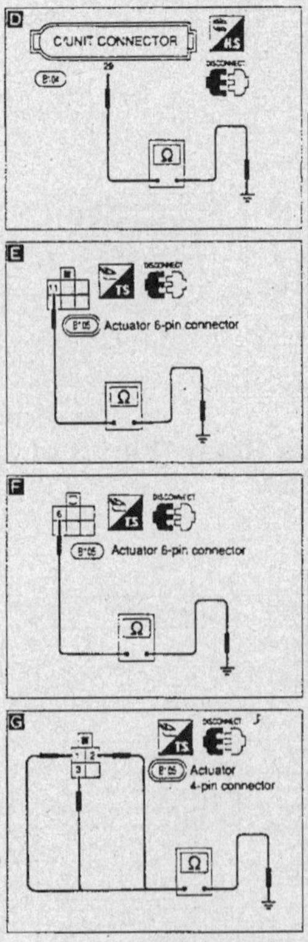
D
C/UNIT CONNECTOR
B104
29
E
11
Actuator 6-pin connector
F
6
Actuator 6-pin connector
G
1
2
3
Actuator 4-pin connector

A

D

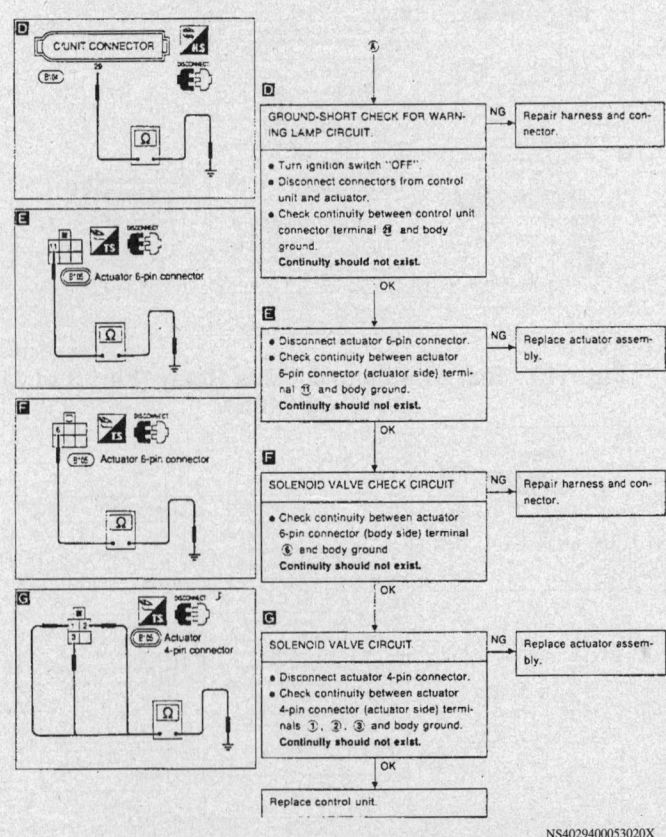

GROUND-SHORT CHECK FOR WARNING LAMP CIRCUIT. — NG → Repair harness and connector.

- Turn ignition switch "OFF".
- Disconnect connectors from control unit and actuator.
- Check continuity between control unit connector terminal 29 and body ground.

Continuity should not exist.

OK ↓

E

- Disconnect actuator 6-pin connector.
- Check continuity between actuator 6-pin connector (actuator side) terminal 11 and body ground.

Continuity should not exist.

— NG → Replace actuator assembly.

OK ↓

F

SOLENOID VALVE CHECK CIRCUIT — NG → Repair harness and connector.

- Check continuity between actuator 6-pin connector (body side) terminal 6 and body ground

Continuity should not exist.

OK ↓

G

SOLENOID VALVE CIRCUIT — NG → Replace actuator assembly.

- Disconnect actuator 4-pin connector.
- Check continuity between actuator 4-pin connector (actuator side) terminals 1, 2, 3 and body ground.

Continuity should not exist.

OK ↓

Replace control unit.

NS4029400053020X

Fig. 119 Test 2: Warning Lamp Stays On Continuously (Part 2 of 3). 1994–96 300ZX

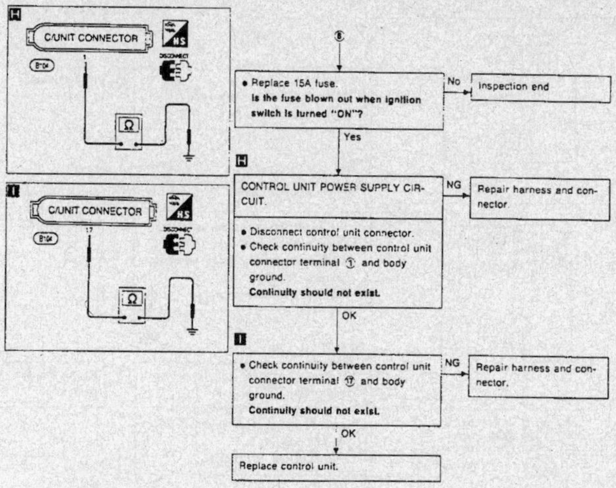
C/UNIT CONNECTOR
• Replace 15A fuse.
Is the fuse blown out when ignition switch is turned "ON"?
No
Inspection end
Yes
CONTROL UNIT POWER SUPPLY CIRCUIT.
• Disconnect control unit connector.
• Check continuity between control unit connector terminal ① and body ground.
Continuity should not exist.
NG
Repair harness and connector.
OK
• Check continuity between control unit connector terminal ⑰ and body ground.
Continuity should not exist.
NG
Repair harness and connector.
OK
Replace control unit.

NS4029400053030X

Fig. 119 Test 2: Warning Lamp Stays On Continuously (Part 3 of 3). 1994–96 300ZX

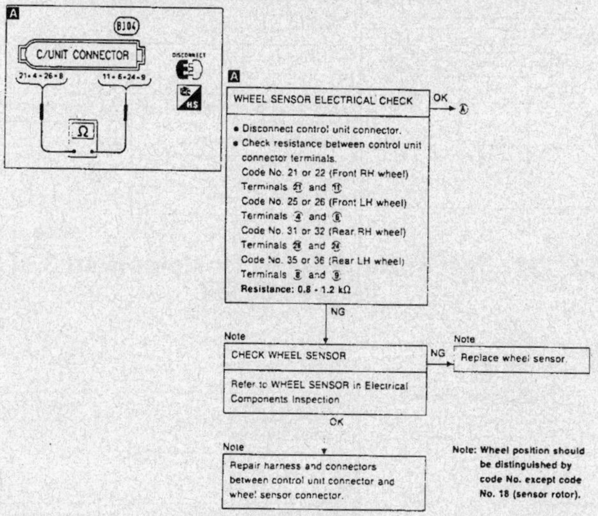
B104
C/UNIT CONNECTOR
WHEEL SENSOR ELECTRICAL CHECK
OK
• Disconnect control unit connector.
• Check resistance between control unit connector terminals.
Code No. 21 or 22 (Front RH wheel)
Terminals ㉑ and ⑪
Code No. 25 or 26 (Front LH wheel)
Terminals ④ and ⑤
Code No. 31 or 32 (Rear RH wheel)
Terminals ㉖ and ㉔
Code No. 35 or 36 (Rear LH wheel)
Terminals ⑧ and ⑨
Resistance: 0.8 - 1.2 kΩ
NG
Note
CHECK WHEEL SENSOR
Refer to WHEEL SENSOR in Electrical Components Inspection
NG
Note
Replace wheel sensor.
OK
Note
Repair harness and connectors between control unit connector and wheel sensor connector.
Note: Wheel position should be distinguished by code No. except code No. 18 (sensor rotor).

NS4029400055010X

Fig. 121 Test 4: Wheel Sensor Or Rotor (Part 1 of 2). 1994–96 300ZX

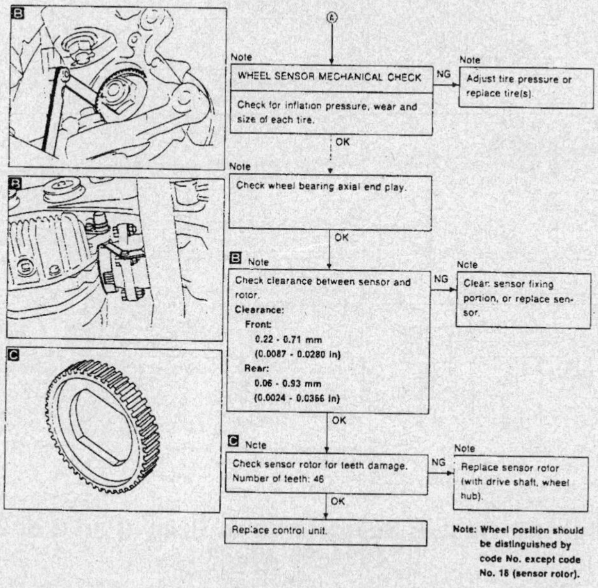
Note
WHEEL SENSOR MECHANICAL CHECK
Check for inflation pressure, wear and size of each tire.
NG
Note
Adjust tire pressure or replace tire(s).
OK
Note
Check wheel bearing axial end play.
OK
Note
Check clearance between sensor and rotor.
Clearance:
Front:
0.22 - 0.71 mm
(0.0087 - 0.0280 in)
Rear:
0.06 - 0.93 mm
(0.0024 - 0.0366 in)
NG
Note
Clean sensor fixing portion, or replace sensor.
OK
Note
Check sensor rotor for teeth damage.
Number of teeth: 46
NG
Note
Replace sensor rotor (with drive shaft, wheel hub).
OK
Replace control unit.
Note: Wheel position should be distinguished by code No. except code No. 18 (sensor rotor).

NS4029400055020X

Fig. 121 Test 4: Wheel Sensor Or Rotor (Part 2 of 2). 1994–96 300ZX

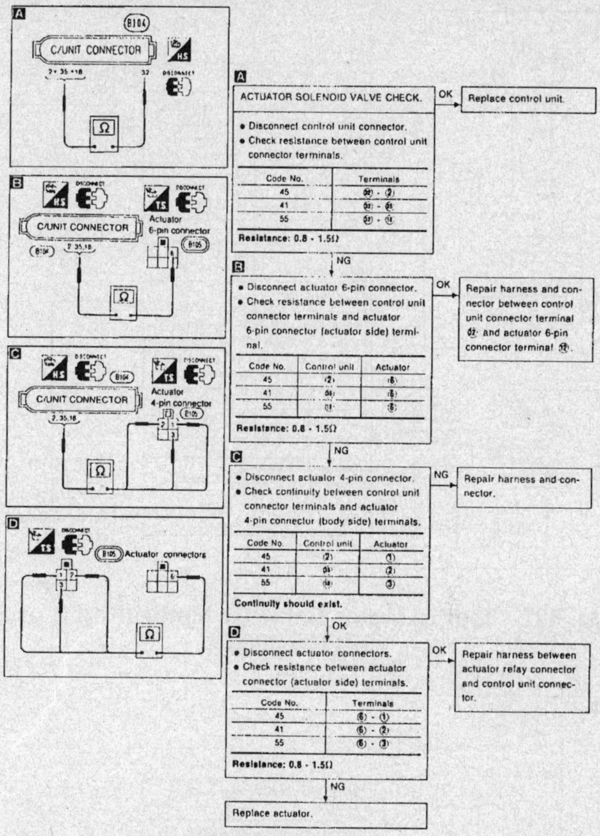
B104
C/UNIT CONNECTOR
ACTUATOR SOLENOID VALVE CHECK.
OK
Replace control unit.
• Disconnect control unit connector.
• Check resistance between control unit connector terminals.
Code No. | Terminals
45
41
55
Resistance: 0.8 - 1.5Ω
NG
Actuator 6-pin connector
• Disconnect actuator 6-pin connector.
• Check resistance between control unit connector terminals and actuator 6-pin connector (actuator side) terminal.
Code No. | Control unit | Actuator
45
41
55
Resistance: 0.8 - 1.5Ω
OK
Repair harness and connector between control unit connector terminal and actuator 6-pin connector terminal.
NG
Actuator 4-pin connector
• Disconnect actuator 4-pin connector.
• Check continuity between control unit connector terminals and actuator 4-pin connector (body side) terminals.
Code No. | Control unit | Actuator
45 | ①
41 | ②
55 | ③
Continuity should exist.
NG
Repair harness and connector.
OK
Actuator connectors
• Disconnect actuator connectors.
• Check resistance between actuator connector (actuator side) terminals.
Code No. | Terminals
45 | ⑥ - ①
41 | ⑥ - ②
55 | ⑥ - ③
Resistance: 0.8 - 1.5Ω
OK
Repair harness between actuator relay connector and control unit connector.
NG
Replace actuator.

NS4029400054000X

Fig. 120 Test 3: Actuator Solenoid Valve. 1994–96 300ZX

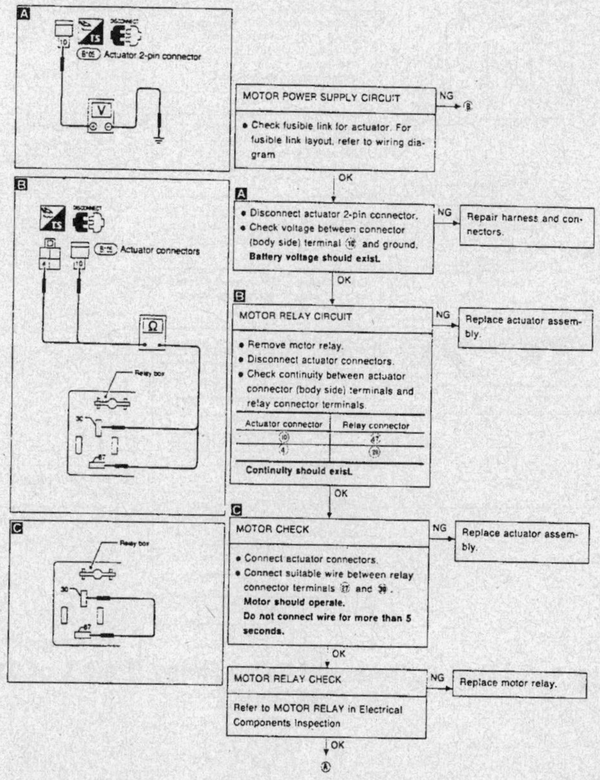
Actuator 2-pin connector
MOTOR POWER SUPPLY CIRCUIT
• Check fusible link for actuator. For fusible link layout, refer to wiring diagram
NG
OK
• Disconnect actuator 2-pin connector.
• Check voltage between connector (body side) terminal ⑩ and ground.
Battery voltage should exist.
NG
Repair harness and connectors.
OK
Actuator connectors
Relay box
MOTOR RELAY CIRCUIT
• Remove motor relay.
• Disconnect actuator connectors.
• Check continuity between actuator connector (body side) terminals and relay connector terminals.
Actuator connector | Relay connector
⑩ | 47
4 | 29
Continuity should exist.
NG
Replace actuator assembly.
OK
MOTOR CHECK
• Connect actuator connectors.
• Connect suitable wire between relay connector terminals ㉗ and ㉚.
Motor should operate.
Do not connect wire for more than 5 seconds.
NG
Replace actuator assembly.
OK
MOTOR RELAY CHECK
Refer to MOTOR RELAY in Electrical Components Inspection
NG
Replace motor relay.
OK

NS4029400056010X

Fig. 122 Test 5: Motor Relay Or Motor (Part 1 of 3). 1994–96 300ZX

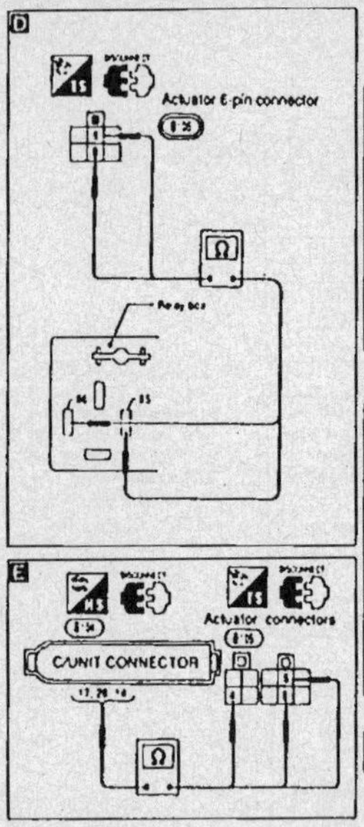
D
Actuator 6-pin connector
Relay box
E
C/UNIT CONNECTOR
Actuator connectors

Ⓐ

D MOTOR RELAY CIRCUIT
- Disconnect actuator 6-pin connector.
- Check continuity between actuator connector (actuator side) terminals and relay connector terminals.

Actuator connector	Relay connector
⑤	㉚
⑥	㉛

Continuity should exist.

NG → Replace actuator assembly.

OK ↓

E CIRCUIT CHECK
- Disconnect control unit connector.
- Check continuity between control unit connector terminals and actuator connector (body side) terminals.

Control unit	Actuator relay
⑰	⑤
㉙	⑤
⑭	⑥

Continuity should exist.

NG → Repair harness and connectors.

OK ↓

Replace control unit — NG → Repair harness and connectors.

NS4029400056020X

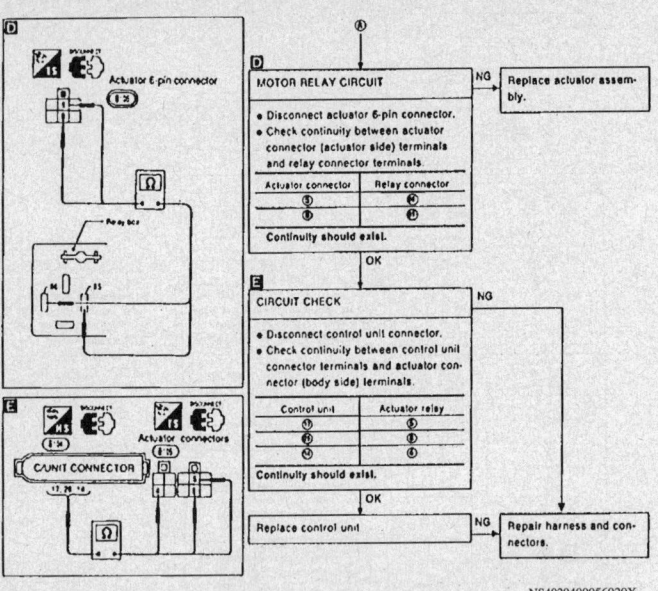

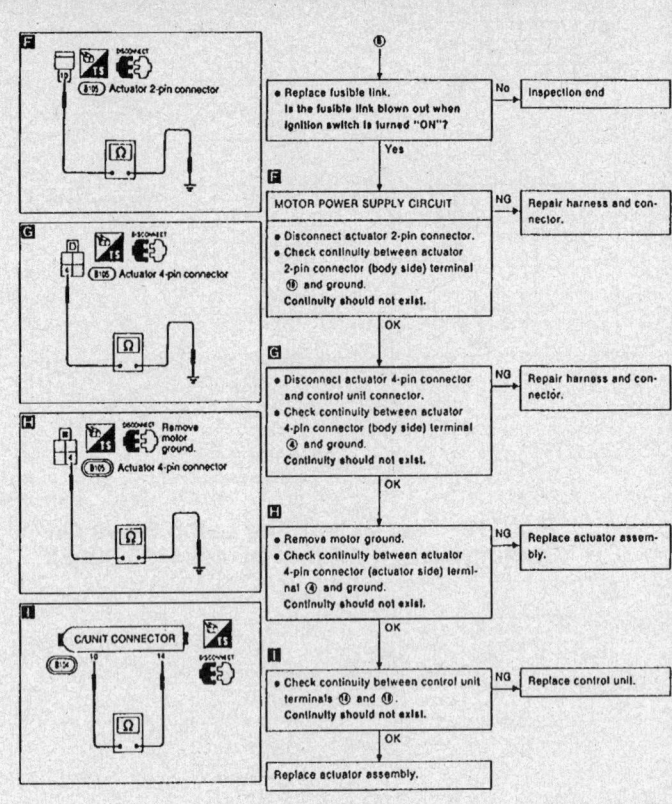

Fig. 122 Test 5: Motor Relay Or Motor (Part 2 of 3). 1994–96 300ZX

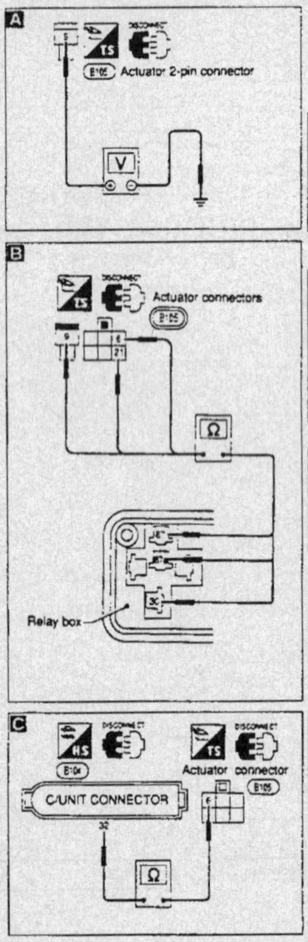
A
Actuator 2-pin connector
B
Actuator connectors
Relay box
C
C/UNIT CONNECTOR
Actuator connector

SOLENOID VALVE POWER SUPPLY CHECK
- Check 20A fuse for actuator. For fuse layout, refer to wiring diagram.

OK ↓

A SOLENOID VALVE POWER SUPPLY CHECK
- Disconnect connectors from actuator.
- Check voltage between actuator 2-pin connector (body side) terminal ⑨ and ground.

Battery voltage should exist.

NG → Repair harness and connector.

OK ↓

SOLENOID VALVE RELAY CHECK

Refer to SOLENOID VALVE RELAY in Electrical Components Inspection

NG → Replace solenoid valve relay.

OK ↓

B SOLENOID VALVE RELAY CIRCUIT CHECK

Check continuity between relay terminals and actuator connector (actuator side) terminals.

Relay terminals	Connector terminals
㊱	⑤
㊲	⑨
㊳	㉑

Continuity should exist.

NG → • Replace actuator.

OK ↓

C CIRCUIT CHECK
- Disconnect control unit connector.
- Check continuity between control unit connector terminal ㉜ and actuator connector (body side) terminal ⑧.

Continuity should exist.

NG → Repair harness and connectors.

OK ↓

Replace control unit.

NS4029400057010X

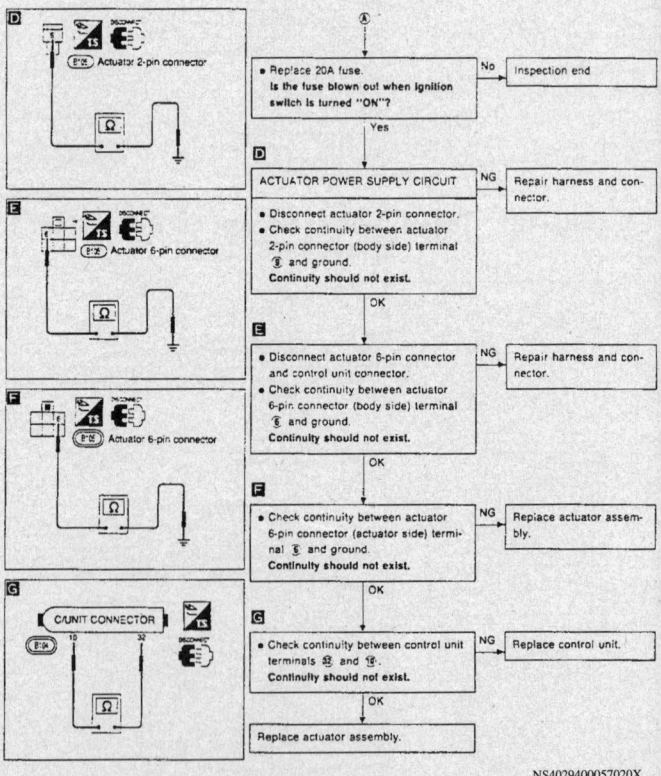

Fig. 123 Test 6: Solenoid Valve Relay (Part 1 of 2). 1994–96 300ZX

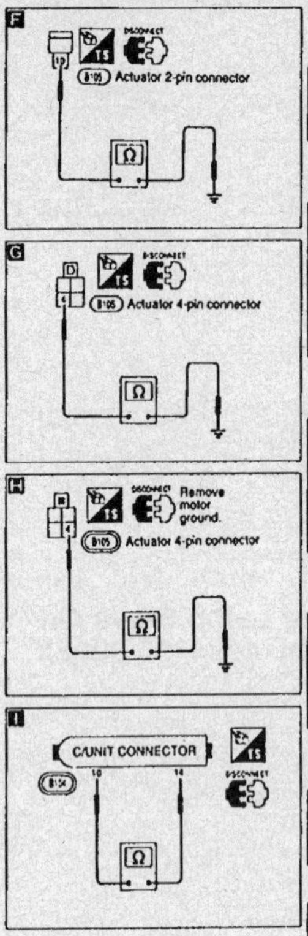
F
Actuator 2-pin connector
G
Actuator 4-pin connector
H
Remove motor ground.
Actuator 4-pin connector
I
C/UNIT CONNECTOR

Ⓑ

- Replace fusible link.

Is the fusible link blown out when ignition switch is turned "ON"?

No → Inspection end

Yes ↓

F MOTOR POWER SUPPLY CIRCUIT
- Disconnect actuator 2-pin connector.
- Check continuity between actuator 2-pin connector (body side) terminal ⑲ and ground.

Continuity should not exist.

NG → Repair harness and connector.

OK ↓

G
- Disconnect actuator 4-pin connector and control unit connector.
- Check continuity between actuator 4-pin connector (body side) terminal ④ and ground.

Continuity should not exist.

NG → Repair harness and connector.

OK ↓

H
- Remove motor ground.
- Check continuity between actuator 4-pin connector (actuator side) terminal ④ and ground.

Continuity should not exist.

NG → Replace actuator assembly.

OK ↓

I
- Check continuity between control unit terminals ⑭ and ⑩.

Continuity should not exist.

NG → Replace control unit.

OK ↓

Replace actuator assembly.

NS4029400056030X

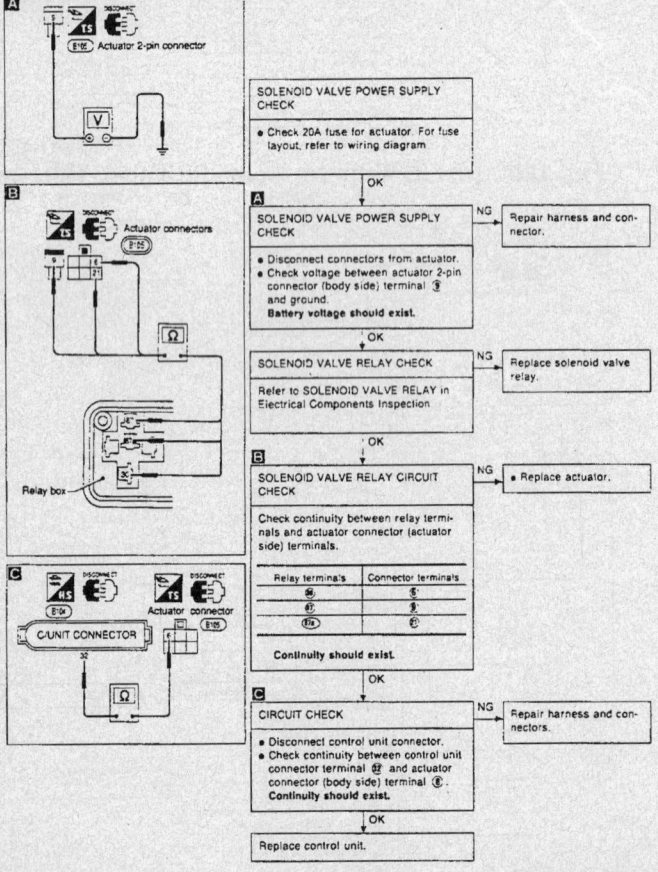

Fig. 122 Test 5: Motor Relay Or Motor (Part 3 of 3). 1994–96 300ZX

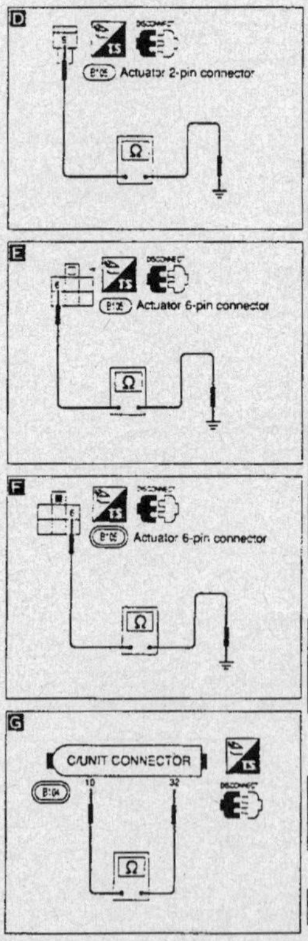
D
Actuator 2-pin connector
E
Actuator 6-pin connector
F
Actuator 6-pin connector
G
C/UNIT CONNECTOR

Ⓐ

- Replace 20A fuse.

Is the fuse blown out when ignition switch is turned "ON"?

No → Inspection end

Yes ↓

D ACTUATOR POWER SUPPLY CIRCUIT
- Disconnect actuator 2-pin connector.
- Check continuity between actuator 2-pin connector (body side) terminal ⑨ and ground.

Continuity should not exist.

NG → Repair harness and connector.

OK ↓

E
- Disconnect actuator 6-pin connector and control unit connector.
- Check continuity between actuator 6-pin connector (body side) terminal ⑧ and ground.

Continuity should not exist.

NG → Repair harness and connector.

OK ↓

F
- Check continuity between actuator 6-pin connector (actuator side) terminal ⑤ and ground.

Continuity should not exist.

NG → Replace actuator assembly.

OK ↓

G
- Check continuity between control unit terminals ㉜ and ⑩.

Continuity should not exist.

NG → Replace control unit.

OK ↓

Replace actuator assembly.

NS4029400057020X

Fig. 123 Test 6: Solenoid Valve Relay (Part 2 of 2). 1994–96 300ZX

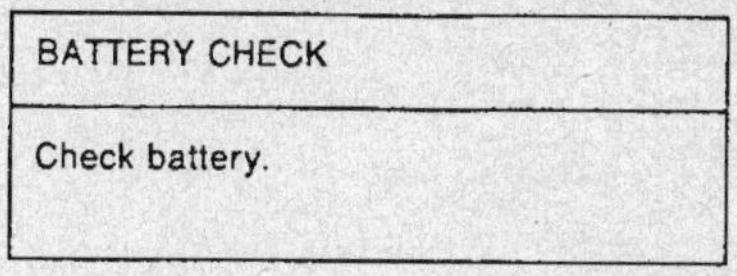
BATTERY CHECK
Check battery.

NS4029400058000X

Fig. 124 Test 7: Power Supply Low Voltage. 1994–96 300ZX

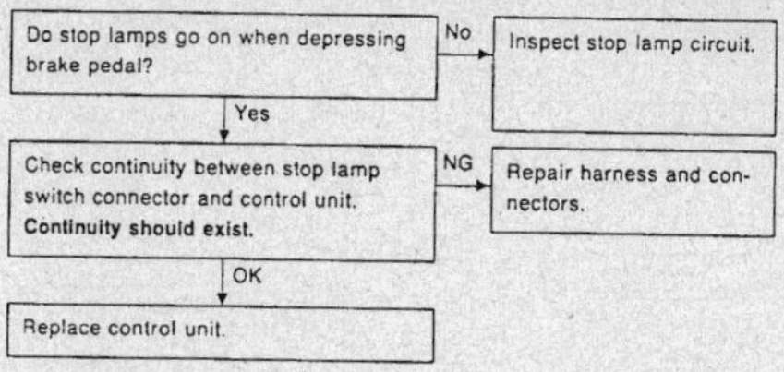
Do stop lamps go on when depressing brake pedal?
No
Inspect stop lamp circuit.
Yes
Check continuity between stop lamp switch connector and control unit. Continuity should exist.
NG
Repair harness and connectors.
OK
Replace control unit.

NS4029400059000X

Fig. 125 Test 8: Stop Lamp Switch Circuit. 1994–96 300ZX

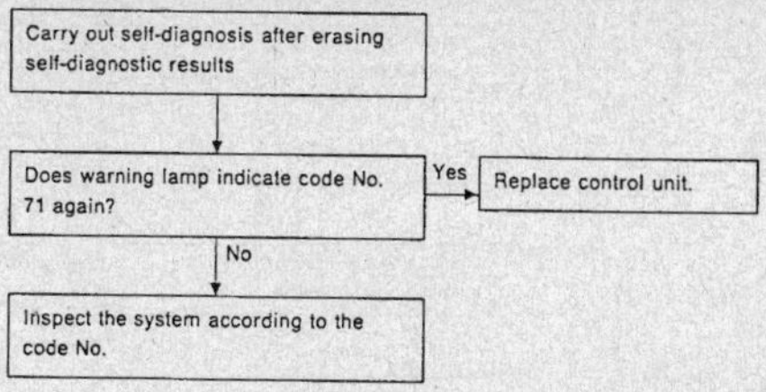
Carry out self-diagnosis after erasing self-diagnostic results
Does warning lamp indicate code No. 71 again?
Yes
Replace control unit.
No
Inspect the system according to the code No.

NS4029400060000X

Fig. 126 Test 9: Control Unit. 1994–96 300ZX

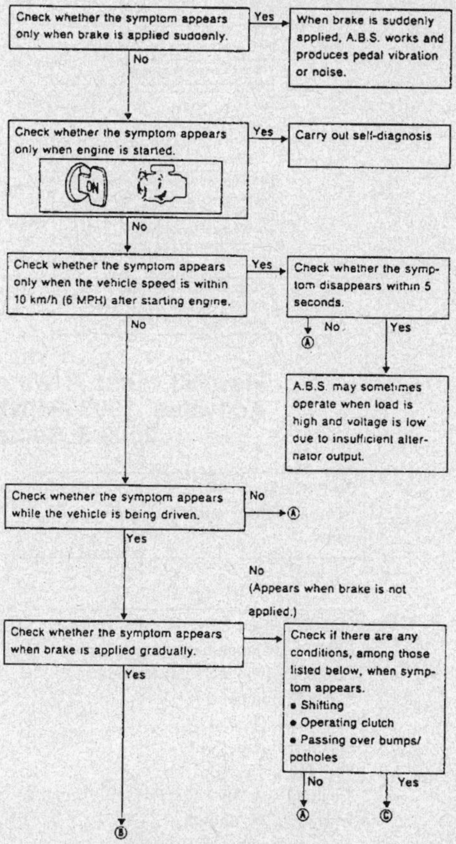
Check whether the symptom appears only when brake is applied suddenly.
Yes
When brake is suddenly applied, A.B.S. works and produces pedal vibration or noise.
No
Check whether the symptom appears only when engine is started.
Yes
Carry out self-diagnosis
ON
No
Check whether the symptom appears only when the vehicle speed is within 10 km/h (6 MPH) after starting engine.
Yes
Check whether the symptom disappears within 5 seconds.
No
Ⓐ
Yes
A.B.S. may sometimes operate when load is high and voltage is low due to insufficient alternator output.
No
Check whether the symptom appears while the vehicle is being driven.
No
Ⓐ
Yes
No (Appears when brake is not applied.)
Check whether the symptom appears when brake is applied gradually.
Check if there are any conditions, among those listed below, when symptom appears.
• Shifting
• Operating clutch
• Passing over bumps/potholes
No
Ⓐ
Yes
Ⓒ
Yes
Ⓑ

NS4029100061010X

Fig. 127 Test 1: Pedal Vibration & Noise (Part 1 of 2). 1993–94 NX 1600, NX 2000 & Sentra

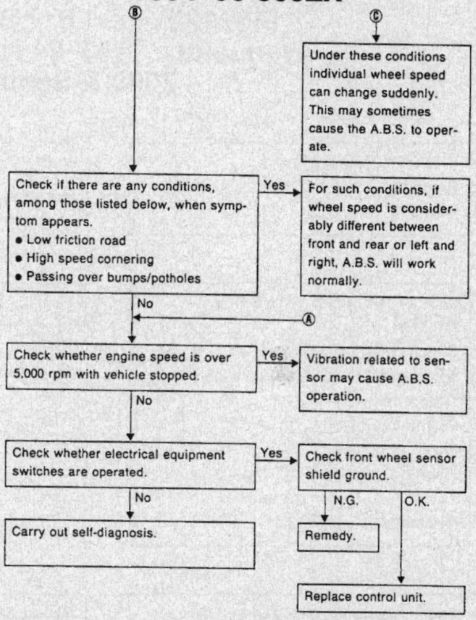
Ⓑ
Ⓒ
Under these conditions individual wheel speed can change suddenly. This may sometimes cause the A.B.S. to operate.
Check if there are any conditions, among those listed below, when symptom appears.
• Low friction road
• High speed cornering
• Passing over bumps/potholes
Yes
For such conditions, if wheel speed is considerably different between front and rear or left and right, A.B.S. will work normally.
No
Ⓐ
Check whether engine speed is over 5,000 rpm with vehicle stopped.
Yes
Vibration related to sensor may cause A.B.S. operation.
No
Check whether electrical equipment switches are operated.
Yes
Check front wheel sensor shield ground.
N.G.
O.K.
Remedy.
No
Carry out self-diagnosis.
Replace control unit.

NS4029100061020X

Fig. 127 Test 1: Pedal Vibration & Noise (Part 2 of 2). 1993–94 NX 1600, NX 2000 & Sentra

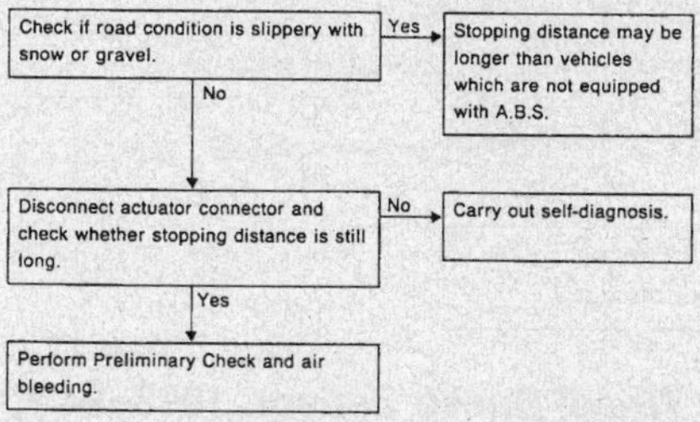
Check if road condition is slippery with snow or gravel.
Yes
Stopping distance may be longer than vehicles which are not equipped with A.B.S.
No
Disconnect actuator connector and check whether stopping distance is still long.
No
Carry out self-diagnosis.
Yes
Perform Preliminary Check and air bleeding.

NS4029100062000X

Fig. 128 Test 2: Long Stopping Distance. 1993–94 NX 1600, NX 2000 & Sentra

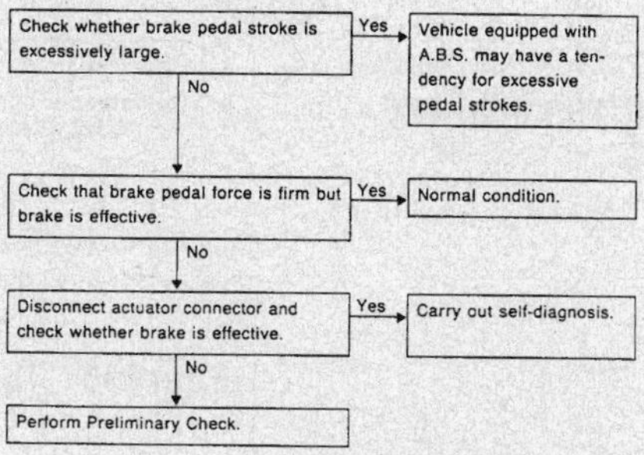
Check whether brake pedal stroke is excessively large.
Yes
Vehicle equipped with A.B.S. may have a tendency for excessive pedal strokes.
No
Check that brake pedal force is firm but brake is effective.
Yes
Normal condition.
No
Disconnect actuator connector and check whether brake is effective.
Yes
Carry out self-diagnosis.
No
Perform Preliminary Check.

NS4029100063000X

Fig. 129 Test 3: Unexpected Pedal Action. 1993–94 NX 1600, NX 2000 & Sentra

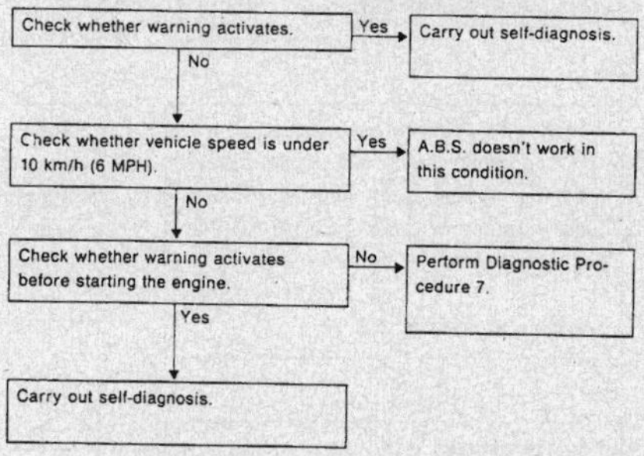
Check whether warning activates.
Yes
Carry out self-diagnosis.
No
Check whether vehicle speed is under 10 km/h (6 MPH).
Yes
A.B.S. doesn't work in this condition.
No
Check whether warning activates before starting the engine.
No
Perform Diagnostic Procedure 7.
Yes
Carry out self-diagnosis.

NS4029100064000X

Fig. 130 Test 4: ABS Doesn't Work. 1993–94 NX 1600, NX 2000 & Sentra

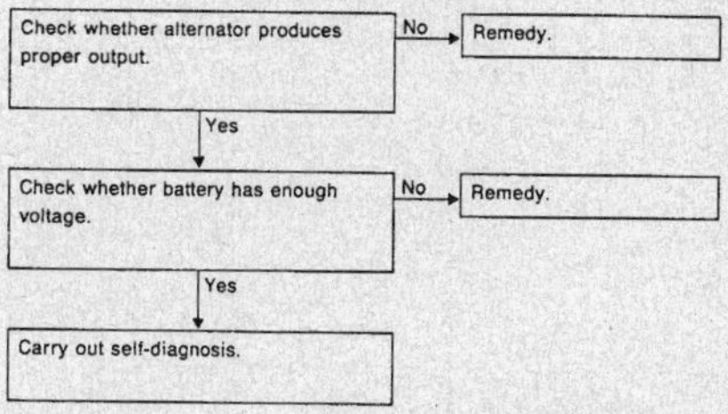
Check whether alternator produces proper output.
No
Remedy.
Yes
Check whether battery has enough voltage.
No
Remedy.
Yes
Carry out self-diagnosis.

NS4029100065000X

Fig. 131 Test 5: ABS Works But Warning Activates. 1993–94 NX 1600, NX 2000 & Sentra

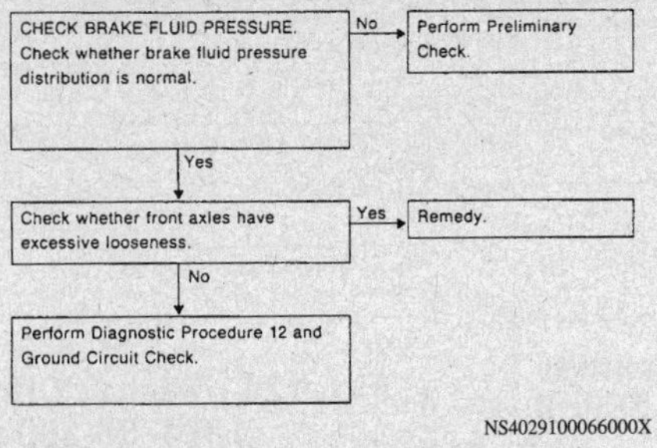

CHECK BRAKE FLUID PRESSURE.
Check whether brake fluid pressure distribution is normal.
No
Perform Preliminary Check.
Yes
Check whether front axles have excessive looseness.
Yes
Remedy.
No
Perform Diagnostic Procedure 12 and Ground Circuit Check.
NS4029100066000X

Fig. 132 Test 6: ABS Works Frequently. 1993–94 NX 1600, NX 2000 & Sentra

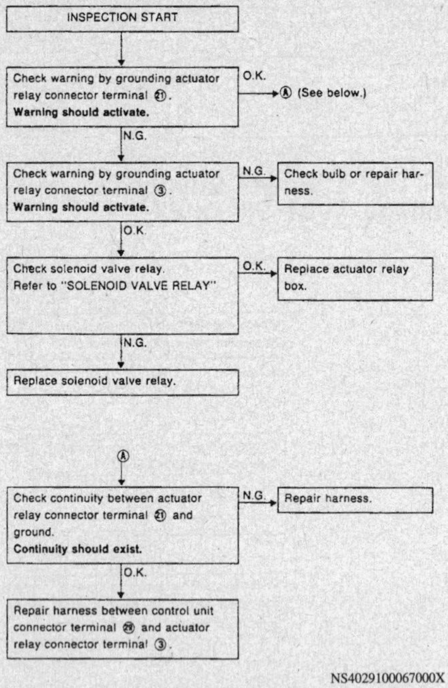

INSPECTION START
Check warning by grounding actuator relay connector terminal (21). Warning should activate.
O.K.
(A) (See below.)
N.G.
Check warning by grounding actuator relay connector terminal (3). Warning should activate.
N.G.
Check bulb or repair harness.
O.K.
Check solenoid valve relay. Refer to "SOLENOID VALVE RELAY"
O.K.
Replace actuator relay box.
N.G.
Replace solenoid valve relay.
(A)
Check continuity between actuator relay connector terminal (21) and ground. Continuity should exist.
N.G.
Repair harness.
O.K.
Repair harness between control unit connector terminal (28) and actuator relay connector terminal (3).
NS4029100067000X

Fig. 133 Test 7: Warning Never Activates. 1993–94 NX 1600, NX 2000 & Sentra

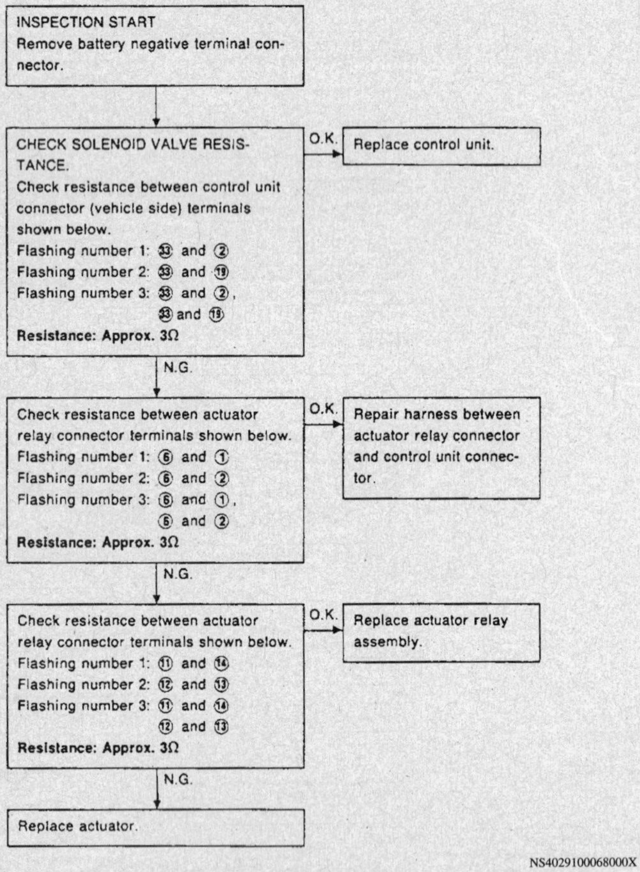

INSPECTION START
Remove battery negative terminal connector.
CHECK SOLENOID VALVE RESISTANCE.
Check resistance between control unit connector (vehicle side) terminals shown below.
Flashing number 1: (33) and (2)
Flashing number 2: (33) and (19)
Flashing number 3: (33) and (2), (33) and (19)
Resistance: Approx. 3Ω
O.K.
Replace control unit.
N.G.
Check resistance between actuator relay connector terminals shown below.
Flashing number 1: (6) and (1)
Flashing number 2: (6) and (2)
Flashing number 3: (6) and (1), (6) and (2)
Resistance: Approx. 3Ω
O.K.
Repair harness between actuator relay connector and control unit connector.
N.G.
Check resistance between actuator relay connector terminals shown below.
Flashing number 1: (11) and (14)
Flashing number 2: (12) and (13)
Flashing number 3: (11) and (14), (12) and (13)
Resistance: Approx. 3Ω
O.K.
Replace actuator relay assembly.
N.G.
Replace actuator.
NS4029100068000X

Fig. 134 Test 8: Actuator Solenoid. 1993–94 NX 1600, NX 2000 & Sentra

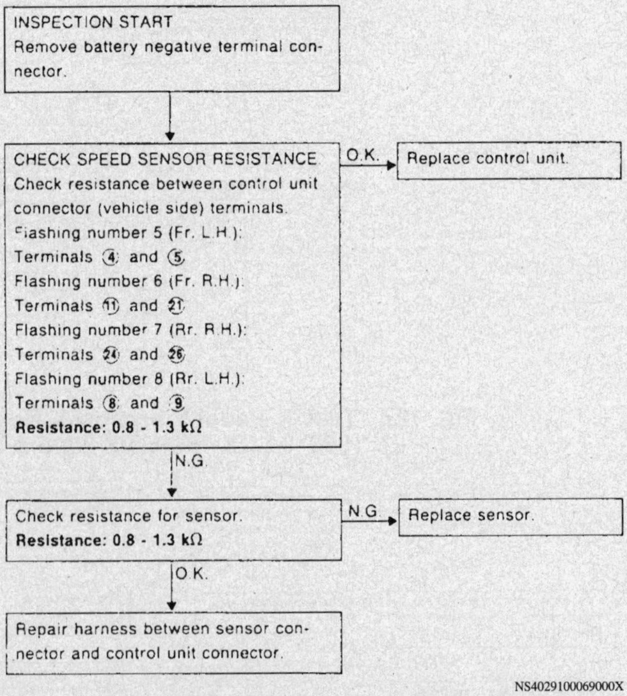

INSPECTION START
Remove battery negative terminal connector.
CHECK SPEED SENSOR RESISTANCE.
Check resistance between control unit connector (vehicle side) terminals.
Flashing number 5 (Fr. L.H.):
Terminals (4) and (5)
Flashing number 6 (Fr. R.H.):
Terminals (11) and (21)
Flashing number 7 (Rr. R.H.):
Terminals (24) and (26)
Flashing number 8 (Rr. L.H.):
Terminals (8) and (9)
Resistance: 0.8 - 1.3 kΩ
O.K.
Replace control unit.
N.G.
Check resistance for sensor.
Resistance: 0.8 - 1.3 kΩ
N.G.
Replace sensor.
O.K.
Repair harness between sensor connector and control unit connector.
NS4029100069000X

Fig. 135 Test 9: Wheel Speed Sensor. 1993–94 NX 1600, NX 2000 & Sentra

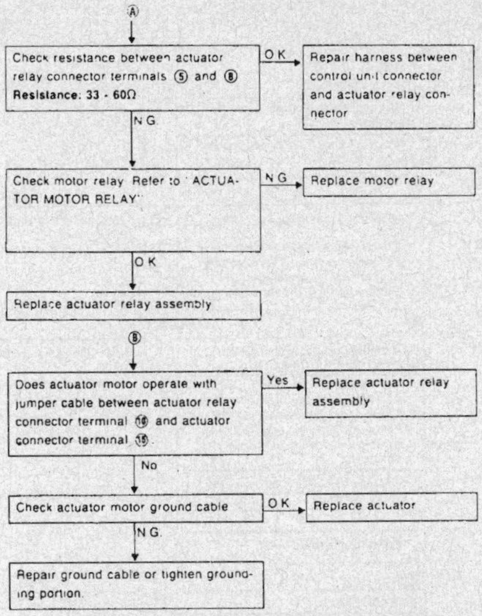
Ⓐ
Check resistance between actuator relay connector terminals ⑤ and ⑧
Resistance: 33 - 60Ω
O.K.
Repair harness between control unit connector and actuator relay connector
N.G.
Check motor relay. Refer to "ACTUATOR MOTOR RELAY".
N.G.
Replace motor relay
O.K.
Replace actuator relay assembly
Ⓑ
Does actuator motor operate with jumper cable between actuator relay connector terminal ⑩ and actuator connector terminal ⑮.
Yes
Replace actuator relay assembly
No
Check actuator motor ground cable
O.K.
Replace actuator
N.G.
Repair ground cable or tighten grounding portion.

NS4029100070010X

Fig. 136 Test 10: Actuator Motor Relay (Part 1 of 2). 1993–94 NX 1600, NX 2000 & Sentra

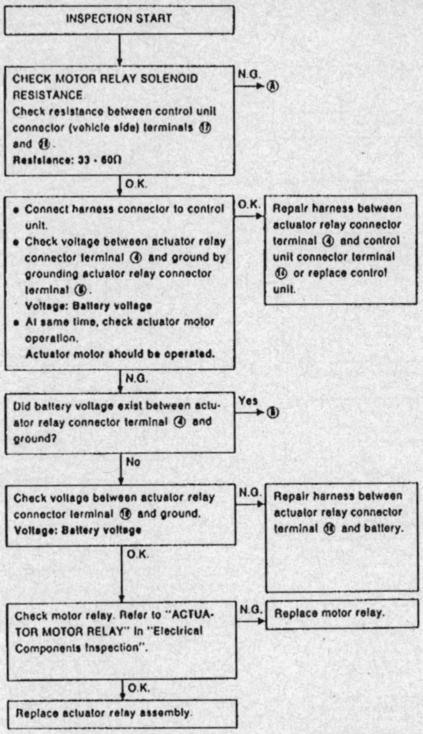
INSPECTION START
CHECK MOTOR RELAY SOLENOID RESISTANCE.
Check resistance between control unit connector (vehicle side) terminals ⑰ and ⑪.
Resistance: 33 - 60Ω
N.G.
Ⓐ
O.K.
• Connect harness connector to control unit.
• Check voltage between actuator relay connector terminal ④ and ground by grounding actuator relay connector terminal ⑧.
Voltage: Battery voltage
• At same time, check actuator motor operation.
Actuator motor should be operated.
O.K.
Repair harness between actuator relay connector terminal ④ and control unit connector terminal ⑭ or replace control unit.
N.G.
Did battery voltage exist between actuator relay connector terminal ④ and ground?
Yes
Ⓑ
No
Check voltage between actuator relay connector terminal ⑱ and ground.
Voltage: Battery voltage
N.G.
Repair harness between actuator relay connector terminal ⑱ and battery.
O.K.
Check motor relay. Refer to "ACTUATOR MOTOR RELAY" in "Electrical Components Inspection".
N.G.
Replace motor relay.
O.K.
Replace actuator relay assembly.

NS4029100070020X

Fig. 136 Test 10: Actuator Motor Relay (Part 2 of 2). 1993–94 NX 1600, NX 2000 & Sentra

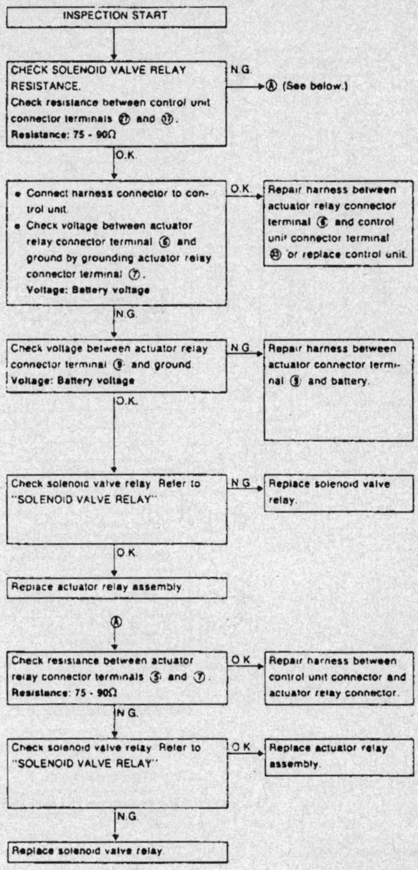
INSPECTION START
CHECK SOLENOID VALVE RELAY RESISTANCE.
Check resistance between control unit connector terminals ⑰ and ⑰.
Resistance: 75 - 90Ω
N.G.
Ⓐ (See below.)
O.K.
• Connect harness connector to control unit.
• Check voltage between actuator relay connector terminal ⑥ and ground by grounding actuator relay connector terminal ⑦.
Voltage: Battery voltage
O.K.
Repair harness between actuator relay connector terminal ⑥ and control unit connector terminal ⑮ or replace control unit.
N.G.
Check voltage between actuator relay connector terminal ⑨ and ground.
Voltage: Battery voltage
N.G.
Repair harness between actuator connector terminal ⑨ and battery.
O.K.
Check solenoid valve relay. Refer to "SOLENOID VALVE RELAY".
N.G.
Replace solenoid valve relay.
O.K.
Replace actuator relay assembly.
Ⓐ
Check resistance between actuator relay connector terminals ③ and ⑦.
Resistance: 75 - 90Ω
O.K.
Repair harness between control unit connector and actuator relay connector.
N.G.
Check solenoid valve relay. Refer to "SOLENOID VALVE RELAY".
O.K.
Replace actuator relay assembly.
N.G.
Replace solenoid valve relay.

NS4029100071000X

Fig. 137 Test 11: Actuator Solenoid Valve Relay. 1993–94 NX 1600, NX 2000 & Sentra

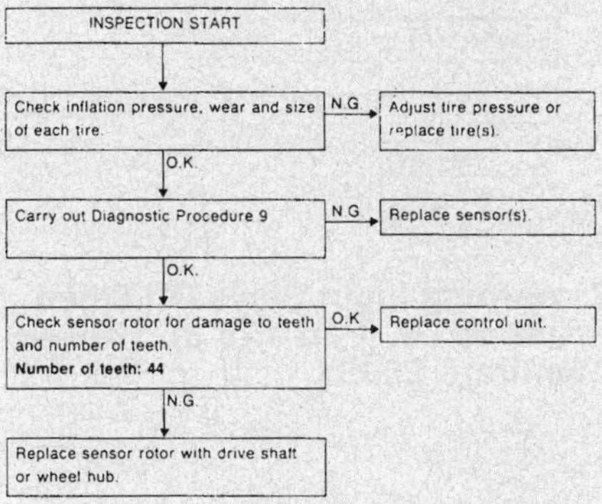
INSPECTION START
Check inflation pressure, wear and size of each tire.
N.G.
Adjust tire pressure or replace tire(s).
O.K.
Carry out Diagnostic Procedure 9
N.G.
Replace sensor(s).
O.K.
Check sensor rotor for damage to teeth and number of teeth.
Number of teeth: 44
O.K.
Replace control unit.
N.G.
Replace sensor rotor with drive shaft or wheel hub.

NS4029100072000X

Fig. 138 Test 12: Sensor & Sensor Rotor. 1993–94 NX 1600, NX 2000 & Sentra

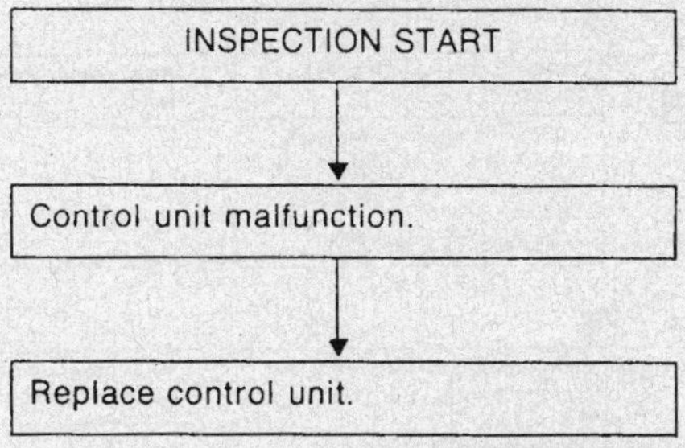
INSPECTION START
Control unit malfunction.
Replace control unit.

NS4029100073000X

Fig. 139 Test 13: Control Unit. 1993–94 NX 1600, NX 2000 & Sentra

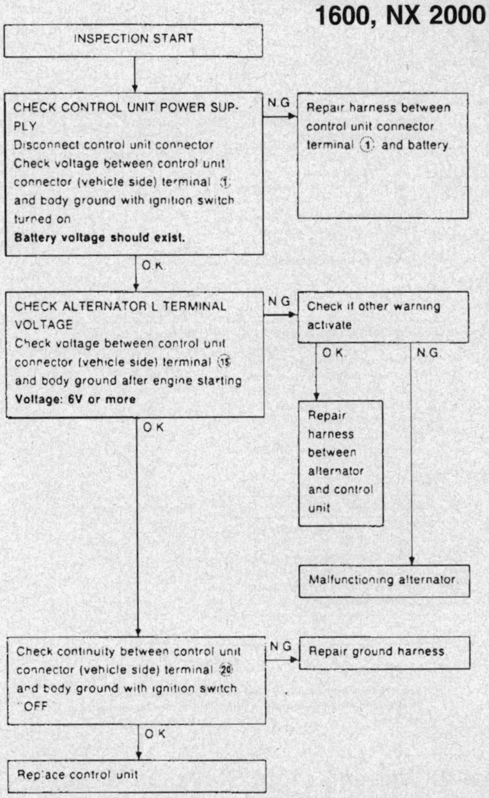
INSPECTION START
CHECK CONTROL UNIT POWER SUPPLY
Disconnect control unit connector
Check voltage between control unit connector (vehicle side) terminal ① and body ground with ignition switch turned on
Battery voltage should exist.
N.G.
Repair harness between control unit connector terminal ① and battery
O.K.
CHECK ALTERNATOR L TERMINAL VOLTAGE
Check voltage between control unit connector (vehicle side) terminal ⑮ and body ground after engine starting
Voltage: 6V or more
N.G.
Check if other warning activate
O.K.
Repair harness between alternator and control unit
N.G.
Malfunctioning alternator.
O.K.
Check continuity between control unit connector (vehicle side) terminal ⑳ and body ground with ignition switch "OFF"
N.G.
Repair ground harness.
O.K.
Replace control unit

NS4029100074000X

Fig. 140 Test 14: Control Unit Or Power Supply & Ground Circuit. 1993–94 NX 1600, NX 2000 & Sentra

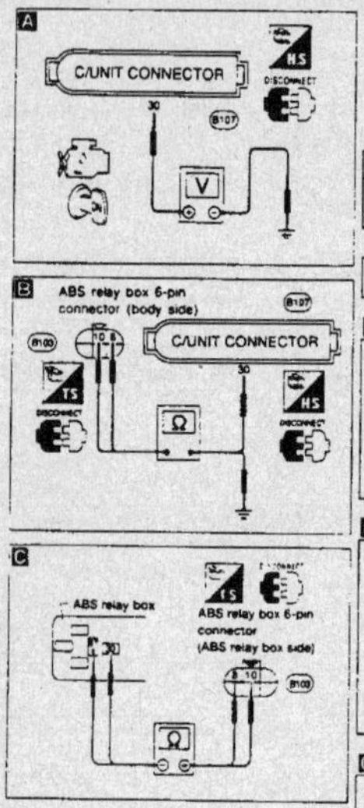
A
C/UNIT CONNECTOR
B107
B
ABS relay box 6-pin connector (body side)
C/UNIT CONNECTOR
C
ABS relay box
ABS relay box 6-pin connector (ABS relay box side)

WARNING LAMP CIRCUIT CHECK
Check 10A fuse for warning lamp. For fuse layout.
NG → Replace fuse

↓ OK

Check warning lamp bulb.
NG → Replace bulb.

↓ OK

A
1. Install 10A fuse and bulb.
2. Disconnect connectors from control unit and ABS relay box.
3. Check voltage between control unit connector terminal ㉚ and ground after turning ignition switch "ON".

Battery voltage should exist after turning ignition switch "ON".

NG → Repair harness and connectors.

↓ OK

B
Check continuity between ABS relay box 6-pin connector (body side) and control unit terminal.

ABS relay box	Control unit
⑩	㉚
⑧	Ground

Continuity should exist.

NG → Repair harness and connectors.

↓ OK

C
1. Remove solenoid valve relay.
2. Check continuity between ABS relay box 6-pin connector (ABS relay box side) and ABS relay box terminals.

ABS relay box connector	ABS relay box terminals
⑩ ⊕	㉚ ⊖
⑧	(87a)

Continuity should exist.
Note: Pay attention to tester polarity*.

NG → Replace ABS relay box.

↓ OK

SOLENOID VALVE RELAY CHECK
NG → Replace solenoid valve relay.

↓ OK

Go to diagnostic procedure 7.

***: Specifications may vary depending on the type of tester. Before performing this inspection, refer to the instruction manual of the tester.**

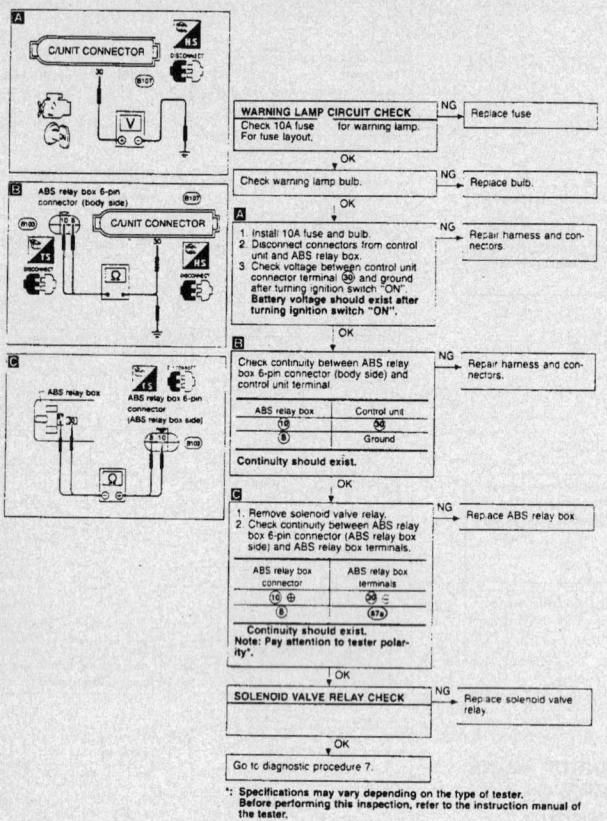

NS4029500161000X

Fig. 141 Test 1: Warning Lamp Does Not Come On When Ignition Switch Is Turned On. 1995–96 Sentra & 200SX

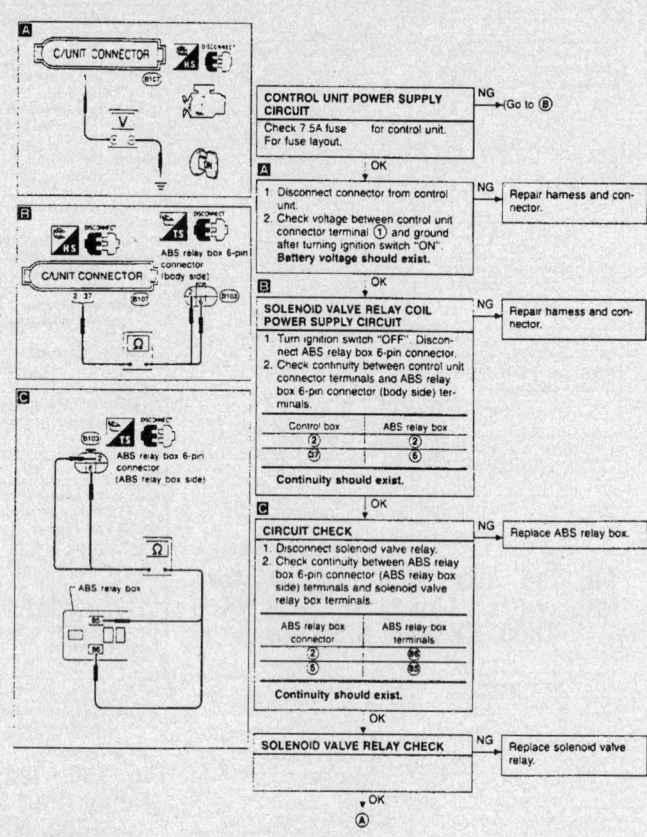

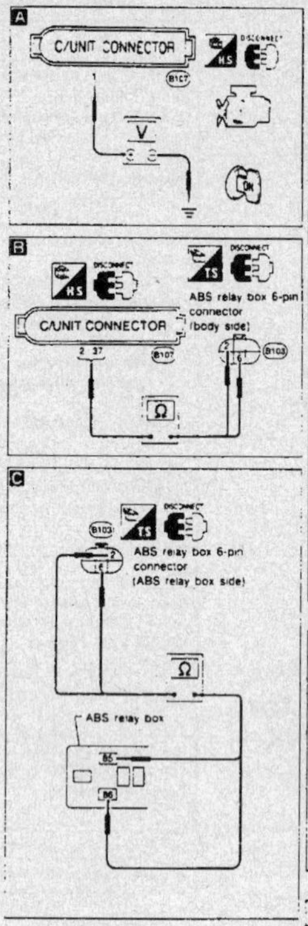
A
C/UNIT CONNECTOR
B
ABS relay box 6-pin connector (body side)
C/UNIT CONNECTOR
C
ABS relay box 6-pin connector (ABS relay box side)
ABS relay box

CONTROL UNIT POWER SUPPLY CIRCUIT
Check 7.5A fuse for control unit. For fuse layout.
NG → (Go to Ⓑ)

↓ OK

A
1. Disconnect connector from control unit.
2. Check voltage between control unit connector terminal ① and ground after turning ignition switch "ON".

Battery voltage should exist.

NG → Repair harness and connector.

↓ OK

B
SOLENOID VALVE RELAY COIL POWER SUPPLY CIRCUIT
1. Turn ignition switch "OFF". Disconnect ABS relay box 6-pin connector.
2. Check continuity between control unit connector terminals and ABS relay box 6-pin connector (body side) terminals.

Control box	ABS relay box
②	②
㊲	⑥

Continuity should exist.

NG → Repair harness and connector.

↓ OK

C
CIRCUIT CHECK
1. Disconnect solenoid valve relay.
2. Check continuity between ABS relay box 6-pin connector (ABS relay box side) terminals and solenoid valve relay box terminals.

ABS relay box connector	ABS relay box terminals
②	(86)
⑤	(85)

Continuity should exist.

NG → Replace ABS relay box.

↓ OK

SOLENOID VALVE RELAY CHECK
NG → Replace solenoid valve relay.

↓ OK

Ⓐ

NS4029500162010X

Fig. 142 Test 2: Warning Light Stays On When Ignition Switch Is Turned On (Part 1 of 3). 1995–96 Sentra & 200SX

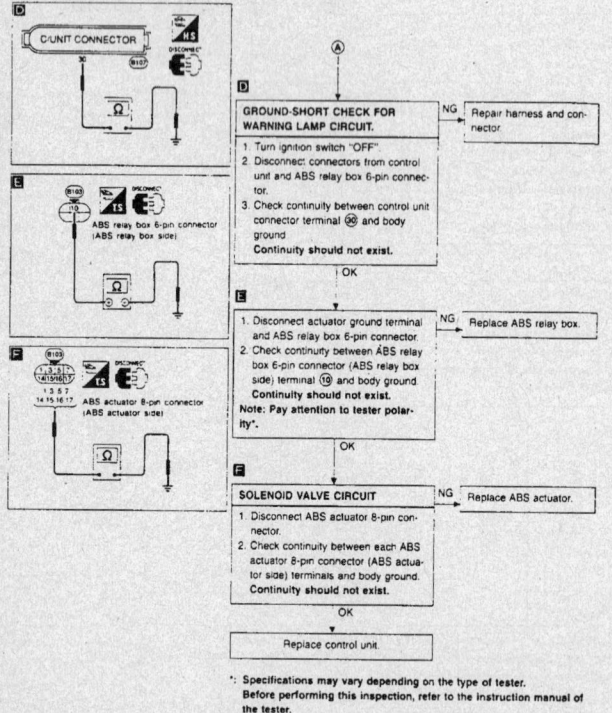

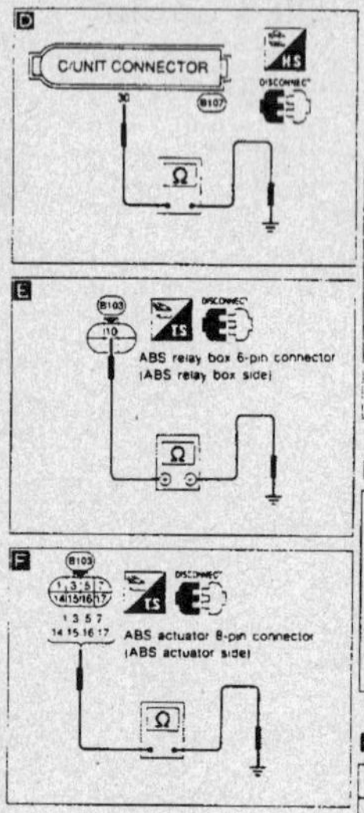
D
C/UNIT CONNECTOR
B107
E
ABS relay box 6-pin connector (ABS relay box side)
F
ABS actuator 8-pin connector (ABS actuator side)

Ⓐ

D
GROUND-SHORT CHECK FOR WARNING LAMP CIRCUIT.
1. Turn ignition switch "OFF".
2. Disconnect connectors from control unit and ABS relay box 6-pin connector.
3. Check continuity between control unit connector terminal ㉚ and body ground

Continuity should not exist.

NG → Repair harness and connector.

↓ OK

E
1. Disconnect actuator ground terminal and ABS relay box 6-pin connector.
2. Check continuity between ABS relay box 6-pin connector (ABS relay box side) terminal ⑩ and body ground

Continuity should not exist.
Note: Pay attention to tester polarity*.

NG → Replace ABS relay box.

↓ OK

F
SOLENOID VALVE CIRCUIT
1. Disconnect ABS actuator 8-pin connector.
2. Check continuity between each ABS actuator 8-pin connector (ABS actuator side) terminals and body ground.

Continuity should not exist.

NG → Replace ABS actuator.

↓ OK

Replace control unit.

***: Specifications may vary depending on the type of tester. Before performing this inspection, refer to the instruction manual of the tester.**

NS4029500162020X

Fig. 142 Test 2: Warning Light Stays On When Ignition Switch Is Turned On (Part 2 of 3). 1995–96 Sentra & 200SX

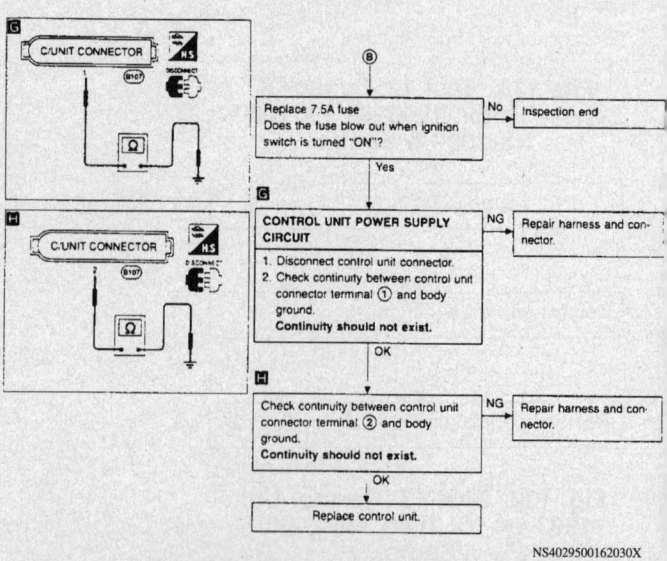

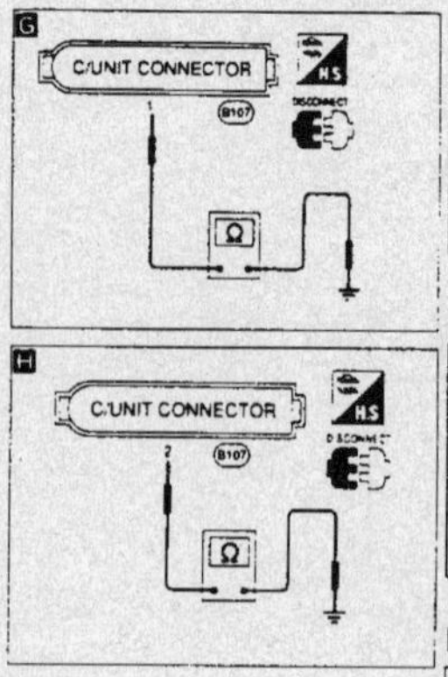
G
C/UNIT CONNECTOR
B107
H
C/UNIT CONNECTOR
B107

Ⓑ

Replace 7.5A fuse
Does the fuse blow out when ignition switch is turned "ON"?
No → Inspection end

↓ Yes

G
CONTROL UNIT POWER SUPPLY CIRCUIT
1. Disconnect control unit connector.
2. Check continuity between control unit connector terminal ① and body ground.

Continuity should not exist.

NG → Repair harness and connector.

↓ OK

H
Check continuity between control unit connector terminal ② and body ground.

Continuity should not exist.

NG → Repair harness and connector.

↓ OK

Replace control unit.

NS4029500162030X

Fig. 142 Test 2: Warning Light Stays On When Ignition Switch Is Turned On (Part 3 of 3). 1995–96 Sentra & 200SX

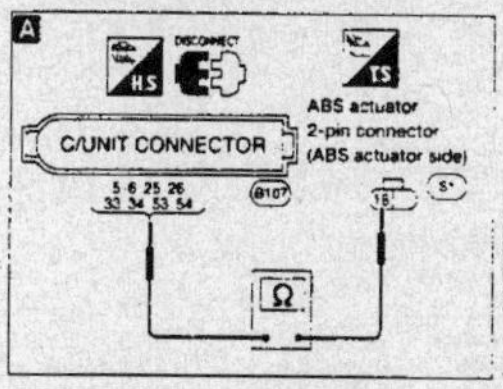
A
DISCONNECT
H.S
T.S
C/UNIT CONNECTOR
ABS actuator
2-pin connector
(ABS actuator side)
B107
18
S1

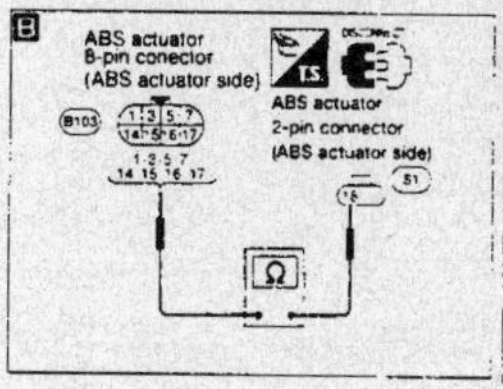
B
ABS actuator
8-pin conector
(ABS actuator side)
DISCONNECT
T.S
B103
ABS actuator
2-pin connector
(ABS actuator side)
18
S1

1. Disconnect connectors from control unit, ABS actuator and ABS relay box. Check terminals for damage or loose connections. Then reconnect connectors.
2. Carry out self-diagnosis again.
Does warning lamp activate again?

No → Inspection end

Yes ↓

A **ABS ACTUATOR SOLENOID VALVE CHECK** — OK → Ⓐ

1. Disconnect connectors from control unit and ABS relay box.
2. Check resistance between control unit connector terminals and ABS actuator 2-pin connector (ABS actuator side) terminal.

Code No	Control unit	ABS actuator	Resistance
41	26	18	4.4 - 6.0Ω
45	33	18	
51	34	18	
55	25	18	
42	54	18	8.5 - 11.0Ω
46	5	18	
52	6	18	
56	53	18	

NG ↓

B

1. Disconnect ABS actuator 8-pin connector.
2. Check resistance between ABS actuator 8-pin connector (ABS actuator side) terminals and ABS actuator 2-pin connector (ABS actuator side) terminal.

OK → Repair harness and connector between control unit connector terminal and ABS actuator 8-pin connector terminal.

Code No.	ABS actuator	ABS actuator	Resistance
41	15	18	4.4 - 6.0Ω
45	14	18	
51	17	18	
55	16	18	
42	3	18	8.5 - 11.0Ω
46	1	18	
52	7	18	
56	5	18	

NG ↓

Replace ABS actuator.

NS4029500163010X

Fig. 143 Test 3: ABS Actuator Solenoid Valve (Part 1 of 2). 1995–96 Sentra & 200SX

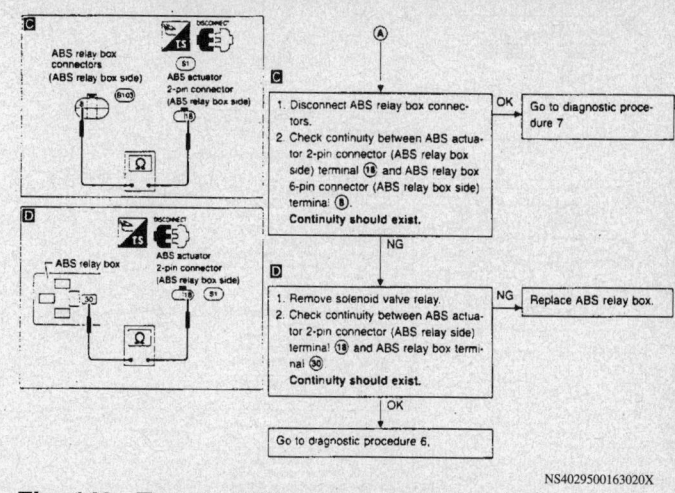

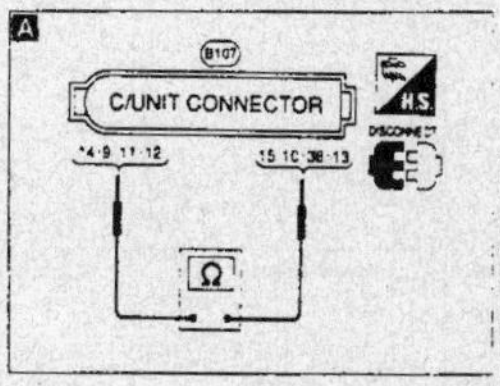
A
B107
C/UNIT CONNECTOR
H.S
DISCONNECT
14 9 11 12
15 10 38 13

1. Disconnect connectors from control unit and wheel sensor of malfunction code No. Check terminals for damage or loose connections. Then reconnect connectors.
2. Carry out self-diagnosis again.
Does warning lamp activate again?

No → Inspection end

Yes ↓

A **WHEEL SENSOR ELECTRICAL CHECK** — OK → Ⓐ

1. Disconnect control unit connector.
2. Check resistance between control unit connector terminals.
   Code No. 21 or 22 (Front RH wheel)
   Terminals ⑭ and ⑮
   Code No. 25 or 26 (Front LH wheel)
   Terminals ⑨ and ⑩
   Code No. 31 or 32 (Rear RH wheel)
   Terminals ⑪ and ㊳
   Code No. 35 or 36 (Rear LH wheel)
   Terminals ⑫ and ⑬
   Resistance: 0.8 - 1.2 kΩ

NG ↓

Note: **CHECK WHEEL SENSOR.** — NG → Note: Replace wheel sensor.

OK ↓

Note: Repair harness and connectors between control unit connector and wheel sensor connector.

Note: Wheel position should be distinguished by code No. except code No. 18 (sensor rotor).

NS4029500164010X

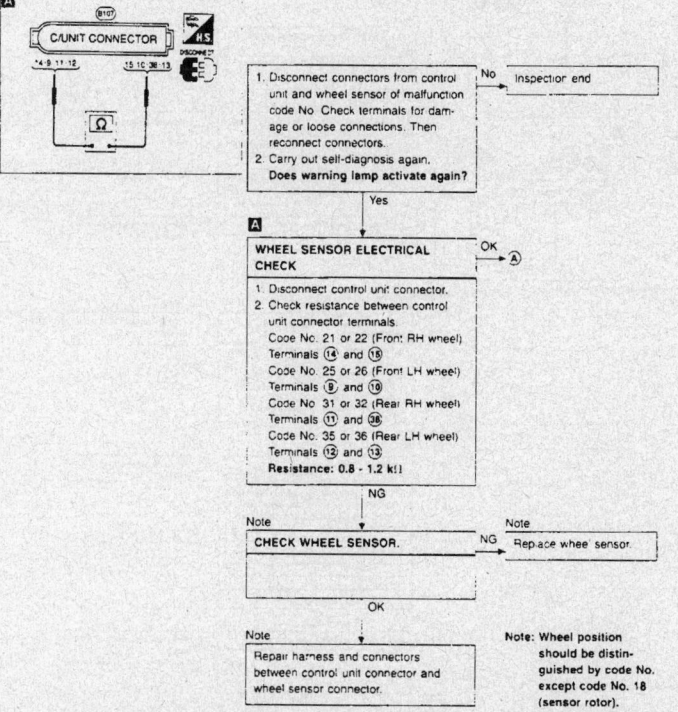

Fig. 144 Test 4: Wheel Sensor Or Rotor (Part 1 of 2). 1995–96 Sentra & 200SX

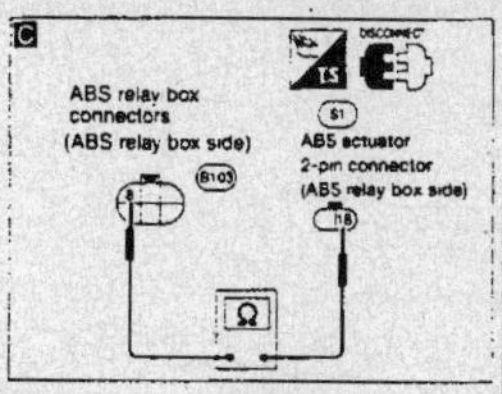
C
DISCONNECT
T.S
ABS relay box
connectors
(ABS relay box side)
B103
S1
ABS actuator
2-pin connector
(ABS relay box side)
18

Ⓐ ↓

C

1. Disconnect ABS relay box connectors.
2. Check continuity between ABS actuator 2-pin connector (ABS relay box side) terminal ⑱ and ABS relay box 6-pin connector (ABS relay box side) terminal ⑧.
Continuity should exist.

OK → Go to diagnostic procedure 7

NG ↓

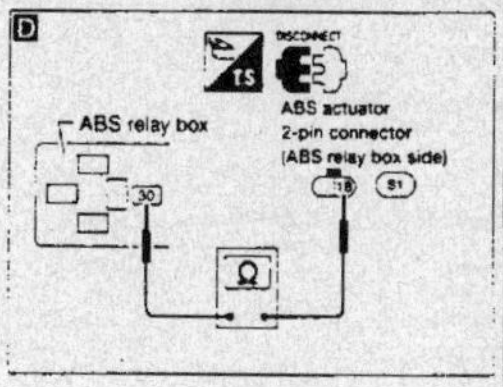
D
DISCONNECT
T.S
ABS relay box
30
ABS actuator
2-pin connector
(ABS relay box side)
18
S1

D

1. Remove solenoid valve relay.
2. Check continuity between ABS actuator 2-pin connector (ABS relay side) terminal ⑱ and ABS relay box terminal ㉚.
Continuity should exist.

NG → Replace ABS relay box.

OK ↓

Go to diagnostic procedure 6.

NS4029500163020X

Fig. 143 Test 3: ABS Actuator Solenoid Valve (Part 2 of 2). 1995–96 Sentra & 200SX

B

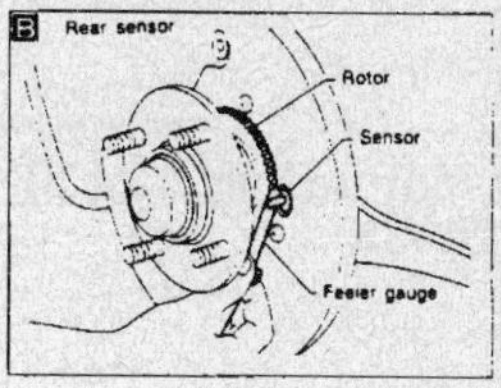
B
Rear sensor
Rotor
Sensor
Feeler gauge

Ⓐ ↓

Note: **WHEEL SENSOR MECHANICAL CHECK**

Check for inflation pressure, wear and size of each tire.

NG → Note: Adjust tire pressure or replace tire(s).

OK ↓

Note: Check wheel bearing axial end play.

OK ↓

B Note: Check clearance between sensor and rotor.
Clearance:
Front
0.1 - 1.1 mm
(0.004 - 0.043 in)
Rear
0.1 - 1.1 mm
(0.004 - 0.043 in)

NG → Note: Clean sensor fixing portion, or replace sensor.

OK ↓

Note: Check sensor rotor for teeth damage. — NG → Note: Replace sensor rotor.

OK ↓

Replace control unit.

Note: Wheel position should be distinguished by code No. except code No. 18 (sensor rotor).

NS4029500164020X

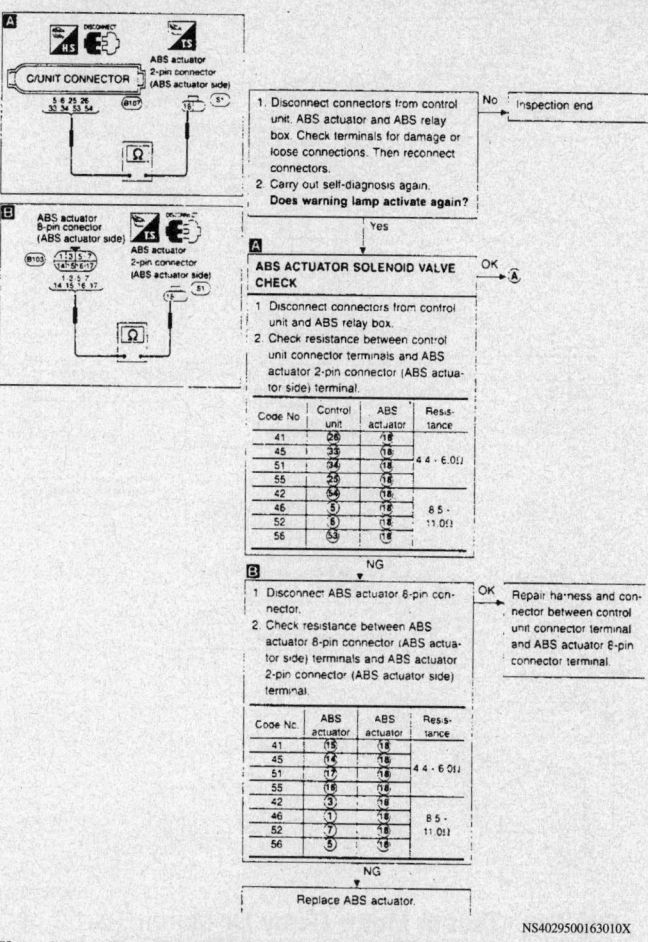

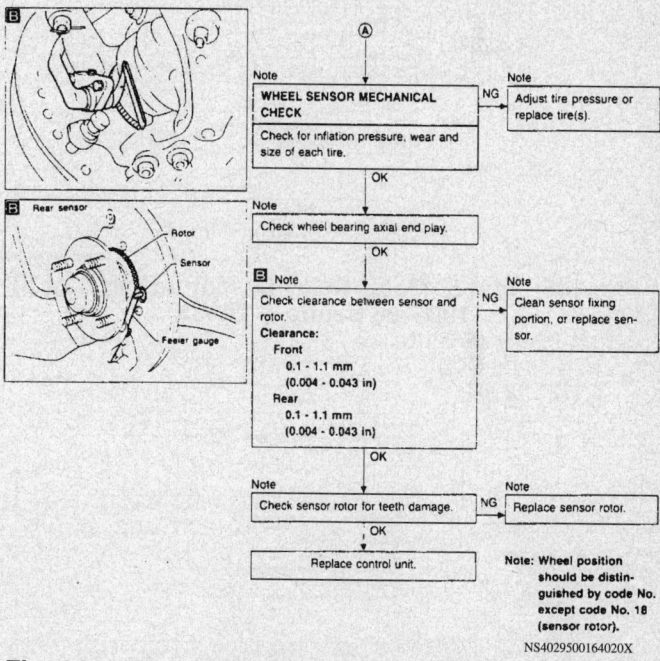

Fig. 144 Test 4: Wheel Sensor Or Rotor (Part 2 of 2). 1995–96 Sentra & 200SX

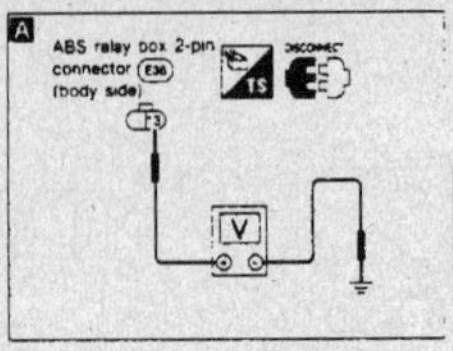
A
ABS relay box 2-pin connector (E36) (body side)
V

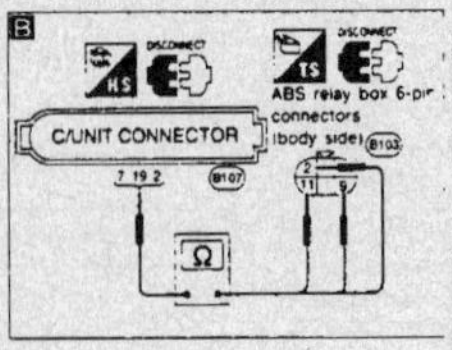
B
ABS relay box 6-pin connectors (body side) (B103)
C/UNIT CONNECTOR
(B107)

MOTOR POWER SUPPLY CIRCUIT — NG → (Go to Ⓑ)
Check fusible link [d] for ABS relay box. For fusible link layout.

↓ OK

1. Disconnect connectors from control unit and ABS actuator. Check terminals for damage or loose connections. Then reconnect connectors.
2. Carry out self-diagnosis again.

Does warning lamp activate again? — No → Inspection end

↓ Yes

A
1. Disconnect ABS relay box 2-pin connector.
2. Check voltage between connector (body side) terminal ⑬ and ground.

Battery voltage should exist. — NG → Repair harness and connectors

↓ OK

B
CIRCUIT CHECK — NG → Repair harness and connectors.
1. Disconnect ABS relay box 6-pin connector and control unit connector.
2. Check continuity between control unit connector terminals and ABS relay box 6-pin connector (body side) terminals.

Control unit	ABS relay box
⑦	⑪
⑲	⑨
②	②

Continuity should exist.

↓ OK

MOTOR RELAY CHECK — NG → Replace motor relay.

↓ OK

MOTOR GROUND CHECK — NG → Repair harness and terminals.

↓ OK

Ⓐ

NS4029500165010X

Fig. 145 Test 5: Motor Relay Or Motor (Part 1 of 3). 1995–96 Sentra & 200SX

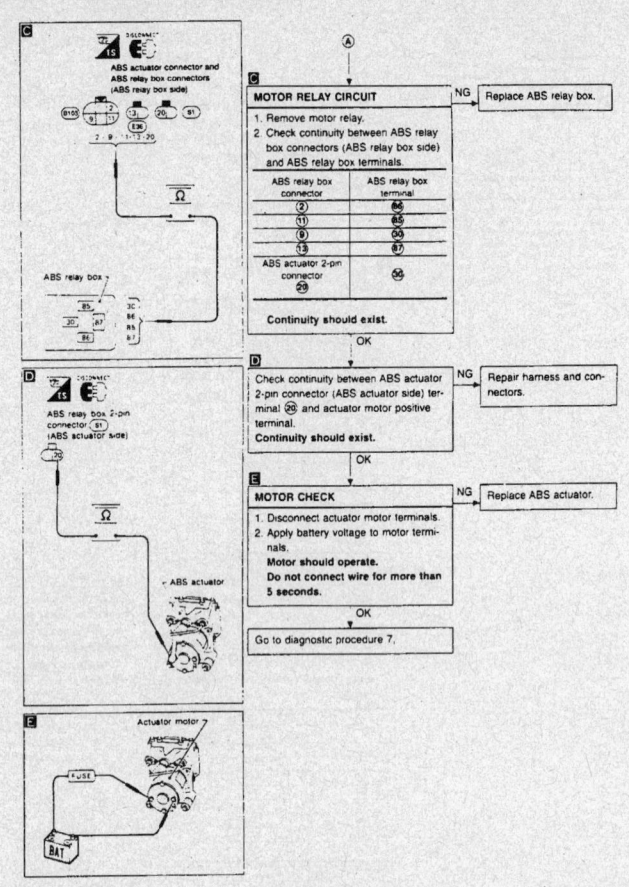

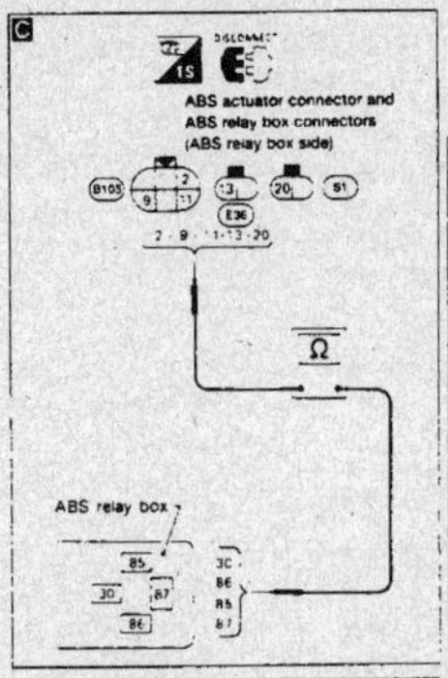
C
ABS actuator connector and ABS relay box connectors (ABS relay box side)
Ω
ABS relay box

Ⓐ

C
MOTOR RELAY CIRCUIT — NG → Replace ABS relay box.
1. Remove motor relay.
2. Check continuity between ABS relay box connectors (ABS relay box side) and ABS relay box terminals.

ABS relay box connector	ABS relay box terminal
②	86
⑪	85
⑨	30
⑬	87
ABS actuator 2-pin connector ⑳	30

Continuity should exist.

↓ OK

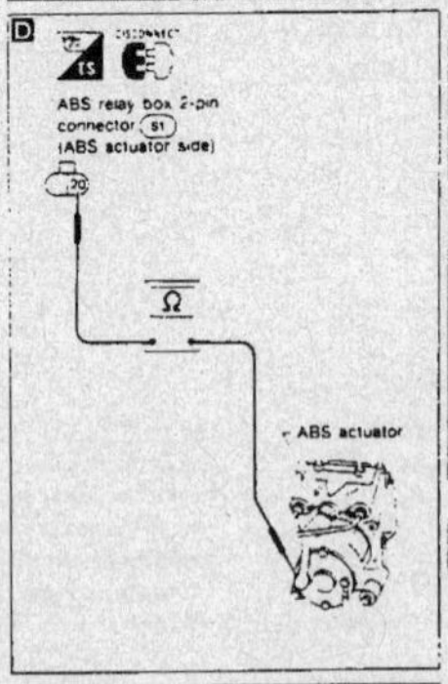
D
ABS relay box 2-pin connector (S1) (ABS actuator side)
Ω
ABS actuator

D
Check continuity between ABS actuator 2-pin connector (ABS actuator side) terminal ⑳ and actuator motor positive terminal.
Continuity should exist. — NG → Repair harness and connectors.

↓ OK

E
MOTOR CHECK — NG → Replace ABS actuator.
1. Disconnect actuator motor terminals.
2. Apply battery voltage to motor terminals.

Motor should operate.
Do not connect wire for more than 5 seconds.

↓ OK

Go to diagnostic procedure 7.

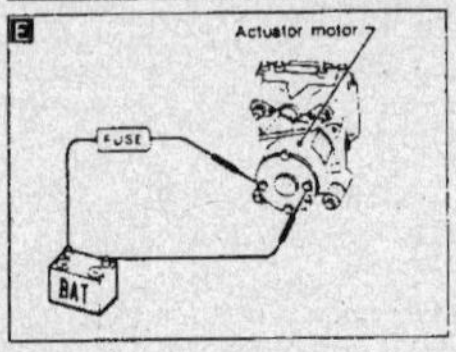
E
Actuator motor
FUSE
BAT

NS4029500165020X

Fig. 145 Test 5: Motor Relay Or Motor (Part 2 of 3). 1995–96 Sentra & 200SX

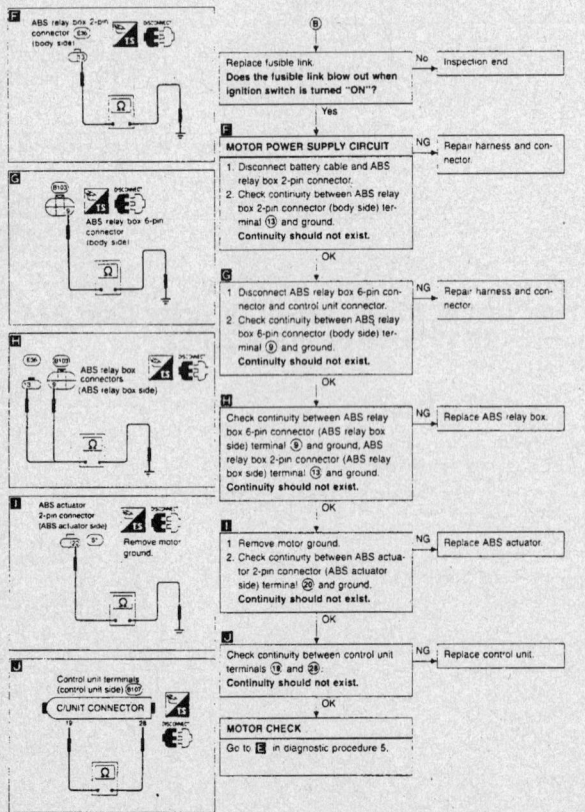

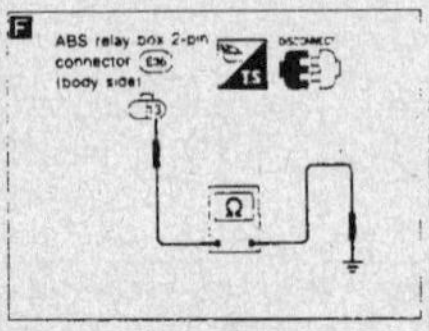
F
ABS relay box 2-pin connector (E36) (body side)
Ω

Ⓑ

Replace fusible link.
Does the fusible link blow out when ignition switch is turned "ON"? — No → Inspection end

↓ Yes

F
MOTOR POWER SUPPLY CIRCUIT — NG → Repair harness and connector.
1. Disconnect battery cable and ABS relay box 2-pin connector.
2. Check continuity between ABS relay box 2-pin connector (body side) terminal ⑬ and ground.

Continuity should not exist.

↓ OK

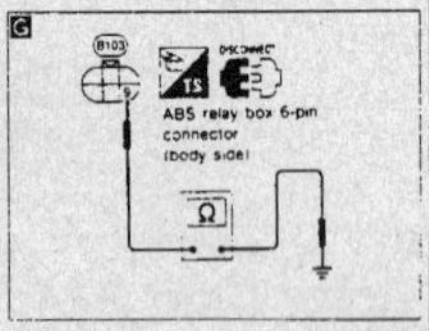
G
(B103)
ABS relay box 6-pin connector (body side)
Ω

G
1. Disconnect ABS relay box 6-pin connector and control unit connector.
2. Check continuity between ABS relay box 6-pin connector (body side) terminal ⑨ and ground.

Continuity should not exist. — NG → Repair harness and connector.

↓ OK

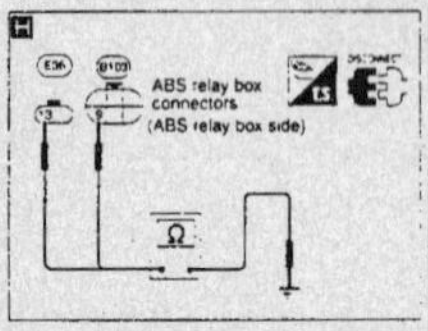
H
(E36) (B103)
ABS relay box connectors (ABS relay box side)
Ω

H
Check continuity between ABS relay box 6-pin connector (ABS relay box side) terminal ⑨ and ground, ABS relay box 2-pin connector (ABS relay box side) terminal ⑬ and ground.
Continuity should not exist. — NG → Replace ABS relay box.

↓ OK

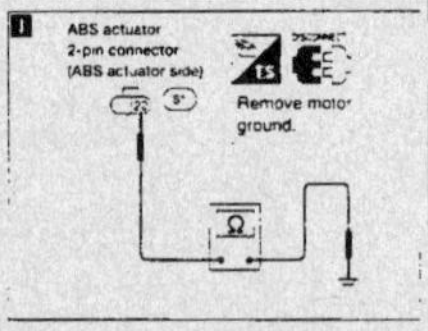
I
ABS actuator 2-pin connector (ABS actuator side)
Remove motor ground.
Ω

I
1. Remove motor ground.
2. Check continuity between ABS actuator 2-pin connector (ABS actuator side) terminal ⑳ and ground.

Continuity should not exist. — NG → Replace ABS actuator.

↓ OK

J
Control unit terminals (control unit side) (B107)
C/UNIT CONNECTOR
19
28
Ω

J
Check continuity between control unit terminals ⑲ and ㉘.
Continuity should not exist. — NG → Replace control unit.

↓ OK

MOTOR CHECK
Go to **E** in diagnostic procedure 5.

NS4029500165030X

Fig. 145 Test 5: Motor Relay Or Motor (Part 3 of 3). 1995–96 Sentra & 200SX

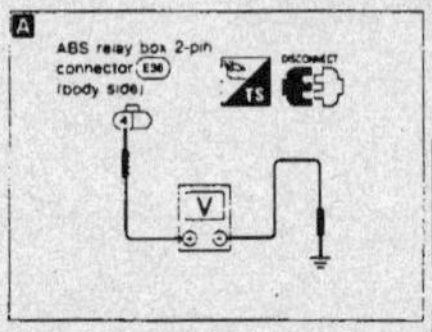
A
ABS relay box 2-pin connector (E36) (body side)
V

SOLENOID VALVE POWER SUPPLY CHECK — NG → Ⓐ
Check fusible link [E]. For fusible link layout.

↓ OK

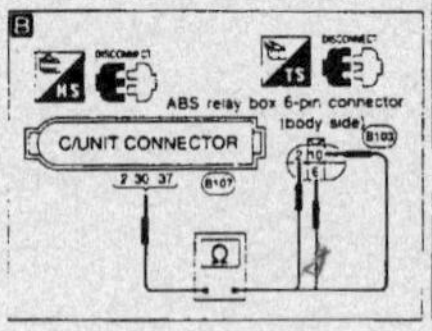
B
ABS relay box 6-pin connector (body side) (B103)
C/UNIT CONNECTOR
(B107)
Ω

1. Disconnect connectors from control unit and ABS actuator. Check terminals for damage or loose connections. Then reconnect connectors.
2. Carry out self-diagnosis again.

Does warning lamp activate again? — No → Inspection end

↓ Yes

GROUND CIRCUIT CHECK — NG → Repair harness and connectors.

↓ OK

A
SOLENOID VALVE POWER SUPPLY CHECK — NG → Repair harness and connector
1. Disconnect connector from ABS relay box.
2. Check voltage between ABS relay box 2-pin connector (body side) terminal ④ and ground.

Battery voltage should exist.

↓ OK

B
CIRCUIT CHECK — NG → Repair harness and connectors.
1. Disconnect control unit connector.
2. Check continuity between control unit connector terminals and ABS relay box 6-pin connector (body side) terminals.

Control unit	ABS relay box
㊲	⑥
②	②
㉚	⑩

Continuity should exist.

↓ OK

SOLENOID VALVE RELAY CHECK — NG → Replace solenoid valve relay.

↓ OK

Ⓑ

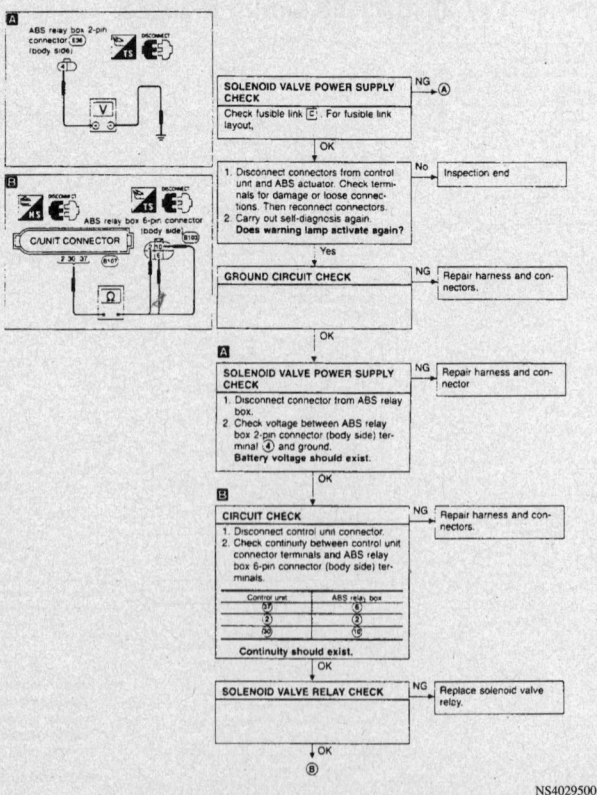

NS4029500166010X

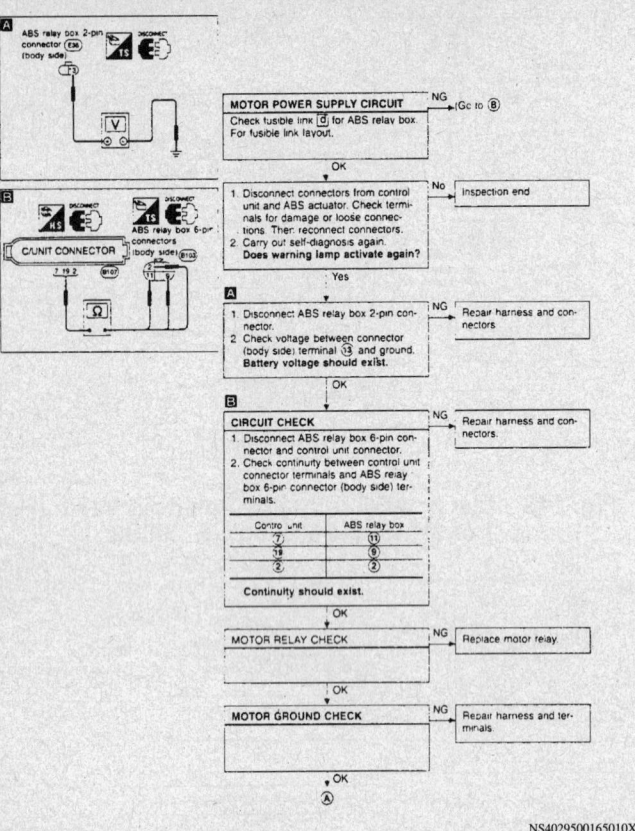

Fig. 146 Test 6: Solenoid Valve Relay (Part 1 of 2). 1995–96 Sentra & 200SX

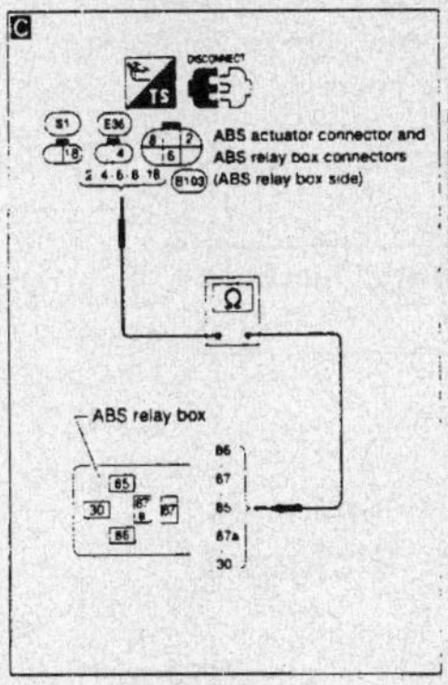
C
DISCONNECT
TS
ABS actuator connector and
ABS relay box connectors
(ABS relay box side)
ABS relay box

C

B ↓

SOLENOID VALVE RELAY CIRCUIT CHECK

Check continuity between ABS relay terminals and ABS actuator connector and ABS relay box connector (ABS relay box side) terminals.

ABS relay box terminal	ABS relay box connector
87	4
87a	8
85	6
86	2
30	ABS actuator connector 18

Continuity should exist.

NG → • Replace ABS relay box.

OK ↓

Go to diagnostic procedure 3.

A ↓

Replace fusible link.
Does the fusible link blow out when ignition switch is turned "ON"?

No → Inspection end

Yes ↓

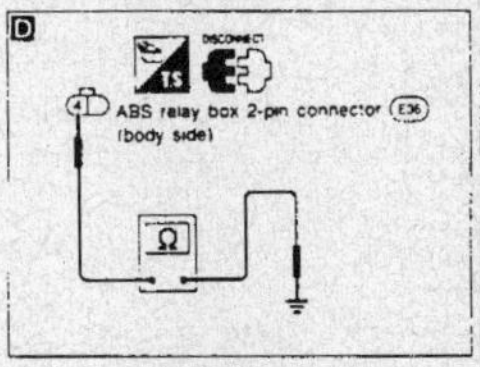
D
DISCONNECT
TS
ABS relay box 2-pin connector E36
(body side)

D

RELAY UNIT POWER SUPPLY CIRCUIT

1. Disconnect ABS relay box 2-pin connector.
2. Check continuity between ABS relay box 2-pin connector (body side) terminal ④ and ground.
Continuity should not exist.

NG → Repair harness and connector.

OK ↓

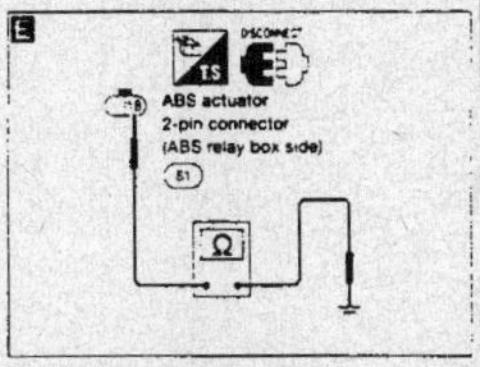
E
DISCONNECT
TS
ABS actuator
2-pin connector
(ABS relay box side)

E

1. Disconnect ABS relay box connectors and control unit connector.
2. Check continuity between ABS actuator 2-pin connector (ABS relay box side) terminal ⑱ and ground.
Continuity should not exist.

NG → Replace ABS relay box.

OK ↓

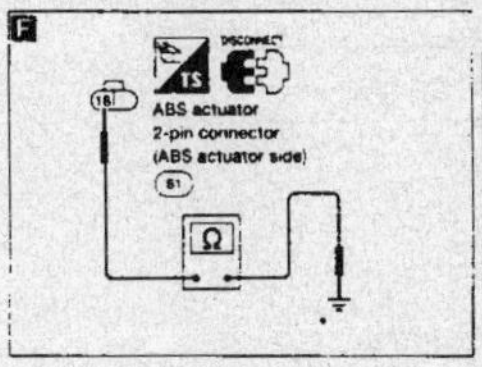
F
DISCONNECT
TS
ABS actuator
2-pin connector
(ABS actuator side)

F

Check continuity between ABS actuator 2-pin connector (ABS actuator side) terminal ⑱ and ground.
Continuity should not exist.

NG → Replace ABS actuator.

OK ↓

Go to diagnostic procedure 3.

NS4029500166020X

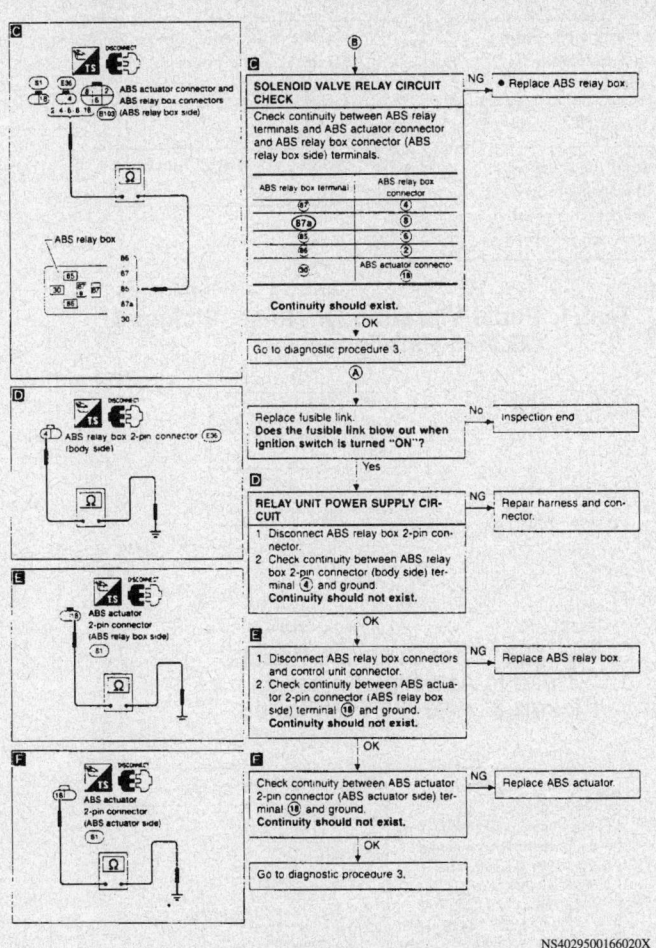

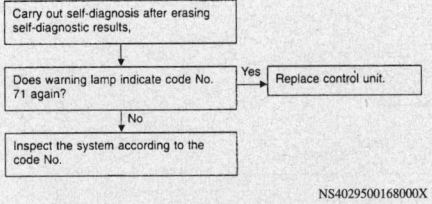

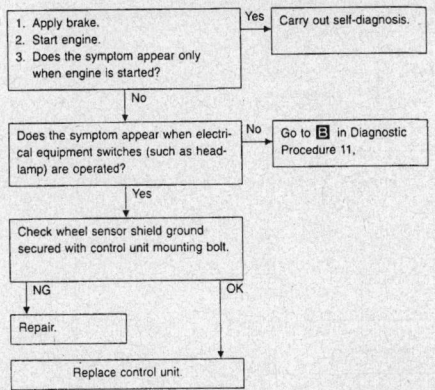

Fig. 146 Test 6: Solenoid Valve Relay (Part 2 of 2). 1995–96 Sentra & 200SX

Carry out self-diagnosis after erasing self-diagnostic results,

↓

Does warning lamp indicate code No. 71 again?

Yes → Replace control unit.

No ↓

Inspect the system according to the code No.

NS4029500168000X

Fig. 148 Test 8: Control Unit. 1995–96 Sentra & 200SX

1. Apply brake.
2. Start engine.
3. Does the symptom appear only when engine is started?

Yes → Carry out self-diagnosis.

No ↓

Does the symptom appear when electrical equipment switches (such as headlamp) are operated?

No → Go to B in Diagnostic Procedure 11,

Yes ↓

Check wheel sensor shield ground secured with control unit mounting bolt.

NG → Repair.

OK → Replace control unit.

NS4029500169000X

Fig. 149 Test 9: Pedal Vibration & Noise. 1995–96 Sentra & 200SX

A
B107
C/UNIT CONNECTOR
DISCONNECT
HS
V

1. Disconnect control unit connectors. Check terminals for damage or loose connections. Then reconnect connectors.
2. Carry out self-diagnosis again.
Does warning lamp activate again?

No → Inspection end

Yes ↓

A

CONTROL UNIT POWER SUPPLY CHECK

1. Disconnect control unit connector.
2. Check voltage between control unit connector terminal ① and ground.
Battery voltage should exist when ignition switch is turned ON.

NG → A (See below.)

OK ↓

CONTROL UNIT GROUND CHECK

NG → Repair harness and connectors.

OK ↓

Replace control unit.

A ↓

Check 7.5A fuse 12

NG → Replace fuse.

OK ↓

Check continuity between battery and control unit connector terminal ①.

NG → Repair harness and connectors.

OK ↓

Check battery.

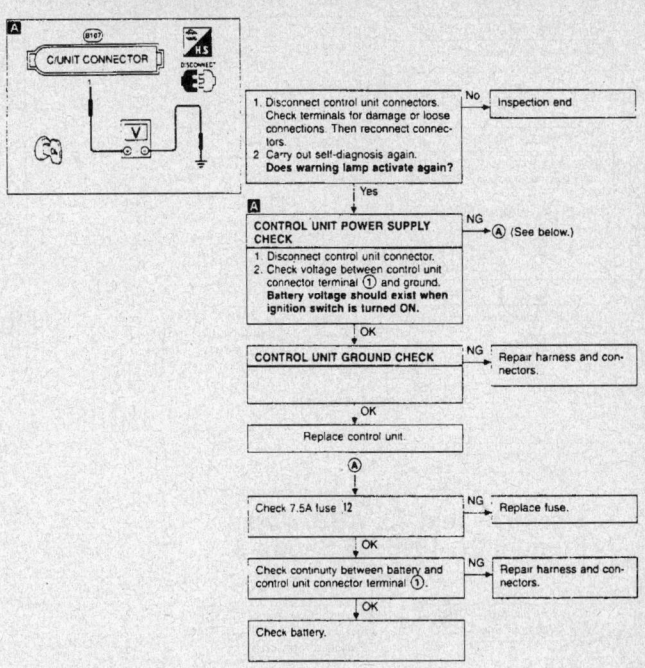

NS4029500167000X

Fig. 147 Test 7: Power Supply Low Voltage. 1995–96 Sentra & 200SX

Disconnect ABS relay box 6-pin connector and check whether stopping distance is still long.

No → Go to B in Diagnostic Procedure 11.

Yes ↓

Perform Preliminary Check and air bleeding.

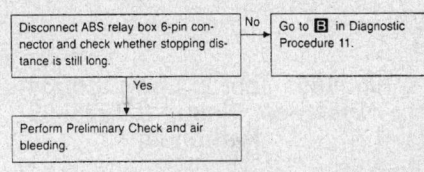

NS4029500170000X

Fig. 150 Test 10: Long Stopping Distance. 1995–96 Sentra & 200SX

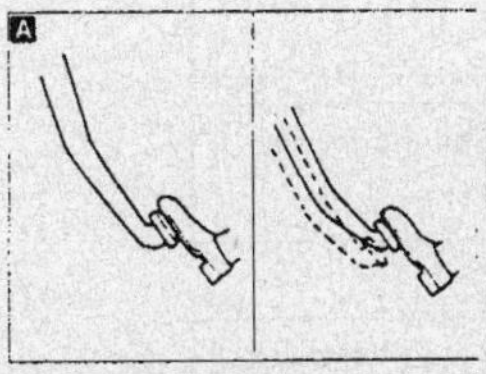
A

A

Check brake pedal stroke. Is stroke excessively large?

Yes → Perform Preliminary Check.

No ↓

Disconnect ABS relay box 6-pin connector and check whether brake is effective.

No → Perform Preliminary Check.

Yes ↓

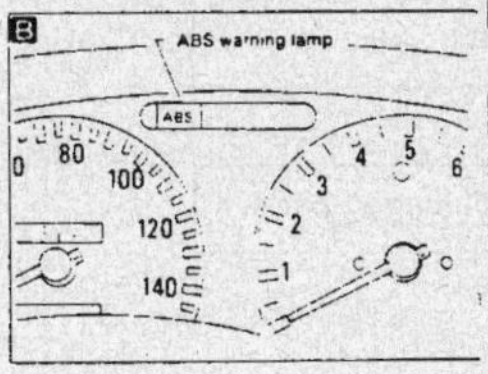
B
ABS warning lamp
ABS
80
100
120
140
2
3
4
5
6

B

Ensure warning lamp remains off while driving

NG → Carry out self-diagnosis.

OK ↓

CHECK WHEEL SENSOR.

1. Check wheel sensor connector for terminal damage or loose connection.
2. Perform wheel sensor mechanical check.
Refer to B in Diagnostic Procedure 4.

NG → Repair.

OK ↓

Replace control unit.

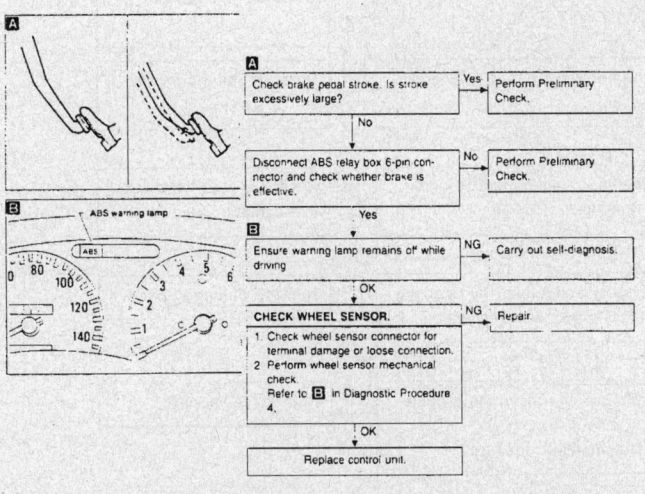

NS4029500171000X

Fig. 151 Test 11: Unexpected Pedal Action. 1995–96 Sentra & 200SX

Does the ABS warning lamp activate?

Yes → Carry out self-diagnosis.

No ↓

Go to B in Diagnostic Procedure 11,

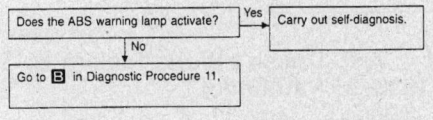

NS4029500172000X

Fig. 152 Test 12: ABS Does Not Work. 1995–96 Sentra & 200SX

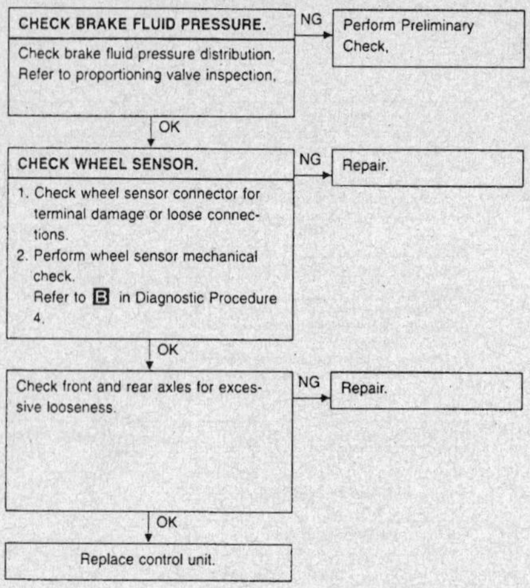
CHECK BRAKE FLUID PRESSURE.
Check brake fluid pressure distribution.
Refer to proportioning valve inspection.
NG
Perform Preliminary Check.
OK
CHECK WHEEL SENSOR.
1. Check wheel sensor connector for terminal damage or loose connections.
2. Perform wheel sensor mechanical check.
Refer to B in Diagnostic Procedure 4.
NG
Repair.
OK
Check front and rear axles for excessive looseness.
NG
Repair.
OK
Replace control unit.

NS4029500173000X

Fig. 153 Test 13: ABS Works Frequently. 1995–96 Sentra & 200SX

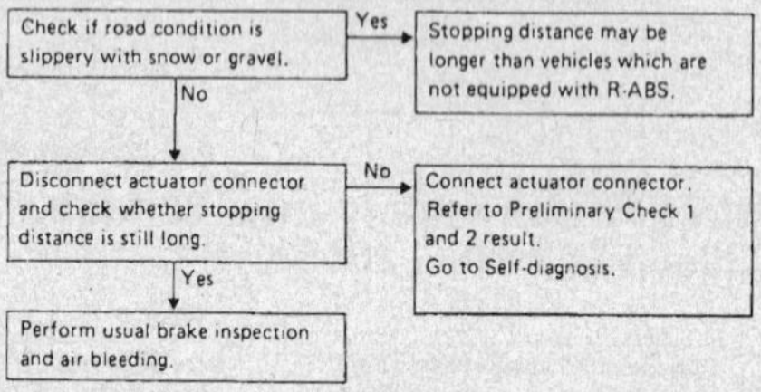
Check if road condition is slippery with snow or gravel.
Yes
Stopping distance may be longer than vehicles which are not equipped with R-ABS.
No
Disconnect actuator connector and check whether stopping distance is still long.
No
Connect actuator connector. Refer to Preliminary Check 1 and 2 result. Go to Self-diagnosis.
Yes
Perform usual brake inspection and air bleeding.

NS4029100076000X

Fig. 155 Test 2: Long Stopping Distance. Pickup & 1993–95 Pathfinder

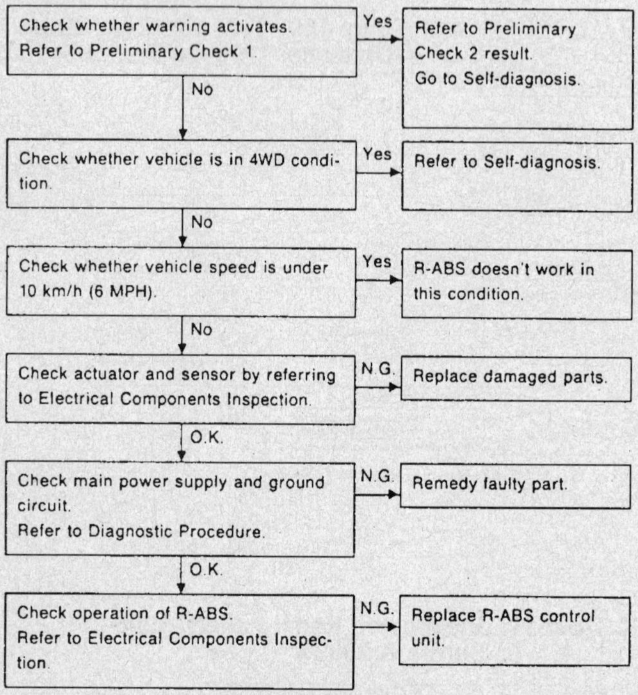
Check whether warning activates. Refer to Preliminary Check 1.
Yes
Refer to Preliminary Check 2 result. Go to Self-diagnosis.
No
Check whether vehicle is in 4WD condition.
Yes
Refer to Self-diagnosis.
No
Check whether vehicle speed is under 10 km/h (6 MPH).
Yes
R-ABS doesn't work in this condition.
No
Check actuator and sensor by referring to Electrical Components Inspection.
N.G.
Replace damaged parts.
O.K.
Check main power supply and ground circuit. Refer to Diagnostic Procedure.
N.G.
Remedy faulty part.
O.K.
Check operation of R-ABS. Refer to Electrical Components Inspection.
N.G.
Replace R-ABS control unit.

NS4029100078000X

Fig. 157 Test 4: ABS Doesn't Work. Pickup & 1993–95 Pathfinder

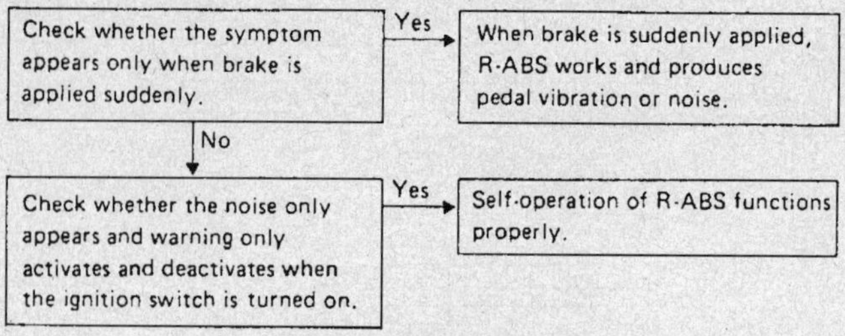
Check whether the symptom appears only when brake is applied suddenly.
Yes
When brake is suddenly applied, R-ABS works and produces pedal vibration or noise.
No
Check whether the noise only appears and warning only activates and deactivates when the ignition switch is turned on.
Yes
Self-operation of R-ABS functions properly.

NS4029100075000X

Fig. 154 Test 1: Pedal Vibration Or Noise. Pickup & 1993–95 Pathfinder

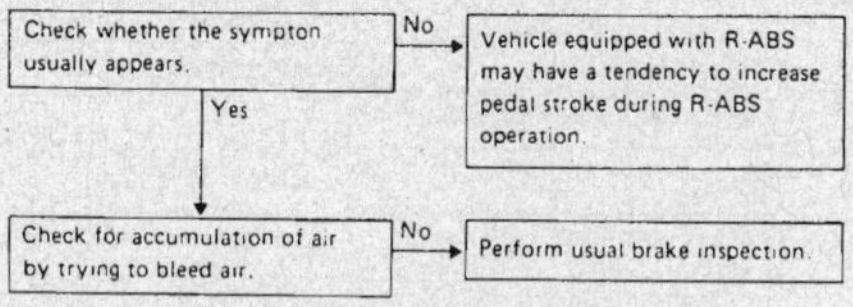
Check whether the sympton usually appears.
No
Vehicle equipped with R-ABS may have a tendency to increase pedal stroke during R-ABS operation.
Yes
Check for accumulation of air by trying to bleed air.
No
Perform usual brake inspection.

NS4029100077000X

Fig. 156 Test 3: Brake Pedal Stroke Is Abnormally Large. Pickup & 1993–95 Pathfinder

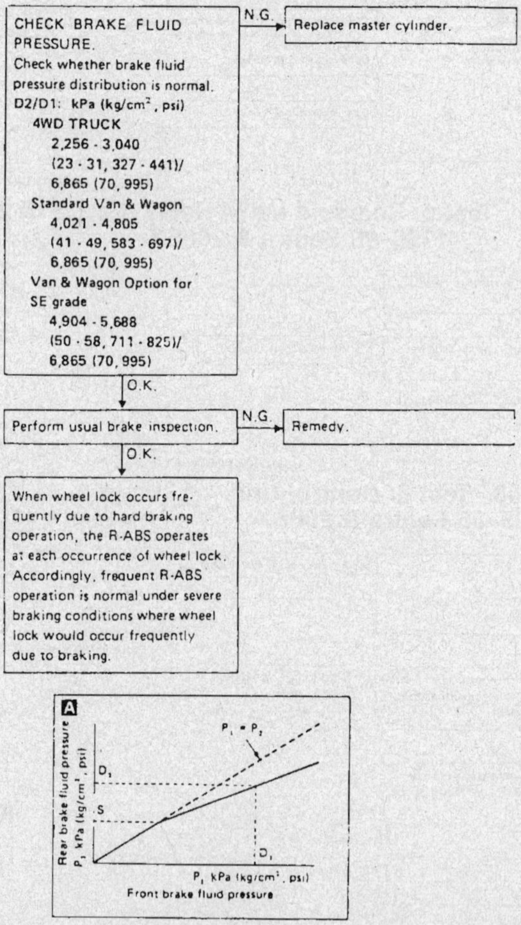
CHECK BRAKE FLUID PRESSURE.
Check whether brake fluid pressure distribution is normal.
D2/D1: kPa (kg/cm², psi)
4WD TRUCK
2,256 - 3,040
(23 - 31, 327 - 441)/
6,865 (70, 995)
Standard Van & Wagon
4,021 - 4,805
(41 - 49, 583 - 697)/
6,865 (70, 995)
Van & Wagon Option for SE grade
4,904 - 5,688
(50 - 58, 711 - 825)/
6,865 (70, 995)
N.G.
Replace master cylinder.
O.K.
Perform usual brake inspection.
N.G.
Remedy.
O.K.
When wheel lock occurs frequently due to hard braking operation, the R-ABS operates at each occurrence of wheel lock. Accordingly, frequent R-ABS operation is normal under severe braking conditions where wheel lock would occur frequently due to braking.
A
Rear brake fluid pressure
P₂ kPa (kg/cm², psi)
P₁ = P₂
D₂
S
D₁
P₁ kPa (kg/cm², psi)
Front brake fluid pressure

NS4029100079000X

Fig. 158 Test 5: ABS Works Frequently. Pickup & 1993–95 Pathfinder

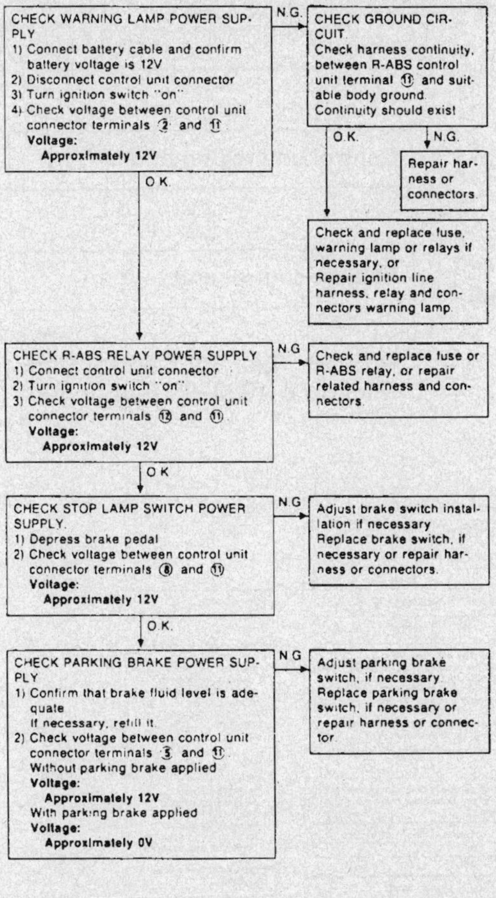
CHECK WARNING LAMP POWER SUPPLY
1) Connect battery cable and confirm battery voltage is 12V
2) Disconnect control unit connector
3) Turn ignition switch "on"
4) Check voltage between control unit connector terminals ② and ⑪
Voltage:
Approximately 12V
N.G.
CHECK GROUND CIRCUIT.
Check harness continuity, between R-ABS control unit terminal ⑪ and suitable body ground.
Continuity should exist
O.K.
N.G.
Repair harness or connectors.
Check and replace fuse, warning lamp or relays if necessary, or
Repair ignition line harness, relay and connectors warning lamp.
O.K.
CHECK R-ABS RELAY POWER SUPPLY
1) Connect control unit connector
2) Turn ignition switch "on".
3) Check voltage between control unit connector terminals ⑫ and ⑪.
Voltage:
Approximately 12V
N.G
Check and replace fuse or R-ABS relay, or repair related harness and connectors.
O.K
CHECK STOP LAMP SWITCH POWER SUPPLY.
1) Depress brake pedal
2) Check voltage between control unit connector terminals ⑧ and ⑪
Voltage:
Approximately 12V
N.G
Adjust brake switch installation if necessary
Replace brake switch, if necessary or repair harness or connectors.
O.K.
CHECK PARKING BRAKE POWER SUPPLY
1) Confirm that brake fluid level is adequate
If necessary, refill it.
2) Check voltage between control unit connector terminals ③ and ⑪.
Without parking brake applied
Voltage:
Approximately 12V
With parking brake applied
Voltage:
Approximately 0V
N.G
Adjust parking brake switch, if necessary
Replace parking brake switch, if necessary or repair harness or connector.
NS4029100080000X

Fig. 159 Test 6: Main Power Supply & Ground circuit. Pickup & 1993–95 Pathfinder

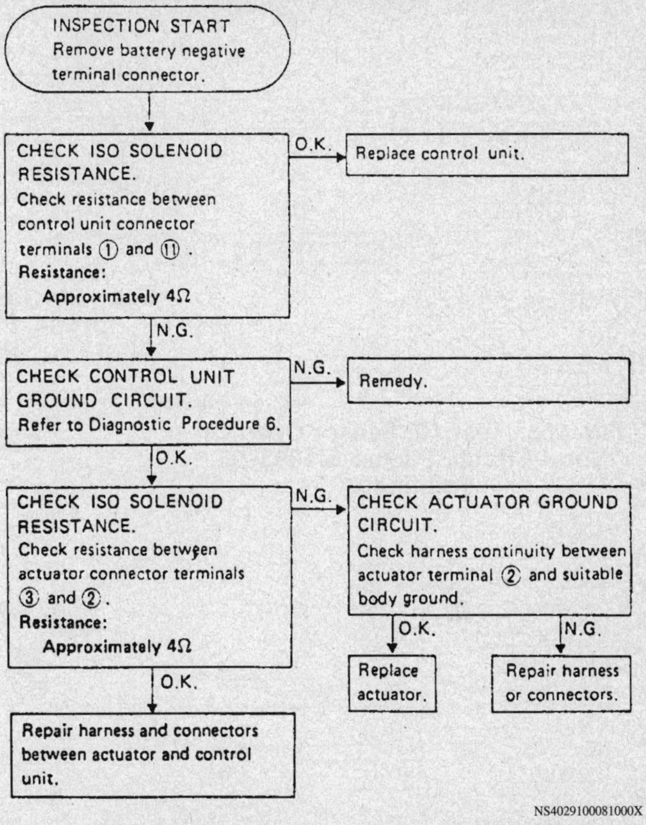
INSPECTION START
Remove battery negative terminal connector.
CHECK ISO SOLENOID RESISTANCE.
Check resistance between control unit connector terminals ① and ⑪.
Resistance:
Approximately 4Ω
O.K.
Replace control unit.
N.G.
CHECK CONTROL UNIT GROUND CIRCUIT.
Refer to Diagnostic Procedure 6.
N.G.
Remedy.
O.K.
CHECK ISO SOLENOID RESISTANCE.
Check resistance between actuator connector terminals ③ and ②.
Resistance:
Approximately 4Ω
N.G.
CHECK ACTUATOR GROUND CIRCUIT.
Check harness continuity between actuator terminal ② and suitable body ground.
O.K.
N.G.
Replace actuator.
Repair harness or connectors.
O.K.
Repair harness and connectors between actuator and control unit.
NS4029100081000X

Fig. 160 Test 7: Actuator ISO Solenoid Short Circuit Or Open. Pickup & 1993–95 Pathfinder

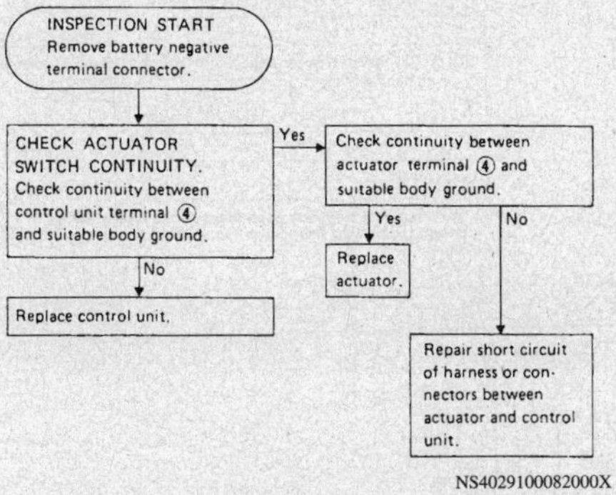
INSPECTION START
Remove battery negative terminal connector.
CHECK ACTUATOR SWITCH CONTINUITY.
Check continuity between control unit terminal ④ and suitable body ground.
Yes
Check continuity between actuator terminal ④ and suitable body ground.
Yes
No
Replace actuator.
No
Replace control unit.
Repair short circuit of harness or connectors between actuator and control unit.
NS4029100082000X

Fig. 161 Test 8: Actuator ISO Solenoid Blocked. Pickup & 1993–95 Pathfinder

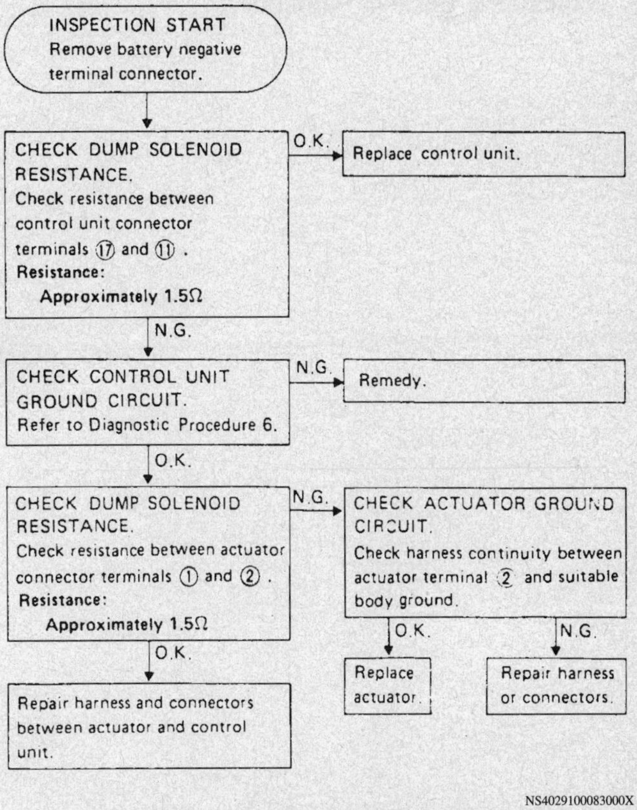
INSPECTION START
Remove battery negative terminal connector.
CHECK DUMP SOLENOID RESISTANCE.
Check resistance between control unit connector terminals ⑰ and ⑪.
Resistance:
Approximately 1.5Ω
O.K.
Replace control unit.
N.G.
CHECK CONTROL UNIT GROUND CIRCUIT.
Refer to Diagnostic Procedure 6.
N.G.
Remedy.
O.K.
CHECK DUMP SOLENOID RESISTANCE.
Check resistance between actuator connector terminals ① and ②.
Resistance:
Approximately 1.5Ω
N.G.
CHECK ACTUATOR GROUND CIRCUIT.
Check harness continuity between actuator terminal ② and suitable body ground.
O.K.
N.G.
Replace actuator.
Repair harness or connectors.
O.K.
Repair harness and connectors between actuator and control unit.
NS4029100083000X

Fig. 162 Test 9: Actuator Dump Solenoid Short Circuit. Pickup & 1993–95 Pathfinder

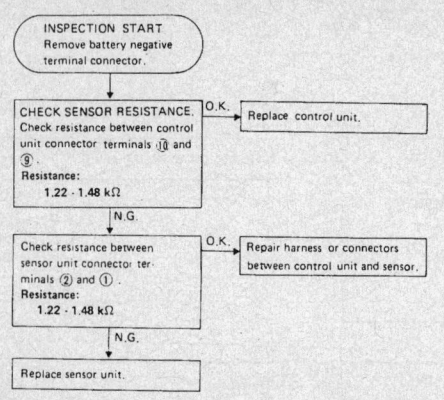

INSPECTION START
Remove battery negative terminal connector.

↓

CHECK SENSOR RESISTANCE.
Check resistance between control unit connector terminals ⑩ and ⑨.
Resistance:
1.22 - 1.48 kΩ
— O.K. → Replace control unit.

↓ N.G.

Check resistance between sensor unit connector terminals ② and ①.
Resistance:
1.22 - 1.48 kΩ
— O.K. → Repair harness or connectors between control unit and sensor.

↓ N.G.

Replace sensor unit.

NS4029100084000X

Fig. 163 Test 10: Sensor Open Or Short Circuit. Pickup & 1993–95 Pathfinder

INSPECTION START

↓

CHECK SENSOR ROTOR TOOTH CONDITION.
1) Remove propeller shaft.
2) Remove companion flange.
3) Check rotor on companion flange.
— N.G. → Replace sensor rotor with companion flange.

↓ O.K.

Replace control unit.

NS4029100085000X

Fig. 164 Test 11: Sensor Signal Erratic. Pickup & 1993–95 Pathfinder

INSPECTION START

↓

Control unit malfunction.

↓

Replace control unit.

NS4029100086000X

Fig. 165 Test 12: Control Unit. Pickup & 1993–95 Pathfinder

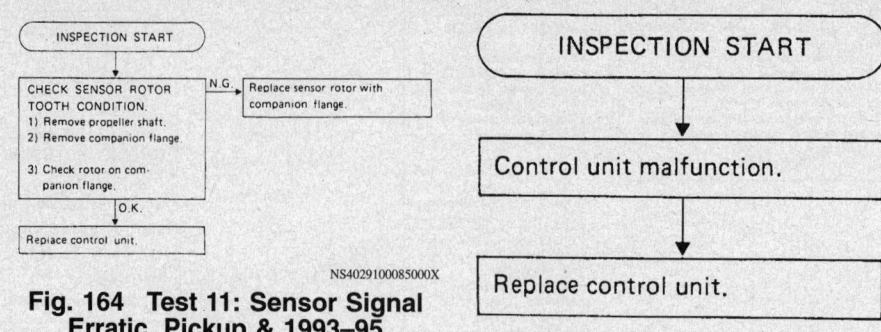

INSPECTION START

↓

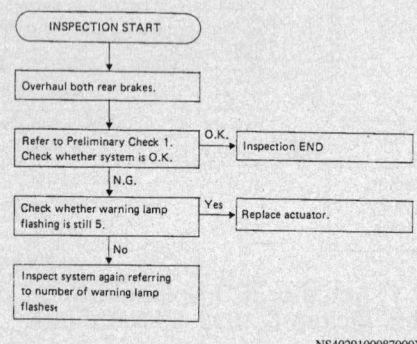

Overhaul both rear brakes.

↓

Refer to Preliminary Check 1.
Check whether system is O.K.
— O.K. → Inspection END

↓ N.G.

Check whether warning lamp flashing is still 5.
— Yes → Replace actuator.

↓ No

Inspect system again referring to number of warning lamp flashes.

NS4029100087000X

Fig. 166 Test 13: Other Problems. Pickup & 1993–95 Pathfinder

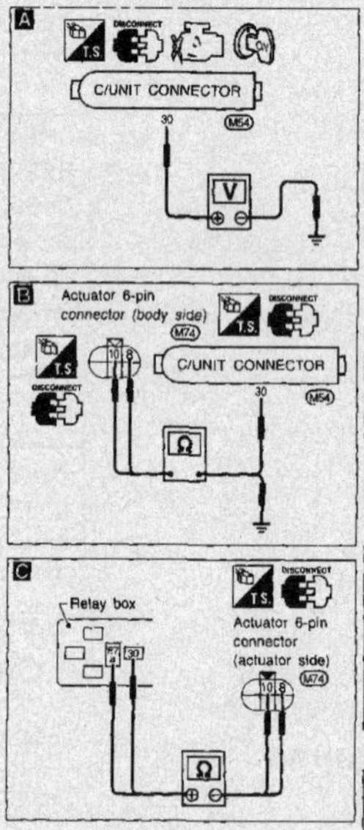

A
DISCONNECT
T.S.
C/UNIT CONNECTOR
30
M54
B
Actuator 6-pin connector (body side)
M74
C/UNIT CONNECTOR
C
Relay box
Actuator 6-pin connector (actuator side)

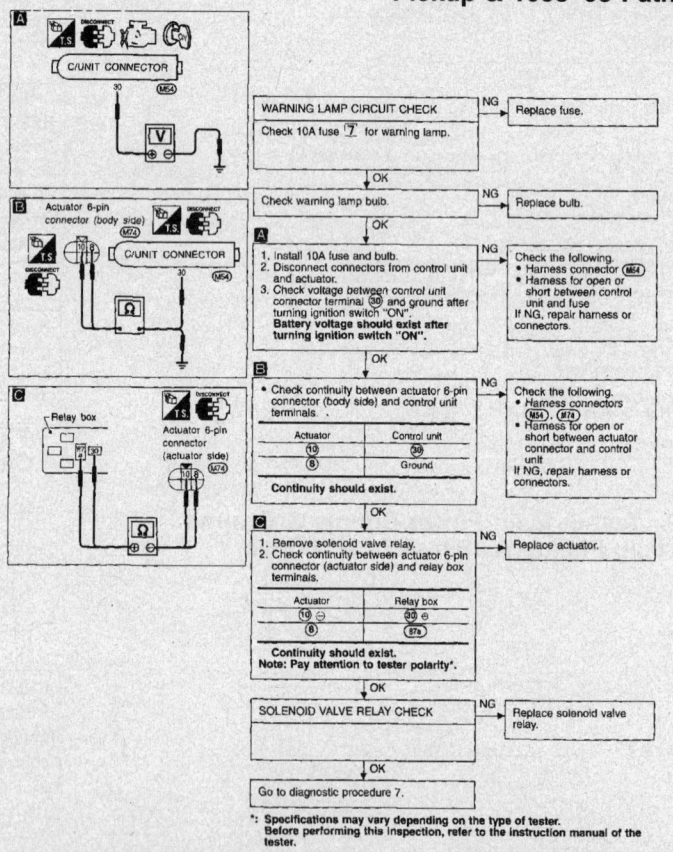

WARNING LAMP CIRCUIT CHECK
Check 10A fuse 7 for warning lamp.
— NG → Replace fuse.

↓ OK

Check warning lamp bulb.
— NG → Replace bulb.

↓ OK

A
1. Install 10A fuse and bulb.
2. Disconnect connectors from control unit and actuator.
3. Check voltage between control unit connector terminal ㉚ and ground after turning ignition switch "ON".
   Battery voltage should exist after turning ignition switch "ON".

— NG → Check the following.
• Harness connector M54
• Harness for open or short between control unit and fuse
If NG, repair harness or connectors.

↓ OK

B
• Check continuity between actuator 6-pin connector (body side) and control unit terminals.

Actuator	Control unit
⑩	㉚
⑧	Ground

Continuity should exist.

— NG → Check the following.
• Harness connectors M54, M74
• Harness for open or short between actuator connector and control unit
If NG, repair harness or connectors.

↓ OK

C
1. Remove solenoid valve relay.
2. Check continuity between actuator 6-pin connector (actuator side) and relay box terminals.

Actuator	Relay box
⑩ ⊖	㉚ ⊕
⑧	87a

Continuity should exist.
Note: Pay attention to tester polarity*.

— NG → Replace actuator.

↓ OK

SOLENOID VALVE RELAY CHECK
— NG → Replace solenoid valve relay.

↓ OK

Go to diagnostic procedure 7.

***: Specifications may vary depending on the type of tester. Before performing this inspection, refer to the instruction manual of the tester.**

NS4029600221000X

Fig. 167 Test 1: Warning Lamp Does Not Work When Ignition Is On. 1996 Pathfinder

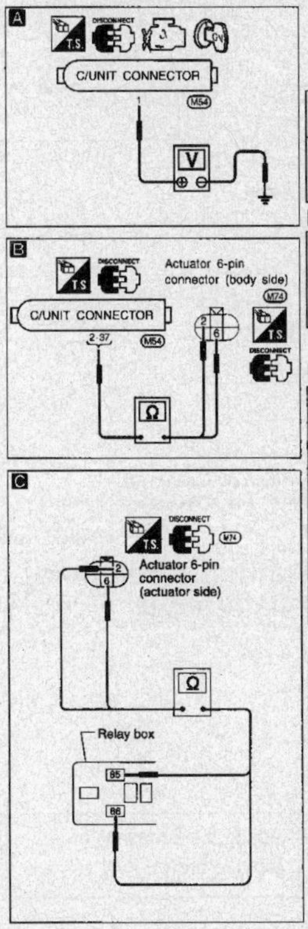
A
C/UNIT CONNECTOR
M54
1
V
B
Actuator 6-pin connector (body side)
M74
C/UNIT CONNECTOR
2 37
M54
2
6
Ω
C
M74
Actuator 6-pin connector (actuator side)
2
6
Ω
Relay box
85
86

CONTROL UNIT POWER SUPPLY CIRCUIT — NG → (Go to Ⓑ.)

Check 7.5A fuse [28] for control unit.

↓ OK

A

1. Disconnect connector from control unit.
2. Check voltage between control unit connector terminal ① and ground after turning ignition switch "ON".

Battery voltage should exist.

NG → Check the following.
- Harness connector (M54)
- Harness for open or short between control unit and fuse

If NG, repair harness or connectors.

↓ OK

B

SOLENOID VALVE RELAY COIL POWER SUPPLY CIRCUIT

1. Turn ignition switch "OFF". Disconnect actuator 6-pin connector.
2. Check continuity between control unit connector terminals and actuator 6-pin connector (body side) terminals.

Control unit	Actuator
②	②
㊲	⑥

Continuity should exist.

NG → Check the following.
- Harness connectors (M54), (M74)
- Harness for open or short between actuator connector and control unit

If NG, repair harness or connectors.

↓ OK

C

CIRCUIT CHECK — NG → Replace actuator.

1. Disconnect solenoid valve relay.
2. Check continuity between actuator 6-pin connector (actuator side) terminals and solenoid valve relay box terminals.

Actuator	Relay box
②	㊱
⑥	㊵

Continuity should exist.

↓ OK

SOLENOID VALVE RELAY CHECK — NG → Replace solenoid valve relay.

↓ OK

Ⓐ

NS4029600222010X

Fig. 168 Test 2: Warning Lamp Stays On When Ignition Switch Is On (Part 1 of 3). 1996 Pathfinder

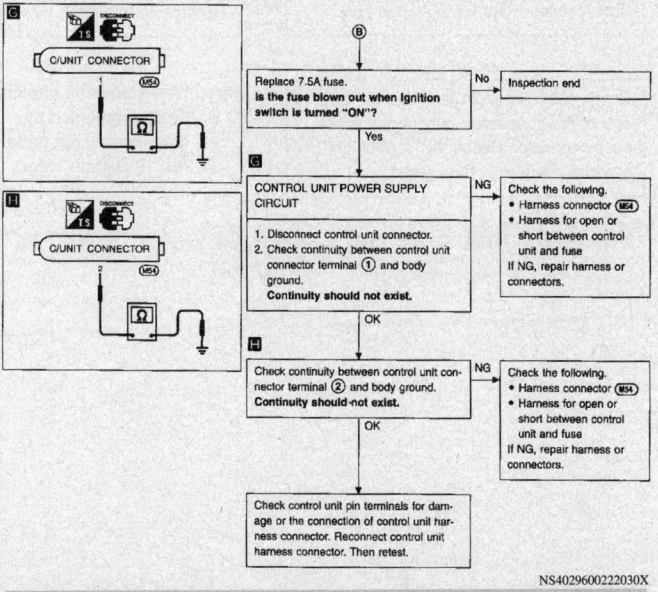

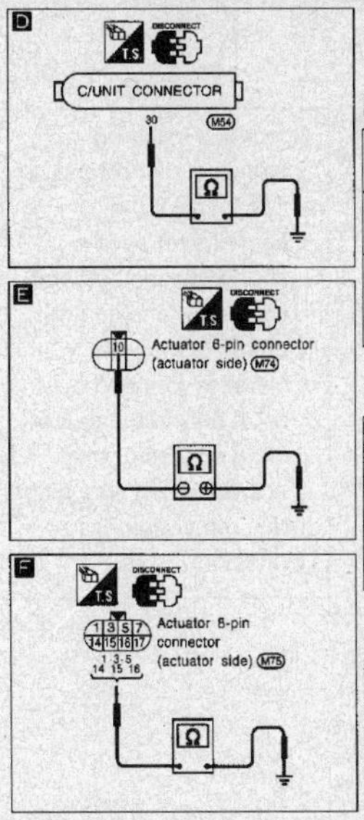
D
C/UNIT CONNECTOR
30
M54
Ω
E
10
Actuator 8-pin connector (actuator side) M74
Ω
F
1 3 5 7
14 15 16 17
Actuator 8-pin connector (actuator side) M75
1 3 5
14 15 16
Ω

Ⓐ

↓

D

GROUND-SHORT CHECK FOR WARNING LAMP CIRCUIT.

1. Turn ignition switch "OFF".
2. Disconnect connectors from control unit and actuator.
3. Check continuity between control unit connector terminal ㉚ and body ground.

Continuity should not exist.

NG → Check the following.
- Harness connector (M54)
- Harness for open or short between control unit and fuse

If NG, repair harness or connectors.

↓ OK

E

1. Disconnect actuator ground terminal and 6-pin connector.
2. Check continuity between actuator 6-pin connector (actuator side) terminal ⑩ and body ground.

Continuity should not exist.

Note: Pay attention to tester polarity*.

NG → Replace relay box.

↓ OK

F

SOLENOID VALVE CIRCUIT

1. Disconnect actuator 8-pin connector.
2. Check continuity between each actuator 8-pin connector (actuator side) terminals and body ground.

Continuity should not exist.

NG → Replace actuator assembly.

↓ OK

Check control unit pin terminals for damage or the connection of control unit harness connector. Reconnect control unit harness connector. Then retest.

***: Specifications may vary depending on the type of tester. Before performing this inspection, refer to the instruction manual of the tester.**

NS4029600222020X

Fig. 168 Test 2: Warning Lamp Stays On When Ignition Switch Is On (Part 2 of 3). 1996 Pathfinder

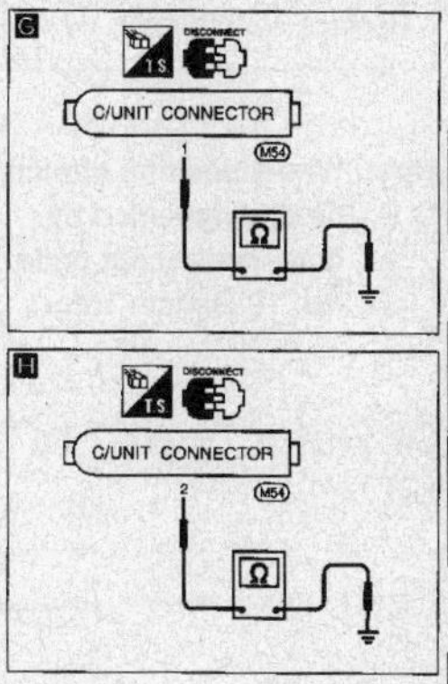
G
C/UNIT CONNECTOR
1
M54
Ω
H
C/UNIT CONNECTOR
2
M54
Ω

Ⓑ

↓

Replace 7.5A fuse.

Is the fuse blown out when ignition switch is turned "ON"?

No → Inspection end

↓ Yes

G

CONTROL UNIT POWER SUPPLY CIRCUIT

1. Disconnect control unit connector.
2. Check continuity between control unit connector terminal ① and body ground.

Continuity should not exist.

NG → Check the following.
- Harness connector (M54)
- Harness for open or short between control unit and fuse

If NG, repair harness or connectors.

↓ OK

H

Check continuity between control unit connector terminal ② and body ground.

Continuity should not exist.

NG → Check the following.
- Harness connector (M54)
- Harness for open or short between control unit and fuse

If NG, repair harness or connectors.

↓ OK

Check control unit pin terminals for damage or the connection of control unit harness connector. Reconnect control unit harness connector. Then retest.

NS4029600222030X

Fig. 168 Test 2: Warning Lamp Stays On When Ignition Switch Is On (Part 3 of 3). 1996 Pathfinder

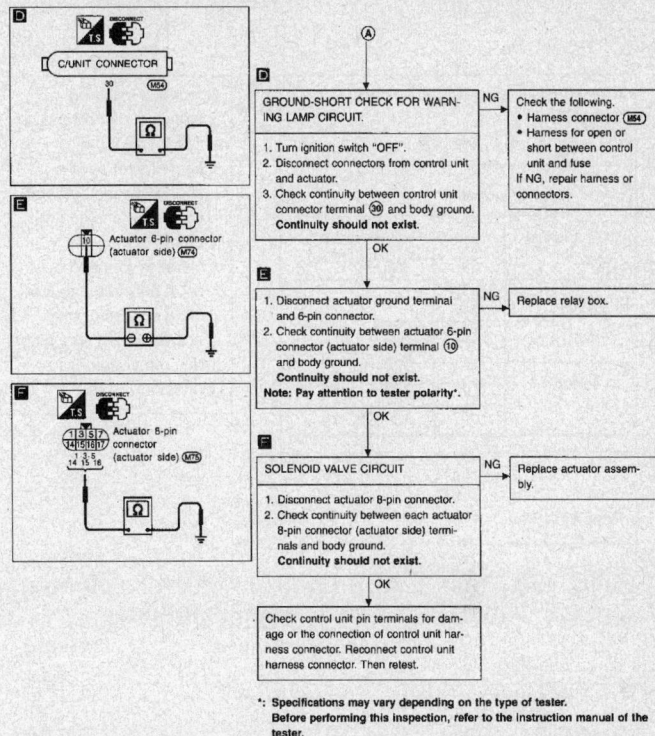

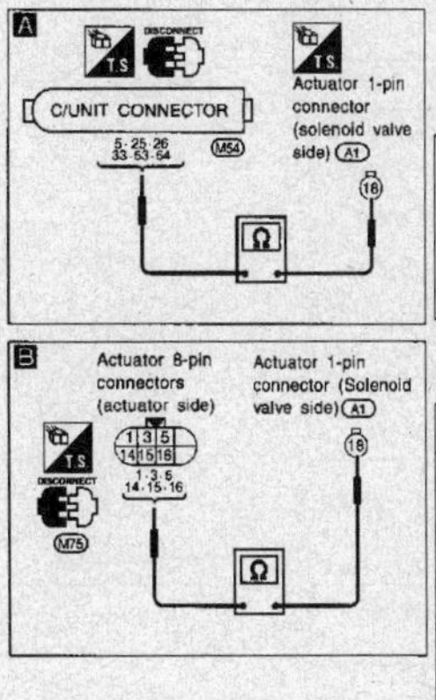
A
Actuator 1-pin connector (solenoid valve side) A1
C/UNIT CONNECTOR
5 25 26
33 53 54
M54
18
Ω
B
Actuator 8-pin connectors (actuator side)
Actuator 1-pin connector (Solenoid valve side) A1
1 3 5
14 15 16
1 3 5
14 15 16
18
M75
Ω

1. Disconnect connectors from control unit and actuator. Check terminals for damage or loose connection. Then reconnect connectors.
2. Carry out self-diagnosis again.

Does warning lamp activate again?

No → Inspection end

↓ Yes

A

ACTUATOR SOLENOID VALVE CHECK — OK → Ⓐ

1. Disconnect connectors from control unit and actuator.
2. Check resistance between control unit connector terminals and actuator 1-pin connector (solenoid valve side) terminal ⑱.

Code No.	Control unit	ABS relay box	Resistance
41	㉖	⑱	3.4 - 6.9Ω
45	㉝	⑱	
55	㉕	⑱	
42	㊵	⑱	6.5 - 13.2Ω
46	⑤	⑱	
56	㊸	⑱	

↓ NG

B

1. Disconnect actuator 8-pin connector.
2. Check resistance between actuator 8-pin connector (actuator side) terminals and actuator 1-pin connector (solenoid valve side) terminal ⑱.

Code No.	ABS actuator	ABS relay box	Resistance
41	⑮	⑱	3.4 - 6.9Ω
45	⑭	⑱	
55	⑯	⑱	
42	③	⑱	6.5 - 13.2Ω
46	①	⑱	
56	⑤	⑱	

OK → Check the following.
- Harness connectors (M54), (M75), (A1)
- Harness for open or short between actuator connector and control unit
- Harness for open or short between actuator 8-pin connector and actuator 1-pin connector

If NG, repair harness or connectors.

↓ NG

Ⓑ

NS4029600223010X

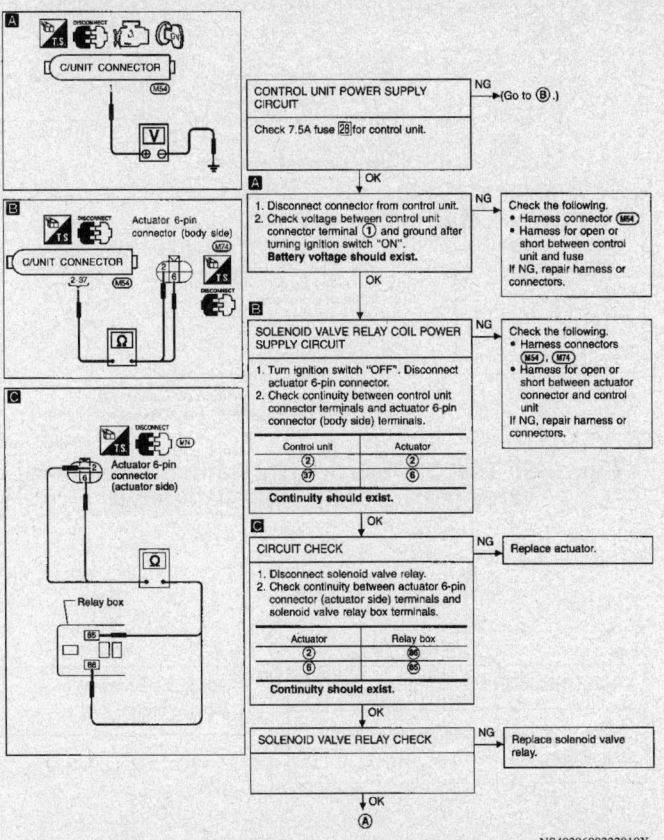

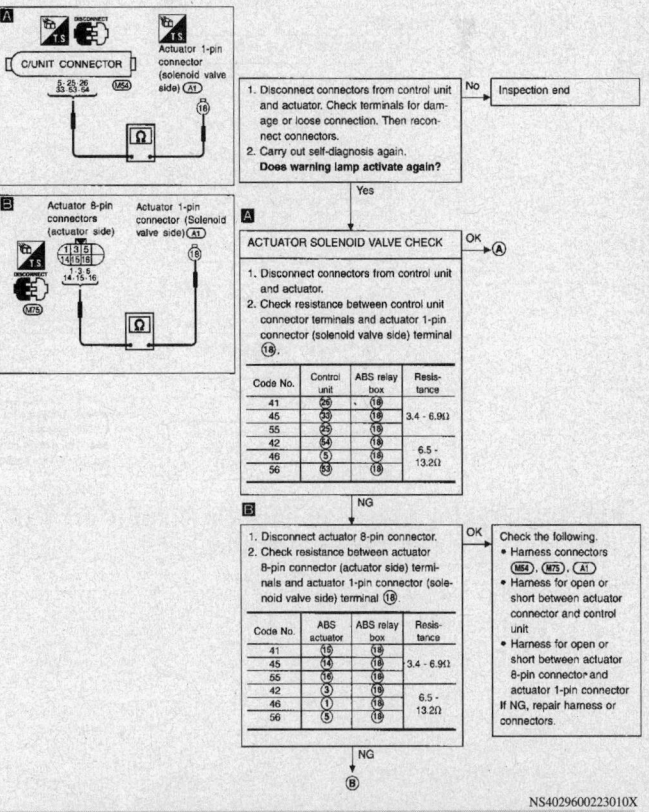

Fig. 169 Test 3: ABS Control Actuator Solenoid Valve (Part 1 of 3). 1996 Pathfinder

(B)

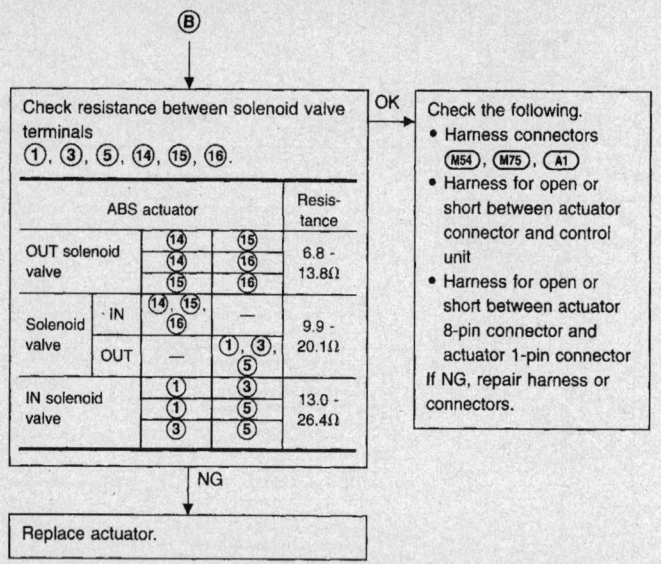

Check resistance between solenoid valve terminals ①, ③, ⑤, ⑭, ⑮, ⑯.

ABS actuator				Resistance
OUT solenoid valve		⑭	⑮	6.8 - 13.8Ω
		⑭	⑯	
		⑮	⑯	
Solenoid valve	IN	⑭, ⑮, ⑯	—	9.9 - 20.1Ω
	OUT	—	①, ③, ⑤	
IN solenoid valve		①	③	13.0 - 26.4Ω
		①	⑤	
		③	⑤	

OK → Check the following.
- Harness connectors (M54), (M75), (A1)
- Harness for open or short between actuator connector and control unit
- Harness for open or short between actuator 8-pin connector and actuator 1-pin connector

If NG, repair harness or connectors.

NG → Replace actuator.

NS4029600223020X

Fig. 169 Test 3: ABS Control Actuator Solenoid Valve (Part 2 of 3). 1996 Pathfinder

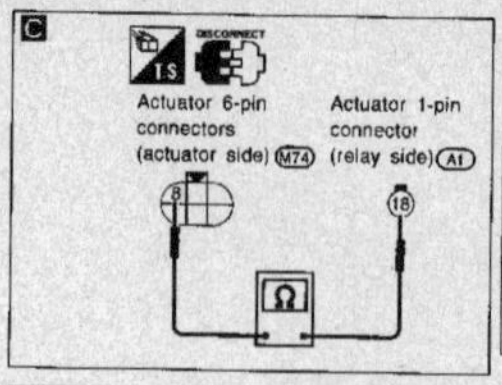
C
DISCONNECT
T.S
Actuator 6-pin connectors (actuator side) (M74)
Actuator 1-pin connector (relay side) (A1)
⑱
Ω

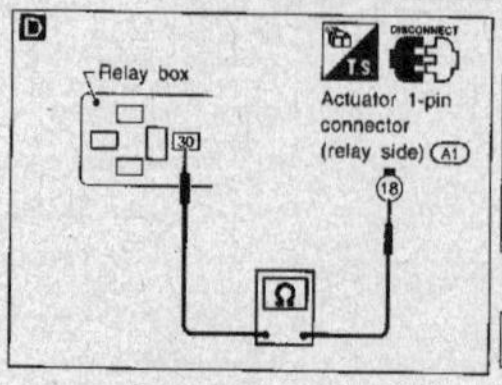
D
Relay box
DISCONNECT
T.S
Actuator 1-pin connector (relay side) (A1)
30
⑱
Ω

(A)

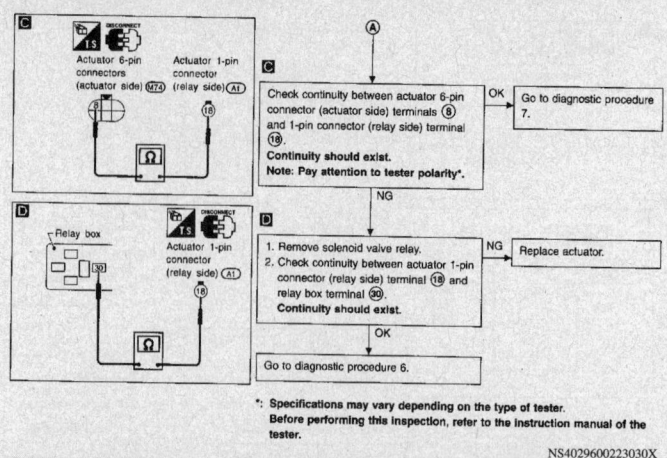

C Check continuity between actuator 6-pin connector (actuator side) terminals ⑧ and 1-pin connector (relay side) terminal ⑱.
Continuity should exist.
Note: Pay attention to tester polarity*.

OK → Go to diagnostic procedure 7.

NG ↓

D
1. Remove solenoid valve relay.
2. Check continuity between actuator 1-pin connector (relay side) terminal ⑱ and relay box terminal ㉚.
Continuity should exist.

NG → Replace actuator.

OK → Go to diagnostic procedure 6.

***: Specifications may vary depending on the type of tester. Before performing this inspection, refer to the instruction manual of the tester.**

NS4029600223030X

Fig. 169 Test 3: ABS Control Actuator Solenoid Valve (Part 3 of 3). 1996 Pathfinder

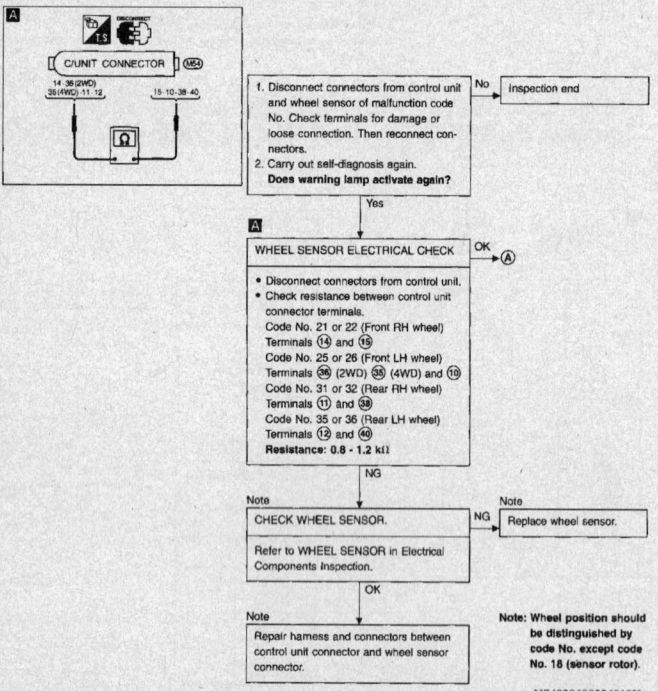

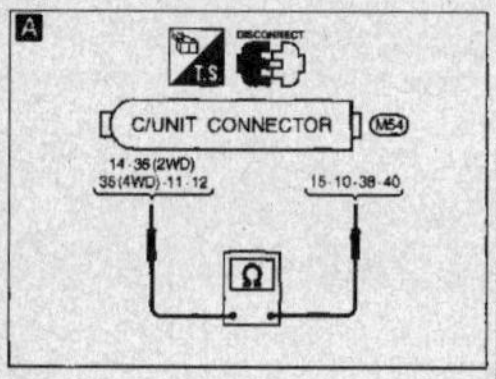
A
DISCONNECT
T.S
C/UNIT CONNECTOR
M54
14 · 36 (2WD)
35 (4WD) · 11 · 12
15 · 10 · 38 · 40
Ω

1. Disconnect connectors from control unit and wheel sensor of malfunction code No. Check terminals for damage or loose connection. Then reconnect connectors.
2. Carry out self-diagnosis again.
Does warning lamp activate again?

No → Inspection end

Yes ↓

A WHEEL SENSOR ELECTRICAL CHECK

- Disconnect connectors from control unit.
- Check resistance between control unit connector terminals.
  Code No. 21 or 22 (Front RH wheel)
  Terminals ⑭ and ⑮
  Code No. 25 or 26 (Front LH wheel)
  Terminals ㊱ (2WD) ㉟ (4WD) and ⑩
  Code No. 31 or 32 (Rear RH wheel)
  Terminals ⑪ and ㊳
  Code No. 35 or 36 (Rear LH wheel)
  Terminals ⑫ and ㊵
  Resistance: 0.8 - 1.2 kΩ

OK → (A)

NG ↓

Note: CHECK WHEEL SENSOR.
Refer to WHEEL SENSOR in Electrical Components Inspection.

NG → Note: Replace wheel sensor.

OK ↓

Note: Repair harness and connectors between control unit connector and wheel sensor connector.

Note: Wheel position should be distinguished by code No. except code No. 18 (sensor rotor).

NS4029600224010X

Fig. 170 Test 4: Wheel Sensor Or Rotor (Part 1 of 2). 1996 Pathfinder

(A)

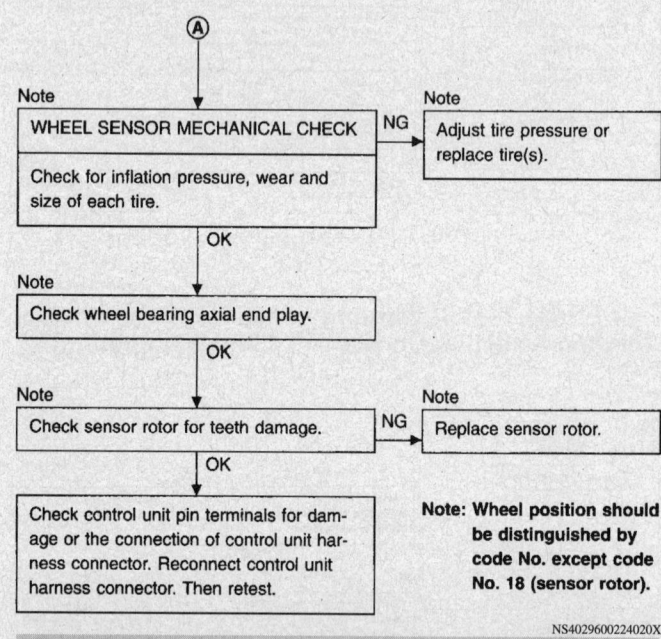

Note: WHEEL SENSOR MECHANICAL CHECK
Check for inflation pressure, wear and size of each tire.

NG → Note: Adjust tire pressure or replace tire(s).

OK ↓

Note: Check wheel bearing axial end play.

OK ↓

Note: Check sensor rotor for teeth damage.

NG → Note: Replace sensor rotor.

OK ↓

Check control unit pin terminals for damage or the connection of control unit harness connector. Reconnect control unit harness connector. Then retest.

Note: Wheel position should be distinguished by code No. except code No. 18 (sensor rotor).

NS4029600224020X

Fig. 170 Test 4: Wheel Sensor Or Rotor (Part 2 of 2). 1996 Pathfinder

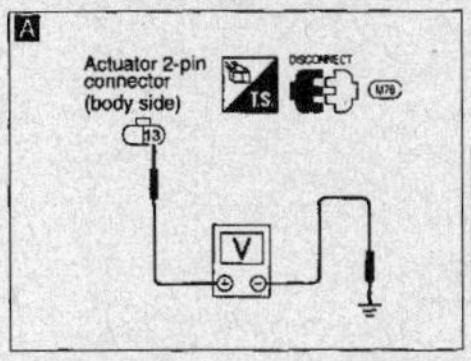

A
Actuator 2-pin connector (body side)
DISCONNECT
T.S.
M76
13
V

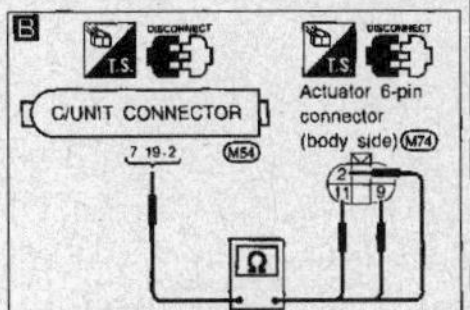

B
DISCONNECT
T.S.
C/UNIT CONNECTOR
7 19 2
M54
Actuator 6-pin connector (body side) M74
2
11
9
Ω

MOTOR POWER SUPPLY CIRCUIT
Check 40A fusible link [d] for actuator.
- NG → (B)
- OK ↓

1. Disconnect connectors from control unit and actuator. Check terminals for damage or loose connection. Then reconnect connectors.
2. Carry out self-diagnosis again.

Does warning lamp activate again?
- No → Inspection end
- Yes ↓

[A]
1. Disconnect actuator 2-pin connector.
2. Check voltage between connector (body side) terminal (13) and ground.

Battery voltage should exist.
- NG → Check the following.
  - Harness connector (M76)
  - Harness for open or short between actuator connector and fuse

  If NG, repair harness or connectors.
- OK ↓

[B]
CIRCUIT CHECK
1. Disconnect actuator 6-pin connector and control unit connector.
2. Check continuity between control unit connector terminals and actuator 6-pin connector (body side) terminals.

Control unit	Actuator
(7)	(11)
(19)	(9)
(2)	(2)

Continuity should exist.
- NG → Check the following.
  - Harness connectors (M54), (M74)
  - Harness for open or short between actuator connector and control unit

  If NG, repair harness or connectors.
- OK ↓

MOTOR RELAY CHECK
Refer to MOTOR RELAY in Electrical Components Inspection.
- NG → Replace motor relay.
- OK ↓

ACTUATOR MOTOR GROUND CHECK
- NG → Check the following.
  - Harness connector (M74)
  - Harness for open or short between actuator connector and ground

  If NG, repair harness or connectors.
- OK ↓ (A)

NS4029600225010X

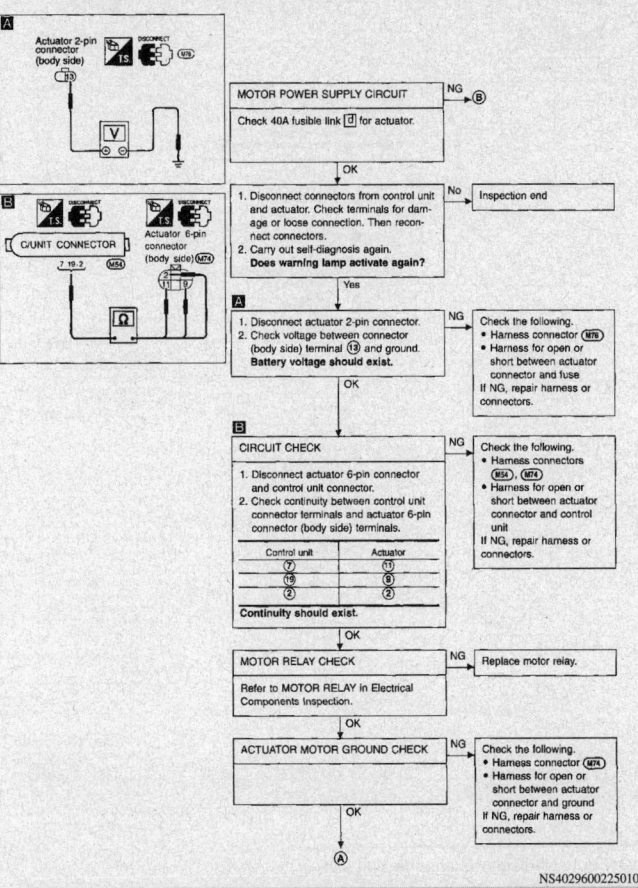

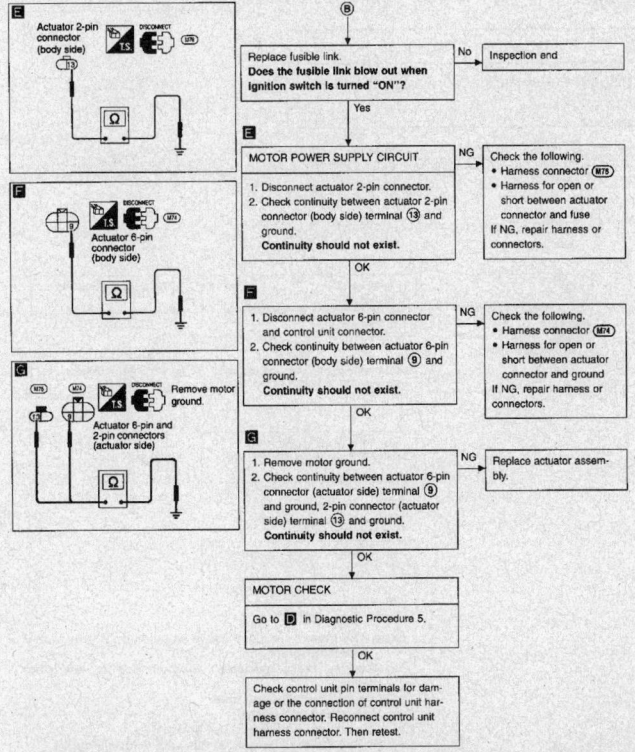

Fig. 171 Test 5: Motor Relay Or Motor (Part 1 of 3). 1996 Pathfinder

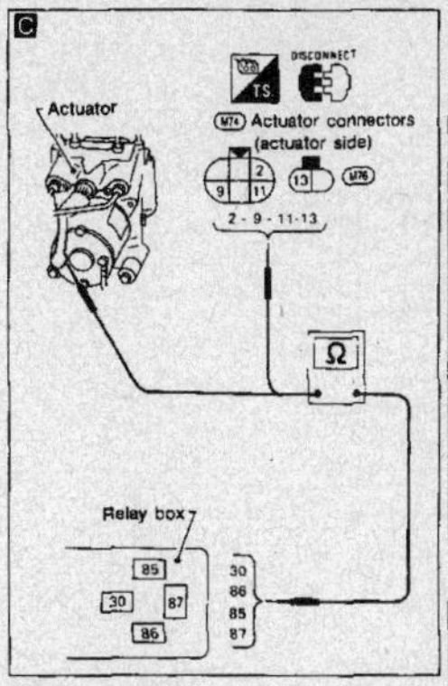

C
Actuator
DISCONNECT
T.S.
M74 Actuator connectors (actuator side)
2
9 11
13
M76
2 · 9 · 11·13
Ω
Relay box
85
30
87
86
30
86
85
87

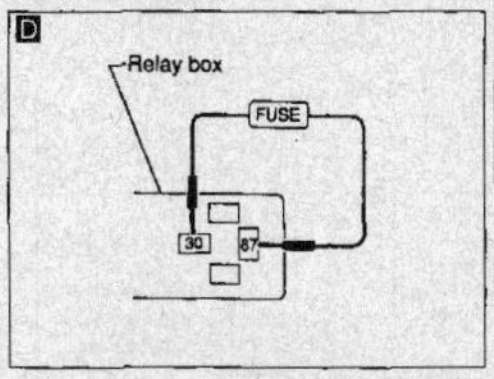

D
Relay box
FUSE
30
87

(A) ↓

[C]
MOTOR RELAY CIRCUIT
1. Remove motor relay.
2. Check continuity between actuator connector (actuator side) terminals and relay connector terminals.

Actuator connector	Relay connector
(2)	(86)
(11)	(85)
(9)	(30)
(13)	(87)
Actuator motor positive terminal	(30)

Continuity should exist.
- NG → Replace relay box assembly.
- OK ↓

[D]
MOTOR CHECK
1. Connect actuator connectors.
2. Connect suitable wire between relay connector terminals (30) and (87).

Motor should operate.
Do not connect wire for more than 5 seconds.
- NG → Replace actuator assembly.
- OK ↓

Go to diagnostic procedure 7.

NS4029600225020X

Fig. 171 Test 5: Motor Relay Or Motor (Part 2 of 3). 1996 Pathfinder

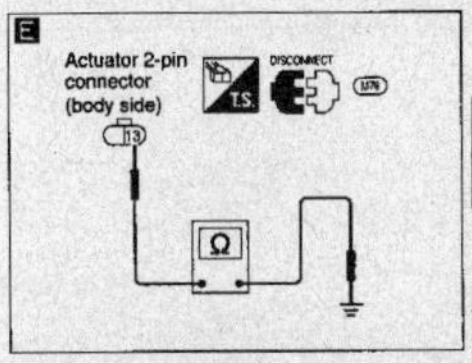

E
Actuator 2-pin connector (body side)
DISCONNECT
T.S.
M76
13
Ω

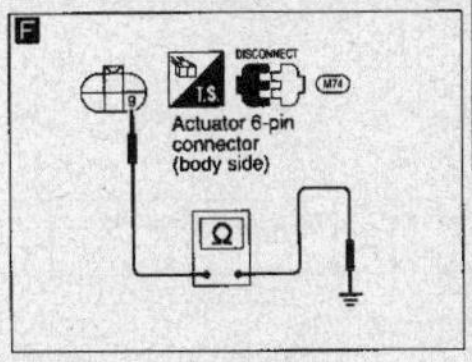

F
9
DISCONNECT
T.S.
M74
Actuator 6-pin connector (body side)
Ω

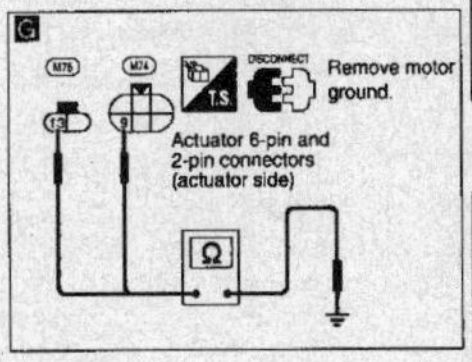

G
M76
M74
DISCONNECT
T.S.
Remove motor ground.
13
9
Actuator 6-pin and 2-pin connectors (actuator side)
Ω

(B) ↓

Replace fusible link.
Does the fusible link blow out when ignition switch is turned "ON"?
- No → Inspection end
- Yes ↓

[E]
MOTOR POWER SUPPLY CIRCUIT
1. Disconnect actuator 2-pin connector.
2. Check continuity between actuator 2-pin connector (body side) terminal (13) and ground.

Continuity should not exist.
- NG → Check the following.
  - Harness connector (M76)
  - Harness for open or short between actuator connector and fuse

  If NG, repair harness or connectors.
- OK ↓

[F]
1. Disconnect actuator 6-pin connector and control unit connector.
2. Check continuity between actuator 6-pin connector (body side) terminal (9) and ground.

Continuity should not exist.
- NG → Check the following.
  - Harness connector (M74)
  - Harness for open or short between actuator connector and ground

  If NG, repair harness or connectors.
- OK ↓

[G]
1. Remove motor ground.
2. Check continuity between actuator 6-pin connector (actuator side) terminal (9) and ground, 2-pin connector (actuator side) terminal (13) and ground.

Continuity should not exist.
- NG → Replace actuator assembly.
- OK ↓

MOTOR CHECK
Go to [D] in Diagnostic Procedure 5.
- OK ↓

Check control unit pin terminals for damage or the connection of control unit harness connector. Reconnect control unit harness connector. Then retest.

NS4029600225030X

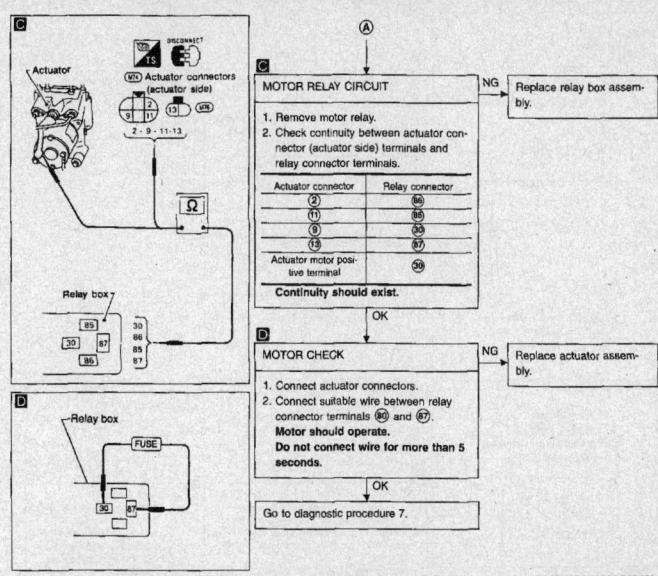

Fig. 171 Test 5: Motor Relay Or Motor (Part 3 of 3). 1996 Pathfinder

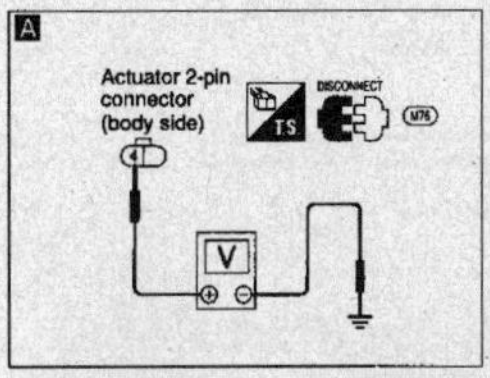

A
Actuator 2-pin connector (body side)
DISCONNECT
T.S.
M76
4
V

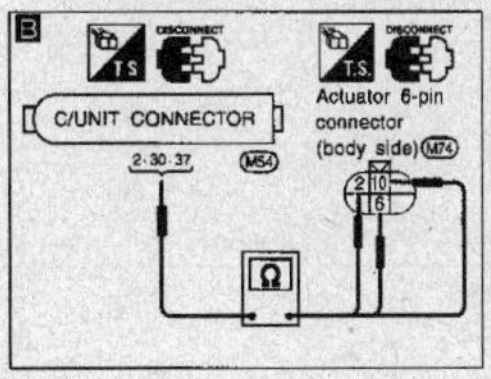

B
DISCONNECT
T.S.
C/UNIT CONNECTOR
2·30 37
M54
Actuator 6-pin connector (body side) M74
2
10
6
Ω

SOLENOID VALVE POWER SUPPLY CHECK
Check 40A fusible link [c].
- NG → (A)
- OK ↓

1. Disconnect connectors from control unit and actuator. Check terminals for damage or loose connection. Then reconnect connectors.
2. Carry out self-diagnosis again.

Does warning lamp activate again?
- No → Inspection end
- Yes ↓

GROUND CIRCUIT CHECK
- NG → Check the following.
  - Harness connectors (M54), (M74)
  - Harness for open or short between actuator harness and ground
  - Harness for open or short between control unit and ground

  If NG, repair harness or connectors.
- OK ↓

[A]
SOLENOID VALVE POWER SUPPLY CHECK
1. Disconnect connectors from actuator.
2. Check voltage between actuator 2-pin connector (body side) terminal (4) and ground.

Battery voltage should exist.
- NG → Check the following.
  - Harness connector (M76)
  - Harness for open or short between actuator connector and fuse

  If NG, repair harness or connectors.
- OK ↓

[B]
CIRCUIT CHECK
1. Disconnect control unit connector.
2. Check continuity between control unit connector terminals and actuator connector (body side) terminals.

Control unit	Actuator
(37)	(6)
(2)	(2)
(30)	(10)

Continuity should exist.
- NG → Check the following.
  - Harness connectors (M54), (M74)
  - Harness for open or short between actuator connector and control unit

  If NG, repair harness or connectors.
- OK ↓

SOLENOID VALVE RELAY CHECK
- NG → Replace solenoid valve relay.
- OK ↓ (B)

NS4029600226010X

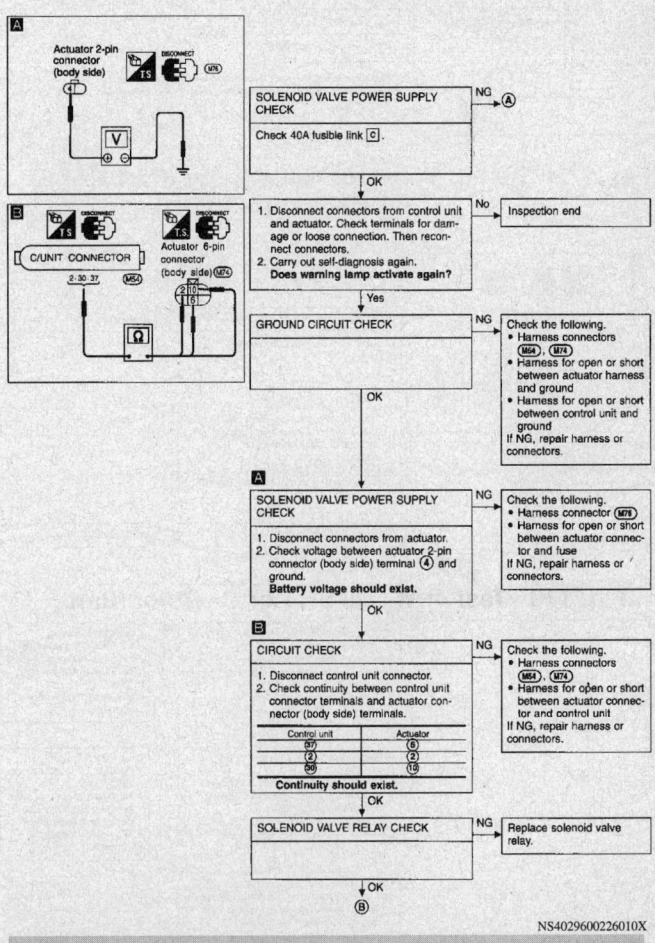

Fig. 172 Test 6: Solenoid Valve Relay (Part 1 of 2). 1996 Pathfinder

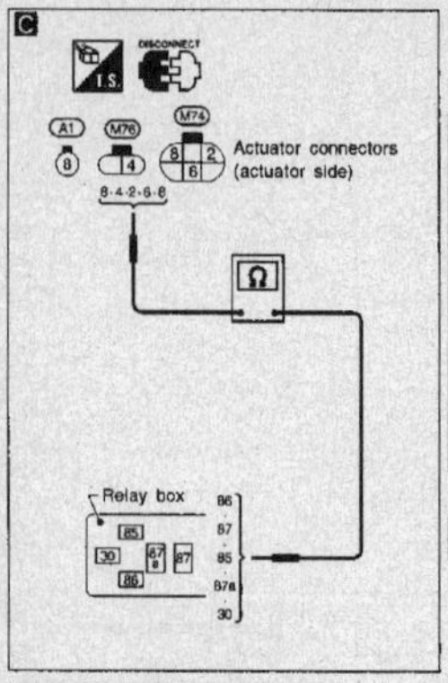
C
DISCONNECT
T.S.
A1
M76
M74
Actuator connectors (actuator side)
8-4-2-6-8
Relay box
86
87
85
87a
30

(B)

C

SOLENOID VALVE RELAY CIRCUIT CHECK — NG → Replace relay box.

Check continuity between relay terminals and actuator connector (actuator side) terminals.

Relay terminals	Actuator connectors
(30) ⊕	(8) ⊖
(87)	(4)
(87a)	(8)
(85)	(6)
(86)	(2)

Continuity should exist.
Note: Pay attention to tester polarity*.

↓ OK

Go to diagnostic procedure 3.

(A)

Replace fusible link.
Is the fusible link blown out when ignition switch is turned "ON"? — No → Inspection end

↓ Yes

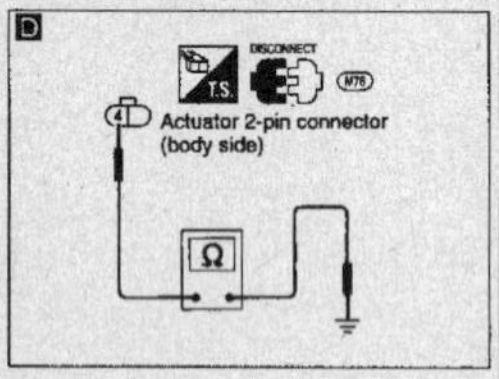
D
DISCONNECT
T.S.
M76
Actuator 2-pin connector (body side)
4

D

ACTUATOR POWER SUPPLY CIRCUIT — NG → Check the following.
- Harness connector (M76)
- Harness for open or short between actuator connector and fuse

If NG, repair harness or connectors.

1. Disconnect actuator 2-pin connector.
2. Check continuity between actuator 2-pin connector (body side) terminal (4) and ground.
   Continuity should not exist.

↓ OK

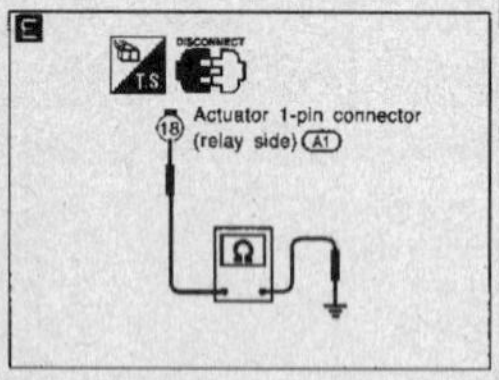
E
DISCONNECT
T.S.
Actuator 1-pin connector (relay side) A1
18

E

1. Disconnect actuator 1-pin and 6-pin connectors and control unit connector.
2. Check continuity between actuator 1-pin connector (relay side) terminal (18) and ground.
   Continuity should not exist.

— NG → Repair relay box.

↓ OK

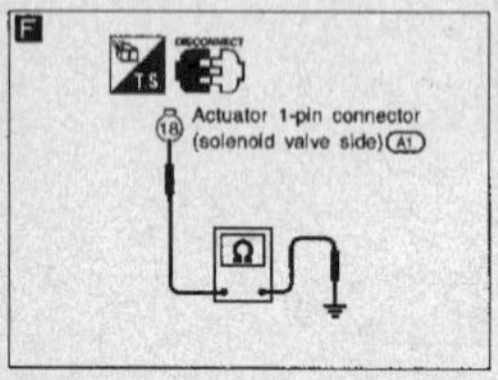
F
DISCONNECT
T.S.
Actuator 1-pin connector (solenoid valve side) A1
18

F

Check continuity between actuator 1-pin connector (solenoid valve side) terminal (18) and ground.
Continuity should not exist. — NG → Replace actuator assembly.

↓ OK

Go to diagnostic procedure 3.

***: Specifications may vary depending on the type of tester. Before performing this inspection, refer to the instruction manual of the tester.**

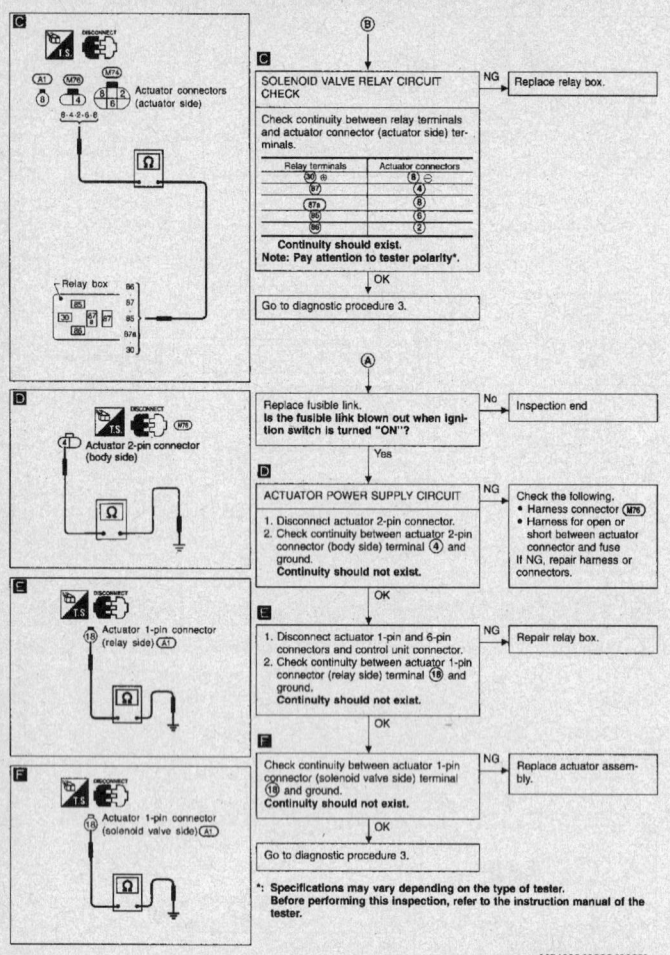

NS4029600226020X

Fig. 172 Test 6: Solenoid Valve Relay (Part 2 of 2). 1996 Pathfinder

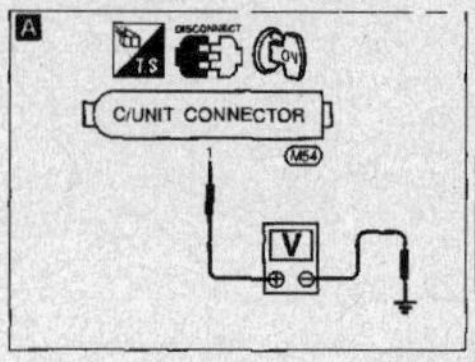
A
DISCONNECT
T.S.
C/UNIT CONNECTOR
M54
V

1. Disconnect control unit connectors. Check terminals for damage or connection. Then reconnect connectors.
2. Carry out self-diagnosis again.
   Does warning lamp activate again?

— No → Inspection end

↓ Yes

A

CONTROL UNIT POWER SUPPLY CHECK — NG → (A)

1. Disconnect control unit connector.
2. Check voltage between control unit connector terminal (1) and ground.
   Battery voltage should exist when ignition switch is turned ON.

↓ OK

CONTROL UNIT GROUND CHECK — NG → Check the following.
- Harness connector (M54)
- Harness for open or short between control unit and ground

If NG, repair harness or connectors.

↓ OK

Check control unit pin terminals for damage or the connection of control unit harness connector. Reconnect control unit harness connector. Then retest.

(A)

Check 7.5A fuse [28]. — NG → Replace fuse.

↓ OK

Check continuity between battery and control unit connector terminal (1). — NG → Check the following.
- Harness connector (M54)
- Harness for open or short between control unit and fuse

If NG, repair harness or connectors.

↓ OK

Check battery.

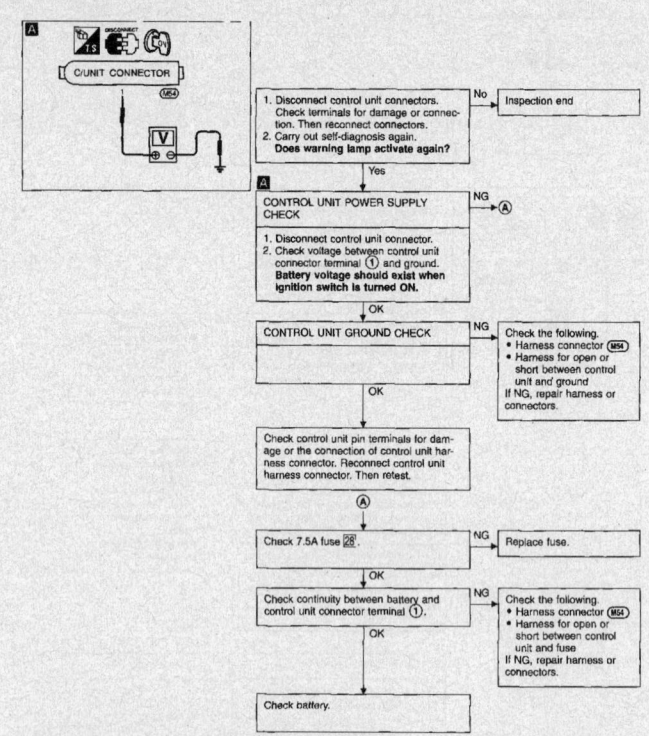

NS4029600227000X

Fig. 173 Test 7: Power Supply Low Voltage. 1996 Pathfinder

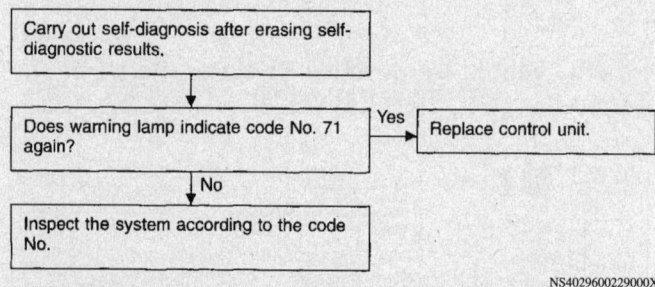

Carry out self-diagnosis after erasing self-diagnostic results.

↓

Does warning lamp indicate code No. 71 again? — Yes → Replace control unit.

↓ No

Inspect the system according to the code No.

NS4029600229000X

Fig. 175 Test 9: Control Unit. 1996 Pathfinder

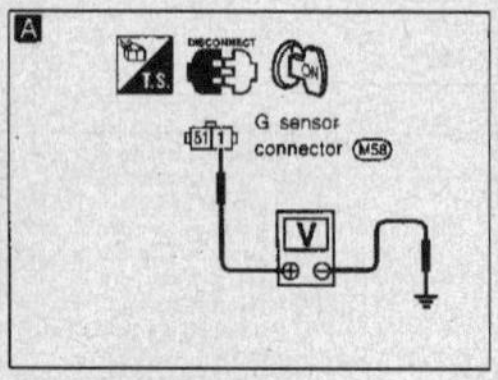
A
DISCONNECT
T.S.
G sensor connector M58
V

G SENSOR POWER SUPPLY CIRCUIT — NG → Replace fuse.

Check 7.5A fuse [28] for control unit.

↓ OK

1. Disconnect connectors from control unit and G sensor. Check terminals for damage or loose connection. Then reconnect connectors.
2. Carry out self-diagnosis again.
   Does warning lamp activate again?

— No → Inspection end

↓ Yes

G SENSOR CHECK — NG → Replace G sensor.

Refer to G SENSOR in Electrical Components Inspection.

↓ OK

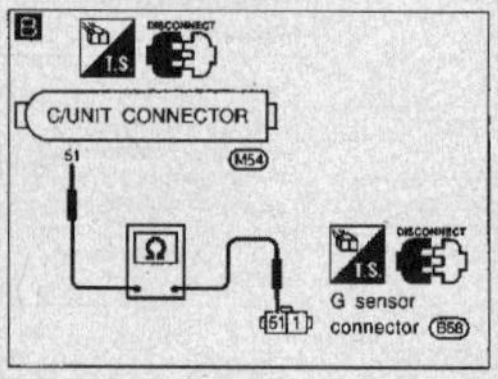
B
DISCONNECT
T.S.
C/UNIT CONNECTOR
51
M54
G sensor connector B56

A

Check voltage between G sensor connector terminal (1) and ground.
Battery voltage should exist. — NG → Check the following.
- Harness connector (M58)
- Harness for open or short between G sensor and fuse

If NG, repair harness or connectors.

↓ OK

B

1. Disconnect harness connector from control unit.
2. Check continuity between control unit connector terminal (51) and G sensor connector terminal (51).
   Continuity should exist.

— NG → Check the following.
- Harness connectors (M54), (M58)
- Harness for open or short between G sensor connector and control unit

If NG, repair harness or connectors.

↓ OK

Check control unit pin terminals for damage or the connection of control unit harness connector. Reconnect control unit harness connector. Then retest.

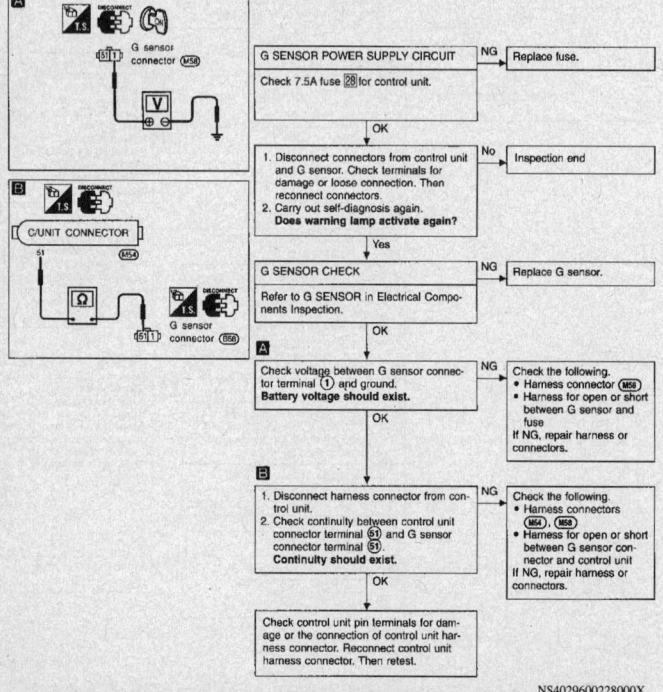

NS4029600228000X

Fig. 174 Test 8: G Sensor. 1996 Pathfinder

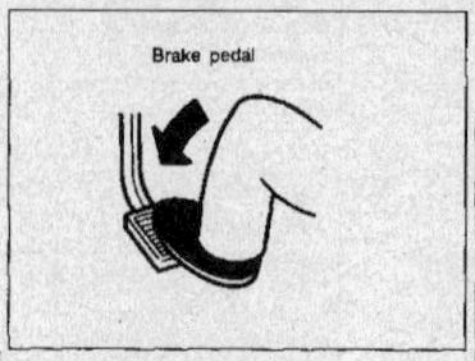
Brake pedal

1. Apply brake.
2. Start engine.
3. Does the symptom appear only when engine is started?

— Yes → Carry out self-diagnosis.

↓ No

Does the symptom appear when electrical equipment switches (such as headlamp) are operated? — No → Go to **E** in Diagnostic Procedure 11.

↓ Yes

Check wheel sensor shield ground secured with control unit mounting bolt.

NG → Repair.

OK → Check control unit pin terminals for damage or the connection of control unit harness connector. Reconnect control unit harness connector. Then retest.

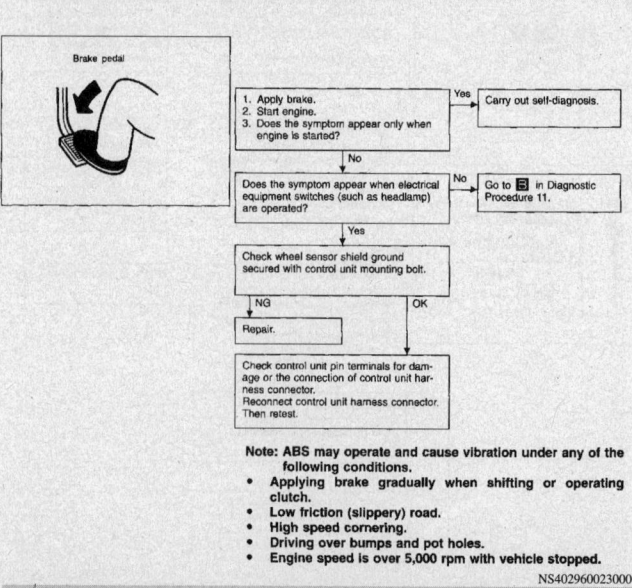

Note: ABS may operate and cause vibration under any of the following conditions.
- **Applying brake gradually when shifting or operating clutch.**
- **Low friction (slippery) road.**
- **High speed cornering.**
- **Driving over bumps and pot holes.**
- **Engine speed is over 5,000 rpm with vehicle stopped.**

NS4029600230000X

Fig. 176 Test 10: Pedal Vibration & Noise. 1996 Pathfinder

Disconnect ABS relay unit 8-pin connector and check whether stopping distance is still long.

- No → Go to B in Diagnostic Procedure 11.
- Yes → Perform Preliminary Check and air bleeding.

Note: Stopping distance may be larger than vehicles without ABS when road condition is slippery.

NS4029600231000X

Fig. 177 Test 11: Long Stopping Distance. 1996 Pathfinder

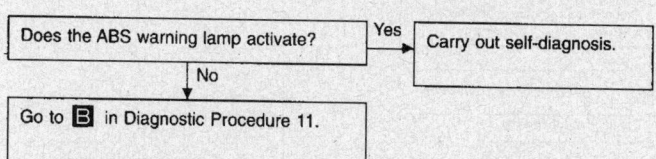

Does the ABS warning lamp activate?

- Yes → Carry out self-diagnosis.
- No → Go to B in Diagnostic Procedure 11.

Note: ABS does not work when vehicle speed is under 10 km/h (6 MPH).

NS4029600233000X

Fig. 179 Test 13: ABS Does Not Work. 1996 Pathfinder

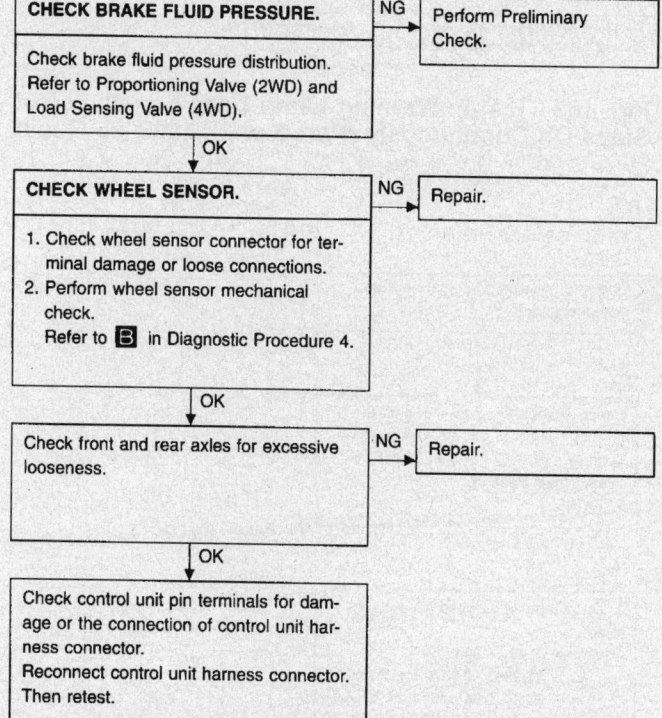

CHECK BRAKE FLUID PRESSURE.

Check brake fluid pressure distribution. Refer to Proportioning Valve (2WD) and Load Sensing Valve (4WD).

- NG → Perform Preliminary Check.
- OK ↓

CHECK WHEEL SENSOR.

1. Check wheel sensor connector for terminal damage or loose connections.
2. Perform wheel sensor mechanical check.
   Refer to B in Diagnostic Procedure 4.

- NG → Repair.
- OK ↓

Check front and rear axles for excessive looseness.

- NG → Repair.
- OK ↓

Check control unit pin terminals for damage or the connection of control unit harness connector.
Reconnect control unit harness connector.
Then retest.

NS4029600234000X

Fig. 180 Test 14: ABS Works Frequently. 1996 Pathfinder

A

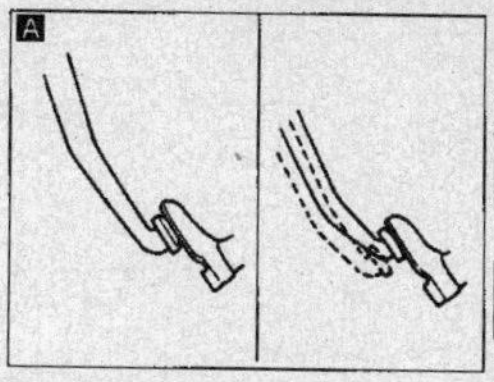

B

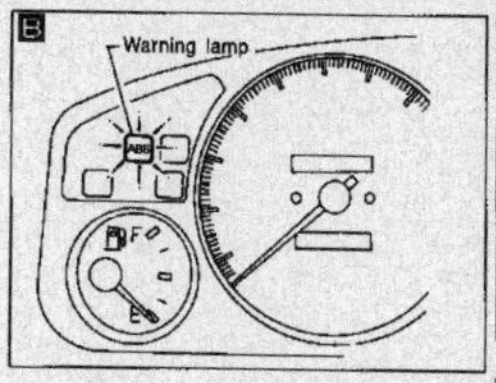
Warning lamp

A

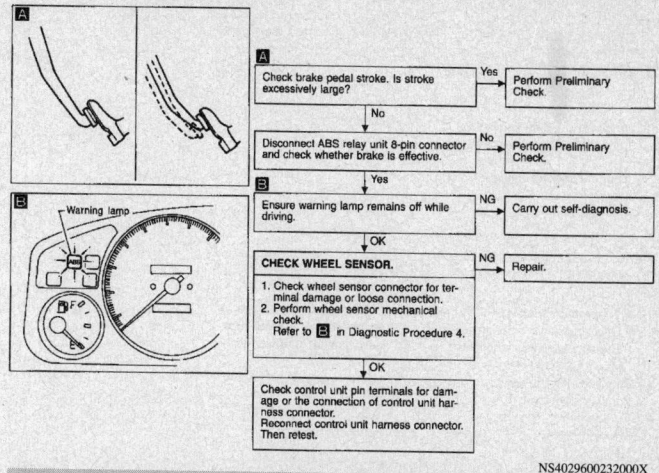

Check brake pedal stroke. Is stroke excessively large?

- Yes → Perform Preliminary Check.
- No ↓

Disconnect ABS relay unit 8-pin connector and check whether brake is effective.

- No → Perform Preliminary Check.
- Yes ↓

B

Ensure warning lamp remains off while driving.

- NG → Carry out self-diagnosis.
- OK ↓

CHECK WHEEL SENSOR.

1. Check wheel sensor connector for terminal damage or loose connection.
2. Perform wheel sensor mechanical check.
   Refer to B in Diagnostic Procedure 4.

- NG → Repair.
- OK ↓

Check control unit pin terminals for damage or the connection of control unit harness connector.
Reconnect control unit harness connector.
Then retest.

NS4029600232000X

Fig. 178 Test 12: Unexpected Pedal Action. 1996 Pathfinder

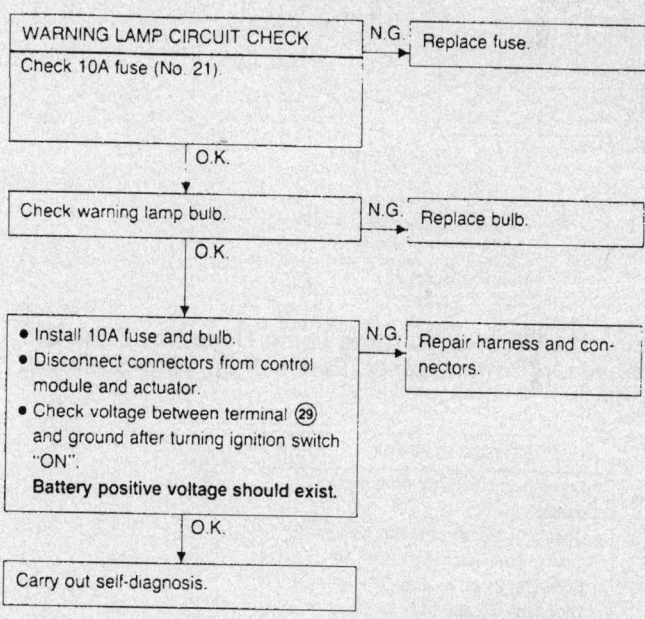

WARNING LAMP CIRCUIT CHECK

Check 10A fuse (No. 21).

- N.G. → Replace fuse.
- O.K. ↓

Check warning lamp bulb.

- N.G. → Replace bulb.
- O.K. ↓

- Install 10A fuse and bulb.
- Disconnect connectors from control module and actuator.
- Check voltage between terminal (29) and ground after turning ignition switch "ON".

Battery positive voltage should exist.

- N.G. → Repair harness and connectors.
- O.K. ↓

Carry out self-diagnosis.

NS4029100105000X

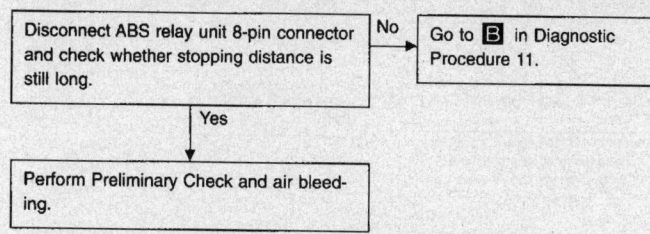

Fig. 181 Test 1: Warning Lamp Does Not Work Before Engine Starts. 1993–95 Quest

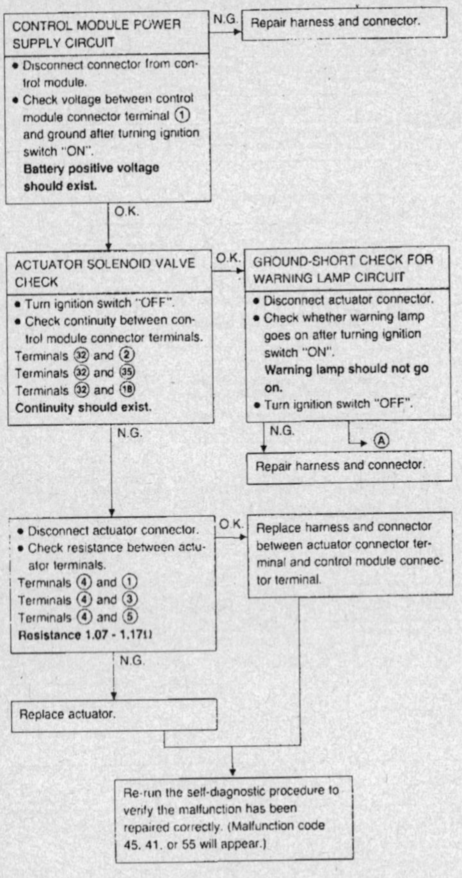
CONTROL MODULE POWER SUPPLY CIRCUIT
• Disconnect connector from control module.
• Check voltage between control module connector terminal ① and ground after turning ignition switch "ON".
Battery positive voltage should exist.
N.G.
Repair harness and connector.
O.K.
ACTUATOR SOLENOID VALVE CHECK
• Turn ignition switch "OFF".
• Check continuity between control module connector terminals.
Terminals ㉜ and ②
Terminals ㉜ and ㉟
Terminals ㉜ and ⑱
Continuity should exist.
O.K.
GROUND-SHORT CHECK FOR WARNING LAMP CIRCUIT
• Disconnect actuator connector.
• Check whether warning lamp goes on after turning ignition switch "ON".
Warning lamp should not go on.
• Turn ignition switch "OFF".
N.G.
Ⓐ
Repair harness and connector.
N.G.
• Disconnect actuator connector.
• Check resistance between actuator terminals.
Terminals ④ and ①
Terminals ④ and ③
Terminals ④ and ⑤
Resistance 1.07 - 1.17Ω
O.K.
Replace harness and connector between actuator connector terminal and control module connector terminal.
N.G.
Replace actuator.
Re-run the self-diagnostic procedure to verify the malfunction has been repaired correctly. (Malfunction code 45, 41, or 55 will appear.)
NS4029100106010X

Fig. 182 Test 2: Warning Lamp Does Not Blink But Stays On Continuously (Part 1 of 2). 1993–95 Quest

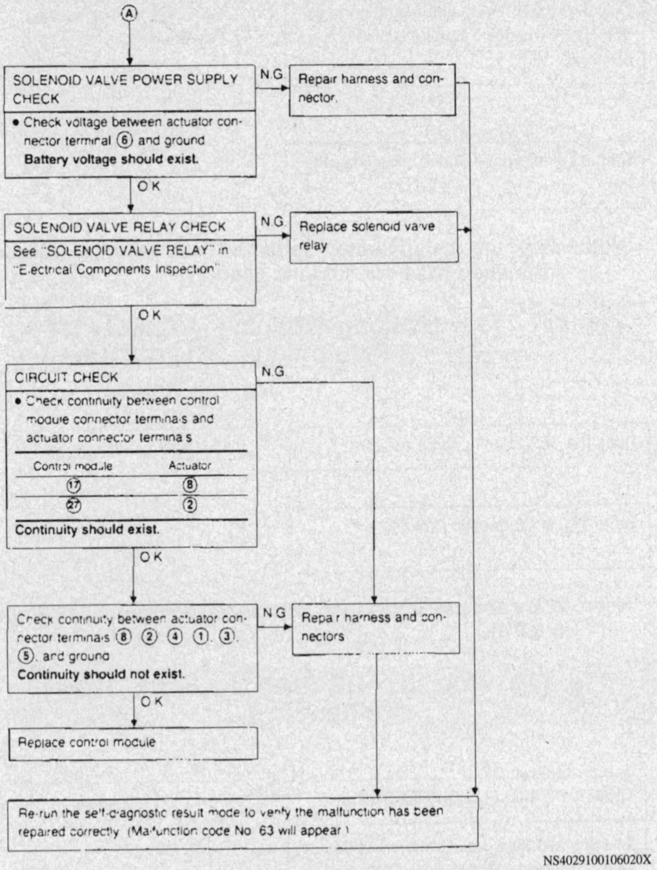
Ⓐ
SOLENOID VALVE POWER SUPPLY CHECK
• Check voltage between actuator connector terminal ⑥ and ground.
Battery voltage should exist.
N.G.
Repair harness and connector.
O.K.
SOLENOID VALVE RELAY CHECK
See "SOLENOID VALVE RELAY" in "Electrical Components Inspection".
N.G.
Replace solenoid valve relay.
O.K.
CIRCUIT CHECK
• Check continuity between control module connector terminals and actuator connector terminals.
Control module | Actuator
⑰ | ⑧
㉗ | ②
Continuity should exist.
N.G.
O.K.
Check continuity between actuator connector terminals ⑧ ② ④ ①, ③, ⑤, and ground.
Continuity should not exist.
N.G.
Repair harness and connectors.
O.K.
Replace control module.
Re-run the self-diagnostic result mode to verify the malfunction has been repaired correctly. (Malfunction code No. 63 will appear.)
NS4029100106020X

Fig. 182 Test 2: Warning Lamp Does Not Blink But Stays On Continuously (Part 2 of 2). 1993–95 Quest

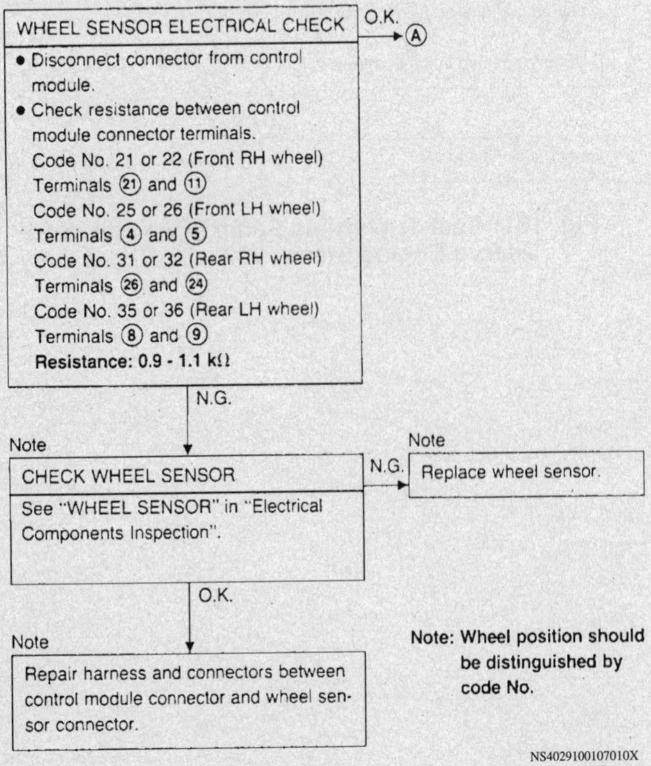
WHEEL SENSOR ELECTRICAL CHECK
• Disconnect connector from control module.
• Check resistance between control module connector terminals.
Code No. 21 or 22 (Front RH wheel)
Terminals ㉑ and ⑪
Code No. 25 or 26 (Front LH wheel)
Terminals ④ and ⑤
Code No. 31 or 32 (Rear RH wheel)
Terminals ㉖ and ㉔
Code No. 35 or 36 (Rear LH wheel)
Terminals ⑧ and ⑨
Resistance: 0.9 - 1.1 kΩ
O.K.
Ⓐ
N.G.
Note
CHECK WHEEL SENSOR
See "WHEEL SENSOR" in "Electrical Components Inspection".
N.G.
Note
Replace wheel sensor.
O.K.
Note
Repair harness and connectors between control module connector and wheel sensor connector.
Note: Wheel position should be distinguished by code No.
NS4029100107010X

Fig. 183 Test 3: Wheel Sensor (Part 1 of 2). 1993–95 Quest

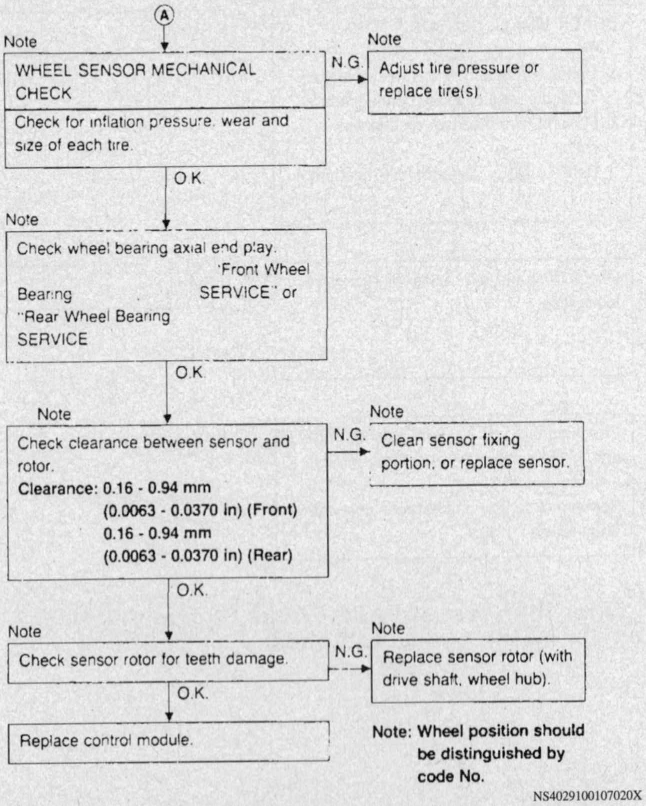
Ⓐ
Note
WHEEL SENSOR MECHANICAL CHECK
Check for inflation pressure, wear and size of each tire.
N.G.
Note
Adjust tire pressure or replace tire(s).
O.K.
Note
Check wheel bearing axial end play.
'Front Wheel Bearing SERVICE' or
"Rear Wheel Bearing SERVICE
O.K.
Note
Check clearance between sensor and rotor.
Clearance: 0.16 - 0.94 mm
(0.0063 - 0.0370 in) (Front)
0.16 - 0.94 mm
(0.0063 - 0.0370 in) (Rear)
N.G.
Note
Clean sensor fixing portion, or replace sensor.
O.K.
Note
Check sensor rotor for teeth damage.
N.G.
Note
Replace sensor rotor (with drive shaft, wheel hub).
O.K.
Replace control module.
Note: Wheel position should be distinguished by code No.
NS4029100107020X

Fig. 183 Test 3: Wheel Sensor (Part 2 of 2). 1993–95 Quest

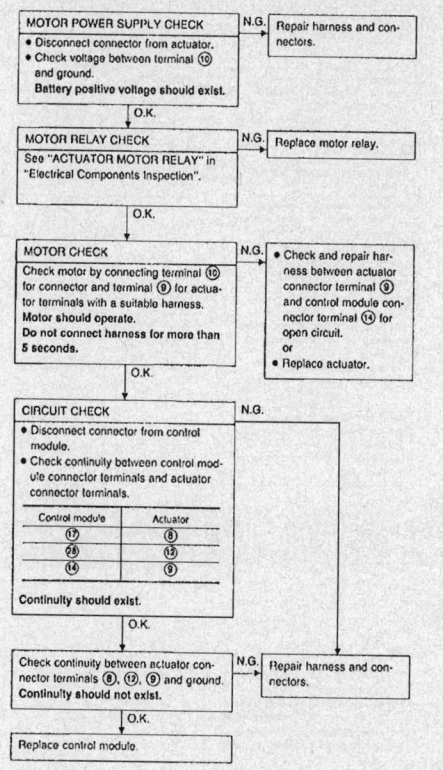

MOTOR POWER SUPPLY CHECK
- Disconnect connector from actuator.
- Check voltage between terminal ⑩ and ground.

Battery positive voltage should exist.

N.G. → Repair harness and connectors.

O.K. ↓

MOTOR RELAY CHECK
See "ACTUATOR MOTOR RELAY" in "Electrical Components Inspection".

N.G. → Replace motor relay.

O.K. ↓

MOTOR CHECK
Check motor by connecting terminal ⑩ for connector and terminal ⑨ for actuator terminals with a suitable harness.
Motor should operate.
Do not connect harness for more than 5 seconds.

N.G. →
- Check and repair harness between actuator connector terminal ⑨ and control module connector terminal ⑭ for open circuit.

or
- Replace actuator.

O.K. ↓

CIRCUIT CHECK
- Disconnect connector from control module.
- Check continuity between control module connector terminals and actuator connector terminals.

Control module	Actuator
⑰	⑧
㉖	⑫
⑭	⑨

Continuity should exist.

N.G. → Repair harness and connectors.

O.K. ↓

Check continuity between actuator connector terminals ⑧, ⑫, ⑨ and ground.
Continuity should not exist.

N.G. → Repair harness and connectors.

O.K. ↓

Replace control module.

NS4029100108000X

Fig. 184 Test 4: Motor Relay Or Motor. 1993–95 Quest

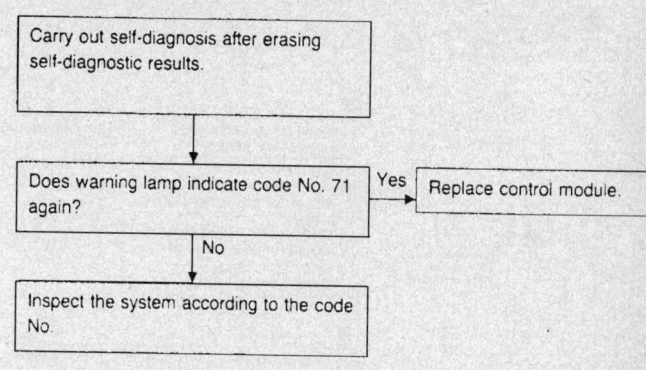

Carry out self-diagnosis after erasing self-diagnostic results.

↓

Does warning lamp indicate code No. 71 again?

Yes → Replace control module.

No ↓

Inspect the system according to the code No.

NS4029100109000X

Fig. 185 Test 5: Control Module. 1993–95 Quest

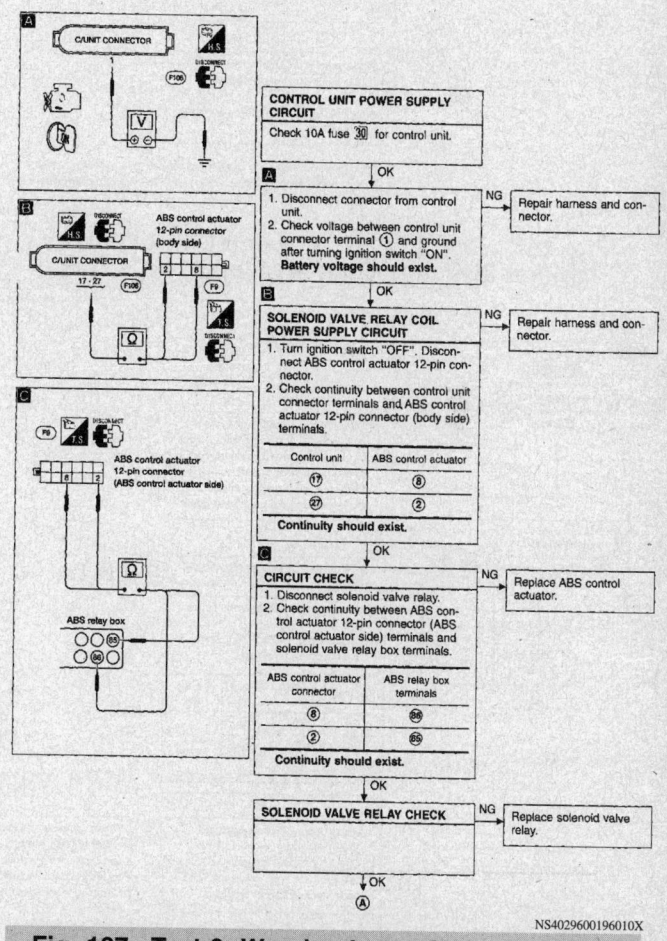

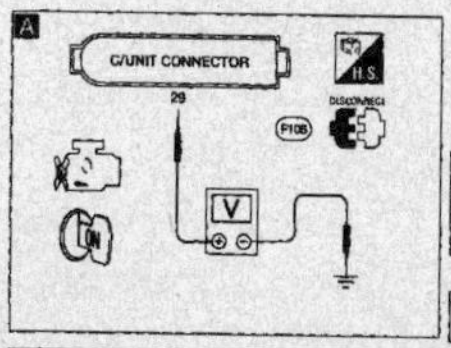

A
C/UNIT CONNECTOR
29
F106
H.S.
DISCONNECT
V

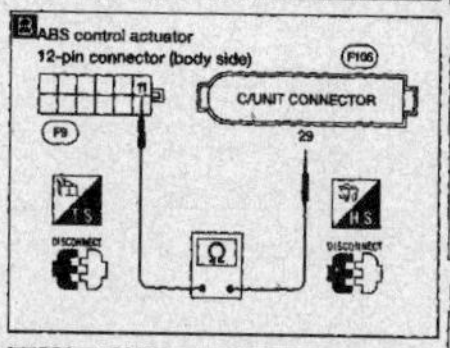

B
ABS control actuator
12-pin connector (body side)
F106
C/UNIT CONNECTOR
F9
29
T.S.
H.S.

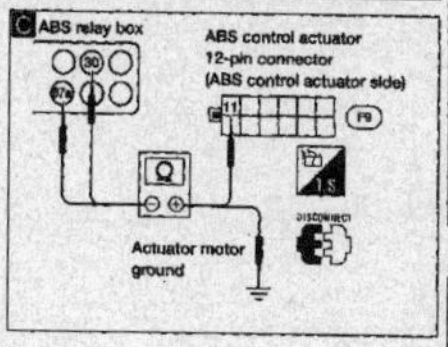

C
ABS relay box
ABS control actuator
12-pin connector
(ABS control actuator side)
F9
Actuator motor ground

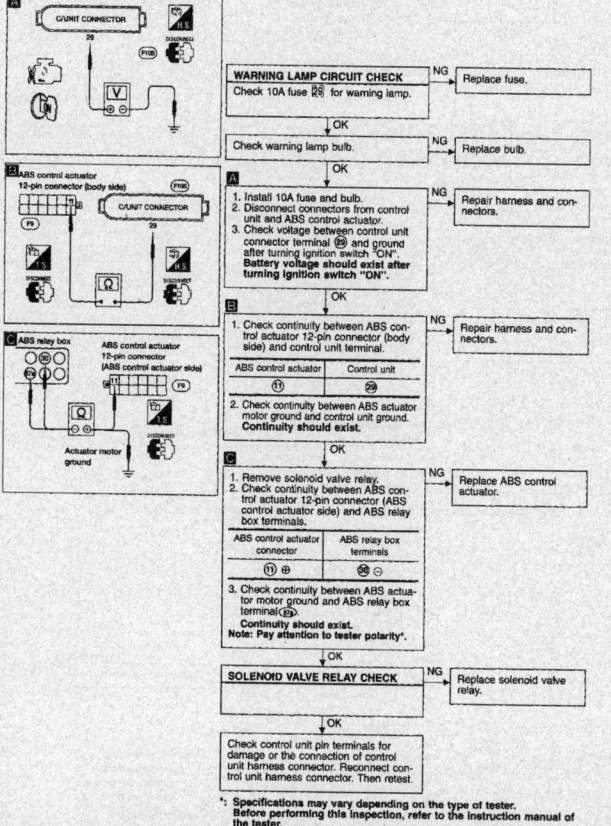

WARNING LAMP CIRCUIT CHECK
Check 10A fuse 29 for warning lamp.

NG → Replace fuse.

OK ↓

Check warning lamp bulb.

NG → Replace bulb.

OK ↓

A
1. Install 10A fuse and bulb.
2. Disconnect connectors from control unit and ABS control actuator.
3. Check voltage between control unit connector terminal ㉙ and ground after turning ignition switch "ON".
Battery voltage should exist after turning ignition switch "ON".

NG → Repair harness and connectors.

OK ↓

B
1. Check continuity between ABS control actuator 12-pin connector (body side) and control unit terminal.

ABS control actuator	Control unit
⑪	㉙

2. Check continuity between ABS actuator motor ground and control unit ground.
Continuity should exist.

NG → Repair harness and connectors.

OK ↓

C
1. Remove solenoid valve relay.
2. Check continuity between ABS control actuator 12-pin connector (ABS control actuator side) and ABS relay box terminals.

ABS control actuator connector	ABS relay box terminals
⑪ ⊕	㉚ ⊖

3. Check continuity between ABS actuator motor ground and ABS relay box terminal (87a).
Continuity should exist.
Note: Pay attention to tester polarity*.

NG → Replace ABS control actuator.

OK ↓

SOLENOID VALVE RELAY CHECK

NG → Replace solenoid valve relay.

OK ↓

Check control unit pin terminals for damage or the connection of control unit harness connector. Reconnect control unit harness connector. Then retest.

*: **Specifications may vary depending on the type of tester. Before performing this inspection, refer to the instruction manual of the tester.**

NS4029600195000X

Fig. 186 Test 1: Warning Lamp Does Not Work When Ignition Is On. 1996 Quest

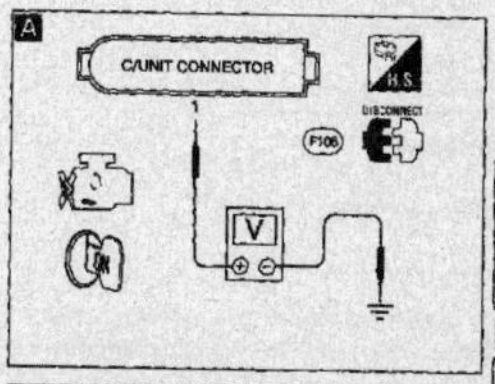

A
C/UNIT CONNECTOR
1
F106
H.S.
DISCONNECT
V

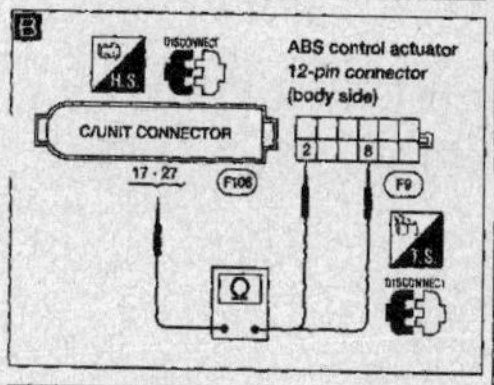

B
H.S.
DISCONNECT
ABS control actuator
12-pin connector
(body side)
C/UNIT CONNECTOR
17 · 27
F106
F9
T.S.
DISCONNECT

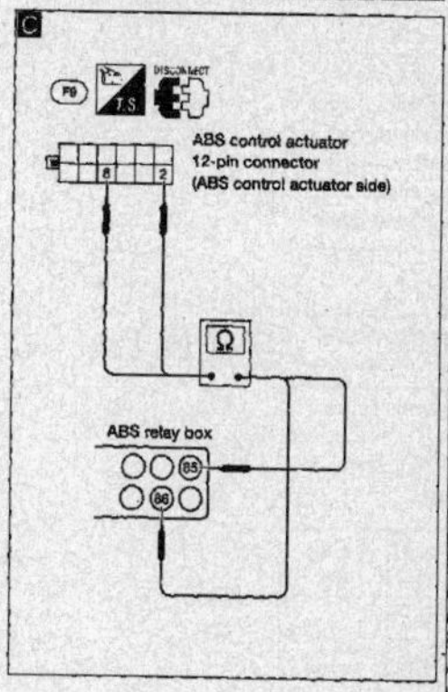

C
F9
T.S.
DISCONNECT
ABS control actuator
12-pin connector
(ABS control actuator side)
ABS relay box

CONTROL UNIT POWER SUPPLY CIRCUIT
Check 10A fuse 30 for control unit.

OK ↓

A
1. Disconnect connector from control unit.
2. Check voltage between control unit connector terminal ① and ground after turning ignition switch "ON".
Battery voltage should exist.

NG → Repair harness and connector.

OK ↓

B
SOLENOID VALVE RELAY COIL POWER SUPPLY CIRCUIT
1. Turn ignition switch "OFF". Disconnect ABS control actuator 12-pin connector.
2. Check continuity between control unit connector terminals and ABS control actuator 12-pin connector (body side) terminals.

Control unit	ABS control actuator
⑰	⑧
㉗	②

Continuity should exist.

NG → Repair harness and connector.

OK ↓

C
CIRCUIT CHECK
1. Disconnect solenoid valve relay.
2. Check continuity between ABS control actuator 12-pin connector (ABS control actuator side) terminals and solenoid valve relay box terminals.

ABS control actuator connector	ABS relay box terminals
⑧	86
②	85

Continuity should exist.

NG → Replace ABS control actuator.

OK ↓

SOLENOID VALVE RELAY CHECK

NG → Replace solenoid valve relay.

OK ↓

Ⓐ

NS4029600196010X

Fig. 187 Test 2: Warning Lamp Stays On When Ignition Switch Is On (Part 1 of 3). 1996 Quest

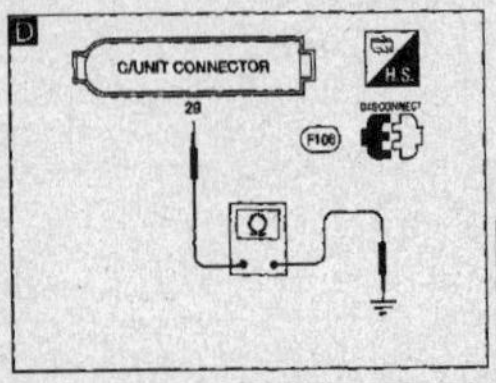
D
C/UNIT CONNECTOR
29
F106
DISCONNECT
H.S.

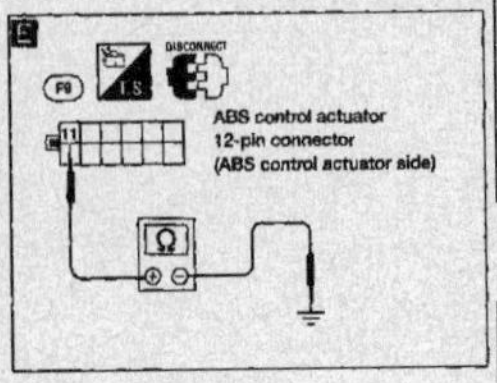
E
F9
DISCONNECT
H.S.
11
ABS control actuator
12-pin connector
(ABS control actuator side)

Ⓐ

D

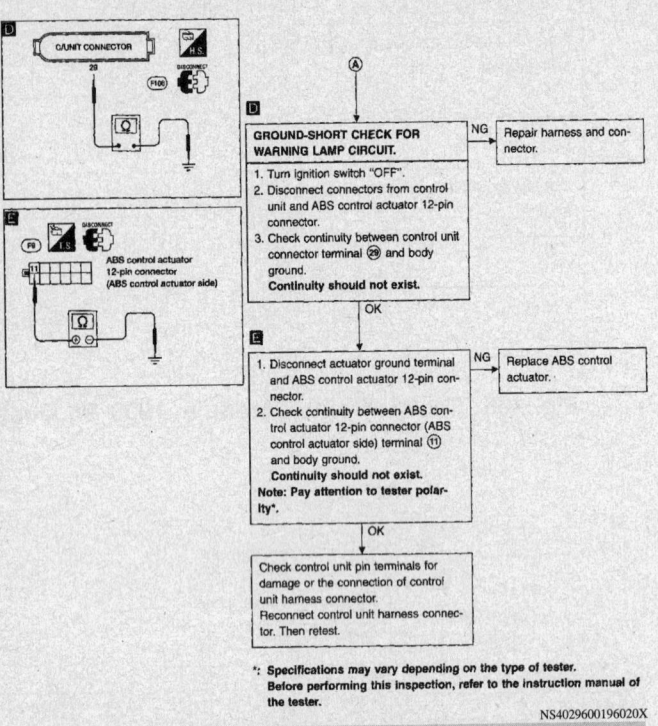

GROUND-SHORT CHECK FOR WARNING LAMP CIRCUIT.

1. Turn ignition switch "OFF".
2. Disconnect connectors from control unit and ABS control actuator 12-pin connector.
3. Check continuity between control unit connector terminal (29) and body ground.
   Continuity should not exist.

NG → Repair harness and connector.

OK ↓

E

1. Disconnect actuator ground terminal and ABS control actuator 12-pin connector.
2. Check continuity between ABS control actuator 12-pin connector (ABS control actuator side) terminal (11) and body ground.
   Continuity should not exist.

Note: Pay attention to tester polarity*.

NG → Replace ABS control actuator.

OK ↓

Check control unit pin terminals for damage or the connection of control unit harness connector.
Reconnect control unit harness connector. Then retest.

***: Specifications may vary depending on the type of tester. Before performing this inspection, refer to the instruction manual of the tester.**

NS4029600196020X

Fig. 187 Test 2: Warning Lamp Stays On When Ignition Switch Is On (Part 2 of 3). 1996 Quest

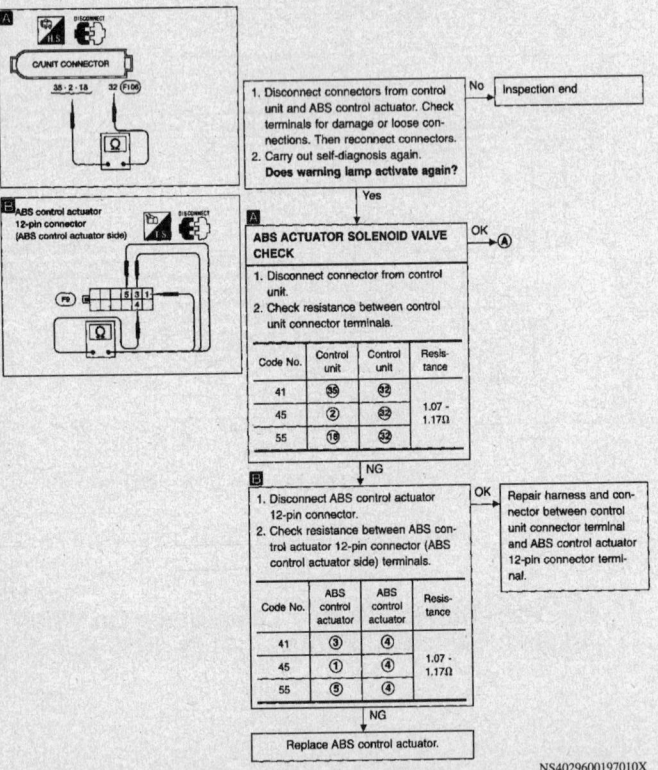

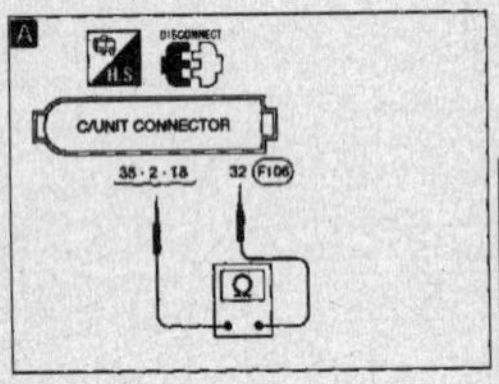
A
DISCONNECT
H.S.
C/UNIT CONNECTOR
35 · 2 · 18
32
F106

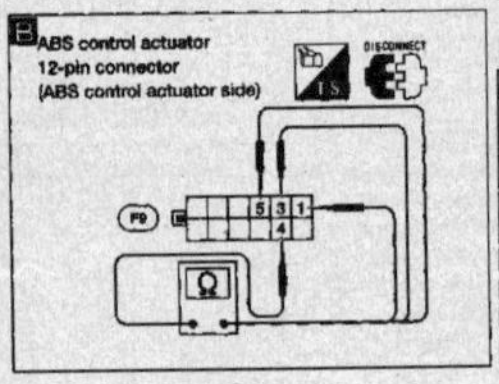
B
ABS control actuator
12-pin connector
(ABS control actuator side)
DISCONNECT
H.S.
F9
5
3
1
4

1. Disconnect connectors from control unit and ABS control actuator. Check terminals for damage or loose connections. Then reconnect connectors.
2. Carry out self-diagnosis again.
   Does warning lamp activate again?

No → Inspection end

Yes ↓

A

ABS ACTUATOR SOLENOID VALVE CHECK

OK → Ⓐ

1. Disconnect connector from control unit.
2. Check resistance between control unit connector terminals.

Code No.	Control unit	Control unit	Resistance
41	(35)	(32)	1.07 - 1.17Ω
45	(2)	(32)	
55	(18)	(32)	

NG ↓

B

1. Disconnect ABS control actuator 12-pin connector.
2. Check resistance between ABS control actuator 12-pin connector (ABS control actuator side) terminals.

Code No.	ABS control actuator	ABS control actuator	Resistance
41	(3)	(4)	1.07 - 1.17Ω
45	(1)	(4)	
55	(5)	(4)	

OK → Repair harness and connector between control unit connector terminal and ABS control actuator 12-pin connector terminal.

NG ↓

Replace ABS control actuator.

NS4029600197010X

Fig. 188 Test 3: ABS Control Actuator Solenoid Valve (Part 1 of 2). 1996 Quest

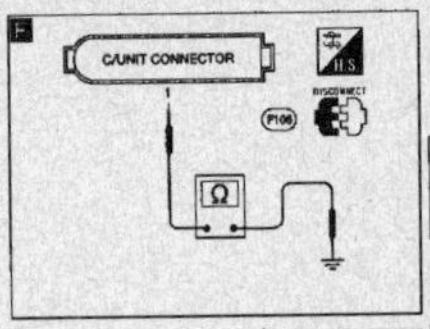
F
C/UNIT CONNECTOR
1
DISCONNECT
H.S.
F106

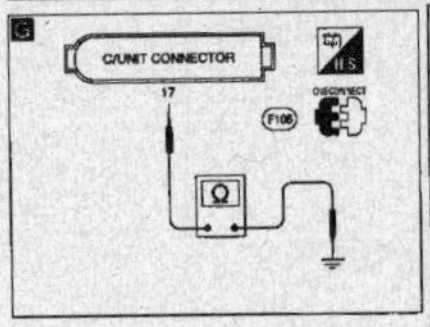
G
C/UNIT CONNECTOR
17
DISCONNECT
H.S.
F106

Ⓑ

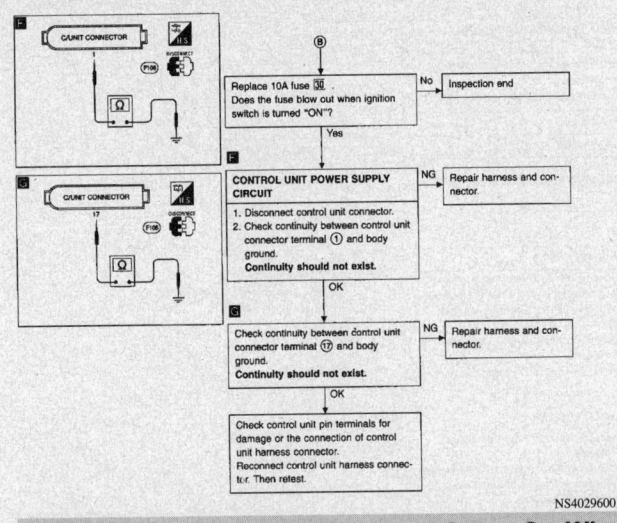

Replace 10A fuse [30].
Does the fuse blow out when ignition switch is turned "ON"?

No → Inspection end

Yes ↓

F

CONTROL UNIT POWER SUPPLY CIRCUIT

1. Disconnect control unit connector.
2. Check continuity between control unit connector terminal (1) and body ground.
   Continuity should not exist.

NG → Repair harness and connector.

OK ↓

G

Check continuity between control unit connector terminal (17) and body ground.
Continuity should not exist.

NG → Repair harness and connector.

OK ↓

Check control unit pin terminals for damage or the connection of control unit harness connector.
Reconnect control unit harness connector. Then retest.

NS4029600196030X

Fig. 187 Test 2: Warning Lamp Stays On When Ignition Switch Is On (Part 3 of 3). 1996 Quest

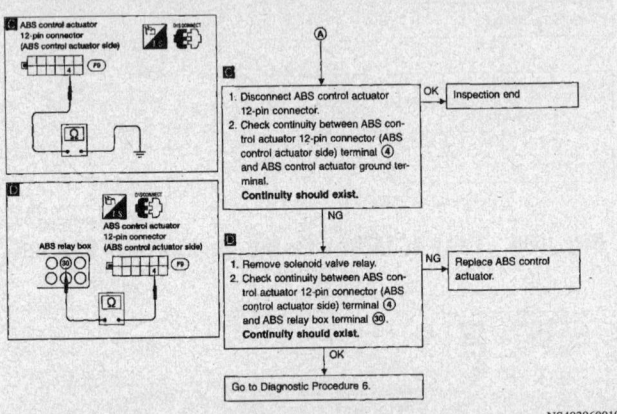

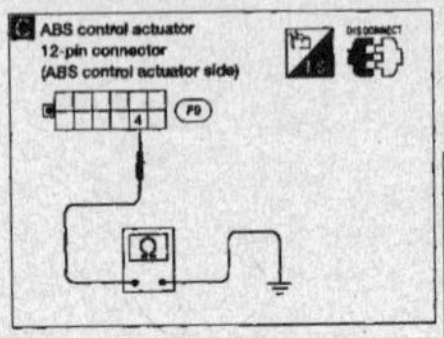
C
ABS control actuator
12-pin connector
(ABS control actuator side)
DISCONNECT
H.S.
4
F9

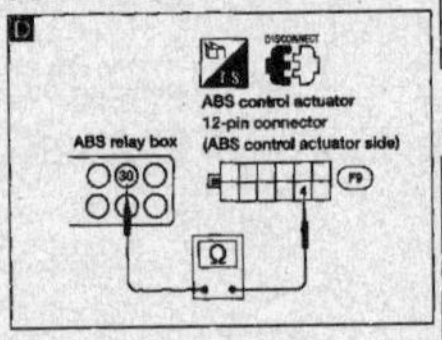
D
DISCONNECT
H.S.
ABS control actuator
12-pin connector
ABS relay box
(ABS control actuator side)
30
4
F9

Ⓐ

C

1. Disconnect ABS control actuator 12-pin connector.
2. Check continuity between ABS control actuator 12-pin connector (ABS control actuator side) terminal (4) and ABS control actuator ground terminal.
   Continuity should exist.

OK → Inspection end

NG ↓

D

1. Remove solenoid valve relay.
2. Check continuity between ABS control actuator 12-pin connector (ABS control actuator side) terminal (4) and ABS relay box terminal (30).
   Continuity should exist.

NG → Replace ABS control actuator.

OK ↓

Go to Diagnostic Procedure 6.

NS4029600197020X

Fig. 188 Test 3: ABS Control Actuator Solenoid Valve (Part 2 of 2). 1996 Quest

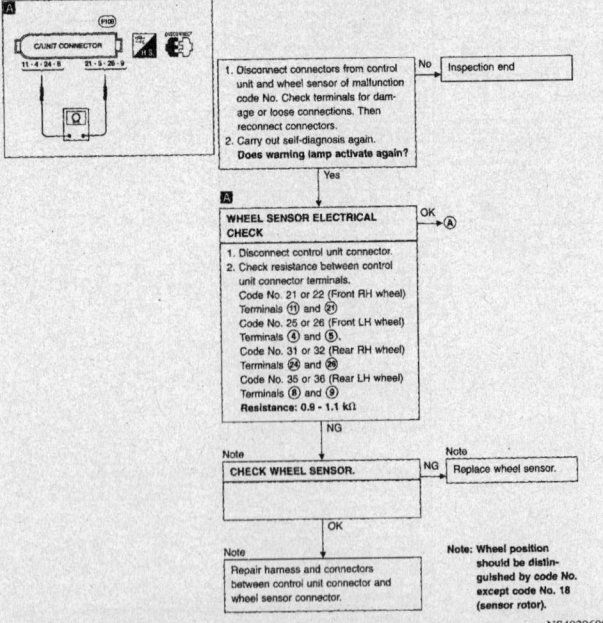

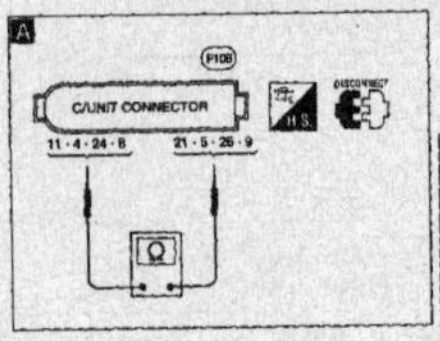
A
F100
C/UNIT CONNECTOR
11 · 4 · 24 · 8
21 · 5 · 26 · 9
DISCONNECT
H.S.

1. Disconnect connectors from control unit and wheel sensor of malfunction code No. Check terminals for damage or loose connections. Then reconnect connectors.
2. Carry out self-diagnosis again.
   Does warning lamp activate again?

No → Inspection end

Yes ↓

A

WHEEL SENSOR ELECTRICAL CHECK

OK → Ⓐ

1. Disconnect control unit connector.
2. Check resistance between control unit connector terminals.
   Code No. 21 or 22 (Front RH wheel)
   Terminals (11) and (21)
   Code No. 25 or 26 (Front LH wheel)
   Terminals (4) and (5).
   Code No. 31 or 32 (Rear RH wheel)
   Terminals (24) and (26)
   Code No. 35 or 36 (Rear LH wheel)
   Terminals (8) and (9)
   Resistance: 0.9 - 1.1 kΩ

NG ↓

Note
CHECK WHEEL SENSOR.

NG → Note: Replace wheel sensor.

OK ↓

Note
Repair harness and connectors between control unit connector and wheel sensor connector.

Note: Wheel position should be distinguished by code No. except code No. 18 (sensor rotor).

NS4029600198010X

Fig. 189 Test 4: Wheel Sensor Or Rotor (Part 1 of 2). 1996 Quest

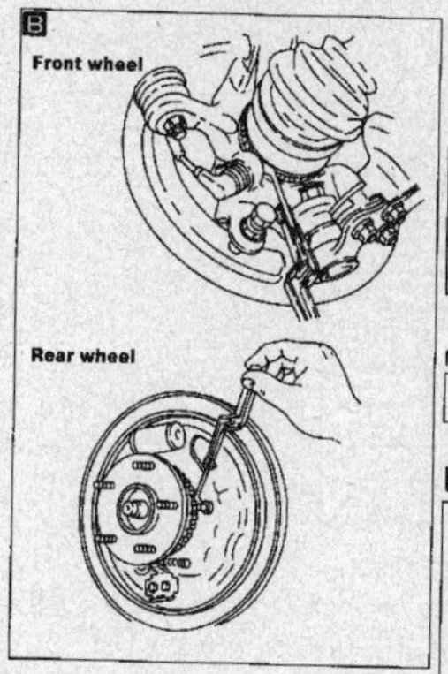
B
Front wheel
Rear wheel

Ⓐ

Note
WHEEL SENSOR MECHANICAL CHECK
Check for inflation pressure, wear and size of each tire.
NG → Note: Adjust tire pressure or replace tire(s).
OK ↓

Note
Check wheel bearing axial end play.
OK ↓

B Note
Check clearance between sensor and rotor.
Clearance:
Front
0.16 - 0.94 mm
(0.0063 - 0.0370 in)
Rear
0.16 - 0.94 mm
(0.0063 - 0.0370 in)
NG → Note: Clean sensor fixing portion, or replace sensor.
OK ↓

Note
Check sensor rotor for teeth damage.
NG → Note: Replace sensor rotor (with drive shaft, wheel hub).
OK ↓

Check control unit pin terminals for damage or the connection of control unit harness connector.
Reconnect control unit harness connector. Then retest.

Note: Wheel position should be distinguished by code No. except code No. 18 (sensor rotor).

NS4029600198020X

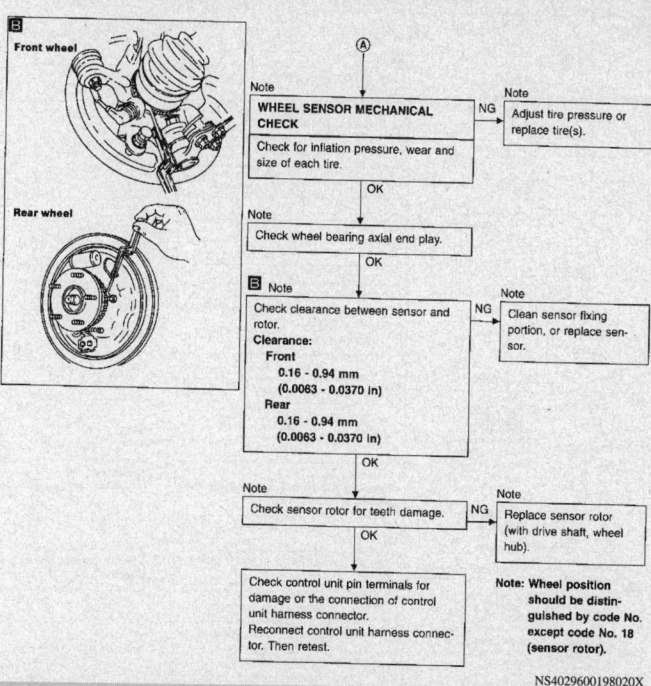

Fig. 189 Test 4: Wheel Sensor Or Rotor (Part 2 of 2). 1996 Quest

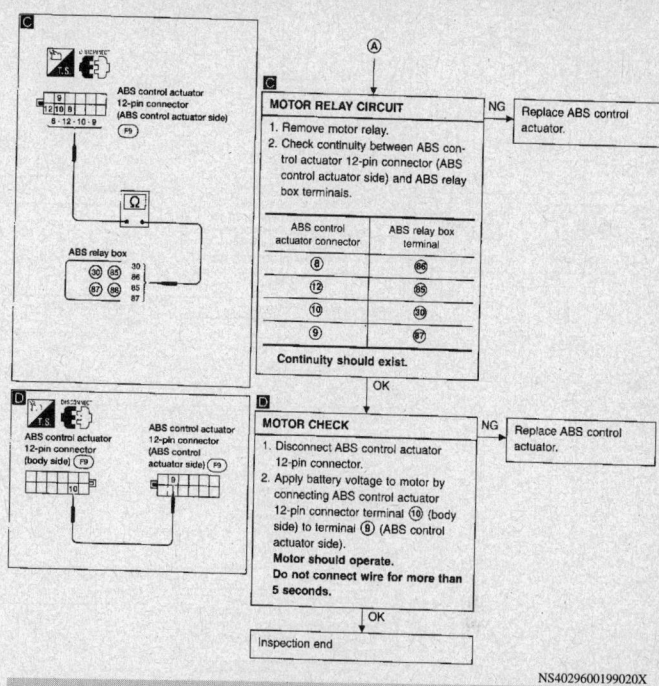

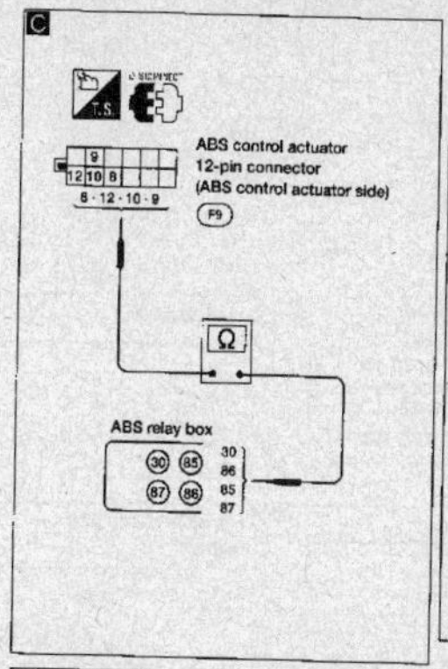
C
ABS control actuator 12-pin connector (ABS control actuator side)
F9
ABS relay box
30
86
85
87

Ⓐ

C
MOTOR RELAY CIRCUIT
1. Remove motor relay.
2. Check continuity between ABS control actuator 12-pin connector (ABS control actuator side) and ABS relay box terminals.

ABS control actuator connector	ABS relay box terminal
⑧	㊱
⑫	㊵
⑩	㉚
⑨	㊷

Continuity should exist.

NG → Replace ABS control actuator.
OK ↓

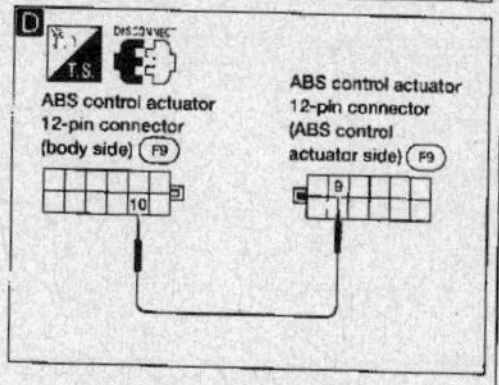
D
ABS control actuator 12-pin connector (body side) F9
ABS control actuator 12-pin connector (ABS control actuator side) F9
10
9

D
MOTOR CHECK
1. Disconnect ABS control actuator 12-pin connector.
2. Apply battery voltage to motor by connecting ABS control actuator 12-pin connector terminal ⑩ (body side) to terminal ⑨ (ABS control actuator side).
Motor should operate.
Do not connect wire for more than 5 seconds.

NG → Replace ABS control actuator.
OK ↓

Inspection end

NS4029600199020X

Fig. 190 Test 5: Motor Relay Or Motor (Part 2 of 3). 1996 Quest

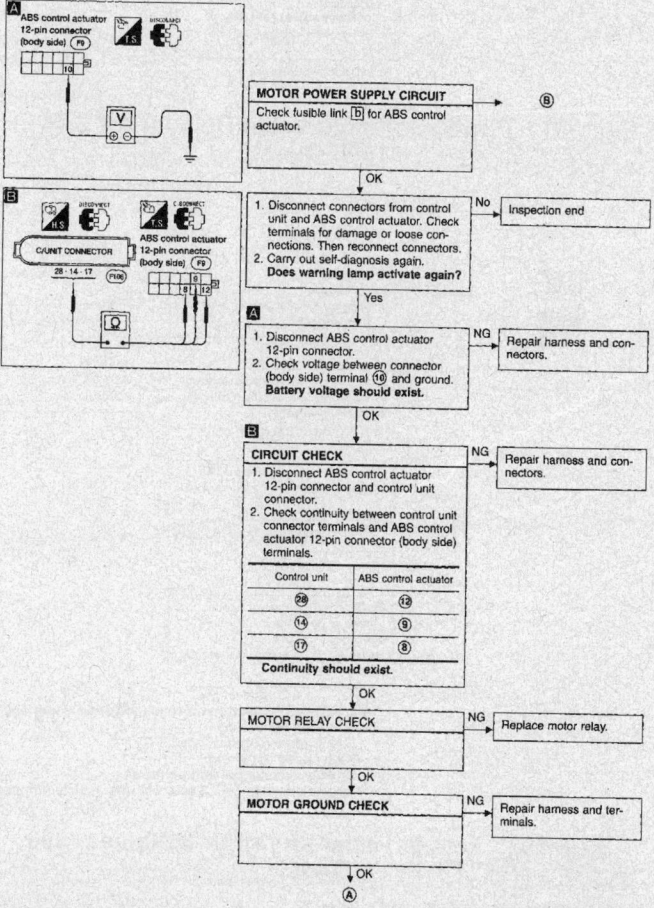

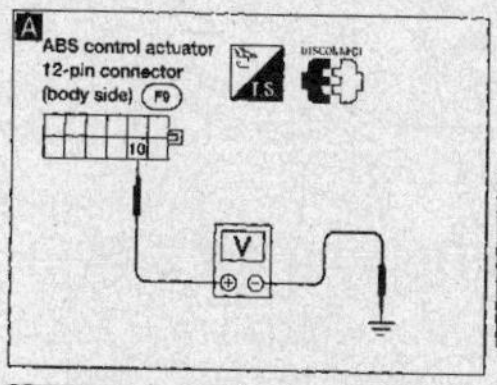
A
ABS control actuator 12-pin connector (body side) F9
10
V

MOTOR POWER SUPPLY CIRCUIT
Check fusible link b for ABS control actuator.
→ Ⓑ
OK ↓

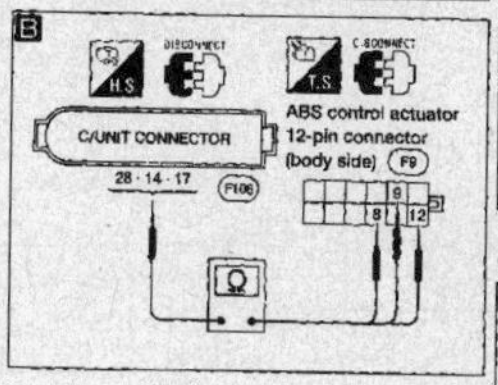
B
H.S.
C/UNIT CONNECTOR
28 · 14 · 17
F106
ABS control actuator 12-pin connector (body side) F9
8
12
Ω

1. Disconnect connectors from control unit and ABS control actuator. Check terminals for damage or loose connections. Then reconnect connectors.
2. Carry out self-diagnosis again.
Does warning lamp activate again?

No → Inspection end
Yes ↓

A
1. Disconnect ABS control actuator 12-pin connector.
2. Check voltage between connector (body side) terminal ⑩ and ground.
Battery voltage should exist.

NG → Repair harness and connectors.
OK ↓

B
CIRCUIT CHECK
1. Disconnect ABS control actuator 12-pin connector and control unit connector.
2. Check continuity between control unit connector terminals and ABS control actuator 12-pin connector (body side) terminals.

Control unit	ABS control actuator
㉘	⑫
⑭	⑨
⑰	⑧

Continuity should exist.

NG → Repair harness and connectors.
OK ↓

MOTOR RELAY CHECK
NG → Replace motor relay.
OK ↓

MOTOR GROUND CHECK
NG → Repair harness and terminals.
OK ↓

Ⓐ

NS4029600199010X

Fig. 190 Test 5: Motor Relay Or Motor (Part 1 of 3). 1996 Quest

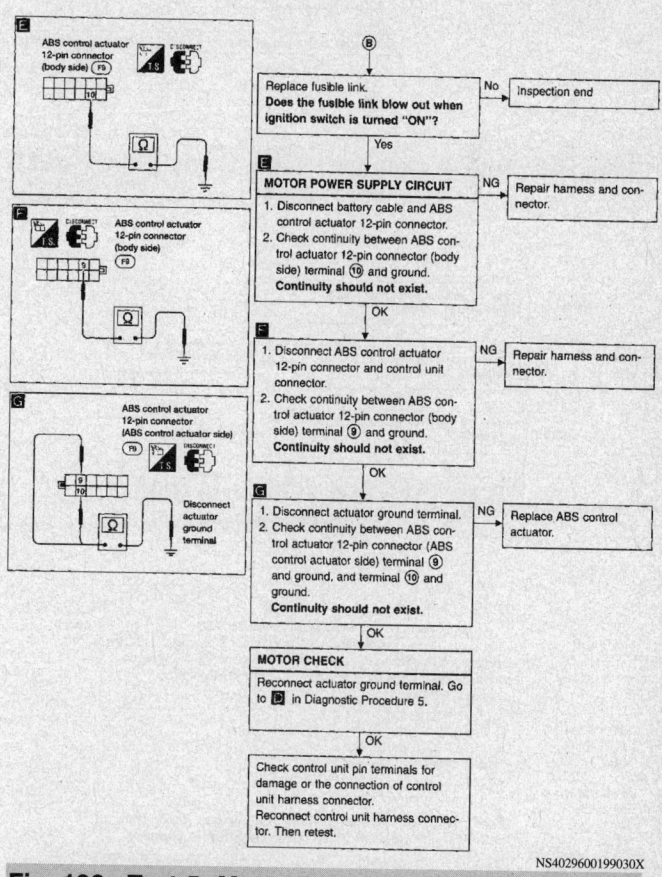

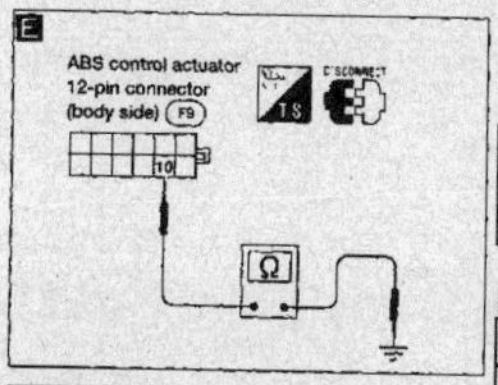
E
ABS control actuator 12-pin connector (body side) F9
10
Ω

Ⓑ

Replace fusible link.
Does the fusible link blow out when ignition switch is turned "ON"?

No → Inspection end
Yes ↓

E
MOTOR POWER SUPPLY CIRCUIT
1. Disconnect battery cable and ABS control actuator 12-pin connector.
2. Check continuity between ABS control actuator 12-pin connector (body side) terminal ⑩ and ground.
Continuity should not exist.

NG → Repair harness and connector.
OK ↓

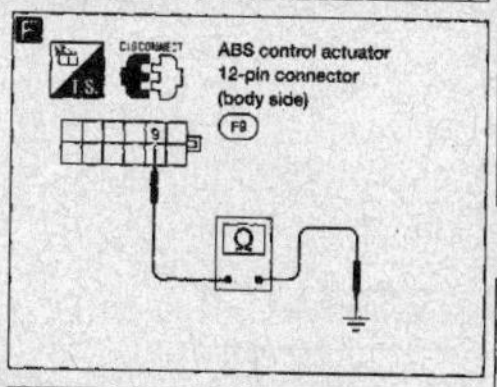
F
ABS control actuator 12-pin connector (body side)
F9
9
Ω

F
1. Disconnect ABS control actuator 12-pin connector and control unit connector.
2. Check continuity between ABS control actuator 12-pin connector (body side) terminal ⑨ and ground.
Continuity should not exist.

NG → Repair harness and connector.
OK ↓

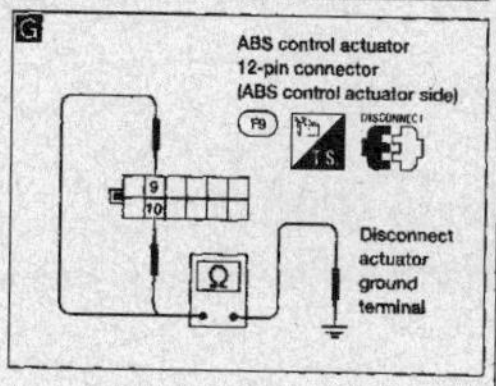
G
ABS control actuator 12-pin connector (ABS control actuator side)
F9
9
10
Ω
Disconnect actuator ground terminal

G
1. Disconnect actuator ground terminal.
2. Check continuity between ABS control actuator 12-pin connector (ABS control actuator side) terminal ⑨ and ground, and terminal ⑩ and ground.
Continuity should not exist.

NG → Replace ABS control actuator.
OK ↓

MOTOR CHECK
Reconnect actuator ground terminal. Go to D in Diagnostic Procedure 5.
OK ↓

Check control unit pin terminals for damage or the connection of control unit harness connector.
Reconnect control unit harness connector. Then retest.

NS4029600199030X

Fig. 190 Test 5: Motor Relay Or Motor (Part 3 of 3). 1996 Quest

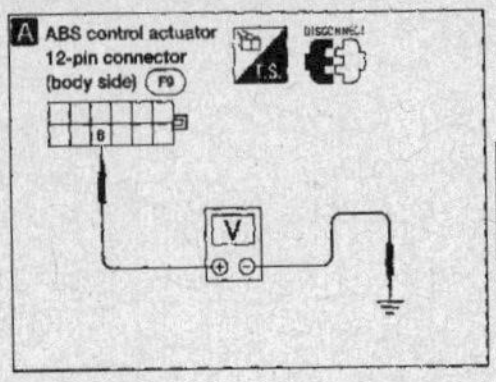
A ABS control actuator
12-pin connector
(body side) F9
V

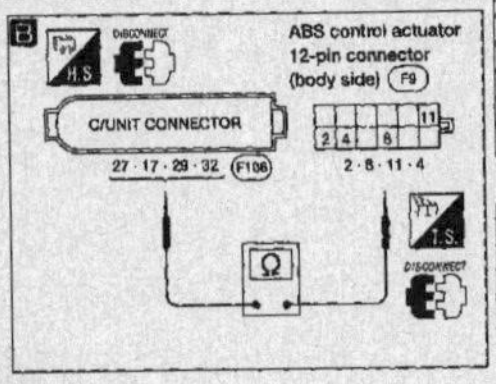
B
ABS control actuator
12-pin connector
(body side) F9
C/UNIT CONNECTOR
27 · 17 · 29 · 32 F106
2 · 8 · 11 · 4
Ω

SOLENOID VALVE POWER SUPPLY CHECK — NG → Ⓐ

Check 20A fuse 43.

↓ OK

1. Disconnect connectors from control unit and ABS control actuator. Check terminals for damage or loose connections. Then reconnect connectors.
2. Carry out self-diagnosis again.
Does warning lamp activate again? — No → Inspection end

↓ Yes

GROUND CIRCUIT CHECK — NG → Repair harness and connectors.

↓ OK

A **SOLENOID VALVE POWER SUPPLY CHECK** — NG → Repair harness and connector.

1. Disconnect 12-pin connector from ABS control actuator.
2. Check voltage between ABS control actuator 12-pin connector (body side) terminal ⑥ and ground.
Battery voltage should exist.

↓ OK

B **CIRCUIT CHECK** — NG → Repair harness and connectors.

1. Disconnect control unit connector.
2. Check continuity between control unit connector terminals and ABS control actuator 12-pin connector (body side) terminals.

Control unit	ABS control actuator
㉗	②
⑰	⑧
㉙	⑪
㉜	④

Continuity should exist.

↓ OK

SOLENOID VALVE RELAY CHECK — NG → Replace solenoid valve relay.

↓ OK

Ⓑ

NS4029600200010X

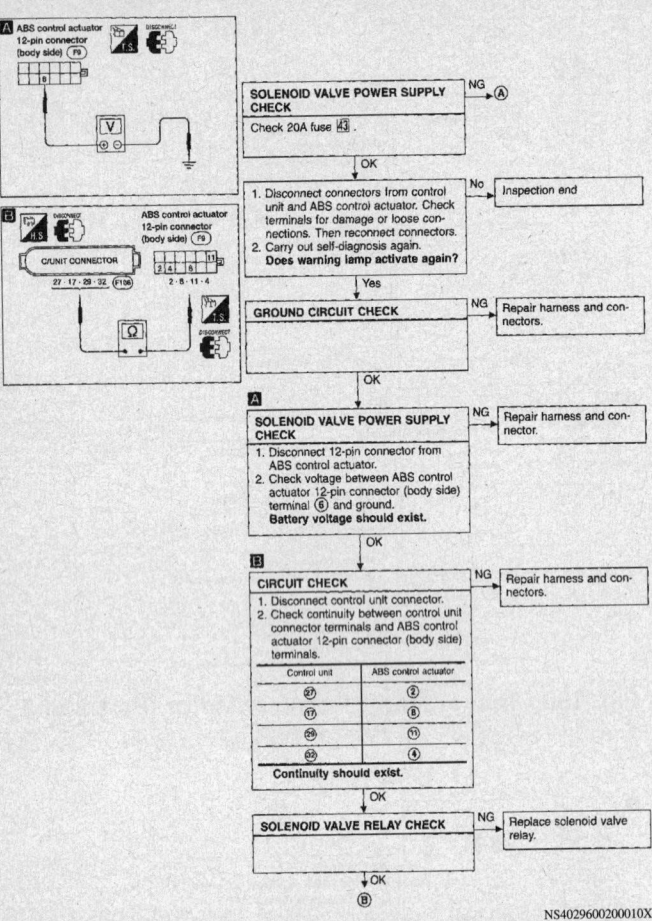

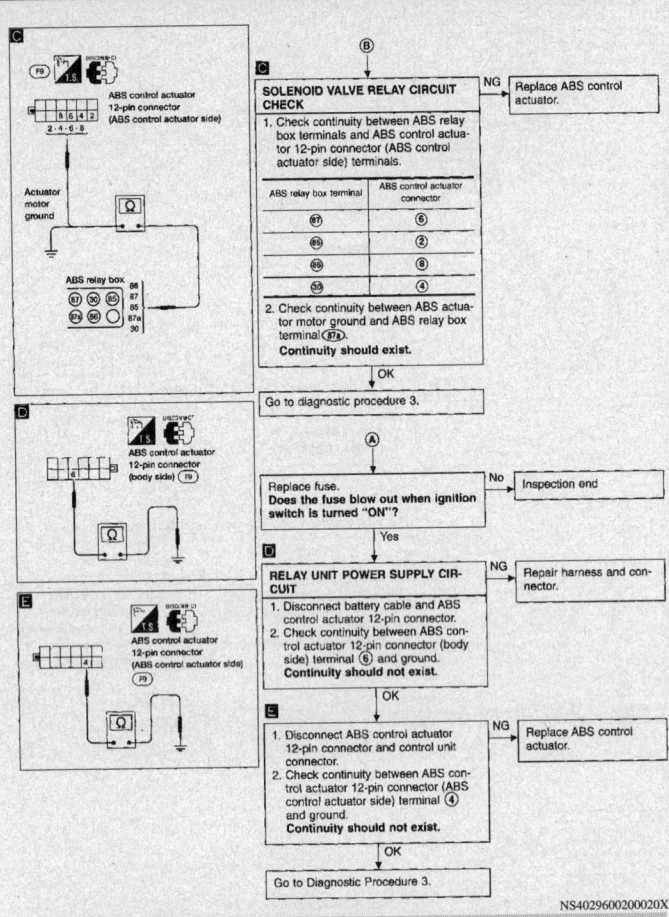

Fig. 191 Test 6: Solenoid Valve Relay (Part 1 of 2). 1996 Quest

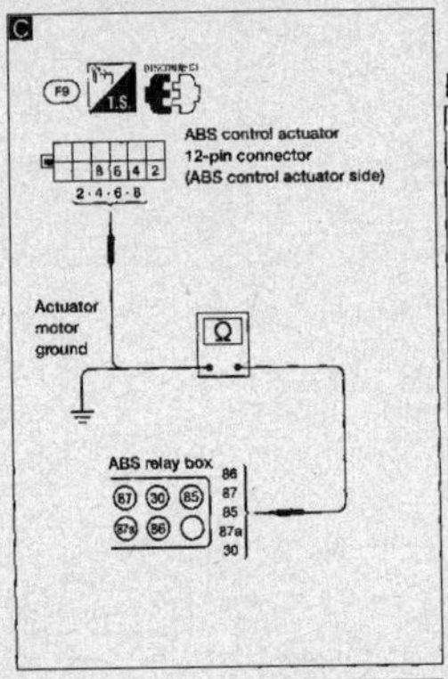
C
F9
T.S.
ABS control actuator
12-pin connector
(ABS control actuator side)
8 6 4 2
2 · 4 · 6 · 8
Actuator
motor
ground
Ω
ABS relay box
87 30 85
87a 86
86
87
85
87a
30

Ⓑ

C **SOLENOID VALVE RELAY CIRCUIT CHECK** — NG → Replace ABS control actuator.

1. Check continuity between ABS relay box terminals and ABS control actuator 12-pin connector (ABS control actuator side) terminals.

ABS relay box terminal	ABS control actuator connector
㊇	⑥
㊅	②
㊆	⑧
㉚	④

2. Check continuity between ABS actuator motor ground and ABS relay box terminal 87a.
Continuity should exist.

↓ OK

Go to diagnostic procedure 3.

Ⓐ

Replace fuse.
Does the fuse blow out when ignition switch is turned "ON"? — No → Inspection end

↓ Yes

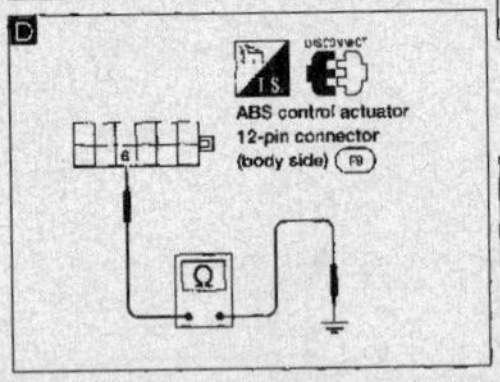
D
T.S.
ABS control actuator
12-pin connector
(body side) F9
Ω

D **RELAY UNIT POWER SUPPLY CIRCUIT** — NG → Repair harness and connector.

1. Disconnect battery cable and ABS control actuator 12-pin connector.
2. Check continuity between ABS control actuator 12-pin connector (body side) terminal ⑥ and ground.
Continuity should not exist.

↓ OK

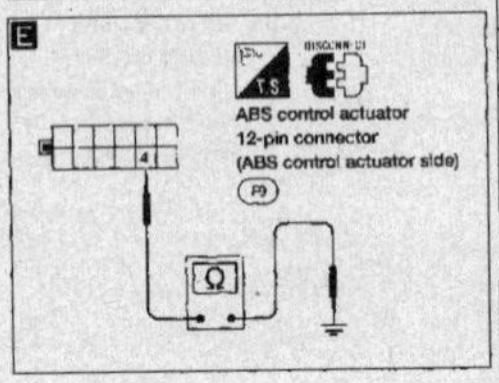
E
T.S.
ABS control actuator
12-pin connector
(ABS control actuator side)
F9
Ω

E
1. Disconnect ABS control actuator 12-pin connector and control unit connector.
2. Check continuity between ABS control actuator 12-pin connector (ABS control actuator side) terminal ④ and ground.
Continuity should not exist. — NG → Replace ABS control actuator.

↓ OK

Go to Diagnostic Procedure 3.

NS4029600200020X

Fig. 191 Test 6: Solenoid Valve Relay (Part 2 of 2). 1996 Quest

Carry out self-diagnosis after erasing self-diagnostic results.

↓

Does warning lamp indicate code No. 71 again? — Yes → Replace control unit.

↓ No

Inspect the system according to the code No.

NS4029600201000X

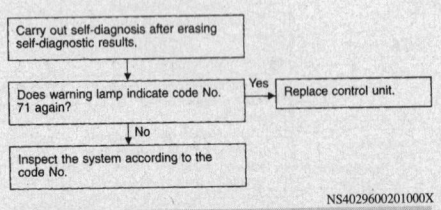

Fig. 192 Test 7: Control Unit. 1996 Quest

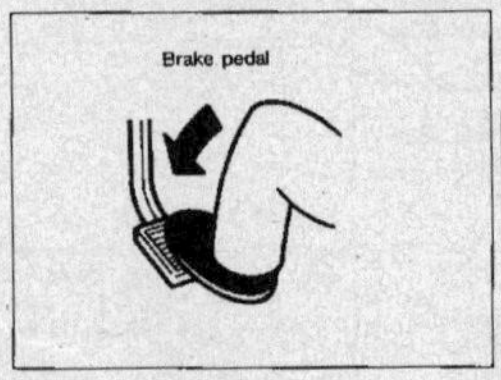
Brake pedal

1. Apply brake.
2. Start engine.
3. Does the symptom appear only when engine is started? — Yes → Carry out Self-diagnosis.

↓ No

Does the symptom appear when electrical equipment switches (such as headlamp) are operated? — No → Go to B in Diagnostic Procedure 10.

↓ Yes

Check wheel sensor shield ground secured with control unit mounting bolt.

NG → Repair.

OK → Check control unit pin terminals for damage or the connection of control unit harness connector. Reconnect control unit harness connector. Then retest.

Note: ABS may operate and cause vibration under any of the following conditions.
- **Low friction (slippery) road.**
- **High speed cornering.**
- **Driving over bumps and pot holes.**
- **Engine speed is over 5,000 rpm with vehicle stopped.**

NS4029600202000X

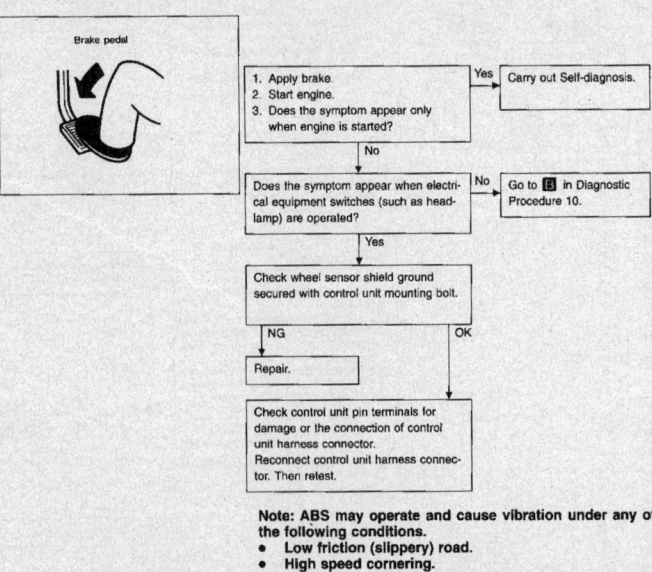

Fig. 193 Test 8: Pedal Vibration & Noise. 1996 Quest

Disconnect ABS control actuator 12-pin connector and check whether stopping distance is still long. — No → Go to B in Diagnostic Procedure 10.

↓ Yes

Perform Preliminary Check and air bleeding.

Note: Stopping distance may be longer than that of vehicles without ABS when road condition is slippery.

NS4029600203000X

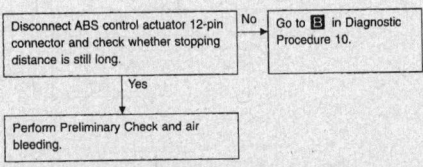

Fig. 194 Test 9: Long Stopping Distance. 1996 Quest

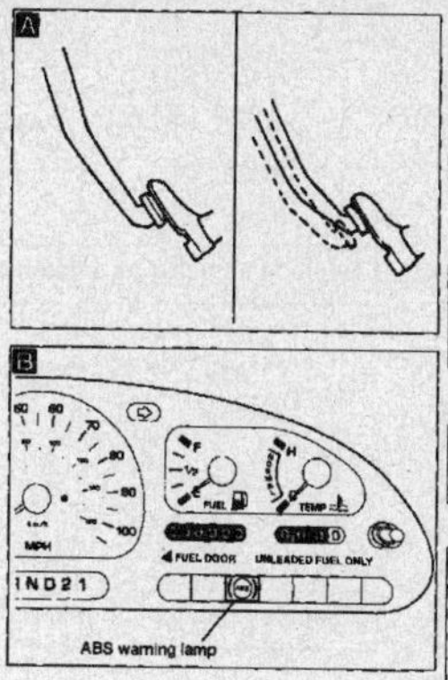
A
B
IND21
ABS warning lamp

A

Check brake pedal stroke. Is stroke excessively large? — Yes → Perform Preliminary Check.

↓ No

Disconnect ABS control actuator 12-pin connector and check whether brake is effective. — No → Perform Preliminary Check.

↓ Yes

B

Ensure warning lamp remains off while driving. — NG → Carry out Self-diagnosis.

↓ OK

CHECK WHEEL SENSOR. — NG → Repair.

1. Check wheel sensor connector for terminal damage or loose connection.
2. Perform wheel sensor mechanical check.
   Refer to B in Diagnostic Procedure 4.

↓ OK

Check control unit pin terminals for damage or the connection of control unit harness connector.
Reconnect control unit harness connector. Then retest.

NS4029600204000X

Fig. 195 Test 10: Unexpected Pedal Action. 1996 Quest

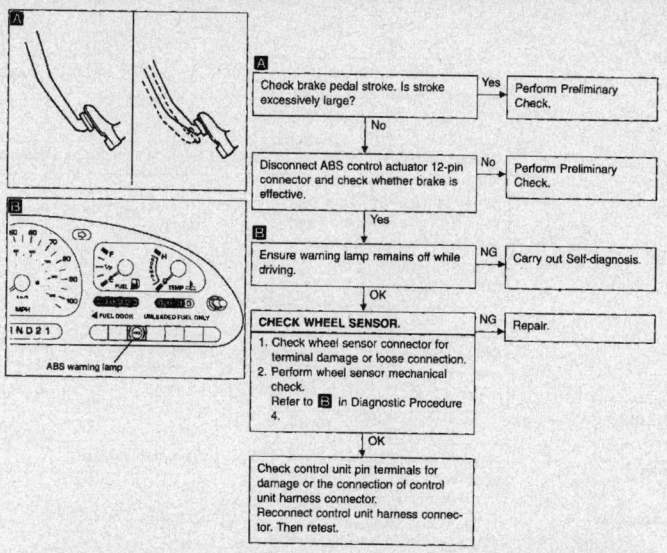

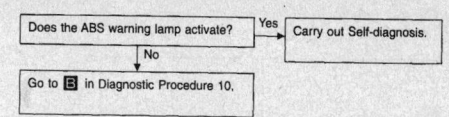

Does the ABS warning lamp activate? — Yes → Carry out Self-diagnosis.

↓ No

Go to B in Diagnostic Procedure 10.

Note: ABS does not work when vehicle speed is under 10 km/h (6 MPH).

NS4029600205000X

Fig. 196 Test 11: ABS Does Not Work. 1996 Quest

CHECK BRAKE FLUID PRESSURE. — NG → Perform Preliminary Check.

Check brake fluid pressure distribution.
Refer to "INSPECTION", "Dual Load Sensing Valve".

↓ OK

CHECK WHEEL SENSOR. — NG → Repair.

1. Check wheel sensor connector for terminal damage or loose connections.
2. Perform wheel sensor mechanical check.
   Refer to B in Diagnostic Procedure 4.

↓ OK

Check front and rear axles for excessive looseness. — NG → Repair.

↓ OK

Check control unit pin terminals for damage or the connection of control unit harness connector.
Reconnect control unit harness connector. Then retest.

NS4029600206000X

Fig. 197 Test 12: ABS Works Frequently. 1996 Quest

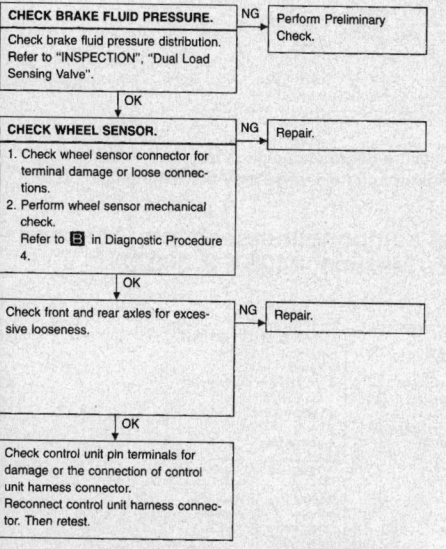

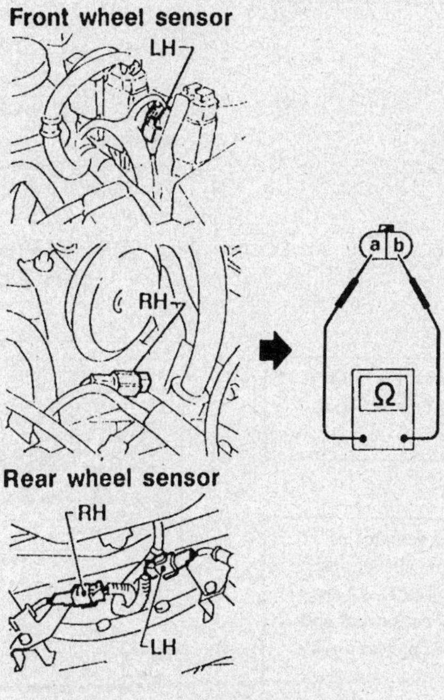
Front wheel sensor
LH
RH
Rear wheel sensor
RH
LH
a
b
Ω

NS4029100110000X

Fig. 198 Wheel sensor inspection. Altima, NX 1600, NX 2000 & Sentra

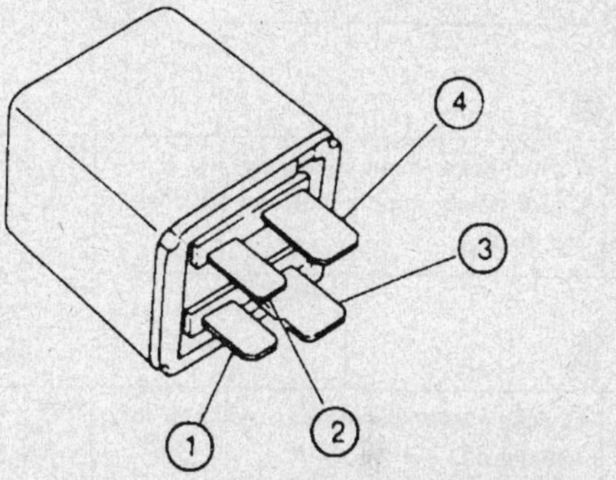
4
3
1
2

NS4029100111000X

Fig. 199 Actuator motor relay terminal locations. Altima, NX 1600, NX 2000, Sentra & 200SX

Condition	Continuity existence between terminals ③ and ④
Battery positive voltage not applied between terminals ① and ②	No
Battery positive voltage applied between terminals ① and ②.	Yes

NS4029100112000X

Fig. 200 Actuator motor relay continuity check. Altima, NX 1600, NX 2000, Sentra & 200SX

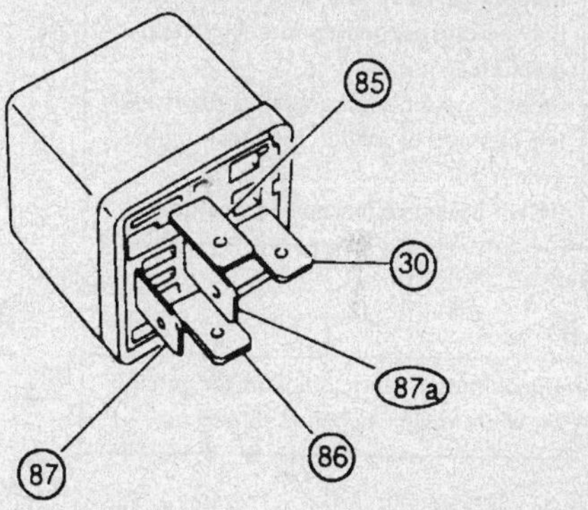
85
30
87a
86
87

NS4029100113000X

Fig. 201 Solenoid valve relay terminal locations. Altima, NX 1600, NX 2000, Sentra & 200SX

Condition	Continuity existence between terminals ㉚ and (87a)	Continuity existence between terminals ㉚ and (87)
Battery positive voltage not applied between terminals (85) and (86)	Yes	No
Battery positive voltage applied between terminals (85) and (86)	No	Yes

NS4029100114000X

Fig. 202 Solenoid valve relay continuity check. Altima, NX 1600, NX 2000, Sentra & 200SX

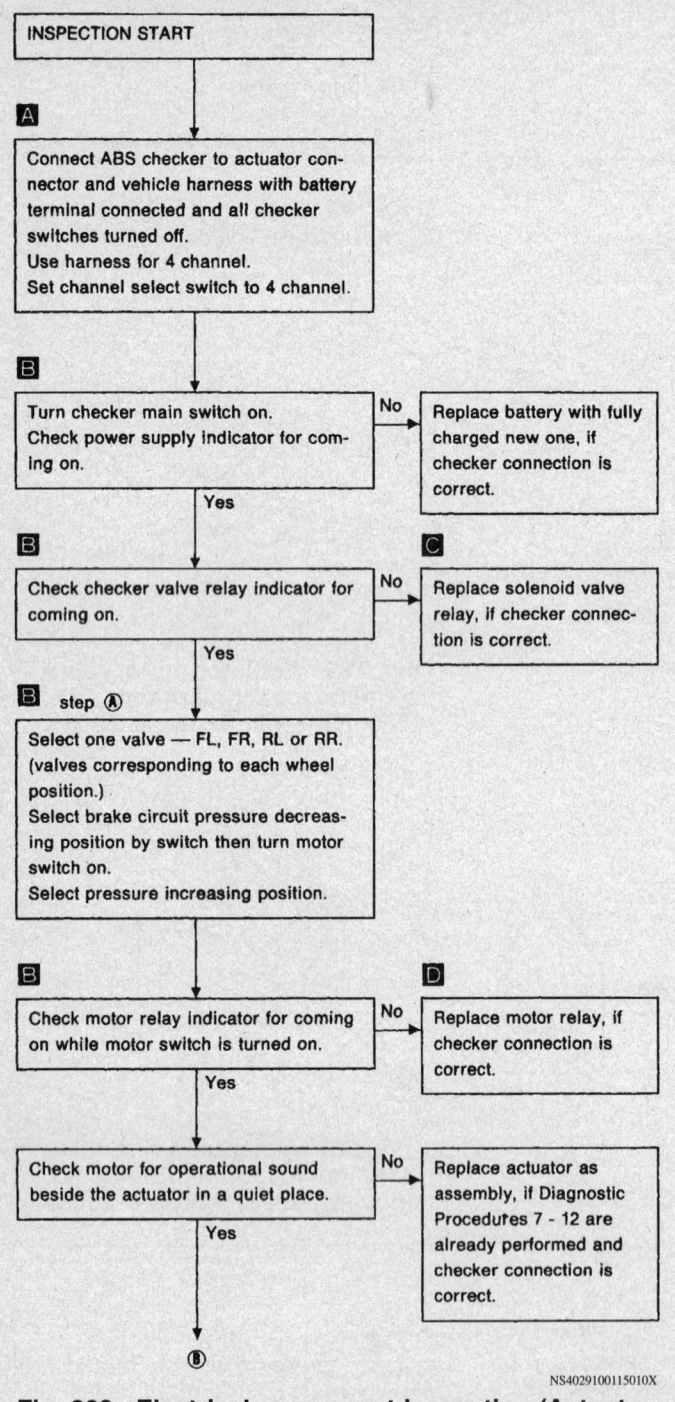

INSPECTION START

A

Connect ABS checker to actuator connector and vehicle harness with battery terminal connected and all checker switches turned off.
Use harness for 4 channel.
Set channel select switch to 4 channel.

B

Turn checker main switch on.
Check power supply indicator for coming on.
- No → Replace battery with fully charged new one, if checker connection is correct.
- Yes ↓

B

Check checker valve relay indicator for coming on.
- No → **C** Replace solenoid valve relay, if checker connection is correct.
- Yes ↓

B step Ⓐ

Select one valve — FL, FR, RL or RR. (valves corresponding to each wheel position.)
Select brake circuit pressure decreasing position by switch then turn motor switch on.
Select pressure increasing position.

B

Check motor relay indicator for coming on while motor switch is turned on.
- No → **D** Replace motor relay, if checker connection is correct.
- Yes ↓

Check motor for operational sound beside the actuator in a quiet place.
- No → Replace actuator as assembly, if Diagnostic Procedures 7 - 12 are already performed and checker connection is correct.
- Yes ↓

Ⓑ

NS4029100115010X

Fig. 203 Electrical component inspection (Actuator, part 1 of 2). Maxima, 240SX & 300ZX

Ⓑ

Bring checker in the vehicle and depress the brake pedal.

Check brake pedal for vibration when motor switch is turned on or while operating solenoid valve selecting switch with motor switch turned on.
N.G.: No vibration
O.K.: Vibration
- N.G. → Replace actuator as assembly.
- O.K. ↓

Check brake pedal for depression when select pressure increases.
- N.G. → Replace actuator as assembly.
- O.K. ↓

Have all wheel positions been checked?
- No → Repeat from step Ⓐ.
- Yes ↓

Actuator works normally

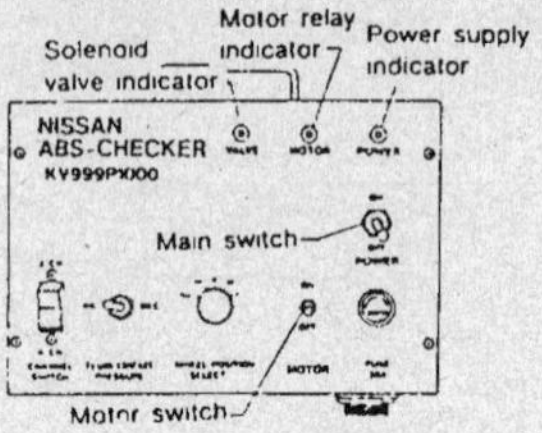
Motor relay indicator
Power supply indicator
Solenoid valve indicator
NISSAN
ABS-CHECKER
KV999PX00
Main switch
Motor switch

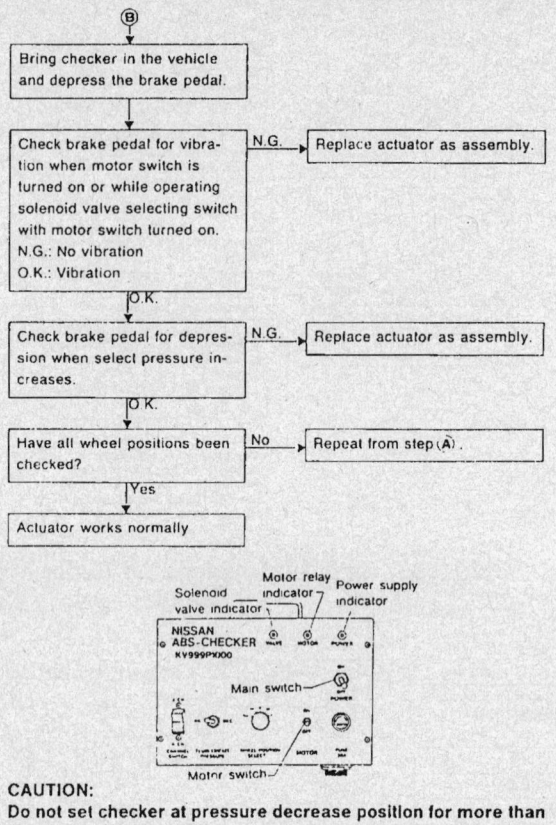

CAUTION:
Do not set checker at pressure decrease position for more than 5 seconds at a time. Actuator solenoid valve may be damaged.

NS4029100115020X

Fig. 203 Electrical component inspection (Actuator, part 2 of 2). Maxima, 240SX & 300ZX

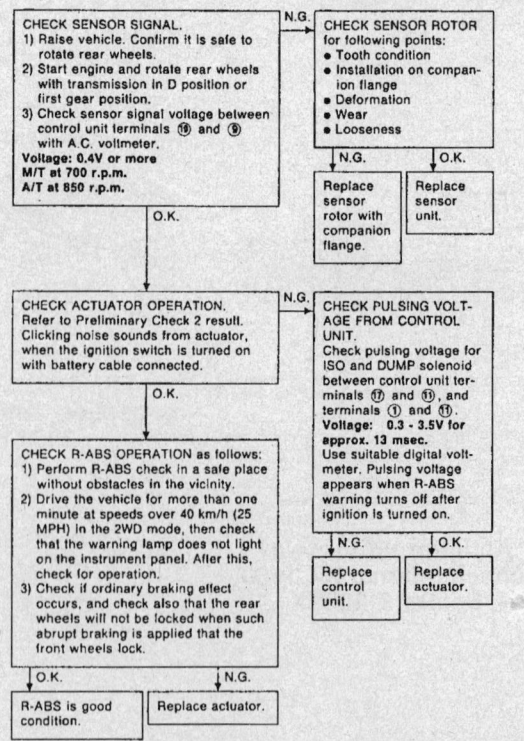

CHECK SENSOR SIGNAL.
1) Raise vehicle. Confirm it is safe to rotate rear wheels.
2) Start engine and rotate rear wheels with transmission in D position or first gear position.
3) Check sensor signal voltage between control unit terminals ⑲ and ⑨ with A.C. voltmeter.

Voltage: 0.4V or more
M/T at 700 r.p.m.
A/T at 850 r.p.m.

- N.G. → CHECK SENSOR ROTOR for following points:
  - Tooth condition
  - Installation on companion flange
  - Deformation
  - Wear
  - Looseness
  - N.G. → Replace sensor rotor with companion flange.
  - O.K. → Replace sensor unit.
- O.K. ↓

CHECK ACTUATOR OPERATION.
Refer to Preliminary Check 2 result.
Clicking noise sounds from actuator, when the ignition switch is turned on with battery cable connected.
- N.G. → CHECK PULSING VOLTAGE FROM CONTROL UNIT.
  Check pulsing voltage for ISO and DUMP solenoid between control unit terminals ⑰ and ⑪, and terminals ① and ⑪.
  Voltage: 0.3 - 3.5V for approx. 13 msec.
  Use suitable digital voltmeter. Pulsing voltage appears when R-ABS warning turns off after ignition is turned on.
  - N.G. → Replace control unit.
  - O.K. → Replace actuator.
- O.K. ↓

CHECK R-ABS OPERATION as follows:
1) Perform R-ABS check in a safe place without obstacles in the vicinity.
2) Drive the vehicle for more than one minute at speeds over 40 km/h (25 MPH) in the 2WD mode, then check that the warning lamp does not light on the instrument panel. After this, check for operation.
3) Check if ordinary braking effect occurs, and check also that the rear wheels will not be locked when such abrupt braking is applied that the front wheels lock.
- O.K. → R-ABS is good condition.
- N.G. → Replace actuator.

NS4029100116000X

Fig. 204 Electrical component inspection (Sensor unit & actuator). Pathfinder & Pickup

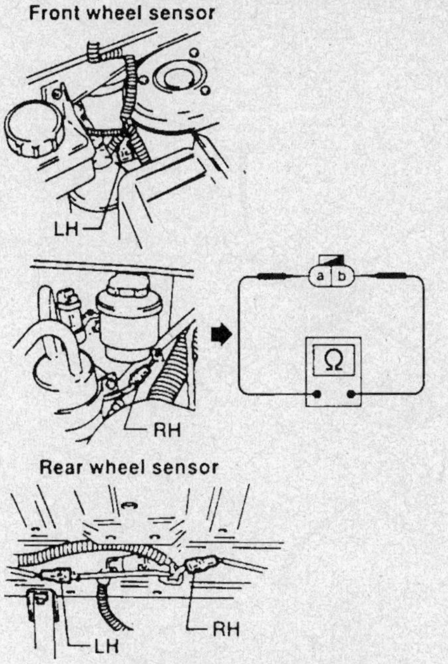
Front wheel sensor
LH
a
b
Ω
RH
Rear wheel sensor
RH
LH

Fig. 205 Wheel sensor inspection. Quest

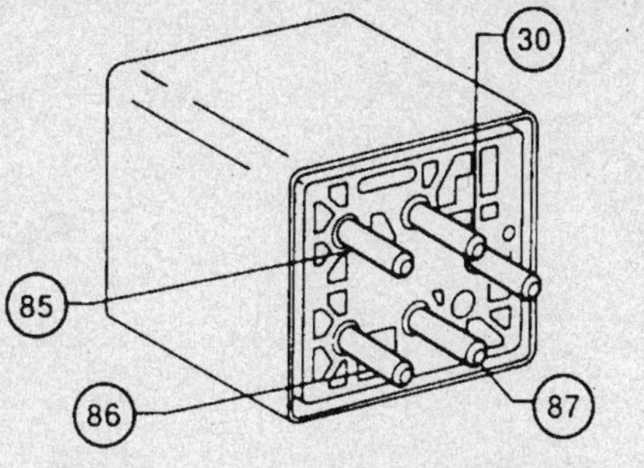
30
85
86
87

Fig. 206 Actuator motor relay terminal locations. Quest

Condition	Continuity existence between terminals (30) and (87)
Battery positive voltage not applied between terminals (85) and (86).	No
Battery positive voltage applied between terminals (85) and (86).	Yes

Fig. 207 Actuator motor relay continuity check. Quest

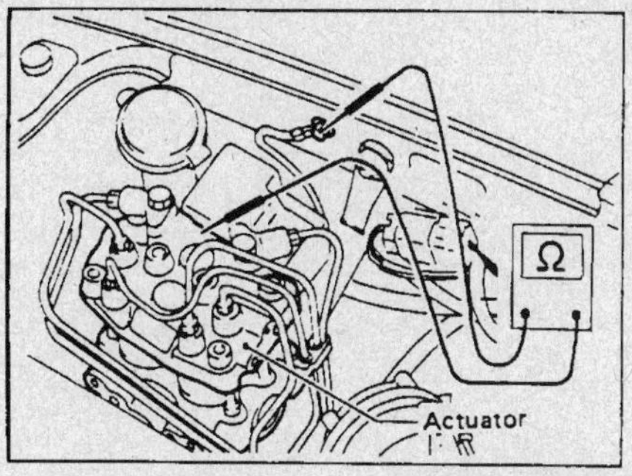
Ω
Actuator

Fig. 210 Actuator motor ground circuit check. Maxima

Condition	Continuity existence between terminals (30) and (87a)	Continuity existence between terminals (30) and (87)
Battery positive voltage not applied between terminals (85) and (86).	Yes	No
Battery positive voltage applied between terminals (85) and (86)	No	Yes

Fig. 209 Solenoid valve relay continuity check. Quest

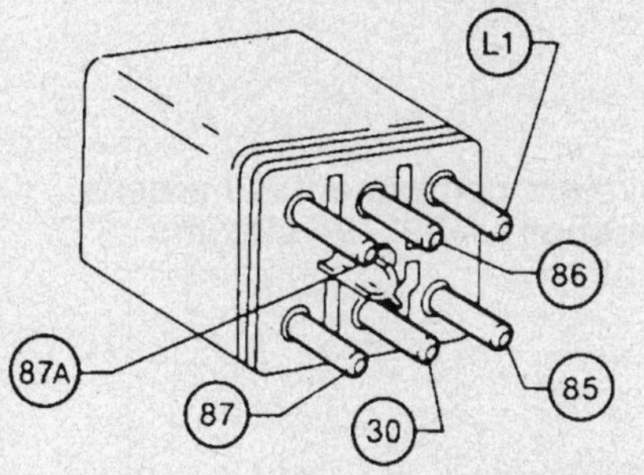
L1
86
87A
85
87
30

Fig. 208 Solenoid valve relay terminal locations. Quest

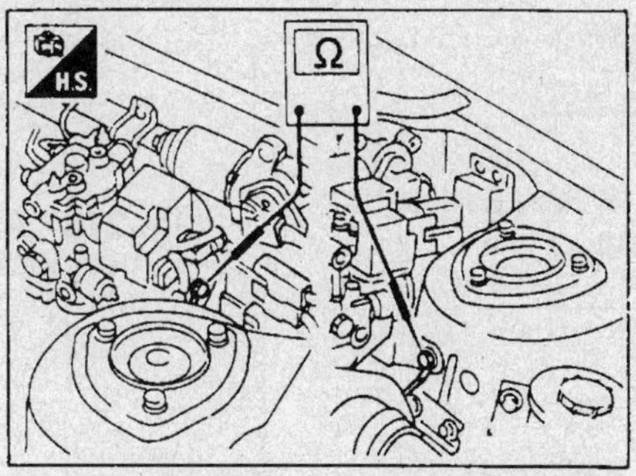
H.S.
Ω

Fig. 212 Actuator motor ground circuit check. 240SX

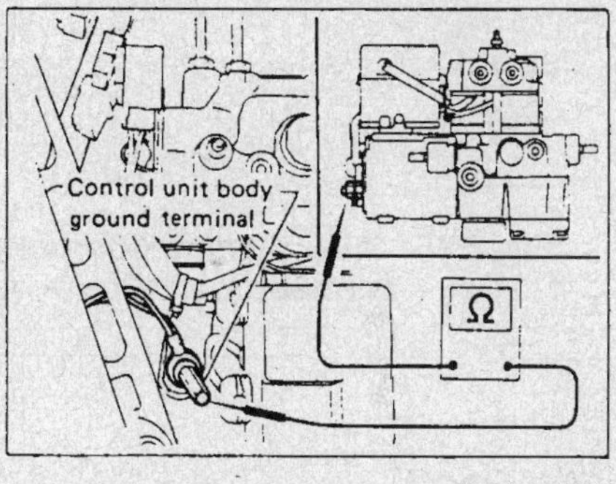
Control unit body ground terminal
Ω

Fig. 213 Actuator motor ground circuit check. 300ZX

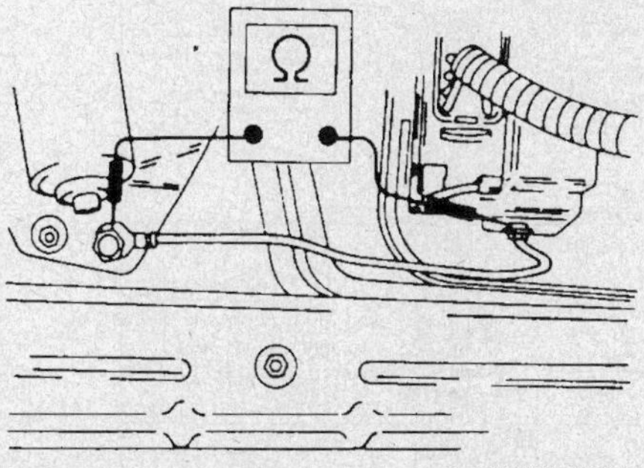
Ω

Fig. 211 Actuator motor ground circuit check. Quest

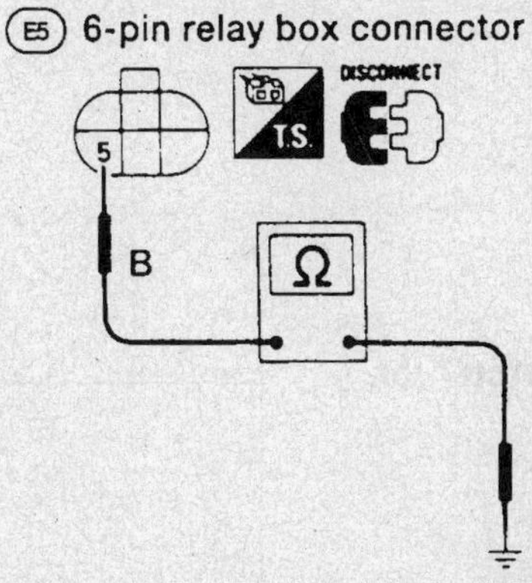
E5 6-pin relay box connector
DISCONNECT
T.S.
5
B
Ω

Fig. 214 Relay box ground circuit check. Altima

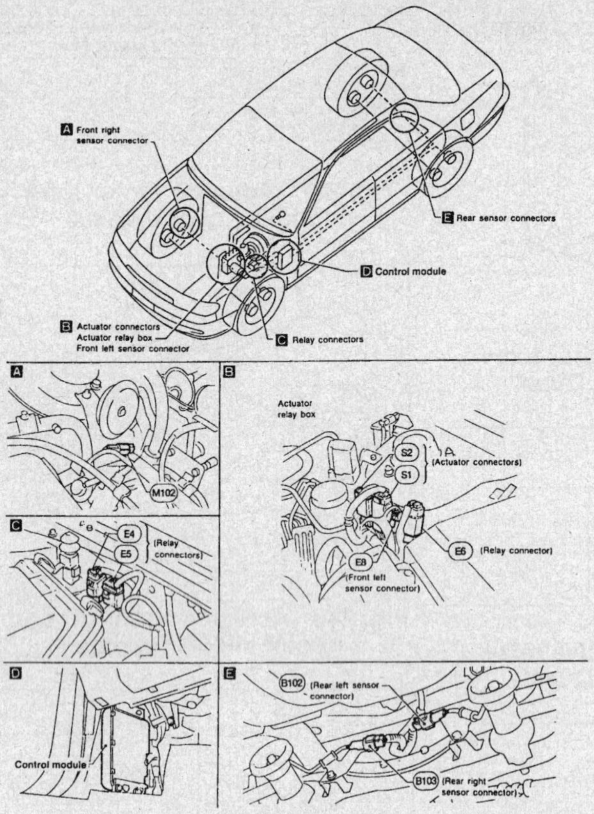
A Front right sensor connector
E Rear sensor connectors
D Control module
B Actuator connectors
Actuator relay box
Front left sensor connector
C Relay connectors
Actuator relay box
(Actuator connectors)
(Relay connectors)
E6 (Relay connector)
E8 (Front left sensor connector)
Control module
B102 (Rear left sensor connector)
B103 (Rear right sensor connector)

NS4029100130000X

Fig. 215 ABS system component & harness connector locations. Altima

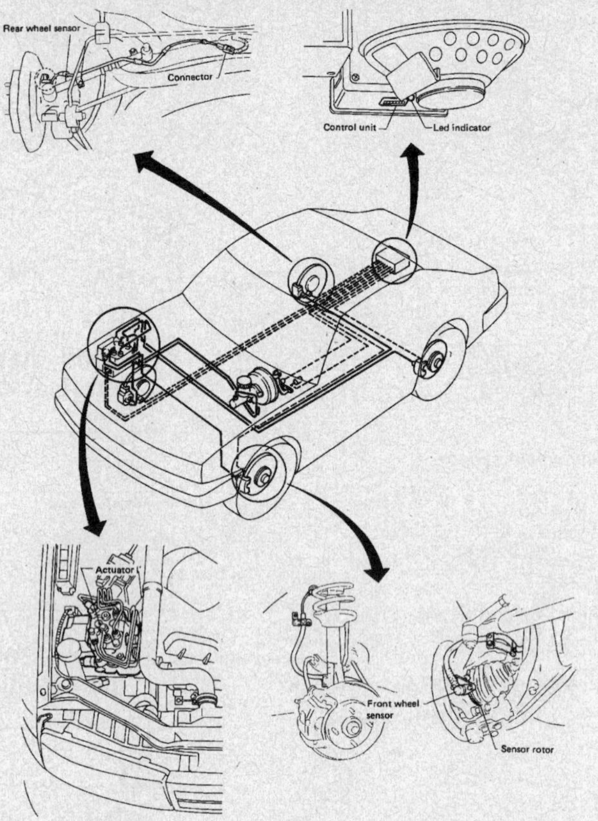
Rear wheel sensor
Connector
Control unit
Led indicator
Actuator
Front wheel sensor
Sensor rotor

NS4029100131000X

Fig. 216 ABS system component & harness connector locations. 1993–94 Maxima

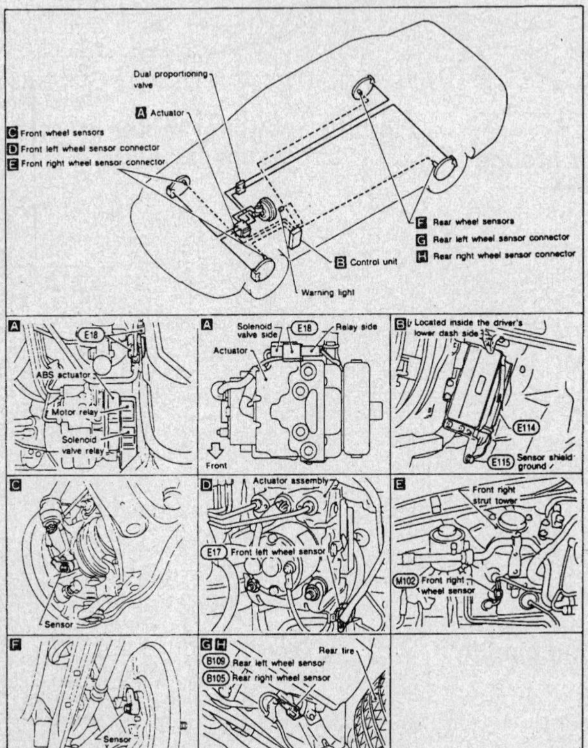
Dual proportioning valve
A Actuator
C Front wheel sensors
D Front left wheel sensor connector
E Front right wheel sensor connector
F Rear wheel sensors
G Rear left wheel sensor connector
H Rear right wheel sensor connector
B Control unit
Warning light
ABS actuator
Motor relay
Solenoid valve relay
Solenoid valve side
Relay side
Front
Located inside the driver's lower dash side
E114
E115 Sensor shield ground
Sensor
Actuator assembly
E17 Front left wheel sensor
Front right strut tower
M102 Front right wheel sensor
Rear tire
B109 Rear left wheel sensor
B105 Rear right wheel sensor

NS4029500187000X

Fig. 217 ABS system component & harness connector locations. 1995–96 Maxima

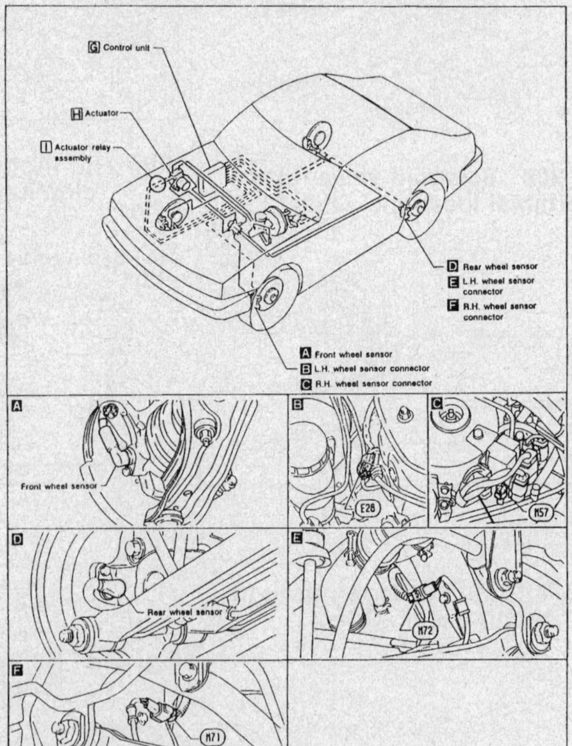
G Control unit
H Actuator
I Actuator relay assembly
D Rear wheel sensor
E L.H. wheel sensor connector
F R.H. wheel sensor connector
A Front wheel sensor
B L.H. wheel sensor connector
C R.H. wheel sensor connector
Front wheel sensor
E28
M57
Rear wheel sensor
M72
M71

NS4029100132010X

Fig. 218 ABS system component & harness connector locations (Part 1 of 2). 1993–94 NX 1600, NX 2000 & Sentra

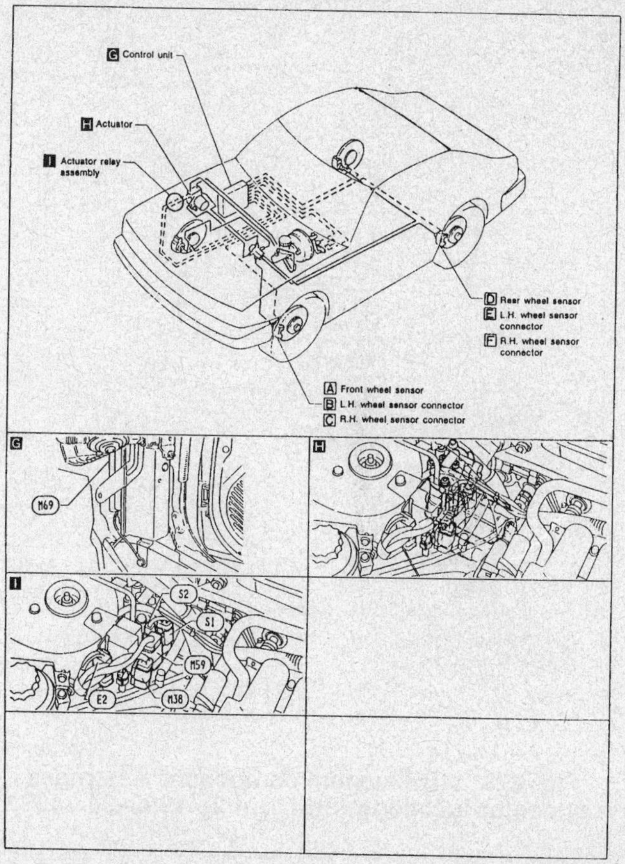
G Control unit
H Actuator
I Actuator relay assembly
D Rear wheel sensor
E L.H. wheel sensor connector
F R.H. wheel sensor connector
A Front wheel sensor
B L.H. wheel sensor connector
C R.H. wheel sensor connector
G
M69
H
I
S2
S1
M59
E2
M38

NS4029100132020X

Fig. 218 ABS system component & harness connector locations (Part 2 of 2). 1993–94 NX 1600, NX 2000 & Sentra

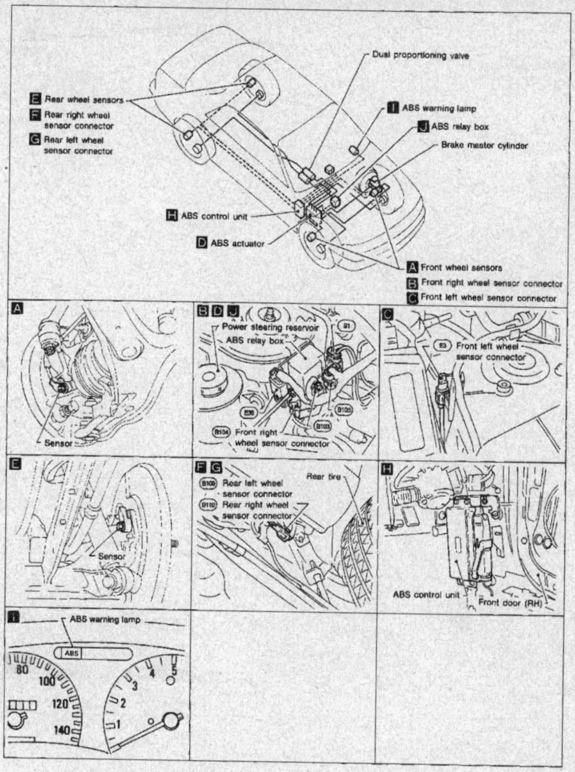
Dual proportioning valve
E Rear wheel sensors
F Rear right wheel sensor connector
G Rear left wheel sensor connector
I ABS warning lamp
J ABS relay box
Brake master cylinder
H ABS control unit
D ABS actuator
A Front wheel sensors
B Front right wheel sensor connector
C Front left wheel sensor connector
A
Sensor
B D J
Power steering reservoir
ABS relay box
Front right wheel sensor connector
C
Front left wheel sensor connector
E
Sensor
F G
Rear tire
Rear left wheel sensor connector
Rear right wheel sensor connector
H
ABS control unit
Front door (RH)
I
ABS warning lamp
ABS

NS4029500188000X

Fig. 219 ABS system component & harness connector locations. 1995–96 Sentra & 200SX

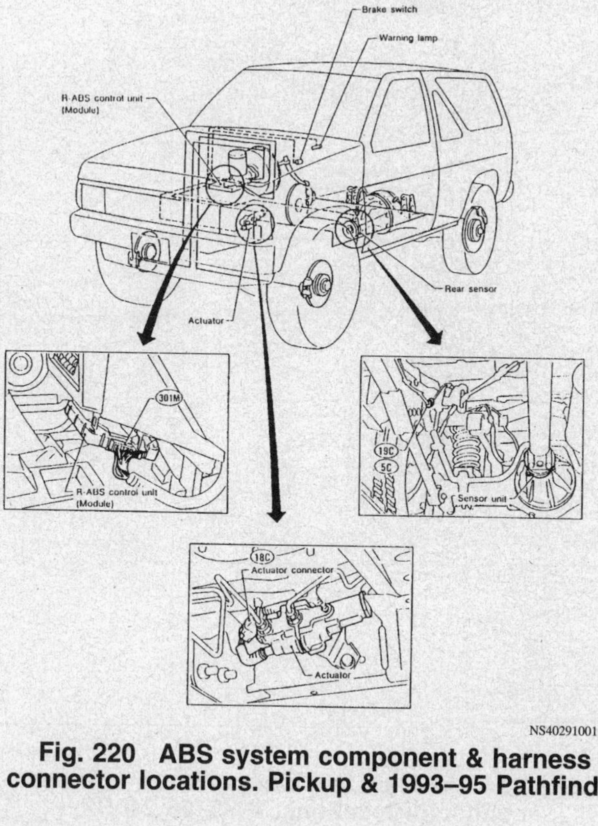
Brake switch
Warning lamp
R-ABS control unit (Module)
Actuator
Rear sensor
301M
R-ABS control unit (Module)
19C
5C
Sensor unit
18C
Actuator connector
Actuator

NS4029100133000X

Fig. 220 ABS system component & harness connector locations. Pickup & 1993–95 Pathfinder

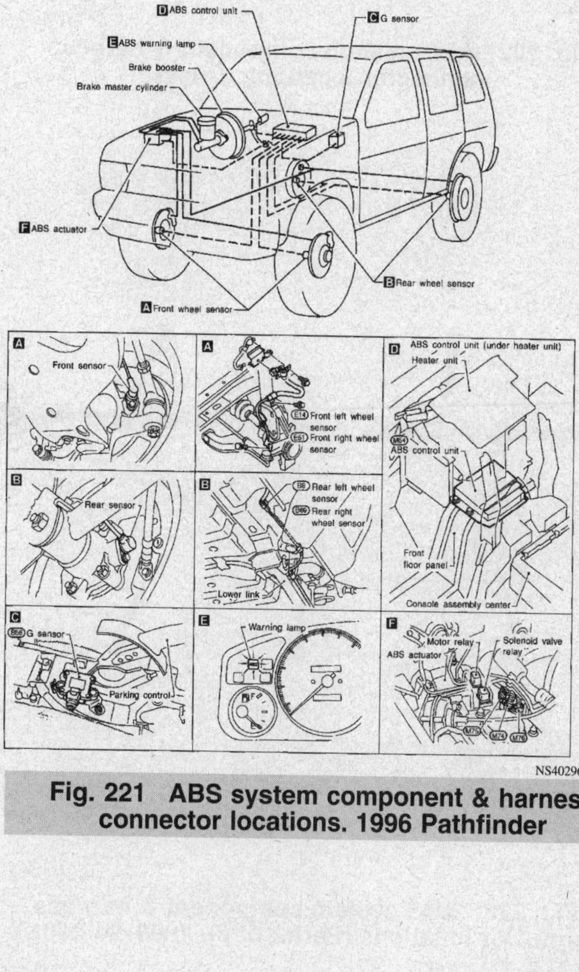
D ABS control unit
C G sensor
E ABS warning lamp
Brake booster
Brake master cylinder
F ABS actuator
B Rear wheel sensor
A Front wheel sensor
A
Front sensor
A
Front left wheel sensor
Front right wheel sensor
D
ABS control unit (under heater unit)
Heater unit
ABS control unit
Front floor panel
Console assembly center
B
Rear sensor
B
Rear left wheel sensor
Rear right wheel sensor
Lower link
C
G sensor
Parking control
E
Warning lamp
F
Motor relay
Solenoid valve relay
ABS actuator

NS4029600235000X

Fig. 221 ABS system component & harness connector locations. 1996 Pathfinder

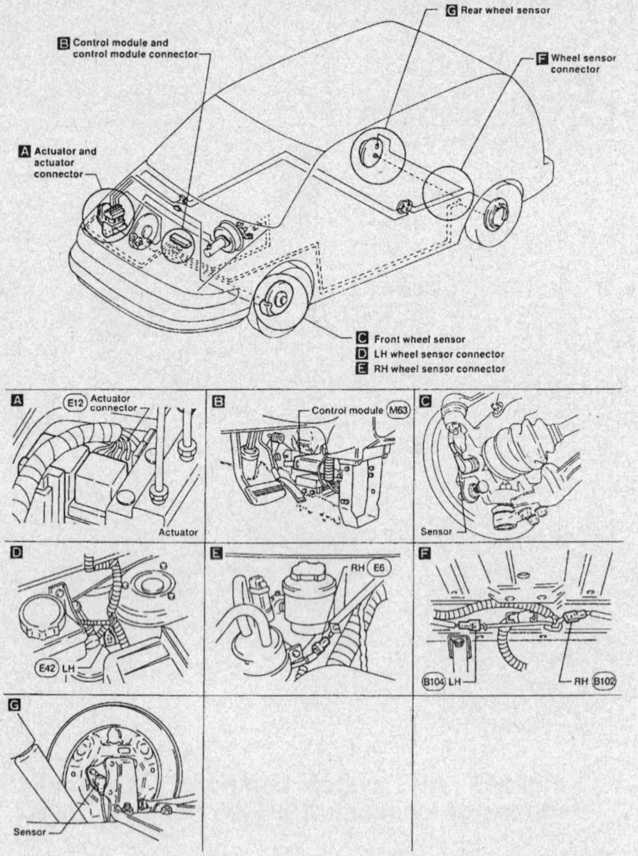
G Rear wheel sensor
B Control module and control module connector
F Wheel sensor connector
A Actuator and actuator connector
C Front wheel sensor
D LH wheel sensor connector
E RH wheel sensor connector
A
E12 Actuator connector
Actuator
B
Control module M63
C
Sensor
D
E42 LH
E
RH E6
F
B104 LH
RH B102
G
Sensor

NS4029100134000X

Fig. 222 ABS system component & harness connector locations. Quest

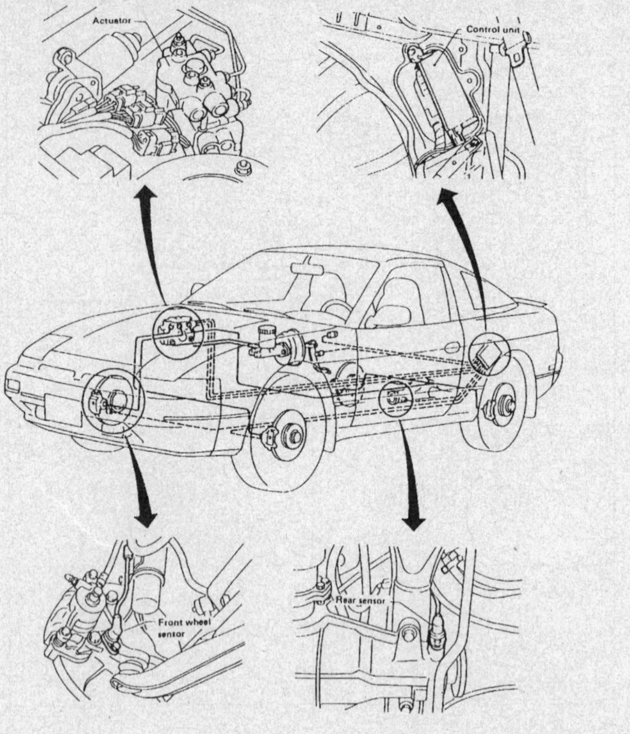
Actuator
Control unit
Front wheel sensor
Rear sensor

NS4029100136010X

Fig. 223 ABS system component & harness connector locations (Part 1 of 2). 1993–94 240SX

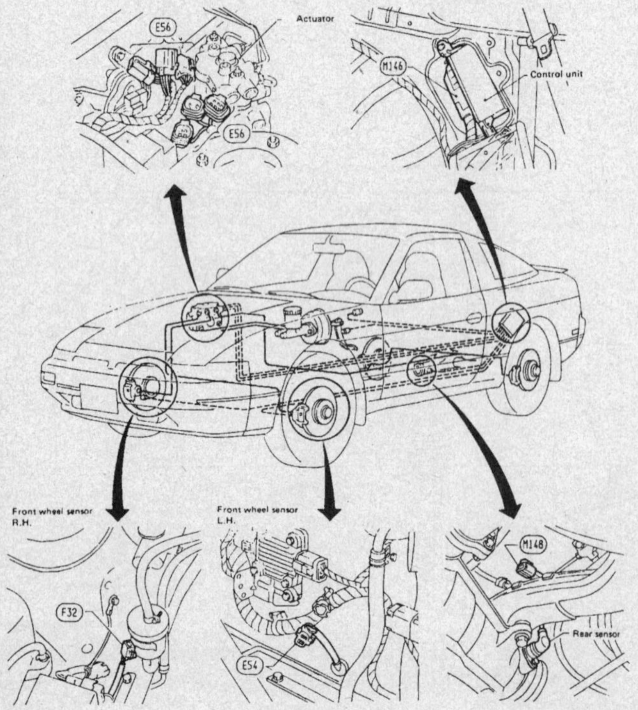
E56
Actuator
E56
M146
Control unit
Front wheel sensor R.H.
Front wheel sensor L.H.
F32
E54
M148
Rear sensor

NS4029100136020X

Fig. 223 ABS system component & harness connector locations (Part 2 of 2). 1993–94 240SX

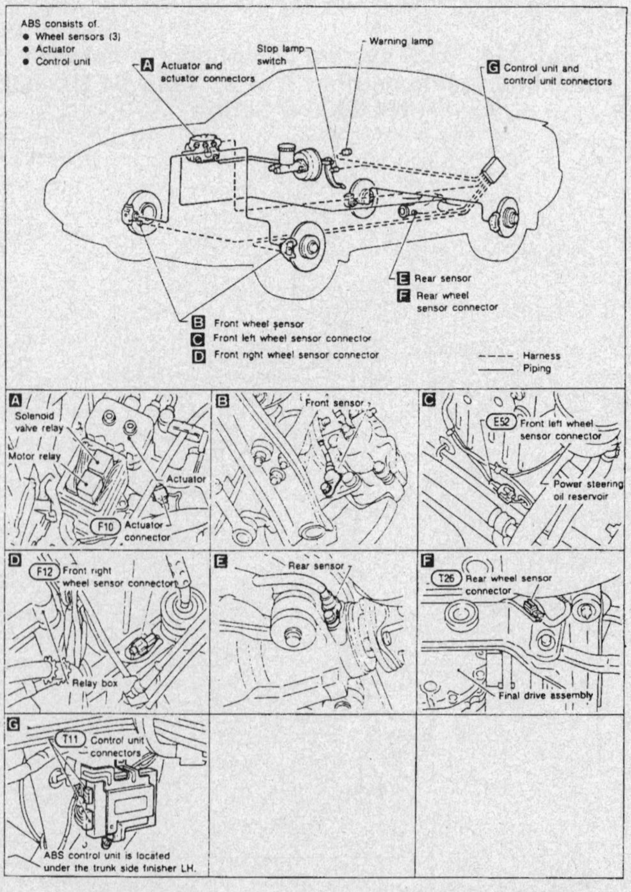
ABS consists of:
• Wheel sensors (3)
• Actuator
• Control unit
A Actuator and actuator connectors
Stop lamp switch
Warning lamp
G Control unit and control unit connectors
E Rear sensor
F Rear wheel sensor connector
B Front wheel sensor
C Front left wheel sensor connector
D Front right wheel sensor connector
Harness
Piping
A
Solenoid valve relay
Motor relay
Actuator
F10 Actuator connector
B
Front sensor
C
E52 Front left wheel sensor connector
Power steering oil reservoir
D
F12 Front right wheel sensor connector
Relay box
E
Rear sensor
F
T26 Rear wheel sensor connector
Final drive assembly
G
T11 Control unit connectors
ABS control unit is located under the trunk side finisher LH.

NS4029500189000X

Fig. 224 ABS system component & harness connector locations. 1995–96 240SX

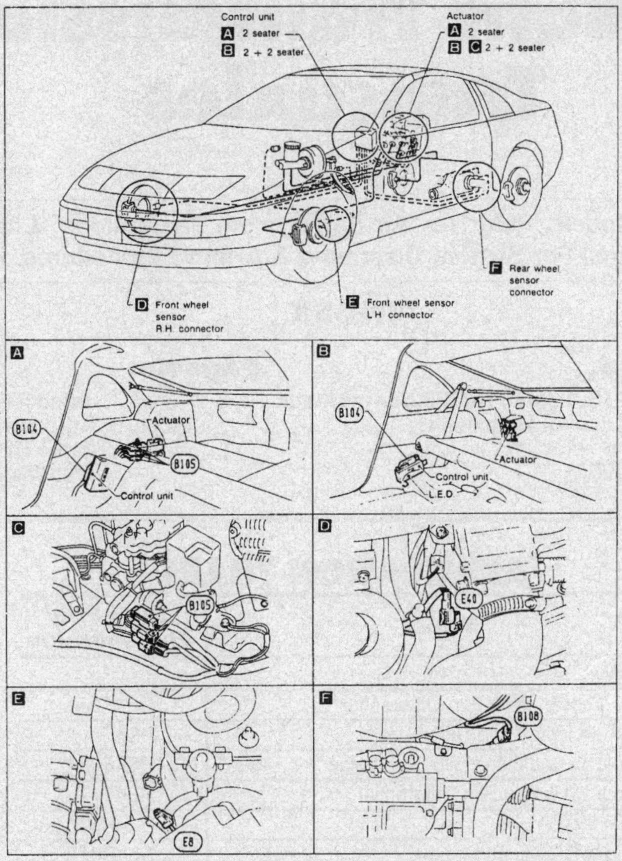
Control unit
A 2 seater
B 2 + 2 seater
Actuator
A 2 seater
B C 2 + 2 seater
F Rear wheel sensor connector
D Front wheel sensor R.H. connector
E Front wheel sensor L.H. connector
A
B104
Actuator
B105
Control unit
B
B104
Actuator
Control unit
L.E.D.
C
B105
D
E40
E
E8
F
B108

NS4029100137000X

Fig. 225 ABS system component & harness connector locations. 300ZX

Automatic Transmissions/ Transaxles

NOTE: On Air Bag Equipped Models, Refer To "Air Bag System Precautions" Located In The Front Of This Manual For System Disarming & Arming Procedures.

INDEX

	Page No.
Application Chart	36-218
Jatco RE4R01A, RE4R03A & RL4R01A Automatic Transmissions	36-220
Jatco RE4F02A Automatic Transaxles	36-228
Jatco RE4F04A & RE4F04V Automatic Transaxles	36-233
Jatco RL4F03A Automatic Transaxles	36-237

APPLICATION CHART

Model	Transaxle/ Transmission
1993	
Altima Less Limited Slip Differential	RE4F04A
Altima w/Limited Slip Differential	RE4F0VA
Maxima Less Limited Slip Differential	RE4F02A
Maxima w/Limited Slip Differential	RE4F04V
Pathfinder	RE4R01A
Pickup w/KA24E Engine	RL4R01A
Pickup w/VG30E Engine	RE4R01A
Quest	RE4F04A
Sentra Less Limited Slip Differential	RL4F03A
Sentra w/Limited Slip Differential	RE4F03V
240SX	RE4R01A
300ZX Less Turbo	RE4R01A
300ZX Turbo	RE4R03A
1994	
Altima Less Limited Slip Differential	RE4F04A
Altima w/Limited Slip Differential	RE4F04V
Maxima Less Limited Slip Differential	RE4F02A
Maxima w/Limited Slip Differential	RE4F04V
Pathfinder	RE4R01A
Pickup w/KA24E Engine	RL4R01A
Pickup w/VG30E Engine	RE4R01A
Quest	RE4F04A
Sentra Less Limited Slip Differential	RL4F03A
Sentra w/Limited Slip Differential	RE4F03V
240SX	RE4R01A
300ZX Less Turbo	RE4R01A
300ZX Turbo	RE4R03A
1995	
Altima Less Limited Slip Differential	RE4F04A
Altima w/Limited Slip Differential	RE4F04V
Maxima Less Limited Slip Differential	RE4F04A
Maxima w/Limited Slip Differential	RE4F04V
Pathfinder	RE4R01A
Pickup w/KA24E Engine	RL4R01A
Pickup w/VG30E Engine	RE4R01A
Quest	RE4F04A

Continued

APPLICATION CHART—Continued

Model	Transaxle/ Transmission
1995	
Sentra & 200SX Less Limited Slip Differential	RL4F03A
Sentra & 200SX w/Limited Slip Differential	RE4F03V
240SX	RE4R01A
300ZX Less Turbo	RE4R01A
300ZX Turbo	RE4R03A
1996	
Altima Less Limited Slip Differential	RE4F04A
Altima w/Limited Slip Differential	RE4F04V
Maxima Less Limited Slip Differential	RE4F04A
Maxima w/Limited Slip Differential	RE4F04V
Pathfinder	RE4R01A
Pickup	RL4R01A
Quest	RE4F04A
Sentra & 200SX w/GA16DE	RL4F03A
Sentra & 200SX w/SR20DE	RE4F03V
240SX	RE4R01A
300ZX Less Turbo	RE4R01A
300ZX Turbo	RE4R03A

Jatco RE4R01A, RE4R03A & RL4R01A Automatic Transmissions

INDEX

	Page No.
Adjustments	36-220
Inhibitor Switch	36-220
Kickdown Switch	36-220
Manual Linkage	36-220
Throttle Wire	36-220
Identification	36-220
In-Vehicle Repairs	36-220
Control Valve Assembly & Accumulators	36-220
Key Interlock Cable, Replace	36-221
Parking Components	36-221
Rear Oil Seal	36-221
Revolution Sensor	36-221
Maintenance	36-220
Fluid Change	36-220
Fluid Check	36-220
Tightening Specifications	36-227
Transmission, Replace	36-221
240SX	36-222
300ZX	36-222
Pathfinder & Pickup	36-221
Troubleshooting	36-220
Brake Transmission Shift Interlock	36-220
Transmission	36-220

IDENTIFICATION

The transmission model number is located on a tag attached to the right side of the transmission case. The transmission model numbers are listed under "Application Chart."

TROUBLESHOOTING

TRANSMISSION

Refer to **Figs. 1 and 2** when troubleshooting the transmission.

BRAKE TRANSMISSION SHIFT INTERLOCK

Pathfinder, Pickup & 240SX

Refer to **Fig. 3** when troubleshooting the brake transmission shift interlock.

300ZX

Refer to **Figs. 4 and 5** when troubleshooting the brake transmission shift interlock.

MAINTENANCE

FLUID CHECK

1. Ensure vehicle is at operating temperature, then park on a level surface and set parking brake.
2. Start engine, then move selector through each gear range ending in "P."
3. Check fluid with engine idling.
4. Fluid level should be within "HOT" range on dipstick.
5. Add fluid as necessary and recheck.

FLUID CHANGE

1. Raise and support vehicle, then remove oil pan to drain fluid.
2. Install oil pan using a new gasket, then fill transmission. **Use caution not to overfill transmission.**

ADJUSTMENTS

MANUAL LINKAGE

4WD Pathfinder & Pickup

1. Place selector lever in Park range.
2. Loosen locknuts, **Fig. 6.**
3. Tighten turnbuckle until it aligns with inner cable, pulling selector lever toward reverse range side without pushing button.
4. Back off turnbuckle one turn and **torque** locknuts to 3–4 ft. lbs.
5. Move selector lever from Park range to 1 range. Ensure lever moves smoothly.

2WD Pathfinder, Pickup, 240SX & 300ZX w/Floor Shift

1. Place selector lever in Park range.
2. Loosen locknuts, **Fig. 7.**
3. Tighten locknut X until it touches trunnion, pulling selector lever toward reverse range side without pushing button.
4. Back off locknut X one turn and **torque** locknut Y to 8–11 ft. lbs.
5. Move selector lever from Park range to 1 range. Ensure lever moves smoothly.

2WD Pickup w/Column Shift

1. Place selector lever in Park range.
2. Loosen locknuts, **Fig. 8.**
3. Tighten locknut A until it touches trunnion, pulling selector lever toward reverse range side without pushing button.
4. Back off locknut A two turns and **torque** locknut B to 8–11 ft. lbs.
5. Move selector lever from Park range to 1 range. Ensure lever moves smoothly.

INHIBITOR SWITCH

1. Remove manual control linkage or cable from manual shaft.
2. Place manual shaft in neutral.
3. Loosen switch attaching bolts.
4. Insert suitable aligning pin, into adjustment holes in inhibitor switch and manual shaft as near vertical as possible.
5. Install control linkage or cable, then tighten attaching bolts.

THROTTLE WIRE

RL4R01A Transmission

1. While pressing lock plate, **Fig. 9,** move adjusting tube in direction "T."
2. Return lock plate, then move throttle drum from P2 to P1 quickly.
3. Ensure throttle wire stroke "L" is within 1.5–1.65 inch between full throttle and idle.
4. **Adjust throttle wire stroke when throttle wire/accelerator wire is installed or after throttle body has been adjusted. Put marks on throttle wire to aid in measuring wire stroke.**

KICKDOWN SWITCH

1. Adjust accelerator cable as follows:
   a. Tighten adjusting nut, **Fig. 10,** until throttle drum starts to move, then back off 1 ½–2 turns and secure with lock nut.
2. Adjust kickdown switch as follows:
   a. Adjust clearance "C", **Fig. 11,** between stopper rubber and end of kickdown switch thread while depressing accelerator pedal fully.
   b. Clearance "C," should be .012–.039 inch.

IN-VEHICLE REPAIRS

CONTROL VALVE ASSEMBLY & ACCUMULATORS

1. **On Pathfinder and Pickup models,** remove front exhaust pipe.
2. **On all models,** raise and support vehicle, then remove oil pan and gasket and drain transmission fluid.
3. Remove fluid temperature sensor, if equipped or necessary.
4. Remove oil strainer, then valve body to case attaching bolts and disconnect harness electrical connector.
5. Remove solenoids and valves from valve body, if necessary.
6. Remove terminal cord assembly, if necessary.
7. Remove accumulator A, B, C and D, if necessary, using compressed air, **Fig. 12.** Cover each piston with a shop towel when removing.
8. Reverse procedure to install. **Always use new sealing parts.**

Symptom Chart

	ON vehicle																				OFF vehicle										
Reference page (AT-)	23, 121		121		47, 49, 64		107		53, 119		55, 66		57, 59		61, 119		119		119		130, 141		158, 162		164		164, 173		168, 177		181
Numbers are arranged in order of probability. Perform inspections starting with number one and work up. Circled numbers indicate that the transmission must be removed from the vehicle.	Fluid level	Control linkage	Inhibitor switch	Throttle position sensor (Adjustment)	Revolution sensor and speed sensor	Engine speed signal	Engine idling rpm	Line pressure	Control valve assembly	Shift solenoid valve A	Shift solenoid valve B	Line pressure solenoid valve	Torque converter clutch solenoid valve	Overrun clutch solenoid valve	Fluid temperature sensor	Accumulator N-D	Accumulator 1-2	Accumulator 2-3	Accumulator 3-4 (N-R)	Ignition switch and starter	Torque converter	Oil pump	Reverse clutch	High clutch	Forward clutch	Forward one-way clutch	Overrun clutch	Low one-way clutch	Low & reverse brake	Brake band	Parking components
Engine does not start in "N", "P" positions.		2	3																	1											
Engine starts in position other than "N" and "P" positions.		1	2																												
Transmission noise in "P" and "N" positions.	1			3	4	5		2													⑦	⑥									
Vehicle moves when changing into "P" position or parking gear does not disengage when shifted out of "P" position.		1																													②
Vehicle runs in "N" position.		1																	2				④		③		⑤				
Vehicle will not run in "R" position (but runs in "D", "2" and "1" positions). Clutch slips. Very poor acceleration.		1						2	4			3											⑤	⑥	⑦		⑧		⑨		
Vehicle braked when shifting into "R" position.	1	2						3	5			4												⑥	⑧		⑨			⑦	
Sharp shock in shifting from "N" to "D" position.				2		5	1	3	7			6			4	8									⑨						
Vehicle will not run in "D" and "2" positions (but runs in "1" and "R" positions).		1																										②			
Vehicle will not run in "D", "1", "2" positions (but runs in "R" position). Clutch slips. Very poor acceleration.	1							2	4			3				5							⑥	⑦	⑧	⑨		⑩			
Clutches or brakes slip somewhat in starting.	1	2		3				4	6			5				7			8		⑬	⑫	⑩		⑨				⑪		
Excessive creep.							1																								
No creep at all.	1							2	3												⑥	⑤			④						
Failure to change gear from "D_1" to "D_2".		2	1		5				4	3																				⑥	
Failure to change gear from "D_2" to "D_3".		2	1		5				4		3													⑥						⑦	
Failure to change gear from "D_3" to "D_4".		2	1		4					3					5															⑥	
Too high a gear change point from "D_1" to "D_2", from "D_2" to "D_3", from "D_3" to "D_4".				1	2					3	4																				
Gear change directly from "D_1" to "D_3" occurs.	1																2													③	
Engine stops when shifting lever into "R", "D", "2" and "1".							1		3				2								④										
Too sharp a shock in change from "D_1" to "D_2".				1				2	4						5		3													⑥	
Too sharp a shock in change from "D_2" to "D_3".				1				2	4									3						⑤						⑥	

NS5029100519010A

Fig. 1 Transaxle troubleshooting chart (Part 1 of 3). RE4R01A & RE4R03A transmissions

	ON vehicle																				OFF vehicle										
Reference page (AT-)	23, 121		121		47, 49, 64		107		53, 119		55, 66		57, 59		61, 119		119		119		130, 141		158, 162		164		164, 173		168, 177		181
Numbers are arranged in order of probability. Perform inspections starting with number one and work up. Circled numbers indicate that the transmission must be removed from the vehicle.	Fluid level	Control linkage	Inhibitor switch	Throttle position sensor (Adjustment)	Revolution sensor and speed sensor	Engine speed signal	Engine idling rpm	Line pressure	Control valve assembly	Shift solenoid valve A	Shift solenoid valve B	Line pressure solenoid valve	Torque converter clutch solenoid valve	Overrun clutch solenoid valve	Fluid temperature sensor	Accumulator N-D	Accumulator 1-2	Accumulator 2-3	Accumulator 3-4 (N-R)	Ignition switch and starter	Torque converter	Oil pump	Reverse clutch	High clutch	Forward clutch	Forward one-way clutch	Overrun clutch	Low one-way clutch	Low & reverse brake	Brake band	Parking components
Too sharp a shock in change from "D_3" to "D_4".				1				2	4										3								⑥			⑤	
Almost no shock or clutches slipping in change from "D_1" to "D_2".	1			2				3	5								4													⑥	
Almost no shock or slipping in change from "D_2" to "D_3".	1			2				3	5									4						⑥						⑦	
Almost no shock or slipping in change from "D_3" to "D_4".	1			2				3	5										4					⑥						⑦	
Vehicle braked by gear change from "D_1" to "D_2".	1																						②	④				⑤	③		
Vehicle braked by gear change from "D_2" to "D_3".	1																													②	
Vehicle braked by gear change from "D_3" to "D_4".	1																						④			③	②				
Maximum speed not attained. Acceleration poor.	1		2						5	3	4										⑪	⑩	⑥	⑦					⑨	⑧	
Failure to change gear from "D_4" to "D_3".	1			2					6	4		5		3													⑧		⑦		
Failure to change gear from "D_3" to "D_2" or from "D_4" to "D_2".	1			2					5	3	4													⑥						⑦	
Failure to change gear from "D_2" to "D_1" or from "D_3" to "D_1".	1			2					5	3	4													⑦				⑥		⑧	
Gear change shock felt during deceleration by releasing accelerator pedal.				1				2	4					3																	
Too high a change point from "D_4" to "D_3", from "D_3" to "D_2", from "D_2" to "D_1".				1	2																										
Kickdown does not operate when depressing pedal in "D_4" within kickdown vehicle speed.				1	2					3	4																				
Kickdown operates or engine overruns when depressing pedal in "D_4" beyond kickdown vehicle speed limit.				2	1					3	4																				
Races extremely fast or slips in changing from "D_4" to "D_3" when depressing pedal.	1			2				3	5			4												⑥	⑦						
Races extremely fast or slips in changing from "D_4" to "D_2" when depressing pedal.	1			2				3	6	5		4													⑧					⑦	
Races extremely fast or slips in changing from "D_3" to "D_2" when depressing pedal.	1			2				3	5			4			6			7						⑩	⑨					⑧	
Races extremely fast or slips in changing from "D_4" or "D_3" to "D_1" when depressing pedal.	1			2				3	5			4													⑥	⑦		⑧			
Vehicle will not run in any position.	1	2						3				4									⑨	⑤		⑥					⑧	⑦	⑩
Transmission noise in "D", "2", "1" and "R" positions.	1																				②										

NS5029100519020A

Fig. 1 Transaxle troubleshooting chart (Part 2 of 3). RE4R01A & RE4R03A transmissions

KEY INTERLOCK CABLE, REPLACE

Removal

1. Unlock slider from adjuster holder and remove rod from cable at shift selector.
2. Remove lock plate and cable from steering lock.

Installation

1. Set key interlock cable to steering lock assembly and install lock plate.
2. Clamp cable to steering column and fix to control cable with band.
3. Set selector lever to P position.
4. Insert interlock rod into adjuster holder.
5. Install casing cap to bracket.
6. Move slider in order to fix adjuster holder to interlock rod.

REAR OIL SEAL

1. Raise and support vehicle, then disconnect driveshaft.
2. **On 4WD Pathfinder and Pickup models,** remove transfer case. Refer to "4 Wheel Drive" section for transfer case removal.
3. **On all models,** use suitable tool to remove old seal.
4. Coat new seal with new transmission fluid and install.
5. Install driveshaft.

REVOLUTION SENSOR

1. Raise and support vehicle.
2. **On 300ZX models,** remove exhaust tube.
3. **On 4WD Pathfinder and Pickup and 240SX models,** proceed as follows:
   a. Support transmission using suitable jack, then remove rear engine mounting crossmember.
   b. Lower transmission as much as possible.
4. **On all models,** remove revolution sensor.
5. Reverse procedure to install.

PARKING COMPONENTS

1. **On 300ZX models,** remove exhaust tube.
2. **On all models,** remove driveshaft.
3. **On 4WD Pathfinder and Pickup models,** remove transfer case. Refer to "4 Wheel Drive" section for transfer case removal.
4. Remove manual control linkage from adapter case.
5. **On 2WD Pickup, 240SX and 300ZX models,** support transmission using a suitable jack, then remove rear engine mounting crossmember.
6. **On 4WD Pathfinder and Pickup models,** support transmission with a suitable jack, then remove adapter case from transmission.
7. **On 2WD Pickup, 240SX and 300ZX models,** remove rear extension housing from transmission.
8. **On all models,** inspect parking components and replace as necessary.
9. Reverse procedure to install.

TRANSMISSION

REPLACE

PATHFINDER & PICKUP

1. Disconnect battery ground cable, then raise and support vehicle.
2. Remove front and rear exhaust pipes.
3. Remove dipstick tube, then disconnect transmission cooler lines from transmission and plug openings.
4. Remove propeller shaft(s) and insert plug into rear oil seal to prevent leakage.
5. **On 4WD models,** disconnect transfer control linkage from transfer case.
6. **On all models,** remove torsion bar springs, as follows:
   a. Remove adjusting nut, then slide back dust cover and remove snap ring from anchor arm.
   b. Remove torque arm attaching nuts, then slide torsion bar forward with torque arm attached and remove from vehicle.

Numbers are arranged in order of probability. Perform inspections starting with number one and work up. Circled numbers indicate that the transmission must be removed from the vehicle.	Fluid level	Control linkage	Inhibitor switch	Throttle position sensor (Adjustment)	Revolution sensor and speed sensor	Engine speed signal	Engine idling rpm	Line pressure	Control valve assembly	Shift solenoid valve A	Shift solenoid valve B	Line pressure solenoid valve	Torque converter clutch solenoid valve	Overrun clutch solenoid valve	Fluid temperature sensor	Accumulator N-D	Accumulator 1-2	Accumulator 2-3	Accumulator 3-4 (N-R)	Ignition switch and starter	Torque converter	Oil pump	Reverse clutch	High clutch	Forward clutch	Forward one-way clutch	Overrun clutch	Low one-way clutch	Low & reverse brake	Brake band	Parking components
	ON vehicle																				OFF vehicle										
Reference page (AT-)	23, 121		121		47, 49, 64		107		53, 119		55, 66		57, 59		61, 119		119		119		130, 141		158, 162		164		164, 173		168, 177		181
Failure to change from "D_3" to "2" when changing lever into "2" position.	.	7	1	2	.	.	.	.	6	5	4	.	.	3	.	.	.	.	.	.	.	.	.	.	.	.	(9)	.	.	(8)	.
Gear change from "2_2" to "2_3" in "2" position.	.	.	1	.	.	.	.	.	.	.	.	.	.	.	.	.	.	.	.	.	.	.	.	.	.	.	.	.	.	.	.
Engine brake does not operate in "1" position.	.	2	1	3	4	.	.	.	6	5	.	.	.	7	.	.	.	.	.	.	.	.	.	.	.	.	(8)	.	(9)	.	.
Gear change from "1_1" to "1_2" in "1" position.		2	1	.	.	.	.	.	.	.	.	.	.	.	.	.	.	.	.	.	.	.	.	.	.	.	.	.	.	.	.
Does not change from "1_2" to "1_1" in "1" position.	.	.	1	.	2	.	.	.	4	3	.	.	.	5	.	.	.	.	.	.	.	.	.	.	.	.	(6)	.	(7)	.	.
Large shock changing from "1_2" to "1_1" in "1" position.	.	.	.	.	.	.	.	.	1	.	.	.	.	.	.	.	.	.	.	.	.	.	.	.	.	.	.	.	(2)	.	.
Transmission overheats.	1	.	.	3	.	.	2	4	6	.	.	5	.	.	.	.	.	.	.	.	(14)	(7)	(8)	(9)	(11)	.	(12)	.	(13)	(10)	.
ATF shoots out during operation. White smoke emitted from exhaust pipe during operation.	1	.	.	.	.	.	.	.	.	.	.	.	.	.	.	.	.	.	.	.	.	.	(2)	(3)	(5)	.	(6)	.	(7)	(4)	.
Offensive smell at fluid charging pipe.	1	.	.	.	.	.	.	.	.	.	.	.	.	.	.	.	.	.	.	.	(2)	(3)	(4)	(5)	(7)	.	(8)	.	(9)	(6)	.
Torque converter is not locked up.	.	.	3	1	2	4	.	6	8	.	.	.	7	.	5	.	.	.	.	.	(9)	.	.	.	.	.	.	.	.	.	.
Torque converter clutch piston slip.	1	.	.	2	.	.	.	3	6	.	.	5	4	.	.	.	.	.	.	.	(7)	.	.	.	.	.	.	.	.	.	.
Lock-up point is extremely high or low.	.	.	.	1	2	.	.	.	4	.	.	.	3	.	.	.	.	.	.	.	.	.	.	.	.	.	.	.	.	.	.
A/T does not shift to "D_4" when driving with overdrive control switch "ON".	.	.	2	1	3	.	.	8	6	4	.	.	.	5	7	.	.	.	.	.	.	.	.	.	.	.	(10)	.	.	(9)	.
Engine is stopped at "R", "D", "2" and "1" positions.	1	.	.	.	.	.	.	.	5	4	3	.	2	.	.	.	.	.	.	.	.	.	.	.	.	.	.	.	.	.	.

NS5029100519030A

Fig. 1 Transaxle troubleshooting chart (Part 3 of 3). RE4R01A & RE4R03A transmissions

ROAD TEST SYMPTOM CHART

Numbers are arranged in order of probability.
Perform inspections starting with number one and working up.
Circled numbers indicate that the transmission must be removed from the vehicle.

☐ : Valve expected to be malfunctioning

Symptom	Condition	Oil level and oil quality	Control linkage	Inhibitor switch and wiring	Throttle wire	Engine idling rpm	Line pressure	Control valve	4th speed cut valve	Pressure regulator valve	Pressure modifier valve	1-2 shift valve	2-3 shift valve	3-4 shift valve	Accumulator control valve	3-2 downshift valve	2-3 throttle modifier valve
		ON VEHICLE															
Sharp shocks in shifting from "N" to "D" range		1	2	.	5	3	4	8									
Shift shocks	When shifting from 1st to 2nd or 2nd to 3rd	1	2	.	4	.	3	7									
	When shifting from 3rd to 4th	1	2	.	4	.	3	6									
	When shifting from D to 2 and 1 range. When O.D. switch is set from "ON" to "OFF"	1	2	.	4	.	3	5									
	When shifting from 2nd to 1st in "1" range	1	2	.	4	.	3	5									
Shift slippage when upshifting	When shifting from 1st to 2nd	1	2	.	4	.	3	6									
	When shifting from 2nd to 3rd	1	2	.	4	.	3	6									
	When shifting from 3rd to 4th	1	2	.	4	.	3	6									
Shift slippage with accelerator pedal depressed	When shifting from 4th to 2nd	1	2	.	5	.	3	7									
	When shifting from 4th to 3rd	1	2	.	4	.	3	6									
	When shifting from 4th to 1st and shifting from 3rd to 1st	1	2	.	5	.	3	7									
Poor power/acceleration	When vehicle starts	1	2	.	5	.	3	10									
	When upshifting	1	2	.	4	.	3	8									
No engine braking	When shifting from "D" to "2" and "1" range	1	2	.	4	.	3	6									
	When O.D. switch is set from "ON" to "OFF"	1	2	.	4	.	3	8									
	When shifting from 2nd to 1st in "1" range	1	2	.	4	.	3	6									
Shift quality	Too low a gear change point from 2nd to 3rd and from 3rd to 2nd.	1	.	.	4	.	2	5									
	Too high a gear change point from 2nd to 3rd and from 3rd to 2nd.	1	.	.	4	.	2	5									
	Too low a gear change point from 2nd to 1st in "1" range.	1	.	.	4	.	2	5									
	Too high a gear change point from 2nd to 1st in "1" range.	1	.	.	4	.	2	5									

NS50291005200010X

Fig. 2 Transaxle troubleshooting chart (Part 1 of 4). RL4R01A transmission

7. Remove second crossmember.
8. Remove speedometer cable from transfer case, then disconnect control cable from transmission.
9. **On 2WD models,** remove speedometer cable from transmission, then disconnect control linkage from selector lever.
10. **On all models,** disconnect transmission harness connectors, then remove starter motor.
11. Remove gusset attaching engine to transmission assembly, then the bolts attaching torque converter to driveplate.
12. Support transmission assembly with a suitable jack and secure to jack, then remove rear mounting bracket from body and transmission assembly.
13. Remove bolts attaching transmission assembly to engine.
14. **On 4WD models,** lower transmission assembly and remove from vehicle.
15. **On 2WD models,** slide transmission assembly backwards, slant and lower assembly, then remove from vehicle.
16. **On all models,** reverse procedure to install.

240SX

1. Disconnect battery ground cable, then raise and support vehicle.
2. Disconnect transmission harness connectors and clamps.
3. Remove dipstick tube, then disconnect transmission cooler line from right side of transmission and plug openings.
4. Disconnect control linkage from selector lever, then remove propeller shaft.
5. Remove heat shield from catalytic converter, then exhaust tube bracket and separate rear exhaust tube from converter.
6. Remove starter motor, then the gussets and end plate.
7. Remove bolts attaching torque converter to driveplate.
8. Support transmission assembly with a suitable jack and secure to jack, then remove rear mounting bracket from body and transmission assembly.
9. Lower transmission as much as possible, then disconnect transmission cooler line from left side of transmission and plug opening.
10. Remove bolts attaching transmission assembly to engine, then lower assembly and remove from vehicle.
11. Reverse procedure to install.

300ZX

1. Disconnect battery ground cable, then raise and support vehicle.
2. Remove exhaust tube, then disconnect transmission harness connectors and clamps.
3. Remove dipstick tube, then disconnect transmission cooler lines from transmission and plug openings.
4. Disconnect control linkage from selector lever, then remove propeller shaft.
5. Remove starter motor if necessary, then the gusset attaching engine to transmission.
6. Remove bolts attaching torque converter to driveplate.
7. Support transmission assembly with a suitable jack and secure to jack, then remove rear mounting bracket from body and transmission assembly.
8. Remove bolts attaching transmission assembly to engine, then lower assembly and remove from vehicle.
9. Reverse procedure to install.

ON VEHICLE																							OFF VEHICLE										
4-2 relay valve	Lock-up control valve	Throttle valve & detent valve	Manual valve	Kickdown modifier valve	1st reducing valve	Overrun clutch reducing valve	3-2 timing valve	Torque converter relief valve	4-2 sequence valve	Governor pressure	Governor valve	Primary governor valve	Secondary governor valve ①	Secondary governor valve ②	O.D. cancel solenoid	Lock-up cancel solenoid	Accumulator N-D	Accumulator 1-2	Accumulator 2-3	Accumulator 3-4 (N-R)	Ignition switch and starter motor	O.D. control switch and wiring	Torque converter	Oil pump	Reverse clutch	High clutch	Forward clutch	Forward one-way clutch	Overrun clutch	Low one-way clutch	Low & reverse clutch	Brake band	Parking components
										.	.				.	.	6	.	.	7	.	.	.	.	9	.	.	.	.	.	.	.	.
										.	.				.	.	.	5	6	.	.	.	.	.	.	.	.	.	.	.	.	.	.
										.	.				.	.	.	.	.	5	.	.	.	.	.	.	.	.	8	.	.	7	.
										.	.				.	.	.	.	.	.	.	.	.	.	.	7	.	.	.	.	.	6	.
										.	.				.	.	.	.	.	.	.	.	.	.	.	.	.	.	.	6	.	.	.
										.	.				.	.	.	5	.	.	.	.	.	.	.	.	.	.	.	.	.	7	.
										.	.				.	.	.	.	5	.	.	.	.	.	.	8	.	.	.	.	.	7	.
										.	.				.	.	.	.	.	5	.	.	.	.	.	8	.	.	.	.	.	7	.
										4	11				.	.	6	8	9	7	.	.	12	13	14	15	17	18	19	20	21	16	.
										.	.				.	.	.	5	6	7	.	.	.	9	.	10	.	.	12	.	13	11	.
										4	8				.	.	.	.	6	.	.	.	.	.	.	9	.	11	.	.	.	10	.
										.	.				.	.	.	.	5	.	.	.	.	.	.	7	8	.	.	.	.	.	.
										4	8				.	.	.	.	6	.	.	.	.	.	.	.	9	.	.	.	.	.	.
										.	.				.	.	.	.	5	.	.	.	.	.	.	.	.	.	7	.	.	.	.
										.	.				7	.	.	.	5	.	.	6	.	.	.	.	.	.	9	.	.	.	.
										.	.				.	.	.	.	.	.	.	.	.	.	.	.	.	.	7	.	8	.	.
										3	6				.	.	.	.	.	.	.	.	.	.	.	.	.	.	.	.	.	.	.
										3	6				.	.	.	.	.	.	.	.	.	.	.	.	.	.	.	.	.	.	.
										3	6				.	.	.	.	.	.	.	.	.	.	.	.	.	.	.	.	.	.	.
										3	6				.	.	.	.	.	.	.	.	.	.	.	.	.	.	.	.	.	.	.

NS50291005200020X

Fig. 2 Transaxle troubleshooting chart (Part 2 of 4). RL4R01A transmission

Numbers are arranged in order of probability. Perform inspections starting with number one and working up.
Circled numbers indicate that the transmission must be removed from the vehicle.

[ ] : Valve expected to be malfunctioning

		ON VEHICLE															
		Oil level and oil quality	Control linkage	Inhibitor switch and wiring	Throttle wire	Engine idling rpm	Line pressure	Control valve	4th speed cut valve	Pressure regulator valve	Pressure modifier valve	1-2 shift valve	2-3 shift valve	3-4 shift valve	Accumulator control valve	3-2 downshift valve	2-3 throttle modifier valve
Shift quality	Failure to change gear from 4th to 2nd with accelerator pedal depressed.	1	.	.	4	.	2	5									
	Failure to change gear from 3rd to 2nd with accelerator pedal depressed.	1	.	.	4	.	2	5									
	Failure to change gear from 1st to 2nd in "D" and "2" range.	1	.	.	4	.	2	5									
	Vehicle does not start from "1st" in "D" and "2" range.	1	.	.	4	.	2	5									
	Failure to change gear to 3rd and 4th in "D" range.	1	.	.	4	.	2	7									
	Changes gear to 1st directly when selector lever is set from "D" to "1" range.	1	.	.	4	.	2	5									
	Changes gear to 2nd in "1" range.	1	.	.	4	.	2	5									
	Too high or low a change point when lock-up operates.	1	.	.	4	.	2	5									
Lock-up quality	Lock-up point is extremely high or low.	1	.	.	4	.	2	5									
	Torque converter does not lock-up.	1	.	.	4	.	2	5									
	Lock-up is not released when accelerator pedal is released.	1	.	.	.	.	.	.									
Engine does not start in "P" and "N" ranges.		.	2	3	.	.	.	.									
Engine starts in ranges other than "P" and "N" ranges.		.	2	3	.	.	.	.									

NS5029100520030X

Fig. 2 Transaxle troubleshooting chart (Part 3 of 4). RL4R01A transmission

ON VEHICLE																							OFF VEHICLE										
4-2 relay valve	Lock-up control valve	Throttle valve & detent valve	Manual valve	Kickdown modifier valve	1st reducing valve	Overrun clutch reducing valve	3-2 timing valve	Torque converter relief valve	4-2 sequence valve	Governor pressure	Governor valve	Primary governor valve	Secondary governor valve (1)	Secondary governor valve (2)	O.D. cancel solenoid	Lock-up cancel solenoid	Accumulator N-D	Accumulator 1-2	Accumulator 2-3	Accumulator 3-4 (N-R)	Ignition switch and starter motor	O.D. control switch and wiring	Torque converter	Oil pump	Reverse clutch	High clutch	Forward clutch	Forward one-way clutch	Overrun clutch	Low one-way clutch	Low & reverse clutch	Brake band	Parking components
										3	6				·	·	·	·	·	·	·	·	·	·	·	·	·	·	·	·	·	·	·
										3	6				·	·	·	·	·	·	·	·	·	·	·	·	·	·	·	·	·	·	·
										3	6				·	·	·	·	·	·	·	·	·	·	·	·	·	·	·	·	·	·	·
										3	6				·	·	·	·	·	·	·	·	·	·	·	·	·	·	·	·	·	·	·
										3	8				6	·	·	·	·	·	·	5	·	·	·	·	·	·	·	·	·	·	·
										3	6				·	·	·	·	·	·	·	·	·	·	·	·	·	·	·	·	·	·	·
										3	6				·	·	·	·	·	·	·	·	·	·	·	·	·	·	·	·	·	·	·
										3	6				·	·	·	·	·	·	·	·	·	·	·	·	·	·	·	·	·	·	·
										3	6				·	·	·	·	·	·	·	·	·	·	·	·	·	·	·	·	·	·	·
										3	6				·	·	·	·	·	·	·	·	7	·	·	·	·	·	·	·	·	·	·
										·	·				·	2	·	·	·	·	·	·	·	·	·	·	·	·	·	·	·	·	·
										·	·				·	·	·	·	·	·	1	·	·	·	·	·	·	·	·	·	·	·	·
										·	·				·	·	·	·	·	·	·	·	·	·	·	·	·	·	·	·	·	·	·

NS5029100520040X

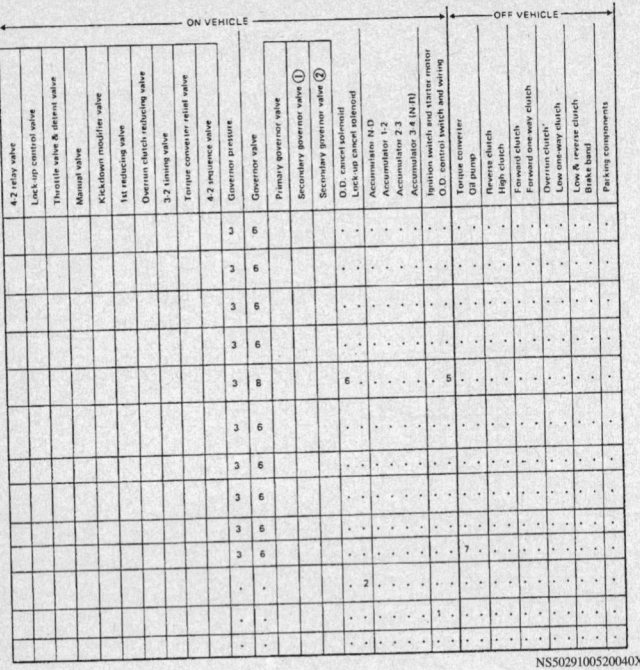

Fig. 2 Transaxle troubleshooting chart (Part 4 of 4). RL4R01A transmission

SYMPTOM 1:

- **Selector lever cannot be moved from "P" position with key in "ON" position and brake pedal applied.**
- **Selector lever can be moved from "P" position with key in "ON" position and brake pedal released.**
- **Selector lever can be moved from "P" position when key is removed from key cylinder.**

SYMPTOM 2:

Ignition key cannot be removed when selector lever is set to "P" position. It can be removed when selector lever is set to any position except "P".

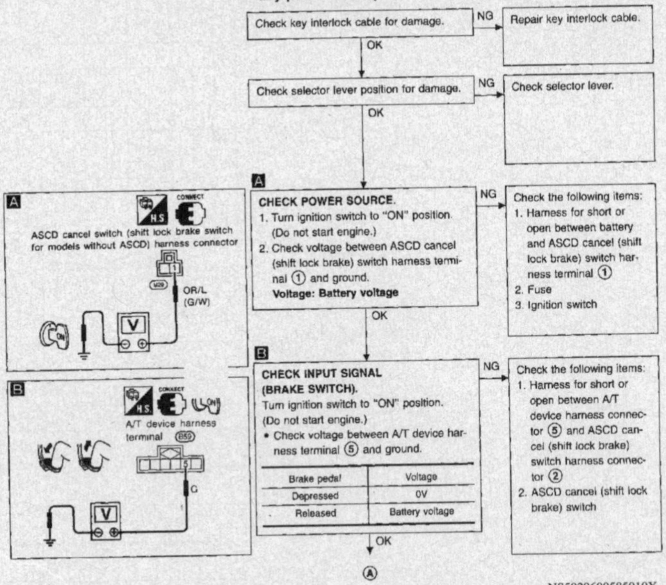
Check key interlock cable for damage.
NG
Repair key interlock cable.
OK
Check selector lever position for damage.
NG
Check selector lever.
OK
A
CHECK POWER SOURCE.
1. Turn ignition switch to "ON" position. (Do not start engine.)
2. Check voltage between ASCD cancel (shift lock brake) switch harness terminal ① and ground.
Voltage: Battery voltage
NG
Check the following items:
1. Harness for short or open between battery and ASCD cancel (shift lock brake) switch harness terminal ①
2. Fuse
3. Ignition switch
OK
B
CHECK INPUT SIGNAL (BRAKE SWITCH).
Turn ignition switch to "ON" position. (Do not start engine.)
• Check voltage between A/T device harness terminal ⑤ and ground.
Brake pedal | Voltage
Depressed | 0V
Released | Battery voltage
NG
Check the following items:
1. Harness for short or open between A/T device harness connector ⑤ and ASCD cancel (shift lock brake) switch harness connector ②
2. ASCD cancel (shift lock brake) switch
OK
Ⓐ
A
CONNECT
H.S.
ASCD cancel switch (shift lock brake switch for models without ASCD) harness connector
OR/L (G/W)
V
B
CONNECT
H.S.
A/T device harness terminal
G
V

NS5029600585010X

Fig. 3 BTSI diagnostic procedure (Part 1 of 2). Pathfinder, Pickup & 240SX

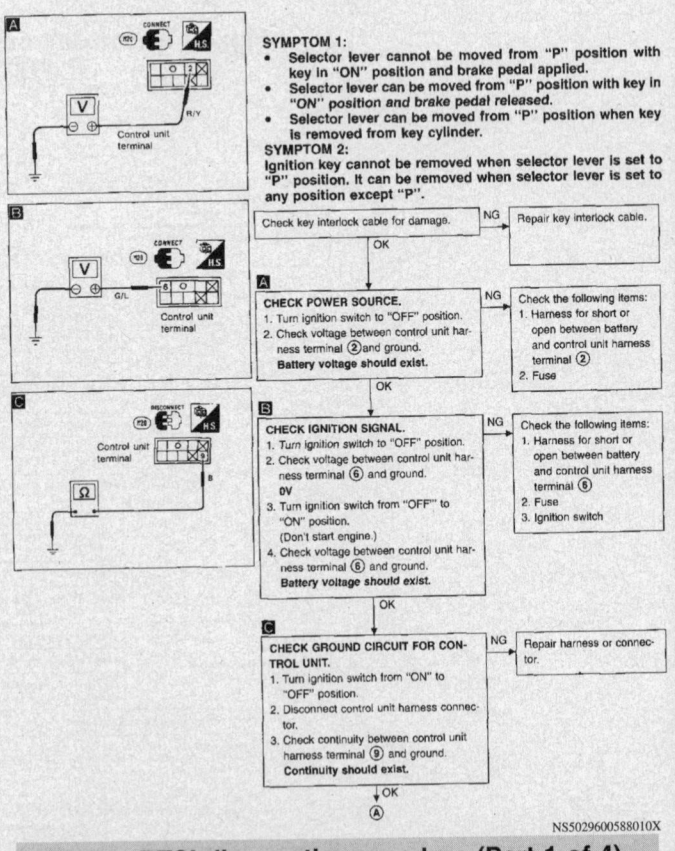

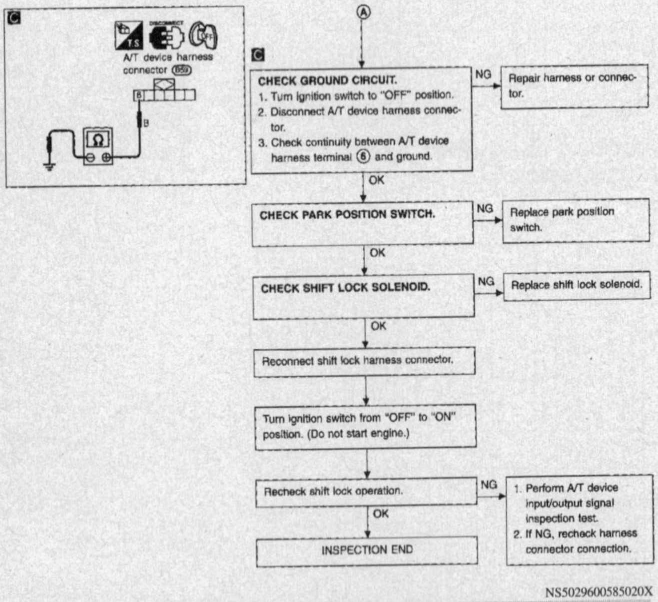
C
DISCONNECT
T.S.
A/T device harness connector
B
Ω
Ⓐ
C
CHECK GROUND CIRCUIT.
1. Turn ignition switch to "OFF" position.
2. Disconnect A/T device harness connector.
3. Check continuity between A/T device harness terminal ⑥ and ground.
NG
Repair harness or connector.
OK
CHECK PARK POSITION SWITCH.
NG
Replace park position switch.
OK
CHECK SHIFT LOCK SOLENOID.
NG
Replace shift lock solenoid.
OK
Reconnect shift lock harness connector.
Turn ignition switch from "OFF" to "ON" position. (Do not start engine.)
Recheck shift lock operation.
NG
1. Perform A/T device input/output signal inspection test.
2. If NG, recheck harness connector connection.
OK
INSPECTION END

NS5029600585020X

Fig. 3 BTSI diagnostic procedure (Part 2 of 2). Pathfinder, Pickup & 240SX

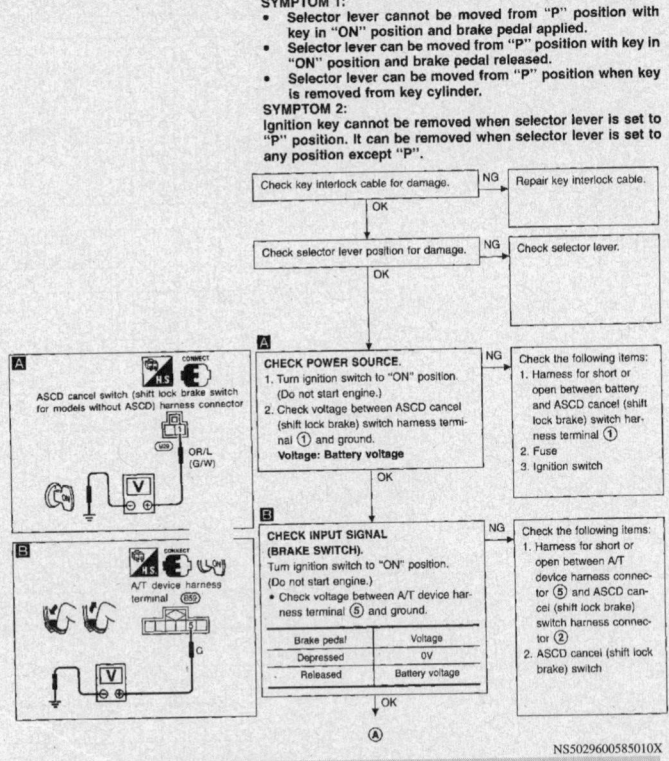

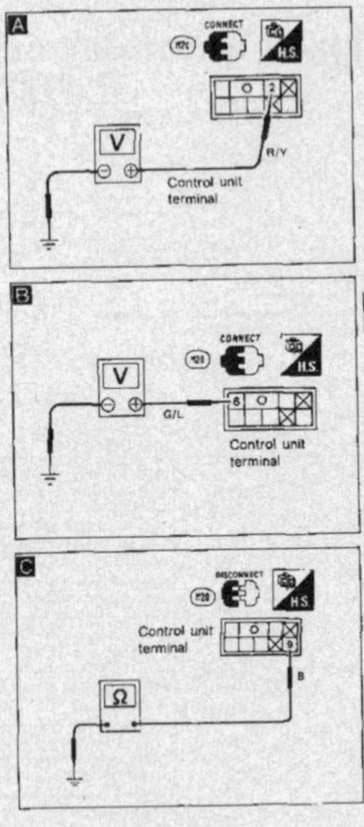
A
CONNECT
H.S.
V
R/Y
Control unit terminal
B
CONNECT
H.S.
V
G/L
Control unit terminal
C
DISCONNECT
H.S.
Control unit terminal
B
Ω

SYMPTOM 1:

- **Selector lever cannot be moved from "P" position with key in "ON" position and brake pedal applied.**
- **Selector lever can be moved from "P" position with key in "ON" position and brake pedal released.**
- **Selector lever can be moved from "P" position when key is removed from key cylinder.**

SYMPTOM 2:

Ignition key cannot be removed when selector lever is set to "P" position. It can be removed when selector lever is set to any position except "P".

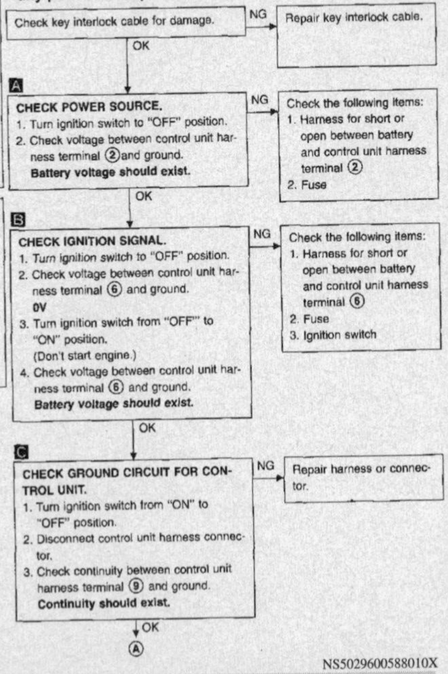
Check key interlock cable for damage.
NG
Repair key interlock cable.
OK
A
CHECK POWER SOURCE.
1. Turn ignition switch to "OFF" position.
2. Check voltage between control unit harness terminal ②and ground.
Battery voltage should exist.
NG
Check the following items:
1. Harness for short or open between battery and control unit harness terminal ②
2. Fuse
OK
B
CHECK IGNITION SIGNAL.
1. Turn ignition switch to "OFF" position.
2. Check voltage between control unit harness terminal ⑥ and ground.
0V
3. Turn ignition switch from "OFF" to "ON" position. (Don't start engine.)
4. Check voltage between control unit harness terminal ⑥ and ground.
Battery voltage should exist.
NG
Check the following items:
1. Harness for short or open between battery and control unit harness terminal ⑥
2. Fuse
3. Ignition switch
OK
C
CHECK GROUND CIRCUIT FOR CONTROL UNIT.
1. Turn ignition switch from "ON" to "OFF" position.
2. Disconnect control unit harness connector.
3. Check continuity between control unit harness terminal ⑨ and ground.
Continuity should exist.
NG
Repair harness or connector.
OK
Ⓐ

NS5029600588010X

Fig. 4 BTSI diagnostic procedure (Part 1 of 4). 300ZX

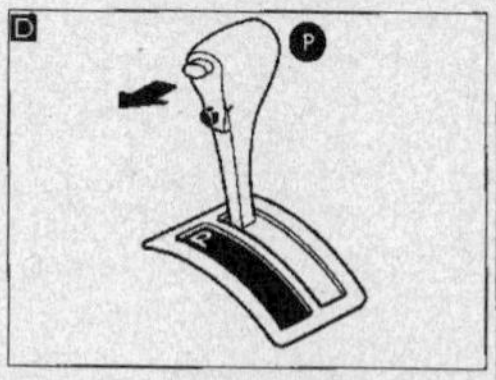
D
P

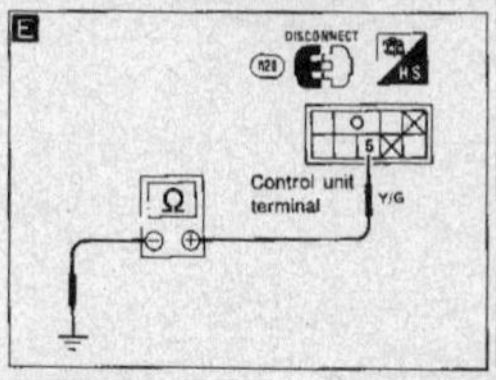
E
DISCONNECT
H.S.
Ω
Control unit terminal
Y/G

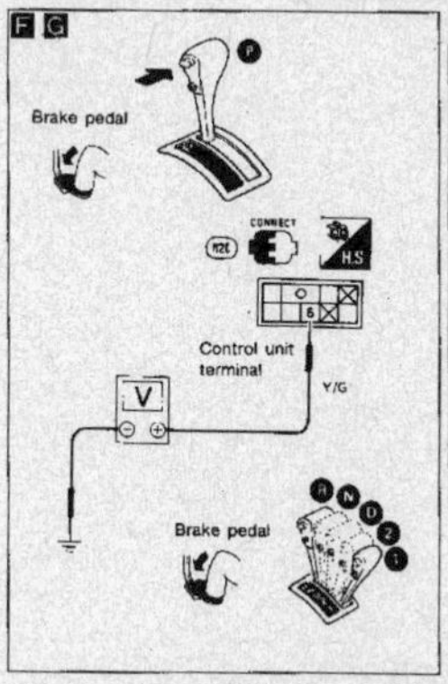
F G
P
Brake pedal
CONNECT
H.S.
Control unit terminal
V
Y/G
Brake pedal

Ⓐ

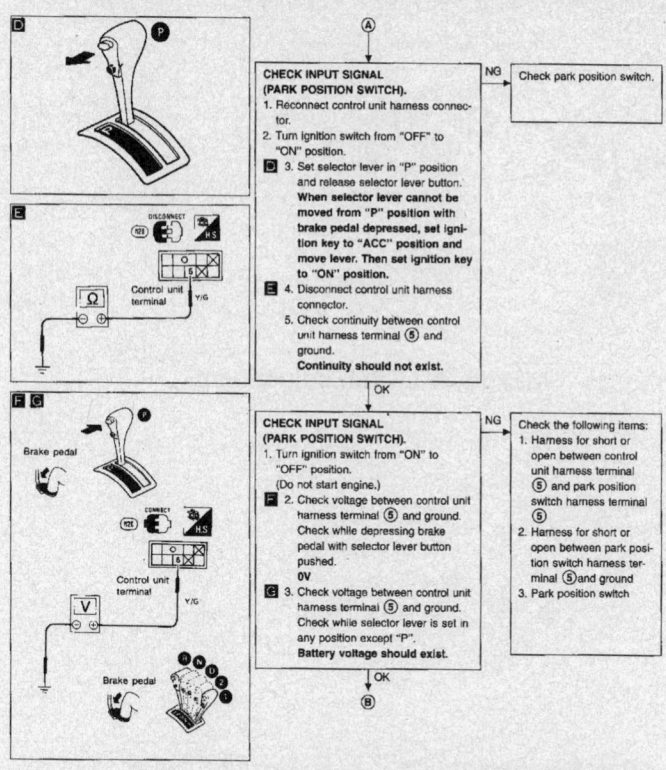

CHECK INPUT SIGNAL (PARK POSITION SWITCH).
1. Reconnect control unit harness connector.
2. Turn ignition switch from "OFF" to "ON" position.
3. [D] Set selector lever in "P" position and release selector lever button. **When selector lever cannot be moved from "P" position with brake pedal depressed, set ignition key to "ACC" position and move lever. Then set ignition key to "ON" position.**
4. [E] Disconnect control unit harness connector.
5. Check continuity between control unit harness terminal ⑤ and ground. **Continuity should not exist.**

NG → Check park position switch.

OK ↓

CHECK INPUT SIGNAL (PARK POSITION SWITCH).
1. Turn ignition switch from "ON" to "OFF" position. (Do not start engine.)
2. [F] Check voltage between control unit harness terminal ⑤ and ground. Check while depressing brake pedal with selector lever button pushed. **0V**
3. [G] Check voltage between control unit harness terminal ⑤ and ground. Check while selector lever is set in any position except "P". **Battery voltage should exist.**

NG → Check the following items:
1. Harness for short or open between control unit harness terminal ⑤ and park position switch harness terminal ⑤
2. Harness for short or open between park position switch harness terminal ⑤and ground
3. Park position switch

OK ↓

Ⓑ

NS5029600588020X

Fig. 4 BTSI diagnostic procedure (Part 2 of 4). 300ZX

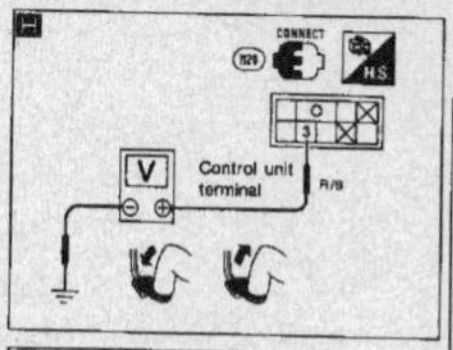
H
CONNECT
H.S.
V
Control unit terminal
R/B

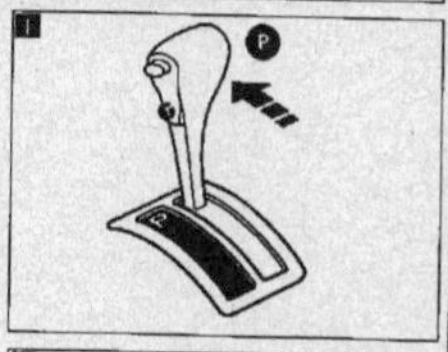
I
P

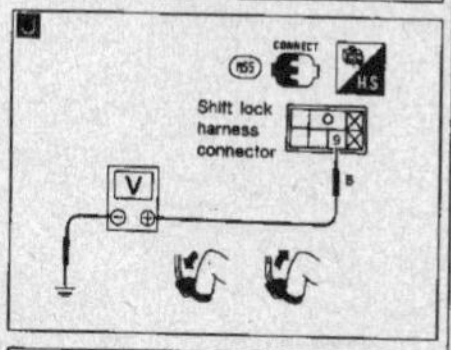
J
CONNECT
H.S.
Shift lock harness connector
V
B

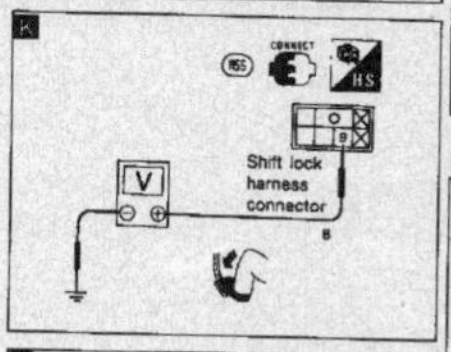
K
CONNECT
H.S.
V
Shift lock harness connector
B

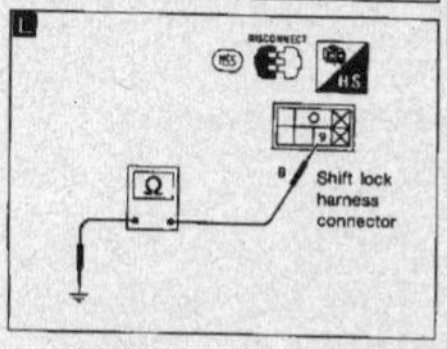
L
DISCONNECT
H.S.
Ω
B
Shift lock harness connector

Ⓑ

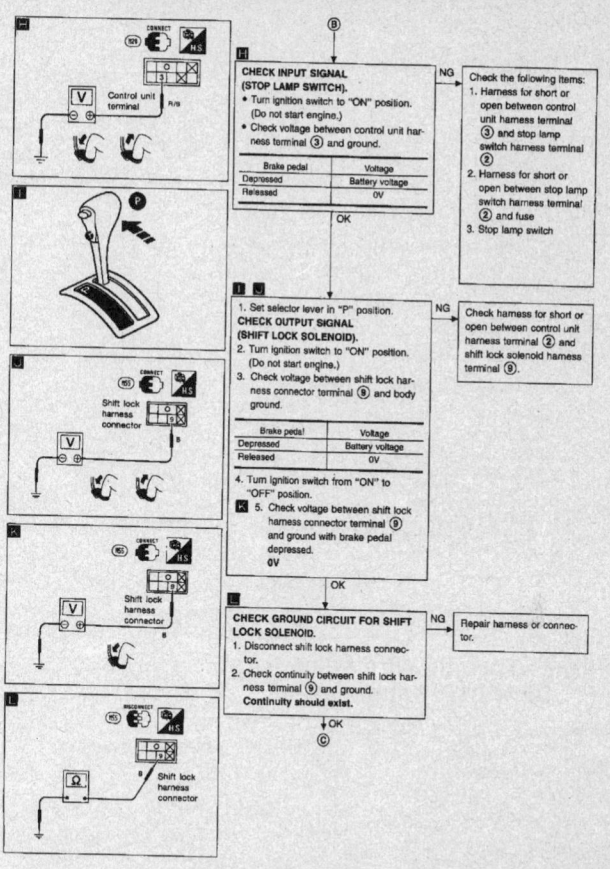

[H] **CHECK INPUT SIGNAL (STOP LAMP SWITCH).**
- Turn ignition switch to "ON" position. (Do not start engine.)
- Check voltage between control unit harness terminal ③ and ground.

Brake pedal	Voltage
Depressed	Battery voltage
Released	0V

NG → Check the following items:
1. Harness for short or open between control unit harness terminal ③ and stop lamp switch harness terminal ②
2. Harness for short or open between stop lamp switch harness terminal ② and fuse
3. Stop lamp switch

OK ↓

[I] [J]
1. Set selector lever in "P" position.

CHECK OUTPUT SIGNAL (SHIFT LOCK SOLENOID).

2. Turn ignition switch to "ON" position. (Do not start engine.)
3. Check voltage between shift lock harness connector terminal ⑨ and body ground.

Brake pedal	Voltage
Depressed	Battery voltage
Released	0V

4. Turn ignition switch from "ON" to "OFF" position.
5. [K] Check voltage between shift lock harness connector terminal ⑨ and ground with brake pedal depressed. **0V**

NG → Check harness for short or open between control unit harness terminal ② and shift lock solenoid harness terminal ⑨.

OK ↓

[L] **CHECK GROUND CIRCUIT FOR SHIFT LOCK SOLENOID.**
1. Disconnect shift lock harness connector.
2. Check continuity between shift lock harness terminal ⑨ and ground. **Continuity should exist.**

NG → Repair harness or connector.

OK ↓

Ⓒ

NS5029600588030X

Fig. 4 BTSI diagnostic procedure (Part 3 of 4). 300ZX

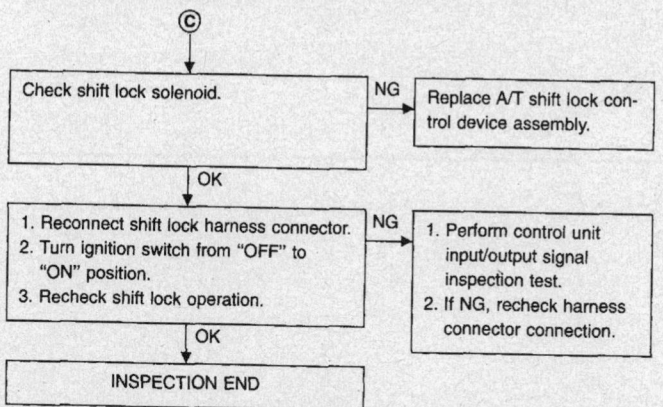

Ⓒ

Check shift lock solenoid.

NG → Replace A/T shift lock control device assembly.

OK ↓

1. Reconnect shift lock harness connector.
2. Turn ignition switch from "OFF" to "ON" position.
3. Recheck shift lock operation.

NG →
1. Perform control unit input/output signal inspection test.
2. If NG, recheck harness connector connection.

OK ↓

INSPECTION END

NS5029600588040X

Fig. 4 BTSI diagnostic procedure (Part 4 of 4). 300ZX

Terminal No. ⊕	Terminal No. ⊖	Item	Condition	Judgment standard
①	⑨	Shift lock signal	[Key ON] When selector lever is set in "P" position and brake pedal is depressed.	Battery voltage
			Except above	0V
②		Power source	Any condition	Battery voltage
③		Stop lamp switch	When brake pedal is depressed.	Battery voltage
			When brake pedal is released.	0V
⑤		Park position switch	• When the key is in key cylinder, selector lever is in "P" position, and selector lever button pushed. • When selector lever is set in any position except "P".	Battery voltage
			Except above	0V
⑥		Ignition signal	[Key ON]	Battery voltage
			Except above	0V

NS5029600589000X

Fig. 5 Shift lock control unit inspection table. 300ZX

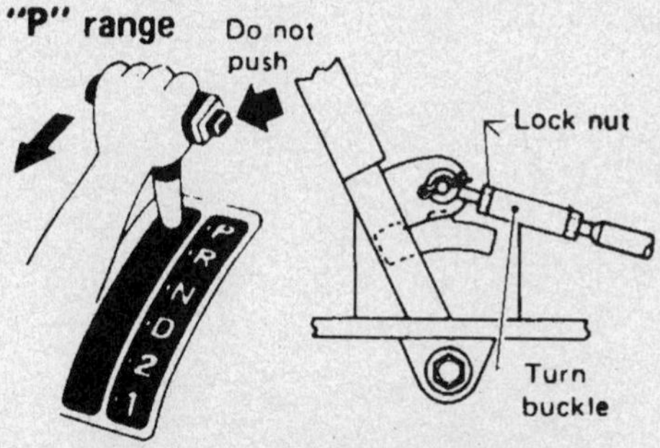
"P" range
Do not push
Lock nut
P R N D 2 1
Turn buckle

NS5028900139000X

Fig. 6 Manual linkage adjustment. 4WD Pathfinder & Pickup

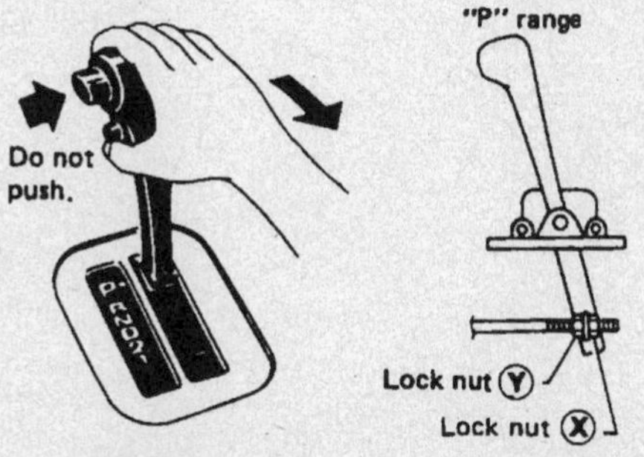
Do not push.
"P" range
Lock nut Ⓨ
Lock nut Ⓧ

NS5028900140000X

Fig. 7 Manual linkage adjustment. 2WD Pathfinder, Pickup, 240SX & 300ZX w/Floor Shift

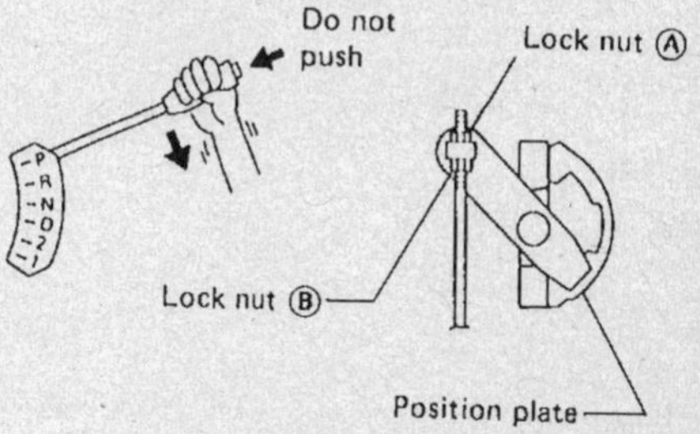
Do not push
Lock nut Ⓐ
P R N D 2 1
Lock nut Ⓑ
Position plate

NS5029000141000X

Fig. 8 Manual linkage adjustment. 2WD Pickup w/column shift

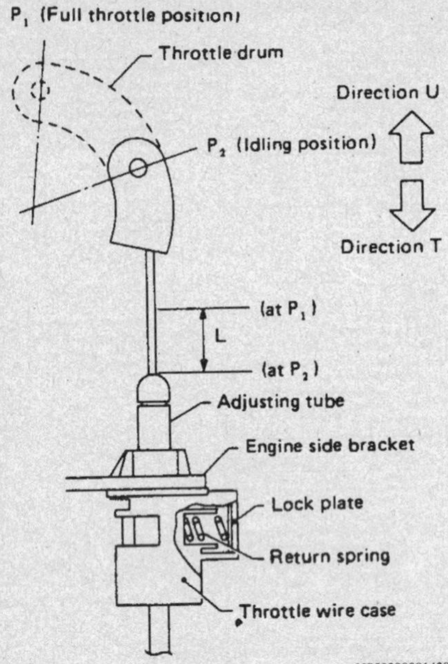

P1 (Full throttle position)
Throttle drum
Direction U
P2 (Idling position)
Direction T
(at P1)
L
(at P2)
Adjusting tube
Engine side bracket
Lock plate
Return spring
Throttle wire case

NS5029000142000X

Fig. 9 Throttle wire adjustment. RL4R01A transmission

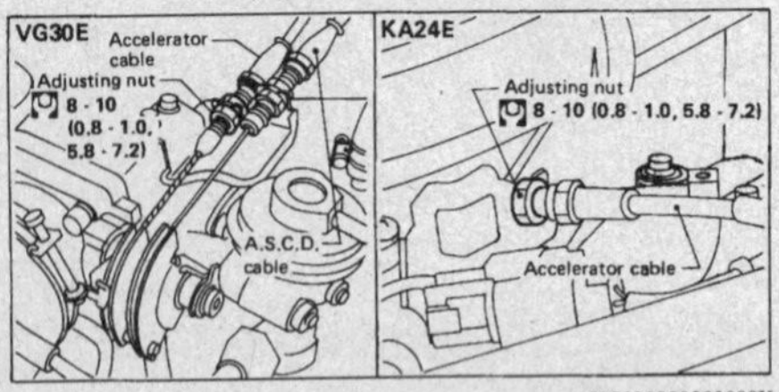

VG30E
Accelerator cable
Adjusting nut
8 - 10 (0.8 - 1.0, 5.8 - 7.2)
A.S.C.D. cable
KA24E
Adjusting nut
8 - 10 (0.8 - 1.0, 5.8 - 7.2)
Accelerator cable

NS5028900283000X

Fig. 10 Accelerator cable adjusting nut

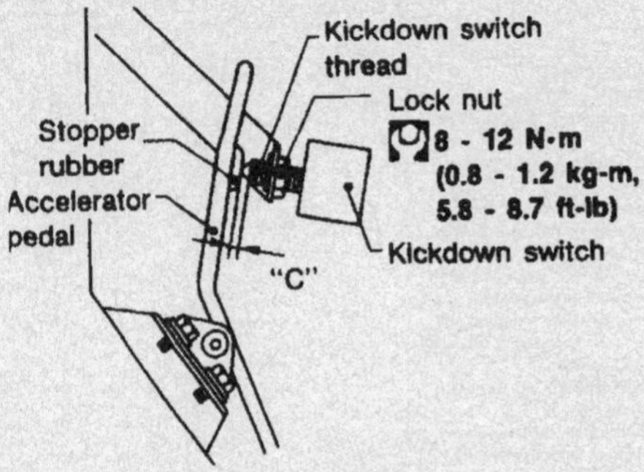

Kickdown switch thread
Lock nut
8 - 12 N·m (0.8 - 1.2 kg-m, 5.8 - 8.7 ft-lb)
Stopper rubber
Accelerator pedal
Kickdown switch
"C"

NS5018900144000X

Fig. 11 Kickdown switch adjustment

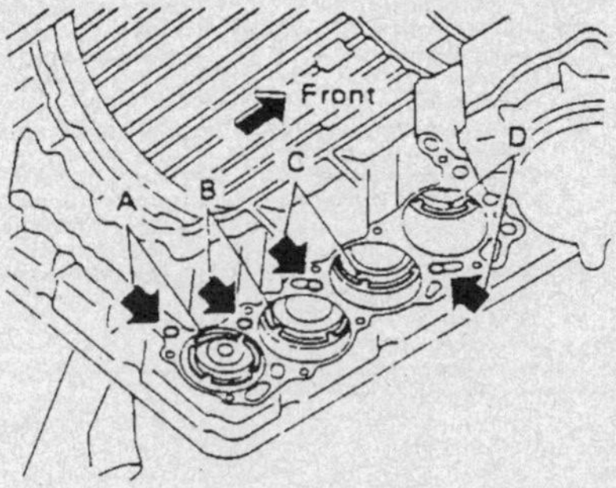

Front
A
B
C
D

NS5029100528000X

Fig. 12 Accumulator A, B, C & D removal

TIGHTENING SPECIFICATIONS

Year	Component	Torque/Ft. Lbs.
1993–96	Control Valve Assembly To Transmission Case	5–7
	Control Valve Lower Body To Upper Body	5–7
	Detent Spring Manual Plate To Transmission	22–29
	Extension Housing To Transmission	14–18
	Inhibitor Switch	12–24①
	Line Pressure Solenoid	5–7
	Oil Cooler Tube Bracket	48–72①
	Oil Pan To Transmission Housing	5–7
	Oil Pump Cover To Oil Pump Housing	12–15
	Oil Strainer To Control Valve	5–7
	Parking Actuator To Extension Housing	17–22
	Revolution Sensor To Extension Housing	48–60①
	Revolution Sensor To Transmission Case	48–60①
	Servo Assembly To Transmission Case	5–7
	Three Unit Solenoid Assembly	5–7
	Torque Converter Housing To Transmission	45–47
	Torque Converter To Driveplate	33–43

① — Inch lbs.

Jatco RE4F02A Automatic Transaxles

NOTE: On Air Bag Equipped Models, Refer To "Air Bag System Precautions" Located In The Front Of This Manual For System Disarming & Arming Procedures.

INDEX

Page No.

Adjustments 36-231
Control Cable 36-231
Inhibitor Switch 36-232
Identification 36-229
In-Vehicle Repairs 36-232
Control Valve, Replace 36-232
Differential Side Oil Seal, Replace 36-232
Maintenance 36-231
Fluid Check 36-231
Tightening Specifications 36-232
Transaxle, Replace 36-232
Troubleshooting 36-229
Almost No Shock Or Clutches Slipping In Change From "D1" To "D2" 36-230
Almost No Shock Or Clutches Slipping In Change From "D2" To "D3" 36-230
Almost No Shock Or Clutches Slipping In Change From "D3" TO "D4" 36-230
Clutches Or Brakes Slip In Starting 36-229
Engine Brake Does Not Operate In "D1" Range 36-231
Engine Does Not Start In "N" & "P" Ranges 36-229
Engine Stalls In "R" And "D" Ranges 36-231
Engine Starts In Range Other Than "N" & "P" 36-229
Engine Stops When Shifting Lever Into "R," "D," "2," & "1" 36-229
Excessive Creep 36-229
Failure To Change From "D3" To "D2" When Changing Lever Into "2" Range 36-231
Failure To Change Gear From "D1" To "D2" 36-229
Failure To Change Gear From "D2" To "D1" Or From "D3" To "D1" 36-230
Failure To Change Gear From "D2" To "D3" 36-229
Failure To Change Gear From "D3" To "D2" Or From "D4" To "D2" 36-230
Failure To Change Gear From "D3" To "D4" 36-229
Failure To Change Gear From "D4" To "D3" 36-230
Fluid Shoots Out During Operation, White Smoke Emitted From Exhaust Pipe During Operation 36-231
Foul Smell At Fluid Fill Pipe 36-231
Gear Change Directly From "D1" To "D3" 36-229
Gear Change Shock Felt During Deceleration By Releasing Accelerator Pedal 36-230
Kickdown Does Not Operate When Depressing Pedal In "D4" Within Kickdown Vehicle Speed 36-230
Kickdown Operates Or Engine Overruns When Depressing Pedal In "D4" Beyond Kickdown Vehicle Speed Limit 36-230
Lock-Up Piston Slip 36-231
Lock-Up Point Is Extremely High Or Low 36-231
Maximum Speed Not Attained, Acceleration Poor 36-230
No Creep At All 36-229
Races Extremely Fast Or Slips In Changing From "D3" To "D2" When Depressing Pedal 36-230
Races Extremely Fast Or Slips In Changing From "D4" Or "D3" To "D1" When Depressing Pedal 36-231
Races Extremely Fast Or Slips In Changing From "D4" To "D2" When Depressing Pedal 36-230
Races Extremely Fast Or Slips In Changing From "D4" To "D3" When Depressing Pedal 36-230
Sharp Shock In Shifting From "N" To "D" Range 36-229
Too High A Change Point From "D4" To "D3," From "D3" To "D2," From "D2" To "D1" 36-230
Too High A Gear Change Point From "D1" To "D2," "D2" To "D3" & "D3" To "D4" 36-229
Too Sharp A Shock In Change From "D1" To "D2" 36-229
Too Sharp A Shock In Change From "D2" To "D3" 36-229
Too Sharp A Shock In Change From "D3" To "D4" 36-230
Torque Converter Does Not Lock Up 36-231
Transaxle Does Not Shift To "D4" When Driving With Overdrive Switch On 36-231
Transaxle Noise In "D," "2," "1" & "R" Ranges 36-231
Transaxle Noise In "P" & "N" Ranges 36-229
Transaxle Overheats 36-231
Vehicle Braked By Gear Change From "D1" To "D2" 36-230
Vehicle Braked By Gear Change From "D2" To "D3" 36-230
Vehicle Braked By Gear Change From "D3" To "D4" 36-230
Vehicle Brakes When Shifting Into "R" Range 36-229
Vehicle Moves In "N" Range 36-229
Vehicle Moves When Changing Into "P" Range Or Parking Gear Does Not Disengage When Shifted Out Of "P" Range 36-229
Vehicle Will Not Move In Any Range 36-231
Vehicle Will Not Move In "D," "1" & "2" Ranges, Clutch Slips & Very Poor Acceleration 36-229
Vehicle Will Not Move In "D" & "2" Ranges 36-229
Vehicle Will Not Move In "R" Range, Clutch Slips & Very Poor Acceleration 36-229

IDENTIFICATION

The transaxle identification serial number is attached on the upper face of the transmission case.

TROUBLESHOOTING

ENGINE DOES NOT START IN "N" & "P" RANGES

1. Faulty ignition switch or starter.
2. Improperly adjusted control linkage.
3. Faulty or incorrectly adjusted inhibitor switch.

ENGINE STARTS IN RANGE OTHER THAN "N" & "P"

1. Improperly adjusted control linkage.
2. Faulty or incorrectly adjusted inhibitor switch.

TRANSAXLE NOISE IN "P" & "N" RANGES

1. Incorrect fluid level.
2. Incorrect line pressure.
3. Incorrect throttle sensor adjustment.
4. Faulty revolution sensor.
5. Faulty speed sensor.
6. Incorrect engine revolution signal.
7. Faulty torque converter.
8. Faulty oil pump.

VEHICLE MOVES WHEN CHANGING INTO "P" RANGE OR PARKING GEAR DOES NOT DISENGAGE WHEN SHIFTED OUT OF "P" RANGE

1. Improperly adjusted control linkage.
2. Faulty parking components.

VEHICLE MOVES IN "N" RANGE

1. Improperly adjusted control linkage.
2. Faulty forward clutch.
3. Faulty reverse clutch.
4. Faulty overrun clutch.

VEHICLE WILL NOT MOVE IN "R" RANGE, CLUTCH SLIPS & VERY POOR ACCELERATION

1. Improperly adjusted control linkage.
2. Incorrect line pressure.
3. Faulty line pressure solenoid.
4. Faulty control valve assembly.
5. Faulty reverse clutch.
6. Faulty high clutch.
7. Faulty forward clutch.
8. Faulty overrun clutch.
9. Faulty low and reverse brake.

VEHICLE BRAKES WHEN SHIFTING INTO "R" RANGE

1. Incorrect fluid level.
2. Improperly adjusted control linkage.
3. Incorrect line pressure.
4. Faulty line pressure solenoid.
5. Faulty control valve assembly.
6. Faulty high clutch.
7. Faulty brake band.
8. Faulty forward clutch.
9. Faulty overrun clutch.

SHARP SHOCK IN SHIFTING FROM "N" TO "D" RANGE

1. Incorrect engine idle RPM.
2. Faulty or incorrectly adjusted throttle sensor.
3. Incorrect line pressure.
4. Faulty fluid temperature sensor.
5. Incorrect engine revolution signal.
6. Faulty line pressure solenoid.
7. Faulty control valve assembly.
8. Faulty N-D accumulator.
9. Faulty forward clutch.

VEHICLE WILL NOT MOVE IN "D" & "2" RANGES

1. Improperly adjusted control linkage.
2. Faulty low one-way clutch.

VEHICLE WILL NOT MOVE IN "D," "1" & "2" RANGES, CLUTCH SLIPS & VERY POOR ACCELERATION

1. Incorrect fluid level.
2. Incorrect line pressure.
3. Faulty line pressure solenoid.
4. Faulty control valve assembly.
5. Faulty N-D accumulator.
6. Faulty reverse clutch.
7. Faulty high clutch.
8. Faulty forward clutch.
9. Faulty forward one-way clutch.
10. Faulty low one-way clutch.

CLUTCHES OR BRAKES SLIP IN STARTING

1. Incorrect fluid level.
2. Improperly adjusted control linkage.
3. Faulty or incorrectly adjusted throttle sensor.
4. Incorrect line pressure.
5. Faulty line pressure solenoid.
6. Faulty control valve assembly.
7. Faulty N-D accumulator.
8. Faulty forward clutch.
9. Faulty reverse clutch.
10. Faulty low and reverse brake.
11. Faulty oil pump.
12. Faulty torque converter.

EXCESSIVE CREEP

Incorrect engine idle RPM.

NO CREEP AT ALL

1. Incorrect fluid level.
2. Incorrect line pressure.
3. Faulty control valve assembly.
4. Faulty forward clutch.
5. Faulty oil pump.
6. Faulty torque converter.

FAILURE TO CHANGE GEAR FROM "D1" TO "D2"

1. Faulty or incorrectly adjusted inhibitor switch.
2. Improperly adjusted control linkage.
3. Faulty shift solenoid "A."
4. Faulty control valve assembly.
5. Faulty revolution sensor.
6. Faulty speed sensor.
7. Faulty brake band.

FAILURE TO CHANGE GEAR FROM "D2" TO "D3"

1. Faulty or incorrectly adjusted inhibitor switch.
2. Improperly adjusted control linkage.
3. Faulty shift solenoid "B."
4. Faulty control valve assembly.
5. Faulty revolution sensor.
6. Faulty speed sensor.
7. Faulty high clutch.
8. Faulty brake band.

FAILURE TO CHANGE GEAR FROM "D3" TO "D4"

1. Faulty or incorrectly adjusted inhibitor switch.
2. Improperly adjusted control linkage.
3. Faulty shift solenoid "A."
4. Faulty revolution sensor.
5. Faulty speed sensor.
6. Faulty fluid temperature sensor.
7. Faulty brake band.

TOO HIGH A GEAR CHANGE POINT FROM "D1" TO "D2," "D2" TO "D3" & "D3" TO "D4"

1. Faulty or incorrectly adjusted throttle sensor.
2. Faulty revolution sensor.
3. Faulty speed sensor.
4. Faulty shift solenoid "A."

GEAR CHANGE DIRECTLY FROM "D1" TO "D3"

1. Incorrect fluid level.
2. Faulty 3-R accumulator.
3. Faulty brake band.

ENGINE STOPS WHEN SHIFTING LEVER INTO "R," "D," "2," & "1"

1. Incorrect engine idle RPM.
2. Faulty lock-up solenoid.
3. Faulty shift solenoid "B."
4. Faulty torque converter.

TOO SHARP A SHOCK IN CHANGE FROM "D1" TO "D2"

1. Faulty or incorrectly adjusted throttle sensor.
2. Incorrect line pressure.
3. Faulty 3-R accumulator.
4. Faulty N-D accumulator.
5. Faulty control valve assembly.
6. Faulty fluid level temperature sensor.
7. Faulty brake band.

TOO SHARP A SHOCK IN CHANGE FROM "D2" TO "D3"

1. Faulty or incorrectly adjusted throttle sensor.

2. Incorrect line pressure.
3. Faulty control valve assembly.
4. Faulty high clutch.
5. Faulty brake band.

TOO SHARP A SHOCK IN CHANGE FROM "D3" TO "D4"

1. Faulty or incorrectly adjusted throttle sensor.
2. Incorrect line pressure.
3. Faulty control valve assembly.
4. Faulty brake band.
5. Faulty overrun clutch.

ALMOST NO SHOCK OR CLUTCHES SLIPPING IN CHANGE FROM "D1" TO "D2"

1. Incorrect fluid level.
2. Faulty or incorrectly adjusted throttle sensor.
3. Incorrect line pressure.
4. Faulty 3-R accumulator.
5. Faulty control valve assembly.
6. Faulty brake band.

ALMOST NO SHOCK OR CLUTCHES SLIPPING IN CHANGE FROM "D2" TO "D3"

1. Incorrect fluid level.
2. Faulty or incorrectly adjusted throttle sensor.
3. Incorrect line pressure.
4. Faulty control valve assembly.
5. Faulty high clutch.
6. Faulty brake band.

ALMOST NO SHOCK OR CLUTCHES SLIPPING IN CHANGE FROM "D3" TO "D4"

1. Incorrect fluid level.
2. Faulty or incorrectly adjusted throttle sensor.
3. Incorrect line pressure.
4. Faulty control valve assembly.
5. Faulty high clutch.
6. Faulty brake band.

VEHICLE BRAKED BY GEAR CHANGE FROM "D1" TO "D2"

1. Incorrect fluid level.
2. Faulty reverse clutch.
3. Faulty low and reverse brake band.
4. Faulty high clutch.
5. Faulty low one-way clutch.

VEHICLE BRAKED BY GEAR CHANGE FROM "D2" TO "D3"

1. Incorrect fluid level.
2. Faulty brake band.

VEHICLE BRAKED BY GEAR CHANGE FROM "D3" TO "D4"

1. Incorrect fluid level.
2. Faulty overrun clutch.
3. Faulty forward one-way clutch.
4. Faulty reverse clutch.

MAXIMUM SPEED NOT ATTAINED, ACCELERATION POOR

1. Incorrect fluid level.
2. Faulty or incorrectly adjusted inhibitor switch.
3. Faulty shift solenoid "A."
4. Faulty shift solenoid "B."
5. Faulty control valve assembly.
6. Faulty reverse clutch.
7. Faulty high clutch.
8. Faulty brake band.
9. Faulty low and reverse brake.
10. Faulty oil pump.
11. Faulty torque converter.

FAILURE TO CHANGE GEAR FROM "D4" TO "D3"

1. Incorrect fluid level.
2. Faulty or incorrectly adjusted throttle sensor.
3. Faulty overrun clutch solenoid.
4. Faulty shift solenoid "A."
5. Faulty line pressure solenoid.
6. Faulty control valve assembly.
7. Faulty low and reverse brake.
8. Faulty overrun clutch.

FAILURE TO CHANGE GEAR FROM "D3" TO "D2" OR FROM "D4" TO "D2"

1. Incorrect fluid level.
2. Faulty or incorrectly adjusted throttle sensor.
3. Faulty shift solenoid "A."
4. Faulty shift solenoid "B."
5. Faulty control valve assembly.
6. Faulty high clutch.
7. Faulty brake band.

FAILURE TO CHANGE GEAR FROM "D2" TO "D1" OR FROM "D3" TO "D1"

1. Incorrect fluid level.
2. Faulty or incorrectly adjusted throttle sensor.
3. Faulty shift solenoid "A."
4. Faulty shift solenoid "B."
5. Faulty control valve assembly.
6. Faulty low one-way clutch.
7. Faulty high clutch.
8. Faulty brake band.

GEAR CHANGE SHOCK FELT DURING DECELERATION BY RELEASING ACCELERATOR PEDAL

1. Faulty engine revolution signal.
2. Incorrect line pressure.
3. Faulty overrun clutch solenoid.
4. Faulty control valve assembly.

TOO HIGH A CHANGE POINT FROM "D4" TO "D3," FROM "D3" TO "D2," FROM "D2" TO "D1"

1. Faulty or incorrectly adjusted throttle sensor.
2. Faulty revolution sensor.
3. Faulty speed sensor.

KICKDOWN DOES NOT OPERATE WHEN DEPRESSING PEDAL IN "D4" WITHIN KICKDOWN VEHICLE SPEED

1. Faulty or incorrectly adjusted throttle sensor.
2. Faulty revolution sensor.
3. Faulty speed sensor.
4. Faulty shift solenoid "A."
5. Faulty shift solenoid "B."

KICKDOWN OPERATES OR ENGINE OVERRUNS WHEN DEPRESSING PEDAL IN "D4" BEYOND KICKDOWN VEHICLE SPEED LIMIT

1. Faulty or incorrectly adjusted throttle sensor.
2. Faulty revolution sensor.
3. Faulty speed sensor.
4. Faulty shift solenoid "A."
5. Faulty shift solenoid "B."

RACES EXTREMELY FAST OR SLIPS IN CHANGING FROM "D4" TO "D3" WHEN DEPRESSING PEDAL

1. Incorrect fluid level.
2. Faulty or incorrectly adjusted throttle sensor.
3. Incorrect line pressure.
4. Faulty line pressure solenoid.
5. Faulty control valve assembly.
6. Faulty high clutch.
7. Faulty forward clutch.

RACES EXTREMELY FAST OR SLIPS IN CHANGING FROM "D4" TO "D2" WHEN DEPRESSING PEDAL

1. Incorrect fluid level.
2. Faulty or incorrectly adjusted throttle sensor.
3. Incorrect line pressure.
4. Faulty line pressure solenoid.
5. Faulty shift solenoid "A."
6. Faulty brake band.
7. Faulty forward clutch.
8. Faulty high clutch.

RACES EXTREMELY FAST OR SLIPS IN CHANGING FROM "D3" TO "D2" WHEN DEPRESSING PEDAL

1. Incorrect fluid level.

2. Faulty or incorrectly adjusted throttle sensor.
3. Incorrect line pressure.
4. Faulty line pressure solenoid.
5. Faulty control valve assembly.
6. Faulty brake band.
7. Faulty forward clutch.
8. Faulty fluid temperature sensor.
9. Faulty high clutch.

RACES EXTREMELY FAST OR SLIPS IN CHANGING FROM "D4" OR "D3" TO "D1" WHEN DEPRESSING PEDAL

1. Incorrect fluid level.
2. Faulty or incorrectly adjusted throttle sensor.
3. Incorrect line pressure.
4. Faulty line pressure solenoid.
5. Faulty control valve assembly.
6. Faulty forward clutch.
7. Faulty forward one-way clutch.
8. Faulty low one-way clutch.

VEHICLE WILL NOT MOVE IN ANY RANGE

1. Incorrect fluid level.
2. Improperly adjusted control linkage.
3. Incorrect line pressure.
4. Faulty line pressure solenoid.
5. Faulty oil pump.
6. Faulty high clutch.
7. Faulty brake band.
8. Faulty low and reverse brake.
9. Faulty torque converter.
10. Faulty parking components.

TRANSAXLE NOISE IN "D," "2," "1" & "R" RANGES

1. Incorrect fluid level.
2. Faulty torque converter.

FAILURE TO CHANGE FROM "D3" TO "D2" WHEN CHANGING LEVER INTO "2" RANGE

1. Faulty or incorrectly adjusted inhibitor switch.
2. Faulty or incorrectly adjusted throttle sensor.
3. Faulty overrun clutch solenoid.
4. Faulty shift solenoid "B."
5. Faulty shift solenoid "A."
6. Faulty control valve assembly.
7. Improperly adjusted control linkage.
8. Faulty brake band.
9. Faulty overrun clutch.

ENGINE BRAKE DOES NOT OPERATE IN "D1" RANGE

1. Faulty or incorrectly adjusted inhibitor switch.
2. Improperly adjusted control linkage.
3. Faulty or incorrectly adjusted throttle sensor.
4. Faulty revolution sensor.
5. Faulty speed sensor.
6. Faulty shift solenoid "A."
7. Faulty control valve assembly.
8. Faulty overrun clutch.
9. Faulty low and reverse brake band.

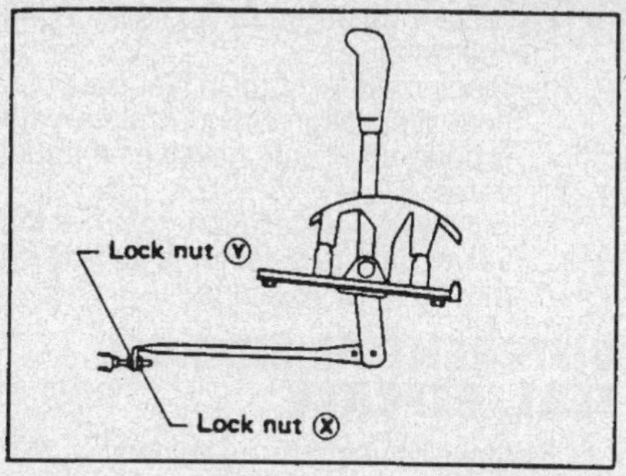
Lock nut (Y)
Lock nut (X)
NS5028900469000X

Fig. 1 Control cable adjustment

TRANSAXLE OVERHEATS

1. Incorrect fluid level.
2. Incorrect engine idle RPM.
3. Faulty or incorrectly adjusted throttle sensor.
4. Incorrect line pressure.
5. Faulty line pressure solenoid.
6. Faulty control valve assembly.
7. Faulty oil pump.
8. Faulty reverse clutch.
9. Faulty high clutch.
10. Faulty brake band.
11. Faulty forward clutch.
12. Faulty overrun clutch.
13. Faulty low and reverse brake.
14. Faulty torque converter.

FLUID SHOOTS OUT DURING OPERATION, WHITE SMOKE EMITTED FROM EXHAUST PIPE DURING OPERATION

1. Incorrect fluid level.
2. Faulty reverse clutch.
3. Faulty high clutch.
4. Faulty brake band.
5. Faulty forward clutch.
6. Faulty overrun clutch.
7. Faulty low and reverse brake.

FOUL SMELL AT FLUID FILL PIPE

1. Incorrect fluid level.
2. Faulty torque converter.
3. Faulty oil pump.
4. Faulty reverse clutch.
5. Faulty high clutch.
6. Faulty brake band.
7. Faulty forward clutch.
8. Faulty overrun clutch.
9. Faulty low and reverse brake.

TORQUE CONVERTER DOES NOT LOCK UP

1. Faulty or incorrectly adjusted throttle sensor.
2. Faulty revolution sensor.
3. Faulty speed sensor.
4. Faulty or incorrectly adjusted inhibitor switch.
5. Faulty fluid temperature sensor.
6. Incorrect line pressure.
7. Faulty lock-up solenoid.
8. Faulty control valve assembly.
9. Faulty torque converter.

LOCK-UP PISTON SLIP

1. Incorrect fluid level.
2. Faulty or incorrectly adjusted throttle sensor.
3. Incorrect line pressure.
4. Faulty lock-up solenoid.
5. Faulty line pressure solenoid.
6. Faulty control valve assembly.
7. Faulty torque converter.

LOCK-UP POINT IS EXTREMELY HIGH OR LOW

1. Faulty or incorrectly adjusted throttle sensor.
2. Faulty revolution sensor.
3. Faulty speed sensor.
4. Faulty lock-up solenoid.
5. Faulty control valve assembly.

TRANSAXLE DOES NOT SHIFT TO "D4" WHEN DRIVING WITH OVERDRIVE SWITCH ON

1. Faulty or incorrectly adjusted throttle sensor.
2. Faulty or incorrectly adjusted inhibitor switch.
3. Faulty revolution sensor.
4. Faulty speed sensor.
5. Faulty shift solenoid "A."
6. Faulty overrun clutch solenoid.
7. Faulty fluid temperature sensor.
8. Faulty control valve assembly.
9. Incorrect line pressure.
10. Faulty brake band.
11. Faulty overrun clutch.

ENGINE STALLS IN "R" AND "D" RANGES

1. Incorrect fluid level.
2. Faulty lock-up solenoid.
3. Faulty shift solenoid "B."
4. Faulty shift solenoid "A."
5. Faulty control valve assembly.

MAINTENANCE

FLUID CHECK

To check fluid, drive vehicle for at least 5 minutes to bring fluid to operating temperature (122–176°F). With vehicle on a level surface and engine idling in Park and parking brake applied, move gear selector through all gear positions and return to P position. Dipsticks may be marked with Hot and Cold ranges. Use cold range if fluid is between (86–120°F).

ADJUSTMENTS

CONTROL CABLE

1. Move selector lever to 1 position. Ensure lever moves smoothly and quietly.
2. Move selector lever back to P position and ensure lever locks properly.
3. Loosen both locknuts, **Fig. 1.** Turn locknut (x) until it touches select rod end while holding rod horizontal, then tighten locknut (y).
4. Ensure proper operation of transaxle selector lever.

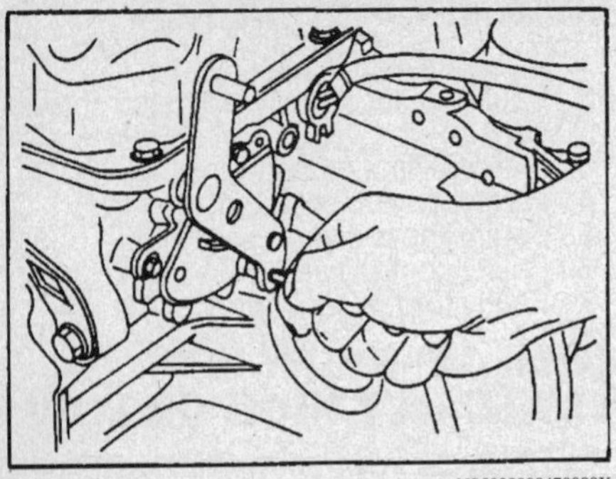

NS5028900470000X

Fig. 2 Inhibitor switch adjustment

INHIBITOR SWITCH

1. Disconnect control cable from manual shaft, then set manual shaft in N position.
2. Loosen inhibitor switch attaching screws.
3. Insert a 0.16 inch diameter pin into adjustment holes in both inhibitor switch and switch lever as near vertical as possible, **Fig. 2,** then tighten switch attaching screws.

IN-VEHICLE REPAIRS

CONTROL VALVE, REPLACE

1. Remove air cleaner, battery and battery bracket.
2. Remove control valve cover.
3. Disconnect control valve electrical connector and remove control valve assembly. **Use care to avoid dropping manual valve from valve body.**
4. Reverse procedure to install, noting the following:
   a. Place manual shaft in Neutral position, then align manual plate with groove in control valve manual valve.
   b. Following installation of control valve, ensure selector lever can be moved to all positions.

DIFFERENTIAL SIDE OIL SEAL, REPLACE

1. Remove driveshafts as follows:
   a. Raise and support vehicle, then disconnect battery ground cable.
   b. Remove wheel and tire assembly, then the wheel bearing locknut while depressing brake pedal.
   c. Remove brake caliper assembly and the tie rod ball joint nut, then separate joint from knuckle.
2. Remove both drive axles using a suitable screwdriver.
3. Remove oil seal.
4. Reverse procedure to install. Lubricate new seal with transaxle fluid before installing.

TRANSAXLE

REPLACE

1. Remove air cleaner assembly and air flow meter, if necessary.
2. Raise and support vehicle.
3. Remove both driveshafts from transaxle.
4. Remove front exhaust pipe attaching bolts, if necessary.
5. Disconnect all cables and electrical connectors from transaxle.

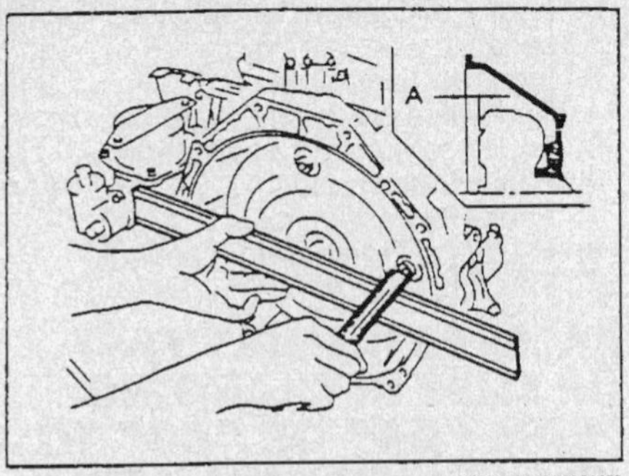
A

NS5029100539000X

Fig. 3 Torque convertor clearance inspection

6. Support engine and transaxle with a suitable jack.
7. Remove starter motor, if necessary.
8. Remove engine mount attaching bolts.
9. Remove engine-to-transaxle attaching bolts, then separate engine from transaxle and lower transaxle assembly from vehicle.
10. Reverse procedure to install, noting the following:
    a. Check driveplate runout by turning crankshaft one full turn with dial indicator probe resting against plate. runout should not exceed .020 inch.
    b. When connecting torque converter to transaxle, measure distance "A," **Fig. 3,** to ensure correct assembly.
    c. After installing converter, rotate crankshaft several times and ensure transaxle rotates freely without binding.

TIGHTENING SPECIFICATIONS

Year	Component	Torque/Ft. Lbs.
1993–94	Bearing Support Retainer	9–14
	Control Cylinder Retaining Bolt	5–6
	Control Valve Body To Transmission Case	5–6
	Control Valve Cover To Valve Body	4–5
	Governor Cap Retaining Bolt	4–5
	Governor Valve Body To Governor Shaft	14–20
	Inhibitor Switch Nut	23–31
	Overdrive Unit Solenoid Assembly	5–7
	Side Bearing Bracket	22–30
	Speedometer Case To Converter Housing	5–6
	Torque Converter To Driveplate	33–43
	Wheel Bearing Locknut	174–231

Jatco RE4F04A & RE4F04V Automatic Transaxles

NOTE: On Air Bag Equipped Models, Refer To "Air Bag System Precautions" Located In The Front Of This Manual For System Disarming & Arming Procedures.

NOTE: Prior To Performing Any Service Operations Listed In This Section, Consult The "Technical Service Bulletins " Section For Related Information.

INDEX

	Page No.
Adjustments	36-233
Control Cable	36-233
Inhibitor Switch	36-233
Identification	36-233
In-Vehicle Repairs	36-233
Control Valve Assembly & Accumulator, Replace	36-233
Key Interlock Cable, Replace	36-234
Maintenance	36-233
Fluid Check	36-233
Precautions	36-233
Air Bag Systems	36-233
Technical Service Bulletins	36-235
1–2 Shift Shudder	36-236
Hard Upshift In All Gears	36-235
Transaxle Overdrive Gear Whine	36-235
Tightening Specifications	36-236
Transaxle, Replace	36-235
Troubleshooting	36-233
Brake Transmission Shift Interlock	36-233
Transaxle	36-233

PRECAUTIONS

AIR BAG SYSTEMS

Refer to "Air Bag System Precautions" in the front of this manual for system disarming and arming procedures.

IDENTIFICATION

The transaxle is identified by a tag stamped into the transaxle case. Refer to **Fig. 1** for transaxle identification tag location.

TROUBLESHOOTING

TRANSAXLE

Refer to **Fig. 2** for transaxle troubleshooting.

BRAKE TRANSMISSION SHIFT INTERLOCK

Refer to **Fig. 3** when troubleshooting the brake transmission shift interlock.

MAINTENANCE

FLUID CHECK

Fluid level should be checked using "HOT" range on dipstick at fluid temperature of 151–171°F after vehicle has been driven approximately 15 minutes under normal driving conditions.

1. Check for fluid leakage.
2. Park vehicle on level surface and set parking brake.

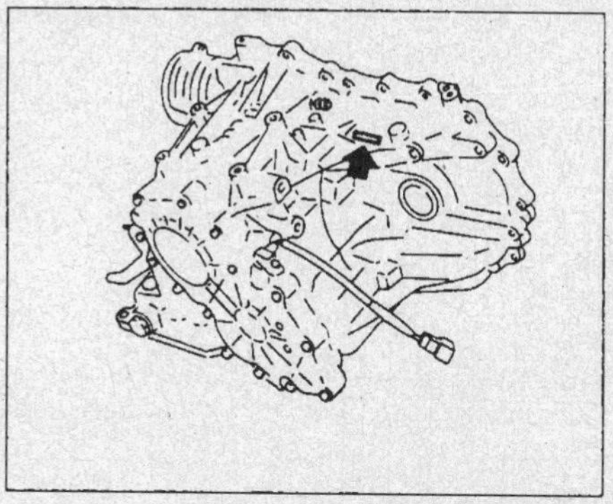

NS5028900518000X

Fig. 1 Transaxle identification

3. Start engine, then move gear selector lever through all gear ranges, ending in Park.
4. Check fluid level with engine idling.
5. If fluid level is low, add Dexron II fluid to charging pipe. **Do not overfill transaxle fluid.**

ADJUSTMENTS

CONTROL CABLE

1. Place selector lever in Park.
2. Loosen locknuts.
3. Tighten locknut, **Fig. 4,** pulling selector lever toward Reverse side.
4. Move selector lever from Park to 1 range. Ensure selector lever moves smoothly.

INHIBITOR SWITCH

1. Remove control cable from manual shaft.
2. Set manual shaft in "N" position.
3. Loosen inhibitor switch fixing bolts.
4. Insert pin into adjustment holes in both inhibitor switch and manual shaft, as near vertical as possible, **Fig. 5.**

IN-VEHICLE REPAIRS

CONTROL VALVE ASSEMBLY & ACCUMULATOR, REPLACE

1. Drain fluid from transaxle, then remove oil and pan.
2. Disconnect transaxle solenoid harness electrical connector.
3. Remove stopper ring from transaxle solenoid harness terminal body.
4. Remove transaxle solenoid harness from transaxle case by pushing on terminal body.
5. Remove control valve assembly by removing fixed bolts, **Fig. 6. Do not drop manual valve, tube connector, tubes or 3-R accumulator return spring.**
6. Remove 3-R and N-D return springs by applying compressed air and holding each piston with a rag, if necessary.
7. Reverse procedure to install, noting the following:
   a. Set manual shaft in Neutral, then align manual plate with groove in manual valve.
   b. Following control valve installation,

	ON vehicle																		OFF vehicle										
Numbers are arranged in order of probability. Perform inspections starting with number one and working up. Circled numbers indicate that the transaxle must be removed from the vehicle.	Fluid level	Control linkage	Inhibitor switch	Throttle position sensor (Adjustment)	Revolution sensor and vehicle speed sensor	Engine speed signal	Engine idling rpm	Line pressure	Control valve assembly	Shift solenoid valve A	Shift solenoid valve B	Line pressure solenoid valve	Torque converter clutch solenoid valve	Overrun clutch solenoid valve	Fluid temperature sensor	Accumulator N-D	Accumulator 3-R	Ignition switch and starter	Torque converter	Oil pump	Reverse clutch	High clutch	Forward clutch	Forward one-way clutch	Overrun clutch	Low one-way clutch	Low & reverse brake	Brake band	Parking components
Engine does not start in "N", "P" positions.		2	3															1											
Engine starts in range other than "N" and "P".		1	2																										
Transaxle noise in "P" and "N" positions.	1			3	4	5		2											⑦	⑧									
Vehicle moves when changing into "P" position or parking gear does not disengage when shifted out of "P" position.		1																											②
Vehicle runs in "N" position.		1																			③		②		④				
Vehicle will not run in "R" position (but runs in "D", "2" and "1" positions). Clutch slips. Very poor acceleration.		1						2	4			3									⑤	⑥	⑦		⑧		⑨		
Vehicle braked when shifting into "R" position.	1	2						3	5			4										⑥	⑧		⑨			⑦	
Sharp shock in shifting from "N" to "D" position.				2		5	1	3	7			6			4	8							⑨						
Vehicle will not run in "D" and "2" positions (but runs in "1" and "R" positions).		1																								②			
Vehicle will not run in "D", "1", "2" positions (but runs in "R" position). Clutch slips. Very poor acceleration.	1							2	4			3				5					⑥	⑦	⑧	⑨		⑩			
Clutches or brakes slip somewhat in starting.	1	2		3				4	6			5				7			⑫	⑪	⑨		⑧				⑩		
Excessive creep.							1																						
No creep at all.	1							2	3										⑥	⑤			④						
Failure to change gear from "D_1" to "D_2".		2	1		5				4	3																		⑥	
Failure to change gear from "D_2" to "D_3".		2	1		5				4		3											⑧						⑦	
Failure to change gear from "D_3" to "D_4".		2	1		4					3					5													⑥	
Too high gear change point from "D_1" to "D_2", from "D_2" to "D_3", from "D_3" to "D_4".				1	2					3	4																		
Gear change directly from "D_1" to "D_3" occurs.	1																2											③	
Engine stops when shifting lever into "R", "D", "2" and "1".							1		3				2						④										
Too sharp a shock in change from "D_1" to "D_2".				1				2	4						5		3											⑥	
Too sharp a shock in change from "D_2" to "D_3".				1				2	3													④						⑤	

NS5029100540010X

Fig. 2 Transaxle troubleshooting chart (Part 1 of 3)

	ON vehicle																		OFF vehicle										
Numbers are arranged in order of probability. Perform inspections starting with number one and working up. Circled numbers indicate that the transaxle must be removed from the vehicle.	Fluid level	Control linkage	Inhibitor switch	Throttle position sensor (Adjustment)	Revolution sensor and vehicle speed sensor	Engine speed signal	Engine idling rpm	Line pressure	Control valve assembly	Shift solenoid valve A	Shift solenoid valve B	Line pressure solenoid valve	Torque converter clutch solenoid valve	Overrun clutch solenoid valve	Fluid temperature sensor	Accumulator N-D	Accumulator 3-R	Ignition switch and starter	Torque converter	Oil pump	Reverse clutch	High clutch	Forward clutch	Forward one-way clutch	Overrun clutch	Low one-way clutch	Low & reverse brake	Brake band	Parking components
Too sharp a shock in change from "D_3" to "D_4".				1				2	3																⑤			④	
Almost no shock or clutches slipping in change from "D_1" to "D_2".	1			2				3	5								4											⑥	
Almost no shock or slipping in change from "D_2" to "D_3".	1			2				3	4													⑤						⑥	
Almost no shock or slipping in change from "D_3" to "D_4".	1			2				3	4													⑤						⑥	
Vehicle braked by gear change from "D_1" to "D_2".	1																				②	④				⑤	③		
Vehicle braked by gear change from "D_2" to "D_3".	1																											②	
Vehicle braked by gear change from "D_3" to "D_4".	1																				④			③	②				
Maximum speed not attained. Acceleration poor.	1		2						5	3	4								⑪	⑩	⑥	⑦					⑨	⑧	
Failure to change gear from "D_4" to "D_3".	1			2					6	4		5		3											⑧		⑦		
Failure to change gear from "D_3" to "D_2" or from "D_4" to "D_2".	1			2					5	3	4											⑥						⑦	
Failure to change gear from "D_2" to "D_1" or from "D_3" to "D_1".	1			2					5	3	4											⑦				⑥		⑥	
Gear change shock felt during deceleration by releasing accelerator pedal.				1				2	4					3															
Too high a change point from "D_4" to "D_3", from "D_3" to "D_2", from "D_2" to "D_1".				1	2																								
Kickdown does not operate when depressing pedal in "D_4" within kickdown vehicle speed.				1	2					3	4																		
Kickdown operates or engine overruns when depressing pedal in "D_4" beyond kickdown vehicle speed limit.				2	1					3	4																		
Races extremely fast or slips in changing from "D_4" to "D_3" when depressing pedal.	1			2				3	5			4										⑥	⑦						
Races extremely fast or slips in changing from "D_4" to "D_2" when depressing pedal.	1			2				3	6	5		4											⑧					⑦	
Races extremely fast or slips in changing from "D_3" to "D_2" when depressing pedal.	1			2				3	5			4			8							⑨	⑦					⑥	
Races extremely fast or slips in changing from "D_4" or "D_3" to "D_1" when depressing pedal.	1			2				3	5			4											⑥	⑦		⑧			
Vehicle will not run in any position.	1	2						3				4							⑨	⑤		⑥					⑧	⑦	⑩
Transaxle noise in "D", "2", "1" and "R" positions.	1																		②										

NS5029100540020X

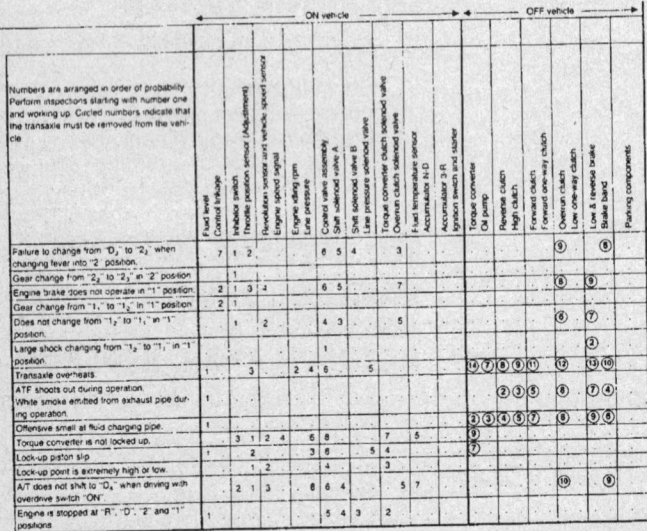

Fig. 2 Transaxle troubleshooting chart (Part 2 of 3)

	ON vehicle																		OFF vehicle										
Numbers are arranged in order of probability. Perform inspections starting with number one and working up. Circled numbers indicate that the transaxle must be removed from the vehicle.	Fluid level	Control linkage	Inhibitor switch	Throttle position sensor (Adjustment)	Revolution sensor and vehicle speed sensor	Engine speed signal	Engine idling rpm	Line pressure	Control valve assembly	Shift solenoid valve A	Shift solenoid valve B	Line pressure solenoid valve	Torque converter clutch solenoid valve	Overrun clutch solenoid valve	Fluid temperature sensor	Accumulator N-D	Accumulator 3-R	Ignition switch and starter	Torque converter	Oil pump	Reverse clutch	High clutch	Forward clutch	Forward one-way clutch	Overrun clutch	Low one-way clutch	Low & reverse brake	Brake band	Parking components
Failure to change from "D_3" to "2_2" when changing lever into "2" position.		7	1	2					6	5	4			3											⑨			⑧	
Gear change from "2_2" to "2_3" in "2" position.			1																										
Engine brake does not operate in "1" position.		2	1	3	4				6	5				7											⑧		⑨		
Gear change from "1_1" to "1_2" in "1" position.		2	1																										
Does not change from "1_2" to "1_1" in "1" position.			1		2				4	3				5											⑥		⑦		
Large shock changing from "1_2" to "1_1" in "1" position.									1																		②		
Transaxle overheats.	1			3			2	4	6			5							⑭	⑦	⑧	⑨	⑪		⑫		⑬	⑩	
ATF shoots out during operation. White smoke emitted from exhaust pipe during operation.	1																				②	③	⑤		⑧		⑦	④	
Offensive smell at fluid charging pipe.	1																		②	③	④	⑤	⑦		⑧		⑨	⑥	
Torque converter is not locked up.			3	1	2	4		6	8				7		5				⑨										
Lock-up piston slip.	1			2				3	6			5	4						⑦										
Lock-up point is extremely high or low.				1	2				4				3																
A/T does not shift to "D_4" when driving with overdrive switch "ON".			2	1	3			8	6	4				5	7										⑩			⑨	
Engine is stopped at "R", "D", "2" and "1" positions.	1								5	4	3		2																

NS5029100540030X

Fig. 2 Transaxle troubleshooting chart (Part 3 of 3)

ensure selector lever can be moved to all positions.

KEY INTERLOCK CABLE, REPLACE

Removal

1. Unlock slider from adjuster holder and remove rod from cable at shift selector.
2. Remove lock plate and cable from steering lock.

Installation

1. Set key interlock cable to steering lock assembly and install lock plate.

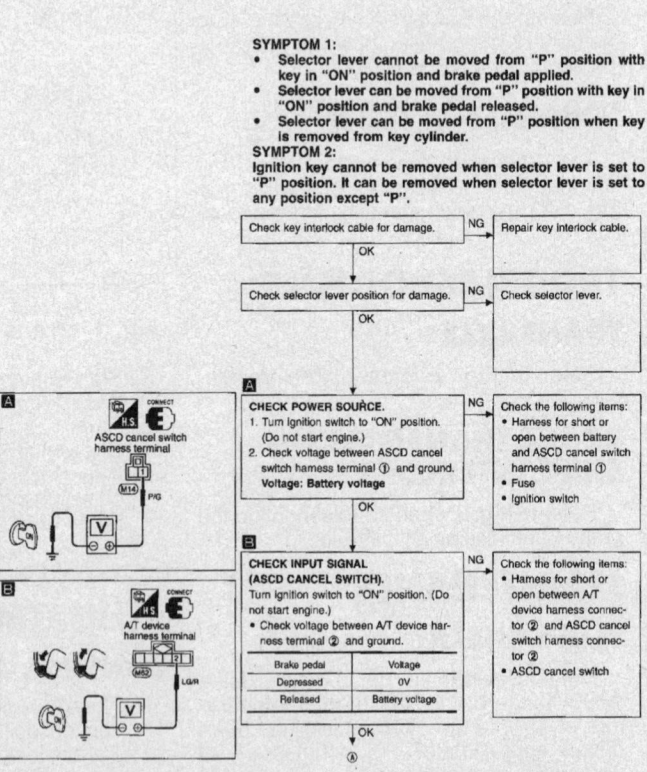

SYMPTOM 1:

- **Selector lever cannot be moved from "P" position with key in "ON" position and brake pedal applied.**
- **Selector lever can be moved from "P" position with key in "ON" position and brake pedal released.**
- **Selector lever can be moved from "P" position when key is removed from key cylinder.**

SYMPTOM 2:

Ignition key cannot be removed when selector lever is set to "P" position. It can be removed when selector lever is set to any position except "P".

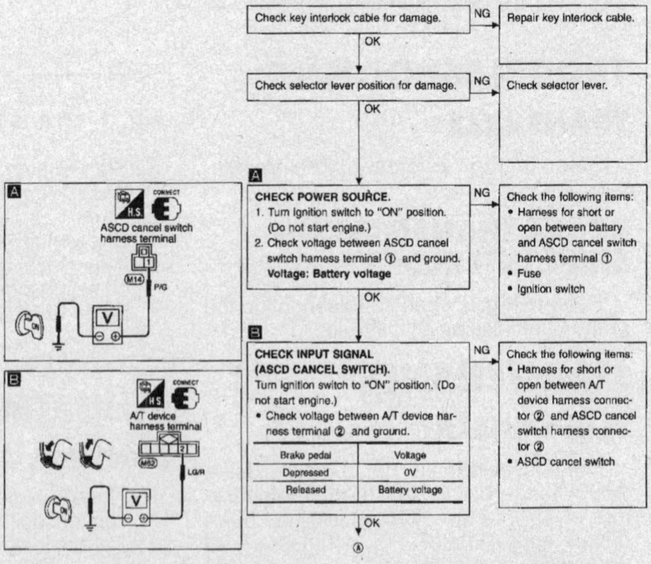
Check key interlock cable for damage.
NG
Repair key interlock cable.
OK
Check selector lever position for damage.
NG
Check selector lever.
OK
A
CHECK POWER SOURCE.
1. Turn ignition switch to "ON" position. (Do not start engine.)
2. Check voltage between ASCD cancel switch harness terminal ① and ground.
Voltage: Battery voltage
NG
Check the following items:
• Harness for short or open between battery and ASCD cancel switch harness terminal ①
• Fuse
• Ignition switch
OK
B
CHECK INPUT SIGNAL (ASCD CANCEL SWITCH).
Turn ignition switch to "ON" position. (Do not start engine.)
• Check voltage between A/T device harness terminal ② and ground.
Brake pedal | Voltage
Depressed | 0V
Released | Battery voltage
NG
Check the following items:
• Harness for short or open between A/T device harness connector ② and ASCD cancel switch harness connector ②
• ASCD cancel switch
OK
Ⓐ
A
CONNECT
H.S.
ASCD cancel switch harness terminal
M14
P/G
V
B
CONNECT
H.S.
A/T device harness terminal
M62
LG/R
V

NS5029600586010X

Fig. 3 BTSI diagnostic procedure (Part 1 of 2)

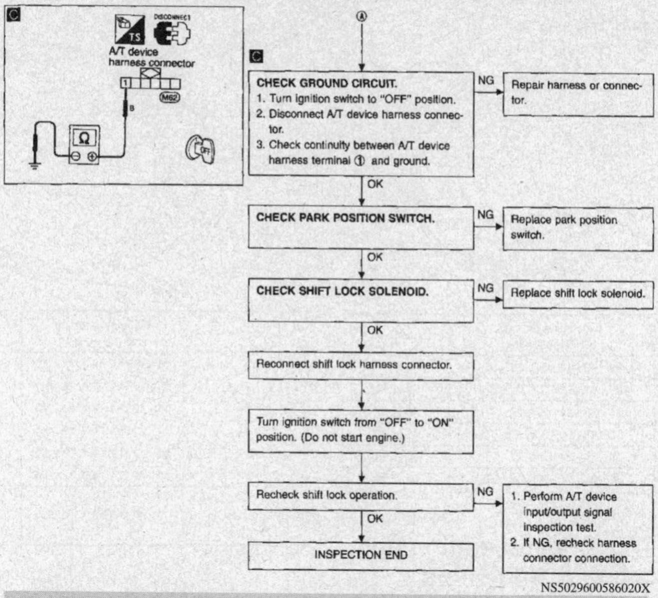
A/T device harness connector
CHECK GROUND CIRCUIT.
1. Turn ignition switch to "OFF" position.
2. Disconnect A/T device harness connector.
3. Check continuity between A/T device harness terminal ① and ground.
NG
Repair harness or connector.
OK
CHECK PARK POSITION SWITCH.
NG
Replace park position switch.
OK
CHECK SHIFT LOCK SOLENOID.
NG
Replace shift lock solenoid.
OK
Reconnect shift lock harness connector.
Turn ignition switch from "OFF" to "ON" position. (Do not start engine.)
Recheck shift lock operation.
NG
1. Perform A/T device input/output signal inspection test.
2. If NG, recheck harness connector connection.
OK
INSPECTION END

NS5029600586020X

Fig. 3 BTSI diagnostic procedure (Part 2 of 2)

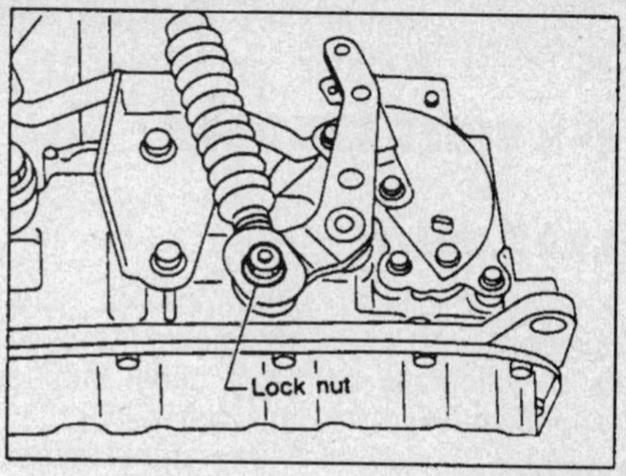
Lock nut

NS5028900522000X

Fig. 4 Control cable adjustment

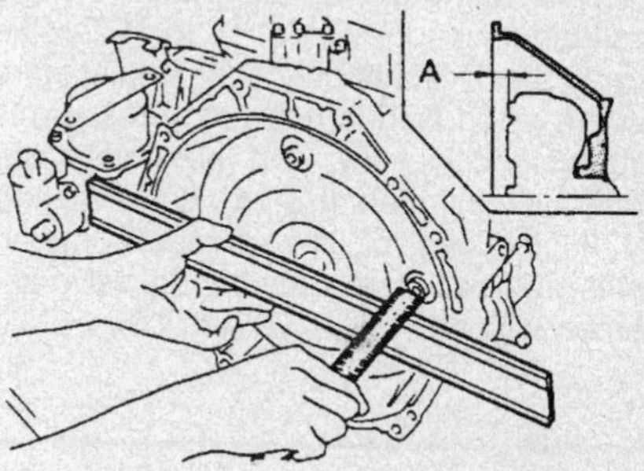
A

NS5029100544000X

Fig. 7 Torque converter clearance measurement

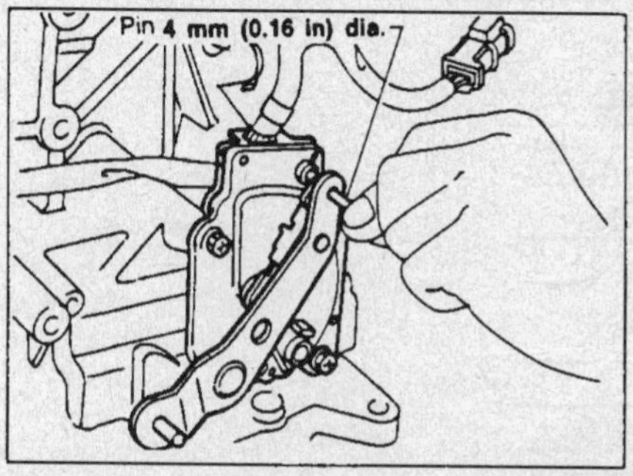
Pin 4 mm (0.16 in) dia.

NS5028900521000X

Fig. 5 Inhibitor switch adjustment

2. Clamp cable to steering column and fix to control cable with band.
3. Set selector lever to P position.
4. Insert interlock rod into adjuster holder.
5. Install casing cap to bracket.
6. Move slider in order to fix adjuster holder to interlock rod.

TRANSAXLE

REPLACE

1. Raise and support front of vehicle. Remove front wheels.
2. Remove wheel bearing locknut. **Do not allow brake hose to stretch or twist.**
3. Remove cotter pin and nut securing lower ball joint to knuckle.
4. Separate lower ball joint from knuckle.
5. Separate driveshaft from knuckle by tapping lightly (use a puller, if necessary). When removing driveshaft, cover boots to prevent damage.
6. Remove right driveshaft from transaxle.
7. Remove left driveshaft with a suitable puller tool. Use caution not to damage pinion mate shaft and side gear.
8. Remove bolts securing torque converter to driveplate by turning crankshaft.

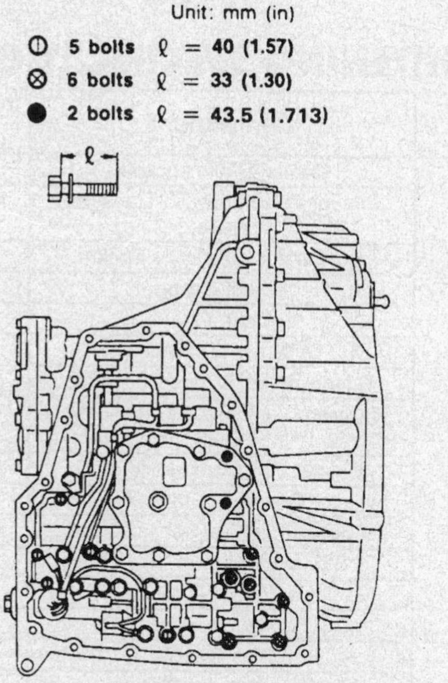
Unit: mm (in)
① 5 bolts ℓ = 40 (1.57)
⊗ 6 bolts ℓ = 33 (1.30)
● 2 bolts ℓ = 43.5 (1.713)
ℓ

NS5028900520000X

Fig. 6 Control valve assembly bolt identification

9. When transaxle is disconnected, scribe matching marks on torque converter and driveplate to ease installation.
10. Reverse procedure to install, noting the following:
    a. When connecting torque converter to transaxle, measure distance "A" shown in **Fig. 7.** Correct distance on Maxima with VE30DE engine is greater than .55 inch. Correct distance on Altima and Maxima with VG30E engine is greater than .75 inch.
    b. Tighten transaxle securing bolts as shown in **Figs. 8 and 9.**
    c. Ensure fluid level is correct. Cycle selector lever through all positions and ensure correct operation.

TECHNICAL SERVICE BULLETINS

TRANSAXLE OVERDRIVE GEAR WHINE

1993–94 Quest

If gear whine is heard between approximately 32–45 mph in overdrive under light throttle acceleration, proceed as follows:

1. Operate vehicle between 32 and 45 mph with overdrive engaged to verify condition. Ensure accelerator pedal is lightly depressed to avoid shifting out of overdrive.
2. If gear whine is heard, press O.D. switch to turn off overdrive.
3. If gear whine is significantly reduced by turning off overdrive, replace sun gear assembly.

HARD UPSHIFT IN ALL GEARS

1993 Quest XE & GXE

Quest minivans with transaxle serial numbers preceding 924X56258; refer to last 5 digits of automatic transaxle serial number (approximate vehicle build date 2/93).

Some Quest minivans may exhibit hard upshifts in all gears when accelerating. This may be due to foreign material entering the solenoid valve bodies during manufacturing. If the transaxle fluid is clean, replace the control valve assembly with part No. 31705-80X20.

1–2 SHIFT SHUDDER

1993 Quest

Quest minivans with transaxle serial numbers up to 4Y59142; refer to last 5 digits of automatic transaxle serial number (approximate vehicle build date 2/93).

Some Quest minivans manufactured prior to the above date may experience a vibration or shudder occurring during the 1–2 shift. Symptoms of this incident include a shudder or vibration at ½ to ⅞ throttle during the 1–2 shift only and usually more severe when fluid is hot. Line pressure is within specifications and no codes are stored. If confirmed, this incident is caused by fluctuations of line pressure during shifts. To resolve, replace control valve assembly with part No. 31705-80X16.

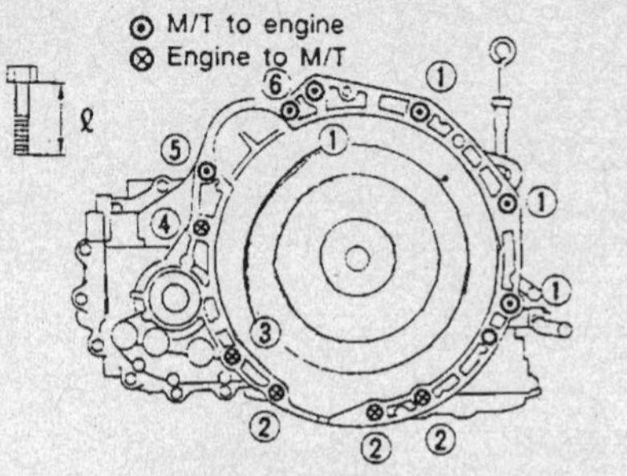

⊙ M/T to engine
⊗ Engine to M/T
ℓ
①
②
③
④
⑤
⑥

Bolt No.	Tightening torque N·m (kg-m, ft-lb)	ℓ mm (in)
1	39 - 49 (4.0 - 5.0, 29 - 36)	45 (1.77)
2	30 - 36 (3.1 - 3.7, 22 - 27)	30 (1.18)
3	30 - 36 (3.1 - 3.7, 22 - 27)	40 (1.57)
4	74 - 83 (7.5 - 8.5, 54 - 61)	45 (1.77)
5	30 - 36 (3.1 - 3.7, 22 - 27)	80 (3.15)
6	30 - 36 (3.1 - 3.7, 22 - 27)	65 (2.56)

NS5029100545000X

Fig. 8 Transaxle to engine bolt location & tightening specifications. Altima

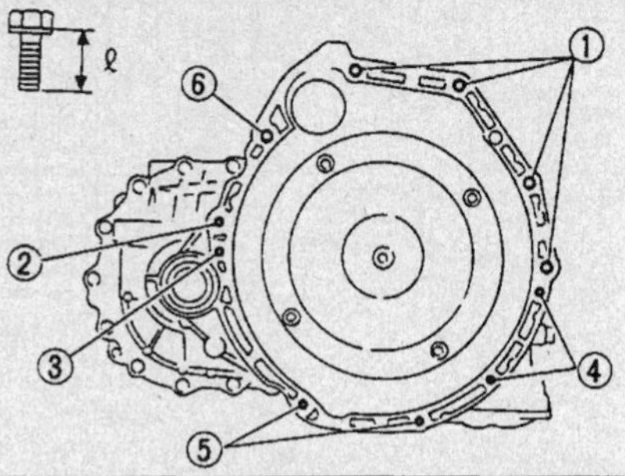

ℓ
①
②
③
④
⑤
⑥

Bolt No.	Tightening torque N·m (kg-m, ft-lb)	ℓ mm (in)
1	39 - 49 (4.0 - 5.0, 29 - 36)	60 (2.36)
2	39 - 49 (4.0 - 5.0, 29 - 36)	60 (2.36)
3	30 - 40 (3.1 - 4.1, 22 - 30)	25 (0.98)
4	30 - 40 (3.1 - 4.1, 22 - 30)	25 (0.98)
5*	30 - 40 (3.1 - 4.1, 22 - 30)	—
6	43 - 58 (4.4 - 5.9, 32 - 43)	115 (4.53)
Front gusset or Rear gusset to engine	30 - 40 (3.1 - 4.1, 22 - 30)	25 (0.98)

*: Nuts and washers.

NS5029100546000X

Fig. 9 Transaxle to engine bolt location & tightening specifications. Maxima

TIGHTENING SPECIFICATIONS

Year	Component	Torque/Ft. Lbs.
1993–96	Control Cable Locknut	23–31
	Control Valve Body To Transaxle Case	5–7
	Converter Housing To Engine	①
	Detent Spring	66②
	Drain Plug	22–29
	Driveplate To Engine	105–112
	Driveplate To Torque Converter	33–43
	Governor Valve Body To Governor Shaft	48–60②
	Gusset To Converter Housing	12–15
	Inhibitor Switch To Transaxle Case	23–35②
	Oil Cooler Pipe To Transaxle Case	22–36
	Oil Strainer To Lower Valve Body	7–9
	Oil Tube To Converter Housing	35–43②
	Revolution Sensor	43–60②
	Side Cover	20–22
	Speedometer Pinion	43–60②
	Transaxle Case To Converter Housing	32–35
	Transaxle Case To Front Cover	14–17

①— Refer to "Transaxle, Replace."

②— Inch lbs.

Jatco RL4F03A Automatic Transaxles

NOTE: On Air Bag Equipped Models, Refer To "Air Bag System Precautions" Located In The Front Of This Manual For System Disarming & Arming Procedures.

INDEX

	Page No.
Adjustments	36-237
Control Cable	36-237
Inhibitor Switch	36-237
Throttle Wire	36-237
Identification	36-237
In-Vehicle Repairs	36-237
Control Valve Assembly & Accumulator	36-237
Differential Side Oil Seal	36-237
Governor Valve	36-238
Key Interlock Cable, Replace	36-238
Maintenance	36-237
Fluid Change	36-237
Fluid Check	36-237
Precautions	36-237
Air Bag Systems	36-237
Tightening Specifications	36-242
Transaxle, Replace	36-238
Troubleshooting	36-237
Brake Transmission Shift Interlock	36-237
Transaxle	36-237

PRECAUTIONS

AIR BAG SYSTEMS

Refer to "Air Bag System Precautions" in the front of this manual for system disarming and arming procedures.

IDENTIFICATION

The transaxle identification serial number is attached on the upper face of the transmission case.

TROUBLESHOOTING

TRANSAXLE

Refer to **Fig. 1,** when troubleshooting the transaxle.

BRAKE TRANSMISSION SHIFT INTERLOCK

Refer to **Figs. 2 through 5,** when troubleshooting the brake transmission shift interlock.

MAINTENANCE

FLUID CHECK

To check fluid, drive vehicle for at least 5 minutes to bring fluid to operating temperature (122–176°F). With vehicle on a level surface and engine idling in Park and parking brake applied, move gear selector through all gear positions and return to P position. Dipsticks may be marked with Hot and Cold ranges. Use cold range if fluid is between (86–120°F).

FLUID CHANGE

1. Raise and support vehicle, then remove drain plug from transaxle oil pan to drain fluid.
2. After fluid has been drained, install drain plug and tighten to specifications.
3. **Fill transmission using caution not to overfill.**

ADJUSTMENTS

THROTTLE WIRE

1. Turn ignition switch to Off position.
2. While pressing lock plate, **Fig. 6,** move adjusting tube in direction "T," then return lock plate.
3. Move throttle drum from P2 to P1 quickly and ensure throttle wire stroke "L" is 1.079–1.236 inch between full throttle and idle.
4. **Adjust throttle wire stroke when throttle wire/accelerator wire is installed and adjusted. Put mark on throttle wire to aid in measuring wire stroke.**

CONTROL CABLE

1. Place selector lever in "P" position, then loosen control cable locknut, **Fig. 7,** and place manual shaft in "P" position.
2. Adjust cable using long hole in control cable at transaxle end, **Fig. 7,** then tighten locknut.
3. Move selector lever from "P" to "1" and ensure selector lever moves smoothly without any sliding noise.

INHIBITOR SWITCH

1. Remove control cable end from manual shaft, then set manual shaft in "N" range.
2. Loosen inhibitor switch attaching bolts, then insert a .157 inch diameter pin into adjustment holes on both inhibitor switch and manual shaft as near vertical as possible.
3. Tighten inhibitor switch attaching bolts, then remove pin from adjusting hole.
4. Install and adjust control cable, then check continuity of inhibitor switch.

IN-VEHICLE REPAIRS

CONTROL VALVE ASSEMBLY & ACCUMULATOR

1. Raise and support vehicle, then remove drain plug from transaxle oil pan to drain fluid.
2. Remove oil pan and gasket.
3. Disconnect transaxle solenoid harness connector.
4. Remove stopper ring from solenoid harness terminal body, then the solenoid harness from transaxle case by pushing on terminal body.
5. Remove control valve assembly attaching bolts, then the control valve assembly.
6. Remove 3-R and N-D accumulators by applying compressed air, if necessary. **Hold pistons with a rag when removing.**
7. Reverse procedure to install noting the following:
   a. Place manual shaft in Neutral, then align manual plate with groove in manual valve.
   b. After installation of control valve assembly, ensure selector lever can be moved to all positions.

DIFFERENTIAL SIDE OIL SEAL

1. Remove driveshafts as follows:
   a. Remove wheel bearing locknut, then the disc brake caliper and position aside.
   b. Remove tie-rod ball joint.
   c. Separate driveshaft from knuckle by lightly tapping it. If it is difficult to remove, use a suitable puller.
   d. Remove right driveshaft from transaxle by prying between transaxle

ROAD TEST SYMPTOM CHART
Numbers are arranged in order of probability. Perform inspections starting with number one and work up.
Circled numbers indicate that the transaxle must be removed from the vehicle.
[ ] : Valve expected to be malfunctioning

		ON VEHICLE														
		Oil level and oil quality	Control cable	Inhibitor switch and wiring	Throttle wire	Engine idling rpm	Line pressure	Control valve	Throttle valve & detent valve	Manual valve	Pressure regulator valve	3-4 shift valve	2-3 shift valve	1-2 shift valve	Overrun clutch control valve	Pressure modifier valve
Sharp shocks in shifting from "N" to "D" range		1	2		5	3	4	7								
Shift shocks	When shifting from 1st to 2nd or 2nd to 3rd	1	2		4		3	6								
	When shifting from 3rd to 4th	1	2		4		3	5								
	When shifting from D to 2 and 1 range. When O.D. switch is set from "ON" to "OFF"	1	2		4		3	5								
	When shifting from 2nd to 1st in "1" range	1	2		4		3	5								
Shift slippage when upshifting	When shifting from 1st to 2nd	1	2		4		3	5								
	When shifting from 2nd to 3rd	1	2		4		3	6								
	When shifting from 3rd to 4th	1	2		4		3	5								
Shift slippage with accelerator pedal depressed	When shifting from 4th to 2nd	1	2		5		3	6								
	When shifting from 4th to 3rd	1	2		4		3	6								
	When shifting from 4th to 1st and shifting from 3rd to 1st	1	2		5		3	6								
Poor power/acceleration	When vehicle starts	1	2		4		3	6								
	When upshifting	1	2		4		3	7								
No engine braking	When shifting from "D" to "2" and "1" range	1	2		4		3	5								
	When O.D. switch is set from "ON" to "OFF"	1	2		4		3	7								
	When shifting from 2nd to 1st in "1" range	1	2		4		3	5								
Shift quality	Too low a gear change point from 2nd to 3rd and from 3rd to 2nd	1			3		2	6								
	Too high a gear change point from 2nd to 3rd and from 3rd to 2nd	1			3		2	6								
	Too low a gear change point from 2nd to 1st in "1" range	1			3		2	6								
	Too high a gear change point from 2nd to 1st in "1" range	1			3		2	6								

NS5029100547010X

Fig. 1 Transaxle troubleshooting chart (Part 1 of 4)

ON VEHICLE																	OFF VEHICLE										
Kickdown modifier valve	1-2 accumulator valve	3-2 timing valve	1st reducing valve	Torque converter relief valve	Throttle modifier valve	4th speed cut valve	Lock-up control valve	4-2 sequence valve	Governor pressure	Governor valve	O.D. cancel solenoid	Lock-up cancel solenoid	Accumulator 3-R	Accumulator N-D	Ignition switch and starter motor	O.D. control switch and wiring	Torque converter	Oil pump	Reverse clutch	High clutch	Forward clutch	Forward one-way clutch	Overrun clutch	Low one-way clutch	Low & reverse clutch	Brake band	Parking components
														6				9	8								
													5					8								7	
																		8					7			6	
																				8			7			6	
																		7							6		
																		7								6	
													5					9		8						7	
																		8		7						6	
									4	7							8	9	10	11	13	14	15	16	17	12	
													5					7		8			10		11	9	
									4	7								11		8		10				9	
														5				9		7	8						
									5	6								9			8						
																							6				
											6					5							8				
																							6	7			
									4	5																	
									4	5																	
									4	5																	
									4	5																	

NS5029100547020X

Fig. 1 Transaxle troubleshooting chart (Part 2 of 4)

case and inner CV housing with a suitable pry bar, **Figs. 8 and 9.**

e. Remove left driveshaft from transaxle by driving shaft out from opposite side using a suitable tool, **Fig. 10. Use caution not to damage pinion mate shaft and side gear.**

2. Remove oil seals using seal puller tool No. ST33290001, or equivalent.
3. Apply ATF to oil seal surface, then install using drift tool No. KV31103000, or equivalent, for transaxle case side and tool No. ST35325000, or equivalent, for converter side.
4. Install oil seals so that dimension "A" and "B," **Fig. 11,** are within .217–.256 inch for dimension "A" and .020 inch or less for dimension "B."
5. Install driveshafts as follows:
   a. Set driveshaft installer tool No. KV38106700, or equivalent, along inner circumference of oil seal.
   b. Insert driveshaft into transaxle ensuring serrations are properly aligned, then remove tool.
   c. Push driveshaft, then press-fit circular clip on driveshaft into circular clip groove of side gear.
   d. Ensure shaft is properly meshed with side gear by attempting to pull flange out of slide joint.
   e. Install driveshaft into knuckle.
   f. Install tie-rod ball joint, disc brake caliper and wheel bearing locknut and tighten as required.

GOVERNOR VALVE

1. Remove governor valve cap snap ring and spacer, then the cap and O-ring.
2. Remove governor valve assembly by pulling upwards.
3. Reverse procedures to install.

KEY INTERLOCK CABLE, REPLACE

Removal

1. Unlock slider from adjuster holder and remove rod from cable at shift selector.
2. Remove lock plate and cable from steering lock.

Installation

1. Set key interlock cable to steering lock assembly and install lock plate.
2. Clamp cable to steering column and fix to control cable with band.
3. Set selector lever to P position.
4. Insert interlock rod into adjuster holder.
5. Install casing cap to bracket.
6. Move slider in order to fix adjuster holder to interlock rod.

TRANSAXLE

REPLACE

1. Remove battery and bracket, then the air duct.
2. Disconnect transaxle solenoid and inhibitor switch harness connectors.
3. Disconnect throttle wire from engine compartment.
4. Raise and support vehicle, then drain ATF from transaxle.
5. Disconnect control cable from transaxle, then the oil cooler hoses.
6. Remove driveshafts, refer to "Differential Side Oil Seal" under "In-Vehicle Repairs."
7. Remove front exhaust tube, then the starter motor from the transaxle.
8. **On Sentra models with SR20DE engine,** remove rear plate cover.
9. **On Sentra models with GA16DE engine,** remove front gussets and rear engine plate.
10. **On all models,** remove bolts attaching torque converter to driveplate.
11. Place a suitable jack under oil pan to support engine.
12. Support transaxle with a suitable jack, then remove mountings from transaxle.
13. Remove bolts attaching engine to transaxle, then lower transaxle while supporting with a jack.

Numbers are arranged in order of probability. Perform inspections starting with number one and work up.
Circled numbers indicate that the transaxle must be removed from the vehicle.

[ ] : Valve expected to be malfunctioning

		ON VEHICLE: Oil level and oil quality	Control cable	Inhibitor switch and wiring	Throttle wire	Engine idling rpm	Line pressure	Control valve	Throttle valve & detent valve	Manual valve	Pressure regulator valve	3-4 shift valve	2-3 shift valve	1-2 shift valve	Overrun clutch control valve	Pressure modifier valve
Shift quality	Failure to change gear from 4th to 2nd with accelerator pedal depressed.	1	.	.	3	.	2	6								
	Failure to change gear from 3rd to 2nd with accelerator pedal depressed.	1	.	.	3	.	2	6								
	Failure to change gear from 1st to 2nd in "D" and "2" range.	1	.	.	3	.	2	6								
	Vehicle does not start from "1st" in "D" and "2" range.	1	.	.	3	.	2	6								
	Failure to change gear to 3rd and 4th in "D" range.	1	.	.	3	.	2	6								
	Changes gear to 1st directly when selector lever is set from "D" to "1" range	1	.	.	3	.	2	6								
	Changes gear to 2nd in "1" range.	1	.	.	3	.	2	6								
Lock-up quality	Lock-up point is extremely high or low.	1	.	.	3	.	2	6								
	Torque converter does not lock-up	1	.	.	3	.	2	7								
	Lock-up is not released when accelerator pedal is released	1	.	.	.	.	.	2								
Engine does not start in "P" and "N" ranges or engine starts in ranges other than "P" and "N" ranges.		.	2	3	.	.	.	.								
Vehicle moves with selector lever in "P" range.		.	1	.	.	.	.	.								

NS5029100547030X

Fig. 1 Transaxle troubleshooting chart (Part 3 of 4)

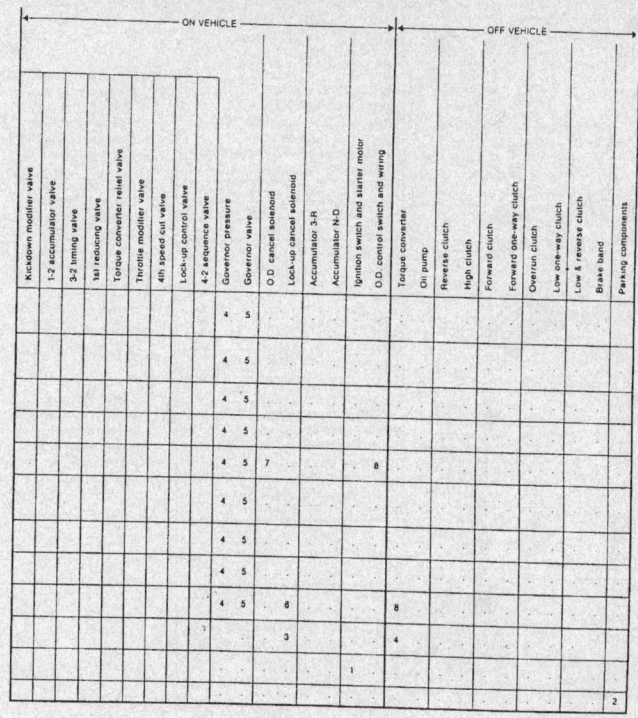

	ON VEHICLE: Kickdown modifier valve	1-2 accumulator valve	3-2 timing valve	1st reducing valve	Torque converter relief valve	Throttle modifier valve	4th speed cut valve	Lock-up control valve	4-2 sequence valve	Governor pressure	Governor valve	O.D. cancel solenoid	Lock-up cancel solenoid	Accumulator 3-R	Accumulator N-D	Ignition switch and starter motor	O.D. control switch and wiring	OFF VEHICLE: Torque converter	Oil pump	Reverse clutch	High clutch	Forward clutch	Forward one-way clutch	Overrun clutch	Low one-way clutch	Low & reverse clutch	Brake band	Parking components
Failure to change gear from 4th to 2nd with accelerator pedal depressed.										4	5																	
Failure to change gear from 3rd to 2nd with accelerator pedal depressed.										4	5																	
Failure to change gear from 1st to 2nd in "D" and "2" range.										4	5																	
Vehicle does not start from "1st" in "D" and "2" range.										4	5																	
Failure to change gear to 3rd and 4th in "D" range.										4	5	7					8											
Changes gear to 1st directly when selector lever is set from "D" to "1" range										4	5																	
Changes gear to 2nd in "1" range.										4	5																	
Lock-up point is extremely high or low.										4	5																	
Torque converter does not lock-up										4	5		6					8										
Lock-up is not released when accelerator pedal is released													3					4										
Engine does not start in "P" and "N" ranges or engine starts in ranges other than "P" and "N" ranges.																1												
Vehicle moves with selector lever in "P" range.																												2

NS5029100547040X

Fig. 1 Transaxle troubleshooting chart (Part 4 of 4)

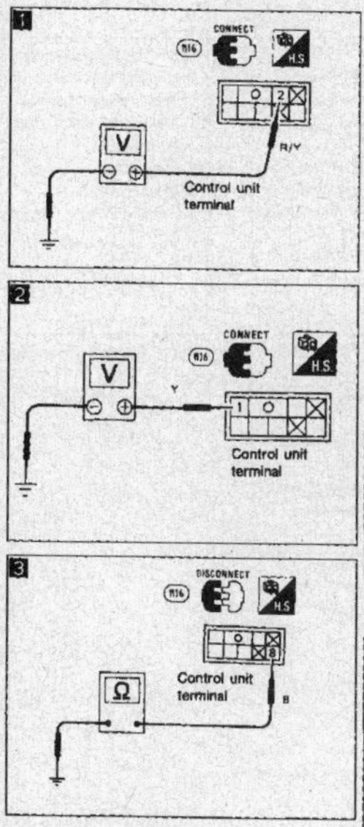

1
CONNECT
H.S.
V
R/Y
Control unit terminal
2
CONNECT
H.S.
V
Y
Control unit terminal
3
DISCONNECT
H.S.
Ω
Control unit terminal
B

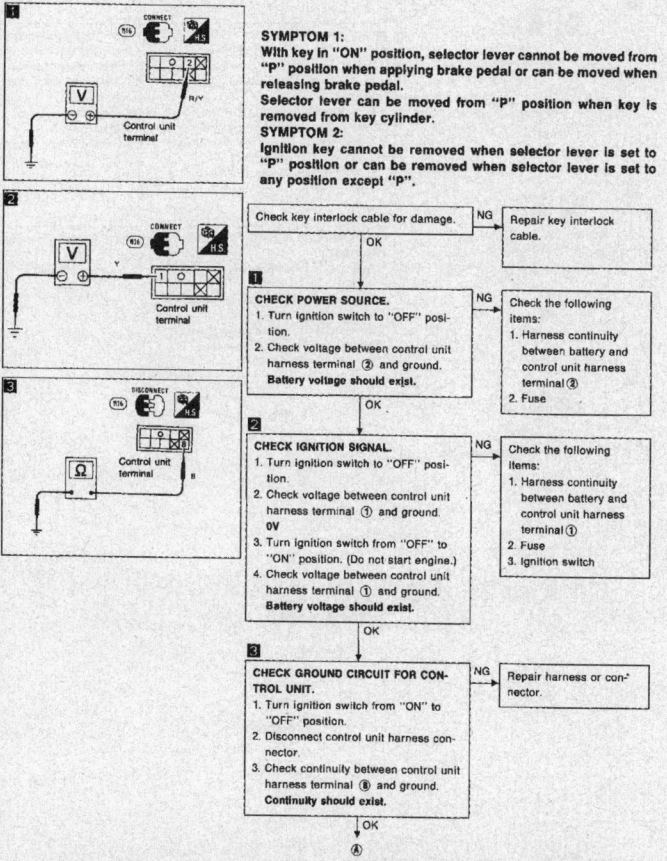

SYMPTOM 1:
With key in "ON" position, selector lever cannot be moved from "P" position when applying brake pedal or can be moved when releasing brake pedal.
Selector lever can be moved from "P" position when key is removed from key cylinder.
SYMPTOM 2:
Ignition key cannot be removed when selector lever is set to "P" position or can be removed when selector lever is set to any position except "P".

Check key interlock cable for damage. — NG → Repair key interlock cable.

↓ OK

1 **CHECK POWER SOURCE.**
1. Turn ignition switch to "OFF" position.
2. Check voltage between control unit harness terminal ② and ground.
Battery voltage should exist.

NG → Check the following items:
1. Harness continuity between battery and control unit harness terminal ②
2. Fuse

↓ OK

2 **CHECK IGNITION SIGNAL.**
1. Turn ignition switch to "OFF" position.
2. Check voltage between control unit harness terminal ① and ground.
0V
3. Turn ignition switch from "OFF" to "ON" position. (Do not start engine.)
4. Check voltage between control unit harness terminal ① and ground.
Battery voltage should exist.

NG → Check the following items:
1. Harness continuity between battery and control unit harness terminal ①
2. Fuse
3. Ignition switch

↓ OK

3 **CHECK GROUND CIRCUIT FOR CONTROL UNIT.**
1. Turn ignition switch from "ON" to "OFF" position.
2. Disconnect control unit harness connector.
3. Check continuity between control unit harness terminal ⑧ and ground.
Continuity should exist.

NG → Repair harness or connector.

↓ OK

Ⓐ

NS5029400587010X

Fig. 2 BTSI diagnostic procedure (Part 1 of 4). 1993–94

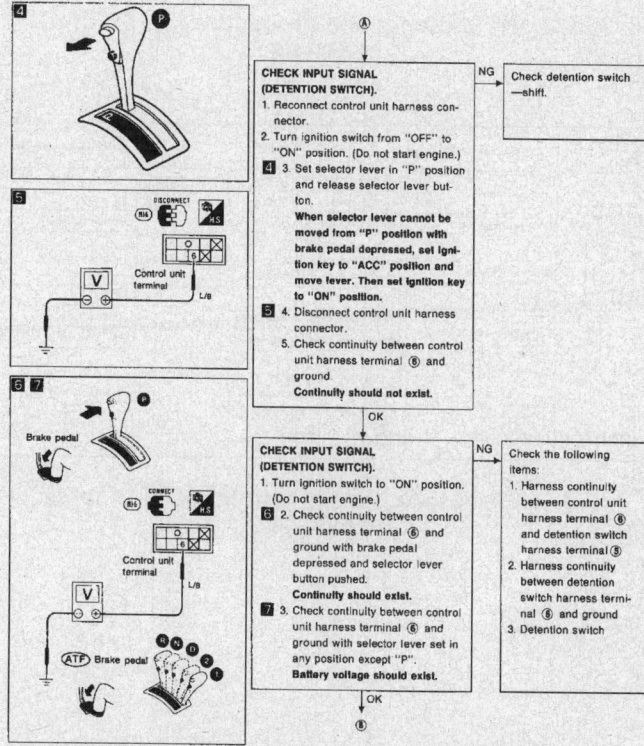

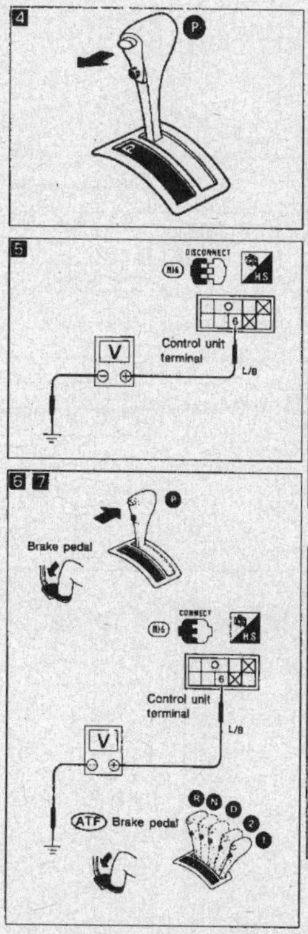

4
P
5
DISCONNECT
H.S.
V
Control unit terminal
L/B
6 7
Brake pedal
CONNECT
H.S.
Control unit terminal
L/B
V
ATF
Brake pedal

Ⓐ

↓

CHECK INPUT SIGNAL (DETENTION SWITCH).
1. Reconnect control unit harness connector.
2. Turn ignition switch from "OFF" to "ON" position. (Do not start engine.)
4 3. Set selector lever in "P" position and release selector lever button.
When selector lever cannot be moved from "P" position with brake pedal depressed, set ignition key to "ACC" position and move lever. Then set ignition key to "ON" position.
5 4. Disconnect control unit harness connector.
5. Check continuity between control unit harness terminal ⑧ and ground.
Continuity should not exist.

NG → Check detention switch —shift.

↓ OK

CHECK INPUT SIGNAL (DETENTION SWITCH).
1. Turn ignition switch to "ON" position. (Do not start engine.)
6 2. Check continuity between control unit harness terminal ⑥ and ground with brake pedal depressed and selector lever button pushed.
Continuity should exist.
7 3. Check continuity between control unit harness terminal ⑥ and ground with selector lever set in any position except "P".
Battery voltage should exist.

NG → Check the following items:
1. Harness continuity between control unit harness terminal ⑥ and detention switch harness terminal ⑤
2. Harness continuity between detention switch harness terminal ⑧ and ground
3. Detention switch

↓ OK

Ⓑ

NS5029400587020X

Fig. 2 BTSI diagnostic procedure (Part 2 of 4). 1993–94

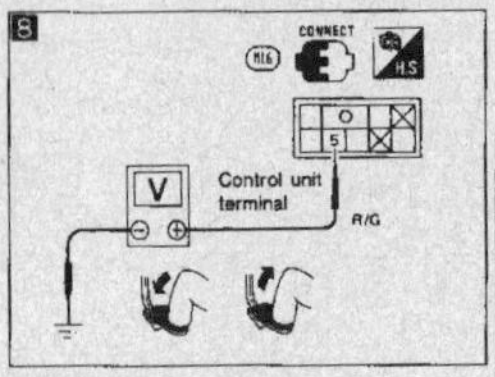
8
CONNECT
H.S
V
Control unit terminal
R/G

Ⓑ

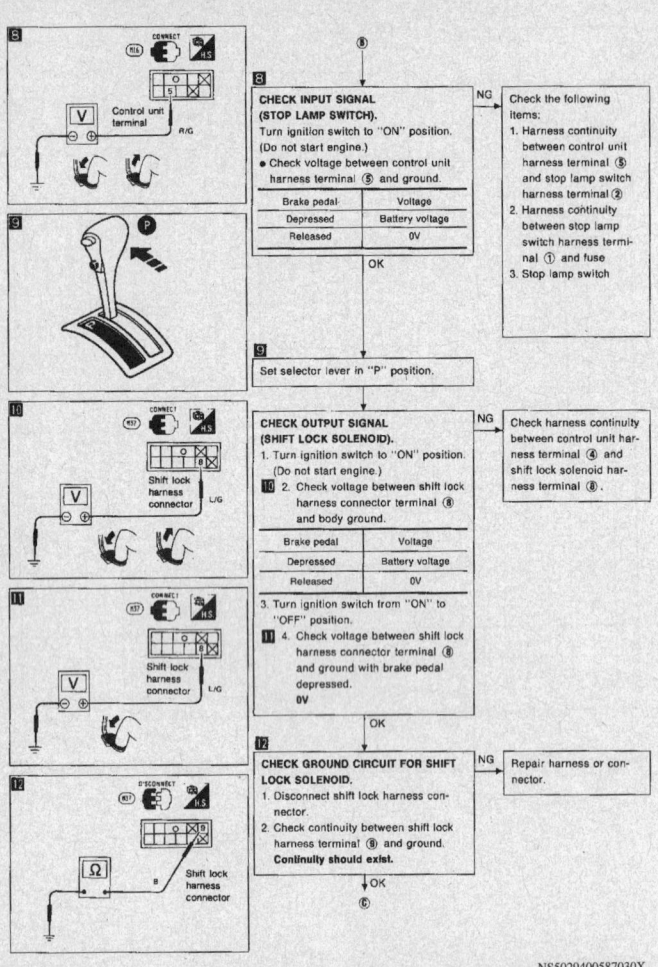

8 CHECK INPUT SIGNAL (STOP LAMP SWITCH).
Turn ignition switch to "ON" position. (Do not start engine.)
- Check voltage between control unit harness terminal ⑤ and ground.

Brake pedal	Voltage
Depressed	Battery voltage
Released	0V

NG → Check the following items:
1. Harness continuity between control unit harness terminal ⑤ and stop lamp switch harness terminal ②
2. Harness continuity between stop lamp switch harness terminal ① and fuse
3. Stop lamp switch

OK ↓

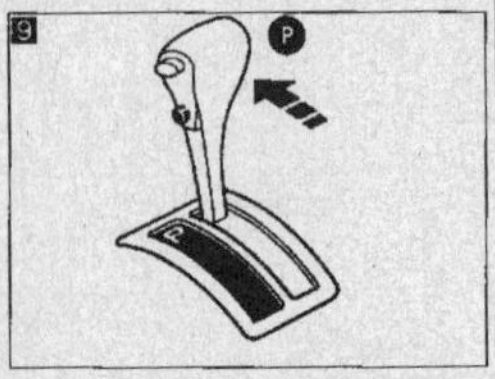
9
P

9 Set selector lever in "P" position.

↓

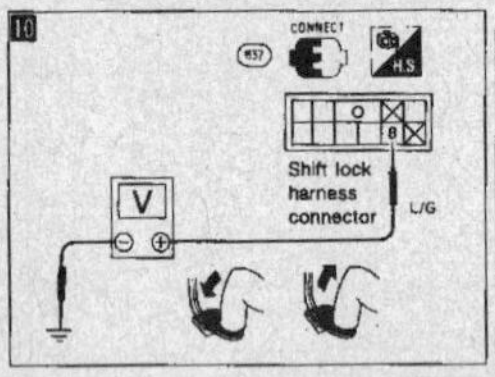
10
CONNECT
H.S
Shift lock harness connector
V
L/G

CHECK OUTPUT SIGNAL (SHIFT LOCK SOLENOID).
1. Turn ignition switch to "ON" position. (Do not start engine.)
2. **10** Check voltage between shift lock harness connector terminal ⑧ and body ground.

Brake pedal	Voltage
Depressed	Battery voltage
Released	0V

3. Turn ignition switch from "ON" to "OFF" position.
4. **11** Check voltage between shift lock harness connector terminal ⑧ and ground with brake pedal depressed. **0V**

NG → Check harness continuity between control unit harness terminal ④ and shift lock solenoid harness terminal ⑧.

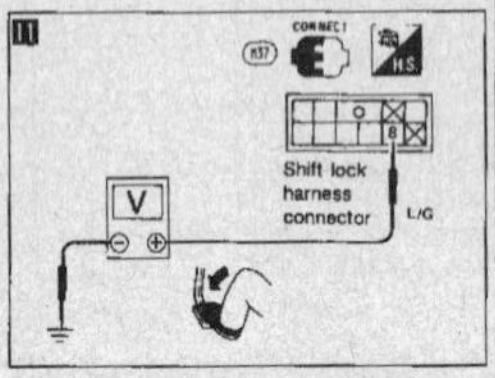
11
CONNECT
H.S
Shift lock harness connector
V
L/G

OK ↓

12 CHECK GROUND CIRCUIT FOR SHIFT LOCK SOLENOID.
1. Disconnect shift lock harness connector.
2. Check continuity between shift lock harness terminal ⑧ and ground. **Continuity should exist.**

NG → Repair harness or connector.

OK ↓ Ⓒ

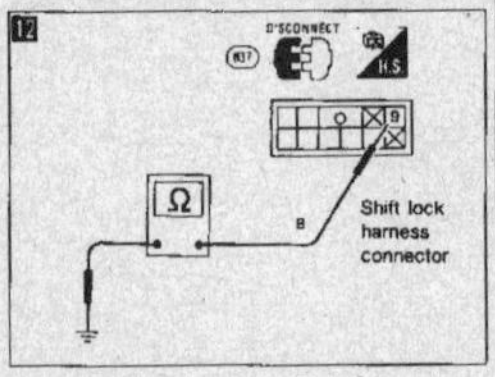
12
DISCONNECT
H.S
Ω
B
Shift lock harness connector

NS5029400587030X

Fig. 2 BTSI diagnostic procedure (Part 3 of 4). 1993–94

Terminal No. ⊕	Terminal No. ⊖	Item	Condition	Judgment standard
1	8	Ignition signal	Ignition switch "ON"	Battery voltage
			Except above	0V
2	8	Power source	Any condition	Battery voltage
4	8	Shift lock signal	• Ignition switch "ON" • When selector lever is set in "P" position and brake pedal is depressed.	Battery voltage
			Except above	0V
5	8	Stop lamp switch	When brake pedal is depressed.	Battery voltage
			When brake pedal is released.	0V
6	8	Detention switch	• When key is inserted into key cylinder and selector lever is set in "P" position with selector lever button pushed. • When selector lever is set in any position except "P".	Battery voltage
			Except above	0V

NS5029400590000X

Fig. 3 Shift lock control unit inspection table. 1993–94

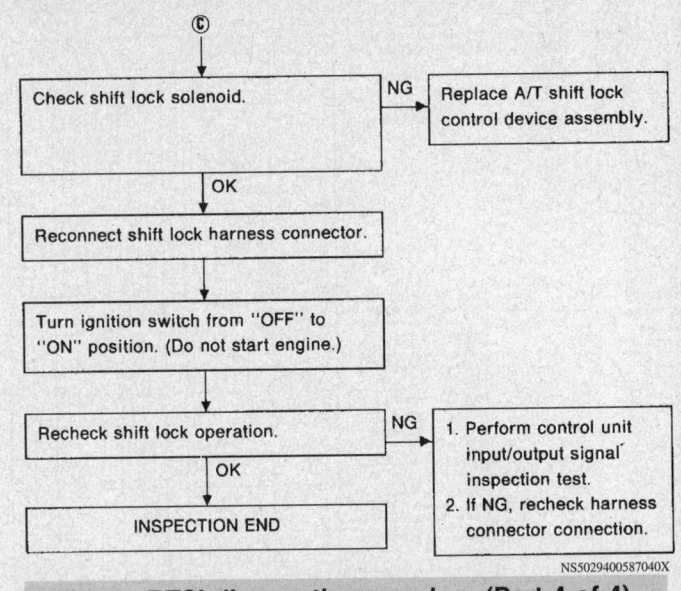

Ⓒ

Check shift lock solenoid.

NG → Replace A/T shift lock control device assembly.

OK ↓

Reconnect shift lock harness connector.

↓

Turn ignition switch from "OFF" to "ON" position. (Do not start engine.)

↓

Recheck shift lock operation.

NG →
1. Perform control unit input/output signal inspection test.
2. If NG, recheck harness connector connection.

OK ↓

INSPECTION END

NS5029400587040X

Fig. 2 BTSI diagnostic procedure (Part 4 of 4). 1993–94

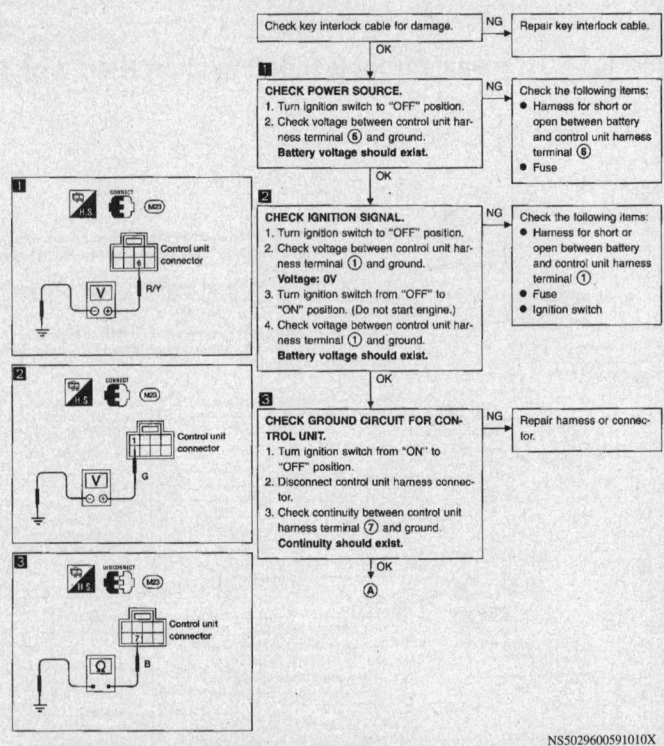

Check key interlock cable for damage.

NG → Repair key interlock cable.

OK ↓

1 CHECK POWER SOURCE.
1. Turn ignition switch to "OFF" position.
2. Check voltage between control unit harness terminal ⑥ and ground. **Battery voltage should exist.**

NG → Check the following items:
- Harness for short or open between battery and control unit harness terminal ⑥
- Fuse

OK ↓

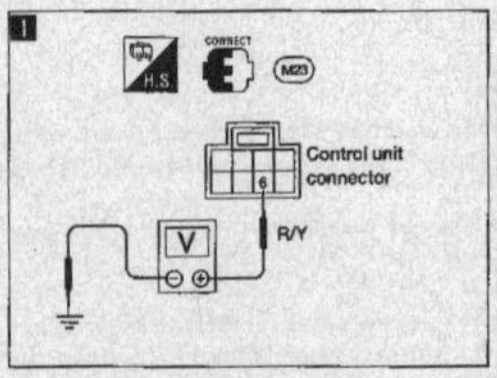
1
H.S
CONNECT
M23
Control unit connector
V
R/Y

2 CHECK IGNITION SIGNAL.
1. Turn ignition switch to "OFF" position.
2. Check voltage between control unit harness terminal ① and ground. **Voltage: 0V**
3. Turn ignition switch from "OFF" to "ON" position. (Do not start engine.)
4. Check voltage between control unit harness terminal ① and ground. **Battery voltage should exist.**

NG → Check the following items:
- Harness for short or open between battery and control unit harness terminal ①
- Fuse
- Ignition switch

OK ↓

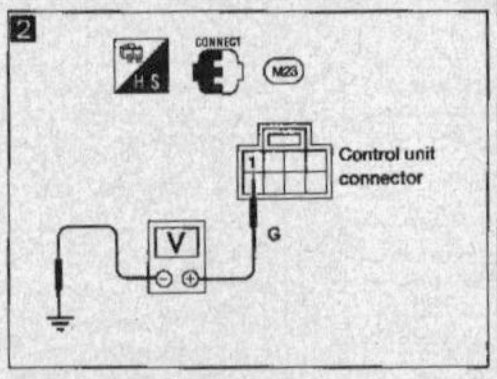
2
H.S
CONNECT
M23
Control unit connector
V
G

3 CHECK GROUND CIRCUIT FOR CONTROL UNIT.
1. Turn ignition switch from "ON" to "OFF" position.
2. Disconnect control unit harness connector.
3. Check continuity between control unit harness terminal ⑦ and ground. **Continuity should exist.**

NG → Repair harness or connector.

OK ↓ Ⓐ

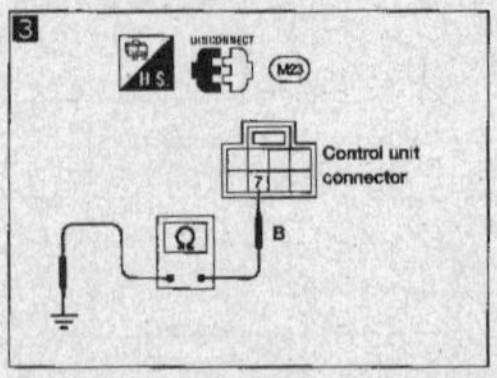
3
H.S
DISCONNECT
M23
Control unit connector
Ω
B

NS5029600591010X

Fig. 4 BTSI diagnostic procedure (Part 1 of 4). 1995–96

4
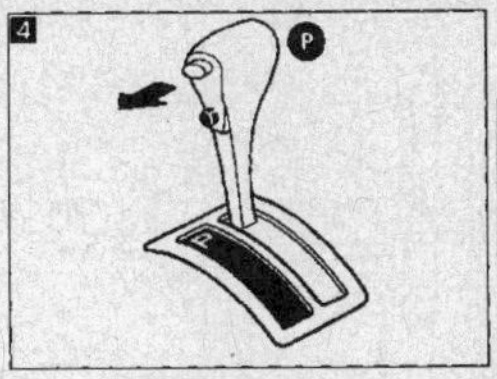

5
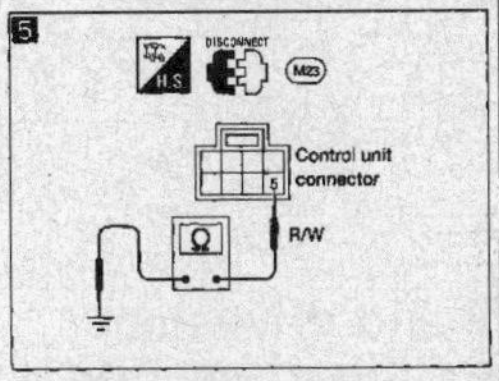
H.S.
DISCONNECT
M23
Control unit connector
5
Ω
R/W

6 7
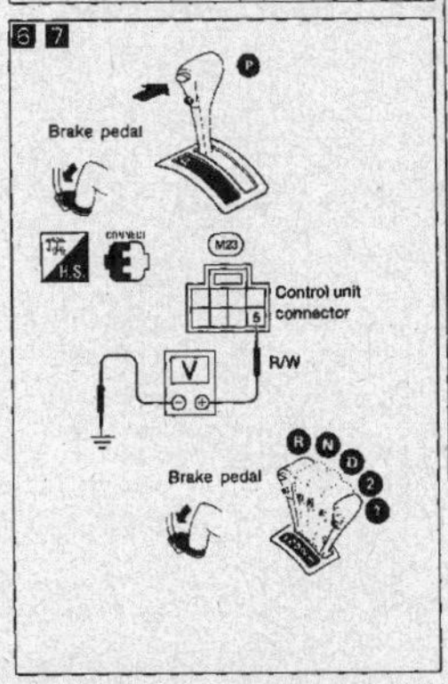
Brake pedal
H.S.
CONNECT
M23
Control unit connector
5
V
R/W
Brake pedal

Ⓐ

CHECK INPUT SIGNAL (PARK POSITION SWITCH).
1. Reconnect control unit harness connector.
2. Turn ignition switch from "OFF" to "ON" position. (Do not start engine.)
3. [4] Set selector lever in "P" position and release selector lever button.
4. [5] Disconnect control unit harness connector.
5. Check continuity between control unit harness terminal ⑤ and ground.

Continuity should not exist.

NG → Check park position switch.

OK ↓

CHECK INPUT SIGNAL (PARK POSITION SWITCH).
1. Turn ignition switch to "ON" position. (Do not start engine.)
2. [5] Check voltage between control unit harness terminal ⑤ and ground. Check while depressing brake pedal with selector lever button pushed. **Voltage: 0V**
3. [7] Check voltage between control unit harness terminal ⑤ and ground. Check while selector lever is set in any position except "P". **When selector lever cannot be moved from "P" position with brake pedal depressed, set ignition key to "ACC" position and move lever. Then set ignition key to "ON" position.** **Battery voltage should exist.**

NG → Check the following items:
- Harness for short or open between control unit harness terminal ⑤ and park position switch harness terminal ②
- Harness for short or open between park position switch harness terminal ① and ground
- Park position switch

OK ↓

Ⓑ

NS5029600591020X

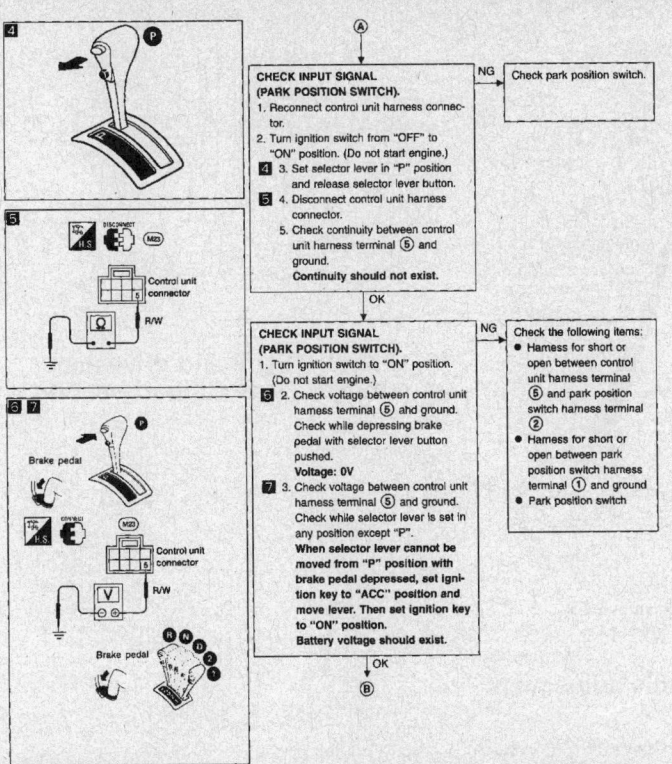

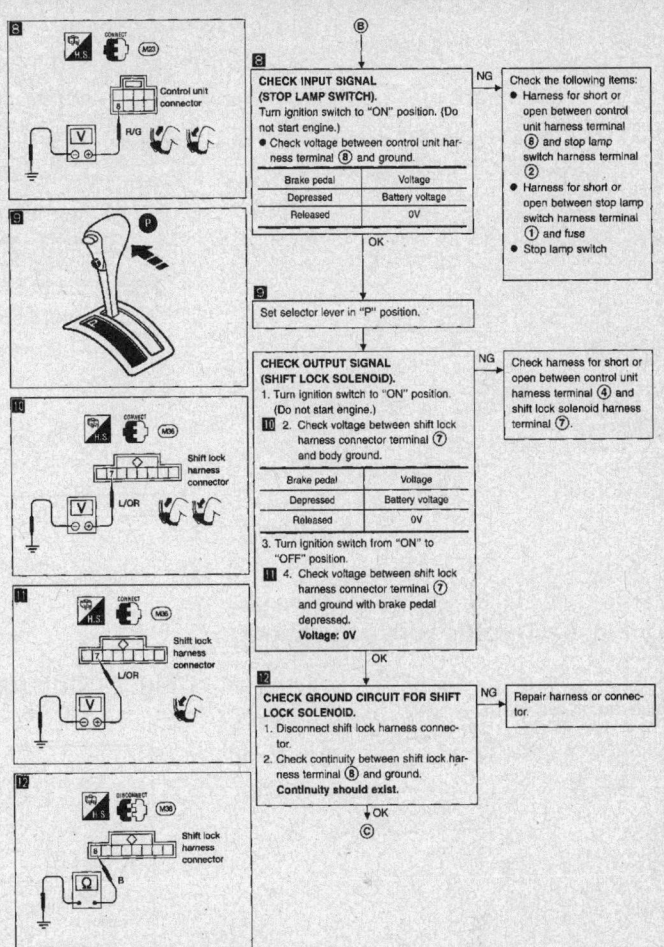

Fig. 4 BTSI diagnostic procedure (Part 2 of 4). 1995–96

8
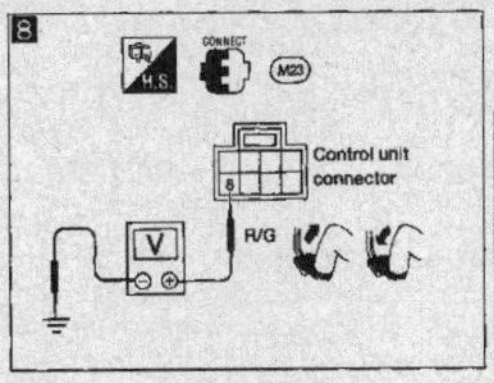
H.S.
CONNECT
M23
Control unit connector
8
V
R/G

9
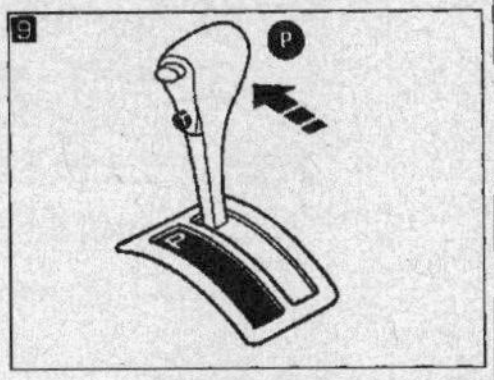

10
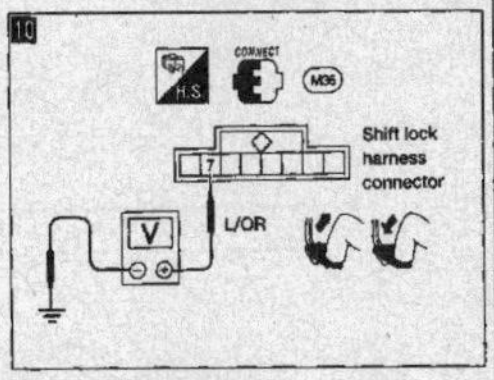
H.S.
CONNECT
M36
7
Shift lock harness connector
V
L/OR

11
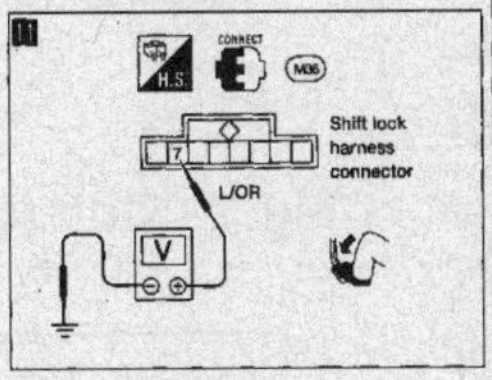
H.S.
CONNECT
M36
7
Shift lock harness connector
L/OR
V

12
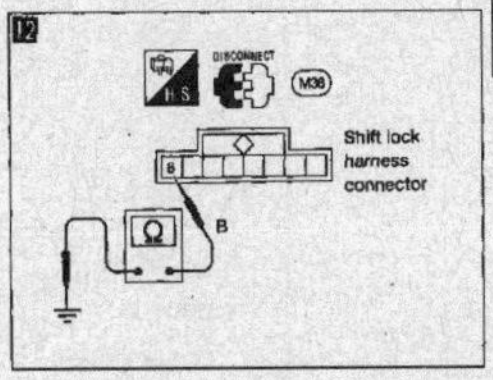
H.S.
DISCONNECT
M36
8
Shift lock harness connector
Ω
B

Ⓑ

[8] **CHECK INPUT SIGNAL (STOP LAMP SWITCH).**
Turn ignition switch to "ON" position. (Do not start engine.)
- Check voltage between control unit harness terminal ⑧ and ground.

Brake pedal	Voltage
Depressed	Battery voltage
Released	0V

NG → Check the following items:
- Harness for short or open between control unit harness terminal ⑧ and stop lamp switch harness terminal ②
- Harness for short or open between stop lamp switch harness terminal ① and fuse
- Stop lamp switch

OK ↓

[9] Set selector lever in "P" position.

CHECK OUTPUT SIGNAL (SHIFT LOCK SOLENOID).
1. Turn ignition switch to "ON" position. (Do not start engine.)
2. [10] Check voltage between shift lock harness connector terminal ⑦ and body ground.

Brake pedal	Voltage
Depressed	Battery voltage
Released	0V

3. Turn ignition switch from "ON" to "OFF" position.
4. [11] Check voltage between shift lock harness connector terminal ⑦ and ground with brake pedal depressed. **Voltage: 0V**

NG → Check harness for short or open between control unit harness terminal ④ and shift lock solenoid harness terminal ⑦.

OK ↓

[12] **CHECK GROUND CIRCUIT FOR SHIFT LOCK SOLENOID.**
1. Disconnect shift lock harness connector.
2. Check continuity between shift lock harness terminal ⑧ and ground.

Continuity should exist.

NG → Repair harness or connector.

OK ↓

Ⓒ

NS5029600591030X

Fig. 4 BTSI diagnostic procedure (Part 3 of 4). 1995–96

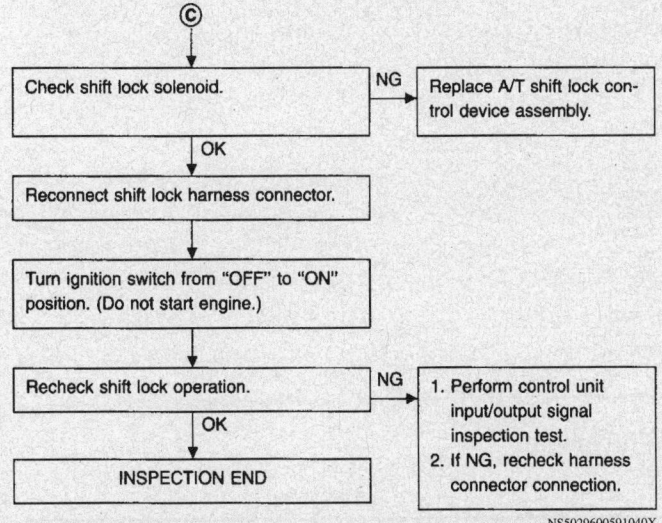

Ⓒ

Check shift lock solenoid. — NG → Replace A/T shift lock control device assembly.

OK ↓

Reconnect shift lock harness connector.

↓

Turn ignition switch from "OFF" to "ON" position. (Do not start engine.)

↓

Recheck shift lock operation. — NG → 1. Perform control unit input/output signal inspection test. 2. If NG, recheck harness connector connection.

OK ↓

INSPECTION END

NS5029600591040X

Fig. 4 BTSI diagnostic procedure (Part 4 of 4). 1995–96

Terminal No. ⊕	Terminal No. ⊖	Item	Condition	Judgement standard
1	7	Ignition signal	• Turn ignition switch to "ON" or "START" position.	Battery voltage
			• Except above	0V
6		Power source	• Any condition	Battery voltage
4		Shift lock signal	• Turn ignition switch to "ON" position • When selector lever is set in "P" position and brake pedal is depressed.	Battery voltage
			• Except above	0V
8		Stop lamp switch	• When brake pedal is depressed.	Battery voltage
			• When brake pedal is released.	0V
5		Park position switch	• When key is in key cylinder, selector lever is in "P" position, and selector lever button pushed. • When selector lever is set in any position except "P".	Battery voltage
			• Except above	0V

NS5029600592000X

Fig. 5 Shift lock control unit inspection table. 1995–96

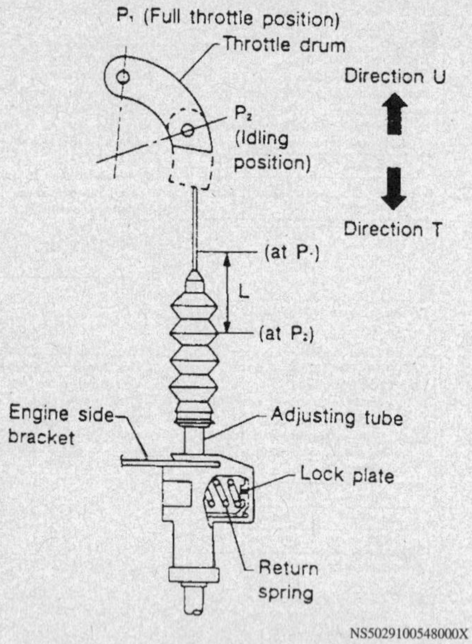
P1 (Full throttle position)
Throttle drum
Direction U
P2 (Idling position)
Direction T
(at P1)
L
(at P2)
Engine side bracket
Adjusting tube
Lock plate
Return spring
NS5029100548000X

Fig. 6 Throttle wire adjustment

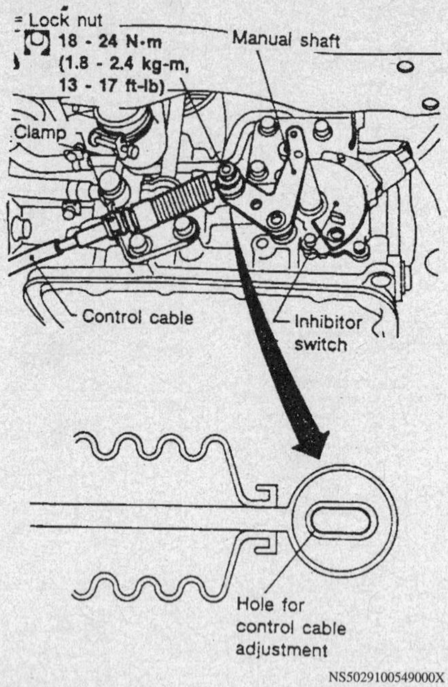
Lock nut
18 - 24 N·m
(1.8 - 2.4 kg-m,
13 - 17 ft-lb)
Manual shaft
Clamp
Control cable
Inhibitor switch
Hole for control cable adjustment
NS5029100549000X

Fig. 7 Control cable adjustment

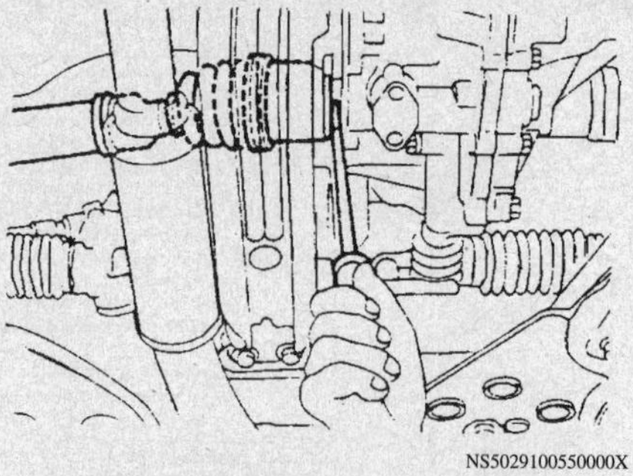
NS5029100550000X

Fig. 8 Righthand driveshaft removal. Less support bearing

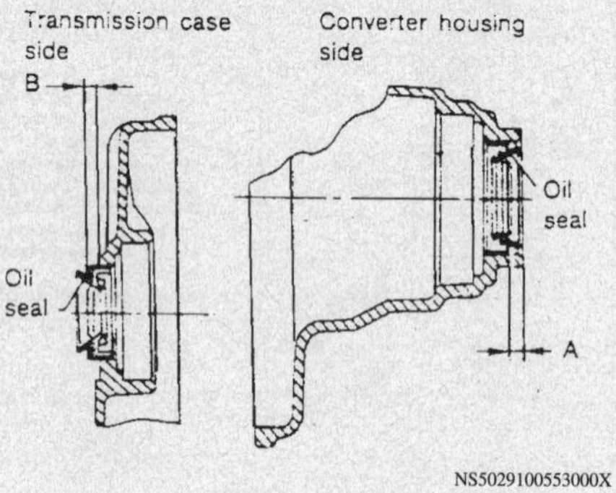
Transmission case side
Converter housing side
B
Oil seal
Oil seal
A
NS5029100553000X

Fig. 11 Differential oil seal dimensions "A" & "B"

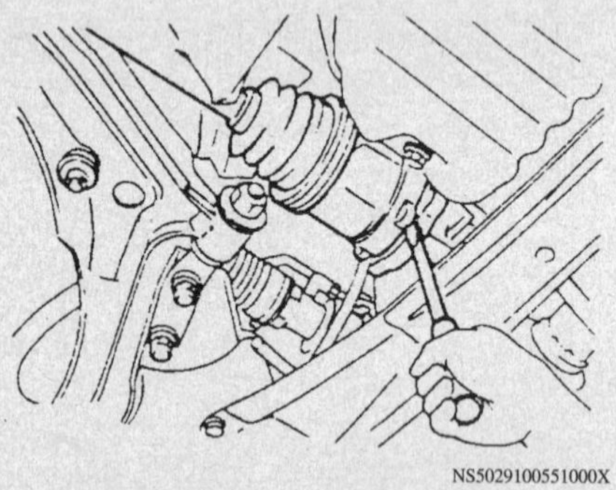
NS5029100551000X

Fig. 9 Righthand driveshaft removal. With support bearing

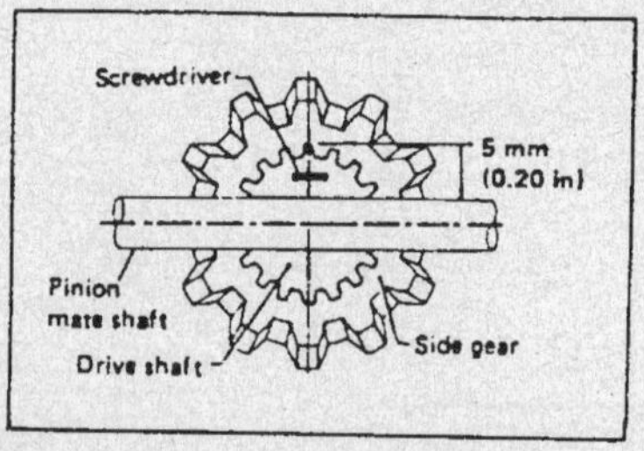
Screwdriver
5 mm
(0.20 in)
Pinion mate shaft
Drive shaft
Side gear

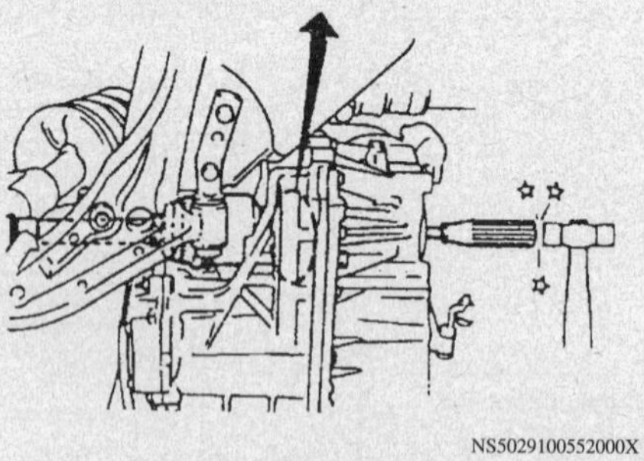
NS5029100552000X

Fig. 10 Lefthand driveshaft removal

TIGHTENING SPECIFICATIONS

Year	Component	Torque/Ft. Lbs.
1993–96	Bearing Retainer To Transaxle Case	14–18
	Control Cable Securing Nut	6–8
	Control Valve Body To Transaxle Case	5–7
	Converter Housing To Engine	①
	Drain Plug	22–29
	Driveplate To Torque Converter	29–36
	Governor Shaft Securing Nut	3–5

Continued

TIGHTENING SPECIFICATIONS—Continued

Year	Component	Torque/Ft. Lbs.
1993–96	Governor Valve Body To Governor Shaft	4–5
	Gusset To Converter Housing	12–15
	Inhibitor Switch To Transaxle Case	1–2
	Low & Reverse Brake Piston Retainer	5–7
	Lower Valve Body To Upper Valve Body	5–7
	Manual Shaft Locknut	23–31
	Oil Cooler Pipe To Transmission Case	22–36
	Oil Pan To Transaxle Case	4–5
	Oil Strainer To Lower Valve Body	7–9
	Oil Tube To Converter Housing	4–5
	Test Plug (Oil Pressure Inspection Hole)	4–7
	Throttle Wire Securing Bolt	2–3
	Transaxle Case To Converter Housing	14–17
	Transaxle Case To Front Cover	14–17

① — Bolts 1.97 inch or longer, 12 — 15 ft. lbs.; bolts 1.77 inch or smaller, 12–15 ft. lbs.

Front Wheel Drive Axles

INDEX

	Page No.
Driveshaft, Replace	36-245
Driveshaft Service	36-245
Assembly & Installation	36-245
Disassembly & Inspection	36-245
Steering Knuckle Service	36-244
Altima & Maxima	36-244
NX 1600, NX 2000, Sentra & 200SX	36-244
Quest	36-244

STEERING KNUCKLE SERVICE

ALTIMA & MAXIMA

Removal

1. Raise and support vehicle and remove wheel.
2. Unfasten brake caliper assembly, leaving brake line attached.
3. Separate driveshaft from steering knuckle by tapping on driveshaft.
4. Disconnect tie-rod from ball joint, then remove lower ball joint attaching nuts.
5. Remove steering knuckle-to-strut attaching bolts.
6. Remove wheel hub and steering knuckle, **Fig. 1,** as an assembly.
7. Separate wheel hub and steering knuckle using a suitable tool, **Fig. 2.**

Assembly & Installation

1. Install outer circlip into groove in steering knuckle, then press bearing outer race into knuckle.
2. Lubricate inner and outer bearing races with suitable grease.
3. Install inner circlip into groove in knuckle.
4. Install bearing inner races, then the outer grease seal.
5. Press hub into steering knuckle.
6. If driveshaft has not been removed from transaxle, adjust bearing preload as follows:
   a. Apply 5.5 tons pressure to bearing with a suitable press.
   b. Spin knuckle several times in each direction, then measure bearing preload using a suitable spring scale.
   c. Preload should measure .4–4.0 lbs. If reading is not within specifications, the wheel bearing must be replaced.
7. If driveshaft has been removed from transaxle, adjust bearing preload as follows:
   a. Position driveshaft in hub and **torque** wheel bearing locknut to 174–231 ft. lbs.
   b. Spin wheel hub several times in each direction, then measure preload using a suitable spring scale.
   c. Preload should measure 1.1–10.1 lbs. If reading is not within specifications, the wheel bearing must be replaced.
   d. Remove wheel bearing nut, then slide driveshaft out of hub.
8. Install inner grease seal into knuckle.
9. Install the assembly in reverse order of removal as outlined previously.

NX 1600, NX 2000, SENTRA & 200SX

Removal

1. Raise and support vehicle.
2. Remove wheel and tire assembly.
3. Remove wheel bearing locknut while depressing brake pedal.
4. Remove caliper.
5. Remove tie rod ball joint from knuckle.
6. Separate driveshaft from knuckle, **Fig. 3.**
7. Support arm assembly, then remove lower strut adjusting bolts. **Make matching marks on strut and adjusting bolt.**
8. Remove lower ball joint to knuckle attaching nut.
9. Separate knuckle from lower ball joint stud, using a suitable tool.
10. Remove steering knuckle.

Disassemble

1. Remove outer hub inner race from knuckle.
2. Remove outside inner race from wheel hub.
3. Remove inner race from wheel bearing.
4. Remove snap ring.
5. Install inner race (inside) of removed wheel bearing, then remove wheel bearing assembly from knuckle.

Inspection

Inspect removed components for excessive wear and/or damage. Replace worn or damaged components as required.

Assemble

1. Press new wheel bearing assembly into knuckle working from outside of knuckle.
2. Install snap ring.
3. Coat seal lip with suitable grease.
4. Press hub into knuckle. **Do not exceed 3.3 tons.**
5. Check bearing preload as follows:
   a. Place press load onto wheel hub shaft (approximately 5 tons).
   b. Spin knuckle several times in both directions.
   c. Ensure wheels bearings operate smoothly.

Installation

Reverse removal procedure to install.

QUEST

Removal

1. Raise and support vehicle, then remove wheel.
2. Remove wheel bearing locknut.
3. Remove brake caliper assembly and brake rotor. Suspend caliper assembly with wire.
4. Using ball joint remover tool No. J25730-A, or equivalent, separate tie-rod ball joint from knuckle.
5. Remove lower strut mounting bolts and nuts, **Fig. 4.**
6. Remove lower ball joint cotter pin and retaining nut.
7. Strike knuckle with a hammer and pull down control arm to separate lower ball joint from knuckle.
8. Separate driveshaft from knuckle by lightly tapping driveshaft. If driveshaft is hard to remove us a suitable puller. **Cover driveshaft boots with a shop towel to protect them during driveshaft removal.**

Disassemble

1. Using a hammer and suitable tool, drive wheel hub out of knuckle.
2. Using a suitable pressing tool, remove wheel bearing inner race from wheel hub.
3. Remove wheel bearing snap ring from knuckle.
4. Using a suitable pressing tool, press wheel bearing out of knuckle.

Assemble

1. Press new wheel bearing into knuckle. **Press only on outer race of wheel bearing.**
2. Install snap ring into groove of knuckle.
3. Install baffle plate and splash guard onto knuckle.
4. Press wheel hub into knuckle, holding wheel bearing inner race as shown in **Fig. 5.**
5. Spin knuckle several turns in both directions, ensure wheel bearings operate smoothly.

Installation

Reverse removal procedure, noting the following:

1. **Torque** lower strut mounting bolts and nuts to 94–108 ft. lbs.

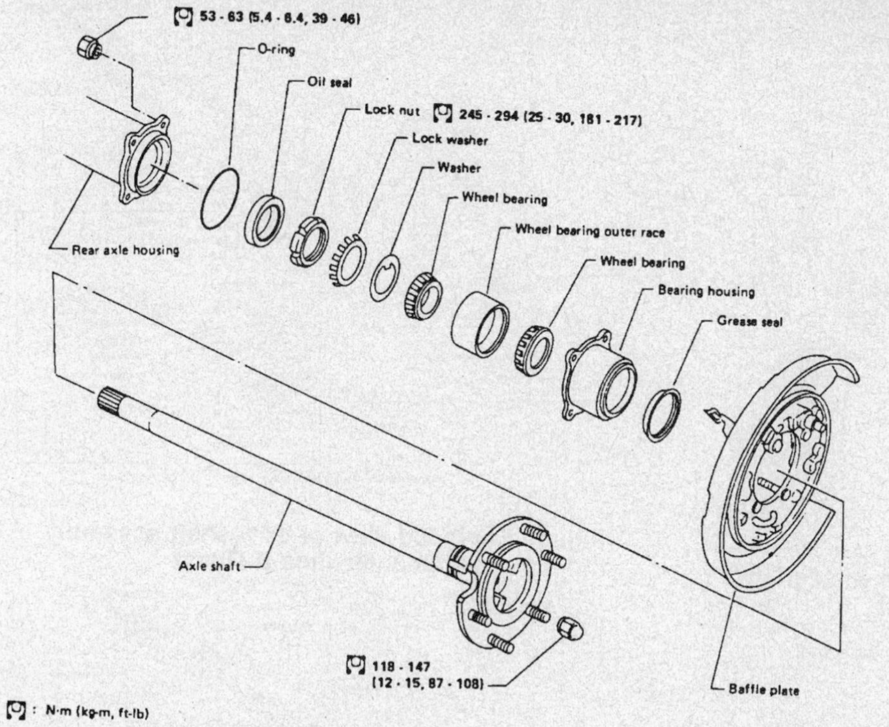
53 - 63 (5.4 - 6.4, 39 - 46)
O-ring
Oil seal
Lock nut
245 - 294 (25 - 30, 181 - 217)
Lock washer
Washer
Wheel bearing
Wheel bearing outer race
Wheel bearing
Bearing housing
Grease seal
Rear axle housing
Axle shaft
118 - 147
(12 - 15, 87 - 108)
Baffle plate
: N·m (kg-m, ft-lb)
NS3039100012000X

Fig. 1 Exploded view of wheel hub & steering knuckle assembly. Altima & Maxima

2. **Torque** tie-rod ball joint nut to 22–29 ft. lbs.
3. **Apply engine oil to threaded portion of driveshaft, then torque wheel bearing locknut to 174–231 ft. lbs.**
4. Check wheel bearing endplay. Endplay should be .002 or less.
5. Ensure wheel bearing operates smoothly.

DRIVESHAFT

REPLACE

1. Raise and support vehicle, then remove wheel.
2. Unfasten brake caliper assembly, leaving brake line attached.
3. Remove tie-rod ball joint from knuckle, then separate driveshaft from steering knuckle by tapping on driveshaft. **When removing driveshafts, cover boots with cloth to prevent damage.**
4. **On models with automatic transaxle,** if replacing both driveshafts, remove righthand driveshaft before removing lefthand driveshaft.
5. **On all models,** use a large screwdriver to pry driveshaft out of transaxle.
6. Reverse procedure to install, noting the following:
   a. Install new oil seal in transaxle.
   b. Use oil seal protector tool Nos. KV38106800 and KV38106700, or equivalents, when inserting driveshaft into transaxle.
   c. After inserting driveshaft, press-fit circular clip into groove of transaxle side gear. **After installing clip, try to pull flange out of side joint by hand. If flange pulls out, circular clip is not properly installed into side gear.**

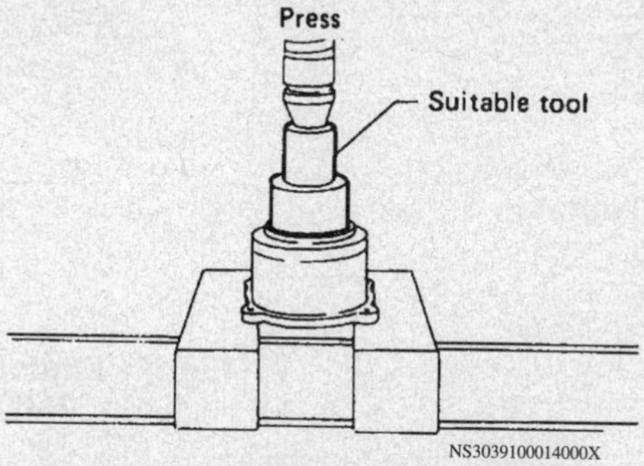
Press
Suitable tool
NS3039100014000X

Fig. 3 Exploded view of wheel hub & steering knuckle assembly. NX 1600, NX 2000, Sentra & 200SX

DRIVESHAFT SERVICE

DISASSEMBLY & INSPECTION

1. Remove boot bands from transaxle side of driveshaft, **Figs. 6 and 7.**
2. Place matching marks on slide joint housing and inner race, before separating joint assembly.
3. **On NX1600, NX2000, Sentra and 200SX models with GA16DE engine,** proceed as follows:
   a. Place matching marks on spider assembly and driveshaft.
   b. Pry off snap ring, then remove spider assembly. **Do not disassemble spider assembly.**
   c. Cover driveshaft serration with tape to prevent any damage to the boot during removal, remove boot from driveshaft.

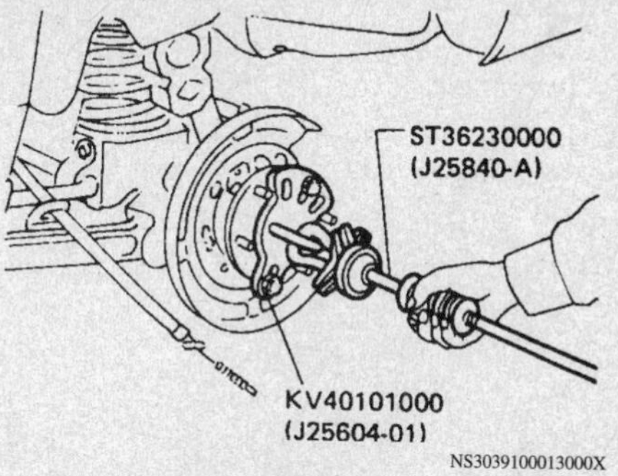
ST36230000
(J25840-A)
KV40101000
(J25604-01)
NS3039100013000X

Fig. 2 Wheel hub removal. Altima & Maxima

4. **On models except NX1600, NX2000, Sentra and 200SX with GA16DE engine,** proceed as follows:
   a. Pry snap ring "A" with a screwdriver, then pull out slide joint housing.
   b. Place matching marks on inner race and driveshaft.
   c. Pry off snap ring "C," then remove ball cage, inner race and balls as a unit.
   d. Cover driveshaft serration with tape to prevent any damage to the boot during removal, remove boot from driveshaft.
5. **On all models,** place matching marks on driveshaft and joint assembly on wheel side of driveshaft.
6. Using a slide hammer, separate joint assembly from driveshaft. **Joint assembly cannot be disassembled.**
7. Remove boot bands, then the dust shield.
8. Using snap ring pliers, remove snap ring.
9. Press support bearing assembly out of driveshaft.
10. Press support bearing out of retainer.
11. Check boots for signs of fatigue, cracks or wear.
12. Check spider assembly for needle bearing and washer damage.
13. Check roller surfaces for scratches, wear or other damage.
14. Check serration for deformation.
15. Check slide joint housing for any damage.
16. Ensure support bearing rolls freely without noise, cracks, pitting or wear.

ASSEMBLY & INSTALLATION

ALTIMA, MAXIMA & QUEST

1. Assemble wheel side of driveshaft in the reverse order of disassembly, noting the following:
   a. When installing new large boot band, lock band in place using a suitable tool.
   b. **On Altima models,** pack boot on driveshaft with 3.53–4.23 ounces of suitable grease.
   c. **On Maxima models,** pack boot on driveshaft with 7.23–7.94 ounces of suitable grease.
   d. **On Quest models,** pack boot on

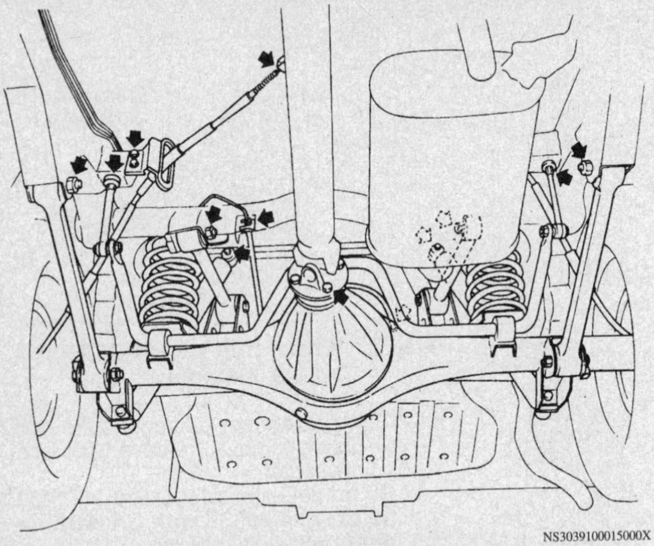
NS3039100015000X

Fig. 4 Exploded view of wheel hub & steering knuckle assembly. Quest

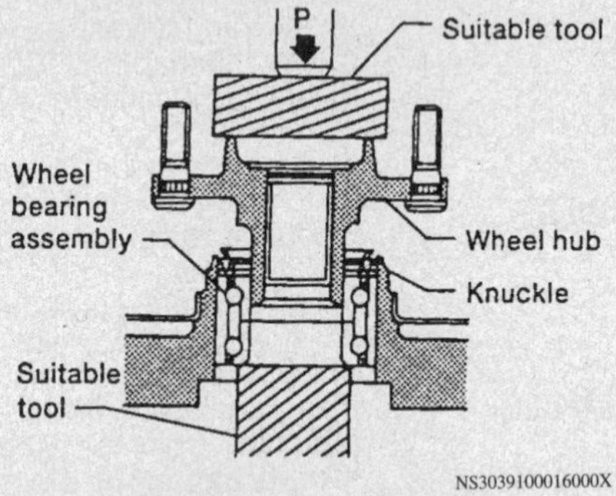
P
Suitable tool
Wheel bearing assembly
Wheel hub
Knuckle
Suitable tool
NS3039100016000X

Fig. 5 Wheel hub installation in knuckle. Quest

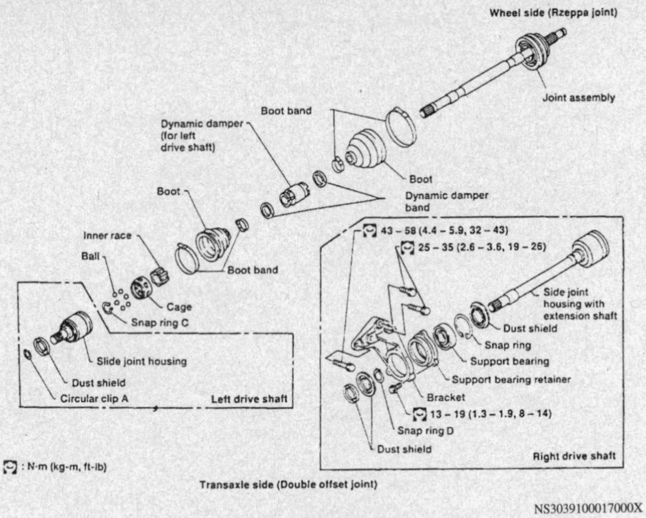
Wheel side (Rzeppa joint)
Joint assembly
Boot band
Dynamic damper (for left drive shaft)
Boot
Dynamic damper band
Boot
Inner race
Ball
Boot band
Cage
Snap ring C
Slide joint housing
Dust shield
Circular clip A
Left drive shaft
43 - 58 (4.4 - 5.9, 32 - 43)
25 - 35 (2.6 - 3.6, 19 - 26)
Side joint housing with extension shaft
Dust shield
Snap ring
Support bearing
Support bearing retainer
Bracket
13 - 19 (1.3 - 1.9, 8 - 14)
Snap ring D
Dust shield
Right drive shaft
: N·m (kg-m, ft-lb)
Transaxle side (Double offset joint)
NS3039100017000X

Fig. 6 Exploded view of driveshaft assembly. Altima, Maxima & Quest

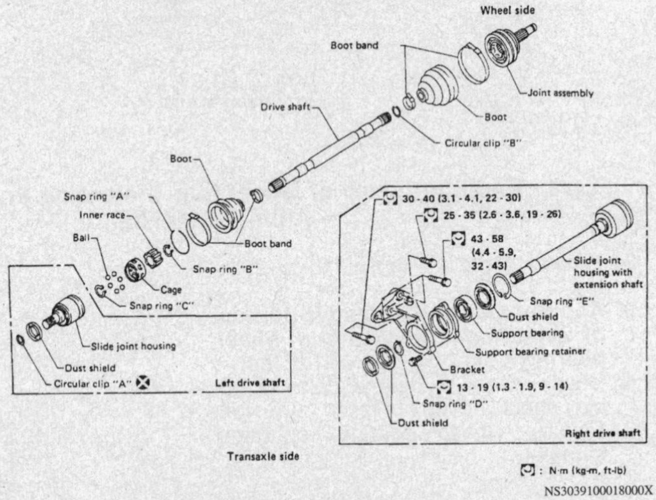
Wheel side
Boot band
Joint assembly
Drive shaft
Boot
Circular clip "B"
Boot
Snap ring "A"
Inner race
Ball
Boot band
Snap ring "B"
Cage
Snap ring "C"
Slide joint housing
Dust shield
Circular clip "A"
Left drive shaft
30 - 40 (3.1 - 4.1, 22 - 30)
25 - 35 (2.6 - 3.6, 19 - 26)
43 - 58 (4.4 - 5.9, 32 - 43)
Slide joint housing with extension shaft
Snap ring "E"
Dust shield
Support bearing
Support bearing retainer
Bracket
13 - 19 (1.3 - 1.9, 9 - 14)
Snap ring "D"
Dust shield
Right drive shaft
Transaxle side
: N·m (kg-m, ft-lb)
NS3039100018000X

Fig. 7 Exploded view of driveshaft assembly. NX 1600, NX 2000, Sentra & 200SX

driveshaft with 6.17–6.88 ounces of suitable grease.

e. **On Altima models,** adjust boot of driveshaft so length L, **Fig. 8,** is 3.327–3.406 inches.

f. **On Maxima models,** adjust boot of driveshaft so length L, **Fig. 8,** is 3.78–3.86 inches.

g. **On Quest models,** adjust boot of driveshaft so length L, **Fig. 8,** is 3.406–3.484 inches.

2. Install dynamic damper from transaxle side while holding it securely.
3. Refer to **Fig. 9** for measurement locations, then adjust driveshaft length as follows:
   a. **On Altima models,** set length "A" on lefthand side driveshaft to 8.0 inches. Set length "A" on righthand side driveshaft to 7.31 inches. Set length "B" on lefthand side driveshaft to 2.76 inches. Set length "B" on righthand side driveshaft to 1.97 inches.
   b. **On Maxima models,** set length "A" to 8.43–8.82 inches. Set length "B" to 1.97 inch.
   c. **On Quest models,** set length "A" to 7.83–8.07 inches. Set length "B" to 2.76 inch.
4. Assemble transaxle side of driveshaft in the reverse order of disassembly, noting the following:
   a. **On Altima models,** pack boot of driveshaft with 5.11–5.82 ounces of suitable grease.
   b. **On Maxima models,** pack boot of driveshaft with 5.64–6.35 ounces of suitable grease.
   c. **On Quest models,** pack boot of driveshaft with 7.41–8.11 ounces of suitable grease.
   d. **On Altima and Maxima models,** adjust boot on driveshaft so length L, **Fig. 8,** is 3.82–3.90 inches.
   e. **On Quest models,** adjust boot on driveshaft so length L, **Fig. 8,** is 3.99–4.07 inches.

NX1600, NX2000, SENTRA & 200SX

GA16DE Engine

1. Assemble transaxle side of driveshaft in reverse order of disassembly, noting the following:
   a. Pack boot with 7.94–8.29 ounces of suitable grease.
   b. Set boot so that it does not swell and deform when its length is set at 4.00–4.07 inches, **Fig. 8.**
   c. Ensure boot is properly installed on driveshaft groove, then lock new larger and smaller boot bands securely.
2. Assemble wheel side of driveshaft in reverse order of disassembly, noting the following:
   a. Pack boot with 5.47–6.17 ounces of suitable grease.
   b. Set boot so that it does not swell and deform when its length is set at 3.78–3.86 inches, **Fig. 8.**
   c. Ensure boot is properly installed on driveshaft groove, then lock new larger and smaller boot bands securely.

SR20DE Engine

1. Assemble transaxle side of driveshaft in reverse order of disassembly, noting the following:
   a. Pack boot with 4.94–5.64 ounces of suitable grease.
   b. Set boot so that it does not swell and deform when its length is set at

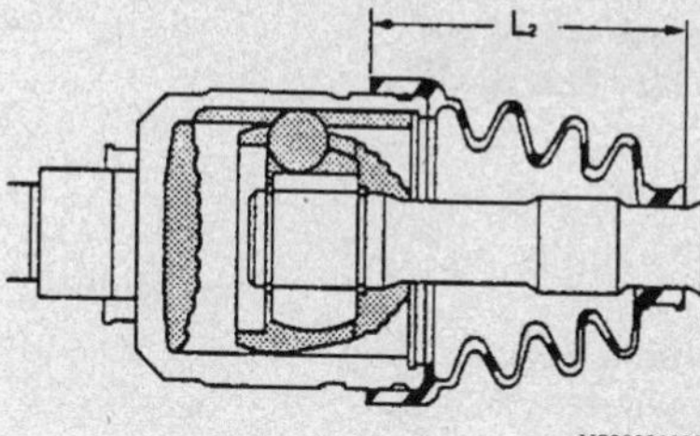
L2
NS3039100019000X

Fig. 8 Axle shaft boot installation

3.82–3.90 inches, **Fig. 8.**
c. Ensure boot is properly installed on driveshaft groove, then lock new larger and smaller boot bands securely.

2. Assemble wheel side of driveshaft in reverse order of disassembly, noting the following:
   a. Pack boot with 3.70–4.41 ounces of suitable grease.
   b. Set boot so that it does not swell and deform when its length is set at 3.917–3.996 inches, **Fig. 8.**
   c. Ensure boot is properly installed on driveshaft groove, then lock new larger and smaller boot bands securely.

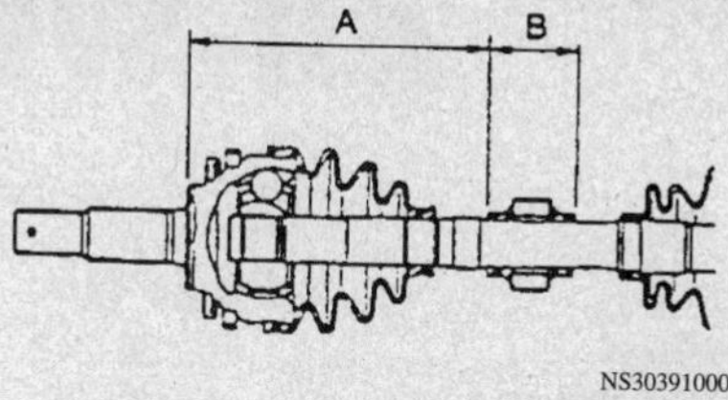
A
B
NS3039100020000X

Fig. 9 Driveshaft length measurement. Altima, Maxima & Quest

All-Wheel Drive Systems

INDEX

	Page No.
Description	36-248
Driveshaft Service	36-248
Assemble	36-248
Disassemble	36-248
On Vehicle Service	36-248
Oil Seal, Replace	36-248

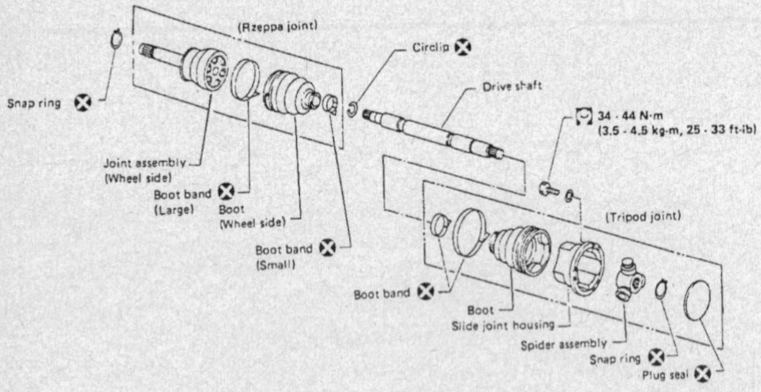

(Rzeppa joint)
Circlip
Drive shaft
Snap ring
Joint assembly (Wheel side)
Boot band (Large)
Boot (Wheel side)
Boot band (Small)
34 - 44 N·m (3.5 - 4.5 kg-m, 25 - 33 ft-lb)
(Tripod joint)
Boot band
Boot
Slide joint housing
Spider assembly
Snap ring
Plug seal
NS3039100021000X

Fig. 1 Exploded view of front driveshaft. KA24E & VG33E engine

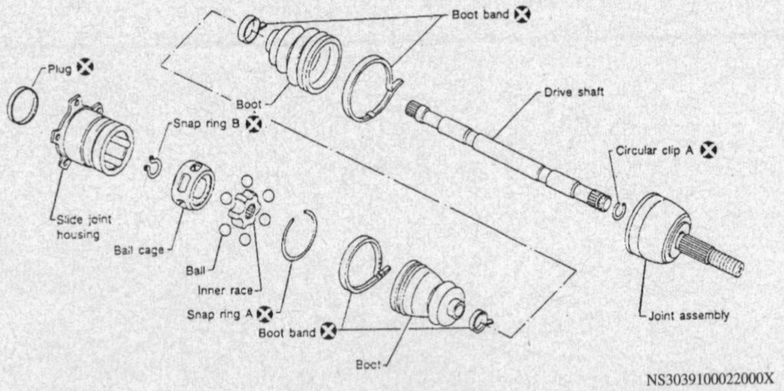

Boot band
Plug
Drive shaft
Boot
Snap ring B
Circular clip A
Slide joint housing
Ball cage
Ball
Inner race
Snap ring A
Boot band
Boot
Joint assembly
NS3039100022000X

Fig. 2 Exploded view of front driveshaft. VG30E engine

DESCRIPTION

All wheel drive models with the KA24E or VG33E engine use a TS82F driveshaft joint type. Models with the VG30E engine use a DS90 type driveshaft joint.

ON VEHICLE SERVICE

OIL SEAL, REPLACE

Front Final Drive

1. Mark then remove front propeller shaft.
2. Loosen drive pinion nut using tool No. J34331, or equivalent.
3. Remove companion flange.
4. Remove front oil seal using a suitable oil seal remover.
5. Reverse procedure to install.

Shift Shaft Oil Seal

1. Mark then remove front propeller shaft.
2. Remove companion flange.
3. Remove transfer control lever from transfer outer shift lever, then the outer shift lever.
4. Remove shift shaft oil seal using a suitable oil seal remover.
5. Reverse procedure to install.

DRIVESHAFT SERVICE

Refer to **Figs. 1 and 2** for driveshaft service.

DISASSEMBLE

TS82F Type

1. Remove plug seal from slide joint housing by lightly tapping around with suitable hammer.
2. Remove boot bands.
3. Put alignment marks in slide joint housing, then move boot and slide joint housing toward wheel side.
4. Put alignment marks on spider assembly and driveshaft.
5. Pry off snap ring, then remove spider assembly. **Do not disassemble spider assembly.**
6. Cover driveshaft serrations with suitable tape then remove boot.

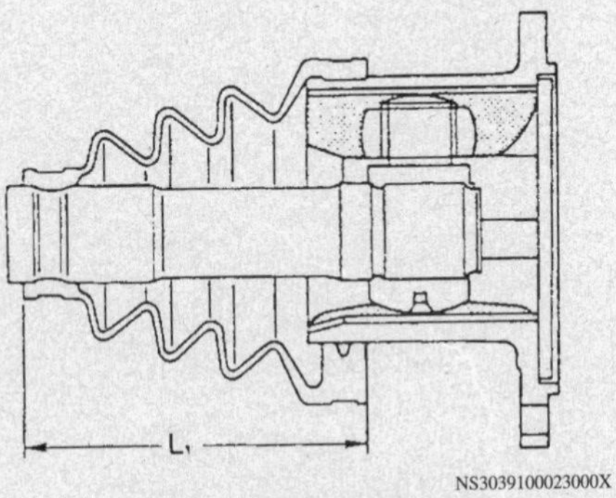

L₁
NS3039100023000X

Fig. 3 Boot length

DS90 Type

1. Remove boot bands.
2. Put alignment marks on slide joint housing and inner race, then separate joint assembly.
3. Pry off snap ring with screwdriver and pull out slide joint housing.
4. Put alignment marks on inner race and driveshaft.
5. Pry off snap ring, then remove ball cage, inner race and balls as a unit.
6. Cover driveshaft serrations with suitable tape then remove boot.

ASSEMBLE

TS82F

1. Cover driveshaft serrations with suitable tape then install boot, new small boot band and side joint housing on driveshaft.
2. Align mating marks then install spider assembly on driveshaft.
3. Install new snap ring.
4. Pack driveshaft boot and joint with 5.29–5.64 oz. of grease.
5. Install boot so that it does not swell and deform when its length is 4.02–4.09 inches, **Fig. 3.**
6. Lock new boot bands securely.
7. Install new plug seal to slide joint housing by lightly tapping it.

DS90 Type

1. Cover driveshaft serrations with suitable tape then install boot and new small boot band on driveshaft.
2. Securely install ball cage, inner race and balls as a unit, ensuring alignment marks match.
3. Install new snap ring.
4. Pack driveshaft with 6.35–7.05 oz. of grease.
5. Align mating marks then install slide joint housing on driveshaft.
6. Install boot so that it does not swell and deform when its length is 3.66–3.74 inches, **Fig. 3.**
7. Lock new boot bands securely.

Drive Axles

INDEX

Page No.

Identification Chart 36-249
Models Less Independent Rear Suspension 36-255
Assemble 36-256
Disassemble 36-255
Inspection 36-256

Page No.

R160 & R180A Differentials 36-250
Assemble 36-250
Disassemble 36-250
Inspection 36-250

Page No.

R200, R200A, R200V & R230V Differentials 36-252
Assembly 36-253
Disassemble 36-252
Inspection 36-253

IDENTIFICATION CHART

Year	Model	Axle Code	Gear Ratio
1993	Pathfinder & Pickup	C200	4.111④⑨⑩
		H190	3.545⑤⑦⑨⑩
			3.700⑤⑥⑨⑩
		H233B	3.700⑤⑦⑪⑭
			3.900⑤⑥⑪⑭
			4.625⑤⑦⑪⑬
			4.375⑤⑥⑪⑬
		H233B	4.375④⑦⑨⑪
			4.625②③④⑥⑪
			4.375②④⑥⑨⑪
			4.625①④⑥⑨⑪
		R180A	4.11④⑧⑩
		R200A	4.375④⑦⑧⑪
			4.375②④⑥⑧⑪
			4.625②④⑥⑧⑪③
			4.625①④⑥⑧⑪
	240SX	R200⑨	4.083
		R200V	4.083
	300ZX	R200V	4.083
		R230V	3.692
1994–95	Pathfinder & Pickup	C200	4.111④⑨⑩
		H190	3.545⑤⑦⑨⑩
			3.700⑤⑥⑨⑩
		H233B	3.700⑤⑦⑪⑭
			3.900⑤⑥⑪⑭
			4.625⑤⑦⑪⑬
			4.375⑤⑥⑪⑬
			4.375④⑦⑨⑪
			4.625②③④⑥⑨⑪
			4.375②④⑥⑨⑪
			4.625①④⑥⑨⑪
		R180A	4.11④⑧⑩
		R200A	4.375④⑦⑧⑪
			4.375②④⑥⑧⑪
			4.625②③④⑥⑧⑪
			4.625①④⑥⑧⑪
	240SX	R200	4.083⑨
		R200V	4.083
	300ZX	R200V	4.083
		R230V	3.692

Continued

IDENTIFICATION CHART—Continued

Year	Model	Axle Code	Gear Ratio
1996	Pathfinder	H233B	4.363⑤⑥⑫
			4.363④⑥⑨⑫
			4.636①④⑥⑨⑫
		R200A	4.363④⑥⑧⑫
			4.636①④⑥⑧⑫
	Pickup	C200A	3.900①⑤⑦⑨⑩
		H190A	3.545②⑤⑦⑨⑩
			4.111⑤⑥⑨⑩
		H233B	4.625④⑨⑩
		R180A	4.625fd④⑩
	240SX	R200	4.083⑨
		R200V	4.083
	300ZX	R200V	4.083
		R230V	3.692

① — SE models.
② — Except SE models.
③ — Models equipped with optional tire size 31 X 10.5R15LT and P235/75.
④ — 4WD.
⑤ — 2WD.
⑥ — Automatic transmission.
⑦ — Manual transmission.
⑧ — Front differential.
⑨ — Limited Slip Differential optional.
⑩ — KA24E engine.
⑪ — VG30E engine.
⑫ — VG33E engine.
⑬ — Heavy duty.
⑭ — Light duty.

R160 & R180A DIFFERENTIALS

DISASSEMBLE

1. **On R180A differentials,** remove extension tube and differential side shaft assembly, then remove differential side flange.
2. **On all models,** remove side retainers, **Fig. 1.**
3. Remove differential case from carrier.
4. When replacing side bearing, extract bearing outer race from side retainer.
5. Loosen drive pinion nut, holding companion flange and pull off companion flange using a suitable puller.
6. Press drive pinion from carrier using a press. Remove drive pinion with rear bearing cone, bearing spacer and adjusting washers.
7. Remove oil seal.
8. Remove pinion bearing with pinion bearing spacer and front bearing cone.
9. Press rear bearing inner race from drive pinion.
10. Drive out front and rear bearing outer races and remove bearing.
11. Remove ring gear.
12. **On R180A differentials,** place match marks on right and left hand side differential cases, then remove bolts and separate them.
13. **On R160 differentials,** remove pinion mate shaft lockpin from ring gear side. **Lockpin is caulked at pin hole mouth on differential case.**
14. **On all models,** remove pinion mate shaft and the pinion mate gears, side gears and thrust washers.

EXTENSION SHAFT & DIFFERENTIAL SIDE SHAFT

R180A Differential

1. Remove differential side shaft assembly from extension tube.
2. Cut rear axle bearing collar with cold chisel being careful not to damage differential side shaft, **Fig. 2.**
3. Reinstall differential side shaft into extension tube and secure with bolts. Remove rear axle bearing by drawing out differential side shaft from rear axle bearing with puller, **Fig. 3.**
4. Remove grease seal.

INSPECTION

Thoroughly clean all disassembled parts, and examine them to see that they are worn, damaged or otherwise faulty, and how they are affected. Repair or replace all faulty parts, whichever is necessary.

1. Check gear teeth for scoring, cracking or chipping, and make sure that tooth contact pattern indicates correct meshing depth. If any fault is evident, replace parts as required. **Drive pinion and drive gear are supplied as a set; therefore, should either part be damaged, replace as a set.**
2. Check pinion gear shaft, and pinion gear for scores and signs of wear, and replace as required. Follow the same procedure for side gear and their seats on differential case.
3. Inspect all bearing races and rollers for scoring, chipping or evidence of excessive wear.
4. Inspect thrust washer faces. Small faults can be corrected with sandpaper. Inspect pinion mate-to-side gear backlash, **Fig. 4.** If clearance between side gear and thrust washer exceeds .0039–.0079 inch, replace thrust washers.
5. Inspect carrier and differential case for cracks or distortion. If either condition is evident, replace faulty parts.

ASSEMBLE

Reverse "Disassemble" procedure to assemble and note the following:

GEAR CASE ASSEMBLY

R160 Differential

1. Assemble pinion mates, side gears and thrust washers in differential case.
2. Install pinion shaft to differential case.
3. Adjust side gear-to-pinion mate backlash by selecting side gear thrust washers. Backlash should be .0039–.0079 inch.
4. Lock pinion shaft lockpin using a punch after secured into place.
5. Apply oil to gear tooth surfaces and thrust surfaces and check if they turn properly.
6. Place ring gear on differential case and **torque** bolts to 65–72 ft. lbs.

R180A Differential

1. Measure clearance between side gear thrust washer and differential case at dimensions A & B, **Fig. 5,** then subtract value B from A. Clearance should be .0039–.0079 inch. If measurement does not fall within specifications, clearance can be adjusted with a side gear thrust washer.
2. Apply gear oil to gear tooth surfaces and thrust surfaces and check if they turn properly.
3. Install left and right hand differential

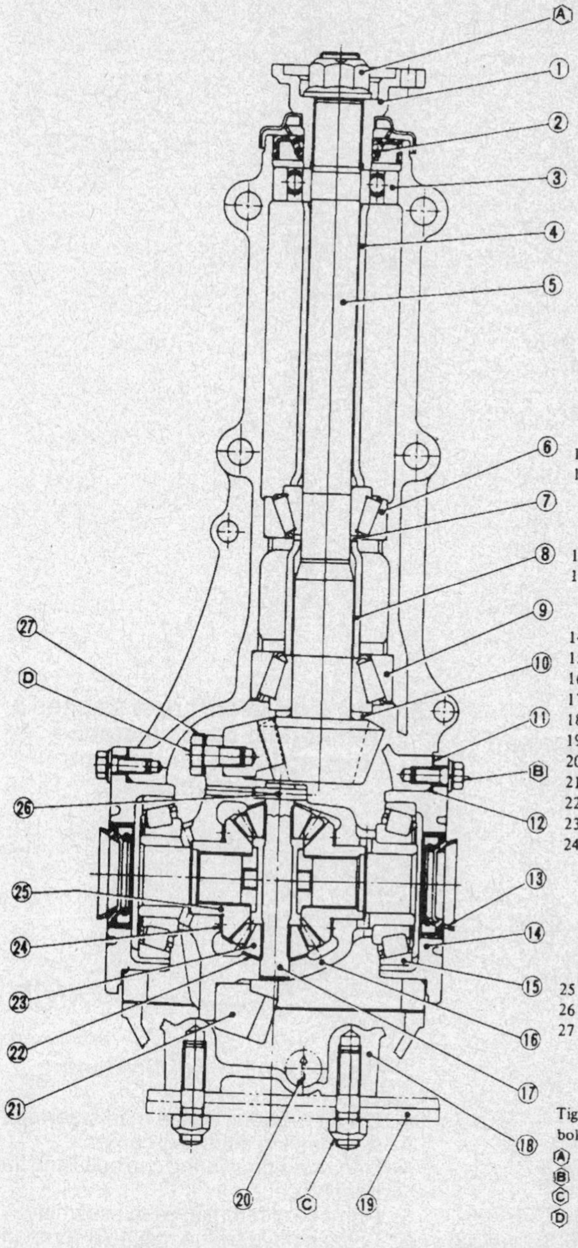
A
B
C
D
1 Companion flange
2 Oil seal
Supply multi-purpose grease to oil seal lip when assembling
3 Front pilot bearing
4 Front pilot bearing spacer
5 Drive pinion
6 Pinion front bearing
7 Pinion bearing adjusting washer
Adjust pinion bearing preload by selecting ⑦ and ⑧
8 Pinion bearing adjusting spacer
9 Pinion rear bearing
10 Pinion height adjusting washer
11 Side retainer adjusting shim
Adjust side bearing preload and ring gear-to-drive pinion backlash by selecting ⑪.
12 O-ring
13 Oil seal
Supply multi-purpose grease to oil seal lip when assembling.
14 Side retainer
15 Side bearing
16 Differential case
17 Pinion mate shaft
18 Rear cover
19 Differential mounting member
20 Breather
21 Ring gear
22 Thrust washer
23 Pinion mate
24 Thrust washer
Adjust the pinion mate-to-side gear backlash (or the clearance between the rear face of side gear and thrust washer) to 0.1 to 0.2 mm (0.0039 to 0.0079 in) by ㉔.
25 Side gear
26 Lock pin
27 Lock strap
Tightening torque (T) of bolts and nuts kg-m (ft-lb)
Ⓐ T : 17 to 20 (123 to 145)
Ⓑ T : 0.9 to 1.2 (6.5 to 8.7)
Ⓒ T : 6 to 8 (43 to 58)
Ⓓ T : 7 to 8 (51 to 58)
NS3039100024000X

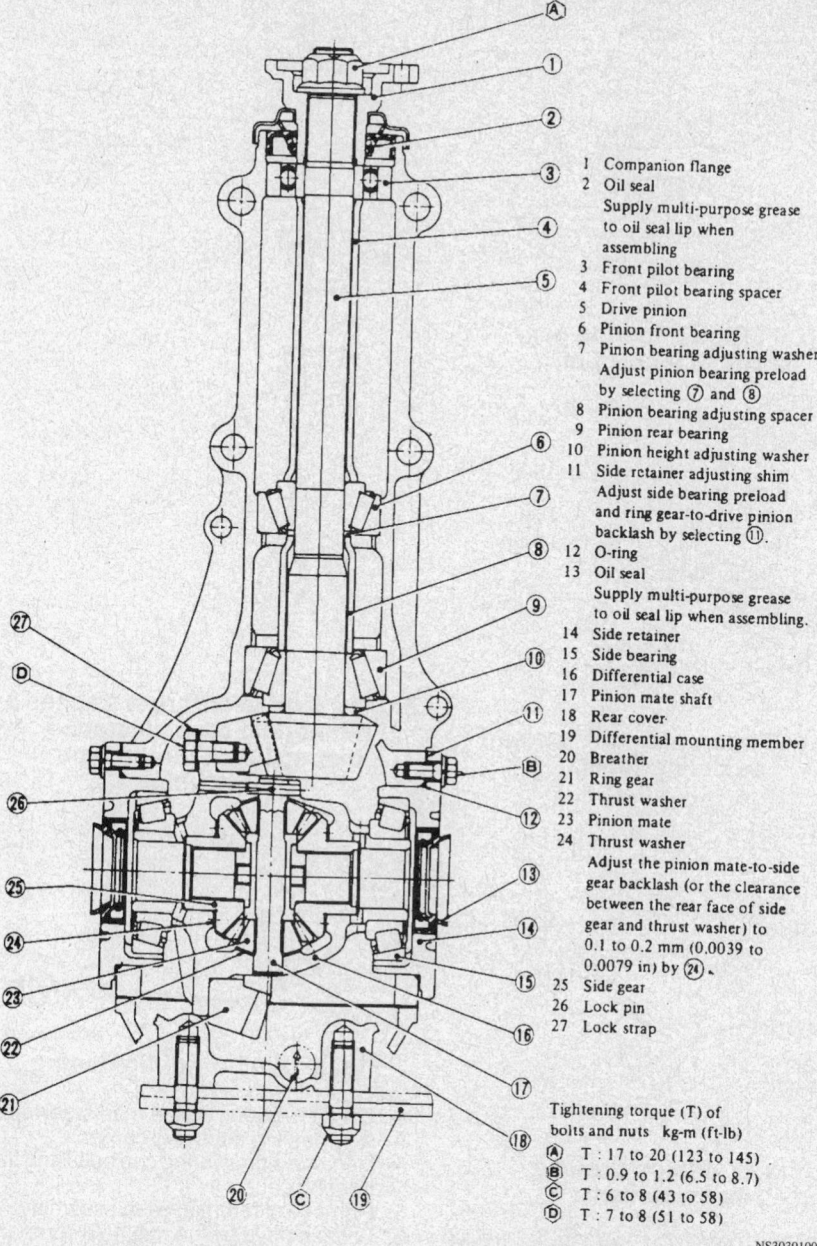

Fig. 1 Cross-sectional view of differential carrier

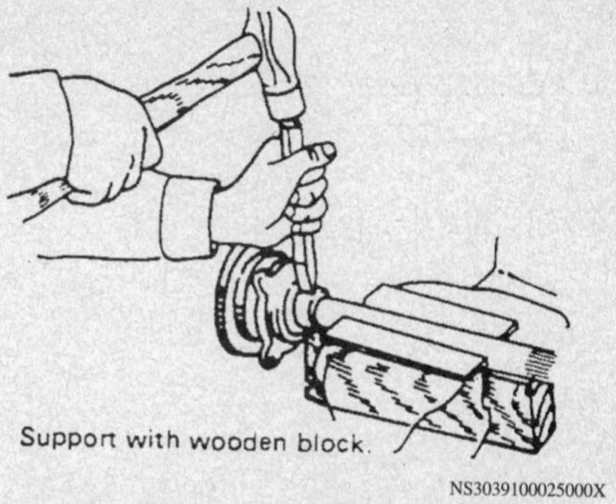
Support with wooden block.
NS3039100025000X

Fig. 2 Cutting axle bearing collar. R180A & R200A differentials

cases together.

EXTENSION TUBE & DIFFERENTIAL SIDE SHAFT

R180A Differential

1. Measure extension tube at dimension A and dimension B, **Fig. 6,** then subtract value B from value A. Axle bearing endplay should be .0039 or less. If it is not, axle bearing endplay can be adjusted with bearing adjusting shims.
2. Using bearing driver tool No. J35764, or equivalent, install grease seal.
3. Install extension tube retainer, axle bearing and axle shaft bearing collar on differential side shaft.
4. Install differential side shaft assembly into extension tube.

DRIVE PINION PRELOAD ADJUSTMENT

Adjust preload of drive pinion with spacer and washer between front and rear bearing cones, regardless of thickness of pinion height adjusting washer.

This adjustment must be performed without oil seal inserted.

1. Press front and rear bearing outer races into gear carrier.
2. Insert pinion height adjusting washer of .1217 inch thickness and rear bearing cone into Dummy Shaft tool No. ST31212000, or equivalent, to make convenient to adjust pinion height, **Fig. 7.**
3. Install drive pinion bearing spacer, washer, front bearing cone, Drive Pinion Dummy Collar tool No. ST31214000, or equivalent, and companion flange on dummy shaft and tighten drive pinion nut using Stopper tool No. ST31852000, or equivalent, **Fig. 8.** Measure pinion bearing preload using Preload Gauge tool No. ST3127S000, or equivalent, and select washer and spacer that will provide required preload, **Fig. 9.**

DRIVE PINION HEIGHT ADJUSTMENT

Adjust pinion height with washer provided between rear bearing cone and back of pinion gear.

1. Install height gauge tool No. ST31211000, or equivalent, on carrier with dummy shaft mounted, **Fig. 10.**
2. Measure the clearance (N) between the tip end of height gauge and the end surface of dummy shaft, using a thickness gauge, **Fig. 10.**
3. The thickness of drive pinion height adjusting washer can be obtained from the following formula: T= WN-(H-D'-S) X 0.01 - 0.20 where T = required thickness of rear bearing adjusting washers in millimeters, W = thickness of washers temporarily inserted in millimeters, N = measured value with thickness gauge in millimeters, H = figure marked on the drive pinion head, D' = figure marked on the dummy shaft, S = figure marked on the height gauge and figures for H, D' and S are dimensional variations in a unit 1/100mm against each standard measurement. **If values signifying H, D' and S are not given, regard them as zero and compute.**
4. Install determined pinion height adjusting washer in drive pinion, and press rear bearing cone in, using Base tool No. ST30901000, or equivalent.
5. Lubricate pinion front and rear bearings. Install drive pinion in gear carrier and the drive pinion bearing spacer and washer, front bearing cone and front bearing pilot spacer, pilot bearing and the front oil seal.
6. Install companion flange on drive pinion and **torque** nut to 123–145 ft. lbs.

SIDE BEARING RETAINER SHIMS

1. If the hypoid gear set, carrier, differential case, side bearing or side bearing retainer has been replaced with a new

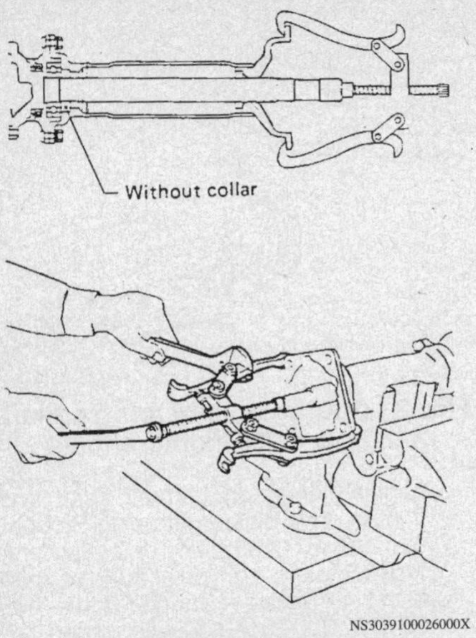
Without collar
NS3039100026000X

Fig. 3 Axle bearing removal. R180A differential

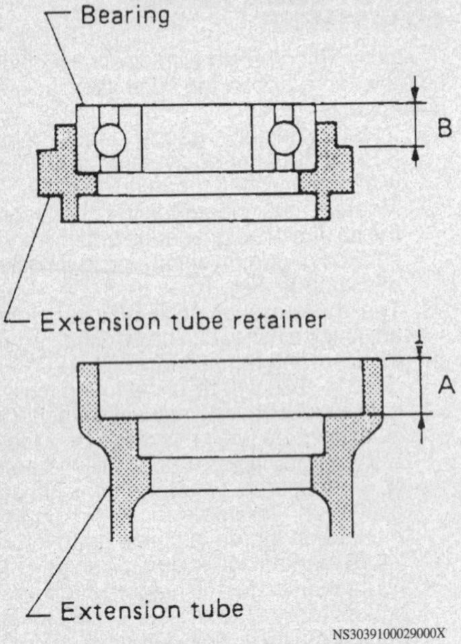
Bearing
B
Extension tube retainer
A
Extension tube
NS3039100029000X

Fig. 6 Axle bearing endplay inspection. R180A & R200A differentials

part, adjust the side bearing preload with adjusting shim. The required thickness of the right and left retainer shims can be obtained from the following formulas: T1= (ACG1-D) X 0.01 0.76-E; T2= (BDG2) X 0.01 0.76-F; where, T1 = required thickness of left side retainer shim in millimeters, **Fig. 11,** T2 = required thickness of right side retainer shim in millimeters, **Fig. 11,** A & B = figures marked on the gear carrier, **Fig. 12,** C & D = figures marked on the differential case, **Fig. 13,** E & F = differences in width of left or right side bearing against the standard width (20mm) in millimeters, **Fig. 14** (measure bearing width using master gauge KV38101900 and weight block

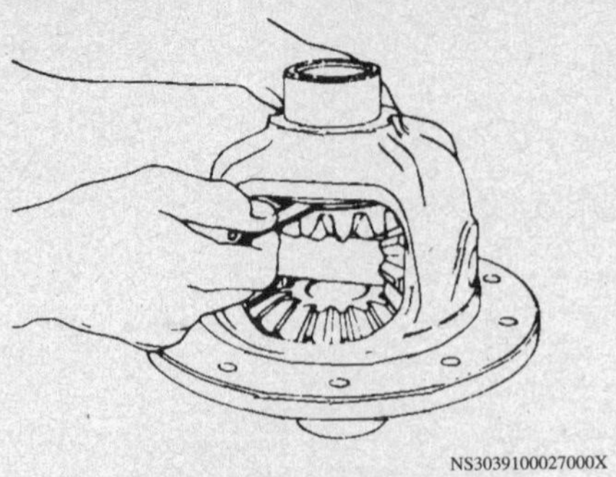
NS3039100027000X

Fig. 4 Pinion to side gear backlash inspection

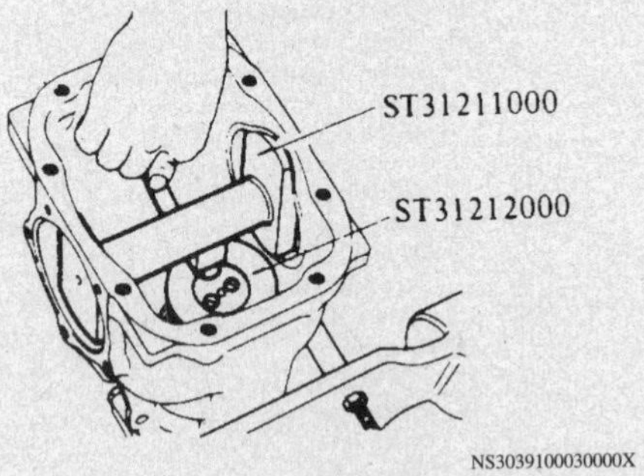
ST31211000
ST31212000
NS3039100030000X

Fig. 7 Pinion height & preload adjusting tools

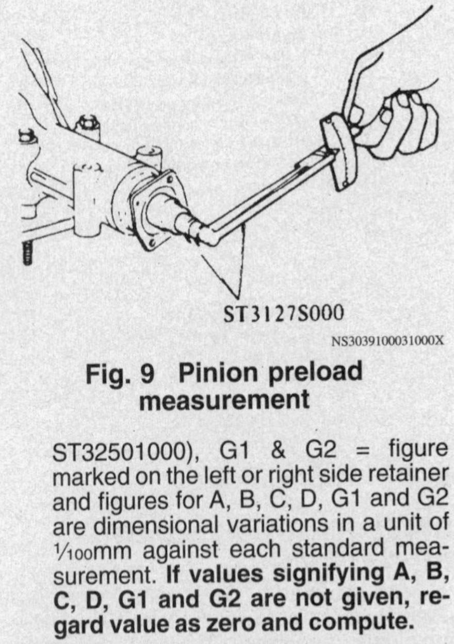
ST3127S000
NS3039100031000X

Fig. 9 Pinion preload measurement

ST32501000), G1 & G2 = figure marked on the left or right side retainer and figures for A, B, C, D, G1 and G2 are dimensional variations in a unit of 1/100mm against each standard measurement. **If values signifying A, B, C, D, G1 and G2 are not given, regard value as zero and compute.**

R200, R200A, R200V & R230V DIFFERENTIALS

DISASSEMBLE

1. **On R200A differentials,** remove extension tube and differential side shaft assembly, then remove differential side flange.
2. **On R200, R200V and R230V differentials,** remove differential side flange, **Fig. 15.**

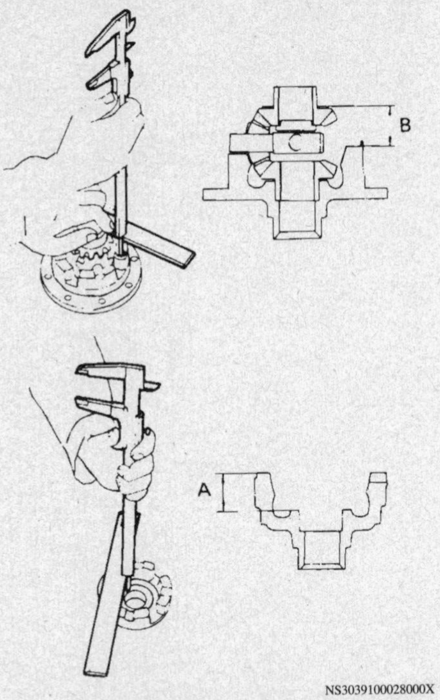
B
A
NS3039100028000X

Fig. 5 Side gear thrust washer & differential case clearance inspection. 4 pinion type differential

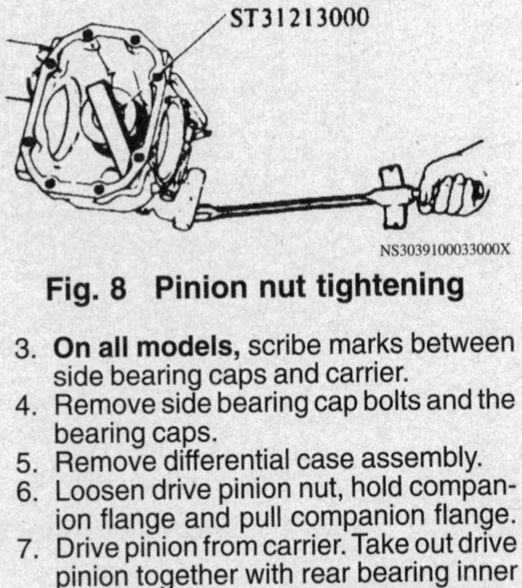
ST31213000
NS3039100033000X

Fig. 8 Pinion nut tightening

3. **On all models,** scribe marks between side bearing caps and carrier.
4. Remove side bearing cap bolts and the bearing caps.
5. Remove differential case assembly.
6. Loosen drive pinion nut, hold companion flange and pull companion flange.
7. Drive pinion from carrier. Take out drive pinion together with rear bearing inner race, bearing spacer and adjusting washer.
8. Remove oil seal.
9. Remove pilot bearing with pilot bearing spacer and front bearing inner race.
10. Remove side oil seal.
11. Press rear bearing inner race from drive pinion.
12. Drive out front and rear bearing outer races.

DIFFERENTIAL SIDE SHAFT

R200A Differential

1. Cut rear axle bearing collar with cold chisel being careful not to damage differential side shaft, **Fig. 2.**
2. Reinstall differential side shaft into extension tube and secure with bolts. Remove rear axle bearing by drawing out

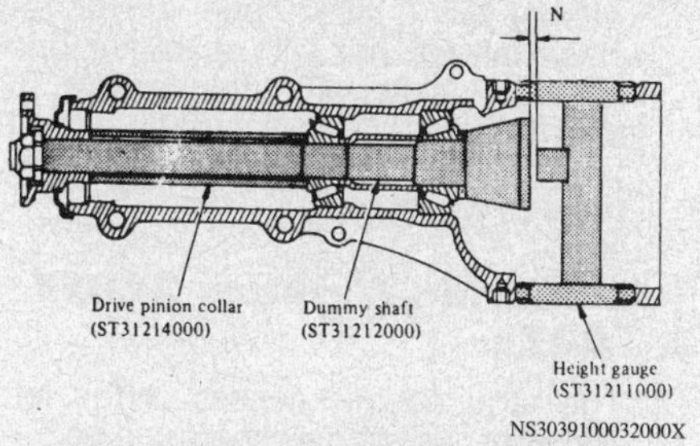
N
Drive pinion collar
(ST31214000)
Dummy shaft
(ST31212000)
Height gauge
(ST31211000)
NS3039100032000X

Fig. 10 Drive pinion height measurement

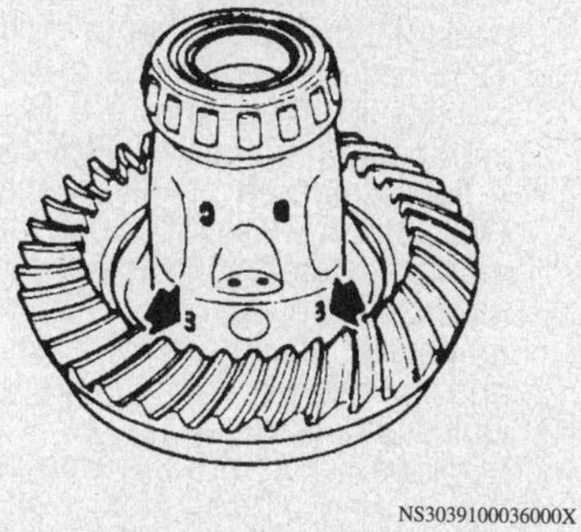
NS3039100036000X

Fig. 13 Location of C & D values

differential side shaft from rear axle bearing with puller, **Fig. 16.**
3. Remove grease and oil seal.

R200 & R200A Differential Case

1. Remove bearing.
2. Remove ring gear.
3. Remove pinion mate shaft lockpin from ring gear side. **Lockpin is caulked at pin hole mouth on differential case.**
4. Remove pinion mate shaft and the pinion mate gears, side gears, thrust washers and thrust block, if equipped.

R200V & R230V Differential Case

1. Remove bearing.
2. Remove ring gear.
3. Place match marks on differential cases A and B.
4. Loosen screws and separate differential cases A and B.

INSPECTION

Refer to "Inspection" as described under "Models w/Independent Rear Suspension," "Except 300ZX w/R200 Differential."

ASSEMBLY

Reverse "Disassembly" procedure to assemble and note the following:

GEAR CASE

R200, R200V & R230V Differentials

1. **On R200 differentials,** assemble pinion mates, side gears, thrust washers, and thrust block, if equipped, in differential case.
2. **On all models,** install pinion shaft to differential case.

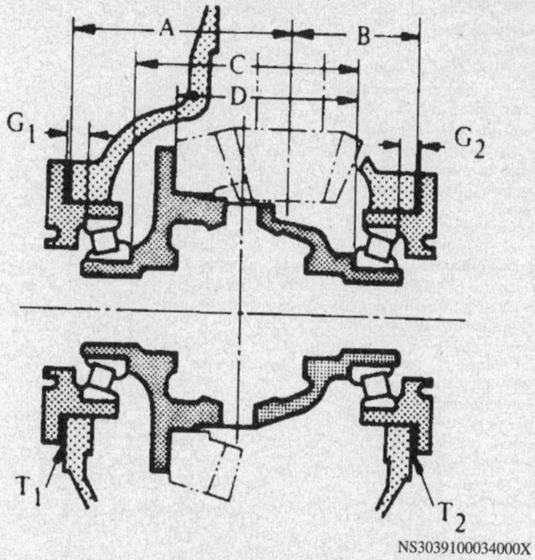
A
B
C
D
G_1
G_2
T_1
T_2
NS3039100034000X

Fig. 11 Side bearing retainer shim thickness

3. Adjust side gear-to-pinion mate backlash or adjust the clearance between the rear face of side gear and thrust washer. Backlash or clearance should be .0039–.0079 inch, .0059 inch with tripod type driveshaft.
4. Lock pinion shaft lockpin.
5. Apply oil to gear tooth surfaces and thrust surfaces and check that they turn properly.
6. **On R200V and R230V differentials,** install differential case A to B.
7. **On all differentials,** place ring gear on differential case and apply a small amount of locking compound to the bolts, then install bolts.
8. **Torque** bolts to 51–58 ft. lbs.
9. Measure bearing width with a standard gauge (21.00mm thickness) and a weight block, about 5.5 lbs., prior to installation, **Fig. 17.**
10. Press side bearing inner race on differential case.

R200A Differential

1. Measure clearance between side gear thrust washer and differential case at dimensions A & B, **Fig. 5,** then subtract value B from A. Clearance should be .0039–.0079 inch. If measurement does not fall within specifications, clearance can be adjusted with a side gear thrust washer.
2. Apply gear oil to gear tooth surfaces and thrust surfaces and check if they turn properly.
3. Install left and right hand differential cases together.

DIFFERENTIAL SIDE SHAFT

R200A Differential

1. Measure extension tube at dimension A and dimension B, **Fig. 6,** then subtract value B from value A. Axle bearing endplay should be .0039 or less. If it is not, axle bearing endplay can be adjusted with bearing adjusting shims.
2. Using driver tool No. J26233, or equivalent, install grease seal.
3. Install extension tube retainer, axle bearing and axle shaft bearing collar on differential side shaft.

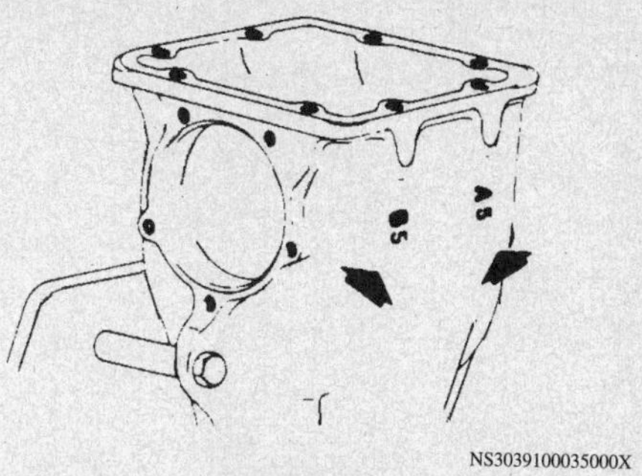
NS3039100035000X

Fig. 12 Location of A & B values

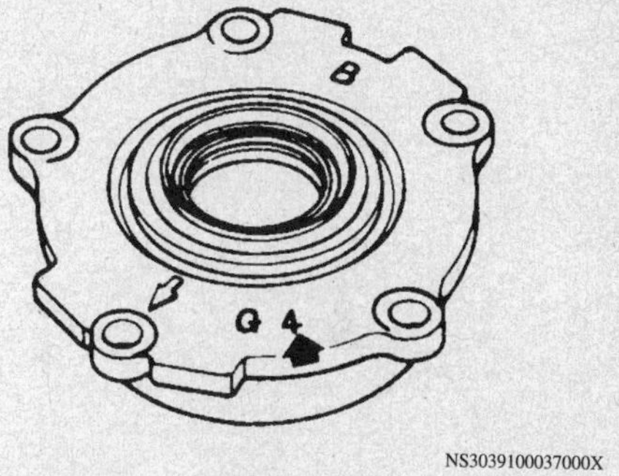
B
G 4
NS3039100037000X

Fig. 14 Location of G1 & G2 values

Drive Pinion Height & Preload, 240SX & 300ZX

1. Before adjusting pinion height and drive pinion bearing preload, set up each tool, rear pinion bearing and front pinion bearing as follows:
   a. Install rear pinion bearing pilot into gauge plate and slide over hex head long bolt, **Fig. 18.**
   b. Slide pinion rear bearing inner race, bearing preload adapter and pinion bearing adjusting spacer over hex head long bolt, **Fig. 19.**
   c. Install hex head long bolt assembly into gear carrier.
   d. Stand front bearing pilot support on workbench with appropriate side up and assemble front pinion bearing pilot, front pinion bearing inner race and lead preload washer, ensuring that all parts are seated, **Fig. 19.**
   e. Install assembly, **Fig. 20,** over hex head long bolt into gear carrier. Install and finger tighten support nut, ensuring that all parts turn freely and that they are properly aligned.
   f. Carefully tighten support nut to obtain preload of 5.2–8.7 inch lbs.
2. Install two side bearing discs with arbor assembly, ensuring that arbor turns freely, **Fig. 21.**
3. Place side bearing discs with arbor assembly into differential carrier, lifting spring loaded plunger and placing it on face of gauge plate, **Fig. 22.**
4. Install bearing caps.
5. Install dial indicator and tighten hold-down clamp, **Fig. 23.**
6. Zero dial indicator by rotating arbor and plunger back and forth while noting highest deflection, then set indicator at zero.

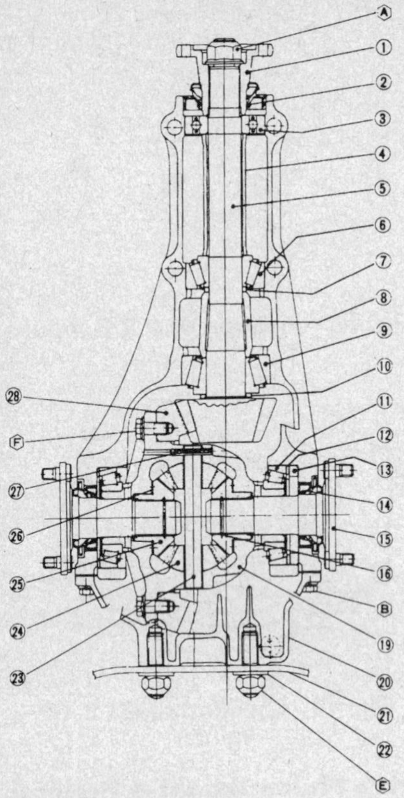
A
1
2
3
4
5
6
7
8
9
10
11
12
13
14
15
16
B
19
20
21
22
E
28
F
27
26
25
24
23

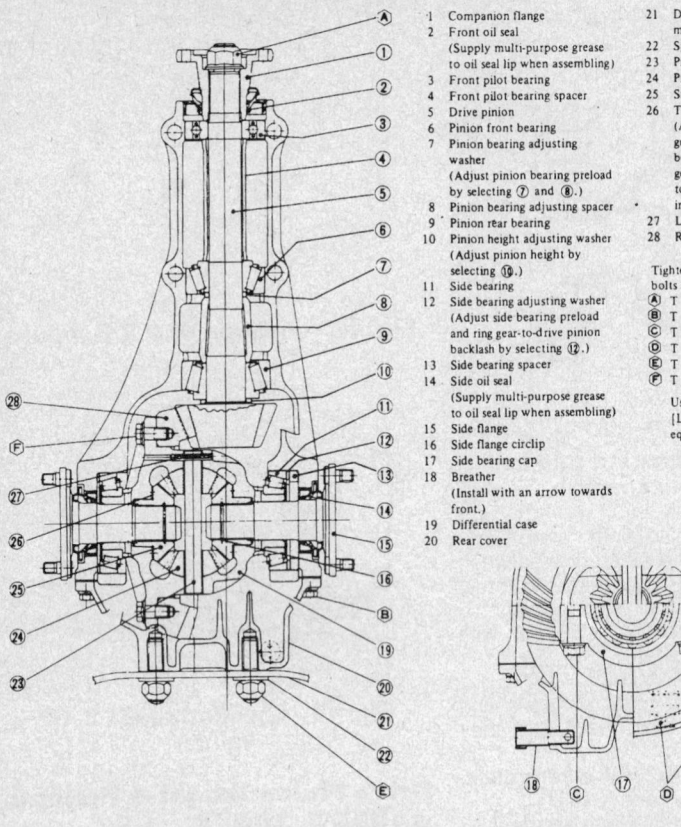

1 Companion flange
2 Front oil seal
(Supply multi-purpose grease to oil seal lip when assembling)
3 Front pilot bearing
4 Front pilot bearing spacer
5 Drive pinion
6 Pinion front bearing
7 Pinion bearing adjusting washer
(Adjust pinion bearing preload by selecting ⑦ and ⑧.)
8 Pinion bearing adjusting spacer
9 Pinion rear bearing
10 Pinion height adjusting washer
(Adjust pinion height by selecting ⑩.)
11 Side bearing
12 Side bearing adjusting washer
(Adjust side bearing preload and ring gear-to-drive pinion backlash by selecting ⑫.)
13 Side bearing spacer
14 Side oil seal
(Supply multi-purpose grease to oil seal lip when assembling)
15 Side flange
16 Side flange circlip
17 Side bearing cap
18 Breather
(Install with an arrow towards front.)
19 Differential case
20 Rear cover
21 Differential rear mounting member
22 Special washer
23 Pinion mate shaft
24 Pinion mate
25 Side gear
26 Thrust washer
(Adjust the pinion mate-to-side gear backlash (or the clearance between the rear face of side gear and thrust washer) to 0.1 to 0.2 mm (0.039 to 0.0079 in) by ㉖.)
27 Lock pin
28 Ring gear

Tightening torque (T) of bolts and nuts kg-m (ft-lb)
Ⓐ T : 19 to 22 (137 to 159)
Ⓑ T : 1.6 to 2.4 (12 to 17)
Ⓒ T : 9.0 to 10.0 (65 to 72)
Ⓓ T : 4.2 to 6.9 (30 to 50)
Ⓔ T : 7.5 to 9.5 (54 to 69)
Ⓕ T : 6.0 to 7.0 (43 to 51)

Using locking agent
[Locktite (stud lock) or equivalent]

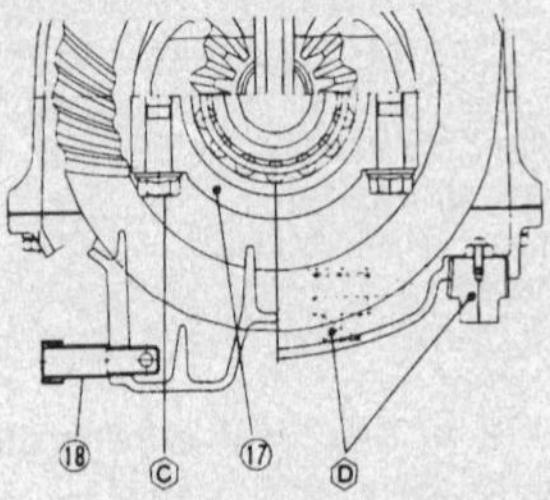
18
C
17
D

NS3039100038000X

Fig. 15 Cross-sectional view of differential carrier

7. Rotate gauge plate until plunger falls off gauge plate and record reading of dial indicator.
8. Note head number on drive pinion head.
9. Calculate washer thickness as follows:
   a. Add dial indicator reading to 3mm.
   b. Using drive pinion head number, subtract it from sum obtained in step 9a if head number is plus (+) or add if head number is minus (-).
   c. Select proper replacement washer equal to total obtained in step 9b. If washer is not available in calculated thickness, use washer whose thickness is closest to calculated thickness.
10. To determine pinion bearing preload, disassemble pinion height/bearing preload tools and measure thickness of lead washer. This is correct size pinion bearing adjusting washer required.
11. If shims are not available in determined thickness, use shims so that total thickness is closest to calculated value. **Sometimes the correct dimension cannot be set with washers only. If this is the case, washers may be used in combination with drive pinion bearing adjusting spacers.**

Side Bearing Washers, Except 240SX & 300ZX

1. If the hypoid gear set, carrier, differential case or side bearing has been replaced with new part, adjust the side bearing preload with adjusting washer. The required thicknesses of the left and right washers can be obtained from the following formulas: T1 = (A-CD-H') X 0.01 2.05; T2 = (B-DH') X 0.01 1.95; where T1 = required thickness of left side washer in millimeters, **Fig. 24,** T2 = required thickness of right side washer in millimeters, **Fig. 24,** A & B = figure marked on the gear carrier, **Fig. 25,** C & D = figure marked on the differential case, **Fig. 26,** E & F = differences in width of left or right side bearing against the standard width (21.00mm) and figures for A, B, C and D are dimensional variations in a unit of 1/100mm against each standard measurement. The decrease or increase in thickness of washers causes change in ring gear-to-pinion backlash. Before calculation, determine "G" value by measuring spacer thickness. If spacer is deformed or scratched, replace. **If values signifying A, B, C and D are not given, regard value as zero and compute.**
2. Install differential case assembly with side bearing outer races into carrier.
3. Insert left and right side bearing preload adjusting washers in place between side bearings and housing.
4. Drive in side bearing spacer between righthand washer and housing.
5. Align mark on bearing cap with that on carrier and install bearing cap on carrier. **Torque** bolts to 65–72 ft. lbs.
6. **Measure** ring gear-to-drive pinion backlash with a dial indicator and adjust to .0051–.0071 inch, **Fig. 27.** If below the specified value, replace left washer with a thinner one and right washer with a thicker one. If over, replace left washer with a thicker one and right washer with a thinner one. **To maintain correct preload at all times, do not change total thickness of washers.**

Side Bearing Washers, 240SX & 300ZX

1. The required thicknesses of the left and right adjusting washers can be obtained from the following formulas: T1 = A - C D E - H 2.05mm; T2 = B - D F G H 1.95mm; where T1 = required thickness of left side washer in millimeters, T2 = required thickness of right side washer in millimeters, A & B = figure marked on gear carrier, **Fig. 25,** C & D = figure marked on differential case, **Fig. 26,** E & F = side bearing measurements as determined in step 2, G = difference between 8.10mm and measured thickness of side spacer and H = figure marked on ring gear.
2. Calculate how far under standard thickness of 21mm the side bearings are using tool Nos. J25407-1, J25407-2 and J25407-3, or equivalents, as follows:
   a. Set weight block, 4 step gauge block and dial indicator on base plate.
   b. Adjust dial indicator to zero.
   c. Carefully slide 4 step gauge block and weight block out from under dial indicator.
   d. Lubricate side bearing and place side bearing on base plate, ensuring that base plate has recess in it and that bearing will turn freely when positioned over recess.
   e. Place weight block on side bearing.
   f. Slide dial indicator onto weight block.
   g. Rotate weight block several times to ensure bearing is properly seated.
   h. Read dial indicator. Indicator should read .10–.30mm. **If needle fluctuates erratically, bearing is either dirty or defective and should be cleaned or replaced as necessary.**
   i. Measurement obtained for left side bearing is measurement E, step 1 and measurement obtained for right side bearing is measurement F.
3. Press in front and rear bearing outer races.
4. Install selected pinion height adjusting washer in drive pinion and press in rear bearing inner race.
5. Set drive pinion assembly in differential carrier and install drive pinion with suitable tool.
6. Apply suitable lubricant to cavity at sealing lips of oil seal, then install front oil seal.
7. Install companion flange and **torque** pinion nut to 137–159 ft. lbs.
8. Turn drive pinion in both directions several times, then measure pinion bearing preload. If preload is not 10–15.2 inch lbs., replace pinion bearing

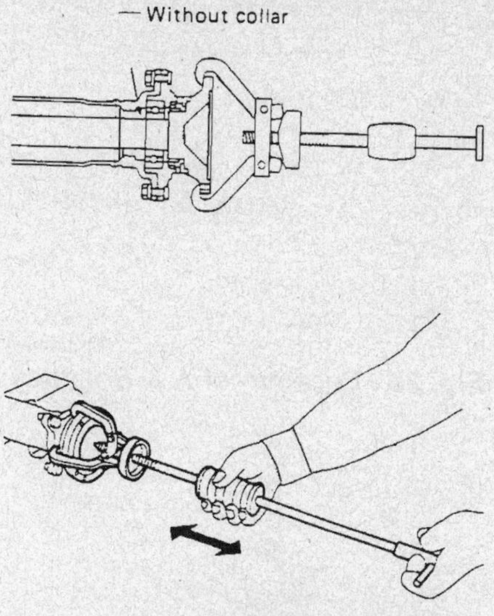
Without collar

NS3039100039000X

Fig. 16 Axle bearing removal. R200A differential

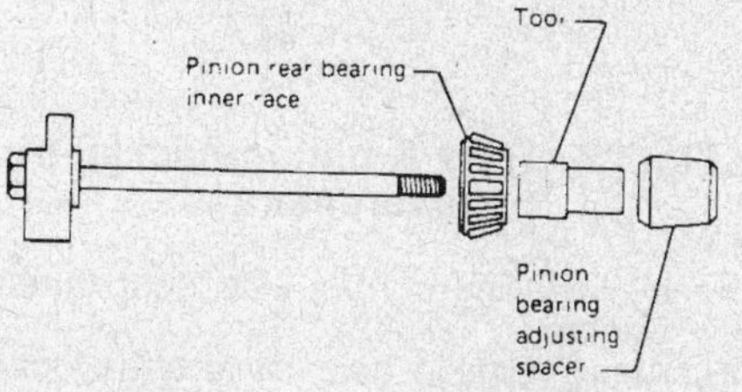
Tool
Pinion rear bearing inner race
Pinion bearing adjusting spacer

Tool number:

Bearing preload adapter (J25269-26)

NS3039100042000X

Fig. 19 Bearing preload adapter & pinion bearing adjusting spacer installation on hex head long bolt

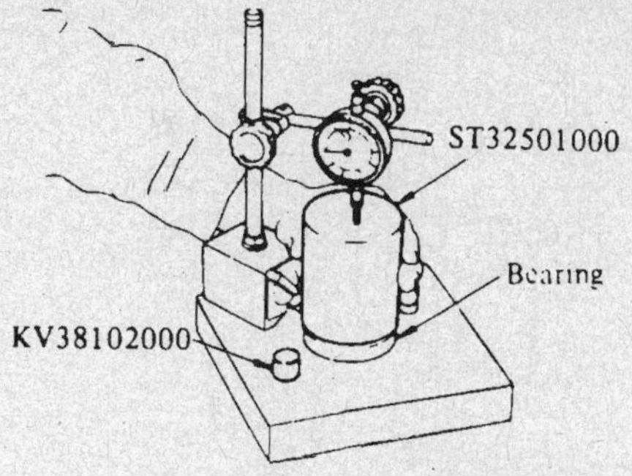
ST32501000
Bearing
KV38102000

NS3039100040000X

Fig. 17 Bearing width measurement

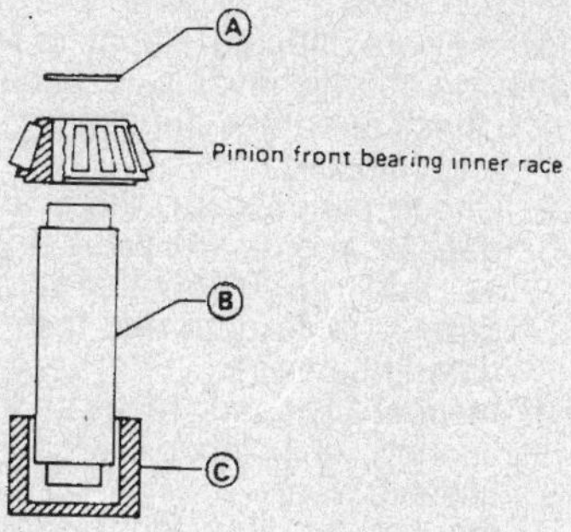
A
Pinion front bearing inner race
B
C

Tool number:

- Ⓐ Lead preload washer (J25269-25)
- Ⓑ Front pinion bearing pilot (J25269-3)
- Ⓒ Front bearing pilot support (J25269-29)

NS3039100043000X

Fig. 20 Front bearing pilot support assembly

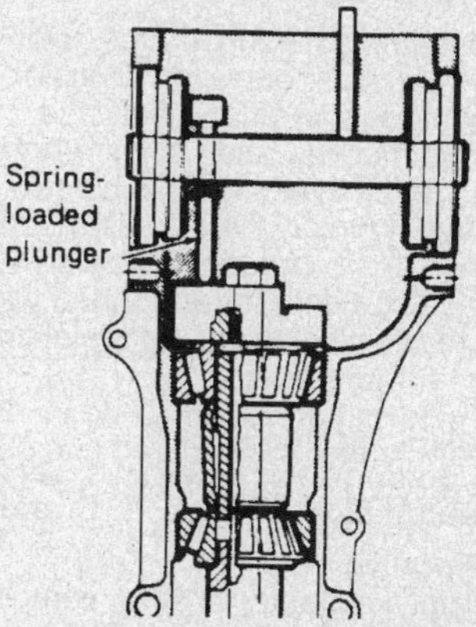
Spring-
loaded
plunger

NS3039100045000X

Fig. 22 Arbor assembly w/discs installation into differential carrier

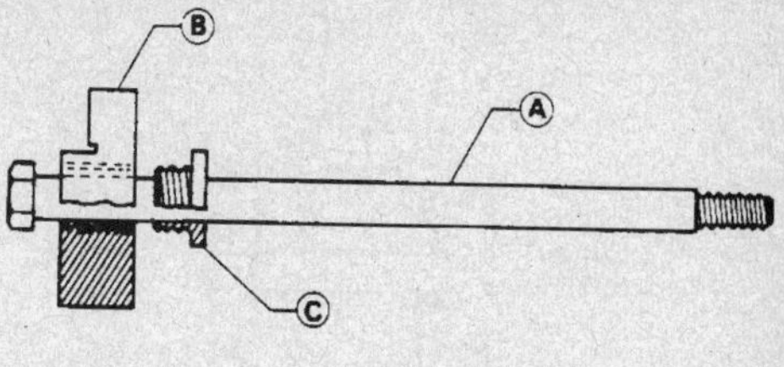
B
A
C

Tool number:

- Ⓐ Hex head long bolt (J25269-23)
- Ⓑ Gauge plate (J25269-1)
- Ⓒ Rear pinion bearing pilot (J25269-2)

NS3039100041000X

Fig. 18 Rear pinion bearing pilot & gauge plate installation on hex head long bolt

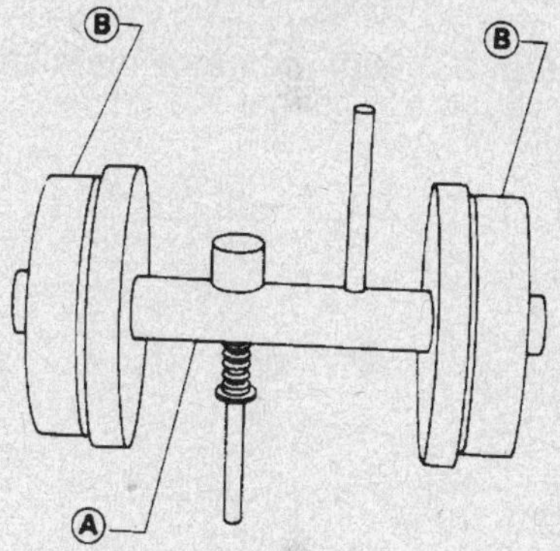
B
B
A

Tool number:

- Ⓐ Arbor assembly (J23597-1)
- Ⓑ Side bearing disc (J25269-4)

NS3039100044000X

Fig. 21 Arbor assembly w/side bearing discs

adjusting washer and spacer with a different thickness.

9. Install differential case assembly with side bearing outer races into gear carrier.
10. Insert selected left and right side bearing adjusting washers in place between side bearings and carrier.
11. Drive in side bearing spacer with suitable tool.
12. Align mark on bearing cap with that on gear carrier and install bearing cap on gear carrier.
13. Apply suitable lubricant to cavity at sealing lips of oil seal, then install side oil seal.
14. Measure ring gear to drive pinion backlash with a dial indicator. If backlash is less than .0051–.0071 inch, decrease thickness of right shim and increase thickness of left shim by same amount. If backlash exceeds .0051–.0071 inch, increase thickness of right shim and decrease thickness of left shim by same amount. **Never change the total amount of shims to prevent changing bearing preload.**
15. Check total preload, which should be 10.9–20.4 inch lbs. If preload is too great, add the same amount of shims to each side. If preload is too small, remove the same amount of shims from each side.
16. Recheck ring gear to drive pinion backlash and check runout of ring gear. If backlash varies excessively in different places, foreign matter may be trapped between ring gear and differential case.
17. If backlash varies greatly, hypoid gear set or differential case needs to be replaced.
18. Install rear cover with gasket.

MODELS LESS INDEPENDENT REAR SUSPENSION

DISASSEMBLE

1. Remove rear cover and scribe alignment marks between side bearing caps and carrier, then remove side bearing caps, side bearing adjuster, if equipped, and differential case.
2. Using suitable tools, remove drive pinion nut, companion flange and drive pinion.
3. Pry out oil seal, being careful not to scratch seal bore, then remove front pinion bearing inner race.
4. Drive out pinion bearing outer race.

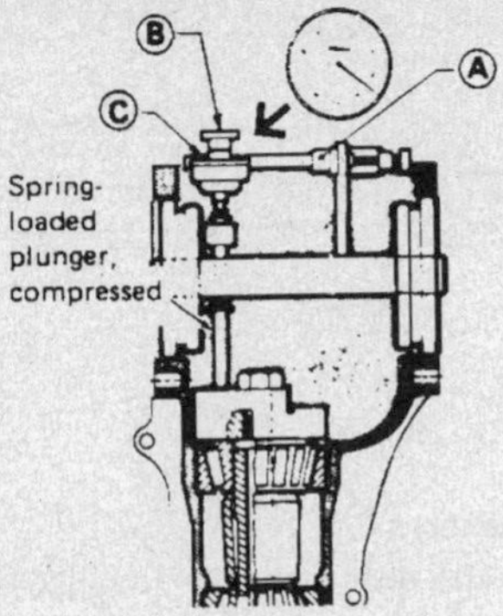
B
C
A
Spring-
loaded
plunger,
compressed

Tool number:

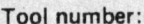

- Ⓐ Hold down clamp (J8001-1)
- Ⓑ Dial indicator clamp (J8001-2)
- Ⓒ Dial indicator (J8001-6)

NS3039100046000X

Fig. 23 Dial indicator installation

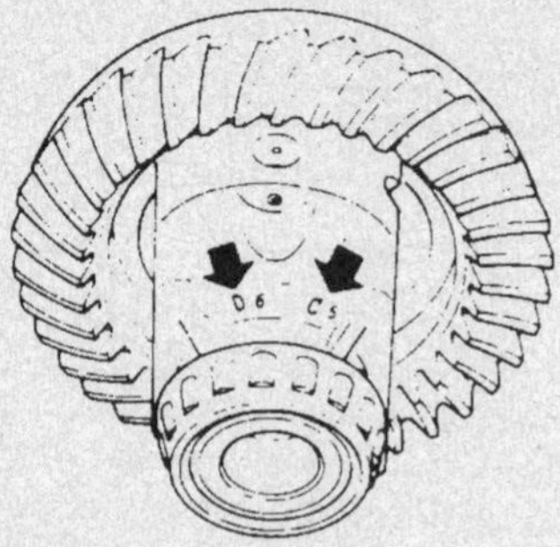
D6
C5

NS3039100049000X

Fig. 26 Location of C & D values

5. Remove collapsible spacer and washer from drive pinion, as required.
6. Press out rear bearing inner race.

DIFFERENTIAL CASE

1. Using suitable tool, remove side bearing inner race.
2. Remove ring gear.
3. **On models with 2 pinion type differential,** proceed as follows:
   a. Drive out pinion mate shaft lockpin from ring gear side.
   b. Remove pinion mate shaft, pinion mate gears, side gears and thrust washers, marking gears and thrust washers so that they can be installed in original position.
4. **On models with 4 pinion type differential,** proceed as follows:
   a. Scribe alignment marks on both lefthand and righthand differential case, then separate lefthand and righthand cases.
   b. Remove side thrust washers, side gear, thrust block if equipped, pinion mate thrust washer, pinion mate gear and pinion mate shaft.

INSPECTION

Thoroughly clean all disassembled parts, and examine them to see if they are worn, damaged or otherwise faulty, and how they are affected. Repair or replace all faulty parts, whichever is necessary.

1. Check gear teeth for scoring, cracking and chipping.
2. Check pinion gear shaft, and pinion gear for scores and wear, and replace as required. Follow the same procedure for side gear and their seats on differential case.
3. Inspect all bearing races and rollers for scoring, chipping or evidence of excessive wear.
4. Inspect thrust washer faces. Small faults can be corrected with sandpaper.
5. Inspect carrier and differential case for cracks or distortion. If either condition is evident, replace faulty parts.

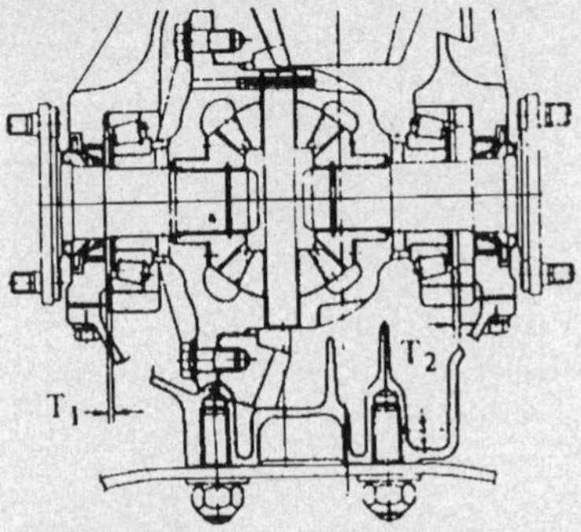
T_1
T_2

NS3039100047000X

Fig. 24 Side bearing washer thickness

ASSEMBLE

Reverse "Disassemble" procedure to assemble. Note the following procedures during assembly.

DIFFERENTIAL CASE ASSEMBLY

2 Pinion Type Differential

1. Assemble pinion mates, side gears, thrust washers, and thrust block, if equipped, in differential case.
2. Install pinion shaft to differential case so that it meets lockpin holes.
3. Adjust pinion mate-to-side gear backlash or the clearance between the rear face of side gear and thrust washer to proper thickness by selecting side gear thrust washer.
4. Lock pinion shaft lockpin using a punch after it is secured into place.
5. Apply oil to gear tooth surfaces and thrust surfaces and check if they turn properly.
6. Apply suitable locking compound to ring gear attaching bolts, then place ring gear on differential case and install bolts and lock washers. **Torque** bolts to 58–72 ft. lbs. on models with 10mm bolts and 98–112 ft. lbs. on models with 12mm bolts, then bend up lock washers, if equipped.

4 Pinion Type Differential

1. Measure clearance between side gear thrust washer and differential case, **Fig. 5.** Clearance (A) and (B) should be .0039–.0079 inch.
2. If clearance is not as specified, adjust by installing correct side gear thrust washer.
3. Apply suitable gear oil to gear tooth surfaces and thrust surfaces, then install thrust washer, pinion mate shaft, pinion mate gear, pinion mate thrust washer, thrust block if equipped and side gear in differential case.
4. Assemble lefthand and righthand differential case, then the ring gear on differential case.
5. Apply suitable locking compound on ring gear attaching bolts, then install bolts. **Torque** attaching bolts in a crisscross pattern to 58–69 ft. lbs. on H233B model axle, 51–58 ft. lbs. for 10mm bolts on C200 model axle and 98–112 ft. lbs. for 12mm bolts on C200 model axle.
6. Press side bearing inner race on differential case using suitable tools.

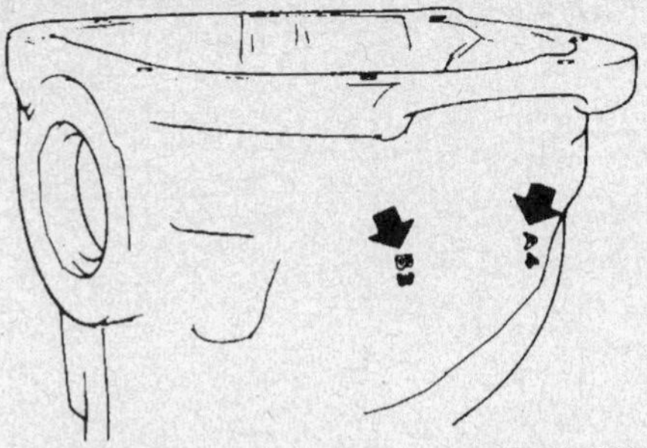
B3
A4

NS3039100048000X

Fig. 25 Location of A & B values

NS3039100050000X

Fig. 27 Ring & pinion backlash measurement

DRIVE PINION HEIGHT, 190 MODEL AXLES

Except Pickup

Adjust the pinion height with washer provided between rear bearing inner race and the back of pinion gear.

1. Press front and rear bearing outer races into gear carrier.
2. Install rear bearing on carrier and install dummy shaft and collar on rear bearing, and place height gauge on carrier, **Fig. 28.**
3. Measure the clearance (N) between the tip end of height gauge and the end surface of dummy shaft, using a thickness gauge, **Fig. 29.**
4. The thickness of drive pinion height adjusting washers can be obtained from the following formula: T = N-(H - D

- S X 0.01) 2.18; where T = required thickness of rear bearing adjusting washers in millimeters, N = measured value with thickness gauge in millimeters, H = figure marked on the drive pinion head, **Fig. 30,** D = figure marked on the dummy shaft, S = figure marked on the height gauge and figures for H, D' and S are dimensional variations in a unit of 1/100mm against each standard measurement. **If values signifying H, D' and S are not given, regard value as zero and compute.**

5. Install determined pinion height adjusting washer in drive pinion, and press rear bearing inner race in.

Pickup

1. Ensure all parts are clean and that bearings are well lubricated.
2. Assemble pinion gear bearings into pinion preload shim selector tool No. J-34309, or equivalent, noting the following:
   a. Front pinion bearing — Ensure front pinion bearing is secured tightly against gauge anvil, then turn front pinion bearing pilot tool No. J-34309-5, or equivalent, to secure bearing in position.
   b. Rear pinion bearing — Rear pinion bearing pilot tool No. J-34309-15, or equivalent, is used to center rear pinion bearing only. Lock bearing to assembly with rear pinion bearing locking seat tool No. J-34309-4, or equivalent.
3. Position pinion preload shim selector tool No. J-34309-1, or equivalent, gauge screw assembly with pinion rear bearing inner cone installed into final drive housing.
4. Assemble front pinion bearing inner cone and gauge anvil tool No. J-34309-2, or equivalent, together with gauge screw tool No. J-34309-1, or equivalent, in final drive housing.
5. Ensure pinion height plate tool No. J-34309-16, or equivalent, will turn a full 360°, then hand tighten the two sections.
6. Turn assembly several times to seat bearings, then measure turning torque at end of gauge anvil. Turning **Torque** should be 9–11 inch lbs.
7. Place pinion height adapter tool No. J-34309-14, or equivalent, onto gauge plate and hand tighten. **Ensure all machined surfaces are clean.**
8. Install side bearing discs tool No. J-25269-18, or equivalent, and arbor into side bearing bores.
9. Install side bearing caps and cap attaching bolts. **Torque** attaching bolts to 36–43 ft. lbs.
10. Using a suitable feeler gauge, select standard pinion height adjusting washer thickness by measuring gap between pinion height adapter tool No. J-34309-14, or equivalent, and arbor.
11. Add or subtract head number on drive pinion head, **Fig. 30,** to measurement found in step 10 to determine the optimum pinion height adjusting washer thickness. **The head number on drive pinion head is in millimeters.**
12. Remove pinion preload selector tool No. J-34309, or equivalent, from final drive housing.

DRIVE PINION HEIGHT, 200 MODEL AXLE

Pathfinder

1. Ensure all parts are clean and that bearings are well lubricated.
2. Assemble pinion gear bearings into pinion preload shim selector tool No. J-34309, or equivalent, noting the following:
   a. Front pinion bearing — Ensure front pinion bearing is secured tightly against gauge anvil tool No. J-34309-2, or equivalent, then turn front pinion bearing pilot tool No. J-34309-5, or equivalent, to secure bearing in position.
   b. Rear pinion bearing — Rear pinion bearing pilot J-34309-15 or equivalent, is used to center rear pinion bearing only. Lock bearing to assembly with rear pinion bearing locking seat tool No. J-34309-4, or equivalent.
3. Position pinion preload shim selector gauge screw assembly tool No. J-34309-1, or equivalent, with pinion rear bearing inner cone installed into final drive housing.
4. Assemble front pinion bearing inner cone and gauge anvil tool No. J-34309-2, or equivalent, together with gauge screw tool No. J-34309-1, or equivalent, in final drive housing.
5. Ensure pinion height plate tool No. J-34309-16, or equivalent, will turn a full 360°, then hand tighten the two sections.
6. Turn assembly several times to seat bearings, then measure turning torque at end of gauge anvil. Turning **torque** should be 9–11 inch lbs.
7. Place pinion height adapter tool No. J-34309-13, or equivalent, onto gauge plate and hand tighten. **Ensure all machined surfaces are clean.**
8. Install side bearing discs tool No. J-25269-4, or equivalent, and arbor into side bearing bores.
9. Install side bearing caps and cap attaching bolts. **Torque** attaching bolts to 65–72 ft. lbs.
10. Using a suitable gauges, select standard pinion height adjusting washer thickness by measuring gap between pinion height adapter tool No. J-34309-13, or equivalent, and arbor.
11. Add or subtract head number on drive pinion head, **Fig. 30,** to measurement found in step 10 to determine the optimum pinion height adjusting washer thickness. **The head number on drive pinion head is in millimeters.**
12. Remove pinion preload selector tool No. J-34309, or equivalent, from final drive housing.

DRIVE PINION HEIGHT & DRIVE PINION PRELOAD

Pickup & Pathfinder w/H233B Model Axle

1. Ensure all parts are clean and that bearings are well lubricated.
2. Assemble pinion gear bearings into pinion preload shim selector tool No. J-34309, or equivalent, noting the following:
   a. Front pinion bearing — Ensure front pinion bearing is secured tightly against gauge anvil tool No. J-34309-2, or equivalent, then turn front pinion bearing pilot tool No. J-34309-5,or equivalent, to secure bearing in position.
   b. Rear pinion bearing — Rear pinion bearing pilot tool No. J-34309-8, or equivalent, is used to center rear pinion bearing only. Lock bearing to assembly with rear pinion bearing locking seat tool No. J-34309-4, or equivalent.
3. Position pinion preload shim selector gauge screw assembly tool No. J-34309-1, or equivalent, with pinion rear bearing inner cone installed into final drive housing.
4. Assemble front pinion bearing inner cone and gauge anvil Tool No. J-34309-2, or equivalent, together with gauge screw tool No. J-34309-1, or equivalent, in final drive housing.
5. Ensure pinion height plate tool No. J-34309-16, or equivalent, will turn a full 360°, then hand tighten the two sections.
6. Turn assembly several times to seat bearings, then measure turning torque at end of gauge anvil. Turning **torque** should be 4–8 inch lbs.
7. Place pinion height adapter tool No. J-34309-12, or equivalent, onto gauge plate and hand tighten. **Ensure all machined surfaces are clean.**
8. Place solid pinion bearing adjusting spacer squarely into recessed portion of gauge anvil and rest its end on gauge screw tool No. J-34209-1, or equivalent.
9. Using a suitable feeler gauge, select correct thickness of pinion bearing preload adjusting washer. **The exact measurement obtained with feeler gauge is thickness of adjusting shim required.**
10. Install side bearing discs tool No. J-25269-18, or equivalent, and arbor into side bearing bores.
11. Install bearing caps and cap attaching bolts. **Torque** attaching bolts to 69–76 ft. lbs.
12. Using a suitable gauge, select standard pinion height adjusting washer thickness by measuring gap between pinion height adapter tool No. J-34309-12, or equivalent, and arbor.
13. Add or subtract head number on drive pinion head, **Fig. 30,** to measurement found in step 10 to determine the optimum pinion height adjusting washer thickness. **The head number on drive**

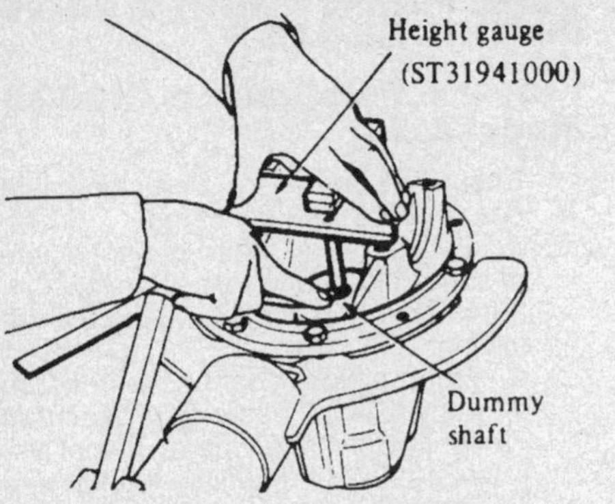
Height gauge
(ST31941000)
Dummy
shaft
NS3039100053000X

Fig. 28 Drive pinion marking

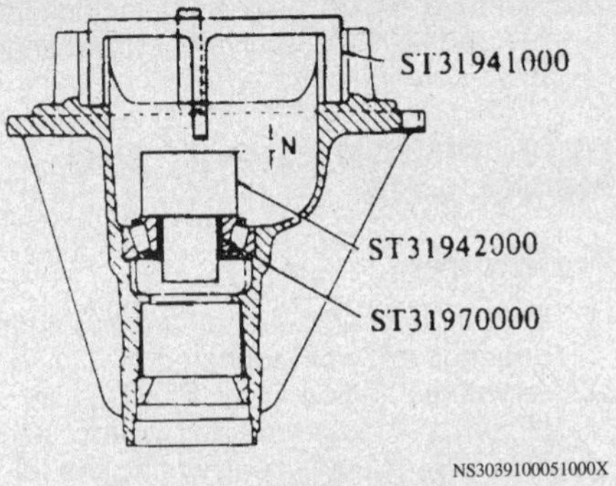
ST31941000
N
ST31942000
ST31970000
NS3039100051000X

Fig. 29 Pinion height adjusting tools installation

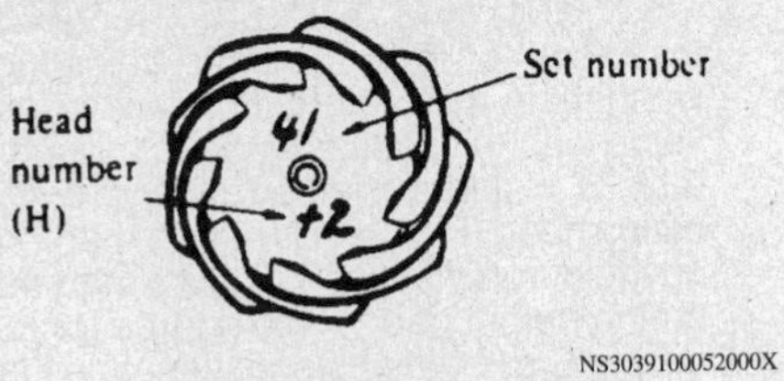
Set number
Head
number
(H)
41
+2
NS3039100052000X

Fig. 30 Pinion height measurement

pinion head is in millimeters.

14. Remove pinion preload selector tool No. J-34309, or equivalent, from final drive housing.

SIDE BEARING PRELOAD & FINAL ASSEMBLY, 190 MODEL AXLE

Except Pickup

1. If hypoid gear set, carrier, differential case or side bearing have been replaced with new ones, adjust the side bearing preload with adjusting shim. The required thickness of adjusting shim can be calculated by the following formulas: T1 = (A - C D - H) X 0.01 0.175 E; T2 = (B - D H) X 0.01 0.150 F; where T1 = required thickness of left side bearing adjusting shim in millimeters, **Fig. 31,** T2 = required thickness of right side bearing adjusting shim in millimeters, **Fig. 31,** A = figure marked on the left side bearing housing of gear carrier, B figure marked on the right side bearing of gear carrier, C & D = figure marked on the differential case, E & F: = differences in width of left or right side bearing against the standard width (20.00mm) in millimeters, H = figure marked on the ring gear and figures for A, B, C, D and H are dimensional variations in a unit of 1⁄100mm against each standard measurement. **If values signifying A, B, C, D and H are not given, regard value as zero and compute.**
2. Install determined side bearing adjusting shim on differential case, and press left and right side bearing inner races in.
3. Install differential case assembly into gear carrier, tapping with a rubber mallet.
4. Align mark on bearing cap with that on gear carrier, and install bearing cap on carrier. **Torque** bolts 36–43 ft. lbs. on all other models.
5. Measure ring gear-to-drive pinion backlash, **Fig. 32.** If backlash is too small, remove shims from left side and add them to right side. To reduce backlash, remove shims from right side and add them to left side.
6. At the same time, check side bearing preload. Bearing preload should be 10.4–17.4 inch lbs.

Pickup

1. Ensure all parts are clean and that bearings are well lubricated with suitable oil.
2. Remove carrier side bearing using a suitable puller, then reinstall all original side bearing adjusting shims on carrier side (away from ring gear).
3. Press on carrier side bearing using suitable tools.
4. Install carrier and bearings into final drive housing.
5. Install side bearing caps and cap attaching bolts. **Torque** attaching bolts to 36–43 ft. lbs. and tap on caps with suitable hammer to seat bearings.
6. Turn carrier several times to seat bearings, then measure carrier turning force with suitable spring scale. Turning force at ring gear bolt should be 8–9 lbs.
7. If turning force is not as specified, correct by adding to or subtracting from the total amount of shim thickness.
8. Press in front and rear bearing outer races, then install selected pinion height adjusting washer in drive pinion and press in rear bearing outer race.
9. Place pinion front bearing inner race in gear carrier.
10. Apply suitable lubricant to cavity at sealing lips of oil seal, then install front oil seal.
11. Install drive pinion washer, collapsible spacer and drive pinion in gear carrier.
12. Install companion flange and hold firmly, then insert pinion into companion flange.
13. Temporarily tighten pinion nut until there is no axial play. **Ensure threaded portion of drive pinion and pinion nut are free from oil or grease.**
14. Tighten pinion nut by degrees until preload is 10–14 inch lbs. **When checking preload, turn drive pinion several times in both directions to seat bearings.**
15. Install differential case assembly with side bearing outer races into gear carrier.
16. Align mark on bearing cap with mark on gear carrier and install bearing cap on gear carrier.
17. Measure ring gear to drive pinion backlash with dial indicator. If backlash is less than .0051–0071 inch, decrease thickness of left shim and increase thickness of right shim by same amount. If backlash exceeds .0051–.0071 inch, increase thickness of right shim and decrease thickness of left shim by same amount. **Never change the total amount of shims to prevent changing bearing preload.**
18. Check total preload, which should be 10–19 inch lbs. If preload is too great, remove same amount of shims from each side. If preload is too small, install same amount of shims on each side.
19. Recheck ring gear to drive pinion backlash and check runout of gear. If backlash varies excessively in different places, foreign matter may be trapped between ring gear and differential case.
20. If backlash varies greatly and ring gear runout is .0031 inch or less, the hypoid gear set or differential case needs to be replaced.

SIDE BEARING PRELOAD & FINAL ASSEMBLY, 200 MODELS AXLE

Pathfinder

1. Ensure all parts are clean and that bearings are well lubricated with suitable oil.
2. Install carrier and bearings into final drive housing.
3. Install side bearing spacer in position on ring gear end of carrier.
4. Install both of the original carrier side bearing preload shims on carrier end (opposite ring gear).
5. Install side bearing caps and cap attaching bolts. **Torque** attaching bolts to 65–72 ft. lbs. and tap on caps with suitable hammer to seat bearings.
6. Turn carrier several times to seat bearings, then measure carrier turning force with suitable spring scale. Turning force at ring gear bolt should be 8–9 lbs.
7. If turning force is not as specified, correct by adding to or subtracting from the total amount of shim thickness.
8. Press in front and rear bearing outer races, then install selected pinion height adjusting washer in drive pinion and press in rear bearing outer race.
9. Place pinion front bearing inner race in gear carrier.
10. Apply suitable lubricant to cavity at sealing lips of oil seal, then install front oil seal.
11. Install drive pinion spacer, drive pinion bearing and drive pinion in gear carrier.
12. Install companion flange into drive pinion using a suitable hammer.
13. **Torque** pinion nut 94 ft. lbs. **Ensure**

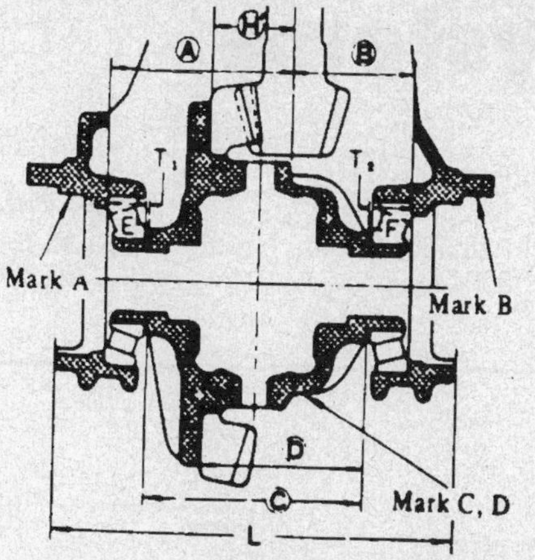
H
A
B
T1
T2
E
F
Mark A
Mark B
D
C
Mark C, D
L
NS3039100054000X

Fig. 31 Side bearing shim thickness

threaded portion of drive pinion and pinion nut are free from oil or grease.

14. Tighten pinion nut by degrees until preload is 10–15 inch lbs. **When checking preload, turn drive pinion several times in both directions to seat bearings.**
15. Install differential case assembly with side bearing outer races into gear carrier.
16. Install right and left side bearing adjusting washers in position between side bearing and carrier, then drive in side bearing spacer using a suitable tool.
17. Align mark on bearing cap with mark on gear carrier and install bearing cap on gear carrier.
18. Measure ring gear to drive pinion backlash with dial indicator. If backlash is less than .0051–.0071 inch, decrease thickness of left shim and increase thickness of right shim by same amount. If backlash exceeds .0051–.0071 inch, increase thickness of right shim and decrease thickness of left shim by same amount. **Never change the total amount of shims to prevent changing bearing preload.**
19. Check total preload, which should be 10–20 inch lbs. If preload is too great, remove same amount of shims from each side. If preload is too small, add same amount of shims to each side.
20. Recheck ring gear to drive pinion backlash and check runout of gear. If backlash varies excessively in different places, foreign matter may be trapped between ring gear and differential case.
21. If backlash varies greatly and ring gear runout is .0031 inch or less, the hypoid gear set or differential case needs to be replaced.

SIDE BEARING PRELOAD & FINAL ASSEMBLY, H233B MODEL AXLE

1. Press in front and rear bearing outer races, then install selected drive pinion adjusting washer in drive pinion and press in rear bearing outer race.
2. Place pinion front bearing inner race in gear carrier.
3. Apply suitable lubricant to cavity at sealing lips of oil seal, then install front oil seal.
4. Install drive pinion spacer, pinion bearing adjusting shim and drive pinion in gear carrier.
5. Install companion flange into drive pinion.
6. Temporarily **torque** pinion nut to 145–181 ft. lbs. **Ensure threaded portion of drive pinion and pinion nut are free from oil or grease.**
7. Measure pinion bearing preload. Preload should be 4–9 inch lbs. **When checking preload, turn drive pinion several times in both directions to seat bearings.**
8. Install differential case assembly with side bearing outer races into gear carrier.
9. Position side bearing adjusters on gear carrier with threads properly engaged, then lightly screw in adjusters.
10. Align mark on bearing cap with mark on gear carrier and install bearing cap on gear carrier. **Do not tighten cap attaching bolts at this point.**
11. Tighten both right and left side bearing adjusters alternately, then measure ring gear backlash with dial indicator. Backlash should be .0059–.0079 inch. If backlash is not as specified, adjust right and left side bearing adjusters by tightening them alternately until specified backlash is obtained.
12. Check total preload, which should be 9–17 inch lbs. If preload is not as specified, adjust right and left side bearing adjusters by tightening them alternately until specified preload is obtained.
13. **Torque** side bearing cap bolts to 69–76 ft. lbs., then place lock finger in position to prevent adjuster rotation during operation.
14. Recheck backlash and ring gear runout of gear. If backlash varies excessively in different places, foreign matter may be trapped between ring gear and differential case.
15. If backlash varies greatly and ring gear runout is .0031 inch or less, the hypoid gear set or differential case needs to be replaced.

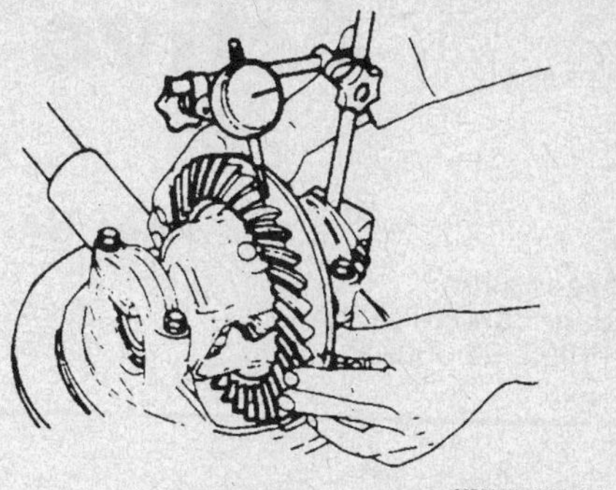
NS3039100055000X

Fig. 32 Ring & pinion backlash measurement

Active Suspension Systems

INDEX

	Page No.
Description	36-260
Diagnosis & Testing	36-261
1995–96 300ZX	36-261
1996 Pathfinder	36-261
Troubleshooting	36-260
Pathfinder	36-260
300ZX	36-260

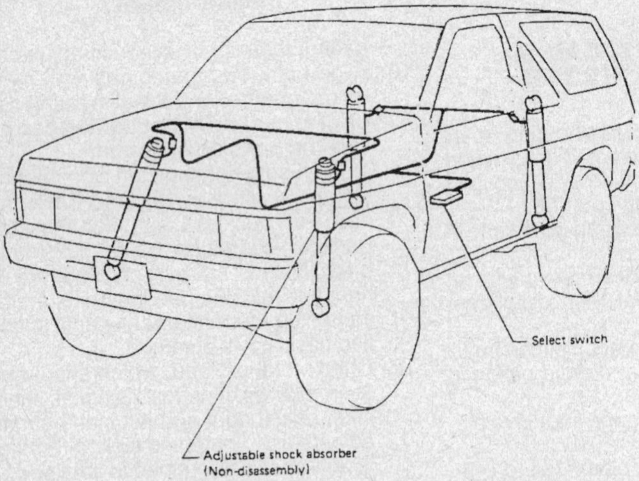

Select switch
Adjustable shock absorber
(Non-disassembly)

NS2019100001000X

Fig. 1 Adjustable shock absorber system components. 1993–95 Pathfinder

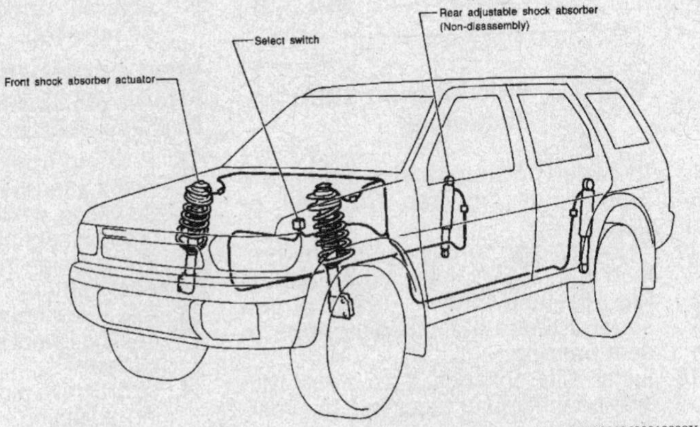

Rear adjustable shock absorber
(Non-disassembly)
Select switch
Front shock absorber actuator

NS2019600010000X

Fig. 2 Adjustable shock absorber system components. 1996 Pathfinder

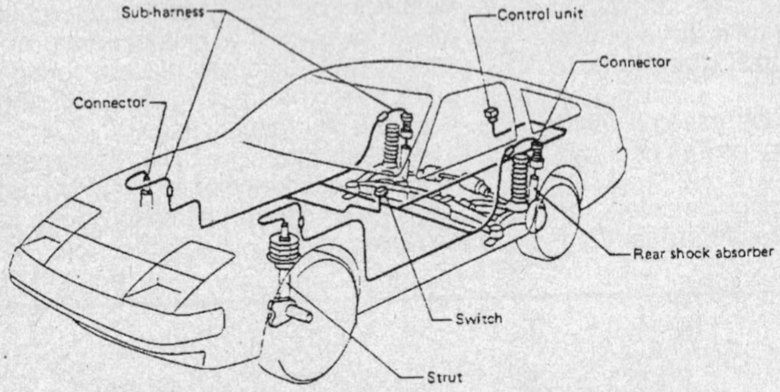

Sub-harness
Control unit
Connector
Connector
Rear shock absorber
Switch
Strut

NS2019100002000X

Fig. 3 Adjustable shock absorber system components. 1993–94 300ZX

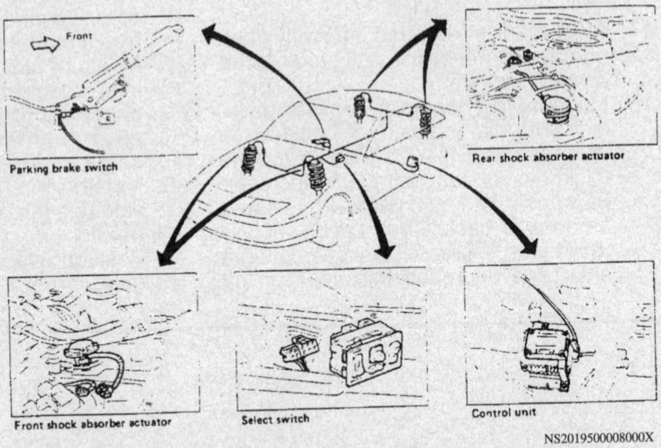

Front
Parking brake switch
Rear shock absorber actuator
Front shock absorber actuator
Select switch
Control unit

NS2019500008000X

Fig. 4 Adjustable shock absorber system components. 1995–96 300ZX

DESCRIPTION

This system, shown in **Figs. 1 through 4,** uses a shock absorber select switch, control unit, shock absorber sensors and control motors to control shock absorber valving. The system allows the driver to select the shock absorber valving that is suitable for various driving conditions.

TROUBLESHOOTING

300ZX

The shock absorber control unit has a self check function to determine whether the control unit is working properly. A malfunction is displayed by an L.E.D. which is located on select switch.

Refer to **Fig. 5** for system troubleshooting charts.

PATHFINDER

Terminal Inspection

1. Disconnect adjustable shock absorber connector.
2. Ensure continuity exists between terminal 3 of connector and body ground.
3. Measure voltage between terminals 2 and 3 then 1 and 3 of the connector and ensure voltage is as specified in **Fig. 6.**

Select Switch Inspection

Disconnect select switch connector, then connect an ohmmeter to switch and test for continuity as shown in **Fig. 7.**

Shock Absorber Inspection

Attach a suitable tool to shock absorber, then check for operating sound of the actuator when select switch is moved from one position to the other.

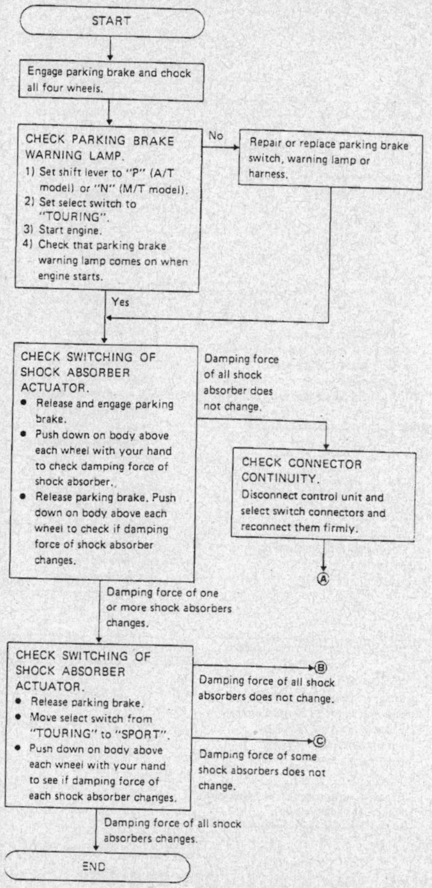
START
Engage parking brake and chock all four wheels.
CHECK PARKING BRAKE WARNING LAMP.
1) Set shift lever to "P" (A/T model) or "N" (M/T model).
2) Set select switch to "TOURING".
3) Start engine.
4) Check that parking brake warning lamp comes on when engine starts.
No
Repair or replace parking brake switch, warning lamp or harness.
Yes
CHECK SWITCHING OF SHOCK ABSORBER ACTUATOR.
• Release and engage parking brake.
• Push down on body above each wheel with your hand to check damping force of shock absorber.
• Release parking brake. Push down on body above each wheel to check if damping force of shock absorber changes.
Damping force of all shock absorber does not change.
CHECK CONNECTOR CONTINUITY.
Disconnect control unit and select switch connectors and reconnect them firmly.
Damping force of one or more shock absorbers changes.
CHECK SWITCHING OF SHOCK ABSORBER ACTUATOR.
• Release parking brake.
• Move select switch from "TOURING" to "SPORT".
• Push down on body above each wheel with your hand to see if damping force of each shock absorber changes.
Damping force of all shock absorbers does not change.
Damping force of some shock absorbers does not change.
Damping force of all shock absorbers changes.
END

NS2019100003010X

Fig. 5 Adjustable shock absorber system suspension troubleshooting charts (Part 1 of 3). 300ZX

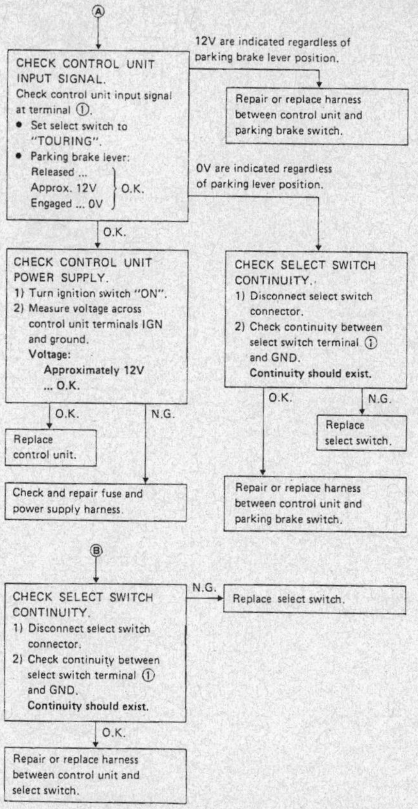
CHECK CONTROL UNIT INPUT SIGNAL.
Check control unit input signal at terminal ①.
• Set select switch to "TOURING".
• Parking brake lever:
Released ... Approx. 12V
Engaged ... 0V
O.K.
12V are indicated regardless of parking brake lever position.
Repair or replace harness between control unit and parking brake switch.
0V are indicated regardless of parking lever position.
CHECK CONTROL UNIT POWER SUPPLY.
1) Turn ignition switch "ON".
2) Measure voltage across control unit terminals IGN and ground.
Voltage:
Approximately 12V ... O.K.
N.G.
Replace control unit.
Check and repair fuse and power supply harness.
CHECK SELECT SWITCH CONTINUITY.
1) Disconnect select switch connector.
2) Check continuity between select switch terminal ① and GND.
Continuity should exist.
Replace select switch.
Repair or replace harness between control unit and parking brake switch.
CHECK SELECT SWITCH CONTINUITY.
1) Disconnect select switch connector.
2) Check continuity between select switch terminal ① and GND.
Continuity should exist.
Replace select switch.
Repair or replace harness between control unit and select switch.

NS2019100003020X

Fig. 5 Adjustable shock absorber system suspension troubleshooting charts (Part 2 of 3). 300ZX

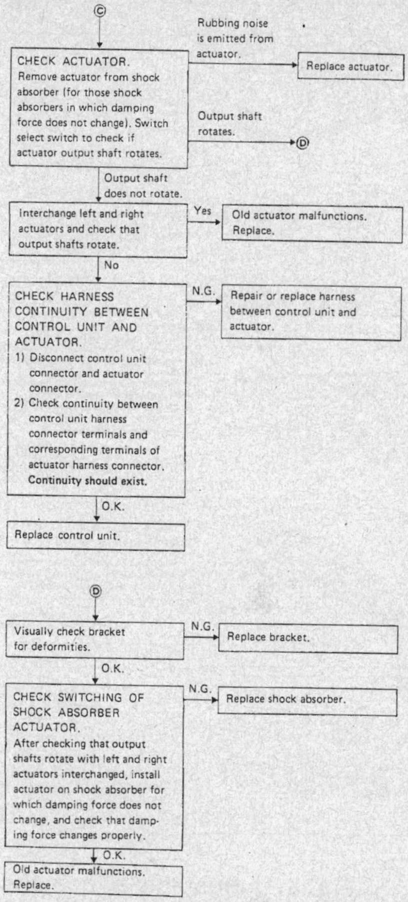
CHECK ACTUATOR.
Remove actuator from shock absorber (for those shock absorbers in which damping force does not change). Switch select switch to check if actuator output shaft rotates.
Rubbing noise is emitted from actuator.
Replace actuator.
Output shaft rotates.
Output shaft does not rotate.
Interchange left and right actuators and check that output shafts rotate.
Yes
Old actuator malfunctions. Replace.
No
CHECK HARNESS CONTINUITY BETWEEN CONTROL UNIT AND ACTUATOR.
1) Disconnect control unit connector and actuator connector.
2) Check continuity between control unit harness connector terminals and corresponding terminals of actuator harness connector.
Continuity should exist.
N.G.
Repair or replace harness between control unit and actuator.
O.K.
Replace control unit.
Visually check bracket for deformities.
Replace bracket.
CHECK SWITCHING OF SHOCK ABSORBER ACTUATOR.
After checking that output shafts rotate with left and right actuators interchanged, install actuator on shock absorber for which damping force does not change, and check that damping force changes properly.
Replace shock absorber.
Old actuator malfunctions. Replace.

NS2019100003030X

Fig. 5 Adjustable shock absorber system suspension troubleshooting charts (Part 3 of 3). 300ZX

DIAGNOSIS & TESTING

1995-96 300ZX

Refer to **Fig. 8** for diagnostic procedures.

1996 PATHFINDER

Refer to **Fig. 9** for diagnostic procedures.

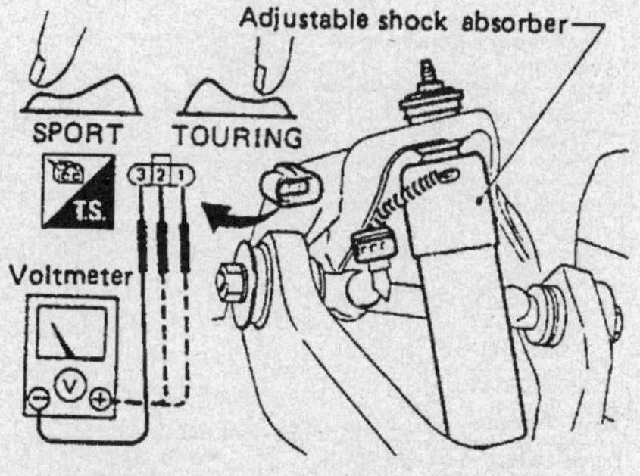
Adjustable shock absorber
SPORT
TOURING
T.S.
3 2 1
Voltmeter

Voltmeter (+)	Voltmeter (−)	Voltage	Select switch position
①	③	Approx. 12V	Push the SPORT end of the switch continuously.
		0	Release the switch.
②		Approx. 12V	Push the TOURING end of the switch continuously.
		Approx. 12V	Release the switch.

NS2019100004000X

Fig. 6 Terminal inspection. Pathfinder

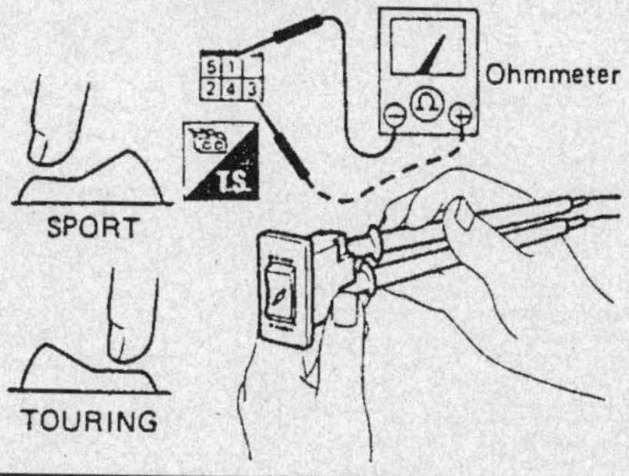
Ohmmeter
SPORT
TOURING
T.S.

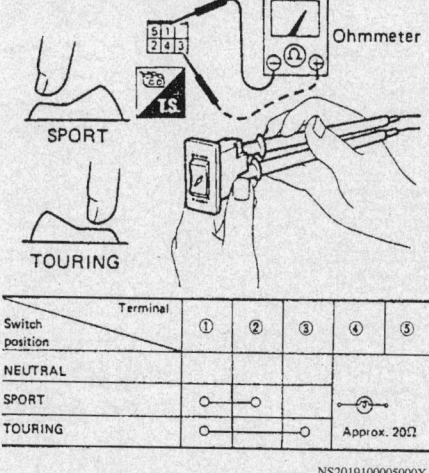

Switch position \ Terminal	①	②	③	④	⑤
NEUTRAL					
SPORT	o—	—o			
TOURING	o—	—	—o		
				Approx. 20Ω	

NS2019100005000X

Fig. 7 Select switch inspection. Pathfinder

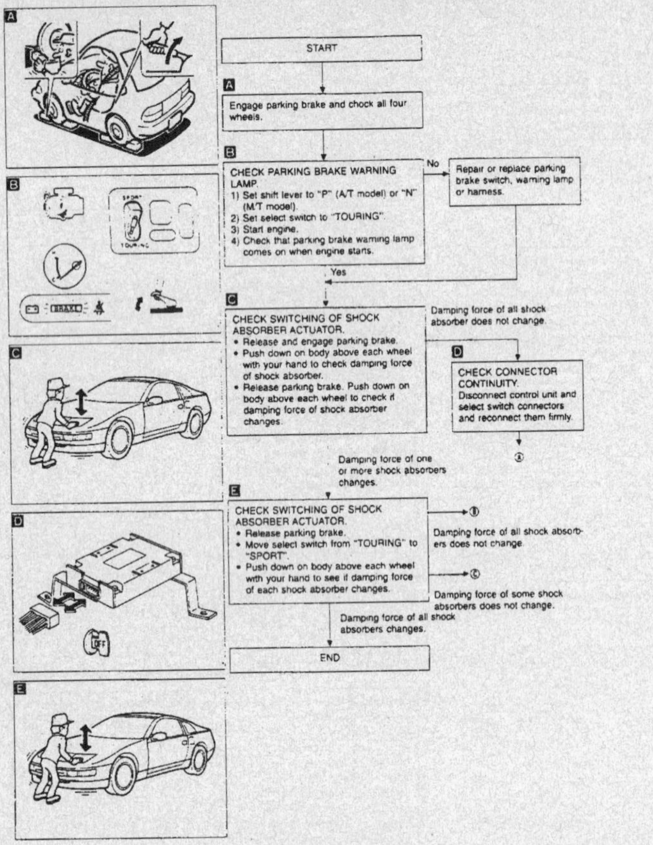
START
A
Engage parking brake and chock all four wheels.
B
CHECK PARKING BRAKE WARNING LAMP.
1) Set shift lever to "P" (A/T model) or "N" (M/T model).
2) Set select switch to "TOURING".
3) Start engine.
4) Check that parking brake warning lamp comes on when engine starts.
No
Repair or replace parking brake switch, warning lamp or harness.
Yes
C
CHECK SWITCHING OF SHOCK ABSORBER ACTUATOR.
• Release and engage parking brake.
• Push down on body above each wheel with your hand to check damping force of shock absorber.
• Release parking brake. Push down on body above each wheel to check if damping force of shock absorber changes.
Damping force of all shock absorber does not change.
D
CHECK CONNECTOR CONTINUITY.
Disconnect control unit and select switch connectors and reconnect them firmly.
Damping force of one or more shock absorbers changes.
E
CHECK SWITCHING OF SHOCK ABSORBER ACTUATOR.
• Release parking brake.
• Move select switch from "TOURING" to "SPORT".
• Push down on body above each wheel with your hand to see if damping force of each shock absorber changes.
Damping force of all shock absorbers does not change.
Damping force of some shock absorbers does not change.
Damping force of all shock absorbers changes.
END

NS2019500009010X

Fig. 8 Adjustable shock absorber system diagnosis (Part 1 of 3). 1995–96 300ZX

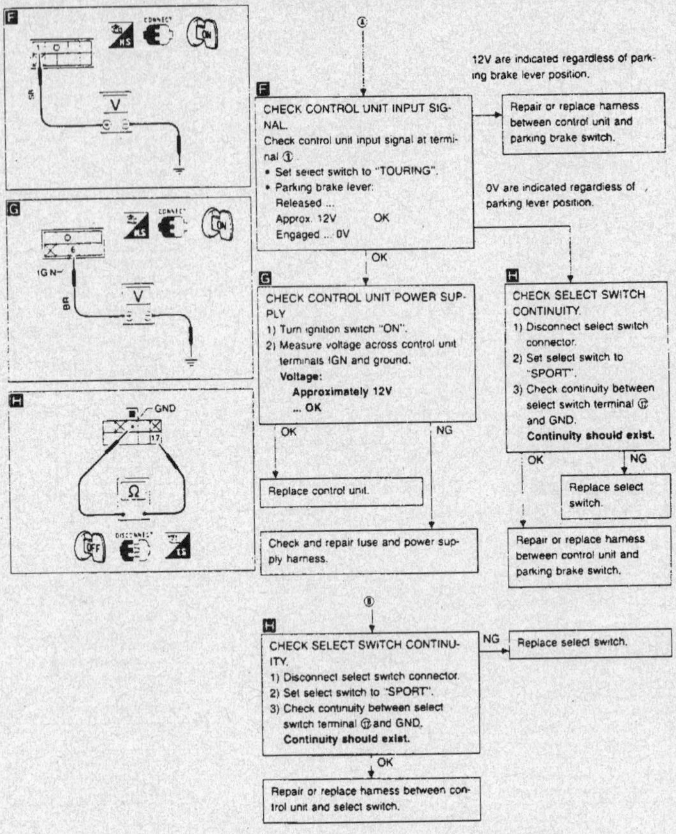
F
CHECK CONTROL UNIT INPUT SIGNAL.
Check control unit input signal at terminal ①.
• Set select switch to "TOURING".
• Parking brake lever:
Released ...
Approx. 12V OK
Engaged ... 0V
12V are indicated regardless of parking brake lever position.
Repair or replace harness between control unit and parking brake switch.
0V are indicated regardless of parking lever position.
OK
G
CHECK CONTROL UNIT POWER SUPPLY
1) Turn ignition switch "ON".
2) Measure voltage across control unit terminals IGN and ground.
Voltage:
Approximately 12V
... OK
H
CHECK SELECT SWITCH CONTINUITY.
1) Disconnect select switch connector.
2) Set select switch to "SPORT".
3) Check continuity between select switch terminal ⑫ and GND.
Continuity should exist.
OK NG
Replace control unit.
Check and repair fuse and power supply harness.
OK NG
Replace select switch.
Repair or replace harness between control unit and parking brake switch.
H
CHECK SELECT SWITCH CONTINUITY.
1) Disconnect select switch connector.
2) Set select switch to "SPORT".
3) Check continuity between select switch terminal ⑫ and GND.
Continuity should exist.
NG
Replace select switch.
OK
Repair or replace harness between control unit and select switch.
GND
IGN
BR

NS2019500009020X

Fig. 8 Adjustable shock absorber system diagnosis (Part 2 of 3). 1995–96 300ZX

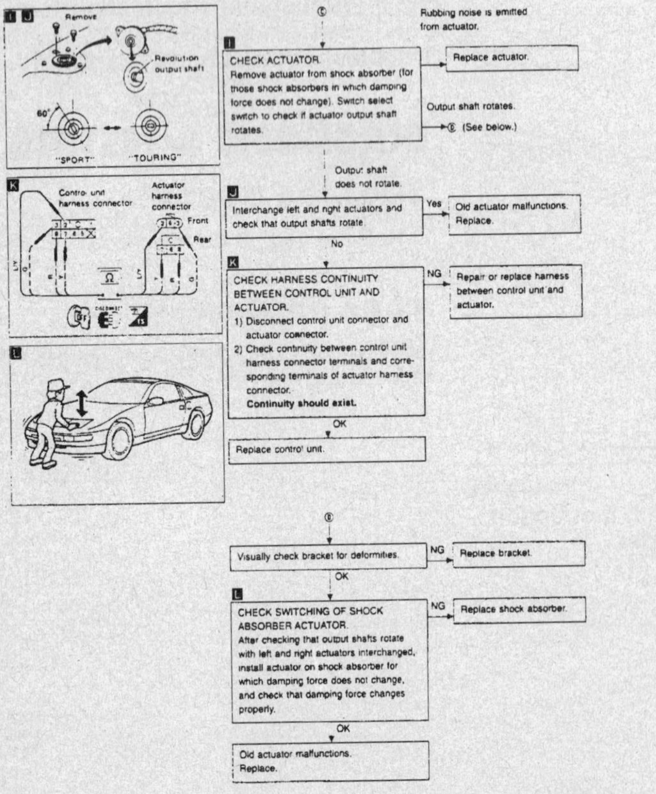
Remove
Revolution output shaft
60°
"SPORT" "TOURING"
Rubbing noise is emitted from actuator.
I
CHECK ACTUATOR.
Remove actuator from shock absorber (for those shock absorbers in which damping force does not change). Switch select switch to check if actuator output shaft rotates.
Replace actuator.
Output shaft rotates.
(See below.)
Output shaft does not rotate.
J
Interchange left and right actuators and check that output shafts rotate.
Yes
Old actuator malfunctions. Replace.
No
Control unit harness connector
Actuator harness connector
Front
Rear
K
CHECK HARNESS CONTINUITY BETWEEN CONTROL UNIT AND ACTUATOR.
1) Disconnect control unit connector and actuator connector.
2) Check continuity between control unit harness connector terminals and corresponding terminals of actuator harness connector.
Continuity should exist.
NG
Repair or replace harness between control unit and actuator.
OK
Replace control unit.
Visually check bracket for deformities.
NG
Replace bracket.
OK
L
CHECK SWITCHING OF SHOCK ABSORBER ACTUATOR.
After checking that output shafts rotate with left and right actuators interchanged, install actuator on shock absorber for which damping force does not change, and check that damping force changes properly.
NG
Replace shock absorber.
OK
Old actuator malfunctions. Replace.

NS2019500009030X

Fig. 8 Adjustable shock absorber system diagnosis (Part 3 of 3). 1995–96 300ZX

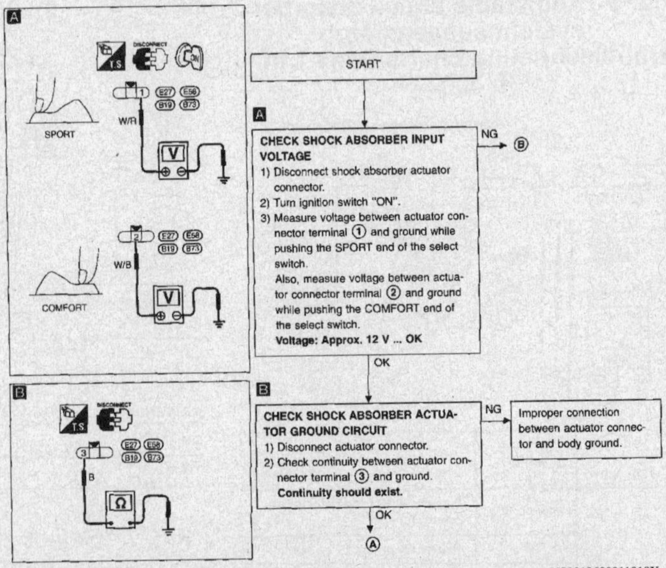
START
SPORT
W/R
COMFORT
W/B
A
CHECK SHOCK ABSORBER INPUT VOLTAGE
1) Disconnect shock absorber actuator connector.
2) Turn ignition switch "ON".
3) Measure voltage between actuator connector terminal ① and ground while pushing the SPORT end of the select switch.
Also, measure voltage between actuator connector terminal ② and ground while pushing the COMFORT end of the select switch.
Voltage: Approx. 12 V ... OK
NG
OK
B
CHECK SHOCK ABSORBER ACTUATOR GROUND CIRCUIT
1) Disconnect actuator connector.
2) Check continuity between actuator connector terminal ③ and ground.
Continuity should exist.
NG
Improper connection between actuator connector and body ground.
OK

NS2019600011010X

Fig. 9 Adjustable shock absorber system diagnosis (Part 1 of 3). 1996 Pathfinder

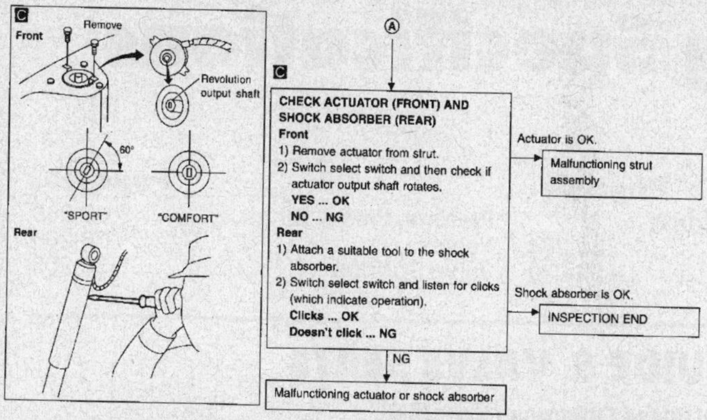
C
Front
Remove
Revolution output shaft
60°
"SPORT"
"COMFORT"
Rear
Ⓐ
C
CHECK ACTUATOR (FRONT) AND SHOCK ABSORBER (REAR)
Front
1) Remove actuator from strut.
2) Switch select switch and then check if actuator output shaft rotates.
YES ... OK
NO ... NG
Rear
1) Attach a suitable tool to the shock absorber.
2) Switch select switch and listen for clicks (which indicate operation).
Clicks ... OK
Doesn't click ... NG
Actuator is OK.
Malfunctioning strut assembly
Shock absorber is OK.
INSPECTION END
NG
Malfunctioning actuator or shock absorber
NS2019600011020X

Fig. 9 Adjustable shock absorber system diagnosis (Part 2 of 3). 1996 Pathfinder

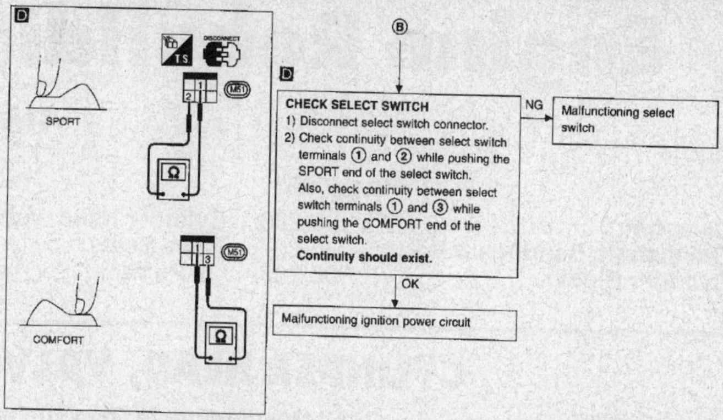
D
DISCONNECT
SPORT
COMFORT
M51
Ⓑ
D
CHECK SELECT SWITCH
1) Disconnect select switch connector.
2) Check continuity between select switch terminals ① and ② while pushing the SPORT end of the select switch.
Also, check continuity between select switch terminals ① and ③ while pushing the COMFORT end of the select switch.
Continuity should exist.
NG
Malfunctioning select switch
OK
Malfunctioning ignition power circuit
NS2019600011030X

Fig. 9 Adjustable shock absorber system diagnosis (Part 3 of 3). 1996 Pathfinder

Engine Rebuilding Specifications

INDEX

	Page No.		Page No.		Page No.
Camshaft	36-266	Cylinder Head, Valve Guide & Valve Seats	36-264	Pistons, Pins & Rings	36-268
Crankshaft, Bearings & Rods	36-267	Oil Pump	36-270	Valves	36-265
Cylinder Block	36-269			Valve Springs	36-265

CYLINDER HEAD, VALVE GUIDE & VALVE SEATS

All Measurements Given In Inches, Unless Otherwise Specified.

Year	Engine	Cylinder Head Warpage Limit	Cylinder Head Overall Thickness②	Valve Guides			Valve Seats	
				Standard Inside Diameter	Stem to Guide Clearance		Seat Width	
					Intake	Exhaust	Intake	Exhaust
1993	GA16DE	.004	4.639–4.646	.2165–.2171	.0008–.0021	.0016–.0028	—	—
	SR20DE	.004	5.390–5.398	.2362–.2369	.0008–.0021	.0016–.0029	—	—
	KA24DE	.004	4.972–4.980	.2756–.2763	.0008–.0021	.0016–.0029	—	—
	VG30DE, VG30DETT	.004	5.433③	.2362–.2369	.0008–.0021	.0016–.0029	—	—
	VG30E	.004	4.205–4.220	①	.0008–.0021	.0016–.0029	.069	.067
	VE30DE	.004	5.469	.2362–.2369	.0008–.0017	.0016–.0025	.042–.053	.050–.061
1994	GA16DE	.004	4.639–4.646	.2165–.2171	.0008–.0021	.0016–.0028	—	—
	SR20DE	.004	5.390–5.398	.2362–.2369	.0008–.0021	.0016–.0029	—	—
	KA24DE	.004	4.972–4.980	.2756–.2763	.0008–.0021	.0016–.0029	—	—
	VG30DE, VG30DETT	.004	5.433③	.2362–.2369	.0008–.0021	.0016–.0029	—	—
	VG30E	.004	4.205–4.220	①	.0008–.0021	.0016–.0029	.069	.067
	VE30DE	.004	5.469	.2362–.2369	.0008–.0017	.0016–.0025	.042–.053	.050–.061
1995–96	GA16DE	.004	4.639–4.646	.2165–.2171	.0008–.0021	.0016–.0028	.042–.053	.042–.066
	SR20DE	.004	5.390–5.398	.2362–.2369	.0008–.0021	.0016–.0029	.055–.067	.067–.079
	KA24DE	.004	4.972–4.980	.2756–.2763	.0008–.0021	.0016–.0029	.058–.064	.071–.079
	VG30DE, VG30DETT	.004	5.433③	.2362–.2369	.0008–.0021	.0016–.0029	—	—
	VG30E, VG33E	.004	4.205–4.220	①	.0008–.0021	.0016–.0029	.069	.067
	VQ30DE	.004	4.972–4.980	.2362–.2369	.0008–.0029	.0016–.0029	.043–.052	.051–.060

① — Intake, .2756–.2763 inch; exhaust, .3150–.3154 inch.
② — Minimum thickness is overall thickness, less warpage limit, combined with amount of grinding of cylinder block gasket surface.
③ — To camshaft center.

VALVE SPRINGS

All Measurements Given In Inches, Unless Otherwise Specified.

Year	Engine	Valve Springs		
		Free Height Inner/ Outer	Assembled Tension Pounds @ Inches Inner/ Outer	Out of Square Limit Inner/Outer
1993–94	GA16DE	①	②	③
	SR20DE	1.943	144.25 @ 1.181	.087
	KA24DE	1.756	123.37 @ 1.024	.075
	VG30DE, VG30DETT	1.697	120.60 @ 1.043	.071
	VG30E	1.736/2.016	57.30 @ .984/117.7 @ 1.181	.075/.087
	VE30DE	1.777	26.90 @ 1.059	.079
1995–96	GA16DE	①	②	③
	SR20DE	1.943	144.25 @ 1.181	.087
	KA24DE	1.756	123.37 @ 1.024	.075
	VG30DE, VG30DETT	1.697	120.60 @ 1.043	.071
	VG30E, VG33E	1.736/2.016	57.30 @ .984/117.70 @ 1.181	.075/.087
	VQ30DE	1.848	102.10 @ 1.085	.079

① — Intake, 2.071 inches; exhaust, 2.154 inches.
② — Intake 110 lbs. at 1.331 inches; exhaust, 122.6 lbs. at 1.346 inches.
③ — Intake, .091 inch; exhaust, .094 inch.

VALVES

All Measurements Given In Inches, Unless Otherwise Specified.

Year	Engine	Valves					
		Stem Diameter		Face Angle, Degrees	Margin Intake/ Exhaust	Clearance	
		Intake	Exhaust			Intake	Exhaust
1993–94	GA16DE	.2152–.2157	.2144–.2150	45 ½	.0350–.0430	.0080–.0190	.0120–.0230
	SR20DE	.2348–.2354	.2341–.2346	45 ½	.0430/.0510	0	0
	KA24DE	.2742–.2748	.2734–.2740	45 ½	①	0	0
	VG30DE, VG30DETT	.2348–.2354	.2341–.2346	45 ½	②	0	0
	VG30E	.2742–.2748	.3136–.3138	45 ½	②	0	0
	VE30DE	.2352–.2354	.2344–.2346	45 ½	.0450/.0570	0	0
1995	GA16DE	.2152–.2157	.2144–.2150	45 ½	.0350–.0430	.0080–.0190	.0120–.0230
	SR20DE	.2348–.2354	.2341–.2346	45 ½	.0430/.0510	0	0
	KA24DE	.2742–.2748	.2734–.2740	45 ½	①	0	0
	VG30DE, VG30DETT	.2348–.2354	.2341–.2346	45 ½	②	0	0
	VG30E	.2742–.2748	.3136–.3138	45 ½	②	.0008–.0021	.0012–0021
	VE30DE	.2352–.2354	.2344–.2346	45 ½	.0450/.0570	0	0
	VQ30DE	.2348–.2354	.2341–.2346	45 ½	③	.0100–.0130	.0110–.0150
1996	GA16DE	.2152–.2157	.2144–.2150	45 ½	.0350–.0430	.0080–.0190	.0120–.0230
	SR20DE	.2348–.2354	.2341–.2346	45 ½	.0430/.0510	0	0
	KA24DE	.2742–.2748	.2734–.2740	45 ½	①	0	0
	VG30DE, VG30DETT	.2348–.2354	.2341–.2346	45 ½	②	0	0
	VG33E	.2742–.2748	.3135–.3138	45 ½	②	0	0
	VE30DE	.2352–.2354	.2344–.2346	45 ½	.0450/.0570	0	0
	VQ30DE	.2348–.2354	.2341–.2346	45 ½	③	.0100–.0130	.0110–.0150

① — Intake margin is .0374–.0492 inch; exhaust is .0453–.0571 inch.
② — Intake margin is .0453–.0571 inch; exhaust is .0531–.0650 inch.
③ — Intake margin is .0370–.0490 inch; exhaust is .0450–.0570 inch.

CAMSHAFT

All Measurements Given In Inches, Unless Otherwise Specified.

Year	Engine Model	Camshaft Journal Outer Diameter	Camshaft Bearing Clearance	Maximum Journal Run-Out	Camshaft Endplay	Lifter Bore Diameter	Lifter Outer Diameter	Lifter To Bore Clearance
1993–94	GA16DE	③	.0018–.0034	.0040	.0045–.0074	1.1811–1.1819	1.1795–1.1801	.0010–.0024
	SR20DE	1.0998–1.1006	.0018–.0034	.0040	.0022–.0055	.6693–.6701	.6685–.6690	.0003–.0016
	KA24DE	③	.0018–.0035	.0016	.0028–.0059	1.3386–1.3394	1.3370–1.3376	.0010–.0024
	VG30DE, VG30DETT	1.0998–1.1006	.0018–.0034	.0040	.0012–.0031	1.2205–1.2213	1.2187–1.2191	.0014–.0026
	VG30E	①②	.0018–.0035	.0040	.0012–.0024	.6299–.6304	.6278–.6282	.0017–.0026
	VE30DE	1.0211–1.0218	.0018–.0034	.0020	.0028–.0058	.6693–.6701	.6685–.6690	.0003–.0016
1995–96	GA16DE	③	.0018–.0034	.0040	.0045–.0074	1.1811–1.1819	1.1795–1.1801	.0010–.0024
	SR20DE	1.0998–1.1006	.0018–.0034	.0040	.0022–.0055	.6693–.6701	.6685–.6690	.0003–.0016
	KA24DE	③	.0018–.0035	.0016	.0028–.0059	1.3386–1.3394	1.3370–1.3376	.0010–.0024
	VG30DE, VG30DETT	1.0998–1.1006	.0018–.0034	.0040	.0012–.0031	1.2205–1.2213	1.2187–1.2191	.0014–.0026
	VG30E, VG33E	①②	.0024–.0041	.0040	.0012–.0024	.6299–.6304	.6278–.6282	.0017–.0026
	VQ30DE	.9226–.9234	.0018–.0034	.0020	.0045–.0074	1.3780–1.3788	1.3764–1.3770	.0010–.0024

① — Journal 1, 1.8866–1.8874 inch; journals 2, 3 & 4, 1.8472–1.8480 inch; journal 5, 1.6701–1.6709 inch.
② — Both right & left side cams.
③ — Journal 1, 1.0998–1.1006 inch; journals 2, 3 ,4 & 5, .9423–.9431 inch.

CRANKSHAFT, BEARINGS & RODS

All Measurements Given In Inches, Unless Otherwise Specified.

Year	Engine Model	Crankshaft				Bearing Clearance		Connecting Rods	
		Standard Journal Diameter		Out Of Round①	Taper①	Main Bearings	Connecting Rod Bearings	Piston Pin Bore Diameter	Side Clearance
		Main Bearing	Crank Pin						
1993–94	GA16DE	⑤	⑪	.0002	.0001	.0007–.0017	.0004–.0014	.7480–.7485	.0079–.0185
	SR20DE	⑫	⑬	.0002	.0002	.0002–.0009	.0008–.0018	.9835–.9843	.0079–.0138
	KA24DE	⑥	⑦	.0002	.0001	.0040	.0035	.8268–.8272	.0240
	VG30DE, VG30DETT④	⑨	⑩	.0002	.0002	.0011–.0022	.0011–.0019	.8661–.8666	.0079–.0138
	VG30E	②	1.9670–1.9675	.0002③	.0002③	.0011–.0022	.0006–.0021	.8261–.8265	.0079–.0138
	VE30DE⑧	②	⑩	.0008	.0008	.0011–.0022	.0011–.0019	.8661–.8666	.0079–.0138
1995–96	GA16DE	⑤	⑪	.0002	.0001	.0007–.0017	.0004–.0014	.7480–.7485	.0079–.0185
	SR20DE	⑫	⑬	.0002	.0002	.0002–.0009	.0008–.0018	.9835–.9843	.0079–.0138
	KA24DE	⑥	⑦	.0002	.0001	.0040	.0035	.8268–.8272	.0240
	VG30DE, VG30DETT④	⑨	⑩	.0002	.0002	.0011–.0022	.0011–.0019	.8661–.8666	.0079–.0138
	VG30E, VG33E	②	1.9670–1.9675	.0002③	.0002③	.0011–.0022	.0006–.0021	.8261–.8265	.0079–.0138
	VE30DE⑧	②	⑩	.0008	.0008	.0011–.0022	.0011–.0019	.8661–.8666	.0079–.0138
	VQ30DE	⑭	⑮	.0001	.0001	.0002–.0007	—	.8658–.8664	.0079–.0138

① — Maximum.
② — Grade 0, 2.4790–2.4793 inches; grade 1, 2.4787–2.4790 inches; grade 2, 2.4784–2.4787 inches.
③ — Standard.
④ — 300ZX.
⑤ — Grade 0, 1.9668–1.9671 inch; grade 1, 1.9665–1.9668 inch; grade 2, 1.9661–1.9665 inch.
⑥ — Grade 0, 2.3609–2.3612 inches; grade 1, 2.3606–2.3609 inches; grade 2, 2.3603–2.3606 inches.
⑦ — Grade 0, 1.9672–1.9675 inch; grade 1, 1.9670–1.9672 inch; grade 2, 1.9668–1.9670 inch.
⑧ — Maxima.
⑨ — Grade 0, 2.4790–2.4793 inch; grade 1, 2.4787–2.4790 inch; grade 2, 2.4784–2.4787 inch.
⑩ — Grade 0, 1.9672–1.9675 inch; grade 1, 1.9670–1.9672 inch; grade 2, 1.9667–1.9670 inch.
⑪ — Grade 0, 1.5735–1.5738 inch; grade 1, 1.5733–1.5735 inch; grade 2, 1.5731–1.5733 inch.
⑫ — Grade 0, 2.1643–2.1646 inch; grade 1, 2.1641–2.1643 inch; grade 2, 2.1639–2.1641 inch; grade 3, 2.1636–2.1639 inch.
⑬ — Grade 0, 1.8885–1.8887 inch; grade 1, 1.8883–1.8885 inch; grade 2, 1.8880–1.8883 inch.
⑭ — Grade 0, 2.3610–2.3612 inch; grade 1, 2.3607–2.3610 inch; grade 2, 2.3605–2.3607 inch; grade 2.3603–2.3605 inch.
⑮ — Grade 0, 1.7704–1.7706 inch; grade 1, 1.7702–1.7704 inch; grade 2, 1.7699–1.7702 inch.

PISTONS, PINS & RINGS

All Measurements Given In Inches, Unless Otherwise Specified.

Year	Engine	Piston Diameter (Std.)	Piston to Cylinder Bore Clear-ance	Piston Pin Diam-eter	Piston Pin to Piston Clear-ance	Piston Ring End Gap		Piston Ring Side Clearance	
						Comp.	Oil	Comp.	Oil
1993–94	GA16DE	⑰	.0006–.0014	.7476–.7481	.0002–.0007	⑦	.0079–.0236	⑧	—
	SE20DE	⑭	.0004–.0012	.8657–.8662	.0002	⑮	.0390	⑯	.0390
	KA24DE	③	.0008–.0016	.8263–.8268	.0002	⑬	.0079–.0272	⑧	—
	VG30DE, VG30DETT②	⑩	⑪	.8657–.8662	.0002	⑫	.0079–.0299	④	—
	VG30E	①	.0006–.0014	.8256–.8261	.0002	⑤	.0079–.0299	④	.0006–.0075
	VE30DE	⑩	.0006–.0014	.8657–.8662	.0002	⑱	.0079–.0272	⑥	—
1995–96	GA16DE	⑰	.0006–.0014	.7476–.7481	.0002–.0007	⑦	.0079–.0236	⑧	—
	SE20DE	⑭	.0004–.0012	.8657–.8662	.0002	⑮	.0390	⑯	.0390
	KA24DE	③	.0008–.0016	.8265–.8267	.0002	⑬	.0079–.0272	⑧	—
	VG30DE, VG30DETT②	⑩	⑪	.8657–.8662	.0002	⑫	.0079–.0299	④	—
	VG30E, VG33E	①	.0010–.0018	.8256–.8261	.0002	⑤	.0079–.0299	④	.0006–.0075
	VQ30DE	⑨	.0004–.0012	.8657–.8662	.0001–.0002	⑲	.0079–.0272	⑧	—

① — Grade No. 1, 3.4238–3.4242 inch; Grade No. 2, 3.4242–3.4246 inch; Grade No. 3, 3.4246–3.4250 inch; Grade No. 4, 3.4250–3.4254 inch; Grade No. 5, 3.4254–3.4258 inch.

② — 300ZX.

③ — Grade No. 1, 3.5027–3.5031 inch; Grade No. 2, 3.5031–3.5035 inch; Grade No. 3, 3.5035–3.5039 inch.

④ — Top, .0016–.0029 inch; second, .0012–.0025 inch.

⑤ — Top, .0083–.0173 inch; second, .0071–.0173 inch.

⑥ — Top. .0016–.0031 inch; second, .0012–.0025 inch.

⑦ — Top, .0079–.0138 inch; second, .0146–.0205 inch.

⑧ — Top, .0016–.0031 inch; second, .0012–.0028 inch.

⑨ — Grade No. 1, 3.6606–3.6601 inch; Grade No. 2, 3.6610–3.6614 inch; Grade No. 3, 3.6614–3.6618 inch.

⑩ — Grade No. 1, 3.4242–3.4246 inch; Grade No. 2, 3.4246–3.4250 inch; Grade No. 3, 3.4250–3.4254 inch.

⑪ — Non-turbo models, .0083–.0157 inch; turbo models, .0010–.0018 inch.

⑫ — Top, .0083–.0157 inch; second, .0197–.0299 inch.

⑬ — Top, .0110–.0205 inch; second, .0177–.0272 inch.

⑭ — Grade No. 1, 3.3850–3.3854 inch; Grade No. 2, 3.3854–3.3858 inch; Grade No. 3, 3.3858–3.3862 inch.

⑮ — Top, .0079–.0118 inch; second, .0138–.0197 inch.

⑯ — Top, .0018–.0031 inch; second, .0012–.0036 inch.

⑰ — Grade No. 1, 2.9911–2.9915 inch; Grade No. 2, 2.9915–2.9919 inch; Grade No. 3, 2.9919–2.9923 inch.

⑱ — Top, .0083–.0157 inch; second, .0197–.0272 inch.

⑲ — Top, .0087–.0161 inch; second, .0197–.0291 inch.

CYLINDER BLOCK

All Measurements Given In Inches, Unless Otherwise Specified.

Year	Engine	Cylinder Bore Diameter (Std.)	Cylinder Bore Taper (Max.)	Cylinder Bore Out of Round (Max.)
1993–94	GA16DE	④	.0004	.0006
	SR20DE	⑤	.0004	.0006
	KA24DE	②	.0004	.0006
	VG30DE, VG30DETT	①	.0006	.0006
	VG30E	①	.0006	.0006
	VE30DE③	①	.0004	.0006
1995	GA16DE	④	.0004	.0006
	SR20DE	⑤	.0004	.0006
	KA24DE	②	.0006	.0006
	VG30DE, VG30DETT	①	.0006	.0006
	VG30E, VG33E	①	.0006	.0006
	VQ30DE	⑦	.0004	.0006
1996	GA16DE	④	.0004	.0006
	SR20DE	⑤	.0004	.0006
	KA24DE	②	.0006	.0006
	VG30DE, VG30DETT	①	.0006	.0006
	VG33E	⑥	.0006	.0006
	VQ30DE	⑦	.0004	.0006

① — Grade No. 1, 3.4252–3.4256 inch; Grade No. 2, 3.4256–3.4260 inch; Grade No. 3, 3.4260–3.4264 inch; Grade No. 4, 3.4264–3.4268 inch; Grade No.5, 3.4268–3.4272 inch.

② — Grade No. 1, 3.5039–3.5043 inch; Grade No.2, 3.5043–3.5047 inch; Grade No. 3, 3.5047–3.5051 inch; Grade No. 4, 3.5051–3.5055 inch; Grade No. 5, 3.5055–3.5059 inch.

③ — Maxima.

④ — Grade No. 1, 2.9921–2.9925 inch; Grade No. 2, 2.9925–2.9929 inch; Grade No. 3, 2.9929–2.9933 inch.

⑤ — Grade No. 1, 3.3858–3.3862 inch; Grade No. 2, 3.3862–3.3866 inch; Grade No. 3, 3.3866–3.3870 inch.

⑥ — Grade No. 1, 3.6024–3.6027 inch; Grade No. 2, 3.6027–3.6031 inch; Grade No. 3, 3.6031–3.6035 inch.

⑦ — Grade No. 1, 3.614–3.6618 inch; Grade No. 2, 3.6618–3.6622 inch; Grade No. 3, 3.6622–3.6626 inch.

OIL PUMP

All Measurements Given In Inches, Unless Otherwise Specified.

Year	Engine Model	Clearances				
		Body To Outer Gear	Inner Gear To Crescent	Outer Gear To Crescent	Housing To Inner Gear	Housing To Outer Gear
1993–94	GA16DE	.0043–.0079	.0085–.0129	.0083–.0126	.0020–.0035	.0020–.0043
	SE20DE	.0043–.0079	①	①	①	①
	KA24DE	.0043–.0079	①	①	①	①
	VG30DE, VG30DETT②	.0043–.0079	.0088–.0131	.0083–.0126	.0020–.0035	.0020–.0043
	VG30E	.0043–.0079	.0047–.0091	.0083–.0126	.0020–.0035	.0020–.0043
	VE30DE③	.0045–.0079	①	①	①	①
1995–96	GA16DE	.0043–.0079	.0085–.0129	.0083–.0126	.0020–.0035	.0020–.0043
	SE20DE	.0043–.0079	①	①	①	①
	KA24DE	.0043–.0079	①	①	①	①
	VG30DE, VG30DETT②	.0043–.0079	.0088–.0131	.0083–.0126	.0020–.0035	.0020–.0043
	VG30E, VG33E	.0043–.0079	.0047–.0091	.0083–.0126	.0020–.0035	.0020–.0043
	VQ30DE	.0045–.0102	.0071	.0020–.0035	.0012–.0075	.0018–.0036

① — Inner gear to outer gear tip clearance, .0016–.0071 inch; cover to inner gear clearance, .0020–.0035 inch; cover to outer gear clearance, .0020–.0043 inch; Inner gear to brazed portion clearance, .0018–.0036 inch.
② — 300ZX.
③ — Maxima.

PORSCHE

INDEX OF SERVICE OPERATIONS

Page No.

AIR BAG SYSTEM PRECAUTIONS 0-8
ALL-WHEEL DRIVE SYSTEMS 37-59
AUTOMATIC TRANSAXLES 37-55
BRAKES
- Anti-Lock Brakes 37-54
- Disc Brakes 37-48
- Hydraulic Brake Systems 37-52
- Power Brake Units 37-53

CLUTCH & MANUAL TRANSAXLE
- Adjustments 37-24
- Clutch, Replace 37-25
- Hydraulic System Service 37-25
- Tightening Specifications 37-26
- Transaxle, Replace 37-25

DRIVE AXLES 37-60
ELECTRICAL
- Air Bags 37-45
- Air Conditioning 37-41
- Alternator, Replace 37-5
- Alternators 37-44
- Blower Motor, Replace 37-6
- Combination Switch, Replace 37-6
- Cooling Fans 37-42
- Cruise Control 37-44
- Dash Gauges 37-43
- Dash Panels 37-47
- Distributor, Replace 37-5
- Evaporator Core, Replace 37-7
- Fuel Pump Relay Location 37-4
- Fuse Panel & Flasher Location 37-4
- Headlamp Switch, Replace 37-5
- Heater Core, Replace 37-6
- Ignition Switch, Replace 37-5
- Instrument Cluster, Replace 37-6
- Neutral Safety Switch, Replace 37-5
- Passive Restraints 37-45
- Precautions 37-4
- Relay Center Location 37-4
- Speed Controls 37-44
- Starter Motors 37-44
- Starter, Replace 37-4
- Steering Wheel, Replace 37-6
- Stop Light Switch, Replace 37-5
- Wiper Motor, Replace 37-6
- Wiper Switch, Replace 37-6
- Wiper Transmission, Replace 37-6

ELECTRICAL SYMBOL IDENTIFICATION 0-139
ENGINE REBUILDING SPECIFICATIONS
- Camshaft 37-61
- Crankshaft, Bearings & Rods 37-61
- Cylinder Block 37-62
- Cylinder Head, Valve Guide & Valve Seats 37-61
- Pistons, Pins & Rings 37-62
- Valves 37-61

FRONT SUSPENSION & STEERING
- Ball Joint, Replace 37-33
- Ball Joint Inspection 37-33
- Control Arm, Replace 37-34
- Manual Steering Gear, Replace 37-37
- Power Steering Gear, Replace 37-36
- Power Steering Pump, Replace 37-37
- Precautions 37-33
- Strut, Replace 37-33
- Tightening Specifications 37-38
- Torsion Bar, Replace 37-35
- Wheel Bearing, Adjust 37-33

REAR AXLE & SUSPENSION
- Coil Spring, Replace 37-28
- Control Arm, Replace 37-28
- Rear Axle, Replace 37-27
- Rear Axle Shaft, Replace 37-27
- Rear Axle Shaft Service 37-28
- Shock Absorber, Replace 37-28
- Strut, Replace 37-28
- Tightening Specifications 37-38
- Torsion Bar, Replace 37-31
- Trailing Arm Service 37-29

SERVICE REMINDER & WARNING LAMP RESET PROCEDURES 0-10
SPECIFICATIONS
- Fluid Capacities & Cooling System Data 37-3
- Front Wheel Alignment Specifications 37-2
- General Engine Specifications 37-2
- Lubricant Data 37-4
- Rear Wheel Alignment Specifications 37-3
- Tune Up Specifications 37-2

VEHICLE IDENTIFICATION 0-1
VEHICLE LIFT POINTS 0-34
VEHICLE MAINTENANCE SCHEDULES 0-69
V8 ENGINE
- Camshaft, Replace 37-23
- Compression Pressures 37-20
- Cooling System Bleed 37-23
- Crankshaft Rear Oil Seal, Replace 37-23
- Cylinder Head, Replace 37-21
- Engine Rebuilding Specifications 37-61
- Engine, Replace 37-20
- Fuel Filter, Replace 37-23
- Fuel Pump, Replace 37-23
- Main & Rod Bearings 37-23
- Oil Pump, Replace 37-23
- Piston & Rod Assembly 37-23
- Pistons, Pins & Rings 37-23
- Precautions 37-20
- Tightening Specifications 37-24
- Timing Belt, Replace 37-21
- Timing Belt, Adjust 37-22
- Valve Guides 37-21

WHEEL ALIGNMENT
- Front Wheel Alignment 37-39
- Rear Wheel Alignment 37-39
- Wheel Alignment Specifications 37-2

WIRE COLOR CODE IDENTIFICATION 0-144
4 CYLINDER ENGINE
- Balance Shaft, Replace 37-11
- Camshaft, Replace 37-10
- Compensating Shaft Drive, Replace 37-12
- Compression Pressure 37-8
- Cooling System Bleed 37-13
- Crankcase 37-13
- Cylinder Head, Replace 37-9
- Engine Mount, Replace 37-8
- Engine Rebuilding Specifications 37-61
- Engine, Replace 37-8
- Fuel Filter, Replace 37-13
- Fuel Pump, Replace 37-13
- Lubricating System Service 37-12
- Oil Pan, Replace 37-12
- Pistons, Pins & Rings 37-12
- Precautions 37-8
- Tightening Specifications 37-13
- Timing Belt, Replace 37-9
- Valve Arrangement 37-9
- Valve Guides 37-9
- Water Pump, Replace 37-13

6 CYLINDER ENGINE
- Compression Pressure 37-14
- Engine Assemble 37-15
- Engine Disassemble 37-15
- Engine Rebuilding Specifications 37-61
- Engine, Replace 37-14
- Fuel Filter, Replace 37-19
- Fuel Pump, Replace 37-19
- Precautions 37-14
- Tightening Specifications 37-19

Specifications

GENERAL ENGINE SPECIFICATIONS

Year	Engine	Fuel System	Bore x Stroke Inch	Compression Ratio	Maximum HP @ RPM	Maximum Torque @ RPM	Normal Oil Pressure, psi
1993	3.0L	MFI	4.09 X 3.46	11.0	236 @ 6200	225 @ 4100	—
	3.6L	MFI	3.49 X 3.01	11.3	247 @ 6100	228 @ 4800	92②
	5.4L	MFI	3.94 X 3.38	10.4	345 @ 5700	369 @ 4250	—
1994–95	3.0L	MFI	4.09 X 3.46	11.0	236 @ 6200	225 @ 4100	43①
	3.6L	MFI	3.49 X 3.01	11.3	270 @ 6100	243 @ 5000	94②
	5.4L	MFI	3.94 X 3.38	10.4	345 @ 5700	369 @ 4250	72③
1996	3.6L	MFI	3.49 X 3.01	11.3	270 @ 6100	243 @ 5000	94②
	3.6L Turbo	MFI	3.49 X 3.01	8.0	400 @ 5750	400 @ 4500	94②

MFI — Multiport Fuel Injection
① — Minimum at 3000 RPM w/oil temperature at 176 to 212°F.
② — Minimum at 5000 RPM w/oil temperature at 176 to 212°F.
③ — Minimum at 4000 RPM w/oil temperature at 176 to 212°F.

TUNE UP SPECIFICATIONS

Year	Model	Spark Plug Gap Inch	Ignition Timing		Curb Idle Speed		Fuel System Pressure, psi	Valve Clearance, inch
			Firing Order	Timing①	Man. Trans.	Auto. Trans.		
1993–94	968	.028	1-3-4-2	③	③	③	53-58	①
	911 Carrera 2/4	.026	1-6-2-4-3-5	④	③	③	51-58	①
	928 GTS	.031	1-3-7-2-6-5-4-8	⑤	⑤	⑤	53-58	①
1995	911 Carrera	.026	1-6-2-4-3-5	③	800	750D	51-58	①
	928 GTS	.031	1-3-7-2-6-5-4-8	10⑥	675	675N	53-58	①
	968	.028	1-3-4-2	10③	840	880N	53-58	①
1996	911 Carrera	.026	1-6-2-4-3-5	③	②	750D	51-58	①
	911 Turbo	.026	1-6-2-4-3-5	③	②	750D	51-58	①

D — Drive
N — Neutral
ATDC — After Top Dead Center
BTDC — Before Top Dead Center
① — Equipped with hydraulic lash adjusters.
② — Models less A/C, 800 RPM; models with A/C, 880 RPM.
③ — Controlled by DME (Digital Motor Electronics) control unit.
④ — Controlled by DME (Digital Motor Electronics) dual ignition control unit.
⑤ — Computer controlled.
⑥ — At idle speed.

FRONT WHEEL ALIGNMENT SPECIFICATIONS

Model	Caster Angle, Degrees		Camber Angle, Degrees		Toe Angle Degrees	Toe Difference Angle @ 20°	Ball Joint Wear
	Limits	Desired	Limits	Desired			
1993							
911 2/4	+3 11/12 to +4 2/3	+4 5/12	−1/6 to +1/6	0	+1/3 to +1/2	—	①
911 Turbo	+4 1/6 to +4 2/3	+4 5/12	−1/6 to +1/6	0	+1/3 to +1/2	−1 5/6 to −5/6	①
928	+4 to +5	+4 1/2	−2/3 to −1/3	−1/2	+1/6 to +1/3	—	①
968	+2 1/4 to +3 3/4	+3	−2/3 to −1/3	0	0 to +1/3	—	①
1994							
911	+4 5/6 to +5 7/12	+5 1/3	−1/2 to −1/6	−1/3	+1/12 to +1/6	−1/2 to −1 1/2	①
928	+4 to +5	+4 1/2	−2/3 to −1/3	−1/2	+1/6 to +1/3	—	①
968	+2 1/4 to +3 3/4	+3	−2/3 to −1/3	0	0 to +1/3	—	①
1995							
911 Carrera	+4 5/6 to +5 7/12	+5 1/3	−2/3 to −1/6	−1/3	0 to +1/6	—	①

Continued

FRONT WHEEL ALIGNMENT SPECIFICATIONS—Continued

Model	Caster Angle, Degrees		Camber Angle, Degrees		Toe Angle Degrees	Toe Difference Angle @ 20°	Ball Joint Wear
	Limits	Desired	Limits	Desired			
1995							
928 GTS	$+4$ to $+5$	$+4$	$-\frac{2}{3}$ to $-\frac{1}{3}$	$-\frac{1}{2}$	$+\frac{1}{6}$ to $\frac{1}{3}$	—	①
968	$\frac{1}{4}$ to $+3$	$+3$	$\frac{1}{6}$ to $+\frac{1}{6}$	0	0 to $\frac{1}{3}$	—	①
1996							
911 Carrera	$+4\frac{5}{6}$ to $+5\frac{7}{12}$	$+5\frac{1}{3}$	$-\frac{2}{3}$ to $-\frac{1}{6}$	$-\frac{1}{3}$	0 to $+\frac{1}{6}$	—	①
911 Turbo	$+4\frac{5}{6}$ to $+5\frac{7}{12}$	$+5\frac{1}{3}$	$-\frac{2}{3}$ to $-\frac{1}{6}$	$-\frac{1}{3}$	0 to $+\frac{1}{6}$	—	①

① — Refer to "Ball Joint Inspection" in "Front Suspension & Steering."

REAR WHEEL ALIGNMENT SPECIFICATIONS

Year	Model	Camber Angle, Deg.		Toe Per Wheel, Deg.①
		Limits	Desired	
1993	911 Carrera 2	$-\frac{1}{2}$ to $-\frac{1}{6}$	$-\frac{1}{3}$	$+\frac{1}{6}$ to $+\frac{1}{3}$
	911 Carrera 4	$-\frac{1}{2}$ to $-\frac{1}{6}$	$-\frac{1}{3}$	$+\frac{1}{6}$ to $+\frac{1}{3}$
	911 Turbo	$-\frac{11}{12}$ to $-\frac{7}{12}$	$-\frac{3}{4}$	$+\frac{1}{6}$ to $+\frac{1}{3}$
	928 GTS	$-\frac{5}{6}$ to $-\frac{1}{2}$	$-\frac{2}{3}$	$+\frac{1}{6}$ to $+\frac{1}{3}$
	968	$-1\frac{1}{12}$ to $-\frac{5}{12}$	$-\frac{3}{4}$	$+\frac{1}{12}$ to $+\frac{1}{4}$
1994–95	911 Carrera	$-1\frac{7}{12}$ to $-1\frac{1}{12}$	$-1\frac{1}{6}$	0 to $+\frac{1}{3}$
	928 GTS	$-\frac{5}{6}$ to $-\frac{1}{2}$	$-\frac{2}{3}$	$+\frac{1}{6}$ to $+\frac{1}{3}$
	968	$-1\frac{1}{12}$ to $-\frac{5}{12}$	$-\frac{3}{4}$	$+\frac{1}{12}$ to $+\frac{1}{4}$
1996	911 Carrera	$-1\frac{7}{12}$ to $-1\frac{1}{12}$	$-1\frac{1}{6}$	0 to $+\frac{1}{3}$
	911 Turbo	$-1\frac{7}{12}$ to $-1\frac{1}{12}$	$-1\frac{1}{6}$	$+\frac{1}{6}$ to $+\frac{1}{3}$

① — Toe-in (+); toe-out (-).

FLUID CAPACITIES & COOLING SYSTEM DATA

Year	Model	Cooling Capacity, Qts.	Fuel Tank Gals.	Engine Oil Refill Qts.	Transmission Oil Pts.	
					Manual①	Auto.
1993	911 2	—	20.3	12.2	7.6	⑥
	911 4	—	20.3	12.1	③	—
	911 Turbo	—	20.3	13.7	3.92	—
	928 GTS	16.9	22.7	8.0	—	⑤
	968	8.4	19.6	7.4	5.8	⑤
1994–95	911	—	⑦	12.2	7.6	21.0①
	928 GTS	16.9	22.7	7.9	—	23.7①
	968	8.4	19.6	7.4	5.8	16.2①
1996	911	—	⑧	10.1	6.3	21.0①
	911 Turbo	—	⑨	10.1	7.4	—

① — Includes final drive.
② — Transmission, 7.72 qts., use Dexron IID/IIE. Final drive, 3.16 qts., use multi-grade gear lube 75W-90 GL-5.
③ — Transmission w/final drive, 8 pts., front transmission 2.56 pts., use multi-grade gear lube 75W-90 GL-5.
④ — With plastic sump, 8.44 qts.
⑤ — Transmission, refill 3 qts., use Dexron IID/IIE. Final drive, 1.3 pts., use multi-grade gear lube 75W-90 GL-5.
⑥ — Transmission, refill 3.2 qts., total capacity 9.5 qts., use Dexron IID/IIE. Final drive, 1.9 pts., use multi-grade gear lube 75W-90 GL-5.
⑦ — Standard tank, 18.9 gallons; optional tank, 14.3 gallons.
⑧ — Standard tank, 16.6 gallons; optional tank, 20.2 gallons.
⑨ — Standard tank, 19.4 gallons; optional tank, 24.2 gallons.

LUBRICANT DATA

Year	Model	Lubricant Type			
		Transmission		Power Steering	Brake System
		Manual	Automatic		
1993–95	911 2	75W-90 GL-5	Dexron IID/IIE/III①	Dexron IID/IIE/III	DOT 3 or 4
	911 4	75W-90 GL-5	—	Dexron IID/IIE/III	DOT 3 or 4
	911 Turbo	75W-90 GL-5	—	Dexron IID/IIE/III	DOT 3 or 4
	968	75W-90 GL-5	—	Dexron IID/IIE/III	DOT 3 or 4 SL
	928 GTS	75W-90 GL-5	Dexron IID/IIE/III	Dexron IID/IIE/III①	DOT 4 Type 200
	911	75W-90 GL-5	Dexron IID/IIE/III①	Dexron IID/IIE/III	DOT 4 Type 200
1996	911	75W-90 GL-5	Dexron IID①	Dexron IID	DOT 4 Type 200
	911 Turbo	75W-90 GL-5	—	Dexron IID	DOT 4 Type 200

① — Final drive, 75W-90 GL-5.

Electrical

NOTE: On Air Bag Equipped Models, Refer To "Air Bag System Precautions" Located In The Front Of This Manual For System Disarming & Arming Procedures.

INDEX

	Page No.
Air Bags	37-45
Air Conditioning	37-41
Alternator, Replace	37-5
911	37-5
Alternators	37-44
Blower Motor, Replace	37-6
928	37-6
968	37-6
Combination Switch, Replace	37-6
928	37-6
968	37-6
Cooling Fans	37-42
Cruise Control	37-44
Dash Gauges	37-43
Dash Panels	37-47
Distributor, Replace	37-5
911 & 928	37-5
Evaporator Core, Replace	37-7
911	37-7
928	37-7
968	37-7
Fuel Pump Relay Location	37-4
Fuse Panel & Flasher Location	37-4
Headlamp Switch, Replace	37-5
928	37-5
968	37-5
Heater Core, Replace	37-6
928	37-6
968	37-7
Ignition Switch, Replace	37-5
911	37-5
928	37-5
Instrument Cluster, Replace	37-6
911	37-6
928	37-6
968	37-6
Neutral Safety Switch, Replace	37-5
928	37-5
Passive Restraints	37-45
Precautions	37-4
Air Bag Systems	37-4
Relay Center Location	37-4
Speed Controls	37-44
Starter Motors	37-44
Starter, Replace	37-4
911 w/ Manual Transmission	37-5
928, 968 & 911 w/Automatic Transmission	37-4
Steering Wheel, Replace	37-6
Installation	37-6
Removal	37-6
Stop Light Switch, Replace	37-5
911	37-5
928	37-5
968	37-5
Wiper Motor, Replace	37-6
911	37-6
968	37-6
Wiper Switch, Replace	37-6
928	37-6
Wiper Transmission, Replace	37-6

PRECAUTIONS

AIR BAG SYSTEMS

Refer to "Air Bag System Precautions" in the front of this manual for system disarming and arming procedures.

FUSE PANEL & FLASHER LOCATION

On 911 models, one fuse panel is located on the lefthand side of the luggage compartment, the other is in the engine compartment. On 968 models, a central fuse panel is located in the engine compartment. On 928 models, the fuse panel is located under the instrument panel on the passenger side.

On 911 models, the flasher is located in the luggage compartment. On 968 models, the flasher is located in the fuse block, at the lefthand side of the engine compartment. On 928 models, the flasher is located in the fuse block, under the righthand side of the instrument panel.

FUEL PUMP RELAY LOCATION

On 911 and 968 models, the fuel pump relay is located in the relay center on the lefthand side of the engine compartment. On 928 models, the fuel pump relay is located on the passenger side footwell relay panel.

RELAY CENTER LOCATION

Refer to "Fuse Panel & Flasher Location" for relay locations.

STARTER

REPLACE

928, 968 & 911 w/AUTOMATIC TRANSMISSION

1. Disconnect battery ground cable.

2. Disconnect battery and alternator wiring.
3. Disconnect ignition lead.
4. Remove starter attaching bolts, then the starter.
5. Reverse procedure to install.

911 w/ MANUAL TRANSMISSION

1. Disconnect battery ground cable, then remove engine guard.
2. Remove air distributor rail mounted on left and right sides of transmission.
3. Separate driveshaft from differential flange.
4. Disconnect solenoid electrical connectors.
5. Remove wire clamp holding solenoid wire to body, then remove tie-wrap from starter.
6. Remove clutch slave cylinder attaching bolts, then position slave cylinder aside. **Do not disconnect slave cylinder hydraulic line.**
7. Using a 10 mm socket, two short extensions tool No. 427, transverse handle tool No. 425, shop made extension pipe and a ratchet, remove upper starter mount nut.
8. Remove bolt from righthand side of starter assembly using transverse handle tool and extension pipe.
9. Use right hand to hold tool in place above transmission, then remove remaining starter bolt with ground cable.
10. Turn starter until solenoid points towards the halfshaft, then remove starter from its support.
11. Reverse procedure to install, noting the following:
    a. Use two tie wraps to attach solenoid to alternator wire.
    b. **Torque** starter attaching bolts and nuts to 29 ft. lbs.
    c. When attaching halfshaft flange to transmission end, make sure mating surfaces are clean and free from grease. Apply a thin coat of copper paste to bolt threads and **torque** to 59 ft. lbs.

ALTERNATOR

REPLACE

911

1. Disconnect battery ground cable.
2. Remove V-Belt cover and belt.
3. Press off fan wheel from alternator/cooling fan assembly using puller tool No. VW202, or equivalent. Adjust both puller hooks as required.
4. Disconnect alternator electrical connector.
5. Disconnect two alternator harness to engine ground wires, **Fig. 1.**
6. Remove alternator retaining screws and the alternator.
7. Install alternator into cooling fan housing. Ensure connections for B+ and terminal D+ are positioned opposite the TDC line mark (located on edge of cooling fan housing).
8. Apply a thin coat of Loctite 270, or equivalent, to alternator shaft, then install alternator cooling fan wheel onto shaft, **torque** fan wheel to 10 ft. lbs.

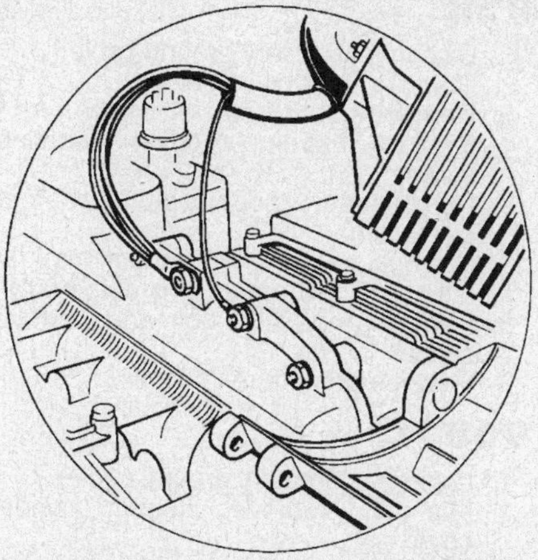
PR1129600002000X

Fig. 1 Alternator harness to engine ground wires. 911

9. Install air guide shroud, then connect alternator harness to engine ground wires.
10. Place alternator with cooling fan housing onto locating pin on crankcase and tighten retaining strap.

DISTRIBUTOR

REPLACE

911 & 928

On Carrera 4 models, a dual distributor is used. Both distributors are connected as one assembly.

1. Set cylinder 1 at Top Dead Center.
2. **On 911 models,** remove heated air elbow, if necessary.
3. **On all models,** remove ignition wires, then the distributor cap(s).
4. Remove distributor electrical and vacuum connectors.
5. Remove distributor hold-down bolt, then distributor.
6. Reverse procedure to install.

IGNITION SWITCH

REPLACE

911

1. Disconnect battery ground cable.
2. Remove ignition switch cover.
3. Drill out shear bolts and remove retaining screw.
4. Pull switch down far enough to allow removal of electrical connectors.
5. Remove ignition/starter switch retaining screws, then the switch.
6. Reverse procedure to install, tightening shear bolts until heads break off.

928

1. Disconnect battery ground cable.
2. Remove steering column switch cover.
3. Remove steering column switch attaching bolt.
4. Disconnect switch electrical connector(s), then remove switch.
5. Reverse procedure to install.

NEUTRAL SAFETY SWITCH

REPLACE

928

1. Place transmission lever in neutral position.
2. Disconnect electrical connections.
3. Remove operating lever retaining bolt.
4. Remove switch mounting bolts.
5. Install switch and mounting bolts.
6. Install operating lever on shaft.
7. Install lugs of driving dog into switch.
8. Install retaining bolt.
9. Install electrical connection.
10. Place transmission lever in neutral position.
11. Loosen adjusting nut.
12. Install 4 mm pin from US8030 tool set through drive dog into locating hole in case.
13. Tighten adjusting screw and remove locating pin.

HEADLAMP SWITCH

REPLACE

968

1. Press retainers on top and bottom of switch together.
2. Remove switch through back of dash.
3. Disconnect switch wiring.
4. Reverse procedure to install.

928

1. Remove switch knob.
2. Compress retaining springs.
3. Remove switch through front of instrument panel.

STOP LIGHT SWITCH

REPLACE

911

1. Disconnect flat electrical connector.
2. Remove retaining screws and remove switch.
3. Reverse procedure to install.

928

1. Disconnect electrical connectors at switch.
2. Remove mounting nuts attaching switch to bracket adjacent to brake pedal.
3. Remove stop light switch.
4. Reverse procedure to install.

968

1. Disconnect electrical connectors at switch.
2. Remove mounting nuts attaching switch to bracket adjacent to brake pedal.
3. Remove stop light switch.
4. Reverse procedure to install.

COMBINATION SWITCH

REPLACE

928

1. Disconnect battery ground cable.
2. Remove steering wheel.
3. Remove cover under steering column switch.
4. Remove steering column mounting bolts.
5. Remove instrument cover mounting screws.
6. Remove instrument cover and disconnect electrical connections.
7. Remove instrument column switch.
8. Reverse procedure to install.

968

1. Disconnect battery ground cable.
2. Manually pull off steering wheel cover.
3. Remove steering column cover mounting screws.
4. Remove steering column switch attaching screws and the steering column cover.
5. Disconnect electrical connector at switch.
6. Disconnect electrical connector for cruise control switch.
7. Reverse procedure to install.

STEERING WHEEL

REPLACE

REMOVAL

1. Remove horn pad.
2. Mark position of steering wheel.
3. Remove nut, then the steering wheel with washer.

INSTALLATION

1. Mount steering wheel with road wheels in straight ahead position or so that marks are positioned in such a manner that steering wheel spokes are horizontal.
2. Install nut and washer, then **torque** to 45 ft. lbs.
3. Align horn wires on horn pad, then press pad on to retaining pins.
4. Check function of horn and turn signal switch.

INSTRUMENT CLUSTER

REPLACE

911

Electrical connections are accessible from luggage compartment.

1. Disconnect battery ground cable.
2. Disconnect electrical connections from instrument to be removed.
3. **On models with mechanical speedometer,** remove flex shaft knurled nut.
4. **On all models,** remove knurled instrument retaining nuts and retaining clamp.
5. Remove instrument from passenger compartment.
6. Reverse procedure to install.

928

1. Disconnect battery ground cable.
2. Remove steering wheel.
3. Remove steering column switch.
4. Remove instrument cover mounting screws.
5. Remove rear window wiper and defogger switch.
6. Disconnect electrical connections.
7. Lift and tilt instrument cluster to rear.
8. Remove mounting bolt and remove cluster.
9. Reverse procedure to install.

968

1. Disconnect battery ground cable.
2. Manually remove steering wheel cover.
3. Remove steering wheel.
4. Remove eight instrument cover attaching screws and the cover.
5. Remove four instrument cluster attaching screws.
6. Pull cluster out far enough to gain access to electrical connectors.
7. Unlock and disconnect electrical connectors at cluster.
8. Remove cluster from vehicle.
9. Reverse procedure to install.

WIPER MOTOR

REPLACE

911

1. Disconnect battery ground cable.
2. Remove luggage compartment cover from rear of compartment.
3. Remove wiper arms.
4. Remove rubber discs located below wiper arms, then the retaining hex nuts.
5. Remove wiper motor with linkage downward and disconnect electrical connector.
6. Remove wiper motor from linkage.
7. Reverse procedure to install.

968

1. Disconnect battery ground cable.
2. Remove windshield wiper arms.
3. Pull off rubber seal with cover from above and loosen cement of cover below windshield.
4. Disconnect wiper motor electrical connector.
5. Remove wiper assembly attaching screws and the assembly.
6. Reverse procedure to install.

WIPER SWITCH

REPLACE

928

Refer to "Combination Switch, Replace" procedure.

WIPER TRANSMISSION

REPLACE

Refer to "Wiper Motor, Replace."

BLOWER MOTOR

REPLACE

928

1. Remove ignition key. Mark relation of hood to hinges (paint or scribe mark) for hood installation alignment. Remove hood from vehicle.
2. Remove right windshield wiper arm assembly.
3. Remove blower cover at cowl. Remove cowl top finish panel outer mounting screws (left and right ends at fender).
4. Remove two clamping screws at rubber connection between blower and A/C-heater unit. Do not attempt to detach A/C-heater end of rubber connection (permanently attached).
5. Disconnect blower harness leads at plug.
6. Remove three blower mounting screws as follows:
   a. Set control switch lever to AIR COND position.
   b. Insert screwdriver through open flap and remove mounting screw.
   c. Remove inner and outer mounting screws at housing.
7. Close main shutoff flap.
8. Lift edge of cowl top finish panel to provide clearance, and lift out blower assembly. Be careful to avoid damaging finish of painted panel.
9. Reverse procedure to install, replacing sealer at rubber connection to A/C-heater unit.

968

1. Remove windshield wiper arms, then the fresh air well cover.
2. Remove fresh air blower mounting screws, then disconnect electrical connectors.
3. Lift blower slightly and disconnect vacuum line, then remove blower.
4. Disconnect connector in holder, then the cable straps.
5. Disconnect vacuum hose, then remove fastening screws and lay blower housing on upper part and separate lower part.
6. Remove blower motor assembly.
7. Reverse procedure to install.

HEATER CORE

REPLACE

928

1. Discharge system refrigerant.
2. On vehicles equipped with electric seat operation, run seats back to rearmost position.
3. Disconnect battery ground strap from body.
4. Remove steering wheel impact pad and disconnect horn leads. Mark relation of steering wheel to shaft (paint mark), remove retaining nut, and remove steering wheel.
5. Remove covers below instrument cowl (pod) and steering column switch.

6. Loosen steering column switch mounting screw.
7. Remove instrument cowl (pod) mounting screws. Lift cowl, disconnect harness plugs at steering column switch, and remove switch.
8. Remove five switches mounted in cowl by removing knobs, then pressing in on spring clips to release switches from cowl. Disconnect harness plugs from switches. Mark for installation.
9. Disconnect harness plugs to printed circuit and mark for installation.
10. Lift cowl off and remove.
11. Remove console and control assembly.
12. Remove bracket for radio and speed control, then place to right side.
13. Remove three retaining screws at instrument panel, then remove steering protection tube.
14. Remove left and right side instrument panel mounting screws. Disconnect side ventilation hoses.
15. Disconnect vacuum line clips. Disconnect yellow and green vacuum lines from actuators at footwell flap and defroster flap.
16. Remove instrument panel.
17. Remove duct hoses from side ventilators to A/C-heater unit.
18. Remove four screws and remove defroster vents.
19. Open vehicle hood. Remove blower cover at right cowl.
20. Remove two clamping screws at rubber connection between blower and A/C-heater unit. Disconnect harness leads at temperature switch.
21. Disconnect wiper linkage at wiper motor to provide clearance.
22. Disconnect harness plugs at resistor block/safety switch. Disconnect violet vacuum line at shutoff flap actuator.
23. Disconnect refrigerant lines at expansion valve, and plug open connections.
24. Disconnect heater hoses at heater core.
25. Remove upper and lower mounting nuts at A/C-heater unit. Disconnect drain hose, then lift out unit from mounting.
26. Separate unit case halves, then remove heater core from case.
27. Reverse procedure to install.

968

1. Drain coolant, then discharge A/C system.
2. Remove windshield wiper arms, then the fresh air well cover.
3. Remove fresh air blower mounting screws, then disconnect electrical connectors.
4. Lift blower slightly and disconnect vacuum line, then remove blower.
5. Remove tray holder and ashtray, then the radio, if equipped.
6. Remove mounting screws on cover frame of center console, then console mounting screws and console.
7. Disconnect horn pad, then remove steering wheel.
8. Remove instrument cover, then unscrew and pull out instrument cluster.
9. Disconnect electrical connections on cluster, then remove cluster.
10. Remove sun visors, trim panel on front roof beam and trim panels on A-pillars.
11. Disconnect and unclip glove compartment light.
12. Remove glove compartment mounting screws and glove compartment.
13. Remove instrument panel mounting screws, then pull air guides out of instrument panel and remove panel.
14. Unclip instrument panel wiring harness, then disconnect connector.
15. Disconnect connector at interior sensor blower, then remove air ducts.
16. Remove drainage hose, then disconnect A/C lines.
17. Remove vacuum lines, then disconnect refrigerant hoses.
18. Remove inside and outside fastening nuts, then the bracket for instrument panel.
19. Remove Heater/A/C unit.
20. Separate unit case halves, then remove heater core from case.
21. Reverse procedure to install.

EVAPORATOR CORE

REPLACE

911

1. Disconnect battery ground cable.
2. Discharge refrigerant from A/C system.
3. Remove right floor mat from passenger compartment.
4. Remove pedal floor board.
5. Remove grating and plastic duct.
6. Remove front luggage compartment pivot bolt, then open flap.
7. Loosen hose clamp from air flex hose, then push hose from evaporator housing.
8. Pull temperature sensor from evaporator housing guide tube.
9. Loosen hose connection from expansion valve.
10. Disconnect blower motor electrical connector.
11. Remove screws from mounting bracket body.
12. Remove evaporator housing from cavity.
13. Reverse procedure to install.

928

1. Remove heater/air conditioner unit as outlined under "Heater Core, Replace."
2. Separate unit case halves, then remove evaporator core from case.
3. Reverse procedure to install.

968

1. Remove heater/air conditioner unit as outlined under "Heater Core, Replace."
2. Separate unit case halves, then remove evaporator core from case.
3. Reverse procedure to install.

4 Cylinder Engine

NOTE: On Air Bag Equipped Models, Refer To "Air Bag System Precautions" Located In The Front Of This Manual For System Disarming & Arming Procedures.

INDEX

	Page No.
Balance Shaft, Replace	37-11
Camshaft, Replace	37-10
Compensating Shaft Drive, Replace	37-12
Compression Pressure	37-8
Cooling System Bleed	37-13
Crankcase	37-13
Cylinder Head, Replace	37-9
Engine Mount, Replace	37-8
Installation	37-8
Removal	37-8
Engine Rebuilding Specifications	37-61
Engine, Replace	37-8
Fuel Filter, Replace	37-13
Fuel Pump, Replace	37-13
Lubricating System Service	37-12
Oil Pan, Replace	37-12
Pistons, Pins & Rings	37-12
Precautions	37-8
Air Bag Systems	37-8
Tightening Specifications	37-13
Timing Belt, Replace	37-9
Valve Arrangement	37-9
Valve Guides	37-9
Water Pump, Replace	37-13

PRECAUTIONS

AIR BAG SYSTEMS

Refer to "Air Bag System Precautions" in the front of this manual for system disarming and arming procedures.

COMPRESSION PRESSURE

1. Disconnect digital Motor Electronics (DME) control unit plug, located in passenger side footwell or connect ignition coil No. 4 terminal to ground with a jumper wire equipped with a 2000 ohm shielding sleeve.
2. Perform compression test with engine at normal operating temperature, spark plugs removed and throttle fully opened.
3. Compression should be 145 psi or higher, with a minimum of 95 psi on any cylinder.

ENGINE MOUNT

REPLACE

REMOVAL

1. Disconnect battery ground cable.
2. Suspend engine from front transport bracket using tool VW10-222, or equivalent and hold firmly in installed position. **It may be necessary to disconnect air flow sensor electrical connector and/or vent hose at air cleaner to gain access to transport bracket.**
3. Raise and support vehicle.
4. Remove splash guard.
5. Disconnect stabilizer mounts at control arms and the stabilizer suspension at side members and remove stabilizer.
6. Remove right engine mount shield attaching nut from front axle crossmember.
7. Remove hydraulic engine mount attaching nut from front axle crossmember.
8. **On models equipped with power steering,** disconnect power steering return line at side member.
9. **On all models,** disconnect universal joint at steering gear, hydraulic engine mount at engine brackets and front axle crossmember at side members. Mark relationship of universal joint to steering gear for proper assembly. Do not loosen control arm mounting bolts.
10. Pull down front axle crossmember far enough to allow removal of engine mount and disconnect driveshaft universal joint at steering gear.
11. Disengage top of engine mount from front axle crossmember.
12. Remove mount toward front of vehicle, turning mount 180° as necessary to facilitate removal.

INSTALLATION

1. Insert mount so that twist is positioned on stop at rear on righthand side and press top of mount into front axle crossmember.
2. Push correctly positioned driveshaft universal joint onto steering gear pinion.
3. Install front axle crossmember, raise crossmember with suitable lifting device to facilitate insertion of bolts, center crossmember and **torque** mounting bolts to 62 ft. lbs.
4. install but do not tighten mount attaching nuts and bolts.
5. Remove tool VW10-222, then connect air flow sensor electrical connector and the air cleaner vent hose.
6. Using new self locking nuts, **torque** to 22 ft. lbs. in order; hydraulic engine mount to front axle crossmember, hydraulic engine mount to engine brackets, universal joint to steering gear.
7. **On models equipped with power steering,** secure return line and, if applicable, the brake pad wear indicator wire on side member.
8. **On all models,** install right engine mount shield, stabilizer and splash guard, **torquing** stabilizer to body and control arms attaching bolts to 17 ft. lbs.

ENGINE

REPLACE

1. Disconnect battery ground cable.
2. Raise and support vehicle.
3. Disconnect positive battery cable and push through splash wall together with rubber grommet.
4. Disconnect two engine wiring harness plugs and remove wire clamps.
5. Disconnect wire plugs from control unit located by steering column.
6. Push wires and plugs through splash wall, then disconnect sensor wire bracket from intake pipe.
7. Disconnect throttle operating cable.
8. Disconnect and remove vacuum hose from brake booster.
9. Remove distributor cap, distributor rotor, and dust cap.
10. Disconnect ground wire at splash wall.
11. Clamp fuel return line and disconnect fuel feed line.
12. Disconnect fuel return line.
13. Attach tool VW 10-222, or equivalent, to front transport bracket of engine and secure engine in installed position.
14. Open heater regulating valve and remove cap from expansion tank.
15. Remove splash shield.
16. Remove exhaust assembly by unscrewing flange, exhaust manifold and exhaust pipe connections, and suspension points.
17. Disconnect oxygen sensor plug and wire in metal lug on firewall.
18. Disconnect electrical connections of starter, then remove starter mounting bolts and the starter.
19. Remove clutch line clamp located on engine.

20. Disconnect clutch slave cylinder from clutch housing, leaving lines connected.
21. Disconnect stabilizer at body and control arms and remove stabilizer.
22. Remove right engine mount shield from front axle crossmember.
23. Unscrew universal joint on steering gear, tie rods on steering arms, upper hydraulic engine mount on engine braces, left and right control arms on front axle crossmember, and remove front axle crossmember with steering from underneath vehicle.
24. **On models with air conditioning,** proceed as follows:
    a. Unscrew poly-rib belt tensioner and remove belt.
    b. Remove compressor from mount, leaving hoses attached, and suspend compressor from spring strut.
25. **On all models,** drain coolant through drain plug bore in radiator.
26. Remove coolant hose from bottom of radiator.
27. Remove upper central tube attaching bolts.
28. Lower vehicle.
29. Remove coolant hose from heater valve, heater coolant return hose, and coolant feed hoses from expansion tank.
30. Remove A/C fast idle hose and the charcoal venting hose.
31. Disconnect vacuum lines at vent valve and thermo valve.
32. Remove upper radiator hose and radiator vent hose.
33. Disconnect electrical connectors of temperature switch and both cooling fans.
34. Remove upper radiator brackets and lift out radiator with cooling fans.
35. Attach tool US 1105, or equivalent, to engine with shorter end toward rear of engine.
36. Lift engine slightly and remove tool VW 10-222.
37. Remove lower central tube mounting bolts.
38. Lower engine, pull forward, and remove from underneath vehicle.
39. Reverse procedure to install.

CYLINDER HEAD

REPLACE

1. Disconnect battery ground cable.
2. Remove cap from expansion tank.
3. Remove splash guard.
4. Drain coolant through coolant drain plug on radiator.
5. Remove drive belt, then the drive belt cover.
6. Turn engine to TDC of cylinder No. 1.
7. Remove distributor cap, distributor rotor, and dust cover.
8. Remove distributor cap mount.
9. Slacken belt tension and pull camshaft belt off of camshaft sprocket.
10. Loosen two mounting bolts on rear drive belt cover.
11. Disconnect fuel lines.
12. Remove plastic cover from fuel collection tube, pull off wire plugs on fuel injectors, and position wiring harness out of way.

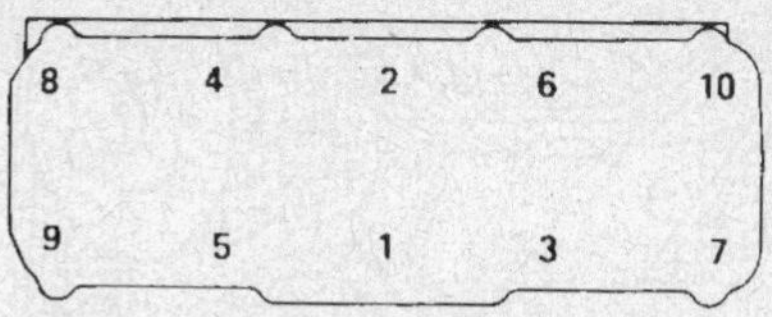
8
4
2
6
10
9
5
1
3
7
PR1069100001000X

Fig. 1 Cylinder head tightening sequence

13. Unscrew aluminum plugs, coolant line, and bolts with attached washers, then remove camshaft housing from cylinder head. **Ensure hydraulic valve tappets do not fall out and are not mixed up.**
14. Remove air cleaner assembly.
15. Remove intake brace attaching bolt.
16. Remove intake distributor by dismantling holder on oil dipstick tube, hose on brake booster, hose on intake distributor, retaining clamp on accelerator cable, and mounting bolts of intake distributor/cylinder head.
17. Remove bolts from flange connecting catalytic converter and exhaust manifold.
18. Remove hose clamp from heater regulating valve and the two screws on neck of cooling circuit.
19. Remove cylinder head attaching bolts in a criss-cross fashion from outside to inside, then remove cylinder head.
20. Reverse procedure to install, noting the following:
    a. Coat threads of cylinder head bolts with engine oil.
    b. Using sequence shown in **Fig. 1, torque** cylinder head bolts in three steps; first step to 15 ft. lbs., second step an additional 60°, third step an additional 90°. **When tightening cylinder head bolts, never lubricate bolts. Only lightly coat stud threads with clean engine oil. The washers must not turn when tightening.**
    c. Wait 30 minutes, then unscrew bolts ½ turn and retighten in sequence, **Fig. 1. Washers must not turn when tightening cylinder head bolts.**
    d. Tighten camshaft housing socket head bolts and aluminum plugs to specification.

VALVE ARRANGEMENT

Front to Rear: E-I-E-I-E-I-E-I

VALVE GUIDES

1. Clean and inspect cylinder head. Cylinder heads whose valve seats or sealing surfaces can no longer be machined are not suitable for replacement of valve guides.
2. Using spot facer, grind off enough of valve guides protruding from camshaft end so that guides are flush with cylinder head. **Be careful not to damage guide collar for spring retainers.**
3. Place cylinder head on tool 9220, or equivalent.
4. Using tool 9224, or equivalent, loosen valve guides from camshaft end by tapping lightly, then press out rest of guides using suitable press.
5. Measure bores in cylinder head with an internal gauge.
6. Using replacement valve guide part No. 92810432852, grind until outside diameter is .0024–.0031 inch greater than bore measurement.
7. Coat valve guides with talcum powder and install by tapping lightly, then, using tool 9221, or equivalent, align valve guides and press into cylinder head against stop from camshaft side. **If suitable equipment is available, cool valve guides in liquid oxygen and press into cylinder head heated to 374°F. Cylinder head should not be heated to 374°F. for longer than 90 minutes.**
8. Using broach, ream out valve guides to .3543–.3549 inch.

TIMING BELT

REPLACE

With timing belt removed, avoid turning camshaft or crankshaft. If movement is required, exercise extreme caution to avoid valve damage cause by piston contact.

1. Disconnect battery ground cable.
2. Remove engine splash shield, then remove air cleaner assembly with air flow sensor.
3. Disconnect vent hose and position aside.
4. Remove distributor cap and position aside.
5. Remove upper and lower timing belt covers.
6. Raise and support vehicle.
7. Ensure bolts of pressure rod are slightly loosened prior to loosening locknuts. Remove the accessory drive belts.
8. Rotate crankshaft in direction of engine rotation until camshaft sprocket TDC mark is aligned with cast mark on distributor cap console. Ensure marks on upper and lower balance shaft sprockets are aligned with marks on rear of timing belt cover. The flywheel TDC mark for No. 1 cylinder must also be aligned with cast boss on clutch housing.
9. Loosen balance shaft timing belt tensioner pulley to release tension belt.
10. Using care, remove balance shaft drive belt.
11. Loosen bolt and nut of camshaft timing belt tensioner at slotted end of tensioner. Use tool 9200 to move tensioner against spring force, then remove camshaft timing belt. Tighten nut and bolt to hold tensioner in the released position.
12. Ensure flywheel TDC mark is aligned with mark on flywheel housing. Also ensure camshaft sprocket mark is aligned with mark on timing belt rear cover, **Fig. 2.**
13. Position camshaft timing belt over

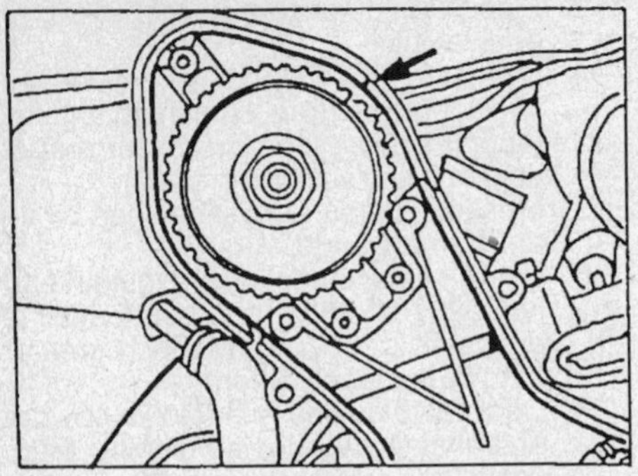

PR1069100002000X

Fig. 2 Camshaft sprocket timing marks

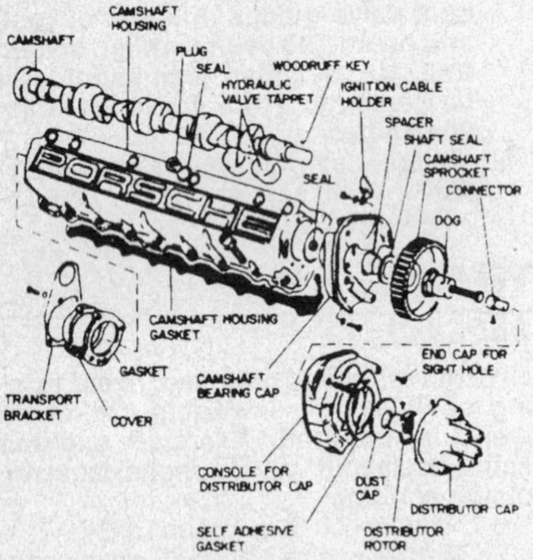
CAMSHAFT HOUSING
CAMSHAFT
PLUG
SEAL
WOODRUFF KEY
HYDRAULIC VALVE TAPPET
IGNITION CABLE HOLDER
SPACER
SHAFT SEAL
CAMSHAFT SPROCKET
CONNECTOR
SEAL
DOG
CAMSHAFT HOUSING GASKET
END CAP FOR SIGHT HOLE
GASKET
CAMSHAFT BEARING CAP
TRANSPORT BRACKET
COVER
CONSOLE FOR DISTRIBUTOR CAP
DUST CAP
DISTRIBUTOR CAP
SELF ADHESIVE GASKET
DISTRIBUTOR ROTOR

PR1069100005000X

Fig. 5 Camshaft housing exploded view

crankshaft sprocket, tensioner sprocket, water pump pulley and camshaft sprocket. Preload belt slightly by hand each time to ensure belt can be placed over camshaft sprocket. Use tool 9200 to move tensioner against spring force, when installing camshaft timing belt.

14. Ensure flywheel TDC mark is aligned with mark on flywheel housing. Also ensure camshaft sprocket mark is aligned with mark on timing belt rear cover.
15. Loosen nut and screw nearest slotted end of tensioner and allow tensioner spring to tension the timing belt.
16. Check mobility at tensioner roller lever by using thumb pressure on toothed side of belt between camshaft sprocket and water pump. Do not rotate crankshaft while tensioner nut and screw are loosened.
17. **Torque** timing belt tensioner screw and nut to 15 ft. lbs.
18. Apply a suitable locking compound to distributor rotor attaching bolt and connector attaching bolt, then install attaching bolts. Ensure distributor dust cap is properly positioned.
19. Ensure flywheel TDC mark is aligned with mark on flywheel housing. Also ensure camshaft sprocket mark is aligned with mark on timing belt rear cover. Rotate both balance shafts until marks on sprockets are aligned with marks on rear timing belt cover.

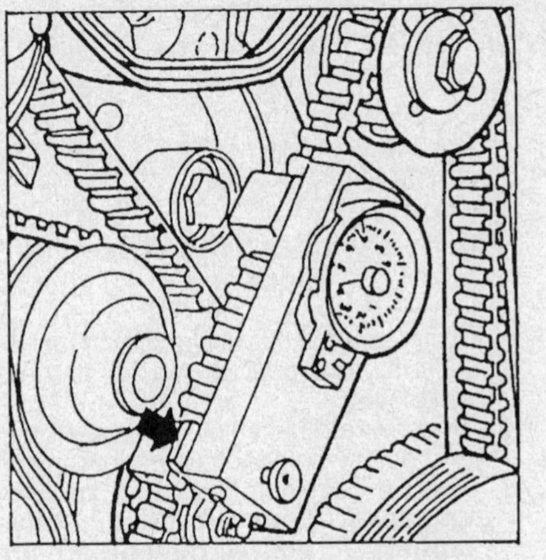

PR1069100003000X

Fig. 3 Positioning tool 9201 on balance shaft timing belt

20. Install balance shaft timing belt over sprockets with color coded tooth facing outward.
21. Pull lockpin form tool 9201 and push gauge pin, opposite lockpin out as far as possible. Align the tool telltale and measuring needles.
22. Slide tool No. 9201 onto balance shaft timing belt, then press tool measuring key until lockpin is heard to engage, **Fig. 3.** Note reading on dial gauge.
23. The tool dial gauge should indicate 2.7 to 3.0 scale graduations. Rotate tensioner roller clockwise to increase balance shaft timing belt tension or counterclockwise to decrease.
24. After completing balance shaft timing belt tensioning, tighten tensioner locknut to specifications.
25. Adjust idle pulley to provide a clearance of .5 mm between belt and pulley at lower balance shaft, when a 0 to 1 mm pretension is applied to the upper run of the timing belt. If adjustment can not be obtained, rotate idler pulley 180 degrees and repeat adjustment. After completing adjustment, Tighten idler pulley nut to specifications.
26. Install accessory drive belts.
27. Install timing belt upper and lower covers. Tighten attaching bolts to specifications.
28. Connect vent hose, then install engine splash shield.
29. Install air cleaner assembly with air flow sensor.
30. Connect battery ground cable.

CAMSHAFT

REPLACE

1. Disassemble balance shaft drive, **Fig. 4,** noting the following:
   a. Handle balance shaft drive belt with care, do not twist or turn. Store separately.
   b. When removing upper balance shaft drive gear attaching bolt, hold gear with tool 9200, or equivalent.
2. Disassemble camshaft drive, noting the following:
   a. When removing camshaft sprocket

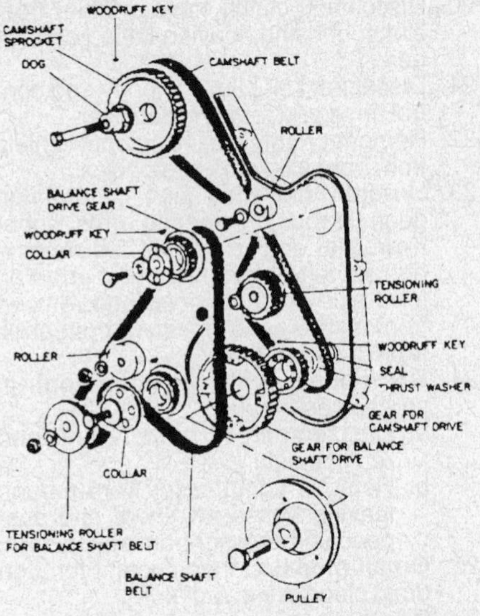
WOODRUFF KEY
CAMSHAFT SPROCKET
DOG
CAMSHAFT BELT
ROLLER
BALANCE SHAFT DRIVE GEAR
WOODRUFF KEY
COLLAR
TENSIONING ROLLER
WOODRUFF KEY
ROLLER
SEAL
THRUST WASHER
GEAR FOR CAMSHAFT DRIVE
GEAR FOR BALANCE SHAFT DRIVE
COLLAR
TENSIONING ROLLER FOR BALANCE SHAFT BELT
BALANCE SHAFT BELT
PULLEY

PR1069100004000X

Fig. 4 Balance shaft drive & camshaft drive exploded view

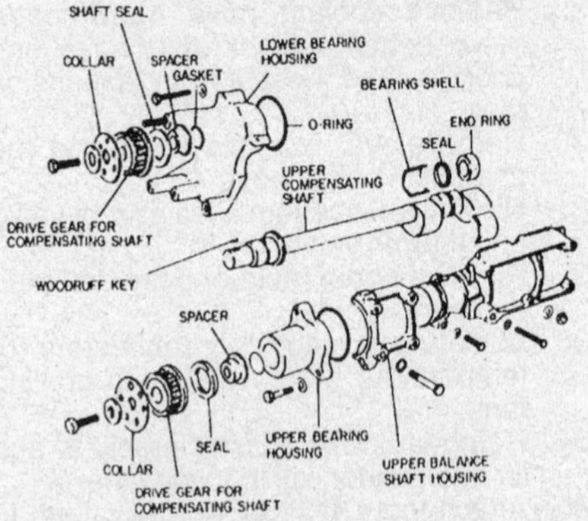
SHAFT SEAL
COLLAR
SPACER
GASKET
LOWER BEARING HOUSING
BEARING SHELL
O-RING
END RING
SEAL
UPPER COMPENSATING SHAFT
DRIVE GEAR FOR COMPENSATING SHAFT
WOODRUFF KEY
SPACER
SEAL
UPPER BEARING HOUSING
COLLAR
DRIVE GEAR FOR COMPENSATING SHAFT
UPPER BALANCE SHAFT HOUSING

PR1069100007000X

Fig. 6 Exploded view of balance shaft drive components

attaching bolt, hold dog with tool 9205, or equivalent.
3. Disassemble camshaft housing, **Fig. 5,** noting the following:
   a. Store valve tappets in order with oil bores facing up.
4. Assemble camshaft housing, noting the following:
   a. Cylinder No. 1 must be at TDC and camshaft sprocket must be aligned with mark when installing camshaft housing.
   b. Never crank engine when camshaft belt is loose or removed.
   c. Apply suitable locking compound to distributor rotor attaching bolt and connector attaching bolt when installing.
   d. Ensure distributor dust cap is correctly positioned.
   e. When installing camshaft sprocket attaching bolt, hold dog with tool 9205, or equivalent and **torque** bolt to 48 ft. lbs. Use only polygon head bolts when assembling.
   f. Install camshaft sprocket with mark aligned.
   g. Lubricate sealing lip of new front

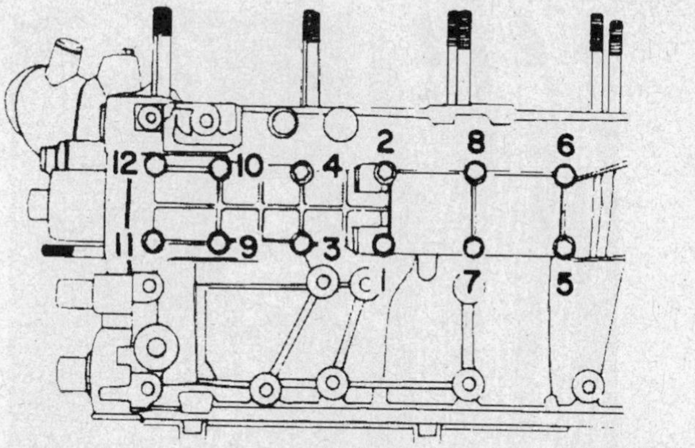
12
10
4
2
8
6
11
9
3
1
7
5

PR1069100008000X

Fig. 7 Balance shaft housing cover attaching bolt tightening sequence

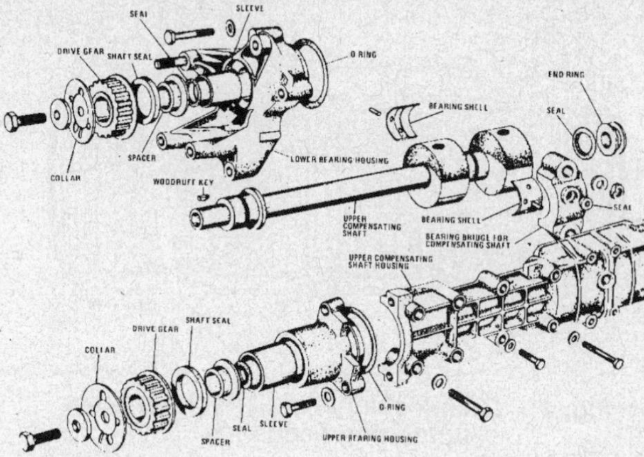

PR1069100009000X

Fig. 8 Exploded view of compensating shaft

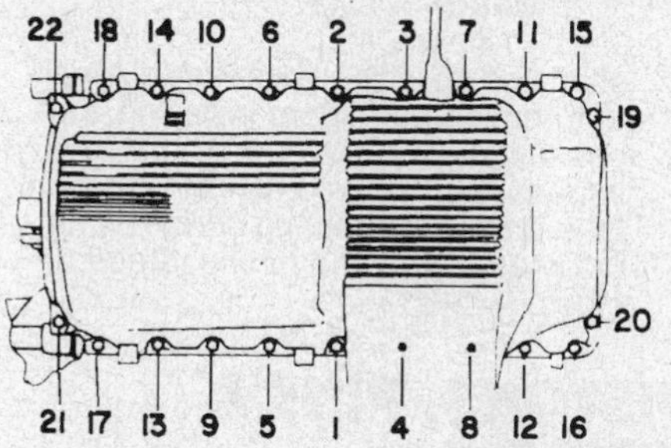
22 18 14 10 6 2 3 7 11 15
19
20
21 17 13 9 5 1 4 8 12 16

PR1099100001000X

Fig. 9 Oil pan bolt tightening sequence

shaft seal and install seal using tool 9202, or equivalent. Install new camshaft bearing cap gasket.

h. Lubricate and install new camshaft bearing cap O-ring.
i. Tighten valve cover attaching bolts.
j. Lubricate camshaft bearings with suitable lubricant.
k. Install new valve cover gasket with "TOP" mark facing up.
l. Install new gasket for rear camshaft housing cover.

5. Installing camshaft timing belt as described under "Timing Belt, Replace."
6. Assemble balance shaft drive.
7. Install balance shaft upper drive gear as follows:
   a. Ensure woodruff key groove of balance shaft faces up and insert woodruff key.
   b. Apply thin coat of Optimoly HT, or equivalent on drive gear bearing surface.
   c. Install drive gear with groove code "O" toward woodruff key.
   d. Install collar with locating tab inserted into unmarked groove of drive gear so that code "O" is visible in large bore of collar.
   e. Coat threads of bolt with suitable locking compound and install bolt and washer.
   f. Using tool 9200 or torque wrench, **torque** bolt to 33 ft. lbs.
8. Install balance shaft lower drive gear as follows:
   a. Ensure woodruff key of balance shaft faces up and insert woodruff key.
   b. Apply thin coat of Optimoly HT, or equivalent on drive gear bearing surface.
   c. Install drive gear with groove code "O" opposite woodruff key.
   d. Install collar with its locating tab inserted into groove "O" of drive gear so that "O" is visible in square opening of collar.
   e. Coat threads of bolt with suitable locking compound and install bolt and washer.
   f. Using tool 9200, or equivalent, **torque** bolt to 33 ft. lbs.
9. Install balance shaft drive belt as follows:
   a. Turn crankshaft clockwise until TDC mark on camshaft sprocket is aligned with mark cast on distributor cap mount.
   b. Ensure TDC marks on flywheel and cast clutch housing are aligned.
   c. Rotate both balance shafts until marks of balance shaft sprockets align with marks on rear drive belt cover.
   d. Install drive belt with color coded tooth facing out. Do not twist belt.
10. Adjust balance shaft portion of drive belt as follows:
   a. Loosen idler pulley so pulley does not contact drive belt.
   b. Turn crankshaft clockwise until TDC mark on camshaft sprocket aligns with cast marking on distributor cap mount.
   c. With engine in this position, TDC marks on flywheel and cast clutch housing must also be aligned properly.
   d. Alignment marks on sprockets should be aligned with marks of rear drive belt cover.
   e. Install tool P9201, or equivalent. Pull out lockpin on tool and push out gauge pin opposite the lockpin completely.
   f. Zero the telltale needle.
   g. Slide tool onto belt. Push in gauge needle until lockpin engages (audible click).
   h. Note reading obtained from dial gauge of tool. **Always zero the telltale needle on gauge tool after the lockpin has engaged (turned counterclockwise) to eliminate incorrect gauge readings.**

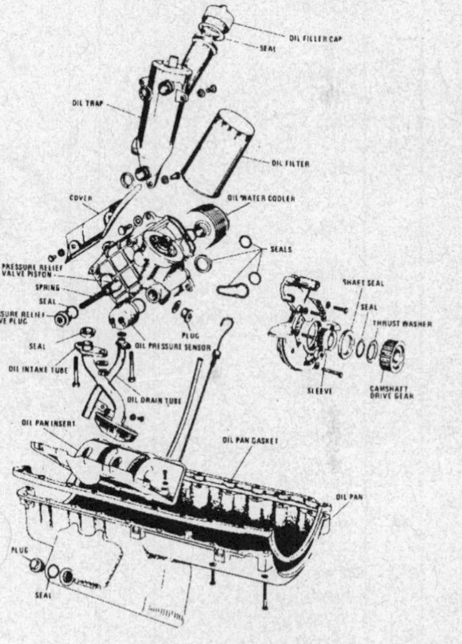

PR1069100006000X

Fig. 10 Exploded view of lubricating system

   i. Reading obtained should be 2.4–3. To adjust, turn tensioner clockwise to tighten or counterclockwise to loosen. After adjustment tighten attaching nut.
   j. After adjusting tension, adjust idler pulley. Using tool 9207 or a .0196 inch (.5 mm) feeler gauge, ensure a clearance of .0196 inch (.5 mm) between drive belt and pulley when upper portion of drive belt is preloaded approximately 0–.039 inch (0–1 mm). With correct clearance obtained, tighten idler pulley attaching nut. If correct clearance cannot be obtained, turn idler pulley 180° and repeat adjustment. After adjustment tighten nut.

BALANCE SHAFT

REPLACE

1. Disassemble balance shaft drive as

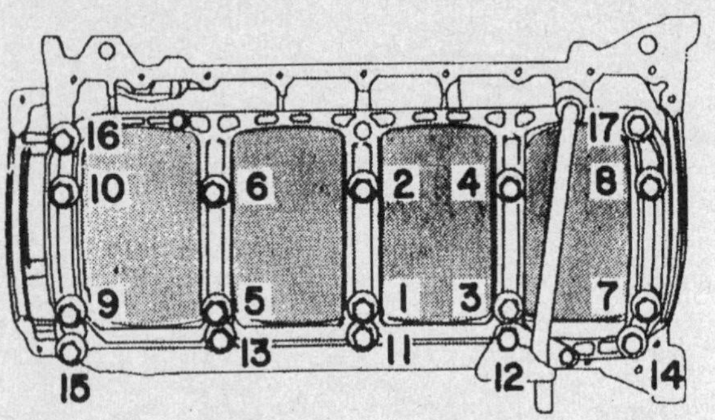
16
17
10
6
2
4
8
9
5
1
3
7
13
11
12
14
15

PR1069100010000X

Fig. 11 Crankcase halves attaching bolts tightening sequence

PR1089100001000X

Fig. 12 Cooling system upper radiator hose air bleeder

No.	Description	Qty.
1	Circlip	1
2	Thermostat	1
3	Seal	1
4	Molded gasket	1
5	Socket head screw M 6 x 70	1
6	Washer	1
7	Socket head screw M 6 x 35	7
7a	Washer	7
8	Bracket	1
9	Hexagon nut M 6	3
10	Washer	3
11	Water pump, assembly	1
12	Gasket	1

12
8
11
9
6
10
5
8
9
7a
7
4
3
2
1

PR1089100002000X

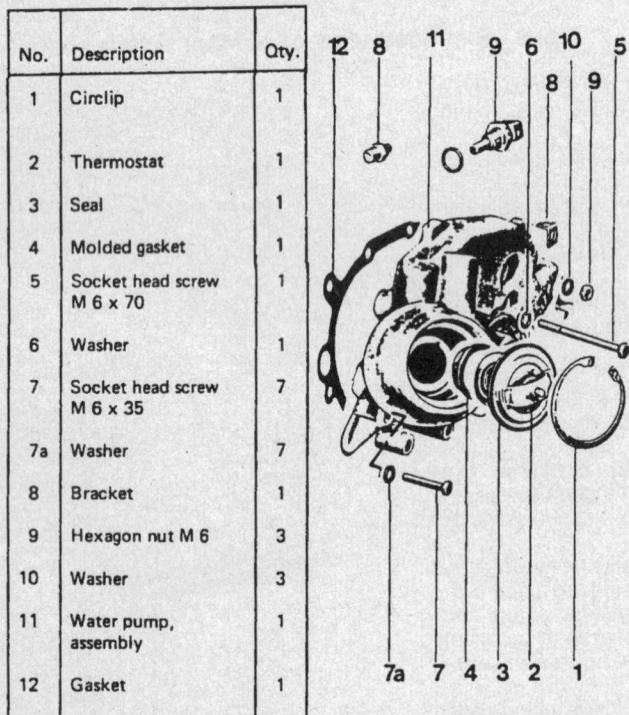

Fig. 13 Water pump and related components

described under "Camshaft, Replace."

2. Disassemble camshaft drive as described under "Camshaft, Replace."
3. When removing and installing balance shaft drive, refer to **Fig. 6.**
4. When installing balance shaft housing, proceed as follows:
   a. Tighten all hexagon head bolts and hexagon nuts finger tight.
   b. Install bearing housing with new lightly oiled O-ring without tightening attaching nuts.
   c. **Torque** bolts in sequence, **Fig. 7. Torque** M6 bolts to 6 ft. lbs. **Torque** M8 stud nuts in two steps to 11 and 22 ft. lbs. **Torque** M8 bolts in two steps to 11 and 14 ft. lbs. Check movement of balance shaft between each tightening step.
5. Refer to "Camshaft, Replace" for assembling camshaft drive, assembling balance shaft drive, installing balance shaft drive gears, and installing and adjusting balance shaft drive belt.

COMPENSATING SHAFT DRIVE

REPLACE

For all operations concerning compensating shaft, **Fig. 8,** other than those mentioned, follow operations as described in "Balance Shaft, Replace."

1. Crankcase upper and lower sections and bearing bridges of compensating shaft are matched and must be installed as set with code numbers matching exactly.
2. When bearing bridges are correctly installed, codes of both bridges should be readable from front.
3. Right side bearing bridges are stamped with a 1 and the left side with a 2.
4. Bearing bridge for left compensating shaft has an oil feed bore for oil supply to turbocharger. When installing compensating shaft cover, it is extremely important to ensure seal is inserted in take-up bore of bearing bridge on naturally aspirated and turbocharged engines.

PISTONS, PINS & RINGS

The cylinder codes are stamped on the engine block and piston codes are stamped on the piston crowns. Piston oversizes are available in 3.9559 inch (100.48 mm), 3.9563 inch (100.49 mm), 3.9567 inch (100.5 mm), 3.9756 inch (100.98 mm), 3.9560 inch (100.99 mm), and 3.9764 inch (101 mm). When installing rings, offset 120°.

OIL PAN

REPLACE

1. Drain crankcase and remove dipstick.
2. Disconnect battery ground cable.
3. Remove oil pan attaching bolts.
4. To loosen pan, strike gently with a soft faced hammer.
5. Disconnect steering at crossmember, if necessary.
6. Remove crossmember and loosen left engine mount bolts, if necessary.
7. Remove pan.
8. Reverse procedure to install. Using sequence shown in **Fig. 9, torque** oil pan bolts in two steps; first step to 36 inch lbs., second step to 90 inch lbs.

LUBRICATING SYSTEM SERVICE

1. When removing lubricating system components, refer to **Fig. 10,** noting the following:
   a. When removing oil pan, be careful not to damage oil intake pipe.
   b. When removing oil trap, intake distributor must be removed.
2. When assembling oil pump, note the following:

a. Install new shaft seal. Apply suitable lubricant to seal lip and install seal together with toothed sleeve and drive in using tool 10-203, or equivalent.
b. **Torque** countersunk screws to 6 ft. lbs.
c. Apply suitable sealant on outside diameter of housing insert.
d. Lubricate inner and outer rotors with suitable oil and ensure punch mark on outer rotor faces out.
e. Apply suitable sealant to face end of oil pump housing.

3. When installing lubricating system components, note the following:
   a. When installing oil dipstick guide tube, use suitable sealant.
   b. When installing new drain plug, use new seal ring and tighten plug to specifications.
   c. Coat threads of oil pan insert attaching bolts with suitable locking compound.
   d. Before installing oil pan insert, open tabs and clean inside.
   e. Coat oil drain pipe attaching bolt with suitable locking compound.
   f. Tighten oil intake pipe attaching bolts to specifications.
   g. When installing camshaft drive gear, ensure belt collar faces balance shaft drive gear.
   h. Replace housing plug seal and **torque** plug to 25 ft. lbs.
   i. Replace oil pressure sensor O-ring seal and **torque** sensor to 25 ft. lbs.
   j. Replace pressure relief valve plug seal and **torque** plug to 33 ft. lbs.
   k. Check pressure relief valve piston for wear or signs of seizure, replacing as necessary.
   l. When installing oil/water cooler, pre-assemble in housing and install together with crankcase upper section.
4. When installing oil pump, note the following:
   a. Align oil pump body surface with upper crankcase section before tightening mounting bolts.
   b. Apply toothed sleeve on sealing lip and seal simultaneously and drive in using tool 10-203, or equivalent.
   c. Coat both sides of gasket in area of corners with sealant before installing oil pan gasket. **New oil pump cannot be installed in older engines.**

CRANKCASE

Crankcase upper and lower sections and balance shaft cover are machined together and must be replaced as a set. Ensure code numbers match and install balance shaft covers so that codes are visible from above. When sealing upper and lower crankcase halves, apply thin coat of suitable locking compound in areas of oil intake and sealing surface in areas of flywheel. **Torque** crankcase connecting stud nuts in sequence, **Fig. 11.**

COOLING SYSTEM BLEED

1. Set heater control lever at "warm" position.
2. Remove bleeder plug, **Fig. 12.**
3. Add coolant slowly until coolant level remains steady at maximum mark on expansion tank.
4. Start engine and run at fast idle speed to reach operating temperature **until radiator fan has cycled on and off.**
5. When no more air bubbles are visible in bleeder opening, replace bleeder plug and tighten hose clamp.
6. Check coolant level, adding coolant if necessary.

WATER PUMP

REPLACE

Refer to **Fig. 13** for water pump replacement.

FUEL PUMP

REPLACE

1. Disconnect battery ground cable, then remove fuel pump cover from bottom right of vehicle.
2. Pinch suction hose with standard clamp, then remove suction hose.
3. Disconnect electrical plug, then remove pressure line from fuel filter.
4. Remove right fuel tank strap at bottom, then the lower guard with fuel pump.
5. Remove fuel line and electrical connector from pump, then loosen hose clamp and remove fuel pump.
6. Reverse procedure to install.

FUEL FILTER

REPLACE

1. Disconnect battery ground cable.
2. Place shop towel over fuel filter line fittings and position a suitable container under fuel filter.
3. Using a back-up wrench on fuel filter fitting, loosen fuel line fittings.
4. Disconnect fuel lines from filter, then loosen filter retaining clamp and remove fuel filter.
5. Reverse procedure to install.

TIGHTENING SPECIFICATIONS

Year	Component	Torque/Ft. Lbs.
1993–95	Balance Shaft Case Cover To Engine Block (Nut)	④
	Balance Shaft Case Cover To Engine Block (Bolt)	④
	Camshaft Sprocket To Camshaft	33
	Connecting Rod Bolt With Smooth Bearing Surface	42
	Connecting Rod Bolt With Ribbed Bearing Surface	55
	Crankcase Upper Sections To Lower Sections	⑥
	Cylinder Head To Engine Block	③
	Flywheel To Crankshaft	66
	Front Axle Crossmember	62
	Gear To Balance Shaft	33
	Gear Wheel To Crankshaft	150
	Idler Pulley Nut	33
	Left And Right Engine Braces To Crankcase	35
	Main Bearing Cap Bolts	⑤

Continued

TIGHTENING SPECIFICATIONS—Continued

Year	Component	Torque/Ft. Lbs.
1993–95	Oil Drain Plug	36
	Oil Intake Pipe	36
	Oil Pan To Crankcase	①
	Oil Pan Insert To Oil Pan	4②
	Spark Plugs	18–22
	Tensioning Roller To Oil Pump Body	33
	Timing Belt Tensioner Locknut	33
	Vibration Damper Or Pulley	151
	Water Pump To Crankcase	5.9②

①— Refer to "Oil Pan, Replace" for tightening procedure.
②— Lock w/Loctite 270, or equivalent.
③— Refer to "Cylinder Head, Replace" for tightening procedure.
④— Refer to "Balance Shaft, Replace" for tightening procedure.
⑤— Hex socket bolt, 32 ft. lbs.; polygon socket bolt, 47 ft. lbs.
⑥— Torque in three steps: (1) 15 ft. lbs., (2) 30 ft. lbs., (3) 55 ft. lbs.

6 Cylinder Engine

NOTE: On Air Bag Equipped Models, Refer To "Air Bag System Precautions" Located In The Front Of This Manual For System Disarming & Arming Procedures.

INDEX

Page No.

Compression Pressure 37-14
Engine Assemble 37-15
Assembling Crankcase Halves.. 37-16
Camshaft Housing Installation... 37-17
Camshaft Installation............ 37-18
Chain Tensioners, Replace...... 37-18
Cylinder Head Installation....... 37-17
Cylinder Installation............. 37-16
Driveshaft Pilot Bearing, Replace 37-16
Flywheel Installation 37-15
Main Bearing No. 1 Oil Seal, Replace 37-16
Main Bearing No. 8 Oil Seal, Replace 37-16
Piston Installation............... 37-16
Rocker Arm Installation 37-17
Split Timing Chain Installation... 37-19
Valve Timing, Adjust 37-18
Valves, Adjust.................... 37-18
Valves, Replace 37-17
Engine Disassemble............. 37-15
Engine Rebuilding Specifications 37-61
Engine, Replace 37-14
Fuel Filter, Replace 37-19
Fuel Pump, Replace 37-19
Front Pump...................... 37-19
Rear Pump 37-19
Precautions...................... 37-14
Air Bag Systems................ 37-14
Tightening Specifications 37-19

PRECAUTIONS

AIR BAG SYSTEMS

Refer to "Air Bag System Precautions" in the front of this manual for system disarming and arming procedures.

COMPRESSION PRESSURE

1. **On non-turbo models,** disconnect digital motor electronics (DME) control unit plug located under driver's seat.
2. **On all models,** perform compression pressure check with engine at normal operating temperature, spark plugs removed and throttle wide open.
3. Compression should be 142–184 psi with a minimum of 107 psi on any cylinder. Pressure should not vary more than 22 psi between cylinders.

ENGINE

REPLACE

1. Raise and support vehicle.
2. Disconnect battery ground cable.
3. Loosen A/C compressor bracket attaching bolts and position aside. **Do not disconnect refrigerant lines.**
4. Remove air cleaner assembly.
5. Label for identification, then disconnect all electrical connectors, vacuum lines and coolant hoses from engine.
6. Disconnect and cap fuel lines, as necessary.
7. Remove rear end cover attaching bolts, then the cover.
8. Pull seal off of retaining edge on body and push forward over selector rod.
9. Raise vehicle and drain engine oil. Disconnect oil hose or oil line on engine and pan.
10. Remove rear stabilizer bar.
11. Disconnect ground strap on body.
12. Disconnect electrical connectors and cables from starter motor.
13. Loosen clutch cable retainer.
14. Remove clutch release lever and spring.
15. Remove positioning lever and spring.
16. Remove release lever from release lever shaft.
17. Remove driveshaft from differential flange.
18. Suspend left driveshaft from vehicle using a suitable piece of wire.
19. Remove rear cowl panel attaching

screws, then the rear cowl panel.
20. Support transaxle assembly with a suitable jack.
21. Loosen transaxle carrier attaching bolts.
22. Loosen engine carrier attaching bolts.
23. Lower support jack slightly, then disconnect electrical connector from shock absorber crossmember as well as plug on air flow sensor.
24. Lower jack with engine/transaxle carefully and roll out toward rear of vehicle. **If vehicle has to be moved after removal of engine/transaxle assembly, suspend driveshafts from vehicle in a horizontal position.**
25. Reverse procedure to install.

ENGINE DISASSEMBLE

When disassembling the engine or when removing components from the engine, never use a lead pencil to place alignment marks on cylinder head assemblies or use a sharp tool to pry off engine components as damage may result. Keep disassembled components in order and on a clean workbench to facilitate assembly.

1. Install engine in suitable working fixture.
2. Remove air filter cover and filter.
3. Remove air injection pump with filter, bracket and hoses, if equipped.
4. Remove EGR valve, connecting pipe and bracket from air distribution/filter housing, if equipped.
5. Disconnect injection system electrical connectors and position connectors clear of intake pipes.
6. Remove throttle control rod and return spring from throttle housing.
7. Remove auxiliary air regulator and auxiliary air valve from right side of engine.
8. Remove all hose clamps and tie wraps.
9. Remove nuts attaching intake manifold and carefully lift manifold off together with air distribution/filter housing fuel distributor, fuel lines and injectors.
10. Mark distributor cap, housing and rotor alignment for assembly, then remove distributor cap, ignition wires and ignition coil.
11. Remove distributor from engine.
12. Disconnect air ducts connecting air blower outlets and heat exchanger inlets and remove together with cover shrouds.
13. Remove all retaining screws for cooling air ducts and cover shrouds.
14. Loosen two screws of band strap on alternator/blower housing.
15. Pull blower housing rearward and remove air guide from alternator.
16. Disconnect electrical connectors at alternator and remove alternator with blower housing and fan.
17. Remove upper air guide with wiring harness.
18. Remove rear engine mount crossmember from engine mount.
19. Remove muffler flange attaching bolts and nuts.

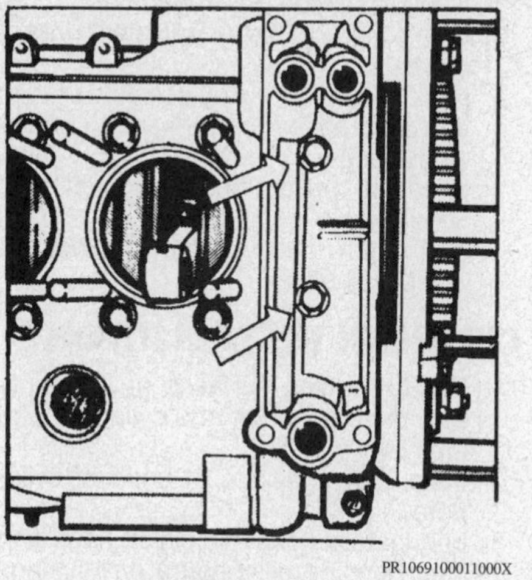
PR1069100011000X

Fig. 1 Bearing No. 1 cap nuts location

20. Loosen muffler straps at rear center mount and remove muffler.
21. Remove engine mount attaching bolts.
22. Remove heat exchangers, removing thermal reactors, catalytic converter, EGR filter with lines and air injection lines as equipped.
23. **On models with air conditioning,** remove compressor bracket from right chain housing cover.
24. **On all models,** disconnect camshaft oil supply lines, then remove both chain housing covers.
25. Remove chain tensioner attaching nuts and pull tensioner out with idler pulley.
26. Using tool P9191, or equivalent, remove camshaft sprocket attaching nuts.
27. Using tool P212, or equivalent, withdraw aligning dowels from chain housing.
28. Remove chain guides from chain housing. **Ensure pistons do not collide with valves when rotating crankshaft or camshafts.**
29. Remove sprocket wheels and wheel flanges.
30. Remove woodruff keys from camshafts.
31. Remove three sealing flange retaining bolts and push out flange with suitable tool.
32. Remove nuts attaching chain housings to crankcase.
33. Remove stud bolts, then the chain guides, from inside of crankcase.
34. Remove oil cooler attaching nuts and the oil cooler.
35. Remove oil pressure relief valve and safety valve.
36. Remove intermediate shaft cover, then the intake and exhaust valve covers.
37. To remove cylinder heads individually, proceed as follows: **When reusing original parts, mark relationship for assembly in original position. The design of the engine allows individual cylinder heads to be removed. Do not place marks of any kind on cylinder head such as lead pencil marks or use a screwdriver to pry off cylinder head or serious engine damage will result. If no work is to be performed on either the cylinder heads or camshaft housings, the entire cylinder head bank can be removed as an assembly.**
    a. Disconnect battery ground cable.
    b. Remove cover plates and heat exchanger only from the side from which it is desired to remove the cylinder head.
    c. Remove rear engine support and exhaust muffler assembly.
    d. Carefully remove camshaft drive only from desired side.
    e. Loosen camshaft housing attaching nuts, then remove spring washers and lift off camshaft housing. **There are three (3) .315 inch (3 X 8 mm) internal hexagon attaching nuts on the camshaft housing.**
    f. Loosen cylinder head attaching nuts and lift cylinder head from engine.
38. To remove camshaft housing and cylinder heads as an assembly, proceed as follows:
    a. Loosen evenly, then remove cylinder head attaching nuts.
    b. Remove cylinder heads with camshaft housing, then cooling air shrouds and cylinders.
39. Remove piston pin retaining clips and drive out piston pin with suitable tool.
40. Remove engine crankcase breather cover, oil pressure sensor, thermostat and oil drain cover with screen.
41. Remove M8 nuts and washers attaching crankcase halves together.
42. Using suitable tools, remove flywheel.
43. Remove nuts from studs at bearing No. 1, **Fig. 1,** then the nuts inside the oil cooler flange on right crankcase half. **Crankcase must be turned so left crankcase half faces upward and right crankcase half can support crankshaft and intermediate shaft.**
44. Remove nut on stud inside left chain housing, **Fig. 2.**
45. Remove attaching bolts, then separate crankcase halves.
46. Remove crankshaft and mount in tool P209a, or equivalent. Label connecting rods according to cylinder, then remove connecting rods.
47. Remove oil pump attaching nuts, then remove oil pump, connecting shaft, intermediate shaft and chains as an assembly.

ENGINE ASSEMBLE

Engine is assembled in reverse order of disassembly, following instructions given for different assembly groups.

FLYWHEEL INSTALLATION

1. Ensure contact surfaces of crankshaft and flywheel are clean.
2. Install and tighten flywheel attaching bolts.

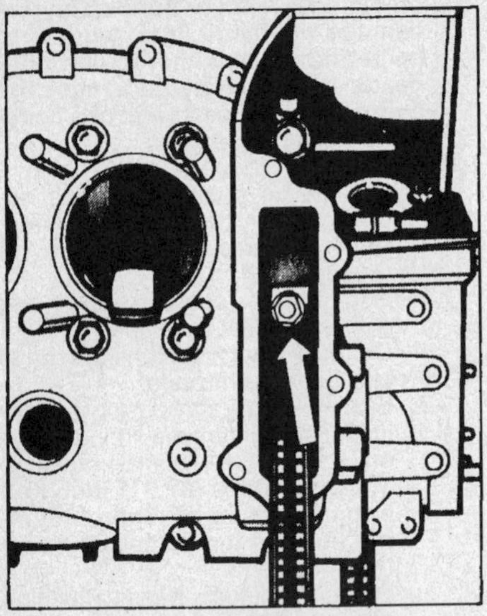

PR1069100012000X

Fig. 2 Left chain housing nut removal

DRIVESHAFT PILOT BEARING, REPLACE

Replace driveshaft pilot bearing with flywheel installed on vehicle.

1. Remove driveshaft pilot bearing attaching bolts.
2. Coat threads of attaching screws with suitable locking compound and **torque** to 7 ft. lbs.

MAIN BEARING NO. 1 OIL SEAL, REPLACE

1. Remove flywheel as previously described.
2. Using screwdriver, pry out oil seal at cutout in left crankcase half.
3. Clean seal contact surface of crankshaft.
4. Coat outer surface of new oil seal with suitable sealing compound.
5. Lubricate sealing lip of new oil seal.
6. Using suitable tools, drive in oil seal until flush with crankcase.
7. Install flywheel as previously described.

MAIN BEARING NO. 8 OIL SEAL, REPLACE

Crankshaft oil seal can be replaced without removing engine from vehicle.

1. Remove drive belt pulley as follows:
   a. Using tool P208b, or equivalent, remove cooling fan pulley attaching nut.
   b. Loosen A/C compressor and remove drive belt.
   c. Loosen and remove drive belt pulley attaching bolt, then remove pulley.
2. Pry out oil seal at cutout in crankshaft bearing No. 8.
3. Clean oil seal contact surface on crankshaft.
4. Coat outer sealing surface of new oil seal with suitable sealant.
5. Lubricate sealing lip of new oil seal and position seal on crankshaft.
6. Using tool P216, or equivalent, install oil seal.
7. Install drive belt pulley as follows:
   a. Clean pulley to crankshaft contact surfaces.
   b. Install pulley on crankshaft and align with locating pin.
   c. Tighten pulley attaching bolt to specifications.

CYLINDER INSTALLATION

1. Ensure mating surfaces at the joints with the crankshaft and cylinder head are clean.
2. Install new gaskets at base of cylinders.
3. Lubricate pistons and piston rings with clean engine oil. Ensure piston rings are installed with "TOP" marking facing upward.
4. Stagger piston ring gaps opposite each other (approximately 90° apart) with oil scraper ring gap to the top.
5. Using tool US1008a, or equivalent, compress piston rings.
6. Apply light coat of clean engine oil to cylinder bore and install cylinder. Ensure studs protruding from crankcase do not contact cylinder cooling fins. **The installed height of the cylinder is divided into two categories. Only cylinders of the same height and bearing the same mark stamped on the lower flange should be installed in the same bank. The mark consists of an equilateral triangle containing a number denoting cylinder height. Do not interchange cylinders.**
7. Install air deflector plates.
8. Install cylinder heads.

PISTON INSTALLATION

1. Ensure connecting rod tolerances are within specifications.
2. Clean piston, removing any heavy oil discoloration on piston crown and in ring grooves, being careful not to damage surfaces. **An uneven blue mark or one sided traces of carbon deposits on piston body at a right angle to piston axis may be caused by a bent connecting rod.**
3. Ensure piston rings are in good condition and that ring gaps and groove clearances are within specifications.
4. Measure piston. Dimensional groups are marked on crowns of pistons.
5. Using tool VW121b, or equivalent, install piston rings with "TOP" mark facing upward.
6. Install piston pin circlip on one side of piston, then insert piston pin from opposite side of piston.
7. Install piston on connecting rod so that larger valve pocket machined on piston faces intake side.
8. Install second circlip so that opening in circlip faces either piston crown or in opposite direction.
9. Install cylinders.

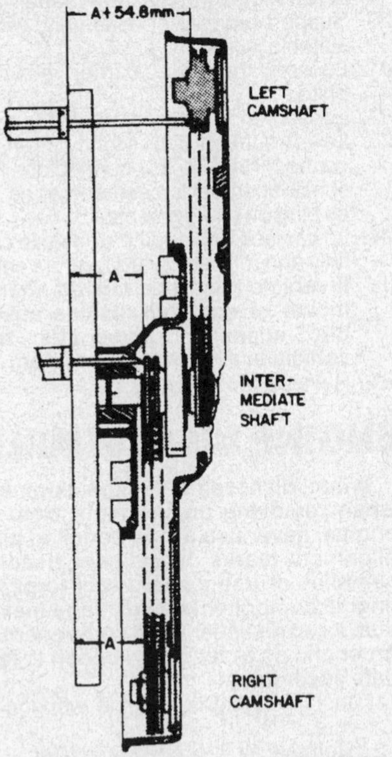
A+54.8mm
LEFT CAMSHAFT
A
INTER-MEDIATE SHAFT
A
RIGHT CAMSHAFT

PR1069100013000X

Fig. 3 Camshaft sprocket alignment

ASSEMBLING CRANKCASE HALVES

1. Clean gasket sealing surfaces of crankcase halves.
2. Bolt together crankcase halves and measure bearing housings in crankcase. Bore diameter should be 2.55095–2.5598 inches.
3. Recondition main bearing bores as necessary.
4. Clean out all oil passages and blow clear using compressed air. An annular groove is cut around main bearing No. 7 through bolt on lefthand crankcase half sealing surface. Keep groove free of dirt or sealing compound.
5. Place intermediate shaft with connecting shaft and oil pump in crankcase without drive chain.
6. Turn intermediate shaft by hand and ensure intermediate shaft, connecting shaft and oil pump turn and mesh smoothly. If any out-of-roundness is visible, gear teeth in mesh must be altered until all parts rotate freely.
7. Remove intermediate shaft with connecting shaft, but do not separate gear wheels.
8. Place drive chains on intermediate shaft chain wheels.
9. Insert sealing ring in oil passage between righthand crankcase half and oil pump housing.
10. Install intermediate shaft with oil pump into righthand crankcase half with new tab washers and nuts, then tighten to specifications and bend up tab washers.
11. Place main bearing shells for bearings

2 through 7 in position in both crankcase halves.
12. Place shells for main bearing No. 1 in position in both crankcase halves.
13. Install crankshaft with bearing No. 8 into right crankcase half.
14. Coat shaft sealing ring at outer extremity with suitable sealant and install flush with exterior of crankcase half.
15. Position and tighten retaining clips for connecting rod and chain.
16. Position sealing rings between oil pump and lefthand crankcase half and the sealing ring linking oil passage between two halves of crankcase.
17. Apply thin coat of suitable sealant to mating surface of crankcase.
18. Install tools P221 and P222, or equivalents in right crankcase half.
19. Install lefthand crankcase half.
20. Assemble through bolts as follows:
    a. Install double chamfer washer in bore so that smoother surface faces crankshaft.
    b. Push on O-ring.
    c. Push through bolt into position from righthand half of crankcase.
    d. Place O-ring on end of through bolt.
    e. Install second double chamfer washer so that smoother surface faces crankshaft.
    f. Install cap nut. **Bearing No. 1 has studs for attachment rather than through bolts. The studs are inserted into the lefthand side below oil cooler flange. Sealing rings and nuts must be installed as described in step 20.**
21. When attaching main bearing No. 7 to stud in chain housing of lefthand crankcase half, use standard washer and nut.
22. Tighten through bolts and studs evenly across crankcase to specifications.
23. Use No. 8 spring washers on all crankcase retaining studs, replacing nuts and **torquing** to 16–18 ft. lbs.
24. Using tools P236 and US1006, or equivalents, install flywheel. Tighten attaching bolts to specifications.
25. Ensure crankshaft turns freely and that chains and connecting rods do not jam.
26. Install pistons, ensuring that flat spot of piston faces intake valve.
27. Cover crankcase openings, then install piston pin retaining circlips so that open end of circlip faces either crankshaft or piston top.
28. Using tool US1008a, or equivalent, compress piston rings.
29. Install new cylinder base gasket on cylinder and carefully push cylinder onto piston until cylinder covers all piston rings.
30. Remove tool and push cylinder into its base in crankcase until it seats on sealing surface.
31. Secure cylinder in position by placing spacer bushings onto two diagonally opposed studs and tightening nuts.
32. Install remaining cylinders.

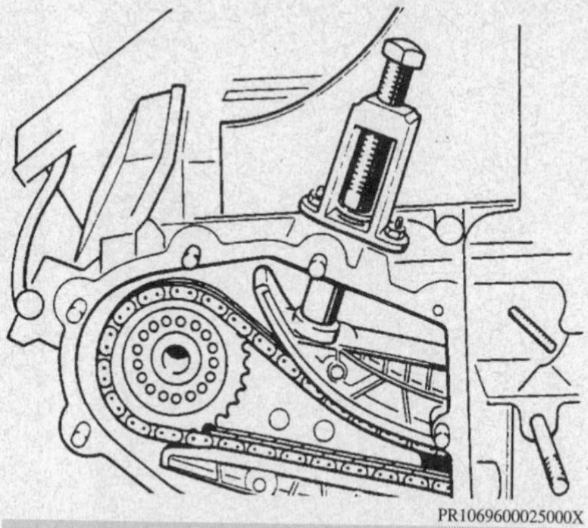
PR1069600025000X

Fig. 4 LH side timing chain tensioner (RH side similar)

CYLINDER HEAD INSTALLATION

Reverse removal step 37 to install cylinder head, noting the following:

1. Before installing cylinder head assembly, ensure head and block surfaces are clean and in good condition.
2. Install a new cylinder head gasket.
3. Threads of cylinder head attaching nuts must be lubricated with "Moly" grease part No. 999 917 728 00, or equivalent, to ensure correct attaching nut torque.
4. Insert washers .413 X .826 X .118 inch (10.5 X 21 X 3 mm) and tighten hexagon nuts. **Tighten cylinder head attaching nuts only lightly to allow movement of cylinder head to properly align camshaft housing.**
5. The mating surface on which the camshaft housing rests is also a sealing surface. No gasket is provided, but the cylinder head face should be coated with suitable sealing compound.
6. Assemble camshaft housing and oil return pipes. Place spring washers and nuts in correct position but do not tighten.
7. Tighten cylinder head attaching nuts.

VALVES, REPLACE

1. Remove cylinder head as previously described.
2. Using tool US1020, or equivalent, compress valve spring.
3. Remove split valve keepers and valve spring retainer.
4. Remove valve springs and spring seat.
5. Remove burrs from valve cotter seats as necessary.
6. Remove valves.
7. Remove valve stem seal and valve spring height adjustment shims.
8. Recondition cylinder head and/or valves as necessary.
9. Check valve springs with standard spring tester. When replacing valve spring, inner and outer spring must be replaced as a set.
10. Check installed length of valve spring as follows:
    a. Install tool P10c, or equivalent, with respective spring retainer and both valve keepers.
    b. Determine indicated value. Installed length of intake valve should be 1.346–1.370 inch. Installed length of exhaust valve should be 1.346–1.370 inch.
    c. If installed length of valve is not within specifications, adjust with correct number of shims. Thickness of shim is .0197 inch.
11. Replace valve stem seals on both intake and exhaust valve guides.
12. Install valve springs. Outer spring is progressively wound and the closely wound coils should be at cylinder head side. **It is not necessary to check installed length of inner springs.**
13. Test valve seating.

CAMSHAFT HOUSING INSTALLATION

The camshaft housing is designed to be fitted to either cylinder block. Press fit cover plate accordingly.

1. Clean sealing surfaces of cylinder heads.
2. Ensure cylinder head studs in cylinder head are firmly seated.
3. Apply very thin coat of suitable sealant on mating surface of camshaft housing.
4. Install oil return tubes into crankcase.
5. Place camshaft housing on cylinder head and oil return tubes. **Cylinder heads may have to be moved slightly to align with camshaft housing.**
6. Place nuts and spring washers on camshaft housing securing studs and loosely tighten.
7. Evenly tighten cylinder head nuts.
8. Install camshaft in camshaft housing.
9. Tighten camshaft housing nuts progressively across cylinder heads. **When tightening camshaft housing, check camshaft for binding in its bearings. If camshaft binds, loosen camshaft housing and retighten in a different order until stresses are relieved and camshaft turns freely.**
10. Install chain guides in crankcase, inserting retaining stud bolts and chain guides at same time.
11. Check for proper positioning of chain guide in groove of stud bolt and tighten to specifications. **Chain guides are installed with longer portion of guide pointing toward nearest gear. Lower right chain guide is brown plastic and remaining five chain guides are black plastic.**
12. Install chain housing gaskets on crankcase.
13. Install chain housings and tighten retaining nuts to specifications.
14. Install remaining chain guides on their respective supports.

ROCKER ARM INSTALLATION

1. Install rockers on shafts. **End rocker arm shafts must always be replaced so that the heads of the Allen head screw securing them face toward cylinders 2 and 5.**
2. Insert rocker shaft until feeler gauge can be passed between camshaft

housing and the rocker into the groove formed on the rocker shaft.
3. Push rocker shaft further in direction of assembly until feeler gauge is held firmly in position then remove feeler gauge.
4. Push rocker arm shaft in an additional .059 inch and tighten.

CAMSHAFT INSTALLATION

1. Install camshaft and ensure it turns freely.
2. Lubricate rotating surfaces with suitable lubricant.
3. Install new sealing ring and O-ring and tighten three attaching screws.
4. Install thrust washer, replacing as necessary.
5. Install spacing washers to same thickness as removed, then install key.
6. Install camshaft sprocket flange.
7. Install camshaft sprockets. Camshaft sprockets are axially offset but are interchangeable. Mount camshaft sprocket on left bank so that deeper recess is visible. Mount camshaft sprocket on right bank so that shallow recess faces back.
8. Tighten camshaft sprocket attaching nut and bolt to specifications.
9. Align camshaft sprockets in relation to drive sprockets as follows:
   a. Push intermediate shaft and camshaft toward flywheel to seat shafts against bearing thrust flanks.
   b. Using straightedge and depth gauge, measure through the hole below the intermediate shaft against front flank of drive sprocket.
   c. Rest straightedge against crankcase inline with camshaft end and measure from near side of straightedge to front flank of drive sprocket.
   d. If measurement obtained in steps b and c differ by more than .01 inch, add or remove spacers between camshaft sprocket flange and thrust plate as necessary.
   e. Push camshaft of cylinders 1 through 3 forward to rest against flank and repeat steps b and c. When checking alignment of camshaft sprocket for cylinders 1 through 3, add 2.157 to distance "A," **Fig. 3.**
   f. Adjust camshaft sprocket for cylinders 4 through 6 so that distance "A," **Fig. 3,** is the same for both sprockets.
10. Install rocker arms, adjust valve timing and adjust valve clearance.

VALVES, ADJUST

When adjusting valve clearances, the valves should be checked in the normal firing order, 1-6-2-4-3-5. The piston of the appropriate cylinder must be at TDC (both intake and exhaust valves closed). TDC markings for each cylinder are located on the belt pulley assembly. Beginning with the No. 1 cylinder, the crankshaft and belt pulley should be turned to the right (normal direction of engine rotation), until both the intake and exhaust valves are closed and the cylinder TDC marking (Z1) on the belt pulley coincides with the mark on the crankcase. To adjust the valves, proceed as follows:

1. Remove valve covers and gaskets, if necessary.
2. Rotate engine until piston of cylinder to be checked is at TDC of compression stroke (in firing order).
3. Using a suitable feeler gauge, check valve clearance.
4. Loosen adjusting screw hexagon nut.
5. Adjust clearance by turning adjusting screw using a suitable screwdriver while holding nut secure. With engine cold, intake and exhaust valve clearance should be .0039 inch (.1 mm).
6. Hold adjusting screw and check to ensure clearance has not changed.
7. Rotate crankshaft in direction of engine rotation until next mark is reached (120°). In this position, check valve clearances for No. 6 cylinder.
8. Turn crankshaft another 120° until piston of No. 2 cylinder is at TDC and check valve clearances.
9. Repeat this procedure until all the valves have been checked.

CHAIN TENSIONERS, REPLACE

Chain tensioners can be replaced without removing engine if muffler and engine rear shrouding are removed.

1. Turn crankshaft to bring No. 1 piston to TDC.
2. Remove chain housing cover.
3. Remove chain tensioner retaining nut and take out tensioner, **Fig. 4.**
4. When installing new chain tensioner, proceed as follows. **Use only chain tensioner, part No. 93010505300, with spacer, part No. 93010551300.**
   a. Push tensioner assembly on shaft of sprocket wheel carrier until half of plunger shaft head is covered by the tensioner arm.
   b. Turn lock ring until hold-down clamp can be removed.
   c. Push chain tensioner fully on sprocket wheel carrier and secure.

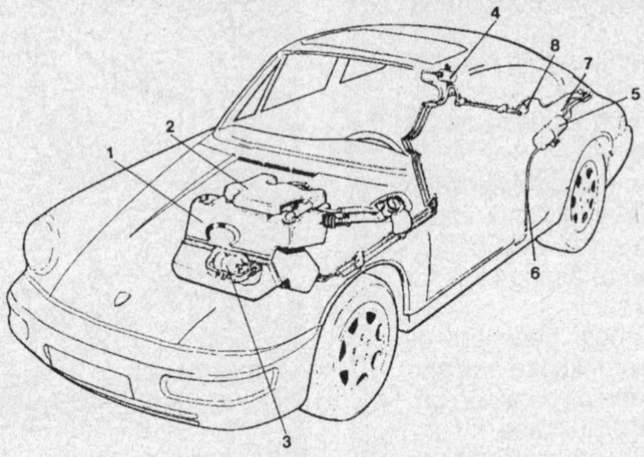
1
2
3
4
5
6
7
8
1 – Fuel tank
2 – Expansion tank
3 – Fuel pump
4 – Fuel filter
5 – Carbon canister
6 – Flushing air pipe
7 – To engine
8 – Fuel return
PR1029100001000X

Fig. 5 Fuel filter location

5. When installing reconditioned chain tensioner, proceed as follows:
   a. Compress tensioner assembly in suitable vise.
   b. Slowly tighten vise until plunger is depressed, then hold piston in depressed position with tool P214, or equivalent.
   c. Install tensioner and remove tool.
6. Tighten chain tensioner retaining nut to specifications.
7. Check valve timing and adjust as necessary.
8. Install chain housing cover.

VALVE TIMING, ADJUST

1. Turn crankshaft until mark "Z1" on pulley is aligned with joint of crankcase or stripe on fan housing.
2. Position both camshafts so that punch marks face up.
3. Insert locating pin in hole in sprocket that is exactly aligned with hole in sprocket flange.
4. Lightly tighten sprocket bolts, holding sprocket with tool 9191, or equivalent.
5. If either camshaft is not positioned with punch mark facing up, proceed as follows:
   a. Remove locating pin from camshaft which is correctly positioned.
   b. Using tool 9191, or equivalent, turn camshaft until punch mark faces up.
   c. Remove sprocket mounting bolt and locating pin and again turn crankshaft to mark "Z1."
6. Adjust valve clearance of intake valves for cylinders No. 1 and 4 to .0039 inch.
7. Using tool 9182, or equivalent, preload timing chains.
8. Using tool P207, or equivalent, mount dial gauge on stud of camshaft housing.
9. Set dial gauge to zero on spring retainer of intake valve for cylinder No. 1 with valve closed and approximately .394 inch preload.
10. Slowly turn crankshaft clockwise and observe dial indicator. Turn crankshaft

until dial indicator reads .061 inch.

11. Remove left sprocket mounting bolt, then, using tool P212, or equivalent, pull out locating spring.
12. Turn crankshaft until mark "Z1" on pulley is exactly aligned with joint of crankcase or stripe on fan housing.
13. Install locating pin and tighten bolt finger tight.
14. Turn crankshaft 720° and check gauge reading. Reading should be .0551–.0669 inch.
15. Using tool P9191, or equivalent, hold camshaft and **torque** bolt to 86 ft. lbs.
16. Set cylinder No. 4 to TDC, then perform steps 8 through 15 on cylinder No. 4.

SPLIT TIMING CHAIN INSTALLATION

Split timing chains can be replaced without removing and disassembling engine. When replacing both chains, they must be replaced one after the other as chains run in opposite directions.

1. Remove spark plugs, then turn crankshaft to mark "Z1" of cylinder No. 1.
2. Remove chain tensioner, sprocket wheel with support, and camshaft gear.
3. Grind open both pins of one link of old chain, protecting engine from grinding dust.
4. Attach new chain with chain lock to end of old chain.
5. Using suitable tool, move camshaft approximately 45° outward.
6. Slowly turn crankshaft in direction of normal engine rotation while keeping chain tensioned.
7. Turn engine until connecting link can be inserted at other end of new chain.
8. Remove old chain and close new chain with connecting link. Insert connecting link from front with shims, then install spring lock with closed end pointing in direction of rotation.
9. Install camshaft gear, sprocket wheel and chain tensioner.
10. Check valve timing and adjust as necessary.

FUEL PUMP

REPLACE

FRONT PUMP

1. Disconnect battery ground cable, then remove bottom guard.
2. Pinch suction hose with standard clamp, then remove suction hose.
3. Remove pump electrical connector, then remove pressure line.
4. Loosen hose strap, then remove fuel pump.
5. Reverse procedure to install.

REAR PUMP

1. Disconnect battery ground cable, then remove pressure line.
2. Remove pump electrical connector, then the suction line.
3. Dismount fuel pump from console.
4. Loosen hose clamp, then remove fuel pump from holder.
5. Reverse procedure to install.

FUEL FILTER

REPLACE

1. Disconnect battery ground cable.
2. Place shop towel over fuel filter line fittings and position a suitable container under fuel filter, **Fig. 5.**
3. Using a back-up wrench on fuel filter fitting, loosen fuel line fittings.
4. Disconnect fuel lines from filter, then loosen filter retaining clamp and remove fuel filter.
5. Reverse procedure to install.

TIGHTENING SPECIFICATIONS

Year	Component	Torque/Ft. Lbs.
1993–96	Camshaft Cover To Camshaft Housing	7
	Camshaft Sprocket Attaching Nut	108
	Camshaft Sprocket Attaching Bolt	86
	Chain Guides	18
	Chain Tensioner Nut	18
	Connecting Rod Bolt	②
	Crankcase	25
	Crankshaft Pulley	③
	Cylinder Heads To Engine Block	①
	Drive Pulley To Camshaft	66
	Dual Mass Flywheel	63
	Engine Carrier Bolts	65
	Flywheel Except Dual Mass	65
	Gear To Balance Shaft	33
	Heat Exchanger To Cylinder Head	15–17
	Knock Sensor To Engine Block	15
	Oil Pan Drain Plug	50
	Oil Pump To Crankcase	17
	Oil Pipe Connections	60–75
	Rocker Arm Shaft	15
	Spark Plugs	15–22
	Timing Chain Tensioner Nut	18
	Vibration Damper Or Pulley	173

① — Except Turbo, torque in two steps: (1) 11 ft lbs., (2) turn bolt 90°. Turbo, torque in 2 steps, (1) 7 ft. lbs.; (2) 24 ft. lbs.

② — Torque in three steps: (1) 11 ft lbs., (2) turn bolt 90°, (3) turn bolt an additional 90°.

③ — Pulley with single groove, 58 ft. lbs.; pulley with double groove, 122 ft. lbs.

V8 Engine

NOTE: On Air Bag Equipped Models, Refer To "Air Bag System Precautions" Located In The Front Of This Manual For System Disarming & Arming Procedures.

INDEX

	Page No.
Camshaft, Replace	37-23
Compression Pressures	37-20
Cooling System Bleed	37-23
Crankshaft Rear Oil Seal, Replace	37-23
Cylinder Head, Replace	37-21
Engine Rebuilding Specifications	37-61
Engine, Replace	37-20
Fuel Filter, Replace	37-23
Fuel Pump, Replace	37-23
Main & Rod Bearings	37-23
Oil Pump, Replace	37-23
Piston & Rod Assembly	37-23
Pistons, Pins & Rings	37-23
Precautions	37-20
Air Bag Systems	37-20
Tightening Specifications	37-24
Timing Belt, Replace	37-21
Timing Belt, Adjust	37-22
Valve Guides	37-21

PRECAUTIONS

AIR BAG SYSTEMS

Refer to "Air Bag System Precautions" in the front of this manual for system disarming and arming procedures.

COMPRESSION PRESSURES

1. Disconnect electronic control unit (ECU) plug or connect ignition coil No. 4 terminal to ground with jumper wire.
2. Perform compression test with engine at operating temperature, spark plugs removed and throttle wide open.
3. Compression pressure should be 114 psi or higher, with a minimum of 95 psi on any cylinder.

ENGINE

REPLACE

1. Disconnect battery ground cable.
2. Remove cross strut.
3. Disconnect windshield washer and heated spray jet hoses and the engine compartment light electrical connector.
4. Disconnect gas pressure prop lock at bottom and remove hood.
5. Remove air cleaner assembly with intake hoses.
6. Remove coolant expansion tank cap and the radiator upper air guide section.
7. Raise and support vehicle.
8. Remove engine splash guard and drain coolant from radiator.
9. Remove water drain plugs on both sides of upper crankcase section.
10. Drain oil from crankcase.
11. Disconnect exhaust pipes and secondary air injection lines at exhaust manifolds.
12. Disconnect engine to body ground wire at engine.

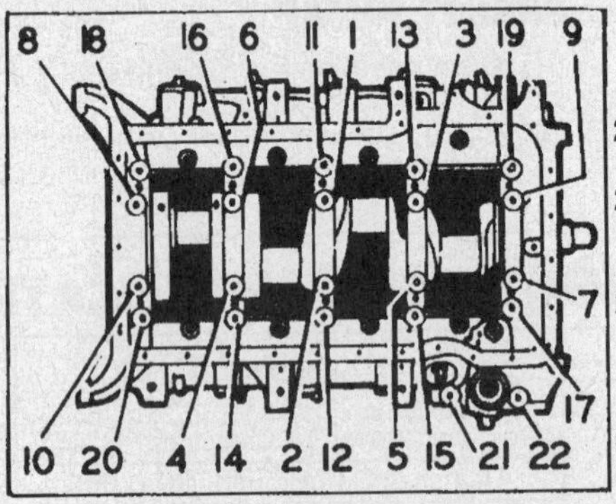
8 18 16 6 11 1 13 3 19 9
7
17
10 20 4 14 2 12 5 15 21 22
PR1069100014000X

Fig. 1 Cylinder head tightening sequence

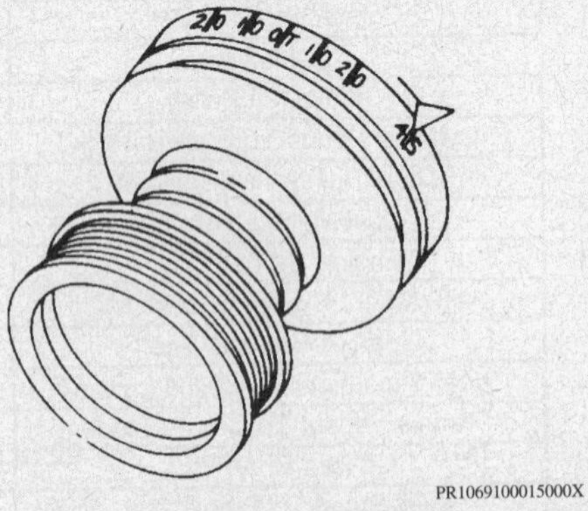
PR1069100015000X

Fig. 2 Aligning 45° BTDC mark

13. Install radiator drain plug. Tighten to specifications.
14. Remove radiator lower air guide section from radiator.
15. Disconnect ventilation hose at alternator.
16. Disconnect electrical connectors at starter.
17. Disconnect starter wiring clamps on steering crossmember and pull forward toward alternator.
18. Remove clutch housing cover.
19. Remove driveplate attaching bolts, loosen clamping sleeve bolt and push driveplate back on central shaft. **Pins for TDC sensor must face down when removing engine.**
20. Remove bolts attaching transaxle mounts.
21. Disconnect automatic transaxle vacuum hose at cylinder head and remove clamp.
22. Remove clutch housing mounting bolts at engine block and push transaxle rearward approximately .197–.236 inch (5–6 mm).
23. Lower vehicle.
24. Disconnect electrical connector at A/C compressor, remove compressor attaching bolts and position compressor out of way with hoses still attached.
25. Remove air pump filter housing.
26. Detach radiator to governor housing coolant hoses at housing.
27. Disconnect engine and automatic transaxle cooling lines at radiator.
28. Disconnect temperature switch electrical connector at radiator.
29. Disconnect vent hose at top left of radiator, then remove radiator attaching bolts and remove radiator from above.
30. Disconnect coolant feed hose on coolant pipe at front right, then disconnect adjacent multiple pin plug and the B+ terminal wire.
31. Remove engine to coolant expansion tank vent hose.
32. Remove hose between heater valve and engine connector.
33. Disconnect fuel feed line.
34. Remove TDC sensor.
35. Disconnect fuel return line.
36. Disconnect ignition lead wires on both sides of distributor cap, then detach both ignition coils and position out of way.
37. Disconnect ground wire at body in front of right ignition coil.
38. Detach flushing valve from holder, the charging valve carbon canister hose and the EZF control unit vacuum hose.
39. Detach vacuum hose at brake booster.
40. Disconnect throttle, cruise control and

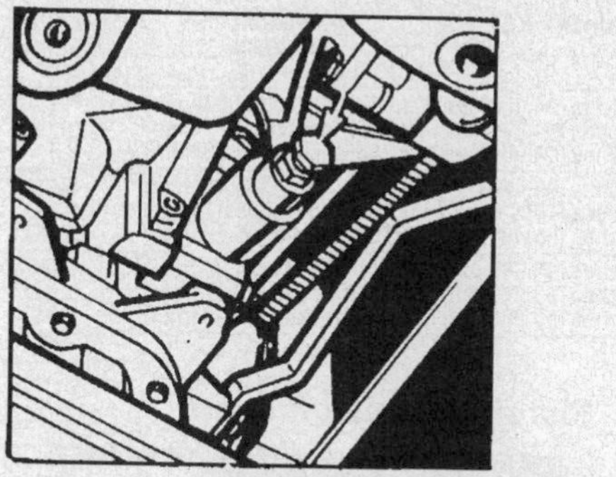

PR1069100016000X

Fig. 3 Adjusting screw location

automatic transaxle cables, then remove retainers and clamp on console and position cables out of way.

41. Disconnect hoses at power steering supply tank, drain oil, loosen hose clamp on tank and remove tank.
42. Remove central electric board cover and disconnect plugs for sensor heating and ignition control units and the oxygen sensor.
43. Disconnect multiple pin plugs at EZF and lefthand control units and the multiple pin plug on right side of central electric board.
44. Push rubber cover out of holder in central electric board and into engine compartment.
45. Raise and support vehicle.
46. Remove attaching bolts for left and right engine mounts.
47. Lower vehicle.
48. Attach suitable lifting equipment to engine lifting eyes and tension slightly.
49. Place wooden block between central tube and crossmember.
50. Tilt engine forward and lift slightly at same time, ensuring engine block and clutch housing have been completely disconnected.
51. Mark installed position of and remove power steering pump pressure hose.
52. Lift engine out of vehicle, ensuring that central electric wire harness does not snag.
53. Reverse procedure to install, noting the following:
    a. Push back transaxle and place wooden block between central tube and crossmember.
    b. Install power steering pump pressure hose in marked position before installing engine.
    c. Ensure central electric wire harness is properly routed.
    d. After lowering engine into hydraulic mounts, remove lifting equipment.
    e. Lift clutch housing and transaxle slightly with suitable jack to move engine into installed position.

CYLINDER HEAD

REPLACE

Cylinder head cannot be replaced unless engine is removed from vehicle.

1. Remove timing chain and camshafts as previously described.
2. Remove cylinder head attaching bolts

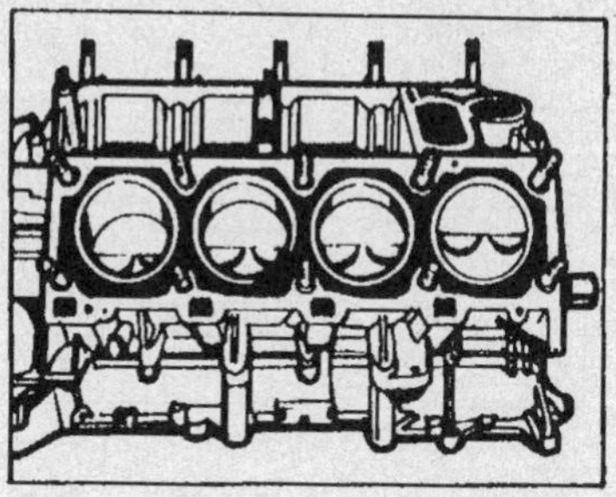

PR1069100017000X

Fig. 4 Piston installation position

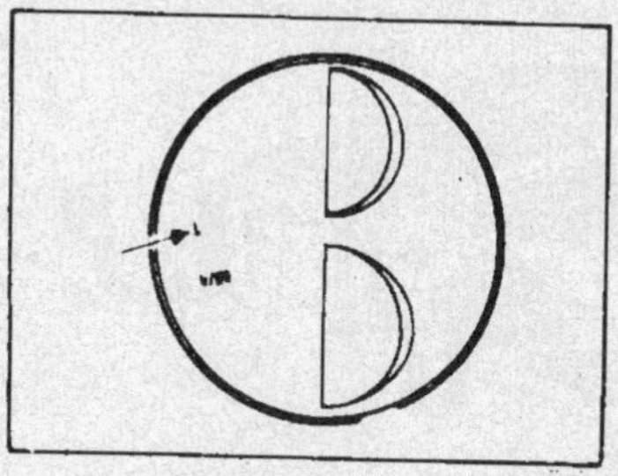

PR1069100019000X

Fig. 6 Piston tolerance group mark

in reverse order of tightening sequence, **Fig. 1,** then the cylinder head.

3. Reverse procedure to install noting the following:
    a. Apply light coat of oil to cylinder head studs.
    b. Install new cylinder head gasket, ensuring "TOP" mark faces up and arrow faces front.
    c. Using sequence shown in **Fig. 1, torque** cylinder head hex head bolts in three steps; first step to 15 ft. lbs., second step an additional 90°, third step an additional 90°.
    d. Using sequence shown in **Fig. 1, torque** cylinder head stud bolts in four steps; first step to 15 ft. lbs., second step an additional 90°, third step an additional 90°, fourth step an additional 90°.

VALVE GUIDES

1. Using suitable tool, machine off protruding valve guides from camshaft side until guides are flush with cylinder head.
2. Place cylinder head on tool 9220, or equivalent.
3. Loosen valve guides from camshaft end with short blows from hammer on tool 9224, or equivalent and press out remainder of guides toward combustion side.
4. Coat valve guides with suitable lubricant, align guides and press into cylinder head against stop from camshaft side. Press fit for valve guides is .0024–.0031 inch (.06–.08 mm). **Valve seat inserts must be machined after replacing valve guides.** Exhaust valve head diameter is changed from 1.259 inch (32 mm) to 1.338 inch (34 mm). The bearing surface on the cylinder head, however, is machined .078

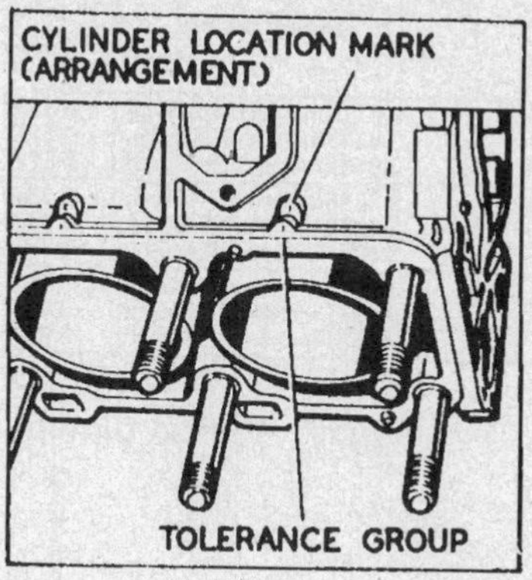
CYLINDER LOCATION MARK
(ARRANGEMENT)
TOLERANCE GROUP

PR1069100018000X

Fig. 5 Cylinder location & tolerance group mark

inch (2 mm) deeper, which is compensated for by the use of .078 inch (2 mm) thicker stepped washers.

TIMING BELT

REPLACE

With timing belt removed, avoid turning camshaft or crankshaft. If movement is required, exercise extreme caution to avoid valve damage cause by piston contact.

1. Disconnect battery ground cable.
2. Remove air cleaner intake hoses.
3. Remove drive belts from alternator, power steering pump, air pump and A/C compressor.
4. Disconnect cables for throttle, cruise control and automatic transaxle, then remove retainers and the clamp on console and position cables out of way.
5. Remove fan console from engine.
6. Disconnect right and left side ignition leads at distributor cap, then remove cap and position out of way.
7. Remove both distributor rotors, then disconnect electrical connectors at A/C compressor and the timing belt tightness indicator.
8. Remove righthand upper timing belt cover.
9. Detach power steering pump and position out of way.
10. Remove clutch slave cylinder; remove clamp from clutch hose holder and remove pushrod, letting cylinder hang by connected hose. **Never operate clutch pedal after removing slave cylinder.**
11. Align mark for 45° before TDC (cylinder No. 1) on vibration damper with red needle, **Fig. 2,** by turning crankshaft clockwise. **Camshafts may be turned without damaging valves after aligning 45° mark.**
12. Lock crankshaft by installing tool 9161/1, or equivalent, securing tool with slave cylinder mounting bolts.
13. Remove crankshaft pulley mounting bolt, then both pulleys, vibration damper and the collar.
14. Remove oil dipstick guide tube.
15. Remove alternator together with console.

	Piston Dia. KS	Cylinder Bore Dia.	Tolerance Group Code
Standard	3.8179 inches (96.975mm)	3.8189 inches (97.00mm)	0
	3.8183 inches (96.985mm)	3.8192 inches (97.01mm)	1
	3.8187 inches (96.995mm)	3.8197 inches (97.02mm)	2
1st Oversize	3.8376 inches (97.475mm)	3.8386 inches (97.50mm)	0 KD 1
	3.8380 inches (97.485mm)	3.8390 inches (97.51mm)	1 KD 1
	3.8384 inches (97.495mm)	3.8394 inches (97.52mm)	2 KD 1
2nd Oversize	3.8573 inches (97.975mm)	3.8583 inches (90.00mm)	0 KD 2
	3.8577 inches (97.985mm)	3.8587 inches (98.01mm)	1 KD 2
	3.8581 inches (97.995mm)	3.8590 inches (98.02mm)	2 KD 2

PR1069100020000X

Fig. 7 Piston dimension chart

	Piston Dia. KS	Cylinder Bore Dia.	Tolerance Group Code
Standard	3.7385 inches (94.960mm)	3.7387 inches (94.964mm)	0
	3.7389 inches (94.970mm)	3.7391 inches (94.974mm)	1
	3.7393 inches (94.980mm)	3.7395 inches (94.984mm)	2
1st Oversize	3.7582 inches (95.460mm)	3.7584 inches (95.464mm)	0 KD 1
	3.7586 inches (95.470mm)	3.7588 inches (95.474mm)	1 KD 1
	3.7590 inches (95.480mm)	3.7592 inches (95.484mm)	2 KD 1
2nd Oversize	3.7779 inches (95.960mm)	3.7781 inches (95.964mm)	0 KD 2
	3.7783 inches (95.970mm)	3.7785 inches (95.974mm)	1 KD 2
	3.7787 inches (95.980mm)	3.7789 inches (95.984mm)	2 KD 2

PR1069100021000X

Fig. 8 Piston dimension chart

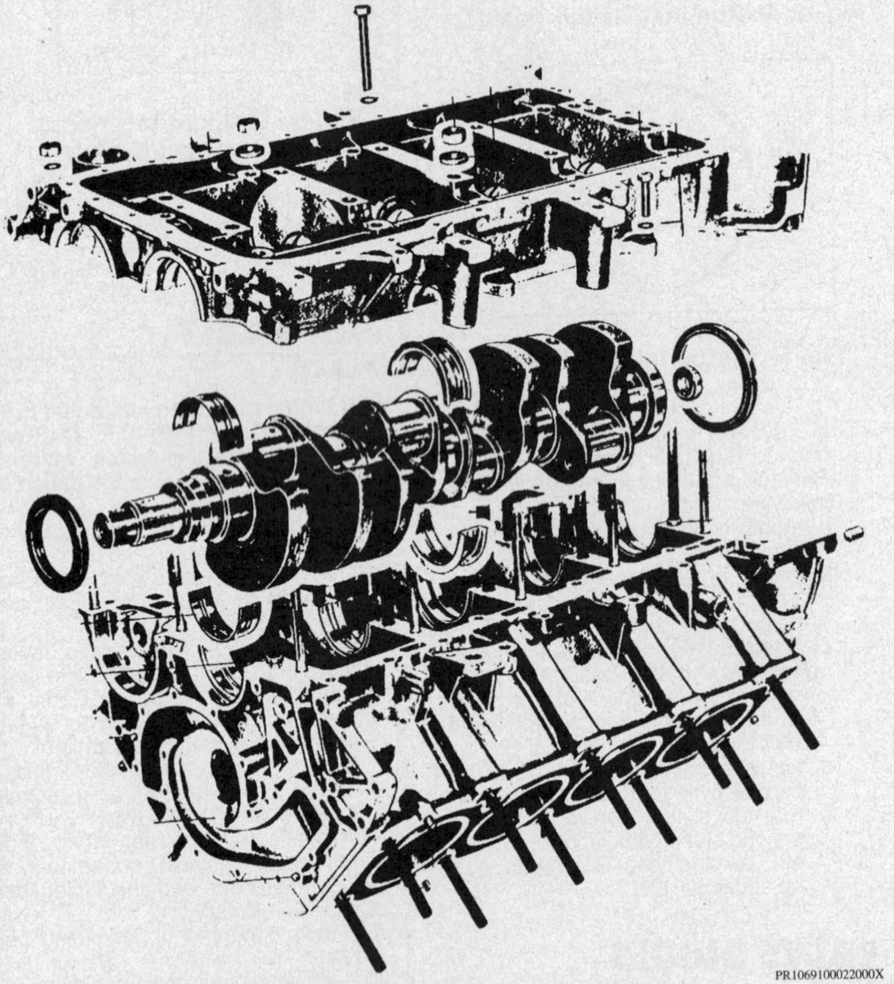

PR1069100022000X

Fig. 9 Crankcase & crankshaft exploded view

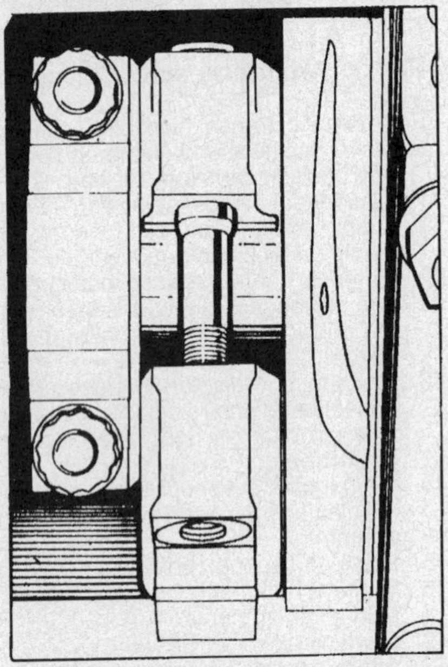

PR1069100023000X

Fig. 10 Connecting rod & cap installation

16. Remove left upper and center timing belt covers.
17. Loosen timing belt with timing belt tensioner.
18. Remove tensioning roller console.
19. Remove timing belt from righthand side over cylinders 1–4 camshaft sprocket, water pump sprocket, cylinders 5–8 camshaft sprocket, oil pump sprocket and crankshaft sprocket.
20. Reverse procedure to install, noting the following:
    a. Install timing belt in reverse order of that described in step 19.
    b. Turn engine in direction of rotation to TDC (cylinder No. 1), then turn camshafts to mark and hold camshafts firmly in position.
    c. Adjust timing belt.

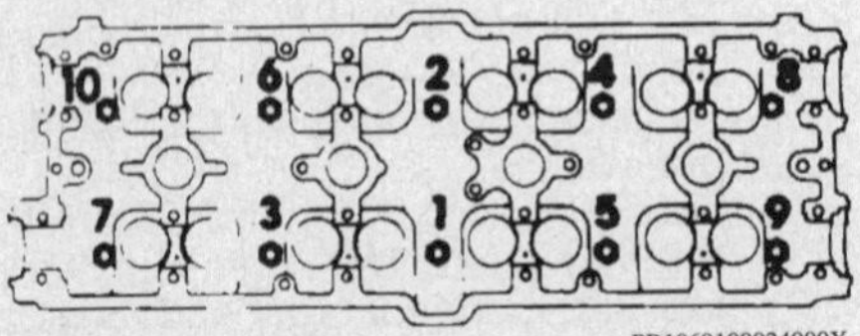
10
6
2
4
8
7
3
1
5
9

PR1069100024000X

Fig. 11 Crankshaft tightening sequence

TIMING BELT

ADJUST

1. Remove air guide hoses.
2. Remove upper air guide section from above.
3. Remove distributor caps and the upper righthand timing belt cover.
4. Detach upper lefthand timing belt cover and push forward.
5. Turn engine in direction of rotation to TDC (cylinder No. 1), ensuring marks on camshaft and flange bearings are aligned.
6. Turn engine 720° until TDC mark is reached again, then continue turning while checking timing belt for wear and/or damage.
7. Prepare tool 9201, or equivalent, for checking by pulling out lockpin and moving testing pin opposite lockpin to starting position, then place drag needle on gauge needle.
8. Slide tool on relaxed section of drive belt with sliding shoes on smooth surface and rollers in tooth gap.
9. Slowly press down on tool case until gauge button resting on air pump bracket engages.
10. Read test value while keeping tool horizontal to timing belt, ensuring tool does not rest on plastic cover. **Sliding shoes must rest on belt with their complete surface. Tool must not be turned or moved on belt while checking. The drag needle must always be placed on the gauge needle after the lockpin has been engaged to eliminate faulty gauge readings. Turn counterclockwise.**

11. Pull out lockpin to disengage gauge tip. Repeat test two or three times.
12. If adjusting value is not 4.7–5.3, adjust as follows:
    a. Loosen adjusting screw locknut and turn adjusting screw until timing belt tightness is correct. Adjusting screw is located on bottom of engine at front righthand side, **Fig. 3. Tightening screw tightens belt and loosening screw loosens belt.**
    b. Tighten locknut, then turn engine 720° and recheck tightness of belt.

CAMSHAFT

REPLACE

1. Disconnect battery ground cable.
2. Remove crossmember.
3. Remove air cleaner assembly with intake hoses.
4. Remove intake air distributor.
5. Remove distributor cap, distributor rotor, timing belt upper section and the cylinder head cover.
6. Turn crankshaft clockwise to align 45° before TDC mark (cylinder No. 1) on vibration damper with cast boss of center timing belt cover. **At 45° mark, camshafts can be turned without damaging valves.**
7. Loosen timing belt with tensioner and remove belt from camshaft sprocket.
8. Remove camshaft attaching bolt, then the sprocket, drive hub and woodruff key from exhaust camshaft.
9. Remove rear timing belt cover.
10. Set marks on camshafts to face up by turning exhaust camshaft with suitable tool.
11. Remove timing chain tensioner. Tensioner piston has spring force. Compress piston for removal and hold together with suitable piece of wire after removing.
12. Secure camshafts in bearings using tool 9226, or equivalent and remove bearing bridges and caps.
13. Release tool uniformly and remove camshafts together with timing chain.
14. Place camshafts in timing chain so that marks on camshafts or cast bosses are aligned with marked chain links, then lubricate bearing surfaces with oil and carefully place timing chain in bearings.
15. Mount camshafts on cylinder head using tool 9226, or equivalent.
16. Install bearing bridges and bearing caps, **torquing** to 7 ft. lbs. **Bearing bridges and caps are machined together with cylinder head and must always be installed in correct position. Ensure codes and pairing numbers match.**
17. Coat sealing surfaces of front and rear double bearing bridges with suitable locking compound.
18. Recheck camshaft position using gauge from tool 9226, or equivalent.
19. Using tools 9233 and 9234, or equivalents, drive seal on to drive end of camshaft. Lubricate sealing lip before installing.
20. Reverse remainder of removal procedure to complete installation, then adjust camshafts as follows:
    a. Turn engine in operating direction to TDC (cylinder No. 1) and ensure both distributor rotors face left, marks on camshaft sprockets and flange bearings are aligned, and marks on camshafts face exhaust side.
    b. Mount dial gauge with holder VW388, or equivalent, on cylinder head. Set dial gauge on hydraulic lifter of cylinder No. 1 intake valve to 0 with 5 mm preload.
    c. Set dial gauge on hydraulic lifter of cylinder No. 6 intake valve and zero indicator. Dial gauge must be aligned perpendicular to intake valve.
    d. Turn crankshaft further from TDC while observing dial gauge. Turn until a value of 1–3 mm lift is obtained and ensure mark for 20° after TDC (cylinder No. 6) is aligned with pointer on timing belt cover. If alignment is not correct, proceed to step e.
    e. Install three M5 X 15 screws in camshaft sprockets to prevent sprockets or camshafts from turning.
    f. Turn crankshaft in operating direction until dial gauge shows 1–3 mm lift.
    g. Remove camshaft attaching bolts while counter holding then remove M5 screws.
    h. Turn crankshaft to 20° after TDC (cylinder No. 6).
    i. Install camshaft sprockets, first installing three M5 X 15 screws, then **torquing** attaching bolts (M10) to 47 ft. lbs.
    j. Turn crankshaft 720°, then recheck adjustment. Reading should be 1–3 mm at 20° after TDC for cylinder No. 6. Repeat adjusting procedures as necessary.
    k. Remove M5 X 15 screws.

PISTON & ROD ASSEMBLY

Install pistons to rods so that valve reliefs face outboard, **Fig. 4.** Install pistons into cylinders of same tolerance group, **Figs. 5 and 6.**

Pistons and piston pins are paired according to weight. Pistons are weighed with piston pins, piston rings and circlips. Piston pins must always remain in corresponding pistons and must not be interchanged within a set of pistons for one engine. If pistons and pins are interchanged, they must be rearranged by checking total weight. Weight of each piston assembly should be 25.3454–25.6278 ounces. **Different tolerance groups could be used in the same engine.**

PISTONS, PINS & RINGS

Refer to **Figs. 7 and 8** for piston standard and oversize. Different tolerance groups can be used in the same engine.

MAIN & ROD BEARINGS

Narrow side of connecting rod and cap face adjacent connecting rod. Wide side faces crankshaft counterweight, **Figs. 9 and 10.** Tighten crankshaft lower section attaching bolts in sequence shown in **Fig. 11.**

CRANKSHAFT REAR OIL SEAL

REPLACE

Refer to **Fig. 9** for service. Align and install seal using tool 9126, or equivalent.

OIL PUMP

REPLACE

1. Hold oil pump drive sprocket using tool 9157 or suitable fixture.
2. Remove oil pump mounting bolts and pump.
3. Reverse procedure to install.

COOLING SYSTEM BLEED

These engines do not require a specified bleed procedure. After filling cooling system, run engine to operating temperature with radiator/pressure cap off. Air will then automatically bled through cap opening.

FUEL PUMP

REPLACE

1. Disconnect battery ground cable, then remove cover off fuel tank bottom.
2. Pinch suction hose with standard clamp, then remove suction hose.
3. Remove pump electrical connector, then remove pressure line.
4. Loosen pump clamp, then remove fuel pump.
5. Reverse procedure to install.

FUEL FILTER

REPLACE

1. Disconnect battery ground cable.
2. Remove cover at fuel tank bottom.
3. Place shop towel over fuel filter line fittings and position a suitable container under fuel filter.
4. Using a back-up wrench on fuel filter fitting, loosen fuel line fittings.
5. Disconnect fuel lines from filter, then loosen filter retaining clamp and remove fuel filter.
6. Reverse procedure to install.

TIGHTENING SPECIFICATIONS

Year	Component	Torque/Ft. Lbs.
1993–95	Camshaft Bearing Caps To Cylinder Head	7
	Connecting Rod Nuts With Ribbed Bearing	55
	Cylinder Head To Engine Block	②
	Cylinder Head Cover	7
	Drive Pulley To Camshaft	213
	Flywheel	66
	Intake Manifold	11
	Main Bearing Cap Bolts	③
	M6 Bolts	5
	M8 Bolts	15
	M10 Bolts	30–35
	Oil Pan Drain Plug	36
	Oil Pump To Crankcase	①
	Radiator Drain Plug	13-17
	Spark Plugs	18–22
	Vibration Damper Or Pulley	170

① — Torque in two steps: (1) 10 ft. lbs., (2) 14 ft. lbs.
② — Refer to "Cylinder Head, Replace" for tightening procedure.
③ — M12 x 1.5 bolts are torqued in three steps: (1) 22 ft. lbs., (2) 41 ft. lbs., (3) 55 ft. lbs. M10 bolts are torqued in two steps: (1) 15 ft. lbs. (2) 37 ft. lbs.

Clutch & Manual Transaxle

INDEX

	Page No.
Adjustments	37-24
Clutch	37-24
Shift Lever	37-24
Clutch, Replace	37-25
911	37-25
928	37-25
968	37-25
Hydraulic System Service	37-25
Clutch System Bleed	37-25
Tightening Specifications	37-26
Transaxle, Replace	37-25
911	37-25
928	37-26
968	37-25

ADJUSTMENTS

CLUTCH

911

Since clutch play cannot be measured accurately at the pedal because of the auxiliary spring, clutch play is measured at the transaxle adjusting lever.

1. Disconnect clutch cable or loosen completely at holder.
2. Using a feeler gauge, adjust clutch play to .047 inch (1.2 mm), and lock adjusting screw.
3. Reconnect the clutch cable.
4. Tighten clutch cable until clutch play is .045 inch (1.0 mm).

928 & 968

The release mechanism is a hydraulic, automatic adjustment type. To ensure correct clutch operation, there must be approximately 3 mm of freeplay at the pedal edge.

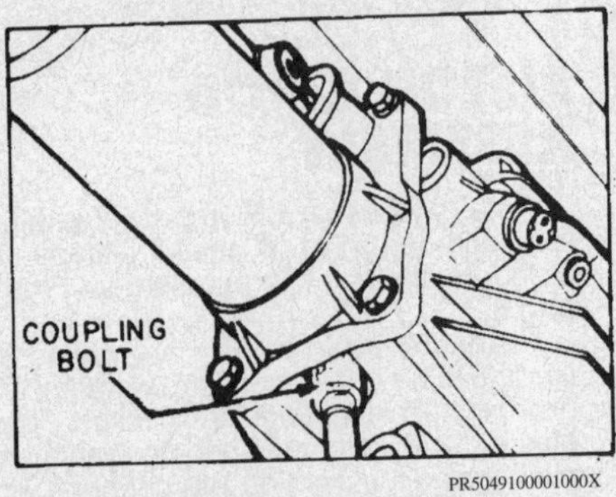

COUPLING BOLT
PR5049100001000X

Fig. 1 Coupling bolt removal

To check for clutch disc wear limit, remove the plastic inspection plug at the clutch slave cylinder. The wear limit has been reached when the front edge of the release lever just appears in the inspection hole.

SHIFT LEVER

911

1. Remove access cover from shift rod tunnel in front of rear seats.
2. Loosen shift rod clamp, then turn shift rod for selector shaft to the right in neutral position.
3. Move shift lever in neutral to the point where lower part of shift lever is positioned vertically and touching left stop.
4. Lightly tighten shift rod clamp.
5. Ensure travel is equal in gears 1 through 4 and that 5th and reverse gears can be easily engaged, adjusting as necessary.
6. **Torque** clamp nut to 18 ft. lbs.
7. Shift into 5th gear, then, with dust boot at shift rod coupling pushed back, ensure rotational play is evident at selector shaft.

968

1. Place shift lever in neutral.
2. Adjust shift lever to an inclination of 85° by moving shift lever console.

HYDRAULIC SYSTEM SERVICE

CLUTCH SYSTEM BLEED

928 & 968

This bleed procedure is outlined using a pressure bleeder.

1. Fill tank to upper edge with brake fluid, then remove restrictor sleeve. Connect bleeder.
2. Switch on bleeder and open bleeder screw on clutch slave cylinder until escaping fluid is without air bubbles. Operate clutch pedal several times during this step.
3. Switch bleeder Off.
4. If necessary because of residual air, unscrew slave cylinder on clutch housing. pushrod against stop in slave cylinder, then release rod. **Never operate clutch pedal with slave cylinder removed.**

CLUTCH

REPLACE

911

1. Remove engine/transaxle assembly from vehicle.
2. Separate engine from transaxle.
3. Loosen clutch attaching bolts alternately and diagonally a little at a time until spring tension is relieved.
4. Remove clutch assembly.
5. Reverse procedure to install.

928

1. Disconnect battery ground cable.
2. Remove lower body brace, if equipped.
3. Loosen clutch slave cylinder attaching bolts.
4. Remove clutch hose bracket.
5. Remove cylinder with line connected.
6. Remove clutch housing cover and starter.
7. Remove catalytic converter.
8. Remove coupling attaching bolts, then push coupling backward on driveshaft.
9. **On models with long coupling assembling,** remove plug from central tube (torque tube) and remove rear bolt. Remove guide tube attaching bolts, then slide guide tube toward flywheel.
10. **On all models,** mark position of pressure plate, intermediate plate and flywheel in relation to each other for installation reference.
11. **On models with dowel pin centered clutches,** drive pins in direction of pressure plate far enough so they are beyond the centering bore on flywheel.
12. **On all models,** loosen clutch attaching bolts 1 to 1½ turns until spring tension is relieved from pressure plate. Disconnect release lever from ball stud.
13. Remove clutch assembly from vehicle.
14. Reverse procedure to install.

968

1. Disconnect battery ground cable.
2. Disconnect ground strap from clutch housing.
3. Disconnect electrical connectors, then remove reference mark sensor and speed sensors.
4. Remove starter harness bracket from clutch assembly.
5. Disconnect exhaust assembly enough to allow clutch removal.
6. Remove heat shield from catalytic converter.
7. Remove splash guard, if equipped.
8. Loosen central tube (torque tube) to rear exhaust pipe bracket attaching bolts.
9. Remove or push back dust cover.
10. Remove shift lever knob retainer.
11. Remove snap ring from shift lever.
12. Pull off selector rod and washer on shift lever bolt.
13. Mark position, then remove shift lever.
14. Press down on insulation and push selector rod forward in cavity.
15. Loosen two uppermost attaching bolts from clutch housing.
16. Remove end cap from central tube (torque tube). Push back protective tube for selector rod far enough, that it is outside of the central tube housing.
17. Remove clamping sleeve attaching bolts.
18. Disconnect joint shafts from transaxle. Do not allow joint shafts to hang.
19. Disconnect back-up light electrical connector.
20. Using a suitable jack lift transmission slightly.
21. Remove transaxle suspension bolts.
22. Lower transaxle with central tube until central tube rests on rear axle cross tube.
23. Remove transaxle to central tube flange attaching bolts. Remove transaxle downward.
24. Remove starter.
25. Pull back on selector rod.
26. Move back central tube far enough until central tube housing rests on transaxle carrier. If central tube cannot be moved out of clutch housing without applying force, secure engine from moving using a suitable hoist and tool VW 10-222, or equivalent.
27. Remove clutch housing guard and right support, if equipped.
28. Remove engine mount nuts and push engine slightly to the right. Remove lower clutch housing attaching bolts.
29. Move out guard and clutch housing with release lever.
30. Remove clutch assembly.
31. Reverse procedure to install.

TRANSAXLE

REPLACE

911

Refer to "Engine, Replace" under 4 Cylinder Engine Section for transaxle replacement procedure since the engine and transaxle are removed as an assembly.

968

1. Disconnect battery ground cable.
2. Remove rear muffler.
3. Disconnect driveshafts at transaxle and suspend from vehicle horizontally.
4. Disconnect electrical connectors at back-up light switch and speedometer drive.
5. Push back dust cover on shift rod and remove lock wire from bolt, then remove bolt.
6. Carefully press shift knob leather cover out of center console and push up.
7. Remove shift lever knob mounting clamp and the knob.
8. Remove circlip from shift lever.
9. Turn shift lever 180°, press down on insulation sheet and push shift rod forward into produced cavity by approximately 12 inches (300 mm).
10. Working through assembly openings, remove clamping sleeve screws, then push clamping sleeve toward transaxle.
11. Press in retainer with large screwdriver and push protective tube back through large opening in case far enough to clear central pipe housing.
12. Place wooden block between cross tube and central pipe to hold transaxle and central pipe in installed position.
13. Place suitable jack under transaxle and attach securely.
14. Remove transaxle suspension mounting bolts.
15. Remove transaxle to central pipe housing attaching bolts.
16. Remove transaxle toward rear of vehicle.
17. Reverse procedure to install, noting the following:
    a. If shift rod protective tube retainers are excessively worn, replace tube.
    b. Place shift rod protective tube in transaxle, **torquing** bolts as follows: M10 X 60, 31 ft. lbs.; M12 X 75 and M12 X 80, 62 ft. lbs.
    c. Push shift rod protective tube forward until retainer engages in transaxle case.
    d. Mount shift rod on intermediate lever and lock clamping bolt with steel wire.
    e. **On models with double point transaxle suspension, torque** bolts as follows: transaxle mount to body, 34 ft. lbs.; mount to bracket and bracket transaxle, 18 ft. lbs.
    f. **On models with single point transaxle suspension, torque** bolts as follows: transaxle carrier to body, 34 ft. lbs.; transaxle mount to carrier, bracket to transaxle mount and

bracket to transaxle, 17 ft. lbs.

928

1. Raise and support vehicle. Loosen rear wheel lug nuts.
2. Remove battery. Remove nuts securing rear springs struts in trunk.
3. Shift transaxle into 5th gear.
4. Remove rubber plug from transaxle inspection hole and disconnect coupling, Fig. 1. **To position coupling for bolt removal, hold one wheel and turn the other.**
5. Shift transaxle into neutral, remove rear wheels then disconnect and suspend brake calipers.
6. From catalytic converter rearward remove exhaust system.
7. Remove heat shields and battery box.
8. Disconnect wiring from back-up light switch and speedometer transmitter, then remove wiring from clips.
9. Pull back shift boot, remove Allen head setscrew from coupling and shift rod from main rod.
10. Disconnect axles from transaxle and support in a horizontal position.
11. Disconnect stabilizer bar from lower control arms.
12. Secure transaxle housing to stabilizer bar with wire.
13. Remove crossmember to transaxle bolts and the two crossmember to frame bolts located near transaxle mounts.
14. Place a transaxle jack under crossmember. Mark crossmember to body location, then remove remaining bolts.
15. Tilt rear axle assembly carefully; make sure spring struts and control arms do not twist. **Support rear axle in a tilted position to keep weight off lower control arm link pins.**
16. Position transaxle jack under transaxle. Disconnect central tube and remove transaxle from stabilizer bar. Move transaxle back to one side, then lower from vehicle.
17. Reverse procedure to install.

TIGHTENING SPECIFICATIONS

Year	Component	Torque/ Ft. Lbs.
911		
1993–96	Bleeder In Case	26
	Brake Caliper Attaching Bolts	43
	Clamp Plate To Transfer Case	7.5
	Differential Cover Housing	11
	Drive Pinion Locknut	177
	Driveshaft Nut	216-252
	Guide Tube To Case	7.5
	Halfshaft Flange Screw	32.5
	Intermediate Case Nut	17
	Lower Shock Absorber Nut	90
	Oil Drain Plug	22
	Oil Filler Plug	22
	Reversing Light Switch To Gearbox	26
	Shift Fork Screw	17
	Transfer Case Nut	17
	Transmission Case Nut	17
	Transmission Side Cover Nut	17
	Tensioning Plate Nut	17
	Upper Shock Absorber Attaching Bolts	18
928		
1993-95	Axle Shaft Flange	59
	Axle Shaft Nut	31
	Brake Caliper Attaching Bolts	61
	Crossmember Attaching Bolts	33
	Halfshaft Castle Nut	217-253
	Spring Strut Self Locking Nut	33
	Toe Adjusting Bolt Locknut	87
	Transmission Mount To Crossmember Attaching Bolts	61
	Upper Strut Retainer Attaching Nuts	42
968		
1993–95	Clutch & Ring Gear	18
	Clutch Housing To Engine	54
	Cover To End Shield	17
	Crankshaft To Flange	30
	Driveshaft To Input Shaft	58
	End Shield To Case	17

Continued

TIGHTENING SPECIFICATIONS—Continued

Year	Component	Torque/ Ft. Lbs.
968		
1993–95	Flywheel To Crankshaft	65
	Guide Sleeve On Housing	11
	Oil Drain Plug	17
	Oil Filler Plug	17
	Reverse Gear To Shield	17
	Reverse Lever To Shield	25
	Shift Lock To Shield and Housing	22
	Shift Shaft Cover To Case	6
	Shift Stop To End Shield	22
	Side Cover To Case	17
	Slave Cylinder To Clutch Housing	15

Rear Axle & Suspension

INDEX

	Page No.
Coil Spring, Replace	37-28
Control Arm, Replace	37-28
928	37-28
Rear Axle, Replace	37-27
928	37-27
Rear Axle Shaft, Replace	37-27
911	37-27
928	37-27
Rear Axle Shaft Service	37-28
928	37-28
Shock Absorber, Replace	37-28
911	37-28
928	37-28
Strut, Replace	37-28
928	37-28
Tightening Specifications	37-31
Torsion Bar, Replace	37-31
911	37-31
Trailing Arm Service	37-29
911	37-29
968	37-30

REAR AXLE

REPLACE

928

1. Remove upper strut retainer attaching nuts from inside luggage compartment.
2. Raise and support vehicle, then remove rear wheel and tire assemblies.
3. Disconnect parking brake cable at connector and pull back out of guide.
4. Remove brake calipers and suspend from body with wire, leaving brake hoses connected.
5. Remove exhaust system components as necessary.
6. Disconnect axle shafts at transmission and suspend from wire in horizontal position on rear axle crossmember.
7. Disconnect stabilizer at lower control arm.
8. Using suitable tool, support transmission from stabilizer bar.
9. Remove two rear axle crossmember mounting bolts and the transmission mount attaching bolts. Note quantity, thickness and location of shims for proper installation.
10. Mark position of toe adjusting eccentric bolts, then remove bolts from rear axle crossmember.
11. Place suitable jack under rear axle crossmember, then mark position of crossmember and remove remaining four attaching bolts.

PR2049100001000X

Fig. 1 Hub removal

12. Carefully lower rear axle, being sure not to twist spring struts, control arms or rear axle crossmember.
13. Reverse procedure to install, noting the following:
    a. Check spring strut seal, repairing as necessary.
    b. Position rear axle, then install mounting bolts and align axle to original position as marked.
    c. Tighten fasteners to specifications.

REAR AXLE SHAFT

REPLACE

911

1. Raise and support vehicle.
2. Remove cotter pin from hub castle nut.
3. Remove castle nut with tools P42a, P36b, P44a, and P296.
4. Remove Allen bolts from axle flanges.
5. Remove axle shaft.
6. Reverse procedure to install. Tighten axle shaft and halfshaft castle nut to specifications.

928

Axle Shaft Bolted On Both Sides

1. Raise and support vehicle, then remove left rear wheel and tire assembly.
2. Remove socket head bolts from drive flanges.
3. Remove righthand axle shaft inward.
4. Remove lefthand axle shaft outward.
5. Reverse procedure to install, ensuring flange surfaces are free of grease, and **torque** socket head bolts to 60 ft. lbs.

Axle Shaft Welded On One Side

1. Raise and support vehicle.

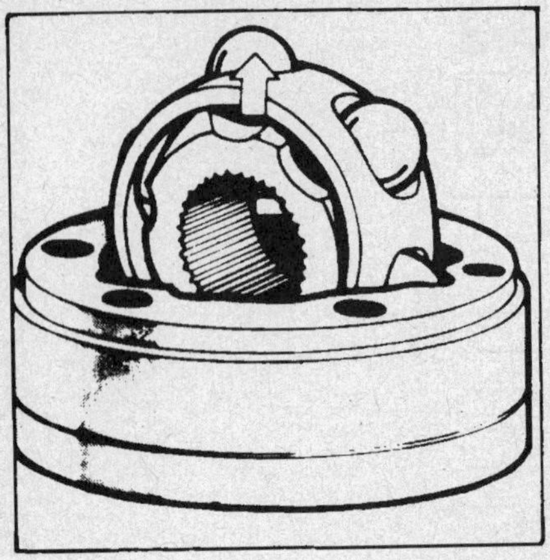

PR2049100002000X

Fig. 2 Ball cage & hub removal

2. Remove socket head bolts on transmission end.
3. Remove wheel cover to gain access, then remove self locking nuts on wheel end.
4. Remove both axle shafts toward inside, lowering rear of left side exhaust assembly as necessary.
5. Run axle shafts into wheel hub on wheel end.
6. Ensure axle shaft flanges are free of grease and install socket head bolts, **torquing** to 60 ft. lbs.
7. **Torque** self locking nuts to 333 ft. lbs.

REAR AXLE SHAFT SERVICE

928

1. Clamp axle shaft in suitable vise.
2. Remove clamp and push dust boot with sealing flange toward inside of axle shaft.
3. Remove circlip.
4. Using suitable tools, press off constant velocity joint.
5. Swing out ball hub and ball cage from joint and press out in direction of arrow, **Fig. 1. Ball hubs and joints are matched. Do not mix.**
6. Tilt ball hub out of ball cage through ball grove, **Fig. 2.**
7. Check joint, ball hub, ball cage and balls for pitting. Replace joint if there is excessive radial play in joint.
8. Place ball hub in ball cage, then press balls into cage, **Fig. 3.**
9. Install hub with cage and balls pointing up, ensuring after swinging in hub into joint that one wide ball groove on joint is together on one side with a narrow groove of hub. **Groove of ball hub and running around periphery of outside diameter on joint must face end of axle shaft.**
10. Swing in ball hub with cage by swinging out hub from cage far enough so that balls are at same distance as grooves, **Fig. 4.**
11. Push hub with balls into joint.
12. Check operation of joint. CV joint has been properly assembled if ball hub

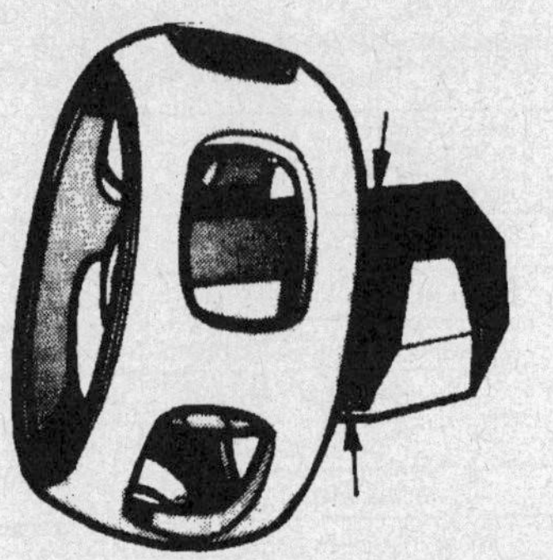

PR2049100003000X

Fig. 3 Ball hub from cage removal

can be pushed back and forth by hand over entire range of travel.

13. Seal large diameter and of new dust boot with suitable adhesive.
14. Using suitable tool, squeeze new clamp between machined shoulders of sealing flange.
15. Replace gasket on flange cover.
16. Push dust boot with sealing flange onto shaft.
17. Pack CV joint from each side with approximately 40 grams of grease supplied in repair kit.
18. Press CV joint onto shaft and install new circlip.
19. Position dust boot correctly, then install clamp.

STRUT

REPLACE

928

1. Remove the three spring strut locknuts in luggage compartment.
2. Raise vehicle and support.
3. Remove wheel.
4. Remove front nut from pivot pin of lower control arm, **Fig. 5. Counterlock and counter hold the rear nut with a separate M14 X 1.5 nut.**
5. Remove stabilizer bar link at control arm.
6. Position strut assembly in vise and install a suitable spring compressor.
7. Remove locknuts and mounting plate with support, **Fig. 6.**
8. Slowly relieve coil spring tension.
9. Check shock absorber for leaks.
10. Reverse procedure to install.

SHOCK ABSORBER

REPLACE

911

1. With vehicle standing on ground, remove shock attaching nut from shock in engine compartment, **Fig. 7.**
2. Raise and support vehicle.
3. Remove shock attaching bolt and nut from trailing arm.
4. Reverse procedure to install, noting the following:
   a. Install shock absorber in shock tower and tighten attaching nut to specification.

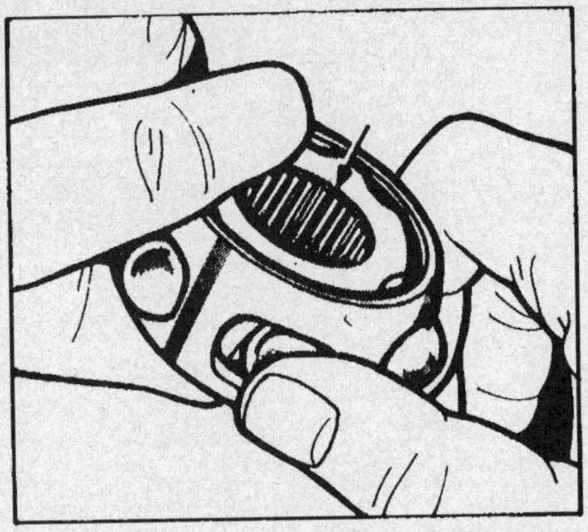

PR2049100004000X

Fig. 4 Ball bearing installation

   b. Tension trailing arm and extend shock absorber to install attaching nut and bolt, tightening to specifications.

928

1. Remove three self-locking nuts from spring strut in luggage compartment.
2. Raise and support vehicle, then remove wheel.
3. Remove front nut on pivot pin of lower control arm, counter holding and counter locking rear nut with a M14 X 1.5 nut then remove pivot.
4. Disconnect stabilizer bar link at control arm.
5. Disassemble and assemble spring strut as shown, **Fig. 6,** noting the following:
   a. Tension coil spring using tool No. VW540, or equivalent, then remove self locking nuts and take out mounting plate with support.
   b. Relax coil spring by loosening clamping pins alternately.
6. Reverse procedure to install, noting the following:
   a. **Torque** spring strut self locking nuts specifications.
   b. Using suitable compound make a new permanently elastic seal on mounting plate 300 mm long and circular in shape.
   c. Ensure lower shock absorber is in proper installed position.

COIL SPRING

REPLACE

Refer to "Strut, Replace" for coil spring replacement.

CONTROL ARM

REPLACE

928

1. Raise and support vehicle.
2. Remove axle shaft with stub axle, **Fig. 8.**
3. Remove brake caliper.
4. Remove brake disc retaining screws and disc.

PR2039100001000X

Fig. 5 Exploded view of rear suspension. 928

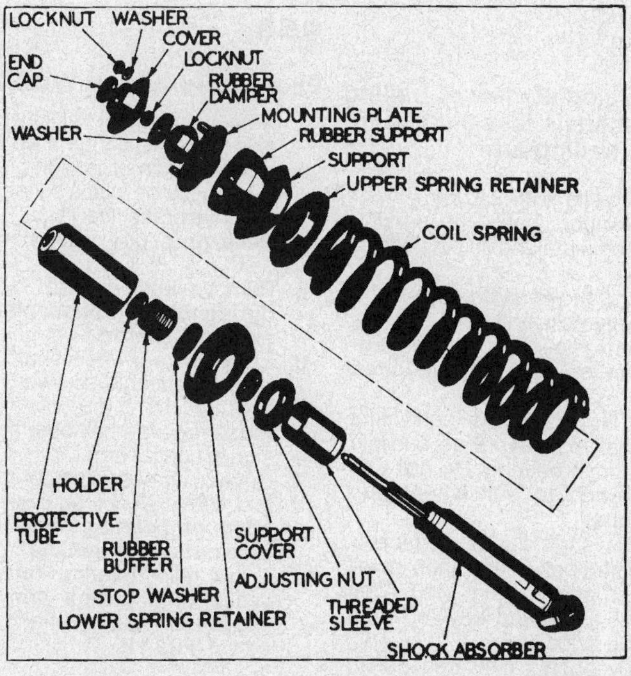
LOCKNUT
WASHER
COVER
END CAP
LOCKNUT
RUBBER DAMPER
MOUNTING PLATE
WASHER
RUBBER SUPPORT
SUPPORT
UPPER SPRING RETAINER
COIL SPRING
HOLDER
PROTECTIVE TUBE
RUBBER BUFFER
SUPPORT COVER
ADJUSTING NUT
STOP WASHER
THREADED SLEEVE
LOWER SPRING RETAINER
SHOCK ABSORBER

PR2039100002000X

Fig. 6 Spring strut. 928 models

5. Remove parking brake shoes and spreader lever.
6. Remove parking brake cable from guide in hub assembly.
7. Remove hub assembly.
8. Remove lower diagonal control arm after removing eccentric bolts and stabilizer bar link bolt, **Fig. 8.**
9. Reverse procedure to install. **Check axle alignment.**

TRAILING ARM SERVICE

911

1. Raise and support vehicle, then remove rear wheels.
2. Depress brake pedal slightly and hold in position.
3. Remove brake line between fixed caliper and brake hose.
4. Remove brake hose clip from rear axle semi-trailing arm, then disconnect brake hose.
5. Loosen brake caliper attaching bolts and remove caliper.
6. Loosen countersunk head bolts on brake disc and remove disc.
7. Support trailing arm with suitable jack and remove shock absorber attaching bolt.

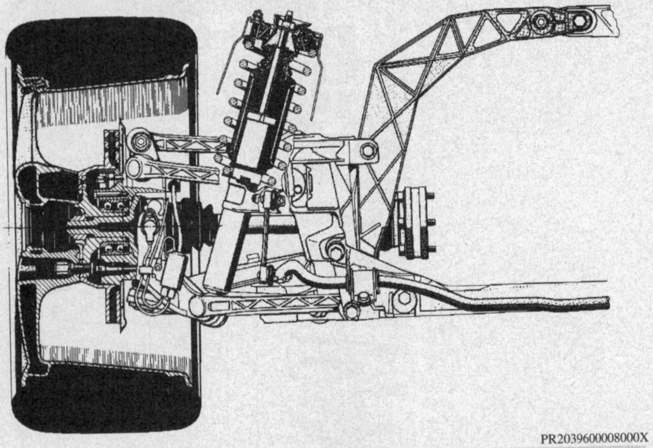

PR2039600008000X

Fig. 7 Rear axle & suspension. 911

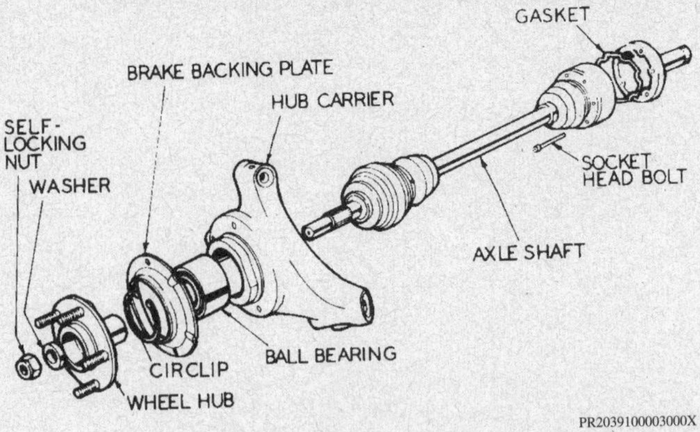
GASKET
BRAKE BACKING PLATE
HUB CARRIER
SELF-LOCKING NUT
WASHER
SOCKET HEAD BOLT
AXLE SHAFT
BALL BEARING
CIRCLIP
WHEEL HUB

PR2039100003000X

Fig. 8 Hub carrier & axle shaft

PR2039100004000X

Fig. 9 Rear wheel hub removal. 911 models

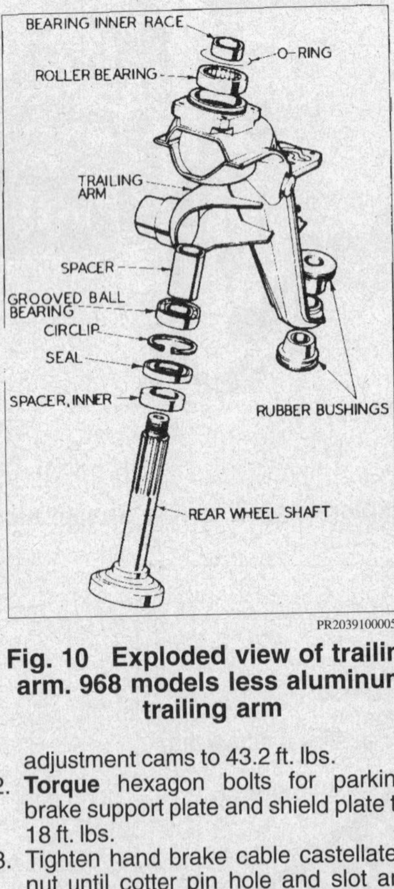
BEARING INNER RACE
O-RING
ROLLER BEARING
TRAILING ARM
SPACER
GROOVED BALL BEARING
CIRCLIP
SEAL
SPACER, INNER
RUBBER BUSHINGS
REAR WHEEL SHAFT

PR2039100005000X

Fig. 10 Exploded view of trailing arm. 968 models less aluminum trailing arm

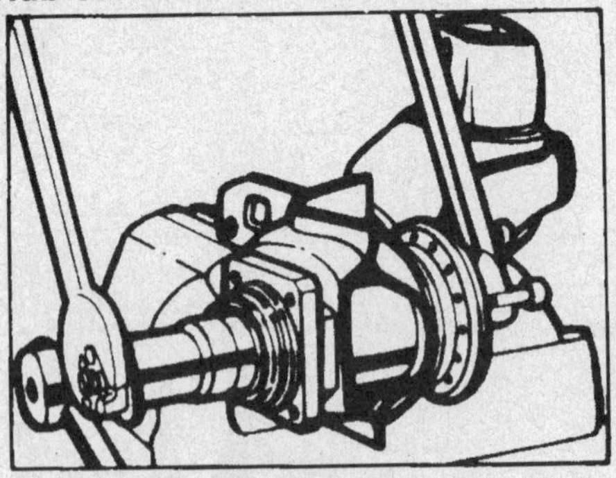

PR2039100006000X

Fig. 11 Axle stub shaft installation

8. Remove cotter pin from castellated nut and remove nut.
9. Remove halfshaft to joint flange attaching bolts, strike with flat chisel near flange gasket to separate halfshaft from joint flange, and remove halfshaft.
10. Drive out axle shaft toward center of vehicle.
11. Using tool No. P297a, or equivalent, drive out rear wheel hub, **Fig. 9.**
12. Remove cotter pin and castellated nut from brake cable end and pull brake cable out toward center of vehicle.
13. Unscrew hexagon nut attaching shield plate.
14. Remove four brake carrier plate attaching nuts and remove brake carrier plate and shield plate.
15. Disconnect hand brake cable guide.
16. Remove attaching bolts and nuts and eccentric bolts of rear axle semi-trailing arm flange.
17. Remove semi-trailing arm pivot bearing attaching nut, then pull out bolt.
18. Press ball bearing out with suitable press.
19. Press in new ball bearing with suitable press, applying pressure to bearing outer race.
20. Install new self locking nut on M14 bolt on trailing arm and **torque** to 43.2 ft. lbs. while lifting arm until lower edge is level with upper edge of spring plate.
21. **Torque** spring plate retaining bolts to 68.4 ft. lbs. and the camber and toe-in adjustment cams to 43.2 ft. lbs.
22. **Torque** hexagon bolts for parking brake support plate and shield plate to 18 ft. lbs.
23. Tighten hand brake cable castellated nut until cotter pin hole and slot are aligned, then install new cotter pin. **Ensure expander clip is positioned correctly.**
24. Using tool No. P298b, or equivalent and driveshaft, pull rear wheel hub into radial ball thrust bearing. **Do not use impact wrench to pull wheel hub into bearings.**
25. Ensure joint shaft flange surface is smooth and free of grease, then install new gasket and **torque** M10 Allen screws to 60 ft. lbs. and M8 Allen head screws to 30 ft. lbs.
26. Tighten driveshaft castellated nut to specifications and install new cotter pin.
27. Tighten shock absorber attaching bolts to specifications.
28. Install brake caliper with new spring washers and tighten attaching bolts to specifications.
29. Bleed brakes and check for leaks.
30. Check hand brake setting, adjusting as necessary.
31. Adjust toe-in and camber.

968

Except Aluminum Trailing Arm

1. Remove constant velocity joint at stub axle mounting flange, **Fig. 10.**
2. Mark location of torsion plate on trailing arm flange with a suitable scribe.
3. Remove brake line.
4. Remove shock absorber attaching bolt.
5. Remove torsion plate. **Use caution during this operation, plate is under extreme tension.**
6. Press out rear wheel shaft.
7. Using a suitable screwdriver, remove seal.
8. Press grooved ball bearings and axle stub in control arm.
9. Drive roller bearing outer race in using tool VW415A, or equivalent. **Flange edge of bearing outer race must face outside of vehicle.**
10. Press roller bearing inner race and spacer into control arm using tool VW454, or equivalent and a castellated nut, **Fig. 11.**

Aluminum Trailing Arm

1. Raise and support vehicle.

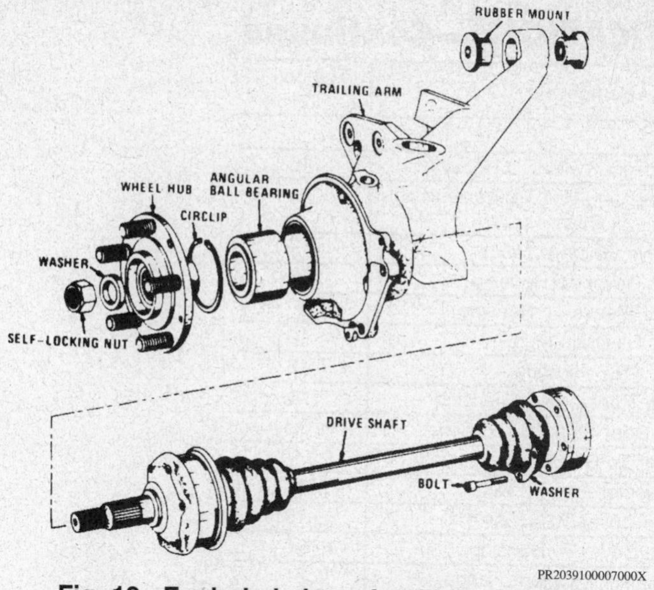
RUBBER MOUNT
TRAILING ARM
WHEEL HUB
ANGULAR BALL BEARING
CIRCLIP
WASHER
SELF-LOCKING NUT
DRIVE SHAFT
BOLT
WASHER
PR2039100007000X

Fig. 12 Exploded view of trailing arm. 968 w/aluminum trailing arm

2. Remove rear wheel, then the self locking nut on driveshaft, **Fig. 12.**
3. Disconnect parking brake cable at parking brake lever.
4. Lift trailing arm slightly with suitable jack, then disconnect vibration damper at trailing arm.
5. Remove axle shaft attaching bolts at transmission and remove complete driveshaft. **When working on left side, push up transmission end of shaft in direction of intermediate shift lever on transmission to remove.**
6. Disconnect brake hose at trailing arm by removing spring lock and unscrewing brake pipe. Plug brake hose or hold brake pedal in slightly depressed position with suitable tool.
7. Remove brake pad wear indicator wiring from holder.
8. Remove brake pad wear indicator wiring plug from its holder and disconnect.
9. Remove brake caliper and the disc.
10. Using tool P297a, or equivalent, drive out rear wheel hub.
11. Remove parking brake shoes and spreader arm, then pull parking brake cable out of trailing arm.
12. Mark position of, then remove trailing arm.
13. Take off brake guard and remove circlip for angular ball bearing.
14. Heat trailing arm to 250–300°F. and, using suitable tools, press out angular ball bearing.
15. If necessary, remove rubber mounts and the bearing inner race.
16. Using suitable tools, set up and align trailing arm.
17. Remove trailing arm from press and heat to 250–300°F., then insert angular ball bearing and press in slightly on aligned bases.
18. If removed, press in new rubber mounts against stops.
19. Install circlip and press in wheel hub.
20. Install trailing arm. **Torque** trailing arm to rear axle strut locknuts to 66 ft. lbs. (camber eccentric) and 76 ft. lbs. and the trailing arm to cross tube locknuts to 45 ft. lbs. **Insert driveshaft before mounting vibration damper on trailing arm on left side.**
21. Adjust parking brake, bleed brakes and check wheel alignment.

TORSION BAR

REPLACE

911

Refer to "Torsion Bar, Adjust" procedure in the "Wheel Alignment" section and "Lower Control Arm, Replace" procedure.

1. Raise and support vehicle.
2. Support radius arm with tool P289.
3. Remove lower shock absorber retaining bolt.
4. Remove control arm retaining and eccentric bolts.
5. Remove radius arm cover retaining bolts.
6. Remove single spacer.
7. Pry radius arm cover with two large screwdrivers.
8. Remove radius arm tool P289.
9. Remove body plug and the radius arm and torsion bar. **Do not mar torsion bar protective paint.**
10. Reverse procedure to install. Refer to "Torsion Bar, Adjust."

TIGHTENING SPECIFICATIONS

Year	Component	Torque/Ft. Lbs.
911		
1993–96	Adjusting Lever To Spring Strut	185
	Camber Eccentric Bolts For Radius Arm	45
	Radius Arm	65
	Radius Arm Bearing Cap	35
	Rear Axle Control Arm	87
	Rear Halfshaft Castellated Nut	217-253
	Shock Absorber Hex Nut	55
	Tracking Eccentric Bolts For Radius Arm	36
	Wheel Hub To Rear Wheel Shaft	335①
	Wheel Hub To Rear Wheel Shaft	345②
	Wheel Nuts	95

Continued

TIGHTENING SPECIFICATIONS—Continued

Year	Component	Torque/Ft. Lbs.
928		
1993–95	Back-Up Light Switch To Housing	16
	Drive Pinion Bearing Unit To Transmission Case	22
	Drive Pinion Locknut	217
	End Cover To Housing	16
	Guide Sleeve To Housing	7
	Oil Drain Plug	16
	Oil Filler Plug	16
	Plug To Transmission Housing	14
	Reverse Gear Stop To Top Cover	6.5
	Ring Gear To Differential Housing	119
	Selector Fork To Rod	18
	Side Cover To Housing	16
	Top Cover To Housing	6.5
	Transmission Output Flange	31
968		
1993–95	Adjusting Lever To Spring Strut	185
	Bearing Flange To Cross Tube	33
	Bearing Flange To Body	50
	Brake Backplate To Steel Trailing Arm	45
	Brake Disc To Wheel Hub	4
	Caliper To Brake Backing Plate	60–65
	Driveshaft Attaching Bolts	30
	Mount To Body	33
	Mount To Strut	15
	Shock Absorber To Body	45
	Shock Absorber To Steel Trailing Arm	45
	Shock Absorber to Aluminum Trailing Arm	90
	Stabilizer To Rear Axle Strut	33
	Stabilizer To Rear Axle Cross Tube	16
	Thrust Bearing To Body	33
	Thrust Bearing To Body Flange	33
	Trailing Arm To Rear Axle Strut	75
	Trailing Arm To Cross Tube	45
	Wheel Hub To Rear Wheel Shaft	335
	Wheel Nuts	95
	Wheel Rim To Hub	96

① — Steel trailing arms.

② — Aluminum trailing arms.

Front Suspension & Steering

NOTE: On Air Bag Equipped Models, Refer To "Air Bag System Precautions" Located In The Front Of This Manual For System Disarming & Arming Procedures.

INDEX

	Page No.
Ball Joint, Replace	37-33
911	37-33
928	37-33
Ball Joint Inspection	37-33
Control Arm, Replace	37-34
911	37-34
928	37-35
968	37-35
Manual Steering Gear, Replace	37-37
911	37-37
968	37-37
Power Steering Gear, Replace	37-36
928	37-36
968	37-36
Power Steering Pump, Replace	37-37
928	37-37
968	37-37
Precautions	37-33
Air Bag Systems	37-33
Strut, Replace	37-33
911	37-33
928	37-33
968	37-33
Tightening Specifications	37-38
Torsion Bar, Replace	37-35
911	37-35
Wheel Bearing, Adjust	37-33

PRECAUTIONS

AIR BAG SYSTEMS

Refer to "Air Bag System Precautions" in the front of this manual for system disarming and arming procedures.

WHEEL BEARING

ADJUST

1. Raise and support vehicle.
2. Remove wheels and axle hub cap.
3. Loosen adjustment nut retaining bolt.
4. While rotating the hub by hand, tighten the adjustment nut slightly.
5. Loosen adjusting nut until brake disc can just be moved using finger pressure on a screwdriver. **Do not support the screwdriver against the hub for use as a lever.**
6. **Torque** the Allen head adjusting nut retainer bolt to 11 ft. lbs.

BALL JOINT INSPECTION

1. Raise and support vehicle.
2. Grasp tire at top and bottom.
3. Shake tire in a side to side motion and check for any ball joint movement.
4. Replace ball joint if any movement is noticed.

BALL JOINT

REPLACE

911

1. Raise and support vehicle.
2. Remove wheel and drive out stud with a suitable hammer and drift.
3. Remove cotter pin and, using tool No. P280b, or equivalent, the four point nut.
4. Coat stud with multi-purpose grease and insert into position. **Check that retaining nut is in front as seen from driving direction and notch in stud points toward wheel spindle.**
5. Seat stud with light hammer, then tighten retaining nut.

928

1. Raise and support vehicle.
2. Remove wheels.
3. Press off ball joints using tool No. VW 267 a, or equivalent.
4. When installing ball joints, apply pressure on the upper control arm with a pry bar. **This is to keep the ball studs from turning and facilitates flange nut installation.**

STRUT

REPLACE

911

1. Raise and support vehicle.
2. Remove wheels and disconnect brake line at hose support bracket.
3. Depress pedal with a suitable device to prevent brake fluid from leaking from reservoir.
4. Remove caliper retaining bolts and complete caliper.
5. Remove grease cap from wheel hub.
6. Loosen bearing adjustment nut and remove brake disc and bearing.
7. Remove disc guard plate.
8. Position aside carpet in luggage compartment covering shock towers.
9. Remove cotter pins and castle nuts from tie rods and ball joints, **Fig. 1.**
10. Remove ball joint from strut using a suitable puller.
11. Remove nut from the top of strut in front luggage compartment.
12. Remove strut and install in vise.
13. Reverse procedure to install.

968

1. Raise and support vehicle.
2. Remove wheels and disconnect brake line at hose support bracket.
3. Support lower control arm and steering knuckle with suitable jack stand.
4. Remove strut retaining and eccentric bolts and strut from steering knuckle.
5. Remove three bearing flange bolts and the shock assembly, **Fig. 2.**
6. Position strut assembly in a suitable spring compressor.
7. Compress spring and remove the strut locknut, stop and flange.
8. Release spring tension and remove the coil spring.
9. Remove components from piston rod.
10. Reverse procedure to install. **Install coil spring in strut unit with straight cut end of spring down.**

928

1. Remove three locknuts from shock tower mount in engine compartment, **Fig. 3.**
2. Raise and support vehicle.
3. Remove wheel and flange locknut.
4. Press off upper ball joint.
5. Remove upper control arm locknuts in engine compartment.
6. Remove strut mounting bolt.
7. Support lower control arm to prevent damage to brake hose.
8. Compress coil spring with a suitable spring compressor and remove strut locknut.
9. Remove washer and upper mounting plate.
10. Carefully remove the tension from coil spring.
11. Remove upper spring retainer, coil spring, and piston rod components.
12. Mark lower spring retainer position for reassembly. Replace struts with major leaks. There are three spring tolerance groups for non-adjustable struts and Boge adjustable struts. Groups are identified by the number of stripes; green for non-adjustable struts, blue for Boge adjustable struts to chassis No. 92A0810714 on 928 models or to chassis No. 92A0820127 on 928S models, and white for Boge adjustable

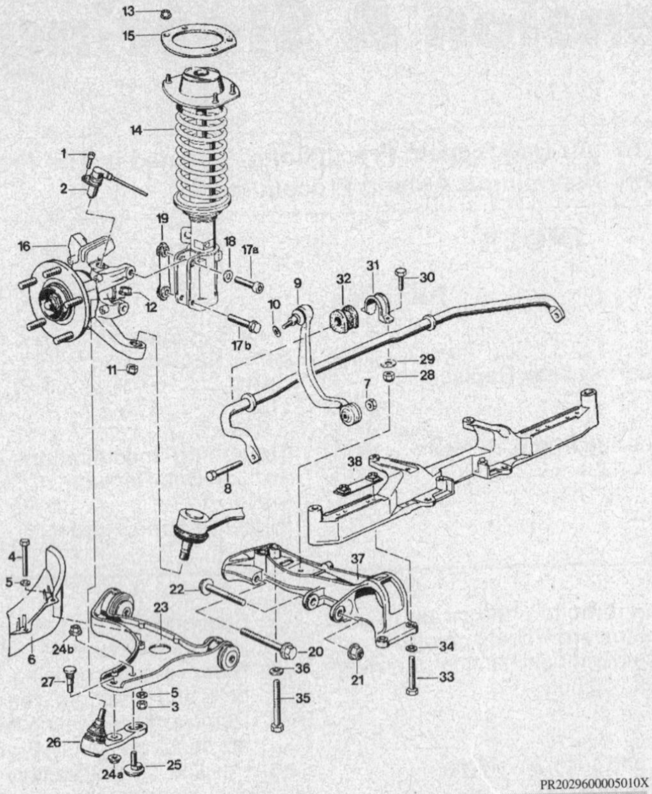

PR2029600005010X

Fig. 1 Front axle & suspension (Part 1 of 3). 911

struts from chassis No. 92A0820128 for 928S models. One stripe is assigned to the 1433–1477 lb. group, two stripes to the 1478–1521 lb. group, and three stripes to the 1522–1565 lb. group. Springs with three white stripes, installed in some models, are no longer available; replace with springs with two white stripes. Bilstein struts are identified by a green and white stripe and are available in only one type. Always replace springs in pairs.

CONTROL ARM

REPLACE

911

1. Raise and support vehicle and remove front wheel.
2. Remove torsion bar adjusting screw and the adjusting arm.
3. Remove ball joint retaining bolt nut and drive out double wedge bolt.
4. Pull ball joint out of strut by pressing control arm downward.
5. Remove hexagon bolts from front transverse control arm bearing and remove protective cap.
6. Remove transverse control arm to subframe attaching bolt and pull control arm toward front.
7. Clamp control arm in suitable vise and remove keeper from slotted locking plate, then remove ball joint nut using tool P280b, or equivalent. **When removing bolt transverse control arms, the subframe retaining bolts must be installed hand tight to hold subframe firmly in position.**
8. Reverse procedure to install, noting the following:
   a. Tighten ball joint slotted nut to specifications, then bend over peg of keeper plate to prevent nut from turning.
   b. Apply light coat of lithium base grease to entire surface of torsion bar and push torsion bar into wishbone. Do not force out the end cap from the wishbone.
   c. Install transverse control arm with torsion bar into subframe. **Torsion bars are preloaded during production. Never interchange torsion bars. Torsion bars are marked on end with "L" for left side or "R" for right side.**
   d. Coat double wedge bolt with suitable grease before installing.
   e. Ensure double wedge is installed so that attaching nut points forward in direction of travel and that notch on face of double wedge bolt and wedge contour point toward wheel stub axle.
   f. Ensure double wedge bolt is properly seated by tapping bolt before tightening.
   g. Slide OWA seal onto torsion bar on rear of subframe.
   h. Using suitable pry bar, push transverse control arm down as far as attached shock absorber strut allows, then slide torsion bar adjusting lever onto torsion bar splines, leaving as little clearance as possible at the lever adjusting point.
   i. Coat threads of adjusting screw with MoS_2 grease, or equivalent

No.	Designation
1	Pan-head screw
2	Rpm sensor
3	Lock nut
4	Screw
5	Washer
6	Air guide
7	Lock nut
8	Screw
9	Stabilizer mount (Figure shows M 030 mount. Standard running gear = mount with 2 ball joints)
10	Washer
11	Lock nut
12	Lock nut
13	Collar lock nut

PR2029600005020X

Fig. 1 Front axle & suspension (Part 2 of 3). 911

No.	Designation
14	Spring strut
15	Gasket
16	Wheel carrier
17a	Pan-head screw M 12
17b	Hexagon head bolt M 14
18	Washer
19	Cage with collar nuts
20	Hexagon-head flange bolt M 12 x 1.5 10.9 120 mm long
21	Collar lock nut M 12 x 1.5
22	Hexagon head flange bolt M 12 x 1.5, 95 mm long

PR2029600005030X

Fig. 1 Front axle & suspension (Part 3 of 3). 911

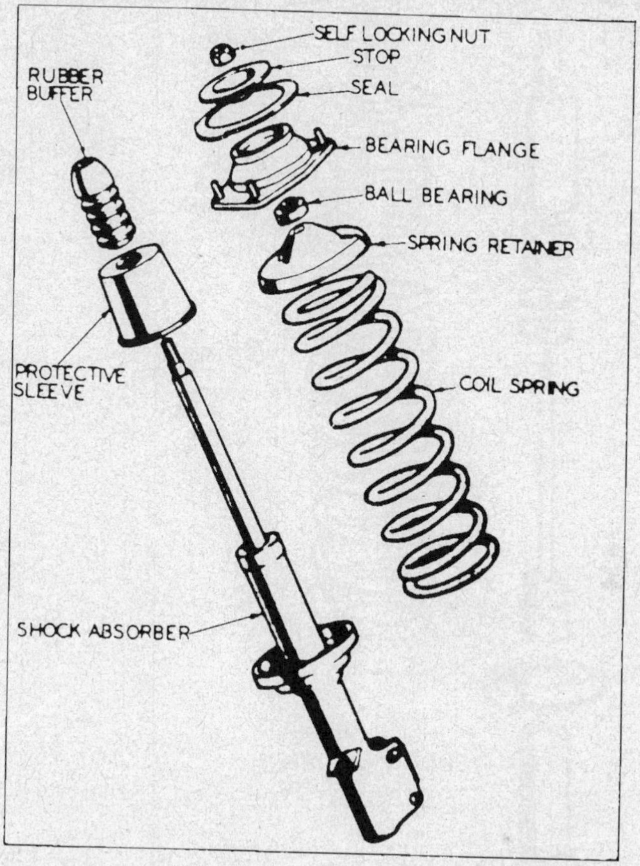
SELF LOCKING NUT
STOP
SEAL
RUBBER BUFFER
BEARING FLANGE
BALL BEARING
SPRING RETAINER
PROTECTIVE SLEEVE
COIL SPRING
SHOCK ABSORBER
PR2029100003000X

Fig. 2 Exploded view of strut. 968 models

and lightly tighten screw in place.

j. Adjust front end height and check wheel alignment.

968

1. Raise and support vehicle.
2. Remove wheels and ball joint bolt, **Fig. 4.**
3. Remove two metal/rubber rear bushing bolts.
4. Remove bushing clamp and bushing.
5. Remove front metal/rubber bushing bolt.
6. Remove control arm.
7. Reverse procedure to install.

928

1. Raise and support vehicle.
2. Remove wheels and disconnect tie rod from steering knuckle, **Fig. 5.**
3. Remove wheel alignment eccentric locknuts and eccentrics.
4. Remove control arm bracket retaining bolts and bracket.
5. Remove tie down bracket retaining bolts and bracket.
6. Reverse procedure to install.

TORSION BAR

REPLACE

911

1. Raise and support vehicle.
2. Remove wheels and torsion bar adjustment screw.
3. Remove seal and torsion bar adjusting lever from torsion bar.
4. Remove forward rubber mount cover.
5. Using a suitable punch, drive torsion bar forward out of lower control arm. **Use caution to avoid damaging the torsion bar splines. Check for rust or damage to the torsion bar finish. Coat torsion bar with lithium grease before installing.**
6. Install torsion bar in lower control arm. **Torsion bars are under tension during production. Torsion bars are marked with either "L" or "R" on their end face. Install bars marked with "L" in lefthand side of vehicle and bars marked with "R" in right-hand side of vehicle.**
7. Install seal on torsion bar.
8. Install adjusting lever on torsion bar as follows:
   a. Using a pry bar, pull the lower control arm as far down as the attached shock absorber strut will allow.
   b. Slide torsion bar adjusting lever with end cap installed onto the torsion bar splines. **Leave as little clearance at the lever adjusting point as possible.**
   c. Coat adjusting screw threads with MoS_2 grease and lightly tighten screw.
9. Check that end cap is properly seated in control arm.
10. Install rubber mount cover bracket.
11. Adjust front end height and check wheel alignment.

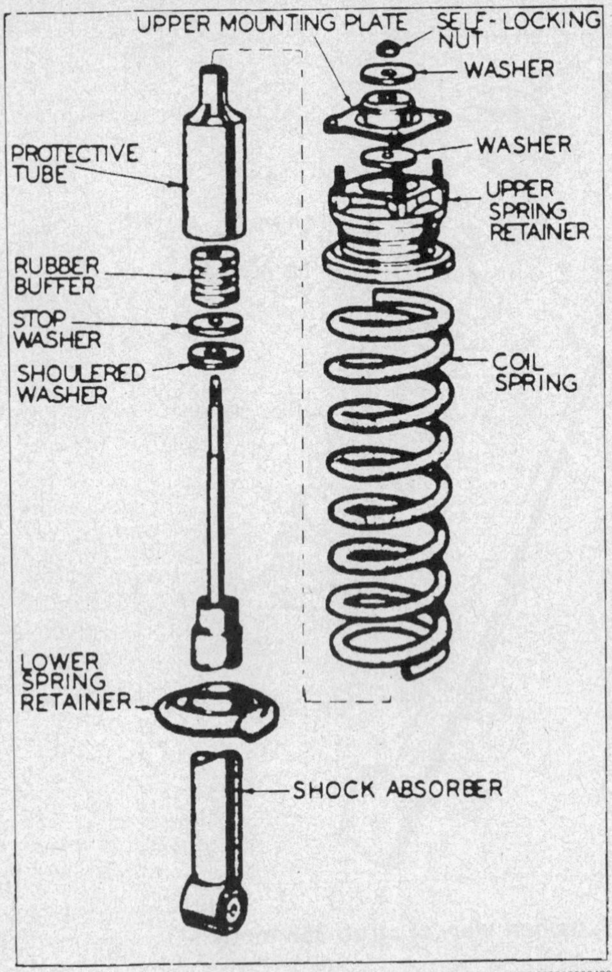
UPPER MOUNTING PLATE
SELF-LOCKING NUT
WASHER
WASHER
PROTECTIVE TUBE
UPPER SPRING RETAINER
RUBBER BUFFER
STOP WASHER
SHOULERED WASHER
COIL SPRING
LOWER SPRING RETAINER
SHOCK ABSORBER

PR2029100004000X

Fig. 3 **Exploded view of strut. 928 non-adjustable strut shown, adjustable strut similar**

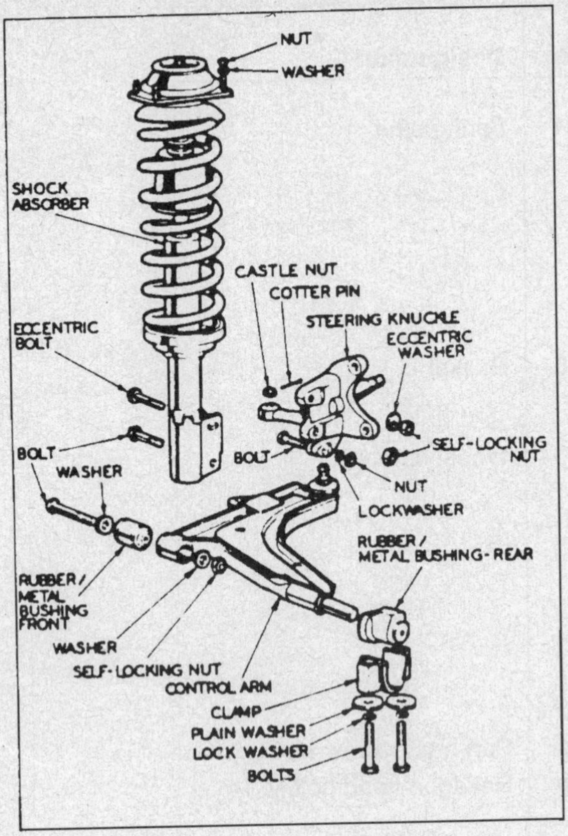
NUT
WASHER
SHOCK ABSORBER
CASTLE NUT
COTTER PIN
STEERING KNUCKLE
ECCENTRIC WASHER
ECCENTRIC BOLT
BOLT
WASHER
BOLT
SELF-LOCKING NUT
NUT
LOCKWASHER
RUBBER / METAL BUSHING-REAR
RUBBER / METAL BUSHING FRONT
WASHER
SELF-LOCKING NUT
CONTROL ARM
CLAMP
PLAIN WASHER
LOCK WASHER
BOLTS

PR2029100001000X

Fig. 4 **Exploded view of front suspension. 968 models**

POWER STEERING GEAR

REPLACE

928

1. Using a suitable siphon drain hydraulic fluid from reservoir.
2. Using a suitable puller, remove tie rods.
3. Remove hose retaining clamp near starter motor.
4. Remove stabilizer bar mounting bolts and allow bar to hang free.
5. Disconnect pressure and return line at steering gear.
6. Remove five reinforcement plate retaining bolts from the engine crossmember.
7. Loosen but do not remove the four steering gear locknuts.
8. Remove universal joint intermediate shaft bolt and disconnect steering intermediate shaft.
9. Remove four steering gear mounting nuts and lower steering gear from vehicle.
10. Reverse procedure to install. Add hydraulic fluid and bleed steering system.

968

1. Raise and support vehicle.
2. Remove stabilizer by disconnecting stabilizer mounts on control arms and stabilizer suspension on side members.
3. Disconnect ground wire on front axle crossmember.
4. Using tool No. 9183, or equivalent and torque wrench, loosen but do not remove tie rods at steering rack, then run rack out of steering gear case on disconnecting side only as far as necessary.
5. Disconnect pressure line on power steering pump, catching hydraulic fluid draining out of pump or tank and power steering gear. Position pressure line connection lower than steering and turn steering wheel from stop to stop several times.
6. Remove bolt on universal joint, then loosen but do not remove four steering gear attaching bolts until shaft can be removed from steering pinion. **Unscrew pressure line clamp on steering gear to gain access to left lower attaching bolt.**
7. Press out tie rods (ball joints) with suitable puller.
8. Disconnect return line at steering gear.
9. Remove four steering gear attaching bolts and remove steering gear toward front of vehicle.
10. If installing new steering gear, mount rubber inserts and clamps in correct position before installing steering gear in vehicle. To facilitate mounting of rubber inserts and clamps, use suitable lubricant that will not deteriorate rubber parts.
11. Connect pressure line to steering gear, **torquing** to 14 ft. lbs.
12. Coat ends of fully extended rack with suitable grease.
13. With steering wheel and steering gear in centered position, slide shaft onto steering gear in correct position. **Steering gear attaching bolts should be screwed in only lightly to facilitate installation.**
14. Attach steering gear.
15. Install tie rods on rack. **Be careful not to damage surface of rack.**
16. After completing installation, fill system with suitable fluid, bleed steering

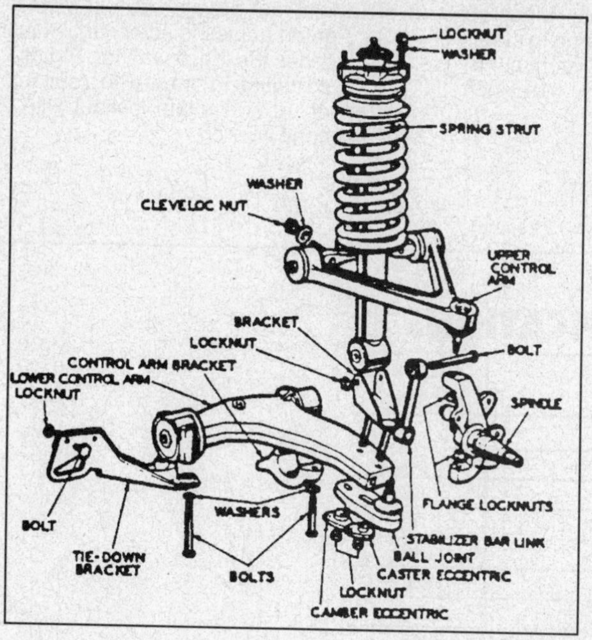
LOCKNUT
WASHER
SPRING STRUT
WASHER
CLEVELOC NUT
UPPER CONTROL ARM
BRACKET
LOCKNUT
BOLT
CONTROL ARM BRACKET
LOWER CONTROL ARM
LOCKNUT
SPINDLE
FLANGE LOCKNUTS
WASHERS
BOLT
TIE-DOWN BRACKET
BOLTS
STABILIZER BAR LINK
BALL JOINT
CASTER ECCENTRIC
LOCKNUT
CAMBER ECCENTRIC

PR2029100002000X

Fig. 5 Front suspension exploded view. 928 models

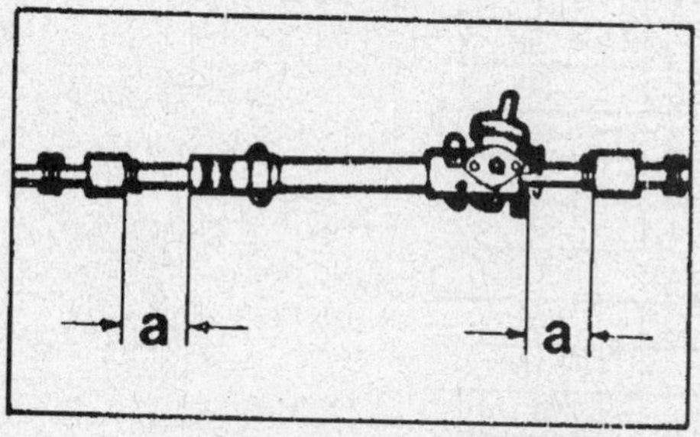
a
a

PR6039100002000X

Fig. 7 Tie rod ends installation

system, check for leaks, and test operation.

17. Adjust toe, if necessary.

POWER STEERING PUMP

REPLACE

928

1. Disconnect battery ground cable.
2. Disconnect intake hose at left side of air cleaner.
3. Remove fluid from power steering pump reservoir.
4. Raise and support vehicle.
5. Remove splash shield.
6. Slightly loosen attaching bolts at front of power steering pump.
7. Remove attaching bolt at rear of power steering pump.
8. Remove power steering drive belt.
9. Remove left upper section of timing belt cover.
10. Disconnect pressure hose at power steering pump.
11. Loosen clamp, then disconnect suction hose at power steering pump.
12. Remove attaching bolts at front of power steering pump, then remove pump and bracket as an assembly.
13. Reverse procedure to install, noting the following:
    a. Position pump by tightening front attaching bolts, then insert but do not tighten rear attaching bolt.
    b. When installing replacement pressure hose, ensure protective ring rests on spring strut mount.
    c. When installing original pressure hose fitted with asbestos sleeve, leave not more than 25 mm between inner wheelwell and hose.
    d. Adjust power steering and alternator drive belts and bleed steering system.

968

1. Disconnect battery ground cable, then remove splash shield.
2. Disconnect pressure line at power steering pump.
3. Loosen clamp, then disconnect suction hose at power steering pump.
4. Disconnect connecting rod at power steering pump, then loosen nut at other end and swing rod downward.
5. Remove power steering pump attaching nut and bolt and remove power

PR6039100001000X

Fig. 6 Centering steering gear

PR6039100003000X

Fig. 8 Steering rack adjustment

steering drive belt.

6. Turn up power steering pump in console and remove spacer from below.
7. Remove power steering pump from console.
8. Reverse procedure to install. Ensure pressure and suction lines are correctly routed to prevent rubbing. Bleed steering system.

MANUAL STEERING GEAR

REPLACE

911

1. Raise and support vehicle.
2. Remove wheels and separate steering shaft at universal joint.
3. Remove castle nuts from tie rod ends.
4. Remove tie rods with a suitable puller.
5. Remove front axle stone shield.
6. Loosen steering gear to auxiliary carrier bolts.
7. Remove torsion bar adjustment screws.
8. Remove torsion bar adjustment levers and seals.
9. Remove lower control arm and auxiliary carrier bolts.
10. Remove carrier and steering gear with tie rods.
11. Reverse procedure to install.

968

1. Raise and support vehicle.
2. Remove wheels and press off tie rods with tool VW 266 H or an equivalent.
3. Remove steering gear universal joint bolt.
4. Remove steering rack retaining bolts.
5. Remove rack.

6. Center steering gear with tool 9116, **Fig. 6. There are two types of steering tie rods. The new design is machined for a distance of .511 inch (13 mm) on the joint for the rubber stop ring. The old design was machined for a .236 inch (6 mm) distance. Only the new version is available for replacement.**
7. Screw tie rods on evenly. Measure from ridge on rubber stop ring to steering housing, **Fig. 7.** Distance "a" should equal 2.55 inches ± .0196 inch (65 mm ± 5 mm).
8. To adjust rack proceed as follows:
   a. Tighten adjusting screw until it just touches the thrust washer, **Fig. 8.**
   b. Hold adjusting screw with a suitable wrench, and rotate locknut with a second wrench.

TIGHTENING SPECIFICATIONS

Year	Component	Torque/Ft. Lbs.
911		
1993–96	Ball Joint Castellated Nut	33
	Ball Joint Hex Nut	33
	Ball Joint Slotted Nut	108
	Brake Disc Hex Bolts	16
	Brake Support	34
	Fixed Caliper Hex Bolt	51
	Hollow Caliper Screw	15
	Shock Absorber Strap Nut	58
	Stabilizer Arm Hex Bolts	18
	Steering Arm Bolts	34
	Steering Box	34
	Steering Wheel Hex Nut	58
	Track Rod Joint Castellated Nut	33
	Wheel Nuts	95
	Wishbone Castellated Nut	54
968		
1993–95	Aluminum Wheel To Brake Disc	96
	Brake Disc To Wheel Hub	18
	Caliper To Steering Knuckle	63
	Cap For Shock Absorber Cartridge	90–130
	Control Arm To Crossmember	45
	Control Arm To Body	33
	Control Arm To Steering Knuckle	37
	Crossmember To Body	63
	Guide Joint To Steel Control Arm	19
	Spring Strut Mount To Spring Strut	60
	Spring Strut To Steering Knuckle	74
	Spring Strut To Body	19
	Stabilizer Clamp To Mount	16
	Stabilizer Mount To Body	16
	Stabilizer Mount To Steel Control Arm	16
	Stabilizer Mount To Aluminum Control Arm	19
	Steel Rim To Brake Disc	96
	Tie-Rod To Steering Knuckle	37
	Wheel Nuts	95

Wheel Alignment

INDEX

	Page No.
Front Wheel Alignment	37-39
Axle Height, Adjust	37-39
Camber & Caster, Adjust	37-39
Rear Wheel Alignment	37-39
Camber Adjustment	37-39
Rear Axle Height Adjustment	37-40
Toe Adjustment	37-40
Torsion Bar Adjustment	37-40
Wheel Alignment Specifications	37-2
Front	37-2
Rear	37-3

FRONT WHEEL ALIGNMENT

Accurate front axle height adjustment is critical to toe-in, camber, and caster adjustments. Ensure tire pressures are at their specified values, fuel tank is full, spare tire is in place, and a weight approximately the same as the driver, positioned on the driver's seat.

AXLE HEIGHT, ADJUST

911

1. Depress front of vehicle several times and allow to rebound to proper height.
2. Measure distance between level floor or ramp to center of wheel hub (dimension a).
3. Value "a" minus 4.25 inches should equal value "b." **Value "b" equals the distance between the torsion bar center and the level surface on which the vehicle is positioned.**
4. Remove torsion bar dust cover at adjusting lever. Use torsion bar centering mark as a reference mark.
5. Loosen or tighten torsion bar adjusting bolt until value "b" is obtained at the torsion bar center.
6. Depress front of vehicle and allow to rebound to proper height. Recheck vehicle height. **The allowable difference in height between left and right sides of the vehicle is .2 inch (5 mm).**

928 Less Adjustable Spring Struts

1. Measure distance from floor to milled surface of lower control arm mount, **Fig. 1.** Distance should be 6.6929–7.4803 inches (170–190 mm) with a maximum left to right difference of .3937 inch (10 mm).
2. Slight adjustment can be made by the installation of spacers underneath the lower spring retainer. Each spacer will increase axle height approximately .3937 inch (10 mm). Never use more than two spacers per spring strut.
3. If axle height can not be adjusted to specifications with spacers, front springs must be replaced. Springs which have approximately 45 lbs. more spring force for the same test strength will increase front axle height by approximately .1969–.5906 inch (5–15 mm).

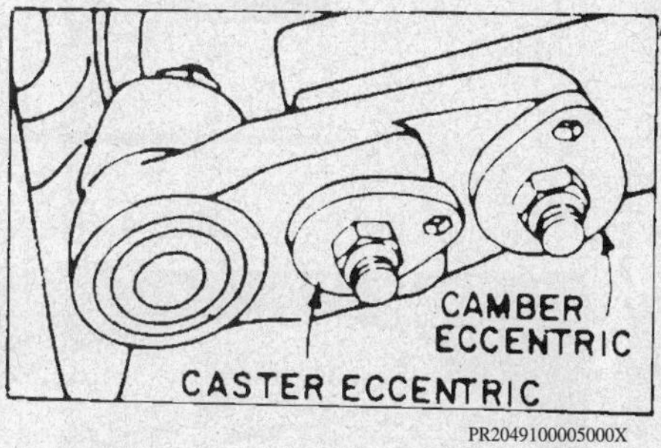
CAMBER
ECCENTRIC
CASTER ECCENTRIC
PR2049100005000X

Fig. 1 Front suspension height check point. 928 models

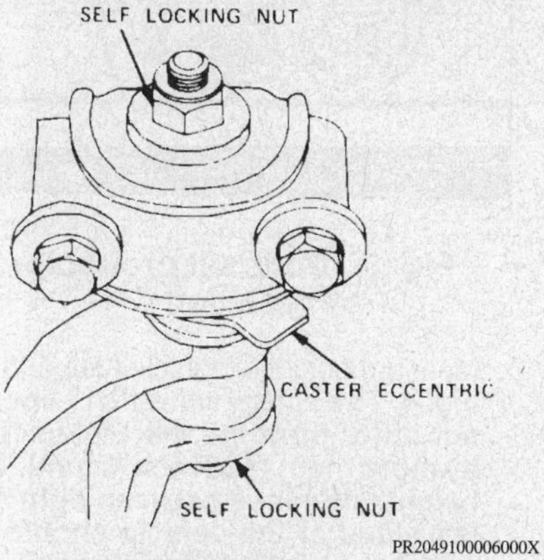
SELF LOCKING NUT
CASTER ECCENTRIC
SELF LOCKING NUT
PR2049100006000X

Fig. 2 Front caster & camber adjustment. 968 models

928 w/Adjustable Spring Struts

1. Measure distance from floor to milled surface of lower control arm mount, **Fig. 1.** Distance should be 6.6929–7.4803 inches (170–190 mm) with a maximum left to right difference of .3937 inch (10 mm).
2. To adjust axle height, turn adjusting nuts at bottom of spring on strut. With vehicle resting on ground, turn wheels against lock accordingly to gain access to adjusting nuts. Turn nuts clockwise to increase height or counterclockwise to decrease height. **The adjusting range for lowering the vehicle is limited by a stop for the adjusting nut on models with Bilstein spring struts. On models with Boge spring struts, the lowest position has been reached when the adjusting nut turns easily.**

CAMBER & CASTER, ADJUST

911

1. Pull front luggage compartment carpeting away from shock towers.
2. Remove sealing compound from pressure plates and movable dish ring.
3. Mark position of single and double hole plates and screws.
4. Position shock absorber strut supporting bearing to adjust caster or camber.
5. **Torque** bolts to 33.8 ft. lbs. and seal plates with a suitable sealing compound.

968

1. Adjust camber by turning eccentric bolt on lower strut mounting.
2. **On models with steel control arms,** adjust caster by moving rear of suspension control arm from side to side.
3. **On models with aluminum control arms,** adjust caster by loosening self locking nuts and turning caster eccentric until caster is within specifications, **Fig. 2,** then **torque** nuts to 62 ft. lbs.

928

On models with aluminum joint carriers, adjust caster and camber by rotating two eccentrics on lower control arm, **Fig. 3.**

On models with steel joint carrier, caster and camber is adjusted in same way, but location of caster and camber eccentrics are opposite those shown in **Fig. 3.**

On models with aluminum joint carrier, always turn caster eccentric from small caster in direction of large caster. When caster is excessive, first turn the eccentric back completely and then adjust to correct value. If specified caster cannot be obtained, opposite side may be corrected to a value of up to 4°30.'

REAR WHEEL ALIGNMENT

CAMBER ADJUSTMENT

911

1. Loosen retaining bolt nuts and eccentric bolt nuts at the rear axle flange.
2. Rotate tracking and camber eccentrics to adjust.
3. Tighten eccentric and retaining nuts.

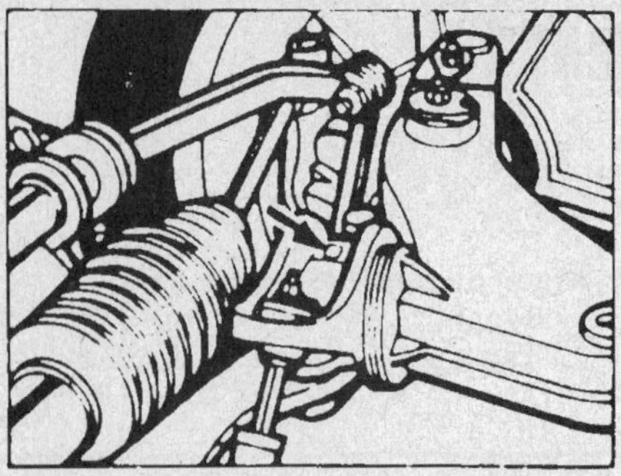

PR2049100007000X

Fig. 3 Front caster & camber adjustment eccentrics. 928 models with aluminum joint carriers

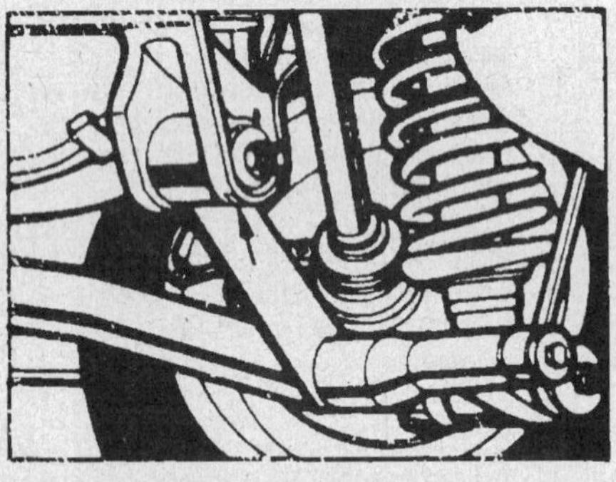

PR2049100009000X

Fig. 5 Rear axle height measurement

928

Camber adjustments are made by rotating the inner control arm bushing eccentric bolt.

968

Camber adjustment is made by loosening joint between spring strut and trailing arm, then turning camber eccentric.

TOE ADJUSTMENT

928

Adjust toe by turning eccentric bolt on front control arm mount.

968

Adjust toe by moving trailing arm in slots of spring strut.

REAR AXLE HEIGHT ADJUSTMENT

911

1. Depress rear of vehicle several times and allow body to rebound.
2. Measure vertical distance between rear wheel center and level section of alignment ramp or level floor (distance a), **Fig. 4.**
3. Value of "a" plus .4724 inch (12 mm) equals value "b." **The value "b" cannot be measured since the torsion bar is off center.**
4. Value "b" less bushing cover radius ($1/2$ diameter) equals value "b1."

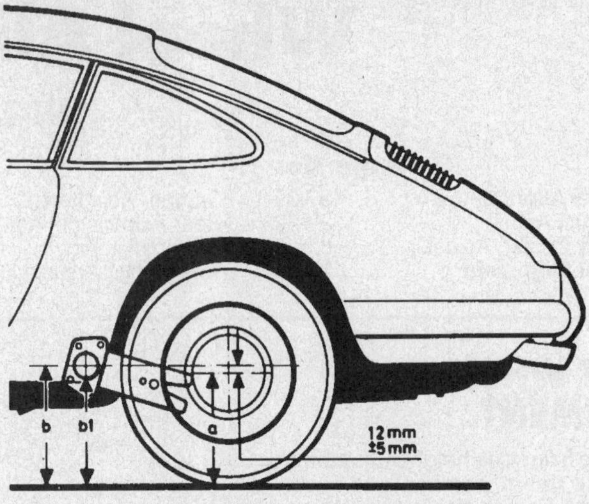
b
b1
a
12 mm
±5 mm

PR2049100008000X

Fig. 4 Rear axle height adjustment

PR2049100010000X

Fig. 6 Door sill protractor position

5. Measure height of vehicle (value "b1"), **Fig. 4. The actual value "b1" should not differ from the calculated "b1" by more than .1968 inch (5 mm). The height difference between right and left sides of the vehicle should be no more than .3145 inch (8 mm).** For example: value "a," 12.40 inches (315 mm) + .47 inch (12 mm) = 12.87 inches (327 mm) – bushing cover radius, 1.18 inches (30 mm) = 11.69 inches (297 mm) = "b1" or vehicle height)
6. If proper suspension height cannot be achieved, proceed as follows:
   a. Check adjustment of front suspension and correct if necessary.
   b. Check rear torsion bar adjustment and correct if necessary.

968

Rear vehicle height can be adjusted on two piece spring plate, without removal of torsion bars. If spring plate angle is as specified, vehicle height will be correct.

928

1. Measure distance from wheel ground surface to measuring surface on crossmember, **Fig. 5.** Height should be 6.4173–7.2047 inches (163–183 mm) with a maximum difference of .3937 inch (10 mm) between left and right side.

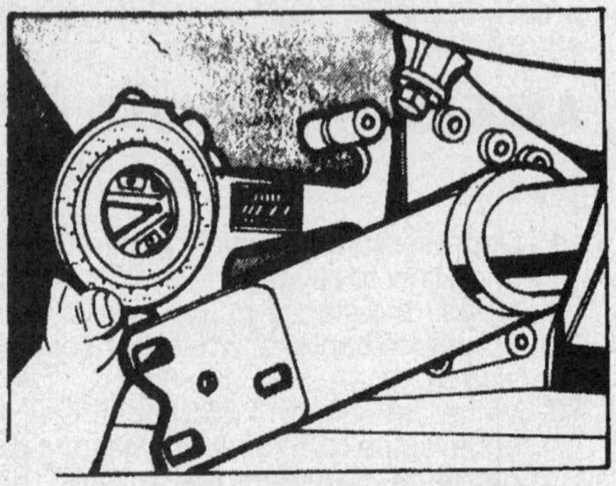

PR2049100011000X

Fig. 7 Torsion plate or radius arm protractor position

2. If height is not within specifications, turn adjusting nut clockwise to raise vehicle or counterclockwise to lower vehicle.

TORSION BAR ADJUSTMENT

If the torsion bar is reset by one spline at its inner end, a 9° change is obtained. If the radius arm is reset by one spline at the outer end of the torsion bar, a change of $8\frac{3}{20}$° is obtained. This arrangement allows a change of $\frac{5}{6}$° if the torsion bar and radius arm are positioned towards each other.

911

1. Install torsion bar into transverse tube.
2. Install radius arm onto outer end of splines.
3. Position a bubble protractor on the lower edge of the door sill, **Fig. 6.**
4. Adjust so that the bubble is in the center of the glass tube.
5. Position protractor on free hanging radius arm and note arm inclination, **Fig. 7.**
6. Adjust arm inclination if necessary.

968

1. Position a bubble protractor on the lower edge of door sill, **Fig. 6.**

2. Rotate bubble level carrier on VW 261,or equivalent protractor to specified torsion plate angle.
3. With torsion plate cover removed, position protractor on torsion plate, **Fig.**

7. Lift the plate enough to remove play from splines.

4. According to angle measurement at door sill, if front of vehicle is lower than rear, add door sill measurement to torsion plate value. If rear of vehicle is lower than front, subtract door sill measurement from torsion plate value.

Air Conditioning

INDEX

	Page No.
A/C Specifications	37-42
Discharging System	37-41
Refrigerant Recovery Procedure	37-41
Oil Charge	37-41
911	37-41
928	37-41
Oil Level Check	37-41
911	37-41
928	37-41
Precautions	37-41

PRECAUTIONS

Some models use refrigerant R-134a in the air conditioning system. Refrigerant R-134a and R-12 are not compatible with each other. Refrigerant oil, refrigerant hoses and other component used in a R-134a refrigerant system also differ from those used with a R-12 refrigerant system. Refer to the "Air Conditioning Specifications" chart to determine refrigerant usage.

DISCHARGING SYSTEM

REFRIGERANT RECOVERY PROCEDURE

The use of refrigerant recovery and recycling stations allows the recovery and reuse of refrigerant after contaminants and moisture have been removed. When servicing systems using R-134a refrigerant, use of specialized recycling equipment is required.

When using a recovery or recycling station, follow the manufacturer's operating instructions, noting the following:

1. **Use extreme caution and observe all safety and service precautions related to use of refrigerants.**
2. Connect refrigerant recycling station hoses to vehicle A/C service ports and recovery station inlet fitting. Hoses used should have shutoff devices or check valve within 12 inches of hose ends to minimize introduction of air into recycling station and to minimize amount of refrigerant release when hoses are disconnected.
3. Turn recycling station On to start recovery process. Allow recycling station to pump refrigerant from A/C system until station pressure gauge indicates vacuum.
4. After vehicle A/C system has been evacuated, close station inlet valve, if equipped.
5. Turn station Off. On some stations the pump will automatically be turned Off by a low pressure switch.
6. Allow vehicle A/C system to remain closed for approximately two minutes. Observe vacuum level indicated on gauge. If pressure does not rise, disconnect recycling station hoses.
7. If system pressure rises, repeat steps 3 through 6 until vacuum level remains stable for two minutes.
8. Service A/C system as necessary, then evacuate and recharge A/C system.

OIL CHARGE

Refrigerant oil used for a R-134a refrigerant system differs from that used with an R-12 refrigerant system. Refer to the "Air Conditioning Specifications" chart to determine refrigerant usage.

928

New compressors are pre-charged with the proper amount of lubricant needed for the entire refrigerant system. If a new compressor is installed and no additional oil has been lost from the system, drain all oil from new compressor, then add 8 ounces of oil to compressor.

When replacing system components, add the following quantities of refrigerant oil to the compressor: condenser, 1 ounce; evaporator, 2 ounces; receiver-drier, .3 ounce.

911

Refer to "Oil Level Check" procedure.

OIL LEVEL CHECK

Refrigerant oil used for a R-134a refrigerant system differs from that used with an R-12 refrigerant system. Refer to the "Air Conditioning Specifications" chart to determine refrigerant usage.

911

1. Start engine and operate air conditioner for several minutes.
2. Stop engine, then discharge refrigerant from system.
3. Remove oil filler plug and rotate compressor rotor on clutch plate until TDC mark is visible.
4. Rotate clutch plate counterclockwise approximately 110°, then insert dipstick at an angle up to the stop.
5. Remove dipstick and read oil level. Oil level should be between the seventh and eleventh graduations on dipstick. Add oil as necessary. **A dipstick can be fabricated from a piece of suitable rod. Oil level should be 13/16 to 1 3/16 inch from end of rod.**
6. Install oil fill plug, then charge refrigerant system.

928

No provision is made for checking oil on these vehicles. Oil is added according to component(s) being replaced. Refer to "Oil Charge."

A/C SPECIFICATIONS

Year	Model	Refrigerant Capacity, Lbs.	Refrigerant Type	Refrigerant Oil		Charging Valve Locations	
				Viscosity	Total System Capacity, Ounces①	High Press.	Low Press.
1993–95	911 2/4	1.84	R-134a	⑥	4.6	②	③
	928 GTS④	⑧	R-12	⑨	9.3	②	③
	928 GTS⑤	⑦	R-134a	⑥	9.3	②	③
	968	1.9	R-134a	⑥	3.9	②	③
1996	911	1.85	R134a	⑥	4.6	②	③

① — Densoil.
② — On high pressure line.
③ — On low pressure line.
④ — To VIN 92 PS 82 0060.
⑤ — From VIN 92 PS 82 0060.
⑥ — Nippondenso oil ND8, or equivalent.
⑦ — Less rear A/C, 1.90 Lbs.; w/rear A/C, 2.31 Lbs.
⑧ — Less rear A/C, 2.09 Lbs.; w/rear A/C, 2.64 Lbs.
⑨ — Densoil 6.

Cooling Fans

INDEX

	Page No.
Component Replacement	37-42
911	37-42
928	37-42
968	37-42

COMPONENT REPLACEMENT

911

Refer to "Alternator, Replace" in electrical section for replacement of engine cooling fan.

928

1. Remove vehicle grille.
2. Disconnect fan harness leads, then remove cable ties from leads where required.
3. Disconnect left and right brackets at condenser.
4. Remove two upper fan housing mounting screws, then the lower mounting screw at crossmember.
5. Remove cable ties at hood lock support area, then the cover from harness.
6. Lift fan out from above, being careful not to damage condenser fins.
7. Reverse procedure to install.

968

1. Remove upper and lower mounting bolts, then the fan assembly.
2. Reverse procedure to install.

Dash Gauges

NOTE: Refer To The "Dash Panel Service" Section For Dash Panel Removal Procedures.

NOTE: Refer To The "Electronic Instrumentation" Section In MOTOR'S "Imported Auto Engine Performance & Driveability Manual" For Information Related To Electronic Instrumentation.

INDEX

Page No.

Gauges 37-43
968 37-43

GAUGES

968

Coolant temperature, oil pressure and fuel gauges can be checked using tester VAG 1301, or equivalent. When using the tester, disconnect the sensor for the gauge being checked. Select proper tester unit setting as listed in **Figs. 1 through 3,** for unit being checked. If gauge indicates incorrect or no value, check gauge wiring for an open or short circuit. If gauge electrical circuit is satisfactory, replace gauge unit. If gauge reading is within one needle width of the indicated reading, replace gauge sending unit.

Gauge Reading °C	Tester Setting	Resistance (Ohms)
40	557–558	287.4
60	247–248	134
80	117–118	69.1
100	55–56	38.5
115	30–31	25.8

Fig. 1 Coolant temperature gauge test specifications. 968

Gauge Reading	Tester Setting	Resistance (Ohms)
RES	105–106	63.2
¼	63–64	42.2
½	21–22	21.2
¾	—	8.6
Full	—	2.8

Fig. 2 Fuel gauge test specifications. 968

Gauge Reading (Bar)	Tester Setting	Resistance (Ohms)
1	37–38	29.6
2	110–111	65.3
3	177–178	98.9
4	246–247	133.6
5	349–350	184

Fig. 3 Oil pressure gauge test specifications. 968

Starter Motors

INDEX

Page No.
Description 37-44

DESCRIPTION

A countershaft mouthed starter is used on models less double mass flywheel. An external bearing starter is used on models with a double mass flywheel. The shaft runs on the bearing located in the transmission case clutch bellhousing. The sintered sleeve in the transmission case, close to the bellhousing must not be lubricated with grease or oil and the sleeve must not be cleaned with solutions.

Alternators

INDEX

Page No.
Alternator Specifications 37-44

ALTERNATOR SPECIFICATIONS

Year	Model	Current Rating Amps.
1993–96	All	115

Speed Control Systems

NOTE: On Air Bag Equipped Models, Refer To "Air Bag System Precautions" Located In The Front Of This Manual For System Disarming & Arming Procedures.

INDEX

Page No.
Component Replacement........ 37-44
Control Unit..................... 37-44
Description 37-44
Precautions...................... 37-44
Air Bag Systems................ 37-44

DESCRIPTION

The cruise control system (Tempostat E) is an electrically controlled system. On 911 models, the cruise control unit is located below the center instrument panel, near the radio. On 928 models, the cruise control unit is located below the center console. On 968 models, the cruise control unit is located below the lefthand side of the instrument panel. The electric connection is made with a 14-pin connector and an additional coding plug (2), the assembly is covered by a cap. On 911 and 968 models, the electric drive servo is located lefthand side of the engine compartment. On 928 models, the electrical drive servo is located in the rear of the lefthand front fender. The electric drive connection is made with a 6-pin plug. A cable is used as a mechanical connection between the drive and throttle valve.

PRECAUTIONS

AIR BAG SYSTEMS

Refer to "Air Bag System Precautions" in the front of this manual for system disarming and arming procedures.

Refer to MOTOR's "Air Bag Manual" for system diagnosis and testing procedures.

COMPONENT REPLACEMENT

CONTROL UNIT

1. Disable air bag system as described in "Precautions."
2. **On 928 models,** remove center console.
3. **On all models,** disconnect control unit electrical connectors.
4. Remove control unit attaching screws, then remove unit.
5. Reverse to install.

Air Bag System

INDEX

	Page No.
Air Bag System Disarming & Arming	37-45
Arming	37-45
Disarming	37-45
Collision Inspection	37-45
Component Service	37-45
Air Bag Assembly Disposal	37-47
Contact Unit, Replace	37-46
Control Unit, Replace	37-46
Driver Side Air Bag Module, Replace	37-45
Front Crash Sensors, Replace	37-46
Passenger Side Air Bag Module, Replace	37-45
Diagnosis & Testing	37-45
Precautions	37-45
Scheduled Maintenance	37-45
Tightening Specifications	37-47

AIR BAG SYSTEM DISARMING & ARMING

DISARMING

1. Place ignition switch in the Off position.
2. Disconnect and cover battery ground cable with electrical tape.
3. Wait 20 minutes before starting any necessary repairs. This is necessary to allow the back-up power supply to the air bag system to discharge.

ARMING

1. Place ignition switch in the Off position.
2. Connect battery ground cable.
3. Place ignition switch in the On position and note air bag warning lamp operation as follows:
   a. **On 1993 928 models,** the warning lamp should be illuminated for approximately 5 seconds after the ignition switch has been placed in the On position and then go Off.
   b. **On 1993 911 and 968 models,** the warning lamp should be illuminated for approximately 2.5 seconds after the ignition switch has been placed in the On position and then go Off.

PRECAUTIONS

Prior to disconnecting any air bag system electrical connectors or servicing any system components or other components located near an air bag system electrical connector, the system must be disarmed. Refer to "Air Bag System Arming and Disarming."

Always observe the following safety measures when working on air bag system:

1. Air bag system components must not be opened or repaired. Always install new components.
2. If air bag module, crash sensor or control unit has been dropped from a height of 18 inches or more, do not install component into vehicle, replace.
3. Always replace air bag system components which have been damaged.
4. Do not leave an undeployed air bag module unattended if work is interrupted. Install into vehicle as soon as unit is removed from packaging.
5. Always place a removed air bag module so that the pad is facing upwards.
6. Air bag module must not be exposed to oil, grease, or cleaning solutions.
7. Do not expose air bag modules to temperatures above 195°F for even brief periods while handling them during a repair process. Keep unit clear of all heat sources.
8. Storage, transportation and disposal of air bag modules are subject to the laws for flammable solids.
9. Deployed air bag modules do not have to be disposed of as a hazardous waste but can disposed of with automotive metal scrap for recycling.
10. Thoroughly wash hands after handling a deployed air bag module.
11. Prior to performing repair or welding procedures in area of an air bag system component, remove the air bag system component.

SCHEDULED MAINTENANCE

Air bag system must be inspected at 4, 8 and 10 years after date of vehicle manufacture, and then every 2 years there after. The vehicle manufacture date is listed on the safety compliance sticker. **On 911 models,** the safety compliance sticker is located on the left door jam. **On 928 models,** the safety compliance sticker is located on the left door sill. **On 968 models,** the safety compliance sticker is located in the engine compartment to the left of the central electronic box.

Inspect air bag system for the following:

1. Check air bag system for stored fault codes.
2. Ensure no stickers or other items have been affixed to the air bag pads.
3. Check condition of air bag system components and wiring and replace components or wiring as necessary.
4. Check whether modifications have been made to system. Also ensure additional electrical equipment has not been connected to the air system wiring.

DIAGNOSIS & TESTING

Refer to MOTOR's Air Bag Manual for complete diagnosis and testing information.

COLLISION INSPECTION

All system components should be inspected for dents, cracks, exposure to excessive heat and other damage. All air bag system wiring should be checked for chaffing and interference with other vehicle components. If air bag system deployment was experience, the air bag modules, control unit, both crash sensors and contact unit should be replaced with new components. On models with passenger side air bag, the instrument panel should also be inspected. When repairing vehicle, system should be disarmed as described under "Air Bag System Disarming and Arming." Also when performing service procedures, do not expose components or wiring to heat guns, welding or spray guns.

COMPONENT SERVICE

DRIVER SIDE AIR BAG MODULE, REPLACE

1. Disarm air bag system as described under "Disarming and Arming Air Bag System."
2. Using a Torx T30 bit, remove air bag module to steering wheel attaching screws.
3. Lift air bag module from steering wheel, then disconnect electrical connector.
4. Reverse procedure to install noting the following:
   a. During installation use new Torx screws. Tighten screws to torque listed in the "Tightening Specifications."
   b. After completing installation, arm air bag system as described under "Air Bag System Disarming And Arming."

PASSENGER SIDE AIR BAG MODULE, REPLACE

911

1. Disarm air bag system as described under "Disarming and Arming Air Bag System."
2. Remove glove compartment.
3. Disconnect passenger side air bag module electrical connectors.
4. Remove the air bag module 8 mm mounting bolt.

5. Remove radio and mounting bracket.
6. Remove A/C and heater control panel and mounting bracket.
7. Remove ashtray.
8. Remove knee bolster.
9. Remove three passenger side air bag flap lower attaching screws.
10. Remove four passenger side air bag flap upper attaching screws.
11. Pull air bag flap forward, then outward and downward.
12. Remove air bag flap to brace attaching screws.
13. Remove the air bag module in a downward direction.
14. Reverse procedure to install, noting the following:
    a. When installing unit, use new attaching nuts and screws.
    b. After completing installation, arm air bag system as described under "Air Bag System Disarming And Arming."

928

1. Disarm air bag system as described under "Disarming and Arming Air Bag System."
2. Remove instrument panel.
3. Remove air bag module attaching screws.
4. Remove the passenger side air bag module.
5. Reverse procedure to install, noting the following:
    a. When installing unit, use new attaching nuts and screws.
    b. After completing installation, arm air bag system as described under "Air Bag System Disarming And Arming."

968

1. Disarm air bag system as described under "Disarming and Arming Air Bag System."
2. Remove glove compartment.
3. Remove air guide hose.
4. Disconnect passenger side air bag module electrical connectors.
5. remove four 5 mm air bag module attaching bolts.
6. Remove the M8 air bag module attaching screw.
7. Remove the passenger side air bag module.
8. Reverse procedure to install, noting the following:
    a. When installing unit, use new attaching nuts and screws.
    b. After completing installation, arm air bag system as described under "Air Bag System Disarming & Arming."

CONTACT UNIT, REPLACE

1. Place front wheels in the straight ahead position.
2. Disarm air bag system as described under "Disarming and Arming Air Bag System."
3. Remove driver side air bag as described under "Driver Side Air Bag Module, Replace."
4. Remove steering wheel retaining nuts.
5. Place alignment marks on steering wheel hub and steering column shaft for use during installation.
6. Using a suitable puller remove steering wheel.
7. Remove steering column upper trim panel.
8. Remove contact unit attaching screws.
9. Disconnect electrical connector and remove contact unit.
10. Reverse procedure to install, noting the following:
    a. Prior to installation, ensure front wheels are in the straight ahead position.
    b. New contact units are locked in the center position. Do not remove the lock until after the contact unit has been installed.
    c. The center position of the contact unit is approximately 4½ turns from either the left or right final stop. The two arrow marks on the contact unit should be aligned when unit is centered.
    d. After completing installation, arm air bag system as described under "Air Bag System Disarming And Arming."

FRONT CRASH SENSORS, REPLACE

1. Disarm air bag system as described under "Disarming and Arming Air Bag System."
2. Disconnect sensor electrical connector.
3. **On 928 models,** proceed as follows:
    a. For left hand sensor, remove tire pressure warning system, mirror and ABS control units.
    b. For right hand sensor, remove LH and EZK control units.
4. **On all models,** using tool No. P9259, remove sensor mounting nuts, then remove sensor.
5. Reverse procedure to install, noting the following:
    a. Prior to installation, ensure sensor mounting contact surface is bare down to the metal.
    b. Use a¼ inch socket to tighten the shear-off bolts.
    c. After completing installation, arm air bag system as described under "Air Bag System Disarming And Arming."

CONTROL UNIT, REPLACE

911

1. Disarm air bag system as described under "Disarming and Arming Air Bag System."
2. Remove center console.
3. Remove glove compartment.
4. Remove the central electric board.
5. Disconnect electrical connectors for left crash sensor, contact unit, right crash sensor, front passenger air bag module and connector to main wiring harness.
6. Remove wiring harness retaining straps.
7. If necessary, guide front crash sensor wiring back into passenger compartment.
8. Using tool 9259, remove control unit shear-off retaining nuts.
9. Using a suitable wrench, remove the remaining attaching nuts, then the control unit with protective cap.
10. Reverse procedure to install, noting the following:
    a. Prior to installation, ensure control mounting contact surface is bare down to the metal.
    b. Use a¼ inch socket to tighten the shear-off bolts.
    c. After completing installation, arm air bag system as described under "Air Bag System Disarming And Arming."

928

1. Disarm air bag system as described under "Disarming and Arming Air Bag System."
2. Remove side panels from left and right side of center condole.
3. Remove kick protector.
4. Disconnect electrical connectors for left crash sensor, contact unit, right crash sensor, front passenger air bag module and connector to main wiring harness.
5. Remove wiring harness retaining straps.
6. Using tool 9259, remove control unit shear-off retaining nuts.
7. Using a suitable wrench, remove the remaining attaching nuts, then the control unit with protective cap.
8. Reverse procedure to install, noting the following:
    a. Prior to installation, ensure control mounting contact surface is bare down to the metal.
    b. Use a¼ inch socket to tighten the shear-off bolts.
    c. After completing installation, arm air bag system as described under "Air Bag System Disarming And Arming."

968

1. Disarm air bag system as described under "Disarming and Arming Air Bag System."
2. Remove glove compartment.
3. Disconnect electrical connectors for left crash sensor, contact unit, right crash sensor, front passenger air bag module and connector to main wiring harness.
4. Remove blower motor to gain access to wiring harness.
5. Remove wiring harness retaining straps.
6. Using tool 9259, remove control unit shear-off retaining nuts.
7. Using a suitable wrench, remove the remaining attaching nuts, then the control unit with protective cap.
8. Reverse procedure to install, noting the following:
    a. Prior to installation, ensure control mounting contact surface is bare down to the metal.
    b. Use a¼ inch socket to tighten the

shear-off bolts.

c. After completing installation, arm air bag system as described under "Air Bag System Disarming And Arming."

AIR BAG ASSEMBLY DISPOSAL

When handling a deployed air bag assembly, a face shield and rubber gloves should be worn. Vehicle interior and A/C, vent, defroster and heater ducts should be vacuumed. If sinus or throat irritation is encountered during air bag removal, exit vehicle and breathe fresh air. If skin irritation is encountered, flush effected area with cool water. If sinus, throat, skin or any other type of irritation continues, consult a physician. After handling a deployed air bag assembly, wash hands and rinse thoroughly with water.

An air bag that has been deployed should be removed as described under "Driver Side Air Bag Module, Replace" or "Passenger Side Air Bag Module, Replace." Prior to removing a deployed air bag assembly, place tape over air bag exhaust vents. After unit has been removed, it should be placed in a heavy duty plastic bag and sealed securely. The sealed plastic bag should then be placed with automotive scrap. To dispose of an air bag assembly that has not been deployed, consult Porsche.

TIGHTENING SPECIFICATIONS

Component	Torque/Ft. Lbs.
911	
Driver Side Air Bag	7
Passenger Side Air Bag	52①
Steering Wheel	32
928	
Control Unit M6 Nuts	7
Driver Side Air Bag	7
Passenger Side Air Bag	7
Steering Wheel	32
968	
Driver Side Air Bag	7
Passenger Side Air Bag	52①
Steering Wheel	32

① — Inch lbs.

Dash Panel Service

NOTE: On Air Bag Equipped Models, Refer To "Air Bag System Precautions" Located In The Front Of This Manual For System Disarming & Arming Procedures.

NOTE: Refer To "Dash Gauges" Section For Related Information.

INDEX

	Page No.
Dash Panel, Replace	37-47
968	37-47
Precautions	37-47
Air Bag Systems	37-47

PRECAUTIONS

AIR BAG SYSTEMS

Refer to "Air Bag System Precautions" in the front of this manual for system disarming and arming procedures.

DASH PANEL

REPLACE

968

1. Pull out tray and ashtray.
2. Loosen center console cover frame attaching screws.
3. Remove radio assembly.
4. Remove center console attaching screws, then remove.
5. Remove instrument cluster.
6. Remove sun visors, front roof beam trim panel, and A-pillar trim panels.
7. Unclip glove compartment light, then disconnect electrical connector.
8. Remove glove compartment attaching screws, then pull off vent hose and remove glove compartment.

9. Remove instrument panel attaching screws on hinge panel.
10. Remove instrument panel to A-pillar attaching screws, then remove I/P bracket attaching screws.
11. Pull air guides out of nozzles, then remove instrument panel.
12. Reverse to install.

Disc Brakes

INDEX

	Page No.
Brake Pad Service	37-48
Front Brake Pads, Replace	37-48
Rear Brake Pads, Replace	37-49
Caliper Service	37-49
911	37-49
928	37-49
968	37-49
Disc Brake Specifications	37-51
Parking Brake Service	37-50
Adjustment	37-50
Tightening Specifications	37-51

BRAKE PAD SERVICE

FRONT BRAKE PADS, REPLACE

911

1. Raise and support vehicle.
2. Using a pair of suitable pliers, remove brake pad pin retainers.
3. Drive pad retaining pins out with a suitable drift and hammer.
4. For pads that are still serviceable, mark their original positions for assembly reference.
5. Remove the pads using tool P86, **Fig. 1.**
6. Position pistons back in caliper using tool P83, **Fig. 2. Brake fluid will be forced back into the reservoir. To prevent overflowing, siphon some fluid from reservoir.**
7. Clean brake pad contact surface in their slots in the caliper. **Do not use mineral solvents or sharp edged tools.**
8. Check dust boots and clamping rings for damage and replace hard or porous boots.
9. Clean brake discs with fine emery cloth.
10. Install new brake pads in caliper slots together with retaining pins, springs, and pin retainers. **Depress brake pedal several times before moving vehicle to properly position caliper pistons.**
11. Check brake fluid level.

911 Turbo

If brake pads are going to be reused, mark pads for installation. Do not interchange pads from inboard to outboard or from left to right wheel assemblies.

1. Disconnect battery ground cable.
2. Raise and support vehicle.
3. Remove wheel and tire assembly.
4. Using suitable pliers, pull out warning contact (wear indicator) from brake pad plate. **Replace wear indicators, if lead core is ground through. The wear indicator is still usable, if only the plastic portion of the indicator has signs of grinding.**
5. Using tool 1966-2, or equivalent, remove brake pads.

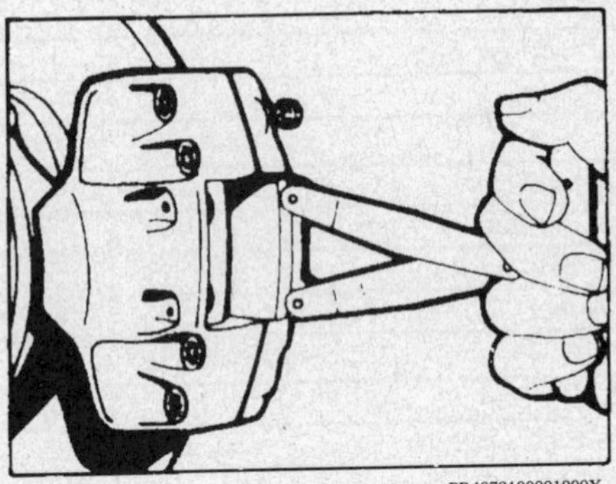

PR4079100001000X

Fig. 1 Brake pads removal

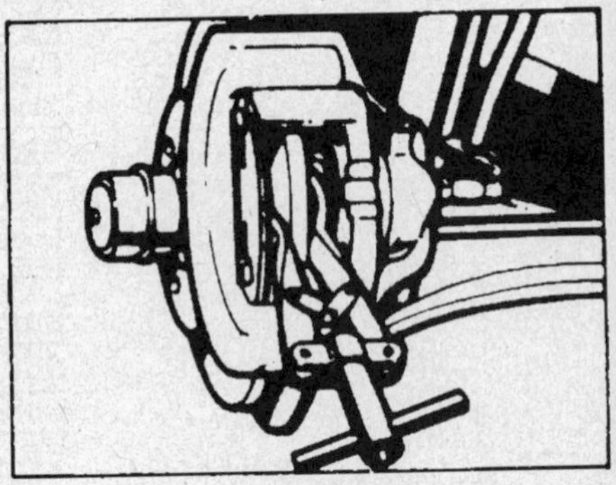

PR4079100002000X

Fig. 2 Positioning caliper pistons

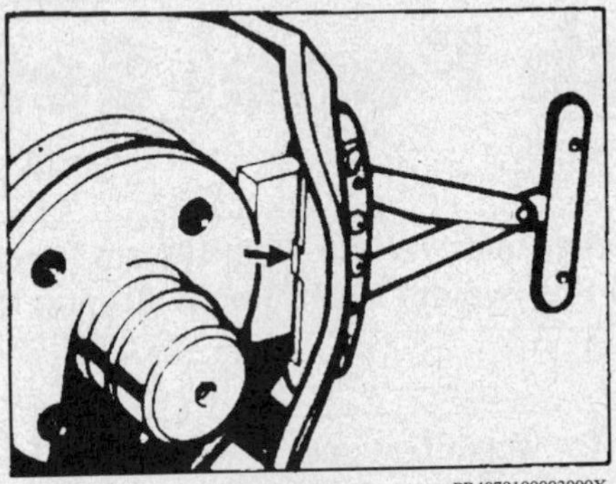

PR4079100003000X

Fig. 3 Outboard brake pads removal

6. Reverse procedure to install.

968

If brake pads are serviceable, pads must be marked for installation in original position.

1. Raise and support vehicle, then remove wheel and tire assembly.
2. Remove retaining pin spring locks, if equipped.
3. Drive out brake paid retaining pins with suitable hammer and drift.
4. Pull brake pad wear indicator warning contact out of pad plate, if equipped.
5. Remove inboard brake pad with tool P86, or equivalent, **Fig. 1.**
6. Using a suitable screwdriver, pry floating frame to full outboard position and remove outboard brake pad. **Outboard brake pad is guided by a tab on the floating caliper frame, Fig. 3.**
7. Replace oil contaminated, cracked or loose pads.
8. Press caliper pistons back into position. **Ensure brake fluid reservoir does not overflow during step 8 by siphoning off any excess.**
9. Clean pad seats and sliding surfaces in caliper. **Do not use cleaning fluids containing mineral oils.**
10. Check that caliper piston is positioned at 20°, if necessary adjust with special pliers. **When using a piston gauge, hold gauge at bottom guide surface of front caliper and top of rear brake caliper, Fig. 4.**
11. Install outboard brake pad and press floating caliper frame toward brake disc so pin engages in groove of pad backplate.
12. Install inboard brake pad.
13. Install retaining pins and cross spring.
14. Press brake pad wear indicator warning contact into inner pad backplate, if equipped.
15. Install retaining pin spring locks, if equipped. **Before moving vehicle, depress brake pedal several times to properly position caliper piston.**

928

1. Raise and support vehicle, then remove wheel and tire assembly.
2. Pull wear sensor warning contact out of inner pad plate.
3. Apply pressure in center of housing retaining spring until it disengages from

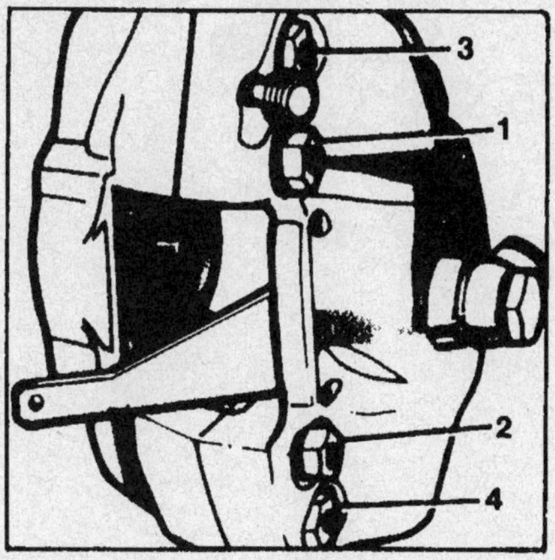
3
1
2
4

PR4079100004000X

Fig. 4 Brake piston position gauge

housing bores and remove spring outward without applying force.
4. Remove dirt on guide pins between holder and housing.
5. Pull plugs out of guide sleeve, then remove guide pins.
6. Pull housing toward outside of vehicle to depress piston slightly, then remove housing and pull inboard brake pad out of piston.
7. Position housing out of way and suspend from vehicle body with wire.
8. Remove outboard brake pad from holder.
9. Using suitable tool, bottom piston in housing.
10. Clean pad gliding surfaces in housing and holder. Do not use mineral solvents or sharp edged tools.
11. Check 20° piston position and adjust with special pliers as necessary.
12. Push brake pad with riveted retaining clip into piston and place other pad on outside of holder's guiding surface on brake disc.
13. Place housing over brake disc and brake pad and install guide pins.
14. Insert plugs in guide sleeves.
15. Insert housing retaining spring, ensuring it engages in housing bore.
16. Insert warning contact.
17. Depress brake pedal several times to position piston and pads.
18. Add brake fluid to master cylinder as necessary.

REAR BRAKE PADS, REPLACE

Refer to "Front Brake Pads, Replace" for rear disc brake service procedures.

CALIPER SERVICE

911

1. Raise and support vehicle.
2. Remove wheels and brake pads.
3. Disconnect brake hydraulic line. **Using a suitable device, depress and hold brake pedal to restrict flow of brake fluid from reservoir.**

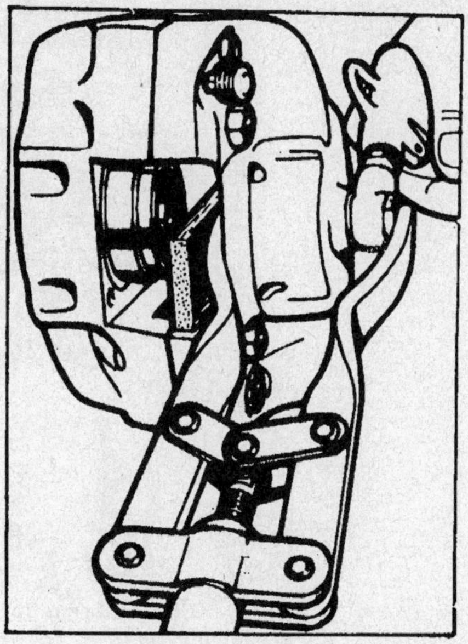

PR4079100005000X

Fig. 5 Brake caliper piston removal

4. Remove caliper retaining bolts, caliper, and metal shield.
5. Loosen bleeder valve and carefully blow hydraulic fluid out of caliper. **The recommended air pressure for fluid removal is 14 psi.**
6. Position the caliper in a soft jaw vise and remove the clamping ring and dust boot.
7. Depress one caliper piston with tool P83 and position a wood block approximately ⅓ inches thick between the tool arm and the piston being removed, **Fig. 5.** Apply pressure. **Start with 29 psi, and raise the pressure as necessary. Keep fingers clear of caliper slot. Repair cylinders one at a time since pressure cannot be built up with one removed.**
8. Remove piston seal with a plastic pin to prevent damage to cylinder bore groove.
9. Clean parts in alcohol. **Disassemble calipers only if the O-rings which seal the fluid passages between both caliper halves are defective and leak.**
10. Check cylinder bore, piston, and slot surfaces for damage.
11. Coat cylinder bore, piston, and piston seal with ATE brake paste.
12. Install piston seal into cylinder bore groove.
13. Position piston into caliper cylinder using aligning tool P84, **Fig. 6.**
14. Remove brake cylinder paste from piston ridge and install dust covers.
15. Install caliper and bleed brake hydraulic system.

928

1. Raise and support vehicle, then remove wheel and tire assembly.
2. Disconnect hydraulic line and the wear indicator warning contact.
3. Remove housing attaching bolts and

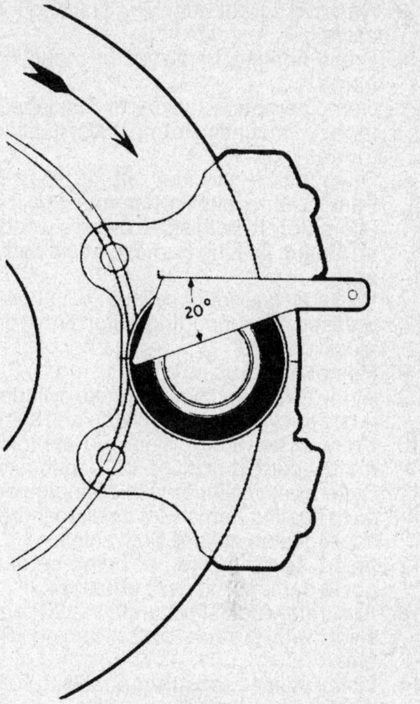
20°

PR4079100006000X

Fig. 6 Aligning piston in caliper cylinder

the housing assembly.
4. Remove housing retaining spring, **Fig. 7.**
5. Pull plugs out of guides and remove guide pins.
6. Remove housing, then take outboard brake pad out of holder and pull inboard brake pad out of piston.
7. Support piston firmly on piece of wood and press piston halfway out of housing with compressed air, take sealing lip of dust cover out of piston groove, then press piston fully out of housing.
8. Remove seal with a plastic needle.
9. Apply a very thin coat of brake cylinder paste on cylinder bore, piston and seal.
10. Push dust cover on inside of piston far enough that large diameter sealing lip extends over piston.
11. Press sealing lip of dust cover into housing groove with piston in approximately correct position, ensuring seal fits properly around its entire periphery.
12. Press piston slowly into housing, ensuring small diameter sealing lip settles in groove of piston.
13. Adjust 20° piston position precisely with piston pliers, ensuring set back surface of piston faces down to brake disc inlet side.
14. bolt holder to housing, insert brake pads and housing retaining springs.
15. Install housing assembly, then connect hydraulic line and wear sensor warning contact.
16. Bleed brake system.

968

1. Raise and support vehicle then remove wheel on side to be serviced.
2. Disconnect hydraulic line at caliper.

3. Remove caliper attaching bolt and the caliper.
4. Press floating frame off of mounting frame.
5. Remove spring guide, if equipped, then run mounting frame out of floating frame.
6. Drive brake cylinder off of floating frame with a plastic hammer applied alternately to both sides using a wooden liner in floating frame to avoid damage.
7. Press piston out of cylinder with compressed air, supporting piston firmly on block of wood.
8. Remove seal using a plastic rod.
9. Apply a very thin seal of brake cylinder paste to cylinder bore, piston and seal.
10. Press piston into cylinder in approximately correct position (20° chamfer).
11. Drive brake cylinder with spring guide on to floating frame with a soft mandrel applied alternately to both sides.
12. Insert mounting frame, being careful not to damage slides, if equipped.
13. Accurately adjust piston to the 20° position with suitable piston turning pliers.
14. Install caliper, **torquing** attaching bolt to 61 ft. lbs.
15. Connect hydraulic lines at caliper.
16. Install wheel and bleed brake system.

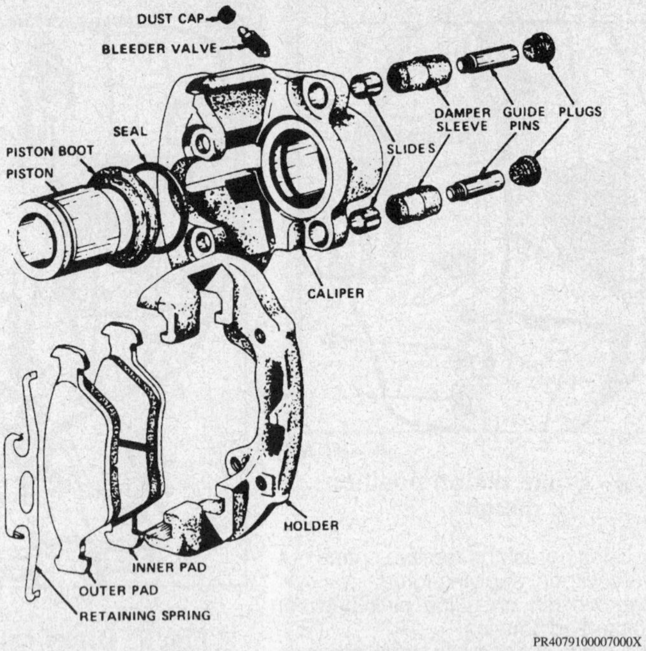
DUST CAP
BLEEDER VALVE
DAMPER SLEEVE
GUIDE PINS
PLUGS
SEAL
PISTON BOOT
PISTON
SLIDES
CALIPER
HOLDER
INNER PAD
OUTER PAD
RETAINING SPRING
PR4079100007000X

Fig. 7 Exploded view of floating brake caliper

PARKING BRAKE SERVICE

ADJUSTMENT

911

1. Raise and support vehicle.
2. Remove rear wheels.
3. Release brake cable tension at adjusting nuts behind disc splash shield.
4. Insert screwdriver into adjustment opening in rear brake disc assembly,
5. Rotate parking brake adjustment sprocket so that disc can no longer be rotated by hand.
6. Repeat step 5 on opposite side.
7. Adjust cable tension until slack is removed by rotating adjustment nuts behind brake disc splash shield.
8. Remove tunnel cover and parking brake lever boot and check position of cable equalizer.
9. Position the equalizer in the two inspection holes when lever is pulled up.
10. To adjust the position of equalizer, rotate the adjustment nuts behind splash shield.
11. After equalizer has been properly positioned, lock adjustment nuts.
12. Back off adjustment sprockets inside each brake drum 4–5 teeth, so that disc rotates freely. **The parking brake should be set when the lever is pulled up 2 clicks.**

928

Adjust parking brake if lever can be pulled beyond eight clicks with average force and no braking effect is noted.

1. Raise and support vehicle.
2. Remove rear wheels.
3. Release parking brake and press pads into rear caliper until disc rotates freely.
4. Remove brake lever boot and rotate adjusting nut on lever/cable connector until cable is tension free.
5. Insert screwdriver into adjustment hole in rear brake disc and rotate adjuster until it stops.
6. Rotate adjuster back until wheel turns freely.
7. Pull up parking brake lever two teeth and rotate adjustment nut under boot until wheels can be rotated by hand.
8. Release parking brake lever and check that wheels rotate freely.
9. Tighten adjuster locknut.

968

1. Raise and support vehicle and remove rear wheels.
2. Release parking brake and press back disc brake pads on rear wheels until brake disc can be turned easily.
3. Loosen adjusting nut on clamp enough to relieve cable tension.
4. Insert screwdriver into hole in disc and turn adjusting device until wheel cannot be turned.
5. Turn adjusting device back until wheel can be turned freely.
6. Pull up parking brake lever two teeth and turn adjusting nut until wheels can still be turned by hand.
7. Ensure wheels cannot be turned by hand at fourth tooth.
8. Release parking brake lever and ensure both wheels turn freely.
9. Lock adjusting nut.
10. Install wheels and lower vehicle.

DISC BRAKE SPECIFICATIONS

Model	Year	Front Disc Brake				Rear Disc Brake			
		Nominal Thickness Inch	Minimum Refinish Thickness Inch	Thickness Variation Parallelism Inch	Lateral Run-Out (T.I.R.) Inch	Nominal Thickness Inch	Minimum Refinish Thickness Inch	Thickness Variation Parallelism Inch	Lateral Run-Out (T.I.R.) Inch
911①	1993–96	1.102	1.047	.0008	.002	.945	.890	.0008	.002
911②	1993–94	—	③	.0008	.002	—	③	.0008	.002
928 GTS②	1993–95	—	③	.0008	.002	—	③	.0008	.002
968④	1993–95	1.102	1.047	.0008	.002	.945	.890	.0008	.002

Continued

DISC BRAKE SPECIFICATIONS—Continued

Model	Year	Front Disc Brake				Rear Disc Brake			
		Nominal Thickness Inch	Minimum Refinish Thickness Inch	Thickness Variation Parallelism Inch	Lateral Run-Out (T.I.R.) Inch	Nominal Thickness Inch	Minimum Refinish Thickness Inch	Thickness Variation Parallelism Inch	Lateral Run-Out (T.I.R.) Inch
968 ⑤	1993–95	1.260	1.205	.0008	.002	.945	.890	.0008	.002

① — Except America Roadster.
② — America Roadster.
③ — Rotor minimum thickness is stamped on rotor.
④ — Standard.
⑤ — Optional.

TIGHTENING SPECIFICATIONS

Year	Component	Torque/ Ft. Lbs.
911 CARRERA 2 & TURBO		
1993–96	Caliper To Rear Axle Arm	43
	Caliper To Steering Knuckle	51
	Disc To Hub Screw	3.6
	Disc To Hub Bolt	17
	Guard & Backplate To Rear Axle Arm	18
	Guard To Backplate	18
	Guard To Knuckle	7
	Nut On Steering Knuckle	11
911 CARRERA 4		
1993–96	Ball Pin To Brake Push-Rod	26
	Caliper To Axles (Front & Rear)	62.5
	Cover Plate To Axles (Front & Rear)	7.5
	Disc To Hub (Front & Rear)	3.5
928		
1993–95	Caliper To Carrier	62
	Caliper To Knuckle	62
	Clamping Nut Panhead Screw	11
	Disc To Hub	7
	Floating Caliper To Bracket	11-15
	Guard To Knuckle	11
	Propshaft/Rear Axle To Wheel Hub	336
968		
1993–95	Backplate To Trailing Arm	43
	Caliper To Backplate Or Trailing Arm	63
	Caliper To Knuckle	63
	Clamping Nut Bolt	9.5-11.5
	Disc To Hub Bolt	3.5
	Disc To Hub Nut	17
	Disc To Hub Screw	7
	Guard To Backplate Or Trailing Arm	7
	Guard To Knuckle	7
	Hub To Rear Wheel Shaft (Aluminum Trailing Arms)	368
	Hub To Rear Wheel Shaft (Steel Trailing Arms)	280-332

Hydraulic Brake Systems

INDEX

Page No.		Page No.		Page No.
Brake System Bleed 37-52	968	37-52	Master Cylinder	37-52
Component Replacement 37-52				

COMPONENT REPLACEMENT

MASTER CYLINDER

911

1. Remove operating rod lockpin.
2. Remove master cylinder mounting bolt located inside on luggage compartment floor plate.
3. Drain brake fluid reservoir with suitable siphon.
4. Disconnect stop light switches, vacuum hose clamp, and brake lines.
5. Remove upper bolt from booster body and booster base retaining nuts.
6. Reverse procedure to install.

928

1. Remove intake hoses and upper section of air cleaner assembly.
2. Drain both chambers of master cylinder by pumping out brake fluid via bleeder valves of front or rear brake calipers.
3. Disconnect vacuum hose with check valve at brake booster.
4. Disconnect vacuum line on branch, electrical connector for warning device, and hose for clutch control.
5. Remove brake fluid tank and disconnect electrical connectors for stop light switches.
6. Disconnect brake lines.
7. Remove master cylinder attaching bolts and the master cylinder.
8. Reverse procedure to install, noting the following:
   a. Replace O-ring between master cylinder and brake booster.
   b. Install master cylinder and connect brake lines.
   c. Press brake fluid tank into sealing plugs in master cylinder.
   d. Fill brake fluid tank with suitable fluid and bleed brake/clutch system.

968

1. Place rags underneath master cylinder and on left wheel housing.
2. Pull brake fluid tank out of master cylinder and catch escaping brake fluid.
3. Place tank with connected clutch hose on wheel house.
4. Disconnect brake lines at master cylinder.
5. Remove master cylinder attaching nuts and the master cylinder.
6. Reverse procedure to install, noting the following:
   a. Install new seal between master cylinder and brake booster and new plugs in the brake fluid tank.
   b. Bleed brakes and clutch.

BRAKE SYSTEM BLEED

Brake fluid is extremely damaging to paint. If fluid should accidentally touch painted surface, immediately wipe fluid from paint and clean painted surface.

1. Fill reservoir to rim with brake fluid, then remove filter insert.
2. Attach pressure bleeder to reservoir, then turn pressure bleeder on.
3. First bleed clutch, then master cylinder if master cylinder or brake fluid tank has been removed.
4. Operate brake pedal firmly several times during bleeding procedure in order to remove all air bubbles in master cylinder.
5. Open bleeder valve of each wheel until escaping brake fluid is without air bubbles.
6. Check for leaks in system after bleeding procedure is completed.

Power Brake Units

INDEX

Page No.

Power Brake Unit Service........ 37-53
Brake Booster, Replace......... 37-53

POWER BRAKE UNIT SERVICE

BRAKE BOOSTER, REPLACE

911

1. Remove brake booster operating rod lockpin.
2. Remove master cylinder attaching bolt from luggage compartment floor plate.
3. Drain brake fluid reservoir.
4. Disconnect electrical connectors for stop light switch, then disconnect vacuum hose at brake booster and the brake lines at master cylinder.
5. Remove brake booster brace upper attaching bolt and the booster base attaching nuts, then remove master cylinder and booster as an assembly. **Brace and operating rod do not have to be disconnected at pedal assembly to remove brake booster.**
6. Reverse procedure to install, noting the following:
   a. Clevis for operating rod must be installed so that clevis clip can be installed from above. **Operating rod must be attached when brake pedal is at its rest position without any force applied to operating lever. The play set at the factory must not be changed.**
   b. **Torque** booster base nuts and the master cylinder bolt to 18 ft. lbs.
   c. **Torque** support to rod bolt to 25 ft. lbs.
   d. Pull brake pedal back to stop.
   e. Loosen nuts on operating rod, then adjust rod until lockpin for operating lever can be installed without tension.
   f. Tighten nuts on operating rod, then bleed brake system.
   g. Check operating rod play at brake pedal by manual operation with engine off. Play must be at least .4 inch (10 mm).

928

1. Remove master cylinder as previously described.
2. Depress brake pedal and clamp master cylinder pushrod.
3. Adjust connector to limit amount of protrusion of brake pushrod from booster, then again depress brake pedal and adjust clamp.
4. Remove connector.
5. Remove cover and the booster attaching bolts.
6. If applicable, remove brake line for right front wheel from holder on cross wall and carefully push toward engine, then route hose for clutch master cylinder and electric wires out of way.
7. Remove booster, removing lower section of air cleaner as necessary to facilitate removal.
8. If necessary, replace gasket between booster and firewall. Use 2 mm thick gasket for ten inch booster and a 4 mm or two 2 mm gaskets for nine inch booster.
9. Install booster, ensuring caps fit properly above control housing.
10. Install brake pressure regulator and the master cylinder, replacing seal between booster and master cylinder.
11. Mount brake pushrod and connector on brake pedal.
12. Pull back brake pedal arm to stop, then loosen locknut on pushrod and adjust pushrod until play of at least .4 inch (10 mm) is obtained.
13. Tighten locknut on pushrod.
14. Bleed brake/clutch system.

968

1. Remove master cylinder as previously described.
2. Disconnect vacuum line at brake booster and remove oil dipstick.
3. Uniformly pry off fuel line holding clip on mounting bolt adjacent to adapter.
4. Remove pushrod lockpin at brake pedal.
5. Disconnect throttle cable at accelerator pedal, then pull down insulation sheet in footwell.
6. Remove brake booster/adapter assembly mounting nuts, then remove brake booster from above at engine compartment end.
7. Screw swivel joint on brake pushrod and adjust so that distance between circumference of larger lip and center of hole of pushrod mounting is 7.28–7.36 inches (185–187 mm).
8. Attach brake booster to adapter in correct position.
9. Install booster in vehicle, guiding in and mounting pushrod swivel joint on brake pedal.
10. Adjust stop light switch as necessary by turning mounting bolts so that distance between switch and brake pedal is .197 inch (5 mm) with pedal in neutral position.
11. Mount fuel line retaining clips.
12. Install master cylinder, using new seal between master cylinder and booster and new plugs for brake fluid reservoir.
13. Bleed brakes and clutch.

Anti-Lock Brakes

NOTE: On Air Bag Equipped Models, Refer To "Air Bag System Precautions" Located In The Front Of This Manual For System Disarming & Arming Procedures.

INDEX

	Page No.
Description	37-54
Diagnosis & Testing	37-54
Precautions	37-54
Air Bag Systems	37-54
System Service	37-54
Brake System Bleed	37-54
Component Replacement	37-54
Electronic Control Unit	37-54
Hydraulic Unit	37-54
Troubleshooting	37-54

PRECAUTIONS

AIR BAG SYSTEMS

Refer to "Air Bag System Precautions" in the front of this manual for system disarming and arming procedures.

DESCRIPTION

The anti-lock braking system prevents the wheels from locking in an emergency stop, until shortly before the vehicle comes to halt, thus assuring full steerability and directional stability. In addition, the system optimizes the braking distance corresponding to the varying degree of grip between the wheel and road surface.

The ABS control unit is matched to the approved tire dimensions. The use of unapproved tires can lead to different wheel speeds which the control unit interprets as different road speeds at the vehicles axles. If the rolling radius exceeds a certain amount, the control unit deactivates the ABS and the ABS pilot lamp illuminates.

The three-channel ABS system manufactured by Bosch has a separate speed sensor at each wheel. A front/rear braking circuit split is used, one braking circuit acts on the front axle (push-rod circuit) with the second acting on the rear axle (floating circuit).

TROUBLESHOOTING

Refer to "Diagnosis & Testing" for troubleshooting procedures.

DIAGNOSIS & TESTING

The electrical control unit has a self-diagnosis testing facility. For this reason, it is not possible or necessary to check the control unit unless the check is carried out as part of an ABS test required for other reasons and only when this test is carried out with the Bosch K7-ETT 016.00/VAG 1516 test equipment.

After any work on the braking system which did not affect parts directly involved in the ABS, a function test check is required. The pilot lamp in the instrument cluster will go out when the engine is started if the ABS system is intact. Repairs include replacing brake pads, brake hoses, brake discs, brake unit, tandem master cylinder, brake cables and parts of the parking brake lines not connected to the hydraulic unit.

If work is performed on the hydraulic unit, electronic control unit, wheel speed sensors or the lines or if units are replaced, a function test must be performed with the ABS tester.

SYSTEM SERVICE

Brake System Bleed

Refer to "Hydraulic Brake System" for bleeding procedure.

Component Replacement

These components are non-serviceable and must be replaced as a unit.

HYDRAULIC UNIT

1. Disconnect battery ground cable.
2. Mark respective positions of wheel and wheel hub for reassembly, then remove right front wheel assembly.
3. Remove wheel-arch inner panel.
4. Disconnect all brake lines, numbers one through six from hydraulic unit.
5. **On all models,** disconnect ground wire, then remove mounting bolts from hydraulic-unit holder.
6. Move hydraulic unit and holder out slightly to gain access to strain relief for 12-pole plug (no. three), then disconnect strain relief and remove plug.
7. Unclip ABS wire harness from hydraulic-unit holder, then remove hydraulic unit with holder.
8. Reverse procedure to install, bleed brake system.

ELECTRONIC CONTROL UNIT

On 968 models, the electronic control unit is located in the passenger side footwell. On 911 Carrera models, the combination ABS and lock control unit is located in the luggage compartment at the right front corner.

968

1. Disengage retaining spring (spring lock), then disconnect plug from electrical control unit.
2. Unscrew retaining nuts, then remove electronic control unit from holder.
3. Reverse procedure to install.

Automatic Transaxles

TABLE OF CONTENTS

	Page No.
TYPE A28 AUTOMATIC TRANSAXLE	37-56
TYPE A50/01 AUTOMATIC TRANSAXLE	37-57

Type A28 Automatic Transaxle

INDEX

	Page No.
Adjustments	37-56
Control Cable	37-56
Selector Lever Cable	37-56
In-Vehicle Repairs	37-56
Governor, Replace	37-56
Vacuum Modulator, Replace	37-56
Valve Body, Replace	37-56
Maintenance	37-56
Fluid Change	37-56
Tightening Specifications	37-56
Transaxle, Replace	37-56
Troubleshooting	37-55
After Installation, Transaxle Has No Power	37-55
Engine Cannot Be Started In Park & Neutral	37-56
No Brake Shifts From 4th To 3rd & 3rd To 2nd	37-56
No Kickdown	37-55
No Power Flow In Any Gear Position	37-55
No Power Flow In Reverse	37-55
No Upshifts	37-55
Poor Acceleration	37-56
Selector Lever Cannot Be Engaged In Reverse & Park	37-56
Shock When Changing Gears	37-55
Shock When Downshifting From 4th To 3rd	37-55
Shock When Engaging Drive Or Reverse	37-55
Shock When Shifting In Partial Load Range	37-55
Slips During 2nd/3rd Shift Or Slips, Then Grabs Hard	37-55
Slips During 3rd/4th Shift	37-55
Slips In All Gears	37-55
Slips In 1st & 2nd Gear	37-55
Slips In 2nd Gear Or Shifts From 1st To 3rd Gear	37-55

TROUBLESHOOTING

SLIPS IN ALL GEARS

1. Incorrect modulating pressure.
2. Faulty modulating pressure control valve.
3. Incorrect vacuum line routing, or vacuum line disconnected.
4. Faulty valve body.
5. Faulty primary pump.

SLIPS IN 2ND GEAR OR SHIFTS FROM 1ST TO 3RD GEAR

1. Faulty valve body.
2. Damaged brake band B 1 piston seal.
3. Damaged brake band B 1 and/or B 1 element.

SLIPS IN 1ST & 2ND GEAR

1. Faulty shift valve B 2.
2. Faulty brake band B 2 piston.
3. Incorrectly adjusted brake band B 2.

SLIPS DURING 2ND/3RD SHIFT OR SLIPS, THEN GRABS HARD

1. Incorrect modulating pressure.
2. Temperature orifice not installed.
3. Damaged shift valve housing.
4. Damaged inner clutch K1 plates.

SLIPS DURING 3RD/4TH SHIFT

1. Incorrect modulating pressure.
2. Damaged shift valve housing.
3. Damaged inner clutch K2 plates.

AFTER INSTALLATION, TRANSAXLE HAS NO POWER

1. Incorrectly installed torque converter.
2. Damaged primary pump.
3. Damaged torque converter.

NO POWER FLOW IN ANY GEAR POSITION

1. Torque converter draining due to leaking and/or defective driveshaft lubricating ring.
2. Check or clean shift valve housing lubricating valve.

NO POWER FLOW IN REVERSE

1. Damaged brake band 3 lined plates and seals.
2. Damaged one-way clutch.

SHOCK WHEN ENGAGING DRIVE OR REVERSE

1. Incorrect idle speed and CO level.
2. Incorrect modulating pressure.
3. Missing shift valve housing check ball (5) spring.
4. Leaking or disconnect vacuum line.
5. Binding shift valve housing pressure acceptance piston.

SHOCK WHEN CHANGING GEARS

1. Incorrect modulating pressure.
2. Leaking or disconnected vacuum line.

SHOCK WHEN DOWNSHIFTING FROM 4TH TO 3RD

1. Damaged B 2 release end seal.
2. Damaged B 2 brake band piston.
3. Damaged B 2 pressure element.

SHOCK WHEN SHIFTING IN PARTIAL LOAD RANGE

1. Incorrectly adjusted control pressure cable.
2. Incorrectly adjusted modulating pressure.
3. Leaking or disconnected vacuum line.

NO UPSHIFTS

1. Incorrect governor pressure.
2. Dirty centrifugal governor.
3. Dirty valve body housing.

NO KICKDOWN

1. No or insufficient power supply to solenoid valve.
2. Faulty solenoid valve.
3. Incorrectly adjusted or damaged control cable.
4. Damaged valve body.

NO BRAKE SHIFTS FROM 4TH TO 3RD & 3RD TO 2ND

1. Incorrectly adjusted control pressure cable.
2. Leaking or disconnected vacuum line.
3. Damaged brake shift piston.

POOR ACCELERATION

1. Incorrect stall speed.
2. Torque converter one-way clutch is slipping.

SELECTOR LEVER CANNOT BE ENGAGED IN REVERSE & PARK

1. Dirty centrifugal governor.
2. Restricted lower cover piston.

ENGINE CANNOT BE STARTED IN PARK & NEUTRAL

1. Incorrectly adjusted selector lever cable and/or starter interlock switch.
2. Damaged starter interlock switch.

MAINTENANCE

FLUID CHANGE

1. Start engine, allow to reach normal operating temperature.
2. Position vehicle on level surface.
3. With engine Off, raise and support vehicle.
4. Remove pan drain plug, then drain into suitable container.
5. To drain torque converter, turn crankshaft until converter drain plug is visible and may be removed.
6. Install drain plugs, then pump most of the fluid into oil pan.
7. With selector lever in P position, start engine and allow to idle.
8. Check and fill to fluid level.
9. Operate service brake and set selector lever to each position, ensuring smooth operation.

ADJUSTMENTS

SELECTOR LEVER CABLE

1. Place selector lever into Neutral position.
2. Place range selector lever on transaxle into Neutral position.
3. Adjust ball end on cable until cable attachment is possible without tension.
4. After adjustment tighten range selector lever attaching bolt.

CONTROL CABLE

1. If necessary, adjust idle speed.
2. Ensure accelerator cable is adjusted correctly, without play.
3. Adjust ball end on control cable until attachment without tension is possible.

IN-VEHICLE REPAIRS

VALVE BODY, REPLACE

1. Disconnect battery ground cable.
2. Raise and support vehicle.
3. Remove drain plug from valve body and allow fluid to drain.
4. Remove valve body oil pan attaching bolts, then the pan.
5. Remove valve body attaching bolts, then the valve body. Note bolt lengths before removing valve body. Three edge bolts are 1.96 inches long and the remaining bolts are 2.16 inches long.
6. Reverse procedure to install.

GOVERNOR, REPLACE

1. Loosen intermediate muffler shield, then position aside as far as possible.
2. Disconnect electrical connectors from starter locking and back-up light switch.
3. Using a suitable tool, pry in cover, then remove snap ring.
4. Loosen axial holder attaching nut.
5. Using a suitable screwdriver, turn axial holder counterclockwise, then pull governor outward.
6. Reverse procedure to install.

VACUUM MODULATOR, REPLACE

1. Loosen intermediate muffler shield, then position aside as far as possible.
2. Disconnect vacuum line from vacuum modulator.
3. Remove holder attaching bolts, then the holder.
4. Remove vacuum modulator assembly.
5. Reverse procedure to install.

TRANSAXLE

REPLACE

1. Disconnect battery ground cable.
2. Disconnect electrical connector located in spare wheelwell.
3. Remove upper and lower air cleaner housings.
4. Remove upper air guide section.
5. Raise and support vehicle.
6. Disconnect control cable from throttle housing.
7. Disconnect oxygen sensor electrical connector.
8. Remove engine air guide.
9. Disconnect, then remove complete exhaust assembly and shields.
10. Remove starter attaching bolts, then suspend starter motor using a suitable piece of wire.
11. Drain fluid from transaxle.
12. Disconnect driveshafts from transaxle, then suspend shafts in a horizontal position.
13. Support transaxle using a suitable jack.
14. Remove rear axle crossmember-to-transaxle suspension attaching bolts.
15. Mark position of toe eccentric nut and rear axle crossmember, then remove rear axle assembly.
16. Remove clamp bolt.
17. Disconnect selector lever cable from transaxle, cable sleeve on holder and case assembly.
18. Disconnect and cap transaxle oil cooler lines.
19. Disconnect vacuum modulator pressure line.
20. Disconnect control pressure cable from transaxle, then remove guide.
21. Disconnect control cable from operating rod.
22. Remove front and rear reinforcement plates.
23. Lift transaxle slightly, then disconnect holding chain.
24. Lower transaxle only far enough so that torque tube-to-transaxle attaching bolts and control cable attaching bolts can be removed.
25. Move torque tube to installed position, mount rear brace with two attaching bolts, then place a suitable block of wood between torque tube and brace.
26. Pull back on transaxle, then carefully lower assembly from vehicle.
27. Reverse procedure to install.

TIGHTENING SPECIFICATIONS

Component	Torque/Ft. Lbs.
Control Cable	87
Drain Plug	10
Tube	6
Transaxle To Crossmember	61
Valve Body	6

Type A50/01 Automatic Transaxle

INDEX

Page No.		Page No.		Page No.	
Adjustments	37-57	Position Switch, Replace	37-58	Fluid Level Check	37-57
Selector Cable	37-57	**Maintenance**	37-57	**Tightening Specifications**	37-58
In-Vehicle Repairs	37-58	Fluid Change	37-57	**Troubleshooting**	37-57
Hydraulic Control Unit, Replace	37-58				

TROUBLESHOOTING

The Tiptronic A50/01 automatic transmission is equipped with a diagnosis system. Detected faults in monitored components are stored in the control unit memory. The control unit will evaluate the information and differentiate between 26 faults. These detected faults can be checked by connecting system tester 9288 to the 19 pin diagnostic connector and by following the tester manufacturers instructions. The fault codes are as follows:

Fault Code 1: Voltage, control unit.
Fault Code 2: Voltage, drive links.
Fault Code 3: Voltage, sensors.
Fault Code 4: Speed signal, DME control unit.
Fault Code 5: Load signal, DME control unit.
Fault Code 6: Throttle plate potentiometer.
Fault Code 7: Change of dwell angle.
Fault Code 8: Solenoid valve 1.
Fault Code 9: Solenoid valve 2.
Fault Code 10: Solenoid valve, torque converter clutch.
Fault Code 11: Pressure regulator.
Fault Code 12: Selector switch transmission.
Fault Code 13: Speed sensor.
Fault Code 14: Transmission temperature sensor.
Fault Code 15: Transmission selector switch.
Fault Code 16: Faulty control unit.
Fault Code 17: Faulty control unit.
Fault Code 18: Faulty control unit.
Fault Code 19: Downshift fault.
Fault Code 20: Rev. limiter.
Fault Code 21: Manual program switch.
Fault Code 22: Tip switch, up and/or downshifting.
Fault Code 23: Kickdown switch.
Fault Code 24: Transverse accel. sensor.
Fault Code 25: Speed signal 1, ABS control unit.
Fault Code 26: Oil cooler blower relay.

MAINTENANCE

FLUID LEVEL CHECK

1. Remove transmission underbody cover.
2. Operate vehicle until transmission fluid temperature is approximately 80°C.

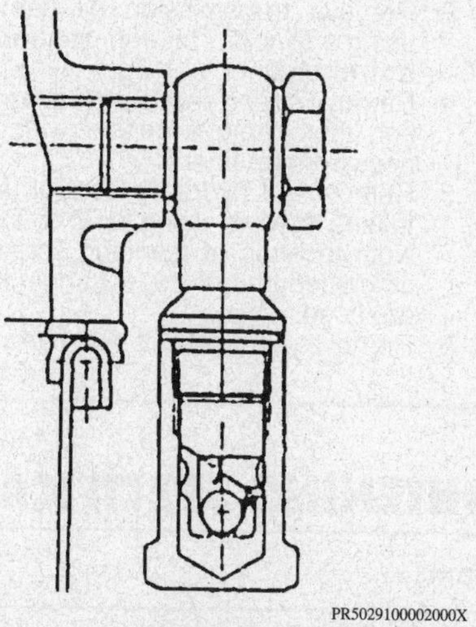
PR5029100002000X

Fig. 1 Transmission quick fill device

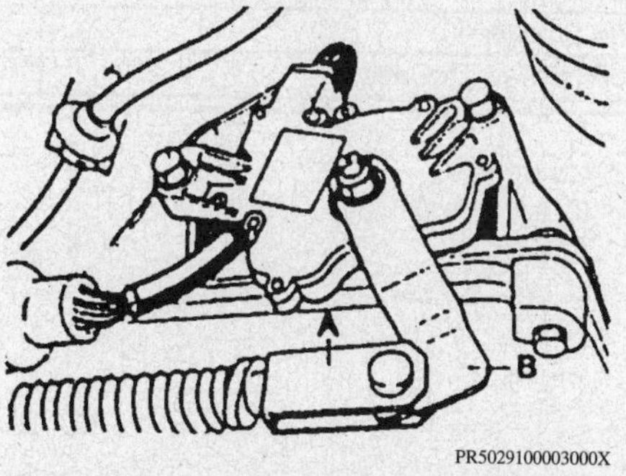
A
B
PR5029100003000X

Fig. 3 Selector cable & actuating lever. A: Cable fork. B: Actuating lever

3. With vehicle on a level surface, place transmission selector lever in Park and apply parking brake. Engine should be operating at idle speed.
4. Transmission fluid level should be between the 80°C Min. and Max. markings on the transmission fluid level indicator.
5. If necessary, add Dexron IID/IIE type automatic transmission fluid through the transmission quick fill device, **Fig. 1.**

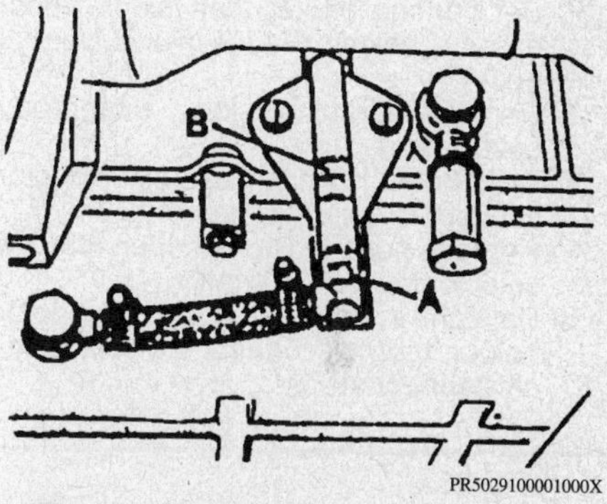
B
A
PR5029100001000X

Fig. 2 Transmission fluid level indicator. A: Fluid level range at 30°C. B: Fluid level range at 80°C

FLUID CHANGE

The transmission fluid should be changed and filter replaced at 25,000 mile intervals.

1. Start engine, allow to reach normal operating temperature.
2. Position vehicle on level surface.
3. With engine Off, raise and support vehicle.
4. Remove drain screw from transmission and allow transmission to drain.
5. Remove transmission oil pan, then remove strainer using a Torx T 27 bit.
6. Clean oil pan and strainer.
7. Position strainer on transmission with a new O-ring, then install.
8. Position transmission oil pan to case with a new seal, then install.
9. Fill transmission, with Dexron IID/IIE type transmission fluid, through the quick fill device to the 30°F level, **Figs. 1 and 2.**
10. Start engine and check fluid as described under checking fluid level.

ADJUSTMENTS

SELECTOR CABLE

1. Place transmission selector lever in the 1 position.
2. Position multi-function switch operating lever to 1 position.
3. Push cable forward, then adjust cable

fork by aligning holes on cable fork head with holes in operating lever, **Fig. 3.** After aligning cable fork and operating lever holes, thread cable fork an additional two turns onto cable threads.
4. Check adjustment by shifting transmission through all ranges.

IN-VEHICLE REPAIRS

POSITION SWITCH, REPLACE

1. Set parking brake, then place transmission selector lever in the Neutral position.
2. Remove transmission underbody cover.
3. Disconnect transmission selector cable from selector lever, **Fig. 3.**
4. Remove nut and washer, then remove selector lever from shaft.
5. Unlatch switch electrical connector holder, then disconnect switch electrical connector.
6. Remove switch attaching screws, then remove the switch.
7. Reverse procedure to install. After completing installation, check selector cable adjustment, as described under "Selector Cable, Adjust."

HYDRAULIC CONTROL UNIT, REPLACE

1. Remove transmission underbody cover.
2. Remove transmission oil pan drain screw and allow transmission fluid to drain.
3. Remove transmission oil pan, then using a Torx T27 bit, remove transmission oil strainer.
4. Remove speed sensor holder and sensor, then remove sensor wiring harness from retainers.
5. Remove 13 hydraulic control unit retaining screws using a Torx T27 bit. Note location of retaining screws, as screw lengths of 65, 80 and 115 mm are used.
6. Remove control unit from transmission, using care not to place tension on wiring harness.
7. Tag wiring harness push on sleeves prior to disconnecting from solenoids. Disconnect push on sleeves from solenoid valves.
8. Remove wiring harness from retaining clamps, then remove valve body from vehicle.
9. Reverse procedure to install noting the following:
   a. Ensure wiring harness push on sleeves are properly seated on solenoid valves.
   b. When mounting hydraulic control unit, ensure pin of notched disc projects into recess of selector slide.
   c. Use care to install hydraulic control unit retaining screws in the same locations as removed.
   d. Position control unit by placing notched disc to position 1 (1st gear), then push control unit back unit it rests against the notched disc.

TIGHTENING SPECIFICATIONS

Component	Torque/Ft. Lbs.
Actuator Shaft	11
Control Unit	6
Position Switch	7.4
Transmission Strainer	6
Transmission Oil Pan To Case	6

All-Wheel Drive Systems

INDEX

	Page No.
Description	37-59

DESCRIPTION

The 911 is equipped with electronically controlled four wheel drive system. Front wheels are driven by a transfer box and a driveshaft running in the central pipe. The four wheel drive system has a permanent division of 31% of the drive torque to the front axle and 69% to the rear axle. The static axle load distribution is 60% to the rear axle and 40% to the front axle. The transverse lock is applied to reduce oversteer while driving the car in curves. The interaxle lock stabilizes the vehicle when accelerating out of a curve, sends more drive torque to the slower turning axle by locking the transfer. The locking effect is increased until equal wheel speeds are restored.

Refer to **Fig. 1,** for all wheel drive component locations.

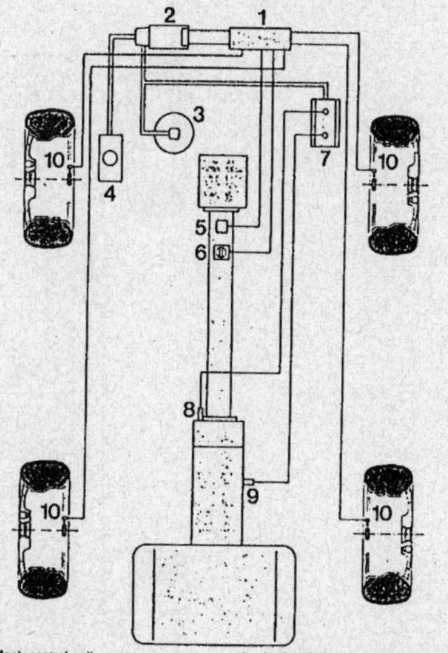

1
2
3
4
5
6
7
8
9
10

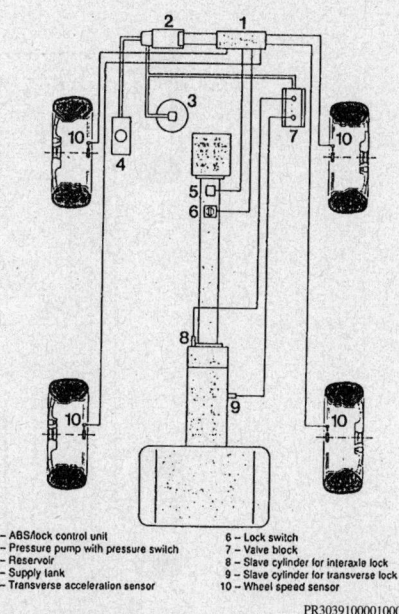

1 – ABS/lock control unit
2 – Pressure pump with pressure switch
3 – Reservoir
4 – Supply tank
5 – Transverse acceleration sensor
6 – Lock switch
7 – Valve block
8 – Slave cylinder for interaxle lock
9 – Slave cylinder for transverse lock
10 – Wheel speed sensor

PR3039100001000X

Fig. 1 AWD component locations

Drive Axles

INDEX

	Page No.
Description	37-60
Diagnosis & Testing	37-60

DESCRIPTION

The 928 limited slip differential is an electronically controlled rear axle traverse differential lock, **Fig. 1.** A high pressure pump, pressure reservoir, solenoid and supply tank are incorporated into the hydraulic system, which is located on a holder in the left rear wheel housing. Power supply (fuse and pump motor relay) are located in the spare tire well.

The anti-lock brake system control unit incorporates an additional platinum board to provide lock control. The control unit uses information from the anti-lock brake system wheel sensors to determine wheel speed, wheel acceleration and deceleration, front to rear axle speed difference and right to left side wheel speed difference. A transverse acceleration sensor, located beneath the drivers seat, is also incorporated. Brake operation is monitored through the stop lamp switch.

When the control unit detects a slipping wheel, the system pressure will increase in steps until the slipping is operating with in the specified wheel speed range. The system will control traction during acceleration and acceleration and deceleration while cornering. A green lock information lamp on the instrument cluster will be illuminated when the locks are in operation and when both rear wheels slip.

DIAGNOSIS & TESTING

The fault code memory of the system can be accessed using tester No. 9268. Follow tester manufacturers instruction to connect tester system and perform test procedures. The test will flash four digit fault codes, **Fig. 2.**

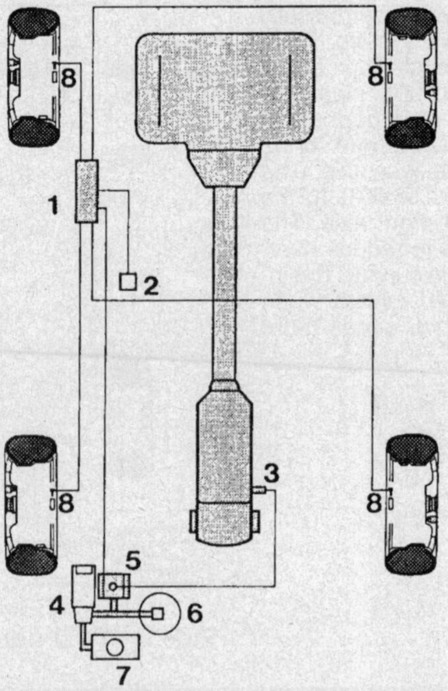
8
8
1
2
3
8
8
5
4
6
7

1 - ABS / lock control unit
2 - Transverse acceleration sensor
3 - Transverse lock slave cylinder
4 - Pressure pump with pressure switch
5 - Block of solenoids
6 - Pressure reservoir
7 - Supply tank
8 - Wheel speed sensor

PR3039100002000X

Fig. 1 Limited slip differential system. 928 models

Explanation of Fault Code Digits

	Display	
1st digit	5	Control unit identification
2nd digit	1	Fault currently exists
	2	Fault was experienced but not currently exist
	5	No faults
3rd digit	1 - 3	Tens digit of fault type
4th digit	1 - 5	Units digit of fault type

PSD Fault Codes

Code (3rd / 4th Digits)	Type of Fault
11	Transverse lock solenoid
12	Transverse acceleration sender - short/break
13	Transverse acceleration sender - not okay
14	Transverse lock - deviation in regulation
15	Control unit - faulty
21	Speed sensor front left
22	Speed sensor front right
23	Speed sensor rear right
24	Speed sensor rear left
31	ABS solenoid front left
32	ABS solenoid front right
33	ABS solenoid rear axle
34	Solenoid relay
35	Return delivery pump

PR3039100003000X

Fig. 2 Limited slip differential system fault codes. 928 models

Engine Rebuilding Specifications

INDEX

	Page No.
Camshaft	37-61
Crankshaft, Bearings & Rods	37-61
Cylinder Block	37-62
Cylinder Head, Valve Guide & Valve Seats	37-61
Pistons, Pins & Rings	37-62
Valves	37-61

CYLINDER HEAD, VALVE GUIDE & VALVE SEATS

All Measurements Given In Inches, Unless Otherwise Specified.

Engine Liter	Year	Cylinder Head Warpage Limit	Valve Guides			Valve Seats		
			Standard Inside Diameter	Stem To Guide Clearance		Seat Angle Degrees	Seat Width	
				Intake	Exhaust		Intake	Exhaust
3.0L	1993–95	.0031①	.3543	.0315	.0315	45	.0669	.0787
3.6L	1993–96	.0059①	.3546	.0039–.0059	.0039–.0079	45	2.0339–2.0346	1.7395–1.7402

① — Maximum.

VALVES

All Measurements Given In Inches, Unless Otherwise Specified.

Engine Liter	Year	Valves				Valve Clearance	
		Stem Diameter		Face Angle	Valve Spring Installed Height	Intake	Exhaust
		Intake	Exhaust				
3.0L	1993–95	.3515	.3524	45	—	③	③
3.6L	1993–96	.3531	.3526	45	①	③	③

① — Intake, 1.358 inch; exhaust, 1.3189 inch.

② — Intake, 1.307–1.330 inch; exhaust, 1.307–1.330 inch.

③ — Equipped w/hydraulic valve lash adjusters.

CAMSHAFT

All Measurements Given In Inches, Unless Otherwise Specified.

Engine Liter	Year	Camshaft Journal Diameter	Maximum Journal Run-out	Camshaft Endplay	Lifter Bore Diameter	Lifter Diameter
3.0L	1993–95	2.3819	.0008	.0039–.0071	1.4963–1.4971	1.4968–1.4974
3.6L	1993–96	1.847–1.848	.0008	.006–.008	—	—

CRANKSHAFT, BEARINGS & RODS

All Measurements Given In Inches, Unless Otherwise Specified.

Engine Liter	Year	Crankshaft Std. Journal Dia.		Bearing Clearance		Endplay	
		Main Bearing	Crank Pin	Main Bearing	Connecting Rod Bearing	Crankshaft	Connecting Rod
3.0L	1993–95	2.7547–2.7555	2.0460–2.0468	.0008–.0039	.0013–.0036	.0043–.0123	.0039–.0157
3.6L	1993–96	2.3611–2.3618	2.1642–2.1650	—	—	—	—

PISTONS, PINS & RINGS

All Measurements Given In Inches, Unless Otherwise Specified.

Engine Liter	Year	Piston Diameter (Std.)	Piston Clearance	Piston Pin Diameter	Piston Ring End Gap		Piston Ring Side Clearance	
					Comp	Oil	Comp.	Oil
3.0L	1993–95	—	.0003–.0013	.9449	.0079–.0177	.0149–.0551	①	②
3.6L	1993–96	3.93579–3.93619	—	.866	.00039–.0079	.0059–.0120	③	.0008–.0019

① — Mahle, .0023–.0040 inch; KS, .0020–.0032 inch.

② — Mahle, .0005–.0049 inch; KS, .0009–.0053 inch.

③ — Top ring .0030–.0040 inch, 2nd ring .0020–.0030 inch.

CYLINDER BLOCK

All Measurements Given In Inches, Unless Otherwise Specified.

Engine Liter	Year	Cylinder Bore Diameter (Std)	Cylinder Bore Out of Round Max.
3.0L	1993–95	4.09	.0008
3.6L	1993–96	3.94	.0016

SAAB

INDEX OF SERVICE OPERATIONS

Page No.

AIR BAG SYSTEM PRECAUTIONS 0-8

AUTOMATIC TRANSMISSION/TRANSAXLES .38-150

BRAKES
- Anti-Lock Brakes............ 38-95
- Disc Brakes.................. 38-87
- Hydraulic Brake Units......... 38-92
- Power Brake Units........... 38-93

CLUTCH & MANUAL TRANSAXLE
- Adjustments 38-34
- Clutch, Replace............. 38-34
- Hydraulic System Service..... 38-34
- Tightening Specifications...... 38-38
- Transaxle, Replace 38-35

ELECTRICAL
- Air Bags.................... 38-71
- Air Conditioning.............. 38-50
- Alternators.................. 38-63
- Blower Motor, Replace........ 38-11
- Coil Pack, Replace 38-7
- Cooling Fans 38-53
- Cruise Control 38-64
- Dash Gauges................ 38-60
- Dash Panels................. 38-79
- Distributor, Replace.......... 38-7
- Evaporator Core, Replace 38-12
- Fuel Pump Relay Location.... 38-6
- Fuse Panel & Flasher Location 38-6
- Heater Core, Replace......... 38-12
- Ignition Lock, Replace 38-7
- Ignition Switch, Replace 38-7
- Instrument Cluster, Replace... 38-10
- Neutral Safety Switch, Replace 38-8
- Passive Restraints........... 38-71
- Precautions.................. 38-6
- Radio, Replace 38-10
- Relay Center Location 38-6
- Speed Controls 38-64
- Starter Motors 38-61
- Starter, Replace 38-7
- Steering Columns............ 38-81
- Steering Wheel, Replace...... 38-9
- Turn Signal Switch, Replace .. 38-9
- Wiper Motor, Replace......... 38-10
- Wiper Switch, Replace........ 38-11
- Wiper Transmission, Replace . 38-11

ELECTRICAL SYMBOL IDENTIFICATION 0-139

ENGINE
- Belt Tension Data............ 38-28
- Camshaft, Replace 38-25
- Cooling System Bleed 38-28
- Crankshaft Seal, Replace..... 38-25
- Cylinder Head, Replace....... 38-19
- Engine Rebuilding Specifications...............38-164
- Engine, Replace 38-14
- Front Cover Seal, Replace.... 38-23
- Fuel Pump, Replace 38-29
- Intake Air Heat Plates, Replace 38-19
- Intake Manifold, Replace...... 38-18
- Main & Rod Bearings 38-25
- Oil Pan, Replace............. 38-26
- Oil Pump, Replace............ 38-27
- Pistons, Pins & Rings......... 38-25
- Precautions.................. 38-14
- Serpentine Drive Belt 38-28
- Tightening Specifications...... 38-31
- Timing Belt, Replace.......... 38-24
- Timing Chain, Replace........ 38-23
- Turbocharger, Replace........ 38-29
- Valve Adjustment 38-22
- Valve Clearance Specifications............... 38-22
- Valve Guides 38-22
- Valve Seats.................. 38-23
- Water Pump, Replace 38-28

FRONT SUSPENSION & STEERING
- Ball Joint, Replace............ 38-44
- Coil Spring, Replace.......... 38-44
- Control Arm, Replace 38-45
- Hub & Bearing, Replace 38-43
- Power Steering 38-84
- Power Steering Gear, Replace 38-46
- Power Steering Pump, Replace 38-47
- Precautions.................. 38-43
- Shock Absorber, Replace 38-44
- Tightening Specifications...... 38-47

FRONT WHEEL DRIVE AXLES.........................38-163

REAR AXLE & SUSPENSION
- Anti-Roll Bar & Bushings, Replace 38-41
- Coil Spring, Replace.......... 38-40
- Hub & Bearing, Replace 38-39
- Panhard Rod & Bushing, Replace 38-41
- Rear Axle, Replace 38-39
- Roll Bar, Replace 38-41
- Shock Absorber, Replace 38-40
- Spring Linkage, Replace...... 38-40
- Tightening Specifications...... 38-42
- Torque Arm & Bushing, Replace 38-40

SERVICE REMINDER & WARNING LAMP RESET PROCEDURES 0-10

SPECIFICATIONS
- Fluid Capacities & Cooling System Data................ 38-4
- Front Wheel Alignment Specifications................ 38-4
- General Engine Specifications................ 38-2
- Lubricant Data............... 38-5
- Rear Wheel Alignment Specifications................ 38-4
- Tune Up Specifications 38-2

VEHICLE IDENTIFICATION. 0-1

VEHICLE LIFT POINTS 0-34

VEHICLE MAINTENANCE SCHEDULES 0-69

WHEEL ALIGNMENT
- Front Wheel Alignment........ 38-49
- Preliminary Inspection 38-49
- Rear Wheel Alignment........ 38-49
- Vehicle Ride Height........... 38-49
- Wheel Alignment Specifications................ 38-4

WIRE COLOR CODE IDENTIFICATION 0-144

Specifications

GENERAL ENGINE SPECIFICATIONS

Year	Engine Liters	Bore X Stroke, Inches (mm)	Comp. Ratio	Maximum Brake H.P. @ RPM	Maximum Torque Ft. Lbs. @ RPM	Normal Oil Pressure, psi①
1993	2.0L③	3.54 X 3.07 (90 X 78)	9.0	160 @ 5500	188 @ 3000	39
	2.1L②	3.66 X 3.07 (93 X 78)	10.1	140 @ 6000	133 @ 2900	39
	2.3L②	3.54 X 3.54 (90 X 90)	10.1	150 @ 5500	156 @ 3800	39
	2.3L③	3.54 X 3.54 (90 X 90)	8.5	200 @ 5000	244 @ 2000	39
1994	2.0L④	3.54 X 3.07 (90 X 78)	9.2	185 @ 5500	195 @ 2100	39
	2.0L②⑦	3.54 X 3.07 (90 X 78)	10.1	130 @ 5500	130 @ 4300	39
	2.0L③⑦	3.54 X 3.07 (90 X 78)	8.8	150 @ 5500	154 @ 2500	39
	2.0L⑦⑧	3.54 X 3.07 (90 X 78)	9.2	185 @ 5500	210 @ 2100	39
	2.3L③④	3.54 X 3.54 (90 X 90)	10.5	150 @ 5700	155 @ 4300	39
	2.3L②⑦	3.54 X 3.54 (90 X 90)	10.5	146 @ 5500	151 @ 3800	39
	2.3L③⑦	3.54 X 3.54 (90 X 90)	9.3	170 @ 5600	192 @ 3200	39
	2.3L⑦⑧	3.54 X 3.54 (90 X 90)	9.25	200 @ 5500	⑤	39
	2.3L⑦⑥	3.54 X 3.54 (90 X 90)	9.25	225 @ 5500	253 @ 1800	39
	2.5L	3.21 X 3.13 (81 X 80)	10.8	170 @ 5900	167 @ 4200	—
1995–96	2.0L④	3.54 X 3.07 (90 X 78)	9.2	185 @ 5500	195 @ 2100	39
	2.0L②⑦	3.54 X 3.07 (90 X 78)	10.1	130 @ 5500	130 @ 4300	39
	2.0L③⑦	3.54 X 3.07 (90 X 78)	8.8	150 @ 5500	154 @ 2500	39
	2.0L⑦⑧	3.54 X 3.07 (90 X 78)	9.2	185 @ 5500	210 @ 2100	39
	2.3L③④	3.54 X 3.54 (90 X 90)	10.5	150 @ 5700	155 @ 4300	39
	2.3L②⑦	3.54 X 3.54 (90 X 90)	10.5	146 @ 5500	151 @ 3800	39
	2.3L③⑦	3.54 X 3.54 (90 X 90)	9.3	170 @ 5600	192 @ 3200	39
	2.3L⑦⑧	3.54 X 3.54 (90 X 90)	9.25	200 @ 5500	⑤	39
	2.3L⑦⑥	3.54 X 3.54 (90 X 90)	9.25	225 @ 5500	253 @ 1800	39
	2.5L	3.21 X 3.13 (82 X 80)	10.8	170 @ 5900	167 @ 4200	—
	3.0L	3.39 X 3.35 (86 X 84)	10.8	210 @ 6200	199 @ 3300	—

① — At 2000 RPM.
② — Non-turbocharged engine.
③ — Turbocharged engine.
④ — 900 series.
⑤ — Manual transaxle, 240 H.P. @ 1800 RPM; automatic transaxle, 218 H.P. @ 1800 RPM.
⑥ — Turbocharged engine w/air cooler, power output 2.
⑦ — 9000 series.
⑧ — Turbocharged engine w/air cooler, power output 1.

TUNE UP SPECIFICATIONS

Year & Engine	Spark Plug Gap, Inch	Ignition Timing			Curb Idle Speed		Fast Idle Speed		Fuel Pressure, psi	Valve Lash, Inch	
		Firing Order Fig.②	Timing, °BTDC	Timing Mark Fig.	Man. Trans.	Auto. Trans.③	Man. Trans.	Auto. Trans.		Intake	Exhaust
1993											
2.0L⑩	.026	⑧	—	④	850	850N	⑤	⑤	—	①	①
2.1L	.026	⑥	14	—	850	850N	⑤	⑤	—	①	①
2.3L Turbo	.043	⑧	—	—	850⑤	850N⑤	⑤	⑤	—	①	①
1994											
2.3L⑩	.003	⑧	—	—	900	900	⑤	⑤	—	①	①
2.3L⑨	.023	⑫	—	—	900	900	⑤	⑤	—	①	①
2.5L	.031	⑪	—	—	900	900	⑤	⑤	—	①	①
1995–96											
2.0L Turbo	.040	⑧	⑤	—	⑤	⑤	⑤	⑤	—	①	①

Continued

TUNE UP SPECIFICATIONS—Continued

Year & Engine	Spark Plug Gap, Inch	Ignition Timing			Curb Idle Speed		Fast Idle Speed		Fuel Pressure, psi	Valve Lash, Inch	
		Firing Order Fig.②	Timing, °BTDC	Timing Mark Fig.	Man. Trans.	Auto. Trans.③	Man. Trans.	Auto. Trans.		Intake	Exhaust
1995–96											
2.3L	.023	⑫	⑤	—	⑤	⑤	⑤	⑤	—	①	①
2.3L Turbo	.040	⑧	⑤	—	⑤	⑤	⑤	⑤	—	①	①
2.5L	.031	⑪	⑤	—	⑤	⑤	⑤	⑤	—	①	①
3.0L	.031	⑦	⑤	—	⑤	⑤	⑤	⑤	—	①	①

BTDC — Before Top Dead Center.
N — Neutral.
① — Equipped w/hydraulic valve lash adjusters.
② — Before disconnecting spark plug wires from distributor cap, determine location of No. 1 wire in cap, as distributor position may have been altered from that shown.
③ — When adjusting idle speed, set parking brake & chock drive wheels.
④ — Mark located on flywheel.
⑤ — Controlled by electronic control unit.
⑥ — Firing Order 1-3-4-2, **Fig. A.**
⑦ — Firing order 1-2-3-4-5-6, 9000 series w/Motronic 5.2L ignition system, **Fig. C.**
⑧ — Firing order, 1–3-4-2, direct ignition system (DIS) Trionic system, **Fig. D.**
⑨ — 16-valve engine, less turbocharger.
⑩ — 16-valve turbocharged engine.
⑪ — Firing order 1-2-3-4-5-6, 900 series w/ Motronic ignition system.
⑫ — Firing order 1-3-4–2, **Fig. B.**

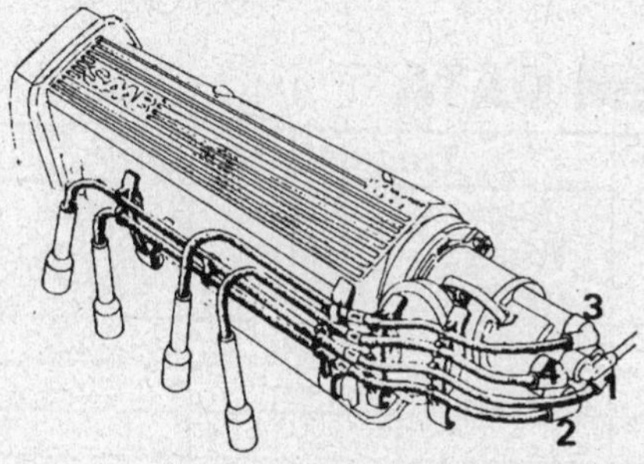
3
4
1
2
SA1139100011000X
Fig. A

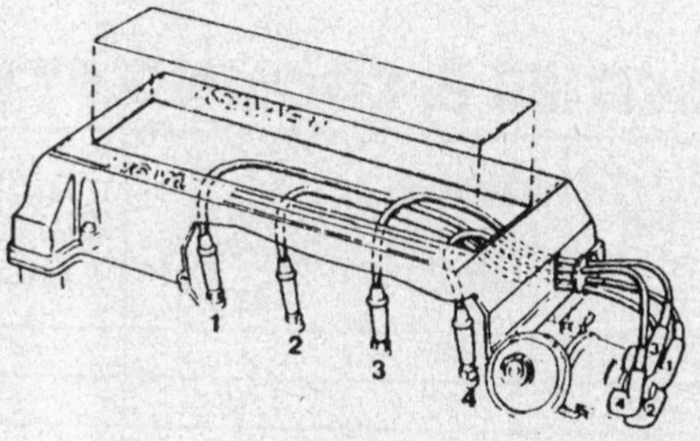
1
2
3
4
SA1139100012000X
Fig. B

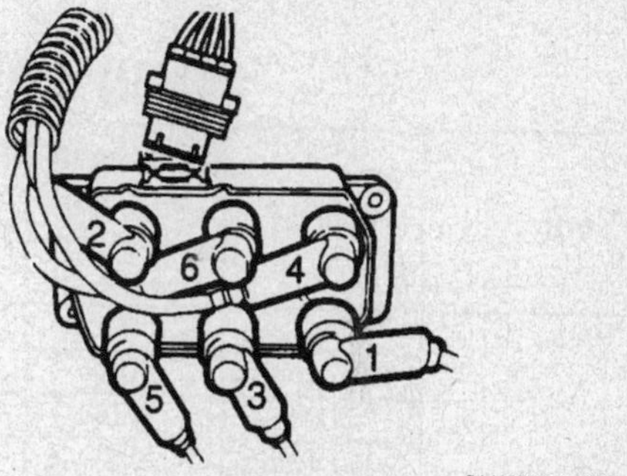
2
6
4
5
3
1
SA1139400024000X
Fig. C

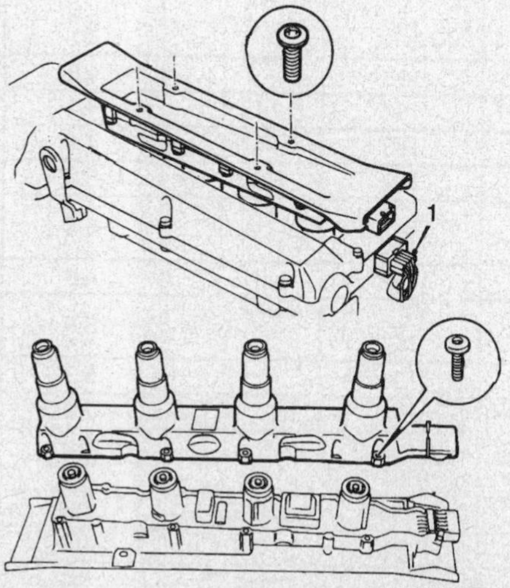
1
SA1139500025000X
Fig. D

FRONT WHEEL ALIGNMENT SPECIFICATIONS

Year	Model	Caster Angle, Degrees		Camber Angle, Degrees		Toe-In, Inch	Toe-Out On Turns, Degrees		Ball Joint Inspection	
		Limits	Desired	Limits	Desired		Inner Wheel	Outer Wheel	Upper	Lower
1993	900	+1.5 to +2.5	+2.00	–.75 to +.25	–.25	.08	21	20	①	①
	9000	+1.15 to +2.15	+1.65	–1.15 to –.15	–.65	.06	21	20	①	①
1994–96	900	+1.6 to +2.6	+2.10	0 to –1	–.5	.06	21	20	①	①
	9000	+1.15 to +2.15	+1.65	–1.15 to -.15	–.65	.06	21	20	①	①

① — Axial play, .08 inch; radial play, .04 inch.

REAR WHEEL ALIGNMENT SPECIFICATIONS

Year	Model	Camber Angle, Degrees		Toe-In, Inch
		Limits	Desired	
1993	900	–.75 to –.25	–.5	.16
1993–96	9000	–.5 to 0	–.25	.10
1994–96	900	–2 to –1.4	–1.7	.04

FLUID CAPACITIES & COOLING SYSTEM DATA

Year	Model	Coolant System Capacity, Qts.	Rad. Cap Relief Pressure, Lbs.	Thermo. Opening Temp., °F	Fuel Tank Capacity, Gals.	Engine Oil Refill, Qts.①	Transmission Oil		
							Man. Trans., Pts.	Auto. Trans., Qts.	Final Drive, Pts.
1993	900	10.5	13–17	180	18	4	6	8.5	2.6②
	900 Turbo	10.5	13–17	180	18	4	6	8.5	2.6②
	9000	9.5	13–17	190	17.4	4.4	5.2	8.4	—
	9000 Turbo	9.5	13–17	180	17.4	4.4	5.2	8.4	—
1994	900 2.3L	8.96	—	192	18	5.3	4	7.6	—
	900 2.0L Turbo	18.96	—	192	18	5.3	4	7.6	—
	900 2.5L	8.44	—	198	18	4.8	4	7.6	—
	9000	9.5	13–17	192	17.4	4.4	3.82	8.7	—
	9000 Turbo	9.5	13–17	180	17.4	4.4	3.82	9.2	—
1995	900 2.3L	8.96	—	192	18	5.3	4	7.6	—
	900 2.0L Turbo	8.96	13–14.5	192	18	5.3	4	7.6	—
	900 2.5L	8.44	13–14.5	192	18	4.8	4	7.6	—
	9000 2.3L Turbo	9.5	13–14.5	192	18	5.8	3.82	9.2	—
	9000 3.0L	9	13–14.5	198	18	5.3	3.82	8.7	—
1996	900 2.0L (J)	8.7	13–14.5	192	18	4.2	4	3.4	—
	900 2.0L (N) Turbo	8.7	13–14.5	192	18	4.2	4	3.4	—
	900 2.3L (B)	8.7	13–14.5	192	18	4.2	4	3.4	—
	900 2.5L (V)	8.9	13–14.5	198	18	4.7	4	3.4	—
	9000 2.3L (M)	9.5	13–14.5	192	17.4	5	4	3.7	—
	9000 2.3L (R)	9.5	13–14.5	192	17.4	5	4	3.7	—
	9000 3.0L (W)	9	13–14.5	198	17.4	4.7	—	3.7	—

① — Includes oil for filter change.
② — Auto. trans. only.

LUBRICANT DATA

Year	Model	Lubricant Type: Transmission, Manual	Lubricant Type: Transmission, Automatic	Rear Axle	Power Steering	Brake System
1993	900	SG 10W-30/ 10W-40 Motor Oil②	ATF Type F or G①	—	Power Steering Fluid③	DOT 4
1993–95	9000	SF 10W-30/ 10W-40 Motor Oil②	Dexron II/IIE/III	—	Power Steering Fluid③	DOT 4
1994–95	900	SE 10W-30/ 10W-40 Motor Oil②	Dexron II/IIE/III	—	Power Steering Fluid③	DOT 4
1996	900	SF CC/CD 10W-30/10W-40 Motor Oil②	Dexron II	—	④	DOT 4
	9000	SF CC/CD 10W-30/10W-40 Motor Oil②	Dexron II	—	⑤	DOT 4

① — Final drive, 80W GL-4/5.
② — Synthetic motor oil must not be used.
③ — Saab power steering fluid part Nos. 4634 or 1890, or equivalent.
④ — Saab power steering fluid part No. (45) 30 09 800.
⑤ — Saab power steering fluid 1890, Part No. (45) 3002995.

Electrical

NOTE: On Air Bag Equipped Models, Refer To "Air Bag System Precautions" Located In The Front Of This Manual For System Disarming & Arming Procedures.

INDEX

	Page No.
Air Bags	38-71
Air Conditioning	38-50
Alternators	38-63
Blower Motor, Replace	38-11
900	38-11
9000	38-11
Coil Pack, Replace	38-7
900 Less Direct Ignition System (DIS)	38-7
900 w/Direct Ignition System (DIS)	38-7
9000 Less Direct Ignition System (DIS)	38-7
9000 w/Direct Ignition System (DIS)	38-7
Cooling Fans	38-53
Cruise Control	38-64
Dash Gauges	38-60
Dash Panels	38-79
Distributor, Replace	38-7
Evaporator Core, Replace	38-12
900	38-12
9000	38-13
Fuel Pump Relay Location	38-6
Fuse Panel & Flasher Location	38-6
900	38-6
9000	38-6
Heater Core, Replace	38-12
900	38-12
9000	38-12
Ignition Lock, Replace	38-7
Ignition Switch, Replace	38-7
900	38-7
9000	38-8
Instrument Cluster, Replace	38-10
900	38-10
9000	38-10
Neutral Safety Switch, Replace	38-8
Passive Restraints	38-71
Precautions	38-6
Air Bag Systems	38-6
Radio Anti-Theft Lock	38-6
Radio, Replace	38-10
Except 1995–96 9000	38-10
1995–96 9000	38-10
Relay Center Location	38-6
900	38-6
9000	38-7
Speed Controls	38-64
Starter, Replace	38-7
900	38-7
9000	38-7
Starter Motors	38-61
Steering Columns	38-81
Steering Wheel, Replace	38-9
Less Air Bag	38-9
With Air Bag	38-9
Turn Signal Switch, Replace	38-9
Wiper Motor, Replace	38-10
900	38-10
9000	38-10
Wiper Switch, Replace	38-11
Wiper Transmission, Replace	38-11
900	38-11
9000	38-11

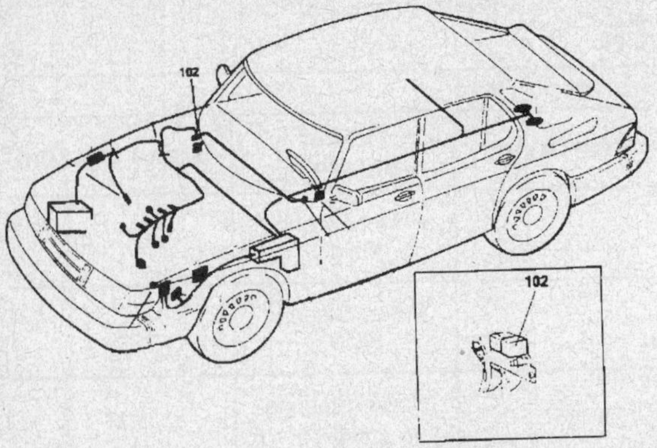
102
102
SA9049300006000X

Fig. 1 Fuel pump relay location. 1993 900 series w/CI fuel system

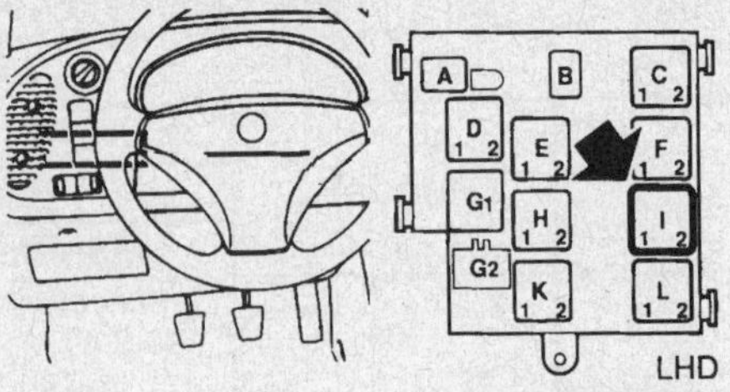
LHD
SA9049300007000X

Fig. 2 Fuel pump relay location. 1994–96 900 series w/Motronic 4.1L fuel system

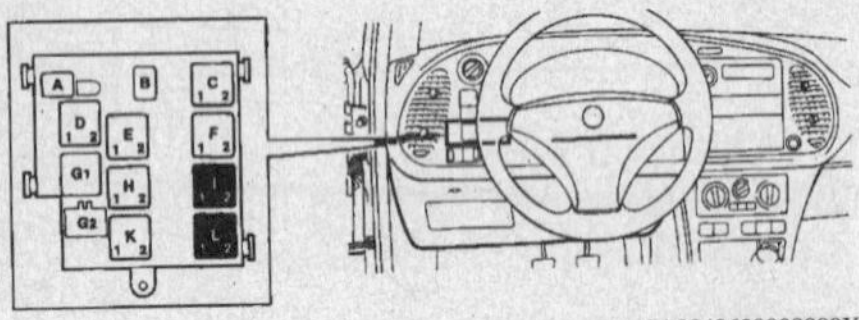
SA9049600008000X

Fig. 3 Fuel pump relay location. 1996 900 series w/Motronic 5.2L fuel system

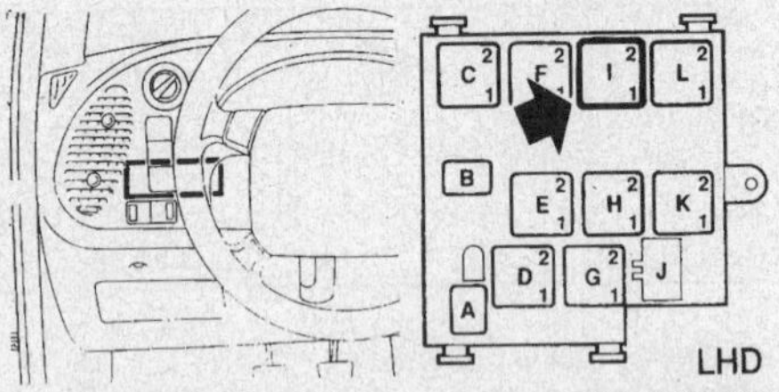
LHD
SA9049400009000X

Fig. 4 Fuel pump relay location. 1994–96 900 series w/Trionic fuel system

PRECAUTIONS

AIR BAG SYSTEMS

Refer to "Air Bag System Precautions" in the front of this manual for system disarming and arming procedures.

RADIO ANTI-THEFT LOCK

9000

1995-96

Radio and cassette player are equipped with an electronic four-digit anti-theft lock. This four-digit code is programmed at manufacturing and cannot be changed. If the battery is disconnected for more than three minutes, if unit is removed or if otherwise cut off from power, the four-digit code must be entered with the quick-selection buttons as follows:

1. Turn radio on, then, when display shows "Code In," enter four-digit code with quick-selection buttons. If code is correct, last-tuned radio frequency is shown on display. If wrong digit has been entered by mistake, all four digits must be entered again. If code is wrong it stays on display.
2. If incorrect four-digit code has been entered, press Band button for more than three seconds to clear display. Display shows "Code In" and new attempt to enter correct code can be made.
3. If wrong code has been used three times in succession, four dashes appear on display and you must wait an hour with radio switched on before trying again.
4. To try again, hold Band button for at least three seconds. "Code In" should appear on display.
5. Correct code must be entered at first attempt, otherwise you must wait another hour with unit switched on before trying again.

FUSE PANEL & FLASHER LOCATION

900

1993

The fuse panel is located on the lefthand wheel housing in the engine compartment. On convertible models, an additional fuse panel is located under the rear lefthand seat. The flasher unit is mounted behind the lefthand side of the instrument panel.

1994-96

The fuse panel is located on the lefthand side of the vehicle, between the door and the instrument panel. Two additional fuse panels are located in the engine compartment. One fuse panel is located at the far left of the engine bay below the windshield, and the other (Maxi fuse box) is located between the battery and the lefthand strut tower. The Integrated Central Electrics (ICE) control module is located on the lefthand side of the vehicle, between the door and the instrument panel.

9000

The fuse panel and flasher are located behind the glove compartment. An additional fuse/relay panel is located in the engine compartment.

FUEL PUMP RELAY LOCATION

On 1993 900 series models, the fuel pump relay (102) is located on the righthand "A" pillar, below fascia, **Fig. 1.** On 1994–96 900 series models, refer to **Figs. 2 through 4** for fuel pump relay location. On 9000 series models, the fuel pump relay is located on the righthand upper instrument panel behind the glove box, **Figs. 5 through 7.**

RELAY CENTER LOCATION

900

1993

The relay panel is located in the electrical distribution box at the lefthand side of the engine compartment.

1994-96

The fuse/relay panel is located in the engine compartment. Some relays are also located in the fuse panel behind the glove compartment.

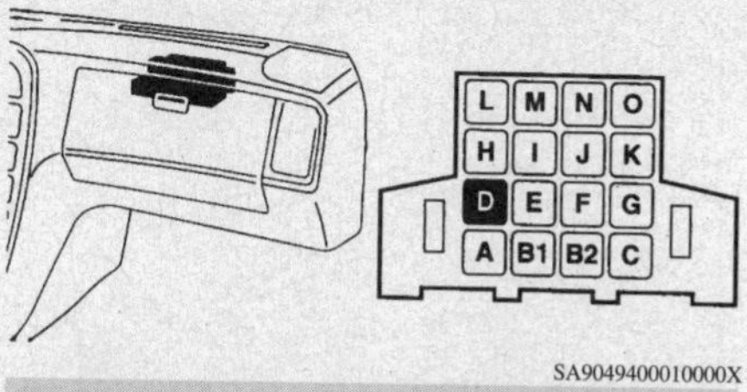
L M N O
H I J K
D E F G
A B1 B2 C
SA9049400010000X

Fig. 5 Fuel pump relay location. 1994–96 9000 series w/Trionic fuel system

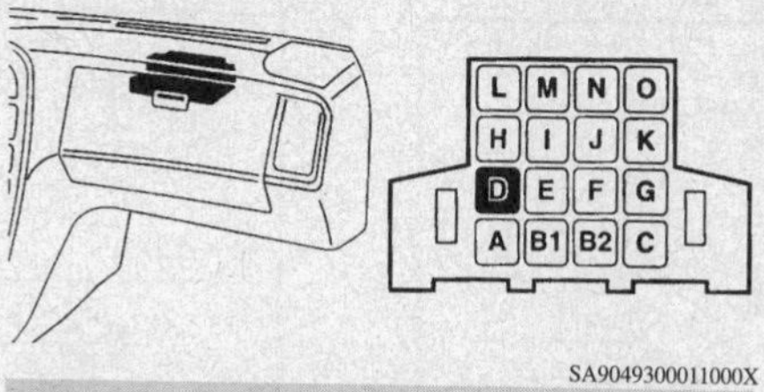
L M N O
H I J K
D E F G
A B1 B2 C
SA9049300011000X

Fig. 6 Fuel pump relay location. 1995 9000 series w/Motronic 2.8L fuel system

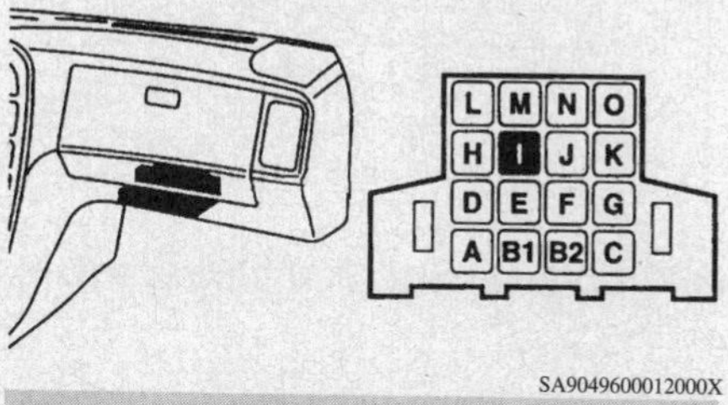
L M N O
H I J K
D E F G
A B1 B2 C
SA9049600012000X

Fig. 7 Fuel pump relay location. 1996 9000 series w/Motronic 5.2L fuel system

9000

The fuse/relay panel is located in the engine compartment. Some relays are also located in the fuse panel behind the glove compartment and in the ABS/TCS fuse box behind the brake fluid reservoir.

STARTER

REPLACE

900

1993

1. Disconnect battery ground cable and electrical connectors from starter motor.
2. Remove two starter motor securing bolts.
3. Move starter motor back, then lift out and remove starter motor from vehicle.
4. Reverse procedure to install.

1994–96

2.0L & 2.3L Engines

1. Disconnect battery ground cable, then remove upper attaching bolt.
2. Raise and support vehicle, then disconnect starter motor cables.
3. Remove lower attaching bolt.
4. Twist exhaust pipe slightly to one side and lift out starter motor.
5. Reverse procedure to install.

2.5L Engine

1. Disconnect battery ground cable.
2. Raise and support vehicle, then snip through cable ties securing wiring around motor.
3. Disconnect starter motor cables.
4. Remove starter motor attaching nuts, then the motor.
5. Reverse procedure to install.

9000

1. **On 1995–96 models,** obtain radio anti-theft code as outlined under "Precautions."
2. **On all models,** disconnect battery ground cable.
3. Disconnect starter motor electrical connectors.
4. Loosen starter motor bracket bar upper attaching bolt. Do not remove bolt.
5. Remove both starter motor to engine block attaching bolts.
6. Remove starter motor from vehicle.
7. Reverse procedure to install.

DISTRIBUTOR

REPLACE

1. **On 1995–96 9000 models,** obtain radio anti-theft code as outlined under "Precautions."
2. **On all models,** disconnect battery ground cable.
3. Disconnect high tension leads from distributor cap.
4. Disconnect Hall sensor and vacuum hose.
5. Remove distributor cap from distributor body.
6. Pry back on distributor retaining clip, then remove distributor.
7. Reverse procedure to install.

COIL PACK

REPLACE

900 LESS DIRECT IGNITION SYSTEM (DIS)

1. Disconnect battery ground cable.
2. Remove engine covers (1), then unplug ignition coil pack electrical connector (2).
3. Remove coil pack mounting bolts (3), then coil pack, **Fig. 8.**
4. Disconnect spark plug wires (4), record position for installation reference.
5. Reverse procedure to install.

900 w/DIRECT IGNITION SYSTEM (DIS)

1. Disconnect battery ground cable.
2. Disconnect DIS coil pack electrical connector (1), **Fig. 9.**
3. Remove DIS coil pack mounting bolts and coil pack from top of cylinder head.
4. Reverse procedure to install.

9000 LESS DIRECT IGNITION SYSTEM (DIS)

1. Disconnect battery ground cable.
2. Remove intake duct and resonating chamber.
3. Disconnect spark plug wires (2).
4. Disconnect ignition coil pack top electrical connector (3).
5. Remove coil pack mounting bolts, then coil pack (5), **Fig. 10.**
6. Reverse procedure to install.

9000 w/DIRECT IGNITION SYSTEM (DIS)

On 9000 series models equipped with DIS, replace coil pack as outlined under "Coil Pack, Replace" in "900 w/Direct Ignition System (DIS)" procedure.

IGNITION LOCK

REPLACE

Refer to "Ignition Switch, Replace" for procedure.

IGNITION SWITCH

REPLACE

900

1993

1. Disconnect battery ground cable, then the wiring harness connector to driver seat heating element.
2. Remove seat.
3. Place automatic transaxle in park or manual transaxle in reverse, then remove ignition key.
4. **On models equipped with automatic transaxle,** remove shift indicator plate and top cover after disconnecting indicator lamp.
5. **On models equipped with manual transaxle,** remove shifter boot and top cover.
6. **On all models,** pull carpet away from shifter cover.
7. Remove center rear console as follows:
   a. Move seats to rear and apply hand brake.
   b. Remove rear ashtray and five console retaining screws.
   c. Disconnect wiring harness connectors and remove console, then remove heater duct.
8. If lock cylinder is to be replaced on manual transaxle models, remove tapered pin from joint between gear lever and selector rod, and disconnect selector rod.
9. Disconnect wiring harness connectors to ignition switch, noting position for reassembly.
10. Disconnect wiring harness connectors to back-up lamp and neutral safety switches.
11. Remove bolts securing gear lever housing using special tool No. 8 912 37, or equivalent.
12. Replace ignition switch as follows:

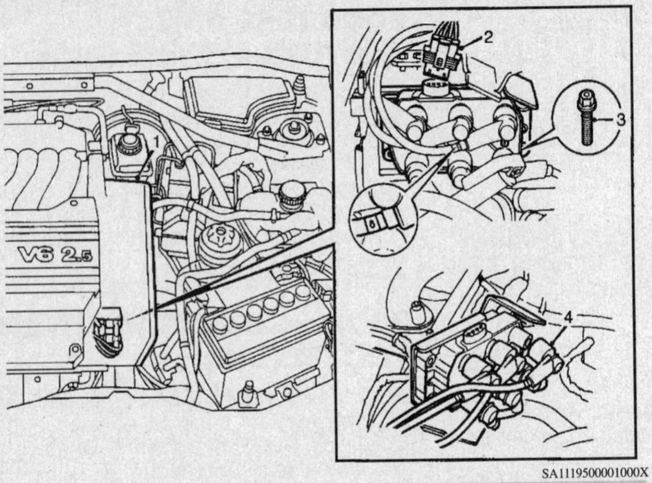
2
3
1
V6 2.5
4
SA1119500001000X

Fig. 8 Coil pack replacement. 900 series less DIS

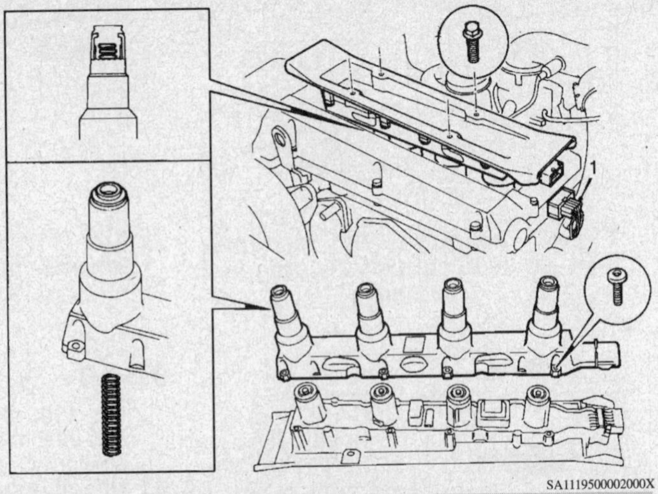
1
SA1119500002000X

Fig. 9 Coil pack replacement. 900 series w/DIS

a. Raise housing slightly, twist to expose cover plate screws, and remove plate.
b. Remove ignition switch retaining screws and switch.
c. Rotate switch to align mark (2) with arrow (3), **Fig. 11.**
d. Ensure key is in lock (L) position and install switch with locating stud (1), **Fig. 11,** in slot on gear lever housing.

13. Replace lock cylinder with key as follows:
    a. **On models equipped with automatic transaxle,** loosen bottom cover screws, then remove cable bracket clip and gear lever housing.
    b. **On models equipped with manual transaxle,** remove gear lever housing assembly.
    c. **On all models,** turn ignition key half way between Lock (L) and garage (G) positions.
    d. Depress lock cylinder retaining pin, **Fig. 12,** with pick, and pull cylinder from housing.
    e. Install lock with key turned half way between Lock (L) and garage (G) positions, ensuring cylinder is aligned with drive gear.
14. Replace lock cylinder with key missing as follows:
    a. Drill out plug covering hole for lock cylinder retaining pin on lefthand side of gear lever housing.
    b. Using punch, drive lock retaining pin in approximately .008 inch, **Fig. 13,** and remove lock cylinder. **Lock cylinder must be replaced after forcing retaining pin.**
    c. Install new lock cylinder as outlined previously.
15. Reverse procedure to install components, then adjust transaxle linkage as necessary.

1994–96

Automatic Transaxle

1. Place selector lever in P position and remove key.
2. Release indicator plate and rubber seal from selector lever housing, then turn it to one side.
3. Release selector lever wire clip.
4. Remove ignition lock switch (4), then the ignition lock (5), **Fig. 14.**
5. Reverse procedure to install, then check play in parking lock.

Manual Transaxle

1. Disconnect battery ground cable.
2. Remove lefthand front seat, middle console side covers and middle console.
3. Remove air duct, then engage transaxle in 4th gear.
4. Remove plastic plug on gearbox, then insert locking pin with ring in uppermost position.
5. Remove clamp holding gear rod in linkage.
6. Engage 3rd gear so gear rod and linkage separate, then remove screws holding gear lever housing.
7. Lift up housing and turn, then remove two clamps holding ignition lock cables in gear lever housing.
8. Disconnect terminal on ignition lock, then pull backward and lift out gear lever housing with gear rod.
9. Remove locking plate holder, then the spring securing locking plate (3), **Fig. 15.**
10. Using screwdriver, click up on rider controlled by ignition lock, then lift up locking plate and plastic fastener (4).
11. Remove ignition lock switch (5), then the ignition lock (6).
12. Reverse procedure to install, noting the following:
    a. Adjust position of locking plate with screw on plate holder. Locking plate should be level with heel in gear lever housing. **Stop should not touch locking plate during adjustment.**
    b. **Torque** gear rod to linkage clamp nut to 16 ft. lbs.

9000

1. **On 1995–96 models,** obtain radio anti-theft code as outlined under "Precautions."
2. **On all models,** disconnect battery ground cable, then remove steering wheel as outlined under "Steering Wheel, Replace."
3. Remove wiper/washer and turn signal switch covers.
4. Remove upper section of instrument panel.
5. Remove air ducts both in and above steering column.
6. Cut off clip securing wiring harness and flexible ducts to steering column.
7. Disconnect wiper/washer and turn signal electrical connectors. Disconnect horn switch and ignition switch leads.
8. Remove upper joint pinch bolt. Loosen remaining bolt and withdraw universal joint from steering column shaft splines.
9. Remove steering wheel adjustment assembly as follows:
    a. Using hammer and drift, tap out tubular dowel.
    b. Remove nut and washer.
    c. Withdraw shaft from clamp.
    d. Lift off upper section of steering wheel adjustment assembly.
10. Remove three attaching screws, then lift off turn signal switch.
11. Remove rubber bushing from housing, then the upper section of the steering column.
12. Remove washer and steering column bearing.
13. Loosen attaching screws, then remove ignition switch.
14. Turn ignition switch key to position 1, then press in locking tab and withdraw lock cylinder.
15. Reverse procedure to install.

NEUTRAL SAFETY SWITCH

REPLACE

1. **On 1995–96 9000 models,** obtain radio anti-theft code as outlined under "Precautions."

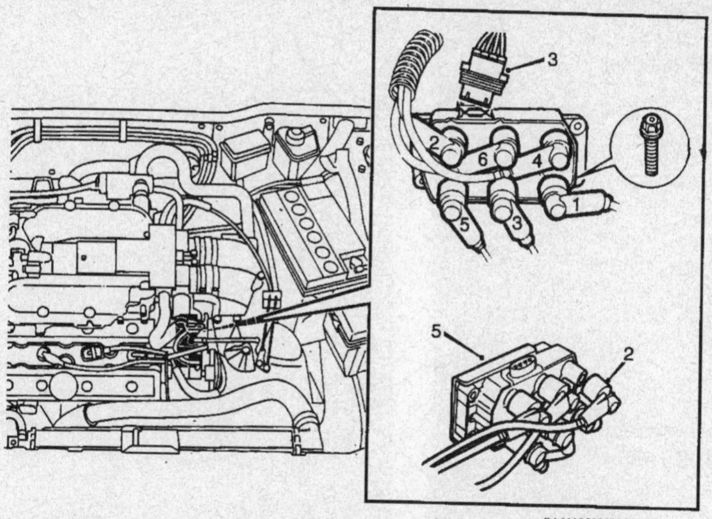
3
2
6
4
1
5
3
5
2

SA1119500003000X

Fig. 10 Coil pack replacement. 9000 series

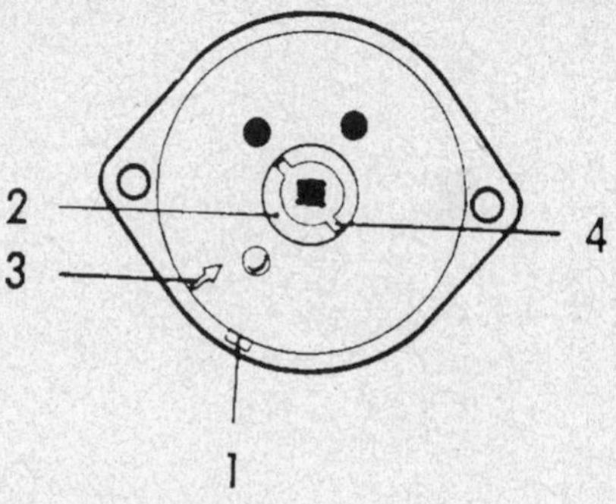
2
3
4
1

IGNITION AND STARTER CONTACT

1. Locating stud
2. Setting mark
3. Mark arrow
4. Gear wheel fitting groove

SA9049100001000X

Fig. 11 Ignition & starter switch contact alignment. 1993 900

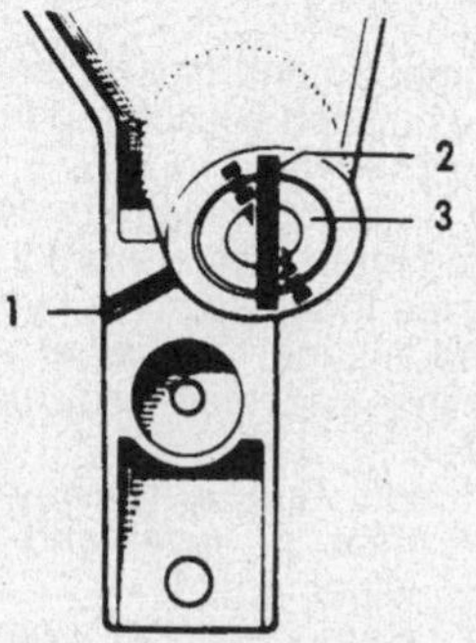
2
3
1

PRESSING IN THE CATCH PIN

1. Hole for catch pin
2. Key
3. Lock cylinder

SA9049100002000X

Fig. 12 Ignition lock cylinder removal w/key. 1993 900

2. **On all models,** disconnect battery ground cable.
3. Loosen locknut and remove shift knob, and remove shift indicator plate and top cover after disconnecting indicator lamp.
4. Pull carpet back from shifter cover assembly.
5. Remove rear ashtray and five screws securing center rear console.
6. Disconnect wiring harness connectors and remove console.
7. Disconnect wiring harness connectors to switch assembly.
8. Remove screws securing switch to shifter assembly, then the switch.
9. Place transaxle selector in neutral and install switch with screws finger tight.
10. Rotate switch until line on switch is aligned with lever, and secure switch.
11. Reconnect wiring harness connectors and reverse procedure to install remaining components.

TURN SIGNAL SWITCH

REPLACE

Switches for direction indicator lights and the wiper/washer system are fitted in a panel mounted on the steering wheel bearing support. The panel can be removed after the cover beneath the support is removed.

STEERING WHEEL

REPLACE

LESS AIR BAG

1. **On 1995–96 9000 models,** obtain radio anti-theft code as outlined under "Precautions."
2. **On all models,** disconnect battery ground cable.
3. Remove safety padding from center of steering wheel.
4. Remove center nut and washer, then install puller tool No. 89 96 258, or equivalent.
5. Remove steering wheel.
6. Using two screwdrivers carefully pry off direction indicator switch.
7. Reverse procedure to install. **Torque** center nut to 21 ft. lbs.

WITH AIR BAG

9000 & 1993 900

1. Position wheels in straight ahead position, then remove two horn pad/air bag module retaining screws from rear of steering wheel.
2. Disconnect horn pad/air bag module electrical connectors, then remove from vehicle.
3. Place match marks on steering shaft and steering wheel, then remove steering wheel nut.
4. Using puller, gently ease steering wheel off of shaft so air bag clock spring is not damaged.
5. Reverse procedure to install, noting the following:
   a. Set wheels in straight ahead position.
   b. Rotate clock spring clockwise until it stops, then rotate counterclockwise 3 ½ turns.
   c. Hold clock spring in position, then thread air bag module and horn wiring through hole in steering wheel.
   d. Align match marks on shaft and steering wheel, then align clock spring with hole in wheel.
   e. **Torque** steering wheel nut to 24–32 ft. lbs.

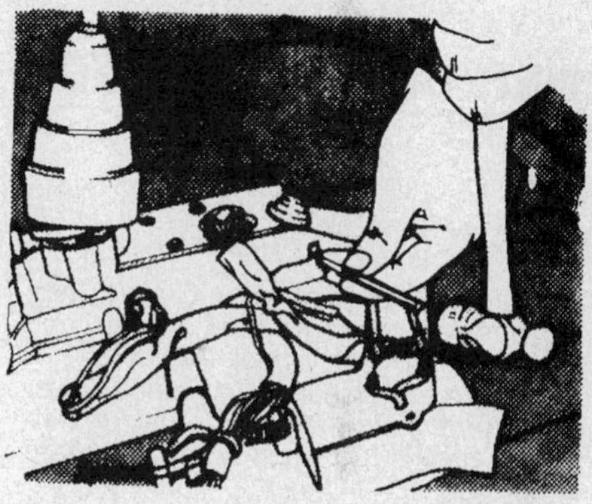

SA9049400003000X

Fig. 13 Ignition lock cylinder removal w/key missing. 1993 900

1994–96 900

1. Disconnect battery ground cable.
2. Remove air bag module retaining screws from underside of steering wheel, then disconnect electrical connector and remove air bag module.
3. Disconnect horn connector, then set wheels in straight ahead position.
4. Loosen steering column, then rock

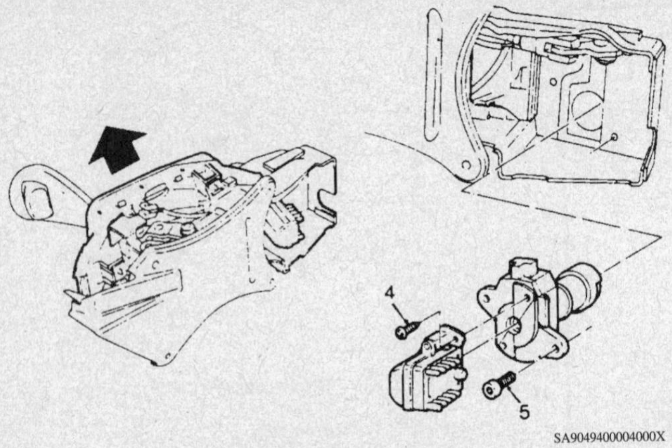
4
5
SA9049400004000X

Fig. 14 Ignition lock switch replacement. 1994–96 900 w/automatic transaxle

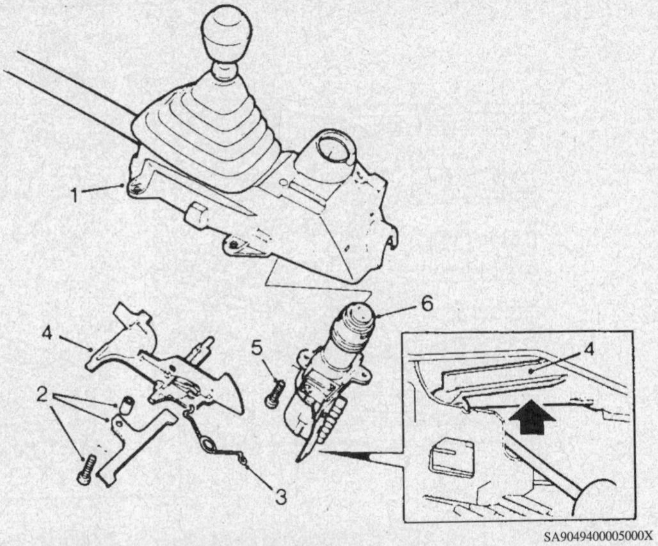
1
6
4
5
4
2
3
SA9049400005000X

Fig. 15 Ignition lock switch removal. 1994–96 900 w/manual transaxle

steering wheel loose and remove.
5. Reverse procedure to install.

INSTRUMENT CLUSTER

REPLACE

900

1993

1. Disconnect battery ground cable, then remove steering wheel as outlined under "Steering Wheel, Replace."
2. Remove four screws securing lower edge of instrument cluster bezel, noting position of each screw for reassembly.
3. Tilt bezel forward, then disconnect electrical connectors and vacuum hoses, if equipped, and remove bezel.
4. Remove lefthand speaker/defroster grille, then disconnect electrical connectors and speedometer cable from cluster.
5. Remove instrument cluster retaining screws and cluster.
6. Reverse procedure to install. **Cluster bezel retaining screws are of different lengths and are not interchangeable. The bezel will be damaged if screws are installed improperly.**

1994–96

1. Remove steering wheel covers.
2. Remove all switches, SID module and audio system from fascia.
3. Mark all connectors for installation reference.
4. Remove nine screws holding front panel.
5. Fold front plate out toward interior.
6. Remove four instrument housing screws.
7. Remove connector(s) from back.
8. Reverse procedure to install.

9000

1. **On 1995–96 models,** obtain radio anti-theft code as outlined under "Precautions."
2. **On all models,** disconnect battery ground cable, then remove both speaker grilles on either side of instrument panel.
3. Remove instrument panel attaching screws, then the panel and duct.
4. Disconnect vacuum hose from turbo pressure gauge, then the speedometer cable and all connectors from instrument cluster.
5. Remove instrument cluster attaching screw, then the instrument cluster.
6. Reverse procedure to install.

RADIO

REPLACE

EXCEPT 1995–96 9000

1. Disconnect battery ground cable.
2. Remove radio knobs and face plate retaining nuts and washers.
3. Remove face plate and radio, then the rear radio support bracket if installed.
4. Remove antenna cable and electrical connections.
5. Reverse procedure to install.

1995–96 9000

1. Obtain radio anti-theft code as outlined under "Precautions."
2. Bend puller arms of radio puller tool No. 8471 161, or equivalent, to a 90° angle and insert into two holes on front of radio unit, **Fig. 16.**
3. Holding puller tool horizontal, pull out radio unit, then disconnect connections.
4. Connect connections, then insert radio unit into dash.

WIPER MOTOR

REPLACE

900

1993

The wiper assembly is an integral unit mounted on the bulkhead in the engine compartment. Two rectangular openings in the bulkhead accommodate the wiper spindles.

These openings are sealed with rubber grommets. Power from the motor is transferred to the spindles by means of a cable and linkage. The wiper arms are fitted in splines and retained by means of a nut, **Fig. 17.**

1. Lift wiper arm away from windshield, then lift cover and remove nut and wiper arm.
2. Remove rubber grommet.
3. Disconnect wiper motor electrical connector, then remove wiper motor bolts and motor assembly.
4. Reverse procedure to install.

1994–96

1. Pry off protective cap at base of wiper arms with screwdriver, then remove nut and lift off arm.
2. Disconnect washer hose for hood from protective cover space between bulkhead partitions.
3. Remove rubber sealing strip from partition.
4. Remove clip for protective cover over space between bulkhead partitions.
5. Raise cover slightly and disconnect washer hose from underside, then remove cover.
6. Remove connector from bracket, then unplug connector.
7. Remove spindle guide covers, then the three bolts securing wiper mechanism.
8. Lift out entire wiper unit, then remove linkages from bracket and motor, **Fig. 18.**
9. Remove three bolts securing motor to bracket and separate motor and bracket, **Fig. 19.**
10. Reverse procedure to install.

9000

1. **On 1995–96 models,** obtain radio antitheft code as outlined under "Precautions."

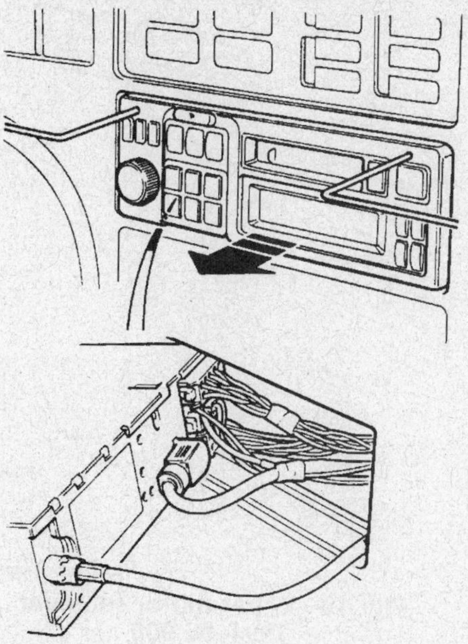

SA9039500001000X

Fig. 16 Radio removal. 1995–96 9000

2. **On all models,** disconnect battery ground cable.
3. Remove wiper arms by lifting covers and removing attaching nuts.
4. Remove rubber grommets from spindles.
5. Remove four bulkhead panel bolts from underneath hood.
6. Remove bulkhead for access to wiper motor.
7. Disconnect wiper motor electrical connectors.
8. Remove spindle nuts.
9. Remove four securing bolts for wiper motor bracket.
10. Push down and pull forward lefthand wiper pushrod.
11. Remove wiper motor with bracket and linkage. **To ease removal, hold electrical connectors under wiper motor bracket as wiper motor is removed.**
12. Remove bracket and linkage from wiper motor.
13. Reverse procedure to install.

WIPER SWITCH

REPLACE

Refer to "Turn Signal Switch, Replace" when replacing wiper switch.

WIPER TRANSMISSION

REPLACE

900

1993

The wiper assembly is an integral unit mounted on the bulkhead in the engine compartment. Two rectangular openings in the bulkhead accommodate the wiper spindles. These openings are sealed with rubber grommets. Power from the motor is transferred to the spindles by means of a cable and linkage. The wiper arms are fitted in splines and retained by means of a nut, **Fig. 17.** Refer to "Wiper Motor, Replace" for wiper transmission replacement procedure.

1994–96

The wiper assembly is an integral unit mounted on the bulkhead in the engine compartment. Power from the motor is transferred to the spindles by the transmission. The transmission is an integral part of the motor. Refer to "Wiper Motor, Replace" for wiper transmission replacement procedure.

9000

Refer to "Wiper Motor, Replace" for wiper transmission and motor replacement.

BLOWER MOTOR

REPLACE

900

1993

1. Disconnect battery ground cable, then remove steering wheel and cluster bezel retaining screws as outlined in "Instrument Cluster, Replace."
2. Tilt panel rearward and disconnect electrical connections and hose connections at vacuum distributor.
3. Remove panel, then the two speaker/defroster grilles.
4. Remove the upper instrument panel retaining screws at base of windshield and under glove compartment and remove panel.
5. Disconnect fan motor electrical connectors.
6. Remove righthand defroster valve housing retaining screws.
7. Remove fan motor retaining screws and fan motor.
8. Reverse procedure to install.

1994–96

1. Pry off protective cap at base of wiper arms with screwdriver, then remove nuts and lift off arms.
2. Remove cover over bulkhead, then disconnect washer hose to hood from protective cover over space between bulkhead partitions.
3. Remove rubber sealing strip from partition.
4. Remove protective cover clip from space between bulkhead partitions.
5. Raise cover slightly, then disconnect washer hose from underside and lift off cover.
6. Remove connector from bracket, then disconnect connector.
7. Remove cover for spindle guides, then the three wiper mechanism attaching bolts and windshield wiper unit.
8. Remove fresh-air filter, then disconnect ventilator fan electrical connector.
9. Remove screw holding electrical connection, then the ventilation fan screws and the ventilation fan.
10. Reverse procedure to install.

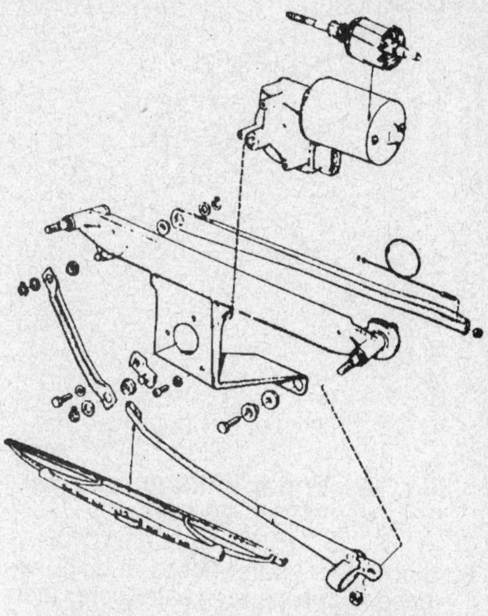

SA9029100001000X

Fig. 17 Exploded view of windshield wiper assembly. 1993 900

9000

1993–94

Less A/C

1. Disconnect battery ground cable, then remove wiper motor cover.
2. Remove air filter and disconnect electrical connectors to blower motor and resistor.
3. Disconnect temperature control cable, then release clips on either side of fan housing.
4. Rotate housing diagonally upwards, then push housing down.
5. Remove assembly by sliding toward righthand side of vehicle.
6. Remove screw in center of housing, then release clips and remove discharge grille.
7. Separate fan housing, then remove screw securing motor and the harness cover.
8. Remove motor and impeller from housing.

With A/C

1. Disconnect battery ground cable, then remove hood.
2. Remove wiper arms, wiper motor and evaporator covers.
3. **On models with automatic climate control,** disconnect wiring from blower motor controller.
4. **On all models,** remove false bulkhead panel and plastic drainage molding below windshield molding.
5. **On models less direct ignition,** remove ignition coil mounting bolts and position coil aside.
6. **On all models,** remove transmission retaining clip, then disconnect electrical connectors and remove wiper motor assembly.
7. Remove rubber lead-through panel for heater hoses and drain several quarts of coolant from cooling system.

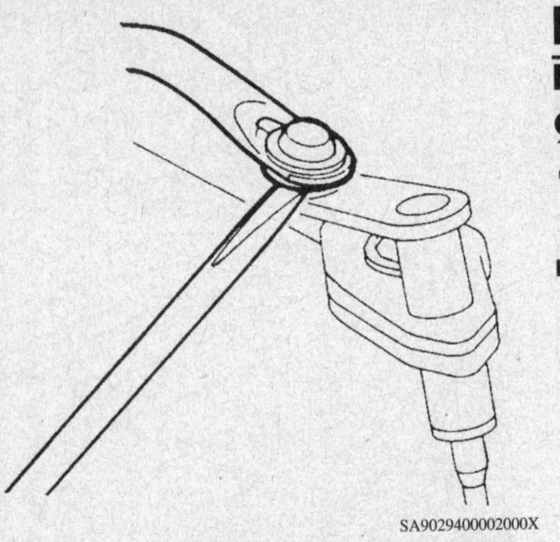
SA9029400002000X

Fig. 18 Wiper linkage removal. 1994–96 900

8. Disconnect heater hoses at quick release couplings for heater core, then remove throttle dashpot assembly.
9. Remove bolts securing cruise control vacuum pump and secure pump aside.
10. Remove evaporator housing retaining screws and refrigerant line clamps.
11. Remove lockwasher and disconnect temperature control cable.
12. Carefully raise evaporator unit and release clips securing blower housing, then remove blower assembly twisting unit diagonally upwards.
13. Remove screw in center of housing, then release clips and remove discharge grille. Separate fan housing.
14. Remove screw securing motor and harness cover, then remove motor and impeller from housing.
15. Reverse procedure to install. **Ensure care is taken not to separate electrical connector from radiator fan unit when installing false bulkhead panel.**

1995–96

1. Remove rubber strip and cover over bulkhead partition space, then disconnect washer hose.
2. Free righthand shield plates, then open brace over A/C lines.
3. Remove evaporator casing screws, then lift evaporator casing forward to gain access to servo motor screws.
4. Remove servo motor screws, then disconnect motor electrical connector and motor.
5. Position motor, then place evaporator casing in position. **Ensure drainage hose is not kinked and water can freely run out of evaporator casing and down drainage hose.**
6. Secure evaporator casing, then plug servo motor connector.
7. Lower brace over A/C lines, then install shield plates.
8. Connect washer hose to cover and secure cover and rubber strip over bulkhead partition space.
9. Calibrate system by pressing Auto and Vent buttons at same time. **When calibrating, all previous diagnostic trouble codes are erased. All stored diagnostic trouble codes should be read before calibration.**

HEATER CORE

REPLACE

900

1993

The heater core and water valve are removed as a unit.

1. Remove cover under switches on steering column.
2. Remove front center console, if equipped, and remove lower section of instrument panel.
3. Remove air diffuser retaining screws.
4. Remove lefthand defroster/speaker grille.
5. Remove control rod from between water valve and control knob by sliding the rod forward until released from knob.
6. Pull rod back to separate from water valve. **Plastic joint at control knob is accessible from underneath once switches below heater controls have been pressed backwards.**
7. Remove lower section of heater housing.
8. Partially drain cooling system, disconnect heater hoses in engine compartment, and plug open fittings on core and water valve.
9. Disconnect brake pedal return spring and depress pedal.
10. Remove heater core and water valve to the rear and downward past brake pedal.
11. Separate water valve and capillary tube, if equipped, from heater core.
12. Reverse procedure to install, using a new gasket between water valve and heater core.

1994–96

1. Install hose clips on hoses by heater core, then remove hoses from heater core.
2. Empty coolant from core using compressed air.
3. Remove glove compartment as follows:
   a. Open glove compartment, then the covers to expose retaining screws.
   b. Remove all retaining screws, retaining bolt and expanding rivet in front edge, then the catch from bulkhead bracket.
   c. Remove glove compartment and disconnect glove compartment lamp connector.
4. Remove center console side panels, then the ignition lock cover.
5. Remove rear ashtray, then the rear air vents and cover.
6. Remove screws attaching rear part of center console.
7. Remove power window switches, then the Automatic Climate Control (ACC) control unit.
8. Remove center console.
9. Cut off cable ties and remove rear air ducts on floor in front of heater core.
10. Open cover on heater core housing, then remove clips holding hoses to heater core.
11. Remove toggle clips on side of heater

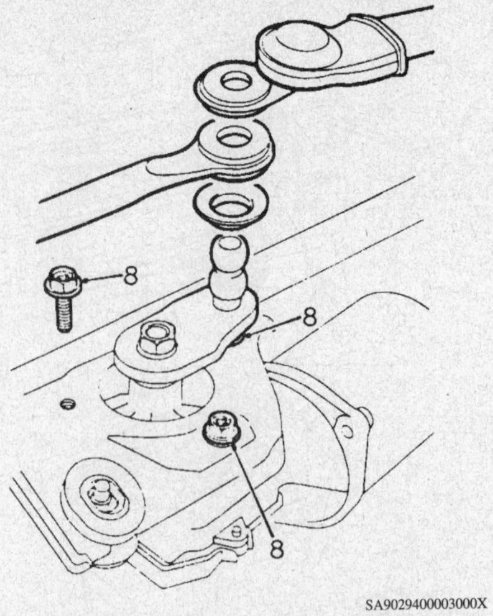
8
8
8
SA9029400003000X

Fig. 19 Wiper motor removal. 1994–96 900

core housing, then pull down hoses and remove heater core.
12. Reverse procedure to install, noting the following:
   a. Refill system with coolant.
   b. **On models equipped with 2.5L engine,** fill system to MAX level, then refit pressure lid. Start engine and run warm, preferably at varying speeds until radiator fan starts. Remove pressure lid and top up to MAX.
   c. **On all models,** refit pressure lid and run engine at varying speeds until radiator fan has started three more times. Switch off engine and top off to MAX level if necessary.

9000

1. **On 1995–96 models,** obtain radio anti-theft code as outlined under "Precautions."
2. **On all models,** disconnect battery ground cable and drain cooling system.
3. Remove blower motor as outlined under "Blower Motor, Replace."
4. Release clips and disconnect heater hoses from heater core.
5. Remove heater core from housing.
6. Reverse procedure to install. Use new O-rings when connecting heater hoses.

EVAPORATOR CORE

REPLACE

900

1993

1. Disconnect battery ground cable, then discharge refrigerant into an approved recovery/recycling device compatible with refrigerant type.
2. Disconnect hoses from evaporator outlet pipe and expansion valve. Cap all open lines.
3. Remove four evaporator mounting

bolts, then the evaporator and expansion valve as a unit.
4. Reverse procedure to install.

1994-96

If the evaporator has one-piece pipes between the evaporator and the lead-through in the bulkhead wall, the pipes must be cut before removal and a new evaporator installed.

1. Drain refrigerant into an approved recovery/recycling device compatible with refrigerant type.
2. Remove glove compartment as follows:
   a. Open glove compartment, then the covers to expose retaining screws.
   b. Remove all retaining screws, retaining bolt and expanding rivet in front edge, then the catch from bulkhead bracket.
   c. Remove glove compartment and disconnect glove compartment lamp connector.
3. Remove center console side panel, then the knee guard.
4. Remove air duct in floor, then the air duct to panel's side vent.
5. **On models equipped with automatic transaxle,** remove gearbox control unit from bracket on bulkhead wall and let hang on its cables.
6. **On all models,** remove evaporator bracket, then disconnect cables. Open cable ties and turn cables to one side.
7. Turn down carpet and remove protective cover.
8. **On models equipped with Automatic Climate Control (ACC),** remove fan control unit attaching screws.
9. **On models equipped with 2.3L engine,** remove screw holding A/C hoses PAD connection to expansion valve. Screw is accessible from engine compartment.
10. **On models equipped with 2.5L engine,** remove screws holding expansion valve, then the valve. Plug valve openings.
11. **On all models,** disconnect electrical connectors, then remove anti-frost thermostat.
12. Cut pipes with plate sheers and pull out evaporator from climate control.
13. Reverse procedure to install. **Torque** expansion valve screws 4 ft. lbs., or block screws 15 ft. lbs.

9000

1. **On 1995–96 models,** obtain radio anti-theft code as outlined under "Precautions."
2. **On all models,** disconnect battery ground cable, then discharge refrigerant into an approved recovery/recycling device compatible with refrigerant type.
3. Remove false bulkhead panel in engine compartment and top bolt from oil filler pipe support.
4. Disconnect refrigerant lines from receiver inlet and evaporator outlet. Plug lines and open fittings.
5. Remove plastic bushing from panel and secure refrigerant lines aside.
6. Remove vacuum pump for cruise control system.
7. Disconnect electrical connectors from fan control unit, air recirculation valve motor, thermostat and pressure switch.
8. Remove bolts securing engine mount bracket and insert rubber mallet between brace and engine.
9. Remove bolts securing evaporator housing.
10. Lift up on end of housing, move assembly toward center, then remove housing assembly from vehicle.
11. Remove fresh air filter and receiver mounting screw.
12. Remove insulation, clip and sensor body, then disconnect capillary tube and expansion valve from evaporator.
13. Remove receiver and expansion valve as an assembly. Plug all open fittings.
14. Remove thermostat assembly and actuating motor for air recirculation valve.
15. Separate housing and remove evaporator.
16. Reverse procedure to install.

Engine

NOTE: On Air Bag Equipped Models, Refer To "Air Bag System Precautions" Located In The Front Of This Manual For System Disarming & Arming Procedures.

INDEX

	Page No.
Belt Tension Data	38-28
Camshaft, Replace	38-25
Cooling System Bleed	38-28
2.0L & 2.3L Engines	38-28
2.5L & 3.0L Engines	38-28
Crankshaft Seal, Replace	38-25
900	38-25
9000	38-26
Cylinder Head, Replace	38-19
900	38-19
9000	38-21
Engine Rebuilding Specifications	38-164
Engine, Replace	38-14
900	38-14
9000	38-16
Front Cover Seal, Replace	38-23
900	38-23
9000	38-23
Fuel Pump, Replace	38-29
900	38-29
9000	38-29
Intake Air Heat Plates, Replace	38-19
900	38-19
Intake Manifold, Replace	38-18
1994–96 900	38-18
9000 & 1993 900	38-18
Main & Rod Bearings	38-25
Oil Pan, Replace	38-26
900	38-26
9000	38-26
Oil Pump, Replace	38-27
900	38-27
9000	38-27
Pistons, Pins & Rings	38-25
Precautions	38-14
Air Bag Systems	38-14
Radio Anti-Theft Lock	38-14
Serpentine Drive Belt	38-28
Routing	38-28
Testing	38-28
Tightening Specifications	38-31
900	38-31
9000	38-32
Timing Belt, Replace	38-24
2.5L Engine	38-24
3.0L Engine	38-24
Timing Chain, Replace	38-23
Except 3.0L Engine	38-23
Turbocharger, Replace	38-29
900	38-29
9000	38-30
Valve Adjustment	38-22
Valve Clearance Specifications	38-22
Valve Guides	38-22
Valve Seats	38-23
Water Pump, Replace	38-28
900	38-28
9000	38-28

PRECAUTIONS

AIR BAG SYSTEMS

Refer to "Air Bag System Precautions" in the front of this manual for system disarming and arming procedures.

RADIO ANTI-THEFT LOCK

9000

1995-96

Radio and cassette player are equipped with an electronic four-digit anti-theft lock. This four-digit code is programmed at manufacturing and cannot be changed. If the battery is disconnected for more than three minutes, if unit is removed or if otherwise cut off from power, the four-digit code must be entered with the quick-selection buttons as follows:

1. Turn radio on, then, when display shows "Code In, " enter four-digit code with quick-selection buttons. If code is correct, last-tuned radio frequency is shown on display. If wrong digit has been entered by mistake, all four digits must be entered again. If code is wrong it stays on display.
2. If incorrect four-digit code has been entered, press Band button for more than three seconds to clear display. Display shows "Code In" and new attempt to enter correct code can be made.
3. If wrong code has been used three times in succession, four dashes appear on display and you must wait an hour with radio switched on before trying again.
4. To try again, hold Band button for at least three seconds. "Code In" should appear on display.
5. Correct code must be entered at first attempt, otherwise you must wait another hour with unit switched on before trying again.

ENGINE

REPLACE

900

1993

On these vehicles, the engine and transaxle must be removed as a complete unit.

1. Scribe hood hinge locations and remove hood.
2. Install spacer tool No. 83 93 209, or equivalent, under upper control arm on righthand side.
3. Disconnect battery positive cable.
4. Drain cooling system.
5. Loosen lug nuts on righthand front wheel.
6. Raise front of vehicle and support with jackstands under forward jacking points.
7. Shift transaxle to R.
8. Remove tapered pin from gear shift rod joint.
9. Disconnect speedometer cable, then remove exhaust pipe-to-clamp bracket attaching bolt from transaxle.
10. Loosen boot bands on inner universal joints and slide boots away.
11. Remove righthand front wheel and tire assembly.
12. Separate ball joint from lower control arm.
13. Separate universal joint and position steering knuckle aside.
14. Disconnect battery positive cable from body clips.
15. Disconnect ground cable from transaxle.
16. Disconnect starter motor leads.
17. Disconnect exhaust pipe from exhaust manifold.
18. Disconnect and plug pressure line from power steering pump.
19. Remove A/C compressor drive belt.
20. Disconnect coolant hoses from heat exchanger valve, expansion tank, thermostat housing and bottom of radiator.
21. Disconnect the following electrical connectors from components on lefthand side of engine:
    a. Air mass meter.
    b. Throttle switch.
    c. AIC actuator.
    d. Injection valves.
    e. Thermostatic switch.
    f. Ground connectors at forward lifting lug.
22. Disconnect the following electrical connectors from components on righthand side of engine:
    a. A/C compressor.
    b. Alternator and regulator.
    c. Blue wire at oil pressure switch.
    d. AIC actuator.
    e. Yellow/white wire at temperature sensor.
    f. Gray wire at knock sensor.
23. Disconnect electrical connector from clip on fuel injection manifold, from rear of engine and from coolant hose between engine and coolant overflow tank.
24. Remove harness from engine compartment and position aside.
25. Remove alternator drive belt, then unfasten alternator and position aside.
26. Disconnect brake servo hose from intake manifold, then unfasten throttle cable.
27. Unfasten A/C compressor and position aside.
28. Disconnect fuel lines from front of fuel injection manifold and fuel pressure regulator.
29. Remove ignition coil, then disconnect turbo pressure line from turbocharger and induction air cooler/throttle housing.
30. Remove auxiliary engine cooling fan.
31. Remove turbocharger air mass meter together with suction pipe.
32. Disconnect vacuum hoses from solenoid valve and the crankcase ventilation from suction pipe.
33. Disconnect electrical connector from Hall switch and coil in distributor.
34. Unfasten Hall switch cable from clips on clutch cover.
35. Disconnect solenoid valve hoses from turbocharger and charging pressure regulator.
36. Disconnect and plug hydraulic line from slave cylinder.
37. Remove engine mounting bolts.
38. Attach lifting equipment to engine and raise engine until lefthand inner universal joint can be disconnected.
39. Continue to raise engine and disconnect oil cooler hoses and power steering pump hose, then remove engine from vehicle.
40. To separate engine and transaxle, proceed as follows:
    a. Drain engine oil.
    b. Remove EGR pipe.
    c. Remove clutch cover, oil dipstick pipe and oil return pipe from turbocharger.
    d. Remove turbocharger bracket.
    e. Using slide hammer tool No. 83 90 270 and joint tool No. 87 90 529, or equivalents, remove clutch shaft.
    f. Remove three slave cylinder retaining bolts.
    g. Remove all engine to transaxle attaching bolts, noting length and position for reassembly.
    h. Release clip for oil filler pipe at intake manifold.
    i. Carefully lift engine off transaxle. At the same time, remove slave cylinder with release bearing guide sleeve and bearing. **If engine and transaxle fail to separate, do not attempt to force them apart without first ensuring all bolts are removed.**
41. Reverse procedure to install, noting the following:
    a. Ensure mating surfaces of engine and transaxle are clean and the two guide sleeves are fitted in transaxle.
    b. Install a new gasket to transaxle mating surface. Apply sealing compound to both sides of gasket and six bolts. Refer to "Oil Pan, Replace." **Ensure bolts are correctly installed, as bolts are different lengths.**

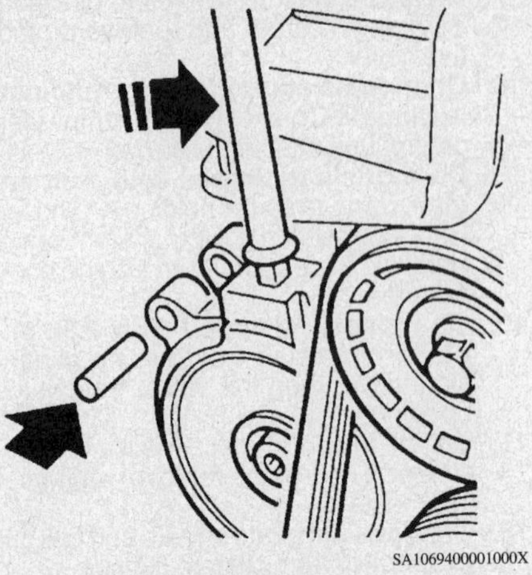
SA1069400001000X
Fig. 1 Belt tensioner loosening. 1994–96 900 w/2.0L & 2.3L engines

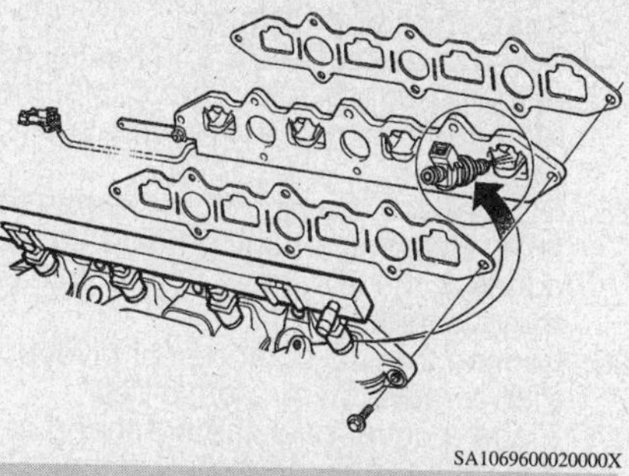

Fig. 2 Intake air heat plate replacement

c. Tighten engine to transaxle bolts to specifications.
d. **Ensure there is at least .4 inch clearance around throttle controls.**

1994–96

2.0L & 2.3L Engines

1. Remove battery, then drain coolant. Remove filler cap on expansion tank to speed draining.
2. Remove air cleaner with hoses, then the cover or resonator.
3. Detach throttle cable and position aside.
4. Remove cruise control unit with cable as follows:
   a. Disconnect cruise control cable from throttle body, then disconnect electrical connector.
   b. Remove cruise control retaining bolts.
   c. Remove cruise control and cable from vehicle.
5. Disconnect fuel hoses using fuel line separator tool No. 83 94 702, or equivalent.
6. Disconnect tank breather hose and position aside.
7. **On turbo models,** remove pressure sensor and place it on engine.
8. **On all models,** disconnect secondary injection vacuum hose, then the brake servo vacuum hose from intake manifold.
9. **On turbo models,** remove boost pressure control and place it on engine.
10. **On all models,** loosen belt tensioner using ratchet handle extension and 6 mm drill, **Fig. 1. Use care to ensure belt tensioner does not break at its end position.**
11. Remove servo pump from bracket and set aside.
12. **On turbo models,** remove pressure pipe between charge air cooler and throttle body.
13. **On all models,** remove coolant hoses, then the secondary air injection hose.
14. Disconnect A/C compressor connector and remove compressor upper retaining bolts.
15. Disconnect positive lead from positive terminal block on engine, then the ground cable from gearbox.
16. **On models equipped with B206i and B234i engines,** remove ignition cable and electrical leads from ignition coil.
17. **On all models,** disconnect gearbox electrical connectors and place on engine.
18. Disconnect oxygen sensor lead and catalytic converter temperature warning lead.
19. **On models equipped with automatic transaxle,** remove breather hose from gearbox, then the selector lever cable.
20. **On models equipped with manual transaxle or Sensonic,** separate selector rod, then the clutch cable or clutch pipe and plug.
21. **On all models,** remove glove compartment.
22. Pull back carpet and unplug central locking system control module, then remove engine wiring.
23. Pull wiring through grommet into engine bay and place on engine. **On turbo models, do not forget lead running to BPC.**
24. Loosen hub nuts on both sides of vehicle, then raise and support vehicle.
25. Remove front wheels, then remove hub nuts.
26. Remove brake calipers and hang from suspension struts.
27. Remove end piece nut, then the steering swivel member nuts.
28. Remove wheel housing covers and spoiler sections.
29. Disconnect front pipe and intermediate pipe, then remove front exhaust pipe from exhaust manifold or turbocharger.
30. Remove catalytic converter from bracket and take down exhaust pipe.
31. **On models equipped with automatic transaxle,** disconnect oil hoses from gearbox and position aside. Plug holes.
32. **On turbo models,** remove pipe between turbocharger and charge air cooler, then disconnect oil hoses from oil cooler. Plug hoses.
33. **On all models,** position suitable lifting table under vehicle so table supports are directly under front engine mountings and gearbox.
34. Remove bolts retaining subframe and front engine mountings, then slightly lower table along with powertrain and sub-frame.
35. Disconnect end pieces and driveshafts on both sides.
36. Remove A/C compressor and hang from tow rope attachment eye.
37. Lower lifting table fully and remove rear engine mounting from gearbox and remove subframe.
38. Reverse procedure to install. Fill cooling system and check for leaks.

2.5L Engine

1. Remove battery, then drain coolant. Remove filler cap on expansion tank to speed draining.
2. Remove two engine covers, then the complete air cleaner assembly by disconnecting hose clip and electrical connectors and removing retaining screws.
3. Disconnect throttle cable and position aside.
4. Remove cruise control unit with cable as follows:
   a. Expose ball in throttle and release cable from clip in bulkhead partition.
   b. Disconnect electrical connectors on cruise control system.
   c. Remove retaining screws.
5. Remove two fuel connections. Plug lines.
6. Disconnect tank breather hose and position aside, then the brake servo vacuum hose.
7. Remove top radiator hose.
8. Remove radiator fan cowl as follows:
   a. Disconnect two electrical connectors, then the power steering pipe from radiator member and battery tray.
   b. Remove fan cowl retaining screws.
   c. Carefully lift out fan cowl.
9. Disconnect bottom radiator hose from engine.
10. Slightly loosen belt pulley bolts, then relieve belt tension and position aside.
11. Remove power steering pump pulley, then the two power steering pump retaining bolts and pump.
12. Disconnect A/C compressor electrical connector and clip, then remove compressor upper retaining bolts.
13. Disconnect radiator hose connected to throttle body at expansion tank.
14. Disconnect hoses connected to heater core at engine and position aside.
15. Disconnect radiator hose from expansion tank at engine.
16. **On models equipped with automatic transaxle,** disconnect two transaxle wiring harness connectors behind battery and place cables on powertrain.
17. **On models equipped with manual transaxle,** remove reversing light switch.
18. **On all models,** disconnect positive battery cable, then disconnect grounding connection on gearbox and tuck cable out of way.
19. **On models equipped with automatic transaxle,** proceed as follows:
   a. Remove breather hose from transaxle casing and plug hole in transaxle casing.
   b. Remove nut securing selector lever cable, then remove cable.
20. **On models equipped with manual transaxle,** proceed as follows:
   a. Engage 4th gear, then separate selector rod.
   b. Engage 3rd gear with gear lever, then disconnect clutch cable.
21. **On all models,** remove engine wiring harness as follows:
   a. Remove glove compartment and air ducts, then fold up carpet.
   b. Remove knee shield, then remove engine wiring harness from inside of vehicle.
   c. From engine bay, pull wiring harness through lead-through into engine bay, then place wiring on engine.
22. Loosen hub center nuts on both front wheels, then raise and support vehicle.
23. Remove both front wheels and remove

hub center nuts.
24. Remove brake calipers and suspend from struts, then the steering swivel joint nuts.
25. Remove cover in righthand wheel housing and spoiler sections.
26. Raise vehicle higher, then unplug oxygen sensor connectors.
27. Remove front exhaust pipe or separate joint between front and center exhaust pipe sections as necessary.
28. Loosen bolt in A/C compressor bracket. **Bolt cannot be removed in this position.**
29. **On models equipped with automatic transaxle,** remove oil pipes from transaxle casing and plug holes.
30. **On all models,** place suitable lifting trolley under vehicle and arrange so trolley holders are directly below front engine mountings and gearbox.
31. Remove subframe retaining bolts, then the front engine mountings from body.
32. Lower trolley about .98 inches along with subframe and powertrain. Ensure steering swivel joints come away and lift out driveshafts.
33. Remove A/C compressor and suspend from tow rope attachment eye with cable ties.
34. Fully lower trolley, then remove rear engine mounting nut. Pull subframe away to rear.
35. Reverse procedure to install, noting the following:
    a. Install new gaskets.
    b. **Ensure gearbox is grounded. Failure to ground gearbox could cause fire.**
    c. Fill cooling system and check for leaks.

9000

1993

1. Raise and support front of vehicle, then remove fill panel from under spoiler.
2. Remove coolant drain plug and drain coolant, then lower vehicle.
3. Remove battery, fuel filter strap, then position filter aside.
4. Remove ABS steady bar, then disconnect all necessary electrical connectors.
5. Remove all cables, ties and clips from the battery shelf.
6. Disconnect ABS five-pin connector, the positive battery lead from the battery shelf terminal block and the negative lead from the terminal block on the wing.
7. Move battery leads aside, then remove the battery shelf.
8. Disconnect electrical connectors and hose from the washer fluid level sensor and pump, then remove two screws and the reservoir.
9. Disconnect electrical connector from the air mass meter, release toggle fasteners on the air cleaner body and turbo inlet hose clip, then lift out the air mass meter and air cleaner top.
10. Disconnect electrical connector from the solenoid valve, remove two screws

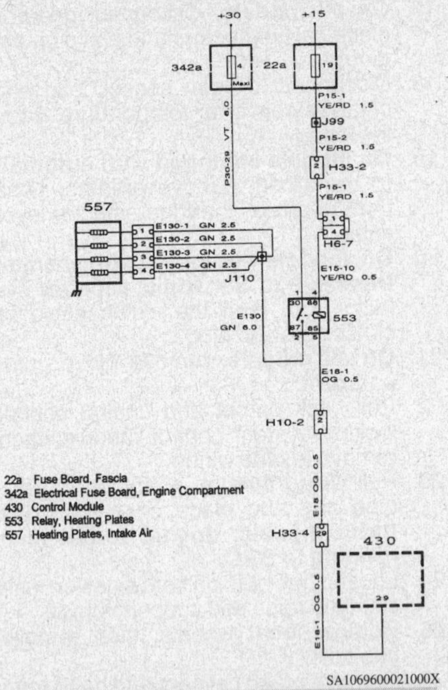
22a Fuse Board, Fascia
342a Electrical Fuse Board, Engine Compartment
430 Control Module
553 Relay, Heating Plates
557 Heating Plates, Intake Air
SA1069600021000X

Fig. 3 Intake air heat plate system wiring diagram. 900 series

and lift valve towards the block.
11. Disconnect the coil high tension lead and the Hall-sensor from the distributor, then remove upper radiator hose.
12. Remove the hose clips from the turbo delivery pipe, disconnect the bypass valve and pressure hose from the transmission, then remove the turbo pipe.
13. Disconnect throttle cable from the linkage, then the fuel return hose from the fuel-pressure regulator. Place hose against the false bulkhead panel.
14. Disconnect fuel supply hose from the fuel rail and position aside. Remove the lefthand cover over the false bulkhead.
15. Remove rubber seal, retaining screws, then the false bulkhead.
16. Disconnect securing strap, then remove ABS control unit and bracket.
17. Disconnect ABS control unit from the lefthand system and position aside.
18. Remove the lefthand system ECU and bracket, then disconnect all the electrical connectors from the engine main wiring harness.
19. Remove the TSI socket. **Use small suitable screwdriver to press back catch on violet/white lead (pin 2) and gray/red lead (pin 1), then remove pins.**
20. Disconnect the vacuum hose between the pressure sensor and the intake manifold, then the heater core hoses.
21. Disconnect the road speed sensor connector, then pull it through the hole in the bottom of the bulkhead panel.
22. Remove the clip securing the kickdown cable to gear selector cable and pipe from the steering servo pump.
23. Disconnect cooler hoses from automatic transmission. **Cap all open hose ends and fittings.**
24. Remove gear selector and rod linkage retaining nut. Slacken the cable, then remove it from the clip and position aside.
25. Disconnect hoses from expansion tank. Remove retaining bolt, then disconnect the electrical connector and remove tank.
26. Loosen the A/C compressor pivot bolt, then remove the A/C drive belt.
27. Place a cover over the righthand section of the radiator crossmember. Disconnect the A/C compressor connector, then the coolant hose from the water pump and lift the compressor and hose onto the radiator crossmember. Secure the compressor aside.
28. Remove the three Lambda lead connectors, then the lambda sensor from the intake manifold.
29. Remove the torque arm, then the top engine mount.
30. Remove the bottom radiator hose, then the turbo delivery pipe.
31. Remove the turbo unit to exhaust attaching nuts, then disconnect lower pipe.
32. Remove to retaining bolts, then loosen the bottom bolts for the oil cooler. Disconnect oil cooler lines, then remove cooler and secure aside. Remove the power steering reservoir
33. Disconnect steering servo delivery hose from the pump. **Cap all open lines and fittings.**
34. Remove intake manifold to charcoal canister vacuum hose, then the nuts from the righthand side engine mounts.
35. Remove lefthand engine mount, then raise and support the vehicle.
36. Remove the front wheels, then the clips for the gaiters over the driveshaft joints.
37. Loosen the MacPherson strut retaining bolts, then disconnect strut from suspension.
38. Separate the driveshaft from the spindle, then cap all ends to prevent contamination.
39. Remove lower cooling fan bolt, lower the vehicle, then remove the top cooling fan bolts and the fan.
40. Attach lifting sling tool No. 83 94 439, or equivalent, to lifting lugs on the engine. Ensure transmission is heavier end when lifted.
41. Disconnect hood struts, then attach extensions tool No. 83 94 439, or equivalent, to lifting sling.
42. Slowly raise engine and transaxle.
43. Reverse procedure to install.

1994–96

2.0L & 2.3L Engines

1. Raise and support vehicle, then remove front wheels.
2. Remove wheel housing trim molding and righthand side front wing liner.
3. Remove middle fill panel from under spoiler.
4. Remove radiator drain plug and drain

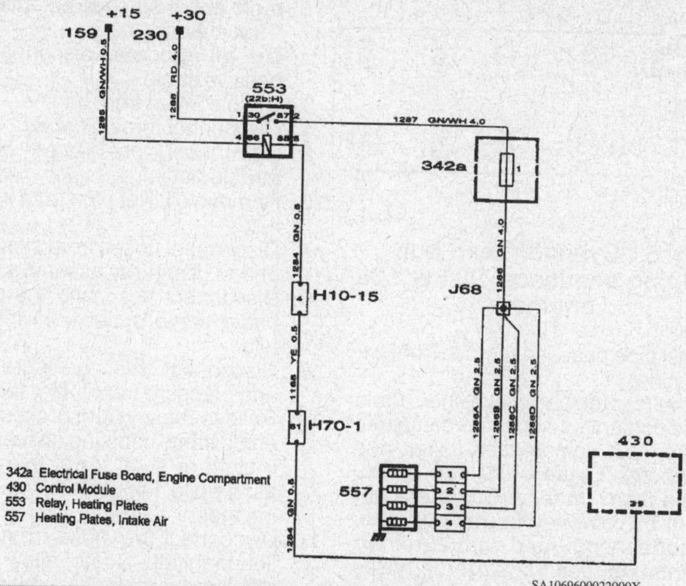
+15
+30
159
230
1285 GN/WH 0.5
1288 RD 4.0
553
(22b:H)
1287 GN/WH 4.0
342a
1284 GN 0.8
1286 GN 4.0
H10-15
J68
1166 YE 0.5
1286A GN 2.5
1286B GN 2.5
1286C GN 2.5
1286D GN 2.5
H70-1
430
342a Electrical Fuse Board, Engine Compartment
430 Control Module
553 Relay, Heating Plates
557 Heating Plates, Intake Air
557
1284 GN 0.8

SA1069600022000X

Fig. 4 Intake air heat plate system wiring diagram. 9000 series

coolant. Lower vehicle and remove filler cap from expansion tank to speed drainage.

5. Remove throttle cable retaining clip and position cable aside.
6. Remove front main fuse box, then the positive cable terminal block.
7. **On 1995–96 models,** obtain radio anti-theft code as outlined under "Precautions."
8. **On all models,** disconnect positive cable, then remove clamp from tray.
9. Disconnect ABS control module electrical connector, then remove battery tray.
10. Disconnect negative cable from gearbox grounding point.
11. Disconnect windshield washer hose and remove bulkhead space cover and rubber molding from bulkhead partition.
12. Remove clamp securing engine wiring harness to bulkhead partition, then disconnect connector.
13. Disconnect pressure sensor electric lead, then place sensor on engine.
14. Remove bulkhead partition, then snip through cable on righthand side.
15. Disconnect pressure sensor cable, then position aside.
16. Remove ABS relay box and brake fluid reservoirs from holders.
17. Snip through cable tie on lefthand side, then disconnect two engine wiring harness connectors.
18. Disconnect control module connector, then snip through cable tie and separate engine wiring harness in connector. Bend wiring up onto engine.
19. Disconnect expansion tank hoses and connector, then remove expansion tank.
20. Loosen automatic belt tensioner by pulling belt hard upward while assistant fits locking yoke tool No. 83 94 448, or equivalent, in place to secure tensioner. Ease belt off A/C compressor pulley.
21. Disconnect A/C compressor electrical connector, then remove retaining bolts and rest compressor on radiator crossmember.
22. Disconnect return fuel hose from fuel pressure sensor and bend hose up against bulkhead partition.
23. Disconnect fuel delivery hose from fuel rail and vacuum hose from evaporative emission canister on intake manifold, then the brake servo hose. Position hose aside.
24. Disconnect interference suppressor cable (ground) from torque arm bracket.
25. Snip through cable ties holding hoses and wiring at upper torque arm, then remove torque arm.
26. Remove torque arm bracket, then disconnect oxygen sensor electrical connector below intake manifold.
27. Disconnect oxygen sensor cable, then remove power steering fluid reservoir. Lower reservoir and siphon off fluid.
28. Disconnect power steering pump suction hose from reservoir and bend it under intake manifold. Stand reservoir on bulkhead.
29. Disconnect solenoid valve connector, then remove solenoid valve from holder and position valve up against engine.
30. Remove intake hose between air cleaner and turbo, then the filter insert from air cleaner.
31. Remove delivery pipe between turbo and charge air cooler.
32. Remove bypass valve from hose, then the delivery pipe between charge air cooler and throttle body with bypass valve.
33. Remove upper coolant hose, then disconnect heat exchanger hoses from engine.
34. Remove coolant hose from water pump, then separate vacuum hose between intake manifold and turbo instrument.
35. Remove kickdown cable, then the gear selector arm from gearbox **Do not separate ball joint.**
36. **On models equipped with manual transaxle,** separate gear selector rod by moving tapered pin.
37. **On all models,** press out gear selector cable rubber bushing from gearbox casing bracket.
38. **On models equipped with manual transaxle,** separate clutch pipe.
39. **On all models,** disconnect oil cooler hoses from gearbox, then remove front exhaust pipe and bolts securing front exhaust pipe to exhaust manifold.
40. Remove catalytic converter top mounting bolt, then raise and support vehicle.
41. Remove catalytic converter mounting bolt, then the front exhaust pipe rear connecting flange bolts. Carefully lower front exhaust pipe, being sure not to damage oxygen sensor.
42. Disconnect two oil cooler hoses from engine, then the power steering pump delivery hose from pump. Plug hose.
43. Remove clips around rubber gaiters secured to driveshaft joints.
44. Remove two strut electric leads, then the brake hoses.
45. Remove bottom strut bolts from steering swivel members.
46. Pull out steering swivel members to separate driveshaft joints. Fit protective caps over both halves of driveshaft joints.
47. Remove radiator fan lower retaining bolt, then lower vehicle and remove radiator fan upper retaining bolts.
48. Disconnect radiator fan wiring harness and remove fan.
49. Remove three engine mounting bolts, then the gas springs from hood. Fit gas spring extension tool No. 83 94 439, or equivalent, on springs.
50. Hook suitable engine lifting yoke to engine lifting eyes and raise engine slightly. Ensure engine is suspended in balance. If it is not, lower engine again and rebalance upper lifting yoke.
51. Reverse procedure to install, noting the following:
    a. **On models equipped with manual transaxle,** insert tapered pin, then install clutch pipes and bleed system.
    b. **On all models,** tighten fasteners to specifications.
    c. **Ensure gearbox is grounded. Failure to ground gearbox could cause fire.**
    d. After refilling cooling system, check for leaks.

3.0L Engine

1. Obtain radio anti-theft code as outlined under "Precautions."
2. Disconnect battery cables, then remove battery.
3. Disconnect front electrical distribution box from battery shelf, then remove distribution box.

4. Disconnect cruise control cable from lever.
5. Remove positive terminal block from battery shelf and take off clamp for positive lead.
6. Pull vacuum hose from battery shelf clamps, then remove cable conduit fastenings and battery shelf bolts.
7. Slightly raise battery shelf and disconnect cruise control electrical connector, then remove battery shelf with cruise control module and cable.
8. Release throttle cable from bracket, then snap out control rod and fold bracket to one side.
9. Remove pipes complete with resonator as follows:
   a. Disconnect hose clamps between inlet pipes and intake manifold.
   b. Disconnect hose clamps between resonator and mass air flow sensor.
   c. Raise pipes and disconnect vacuum hoses and electrical connectors.
10. Disconnect secondary air injection hoses from check valves and cut cable tie at resonator bracket.
11. Remove bulkhead plate seal, then the cover, disconnecting washer hoses.
12. Disconnect fuel pipe clamps from bulkhead plate, then remove bulkhead plate bolts and raise plate.
13. Disconnect Motronic control module electrical connector and separate engine wiring harness, pulling wiring through engine compartment and removing bulkhead plate.
14. Disconnect torque arm engine mounting lead, then remove power steering servo oil reservoir and torque arm.
15. Turn power steering belt tensioner pulley forward to release load from tensioner, then move belt to one side.
16. Disconnect power steering servo pump and remove clamp from servo pipe, then position pump and reservoir aside.
17. **On models equipped with automatic transaxle,** disconnect gear selector cable.
18. **On all models,** disconnect rear oxygen sensor and release electrical connectors from bracket.
19. **On models equipped with automatic transaxle,** disconnect oil hoses from transaxle. Plug hoses and install bolts into transaxle.
20. **On all models,** disconnect fuel hoses, then ease expansion tank lid.
21. Slightly raise and support vehicle, then remove both front wheels.
22. Disconnect steering knuckle housings from MacPherson struts and remove clamps around inner universal joint gaiters. Pull universal joints apart and install covers over halves.
23. Raise vehicle further and support, then remove oxygen sensor, knock sensor and crankshaft position sensor lead clamp from cylinder block.
24. Disconnect oxygen sensor, knock sensor and crankshaft position sensor electrical connectors, then remove from bracket.
25. Separate exhaust pipe at front joint, then remove exhaust manifold to front exhaust pipe nuts and remove front exhaust pipe.

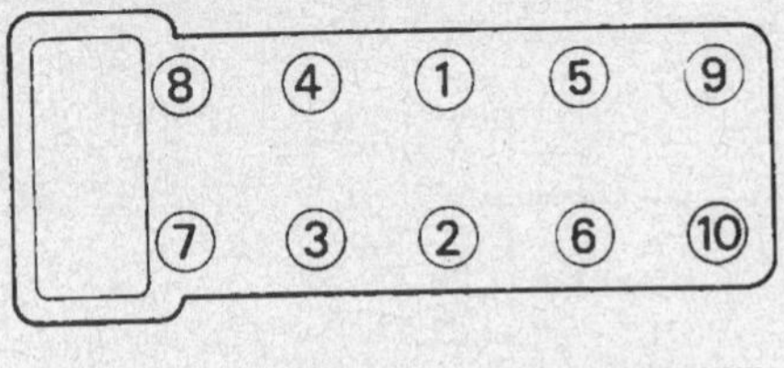
8
4
1
5
9
7
3
2
6
10

SA1069100002000X

Fig. 5 Cylinder head bolt tightening sequence. 900 w/2.3L engine

26. Remove center air shield, then drain engine coolant into suitable container.
27. Loosen A/C compressor lower and upper bolts. **These bolts can be accessed from under A/C system but cannot be removed in this position.**
28. **On models equipped with automatic transaxle,** pull transaxle oil hoses forward.
29. **On all models,** lower vehicle and disconnect upper, then the lower radiator hoses from engine. Pull lower radiator hoses forward.
30. Disconnect heat exchanger hoses, then the expansion tank hose.
31. Raise power steering servo pump and oil reservoir, then the brake servo vacuum hose from intake manifold.
32. Disconnect positive lead from positive terminal block, then the grounding lead from gearbox.
33. Remove A/C compressor bolts, then the compressor.
34. Disconnect rear and righthand engine mounting and install extender tool No. 83 94 439, or equivalent, on engine hood gas springs.
35. Install lifting yoke tool No. 83 92 409, or equivalent, on suitable engine lift and engine, then remove lefthand engine mounting.
36. Lift engine slightly, then remove resonator bracket.
37. Remove engine from vehicle.
38. Reverse procedure to install, noting the following:
    a. Adjust throttle cable adjusting screw so stops on throttle body are no more than .0118 inch from end position, as checked with suitable feeler gauge. Adjusting screw is on front underside of throttle cable control bracket.
    b. Fill cooling system with suitable coolant as specified.
    c. Fill engine with suitable engine oil as specified.
    d. Bleed cooling system as outlined under "Cooling System Bleed," then test drive vehicle.

INTAKE MANIFOLD

REPLACE

9000 & 1993 900

Except 3.0L Engine

1. **On 1995–96 9000 models,** obtain radio anti-theft code as outlined under "Precautions."
2. **On all models,** disconnect battery positive cable.
3. Drain coolant from engine.
4. Disconnect throttle cable.
5. Disconnect pre-heater hose from throttle body.
6. Remove oil filler pipe from intake manifold.
7. Disconnect hoses from signal converter and distributor assembly.
8. Disconnect hose and tee piece from brake servo outlet from intake manifold.
9. Disconnect fuel pressure regulator and pressure transmitter tee hoses.
10. Relieve fuel system pressure by loosening banjo coupling on fuel filter. Hold a cloth or shop towel round the coupling while doing this to soak up escaping fuel.
11. Disconnect fuel hose from fuel injection manifold. Do not allow fuel to drip onto starter motor assembly.
12. Disconnect fuel return line from fuel pressure regulator outlet.
13. Disconnect turbocharger pressure pipe from throttle body.
14. Disconnect throttle switch, auxiliary air valve, temperature sensor (NTC resistor) and injection valve electrical connectors.
15. Loosen intake manifold to throttle body attaching bracket bar bolts.
16. Disconnect breather hose from camshaft cover.
17. Loosen intake manifold attaching bolts, then lift intake manifold assembly from engine.
18. Reverse procedure to install. Tighten intake manifold bolts to specifications.

3.0L Engine

For intake manifold replacement, refer to "Cylinder Head, Replace."

1994–96 900

2.0L & 2.3L Engines

1. **On turbo models,** remove cowl.
2. **On non-turbo models,** remove resonator.
3. **On all models,** remove crankcase breather hose and idle adjusting valve.
4. Disconnect pressure and return fuel lines from fuel injection manifold using fuel line separator tool No. 83 94 702, or equivalent.
5. Remove four fuel injection manifold retaining bolts (two at each end), then the two protective covers.
6. Disconnect injector electrical leads, then carefully remove fuel injection manifold.
7. Remove injector to injection manifold locking clips, then the injector.
8. **On turbo models equipped with intake air heat plates,** remove heat plate assembly as outlined under "Intake Air Heat Plates, Replace."
9. **On all models,** reverse procedure to install. Lubricate all O-rings with petroleum jelly before installing.

2.5L Engine

1. Remove engine protective covers, then the hose clip securing rubber duct.
2. Disconnect IAC valve hose and rear knock sensor electrical connector from duct.
3. Remove rubber duct, then the intake manifold retaining bar and cable conduits.
4. Disconnect throttle and cruise control cables from throttle lever and bracket.
5. Disconnect brake servo and crankcase breather vacuum hoses.
6. Remove seven nuts securing upper half of intake manifold, then lift upper half of inlet manifold and support with rubber mallet.
7. Disconnect connectors from injectors, then remove fuel lines and vacuum hose from pressure regulator.
8. Remove seven fuel injection manifold retaining bolts, then use screwdriver to jiggle out manifold.
9. Remove injectors from fuel injection manifold, then the pressure regulator.
10. Reverse procedure to install, noting the following:
    a. Inspect O-rings at both ends of injectors and smear with petroleum jelly to ease installation.
    b. Tighten all manifold flange bolts and inlet manifold retaining bar to specifications.
    c. Ensure pressure regulator vacuum hose is connected to front nipple on throttle body in front of butterfly.

INTAKE AIR HEAT PLATES

REPLACE

900

On the low emission version of the turbo equipped engine, intake air heat plates have been added to further minimize exhaust emission, **Fig. 2.** The four intake air heat plates are integrated in one assembly, mounted between the intake manifold and cylinder head. During warm-up, the intake air heat plates vaporize injected fuel. This vaporization of fuel reduces the need for fuel enrichment, thereby reducing exhaust emissions. Heating of the intake air heat plates begins upon start-up and ceases when engine temperature reaches 185°F or four minutes after start-up.

There are no diagnostic trouble codes for the intake air heat plate system. When troubleshooting intake air heat plate assembly electrical circuits, refer to **Figs. 3 and 4.**

1. Disconnect battery ground cable.
2. Drain engine coolant.
3. Remove charge air bypass hose, turbocharger delivery pipe and charge air cooler. Plug charge air cooler to prevent dirt contamination.
4. Remove oil dipstick tube, then crankcase ventilation and vacuum hoses from camshaft cover.
5. Remove engine lift brackets and disconnect electrical connectors.

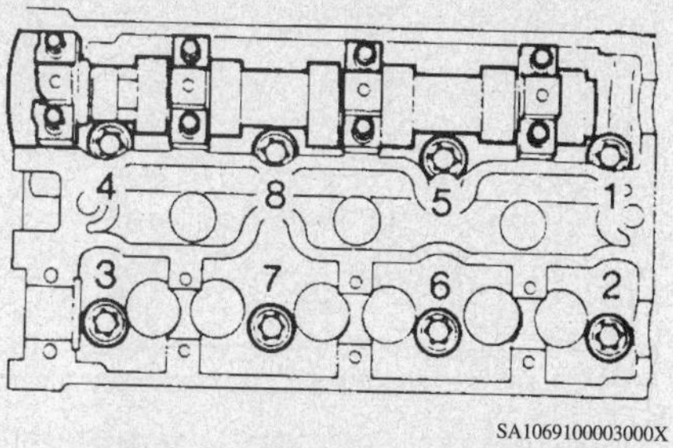
4
8
5
1
3
7
6
2
SA1069100003000X

Fig. 6 Cylinder head bolt tightening sequence. 900 w/2.5L engine

6. Remove throttle body preheating hoses.
7. Remove engine coolant manifold to thermostat housing bolts.
8. Disconnect engine temperature sensor electrical connector at intake manifold.
9. Remove intake manifold bolts, then intake manifold and intake air heat plates.
10. Reverse procedure to install, noting the following:
    a. Align intake air heat plates with intake manifold and new gaskets.
    b. Install air heat plate assembly and bolts, then tighten assembly bolts to specifications.
    c. Check and fill engine coolant to proper level.

CYLINDER HEAD

REPLACE

900

1993

1. Scribe hood hinge locations and remove hood.
2. Disconnect battery cables and remove battery from engine compartment.
3. Drain engine coolant from radiator and block.
4. **On models with turbocharger,** proceed as follows:
    a. Remove distributor and distributor heat shield.
    b. Disconnect suction pipe, pressure pipe and oil supply pipe from turbocharger. **Oil supply pipe must also be disconnected from engine block.**
    c. Disconnect solenoid at turbocharger and charging pressure regulator.
    d. Disconnect turbocharger support bracket from transaxle.
    e. Remove oil dipstick pipe.
    f. Disconnect oil return pipe from turbocharger.
    g. Disconnect exhaust pipe from turbocharger.
    h. Remove nuts, spacer sleeves and washers from exhaust manifold.
    i. Lower exhaust manifold until clear of studs, then remove exhaust manifold and turbocharger unit as an assembly.
5. **On models less turbocharger,** disconnect exhaust pipe from exhaust manifold, then remove exhaust manifold.
6. **On all models,** remove tensioner pulley and compressor drive belt.
7. Remove power steering pump drive belt and position pump aside.
8. Unfasten wiring harness clips from cylinder head.
9. Remove two engine front cover to cylinder head attaching bolts.
10. Remove righthand side engine mount to cylinder head bolts and spacers.
11. Disconnect hose between thermostat housing and radiator at the thermostat housing end.
12. Remove fuel pressure regulator, then disconnect ground wires for lefthand system.
13. Remove AIC actuator, then the A/C compressor bracket from cylinder head.
14. Remove intake manifold as an assembly with injection valves and fuel injection manifold.
15. Disconnect electrical connector from temperature sender.
16. Remove lid on valve cover and ignition cables together with distributor cap.
17. Remove valve cover. Disconnect crankcase ventilation hose and remove rubber plug halves from cylinder head.
18. Unfasten A/C compressor and position aside.
19. Align flywheel (0) mark with line on clutch cover and notches on camshaft with marks on bearing cap, then remove chain tensioner, camshaft sprockets and timing chain.
20. Raise engine to lift cylinder head off engine mounts, then remove cylinder head attaching bolts.
21. Install guide pin in one of bolt holes and remove cylinder head. **Ensure pivoting guide for timing chain is not damaged during removal.**
22. Rotate crankshaft so (0) mark on flywheel is aligned with timing mark on end plate.
23. Align notches on camshaft with marks on bearing cap.
24. Reverse procedure to install, noting the following:
    a. **On cylinder heads with 17 mm bolts, torque** cylinder head bolts in sequence, **Fig. 5,** first to 44 ft. lbs., then to 70 ft. lbs. Warm engine to operating temperature, then allow engine to cool for 30 minutes. Loosen all cylinder head bolts, then **torque** bolts in sequence, **Fig. 5,** to 70 ft. lbs. Then **torque** an additional 90°.
    b. **On cylinder heads with 15 mm or Torx bolts, torque** cylinder head bolts in sequence, **Fig. 5,** first to 44 ft. lbs., then to 59 ft. lbs. Then **torque** an additional 90°.
    c. **On all cylinder heads,** install two bolts on underside of head and **torque** to 15 ft lbs.
    d. Install camshaft sprocket for exhaust valve camshaft first. Ensure chain between camshaft and crankshaft sprockets is tight, then install camshaft sprocket for inlet

valve camshaft.

e. Adjust chain tension with camshaft sprocket center bolts not fully tightened. Tighten tensioner bolt, then release tensioner by pressing pivoting guide firmly against it. Depress pivoting guide to verify proper tensioner operation, then rotate engine two complete turns. Ensure crankshaft and camshafts are still properly aligned, then tighten sprocket bolts to specifications.

1994-96

2.0L & 2.3L Engines

1. Drain coolant, then disconnect battery ground cable.
2. **On B206i and B234i engines,** disconnect mass air flow sensor and inlet hose.
3. **On all engines,** remove air cleaner.
4. **On turbo models,** remove bypass hose and inlet hose. Plug inlet pipe.
5. **On all models,** remove cover or resonator.
6. **On turbo models,** remove pressure pipe between charge air cooler and throttle body. Plug hose at charge air cooler end.
7. **On all models,** loosen belt tensioner using ratchet handle extension and 6 mm drill bit, **Fig. 1.** Remove belt.
8. Disconnect servo pump and position aside.
9. **On turbo models,** proceed as follows:
   a. Remove crankcase breather valve and inlet pipe.
   b. Remove turbocharger nuts and washers, then the turbocharger steady bar bolts.
   c. Disconnect coolant hoses from cylinder head and remove water pipe for cooling turbocharger from cylinder head.
   d. Disconnect ignition discharge module connector.
10. **On non-turbo models,** remove exhaust manifold.
11. **On all models,** remove bracket for dipstick tube and remove tube.
12. Disconnect crankcase breather and vacuum hoses from camshaft cover, then remove lifting eyes at intake manifold and move bracket for electrical connections to one side.
13. Disconnect throttle body preheating hose and bolts securing water pipe to thermostat housing cover.
14. Disconnect throttle body preheating hose, then remove water pipe to thermostat housing cover bolts.
15. Disconnect temperature sensor electrical connector, located next to intake manifold.
16. Remove intake manifold steady bar bolts, then the intake manifold.
17. **On turbocharged models equipped with intake air heat plates,** remove intake air heat plates as outlined under "Intake Air Heat Plates, Replace" procedures.
18. **On B206i and B234i engines,** remove cover plate, ignition cables and distributor cap.
19. **On all other engines,** remove ignition discharge module.
20. **On all engines,** remove spark plugs, then the camshaft cover. Line up 0° mark on flywheel with timing mark and ensure timing marks on camshafts are also in line.
21. Remove chain tensioner, then the camshaft sprockets. Position chain so it will not obstruct cylinder head removal.
22. Remove cylinder head by starting with timing cover bolts and continuing in **reverse** order of tightening, **Fig. 5.**
23. Ensure timing chain does not obstruct removal, then remove cylinder head.
24. Reverse procedure to install. When installing cylinder head and tightening cylinder head bolts, **torque** bolts in sequence, **Fig. 5,** first to 44 ft. lbs., then to 59 ft. lbs., and finally an additional 90°.

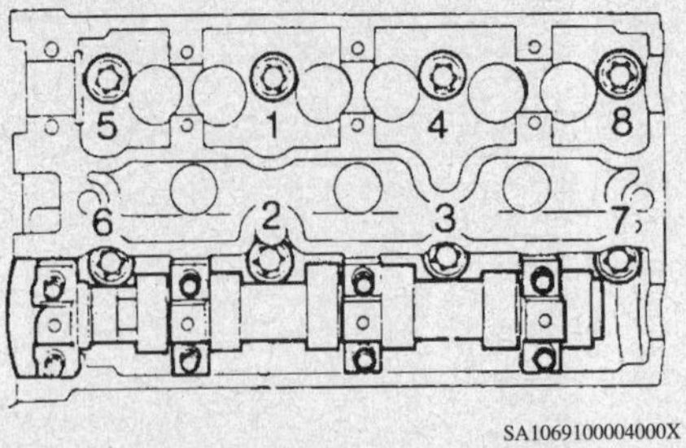
5
1
4
8
6
2
3
7
SA1069100004000X

Fig. 7 Bearing cap bolt tightening sequence. 900 w/2.5L engine

2.5L Engine

The camshaft sprockets must not be rotated because the valves could then touch the pistons or each other and be damaged. The crankshaft should be turned only when the camshaft sprockets of both cylinder heads are locked with suitable locking tools.

1. Drain coolant, then disconnect battery ground cable.
2. Raise and support vehicle, then remove two bolts securing front exhaust pipe to rear part of engine.
3. Lower vehicle to floor and remove air cleaner and mass air flow sensor.
4. Remove engine covers, then the intake manifold. Plug holes with paper.
5. Remove hose from fuel pressure regulator, IAC valve connector, TCS throttle body connector and throttle connector.
6. Remove coolant hoses from throttle body and hose from EVAP canister purge valve, then lift away induction manifold.
7. Remove fuel lines, then plug connections.
8. Remove center induction manifold screws, then the manifold complete with fuel rail. Lay aside.
9. Remove gasket to gain access to lower intake manifold retaining bolts, then remove lower section and plug with paper.
10. Disconnect electrical connectors and radiator hose, then remove coolant bridge.
11. Disconnect HT leads.
12. Remove oxygen sensor from holder, then the crankcase breather housing from lefthand side of engine. Plug holes with paper.
13. Remove ignition coil, then disconnect HT leads from righthand side of engine.
14. Remove ignition coil bracket, camshaft position sensor and oxygen sensor connection from righthand side of engine. Lay bracket aside.
15. Remove top radiator hose at engine, then the lifting eye on righthand side of engine.
16. Slightly loosen pulley bolts, then remove multigroove drive belt, tensioner, power steering pump pulley, water pump pulley and cover.
17. Remove righthand front wheel and cover in wheel housing.
18. Remove crankshaft pulley. Loosen six bolts, but do not remove center bolt.
19. Put No. 1 cylinder in compression position, or Before Top Dead Center (BTDC). Markings on camshaft sprockets and timing cover should be in alignment as well as marking on crankshaft. Insert suitable locking tools for camshaft sprockets on cylinder heads.
20. Mark rotating direction of belt at camshaft markings and crankshaft marking.
21. Remove tensioning roller and two adjusting rollers, then the belt.
22. Turn crankshaft back 60° BTDC, then remove bracket holding middle adjusting roller and tensioning roller.
23. Remove valve cover. Ensure O-rings are in place and they do not fall into engine.
24. Remove camshaft sprockets and remove timing cover screws in cylinder head. Camshaft sprockets are marked 1, 2, 3 and 4. **If using open-end spanner to hold camshaft when removing sprockets, ensure jaws are not too long as they may damage casting and cause tappet to jam.**
25. Remove bearing caps on exhaust camshaft. **Finish removal of bearing cap where valve tappets are under load. Pay attention to marking on bearing cap. Loosen bolts in stages, ½ to 1 turn at a time. Remove camshaft seal and lift out camshaft.**
26. Remove cylinder head bolts in order, **Fig. 6.** First loosen ¼ turn, then ½ turn.
27. Remove cylinder head. Use care when putting head down, as intake camshaft is still in place and valve stems could be accidentally bent.
28. Remove intake camshaft, exhaust manifold and tappets.
29. Reverse procedure to install, noting the following:
   a. Ensure crankshaft is positioned at BTDC.
   b. Clean all contact surfaces and fit gasket. Note guides for gasket and gasket is marked OBEN/TOP.
   c. **Torque** new cylinder head bolts in sequence, **Fig. 6,** first to 19 ft. lbs.; second, an additional 90°; third, 90°; and fourth, 90° again.
   d. **Torque** bearing cap bolts in sequence, **Fig. 7,** in stages, ½ to 1 turn per stage, to 6 ft. lbs.

e. Fit camshaft sprockets correctly, **Fig. 8,** then tighten to specifications.

9000

1993

1. Raise and support front of vehicle.
2. Remove righthand wheel.
3. Remove front wheel liner assembly.
4. Drain coolant from engine.
5. Disconnect battery ground cable.
6. Remove expansion tank.
7. Remove power steering fluid reservoir from mountings and position aside, leaving hoses attached.
8. Loosen A/C compressor drive belt, then disconnect electrical connectors and position compressor aside. **Do not disconnect refrigerant lines.**
9. Loosen front exhaust pipe flange, then disconnect rubber hangers.
10. **On models with turbocharger,** proceed as follows:
    a. Remove turbocharger support bar, then the oil return line.
    b. Disconnect intercooler hose from turbocharger assembly.
    c. Disconnect oil supply line from turbocharger assembly. Remove clip attaching pipe to cylinder head.
    d. Remove exhaust manifold with turbocharger attached, while pushing oil return pipe out of the way.
11. **On models without turbocharger,** remove exhaust manifold.
12. **On all models,** label, disconnect and cap all vacuum lines, fuel lines, oil lines and electrical connectors from cylinder head and distributor assembly.
13. Disconnect coolant lines and hoses from cylinder head.
14. Remove engine stay bracket.
15. Remove engine stay bracket from cylinder head.
16. Remove intake manifold from cylinder head.
17. Disconnect breather hose from camshaft cover.
18. Remove spark plug inspection plates.
19. Remove camshaft cover attaching bolts, then the camshaft cover.
20. Turn crankshaft in normal direction of rotation until zero (0) mark on crankshaft and engine block align and camshaft timing marks are also aligned properly.
21. With crankshaft and camshaft timing marks properly aligned, remove camshaft sprockets and timing chain tensioner.
22. Remove the two cylinder head bolts adjacent to the timing case cover. Bolts are accessible from below.
23. Remove the ten, Torx-type cylinder head attaching bolts.
24. Install a guide pin in the drilled hole in the top righthand corner of the cylinder head. Ensure timing chain is positioned correctly, so that the pivoting chain guide will not obstruct the cylinder head and carefully lift cylinder head from engine block.
25. Reverse procedure to install. When installing cylinder head and torquing cylinder head bolts, proceed as follows:
    a. **Torque** cylinder head bolts in sequence, first to 44 ft. lbs., then to 59 ft. lbs.
    b. **Torque** all bolts in sequence an additional 90°.

1994–96

2.0L & 2.3L Engines

1. Raise and support vehicle, then drain engine coolant. Lower vehicle and remove filler cap to speed drainage.
2. **On 1995–96 models,** obtain radio anti-theft code as outlined under "Precautions."
3. **On all models,** disconnect battery ground cable.
4. Remove throttle control retaining clip, then bend up lever and remove control.
5. Disconnect coolant level sensor connector, then remove coolant tank. Disconnect coolant hoses so they are with tank.
6. Remove belt.
7. Disconnect A/C compressor electrical connector, then remove retaining bolts and rest compressor on radiator crossmember.
8. Remove A/C compressor bracket.
9. Snip through cable ties holding hoses and wiring at upper torque arm, then remove interference suppressor cable (ground), torque arm and two cylinder head upper bolts.
10. Disconnect ignition discharge module connector, then the temperature sensor connector.
11. **On turbo models,** remove turbo pressure pipe between charge air cooler and throttle body.
12. **On all models,** remove radiator hose from throttle body, then the upper radiator hose from cylinder head.
13. Disconnect heat exchanger hose and water temperature sensor connector from cylinder head.
14. Disconnect crankcase breather and vacuum hoses from camshaft cover.
15. **On turbo models,** remove turbo intake hose.
16. **On all models,** disconnect solenoid valve connector, then remove solenoid valve from holder and bend valve up against engine.
17. Remove vacuum hose at bypass valve and remove bypass valve.
18. Remove bolts securing front exhaust pipe to exhaust manifold, then the bolt from bracket on top of catalytic converter using suitable extension bar.
19. Raise and support vehicle, then remove bolt from catalytic converter bracket.
20. Remove front exhaust pipe rear connecting flange bolts, then disconnect oxygen sensor cable at exhaust pipe and feed it into engine bay.
21. Carefully lower front exhaust pipe, then remove oil drain pipe.
22. Lower vehicle.
23. **On turbo models,** remove coolant pipe between turbo and cylinder head, then the turbo oil delivery pipe and coolant pipe between turbo and water pump.

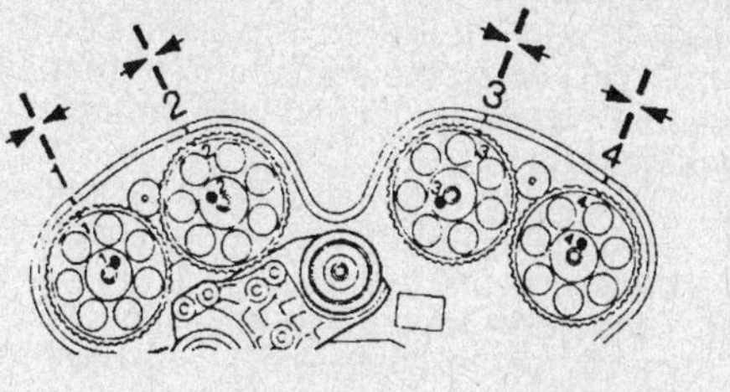
1
2
3
4

SA1069400005000X

Fig. 8 Camshaft sprocket installation. 900 w/2.5L engine

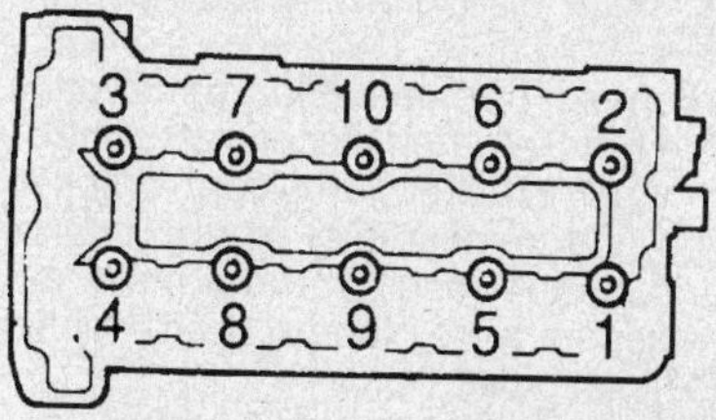
3 7 10 6 2
4 8 9 5 1

SA1069100006000X

Fig. 9 Cylinder head bolt loosening sequence. 1994–96 9000 w/2.0L & 2.3L engines

24. **On all models,** remove oil return pipe.
25. **On turbo models,** remove two hoses between solenoid valve and turbo, then the delivery pipe between turbo and charge air cooler.
26. **On all models,** remove seven bolts and five washers securing manifold to cylinder head.
27. Remove manifold and turbo unit.
28. Remove gasket, then the intake manifold from cylinder head as follows:
    a. Remove lifting eye, then the oil filler pipe bracket.
    b. Remove fuel rail retaining bolts, then the fuel rail with nozzles.
    c. Remove intake manifold retaining bolts, then the gasket.
    d. Remove water pipe bracket on thermostat housing, then the intake manifold.
    e. Remove ignition discharge module and spark plugs.
29. Remove camshaft cover, then line up crankshaft with 0° mark and ensure timing marks on camshafts are also in alignment.
30. Remove power steering fluid reservoir, then the chain tensioner.
31. Unscrew camshaft sprocket bolts and remove sprockets from camshafts.
32. Hold up chain and lower chain guide to middle of engine.
33. Remove two timing cover to cylinder head bolts.
34. Unscrew cylinder head bolts in sequence, **Fig. 9.**
35. Reverse procedure to install. **Torque** cylinder head bolts in sequence, **Fig. 5,** first to 44 ft. lbs., then to 59 ft. lbs. Then **torque** bolts an additional 90°.

3.0L Engine

The camshafts must not be rotated because the valves could touch the pistons or each other, causing damage.

The crankshaft may only be turned between 0° and 60° Before Top Dead Center (BTDC) when the camshafts of both cylinder heads are locked with suitable locking tools.

1. Obtain radio anti-theft code as outlined under "Precautions," then disconnect battery ground cable.
2. Raise and support vehicle, then remove rear exhaust pipe to exhaust manifold nuts.
3. Remove center air shield, then drain engine coolant into suitable container.
4. Lower vehicle and remove engine covers, then disconnect cruise control cable.
5. Disconnect throttle cable from throttle cable bracket, then disconnect control rod and bracket. Position bracket aside. Disconnect inlet pipe to intake manifold and resonator and mass air flow sensor hose clamps, then slightly raise inlet pipes.
6. Disconnect vacuum hoses and electrical connectors, then remove pipes complete with resonator.
7. Remove intake manifold bolts, then disconnect throttle body preheater hoses, crankcase ventilation hose and vacuum hoses from intake manifold. **Note where hoses are connected.**
8. Disconnect IAC valve electrical connector, then the fuel pressure regulator hose and remove wiring harness conduit from under throttle body.
9. Disconnect throttle position indicator electrical connector and ignition coil, then the TCS throttle body electrical connector.
10. Lift off intake manifold. Plug openings with paper.
11. Disconnect injector electrical connector, then the camshaft position sensor.
12. Disconnect fuel lines and plug openings, then remove center intake manifold bolts. Secure center intake manifold with fuel rail aside.
13. Mark position of lower part of intake manifold and remove. Plug openings with paper.
14. Remove coolant bridge and bend aside.
15. **If removing rear cylinder head,** proceed as follows:
    a. Disconnect ignition leads 1–3–5.
    b. Remove oxygen sensor from holder, then the crankcase ventilation housing. Plug all openings with paper.
16. **If removing front cylinder head,** proceed as follows:
    a. Disconnect ignition leads 2–4–6, then the ignition coil. Bend coil aside and remove ignition coil bracket.
    b. Remove lifting eye and heat shield over exhaust manifold.
17. **On both cylinder heads,** remove power steering servo oil reservoir, then disconnect torque arm engine mounting lead and remove torque arm.
18. Remove servo line clamp from torque arm engine mounting, then the engine mounting.
19. Disconnect expansion tank upper

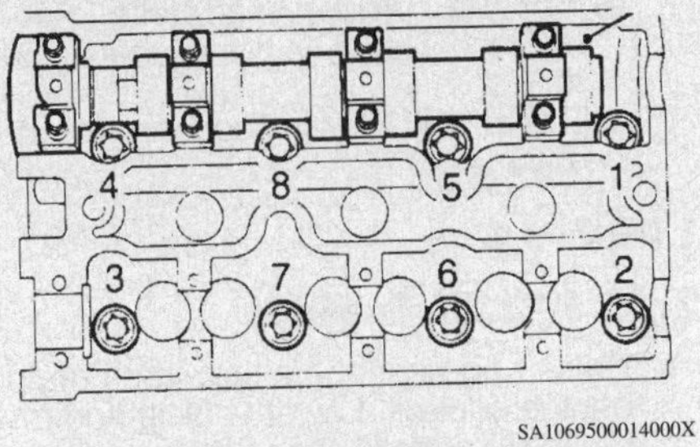
4
8
5
1
3
7
6
2
SA1069500014000X

Fig. 10 Front cylinder head bolt removal sequence. 9000 w/3.0L engine

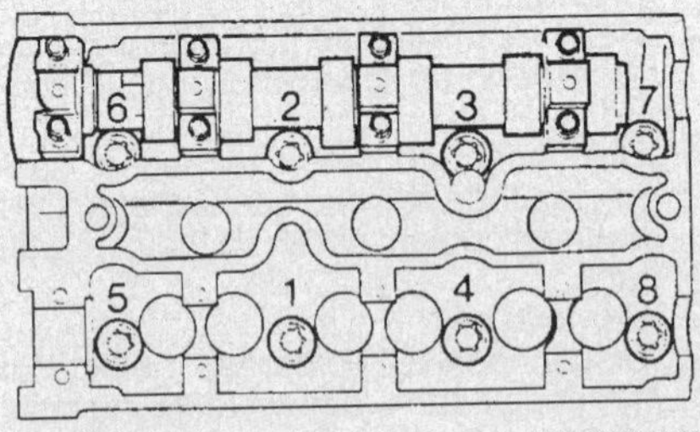
6
2
3
7
5
1
4
8
SA1069500016000X

Fig. 12 Front cylinder head bolt tightening sequence. 9000 w/3.0L engine

hose, then the upper part of generator air intake.

20. Slightly loosen pulley bolts, then remove power steering belt, belt tensioner, power steering servo pump, coolant pump pulley and timing cover.
21. Remove six crankshaft pulley outer bolts, then the pulley. **Do not remove center bolt.**
22. Zero engine, then insert suitable locking tool for camshaft sprocket on cylinder head. **Markings on camshaft sprocket and timing cover should align, as should marking on crankshaft.**
23. Mark toothed belt direction of rotation, then release belt from tension and remove belt. **For easier installation, mark belt at both camshaft marking and crankshaft marking.**
24. Remove adjuster pulley bolts, then turn crankshaft back to 60° BTDC and remove bracket holding upper adjuster and tensioner pulleys.
25. Remove timing cover. **Ensure O-rings are in position and do not fall into engine.**
26. Remove cylinder head camshaft sprockets, then the timing cover bolts in cylinder head, noting the following:
    a. **On rear cylinder head,** camshaft sprockets are marked "1" and "2."
    b. **On front cylinder head,** camshaft sprockets are marked "3" and "4."
    c. **On both cylinder heads, ensure open-ended wrench used as holding tool to remove camshaft sprockets does not have jaws which are too long. There is a risk of damaging casting, causing tappet to lock.**
27. Remove exhaust camshaft bearing caps, noting the following:

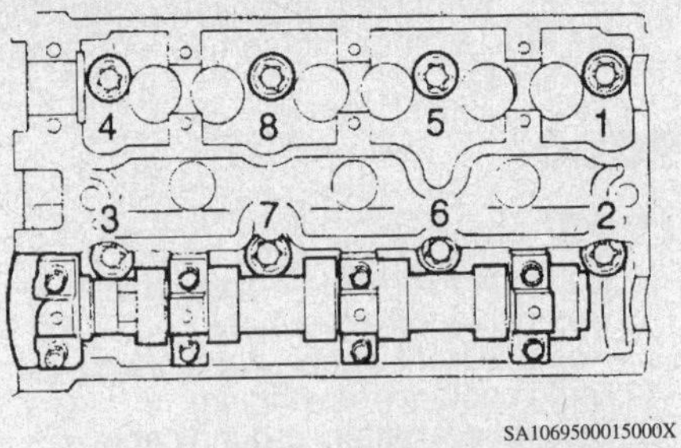
4
8
5
1
3
7
6
2
SA1069500015000X

Fig. 11 Rear cylinder head bolt removal sequence. 9000 w/3.0L engine

    a. **It is important to finish removal at bearing cap where valve depressors are compressed.**
    b. Note marking on bearing caps.
    c. Remove bolts in stages of ½ to one turn and lift out camshaft.
28. Remove cylinder head bolts in order specified, **Figs. 10 and 11. First loosen ¼ turn, then ½ turn.**
29. Remove cylinder head. **Use care when putting down cylinder head as intake camshaft is still in place and valve stems could accidently bend.**
30. Reverse procedure to install, noting the following:
    a. Before installing, ensure crankshaft is positioned at 60° BTDC, then clean all contact surfaces and install gasket. Note guides for gasket.
    b. **Torque** cylinder head bolts in order specified, **Figs. 12 and 13,** in four steps: first to 19 ft. lbs., next an additional 90°, then another 90°, and finally, 90° more.
    c. Ensure camshaft sprocket locating pins are in correct position. If locating pins are hollow, change them for solid pins. Fit camshaft sprockets in correct relation to locating pins, **Fig. 14.**
    d. Adjust kickdown and throttle cables.
    e. Fill radiator with suitable coolant according to specifications and check system for leaks.
    f. Check oil and fluid levels and adjust as necessary, then bleed cooling system as outlined under "Cooling System Bleed."
    g. Test drive vehicle.

VALVE CLEARANCE SPECIFICATIONS

Hydraulic valve lifters are used on all engines and no adjustment is required.

VALVE ADJUSTMENT

Hydraulic valve lifters are used on all engines and no adjustment is required.

VALVE GUIDES

Before removing valve guide, flush cylinder head with hot water. Remove guide using jackscrew and pull rod tool No. 83 93 811 with spacer No. 8393829 and nut No.

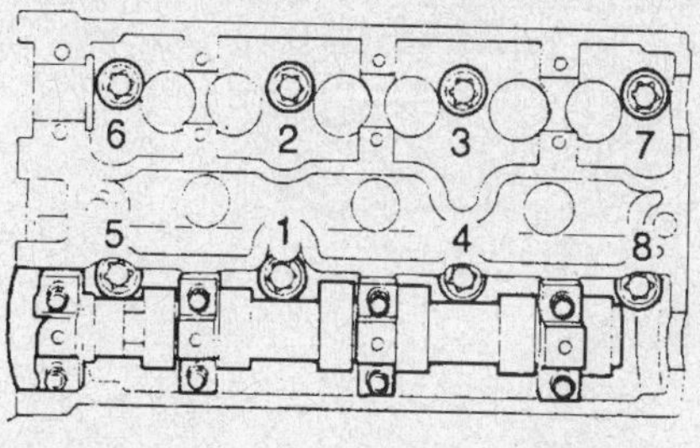
6
2
3
7
5
1
4
8
SA1069500017000X

Fig. 13 Rear cylinder head bolt tightening sequence. 9000 w/3.0L engine

8393845, or equivalents. Install guide from top after flushing cylinder head with hot water and cooling guide with cold water. Install guide using jackscrew and pull rod tool No. 83 93 811 with stop No. 8393837, centering sleeve No. 8390379 and nut No. 8393845, or equivalents. Center tool in valve seat and draw guide into position using tool.

VALVE SEATS

Machine valve seats as necessary using a 60 milling cutter. Width of intake valve seat should measure 1–1.5 mm and width of exhaust valve seat should measure 1.5–2 mm.

Only a limited amount of material can be removed from exhaust valve face, since the stellite coating must be preserved as much as possible. Consequently, if valve is badly pitted or worn, it should be replaced.

FRONT COVER SEAL

REPLACE

900

1993

1. Remove engine drive belts.
2. Using clamp tool No. 83 92 987, or equivalent, secure crankshaft from turning, then remove crankshaft pulley attaching bolt.
3. Remove crankshaft pulley.
4. Using screwdriver, pry out old front seal from crankshaft.
5. Before installing, lubricate lip of new seal with engine oil, then using installer tool No. 83 93 349, or equivalent, and crank pulley bolt, install new front seal onto crankshaft.
6. Install crankshaft pulley and tighten pulley attaching bolt to specifications.
7. Install and tension drive belts.

1994–96

1. Remove air cleaner and mass air flow sensor.
2. Slightly loosen pulley bolts, then remove drive belt, tensioner, power steering pump pulley, water pump pulley and cover.
3. Remove front righthand wheel and cover in wheel housing.
4. Remove crankshaft pulley. Loosen six bolts, but do not remove center bolt.
5. Position No. 1 cylinder in compression position. Markings on camshaft sprockets and timing cover should be in alignment as well as marking on crankshaft. Insert suitable locking tools for camshaft sprockets on cylinder heads.
6. Before removing belt, mark direction of rotation at camshaft markings and crankshaft marking.
7. Remove tensioning roller and two adjusting rollers, then the belt.
8. Turn crankshaft back 60° Before Top Dead Center (BTDC).
9. Raise and support vehicle and remove protective plate for flywheel.
10. Install flywheel stop, then remove crankshaft pulley and spacer ring.
11. Pry out seal, using care not to damage crankshaft sealing surface.
12. Fit inner part of crankshaft seal assembly tool No. 83 94 942, or equivalent, on crankshaft, then lubricate seal and fit onto shaft. Tap seal into place using outer part of tool.
13. Install spacer ring and crankshaft pulley. Tighten crankshaft pulley to specifications.
14. Install cover in wheel housing, then the front righthand wheel. Tighten wheel bolt to specifications.
15. Install cover, water pump pulley, power steering pump pulley, belt tensioner and multigroove drive belt.
16. Install air cleaner and mass air flow sensor.

9000

1. Raise and support front of vehicle.
2. Remove front fender inner liner.
3. Loosen accessory attaching bolts, then remove drive belts.
4. Using clamp tool No. 83 93 993, or equivalent, secure crankshaft from turning, then remove crankshaft pulley attaching bolt.
5. Remove crankshaft pulley.
6. Using screwdriver, pry out old front seal from crankshaft.
7. Using installer tool No. 83 93 349, or equivalent, install new front seal onto crankshaft.
8. Install crankshaft pulley and tighten pulley attaching bolt to specifications.
9. Install and tension drive belts.
10. Install fender liner and wheel, then tighten attaching bolts and lower vehicle.

TIMING CHAIN

REPLACE

EXCEPT 3.0L ENGINE

The camshaft timing mechanism is comprised of a chain and sprockets. The chain has two guides, one fixed and one pivoting. The pivoting guide maintains tension in the chain aided by a hydraulic chain tensioner.

1. Remove engine from vehicle as outlined in "Engine, Replace."
2. Remove breather hose for crankcase ventilation from valve cover.
3. Disconnect vacuum hose and Hall transducer from distributor, then remove distributor cap with ignition wires.
4. Remove spark plug inspection cover and clips for plug wires.
5. Remove valve cover.
6. Rotate engine until (0) mark on flywheel is aligned with pointer, **Fig. 15. Ensure camshaft timing marks are also correctly aligned.**
7. Remove chain tensioner.
8. Remove camshaft sprockets.
9. Remove crankshaft pulley, then the belt tensioner.
10. Remove water pump pipe.
11. Remove oil pipes, then the water pump pulley.
12. Remove water pump and three bolts in block.
13. Remove oil pump.
14. Remove timing cover.
15. Remove pivoting chain guide. **Do not remove fixed chain guide.**
16. Remove timing chain and sprocket with oil pump drive dog. **Do not rotate camshafts or crankshaft with timing chain removed.**
17. Reverse procedure to install, noting the following:
    a. Install timing chain around crankshaft sprocket, then install chain and sprocket on exhaust valve camshaft. **Ensure chain is taut between crankshaft and exhaust valve camshaft sprockets.**
    b. Install chain and sprocket on intake valve camshaft. **Maintain chain tension between camshaft sprockets while installing.**
    c. Set chain tensioner by pushing and turning adjuster simultaneously, then install chain tensioner. **Ensure copper gasket is in good condition and sealing surface is clean and free of burrs.**
    d. Using wrench, release chain tensioner by pressing pivoting chain guide against tensioner, then press pivoting guide against chain to give basic tension. **Ensure chain is correctly positioned in guides.**
    e. Check that chain tensioner maintains tension on chain when pressure on chain guide is released and that basic setting stop for tensioner holds chain guide tight against chain. **A limited amount of play will be present until hydraulic pressure develops with engine running.**
    f. Rotate engine two complete turns, ensuring crankshaft and camshafts

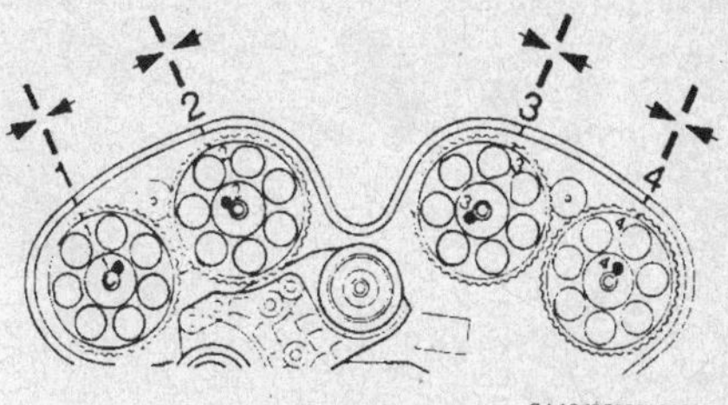
1
2
3
4
SA1069500018000X

Fig. 14 Camshaft sprocket alignment. 9000 w/3.0L

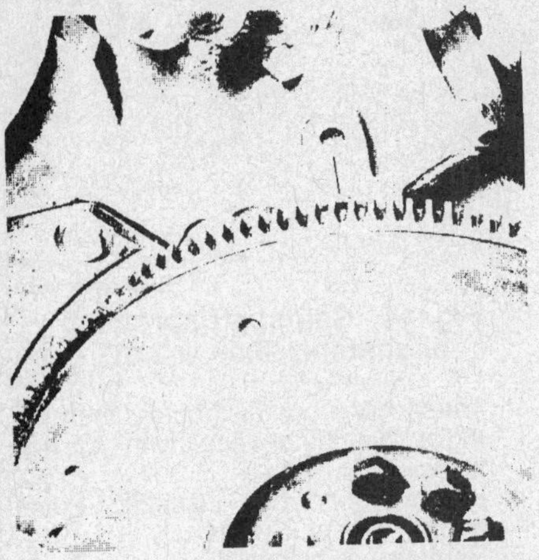
SA1069100007000X

Fig. 15 Flywheel timing mark alignment

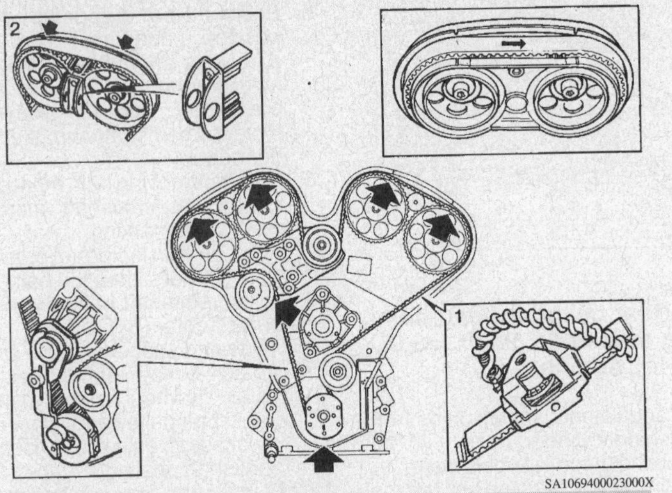
2
1
SA1069400023000X

Fig. 16 Timing belt timing mark alignment. 2.5L engine

are properly aligned.

TIMING BELT

REPLACE

2.5L ENGINE

With the timing belt removed, avoid turning the camshaft or crankshaft. If movement is required, exercise extreme caution to avoid valve damage caused by piston contact.

1. Disconnect battery ground cable.
2. Remove air cleaner assembly.
3. Remove accessory drive belt and tensioner.
4. Remove power steering pump pulley.
5. Remove water pump pulley. Using engine bracket as fulcrum, move engine slightly to the left during pulley removal.
6. Remove timing belt cover.
7. Raise and suitably support vehicle.
8. Remove righthand front wheel and splash shield.
9. Remove crankshaft pulley attaching bolts and pulley. **Do not remove center crankshaft pulley bolt.**
10. Position No. 1 cylinder at TDC of compression stroke. Ensure crankshaft and camshaft sprocket timing marks are aligned, **Fig. 16.**
11. Install Saab locking insert tool No. 83–94–926 (2), or equivalent, to hold camshaft and crankshaft sprockets in position.
12. Loosen timing belt tensioner pulley bolt and two adjusting rollers.
13. Remove timing belt.
14. Install timing belt. Move tensioner pulley in counterclockwise direction to prevent timing belt from slipping off sprockets.
15. Install Saab timing belt tension tool No. 83–93–985 (1), or equivalent, to timing belt, **Fig. 16.**
16. Finger tighten center bolts of adjusting rollers.
17. Adjust lower adjusting roller in counterclockwise direction to tension timing belt to 275–300 Nm.
18. Adjust tensioner pulley until tensioner marks are aligned.
19. Remove camshaft sprocket locking tools for camshaft sprockets Nos. 1 and 2.
20. Turn crankshaft two revolutions in normal direction of rotation. **Ensure crankshaft and camshaft timing marks are aligned, Fig. 16.** Use locking tool to check crankshaft and camshaft sprockets for proper alignment. Also check tensioner pulley marks for proper alignment.
21. **Torque** tensioner pulley and lower adjusting roller bolts to 15 ft. lbs. **Torque** upper center roller bolt to 30 ft. lbs.
22. Install crankshaft pulley bolt, then tighten to specifications.
23. Install splash shield, then righthand front wheel assembly and **torque** wheel lug nuts to 89 ft. lbs.
24. Lower vehicle, then install timing belt cover.
25. Install water pump and power steering pump pulleys.
26. Install accessory drive belt tensioner.
27. Install accessory drive belt.
28. Install air cleaner assembly and battery ground cable.

3.0L ENGINE

With the timing belt removed, avoid turning the camshaft or crankshaft. If movement is required, exercise extreme caution to avoid valve damage caused by piston contact.

Removal

Each cylinder head has twin overhead camshafts with a large-diameter base circle, providing a large amount of lift with little stress. All four camshafts are driven by an internally-cogged belt with self-adjusting belt tensioner. The belt assembly also includes two adjuster rollers.

1. Lift power steering servo oil reservoir and free lead from torque arm engine mounting, then remove torque arm.
2. Remove servo line clamp from torque arm engine mounting and remove engine mounting.
3. Slightly loosen power steering pump pulley bolts, then release load from belt tensioner by turning belt tensioner pulley screw forward in vehicle.
4. Remove belt from coolant pump pulley and carefully release belt tensioner.
5. Disconnect expansion tank hoses, then remove coolant pump pulley.
6. Remove upper portion of generator air intake, then the belt tensioner and power steering servo pump.
7. Remove timing cover.
8. Remove six crankshaft pulley bolts, then the pulley. **Do not remove center bolt.**
9. Zero engine, noting the following:
   a. Marks on camshaft sprockets and timing cover should align, **Fig. 17.**
   b. Markings on crankshaft and timing cover should align, **Fig. 17.**
   c. Install locking tool Nos. KM-800-1 and KM-800-2, or equivalents, for camshaft sprockets on cylinder heads and locking tool No. KM-800-10, or equivalent, for crankshaft.
10. Release belt from tension and remove, then remove adjuster pulley bolts. **Before removing belt, mark direction of rotation. Markings can be made at both camshaft and crankshaft.**

Installation

1. Install toothed belt in marked direction of rotation as follows:
   a. Holding belt in position, lightly adjust tensioner roller by hand so belt does not disengage. Adjust counter clockwise.
   b. Install piece of toothed belt and belt tension meter tool No. 83 93 985, or equivalent, to measure belt tension.
   c. Lightly turn center bolt on adjuster rollers.
   d. Adjust lower roller counter clockwise to tension of 62–67 lbs. **This belt tension adjustment is only preparatory measure and must**

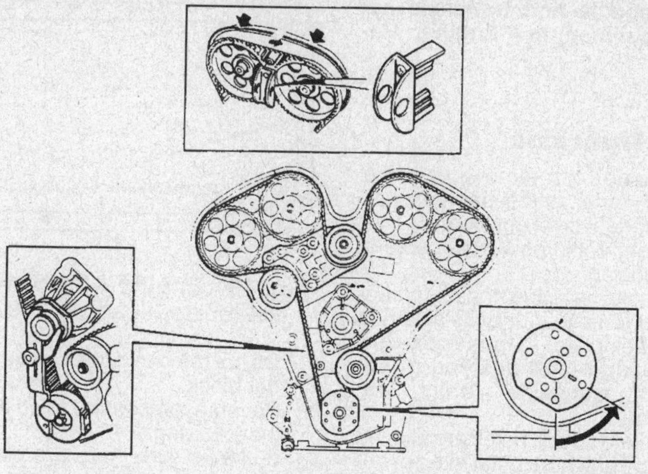
SA1069500019000X

Fig. 17 Camshaft & crankshaft alignment for timing chain removal. 3.0L engine

not be used as check when belt is finally adjusted.

2. Adjust tensioning pulley with suitable Allen wrench until two marks are aligned. Tighten tensioning pulley to specifications.
3. Remove locking tool for camshaft sprockets 1 and 2, then adjust upper adjusting roller counterclockwise until No. 2 sprocket moves .039–.079 inch clockwise. Tighten sprockets to specifications, then remove upper locking tool.
4. Turn engine two revolutions to just before zero marking and install suitable locking tool to crankshaft.
5. Carefully turn crankshaft in direction of engine rotation until arm is against coolant pump flange. Tighten crankshaft.
6. Position tool No. KM-800-20, or equivalent, and ensure markings on camshaft sprocket are aligned with markings on tool and edge of belt meets edge of sprocket. Also ensure tensioning roller marks are aligned.
7. Install crankshaft pulley, then the timing cover.
8. Install power steering servo pump, then the belt tensioner.
9. Install upper portion of generator air intake.
10. Install coolant pump pulley, then connect upper hose to expansion tank.
11. Relieve load from belt tensioner by turning belt tensioner pulley locking bolt forward in vehicle.
12. Fit belt on coolant pump pulley and check other pulleys, then carefully release belt tensioner.
13. Install torque arm engine mounting, then the servo line clamp.
14. Install torque arm, then bolt lead to torque arm engine mounting and install power steering servo oil reservoir.

CAMSHAFT

REPLACE

1. Remove breather hose for crankcase ventilation from valve cover.
2. Disconnect vacuum hose and Hall transducer from distributor, then remove distributor cap with ignition wires.
3. Remove spark plug inspection cover and clips for plug wires.
4. Remove valve cover.
5. Rotate engine until (0) mark on flywheel is aligned with pointer, **Fig. 15. Ensure camshaft timing marks are also correctly aligned.**
6. Remove distributor.
7. Remove camshaft sprockets with chain.
8. Remove oil pipes, then the camshaft bearing caps and camshafts.
9. Reverse procedure to install.

PISTONS, PINS & RINGS

The type pistons used varies with the engine compression ratio. Either Mahle or Karl Schmidt pistons may be fitted to the engine, but pistons of different makes should not be installed in the same engine as an imbalance condition may be created.

Pistons and rings are available in standard, 0.020 inch (0.5 mm) oversize and 0.040 inch (1 mm) oversize. Standard size pistons are supplied in 3 different size classes, and all pistons and cylinder bores should be measured prior to installation. Pistons should be measured at right angles to the piston pin hole at a point 0.63 inch (16 mm) above lower edge of skirt for Mahle pistons, or 1.03 inch (26 mm) above edge of skirt for Schmidt pistons.

Measure piston installation clearance using a spring gauge and feeler gauges ½ inch wide. Clearance should be measured with piston installed in a lightly oiled bore, without rings, at right angle to piston pin bore. When indication on spring gauge used to pull feeler gauge between piston and bore is 1.8–2.6 lbs., piston clearance is equal to the thickness of the feeler gauge used.

Piston ring gap should be measured in the finished bore, using feeler gauges. Push each ring into bore using an inverted piston to properly position rings. New rings fitted to a worn cylinder bore should be checked at the bottom of the piston travel, as the cylinder will be narrowest at this point.

Install piston and rod assemblies with FRONT mark or notch pointing toward timing cover, **Fig. 18.** Piston and rod should be assembled so reference stampings on connecting rod, **Fig. 18,** face exhaust side of engine. Use a piston ring installation tool to position the lower compression ring with the side marked "top" uppermost. Rotate compression rings so that gaps in alternate rings are 180° in relation to each other, positioned over the ends of the piston pins. Make sure that the ring gaps of the top and bottom rings in the three piece scraper ring are staggered.

MAIN & ROD BEARINGS

Rod and main bearings are available in standard size and under sizes of .010 inch (.25 mm), .020 inch (.5 mm), .030 inch (.75 mm) and .040 inch (1 mm).

CRANKSHAFT SEAL

REPLACE

900

1993

1. Remove clutch and flywheel, as outlined under "Clutch, Replace."
2. Using screwdriver, pry out old oil seal.
3. Before installing, lubricate lip of new seal with engine oil, then install seal using installer tool No. 83 92 540, or equivalent.
4. Reinstall clutch and flywheel, then tighten flywheel bolts to specifications.

1994–96

2.0L & 2.3L Engines

1. Loosen belt tensioner using ratchet handle extension and 6 mm drill bit, **Fig. 1. Use care to ensure belt tensioner does not break at its end position.**
2. Raise and support vehicle, then remove front righthand wheel and cover.
3. Remove protective plate and fit flywheel locking segment tool No. 83 94 868, or equivalent, on flywheel ring gear.
4. Remove crankshaft pulley, then use screwdriver to break off old seal.
5. Fit new seal using assembly tool No. 83 94 876, or equivalent.
6. Install crankshaft pulley. Tighten to specifications.
7. Install drive belt and check position of belt on all pulleys, then install cover.
8. Install wheel, then lower vehicle and tighten wheel nuts to specifications.
9. Loosen belt tensioner as outlined earlier.
10. Run engine at idle speed, then turn off and check if drive belt is correctly positioned.

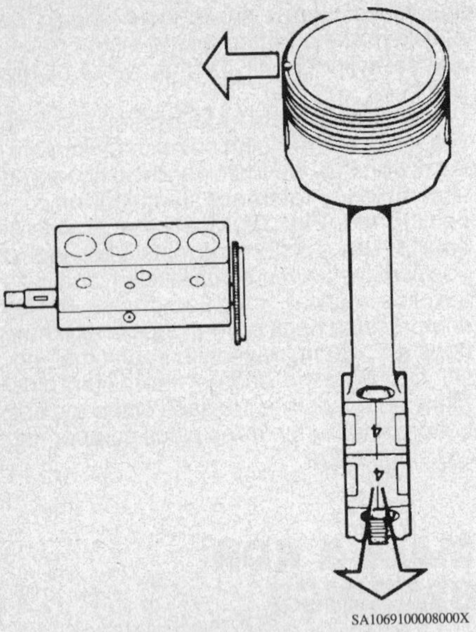
SA1069100008000X

Fig. 18 Piston & connecting rod installation

2.5L Engine

1. Remove transaxle as outlined under "Clutch & Manual Transaxle" or "Automatic Transaxles."
2. **On models equipped with manual transaxle,** remove clutch, pressure plate and flywheel.
3. **On models equipped with automatic transaxle,** remove driver disc.
4. **On all models,** pry seal out using care not to damage sealing surface.
5. Lubricate sealing lips.
6. Insert rear crankshaft seal assembly kit tool No. 83 94 934, or equivalent, to tap seal into place. Ensure sealing lips fit correctly on crankshaft.
7. **On models equipped with manual transaxle,** install flywheel, then the clutch and gearbox as outlined in "Clutch and Manual Transaxle" section.
8. **On models equipped with automatic transaxle,** install driver disc, then the automatic transaxle as outlined under "Automatic Transaxles."

9000

1. Remove transaxle, clutch and flywheel as outlined under "Clutch, Replace," in "Clutch and Manual Transaxle " section.
2. Using screwdriver, pry out old oil seal.
3. Before installing, lubricate lip of new seal with engine oil, then install seal using installer tool No. 83 92 540, or equivalent.
4. Reinstall transaxle, clutch and flywheel, tighten flywheel bolts to specifications.

OIL PAN

REPLACE

900

The engine oil pan is an integral part of engine case. To remove the oil pan, remove the engine and transaxle assembly as outlined in "Engine, Replace."

1993

Automatic Transaxle

1. Drain engine oil, remove flywheel cover and starter, and support assembly in an upright level position.
2. Disconnect throttle downshift cable at throttle housing.
3. Remove bolts securing engine to transaxle, and remove four bolts securing flywheel (flex plate) to torque converter. **Note length and position of engine to transaxle bolts for reassembly.**
4. Turn flex plate so bolt holes are aligned with vertical and horizontal axes of engine.
5. Lift engine from transaxle, taking care not to disturb torque converter.
6. Install torque converter support tool No. 87 90 255, or equivalent.
7. Reverse procedure to install, applying sealer to bolts and areas shown by arrows, **Fig. 19.**
8. Tighten engine to transaxle bolts to specifications.

Manual Transaxle

1. Drain engine oil, then remove clutch cover and starter motor and support assembly in upright level position.
2. Remove clutch shaft as outlined in "Clutch, Replace. "
3. Remove clutch slave cylinder.
4. Remove bolts securing engine to transaxle and lift engine from transaxle, removing release bearing guide sleeve as assemblies are separated. **Note length and position of engine to transaxle bolts for reassembly.**
5. Reverse procedure to install, using sealer on areas shown by arrows, **Fig. 19.** Tighten engine to transaxle bolts to specifications.

1994–95

2.0L & 2.3L Engines

1. Remove dipstick and stuff cloth into end of dipstick tube, then raise engine slightly with suitable lift.
2. Disconnect oxygen sensor leads, then disconnect cable clamp and remove clip.
3. Raise and support vehicle, then drain oil and position suitable lifting table under engine.
4. Remove front wheels and spoiler sections, then disconnect joint between front exhaust pipe and intermediate pipe.
5. Remove exhaust pipe from turbocharger or exhaust manifold.
6. Remove catalytic converter from its bracket, then the exhaust pipe.
7. Remove steering swivel member end pieces, then the rear engine mounting.
8. Raise lifting table, then remove other bolts and subframe.
9. Disconnect oil level sensor connector and pull cable out of its clamps.
10. Remove protective plate and oil pan.

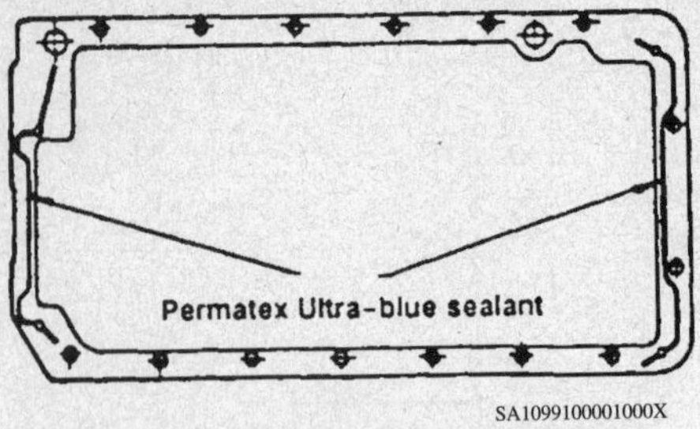
Permatex Ultra-blue sealant
SA1099100001000X

Fig. 19 Engine & transaxle bolt sealer application. 1993 900

Do not remove guide sleeve from cylinder block.

11. Reverse procedure to install, noting the following:
    a. Make sure there are no impurities or foreign matter in pan, then thoroughly clean flange with benzine.
    b. Apply even bead of Loctite 518, or equivalent, along flange before installing pan.

2.5L Engine

1. Raise and support vehicle, then drain oil and remove subframe.
2. Remove oil pan bolts, then the pan.
3. Remove oil strainer holder bolts, then the oil suction pipe retaining bolts in oil pump.
4. Remove strainer, noting oil suction pipe O-ring.
5. Remove anti-slosh baffles.
6. Reverse procedure to install, noting the following:
    a. Apply Loctite 242, or equivalent, to oil suction pipe and pan bolts.
    b. Apply suitable sealing compound to joint at engine to oil pan mating surface.

9000

1994–96

2.0L & 2.3L Engines

1. **On 1995–96 models,** obtain radio anti-theft code as outlined under "Precautions."
2. **On all models,** disconnect battery ground cable, then raise and support vehicle.
3. Remove front righthand wheel, then the righthand wheel housing trim molding.
4. Remove righthand front fender liner.
5. Loosen automatic belt tensioner by pulling belt hard upward while an assistant secures tensioner with locking yoke tool No. 83 94 448, or equivalent.
6. **On turbo models,** remove three bolts securing exhaust pipe to turbo.
7. **On all models,** disconnect oxygen sensor connector and cable, then remove front exhaust pipe.
8. Drain oil from oil pan, then disconnect oil level sensor connector and remove sensor cable from pan.
9. Remove bolts from rear engine mounting and righthand engine mounting.
10. Remove five oil pan front retaining bolts, then remove clip around rubber

gaiter on righthand driveshaft universal joint.
11. Remove two electric leads, brake hose and strut lower bolts from steering swivel member.
12. Pull away steering swivel member to separate driveshaft joint. Install protective caps.
13. Remove driver bracket retaining bolts from engine, then the driver.
14. Remove crankcase breather hose, ground cable from torque arm, then the torque arm.
15. Move lifting eye from rear position to front position.
16. Lift engine and remove protective plate from gearbox.
17. Raise vehicle and remove remaining bolts from pan, then the pan.
18. Reverse procedure to install. Apply sealing compound Loctite 518, or equivalent, to joint surfaces of pan and cylinder block.

3.0L Engine

1. Raise and support vehicle, then drain engine oil into suitable container.
2. Remove front exhaust pipe from both exhaust manifolds, then pull front exhaust pipe down a little.
3. Remove cover plate.
4. Remove oil pan bolts, then the oil pan.
5. Reverse procedure to install, noting the following:
   a. Install oil pan bolts. **Torque,** in sequence shown, **Fig. 20,** to 11 ft. lbs.
   b. Apply suitable sealant to oil pan bolts.

OIL PUMP

REPLACE

900

1993

1. Clean pump area.
2. Remove crankshaft pulley retaining bolt. **Retain crankshaft by installing locking device tool No. 83 92 987, or equivalent, on flywheel ring gear.**
3. Remove pump retaining bolts, then the pump.
4. Apply lubricant to gear wheels.
5. Install ring gear with mark on face visible.
6. Install new sealing ring in pump body groove, then the dowel.
7. To facilitate positioning gear on driving plate, pull pump gear slightly outward.
8. Ensure oil pump is primed with oil prior to installation.
9. Install centering tool No. 83 93 589, or equivalent, in oil pump.
10. Install oil pump with centering tool No. 83 93 589, or equivalent, in place.
11. Install crankshaft pulley bolt and tighten to center oil pump.
12. Install oil pump retaining bolts and tighten to specifications.
13. Remove crankshaft pulley bolt and centering tool No. 83 93 589, or equivalent.
14. Install crankshaft pulley and bolts.

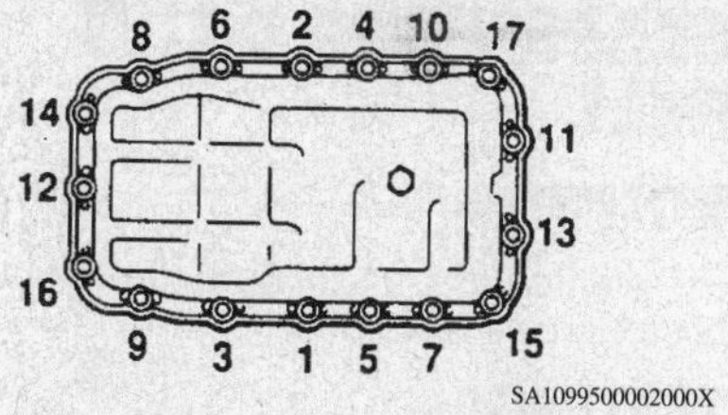

8
6
2
4
10
17
14
11
12
13
16
9
3
1
5
7
15
SA1099500002000X

Fig. 20 Oil pan bolt tightening sequence. 3.0L engine

1994-95

2.0L & 2.3L Engines

1. Disconnect air cleaner and position aside.
2. Loosen belt tensioner with ratchet handle extension and 6 mm drill, **Fig. 1.**
3. Raise and support vehicle, then remove front righthand wheel.
4. Remove crankshaft pulley and oil pump circlip.
5. Remove pump cover using large pair of slip-joint pliers, then the pump gears.
6. Reverse procedure to install, noting the following:
   a. Ensure marking on oil pump ring gear faces outward.
   b. Insert pump gears and place pump cover correctly with aid of arrows.
   c. Tighten crankshaft pulleys and wheel bolts to specifications.

2.5L Engine

1. Disconnect battery ground cable, then remove air cleaner and mass air flow sensor.
2. Slightly loosen pulley bolts, then remove drive belt, belt tensioner, power steering pump pulley, water pump pulley and cover.
3. Remove power steering pump from bracket and set aside.
4. Remove front righthand wheel and cover in wheelhousing.
5. Remove crankshaft pulley by loosening six bolts. Do not remove center bolt.
6. Position No. 1 cylinder in compression position. Markings on camshaft sprockets and timing cover should be in alignment as well as marking on crankshaft. Insert locking tools for camshaft sprockets on both cylinder heads.
7. Mark direction of belt rotation at camshaft and crankshaft markings.
8. Remove tensioning roller, two adjusting rollers and toothed belt.
9. Turn crankshaft back 60° Before Top Dead Center (BTDC).
10. Remove bracket holding middle adjusting roller and tensioning roller.
11. Remove timing cover retaining bolts. Use suitable open-ended spanner to rotate camshaft sprocket No. 1 so timing cover retaining bolt located behind sprocket can be removed. Use care to ensure camshaft does not snap.
12. Turn camshaft sprocket back to zero position, then remove bolt behind sprocket No. 2 the same way.
13. Install suitable lifting sling and yoke, then raise and support vehicle.
14. Remove spoiler sections, front exhaust pipe and protective plate, then install flywheel stop.
15. Remove flywheel pulley, then the subframe.
16. Remove alternator, then the A/C compressor. Hang up compressor.
17. Drain oil, then remove oil pan, soil strainer and anti-slosh baffles.
18. Remove oil pressure switch cable, then lower vehicle and place stand under front of engine.
19. Remove engine mounting and bracket, then the oil pump housing.
20. Remove cover, then the two impellers.
21. Check oil pressure relief valve and control valve.
22. Reverse procedure to install, noting the following:
    a. Markings on impellers should face outward.
    b. Install new gasket to pump housing.
    c. Apply Loctite 242, or equivalent, to anti-slosh baffle, oil suction pipe and oil pan bolts.
    d. Tighten fasteners to specifications.

9000

1993

1. Raise and support front of vehicle.
2. Remove front fender inner liner and righthand side wheel.
3. Remove drive belts.
4. Secure crankshaft from turning, then remove crankshaft pulley attaching bolt.
5. Remove oil pump cover attaching bolts, then the oil pump.
6. To install, proceed as follows:
   a. Ensure pump O-ring is not damaged.
   b. Install oil pump and tighten attaching bolt to specifications.
   c. Install crankshaft pulley and drive belts.
   d. Install fender inner liner and wheel.
   e. Lower vehicle.

1994-95

2.0L & 2.3L Engines

1. Raise and support vehicle, then remove front righthand wheel.
2. Remove wheel housing trim molding and front fender liner.
3. Loosen automatic belt tensioner by pulling belt hard upward while an assistant secures tensioner with locking yoke tool No. 83 94 488, or equivalent.
4. Remove protective plate from gearbox, then lock flywheel with flywheel holder tool No. 83 94 868, or equivalent.
5. Lift belt off crankshaft pulley, then remove crankshaft pulley.
6. If replacing crankshaft seal, pry out seal with screwdriver.
7. Remove retaining ring with chamfer facing outward.
8. Note markings on oil pump, then remove pump.
9. Reverse procedure to install. Ensure

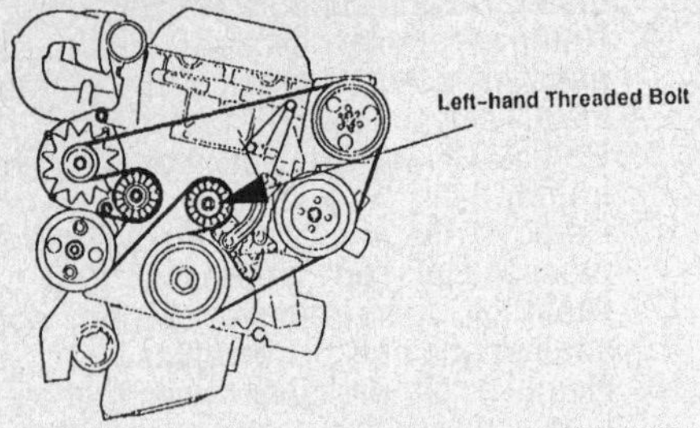
Left-hand Threaded Bolt
SA1069100009000X

Fig. 21 Serpentine drive belt routing. 1993

oil pump arrows are opposite each other.

3.0L Engine

1. Remove timing belt as outlined under "Timing Belt, Replace."
2. Remove bracket holding upper adjuster pulley and tensioner pulley.
3. Remove coolant pump, then lock camshaft sprockets with locking tool Nos. KM-800-1 and KM-800-2, or equivalents, and remove camshaft sprockets.
4. Remove rear timing cover.
5. Raise and support vehicle, then disconnect front exhaust pipe from both exhaust manifolds.
6. Remove protective plate, then install holder tool No. 83 95 063, or equivalent, and remove crankshaft pulley.
7. Remove alternator, then the A/C compressor. Hang A/C compressor aside.
8. Drain engine oil, then remove oil pan and strainer.
9. Disconnect oil pressure switch cable, then lower vehicle and place suitable wood block under front edge of engine block.
10. Remove A/C compressor bracket, then the oil pump housing.
11. Remove cover, then the two impellers.
12. Check oil pressure release valve and oil pressure control valve
13. Reverse procedure to install.

BELT TENSION DATA

Model	Belt	New Lbs.	Used Lbs.
900	A/C	110–130	75–85
900	Alt.②	110–130	75–85
900	Alt.③	110–130④	⑤
900	Power Steer.	90–110	65–75
9000①	A/C	110–130	75–85
9000①	Alt.	170–190	110–130

①— 4-cylinder engine, less balancer shafts.

②— Single belt.

③— Double belt.

④— Check belts separately.

⑤— When checking one belt, 65–75 ft. lbs.; when checking both belts together, 140–150 ft. lbs.

SERPENTINE DRIVE BELT

ROUTING

Refer to **Figs. 21 through 24** for routing of serpentine drive belt.

TESTING

Check performance of belt tensioner by pressing and pulling belt. Belt should return smoothly to tensioned position. Tension of belt should be a minimum of 40 ft. lbs.

COOLING SYSTEM BLEED

2.0L & 2.3L ENGINES

These engines do not require a specific bleed procedure. After filling cooling system, run engine to operating temperature with the radiator/pressure cap off. Air will then be automatically bled through cap opening.

2.5L & 3.0L ENGINES

1. Fill system to MAX level, then fit pressure lid.
2. Start engine and run warm, preferably at varying speeds, until radiator fan starts.
3. Remove pressure lid and top up to MAX level.
4. Refit pressure lid and run engine at varying speeds until radiator fan starts three more times.
5. Switch off engine and top up to MAX level if necessary.

WATER PUMP

REPLACE

900

1993

1. Disconnect battery ground cable and drain cooling system.
2. Release tension and remove water pump drive belt.
3. Remove pulley retaining bolts and pulley.
4. Remove pump retaining bolts and pump.
5. Reverse procedure to install and refill cooling system to specifications.

1994–96

2.0L & 2.3L Engines

1. Drain coolant, then remove air cleaner. Open expansion tank lid to speed drainage.
2. **On turbo models,** disconnect intake hose and plug pipe, then remove bypass hose and pressure pipe between charge air cooler and throttle body.
3. **On all models,** loosen belt tensioner with ratchet extension and 6 mm drill, **Fig. 1.**
4. Disconnect steering servo pump with console and hang on radiator crossmember.

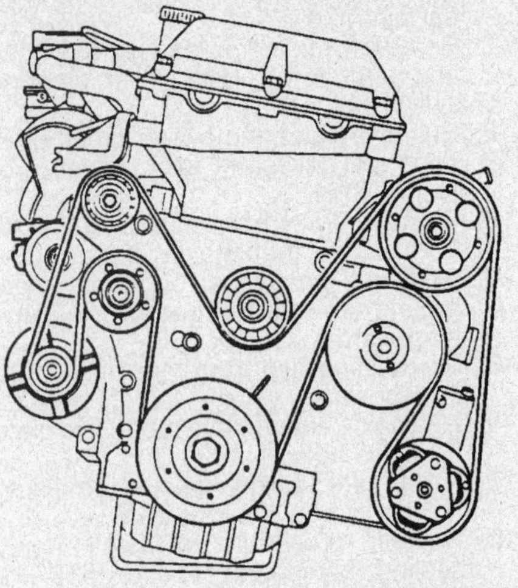
SA1069400010000X

Fig. 22 Serpentine drive belt routing. 1994–96 900 w/2.0L & 2.3L engines

5. Disconnect coolant hoses and pipes from pump, then remove screw holding coolant pipe to front lefthand corner of engine.
6. Remove hose connecting throttle body to coolant pipe, then remove screws on thermostat housing. Move pipes to one side.
7. **On turbo models,** remove boost pressure control valve and move to one side.
8. **On all models,** remove coolant pipe.
9. Remove sleeve with O-rings, then the coolant pump from pump housing.
10. Reverse procedure to install.

2.5L Engine

1. Drain coolant, then remove air cleaner, complete with hoses. Open expansion tank lid to speed drainage.
2. Loosen belt tensioner by turning belt tensioner securing screw with suitable 15 mm open-ended spanner forward in vehicle.
3. Remove belt from coolant pump pulley and slowly release tensioner, then remove belt tensioner and servo pump pulley.
4. Remove coolant pump pulley by pressing motor to left and using motor console as support.
5. Remove cam belt cover, then the coolant pump.
6. Reverse procedure to install, noting the following:
   a. Tighten servo pump pulley and belt tensioner to specifications.
   b. Bleed system as outlined under "Cooling System Bleed."

9000

1. Raise and support vehicle, then remove righthand wheel.
2. Remove front wheelwell liner for access to water pump.
3. Drain coolant.
4. Loosen drive belt and remove water pump pulley.
5. Remove belt tensioner pulley.

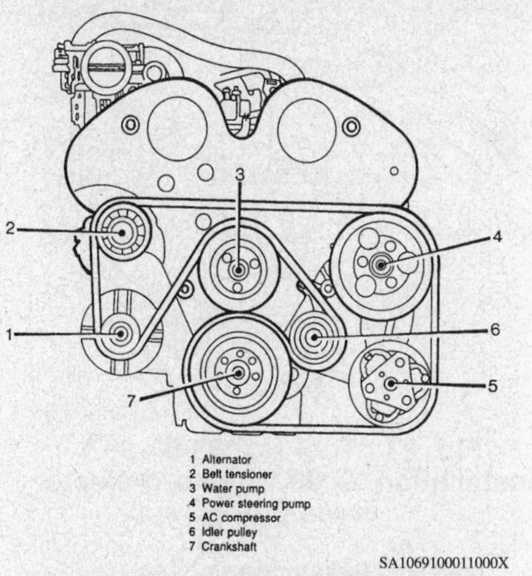
1
2
3
4
5
6
7
1 Alternator
2 Belt tensioner
3 Water pump
4 Power steering pump
5 AC compressor
6 Idler pulley
7 Crankshaft
SA1069100011000X

Fig. 23 Serpentine drive belt routing. 1994–96 900 w/2.5L engine

6. Remove clips securing oil lines.
7. Remove clip securing water pipe to block.
8. Disconnect hoses from pump and remove pump attaching bolts, then the pump.
9. Reverse procedure to install, tighten bolts and refill cooling system to specifications.

FUEL PUMP

REPLACE

The fuel system on models with fuel injection is under constant pressure. Exercise caution when disconnecting fuel lines to release pressure slowly and prevent fuel from spraying.

900

1993

1. Disconnect battery ground cable.
2. Remove panel at rear of luggage compartment floor.
3. Lift fuel pump cover, then disconnect electrical connectors from fuel pump, feed pump and fuel flow transmitter and remove cover.
4. Disconnect fuel line from pump, then remove clamp around pump sealing collar.
5. Lift out fuel pump and container.
6. Disconnect return fuel line from container and feed pump electrical connector from gland in tank.
7. Remove fuel pump and strainer from fuel container.
8. Reverse procedure to install.

1994–96

1. Using suitable tank draining unit, drain fuel tank through fuel filler pipe.
2. Raise and support vehicle. Ensure righthand rear support is positioned as far out as possible so it won't obstruct work.
3. Remove rubber hoses from tank and plug tank.
4. Remove clamp securing fuel filter.

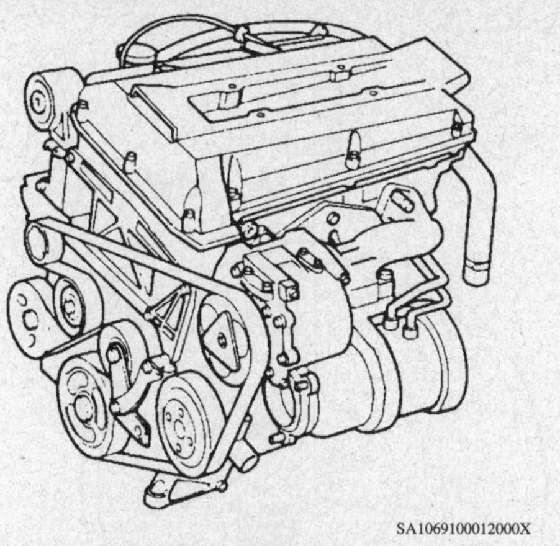
SA1069100012000X

Fig. 24 Serpentine drive belt routing. 1994–96 9000

5. Support tank with suitable pillar lift, then remove metal strap nuts and straps.
6. Carefully lower tank, righthand side first, until top becomes visible.
7. Disconnect fuel pump connectors, then the fuel pump pressure and return lines.
8. Lower tank to convenient working height, then use fuel pump tool No. 83 94 462, or equivalent, to remove screw ring from top of fuel pump.
9. Lift pump until top of it is about 50 mm above tank, then turn pump clockwise about 80°. Carefully remove pump.
10. Reverse procedure to install. Tighten fasteners to specifications.

9000

Bosch Non-Ejector Type Pump

1. **On 1995–96 models,** obtain radio anti-theft code as outlined under "Precautions."
2. **On all models,** disconnect and tape battery positive cable.
3. Lift up rear section of luggage compartment floor, then remove two floor to panel attaching screws and lift out floor panel.
4. Using an Allen wrench, loosen two bayonet attaching screws, then remove fuel pump cover.
5. Disconnect electrical connectors from fuel pump, feed pump and fuel gauge transmitter.
6. Loosen, then remove fuel pipe banjo coupling. Retain washers.
7. Remove fuel pump rubber collar clip.
8. Remove fuel pump and suction reservoir.
9. Reverse procedure to install, noting the following:
   a. Install fuel pump in rubber collar so lip of collar is 1.97 inches (50 mm) above top edge of pump as shown, **Fig. 25.**
   b. Ensure relief valve on reservoir is turned 45°±10° from mark, **Fig. 26.**
   c. Adjust overall length of fuel pump to 9.84 inches (250 mm), **Fig. 25.**

Walbro Ejector Type Pump

1. **On 1995–96 models,** obtain radio anti-theft code as outlined under "Precautions."
2. **On all models,** disconnect and tape battery positive cable.
3. Lift up rear section of luggage compartment floor, then remove two floor to panel attaching screws and lift out floor panel.
4. Remove pump cover, then disconnect wiring harness.
5. Disconnect fuel lines. Position lines aside.
6. Install tool No. 83 94 397, or equivalent, **Fig. 27.**
7. Install chain through load securing eyes, **Fig. 28,** then tighten chain.
8. Loosen screw top, then remove tool.
9. Remove screw top, then the seal.
10. Remove fuel pump from fuel tank, tilting top to right.
11. Reverse procedure to install, noting the following:
    a. Ensure bottom of pump is between ribs on bottom of tank.
    b. Ensure mark on top of pump aligns with mark on top of tank.
    c. Using tool No. 83 94 397, or equivalent, **torque** screw top to 40 ft. lbs. Do not allow pump to turn when tightening screw top.

TURBOCHARGER

REPLACE

900

1993

1. Disconnect both battery cables, then remove battery.
2. Disconnect electrical and vacuum connections from distributor, then remove distributor.
3. Remove distributor heat shield.
4. Disconnect suction pipe, pressure pipe and oil supply pipe from turbocharger. **Oil supply pipe must also be disconnected from engine block.**
5. Disconnect solenoid at turbocharger and charging pressure regulator.
6. Disconnect turbocharger support bracket from transaxle.
7. Remove oil dipstick pipe.
8. Disconnect oil return pipe from turbocharger.
9. Disconnect exhaust pipe from turbocharger.
10. Remove nuts, spacer sleeves and washers from exhaust manifold.
11. Lower exhaust manifold until clear of studs, then remove exhaust manifold and turbocharger unit as an assembly.
12. Mount the assembly in vise and remove nuts attaching turbocharger and exhaust manifold.
13. Separate turbocharger from exhaust manifold.
14. Reverse procedure to install, noting the following:
    a. Install new gaskets on mating surfaces.
    b. Install new nuts for exhaust manifold and new locking nuts connecting exhaust pipe to turbocharger.

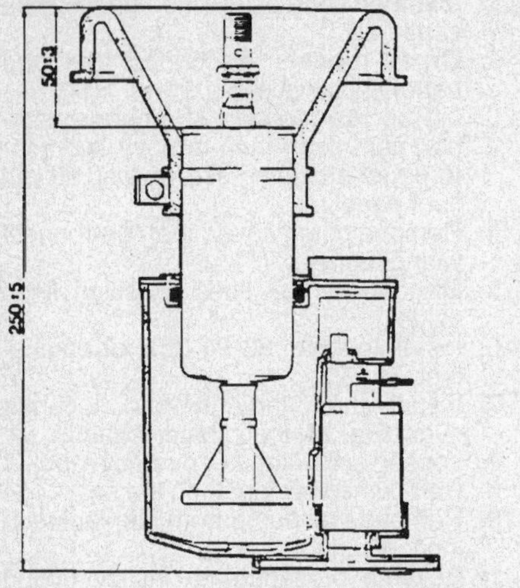
50±3
250±5
SA1029100001000X

Fig. 25 Fuel pump installation. 9000 w/Bosch non-ejector type pump

1994–96

1. Drain coolant. Remove expansion tank lid to speed drainage.
2. Raise and support vehicle, then remove air pipe and hose between turbocharger and charge air cooler.
3. Disconnect joint between front exhaust pipe and intermediate pipe, then loosen screw holding exhaust pipe to engine.
4. Remove front exhaust pipe from turbocharger and hang pipe to oxygen sensor cable is not damaged.
5. Break seal and remove wastegate locking ring.
6. Remove turbocharger stay, then the oil return pipe. Plug pipe with rag.
7. Disconnect oil pipe on oil filter, then lower vehicle.
8. Remove hoses to boost pressure control valve, noting their positions.
9. Remove intake hose with bypass hose.
10. Remove wastegate diaphragm nuts, then the intake pipe together with crankcase ventilation pipe.
11. Remove oil pipe to turbocharger, then the lower coolant pipe.
12. Remove upper coolant pipe screw from turbocharger, then the turbocharger.
13. Reverse procedure to install, noting the following:
    a. Lubricate three pin screws on turbocharger with Molycote 1000, or equivalent, before installing front exhaust pipe.
    b. Tighten turbocharger to specifications.
    c. Ensure turbo system is working properly.

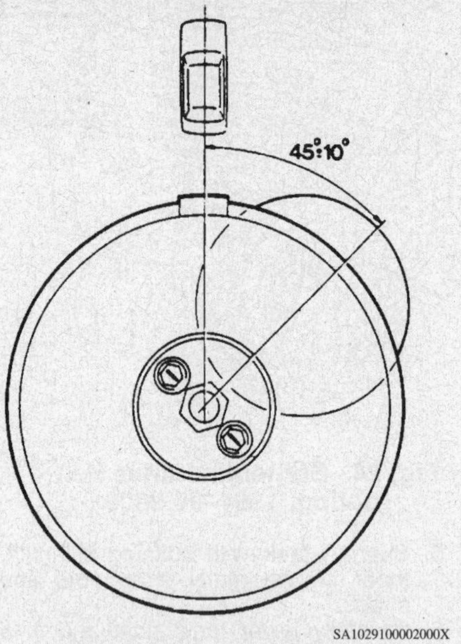
45°±10°
SA1029100002000X

Fig. 26 Fuel pump relief valve positioning. 9000 w/Bosch non-ejector type pump

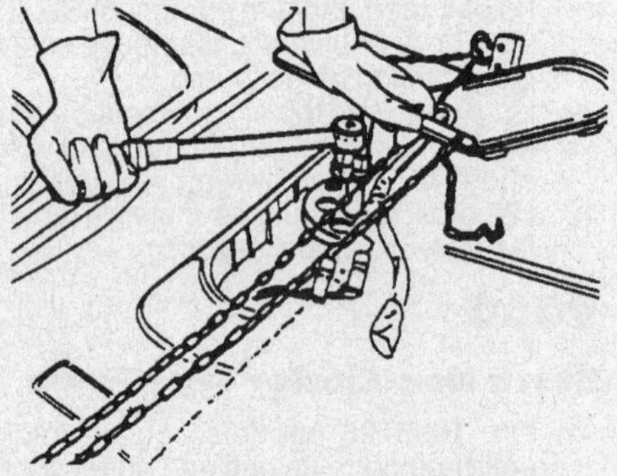
SA1029100004000X

Fig. 28 Load securing chain installation. 9000 w/Walbro ejector type pump

9000

1. Loosen A/C compressor belt tensioner, then remove A/C compressor drive belt.
2. Disconnect upper pipe coupling on oil cooler, then remove clips attaching pipe to radiator.
3. Remove A/C compressor mounting bolts, then insert piece of sheet metal to protect oil cooler and position A/C compressor aside.
4. Disconnect solenoid valve electrical connector, then remove solenoid valve from mounting on radiator.
5. Disconnect radiator cooling fan electrical connector, then remove mounting

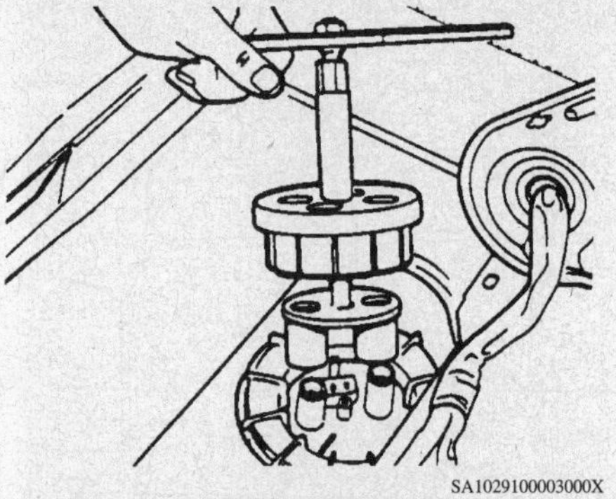
SA1029100003000X

Fig. 27 Tool No. 83-94-397 installation. 9000 w/Walbro ejector type pump

bolts and radiator cooling fan.

6. Disconnect air mass meter electrical connector and remove clips securing air mass meter to air cleaner cover, then pull rubber socket connector off turbocharger and position air mass meter aside.
7. Disconnect pressure pipe from turbocharger.
8. Remove bolts securing oil pipe to turbocharger, then unbolt clutch slave cylinder and remove clip securing oil pipe to cylinder head.
9. Disconnect oil pipe banjo coupling from engine block, then remove clip on intake manifold.
10. Disconnect exhaust pipe from turbocharger.
11. Disconnect exhaust pipe front rubber hangers.
12. Remove support bracket between oil pan and turbocharger.
13. Remove attaching bolts for oil return pipe at engine block. **Cover exposed hole to prevent nuts or washers from exhaust manifold entering engine during removal.**
14. Remove nuts and washers securing exhaust manifold to cylinder head.
15. Lower exhaust manifold until clear of studs, then remove exhaust manifold and turbocharger unit as an assembly.
16. Mount assembly in vise and remove nuts attaching turbocharger and exhaust manifold.
17. Separate turbocharger from exhaust manifold.
18. Reverse procedure to install, noting the following:
    a. Install new locknuts attaching turbocharger to exhaust manifold with locking flanges turned inward, then tighten to specifications.
    b. Tighten exhaust manifold nuts to specifications.
    c. Adjust A/C drive belt tension.

TIGHTENING SPECIFICATIONS

900

Year	Component	Torque/Ft. Lbs.
1993	Big-End Bearings	41
	Camshaft Bearing Cap Bolts	11
	Camshaft Cover	11
	Camshaft Sprocket Bolts	47
	Crankshaft Pulley Bolts	130
	Cylinder Head Bolts	①
	Distributor Bolts	13
	Engine To Transaxle Bolts	19
	Exhaust Manifold Nuts (Non Turbo)	13
	Exhaust Manifold Nuts (Turbo)	19
	Flywheel Bolts (17 mm Bolts)	44
	Flywheel Bolts (19 mm Bolts)	63
	Intake Manifold Attaching Bolts	16
	Main Bearings	81
	Oil Pump Bolts	6
	Rear Engine Plate (Flywheel End)	19
	Spark Plugs	21
	Thermostat Housing Cover	16
	Throttle Housing	16
	Timing Chain Tensioner Bolt	47
	Timing Cover Bolts	19
	Valve Cover Bolts	4
	Valve Cover Bolts	11
1994–96②	Camshaft Sprocket Bolts	47
	Camshaft Cover Bolts	11
	Chain Tensioner	47
	Chain Tensioner Pushrod & Spring	16
	Cover Plate	21
	Crankshaft Pulley	130
	Cylinder Head Bolts	①
	Front Engine Mounting Bolts	54
	Front Exhaust Pipe Nuts	16
	Front Subframe Retaining Bolts	85
	Fuel Pump Screw Ring	55
	Gearbox Oil Hoses	19
	Ignition Discharge Module	21
	Intake Manifold	16
	Middle Subframe Retaining Bolts	141
	Oil Cooler	13
	Oil Pan Bolts	16
	Rear Subframe Retaining Bolts	81⑤
	Selector Lever Cable	16
	Selector Rod	16
	Spark Plugs	21
	Timing Cover To Cylinder Head Cover Bolts	16
	Turbocharger	16
	Turbocharger Nuts	16

Continued

900—Continued

Year	Component	Torque/Ft. Lbs.
1994–96③	Anti-Slosh Baffle Bolts	6
	Bearing Cap Bolts	①
	Belt Tensioner	30
	Camshaft Sprockets	37④
	Center Intake Manifold To Fuel Rail	15
	Coolant Bridge Connections	22
	Crankshaft Pulley	15
	Cylinder Head Bolts	①
	Front Engine Mounting Bolts	54
	Front Subframe Retaining Bolts	85
	Fuel Injection Manifold	15
	Intake Manifold	16
	Intake Manifold Retaining Bar	15
	Lower Adjusting Roller	15
	Middle Subframe Retaining Bolts	141
	Oil Pan Bolts	11
	Oil Suction Pipe Bolts	6
	Radiator Hose Connections	22
	Rear Engine Mounting Bolts	35
	Rear Subframe Retaining Bolts	81⑤
	Servo Pump Pulley	6
	Tensioning Roller	15
	Transaxle Oil Pipe Connections	19
	Upper Adjusting Roller	30

① — Refer to "Cylinder Head, Replace" for procedure.
② — 4–cylinder engines.
③ — 6–cylinder engine.
④ — Plus an additional 60°.
⑤ — Plus an additional 75°.

9000

Year	Component	Torque/Ft. Lbs.
1993–96⑤	Balance Shaft Idler Wheel Sprocket③	17
	Balance Shaft Sprockets③	47
	Big-End Bearings②	41
	Big-End Bearings③	15④
	Camshaft Bearing Caps	11
	Camshaft Cover Attaching Bolts	11
	Camshaft Sprocket Bolts	47
	Crankshaft Pulley②	129
	Crankshaft Pulley③	129
	Cylinder Head Bolts	①
	Distributor Bolt②	13
	Engine Mounting Bolts⑤	⑤
	Engine To Transaxle Bolts	40-75
	Exhaust Manifold Nuts (Non-Turbo)	13
	Exhaust Manifold Nuts (Turbo)②	19
	Exhaust Manifold Nuts (Turbo)③	18
	Flywheel Bolts (17 mm Bolt)②	44
	Flywheel Bolts (19 mm Bolt)	63
	Intake Manifold Attaching Bolts	16
	Main Bearings②	81
	Main Bearings③	15④
	Oil Pan Bolts	16

Continued

9000—Continued

Year	Component	Torque/Ft. Lbs.
1993–96⑤	Oil Pan Drain Plug	19
	Oil Pump Bolts	6
	Spark Plugs	21
	Thermostat Housing	16
	Throttle Housing	16
	Timing Chain Tensioner	47
	Timing Cover②	18
	Timing Cover③	15
	Valve Cover Bolts	11
	Water Pump Pulley Bolts	6
	Water Pump Retaining Bolts	15
1995–96⑥	Belt Tensioning Pulley	15
	Camshaft Bearing Cap Bolts	6
	Camshaft Sprocket	37⑧
	Center Intake Manifold Bolts	16
	Coolant Bridge Bolts	22
	Crankshaft Pulley	15
	Cylinder Head Bolts	①
	Engine Mounting Bolts	29
	Intake Manifold Bolts	15
	Lower Intake Manifold Bolts	15
	Lower Roller Counter	30
	Oil Pump Housing Bolts	5
	Oil Pump Housing Lid Bolts	5
	Oil Pressure Release Valve	⑦
	Power Steering Pump Belt Tensioner	30
	Spark Plugs	19
	Steering Swivel Member To MacPherson Struts	68
	Tensioning Pulley	15

① — Refer to "Cylinder Head, Replace" for procedure.
② — 4–cylinder engine less balancer shafts.
③ — 4–cylinder engine w/balancer shafts.
④ — Tighten an additional 70°.
⑤ — 4–cylinder engines.
⑥ — 6–cylinder engine.
⑦ — Aluminum grommet, 15 ft. lbs.; copper grommet, 21 ft. lbs.
⑧ — Tighten an additional 60°.

Clutch & Manual Transaxle

INDEX

	Page No.
Adjustments	38-34
Clutch Pedal	38-34
Shift Linkage	38-34
900	38-34
9000	38-34
Clutch, Replace	38-34
900	38-34
9000	38-35
Hydraulic System Service	38-34
Clutch Bleed	38-34
Master Cylinder, Replace	38-34
Slave Cylinder, Replace	38-34
Tightening Specifications	38-38
Transaxle, Replace	38-35
900	38-35
9000	38-37

ADJUSTMENTS

Clutch Pedal

No adjustment is necessary since clutch adjustment is automatic. On hydraulic clutches, the sliding lock ring on the slave cylinder moves along the piston to compensate for clutch disc wear.

Shift Linkage

900

1993

Tapered Pin Gearshift Rod Joint

1. Place gear shift lever in R, then turn ignition key to locked position.
2. Gear shift rod freeplay should be .12–.16 inch (3–4 mm).
3. Adjust freeplay by positioning gear lever housing forward or backward until freeplay is within specification. Use key tool No. 87 90 370, or equivalent, to remove gear lever housing attaching bolts.

Clamped Gearshift Rod Joint

1. Pry out and lift rubber boot from console.
2. Loosen pinch bolt at selector rod joint.
3. Lock gear selector lever in reverse by inserting a .16 inch (4 mm) drill bit through holes in gear selector lever and gear selector lever housing.
4. Connect the selector rod to selector rod joint and tighten pinch bolt to specification.

1994–96

1. Place gear lever in 4th gear.
2. Remove gearbox plastic plug and fit locking pin tool No. 87 92 335, or equivalent, so 4th gear is fixed in gearbox. Locking pin ring should be all the way up.
3. Remove gaiter on gear lever and check that locking pin tool can be inserted into hole in lever housing. locking pin ring should be down in the hole. If it is not possible to insert locking pin, continue this procedure to adjust lever. If no adjustment is necessary, remove locking pin tool.
4. Remove clamp holding gear rod in linkage on gearbox, then ensure gear lever is in 4th gear.
5. Insert locking pin tool in gear lever housing. locking pin ring should be down in hole.
6. Tighten gear rod to linkage clamp nut to specifications.
7. Remove locking pin from gearbox, then install plastic plug.
8. Remove locking pin from gear lever housing and install gaiter.
9. Test shift linkage by changing gears.

9000

1. Pry out and lift rubber boot from console.
2. Place gear shift lever in reverse by inserting a .16 inch (4 mm) drill through fixing holes in gear lever housing.
3. Connect selector rod to selector rod joint, then tighten pinch bolt to specifications.
4. Remove drill, then reinstall rubber boot.

HYDRAULIC SYSTEM SERVICE

SLAVE CYLINDER, REPLACE

1. Remove transaxle as outlined in "Transaxle, Replace."
2. Remove release bearing from slave cylinder.
3. Disconnect pressure pipe and remove bleed nipple.
4. Remove three slave cylinder retaining bolts, then the slave cylinder.
5. Reverse procedure to install, noting the following:
   a. Use new O-rings.
   b. Bleed clutch hydraulic system as outlined in "Clutch Bleed."

MASTER CYLINDER, REPLACE

900

1. Remove clip securing hydraulic tube from master cylinder, then disconnect tube from cylinder.
2. Remove knee shield from under left-hand side of instrument panel.
3. Remove clevis pin connecting pushrod to clutch pedal.
4. Remove master cylinder retaining nuts from inside of bulkhead, then the master cylinder from engine compartment side.
5. Disconnect hydraulic supply hose from master cylinder and secure it in a raised position so that fluid will not runout.
6. Reverse procedure to install. Bleed clutch hydraulic system as outlined in "Clutch Bleed."

9000

1. Remove trim panel from under left-hand side of instrument panel.
2. Remove clip, then the clevis pin connecting clutch pedal to master cylinder pushrod.
3. Place sheet of cardboard under clutch pedal to prevent hydraulic fluid from dripping on carpet.
4. Disconnect supply hose from cylinder and plug end of hose.
5. Disconnect hydraulic hose from cylinder, then remove retaining bolts and cylinder.
6. Reverse procedure to install. Bleed clutch hydraulic system as outlined in "Clutch Bleed."

CLUTCH BLEED

1. Attach clear vinyl hose to bleed nipple of slave cylinder, then place opposite end of hose into a clear container.
2. Fill fluid reservoir and open bleed nipple ½ turn.
3. Attach suitable cooling system pressure tester to the fluid reservoir.
4. Pump pressure tester until all air bubbles are gone from system.
5. Close bleed nipple, refill reservoir and ensure clutch operates properly.

CLUTCH

REPLACE

900

1993

An inspection opening has been included in the clutch housing to check clutch wear.

1. Perform clutch inspection as follows:
   a. Remove plug from inspection opening in clutch cover.
   b. Depress and release clutch pedal and ensure release bearing is in contact with pressure plate fingers.
   c. Measure clearance between front edge of plastic sleeve and edge of release bearing.
   d. Clearance should be .08–.35 inch.

If clearance is less than .08 inch, clutch should be replaced.
2. Disconnect battery ground cable.
3. Remove bolts securing clutch housing and remove housing.
4. With clutch pedal depressed (clutch released), insert spacer tool No. 83 90 023, or equivalent, between pressure plate diaphragm spring and housing. **If clutch cannot be released in normal manner, use lever tool No. 83 93 175, or equivalent, to depress diaphragm spring.**
5. Remove lock ring, seal cap, and plastic propeller from clutch shaft at gear housing.
6. Remove clutch shaft, using lever tool No. 83 93 175, or equivalent, and an M8 bolt of suitable length.
7. Remove three bolts securing slave cylinder, then the six bolts securing pressure plate to flywheel.
8. Remove clutch disc, pressure plate, and release mechanism as an assembly, then separate components. **It is not necessary to disconnect hydraulic hose to slave cylinder.**
9. Check condition of clutch shaft seal in gear housing, and replace as needed.
10. Position new clutch disc, pressure plate, and release mechanism on flywheel, ensuring hardened face of release bearing faces flywheel, and install two pressure plate retaining bolts finger tight.
11. Insert clutch shaft, ensuring shaft engages clutch disc and pilot bearing.
12. Using hammer, drive clutch shaft into place, ensuring lock ring engages groove in gear housing.
13. Reverse procedure to complete installation, noting the following:
    a. Depress clutch pedal to remove spacer tool from pressure plate. **Do not depress pedal farther than necessary to remove spacer. Slave cylinder seal may be forced out of position, causing fluid leakage.**
    b. Depress clutch pedal and position plastic sleeve against release bearing.

1994–96

1. Remove transaxle as outlined under, "Manual Transaxle, Replace."
2. Install flywheel holder tool No. 83 94 868, or equivalent, to lock flywheel.
3. Remove pressure plate screws, then the clutch.
4. Inspect clutch as follows:
    a. Check clutch plate contact surface in flywheel. If surface is blue annealed and has small cracks, it is satisfactory. If there are deep scratches, flywheel should be turned in lathe or replaced.
    b. Check pressure plate in spring unit for any scratches or deformity. Replace pressure plate if surfaces are uneven.
    c. Check wear on clutch plate and replace as necessary.
5. Place plate and pressure plate on flywheel and loosely attach screws.
6. Center plate with centering drift tool No. 87 92 327, or equivalent. Tighten screws alternately to specifications.
7. Install manual transaxle as outlined under "Manual Transaxle, Replace."

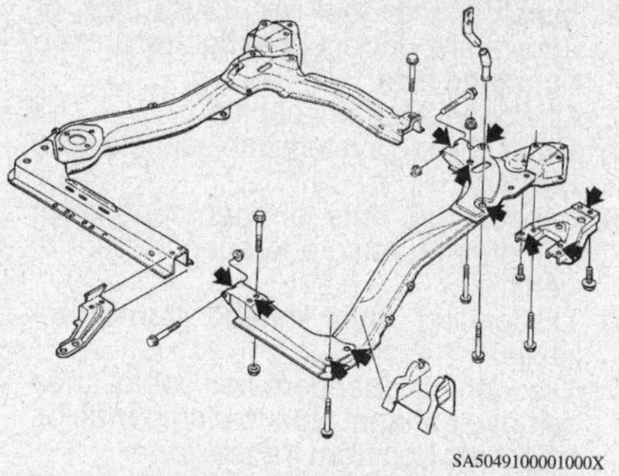
SA5049100001000X

Fig. 1 Subframe mounting bolts. 9000

9000

An inspection opening has been included in the clutch housing to check clutch wear.

1. Perform clutch inspection as follows:
    a. Remove plug from inspection opening in clutch cover.
    b. Depress and release clutch pedal and ensure release bearing is in contact with pressure plate fingers.
    c. Measure clearance between front edge of plastic sleeve and edge of release bearing.
    d. Clearance should be .08–.35 inch. If clearance is less than .08 inch, clutch should be replaced.
2. Raise and support front of vehicle.
3. **On 1995–96 models,** obtain radio anti-theft code as outlined under "Precautions."
4. **On all models,** disconnect battery cables, then remove battery.
5. Remove washer fluid reservoir, then disconnect positive lead from terminal block.
6. Remove fuel filter, terminal block, then the battery shelf.
7. Disconnect electrical connector from air mass meter, then remove meter.
8. Remove air cleaner intake duct, then disconnect Hall transmitter lead from distributor.
9. Remove cover and filter element from air cleaner, then the air cleaner body.
10. Remove turbo pressure pipe, then disconnect battery ground lead and backup lamp switch from gearbox.
11. Attach clamp to hose in slave cylinder pressure line, then tighten clamp securely and disconnect pressure line between pipe and hose. Remove oil supply pipe clamp.
12. Disconnect lefthand engine mount, then support engine using engine lifting tool No. 83 93 977, or equivalent.
13. Remove lefthand front wheel and wing insert panel, then separate suspension arm from lower ball joint.
14. Disconnect speedometer cable, then carefully remove cable as not to allow drive to fall into transaxle.
15. Separate selector rod joint halves, then remove clip from dust cover on intermediate driveshaft.
16. Disconnect intake manifold brace, then remove starter motor attaching bolts and starter.
17. Remove engine to transaxle attaching bolts, except bolt positioned at top flange between engine and transaxle. Insert locating dowel tools No. 8392128, or equivalents, in bolt holes.
18. Loosen two subframe pivot mountings, then remove four attaching bolts, **Fig. 1.**
19. Remove attaching bolts and screws from subframe attaching point, then remove wheel arch bracket lower attaching point attaching bolts, allowing subframe to hang from anti-roll bar.
20. Remove rubber boot to U-joint retaining clip, then the driveshaft and install protective covers on open ends of boot and driver cup.
21. Attach lifting sling to transaxle, then remove last attaching bolt. Withdraw transaxle, and allow to hang from sling.
22. Install flywheel lock tool No. 86 92 987, or equivalent, to top of locating dowel, then lift off clutch assembly and remove driven plate.
23. Reverse procedure to install. Tighten bolts to specifications.

TRANSAXLE

REPLACE

900

1993

Except Turbo 16 Engine

1. Disconnect battery ground cable, then drain coolant into suitable container.
2. Disconnect windshield washer hose and hood hinge links. Scribe hood hinge reference marks, then remove hood.
3. Disconnect and/or remove the following components:
    a. Upper radiator hose and engine ground straps.
    b. Wiring harness connectors to distributor and ignition coil and distributor high tension lead.
    c. Disconnect hoses, then remove preheater valve.
    d. Hoses to vacuum pump, crankcase ventilation system and brake booster.
    e. Hydraulic hose to clutch slave cylinder. **Plug hose and cylinder openings to prevent contamination.**
    f. Main harness connector at rear of engine.
    g. Wiring harness connectors at alternator and oil pressure switch.
    h. Heater and expansion tank hoses.
    i. Lower radiator hose and throttle cable at housing and bracket.
    j. Wiring harness connector to oxygen sensor.
    k. Fuel lines to engine. **Prior to removal, clean area surrounding fuel lines to prevent contamination. After fuel line removal, plug openings to prevent fuel spillage.**

l. Oil cooler hoses. **Plug hoses and fittings.**
m. Remove power steering pump and set aside.
n. Wiring harness connectors to APC solenoid, if equipped.
o. Remove APC solenoid, if equipped.
p. Wiring harness connector to knock sensor, if equipped.
q. Remove compressor mounting bolts and secure compressor in righthand wheel housing, then disconnect A/C wiring harness connectors and remove auxiliary fan.

4. Remove clamps and boots from inner ends of driveshafts.
5. Place spacer tool No. 83 93 209, or equivalent, between upper control arm underside and car body. Insert tool from wheel housing side and ensure it is properly positioned to unload suspension when vehicle is raised.
6. Raise and support front of vehicle.
7. Unbolt lower control arm from steering knuckle, then pull knuckle and axle assembly outward and support against outer end of lower control arm.
8. Disconnect shift linkage from transaxle.
9. Disconnect exhaust pipe from engine.
10. Remove speedometer cable from engine.
11. Remove rear engine mounting bolts.
12. Loosen front engine mounting nut enough to allow mount to be lifted out of bracket.
13. **On models with power steering,** disconnect hydraulic hoses at servo pump and plug exposed openings.
14. **On all models,** install suitable lifting device on engine and raise engine/transaxle assembly slightly. Move engine/transaxle assembly from side to side to free universal joints, then remove assembly.
15. Remove engine/transaxle assembly from chassis. Place protective cover on universal joints and boots to prevent entry of dirt.
16. It is not necessary to separate engine/transaxle assembly to overhaul transaxle. If transaxle is to be overhauled while attached to engine, the flywheel and starter must be removed. If transaxle separation is desired, use the following procedure:
    a. Clean engine/transaxle assembly.
    b. Drain engine oil, then remove ring gear cover.
    c. Using slide hammer No. 83 90 270 and joint No. 87 90 529, or equivalents, remove clutch shaft.
    d. Remove slave cylinder attaching bolts, then engine to transaxle attaching bolts.
    e. Carefully separate transaxle from engine. **Do not force engine and transaxle apart without first ensuring all bolts have been removed.**
17. Reverse procedure to install. Tighten bolts to specifications.

Turbo 16 Engine

1. Scribe hood hinge reference marks, then remove hood.
2. Install spacer tool No. 83 93 209, or equivalent, under upper control arm on righthand side.
3. Disconnect battery cables.
4. Drain cooling system into suitable container.
5. Loosen lug nuts on righthand front wheel, then raise and support front of vehicle.
6. Disconnect shift linkage from transaxle.
7. Disconnect speedometer cable, then remove exhaust pipe to clamp bracket attaching bolt from transaxle.
8. Loosen boot clamps on inner ends of drive axles, and slide boots outward.
9. Remove righthand front wheel and tire assembly.
10. Separate ball joint from lower control arm.
11. Separate universal joint and position steering knuckle aside.
12. Disconnect battery positive cable from body clips.
13. Disconnect ground cable from transaxle.
14. Disconnect starter motor wiring.
15. Disconnect exhaust pipe from exhaust manifold.
16. Disconnect pressure line from power steering pump, then plug open fittings.
17. **On models with A/C,** remove A/C compressor drive belt.
18. **On all models,** disconnect coolant hoses from heat exchanger valve, expansion tank, thermostat housing and bottom of radiator.
19. Disconnect the following electrical connectors from components on lefthand side of engine:
    a. Air mass meter.
    b. Throttle switch.
    c. AIC actuator.
    d. Injection valves.
    e. Thermostatic switch.
    f. Ground connections at forward lifting lug.
20. Disconnect the following electrical connectors from components on righthand side of engine:
    a. A/C compressor, if equipped.
    b. Alternator and regulator.
    c. Blue wire at oil pressure switch.
    d. AIC actuator.
    e. Yellow/white wire at temperature sensor.
    f. Gray wire at knock sensor.
21. Disconnect electrical connector from clip on fuel injection manifold, from rear of engine, from coolant hose between engine and coolant overflow tank.
22. Remove harness from engine compartment, then position aside.
23. Remove alternator drive belt, then the alternator. Position alternator aside.
24. Disconnect brake servo hose from intake manifold, then the throttle cable.
25. **On models with A/C,** disconnect compressor, then position compressor aside.
26. **On all models,** disconnect fuel lines from front of fuel injection manifold and fuel pressure regulator.
27. Remove ignition coil, then disconnect turbo pressure line from turbocharger and induction air cooler/throttle housing.
28. Remove auxiliary fan.
29. Remove turbocharger air mass meter together with suction pipe.
30. Disconnect vacuum hoses from solenoid valve and crankcase ventilation system from suction pipe.
31. Disconnect electrical connector from Hall switch and coil in distributor.
32. Unfasten Hall switch cable from clips on clutch cover.
33. Disconnect solenoid valve hoses from turbocharger and charging pressure regulator.
34. Disconnect hydraulic hose from clutch slave cylinder, then plug all open fittings.
35. Remove engine mounting bolts.
36. Attach suitable lifting device to engine/transaxle assembly, then raise assembly until lefthand inner universal joint can be disconnected. Disconnect universal joint.
37. Continue to raise engine/transaxle assembly, then disconnect oil cooler hoses and power steering pump hose.
38. Remove engine/transaxle assembly from chassis. Place protective covers on universal joints and boots to prevent entry of dirt.
39. It is not necessary to separate engine/transaxle assembly to overhaul the transaxle. If transaxle is to be overhauled while attached to engine, flywheel and starter must be removed. If transaxle separation is desired, use the following procedure:
    a. Clean engine/transaxle assembly.
    b. Drain engine oil, then remove ring gear cover.
    c. Use slide hammer No. 83 90 270 and joint 87 90 529, or equivalents, to remove clutch shaft.
    d. Remove slave cylinder attaching bolts, then the engine to transaxle attaching bolts.
    e. Carefully separate transaxle from engine. **Do not force engine and transaxle apart without first ensuring all bolts have been removed.**
40. Reverse procedure to install. Tighten bolts to specifications.

1994-96

1. Place vehicle on ramp and engage 4th gear.
2. Disconnect battery ground cable, then remove battery.
3. Disconnect battery ground cable from gearbox.
4. **On models equipped with 2.5L engine,** remove two shields over engine, then the strap holding battery positive cable in radiator hose.
5. **On models equipped with 2.3L engine,** disconnect front clamp holding positive cable.
6. **On all models,** disconnect terminal to rear light switch.
7. Disconnect clutch wire from clutch lever, then release clutch wire rubber damper from fastener on gearbox.
8. **On models equipped with 2.5L engines,** cut off straps, then disconnect

two oxygen sensor connectors and remove from fasteners.

9. Install holder tool No. 83 94 835, or equivalent, in engine's two lifting eyes.
10. **On models equipped with 2.3L engines,** remove oxygen sensor, then push out rubber bushing from lefthand lifting eye.
11. Push out rubber bushing from lefthand lifting eye.
12. **On all models,** place yoke tool No. 83 93 850, or equivalent, on wheel housings. Ensure yoke is in close contact with fender edges.
13. Take up load of engine and gearbox.
14. Remove plastic plug on gearbox and install locking pin tool No. 87 92 335, or equivalent, with ring facing upward, to secure gear position.
15. Disconnect clamp holding gear rod in linkage on gearbox.
16. Engage 3rd gear so gear rod is released from linkage, then install locking pin. locking pin ring should be down in hole.
17. Raise and support vehicle, then remove front wheels.
18. Remove front exhaust pipe, then the lefthand and righthand spoilers below bumper.
19. Remove plastic seal at bottom of righthand inner fender.
20. Remove ball bolts on both sides, then place mobile jack tool No. 83 94 793, or equivalent, with mother fixture tool No. 83 94 801, or equivalent, under vehicle.
21. Place front holder tool No. 83 94 819, or equivalent, in mother fixture and fit guide pins.
22. Place rear holders tool No. 83 94 827, or equivalent, on mother fixture and install small bosses.
23. Fit mobile jack up against carrying frame, then remove two rear engine support nuts.
24. Remove carrying frame screws, then place washer under two rear screws in safe place.
25. Lower mobile jack with carrying frame.
26. Remove oil drain plug and drain oil from gearbox, then install plug using thread-sealing liquid. Tighten drain plug to specifications.
27. Remove lefthand driveshaft using removal tool No. 89 96 654, or equivalent, then suspend shaft using securing straps.
28. Fit cover tool No. 87 92 244, or equivalent, to gearbox, then pull out righthand driveshaft from intermediate shaft with removal tool. Suspend shaft with securing straps.
29. **On models equipped with 2.3L engine,** remove two intermediate shaft bearing to bearing bracket screws, then pull out shaft.
30. **On models equipped with 2.5L engine,** remove intermediate shaft with bearing bracket.
31. **On all models,** install sealing cover No. 8792244, or equivalent, to gearbox.
32. Remove splash plate behind flywheel, then the two engine bracket screws.
33. Remove three gearbox bracket screws from gearbox.
34. Remove engine/gearbox parting surface screws, accessible from outside.
35. **On models equipped with 2.3L engine,** remove bottom starter motor nut.
36. **On all models,** lower vehicle, then remove two outer gearbox screws so gearbox hangs on middle screw.
37. Fit lifting bracket tool No. 87 92 368 and wire tool No. 87 92 251, or equivalents, on gearbox parting surface, then connect suitable engine hoist.
38. Lower entire powertrain about 1.97 inches, then remove last screw.
39. Pull out and lower gearbox, then remove rear engine bracket console.
40. Reverse procedure to install. Ensure rear engine bracket console and its linkage has been installed, if removed.

9000

2.0L ENGINE

1. Raise and support front of vehicle.
2. **On 1995–96 models,** obtain radio anti-theft code as outlined under "Precautions."
3. **On all models,** disconnect battery cables, then the battery.
4. Disconnect air intake duct from inside fender wheel housing.
5. Remove washer fluid reservoir, then disconnect positive cable from terminal block.
6. Remove fuel filter, terminal block, then the battery shelf.
7. Disconnect air mass meter electrical connector, then remove mass meter. **Handle mass meter very carefully.**
8. Disconnect bayonet coupling at air intake duct, then remove air intake duct from air cleaner.
9. Disconnect Hall sensor cable from distributor.
10. Remove air cleaner assembly, then the turbo delivery pipe.
11. Disconnect ground cable and back-up light switch wire connector from transaxle.
12. Attach suitable clamp around clutch slave cylinder hydraulic line and tighten enough to prevent fluid loss. Disconnect hydraulic line from slave cylinder and remove support clip.
13. Remove lefthand side engine mounting nut and bolt.
14. Position lifting beam tool No. 83 93 977, or equivalent, on fender edges, then attach to engine for support.
15. Remove lefthand front wheel and fender insert panel.
16. Separate lefthand front lower control arm from lower ball joint.
17. Disconnect speedometer cable. **Use caution when removing cable not to drop pinion into gearbox.**
18. Disconnect shift linkage from selector rod joint.
19. Remove intermediate driveshaft dust cover clamp.
20. Remove steady bar to intake manifold attaching bolt, remove starter motor, then push steady bar aside. Allow starter motor to hang by electrical leads.
21. Remove all but top flywheel housing to engine block attaching bolts, installing locating dowels tool No. 83 92 128, or equivalent.
22. Loosen subframe pivot mounting nuts, then remove front, then rear subframe mounting.
23. Remove wheel arch bracket lower mounting to subframe attaching bolt and allow subframe to hang from stabilizer bar.
24. Loosen stabilizer bar to lower control arm attaching nut and allow lower control arm to hang, then remove lefthand side stabilizer bar bracket from subframe.
25. Loosen inboard universal joint boot clamp, then remove driveshaft and universal joint from drive cup. Cover drive cup and universal joint to prevent contamination.
26. Attach suitable lifting device to transaxle and remove remaining engine to transaxle attaching bolt.
27. Pull transaxle away from engine and lower to ground.
28. Reverse procedure to install. Tighten bolts to specifications.

2.3L ENGINE

1. **On 1995–96 models,** obtain radio anti-theft code as outlined under "Precautions."
2. **On all models,** disconnect battery cables, then remove battery.
3. Remove washer fluid container.
4. Remove holder with connectors, terminal blocks and positive battery cable. **If car is equipped with ABS braking system, release stay for hydraulic unit.**
5. Remove battery tray, then bolts for cover over bulkhead.
6. Remove rubber strip, then lift cover and disconnect washer hoses from nozzle, then remove cover.
7. Separate speedometer cable connector, then pull speedometer cable and washer hose through rubber grommet.
8. Disconnect electrical connectors from air mass meter and air intake temperature sensor, then disconnect hose on air delivery pipe from bypass valve.
9. Remove delivery pipe between throttle housing and intercooler.
10. Remove starter motor retaining nuts, then secure starter motor to steering gear.
11. Separate selector rod universal joint, then the selector rod.
12. Pinch slave cylinder pressure hose using suitable clamping tongs, then separate pressure line.
13. Remove upper bolts for stay at wheel housing, then release lefthand engine mount.
14. Position lifting beam tool No. 83 93 977, or equivalent, on fender edges, then attach to engine for support.
15. Disconnect negative battery cable from battery and reversing light switch connector from gearbox.
16. Separate suspension arm from ball joint, then remove anti-roll bar.
17. Remove lower bolt for stay at wheel housing, then the three bottom bolts

from joint between engine and gearbox.
18. Remove center and lefthand skirts from spoiler.
19. Separate subframe at front and rear, then lower, using suitable jack.
20. Remove universal joint, then lower vehicle.
21. Attach suitable lifting device to transaxle and remove remaining engine to transaxle attaching bolt.
22. Pull transaxle away from engine and lower to ground.
23. Reverse procedure to install. Tighten bolts to specifications.

TIGHTENING SPECIFICATIONS

Component	Torque/Ft. Lbs.
1993 900	
Ball Joint Nut	15–20
Engine Mount Bolts	52
Flywheel (17 mm Bolts)	44
Flywheel (19 mm Bolts)	63
Pressure Plate Bolts	10–19
Reverse Light Switch	15–17
Selector Rod Joint Pinch Bolt	22–25
Servo Pump Coupling	15–25
Slave Cylinder Mounting Bolts	5–10
Subframe Bolts	32–42
Transaxle Drain Plug	29–43
Transaxle To Engine Attaching Bolts	40–74
1994–96 900	
Ball Bolt To Link Arm Nuts	55
Clutch Plate Screws	16
Engine Bracket Screws	54
Engine/Gearbox Parting Surface Screws	50
Front Carrying Frame	85
Gearbox Bracket Screws	30
Gearbox Parting Surface Screw	16
Gear Rod To Linkage Clamp Nut	16
Intermediate Shaft Bearing Screws	15
Middle Carrying Frame	141
Rear Carrying Frame	81
Transaxle Drain Plug	37
9000	
Control Arm To Lower Ball Joint	15–20
Engine Mount Bolts	52
Flywheel (17 mm Bolts)	44
Flywheel (19 mm Bolts)	63
Front Sway Bar Pinch-Bolt	30–40
Master Cylinder Pressure Line	11–14
Pressure Line Clamp Bolt	13–20
Reverse Light Switch	15–17
Selector Rod Joint Pinch Bolt	22–25
Slave Cylinder Mounting Bolts	6–8
Slave Cylinder Pressure Line	11–14
Starter Motor Attaching Bolts	28–35
Subframe Attaching Bolts	32–42
Sway Bar	30–40
Transaxle Drain Plug	30–44
Transaxle To Engine Bolts	40–75

Rear Axle & Suspension

INDEX

	Page No.
Anti-Roll Bar & Bushings, Replace	38-41
9000	38-41
Coil Spring, Replace	38-40
900	38-40
9000	38-40
Hub & Bearing, Replace	38-39
1994–96 900	38-39
9000 & 1993 900	38-39
Panhard Rod & Bushing, Replace	38-41
Rear Axle, Replace	38-39
900	38-39
9000	38-39
Roll Bar, Replace	38-41
900	38-41
Shock Absorber, Replace	38-40
900	38-40
9000	38-40
Spring Linkage, Replace	38-40
900	38-40
9000	38-40
Tightening Specifications	38-42
Torque Arm & Bushing, Replace	38-40

REAR AXLE

REPLACE

900

1993

1. Raise and support vehicle, then remove rear wheels,
2. Remove panhard rod from rear axle. Position rod aside.
3. Clamp brake hose(s) with pliers, then disconnect hose(s) from block and bracket on rear axle.
4. **On models equipped with anti lock brakes,** disconnect wheel sensor leads from bracket at trailing end of spring link, then remove wheel sensors.
5. **On all models,** disconnect hand brake cables from calipers.
6. Place jacks under spring links, then remove bolts from spring link rear mountings.
7. Place jack under center of rear axle, then unbolt torque arm mountings.
8. Use jack to lift axle out of spring link mountings.
9. Reverse procedure to install. Insert bolt in mounting on rear axle with head toward fuel tank.

1994–96

1. Use brake clamp to hold brake pedal in depressed position.
2. Raise and support vehicle, then remove rear wheels.
3. Disconnect speed sensor connectors and cables from spring link.
4. Remove return springs from levers on both sides, then the lefthand parking brake cable from lever, holder and equalizing sleeve.
5. Remove righthand parking brake cable from lever and holder.
6. Remove rear silencer, then the anti-roll bar. Collect nut washers.
7. Remove lefthand and righthand rear brake pipes, **Fig. 1.** Plug brake calipers and hose connections.
8. Remove retaining clips for brake hose connections and press them out of holder.
9. Use suitable high-lift jack to slightly press up spring link on one side.
10. Remove damper lower retaining bolt, then the jack.
11. Carefully force spring link down using crowbar, then remove coil spring and spacer.
12. Remove four hub assembly retaining nuts, then the hub assembly and spacer, **Fig. 1.**
13. Place jack under spring link on other side of vehicle, then slightly press up spring link.
14. Remove damper lower retaining bolt.
15. Carefully release and lower spring link, then remove coil spring and spacer.
16. Remove four hub assembly retaining nuts, then the hub assembly with spacer.
17. Position jack under rear axle, then remove rear axle retaining bolts.
18. Lower rear axle, then place on workbench.
19. Remove inner anti-roll bar and bushing.
20. Remove brake hose and brake cable holder.
21. Reverse procedure to install, noting the following:
    a. Install new bushings.
    b. Using jack, raise spring link to about 14.55 inches (37 cm) between edge of wheel arch and upper edge of hub center, then tighten bolts to specifications.
    c. Ensure marking on coil spring faces rearward.

9000

1. Raise and support vehicle, then disconnect hand brake cables from levers on brake calipers.
2. Unscrew clips attaching cables to spring links.
3. Remove or disconnect righthand side components as follows:
    a. **On models equipped with anti-lock brakes,** remove ABS sensor from hub and release ABS lead from clips on spring link.
    b. **On all models,** remove screw plug from over adjusting screw and slightly back off adjusting screw.
    c. Remove brake caliper and disc backplate mounting bolts, then brake caliper. Hang caliper on torque arm.
    d. Disconnect panhard rod from rear axle. Position rod aside.
    e. Position jack under spring link and raise link enough to relieve load on mountings.
    f. Remove bolt from spring link rear mounting, then lower jack under spring link and remove coil spring.
4. Repeat previous step for lefthand side components.
5. Disconnect torque arms from rear axle, then place jack under middle of rear axle. Slightly raise rear axle.
6. Disconnect lower mountings for dampers and anti-roll bar.
7. Lower rear axle from vehicle.
8. Reverse procedure to install.

HUB & BEARING

REPLACE

9000 & 1993 900

1. Raise rear of vehicle and support at frame.
2. Remove rear wheels, then disconnect hand brake cable from caliper.
3. **On vehicles with anti lock brakes,** disconnect wheel sensor from hub and release lead from bracket on trailing end of spring link.
4. **On all models,** remove screw plug, then slightly unscrew adjusting screw in caliper.
5. Remove caliper from mounting. Hang caliper from torque arm.
6. Remove brake disc, dust cap, locknut and washer.
7. Remove hub assembly, using puller if necessary. **Hub, bearing, and seals are an integral unit and must be serviced as an assembly.**
8. Reverse procedure to install. Tighten bolt and nut to specifications.

1994–96 900

The wheel bearings are incorporated in the hub and are not part of a shaft or subaxle assembly. The bearings are of double-row, angular contact type which are permanently lubricated and maintenance free. They cannot be replaced individually.

1. Raise and support vehicle, then press back brake pistons using slip joint pliers.
2. Remove two brake caliper retaining bolts, then disconnect brake pipe if necessary. Suspend brake caliper aside with cable tie.
3. Back off brake shoe adjusting screw.

4. Remove lever return spring, then disconnect parking brake cable from lever.
5. Remove brake disc retaining bolts, then the brake disc.
6. Disconnect speed sensor connector, then remove four wheel hub retaining bolts.
7. Remove wheel hub, back plate and spacer, then separate wheel hub from back plate.
8. Reverse procedure to install, noting the following:
   a. Clean contact surfaces with wire brush.
   b. Secure brake disc locking screw with Loctite, or equivalent.

SHOCK ABSORBER

REPLACE

900

1993

1. Raise and support vehicle, then remove rear wheels.
2. Place jack under spring link to relieve load on damper.
3. Remove nut and bolt from lower damper mounting.
4. Remove jack, then the shock absorber upper mounting nut and bushing.
5. Reverse procedure to install. Tighten bolts and nuts to specifications.

1994–96

1. Cut flap in luggage compartment carpeting to gain access to shock absorber upper mounting.
2. Remove nut, washer and bushing from upper mounting point.
3. Raise and support vehicle, then remove rear wheel.
4. Remove shock absorber lower mounting retaining bolt, then the shock absorber.
5. Reverse procedure to install. Insert shock absorber upper mounting through hole in body.

9000

1. Raise vehicle at rear jacking point.
2. Support using jackstands placed under rear mountings of spring links.
3. Raise vehicle enough to relieve load on shocks and sway bar.
4. Remove rear wheels.
5. Remove lower shock mounting bolts.
6. From inside vehicle, remove panel over spare tire, then fold back carpet.
7. Remove nut, cap and bushing from top of shocks, then remove shocks.
8. Reverse procedure to install.

COIL SPRING

REPLACE

900

1993

1. Raise and support vehicle, then remove rear wheels.
2. Remove parking brake cable bracket from spring link.

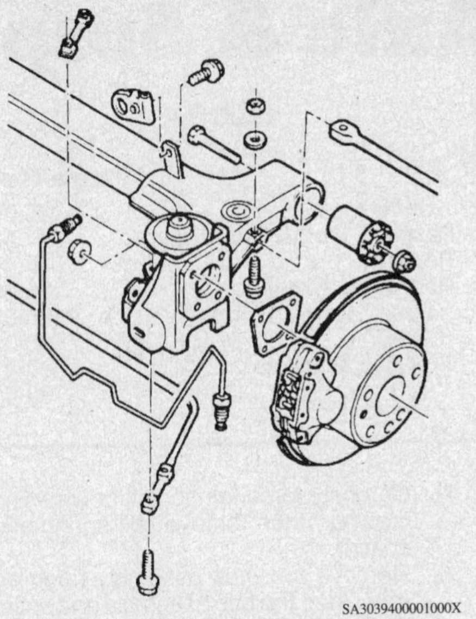
SA3039400001000X

Fig. 1 Rear axle components. 1994–96 900

3. **On models with anti-lock brakes,** release ABS lead from clips and brackets.
4. **On all models,** position jack under spring link, **Fig. 2.**
5. Support spring link with jack and remove lower end of shock absorber.
6. Remove nut and bolt from spring link rear mounting.
7. **On vehicles equipped with anti-roll bar,** disconnect anti-roll bar and swivel bar down.
8. **On all models,** position another jackstand under rear axle. Use care is not to damage brake lines.
9. Slowly lower jackstand under spring link, then remove coil spring.
10. Reverse procedure to install.

1994–96

1. Raise and support vehicle, then remove wheel.
2. Place jack under spring link, then remove jack.
3. Place crowbar or other suitable tool in damper mounting bracket and carefully lever spring link downward.
4. Remove coil spring.
5. Reverse procedure to install, noting the following:
   a. Press spring link down and position coil spring with spring support on it.
   b. Marking on coil spring should face rearward.
   c. Tighten damper lower mounting bolt and wheel bolts to specifications.

9000

1. Raise and support vehicle.
2. Remove rear wheel and position jack under spring link, **Fig. 3.**
3. Remove parking brake cable bracket from spring link.
4. **On models with anti-lock brakes,** release ABS lead from clips.
5. **On all models,** remove bolt attaching rear of spring link to rear axle.
6. Lower spring link, then remove spring.
7. Reverse procedure to install.

SPRING LINKAGE

REPLACE

900

1. Remove coil spring as outlined under "Coil Spring, Replace."
2. **On vehicles with anti-roll bar,** remove spring link front mounting bolt and anti-roll bar.
3. **On all models,** remove two bolts attaching front spring link mounting bracket to body, then the spring link.
4. Remove front bushing by pressing out using a sleeve applied to tube of bushing.
5. Remove rear bushing using bushing remover No. 89-96-274, or equivalent.
6. Reverse procedure to install. Lubricate new bushings with petroleum jelly.

9000

Spring Links, Replace

1. Remove coil spring as outlined under "Coil Spring, Replace."
2. Remove spring link front bracket mounting bolts, then the link.
3. Reverse procedure to install.

Spring Link Front Bushing, Replace

1. Remove rear wheel and position jack under spring link.
2. Disconnect spring link from bushing and bracket.
3. Remove bracket from underside of body.
4. Install new bushing and bracket onto spring link, then the spring link to underside of body.
5.

Spring Link Rear Bushing, Replace

1. Remove coil spring as outlined under "Coil Spring, Replace."
2. Clean bushing and surrounding area, then apply petroleum jelly to all visible parts of bushing.
3. Position bushing remover tool No. 89 96 506, or equivalent, as shown, **Fig. 4.**
4. Press out bushings.
5. Reverse procedure to install.

TORQUE ARM & BUSHING

REPLACE

1. Raise and support vehicle
2. Remove torque arm mounting nuts, then the torque arm.
3. Press out rear bushing using 24 mm socket as support and 14 mm socket applied to inner spacer.
4. Press out front bushings using 30 mm socket and tool No. 89 96 464, or equivalent, as support.
5. Reverse procedure to install.

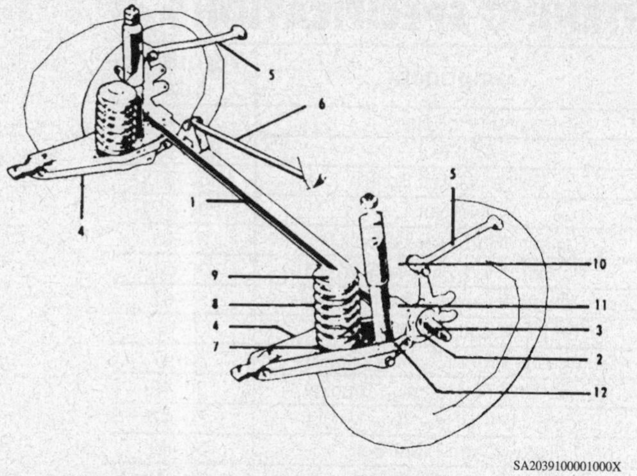

1. Rear axle
2. End piece
3. Stub axle
4. Spring links
5. Torsion bar
6. Panhard rod
7. Spring seat
8. Coil spring
9. Spring insulator
10. Rubber buffer
11. Stop
12. Shock absorber

SA2039100001000X

Fig. 2 Rear suspension assembly. 1993 900

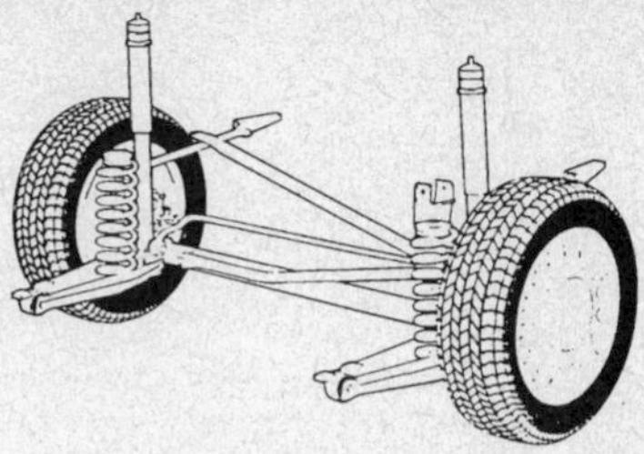

SA2039100002000X

Fig. 3 Rear suspension assembly. 9000

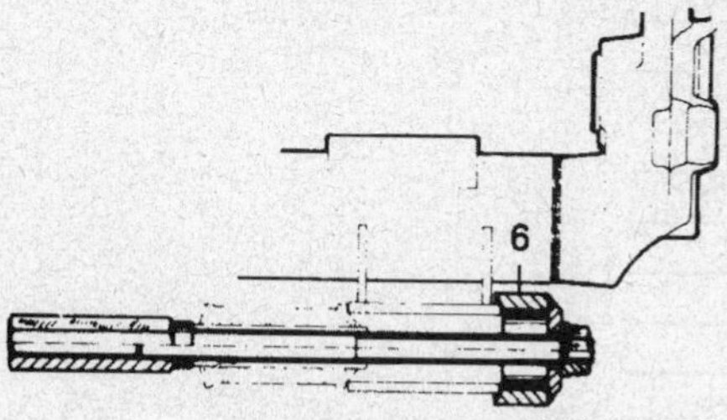

SA2039100003000X

Fig. 4 Spring link rear bushing removal. 9000

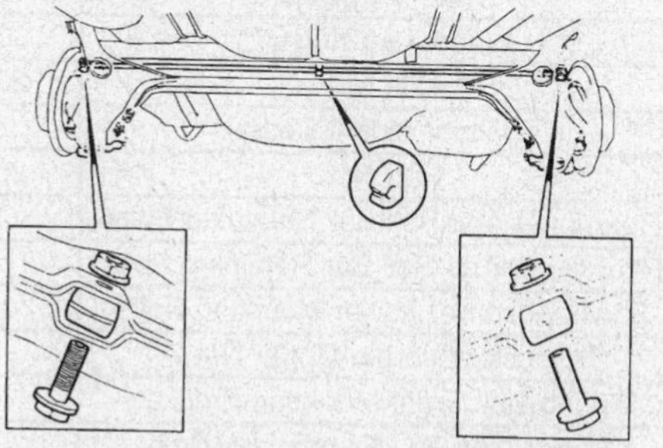

SA3039400002000X

Fig. 5 Rear inner anti-sway bar replacement. 1994–96 900

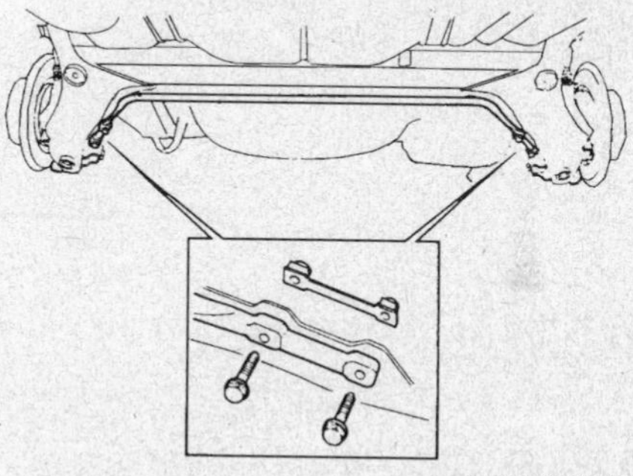

SA3039400003000X

Fig. 6 Rear outer anti-sway bar replacement. 1994–96 900

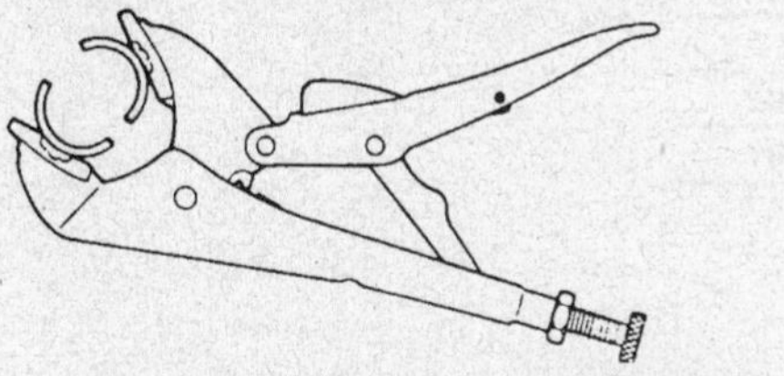

SA3039100004000X

Fig. 7 Anti-roll bar bushing installer fabrication. 9000

ROLL BAR

REPLACE

900

1993

1. Raise and support vehicle, then place jacks under both spring links.
2. Remove righthand and lefthand spring link rear mounting nuts.
3. Swivel anti-roll bar downward, then press anti-roll bar link arms inward to remove bar. If bolt in front mounting is fitted with the head on inboard side, the spring link will have to be removed.
4. Reverse procedure to install, torquing all bolts and nuts to specifications.

1994–96

Inner

1. Raise and support vehicle, then remove one of rear wheels.
2. Remove inner anti-roll bar retaining bolts, **Fig. 5.**
3. Remove anti-roll bar from vehicle.
4. Coat anti-roll bar with thin coat of grease, then slide into rear axle.
5. Install retaining bolts. Tighten to specifications.
6. Ensure rubber block is properly positioned in center of bar, **Fig. 5.**
7. Install wheel, then lower vehicle.

Outer

1. Raise and support vehicle, then remove four outer anti-roll bar bolts, **Fig. 6.**
2. Lower outer anti-roll bar.
3. Position anti-roll bar on vehicle.
4. Install anti-roll bar bolts. Tighten to specifications.
5. Lower vehicle.

ANTI-ROLL BAR & BUSHINGS

REPLACE

9000

1. Raise and support vehicle.
2. Place jack under rear axle, then slightly lift rear axle.
3. Remove outboard mountings of anti-roll bar.
4. Disconnect anti-roll bar from link arms, then remove bar.
5. Remove U clamps from anti-roll bar.
6. Remove bushings using bushing remover tool No. 89 96 274, or equivalent.
7. To install bushings fabricate tool as follows:
   a. Parts necessary to fabricate tool: self grip pliers with jaw opening of at least 35 mm and 20 mm length of water pipe with inside diameter of 27 mm and thickness of 3–4 mm.
   b. Cut piece of pipe into two equal halves.
   c. Position two halves in jaws of pliers so they are flush with edges of jaws on one side.
   d. Weld two halves to jaws, **Fig. 7.**
8. Lubricate bushing and seating surface of anti-roll bar.
9. Assemble tool complete with bushings, bolt, sleeve and nut, then press bushing into place. Remove tool.
10. Install U clamps to anti-roll bar.
11. Connect anti-roll bar to link arms, then install outboard mountings. Tighten fasteners to specifications.
12. Slowly lower rear axle, then the vehicle.

PANHARD ROD & BUSHING

REPLACE

1. Raise and support vehicle.
2. Disconnect panhard rod from rear axle and body.
3. **On 900 models,** press out bushing using suitable sleeve and base.
4. **On 9000 models,** press out bushing using a 14 mm socket and tool No. 89 96 464, or equivalent, as a support.
5. **On all models,** reverse procedure to install.

TIGHTENING SPECIFICATIONS

Year	Component	Torque/Ft. Lbs.
1993–96③	Anti-Roll Bar	59–67
	Axle Nut	207–221
	Caliper Mount Bolts	52–81
	Hub Nut	207–221
	Panhard Rod To Axle Bolt①	37–63
	Panhard Rod To Axle Bolt②	30–51
	Shock Absorber Lower Mounting Bolts①	59–67
	Shock Absorber Upper Nut	7–15
	Spring Link Front Mounting Bracket	30–47
	Spring Link To Mounting Bracket	30–40
	Spring Link To Rear Axle Mount	30–47
	Torque Arm Front Bolt	30–40
	Torque Arm Rear Bolt	15–20
	Wheel Lug Bolts	78–92
	Wheel Lug Nuts②	66–81
1994–96②	Axle Nut	207–221
	Caliper Mount Bolts	52-81
	Hub Nut	207–221
	Rear Inner Anti-Roll Bar Retaining Bolts	44
	Rear Outer Anti-Roll Bar Retaining Bolts	18
	Shock Absorber Lower Mounting Bolts	46
	Shock Absorber Upper Nut	7–15
	Spring Link Front Mounting Bracket	30–47
	Spring Link To Mounting Bracket	30–40
	Spring Link To Rear Axle Mount	30–47
	Tie Down Bracket Bolt	18
	Wheel Lug Bolts	78–92
	Wheel Lug Nuts	66–81

① — 9000.
② — 900.
③ — Except 1994–96 900.

Front Suspension & Steering

NOTE: On Air Bag Equipped Models, Refer To "Air Bag System Precautions" Located In The Front Of This Manual For System Disarming & Arming Procedures.

INDEX

	Page No.
Ball Joint, Replace	38-44
900	38-44
9000	38-44
Coil Spring, Replace	38-44
900	38-44
9000	38-44
Control Arm, Replace	38-45
Lower	38-45
Upper	38-45
Hub & Bearing, Replace	38-43
900	38-43
9000	38-43
Power Steering	38-84
Power Steering Gear, Replace	38-46
900	38-46
9000	38-46
Power Steering Pump, Replace	38-47
900	38-47
9000	38-47
Precautions	38-43
Air Bag Systems	38-43
Shock Absorber, Replace	38-44
900	38-44
9000	38-44
Tightening Specifications	38-47
900	38-47
9000	38-48

PRECAUTIONS

AIR BAG SYSTEMS

Refer to "Air Bag System Precautions" in the front of this manual for system disarming and arming procedures.

HUB & BEARING

REPLACE

900

1993

1. Position spacer tool No. 83 93 209, or equivalent, under upper control arm.
2. Raise and support vehicle, then remove wheel.
3. Remove hub center retaining nut and thrust washer.
4. Rotate brake rotor so recess in edge of rotor lines up with brake pads, then remove brake pads.
5. Remove brake caliper and hang it to one side so that brake hose and pipe are not damaged.
6. Remove brake rotor from hub.
7. Use taper breaker tool No. 89 95 409, or equivalent, to remove tie rod end from control arm.
8. Remove bolts securing upper and lower ball joints in control arms, then remove steering knuckle housing with hub from control arms and driveshaft.
9. Use sleeve tools Nos. 7841067 and 8996449 and support plate tool No. 89 96 456, or equivalents, to press off hub. Pull inner bearing race off hub using suitable universal puller. If there are no recesses for puller, chisel off race. **Pressing off hub destroys bearing, so it must be replaced.**
10. Remove circlips from steering knuckle housing and press out bearing using sleeve tool Nos. 8390114 and 8996449 and support plate tool No. 89 96 456, or equivalents.
11. To assemble, lubricate bearing recess in steering knuckle housing with Molycote Paste G, or equivalent.
12. Use sleeve tool No. 83 90 114 and support tool No. 89 96 464, or equivalents, to press in bearing until it contacts circlip.
13. Install outer circlip.
14. Use sleeve tool No. 83 90 114 and support tool No. 89 96 464, or equivalents, to press hub into bearing.
15. Lubricate driveshaft splines with Molycote Paste G, or equivalent, then install driveshaft into hub.
16. Replace steering knuckle housing by installing the ball joints to upper and lower control arms.
17. Install hub nut, thrust washer, brake rotor, brake caliper and brake pads.
18. Install tie rod to control arm.
19. Install wheel, then lower vehicle and tighten hub nut to specifications. Lock hub by punching flange into stub axle groove.
20. Remove spacer tool No. 83 93 209, or equivalent, from below upper control arm.
21. Pump brake pedal until brakes begin to operate. **Do not move vehicle until brakes are operating properly.**

1994-96

The wheel bearings are incorporated in the hub and are not part of a shaft or sub-axle assembly. The bearings are of double-row, angular contact type which are permanently lubricated and maintenance free. They cannot be replaced individually.

1. Remove shock absorber as outlined under "Shock Absorber, Replace."
2. Place two pieces of flat or square bar under shock absorber.
3. Press front wheel hub off wheel bearing using front wheel bearing drift tool No. 89 96 704, or equivalent.
4. Remove circlips from shock absorber.
5. Remove wheel bearing from steering swivel member using wheel bearing drift tool No. 89 96 704, or equivalent.
6. Install outer circlip on steering swivel member. Opening in circlip should face downward.
7. Press wheel bearing in until it abuts circlip, using front wheel bearing drift tool No. 89 96 704, or equivalent.
8. Lubricate baring seat and outside of bearing with suitable grease.
9. Install inner circlip on steering swivel member. Opening in circlip should face downward.
10. Install hub in wheel bearing using front wheel bearing drift tool No. 89 96 704, or equivalent.
11. Install shock absorber as outlined under "Shock Absorber, Replace."

9000

1. Loosen hub center nut and wheel attaching bolts.
2. Raise and support front of vehicle, then remove wheel.
3. Remove hub center nut and thrust washer.
4. Remove brake hose from retaining clip, then the caliper. Position aside.
5. Remove locating stud, then the brake rotor.
6. Gently push in on driveshaft, then remove four hub-to-steering spindle attaching bolts.
7. Remove hub and backing plate. **Wheel bearings are an integral part of hub assembly. If the wheel bearings are defective, hub assembly must be replaced.**
8. Reverse procedure to install, noting the following:
   a. Ensure slot in hub faces upward.
   b. Tighten hub to steering spindle bolts to specifications.
   c. Tighten caliper bolts to specifications.
   d. Tighten hub center nut to specifications.

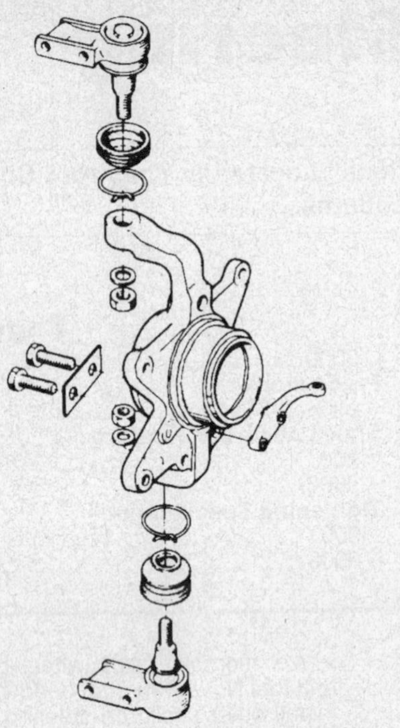
SA2029100012000X

Fig. 1 Exploded view of ball joint & steering knuckle. 1993 900

BALL JOINT

REPLACE

900

1993

1. Raise and support vehicle.
2. Clean ball joint and surrounding area.
3. Remove brake caliper and position aside. **Maximum travel of control arm is limited by shock absorber. Remove weight from travel stop before loosening shock absorber.**
4. Position jack under outer end of lower control arm and raise slightly. Remove lower shock absorber mounting.
5. Lower jack so driveshaft meets body flush at grommet aperture. Leave jack in position to provide support when removing ball joint.
6. Remove nut on ball joint in steering knuckle housing, **Fig. 1.** Remove bolt using puller tool No. 89 95 409, or equivalent.
7. Separate ball joint from control arm. Position jackstand under steering knuckle housing to prevent damage to brake hose.
8. Install new ball joint and bolt in steering knuckle housing.
9. Install ball joints to control arm using new locknuts.
10. Raise control arm slightly using jack and install shock absorber.
11. Install wheel and lower vehicle.

1994–96

1. Raise and support vehicle, then remove wheels.
2. Remove anti-roll bar nut.
3. Use puller tool No. 89 96 696, or equivalent, to press ball joint stud out of swivel member, **Fig. 2.**
4. Remove ball joint nut, then bend support arm/suspension arm down.
5. Remove locking ring securing rubber gaiter, then the gaiter.
6. Reverse procedure to install, noting the following:
   a. Pack new rubber gaiter with suitable grease.
   b. Tighten ball joint nut and anti-roll bar nut to specifications.

9000

1. Raise and support vehicle, then remove wheels.
2. Remove bolts attaching ball joint to spindle.
3. Remove bolts attaching ball joint to lower control arm.
4. Remove ball joint.
5. Reverse procedure to install. Tighten ball joint to spindle nut to specifications.

COIL SPRING

REPLACE

900

1993

1. Remove upper shock absorber retaining nuts, **Fig. 3. Suspension travel is limited by a stop built into the shock absorber. Therefore, the shock absorber must be removed prior to raising the vehicle, or by using a jack to lift the outer end of the control arm.**
2. Raise and support vehicle and remove front wheel.
3. Install spring compressor tool No. 89 95 839, or equivalent, on lower spring cup and second free coil from top of spring. **Ensure compressor is properly seated prior to compressing spring.**
4. Compress spring to obtain 1 ½ inches of clearance at upper coil, then remove spring.
5. Remove spacers and upper cone, noting position for reassembly.
6. Reverse procedure to install.

1994–96

Refer to "Shock Absorber, Replace" for front spring replacement.

9000

Refer to "Shock Absorber, Replace" for front spring replacement.

SHOCK ABSORBER

REPLACE

900

1993

1. Remove upper shock nut.
2. Raise and support vehicle, using jackstands.
3. Disconnect shock absorber at lower mountings, **Fig. 3.**
4. Remove shock absorber from vehicle.

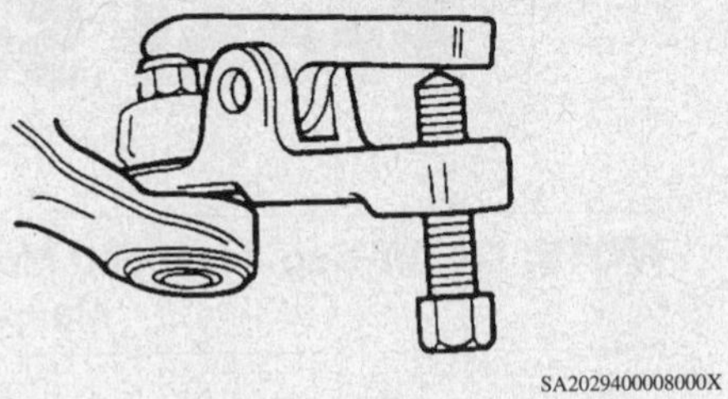
SA2029400008000X

Fig. 2 Ball joint removal. 1994–96 900

5. Reverse procedure to install.

1994–96

1. Slightly loosen hub center nut when all four wheels are on ground.
2. Raise and support vehicle, then remove five wheel bolts and wheel.
3. Remove hub center nut, then the wheel sensor, **Fig. 4.**
4. Press back brake piston using slip-joint pliers, **Fig. 4.**
5. Remove caliper from steering swivel member, **Fig. 4,** then suspend in wheel housing with cable tie.
6. Remove brake disc and back plate, **Fig. 4,** then slightly loosen tie rod end nut.
7. Press out tie rod end nut using puller tool No. 89 96 696, or equivalent.
8. Remove nut and tie rod end bolt, then the anti-roll bar to swinging arm nut.
9. Remove outer ball joint nut.
10. Press ball joint out of steering swivel member using puller tool No. 89 96 696, or equivalent, installed on spring link.
11. Remove nut and discard. This self-locking nut must not be reused.
12. Remove three upper mounting nuts for MacPherson strut, then the strut.
13. Clamp MacPherson strut in vice.
14. Compress spring using spring compressor tool No. 88 18 791 and holder tool No. 88 18 809, or equivalents.
15. Hold piston rod and remove nut using MacPherson strut socket tool No. 89 96 662, or equivalent. **This is a self-locking nut and must not be reused.**
16. Remove mounting and top spring seat, then the coil spring, gaiter and compression stop.
17. Unscrew damper using wrench tool No. 89 96 670, or equivalent, then remove damper from strut.
18. Reverse procedure to install, noting the following:
    a. Screw damper in place using wrench tool No. 89 96 670, or equivalent.
    b. Lower end of coil spring should abut against stop in bottom of spring cup.
    c. Position MacPherson strut on vehicle and install three retaining nuts on top mounting. Tighten nuts alternately, according to specifications.
    d. Always use new hub center nut with self-locking threads.

9000

1. Raise and support vehicle.
2. Remove brake line from strut.

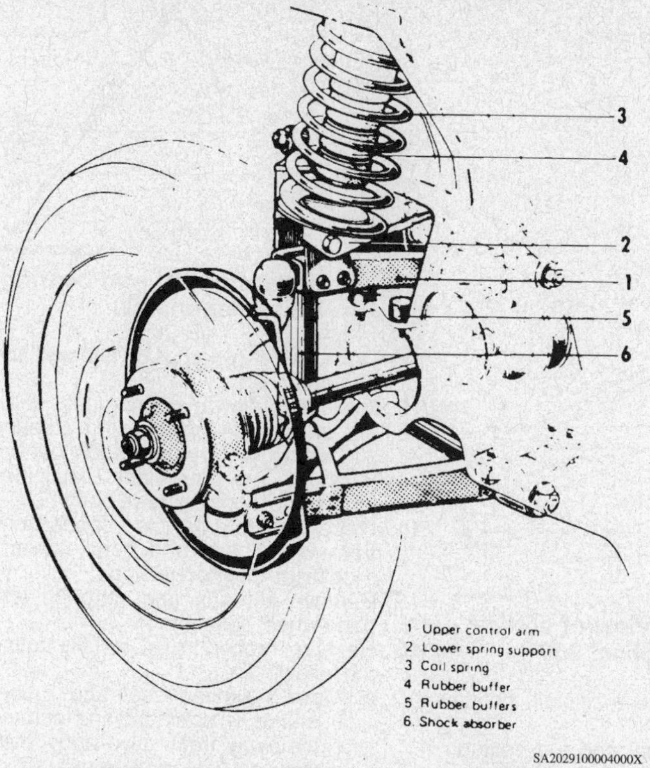
3
4
2
1
5
6
1 Upper control arm
2 Lower spring support
3 Coil spring
4 Rubber buffer
5 Rubber buffers
6 Shock absorber
SA2029100004000X

Fig. 3 Front suspension. 1993 900

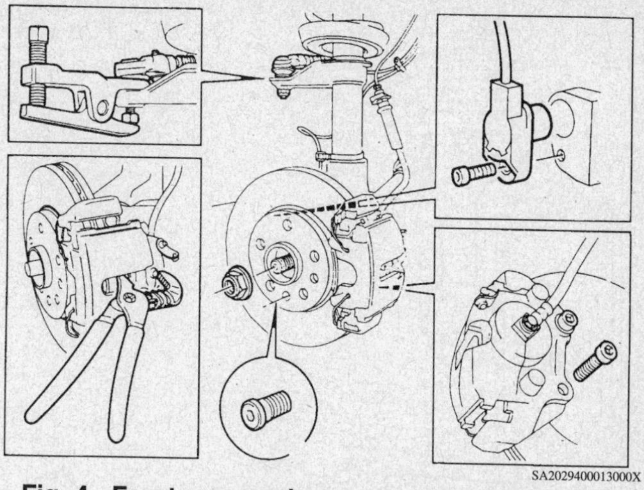
SA2029400013000X

Fig. 4 Front suspension assembly. 1994–96 900

3. Remove bolts attaching strut to spindle, **Fig. 5.**
4. Remove three bolts attaching top of strut, then the strut assembly from vehicle.
5. Compress spring.
6. Remove top nut, then the upper fixture and spring cup.
7. Remove spring and lower spring cup.
8. Remove compression stop and boot.
9. Remove strut damper assembly. **Damper is an integral part of strut, not an insert, and therefore cannot be replaced separately.**
10. Reverse procedure to install, noting the following:
    a. Distance between boot and lower spring cup should be approximately .5 inch (12 mm).
    b. Rotate boot until mark at bottom of boot is aligned with kingpin mounting and groove in spring cap.
    c. Install top spring cup with notch aligned with mark on boot. **Ensure marks are aligned with kingpin mounting.**
    d. Tighten three top nuts to specifications.
    e. Tighten top nut securing spring to specifications.
    f. Tighten bolts securing strut to spindle to specifications.

CONTROL ARM

REPLACE

UPPER

900

1. If lefthand control arm is to be replaced, remove engine and transaxle assembly.
2. Remove top shock absorber nut.
3. Raise and support vehicle.
4. Remove wheel and shock absorber, **Fig. 3.**
5. Compress coil spring using spring compressor tool No. 89 95 839, or equivalent.
6. Remove bolts securing upper ball joint to control arm. **Support steering knuckle to prevent brake lines from being damaged.**
7. Remove bolts securing control arm bearings, **Fig. 6,** then the control arm and spring.
8. Remove nuts securing bearings to control arm, then the bearings and rubber bushings.
9. Press new bushings into bearings using press tool No. 78 41 331, or equivalent. **Do not use oil or grease to ease installation. If lubrication is necessary, use a soap and water solution.**
10. Reinstall bearing assemblies. Tighten nuts to specifications, noting proper angle between control arm and bearing, **Fig. 7.**
11. Reverse procedure to install. Road test vehicle, then check alignment.

LOWER

900

1993

1. Remove upper shock nut.
2. Raise and support vehicle, then remove wheel and shock.
3. Disconnect lower ball joint from control arm.
4. Disconnect lower control arm attaching screws beneath engine compartment floor.
5. Remove lower control arm with brackets, **Fig. 6.**
6. Remove bearing retaining nuts, then the bearings and rubber bushings.
7. Press new bushings into bearings using press tool No. 78 41 349, or equivalent. **Do not use oil or grease to ease installation. If lubrication is necessary, use soap and water solution.**
8. Reinstall bearing assemblies. Tighten nuts to specifications, noting proper angle between control arm and bearing, **Fig. 8.**
9. Reverse procedure to install control arm. Road test vehicle, then check alignment.

1994–96

1. Raise vehicle and remove appropriate front wheel.
2. Remove anti-roll bar nut.
3. Loosen ball joint nut, then install puller tool No. 89 96 696, or equivalent, to press out ball joint, **Fig. 2.**
4. Remove ball joint nut, then the support arm to suspension arm nut, **Fig. 9.**
5. Reverse procedure to install. When replacing suspension arm, new self-locking nut must be installed.

9000

1. Raise and support vehicle, then remove wheel.
2. Remove nut securing sway bar link to control arm, **Fig. 5,** then the upper securing bolt for sway bar link.
3. Press down on control arm and remove sway bar link.
4. Remove two nuts at front of control arm securing arm to frame.
5. Remove two rear bolts securing reinforcement member to frame.
6. Remove two bolts securing control arm rear pivot to frame, then the control arm.
7. Reverse procedure to install, noting the following:

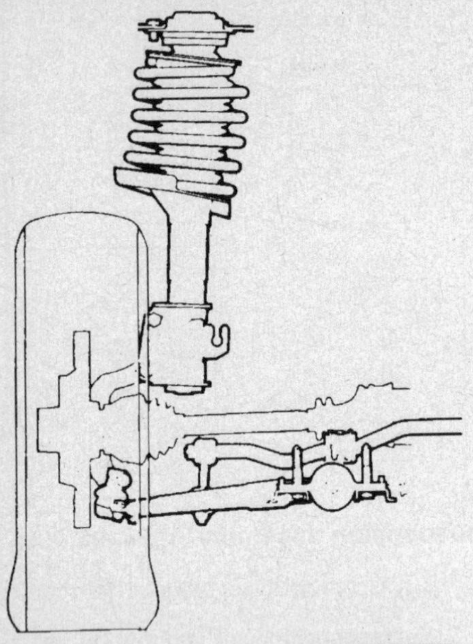
SA2029100010000X

Fig. 5 Front suspension. 9000

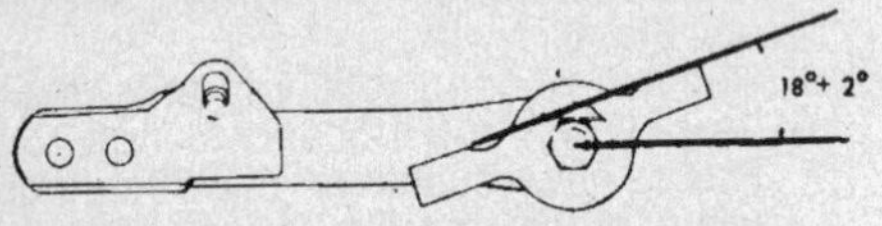
18°+ 2°
SA2029100007000X

Fig. 8 Lower control arm bearing installation. 900

a. To facilitate control arm installation, leave nuts for bushing in rear pivot loose until arm is installed, **Fig. 10.**

8. Road test vehicle, then check alignment.

POWER STEERING GEAR

REPLACE

900

1993

1. Disconnect hydraulic lines from gear and plug lines and open fittings.
2. Remove clamp bolt where joint of steering column shaft is connected to steering gear.
3. Raise and support vehicle.
4. Remove front wheels and tie rod end nuts.
5. Separate tie rod ends from steering arms using puller tool No. 89 95 409, or equivalent.
6. From under vehicle, remove the two steering gear bolts.
7. Separate steering column joint from steering gear, then position steering gear to side and remove by guiding it diagonally downward through opening in engine compartment floor. **Use caution to avoid damaging rubber bellows on edges of lower body work.**
8. Loosen tie rod end locknuts, then remove tie rod ends.

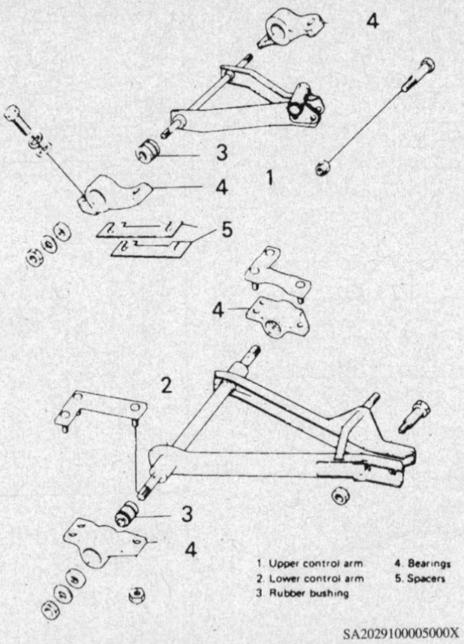
1
2
3
4
5
1. Upper control arm
2. Lower control arm
3. Rubber bushing
4. Bearings
5. Spacers
SA2029100005000X

Fig. 6 Exploded view of control arm assemblies. 900

9. Reverse procedure to install, noting the following:
   a. Check fluid level and toe setting. Adjust as necessary.
   b. Bleed power steering system by turning steering wheel from lock to lock several times with engine running at idle.

1994–96

1. Remove hose connected to return pipe on steering system, then plug hose.
2. Fit length of hose onto pipe and place other end in suitable container that will hold at least .53 quarts (.5 liters).
3. Turn steering wheel to full left lock and full right lock until all fluid has runout of steering system.
4. Remove length of hose from return pipe and refit return hose.
5. Disconnect battery ground cable, then remove main fuse box.
6. Remove lower lefthand section of instrument panel, then the bolt from steering column shaft joint, **Fig. 11.**
7. Turn steering wheel to straight ahead position. **Fix steering wheel so it will not move out of straight-ahead position to avoid twisting and breaking coil spring. Tape steering wheel to instrument panel with suitable heavy-duty adhesive fabric type tape.**
8. Separate joint on steering column shaft from steering gear, then remove tie rod from steering gear.
9. Raise and support vehicle, then remove front lefthand wheel.
10. Remove tie rod from MacPherson strut using puller tool No. 89 96 696, or equivalent, then press out ball joint, **Fig. 2.**
11. Remove tie rod and lower vehicle to floor.

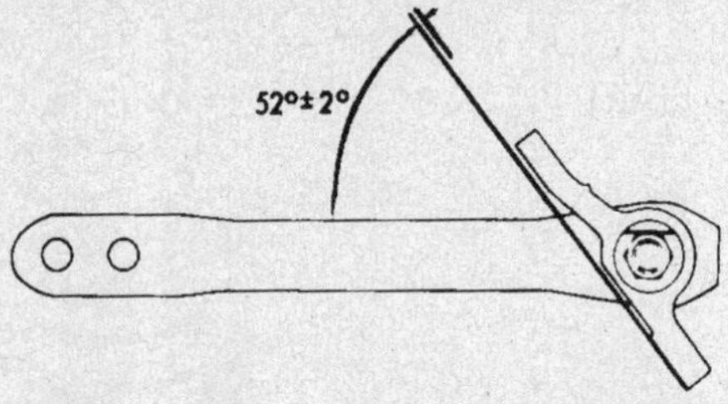
52°± 2°
SA2029100006000X

Fig. 7 Upper control arm bearing installation. 900

12. Remove fixing clamps on lefthand and righthand sides.
13. Disconnect power steering gear delivery and return pipes using steering system hydraulic pipe wrench tool No. 87 91 287, or equivalent. Plug pipes and connections on valve body.
14. Disconnect internal pipe connections from valve body and bend upward. Plug pipes and connections.
15. Remove steering gear through lefthand wheel housing.
16. Reverse procedure to install, noting the following:
    a. Move bulkhead seal and rubber bushings on righthand and lefthand sides away from valve body, then disconnect internal pipes from steering gear and plug them.
    b. If steering wheel has moved, coil spring must be readjusted as outlined in "Air Bag Systems."

9000

1. Remove steering column lower clamp attaching bolt, then loosen upper clamp attaching bolt and remove intermediate shaft.
2. From inside vehicle, remove floor panel covering, then the cover plate, gasket, seal and plastic bushing.
3. Raise and support front of vehicle, then remove wheel assemblies.
4. Remove lefthand fender rear undercover.
5. Remove tie rod ends from steering arms, using puller tool No. 89 95 409, or equivalent.
6. Clean surfaces of hydraulic line connectors at pump reservoir, then drain reservoir fluid.
7. Disconnect servo pump hoses, then the reservoir return hose. **Cap all line and reservoir openings to prevent entry of foreign material.**
8. Remove steering gear attaching bolts, then the vertical brace between engine and body subframe.
9. Remove steering gear through lefthand wheelwell, using care not to damage brake components, gear unit or surrounding components.
10. Reverse procedure to install, noting the following:
    a. Check fluid level and toe setting, adjusting as necessary.
    b. Bleed power steering system by turning steering wheel from lock to

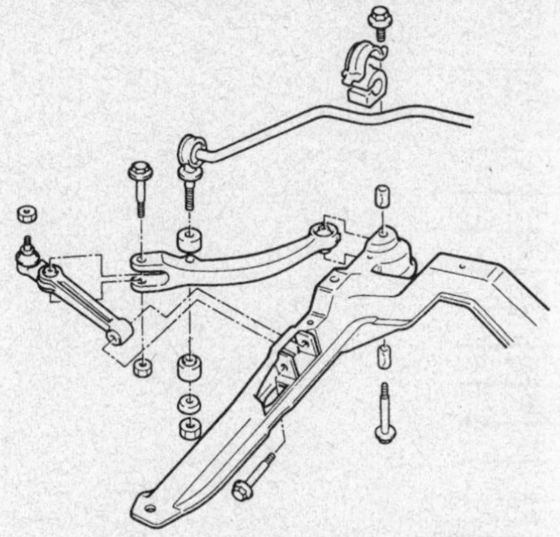
SA2029400009000X

Fig. 9 Exploded view of suspension arm. 1994–96 900

lock several times with engine running at idle.

POWER STEERING PUMP

REPLACE

900

1993

1. Disconnect battery ground cable.
2. Clean area around hose connections, then disconnect return line at pump and drain fluid into a container.
3. Remove pump as follows:
   a. Loosen pivot and adjusting bolts and remove drive belt.
   b. Remove pivot bolt and bolt securing adjusting bracket to engine.
   c. Disconnect and plug pressure line, then remove pump and brackets. **Hold hex fitting on pump with second wrench when disconnecting pressure line.**
4. Remove pump pulley with puller tool No. 89 96 423, or equivalent.
5. Remove bolts securing brackets to pump and remove brackets.
6. Reverse procedure to install, noting the following:
   a. Press pulley onto pump shaft using installer tool No. 899 64 15, or equivalent. **Shaft should be flush with hub.**
   b. Adjust drive belt tension to specifications.
   c. Fill reservoir, then bleed system by turning steering wheel from lock to lock with engine running at idle.
   d. Refill system to full mark on dipstick.

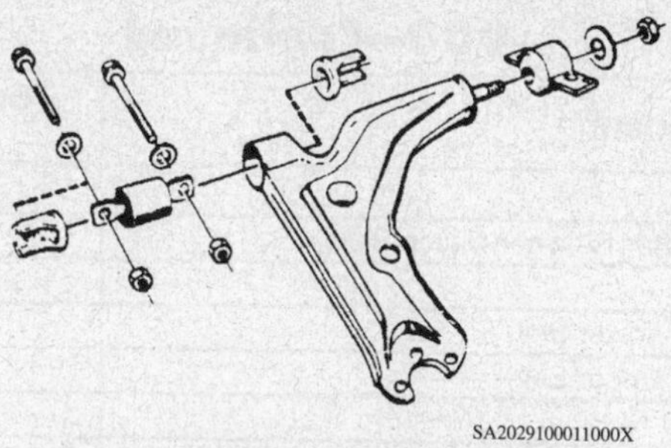
SA2029100011000X

Fig. 10 Exploded view of lower control arm assembly. 9000

1994–96

1. Drain power steering fluid from pump as follows:
   a. Disconnect hose from return pipe, then plug hose.
   b. Connect length of hose to return pipe and place other end in suitable container that holds at least 1.06 quarts (1 liter).
   c. Start engine and allow hydraulic fluid to be pumped out of steering gear.
   d. Turn steering wheel from full lock to full lock position, then switch off engine when no more fluid runs into container. **Never allow pump to run dry.**
2. Remove hose and container, then reconnect return hose to pipe connection.
3. Remove air cleaner, then the belt from belt pulley.
4. Remove delivery pipe and suction hose from pump.
5. Remove pump retaining bolts, then the pump.
6. Reverse procedure to install, noting the following:
   a. Tighten pump retaining bolts to specifications.
   b. Fill pump reservoir with power steering fluid, then start engine and turn steering wheel two or three times from full lock to full lock position.
   c. Switch off engine and top off fluid reservoir.

9000

1. Siphon power steering fluid from reservoir.
2. **On 1995–96 models,** obtain radio anti-theft code as outlined under "Precautions."
3. **On all models,** disconnect battery ground cable.

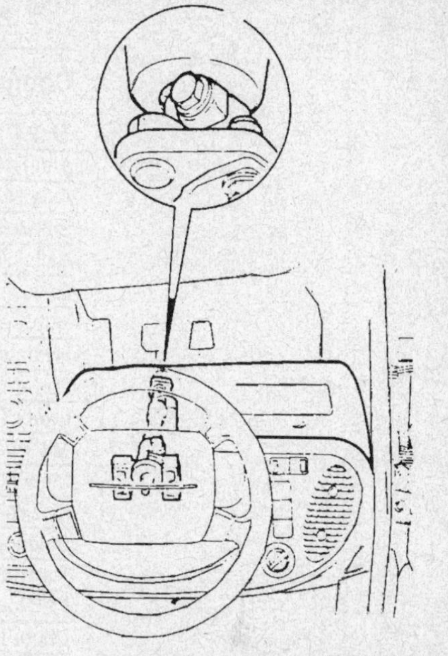
SA6039100001000X

Fig. 11 Steering column shaft joint. 1994–96 900

4. Raise and support vehicle, then remove righthand front wheel and inner fender liner.
5. Loosen, then remove drive belt.
6. Remove bracket for engine oil filler pipe.
7. Remove engine support.
8. Clean area around hose connections, then disconnect hoses and cap openings.
9. Remove power steering pump. **One of pump attaching bolts is located behind pulley and is accessible through hole in pulley.**
10. Using puller tool No. 899 64 23, or equivalent, remove pump pulley from shaft.
11. Reverse procedure to install, noting the following:
    a. Press pulley onto pump shaft using installer tool No. 899 64 15, or equivalent. **Ensure distance between end plate of pump body and outer pulley rim is 4.23 inches (107.5 mm).**
    b. Adjust drive belt tension to specifications.
    c. Fill reservoir, then bleed system by turning steering wheel from lock to lock with engine running at idle.
    d. Refill system to full mark on dipstick.

TIGHTENING SPECIFICATIONS

900

Component	Torque/Ft. Lbs.
1993	
Anti-Roll Bar Anchor Bolt	15–19

Continued

900—Continued

Component	Torque/Ft. Lbs.
1993	
Anti-Roll Bar Retainer Clamp Bolts	15–19
Axle Nut	214–229
Ball Joint Lower Bolt	15–19
Ball Joint Upper Bolt	31–41
Driveshaft Nut	214–229
Hub Center Nut	214–229
Hydraulic Line Couplings	15–25
Lower Control Arm Bearing Retaining Nuts	70–77
Lower Control Arm Bushing Bolt	51–69
MacPherson Strut Lower Mounting Bolts	56–76
MacPherson Strut Tower Cap Nut	49–59
MacPherson Strut Upper Mounting Bolts	29–39
Steering Shaft Clamp Bolts	26–30
Tie Rod End Locknuts	44–60
Tie Rod To Steering Arm Nuts	37–44
Upper Control Arm Bearing Retaining Nut	54–66
Wheel Bolts	65–79
1994–96	
Anti-Roll Bar Nut	7
Axle Nut	214
Ball Joint Nut	55
Damper	159
Driveshaft Nut	214
Hub Center Nut	214
MacPherson Strut Top Mounting Retaining Nuts	13
Steering Arm To Subframe Bolt	85
Support Arm To Subframe Bolt	①
Support Arm To Suspension Arm Bolt	68
Tie Rod To Steering Gear Bolts	68
Wheel Bolts	78–96

① — **Torque** to 74 ft. lbs., then an additional 82°.

9000

Component	Torque/Ft. Lbs.
Anti-Roll Bar Anchor Bolt	15–19
Anti-Roll Bar Retainer Clamp Bolts	15–19
Axle Nut	194–208
Ball Joint Lower Bolt	15–19
Ball Joint To Spindle Nut	32–41
Ball Joint Upper Bolt	31–41
Caliper Bolts	51–79
Driveshaft Nut	195–208
Hub Center Nut	195–208
Hub To Steering Spindle	40–43
Hydraulic Line Couplings	14–26
Lower Control Arm Bushing Bolt	51–69
MacPherson Strut Lower Mounting Bolts	56–76
MacPherson Strut Tower Cap Nut	49–59
MacPherson Strut Upper Mounting Bolts	29–39
Shock Absorber Tower Nut	49–59
Shock Absorber Upper Nuts	16–21
Steering Gear Attaching Bolts	46–56
Steering Shaft Clamp Bolts	26.5–32

Continued

9000—Continued

Component	Torque/Ft. Lbs.
Strut To Spindle Bolts	56–75
Tie Rod End Locknuts	46–56
Tie Rod End To Steering Arm Nuts	36–46
Wheel Bolts	65–79

Wheel Alignment

INDEX

	Page No.
Front Wheel Alignment	38-49
Camber	38-49
Caster	38-49
Kingpin Inclination	38-49
Toe-In	38-49
Preliminary Inspection	38-49
Rear Wheel Alignment	38-49
Camber	38-49
Toe-In	38-49
Vehicle Ride Height	38-49
9000	38-49
Wheel Alignment Specifications	38-4

PRELIMINARY INSPECTION

1. Ensure tires are inflated to correct pressure and check for uneven wear.
2. Check front wheel bearings, suspension arm bearing, ball joints and track rods for damage. Replace components as necessary.
3. Check rack and pinion steering gear and adjust as necessary.
4. Check shock absorbers for damage. Replace as necessary.
5. Rock vehicle backward and forward, then bounce it upward and downward to settle it prior to alignment.
6. Ensure vehicle is unloaded and on an alignment rack according to manufacturer's instructions. **When measuring equipment is attached directly to outer end of driveshaft and front wheels are on turntables, apply brake to prevent improper vehicle movement.**

FRONT WHEEL ALIGNMENT

CAMBER

900

1993

Camber is adjusted by placing shims or spacers under the two upper control arm bearing brackets. Place the same thickness under both front and rear brackets.

1994–96

The camber cannot be adjusted. If setting is outside the specified limits, it must be corrected by replacing defective components.

9000

Camber is preset during production and is not adjustable. If front camber is not within specified limits, check and replace defective components.

CASTER

900

1993

To increase the caster, transfer shims from front upper control arm bracket to rear upper control arm bracket. To decrease the caster, transfer shims from back to front.

1994

The caster cannot be adjusted. If setting is outside the specified limits, it must be corrected by replacing defective components.

9000

Caster cannot be adjusted. If setting is not within specified limits, defective components must be replaced.

TOE-IN

1. Roll vehicle straight forward on level floor and stop without using brakes.
2. Take reading at dimension "A," **Fig. 1**, using toe-in gauge between the front wheel rims level with axle. Mark measurement parts with chalk.
3. Roll vehicle forward until chalk marks are level with, but behind, axles and take reading of B, **Fig. 1.** Any necessary adjustment is made by altering length of tie rod.
4. Remove rubber bellows to track rod retaining clip.
5. Push rubber bellows toward steering gear housing to expose groove in which bellows seals.
6. Measure distance A, **Fig. 1.** Distance A should not exceed 3.94 inches (100 mm) on 1993 900 models, 2.03 inches (52 mm) on 1994 900 models, or 5.51 inches (140 mm) on 9000 models.
7. Perform steps 4 through 6 on opposite side of vehicle, then compare measurements calculated at each side of vehicle. **Difference between measurements must not exceed .079 inch (2 mm) on 9000 and 1993 900 models, or .114 inch (3 mm) on 1994 900 models.**
8. If necessary to adjust, loosen nut on outer end of tie rod, then rotate tie rod until distance A, is as specified.
9. **Torque** tie rod end locknuts to 46–56 ft. lbs.

KINGPIN INCLINATION

Kingpin inclination is preset and not adjustable. If kingpin inclination is incorrect, but camber is satisfactory, check for a faulty steering swivel member. Replace if necessary.

REAR WHEEL ALIGNMENT

CAMBER

Camber cannot be adjusted. If setting is not within specified limits, defective components must be replaced.

TOE-IN

Rear toe-in is not adjustable. If setting is not within specified limits, check and replace defective components.

VEHICLE RIDE HEIGHT

9000

When measuring vehicle ride height, refer to vehicle ride height dimension and measurement chart, **Figs. 3 and 4.**

1. Roll vehicle forward, then backward approximately 3 feet.
2. Depress front of vehicle, then release.
3. Measure height and record results.
4. Repeat step 1.
5. Pull up on front of vehicle, then release.
6. Measure height and record results.
7. Calculate an average of the two measurements. Maximum tolerance for variation is .393 inch.

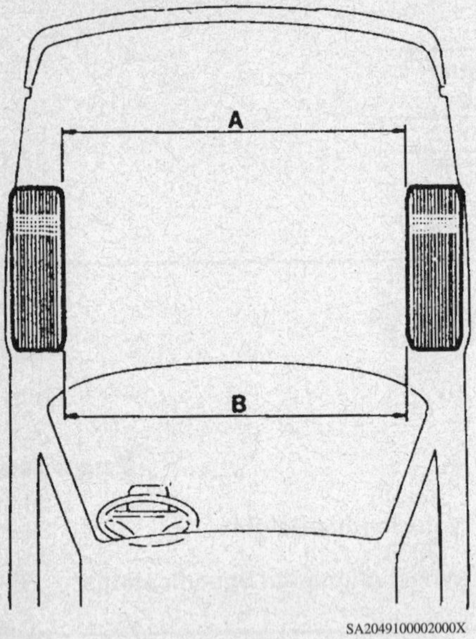
A
B

Fig. 1 Toe-in adjustment vehicle position

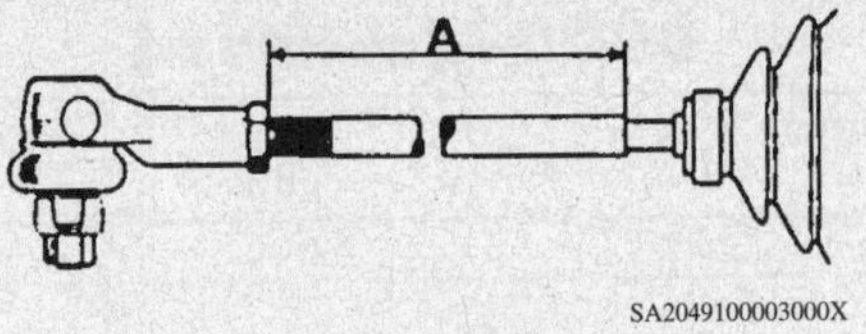
A

Fig. 2 Toe-in adjustment

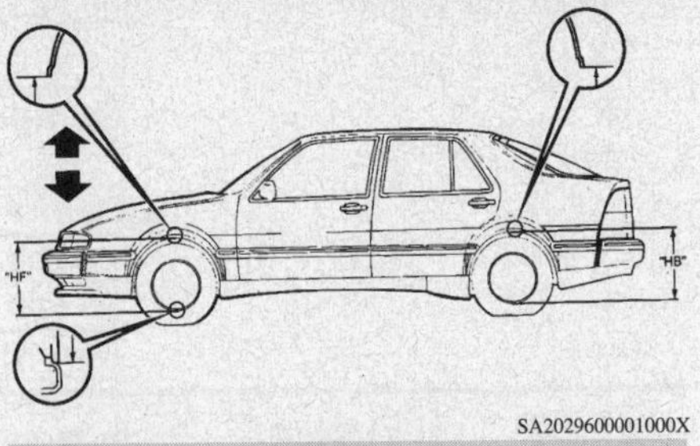

Fig. 3 Vehicle ride height dimension

Year	Model	HF, Inch	HB, Inch
1993–95	Standard	23.5	22.7
1993–95	Standard CS	23.8	22.7
1993–95	Sport	23.7	23.2
1993–95	Sport CS	24.0	23.2
1996	Standard CS	23.4	22.7
1996	Sport	23.4	22.9

Fig. 4 Vehicle ride height measurement

Air Conditioning

NOTE: On Air Bag Equipped Models, Refer To "Air Bag System Precautions" Located In The Front Of This Manual For System Disarming & Arming Procedures.

INDEX

	Page No.
A/C Specifications	38-52
Belt Tension	38-52
Oil Charge	38-52
R-12 Systems	38-52
R134a Systems	38-52
Performance Test	38-51
R-12 Systems	38-51
R134a Systems	38-51
Precautions	38-50
Air Bag Systems	38-50
R-12 Systems	38-50
R134a Systems	38-50
Refrigerant Recovery	38-51

PRECAUTIONS

AIR BAG SYSTEMS

Refer to "Air Bag System Precautions" in the front of this manual for system disarming and arming procedures.

R-12 SYSTEMS

The Freon refrigerant used in A/C systems is colorless and odorless both as a gas and a liquid. Since Freon boils (vaporizes) at -21.7°F, it will usually be in a vapor state when being handled in a repair shop. If a portion of the liquid coolant should come in contact with the hands or face, note that its temperature momentarily will be at least -22°F.

Protective goggles should be worn when opening any refrigerant lines. If liquid coolant does touch the eyes, bathe eyes quickly in cold water. Then apply bland disinfectant oil to the eyes. See an eye doctor.

When checking a system for leaks with a torch type leak detector, do not breathe vapors coming from the flame. Do not discharge the refrigerant in the area of the live flame. A poisonous phosphene gas is produced when refrigerant is burned. While a small amount of this gas produced by a leak detector is not harmful unless inhaled directly at the flame, the quantity of refrigerant released into the air when a system is purged can be extremely dangerous if allowed to come in contact with an open flame. When purging a system, ensure the hose is directed to a well ventilated area where no flame is present.

Never allow temperature of refrigerant drums to exceed 125°F. The increase in temperature will cause a corresponding rise in pressure which may cause the safety plug to release or the drum to burst.

If it is necessary to heat a drum of refrigerant when charging a system, the drum should be placed in water that is no hotter than 125°F. never use a torch or other open flame. If possible, a pressure release mechanism should be attached before the drum is heated.

R134a SYSTEMS

Avoid breathing A/C refrigerant and lubricant vapor or mist. Exposure may irritate eyes, nose and/or throat. Wear eye protection when servicing the refrigerant system. Serious eye injury can result from eye contact with refrigerant.

Do not expose refrigerant to open flame. Poisonous gas is created when refrigerant is burned. An electronic type leak detector is recommended.

If accidental system discharge occurs, ventilate work area before resuming service. Large amounts of refrigerant released

No cooling	Little cooling	Erratic cooling	Noise in system	Possible cause	Check/remedy
				Electrical faults:	
X				Blow fuse	Check the fuses
X				Poor connection or earthing (Compressor not running)	Check all leads
X				Compressor clutch burnt out	Change the clutch
X				Fan motor not running	Check electrical connections and fan motor
	X	X		Fan motor running erratically (Play or fractured component in motor)	Check and change if necessary
		X	X	Break or poor contact in the compressor clutch winding (clutch slips in and out)	Change the clutch
			X	Fan motor whining or touching casing	Check
				Mechanical faults:	
X	X		X	Slack drive belt	Adjust or change the belt
	X			Blockage in air duct	Check and clean
			X	Clutch bearing worn or out of true	Change the bearing
	X		X	Compressor worn or insecurely fitted	Overhaul the compressor and tighten fixings

SA7029100003010X

Fig. 1 A/C troubleshooting chart (Part 1 of 2). R-12

Symptom

No cooling	Little cooling	Erratic cooling	Noise in system	Possible cause	Check/remedy
				System faults:	
X				Anti-frost thermostat fails to make circuit to fitted, compressor	Check that the thermostat is fully inserted in the evaporator. If correctly change the thermostat
X				Expansion valve stuck open	Change the expansion valve
X				Leak in system	Recharge the system and test for and repair any leaks
X				Blockage in hose or component	Check the flow through each component
X				System starved of refrigerant	Recharge the system
	X			Air filter clogged on inlet side	Change the filter
	X		X	Insufficient refrigerant in the system (whistling noise from expansion valve on evaporator - bubbles visible in the sight glas)	Drain the system and recharge
	X			Expansion valve capillary tube damaged (Tube empty of medium)	Change the expansion valve
	X			Receiver clogged	Change the receiver
	X	X		Moisture in the system. Cooling good initially (for a few minutes) and then deteriorating. Alternatively, deterioration at bigh ambient temperature	Drain the system, change the receiver and recharge with refrigerant
	X			Air in the system (Bubbles visible in sight glass)	Drain the system, change the receiver and refrigerant
		X		Frosting on air side of evaporator	Make sure that the capillary tube for the anti-frost thermostat is correctly located between the fins on the evaporator. If so, change the thermostat
		X		Play in anti-frost thermostat	Check the thermostat and change if necessary
		X		Coil on expansion valve capillary tube not making good contact with evaporator outlet pipe or poorly insulated from air temperature	Check the contact and insulation
		X		Interval between cut-in and cut-out temperature of anti-frost thermostat too great	Change the thermostat
			X	**System flooded:** Causes rumbling noise or vibration in high-pressure line, gurgling noise in compressor, excessive compressor and suction pressure, hissing noise in expansion valve and bubbles or vapour in sight glass. If the compressor valves have been damaged by an excess charge of refrigerant in the system, the compressor pressure will be too low	Drain the system and recharge
			X	Excessive moisture in the system can cause noise in the expansion valve	Drain the system. Change the receiver and recharge the system with refrigerant

SA7029100003020X

Fig. 1 A/C troubleshooting chart (Part 2 of 2). R-12

in a closed work area will displace the oxygen and cause suffocation.

The evaporation rate of R-134a refrigerant at average temperature and altitude is extremely high. As a result, anything that comes in contact with the refrigerant will freeze. Always protect skin or delicate objects from direct contact with refrigerant.

Liquid refrigerant is corrosive to metal surfaces. Follow operating instructions supplied with equipment being used.

PERFORMANCE TEST

R-12 SYSTEMS

1. Connect manifold gauge set to high and low pressure fittings of A/C system.
2. Insert a suitable thermometer approximately four inches into center dash vent and position thermometer at blower inlet to measure ambient temperature.
3. Start engine and run engine at 2000 RPM.
4. **On models with manual A/C,** set temperature control to COLD, air distribution to VENT, air inlet to RECIRCULATION and blower to RUN position 4. Engage A/C.
5. **On models with Automatic Climate Control (ACC),** set temperature control to LO and manually set air distribution control to VENT, air inlet to RECIRCULATION and blower speed to RUN position 3.
6. **On all models,** close doors, windows and hood.
7. Allow compressor clutch to cycle several times and observe discharge temperature at center vent. Discharge temperature should be as follows:
   a. If ambient temperature is 68°F, discharge temperature should be 43–50°F.
   b. If ambient temperature is 86°F, discharge temperature should be 43–50°F.
   c. If ambient temperature is 104°F, discharge temperature should be 50–54°F.
8. If system fail to operate as specified, refer to system troubleshooting **Fig. 1.**

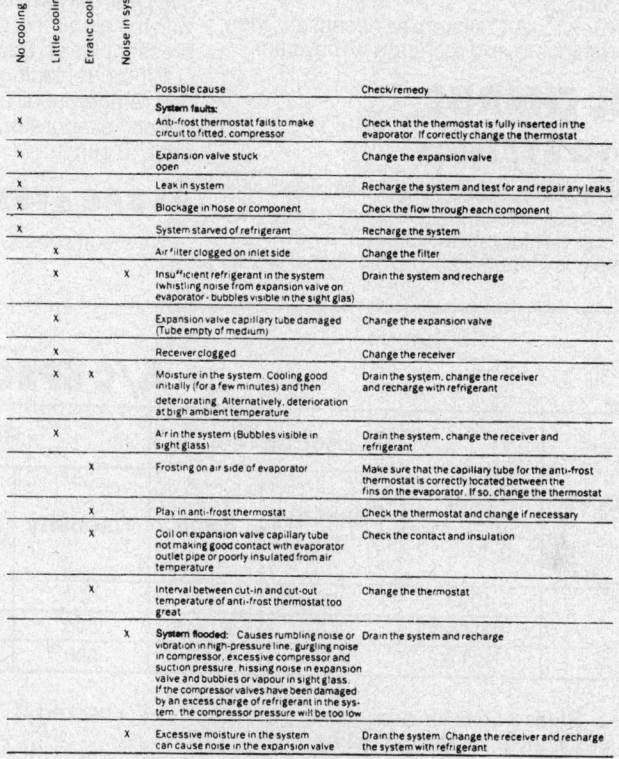

R134a SYSTEMS

Temperature Readings

1. Ensure doors and windows are closed and engine speed is between 1500-2000 RPM.
2. Ensure all vent panels are open.
3. **On models with Automatic Climate Control,** select Lo position on ACC control unit and max fan speed.
4. **On models with manual A/C,** set fan speed to position 4, air distribution to Vent position and recirculation to On position.
5. **On all models,** measure temperature 4 inches inside center panel outlet. Take reading after five minutes.
6. Temperature should be between 43–54°F. Difference between turn on and turn off temperature should be 33–39°F.

Pressure Reading

1. Ensure both valves for the low pressure hose and valve for the high pressure hose on gauge stank are closed.
2. Connect hoses to compressor, then open valves on both snap-on couplings.
3. Start engine.
4. With an engine speed of 1500-2000 RPM and ambient temperature of 68°F, pressure reading should be as follows:
   a. Low-pressure side should read, 14.5–43.5 psi.
   b. High-pressure side should read, 174-239 psi.

REFRIGERANT RECOVERY

Using refrigerant recovery and recycling stations allows the recovery and reuse of refrigerant after moisture and contaminants have been removed.

When using a recovery or recycling station, follow the manufacturers' operating instructions, noting the following:

1. **Use extreme caution and observe all safety and service precautions related to use of refrigerants.**
2. Connect refrigerant recycling station hose(s) to vehicle A/C service port(s) and recovery station inlet fitting. Hoses used should have shutoff devices or check valve within 12 inches of hose ends to minimize introduction of air into recycling station and to limit amount of refrigerant release when hose(s) is disconnected.
3. Turn recycling station on to start recovery process. Allow recycling station to pump refrigerant from A/C system until pressure gauge indicates vacuum.
4. After vehicle A/C system has been evacuated, close station inlet valve, if equipped.
5. Turn station off. On some stations the pump will automatically be turned off by a low pressure switch.
6. Allow vehicle A/C system to remain closed for approximately two minutes. Observe vacuum level indicated on gauge. If pressure does not rise, disconnect recycling station hose(s).
7. If system pressure rises, start recovery

process again and continue until vacuum level remains stable for two minutes.

8. Service A/C system as necessary, then evacuate and recharge A/C system.

OIL CHARGE

R-12 SYSTEMS

New compressors are pre-charged with the proper amount of lubricant needed for the entire refrigerant system. If a new compressor is installed and no additional oil has been lost from the system, drain and measure amount of oil present in old compressor. Drain oil from new compressor, then fill with the amount of oil drained from old compressor plus an additional .8 ounce.

When replacing system components, add refrigerant oil as follows: condenser, .6 ounce; evaporator, 1.4 ounces; receiver-drier, .6 ounce.

R134a SYSTEMS

New compressors are pre-charged with the proper amount of lubricant needed for the entire refrigerant system. If a new compressor is installed and no additional oil has been lost from the system, drain 4.4 ounces from new compressor.

When servicing A/C system, add refrigerant oil as follows: purging refrigerant, .67 ounce, burst A/C hose, 1.35 ounces, A/C hose replacement, .67 ounce, condenser, 1.35 ounces, evaporator, 1.35 ounces, receiver-drier, 1.35 ounces, expansion valve, .67 ounce.

A/C SPECIFICATIONS

Model	Year	Refrigerant		Refrigerant Oil①			Compressor Clutch Air Gap, Inch	Charging Valve Locations	
		Capacity, Lbs.	Type	Viscosity	Total System Capacity, Ounces	Compressor Oil Level Check, Inches		High Press.	Low Press.
900	1993	2.2	R-12	500	5.60	②	.016–.031	③	③
	1994-96	1.6	R134a	500	6.78	②	—	③	③
9000	1993-96	2.09	R-134a	500	6.76	②	—	③	③

① — Suniso 5GS, or equivalent.
② — Oil level inches cannot be checked.
③ — On accumulator.

BELT TENSION

Use a suitable tension gauge to measure and adjust belt tension. If a new belt is installed, tension should be adjusted to 110–130 lbs. If adjusting a used belt, tension should be 75–85 lbs.

Cooling Fans

NOTE: On Air Bag Equipped Models, Refer To "Air Bag System Precautions" Located In The Front Of This Manual For System Disarming & Arming Procedures.

NOTE: Electrical Symbol & Wire Color Code Identification Located In The Front Of This Manual May Be Used As An Aid When Using Wiring Circuits Found In This Section.

INDEX

	Page No.
Component Replacement	38-55
Electric Cooling Fan, Replace	38-55
Description	38-53
900	38-53
9000	38-54
Precautions	38-53
ACC Air Flap Stepper Motor Calibration	38-53
Air Bag Systems	38-53
Radio Anti-Theft Lock	38-53
System Diagnosis & Testing	38-54
1994–96 900	38-54
Troubleshooting	38-54
9000 & 1993 900	38-54

PRECAUTIONS

AIR BAG SYSTEMS

Refer to "Air Bag System Precautions" in the front of this manual for system disarming and arming procedures.

RADIO ANTI-THEFT LOCK

9000

1995-96

Radio and cassette player are equipped with an electronic four-digit anti-theft lock. This four-digit code is programmed at manufacturing and cannot be changed. If the battery is disconnected for more than three minutes, if unit is removed or if otherwise cut off from power, the four-digit code must be entered with the quick-selection buttons as follows:

1. Turn radio on, then, when display shows "Code In, " enter four-digit code with quick-selection buttons. If code is correct, last-tuned radio frequency is shown on display. If wrong digit has been entered by mistake, all four digits must be entered again. If code is wrong it stays on display.
2. If incorrect four-digit code has been entered, press Band button for more than three seconds to clear display. Display shows "Code In" and new attempt to enter correct code can be made.
3. If wrong code has been used three times in succession, four dashes appear on display and you must wait an hour with radio switched on before trying again.
4. To try again, hold Band button for at least three seconds. "Code In" should appear on display.
5. Correct code must be entered at first attempt, otherwise you must wait another hour with unit switched on before trying again.

ACC AIR FLAP STEPPER MOTOR CALIBRATION

The ACC stepper motors do not have a feedback function. Whenever power to the ACC control module is interrupted or a stepper motor is serviced, it is necessary to calibrate the flap stepper motors to their end position. This calibration may be accomplished using the ISAT or other suitable scan tool or by placing the system into a self-test mode.

ISAT METHOD

Connect the ISAT or suitable scan tool to the green connector found under the left seat using the correct interface cable. Start vehicle to maintain correct system voltage during calibration procedure. Select "ACC" mode, then select "Calibrate" from menu. Follow ISAT menu steps to calibrate stepper motors by entering ISAT diagnostic trouble code 900.

ACC CONTROL PANEL METHOD

Retrieve any stored diagnostic trouble codes from memory. Refer to "System Diagnosis and Testing."

Start vehicle to ensure correct system voltage during calibration. Press and hold the "Auto" and "Vent " buttons for approximately one second. This puts the system into self-test mode. The system will check for any current diagnostic trouble codes and display them while cycling flap motors to their calibration positions. The vehicle must remain running for at least 35 seconds for a complete sequence to occur.

Turn off engine and wait at least 30 seconds before turning ignition switch to On position or restarting vehicle.

DESCRIPTION

900

1993

The electric cooling fan is mounted behind the radiator assembly and is thermostatically controlled. When engine coolant temperature has reached about 92°C (198°F), the temperature switch will close its contacts, allowing the electric cooling fan to operate. On models with A/C, the circuit is equipped with a crimped branch connection, because fan operation is also controlled by A/C operation. When engine coolant temperature decreases, the temperature switch opens its contacts, de-energizing the electric cooling fan.

These vehicles are also equipped with a time-delay relay, which limits cooling fan running time after engine has been shutoff. The relay that controls this function is always energized when the engine is running. When the engine is switched off, the supply to the relay coil will be interrupted. After about 10 minutes, the relay will trip the supply to the fan motor, even if temperature switch is still closed.

1994-95

Vehicles are equipped with either a one- or two-speed cooling fan, which is located behind the radiator and is powered by an electric motor. A relay in relay position G in the distribution center of the engine compartment is used for the one-speed cooling fan and also for the two-speed fan when it is running at low speed. In relay position I in the distribution center of the engine compartment, is the relay used for the two-speed fan when it is operated at high speed.

The cooling fan is controlled by the Integrated Central Electronics (ICE) system. ICE starts and stops the cooling fan at programmed coolant temperatures by grounding the relay. The ICE reads temperature for 20 minutes after the ignition has been turned off. The cooling fan can run at low speed during that time for a maximum of three minutes.

On models equipped with air conditioning, the ICE starts the cooling fan at low

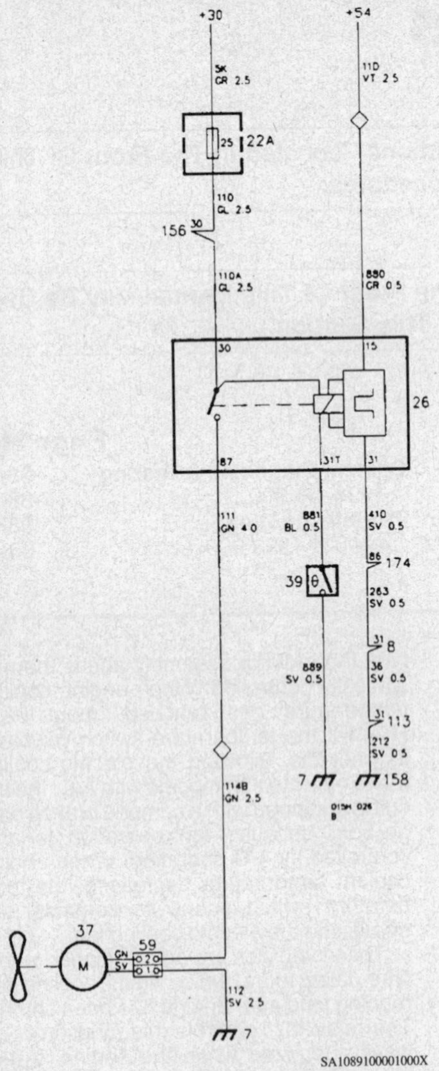
+30
+54
22A
156
26
39
174
8
113
7
158
37
59
7
SA1089100001000X

Fig. 1 Cooling fan wiring circuit. 1993 900

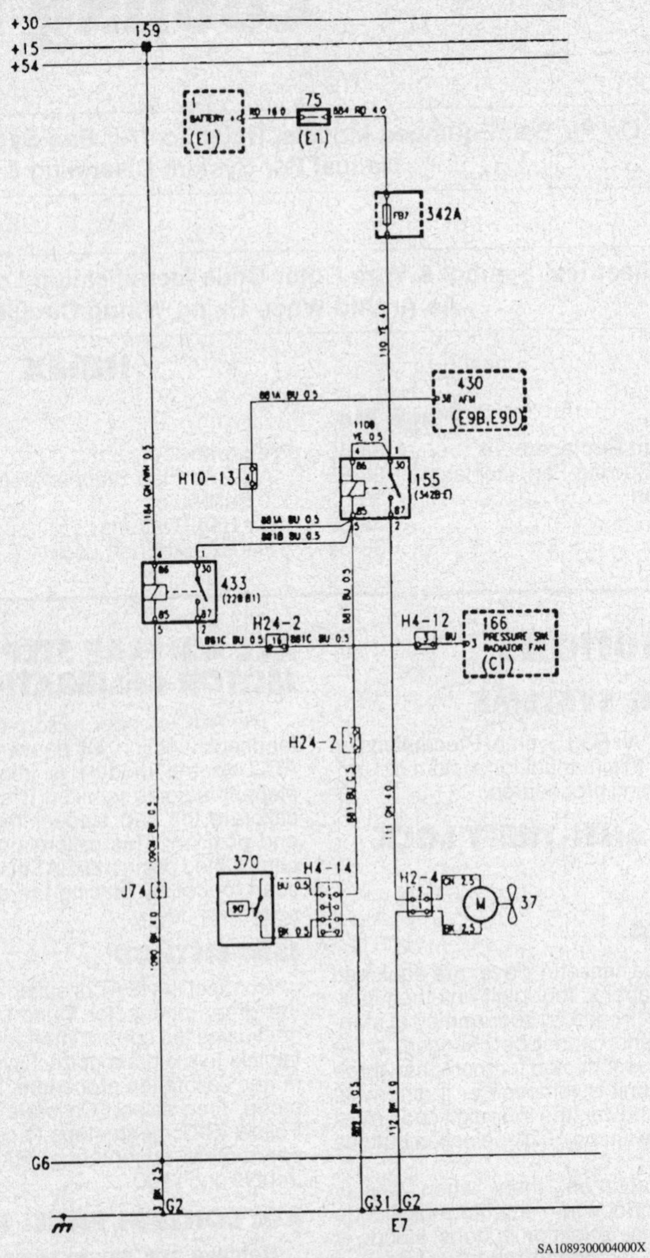
+30
+15
+54
159
75
342A
430
H10-13
155
433
H24-2
H4-12
166
PRESSURE SW.
RADIATOR FAN
(C1)
H24-2
370
H4-14
J74
H2-4
37
G6
G2
G31
G2
E7
SA1089300004000X

Fig. 2 Cooling fan wiring circuit. 1993–95 9000 w/single-speed fan

speed when the pressure switch on the desiccant container closes (approximately 240 psi).

9000

The electric cooling fan is mounted behind the radiator assembly and is thermostatically controlled. Vehicles with manual transaxles have a one-speed cooling fan. When engine coolant temperature reaches about 90°C (194°F), the temperature switch closes its contacts, allowing the electric cooling fan to operate. Vehicles with automatic transaxles are equipped with a two-speed cooling fan for more efficient cooling. The temperature fan switch has two pairs of contacts. One set closes at 90°C (194°F) and the other when it reaches 110°C (230°F). Models equipped with A/C, have an auxiliary cooling fan. This fan is controlled by a time-delay relay that also turns on the compressor.

These vehicles are also equipped with a time-delay relay, which limits cooling fan running time after engine has been shutoff. The relay that controls this function is always energized when the engine is running. When the engine is switched off, the supply to the relay coil will be interrupted. After about 10 minutes, the relay will trip the supply to the fan motor, even if temperature switch is still closed.

TROUBLESHOOTING

9000 & 1993 900

When checking these systems refer to wiring circuits **Figs. 1 through 3.**

1. Check cooling fan fuse and ensure supply to it is live.
2. Check for voltage at temperature switch.
3. Check radiator fan operation by connecting jumper wire across temperature switch terminals.
4. Run engine until it reaches normal operating temperature and ensure temperature switch turns fan on.
5. Check connectors, cable harnesses and ground connections.

SYSTEM DIAGNOSIS & TESTING

1994-96 900

Refer to **Fig. 4** for cooling fan wiring circuit and **Figs. 5 and 6** for connector view and terminal identification.

For diagnostic testing, refer to **Figs. 7 through 14.** Follow equipment manufacturer's instructions for using test equipment.

1. **Never remove ICE signal ground on A pillar without first disconnecting battery, as the control module could be seriously damaged.**
2. SDA MkII should never be connected to ISAT scan tool.
3. Data link connector is located by steering column under fascia.
4. During diagnosis, ignition key should always be in drive position.
5. If it is not possible to connect ISAT and cooling system, first check that fuse Nos. 3 or 4 in engine compartment distribution center is intact and is receiving power, then check cable between ICE control module connection No. 60 and data link connector pin No. 8.
6. Check that there is power and correct ground in data link connector and connector pins are undamaged and securely fitted.
7. To avoid damage to control module and components, always check that ignition is switched off before connector(s) is disconnected.
8. Check for correct control module ground connection and power supply.
9. If necessary, remove connectors and check that connections and pins are undamaged and securely fitted. Reconnect connectors and erase all diagnostic trouble codes. If possible, start vehicle and check if faults are still there.
10. All signals around 12-volt level are proportional to battery voltage and levels should only be used as a guide.
11. The 0-volt signals designate ground, but could give indication of measurable voltage on sensitive multimeter.
12. Never switch from one unit of measurement to another without first disconnecting instrument measuring cables.
13. After performing function check, always erase fault memory with "CLEAR DIAGNOSTIC TROUBLE CODES" command.

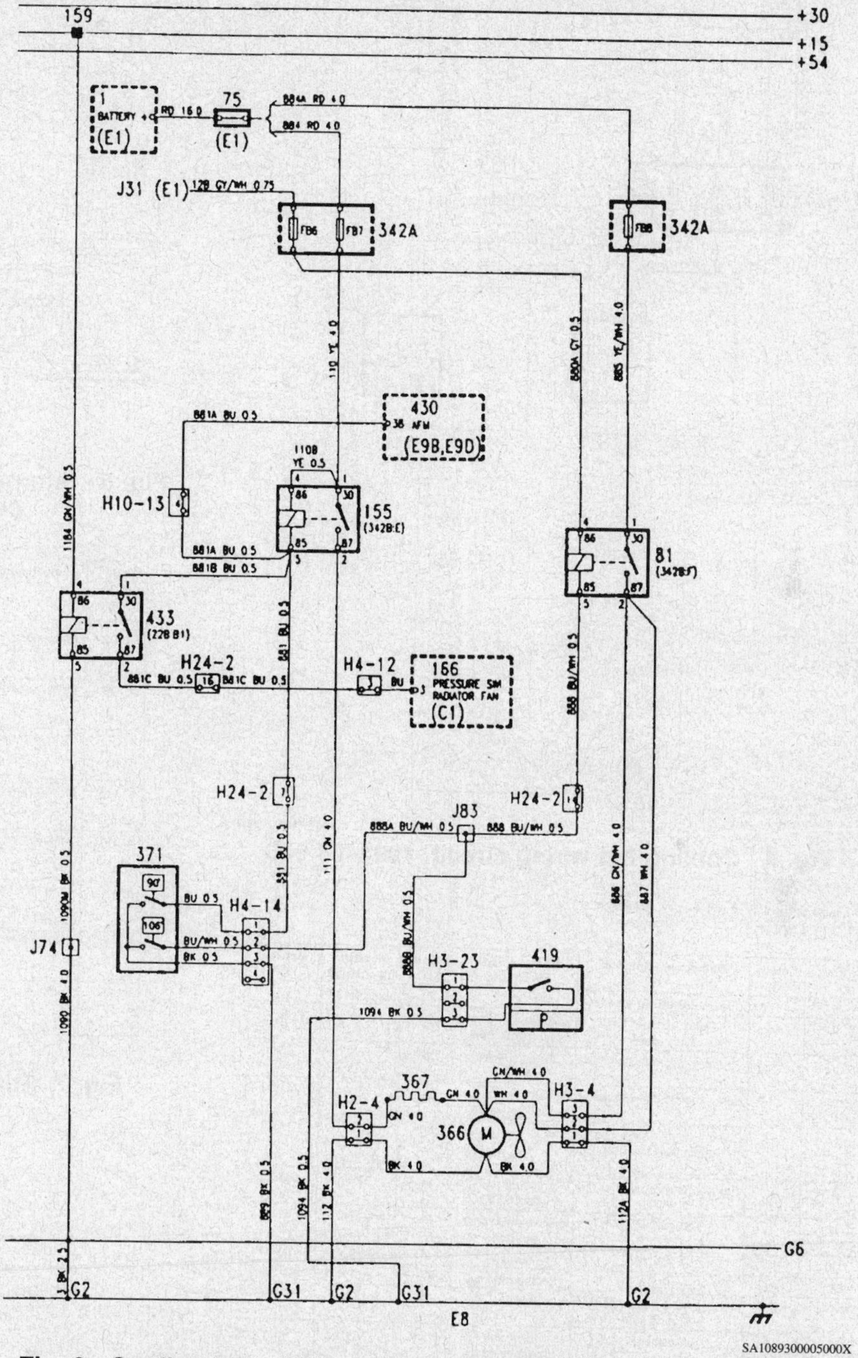
159
+30
+15
+54
BATTERY
(E1)
75
(E1)
J31 (E1)
342A
342A
430
38 AFM
(E9B,E9D)
H10-13
155
(342B:E)
81
(342B:F)
433
(228 B1)
H24-2
H4-12
166
PRESSURE SW
RADIATOR FAN
(C1)
H24-2
H24-2
J83
371
H4-14
J74
H3-23
419
367
H2-4
H3-4
366
G6
G2
G31
G2
G31
G2
E8
SA1089300005000X

Fig. 3 Cooling fan wiring circuit. 1993–95 9000 w/two-speed fan

COMPONENT REPLACEMENT

ELECTRIC COOLING FAN, REPLACE

9000 & 1993 900

Main Fan

Do not attempt to remove the electric cooling fan with engine hot. The electric cooling fan operates in conjunction with engine coolant operating temperatures. Ensure engine coolant temperature drops enough to safely permit electric cooling fan removal.

1. **On 1995–96 9000 models,** obtain radio anti-theft code as outlined under "Precautions."
2. **On all models,** open hood and disconnect battery ground cable.
3. Disconnect electric cooling fan and thermoswitch electrical connectors.
4. Remove electric cooling fan-to-radiator attaching bolts. **If necessary, loosen radiator attaching bolts and move radiator back to allow sufficient clearance for fan removal. On some models it also may be necessary to disconnect radiator hose(s) to allow sufficient clearance for fan removal.**
5. Remove electric cooling fan from vehicle.
6. Reverse procedure to install.

Auxiliary Fan

1. **On 1995–96 9000 models,** obtain radio anti-theft code as outlined under "Precautions."
2. **On all models,** disconnect battery ground cable.
3. Remove front spoiler and grill.
4. Remove screws from tops of radiator support member bars, then the lower radiator support member attaching screws.
5. Remove light cluster retaining screw and pull light forward slightly.
6. Remove headlights, then ignition coil attaching screws. Position coil out of the way.
7. Remove cooler battery to radiator support attaching screw.
8. Remove radiator support attaching bolts, then unplug horn electrical connectors.

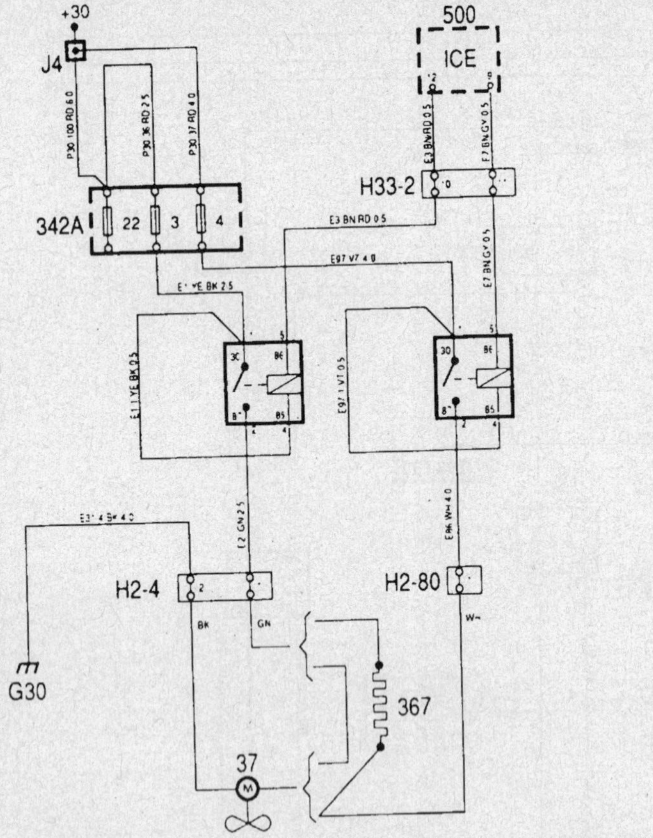
+30
J4
500
ICE
H33-2
342A
22
3
4
H2-4
H2-80
G30
367
37

SA1089400006000X

Fig. 4 Cooling fan wiring circuit. 1994–96 900

The table below only shows the pins which concern the cooling system.

Pin	Colour	Component/function	Measurement conditions	In/Out	Measure-ment result	Between X-Y
5		Coolant temperature sensor		In	about 0-12 V	5-58
9		Relay, radiator fan high speed	Radiator fan high speed activated	Out	12 V	47-9
10		Idling increase signal	Idling increase activated	Out	12 V	47-10
12		Relay, radiator fan low speed	Radiator fan low speed activated	Out	12 V	47-12
14		Coolant temperature signal (main instrument 2)		Out/ PWM	about 122 Hz 8-92 %duty	14-70
22		Pressure switch radiator fan A/C	If pressure switch is closed (>15 bar)	In	12 V	47-22
41		Supply +54	Ignition key in drive position	In	12 V	41-70
47		Power +30	Always	In	<0.5 V	B+-47
53		Signal ground	Engine running	In	<0.1 V	53-Batt-
58		Coolant temperature sensor, ground side	Always	In	12 V	47-58
60		Diagnosis	ISAT not connected ISAT connected + contact with ICE	In/Out	0 V 12 V	60-70
61		Coolant temperature signal (main instrument 1)		Out	500 Hz 8-92%duty	61-70
65		Power B	Key in position B	In	12 V	65-70
69		Pressure switch A/C cool	Pressure switch closed (>22 bar)	In	12 V	47-69
70		Power ground	Engine running	In	<0.1 V	70-Batt-

SA1089400008000X

Fig. 6 ICE control module connector pin identification. 1994–96 900

9. Lift out radiator support and position aside.
10. Remove cooling fan retaining nut and screws.

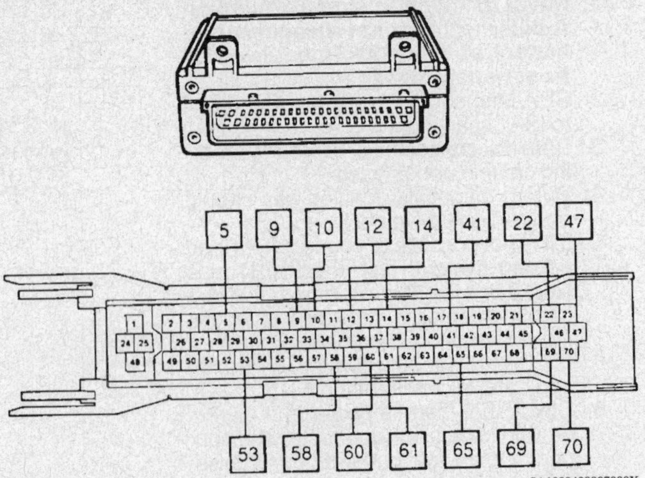
5
9
10
12
14
41
22
47
53
58
60
61
65
69
70

SA1089400007000X

Fig. 5 Internal Central Electric (ICE) control module connector view. 1994–96 900

Diag-nostic trouble code	Faulty function/component	Test on the ISAT display
B1102	Relay, radiator fan high speed	FAULT XX P1 B1102 RAD FAN HIGH SPEED RELAY SHORT TO BATTERY +
B1103	Relay, radiator fan high speed	FAULT XX P1 B1103 RAD FAN HIGH SPEED RELAY SHORT TO GR BREAK
B1104	Relay, radiator fan low speed	FAULT XX P1 B1104 RAD FAN LOW SPEED RELAY SHORT TO BATTERY +
B1105	Relay, radiator fan low speed	FAULT XX P1 B1105 RAD FAN LOW SPEED RELAY SHORT TO GR BREAK
B1311	Temperature sensor, coolant	FAULT XX P1 B1311 COOLANT TEMP SENSOR OUTSIDE LIMIT
B1412	Idling increase function	FAULT XX P1 B1412 IDLING INCREASE SHORT TO BATTERY
B1417	Temperature gauge, coolant	FAULT XX P1 B1417 COOLANT TEMP GAUGE SIGNAL SHORT TO BATTERY
B1422	Temperature gauge, coolant	FAULT XX P1 B1422 COOLANT TEMP GAUGE SIGNAL SHORT TO BATTERY

SA1089400009000X

Fig. 7 Diagnostic trouble codes. 1994–96 900

11. Reverse procedure to install.

1994–96 900

1. Disconnect and remove battery.
2. **On models equipped with Sensonic,** remove battery shelf.
3. **On all models,** separate radiator fan electrical connections.
4. Disconnect servo pump oil pipes and radiator breather hose clips from radiator crossmember. Turn oil pipe to one side.
5. Remove two radiator fan cover screws, then the cover.
6. Remove radiator fan to fan cover screws.
7. **On models equipped with two-speed cooling fan,** disconnect resistor.
8. **On all models,** disconnect fan cover contacts, then remove fan.
9. Reverse procedure to install.

Diagnostic trouble code	Reason for fault	Fault symptom
B1102	Short to battery +	Radiator fan does not work.
B1103	Short to ground, open circuit.	Radiator fan running continuously at high speed even when ignition is switched off.
B1104	Short to battery +	Radiator fan does not work.
B1105	Short to ground, open circuit	Radiator fan running continuously at low speed even when the ignition is switched off, or does not work.
B1311		Radiator fan running all the time.
B1412	Short to battery +	No increase in idling speed when radiator fan starts.
B1417	Short to battery +	Temperature gauge always shows cold engine.
B1422	Short to battery +	Temperature gauge always shows cold engine.

SA1089400010000X

Fig. 8 Diagnostic trouble code symptoms. 1994–96 900

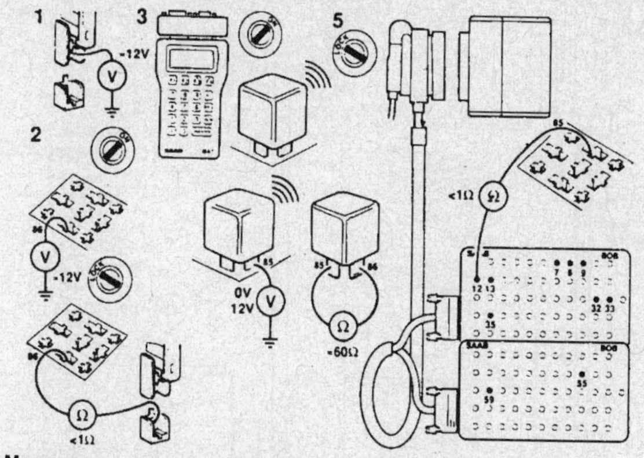

1
-12V
3
5
2
-12V
0V
12V
<1Ω
-60Ω

Measures

1 Check that fuses 3 (1-speed radiator fan or 2-speed radiator fan, low speed) and 4 (2-speed radiator fan, high speed) in the engine compartment's distribution centre are intact and that there is power to the fuses.

2 With the ignition key in drive position, check that there is power to the control coil on relay connection 86. The relay for the 1-speed radiator fan and the 2-speed radiator fan low speed position is situated in relay position G in the engine compartment. There is a relay for the 2-speed radiator fan high speed position in relay position I in the engine compartment.

If there is no power, check the wiring between the fuse and the relay for any open circuits/short circuits.

3 Connect ISAT and select "ACTIVATE RELAY" on the menu. Depending upon which relay is to be checked, select the next activation command like "RADIATOR LOW".

Check connection 85 on the relay with a voltmeter, i.e the relay should be in place but slightly raised. Repeat point 3 and read the voltmeter as follows:

Relay activated— 0 V

Relay not activated—12 V

If the voltages are not correct, remove the relay and check that the resistance between pins 85 and 86 is 50-100 Ohm.

If this is not the case, fit a new relay.

4 If the resistance is correct, check that the pins for each connection in the relay holder are securely fitted and that the relay is properly pressed down.

5 When the ignition is switched off, a BOB can be connected to the ICE wiring (control module disconnected). Check the cable between the ICE control module's connection 9 (2-speed radiator fan, high speed) or 12 (1-speed radiator fan and 2-speed radiator fan, low speed) and the relay holder's connection 85 as regards an open circuit/short circuit to ground.

Attend to any faulty wiring or connector.

SA1089400011000X

Fig. 9 Codes B1102 through 1105: Radiator fan does not work or radiator fan is running continuously at high or low speed when ignition is switched off. 1994–96 900

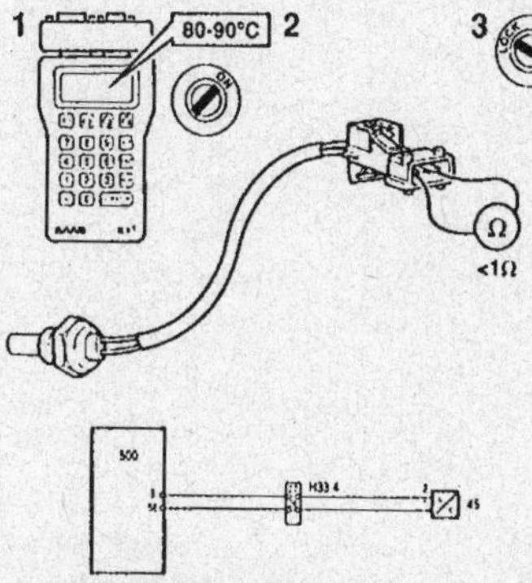

1
80-90°C
2
<1Ω

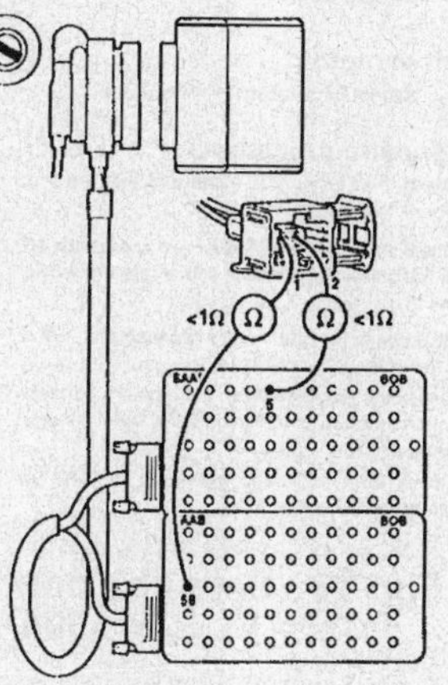

3
<1Ω
<1Ω

Fault symptom

Radiator fan running all the time

Diagnostic procedure

1 Select "OBTAIN READOUTS" on the ISAT menu followed by "COOLANT TEMP.". Read the result on ISAT.

The coolant temperature should be 80-90°C (176-194°F) when the engine is warm. If there is a fault in the circuit, ISAT will show 215°C (419°F).

2 Check the resistance on the coolant temperature sensor's connector and compare with the table.

If the resistance is not correct, the fault is in the temperature sensor. Fit a new temperature sensor.

If the resistance is correct, connect a BOB and check the cable between ICE connections 5 and 58 respectively and coolant temperature sensor connections 2 and 1 respectively as regards open circuits/short circuits.

°C	°F	Resistance kOhm
-30	-22	24
20	68	2
30	86	1.6
50	122	0.8
85	185	0.3
110	230	0.14
130	266	0.1

SA1089400012000X

Fig. 10 Code B1311: Cooling temperature lower than -76°F or higher than 320°F. 1994–96 900

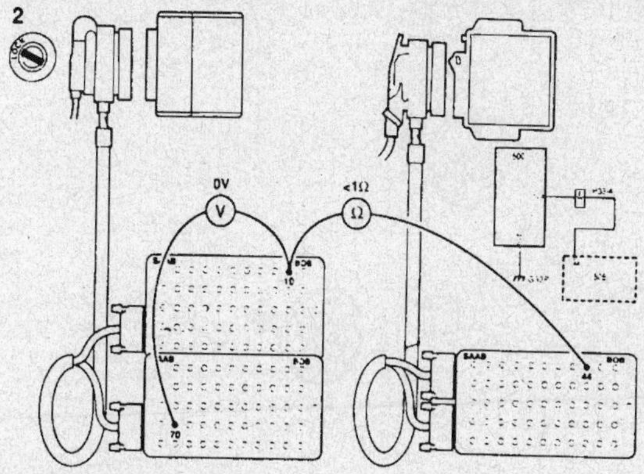

2
0V
<1Ω

Fault symptom

Idling speed does not increase when the radiator fan starts.

The engine speed could drop causing it to stall.

Diagnostic procedure

1 Connect a BOB and a voltmeter. Select "ACT OTHER FUNCT" on ISAT followed by "IDLING INCREASE".

Check that the voltage is 0 V at "ON" and 12 V at "OFF".

2 If that is not the case, check the cable between ICE connection 10 and MOTRONIC engine control module's pin 44 for any short circuit to positive voltage.

3 Connect the ICE control module and ground pin 44 on the MOTRONIC engine control module.

Measure with a voltmeter and repeat point 1.

4 If the voltmeter shows 0 V, fault in the engine control system.

If the voltmeter shows a voltage which is not 0 V, fault in ICE

SA1089400013000X

Fig. 11 Code B1412: Idling speed increase short-circuited to battery . 1994–96 900

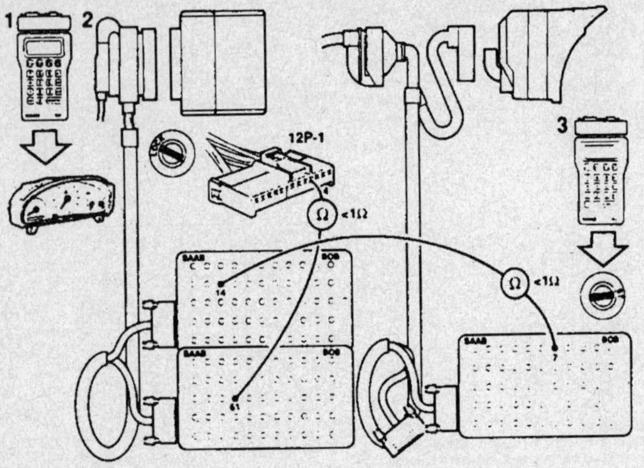
1
2
12P-1
<1Ω
<1Ω
3
SAAB
BOB
14
61
7

Fault symptom

Temperature gauge always shows cold engine.

Diagnostic procedure

1 Check that there are no diagnostic trouble codes stored in the main instrument. If there are diagnostic trouble codes, fault in main instrument

2 Connect a BOB and check the wiring for any short circuit to positive voltage between:

- ICE connection 61 and connection 4 in main instrument 1.
- ICE connection 14 and connection 7 in main instrument 2.

3 Clear the diagnostic trouble code, start the car and check if the diagnostic trouble code reappears.

SA1089400014000X

Fig. 12 Code B1417 & B1422: Short circuit to battery. 1994–96 900

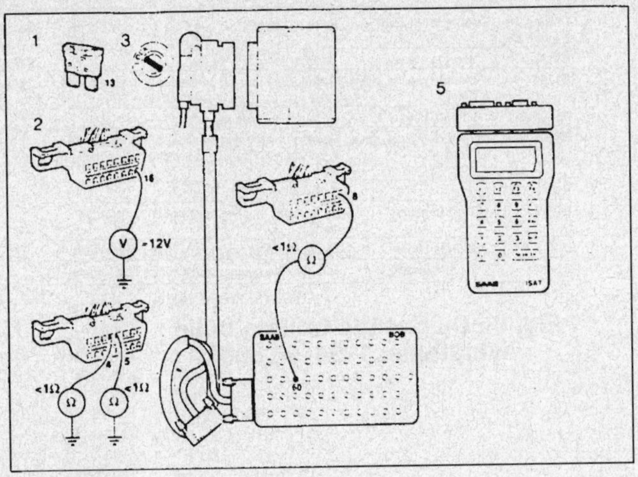
1
3
2
5
16
≈12V
<1Ω
8
<1Ω
<1Ω
60
SAAB
BOB
ISAT

Fault symptom

Contact cannot be established with ISAT

Diagnostic procedure

1 Check that fuse 13 is intact and that there is power to the fuse.

2 Check that there is 12 V between connection 16 in the data link connector and a safe grounding point.

Also check the grounding in connections 4 and 5.

3 Check the wiring between the data link connector and the ICE control module for open circuits/short circuits.

4 Check ISAT, SDA and the wiring for ISAT by testing with another ISAT.

SA1089400015000X

Fig. 13 Data link connector functional check. 1994–96 900

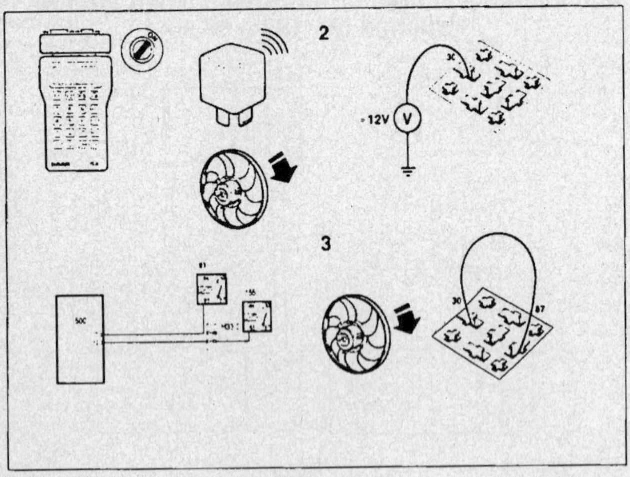
2
≈12V
3
30
87

Radiator fan

1 Connect ISAT and select "READ FAULT CODES" on the menu.

2 To start the radiator fan, select "ACTIVATE RELAY" on the menu followed by "RADIATOR FAN, LOW".

If the car is equipped with a 2-speed radiator fan, select "ACTIVATE RELAY" followed by "RADIATOR FAN, LOW".

If the radiator fan does not work, check that there is 12 V on connection 30 on the relay holder for each radiator fan relay.

3 Strap between connections 30 and 87 in the relay holder.

If the radiator fan works, the fault is in the relay. Fit a new relay.

If the radiator fan does not work, continue with point 4.

SA1089400016010X

Fig. 14 Cooling System Functional Check (Part 1 of 8). 1994–96 900

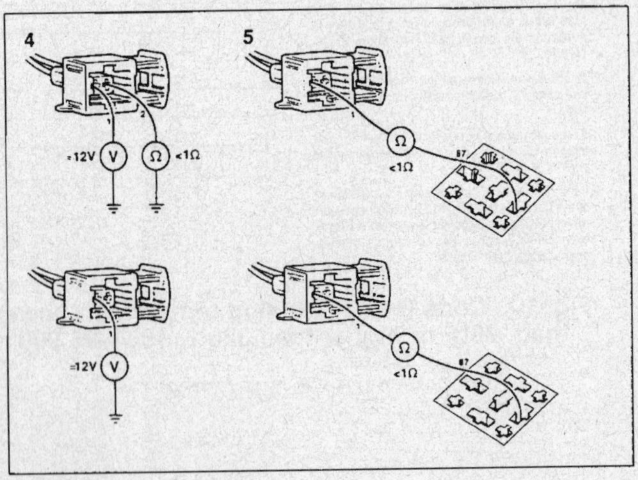
4
5
≈12V
<1Ω
<1Ω
87
≈12V
<1Ω
87

4 Disconnect the radiator fan's connector and check that there is:

- 12 V between pin 1 and a safe grounding point.
- a resistance which is less than 1 Ohm between pin 2 and a safe grounding point.

5 If that is not the case, check the wiring for short circuits open circuits between the connection 87 on the relay holder and connector 1 on the radiator fan.

6 If the fan does not work in spite of these checks, fit a new radiator fan.

SA1089400016020X

Fig. 14 Cooling System Functional Check (Part 2 of 8). 1994–96 900

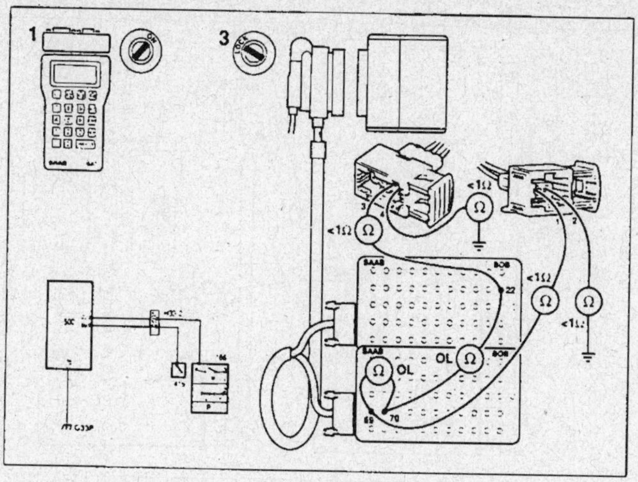

<1Ω
OL

Pressure switch A C

1 Connect ISAT and select "OBTAIN READ-OUTS" followed by "PRESS. SWITCH 1 AC". For certain markets the car is equipped with an extra pressure switch, in which in which case select "PRESS. SWITCH 2 AC".

"OPEN "→ The fan should not be activated

" CLOSED "→ The fan should be activated

2 If this is not correct, disconnect the pressure switch and clamp between the connector's pins and repeat point 1.

3 If this does not work, connect a BOB and check the wiring for any open circuits short circuits as follows:

Pressure switch 1

- between connection 22 on the ICE and connection 3 on the pressure switch.
- between connection 4 on the pressure switch and a safe grounding point.

Pressure switch 2

- between connection 69 on the ICE and connection 1 on the pressure switch.
- between connection 2 on the pressure switch and a safe grounding point.

4 If there is no fault in the wiring, replace the pressure switch.

SA1089400016030X

Fig. 14 Cooling System Functional Check (Part 3 of 8). 1994–96 900

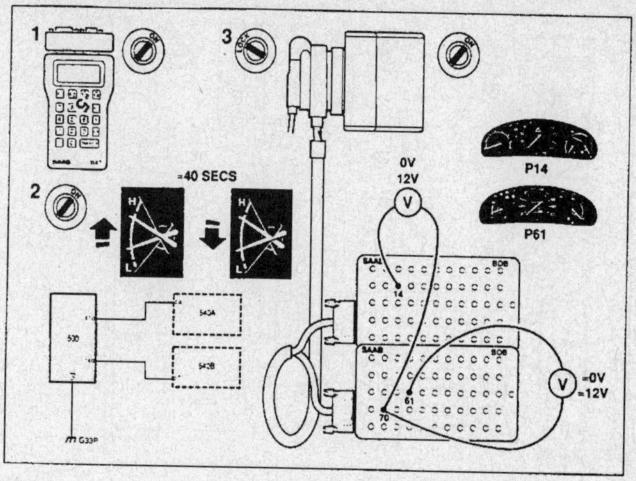

≈40 SECS
0V
12V
P14
P61
≈0V
≈12V

The temperature in the cooling system

1 Connect ISAT and select "READ FAULT CODES" on the menu.

2 Check the temperature gauge in the main instrument by first selecting "ACT INSTR FUNCT" followed by "SIM.COOL.TEMP. 2" or "SIM.COOL.TEMP. 1". The ICE will now simulate a temperature in the cooling system between -30 and +130°C (-22 and→+266°F) for 40 seconds.

Read the temperature gauge in the car.

3 Connect a BOB and connect a voltmeter between connections 70 and 61 for main instrument 1 or between connections 70 and 14 for main instrument 2. Then select "ACT INSTR FUNCT" followed by "TEMP.GAUGE.OUT. 1" or "TEMP.GAUGE.OUT. 2". The measured voltage should be

- about 0 V at "ON"
- about 12 V at "OFF"

SA1089400016040X

Fig. 14 Cooling System Functional Check (Part 4 of 8). 1994–96 900

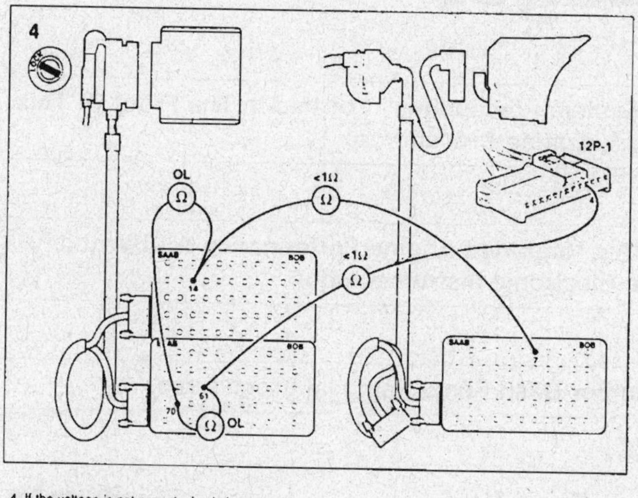

4
OL
<1Ω
12P-1

4 If the voltage is not correct, check the wiring for any open circuits/short circuits as follows:

- between connection 61 on the ICE and connection 4 on the main instrument (main instrument 1)
- between connection 14 on the ICE and connection 7 on the main instrument (main instrument 2).

SA1089400016050X

Fig. 14 Cooling System Functional Check (Part 5 of 8). 1994–96 900

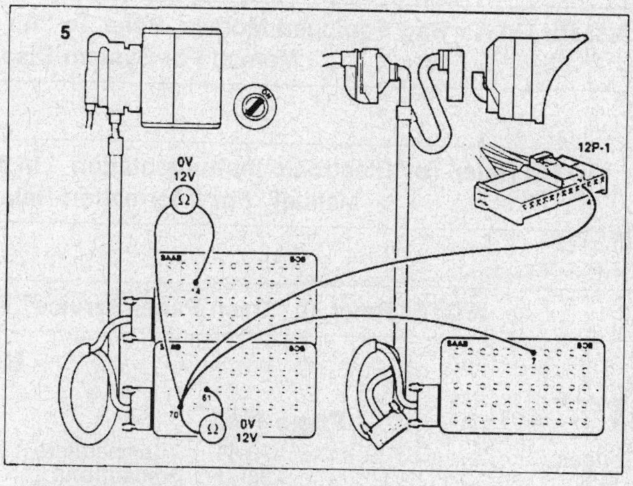

5
12P-1
0V
12V

5 If the cables are intact, the fault is probably in one of the control modules.

Connect the ICE control module and repeat points 2 and 3 at the same time as connection 4 (main instrument 1) or 7 (main instrument 2) is grounded.

Measured voltage should be 0 V at "ON" and *12 V at "OFF".

If the voltage is correct, the fault is probably in the main instrument

If the signal is faulty, the fault is probably in ICE

SA1089400016060X

Fig. 14 Cooling System Functional Check (Part 6 of 8). 1994–96 900

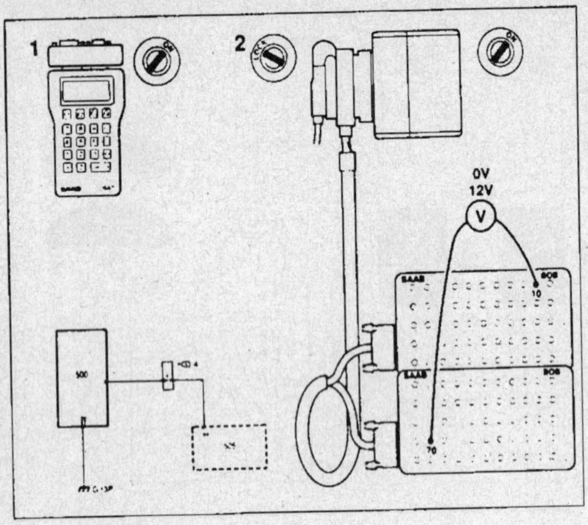
1
2
0V
12V
V
10
70

Checking the idling speed increase (only in MOTRONIC 2.10.2)

1 Connect ISAT and select "READ FAULT CODES" on the menu.

2 Connect a BOB and measure with a voltmeter between connections 10 and 70. Check the idling speed increase function by selecting "ACT OTHER FUNCT" on the menu followed by "IDLING INCREASE".

Check on the voltmeter that the voltage falls to about 0 V at "ON" and that it rises to about 12 V at "OFF".

SA1089400016070X

Fig. 14 Cooling System Functional Check (Part 7 of 8). 1994–96 900

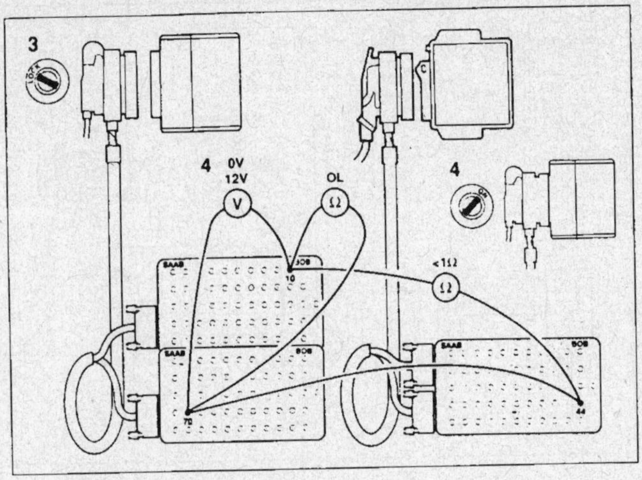
3
4
0V
12V
V
OL
Ω
4
<1Ω
10
70
44

3 If it does not work, check the wiring between the ICE control module and the engine control system's control module (both control modules disconnected) for any open circuits/short circuits.

4 Connect the engine control system's control module and repeat point 2.

The voltage should be 0 V at "ON" and 12 V at "OFF".

If the voltage is correct, the fault is in the engine control system

SA1089400016080X

Fig. 14 Cooling System Functional Check (Part 8 of 8). 1994–96 900

Dash Gauges

NOTE: On Air Bag Equipped Models, Refer To "Air Bag System Precautions" Located In The Front Of This Manual For System Disarming & Arming Procedures.

NOTE: Refer To "Electronic Instrumentation " In MOTOR's "Imported Engine Performance & Driveability Manual" For Information Related To Electronic Instrumentation.

NOTE: Refer To "Dash Panel Service" Section For Dash Panel Removal Procedures.

INDEX

	Page No.
Gauges	38-61
Fuel	38-61
Temperature	38-61
Precautions	38-61
Air Bag Systems	38-61

PRECAUTIONS

AIR BAG SYSTEMS

Refer to "Air Bag System Precautions" in the front of this manual for system disarming and arming procedures.

GAUGES

FUEL

900

1993

The fuel gauge for fuel reserve will be operative when the ignition switch is in the drive position.

1. Check fuse 22 and that power is supplied to it.
2. Check that terminals of fuel gauge and fuel level transmitter are live.
3. Check connectors, cable harnesses and ground connections of fuel level transmitter.
4. Resistance of fuel level transmitter are as follows:
   a. With fuel tank full, 2.4–8.0 ohms.
   b. With fuel tank empty, 63.3–67.5 ohms.

1994

The fuel gauge is operative when the ignition switch is in drive position.

1. Disconnect connector to fuel level transmitter, located under cover in rear seat.
2. Measure resistance between connector pins. Resistance should be 2–4.5 ohms. If resistance is outside this range, there is a fault in transmitter or its connecting cable. If resistance is correct, continue this procedure.
3. Check wiring between fuel level transmitter and main instrument. Disconnect main instrument and three connectors.
4. Connect connector to fuel level transmitter. Measure between pin 6 (black 12-pin connector) and pin 1 (14-pin connector) in connectors to instrument for any open or short circuits. Resistance should be 2-4.5 ohms. If resistance is outside range, there is fault in wiring. If resistance is correct, continue this procedure.
5. Check foil circuits at back of main instrument by measuring between terminal 6 (12p-2) and screw marked "F SIG" and between terminal 1 (14p) and screw marked "GND" behind fuel gauge on main instrument for any open circuits.
6. If circuits are intact and fuel gauge does not work, fault is probably in fuel gauge. Install new main instrument. If there is an open circuit, change foil.

9000

The fuel gauge is monitored by the EDU 1/2 trip computer. In the event of a fault "Err" may light up on the computer display.

1. Check fuse 13 and that power is supplied to it.
2. Ensure fuel gauge terminals have power supplied to them.
3. Check connectors, cable harnesses and ground connections.
4. Resistance of fuel level transmitter are as follows:
   a. With fuel tank full, 350 ohms.
   b. With fuel tank empty, 35 ohms.

TEMPERATURE

900

1993

1. Check fuse 22 and that power is supplied to it.
2. Check that temperature gauge has power supplied to it.
3. Ensure open does not exist in coolant temperature transmitter.
4. Check connectors, cable harnesses and ground connections.
5. Resistance of temperature transmitter should be 46.9–55.5 ohms at 194°F.

1994-95

1. Check foil circuits at back of instrument by measuring between terminal 4 (12p-1) and screw marked "T-SIG" in main instrument for any open circuits.
2. If cables are intact and temperature gauge does not work, fault is in temperature gauge. Install new main instrument.
3. If there is an open circuit, change foil.

Starter Motors

INDEX

	Page No.
Description	38-61
Diagnosis & Testing	38-61
Bench	38-62
In-Vehicle	38-61
Starter Specifications	38-63

DESCRIPTION

The starter motor used on both the 900 and 9000 models is a gear reduction starter. This starter, **Fig. 1,** uses six permanent magnets in place of conventional wound field magnets to reduce electrical and starting resistance. The gear reduction system uses a planetary gear train to transmit armature rotation to the pinion shaft.

DIAGNOSIS & TESTING

IN-VEHICLE

Before beginning any tests, ensure battery is fully charged and that all connections are satisfactory.

AMPERAGE DRAW TEST

9000 & 1993 900

1. Run engine until it reaches normal operating temperature, then turn engine off.
2. Connect suitable battery-starter tester according to manufacturer's instructions.
3. Turn battery-starter tester control knob to OFF position.
4. Turn voltmeter selector knob to "16 Volt" position.
5. Turn battery-starter function selector to STARTER TEST (0–500 amp scale).
6. Connect red positive ammeter lead to positive battery terminal and black negative ammeter lead to negative battery terminal.
7. Connect red positive voltmeter lead to positive battery terminal and black negative voltmeter lead to negative terminal.
8. Connect remote starter switch according to manufacturer's instructions. **Do not crank engine excessively during testing.**
9. Disconnect coil wire from distributor cap and secure it to good ground.
10. Crank engine and observe voltmeter reading, then stop cranking engine.
11. Turn tester control knob clockwise until voltmeter reading is the same as when engine was being cranked. Ammeter should read between 105–210 amps.

STARTER RESISTANCE TEST

9000 & 1993 900

1. Disconnect positive battery cable and connect 0–300 scale ammeter between disconnected lead and terminal post.
2. Connect voltmeter between positive post on battery and starter relay terminal on starter solenoid.

3. Crank engine while observing readings on voltmeter and ammeter. A voltage reading exceeding .3 volts indicates a high resistance caused by loose circuit connections, faulty cable, burned starter relay or solenoid switch contacts. High current combined with slow cranking speed indicates a need for starter repair.
4. Reconnect positive battery lead.

GROUND TEST

1. Connect voltmeter positive lead to starter through bolt and negative voltmeter lead to battery negative post.
2. Crank engine with remote starter switch and observe voltmeter reading.
3. If voltmeter reading exceeds .2 volt, isolate points of excessive voltage loss by leaving negative lead connected to negative battery post and repeating test at the following locations:
   a. Voltmeter positive lead to starter drive housing.
   b. Voltmeter positive lead to ground terminal at engine.
   c. Voltmeter positive lead to cable clamp at battery.
4. Small changes in voltmeter reading should occur every time lead position is changed. A large change in voltage reading would indicates last part eliminated in test is at fault.

STARTER SOLENOID TEST

9000 & 1993 900

1. Connect heavy jumper wire on starter relay between battery and solenoid terminals.
2. If engine cranks, perform "Starter Relay Test."
3. If engine does not crank or solenoid chatters, check wiring and connectors from relay to starter solenoid.

BASIC CHECKS

1994-95 900

1. Use voltmeter to check that at least 12 volts is present directly across battery terminals. If it is not, test battery.
2. Use voltmeter to check that at least 12 volts is present across terminal 30 on starter motor and negative battery terminal.
3. Use voltmeter to check that operating voltage is present on +50 terminal. If it is not, check wiring between battery and starter motor.

CHECKING STARTER MOTOR WHILE IN OPERATION

1994-95 900

1. Connect voltmeter across battery terminals.

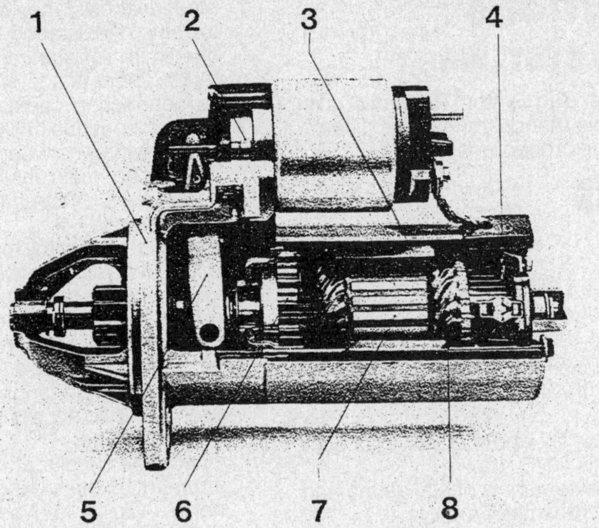
1
2
3
4
5
6
7
8
1 Pinion bracket assembly
2 Solenoid
3 Permanent magnets
4 Brush-holder assembly
5 Pinion-engaging lever
6 Planetary gear train
7 Armature
8 Stator frame
SA1129100001000X

Fig. 1 Cross-sectional view of starter motor

2. Start engine and read off instrument.
3. If voltmeter shows less than 10 volts, battery must be recharged.

VOLTAGE DROP IN CIRCUIT

1994-95 900

1. Connect voltmeter across the following:
   a. Positive battery terminal and terminal 30 on starter motor.
   b. Positive battery terminal and terminal 50 on starter motor (voltage in starting position only).
   c. Negative battery terminal and starter motor casing.
2. Start engine and read off voltmeter. Reading should not exceed .2–.3 volts.
3. If circuit shows higher reading it should be checked to determine reason for excessive voltage drop.

BENCH

STARTER SOLENOID

9000 & 1993 900

1. Disconnect field coil wire from field coil terminal.
2. Check for continuity between solenoid terminal and field coil terminal. There should be continuity.
3. Check for continuity between solenoid terminal and solenoid housing. There should be continuity.
4. If continuity does not exist in either test, replace solenoid assembly.

STARTER RELAY TEST

9000 & 1993 900

1. Place transaxle in neutral and apply parking brake.
2. Check for battery voltage between starter relay battery terminal and ground.
3. Connect jumper wire on starter relay between battery and ignition terminals.
4. If engine does not crank, connect second jumper wire to starter relay between ground terminal and good ground, repeat test.
5. If engine now cranks, transaxle linkage is improperly adjusted or neutral switch is defective.
6. If engine does not crank now, starter relay is defective.

STARTER SPECIFICATIONS

Year	Model	Starter Number	Brush Spring Tension Oz.	No Load Test			Load Test		
				Amps	Volts	RPM	Amps	Volts	RPM
1993	900 & 9000	0 001 108 038	—	70	12	3000①	315	9	1700①
1994-96	900②	0 001 108 151	—	80	12	3000	310	9	1630
	900③	0 001 108 080	—	80	12	3300	295	9	1650
	9000	0 001 108 038	—	70	12	3000①	315	9	1700①

① — Minimum.
② — 2.3L engine.
③ — 2.5L engine.

Alternators

INDEX

Page No.

Alternator Specifications 38-64
Diagnosis & Testing 38-63
In-Vehicle 38-63
Troubleshooting 38-63
Alternator Not Charging 38-63
Current Too High 38-63
Insufficient Or Irregular Power Supply 38-63
Noisy Alternator 38-63

TROUBLESHOOTING

ALTERNATOR NOT CHARGING

1. Drive belt slipping.
2. Open in charging or ground circuits.
3. Defective brushes, regulator or diodes.
4. Broken excitation circuit or rotor winding.
5. Open stator ground circuit.

INSUFFICIENT OR IRREGULAR POWER SUPPLY

1. Drive belt slipping.
2. Defective brushes, regulator, or diode rectifiers.
3. Partial short circuit in rotor.
4. Poor stator to ground connection.

CURRENT TOO HIGH

1. Defective regulator.
2. Poor contact between regulator and alternator.

NOISY ALTERNATOR

1. Worn drive belt.
2. Pulley fitted incorrectly.
3. Loose alternator brackets.
4. Alternator and crankshaft pulleys misaligned.
5. Worn or defective bearings.
6. Short circuit in diode rectifier.

DIAGNOSIS & TESTING

IN-VEHICLE

9000 & 1993 900

When measuring charging current, never disconnect battery leads with engine running. Avoid applying any mechanical stress where leads extend from the diode holder, do not bend or apply pressure to wire where it is joined to the terminal.

1. Connect a volt/amp meter to system following manufacturers' instructions. **Alternator output voltage should be checked between battery positive post and alternator ground.**
2. Connect a tachometer to engine, start and run engine until it reaches normal operating temperature.
3. Apply current load to alternator and set engine to run at following speeds:
   a. 55 amp alternator, 900 RPM.
   b. 65 amp alternator, 950 RPM.
   c. 70 amp Motorola alternator, 800 RPM.
   d. 70 amp Bosch alternator, 850 RPM.
   e. 80 amp alternator, 800 RPM.
4. Compare output readings with those listed in under "Rated Hot Output" column of "Alternator Specifications " chart.
5. If output is not within specifications, check drive belt, feed and ground circuits. Repair as required.
6. If wiring and drive belt are satisfactory, repair or replace alternator as necessary.

1994-95 900

Never start the engine while carrying out this test procedure, as the alternator could be permanently damaged.

1. If lamp fails to light up when ignition is switched on, ground D terminal on alternator while ignition is still switched on.
2. If lamp lights up, electrical system is satisfactory and alternator is faulty.
3. Connect voltmeter across battery terminals.
4. Run engine at medium-high RPM for several minutes and read voltmeter. Reading should be 13.5–14 volts.
5. Connect ammeter to alternator output circuit (B) or use clip-on ammeter.
6. Run engine at about 2500 RPM.
7. Apply maximum electrical load to alternator either by connecting special carbon film resistor to it or by switching on all of vehicle's electrical equipment.
8. Read ammeter. Reading should be 45-90 amps for 2.3L engine and 60-120 amps for 2.5L engine.
9. Connect voltmeter across battery positive terminal and alternator B terminal.
10. Run engine at 2500 RPM and apply electrical load to alternator by switching on all lights.
11. Read instrument, then connect voltmeter across battery negative terminal and alternator B- terminal (ground).
12. Run engine at 2500 RPM and apply electrical load again. Read instrument.
13. Readings taken above should not exceed .5 volts. If higher reading is obtained, check relevant circuit for shorting or continuity.

ALTERNATOR SPECIFICATIONS

Year	Alternator					Regulator
	Model	Rated Hot Output		Output @ 14 Volts		
		Amps	Volts	Amps @ RPM①	Amps @ RPM①	
1993	Bosch K1-14V 55A 20	55	14	36.0 @ 2000	55 @ 6000	Integral
	Bosch K1-14V 65A 21	65	14	44.0 @ 2100	65 @ 6000	Integral
	Bosch K1-14V 70A 20	70	14	46.0 @ 2000	70 @ 6000	Integral
	Bosch N1-14V 80A 19	80	14	54.0 @ 1900	80 @ 6000	Integral
	Bosch N1-14V 40/115A	115	14	40.0 @ 1500	115 @ 6000	Integral
	Motorola 70A	70	14	36.5 @ 1800	71 @ 6000	Integral
1994-96②	Bosch KC-14V 40-70A	70	14	40.0 @ 1800	70 @ 6000	Integral
	Bosch KC-14V 45-90A	90	14	45.0 @ 1800	90 @ 6000	Integral
	Bosch NC-14V 60-120A	120	14	60.0 @ 1800	120 @ 6000	Integral

① — Alternator RPM.
② — 900.

Speed Control Systems

NOTE: Electrical Symbol & Wire Color Code Identification Located In The Front Of This Manual May Be Used As An Aid When Using Wiring Circuits Found In This Section.

INDEX

Page No.
Description 38-64
1993–94 38-64
1995–96 38-64
System Diagnosis & Testing 38-65
900 38-65
9000 38-65

DESCRIPTION

1993-94

The speed control system consists of a speed transmitter, selector switch, electronic control unit, vacuum pump with valve, vacuum regulator and pedal switches

The system is turned on by the selector switch. When the selector is switched to the On position power is supplied to the control unit terminal 9 from terminal 1 through the pedal switches, **Figs. 1 and 2.** Power is supplied to the vacuum pump and valve from the control unit terminals 6 and 7. Grounding is through terminal 1 on the control unit.

When the Set button is depressed, power is supplied to terminal 3 of the control unit and vehicle speed is sensed by the speed transmitter. The value is supplied to the control unit and is stored in the unit's memory.

The vacuum pump generates vacuum in the vacuum regulator, corresponding to selected vehicle speed. The vacuum regulator is connected by a chain to the throttle linkage. Vehicle speed is continuously sensed and compared with the stored value. If vehicle speed deviates, the vacuum pump/valve increases or decreases the vacuum in the regulator and the throttle linkage is adjusted accordingly.

When the vacuum pump is not running, the vacuum valve is closed and vacuum in the system remains constant. When terminals 6 and 7 on the control unit are open (not energized), the vacuum pump will be inoperative and the valve will be open, causing the vacuum in the regulator to drop and the accelerator setting to be reduced.

If either the brake or clutch pedal are depressed, the voltage supply will be turned off by the corresponding pedal switch. At the same time, a valve in the pedal switches will open and vacuum will be released.

If a fault should arise in either of the pedal switches, the speed control system will be switched out by the brake light switch.

1995-96

On 900 models, the cruise control system consists of the cruise control module, cruise control switches, brake and clutch pedal switches, brake lights switch, speed signal from the ABS control module, cruise control signal active to engine management system, **Fig. 3.**

On 9000 models, the speed control system consists of the cruise control module, cruise control switches, brake and clutch pedal switches, brake lights switch, speed signal from the speedometer and the cruise control active signal to the engine management system, **Fig 4.**

The driver sets the speed control system using the switch on the combination switch. The system will disengage automatically when either the clutch pedal or brake pedal is pressed, when the switch is moved to the Off or Tip position, when the selector lever is in the N position or when the traction control system is activated.

The control module incorporates an electric stepping motor which mechanically

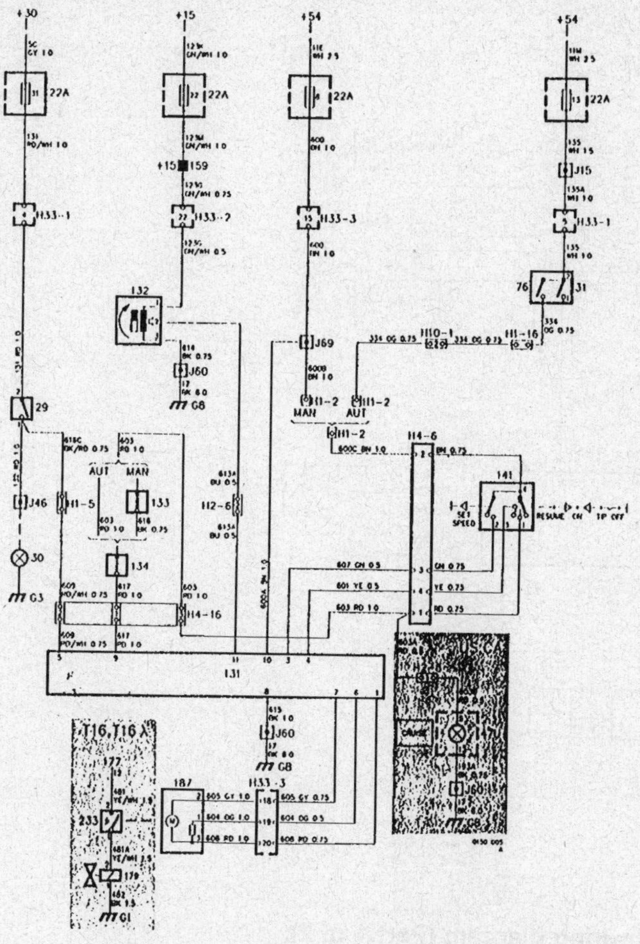

SA1109200001000X

Fig. 1 Speed control wiring diagram. (Part 1 of 2) 1993 900

Component location list

- 22A Fuse holder in dashboard
- 29 Brake light switch on pedal assembly
- 30 Brake light bulbs, in RH and LH rear light clusters.
- 47U CRUISE indicator lamp in main instrument display panel.
- 76 Idling speed compensation switch in selector lever position sensor 239 on gearbox
- 133 Clutch pedal switch for Cruise Control
- 134 Brake pedal switch
- 141 Cruise Control switch on dipswitch stalk on left-hand side of steering column
- 239 Selector lever position sensor on gearbox
- 430 TRIONIC control module below right-hand A pillar in cabin
- 500 ICE control module above relay holder 22B next to steering column under dashboard
- 502 TCM control module on bulkhead partition behind glove box
- 507 TCS control module under right-hand front seat
- 508 Control module for the Cruise Control system on a bracket in the engine bay on the right-hand side in the space between the bulkhead partitions.
- 509 SENSONIC control module on bulkhead partition behind glove box
- 540 Main instrument panel on dashboard.
- 540A Main instrument panel 1 without rev counter (tachometer) on dashboard
- 540B Main instrument panel 2 with rev counter (tachometer) on dashboard
- 547 ABS control module on brake unit in engine bay

10-pin connectors

- H10-1 Mounted on a bracket in the engine bay behind the battery
- H10-3 Mounted on a bracket in the engine bay behind the battery

33-pin connectors

- H33-1 Blue 33-pin connector on a bracket below the left-hand A pillar
- H33-2 Black 33-pin connector on a bracket below the left-hand A pillar
- H33-4 Behind the glove box on a bracket on the bulkhead partition
- G3 Grounding point in luggage compartment on left-hand side
- G33P Power ground on a bracket below the left-hand A pillar
- G33S Signal ground on a bracket below the left-hand A—pillar

SA1109400004020X

Fig. 1 Speed control wiring diagram (Part 2 of 2). 1994-94 900

regulates the cruise control cable connected to the throttle body, either retracting it or extending it according to the speed of the vehicle.

SYSTEM DIAGNOSIS & TESTING

900

1993

1. With ignition switch and selector in On position, check the following:
   a. **On models equipped with manual transmission,** fuse No. 8 is satisfactory and power is supplied to fuse.
   b. **On models equipped with automatic transmission,** fuses No. 8 and 13 is satisfactory and power is supplied to fuse.
   c. Fuse 76 is satisfactory and power is supplied to fuse.
   d. **On all models,** power is supplied to terminal 4 of selector and terminal 9 of the control unit.
   e. That there is voltage at terminal 1 of speed transmitter.
2. With ignition switch On and selector in Set position, check voltage at terminal 2 of selector and at terminal 3 of control unit.
3. With ignition switch On and selector in Resume position, check voltage at terminals 1 and 3 of selector and at terminals 4 and 9 of control unit.
4. Test vacuum pump by grounding pin 3 and applying voltage to pin 2.
5. Test vacuum valve by grounding pin 3 and applying voltage to pin 1.

1994-95

Refer to **Figs. 5 and 6** when testing the speed control system.

9000

1993-94

1. With ignition switch and selector in On position, check the following:
   a. **On models with manual transmission,** fuse No. 2 is satisfactory and power is supplied to fuse.
   b. **On all models,** fuse No. 9 is satisfactory and power is supplied to fuse.
   c. **On models with automatic transmission,** switch 76 is satisfactory and power is supplied to fuse.
   d. **On all models,** power is supplied to terminal 4, (cable marked 600B), of selector and terminal 9 of the control unit.
   e. That there is voltage at terminal 1 of speed transmitter.
2. With ignition switch On and selector in A-B SET position, check voltage at terminal 2 of selector and at terminal 3 of control unit.
3. With ignition switch On and selector in RESUME position, check voltage at terminals 1 and 3 of selector and at terminal 4 of control unit.
4. Test vacuum pump by grounding pin 3 and applying voltage to pin 2.
5. Test vacuum valve by grounding pin 3 and applying voltage to pin 1.

1995-96

Refer to **Figs. 7 and 8** when testing the speed control system.

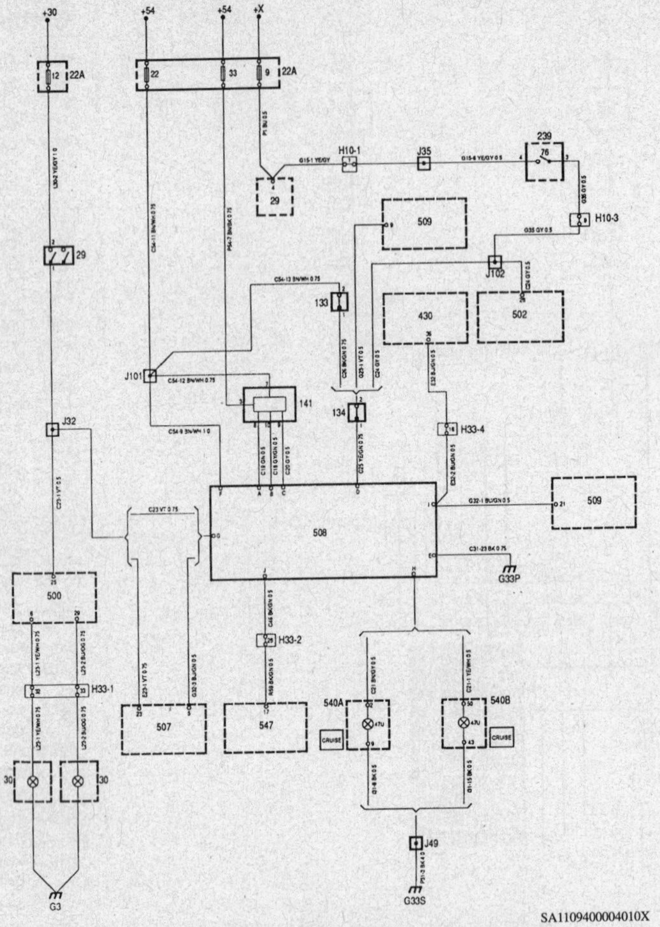
+30
+54
+54
+X
22A
22A
29
H10-1
J35
239
H10-3
509
J102
133
430
502
J101
141
134
J32
H33-4
508
509
G33P
500
H33-2
H33-1
507
547
540A
540B
CRUISE
CRUISE
30
30
J49
G3
G33S
SA1109400004010X

Fig. 1 Speed control wiring diagram (Part 1 of 2). 1994 900

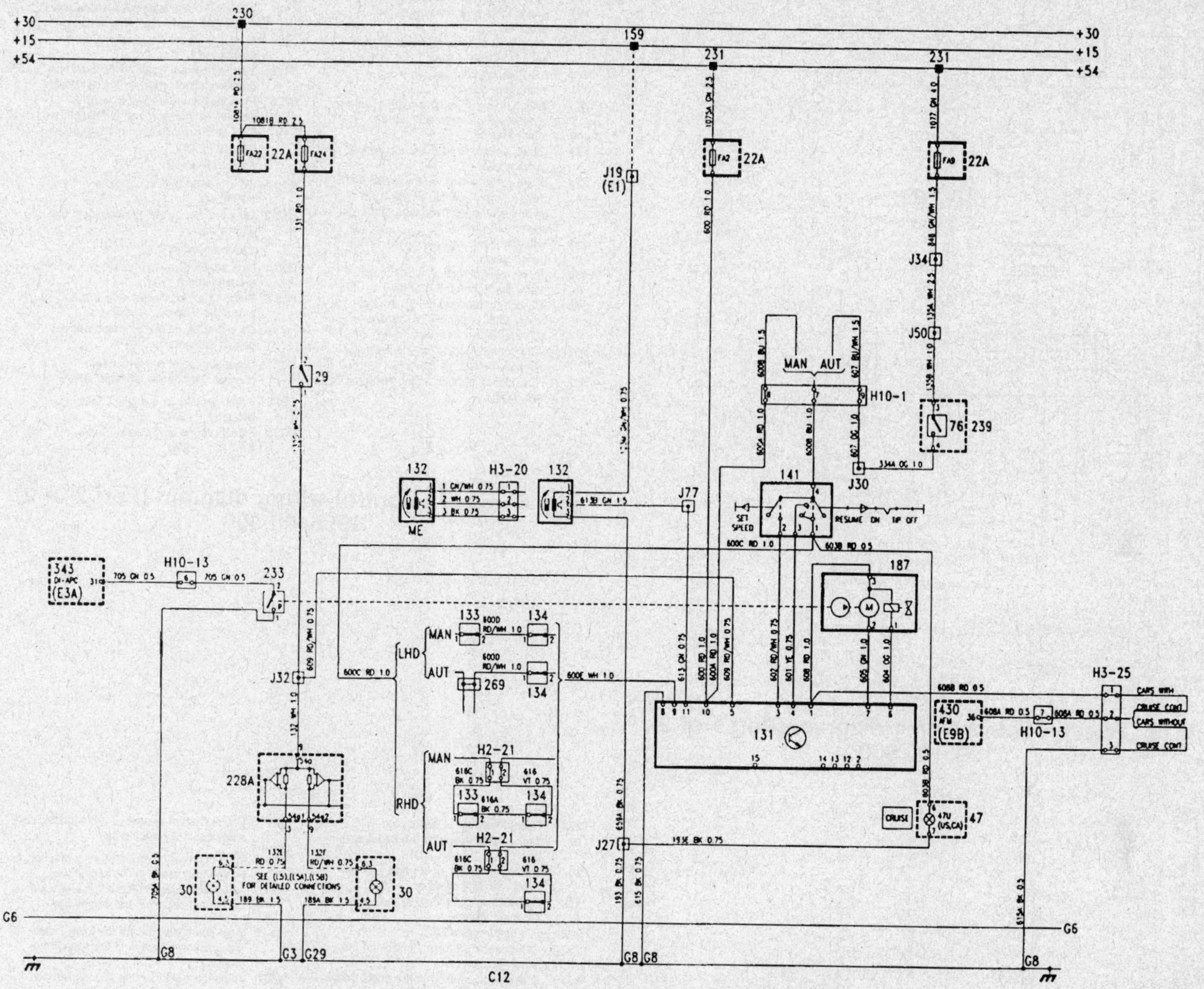

SA1109300003000X

Fig. 2 Speed control wiring diagram. 1993-94 9000

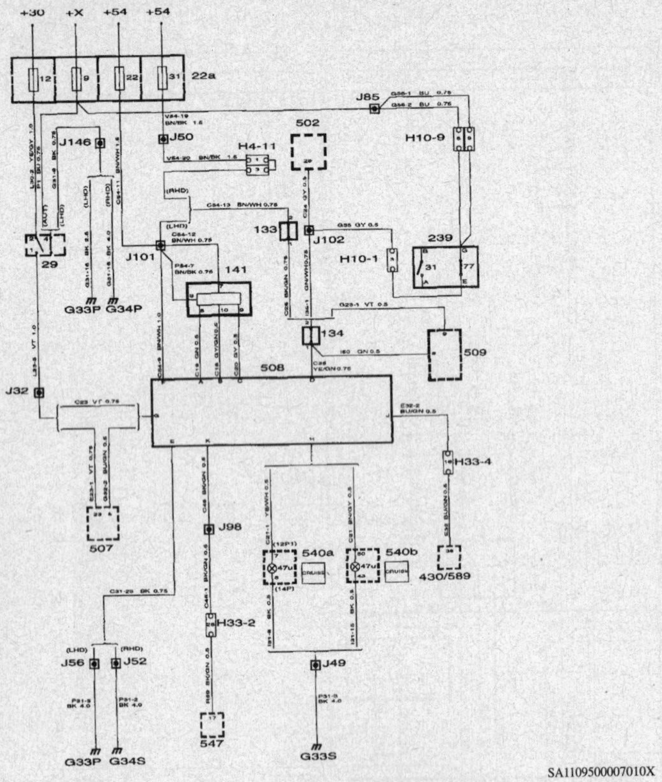

SA1109500007010X

Fig. 3 Speed control wiring diagram (Part 1 of 2). 1995–96 900

- 22A Fuse holder in the dashboard
- 29 Brake lights switch on the pedal assembly
- 30 Brake light bulbs, right-hand and left-hand rear light clusters
- 47U CRUISE indicator lamp in main instrument display
- 76 Switch, idling speed increase, in selector lever position sensor 239 on the transmission.
- 133 Clutch switch, Cruise Control, on the clutch pedal
- 134 Brake pedal switch, on the brake pedal
- 141 Cruise Control switch, on the lights switch, on the left-hand side of the steering column
- 239 Selector lever position sensor, on the transmission
- 430 Trionic control module, in the cabin, below the right-hand A pillar
- 500 ICE control module, on top of relay holder 22B, under the dashboard adjacent to the steering wheel
- 502 TCM control module, on the bulkhead partition, behind the glove box
- 507 TCS control module, under the right-hand front seat
- 508 Cruise Control system control module, on a bracket in the false bulkhead space, in the engine bay on the right-hand side
- 540 Main instrument display panel on the dashboard
- 540A Main instrument display 1, without rev counter (tachometer), on the dashboard
- 540B Main instrument display 2, with rev counter (tachometer), on the dashboard
- 547 ABS control module, on the brake unit in the engine bay

10-pin connectors

- H10-1 On a bracket behind the battery in the engine bay
- H10-3 On a bracket behind the battery in the engine bay

33-pin connectors

- H33-1 Blue 33-pin connector on a bracket below the left-hand A pillar
- H33-2 Black 33-pin connector on a bracket below the left-hand A pillar
- H33-4 On a bracket on the bulkhead partition behind the glove box
- G3 Grounding point in the luggage compartment on the left-hand side
- G33P Power ground on a bracket below the left-hand A pillar
- G33S Signal ground on a bracket below the left-hand A pillar

SA1109500007020X

Fig. 3 Speed control wiring diagram (Part 2 of 2). 1995–96 900

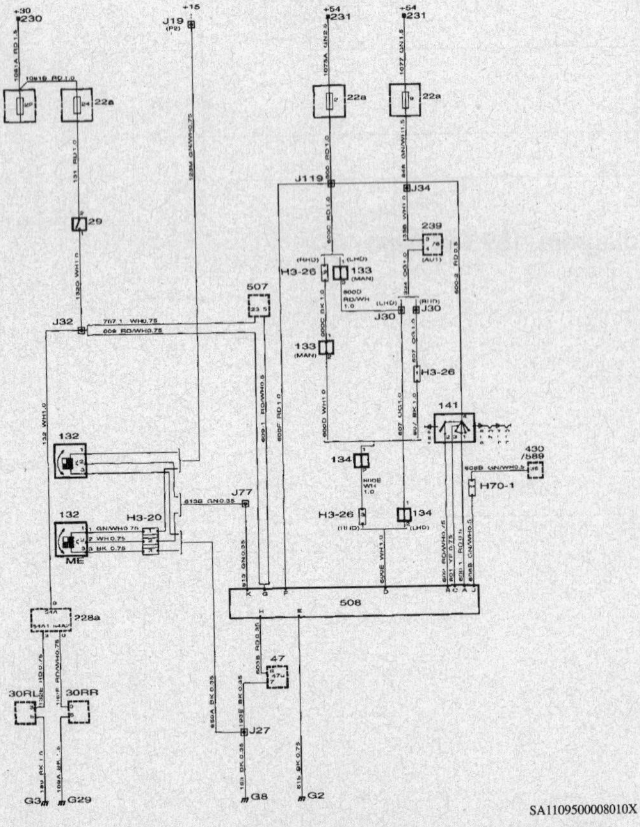

SA1109500008010X

Fig. 4 Speed control wiring diagram (Part 1 of 2). 1995–96 9000

- 22A Fuse holder in the dashboard
- 29 Brake lights switch on the pedal assembly
- 30 Brake light bulbs, right-hand and left-hand rear light clusters
- 47U CRUISE indicator lamp in the main instrument display
- 228A Filament monitor
- 133 Clutch switch, Cruise Control, on the clutch pedal
- 134 Brake pedal switch, on the brake pedal
- 141 Cruise Control switch, on the lights stalk, on the left-hand side of the steering column
- 239 Selector lever position sensor, under the selector lever
- 430 TRIONIC control module, in the cabin, below the right-hand A pillar
- 132 Speedometer, in the main instrument display
- 507 TCS control module, under the left-hand front seat
- 508 Cruise Control system control module, on a bracket in the engine bay
- H10-1 10-pin connector, mounted on a bracket behind the battery in the engine bay
- H10-3 10-pin connector, mounted on a bracket behind the battery in the engine bay
- H3-20 3-pin connector, behind the main instrument display adjacent to the speedometer (ME)
- H70-1 70-pin connector, in the false bulkhead space
- H3-26 3-pin connector, above the pedal assembly adjacent to the pedal switches
- G3 Grounding point, luggage compartment
- G8 Grounding point, dashboard
- G2 Grounding point, battery tray
- G29 Grounding point, right-hand rear light cluster

SA1109500008020X

Fig. 4 Speed control wiring diagram (Part 2 of 2). 1995–96 9000

		CRUISE lamp	Item checked
1	Engine switched off and handbrake applied		
2	Automatic transmission: selector lever in position N (P, R) Manual gearbox: clutch pedal depressed		
3	Move the switch to the TIP position and hold it there while the engine starts.		
	The CRUISE lamp should light up to confirm that you are in diagnosis mode.	Lights up Remains out	
4	Release the TIP button	Goes out Remains on	TIP function
5	Press the SET button	Lights up Remains out	SET function
	Release the SET button	Goes out Remains on	SET function
7	Move the switch to the RES/— position	Lights up Remains out	RESUME function
8	Release RES/—	Goes out Remains on	RESUME function
9	Move the switch to the ON/OFF position	Lights up Remains out	ON/OFF function
10	Release ON/OFF	Goes out Remains on	ON/OFF function
11	Automatic transmission: shift to D (3, 2, 1) Manual gearbox: release the clutch pedal	Lights up Remains out	Automatic transmission: Selector lever position sensor Manual gearbox: Clutch pedal switch

SA1109400005010X

Fig. 5 Speed control fault diagnosis (Part 1 of 2). 1994 900

		CRUISE lamp	Item checked
12	Depress the brake pedal	Goes out Remains on	Brake pedal switch Automatic transmission Manual gearbox
13	Release the brake pedal	Lights up Remains out	Brake pedal switch Automatic transmission Manual gearbox
14	Automatic transmission: shift to N (P, R) Manual gearbox: depress the clutch pedal	Goes out Remains on	Automatic transmission: Selector lever position sensor Manual gearbox: Clutch pedal switch
15	Depress the brake pedal and keep it depressed for about five seconds. After about five seconds	Lights up Remains out Goes out Remains on	Brake light switch Brake light switch
16	Release the brake pedal	Slight increase in engine idling speed No increase in engine idling speed	Stepping motor
17	Drive off slowly	Lamp flashes in time with the speed Lamp does not flash	Speed signal

SA1109400005020X

Fig. 5 Speed control fault diagnosis (Part 2 of 2). 1994–95 900

F G H I J
E D C B A

Pin	Colour	Component/function	Test conditions	Input/Output	Test value	Across X—Y
1 (A)	Green	Switch	Switch held in ON/OFF position Ignition switched on	Input	12 V	1-5
2 (B)	Grey/green	Switch	Switch held in ON/OFF position Ignition switched on	Input	12 V	2-5
3 (C)	Grey	Switch	Switch held in ON/OFF position Ignition switched on	Input	12 V	3-5
4 (D)	Yellow/green	Pedal switches				
		Brake switch	Automatic transmission D, 1, 2, 3 Pedal not depressed Pedal depressed	Input	12 V 0 V	4-5
			Manual gearbox Pedal not depressed Pedal depressed	Input	12 V 0 V	4-5
		Clutch pedal switch	Manual gearbox Pedal not depressed Pedal depressed	Input	12 V 0 V	4-5
5 (E)	Black	Power ground		Input	12 V	5-batt+
6 (F)	Brown/white	Ignition +54	Ignition switched on	input	12 V	6-5
7 (G)	Violet or Blue/green	Brake light switch	Brake pedal depressed Brake pedal not depressed	Input	12 V 0 V	7-5
8 (H)	Brown/yellow or Yellow/white	CRUISE lamp	Lamp out Lamp on	Output	0 V 12 V	8-5
9 (J)	Blue/green	Communication with other systems	In diagnosis mode ON/OFF SET RESUME	Output	12 V	9-5
10 (K)	Black/green	Speed signal	Left-hand front wheel spinning 1/2 rev/sec	Input	approx. 15 Hz	10-5

SA1109400006000X

Fig. 6 Speed control module connector test values. 1994–95 900

	Action	CRUISE lamp	Item checked
1	Engine switched off and handbrake applied.		
2	Automatic transmission: selector lever in position N (P, R). Manual gearbox: clutch pedal depressed.		
3	Press the SET and RES buttons simultaneously and keep them depressed while the engine starts.		
	The CRUISE lamp should light up to confirm that you are in diagnostics mode.	Lights up Remains out	On function SET function RESUME function Cruise lamp
4	First release the SET button and then the RES button.	Goes out Remains on	SET function RESUME function
5	Press the SET button.	Lights up Remains out	SET function
	Release the SET button.	Goes out Remains on	SET function
7	Move the switch to the RES/- position.	Lights up Remains out	RESUME function
8	Release RES/-.	Goes out Remains on	RESUME function
9	Move the switch to the TIP/OFF position.	Lights up Remains out	TIP/OFF function
10	Release TIP/OFF.	Goes out Remains on	TIP/OFF function
11	Automatic transmission: shift to D (3, 2, 1). Manual gearbox: release the clutch pedal.	Lights up Remains out	Automatic transmission: Selector lever position sensor Manual gearbox: Clutch pedal switch

SA1109500009010X

Fig. 7 Speed control fault diagnosis (Part 1 of 2). 1995–96 9000

	Action	CRUISE lamp	Item checked
12	Depress the brake pedal.	Goes out Remains on	Brake pedal switch Automatic transmission Manual gearbox
13	Release the brake pedal.	Lights up Remains out	Brake pedal switch Automatic transmission Manual gearbox
14	Automatic transmission: shift to N (P, R). Manual gearbox: depress the clutch pedal.	Goes out Remains on	Automatic transmission: Selector lever position sensor Manual gearbox: Clutch pedal switch
15	Depress the brake pedal and keep it depressed for about five seconds. After about five seconds:	Lights up Remains out Goes out Remains on	Brake lights switch Control module
16	Release the brake pedal.	Slight increase in engine idling speed No increase in engine idling speed	Stepping motor/ cable
17	Drive off slowly.	Lamp flashes in time with the speed. Lamp does not flash.	Speed signal

SA1109500009020X

Fig. 7 Speed control fault diagnosis (Part 2 of 2). 1995–96 9000

F G H J K
E D C B A

Pin	Colour	Component/function	Test conditions	Input/ Output	Test reading	Across X—Y
1 (A)	Green	Switches	Switch set to ON position Ignition switched on	Input	Batt+	1-5
2 (B)	Grey/ green	Switches	Switch held in SET position Ignition switched on	Input	Batt+	2-5
3 (C)	Grey	Switches	Switch held in RES position Ignition switched on	Input	Batt+	3-5
4 (D)	Yellow/ green	Pedal switches				
		Brake pedal switch	Automatic transmission D, 1, 2, 3 Pedal not depressed Pedal depressed	Input	Batt+ 0 V	4-5
			Manual gearbox Pedal not depressed Pedal depressed	Input	Batt+ 0 V	4-5
		Clutch pedal switch	Manual gearbox Pedal not depressed Pedal depressed	Input	Batt+ 0 V	4-5
5 (E)	Black	Power ground		Input	Batt+	5-batt+
6 (F)	Brown/ white	Ignition +54	Ignition switched on	Input	Batt+	6-5
7 (G)	Violet or Blue/ green	Brake lights switch	Brake pedal depressed Brake pedal not depressed	Input	Batt+ 0 V	7-5
8 (H)	Brown/ yellow or Yellow/ white	CRUISE indicator lamp	Lamp out Lamp on	Output	0 V Batt+	8-5
9 (J)	Blue/ green	Communication with Tronic	In diagnostics mode ON/OFF SET RESUME	Output	Batt+	6-9
10 (K)	Black/ green	Speed signal	Car driven slowly forward	Input	approx. 6 V	10-5

SA1109500010000X

Fig. 8 Speed control module connector test values. 1995–96 9000

Air Bag System

NOTE: Electrical Symbol & Wire Color Code Identification Located In The Front Of This Manual May Be Used As An Aid When Using Wiring Circuits Found In This Section.

NOTE: Prior To Performing Any Service Operations Listed In This Section, Consult The "Technical Service Bulletins " Section For Related Information.

INDEX

	Page No.
Air Bag System Disarming & Arming	38-71
Arming	38-71
Disarming	38-71
Collision Inspection	38-74
Component Locations	38-74
Component Service	38-74
Air Bag Module, Replace	38-74
Air Bag Or Seat Belt Pretensioner Assembly Disposal	38-76
Contact Unit, Replace	38-75
Control Module, Replace	38-76
Front Sensors, Replace	38-76
Pyrotechnical Seat Belt Pretensioner, Replace	38-76
Description & Operation	38-71
Components	38-71
System	38-71
Diagnosis & Testing	38-74
Precautions	38-73
Air Bag Systems	38-73
Radio Anti-Theft Lock	38-74
Scheduled Maintenance	38-74
Technical Service Bulletins	38-77
Passenger Air Bag Squeak	38-78
SRS Lamp On	38-77
Pre-1994 900 & Pre-1995 Convertible	38-78
1993-94 9000	38-77
Tightening Specifications	38-78
Wire Harness & Connector Repair	38-74

AIR BAG SYSTEM DISARMING & ARMING

DISARMING

1. Disconnect battery ground cable.
2. Prior to performing any service or diagnostic procedure, wait at least 20 minutes for back up power supply to deplete.

ARMING

1. Connect battery ground cable. **Ensure no one is inside vehicle when connecting battery ground cable.**
2. Turn ignition On and note SRS warning lamp operation. The SRS warning lamp should light for about six seconds, and then go off. If lamp remains illuminated or fails to light, refer to "Diagnosis and Testing."

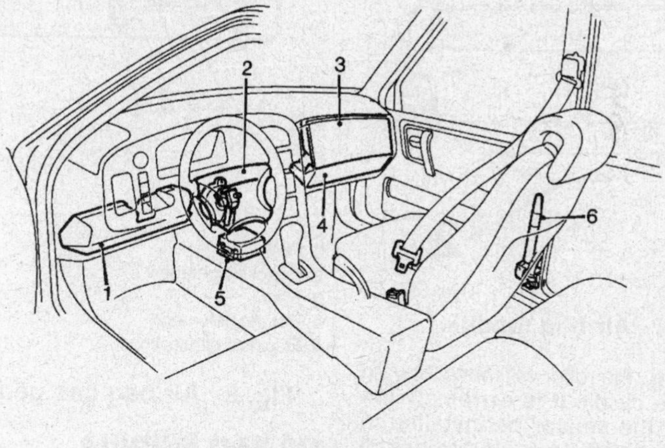

1
2
3
4
5
6
1. Knee shields, driver side
2. Airbag, steering wheel
3. Airbag, passenger side
4. Knee shield, passenger side
5. SRS control module
6. Pyrotechnical belt tensioner
SA8019400032000X

Fig. 1 SRS system components. 900 & 1995–96 9000

DESCRIPTION & OPERATION

SYSTEM

900 & 1995–96 9000

This system consists of a safety sensor, control module, driver and passenger air bag modules, and pyrotechnical seat belt pretensioners, **Fig. 1.**

The air bag(s) and pyrotechnical seat belt pretensioner(s) will activate when the safety sensor is subjected to a force equivalent to a frontal collision at approximately 15 mph.

1994 9000

This system consists of two front parallel-connected sensors, a safety sensor, control module, driver air bag module and pyrotechnical seat belt pretensioner. When equipped, there is also a passenger air bag and pyrotechnical seat belt pretensioner, **Fig. 2.**

The air bag(s) and seat belt pretensioner(s), if equipped, will activate when at least one of the two front sensors and the safety sensor are subjected to a force equivalent to a frontal collision at approximately 15 mph.

COMPONENTS

FRONT SENSORS

1994 9000

The front sensor consist of a contact roller which is held in position by a spring, **Fig. 3.** When the roller is subjected to a force in

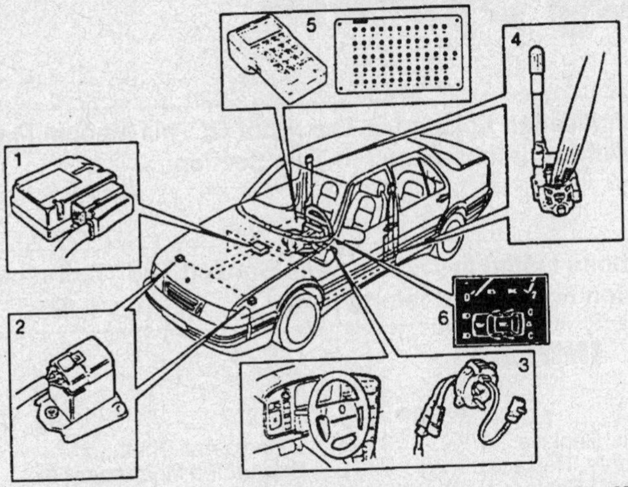
1
2
3
4
5
6

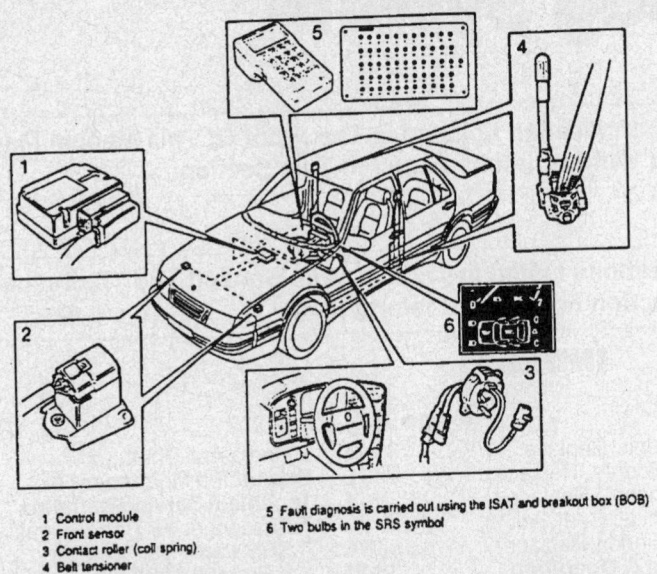

1 Control module
2 Front sensor
3 Contact roller (coil spring)
4 Belt tensioner
5 Fault diagnosis is carried out using the ISAT and breakout box (BOB)
6 Two bulbs in the SRS symbol

SA8019400033000X

Fig. 2 SRS system components. 1994 9000

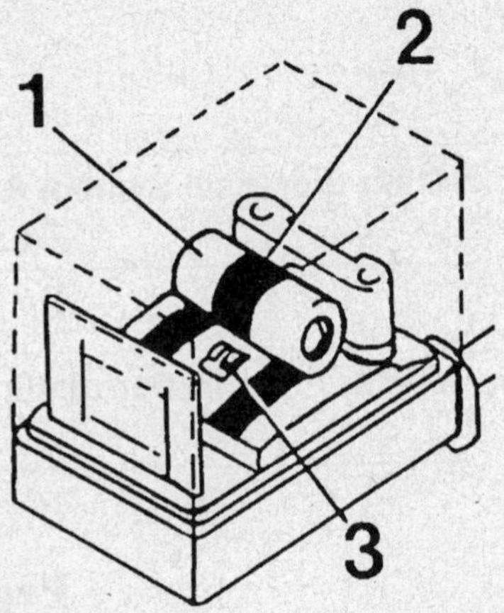
1
2
3

1 Contact roller
2 Contact surface
3 Contact

SA8019400034000X

Fig. 3 Front sensor assembly. 1994 9000

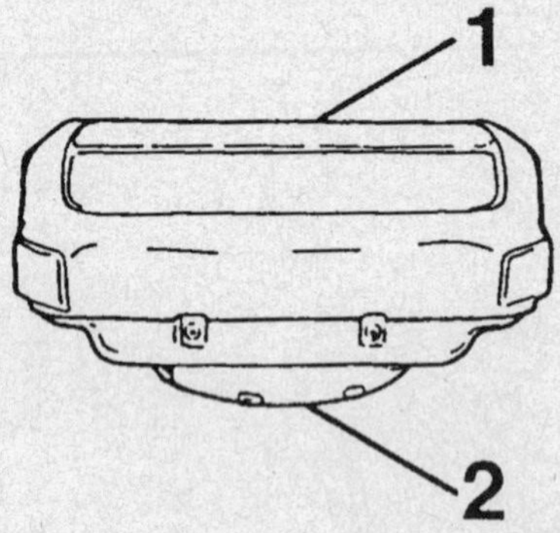
1
2

SA8019400035000X

Fig. 4 Air bag module

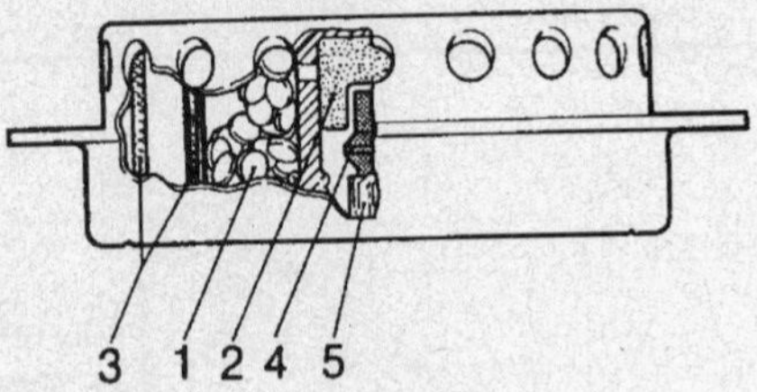
3 1 2 4 5

1 Fuel
2 Explosive charge
3 Filter
4 Electric detonator
5 Electrical connection

SA8019400036000X

Fig. 5 Air bag gas generator

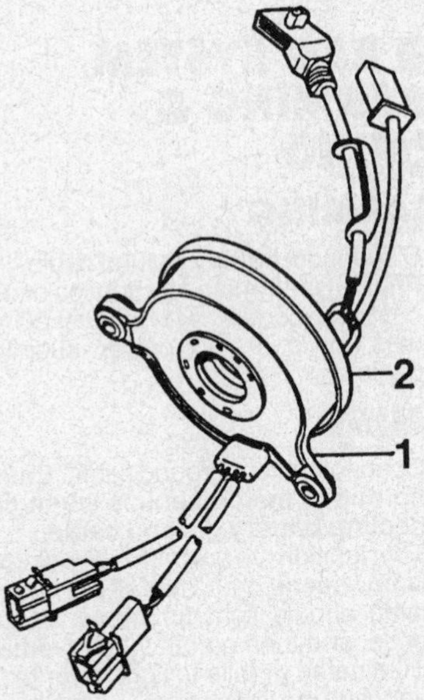
2
1

1 Fixed part
2 Movable part

SA8019400037000X

Fig. 6 Contact unit

excess of 16 g., the roller will move forward and close the circuit. **It is extremely important that the sensor be installed in the proper direction to avoid accidental deployment.**

CONTROL MODULE

The control module contains the safety sensor, a capacitor pack and the diagnostic unit. **It is important that the control module be mounted facing in proper direction.**

The diagnostic unit continuously monitors the air bag system. If a system fault or condition should occur, the SRS warning lamp will light. The symbol will flash for about 10 minutes, then the lamp will remain On steadily until the ignition is turned Off. If a condition is still present the next time the ignition is turned On, the SRS lamp will again flash for approximately 10 minutes. Condition indications are stored as DTCs in the diagnostic unit memory.

AIR BAG MODULE

Driver

The driver air bag module, located in the steering wheel pad, contains the gas generator and air bag, **Fig. 4.** The gas generator consists of an aluminum case with a center compartment and two annular compartments, **Fig. 5.** The center compartment has an electric detonator and an explosive charge, and communicates with the inner annular compartment.

Passenger

The passenger air bag module, located under a panel in the instrument panel pad above the glove compartment, contains the gas generator and air bag, **Fig. 4.** The gas generator consists of an aluminum case with a center compartment and two annular compartments, **Fig. 5.** The center compartment has an electric detonator and an explosive charge, and communicates with the inner annular compartment.

PYROTECHNICAL SEAT BELT PRETENSIONER

The pyrotechnical seat belt pretensioner is located in the seat belt retractor units found in the vehicle "B" pillar. The unit contains a gas generator and piston, which in a collision will automatically tighten the seat belt and shoulder harness.

CONTACT UNIT

The contact unit, **Fig. 6,** is located between the steering wheel and the steering column bracket. The contact unit is used to transmit testing and firing signals to the air bag unit. It also supplies current to the horn and turn signal switches. The unit consists of a fixed and moving part. A coiled plastic strip with four conductors is located between the fixed and movable parts. The movable part can be rotated the number of turns listed on the label in either direction from the center position. If the movable part is rotated beyond these limits, the plastic coil strip may break, rendering the air bag system inoperative.

SRS WARNING LAMP

The warning lamp is located in the combined instrument panel on 900 models and in the pictogram on 9000 models. This lamp will light for approximately six seconds when the ignition is turned on, and will go out if there are no SRS conditions.

PRECAUTIONS

AIR BAG SYSTEMS

The SRS must be disarmed prior to disconnecting any SRS electrical connectors or servicing any system components located near them. Refer to "Air Bag System Disarming and Arming."

1. SRS components must not be opened or repaired. Always install new components.
2. Always replace SRS system components which have been damaged.
3. SRS wiring cannot be repaired or spliced. If damaged, replace the wiring harness.
4. When performing body work or welding repairs, always disconnect the driver's air bag and seat belt pretensioner electrical connectors.
5. The air bag must not be stored at temperatures higher than 158°F. There is a risk of self-detonation at temperatures above 275°F.
6. Do not paint air bag unit cover to correct cosmetic flaws. It must be replaced.
7. The contact unit must not be turned more than number of turns listed on the label in either direction from center as contact unit damage may result.
8. Do not leave an undeployed air bag module or seat belt pretensioner unattended if work is interrupted. Install into vehicle as soon as unit is removed from packaging.
9. The SRS must be inspected every 10 years.
10. Handle air bag module carefully so that it is not exposed to impacts or vibrations.
11. Air bag must be stored and carried with its metal case facing downward to prevent injury in event of accidental detonation.

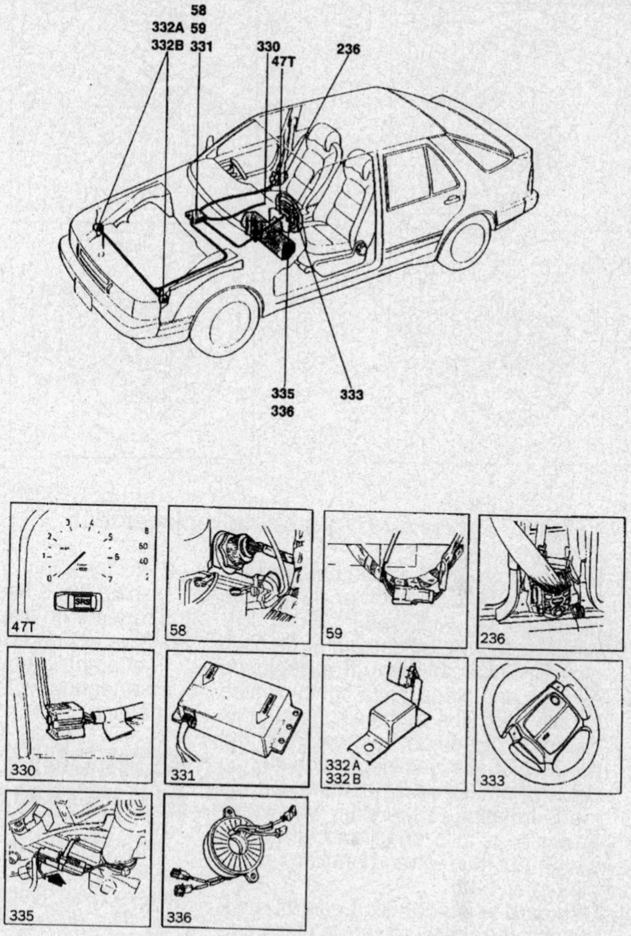
58
332A 59
332B 331
330
47T
236
335
336
333
47T
58
59
236
330
331
332 A
332 B
333
335
336

SA8019400042010X

Fig. 7 SRS component locations (Part 1 of 2). 1994 9000

47T	Airbag warning lamp in pictogram
58	12-pin connector
59	2-pin connector (orange). The male pins are short-circuited when the connector is separated.
236	Seat-belt tensioner, right-hand
330	Test outlet, 10-pin, airbag
331	Electronic unit, airbag
332 A	Front sensor, left-hand
332 B	Front sensor, right-hand
333	Steering wheel pad, airbag
334	Ground point for electronic unit and test outlet
335	2-pin connector (orange). The male pins are short-circuited when the connector is separated.
336	Contact unit (coil spring)

SA8019400042020X

Fig. 7 SRS component locations (Part 2 of 2). 1994 9000

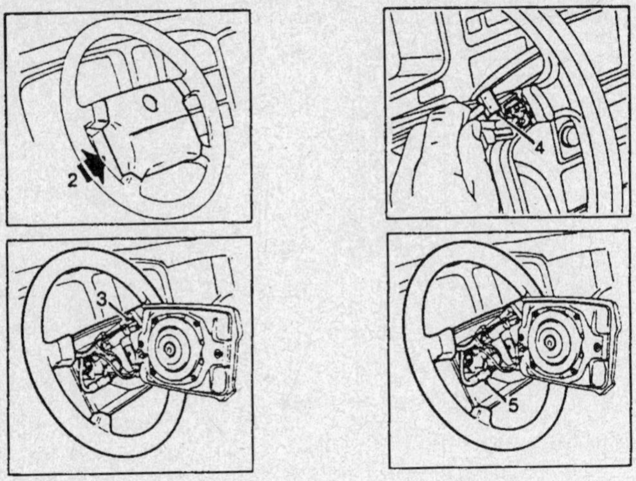
2
4
3
5

SA8019400049000X

Fig. 8 Driver air bag module replacement

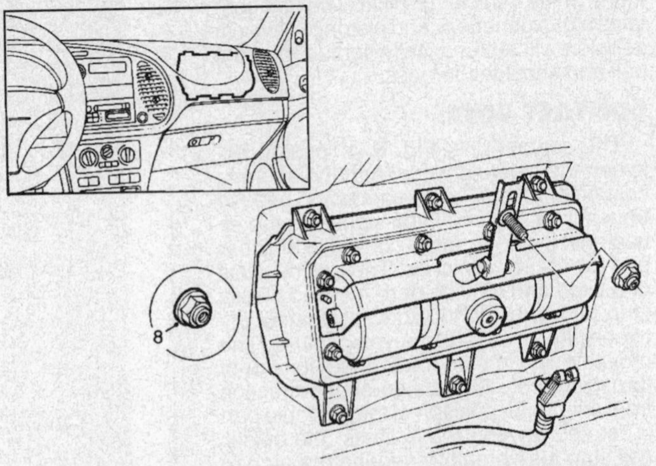
8

SA8019400050000X

Fig. 9 Passenger air bag module replacement. 900

12. Do not store air bag together with petroleum products or other flammable materials.
13. Wear safety goggles and protective gloves during removal of a deployed air bag, and place it in a tightly sealed plastic bag. The surface may contain deposits of sodium hydroxide, a by-product of the gas generated during deployment. Because sodium hydroxide is irritating to the skin, wash your hands in a mild soap and lukewarm water solution after handling a deployed air bag.
14. Use care when handling control module as it is sensitive to static electricity. Do not touch or allow foreign objects to come into contact with connector pins.

RADIO ANTI-THEFT LOCK

9000

1995–96

Radio and cassette player are equipped with an electronic four-digit anti-theft lock. This four-digit code is programmed at manufacturing and cannot be changed. If the battery is disconnected for more than three minutes, if unit is removed or if otherwise cut off from power, the four-digit code must be entered with the quick-selection buttons as follows:

1. Turn radio on, then, when display shows "Code In, " enter four-digit code with quick-selection buttons. If code is correct, last-tuned radio frequency is shown on display. If wrong digit has been entered by mistake, all four digits must be entered again. If code is wrong it stays on display.
2. If incorrect four-digit code has been entered, press Band button for more than three seconds to clear display. Display shows "Code In" and new attempt to enter correct code can be made.
3. If wrong code has been used three times in succession, four dashes appear on display and you must wait an hour with radio switched on before trying again.
4. To try again, hold Band button for at least three seconds. "Code In" should appear on display.
5. Correct code must be entered at first attempt, otherwise you must wait another hour with unit switched on before trying again.

SCHEDULED MAINTENANCE

The SRS must be inspected every 10 years. The SRS should be inspected for stored DTCs. Refer to "Diagnosis and Testing." The air bag module, steering wheel, contact unit, control module, front sensors and brackets, wiring harnesses and seat belt pretensioner(s), if equipped, should be inspected for wear and damage and replaced as necessary. Refer to "Component Service " for replacement procedures.

WIRE HARNESS & CONNECTOR REPAIR

The SRS wiring harness should not be spliced. If wiring harness insulation is damaged, but the copper conductor is in satisfactory condition, the insulation may be replaced.

COMPONENT LOCATIONS

Refer to **Figs. 1, 2 and 7** for SRS component locations.

DIAGNOSIS & TESTING

Refer to **MOTOR's "Air Bag Manual"** for complete diagnosis and testing information.

COLLISION INSPECTION

If SRS deployment has occurred, the air bag module, contact unit, control module or control module, front sensors and seat belt pre-tensioner(s), if equipped, must be replaced. Refer to "Component Service " for replacement procedures. The SRS wiring circuit, sensor brackets, steering wheel, steering column bracket, steering shaft, knee bolster and cable should be inspected for damage and replaced as necessary.

Wear safety goggles and protective gloves during removal of a deployed air bag. Place air bag in a tightly sealed plastic bag. The sealed plastic bag should then be placed with automotive scrap. Vehicle interior and A/C, vent, defroster and heater ducts should be vacuumed.

The air bag surface may contain deposits of sodium hydroxide, a by-product of the gas generated during deployment. Because sodium hydroxide is irritating to the skin, wash your hands in mild soap solution and lukewarm water after handling a detonated air bag. If sinus or throat irritation is encountered during air bag removal, exit vehicle and breathe fresh air. If skin irritation is encountered, flush effected area with cool water. If sinus, throat, skin or any other type of irritation continues, consult a physician.

COMPONENT SERVICE

Prior to performing any service procedures, disarm SRS system as outlined under "Air Bag System Disarming and Arming." After a component has been replaced it may be necessary to clear the diagnostic trouble code from the control module memory.

It may be necessary to clear the DTCs from the control module memory after component has been installed.

AIR BAG MODULE, REPLACE

DRIVER

1. Disarm SRS as outlined under "Air Bag System Disarming and Arming."
2. Remove air bag module to steering wheel retaining screws, **Fig. 8.**
3. Disconnect air bag connector, then remove air bag module.

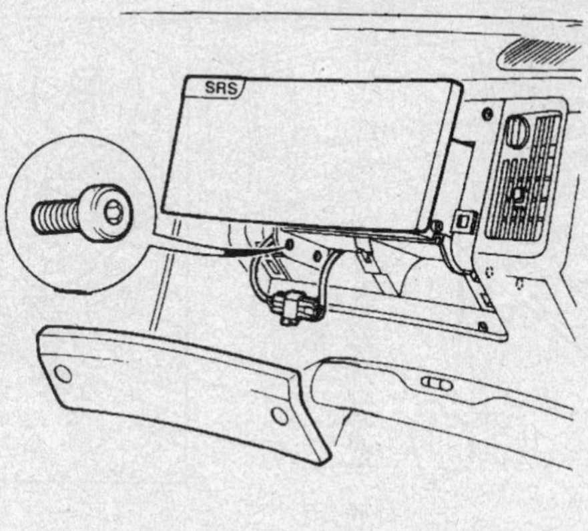
SRS
SA8019400051000X

Fig. 10 Passenger air bag module replacement. 9000

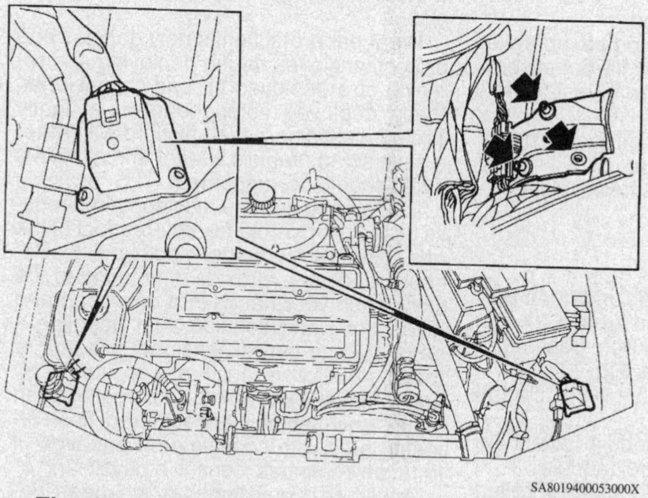
SA8019400053000X

Fig. 12 Front sensor replacement. 1994 9000

4. Reverse procedure to install. Tighten retaining screws to specifications.

PASSENGER

900

1. Disarm SRS as outlined under "Air Bag System Disarming and Arming."
2. Remove glove box lid, then remove and disconnect clove box lamp.
3. Remove screws and push clips retaining glove box, then remove glove box.
4. Disconnect air bag connector **Fig 9.**
5. Remove nut retaining air bag stay to support member, then remove nuts holding air bag to instrument panel.
6. Reverse procedures to install, noting the following:
   a. Tighten nuts to specifications.
   b. Use a suitable sealing compound on right upper and left lower nuts.

9000

1. Disarm air bag system as outlined under "Air Bag System Disarming and Arming."
2. Remove trim caps and retaining screws for lower cover, **Fig. 10.**
3. Pry out lower cover clips using trim tool No. 82 92 997 or equivalent, then remove cover.
4. Disconnect air bag connector.
5. Remove air bag mounting screws, then grasp air bag at rear and pull assembly from instrument panel. Trim panel also has mounting clips.
6. Reverse procedures to install, noting the following:
   a. Ensure all trim clips are firmly seated.
   b. Tighten screws to specifications.

CONTACT UNIT, REPLACE

900

REMOVAL

1. Disarm SRS as outlined under "Air Bag System Disarming and Arming."
2. Remove air bag module as outlined under "Air Bag Module, Replace."
3. Position front wheels in straight-ahead position, then disconnect horn connector.
4. Remove steering wheel, then both steering column covers.
5. Disconnect connectors for horn and contact unit **Fig. 11.**
6. Remove contact unit retaining screws.

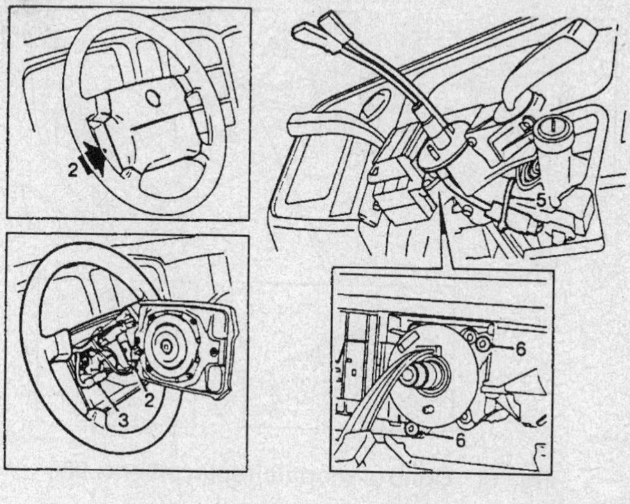
2
5
2
3
6
6
SA8019400052000X

Fig. 11 Contact roller unit replacement. 900

7. Remove contact unit.

INSTALLATION

1. Remove transit safety, if any, from contact unit.
2. Install contact unit on bracket, then connect electrical connectors.
3. Install and tighten mounting screws to specifications.
4. Install both steering column covers.
5. Set contact unit to center position as follows:
   a. Ensure front wheels are in straight-ahead position.
   b. Turn contact unit clockwise as far as possible, then turn counterclockwise two and one half turns.
6. Install steering wheel. **Torque** nut to 24-32 ft. lbs.
7. Connect horn connector.
8. Install air bag module as outlined under "Air Bag Module, Replace."
9. Arm SRS as outlined under "Air Bag System Disarming and Arming."

9000

1. Disarm SRS as outlined under "Air Bag System Disarming and Arming."
2. Remove air bag module as outlined under "Air Bag Module."
3. Position front wheels in straight-ahead position, then disconnect horn connector.
4. Remove steering wheel, then steering column covers.
5. Disconnect horn connector, then cut strap and disconnect contact unit connector.
6. Remove contact unit mounting screws, then the contact unit, **Fig. 11.**
7. Reverse procedure to install. Adjust contact unit (coil spring) as follows:
   a. Ensure front wheels are in straight-ahead position.
   b. Rotate contact unit clockwise to end position, then rotate counterclockwise then number of turns listed on label.

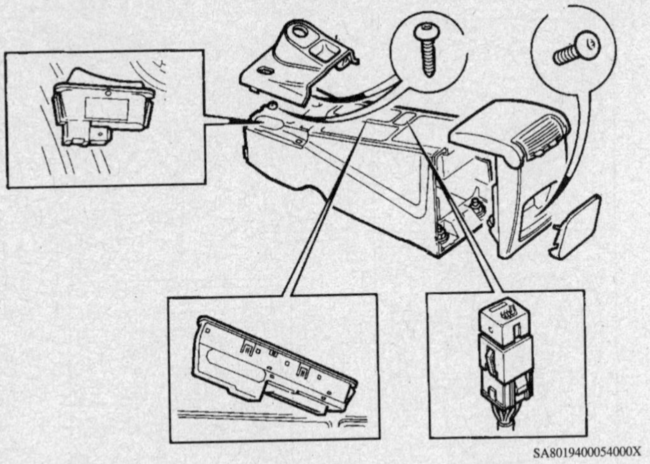
SA8019400054000X

Fig. 13 Control module replacement. 900

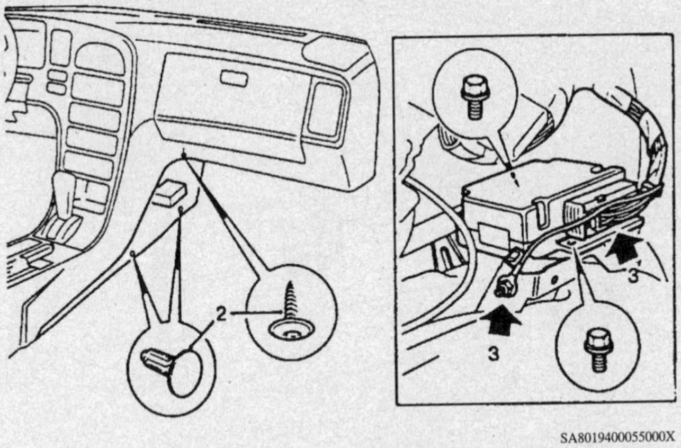
2
3
3
SA8019400055000X

Fig. 14 Control module replacement. 9000

FRONT SENSORS, REPLACE

1994 9000

1. Disarm SRS as outlined under "Air Bag System Disarming and Arming."
2. **On lefthand side,** position electrical distribution box aside.
3. **On both sides,** cut retaining strap and disconnect connector.
4. Using Torx bit 84 71 120 or equivalent, remove sensor, **Fig. 12.**
5. Reverse procedure to install, noting the following:
   a. Ensure a good ground is obtained for sensor.
   b. Lubricate threads of new mounting screw with silicone dielectric compound or other suitable lubricant having good conductivity and high viscosity.
   c. Install sensor with arrow markings on sensor pointing forward.
   d. Tighten attaching screws to specifications.

CONTROL MODULE, REPLACE

Use care when handling control module as it is sensitive to static electricity. Do not touch or allow foreign objects to come in contact with connector pins.

900

1. Disarm SRS as outlined under "Air Bag System Disarming and Arming."
2. Apply parking brake.
3. Remove center console as follows:
   a. Remove ignition switch cover, loosen front lefthand edge first, then rear, then pry out front, **Fig. 13.**
   b. Disconnect ignition switch lamp, then remove front console retaining screws.
   c. Remove rear ash tray, then remove rear cover screw and rear cover.
   d. Remove rear retaining nuts, then loosen center console by lifting and pulling back slightly.
   e. Remove and disconnect interior lamp turn, heated seat turn and power window turn.
   f. Lift out center console.
4. Cut cable ties and unplug orange connector, then disconnect ground connections where needed.
5. Remove control module bracket mounting screws, then lift out assembly. Reverse procedure to install, noting the following:
   a. Ensure arrow markings on control module face forward.
   b. Tighten attaching screws to specifications.

9000

1. Disarm SRS as outlined under "Air Bag System Disarming and Arming."
2. Remove carpet panel from passenger side of center console, **Fig. 14.**
3. Disconnect connector from control module.
4. Remove control module attaching screws, then the control module.
5. Reverse procedure to install. Tighten attaching screws to specifications.

PYROTECHNICAL SEAT BELT PRETENSIONER, REPLACE

1. Disarm SRS as outlined under "Air Bag System Disarming and Arming."
2. Position front seat forward, then position the seat backrest forward.
3. Remove door sill plate.
4. Release bottom edge of seat belt guide cover, then remove guide cover.
5. Remove seat belt guide from B-pillar.
6. Remove seat belt guide from B-pillar, then remove trim panel.
7. Remove cover from seat belt pretensioner.
8. Disconnect connector at seat belt pretensioner.
9. Remove seat belt reel attaching bolts, then remove seat belt reel.
10. Reverse procedure to install, noting the following:
    a. Tighten attaching bolts to specifications.

AIR BAG OR SEAT BELT PRETENSIONER ASSEMBLY DISPOSAL

In the event an air bag assembly or seat belt pretensioner must be discarded, it is recommended that the unit be triggered without removing the system from the vehicle.

Wear ear protection, safety goggles and protective gloves during deploying and removal of a deployed air bag or tensioner. Place deployed components in a tightly sealed plastic bag, then discard with automotive scrap. Vehicle interior and all HVAC ducts should be vacuumed.

The air bag surface may contain deposits of sodium hydroxide, a by-product of the gas generated during deployment. Because sodium hydroxide is irritating to the skin, wash your hands in a mild soap and lukewarm water solution after handling a detonated air bag or tensioner. If sinus or throat irritation is encountered during air bag removal, exit vehicle and breathe fresh air. If skin irritation is encountered, flush affected area with cool water. If any type of irritation continues, consult a physician.

An air bag unit that has not been deployed must be deployed prior to disposal.

AIR BAG DEPLOYMENT

1. Locate vehicle in an open area outdoors.
2. Disconnect battery ground cable.
3. Remove bottom steering column cover, then disconnect orange two-terminal connector.
4. **On 1995–96 9000 models,** connect deployment device No. 84 71 104, and cable No. 86 11 477 or equivalent, to the disconnected two terminal orange connector, **Fig. 15.**
5. **On all other models,** connect deployment device 84 71 104, or an equivalent electrical connector to the disconnected two terminal orange connector, **Fig. 15.**
6. **On all models,** ensure all vehicle windows and doors are closed after connecting deployment device.
7. Connect deployment device to a fully charged 12 volt battery positioned approximately 30 ft. from vehicle. **Ensure no people, animals or objects are within 30 feet of the vehicle.**
8. Press deployment tool button to detonate air bag. When air bag detonation occurs, an explosion will be heard and white smoke will be visible in passenger compartment. **After air bag has**

detonated, allow SRS system components 30 minutes to cool before handling.

9. If air bag fails to detonate, disconnect deployment device from battery and carefully inspect connections. Also inspect battery state of charge. If connections and battery are satisfactory, contact Saab for further information.

SEAT BELT PRETENSIONER DEPLOYMENT

1. Locate vehicle in an open area outdoors.
2. Disconnect battery ground cable.
3. Position front seat forward, then position seat backrest forward.
4. Remove door sill plate.
5. Release bottom edge of seat belt guide cover, then remove guide cover.
6. Remove seat belt guide from B-pillar.
7. Remove seat belt guide from B-pillar, then remove trim panel.
8. Remove cover from seat belt pretensioner.
9. Disconnect connector at pretensioner.
10. **On 1995–96 9000 models,** connect deployment device No. 84 71 104, and cable No. 86 11 469 to tensioner, **Fig. 16.**
11. **On all other models,** connect deployment device harness No. 85 80 052 or equivalent, to tensioner, **Fig. 16.**
12. Position upper seat belt guide on mounting. Ensure seat belt runs freely through guide and can be taken up approximately seven inches without causing damage.
13. Route outer end of deployment device harness No. 85 80 052 or equivalent, to engine compartment.
14. Ensure all doors and windows are closed.
15. Connect deployment device harness to vehicle battery. Ensure vehicle battery is sufficiently charged, and that nobody is inside vehicle.
16. While standing in front of vehicle, depress deployment device button.
17. Disconnect deployment device from vehicle battery. **After seat belt pretensioner has detonated, allow SRS system components 30 minutes to cool before handling.**

TECHNICAL SERVICE BULLETINS

SRS LAMP ON

1993–94 9000

On these models, the SRS lamp may light and DTCs OE S, OF S, 10 S, 11 S, 12 S, 13 S, 14 S, 23A24, 25321, 25322, 25341 and 25342 may be stored.

This condition may be caused by a wiring harness. To correct this condition, install new wiring harness (leave old harness in place) as follows:

1. Disarm air bag system. Refer to "Air Bag System Disarming and Arming" for procedure.
2. **On 1993–94 models,** install front sensor harness, Part No. 44 33 165, as follows:

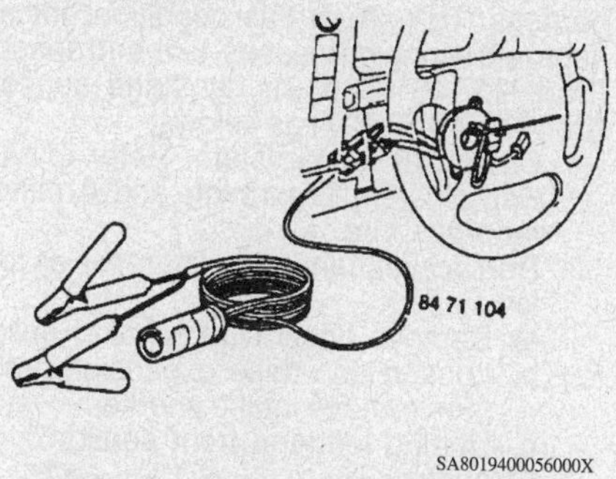
84 71 104
SA8019400056000X

Fig. 15 Deployment tool & harness to air bag connection

a. Remove false bulkhead space cover and partition, then remove lefthand underdash insulating materials.
b. Protect pins on new wiring harness loose ends with tape, then position harness in engine compartment. Branch should be in front of bulkhead rubber grommet. Three-pin lead is for lefthand front sensor, four-pin lead is for righthand.
c. Remove cable conduit cover beside battery and place harness in conduit, then run harness to lefthand front sensor.
d. Remove old harness connector from sensor and tie back.
e. Plug new harness into sensor and secure with cable tie about 3.934 inches away.
f. Install righthand harness through bulkhead rubber grommet, then run harness behind front partition bottom of false bulkhead space to righthand side.
g. Run cable under leads and hoses. Remove screw, bend sheet metal in front of HVAC unit to make harness running easier, then install the screw.
h. Secure harness away from wiper arm mechanism.
i. Unplug four-pin connector and plug new harness into righthand front sensor.
j. In engine compartment, lift ABS main fuse box to locate three inch diameter rubber grommet in bulkhead above pedal assembly.
k. Remove grommet from passenger compartment and remove leads.
l. Drill .397 inch hole in grommet (predrilled at rear) and cut slit to hole from outside similar to others.
m. Coat wiring harnesses with silicone spray (harness has shrink tubing at places where it passes through rubber grommet), then install new and old wiring harnesses through grommet from engine compartment and install grommet.
n. Secure harness to electronic holder righthand front corner and air duct above pedal assembly.
o. Remove center console righthand side panel and install wiring harness, then fasten to air duct to SRS control module. Ensure harness

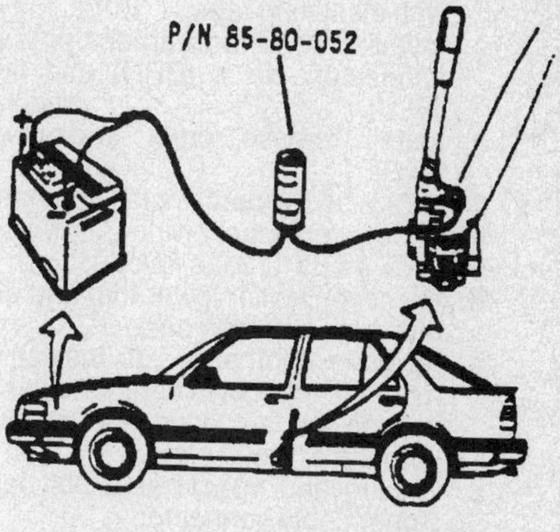
P/N 85-80-052
SA8019400057000X

Fig. 16 Deployment tool & harness to seat belt pretensioner connection

clears pedals and steering column.
p. Unplug SRS control module connector and remove pins 7 (YLW/RED), 8 (GRN/RED), 26 (BLU/RED), 9 (GRY/WHT), 10 (BLK/WHT) and 27 (BRN/WHT).
q. Cut pins off and wrap lead ends with insulating tape.
r. Install new harness pins in connector: pin 7(YLW/RED), eight (GRN/RED), 26 (BLU/RED), 9 (GRY/WHT), 10 (BLK/WHT) and 27 (BRN/WHT).
s. Install remove parts and clear DTCs.

3. **On 1993–94 models,** install four-pin connector to righthand front sensor wiring harness, Part No. 46 63 035 as follows:
   a. Unplug righthand front sensor connector and run new wiring harness along righthand side of engine compartment, fastening with cable ties.
   b. Remove false bulkhead space cover and install harness in rubber grommet and run it to bulkhead space.
   c. Unplug old harness and plug new harness into four-pin connector.
   d. Install remove parts and clear DTCs.
4. **On 1993–94 models,** install lefthand seat belt tensioner wiring harness, Part No. 44 33 181, as follows:
   a. Remove B-pillar lower trim and detach seat belt tensioner.
   b. Remove lefthand side insulating material, fold down lefthand panel section forward edge and remove lefthand sill scuff plate.
   c. Unplug and cut off seat belt tensioner cable connector.
   d. Run new wiring harness behind seat belt reel and plug connector into tensioner, then place wiring into cable conduit and secure under other wiring harness.
   e. Run harness along air duct to SRS control module, then unplug connector and remove pins four (BRN) and five (BLU).

f. Cut pins off and wrap leads ends with insulating tape.
g. Install new wiring harness pins in connector: pin 4 (BRN) and five (BLU).
h. Install remove parts and clear DTCs.

5. **On 1993–94 models,** install righthand seat belt tensioner wiring harness, Part No. 44 33 173, as follows:
   a. Remove B-pillar lower trim and detach seat belt tensioner.
   b. Remove righthand side insulating material, fold down righthand panel section forward edge and remove lefthand sill scuff plate.
   c. Unplug and cut off seat belt tensioner cable connector.
   d. Run new wiring harness behind seat belt reel and plug connector into tensioner, then place wiring into cable conduit and secure under other wiring harness.
   e. Run harness behind carpet to SRS control module, then unplug connector and remove pins 23 (BLU/WHT) and 24 (YLW/WHT).
   f. Cut pins off and wrap leads ends with insulating tape.
   g. Install new wiring harness pins in connector: pin 23 (BLU/WHT) and 24 (YLW/WHT).
   h. Install remove parts and clear DTCs.

SRS LAMP ON

Pre-1994 900 & Pre-1995 900 Convertible

On these models, the SRS lamp may light with DTCs OE S, OF S, 10 S, 11 S, 12 S, 13 S and 14 S.

This condition may be caused by a wiring harness. To correct this condition, install separate wiring harnesses, lefthand sensor (Part No. 46 63 019), righthand sensor, (Part No. 46 63 027) as follows:

1. Disarm air bag system. Refer to "Air Bag System Disarming and Arming" for procedure.
2. Replace lefthand wiring harness as follows:
   a. Remove driver side speaker grille.
   b. Loosen and raise expansion tank, then remove intake snorkel.
   c. Unplug lefthand front sensor connector.
   d. Follow wiring to bulkhead and cut at rubber grommet, then remove harness.
   e. Plug new harness connector into lefthand front sensor.
   f. Fasten harness in place along old wiring harness route, then inset through bulkhead.
   g. Fish harness up using steel wire inserted through speaker grille.
   h. Unplug old and plug new harness into control module.
   i. Install parts removed and clear DTCs.
3. Replace righthand wiring harness as follows:
   a. Remove driver side speaker grille and radio compartment.
   b. Cut cable ties hold old wiring harness to dashboard.
   c. Unplug righthand front sensor connector.
   d. Remove wiring from clamp to bulkhead rubber grommet.
   e. Plug new harness connector into righthand front sensor.
   f. Fasten harness in place along old wiring harness route.
   g. Cut old harness about 12 inches from rubber grommet.
   h. Remove pins from new wiring harness four-pin connector and inset into old wiring harness sleeve, then tape two harnesses together.
   i. Coat harness with silicone spray, then unplug old harness from control module and pull it to bring new harness to control module.
   j. Install pins into new harness connector (pin 1 to BLK/WHT, pin 2 to BRN/WHT and pin 3 to GRY/WHT), then connect to control module.
   k. Install new cable ties and install parts removed, then clear DTCs.

PASSENGER AIR BAG SQUEAK

1994 9000

On these models, built between VIN R1000061 through R1005992, there may be an annoying squeak from the passenger air bag area.

This condition may be caused by an unwrapped air bag harness. To correct this condition, proceed as follows:

1. Inspect passenger air bag harness for manufacturer's tag.
2. If harness is marked "UT-MAI" on red tag, remove plastic caps and screws for lower righthand dash panel, then remove panel.
3. Release connector from mount and carefully draw harness out as far as possible.
4. Start at HVAC unit and wrap cloth tape as tightly as possible to connector.
5. Install harness with wrapped area resting on top of knee pad.

TIGHTENING SPECIFICATIONS

Component	Torque/Ft. Lbs.
900	
Air Bag Module Retaining Screws	4.1–5.3
Control Module	4.4–6.6
Front Sensor	4.4–6.6
Steering Wheel Retaining Nut	24–32
9000	
Air Bag Module Retaining Screws	4.1–5.3
Control Module	6.6
Front Sensor	6
Steering Wheel Retaining Nut	22.1
Seat Belt Reel Retaining Bolt	19–50
Seat Belt Guide At B-Pillar	18–29
Seat Belt Anchor Point At Seat	19–50

Dash Panel Service

NOTE: On Air Bag Equipped Models, Refer To "Air Bag System Precautions" Located In The Front Of This Manual For System Disarming & Arming Procedures.

NOTE: Refer To "Dash Gauges" Section For Dash Panel For Related Information.

INDEX

	Page No.
Dash Panel, Replace	38-79
900	38-79
9000	38-81
Precautions	38-79
Air Bag Systems	38-79
Radio Anti-Theft Lock	38-79

PRECAUTIONS

AIR BAG SYSTEMS

Refer to "Air Bag System Precautions" in the front of this manual for system disarming and arming procedures.

RADIO ANTI-THEFT LOCK

9000

1995-96

Radio and cassette player are equipped with an electronic four-digit anti-theft lock. This four-digit code is programmed at manufacturing and cannot be changed. If the battery is disconnected for more than three minutes, if unit is removed or if otherwise cut off from power, the four-digit code must be entered with the quick-selection buttons as follows:

1. Turn radio on, then, when display shows "Code In, " enter four-digit code with quick-selection buttons. If code is correct, last-tuned radio frequency is shown on display. If wrong digit has been entered by mistake, all four digits must be entered again. If code is wrong it stays on display.
2. If incorrect four-digit code has been entered, press Band button for more than three seconds to clear display. Display shows "Code In" and new attempt to enter correct code can be made.
3. If wrong code has been used three times in succession, four dashes appear on display and you must wait an hour with radio switched on before trying again.
4. To try again, hold Band button for at least three seconds. "Code In" should appear on display.
5. Correct code must be entered at first attempt, otherwise you must wait another hour with unit switched on before trying again.

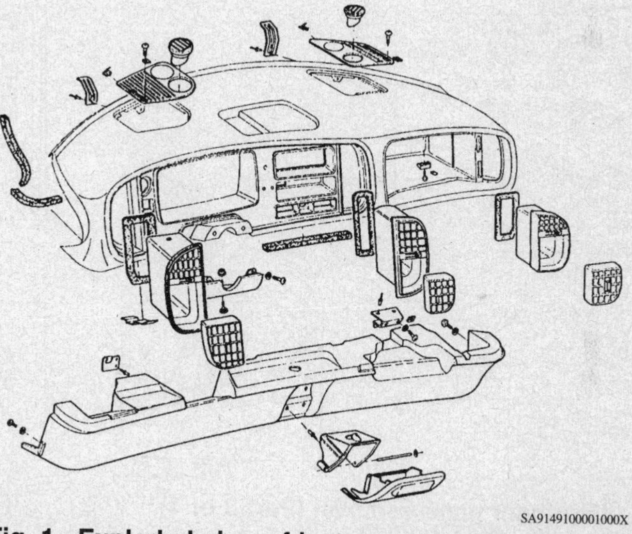
SA9149100001000X

Fig. 1 Exploded view of instrument panel. 1993 900

DASH PANEL

REPLACE

900

1993

1. Disconnect battery ground cable.
2. Remove lefthand seat, then the trim cover below steering column, **Fig. 1.**
3. **On models with center console,** remove console as follows:
   a. Squeeze together rubber boot on gear lever to free retaining bolts and slide boot up.
   b. Remove four ashtray holder attaching screws, then the bolt securing holder to instrument panel.
   c. Disconnect ashtray bulb electrical connector, then remove ashtray holder from console and instrument panel.
   d. Remove six console to frame and console to vehicle body attaching screws, then the console and frame assembly from vehicle.
4. **On all models,** remove instrument panel lower trim panel.
5. Remove locking screw for upper joint of intermediate shaft in steering assembly.
6. Unhook brake and clutch pedal return springs, then disconnect instrument panel electrical connectors.
7. Remove speaker/defroster grills and remove screws in upper section of panel.
8. Disconnect speedometer cable, then lead from righthand door switch and pull lead into passenger compartment.
9. Remove instrument panel attaching bolts, then disconnect heater housing vacuum connections located in engine compartment.
10. Remove instrument panel from vehicle.
11. Reverse procedure to install.

1994-96

1. Disconnect battery ground cable, then pull back steering wheel to full extent.
2. Remove air bag module screws from

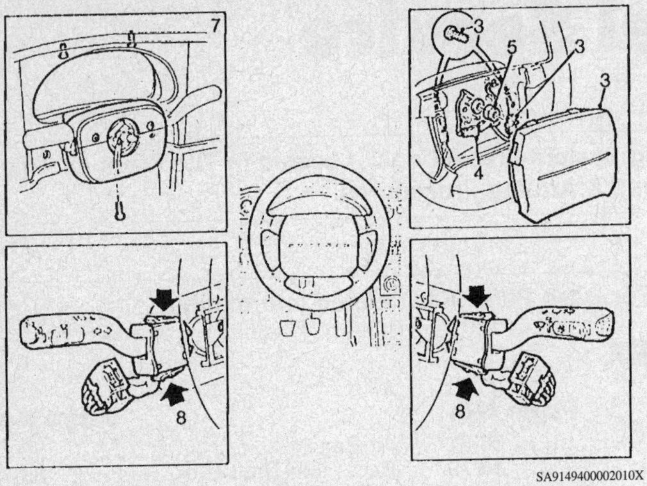
7
3
5
3
3
4
8
8
SA9149400002010X

Fig. 2 Instrument panel removal (Part 1 of 4). 1994–96 900

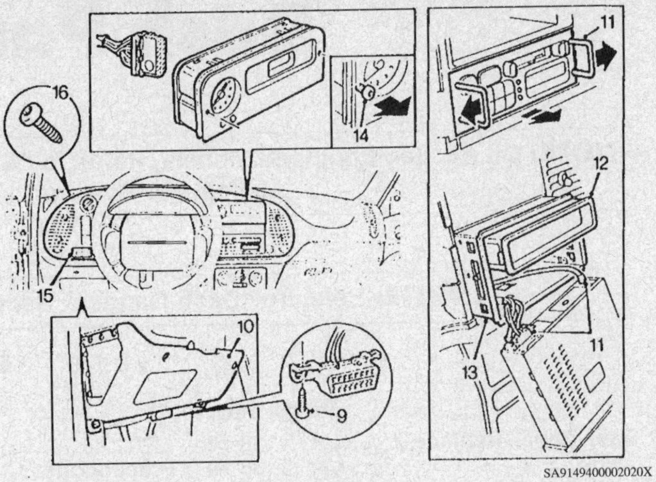
16
11
14
12
15
10
9
13
11
SA9149400002020X

Fig. 2 Instrument panel removal (Part 2 of 4). 1994–96 900

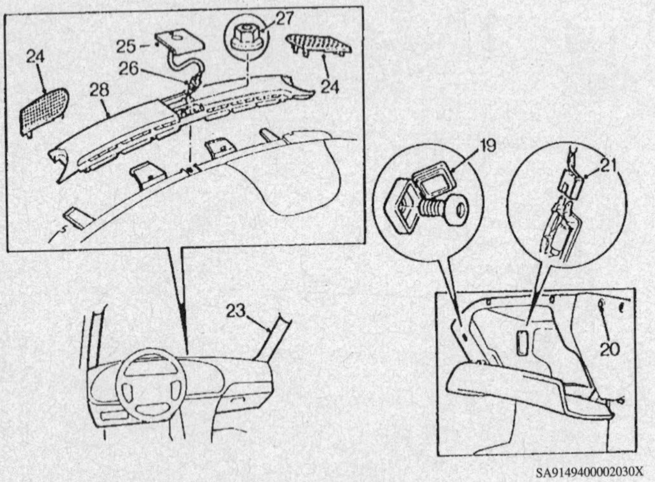
27
25
24
26
28
24
19
21
23
20
SA9149400002030X

Fig. 2 Instrument panel removal (Part 3 of 4). 1994–96 900

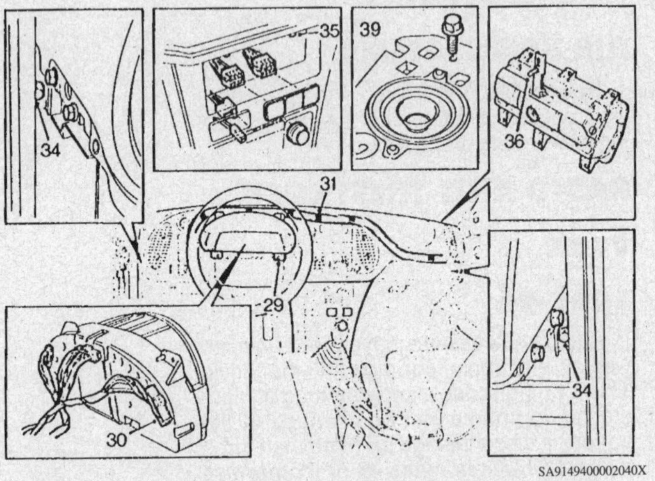
35
39
34
36
31
29
30
34
SA9149400002040X

Fig. 2 Instrument panel removal (Part 4 of 4). 1994–96 900

under side of steering wheel, then disconnect connector and remove module (3), **Fig. 2.**

3. Disconnect horn connector (4), then turn steering wheel so front wheels point straight ahead.
4. Loosen steering column nut (5) but do not remove.
5. Rock steering wheel loose, then pull out connectors and unscrew steering column nut.
6. Remove screws securing upper and lower sections of cowl, then the cowl (7).
7. Press in two clips on each mounting (8), then pull steering column controls straight out. Disconnect electrical connectors.
8. Remove diagnostic socket (9) located under lefthand side of dashboard.
9. Remove screws securing lower dashboard section (10), then the expanding rivets in front edge. To remove expanding rivets, press center pin further into rivet.
10. Release radio with forks (11), then remove.
11. Remove storage compartment (12), then the radio contact box (13), using screwdriver.
12. Remove auxiliary instrument panel (SID unit) with suitable extraction screws (14). Disconnect connector.
13. Remove light switch and headlamp beam control switch (15) by pressing out from behind.
14. Remove instrument panel retaining screws.
15. Loosen top of instrument panel. Ensure short side clips release and go clear.
16. Lift out panel, then disconnect all instrument panel electrical connectors.
17. Open glove compartment, then open covers to remove retaining screws (19).
18. Remove other glove compartment retaining screws (20), retaining bolt and expanding rivet in front edge and remove catch from bulkhead bracket.
19. Remove glove compartment and disconnect electrical connector for glove compartment lamp (21).
20. Pull A-pillar rubber moldings away and remove pillar trim (3).
21. Remove lefthand and righthand speaker grilles (24) using screwdriver.
22. Pull sun sensor surround (25) slightly rearward, then lift to remove.
23. **On models equipped with ACC and/or alarm,** disconnect sun sensor and/or alarm electrical connector (26).
24. **On all models,** remove defroster cover retaining nut (27), then the defroster by lifting rear edge straight up, then move sideways to clear lugs on dashboard.
25. Remove main instrument panel retaining screws (29), then pull straight out. Disconnect electrical connector (30).
26. Snip cable ties to release wiring harness underneath dashboard (31). Cable tie on passenger side can be opened.
27. Remove lefthand floor duct, then the two fuse holder retaining screws and fuse holder. Let fuse holder hang down.
28. Remove dashboard retaining bolts from A pillar (34).
29. Press out heating control panel (35) and remove expanding rivets securing dashboard to center console. Press

about 3 mm into center pin, then remove.
30. Disconnect passenger side air bag electrical connector and nut securing stay (36).
31. Remove righthand and center air vent ducts.
32. Disconnect cable ties holding speaker wiring on righthand side, then the speaker connectors.
33. Remove retaining bolts from each side of speakers (39), then carefully remove dashboard.
34. Reverse procedure to install, noting the following:
    a. **Torque** passenger side air bag stay nut to 15 ft. lbs.
    b. When installing steering wheel, turn contact unit (coil spring) counterclockwise to end position, then back 2.5 turns.

9000

1. **On 1995–96 models,** obtain radio anti-theft code as outlined under "Precautions."
2. **On all models,** disconnect battery ground cable.
3. Remove speaker grilles, then instrument panel top trim panel.
4. Remove glove compartment, then the air vent.
5. Remove fuse panel retaining screws, then pull it forward.

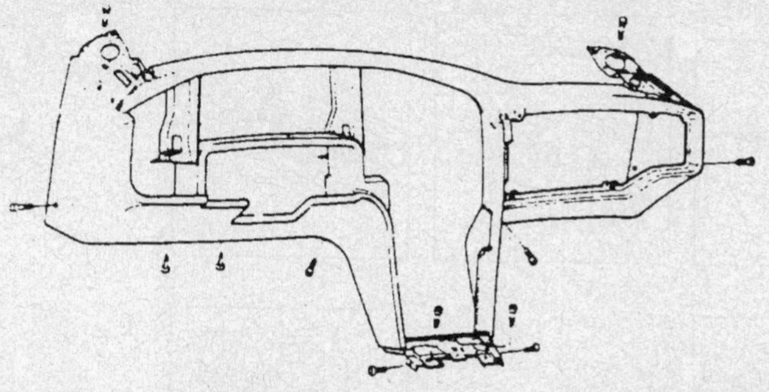
SA9149100003000X

Fig. 3 Instrument panel retaining bolt removal. 9000

6. Remove ashtray and ashtray housing.
7. Remove steering column trim covers, then instrument panel attaching bolts located behind steering wheel.
8. Lift rubber insulator around gearshift, then remove center console retaining screws.
9. Remove middle air vent from instrument panel.
10. **On models with standard A/C,** remove control panel as follows:
    a. Press in four control panel retaining clips.
    b. Pull panel out of instrument panel.
    c. Disconnect ball joint and link rod for air distribution.
    d. Remove gear housing for temperature control valve and disconnect all electrical connectors.
11. **On models with automatic climate control,** pull rearward on climate control unit. Remove panel vent and disconnect electrical connectors.
12. **On all models,** remove steering wheel.
13. Remove instrument panel to instrument cluster attaching screws.
14. Remove trim from under instrument panel.
15. Remove all instrument panel retaining screws, **Fig. 3.**
16. Remove instrument panel from vehicle.

Steering Columns

NOTE: On Air Bag Equipped Models, Refer To "Air Bag System Precautions" Located In The Front Of This Manual For System Disarming & Arming Procedures.

INDEX

	Page No.
Precautions	38-81
Air Bag Systems	38-81
Radio Anti-Theft Lock	38-81
Steering Column, Replace	38-81
900	38-81
9000	38-82
Steering Column Service	38-84
900	38-84
9000	38-84

PRECAUTIONS

AIR BAG SYSTEMS

Refer to "Air Bag System Precautions" in the front of this manual for system disarming and arming procedures.

RADIO ANTI-THEFT LOCK

9000

1995–96

Radio and cassette player are equipped with an electronic four-digit anti-theft lock. This four-digit code is programmed at manufacturing and cannot be changed. If the battery is disconnected for more than three minutes, if unit is removed or if otherwise cut off from power, the four-digit code must be entered with the quick-selection buttons as follows:

1. Turn radio on, then, when display shows "Code In," enter four-digit code with quick-selection buttons. If code is correct, last-tuned radio frequency is shown on display. If wrong digit has been entered by mistake, all four digits must be entered again. If code is wrong it stays on display.
2. If incorrect four-digit code has been entered, press Band button for more than three seconds to clear display. Display shows "Code In" and new attempt to enter correct code can be made.
3. If wrong code has been used three times in succession, four dashes appear on display and you must wait an hour with radio switched on before trying again.
4. To try again, hold Band button for at least three seconds. "Code In" should appear on display.
5. Correct code must be entered at first attempt, otherwise you must wait another hour with unit switched on before trying again.

STEERING COLUMN

REPLACE

900

1993

1. Remove radio and radio contact box.

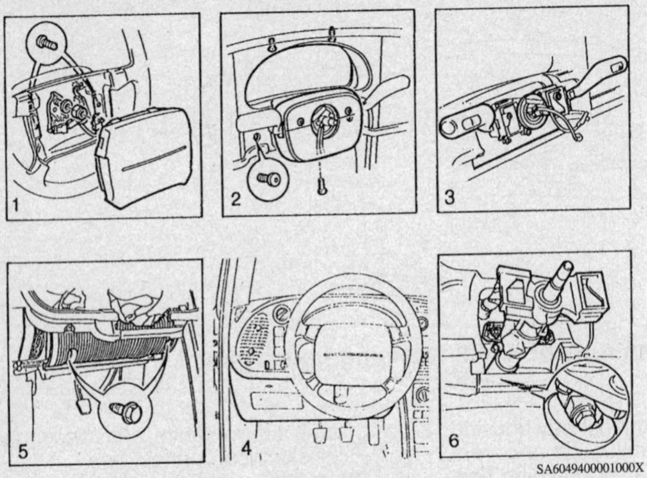
1
2
3
5
4
6
SA6049400001000X

Fig. 1 Steering column replacement. 1994–96 900

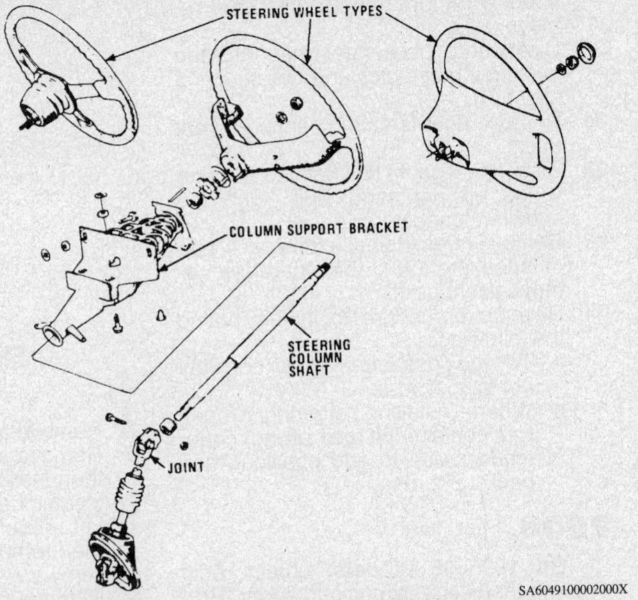
STEERING WHEEL TYPES
COLUMN SUPPORT BRACKET
STEERING COLUMN SHAFT
JOINT
SA6049100002000X

Fig. 2 Exploded view of steering column. 1993 900

2. Remove center console as follows:
   a. Remove rubber dust excluder between center console and gear lever, then the ashtray.
   b. Remove ashtray holder mounting screws, then the holder.
   c. Remove four center console lower mounting screws, then withdraw console slightly and remove two upper retaining screws.
   d. Remove center console.
3. Remove bottom steering column bearing cover, then the knee guard.
4. Remove floor air duct mounting screws, then place duct aside.
5. Remove steering wheel center pad (air bag module) mounting screws, then disconnect air bag electrical connector. Remove center pad.
6. Position front wheels in straight ahead position, then disconnect horn connector.
7. Remove steering wheel.
8. Remove holder for wiper and indicator stalk switches. Mark and remove switch connectors.
9. **On models equipped with cruise control,** disconnect cruise control connector.
10. **On all models,** remove cable ties holding wiring to steering column. Disconnect horn and contact unit electrical connector.
11. Remove wear guard on right side of steering column.
12. Unhook spring from pedal assembly and remove defroster hose.
13. Separate cruise control vacuum hose at T piece.
14. Remove nut and bolt from clamping joint on steering column shaft.
15. Remove steering column retaining bolts and washers. Lower steering column and withdraw it from intermediate steering column shaft.
16. Reverse removal procedure to install, noting the following:
   a. Coat steering column retaining bolts with Loctite and **torque** to 15-20 ft. lbs.
   b. **Torque** clamping joint bolt to 20-25 ft. lbs.
   c. Ensure front wheels are in straight ahead position.
   d. Set contact unit to center position by turning contact unit clockwise as far as possible, then turn it counterclockwise the number of turns indicated by yellow label on contact unit connecting cable.
   e. **Torque** steering wheel nut to 24-32 ft. lbs.
   f. **Torque** steering wheel center pad (air bag module) mounting screws to 4–5 ft. lbs.

1994-96

1. Remove steering wheel (1) as outlined under “Steering Wheel, Replace” under “Electrical.”
2. Remove upper and lower sections of steering wheel cowling (2), then the coil spring and two retaining screws (3), **Fig. 1.** Disconnect electrical connectors.
3. Remove all switches from steering column as well as the fixing cable from bearing housing.
4. Remove lower part of dashboard (4), then the two knee protection member retaining bolts and member (5).
5. Remove locking bolt from steering column shaft joint and lift joint off pinion shaft (6).
6. Remove steering column assembly retaining bolt above ventilation duct, then the retaining nuts under instrument panel.
7. Remove steering column assembly.
8. Reverse procedure to install, noting the following:
   a. After fitting steering column shaft joint onto pinion shaft, lock adjusting lever.
   b. **Torque** steering wheel nut to 22 ft. lbs.

9000

Removal

1. Remove left front door sill plate, then, using ignition switch, stop wipers at straight up position.
2. **On 1995–96 models,** obtain radio anti-theft code as outlined under “Precautions.”
3. **On all models,** disconnect battery ground cable, then remove A pillar trim.
4. Remove speaker grilles, then disconnect burglar alarm LED connector.
5. Disconnect sun sensor connector, located in the right speaker grille, then remove gaskets.
6. Remove eight screws from top of dash panel. One screw is located behind rubber plug inside glove compartment door.
7. Remove glove compartment as follows:
   a. Drop glove compartment door to its lower position by prying out hinge arms to release stop cleats.
   b. Remove glove compartment retaining screws.
   c. Pull out glove compartment together with right ventilation air outlet. Pry outlet out carefully with screwdriver. Note positions of clips. Disconnect cable from glove compartment light and light switch.
8. Remove electrical distribution box mounting screw, then position box aside.
9. Remove ashtray, then bend down two locking tabs at top of ashtray holding. Pull out holder and disconnect electrical connectors.
10. Remove lower radio basket and disconnect electrical connections.
11. Remove upper radio basket and disconnect antenna cable and electrical connections.
12. Press out ACC control unit and disconnect connectors.
13. Remove steering wheel center pad (air bag module) mounting screws, then disconnect air bag electrical connector and remove center pad.

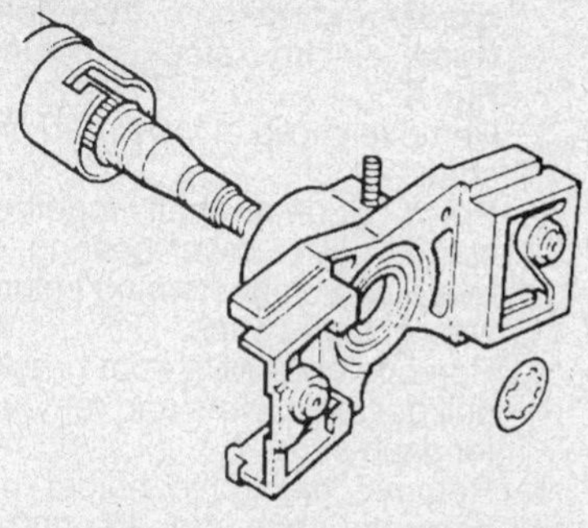
SA6049400003000X

Fig. 3 Bearing housing & bolt replacement. 1994–96 900

14. Position wheels in straight ahead position, then disconnect horn connector.
15. Remove steering wheel, then the top and bottom steering column covers.
16. Remove cover plates over interior temperature sensor and unused openings.
17. Carefully pry at edges of interior temperature sensor while pressing it inward.
18. Press out all switches and disconnect connectors.
19. Remove clock/DCC instrument, then disconnect connectors.
20. Remove direction indicator/light switch upper connector, then the washer/wiper switch connector. Remove stalk switches, then the two remaining direction indicator/light switch connectors.
21. Remove instrument panel as follows:
    a. Remove five instrument panel retaining screws, then the cover plate around gearshaft lever. One instrument panel screw is located under the rubber cover at gearshaft lever.
    b. Pull out instrument panel slightly, then carefully pry up plastic catches locking panel to middle ventilation air outlet.
    c. Lift out panel in middle and pull it out of bracket at outer side.
22. Cut straps and separate connectors from horn and contact unit (coil spring).
23. Remove contact unit mounting screws, then the contact unit.
24. Remove stalk switch holder.
25. Remove instrument cluster (combined instrument) as follows:
    a. Remove cluster mounting screws.
    b. Remove hose to boost pressure gauge and turn cluster so its glass faces windshield.
    c. Remove connectors and rubber supports from cluster and lift out.
26. Remove left and right sound baffles, floor ducts and carpeted center console panels.
27. Remove screws holding side defroster outlets to dash panel, then disconnect speaker leads.
28. Remove burglar alarm control unit from panel and leave it hanging by its cables.
29. Remove dash panel retaining screws. Two screws are located under plastic cover on center console. Cut straps holding safety cable to panel.
30. Place gearshift lever in reverse position and carefully move lower part of dash panel. Move gearshift lever forward and lift dash panel out of vehicle.
31. Cut strap and remove left air duct, then the left ventilation air outlet.
32. Remove inner part of left ventilation air outlet.
33. Remove defroster outlet for left of windshield, then position wiring harness on left side of steering column aside.
34. Disconnect connector from ignition switch and remove strap securing cable. Remove strap securing wiring harness to right side of steering column.
35. Disconnect clamped joint and remove screw between universal joint and intermediate shaft.
36. Remove safety cable from bracket on tunnel. Detach cable from retainer on other side.
37. Remove holder for wiring harness, then the metal clips between steering column and dash panel crossmember. These clips do not have to be reinstalled.
38. Remove two screws holding electronic holder on steering column.
39. From engine compartment, remove cover from left portion of firewall space.
40. Lift plastic casing and remove clip holding ABS control unit. Remove strap and cable, then position control unit aside.

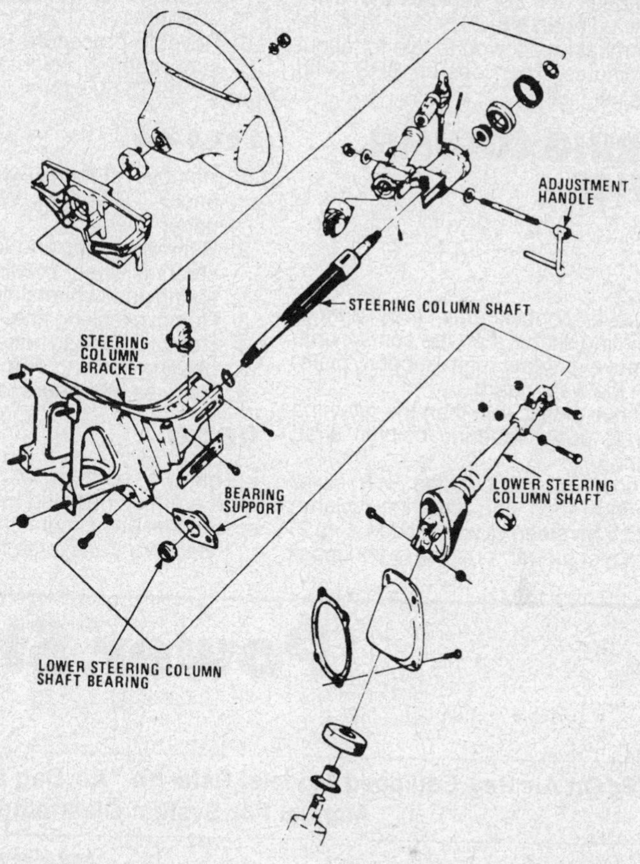
ADJUSTMENT HANDLE
STEERING COLUMN SHAFT
STEERING COLUMN BRACKET
BEARING SUPPORT
LOWER STEERING COLUMN SHAFT
LOWER STEERING COLUMN SHAFT BEARING
SA6049100004000X

Fig. 4 Exploded view of steering column. 9000

41. Position ABS electrical distribution box aside. Remove ABS control unit mounting bracket and position LH control unit aside.
42. Pry off plastic bushing that holds link rod to left wiper spindle, then remove steering column mounting nuts.
43. Disengage vacuum hose from steering column and lift column out of vehicle. Note location of washers.

Installation

Reverse removal procedure to install, noting the following:

1. **Torque** standard steering column nuts to 15–20 ft. lbs. and green chromated nuts to 11-16 ft. lbs.
2. Adjust clearance between upper intermediate shaft universal joint and steering column .118–.197 inch (3–5 mm), then **torque** universal joint bolt to 17-22 ft. lbs.
3. **Torque** safety cable to 1 ft. lbs.
4. Adjust contact unit (coil spring) as follows:
    a. Ensure front wheels are in straight ahead position.
    b. Rotate contact unit counterclockwise to end position. Then rotate it clockwise about 3½ turns.
5. **Torque** steering wheel nut to 22 ft. lbs.
6. **Torque** air bag module to 4–5 ft. lbs.
7. Start vehicle. Ensure SRS lamp illuminates for approximately 6 seconds

then goes out. For vehicles with electronic unit part No. 9124074, then engine must be allowed to idle for about 15 minutes. Then ensure SRS lamp does not flash.

STEERING COLUMN SERVICE

900

1993

1. Remove contact unit (coil spring) mounting screw, then the contact unit.
2. Remove contact unit support plate, then the wear guard.
3. Remove plastic nut, then the retaining ring at upper steering column shaft bearing.
4. Remove rubber bushing with lower bearing, then the steering column shaft from steering wheel cage, **Fig. 2.**
5. Remove rubber bushing with upper steering column shaft bearing and washer.
6. Reverse procedure to assemble. Ensure steering column shaft length is 16.42–16.50 inch.

1994–96

1. Remove steering wheel as outlined under "Steering Wheel, Replace" under "Electrical."
2. Remove upper and lower sections of steering wheel cowling, then the coil spring and two retaining screws.
3. Remove locking ring.
4. Remove bearing housing bolt, then the bearing housing, **Fig. 3.**
5. Reverse procedure to install.

9000

The two sections of steering column shaft are matched and must not be pulled apart under any circumstances.

1. Remove transverse bolt together with spacer and washers, then detach universal joint from steering column shaft, **Fig. 4.**
2. Remove circlip at lower end of column shaft.
3. Press column shaft together so it comes out of lower bearing, then remove complete steering column shaft with ignition switch.
4. Remove slide rails from bracket, then drill out blind rivets and remove holder for dash panel.
5. Remove electronic holder mounting brackets, then the steering column shaft bearing housing and clip for vacuum tube.
6. Drill out blind rivets that hold knee guard, then remove knee guard with safety cable.
7. Reverse procedure to assemble, noting the following:
   a. **Torque** universal joint to 17-22 ft. lbs.
   b. **Torque** transverse bolt to 15 ft. lbs.

Power Steering

NOTE: On Air Bag Equipped Models, Refer To "Air Bag System Precautions" Located In The Front Of This Manual For System Disarming & Arming Procedures.

INDEX

	Page No.
Power Steering System Service	38-84
Power Steering Gear Service	38-84
Precautions	38-84
Air Bag Systems	38-84

PRECAUTIONS

AIR BAG SYSTEMS

Refer to "Air Bag System Precautions" in the front of this manual for system disarming and arming procedures.

POWER STEERING SYSTEM SERVICE

POWER STEERING GEAR SERVICE

900

1993

1. Remove locknuts and tie rod ends.
2. Remove rubber bellows and breather tube, **Fig. 1.**
3. Disconnect hydraulic lines between steering valve and hydraulic cylinder from steering gear.
4. Remove radial adjustment locknut from rack and remove adjusting plug and spring.
5. Tap steering knuckle housing carefully against workbench to remove bearing piston.
6. Remove cover under steering valve and remove nut on shaft. **Use an 11⁄16 inch socket or soft jawed vise to grip top of steering valve shaft.**
7. Remove dust cover snap ring from upper end of steering valve.
8. Press steering valve out of steering gear housing. The needle bearing, bearing support, hydraulic seal, and dust cover will come free with valve. **Knocking or tapping valve unit may result in damage.**
9. Remove inner ball joint furthest from pinion as follows:
   a. Clamp rack in soft jawed vise.
   b. Push plastic sleeve (end stop) covering ball joint's flats out of way.
   c. Unscrew ball joint.
10. Remove snap ring from end of hydraulic cylinder as follows:
    a. Push rack as far toward hydraulic cylinder as possible.
    b. Install sleeve tool No. 8996407, or equivalent, over rack, and press in spring seal housing by screwing in inner ball joint.
    c. Press in wire end of snap ring through small hole in steering gear housing.
    d. Pry off snap ring using two screwdrivers or wire hook made from a 1 mm piano wire.
    e. Remove ball joint and sleeve tool.
11. Remove ball joint nearest pinion.
12. Press out rack together with hydraulic seal, washer and bushing. **Before removing bushing and hydraulic seal from rack, remove any burrs on end of rack using fine file.**
13. Remove inner rack seal using seal removal tool No. 8996399, or equivalent, and long drift.
14. Remove snap ring and lower pinion bearing.
15. Remove sealing ring and bushing on top of pinion. **Lubricate pinion, rack teeth, bearing and dust cover seal with 2.1 oz. (60 g) of lithium grease equivalent to Shell EP2, B2, Code 71303. Lubricate hydraulic components with Texaco power steering fluid 4634, part No. (45) 3009800 or equivalent.**
16. Install lower pinion bearing and snap ring. **Enclosed side of bearing should face down. Chamfer of snap ring should face out.**
17. Install upper bushing for pinion and hydraulic seal using sleeve tool No. 8996407, or equivalent. **Do not apply force greater than 38 lbs. per sq. inch.**

18. Install inner hydraulic seal to rack. Prevent sealing lip from being damaged by rack teeth using sleeve No. 8995938, or equivalent.
19. Install rack in housing, then press in inner hydraulic seal using rack pinion, using care not to apply force greater than 32 lbs. per sq. inch. **Avoid withdrawing rack too far after inner seal has been fitted.**
20. Install bushing in cylinder with small bore facing inward. Install washer against bushing.
21. Install new O-ring on outer hydraulic seal support. Inspect old seal and install if free of defects. If seal is to be replaced, install using sleeve tool No. 8996407, or equivalent.
22. Slide sealing ring support carefully onto rack and avoid damaging sealing lip. Press in sealing ring support using sleeve tool No. 8390148, or equivalent.
23. Push in rack so it extends same amount on both sides. Rotate rack so pinion meshes in teeth.
24. Assemble steering gear as follows:
    a. Hold valve unit so groove in end of shaft (for tensioning screw) points toward left at 9 o'clock position in relation to direction of movement of vehicle when pinion engages rack.
    b. Insert pinion. Valve unit should then rotate so groove in end of shaft in withdrawn position, points to front (12 o'clock when rack is centralized).
25. Install nut at pinion. Grip top end of shaft using an 11⁄16 inch socket or soft-jawed vise. **Torque** nut to 22–34 ft. lbs.
26. Install cover, washer, needle bearing, sealing ring, dust cover and snap ring at top of steering valve. Protect sealing lips using protective sleeve of plastic film or metal foil. Use sleeve tool No. 7841067, or equivalent, to insert seal.
27. Install radial bearing piston, then the spring and adjusting plug. **To set radial adjustment, screw adjusting plug all way down (clockwise), then back off (counterclockwise) 30°–50°.**
28. **Torque** locknut to 48–55 ft. lbs. Install new seal using sleeve tool No. 8996407, or equivalent.
29. Slide on plastic sleeves (end stops), then install inner ball joints and tie rods onto rack ends. Install rack in soft vise and **torque** ball joints to 59–72 ft. lbs. **Torsional force should not be exerted on pinion.**
30. Lock inner ball joints by driving flange into two surfaces of rack using drift. **If old joint is to be reused, previous locking mark must be offset 90°. Install shim, Fig. 2, between joint and shoulder of rack.**
31. Install snap ring for sealing ring support in end of hydraulic cylinder:
    a. Using an 11⁄16 inch socket, turn pinion so inner ball joint presses against sealing ring support.
    b. Press in support and, at same time, install sealing ring in groove using thin screwdriver.
32. Install rubber bellows and breather tube between two.

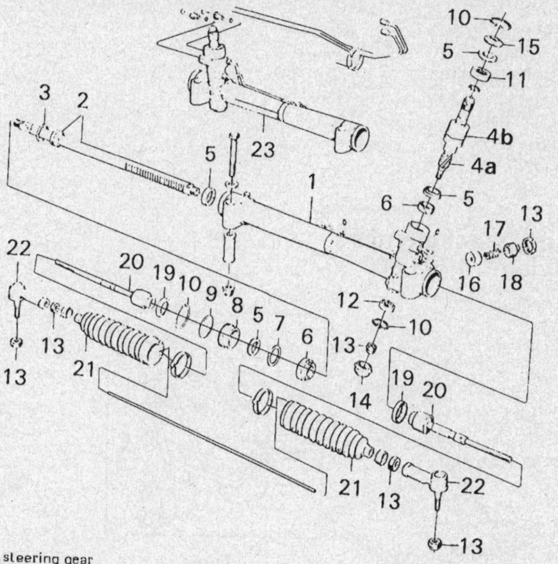

10
5
15
11
3
2
5
23
4b
4a
1
6
5
13
17
22
20
19
10
9
8
5
7
6
16
18
12
10
13
13
21
13
14
19
20
21
13
22
13

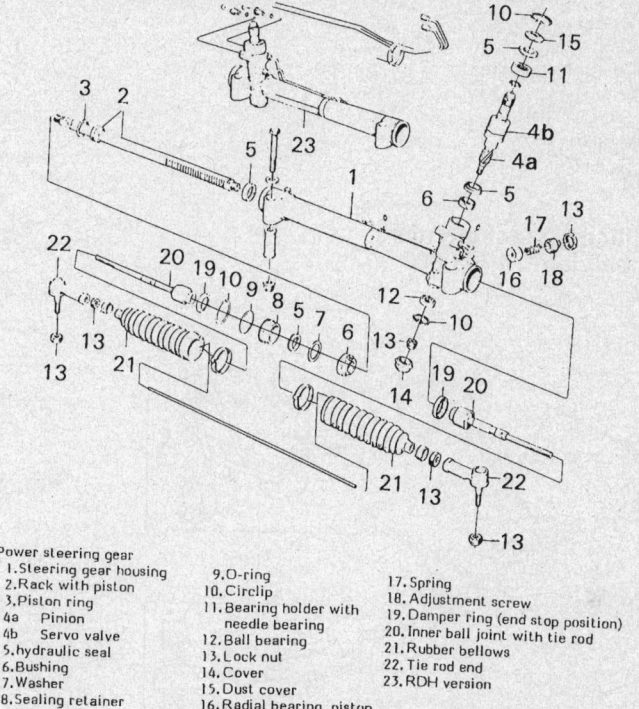

Power steering gear
1. Steering gear housing
2. Rack with piston
3. Piston ring
4a Pinion
4b Servo valve
5. hydraulic seal
6. Bushing
7. Washer
8. Sealing retainer
9. O-ring
10. Circlip
11. Bearing holder with needle bearing
12. Ball bearing
13. Lock nut
14. Cover
15. Dust cover
16. Radial bearing, piston
17. Spring
18. Adjustment screw
19. Damper ring (end stop position)
20. Inner ball joint with tie rod
21. Rubber bellows
22. Tie rod end
23. RDH version

SA6029100001000X

Fig. 1 Exploded view of power steering gear assembly. 1993 900

33. Install hydraulic lines between steering valve and hydraulic cylinder, **torquing** to 14–22 ft. lbs.
34. Install tie rod ends and **torque** lock-nuts to 44–60 ft. lbs.

1994-96

1. Remove hose connected to return pipe on steering system, then plug hose.
2. Fit length of hose onto pipe and replace other end in suitable container that will hold at least .53 quarts.
3. Turn steering wheel to full left lock and full right lock until all fluid has runout of steering system.
4. Remove hose from return pipe and install return hose.
5. Disconnect battery ground cable, then remove main fuse box.
6. Remove lower section of lefthand dashboard.
7. Remove bolt from joint on steering column shaft (1), **Fig. 3,** then turn steering wheel to straight-ahead position.
8. Fix steering wheel so it will not move out of this position. If steering wheel moves, coil spring may twist and break. One method is to tape steering wheel to dashboard with suitable heavy-duty fabric adhesive tape.
9. Separate joint on steering column shaft from steering gear, then remove track rod from steering gear (2).
10. Raise and support vehicle, then remove front lefthand wheel.
11. Remove track rod from MacPherson strut using puller tool No. 89 96 696, or equivalent, to press out ball joint (3).
12. Lift out track rod and lower vehicle to floor.
13. Remove fixing clamps from both sides (4).
14. Disconnect delivery and return pipes from steering gear (5), using steering system hydraulic pipe wrench tool No. 87 91 287, or equivalent. Plug pipes and connections on valve body and note cable holder on righthand side.
15. Disconnect both internal pipe connections from valve body and bend upward. Plug pipes and connections.
16. Remove steering gear through lefthand wheel housing.
17. Move bulkhead seal and rubber bushes on both sides away from valve body if installing new steering gear.
18. Disconnect internal pipes from steering gear and plug them if installing new steering gear.
19. Lift steering gear into place through lefthand wheel housing.
20. Remove plugs and connect pipes to valve body.
21. Remove plugs and connect delivery and return pipes using steering system hydraulic wrench tool No. 87 91 287, or equivalent.
22. Mount fixing clamps on both sides. Note cable holder on righthand side.
23. Install track rod to steering swivel member, then **torque** connection to 44 ft. lbs.
24. Install both track rods to steering gear and **torque** connections to 68 ft. lbs.
25. Install steering column shaft joint to steering gear, then remove tape holding steering wheel in position. **If steering wheel has moved, coil spring must be readjusted. Refer to "Passive Restraints."**

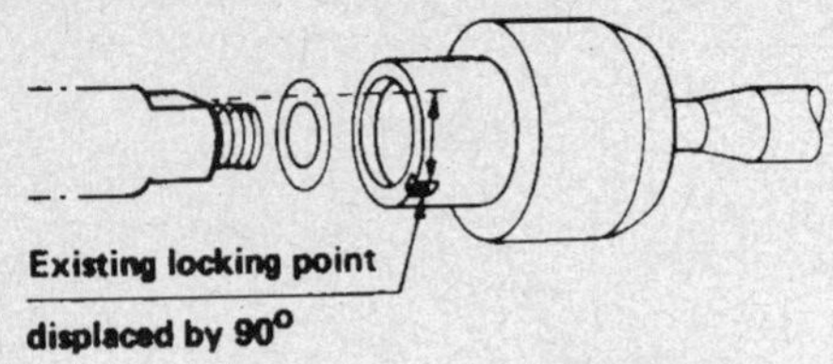
Existing locking point
displaced by 90°

SA6029100002000X

Fig. 2 Positioning locking mark on inner ball joint. 1993 900

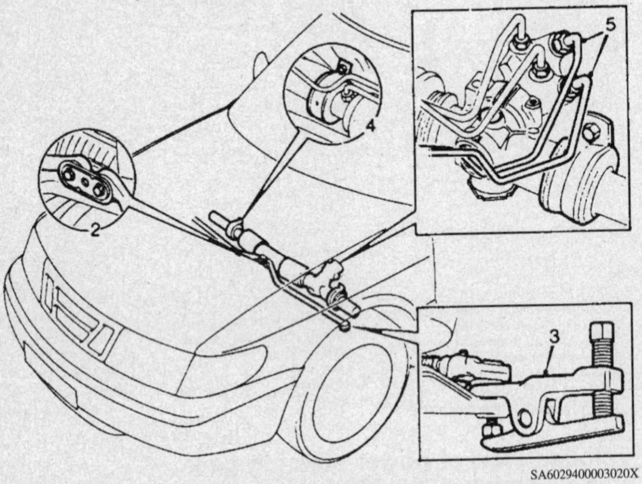
5
4
2
3

SA6029400003020X

Fig. 3 Power steering gear removal (Part 2 of 2). 1994–96 900

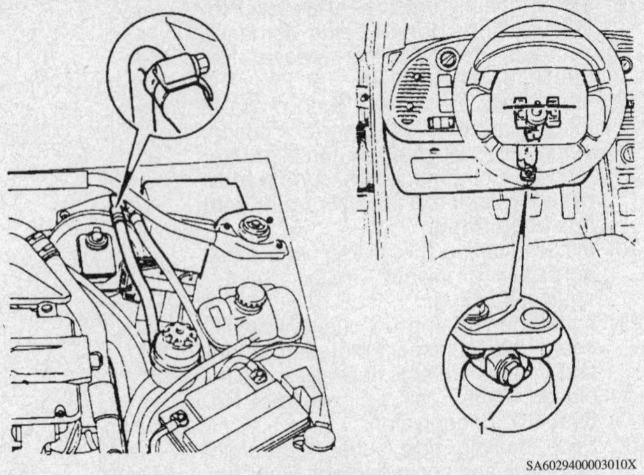
1

SA6029400003010X

Fig. 3 Power steering gear removal (Part 1 of 2). 1994–96 900

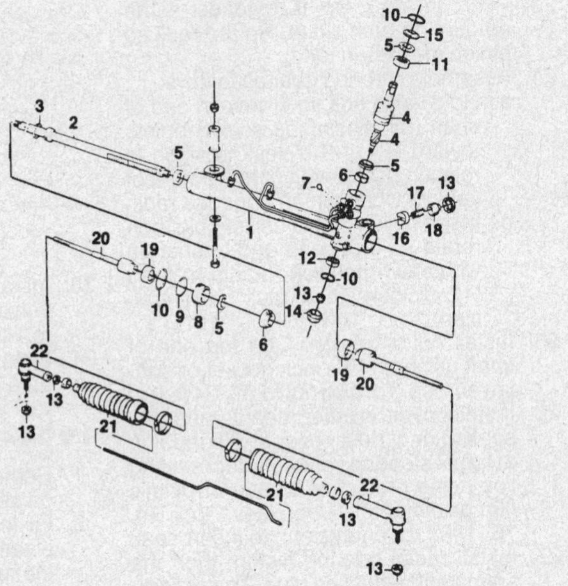

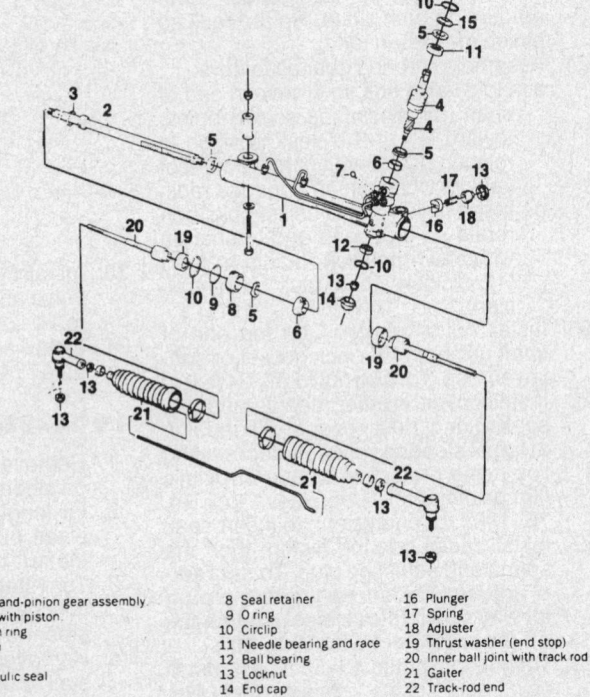

1 Rack-and-pinion gear assembly
2 Rack with piston
3 Piston ring
4a Pinion
4b Valve
5 Hydraulic seal
6 Bush
7 O ring
8 Seal retainer
9 O ring
10 Circlip
11 Needle bearing and race
12 Ball bearing
13 Locknut
14 End cap
15 Dust cap
16 Plunger
17 Spring
18 Adjuster
19 Thrust washer (end stop)
20 Inner ball joint with track rod
21 Gaiter
22 Track-rod end

SA6029100004000X

Fig. 4 Exploded view of power steering gear assembly. 9000

26. Install lower lefthand section of dashboard.
27. Install main fuse box, then connect battery ground cable.
28. Fill hydraulic fluid reservoir with hydraulic fluid, then start engine.
29. Turn steering wheel two or three times from full lock to full lock. Switch off engine and top off fluid reservoir.
30. Install wheel, then lower vehicle.
31. Check toe-in and adjust if necessary.

9000

1. Thoroughly clean rack and pinion gear.
2. Loosen locknuts, then remove tie rod ends.
3. Remove boots and pressure equalizing pipe, **Fig. 4.**
4. Disconnect and cap all hydraulic lines.
5. Loosen rack radial adjuster locknut, then remove plunger and spring.
6. Tap rack and pinion gear gently to free plunger. Plunger may also be removed using snap ring pliers.
7. Remove cover from valve bottom.
8. Remove nut from shaft. **Use an 9/16 inch open end wrench to hold valve shaft.**
9. Remove snap ring from upper end of valve.
10. Using sleeve and support tools Nos. 8790644 and 8391849, or equivalents, press out control valve. **Do not attempt to remove valve by tapping or knocking it out.**
11. Remove righthand side inner ball joint as follows:
    a. Clamp rack into vise.
    b. Slide back thrust washer from ball joint flats.
    c. Using crow's foot wrench tool No. 89966480, or equivalent, loosen ball joint. **Never hold pinion when loosening or tightening ball joint.**
12. Remove snap ring from hydraulic cylinder end, using drift to depress snap ring.
13. Remove lefthand side inner ball joint in same manner.
14. Withdraw rack completely with hydraulic seal and bushing attached.
15. Using seal removal tool No. 8996399, or equivalent, and drift, remove inner hydraulic seal.
16. Remove snap ring and lower pinion bearing.
17. Remove sealing ring and bushing from other end of pinion. **Lubricate pinion, rack teeth, bearing and dust seal with 2.1 oz. (60 g.) of lithium grease equivalent to Shell EP, B2, Code 71303. Lubricate hydraulic components using Saginaw hydraulic fluid or equivalent.**
18. Install lower pinion bearing.
19. Using sleeve tool No. 8996407, or equivalent, install upper bushing and hydraulic seal. **Do not exceed force of 118 lbs., when install bushing and hydraulic seal.**
20. Using sleeve tool No. 8995938, or equivalent, install inner hydraulic seal

5into rack. **Use caution not to damage sealing lip.**

21. Install rack into housing and press inner hydraulic seal into position using rack piston. **Do not exceed of force of 100 lbs. when installing rack. If excessive force is used, piston may separate from rack assembly. Ensure not to withdraw rack too far after the inner seal has been installed or damage to inner sealing ring will result.**
22. Install new O-ring onto seal retainer and check hydraulic seal, then install seal if it is free of defects. If seal is to be replaced, install using sleeve tool No. 8996407, or equivalent.
23. Install seal retainer onto rack. **Use caution not to damage sealing lip.**
24. Insert rack so equal length protrudes at either end. Twist rack until pinion teeth mesh with those on rack.
25. Install control valve as follows:
    a. Hold valve body with slot in end of strut pointing to left as teeth are enmeshed.
    b. Insert pinion and rotate valve body so slot in end of the shaft is pointing forward when shaft is inserted.
26. Install locknut and cover. **Torque** locknut to 21–32 ft. lbs.
27. Install bearing race and needle bearing, hydraulic seal, duct cap and snap ring onto upper end of control valve.
28. Install plunger, spring, adjusting screw and locknut onto radial adjuster.
29. Adjust adjusting screw as follows:
    a. Turn adjusting screw completely inward.
    b. Back off adjusting screw 40–60°.
    c. Tighten adjusting screw locknut.
    d. **Torque** locknut to 47–54 ft. lbs.
30. Clamp rack assembly into vise, then slide thrust washers into position and install inner ball joints complete with track rods. Clamp toothed end of rack into vise.
31. When installing ball joints, special washer must be installed which will move slot through 90°, **Fig. 2.**
32. Using crowsfoot wrench tool No. 8996480, or equivalent, and torque wrench, **torque** ball joint to 58–73 ft. lbs.
33. Secure inner ball joints by tapping tabs against two flats on rack.
34. Install snap ring seal retainer at end of hydraulic cylinder.
35. Install rubber boots and ventilation pipe.
36. Connect hydraulic lines between control valve and hydraulic cylinder.
37. **Torque** line fittings to 15–21 ft. lbs.
38. Install locknuts and tie rod ends. **Torque** locknuts to 46–56 ft. lbs.

Disc Brakes

INDEX

	Page No.
Adjustments	38-90
Parking Brake	38-90
Parking Brake Cable Equalization	38-90
Parking Brake Shoes	38-90
Brake Pad Service	38-87
Front	38-87
Rear	38-88
Caliper Service	38-88
Caliper Overhaul	38-89
Front	38-89
Rear	38-90
Caliper, Replace	38-88
Front	38-88
Rear	38-88
Disc Brake Specifications	38-91
Precautions	38-87
Air Bag Systems	38-87
Radio Anti-Theft Lock	38-87
Tightening Specifications	38-91

PRECAUTIONS

AIR BAG SYSTEMS

Refer to "Air Bag System Precautions" in the front of this manual for system disarming and arming procedures.

RADIO ANTI-THEFT LOCK

9000

1995–96

Radio and cassette player are equipped with an electronic four-digit anti-theft lock. This four-digit code is programmed at manufacturing and cannot be changed. If the battery is disconnected for more than three minutes, if unit is removed or if otherwise cut off from power, the four-digit code must be entered with the quick-selection buttons as follows:

1. Turn radio on, then, when display shows "Code In, " enter four-digit code with quick-selection buttons. If code is correct, last-tuned radio frequency is shown on display. If wrong digit has been entered by mistake, all four digits must be entered again. If code is wrong it stays on display.
2. If incorrect four-digit code has been entered, press Band button for more than three seconds to clear display. Display shows "Code In" and new attempt to enter correct code can be made.
3. If wrong code has been used three times in succession, four dashes appear on display and you must wait an hour with radio switched on before trying again.
4. To try again, hold Band button for at least three seconds. "Code In" should appear on display.
5. Correct code must be entered at first attempt, otherwise you must wait another hour with unit switched on before trying again.

BRAKE PAD SERVICE

FRONT

900

1993

1. Raise and support vehicle, then remove front wheels.
2. Using pliers, simultaneously push in brake piston and press caliper outward to release pads from rotor.
3. Remove upper guide pin bolt, **Fig. 1.**
4. Pivot caliper downward, then remove brake pads.
5. Reverse procedure to install, noting the following:
    a. Clean surfaces between pads and carrier.
    b. Press pistons fully into bores, taking care not to damage dust boots.
    c. Ensure guide pins slide freely and dust covers are in good condition.
    d. Pump brake pedal to move pads to operating positions. **Do not move vehicle until brakes are operating properly.**

1994–96

Because the brakes are self-adjusting, it is impossible to tell from the brake pedal stroke whether the linings are worn. The lining thickness should be checked at specified intervals as outlined in "Vehicle Maintenance Schedule" section.

When vehicle is serviced, the brake pads must be replaced before lining thickness falls below .2 inches (5 mm).

1. Raise and support vehicle, then remove wheel.
2. Press piston back with suitable pliers (1), then remove clip from caliper (2), **Fig. 2.**
3. Remove dust caps from guide pins, then the guide pins (3).
4. Lift brake caliper off brake disc and bind it in spring strut with tie.

5. Remove brake pads (4).
6. Reverse procedure to install, noting the following:
   a. Clean inside of brake caliper with soft metal brush and check dust covers.
   b. Tighten guide brake caliper pins and wheel studs to specifications.
   c. After lowering vehicle, press out brake pads by depressing brake pedal.
   d. Check brake fluid and correct if necessary.

9000

1. Raise and support vehicle, then remove front wheels.
2. Remove dust caps, **Fig. 3,** then both guide pin bolts, using a 7 mm Allen wrench or hex bit adapter.
3. Remove pad retainer, then the caliper and pads.
4. Reverse procedure to install brake pads, noting the following:
   a. Clean surfaces between pads and carrier.
   b. Press pistons fully into bores, taking care not to damage dust boots.
   c. Ensure guide pins slide freely and dust covers are in good condition.
   d. Pump brake pedal to move pads to operating positions. **Do not move vehicle until brakes are operating properly.**

REAR

900

1993

1. Raise and support vehicle, then remove rear wheels.
2. Ensure parking brake is released, then remove pad retainer, **Fig. 4.**
3. Remove parking brake cable from lever.
4. Remove plug for adjusting screw, then back off adjusting screw so pads clear rotor.
5. Remove dust caps, then remove guide pin bolts.
6. Remove caliper, then the brake pads.
7. Reverse procedure to install, noting the following:
   a. Clean surfaces between pads and carrier.
   b. Press pistons fully into bores, taking care not to damage dust boots.
   c. Ensure guide pins slide freely and dust covers are in good condition.
   d. Tighten guide pin bolts to specifications.
   e. Turn adjusting screw in until rotor is locked, then back off adjusting screw ¼– ½ turn. **Ensure rotor turns freely.**
   f. Ensure clearance between parking brake lever and stop is .04±.02 inch (1±.5 mm).
   g. Adjust parking brake as necessary.

1994-96

Because the brakes are self-adjusting, it is impossible to tell from the brake pedal stroke if the linings are worn. The lining thickness should be checked at specified intervals as outlined in "Vehicle Maintenance Schedule" section.

When vehicle is serviced, the brake pads must be replaced before lining thickness falls below .2 inches (5 mm).

Refer to **Fig. 5** when replacing rear brake pads.

1. Raise and support vehicle, then remove wheel.
2. Press pistons back with suitable pliers (1), then remove pins and keep lock spring (2).
3. Remove brake pads. If pads are jammed, use brake pad remover tool No. 89 95 771, or equivalent (3), to remove.
4. Reverse procedure to install, noting the following:
   a. Clean surfaces where brake pads are in contact with brake caliper using soft metal brush, then check dust covers.
   b. Tighten wheel studs to specifications.
   c. Adjust brake pad clearance by fully depressing brake pedal several times.
   d. Check brake fluid level and correct if necessary.

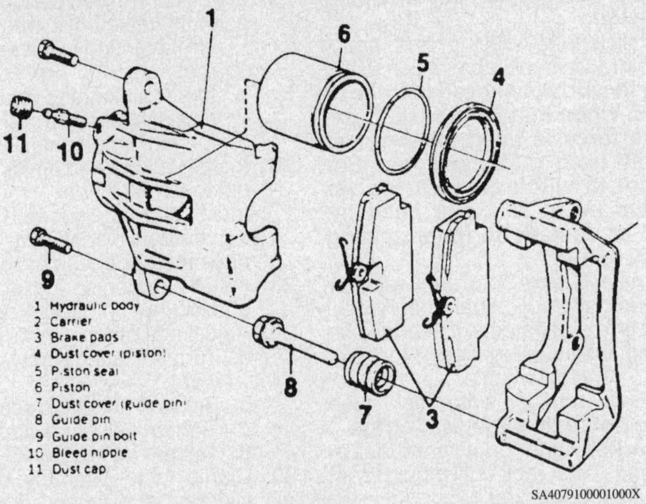
1
6
5
4
11
10
9
8
7
3
1 Hydraulic body
2 Carrier
3 Brake pads
4 Dust cover (piston)
5 Piston seal
6 Piston
7 Dust cover (guide pin)
8 Guide pin
9 Guide pin bolt
10 Bleed nipple
11 Dust cap
SA4079100001000X

Fig. 1 Exploded view of front disc brake caliper. 1993 900

9000

1. Raise and support vehicle, then remove rear wheels.
2. Ensure parking brake is released, then remove pad retainer, **Fig. 4.**
3. Remove parking brake cable from lever.
4. Remove both guide pin bolts.
5. Remove caliper, then the brake pads.
6. Reverse procedure to install, noting the following:
   a. Clean surfaces between pads and carrier.
   b. Remove plug from adjusting screw and retract piston by turning adjusting screw.
   c. Ensure guide pins slide freely and dust covers are in good condition.
   d. Turn adjusting screw in until rotor is locked, then back off adjusting screw ¼– ½ turn. **Ensure rotor turns freely.**
   e. Ensure clearance between parking brake lever and stop is .04±.02 inch (1±.5 mm).
   f. Adjust parking brake as necessary.

CALIPER SERVICE

Caliper, Replace

FRONT

900

1. Remove brake pads as outlined previously.
2. Loosen brake hose at caliper.
3. Press brake pedal fully to floor and secure in that position.
4. Remove upper guide pin bolt, then disconnect brake hose at caliper and plug hose and fitting.
5. Remove caliper.
6. Reverse procedure to install and bleed brake system.

9000

1. Remove brake pads as outlined previously.
2. Loosen brake hose at caliper.
3. Press brake pedal fully to the floor and secure in that position.
4. Disconnect brake hose at caliper and plug hose and fitting.
5. Remove caliper.
6. Reverse procedure to install. Bleed brake system.

REAR

900

1993

1. Remove brake pads as previously outlined.
2. Disconnect brake hose at caliper and plug hose and fitting.
3. Remove caliper.
4. Reverse procedure to install and bleed brake system.

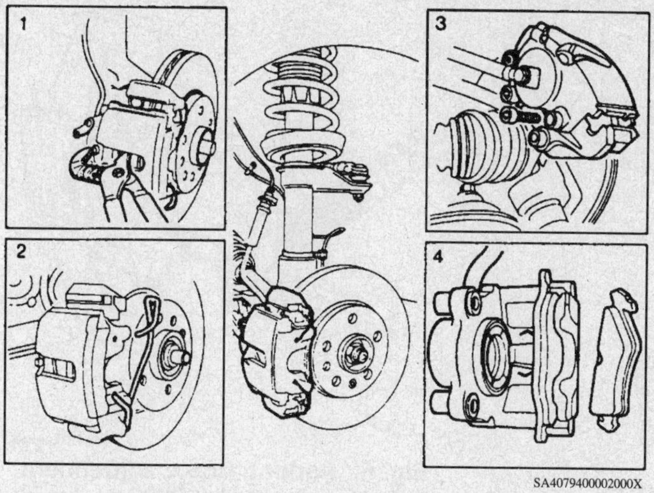
1
2
3
4
SA4079400002000X

Fig. 2 Front brake pad replacement. 1994-96 900

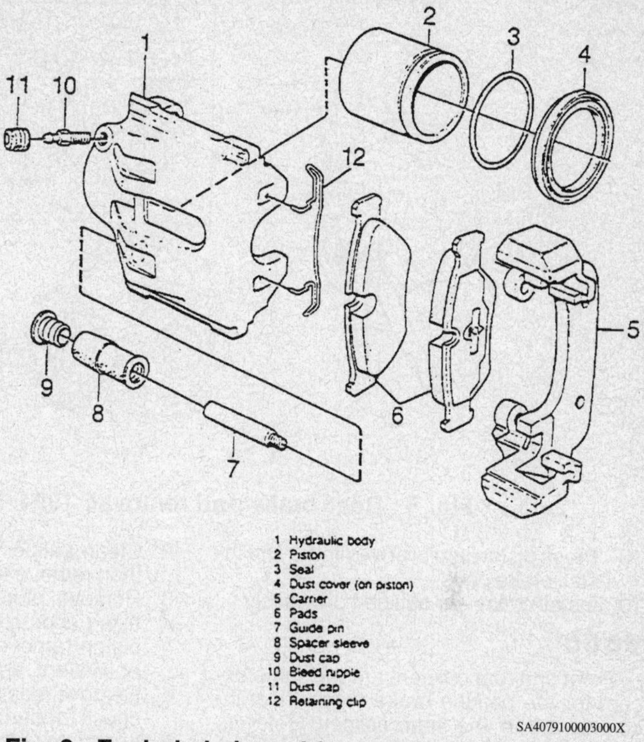
1 Hydraulic body
2 Piston
3 Seal
4 Dust cover (on piston)
5 Carrier
6 Pads
7 Guide pin
8 Spacer sleeve
9 Dust cap
10 Bleed nipple
11 Dust cap
12 Retaining clip
SA4079100003000X

Fig. 3 Exploded view of front disc brake caliper. 9000

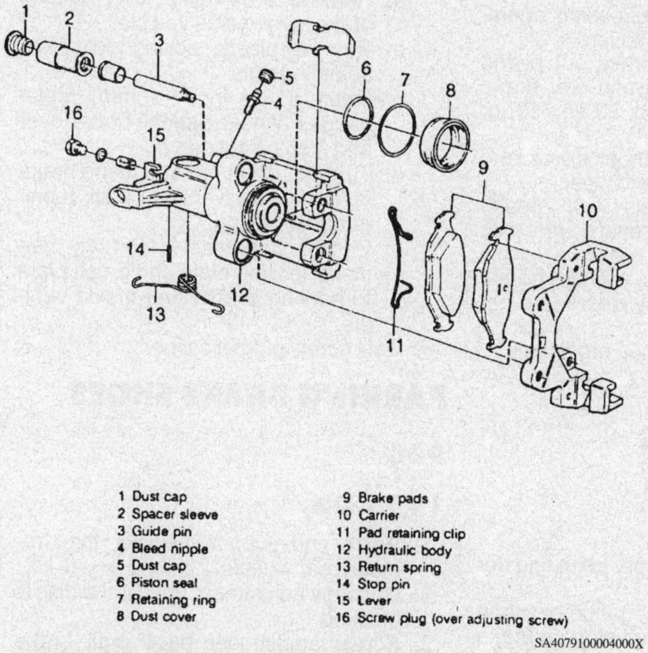
1 Dust cap
2 Spacer sleeve
3 Guide pin
4 Bleed nipple
5 Dust cap
6 Piston seal
7 Retaining ring
8 Dust cover
9 Brake pads
10 Carrier
11 Pad retaining clip
12 Hydraulic body
13 Return spring
14 Stop pin
15 Lever
16 Screw plug (over adjusting screw)
SA4079100004000X

Fig. 4 Exploded view of rear disc brake caliper

5. Adjust parking brake as necessary.

1994-96

1. Raise and support vehicle, then remove wheel.
2. Press out brake pistons with suitable pliers.
3. Depress brake pedal with brake clamp.
4. Disconnect brake pipe from brake caliper, then plug pipes and brake caliper.
5. Remove pins and locking spring, then the brake pads.
6. Remove two brake caliper securing bolts, then the caliper.
7. Reverse procedure to install, noting the following:
   a. Bleed brake system as outlined under "Hydraulic Brake Systems."
   b. Tighten wheel studs to specifications.

9000

1. Remove brake pads as outlined previously.
2. Disconnect brake hose at caliper and plug hose and fitting.
3. Remove caliper.
4. Reverse procedure to install, noting the following:
   a. Bleed brake system.
   b. Adjust parking brake as necessary.

Caliper Overhaul

FRONT

900

1993

1. Remove caliper, clean housing and mount in vise.
2. Remove piston, **Fig. 1,** by applying compressed air through brake line hole, using a piece of wood as a stop to prevent piston from being damaged.
3. Remove dust cover, then remove piston seal from bore.
4. Wash parts in solvent, rinse with clean brake fluid and blow dry with compressed air. Wipe piston clean for inspection, and if found defective, replace as an assembly.
5. Reverse procedure to assemble, noting the following:
   a. Prior to installing piston seal, lubricate seal with grease included in seal kit and pack dust cover with grease.
   b. Ensure dust cover is correctly installed in groove in cylinder.
   c. Install piston, taking care not to damage dust cover.
   d. Install caliper and bleed brake system.

1994-96

1. Remove brake caliper as outlined previously.
2. Remove brake pads, then clean hydraulic body.
3. Force piston out with compressed air through hose connection.
4. Remove dust cover and piston seal.
5. Check for damage due to wear.
6. Lubricate piston seal with grease supplied in kit, then fill dust cover with grease.
7. Position new piston seal in groove on brake cylinder, then slip dust cover onto piston.
8. Press dust cover collar into brake cylinder groove.

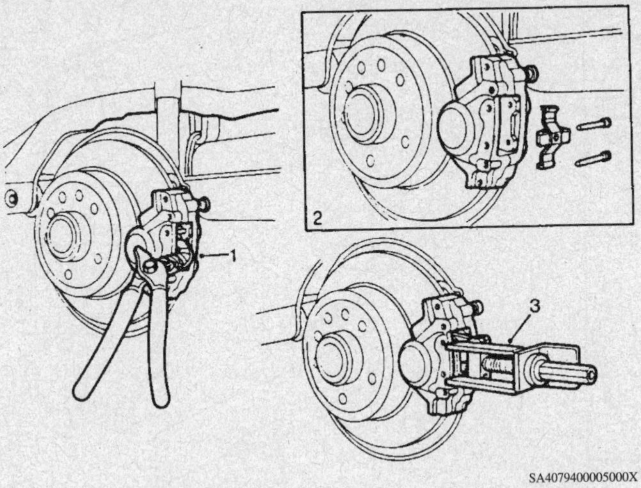
1
2
3
SA4079400005000X

Fig. 5 Rear brake pad removal. 1994–96 900

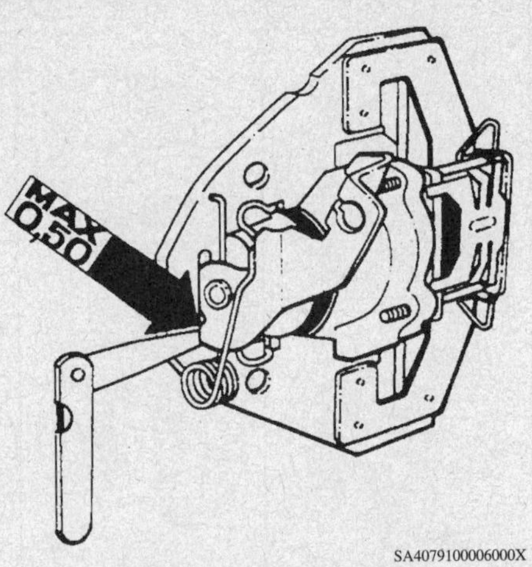
MAX
0,50
SA4079100006000X

Fig. 6 Parking brake adjustment clearance. 9000

9. Press piston into brake cylinder and install brake pads.
10. Install caliper as outlined previously.

9000

Front and rear calipers are the same except for the parking brake mechanism incorporated in the rear caliper. Refer to "Rear" for service procedure.

REAR

9000 & 1993 900

1. Remove caliper and clean housing.
2. Remove dust caps and bushings.
3. Remove spring from parking brake lever.
4. Remove dust cover retainer, then the dust cover.
5. Remove plug for adjusting screw, then the piston adjusting screw.
6. Remove piston seal.
7. Wash parts in solvent, then rinse with clean brake fluid and blow dry with compressed air.
8. Replace any components found defective.
9. Reverse procedure to assemble, noting the following:
   a. Prior to installing piston seal, lubricate seal with grease included in seal kit and pack dust cover with grease.
   b. Ensure dust cover is correctly installed in groove in cylinder.
   c. Install caliper, then turn adjusting screw in until rotor is locked. Back off adjusting screw ¼– ½ turn. **Ensure rotor turns freely.**
   d. Ensure clearance between parking brake lever and stop is .04±.02 inch (1±.5 mm).
   e. Bleed brake system, then adjust parking brake as necessary.

1994–96 900

1. Remove brake caliper as outlined previously.
2. Clean caliper with degreasing agent, then remove two dust covers.
3. Remove plugs and press out piston using compressed air and rear brake piston removal tool No. 89 96 712, or equivalent, as a dolly.
4. Remove seals in cylinder bores and check for damage due to wear.
5. Lubricate piston seals with grease supplied in kit, then fill dust covers with grease.
6. Install piston seals into cylinder bores, then the pistons into cylinders.
7. Install dust covers.
8. Install caliper as outlined previously.

ADJUSTMENTS

PARKING BRAKE

900

1. Raise rear seat, then pry adjusting device apart.
2. Insert a .08 inch feeler gauge between parking brake lever and stop on brake caliper.
3. Screw locknut against adjusting sleeve until feeler gauge drops out.
4. Apply and release parking brake lever a few times to settle adjusting device.
5. Ensure clearance between lever and stop is .02–.08 inch.
6. Lower rear seat.

9000

1. Release parking brake.
2. Remove screw plug from adjusting screw on back side of rear caliper, **Fig. 6.**
3. Tighten adjusting screw, then back off ¼– ½ turn. **Ensure rotor turns freely.**
4. Ensure clearance between parking brake lever and stop is .04±.02 inch. (1±.5 mm).
5. If clearance is not as specified, proceed as follows:
   a. Remove brush seal from parking brake lever inside vehicle.
   b. Remove plastic locking plate from adjusting nuts.
   c. Insert a .04 inch (1 mm) feeler gauge between parking brake lever and stop on caliper.
   d. Turn adjusting nut at parking brake lever (inside vehicle) until feeler gauge drops out.
   e. Ensure clearance is correct, then install locking plate and brush plate to parking brake lever inside vehicle.
6. Refit screw plug at caliper.

PARKING BRAKE SHOES

900

1994–96

1. Raise and support vehicle, then remove rear wheels.
2. Unscrew adjustment until brake disc is blocked.
3. Screw adjustment back until brake disc drags slightly but can be turned.
4. Carry out same method on other rear wheel, then install rear wheels.
5. Pull parking brake to sixth notch and ensure both wheels are locked.
6. Check parking brake as well, then adjust cable equalization if necessary as outlined under "Parking Brake Cable Equalization."

PARKING BRAKE CABLE EQUALIZATION

1. Set parking brake at notch 2.
2. Raise and support vehicle, then tighten adjusting nut on link rod (wire equalization) until brake starts to act.
3. Lower vehicle slightly, then release parking brake and tighten again. Wheels must be locked at sixth notch.

DISC BRAKE SPECIFICATIONS

Year	Model	Nominal Thickness	Minimum Refinish Thickness	Thickness Variation (Parallelism)	Lateral Runout (TIR)	Caliper Bore Diameter, Inches
1993–96	900①	.930	.850	.0006	.003	2.13
	900②	.350	.320	.0006	.003	1.30
	9000①	.980	.910	.0006	.003	2.24
	9000②	.350	.290	.0006	.003	1.26

① — Front brakes.
② — Rear brakes.

TIGHTENING SPECIFICATIONS

Year	Component	Torque/Ft. Lbs.
1993-96	Caliper Mounting Bolts①	52-81
	Caliper Mounting Bolts④②	52-67
	Caliper Mounting Bolts③②	30-40
	Hub Carrier To Hub	51-80
	Hub Nut①	195-208
	Hub Nut②	207-221
	Guide Pin③①	22-26
	Guide Pin③②	18-22
	Wheel Lug Bolts	78-92
	Wheel Lug Nuts③	66-81
1994-96③	Brake Caliper Guide Pins	78
	Wheel Studs	87

① — Front brakes.

② — Rear brakes.

③ — 900.

④ — 9000.

Hydraulic Brake Systems

INDEX

	Page No.
Brake System Bleed	38-92
1994–96 900	38-92
9000 & 1993 900	38-92
Component Replacement	38-92
Master Cylinder, Replace	38-92
Component Service	38-92
Master Cylinder Overhaul	38-92
Description	38-92

DESCRIPTION

When the brake pedal is depressed, pedal pressure assisted by power from the servo unit pushes the input rod into the master cylinder. The input rod pushes the primary plunger up the bore which closes the cutoff port to the fluid reservoir. This creates pressure ahead of the primary plunger. This pressure also acts on the secondary plunger, pushing it up the bore and closing the cutoff port from the secondary chamber. The pressure in both circuits increases and, because the plungers are the same size, pressure in each circuit is the same. Fluid pressure is directed to the brake system, which advances the piston in each individual caliper. When the pedal is released, the plungers in the master cylinder retract and cutoff ports are opened. The pressure is exhausted and the piston seal in each caliper returns the piston to its retracted position.

If there is a fluid leak in the primary circuit, the input rod pushes the primary plunger up the bore until it acts mechanically on the secondary plunger. The secondary plunger closes the cutoff port, allowing hydraulic pressure to build up in the secondary circuit. If a leak should occur in the secondary circuit, the secondary plunger will be pushed right up the bore until it reaches the end of the cylinder. In either case, greater pedal movement will be required to achieve desired braking effect.

COMPONENT REPLACEMENT

MASTER CYLINDER, REPLACE

900

1. Drain brake fluid from fluid reservoir.
2. Disconnect hydraulic lines from cylinder.
3. Temporarily plug these lines to avoid loss of fluid.
4. Disconnect brake/warning switch connector on filler cap.
5. Remove the two nuts connecting cylinder to brake booster, then the master cylinder.
6. Reverse procedure to install, then bleed brake system.

9000

1. **On 1995–96 9000 models,** obtain anti-theft code as outlined under "Precautions."
2. Disconnect battery cables and remove battery.
3. Disconnect fuel filter mounting and move to one side.
4. Drain brake fluid reservoir, then remove lines with adapters from master cylinder and move toward reservoir.
5. Disconnect brake lines.
6. Remove attaching nuts and master cylinder.
7. Reverse procedure to install, then bleed brake system.

COMPONENT SERVICE

MASTER CYLINDER OVERHAUL

When working on any hydraulic brake components it is extremely important to keep the work area clean. Clean any parts that are to be reused with new brake fluid or a cleaning fluid specifically designed for hydraulic components. Wipe all parts dry using clean lint-free paper or cloth. Gaskets, seals, O-rings and rubber components should not be reused. Prior to assembly, all components should be generously lubricated with clean brake fluid.

Disassemble

1. Clamp master cylinder in soft-jaw vice.
2. Remove rubber seals from brake hose connections.
3. Carefully push primary plunger up bore at bulkhead end and remove stop pin from secondary plunger, **Fig. 1.**
4. Remove plunger assemblies and loose plastic bleed cup from cylinder bore.

Assemble

1. Fit new seals to secondary plunger, **Fig. 2. Because the primary assembly is fitted with captive plastic bleed cup, if a seal is worn the entire plunger assembly must be replaced.**
2. Install spring and spring retainer onto secondary plunger.
3. Lubricate seals and cylinder bore with brake fluid, then install secondary plunger plastic bleed cup.
4. Insert secondary plunger, then the primary plunger into cylinder bore, taking care not to damage seals.
5. Push primary plunger up bore and install secondary plunger stop pin.
6. Install master cylinder and bleed brake system.

BRAKE SYSTEM BLEED

9000 & 1993 900

1. Ensure brake fluid reservoir is full.
2. Connect transparent hose to bleed nipple of brake caliper.
3. Place other end of hose into clear container.
4. Depress brake pedal, then open bleed nipple. Close nipple as soon as pedal reaches floor. Repeat this until no air bubbles are visible in fluid.
5. Repeat previous step at each brake caliper, then refill fluid reservoir. **On models with Anti-Lock Brake Systems (ABS), front calipers must be bled before rear calipers.**

1994–96 900

1. Unscrew cover of brake fluid reservoir and top off with brake fluid.
2. Connect topping-off fitting from brake bleeding unit kit tool No. 88 19 096, or equivalent, to brake fluid reservoir.
3. Position hose with one end on topping-off fitting and other end in bottle filled with clean brake fluid.
4. Raise and support vehicle, then connect brake bleeder hose to front left wheel and open nipple. Draw off approximately .1 quart brake fluid. Repeat at front right wheel.
5. Move brake bleeder to rear left wheel and open nipple. Draw off approximately .05 quart brake fluid. Repeat at rear right wheel.
6. Lower vehicle, then check brake operation. Depress brake pedal and check that it does not drop.
7. Remove topping-off fitting, hose and bottle.
8. Adjust brake fluid level.

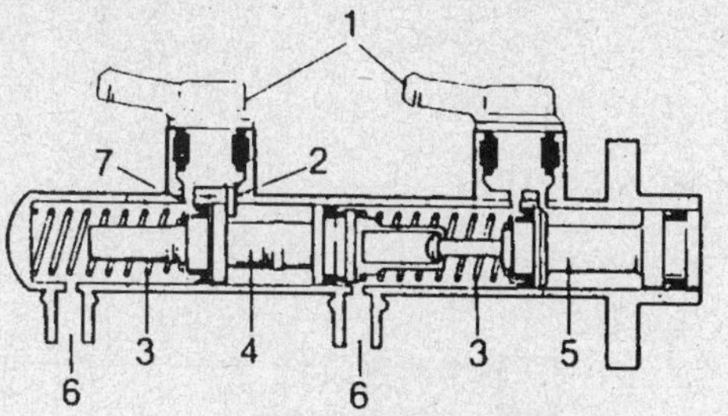
1
7
2
3
4
3
5
6
6

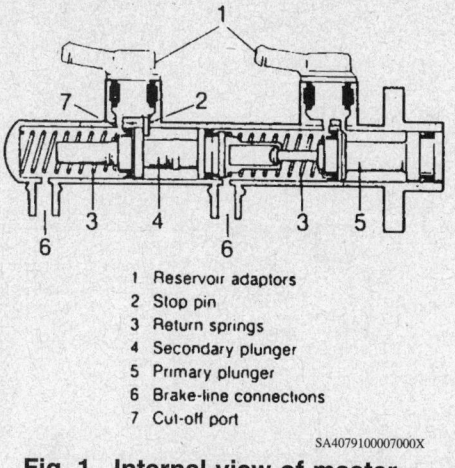

1 Reservoir adaptors
2 Stop pin
3 Return springs
4 Secondary plunger
5 Primary plunger
6 Brake-line connections
7 Cut-off port

SA4079100007000X

Fig. 1 Internal view of master cylinder

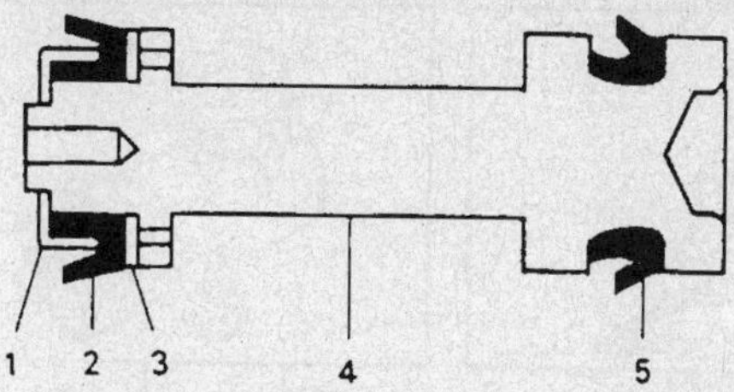
1
2
3
4
5

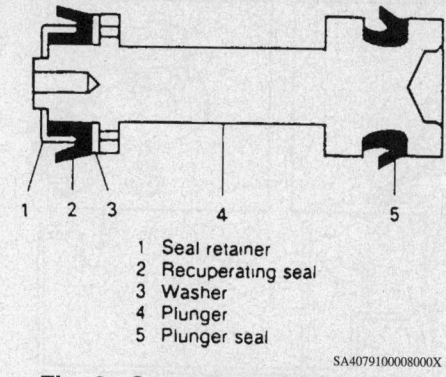

1 Seal retainer
2 Recuperating seal
3 Washer
4 Plunger
5 Plunger seal

SA4079100008000X

Fig. 2 Secondary plunger seal installation

Power Brake Units

NOTE: Electrical Symbol & Wire Color Code Identification Located In The Front Of This Manual May Be Used As An Aid When Using Wiring Circuits Found In This Section.

INDEX

	Page No.		Page No.		Page No.
Description	38-93	Power Brake Unit Service	38-94	Vacuum Pump	38-94
Operation	38-93	Replacement	38-94		

DESCRIPTION

The servo (booster) unit, **Fig. 1,** provides power assistance to the pedal effort applied. The servo obtains its power from vacuum created in the engine inlet manifold and provides assistance in a ratio of about 4 to 1. Should a vacuum failure occur, the two pushrods will act as a single rod, allowing brakes to work conventionally but with a much greater pedal effort.

OPERATION

When the brake pedal is depressed, then input rod pushes the control piston and diaphragm forward, closing the vacuum port. As the input rod continues to move forward, the control piston opens the atmospheric port, allowing atmospheric pressure to enter through the filter and into the rear shell behind the diaphragm. Since vacuum is still present at the front of the diaphragm, the pressure assists the input rod in pushing the diaphragm forward and the output rod to actuate the master cylinder.

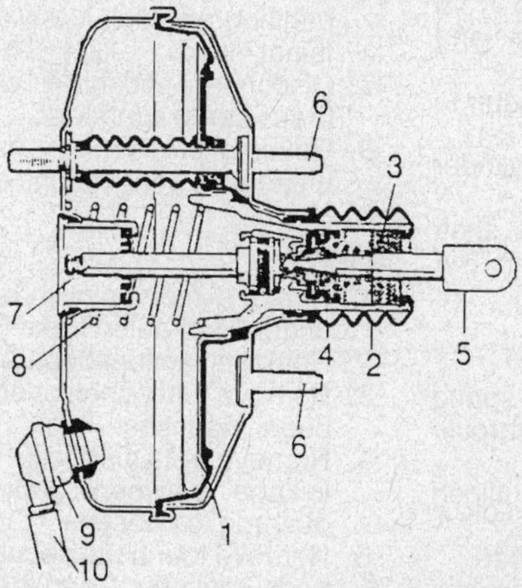
6
3
7
8
4
2
5
6
9
1
10

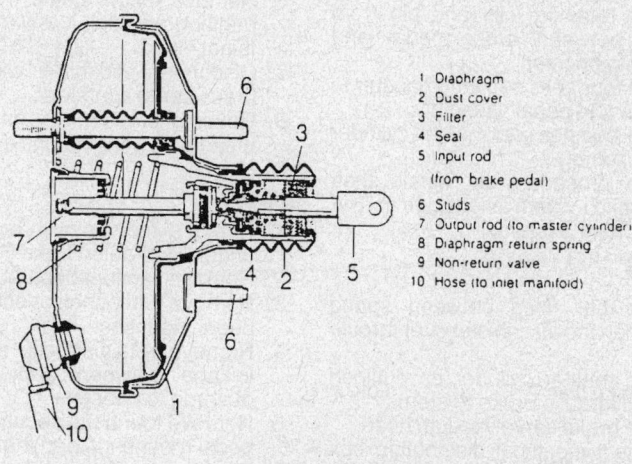

1 Diaphragm
2 Dust cover
3 Filter
4 Seal
5 Input rod (from brake pedal)
6 Studs
7 Output rod (to master cylinder)
8 Diaphragm return spring
9 Non-return valve
10 Hose (to inlet manifold)

SA4039100001000X

Fig. 1 Power brake booster (servo)

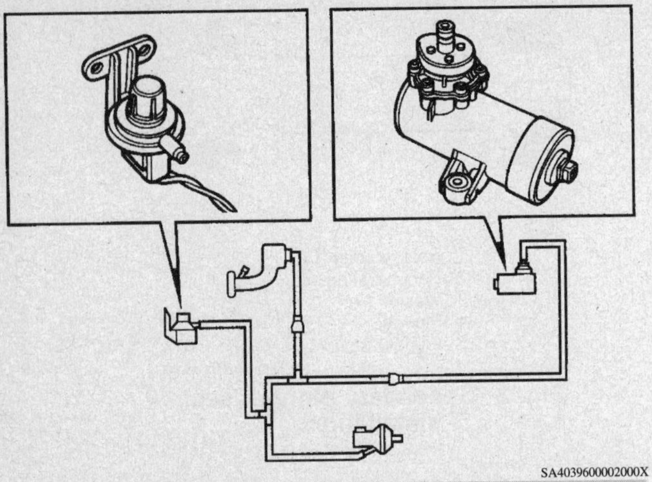

SA4039600002000X

Fig. 2 Brake vacuum pump. 1996 9000 w/2.0L light pressure turbo engine & automatic transmission

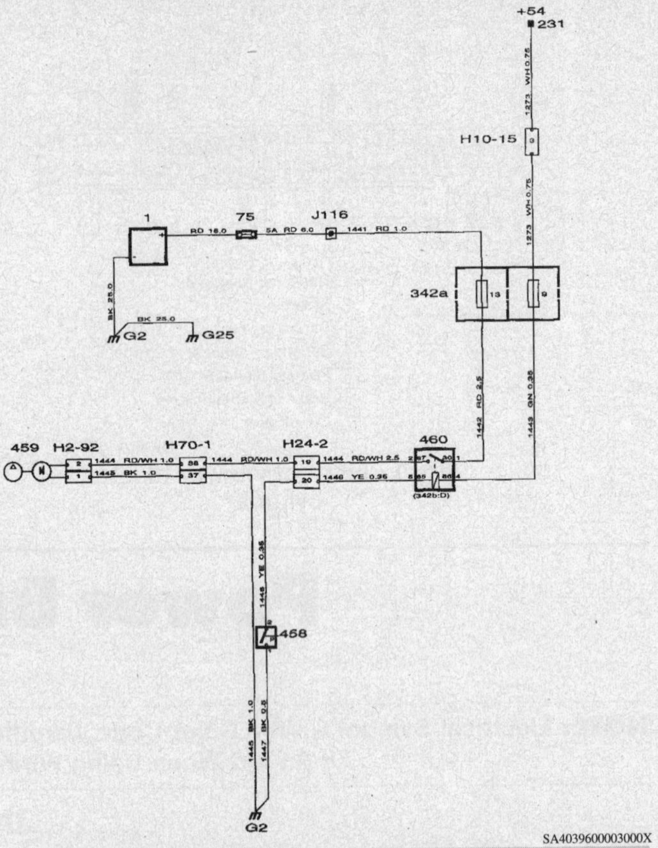

+54
231
H10-15
1
75
J116
342a
G2
G25
459
H2-92
H70-1
H24-2
460
458
G2

SA4039600003000X

Fig. 3 Brake vacuum pump wiring diagram. 1996 9000 w/2.0L light pressure turbo engine & automatic transmission

POWER BRAKE UNIT SERVICE

REPLACEMENT

900

1993

1. Remove steering column trim cover.
2. Remove ashtray, then the lower dash panel.
3. Remove vacuum hose from booster.
4. Remove wiring harness from booster.
5. Disconnect brake lines from master cylinder.
6. Temporarily plug these lines to avoid loss of fluid.
7. Remove retaining clip and pin from linkage between brake pedal and pushrod to booster.
8. Remove four bolts securing booster to bulkhead and pedal assembly.
9. Remove booster and master cylinder as an assembly.
10. Reverse procedure to install, then bleed brake system as outlined in "Hydraulic Brake Systems."

1994–96

1. Remove bar fixed between spring struts, then the air canister over throttle body.
2. Remove master cylinder as outlined under "Hydraulic Brake Systems."
3. Remove brake servo vacuum hose.
4. Disconnect electrical distribution box and move aside.
5. Remove four brake servo retaining nuts from bracket.
6. Remove rubber gaiter from bulkhead partition and pull it toward servo container.
7. Disconnect pushrod clip, then the brake servo container.
8. Reverse procedure to install. Ensure brake pipe connections do not leak.

9000

1. Remove master cylinder as outlined under "Hydraulic Brake Systems."
2. Remove vacuum hose from booster.
3. Remove trim panel for access to brake pedal mounting.
4. Remove retaining clip and pin from linkage between brake pedal and pushrod to booster.
5. Remove four bolts securing booster to pedal mounting, then the booster.
6. Reverse procedure to install, then bleed brake system as outlined in "Hydraulic Brake Systems."

VACUUM PUMP

1996 9000

1996 series 9000 models equipped with 2.0L Light Pressure Turbo engine and automatic transmission, have been fitted with a brake vacuum pump, **Fig. 2.** Whenever the engine is unable to provide adequate vacuum, due to certain driving conditions, the vacuum pump supplies vacuum to the brake servo.

When vacuum is less than .035 bar, the pump starts operation. When vacuum reaches .04 bar the pump switches Off. The pump is located on the rear of the engine against the bulkhead.

When troubleshooting vacuum pump electrical system, refer to vacuum pump wiring diagram, **Fig. 3.**

Anti-Lock Brakes

INDEX

	Page No.
Application Chart	38-95
Mark II Anti-Lock Brake System Less Traction Control	38-95
Mark II Anti-Lock Brake System w/Traction Control	38-104
Mark IV Anti-Lock Brake System	38-115
1994-95 900 Anti-Lock Brake System	38-124
1996 900 Bosch 5.3 Anti-Lock Brake System	38-135

Application Chart

Model	Type
1993	
900	Mark II
9000①	Mark II
9000②	Mark IV
1994-95	
900	1994-95 900
9000①	Mark II
9000②	Mark IV
1996	
900	ABS 5.3
9000①	Mark II
9000②	Mark IV

① — Turbo models w/traction control and manual transaxle.
② — Except turbo models w/traction control and manual transaxle.

Mark II Anti-Lock Brake System Less Traction Control

NOTE: On Air Bag Equipped Models, Refer To "Air Bag System Precautions" Located In The Front Of This Manual For System Disarming & Arming Procedures.

NOTE: Electrical Symbol & Wire Color Code Identification Located In The Front Of This Manual May Be Used As An Aid When Using Wiring Circuits Found In This Section.

INDEX

	Page No.
Description	38-96
Components	38-96
System	38-96
Diagnosis & Testing	38-96
Accessing Diagnostic Trouble Codes	38-96
Diagnostic Trouble Code Interpretation	38-98
Precautions	38-96
Air Bag Systems	38-96
Radio Anti-Theft Lock	38-96
System Service	38-100
Brake System Bleed	38-100
Component Replacement	38-101
Accumulator, Replace	38-102
Brake Fluid Reservoir, Replace	38-101
ECU, Replace	38-103
Hydraulic Unit, Replace	38-101
Pressure Switch, Replace	38-102
Pump & Motor Unit, Replace	38-103
Pump Delivery Line, Replace	38-102
Valve Block, Replace	38-103
Wheel Sensors, Replace	38-103
Troubleshooting	38-96

PRECAUTIONS

AIR BAG SYSTEMS

Refer to "Air Bag System Precautions" in the front of this manual for system disarming and arming procedures.

RADIO ANTI-THEFT LOCK

9000

1995-96

Radio and cassette player are equipped with an electronic four-digit anti-theft lock. This four-digit code is programmed at manufacturing and cannot be changed. If the battery is disconnected for more than three minutes, if unit is removed or if otherwise cut off from power, the four-digit code must be entered with the quick-selection buttons as follows:

1. Turn radio on, then, when display shows "Code In, " enter four-digit code with quick-selection buttons. If code is correct, last-tuned radio frequency is shown on display. If wrong digit has been entered by mistake, all four digits must be entered again. If code is wrong it stays on display.
2. If incorrect four-digit code has been entered, press Band button for more than three seconds to clear display. Display shows "Code In" and new attempt to enter correct code can be made.
3. If wrong code has been used three times in succession, four dashes appear on display and you must wait an hour with radio switched on before trying again.
4. To try again, hold Band button for at least three seconds. "Code In" should appear on display.
5. Correct code must be entered at first attempt, otherwise you must wait another hour with unit switched on before trying again.

DESCRIPTION

SYSTEM

This Anti-Lock Brake System (ABS), **Fig. 1,** is a triple-circuit system, with split circuits and individual monitoring and control for each front wheel and for the two rear wheels together.

Signals from the four wheel sensors are sent to the ECU, which continuously monitors the speed, acceleration and deceleration of the wheels, road speed and tire slip. If a wheel is about to lock up, the ECU sends signals to the solenoid valves for the wheel that is slipping. This signal modulates the amount of hydraulic brake pressure sent to that wheel. By preventing lock up, the ABS system provides the shortest possible stopping distance without losing steering control.

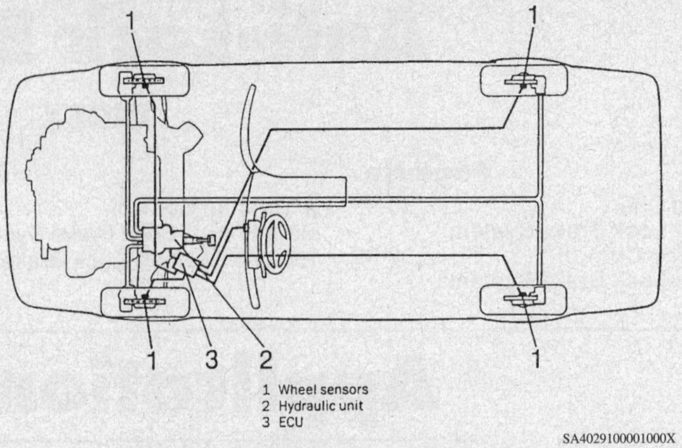
1
1
1
3
2
1
1 Wheel sensors
2 Hydraulic unit
3 ECU
SA4029100001000X

Fig. 1 Anti-lock brake system

COMPONENTS

Hydraulic Unit

The hydraulic unit replaces the conventional master cylinder and vacuum-operated servo. This unit is comprised of a master cylinder, hydraulic servo cylinder, brake fluid reservoir, independent pump for hydraulic pressure and a valve block which modulates pressure to the individual calipers. The valve block contains six solenoid valves, three inlet and three outlet, this gives each brake circuit one inlet and one outlet valve.

If the ABS system should become inoperative for any reason, all the solenoid valves will be de-energized and the brake system will operate in the same way as a conventional braking system.

Electronic Control Unit (ECU)

The ECU processes the signals from wheel sensors. If any of the wheel sensors detect a lock up tendency, the ECU sends signals directly to the valve block in the hydraulic unit. The ECU is located at the rear lefthand side of the engine compartment.

Relay & Fuse Box

The relays and fuses of the ABS system are housed in a special fuse box located near the ECU. The fuse box contains a system relay and fuse for the ECU, relay and fuse for the pump motor and an additional fuse for the ECU.

Brake Warning & ABS Warning Lights

As on cars with conventional brakes, the brake warning light will come on if level in the fluid reservoir falls below the MIN mark. However, if there is a pressure drop in the accumulator both the brake warning and the ABS warning lights will come on. The ABS warning light will also come on if there is an additional drop of fluid in the reservoir, a malfunction in the ECU, an open circuit in the electrical system or a weak signal being received from the wheel sensors. The ABS system is inoperative when the ABS warning light is on.

Wheel Sensors

The wheel sensors are mounted near a toothed sensor wheel at each wheel. Each time a tooth on the sensor wheel passes the sensor, it distorts a magnetic field, which causes a signal to be sent to the ECU. Although the sensors are mounted differently in the front (radially) and rear (axially), they operate exactly the same.

TROUBLESHOOTING

Perform the following quick checks:

1. Check brake fluid level, noting the following:
   a. Ensure accumulator is fully charged with fluid.
   b. Turn ignition switch to On position and check fluid level after hydraulic pump cuts out.
   c. Fill as necessary with DOT 4 brake fluid to bring level to MAX mark on side of reservoir.
2. Inspect all fuses in fuse panel adjacent to ABS system ECU.
3. Ensure relays for ECU and pump motor have been properly installed.
4. Check all electrical connectors and ensure sensor lead connectors are making good contact.
5. Check all ground points.

DIAGNOSIS & TESTING

ACCESSING DIAGNOSTIC TROUBLE CODES

To access diagnostic trouble codes and perform system service, a SAAB ABS system tester will be required. The tester, **Fig. 2,** can perform three different sets of tests. These tests include; automatic testing of each wheel sensor and hydraulic pressure (Test Mode), manual valve testing (Valve Test Mode) and manual testing of each wheel sensor and hydraulic pressure (Monitor Mode).

The tester display, **Fig. 3,** is divided into three zones; test prompts; measured values and diagnostic trouble codes, with overview of test items; valve and ABS-version monitor. The test prompts display, displays driving instructions for the operator during testing. The measured values and diagnostic trouble codes display, shows instantaneous values for wheel speed, wheel sensor signal amplitude, sensor-wheel eccentricity and which wheel the values refer to. A check is also made of the relays, accumulator pressure if pressure sensor is connected and the diagnostic trouble codes are displayed at the end of

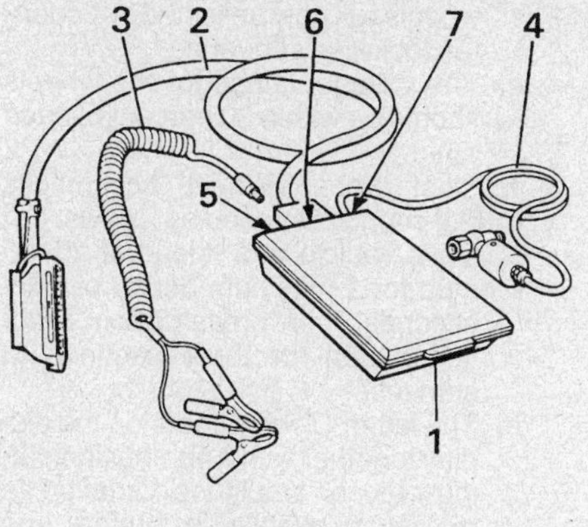
3
2
6
7
4
5
1

1 Tester unit
2 Test lead with two-way 35-pin connector
3 Power supply lead
4 Pressure sensor with connecting lead
5 Port for power supply
6 Port for test lead
7 Port for pressure-sensor lead

SA4029100002000X

Fig. 2 ABS system tester

the run. The valve monitoring display, shows which valves are operating during test whenever ABS-system version is selected.

The tester control panel has three buttons to control the function of the ABS tester. Button A is used to start the test cycle and to run through the diagnostic trouble codes. Button B is used to select the program that measures wheel sensor signal strength, tests the operation of wheel sensors and measures accumulator pressure (if pressure sensor is connected). Button C is used to select the program that measures sensor wheel eccentricity, test the operation of the wheel sensors and to measure accumulator pressure (if pressure sensor is connected). Buttons B and C can be pressed simultaneously to select ABS-system version.

CONNECTING ABS-SYSTEM TESTER

1. Perform system checks as outlined under "Troubleshooting."
2. Switch ignition off, then remove ECU cover located at rear lefthand corner of engine compartment.
3. Release ECU retaining clips, then disconnect ECU.
4. Connect tester lead between ECU and ABS wiring harness connector using a two-way 35-pin connector.
5. Support ECU and connectors using vinyl ties, then run tester electrical lead through driver window.
6. Connect power supply lead to battery negative terminal, then the positive terminal.
7. Run power lead through the window and connect it to the tester, **Fig. 4. Ensure connector is installed correctly at the tester, if connector is installed upside down, tester circuitry may be burnt out.**
8. Tester will now automatically select ABS-type 1. **Always switch off the ignition before unplugging test lead connector from the ECU. Failure to do so can result in ECU circuitry being burnt out.**

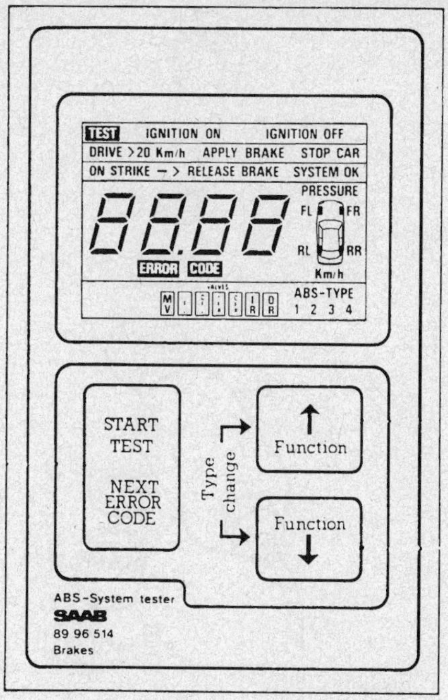
TEST IGNITION ON IGNITION OFF
DRIVE >20 Km/h APPLY BRAKE STOP CAR
ON STRIKE —> RELEASE BRAKE SYSTEM OK
PRESSURE
FL FR
RL RR
ERROR CODE
Km/h
ABS-TYPE
1 2 3 4
START TEST
NEXT ERROR CODE
Type change
Function
Function
ABS-System tester
SAAB
89 96 514
Brakes

SA4029100003000X

Fig. 3 ABS tester display

Test Mode

1. Ensure tester is in "Monitor Mode." **This is the mode the tester enters automatically after "ABS-System Version" has been selected.**
2. Drive the vehicle at about 6 mph and press START TEST button.
3. The word TEST will now start to flash on the display, indicating that "TEST MODE" has been started.
4. If tester will not enter TEST MODE, remain in MONITOR MODE and check wheel sensor signal strength for each wheel as outlined in "Monitor Mode."
5. Drive vehicle for at least three minutes at a speed of approximately 42 mph. **Test results will not be affected by the vehicle stopping and starting.**
6. Test cycle for each wheel takes about two seconds.
7. Tester will beep each time a fault is detected, testing will continue until tester is switched off or START TEST button is pressed for approximately three seconds.
8. To read test results, proceed as follows:
   a. Stop vehicle but do not turn off the ignition switch, wait until display indicates FR, FL, RL, or RR and press START TEST button.
   b. If no faults have been detected, display will read SYSTEM OK.
   c. If any faults have been detected, ERROR will appear on the display followed by a figure indicating the number of faults found.
   d. To read diagnostic trouble codes, press NEXT ERROR CODE button and diagnostic trouble codes will be displayed. Press button again to read each successive diagnostic trouble code.
   e. If several diagnostic trouble codes are displayed together they must be investigated and repaired in the order, **Fig. 5.**

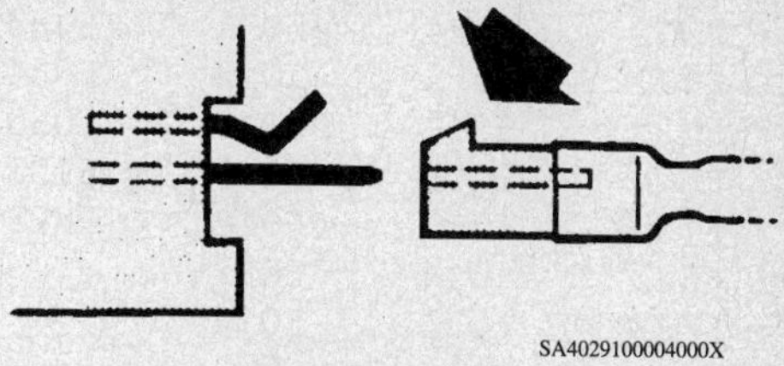

SA4029100004000X

Fig. 4 Tester power lead connection

9. To diagnose and repair diagnostic trouble codes, refer to "Diagnostic Trouble Code Interpretation."
10. To return to MONITOR MODE, press one of the function buttons.

Valve Test Mode

During this test you will need to stop the vehicle abruptly several times. Use roads that are lightly traveled or deserted.

1. Ensure tester is in MONITOR MODE, vehicle is not moving and engine at idle speed.
2. Press one of the function buttons to enter VALVE TEST MODE. The ABS warning light on the instrument panel will come on and stay on during the test sequence.
3. Press START TEST button, TEST will now flash on the display, indicating test sequence has begun.
4. Tester will beep each time a fault is detected.
5. Inlet valves will be tested in this order; IFL-Inlet Front Left, IFR-Inlet Front Right, IR-Inlet Rear. **When rear inlet valve is to be tested, choose a place to stop the vehicle where it can remain parked while the remaining valves are tested.**
6. To test inlet valves, proceed as follows:
   a. System prompt DRIVE 20km/h, drive vehicle between 13-19 mph.
   b. System prompt STOP CAR & RELEASE BRAKE, take foot off accelerator and let car coast. **Do not touch brake pedal. Use the parking brake or depress clutch pedal several times to slow vehicle down.**
   c. When the vehicle reaches 11 mph, APPLY BRAKE prompt will appear on the screen. Press down hard on the brake pedal as soon as the prompt appears. Test will now measure the wheel retardation as the vehicle slows down.
   d. System prompt RELEASE BRAKE, release brake pedal as soon as the vehicle has stopped. **Do not touch brake pedal again.**
   e. After test sequence for inlet valves has been completed, tester will automatically continue the next test sequence.
7. Outlet valves will be tested in this order; OR-Outlet Rear, OFR-Outlet Front Right, OFL-Outlet Front Left, MV-Main Valve. **During the test for**

E002	EE24	E001	E033
E422	EE25	E009	E034
E523	E011	E010	E035
E624	E008	E015	E132
E725	E320	E016	PRES
EE22	E014	E017	
EE23	E032	E018	

SA4029100005000X

Fig. 5 Diagnostic trouble code repair sequence

the main valve, the brake pedal will pulsate strongly.

8. To test outlet valves and main valve, proceed as follows:
   a. Ensure vehicle is parked and engine off.
   b. System prompt IGNITION ON, turn key to DRIVE position.
   c. System prompt RELEASE BRAKE. **Do not touch brake pedal.** After approximately five seconds, pump will have raised pressure in accumulator to 2610 psi and RELEASE BRAKE will disappear from screen.
   d. System prompt APPLY BRAKE, press down hard on the brake pedal as soon as the prompt appears.
   e. System prompt ON STRIKE- & IGNITION OFF, brake pedal should pulsate or there should be excessive pedal travel when pedal is depressed. If pedal responds as outlined, turn ignition switch off within 10 seconds to send acknowledgment to the tester. **If brake pedal does not respond as outlined, do not turn off ignition at this time.** Wait approximately 20 seconds for system prompt RELEASE BRAKE to appear on the screen.
9. If system does not detect any faults, display will read SYSTEM OK.
10. If any faults have been detected, ERROR will appear on the display followed by a figure indicating the number of faults found.
11. To read diagnostic trouble codes, press NEXT ERROR CODE button and diagnostic trouble codes will be displayed. Press button again to read each successive diagnostic trouble code.
12. If several diagnostic trouble codes are displayed together they must be investigated and repaired in the order, **Fig. 5.**
13. To diagnose and repair diagnostic trouble codes, refer to "Diagnostic Trouble Codes."
14. To return to MONITOR MODE, press one of the function buttons.

Monitor Mode

1. After tester has been powered up and ABS-System Version selected, tester will automatically enter MONITOR MODE.
2. MONITOR MODE can be used to test wheel speed, wheel signal strength, sensor wheel eccentricity (out-of-round) and accumulator pressure (if

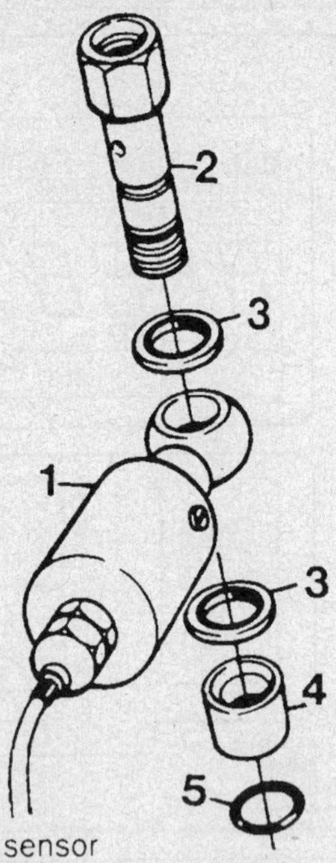
1
2
3
3
4
5

1 Pressure sensor
2 Fitting with groove for 'O' ring
3 Washer
4 Sleeve
5 'O' ring

SA4029100006000X

Fig. 6 Pressure sensor connection

pressure sensor is connected).

3. Tester will beep each time a fault is found.
4. To test Road-Wheel speed, proceed as follows:
   a. Drive vehicle at a steady speed.
   b. Km/h will appear on display together with a number, indicating speed of wheel.
   c. The tester will begin the test with the FR (front right) wheel, which will be indicated on the display screen.
   d. To test speed of other wheels, press top FUNCTION button, wheels will now be tested in a counterclockwise sequence.
   e. Values for wheel speed should be approximately the same.
5. To test accumulator pressure, connect pressure sensor as outlined in "Connecting Pressure Sensor." Working pressure of the accumulator will be displayed in bar. **Some of the valve segments may flash during this test, this is quite normal and can be disregarded.**
6. To test Wheel-Sensor signal strength, proceed as follows:
   a. Drive vehicle at a steady speed, then press top FUNCTION button for about three seconds.
   b. The letter "A" will be displayed along with a value proportional to signal voltage.
   c. The tester will begin the test with the FR (front right) wheel, which will be indicated on the display screen.
   d. To test speed of other wheels, press top FUNCTION button, wheels will now be tested in a counterclockwise sequence.
   e. The voltage values for the wheels should be within 20 percent of each other.
7. To test Sensor-Wheel eccentricity (out-of-round), proceed as follows:
   a. Drive vehicle at a speed of 25–30 mph for a minimum period of sixty seconds, then press bottom function button for three seconds to start test.
   b. The letter "E" will appear on the display together with a number indicating ratio of amplitude variation to maximum amplitude during one revolution of the wheel. **This value should not be higher than 6.**
   c. The front right wheel sensor will the first one tested, to test the other wheels press top FUNCTION button.
   d. Other wheel sensors will now be tested in counterclockwise direction.

CONNECTING PRESSURE SENSOR

It is not necessary to connect the pressure tester unless a pressure related fault is detected.

The system must be depressurized before work is started. To do this, with ignition switch off depress brake pedal approximately 20 times until positive resistance is felt in the pedal.

1. Remove ABS fuse/relay box.
2. Using an 8 mm Allen key, remove accumulator.
3. Connect pressure hose to accumulator port on hydraulic unit.
4. Fit pressure sensor onto hose, **Fig. 6.**
5. Set accumulator onto pressure sensor, then place accumulator where it will not obstruct closing of the hood.
6. Loosely refit the fuse box.
7. Reverse procedure to disconnect pressure sensor.

DIAGNOSTIC TROUBLE CODE INTERPRETATION

When performing diagnostic trouble code diagnosis and repair, refer to **Figs. 7 and 8** for diagnostic trouble code identification and **Figs. 9 and 10** for ABS wiring circuits. If several diagnostic trouble codes are displayed together they must be investigated and repaired in specified order, **Fig. 5.**

DIAGNOSTIC TROUBLE CODE E001

1. Diagnostic trouble code E001 indicates a no ground condition between pin 1 of the ECU and ground point 301 on 9000 models or ground point 93 on 900 models.
2. Check wiring between pin 1 and grounding points, repair as necessary.
3. Check grounding point for good contact.

DIAGNOSTIC TROUBLE CODE E002

1. Diagnostic trouble code E001 indicates no battery voltage at ECU pin 2.
2. **On 900 models,** proceed as follows:
   a. Check 10 amp ABS fuse in ABS fuse panel and fuse 10 in vehicle fuse panel.
   b. Ensure battery voltage is at least 10 volts.
   c. Check wiring between ECU pin 2 and terminal 87 of the ignition switch relay, repair as necessary.
   d. Check wiring between terminal 30 of the ignition switch relay and connector 75, repair as necessary.
3. **On 9000 models,** proceed as follows:
   a. Check 10 amp fuse on ABS fuse panel.
   b. Ensure battery voltage is at least 10 volts.
   c. Check wiring between terminal 54 of the ignition switch and pin 2 of the ECU, repair as necessary.

DIAGNOSTIC TROUBLE CODE E320

1. This diagnostic trouble code indicates that the system relay is defective.
2. Check signals from wheel sensors as outlined in "Monitor Mode." A break in circuitry indicated by a zero reading on the tester can cause a diagnostic trouble code E320. Repair any fault following procedures given in "Diagnostic Trouble Codes E422, E523, E624 or E725."
3. Check valves as outlined in "Valve Test Mode."
4. Check 30 amp ABS fuse and 30 amp PUMP fuse on the ABS fuse panel.
5. Check wiring from ECU pins 3 and 20 to pin 30 on the system relay, repair as necessary.
6. Check wiring between connector 75 and pin 87 on the system relay, repair as necessary.
7. **On 900 models,** check wiring between ground point 93 and pin 87 A on system relay, repair as necessary.
8. **On 9000 models,** check wiring between ground point 300 (hydraulic unit) and pin 87 A on system relay, repair as necessary.
9. **On all models,** check wiring between ECU pin 8 and pin 86 on the system relay, repair as necessary.
10. **On 900 models,** check wiring between ground point 93 and pin 85 on the system relay, repair as necessary.
11. **On 9000 models,** check wiring between ground point 301 (ECU) and pin 85 on the system relay, repair as necessary.
12. **On 900 models,** check wiring between ground point 93 and ground point 300, repair as necessary.
13. **On 9000 models,** check wiring between ground point 301 and ground point 7, repair as necessary.
14. **On all models,** check system relay for a break or short circuit between pins 85 and 86.
15. If system relay wire circuit is satisfactory, replace system relay.

Error code	ECU pin no	Malfunction indicated
E001	1	No earth connection
E002	2	Battery voltage low or absent
E320	3, 20	System relay function
E422	4, 22	No signal from right rear wheel sensor
E523	5, 23	No signal from front left wheel sensor
E624	6, 24	No signal from left rear wheel sensor
E725	7, 25	No signal from right front wheel sensor
E008	8	Systemrelay-controlsignalmissing
E009	9	Brake fluid level low: hydraulic pressure low
E010	10	ECU defective
E011	11	No earth connection
E014	14	Pump relay/pressure switch defective
E015	15	Right front inlet valve
E016	16	Rear outlet valve
E017	17	Rear inlet valve
E018	18	Main valve
EE22	Sensor	Right rear sensor wheel runout
EE23	Sensor	Left front sensor wheel runout
EE24	Sensor	Left rear sensor wheel runout
EE25	Sensor	Right front sensor wheel runout
E032	32	Pump relay defective
E132	1, 32	Pump running continuously
E033	33	Left front outlet valve
E034	34	Right front outlet valve
E035	35	Left front inlet valve
PRES	ext	Low accumulator pressure

SA4029100007000X

Fig. 7 Diagnostic trouble code & ECU pin identification. 900

DIAGNOSTIC TROUBLE CODES E422, E523, E624 & E725

1. These diagnostic trouble codes indicate the following wheel sensor faults:
   a. Diagnostic trouble code E422, no signal from the right rear wheel sensor to pins 4 and 22 of ECU.
   b. Diagnostic trouble code E523, no signal from the left front wheel sensor to pins 5 and 23 of ECU.
   c. Diagnostic trouble code E624, no signal from the left rear wheel sensor to pins 6 and 24 of ECU.
   d. Diagnostic trouble code E725, no signal from the right front wheel sensor to pins 7 and 25 of ECU.
2. Check wiring from ECU pins to wheel sensor, then repair as necessary.
3. Ensure gap between sensor wheel and sensor is .026 inch.
4. If wiring and gap are satisfactory, replace sensor.

DIAGNOSTIC TROUBLE CODE E008

1. This diagnostic trouble code indicates there is no control signal to system relay.
2. Check signals from wheel sensors as outlined in "Monitor Mode," repair as necessary.
3. Check valves as outlined in "Valve Test Mode," repair as necessary.
4. Check 30 amp fuse on ABS fuse panel.
5. Check for a short circuit or break in wiring between pin 8 of the ECU and pin 86 of the system relay.
6. Check system relay for a break or short circuit between pins 85 and 86.
7. **On 900 models,** check wiring between pin 85 on system relay and ground point 93, then the wiring between ECU pins 3 and 20 to pin 30 on the system relay, repair as necessary.
8. **On 9000 models,** check wiring between pin 85 on system relay and ground point 301, repair as necessary.
9. **On all models,** if wiring and grounds are satisfactory, replace ECU.

DIAGNOSTIC TROUBLE CODE E009

1. This diagnostic trouble code indicates either the hydraulic pressure or fluid level are low.
2. Fill fluid reservoir and check accumulator pressure.

DIAGNOSTIC TROUBLE CODE E010

1. This diagnostic trouble code indicates the ECU is defective.
2. **On 900 models,** proceed as follows:
   a. Check 30 amp fuse in ABS fuse panel.
   b. Check valves as outlined in "Valve Test Mode."
   c. Check wheel sensors as outlined in "Monitor Mode."
   d. Check wiring between ECU pin 10 and pin of the pressure switch.
   e. Check wiring between pin 3 of the pressure switch and pin 2 on the fluid level indicator.
   f. Check wiring between pin 1 of the fluid level indicator and ECU pin 9.
   g. Check function of the pressure switch, contacts 3 and 5 should be closed when pressure is above 105 bar (1523 psi).
   h. Check function of fluid level indicator.
   i. Check wiring from ECU pins 3 and 20 to pin 30 on the system relay.
   j. Check wiring between connector 75 and pin 87 on the system relay.
   k. Check wiring between ECU pin 8 and pin 86 on system relay.
   l. Check for break or short circuit between pins 85 and 86 on the system relay.
   m. Check wiring between pin 85 of system relay and ground point 93.
   n. If fuses and wiring are satisfactory, replace ECU.
3. **On 9000 models,** proceed as follows:
   a. Check wiring between pin 10 of the ECU and pin 5 of the pressure switch.
   b. Check wiring between pin 3 of the pressure switch and pin 2 of the fluid level indicator.
   c. Check wiring between pin 1 of the fluid level indicator and pin 9 of the ECU.
   d. Check function of the pressure switch, contacts 3 and 5 should be closed if pressure is above 105 bar (1523 psi).
   e. Check function of fluid level indicator.
   f. If pressure switch, fluid level indicator and wiring are satisfactory, replace ECU.

DIAGNOSTIC TROUBLE CODE E011

1. This diagnostic trouble code indicates there is a break in continuity between pin 11 of the ECU and pin 1 on the valve block connector.

Error code	ECU pin no	Malfunction indicated
E001	1	No earth connection
E002	2	Battery voltage low
E008	8	No control signal to system relay
E009	9	Brake fluid level or hydraulic pressure low
E010	10	ECU defective
E011	11	No earth connection
E014	14	Pump relay/pressure switch defective
E015	15	Right front inlet valve
E016	33	Rear outlet valve
E017	17	Rear inlet valve
E018	18	Main valve
E032	32	Pump relay defective
E033	16	Left front outlet valve
E034	34	Right front outlet valve
E035	35	Left front inlet valve
E132	1, 32	Pump running continuously
E320	3, 20	System relay defective
E422	4, 22	No signal from right rear wheel sensor
E523	5, 23	No signal from front left wheel sensor
E624	6, 24	No signal from left rear wheel sensor
E725	7, 25	No signal from right front wheel sensor
EE22	Sensor	Right rear sensor wheel runout
EE23	Sensor	Left front sensor wheel runout
EE24	Sensor	Left rear sensor wheel runout
EE25	Sensor	Right front sensor wheel runout
PRES	ext	Hydraulic pressure to pressure switch low

SA4029100008000X

Fig. 8 Diagnostic trouble code & ECU pin identification. 9000

2. Check wiring between ECU pin 11 and pin 1 of valve block connector, repair as necessary.
3. Ensure ground point 300 of the hydraulic unit is secure.

DIAGNOSTIC TROUBLE CODE E014

1. This diagnostic trouble code indicates a defective pump relay or pressure switch, this diagnostic trouble code is tripped if terminal 14 of the ECU has sensed continuous pump operation for more than 90 seconds during testing.
2. **On 900 models,** check 10 amp ABS fuse on ABS fuse panel and 10 amp fuse on main fuse panel.
3. **On 9000 models,** check 10 amp ABS fuse on ABS fuse panel.
4. **On all models,** if pressure is below 140 bar (2030 psi), check that switch between terminals 1 and 4 on the pressure switch is closed.
5. **On 900 models,** check wiring between connector 75 and pin 86 on the pump relay.
6. **On 9000 models,** check wiring between 54 terminal of the ignition switch and pin 86 on the pump relay.
7. **On all models,** check wiring between pin 85 on the pump relay and pin 4 on the pressure switch.
8. **On 900 models,** check wiring between pin 1 on the pressure switch and ground point 93.
9. **On 9000 models,** check wiring between pin 1 on the pressure switch and ground point 7.
10. **On all models,** check wiring between pin 85 on the pump relay and pin 14 on the ECU.
11. If wiring is satisfactory, replace pump relay.

DIAGNOSTIC TROUBLE CODES E015, E016, E017, E018, E033, E034 & E035

1. These diagnostic trouble codes indicate the following inlet and outlet valve faults:
   a. Diagnostic trouble code E015, right front inlet valve is defective.
   b. Diagnostic trouble code E016, rear outlet valve is defective.
   c. Diagnostic trouble code E017, rear inlet valve is defective.
   d. Diagnostic trouble code E018, main valve is defective.
   e. Diagnostic trouble code E033, front left outlet valve is defective.
   f. Diagnostic trouble code E034, front right outlet valve is defective.
   g. Diagnostic trouble code E035, front left inlet valve is defective.
2. Check wiring as follows:
   a. Diagnostic trouble code E015, check between pin 7 of the valve block connector and pin 15 of the ECU.
   b. Diagnostic trouble code E016, check between pin 4 of the valve block connector and pin 33 of the ECU.
   c. Diagnostic trouble code E017, check between pin 5 of the valve block connector and pin 17 of the ECU.
   d. Diagnostic trouble code E018, check between main valve connector and pin 18 of the ECU.
   e. Diagnostic trouble code E033, check between pin 3 of the valve block connector and pin 16 of the ECU.
   f. Diagnostic trouble code E034, check between pin 6 of the valve block connector and pin 34 of the ECU.
   g. Diagnostic trouble code E034, check between pin 2 of the valve block connector and pin 35 of the ECU.
3. If wiring is satisfactory, replace valve block.

DIAGNOSTIC TROUBLE CODES EE22, EE23, EE24 & EE25

1. These error codes indicate sensor wheel runout, replace sensor wheel as follows:
   a. Diagnostic trouble code EE22, right rear sensor wheel.
   b. Diagnostic trouble code EE23, left front sensor wheel.
   c. Diagnostic trouble code EE24, left rear sensor wheel.
   d. Diagnostic trouble code EE25, right front sensor wheel.

DIAGNOSTIC TROUBLE CODE E032

1. This diagnostic trouble code indicates a defective pump relay. This diagnostic trouble code is triggered if signal level at pins 14 and 32 of the ECU has been the same for more than 40 seconds.
2. Check 30 amp fuse of the ABS fuse panel.
3. Check wiring between connector 75 and pin 30 on the pump relay.
4. Check wiring between pin 32 of the ECU and pin 87 on the pump relay.
5. Check wiring between pin 87 on the pump relay and pin 1 on the pump motor.
6. Check for break in circuit continuity or short circuit between pins 85 and 86 of the pump relay.
7. **On 900 models,** check wiring between pin 2 on pump motor and ground point 93.
8. **On 9000 models,** check wiring between pin 2 on pump motor and ground point 7.
9. **On all models,** if wiring is satisfactory, replace pump relay.

DIAGNOSTIC TROUBLE CODE E132

1. This diagnostic trouble code indicates hydraulic pump is running continuously. This diagnostic trouble code can be triggered only if ECU terminal 32 has been energized for more than 90 seconds during testing.
2. Check wiring between pin 14 on the ECU and pin 85 on the pump relay.
3. Check wiring between pin 85 on the pump relay and pin 4 on the pressure switch.
4. If hydraulic pressure is higher than 180 bar (2610 psi), check if switch between pins 1 and 4 on the pressure switch is open.
5. If switch is not open and wiring is satisfactory, replace pump relay.

DIAGNOSTIC TROUBLE CODE PRES

1. This diagnostic trouble code indicates hydraulic pressure to pressure switch is low.
2. Ensure pressure switch connections are satisfactory.
3. Check level in brake fluid reservoir.
4. **On 900 models,** check wiring between pin 1 on the pump and ground point 93.
5. **On 9000 models,** check wiring between pin 1 on the pump and ground point 7.
6. **On all models,** if pressure switch connections, brake fluid level and wiring are satisfactory, replace pump.

SYSTEM SERVICE

Brake System Bleed

Front brake calipers must be bled first.

1. Fill fluid reservoir to the top.
2. Connect a length of transparent hose to right front caliper bleed nipple and place other end of hose into a clear container.
3. While depressing brake pedal, open bleed nipple. Repeat until there are no more air bubbles visible in hose.
4. Connect hose to left front caliper and repeat bleed process.
5. Connect hose to rear caliper, switch on ignition and repeat bleed process. **Pump motor must not run for more than two minutes at a time. After motor has been running, let it cool for approximately 10 minutes.** Repeat on the other rear caliper, then fill fluid reservoir.

Component Replacement

BRAKE FLUID RESERVOIR, REPLACE

1. Remove accumulator as outlined in "Accumulator, Replace."
2. Remove hydraulic unit as outlined in "Hydraulic Unit, Replace."
3. Disconnect pump inlet hose from brake fluid reservoir, then remove reservoir to hydraulic unit attaching screw.
4. Lift reservoir off hydraulic unit, then remove rubber bushings from hydraulic unit. **Take care not to lose spacer and O-ring on rear connection.**
5. Reverse procedure to install, noting the following:
   a. Install two new rubber bushings into hydraulic unit.
   b. Bleed brake system as outlined in "Brake System Bleed."
   c. Switch ignition on and ensure brake-warning and ABS-warning lights go off.

HYDRAULIC UNIT, REPLACE

Prior to beginning work, system must be depressurized. To depressurize the system, turn ignition switch off and press brake pedal down about 20 times until positive resistance is felt in the pedal. The hydraulic unit and its connections must also be thoroughly cleaned, to prevent dirt from entering the hydraulic system.

900

1. Remove lower trim panel from under the steering wheel.
2. Remove heater duct, sound insulation from behind brake pedal, disconnect lefthand side defroster hose.
3. Remove hydraulic pushrod pin retaining clip, then the pin from the pushrod.
4. Remove air intake hose and coolant tank retaining bolts, then position coolant tank aside.
5. Disconnect hydraulic unit electrical connectors.
6. Remove retaining bolt from bracket between hydraulic unit and front assembly, then move bracket and electrical leads out of the way.
7. Siphon as much fluid as possible from reservoir.
8. **On models with manual transaxle,** disconnect and plug hose for clutch cylinder.
9. **On all models,** unplug electrical connector for the pump motor at the hydraulic unit.
10. Label brake hydraulic pipes and large bore return pipe.
11. Disconnect brake pipes from valve block, then plug all pipes to prevent dirt from entering system.
12. Remove hydraulic unit retaining nuts, then the hydraulic unit.
13. Reverse procedure to install, noting the following:
    a. **Torque** hydraulic unit retaining nuts to 16–22 ft. lbs.
    b. Switch ignition on and ensure pump is operating.
    c. Bleed brake system as outlined in "Brake System Bleed."

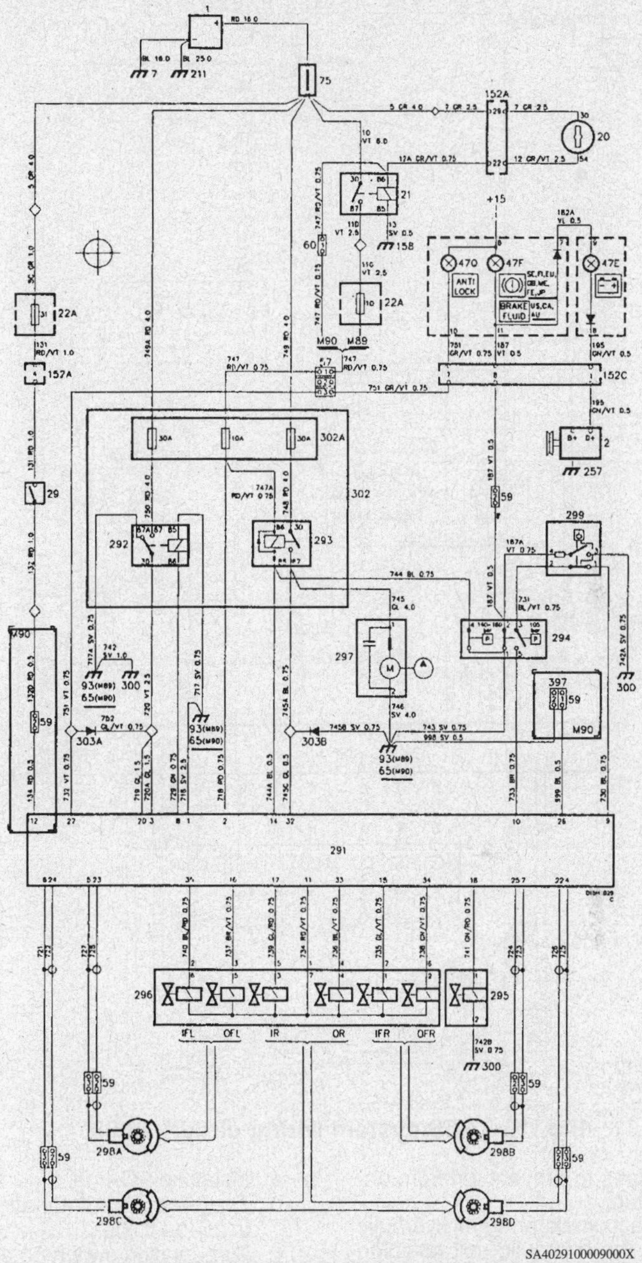

SA4029100009000X

Fig. 9 ABS system wiring circuit. 900

9000

1. Remove lower trim panel from under the steering wheel.
2. Remove hydraulic pushrod pin retaining clip, then the pin from the pushrod.
3. To gain access to the hydraulic unit, remove the following:
   a. Disconnect battery leads and remove battery.
   b. Two clips for positive battery lead at bottom of battery shelf.
   c. Terminal block with leads from battery shelf.
   d. Bracket and connector at rear of battery shelf.
   e. Fuel filter from battery shelf, then the battery shelf.
4. Remove steady bar between fender and subframe.
5. Position fuel filter aside, then siphon as much fluid as possible from reservoir.
6. Remove lefthand front wheel and wheelwell liner.
7. Remove steady bar between fender and subframe.
8. Disconnect hydraulic unit electrical connectors.
9. Remove ground lead retaining clip and ground lead.
10. **On models with manual transaxle,** disconnect and plug hose for clutch cylinder.
11. **On all models,** label brake hydraulic pipes, then disconnect brake pipes from valve block.

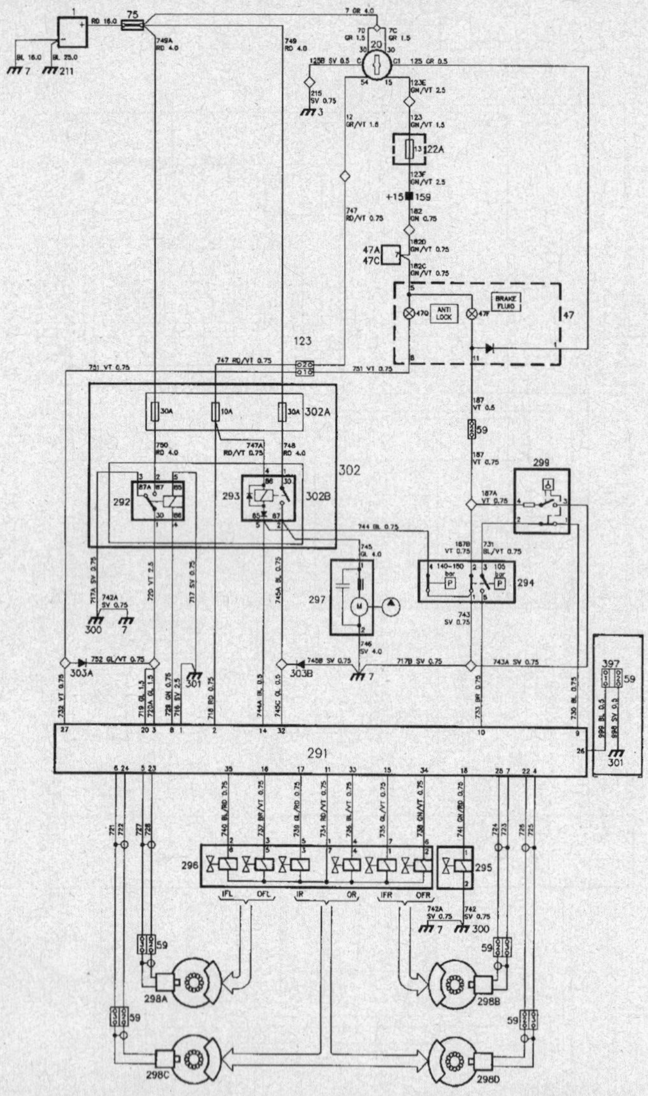

SA4029100010000X

Fig. 10 ABS system wiring circuit. 9000

12. Plug all pipes to prevent dirt from entering system.
13. Remove accumulator from hydraulic unit, then the hydraulic unit retaining nuts and hydraulic unit from bulkhead.
14. Reverse procedure to install, noting the following:
    a. **Torque** hydraulic unit retaining nuts to 16–22 ft. lbs.
    b. **Torque** accumulator to hydraulic unit retaining nuts to 25–34 ft. lbs.
    c. Switch ignition on and ensure pump is operating.
    d. Bleed brake system as outlined in "Brake System Bleed."

ACCUMULATOR, REPLACE

900

1. **Depressurize system as outlined in "Hydraulic Unit, Replace," prior to beginning work.**
2. Using an 8 mm Allen key, remove accumulator retaining bolt.
3. Remove accumulator from vehicle.
4. Reverse procedure to install, noting the following:
    a. Install new O-ring.
    b. **Torque** accumulator attaching bolt to 25–34 ft. lbs.
    c. Turn ignition switch on and ensure brake and ABS warning lights go off.

9000

1. **Depressurize system as outlined in "Hydraulic Unit, Replace," prior to beginning work.**
2. Disconnect battery leads, then remove battery.
3. Remove fuel filter from battery shelf, then position aside.
4. Remove accumulator from vehicle.
5. Reverse procedure to install, noting the following:
    a. Install new O-ring.
    b. **Torque** accumulator attaching bolt to 25–34 ft. lbs.
    c. Turn ignition switch on and ensure brake and ABS warning lights go off.

PRESSURE SWITCH, REPLACE

900

1. **Depressurize system as outlined in "Hydraulic Unit, Replace," prior to beginning work.**
2. Remove rubber damper from pump delivery pipe.
3. Disconnect pressure switch electrical connector.
4. Using socket tool No. 89 96 571, or equivalent, remove pressure switch.
5. Reverse procedure to install, noting the following:
    a. Fit new O-ring onto pressure switch.
    b. **Torque** pressure switch to 15–19 ft. lbs.
    c. Switch ignition on to ensure brake and ABS warning lights go off.

9000

1. **Depressurize system as outlined in "Hydraulic Unit, Replace," prior to beginning work.**
2. Remove rubber covering from delivery pipe.
3. Disconnect pressure switch electrical connector.
4. Using socket tool No. 89 96 571, or equivalent, remove pressure switch.
5. Reverse procedure to install, noting the following:
    a. Fit new O-ring onto pressure switch.
    b. **Torque** pressure switch to 15–19 ft. lbs.
    c. Switch ignition on to ensure brake and ABS warning lights go off.

PUMP DELIVERY LINE, REPLACE

900

1. **Depressurize system as outlined in "Hydraulic Unit, Replace," prior to beginning work.**
2. Remove air intake, then remove coolant expansion tank retaining bolt and position tank aside.
3. Siphon hydraulic fluid from the fluid reservoir.
4. Disconnect electrical connector for fluid level indicator.
5. **On models with manual transaxle,** disconnect and plug end of hose for clutch cylinder.
6. **On all models,** remove reservoir retaining screw, then lift reservoir off of hydraulic unit.
7. Disconnect rear brake pipe on the hydraulic unit to gain access to pump delivery pipe coupling.
8. Remove pump delivery pipe, plug two openings for pipe unit.
9. Reverse procedure to install, bleed brake system as outlined in "Brake System Bleed."

9000

1. Remove hydraulic unit as outlined in

"Hydraulic Unit, Replace."
2. Remove pump delivery pipe from hydraulic unit and plug both openings.
3. Reverse procedure to install, bleed brake system as outlined in "Brake System Bleed."

PUMP & MOTOR UNIT, REPLACE

900

1. Remove hydraulic unit as outlined in "Hydraulic Unit, Replace."
2. Remove pump delivery pipe from pump unit.
3. Pry back catch and unplug motor electrical connector.
4. Disconnect inlet hose from pump unit, then remove screw at front of pump unit.
5. Remove dampers, spacers and washers.
6. Remove pump and motor from rear mounting, then the pressure switch.
7. Reverse procedure to install, noting the following:
   a. Install a new O-ring on the pressure switch.
   b. Assemble dampers, washers and spacers, **Fig. 11,** then install front securing screw.
   c. Bleed brake system as outlined in "Brake System Bleed."

9000

1. Remove hydraulic unit as outlined in "Hydraulic Unit, Replace."
2. Remove pump delivery pipe from pump, then plug port in pump unit.
3. Release catch and unplug electrical connector.
4. Disconnect pump inlet hose from pump.
5. Remove securing bolt from front of pump unit. **When removing washers, note their position for assembly reference.**
6. Lift pump unit out of rear mounting, then remove pressure switch.
7. Reverse procedure to install, noting the following:
   a. Install a new O-ring, then **torque** pressure switch to 15–19 ft. lbs.
   b. Position washers in order they were removed, then install securing bolt.
   c. Bleed brake system as outlined in "Brake System Bleed."
   d. Switch ignition on to ensure brake and ABS warning lights go off.

VALVE BLOCK, REPLACE

900

1. **Depressurize system as outlined in "Hydraulic Unit, Replace," prior to beginning work.**
2. Remove air intake, then remove coolant expansion tank retaining bolt and position tank aside.

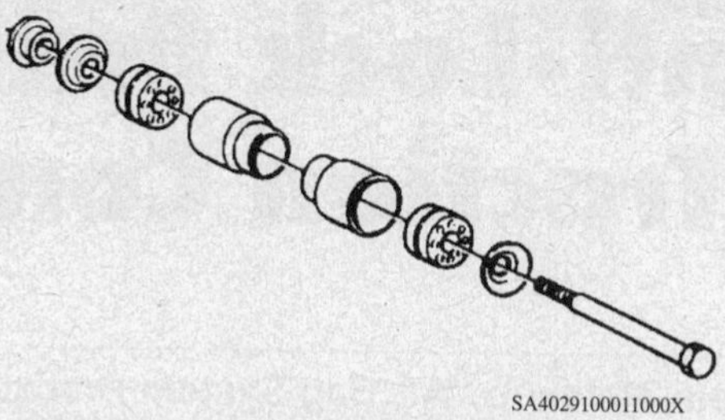
SA4029100011000X

Fig. 11 Pump/motor unit damper, washer & spacer installation. 900

3. Siphon hydraulic fluid from the fluid reservoir.
4. Disconnect electrical connector on valve block.
5. Disconnect brake hydraulic pipes from underside of valve block.
6. Disconnect remaining brake hydraulic pipes and large bore return pipe from valve block.
7. Loosen nut on cover underneath brake hydraulic pipes.
8. Pull brake pipes and return pipe away from valve body, then plug ends of pipes.
9. Cut tie that secures wiring harness to valve block.
10. Remove three retaining nuts and remove valve block.
11. Reverse procedure to install, bleed brake system as outlined in "Brake System Bleed," then switch ignition on to ensure brake and ABS warning lights go off.

ECU, REPLACE

1. Disconnect battery ground cable.
2. **On 9000 models,** remove cover from rear lefthand side of engine compartment.
3. **On all models,** remove ECU attaching bolts.
4. Disconnect ECU electrical connector, then remove ECU.
5. Reverse procedure to install.

WHEEL SENSORS, REPLACE

900

Front

1. Disconnect battery ground cable.
2. Disconnect sensor lead connector for each wheel, lead connectors are located in the engine compartment.
3. Raise and support front of vehicle, then remove wheel.
4. Pull sensor lead from guide and rubber grommet on wheelwell.
5. Remove sensor retaining screw from caliper, then the sensor.
6. Reverse procedure to install, bleed brake system as outlined in "Brake System Bleed," then switch ignition on to ensure brake and ABS warning lights go off.

Rear

1. Disconnect battery ground cable.
2. Disconnect sensor lead located under the rear seat.
3. Raise and support rear of vehicle, then remove wheel.
4. Pull sensor lead through rubber grommet on floor.
5. Remove parking brake cable to suspension arm securing clip.
6. Release sensor lead from guide on back of suspension arm.
7. Remove sensor retaining screw from caliper, then the sensor.
8. Reverse procedure to install, bleed brake system as outlined in "Brake System Bleed," then switch ignition on to ensure brake and ABS warning lights go off.

9000

Front

1. Disconnect battery ground cable.
2. Disconnect sensor lead connector for each wheel, lead connectors are located in the engine compartment.
3. Remove cover over space behind false bulkhead panel at rear lefthand side of engine compartment.
4. Lift rubber molding on false bulkhead panel and remove plastic clip on the panel.
5. Remove cover from fresh air filter at false bulkhead panel on the rear righthand side of engine compartment.
6. Undo pipe clips for A/C flow and return pipes, then raise A/C pipes and pull sensor lead through.
7. Loosen bolt securing false bulkhead panel and raise panel enough to allow sensor lead to be pulled under the panel.
8. Raise and support vehicle, then remove wheel assembly.
9. Remove wheelwell liner rear section, then cut through tie holding sensor lead to top bracket.
10. Pull sensor lead through rubber grommet on wheelwell.
11. Remove sensor retaining bolt and sensor.
12. Reverse procedure to install.

Rear

1. Disconnect battery ground cable.
2. Tilt rear seat forward and remove cover.
3. Disconnect sensor lead connector.
4. Raise and support rear of vehicle, then remove rear wheel.
5. Undo clip and pull sensor lead through rubber grommet on floor.
6. Remove sensor retaining bolt and sensor.
7. Reverse procedure to install.

Mark II Anti-Lock Brake System w/Traction Control

NOTE: On Air Bag Equipped Models, Refer To "Air Bag System Precautions" Located In The Front Of This Manual For System Disarming & Arming Procedures.

NOTE: Electrical Symbol & Wire Color Code Identification Located In The Front Of This Manual May Be Used As An Aid When Using Wiring Circuits Found In This Section.

INDEX

	Page No.
Description	38-104
Components	38-105
System	38-104
Diagnosis & Testing	38-105
Accessing Diagnostic Trouble Codes	38-105
Diagnostic Trouble Code Interpretation	38-106
TC/ABS Control Unit Pin Tests	38-113
Precautions	38-104
Air Bag Systems	38-104
Radio Anti-Theft Lock	38-104
System Service	38-114
Brake System Bleed	38-114
Calibrating ETS ECU	38-114
Component Replacement	38-114
Control Valve For Turbo Bypass Valve	38-114
Non-Return Valve	38-114
Safety Valve	38-114
TC/ABS ECU	38-114
TC/ABS Hydraulic Unit	38-114
Troubleshooting	38-105

PRECAUTIONS

AIR BAG SYSTEMS

Refer to "Air Bag System Precautions" in the front of this manual for system disarming and arming procedures.

RADIO ANTI-THEFT LOCK

9000

1995-96

Radio and cassette player are equipped with an electronic four-digit anti-theft lock. This four-digit code is programmed at manufacturing and cannot be changed. If the battery is disconnected for more than three minutes, if unit is removed or if otherwise cut off from power, the four-digit code must be entered with the quick-selection buttons as follows:

1. Turn radio on, then, when display shows "Code In," enter four-digit code with quick-selection buttons. If code is correct, last-tuned radio frequency is shown on display. If wrong digit has been entered by mistake, all four digits must be entered again. If code is wrong it stays on display.
2. If incorrect four-digit code has been entered, press Band button for more than three seconds to clear display. Display shows "Code In" and new attempt to enter correct code can be made.
3. If wrong code has been used three times in succession, four dashes appear on display and you must wait an hour with radio switched on before trying again.
4. To try again, hold Band button for at least three seconds. "Code In" should appear on display.
5. Correct code must be entered at first attempt, otherwise you must wait another hour with unit switched on before trying again.

DESCRIPTION

SYSTEM

Traction Control System (TCS) prevents wheel spin when the vehicle is accelerating on a slippery surface.

The TCS system for manual transaxles consists of two subsystems, Anti-Lock Braking System (ABS) and Electronic Throttle System (ETS).

The TCS system utilizes many of the components in the ABS system. The major difference is the addition of the Electronic Throttle System.

The Manual transaxle TCS has the capability to apply the front brakes independently during low speed wheel spin and also the ability to close the throttle butterfly to reduce wheel spin at any speed.

TRACTION CONTROL SYSTEM OPERATION

This system uses the speed of the rear wheels as a reference speed against the speed of each front wheel. If the speed of a front wheel exceeds that of the reference speed from the rear wheels, the condition is known as wheel spin. The magnitude of the spin together with the speed of the vehicle determine how the system operates.

To enable the vehicle to achieve maximum traction, a certain amount of wheel spin, which varies depending on the speed of the car, is allowed.

Low Speed Operating Mode

The front wheel having the poorer grip (lower friction) starts to spin first.

When wheel spin has reached a speed of just under 10 mph, TCS control is initiated and the TC/ABS system applies the brake for that wheel. As brake is applied to the wheel, additional torque is transferred to the other wheel, which still is maintaining good traction. If the road surface is very slippery, the other wheel may also start to spin, if it does, once it is spinning at a speed of about 4 mph, the amount of throttle is reduced electronically, inhibiting further wheel spin.

So the system is able to provide the optimum combination of traction and steering precision with the same traction or mobility as that provided by a conventional limited-slip differential.

The upper limit for the amount of wheel spin allowed before the TCS takes over is gradually reduced up to a speed of about 12 mph, after which it remains constant regardless of how much throttle is used, although the upper limit for braking will then be increased.

High Speed Operating Mode (Over 25 MPH)

Once the vehicle reaches a speed of about 25 mph, the system switches mode and initiates throttle control when the first wheel starts spinning. Traction control by application of the brake will be initiated for the other wheel if the amount of wheel spin is great enough.

Up to a speed of about 37 mph, wheel spin of up to just under 2 mph is allowed, after which an increase of about 5 percent

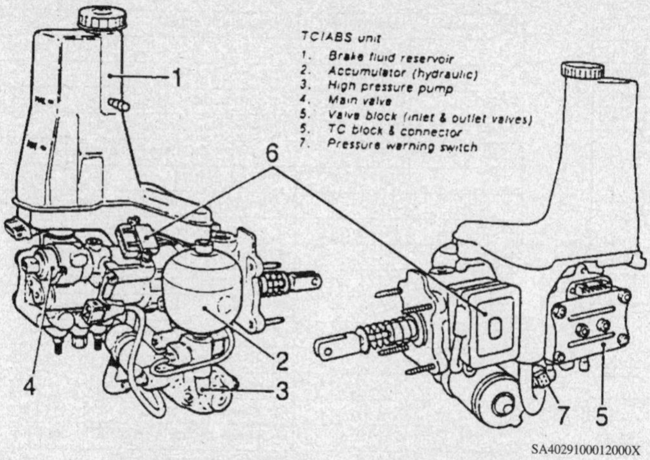
TC/ABS unit
1. Brake fluid reservoir
2. Accumulator (hydraulic)
3. High pressure pump
4. Main valve
5. Valve block (inlet & outlet valves)
5. TC block & connector
7. Pressure warning switch
1
2
3
4
5
6
7
SA4029100012000X

Fig. 1 Hydraulic unit components

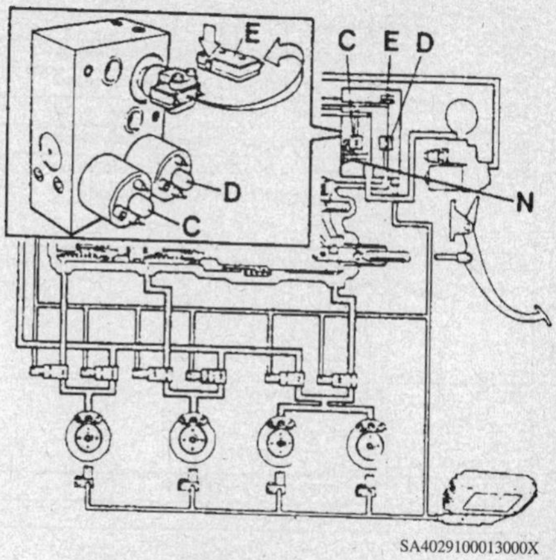
C
E
D
N
SA4029100013000X

Fig. 2 TCS valve block components

relative to the increased speed of the vehicle will be allowed.

So at speed of 87 mph, for instance, wheel spin of approximately 4.4 mph will be allowed before electronic control of the throttle is initiated.

System Interaction

Conventional operation of the ABS system is the same as before, but an additional valve block (TC block) for the anti-spin function has been added onto the hydraulic unit.

The TC block, together with the main valve, wheel sensors, and inlet and outlet valves are the main components of the TC/ABS system. The system is equipped with indicator/warning lights for monitoring and checking of the system. These warning lights indicate when the system is operating and provide a warning if a fault should occur.

The wheel sensors send wheel speed information to the ABS ECU. Using the average speed of the rear wheels as a reference value, the ECU continuously monitors the amount of wheel spin in the front wheels (speed above reference value for rear wheels).

When the system detects a tendency for wheel spin, and the TCS calls for braking of the front wheel concerned, pressure is directed from the accumulator through the TC block and main valve to the front wheel circuits. The inlet and outlet valves then control the TCS initiated braking.

COMPONENTS

ELECTRONIC CONTROL UNIT (TC/ABS ECU)

The ECU is programmed to detect both permanent and intermittent faults. Faults detected by the ECU are stored in an EEPROM chip, so the diagnostic trouble codes remain in memory even when power supply is switched off or interrupted.

TC/ABS HYDRAULIC UNIT

The main components of the hydraulic unit, **Fig. 1,** are the brake fluid reservoir, fluid level switch, accumulator and a pressure warning switch.

TCS VALVE BLOCK

In contrast to the conventional ABS unit. the TC/ABS unit has a separate valve block (TC block), **Fig. 2,** to direct accumulator pressure for TC controlled braking to the appropriate wheel.

The pressure is directed to the front wheel circuits through the main valve and is modulated by the inlet and outlet valves for the front wheel indicating spin.

The TC block, **Fig. 2,** includes two control valves (C and D), a pressure reducing valve (N) and a pressure switch (E). The function of the control valve is to direct hydraulic pressure as required, depending on whether braking is TCS controlled or required for modulation in conjunction with ABS control.

TROUBLESHOOTING

1. The diagnostic socket (green) is located below the righthand front seat.
2. During fault diagnosis, the ignition switch must always be in the On position.
3. The ISAT system number for the TC/ABS system is number 3.
4. Always read off and note down all stored diagnostic trouble codes before disconnecting the battery or ECU.
5. If communication cannot be established between ISAT and the ECU, check the leads between ECU pins 23 and 42 and the diagnostic socket. Also check that the power feed and ground circuits to the diagnostic socket are good and the connector pins are not damaged.
6. Once diagnostic trouble codes stored in the systems's ECU have been transferred to ISAT, the diagnosis function is finished. The technician should next enter any command codes which apply to the problem which exists. It is sometimes quite helpful to enter All command codes to check the status of certain signals and components before proceeding with the detailed diagnostic procedure.
7. To avoid doing damage to the ECU, ensure the ignition is off before unplugging the connector.
8. Before tracing faults on a vehicle's electronic systems, always start by checking that the grounding circuits for the ECU concerned are good and that all nominal voltage levels are correct.
9. Unplug connectors and plugs to check the pins are undamaged and not loose. After checking, plug in all connectors and clear all diagnostic trouble codes. Start engine or drive vehicle again to check that the fault or faults persist.
10. When first detected, a fault will be assigned a permanent diagnostic trouble code. If the fault later disappears, the fault will be classified as intermittent.
11. All signals around the 12 volt level are proportional to battery voltage. These levels must therefore be taken only as a rough guide.
12. Zero voltage signal levels indicate ground, although a sensitive multimeter may indicate a value slightly above zero volts.
13. When ISAT command codes are being used to test the system while the vehicle is being driven, communication between ISAT and the ECU will be broken if the speed of the vehicle exceeds 12 mph.
14. If no diagnostic trouble codes can be read from the system even though the warning lights are On, start by checking the safety circuit (pin 8 and 51).
15. Never use the breakout box when vehicle is being driven.

DIAGNOSIS & TESTING

ACCESSING DIAGNOSTIC TROUBLE CODES

Command codes instruct the ECU to perform certain functions while diagnosing diagnostic trouble codes.

Refer to **Fig. 3,** for ISAT command codes.

The ECU connector on the wiring loom is in the form of a molded plug, test probes cannot be connected to the back of the connector.

Use breakout box 8611006 with test lead set 8611030, which should be connected between the ECU and the connector.

All measurements on the system must be made with breakout box connected.

Code	Function/Component	Display Text
259	Reads speed signal from LF wheel sensor	e.g. 80020 = 20 km/h
25A	Reads speed signal from RF wheel sensor	e.g. 80020 = 20 km/h
25B	Reads speed signal from LR wheel sensor	e.g. 80020 = 20 km/h
25C	Reads speed signal from RR wheel sensor	e.g. 80020 = 20 km/h
200	Shows status of TC-block pressure switch (Manual transmission TCS version only)	8B100 = closed (brake released) 8B000 = open (brake applied)
201	Shows status of pressure and level-warning switch (safety circuit)	8B100 = closed (system OK) 8B000 = open (low fluid level or low pressure or open circuit)
202	Shows status of brake-light switch	8B100 = closed (brake applied) 8B000 = open (brake released)
800	Terminate communications	
900	Clear all fault codes	

SA4029100014000X

Fig. 3 Command code chart

To access diagnostic trouble codes, connect ISAT tester to diagnostic socket (green), located under righthand front seat, then follow instructions included with tester.

DIAGNOSTIC TROUBLE CODE INTERPRETATION

Refer to **Fig. 4** for diagnostic trouble code identification, and **Fig. 5** for system wiring diagram.

DIAGNOSTIC TROUBLE CODE 3/22251

If another diagnostic trouble code other than 32251 or 22251 exists, diagnose that diagnostic trouble code(s) first.

1. Ensure battery voltage is present at pins 3, 33 and 35.
   a. If no voltage is present at all pins, check ABS 30A fuse for the 30 feed (fuse box at bulkhead), RD lead from fuse to system relay and to terminal block on battery shelf.
   b. If voltage is present at one of the pins, check lead from ECU pin to system relay.
   c. If voltage is present at pin 35 only, check system relay operating circuit and that no other diagnostic trouble codes exist for faults that could cause exciter circuit to be open.
2. If no voltage is present at pins 34, 3 and 33, check 10A fuse (ABS).
   a. If fuse is good, check live feed to pin 53. If no voltage is present at pin 53, go to step e.
   b. If voltage is present at pin 53, check GN lead between pin 86 on system relay and ECU pin 34.
   c. Ensure voltage is present at system relay pin 85. If not, go to step f.
   d. If voltage exists, try a new system relay.
   e. If no voltage exits at pin 53, check RD/WH lead as far as the fuse, and the feed in the lead from pin 54 of ignition switch to the live side of ABS fuse.
   f. Check BK lead from pin 85 on system relay through pump relay to 10A fuse.
3. If there is battery voltage at pin 34 but not at pins 3 and 33, operating circuit is satisfactory but ECU has failed to ground the circuit because of another fault in ABS system.
4. If battery voltage is reaching pin 34 but diagnostic trouble code 3/22251 is still being generated, check resistance across relay pins 85 and 86. Resistance should be approximately 75 ohms.

DIAGNOSTIC TROUBLE CODE 36522

There are three different conditions associated with diagnostic trouble code 36522 and the safety circuit. For complete test procedure of this circuit, follow the fault tracing procedure for all three conditions.

Short To 12V

1. With ignition in Drive position, enter ISAT command code 201. If display shows 8B100, it indicates continuity from pin 8 to pin 51. If display shows 8B000, it indicates an open circuit.
2. With ignition in Off position, remove ECU and connect breakout box. With ignition in Drive position, ensure voltage exists across pin 8 and ground and across pin 51 and ground.
   a. If voltage exists, check circuit between pins 8 and 51 for short to 12V.
   b. If voltage does not exist, turn ignition to Off position, fit and connect ECU, then clear diagnostic trouble code and see if it is regenerated.
3. If diagnostic trouble code 36522 is regenerated, continue with "Short To Ground" test procedure. If no other faults are found after test procedure is completed, replace ECU.

Short To Ground

1. With ignition in Drive position, enter ISAT command code 201. If display shows 8B100, it indicates continuity from pin 8 to pin 51. If display shows 8B000, it indicates an open circuit.
2. Turn ignition to Off position, remove ECU and connect breakout box.
3. Measure resistance across pin 8 and ground and across pin 51 and ground. Resistance should be infinity.
4. If resistance is not infinity, check leads and connections for short to ground.

Open Circuit

1. With ignition in On position, ensure pump is running and check brake fluid level.

Permanent	Intermittent	Component/signal
	775B1	ECU fault
	775B2	ECU fault (RAM)
E7061	F7061	No communication with ETS
32251	22251	System-relay function faulty
35321	25321	Brake-light switch function faulty
	36521	Pressure switch function faulty
	36522	Safety circuit, pins 8-51, open or shorted
44221	24221	LF wheel-sensor signal absent
44222	24222	RF wheel-sensor signal absent
44223	24223	LR wheel-sensor signal absent
44224	24224	RR wheel-sensor signal absent
	2422A	LF wheel-sensor signal faulty (>40 km h)
	2422B	RF wheel-sensor signal faulty (>40 km h)
	2422C	LR wheel-sensor signal faulty (>40 km h)
	2422D	RR wheel-sensor signal faulty (>40 km h)
	24291	LF wheel-sensor signal faulty (<40 km h)
	24292	RF wheel-sensor signal faulty (<40 km h)
	24293	LR wheel-sensor signal faulty (<40 km h)
	24294	RR wheel-sensor signal faulty (<40 km h)
	24251	LF wheel-sensor signal faulty (compare wheel speed)
	24252	RF wheel-sensor signal faulty (compare wheel speed)
	24253	LR wheel-sensor signal faulty (compare wheel speed)
	24254	RR wheel-sensor signal faulty (compare wheel speed)
53427	33427	Main valve fault
53428	33428	NC TC-block valve fault
53429	33429	NO TC-block valve fault
53421	33421	LF inlet valve fault
53422	33422	LF outlet valve fault
53423	33423	RF inlet valve fault
53424	33424	RF outlet valve fault
53425	33425	Rear inlet valve fault
53426	33426	Rear outlet valve fault
	234B1	LF outlet valve hydraulic fault
	234B2	RF outlet valve hydraulic fault
	234B3	Rear outlet valve hydraulic fault
	234B4	Rear outlet valve hydraulic fault
		Warning light diagnostics

SA4029100015000X

Fig. 4 TC/ABS diagnostic trouble code chart

Component Location	Description
22A	Fuse panel In glovebox
47A	Fuel gauge In instrument cluster
47C	Coolant temperature gauge In instrument cluster
47F	Brake fluid level warning lamp In the instrument cluster on the circuit board for indicating and warning lamps
47Q	Anti-lock brakes (ABS) warning lamp In the instrument cluster on the circuit board for indicating and warning lamps
291	Control unit, ABS In left rear corner engine compartment on battery bracket
292	Main relay, ABS In the left rear corner of engine compartment in the ABS relay/fuse box
293	Pump relay, ABS In the left rear corner of engine compartment in the ABS relay/fuse box
294	Pressure switch, ABS In the rear of the engine compartment on the brake hydraulic unit
296	Valve block, ABS In the rear of the engine compartment on the brake hydraulic unit
297	Hydraulic pump motor, ABS In the rear of the engine compartment on the brake hydraulic unit
298A	Left front wheel sensor On the left-hand steering knuckle housing
298B	Right front wheel sensor On the right-hand steering knuckle housing
298C	Left rear wheel sensor On the left-hand rear wheel hub
298D	Right rear wheel sensor On the right-hand rear wheel hub
299	Brake fluid level sensor, ABS In the rear of the engine compartment in the brake fluid reservoir
302A	Relay and fuse box, ABS In the left rear corner of the engine compartment on the false bulkhead
303A, 303B	Diode, ABS Inside the ABS relay/fuse box under the relay/fuse holders

SA4029100016010X

Fig. 5 TC/ABS wiring diagram (Part 1 of 3)

Component Location	Description
347	ISAT diagnostic plug for engine systems (black) Under forward edge of right front seat behind trim plate
348	ISAT diagnostic plug for chassis systems (green) Under forward edge of right front seat behind trim plate
376	ETS electronic control unit Under left front seat
382	TC/ABS electronic control unit In left rear corner of engine compartment on battery bracket
383	TC valve block In the engine compartment on the brake hydraulic unit
385	Diode
397	Diagnostic test socket, ABS (1990 model) In engine compartment under the false bulkhead to the left of the ABS control unit
414	ASR electronic control unit Under left front seat on top of ETS electronic control unit
H2-12	2-pole connector In the left rear corner of engine compartment to the left of the brake fluid reservoir
H2-46	2-pole connector In the engine compartment under false bulkhead to the extreme left
H2-47	2-pole connector In the engine compartment under false bulkhead to the extreme right
H2-48	2-pole connector Beneath floor under left side of rear seat, access through foam plug
H2-49	2-pole connector Beneath floor under right side of rear seat, access through foam plug
H10-8	10-pole connector (347) Under forward edge of right front seat behind trim plate (black)
H10-9	10-pole connector (348) Under forward edge of right front seat behind trim plate (green)
H10-12	10-pole connector In left rear corner of engine compartment below ABS fuse/relay box

SA4029100016020X

Fig. 5 TC/ABS wiring diagram (Part 2 of 3)

a. If brake fluid level is low, check system for leaks. Add brake fluid if necessary to bring to correct level.
b. If pump is not running or pressure is below 1522 psi, check fuse for pump (ABS 30A) and pump relay operating circuit (ABS 10A).
c. If fluid level, pump and pressure are satisfactory, go to next step and check safety circuit.

2. With ignition in Drive position, enter ISAT command code 201. If display shows 8B100, it indicates circuit continuity. If display shows 8B000, it indicates an open circuit. With ignition in Off position, connect breakout box. Measure resistance across pins 8 and 51 to determine whether circuit has continuity or is open.
3. If circuit is open, check circuit continuity as follows:
   a. Between ECU pin 8 and pin 1 on reservoir switch.
   b. Between pins 1 and 2 on reservoir switch.
   c. Between pin 2 at reservoir and pin 3 on pressure-warning switch.
   d. Between pins 3 and 5 on pressure-warning switch.
   e. Between pin 5 on pressure-warning switch and ECU pin 51.
4. Discharge accumulator, then with ignition in On position, check for battery voltage at pin 14 (pump relay operation).
   a. If voltage does not exist, go to step 6.
   b. If voltage exists, switch ignition to Off position, check motor winding by measuring resistance across pin 14 and ground.
   c. Resistance should be approximately 10 ohms. If not, check resistance across pins 1 and 2 on motor.
   d. If resistance is as specified, check YE lead between pin 1 on motor and pin 87 on pump relay, then BK lead between pin 2 on motor and grounding point G2.
   e. Check diode circuit between pin 87 on pump relay and ground by removing relay and disconnecting pump connector before measuring resistance.
   f. Ensure diode has continuity in one direction and no continuity in the other direction.
5. If the fault has not been found at this point of diagnosis, replace pump.
6. With ignition in On position and pump not running, ensure battery voltage is reaching ECU pin 50. If not, check that voltage is reaching pins 85 and 86 on pump relay and the 10-A fuse. Ensure circuit continuity in leads from pin 86 on pump relay via fuse holder to pin 54 on ignition switch.
7. If voltage exists at pin 86 but not at pin 85, replace pump relay.
8. If battery voltage exists at pin 50, exciter circuit is satisfactory but is not being grounded by pressure-warning switch.
   a. With ignition in Off position, accumulator discharged and ECU connector disconnected, ensure pressure-warning switch is closed by measuring circuit continuity between pin 50 and ground.
   b. If a fault is found in circuit, check BU lead between pump relay pin 85 and pin 4 on pressure-warning switch, between pins 4 and 1 on switch, then check BK lead between pin 1 on switch and ground.
9. If continuity does not exist between pins 1 and 4 on pressure-warning switch connector, replace switch.

DIAGNOSTIC TROUBLE CODES 4/24221, 2422A, 24251 & 24291

1. Raise and support vehicle.
2. With ignition in Drive position, enter ISAT command code 259. The diagnostic trouble code displayed will be between 80002 and 80020 (0–20 km/h), depending on whether wheel is stationary or being rotated by hand.
3. With AC range selected on multimeter, signal can also be measured by connecting probes across pins 30 and 48. Voltage should be approximately 0.1–0.5V AC as wheel is rotated by hand.
4. With ignition in Off position and ECU connector disconnected, check sensor

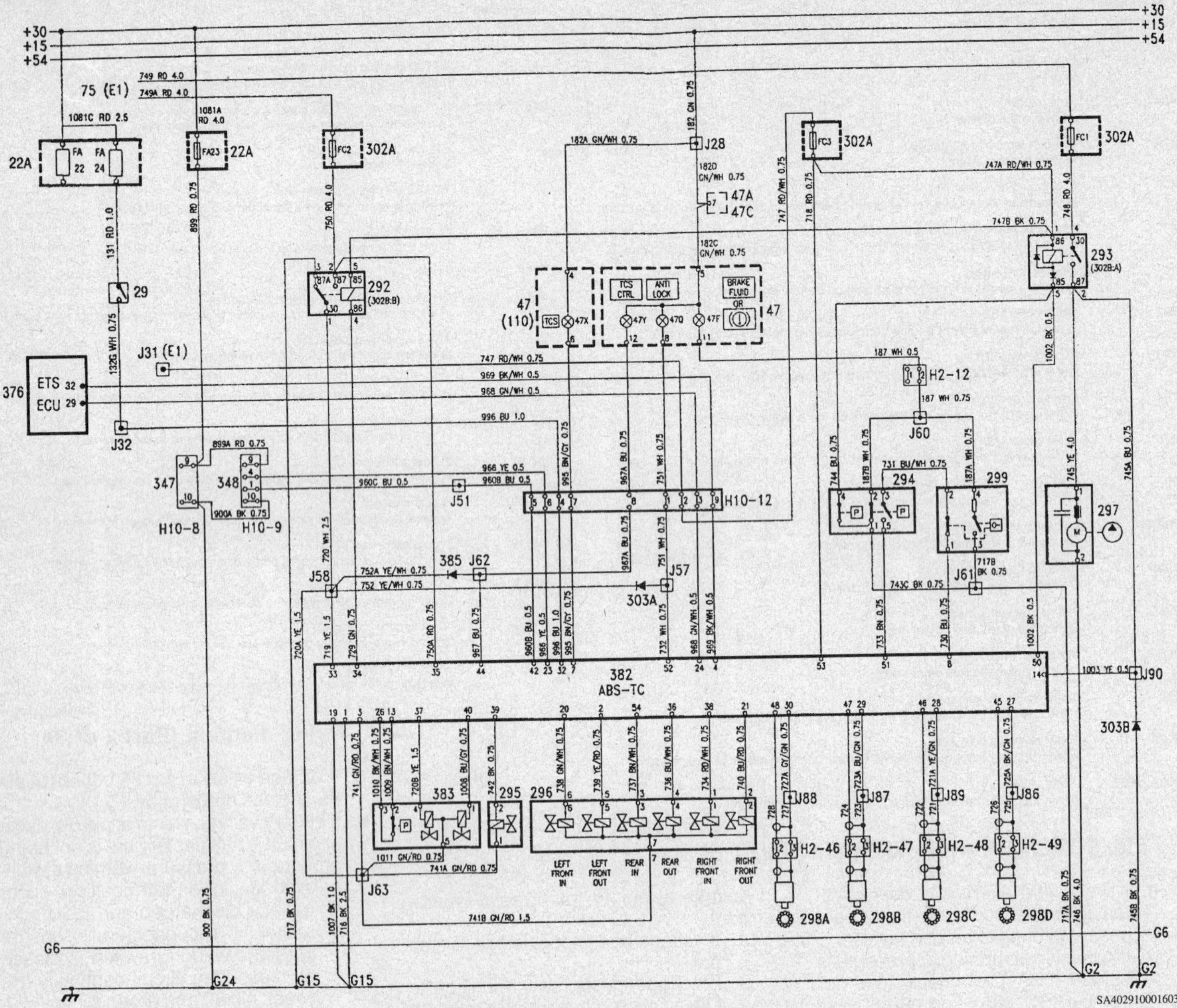

+30
+15
+54
75 (E1)
22A
FA 22
FA 24
29
J31 (E1)
376
ETS
ECU
J32
347
348
H10-8
H10-9
292
(302B:B)
302A
385
J62
J58
J51
47
(110)
TCS CTRL
ANTI LOCK
BRAKE FLUID OR
J28
47A
47C
H10-12
303A
J57
382
ABS-TC
H2-12
J60
294
299
293
(302B:A)
297
J61
J90
303B
383
295
296
LEFT FRONT IN
LEFT FRONT OUT
REAR IN
REAR OUT
RIGHT FRONT IN
RIGHT FRONT OUT
J63
J88
J87
J89
J86
H2-46
H2-47
H2-48
H2-49
298A
298B
298C
298D
G6
G24
G15
G2
SA4029100016030X

Fig. 5 TC/ABS wiring diagram (Part 3 of 3)

winding for continuity by measuring resistance across pins 30 and 48. Resistance should be approximately 1100 ohms.

5. Check leads between sensor and pins 30 and 48 on TC/ABS-system ECU for shorting. Check for poor contact in connectors. Resistance should be as follows:
   a. Pin 30 and ground: infinity.
   b. Pin 48 and ground: infinity.
6. When testing for short to 12V, voltage should be as follows:
   a. Pin 30 and ground: 0V DC (indicates no short to 12V).
   b. Pin 48 and ground: 0V DC (indicates no short to 12V).
7. Ensure left front wheel sensor is properly installed.
8. Ensure sensor wheel is not damaged and is properly installed. Check for play in wheel bearings.
9. Check clearance between sensor and sensor wheel.
10. Ensure ECU pins 1 and 19 are properly grounded.
11. If no fault has been found, test drive vehicle to see if diagnostic trouble code is regenerated. If so, try a known good ECU.

DIAGNOSTIC TROUBLE CODES 4/24222, 2422B, 24252 & 24292

1. Raise and support vehicle.
2. With ignition in Drive position, enter ISAT command code 25A. The code displayed will be between 80002 and 80030 (0–20 km/h), depending on whether wheel is stationary or being rotated by hand.
3. With AC range selected on multimeter, signal can also be measured by connecting probes across pins 29 and 47.
4. With ignition in Off position and ECU connector disconnected, check sensor winding for continuity by measuring resistance across pins 29 and 47. Resistance should be approximately 1100 ohms.
5. Check leads between sensor and pins 29 and 47 on TC/ABS-system ECU for shorting. Check for poor contact in connectors. Resistance should be as follows:
   a. Across pin 29 and ground: infinity.
   b. Across pin 47 and ground: infinity.
6. When testing for short to 12V, voltage should be as follows:
   a. Across pin 29 and ground: 0V DC (indicates no short to 12V).
   b. Across pin 47 and ground: 0V DC (indicates no short to 12V).
7. Ensure right front wheel sensor is properly installed.
8. Ensure sensor wheel is not damaged and is properly installed. Check for play in wheel bearings.
9. Check clearance between sensor and sensor wheel. Clearance should be 0.45–1.55 mm.
10. Ensure ECU pins 1 and 19 are properly grounded.

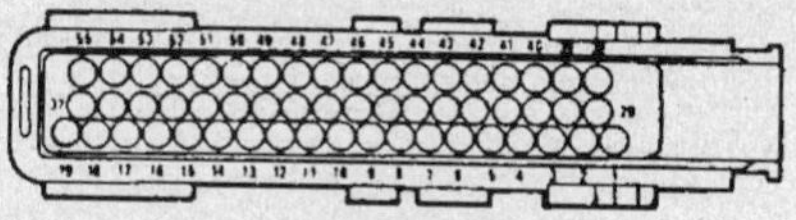

Voltage Checks

The following signals must be tested with the breakout box connected, all system components connected and the ignition switched on. All tests should be made at the breakout box.

Pin#	Circuit/Function	Wire Color	Test
1	Ground	Black	Check voltage drop to ground should be less than 0.1 volts (Ignition must be on to check voltage drop).
2	Left front outlet valve (ECU energizes valve by providing ground)	Yellow/Red	See resistance testing procedure
3	Power in from system relay	Green/Red -or- Yellow/White	System operational (relay activated) = battery volts Relay de-energizes (fault in system) = less than 2 volts
4*	Communication between TC/ABS and ETS (digital signal to ETS pin #32)	Black/White	Engine running = approx. 5 volts D.C. (A reading close to 0 or close to 10 volts indicates a problem in this wire/circuit.) A logic probe should also indicate a continuous 'PULSE' signal.
5	Not used		
6	Not used		
7*	TCS indicator light (ECU provides ground for bulb when system is operating in TCS mode)	Brown Red	Light off = approx. battery volts Light on = approx. 0 volts
8	Pressure/fluid safety circuit (with pin #51)	Blue	System O.K. (switches closed) = 5 to 10 volts Fault (switch open) = 0 volts

* Manual Transmission TCS Version Only
‡ Automatic Transmission TCS Version Only

SA4029100017010X

Fig. 6 TC/ABS control unit pin voltage check (Part 1 of 5)

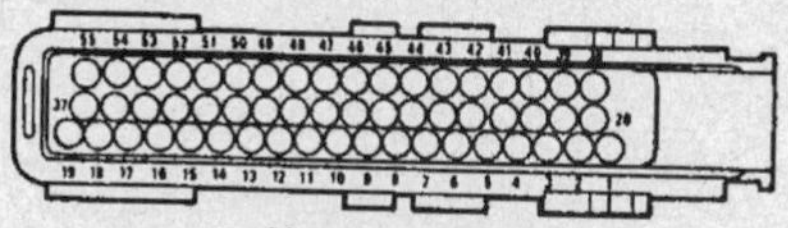

Voltage Checks

The following signals must be tested with the breakout box connected, all system components connected and the ignition switched on. All tests should be made at the breakout box.

Pin#	Circuit/Function	Wire Color	Test
9‡	RR wheel speed signal (digital output to ASR ECU)	Green	Using a Logic Probe: –You should find a steady 'PULSE' at each wire with the ignition ON and the wheel NOT turning (this is a test pulse). –The frequency of the 'PULSE' should increase as the speed of each wheel increases.
10‡	LF wheel speed signal (digital output to ASR ECU)	Yellow	
11‡	RF wheel speed signal (digital output to ASR ECU)	Blue	
12‡	LR wheel speed signal (digital output to ASR ECU)	Grey	
13*	TC block pressure switch (voltage signal into switch)	Brown/White	Brake off = approx. 8 volts (switch closed) Brake applied = approx. 10 volts (switch open)
14	Pump relay pin 87 (monitors the status of relay contacts)	Yellow	Pump relay energizes = battery volts Pump relay de-energizes = 0 volts
15	Not used		
16	Not used		
17	Not used		
18	Not used		
19	Ground	Black	Check voltage drop to ground. Should be less than 0.1 volt (ignition must be on to check voltage drop).
20	Left front inlet valve (ECU energizes valve by providing ground)	Green/White	See resistance testing procedure
21	Right front outlet valve (ECU energizes valve by providing ground)	Blue/Red	See resistance testing procedure

* Manual Transmission TCS Version Only
‡ Automatic Transmission TCS Version Only

SA4029100017020X

Fig. 6 TC/ABS control unit pin voltage check (Part 2 of 5)

11. If no fault has been found, test drive vehicle to see if diagnostic trouble code is regenerated. If so, try a known good ECU.

DIAGNOSTIC TROUBLE CODES 4/24223, 2422C, 24253 & 24293

1. Raise and support vehicle.
2. With ignition in Drive position, enter ISAT command code 25B. The code displayed will be between 80002 and 80020 (0–20 km/h), depending on whether wheel is stationary or being rotated by hand.
3. With AC range selected on multimeter, signal can also be measured by connecting probes across pins 28 and 46. Voltage should be approximately 0.1–0.5V AC as wheel is rotated by hand.
4. With ignition in Off position and ECU connector disconnected, check sensor winding for continuity by measuring resistance across pins 28 and 46. Resistance should be approximately 1100 ohms.
5. Check leads between sensor and pins 28 and 46 on TC/ABS-system ECU for shorting. Check for poor contact in connectors. Resistance should be as follows:
   a. Across pin 28 and ground: infinity.
   b. Across pin 46 and ground: infinity.
6. When testing for short to 12V, voltage should be as follows:
   a. Across pin 28 and ground: 0V DC (indicates no short to 12V).
   b. Across pin 46 and ground: 0V DC (indicates no short to 12V).
7. Ensure left rear wheel sensor is properly installed.
8. Ensure sensor wheel is not damaged and is properly installed.
9. Check clearance between sensor and sensor wheel. Clearance should be 0.45–1.55 mm.
10. Ensure ECU pins 1 and 19 are properly grounded.
11. If no fault has been found, test drive vehicle to see if diagnostic trouble code is regenerated. If so, try a known good ECU.

DIAGNOSTIC TROUBLE CODES 4/24224, 2422D, 24254 & 24294

1. Raise and support vehicle.
2. With ignition in Drive position, enter ISAT command code 25C. The code displayed will be between 80002 and 80020 (0–20 km/h), depending on whether wheel is stationary or being rotated by hand.
3. With AC range selected on multimeter, signal can also be measured by connecting probes across pins 27 and 45. Voltage should be approximately 0.1–0.5V AC as wheel is rotated by hand.
4. With ignition in Off position and ECU connector disconnected, check sensor winding for continuity by measuring resistance across pins 27 and 45. Resistance should be approximately 1100 ohms.
5. Check leads between sensor and pins 27 and 45 on TC/ABS-system ECU for shorting. Check for poor contact in connectors. Resistance should be as follows:
   a. Across pin 27 and ground: infinity.
   b. Across pin 45 and ground: infinity.
6. When testing for short to 12V, voltage should be as follows:
   a. Across pin 27 and ground: 0V DC (indicates no short to 12V).
   b. Across pin 45 and ground: 0V DC (indicates no short to 12V).
7. Ensure right rear wheel sensor is properly installed.
8. Ensure sensor wheel is not damaged and is properly installed.
9. Check clearance between sensor and sensor wheel. Clearance should be 0.45–1.55 mm.
10. Ensure ECU pins 1 and 19 are properly grounded.
11. If no fault has been found, test drive vehicle to see if diagnostic trouble code is regenerated. If so, try a known good ECU.

DIAGNOSTIC TROUBLE CODE 5/33421

1. With ECU connector disconnected, check resistance in circuit between pin 3 and pin 20 of TC/ABS-system ECU using breakout box. Resistance should be 5–7 ohms.
   a. If circuit is good, clear diagnostic trouble code and test drive vehicle to see if diagnostic trouble code is regenerated. If so, try a known good ECU.

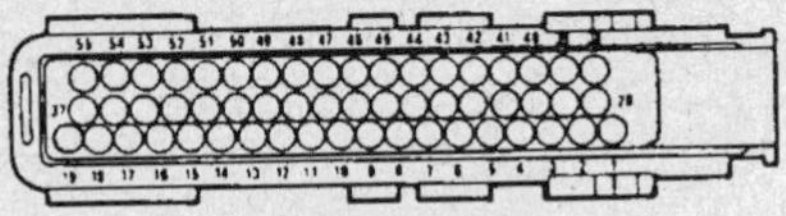

Voltage Checks

The following signals must be tested with the breakout box connected, all system components connected and the ignition switched on. All tests should be made at the breakout box.

Pin#	Circuit/Function	Wire Color	Test
9‡	RR wheel speed signal (digital output to ASR ECU)	Green	Using a Logic Probe:
10‡	LF wheel speed signal (digital output to ASR ECU)	Yellow	–You should find a steady 'PULSE' at each wire with the ignition ON and the wheel NOT turning (this is a test pulse).
11‡	RF wheel speed signal (digital output to ASR ECU)	Blue	–The frequency of the 'PULSE' should increase as the speed of each wheel increases.
12‡	LR wheel speed signal (digital output to ASR ECU)	Grey	
13*	TC block pressure switch (voltage signal into switch)	Brown/White	Brake off = approx. 8 volts (switch closed) Brake applied = approx. 10 volts (switch open)
14	Pump relay pin 87 (monitors the status of relay contacts)	Yellow	Pump relay energizes = battery volts Pump relay de-energizes = 0 volts
15	Not used		
16	Not used		
17	Not used		
18	Not used		
19	Ground	Black	Check voltage drop to ground. Should be less than 0.1 volt (ignition must be on to check voltage drop).
20	Left front inlet valve (ECU energizes valve by providing ground)	Green/White	See resistance testing procedure
21	Right front outlet valve (ECU energizes valve by providing ground)	Blue/Red	See resistance testing procedure

* Manual Transmission TCS Version Only
‡ Automatic Transmission TCS Version Only

SA4029100017030X

Fig. 6 TC/ABS control unit pin voltage check (Part 3 of 5)

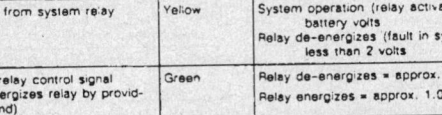

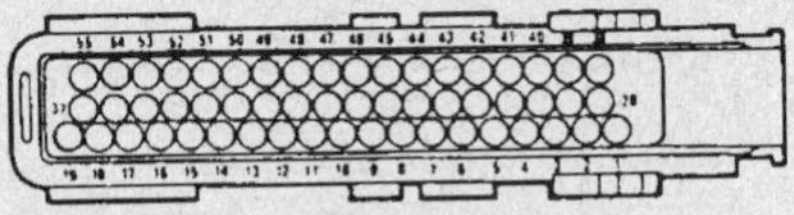

Voltage Checks

The following signals must be tested with the breakout box connected, all system components connected and the ignition switched on. All tests should be made at the breakout box.

Pin#	Circuit/Function	Wire Color	Test
32	Brake light signal (from brake light switch)	Blue	Brake off – 0 volts Brake applied = Battery volts
33	Power in from system relay	Yellow	System operation (relay activated) = battery volts Relay de-energizes (fault in system) = less than 2 volts
34	System relay control signal (ECU energizes relay by providing ground)	Green	Relay de-energizes = approx. battery volts Relay energizes = approx. 1.0 volt or less
35*	+30 Constant power	Red	Battery voltage all the time
36	Rear outlet valve (ECU energizes valve by providing ground)	Blue/White	See resistance testing procedure
37*	TC block normally open valve (ECU energizes valve by providing ground)	Yellow	See resistance testing procedure
38	Right front inlet valve (ECU energizes valve by providing ground)	Red/White	See resistance testing procedure
39	Main valve (ECU energizes valve by providing ground)	Black	See resistance testing procedure
40*	TC block normally closed valve (ECU energizes valve by providing ground)	Blue Gray	See resistance testing procedure
41	Not used		
42	Diagnostic "K" lead (reply from control unit to ISAT)	Blue	
43	Not used		
44*	TCS control warning light	Blue	Light off = approx. battery volts Light on = less than 2 volts

* Manual Transmission TCS Version Only

SA4029100017040X

Fig. 6 TC/ABS control unit pin voltage check (Part 4 of 5)

b. If circuit is faulty, continue to next step.

2. Check for continuity in left front inlet valve winding by measuring resistance across pins 6 and 7 on valve body. Resistance should be 5–7 ohms. If not, replace hydraulic unit.
3. Check lead between pin 6 on valve connector and pin 20 on TC/ABS-system ECU for a broken or short circuit.
4. Check lead between pin 7 on valve connector and pin 30 on system relay for a broken or short circuit.

DIAGNOSTIC TROUBLE CODE 5/33422

1. With ECU connector disconnected, check resistance in circuit between pin 3 and pin 2 of TC/ABS-system ECU using breakout box. Resistance should be 3–4 ohms.
   a. If circuit is good, clear diagnostic trouble code and test drive vehicle to see if diagnostic trouble code is regenerated. If so, try a known good ECU.
   b. If circuit is faulty, go to step 2.
2. Check for continuity in left front outlet valve winding by measuring resistance across pins 5 and 7 on valve body. Resistance should be 3–4 ohms. If not, replace hydraulic unit.
3. Check lead between pin 5 on valve connector and pin 2 on TC/ABS-system ECU for a broken or short circuit.
4. Check lead between pin 7 on valve connector and pin 30 on system relay for a broken or short circuit.

DIAGNOSTIC TROUBLE CODE 5/33423

1. With ECU connector disconnected, check resistance in circuit between pin 3 and pin 38 of TC/ABS-system ECU using breakout box. Resistance should be 5–7 ohms.
   a. If circuit is good, clear diagnostic trouble code and test drive vehicle to see if diagnostic trouble code is regenerated. If so, try a known good ECU.
   b. If circuit is faulty, go to step 2.
2. Check for continuity in right front inlet valve winding by measuring resistance across pins 1 and 7 on valve body. Resistance should be 5–7 ohms. If not, replace hydraulic unit.
3. Check lead between pin 1 on valve connector and pin 38 on TC/ABS-system ECU for a broken or short circuit.
4. Check lead between pin 7 on valve connector and pin 30 on system relay for a broken or short circuit.

DIAGNOSTIC TROUBLE CODE 5/33424

1. With ECU connector disconnected, check resistance in circuit between pin 3 and pin 21 of TC/ABS-system ECU using breakout box. Resistance should be 3–4 ohms.
   a. If circuit is good, clear diagnostic trouble code and test drive vehicle to see if diagnostic trouble code is regenerated. If so, try a known good ECU.
   b. If circuit is faulty, go to step 2.
2. Check for continuity in right front outlet valve winding by measuring resistance across pins 2 and 7 on valve body. Resistance should be 3–4 ohms. If not, replace hydraulic unit.
3. Check lead between pin 2 on valve connector and pin 21 on TC/ABS-system ECU for a broken or short circuit.
4. Check lead between pin 7 on valve connector and pin 30 on system relay for a broken or short circuit.

DIAGNOSTIC TROUBLE CODE 5/33425

1. With ECU connector disconnected, check resistance in circuit between pin 3 and pin 54 of TC/ABS-system ECU using breakout box. Resistance should be 5–7 ohms.
   a. If circuit is good, clear diagnostic trouble code and test drive vehicle to see if diagnostic trouble code is regenerated. If so, try a known good ECU.
   b. If circuit is faulty, go to step 2.
2. Check for continuity in rear inlet valve winding by measuring resistance across pins 3 and 7 on valve body. Resistance should be 5–7 ohms. If not, replace hydraulic unit.

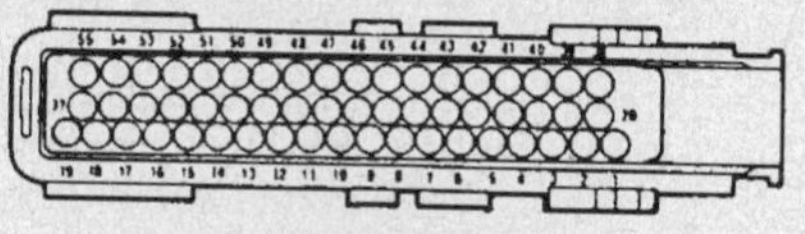

Voltage Checks

The following signals must be tested with the breakout box connected, all system components connected and the ignition switched on. All tests should be made at the breakout box.

Pin#	Circuit/Function	Wire Color	Test
45	Right rear wheel sensor signal	Green	Connect A.C. voltmeter between pin 45 and 27. With wheel rotating one revolution per second, sensor should produce approximately 0.1 to 0.5 volts A.C.
46	Left rear wheel sensor signal	Green	Connect A.C. voltmeter between pin 46 and 28. With wheel rotating one revolution per second, sensor should produce approximately 0.1 to 0.5 volts A.C.
47	Right front wheel sensor signal	Green	Connect A.C. voltmeter between pin 47 and 29. With wheel rotating one revolution per second, sensor should produce approximately 0.1 to 0.5 volts A.C.
48	Left front wheel sensor signal	Green	Connect A.C. voltmeter between pin 48 and 30. With wheel rotating one revolution per second, sensor should produce approximately 0.1 to 0.5 volts A.C.
49	Not used		
50	Pump relay pin 85 (monitors the status of relay "pull-down")	Black	Relay "pulldown" circuit de-energized (pressure switch open) = approx battery volts Relay "pulldown" circuit energizes (pressure switch closed) = less than 1 volt
51	Pressure-fluid safety circuit (with pin #8)	Brown	System O.K. (switches closed) = 5 to 10 volts Fault (switch open) = approx. 1.5 volts
52	Anti-lock warning light	White	Light off = approx. battery volts Light on = less than 2 volts
53	+54 Switched power input	Red	Battery volts with ign. in "Run" pos. only.
54	Rear inlet valve (ECU energizes valve by providing ground)	Brown/White	See resistance testing procedure
55	Not used		

* Manual Transmission TCS Version Only

SA4029100017050X

Fig. 6 TC/ABS control unit pin voltage check (Part 5 of 5)

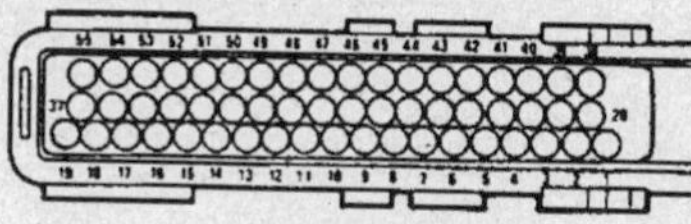

Resistance Checks

The following resistance values must be tested with the breakout box connected, the ECU DISCONNECTED and the ignition switched OFF. All tests should be made at the breakout box.

Pin#	Circuit/Function	Wire Color	Test
1	Ground	Black	Less than 1 ohm resistance to battery negative.
2	Left front outlet valve (ECU energizes valve by providing ground)	Yellow/Red	Resistance from ECU pin 2 to ECU pin 3 should be 3 - 4 ohms.
3	Power in from system relay	Green/Red -or- Yellow/White	Check for continuity to system relay pin 30.
4*	Communication between TC/ABS and ETS (digital signal to ETS pin #32)	Black/White	Check for: -Continuity to ETS Pin #32 -No continuity to ground
5	Not used		
6	Not used		
7*	TCS indicator light (ECU provides ground for bulb when system is operating in TCS mode)	Brown/Red	See voltage test procedure.
8	Pressure/fluid safety circuit (with pin #51)	Blue	Check for continuity between ECU pin 8 and ECU pin 51 with accumulator charged.
9‡	RR wheel speed signal (digital output to ASR ECU)	Green	See voltage test procedure.
10‡	LF wheel speed signal (digital output to ASR ECU)	Yellow	See voltage test procedure.
11‡	RF wheel speed signal (digital output to ASR ECU)	Blue	See voltage test procedure.
12‡	LR wheel speed signal (digital output to ASR ECU)	Grey	See voltage test procedure.

* Manual Transmission TCS Version Only
‡ Automatic Transmission TCS Version Only

SA4029100018010X

Fig. 7 TC/ABS control unit pin resistance check (Part 1 of 4)

3. Check lead between pin 3 on valve connector and pin 54 on TC/ABS-system ECU for a broken or short circuit.
4. Check lead between pin 7 on valve connector and pin 30 on system relay for a broken or short circuit.

DIAGNOSTIC TROUBLE CODE 5/33426

1. With ECU connector disconnected, check resistance in circuit between pin 3 and pin 36 of TC/ABS-system ECU using breakout box. Resistance should be 3–4 ohms.
   a. If circuit is good, clear diagnostic trouble code and test drive vehicle to see if diagnostic trouble code is regenerated. If so, try a known good ECU.
   b. If circuit is faulty, go to step 2.
2. Check for continuity in rear outlet valve winding by measuring resistance across pins 4 and 7 on valve body. Resistance should be 3–4 ohms. If not, replace hydraulic unit.
3. Check lead between pin 4 on valve connector and pin 36 on TC/ABS-system ECU for a broken or short circuit.
4. Check lead between pin 7 on valve connector and pin 30 on system relay for a broken or short circuit.

DIAGNOSTIC TROUBLE CODE 5/33427

1. With ECU connector disconnected, check resistance in circuit between pin 3 and pin 39 of TC/ABS-system ECU using breakout box. Resistance should be 4–5 ohms.
   a. If circuit is good, clear diagnostic trouble code and test drive vehicle to see if diagnostic trouble code is regenerated. If so, try a known good ECU.
   b. If circuit is faulty, go to step 2.
2. Check for continuity in main-valve winding by measuring resistance across pins 1 and 2 on valve body. Resistance should be 4–5 ohms. If not, replace hydraulic unit.
3. Check GN/RD lead between pin 1 on main valve and pin 3 on TC/ABS-system ECU for a broken or short circuit.
4. Check BK lead between pin 2 on main valve and pin 39 on TC/ABS-system ECU for a broken or short circuit.

DIAGNOSTIC TROUBLE CODE 5/33428

1. With ECU connector disconnected, check resistance in circuit between pin 3 and pin 40 of TC/ABS-system ECU using breakout box. Resistance should be 6–8 ohms.
   a. If circuit is good, clear diagnostic trouble code and test drive vehicle to see if diagnostic trouble code is regenerated. If so, try a known good ECU.
   b. If circuit is faulty, go to step 2.
2. Check for continuity in TC-valve (NC) winding by measuring resistance across pins 1 and 5 on valve connector. Resistance should be 6–8 ohms. If not, replace hydraulic unit.
3. Check lead between pin 1 on TC block and pin 40 on TC/ABS-system ECU for a broken or short circuit.
4. Check lead between pin 5 on TC block and pin 3 on TC/ABS-system ECU for a broken or short circuit.

DIAGNOSTIC TROUBLE CODE 5/33429

1. With ECU connector disconnected, check resistance in circuit between pin 3 and pin 37 of TC/ABS-system ECU using breakout box. Resistance should be 6–8 ohms.
   a. If circuit is good, clear diagnostic trouble code and test drive vehicle to see if diagnostic trouble code is regenerated. If so, try a known good ECU.
   b. If circuit is faulty, go to step 2.
2. Check for continuity in TC-valve (NC) winding by measuring resistance across pins 4 and 5 on valve-block connector. Resistance should be 6–8 ohms.
3. Check lead between pin 4 on TC block and pin 37 on TC/ABS-system ECU for a broken or short circuit.
4. Check lead between pin 5 on TC block and pin 3 on TC/ABS-system ECU for a broken or short circuit.

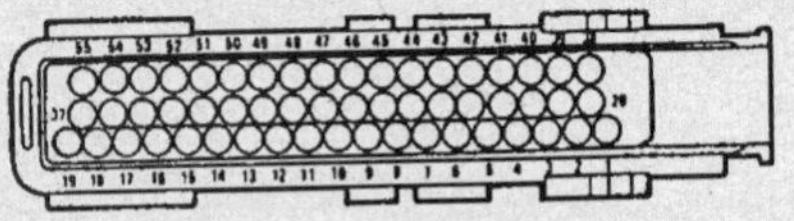

Resistance Checks

The following resistance values must be tested with the breakout box connected, the ECU DISCONNECTED and the ignition switched OFF. All tests should be made at the breakout box.

Pin #	Circuit/Function	Wire Color	Test
13*	TC block pressure switch (voltage signal into switch)	Brown/White	Check for continuity from ECU pin 13 to ECU pin 26 with brake pedal released.
14	Pump relay pin 87 (monitors the status of relay contacts)	Yellow	Check for continuity to pump relay pin #87.
15	Not used		
16	Not used		
17	Not used		
18	Not used		
19	Ground	Black	Less than 1 ohm resistance to battery negative.
20	Left front inlet valve (ECU energizes valve by providing ground)	Green/White	Resistance from ECU pin 20 to ECU pin 3 should be 5 – 7 ohms.
21	Right front outlet valve (ECU energizes valve by providing ground)	Blue/Red	Resistance from ECU pin 21 to ECU pin 3 should be 3 – 4 ohms.
22	Not used		
23	Diagnostic "L" lead (request from ISAT to control unit)	Yellow	
24*	Communication between TC/ABS and ETS (digital signal to ETS pin #29)	Green/White	Check for: -Continuity to ETS pin #29 -No continuity to ground
25	Not used		

* Manual Transmission TCS Version Only
‡ Automatic Transmission TCS Version Only

SA4029100018020X

Fig. 7 TC/ABS control unit pin resistance check (Part 2 of 4)

DIAGNOSTIC TROUBLE CODES 234B1, 234B2, 234B3 & 234B4

1. Perform diagnosis for any other diagnostic trouble codes first.
2. Check wheel sensors. Refer to wheel sensor diagnostic trouble code diagnosis.
3. Replace hydraulic unit.

DIAGNOSTIC TROUBLE CODE 775B1

1. Clear diagnostic trouble code and test drive vehicle to see if diagnostic trouble code is regenerated.
2. If diagnostic trouble code is regenerated, check grounding circuits to pin 1 and pin 19 of ECU. Ensure ground G15 grounding point is making good connection.
3. Try a known good ECU.

DIAGNOSTIC TROUBLE CODE 775B2

1. Clear diagnostic trouble code and test drive vehicle to see if diagnostic trouble code is regenerated.
2. If diagnostic trouble code is regenerated, try a known good ECU.

DIAGNOSTIC TROUBLE CODE E/F7061

This diagnostic trouble code is usually generated by the presence of another fault. Perform diagnosis for any other codes first.

1. Disconnect ETS-system connector.
2. With ignition in On position and engine not running, check reference voltage from pin 4 of TC/ABS-system ECU to pin 32 of ETS connector. Voltage should be approximately 10V DC
   a. If voltage is as specified, go to step 3.
   b. If voltage is close to 0, check for a short to ground in the wire.
   c. If no shorts are found, try a new TC/ABS ECU.
   d. If voltage is as specified at TC/ABS ECU but no voltage exists at ETS connector, check for an open circuit in the wire.
3. With ignition in Off position, connect ETS ECU and start engine. Check communication signal with a DC voltmeter or a Logic Probe. Voltage should be approximately 5V DC, or Logic Probe reading should be a continuous "pulse."
4. If voltage was as specified in step 2 but not in step 3, try a new ETS ECU. Ensure no other diagnostic trouble codes were present in either the ETS system or the TC/ABS system.
5. With ignition in Off position, disconnect TC/ABS-system ECU.
6. With ignition in On position and engine not running, check reference voltage from pin 29 of ETS-system ECU to pin 24 of TC/ABS connector. Voltage should be approximately 10V DC.
   a. If voltage is as specified, go to step 7.
   b. If voltage is close to 0, check for a short to ground in the wire.
   c. If no shorts are found, try a new ETS ECU.
   d. If voltage is as specified at ETS ECU but no voltage exists at TC/ABS connector, check for an open circuit in the wire.
7. With ignition in Off position, connect TC/ABS ECU and start engine. Check communication signal with a DC voltmeter or a Logic Probe. Voltage should be approximately 5V DC, or Logic Probe reading should be a continuous "Pulse."
8. If voltage was as specified in step 6 but not in step 7, try a new TC/ABS ECU. Ensure no other diagnostic trouble codes were present in either the ETS system or the TC/ABS system.

DIAGNOSTIC TROUBLE CODE 3/25321

This fault may also be generated if the pressure switch in the TC block is faulty. Refer to TC block test procedure.

1. With ignition in Drive position, enter ISAT command code 202. When brake pedal is applied, ISAT should display 85100; with foot off pedal, ISAT should display 8B000. Measure voltage at pin 32: this should be battery voltage when the pedal is applied and 0V with foot off. If not voltage is reaching the pin, go to step 2. If signal is correct, perform test procedure for pressure switch in TC block.
2. Check fuse No. 24. Ensure brake lights are working properly.
   a. Ensure voltage is reaching brake light switch.
   b. If voltage is not reaching brake light switch, check RD lead between switch and fuse holder.
3. Check lead between ECU connector pin 32 and brake light switch.
4. Perform test procedure for pressure switch in TC block as outlined under "Diagnostic Trouble Code 36521."
5. Replace brake light switch.

DIAGNOSTIC TROUBLE CODE 36521

With ISAT Tester

1. With ignition in Drive position, enter ISAT command code 200.
2. With brake pedal applied, pressure switch should be open, indicated on ISAT display by 8D000.
3. With brake pedal released, switch should be closed, indicated by 8B100.
4. If signal is correct, perform test procedure for brake light switch.

Less ISAT Tester

1. Switch on ignition and wait for pump to build up pressure in the accumulator. After system has pressurized, switch off ignition and unplug ECU connector.
2. Using a multimeter, ensure circuit across pins 13 and 26 is closed, and that it opens when the brake pedal is applied. If circuit is not as specified, check the following:
   a. BN/WH lead between pin 13 on ECU connector and pin 2 on TC block connector.

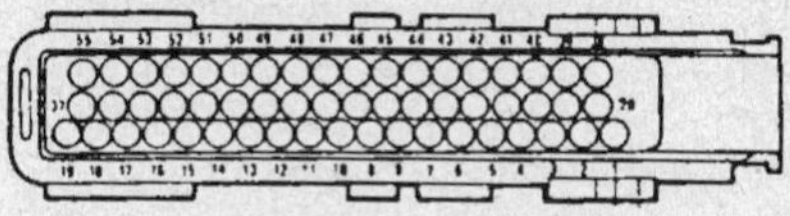

Resistance Checks

The following resistance values must be tested with the breakout box connected, the ECU DISCONNECTED and the ignition switched OFF. All tests should be made at the breakout box.

Pin#	Circuit/Function	Wire Color	Test
26*	TC block pressure switch (voltage signal from switch)	Black/White	Check for continuity from ECU pin 26 to ECU pin 13 with brake pedal released.
27	Shield, RR wheel sensor	Black/Green	Resistance from ECU pin 27 to ECU pin 45 should be approx. 1100 ohms.
28	Shield, LR wheel sensor	Yellow/Green	Resistance from ECU pin 28 to ECU pin 46 should be approx. 1100 ohms.
29	Shield, RF wheel sensor	Blue Green	Resistance from ECU pin 29 to ECU pin 47 should be approx. 1100 ohms.
30	Shield, LF wheel sensor	Gray/Green	Resistance from ECU pin 30 to ECU pin 48 should be approx. 1100 ohms.
31	Not used		
32	Brake light signal (from brake light switch)	Blue	See voltage test procedure.
33	Power in from system relay	Yellow	Check for continuity to system relay pin 30.
34	System relay control signal (ECU energized relay by providing ground)	Green	Check for continuity with system relay pin 86.
35*	+30 Constant power	Red	See voltage test procedure.
36	Rear outlet valve (ECU energizes valve by providing ground)	Blue White	Resistance from ECU pin 36 to ECU pin 3 should be 3 - 4 ohms.
37*	TC block normally open valve (ECU energizes valve by providing ground)	Yellow	Resistance from ECU pin 37 to ECU pin 3 should be 6 - 8 ohms.
38	Right front inlet valve (ECU energizes valve by providing ground)	Red White	Resistance from ECU pin 38 to ECU pin 3 should be 5 - 7 ohms.
39	Main valve (ECU energized valve by providing ground)	Black	Resistance from ECU pin 39 to ECU pin 3 should be 4 - 5 ohms.

* Manual Transmission TCS Version Only

SA4029100018030X

Fig. 7 TC/ABS control unit pin resistance check (Part 3 of 4)

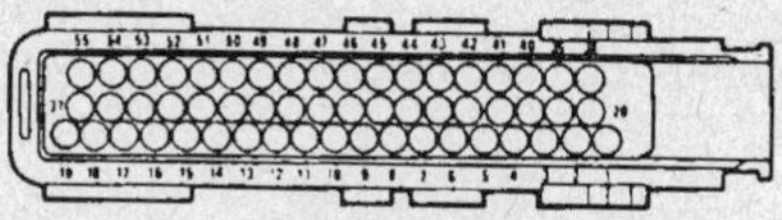

Resistance Checks

The following resistance values must be tested with the breakout box connected, the ECU DISCONNECTED and the ignition switched OFF. All tests should be made at the breakout box.

Pin#	Circuit/Function	Wire Color	Test
40*	TC block normally closed valve (ECU energized valve by providing ground)	Blue/Gray	Resistance from ECU pin 40 to ECU pin 3 should be 6 - 8 ohms.
41	Not used		
42	Diagnostic "K" lead (reply from control unit to ISAT)	Blue	
43	Not used		
44*	TCS control warning light	Blue	See voltage test procedure.
45	Right rear wheel sensor output signal	Green	Resistance from ECU pin 45 to ECU pin 27 should be approx. 1100 ohms.
46	Left rear wheel sensor output signal	Green	Resistance from ECU pin 46 to ECU pin 28 should be approx. 1100 ohms.
47	Right front wheel sensor output signal	Green	Resistance from ECU pin 47 to ECU pin 29 should be approx. 1100 ohms.
48	Left front wheel sensor output signal	Green	Resistance from ECU pin 48 to ECU pin 30 should be approx. 1100 ohms.
49	Not used		
50	Pump relay pin 85 (monitors the status of relay "pull-down")	Black	Check for continuity to pump relay pin 85. Also should have continuity to ground with pressure switch closed (accumulator discharged).
51	Pressure/fluid safety circuit (with pin #8)	Brown	Check for continuity between ECU pin 8 and ECU pin 51 with accumulator charged.
52	Anti-lock warning light	White	See voltage test procedure.
53	+54 Switched power input	Red	See voltage test procedure.
54	Rear inlet valve (ECU energizes valve by providing ground)	Yellow/Red	Resistance from ECU pin 54 to ECU pin 3 should be 5 - 7 ohms
55	Not used		

* Manual Transmission TCS Version Only

SA4029100018040X

Fig. 7 TC/ABS control unit pin resistance check (Part 4 of 4)

b. BK/WH lead between ECU pin 26 and TC block connector pin 3.
3. If pressure switch on TC block is faulty, replace hydraulic unit.
4. Perform brake light test procedure.
5. If not faults are found, replace ECU.

WARNING & INDICATOR LIGHTS

Anti-Lock Light

1. With ECU connector plugged in and ignition in Drive position, ensure battery voltage at pin 52 exists. If not, check bulb and lead between ECU pin 52 and pin 8 on main instrument panel (H10-12).
2. With ignition Off and connectors for ECU and system relay unplugged, check circuit between ECU pin 52 and ECU pin 33. Ensure diode prevents current flow toward pin 52.

TCS CTRL Light

1. With ignition in Drive position, ensure battery voltage at pin 52 exists. If not, check bulb and lead between ECU pin 44 and pin 12 on main instrument panel (H10-12).
2. With ignition Off and connectors for ECU and system relay unplugged, check circuit between ECU pin 52 and ECU pin 33. Ensure diode prevents current flow towards pin 44.

Brake Fluid Light

1. Ensure light is working by turning ignition to a point between Start and Drive positions. If light does not illuminate, check bulb in panel.
2. If light fails to illuminate when pressure is low, proceed as follows:
   a. With pressure warning switch connector (294) unplugged and ignition in Drive position, ensure battery voltage is at pin 2 of pressure switch connector. If not, check WH lead between pin 2 on connector and pin 11 on instrument panel.
   b. If voltage is at pin 2, switch off ignition and depressurize system.
   c. Check resistance across pins 1 and 2 on pressure warning switch. Reading should indicate circuit continuity. If not, replace switch.
   d. If switch is satisfactory, check BK lead between pin 1 of pressure switch connector and ground.
3. If light fails to illuminate when fluid level is low, proceed as follows:
   a. With connector for level warning switch (299) unplugged and ignition in Drive position, ensure battery voltage is at pin 4 of reservoir switch connector. If not, check WH lead between pin 4 on connector and pin 11 on instrument panel. If voltage exists at pin 4, switch off ignition and proceed to step b.
   b. Check level switch by verifying that circuit is closed when the float is pressed down, and that the circuit is open when the float is up. If values are unsatisfactory, replace reservoir. If values are satisfactory, proceed to step c.
   c. Check BK lead by measuring resistance across pin 3 of reservoir switch connector and ground.

TCS Light

1. With ignition in Drive position, ensure battery voltage is at ECU pin 7. If battery voltage does not exist, proceed as follows:
   a. Ensure bulb is good.
   b. Circuit continuity exists in BN/GY lead between ECU pin 7 and pin 6 on tachometer connector.
   c. Ensure there is a live feed to pin 4 on rev counter.
2. If TCS light fails to illuminate when the system is operating and no other warning lights are on, replace ECU.

TC/ABS CONTROL UNIT PIN TESTS

VOLTAGE CHECKS

Refer to **Fig. 6** for voltage checks.

RESISTANCE CHECKS

When an intermittent fault is suspected, wiggle wires and connectors related to the pin being tested.

In cases where resistance specifications

indicate a range such as "3 to 4 ohms," good judgement must be used before condemning a circuit which indicates 4.1 ohms for example.

Refer to **Fig. 7,** for resistance checks.

SYSTEM SERVICE

CALIBRATING ETS ECU

Calibration must be carried out after replacing any major system component, such as ETS ECU, TC/ABS ECU, pedal potentiometer or throttle housing.

1. Start and run engine until normal operating temperature is reached. If the engine will not run correctly during warm up cycle, establish ISAT communications and enter command code 974 in order to enter basic data and enable warm up to be completed.
2. Switch off engine. Connect ISAT and capacitor lead, part No. 86-11-048, to Black diagnostic connector.
3. Turn ignition On, select DIAG, ONE system from menu, and enter system number 3. Check if any diagnostic trouble codes are stored in memory. If diagnostic trouble codes are present, repair as necessary, then erase diagnostic trouble codes before proceeding.
4. To enter the base line setting, enter command code 971. ISAT will display 8A971. After several seconds, the display will change to 8D971, indicating that the basic setting has been made and the system is ready for calibration.
5. With ignition On, engine Off, enter command code 973.
   a. Once the TCS CTRL light illuminates, start engine. **Do not touch pedals.**
   b. Wait for idle to stabilize at approximately 850 RPM.
   c. The ECU will raise engine speed to approximately 3000 RPM.
6. The calibration procedure will be discontinued if a pedal is depressed or vehicle starts to roll.
7. When calibration process is complete, the TCS CTRL light will shutoff. Terminate ISAT communications and shutoff engine. Check if any diagnostic trouble codes were stored during calibration procedure.

Brake System Bleed

Front brake calipers must be bled first.

1. Fill fluid reservoir to the top.
2. Connect a length of transparent hose to right front caliper bleed nipple and place other end of hose into a clear container.
3. While depressing brake pedal, open bleed nipple.
4. Repeat step 3 until there are no more air bubbles visible in the hose.
5. Connect hose to left front caliper and repeat steps 3 and 4.
6. Connect hose to rear caliper, switch on ignition and repeat steps 3 and 4. **Pump motor must not run for more than two minutes at a time. After motor has been running, let it cool for approximately 10 minutes.**
7. Repeat step 6 on the other rear caliper, then fill fluid reservoir.

Component Replacement

TC/ABS ECU

1. **On 1995–96 9000 models,** obtain radio anti-theft code as outlined under "Precautions."
2. **On all models,** disconnect battery ground cable.
3. Remove two mounting screws, then lift out ECU and disconnect connector.
4. Reverse procedure to install.

CONTROL VALVE FOR TURBO BYPASS VALVE

This valve is located inside the engine compartment, on the lefthand inner fender.

1. Remove two mounting nuts.
2. Unplug electrical connector, then disconnect three signal hoses. Keep color coded rings on valve ports when hoses are disconnected.
3. Reverse procedure to install.

SAFETY VALVE

This valve is mounted on the false bulkhead panel on right side of car.

1. Remove two mounting nuts.
2. Unplug connector, then disconnect vacuum hoses. Keep color coded rings on valve ports when hoses are disconnected.
3. Reverse procedure to install.

NON-RETURN VALVE

This valve is installed in the vacuum hose between the safety valve and inlet manifold.

1. Disconnect vacuum hoses.
2. To install, reconnect vacuum hoses. Ensure white end of valve is pointed towards the safety valve.

TC/ABS HYDRAULIC UNIT

Before beginning this procedure, depressurize accumulator in the TC/ABS hydraulic unit by repeatedly depressing the brake pedal until a dramatic increase in resistance is felt (at least 20 times). Failure to perform this step could result in serious injury.

1. Remove lower dash panel to gain access to top of pedal assembly.
2. Remove pin retaining clip, then withdraw pin from hydraulic unit pushrod.
3. **On 1995–96 9000 models,** obtain radio anti-theft code as outlined under "Precautions."
4. **On all models,** disconnect battery leads, then remove battery.
5. Remove clips securing positive lead to battery shelf, then the terminal block (with leads) from battery shelf.
6. Remove connectors at rear of battery shelf, then nuts for the brace.
7. Position TC/ABS ECU aside.
8. Remove battery shelf, then release ABS fuse/relay panel. Position panel aside.
9. Siphon fluid from reservoir, then remove lefthand front wheel and fender liner.
10. Remove brace between engine subframe and wheel housing.
11. Cut tie strap and disconnect all electrical leads from hydraulic unit.
12. Remove mount for battery shelf at hydraulic unit.
13. Disconnect hose for clutch cylinder, then plug end of hose. Do not spill any brake fluid as this could allow air to get into clutch system.
14. Disconnect and plug brake lines from valve block, then remove accumulator.
15. Remove four hydraulic unit mounting nuts, located on bulkhead behind pedal assembly.
16. Remove hydraulic unit.
17. Reverse procedure to install, noting the following:
    a. **Torque** hydraulic unit mounting nuts to 19 ft. lbs.
    b. **Torque** accumulator to 28 ft. lbs.

Mark IV Anti-Lock Brake System

NOTE: On Air Bag Equipped Models, Refer To "Air Bag System Precautions" Located In The Front Of This Manual For System Disarming & Arming Procedures.

NOTE: Electrical Symbol & Wire Color Code Identification Located In The Front Of This Manual May Be Used As An Aid When Using Wiring Circuits Found In This Section.

INDEX

	Page No.
Description	38-115
Components	38-115
System	38-115
Diagnosis & Testing	38-116
Accessing Diagnostic Trouble Codes	38-116
Component Testing	38-122
Diagnostic Trouble Code Interpretation	38-117
Precautions	38-115
Air Bag Systems	38-115
Radio Anti-Theft Lock	38-115
System Service	38-122
Brake System Bleed	38-122
Component Replacement	38-122
ABS Electronic Control Unit (ECU), Replace	38-123
Front Wheel Sensors, Replace	38-123
Hydraulic Unit, Replace	38-122
Master Cylinder, Replace	38-123
Rear Wheel Sensors, Replace	38-123
Travel Sensor, Replace	38-123
Vacuum Operated Servo	38-123
Fluid Change	38-122
Troubleshooting	38-116

PRECAUTIONS

AIR BAG SYSTEMS

Refer to "Air Bag System Precautions" in the front of this manual for system disarming and arming procedures.

RADIO ANTI-THEFT LOCK

9000

1995-96

Radio and cassette player are equipped with an electronic four-digit anti-theft lock. This four-digit code is programmed at manufacturing and cannot be changed. If the battery is disconnected for more than three minutes, if unit is removed or if otherwise cut off from power, the four-digit code must be entered with the quick-selection buttons as follows:

1. Turn radio on, then, when display shows "Code In," enter four-digit code with quick-selection buttons. If code is correct, last-tuned radio frequency is shown on display. If wrong digit has been entered by mistake, all four digits must be entered again. If code is wrong it stays on display.
2. If incorrect four-digit code has been entered, press Band button for more than three seconds to clear display. Display shows "Code In" and new attempt to enter correct code can be made.
3. If wrong code has been used three times in succession, four dashes appear on display and you must wait an hour with radio switched on before trying again.
4. To try again, hold Band button for at least three seconds. "Code In" should appear on display.
5. Correct code must be entered at first attempt, otherwise you must wait another hour with unit switched on before trying again.

DESCRIPTION

SYSTEM

The Anti-Lock Brake System (ABS), **Fig. 1**, has been developed to provide optimum braking, with no loss of directional stability, under widely varying conditions. The braking system is divided into two separate diagonal brake circuits. One circuit comprises the right front wheel and left rear wheel (primary circuit), while the other comprises the left front wheel and right rear wheel (secondary circuit).

COMPONENTS

HYDRAULIC UNIT

The hydraulic unit consists of a valve block, master cylinder, hydraulic pump and electric motor in one unit. The hydraulic unit is secured in a vacuum-operated servo (brake pressure booster). The brake fluid reservoir is separate from the hydraulic unit.

Electric Motor

The electric motor, part of the hydraulic unit, drives the hydraulic pump is a direct current motor with a built-in speed sensor so the ECU can receive information that the pump motor is running. The motor can be replaced only as a complete unit with pump and valve block.

Hydraulic Pump

The pump unit, part of the hydraulic unit, delivers brake fluid under ABS control to the brake circuits. Pressure of the brake fluid is determined by brake pressure in the master cylinder, which in turn is proportional to the pedal force applied. The hydraulic pump can be replaced only as a complete unit with motor and valve block.

Master Cylinder

The master cylinder, part of the hydraulic unit, consists of a tandem cylinder made of aluminum. Two central valves open the port to the brake fluid reservoir in the brakes Off position so that the sealing rings are not damaged during braking when ABS is activated. These central valves replace cutoff ports to prevent damage to the sealing ring when ABS is activated. The central valves are made of steel to withstand the high pressure in the master cylinder.

Valve Block

The valve block, part of the hydraulic unit, modulates the pressure to the brake calipers when the ABS system is operative. The valve block contains eight solenoid valves: four inlet valves and four outlet valves. Each brake circuit has one inlet and one outlet valve per wheel.

BRAKE FLUID RESERVOIR

The reservoir contains five chambers. One chamber for the clutch (manual transmission only). On vehicles with automatic transmission this chamber is plugged. Two chambers for the primary circuit. One formaster cylinder and one to supply the hydraulic pump. Two chambers for the secondary circuit. One for the master cylinder and one to supply the hydraulic pump.

A safety function is incorporated in the design of the chambers. In the event of a leak in one of the circuits, sufficient brake fluid will always remain for the other circuit and full braking effect will be maintained.

TRAVEL SENSOR

The travel sensor is mounted on the vacuum servo and consists of a set of resistors connected in series which are read by a sliding contact. This enables the travel sensor to detect a total of seven pedal position points for evaluation by the ECU.

A pump test begins every time the car exceeds 19 mph after starting. The pump then runs for around 300 msec.

If the pedal has reached the seventh position of the travel sensor, the pump will be started regardless of whether braking requires ABS or not. If the ECU does not modulate the pedal to the preceding position, the ABS warning light will come On. If the ECU then detects a defect in the power supply, the ABS will be completely inoperative.

ELECTRONIC CONTROL UNIT (ECU)

The ECU processes the signals from the wheel sensors and, on detecting any lock-up tendency in one or more wheels, sends signals to the solenoid valves in the valve block. the pump starts and stops as required. The ECU is located in the engine compartment on the side of the battery tray.

BRAKE WARNING & ABS WARNING LIGHTS

The brake warning light will come On if the level in the fluid reservoir falls below the MIN mark.

The ABS warning light will come On under the following conditions: malfunction in the ECU, break in circuit continuity or weak signals being received from the wheel sensors. The ABS is always inoperative when the ABS warning light is On, and the vehicle will then have standard power assisted brakes.

FRONT WHEEL SENSOR & SENSOR WHEELS

The front wheel sensors are mounted radially relative to the trigger wheel and operate on the same principle as a generator. Each time a tooth on the rotating sensor wheel passes the sensor, it distorts a magnetic field, causing a signal to be sent to the ECU, which processes the signals to produce the control information it requires, such as wheel speed, retardation and slip.

REAR WHEEL SENSORS & SENSOR WHEELS

The rear wheel sensors are mounted axially relative to the trigger wheel: the trigger wheels are therefore of a different design to those for the front wheels, although they operate in exactly the same way.

TROUBLESHOOTING

1. The diagnostic socket (green) is located below the righthand front seat.
2. During fault diagnosis, the ignition switch must always be in the On position.
3. The ISAT system number for the ABS system is number 3.
4. Always read off and note down all stored diagnostic trouble codes before disconnecting the battery or ECU.
5. If communication cannot be established between ISAT and the ECU, check the leads between ECU pins 23 and 42 and the diagnostic socket. Also check that the power feed and ground circuits to the diagnostic socket are good and the connector pins are not damaged.
6. Once diagnostic trouble codes stored in the systems's ECU have been transferred to ISAT, the diagnosis function is finished. The faults are now available in the form of five-figure trouble codes.
7. To avoid doing damage to the ECU, ensure the ignition is off before unplugging the connector.
8. Before tracing faults on a vehicle's electronic systems, always start by checking that the grounding circuits for the ECU concerned are good and that all nominal voltage levels are correct.
9. Unplug connectors and plugs to check the pins are undamaged and not loose. After checking, plug in all connectors and clear all diagnostic trouble codes. Start engine or drive car again to check that the fault or faults persist.
10. When first detected, a fault will be assigned a continuous diagnostic trouble code. If the fault later disappears, the fault will be classified as intermittent.
11. All signals around the 12 volt level are proportional to battery voltage. These levels must therefore be taken only as a rough guide.
12. Zero voltage signal levels indicate ground, although a sensitive multimeter may indicate a value slightly above zero volts.
13. When ISAT command codes are being used to test the system while the car is being driven, communication between ISAT and the ECU will be broken if the speed of the car exceeds 12 mph.
14. Never use the breakout box when car is being driven.

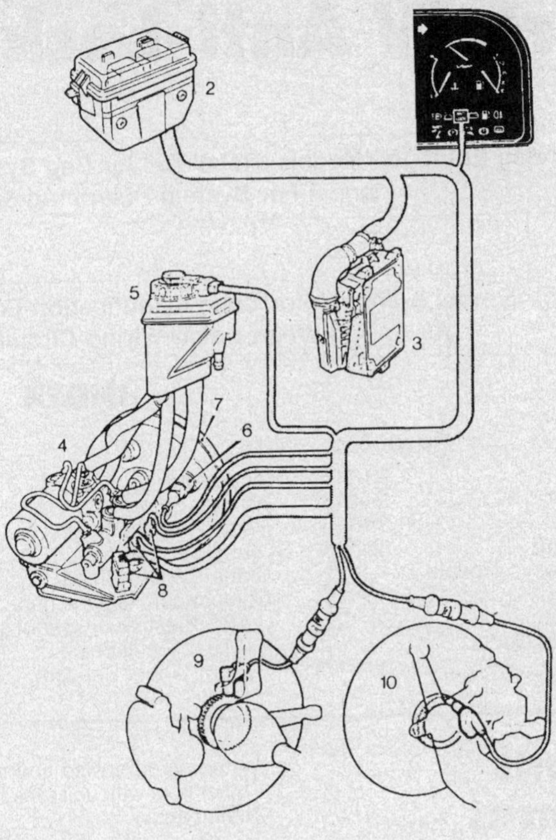
1
2
3
4
5
6
7
8
9
10

1 ABS warning lights
2 ABS relay box
3 ECU
4 Hydraulic unit
5 Brake fluid reservoir
6 Travel sensor
7 Vacuum-operated servo
8 ABS connectors
9 Wheel sensor, front wheel
10 Wheel sensor, back wheel

SA4029100019000X

Fig. 1 Anti-Lock brake system components

DIAGNOSIS & TESTING

ACCESSING DIAGNOSTIC TROUBLE CODES

Command codes instruct the ECU to perform certain functions while accessing diagnostic trouble codes.

Refer to **Fig. 2** for ISAT command codes.

The ECU connector on the wiring loom is in the form of a molded plug, test probes cannot be connected to the back of the connector.

Use breakout box 8611006 with test lead set 8611030, which should be connected between the ECU and the connector.

ABS command codes

Code	Function/component	Display text
100	Reads all stored trouble codes	
201	Travel sensor	8B X00 (X = 1-7)
202	Brake light switch	8B 000/100 (100 = Closed, 000 = Open)
259	Left front wheel speed	8B 0XX (XX = km/h)
25A	Right front wheel speed	8B 0XX
25B	Left rear wheel speed	8B 0XX
25C	Right rear wheel speed	8B 0XX
800	Communication completed	
900	Clear all trouble codes	11111

SA4029100020000X

Fig. 2 ABS command codes

All measurements on the system must be made with breakout box connected.

To access diagnostic trouble codes, connect ISAT tester to diagnostic socket (green), located under righthand front seat, then follow instructions included with tester.

DIAGNOSTIC TROUBLE CODE INTERPRETATION

Refer to **Fig. 3** for diagnostic trouble codes identification and **Figs. 4 and 5** for system wiring diagram.

DIAGNOSTIC TROUBLE CODE 4/22251

If another diagnostic trouble code other than 42251 exists, diagnose this diagnostic trouble code first.

1. Ensure battery voltage is present at pins 3 and 33.
   a. If no voltage is present at either pin, check ABS 30A fuse for the +30 supply in main fuse box on bulkhead and red wire from fuse to main relay and to distribution block on battery tray.
2. If there is no voltage at any pins, check wire from ECU to main relay from pin concerned.
3. With 0 volts on pin 34 and no voltage at pins 3 and 33, check that 10A ABS fuse is intact.
   a. If fuse is satisfactory, check power supply to pin 53. If there is no voltage, proceed to step e.
   b. If there is voltage at pin 53, check green wire between pin 85 of system relay and pin 34 of ECU.
   c. Check there is voltage at pin 86 of system relay. If voltage is no present, proceed to step f.
   d. If there is voltage, install new system relay.
   e. If there is no voltage at pin 53 either, check red and white wire as far as fuse. Also check that power is supplied from pin 54 of ignition switch in grey and white wire as far as supply side of ABS fuse.
   f. Check red and white wire between 86 on system relay via pump relay to 10A fuse.
4. If there is battery voltage on pin 34 but no voltage on pins 3 and 33, the control circuit is correct but the ECU has not grounded the circuit due to a different fault in the ABS system.

DIAGNOSTIC TROUBLE CODES 4/24221, 2422A, 24251 & 24291

1. Raise and support vehicle.
2. With ignition in Drive position, enter command code 259 on ISAT. 8B OXX will show on display.
3. With a multimeter set to AC, take reading across pins 30 and 48. Reading should be 150-700 mV.
4. With ignition turned off and connector of ECU removed, check sensor winding for breaks in continuity by measuring resistance between pins 30 and 48. Resistance must be approximately 1000 ohms.
5. Check wires between sensor and pins 30 and 48 of ABS ECU for short circuits and for poor contact in connector as follows:
   a. Between pin 30 and ground. Resistance should be infinity and voltage should be 0 volts.
   b. Between pin 48 and ground. Resistance should be infinity and voltage should be 0 volts.
6. Ensure left front wheel sensor is firmly in position.
7. Check sensor wheel is not damaged and is firmly in position. Also check that there is no bearing clearance.
8. Ensure gap between sensor and sensor wheel is .0255 inch (.65 mm).
9. Ensure ECU has a satisfactory ground connection at pin 1 and pin 19.
10. If no fault is discovered, test drive vehicle and check if diagnostic trouble code is triggered again. If diagnostic trouble code persists, proceed to "Guidelines for ECU replacement."

DIAGNOSTIC TROUBLE CODES 4/24222, 2422B, 24252 & 24292

1. Raise and support vehicle.
2. With ignition in Drive position, enter command code 25A on ISAT. 8B OXX will show on display.
3. With a multimeter set to AC, take reading across pins 29 and 47. Reading should be 150-700 mV.
4. With ignition turned off and connector of ECU removed, check sensor winding for breaks in continuity by measuring resistance between pins 29 and 47. Resistance must be approximately 1000 ohms.
5. Check wires between sensor and pins 29 and 47 of ABS ECU for short circuits and for poor contact in connector as follows:
   a. Between pin 29 and ground. Resistance should be infinity and voltage should be 0 volts.
   b. Between pin 47 and ground. Resistance should be infinity and voltage should be 0 volts.
6. Ensure right front wheel sensor is firmly in position.
7. Check sensor wheel is not damaged and is firmly in position. Also check that there is no bearing clearance.
8. Ensure gap between sensor and sensor wheel is .0255 inch (.65 mm).
9. Ensure ECU has a satisfactory ground connection at pin 1 and pin 19.
10. If no fault is discovered, test drive vehicle and check if diagnostic trouble code is triggered again. If diagnostic trouble code persists, proceed to "Guidelines for ECU replacement."

DIAGNOSTIC TROUBLE CODES 4/24223, 2422C, 24253 & 24293

1. Raise and support vehicle.
2. With ignition in Drive position, enter command code 25B on ISAT. 8B OXX will show on display.
3. With a multimeter set to AC, take reading across pins 28 and 46. Reading should be 150-700 mV.
4. With ignition turned off and connector of ECU removed, check sensor winding for breaks in continuity by measuring resistance between pins 28 and 46. Resistance must be approximately 1000 ohms.
5. Check wires between sensor and pins 28 and 46 of ABS ECU for short circuits and for poor contact in connector as follows:
   a. Between pin 28 and ground. Resistance should be infinity and voltage should be 0 volts.
   b. Between pin 46 and ground. Resistance should be infinity and voltage should be 0 volts.
6. Ensure left rear wheel sensor is firmly in position.
7. Check sensor wheel is not damaged and is firmly in position. Also check that there is no bearing clearance.
8. Ensure gap between sensor and sensor wheel is .0255 inch (.65 mm).
9. Ensure ECU has a satisfactory ground connection at pin 1 and pin 19.
10. If no fault is discovered, test drive vehicle and check if diagnostic trouble code is triggered again. If diagnostic trouble code persists, proceed to "Guidelines for ECU replacement."

DIAGNOSTIC TROUBLE CODES 4/24224, 2422D, 24254 & 24294

1. Raise and support vehicle.
2. With ignition in Drive position, enter command code 25C on ISAT. 8B OXX will show on display.
3. With a multimeter set to AC, take reading across pins 27 and 45. Reading should be 150-700 mV.
4. With ignition turned off and connector

of ECU removed, check sensor winding for breaks in continuity by measuring resistance between pins 27 and 45. Resistance must be approximately 1000 ohms.

5. Check wires between sensor and pins 27 and 45 of ABS ECU for short circuits and for poor contact in connector as follows:
   a. Between pin 27 and ground. Resistance should be infinity and voltage should be 0 volts.
   b. Between pin 45 and ground. Resistance should be infinity and voltage should be 0 volts.
6. Ensure right rear wheel sensor is firmly in position.
7. Check sensor wheel is not damaged and is firmly in position. Also check that there is no bearing clearance.
8. Ensure gap between sensor and sensor wheel is .0255 inch (.65 mm).
9. Ensure ECU has a satisfactory ground connection at pin 1 and pin 19.
10. If no fault is discovered, test drive vehicle and check if diagnostic trouble code is triggered again. If diagnostic trouble code persists, proceed to "Guidelines for ECU replacement."

DIAGNOSTIC TROUBLE CODE 5/33421

1. With ECU disconnected, check circuit between pin 20 and pin 3 of ABS ECU. Resistance should be approximately 7 ohms. If circuit is satisfactory, clear diagnostic trouble code and test drive vehicle. Check if diagnostic trouble code is triggered again. If diagnostic trouble code persists, proceed to "Guidelines for ECU replacement." If circuit is unsatisfactory, proceed to step 2.
2. Check winding of left front inlet valve is intact by measuring resistance between pins 7 and 10 or 1 on valve body. Resistance should be approximately 7 ohms. If resistance is not as specified, install new hydraulic unit. If resistance is now correct, fault is in the wiring harness, proceed to step 3.
3. Check green and white wire between pin 7 on connector of valve housing and pin 20 on ABS ECU for break in continuity.
4. Check green and white wire between pin 10 or 1 on connector of valve housing and pin 3 on ABS ECU for break in continuity.

DIAGNOSTIC TROUBLE CODES 5/33422 & 334B1

1. With ECU disconnected, check circuit between pin 2 and pin 3 of ABS ECU. Resistance should be 3-4 ohms. If circuit is satisfactory, clear diagnostic trouble code and test drive vehicle. Check if diagnostic trouble code is triggered again. If diagnostic trouble code persists, proceed to "Guidelines for ECU replacement." If circuit is unsatisfactory, proceed to following step.
2. Check winding of left front outlet valve is intact by measuring resistance between pins 6 and 10 or 1 on valve body. Resistance should be 3-4 ohms. If resistance is not as specified, install new hydraulic unit. If resistance is now correct, fault is in the wiring harness, proceed to following step.
3. Check yellow and red wire between pin 6 on connector of valve housing and pin 2 on ABS ECU for break in continuity.
4. Check wire between pin 10 or 1 on connector of valve housing and pin 3 on ABS ECU for break in continuity.

DIAGNOSTIC TROUBLE CODE 5/33423

1. With ECU disconnected, check circuit between pin 38 and pin 3 of ABS ECU. Resistance should be approximately 7 ohms. If circuit is satisfactory, clear diagnostic trouble code and test drive vehicle. Check if diagnostic trouble code is triggered again. If diagnostic trouble code persists, proceed to "Guidelines for ECU replacement." If circuit is unsatisfactory, proceed to step 2.
2. Check winding of right front inlet valve is intact by measuring resistance between pins 9 and 10 or 1 on valve body. Resistance should be approximately 7 ohms. If resistance is not as specified, install new hydraulic unit. If resistance is now correct, fault is in the wiring harness, proceed to step 3.
3. Check red and white wire between pin 1 on connector of valve housing and pin 38 on ABS ECU for break in continuity.
4. Check wire between pin 10 or 1 on connector of valve housing and pin 3 on ABS ECU for break in continuity.

ABS trouble codes

Continuous	Intermittent	Component/Signal
	775B1	ECU fault
	775B2	ECU fault,-RAM
42251	22251	System relay, defective
44221	24221	No signal from front left wheel sensor
44222	24222	No signal from right front wheel sensor
44223	24223	No signal from left rear wheel sensor
44224	24224	No signal from right rear wheel sensor
	2422A	Incorrect signal from left front wheel sensor (>40 km/h)
	2422B	Incorrect signal from right front wheel sensor (>40 km/h)
	2422C	Incorrect signal from left rear wheel sensor (>40 km/h)
	2422D	Incorrect signal from right rear wheel sensor (>40 km/h)
	24291	Incorrect signal from left front wheel sensor (<40 km/h)
	24292	Incorrect signal from right front wheel sensor (<40 km/h>
	24293	Incorrect signal from left rear wheel sensor (<40 km/h)
	24294	Incorrect signal from right rear wheel sensor (<40 km/h)
	24251	Incorrect signal from left front wheel sensor (compare wheel speed)
	24252	Incorrect signal from right front wheel sensor (compare wheel speed)
	24253	Incorrect signal from left rear wheel sensor (compare wheel speed)
	24254	Incorrect signal from right rear wheel sensor (compare wheel speed)
53421	33421	Left front inlet valve inoperative
53422	33422	Left front outlet valve inoperative
53423	33423	Right front inlet valve inoperative
53424	33424	Right front outlet valve inoperative
53425	33425	Left rear inlet valve inoperative
53426	33426	Left rear outlet valve inoperative
53427	33427	Right rear inlet valve inoperative
53428	33428	Right rear outlet valve inoperative
	334B1	Left front outlet valve hydraulic fault
	334B2	Right front outlet valve, hydraulic fault
	334B3	Left rear outlet valve, hydraulic fault
	334B4	Right rear outlet valve, hydraulic fault
45721	25721	Travel sensor fault
	24791	Pump fault. Does not operate despite control signal
44792	24792	Pump fault. Operates without control signal
E75B1		Hydraulic fault

SA4029100021000X

Fig. 3 ABS diagnostic trouble codes

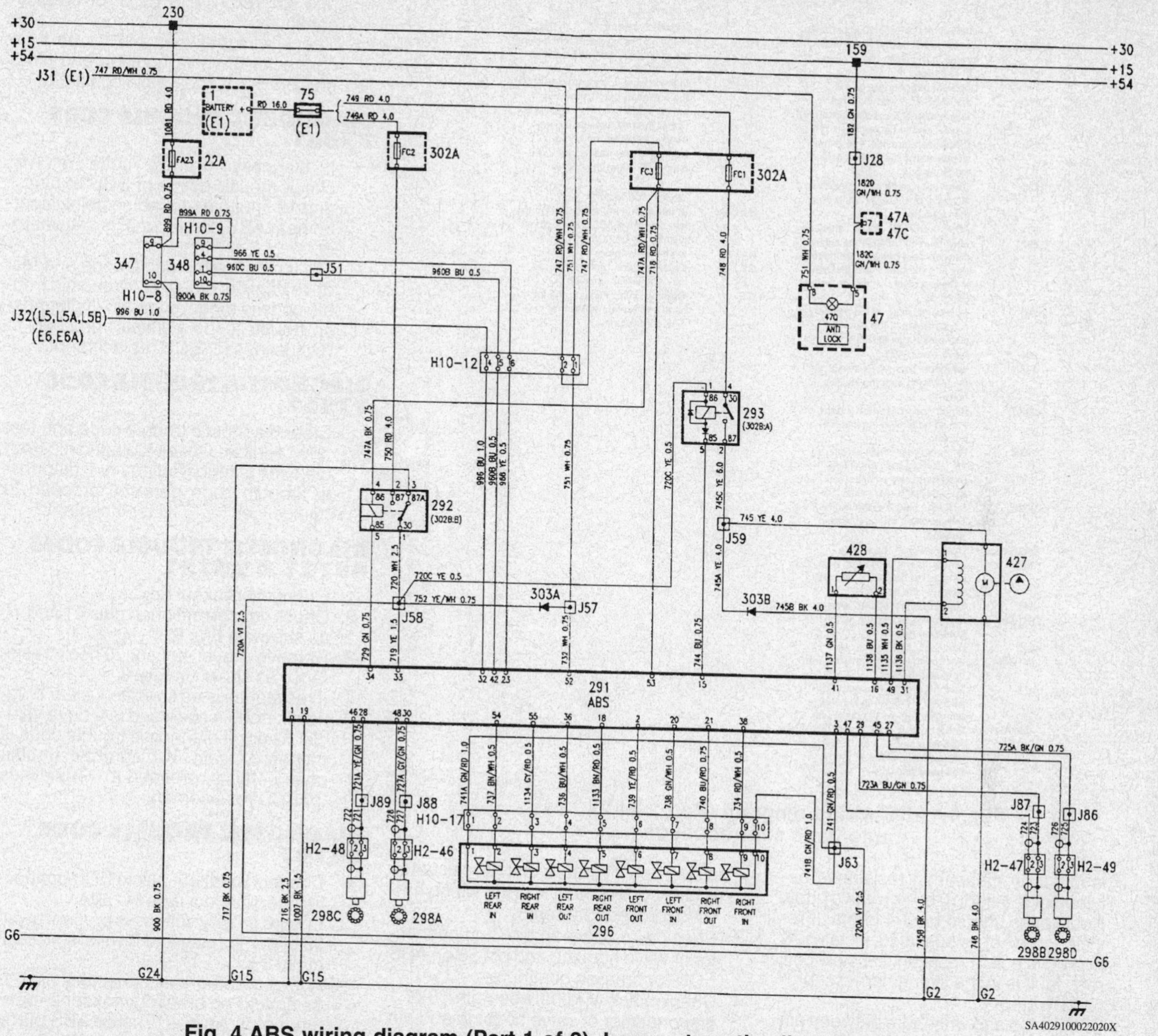
+30
+15
+54
230
159
J31 (E1)
BATTERY
(E1)
75
22A
302A
J28
47A
47C
47
ANTI LOCK
347
348
H10-8
H10-9
J51
J32(L5,L5A,L5B)
(E6,E6A)
H10-12
293
292
J59
428
427
303A
J57
303B
J58
291
ABS
J89
J88
H10-17
H2-48
H2-46
298C
298A
LEFT REAR IN
RIGHT REAR IN
LEFT REAR OUT
RIGHT REAR OUT
LEFT FRONT OUT
LEFT FRONT IN
RIGHT FRONT OUT
RIGHT FRONT IN
296
J63
J87
J86
H2-47
H2-49
298B
298D
G6
G24
G15
G2
SA4029100022020X

Fig. 4 ABS wiring diagram (Part 1 of 2). Less automatic slip reduction

DIAGNOSTIC TROUBLE CODES 5/33424 & 334B2

1. With ECU disconnected, check circuit between pin 21 and pin 3 of ABS ECU. Resistance should be 3-4 ohms. If circuit is satisfactory, clear diagnostic trouble code and test drive vehicle. Check if diagnostic trouble code is triggered again. If diagnostic trouble code persists, proceed to "Guidelines for ECU replacement." If circuit is unsatisfactory, proceed to step 2.
2. Check winding of right front outlet valve is intact by measuring resistance between pins 8 and 10 or 1 on valve body. Resistance should be 3-4 ohms. If resistance is not as specified, install new hydraulic unit. If resistance is now correct, fault is in the wiring harness, proceed to step 3.
3. Check blue and red wire between pin 8 on connector of valve housing and pin 2 on ABS ECU for break in continuity.
4. Check wire between pin 10 or 1 on connector of valve housing and pin 3 on ABS ECU for break in continuity.

DIAGNOSTIC TROUBLE CODE 3/53425

1. With ECU disconnected, check circuit between pin 54 and pin 3 of ABS ECU. Resistance should be approximately 7 ohms. If circuit is satisfactory, clear diagnostic trouble code and test drive vehicle. Check if diagnostic trouble code is triggered again. If diagnostic trouble code persists, proceed to "Guidelines for ECU replacement." If circuit is unsatisfactory, proceed to step 2.
2. Check winding of left rear inlet valve is intact by measuring resistance between pins 2 and 10 or 1 on valve body. Resistance should be approximately 7 ohms. If resistance is not as specified, install new hydraulic unit. If resistance is now correct, fault is in the wiring harness, proceed to step 3.
3. Check brown and white wire between pin 2 on connector of valve housing and pin 54 on ABS ECU for break in continuity.
4. Check wire between pin 10 or 1 on connector of valve housing and pin 3 on ABS ECU for break in continuity.

DIAGNOSTIC TROUBLE CODES 5/33426 & 334B3

1. With ECU disconnected, check circuit between pin 36 and pin 3 of ABS ECU. Resistance should be 3-4 ohms. If circuit is satisfactory, clear diagnostic trouble code and test drive vehicle. Check if diagnostic trouble code is triggered again. If diagnostic trouble code persists, proceed to "Guidelines for ECU replacement." If circuit is unsatisfactory, proceed to step 2.
2. Check winding of left rear outlet valve

1	Battery in the engine compartment
22A	Fuse holder behind the access panel in the glove box
47A	Fuel gauge
47C	Coolant temperature gauge
47Q	ABS/ABS-TCS warning lamp
75	Distribution block, positive battery supply, on the battery tray
159	Distribution terminal +15 in the electrical distribution box behind the glove box
230	Distribution terminal +30 in the electrical distribution box behind the glove box
291	ABS control unit on the battery tray
292	Main relay for ABS, in the engine compartment between the battery tray and the brake fluid reservoir, in the electrical distribution board (302B:B)
293	ABS pump relay, in the engine compartment in the electrical distribution box (302B:A)
296	Valve block, ABS
298A	Left-hand front wheel sensor, on the left-hand steering knuckle housing
298B	Right-hand front wheel sensor, on the left-hand steering knuckle housing
298C	Left-hand rear wheel sensor, on the left-hand rear wheel hub
298D	Right-hand rear wheel sensor, on the right-hand rear wheel hub
302A	ABS fuse holder in the engine compartment on the bulkhead partition
303A/ 303B	Diode, ABS, in the engine compartment, in the ABS electrical distribution box under the relay board, in the casing
347 (H10-8)	Diagnostic test socket, engine electronics, under the right-hand front seat (black)
348 (H10-9)	Diagnostic test socket, car electronics, under the right-hand front seat (green)
427	Motor for hydraulic pump (ABS/ ABS-ASR Mark IV) in the engine compartment on the brake unit
428	Pedal position transmistter (ABS/ ABS-ASR Mark IV) on the vacuum servo which is located on the bulkhead partition
	2-pole connector
H2-46	In the engine compartment behind the bulkhead partition on the extreme left
H2-47	In the engine compartment behind the bulkhead partition on the extreme right
H2-48	Under the rear seat on the left-hand side under the carpet
H2-49	Under the rear seat on the right-hand side under the carpet
	10-pole connector
H10-12	In the engine compartment on the left, below the ABS 302 electrical distribution box
H10-17	On the valve block
G2	Earthing point, battery tray, on left-hand wheel housing
G15	Earthing point, ABS, on the left-hand structuiral member, at the ABS control unit

SA4029100022010X

Fig. 4 ABS wiring diagram (Part 2 of 2). Less automatic slip reduction

is intact by measuring resistance between pins 4 and 10 or 1 on valve body. Resistance should be 3-4 ohms. If resistance is not as specified, install new hydraulic unit. If resistance is now correct, fault is in the wiring harness, proceed to step 3.

3. Check blue and white wire between pin 4 on connector of valve housing and pin 36 on ABS ECU for break in continuity.
4. Check wire between pin 10 or 1 on connector of valve housing and pin 3 on ABS ECU for break in continuity.

DIAGNOSTIC TROUBLE CODE 5/33427

1. With ECU disconnected, check circuit between pin 55 and pin 3 of ABS ECU. Resistance should be approximately 7 ohms. If circuit is satisfactory, clear diagnostic trouble code and test drive vehicle. Check if diagnostic trouble code is triggered again. If diagnostic trouble code persists, proceed to "Guidelines for ECU replacement." If circuit is unsatisfactory, proceed to step 2.
2. Check winding of right rear inlet valve is intact by measuring resistance between pins 3 and 10 or 1 on valve body. Resistance should be approximately 7 ohms. If resistance is not as specified, install new hydraulic unit. If resistance is now correct, fault is in the wiring harness, proceed to step 3.
3. Check wire between pin 3 on connector of valve housing and pin 55 on ABS ECU for break in continuity.
4. Check black wire between pin 10 or 1 on connector of valve housing and pin 3 on ABS ECU for break in continuity.

DIAGNOSTIC TROUBLE CODES 5/33428 & 334B4

1. With ECU disconnected, check circuit between pin 18 and pin 3 of ABS ECU. Resistance should be 3-4 ohms. If circuit is satisfactory, clear diagnostic trouble code and test drive vehicle. Check if diagnostic trouble code is triggered again. If diagnostic trouble code persists, proceed to "Guidelines for ECU replacement." If circuit is unsatisfactory, proceed to step 2.
2. Check winding of right rear outlet valve is intact by measuring resistance between pins 5 and 10 or 1 on valve body. Resistance should be 3-4 ohms. If resistance is not as specified, install new hydraulic unit. If resistance is now correct, fault is in the wiring harness, proceed to step 3.
3. Check brown and white wire between pin 5 on connector of valve housing and pin 18 on ABS ECU for break in continuity.
4. Check wire between pin 10 or 1 on connector of valve housing and pin 3 on ABS ECU for break in continuity.

DIAGNOSTIC TROUBLE CODE 775B1

1. If diagnostic trouble code returns, check ground points of ECU at pins 1 and 19 and that grounding point, located near ABS control unit, is satisfactory.
2. Clear diagnostic trouble code and test drive vehicle. Check if diagnostic trouble code is triggered again. If diagnostic trouble code persists, proceed to "Guidelines for ECU replacement."

DIAGNOSTIC TROUBLE CODE 775B2

1. Clear diagnostic trouble code and test drive vehicle. Check if diagnostic trouble code is triggered again. If diagnostic trouble code persists, proceed to "Guidelines for ECU replacement."

DIAGNOSTIC TROUBLE CODES 45721 & 25721

1. Connect breakout box.
2. Check voltage between pins 41 and 16 as shown in **Fig. 6.**
3. Remove travel sensor. Check resistance as shown in **Fig. 6.**
4. If resistance is as specified, clear diagnostic trouble code and test drive vehicle. Check if diagnostic trouble code is triggered again. If diagnostic trouble code persists, proceed to "Guidelines for ECU replacement."

DIAGNOSTIC TROUBLE CODE 24791

1. Connect breakout box to ECU connector, then inspect fuse FC 30A.
2. Ensure battery voltage is present at pin 30 of pump relay and 0 volts is present at pin 87.
3. Activate pump by connecting pins 1, 34 and 15 on breakout box for a maximum of 2 minutes. Ensure ABS pump relay clicks.
4. Check pins 49 and 31 on breakout box. With motor running reading should be approximately .7 volt AC. With motor stationary reading should be 0 volt.
5. Check pin 2 with relay operated. If battery voltage is present, check ground. If ground is satisfactory, install new pump.

DIAGNOSTIC TROUBLE CODES 44792 & 24792

1. Unplug ECU and connect breakout box to its connector.
2. Ensure pump motor and speed sensor are operative. Refer to "Diagnostic Trouble Code 24791."
3. Check travel sensor.
4. Check voltage at pin 15 of breakout box. Battery voltage should be present. If voltage is not as specified, clear diagnostic trouble code and test drive vehicle. Check if diagnostic trouble code is triggered again. If diagnostic trouble code persists, proceed to

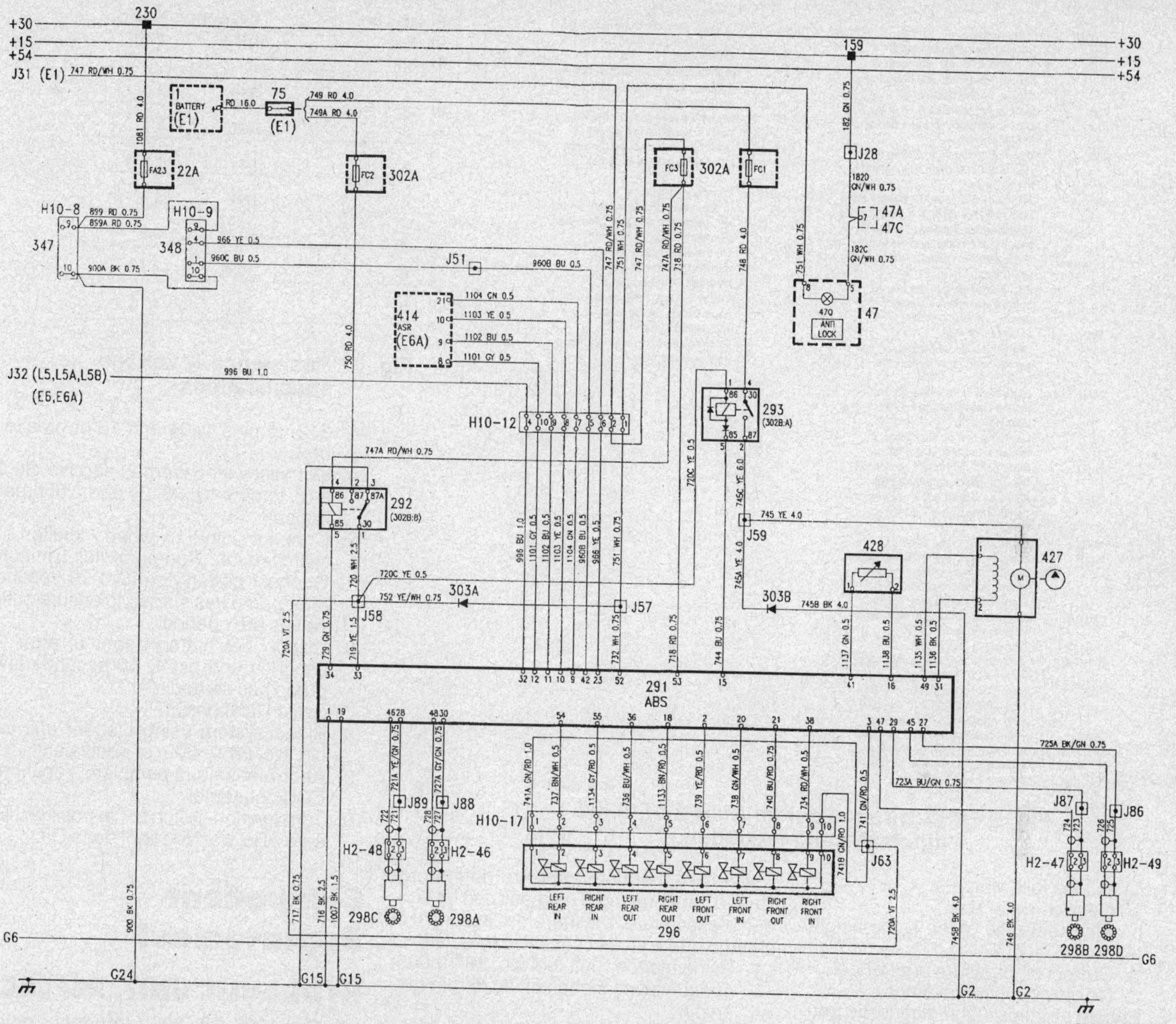
+30
+15
+54
230
159
J31 (E1)
BATTERY
(E1)
75
22A
302A
FC1
J28
47A
47C
47
ANTI LOCK
H10-8
H10-9
347
348
J51
414
ASR
(E6A)
J32 (L5,L5A,L5B)
(E6,E6A)
H10-12
293
292
J59
428
427
303A
303B
J58
J57
291
ABS
J89
J88
H10-17
H2-48
H2-46
J63
J87
J86
H2-47
H2-49
LEFT REAR IN
RIGHT REAR IN
LEFT REAR OUT
RIGHT REAR OUT
LEFT FRONT OUT
LEFT FRONT IN
RIGHT FRONT OUT
RIGHT FRONT IN
296
298C
298A
298B
298D
G6
G24
G15
G2
SA4029100023020X

Fig. 5 ABS diagram (Part 1 of 2). w/ automatic slip reduction

"Guidelines for ECU replacement. "

DIAGNOSTIC TROUBLE CODES E75B1

1. Ensure there is brake fluid in system and thickness of brake pads is within specification. Check master cylinder operation and all hoses for damage or swelling.
2. Check voltage between pins 41 and 16 as shown in **Fig. 6.**
3. Remove travel sensor. Check resistance as shown in **Fig. 6.**
4. If resistance is as specified, clear diagnostic trouble code and test drive vehicle. Check if diagnostic trouble code is triggered again. If diagnostic trouble code persists, proceed to "Guidelines for ECU replacement. "

WARNING LIGHTS

Anti-Lock Light

1. With ECU connector connected and ignition switch in Drive position, check there is battery voltage at pin 52. If voltage is not present, check bulb is intact and white wire between pins 52 and 8 of main instrument display panel.
2. With ignition in Off position and ECU main relay disconnected, check circuit between pins 52 and 33.
3. Ensure diode is nonconducting to pin 52.

Brake Fluid Level Light

1. **If light comes on when car is started,** proceed as follows:
   a. With ignition On, check for battery voltage at pin 2 on brake fluid reservoir. If voltage is not present at 2, check pin 5 on combined instrument. If battery voltage is present at pin 5, there is no fault in power supply.
   b. Check light. If light is intact, install a new circuit.
   c. Ensure pin 1 is grounded. If not, check ground supply. If ground is found at supply, install new float.
   d. If no voltage is present at pin 5 on combined instrument, there is a fault in power supply.
2. **If light does not come on when care is started,** proceed as follows:
   a. Ensure lamp comes on when float is pressed down in reservoir.
   b. Check pin 1 of main instrument display panel. Test position of ignition switch equals 0 volt. If voltage reading is as specified, replace circuit board. If voltage is present, check ground on ignition switch. If switch is grounded, install new ignition switch. If switch is not grounded, check grounding path.

GUIDELINES FOR ECU REPLACEMENT

When all checks have been carried out according to diagnostic trouble code diagnosis without any faults being discovered, it is logical to assume the ECU is defective. The following steps must therefore be carried out carefully before the ABS ECU is identified as the cause of the fault.

47A	Fuel gauge
47C	Coolant temperature gauge
47Q	ABS/ABS-TCS warning lamp
75	Distribution block, positive battery supply, on the battery tray
159	Distribution terminal + 15 in the electrical distribution box behind the glove box
230	Distribution terminal + 30 in the electrical distribution box behind the glove box
291	ABS control unit on the battery tray
292	Main relay for ABS, in the engine compartment between the battery tray and the brake fluid reservoir, in the electrical distribution board (302B:B)
293	ABS pump relay, in the engine compartment in the electrical distribution box (302B:A)
296	Valve block, ABS
298A	Left-hand front wheel sensor, on the left-hand steering knuckle housing
298B	Right-hand front wheel sensor, on the left-hand steering knuckle housing
298C	Left-hand rear wheel sensor, on the left-hand rear wheel hub
298D	Right-hand rear wheel sensor, on the right-hand rear wheel hub
302A	ABS fuse holder in the engine compartment on the bulkhead partition
303A/ 303B	Diode, ABS, in the engine compartment, in the ABS electrical distribution box under the relay board, in the casing
347 (H10-8)	Diagnostic test socket, engine electronics, under the right-hand front seat (black)
348 (H10-9)	Diagnostic test socket, car electronics, under the right-hand front seat (green)
427	Motor for hydraulic pump (ABS/ ABS-ASR Mark IV) in the engine compartment on the brake unit
428	Pedal position transmistter (ABS/ ABS-ASR Mark IV) on the vacuum servo which is located on the bulkhead partition
	2-pole connector
H2-46	In the engine compartment behind the bulkhead partition on the extreme left
H2-47	In the engine compartment behind the bulkhead partition on the extreme right
H2-48	Under the rear seat on the left-hand side under the carpet
H2-49	Under the rear seat on the right-hand side under the carpet
	10-pole connector
H10-12	In the engine compartment on the left, below the ABS 302 electrical distribution box
H10-17	On the valve block
G2	Earthing point, battery tray, on left-hand wheel housing
G15	Earthing point, ABS, on the left-hand structuiral member, at the ABS control unit
G24	Earthing point, on the right-hand front seat member

SA4029100023010X

Fig. 5 ABS wiring diagram (Part 2 of 2). w/ automatic slip reduction

Position of travel sensor	Resistance Ohms	Voltage Volts
1	250	1.0
2	437	1.7
3	564	2.3
4	691	2.8
5	817	3.3
6	1034	4.1
7	OL	10.0

SA4029100024000X

Fig. 6 Resistance & voltage specifications

1. Check the following:
   a. Correct wheel size.
   b. All wheels are of the same height/ width.
   c. Correct air pressure in all wheels.
   d. No play in wheel bearings.
2. Ensure all steps in the diagnostic trouble code diagnosis have been carried out.
3. Study wiring diagram of the circuit concerned and familiarize yourself with how it works.
4. Inspect all ground points. Check power ground and signal ground are electrically separated.
5. Check power supply to ECU.
6. Clear diagnostic trouble code. Test drive vehicle again. If original diagnostic trouble code persists, The ABS ECU must be replaced.

COMPONENT TESTING

ABS ECU VOLTAGE TEST USING BREAKOUT BOX

Refer to **Fig. 7,** for voltage specifications.

SYSTEM SERVICE

FLUID CHANGE

All brake fluid deteriorates after a time through oxidation and absorption of water. This lower the boiling point of the fluid, which may therefore vaporize during prolonged hard braking. The result can be sudden brake failure. It is therefore essential to change brake fluid at specified intervals.

1. Using bleeder unit tool No. 88 19 096, or equivalent, siphon off fluid from reservoir.
2. Fill reservoir with DOT 4 brake fluid.
3. Using bleeder unit to drain each individual wheel. The following quantities must be drained from each wheel:
   a. Right front wheel, 1 quart.
   b. Left rear wheel, .5 quart.
   c. Left front wheel, 1 quart.
   d. Right rear wheel, .5 quart.
4. Fill system with new brake fluid to bring level up to MAX mark on side of reservoir. Also change fluid in clutch system.

Brake System Bleed

Brake system must be bled when the hydraulic unit is replaced.

Brakes must be bled in the following sequence: right front, left rear, left front and right rear wheels.

1. Unscrew cover of brake fluid reservoir, then connect topping-up assembly (part of brake bleed unit kit part No. 88 19 096) to reservoir.
2. Disconnect ECU connector. Plug connector of breakout box into ABS connector for ECU.
3. Connect wiring loom 1, part No. 86 11 212, to pins 1, 34 and 15 of breakout box.
4. Connect wiring loom 2, part No. 86 11 212, to pins 18, 36, 21 and 2 of breakout box.
5. Connect pin 1 when ignition is switched On. Run pump for 1 minute. Connect battery terminal 20 seconds after pump has started to ensure outlet valves are opened.
6. Disconnect battery terminal after 20 seconds and pin 1, 60 seconds after pump has started.
7. Switch ignition Off.
8. Bleed system using bleeder unit tool No. No. 88 19 096, or equivalent.
9. After bleeding is complete, reconnect ECU connector.
10. Turn ignition switch to On position. Ensure ABS warning light goes Off.

Component Replacement

HYDRAULIC UNIT, REPLACE

1. **On 1995–96 9000 models,** obtain radio anti-theft code as outlined under "Precautions."
2. **On all models,** disconnect battery cables, then remove bolt securing battery to tray.
3. Remove battery, then disconnect main fuse box by lifting straight up.
4. Remove battery tray mounting bolts and screws, then the battery tray.
5. Unplug connector from ECU on side of battery tray, then disconnect ABS wiring loom clip.
6. Remove throttle cable from throttle housing, then the ABS main fuse box and brake fluid reservoir from their brackets.
7. Using brake bleeder unit part No. 88 19 096, or equivalent, siphon brake fluid out of reservoir.
8. **On models with manual transaxle,** disconnect clutch cylinder hose from reservoir.
9. **On all models,** mark and remove four brake pipes. Plug ends of valve block and brake pipes.
10. Disconnect hydraulic unit connectors, then the travel sensor connector.

Pin no.	Wire colour	Component/function	In-put	Out-put	Voltage (V)	Remarks
1	BK	Earth 1	X		0	G 15
2	YE/RD	Left front outlet valve		X	Pwm neg	Ref 12V
3	GN/RD	REF voltage	X		Batt.	
4						Not connected
5						Not connected
6						Not connected
7						Not connected
8						Not connected
9	GN	ASR right rear		X		To ASR
10	YE	ASR left front		X		To ASR
11	BU	ASR right front		X		To ASR
12	GY	ASR left rear		X		To ASR
13						Not connected
14						Not connected
15	BU	Pump relay Pin 85		X	0v	Relay earth Ref 12V (off)
16	BU	Travel sensor	X		1-10V	Depending on position
17						Not connected
18	BN/RD	Right rear outlet valve		X	Pwm neg	Ref 12V
19	BK	Earth 2	X		0	G 15
20	GN/WH	Left front inlet valve		X	Pwm neg	Ref 12V
21	BU/RD	Right front outlet valve		X	Pwm neg	Ref 12V
22						Not connected
23	YE	Diagnostic lead L	X			Pin 4
24						Not connected
25						Not connected
26						Not connected

SA4029100025010X

Fig. 7 ABS ECU voltage specifications (Part 1 of 2)

Pin no.	Wire colour	Component/function	In-put	Out-put	Voltage (V)	Remarks
27	BK/GN	Right rear wheel sensor		X	0V	Ref earth
28	YE/GN	Left front wheel sensor		X	0V	Ref earth
29	BU/GN	Right front wheel sensor		X	0V	Ref earth
30	GN/GY	Left front wheel sensor		X	0V	Ref earth
31	BK	Pump sensor		X	approx. 0.7 AC	Active
32	BU	Brake light switch	X		12V	0V off
33	YE	Power supply +30	X		12 V	Via main relay
34	GN	Main relay earth		X	0V	Ref 12V Pin 85
35						Not connected
36	BU/WH	Left rear outlet valve		X	Pwm neg	Ref 12V
37						Not connected
38	RD/WH	Right front inlet valve		X	Pwm neg	Ref 12V
39						No connection activated
40						Not connected
41	GN	Travel sensor		X	0V	Earth
42	BU	Diagnostic lead K		X		Pin 1
43						Not connected
44						Not connected
45	GN	Right rear wheel sensor	X		0.15-0.70	AC sine wave
46	GN	Left rear wheel sensor	X		0.15-0.70	AC sine wave
47	GN	Right front wheel sensor	X		0.15-0.70	AC sine wave
48	GN	Left front wheel sensor	X		0.15-0.70	AC sine wave
49	WH	Pump sensor	X		approx. 0.7 AC	Signal
50						Not connected
51						Not connected
52	WH	ANTI LOCK warning light earth		X	0V	Ref 12V off
53	RD	Power supply +54	X		12v	+54
54	BN/WH	Left rear inlet valve		X	Pwm neg	Ref 12V
55	GY/RD	Right rear inlet valve		X	Pwm neg	Ref 12V

SA4029100025020X

Fig. 7 ABS ECU voltage specifications (Part 2 of 2)

11. Remove hydraulic unit mounting nuts, then the unit.
12. Reverse procedure to install. Bleed brake system as outlined under "Brake System Bleed."

MASTER CYLINDER, REPLACE

1. Clean around ends of brake pipes.
2. **On 1995–96 9000 models,** obtain radio anti-theft code as outlined under "Precautions."
3. **On all models,** disconnect battery cables, then remove bolt securing battery to tray.
4. Remove battery, then disconnect main fuse box by lifting straight up.
5. Remove battery tray mounting bolts and screws, then the battery tray.
6. Drain brake fluid reservoir, then disconnect brake pipes from master cylinder.
7. Remove securing bolt from below master cylinder.
8. Remove nuts mounting master cylinder to vacuum operated servo.
9. Remove master cylinder assembly, then disconnect hose from master cylinder.
10. Reverse procedure to install, then bleed brake system as outlined under "Brake System Bleed."

VACUUM OPERATED SERVO

1. Remove ABS hydraulic unit as outlined under "Hydraulic Unit, Replace."
2. Disconnect lower dash panel by pressing locking pins on 5 plastic clips with a flat head screwdriver.
3. Disconnect clip and pin from pushrod.
4. Remove vacuum servo mounting nuts, then disconnect vacuum hose and travel sensor connector from servo.
5. Remove servo unit. When changing vacuum servo unit, travel sensor must be transferred to new servo unit. Adjusting sleeve having same color as mark servo should be installed on travel sensor.
6. Reverse procedure to install.

ABS ELECTRONIC CONTROL UNIT (ECU), REPLACE

1. **On 1995–96 9000 models,** obtain radio anti-theft code as outlined under "Precautions."
2. **On all models,** disconnect battery cables, then disconnect ABS wiring loom clip.
3. Disconnect ECU electrical connector.
4. Remove ECU mounting bolts, then the ECU.
5. Reverse procedure to install.

TRAVEL SENSOR, REPLACE

1. Remove rubber elbow from throttle housing.
2. Remove ABS main fuse box and brake fluid reservoir.
3. Disconnect connectors from hydraulic unit, then remove circlip below travel sensor.
4. Remove travel sensor, then the O-ring from sensor.
5. Reverse procedure to install. Adjusting sleeve should have same color as mark on vacuum servo.

FRONT WHEEL SENSORS, REPLACE

1. Disconnect sensor connector (one for each wheel) by pushing halves together to release catches:
   a. Lift rubber molding on bulkhead panel. Remove cover over space behind bulkhead panel. Remove plastic clip at panel.
   b. On right side, raise A/C pipes and pull sensor lead through.
2. Raise and support vehicle, then remove front wheel(s).
3. Remove rear section of wing liner.
4. Cut cable tie securing sensor lead to top bracket. Pull sensor lead through rubber grommet in wheel housing.
5. Remove sensor mounting bolt, then the sensor.
6. Reverse procedure to install. Turn steering wheel from lock to lock to ensure sensor lead cannot rub against any front assembly components.

REAR WHEEL SENSORS, REPLACE

1. Tilt rear seat forward and remove cover on left and/or right side of floor.
2. Unplug sensor connector from brackets by clipping tie on top bracket.
3. Raise and support vehicle, then remove rear wheel(s).
4. Disconnect clip and pull sensor lead through rubber grommet in floor.
5. Remove sensor mounting bolt, then the sensor.
6. Reverse procedure to install.

1994–95 900 Anti-Lock Brake System

NOTE: On Air Bag Equipped Models, Refer To "Air Bag System Precautions" Located In The Front Of This Manual For System Disarming & Arming Procedures.

NOTE: Electrical Symbol & Wire Color Code Identification Located In The Front Of This Manual May Be Used As An Aid When Using Wiring Circuits Found In This Section.

INDEX

	Page No.
Description	38-124
Components	38-124
System	38-124
Diagnosis & Testing	38-125
ABS Measured Data	38-125
Accessing Diagnostic Trouble Codes	38-126
Diagnostic Trouble Code Interpretation	38-126
Flashing Codes	38-125
Diagnostic Chart Index	38-127
Precautions	38-124
Air Bag Systems	38-124
System Service	38-126
Brake System Bleed	38-126
Component Replacement	38-126
ABS Control Module, Replace	38-126
Hydraulic Unit, Replace	38-126
Wheel Sensors, Replace	38-126
Troubleshooting	38-125
Checking Break In Continuity/ Short Circuit	38-125

PRECAUTIONS

AIR BAG SYSTEMS

Refer to "Air Bag System Precautions" in the front of this manual for system disarming and arming procedures.

DESCRIPTION

SYSTEM

The Anti-Lock Brake System (ABS) is a two-circuit, three-port brake system, **Fig. 1.**

Four wheel sensors at the wheels send signals to an electronic control unit, which continuously calculates on the basis of the wheel acceleration (speed increase), wheel deceleration (speed decrease), the speed of the vehicle and the slip of the wheels (degree of wheel lock-up). If any wheel approaches the limit for lock-up, the control unit passes signals to solenoid valves in the valve block for the wheel concerned. The pressure in the brake circuit for the wheel is controlled in this way so the maximum possible braking power is transmitted to the road surface at all times with no loss of steering ability.

COMPONENTS

HYDRAULIC UNIT

The hydraulic unit consists of the valve block with three 3/3 solenoid valves (1 valve for front right wheel, 1 for front left wheel and 1 for both rear wheels), equalization valve and control module with main and pump relays and return pump.

When the ignition key is turned to drive position and the wheels start to rotate, the return pump is always tested by the control module starting the pump for approximately .5 seconds.

The master cylinder is separated from the hydraulic unit and is connected via two pipes from the primary and secondary circuits.

CONTROL MODULE

The control module forms an integral unit with the ABS unit and has a 25-pin connector.

The control module always receives information on the speed of the wheels through input signals from the wheel sensors.

If any of the wheels has greater deceleration on braking than the others, the control module controls the solenoid valves so the hydraulic brake pressure can be kept constant or reduced, and every wheel can obtain the maximum from the friction of the road surface.

The control module incorporates the main relay, the pump relay, a 4-pin connector for voltage measurement and ground and a 6-pin connector for solenoid valves.

WHEEL SENSORS

The wheel sensors are mounted near a toothed sensor wheel at each wheel. Each time a tooth on the sensor wheel passes the sensor, it distorts a magnetic field, which causes a signal to be sent to the Engine Control Unit (ECU).

The rear wheel sensor is designed differently than the front, in that it is less sensitive to wheel bearing play and starts to pass information to the control module at very low wheel speeds.

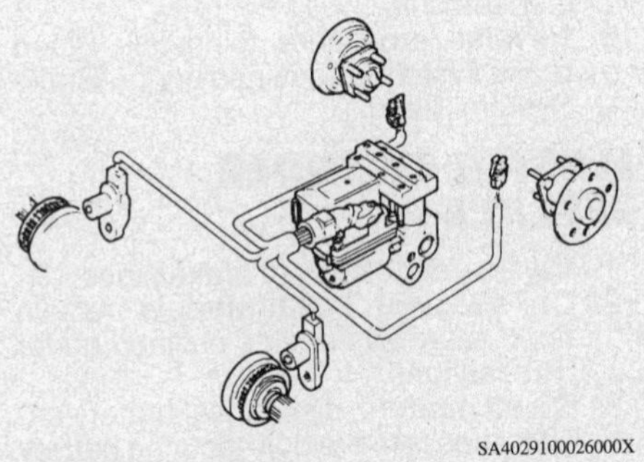
SA4029100026000X

Fig. 1 Anti-lock brake system

SOLENOID VALVES

Normal Position (Pressure Build-Up)

In normal position, **Fig. 2,** the solenoid valve is de-energized. The piston is pressed down toward the normal position of the return spring. The brake fluid is now able to flow freely from the master cylinder out through the solenoid valve to the wheel cylinder. This position is the normal position in braking without ABS control and the pressure build-up position in ABS control.

In ABS control, the control module can run up to ten control cycles per second.

Pressure Holding Position

In this position, **Fig. 3,** the solenoid valve has received around half the current from the ABS control module. The piston has moved into the pressure holding position by rising slightly and the passage from the master cylinder to the wheel cylinder is consequently closed.

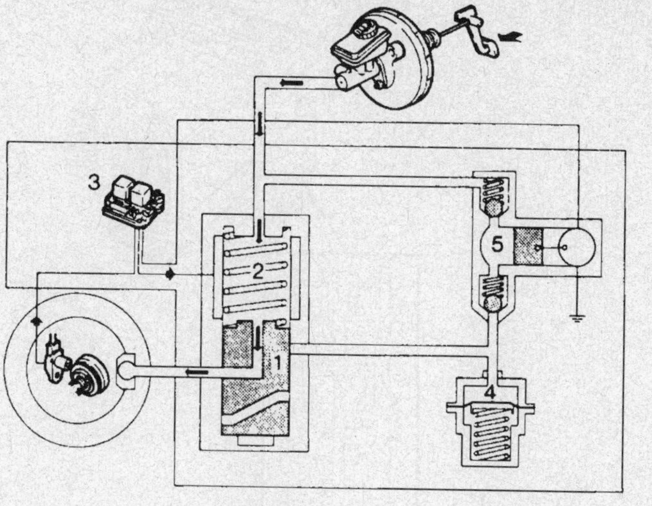
3
5
2
1
4

1 Piston
2 Return spring
3 Control module
4 Pressure accumulator
5 Return pump

SA4029100027000X

Fig. 2 Solenoid valve in normal position (pressure build-up)

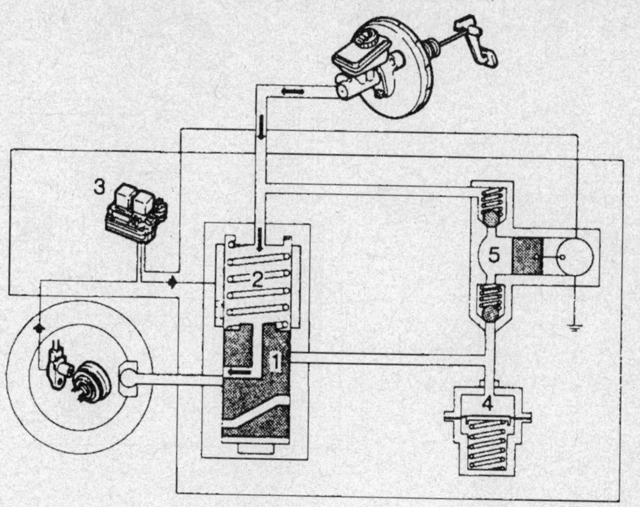
3
5
2
1
4

1 Piston
2 Return spring
3 ECU
4 Pressure accumulator
5 Return pump

SA4029100028000X

Fig. 3 Solenoid valve in pressure holding position

This is one of the three positions with which the control module operates under ABS control.

Pressure Relief

In this position, **Fig. 4,** the solenoid valve obtains full current from the control module. The piston in the valve has risen to the pressure relief position and opens the channel from the wheel cylinder to the pressure accumulator which can quickly receive pressure from the wheel cylinder. The control module energizes the return pump and the pressure can be pumped back to the master cylinder.

EQUALIZATION VALVE

In addition to the solenoid valve, there is an equalization valve, **Fig. 5,** for the rear wheel circuit so both rear wheels can be operated with only one solenoid valve.

The equalization valve ensures both rear wheels receive the same brake pressure in ABS control. This means the vehicle has good directional stability.

In the case of ABS control of the rear wheels, the solenoid valve moves to the pressure holding position. The channel to the rear right wheel is now blocked. If the pressure from the master cylinder rises, a pressure difference develops below and above the piston (1). The piston is raised and the valve (2) closes the pressure to the rear left wheel. If the pressure to the rear right wheel drops (pressure relief), a greater pressure difference develops above and below the piston (1), and the piston is lifted further upward until the pressure for the right and left rear wheels has balanced out.

BRAKE LIGHT SWITCH

The control module receives voltage from the brake light switch to pin 23 if the brake is activated. For example, the brake light switch is used if the surface is very slippery and the driver decides to pump-brake.

Every time the driver depresses the brake pedal, (when power is fed to the ECU from the brake light switch), ABS control restarts from its starting position.

TROUBLESHOOTING

CHECKING BREAK IN CONTINUITY/SHORT CIRCUIT

BREAK IN CONTINUITY

Resistance Measurement

1. Ensure component or cable to be checked is not live.
2. With instrument set for resistance measurement, connect the measuring cables to each end of the component or cable to be checked.
3. Resistance for wiring must normally be less than 1 ohm. Specified value applies to components.

Voltage Measurement

1. Switch on any load.
2. With instrument set for voltage measurement, connect black measuring cable to safe ground and red measuring cable to lead side.
3. In case of output from control module/switch, measure away from these and gradually move out toward load. When load disappears, you have just passed break in continuity.
4. In case of input to control module/consumer, measure away from current source and gradually move in toward control module/consumer. When voltage disappears, you have just passed break in continuity.

SHORT-CIRCUIT TO GROUND

Resistance Measurement

1. Ensure lead to be checked is not live and that any load has been disconnected.
2. With instrument set for resistance measurement, connect one measuring cable to load side of lead and the other to safe ground.
3. Move carefully on wiring and check at same time that instrument shows infinite resistance the whole time.

DIAGNOSIS & TESTING

ABS MEASURED DATA

Refer to **Figs. 6 and 7** for ABS measured data.

1. Measurements must be performed using Breakout Box (BOB) connected 3between control module and control module connector.
2. Several voltage levels must be regarded as guide values. Apply common sense in judging whether a measured value is correct or faulty.
3. If any measured value is faulty, use the wiring diagram, **Fig. 8,** to find out which leads, connectors or components should be checked more closely.

FLASHING CODES

To begin flashing code diagnosis, ground pin 24 in 25-pin connector of control module, **Fig. 6,** before ignition is turned on. Refer to **Fig. 9** for description of flashing codes.

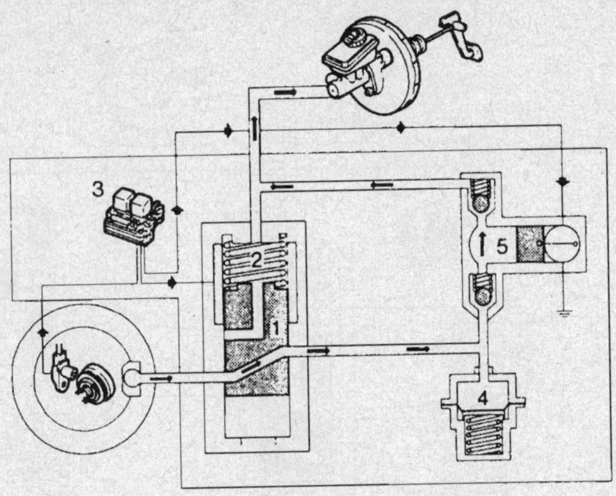
3
2
1
5
4
1 Piston
2 Return spring
3 Control module
4 Pressure accumulator
5 Return pump
SA4029100029000X

Fig. 4 Solenoid valve in pressure relief position

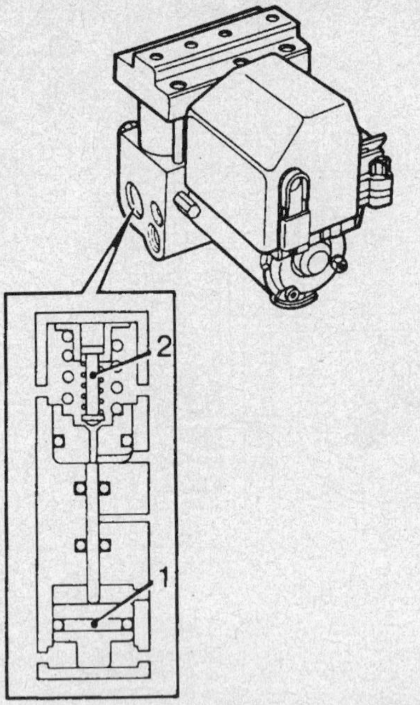
2
1
SA4029100030000X

Fig. 5 Rear wheel equalization valve

ACCESSING DIAGNOSTIC TROUBLE CODES

The ABS control module communicates with ISAT, **Fig. 10,** through pin 11 (K cable).

Any diagnostic trouble codes stored in the control module can be read out by means of ISAT. ISAT can also command the control module to control the solenoid valves or read the wheel speed.

With the ignition on and ISAT connected, the voltage on pin is approximately 10 volts. The diagnostic testing socket is located below the lower lefthand instrument panel fascia.

Operation

The ISAT features a system where clear text under a number of menu options enables the user to directly select the desired command with the keypad. The structure of the ABS command menus, **Fig. 11,** provides six main menus. Three of these menus have varying numbers of commands in a submenu.

When a system function is activated with ISAT, it means the ABS control module is performing something which is not functionally normal. diagnostic trouble codes can be put into other systems which are dependent on the ABS.

The Activate functions must always be used with caution. Always deactivate an activated function before proceeding in the ISAT menu. Always clear any diagnostic trouble codes recorded in ABS or any other system after work has been completed.

DIAGNOSTIC TROUBLE CODE INTERPRETATION

When performing diagnostic trouble code diagnosis and repair, refer to **Fig. 8** for ABS wiring circuit and **Fig 12** for diagnostic trouble code identification.

Refer to **Fig. 13** for explanation of valve test, Front Left (FL) and Front Right (FR). The rear valve test is similar to the front valve test, but is simpler. Refer to **Fig. 13** for an explanation for the rear valve test, noting that only displays 1, 2, and 8-12 apply.

Refer to **Figs. 14 through 28** for diagnostic trouble code diagnostic routines.

SYSTEM SERVICE

Brake System Bleed

1. Unscrew cover of brake fluid reservoir and top off with brake fluid.
2. Connect topping-off fitting from brake bleeding unit kit tool No. 88 19 096, or equivalent, to brake fluid reservoir.
3. Position hose with one end on topping-off fitting and other end in bottle filled with clean brake fluid.
4. Raise and support vehicle, then connect brake bleeder hose to front left wheel and open nipple. Draw off approximately .1 quart brake fluid. Repeat this at front right wheel.
5. Move brake bleeder to rear left wheel and open nipple. Draw off approximately .05 quart brake fluid. Repeat this at rear right wheel.
6. Lower vehicle, then check brake operation. Depress brake pedal and check that it does not drop.
7. Remove topping-off fitting, hose and bottle.
8. Adjust brake fluid level.

Component Replacement

HYDRAULIC UNIT, REPLACE

Refer to **Fig. 29** when replacing hydraulic unit.

1. Remove bar fixed between spring struts.
2. Remove black plastic cover screw, then the cover.
3. Disconnect electrical connector and electrical connection (1), then the ground cable (2).
4. Remove brake pipe connections and plug holes (3).
5. Remove three hydraulic unit to bracket nuts (4). Disconnect steering servo reservoir (5) to improve access if necessary.
6. Remove hydraulic unit.
7. Reverse procedure to install. Bleed brake system as outlined under "Brake System Bleed."

ABS CONTROL MODULE, REPLACE

1. Disconnect battery ground cable, then remove hydraulic unit cover.
2. Disconnect 4-pin plug connector and electrical connector, then the 6-pin plug connector.
3. Remove six control module securing bolts, then the control module from hydraulic unit.
4. Reverse procedure to install. Start vehicle and check that warning lamps go out.

WHEEL SENSORS, REPLACE

Front

1. Disconnect battery ground cable, then raise and support vehicle.
2. Remove wheel, then clean around wheel sensor with soft steel brush.
3. Remove wheel sensor securing bolt and disconnect sensor.
4. Disconnect sensor cable from bracket in wheel arch, then disconnect connector.
5. Reverse procedure to install.

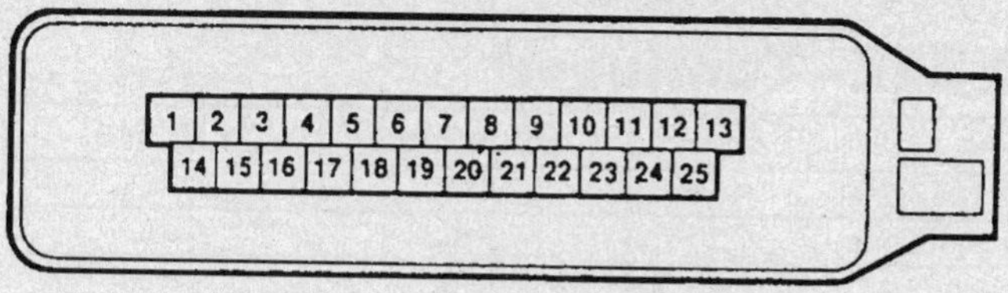
1
2
3
4
5
6
7
8
9
10
11
12
13
14
15
16
17
18
19
20
21
22
23
24
25

SA4029100031000X

Fig. 6 ABS control module connector view

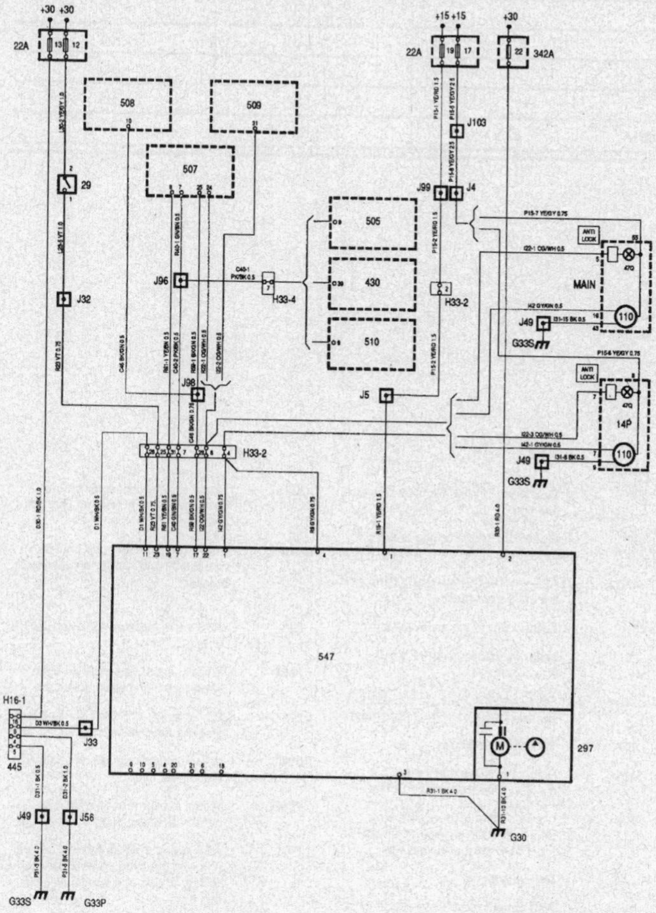
+30 +30
22A
508
509
507
29
J32
J96
H33-4
505
430
510
J98
H33-2
+15 +15
+30
342A
J103
J99
J4
H33-2
MAIN
J49
G33S
110
14P
J5
547
297
H16-1
J33
445
J49
J56
G33S
G33P
G30

SA4029100033010X

Fig. 8 ABS system wiring circuit (Part 1 of 3)

> = Greater than < = Less than
≈ = Approximately equal to ~ = AC voltage

Pin	Colour	Component/ Function	Input/ Output	Measuring conditions	Measured value	Be-tween X-Y
1	GY/GN	MIL	Output	MIL lit	0	1-3
				MIL not lit	Batt+	
2						
3						
4	GN	Wheel sensor FL	Input	Rotate the wheel 1 rev/sec	>100mV~	4-5
5	GN	Wheel sensor FL	Input	Rotate the wheel 1 rev/sec	>100mV~	5-4
6	BN/RD	Wheel sensor RR	Input	Rotate the wheel 1 rev/sec	>100mV~	6-18
7	GN/BN	Wheel speed FR	Output	Rotate the wheel	0/10V	7-B-
8						
9	BU/WH	Wheel sensor RL	Input	Rotate the wheel 1 rev/sec	>100mV~	9-10
10	BU/WH	Wheel sensor RL	Input	Rotate the wheel 1 rev/sec	>100mV~	10-9
11	WH/BK	Diagnostic contact	Input Output	Ignition on ISAT connected	≈10V	11-B-
12						
13						
14						
15						
16						
17	BK/GN	Wheel speed FL	Output	Rotate the wheel	0/10V	17-B-
18	BN/RD	Wheel sensor RR	Input	Rotate the wheel 1 rev/sec	>100mV~	18-6
19	YE/BN	Wheel speed RR	Output	Rotate the wheel	0/10V	19-B-
20	GN/RD	Wheel sensor FR	Input	Rotate the wheel 1 rev/sec	>100mV~	20-21
21	GN/RD	Wheel sensor FR	Input	Rotate the wheel 1 rev/sec	>100mV~	21-20
22	OG/WH	Wheel speed RL	Output	Rotate the wheel	0/10V	22-B-
23	WT	Brake light switch	Input	Brake activity	Batt+	23-B-
24						
25						

SA4029100032000X

Fig. 7 ABS control module connector pins measured data

Rear

1. Raise and support vehicle, then remove wheel.
2. Force brake pistons back with suitable pliers, then depress brake pedal with brake clamp.
3. Remove two brake caliper securing bolts, then the brake pipe from clip. Bind brake caliper in tie.
4. Loosen brake shoe adjustment.
5. Remove lever return spring, then disconnect parking brake cable from lever.
6. Remove brake disc securing bolt, then the brake disc.
7. Disconnect speed sensor connector.
8. Remove four wheel hub retaining nuts, then the wheel hub, disc backing plate and spacer strip.
9. Remove wheel hub from disc backing plate
10. Reverse procedure to install. Tighten fasteners to specifications.

DIAGNOSTIC CHART INDEX

Code	Description	Page No.	Fig. No.
Code B1195	Main Relay Circuit, Faulty	38-131	14
Code B1371	Wheel Sensor Front Left, Signal Faulty Or No Signal	38-131	15
Code B1372	Wheel Sensor Front Left, Signal Faulty Or No Signal	38-131	15
Code B1376	Wheel Sensor Front Right, Signal Faulty Or No Signal	38-131	16
Code B1377	Wheel Sensor Front Right, Signal Faulty Or No Signal	38-131	16
Code B1381	Wheel Sensor Rear Left, Signal Faulty Or No Signal	38-131	17
Code B1382	Wheel Sensor Rear Left, Signal Faulty Or No Signal	38-131	17

Continued

DIAGNOSTIC CHART INDEX—Continued

Code	Description	Page No.	Fig. No.
Code B1386	Wheel Sensor Rear Right, Signal Faulty Or No Signal	38-132	18
Code B1387	Wheel Sensor Rear Right, Signal Faulty Or No Signal	38-132	18
Code B1390	Wheel Sensor, Wrong Number Of Teeth	38-132	19
Code B1532	Battery Voltage, Low	38-132	20
Code B1605	Control Module Fault	38-132	21
Code B2450	solenoid Valve Front Left, Faulty	38-133	22
Code B2455	Solenoid Valve Front Right, Faulty	38-133	23
Code B2460	Solenoid Valve Rear, Faulty	38-133	24
Code B2465	Pump Motor, Faulty	38-133	25
Code B2470	Brake Light Switch, No Signal	38-134	26
—	Fault Tracing Wheel Speed Signals	38-134	27

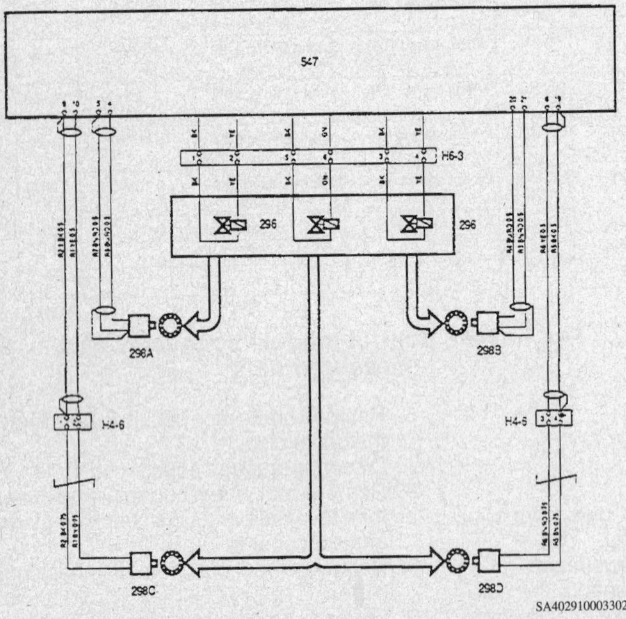
547
H6-3
296
296
298A
298B
H4-6
H4-6
298C
298D
SA4029100033020X

Fig. 8 ABS system wiring circuit (Part 2 of 3)

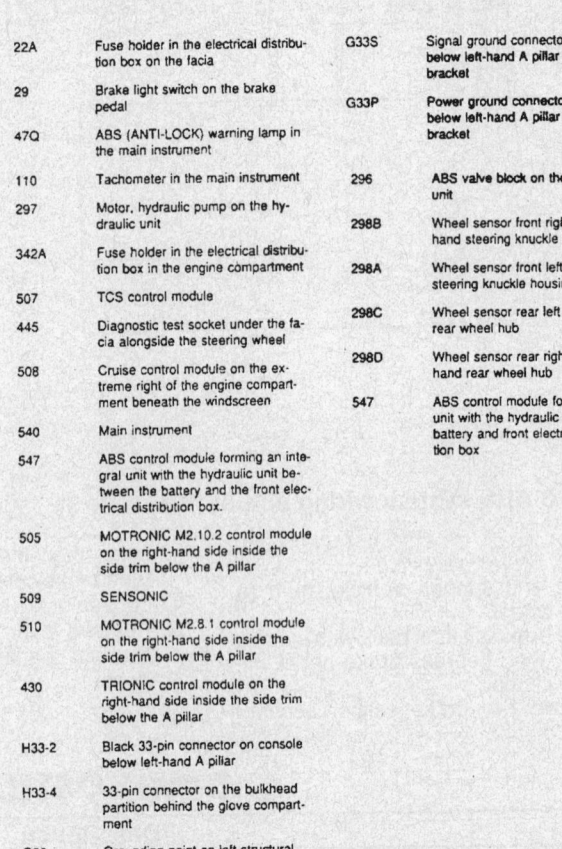

22A	Fuse holder in the electrical distribution box on the facia
29	Brake light switch on the brake pedal
47Q	ABS (ANTI-LOCK) warning lamp in the main instrument
110	Tachometer in the main instrument
297	Motor, hydraulic pump on the hydraulic unit
342A	Fuse holder in the electrical distribution box in the engine compartment
507	TCS control module
445	Diagnostic test socket under the facia alongside the steering wheel
508	Cruise control module on the extreme right of the engine compartment beneath the windscreen
540	Main instrument
547	ABS control module forming an integral unit with the hydraulic unit between the battery and the front electrical distribution box.
505	MOTRONIC M2.10.2 control module on the right-hand side inside the side trim below the A pillar
509	SENSONIC
510	MOTRONIC M2.8.1 control module on the right-hand side inside the side trim below the A pillar
430	TRIONIC control module on the right-hand side inside the side trim below the A pillar
H33-2	Black 33-pin connector on console below left-hand A pillar
H33-4	33-pin connector on the bulkhead partition behind the glove compartment
G30	Grounding point on left structural member behind the battery
G33S	Signal ground connector bracket, below left-hand A pillar on connector bracket
G33P	Power ground connector bracket, below left-hand A pillar on connector bracket
296	ABS valve block on the hydraulic unit
298B	Wheel sensor front right on right-hand steering knuckle housing
298A	Wheel sensor front left on left-hand steering knuckle housing
298C	Wheel sensor rear left on left-hand rear wheel hub
298D	Wheel sensor rear right on right-hand rear wheel hub
547	ABS control module forming integral unit with the hydraulic unit between battery and front electrical distribution box

SA4029100033030X

Fig. 8 ABS system wiring circuit (Part 3 of 3)

Code	Location of fault	Nature of fault
12	Flashing code diagnosis starts	
16	Valve, front left	Faulty
17	Valve, front right	Faulty
18	Valve rear	Faulty
19	Valve relay	Faulty
25	Wheel sensor	Wrong number of teeth
35	Pump motor	Faulty
37	Brake light switch	No signal
39	Wheel sensor, front left	Signal faulty
41	Wheel sensor, front left	No signal
42	Wheel sensor, front right	Signal faulty
43	Wheel sensor, front right	No signal
44	Wheel sensor, rear left	Signal faulty
45	Wheel sensor, rear left	No signal
46	Wheel sensor, rear right	Signal faulty
47	Wheel sensor, rear right	No signal
48	Battery voltage (UVR)	Too low
55	Control module	Faulty
56	Flashing code diagnosis	Application fault

SA4029100034000X

Fig. 9 ABS flashing codes

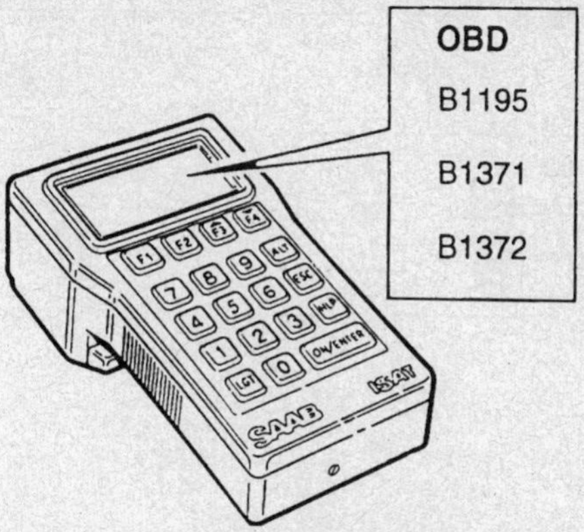
OBD
B1195
B1371
B1372
SAAB
ISAT

SA4029100035000X

Fig. 10 ISAT ABS diagnostic tool

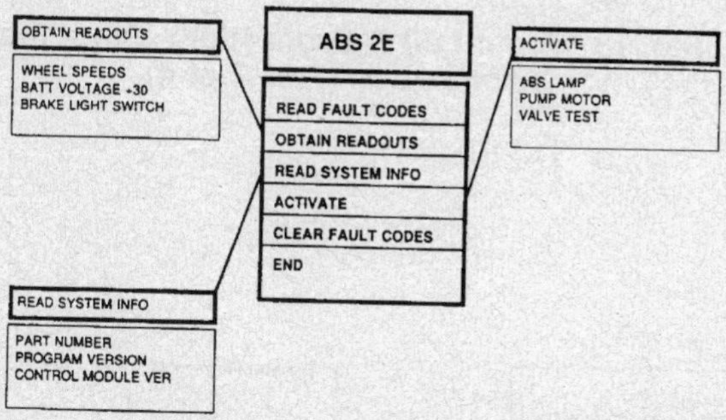
OBTAIN READOUTS
WHEEL SPEEDS
BATT VOLTAGE +30
BRAKE LIGHT SWITCH
ABS 2E
READ FAULT CODES
OBTAIN READOUTS
READ SYSTEM INFO
ACTIVATE
CLEAR FAULT CODES
END
ACTIVATE
ABS LAMP
PUMP MOTOR
VALVE TEST
READ SYSTEM INFO
PART NUMBER
PROGRAM VERSION
CONTROL MODULE VER

SA4029100036000X

Fig. 11 ISAT diagnostic menus

Fault code	Faulty operation/component	ANTI-LOCK	Text on ISAT display
B1195	Main relay circuit, faulty	LIT	FAULT XX B1195 MAIN RELAY CIRCUIT FAULTY
B1371	Wheel sensor front left, faulty signal	LIT	FAULT XX B1371 WHEEL SENSOR FL SIGNAL FAULTY
B1372	Wheel sensor front left, no signal	LIT	FAULT XX B1372 WHEEL SENSOR FL NO SIGNAL
B1376	Wheel sensor front right, signal faulty	LIT	FAULT XX B1376 WHEEL SENSOR RF SIGNAL FAULTY
B1377	Wheel sensor front right, no signal	LIT	FAULT XX B1377 WHEEL SENSOR FR NO SIGNAL
B1381	Wheel sensor rear left, signal faulty	LIT	FAULT XX B1381 WHEEL SENSOR FR SIGNAL FAULTY
B1382	Wheel sensor rear left, no signal	LIT	FAULT XX B1382 WHEEL SENSOR RL NO SIGNAL
B1386	Wheel sensor rear right, signal faulty	LIT	FAULT XX B1386 WHEEL SENSOR RR SIGNAL FAULTY
B1387	Wheel sensor rear right, no signal	LIT	FAULT XX B1387 WHEEL SENSOR RR NO SIGNAL
B1390	Wheel sensor, wrong number of teeth	LIT	FAULT XX B1390 WHEEL SENSOR WRONG NO. OF TEETH
B1532	Battery voltage, low	LIT	FAULT XX B1532 BATTERY VOLTAGE LOW
B1605	Control module fault	LIT	FAULT XX B1605 CONTROL MODULE FAULT

SA4029100037010X

Fig. 12 ABS Diagnostic Trouble Codes (Part 1 of 2)

Fault code	Faulty operation/component	ANTI-LOCK	Text on ISAT display
B2450	Solenoid valve front left, faulty	LIT	FAULT XX B2450 SOLENOID VALVE FL FAULTY
B2455	Solenoid valve front right, faulty	LIT	FAULT XX B2455 SOLENOID VALVE FR FAULTY
B2460	Solenoid valve rear, faulty	LIT	FAULT XX B2460 SOLENOID VALVE REAR FAULTY
B2465	Pump motor, faulty	LIT	FAULT XX B2465 PUMP MOTOR FAULTY
B2470	Brake light switch, no signal	LIT	FAULT XX B2470 BRAKE LIGHT SWITCH NO SIGNAL

SA4029100037020X

Fig. 12 ABS Diagnostic Trouble Codes (Part 2 of 2)

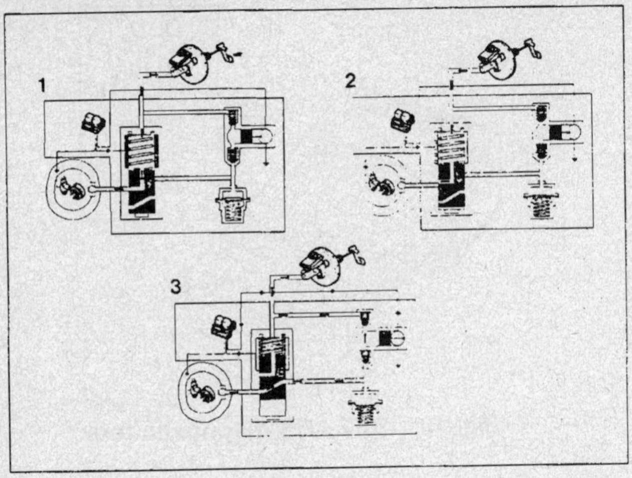
1
2
3

ISAT DISPLAY 1

ACTIVATE
=> VALVE TEST FL
VALVE TEST FR
VALVE TEST REAR

1 Select VALVE TEST in the ACTIVATE menu.

Caution

The test can only be carried out if the car is stationary.

ISAT DISPLAY 2

VALVE TEST FL
NORMAL POSITION
WHEEL ROTATING?
YES NO

2 The test starts with a check that the valve is not locked for example in HOLDING PRESSURE POSITION but is in the NORMAL POSITION (see Fig. 1).
Select YES using key F1 and NO using key F2

SA4029100038010X

Fig. 13 Front Left & Front Right Valve Test Explanation (Part 1 of 4)

ISAT DISPLAY 3

VALVE TEST FL
NORMAL POSITION
BRAKE AND HOLD
PRESS ON/ENTER

3 Depressing the pedal causes pressure to be pumped from the master cylinder through the valve to the wheel cylinder. If the passage is open, the wheel locks (see Fig. 1).

ISAT DISPLAY 4

VALVE TEST FL
NORMAL POSITION
WHEEL LOCKED?
YES NO

4 ISAT asks where the brake locks normally. The wheel must be locked. If you respond with yes, the valve moves to the HOLDING PRESSURE POSITION (see Fig. 2).

ISAT DISPLAY 5

VALVE TEST FL
HOLDING PRESSURE
RELEASE BRAKE
PRESS ON/ENTER

5 The valve holds the pressure which built up in stage 3 even if the brake is released (see Fig. 2).

ISAT DISPLAY 6

VALVE TEST FL
HOLDING PRESSURE
WHEEL LOCKED?
YES NO

6 The wheels must be locked. If you respond with YES, the valve moves to the NORMAL POSITION and the brake fluid pressure can return to the brake fluid reservoir.

SA4029100038020X

Fig. 13 Front Left & Front Right Valve Test Explanation (Part 2 of 4)

ISAT DISPLAY 7

VALVE TEST FL
NORMAL POSITION
WHEEL ROTATING?
YES NO

7 The wheel must rotate freely.
If you respond with YES, the valve moves to the HOLDING PRESSURE POSITION and the passage from the master cylinder to the wheel cylinder is closed (see Fig. 2).

ISAT DISPLAY 8

VALVE TEST FL
HOLDING PRESSURE
BRAKE AND HOLD
PRESS ON/ENTER

8 The valve has moved to the HOLDING PRESSURE POSITION.
The passage is closed and no brake pressure to the wheels is obtained.

ISAT DISPLAY 9

VALVE TEST FL
HOLDING PRESSURE
WHEEL ROTATING?
YES NO

9 The wheel must rotate freely.
If you respond with YES, the valve moves to the NORMAL position and the passage opens (see Fig. 1). The brake pressure can pass to the wheel.

ISAT DISPLAY 10

VALVE TEST FL
NORMAL POSITION
WHEEL LOCKED?
YES NO

10 The wheel must be locked.
If you respond with YES, the valve moves to the PRESSURE RELIEVED POSITION (see Fig. 3) and the return pump starts. The brake fluid pressure returns from the wheel cylinder by means of the return pump.

SA4029100038030X

Fig. 13 Front Left & Front Right Valve Test Explanation (Part 3 of 4)

ISAT DISPLAY 11

VALVE TEST FL
PRESSURE RELIEVED
WHEEL ROTATING?
YES NO

11 The wheel must rotate freely.

ISAT DISPLAY 12

TEST OK
PRESS ON/ENTER

12 The last display shows that the test is finished.

ISAT DISPLAY 13

VALVE TEST FL
FAULT IN TEST
SEE SERVICE
MANUAL
PRESS ON/ENTER

13 If any fault arises when the test is in progress or if you respond with YES to any of the questions, this display appears.

SA4029100038040X

Fig. 13 Front Left & Front Right Valve Test Explanation (Part 4 of 4)

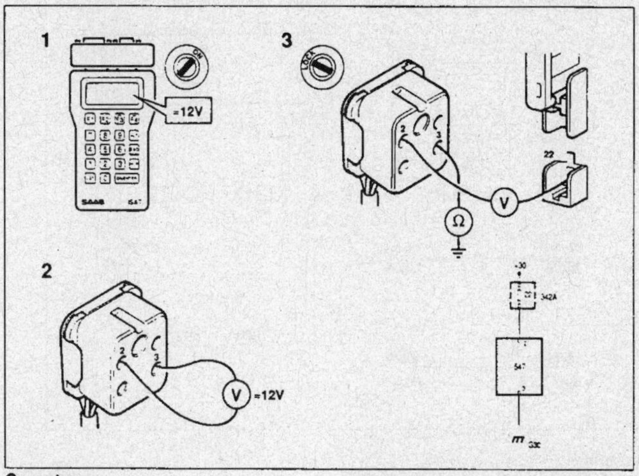
1
3
=12V
V
Ω
22
2
V =12V

Symptom

ABS warning lamp is lit, ABS inoperative.

Condition

Fault is recorded with ignition on and subsequent connection test if the battery voltage is less than 5V for more than 30 seconds, or during driving if the battery voltage is less than 5V for longer than 20 milliseconds.

Action

1 Check the voltage to the control module by using the ISAT command "BATT VOLTAGE +30" in the "OBTAIN READOUTS" menu.

The voltage must be at least equal to Batt+.

If the voltage is correct, go to item 4. If the voltage is wrong, check fuse 22. Replace the fuse if necessary. If the fuse is intact, continue with the next item.

2 Disconnect the 4-pin connector from the control module with the ignition turned off. Measure where there is voltage between pins 2 and 3 of the connector.

If there is voltage (approx. 12V), move on to item 4, otherwise continue with the next item.

3 Check the wire between pin 2 in the 4-pin connector and fuse 22 for short-circuit or break in continuity. Check the ground lead between pin 3 and grounding point G-30 as well.

4 Clear the fault code if no fault is discovered despite the above checks. Test-drive the car and check whether the fault code re-appears. If so, go to Fig. 28 for further action.

SA4029100039000X

Fig. 14 Code B1195: Main Relay Circuit, Faulty

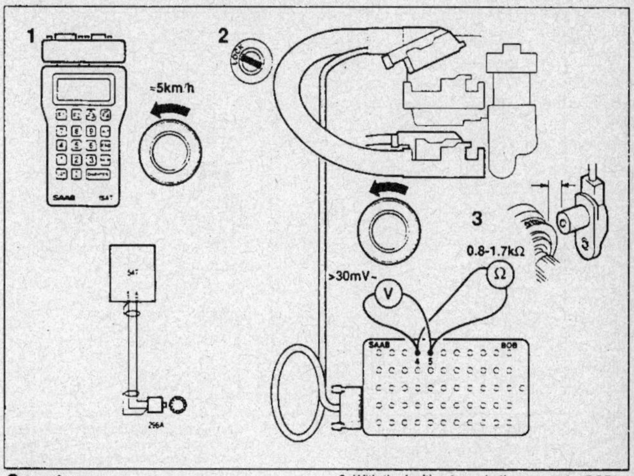
1
2
≈5km/h
3
0.8-1.7kΩ
>30mV~
V
Ω
SAAB
BOB
4 5

Symptom

ABS warning lamp is lit, ABS inoperative.

Condition

Fault is recorded in case of break of continuity after max. 150 milliseconds both when the car is stationary and when the car is being driven.

Fault is recorded in case of faulty signal after max. 20 seconds at a speed >10 km/h.

Action

1 Raise the car, and check wheel sensor for front left wheel with ISAT command "WHEEL SPEEDS" on the "OBTAIN READOUTS" menu.

All four wheel speeds are shown on the display.

Rotate the front left wheel by hand. The ISAT display must show approx. 5 km/h.

If the values are correct, go to item 4.

If the values are incorrect, continue with the next item.

2 With the ignition turned off, connect the BOB to the cable connector of the ABS unit. Rotate the front left wheel at 1 rev./sec. and measure the AC voltage between pins 4 and 5. The correct value must be greater than 100mV. The voltage must increase with wheel speed. If the values are correct, go to item 4. If the values are incorrect, continue with the next item.

3 Check the resistance in the wheel sensor by measuring between pins 4 and 5. The correct resistance must be 0.8—1.7 KOhm. If the values agree, check the distance between the wheel sensor and the gear wheel. Check the gear wheel also for signs of damage. Check the wheel bearing clearance as well. If the resistance is correct, check the wire between pins 4 and 5 of the ABS unit and the wheel sensor for break in continuity or short circuit. Replace the wheel sensor if necessary.

4 If no faults have been discovered despite the above checks, clear the fault codes, test-drive the car and see whether the fault codes reappear.

5. Go to Fig. 28 for further action.

SA4029100040000X

Fig. 15 Codes B1371 & B1372: Wheel Sensor Front Left, Signal Faulty Or No Signal

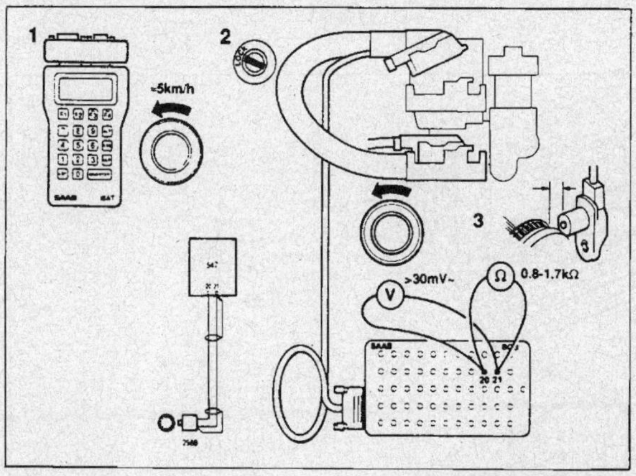
1
2
≈5km/h
3
>30mV~
V
Ω
0.8-1.7kΩ
SAAB
20 21

Symptom

ABS warning lamp is lit, ABS inoperative.

Condition

Fault is recorded in case of break of continuity after max. 150 milliseconds both when the car is stationary and when the car is being driven.

Fault is recorded in case of faulty signal after max. 20 seconds at a speed >10 km/h.

Action

1 Raise the car, and check wheel sensor for front left wheel with ISAT command "WHEEL SPEEDS" on the "OBTAIN READOUTS" menu.

All four wheel speeds are shown on the display.

Rotate the front right wheel by hand. The ISAT display must show approx. 5 km/h.

If the values are correct, go to item 4. If the values are incorrect, continue with the next item.

2 With the ignition turned off, connect the BOB to the cable connector of the ABS unit. Rotate the front left wheel at 1 rev./sec. and measure the AC voltage between pins 20 and 21. The correct value must be greater than 100mV. The voltage must increase with wheel speed. If the values are correct, go to item 4. If the values are incorrect, continue with the next item.

3 Check the resistance in the wheel sensor by measuring between pins 20 and 21. The correct resistance must be 0.8—1.7 KOhm. If the values agree, check the distance between the wheel sensor and the gear wheel. Check the gear also for signs of damage. Check the wheel bearing clearance as well. If the resistance is correct, check the wire between pins 20 and 21 of the ABS unit and the wheel sensor for break in continuity or short circuit. Replace the wheel sensor if necessary.

4 If no faults have been discovered despite the above checks, clear the fault codes, test-drive the car and see whether the fault codes reappear.

5. Go to Fig. 28 for further action.

SA4029100041000X

Fig. 16 Codes B1376 & B1377: Wheel Sensor Front Right, Signal Faulty Or No Signal

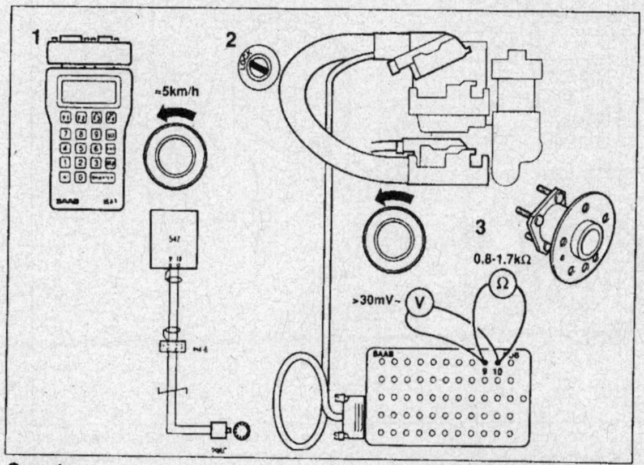
1
2
≈5km/h
3
0.8-1.7kΩ
Ω
>30mV~
V
SAAB
9 10

Symptom

ABS warning lamp is lit, ABS inoperative.

Condition

Fault is recorded in case of break of continuity after max. 150 milliseconds both when the car is stationary and when the car is being driven.

Fault is recorded in case of faulty signal after max. 20 seconds at a speed >10 km/h.

Action

1 Raise the car, and check wheel sensor for front left wheel with ISAT command "WHEEL SPEEDS" on the "OBTAIN READOUTS" menu.

All four wheel speeds are shown on the display.

Rotate the rear left wheel by hand. The ISAT display must show approx. 5 km/h.

If the values are correct, go to item 4. If the values are incorrect, continue with the next item.

2 With the ignition turned off, connect the BOB to the cable connector of the ABS unit. Rotate the front left wheel at 1 rev./sec. and measure the AC voltage between pins 9 and 10. The correct value must be greater than 100mV. The voltage must increase with wheel speed. If the values are correct, go to item 4. If the values are incorrect, continue with the next item.

3 Check the resistance in the wheel sensor by measuring between pins 9 and 10. The correct resistance must be 0.8—1.7 KOhm. If the values agree, check the distance between the wheel sensor and the gear wheel. Check the gear also for signs of damage. Check the wheel bearing clearance as well. If the resistance is correct, check the wire between pins 9 and 10 of the ABS unit and the wheel sensor for break in continuity or short circuit. Replace the wheel sensor if necessary.

4 If no faults have been discovered despite the above checks, clear the fault codes, test-drive the car and see whether the fault codes reappear.

5. Go to Fig. 28 for further action.

SA4029100042000X

Fig. 17 Codes B1381 & B1382: Wheel Sensor Rear Left, Signal Faulty Or No Signal

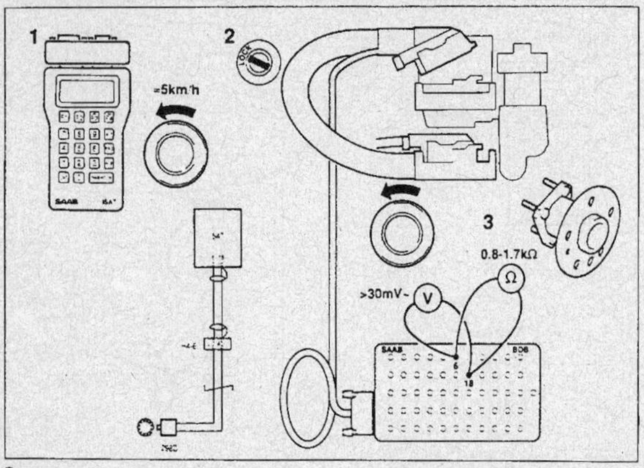
1
2
≈5km/h
3
0.8-1.7kΩ
>30mV~
V
Ω
SAAB
BOB

Symptom

ABS warning lamp is lit, ABS inoperative.

Condition

Fault is recorded in case of break of continuity after max. 150 milliseconds both when the car is stationary and when the car is being driven.
Fault is recorded in case of faulty signal after max. 20 seconds at a speed >10 km/h.

Action

1 Raise the car, and check wheel sensor for rear right wheel with ISAT command "WHEEL SPEEDS" on the "OBTAIN READOUTS" menu.

All four wheel speeds are shown on the display.

Rotate the front left wheel by hand. The ISAT display must show approx. 5 km/h.

If the values are correct, go to item 4. If the values are incorrect, continue with the next item.

2 With the ignition turned off, connect the BOB to the cable connector of the ABS unit. Rotate the front left wheel at 1 rev./sec. and measure the AC voltage between pins 6 and 18. The correct value must be greater than 100mV. The voltage must increase with wheel speed. If the values are correct, go to item 4. If the values are incorrect, continue with the next item.

3 Check the resistance in the wheel sensor by measuring between pins 6 and 18. The correct resistance must be 0.8—1.7 KOhm. If the values agree, check the distance between the wheel sensor and the gear wheel. Check the gear also for signs of damage. Check the wheel bearing clearance as well. If the resistance is correct, check the wire between pins 6 and 18 of the ABS unit and the wheel sensor for break in continuity or short circuit. Replace the wheel sensor if necessary.

4 If no faults have been discovered despite the above checks, clear the fault codes, test-drive the car and see whether the fault codes reappear.

5. Go to Fig. 28 for further action.

SA4029100043000X

Fig. 18 Codes B1386 & B1387: Wheel Sensor Rear Right, Signal Faulty Or No Signal

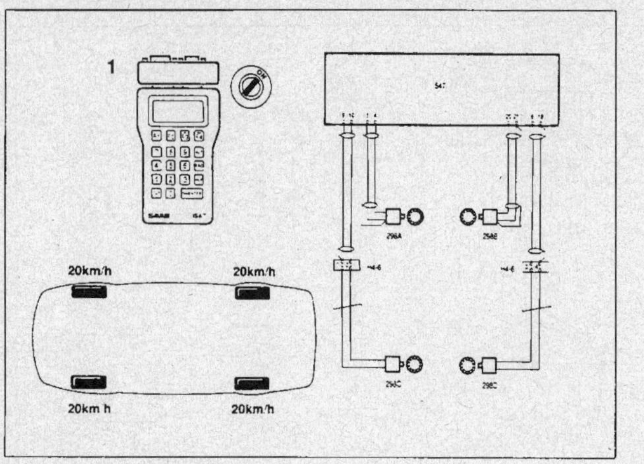
1
20km/h
20km/h
20km h
20km/h

Symptom

ABS warning lamp, ABS inoperative.

Condition

A fault is recorded if the speed of a wheel is at least 25%higher than the calculated speed of the car over a period of more than 2 minutes or a wheel has slip >4.5%for a period of more than 2 minutes. The system is additionally closed down if ABS control is obtained for a period of more than 1 minute.

Action

1 Check the wheel sensors with the ISAT command "WHEEL SPEEDS" on the "OBTAIN READOUTS" menu

All four wheel speeds are shown on the display.

Drive the car at a steady speed, for example 20 km/h and check that all the wheels show the same speed.

If any fault is discovered, go to Fig. 15, 16, 17 or 18 for further action.

SA4029100044000X

Fig. 19 Code B1390: Wheel Sensor, Wrong Number Of Teeth

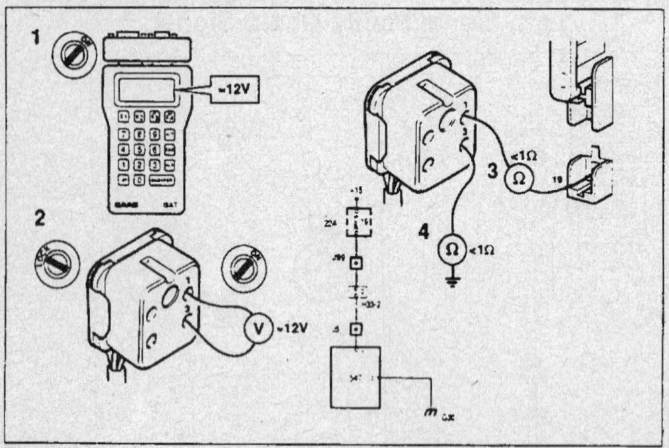
1
≈12V
2
V
≈12V
3
Ω
<1Ω
4
Ω
<1Ω

Symptom

ABS warning lamp is lit, ABS inoperative.

Condition

Fault is recorded after max. 60 seconds when the system does not control if the battery voltage is between 5V and 9.8V.
Fault is recorded after max. 60 seconds when the system does not control if the battery voltage is between 5V and 8.6V.

Action

1 Check the +15 voltage to the control module by using the ISAT command "BATT VOLTAGE +30" on the "OBTAIN READOUTS" menu.

The voltage must be equal to Batt+.

If the voltage is correct, go to item 4. If the voltage is incorrect, continue with the next item.

2 Unplug the 4-pin connector from the control module with the ignition turned off. With the ignition on, check that there is voltage by measuring between pins 1 and 3 on the connector.

If there is voltage (approx. 12V), proceed to item 4.

If there is no voltage, check fuse 19. Replace the fuse if necessary. If the fuse is intact, continue with the next item.

3 Check the wire between pin 1 in the 4-pin connector and fuse 19 for short-circuit or break in continuity. Check ground lead between pin 3 and grounding point G-30 as well.

4 If no fault has been discovered despite the above checks, clear the fault code. Test-drive the car and see whether the fault code reappears. If so, go to Fig. 28 for further action.

SA4029100045000X

Fig. 20 Code B1532: Battery Voltage Low

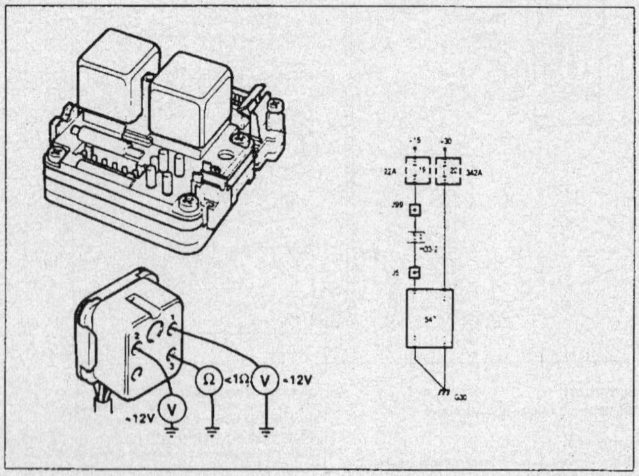
Ω
<1Ω
V
≈12V
V
≈12V

Symptom

ABS warning lamp is lit, ABS inoperative.

Condition

A fault is recorded in the case of an internal fault in the control module when the ignition is turned on during driving.

Action

1 Check whether the positive power supplies and ground connections of the control module have a poor contact.

2 Clear the fault code, test-drive the car and check whether the fault is recorded again. If so, go to Fig. 28 for further action.

SA4029100046000X

Fig. 21 Code B1605: Control Module Fault

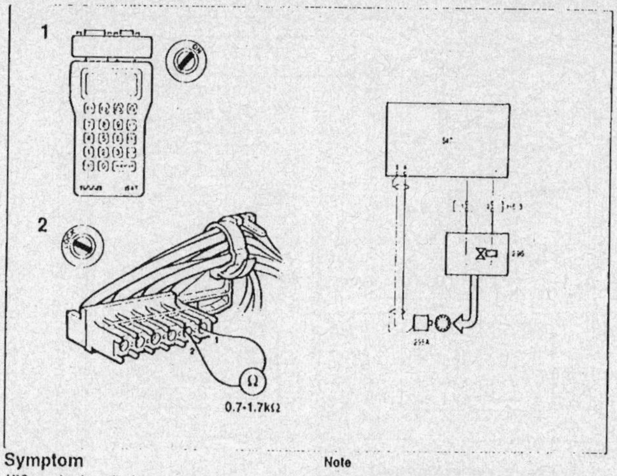
1
2
0.7-1.7kΩ

Symptom
ABS warning lamp lit, ABS inoperative.

Condition
The fault code is recorded when the ignition is turned on and the control module carries out a connection test on the solenoid valves. The main relay is briefly activated twice and then breaks again. The pilot lamp goes out for a short time before remaining lit.

Action
1 Raise the car, and check the solenoid valve of the front left wheel with ISAT command "VALVE TEST FL" on the "ACTIVATE" menu.

Read page 590-31 for a description of the ISAT test sequence for the solenoid valves.

If the test shows "TEST OK", go to item 3. If not, continue with the next item.

2 Remove the cover of the control module. Unplug the 6-pin connector of the solenoid valve from the control module.

Note
The connector is firmly seated

Measure the resistance in the coil of the solenoid valve by measuring on pins 1 and 2 of the connector.

The resistance must be approx. 0.7 to 1.7 Ohms.

If the resistance is incorrect, replace the hydraulic unit.

If the resistance is correct, continue with the next item

3 Clear the fault, test-drive the car and check whether the fault code re-appears. If so, go to Fig. 28 for further action.

SA4029100047000X

Fig. 22 Code B2450: Solenoid Valve Front Left, Faulty

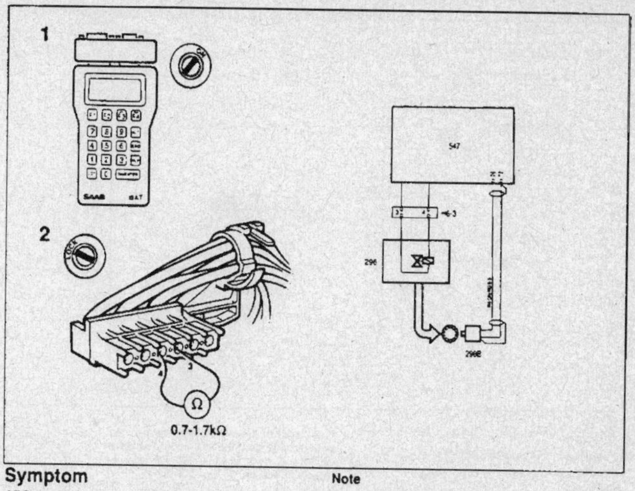
1
2
0.7-1.7kΩ

Symptom
ABS warning lamp lit, ABS inoperative.

Condition
The fault code is recorded when the ignition is turned on and the control module carries out a connection test on the solenoid valves. The main relay is briefly activated twice and then breaks again. The pilot lamp goes out for a short time before remaining lit.

Action
1 Raise the car, and check the solenoid valve of the front left wheel with ISAT command "VALVE TEST FL" on the "ACTIVATE" menu.

Read page 590-11 for a description of the ISAT test sequence for the solenoid valves.

If the test shows "TEST OK", go to item 3. If not, continue with the next item.

2 Remove the cover of the control module. Unplug the 6-pin connector of the solenoid valve from the control module.

Note
The connector is firmly seated.

Measure the resistance in the coil of the solenoid valve by measuring on pins 3 and 4 of the connector.

The resistance must be approx. 0.7 to 1.7 Ohms.

If the resistance is incorrect, replace the hydraulic unit.

If the resistance is correct, continue with the next item

3 Clear the fault, test-drive the car and check whether the fault code re-appears. If so, go to Fig. 28 for further action.

SA4029100048000X

Fig. 23 Code B2455: Solenoid Valve Front Right, Faulty

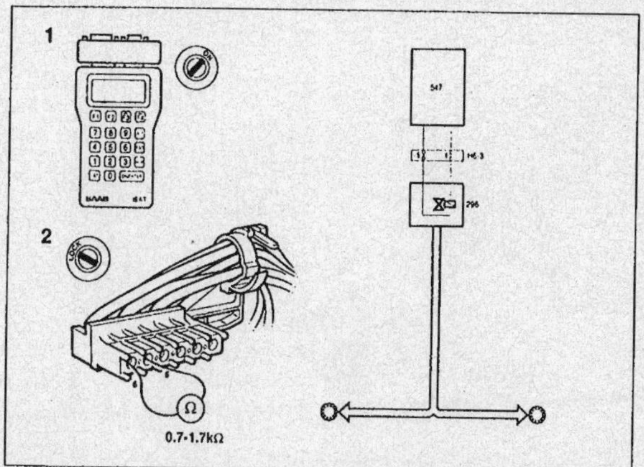
1
2
0.7-1.7kΩ

Symptom
ABS warning lamp lit, ABS inoperative.

Condition
The fault code is recorded when the ignition is turned on and the control module carries out a connection test on the solenoid valves. The main relay is briefly activated twice and then breaks again. The pilot lamp goes out for a short time before remaining lit.

Action
1 Raise the car, and check the solenoid valve of the front left wheel with ISAT command "VALVE TEST FL" on the "ACTIVATE" menu.

Read page 590-15 for a description of the ISAT test sequence for the solenoid valves.

If the test shows "TEST OK", go to item 3. If not, continue with the next item.

2 Remove the cover of the control module. Unplug the 6-pin connector of the solenoid valve from the control module.

Note
The connector is firmly seated

Measure the resistance in the coil of the solenoid valve by measuring on pins 5 and 6 of the connector.

The resistance must be approx. 0.7 to 1.7 Ohms.

If the resistance is incorrect, replace the hydraulic unit.

If the resistance is correct, continue with the next item

3 Clear the fault, test-drive the car and check whether the fault code re-appears. If so, go to Fig. 28 for further action.

SA4029100049000X

Fig. 24 Code B2460: Solenoid Valve Rear, Faulty

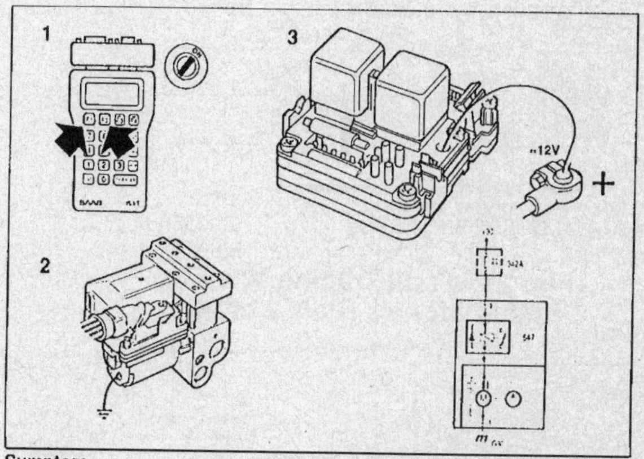
1
2
3
≈12V
+

Symptom
ABS warning lamp lit, no ABS function.

Condition
The pump motor is tested after the car has started and wheels have begun to rotate (v>6 km/h). It is then continuously monitored.

Faults are recorded:

- if the power supply to the motor in the 100 milliseconds falls below a particular level after activation from the pump motor relay has stopped.
- if the power supply to the motor remains above a particular level for more than 5 seconds without activation from the pump motor relay.

Action
1 Check with the ISAT command "PUMP MOTOR" on the "ACTIVATE" menu.

Press "ON" and check that the motor is activated. Then press "OFF".

If the motor is activated, proceed to item 3. If not, proceed to the next item.

2 Check whether the motor ground cable has a break in continuity or poor contact.

3 Apply battery voltage to the positive power supply of the motor via the screw on the front of the control module with the ignition turned off.

If the motor is activated, clear the fault code. Test-drive the car and see whether the fault code re-appears.

If the motor does not operate, replace the motor. If so, go to Fig. 28 for further action.

SA4029100050000X

Fig. 25 Code B2465: Pump Motor, Faulty

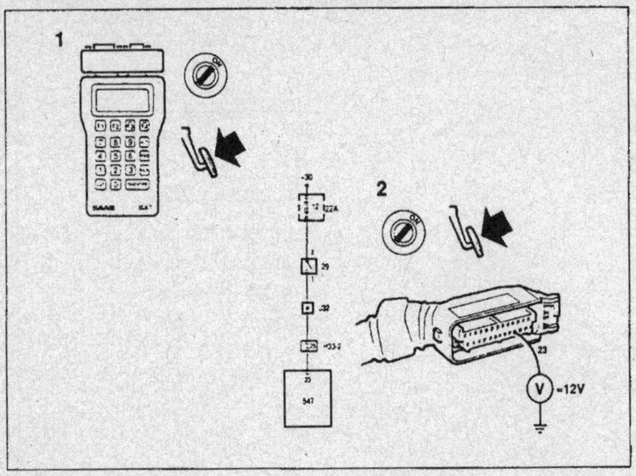
1
2
=12V

Symptom

ABS warning lamp lit, no ABS function.

Condition

Fault is recorded in case of a break in lead continuity for more than 700 seconds.
(If a fault occurs, the system closes down immediately. If the system is controlling, it does not close down until control has been completed. Fault codes are stored when the system is closed off.)

Action

1 Check with the ISAT command "BRAKE LIGHT SWITCH" on the "OBTAIN READOUTS" menu.

Depress the brake with the ignition on. ISAT shows "ON".

If ISAT shows "ON", proceed to page 590-31 for further action.

If ISAT shows "OFF", connect the BOB cable and check for any break in the cable between pin 23 of the control module and the brake light switch.

If no break in the cable is discovered, check whether the brake light switch is defective.

2 If no fault has been discovered despite the above checks, clear the fault code. Test-drive the car and check whether the fault code reappears. If so, go to Fig. 28 for further action.

SA4029100051000X

Fig. 26 Code B2470: Brake Light Switch, No Signal

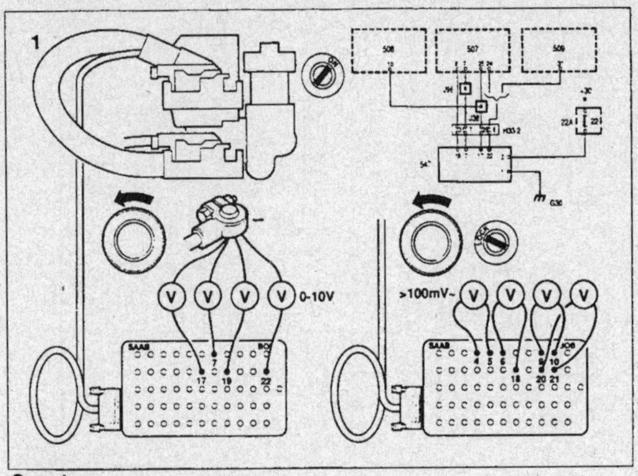
1
0-10V
>100mV~

Symptom

Fault code in any of the other electronic systems of the car that there is no speed signal.

Action

1 With the ignition off, connect the BOB to the control module and wiring.
Raise the car.

With the ignition on, rotate the wheels gently and measure between the respective pins (see table) 7, 17, 19 and 22 and Batt- that the voltage alternates between 0 and 10V.

If the voltage alternates between 0 and 10V, go to item 3. If not, continue with the next item.

2 Rotate the wheels at approx. 1 rev./sec. and measure with the voltmeter the AC voltage between pins (see table) 4 and 5, 6 and 18, 9 and 10 and 20 and 21 >100mV~.
If value is incorrect or there is no value, continue to Figs. 15, 16, 17 and 18 for wheel sensor fault tracing.
If the value is correct, go to the next item.

SA4029100052010X

Fig. 27 Fault Tracing Wheel Speed Signals (Part 1 of 2)

	Wheel speed output signal Pin	Wheel sensor input Pin
Front right wheel	7	20-21
Front left wheel	17	4-5
Rear right wheel	19	6-18
Rear left wheel	22	9-10

3 If there is input from the wheel sensors but no output signal on wheel speed, go to Fig. 28 for further action.

SA4029100052020X

Fig. 27 Fault Tracing Wheel Speed Signals (Part 2 of 2)

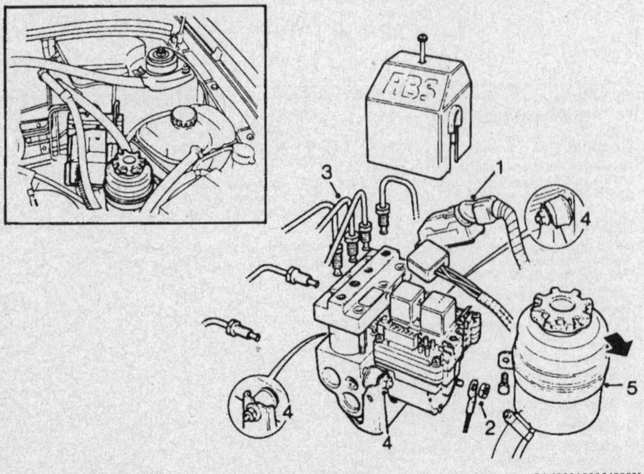
ABS
1
2
3
4
5

SA4029100054000X

Fig. 29 Hydraulic unit replacement

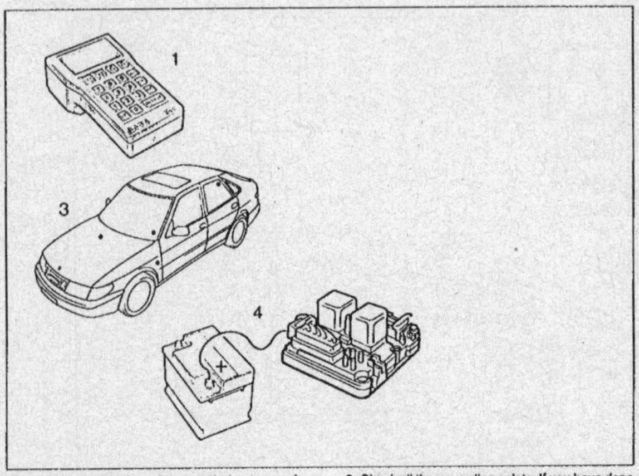
1
3
4

When all the checks have been carried out according to the action programme under the fault code concerned without any fault having been discovered, it is logical to assume that the control module is faulty.
In view of the fact that the control module is a very high-quality and expensive component, it is important to diagnose the fault as far as possible.
Carefully run through the following items before finally identifying the ABS control module as the cause of the fault.

1 Check the following:

- Correct wheel size
- All the wheels have the same height/width
- Correct air pressure in all the wheels
- No play in the wheel bearings

Check also once more that all the checks in the fault-tracing routine concerned have been carried out.

2 Study the wiring diagram of the circuit concerned and examine its function.

3 Check all the grounding points. If you have done this previously, do it once more. Check that power ground and signal ground are electrically and physically separated.

4 Check the power supply to the control module.

5 Clear the fault code. Test the car again. If the original fault remains despite this, the ABS control module must be replaced.

SA4029100053000X

Fig. 28 Action To Be Taken Before Replacing Control Module

1996 900 Bosch 5.3 Anti-Lock Brake System

NOTE: On Air Bag Equipped Models, Refer To "Air Bag System Precautions" Located In The Front Of This Manual For System Disarming & Arming Procedures.

NOTE: Electrical Symbol & Wire Color Code Identification Located In The Front Of This Manual May Be Used As An Aid When Using Wiring Circuits Found In This Section.

INDEX

	Page No.
Description	38-135
Components	38-135
System	38-135
Diagnosis & Testing	38-136
ABS Measured Data	38-136
Accessing Diagnostic Trouble Codes	38-136
Diagnostic Trouble Code Interpretation	38-137
Diagnostic Chart Index	38-141
Precautions	38-135
Air Bag Systems	38-135
System Service	38-137
ABS Control Module, Replace	38-137
Brake System Bleed	38-137
Component Replacement	38-137
Hydraulic Unit, Replace	38-137
Wheel Sensors, Replace	38-137
Troubleshooting	38-136
Checking Break In Continuity/ Short Circuit	38-136

PRECAUTIONS

AIR BAG SYSTEMS

Refer to "Air Bag System Precautions" in the front of this manual for system disarming and arming procedures.

DESCRIPTION

SYSTEM

The Anti-Lock Brake System (ABS) is a two-circuit, four-port brake system, **Fig. 1.**

Four wheel sensors at the wheels send signals to an electronic control unit, which continuously calculates on the basis of the wheel acceleration (speed increase), wheel deceleration (speed decrease), the speed of the vehicle and the slip of the wheels (degree of wheel lock-up). If any wheel approaches the limit for lock-up, the control unit passes signals to solenoid valves in the valve block for the wheel concerned. The pressure in the brake circuit for the wheel is controlled in this way so the maximum possible braking power is transmitted to the road surface at all times with no loss of steering ability.

Electronic Brake-Force Distribution (EBD), a built in function of the electronic control module, controls the rear electromagnetic intake valves to provide maximum braking power at the rear wheels without front wheel lock-up.

COMPONENTS

HYDRAULIC UNIT

The hydraulic unit consists of the valve block with eight boost pressure control valves (1 intake and outlet valve for each wheel and an electronic control module with main and pump relays and return pump.

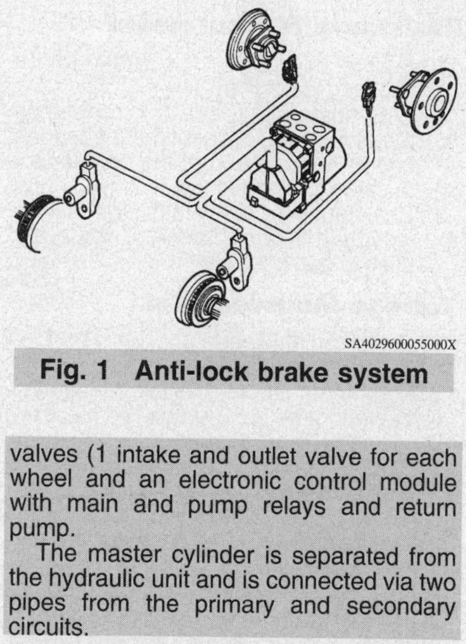
SA4029600055000X

Fig. 1 Anti-lock brake system

The master cylinder is separated from the hydraulic unit and is connected via two pipes from the primary and secondary circuits.

ELECTRONIC CONTROL MODULE

The electronic control module forms an integral unit with the ABS hydraulic unit and has a 26/31-pin connector.

The control module receives wheel speed information through input signals from the wheel sensors.

If any of the wheels has greater deceleration on braking than the others, the control module controls the solenoid valves so the hydraulic brake pressure can be kept constant or reduced to each wheel, while receiving maximum friction from the road surface.

WHEEL SENSORS

The wheel sensors are mounted near a toothed sensor wheel at each wheel. Each time a tooth on the sensor wheel passes the sensor, it interrupts a magnetic field, which causes a signal to be sent to the Electronic Control Unit (ECU).

The rear wheel sensor is designed differently than the front, in that it is less sensitive to wheel bearing play and starts to pass information to the control module at very low wheel speeds.

SOLENOID VALVES

Normal Position (Pressure Build-Up)

In normal position, **Fig. 2,** the solenoid valve is de-energized. The piston is pressed down toward the normal position of the return spring. The brake fluid is now able to flow freely from the master cylinder out through the solenoid valve to the wheel cylinder. This position is the normal position in braking without ABS control and the pressure build-up position in ABS control.

Pressure Holding Position

In this position, **Fig. 3,** the solenoid valve has received around half the current from the ABS control module. The piston has moved into the pressure holding position by rising slightly and the passage from the master cylinder to the wheel cylinder is consequently closed.

This is one of the three positions with

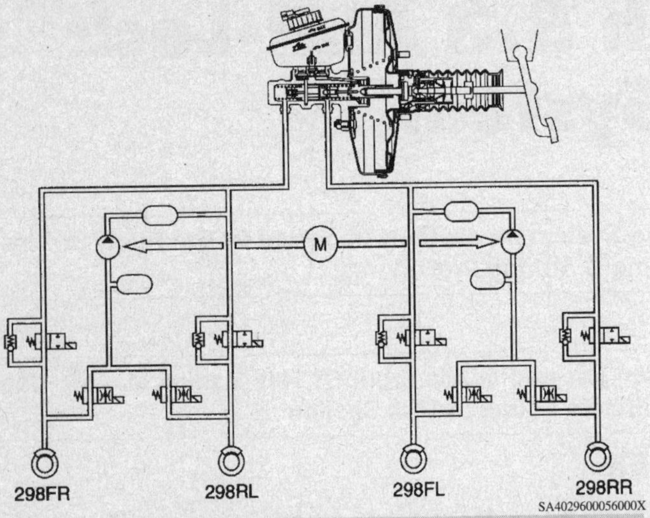
M
298FR
298RL
298FL
298RR
SA4029600056000X

Fig. 2 Solenoid valve in normal position (pressure build-up)

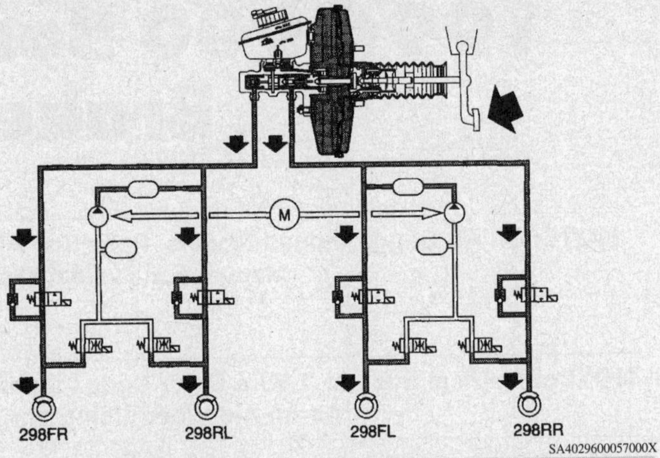
M
298FR
298RL
298FL
298RR
SA4029600057000X

Fig. 3 Solenoid valve in pressure holding position

which the control module operates under ABS control.

Pressure Relief

In this position, **Fig. 4,** the solenoid valve obtains full current from the control module. The piston in the valve has risen to the pressure relief position and opens the channel from the wheel cylinder to the pressure accumulator which can quickly receive pressure from the wheel cylinder. The control module energizes the return pump and the pressure can be pumped back to the master cylinder.

EQUALIZATION VALVE

In addition to the solenoid valve, there is an equalization valve, **Fig. 5,** for the rear wheel circuit so both rear wheels can be operated with only one solenoid valve.

The equalization valve ensures both rear wheels receive the same brake pressure in ABS control. This means the vehicle has good directional stability.

In the case of ABS control of the rear wheels, the solenoid valve moves to the pressure holding position. The channel to the rear right wheel is now blocked. If the pressure from the master cylinder rises, a pressure difference develops below and above the piston (1). The piston is raised and the valve (2) closes the pressure to the rear left wheel. If the pressure to the rear right wheel drops (pressure relief), a greater pressure difference develops above and below the piston (1), and the piston is lifted further upward until the pressure for the right and left rear wheels has balanced out.

BRAKE LIGHT SWITCH

The control module receives voltage from the brake light switch, when the brake is activated. For example, the brake light switch is used if the surface is very slippery and the driver decides to apply the brake.

Every time the driver depresses the brake pedal, when power is fed to the ECU from the brake light switch, the ABS control restarts from its starting position.

TROUBLESHOOTING

CHECKING BREAK IN CONTINUITY/SHORT CIRCUIT

BREAK IN CONTINUITY

Resistance Measurement

1. Ensure component or cable to be checked is not live.
2. With instrument set for resistance measurement, connect the measuring cables to each end of the component or cable to be checked.
3. Resistance for wiring must normally be less than 1 ohm. Specified value applies to components.

Voltage Measurement

1. Switch on any load.
2. With instrument set for voltage measurement, connect black measuring cable to safe ground and red measuring cable to lead side.
3. In case of output from control module/ switch, measure away from these and gradually move out toward load. When load disappears, you have just passed break in continuity.
4. In case of input to control module/ consumer, measure away from current source and gradually move in toward control module/consumer. When voltage disappears, you have just passed break in continuity.

SHORT-CIRCUIT TO GROUND

Resistance Measurement

1. Ensure lead to be checked is not live and that any load has been disconnected.
2. With instrument set for resistance measurement, connect one measuring cable to load side of lead and the other to safe ground.
3. Move carefully on wiring and check at same time that instrument shows infinite resistance the whole time.

DIAGNOSIS & TESTING

ABS MEASURED DATA

Refer to **Figs. 6 and 7.**

1. Several voltage levels must be regarded as guide values. Apply common sense in judging whether a measured value is correct or faulty.
2. If any measured value is faulty, use the wiring diagram, **Fig. 8,** to find out which leads, connectors or components should be checked more closely.

ACCESSING DIAGNOSTIC TROUBLE CODES

The ABS control module communicates with ISAT, **Fig. 9,** through pin 11 and is bidirectional.

Any diagnostic trouble codes stored in the control module can be read out by means of ISAT. ISAT can also command the control module to control the solenoid valves or read the wheel speed.

With the ignition on and ISAT connected, the voltage on pin is approximately 10 volts. The diagnostic testing socket (data link connector) is located below the lower left-hand instrument panel fascia.

Operation

The ISAT features a system where clear text under a number of menu options enables the user to directly select the desired command with the keypad. The structure of the ABS command menus, **Fig. 10,** provides six main menus. Three of these menus have varying numbers of commands in a submenu.

When a system function is activated with ISAT, it means the ABS control module is performing something which is not functionally normal. diagnostic trouble codes can be put into other systems which are dependent on the ABS.

The Activate functions must always be used with caution. Always deactivate an activated function before proceeding in the ISAT menu. Always clear any diagnostic trouble codes recorded in ABS or

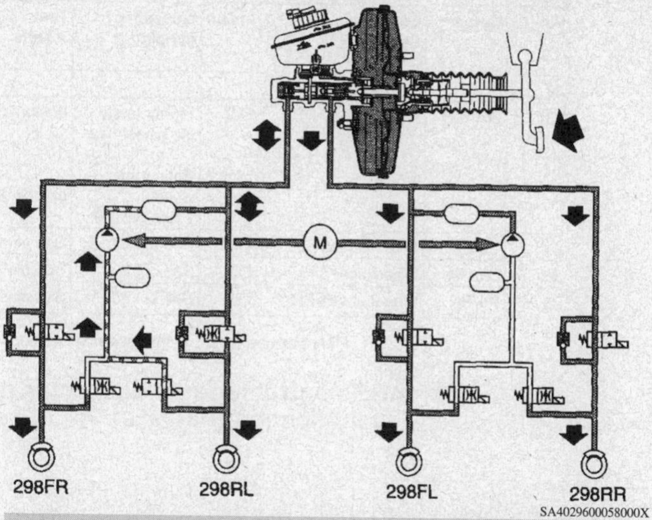
M
298FR
298RL
298FL
298RR
SA4029600058000X

Fig. 4 Solenoid valve in pressure relief position

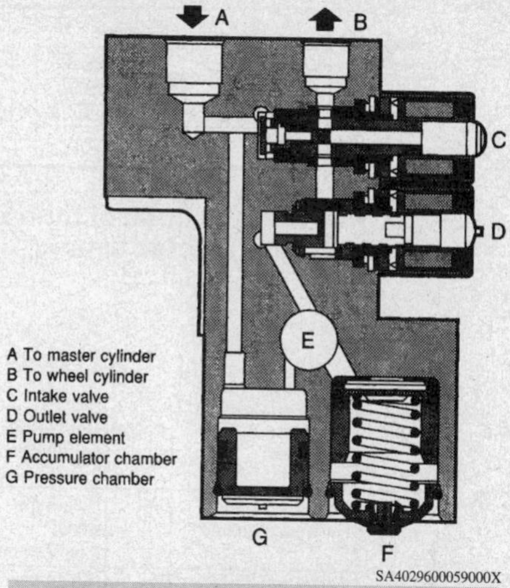
A
B
C
D
E
G
F
A To master cylinder
B To wheel cylinder
C Intake valve
D Outlet valve
E Pump element
F Accumulator chamber
G Pressure chamber
SA4029600059000X

Fig. 5 Equalization valve replacement

any other system after work has been completed.

DIAGNOSTIC TROUBLE CODE INTERPRETATION

When performing diagnostic trouble code diagnosis and repair, refer to **Fig. 8** for ABS wiring circuit and **Fig. 11** for diagnostic trouble code identification.

Refer to **Fig. 12** for valve test interpretation and **Fig. 13** for front left (FL) and front right (FR) valve test interpretation.

Refer to **Figs. 14 through 32** for diagnostic trouble code diagnostic routines.

SYSTEM SERVICE

Brake System Bleed

1. Unscrew cover of brake fluid reservoir and top off with brake fluid.
2. Connect topping-off fitting from brake bleeding unit kit tool No. 88 19 096, or equivalent, to brake fluid reservoir.
3. Position hose with one end on topping-off fitting and other end in bottle filled with clean brake fluid.
4. Raise and support vehicle, then connect brake bleeder hose to front left wheel and open nipple. Draw off approximately .1 quart brake fluid. Repeat this at front right wheel.
5. Move brake bleeder to rear left wheel and open nipple. Draw off approximately .05 quart brake fluid. Repeat this at rear right wheel.
6. Lower vehicle, then check brake operation. Depress brake pedal and check that it does not drop.
7. Remove topping-off fitting, hose and bottle.
8. Adjust brake fluid level.

Component Replacement

HYDRAULIC UNIT, REPLACE

1. Disconnect battery ground cable.
2. Remove black plastic cover screw, then the cover, **Fig. 33.**
3. Disconnect electrical connector and electrical connection, then the ground cable.
4. Remove brake pipe connections and plug holes.
5. Remove two hydraulic unit to bracket bolts.
6. Remove hydraulic unit.
7. Reverse procedure to install. Bleed brake system as outlined under "Brake System Bleed."

ABS CONTROL MODULE, REPLACE

1. Disconnect battery ground cable, then remove hydraulic unit cover.
2. Remove electrical boot, then disconnect two-pole electrical connector.
3. Remove six control module securing bolts, then the control module from hydraulic unit. Leave washers on hydraulic unit.
4. Reverse procedure to install. Start vehicle and check that warning lamps go out.

WHEEL SENSORS, REPLACE

Front

1. Disconnect battery ground cable, then raise and support vehicle.
2. Remove wheel, then clean around wheel sensor with soft steel brush.
3. Remove wheel sensor securing bolt and disconnect sensor.
4. Disconnect sensor cable from bracket in wheel arch, then disconnect connector.
5. Reverse procedure to install.

Rear

1. Raise and support vehicle, then remove wheel.
2. Force brake pistons back with suitable pliers, then depress brake pedal with brake clamp.
3. Remove two brake caliper securing bolts, then the brake pipe from clip. Bind brake caliper in tie.
4. Loosen brake shoe adjustment.
5. Remove lever return spring, then disconnect parking brake cable from lever.
6. Remove brake disc securing bolt, then the brake disc.
7. Disconnect speed sensor connector.
8. Remove four wheel hub retaining nuts, then the wheel hub, disc backing plate and spacer strip.
9. Remove wheel hub from disc backing plate
10. Reverse procedure to install. Tighten fasteners to specifications.

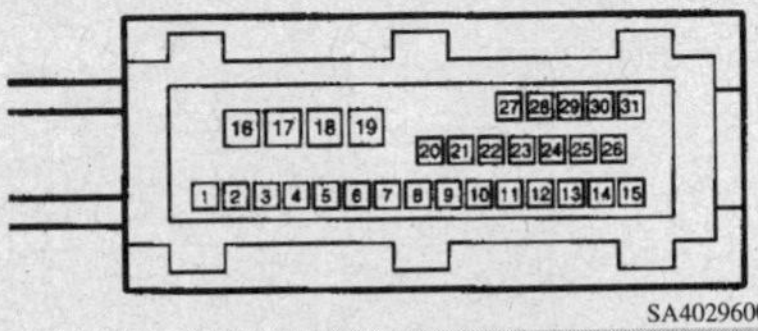
16 17 18 19
27 28 29 30 31
20 21 22 23 24 25 26
1 2 3 4 5 6 7 8 9 10 11 12 13 14 15
SA4029600060000X

Fig. 6 ABS control module connector view

Pin	Colour	Component/ Operation	In/Out	Measuring conditions	Test results	Be- tween X-Y
1	YE	Wheel sensor RR Reference ground	In	Rotate the wheel 1 turn/second	L100 mVac	1-2
2	BK	Wheel sensor RR Signal input	In	Rotate the wheel 1 turn/second	L100 mVac	2-1
3	BK	Wheel sensors FR reference ground	In	Rotate the wheel 1 turn/second	L100 mVac	3-5
4		No connection				
5	YE	Wheel sensor FR Signal input	In	Rotate the wheel 1 turn/second	L100 mVac	5-3
6	BK	Wheel sensor FL reference ground	In	Rotate the wheel 1 turn/second	L100 mVac	6-7
7	YE	Wheel sensors FL Signal input	In	Rotate the wheel 1 turn/second	L100 mVac	7-6
8	BK	Wheel sensor RL Reference ground	In	Rotate the wheel 1 turn/second	L100 mVac	8-9
9	YE	Wheel sensors RL Signal input	In	Rotate the wheel 1 turn/second	L100 mVac	9-8
10		No connection				
11	WH/BK	Data link	In/Out			
12		No connection				
13		No connection				
14	VT	Brake Light Switch	In	Brake activity	B+	14-16
15	YE/RD	+15 voltage	In	Ignition timing on	<0,5V	15-B+
16	BK	Power ground	In		B+	16-B+
17	RD	+30 voltage	In		<0,5V	17-B+
18	RD	+30 voltage	In		<0,5V	18-B+
19	BK	Ground	In		B+	19-B+
20		No connection				
21	GY/GN	Warning lamp ABS	In	Ignition timing on	<0,5V	21-B+

SA4029600061010X

Fig. 7 ABS control module connector pin identification (Part 1 of 2)

Pin	Colour	Component/ Operation	In/Out	Measuring conditions	Test results	Be- tween X-Y
22		No connection				
23	OG/WH	Wheel speed RL	Out	Slowly rotate the wheel Rotate the wheel 1 turn/second	0/approx. 12 V approx. 6 V	*)
24	YE/BN	Wheel speed RR	Out	See pin 23	See pin 23	*)
25	BK/GN	Wheel speed FL	Out	See pin 23	See pin 23	*)
26	PK/BK	Wheel speed FR	Out	See pin 23	See pin 23	*)

*) = Must be tested at the receiving components.

SA4029600061020X

Fig. 7 ABS control module connector pin identification (Part 2 of 2)

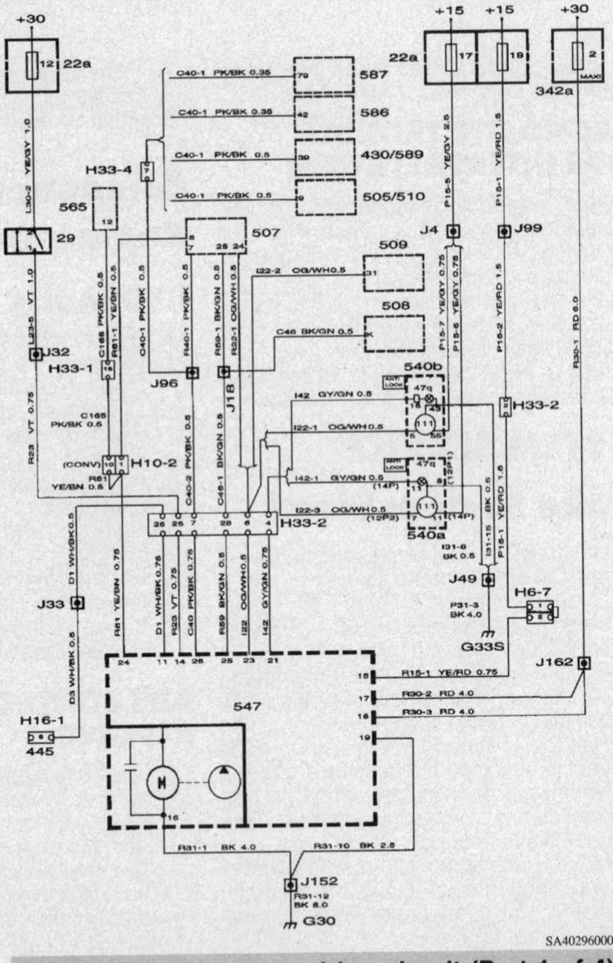
+30
+15
+15
+30
22a
22a
342a
587
586
430/589
505/510
507
509
508
540b
540a
565
29
H33-4
H33-1
H33-2
H10-2
J32
J96
J18
J4
J99
J33
J49
J162
J152
H6-7
H16-1
445
G33S
G30
547
M
SA4029600062010X

Fig. 8 ABS system wiring circuit (Part 1 of 4)

22a	Fuse board in electrical distribution box, facia
29	Brake light switch for brake pedal
47q	ABS Warning lamp in main instrument
111	Electronic speedometer
342a	Fuse board in electrical distribution box in engine compartment
430	Trionic electronic control module on the right side inside the side trim below the A-pillar
445	Data Link Connector, 16 pole, CARB
505	Motronic electronic control module M2.10.3 on the right side inside the side trim below the A-pillar
507	Electronic control module TCS V6
508	The electronic control module cruise control to the far right in the engine compartment below the windscreen.
509	Saab Sensonic electronic control module behind the glove compartment on the bulk head partition.
510	Electronic control module Motronic M2.8.1 on the right side inside the side trim under the A-pillar.
540a	Main instrument, low specification.
540b	Main instrument, high specification
547	ABS electronic control module integrated in hydraulic brake unit between the battery and the front electrical distribution box.
586	Motronic electronic control module 4.1 OBDII
587	Motronic electronic control module 5.2 OBDII
589	Electronic control module, Saab Trionic OBDII
H6-7	6 pole connectors
H10-2	10-pole connectors below the left A-pillar
H16-1	Data link connector under the facia at the steering column
H33-2	Black 33-pole connectors on the bracket below the left A-pillar
H33-4	33-pole connectors on the bulkhead partition at the back of the glove compartment
G30	Grounding point left structural member behind the battery
G33S	Signal ground connector bracket, below the left A-pillar on connector bracket.
J4	Crimp (LHD):Approx. 450 mm from the rheostat towards the main instrument (RHD):Approx. 240 mm from the rheostat towards the main instrument
J18	Crimp (LHD):Approx. 145 mm from the connectors H33-2 (RHD):Approx. 170 mm from the connectors H33-2 towards grounding point G33
J32	Crimp (LHD):Approx. 210 mm from the brake light switch towards the rheostat (RHD):Approx. 60 mm from branching rheostat towards the ICE electronic control module (CONV):Approx. 150 mm from branching electrically heated rear window towards the luggage compartment
J33	Crimp (LHD):Approx. 90 mm from the connectors H33-3 (RHD):Approx. 450 mm from the connectors H33-2 against SID
J49	Crimp (LHD):Approx. 390 mm from the rheostat against the connector bracket, left A-pillar (RHD):Approx. 150 mm from branching SID against the main instrument
J96	Crimp (LHD):Approx. 110 mm from branching ICE electronic control module against the brake light switch (RHD):Approx. 290 mm from the connectors H33-4 towards the grounding point G34
J99	Crimp (LHD):Approx. 270 mm from the grounding point G33 against the ICE (RHD):Approx. 340 mm from the connectors H33-4 against the grounding point G34
J152	Crimp approx. 60 mm from the branching washer fluid pump against the electrical distribution box
J162	Crimp approx. 250 mm from the ABS electronic control module

SA4029600062020X

Fig. 8 ABS system wiring circuit (Part 2 of 4)

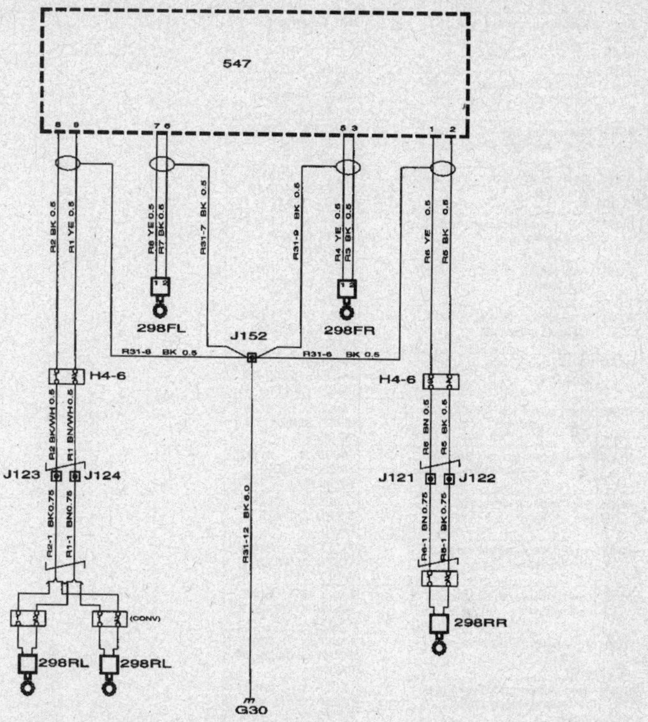
547
298FL
298FR
J152
H4-6
J123
J124
J121
J122
298RL
(CONV)
298RR
G30

SA4029600062030X

Fig. 8 ABS system wiring circuit (Part 3 of 4)

298 FR	Wheel sensor front right on steering swivel member
298 FL	Wheel sensors front left on steering swivel member
298 RL	Wheel sensors rear left on rear left wheel hub
298 RR	Wheel sensors rear right on rear right wheel hub
547	ABS electronic control module integrated in hydraulic brake unit between the battery and the front electrical distribution box
H4-6	4-pole connector on the bracket below the left A-pillar
G30	Grounding point left structural member behind the battery
J121	Crimp (3d/5D):Approx. 510 mm from branching fuel pump against the connector bracket left A-pillar (CONV):Approx. 640 mm from branching fuel pump against connector bracket left A-pillar
J122	Crimp (3d/5D):Approx. 535 mm from branching fuel pump against the connector bracket left A-pillar (CONV):Approx. 665 mm from branching fuel pump against connector bracket left A-pillar
J123	Crimp (3d/5D):Approx. 610 mm from branching fuel pump against the connector bracket left A-pillar (CONV):Approx. 715 mm from branching fuel pump against connector bracket left A-pillar
J124	Crimp (3d/5D):Approx. 585 mm from branching fuel pump against the connector bracket left A-pillar (CONV):Approx. 740 mm from branching fuel pump against connector bracket left A-pillar
J152	Crimp approx. 60 mm from the branching washer fluid pump against the electrical distribution box

SA4029600062040X

Fig. 8 ABS system wiring circuit (Part 4 of 4)

SA4029600063000X

Fig. 9 ISAT ABS diagnostic tool

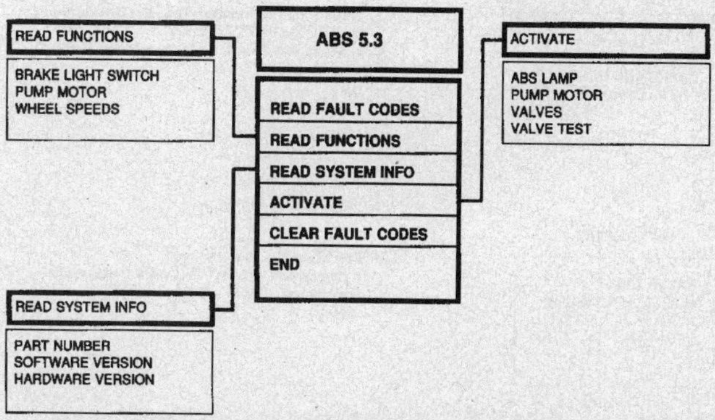
READ FUNCTIONS
BRAKE LIGHT SWITCH
PUMP MOTOR
WHEEL SPEEDS
ABS 5.3
READ FAULT CODES
READ FUNCTIONS
READ SYSTEM INFO
ACTIVATE
CLEAR FAULT CODES
END
ACTIVATE
ABS LAMP
PUMP MOTOR
VALVES
VALVE TEST
READ SYSTEM INFO
PART NUMBER
SOFTWARE VERSION
HARDWARE VERSION

SA4029600064000X

Fig. 10 ISAT diagnostic menus

Diag-nostic Trouble Code	Function/component fault	ABS	ISAT display text
B1371	Wheel sensor front left, faulty signal	ON	FAULT XX B1371 WHEEL SENSOR FL SIGNAL FAULTY
B1372	Wheel sensor front left, Signal faulty (open-circuit)	ON	FAULT XX B1372 WHEEL SENSOR FL NO SIGNAL
B1376	Wheel sensor front right, signal faulty	ON	FAULT XX B1376 WHEEL SENSOR FR SIGNAL FAULTY
B1377	Wheel sensor front right, no signal (open-circuit)	ON	FAULT XX B1376 WHEEL SENSOR FR NO SIGNAL
B1381	Wheel sensor rear left, signal faulty	ON	FAULT XX B1381 WHEEL SENSOR RL SIGNAL FAULTY
B1382	Wheel sensor rear right, no signal (open-circuit)	ON	FAULT XX B1382 WHEEL SENSOR RL NO SIGNAL
B1386	Wheel sensor rear right, signal faulty	ON	FAULT XX B1386 WHEEL SENSOR RR SIGNAL FAULTY
B1387	Wheel sensor rear right, no signal (open-circuit)	ON	FAULT XX B1387 WHEEL SENSOR RR NO SIGNAL
B1390	Wheel sensor, incorrect teeth number at a wheel sensor	ON	FAULT XX B1390 WHEEL SENSOR WRONG NO. OF TEETH
B2415	Boost pressure control valve rear left, faulty	ON	FAULT XX B2415 SOLENOID VALVE RL FAULTY
B2450	Boost pressure control valve front left, faulty	ON	FAULT XX B2450 SOLENOID VALVE FL FAULTY
B2455	Boost pressure control valve front right, faulty	ON	FAULT XX B2455 SOLENOID VALVE FR FAULTY
B2485	Boost pressure control valve rear right, faulty	ON	FAULT XX B2485 SOLENOID VALVE RR FAULTY
B1540	Boost pressure control valve, no voltage supply (open-circuit)	ON	FAULT XX B1540 SOLENOID VALVES NO VOLTAGE

SA4029600065010X

Fig. 11 ABS Diagnostic Trouble Codes (Part 1 of 2)

Diag-nostic Trouble Code	Function/component fault	ABS	ISAT display text
B1605	Electronic control module fault	ON	FAULT XX B1605 CONTROL MODULE INTERNAL FAULT
B1532	Battery voltage, low voltage rating	ON	FAULT XX B1532 BATTERY VOLTAGE LOW
B2470	Brake light switch, no signal (open-circuit)	ON	FAULT XX B2470 BRAKE LIGHT SWITCH NO SIGNAL
B2465	Pump motor, faulty	ON	FAULT XX B2465 PUMP MOTOR FAULTY

SA4029600065020X

Fig. 11 ABS Diagnostic Trouble Codes (Part 2 of 2)

ISAT DISPLAY 1

ACTIVATE
VALVE TEST FL
VALVE TEST FR
VALVE TEST RL
VALVE TEST RR

1 Select VALVE TEST in the ACTIVATE menu.

Caution

The test can only be started when the car is standing still.

ISAT DISPLAY 2

VALVE TEST FL
NORMAL POSITION
ROTATE WHEEL! OK?
YES NO

2 Rotate the wheel by hand. The wheel should rotate freely.
If you respond YES the intake valve and passage from the master cylinder to the wheel cylinder is closed.

ISAT DISPLAY 3

VALVE TEST FL
HOLDING PRESSURE
BRAKE AND HOLD!
PRESS ON/ENTER

3 The intake valve is closed. The valve has moved to HOLDING PRESSURE position. The passage is closed and there is no brake pressure to the wheels.

ISAT DISPLAY 4

VALVE TEST FL
HOLDING PRESSURE
ROTATE WHEEL! OK?
YES NO

4 The wheel should rotate freely.
If you respond YES the intake valve and passage are opened. Brake pressure can go to the wheels.

SA4029600066000X

Fig. 12 Valve Test Interpretation

ISAT DISPLAY 5

VALVE TEST FL
NORMAL POSITION
WHEEL LOCKED?
YES NO

5 The wheel should be locked
If you respond with YES the outlet valve opens and the return pump starts. Brake fluid pressure returns from the wheel cylinder with the aid of the return pump.

ISAT DISPLAY 6

VALVE TEST FL
PRESSURE RELIEVED
ROTATE WHEEL! OK?
YES NO

6 The wheel should rotate freely.

ISAT DISPLAY 7

TEST OK
PRESS ON/ENTER

7 The last display shows that the test is accomplished.

ISAT DISPLAY 8

VALVE TEST FL
FAULT IN TEST
SEE SERVICE MANUAL
PRESS ON/ENTER

8 If a fault arises when the test is in progress or you answer NO to any of the questions this display is shown.

SA4029600067000X

Fig. 13 Front Left & Front Right Valve Test Interpretation

DIAGNOSTIC CHART INDEX

Code	Description	Page No.	Fig. No.
Code B1371	Wheel Sensor Front Left, Signal Faulty	38-141	14
Code B1372	Wheel Sensor Front Left, Signal Faulty Open Circuit	38-142	15
Code B1376	Wheel Sensor Front Right, Signal Faulty Or No Signal	38-142	16
Code B1377	Wheel Sensor Front Right, Signal Faulty Open Circuit	38-143	17
Code B1381	Wheel Sensor Rear Left, Signal Faulty Or No Signal	38-143	18
Code B1382	Wheel Sensor Rear Left, Signal Faulty Open Circuit	38-144	19
Code B1386	Wheel Sensor Rear Right, Signal Faulty	38-144	
Code B1387	Wheel Sensor Rear Right, No Signal Open Circuit	38-145	21
Code B1390	Wheel Sensor, Wrong Number Of Teeth	38-145	22
Code B1532	Battery Voltage Low	38-147	26
Code B1540	Boost Pressure Control Valve, No Voltage Supply Open Circuit	38-146	24
Code B1605	Electronic Control Module Fault	38-146	25
Code B2415	Boost Pressure Control Valve Rear Left, Faulty	38-146	23
Code B2450	Boost Pressure Control Valve Rear Left, Faulty	38-146	23
Code B2455	Boost Pressure Control Valve Rear Left, Faulty	38-146	23
Code B2485	Boost Pressure Control Valve Rear Left, Faulty	38-146	23
Code B2470	Brake Light Switch No Signal Open Circuit	38-147	27
Code B2465	Pump Motor Faulty	38-147	28
—	ABS Lamp Not Operating	38-148	29
—	ABS Lamp On At All Times	38-148	30
—	No Wheel Speed Signal	38-149	31
—	Test Procedure Prior To ECM Replacement	38-149	32

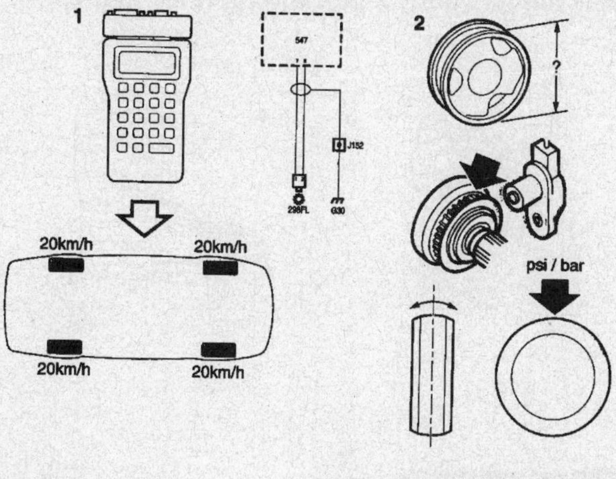

1
2
20km/h
20km/h
20km/h
20km/h
?
psi / bar

Fault symptom

ABS warning lamp on, no ABS function.

Condition

Fault registered as open-circuit with a speed of 40 km/h.

Diagnostic help

- The front left wheel sensor can be read by ISAT.
  - Select "READ FUNCTIONS"
  - Select "WHEEL SPEEDS"

The current wheel speed in km/h is displayed.

- If the front assembly of the vehicle is lifted the ISAT should display approx. 5 km/h if the left front wheel is rotated by hand at approx. 1 turn per second.

Diagnostic procedure

1 **Diagnostic Trouble Code inspection**
- Connect the ISAT Scan Tool.
- Start and test drive the car at an even speed. Read WHEEL SPEEDS in accordance with diagnostic help. Compare the four wheel speeds shown.

Does the front left wheel speed have a faulty rating?

YES Continue with point 2.

NO Continue with point 4.

2 **Mechanical size inspection.**
- Check that:

- wheel size and tyre pressure are correct.
- there is no wheel bearing play.
- the toothed wheel is not damaged.

Is the inspection OK?

YES Continue with point 3.

NO Rectify the fault

SA4029600068010X

Fig. 14 Code B1371: Wheel Sensor Front Left, Signal Faulty (Part 1 of 2)

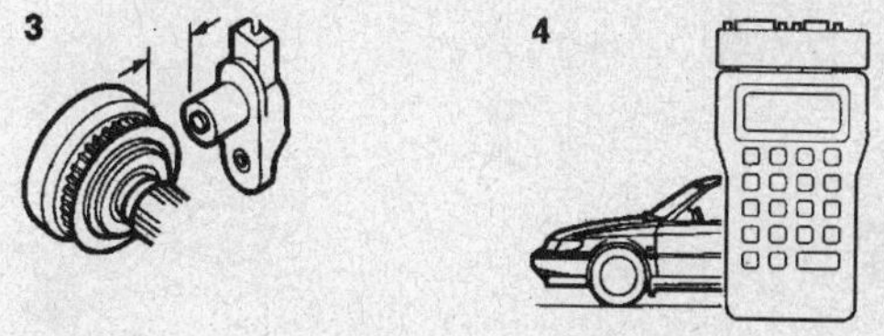

3
4

3 **Toothed wheel air gap inspection**
- Check that the air gap between the toothed wheel and the wheel sensor is 0.6±0.3 mm.

Is the air gap correct?

YES Continue with point 4.

NO Rectify the fault

4 **Final inspection**
- Erase the diagnostic trouble code.
- Carry out the driving cycle, drive the car with various load and engine speeds for 5 minutes.
- Read the diagnostic trouble code.

Is the diagnostic trouble code stored?

YES Continue With "Test Procedure Prior To Replacing ECM"

NO The diagnostic procedure performed is right or the fault is of intermittent character.

SA4029600068020X

Fig. 14 Code B1371: Wheel Sensor Front Left, Signal Faulty (Part 2 of 2)

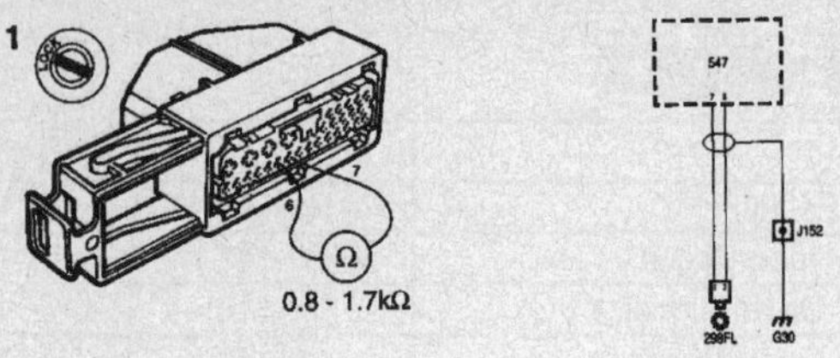
1
0.8 - 1.7kΩ
547
J152
298FL
G30

Fault symptom

ABS warning lamp on, no ABS function.

Condition

Fault registered as open-circuit

Diagnostic help

- The front left wheel sensor can be read by ISAT.
  - Select "READ FUNCTIONS"
  - Select "WHEEL SPEEDS"

The current wheel speed in km/h is displayed.

- If the front assembly of the vehicle is lifted the ISAT should display approx. 5 km/h if the left front wheel is rotated by hand at approx. 1 turn per second.

Diagnostic procedure

1 **Wheel sensor resistance check**

- Disconnect the electronic control module connector.
- Take a resistance reading from the electronic control module sensor connector between pin 6 and 7. The resistance should be 0.8-1.7 kOhm

Is the resistance correct?

YES Continue with point 3.

NO Continue with point 2.

SA4029600069010X

Fig. 15 Code B1372: Wheel Sensor Front Left, Signal Faulty Open Circuit (Part 1 of 2)

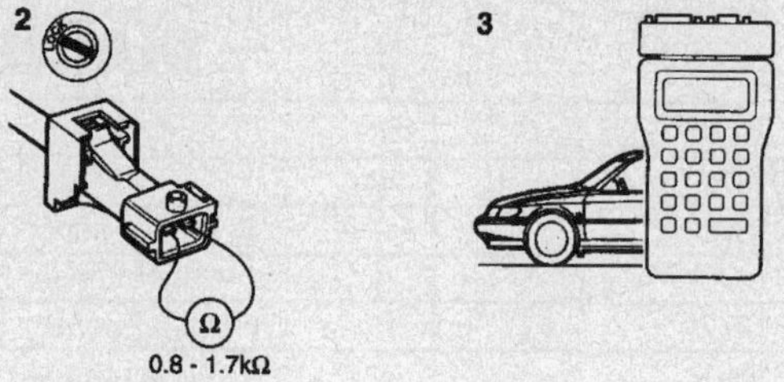
2
3
0.8 - 1.7kΩ

2 **Wheel sensor resistance check**

- Disconnect the wheel sensors connector (2 pin connector located at the left wheel house in the engine compartment).
- Take a resistance reading in the wheel sensor connector between the two connector pins. The resistance should be 0.8-1.7 kOhm

Is the resistance rating correct?

YES Check and rectify the wiring including the connection between the electronic control module and the wheel sensor connector.

NO Check and possibly rectify the wiring including the connector to the wheel sensor. If there is no relevant reason for the fault, change the wheel sensor.

3 **Final inspection**

- Erase the diagnostic trouble code.
- Perform the driving cycle, drive the car at varying loads and engines speeds for 5 minutes.
- Read diagnostic trouble codes.

Is the diagnostic trouble code stored?

YES Continue Test Procedure Prior To Replacing ECM

NO The diagnostic procedure taken is right.

SA4029600069020X

Fig. 15 Code B1372: Wheel Sensor Front Left, Signal Faulty Open Circuit (Part 2 of 2)

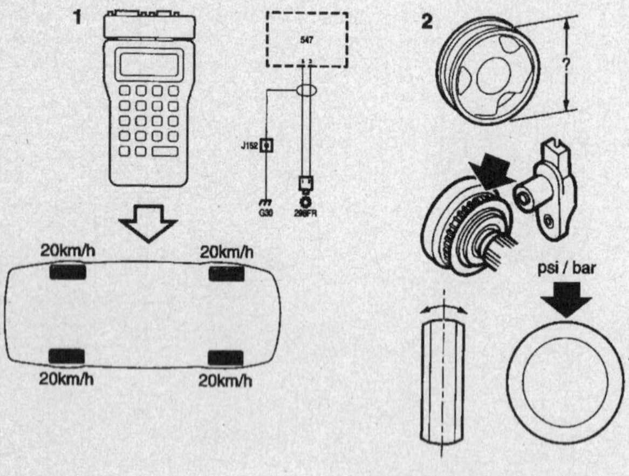
1
547
J152
G30
298FR
20km/h
20km/h
20km/h
20km/h
2
?
psi / bar

Fault symptom

ABS warning lamp on, no ABS function.

Condition

Fault registered as open-circuit with a speed of 40 km/h.

Diagnostic help

- The front right wheel sensor can be read by ISAT.
  - Select "READ FUNCTIONS"
  - Select "WHEEL SPEEDS"

The current wheel speed in km/h is displayed.

- If the front assembly of the vehicle is lifted the ISAT should display approx. 5 km/h if the right front wheel is rotated by hand at approx. 1 turn per second.

Diagnostic procedure

1 **Diagnostic Trouble Code inspection**

- Connect the ISAT Scan Tool.
- Start and test drive the car at an even speed. Read WHEEL SPEEDS in accordance with diagnostic help. Compare the four wheel speeds shown.

Does the front right wheel speed have a faulty rating?

YES Continue with point 2.

NO Continue with point 4.

2 **Mechanical size inspection.**

- Check that:

- wheel size and tyre pressure are correct.
- there is no wheel bearing play.
- the toothed wheel is not damaged.

Is the inspection OK?

YES Continue with point 3.

NO Rectify the fault

SA4029600070010X

Fig. 16 Code B1376: Wheel Sensor Front Right, Signal Faulty Or No Signal (Part 1 of 2)

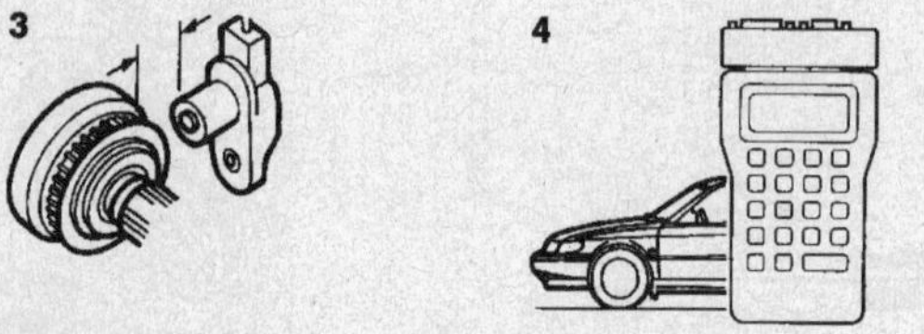
3
4

3 **Toothed wheel air gap inspection**

- Check that the air gap between the toothed wheel and the wheel sensor is 0.6±0.3 mm.

Is the air gap correct?

YES Continue with point 4.

NO Rectify the fault

4 **Final inspection**

- Erase the diagnostic trouble code.
- Carry out the driving cycle, drive the car with various load and engine speeds for 5 minutes.
- Read the diagnostic trouble code.

Is the diagnostic trouble code stored?

YES Continue With "Test Procedure Prior To Replacing ECM"

NO The diagnostic procedure performed is right or the fault is of intermittent character.

SA4029600070020X

Fig. 16 Code B1376: Wheel Sensor Front Right, Signal Faulty Or No Signal (Part 2 of 2)

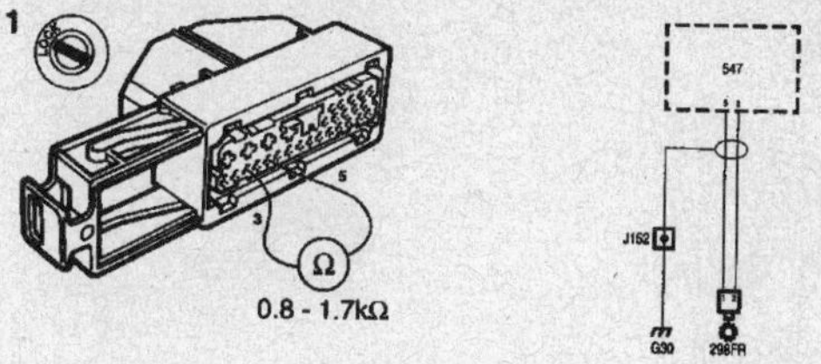
1
0.8 - 1.7kΩ
547
J152
G30
298FR

Fault symptom

ABS warning lamp on, no ABS function.

Condition

Fault registered as open-circuit

Diagnostic help

- The front right wheel sensor can be read by ISAT.
  - Select "READ FUNCTIONS"
  - Select "WHEEL SPEEDS"

The current wheel speed in km/h is displayed.

- If the front assembly of the vehicle is lifted the ISAT should display approx. 5 km/h if the right front wheel is rotated by hand at approx. 1 turn per second.

Diagnostic procedure

1 **Wheel sensor resistance check**

- Disconnect the electronic control module connector.
- Take a resistance reading at the electronic control module sensor connector between pin 3 and 5. The resistance should be 0.8-1.7 kOhm

Is the resistance correct?

YES Continue with point 3.

NO Continue with point 2.

SA4029600071010X

Fig. 17 Code B1377: Wheel Sensor Front Right, Signal Faulty Open Circuit (Part 1 of 2)

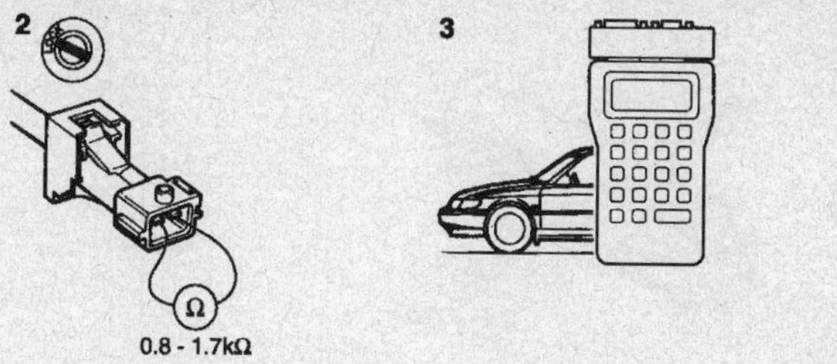
2
3
0.8 - 1.7kΩ

2 **Wheel sensor resistance check**

Remove the wheel sensor connector (2 pin connector located at the right of the wheel housing in the engine compartment).

- Take a resistance reading in the wheel sensor connector between the two connector pins. The resistance should be 0.8-1.7 kOhm

Is the resistance rating correct?

YES Check and rectify the wiring including the connection between the electronic control module and the wheel sensor connector.

NO Check and possibly rectify the wiring including the connector to the wheel sensor. If there is no relevant reason for the fault, change the wheel sensor.

3 **Final inspection**

- Erase the diagnostic trouble code.
- Perform the driving cycle, drive the car at varying loads and engines speeds for 5 minutes.
- Read diagnostic trouble codes.

Is the diagnostic trouble code stored?

YES Continue Test Procedure Prior To Replacing ECM

NO The diagnostic procedure taken is right.

SA4029600071020X

Fig. 17 Code B1377: Wheel Sensor Front Right, Signal Faulty Open Circuit (Part 2 of 2)

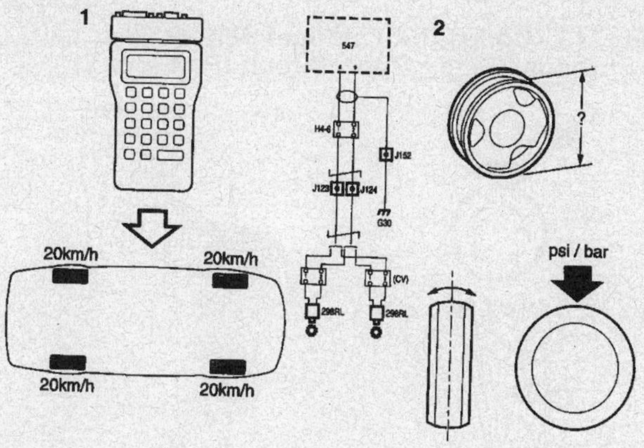
1
2
547
20km/h
20km/h
20km/h
20km/h
?
psi / bar

Fault symptom

ABS warning lamp on, no ABS function.

Condition

Fault registered at a speed of l10 km/h.

Diagnostic help

- The rear left wheel sensor can be read by ISAT.
  - Select "READ FUNCTIONS"
  - Select "WHEEL SPEEDS"

The current wheel speed in km/h is displayed.

- If the rear assembly of the vehicle is lifted the ISAT should display approx. 5 km/h if the left rear wheel is rotated by hand at approx. 1 turn per second.

Diagnostic procedure

1 **Diagnostic Trouble Code inspection**

- Connect the ISAT Scan Tool.
- Start and test drive the car at an even speed. Read WHEEL SPEEDS in accordance with diagnostic help. Compare the four wheel speeds shown.

Does the rear left wheel speed show a faulty rating?

YES Continue with point 2.

NO Continue with point 4.

2 **Mechanical size inspection.**

- Check that:

- wheel size and tyre pressure are correct.
- there is no wheel bearing play.

Is the inspection OK?

YES Continue with point 3.

NO Rectify the fault

SA4029600072010X

Fig. 18 Code B1381: Wheel Sensor Rear Left, Signal Faulty Or No Signal (Part 1 of 2)

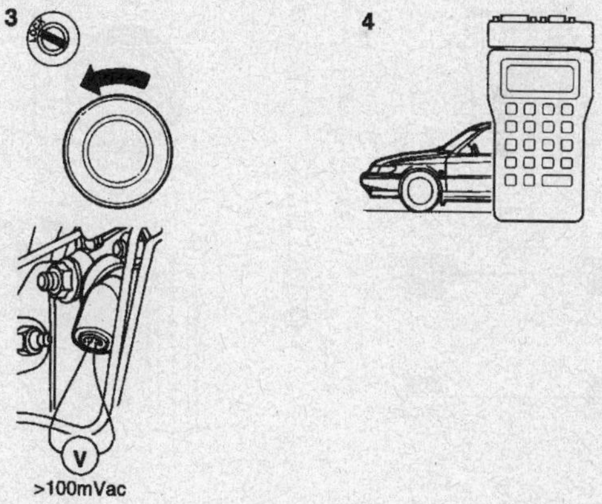
3
4
V
>100mVac

3 **Wheel sensor signal check**

- *Lift the rear suspension of the vehicle.*
- Take a voltage measurement, mVac, at the wheel sensors connector. Connect a voltmeter between the connector pins. Rotate the rear left wheel at approx. 1 turn per second. The wheel sensor voltage should be l100 mVac.

Is the voltage OK?

YES Continue with point 4.

NO Change wheel sensor.

4 **Final inspection**

- Erase the diagnostic trouble code.
- Carry out the driving cycle, drive the car with various load and engine speeds for 5 minutes.
- Read the diagnostic trouble code.

Is the diagnostic trouble code stored?

YES Continue With "Test Procedure Prior To Replacing ECM"

NO The diagnostic procedure performed is right or the fault is of intermittent character.

SA4029600072020X

Fig. 18 Code B1381: Wheel Sensor Rear Left, Signal Faulty Or No Signal (Part 2 of 2)

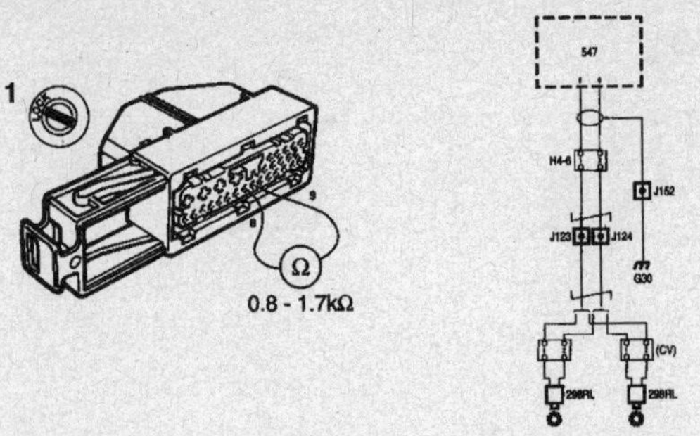

1
0.8 - 1.7kΩ
547
H4-6
J152
J123
J124
G30
(CV)
298RL
298RL

Fault symptom
ABS warning lamp on, no ABS function.

Condition
Fault registered as open-circuit

Diagnostic help

- The rear left wheel sensor can be read by ISAT.
  - Select "READ FUNCTIONS"
  - Select "WHEEL SPEEDS"

The current wheel speed in km/h is displayed.

- If the rear assembly of the vehicle is lifted the ISAT should display approx. 5 km/h if the left rear wheel is rotated by hand at approx. 1 turn per second.

Diagnostic procedure

1 **Wheel sensor resistance check**
- Disconnect the electronic control module connector.
- Take a resistance reading at the electronic control module sensor connector between pin 8 and pin 9. The resistance should be 0.8-1.7 kOhm.

Is the resistance rating correct?

YES Continue with point 3.
NO Continue with point 2.

SA4029600073010X

Fig. 19 Code B1382: Wheel Sensor Rear Left, Signal Faulty Open Circuit (Part 1 of 2)

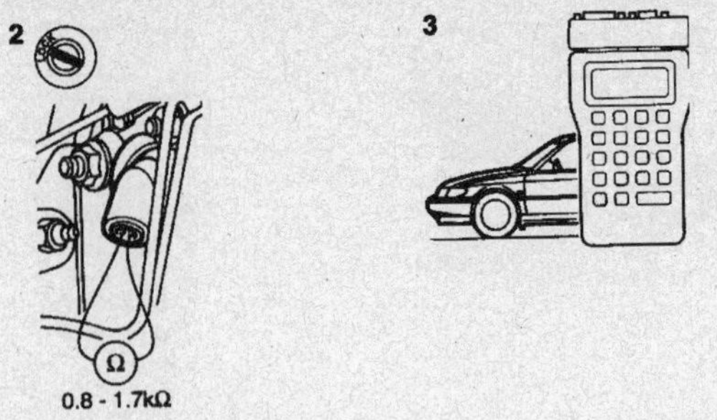

2
3
0.8 - 1.7kΩ

2 **Wheel sensor resistance check (cont.)**
- Remove the wheel sensor connector. The connector is integrated into the wheel sensor, against the wheel bearing rear side.
- Take a resistance reading at the wheel sensor switch between two connector pins. The resistance should be 0.8-1.7 kOhm.

Is the resistance rating correct?

YES Check and rectify the wiring including the connection between the electronic control module and the wheel sensor.
NO Inspect the wheel sensor connector for damp and corrosion. If there is no obvious fault cause, change the wheel sensor.

3 **Final inspection**
- Erase the diagnostic trouble code.
- Carry out the driving cycle, drive the car with various load and engine speeds for 5 minutes.
- Read the diagnostic trouble code.

Is the diagnostic trouble code stored?

YES Continue With "Test Procedure Prior To Replacing ECM"
NO The diagnostic procedure taken is right.

SA4029600073020X

Fig. 19 Code B1382: Wheel Sensor Rear Left, Signal Faulty Open Circuit (Part 2 of 2)

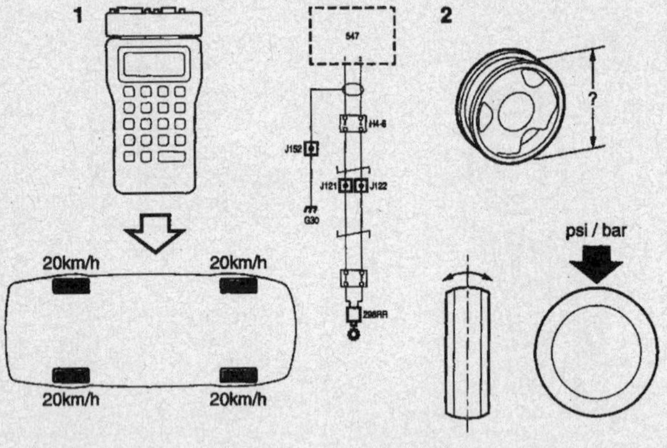

1
2
20km/h
20km/h
20km/h
20km/h
547
H4-6
J152
J121
J122
G30
298RR
?
psi / bar

Fault symptom
ABS warning lamp on, no ABS function.

Condition
Fault registered at a speed of l10 km/h.

Diagnostic help

- The rear right wheel sensor can be read by ISAT.
  - Select "READ FUNCTIONS"
  - Select "WHEEL SPEEDS"

The current wheel speed in km/h is displayed.

- If the rear assembly of the vehicle is lifted the ISAT should display approx. 5 km/h if the right rear wheel is rotated by hand at approx. 1 turn per second.

Diagnostic procedure

1 **Diagnostic Trouble Code inspection**
- Connect the ISAT Scan Tool.
- Start and test drive the car at an even speed. Read WHEEL SPEEDS in accordance with diagnostic help. Compare the four wheel speeds shown.

Does the rear right wheel speed have an incorrect reading?

YES Continue with point 2.
NO Continue with point 4.

2 **Mechanical size inspection.**
- Check that:
- wheel size and tyre pressure are correct.
- there is no wheel bearing play.

Is the inspection OK?

YES Continue with point 3.
NO Rectify the fault

SA4029600074010X

Fig. 20 Code B1386: Wheel Sensor Rear Right, Signal Faulty (Part 1 of 2)

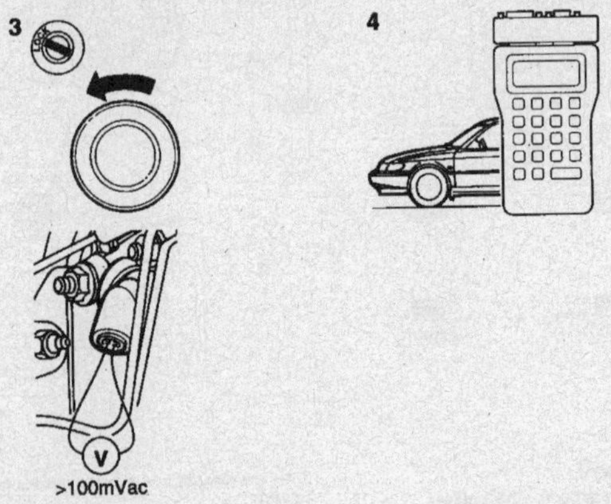

3
4
>100mVac

3 **Wheel sensor signal check**
- Lift the rear suspension of the vehicle.
- Take a voltage reading, mVac, at the wheel sensor connector. Connect a voltmeter between the connector pins. Rotate the rear right wheel at approx. 1 turn per second. The wheel sensor voltage should be l100 mVac.

Is the voltage OK?

YES Continue with point 4.
NO Change wheel sensor.

4 **Final inspection**
- Erase the diagnostic trouble code.
- Carry out the driving cycle, drive the car with various load and engine speeds for 5 minutes.
- Read the diagnostic trouble code.

Is the diagnostic trouble code stored?

YES Continue With "Test Procedure Prior To Replacing ECM"
NO The diagnostic procedure performed is right or the fault is of intermittent character.

SA4029600074020X

Fig. 20 Code B1386: Wheel Sensor Rear Right, Signal Faulty (Part 2 of 2)

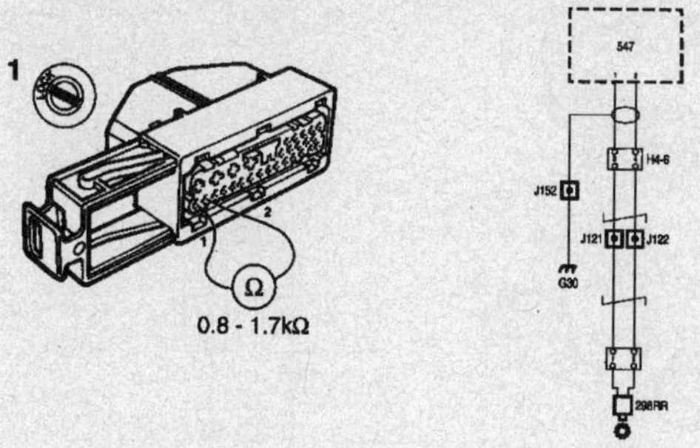
1
0.8 - 1.7kΩ
547
H4-6
J152
J121
J122
G30
298RR

Fault symptom
ABS warning lamp on, no ABS function.

Condition
Fault registered as open-circuit

Diagnostic help
- The rear right wheel sensor can be read by ISAT.
  - Select "READ FUNCTIONS"
  - Select "WHEEL SPEEDS"

The current wheel speed in km/h is displayed.
- If the rear assembly of the vehicle is lifted the ISAT should display approx. 5 km/h if the right rear wheel is rotated by hand at approx. 1 turn per second.

Diagnostic procedure
1 **Wheel sensor resistance check**
- Disconnect the electronic control module connector.
- Take a resistance reading at the electronic control module sensor connector between pins 1 and 2. The resistance should be 0.8-1.7 kOhm.

Is the resistance rating correct?

YES Continue with point 3.
NO Continue with point 2.

SA4029600075010X

Fig. 21 Codes B1387: Wheel Sensor Rear Right, No Signal Open Circuit (Part 1 of 2)

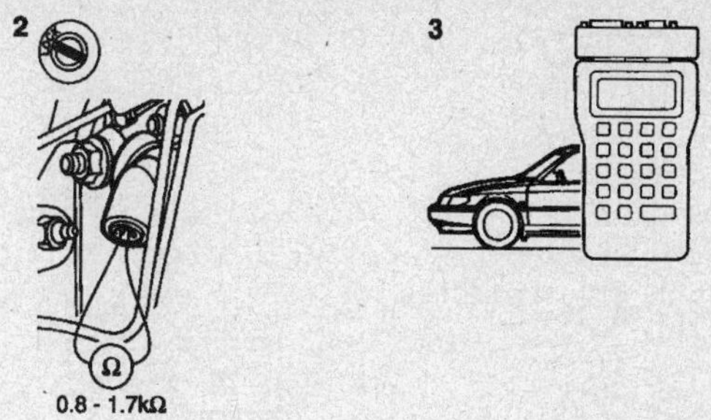
2
0.8 - 1.7kΩ
3

2 **Wheel sensor resistance check (cont.)**
- Remove the wheel sensor connector. The sensor connector is integrated in the wheel sensor against the rear side of the wheel sensor.
- Take a resistance reading at the wheel sensor switch between two connector pins. The resistance should be 0.8-1.7 kOhm.

Is the resistance rating correct?

YES Check and rectify the wiring including the connection between the electronic control module and the wheel sensor.
NO Inspect the wheel sensor connector for damp and corrosion. If there is no obvious fault cause, change the wheel sensor.

3 **Final inspection**
- Erase the diagnostic trouble code.
- Carry out the driving cycle, drive the car with various load and engine speeds for 5 minutes.
- Read the diagnostic trouble code.

Is the diagnostic trouble code stored?

YES Continue With "Test Procedure Prior To Replacing ECM"
NO The diagnostic procedure taken is right.

SA4029600075020X

Fig. 21 Codes B1387: Wheel Sensor Rear Right, No Signal Open Circuit (Part 2 of 2)

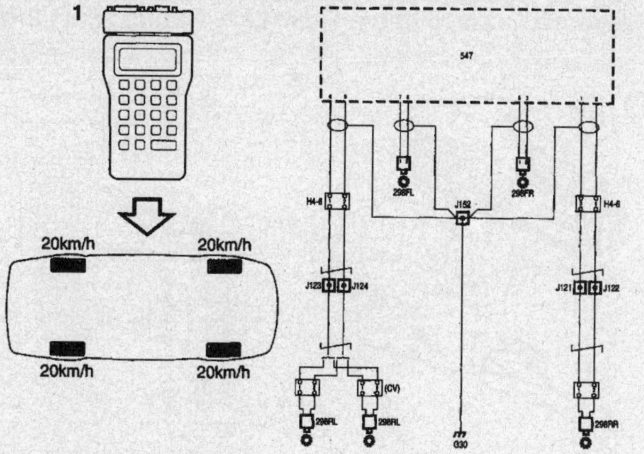
1
20km/h
20km/h
20km/h
20km/h
547
H4-6
J152
J123
J124
J121
J122
298FL
298FR
298RL
298RR
G30
(CV)

Fault symptom
ABS warning lamp on, no ABS function.

Condition
The wheel speed is compared to a reference speed (= filtrated mean value of all wheel speeds).
- a wheel speed l25% higher than the reference speed for 20 seconds.
- Two wheel speeds l6% higher than the reference speed for 80 seconds.
- A wheel speed <6% lower than the reference speed for 20 seconds, or two wheel speeds for 10 seconds.
- Continual ABS modulation for more than 60 seconds.

Diagnostic help
- Any particular wheel speed sensor can be read by the ISAT Scan Tool.
  - Select "READ FUNCTIONS"
  - Select "WHEEL SPEEDS"

The current wheel speed in km/h is displayed.

SA4029600076010X

Fig. 22 Code B1390: Wheel Sensor, Wrong Number Of Teeth (Part 1 of 2)

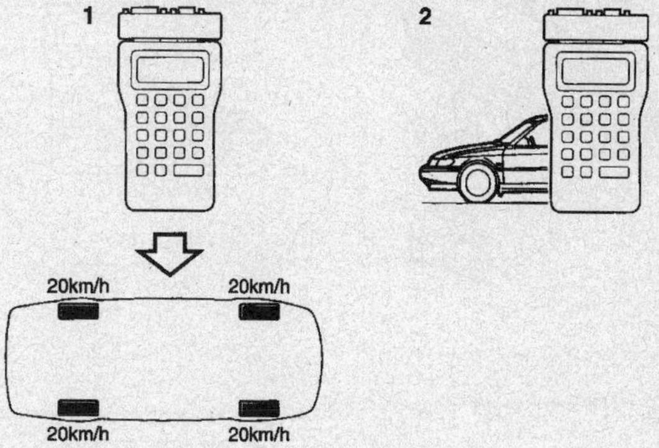
1
2
20km/h
20km/h
20km/h
20km/h

Diagnostic procedure
1 **Diagnostic Trouble Code inspection**
- Connect the ISAT Scan Tool.
- Start and test drive the car at an even speed. Read WHEEL SPEEDS according to the Diagnostic help. Compare the four displayed wheel speeds. All wheel speed ratings should be the same.

Does the ISAT display the correct rating?

YES Continue with point 2.
NO Displays FL faulty reading, continue fault diagnosis according to B1371
Displays FR faulty reading, continue fault diagnosis according to B1376
Displays RL faulty reading, continue fault diagnosis according to B1381
Displays RR faulty reading, continue fault diagnosis according to B1386.

2 **Final inspection**
- Erase the diagnostic trouble code.
- Carry out the driving cycle, drive the car with various load and engine speeds for 5 minutes.
- Read the diagnostic trouble code.

Is the diagnostic trouble code stored?

YES Continue on Test Procedure Prior To Replacing ECM
NO The diagnostic procedure performed is right or the fault is of intermittent character.

SA4029600076020X

Fig. 22 Code B1390: Wheel Sensor, Wrong Number Of Teeth (Part 2 of 2)

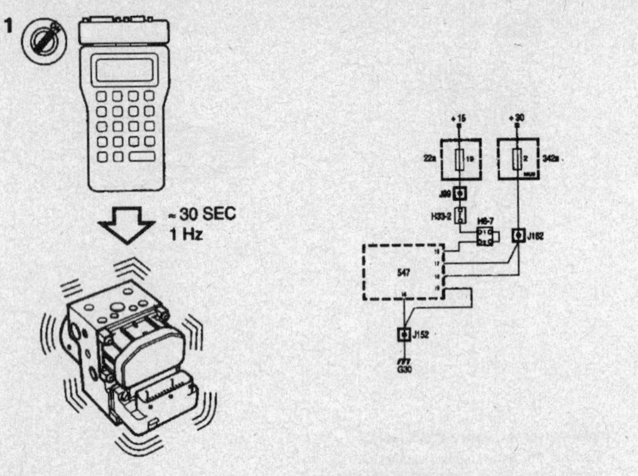
1
≈ 30 SEC
1 Hz
+15
+30
547
J152
G30

Fault symptom

ABS warning lamp on, no ABS function.

Condition

- The ignition timing is in the On position.
- The electronic control module makes a boost pressure control valve connection test.

Diagnostic help

The boost pressure control valves can be activated with the ISAT Scan Tool.

- Select "ACTIVATE"
- Select "VALVES"

Particular valves can be identified in the sub menu. The selected valve is activated within approx. 30 seconds with a frequency of 1 Hz.

Diagnostic procedure

1 **Valve check**

- Connect the ISAT Scan Tool. The ignition timing is in the ON position
- First activate the "INTAKE" and then after the activation period is over activate the "OUTLET" Listen if the valves click.

Do the valves click?

YES Continue with point 3.

NO Continue with point 2.

SA4029600077010X

Fig. 23 Code B2415, 2450, 2455 & 2485: Boost Pressure Control Valve Rear Left, Faulty (Part 1 of 2)

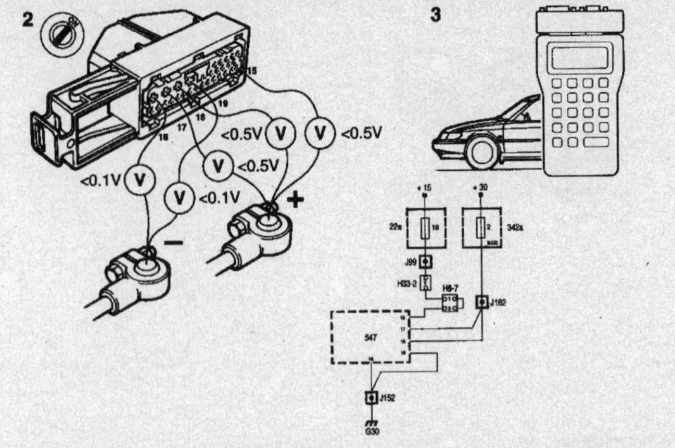
2
3
<0.5V
<0.5V
<0.5V
<0.1V
<0.1V
+
−
+15
+30
547
J152
G30

2 **Electronic control module ground and voltage supply check**

- Disconnect the electronic control module connector. The ignition timing is in the On position. Take a voltage reading at the electronic control module sensor connector. Connect the voltmeter,

- between B+ and pin 15 = <0.5V
- between B+ and pin 17 = <0.5V
- between B+ and pin 18 = <0.5V
- between pin 16 and B- = <0.1V
- between pin 19 and B- = <0.1V

Are the voltage ratings OK?

YES Continue with point 3.

NO Check and rectify the wiring including the connector and grounding points.

3 **Final inspection**

- Erase the diagnostic trouble code.
- Carry out the driving cycle, drive the car with various load and engine speeds for 5 minutes.
- Read the diagnostic trouble code.

Is the diagnostic trouble code stored?

YES Continue on Test Procedure Prior To Replacing ECM

NO The diagnostic procedure performed is right or the fault is of intermittent character.

SA4029600077020X

Fig. 23 Code B2415, 2450, 2455 & 2485: Boost Pressure Control Valve Rear Left, Faulty (Part 2 of 2)

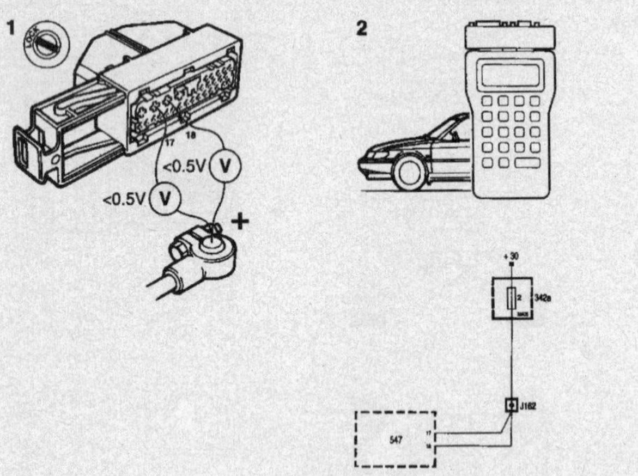
1
2
<0.5V
<0.5V
+
+30
547
J162

Fault symptom

ABS warning lamp on, no ABS function.

Condition

- If three or more valves lack voltage supply.
- If the internal voltage relay is out of order.
- The electronic control module lacks a +30-voltage supply (connector pins 17 and 18).

Diagnostic procedure

1 **+30 voltage supply check**

- Remove the electronic control module connector. Take a voltage measurement at the electronic control module sensor connector. Connect the voltmeter

- between pin 17 and B+ = < 0.5 V
- between pin 18 and B+ = < 0.5 V.

Are the voltage ratings OK?

YES Continue with point 2.

NO Check and possibly rectify the wiring between pin 17 and 18 of the electronic control module and the MAXI 2 fuse. If the wiring is correct, continue fault diagnosis in Service Manual 3:2 Electrical system, power supply +30.

2 **Final inspection**

- Erase the diagnostic trouble code.
- Carry out the driving cycle, drive the car with various load and engine speeds for 5 minutes.
- Read the diagnostic trouble code.

Is the diagnostic trouble code stored?

YES "Test Procedure Prior To Replacing ECM"

NO The diagnostic procedure performed is right or the fault is of intermittent character.

SA4029600078000X

Fig. 24 Code B1540: Boost Pressure Control Valve, No Voltage Supply Open Circuit

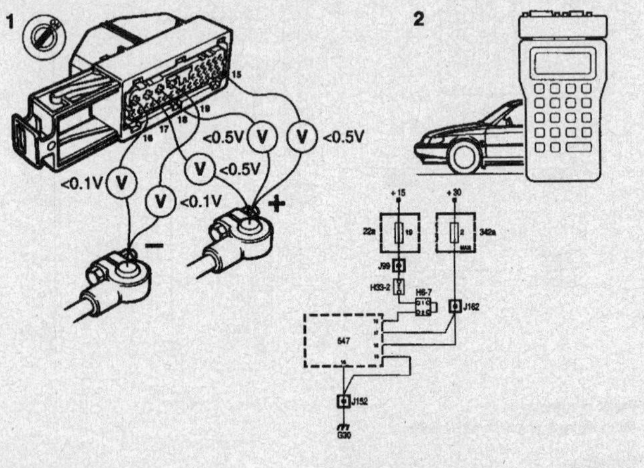
1
2
<0.5V
<0.5V
<0.5V
<0.1V
<0.1V
+
−
+15
+30
547
J152
G30

Fault symptom

ABS warning lamp on, no ABS function.

Condition

Fault registered as an internal program fault.

Diagnostic procedure

1 **Electronic control module ground and voltage supply check**

- Disconnect the electronic control module connector. The ignition timing is in the On position. Take a voltage reading at the electronic control module sensor connector. Connect the voltmeter,

- between pin 15 and B+ = <0.5V
- between pin 17 and B+ = <0.5V
- between pin 18 and B+ = <0.5V
- between pin 16 and B- = <0.1V
- between pin 19 and B- = <0.1V

Are the voltage ratings OK?

YES Continue with point 2.

NO Check and rectify the wiring including the connector and grounding points.

2 **Final inspection**

- Erase the diagnostic trouble code.
- Carry out the driving cycle, drive the car with various load and engine speeds for 5 minutes.
- Read the diagnostic trouble code.

Is the diagnostic trouble code stored?

YES

NO The diagnostic procedure performed is right or the fault is of intermittent character.

SA4029600079000X

Fig. 25 Code B1605: Electronic Control Module Fault

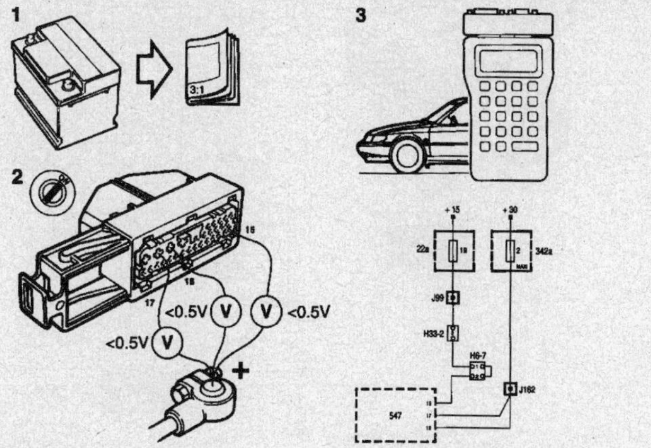
1
3:1
2
3
<0.5V
<0.5V
<0.5V
+15
+30
22a
342a
J99
H33-2
H6-7
547
J162

Fault symptom
ABS warning lamp on, no ABS function.

Condition
- Battery voltage <9V for more than 0.5 seconds.
- Wheel speeds over 6 km/h.

Diagnostic procedure
1 **Battery check**
- Check the condition of the battery.

Is the condition of the battery OK?
YES Continue with point 2.
NO Rectify the fault

2 **Electronic control module voltage supply check**
- Remove the electronic control module connector. The ignition should be in the ON position. Take a voltage measurement at the sensor connector. Connect the voltmeter
- between pin 17 and B+ = <0.5V
- between pin 18 and B+ = <0.5V
- between pin 15 and B+ = <0.5V

Are the voltage ratings OK?
YES Continue with point 3.
NO Check and rectify the wiring including the connector.

3 **Final inspection**
- Erase the diagnostic trouble code.
- Carry out the driving cycle, drive the car with various load and engine speeds for 5 minutes.
- Read the diagnostic trouble code.

Is the diagnostic trouble code stored?
YES Continue "Test Procedure Prior To Replacing ECM"
NO The diagnostic procedure performed is right or the fault is of intermittent character.

SA4029600080000X

Fig. 26 Code B1532: Battery Voltage Low

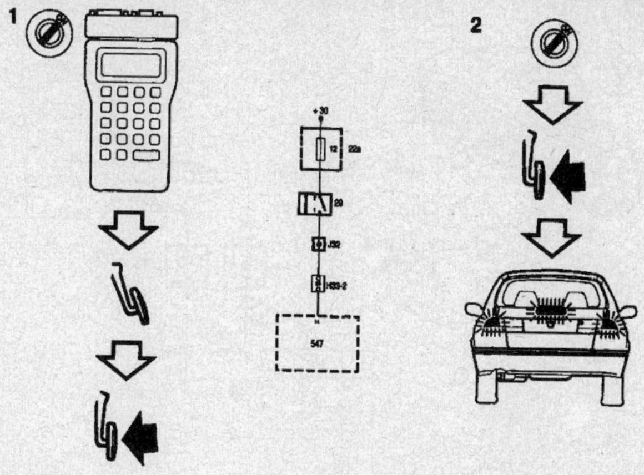
1
2
+30
22a
29
J32
H33-2
547

Fault symptom
No sumptoms.

Condition
Fault registered with open circuit for longer than 1 second.

Diagnostic help
Brake light switch position ON/OFF, can be read with the ISAT Scan Tool.
- Select "READ FUNCTIONS"
- Select "BRAKE LIGHT SWITCH"

Diagnostic procedure
1 **Brake light switch inspection.**
- Connect the ISAT Scan Tool. The ignition timing is in the ON position
- Check the brake light switch in accordance with Diagnostic help and depress and release the brake pedal.

Does the ISAT display the correct rating?
YES Continue with point 3.
NO Continue with point 2.

2 **Brake lights inspection.**
- Check that the brake light functions when the brake pedal is depressed.

Does the brake light function?
YES Check and rectify the cable including the connector between pin 14 of the electronic control module and brake light switch.
NO Continue the fault diagnosis

SA4029600081010X

Fig. 27 Code B2470: Brake Light Switch No Signal Open Circuit (Part 1 of 2)

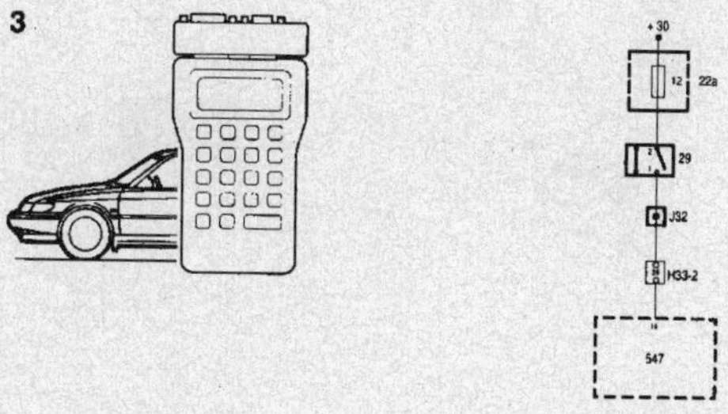
3
+30
22a
29
J32
H33-2
547

3 **Final inspection**
- Erase the diagnostic trouble code.
- Perform a driving cycle, drive the car with varying loads and engine speed and use the brake pedal.
- Read the diagnostic trouble code.

Is the diagnostic trouble code stored?
YES With "Test Procedure Prior To Replacing ECM"
NO The diagnostic procedure performed is right or the fault is of intermittent character.

SA4029600081020X

Fig. 27 Code B2470: Brake Light Switch No Signal Open Circuit (Part 2 of 2)

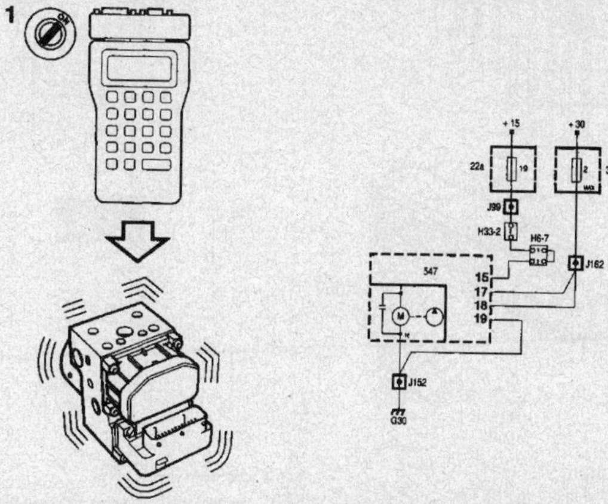
1
+15
+30
22a
342a
J99
H33-2
H6-7
547
J162
15
17
18
19
J152
G30

Fault symptom
ABS warning lamp on, no ABS function.

Condition
- The pump motor is tested after the car has started and the wheels start to rotate (Vl6 km/h). Then observe it continually.

Diagnostic help
The pump motor can be rotated with the ISAT Scan Tool.
- Select "ACTIVATE"
- Select "PUMP MOTOR"
- If the ABS electronic control module has no ground connection (connector pin 16) a diagnostic trouble code is registered.

Diagnostic procedure
1 **Pump motor inspection**
- Connect the ISAT Scan Tool. The ignition timing is in the ON position
- Activate the pump motor in accordance with Diagnostic help. Listen if the motor comes on/off.

Does the pump motor work?
YES Continue with point 3.
NO Inspect the 2 pole sensor connector for any open-circuit. If the conductors are correct continue with point 2.

SA4029600082010X

Fig. 28 Code B2465: Pump Motor Faulty (Part 1 of 2)

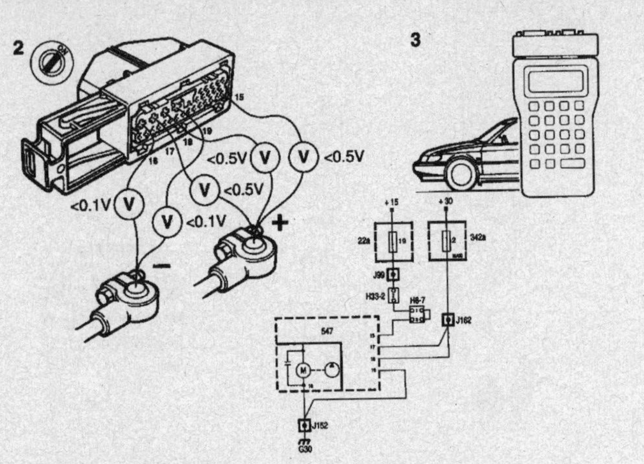
2
3
<0.5V
<0.5V
<0.5V
<0.1V
<0.1V
+
-
+15
+30
22a
342a
J99
H33-2
H6-7
J162
547
J152
G30

2 **Electronic control module ground and voltage supply check**

- Disconnect the electronic control module connector.
  The ignition timing is in the On position.
  Take a voltage reading at the electronic control module sensor connector. Connect the voltmeter,

- between B+ and pin 15 = <0.5V
- between B+ and pin 17 = <0.5V
- between B+ and pin 18 = <0.5V
- between pin 16 and B- = <0.1V
- between pin 19 and B- = <0.1V

Are the voltage ratings OK?

YES Continue with point 3.

NO Check and rectify the wiring including the connector and grounding points.

3 **Final inspection**

- Erase the diagnostic trouble code.
- Carry out the driving cycle, drive the car with various load and engine speeds for 5 minutes.
- Read the diagnostic trouble code.

Is the diagnostic trouble code stored?

YES Test Procedure Prior To Replacing ECM

NO The diagnostic procedure performed is right or the fault is of intermittent character.

SA4029600082020X

Fig. 28 Code B2465: Pump Motor Faulty (Part 2 of 2)

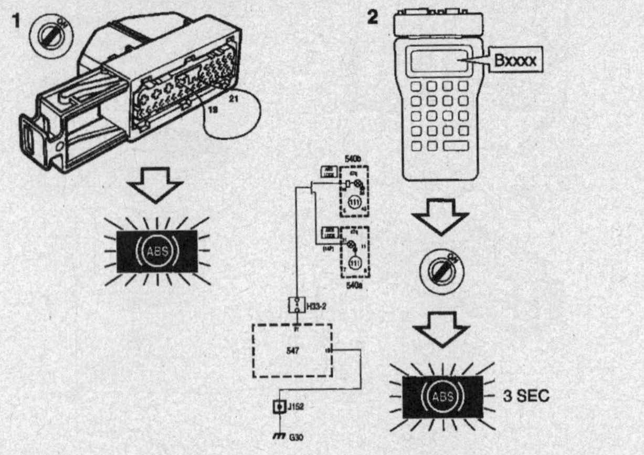
1
2
Bxxxx
3 SEC
540b
540a
H33-2
547
J152
G30

Fault symptom

The lamp test is carried out with the ignition timing on.
ABS-lamp should be on for approx. 3 seconds.
ABS lamps fails to come on.

Condition

- Open-circuit in the electrical circuit.

Diagnostic help

ABS lamp can be activated with the ISAT Scan Tool
Select "ACTIVATE"
Select "ABS LAMP"

Diagnostic procedure

1 **ABS lamp operation check**

- Remove electronic control module connector
  The ignition timing is in the ON position.
- Interconnect a loop between pin 21 and pin 19 in the electronic control module sensor connector.
  The ABS lamp should come on.

Does the lamp come on?

YES Check the electronic control module connector for damp, corrosion and dislodged contact pins. Continue with point 2..

NO Inspect the cable between pin 21 of the ABS electronic control module and pin 16 of the main instrument. If the cable is not faulty, continue the fault diagnosis

2 **Final inspection**

- Make a operations check of the ABS lamp with the ignition timing switched on.

Does the lamp come on?

YES The diagnostic procedure taken is right.

NO on Test Procedure Prior To Replacing ECM

SA4029600083000X

Fig. 29 ABS Lamp Not Operating

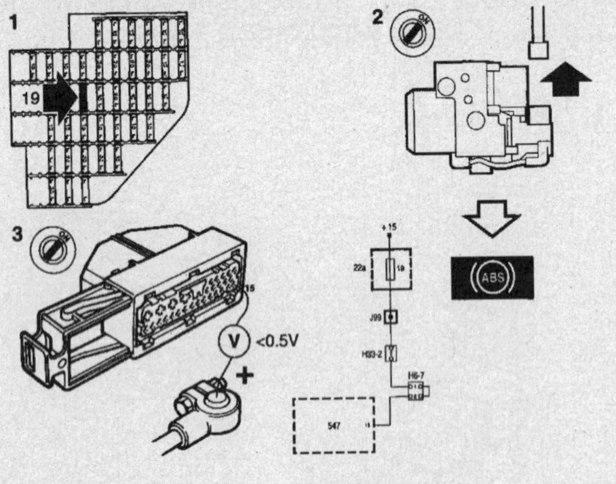
1
19
2
3
<0.5V
+
+15
22a
J99
H33-2
H6-7
547

Fault symptom

The ABS lamp is on constantly.

Condition

- Short circuit to ground in the electrical circuit.
- The ABS electronic control module faults +15 voltage (pin 15).

Diagnostic procedure

1 **Inspection of fuses**

- Check that fuse 19 is intact.

Is fuse 19 intact?

YES Continue with point 2.

NO Replace fuse.

2 **ABS lamp operation check**

- Disconnect the electronic control module connector.
  The ignition timing is in the On position.

Is the ABS lamp on?

YES Inspect the conductors between pin 21 of the electronic control module and pin 16 of the main instrument.
If the cable is not faulty, continue fault diagnosis

NO Continue with point 3.

3 **The electronic control module +15 voltage supply check.**

- The ignition timing is in the ON position.
  Take a voltage measurement between B+ and the electronic control module sensor connector, pin 15.
  The voltage should be <0.5V.

Is the voltage correct?

YES Continue with point 5.

NO Continue with point 4.

SA4029600084010X

Fig. 30 ABS Lamp On At All Times (Part 1 of 2)

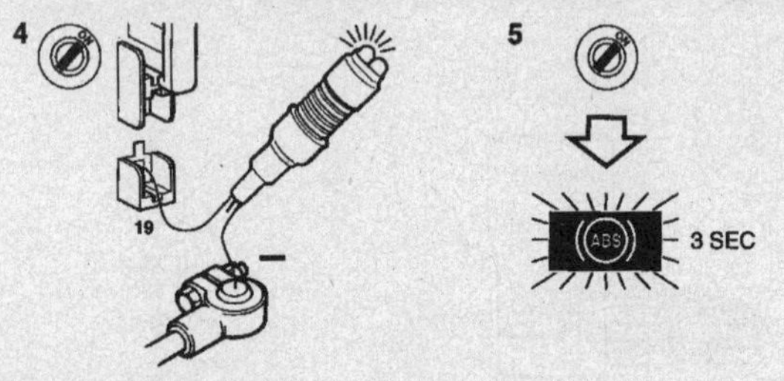
4
5
19
-
3 SEC

4 **Check the +15-voltage supply**

- Check that there is a +15-voltage at fuse 19.
  The ignition timing is in the ON position.
  Connect the test lamp between fuse 19 and a definite grounding point.

Does the test lamp come on?

YES Check and rectify the cable including the connector between fuse 19 and pin 15 of the electronic control module.

NO Continue fault diagnosis

5 **Final inspection**

- Make a operations check of the ABS lamp with the ignition timing switched on.

Does the ABS lamp operate correctly?

YES The diagnostic procedure taken was correct

NO Continue With "Test Procedure Prior To Replacing ECM"

SA4029600084020X

Fig. 30 ABS Lamp On At All Times (Part 2 of 2)

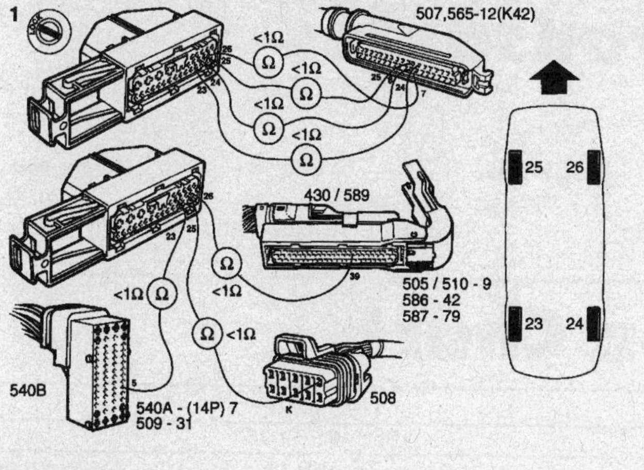
1
507,565-12(K42)
<1Ω
<1Ω
<1Ω
<1Ω
430 / 589
505 / 510 - 9
586 - 42
587 - 79
<1Ω
<1Ω
<1Ω
540B
540A - (14P) 7
509 - 31
508
25
26
23
24

Fault symptom

The diagnostic trouble code for one of the other electronic systems in the car displays that there is no speed signal.

Condition

- Open/short-circuit in the electrical circuit.

Diagnostic procedure

1 **Cable inspection**

- Remove the electronic control module connector.
Remove the connector to the electronic control module that detected the faulty wheel speed.
Make a continuity test on the cables between the respective electronic control module.

Is the cable OK?

YES Continue with point 2.

NO Rectify the fault

SA4029600085010X

Fig. 31 No Wheel Speed Signal (Part 1 of 2)

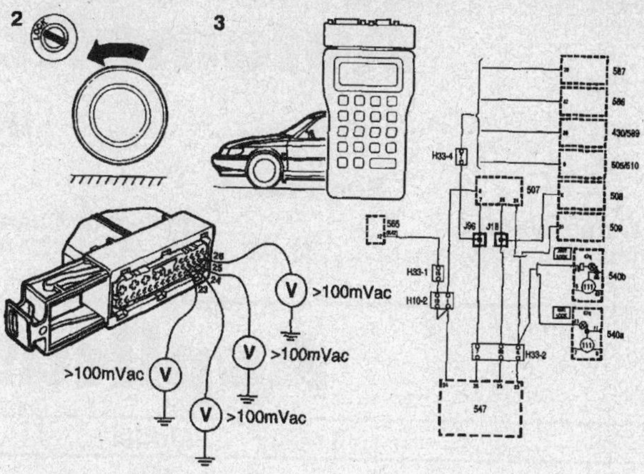
2
3
>100mVac
>100mVac
>100mVac
>100mVac

2 **Wheel speed signal check**

- Connect the ABS electronic control module
Lift the car
Take a voltage measurement, mVac, at the particular connector pin that detected the faulty wheel speed in the electronic control module.
Rotate the wheel concerned by hand at 1 turn a second. The voltmeter should show a reading of I100 mVac.

Is the voltage OK?

YES Continue the fault diagnosis in the appropriate service manual

NO Continue with point 3.

3 **Final inspection**

- *Make an operation check.*

- Erase the diagnostic trouble code in the system concerned
- Drive the car with varying loads and engine speeds for approx. 5 minutes.
  - *Check if the fault symptom remains.*

Do the fault symptoms remain?

YES Continue With "Test Procedure Prior To Replacing ECM"

NO The diagnostic procedure taken is right.

SA4029600085020X

Fig. 31 No Wheel Speed Signal (Part 2 of 2)

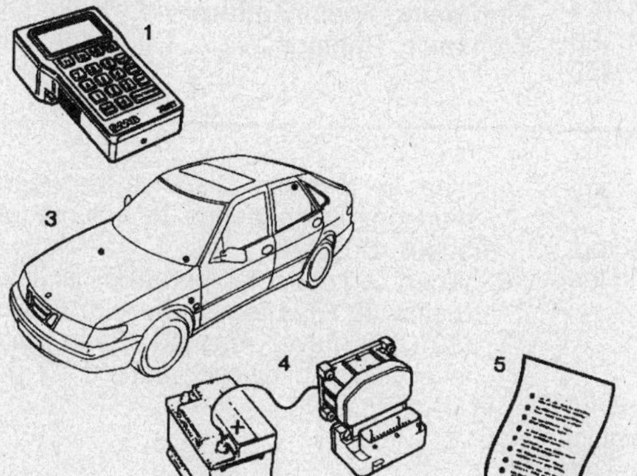
1
3
4
5

When all tests have been completed in accordance with the rectification program to the particular diagnostic trouble code or through service manual fault diagnosis, without any fault being traced, it is natural to assume that the electronic control module is faulty.

Observe the following points before you definitely identify the ABS electronic control module as the cause of the problem.

1 Check once again that all tests in the codes fault diagnostic scheme have been carried out.

2 Study the particular circuits wiring diagram and familiarise yourself with its operation.

wiring diagram.

3 When fitting or removing the electronic control module be aware of its sensitivity to electrostatic discharge.

4 Check all grounding points and the voltage supply to the electronic control module. If you have checked this before, check it once again.

5 If the suggested diagnostic procedure routine fails to correctly rectify the problem, attempt to trace the problem through testing and analyse "Test reading, electronic control module connections".

6

Be very reluctant to change the electronic control module.

Think through all likely fault reasons before replacing the electronic control module!

7 If the original fault remains, despite that, the ABS electronic control module must be changed.

SA4029600086000X

Fig. 32 Test Procedure Prior To ECM Replacement

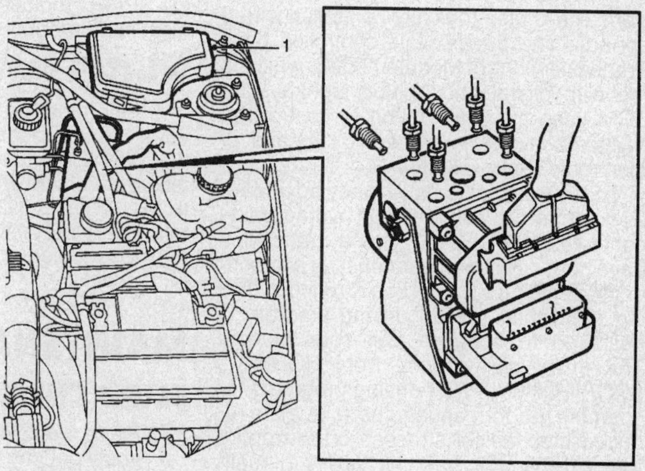
1

SA4029600087000X

Fig. 33 Hydraulic unit replacement

Automatic Transaxles

INDEX

	Page No.
Aisin-Warner 50-40LE Automatic Transaxle	38-150
Application Chart	38-150
Borg-Warner 37 Automatic Transaxle	38-155
ZF4-HP-18 Automatic Transaxle	38-159

Application Chart

Year	Model	Transaxle
1993	900	Borg-Warner 37
	9000	ZF 4-HP-18
1994-96	900	Aisin-Warner 50-40 LE
	9000	ZF 4-HP-18

Aisin-Warner 50-40LE Automatic Transaxle

INDEX

	Page No.
Adjustments	38-150
Kickdown Function	38-151
Shift-Lock Solenoid, Replace	38-150
Transaxle Range Switch	38-150
Description	38-150
Sport Switch	38-150
Winter Switch	38-150
In-Vehicle Repairs	38-151
Solenoid	38-151
Valve Housing	38-151
Maintenance	38-150
Fluid Check	38-150
Shift Lock System	38-154
Diagnosis & Testing	38-154
Solenoid, Replace	38-154
Tightening Specifications	38-154
Transaxle, Replace	38-151

DESCRIPTION

The Aisin-Warner 50-40LE automatic transaxle is electronically-controlled with 4 speeds. The transaxle is controlled by a Transaxle Control Module (TCM), which is fed with digital and analog signals. The TCM uses this information to control the transaxle hydraulic system by means of electronic control signals.

These transaxles have many advantages compared to conventional hydraulically-controlled transaxles. These transaxles have better quality of gear shifting and softer gear shifting since torque is reduced during gear shifting. The driving program is designed to optimize fuel consumption. The driver can choose from NORMAL, SPORT OR WINTER driving programs for optimum performance. There is also reduced mechanical stresses on the entire transaxle and it has the ability of self-diagnosis and to store diagnostic codes.

SPORT SWITCH

A spring-loaded switch in the selector knob allows the driver to switch between NORMAL and SPORT gear shifting programs. NORMAL is always connected from the start. The SPORT program means the transaxle stays longer in each gear than normal and the gear shifting points are adapted for performance.

When the SPORT program is selected, the SPORT indicator lamp comes on in the main instrument.

WINTER SWITCH

A spring-loaded switch in the selector lever's console enables the driver to select the WINTER gear shifting program. This aids the vehicle when starting on slippery roads. When activated, the transaxle is automatically prevented from engaging in first and second gears. The vehicle is started in third gear.

MAINTENANCE

FLUID CHECK

1. Place vehicle on level surface and apply parking brake.
2. Transaxle fluid should be at operating temperature (176°F or 80°C). This is reached after driving about 12.4 miles.
3. Clean fluid dipstick with lint-free cloth, then reinsert.
4. Fluid level should read between MIN and MAX markings on side of oil dipstick marked °C.
5. If necessary, top off fluid with Dexron II type automatic transaxle fluid through pipe in dipstick. Distance between markings corresponds to volume of about .42 quarts.
6. When outdoor temperature is low (below 32°F), a temperature of 176°F (80°C) is never reached. Read fluid level on side of dipstick marked °C.

ADJUSTMENTS

TRANSAXLE RANGE SWITCH

If arrow on transaxle lever does not correspond to marking on transaxle range switch, adjust the switch.

1. Remove dipstick from lever.
2. Loosen transaxle range switch screw.
3. Turn switch so marking corresponds to arrow on lever, then tighten screw to specifications.
4. Install dipstick to lever.

SHIFT-LOCK SOLENOID, REPLACE

1. Remove floor and center consoles.
2. Release wiring by cutting cable tie.
3. Loosen solenoid screws.

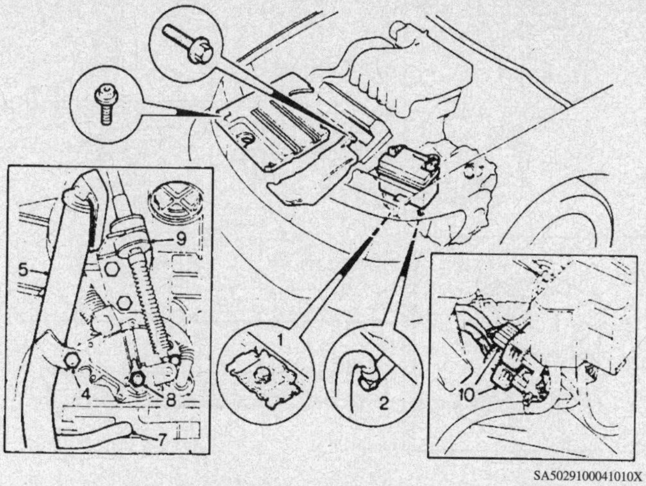
9
5
1
2
10
4
8
7
SA5029100041010X
Fig. 1 Transaxle removal (Part 1 of 5)

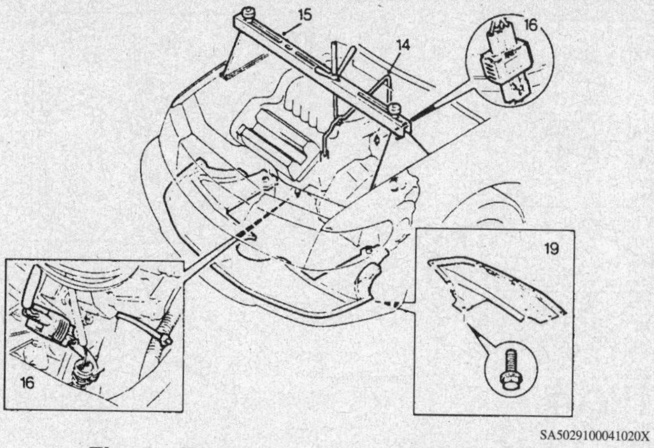
15
14
16
19
16
SA5029100041020X
Fig. 1 Transaxle removal (Part 2 of 5)

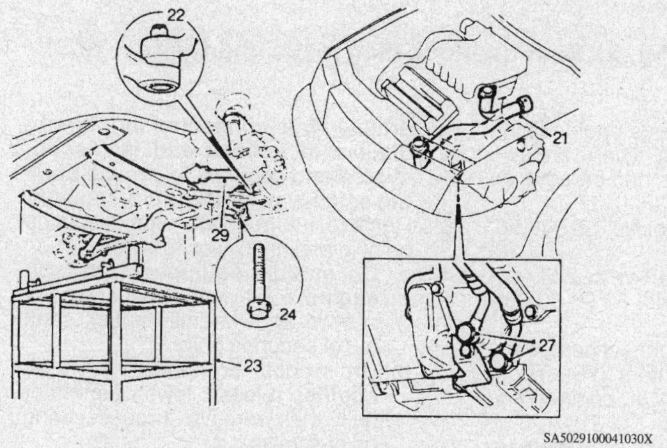
22
21
29
24
23
27
SA5029100041030X
Fig. 1 Transaxle removal (Part 3 of 5)

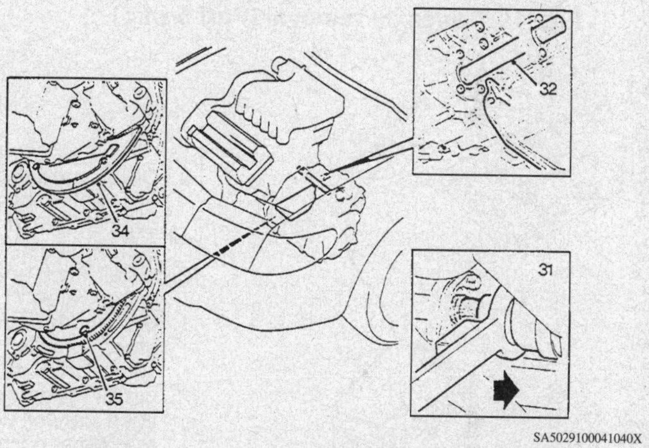
32
34
31
35
SA5029100041040X
Fig. 1 Transaxle removal (Part 4 of 5)

4. When hook is in bottom position, distance to pin should be 1-2 mm.
5. Tighten solenoid screws to specification, then install floor and center consoles.

KICKDOWN FUNCTION

1. **On models equipped with 2.3L engine,** remove resonator.
2. **On all models,** press down on accelerator pedal so it exactly reaches kickdown switch.
3. Check that it is easy to press pedal to kick-down switch. If it is not, throttle cable may be improperly adjusted.
4. Check that throttle is fully open. If not, continue this procedure to adjust throttle cable.
5. Release accelerator pedal and check for slack in throttle cable. If there is no slack, remove lower part of fascia and adjust with help of accelerator pedal setting screw on upper part of pedal.
6. Start vehicle and check idling speed.
7. Install lower part of fascia, then the resonator.

IN-VEHICLE REPAIRS

VALVE HOUSING

1. **On models equipped with 2.5L engine,** remove engine cover.
2. **On all models,** remove transaxle venting hose.
3. Install suitable lift to engine, then raise and support vehicle.
4. Remove spoiler shields, then the engine mounting securing bolts.
5. Remove grounding cable and engine console securing bolts.
6. Place oil pan under transaxle, then remove cooling hoses. Plug hoses and turn to one side.
7. Remove transaxle temperature sensor to valve housing cover bolt.
8. Remove eight remaining bolts.
9. Remove valve housing cover and turn it to right of engine mounting. Use rubber mallet to knock out cover.
10. Remove nine valve housing securing screws. **Start with two screws at bottom left holding cover for oil channels. Save two upper screws for last.**
11. Carefully remove selector lever manual valve from lifting eye.
12. Carefully remove valve housing. **Ensure two O-rings from inside valve housing do not fall out.**
13. Reverse procedure to install, noting the following:
    a. Clean any old sealant residue from contact surfaces of valve housing cover and transaxle. Place string of sealant on transaxle contact surface.
    b. Ensure all oil is removed from surface so sealant will adhere in thin and even layer. If transaxle has been removed, sealant can be applied to contact surface of cover.

SOLENOID

1. Remove valve housing cover as outlined under "Valve Housing."
2. Disconnect solenoid electrical connector.
3. Remove solenoid screw, then the solenoid with screwdriver.
4. Reverse procedure to install. Tighten solenoid screw to specifications.

TRANSAXLE

REPLACE

1. Remove battery, then the battery negative cable secured to automatic transaxle valve housing. Negative cable securing bolt also secures valve housing.
2. **On models equipped with 2.3L engine,** remove cable securing point from dipstick.
3. **On all models,** remove dipstick securing screw (4), then pull dipstick and dipstick sleeve straight up (5), **Fig. 1.** Plug dipstick hole on transaxle.

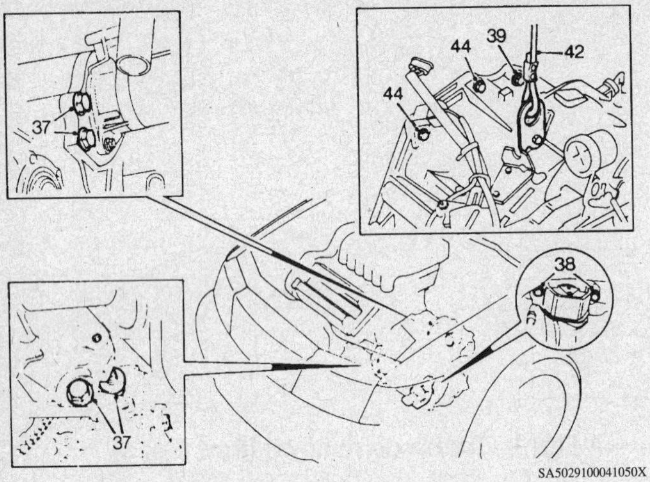
37
44
39
42
44
38
37
SA5029100041050X

Fig. 1 Transaxle removal (Part 5 of 5)

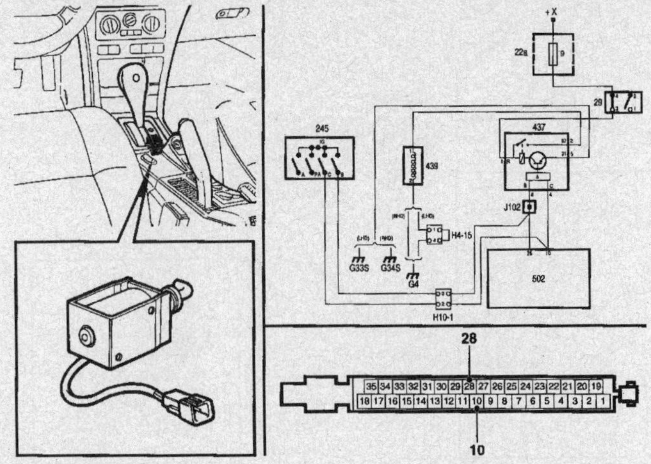
+X
22a
29
245
437
439
J102
H4-15
G33S
G34S
G4
502
H10-1
28
10

Fault symptom

The selector lever cannot be moved away from position P.

SA5029600070010X

Fig. 2 Shift interlock diagnostic chart (Part 1 of 6)

1

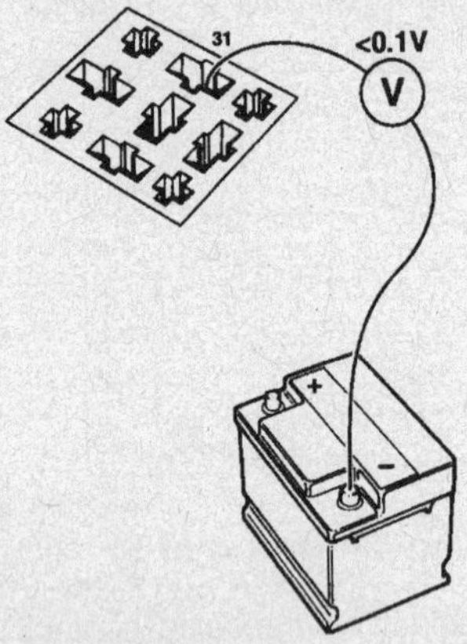
31
<0.1V
V
+
-

Procedure

1 **Check the relay's connection to ground**

- Remove the shift-lock relay, mounted in the main fuse box in the dashboard.
- Check the relay's connection to ground and rectify it if necessary.
- Connect a voltmeter to pin 31 of the relay socket and battery negative (B-). The reading obtained should be less than 0.1 V.

Is the voltage reading OK?

YES Continue with point 2.

NO Check and repair or replace the lead between pin 31 of the relay socket and grounding point G34S (RHD) or G33S (LHD). Then proceed to point 6.

SA5029600070020X

Fig. 2 Shift interlock diagnostic chart (Part 2 of 6)

4. Remove venting hose (7), then the selector lever arm (8) from transaxle.
5. Remove wire from transaxle securing point (9), then move wire to one side.
6. Disconnect transaxle electrical connectors (one gray and one black,10).
7. Disconnect straps holding cables on transaxle.
8. **On models equipped with 2.3L engine,** remove engine air filter housing.
9. **On all models,** remove engine lifting eye rubber bushings. There are two eyes on 2.5L engines and one eye on 2.3L engines.
10. Install lifting beam tool No. 83 948 50, or equivalent (14).
11. **On models equipped with 2.5L engine,** fit holder tool No. 83 94 835, or equivalent (15).
12. **On all models,** disconnect heated oxygen sensor connectors (16). There are two sensors on 2.5L engines and one on 2.3L engines.
13. Raise and support vehicle, then remove both front wheels.
14. Remove spoiler shields and middle spoiler shield in front right wheel housing secured by three screws (19).
15. **On models equipped with 2.3L engine,** remove heated oxygen sensor cable securing point from front end of engine.
16. **On all models,** remove front part of exhaust pipe (21).
17. Disconnect subframe securing point for wheel housing pivots, then remove two subframe securing points on engine (22).
18. Install suitable lifting device under subframe (23), then remove six remaining subframe securing screws (24).
19. Lower lifting device about 2 cm, then release frame from pivots and remove.
20. Remove transaxle oil cooler inlet and outlet hoses (27). Plug inlet and outlet holes on transaxle. Plug hoses and turn upward.
21. Remove left driveshaft (29) from transaxle by releasing from splines and carefully pulling straight out from splines by hand. Plug driveshaft inlet hole on transaxle with plastic plug.
22. Secure driveshaft to vehicle body so it does not hang in way to be damaged when vehicle is lowered.
23. Separate right driveshaft from intermediate shaft securing point in engine, including spacers (31). **Right driveshaft is connected to intermediate with splines and is disconnected and secured to vehicle body the same way as the left driveshaft.**
24. Remove intermediate shaft securing point in engine (32) as follows:
    a. **On models equipped with 2.5L engine,** remove two securing point screws and carefully knock shaft out of securing point.
    b. **On models equipped with 2.3L engine,** release lower generator bolt, then remove three securing point screws.
    c. Turn generator upward and force out securing point to free two guide pins.
    d. Pull out intermediate shaft with securing point.
25. **On all models,** plug inlet hole with plastic plug.
26. Remove two screws, then the actuator cover between engine and transaxle (34) to free torque converter securing point on actuator.
27. Remove six torque converter to actuator screws (35). **Engine must be turned to reach all screws.**
28. Install special tool to hold torque converter in place while removing transaxle. For 2.5L engines, use specially made grip. For 2.3L engines, use torque converter fixing tool No. 87 92 277, or equivalent.
29. Remove lower transaxle to engine securing bolts (37). 2.3L engines have two bolts, and 2.5L engines have four bolts.
30. Remove front engine mounting bolts (38), then the rear bolt from three upper securing bolts (39).
31. Lower vehicle.
32. Lower engine and transaxle with lifting beam to create gap of about 10 cm between vehicle body and transaxle front mounting. Gap can be seen from front lefthand wheel housing.
33. Install lifting wire tool No. 87 92 251, or

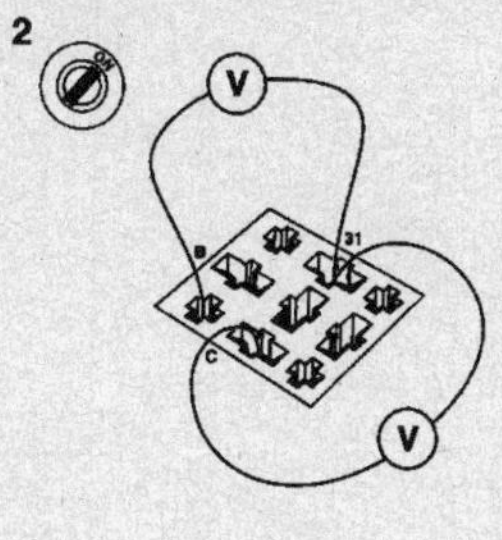
2
V
B
31
C
V

2 **Check the relay's signal inputs**

- Check and, if necessary, rectify the relay's inputs from the gear selector position sensor.
- With the ignition switch turned to the ON position, connect a voltmeter to the relay socket across
  • pin B - pin 31
  • pin C - pin 31
  and move the selector lever through all gear positions. Nominal voltage readings are as in the following table:

	pin B - pin 31	pin C - pin 31
P	< 0.5 V	< 0.5 V
R	12 V	< 0.5 V
N	12 V	< 0.5 V
D	12 V	12 V
3	12 V	12 V
2	< 0.5 V	12 V
1	< 0.5 V	12 V

A fault in connections B and C can generate diagnostic trouble code P0705. The CHECK GEARBOX lamp is on and the system's emergency operation program (limp home mode) has been activated.

Are the voltage readings OK?

YES Continue with point 3.

NO Check and, if necessary, rectify the wiring harness between pins B and C of the relay socket and contacts B and C of the gear selector position sensor. If the wiring harness is OK, the gear selector position sensor will have to be adjusted.
Then proceed to point 6.

SA5029600070030X

Fig. 2 Shift interlock diagnostic chart (Part 3 of 6)

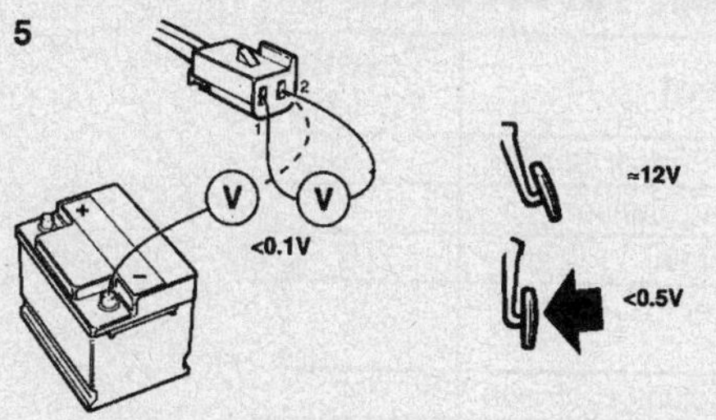
5
2
1
V
V
<0.1V
≈12V
<0.5V

5 **Check the lifting electromagnet's wiring**

- Check and, if necessary, rectify the lifting electromagnet and associated wiring.
  The lifting electromagnet is located in the selector lever housing.
- Unplug the lifting electromagnet's connector.
- Connect a voltmeter to the female connector across
  • pin 2 and battery negative (B-). Should be less than 0.1 V.
  • pins 1 and 2. Should be ≈ B+ (battery positive) when the brake pedal is not depressed and less than 0.5 V when it is depressed.

Are the voltage readings OK?

YES Change the lifting electromagnet and continue with point 6.

NO Change the shift-lock relay and continue with point 6.

6 **Final check**

Check whether the fault symptom persists.

Does the fault symptom persist?

YES Continue as described under "Before changing an electronic control module".

NO The remedial action taken was correct.

SA5029600070060X

Fig. 2 Shift interlock diagnostic chart (Part 6 of 6)

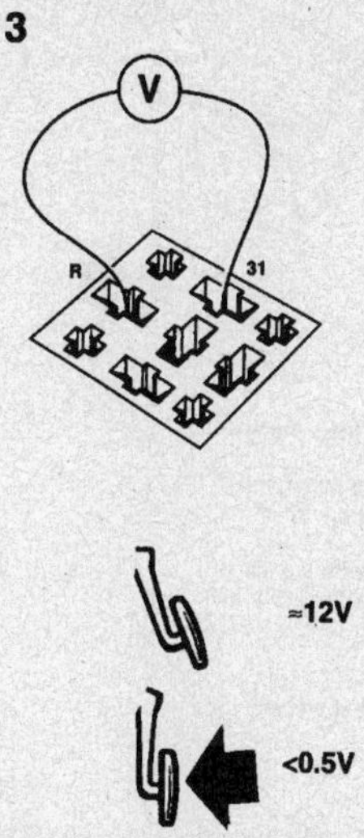
3
V
R
31
≈12V
<0.5V

3 **Check the relay's input from the brake light switch.**

With the ignition switch in the ON position, connect a voltmeter to the relay socket across pins R and 31. Depress the brake pedal.
With the brake pedal not depressed, a reading of battery positive (B+) should be obtained. With the brake pedal depressed, a reading of less than 0.5 V should be obtained.

Are the readings correct?

YES Continue with point 4.

NO Check
- that fuse 9 is intact and supplied with power, using a test lamp.
- the brake light switch. It might have to be adjusted or changed.
- the wiring
and proceed to point 6.

SA5029600070040X

Fig. 2 Shift interlock diagnostic chart (Part 4 of 6)

equivalent, to transaxle rear securing holes (42), then the wire to lifting device.

34. Tighten with lifting device, then remove remaining two upper securing bolts (44).
35. Remove transaxle from engine by carefully inching it loose and lifting it down.
36. Unhook lifting wire from device, then raise and support vehicle and pull out transaxle.
37. Remove lifting wire from transaxle, then the tool holding torque converter in place.
38. Reverse procedure to install, noting the following:
    a. Ensure no cables are in the way when transaxle is lifted into vehicle.
    b. Check upper generator bolt after transaxle has been installed.
    c. After installing driveshaft, check that spline connections has "clicked in" by pulling at wheel housing.
    d. **On models equipped with 2.3L engine,** ensure oxygen sensor cable is pulled behind lower water pipe so cable cannot move forward onto exhaust pipe.
    e. **On models equipped with 2.5L**

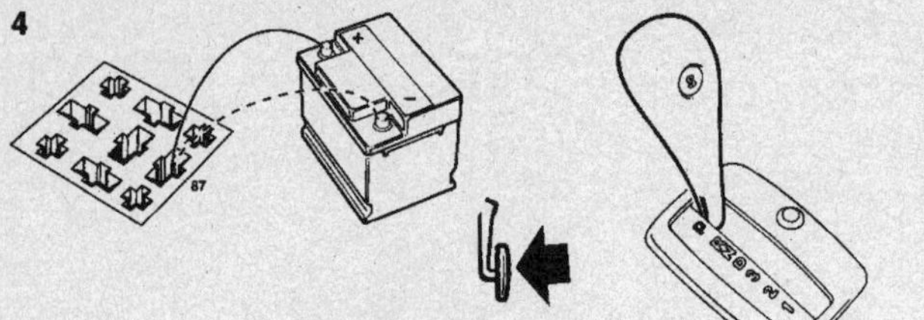
4
87

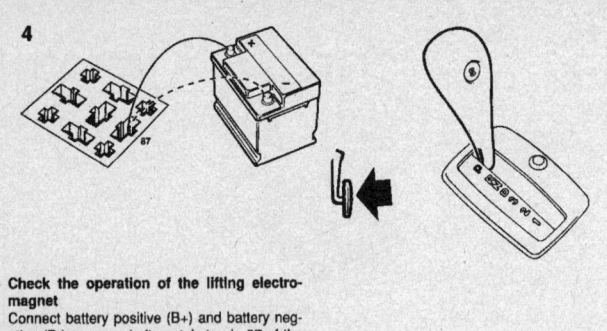

4 **Check the operation of the lifting electromagnet**
Connect battery positive (B+) and battery negative (B-) or ground alternately to pin 87 of the relay socket.
Battery positive (B+) should activate the lifting electromagnet and battery negative (B-) or ground should cause it to release.

Does the electromagnet work?

YES — Change the shift-lock relay and proceed to point 6.

NO — Continue with point 5.

SA5029600070050X

Fig. 2 Shift interlock diagnostic chart (Part 5 of 6)

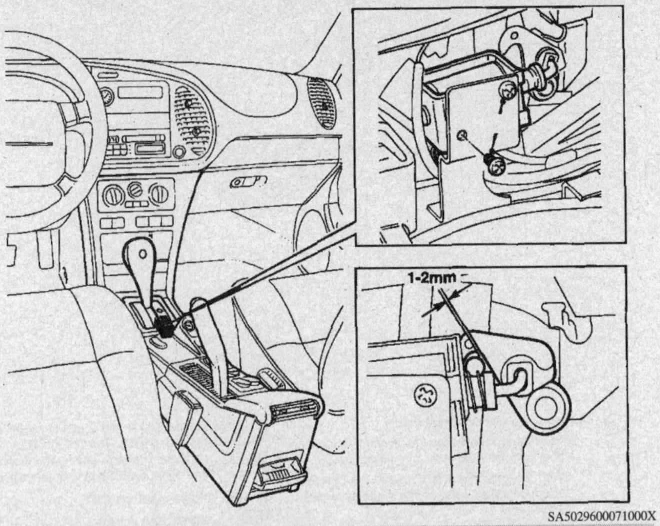
1-2mm

SA5029600071000X

Fig. 3 Shift interlock solenoid replacement

engine, ensure front oxygen sensor cable is pulled behind lower water pipe so cable cannot move forward onto exhaust pipe.

SHIFT LOCK SYSTEM

DIAGNOSIS & TESTING

When performing diagnosis and testing of shift lock system, refer to **Fig. 2.**

SOLENOID, REPLACE

1. Disconnect battery ground cable.
2. Remove floor center console.
3. Remove shift lock solenoid, **Fig. 2.**
4. Reverse procedure to install noting the following:
   a. Measure distance between hook and pin when hook is in bottom position. Distance should be 1–2 mm.
   b. Install solenoid and consoles.

TIGHTENING SPECIFICATIONS

Year	Component	Torque/ Ft. Lbs.
1994-96	Input Shaft To Speed Sensor Screw	5
	Output Speed Shaft Sensor	5
	Solenoid Screw	5
	Torque Converter Cover To Actuator Screws	5
	Torque Converter To Actuator Screws	37
	Transaxle Fluid Temperature Sensor Cover Screw	19
	Transaxle Fluid Temperature Sensor Screw	19
	Transaxle Range Switch	19
	Transaxle To Oil Cooler Hose	16
	Transaxle Upper Securing Bolts	55
	Valve Housing Cover Screws	19
	Valve Housing Screws	5

Borg-Warner 37 Automatic Transaxle

INDEX

	Page No.
Adjustments	38-156
Downshift Cable, Adjust	38-157
Front Band, Adjust	38-157
Manual Linkage, Adjust	38-156
Rear Band, Adjust	38-157
Identification	38-155
In-Vehicle Repairs	38-157
Governor Assembly	38-157
Valve Body	38-157
Maintenance	38-156
Fluid Change	38-156
Fluid Check	38-156
Precautions	38-155
Radio Anti-Theft Lock	38-155
Tightening Specifications	38-158
Transaxle, Replace	38-157

	Page No.
Troubleshooting	38-155
Delayed Or No 1-2 Shift	38-155
Delayed Or No 2-3 Shift	38-155
Drag Or Binding On 2-3 Shift	38-155
Drags In R	38-156
Drive In 1 But Not In D Or 2	38-155
Harsh Engagement In D, 1, 2 & R	38-155
Harsh Gear Shifts	38-155
Loss Of Performance & Overheating In D	38-156
No Drive In D, 2, 1 & R	38-155
No Drive In R	38-156
No Park	38-156
No 2-1 Downshift	38-156

	Page No.
No 3-2 Downshift	38-156
Slip, Breakaway Noise Or Shudder On Acceleration In 1	38-156
Slip, Breakaway Noise Or Shudder On Acceleration In R	38-156
Slip, Breakaway Noise Or Shudder On Full Throttle Acceleration In D Or 2	38-156
Slips In R	38-156
Slips On 1-2 Shift	38-155
Slips On 2-3 Shift	38-155
Transaxle Downshifts Too Easily	38-156
Transaxle Will Not Downshift	38-156

PRECAUTIONS

RADIO ANTI-THEFT LOCK

9000

1995-96

Radio and cassette player are equipped with an electronic four-digit anti-theft lock. This four-digit code is programmed at manufacturing and cannot be changed. If the battery is disconnected for more than three minutes, if unit is removed or if otherwise cut off from power, the four-digit code must be entered with the quick-selection buttons as follows:

1. Turn radio on, then, when display shows "Code In, " enter four-digit code with quick-selection buttons. If code is correct, last-tuned radio frequency is shown on display. If wrong digit has been entered by mistake, all four digits must be entered again. If code is wrong it stays on display.
2. If incorrect four-digit code has been entered, press Band button for more than three seconds to clear display. Display shows "Code In" and new attempt to enter correct code can be made.
3. If wrong code has been used three times in succession, four dashes appear on display and you must wait an hour with radio switched on before trying again.
4. To try again, hold Band button for at least three seconds. "Code In" should appear on display.
5. Correct code must be entered at first attempt, otherwise you must wait another hour with unit switched on before trying again.

IDENTIFICATION

Refer to **Fig. 1** for transaxle identification.

TROUBLESHOOTING

HARSH ENGAGEMENT IN D, 1, 2 & R

1. High idle speed.
2. Improperly adjusted downshift cable.
3. Incorrect line pressure or pressure rise.

DRIVE IN 1 BUT NOT IN D OR 2

1. Improperly adjusted manual linkage.
2. Incorrect fluid level.
3. Improperly adjusted downshift cable.
4. Dirty valve body passages.
5. Worn front clutch and seals.
6. Worn forward sun gear sealing rings.
7. Leaking or missing driven shaft cup plug.
8. Worn or damaged front pump and drive tangs.
9. Leaking pump inlet pipe.
10. Defective one-way clutch.

NO DRIVE IN D, 2, 1 & R

1. Improperly adjusted manual linkage.
2. Incorrect fluid level.
3. Incorrect downshift cable adjustment.
4. Dirty valve body passages.
5. Worn front clutch and seals.
6. Worn forward sun gear sealing rings.
7. Leaking or missing driven shaft cup plug.
8. Worn or damaged front pump and drive tangs.
9. Defective one-way clutch.
10. Leak at pump inlet pipe.

DELAYED OR NO 1-2 SHIFT

1. Incorrect downshift cable adjustment.
2. Dirty governor passages.
3. Dirty valve body passages.
4. Incorrect front band adjustment.
5. Leaking front servo seals or tubes.

SLIPS ON 1-2 SHIFT

1. Improper fluid level.
2. Incorrect downshift cable adjustment.
3. Incorrect front band adjustment.
4. Leaking front servo seals or tubes.
5. Worn front band.
6. Dirty valve body or sticking valves.

DELAYED OR NO 2-3 SHIFT

1. Incorrect downshift cable adjustment.
2. Dirty governor passages.
3. Dirty valve body passages.
4. Incorrect front band adjustment.
5. Leaking front servo seals or tubes.
6. Leaking or damaged rear clutch valve, seals or tubes.

SLIPS ON 2-3 SHIFT

1. Improper fluid level.
2. Incorrect downshift cable adjustment.
3. Incorrect front band adjustment.
4. Dirty valve body passages.
5. Leaking or damaged rear clutch valve, seal or tubes.

HARSH GEAR SHIFTS

1. Incorrect downshift cable adjustment.
2. Incorrect fluid pressure.

DRAG OR BINDING ON 2-3 SHIFT

1. Incorrect front band adjustment.
2. Leaking front servo seals or tubes.

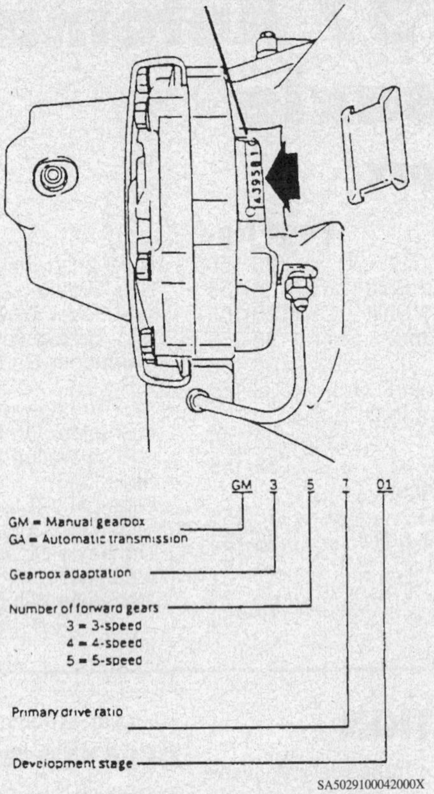
GM 3 5 7 01
GM = Manual gearbox
GA = Automatic transmission
Gearbox adaptation
Number of forward gears
3 = 3-speed
4 = 4-speed
5 = 5-speed
Primary drive ratio
Development stage
SA5029100042000X

Fig. 1 Transaxle identification

SLIP, BREAKAWAY NOISE OR SHUDDER ON FULL THROTTLE ACCELERATION IN D OR 2

1. Incorrect manual linkage adjustment.
2. Improper fluid level.
3. Incorrect downshift cable adjustment.
4. Dirty valve body passages.
5. Worn front clutch and seals.
6. Worn forward sun gear sealing rings.
7. Leaking or missing driven shaft cup plug.

LOSS OF PERFORMANCE & OVERHEATING IN D

1. Defective torque converter.

TRANSAXLE DOWNSHIFTS TOO EASILY

1. Incorrect downshift cable adjustment.

TRANSAXLE WILL NOT DOWNSHIFT

1. Incorrect downshift cable adjustment.
2. Dirty valve body passages.
3. Dirty governor valve passages.

NO 3-2 DOWNSHIFT

1. Incorrect manual linkage adjustment.
2. Incorrect front band adjustment.
3. Leaking front servo seals or tubes.
4. Worn front band.
5. Leaking or damaged rear clutch valve, seals or tubes.

NO 2-1 DOWNSHIFT

1. Improperly adjusted manual linkage.
2. Improper fluid level.
3. Improperly adjusted downshift cable.
4. Incorrect fluid pressures.
5. Incorrect rear band adjustment.
6. Leaking rear servo seals or tubes.
7. Worn rear band.

SLIP, BREAKAWAY NOISE OR SHUDDER ON ACCELERATION IN 1

1. Incorrect manual linkage adjustment.
2. Incorrect downshift cable adjustment.
3. Dirty valve body passages.
4. Worn front clutch and seals.
5. Worn forward sun gear sealing rings.
6. Leaking or missing driven shaft cup plug.

SLIP, BREAKAWAY NOISE OR SHUDDER ON ACCELERATION IN R

1. Incorrect manual linkage adjustment.
2. Improper fluid level.
3. Incorrect downshift cable adjustment.
4. Dirty valve body passages.
5. Leaking or damaged rear clutch valve, seals or tubes.

SLIPS IN R

1. Incorrect manual linkage adjustment.
2. Improper fluid level.
3. Incorrect downshift cable adjustment.
4. Incorrect rear band adjustment.
5. Leaking rear servo seals or tubes.
6. Worn rear band.

DRAGS IN R

1. Incorrect front band adjustment.

NO DRIVE IN R

1. Incorrect manual linkage adjustment.
2. Improper fluid level.
3. Incorrect downshift cable adjustment.
4. Incorrect rear band adjustment.
5. Dirty valve body passages.
6. Leaking rear servo seal or tubes.
7. Worn rear band.
8. Leaking or damaged rear clutch valve, seal or tubes.

NO PARK

1. Incorrect manual linkage adjustment.
2. Damaged or missing parking pawl, gear or internal linkage.

MAINTENANCE

FLUID CHECK

1. Ensure vehicle is on level surface.
2. Apply parking brake firmly.
3. Start engine and allow to reach normal operating temperature.
4. Shift selector lever through all positions, then place lever in park position. Do not shutdown engine during fluid level checks.
5. Clean all dirt and from dipstick cap before removing dipstick from filler tube.
6. Pull dipstick from tube, wipe clean and replace completely back in tube.
7. Remove transaxle dipstick to check fluid level, add specified fluid to raise level to full mark on dipstick. Do not overfill.

FLUID CHANGE

1. Raise and support vehicle.
2. Clean area around final drive unit and transaxle case drain plugs.
3. Using a suitable oil drain pan, remove drain plugs and completely drain fluid.
4. After fluid has stopped draining, reinstall oil drain plugs.
5. Add recommended fluid to transaxle pan through filler tube.
6. Refer to "Fluid Check" for final fluid level check.

ADJUSTMENTS

MANUAL LINKAGE, ADJUST

1. Place gearshift selector lever in N. Depress pawl button and move lever back and forth slightly until valve locks in Neutral position.
2. Hold shift lever perfectly still with pawl button depressed, and loosen cable from lever using hexagon bit adapter tool No. 8790883, or equivalent. **To gain access to cable setscrew, lift carpet.**
3. Release pawl button and move shift lever to N position.
4. Using hex bit tool No. 8790883, or equivalent, and torque wrench, tighten selector cable setscrew to specification. A notch indicating the exact location of N eases the gear selector cable adjustment.

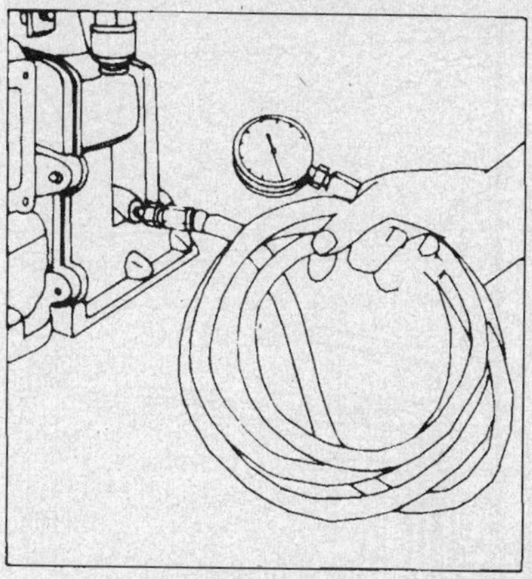

SA5029100043000X

Fig. 2 Transaxle pressure gauge connection

DOWNSHIFT CABLE, ADJUST

1. Connect a tachometer to engine and an oil pressure gauge to transaxle, **Fig. 2.**
2. Block drive wheels and apply brakes.
3. Start engine and ensure idle speed is 850 RPM.
4. Release throttle cable from throttle spindle lever and ensure throttle cable is not binding.
5. Pull cable out as far as possible to obtain maximum line pressure, then return cable to original position. If pressure does not return to basic setting, or remains above 70 psi when cable is released, the throttle must be cleaned and adjusted as necessary.
6. Attach throttle cable to spindle lever, **Fig. 3,** then place gear selector in D. Ensure cable is released so lowest pressure is obtained, then increase pressure 1.4 psi by adjusting throttle cable as necessary.
7. Shift transaxle into Park and note gauge reading. Pressures should now be 59–69 psi.

FRONT BAND, ADJUST

Up To Serial Nos. 001-1700 & 002-2800

1. Remove rear bottom cover, then loosen locknut and install .25 inch spacer (part No. 8790073) between adjusting screw and piston rod.
2. Tighten adjusting screw to specification, then back off screw one turn.
3. Tighten locknut to specification while holding adjusting screw in position.

Beginning Serial Nos. 001-1701 & 002-2801

1. Remove rear bottom cover, then loosen locknut and install .35 inch spacer (part No. 8791030) between adjusting screw and piston rod.
2. Tighten adjusting screw to specification, then tighten locknut to specification while holding adjusting screw in position.

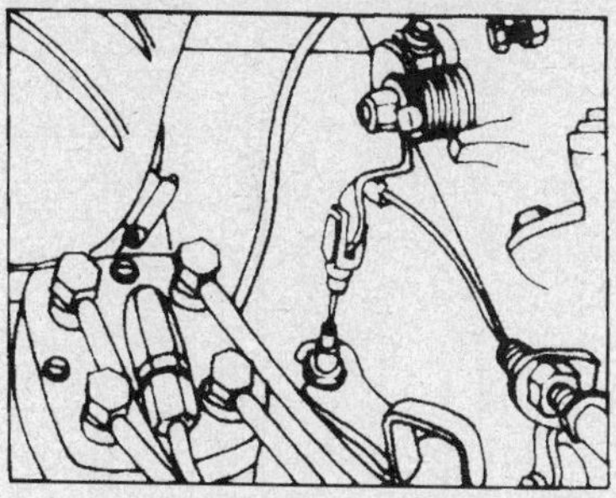

SA5029100044000X

Fig. 3 Downshift cable adjustment

REAR BAND, ADJUST

1. Loosen adjusting nut several turns.
2. Tighten adjusting screw to specification, then back off screw 1–1 ¼ turns.
3. Tighten locknut while holding adjusting screw in position, **Fig. 4.**

IN-VEHICLE REPAIRS

GOVERNOR ASSEMBLY

1. Place gearshift selector in N, then drain transaxle fluid.
2. Remove rear oil pan attaching bolts to allow residual fluid to drain.
3. Invert oil pan and remove rearward over crossmember.
4. Remove governor attaching bolts and the governor. It may be necessary to turn front wheels to gain access to governor attaching bolts.
5. Reverse procedure to install.

VALVE BODY

Up To & Including Serial Nos. 001-1700 & 002-2800

1. Raise and support vehicle.
2. Remove engine and transaxle support member, then drain transaxle fluid.
3. Remove front cover attaching bolts and the front cover.
4. Remove oil pipes 13 and 14 for front servo band from drain valve, **Fig. 5.**
5. Remove level pipes. Note position of O-ring for installation reference.
6. Remove oil strainer and magnet.
7. Remove oil pipes 5 through 12, then disconnect throttle cable.
8. Remove four valve body attaching bolts, then the valve body and accumulator as an assembly. Use care to avoid damaging oil pressure and lubrication pipes running between valve body and oil pump.
9. Reverse procedure to install. **If 2-3 drain valve was removed, install it together with pipes 15 and 16 before mounting the valve body.**

Serial Nos. above 001-1700 & 002-2800

1. Raise and support vehicle.
2. Remove engine and transaxle support member, then drain transaxle fluid.
3. Remove front cover attaching bolts and the front cover.

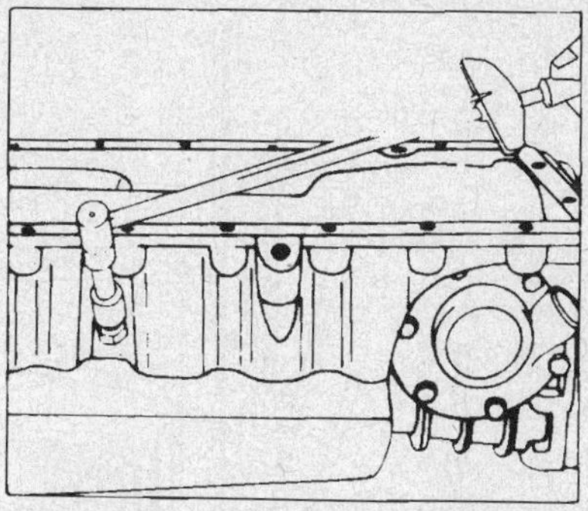

SA5029100045000X

Fig. 4 Rear band adjustment

4. Remove overflow pipes, oil pump strainer, magnet and pipes 13, 14 and 15, **Fig. 6.**
5. Remove pipe support 18, then pipes 5 through 12.
6. Disconnect throttle cable.
7. Remove two valve body attaching bolts and the valve body. Use care to avoid damaging oil pressure and lubrication pipes running between valve body and oil pump.
8. Reverse procedure to install. **If 2-3 drain valve was removed, install it together with pipes 16 and 17 before mounting the valve body.**

TRANSAXLE

REPLACE

The engine and transaxle are removed as an assembly.

1. Remove engine/transaxle assembly, as outlined under "Engine, Replace."
2. Separate engine from transaxle, proceed as follows:
   a. Drain engine oil.
   b. Remove ring gear cover, then the starter motor.
   c. Disconnect throttle cable from throttle valve housing.
   d. Remove clip securing oil filler pipe to intake manifold.
   e. Remove all engine to transaxle attaching bolts, noting length and position for assembly reference.
   f. Remove bolts securing flywheel ring gear to torque converter.
   g. Rotate driver disc so plate angles are horizontal.
   h. Carefully lift engine off transaxle. **If engine and transaxle fail to separate, do not attempt to force them apart without first ensuring all bolts are removed.**
   i. Secure torque converter using support tool No. 8790255, or equivalent.
3. Reverse procedure to install, noting the following:
   a. Ensure mating surfaces of engine and transaxle are clean and the two guide sleeves are fitted in transaxle case.
   b. Install a new gasket to transaxle mating surface. Apply sealing compound to both sides of gasket and six bolts. Refer to "Oil Pan, Replace." **Ensure bolts are correctly**

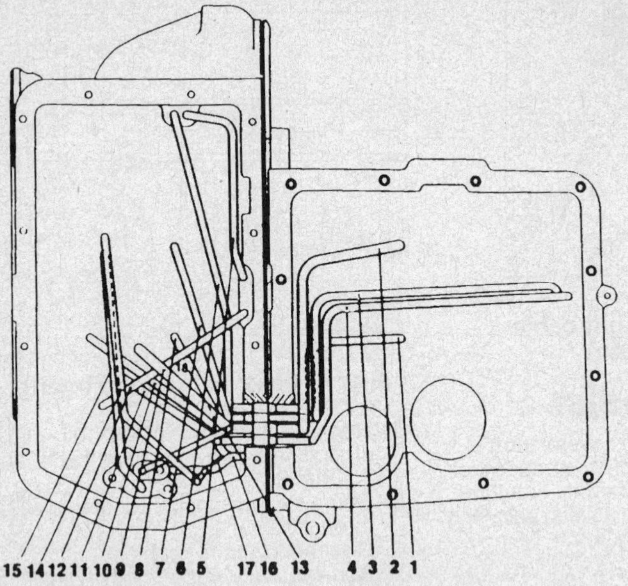
15 14 12 11 10 9 8 7 6 5 17 16 13 4 3 2 1

1. REAR LUBRICATION
2. REAR CLUTCH
3. GOVERNOR SUPPLY
4. GOVERNOR RETURN
5. FRONT LUBRICATION
6. REAR LUBRICATION
7. GOVERNOR SUPPLY
8. REAR BRAKE SERVO (OUTER HOLE)
9. REAR CLUTCH
10. REAR BRAKE SERVO (INNER HOLE)
11. GOVERNOR RETURN
12. FRONT CLUTCH
13. REAR CLUTCH, 3-2 DRAIN VALVE, BRANCH PIPE 9
14. FRONT BRAKE SERVO, RELEASE SIDE, VALVE BODY BRANCH PIPE 9
15. FRONT BRAKE SERVO, APPLY SIDE, VALVE BODY 3-2 DRAIN VALVE
16. FRONT BRAKE BAND, RELEASE SIDE 3-2 DRAIN VALVE
17. FRONT BRAKE BAND, APPLY SIDE, 3-2 VALVE
18. PIPE SUPPORT

SA5029100046000X

Fig. 5 Oil pipe installation locations. Up to & including serial Nos. 001-1700 & 002-2800

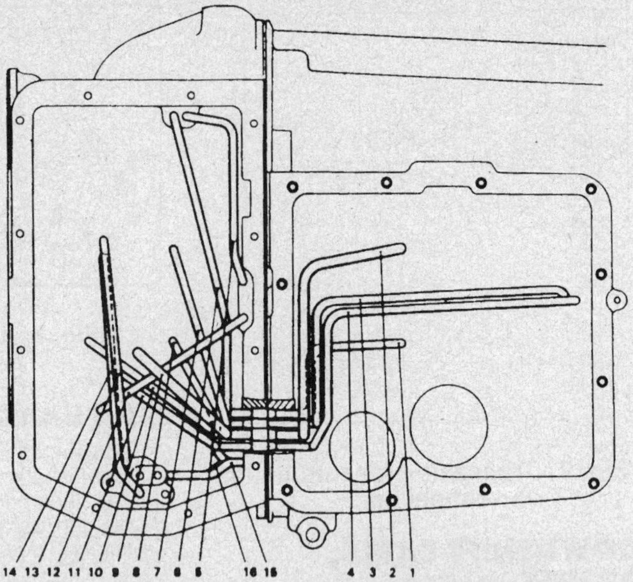
14 13 12 11 10 9 8 7 6 5 16 15 4 3 2 1

1. REAR LUBRICATION
2. REAR CLUTCH
3. GOVERNOR, SUPPLY
4. GOVERNOR, RETURN
5. FRONT LUBRICATION
6. REAR LUBRICATION
7. GOVERNOR, SUPPLY
8. REAR SERVO BAND (OUTER HOLE)
9. REAR CLUTCH
10. REAR SERVO BAND (INNER HOLE)
11. RETURN FROM GOVERNOR
12. FRONT CLUTCH
13. FRONT SERVO BAND (RELEASE SIDE, INNER HOLE, DRAIN VALVE
14. FRONT SERVO BAND (APPLY SIDE, OUTER HOLE, DRAIN VALVE
15. FRONT SERVO BAND, RELEASE SIDE
16. FRONT SERVO BAND, APPLY SIDE

SA5029100047000X

Fig. 6 Oil pipe installation locations. Serial Nos. above 001-1700 & 002-2800

installed, as bolts are different lengths.

c. Tighten engine to transaxle and power steering coupling bolts to specifications.

d. **Ensure there is at least .4 inch (10 mm) clearance around the throttle controls.**

TIGHTENING SPECIFICATIONS

Component	Torque/Ft. Lbs.
Engine To Transaxle	16-20
Front Band Adjusting Screw	12①
Front Band Adjusting Screw Locknut	17
Power Steering Coupling	15-25
Rear Band Adjusting Screw	10
Selector Cable Setscrew	20①

① — Inch lbs.

ZF 4-HP-18 Automatic Transaxle

INDEX

	Page No.
Adjustments	38-160
Brake Band Mechanism	38-160
Selector Lever	38-160
Throttle Cable	38-160
Identification	38-159
In-Vehicle Repairs	38-161
Governor Assembly	38-161
Valve Body	38-161
Maintenance	38-160
Fluid Change	38-160
Fluid Check	38-160
Tightening Specifications	38-162
Transaxle, Replace	38-161
2.0L Engine	38-161
2.3L Engine	38-161
Troubleshooting	38-159
Car Pulls Away In Neutral Position	38-159
Downshift Too Harsh	38-160
Engine Cannot Be Started	38-159
Engine Speed Flares On 4-3 Downshift	38-160
Engine Speed Flares Up On 4-3 Downshift At Part Throttle	38-160
Erratic Or Hard Shifts	38-159
Full Throttle Kickdown Shifting Too Harsh	38-160
Full Throttle Kickdown Shifting Too Slow	38-160
Harsh Jerk When Selector Lever Is Moved From N To D	38-159
Harsh Jerk When Selector Lever Moved From P To R	38-159
High Shift Point	38-160
Incorrect Full Throttle Shift Points	38-160
Incorrect Shifting Speed On Roll Out	38-160
Leakage Between Gearbox & Converter Housing	38-160
Manual Downshift Inoperative	38-160
No Drive	38-159
No Electrical Fault But Reversing Lights Do Not Light Up	38-159
No Forward/Reverse Drive, Loud Noise	38-160
No Kickdown Shift	38-160
No 1-2 Upshift	38-159
No 1-2/2-1 Shift	38-159
No 2-3 Upshift	38-159
No 2-3/3-2 Shift	38-159
No 3-4 Upshift	38-159
No 3-4/4-3 Shift	38-159
Noise In All Selector Lever Positions	38-160
Oil Dripping From Converter Housing	38-160
Parking Pawl Does Not Engage Or Slips	38-159
Reverse Gear Does Not Engage	38-159
Slipping Or Shuddering When Pulling Away	38-159
Slipping Or Vibrations When Pulling Away	38-159
Speed Dependent Noise	38-160
Throttle Cable Jams	38-160
Transaxle Binding Can Only Be Driven In Locked 1st Position	38-160
Vehicle Pulls Away In 2nd Gear	38-159
Vehicle Pulls Away In 3rd Gear	38-160

IDENTIFICATION

Refer to **Fig. 1** for transaxle identification.

TROUBLESHOOTING

ERRATIC OR HARD SHIFTS

A transaxle that exhibits erratic or hard shifts, noise when shifting, particularly on 2–3 upshift and/or clutch slipping tendencies, may indicate a radiator oil cooler failure. Refer to "Valve Body" in "In-Vehicle Repairs" section to inspect for antifreeze contamination of the transaxle.

PARKING PAWL DOES NOT ENGAGE OR SLIPS

1. Selector control or cable in correctly adjusted.
2. Excessive play at parking pawl washer.
3. Segment incorrectly fitted.
4. Excessive friction in the parking pawl mechanism.

ENGINE CANNOT BE STARTED

1. Start inhibitor switch faulty.
2. Excessive play in selector lever shaft.

REVERSE GEAR DOES NOT ENGAGE

1. Selector control or selector cable between selector lever and transaxle incorrectly adjusted.
2. Oil filter clogged.
3. Clutch B faulty.
4. Brake D faulty. No back-off braking will be obtained in position 1.
5. Binding governor.
6. Inhibitor valve 1 and R binding.

SLIPPING OR VIBRATIONS WHEN PULLING AWAY

1. Clutch B or brake D damaged.
2. Oil supply circuit to clutch B leaking.

HARSH JERK WHEN SELECTOR LEVER MOVED FROM P TO R

1. Accumulator D defective.

NO ELECTRICAL FAULT BUT REVERSING LIGHTS DO NOT LIGHT UP

1. Start inhibitor switch is defective.

CAR PULLS AWAY IN NEUTRAL POSITION

1. Selector control or cable incorrectly adjusted.

NO DRIVE

1. Selector control or cable incorrectly adjusted.
2. Oil filter clogged.
3. 3–4 shift timing valve binding.
4. Converter relief valve binding.
5. Clutch A defective.
6. 1st Gear one-way clutch slipping.

SLIPPING OR SHUDDERING WHEN PULLING AWAY

1. Clutch A damaged.
2. Seal on turbine shaft damaged.
3. O-ring of clutch A piston damaged.

HARSH JERK WHEN SELECTOR LEVER IS MOVED FROM N TO D

1. Accumulator A binding or spring failed.
2. Ball in 3–4 shift timing valve leaking.
3. Clutch A damaged.

NO 1-2/2-1 SHIFT

1. Governor binding.
2. 1–2 Upshift valve binding.

NO 1-2 UPSHIFT

1. Brake C or band C1 damaged.

NO 2-3/3-2 SHIFT

1. Governor binding.
2. 2–3 Upshift valve binding.

NO 2-3 UPSHIFT

1. Clutch E damaged.
2. Seal on engine or turbine shaft leaking.
3. Oil supply to clutch E leaking.

NO 3-4/4-3 SHIFT

1. Governor binding.
2. 3–4 upshift valve binding.

NO 3-4 UPSHIFT

1. Brake band C1 defective, and 1–2 upshift also faulty.
2. Brake Band C1 is not preloaded.
3. 2–3–4 Shift valve binding.
4. Position 3 valve binding.

VEHICLE PULLS AWAY IN 2ND GEAR

1. Governor bushing binding.

2. 1–2 Upshift valve binding.
3. Brake band C1 tightened too hard.
4. Center seal on governor flange defective.
5. Brake band C1 does not release unit.

VEHICLE PULLS AWAY IN 3RD GEAR

1. Center seal on governor flange defective.
2. Governor binding.
3. 1–2 And 2–3 upshift valves binding.
4. Intermediate plate leaking, clutch B permanently applied.
5. 2—3 Shift valve binding.
6. 2–3–4 Shift valve binding.
7. 1–2–3 Shift valve binding.

TRANSAXLE BINDING CAN ONLY BE DRIVEN IN LOCKED 1ST POSITION

1. Stuck governor.

INCORRECT SHIFTING SPEED ON ROLL OUT

1. Governor fouled.
2. Shift valves binding.
3. Leakage within governor range.

INCORRECT FULL THROTTLE SHIFT POINTS

1. Throttle cable incorrectly adjusted.

NO KICKDOWN SHIFT

1. Throttle cable incorrectly adjusted.

HIGH SHIFT POINT

1. Governor unbalance.

DOWNSHIFT TOO HARSH

1. Accumulator function defective.
2. Modulation pressure too high.
3. Clutch plates damaged.

FULL THROTTLE KICKDOWN SHIFTING TOO SLOW

1. Accumulator function defective.
2. Modulation pressure too low.
3. Clutch plates damaged.

FULL THROTTLE KICKDOWN SHIFTING TOO HARSH

1. Incorrect modulation pressure.
2. Accumulator function defective.

ENGINE SPEED FLARES UP ON 4-3 DOWNSHIFT AT PART THROTTLE

1. Throttle cable incorrectly adjusted.
2. Transaxle does not disengage.
3. Orifice control valve binding in the braking position.
4. 3-4 Shift timing valve binding.
5. Brake band incorrectly adjusted.

ENGINE SPEED FLARES ON 4-3 DOWNSHIFT

1. Improper operation of timing valve and 4-3 downshift valve.
2. Clutch A damaged.

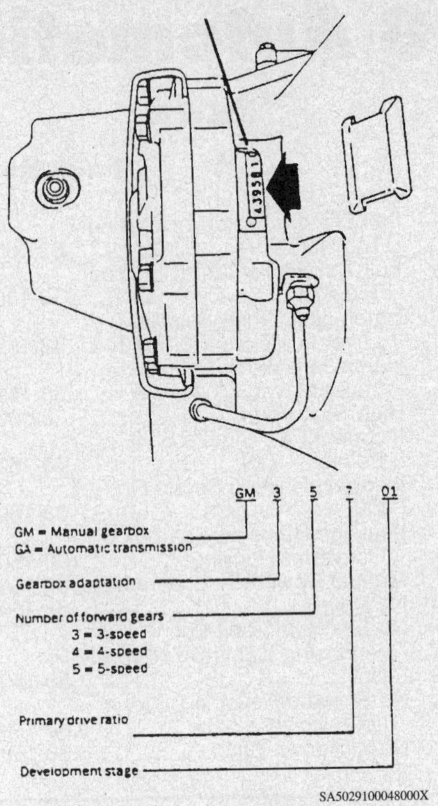

GM 3 5 7 01
GM = Manual gearbox
GA = Automatic transmission
Gearbox adaptation
Number of forward gears
3 = 3-speed
4 = 4-speed
5 = 5-speed
Primary drive ratio
Development stage
SA5029100048000X

Fig. 1 Transaxle identification

3. Accumulator function for clutch A and 4–3 shift timing valve defective.
4. Boost pressure supply incorrect.

MANUAL DOWNSHIFT INOPERATIVE

1. Inhibitor valve 2 binding.
2. Governor binding.

THROTTLE CABLE JAMS

1. Nipple in throttle cam unhooked.
2. Throttle cam deformed.
3. Throttle cam spring broken.
4. High friction in throttle cable sheath.
5. Kickdown valve binding.

NO FORWARD/REVERSE DRIVE, LOUD NOISE

1. Driveplate between converter and flywheel damaged.
2. Pump drive failure.

OIL DRIPPING FROM CONVERTER HOUSING

1. Seal in converter housing damaged.
2. Converter leaking at welded joint.

LEAKAGE BETWEEN GEARBOX & CONVERTER HOUSING

1. Converter housing retaining bolts loose.

NOISE IN ALL SELECTOR LEVER POSITIONS

1. Oil level too low.
2. Valve body leaking.
3. Oil filter clogged.

SPEED DEPENDENT NOISE

1. Bearing adjustment of the intermediate gear has changed or is incorrect.
2. Bearing setting of the differential has changed or is incorrect.

MAINTENANCE

FLUID CHECK

1. Ensure vehicle is on level surface.
2. Apply parking brake firmly.
3. Start engine and allow to reach normal operating temperature.
4. Shift selector lever through all positions, then place lever in park position. Do not shutdown engine during fluid level checks.
5. Clean all dirt and from dipstick cap before removing dipstick from filler tube.
6. Pull dipstick from tube, wipe clean and replace completely back in tube.
7. Remove transaxle dipstick to check fluid level, add specified fluid to raise level to full mark on dipstick. Do not overfill.

FLUID CHANGE

1. Raise and support vehicle.
2. Remove hose connector for oil cooler return from front of transaxle. Place a suitable drain pan under vehicle to collect oil.
3. When fluid has stopped draining, reinstall oil cooler return hose.
4. Add recommended fluid to transaxle pan through filler tube.
5. Refer to "Fluid Check," for final fluid level check.

ADJUSTMENTS

THROTTLE CABLE

1. Verify crimp is correctly positioned by opening throttle to point where kickdown cam in transaxle begins to engage.
2. Measure from end of cable housing to crimp, distance should be 1.53 inches or (39 mm), **Fig. 2.**
3. If distance is incorrect, move crimp.
4. Close throttle and measure same clearance again.
5. Distance should be .098 inch or (2.5 mm).
6. If incorrect, dimension can be brought within specification by adjusting two nuts which lock cable assembly to throttle housing bracket.

BRAKE BAND MECHANISM

1. Fit O-ring to parallel pin and fit pin into gearbox.
2. Screw in adjusting screw and tighten to specification.
3. Make a mark on adjusting screw and gearbox.
4. Back off adjusting screw two turns.
5. Hold adjusting screw and tighten locknut to specification.

SELECTOR LEVER

1. Loosen nut on adjustment mechanism in front of selector lever, **Fig. 3.**

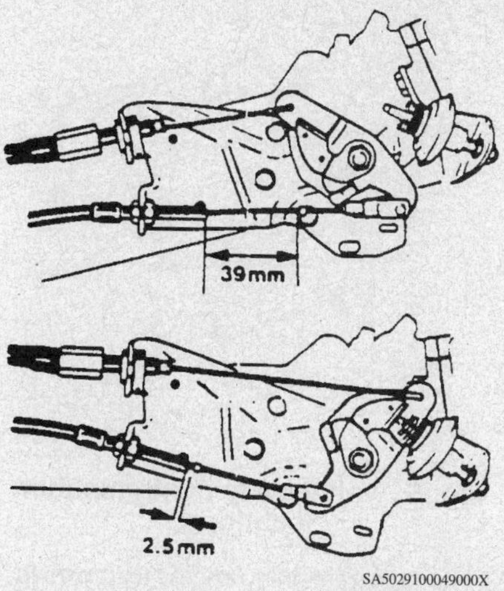
39mm
2.5mm
SA5029100049000X

Fig. 2 Throttle cable adjustment

2. Place lever on transaxle to N position.
3. Place selector lever in N position.
4. Tighten nut to specification.

IN-VEHICLE REPAIRS

GOVERNOR ASSEMBLY

1. Remove lefthand front wheel and wing liner assembly.
2. Remove side cover attaching bolts, then the side cover and gasket.
3. Remove screw on pinion shaft. **The parking pawl must be engaged.**
4. Remove gearwheel with inner race of taper roller bearing from pinion shaft.
5. Remove outer race of taper bearing, heat may be required.
6. Remove governor and governor housing as an assembly.
7. Reverse procedure to install noting the following:
   a. Apply petroleum jelly to seals before installing governor.
   b. Tighten bolt on pinion shaft to specification.
   c. Tighten side cover bolts to specification.

VALVE BODY

The following procedure has been revised by a Technical Service Bulletin:

1. **On 1995–96 9000 models,** obtain radio anti-theft code as outlined under "Precautions."
2. **On all models,** disconnect battery cables, then remove battery and shelf.
3. Remove oil dipstick.
4. Remove valve body cover retaining screws, then the valve body cover, **Fig. 4.**
5. Inspect valve body for antifreeze contamination. Inspect for any of the following indications:
   a. Separated droplets of antifreeze or pink, milky emulsion in the recesses of the valve body assembly, screw heads, or main case, **Fig. 5.** Probing and stirring may be necessary to provide a complete inspection.
   b. Rust formation and/or sludge accumulation on old style metal vent.
   c. Rust formation and/or sludge accumulation on underside of valve body cover.
   d. Rust formation on steel separator plates of valve body assembly.
6. Remove valve body retaining screws.
7. Remove oil tubes, then the valve body.
8. Reverse procedure to install noting the following:
   a. Set selector mechanism in position 1.
   b. Set selector rod in valve body to position 1, fully inserted.
   c. Tighten valve body retaining screws to specification.
   d. Replace all oil tube O-rings.

TRANSAXLE

REPLACE

2.0L ENGINE

1. Raise and support vehicle.
2. **On 1995–96 9000 models,** obtain radio anti-theft code as outlined under "Precautions."
3. **On all models,** disconnect battery cables.
4. Remove battery, then the washer fluid container.
5. Remove holder with connectors, terminal block and positive cable from battery tray. **On vehicles equipped with ABS brakes, release stay for hydraulic unit.**
6. Remove battery tray, then disconnect connector from air mass meter.
7. Disconnect connector for intake air temperature sensor on delivery pipe between throttle housing and intercooler. Remove hose on delivery pipe from bypass valve, and hose between transaxle and delivery pipe.
8. Remove delivery pipe between throttle housing and intercooler.
9. Remove starter motor retaining nuts, then secure starter motor to steering gear.
10. Remove throttle cable, then the oil cooler hoses for transaxle.
11. Disconnect selector cable, then remove bolts securing bulkhead cover.
12. Remove rubber strip, lift cover, then disconnect hoses from nozzle and remove cover.
13. Disconnect speedometer cable connector. Remove washer hose, then the speedometer cable through rubber grommet.
14. Disconnect negative battery cable from gearbox, then remove bolt securing top end of stay to wheel housing.
15. Position lifting beam tool No. 83 93 977, or equivalent, on fender edges, then attach to engine for support.
16. Remove lefthand front wheel, then the wheel housing liners.
17. Remove bolts securing torque converter to driveplate, through starter opening.
18. Separate suspension arm from ball joint, then remove anti roll bar.
19. Release lefthand engine mount, then remove lower bolt securing stay to wheel housing.

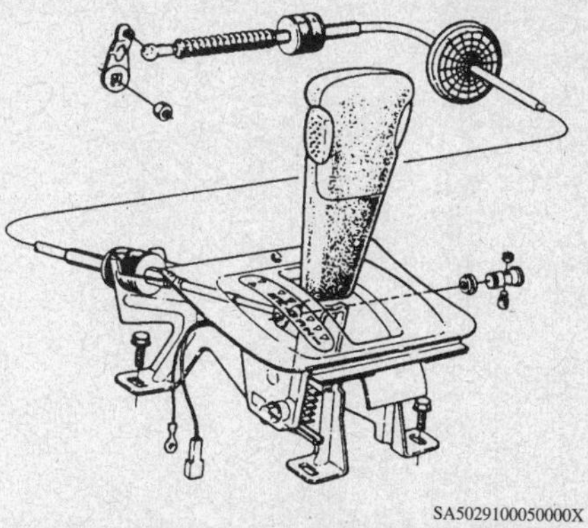
SA5029100050000X

Fig. 3 Selector lever adjustment

20. Remove center and lefthand skirts under spoiler.
21. Split subframe at front and rear, then lower using suitable jack.
22. Separate universal joint.
23. Remove bolts at bottom of gearbox joint face, then lower vehicle.
24. Install converter fixing tool No. 87 91 816, or equivalent, to keep torque converter in place.
25. Remove vent on gearbox cover and plug hole.
26. Install gearbox lifting yoke tool No. 87 91 451, or equivalent, to transaxle.
27. Remove remaining bolts from joint face and lower transaxle to ground.
28. Reverse procedure to install noting the following:
   a. Ensure driveshaft is in position in the righthand driver and aluminum tube is pressed into seal.
   b. Apply Loctite to torque converter bolt threads before installing.

2.3L ENGINE

1. **On 1995–96 9000 models,** obtain radio anti-theft code as outlined under "Precautions."
2. **On all models,** remove battery, then the washer reservoir.
3. Remove terminal block and positive cable from battery tray.
4. **On models with ABS,** release stay for hydraulic unit.
5. **On all models,** Remove battery tray, then disconnect air mass meter electrical connector.
6. Disconnect connector for intake air temperature sensor on delivery pipe between throttle housing and intercooler. Remove hose on delivery pipe from bypass valve, and hose between transaxle and delivery pipe.
7. Remove delivery pipe between throttle housing and intercooler.
8. Dismount starter motor and place on steering gear.
9. Remove throttle cable, then oil cooler hoses from transaxle.
10. Disconnect selector cable, then remove bulkhead cover mounting bolts.
11. Remove bulkhead cover rubber strip. Lift cover and disconnect hoses from nozzle, then remove cover.
12. Disconnect speedometer cable connector. Withdraw washer hose, then

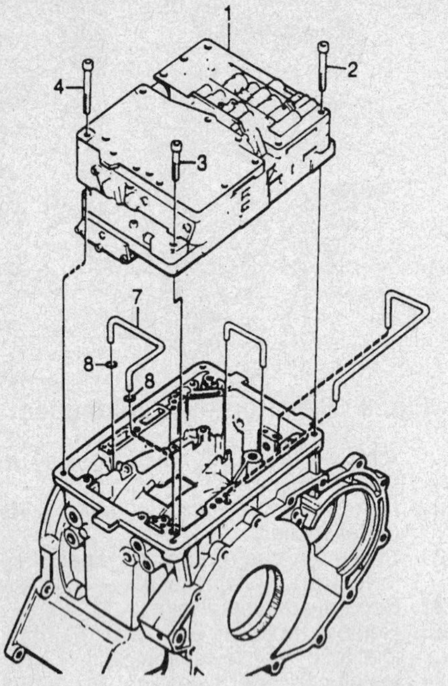
1
2
3
4
7
8
8

SA5029100051000X

Fig. 4 Valve body assembly

the speedometer cable through rubber grommet.

13. Disconnect battery negative cable from gear case, then remove bolt securing top end of stay to wheel housing.
14. Install engine lifting fixture tool No. 83 93 977, or equivalent, then raise and support vehicle.
15. Remove left front wheel, then the wheel housing liners.
16. Remove torque converter to driveplate mounting bolts, then the bolts through the starter motor opening.
17. Separate suspension arm from ball joint, then remove anti-roll bar.
18. Release lefthand engine mounting, then remove lower bolt securing stay to wheel housing.
19. Remove center and lefthand skirt under spoiler. Split subframe at front and rear, then lower subframe.
20. Separate universal joint, then remove 3 bolts at bottom of gear case joint face.
21. Lower vehicle, then install torque converter holding fixture tool No. 87 91 816, or equivalent.
22. Remove vent on gear case cover and plug hole, then install tool No. 87 91 451, or equivalent, and hook tool hoist into tool. It is easier to lower transaxle if lifting beam tool No. 83 92 977, or equivalent, is removed.

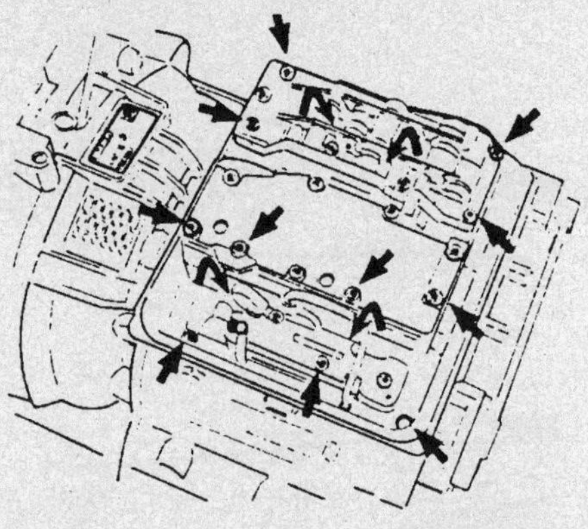

SA5029100052000X

Fig. 5 Valve body contamination locations

23. Remove remaining engine to transaxle mounting bolts, then lower transaxle.
24. Reverse procedure to install. Apply Loctite 242 to torque converter to driveplate bolts.

TIGHTENING SPECIFICATIONS

Component	Torque/Ft. Lbs.
Brake Band Adjusting Screw	7
Brake Band Adjusting Screw Locknut	59
Pinion Shaft Bolt	110
Selector Lever Nut	4-7
Side Cover Bolts	7
Valve Body Retaining Screws	7

Front Wheel Drive Axles

INDEX

	Page No.		Page No.		Page No.
CV Joint, Replace	38-163	9000 & 1993 900	38-163	900	38-163
1994–96 900	38-164	**Driveshaft, Replace**	38-163	9000	38-163

DRIVESHAFT

REPLACE

900

1993

1. Position spacer tool No. 8393209, or equivalent, between upper control arm and body.
2. Loosen hub nut, then the wheel nuts.
3. Raise and support vehicle, then remove wheel.
4. Rotate brake rotor so recess in edge of rotor is aligned with brake pads.
5. Remove brake pads.
6. Remove brake caliper, position and support caliper so brake hose and pipe are not damaged.
7. Remove brake rotor from hub.
8. Using taper breaker tool No. 8995409, or equivalent, remove tie rod end from control arm.
9. Remove bolts securing upper and lower ball joints to control arms, then remove hub nut and thrust washer.
10. Pull steering knuckle housing (with hub) off driveshaft and control arms.
11. Loosen large clamp around boot of inner CV joint, then separate inner CV joint and driver.
12. Remove drive axle assembly through opening in wheel housing. **Cover inner CV boot and driver.**
13. Remove inner and outer CV joints as outlined under "CV Joints, Replace."
14. Reverse procedure to install, noting the following:
    a. **Torque** hub nut to 195–208 ft. lbs.
    b. Pump brake pedal to advance brake pads to operating position. **Do not move vehicle until brakes are operating properly.**

1994–96

1. Remove dust cap and loosen hub center nut (1), **Fig. 1. Do not completely remove nut.**
2. Raise and support vehicle, then remove wheel.
3. Remove hub center nut (1), then the ball joint nut (2).
4. Remove ball joint using ball joint tool No. 89 96 696, or equivalent.
5. Remove anti-roll bar nut (4) and collect washer and rubber bushing.
6. Press spring link down.
7. Tap driveshaft out of hub using rubber mallet, then move MacPherson strut aside and pull out driveshaft. Use care to avoid stretching brake hoses and sensor cables.
8. Remove driveshaft joint from intermediate shaft using driveshaft dismantling tool No. 89 96 654, or equivalent.
9. Reverse procedure to install, noting the following:
    a. **Torque** ball joint to 55 ft. lbs.
    b. **Torque** anti-roll bar nut to 7 ft. lbs.
    c. **Torque** wheel bolts to 87 ft. lbs.
    d. Install new hub center nut and **torque** to 214 ft. lbs. It is self-locking and should not be reused.

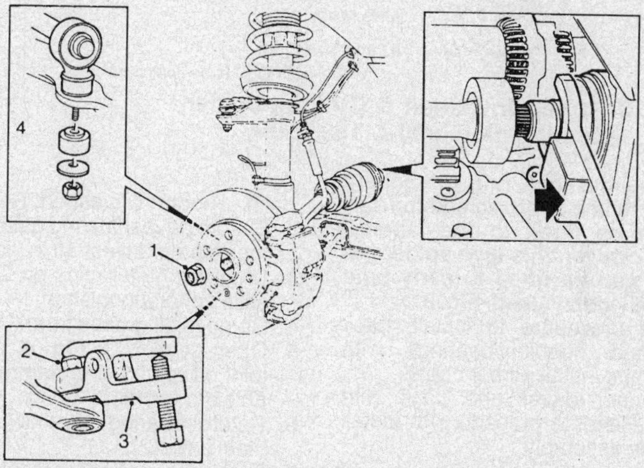

4
1
2
3
SA3039400005000X

Fig. 1 Driveshaft removal. 1994–96 900

9000

1. Loosen hub nut.
2. Raise and support vehicle and remove wheels.
3. Remove wheelwell liners.
4. Remove strut-to-steering member attaching bolts. Disconnect brake line from strut.
5. Remove clamp securing inboard dust boot, then separate the two halves of joint. **Cover boot and driver.**
6. Remove hub nut and thrust washer, then the drive axle assembly.
7. Remove inner and outer CV joints as outlined under "CV Joint, Replace."
8. Reverse procedure to install, noting the following:
    a. **Torque** strut-to-steering member bolts to 56–75 ft. lbs.
    b. **Torque** hub nut to 195–208 ft. lbs.

CV JOINT

REPLACE

9000 & 1993 900

1. Remove drive axle assembly as outlined under "Driveshaft, Replace."

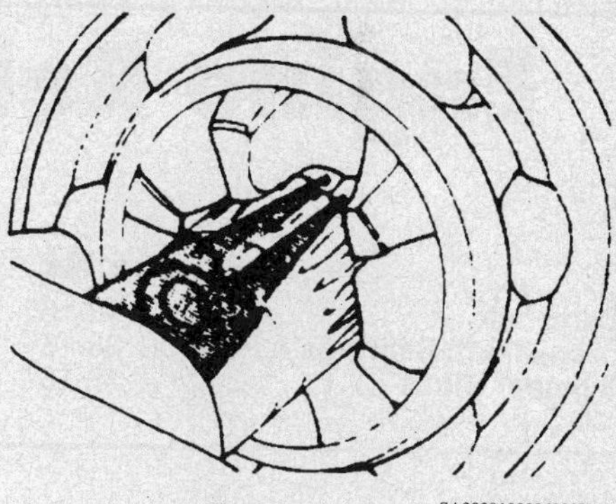

SA3039100006000X

Fig. 2 Outer CV joint removal. 9000 & 1993 900

Inner driver is retained in differential bearing carrier with a snap ring. If replacement is necessary, bearing carrier must be removed and differential clearances must be checked during reassembly.

2. Remove outer joint from shaft as follows:
    a. Release clamp securing boot to outer joint and slide boot toward center of shaft.
    b. Open retaining clip, **Fig. 2,** and remove joint from end of shaft.
3. Rubber boots can be removed, if necessary, by sliding off outer end of shaft.
4. To remove inner joint spider assembly, remove retaining clip and press spider from shaft, using a spacer. **The intermediate shaft uses a tapered shoulder as an inner stop for the spider,**

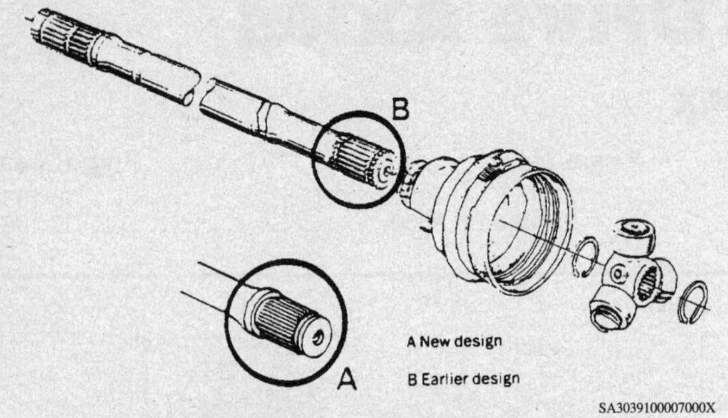
B
A
A New design
B Earlier design
SA3039100007000X

Fig. 3 Inner driveshaft & CV joint spider identification. 900 & 1993 900

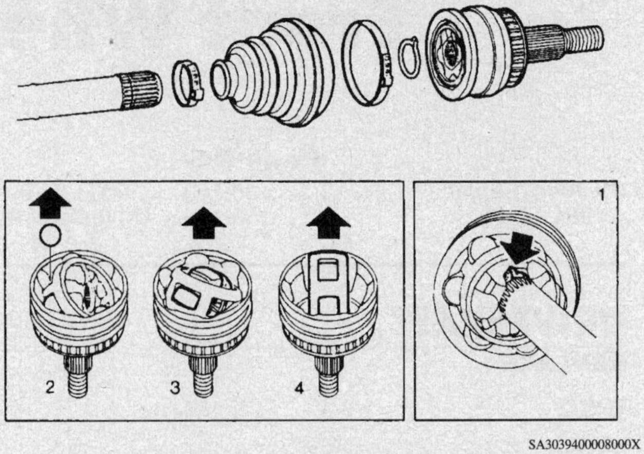
1
2
3
4
SA3039400008000X

Fig. 4 CV joint removal. 1994–96 900

replacing the lock ring previously used. Only the conforming type spider can be fitted to the tapered shaft. However, this type spider assembly can be fitted to early type shaft previously used, Fig. 3.

5. Reverse procedure to install, pack joints and needle bearings with grease, and install rubber boots.
6. Clean inner driver and pack with grease. Reverse procedure to install drive axle assembly.

1994–96 900

1. Remove driveshaft assembly as outlined under "Driveshaft, Replace."
2. Ensure driveshaft and gaiter are clean, then clamp driveshaft in vice.
3. Unfasten gaiter clips on CV joint and slide gaiter along shaft.
4. Remove all grease from CV joint.
5. Open circlip (1), **Fig. 4,** and tap CV joint off shaft using hammer and suitable brass drift.
6. Rotate bearing to allow removal of steel balls (2).
7. Rotate inner cage for steel balls to permit removal of outer race (3).
8. Remove outer race (4), then wipe balls and other parts clean.
9. Install new rubber gaiter onto driveshaft, then position outer race in CV joint.
10. Fit inner cage in outer race and rotate it so steel balls can be inserted, then press each ball into place.
11. Pack CV joint with .18 lbs. fresh Molycote Rapid G VN24612C grease or equivalent.
12. Press driveshaft into CV joint.
13. Position new rubber gaiter correctly and secure with new clips.

Engine Rebuilding Specifications

INDEX

	Page No.
Camshaft	38-165
Crankshaft, Bearings & Rods	38-166
Cylinder Block	38-167
Cylinder Head, Valve Guide & Valve Seats	38-164
Oil Pump	38-168
Pistons, Pins & Rings	38-166
Valves	38-164

CYLINDER HEAD, VALVE GUIDE & VALVE SEATS

All measurements given in inches, unless otherwise specified.

Engine Liter	Year	Cylinder Head Height		Valve Stem To Guide Clearance①		Valve Seat Angle, Degrees	Valve Seat To Face Contact Area	
		Nominal	Minimum	Intake	Exhaust		Intake	Exhaust
2.0L SOHC	1993	3.652	3.634	.02	.02	44.5	.06	.06
2.0L DOHC	1993	5.533	5.514	.02	.02	44.5	.06	.06
2.0L	1994-96	5.490	5.470	.02	.02	44.5	.04-.06	.06-.08
2.1L	1993	5.533	5.514	.02	.02	44.5	.06	.06
2.3L	1993	5.530	5.520	.02	.02	44.5	.06	.06
2.3L	1994-96	5.490	5.470	.10	.10	44.5	.08	.07
2.5L	1994-96	—	—	—	—	45.2	—	—
3.0L	1995-96	5.280	5.270	—	—	45.3	.04-.06	.06-.07

SOHC — Single Overhead Cam.
DOHC — Dual Overhead Cam.

① — Measured w/valve guide head raised .12 inch above seat.

VALVES

All measurements given in inches, unless otherwise specified.

Engine Liter	Year	Valves			Valve Clearance
		Stem Diameter		Face Angle, Degrees	
		Intake	Exhaust		
2.0L SOHC	1993	.3134-.3140	.3132-.3142	44.5	①②
2.0L DOHC	1993	.2740-.2746	.2738-.2748	44.5	③
2.0L	1994-96	.2740-.2746	.2742-.2748	44.5	—
2.1L	1993	.2740-.2746	.2738-.2748	44.5	③
2.3L	1993–96	.2740–.2746	.2738-.2748	44.5	③
2.5L	1994-96	.2344–.2350	.2341–.2346	45.3	③
3.0L	1995-96	.2344-.2350	.2340-.2346	45.3	③

SOHC — Single Overhead Cam.
DOHC — Dual Overhead Cam.
① — Intake valves, .009-.017 inch; exhaust valves, .017–.019 inch.
② — Measure valve clearance on cold engine or 30 minutes after running engine at operating temperature.
③ — Not adjustable.

CAMSHAFT

All measurements given in inches, unless otherwise specified.

Engine Liter	Year	Camshaft		Cam Follower		
		Bearing Diameter	Endplay	Cam Follower Height	Cam Follower Diameter	Cam Follower Bore In Cylinder Head
2.0L SOHC	1993	1.1394	.003–.010	1.30	1.4909–1.4953	1.4961–1.4967
2.0L DOHC	1993	1.1387–1.1392	.003–.014	1.02	1.2976–1.2984	1.2992–1.2998
2.0L	1994-96	1.1395-1.1400	.003-.014	1.02	1.2976-1.2992	1.3002-1.3008
2.1L	1993	1.1387–1.1392	.003–.014	1.02	1.2976–1.2984	1.2992–1.2998
2.3L	1993	1.1387–1.1392	.003–.014	1.02	1.2976–1.2982	1.2992–1.2998
2.3L	1994-96	1.1395-1.1400	.003-.014	1.02	1.2976-1.2992	1.3002-1.3008
2.5L	1994-96	—	—	—	—	—
3.0L	1995-96	—	.002-.006	—	—	—

SOHC — Single Overhead Cam.
DOHC — Dual Overhead Cam.

CRANKSHAFT, BEARINGS & RODS

All measurements given in inches, unless otherwise specified.

Engine Liter	Year	Crankshaft					Bearing Clearance		Connecting Rod Pin Bushing Bore Diameter
		Standard Journal Diameter		Out of Round	Taper	Endplay	Main Bearings	Connecting Rod Bearings	
		Main Bearing	Crank Pin						
2.0L	1993	2.2827–2.2835	2.0465–2.0472	.0019	.0019	.0031–.0110	.0008–.0024	.0010–.0024	.9451–.9453
2.0L	1994-96	2.2845-2.2952	2.0481-2.0488	.0002	.0002	.0020-.0120	.0006-.0024	—	.9458-.9460
2.1L	1993	2.2827–2.2835	2.0465–2.0472	.0019	.0019	.0031–.0110	.0008–.0024	.0010–.0024	.9451–.9453
2.3L	1993	2.2827–2.2835	2.0465–2.0472	.0019	.0019	.0020–.0120	.0008–.0024	.0010–.0024	.9451–.9453
2.3L①	1994-96	2.2827–2.2835	2.0465–2.0472	.0002	.0002	.0020–.0120	.0006–.0024	—	.9450–.9453
2.3L②	1994-96	2.2845-2.282	2.0481-2.0488	.0002	.0002	.0020-.0120	.0006-.0024	—	.9458-.9460
2.5L	1994-96	2.6760–2.6770	1.9270–1.9286	—	—	.0039-.0079	.0005-.0017	—	—
3.0L	1995-96	2.6764-2.6770	1.9280-1.9286	.0001	—	.0039-.0299	.0006-.0017	.0005-.0024	—

① — 900.
② — 9000.

PISTONS, PINS & RINGS

All measurements given in inches, unless otherwise specified.

Engine Liter	Year	Piston Diameter (Standard)	Piston Clearance	Piston Pin Diameter	Piston Pin To Piston Clearance	Piston Ring End Gap①		Piston Ring Side Clearance	
						Comp.	Oil	Comp.	Oil
900									
2.0L③	1993–96	④⑤	.0004–.0014	.9448	.0002–.0006	⑥	.015	.002–.003	—
2.0L⑧	1993–96	⑤⑨	.0002–.0012	.9448	.0002–.0006	⑥	.015	.002–.003	—
2.1L	1993	⑤⑫	.0004–.0013	.9448	.0001–.0004	⑥	.015	.002–.003	—
2.3L	1994–96	⑤⑮	.0004-.0015	.9448	⑯	.0350	⑰	—	
2.5L	1994–96	⑱	—	.8264–.8268	—	.0118-.0197	.012-.020	—	—
9000									
2.0L	1993	⑤⑪	.0008–.0020	.9448	.0002–.0006	⑭	.0149	⑦	—
2.0L	1994-96	⑤⑲	.0004-.0015	—	—	⑳	.0150-.0552	㉑	—
2.3L	1993	⑤⑬	.0002–.0016	.9448	.0002–.0006	⑩	.0149	②	—
2.3L	1994-96	⑤⑮	.0004-.0015	.9448	⑯	⑰	.0150-.00550	.002-.003	.0016-.0028
3.0L	1995-96	㉒	.0010-.0002	.8264-.8267	—	.0118-.0197	.0157-.0551	—	—

① — Minimum.
② — Top ring, .0020–.0033 inch; 2nd ring, .0014–.0028 inch.
③ — Except Turbo.
④ — Piston class A, 3.5451–3.5454 inches; piston class AB, 3.5454–3.5456 inches; piston class B, 3.5456–3.5460 inches; piston class C, 3.5460–3.5466 inches.
⑤ — Piston class is stamped on piston crown.
⑥ — Top ring, .014 inch; 2nd ring, .012 inch.
⑦ — Top ring, .0019–.0032 inch; 2nd ring, .0016–.0028 inch.
⑧ — Turbo.
⑨ — Piston class A, 3.5451–3.5455 inches; piston class AB, 3.5455–3.5458 inches; piston class B, 3.5458–3.5462 inches; piston class C, 3.5462–3.5468 inches.
⑩ — Top ring, .012 inch; 2nd ring, .0118 inch.
⑪ — Piston class A, 3.5417–3.5421 inches; piston class AB, 3.5421–3.5424 inches; piston class B, 3.5424–3.5427 inches; piston class C, 3.5427–3.5434 inches.
⑫ — Piston class A, 3.6263–3.6267 inches; piston class B, 3.6267–3.6271 inches; piston class B+, 3.6271–3.6275 inches.
⑬ — Piston class A, 3.5422–3.5425 inches; piston class AB, 3.5425–3.5429 inches; piston class B, 3.5429–3.5432 inches; piston class C, 3.5432–3.5438 inches.
⑭ — Top ring, .0138 inch; 2nd ring, .0118 inch.
⑮ — Piston class A, 3.5028–3.5425 inches; piston class AB, 3.5425–3.5429 inches; piston class B, 3.5429–3.5433 inches; piston class C, 3.5433–3.5438 inches.
⑯ — Top ring, .0118–.0197 inch; 2nd ring, .0059–.0256 inch.
⑰ — Top ring, .0012–.020 inch; 2nd ring, .0059-.0256 inch.
⑱ — Piston class 8, 3.2102–3.2106 inches; piston class 99, 3.2106–3.2110 inches; piston class 00, 3.2110–3.2114 inches; piston class 01, 3.2114–3.2118 inches; piston class 02, 3.2118–3.2122 inches.
⑲ — Piston class A, 3.5449–3.5452 inches; piston class AB, 3.5452–3.5456 inches; piston class B, 3.5456–3.5460 inches; piston class C, 3.5460–3.5465 inches.
⑳ — Top ring, .0138–.0189 inch; second ring, .0099–.0150 inch.
㉑ — Top ring, .0020–.0032 inch; second ring, .0013–.0028 inch.
㉒ — Piston class 8, 3.3835–3.3839 inches; piston class 99, 3.3839–3.3843 inches; piston class 00, 3.3843–3.38465 inches; piston class 01, 3.3847–3.3850 inches; piston class 02, 3.3850–3.3854 inches.

CYLINDER BLOCK

All measurements given in inches, unless otherwise specified.

Engine Liter	Year	Cylinder Bore Diameter (Standard)
2.0L	1993	①
2.0L⑤	1994-96	⑦
2.0L⑥	1994-96	⑧
2.1L	1993	②
2.3L	1993	①
2.3L	1994-96	⑧
2.5L	1994-96	④
3.0L	1995-96	③

① — Cylinder class A, 3.5433–3.5437 inches; cylinder class B, 3.5437–3.5441 inches. Cylinder class is stamped on cylinder plane.
② — Cylinder class A, 3.6270–3.6227 inches; cylinder class B, 3.6274–3.6278 inches. Cylinder class is stamped on cylinder plane.
③ — Cylinder class 8, 3.38484–3.38524 inches; cylinder class 99, 3.38524–3.38563 inches; cylinder class 00, 3.38563–3.38602 inches; cylinder class 01, 3.38602–3.38642; class 02, 3.38642–3.38681 inches. Cylinder class is stamped on cylinder plane.
④ — Cylinder class 8, 3.2116–3.2120 inches; cylinder class 9, 3.2120–3.2124 inches; cylinder class 00, 3.2124–3.2128 inches; cylinder class 01, 3.2128–3.2134; cylinder class 02, 3.2134–3.2136. Cylinder class is stamped on cylinder plane.
⑤ — Less twin balance shafts.
⑥ — Twin balance shafts.
⑦ — Cylinder class A, 3.5460–3.5464 inches; cylinder class B, 3.5464–3.5468 inches. Cylinder class is stamped on cylinder plane.
⑧ — Cylinder class A, 3.5460–3.5465 inches; cylinder class B, 3.5461–3.5468 inches. Cylinder class is stamped on cylinder plane.

OIL PUMP

All measurements given in inches, unless otherwise specified.

Engine Liter	Year	Gear To Body Clearance	Relief Valve Opening Pressure, psi	Engine Oil Pressure @ 2000 RPM①	Engine To Oil Cooler Thermostat Opening Temperature °F
2.0L SOHC	1993	.0012–.0031	65–72	39	—
2.0L DOHC	1993	.0012–.0031	52–75	39	194
2.0L②	1994-96	.0012-.0031	52-75	39	194
2.0L③	1994-96	.0012-.0031	44	39	225
2.1L	1993	—	—	—	—
2.3L	1993	.0012–.0031	51	39	167
2.3L④	1994-96	—	55	39	176
2.3L⑤	1994-96	.0012-.0031	44	39	225
2.5L	1994-96	—	64	—	—
3.0L	1995-96	—	64	—	—

SOHC — Single Overhead Cam.
DOHC — Dual Overhead Cam.

① — At engine temperature of 176°F, using 10W-30 engine oil.
② — Less twin balance shafts.
③ — Twin balance shafts.
④ — 900.
⑤ — 9000.

SUBARU

INDEX OF SERVICE OPERATIONS

Page No.

ACTIVE SUSPENSION SYSTEMS 39-188
AIR BAG SYSTEM PRECAUTIONS 0-8
ALL-WHEEL DRIVE SYSTEMS 39-180
AUTOMATIC TRANSMISSIONS/ TRANSAXLES 39-158
BRAKES
- Anti-Lock Brakes 39-125
- Disc Brakes 39-114
- Drum Brakes 39-119
- Hydraulic Brake Systems 39-122
- Power Brake Units 39-124

CLUTCH & MANUAL TRANSMISSION
- Adjustments 39-37
- Clutch, Replace 39-38
- Hydraulic System Service 39-37
- Tightening Specifications 39-39
- Transaxle, Replace 39-38

DRIVE AXLES 39-184
ELECTRICAL
- Air Bags 39-85
- Air Conditioning 39-60
- Alternators 39-72
- Blower Motor, Replace 39-9
- Coil Pack, Replace 39-6
- Combination Switch, Replace 39-7
- Cooling Fans 39-65
- Cruise Control 39-75
- Dash Gauges 39-68
- Dash Panels 39-96
- Distributor, Replace 39-6
- Evaporator Core, Replace 39-10
- Fuel Pump Relay Location 39-6
- Fuse Panel & Flasher Location 39-6
- Headlamp Switch, Replace 39-7
- Heater Core, Replace 39-9
- Ignition Switch, Replace 39-6
- Instrument Cluster, Replace 39-8
- Neutral Safety Switch, Replace 39-7
- Passive Restraints 39-85
- Precautions 39-6
- Radio, Replace 39-9
- Relay Center Location 39-6
- Speed Controls 39-75
- Starter Motors 39-70
- Starter, Replace 39-6
- Steering Columns 39-102
- Steering Wheel, Replace 39-8
- Stop Light Switch, Replace 39-7
- Turn Signal Switch, Replace 39-8
- Wiper Motor, Replace 39-9
- Wiper Switch, Replace 39-9
- Wiper Systems 39-81
- Wiper Transmission, Replace 39-9

ELECTRICAL SYMBOL IDENTIFICATION 0-139
ENGINE
- Belt Tension Data 39-28
- Compression Pressures 39-10
- Cooling System Bleed 39-28
- Engine Rebuilding Specifications 39-191
- Engine, Replace 39-11
- Engine Service 39-14
- Fuel Filter, Replace 39-30
- Fuel Pump, Replace 39-29
- Precautions 39-10
- Radiator, Replace 39-29
- Thermostat, Replace 39-28
- Tightening Specifications 39-34
- Valve Clearance Specifications 39-28
- Water Pump, Replace 39-28

FRONT SUSPENSION & STEERING
- Ball Joint, Replace 39-50
- Ball Joint Inspection 39-50
- Control Arm, Replace 39-52
- Crossmember, Replace 39-52
- Hub & Bearing, Replace 39-49
- Manual Steering Gear, Replace 39-54
- Manual Steering Gears 39-104
- Power Steering 39-106
- Power Steering Gear, Replace 39-53
- Power Steering Pump, Replace 39-54
- Stabilizer Bar, Replace 39-52
- Strut, Replace 39-50
- Tightening Specifications 39-56
- Wheel Hub & Steering Knuckle, Replace 39-49

FRONT WHEEL DRIVE AXLES 39-179
REAR AXLE & SUSPENSION
- Hill Holder 39-47
- Hub & Bearing, Replace 39-40
- Rear Suspension, Replace 39-41
- Stabilizer Bar, Replace 39-48
- Strut, Replace 39-45
- Tightening Specifications 39-48
- Wheel Bearing, Adjust 39-41

SERVICE REMINDER & WARNING LAMP RESET PROCEDURES 0-10
SPECIFICATIONS
- Fluid Capacities & Cooling System Data 39-5
- Front Wheel Alignment Specifications 39-4
- General Engine Specifications 39-2
- Lubricant Data 39-5
- Rear Wheel Alignment Specifications 39-4
- Tune Up Specifications 39-2

VEHICLE IDENTIFICATION 0-1
VEHICLE LIFT POINTS 0-34
VEHICLE MAINTENANCE SCHEDULES 0-69
WHEEL ALIGNMENT
- Front Wheel Alignment 39-57
- Rear Wheel Alignment 39-57
- Vehicle Ride Height 39-57
- Wheel Alignment Specifications 39-4

WIRE COLOR CODE IDENTIFICATION 0-144

Specifications

GENERAL ENGINE SPECIFICATIONS

Year	Engine Liters	Fuel System	Bore x Stroke Inch (mm)	Compression Ratio	Max. H.P. @ RPM	Max. Torque @ RPM	Normal Oil Pressure
1993–94	1.2L	MPFI	3.07 x 3.27 (78 x 83)	9.1	73 @ 5600	71 @ 2800	④
	1.8L①	SPFI	3.62 x 2.64 (92 x 67)	9.5	90 @ 5200	101 @ 2800	⑤
	1.8L②	MPFI	3.62 x 2.64 (92 x 67)	7.7	115 @ 5200	134 @ 2800	⑤
	1.8L	MPFI	3.46 x 2.95 (87.9 x 75)	9.5	110 @ 5600	110 @ 4400	③
	2.2L①	MPFI	3.82 x 2.95 (97 x 75)	9.5	130 @ 5600	137 @ 4400	③
	2.2L②	MPFI	3.82 x 2.95 (97 x 75)	8.0	160 @ 5600	181 @ 2800	③
	3.3L	MPFI	3.82 x 2.95 (97 x 75)	10.0	230 @ 5400	228 @ 4400	③
1995	1.8L	MPFI	3.46 x 2.95 (87.9 x 75)	9.5	110 @ 5600	110 @ 4400	③
	2.2L①	MPFI	3.82 x 2.95 (97 x 75)	9.5	130 @ 5600	137 @ 4400	③
	2.2L②	MPFI	3.82 x 2.95 (97 x 75)	9.5	135 @ 5400	140 @ 4400	⑥
	3.3L	MPFI	3.82 x 2.95 (97 x 75)	10.0	230 @ 5400	228 @ 4400	③
1996	1.8L	MPFI	3.46 x 2.95 (87.9 x 75)	9.5	110 @ 5600	110 @ 4400	③
	2.2L②	MPFI	3.82 x 2.95 (97 x 75)	9.5	135 @ 5400	140 @ 4400	⑥
	2.5L	MPFI	—	—	—	—	—
	3.3L	MPFI	3.82 x 2.95 (97 x 75)	10.0	230 @ 5400	228 @ 4400	③

① — Except Turbocharged.
② — Turbocharged.
③ — Discharge performance I, 14 psi @ 600; Discharge performance II, 43 @ 5000.
④ — Discharge performance I, 30 psi @ 1500; Discharge performance II, 47 @ 3000.
⑤ — Discharge performance I, 14 psi @ 550; Discharge performance II, 43 @ 5000.
⑥ — Legacy discharge performance I, 14 psi @ 800; Legacy discharge performance II, 43 @ 5000. Impreza discharge performance I, 14 psi @ 600; Impreza discharge performance II, 43 @ 5000.

TUNE UP SPECIFICATIONS

Year & Model	Spark Plug Gap Inch	Ignition			Curb Idle Speed③		Fast Idle Speed③		Fuel Pressure, psi	Valve Lash, Inch	
		Firing Order②	Timing °BTDC	Timing Mark	Man. Trans.	Auto. Trans.	Man. Trans.	Auto. Trans.		Intake	Exhaust
1993–94											
1.2L	.041	1-3-2.	5①	B	700④	700N④	⑫	⑫	31–34⑤	⑨	⑨
1.8L	.041	A	20	C	700	700N	⑫	⑫	34–38⑩	⑨	⑨
1.8L	.041	A	20	C	700	700N	⑫	⑫	26–30⑤	⑨	⑨
2.2L	.041	A	15	C	700	700N	⑫	⑫	26–30⑤	⑨	⑨
2.2L	.041	A	20①⑥	D	700	700N	⑫	⑫	20–24⑧	⑨	⑨
3.3L	.041	⑦	20	—	—	610N	—	⑫	26–30⑤	⑨	⑨
1995											
1.8L	.041	A	20	C	700	700N	⑫	⑫	34–38⑩	⑨	⑨

Continued

TUNE UP SPECIFICATIONS—Continued

Year & Model	Spark Plug Gap Inch	Ignition			Curb Idle Speed③		Fast Idle Speed③		Fuel Pressure, psi	Valve Lash, Inch	
		Firing Order②	Timing °BTDC	Timing Mark	Man. Trans.	Auto. Trans.	Man. Trans.	Auto. Trans.		Intake	Exhaust
1995											
2.2L	.041	A	⑪	C	700	700N	⑫	⑫	34–38⑩	⑨	⑨
3.3L	.041	⑦	20	—	—	610N	⑫	⑫	26–30⑤	⑨	⑨
1996											
1.8L	.041	A	20	C	700	700N	⑫	⑫	34–38⑩	⑨	⑨
2.2L	.041	A	⑪	C	700	700N	⑫	⑫	36	⑨	⑨
3.3L	.041	⑦	20	—	—	610N	—	⑫	26–30⑤	⑨	⑨

BTDC — Before Top Dead Center
C — Cold
MPFI — Multi-Point Fuel Injection
N — Neutral
SPFI — Single-Point Fuel Injection
① — Connect test mode connectors.
② — Before disconnecting spark plug wires from distributor cap, determine location of number 1 wire in cap, as distributor position may have been altered from that shown.
③ — When adjusting idle speed, set parking brake & chock drive wheels.
④ — Connect test mode & read memory connectors.
⑤ — Remove fuel pump connector, start engine & allow to stall, then crank for five seconds & turn ignition switch to Off. Place shop towel under fuel filter, then install suitable fuel pressure gauge between fuel filter & hose. Install fuel pump connector, start engine & note fuel pressure at idle.
⑥ — Less vacuum.
⑦ — Firing order 1-6-3-2-5-4.
⑧ — Remove fuel pump connector, start engine & allow to stall, then crank for five seconds & turn ignition switch to Off. Place shop towel under fuel delivery pipe, then install suitable fuel pressure gauge between throttle chamber & hose. Install fuel pump connector, start engine & note fuel pressure at idle.
⑨ — Equipped w/hydraulic valve lash adjusters.
⑩ — Remove fuel pump connector, start engine & allow to stall, then crank for five seconds & turn ignition switch to Off. Place shop towel under fuel filter, then install suitable fuel pressure gauge between fuel filter & hose. Install fuel pump connector, start engine, disconnect pressure regulator vacuum hose from collector chamber & note fuel pressure at idle.
⑪ — Man. trans., 14 BTDC; auto. trans. 20 BTDC.
⑫ — Controlled by ECU.

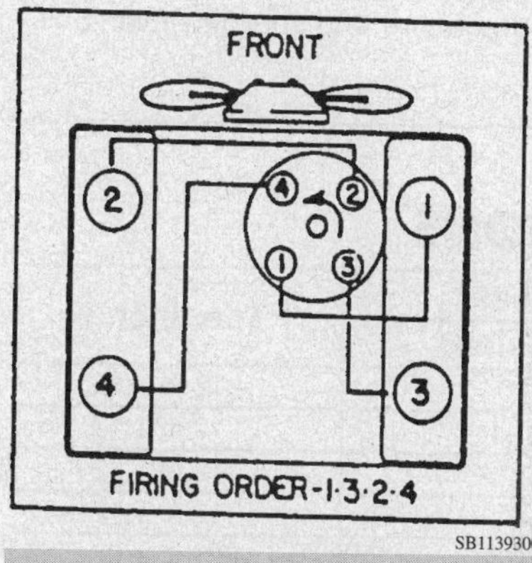
FRONT
FIRING ORDER-1·3·2·4
SB1139300002000X

Fig. A

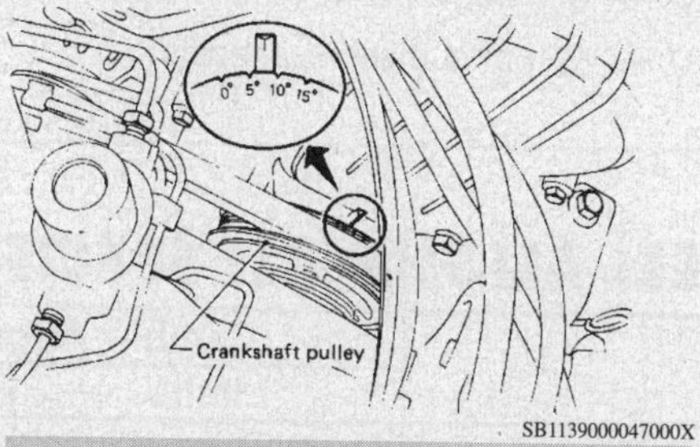
0° 5° 10° 15°
Crankshaft pulley
SB1139000047000X

Fig. B

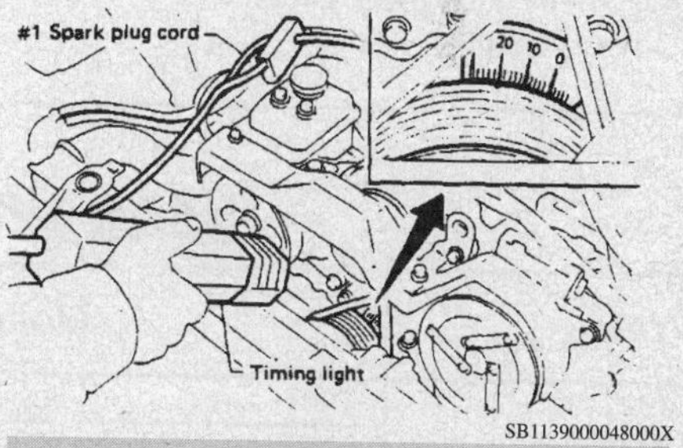
#1 Spark plug cord
Timing light
SB1139000048000X

Fig. C

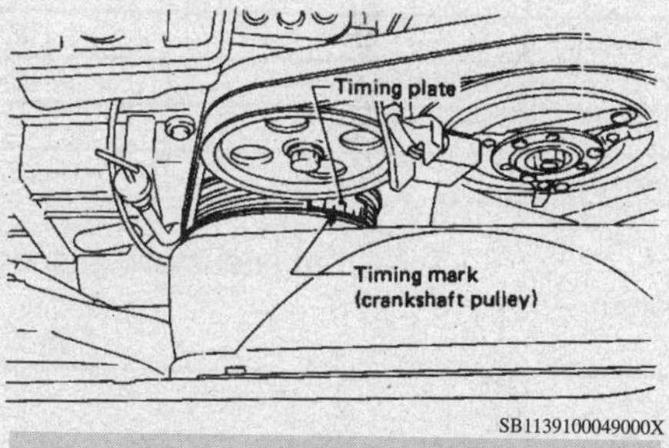
Timing plate
Timing mark
(crankshaft pulley)
SB1139100049000X

Fig. D

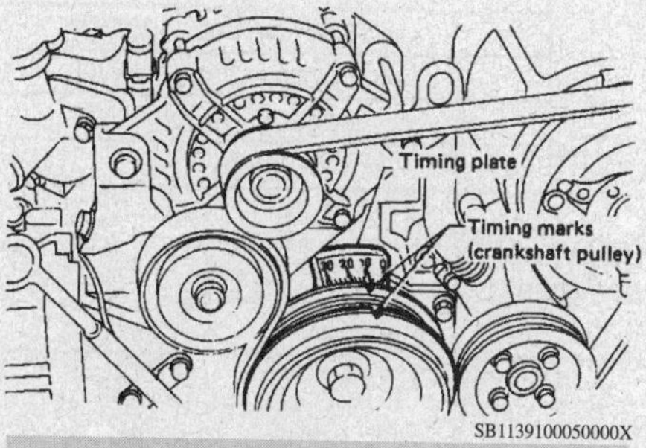
Timing plate
Timing marks
(crankshaft pulley)
SB1139100050000X

Fig. E

FRONT WHEEL ALIGNMENT SPECIFICATIONS

Year	Model	Caster Angle, Degrees		Camber Angle, Degrees		Toe, Inch①	Ball Joint Inspection	
		Limits	Desired	Limits	Desired		Upper	Lower
1993–94	Justy	+1 ½ to +3 ½	+2 ½	−⅓ to +1 ⅔	+ ⅔	+.08	④	④
	Legacy Sedan FWD Except Turbo	+2 1⁄12 to +4 1⁄12	+3 1⁄12	− ¾ to + ¼	− ¼	0	④	④
	Legacy Sedan FWD Turbo	+1 ⅚ to +3 ⅚	+2 ⅚	− ¾ to + ¼	− ¼	0	④	④
	Legacy Sedan 4WD Except Turbo②	+2 to +4	+3	− ½ to + ½	0	0	④	④
	Legacy Sedan 4WD Turbo②	+1 ⅚ to +3 ⅚	+2 ⅚	− ¾ to + ¼	− ¼	0	④	④
	Legacy Wagon FWD	+1 ⅚ to +3 ⅚	+2 ⅚	− ¾ to + ¼	− ¼	0	④	④
	Legacy Wagon 4WD②	+1 ¾ to +3 ¾	+2 ¾	− ½ to + ½	0	0	④	④
	Legacy③	+2 to +4	+3	− ½ to + ½	0	0	④	④
	Loyale Sedan & 3 Door FWD	+1 ¾ to +3 ¼	+2 ½	0 to +1 ½	+ ¾	+.08	④	④
	Loyale Sedan & 3 Door 4WD	− ¾ to + ¾	0	+ 11⁄12 to +2 5⁄12	+1 ⅔	−.20	④	④
	Loyale Wagon FWD	+1 ⅓ to +2 ⅚	+2 1⁄12	+ ¼ to +1 ¾	+1	+.08	④	④
	Loyale Wagon 4WD	− ¾ to + ¾	0	+1 to +2 ½	+1 ¾	−.20	④	④
	SVX	+4 1⁄12 to +5 7⁄12	+4 ⅚	−1 ⅙ to + ⅓	− 5⁄12	0	④	④
1993–96	Impreza	+2 to +4	+3	− ½ to + ½	0	0	④	④
1995–96	Legacy	+2 1⁄12 to +4 1⁄12	+3 1⁄12	-7⁄12 to +5⁄12	-1⁄12	0	④	④
	SVX	+4 1⁄12 to +5 7⁄12	+4 ⅚	−1 ⅙ to + ⅓	− 5⁄12	0	④	④

FWD — Front Wheel Drive
4WD — Four Wheel Drive
① — Toe-in (+); toe-out (-).
② — With conventional suspension.
③ — With pneumatic suspension.
④ — Refer to "Ball Joint Inspection" for procedure and specification.

REAR WHEEL ALIGNMENT SPECIFICATIONS

Year	Model	Camber Angle, Degrees		Toe, Inch①
		Limits	Desired	
1993–94	Justy	−1 to +1	0	−.12 to +.12
	Legacy Sedan②	−2 to +0	−1	−.12 to +.12
	Legacy Wagon②	−1 ⅚ to + ⅙	− ⅚	−.12 to +.12
	Legacy③	−2 to + 0	−1	−.12 to +.12
	Loyale	− ¾ to + ¾	0	−.08 to +.08
	SVX	−1 5⁄12 to + 1⁄12	− ⅔	−.12 to +.12
1993–96	Impreza AWD	−1 ⅔ to -⅙	− 11⁄12	−.12 to +.12
	Impreza FWD	−1 7⁄12 to −1⁄12	− ⅚	−.12 to +.12
1995–96	Legacy Sedan AWD	-1 ¾ to -¼	-1	−.12 to +.12
	Legacy Sedan FWD	-1 ⅔ to -⅙	-11⁄12	−.12 to +.12
	Legacy Wagon AWD	-1 ⅔ to -⅙	-11⁄12	−.12 to +.12
	Legacy Wagon FWD	-1 ½ to 0	-¾	−.12 to +.12
	SVX	−1 5⁄12 to +1⁄12	− ⅔	−.12 to +.12

FWD — Front Wheel Drive
4WD — Four Wheel Drive
① — Toe-in (+); toe-out (-).
② — With conventional suspension.
③ — With pneumatic suspension.

FLUID CAPACITIES & COOLING SYSTEM DATA

Year	Model	Cooling Capacity Qts. With Heater	Cooling Capacity Qts. With A/C	Radiator Cap Relief Pressure Lbs.	Thermo. Opening Temp. °F	Fuel Tank Gals.	Engine Oil Refill Qts.	Transmission Oil 4 Spd. Pts.	Transmission Oil 5 Spd. Pts.	Transmission Oil Auto. Trans. Qts.	Rear Axle Oil Pts.
1993	Impreza⑪	6.2	6.2	13	173	13.2	4.2	—	5.4	8.4⑦	—
	Impreza⑥	6.2	6.2	13	173	13.2	4.2	—	7.4	8.4⑦	1.6
1993–94	Justy⑪	5.2	5.2	13	185	9.2	3	—	5	3.5	—
	Justy④	5.2	5.2	13	185	9.2	3.2	—	7.2	4.4	1.6
	Legacy⑪	6.2	6.2	13	173	15.9	4.8	—	7	8.8	—
	Legacy⑥	③	③	13	173	15.9	4.8	—	7.4	①⑦	1.6
	Loyale⑪	5.8	5.8	13	190	15.9	4.2	—	5.4	6.6②	—
	Loyale⑥	5.8	5.8	13	190	15.9	4.2	—	7	7⑦	1.6
	SVX	7.9	7.9	13	173	18.5	6.3	—	—	10.2⑦	1.8
1994	Impreza⑪	6.2	6.2	13	173	13.2	4.2	—	5.4	8.4⑦	—
	Impreza⑥	6.2	6.2	13	173	13.2	4.2	—	8.4	8.4⑦	1.6
1995	Impreza⑪	6.6	6.6	13	173	13.2	4.2	—	7	8.4⑦	—
	Impreza⑥	6.6	6.6	13	173	13.2	4.2	—	8.4	8.4⑦	1.6
	Legacy⑪	6.4	6.4	13	173	15.9	4.2	—	7	8.4⑦	—
	Legacy⑥	6.4	6.4	13	173	15.9	4.2	—	8.4	8.4⑦	1.6
	SVX	7.9	7.9	13	173	18.5	6.3	—	—	10.2⑦	1.8
1996	Impreza	6.3	6.3	—	—	13.2	⑤	—	7.4	⑧	—
	Legacy L, LS & LSi	6.3	6.3	—	—	15.9	⑨	—	⑩	7.5	—
	Legacy Outback	6.3	6.3	—	—	15.9	④	—	—	—	—
	Legacy 2.5 GT	6	6	—	—	15.9	4.7	—	—	—	—
	SVX	7.4	7.4	—	—	18.5	6.3	—	—	10	—

4WD — Four wheel drive
① — Except Sport Sedan & Touring Wagon, 8.8 qts.; Sport Sedan & Touring Wagon, 9.4 qts.
② — Differential, 3 pts.
③ — Sedan, 6.2 qts.; Wagon, 6.3 qts.; Sport Sedan & Touring Wagon, 7.4 qts.
④ — 2.2L engine, 4.4 qts.; 2.5L engine, 4,7 qts.
⑤ — 1.8L engine, 4.2 qts.; 2.2L engine, 4.4 qts.
⑥ — 4WD.
⑦ — Differential, 2.6 pts.
⑧ — Less AWD, 8.4 qts.; w/AWD, 8.75 qts.
⑨ — Less LSi, 4.4 qts.; LSi models, 4.7 qts.
⑩ — Less AWD, 7 pts.; w/AWD, 7.6 pts.
⑪ — Except 4WD.

LUBRICANT DATA

Year	Model	Lubricant Type: Transmission Manual	Transmission Automatic	Transfer Case	Rear Axle	Power Steering	Brake System
1993–94	All	80W-90 GL-5	Dexron II/IIE①	—	80W-90 GL-5	Dexron II/IIE	DOT 3
1995–96	Impreza	80W-90 GL-5	Dexron IIE/III①	—	80W-90 GL-5	Dexron II/IIE	DOT 3 or 4
	Legacy	75W-90 GL-5	Dexron IIE/III①	—	75W-90 GL-5	Dexron II/IIE	DOT 3 or 4
	SVX	—	Dexron IIE/III①	—	75W-90 GL-5	Dexron II/IIE	DOT 3 or 4

① — Final drive, 80W-90 GL-5.

Electrical

NOTE: On Air Bag Equipped Models, Refer To "Air Bag System Precautions" Located In The Front Of This Manual For System Disarming & Arming Procedures.

INDEX

	Page No.
Air Bags	39-85
Air Conditioning	39-60
Alternators	39-72
Blower Motor, Replace	39-9
Impreza & SVX	39-9
Justy	39-9
Legacy	39-9
Loyale	39-9
Coil Pack, Replace	39-6
Combination Switch, Replace	39-7
Impreza	39-7
Justy & Loyale	39-7
SVX & 1993–94 Legacy	39-8
1995–96 Legacy	39-8
Cooling Fans	39-65
Cruise Control	39-75
Dash Gauges	39-68
Dash Panels	39-96
Distributor, Replace	39-6
Justy	39-6
Evaporator Core, Replace	39-10
Fuel Pump Relay Location	39-6
Fuse Panel & Flasher Location	39-6
Headlamp Switch, Replace	39-7
Heater Core, Replace	39-9
Except Justy	39-9
Justy	39-10
Ignition Switch, Replace	39-6
Impreza	39-7
Justy & Loyale	39-6
Legacy	39-7
Instrument Cluster, Replace	39-8
Impreza	39-8
Justy	39-8
Legacy	39-8
Loyale	39-8
SVX	39-8
Neutral Safety Switch, Replace	39-7
Except 4-Speed Automatic Transaxle	39-7
4-Speed Automatic Transaxle	39-7
Passive Restraints	39-85
Precautions	39-6
Air Bag Systems	39-6
Radio, Replace	39-9
Except SVX & 1995–96 Legacy	39-9
SVX	39-9
1995–96 Legacy	39-9
Relay Center Location	39-6
Speed Controls	39-75
Starter Motors	39-70
Starter, Replace	39-6
Steering Columns	39-102
Steering Wheel, Replace	39-8
Stop Light Switch, Replace	39-7
Turn Signal Switch, Replace	39-8
Wiper Motor, Replace	39-9
Front	39-9
Rear	39-9
Wiper Switch, Replace	39-9
Wiper Systems	39-81
Wiper Transmission, Replace	39-9
Except Legacy	39-9
Legacy	39-9

PRECAUTIONS

AIR BAG SYSTEMS

Refer to "Air Bag System Precautions" in the front of this manual for system disarming and arming procedures.

FUSE PANEL & FLASHER LOCATION

There are two fuse/relay panels. The engine compartment fuse/relay panel is located in the engine compartment, near the battery. The passenger compartment fuse/relay panel is located below the lefthand side of the instrument panel.

On Impreza models, the hazard and turn signal flasher is located behind the center of the instrument panel.

On Justy models, the hazard and turn signal flasher is located behind the lefthand side of the instrument panel.

On SVX models, the hazard and turn signal flasher is located behind the lefthand side of the instrument panel, near the brake pedal bracket.

On Loyale and 1993–94 Legacy models, the hazard and turn signal flasher is located behind the righthand side of the instrument panel, near the glove compartment.

On 1995–96 Legacy models, the hazard and turn signal flasher is located below the lefthand side of the instrument panel, near the instrument panel wiring harness.

FUEL PUMP RELAY LOCATION

On Loyale models, the fuel pump relay is located inside the I/P.

On Justy models, refer to **Fig. 1,** for fuel pump relay location.

On SVX models, refer to **Fig. 2,** for fuel pump relay location.

On Impreza and Legacy models, refer to **Fig. 3,** for fuel pump relay location (2).

RELAY CENTER LOCATION

Relays are located on both fuse/relay panels, refer to "Fuse Panel & Flasher Location" for relay center location.

STARTER

REPLACE

1. Disconnect battery ground cable.
2. Disconnect battery cable and solenoid wiring at starter.
3. Remove starter retaining bolts, then the starter from bellhousing.
4. Reverse procedure to install.

DISTRIBUTOR

REPLACE

JUSTY

1. Number spark plug wires for installation reference, then remove spark plug wires from distributor cap.
2. Remove distributor cap, mark position of rotor for assembly reference.
3. Remove distributor retaining bolts, then the distributor from engine.
4. Reverse procedure to install, align rotor reference marks and adjust ignition timing to specification.

COIL PACK

REPLACE

1. Disconnect battery ground cable.
2. Disconnect coil pack electrical connector, **Fig. 4.**
3. Disconnect spark plug wires from coil pack, noting wire position for installation.
4. Remove coil pack attaching bolts and remove coil pack.
5. Reverse procedure to install.

IGNITION SWITCH

REPLACE

JUSTY & LOYALE

1. Remove steering wheel as outlined in "Steering Wheel, Replace."
2. Remove mast jacket plastic cover held by four screws to expose the switch mounting.
3. Drill two rounded bolt heads then remove bolts with an easy-out.
4. Remove two bolts with conventional hex heads.

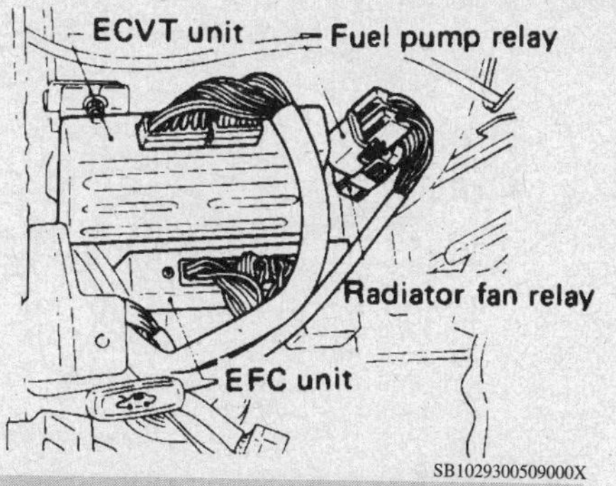
ECVT unit
Fuel pump relay
Radiator fan relay
EFC unit
SB1029300509000X

Fig. 1 Fuel pump relay location. Justy

5. Pull out switch with clamps.
6. Reverse procedure to install, noting the following:
   a. Refit new switch with clamp. If clamp bolts are same as original equipment, they will have a double-head. The top portion permits tightening with a wrench, and when the necessary torque is reached, the top portion can be snapped off, leaving only the tamper-resistant lower head.

IMPREZA

1. Remove upper and lower steering column covers, then the knee protector.
2. Remove instrument cluster visor, then disconnect ignition switch electrical connectors.
3. Using a drift or hammer, hit torn bolt head to loosen and remove ignition switch.
4. Reverse procedure to install. Tighten switch mounting bolts until heads twist off.

LEGACY

1993-94

1. Disconnect negative battery cable.
2. Remove lower instrument panel cover, then lower and upper steering column covers.
3. Disconnect body harness electrical connector.
4. Remove steering column as follows:
   a. Raise and support vehicle.
   b. Remove front wheels.
   c. Remove steering shaft universal joint.
   d. Remove two steering shaft to instrument panel retaining bolts.
   e. Pull steering shaft out from toe board.
5. Cut upper to lower ignition key switch retaining bolt.
6. Tap cutoff surface of bolt with a hammer and punch, then remove the switch.
7. Reverse procedure to install noting the following:
   a. Tighten ignition key switch retaining bolt until head twists off.
   b. **Torque** steering shaft to instrument panel retaining bolts to 14–22 ft. lbs. **Ensure left side of column is tightened together with ground terminal, and coating plates are properly positioned.**
   c. **Torque** universal joint to 15–20 ft. lbs. **Tighten long yoke side first.**

①
Fuel pump relay
Main relay
SB1029300510000X

Fig. 2 Fuel pump relay location. SVX

1995-96

1. Remove upper and lower steering column covers.
2. Remove instrument panel lower cover.
3. Disconnect ignition switch electrical connector from main body harness.
4. Using a suitable hammer and punch hit the torn bolt head to loosen and remove ignition switch.
5. Reverse procedure to install. Tighten connecting bolt until head twist off.

NEUTRAL SAFETY SWITCH

REPLACE

EXCEPT 4-SPEED AUTOMATIC TRANSAXLE

1. Disconnect battery ground cable.
2. Remove hand brake cover and center console.
3. Disconnect indicator light and neutral safety switch electrical connections.
4. Remove selector lever assembly retaining screws and lever assembly.
5. Remove safety switch retaining screws and switch from the selector lever assembly.
6. Reverse procedure to install.

4-SPEED AUTOMATIC TRANSAXLE

1. Disconnect battery ground cable.
2. Detach cable from select lever.
3. Remove three inhibitor switch to transaxle retaining bolts.
4. Disconnect switch electrical connector and remove inhibitor switch.
5. Install new inhibitor switch and lightly install retaining bolts.
6. Adjust switch as follows:
   a. Ensure select lever is set in the N position.
   b. Insert stopper pin, tool No. 499267300, or equivalent, into the inhibitor switch lever and switch body.
   c. **Torque** retaining bolts to 3 ft. lbs., then remove the stopper pin.
   d. Attach cable to select lever, then check for proper operation.

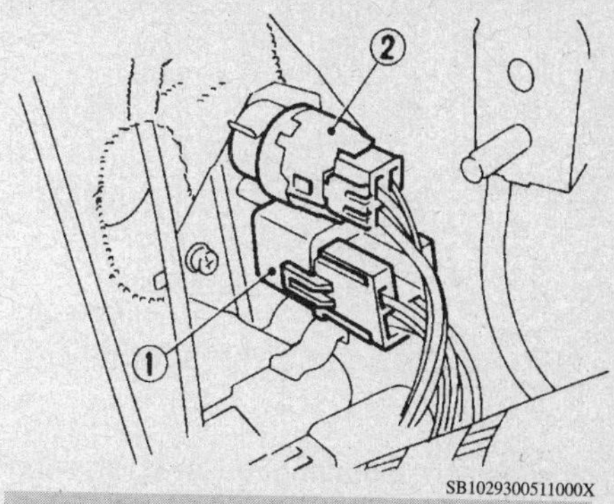
②
①
SB1029300511000X

Fig. 3 Fuel pump relay location. Impreza & Legacy

HEADLAMP SWITCH

REPLACE

Refer to "Combination Switch, Replace." for procedure.

STOP LIGHT SWITCH

REPLACE

Switch is located on bracket under dashboard, near top of brake pedal.

1. Disconnect battery ground cable.
2. Remove locknut on pedal side of bracket.
3. Push switch through bracket and remove wiring connector.
4. Reverse procedure to install.

COMBINATION SWITCH

REPLACE

JUSTY & LOYALE

1. Remove steering wheel as outlined under "Steering Wheel, Replace."
2. Remove screws securing lower steering column cover and the cover.
3. Remove steering column upper mounting screws and pull down on column as needed, then remove upper column cover.
4. Release switch harness retaining straps and remove combination switch mounting screws.
5. Disconnect electrical connectors and remove combination switch assembly.
6. Reverse procedure to install noting the following:
   a. **On models equipped with key interlock,** do not position combination switch harness over key interlock release knob. Ensure release knob is accessible after installing lower column cover.

IMPREZA

Less Air Bag

1. Remove steering wheel as outlined under "Steering Wheel, Replace."

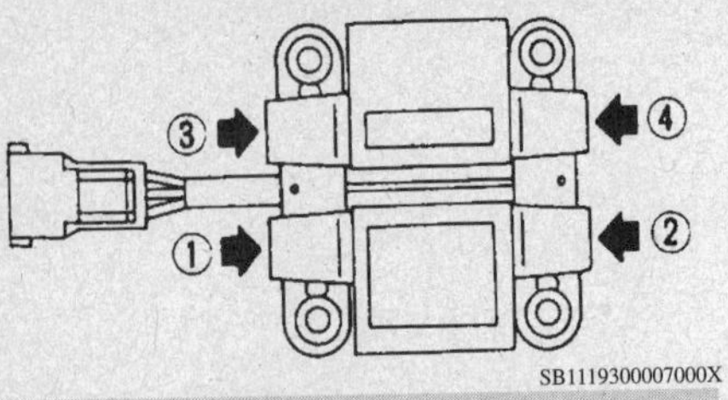
③
④
①
②
SB1119300007000X

Fig. 4 Coil pack replacement

2. Remove mounting bolts to steering column covers, then the covers.
3. Remove knee protector, then disconnect combination switch electrical connector.
4. Remove combination switch mounting screws, then the switch.
5. Reverse procedure to install, noting the following:
   a. When routing combination switch harness around steering system, do not place it over key interlock release knob.
   b. After installing lower column cover, ensure key interlock release knob is accessible.

With Air Bag

1. Remove column lower cover, then disconnect air bag connectors located below steering column.
2. Disconnect combination switch electrical connectors.
3. Position front wheels in straight ahead position, then remove covers from both side of steering column.
4. Using T30 Torx bit, remove four Torx bolts located below steering wheel side covers.
5. Disconnect air bag and horn connectors on back side of air bag module. Remove air bag module and place it with pad side facing upward.
6. Using suitable puller, remove steering wheel.
7. Remove steering column cover.
8. Remove combination switch mounting bolts, then the switch.
9. Reverse procedure to install, noting the following:
   a. Before installing switch, ensure switch is off and front wheels are in straight ahead position.
   b. Align column cover and center roll connector as shown in **Fig. 5.**

SVX & 1993-94 LEGACY

1. Remove air bag module as outlined under "Air Bag Systems" section of this chapter.
2. **On all models,** disconnect negative battery cable.
3. Raise and support vehicle, then remove front wheels.
4. Remove steering shaft universal joint, then the lower instrument panel trim panel.
5. Disconnect electrical connectors for ignition switch and combination switch.
6. Remove two steering shaft to instrument panel retaining bolts.
7. Pull steering shaft out from toe board.
8. **On models less air bags,** remove horn pad.
9. **On all models,** remove steering wheel as outlined under "Steering Wheel, Replace."
10. Remove steering column upper and lower covers, then two combination switch mounting bolts.
11. Remove combination switch.
12. Reverse procedure to install.
13. **On models with air bags,** align center of roll connector, **Fig. 5.**

1995-96 LEGACY

1. Remove steering wheel as outlined under "Steering Wheel Replace."
2. Remove upper and lower steering column covers.
3. Remove instrument panel lower cover.
4. Disconnect combination switch electrical connector from main body harness, then undo hold down band.
5. Remove switch.
6. Reverse procedure to install.

TURN SIGNAL SWITCH

REPLACE

Refer to "Combination Switch, Replace" for procedure.

STEERING WHEEL

REPLACE

1. **On models equipped with air bags,** remove air bag module as outlined in the "Air Bag System" section.
2. **On all models,** disconnect negative battery cable.
3. Remove steering wheel trim pad.
4. Mark steering wheel for reference during assembly.
5. Remove steering wheel retaining nut.
6. Using a suitable puller, separate steering wheel from steering shaft.
7. Reverse procedure to install.

INSTRUMENT CLUSTER

REPLACE

JUSTY

1. Disconnect battery ground cable.
2. Remove four clips, one tapping screw, the choke knob and dress nut, then the trim panel.
3. Remove clips and tapping screws, then the visor.
4. Remove four instrument cluster tapping screws.
5. Separate the speedometer cable and all electrical connectors from the instrument cluster.
6. Remove instrument cluster from dash panel.

LEGACY

1993-94

1. Disconnect negative battery cable.
2. Loosen steering column to instrument panel retaining bolts and suspend the steering column.
3. Remove visor ventilation grille.

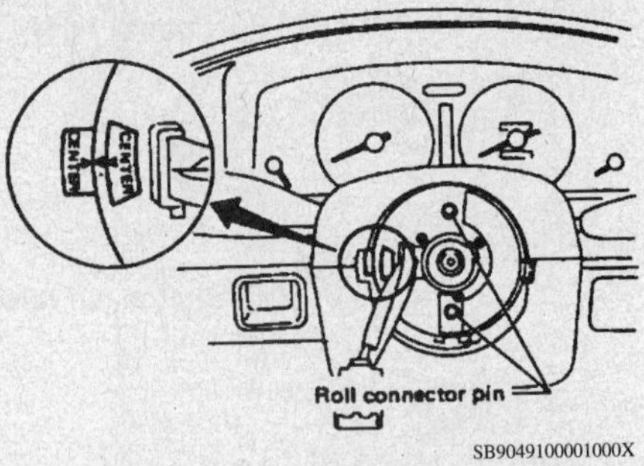
CENTER
Roll connector pin
SB9049100001000X

Fig. 5 Aligning tool connector. Legacy & SVX w/air bag

4. Remove and disconnect all switches necessary to facilitate cluster removal.
5. Remove cup holder and visor.
6. Remove combination meter retaining screws.
7. Pull meter out from dash panel enough to disconnect speedometer and connector, then tilt combination meter and remove from instrument panel.
8. Reverse procedure to install.

1995-96

1. Tilt steering wheel down fully.
2. Remove screws from instrument cluster trim visor and pull out visor part way, then disconnect electrical connections and remove trim visor.
3. Remove screws from instrument cluster and pull out cluster part way, then disconnect electrical connections and remove Instrument cluster.
4. Reverse procedure to install.

LOYALE

1. Disconnect battery ground cable.
2. Remove knobs from wiper switch and upper and lower switches on right side switch panel.
3. Remove screws securing instrument cluster bezel and switch panel, disconnect electrical connectors, then remove panel and bezel.
4. Remove cluster retaining screws and pull cluster away from instrument panel.
5. Disconnect electrical connectors and speedometer cable, taking care not to damage speed sensor assembly, then remove cluster.
6. Reverse procedure to install.

IMPREZA

1. Tilt steering wheel to lowest position, then remove instrument cluster visor.
2. Disconnect cluster electrical connector.
3. Remove cluster mounting screws, then slightly pull out cluster.
4. Disconnect connector and speedometer cable from back of cluster, then remove cluster.
5. Reverse procedure to install.

SVX

1. Tilt steering wheel to lowest position, then retract steering wheel back.
2. Remove lower cover.
3. Push switch box assembly from rear

side of switch, then disconnect connector and remove switch box assembly.
4. Remove visor, then disconnect clock connector.
5. Remove instrument cluster mounting screws, then the instrument cluster.
6. Reverse procedure to install.

RADIO

REPLACE

EXCEPT SVX & 1995-96 LEGACY

1. Disconnect battery ground cable.
2. As equipped, remove cup holder and ashtray.
3. Disconnect center instrument panel trim plate.
4. Remove radio mounting screws.
5. Disconnect electrical connectors and antenna lead, then remove radio.
6. Reverse procedure to install.

SVX

1. Tilt steering wheel to lowest position, then retract steering wheel back.
2. Remove lower cover.
3. Push switch box assembly from rear side of switch, then disconnect connector and remove switch box assembly.
4. Remove visor, then disconnect clock connector.
5. Remove center ventilation grille, then the auto A/C amplifier.
6. Remove radio inner panel, then the center panel.
7. Remove lefthand cowl panel. Roll carpet and disconnect antenna feeder cables.
8. Remove ashtray, then the radio mounting screws.
9. Close radio panel, slide radio outward and disconnect electrical connector.
10. Remove radio.
11. Reverse procedure to install.

1995-96 LEGACY

1. Remove hand brake cover and console cover.
2. Remove center panel mounting screws, then center panel.
3. Remove radio mounting screws, then radio.
4. Disconnect electrical connectors and antenna feeder cord.
5. Reverse procedure to install.

WIPER MOTOR

REPLACE

FRONT

1. Disconnect battery ground cable.
2. Remove weatherstrip and nets.
3. Disconnect wiper motor electrical connector.
4. Remove wiper motor attaching bolts.
5. Remove wiper motor link attaching nut, and separate link from motor.
6. Remove wiper motor from vehicle.
7. Reverse procedure to install.

REAR

1. Disconnect battery ground cable.
2. Remove wiper arm from the shaft.
3. Remove cap and nut from wiper arm mounting.
4. Remove back door or rear gate inner trim.
5. Disconnect wiper motor electrical connections.
6. Disconnect washer hoses at joint, if equipped.
7. Remove wiper motor retaining bolts and the motor.
8. Reverse procedure to install.

WIPER SWITCH

REPLACE

Refer to "Combination Switch, Replace" for procedure.

WIPER TRANSMISSION

REPLACE

EXCEPT LEGACY

1. Remove wiper motor as outlined under "Windshield Wiper Motor, Replace."
2. Remove transaxle mounting bolts.
3. Remove wiper link from service hole in front panel.
4. Reverse procedure to install.

LEGACY

1. Remove wiper motor as outlined under "Windshield Wiper Motor, Replace."
2. Remove left side transaxle mounting nuts, then separate left and right wiper links at center joint. To separate links pry with standard screwdriver inserted into service hole in front panel.
3. Remove right side transaxle mounting nuts, right side transaxle mounting nuts.
4. Remove wiper links from service holes in front panel.
5. Reverse procedure to install. To assemble wiper links, push using grip of screwdriver.

BLOWER MOTOR

REPLACE

LOYALE

1. Disconnect battery ground cable.
2. Remove passenger side trim panel.
3. Remove glove compartment pocket.
4. Remove pocket frame.
5. **On models less A/C,** remove heater duct.
6. **On models with A/C,** separate evaporator from blower assembly.
7. **On all models,** disconnect blower vacuum hose from instrument panel vacuum hose.
8. Disconnect blower motor and resistor electrical connectors.
9. Remove blower attaching bolts and nuts.
10. Remove ventilation duct bracket and the blower motor assembly.
11. Reverse procedure to install, noting the following:
    a. Fitting length of vacuum hose must exceed .31 inch.
    b. **Torque** blower attaching nuts and bolts to 4.0–6.9 ft. lbs.

LEGACY

1. Disconnect battery ground cable.
2. Remove glove compartment.
3. Remove heater duct.
4. Disconnect intake door motor and blower motor electrical connectors.
5. Remove blower motor retaining bolts and the blower motor.
6. Reverse procedure to install.

JUSTY

1. Disconnect battery ground cable.
2. Open glove compartment then, while pulling stopper clips inward, lower the glove compartment.
3. Separate heater duct from blower assembly.
4. Disconnect blower motor and resistor electrical connectors.
5. Disconnect inside-outside air control cable at blower assembly.
6. Remove blower assembly attaching bolts, then the blower assembly.
7. Remove blower motor attaching screws, then the blower motor.
8. Reverse procedure to install.

IMPREZA & SVX

1. Remove glove compartment.
2. **On SVX models,** remove glove compartment support bracket.
3. **On all models,** disconnect blower motor electrical connector, then remove motor cool hose.
4. Remove motor mounting screws, then the motor assembly.
5. Reverse procedure to install.

HEATER CORE

REPLACE

EXCEPT JUSTY

1. Disconnect battery ground cable.
2. Disconnect inlet and outlet heater hoses in engine compartment. Drain as much coolant as possible from heater unit and plug disconnected hoses.
3. Disconnect heater control and mode door cables, then vacuum hose from heater unit joint as equipped.
4. Remove instrument panel as outlined under "Dash Panel Service."
5. **On Impreza models,** remove steering column support beam.
6. **On Impreza and Legacy models,** remove evaporator as outlined under "Evaporator Core, Replace."
7. **On all models,** remove heater unit.
8. Remove heater core from heater unit.
9. Reverse procedure to install, noting the following:
    a. **On Legacy and Loyale models,** fitted length of heater hose to pipe is .79–.98 inch.
    b. **On Impreza models,** fitted length of heater hose to pipe is .99–1.18 inch.
    c. **On Loyale and SVX models,** fitted

length of vacuum hose must exceed .31 inch.

d. **On all models, torque** heater unit attaching bolts to 4.0–6.9 ft. lbs.

JUSTY

1. Disconnect battery ground cable.
2. Remove radiator drain plug and allow coolant to drain.
3. Loosen heater hose clamps, then remove inlet and outlet hoses from the heater unit.
4. Separate left and right defroster ducts from nozzles and remove ducts from the heater unit.
5. Disconnect blower motor and fan switch electrical connectors.
6. Disconnect heater unit air mix and mode cables.
7. Remove heater unit to instrument panel attaching bolt.
8. Open glove compartment then, while pulling stopper clips inward, lower the glove compartment.
9. Disconnect inside-outside air control cable at blower assembly.
10. Remove instrument panel as follows:
    a. Remove steering wheel as outlined under "Steering Wheel, Replace."
    b. Remove defroster duct.
    c. Disconnect heater control cable from inside-outside air selector rod at heater unit.
    d. Disconnect speedometer cable.
    e. Disconnect electrical harness connector.
    f. Remove instrument panel attaching bolt covers, the attaching bolts, then the instrument panel.
11. Remove blower assembly and heater unit attaching bolts.
12. Carefully remove heater unit.
13. Remove heater core cushion.
14. Loosen and remove heater core holder.
15. Remove heater core from heater unit.
16. Reverse procedure to install.

EVAPORATOR CORE

REPLACE

1. Disconnect battery ground cable.
2. **On Loyale models,** remove spare tire.
3. **On all models,** properly discharge A/C system.
4. Disconnect discharge and suction pipes and remove grommets from evaporator.
5. Remove undercover trim, if necessary.
6. Remove glove compartment, then the glove compartment support bracket, if necessary.
7. **On SVX models,** remove time control unit, then disconnect fan control amplifier harness.
8. **On all models,** disconnect electrical connector from evaporator.
9. Remove evaporator retaining bands or bolts, then the evaporator assembly.
10. Remove upper to lower evaporator case retaining bolts or clamps, then remove evaporator core from case.
11. Reverse procedure to install.

Engine

NOTE: On Air Bag Equipped Models, Refer To "Air Bag System Precautions" Located In The Front Of This Manual For System Disarming & Arming Procedures.

INDEX

	Page No.
Belt Tension Data	39-28
Impreza & Legacy	39-28
Justy & Loyale	39-28
SVX	39-28
Compression Pressures	39-10
Cooling System Bleed	39-28
Engine Rebuilding Specifications	39-191
Engine, Replace	39-11
Impreza	39-11
Justy	39-11
Legacy	39-12
Loyale	39-13
SVX	39-13
Engine Service	39-14
Impreza w/1.8L & 2.2L Engines	39-20
Loyale w/1.8L Engine	39-16
1.2L Engine	39-14
3.3L Engine	39-24
Fuel Filter, Replace	39-30
Impreza, Legacy & SVX	39-30
Justy	39-30
Loyale	39-30
Fuel Pump, Replace	39-29
Impreza & Legacy	39-29
Justy & Loyale	39-29
SVX	39-30
Precautions	39-10
Air Bag Systems	39-10
Fuel System Pressure Relief	39-10
Radiator, Replace	39-29
Except Justy	39-29
Justy	39-29
Thermostat, Replace	39-28
Tightening Specifications	39-34
Impreza w/1.8L & 2.2L Engine	39-35
Loyale w/1.8L Engine	39-34
1.2L Engine	39-34
3.3L Engine	39-36
Valve Clearance Specifications	39-28
Water Pump, Replace	39-28
Impreza w/1.8L & 2.2L Engine	39-29
Loyale w/1.8L Engine	39-28
1.2L Engine	39-28
3.3L Engine	39-29

PRECAUTIONS

AIR BAG SYSTEMS

Refer to "Air Bag System Precautions" in the front of this manual for system disarming and arming procedures.

FUEL SYSTEM PRESSURE RELIEF

1. **On Impreza, Legacy & SVX models,** fold down rear seat back and remove floor mat, then remove access hole cover.
2. **On Loyale and Justy models,** raise and support vehicle.
3. **On all models,** disconnect fuel pump electrical connection.
4. Start engine and run until engine stalls.
5. After engine stalls crank engine for five more seconds, then place ignition switch in OFF position.
6. Reconnect fuel pump electrical connector.

COMPRESSION PRESSURES

When checking compression pressures, ensure engine is at normal operating temperature and battery is completely charged. Remove all spark plugs and open

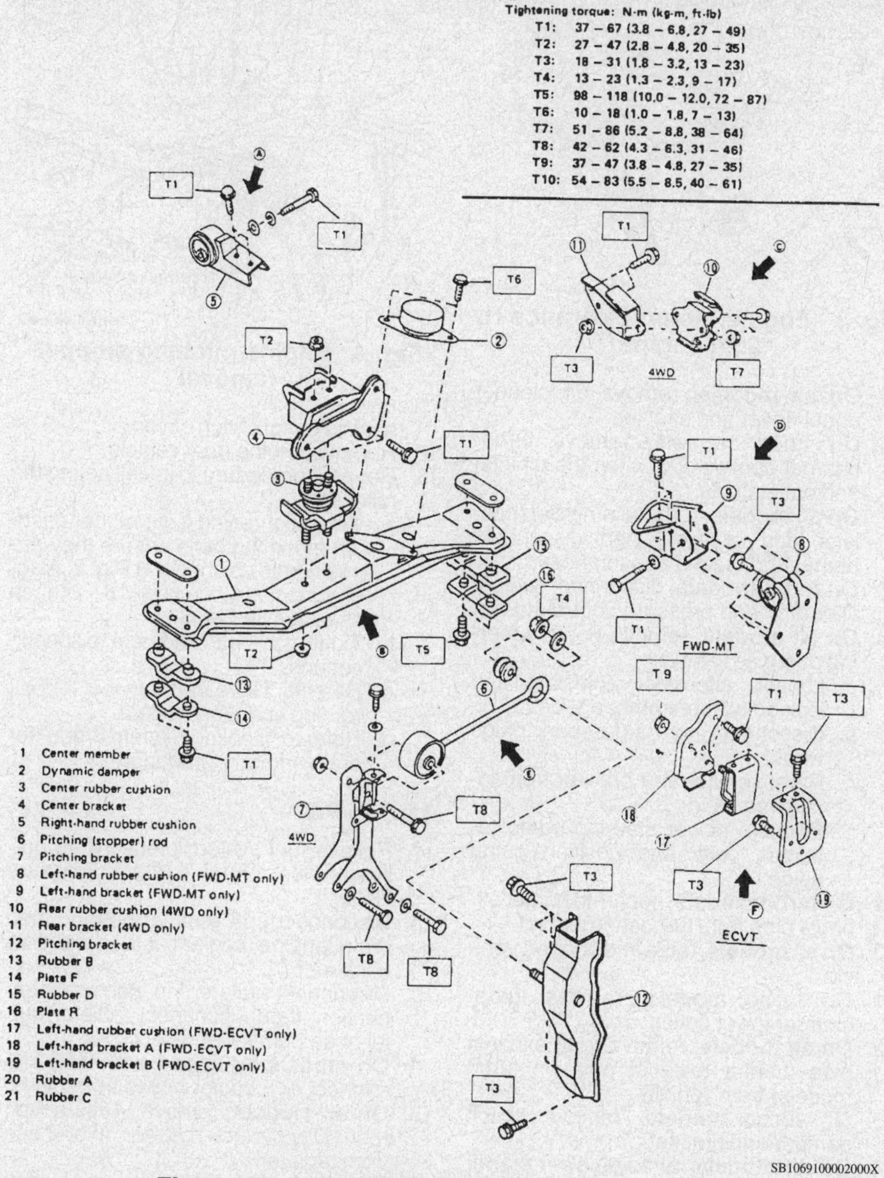
Tightening torque: N·m (kg-m, ft-lb)
T1: 37 – 67 (3.8 – 6.8, 27 – 49)
T2: 27 – 47 (2.8 – 4.8, 20 – 35)
T3: 18 – 31 (1.8 – 3.2, 13 – 23)
T4: 13 – 23 (1.3 – 2.3, 9 – 17)
T5: 98 – 118 (10.0 – 12.0, 72 – 87)
T6: 10 – 18 (1.0 – 1.8, 7 – 13)
T7: 51 – 86 (5.2 – 8.8, 38 – 64)
T8: 42 – 62 (4.3 – 6.3, 31 – 46)
T9: 37 – 47 (3.8 – 4.8, 27 – 35)
T10: 54 – 83 (5.5 – 8.5, 40 – 61)
4WD
FWD-MT
ECVT
1 Center member
2 Dynamic damper
3 Center rubber cushion
4 Center bracket
5 Right-hand rubber cushion
6 Pitching (stopper) rod
7 Pitching bracket
8 Left-hand rubber cushion (FWD-MT only)
9 Left-hand bracket (FWD-MT only)
10 Rear rubber cushion (4WD only)
11 Rear bracket (4WD only)
12 Pitching bracket
13 Rubber B
14 Plate F
15 Rubber D
16 Plate R
17 Left-hand rubber cushion (FWD-ECVT only)
18 Left-hand bracket A (FWD-ECVT only)
19 Left-hand bracket B (FWD-ECVT only)
20 Rubber A
21 Rubber C
SB1069100002000X

Fig. 1 Exploded view of engine mount. Justy

throttle fully. Remove ignition coil harness, then install a suitable compression gauge. Crank engine and note compression gauge reading when gauge pointer is steady. Perform at least two measurements per cylinder to ensure compression readings are correct. The maximum compression difference between cylinders is 14 psi. Compression pressures should be 135–156 psi at 300 RPM.

ENGINE

REPLACE

IMPREZA

1. Place vehicle on lift and open hood.
2. Relieve fuel system pressure as outlined under "Fuel System Pressure Relief" in this section.
3. Disconnect battery cables and remove battery, then drain coolant.
4. Remove radiator assembly as follows:
   a. Disconnect radiator fan motor connector, then radiator hose from thermostat cover.
   b. **On models equipped with automatic transaxle,** disconnect transaxle cooler hoses from pipes.
   c. **On all models,** remove V-belt cover, then disconnect radiator inlet hose from radiator.
   d. Remove radiator upper bracket, then the radiator assembly.
5. Discharge A/C system, then disconnect A/C hoses from compressor.
6. Disconnect mass air flow sensor connector. Remove air intake duct with air cleaner upper cover, then air cleaner element.
7. Remove canister and bracket.
8. **On models equipped with A/C,** disconnect FICD solenoid valve and compressor connectors.
9. **On all models,** disconnect engine harness and oxygen sensor connectors.
10. Disconnect engine ground terminal and alternator connector and terminal.
11. Disconnect accelerator and cruise control cables.
12. **On models equipped with manual transaxle,** disconnect clutch release spring, clutch cable and hill holder cable. Disconnect hill holder on release fork side and transfer it to PHV side.
13. **On all models,** disconnect cruise control and brake booster vacuum hoses, then the heater hoses.
14. Remove power steering pump from bracket. Position pump on right side wheel apron.
15. Raise and support vehicle, then remove front and center exhaust pipes.
16. Remove lower engine to transaxle mounting bolts, then the front cushion to front crossmember mounting nuts.
17. **On models equipped with automatic transaxle,** separate torque converter from driveplate as follows:
    a. Lower vehicle, then remove service hole plug.
    b. Remove torque converter to driveplate bolts.
    c. Remove other bolt while rotating engine using crankshaft pulley wrench tool No. 499977000, or equivalent.
18. **On all models,** remove pitching stopper, then disconnect fuel and evaporation hoses.
19. Support engine with suitable lifting device and transaxle with jack.
20. Remove upper transaxle to engine mounting bolts.
21. Remove engine from vehicle as follows:
    a. Slightly raise engine, then the transaxle with jack.
    b. Move engine horizontally until mainshaft is withdrawn from clutch cover.
    c. Slowly move engine away from engine compartment.
22. Reverse procedure to install.

JUSTY

The engine and transaxle are removed as an assembly on these vehicles.

1. Disconnect battery ground cable and drain cooling system.
2. Remove front bumper and grille.
3. Disconnect hoses and all electrical connections, then remove radiator.
4. Disconnect hood release cable, then remove upper radiator support.
5. Remove air cleaner assembly.
6. Disconnect hoses from carburetor, heater unit, brake booster and AWD to front wheel drive changeover, if equipped. Mark all hoses to aid installation.
7. Disconnect clutch cable from clutch housing and accelerator cable from carburetor.
8. Disconnect speedometer cable at transaxle.
9. Disconnect ignition coil to distributor electrical connections at distributor.
10. Remove pitching stopper rod from bracket.
11. Raise and support vehicle, then remove engine undercovers.

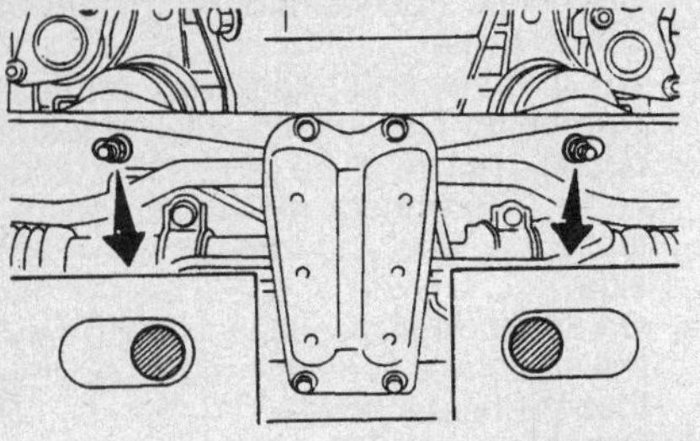
SB1069100003000X

Fig. 2 Front rubber cushion installation. 2.2L engine

12. Disconnect exhaust pipes from manifold, then the gearshift rod from transaxle.
13. Disconnect propeller shaft from transaxle, if applicable. Cap opening to prevent loss of fluid.
14. Remove transverse link.
15. Using suitable drift, remove spring pin and disconnect front axle from transaxle.
16. Support engine using suitable hoist, then remove engine/transaxle mounting brackets.
17. Raise engine slightly, then remove center member and crossmember.
18. Lift engine/transaxle assembly out of vehicle.
19. Reverse procedure to install noting the following:
    a. Refer to "Tightening Specifications" and **Fig. 1** for tightening specifications.
    b. Refer to "Drive Belt Service" for belt routing and tension data.
    c. Refer to "Cooling System Bleed" for drain and refill procedure.

LEGACY

1993–94

1. Relieve fuel system pressure as outlined under "Fuel System Pressure Relief" in this section.
2. Disconnect battery cables from battery, then remove battery from vehicle.
3. Drain cooling system.
4. **On non-turbo models,** remove manifold cover.
5. **On all models,** disconnect radiator hoses from engine, then the radiator cooling fan motor electrical connectors.
6. Remove V-belt cover, then the reservoir tank.
7. Remove radiator retaining brackets. Lift and position radiator slightly to the left.
8. Disconnect automatic transaxle fluid cooler hoses from radiator.
9. Remove radiator from vehicle.
10. **On models equipped with A/C,** properly discharge A/C system.
11. Disconnect and plug discharge and suction hoses. **Ensure care is taken not to loose O-ring in low pressure hose.**
12. **On non-turbo models,** remove air intake duct.
13. **On turbo models,** remove resonator chamber.

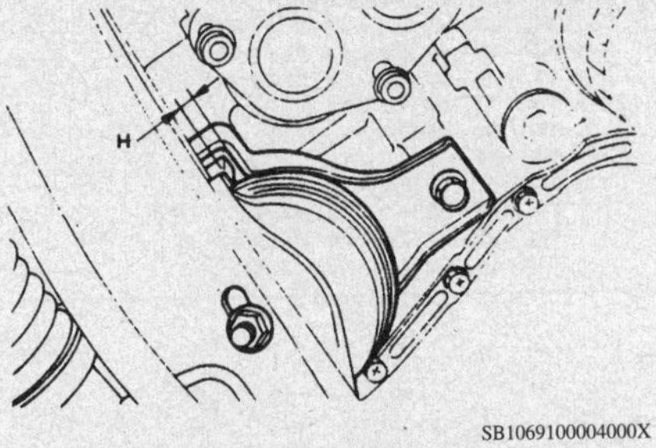
H
SB1069100004000X

Fig. 3 Engine mount clearance H. 2.2L engine

14. **On all models,** remove air cleaner upper cover and air filter.
15. **On turbo models,** remove turbocharger cooling duct, then the air inlet and outlet ducts.
16. **On all models,** remove emission canister and bracket, then disconnect heater and brakes booster hoses.
17. **On turbo models,** disconnect coolant filler tank and pressure control hoses.
18. **On all models,** remove power steering pump as follows:
    a. Loosen alternator adjusting and lock bolts, then remove V-belt.
    b. Disconnect right side spark plugs wires.
    c. Remove pipe and bracket from intake manifold.
    d. Remove power steering pump retaining bolts and position pump aside.
19. **On turbo models,** separate center exhaust pipe from turbocharger unit.
20. **On all models,** raise and support vehicle.
21. **On turbo models,** remove turbocharger lower cover.
22. **On all models,** remove front exhaust pipe (center exhaust pipe on turbo models) from vehicle.
23. **On turbo models,** remove clutch damper and bracket.
24. **On all models,** remove lower starter mounting nut, then the lower transaxle to engine nuts.
25. Remove front cushion rubber to front crossmember mounting nuts, then the starter.
26. **On turbo models,** separate clutch release fork from release bearing as follows:
    a. Remove clutch operating cylinder from transaxle.
    b. Using 10 mm hex wrench, remove plug.
    c. Screw 6 mm diameter bolt into release fork shaft, then remove shaft.
    d. Raise release fork and unfasten release bearing tabs to free fork.
27. **On models equipped with automatic transaxle,** separate torque converter from driveplate.
28. **On all models,** remove pitching stopper, then disconnect fuel hoses.
29. Support engine with suitable lifting device and transaxle with suitable stand.
30. Remove upper side transaxle to engine bolt.
31. Slightly raise engine and transaxle. Move engine horizontally until mainshaft is out of clutch cover.

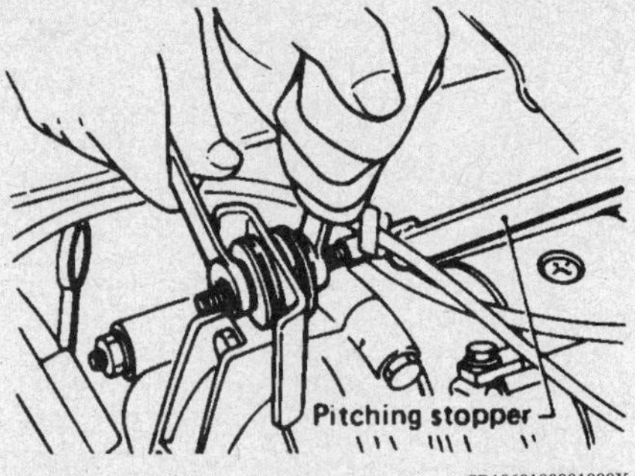
Pitching stopper
SB1069100001000X

Fig. 4 Engine pitching stopper removal

32. Remove engine from vehicle.
33. Reverse procedure to install noting the following:
    a. When tightening front rubber cushion mounting bolts ensure they are positioned as shown in **Fig. 2.** Also, ensure clearance H is .16–.24 inch as shown in **Fig. 3.**
    b. Tighten all bolts and nuts to specifications.
    c. Refer to "Drive Belt Service" for belt routing and tension data.
    d. Refer to "Cooling System Bleed" for drain and refill procedure.

1995–96

1. Relieve fuel system pressure as outlined under "Fuel System Pressure Relief."
2. Disconnect and remove battery, then drain engine coolant into a suitable container.
3. Disconnect radiator fan electrical connection, then disconnect radiator outlet hose from thermostat cover.
4. **On models equipped with A/T,** disconnect ATF cooler hoses from pipes.
5. **On all models,** remove V-belt cover, then Disconnect radiator inlet hose from radiator.
6. Remove radiator upper bracket, then radiator assembly.
7. **On models equipped with A/C,** discharge and recover system refrigerant, then disconnect A/C pressure hoses from compressor.
8. **On all models,** disconnect mass air flow electrical connection, then remove air intake duct, air cleaner upper cover and air cleaner element.
9. Remove emissions canister and bracket.
10. Disconnect all cables, electrical connections and hoses. **Label all connections for installation reference.**
11. Loosen power steering pump lock bolt and slider bolt, then remove front side V-belt.
12. Remove power steering pipe with bracket from intake manifold.
13. Remove mounting bolts and power steering pump. Place pump on right side wheel apron.
14. Raise and support vehicle, then remove front exhaust pipe to engine mounting nuts.
15. Disconnect electrical connection from

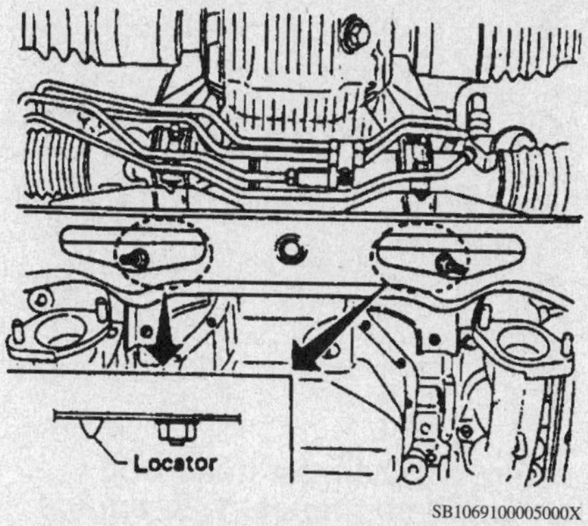
Locator

SB1069100005000X

Fig. 5 Front rubber cushion installation. 3.3L engine

rear oxygen sensor then, separate center and rear exhaust pipes.

16. Remove center exhaust pipe mounting bolt from hanger bracket, then remove front and center exhaust pipe.
17. Remove lower transaxle to engine mounting nuts, then remove front cushion rubber to front crossmember nuts.
18. **On models equipped with A/T,** lower vehicle and remove torque converter service hole plug.
19. Remove torque converter to drive plate mounting bolts, then remove all other bolts from torque converter while rotating engine with crank pulley wrench tool No. 499977000, or equivalent.
20. **On all models,** remove engine pitching stopper, then disconnect fuel delivery hose, return hose and evaporation hose.
21. Support transaxle with suitable jack, then remove upper transaxle to engine mounting nuts.
22. Remove engine.
23. Reverse procedure to install.

LOYALE

1. Remove spare tire from engine compartment.
2. Relieve fuel system pressure as outlined under "Fuel System Pressure Relief" in this section.
3. Disconnect battery ground cable from battery and engine.
4. Remove spare support clamp and the support.
5. Disconnect vacuum hoses from charcoal canister, then remove upper air cleaner case and filter and disconnect electrical connector.
6. Disconnect fuel delivery, return and evaporation hoses.
7. **On models equipped with automatic transaxle,** disconnect diaphragm vacuum hose.
8. **On all models,** disconnect wire harness connectors between engine and body.
9. Disconnect accelerator cable from carburetor or throttle body.
10. **On models equipped with manual transaxle,** remove release lever spring, then disconnect hill holder cable, if equipped.

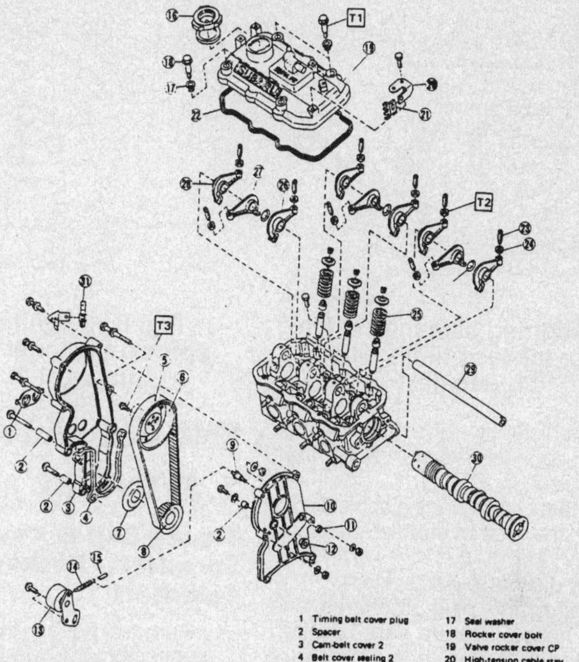

Tightening torque: N-m (kg-m, ft-lb)
T1: 6.9 – 7.8 (0.70 – 0.80, 5.1 – 5.8)
T2: 17 – 23 (1.7 – 2.3, 12 – 17)
T3: 11.3 – 12.3 (1.15 – 1.25, 8.3 – 9.0)

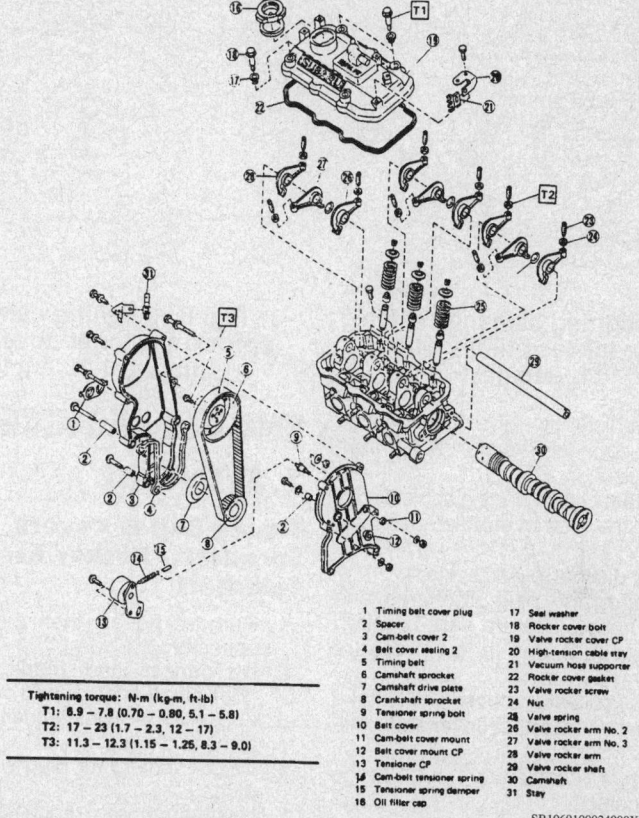

1 Timing belt cover plug
2 Spacer
3 Cam-belt cover 2
4 Belt cover sealing 2
5 Timing belt
6 Camshaft sprocket
7 Camshaft drive plate
8 Crankshaft sprocket
9 Tensioner spring bolt
10 Belt cover
11 Cam-belt cover mount
12 Belt cover mount CP
13 Tensioner CP
14 Cam-belt tensioner spring
15 Tensioner spring damper
16 Oil filler cap
17 Seal washer
18 Rocker cover bolt
19 Valve rocker cover CP
20 High-tension cable stay
21 Vacuum hose supporter
22 Rocker cover gasket
23 Valve rocker screw
24 Nut
25 Valve spring
26 Valve rocker arm No. 2
27 Valve rocker arm No. 3
28 Valve rocker arm
29 Valve rocker shaft
30 Camshaft
31 Stay

SB1069100024000X

Fig. 6 Exploded view of timing belt & valve system components. 1.2L engine

11. **On all models,** remove pitching stopper rod, **Fig. 4.**
12. **On models equipped with turbocharged engine,** proceed as follows:
    a. Remove transaxle heat shield, then the turbocharger side heat shield.
    b. Raise and support vehicle.
    c. Loosen front exhaust pipe connection, then lower vehicle and remove heat shield cover from center exhaust pipe.
    d. Disconnect center exhaust pipe from turbocharger.
    e. Raise and support vehicle.
    f. Disconnect center exhaust pipe from rear exhaust pipe, then unfasten and remove center exhaust pipe and lower vehicle.
13. **On models equipped with automatic transaxle,** remove timing hole plug, then the four torque converter to driveplate attaching bolts.
14. **On all models,** drain cooling system, then disconnect radiator hoses and remove radiator from vehicle.
15. Disconnect heater hoses from engine.
16. Unfasten power steering pump, if equipped, and position aside.
17. Raise and support vehicle.
18. **On models equipped with nonturbocharged engine,** proceed as follows:
    a. Disconnect front exhaust pipe from engine. **Leave one nut installed to temporarily hold exhaust pipe.**
    b. Disconnect front exhaust pipe from rear exhaust pipe.
    c. Unfasten and remove front exhaust pipe.
19. **On all models,** remove engine mount.
20. Remove lower engine to transaxle attaching nuts, the lower vehicle.
21. Support engine using suitable lifting equipment.
22. Remove upper engine to transaxle attaching bolts and nuts.
23. Support transaxle with a suitable jack, then raise engine and transaxle slightly.
24. **On models equipped with manual transaxle,** move engine back until mainshaft clears clutch cover.
25. **On all models,** carefully lift engine and remove from vehicle.
26. Reverse procedure to install noting the following:
    a. Tighten bolts and nuts to specifications.
    b. Refer to "Drive Belt Service" for belt routing and tension data.
    c. Refer to "Cooling System Bleed" for drain and refill procedure.

SVX

1. Relieve fuel system pressure as outlined under "Fuel System Pressure Relief" in this section.
2. Disconnect battery ground cable, then raise and support vehicle.
3. Remove undercover, then drain cooling system.
4. Disconnect radiator hose from thermostat, then the transaxle lines from radiator.

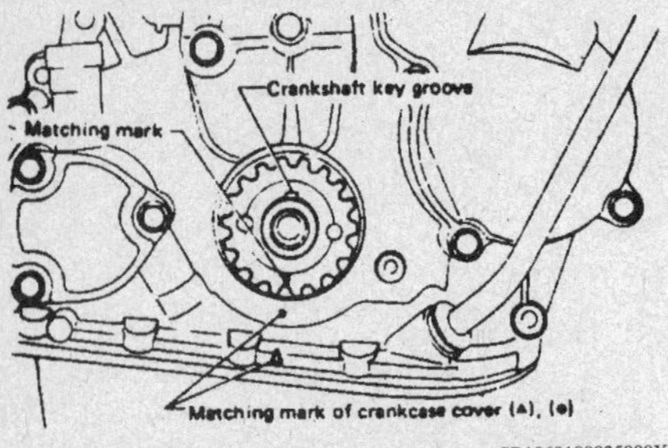
Crankshaft key groove
Matching mark
Matching mark of crankcase cover (▲), (●)
SB1069100025000X

Fig. 7 Aligning camshaft drive pulley & crankcase timing marks. 1.2L engine

5. Lower vehicle. Remove V belt cover, then disconnect radiator hose from water pipe.
6. Disconnect cooling fans electrical connectors, then remove radiator assembly.
7. Properly discharge A/C system.
8. Disconnect and plug discharge and suction hoses. **Ensure care is taken not to loose O-ring in low pressure hose.**
9. Remove collector cover, air intake boot, air cleaner upper cover and air filter.
10. Disconnect accelerator and cruise control cables.
11. Disconnect the following electrical connectors; engine harness, ignition coil, oxygen sensors, vehicle speed sensor 2, power steering, engine ground, alternator and A/C compressor.
12. Disconnect brakes booster, heater and power steering hoses.
13. Remove emission canister and bracket, then raise and support vehicle.
14. Remove oxygen sensor, then the front exhaust pipe and rear catalyst converter.
15. Disconnect transaxle cooler hose from pipe on transaxle.
16. Remove lower starter mounting nut, then the lower transaxle to engine nuts.
17. Remove front cushion rubber to front crossmember mounting nuts, then separate torque converter from driveplate.
18. Remove pitching stopper from bracket, then disconnect fuel hoses.
19. Support engine with suitable lifting device and transaxle with suitable stand.
20. Remove upper side transaxle to engine bolts.
21. Slightly raise engine and transaxle, then remove engine from vehicle.
22. Reverse procedure to install noting the following:
    a. When tightening front rubber cushion mounting bolts ensure they are positioned as shown in **Fig. 5.**
    b. Tighten bolts and nuts to specification.
    c. Refer to "Drive Belt Service" for belt routing and tension data.
    d. Refer to "Cooling System Bleed" for drain and refill procedure.

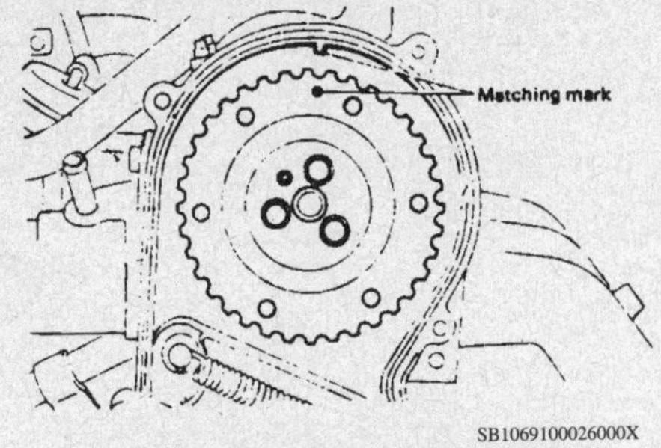
Matching mark
SB1069100026000X

Fig. 8 Aligning camshaft sprocket & inner cover timing marks. 1.2L engine

ENGINE SERVICE

1.2L ENGINE

Timing Belt & Covers, Sprockets, Rocker Assembly & Camshaft

1. Remove hoses, then the air cleaner assembly.
2. Disconnect and mark all vacuum hoses to distributor and carburetor.
3. Loosen alternator adjusting bolt, then remove drive belt.
4. Disconnect spark plug wires at spark plugs.
5. Using spanner wrench 499205500, or equivalent, hold crankshaft pulley in position, then remove retaining bolt and pulley.
6. Remove No. 2 (outer) timing belt cover, **Fig. 6.**
7. Loosen timing belt tensioner bolt ½ turn, then rotate tensioner clockwise and retighten bolt.
8. Remove camshaft driveplate from drive pulley, then mark direction of rotation and remove timing belt.
9. Remove belt tensioner and spring, then the camshaft drive pulley from crankshaft snout.
10. Using spanner wrench 499205500, or equivalent, hold camshaft sprocket in position, then remove retaining bolts and sprocket.
11. Remove inner belt cover and cover mount, then disconnect PCV hose from rocker cover.
12. Remove rocker cover and gasket, then the distributor mounting bolt and distributor.
13. Loosen valve adjusting screw locknuts and adjusting screws. Ensure screws protrude from rocker arm at least .040 inch after loosening.
14. Remove rocker shaft retaining bolt, pull rocker shaft out of cylinder head, then remove rocker arms and spring washers, noting removal sequence.
15. Carefully slide camshaft out of cylinder head.
16. Clean all parts with suitable solvent and check for excessive wear or damage. Replace components as necessary.
17. Lubricate camshaft, then install into cylinder head.
18. Install rocker arms, spring washers and rocker shaft in sequence, as noted during removal, then install rocker shaft retaining bolt.
19. Install distributor. **The coupling groove on camshaft and distributor coupling are offset .031 inch respectively from their axial centers. When installing distributor, ensure offset is positioned correctly.**
20. Install inner belt cover and cover mount, then the camshaft sprocket. Tighten bolts to specifications.
21. Install camshaft drive pulley, flanged side inward, and plate onto crankshaft snout, then align marks on pulley and crankcase as shown in **Fig. 7.**
22. Install belt tensioner and spring, rotate tensioner clockwise, then tighten bolt.
23. Align camshaft sprocket timing mark with mark on inner cover, **Fig. 8,** then install timing belt.
24. Loosen tensioner bolt until tensioner swings against timing belt, then tighten the lower left, then the right tensioner bolts in that order.
25. Install camshaft drive pulley plate onto crankshaft.
26. Install No. 2 (outer) timing belt cover and clamp, then the crankshaft pulley and retaining bolt. Using spanner wrench 499205500, or equivalent, hold crankshaft pulley in position, then tighten retaining bolt to specifications.
27. Adjust valve clearance, proceed as follows:
    a. Rotate crankshaft in normal direction of rotation until cylinder to be adjusted is at TDC compression stroke.
    b. Insert suitable feeler gauge between rocker arm and valve, then turn adjusting screw until slight drag can be felt at gauge.
    c. While holding adjusting screw, **torque** locknut to 12–17 ft. lbs.
    d. Rotate crankshaft and adjust remaining valves as outlined above.
28. Install rocker cover, then reconnect PCV hose.
29. Reconnect spark plug wires, then install drive belt.
30. Reconnect vacuum hoses to carburetor and distributor, then reinstall air cleaner assembly.

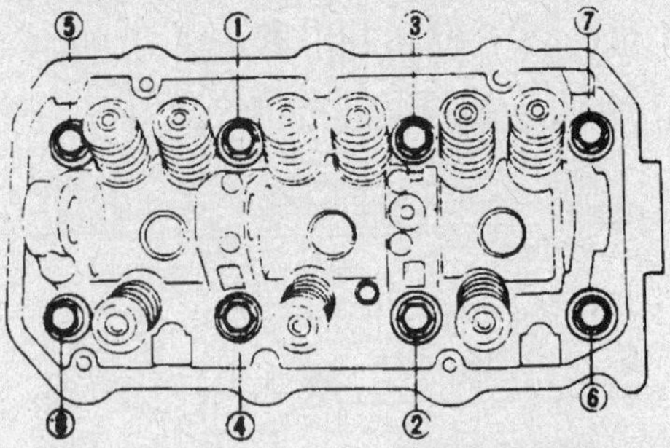
5
1
3
7
8
4
2
6
SB1069100027000X

Fig. 9 Cylinder head bolt tightening sequence. 1.2L engine

Cylinder Head, Valves & Springs

1. Remove timing belt cover, timing belt,

rocker assembly and camshaft as outlined previously.
2. Remove exhaust manifold, then disconnect wiring harnesses from intake manifold.
3. Remove air suction valve and pipe, if applicable.
4. Remove intake manifold attaching bolts, then the intake manifold together with carburetor.
5. Remove cylinder head bolts in reverse sequence as that shown in **Fig. 9,** then remove cylinder head from crankcase.
6. Using suitable valve spring compressor tool, or equivalent, compress valve springs and remove retainer keys.
7. Remove retainers, springs, valves and valve seals.
8. Coat valve seals with engine oil, then install seals using seal installation tool 398852100, or equivalent. **Intake and exhaust seals are not interchangeable. Intake seals measure .512 inch high, while exhaust seals are .425 inch high. Ensure seals are installed correctly.**
9. Coat valve stems with engine oil, then install valves into guides.
10. Install springs, with close-coiled end facing cylinder head, and retainers, then compress spring and install retainer key. Tap retainer lightly with mallet to seat key.
11. Install cylinder head onto crankcase using new gaskets.
12. Apply engine oil to head bolt threads, then install bolts through cylinder head and into crankcase.
13. **Torque** each cylinder head bolts to specifications in three steps in sequence shown, **Fig. 9.** First step to 29 ft. lbs., then 54 ft. lbs., then back off head bolts 90°, and finally retorque in sequence to 51–7 ft. lbs.
14. Install intake manifold and carburetor assembly. Tighten bolts to specifications.
15. Install air suction valve and pipe, if applicable, then reconnect wiring harnesses at intake manifold.
16. Install exhaust manifold and tighten bolts to specifications.
17. Install camshaft, rocker assembly, timing belt and timing belt cover as outlined previously.

Crankcase, Crankshaft, Balancer Shaft, Pistons & Oil Pump

1. Remove timing belt cover, timing belt, rocker assembly, camshaft and cylinder head as outlined previously.
2. Remove oil filter, then the alternator, wiring harness and alternator bracket.
3. Remove engine mounting bracket and mounting stay.
4. Lock flywheel with suitable tool, then remove attaching bolts and flywheel.
5. Remove oil dipstick and dipstick tube, then the flywheel housing.
6. Remove oil pan attaching bolts and the oil pan.
7. Remove water pump cover and impeller, then the water pipe, **Fig. 10.** Use a screwdriver to prevent balancer shaft

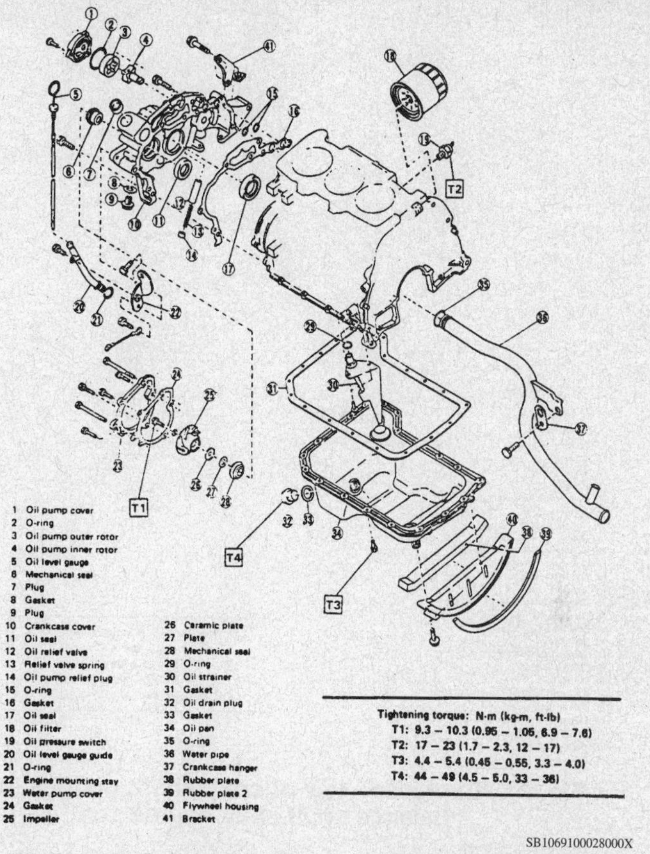

T1
T2
T3
T4
1 Oil pump cover
2 O-ring
3 Oil pump outer rotor
4 Oil pump inner rotor
5 Oil level gauge
6 Mechanical seal
7 Plug
8 Gasket
9 Plug
10 Crankcase cover
11 Oil seal
12 Oil relief valve
13 Relief valve spring
14 Oil pump relief plug
15 O-ring
16 Gasket
17 Oil seal
18 Oil filter
19 Oil pressure switch
20 Oil level gauge guide
21 O-ring
22 Engine mounting stay
23 Water pump cover
24 Gasket
25 Impeller
26 Ceramic plate
27 Plate
28 Mechanical seal
29 O-ring
30 Oil strainer
31 Gasket
32 Oil drain plug
33 Gasket
34 Oil pan
35 O-ring
36 Water pipe
37 Crankcase hanger
38 Rubber plate
39 Rubber plate 2
40 Flywheel housing
41 Bracket
Tightening torque: N·m (kg-m, ft-lb)
T1: 9.3 – 10.3 (0.95 – 1.05, 6.9 – 7.6)
T2: 17 – 23 (1.7 – 2.3, 12 – 17)
T3: 4.4 – 5.4 (0.45 – 0.55, 3.3 – 4.0)
T4: 44 – 49 (4.5 – 5.0, 33 – 36)
SB1069100028000X

Fig. 10 Exploded view of crankcase, oil pump & water pump. 1.2L engine

from rotating when removing impeller.
8. Remove oil pump cover attaching bolts, then the cover and inner and outer rotors.
9. Remove crankcase cover.
10. Remove connecting rod cap nuts, then tap piston/rod assemblies from underneath with hammer handle and remove assemblies from crankcase.
11. Remove balancer chain, then chain guide and oil pump sprocket, **Fig. 11.**
12. Remove main bearing cap attaching bolts, then the caps and crankshaft.
13. Carefully remove balancer shaft from crankcase.
14. Press piston pins from connecting rod small end using suitable tool.
15. Ensure all components are clean and free from foreign material, and that oil passages are clear. Coat all friction surfaces with oil or suitable assembly lubricant.
16. Assemble piston to connecting rod so that intake valve recesses on piston and crescent mark on connecting rod are positioned as shown, **Fig. 12.**
17. Install rings onto pistons. **Ensure R1 (top ring) and R2 (second ring) marks on compression rings face upward.**
18. Install balancer shaft and oil pump sprocket, then temporarily install chain guide. If replacing chain and/or chain guide, always replace them in the following combinations:
   a. If replacing chain only, replacement chain should have green color identification.
   b. If replacing chain guide only, and original chain guide is white, replacement guide should have white color identification. If original chain guide is blue, replacement guide should have blue color identification. If original chain guide is green, replacement guide should have white or blue color identification.
   c. If replacing chain and chain guide, and original chain guide is white or blue, replacement guide should be same as original, and replacement chain should have green color identification.
19. Install main bearing halves into crankcase.
20. Install chain and crankshaft, then align marks on sprockets with gold links on chain as shown in **Fig. 13.**
21. Install main bearing caps with arrows facing front of engine. Tighten bolts to specifications.
22. Position ring end gaps as shown, **Fig. 14,** then install piston/rod assemblies into cylinders. Ensure intake valve recesses on piston face intake manifold side of engine.
23. Install connecting rod bearing caps. Tighten nuts to specifications.
24. Install rear oil seal using suitable tools.
25. Install crankcase cover together with air suction manifold bracket.
26. Install oil pump inner rotor, outer rotor and cover. Ensure inner rotor shaft

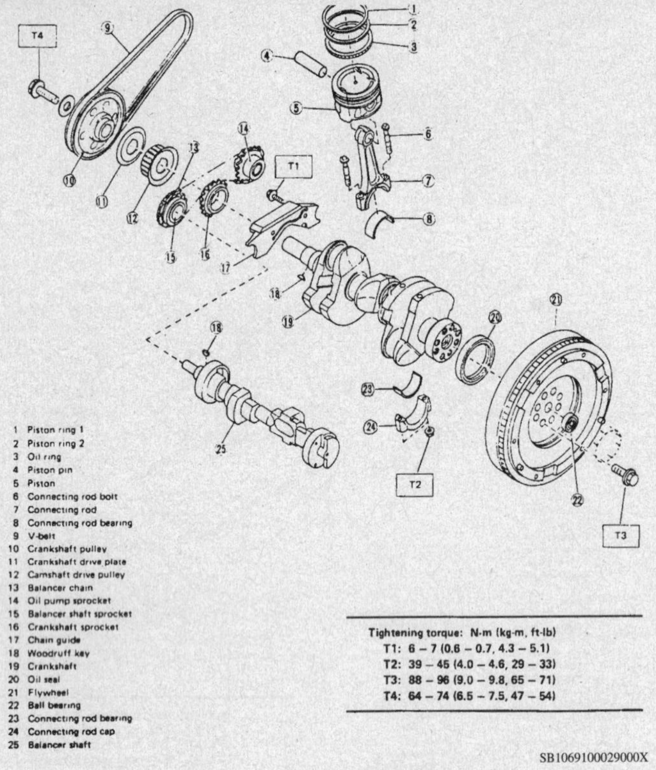
T4
T1
T2
T3
1 Piston ring 1
2 Piston ring 2
3 Oil ring
4 Piston pin
5 Piston
6 Connecting rod bolt
7 Connecting rod
8 Connecting rod bearing
9 V-belt
10 Crankshaft pulley
11 Crankshaft drive plate
12 Camshaft drive pulley
13 Balancer chain
14 Oil pump sprocket
15 Balancer shaft sprocket
16 Crankshaft sprocket
17 Chain guide
18 Woodruff key
19 Crankshaft
20 Oil seal
21 Flywheel
22 Ball bearing
23 Connecting rod bearing
24 Connecting rod cap
25 Balancer shaft
Tightening torque: N·m (kg-m, ft-lb)
T1: 6 – 7 (0.6 – 0.7, 4.3 – 5.1)
T2: 39 – 45 (4.0 – 4.6, 29 – 33)
T3: 88 – 96 (9.0 – 9.8, 65 – 71)
T4: 64 – 74 (6.5 – 7.5, 47 – 54)
SB1069100029000X

Fig. 11 Exploded view of crankshaft, pistons, & balance shaft. 1.2L engine

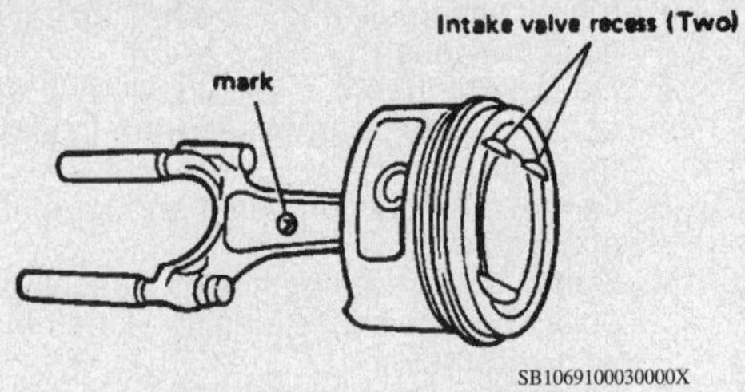
Intake valve recess (Two)
mark
SB1069100030000X

Fig. 12 Assembling piston to connecting rod. 1.2L engine

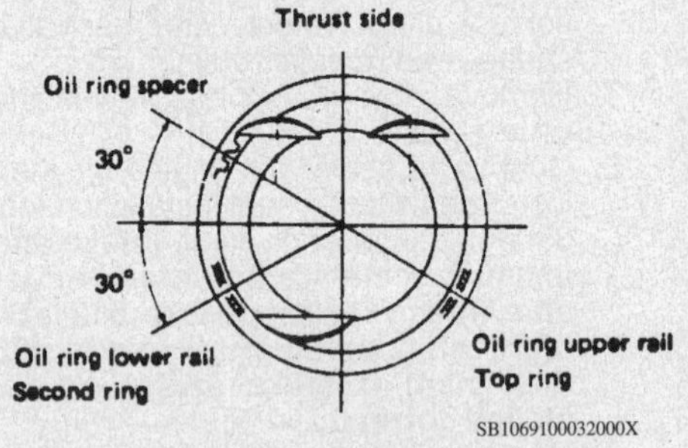
Thrust side
Oil ring spacer
30°
30°
Oil ring lower rail
Second ring
Oil ring upper rail
Top ring
SB1069100032000X

Fig. 14 Piston ring installation. 1.2L engine

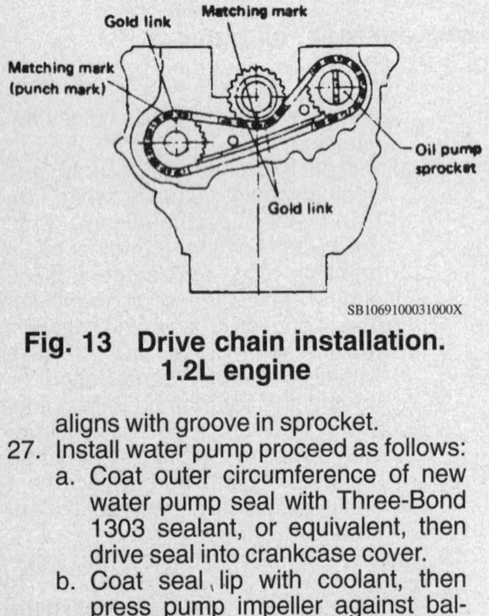
Gold link
Matching mark
Matching mark (punch mark)
Oil pump sprocket
Gold link
SB1069100031000X

Fig. 13 Drive chain installation. 1.2L engine

aligns with groove in sprocket.

27. Install water pump proceed as follows:
    a. Coat outer circumference of new water pump seal with Three-Bond 1303 sealant, or equivalent, then drive seal into crankcase cover.
    b. Coat seal lip with coolant, then press pump impeller against balancer shaft and measure tip clearance. Tip clearance should be .012–.035 inch. If clearance is not as specified, add spacers as required.
    c. Position screwdriver between balancer shaft weight and crankcase, then install impeller attaching bolt and tighten to specifications.
    d. Install water pump cover using new gasket.
28. Install oil pan with new gasket. Tighten bolts to specifications.
29. Install flywheel housing.
30. Install oil dipstick tube and dipstick.
31. Install flywheel and attaching bolts. Lock flywheel using suitable tool and tighten attaching bolts to specifications.
32. Install oil filter, engine mounting bracket and mounting stay.
33. Install alternator mounting bracket and alternator.
34. Install cylinder head, camshaft, rocker assembly, timing belt and timing belt cover as outlined previously.

LOYALE w/1.8L ENGINE

Disassembly

1. Remove air intake duct.
2. **On turbocharged models,** disconnect coolant hoses from turbocharger, then remove turbocharger and front exhaust pipe.
3. **On all models,** mount engine in suitable stands, drain coolant and engine oil, then reinstall drain plugs.
4. Disconnect high tension leads from spark plugs and ignition coil, and remove leads from support bracket.
5. Remove PCV and distributor vacuum hoses, wiring harness clips and ground terminal fastener, disconnect connectors and remove wiring harness.
6. Remove hold-down bolts and the distributor.
7. **On models less A/C,** loosen water pump pulley nut, then remove alternator and drive belt.
8. **On all models,** disconnect electrical connector from oil pressure switch and air bleed hose from intake manifold.
9. Remove EGR pipe clamps, EGR cover and the EGR pipe.
10. Remove intake manifold assembly.
11. Remove power steering pump and alternator brackets.
12. **On turbocharged models,** remove knock sensor.
13. Remove fuel injectors, if equipped.
14. **On all models,** remove oil filler pipe, water pipes and air bleed hoses. **On models equipped with AWD,** remove the stiffener.
15. **On all models,** remove crankshaft pulley bolt. To prevent crank from turning, insert a screwdriver through the timing hole.
16. Remove crankshaft pulley by tapping it lightly with a suitable soft-faced hammer.
17. Remove oil pump and filter assembly.
18. Remove water pump pulley and pulley cover.
19. Remove dipstick and dipstick tube, **Fig. 15.**
20. **On turbocharged models,** remove timing belt cover plate, then, **on all models,** the left and right front timing belt covers, **Fig. 16.**
21. Loosen bolts securing timing belt tensioner to No. 1 cylinder, rotate tensioner to fully released position, then retighten bolts, **Fig. 17.**
22. Mark rotational direction, then remove timing belt.
23. Loosen bolts securing tensioner 2 to No. 2 cylinder, rotate tensioner to fully relaxed position using wrench 499007000, or equivalent, then retighten bolts.
24. Remove first crankshaft sprocket.
25. Mark rotational direction of remaining belt, then remove belt and second crankshaft sprocket.
26. Remove both belt tensioner assemblies along with tensioner springs.
27. Secure camshaft sprockets with suitable wrench, then remove sprocket retaining bolts and the sprockets.
28. Remove remaining timing belt covers.

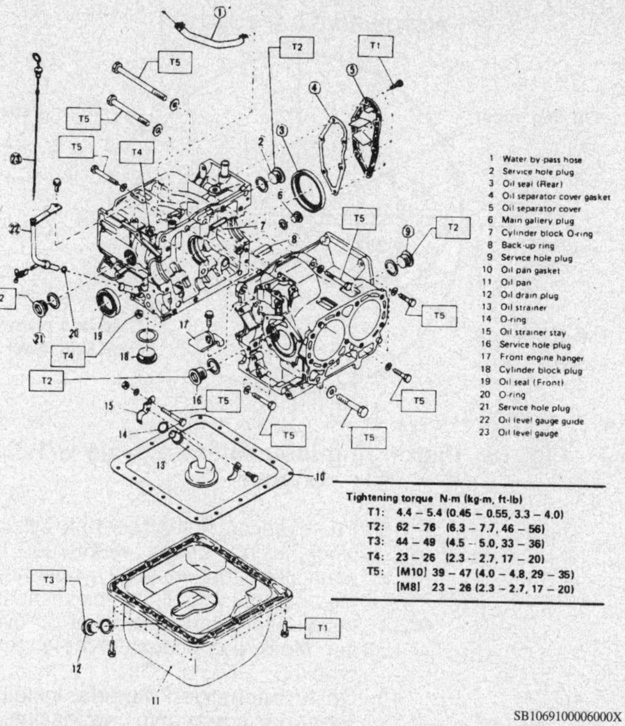
1 Water by-pass hose
2 Service hole plug
3 Oil seal (Rear)
4 Oil separator cover gasket
5 Oil separator cover
6 Main gallery plug
7 Cylinder block O-ring
8 Back-up ring
9 Service hole plug
10 Oil pan gasket
11 Oil pan
12 Oil drain plug
13 Oil strainer
14 O-ring
15 Oil strainer stay
16 Service hole plug
17 Front engine hanger
18 Cylinder block plug
19 Oil seal (Front)
20 O-ring
21 Service hole plug
22 Oil level gauge guide
23 Oil level gauge
Tightening torque N·m (kg-m, ft-lb)
T1: 4.4 – 5.4 (0.45 – 0.55, 3.3 – 4.0)
T2: 62 – 76 (6.3 – 7.7, 46 – 56)
T3: 44 – 49 (4.5 – 5.0, 33 – 36)
T4: 23 – 26 (2.3 – 2.7, 17 – 20)
T5: [M10] 39 – 47 (4.0 – 4.8, 29 – 35)
[M8] 23 – 26 (2.3 – 2.7, 17 – 20)
SB1069100006000X

Fig. 15 Exploded view of cylinder block assembly. Loyale w/1.8L engine

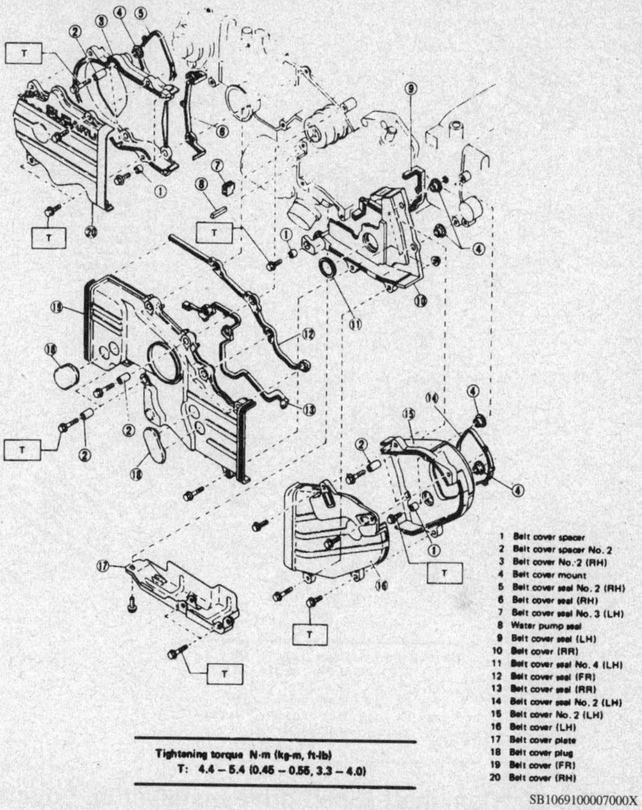
1 Belt cover spacer
2 Belt cover spacer No. 2
3 Belt cover No. 2 (RH)
4 Belt cover mount
5 Belt cover seal No. 2 (RH)
6 Belt cover seal (RH)
7 Belt cover seal No. 3 (LH)
8 Water pump seal
9 Belt cover seal (LH)
10 Belt cover (RR)
11 Belt cover seal No. 4 (LH)
12 Belt cover seal (FR)
13 Belt cover seal (RR)
14 Belt cover seal No. 2 (LH)
15 Belt cover No. 2 (LH)
16 Belt cover (LH)
17 Belt cover plate
18 Belt cover plug
19 Belt cover (FR)
20 Belt cover (RH)
Tightening torque N·m (kg-m, ft-lb)
T: 4.4 – 5.4 (0.45 – 0.55, 3.3 – 4.0)
SB1069100007000X

Fig. 16 Exploded view of timing belt cover assembly. Loyale w/1.8L engine

29. Remove water pump, hose and pipe as an assembly.
30. Align oil pump sprocket notch with retaining bolt, then remove bolts and pump rotor assembly from cylinder block.
31. Remove clutch assembly and flywheel or automatic transaxle flex plate, as equipped, then the flywheel housing.
32. Remove spark plugs, camshaft covers and cover gaskets.
33. Evenly loosen bolts securing camshaft cases, then remove case, camshaft support and camshaft assemblies.
34. Remove rocker arms and hydraulic lifters, keeping components in proper order for assembly. **Do not store lifters on their sides; keep them upright.**
35. **On turbocharged models,** remove turbocharger cooling pipe, union and gasket from cylinder head.
36. **On all models,** remove cylinder head retaining bolts and the cylinder heads.
37. Remove service access plugs from cylinder block, then rotate crankshaft to bring Nos. 1 and 2 pistons to BDC.
38. Remove piston pin retainers through service openings, then withdraw piston pins using suitable remover.
39. Rotate crankshaft to position Nos. 3 and 4 pistons at BDC, then remove piston pin retainers and piston pins.
40. Remove all cylinder block retaining bolts except 10mm bolt under center crankshaft journal, and loosen the 10mm bolt until it can be turned by hand.
41. Position cylinder block assembly with cylinders No. 3 and 4 facing up, then separate left and right halves of block, **Fig. 15.**
42. Remove coolant passage O-ring and back-up ring from lefthand cylinder block, and front and rear oil seals from crankshaft.
43. Remove crankshaft and connecting rod assembly.
44. Mark and remove pistons from cylinder block halves, and mate pistons with respective pins. **Keep all components in order to ensure proper assembly. Components that are to be reused should be installed in original position.**
45. Remove main bearings from crankcase halves.
46. Remove oil relief plug, oil relief pipe and spring and the oil relief valve from camshaft case.

Assembly

Ensure all components are clean and free from foreign material, and that oil passages are clear. Coat all friction surfaces with oil or suitable assembly lubricant, and coat seal lips with grease prior to assembly. Replace all gaskets, seals and damaged fasteners during assembly. Components that are to be reused should be installed in original position.

1. Install connecting rods as follows:
   a. Seat bearings in connecting rods and rod caps. Ensure connecting rod and cap matching marks are aligned, and install connecting rod assemblies with crescent shaped mark facing forward.
   b. Lubricate connecting rod bolt threads and ensure bolts are properly seated in cap and that caps are fully seated against connecting rods.
   c. Evenly tighten connecting rod nuts to specifications.
2. Install piston ring and pin, proceed as follows:
   a. Install oil ring spacer, upper rail, then the lower rail.
   b. Using a suitable piston ring expander, install the second ring, then the top ring. **Install compression rings with "N" or "R" mark facing up.**
   c. Stagger ring and oil expander gaps as shown in **Fig. 18.**
   d. Install pin retainer in each piston as shown in **Fig. 19.**
3. Install valves as follows:
   a. Coat valve stems with oil prior to installation and take care not to damage seal lips when inserting valves.
   b. Install valve springs with close-coiled end toward cylinder head.
   c. After releasing spring tension against valve key, tap valve stem with suitable mallet to ensure keys are seated in retainer and valve stem grooves.
4. Press new seals into camshaft support plates and install new O-rings.
5. Install oil pressure relief valve, spring, pipe and plug, and tighten plug to specifications.
6. Install woodruff key and press on distributor drive gear, if removed, securing camshaft in suitable holder. **When pressing on distributor drive gear,**

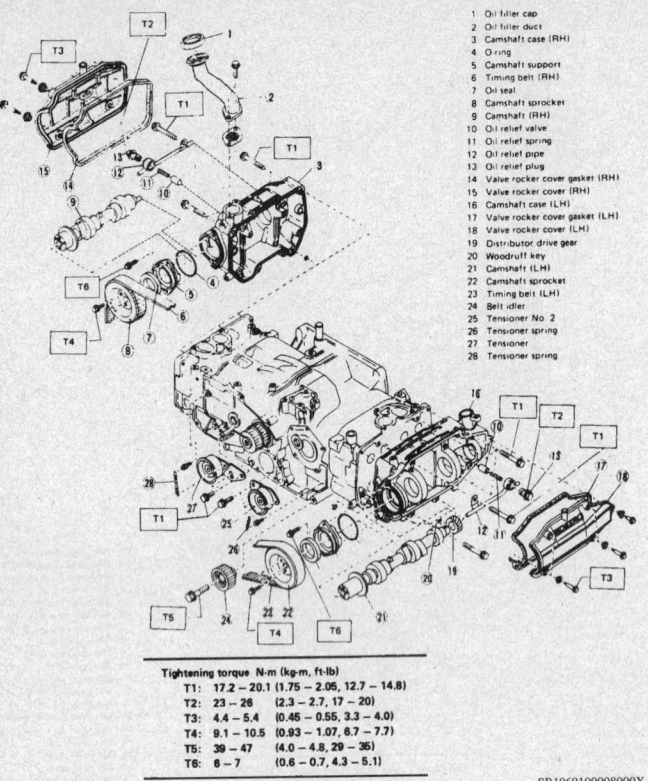

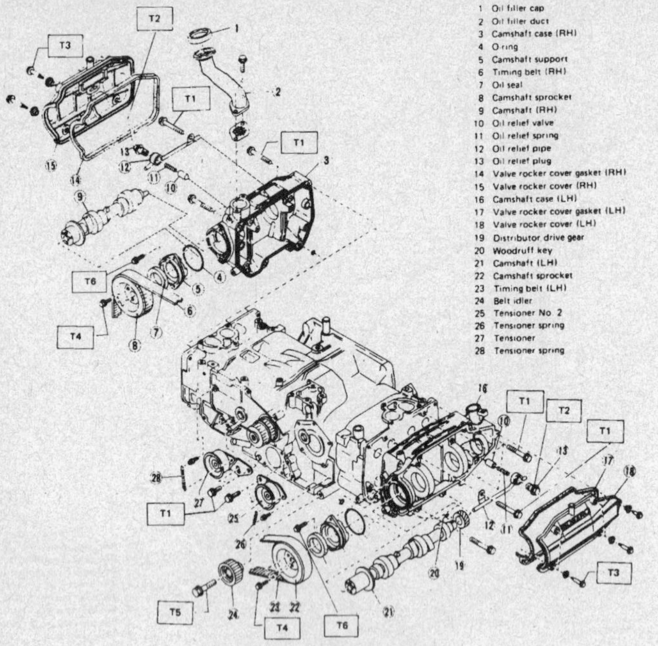
T1
T2
T3
T4
T5
T6
1 Oil filler cap
2 Oil filler duct
3 Camshaft case (RH)
4 O-ring
5 Camshaft support
6 Timing belt (RH)
7 Oil seal
8 Camshaft sprocket
9 Camshaft (RH)
10 Oil relief valve
11 Oil relief spring
12 Oil relief pipe
13 Oil relief plug
14 Valve rocker cover gasket (RH)
15 Valve rocker cover (RH)
16 Camshaft case (LH)
17 Valve rocker cover gasket (LH)
18 Valve rocker cover (LH)
19 Distributor drive gear
20 Woodruff key
21 Camshaft (LH)
22 Camshaft sprocket
23 Timing belt (LH)
24 Belt idler
25 Tensioner No. 2
26 Tensioner spring
27 Tensioner
28 Tensioner spring

Tightening torque N·m (kg-m, ft-lb)

T1:	17.2 – 20.1	(1.75 – 2.05, 12.7 – 14.8)
T2:	23 – 26	(2.3 – 2.7, 17 – 20)
T3:	4.4 – 5.4	(0.45 – 0.55, 3.3 – 4.0)
T4:	9.1 – 10.5	(0.93 – 1.07, 6.7 – 7.7)
T5:	39 – 47	(4.0 – 4.8, 29 – 35)
T6:	6 – 7	(0.6 – 0.7, 4.3 – 5.1)

SB1069100008000X

Fig. 17 Camshaft & belt drive installation. Loyale w/1.8L engine

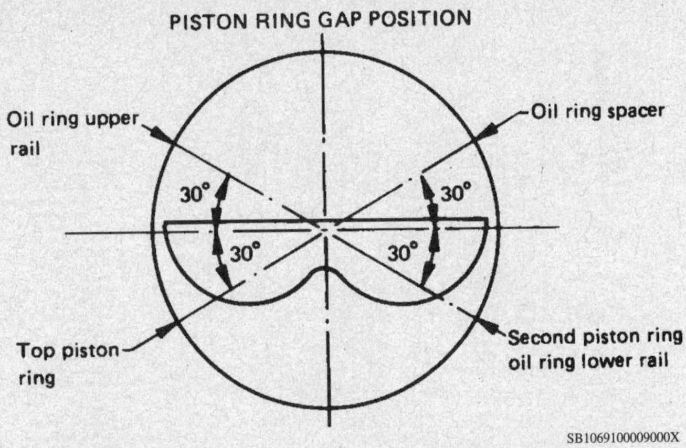
PISTON RING GAP POSITION
Oil ring upper rail
Oil ring spacer
30°
30°
30°
30°
Top piston ring
Second piston ring
oil ring lower rail

SB1069100009000X

Fig. 18 Piston ring installation. Loyale w/1.8L engine

do not support camshaft on end, as shaft may be distorted.

7. To install camshaft and crankshaft proceed as follows:
   a. Insert camshafts into cases, then install support plate, seal and O-ring assemblies, **Fig. 16.** Tighten bolts and nuts to specifications.
   b. Mount cylinder block halves on stands 498027000, or equivalent, installing bolts marked "R" into cylinder 1 and 3 section and bolts marked "L" into cylinder 2 and 4 section.
   c. Seat main bearings into cylinder block webs, ensuring that tangs are properly engaged and that oil holes are properly aligned.
   d. Install coolant passage O-ring and support ring in groove in lefthand cylinder block.
   e. Install crankshaft assembly into lefthand cylinder block.
   f. Apply liquid gasket compound Three-bond 1215, or equivalent to cylinder block mating surfaces, then align connecting rods and install righthand cylinder block assembly, ensuring that O-ring remains in place.
   g. Tighten cylinder block bolts evenly, then lay block down and tighten bolts to specifications.
8. Install piston, proceed as follows:
   a. Position cylinder block with cylinders 3 and 4 facing downward and rotate crankshaft until Nos. 1 and 2 connecting rods are at BDC. **Take care not to mar cylinder walls when positioning connecting rods.**
   b. Coat pistons and cylinder walls with assembly lubricant, install pistons No. 1 and 2, align pin bores in pistons and connecting rods using pin guide 399284300, or equivalent, **Fig. 20,** piston pins and retainers.
   c. Invert cylinder block assembly, rotate crankshaft to position Nos. 3 and 4 connecting rods, then install Nos. 3 and 4 pistons, pins and retainers as outlined previously.
   d. Apply Fuji-bond C sealer, or equivalent to service access plugs, install new aluminum sealing gaskets and access plugs. Tighten plugs to specifications.
9. Install cylinder head, proceed as follows:
   a. Install new cylinder head gaskets and the cylinder heads, dip head bolts in oil and install all bolts hand tight.
   b. Tighten cylinder head bolts to specifications following sequence shown in **Fig. 21. Torque** each cylinder head bolt in three steps to 22 ft. lbs., then 43 ft. lbs., and finally 47 ft. lbs.
10. **On turbocharged models,** install turbocharger coolant pipe and union along with new gasket and tighten to specifications.
11. **On all models,** secure oil strainer to cylinder block with new retaining clips.
12. Install oil pan and clutch housing cover with gasket positioned in between. Tighten bolts to specifications.
13. Press rear crankshaft seal into cylinder block using driver 499587000, or equivalent, then install flywheel housing and tighten bolts to specifications.
14. Install pitch stopper bracket on cylinder block and mount clip No. 3 on bracket.
15. **On turbocharged models,** install oil separator cover and new gasket on righthand cylinder block. Tighten bolts to specifications.
16. Install flywheel or flex plate and reinforcement. Tighten bolts to specifications.
17. **On manual transaxle models,** install clutch and pressure plate assembly, ensuring that "0" markings on flywheel and pressure plate are spaced 180° apart, insert suitable alignment tool and evenly tighten pressure plate bolts to specifications.
18. **On all models,** press seal into water pump, then install water pump along with new gasket.
19. Install oil pump, proceed as follows:
   a. Ensure excess sealer is removed from oil pump rotor housing in cylinder block.
   b. Apply small amount of Three-bond 1215 sealer, or equivalent to split line in housing as shown by arrows in **Fig. 22.**
   c. Liberally coat housing with oil, then install outer rotor into housing in direction shown in **Fig. 22.**
   d. Position oil pump pulley as shown in **Fig. 22,** then install pulley and front housing and ensure pulley rotates smoothly.
   e. Install pressure switch or pressure gauge on oil pump, ensure gauge lead is properly routed along side of Nos. 1 and 3 cylinders.
20. Install belt cover seal lefthand No. 3 on cylinder block, **Fig. 16.**
21. Press new front crankshaft seal into block using suitable driver.
22. Install camshaft housing, proceed as follows:
   a. Insert hydraulic lifters into proper bores, coat rocker arms with grease to aid retention, then mount rocker arms over lifters and valve stems.

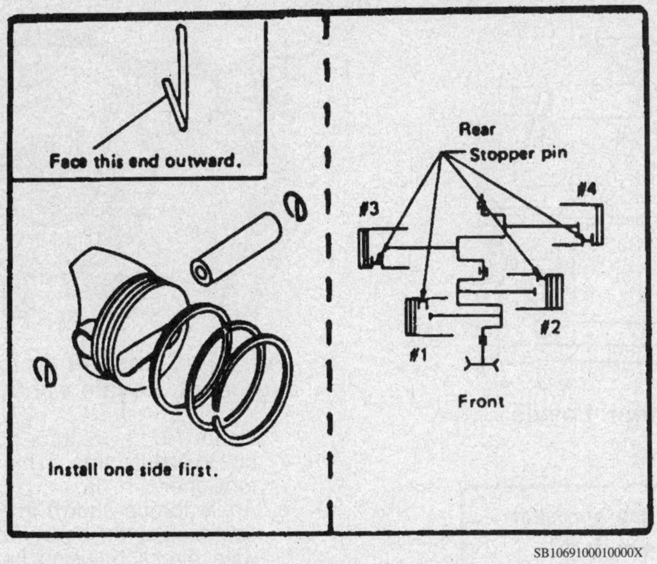
Face this end outward.
Install one side first.
Rear
Stopper pin
#3
#4
#2
#1
Front
SB1069100010000X

Fig. 19 Piston pin retainer installation. Loyale w/1.8L engine

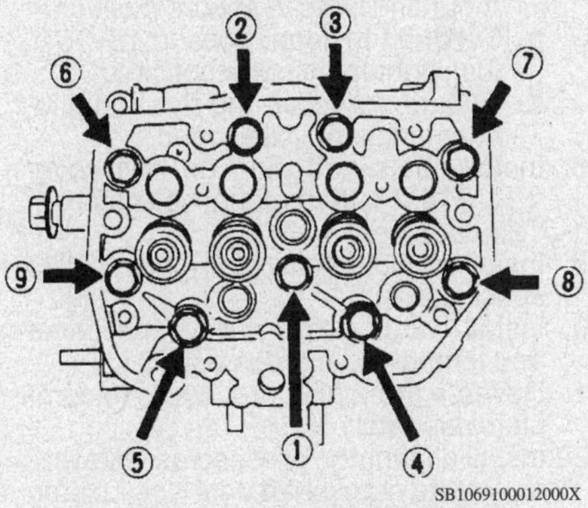
SB1069100012000X

Fig. 21 Cylinder head bolt tightening sequence. Loyale w/1.8L engine

b. Rotate crankshaft until timing mark on flywheel is aligned with pointer on housing and orient each camshaft pin so that pin faces up when assembly is installed on engine.
c. Install O-ring, if used and apply Three-bond sealer 1215, or equivalent to camshaft housing sealing groove.
d. Install camshaft and housing assemblies torquing retaining bolts evenly to specifications.
e. Install camshaft covers with gaskets torquing retaining bolts evenly to specifications.

23. Install timing belt cover as follows:
 a. Install belt cover lefthand seal, belt cover No. 4 lefthand seal and belt cover mount on cover RR, then mount assembly on cylinder block ensuring that spacers are properly positioned, **Fig. 16,** and **torque** bolts to 4 ft. lbs.
 b. Install belt cover No. 2 lefthand seal and mount on belt cover No. 2 lefthand, then mount assembly on cylinder block and camshaft housing, **Fig. 16,** and **torque** bolts to 4 ft. lbs.
 c. Install belt cover righthand seal, No. 2 righthand seal and mount on belt cover No. 2 righthand, then mount assembly on cylinder head and camshaft cover, **Fig. 16,** and **torque** bolts to 4 ft. lbs.
 d. Install camshaft sprockets and retaining bolts. While holding sprocket in position with a suitable wrench, tighten retaining bolts evenly to specifications.
24. Install belt tensioner, proceed as follows:
 a. Connect tensioner spring to tensioner and mount assembly on righthand cylinder block, temporarily hand tightening bolts, **Fig. 17.**
 b. Connect tensioner spring to mounting stud, tighten inner tensioner mounting bolt, then loosen bolt ½ turn.
 c. Push tensioner down to stop, then tighten inner tensioner mounting bolt to secure position.
25. Install No. 2 belt tensioner, proceed as follows:
 a. Connect tensioner spring to tensioner and mount assembly on lefthand cylinder block, temporarily hand tightening bolts, **Fig. 17.**
 b. Connect tensioner spring to mounting stud, tighten upper tensioner mounting bolt, then loosen bolt ½ turn.
 c. Raise tensioner to stop using suitable lever, then tighten lower tensioner mounting bolt to secure position.
26. Install No. 2 timing belt, proceed as follows:
 a. Install belt idler on cylinder block taking care not to damage seal, and **torque** bolts to 29–35 ft. lbs., **Fig. 17.**
 b. Install sprocket No. 2 on crankshaft.
 c. Ensure center mark on flywheel is aligned with housing pointer, **Fig.**

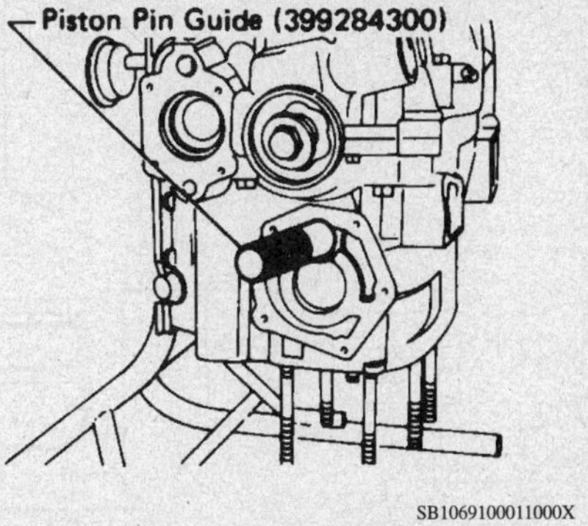
Piston Pin Guide (399284300)
SB1069100011000X

Fig. 20 Service hole location & piston pin guide tool

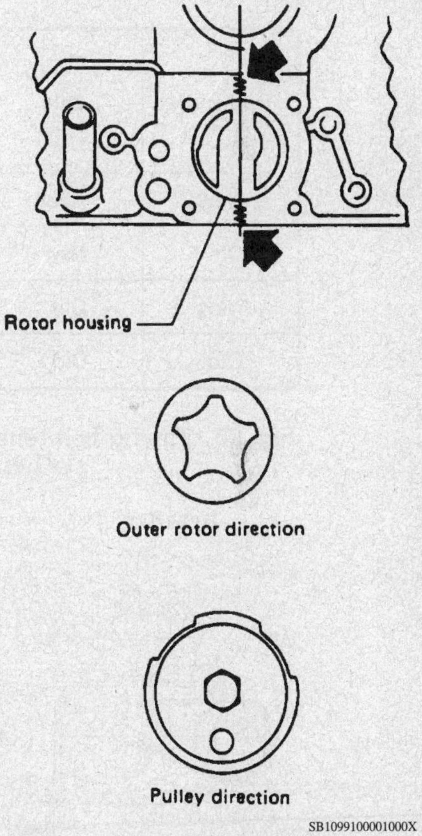
Rotor housing
Outer rotor direction
Pulley direction
SB1099100001000X

Fig. 22 Oil pump installation. Loyale w/1.8L engine

23, and that timing mark on camshaft sprocket is aligned with notch in belt cover, **Fig. 24.**
 d. Route timing belt No. 2 over crankshaft sprocket, oil pump sprocket, belt idler and camshaft sprocket in order, noting belt rotation direction and avoiding downward slackening of belt.
 e. Loosen lower mounting bolt on tensioner No. 2, ½ turn, and press in on belt to ensure smooth movement of belt tensioner.
 f. Apply torque shown in **Fig. 25** to camshaft sprocket in counterclockwise direction using belt tension wrench 499437000.

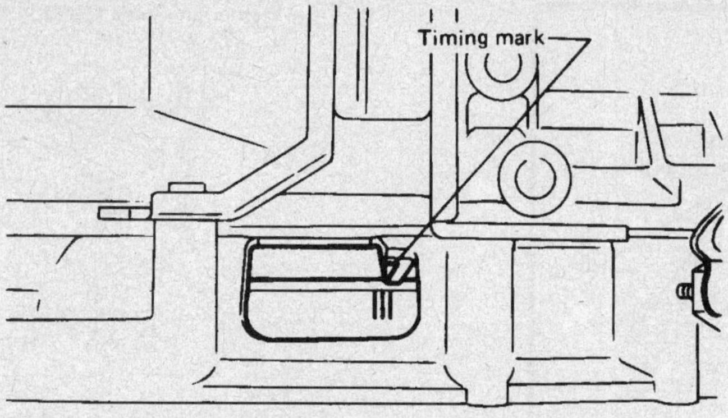
Timing mark
SB1069100013000X

Fig. 23 Flywheel timing mark alignment. Loyale w/1.8L engine

Head gasket	Belt	Torque to cam sprocket N·m (kg-m, ft-lb)	
		Right side	Left side (No. 2)
New	New	25 (2.5, 18)	34 (3.5, 25)
Old	New		25 (2.5, 18)
New	Old		
Old	Old		

SB1069100015000X

Fig. 25 Timing belt tension specifications. Loyale w/1.8L engine

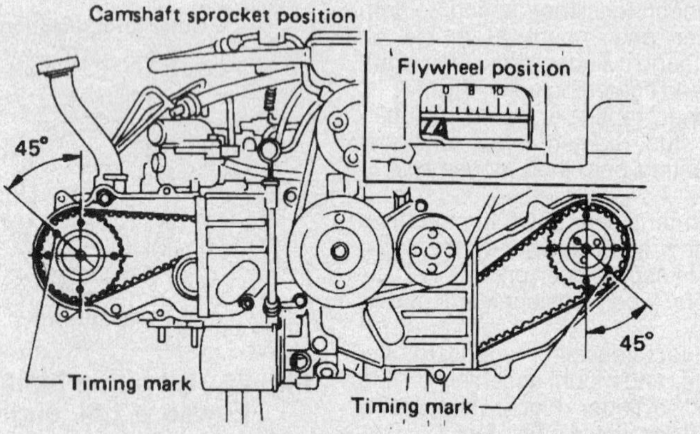
Camshaft sprocket position
Flywheel position
45°
45°
Timing mark
Timing mark
SB1069100016000X

Fig. 26 Timing mark alignment for distributor installation. Loyale w/1.8L engine

g. While holding tension on camshaft sprocket, temporarily tighten tensioner No. 2 mounting bolts to secure position. **Applying torque to camshaft sprocket sets belt tension to specifications. Care must be taken not to apply excessive force to sprocket, as excessive tension will reduce belt life.**

h. **Torque** tensioner No. 2 mounting bolts to 13–15 ft. lbs., tightening lower mounting bolt first.

i. Ensure camshaft and flywheel timing marks are still properly aligned, **Figs. 23 and 24.**

27. Install righthand timing belt, proceed as follows:
    a. Rotate crankshaft 1 revolution in clockwise direction from position where No. 2 belt was installed, realigning center flywheel timing mark with pointer, **Fig. 23.**
    b. Install sprocket on crankshaft and align timing mark on camshaft sprocket with notch in belt cover.
    c. Install timing belt over crankshaft and camshaft sprockets, noting direction of rotation and avoiding slack on upper run of belt.
    d. Loosen inner bolt securing tensioner No. 1, ½ turn, pushing on belt to ensure smooth movement of tensioner.

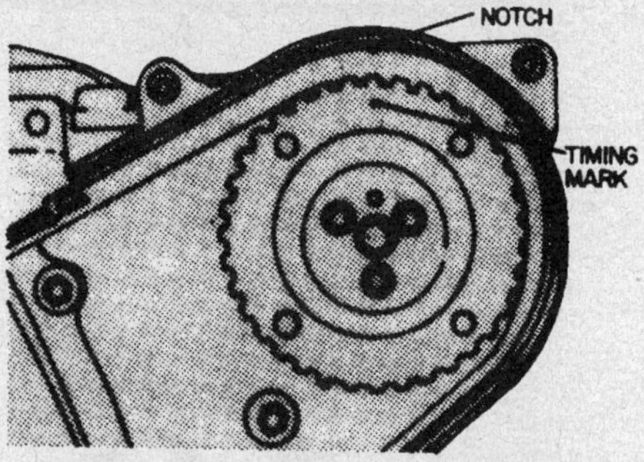
NOTCH
TIMING MARK
SB1069100014000X

Fig. 24 Camshaft timing mark alignment. Loyale w/1.8L engine

    e. Apply torque shown in **Fig. 25** to camshaft sprocket in counterclockwise direction, using belt tension wrench 499437000.
    f. While holding tension on sprocket, temporarily tighten tensioner mounting bolts to secure position.
    g. **Torque** tensioner bolts to 13–15 ft. lbs., tightening outer bolt first.
    h. Ensure sprocket and flywheel timing marks are still aligned.
28. Install seals and plug on belt cover "FR," **Fig. 16,** then mount belt cover on cylinder block.
29. Install crankshaft pulley. Tighten bolt to specifications.
30. Install water pump pulley and cover and temporarily tighten bolts.
31. Reverse remaining procedure to complete assembly.
32. Install distributor, proceed as follows:
    a. Rotate crankshaft until No. 1 piston is at TDC on compression stroke with timing marks aligned as shown in **Fig. 26.**
    b. Align matching marks on distributor drive gear and housing to position distributor in firing position for No. 1 cylinder.
    c. Insert distributor and ensure rotor contact points toward No. 1 cylinder contact in cap.

IMPREZA w/1.8L & 2.2L ENGINES

Timing Belt, Tensioner & Idler

1. Remove drive belt, **Fig. 27.**
2. Lock crankshaft using crankshaft pulley wrench tool No. 499977000, or equivalent, then remove pulley retaining bolt and pulley.
3. Remove lefthand, righthand and front belt covers.
4. Ensure timing belt rotation arrows and alignment marks are visible prior to belt removal, **Fig. 28.** If original marks are faded, new alignment marks can be made as follows:
    a. Align camshaft and crankshaft sprockets with notches in belt cover and cylinder block, **Fig. 29.**
    b. Mark timing belt in relation to sprockets, **Fig. 30. Ensure "Z" dimension equals 44 tooth length**

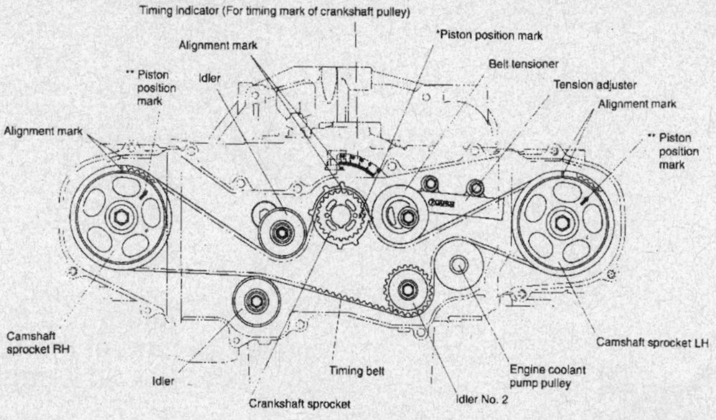
Timing indicator (For timing mark of crankshaft pulley)
Alignment mark
*Piston position mark
** Piston position mark
Idler
Belt tensioner
Tension adjuster
Alignment mark
** Piston position mark
Alignment mark
Camshaft sprocket RH
Camshaft sprocket LH
Idler
Timing belt
Engine coolant pump pulley
Crankshaft sprocket
Idler No. 2
SB1069300067000X

Fig. 27 Timing belt replacement. Impreza w/1.8L & 2.2L engines

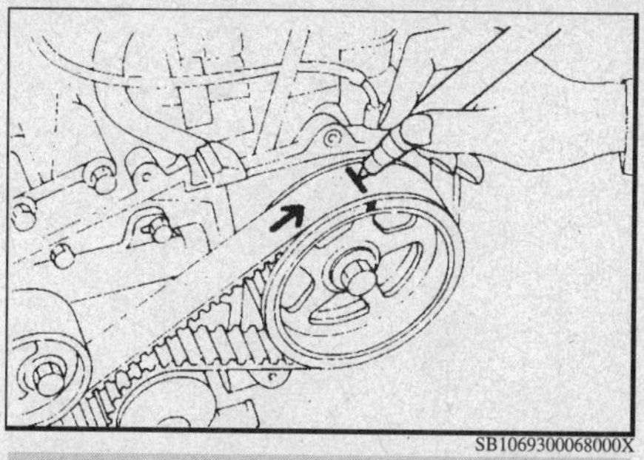
SB1069300068000X

Fig. 28 Timing belt rotation mark. Impreza w/1.8L & 2.2L engines

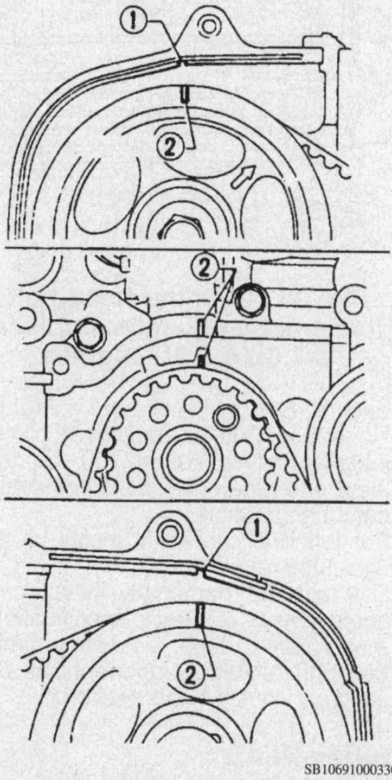
①
②
②
①
②
SB1069100033000X

Fig. 29 Timing belt camshaft alignment marks. Impreza w/1.8L & 2.2L engines

and "Z2" dimension equals 40.5 tooth length.

5. Loosen tensioner adjuster mounting bolts, **Fig. 31.**
6. Remove belt idler, belt idler No. 2, timing belt, spacer, belt tensioner and tensioner adjuster.
7. Lock camshaft sprocket using camshaft sprocket wrench tool No. 499207100, or equivalent, then remove sprocket retaining bolt and sprocket. **Do not mix lefthand and righthand camshaft sprockets.** Lefthand sprocket can be identified by a projection used to monitor cam angle sensor.
8. Remove No. 2 lefthand and righthand belt covers.
9. Remove tensioner bracket.
10. Install No. 2 righthand and lefthand belt covers. Tighten bolts to specification.
11. Install tensioner bracket and tighten bolts to specifications.
12. Install crankshaft sprocket.
13. Install righthand, then the lefthand camshaft sprockets. Lock sprocket using tool No. 499207100, or equivalent and tighten bolt to specifications. **Lefthand sprocket can be identified by a projection used to monitor cam-angle sensor.**
14. Vertically push tensioner adjuster rod into adjuster body using a suitable press, then completely insert stopper pin .059 inch diameter into tensioner adjuster to hold rod in place. **Do not allow press pressure to exceed 2205 lbs.**
15. Install tensioner adjuster. Ensure adjuster is positioned completely to the right and tighten retaining bolts.
16. Install belt tensioner and tighten bolts to specifications.
17. Install belt idler and tighten bolts to specifications.
18. Using sprocket wrench, turn sprockets to position alignment marks at the top.
19. Install timing belt. Position timing belt with rotation arrows facing in correct direction and sprocket and belt alignment marks properly aligned, **Fig. 32.**
20. Install belt idler No. 2, then the belt idler. Tighten bolts to specifications.
21. Loosen tensioner adjuster retaining bolts, position adjuster completely to the left and tighten retaining bolts to specifications.
22. Ensure timing marks are properly aligned, then remove stopper pin from tension adjuster.
23. Install front, lefthand and righthand belt covers.
24. Install crankshaft pulley. Lock crankshaft using tool No. 499977000, or equivalent and tighten pulley retaining bolt to specifications.
25. Install drive belt. Refer to "Drive Belt Service " for belt routing and tension data.

Valve Rocker Assembly

1. Disconnect PCV hose.
2. Remove valve cover.

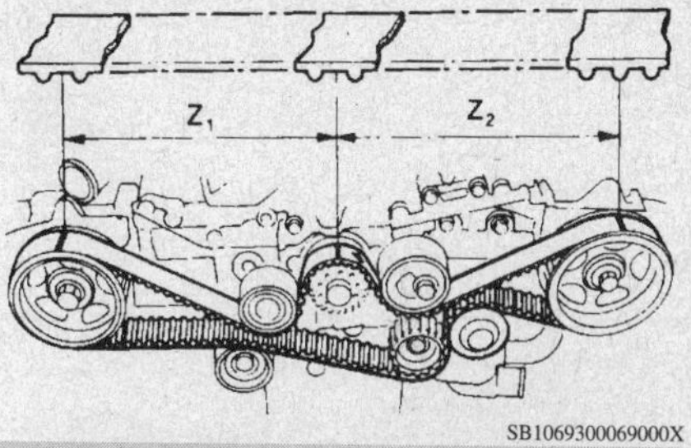
Z_1
Z_2
SB1069300069000X

Fig. 30 Timing belt tooth to sprocket alignment. Impreza w/1.8L & 2.2L engines

3. Loosen valve rocker assembly bolt No. 1 as shown **Fig. 33. Do not remove bolt at this time.**
4. Remove remainder of valve rocker assembly bolts in numerical order as shown **Fig. 33. Use caution not to gouge dowel pin.**
5. Remove bolt No. 1 and the rocker assembly. Position rocker arms with air vents facing upward.
6. Remove rocker shaft retaining bolts, rocker arms, springs and shaft supports from rocker shaft. Position rocker arms with air vents facing upward. Separate valve lash adjuster from valve rocker only if air bleeding or replacement is required. **Keep all parts in order of removal for proper installation.**
7. Bleed valve lash adjuster as follows:
   a. Submerge lash adjuster in a container of clean engine oil, then press check ball inward using a .08 inch diameter round bar.
   b. While holding check ball inward, manually move plunger up and down at one second intervals until air bubbles disappear.
   c. Release check ball and quickly push plunger in and lock it. Replace lash adjuster if plunger will not lock. **Allow valve lash adjuster to soak in engine oil until it is to be installed.**
8. Dip lash adjuster and rocker arm in clean engine oil and assemble them. **Fill rocker arm oil reservoir chamber with clean engine oil. Carefully install a new valve lash adjuster O-ring so as not to scratch it. Do not rotate lash adjuster during installation.**

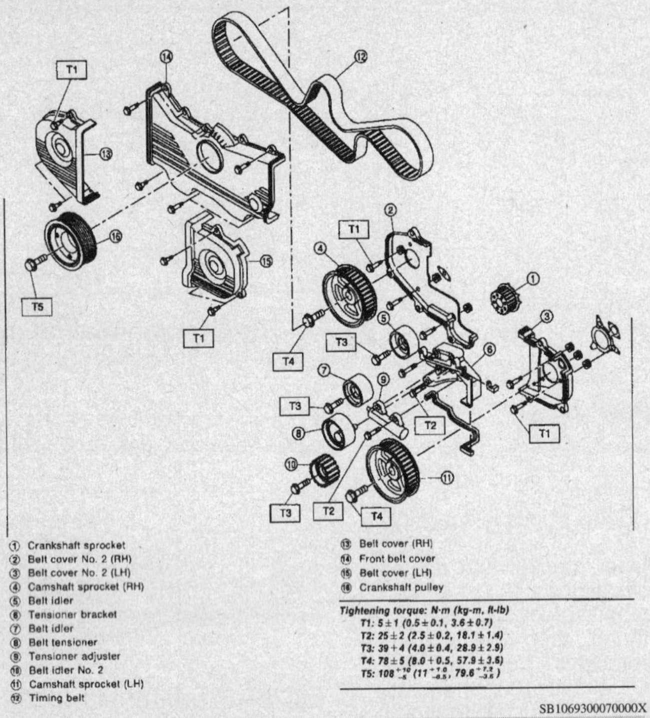
T1
T5
T1
T1
T4
T3
T3
T2
T1
T3
T2
T4
① Crankshaft sprocket
② Belt cover No. 2 (RH)
③ Belt cover No. 2 (LH)
④ Camshaft sprocket (RH)
⑤ Belt idler
⑥ Tensioner bracket
⑦ Belt idler
⑧ Belt tensioner
⑨ Tensioner adjuster
⑩ Belt idler No. 2
⑪ Camshaft sprocket (LH)
⑫ Timing belt
⑬ Belt cover (RH)
⑭ Front belt cover
⑮ Belt cover (LH)
⑯ Crankshaft pulley
Tightening torque: N·m (kg-m, ft-lb)
T1: 5±1 (0.5±0.1, 3.6±0.7)
T2: 25±2 (2.5±0.2, 18.1±1.4)
T3: 39+4 (4.0±0.4, 28.9±2.9)
T4: 78±5 (8.0+0.5, 57.9±3.6)
T5: 108 +10 −5 (11 +1.0 −0.5, 79.6 +7.2 −3.6)
SB1069300070000X

Fig. 31 Timing belt tensioner replacement. Impreza w/1.8L & 2.2L engines

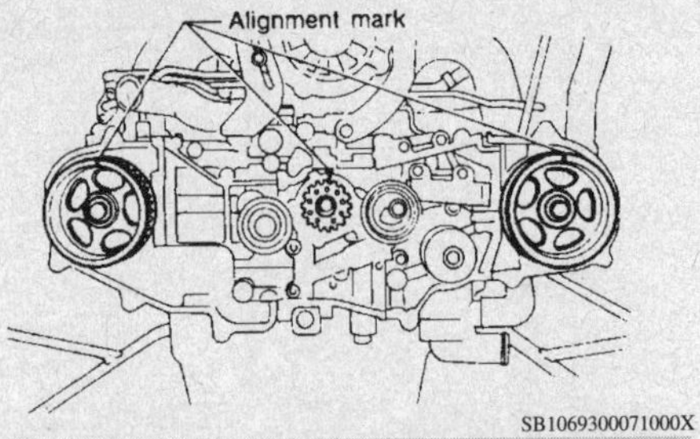
Alignment mark
SB1069300071000X

Fig. 32 Timing belt crankshaft pulley alignment mark. Impreza w/1.8L & 2.2L engines

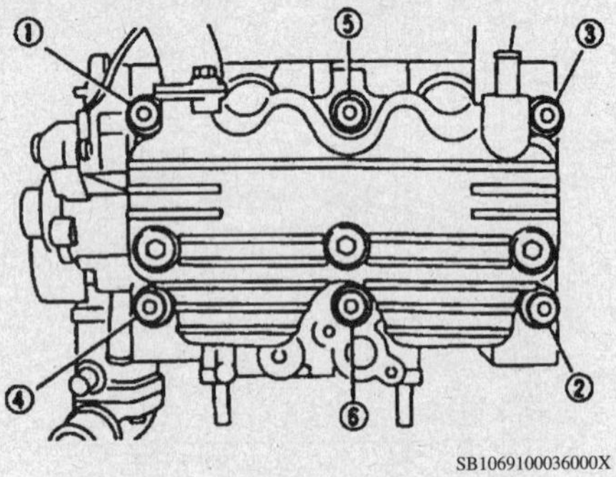
SB1069100036000X

Fig. 35 Cylinder head bolt loosening sequence. Impreza w/1.8L & 2.2L engines

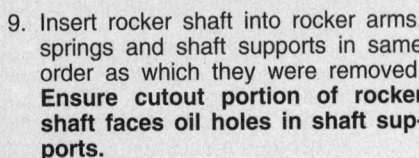

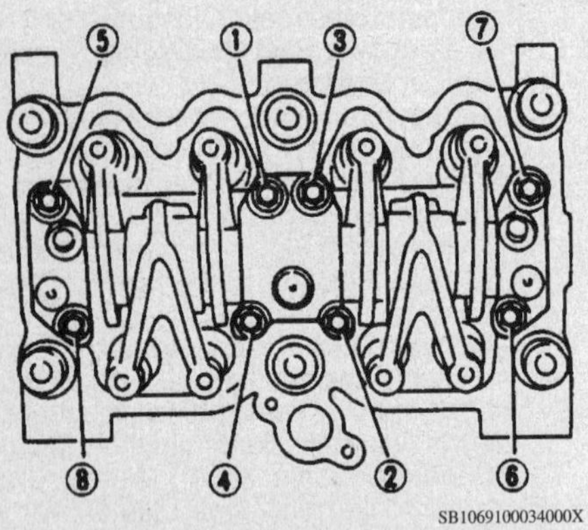
SB1069100034000X

Fig. 33 Rocker assembly bolt loosening sequence. Impreza w/1.8L & 2.2L engines

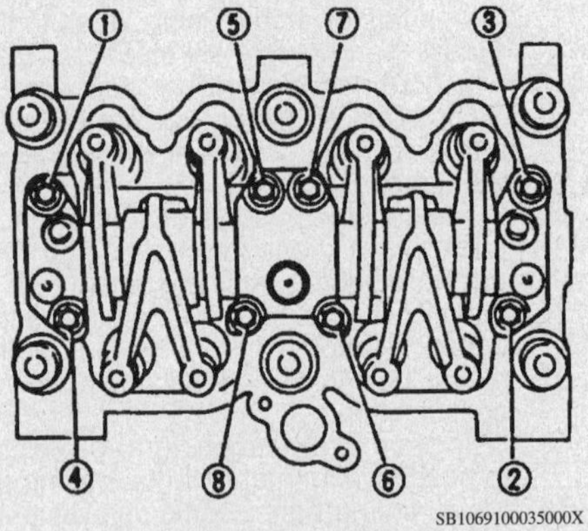
SB1069100035000X

Fig. 34 Rocker assembly bolt tightening sequence. Impreza w/1.8L & 2.2L engines

9. Insert rocker shaft into rocker arms, springs and shaft supports in same order as which they were removed. **Ensure cutout portion of rocker shaft faces oil holes in shaft supports.**
10. Align rocker shaft lock holes and install retaining bolts. Tighten bolts to specifications.
11. Install valve rocker assembly. Equally tighten rocker assembly bolts 1 through 4 as shown **Fig. 34. Use caution not to gouge dowel pin.**
12. Tighten rocker assembly bolts 5 through 8, then bolts 1 through 4 to specifications as shown **Fig. 34.**
13. Install rocker cover. Tighten bolts to specifications.
14. Install PCV valve.

Camshaft

1. Remove timing belt and related components as outlined previously in this section.
2. Remove valve rocker assembly as outlined previously in this section.
3. For lefthand camshaft, remove cam-angle sensor.
4. For lefthand camshaft, remove oil dipstick tube retaining bolt.
5. For either side, remove camshaft support and camshaft. Separate O-ring and oil seal from camshaft support.
6. Coat camshaft journals with clean engine oil, then install camshaft.
7. Install O-ring to camshaft support.
8. Install camshaft support and tighten to specifications.
9. Coat new oil seal lips with a suitable lubricant, then using oil seal guide tool No. 499597000, or equivalent, oil seal installer tool No. 499587100, or equivalent and a hammer, install oil seal to camshaft support.
10. For lefthand camshaft, install oil dipstick tube retaining bolt.
11. For lefthand camshaft, install cam-angle sensor. Tighten to specifications.
12. Install valve rocker assembly, timing belt and related components as outlined previously in this section.

Cylinder Head

1. Remove drive belt, power steering pump, alternator and bracket.
2. Remove timing belt and related components as outlined previously in this section.
3. Remove valve rocker assembly as outlined previously in this section.
4. Remove camshaft as outlined previously in this section.
5. Disconnect spark plug wires, oil pressure switch electrical connector and blow-by hose.
6. Remove connector bracket retaining bolts, crank-angle and knock sensors.
7. Remove intake manifold and gasket.
8. Remove water pipe.
9. Separate cylinder head from cylinder block as follows:
   a. Loosen cylinder head retaining bolts No. 1 and 3 as shown, **Fig. 35. Do not remove bolts at this time.**
   b. Remove remainder of cylinder head retaining bolts in numerical order as shown **Fig. 35.**

c. Using a plastic hammer, tap on cylinder head while separating it from cylinder block.
d. Remove bolts No. 1 and 3 with cylinder head and gasket.
10. Remove valves from cylinder head using valve spring remover tool No. 499718000, or equivalent. **Use caution not to damage oil seals. Keep all parts in order of removal for proper installation.**
11. For lefthand cylinder head, remove plug only if service is needed.
12. For lefthand cylinder head, install plug using oil seal installer tool No. 499587100, or equivalent.
13. For either cylinder head, install valves as follows:
a. Coat valve stem with clean engine oil and insert valve into valve guide. **Use caution not to damage oil seal lip. Install all parts in same order as which they were removed.**
b. Install valve spring with closed coil end facing cylinder head seat.
c. Use valve spring remover tool No. 499718000, or equivalent to compress valve spring and install retainer. Seat valve spring retainer by tapping it with a soft hammer.
14. Install camshaft and valve rocker assemblies as outlined previously in this section.
15. Install cylinder head with new gasket.
16. **On 2.2L engine,** using sequence shown in **Fig. 36,** tighten cylinder head bolts as follows:
a. Coat bolt threads and washers with clean engine oil.
b. **Torque** all six bolts to 22 ft. lbs.
c. **Torque** all bolts to 51 ft. lbs.
d. Loosen all bolts 180°, then loosen an additional 180°.
e. **On non-turbo models, torque** bolts 1 and 2 to 25 ft. lbs.
f. **On turbo models, torque** bolts 1 and 2 to 27.1 ft. lbs.
g. **On non-turbo models, torque** bolts 3, 4, 5 and 6 to 11 ft. lbs.
h. **On turbo models, torque** bolts 3, 4, 5 and 6 to 14 ft. lbs.
i. **On all models,** tighten all bolts an additional 80°–90° in sequence. **Do not tighten bolts more than 90°.**
j. Tighten all bolts an additional 80°–90° in sequence. **Ensure total retightening angle does not exceed 180°.**
17. **On Impreza 1.8L engine,** using sequence shown in **Fig. 36,** tighten cylinder head bolts as follows:
a. Coat bolt threads and washers with clean engine oil.
b. **Torque** all cylinder head bolts to 22 ft. lbs., then again to 51 ft. lbs.
c. Loosen all bolts 180°, then loosen an additional 180°.
d. **Torque** bolts 1 and 2 to 25 ft. lbs.
e. **Torque** bolts 3, 4, 5 and 6 to 11 ft. lbs.
f. Tighten all bolts an additional 80–90.° **Do not tighten bolts more than 90.°**
g. Tighten all bolts an additional 80°–90°. **Ensure total retightening**

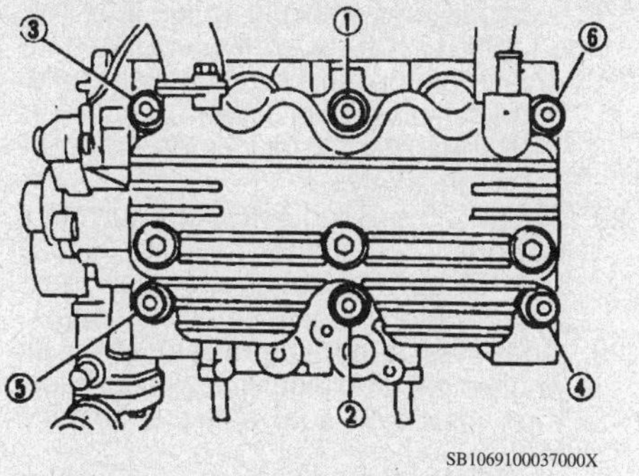

③
①
⑥
⑤
②
④
SB1069100037000X

Fig. 36 Cylinder head bolt tightening sequence. Impreza 1.8L & 1993–94 2.2L engines

angle does not exceed 180°.
18. **On all models,** install timing belt and related components as outlined previously in this section.
19. Install water pipe.
20. Install intake manifold and gasket.
21. Install connector bracket retaining bolts, crank-angle and knock sensors.
22. Connect spark plug wires, oil pressure switch electrical connector and blow-by hose.
23. Install power steering pump, alternator and bracket.
24. Install drive belt. Refer to "Drive Belt Service " for belt routing and tension data.

Cylinder Block

1. Separate cylinder head from cylinder block as outlined under "Cylinder Head" procedure.
2. Remove flywheel or driveplate housing cover.
3. Lock crankshaft using crankshaft stopper tool No. 498497100, or equivalent, then remove flywheel or driveplate.
4. Remove oil separator cover.
5. Remove water pump.
6. Remove oil pump retaining bolts, then using a flat blade screwdriver, separate oil pump from cylinder block. **Use caution not to scrape mating surfaces.**
7. Position cylinder block with No. 2 and 4 pistons facing upward.
8. Remove oil pan retaining bolts, then using oil pan cutter tool, or equivalent, separate oil pan from cylinder block. **Use caution not to scrape mating surfaces.**
9. Remove oil strainer stay, oil strainer, baffle plate and oil filter.
10. Remove pistons as follows:
a. Remove service hole cover and plugs from both sides of crankcase.
b. Rotate crankshaft until pistons for No. 1 and No. 2 cylinders are at BDC.
c. Working through access holes, remove piston pin circlips for No. 1 and No. 2 pistons.
d. Using piston pin remover tool No. 499097500, or equivalent, withdraw piston pins for No. 1 and No. 2 pistons.
e. Repeat step 10 for cylinders 3 and 4 respectively.
11. Separate crankcase as follows:
a. Remove crankcase half retaining bolts from No. 2 and 4 cylinder side of block.
b. Loosen crankcase half retaining bolts from No. 1 and 3 cylinder side of block. Do not remove bolts at this time.
c. Position crankcase so that cylinders No. 1 and 3 face upward.
d. Remove retaining bolts and separate crankcase halves. **Use caution so connecting rod will not damage cylinder block.**
12. Remove rear oil seal.
13. Remove crankshaft and connecting rod assembly.
14. Remove crankshaft bearings from crankcase halves keeping them in order.
15. Mark and remove pistons from crankcase halves, and mate pistons with respective pins.
16. Remove connecting rod caps and rod bearings. **Keep all components in order to ensure proper assembly. Components that are to be reused should be installed in original position.**
17. Remove piston rings using a piston ring expander. Remove oil ring by hand.
18. Remove circlip.
19. Ensure all components are clean and free from foreign material, and that oil passages are clear. Coat all friction surfaces with oil or suitable assembly lubricant.
20. Install connecting rods, proceed as follows:
a. Seat connecting rod bearings in caps and rods, then coat bearing with clean engine oil.
b. Ensure connecting rod and cap matching marks are aligned, and install connecting rod assemblies with mark facing forward.
c. Lubricate connecting rod bolt threads and ensure bolts are properly seated in cap and that caps are fully seated against connecting rods.
d. Evenly tighten connecting rod nuts to specifications.
21. Install main bearings into crankcase halves, then coat bearing with clean engine oil.
22. Install crankshaft into lefthand crankcase.
23. Clean crankcase half mating surfaces with suitable solvent, then apply a thin bead of Three-Bond 1215, or equivalent sealant to one crankcase half. Ensure sealant does not enter oil or coolant passages.
24. **On 1993–94 2.2L engine,** guide righthand crankcase half onto left case, then install and tighten retaining bolts as follows:
a. **Torque** bolts on No. 1 and 3 cylinder side of block to 14–22 ft. lbs.
b. Position cylinder block horizontally.
c. Tighten all retaining bolts to specifications as shown in **Fig. 37,** beginning with No. 1 and 3 cylinder side of block.

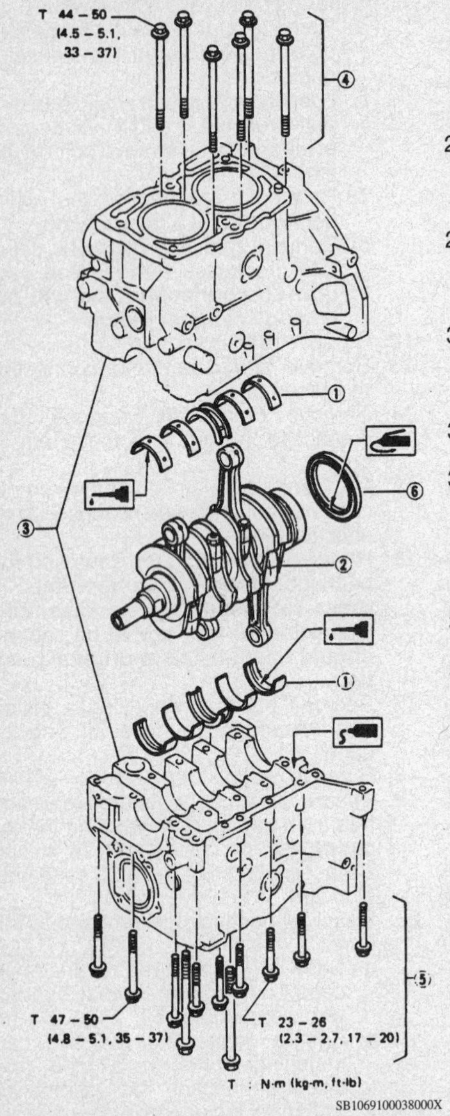
T 44 – 50
(4.5 – 5.1,
33 – 37)
T 47 – 50
(4.8 – 5.1, 35 – 37)
T 23 – 26
(2.3 – 2.7, 17 – 20)
T : N·m (kg-m, ft-lb)
SB1069100038000X

Fig. 37 Crankcase bolt tightening specifications. 2.2L engine

25. **On Impreza 1.8L & 1995–96 2.2L engines,** guide righthand crankcase half onto left case, then install and tighten retaining bolts as follows:
    a. **Torque** 10 mm bolts in sequence shown in **Fig. 38,** to 33–37 ft. lbs.
    b. Tighten 8 mm and 6 mm bolts in sequence shown in **Fig. 39. Torque** bolts 1 through 7 to 17–20 ft. lbs. and bolt 8 to 4.7 ft. lbs.
26. **On all engines,** install piston rings onto pistons, positioning end gaps as shown, **Figs. 40 and 41.** After installation, bend pawl of upper oil ring rail upward and attach to hole in piston.
27. Install piston, proceed as follows:
    a. Prior to insertion, coat piston, pin guide and piston pin with clean engine oil.
    b. With No. 1 and 2 cylinders facing upward, turn crankshaft until No. 1 and 2 connecting rods are positioned at BDC.
    c. Insert piston into cylinder, align piston pin hole and connecting rod small end with pin guide tool No. 499017100, or equivalent, then install piston pin through access hole.
    d. Install piston pin circlip.
    e. Repeat step 26 for cylinders 3 and 4 respectively.
28. Apply Three-Bond 1105, or equivalent sealant, then install service access hole plugs and cover with new gaskets. Tighten plugs to specifications.
29. Coat outside surface of rear seal with engine oil, and seal lip with grease, then install oil seal using a suitable tool.
30. Apply Three-Bond 1207C, or equivalent sealant, then install oil separator cover with new gasket and Tighten to specifications.
31. Install flywheel or driveplate and tighten bolts to specifications.
32. Apply Three-Bond 1215, or equivalent sealant to oil pump to cylinder block mating surface. Align flat surface of inner rotor with crankshaft and install oil pump assembly with new seal and O-ring. Tighten bolts to specifications.
33. Install water pump with new gasket. Tighten bolts to specifications.
34. Install baffle plate, oil strainer, stay and oil pan. Tighten bolts to specifications.
35. Install oil filter.
36. Install flywheel or driveplate housing cover.
37. Finalize installation by performing steps 14 through 22 of cylinder head service procedure.

3.3L ENGINE

Timing Belt, Tensioner & Idler

1. Remove drive belt, power steering pump, alternator and drive belt cover bracket.
2. Remove power steering pump bracket, A/C belt tensioner, A/C compressor and bracket.
3. Lock crankshaft using crankshaft pulley wrench tool No. 499977000, or equivalent, then remove pulley retaining bolt and pulley.
4. Remove lefthand, righthand and front belt covers.
5. Ensure timing belt rotation arrows and alignment marks are visible prior to belt removal. If original marks are faded, new alignment marks can be made as follows:
    a. Align camshaft and crankshaft sprockets with notches in belt cover and cylinder block.
    b. Mark timing belt in relation to sprockets.
6. Loosen tensioner adjuster mounting bolts.
7. Remove belt idler, belt idler No. 2, timing belt, spacer, belt tensioner and tensioner adjuster.
8. Lock camshaft sprocket using camshaft sprocket wrench tool No. 499207100, or equivalent, then remove sprocket retaining bolt and sprocket.
9. Remove No. 2 lefthand and righthand belt covers.
10. Remove tensioner bracket.
11. Install tensioner bracket. Tighten bolts to specifications.

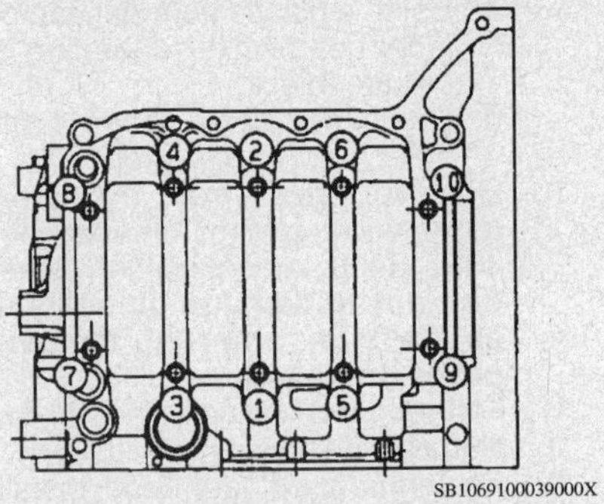
SB1069100039000X

Fig. 38 Crankcase 10 mm bolt tightening sequence. Impreza w/1.8L & 1995–96 2.2L engines

12. Install No. 2 righthand and lefthand belt covers.
13. Install crankshaft sprocket.
14. Install righthand, then the lefthand camshaft sprockets. Lock sprocket using tool No. 499207100, or equivalent and tighten bolt to specifications. **Lefthand sprocket can be identified by a projection used to monitor cam-angle sensor.**
15. Vertically push tensioner adjuster rod into adjuster body using a suitable press, then completely insert stopper pin .059 inch diameter into tensioner adjuster to hold rod in place. **Do not allow press pressure to exceed 2205 lbs.**
16. Install tensioner adjuster. Ensure adjuster is positioned completely to the right and tighten retaining bolts.
17. Install belt tensioner. Tighten bolts to specifications.
18. Install belt idler. Tighten bolts to specifications.
19. Using sprocket wrench, turn sprockets to position alignment marks at the top.
20. Install timing belt. Position timing belt with rotation arrows facing in correct direction and sprocket and belt alignment marks properly aligned.
21. Install belt idler No. 2, then the belt idler. Tighten bolts to specifications.
22. Loosen tensioner adjuster retaining bolts, position adjuster completely to the left and tighten retaining bolts to specifications.
23. Ensure timing marks are properly aligned, then remove stopper pin from tension adjuster.
24. Install front, lefthand and righthand belt covers.
25. Install crankshaft pulley. Lock crankshaft using tool No. 499977000, or equivalent and tighten pulley retaining bolt to specifications.
26. Install drive belt. Refer to "Drive Belt Service " for belt routing and tension data.
27. Install power steering pump bracket, A/C belt tensioner, A/C compressor and bracket.
28. Install drive belt, power steering pump, alternator and drive belt cover bracket.

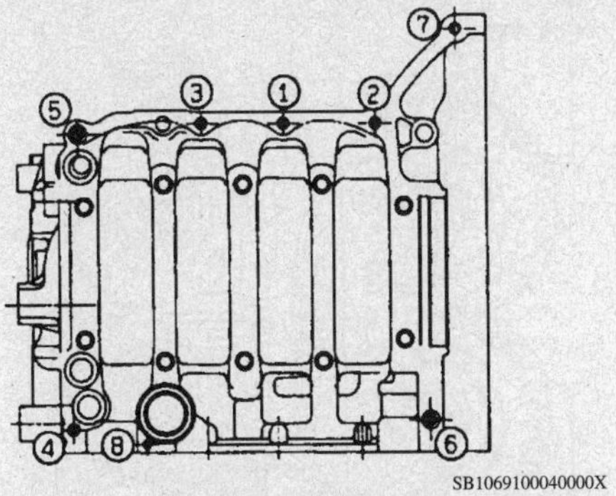
7
5
3
1
2
4
8
6
SB1069100040000X

Fig. 39 Crankcase 8 mm & 6 mm bolt tightening sequence. Impreza w/1.8L & 1995–96 2.2L engines

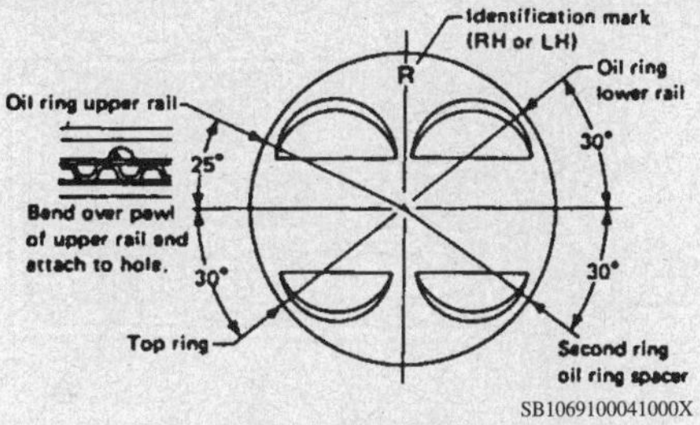
Identification mark (RH or LH)
Oil ring upper rail
Oil ring lower rail
R
25°
30°
Bend over pawl of upper rail and attach to hole.
30°
30°
Top ring
Second ring oil ring spacer
SB1069100041000X

Fig. 40 Piston ring installation. Impreza w/1.8L, 3.3L & 1993–94 2.2L engines

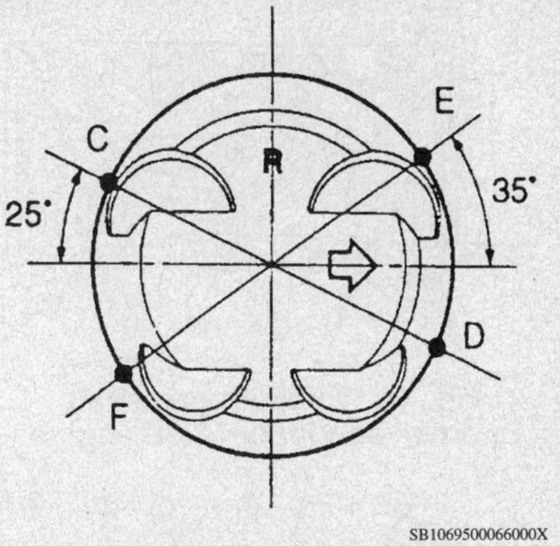
E
C
R
35°
25°
D
F
SB1069500066000X

Fig. 41 Piston ring installation. 1995–96 2.2L engine

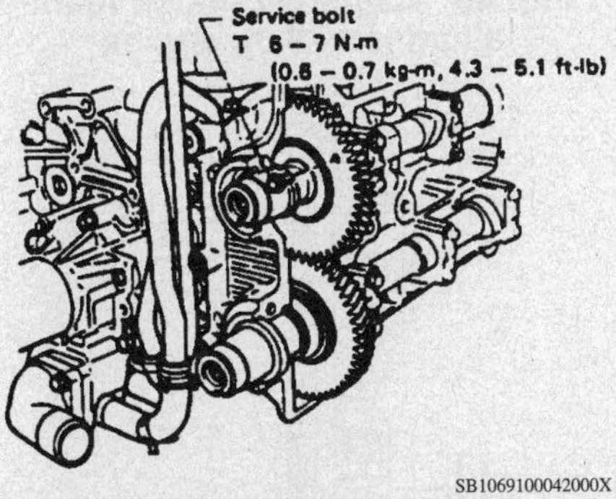
Service bolt
T 6 – 7 N·m
(0.6 – 0.7 kg-m, 4.3 – 5.1 ft-lb)
SB1069100042000X

Fig. 42 Securing camshaft. 3.3L engine

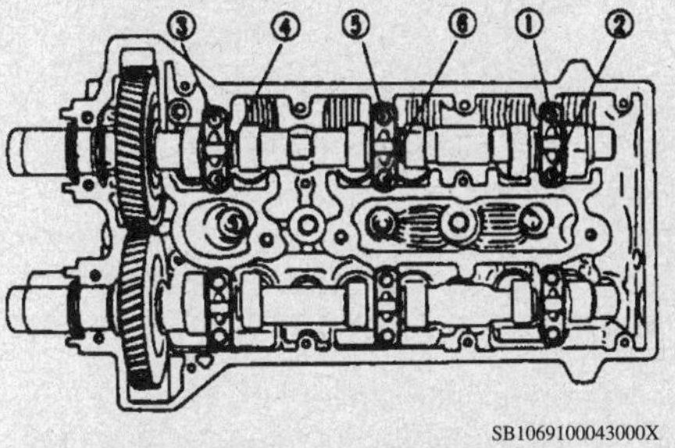
3
4
5
6
1
2
SB1069100043000X

Fig. 43 Intake camshaft removal sequence. 3.3L engine

Camshafts

1. Remove timing belt and related components as outlined previously in this section.
2. Disconnect cam angle sensor and ignition coil connectors.
3. Remove cam angle sensor and bracket, then fully loosen ignition coil mounting bolts.
4. Disconnect blow-by hose, then remove cylinder head cover and gasket.
5. Remove front camshaft cap, camshaft oil seal and plug.
6. Remove intake and exhaust camshafts as follows:
   a. **On lefthand side camshafts,** rotate intake camshaft (upper) and exhaust camshaft (lower) so notch at front end of each camshaft faces directly downward.
   b. **On righthand side camshafts,** rotate intake camshaft (upper) and exhaust camshaft (lower) so notch at front end of each camshaft faces directly upward.
   c. **On either side,** looking from rear side of camshaft gears, ensure match marks on gears are aligned.
   d. Install .24 inch diameter bolt to sub-gear mounting bolt hole of intake camshaft gear to secure gear train, **Fig. 42.**
   e. Loosen bolts on intake camshaft caps equally, a little at a time, in sequence shown in **Fig. 43.** Ensure as bolts are loosened, clearance between camshaft journal and cylinder head journal bearing increases evenly. If not, tighten bolts by reversing sequence in **Fig. 43,** and repeat this step.
   f. Remove camshaft caps while holding intake camshaft, then remove camshaft. If intake camshaft is hard to remove, rotate exhaust camshaft counterclockwise.
   g. Arrange caps in correct order. Caps must be installed in their original positions.
   h. Loosen bolts on exhaust camshaft caps equally, a little at a time, in sequence shown in **Fig. 44.** Ensure as bolts are loosened, clearance between camshaft journal and cylinder head journal bearing increases evenly. If not, tighten bolts by reversing sequence in **Fig. 44,** and repeat this step.
   i. Remove camshaft caps while holding exhaust camshaft, then remove camshaft. Arrange caps in correct order. Caps must be installed in their original positions.
7. Remove hydraulic lash adjuster. Arrange adjusters in correct order. Adjusters must be installed in their original positions.
8. Service intake camshaft as follows:
   a. Using a rag, secure shaft portion of camshaft in vice, then remove bolt installed in sub-gear.
   b. Using camshaft gear wrench No. 49920-7200, or equivalent, turn sub-gear clockwise, then remove snap ring.
   c. Remove wave washer, sub-gear and gear spring.
   d. Reverse step 8 to assembly intake camshaft.
9. Install exhaust camshaft as follows:
   a. Install lash adjusters. Apply coat of clean engine oil to adjuster surface.
   b. Apply coat of clean engine oil to camshaft journals.
   c. Set exhaust camshaft on cylinder head with front end notch of camshaft facing directly downward.
   d. Attach camshaft caps in their original positions. Fully hand tighten cap bolts.
   e. Tighten cap bolts equally, a little at a time, in sequence shown in **Fig. 45,** to specifications. Ensure as bolts are tightened, clearance between camshaft journal and cylinder head journal bearing decreases evenly. If not, loosen bolts by reversing sequence in **Fig. 45,** and repeat this step.
10. Install intake camshaft as follows:
    a. Install lash adjusters. Apply coat of clean engine oil to adjuster surface.
    b. Apply coat of clean engine oil to camshaft journals.
    c. **On lefthand side camshafts,** align intake camshaft match mark with match mark of exhaust camshaft. Ensure notch on front end of camshafts are facing same direction (downward), **Fig. 46.**
    d. **On righthand side camshafts,** align intake camshaft match mark with match mark of exhaust camshaft. Ensure notch on front end of camshafts are facing same direction (upward), **Fig. 46.**
    e. **On either side,** attach camshaft caps in their original positions. Fully hand tighten cap bolts. Ensure match marks on rear side of camshaft gears are aligned.
    f. Tighten cap bolts equally, a little at a time, in sequence shown in **Fig. 47,** to specifications. Ensure as bolts are tightened, clearance between camshaft journal and cylinder head journal bearing decreases evenly. If not, loosen bolts by reversing sequence in **Fig. 47,** and repeat this step.
11. Remove sub-gear securing bolt from intake camshaft gear.
12. Apply fluid packing for mating surface of front camshaft cover, then install camshaft cover.
13. Using oil seal guide No. 49959-7000

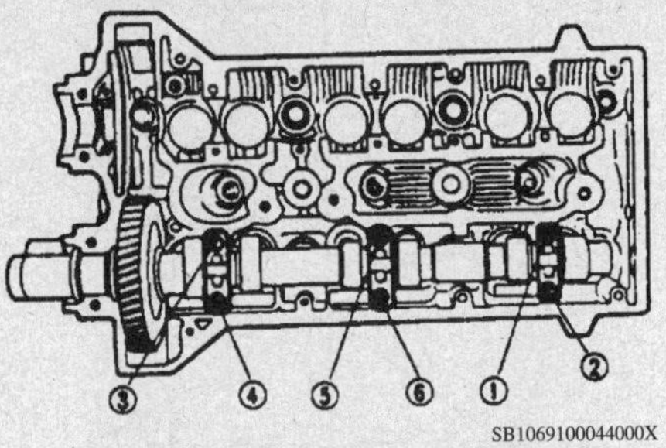
③
④
⑤
⑥
①
②
SB1069100044000X

Fig. 44 Exhaust camshaft removal sequence. 3.3L engine

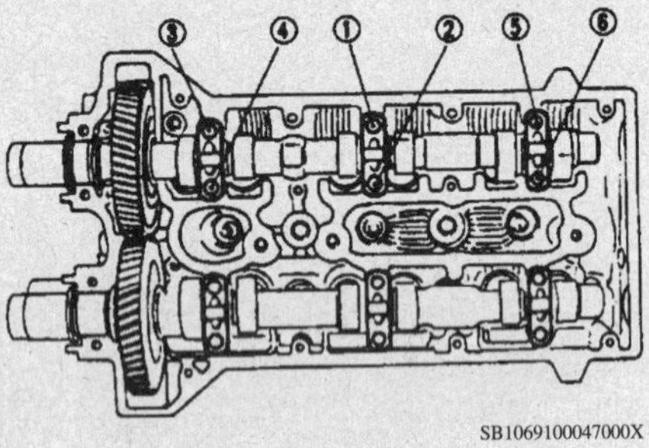
③
④
⑤
⑥
①
②
SB1069100047000X

Fig. 47 Intake camshaft installation sequence. 3.3L engine

and oil seal installer No. 49958-7300, or equivalents, lubricate and install new camshaft oil seal.

14. Using plug installer No. 49803-7100, or equivalent, install camshaft plug.
15. **On lefthand side camshafts,** install cylinder head cover. Apply soapy water over A and B shown in **Fig. 48.**
16. **On righthand side camshafts,** install cylinder head cover. Apply soapy water over A shown in **Fig. 48.**
17. **On either side,** connect blow-by hose, then install ignition coils and cam angle sensor.

Cylinder Head

1. Remove timing belt and related components as outlined previously in this section.
2. Remove intake manifold as follows:
   a. Remove EGR valve, EGR pipe and backpressure transducer, then disconnect auxiliary air control valve connector.
   b. Disconnect blow-by, auxiliary air control valve and PCV hoses, then two water hoses from throttle body.
   c. Remove collector, then intake manifold assembly.
3. Remove exhaust manifold and gasket.
4. Remove cylinder head cover and camshafts as outlined previously in this section.
5. Remove dipstick, then heater pipe.
6. Separate cylinder head from cylinder block as follows:
   a. Remove cylinder head bolts in sequence shown in **Fig. 49. Leave bolts 5 and 8 engaged by four threads to prevent cylinder head from falling.** Cylinder head bolts come in two different lengths.
   b. Using plastic hammer, tap on cylinder head while separating it from

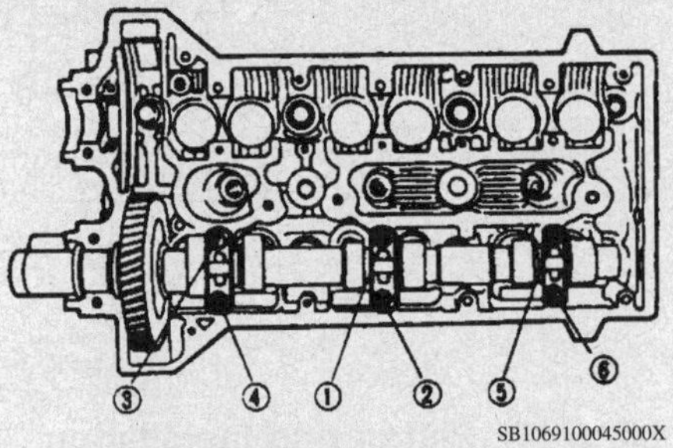
③
④
①
②
⑤
⑥
SB1069100045000X

Fig. 45 Exhaust camshaft installation sequence. 3.3L engine

cylinder block.
   c. Remove bolts 5 and 8 with cylinder head and gasket.
7. Remove hydraulic lash adjuster. Arrange adjusters in correct order. Adjusters must be installed in their original positions.
8. Using valve spring remover No. 49971-8000, or equivalent, compress valve spring, then remove spring retainer key.
9. Remove valves from cylinder head. **Use caution not to damage oil seals. Keep all parts in order of removal for proper installation.**
10. Install valve as follows:
   a. Coat valve stem with clean engine oil and insert valve into valve guide. **Use caution not to damage oil seal lip. Install all parts in same position as they were removed from.**
   b. Install valve spring with closed coil end facing cylinder head seat.
   c. Use valve spring remover tool No. 499718000, or equivalent to compress valve spring and install retainer key. Seat valve spring retainer by tapping it with a soft hammer.
11. Apply coat of clean engine oil to hydraulic lash adjuster sliding surface, then install adjusters.
12. Install cylinder head with new gasket. Using sequence shown in **Fig. 50,** tighten cylinder head bolts as follows:
   a. Coat bolt threads and washers with clean engine oil.
   b. **Torque** all cylinder head bolts to 22 ft. lbs.
   c. **Torque** all bolts to 51 ft. lbs.
   d. Loosen all bolts 180°, then loosen an additional 180°.
   e. **Torque** all bolts to 20 ft. lbs.
   f. Tighten bolts 1, 2, 3 and 4, 80°–90° in sequence. **Do not tighten bolts more than 90°.**
   g. **Torque** bolts 5, 6, 7 and 8 in sequence to 33 ft. lbs.
   h. Tighten all bolts an additional 80°–90° in sequence. **Ensure total retightening angle (steps f and h) does not exceed 180°**
13. Install camshafts, cylinder head covers and related parts.
14. Install exhaust manifold and gasket, then the collector and intake manifold assembly.
15. Connector blow-by, auxiliary air control valve and PCV hoses, then two water

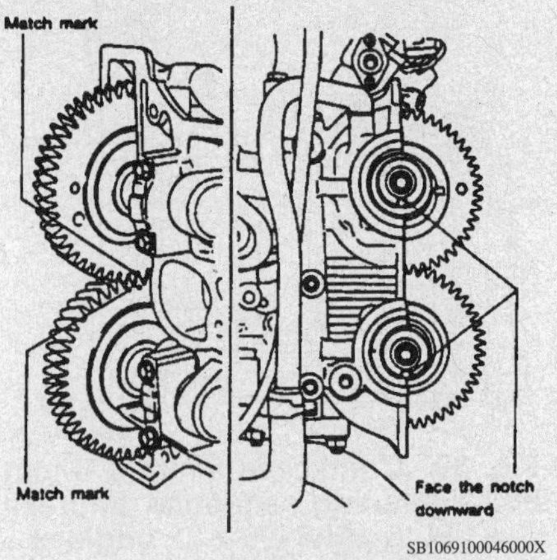
Match mark
Match mark
Face the notch downward
SB1069100046000X

Fig. 46 Camshaft match mark alignment. 3.3L engine

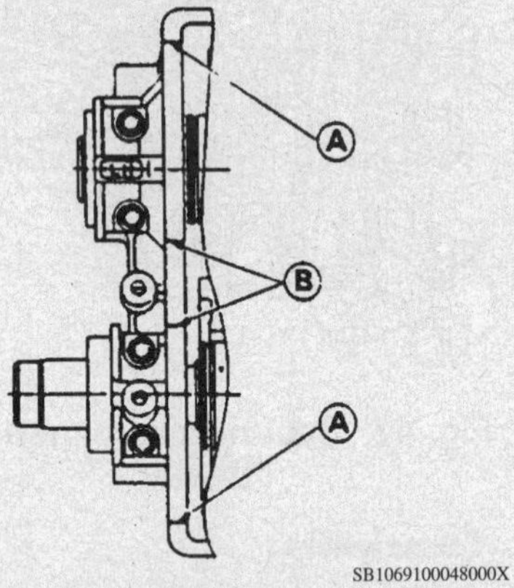
A
B
A
SB1069100048000X

Fig. 48 Cylinder head cover lube points. 3.3L engine

hoses from throttle body.

16. Install EGR valve, EGR pipe and backpressure transducer, then connect auxiliary air control valve connector.
17. Install timing belt and related components as outlined previously in this section.

Cylinder Block

1. Remove cylinder head and related components as outlined previously in this section.
2. Remove crank angle and knock sensors.
3. Lock crankshaft using crankshaft stopper tool No. 498497200, or equivalent, then remove driveplate.
4. Remove oil separator cover.
5. Remove water bypass pipe and pump.
6. Remove oil pump retaining bolts, then using a flat blade screwdriver, separate oil pump from cylinder block. **Use caution not to scrape mating surfaces.**
7. Position cylinder block with No. 2, 4 and 6 pistons facing upward.
8. Remove oil pan retaining bolts, then using oil pan cutter tool separate oil pan from cylinder block. **Use caution not to scrape mating surfaces.**
9. Remove oil strainer, baffle plate and oil filter.
10. Remove pistons as follows:

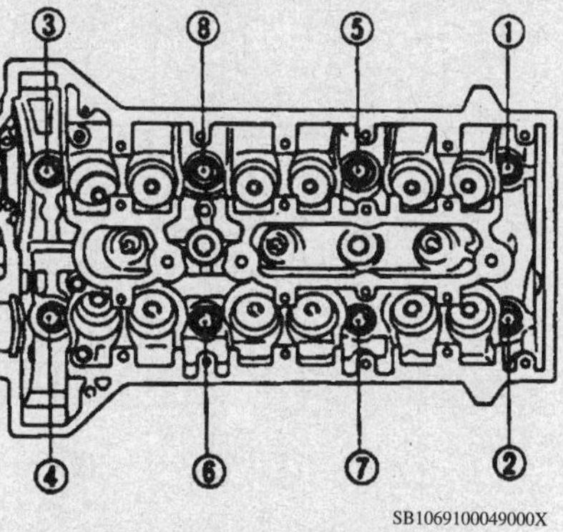
3
8
5
1
4
6
7
2
SB1069100049000X

Fig. 49 Cylinder head removal sequence. 3.3L engine

a. Remove service hole cover and plugs from both sides of crankcase.
b. Rotate crankshaft until pistons for No. 1 and No. 2 cylinders are at BDC.
c. Working through access holes, remove piston pin circlips for No. 1 and No. 2 pistons.
d. Using piston pin remover tool No. 499097500, or equivalent, withdraw piston pins for No. 1 and No. 2 pistons.
e. Rotate crankshaft until pistons for No. 3 and No. 4 cylinders are at BDC, then remove piston circlip in same manner through service hole of No. 1 and No. 2 cylinders.
f. Rotate crankshaft until pistons for No. 5 and No. 6 cylinder are at BDC, then remove piston circlip in same manner through service hole of No. 5 and No. 6 cylinders.

11. Separate crankcase as follows:
    a. Remove crankcase half retaining bolts from No. 1, 3 and 5 cylinder side of block.
    b. Loosen crankcase half retaining bolts from No. 2, 4 and 6 cylinder side of block. Do not remove bolts at this time.
    c. Position crankcase so that cylinders No. 2, 4 and 6 face upward.
    d. Remove retaining bolts and separate crankcase halves. **Use caution so connecting rod will not damage cylinder block.**
12. Remove rear oil seal.
13. Remove crankshaft and connecting rod assembly.
14. Remove crankshaft bearings from crankcase halves keeping them in order.
15. Mark and remove pistons from crankcase halves, and mate pistons with respective pins.
16. Remove connecting rod caps and rod bearings. **Keep all components in order to ensure proper assembly. Components that are to be reused should be installed in original position.**
17. Remove piston rings using a piston ring expander. Remove oil ring by hand.
18. Remove circlip.
19. Ensure all components are clean and free from foreign material, and that oil passages are clear. Coat all friction surfaces with oil or suitable assembly lubricant.
20. Install connecting rods, proceed as follows:
    a. Seat connecting rod bearings in caps and rods, then coat bearing with clean engine oil.
    b. Ensure connecting rod and cap matching marks are aligned, then install connecting rod assemblies with mark facing forward.
    c. Lubricate connecting rod bolt threads and ensure bolts are properly seated in cap and that caps are fully seated against connecting rods.
    d. Evenly tighten connecting rod nuts to specifications.
21. Install piston ring, proceed as follows:
    a. Install oil ring spacer, upper rail and lower rail by hand, then the second ring and top ring with ring expander.
    b. Position ring end gaps as shown in **Fig. 40.**
22. Install main bearings into crankcase halves, then coat bearing with clean engine oil.
23. Install crankshaft on No. 1, 3, and 5 cylinder block half.
24. Clean crankcase half mating surfaces with suitable solvent, then apply a thin bead of Three-Bond 1215, or equivalent sealant to No. 1, 3 and 5 crankcase half. Ensure sealant does not enter oil or coolant passages.
25. Install O-rings on grooves of No. 1, 3 and 5 cylinder block.
26. Guide No. 2, 4 and 6 crankcase half onto No. 1, 3 and 5 case, then install and tighten retaining bolts as follows:
    a. **Torque** bolts on No. 2, 4 and 6 cylinder side of block in sequence shown in **Fig. 51,** to 11 ft. lbs.
    b. Tighten small bolt in crankcase, then position cylinder block horizontally.
    c. **Torque** bolts on No. 1, 3 and 5 cylinder side of block to 11 ft. lbs. using sequence shown in **Fig. 52.**
    d. **Torque** No. 2, 4 and 6 cylinder side of block a second time to 11 ft. lbs. using sequence shown in **Fig. 51.**
    e. Tighten bolts an additional 90°–110° on No. 2, 4 and 6 cylinder side of block in sequence shown in **Fig. 51.**
    f. Tighten bolts an additional 90°–110° on No. 1, 3 and 5 cylinder side of block in sequence shown in **Fig. 52.**
    g. Tighten other connecting bolts to specifications.
27. Using oil seal installer No. 499587200 and oil seal guide No. 499597100, or equivalents, install rear oil seal.
28. Install pistons, proceed as follows:
    a. Prior to insertion, coat piston, pin guide and piston pin with clean engine oil.
    b. With No. 1 and 2 cylinders facing upward, turn crankshaft until No. 3 and 4 connecting rods are positioned at BDC.
    c. Insert piston into cylinder, align piston pin hole and connecting rod small end with pin guide tool No. 499017100, or equivalent, then install piston pin through access hole.

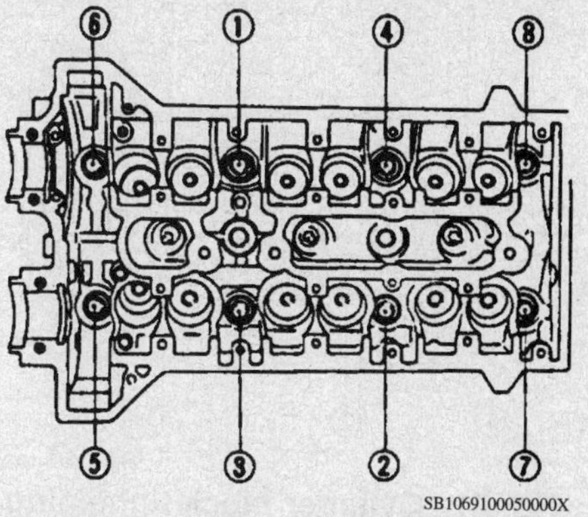
6
1
4
8
5
3
2
7
SB1069100050000X

Fig. 50 Cylinder head installation sequence. 3.3L engine

    d. Install new piston pin circlip.
    e. Repeat step 28 for cylinders 1 and 2, then 5 and 6 respectively.
29. Apply Three-Bond 1105, or equivalent sealant, then install service access hole plugs and cover with new gaskets.
30. Install baffle plate, oil strainer and O-ring.
31. Apply Three-Bond 1207F, or equivalent sealant, then install oil pan.
32. Apply Three-Bond 1215B, or equivalent sealant, then install separator cover with new gasket.
33. Install driveplate.
34. Remove front oil seal, then install new seal using oil seal installer No. 499587100, or equivalent.
35. Apply Three-Bond 1215B, or equivalent sealant to oil pump to cylinder block mating surface. Align flat surface of inner rotor with crankshaft and install oil pump assembly with new seal and O-ring.
36. Install water pump with new gasket, water pipe and water bypass.
37. Install oil filter.
38. Apply coat of clean engine oil to hydraulic lash adjuster sliding surface, then install adjusters.
39. Install cylinder head with new gasket. Using sequence shown in **Fig. 49,** tighten cylinder head bolts as follows:
    a. Coat bolt threads and washers with clean engine oil.
    b. **Torque** all bolts in sequence to 22 ft. lbs.
    c. **Torque** all bolts in sequence to 51 ft. lbs.
    d. Back off all bolts 180°, then back all bolts of an additional 180°.
    e. **Torque** all bolts in sequence to 20 ft. lbs.
    f. **Torque** bolts 1, 2, 3 and 4, an additional 80°–90° in sequence. **Do not tighten bolts more than 90°.**
    g. **Torque** bolts 5, 6, 7 and 8 in sequence to 33 ft. lbs.
    h. Tighten all bolts an additional 80°–90° in sequence. **Ensure total retightening angle (steps f and h) does not exceed 180°**

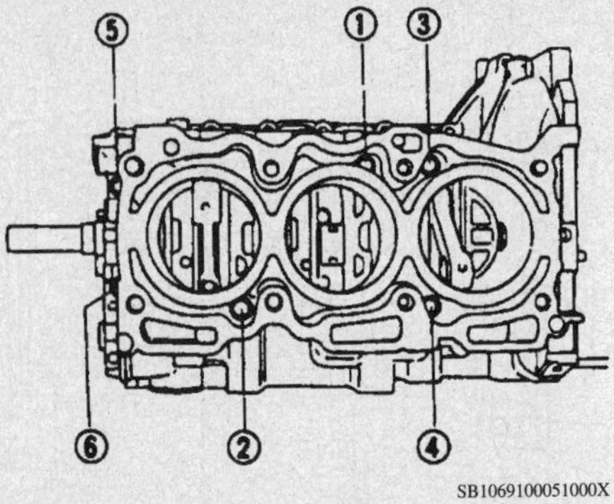
5
1
3
6
2
4
SB1069100051000X

Fig. 51 Cylinder block tightening sequence (No. 2, 4 & 6 cylinder block side). 3.3L engine

40. Install camshafts, cylinder head covers and related parts.
41. Install exhaust manifold and gasket, then the collector and intake manifold assembly.
42. Connector blow-by, auxiliary air control valve and PCV hoses, then two water hoses from throttle body.
43. Install EGR valve, EGR pipe and backpressure transducer, then connect auxiliary air control valve connector.
44. Install timing belt and related components as outlined previously in this section.

VALVE CLEARANCE SPECIFICATIONS

When measuring valve clearance, refer to "Valve Lash" under "Tune Up Specifications."

BELT TENSION DATA

Refer to **Figs. 53 through 56** for drive belt routing and tension data.

IMPREZA & LEGACY

Where applicable, always replace drive belts in pairs.

Front Drive Belt

1. Loosen upper soldier lock and slide bolts, **Fig. 57.**
2. Remove drive belt.
3. Install drive belt, then tighten upper soldier slide bolt, **Fig. 58,** until proper belt tension is achieved, **Fig. 55.**
4. Tighten upper soldier lock bolt, **Fig. 57.**
5. For new belt installation, readjust belt tension to specifications after running engine for five minutes.

Second Drive Belt

1. Remove front drive belt as outlined previously.
2. Loosen lower soldier lock and slide bolts, **Fig. 57.**
3. Remove drive belt.
4. Install drive belt, then tighten lower soldier slide bolt, **Fig. 57,** until proper belt tension is achieved, **Fig. 55.**
5. Tighten lower soldier lock bolt, **Fig. 57.**
6. Install front drive belt as outlined previously.

JUSTY & LOYALE

Where applicable, always replace drive belts in pairs.

First Drive Belt

1. Loosen alternator mount and slide bolts, **Fig. 59.**
2. Remove drive belt.
3. Install drive belt. When proper belt tension is achieved, as specified in **Figs. 53 and 54,** tighten alternator slide and mount bolts, **Fig. 59.**
4. For new belt installation, readjust belt tension to specifications after running engine for five minutes.

Second Drive Belt

1. Loosen idler pulley retaining bolt and nut, **Fig. 60.**
2. Remove drive belt.
3. Install drive belt. When proper belt tension is achieved, as specified in **Figs. 53 and 54,** tighten idler pulley retaining bolt and nut, **Fig. 60.**
4. For new belt installation, readjust belt tension to specifications after running engine for five minutes.

SVX

Front Drive Belt

1. Remove drive belt cover, then loosen locknut and slider bolt, **Fig. 61.**
2. Remove front drive belt.
3. Install drive belt. When proper belt tension is achieved, as specified in **Fig. 56,** tighten locknut.
4. For new belt installation, readjust belt tension to specifications after running engine for five minutes.
5. Install drive belt cover.

Rear Drive Belt

1. Remove front drive belt as outlined previously.
2. Loosen locknut and bolt, **Fig. 62.**
3. Remove rear drive belt.
4. Install drive belt. When proper belt tension is achieved, as specified in **Fig. 56,** tighten lockbolt.
5. Install front drive belt as outlined previously.

COOLING SYSTEM BLEED

1. With engine cool, open radiator drain plug and drain coolant into a suitable container.
2. Remove radiator pressure cap. **Never open cap with engine hot.**
3. Remove and drain coolant reservoir.
4. If equipped, remove drain plug(s) from engine. When coolant is completely drained, install the plug(s).
5. Close radiator drain plug.
6. Install coolant reservoir.
7. **On Impreza 1.8L and 2.2L engine,** remove air vent plug from radiator, **Fig. 63.**
8. **On all engines,** slowly add coolant to radiator until fluid level reaches filler neck.

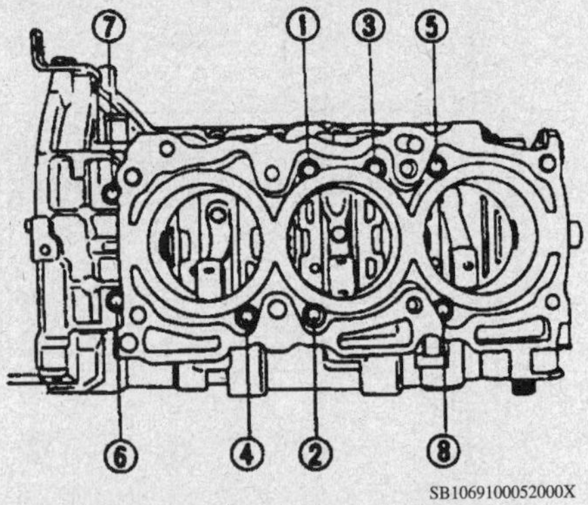
7
1
3
5
6
4
2
8
SB1069100052000X

Fig. 52 Cylinder block tightening sequence (No. 1, 3 & 5 cylinder block side). 3.3L engine

9. Slowly add coolant to reservoir until fluid level reaches Full mark.
10. Install radiator and reservoir caps.
11. Start and run engine at 2000–3000 RPM. When operating temperature is achieved, stop the engine.
12. With engine cool, remove radiator and reservoir caps. **Never open cap with engine hot.**
13. Add coolant as needed until fluid level is as specified in steps 8 and 9.
14. Install radiator and reservoir caps.
15. **On Impreza 1.8L and 2.2L engine,** install air vent plug.

THERMOSTAT

REPLACE

1. Remove thermostat housing mounting bolts, then the housing and gasket.
2. Remove thermostat.
3. Reverse procedure to install. **When installing thermostat, ensure jiggle pin is facing upward.**

WATER PUMP

REPLACE

1.2L ENGINE

1. Disconnect battery ground cable.
2. Drain cooling system. Refer to "Cooling System Bleed."
3. Drain engine oil.
4. Remove oil dipstick tube.
5. Loosen alternator mount and slide bolts, then remove drive belt. Refer to "Drive Belt Service."
6. Remove alternator.
7. Refer to "Engine Service" for removal of crankshaft pulley, cam belt cover No. 2, cam belt tensioner and spring, camshaft driveplate and belt, camshaft drive and driven pulleys, cam belt cover and mount, flywheel housing, oil pan and gasket.
8. Remove water pump and crankcase cover assembly, **Fig. 64.**
9. Reverse procedure to install. Tighten bolts to specifications.

LOYALE w/1.8L ENGINE

1. Disconnect battery ground cable.
2. Drain cooling system. Refer to "Cooling System Bleed."

Type	Pulley arrangement	Tension mm (in)/98 N (10 kg, 22 lb) New belt	Tension mm (in)/98 N (10 kg, 22 lb) Existing belt
Basic model	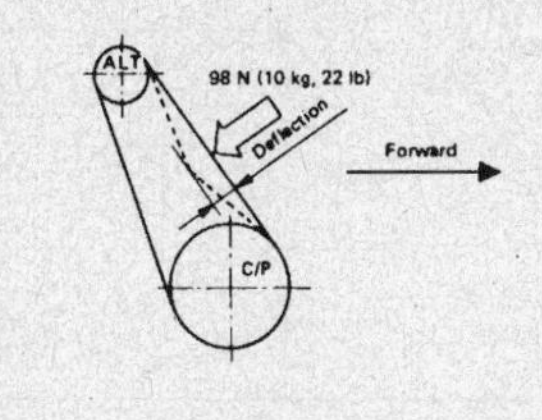	8 – 9 (0.31 – 0.35)	9 – 10 (0.35 – 0.39)
Air conditioner equipped model	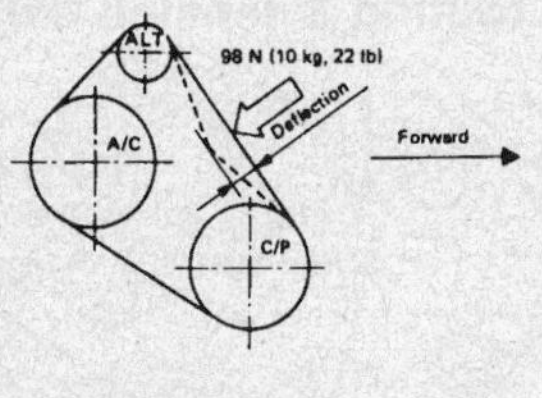	10 – 11 (0.39 – 0.43)	11.5 – 12.5 (0.453 – 0.492)

C/P: Crankshaft pulley
ALT: Alternator pulley
A/C: Air conditioner compressor pulley

SB1069100053000X

Fig. 53 Drive belt routing & tension data. Justy

Type	Pulley arrangement	Tension mm (in)/98 N (10 kg, 22 lb) New belt	Tension mm (in)/98 N (10 kg, 22 lb) Existing belt
Power steering equipped model	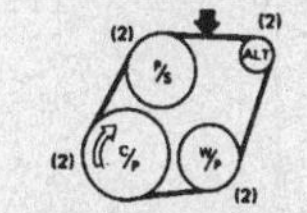	7 – 9 (0.28 – 0.35)	9 – 11 (0.35 – 0.43)
Power steering and air conditioner equipped model	HITACHI / PANASONIC 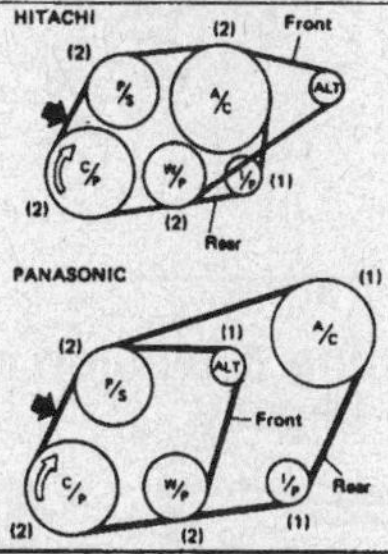	7.5 – 8.5 (0.295 – 0.335)	

Figures in parentheses refer to the number of grooves in pulleys.
C/P : Crankshaft pulley P/S : Power steering oil pump pulley
W/P : Water pump pulley A/C : Air conditioner compressor pulley
ALT : Alternator pulley I/P : Idler pulley

SB1069100054000X

Fig. 54 Drive belt routing & tension data. Loyale

3. Loosen alternator mount and slide bolts and remove drive belt. Refer to "Drive Belt Service."
4. Remove alternator.
5. Disconnect radiator outlet hose.
6. Disconnect water bypass hose from pipe.
7. Unfasten oil pressure switch electrical harness.
8. Remove oil dipstick tube.
9. Remove water pump pulley.
10. Remove crankshaft pulley using stopper tools Nos. 498227700 or 498497000, or equivalents.
11. **On turbo models,** proceed as follows:
    a. Raise and support vehicle.
    b. Remove belt cover plate.
    c. Lower vehicle.
12. **On all models,** remove water pipe.
13. Remove timing belt covers.
14. Remove water pump retaining bolts, **Fig. 65,** then the pump and timing plate assembly.
15. Reverse procedure to install. Tighten bolts to specifications.

IMPREZA w/1.8L & 2.2L ENGINE

1. Disconnect battery ground cable.
2. Drain cooling system. Refer to "Cooling System Bleed."
3. Disconnect radiator outlet hose.
4. Remove radiator cooling fan motor assembly.
5. Remove drive belt(s). Refer to "Drive Belt Service."
6. Refer to "Engine Service" for removal of the timing belt, tensioner adjuster, lefthand camshaft pulley, lefthand rear timing belt cover and the tensioner bracket.
7. Disconnect heater and radiator hose from water pump.
8. Remove water pump retaining bolts **Fig. 66,** then the pump.
9. Reverse procedure to install. Tighten water mounting bolts in two step in sequence, **Fig. 67,** and to specification, **Fig. 66.**

3.3L ENGINE

1. Disconnect battery ground cable, then drain cooling system.
2. Disconnect radiator outlet hose, then the radiator fan motor electrical connector.
3. Remove radiator bracket, then the radiator sub fan motor assembly.
4. Remove drive belts, then the timing belt.
5. Remove tensioner adjuster, then the cam angle sensor.
6. Remove left side camshaft pulley, then the left side rear timing belt cover.
7. Remove tensioner bracket, then disconnect radiator and heater hose from water pump.
8. Remove water pump.
9. Reverse procedure to install, tighten water pump bolts in sequence shown in **Fig. 68,** to specification.

RADIATOR

REPLACE

EXCEPT JUSTY

1. Disconnect battery cables, then remove battery from vehicle.
2. **On SVX models,** raise and support vehicle, then remove lower cover.
3. **On all models,** drain engine coolant.
4. Disconnect radiator outlet hoses, then ATF cooler hoses, **Figs. 69 through 73.**
5. **On SVX models,** lower vehicle.
6. **On all models,** remove drive belt cover, then disconnect inlet hoses.
7. **On SVX and 1993–94 Legacy models,** remove reservoir tank and overflow hose.
8. **On all models,** disconnect electrical connections from radiator main fan and sub fan if equipped.
9. Remove radiator upper brackets. **On Impreza and 1995–96 Legacy models place left upper radiator bracket between grille and body.**
10. Remove radiator assembly.
11. Reverse procedure to install. Refill and bleed cooling system as outlined under "Cooling System Bleed" in this section.

JUSTY

1. Drain engine coolant.
2. Remove inlet and outlet hoses from radiator, **Fig. 74.**
3. Disconnect radiator fan electrical connection.
4. Remove radiator brackets.
5. **On models equipped with electronically controlled variable transaxles (ECTV),** loosen oil cooler hose on transaxle side and disconnect hose from pipe.
6. Remove radiator. **On models equipped with ECTV,** remove radiator and oil cooler as an assembly.
7. Reverse procedure to install. Refill and bleed cooling system as outlined under "Cooling System Bleed" in this section.

FUEL PUMP

REPLACE

IMPREZA & LEGACY

1. Relieve fuel system pressure as outlined under "Fuel System Pressure Relief" in this section.
2. Remove access hole lid, then disconnect fuel hoses.
3. Remove fuel pump mounting nuts, then the fuel pump.
4. Reverse procedure to install.

JUSTY & LOYALE

1. Relieve fuel system pressure as outlined under "Fuel System Pressure Relief" in this section.
2. Raise and support vehicle.
3. Clamp portion of hose connecting pipe and pump, to prevent fuel from flowing out.
4. Loosen hose clamp, then disconnect hose.

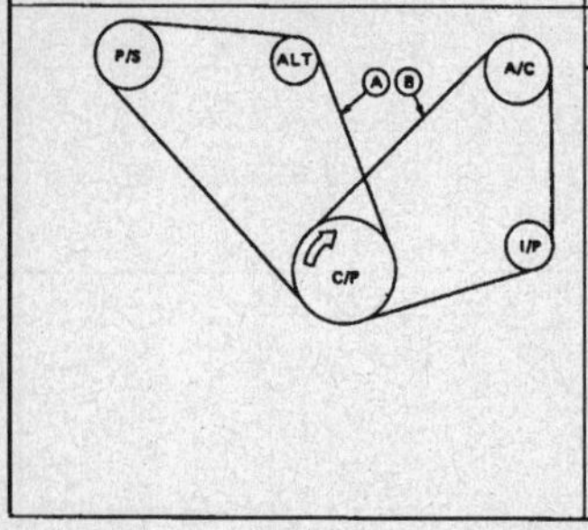
Pulley arrangement
P/S
ALT
A
B
A/C
I/P
C/P

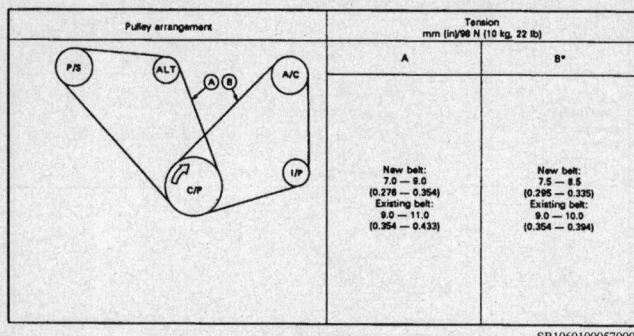

Tension mm (in)/98 N (10 kg, 22 lb) A	B*
New belt: 7.0 — 9.0 (0.276 — 0.354) Existing belt: 9.0 — 11.0 (0.354 — 0.433)	New belt: 7.5 — 8.5 (0.295 — 0.335) Existing belt: 9.0 — 10.0 (0.354 — 0.394)

SB1069100057000X

Fig. 55 Drive belt routing & tension data. Impreza & Legacy

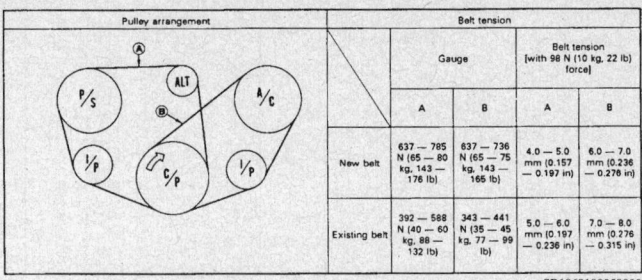

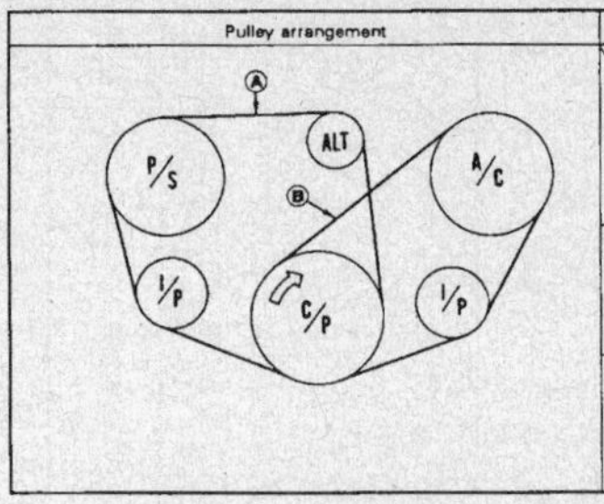
Pulley arrangement
A
P/S
ALT
B
A/C
I/P
C/P
I/P

Belt tension	Gauge		Belt tension [with 98 N (10 kg, 22 lb) force]	
	A	B	A	B
New belt	637 — 785 N (65 — 80 kg, 143 — 176 lb)	637 — 736 N (65 — 75 kg, 143 — 165 lb)	4.0 — 5.0 mm (0.157 — 0.197 in)	6.0 — 7.0 mm (0.236 — 0.276 in)
Existing belt	392 — 588 N (40 — 60 kg, 88 — 132 lb)	343 — 441 N (35 — 45 kg, 77 — 99 lb)	5.0 — 6.0 mm (0.197 — 0.236 in)	7.0 — 8.0 mm (0.276 — 0.315 in)

SB1069100059000X

Fig. 56 Drive belt routing & tension data. SVX

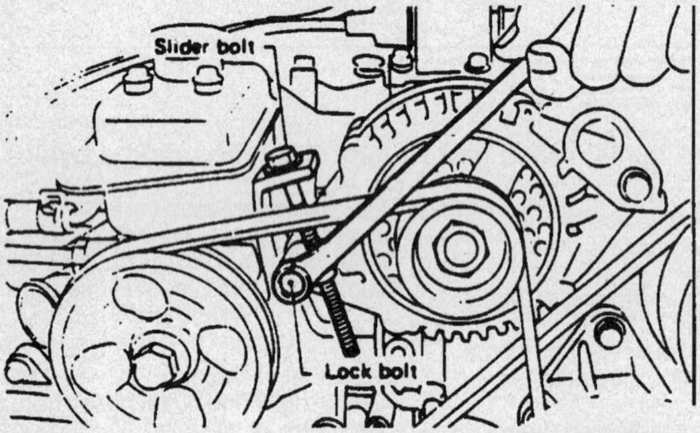
Slider bolt
Lock bolt

SB1069100062000X

Fig. 57 Upper soldier lock & slide bolt location

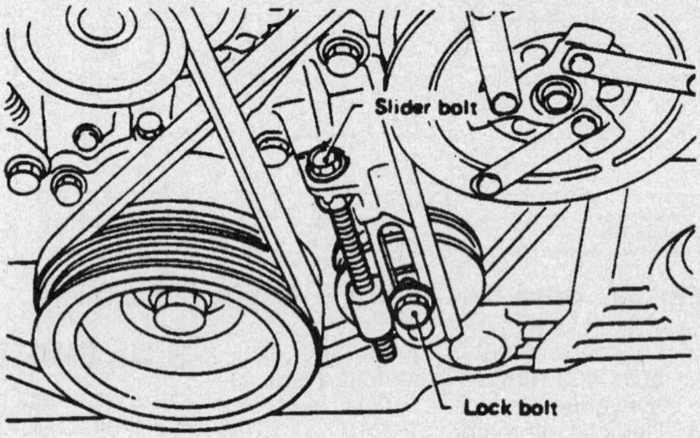
Slider bolt
Lock bolt

SB1069100063000X

Fig. 58 Lower soldier lock & slide bolt location

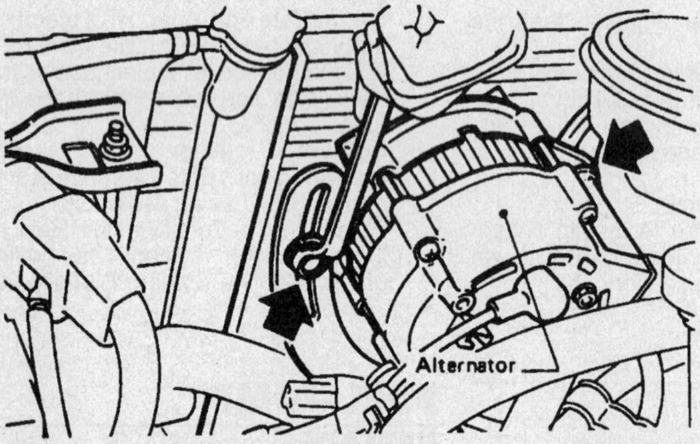
Alternator

SB1069100060000X

Fig. 59 Alternator mount & slide bolt location

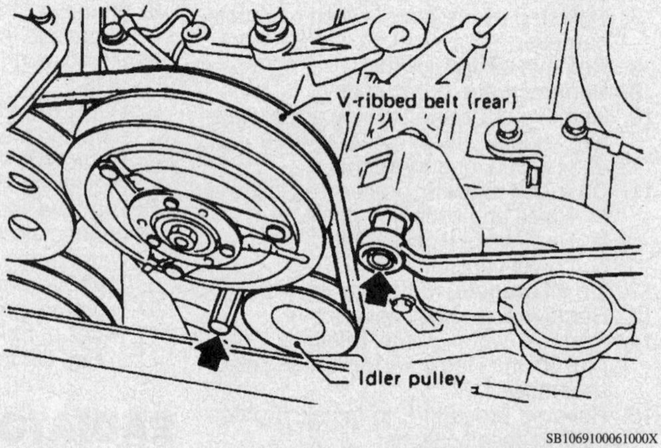
V-ribbed belt (rear)
Idler pulley

SB1069100061000X

Fig. 60 Idler pulley retaining bolt & nut location

5. Remove pump bracket attaching bolts, then remove pump together with pump damper.

SVX

1. Relieve fuel system pressure as outlined under "Fuel System Pressure Relief" in this section.
2. Disconnect fuel hoses from top of fuel tank.
3. Remove fuel tank as follows:
   a. Raise and support vehicle, then remove rear exhaust pipe and muffler assembly.
   b. Separate rear axle shaft from differential, then remove propeller shaft and rear differential assembly.
   c. Remove rear sub frame, then separate fuel filler duct from pipe.
   d. Disconnect fuel hoses from pipes.
   e. Support fuel tank, then remove support bands.
   f. Remove fuel tank from vehicle.
4. Remove fuel pump in numbered sequence shown in **Fig. 75.**
5. Reverse procedure to install.

FUEL FILTER

REPLACE

JUSTY

1. Relieve fuel system pressure as outlined under "Fuel System Pressure Relief" in this section.
2. Raise and support vehicle.
3. Remove clamp screws, then disconnect fuel hoses.
4. Remove fuel filter bracket mounting bolts, **Fig. 76,** then the fuel filter.
5. Reverse procedure to install.

IMPREZA, LEGACY & SVX

1. Relieve fuel system pressure as outlined under "Fuel System Pressure Relief" in this section.
2. Disconnect hoses from fuel filter, **Fig. 77,** then remove filter from holder and vehicle.
3. Reverse procedure to install.

LOYALE

1. Relieve fuel system pressure as outlined under "Fuel System Pressure Relief" in this section.

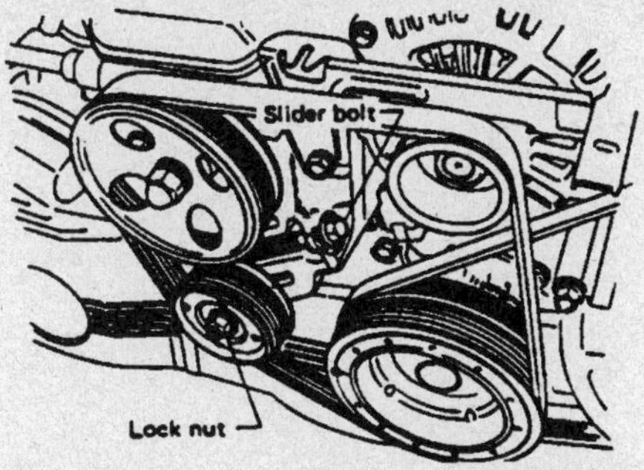
Slider bolt
Lock nut
SB1069100064000X

Fig. 61 Front drive belt removal. SVX

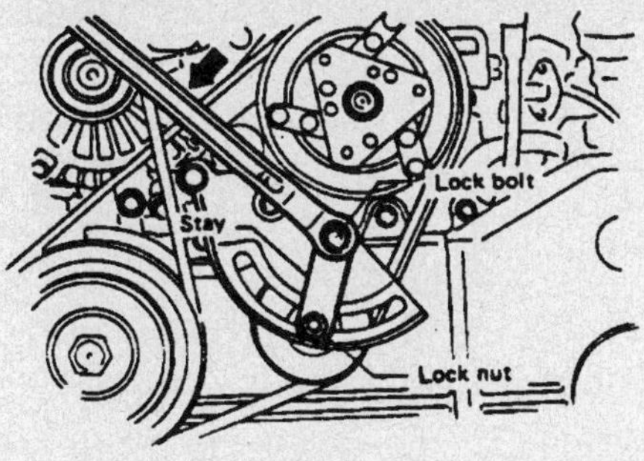
Lock bolt
Stay
Lock nut
SB1069100065000X

Fig. 62 Rear drive belt removal. SVX

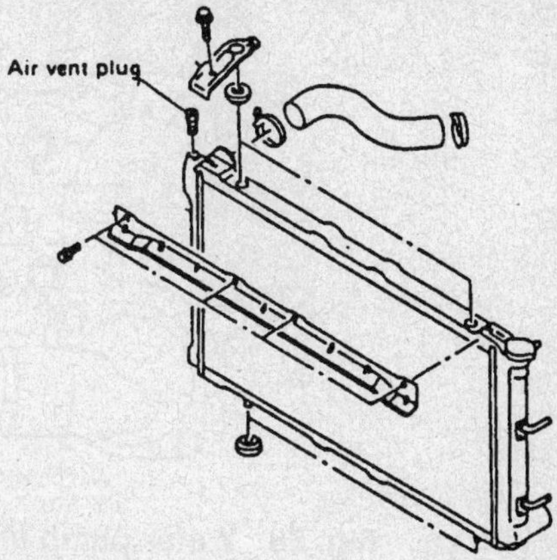
Air vent plug
SB1089100001000X

Fig. 63 Air vent plug location

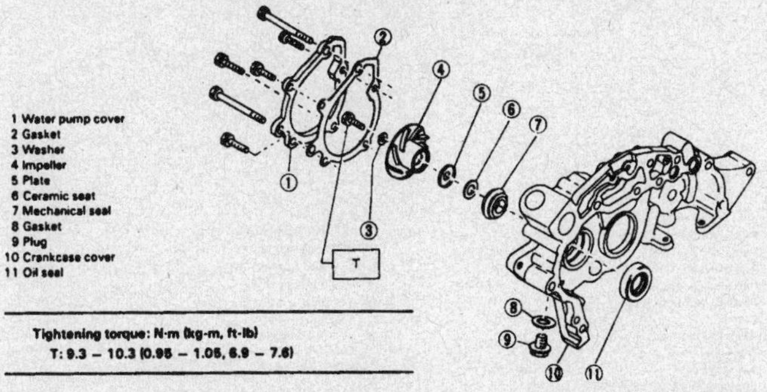
1 Water pump cover
2 Gasket
3 Washer
4 Impeller
5 Plate
6 Ceramic seat
7 Mechanical seal
8 Gasket
9 Plug
10 Crankcase cover
11 Oil seal
T
Tightening torque: N·m (kg-m, ft-lb)
T: 9.3 – 10.3 (0.95 – 1.05, 6.9 – 7.6)
SB1089100002000X

Fig. 64 Water pump assembly replacement. 1.2L engine

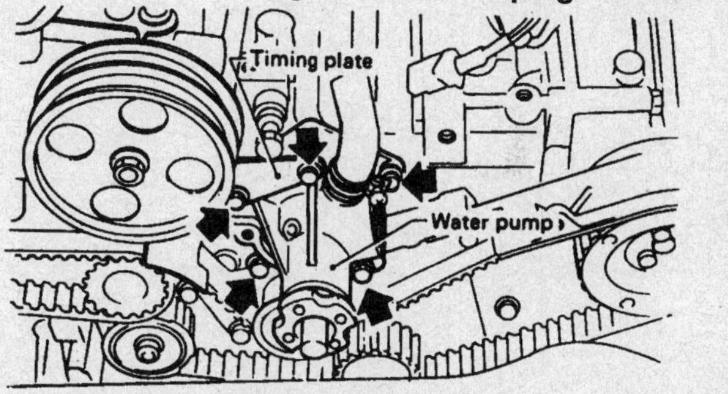
Timing plate
Water pump
SB1089100003000X

Fig. 65 Water pump assembly replacement. Loyale w/1.8L engine

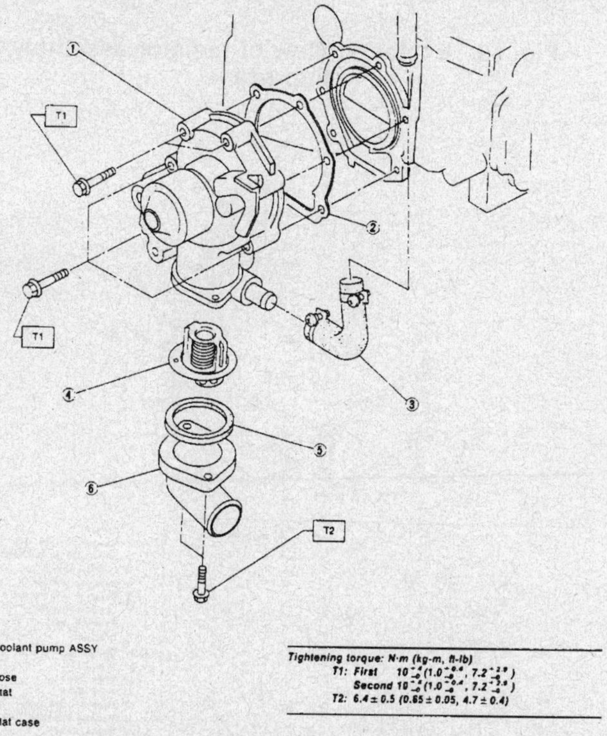
T1
T1
T2
① Engine coolant pump ASSY
② Gasket
③ Heater hose
④ Thermostat
⑤ Gasket
⑥ Thermostat case
Tightening torque: N·m (kg-m, ft-lb)
T1: First 10^{+4}_{-0} ($1.0^{+0.4}_{-0}$, $7.2^{+2.9}_{-0}$)
Second 10^{+4}_{-0} ($1.0^{+0.4}_{-0}$, $7.2^{+2.9}_{-0}$)
T2: 6.4 ± 0.5 (0.65 ± 0.05, 4.7 ± 0.4)
SB1089500023000X

Fig. 66 Water pump assembly replacement. Impreza w/1.8L & 2.2L engines

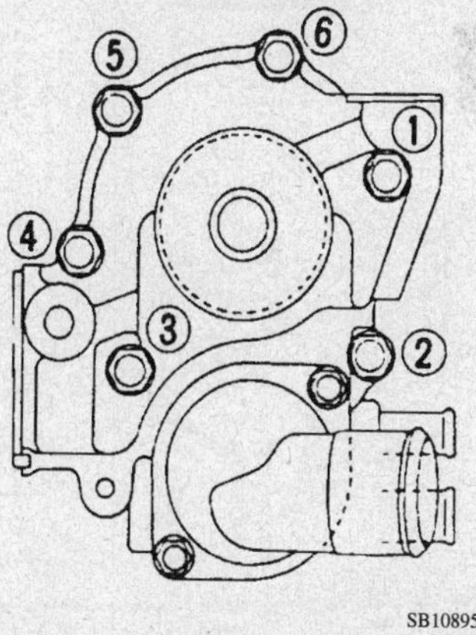
SB1089500024000X

Fig. 67 Water pump bolt tightening sequence. Impreza w/1.8L & 2.2L engines

2. Disconnect hoses from fuel filter, **Fig. 78,** then remove filter from holder and vehicle.

3. Reverse procedure to install.

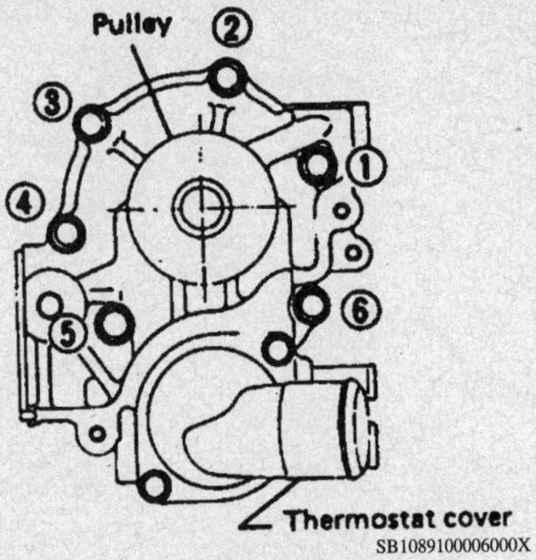
Pulley
Thermostat cover

SB1089100006000X

Fig. 68 Water pump assembly replacement. 3.3L engine

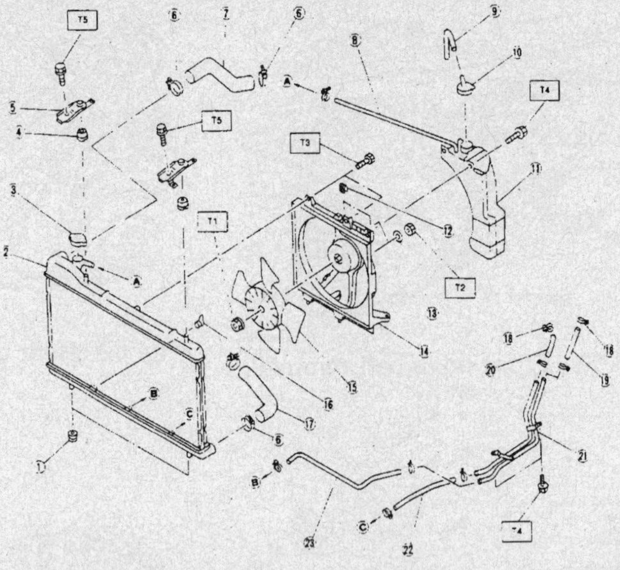

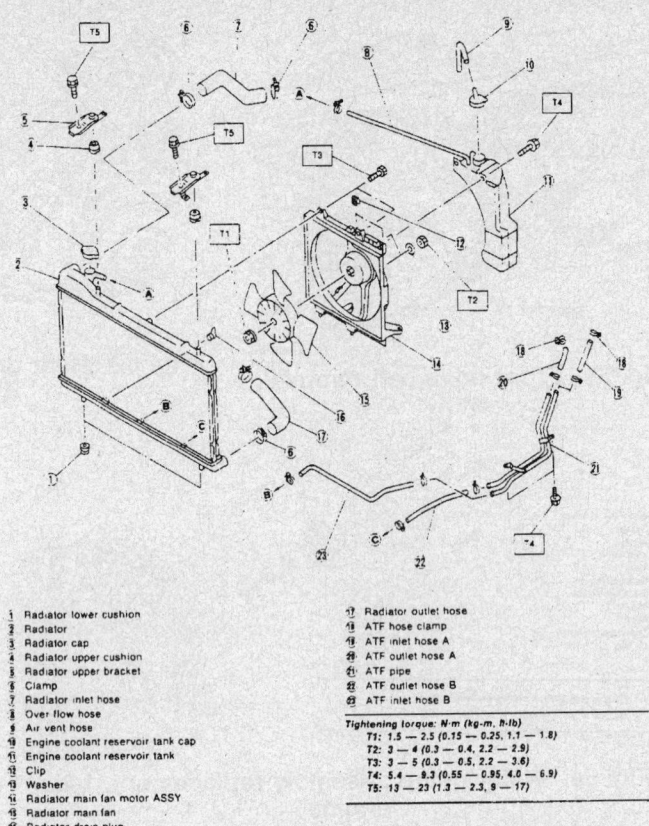

1 Radiator lower cushion
2 Radiator
3 Radiator cap
4 Radiator upper cushion
5 Radiator upper bracket
6 Clamp
7 Radiator inlet hose
8 Over flow hose
9 Air vent hose
10 Engine coolant reservoir tank cap
11 Engine coolant reservoir tank
12 Clip
13 Washer
14 Radiator main fan motor ASSY
15 Radiator main fan
16 Radiator drain plug
17 Radiator outlet hose
18 ATF hose clamp
19 ATF inlet hose A
20 ATF outlet hose A
21 ATF pipe
22 ATF outlet hose B
23 ATF inlet hose B

Tightening torque: N·m (kg-m, ft-lb)
T1: 1.5 — 2.5 (0.15 — 0.25, 1.1 — 1.8)
T2: 3 — 4 (0.3 — 0.4, 2.2 — 2.9)
T3: 3 — 5 (0.3 — 0.5, 2.2 — 3.6)
T4: 5.4 — 9.3 (0.55 — 0.95, 4.0 — 6.9)
T5: 13 — 23 (1.3 — 2.3, 9 — 17)

SB1089500025000X

Fig. 69 Exploded view of radiator assembly. Impreza

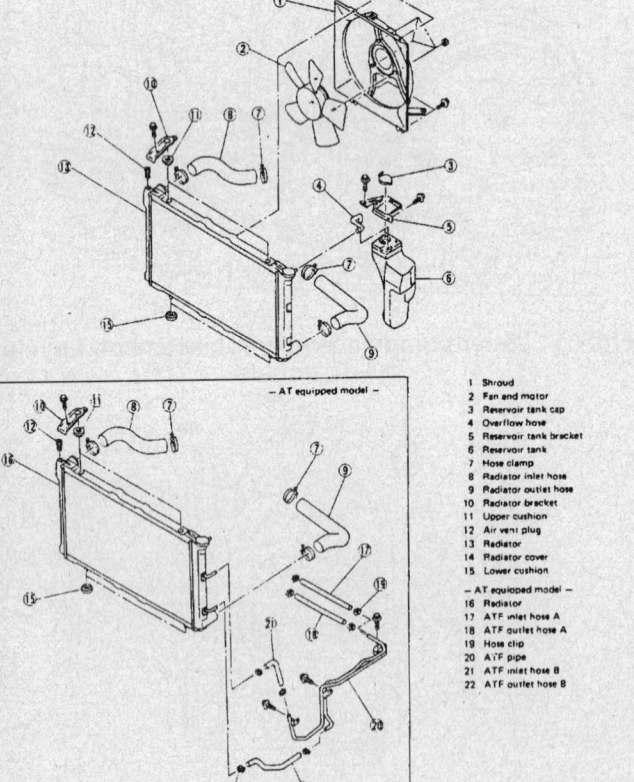

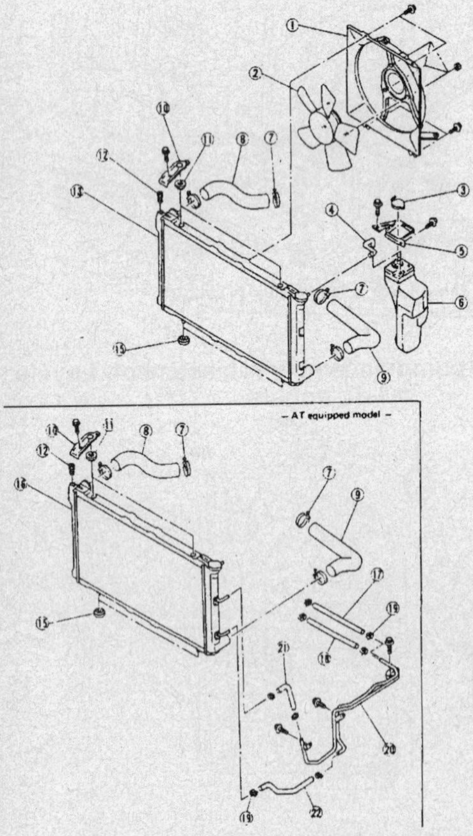
– AT equipped model –

1 Shroud
2 Fan and motor
3 Reservoir tank cap
4 Overflow hose
5 Reservoir tank bracket
6 Reservoir tank
7 Hose clamp
8 Radiator inlet hose
9 Radiator outlet hose
10 Radiator bracket
11 Upper cushion
12 Air vent plug
13 Radiator
14 Radiator cover
15 Lower cushion
– AT equipped model –
16 Radiator
17 ATF inlet hose A
18 ATF outlet hose A
19 Hose clip
20 ATF pipe
21 ATF inlet hose B
22 ATF outlet hose B

SB1089500026000X

Fig. 70 Exploded view of radiator assembly. Legacy less turbo

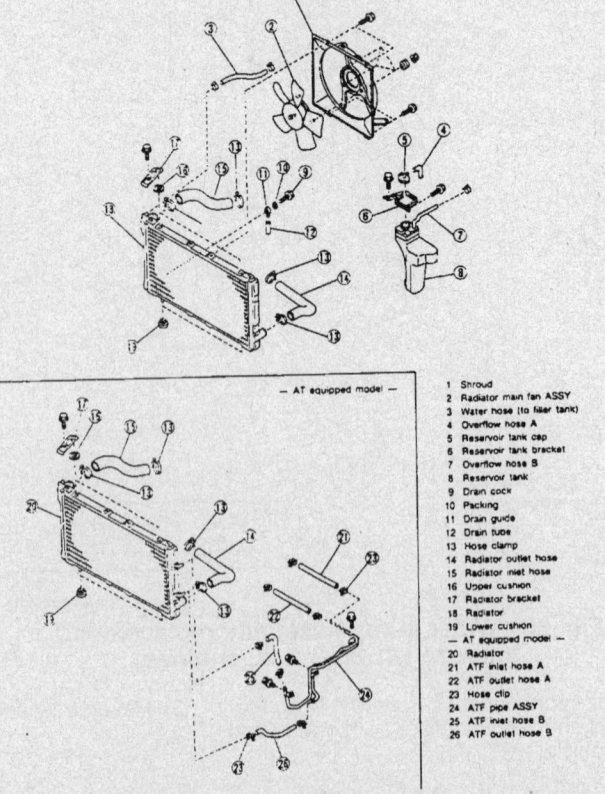

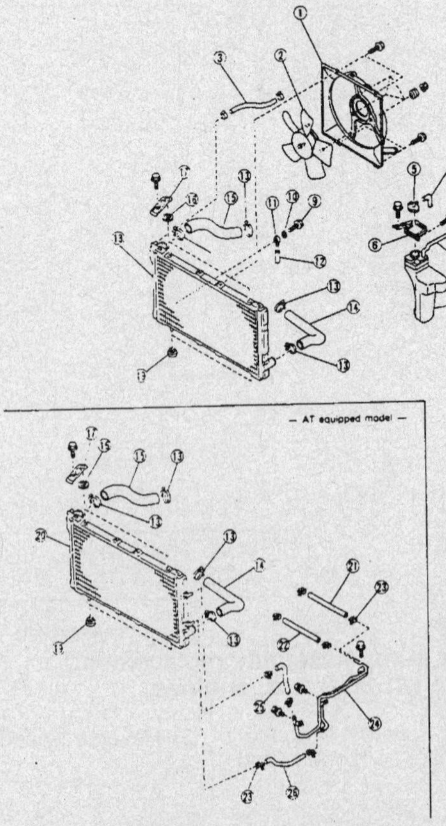
– AT equipped model –

1 Shroud
2 Radiator main fan ASSY
3 Water hose (to filler tank)
4 Overflow hose A
5 Reservoir tank cap
6 Reservoir tank bracket
7 Overflow hose B
8 Reservoir tank
9 Drain cock
10 Packing
11 Drain guide
12 Drain tube
13 Hose clamp
14 Radiator outlet hose
15 Radiator inlet hose
16 Upper cushion
17 Radiator bracket
18 Radiator
19 Lower cushion
— AT equipped model —
20 Radiator
21 ATF inlet hose A
22 ATF outlet hose A
23 Hose clip
24 ATF pipe ASSY
25 ATF inlet hose B
26 ATF outlet hose B

SB1089500027000X

Fig. 71 Exploded view of radiator assembly. Legacy w/turbo

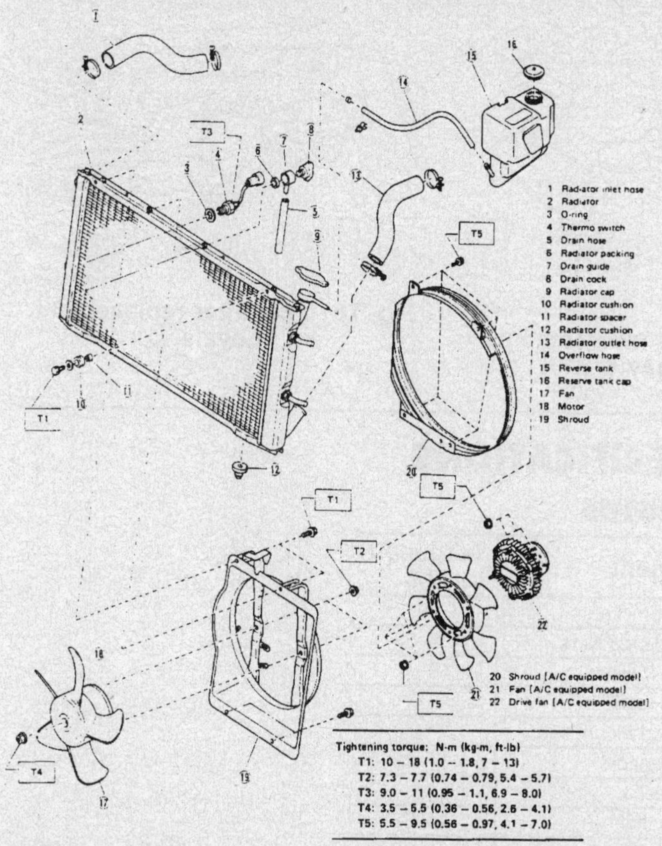
1 Radiator inlet hose
2 Radiator
3 O-ring
4 Thermo switch
5 Drain hose
6 Radiator packing
7 Drain guide
8 Drain cock
9 Radiator cap
10 Radiator cushion
11 Radiator spacer
12 Radiator cushion
13 Radiator outlet hose
14 Overflow hose
15 Reverse tank
16 Reserve tank cap
17 Fan
18 Motor
19 Shroud
20 Shroud (A/C equipped model)
21 Fan (A/C equipped model)
22 Drive fan (A/C equipped model)
Tightening torque: N-m (kg-m, ft-lb)
T1: 10 – 18 (1.0 – 1.8, 7 – 13)
T2: 7.3 – 7.7 (0.74 – 0.79, 5.4 – 5.7)
T3: 9.0 – 11 (0.95 – 1.1, 6.9 – 8.0)
T4: 3.5 – 5.5 (0.36 – 0.56, 2.6 – 4.1)
T5: 5.5 – 9.5 (0.56 – 0.97, 4.1 – 7.0)

SB1089500028000X

Fig. 72 Exploded view of radiator assembly. Loyale

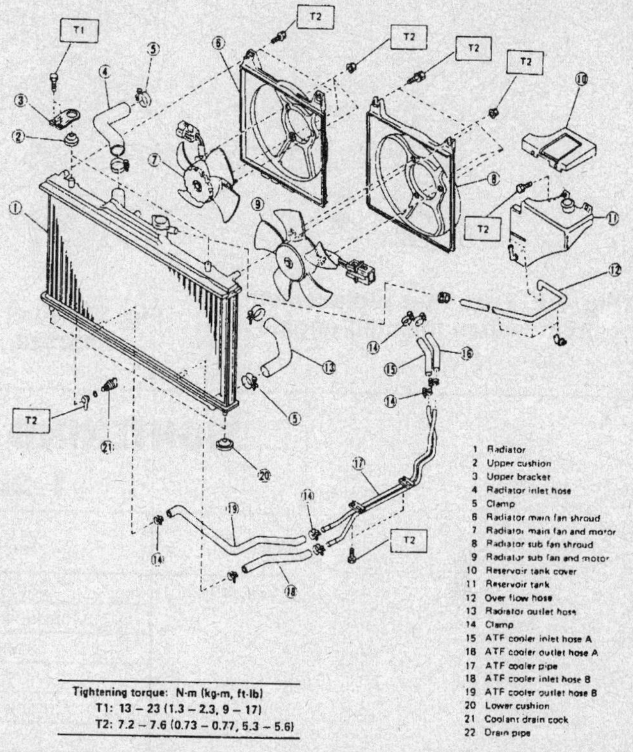
1 Radiator
2 Upper cushion
3 Upper bracket
4 Radiator inlet hose
5 Clamp
6 Radiator main fan shroud
7 Radiator main fan and motor
8 Radiator sub fan shroud
9 Radiator sub fan and motor
10 Reservoir tank cover
11 Reservoir tank
12 Over flow hose
13 Radiator outlet hose
14 Clamp
15 ATF cooler inlet hose A
16 ATF cooler outlet hose A
17 ATF cooler pipe
18 ATF cooler inlet hose B
19 ATF cooler outlet hose B
20 Lower cushion
21 Coolant drain cock
22 Drain pipe
Tightening torque: N-m (kg-m, ft-lb)
T1: 13 – 23 (1.3 – 2.3, 9 – 17)
T2: 7.2 – 7.6 (0.73 – 0.77, 5.3 – 5.6)

SB1089500029000X

Fig. 73 Exploded view of radiator assembly. SVX

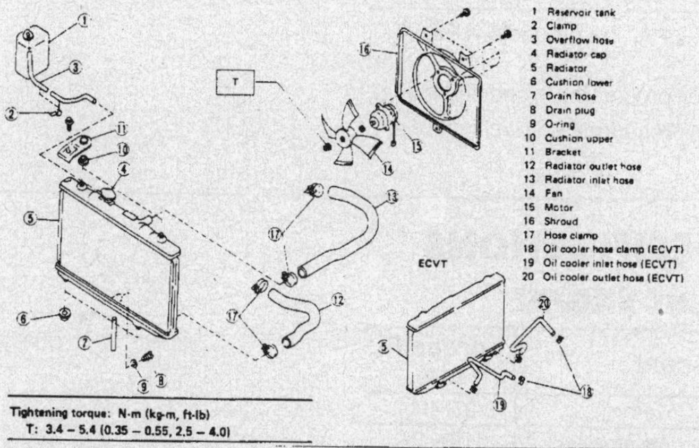
1 Reservoir tank
2 Clamp
3 Overflow hose
4 Radiator cap
5 Radiator
6 Cushion lower
7 Drain hose
8 Drain plug
9 O-ring
10 Cushion upper
11 Bracket
12 Radiator outlet hose
13 Radiator inlet hose
14 Fan
15 Motor
16 Shroud
17 Hose clamp
18 Oil cooler hose clamp (ECVT)
19 Oil cooler inlet hose (ECVT)
20 Oil cooler outlet hose (ECVT)
ECVT
Tightening torque: N-m (kg-m, ft-lb)
T: 3.4 – 5.4 (0.35 – 0.55, 2.5 – 4.0)

SB1089500030000X

Fig. 74 Exploded view of radiator assembly. Justy

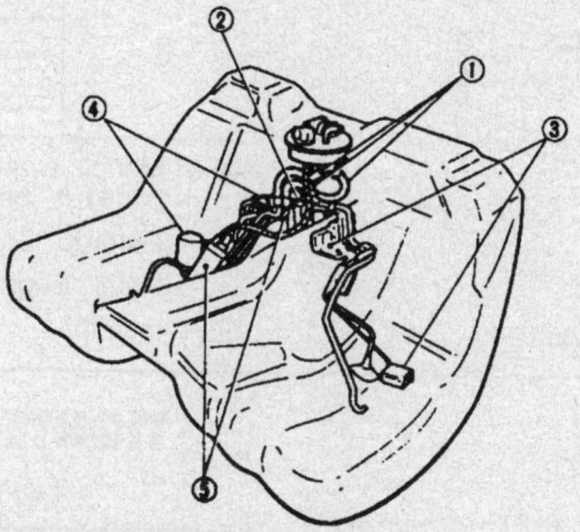

(1) Disconnect hoses and harness connector, and remove fuel tank cap.
(2) Remove bracket cover for installing each assembly bracket onto tank inner.
(3) Take out fuel meter unit LH.
(4) Take out fuel meter unit RH.
(5) Take out fuel pump ASSY.

SB1029100001000X

Fig. 75 Fuel pump replacement. SVX

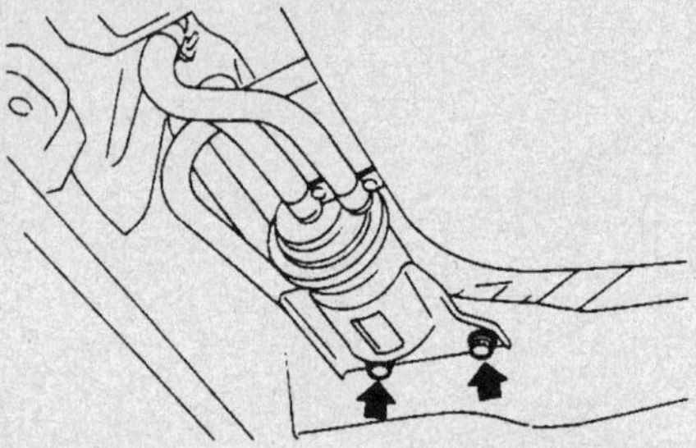

SB1029100003000X

Fig. 76 Fuel filter replacement. Justy w/fuel injected engine

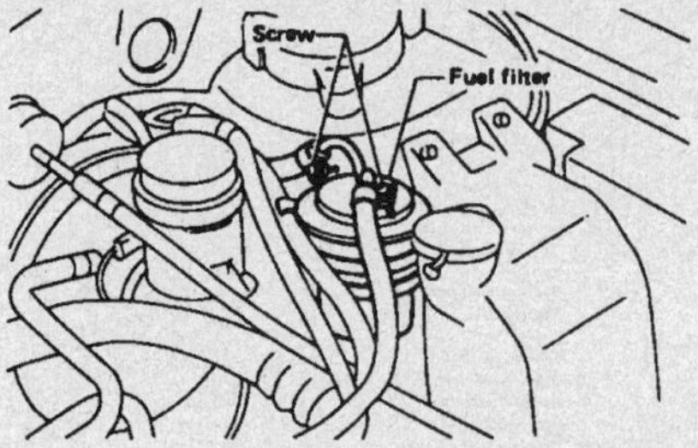
Screw
Fuel filter

SB1029100004000X

Fig. 77 Fuel filter replacement. Impreza, Legacy & SVX

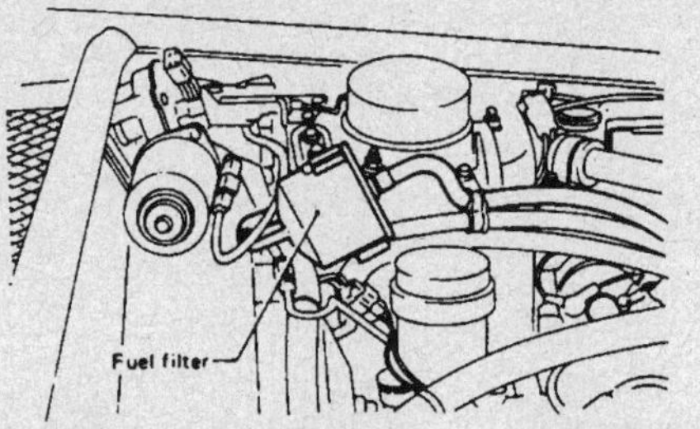
Fuel filter

SB1029100005000X

Fig. 78 Fuel filter replacement. Loyale

TIGHTENING SPECIFICATIONS

1.2L ENGINE

Year	Component	Torque/Ft. Lbs.
1993–94	Camshaft Sprocket	9
	Connecting Rod Cap Nuts	29–33
	Crankshaft Pulley	58–72
	Cylinder Head	②
	Engine & Trans Mount	③
	Exhaust Manifold	14–22
	Flywheel	①
	Intake Manifold	14–22
	Main Bearing Caps	30–35
	Oil Pan	48④
	Rocker Arm Cover	5–6
	Spark Plugs	13–17
	Water Pump Assembly	7–8

① — Models w/manual trans. 65–71 ft. lbs.; models w/ECVT 54–61 ft. lbs.

② — Refer to “Engine Service” for procedure & specifications.

③ — Refer “Engine, Replace” for procedure & specifications.

④ — Inch lbs.

TIGHTENING SPECIFICATIONS

LOYALE w/1.8L ENGINE

Year	Component	Torque/Ft. Lbs.
1993–94	Camshaft Covers	37–49④
	Camshaft Housing Assemblies	13–15
	Camshaft Sprockets	①
	Camshaft Support Plate	7–8
	Center Exhaust Pipe To Rear Exhaust Pipe	9–17
	Center Exhaust Pipe To Transmission	18–25
	Center Exhaust Pipe To Turbocharger	18–25
	Clutch Housing Cover	48④
	Connecting Rod Cap Nuts	29–31
	Crankcase Halves	②
	Crankshaft Pulley	66–79
	Cylinder Head	③
	Driveplate	51–55
	Engine To Transmission	34–40
	Exhaust Manifold	19–22

Continued

TIGHTENING SPECIFICATIONS

LOYALE w/1.8L ENGINE—Continued

Year	Component	Torque/Ft. Lbs.
1993–94	Fan Drive To Water Pump Pulley	4–7
	Fan To Drive	4–7
	Flywheel	51–55
	Flywheel Housing	25–30
	Front Engine Mount	17–27
	Front Exhaust Pipe To Bracket	18–25
	Front Exhaust Pipe To Cylinder Head	19–22
	Front Exhaust Pipe To Rear Exhaust Pipe	9–17
	Intake Manifold	13–16
	Oil Pan	48④
	Oil Pressure Relief Plug	17–20
	Oil Pressure Switch/Gauge	16–20
	Oil Separator Cover	48④
	Pitching Stopper Rod To Body	27–49
	Pitching Stopper To Engine Or Transmission	33–40
	Power Steering Pump	22–36
	Power Steering Pump Pulley	31–46
	Pressure Plate	12
	Radiator	7–13
	Rocker Arm Cover	40–48④
	Rocker Arm Shaft Or Camshaft Bracket	13–15
	Service Access Plugs	46–56
	Shroud	4–7
	Spark Plugs	13–17
	Timing Belt Covers	③
	Timing Belt Idler	③
	Timing Belt Tensioner	③
	Torque Converter	17–20
	Turbocharger Coolant Pipe To Cylinder Head	16–18
	Water Pump Assembly	7–8

① — Torque to 7–8 ft. lbs. in several steps.

② — 6 mm bolts, 3.3–4 ft. lbs.; 8 mm bolts, 17–20 ft. lbs.; 10 mm bolts, 29–35 ft. lbs.

③ — Refer to "Engine Service" for procedure & specifications.

④ — Inch lbs.

TIGHTENING SPECIFICATIONS

IMPREZA w/1.8L & 2.2L ENGINE

Year	Component	Torque/Ft. Lbs.
1993–96	A/C Hoses	13–23
	Baffle Plate	43.2②
	Cam-Angle Sensor	43.2②
	Camshaft Sprockets	54–61
	Center Exhaust Pipe To Front Catalytic Converter	22–29
	Center Exhaust Pipe To Hanger Bracket	22–29

Continued

TIGHTENING SPECIFICATIONS

IMPREZA w/1.8L & 2.2L ENGINE—Continued

1993–96	Center Exhaust Pipe To Rear Exhaust Pipe	9–17
	Connecting Rod	32–34
	Crankcase Halves	①
	Crankshaft Pulley	66–79
	Cylinder Head	①
	Driveplate	51–55
	Engine Mount	40–61
	Engine To Transmission	34–40
	Flywheel	51–55
	Front Exhaust Pipe To Front Catalytic Converter	19–26
	Front Exhaust Pipe To Cylinder Head	18–25
	Lefthand Lower Camshaft Support	7
	Lefthand Upper Camshaft Support	12
	Oil Pan	43②
	Oil Pump	56②
	Oil Separator Cover	56②
	Oil Strainer	7
	Oil Strainer Stay	7
	Pitching Stopper Rod To Body	35–49
	Pitching Stopper Rod To Engine Or Transmission	33–40
	Power Steering Pump	22–36
	Radiator	9–11
	Righthand Camshaft Support	12
	Rocker Arm Assembly	9
	Rocker Cover	43②
	Rocker Shaft	43②
	Service Access Hole Cover	43②
	Service Access Hole Plugs	46–56
	Tensioner Bracket	17–20
	Timing Belt Covers	43②
	Timing Belt Idler	26–32
	Timing Belt Tensioner	26–32
	Timing Belt Tensioner Adjuster	17–20
	Torque Converter	17–20
	Water Pump	①

① — Refer to "Engine Service" for procedure & specifications.

② — Inch lbs.

TIGHTENING SPECIFICATIONS

3.3L ENGINE

Year	Component	Torque/Ft. Lbs.
1993–96	Baffle Plate	36–48②
	Camshaft Sprockets	80–94
	Connecting Rod Nut	32–34
	Crankshaft Pulley	108–123
	Cylinder Block	①
	Cylinder Head Bolt	①
	Cylinder Head Cover	48②
	Driveplate Reinforcement	51–55

Continued

TIGHTENING SPECIFICATIONS

3.3L ENGINE—Continued

1993–96	Exhaust Camshaft Cap	7–8
	Front Camshaft Cap	8
	Intake Camshaft Cap	7–8
	Oil Filter	9–12
	Oil Level Gauge Guide	52–62②
	Oil Pan	40–48②
	Oil Pump	52–61②
	Oil Pump Cover	35–61②
	Oil Pump Relief Valve Plug	30–35
	Oil Separator Cover	52–61②
	Oil Strainer	7–8
	Service Hole Cover	52–61②
	Service Hole Plug	46–56
	Thermostat Housing	52–61②
	Timing Belt Covers	48②
	Timing Belt Idler	26–32
	Timing Belt Tension Adjuster	17–20
	Timing Belt Tensioner	26–32
	Timing Belt Tensioner Bracket	17–20
	Water Pipe	7–10
	Water Pump	7–10

① — Refer to "Engine Service" for procedure & specifications.
② — Inch lbs.

Clutch & Manual Transmission

INDEX

	Page No.
Adjustments	39-37
Clutch Pedal	39-37
Hill Holder	39-37
Clutch, Replace	39-38
Hydraulic System Service	39-37
Clutch Bleed	39-37
Operating Cylinder, Replace	39-37
Tightening Specifications	39-39
Impreza & Legacy	39-40
Justy	39-39
Loyale	39-40
Transaxle, Replace	39-38
Impreza	39-38
Justy	39-38
Legacy	39-38
Loyale	39-39

ADJUSTMENTS

HILL HOLDER

For Hill Holder adjustments, refer to the "Rear Axle & Suspension" section.

CLUTCH PEDAL

Except Justy

1. Remove clutch fork return spring.
2. Turn adjusting nut at fork end, **Fig. 1,** to obtain an endplay of .08–.12 inch on FWD Loyale, or .12–.16 inch on Impreza, Legacy, AWD Loyale. **When performing adjustment, use care not to twist clutch cable.**
3. Check to ensure clutch release lever full stroke measures .67–.71 inch on FWD Loyale models, or .94–1.02 inch on Impreza or 1.004–1.063 inch on Legacy and AWD Loyale.

Justy

1. Remove clutch fork return spring.
2. Turn adjusting nut to obtain an endplay of .08–.16 inch (2–4 mm) at center of cable joints.
3. Secure fork to cable with locknut, then reattach return spring.
4. Depress clutch and check for proper operation. If gear clash is evident, repeat adjustment.

HYDRAULIC SYSTEM SERVICE

CLUTCH BLEED

Clutch pedal adjustment for hydraulic application type systems is completed by bleeding clutch system.

1. Install one end of vinyl tube into air bleeder of clutch damper. Place other end in suitable container.
2. Slowly depress and hold clutch pedal, then open bleeder for 1 to 2 seconds.
3. Close bleeder, then release clutch pedal. **Do not release clutch pedal with bleeder open.**
4. Repeat steps 2 and 3 until there are no air bubbles in vinyl tube. Tighten bleeder screw.
5. Repeat procedure using bleeder on operating cylinder.
6. Ensure no leaks are evident in system.

OPERATING CYLINDER, REPLACE

1. Disconnect and plug clutch pipe from operating cylinder.
2. Remove operating cylinder from transaxle.
3. Reverse procedure to install.

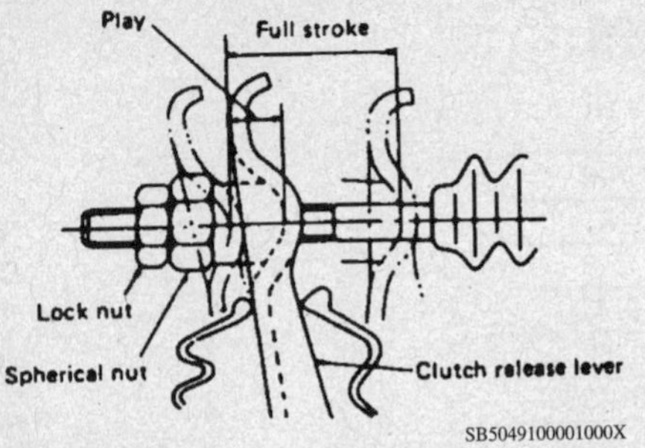
Play
Full stroke
Lock nut
Spherical nut
Clutch release lever
SB5049100001000X

Fig. 1 Clutch pedal adjustments

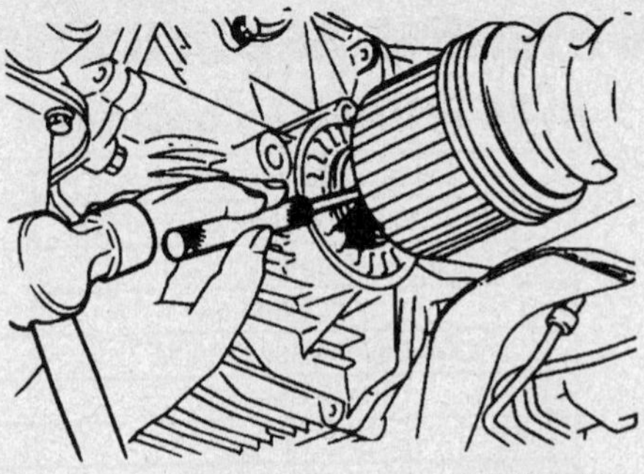
SB5038900002000X

Fig. 2 Spring pin removal

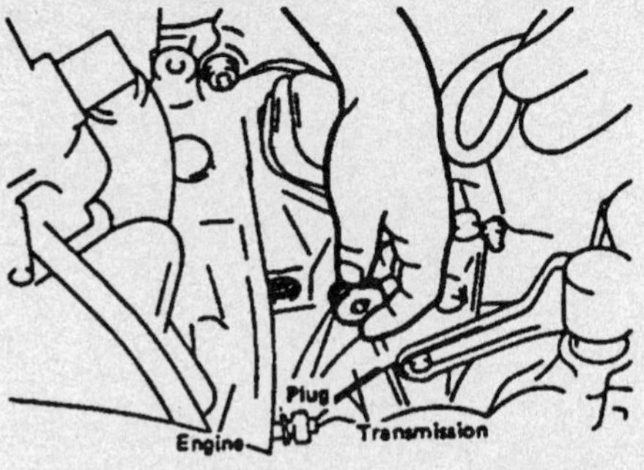
Plug
Engine
Transmission
SB5038900003000X

Fig. 3 Plug removal. Legacy

CLUTCH

REPLACE

1. Remove transaxle as outlined under "Transaxle, Replace."
2. Remove six attaching bolts from pressure plate, then remove pressure plate and clutch disc.
3. When installing, apply light coat of grease to transaxle main driveshaft spline.
4. Install clutch disc guide into clutch disc. Then install on flywheel by inserting end of guide into needle bearing.
5. **On Loyale models,** position the clutch cover so that there is a gap of 120° or more between "O" marks on the flywheel and the pressure plate. ("O" marks indicate the directions of residual unbalance.) Tighten pressure plate bolts one or two turns at a time in a diagonal pattern reaching a final torque of 10.5–12.7 ft. lbs.
6. Remove clutch disc guide and reinstall transaxle.

TRANSAXLE

REPLACE

IMPREZA

1. Raise and support hood, then disconnect battery ground cable.
2. Remove manifold cover and air intake duct.
3. Disconnect oxygen sensor, transaxle harness and ground connectors.
4. Disconnect clutch release spring, clutch cable, hill holder and speedometer cable as equipped.
5. Remove starter, then the pitching stopper and bracket.
6. Remove transaxle oil level gauge, then the transaxle connector bracket.
7. Install engine support fixture tool No. 41099AA000, or equivalent, then remove right upper side of transaxle to engine bolts.
8. Remove exhaust system as follows:
   a. Raise and support vehicle.
   b. Remove front exhaust pipe, then center exhaust pipe.
   c. **On AWD models,** remove rear exhaust pipe.
9. **On AWD models,** remove propeller shaft as follows:
   a. Remove front cover of rear differential mount, then separate propeller shaft from rear differential.
   b. Remove bolts holding center bearing onto body, then the propeller shaft.
10. **On all models,** remove gear shift rod and stay from transaxle.
11. Remove gear selector cable from selector lever and cable bracket.
12. Remove stabilizer clamp to crossmember bolts.
13. Remove front driveshaft from transaxle as follows:
    a. Remove and lower transverse link from housing.
    b. Remove spring pin and separate front driveshaft from each side of transaxle.
14. Remove lower side transaxle to engine nuts.
15. Place suitable transaxle jack stand under transaxle.
16. Remove transaxle rear crossmember.
17. Remove transaxle from vehicle. Move transaxle jack toward rear until mainshaft is withdrawn from clutch cover.
18. Reverse procedure to install, tighten all bolts/nuts to specifications.

JUSTY

1. Disconnect battery ground cable, then remove air cleaner.
2. Disconnect starter electrical connections and remove starter.
3. **On AWD models,** disconnect hoses at changeover actuator.
4. **On all models,** disconnect speedometer cable and all electrical connections at transaxle.
5. Disconnect distributor to ignition coil high tension lead.
6. Disconnect clutch cable from transaxle, then remove cable bracket and attach lifting hook where bracket was positioned.
7. Remove pitching stopper and brackets between transaxle and body.
8. Support engine using suitable tools, then raise vehicle.
9. Support transaxle with suitable jack, then remove undercovers.
10. Disconnect rear exhaust pipe from front pipe and vehicle body.
11. Remove center member and transverse link.
12. Using a drift and hammer, drive out spring pin, then disconnect axle shafts from transaxle, **Fig. 2.**
13. Remove attaching bolts, then transaxle mounting bracket.
14. Disconnect gearshift rod, stay and propeller shaft, if applicable, from transaxle.
15. Remove transaxle to engine attaching bolts, then disengage transaxle from engine.
16. Lift transaxle carefully and remove from vehicle.
17. Reverse procedure to install.

LEGACY

1. Raise and support hood, then disconnect battery ground cable.
2. **On non-turbo models,** remove manifold cover and air intake duct.
3. **On turbo models,** remove resonator chamber, then air inlet and outlet ducts, turbocharger cooling duct.
4. **On all models,** disconnect oxygen sensor, transaxle harness and ground connectors.
5. **On 1995–96 models,** disconnect neutral position switch, back-up lamp switch, and vehicle speed sensor.
6. **On all models,** disconnect clutch release spring, clutch cable, hill holder and speedometer cable as equipped.
7. Remove starter, then the pitching stopper and bracket.
8. **On turbo models,** remove clutch operating cylinder from transaxle case, then the plug **Fig. 3.**
9. **On turbo models,** install a 6 mm bolt into bolt hole of release fork shaft, then drive out release fork shaft.
10. **On turbo models,** raise release fork to separate from release bearing tabs.
11. **On all models,** remove transaxle oil level gauge, then the transaxle connector bracket.
12. Install engine support fixture No. 41099AA000, or equivalent, then remove right upper side of transaxle to engine bolts.
13. Remove exhaust system as follows:
    a. **On turbo models,** separate center exhaust pipe from turbocharger.
    b. **On all models,** raise and support vehicle.
    c. **On non-turbo models,** remove front exhaust pipe.
    d. **On 1995–96 models,** disconnect rear oxygen sensor, then remove center exhaust pipe.
    e. **On turbo models,** remove turbocharger lower cover, then center exhaust pipe.
    f. **On AWD models,** remove rear exhaust pipe.

14. **On AWD models,** remove propeller shaft as follows:
    a. Remove front cover of rear differential mount, then separate propeller shaft from rear differential.
    b. Remove bolts holding center bearing onto body, then the propeller shaft.
15. **On all models,** remove gear shift rod and stay from transaxle.
16. **On turbo models,** remove clutch damper from transaxle case.
17. **On all models,** remove stabilizer clamp to crossmember bolts.
18. Remove front driveshaft from transaxle as follows:
    a. Remove and lower transverse link from housing.
    b. Remove spring pin and separate front driveshaft from each side of transaxle.
19. Remove lower side transaxle to engine nuts.
20. Place suitable transaxle jack stand under transaxle.
21. Remove transaxle rear crossmember.
22. Remove transaxle from vehicle. Move transaxle jack toward rear until mainshaft is withdrawn from clutch cover.
23. Reverse procedure to install, noting the following:
    a. Ensure cutout portion of release fork shaft contacts spring pin.
    b. Tighten all bolts/nuts to specifications.

LOYALE

1. Raise and support hood, then remove spare tire and support.
2. Disconnect battery ground cable.
3. Remove hill-holder cable, clutch cable and return spring.
4. Disconnect electrical connectors and vacuum hoses from the following as equipped: oxygen sensor, neutral switch, back-up light, transaxle cord and differential lock vacuum hose.
5. Remove pitching stopper rod, then install engine support assembly 926610000 to pitching stopper rod bracket.

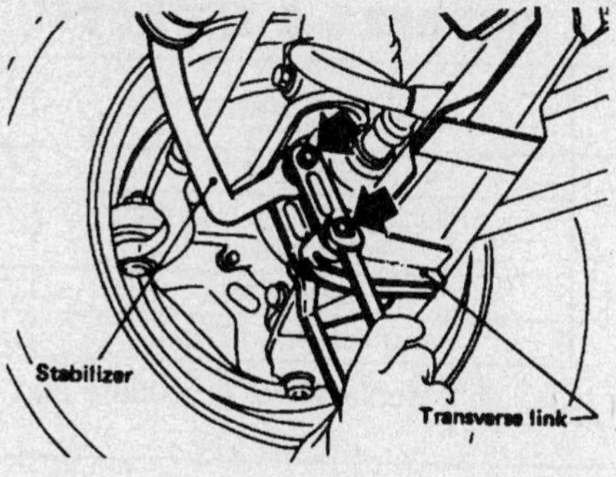
Stabilizer
Transverse link
SB5038900001000X

Fig. 4 Stabilizer from transverse link removal

6. Remove starter motor attaching bolts, then the starter motor.
7. Remove right side engine to transaxle attaching nut and bolt.
8. **On turbocharged models,** remove exhaust system as follows:
    a. Remove turbo upper heat shield and accelerator cable cover.
    b. Raise and support vehicle, then loosen two front exhaust pipe attaching bolts.
    c. Lower vehicle, then remove turbo lower heat shield.
    d. Separate center exhaust pipe from turbocharger.
    e. Raise and support vehicle, then separate center exhaust pipe from rear pipe.
    f. Disconnect the center exhaust pipe from transaxle by removing hanger bolt.
    g. **On AWD models,** separate muffler from rear exhaust pipe.
9. **On models less turbocharger,** remove exhaust system as follows:
    a. Raise and support vehicle.
    b. Remove front exhaust pipe to engine retaining nuts. Leave one nut attached to temporarily support the exhaust pipe.
    c. Separate front exhaust pipe from rear pipe.
    d. Disconnect front exhaust pipe from transaxle by removing hanger bolt.
    e. Remove remaining exhaust pipe to engine retaining nut, then exhaust pipe.
    f. **On AWD models,** separate muffler from rear exhaust pipe.
10. **On all models,** remove rigid crossmember.
11. **On AWD models,** remove propeller shaft. **Plug opening at rear extension to prevent oil from flowing out.**
12. **On all models,** remove gear shift system as follows:
    a. Remove spring.
    b. Disconnect rod from transaxle.
    c. Disconnect stay from transaxle.
13. **On AWD models,** disconnect select rod from transfer rail.
14. **On all models,** loosen nut and bolt on lower side of plate, **Fig. 4,** then separate stabilizer from transverse link.
15. Remove bolt attaching transverse link to front crossmember on each side.
16. Remove hand brake cable bracket from transverse link. Remove transverse link attaching nut and bolt, then lower transverse link.
17. Using a drift and hammer, remove spring pin and separate axle shaft from driveshaft, on each side. **Fig. 2.**
18. Remove engine to transaxle attaching nuts, then position transaxle jack under transaxle.
19. Remove rear rubber cushion attaching nuts, then the rear and rigid crossmembers.
20. Move transaxle jack rearward until mainshaft is withdrawn from clutch cover.
21. Reverse procedure to install.

TIGHTENING SPECIFICATIONS

JUSTY

Year	Component	Torque/Ft. Lbs.
1993–94	Clutch Release Fork Pivot	11–18
	Flywheel	65–71
	Pressure Plate	7–8
	Speedometer Gear	10–13

IMPREZA & LEGACY

Year	Component	Torque/Ft. Lbs.
1993–96	Flywheel	51–56
	Pitching Stopper Rod To Transmission	33–40
	Pressure Plate	①
	Transmission To Engine	34–40

① — Refer to "Clutch, Replace" for procedure and specifications.

LOYALE

Year	Component	Torque/Ft. Lbs.
1993–94	Clutch Release Fork Pivot	11–18
	Crossmember To Body	65–87
	Flywheel	51–55
	Pressure Plate	①
	Rear Transmission Mounts To Transmission	13–23
	Transmission Case To Engine Adapter	34–40
	Transmission Mounts To Crossmember	20–35

① — Refer to "Clutch, Replace" for procedure and specifications.

Rear Axle & Suspension

INDEX

	Page No.
Hill Holder	39-47
Adjustment	39-48
Inspection	39-47
Installation	39-47
Removal	39-47
Hub & Bearing, Replace	39-40
Impreza & Legacy	39-40
Justy & Loyale	39-40
SVX	39-41
Rear Suspension, Replace	39-41
Impreza	39-44
Justy	39-42
Legacy	39-42
Loyale	39-41
SVX	39-43
Stabilizer Bar, Replace	39-48
Strut, Replace	39-45
Impreza	39-46
Justy	39-45
Legacy	39-46
Loyale	39-45
SVX	39-46
Tightening Specifications	39-48
Wheel Bearing, Adjust	39-41
Justy & FWD Loyale	39-41

HUB & BEARING

REPLACE

JUSTY & LOYALE

1. Raise and support vehicle.
2. Remove rear wheels.
3. Remove bearing cap.
4. **On all except AWD,** flatten lock washer, then remove axle nut, lock washer and lock plate. Discard lock washer.
5. **On AWD models,** remove cotter pin and castle nut.
6. **On models equipped with disc brakes,** unfasten caliper assembly and position aside.
7. **On all models,** remove hub and drum or hub and rotor assembly.
8. Reverse procedure to install noting the following:
   a. **On all except AWD,** install hub using new lock washer. Adjust wheel bearing as outlined under "Wheel Bearing, Adjust."
   b. **On AWD,** Refer to "Tightening Specifications" for tightening specifications.

IMPREZA & LEGACY

1. Disconnect battery ground cable, then raise and support vehicle.
2. Remove rear wheel caps, then rear wheels. Loosen and retighten axle nut after removing wheels from vehicle.
3. **On FWD models,** using screwdriver, pry hub cap off.
4. **On all models,** unlock and remove axle nut, then return parking brake and loosen adjuster.
5. **On models equipped with disc brakes,** remove disc brake caliper and suspend caliper from strut, then remove disc rotor from hub. If rotor seizes on hub, drive off rotor by installing 8 mm bolt into hole in rotor.
6. **On models equipped with drum brakes,** remove brake drum from hub.
7. If it is difficult to remove brake drum, then remove adjusting hole cover from back plate and turn adjusting screw until brake shoe separates from drum.
8. If drum is difficult to remove, drive it out by installing 8 mm bolt into hole in brake drum.
9. **On all models,** disconnect parking brake cable end.
10. **On 1993–94 Legacy models equipped with AWD,** remove stabilizer clamp.
11. **On all models,** remove lateral link assembly to rear housing attaching bolts. Discard self-locking nut.
12. Remove trailing link assembly to rear housing attaching bolts. Discard self-locking nut.

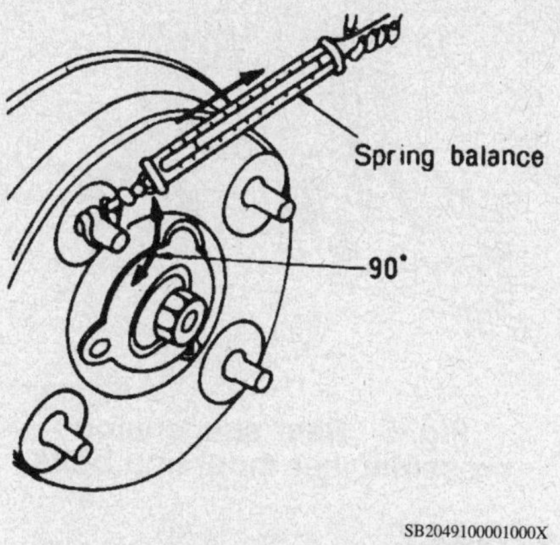
Spring balance
90°
SB2049100001000X

Fig. 1 Checking rear wheel bearing adjustment

13. **On AWD models,** remove rear driveshafts as follows:
    a. **On 1993–94 models,** remove and discard spring pin which secures rear differential spindle to double offset joint (DOJ).
    b. **On 1993–94 models,** remove DOJ from rear differential spindle.
    c. **On all models,** disengage bell joint from housing splines, then remove rear driveshaft assembly.
14. **On all models,** remove lower strut to rear housing mounting bolts, then separate strut from housing.
15. **On models with anti-lock brakes,** remove rear ABS sensor from back plate.
16. **On all models,** remove rear housing (hub) from vehicle.
17. Reverse procedure to install.

SVX

1. Move select lever to Park position, then set parking brake.
2. Raise and support vehicle, then remove rear wheels. Loosen and retighten axle nut after removing wheels from vehicle.
3. Remove hub cap, then unlock and remove axle nut.
4. Return parking brake lever, then remove console box lid.
5. Loosen parking brake adjuster nut, then remove stabilizer link.
6. Remove ABS sensor and clamp, then disconnect parking brake cable clamp.
7. Disconnect brake hose from strut, then loosen caliper mounting bolts.
8. Disconnect trailing link and lateral link from housing.
9. Remove lower strut to housing mounting bolts, then the caliper assembly. Suspend caliper from strut.
10. Remove disc rotor from hub. If rotor seizes on hub, drive off rotor using 8 mm bolt into hole in rotor.
11. Remove parking brake lining, then disconnect cable from lining.
12. Remove parking brake cable clamp, then the cable from backing plate.
13. Separate strut from housing, then remove driveshaft from housing.
14. Remove rear housing (hub) mounting bolts, then the housing.

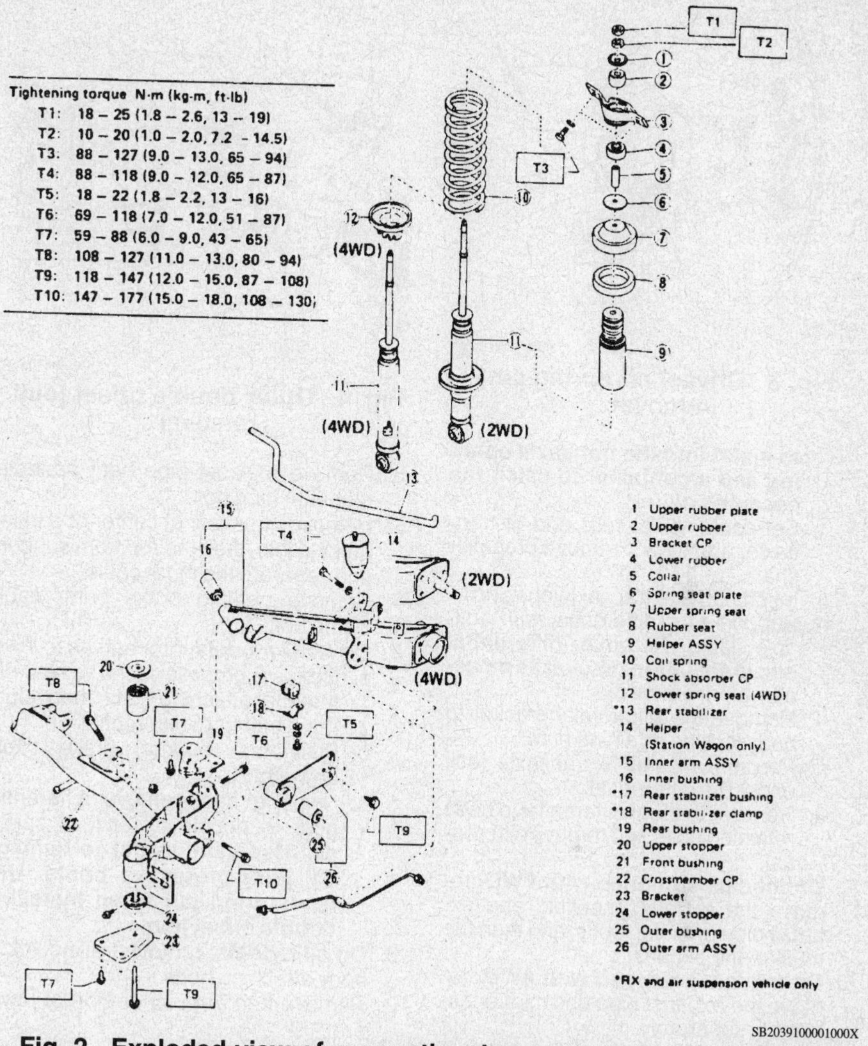
Tightening torque N·m (kg-m, ft-lb)
T1: 18 – 25 (1.8 – 2.6, 13 – 19)
T2: 10 – 20 (1.0 – 2.0, 7.2 – 14.5)
T3: 88 – 127 (9.0 – 13.0, 65 – 94)
T4: 88 – 118 (9.0 – 12.0, 65 – 87)
T5: 18 – 22 (1.8 – 2.2, 13 – 16)
T6: 69 – 118 (7.0 – 12.0, 51 – 87)
T7: 59 – 88 (6.0 – 9.0, 43 – 65)
T8: 108 – 127 (11.0 – 13.0, 80 – 94)
T9: 118 – 147 (12.0 – 15.0, 87 – 108)
T10: 147 – 177 (15.0 – 18.0, 108 – 130)
(4WD)
(2WD)
1 Upper rubber plate
2 Upper rubber
3 Bracket CP
4 Lower rubber
5 Collar
6 Spring seat plate
7 Upper spring seat
8 Rubber seat
9 Helper ASSY
10 Coil spring
11 Shock absorber CP
12 Lower spring seat (4WD)
*13 Rear stabilizer
14 Helper (Station Wagon only)
15 Inner arm ASSY
16 Inner bushing
*17 Rear stabilizer bushing
*18 Rear stabilizer clamp
19 Rear bushing
20 Upper stopper
21 Front bushing
22 Crossmember CP
23 Bracket
24 Lower stopper
25 Outer bushing
26 Outer arm ASSY
*RX and air suspension vehicle only
SB2039100001000X

Fig. 2 Exploded view of conventional rear suspension assembly. Loyale

15. Reverse procedure to install.

WHEEL BEARING

ADJUST

JUSTY & FWD LOYALE

1. **On FWD Loyale models, torque** axle nut to approximately 36 ft. lbs.
2. **On Justy models, torque** axle nut to approximately 29 ft. lbs.
3. **On all models,** loosen axle nut ⅛ to ¹⁄₁₀ turn.
4. Measure starting force using a spring scale as shown in **Fig. 1.** On all except Justy, reading should be 1.9–3.2 lbs. On Justy, reading should be 3.1–4.4 lbs.
5. Bend lock plate to locknut in position, then install bearing cap and gasket.

REAR SUSPENSION

REPLACE

LOYALE

Refer to **Fig. 2** when performing the following procedure.

1. Remove the two upper shock absorber retaining bolts. **Lift vehicle slightly and use an extension to facilitate upper shock absorber bolts removal.**
2. Raise and support vehicle.
3. Remove rear wheels.
4. **On models equipped with AWD,** disconnect rear drive system as follows:
    a. Using a drift and hammer, drive out driveshaft spring pins, **Fig. 3.**
    b. Remove outer driveshaft DOJ from rear axle spindle by pushing inside of DOJ toward rear differential and pushing rear brake drum downward, **Fig. 4. DOJ designates double offset joint.**
    c. Remove inner end of driveshaft.
    d. Perform same procedure as previously described on opposite driveshaft.
    e. Remove the four propeller shaft to rear differential retaining bolts. **When propeller shaft is removed from transaxle, oil will flow from transaxle. Prepare a suitable cap**

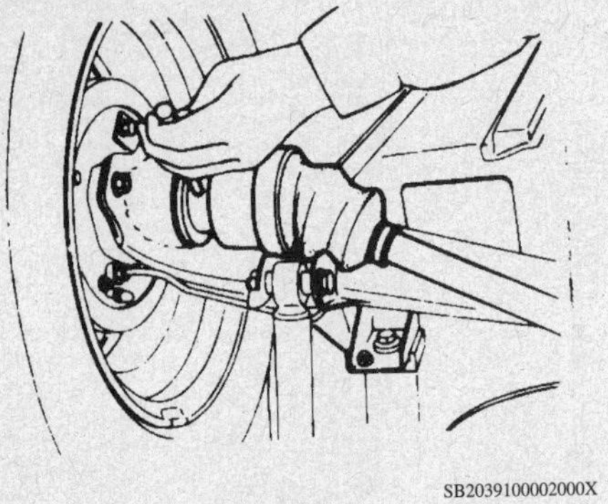
SB2039100002000X

Fig. 3 Driveshaft spring pin removal

to insert into the transaxle opening and a container to catch the escaping oil.

f. Set container at rear end of transaxle, and slowly remove propeller shaft.
g. Insert cap into transaxle opening.
h. Support rear differential with suitable jack. **Remove differential and installation bracket as an assembly from body.**
i. Remove the differential bracket to body locking retaining nuts.
j. Position a suitable transaxle jack under the differential.
k. Remove the four differential to body retaining bolts and remove differential.

5. **On models equipped with FWD,** remove the exhaust manifold and exhaust pipe retaining bolts, and then the muffler and exhaust pipe.
6. **On models equipped with AWD,** remove the exhaust pipe and muffler assembly separately.
7. **On all models,** remove the exhaust covers.
8. Disconnect brake hose and pipe at inner arm side bracket by loosening flare nut.
9. Perform the same procedure on the opposite side.
10. Position suitable jack under center of rear crossmember.
11. Remove retaining bolts, **Fig. 5,** from both ends of crossmember.
12. Slowly lower jack and withdraw suspension assembly from under vehicle.
13. Reverse procedure to install. Refer to **Fig. 2** for tightening specifications.

JUSTY

Refer to **Fig. 6,** when performing the following procedures.

REAR SUSPENSION ASSEMBLY

When removing brake parts, lower arm, strut, rear axle and trailing link, do not remove crossmember from frame.

1. Raise and support vehicle.
2. Remove rear wheels.
3. Using a line wrench, disconnect brake hose from frame bracket. **Cap brake hose to prevent fluid contamination and leakage.**
4. Separate and remove rear exhaust pipe from the muffler and pipe hanger.

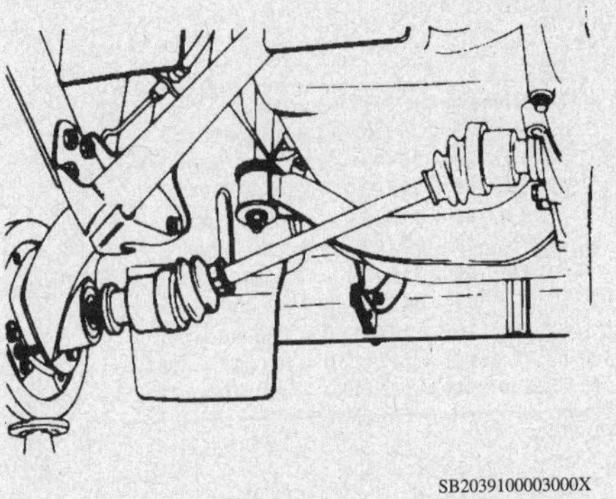
SB2039100003000X

Fig. 4 Outer double offset joint removal

5. Remove exhaust pipe heat protector rear attaching bolt.
6. Remove equalizer at center of parking brake cable, then the rod from support, and separate the inner cable.
7. Remove parking brake outer cable clamp bolt.
8. **On AWD models,** proceed as follows:
   a. Remove propeller shaft to rear differential attaching bolts, then separate shaft from differential.
   b. Pull inner parking brake cable downward.
   c. Using a drift, remove differential gear to double offset joint spring pin. **Use caution not to damage CV joint protective boots. Use new spring pin when installing double offset joint.**
9. **On all models,** remove trailing link to body attaching bolts.
10. Remove bolt from inner side of lower arm.
11. Remove coil spring.
12. Support left and right side brake drums. **Use caution not to damage backing plates.**
13. Reverse procedure to install. Refer to **Fig. 6** for tightening specifications.
14. Ensure hydraulic brake system is properly bled.

CROSSMEMBER

1. Raise and support vehicle.
2. Remove rear wheels.
3. Remove strut to axle mount attaching bolts.
4. While pushing lower arm downward, remove the coil spring.
5. Remove lower arm inner bushing bolt.
6. **On AWD models,** using a jack raise the rear differential. **Pad the jack to prevent damage to differential.**
7. **On AWD models,** remove rear differential bushing to crossmember attaching bolt.
8. **On all models,** remove crossmember to body attaching bolts.
9. Separate muffler from hanger, then while pushing downward on muffler, pull the crossmember.
10. Reverse procedure to install. Refer to **Fig. 6** for tightening specifications.

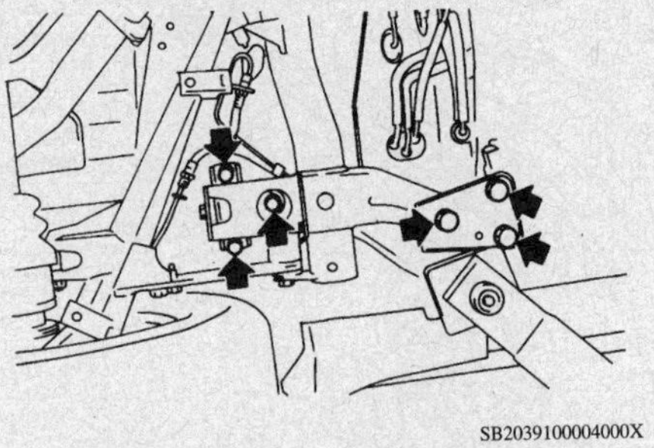
SB2039100004000X

Fig. 5 Rear suspension crossmember mounting bolts

LEGACY

Refer to **Figs. 7 and 8** when performing the following procedures.

TRAILING LINK

1. Raise and support vehicle.
2. Remove rear wheels.
3. Remove parking brake cable clamp and ABS sensor harness clamp from trailing link, if equipped.
4. Remove retaining bolts and the trailing link.
5. Reverse procedure to install. Refer to **Figs. 7 and 8** for tightening specifications.

LATERAL LINK

FWD Models

1. Raise and support vehicle, then remove rear wheels.
2. Separate stabilizer link from lateral link.
3. Scribe an aligning mark on adjusting bolt, adjusting wheel and crossmember.
4. Remove bolts securing lateral links to housing.
5. Turn lateral link cap counterclockwise until it contacts stopper, then remove.
6. Loosen self locking nut while holding adjusting bolt with a suitable wrench. **Self locking nut must be loosened before turning adjusting nut.**
7. Remove left lateral links as follows:
   a. Remove adjusting bolt, then front and rear lateral links.
8. Remove right lateral links as follows:
   a. Support crossmember with suitable jackstand, then remove crossmember to vehicle body mounting bolts.
   b. Lower jackstand until adjusting bolt can be removed, then remove adjusting bolt, front and rear lateral links.
9. Reverse procedure to install.

AWD Models

1. Raise and support vehicle, remove rear wheels.
2. Separate stabilizer link from lateral link.
3. Remove parking brake cable clamp and ABS sensor harness clamp from trailing link, if equipped.
4. Loosen trailing link to body retaining bolt.

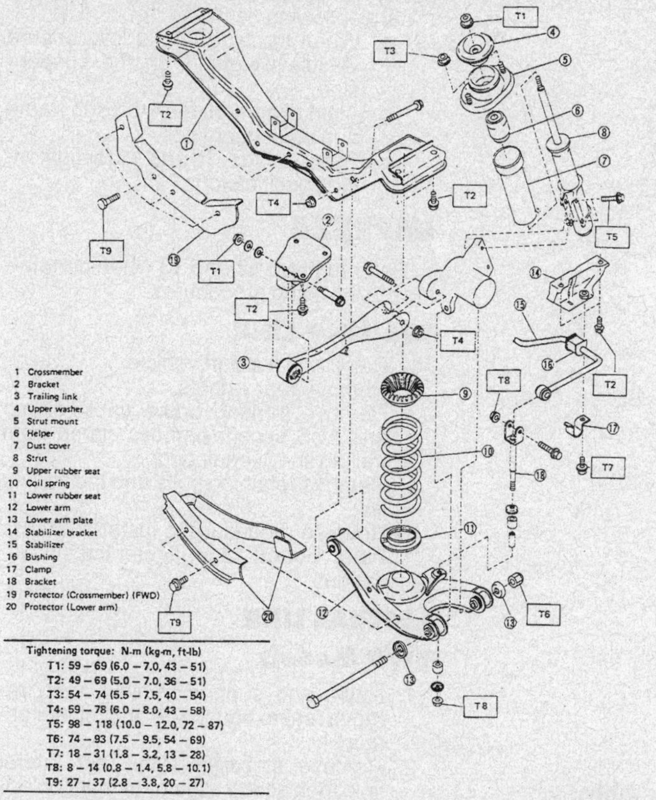
1 Crossmember
2 Bracket
3 Trailing link
4 Upper washer
5 Strut mount
6 Helper
7 Dust cover
8 Strut
9 Upper rubber seat
10 Coil spring
11 Lower rubber seat
12 Lower arm
13 Lower arm plate
14 Stabilizer bracket
15 Stabilizer
16 Bushing
17 Clamp
18 Bracket
19 Protector (Crossmember) (FWD)
20 Protector (Lower arm)
Tightening torque: N-m (kg-m, ft-lb)
T1: 59 – 69 (6.0 – 7.0, 43 – 51)
T2: 49 – 69 (5.0 – 7.0, 36 – 51)
T3: 54 – 74 (5.5 – 7.5, 40 – 54)
T4: 59 – 78 (6.0 – 8.0, 43 – 58)
T5: 98 – 118 (10.0 – 12.0, 72 – 87)
T6: 74 – 93 (7.5 – 9.5, 54 – 69)
T7: 18 – 31 (1.8 – 3.2, 13 – 28)
T8: 8 – 14 (0.8 – 1.4, 5.8 – 10.1)
T9: 27 – 37 (2.8 – 3.8, 20 – 27)
SB2039100007000X

Fig. 6 Exploded view of rear suspension assembly. Justy

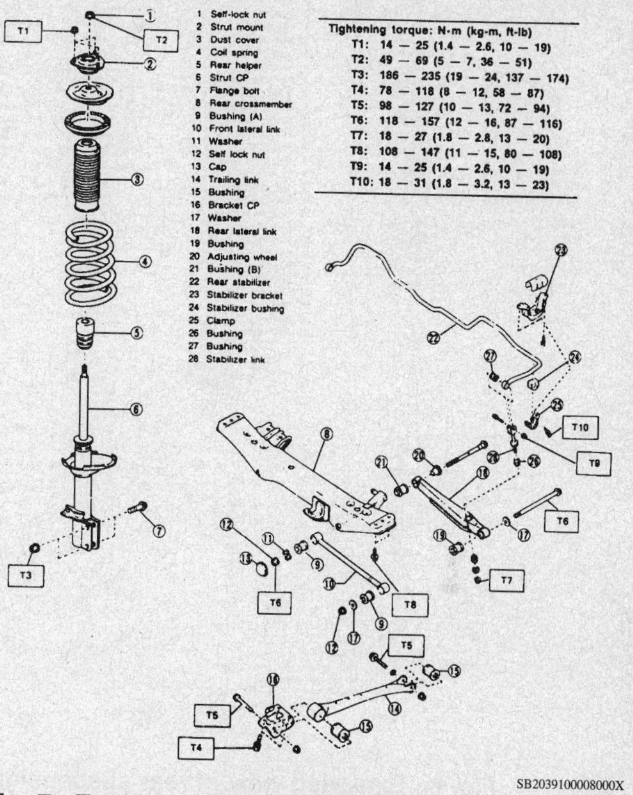
1 Self-lock nut
2 Strut mount
3 Dust cover
4 Coil spring
5 Rear helper
6 Strut CP
7 Flange bolt
8 Rear crossmember
9 Bushing (A)
10 Front lateral link
11 Washer
12 Self lock nut
13 Cap
14 Trailing link
15 Bushing
16 Bracket CP
17 Washer
18 Rear lateral link
19 Bushing
20 Adjusting wheel
21 Bushing (B)
22 Rear stabilizer
23 Stabilizer bracket
24 Stabilizer bushing
25 Clamp
26 Bushing
27 Bushing
28 Stabilizer link
Tightening torque: N·m (kg-m, ft-lb)
T1: 14 — 25 (1.4 — 2.6, 10 — 19)
T2: 49 — 69 (5 — 7, 36 — 51)
T3: 186 — 235 (19 — 24, 137 — 174)
T4: 78 — 118 (8 — 12, 58 — 87)
T5: 98 — 127 (10 — 13, 72 — 94)
T6: 118 — 157 (12 — 16, 87 — 116)
T7: 18 — 27 (1.8 — 2.8, 13 — 20)
T8: 108 — 147 (11 — 15, 80 — 108)
T9: 14 — 25 (1.4 — 2.6, 10 — 19)
T10: 18 — 31 (1.8 — 3.2, 13 — 23)
SB2039100008000X

Fig. 7 Exploded view of rear suspension assembly. FWD Legacy

5. Remove trailing link to housing retaining bolt.
6. Remove axle shaft as outlined in the "Rear Drive Axle" section.
7. Scribe an aligning mark on adjusting bolt, adjusting wheel and crossmember.
8. Loosen front lateral link retaining bolts.
9. Remove rear then front lateral links. **Self locking nut must be loosened before turning adjusting nut.**
10. Reverse procedure to install noting the following:
    a. Install DOJ with new spring pins.
    b. Refer to **Figs. 7 and 8** for tightening specifications.

CROSSMEMBER

FWD Models

1. Raise and support vehicle.
2. Remove rear wheels.
3. Disconnect lateral links from housing.
4. Remove exhaust pipe and muffler.
5. Remove four crossmember to body mounting bolts, then crossmember.
6. Reverse procedure to install, noting the following:
    a. Self-locking nut must be replaced.
    b. When tightening adjusting bolt, always tighten the nut and not the bolt.
    c. Tighten rubber bushings with vehicle on ground and at curb weight.
    d. Refer to **Figs. 7 and 8** for tightening specifications.

1993–94 AWD Models

1. Raise and support vehicle.
2. Remove rear wheels.
3. Separate front exhaust pipe and rear exhaust pipe.
4. Remove exhaust pipe and muffler.
5. Remove front cover of rear differential.
6. Remove propeller shaft.
7. Remove heat shielding cover.
8. Remove rear stabilizer.
9. Remove parking brake cable clamps and bracket.
10. Remove lower differential bracket .
11. Position suitable transaxle jack under rear differential.
12. Remove nuts connecting rear differential to rear member.
13. Remove rear differential front mount to body mounting bolts.
14. lower transaxle jack, then mover rear differential forward and remove bolts from rear member.
15. Remove rear driveshaft from differential. Suspend shaft with a wire or rope.
16. Remove rear differential member from crossmember.
17. Scribe an alignment mark on rear lateral link cam bolt and crossmember, then remove front and rear lateral links.
18. Reverse procedure to install. Refer to **Figs. 7 and 8** for tightening specifications.

1995–96 AWD Models

1. Raise and support vehicle.
2. Remove rear wheels.
3. Separate front exhaust pipe and rear exhaust pipe.
4. Remove exhaust pipe and muffler.
5. **On all sedan models,** remove crossmember reinforcement lower.
6. Remove rear differential.
7. Place a suitable transaxle jack under rear crossmember, then remove crossmember to body mounting bolts and crossmember.
8. Scribe an alignment mark on rear lateral link cam bolt and crossmember, then remove front and rear lateral links.
9. Reverse procedure to install, noting the following:
    a. Tighten rubber bushings with vehicle on ground and at curb weight.
    b. Adjust rear wheel alignment if necessary.
    c. Refer to **Figs. 7 and 8** for tightening specifications.

SVX

Refer to **Fig. 9** when performing the following procedures.

TRAILING LINK

1. Raise and support vehicle, then remove rear wheels.
2. Disconnect ABS sensor clamp, then parking brake cable bracket.
3. Remove trailing link mounting screws, then the trailing link.
4. Reverse procedure to install, noting the following:
    a. When torquing trailing arm, ensure vehicle weight is on the suspension.

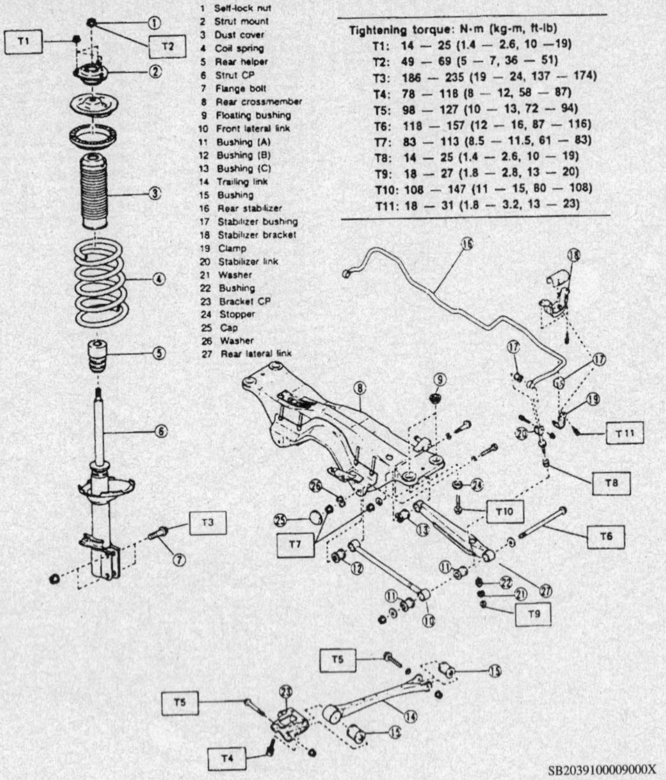
1 Self-lock nut
2 Strut mount
3 Dust cover
4 Coil spring
5 Rear helper
6 Strut CP
7 Flange bolt
8 Rear crossmember
9 Floating bushing
10 Front lateral link
11 Bushing (A)
12 Bushing (B)
13 Bushing (C)
14 Trailing link
15 Bushing
16 Rear stabilizer
17 Stabilizer bushing
18 Stabilizer bracket
19 Clamp
20 Stabilizer link
21 Washer
22 Bushing
23 Bracket CP
24 Stopper
25 Cap
26 Washer
27 Rear lateral link
Tightening torque: N·m (kg-m, ft-lb)
T1: 14 — 25 (1.4 — 2.6, 10 —19)
T2: 49 — 69 (5 — 7, 36 — 51)
T3: 186 — 235 (19 — 24, 137 — 174)
T4: 78 — 118 (8 — 12, 58 — 87)
T5: 98 — 127 (10 — 13, 72 — 94)
T6: 118 — 157 (12 — 16, 87 — 116)
T7: 83 — 113 (8.5 — 11.5, 61 — 83)
T8: 14 — 25 (1.4 — 2.6, 10 — 19)
T9: 18 — 27 (1.8 — 2.8, 13 — 20)
T10: 108 — 147 (11 — 15, 80 — 108)
T11: 18 — 31 (1.8 — 3.2, 13 — 23)
SB2039100009000X

Fig. 8 Exploded view of rear suspension assembly. AWD Legacy

b. Refer to **Fig. 9** for tightening specifications.

LATERAL LINK

1. Raise and support vehicle, then remove rear wheels.
2. Remove rear exhaust pipe, then the stabilizer link.
3. Remove parking brake cable, then the ABS sensor harness bracket.
4. Disconnect parking brake cable clamp.
5. Disconnect trailing link and lateral link from housing (hub).
6. Using driveshaft remover No. 28099PA100, or equivalent, separate DOJ from differential. Use bolt on side bearing retainer as a support for tool.
7. Place mark on alignment adjustment bolt, then remove lateral link from sub frame.
8. Reverse procedure to install, noting the following:
   a. When torquing lateral link, ensure vehicle weight is on the suspension.
   b. Align alignment mark when installing adjustment bolt.
   c. Refer to **Fig. 9** for tightening specifications.

SUB FRAME

1. Raise and support vehicle, then remove rear wheels.
2. Position shift lever in Neutral position, then release parking brakes.
3. Remove rear exhaust pipe and muffler.
4. Remove propeller shaft as follows:
   a. Remove front exhaust cover, then propeller shaft to rear differential mounting bolts.
   b. Remove bolts holding center bearing to body, then remove propeller shaft.
5. Remove rear differential as follows:
   a. Using driveshaft remover No. 28099PA100, or equivalent, separate DOJ from differential. Use bolt on side bearing retainer as a support for tool.
   b. Remove bracket to rear differential member mounting bolts, then support differential with suitable jack.
   c. Remove mounting bolts for bracket/rear differential to rear differential member.
   d. Remove self locking nuts which connect rear differential to rear sub frame.
   e. Slowly lower jack, move rear differential forward and remove bolts from rear sub frame.
   f. Remove rear differential assembly from body.
6. Remove fuel tank cover, then the differential member.
7. Remove stabilizers and brackets, then the trailing links.
8. Remove ABS sensor connector from backing plate and sub frame.
9. Place suitable jack under sub frame, then remove sub frame brackets. More than one person is needed to remove sub frame brackets.
10. Place alignment marks on adjustment bolt and sub frame.
11. Remove sub frame, then remove lateral links from frame.
12. Reverse procedure to install, noting the following:
    a. When torquing lateral link, ensure vehicle weight is on the suspension.
    b. Align alignment mark on sub frame and adjustment bolt.
    c. Refer to **Figs. 10 and 11** for tightening specifications.

IMPREZA

Refer to **Figs. 12 and 13** when performing the following procedures.

TRAILING LINK

1. Raise and support vehicle.
2. Remove rear wheels.
3. Remove parking brake cable clamp and ABS sensor harness clamp from trailing link, if equipped.
4. Remove retaining bolts and the trailing link.
5. Reverse procedure to install. Refer to **Figs. 12 and 13** for tightening specifications.

LATERAL LINK

FWD Models

1. Raise and support vehicle, then remove rear exhaust pipe and muffler assembly.
2. Remove stabilizer from rear lateral link, then scribe alignment mark on adjusting bolt, adjusting wheel and crossmember.
3. Remove lateral links to housing mounting bolts.
4. Turn cap (lateral link) counterclockwise until it contacts stopper, then remove cap.
5. While holding adjusting bolt head with wrench, loosen self-locking nut.
6. **On left lateral link,** remove adjusting bolt, then front and rear lateral links.
7. **On right lateral link,** remove bolt securing crossmember to body, then adjusting bolt, front and rear lateral links.
8. Reverse procedure to install. Refer to **Fig. 12,** for tightening specifications.

AWD Models

1. Raise and support vehicle, then remove rear wheels.
2. Remove stabilizers, then ABS sensor harness from trailing link.
3. Loosen trailing link to housing retaining bolt, then remove double offset joint from differential.
4. Scribe alignment mark on adjusting bolt and crossmember.
5. Remove outer lateral link bolt on housing side.
6. Remove lateral links to crossmember mounting bolts, then remove lateral links.
7. Reverse procedure to install. Refer to **Fig. 13,** for tightening specifications.

CROSSMEMBER

FWD Models

1. Disconnect lateral links from housing.
2. Remove rear exhaust pipe and muffler assembly.
3. Remove heat shield cover.

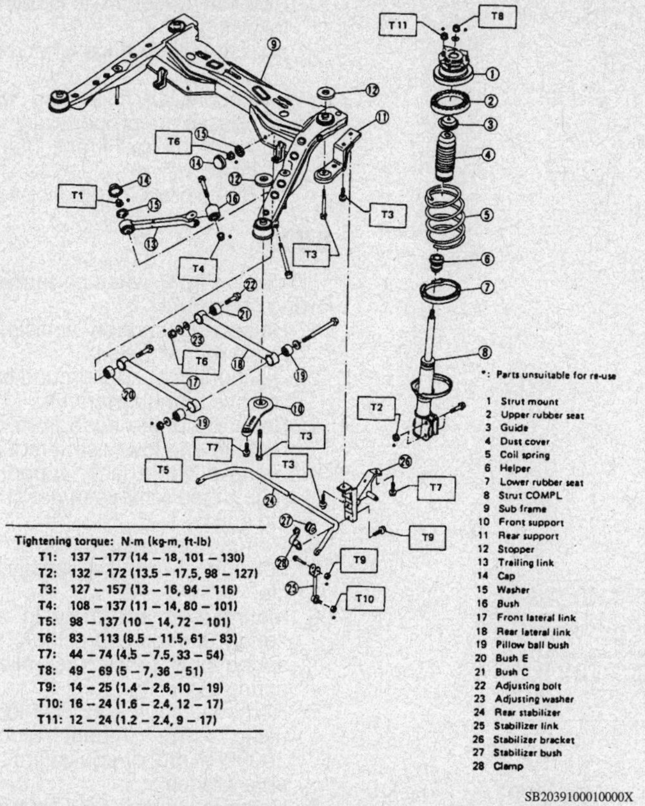

T11
T8
T6
T1
T4
T3
T2
T5
T7
T9
T10
*: Parts unsuitable for re-use
1 Strut mount
2 Upper rubber seat
3 Guide
4 Dust cover
5 Coil spring
6 Helper
7 Lower rubber seat
8 Strut COMPL
9 Sub frame
10 Front support
11 Rear support
12 Stopper
13 Trailing link
14 Cap
15 Washer
16 Bush
17 Front lateral link
18 Rear lateral link
19 Pillow ball bush
20 Bush E
21 Bush C
22 Adjusting bolt
23 Adjusting washer
24 Rear stabilizer
25 Stabilizer link
26 Stabilizer bracket
27 Stabilizer bush
28 Clamp
Tightening torque: N·m (kg-m, ft-lb)
T1: 137 – 177 (14 – 18, 101 – 130)
T2: 132 – 172 (13.5 – 17.5, 98 – 127)
T3: 127 – 157 (13 – 16, 94 – 116)
T4: 108 – 137 (11 – 14, 80 – 101)
T5: 98 – 137 (10 – 14, 72 – 101)
T6: 83 – 113 (8.5 – 11.5, 61 – 83)
T7: 44 – 74 (4.5 – 7.5, 33 – 54)
T8: 49 – 69 (5 – 7, 36 – 51)
T9: 14 – 25 (1.4 – 2.6, 10 – 19)
T10: 16 – 24 (1.6 – 2.4, 12 – 17)
T11: 12 – 24 (1.2 – 2.4, 9 – 17)
SB2039100010000X

Fig. 9 Exploded view of rear suspension. SVX

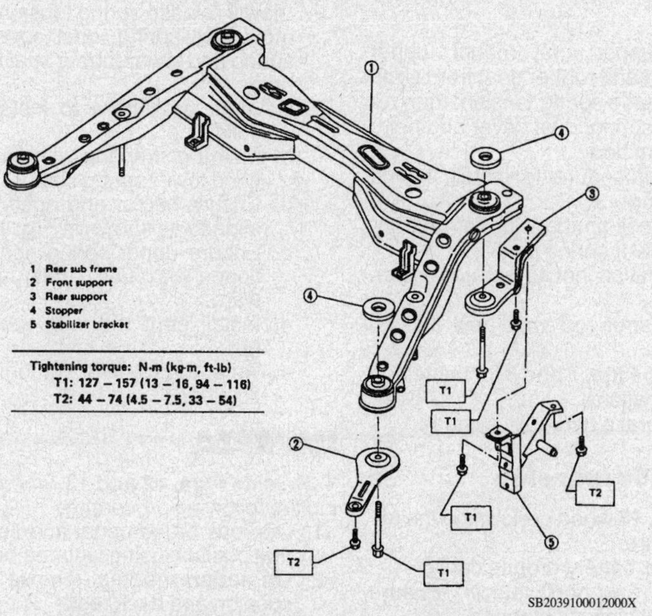

1 Rear sub frame
2 Front support
3 Rear support
4 Stopper
5 Stabilizer bracket
Tightening torque: N·m (kg-m, ft-lb)
T1: 127 – 157 (13 – 16, 94 – 116)
T2: 44 – 74 (4.5 – 7.5, 33 – 54)
T1
T2
SB2039100012000X

Fig. 11 Exploded view of sub frame. SVX

4. Remove crossmember mounting bolts then the crossmember.
5. Reverse procedure to install. Refer to **Fig. 12,** for tightening specifications.

AWD Models

1. Raise and support vehicle, then remove rear wheels.
2. Remove rear exhaust pipe and muffler assembly.
3. Remove rear differential, then place transaxle jack under crossmember.
4. Remove crossmember mounting bolts, then the crossmember.
5. Scribe alignment mark on lateral link cam bolt and crossmember, then remove lateral links.
6. Reverse procedure to install. Refer to **Fig. 13,** for tightening specifications.

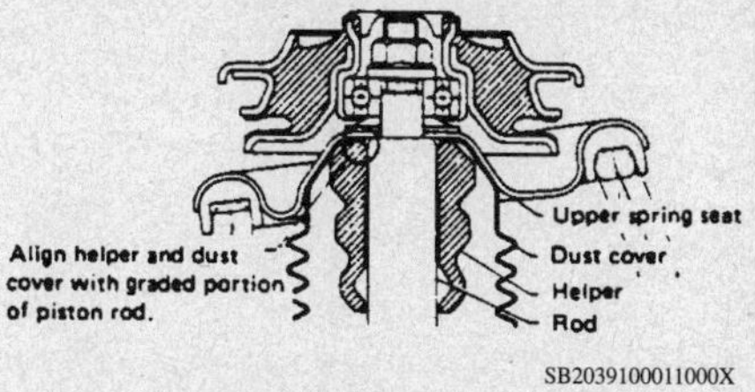

Align helper and dust cover with graded portion of piston rod.
Upper spring seat
Dust cover
Helper
Rod
SB2039100011000X

Fig. 10 Helper and dust cover alignment. SVX

STRUT

REPLACE

LOYALE

Refer to **Fig. 2** when performing the following procedure.

1. Raise and support vehicle. Ensure rear suspension is unloaded.
2. Remove two upper strut assembly mounting bolts.
3. Remove lower mounting bolt and the strut assembly.
4. Mount assembly in suitable spring compressor. Ensure projections on compressor are seated on inner diameter of spring.
5. Compress spring until tension is relieved from spring seats.
6. Remove strut rod retaining nut.
7. Remove body mounting bracket, plate and upper spring seat as an assembly.
8. Slowly release spring tension, then remove coil spring from strut body.
9. Remove helper assembly from strut.
10. Reverse procedure to install, noting the following:
    a. Mount coil spring with flat face toward lower spring seat.
    b. Ensure body mounting bracket is properly aligned and that rubber seat does not extrude from spring seat.
    c. Ensure upper end of spring is fully seated in upper seat.
    d. Refer to **Fig. 2.** for tightening specifications.

JUSTY

Refer to **Fig. 6,** when performing the following procedure.

1. Raise and support vehicle.
2. Remove rear wheels.
3. Remove upper strut mount trim cover.
4. Remove strut to body attaching nuts.
5. While pushing lower arm downward, remove the coil spring.
6. Remove strut to axle mount attaching bolts, then the strut assembly.
7. Wrap strut bracket with a cloth, then lightly clamp the bracket in a suitable vise.
8. Using hexagon head, and box end type wrenches, remove strut mount to piston rod attaching nut.
9. Remove strut mount and associated parts.

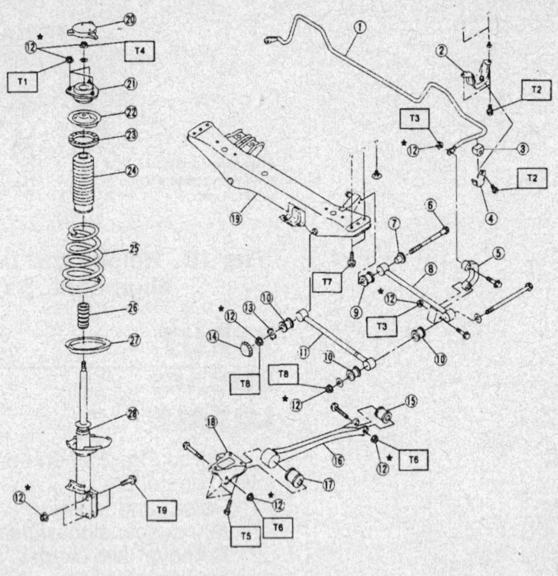

1. Stabilizer
2. Stabilizer bracket
3. Stabilizer bushing
4. Clamp
5. Stabilizer link
6. Adjusting bolt
7. Adjusting wheel
8. Rear lateral link
9. Bushing (D)
10. Bushing (A)
11. Front lateral link
12. Self-locking nut
13. Washer
14. Cap
15. Trailing link rear bushing
16. Trailing link
17. Trailing link front bushing
18. Trailing link bracket
19. Crossmember
20. Cap
21. Strut mount
22. Spring seat
23. Rubber seat upper
24. Dust cover
25. Coil spring
26. Helper
27. Rubber seat lower
28. Damper strut

Tightening torque: N·m (kg-m, ft-lb)
T1: 20 ± 6 (2.0 ± 0.6, 14.5 ± 4.3)
T2: 25 ± 7 (2.5 ± 0.7, 18.1 ± 5.1)
T3: 44 ± 6 (4.5 ± 0.6, 32.5 ± 4.3)
T4: 59 ± 10 (6.0 ± 1.0, 43 ± 7)
T5: 98 ± 20 (10.0 ± 2.0, 72 ± 14)
T6: 113 ± 15 (11.5 ± 1.5, 83 ± 11)
T7: 127 ± 20 (13.0 ± 2.0, 94 ± 14)
T8: 137 ± 20 (14.0 ± 2.0, 101 ± 14)
T9: 196^{+39}_{-10} ($20.0^{+4.0}_{-1.0}$, 145^{+29}_{-7})

SB2039100013000X

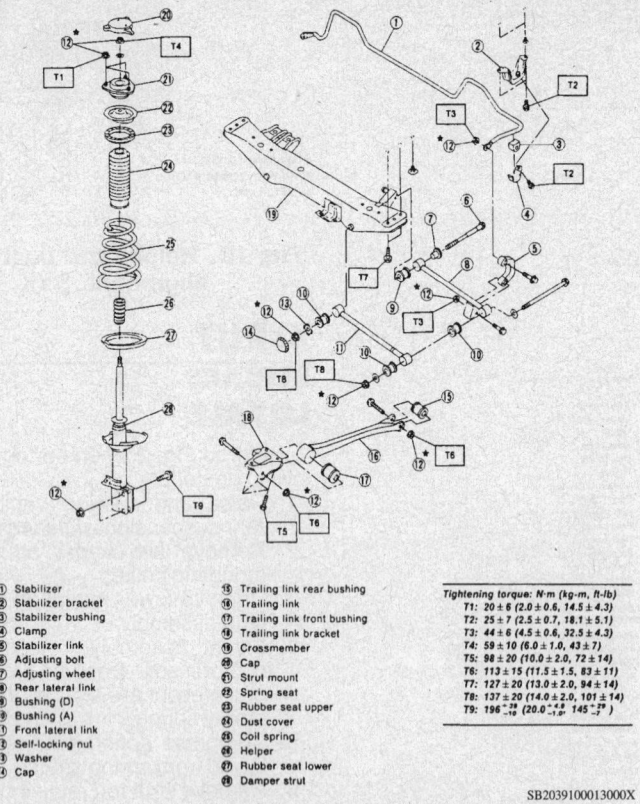

Fig. 12 Exploded view of rear suspension assembly. FWD Impreza

10. Reverse procedure to install. Refer to **Fig. 6,** for tightening specifications.

LEGACY

Conventional Suspension

Refer to **Figs. 7 and 8** when performing the following procedure.

1. **On sedan models,** remove rear seat cushion and back rest.
2. **On 1993–94 wagon models** remove rear speaker grill.
3. **On 1995–96 wagon models** remove strut cap of rear quarter trim.
4. **On all models,** raise and support vehicle.
5. Remove rear wheels.
6. Disconnect brake hose from brake caliper.
7. **On models equipped with disc brakes,** remove union bolt from brake calliper.
8. **On models equipped with drum brakes,** disconnect brake hose from brake pipe strut, then disconnect brake hose from drum brake.
9. **On all models,** remove lower and upper strut mount retaining bolts, then the strut assembly.
10. Mount strut assembly in a suitable spring compressor. Ensure projections on compressor are seated on inner diameter of spring.
11. Compress spring until tension is relieved from spring seats.
12. Remove strut rod self-locking nut using a suitable socket wrench and strut mount socket tool No. 927760000, or equivalent.
13. Remove upper strut mount, upper spring seat and rubber seat from strut.
14. Slowly release spring tension, then remove coil spring, dust cover and helper from strut body.
15. Reverse procedure to install, noting the following:
    a. Mount coil spring with flat face toward lower spring seat.
    b. Use caution not to scratch piston rod.
    c. Install strut rod with new locking nut.
    d. Refer to **Figs. 7 and 8** for tightening specifications.
    e. Bleed brake hydraulic system.

Pneumatic Suspension

Refer to **Fig. 14** when performing the following procedure.

1. Disconnect battery ground cable.
2. Raise and support vehicle. Ensure rear suspension is unloaded.
3. Remove rear wheels.
4. Disconnect brake hose from caliper.
5. Remove upper rear quarter trim panel stereo cover.
6. Disconnect air line from rear suspension solenoid valve using air pipe remover tool as shown in **Fig. 15.**
7. Remove rear suspension solenoid valve.
8. Withdraw height sensor harness from access hole in body, then disconnect electrical connector.
9. Remove strut mount retaining bolts and the strut assembly.
10. Reverse procedure to install noting the following:
    a. Use new O-rings when connecting air lines.
    b. Ensure air lines and wiring harnesses are properly aligned.
    c. Refer to **Fig. 14** for tightening specifications.
    d. Bleed brake hydraulic system.

SVX

Refer to **Fig. 9,** when performing the following procedure.

1. Raise and support vehicle, then remove rear wheels.
2. Disconnect battery ground cable, then remove rear quarter trim.
3. Separate brake hose from strut, then remove one lower strut mounting bolt.
4. Using suitable jack, support housing (hub), then remove upper strut mounting bolts.
5. Remove remaining lower mounting bolt, then the strut assembly from vehicle.
6. Mount strut assembly in a suitable spring compressor, then compress spring until tension is relieved from spring seats.
7. Remove strut rod self-locking nut using strut mount socket No. 20099PA000, or equivalent and a suitable wrench.
8. Remove upper strut mount, upper spring seat and upper rubber seat.
9. Slowly release spring tension, then remove coil spring, dust cover, helper spring and lower rubber seat from strut body.
10. Reverse procedure to install, noting the following:
    a. Mount coil spring with flat face toward lower spring seat.
    b. Ensure helper and dust cover are aligned as shown in **Fig. 10.**
    c. Ensure upper spring seat is positioned with "Out " mark facing outward.
    d. Install strut rod with new locking nut.
    e. Refer to **Fig. 9** for tightening specifications.

IMPREZA

Refer to **Figs. 12 and 13,** when performing the following procedure.

1. Depress brake pedal and secure it in that position using wooden block.
2. **On sedan models,** remove rear seat cushion and back rest.
3. **On wagon models,** remove rear speaker grille and service hole cap.
4. **On all models,** remove strut mount cap, then raise and support vehicle.
5. Remove rear wheels and brake hose clip.
6. **On models with rear disc brakes,** remove union bolt from caliper.
7. **On models with rear drum brakes,** disconnect brake hose from brake pipe on strut and brake pipe from drum brake.
8. Remove lower and upper strut mounting bolts, then remove strut from vehicle.

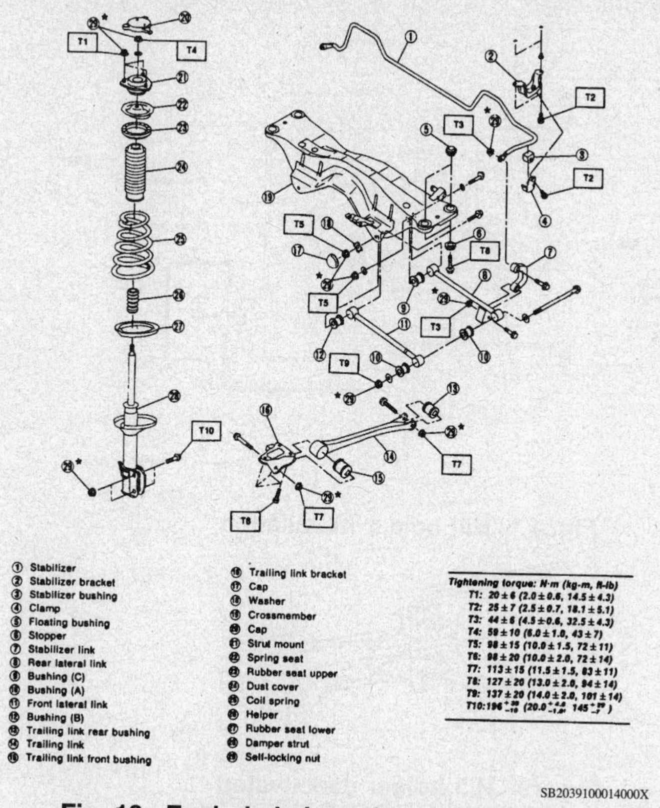

T1
T2
T3
T4
T5
T6
T7
T8
T9
T10
① Stabilizer
② Stabilizer bracket
③ Stabilizer bushing
④ Clamp
⑤ Floating bushing
⑥ Stopper
⑦ Stabilizer link
⑧ Rear lateral link
⑨ Bushing (C)
⑩ Bushing (A)
⑪ Front lateral link
⑫ Bushing (B)
⑬ Trailing link rear bushing
⑭ Trailing link
⑮ Trailing link front bushing
⑯ Trailing link bracket
⑰ Cap
⑱ Washer
⑲ Crossmember
⑳ Cap
㉑ Strut mount
㉒ Spring seat
㉓ Rubber seat upper
㉔ Dust cover
㉕ Coil spring
㉖ Helper
㉗ Rubber seat lower
㉘ Damper strut
㉙ Self-locking nut
Tightening torque: N·m (kg-m, ft-lb)
T1: 20 ± 6 (2.0 ± 0.6, 14.5 ± 4.3)
T2: 25 ± 7 (2.5 ± 0.7, 18.1 ± 5.1)
T3: 44 ± 6 (4.5 ± 0.6, 32.5 ± 4.3)
T4: 59 ± 10 (6.0 ± 1.0, 43 ± 7)
T5: 98 ± 15 (10.0 ± 1.5, 72 ± 11)
T6: 98 ± 20 (10.0 ± 2.0, 72 ± 14)
T7: 113 ± 15 (11.5 ± 1.5, 83 ± 11)
T8: 127 ± 20 (13.0 ± 2.0, 94 ± 14)
T9: 137 ± 20 (14.0 ± 2.0, 101 ± 14)
T10: 196 (20.0 145)
SB2039100014000X

Fig. 13 Exploded view of rear suspension assembly. AWD Impreza

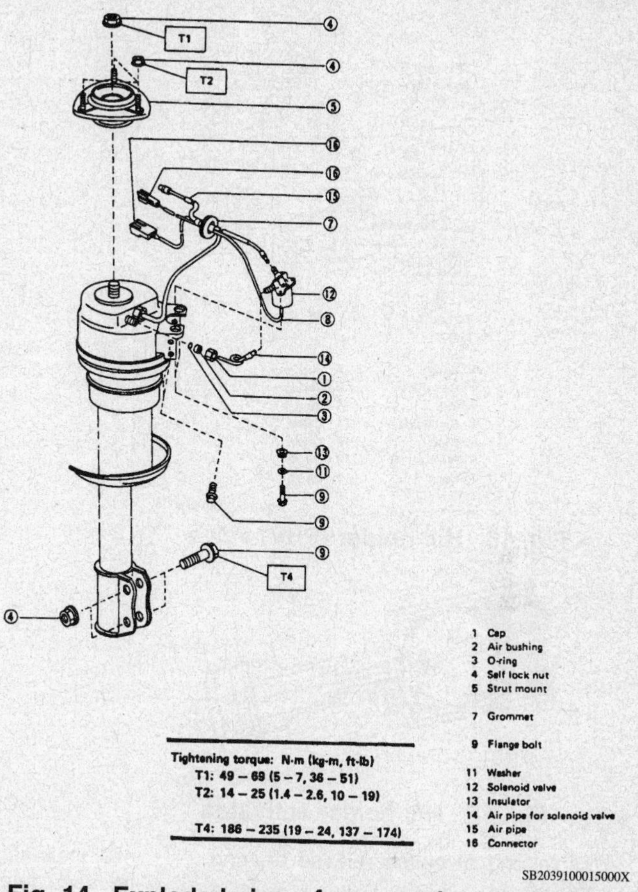

T1
T2
T4
1 Cap
2 Air bushing
3 O-ring
4 Self lock nut
5 Strut mount
7 Grommet
9 Flange bolt
11 Washer
12 Solenoid valve
13 Insulator
14 Air pipe for solenoid valve
15 Air pipe
16 Connector
Tightening torque: N·m (kg-m, ft-lb)
T1: 49 – 69 (5 – 7, 36 – 51)
T2: 14 – 25 (1.4 – 2.6, 10 – 19)
T4: 186 – 235 (19 – 24, 137 – 174)
SB2039100015000X

Fig. 14 Exploded view of pneumatic suspension system components. Legacy

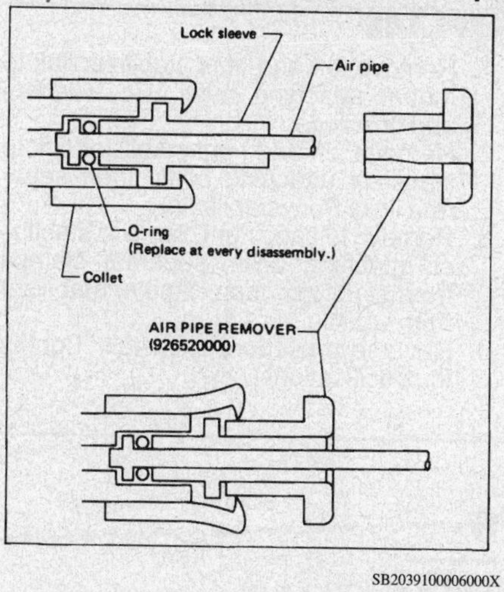

Lock sleeve
Air pipe
O-ring
(Replace at every disassembly.)
Collet
AIR PIPE REMOVER
(926520000)
SB2039100006000X

Fig. 15 Air line replacement

9. Mount strut assembly in a suitable spring compressor, then compress spring until tension is relieved from spring seats.
10. Remove strut rod self-locking nut using strut mount socket No. 9277600000, or equivalent and a suitable wrench.
11. Remove upper strut mount, upper spring seat and upper rubber seat.
12. Slowly release spring tension, then remove coil spring, dust cover and helper spring.
13. Reverse procedure to install, noting the following:
    a. Mount coil spring with flat end towards top side and inclined end towards bottom side.
    b. Ensure upper spring seat is positioned with "Out " mark facing outward.
    c. Install strut rod with new locking nut.
    d. Refer to **Figs. 12 and 13** for tightening specifications.

HILL HOLDER

The Hill holder is essentially a Pressure Hold Valve (PHV), **Fig. 16,** built into one brake circuit, that maintains hydraulic pressure in the brake circuit when the vehicle is facing uphill and the clutch pedal is depressed, **Fig. 17.**

The PHV lever, **Fig. 16,** is connected through a linkage to the clutch pedal and controlled by a camshaft which provides the motion to the PHV driveshaft. The PHV driveshaft controls the clearance between the PHV inertia controlled ball and seal.

When the clutch pedal is depressed, the PHV driveshaft is pulled into the seal, allowing the ball free movement. If the vehicle is facing uphill, inertia will cause the ball to roll onto the seal, **Fig. 18,** thereby holding hydraulic pressure. When the clutch is released, **Fig. 19,** the driveshaft is forced into the ball chamber, unsealing the ball and releasing hydraulic pressure.

REMOVAL

1. Drain primary side of master cylinder.
2. Remove cable adjusting nut and clamp from clutch release bearing fork, then disconnect cable from engine bracket.
3. Remove cable from PHV.
4. Separate connector bracket from PHV, then remove brake lines using a suitable flare wrench.
5. Remove PHV bracket to frame retaining bolts and the PHV. **Do not allow any dirt to enter PHV.**

INSPECTION

1. Inspect PHV cable boots and outer casing for damage, replace as necessary.
2. Inspect PHV cable inner core for corrosion and wear, replace as necessary.
3. Inspect PHV return spring for damage or corrosion.
4. Tilt PHV assembly and listen for ball rolling to ensure free operation.
5. Operate lever to ensure smooth operation. **Do not attempt to disassemble PHV. If unit is defective, it should be replaced.**

INSTALLATION

To install, reverse removal procedure, noting the following:

1. Apply lubricant to hooked portion of return spring, cable end of lever and

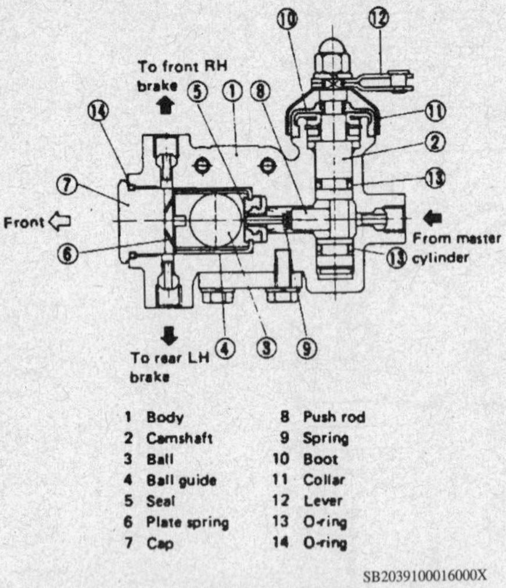

To front RH brake
Front
From master cylinder
To rear LH brake
1 Body
2 Camshaft
3 Ball
4 Ball guide
5 Seal
6 Plate spring
7 Cap
8 Push rod
9 Spring
10 Boot
11 Collar
12 Lever
13 O-ring
14 O-ring
SB2039100016000X

Fig. 16 Hill holder (PHV) valve

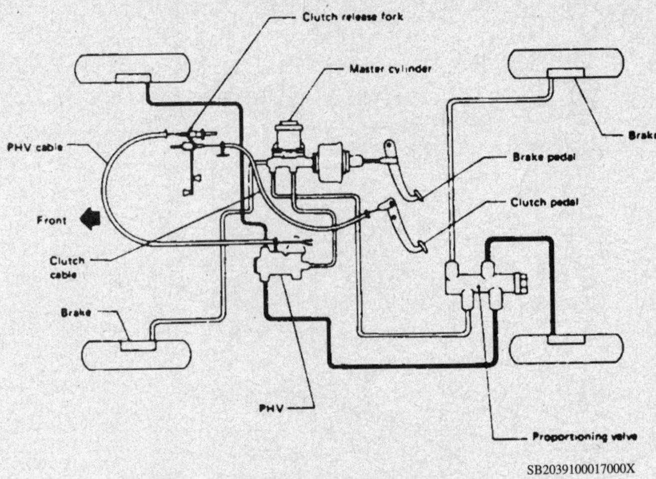

Clutch release fork
Master cylinder
Brake
PHV cable
Brake pedal
Clutch pedal
Front
Clutch cable
Brake
PHV
Proportioning valve
SB2039100017000X

Fig. 17 Hill holder installation

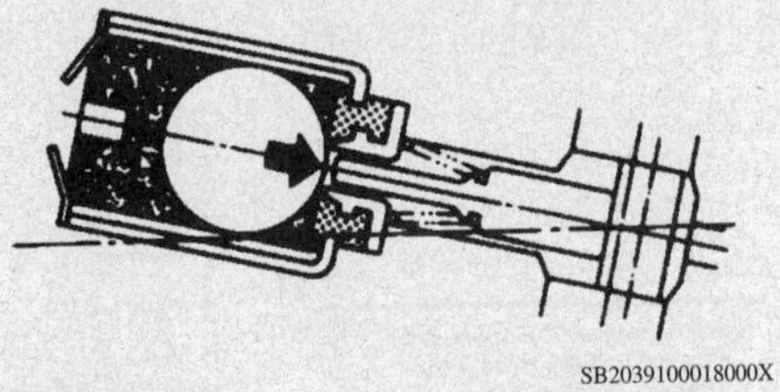

SB2039100018000X

Fig. 18 Hill holder activated

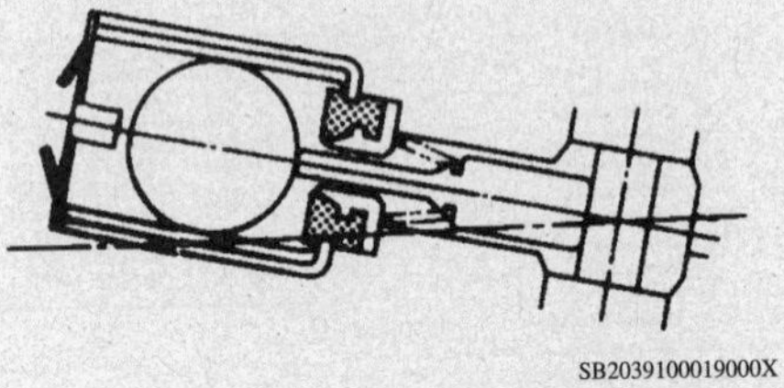

SB2039100019000X

Fig. 19 Hill holder deactivated

cable end at clutch release bearing fork.

2. Bleed brakes after installation.

ADJUSTMENT

After replacing PHV cable or clutch cable, operate clutch pedal approximately 30 times to seat new parts prior to making any adjustments.

1. Ensure clutch is adjusted properly. Refer to "Clutch and Manual Transmission" section.
2. Road test vehicle to determine Hill holder performance on an uphill road of 3° inclination or more. If Hill holder is released late (engine tends to stall), loosen adjustment nut gradually, until smooth starting is obtained. If Hill holder releases early (vehicle rolls down incline), tighten adjustment nut until Hill holder releases late (engine tends to stall), then loosen adjustment nut gradually, until smooth starting is obtained.
3. Tighten to specifications.

STABILIZER BAR

REPLACE

1. Remove left and right stabilizer link to mount attaching nuts with washers and bushings.
2. Remove left and right stabilizer link to stabilizer attaching bolts, then separate links from stabilizer.
3. Remove left and right clamp to stabilizer attaching bolts, separate clamps from stabilizer, then remove stabilizer from vehicle.
4. Reverse procedure to install. Tighten to specifications.

TIGHTENING SPECIFICATIONS

Year	Component	Torque/Ft. Lbs.
1993–96	Axle nut①②	③
	Axle nut①④	145
	Axle nut⑤⑦	123–152
	Hill Holder Adjustment Nut	22–39⑧
	Hub Nut	145
	Lug Nuts	58–72
	Parking Brake Adjustment Locknut	40–65⑧
	Stabilizer Clamps①	13–16
	Stabilizer Clamps⑥	13–28
	Stabilizer Clamps⑤⑦	10–19
	Stabilizer Link To Mount①⑥	6–10
	Stabilizer Link To Mount⑤⑦	13–17

Continued

TIGHTENING SPECIFICATIONS—Continued

Year	Component	Torque/Ft. Lbs.
1993–96	Stabilizer Link To Stabilizer①⑥	6–10
	Stabilizer Link To Stabilizer⑤⑦	10–19
	Strut Assembly	③
	Suspension Assembly	③

① — Except Legacy.
② — Except AWD.
③ — Refer to "Wheel Bearing, Adjust" for procedure & specifications.
④ — AWD.
⑤ — Legacy.
⑥ — Justy.
⑦ — SVX.
⑧ — Inch lbs.

Front Suspension & Steering

NOTE: On Air Bag Equipped Models, Refer To "Air Bag System Precautions" Located In The Front Of This Manual For System Disarming & Arming Procedures.

INDEX

Page No.

Ball Joint Inspection 39-50
Ball Joint, Replace 39-50
Control Arm, Replace 39-52
Lower 39-52
Crossmember, Replace 39-52
Impreza & Legacy 39-53
Justy 39-53
Loyale 39-52
Hub & Bearing, Replace 39-49
Justy & Loyale 39-49
Legacy 39-49
Manual Steering Gear, Replace .. 39-54
Loyale & Justy 39-54
Manual Steering Gears 39-104
Power Steering 39-106
Power Steering Gear, Replace ... 39-53
Except SVX 39-53
SVX 39-54
Power Steering Pump, Replace .. 39-54
Impreza & Legacy 39-54
SVX 39-54
Stabilizer Bar, Replace 39-52
Except SVX 39-52
SVX 39-52
Strut, Replace 39-50
Impreza 39-51
Justy 39-51
Loyale & Legacy 39-50
SVX 39-51
Tightening Specifications 39-56
Wheel Hub & Steering Knuckle, Replace 39-49
Impreza 39-50
SVX 39-49

HUB & BEARING

REPLACE

JUSTY & LOYALE

1. Raise and support vehicle.
2. Remove front wheels.
3. Remove grease cap and cotter pin, then loosen axle castle nut.
4. Remove caliper and position aside. Leave brake line attached to caliper.
5. Remove caliper mounting bracket.
6. Remove axle castle nut and washer, then the hub and rotor assembly.
7. Reverse procedure to install. Tighten bolts and nuts to specifications.

LEGACY

1. Remove front driveshaft as outlined in the "Front Wheel Drive" section.
2. Remove disc brake caliper with support and the disc brake rotor from housing.
3. Separate tie-rod end and ball joint from housing.
4. If equipped, remove ABS sensor from housing.
5. Remove transverse link ball joint from housing.
6. Scribe an alignment mark on camber adjusting bolt head.
7. Remove strut to housing retaining bolts and the housing assembly.
8. Reverse procedure to install, Tighten to specifications.

WHEEL HUB & STEERING KNUCKLE

REPLACE

SVX

Refer to **Fig. 1** when performing the following procedure.

1. Raise and support vehicle, then remove front wheels.
2. Remove hub caps, then unlock axle nut.
3. Using a suitable socket, remove axle nut. **Do not remove axle nut with wheel installed.**
4. Remove ball joint retaining bolts, then disconnect ABS sensor from knuckle.
5. Disconnect brake hose clamp from strut, then scribe alignment mark on camber adjusting bolt and remove strut mounting nuts. **Do not remove strut bolts at this time.**
6. Disconnect brake caliper from knuckle and secure to strut with wire.
7. Remove driveshaft from knuckle. If it is difficult to remove, use remover tool No. 926470000 and plate tool No. 28099PA110, or equivalents.
8. Remove brake rotor from hub. If rotor is seized, install two 8 mm bolts in screw holes to remove.
9. Using a suitable puller, disconnect tie rod from knuckle, then remove knuckle and hub assembly.
10. Support knuckle and hub assembly using hub stand tool No. 28099PA080, or equivalent, then attach hub remover

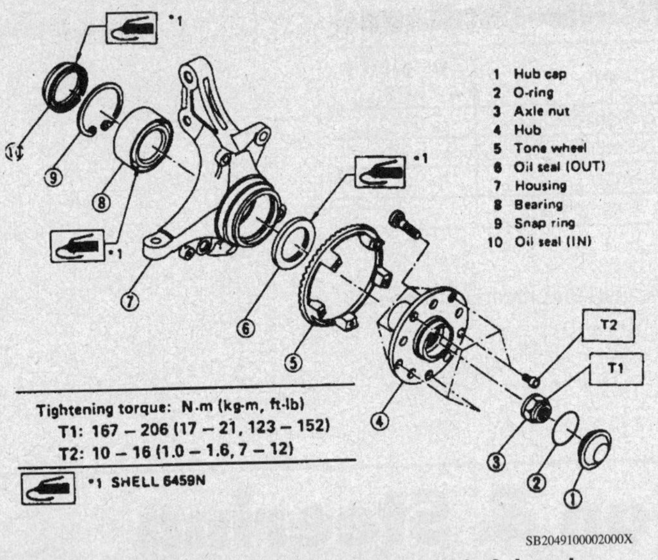
1 Hub cap
2 O-ring
3 Axle nut
4 Hub
5 Tone wheel
6 Oil seal (OUT)
7 Housing
8 Bearing
9 Snap ring
10 Oil seal (IN)
T2
T1
Tightening torque: N·m (kg-m, ft-lb)
T1: 167 – 206 (17 – 21, 123 – 152)
T2: 10 – 16 (1.0 – 1.6, 7 – 12)
*1 SHELL 6459N
SB2049100002000X

Fig. 1 Exploded view of knuckle, hub & bearing. Impreza & SVX

front tool No. 28099PA040, or equivalent to knuckle and drive hub out of knuckle.

11. If inner bearing race remains in hub, remove using a suitable tool.
12. Remove brake backing plate from knuckle, then using a suitable screwdriver, remove inner and outer oil seals.
13. Remove snap ring, then support knuckle using housing stand front tool No. 28099PA010, or equivalent.
14. Using bearing installer front tool No. 28099PA000, or equivalent, press inner race to drive out bearing. **Do not remove outer race unless it is damaged.**
15. Using housing stand front tool No. 28099PA010 and bearing installer front tool No. 28099PA000, or equivalents, press outer race to install new bearing.
16. Install snap ring, then using oil seal installer front tool No. 28099PA030, or equivalent, press inner oil seal until it contacts circlip.
17. Using oil seal installer front tool No. 28099PA030, or equivalent, press outer oil seal until it contacts bottom of housing.
18. Install brake backing plate, attach hub assembly to hub stand, then using hub installer front, press hub assembly into knuckle.
19. Assemble steering knuckle assembly to vehicle by reversing steps 1 through 9.

IMPREZA

Refer to **Fig. 1** when performing the following procedure.

1. Disconnect battery ground cable, then raise and support vehicle.
2. Remove front wheels, then unlock axle nut.
3. Using a suitable socket, remove axle nut. **Do not remove axle nut with wheel installed.**
4. Remove stabilizer link, then double offset joint from transaxle spindle.
5. Remove driveshaft from knuckle. If it is difficult to remove, use remover tool No. 926470000 and plate tool No. 927140000, or equivalents.
6. Disconnect brake caliper from knuckle and secure to strut with wire.
7. Remove brake rotor from hub. If rotor is seized, install two 8 mm bolts in screw holes to remove.
8. Using a suitable puller, disconnect tie rod from knuckle.
9. **On models with ABS,** remove ABS sensor assembly.
10. **On all models,** disconnect ball joint from knuckle.
11. Scribe alignment mark on camber adjustment bolt head, then remove knuckle to strut mounting bolts.
12. Remove knuckle assembly from vehicle.
13. Support knuckle using knuckle stand tool No. 927080000, or equivalent.
14. Using hub remover tool No. 927060000, or equivalent, press hub out of knuckle. If inner bearing race remains in hub, remove it with a suitable tool.
15. Remove disc cover from housing, then using standard screwdriver, remove outer and inner oil seals.
16. Remove snap ring.
17. Support hub using hub stand tool No. 927400000, or equivalent, then using bearing remover tool No. 927100000, or equivalent, press out inner race and bearing.
18. **On models with ABS,** remove tone wheel.
19. Install tone wheel.
20. **On all models,** Using hub stand and bearing remover, press new bearing into place. Always press outer race when installing bearing.
21. Install snap ring. Using hub stand and oil seal installer tool No. 927410000, or equivalent, press outer seal until it contacts bottom of housing and inner seal until it contacts circlip.
22. Install disc cover and **torque** bolts to 7–13 ft. lbs.
23. Install hub in hub stand. Using hub installer tool No. 927120000, or equivalent, press bearing into hub.
24. Assemble steering knuckle assembly to vehicle by reversing steps 1 through 14.

BALL JOINT INSPECTION

1. Measure dimension "L," with 154 lbs. of download pressure placed on ball joint in the direction of "L," **Fig. 2.**
2. Measure dimension "L," with 154 lbs. of upload pressure placed on ball joint in the direction of "L," **Fig. 3.**
3. Calculate ball joint play using the following formula:
   a. S=L2–L1
   b. Ball joint play "S" equals .012 inch.
   c. Ball joint play should not exceed .012 inch.
   d. If ball joint play exceeds calculated figure, then replace with new ball joint.

BALL JOINT

REPLACE

Refer to **Figs. 4 through 8** when performing the following procedure.

1. Raise and support vehicle.
2. Remove front wheels.
3. Remove cotter pin and castle nut from ball stud, then disconnect ball stud from transverse link.
4. Remove ball joint to housing retaining bolt and the ball joint.
5. Reverse procedure to install. Refer to **Figs. 4 through 8,** for tightening specifications.

STRUT

REPLACE

LOYALE & LEGACY

Conventional Suspension

Refer to **Figs. 4 and 5,** when performing the following procedure.

1. Raise and support vehicle.
2. Remove front wheels.
3. **On Legacy models,** remove union bolts from caliper.
4. **On all models,** disconnect brake hose from caliper.
5. Remove brake hose to strut bracket retaining clip, then separate brake hose from strut bracket.
6. **On Loyale models,** proceed as follows:
   a. Remove bolts securing strut and strut bracket to axle housing.
   b. Carefully remove strut from housing with housing positioned downward.
7. **On Legacy models,** scribe an alignment mark on camber adjusting bolt.
8. **On models equipped with anti-lock brakes,** remove ABS sensor.

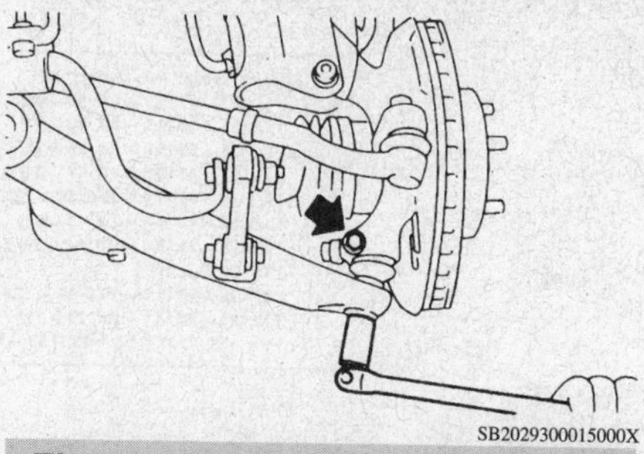
SB2029300015000X

Fig. 2 Ball joint play download dimension measurement

9. **On all models,** remove strut to body mounting bolts.
10. Remove strut assembly from vehicle.
11. Properly position strut assembly in spring compressor tool, then compress spring until it separates from upper seat.
12. **On Loyale models,** position spanner tool No. 925651000, or equivalent, to upper spring seat holes, then remove strut rod self-locking nut using a 17mm box wrench.
13. **On Legacy models,** remove strut rod self-locking nut using socket tool No. 927760000, or equivalent.
14. **On all models,** remove strut mount and associated parts.
15. Carefully release spring compressor tool.
16. Remove coil spring, then the strut from spring compressor tool.
17. Remove dust cover and helper from strut rod.
18. Reverse procedure to install, noting the following:
    a. Refer to **Figs. 4 and 5** for tightening specifications.
    b. Ensure hydraulic brake system is properly bled.
    c. Check and adjust wheel alignment as needed.

Pneumatic Suspension

Service on air spring strut assemblies is limited to replacement of the upper mount and the entire strut assembly. When performing the following procedure, refer to **Fig. 9.**

1. Ensure height control switch is turned Off and vehicle height is in "Normal" low position.
2. Disconnect battery negative cable.
3. Raise and support vehicle.
4. Remove front wheels.
5. Disconnect brake hose from caliper.
6. Remove brake hose to strut bracket retaining clip, then separate brake hose from strut bracket.
7. **On models equipped with anti-lock brakes,** remove ABS sensor.
8. **On Legacy models,** proceed as follows:
    a. Disconnect air line from solenoid valve.
    b. Disconnect solenoid valve electrical connector.
    c. Remove strut bracket to axle housing attaching bolts.
9. **On all models,** remove strut to shock tower retaining bolts and the strut assembly from vehicle.
10. Ensure all air has been discharged from air spring chamber, then remove strut mount retaining nut while holding strut shaft with spanner wrench tool No. 926510000, or equivalent. **Strut rod must be properly secured with spanner wrench to prevent damaging diaphragm.**
11. Reverse procedure to install noting the following:
    a. Refer to **Fig. 9,** for tightening specifications.
    b. Install air lines with new O-rings lightly lubricated with multi-purpose grease.
    c. Ensure hydraulic brake system is properly bled.
    d. Check and adjust wheel alignment as needed.

JUSTY

Refer to **Fig. 6,** when performing the following procedure.

1. Raise and support vehicle.
2. Remove front wheels.
3. Disconnect brake hose from strut bracket.
4. Remove bolts securing strut and strut bracket to housing. Carefully remove strut from housing with housing positioned downward.
5. Remove strut to shock tower retaining nuts and the strut assembly.
6. Properly position strut assembly in spring compressor tool. Compress spring and remove strut mount retaining nut.
7. Remove strut from spring compressor tool.
8. Remove upper washer, mount, lower washer, O-ring, strut washer, oil seal, lower strut washer, spring seat, dust cover, spring and helper bumper from strut.
9. Inspect all components for wear, and replace as necessary. **The strut assembly itself is not repairable. If strut shows signs of excessive leakage, or is damaged, it should be replaced.**
10. Reverse procedure to install, noting the following:
    a. Refer to **Fig. 6** for tightening specifications.
    b. Ensure hydraulic brake system is properly bled.

SVX

Refer to **Fig. 10,** when performing the following procedure.

1. Raise and support vehicle, then remove front wheels.
2. Remove stabilizer link, then disconnect ABS sensor clamp and brake hose clamp from strut.
3. Scribe an alignment mark on camber adjusting bolt and remove strut mounting nuts. **Do not remove strut bolts at this time.**
4. Support knuckle assembly with a suitable jack, then remove strut mount cap and three upper strut mounting nuts.

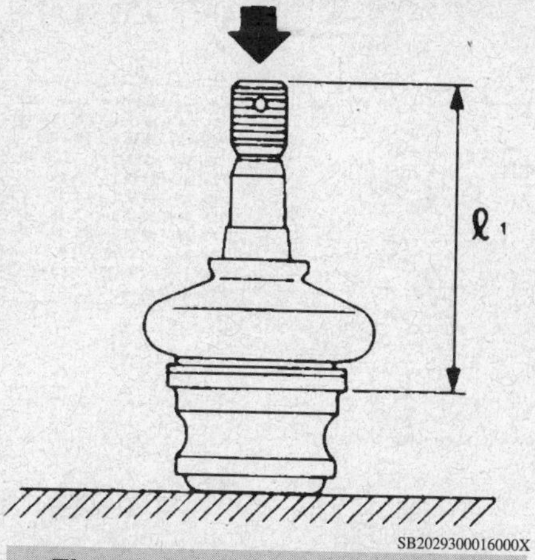
ℓ1
SB2029300016000X

Fig. 3 Ball joint play upload dimension measurement

5. Remove bolts from lower strut mounting, then the strut assembly from vehicle.
6. Compress coil spring using a suitable coil spring compressor, then remove self-locking nut using strut mount socket tool No. 20099PA000, or equivalent.
7. Remove strut mount, upper spring seat and upper rubber seat from strut assembly.
8. Remove coil spring, dust cover, helper spring and lower rubber seat.
9. Install lower rubber seat to spring seat, then install coil spring so that its end face fits into spring seat as shown in **Fig. 11.**
10. Install helper and dust cover to piston rod, ensuring helper and dust cover are aligned with graded section of piston rod as shown in **Fig. 12.**
11. Pull piston fully upward, then install rubber seat and spring seat, ensuring upper spring seat is positioned with "OUT" mark facing outward.
12. Install strut mount to piston rod, then a new self-locking nut and temporarily tighten.
13. Loosen coil spring carefully, then while fixing spring seat, tighten self-locking nut to specifications.
14. Assemble strut assembly to vehicle by reversing steps 1 through 5.

IMPREZA

Refer to **Fig. 7,** when performing the following procedure.

1. Raise and support vehicle, then remove front wheels.
2. Disconnect brake hose from caliper, then disconnect brake hose from strut.
3. Scribe alignment mark on camber adjusting bolt, then remove ABS sensor harness, if equipped.
4. Remove lower strut mounting bolts, then the upper strut mounting bolts.
5. Remove strut from vehicle.
6. Compress coil spring using a suitable coil spring compressor, then remove self-locking nut using strut mount socket tool No. 927760000, or equivalent.

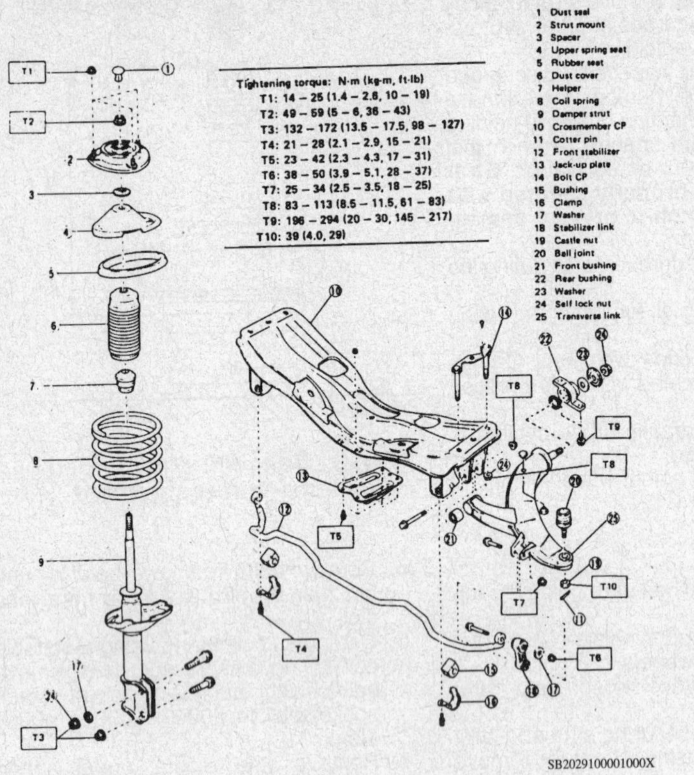
Tightening torque: N·m (kg-m, ft-lb)
T1: 14 – 25 (1.4 – 2.6, 10 – 19)
T2: 49 – 59 (5 – 6, 36 – 43)
T3: 132 – 172 (13.5 – 17.5, 98 – 127)
T4: 21 – 28 (2.1 – 2.9, 15 – 21)
T5: 23 – 42 (2.3 – 4.3, 17 – 31)
T6: 38 – 50 (3.9 – 5.1, 28 – 37)
T7: 25 – 34 (2.5 – 3.5, 18 – 25)
T8: 83 – 113 (8.5 – 11.5, 61 – 83)
T9: 196 – 294 (20 – 30, 145 – 217)
T10: 39 (4.0, 29)
1 Dust seal
2 Strut mount
3 Spacer
4 Upper spring seat
5 Rubber seat
6 Dust cover
7 Helper
8 Coil spring
9 Damper strut
10 Crossmember CP
11 Cotter pin
12 Front stabilizer
13 Jack-up plate
14 Bolt CP
15 Bushing
16 Clamp
17 Washer
18 Stabilizer link
19 Castle nut
20 Ball joint
21 Front bushing
22 Rear bushing
23 Washer
24 Self lock nut
25 Transverse link
SB2029100001000X

Fig. 4 Front suspension assembly. Legacy

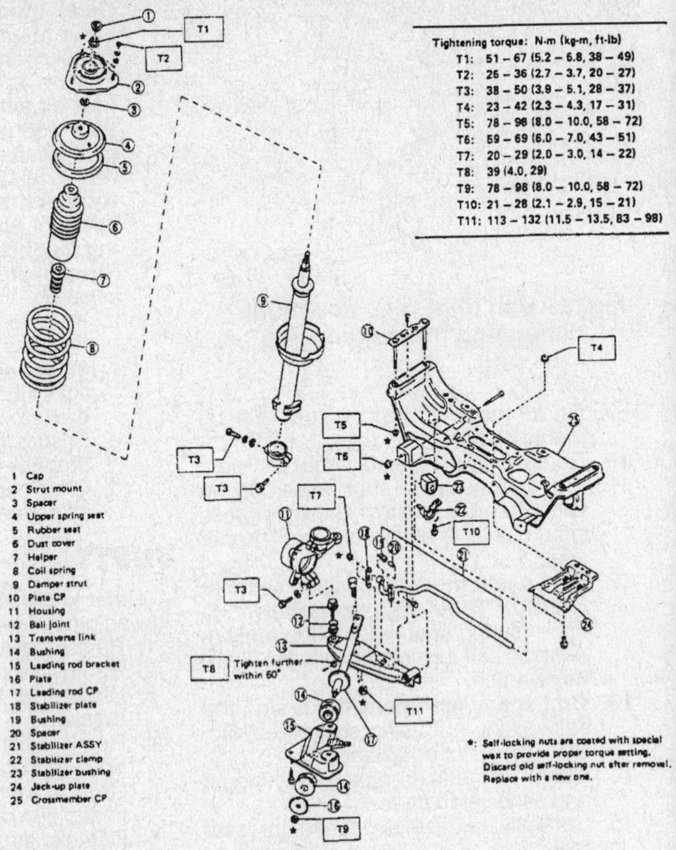
Tightening torque: N·m (kg-m, ft-lb)
T1: 51 – 67 (5.2 – 6.8, 38 – 49)
T2: 26 – 36 (2.7 – 3.7, 20 – 27)
T3: 38 – 50 (3.9 – 5.1, 28 – 37)
T4: 23 – 42 (2.3 – 4.3, 17 – 31)
T5: 78 – 98 (8.0 – 10.0, 58 – 72)
T6: 59 – 69 (6.0 – 7.0, 43 – 51)
T7: 20 – 29 (2.0 – 3.0, 14 – 22)
T8: 39 (4.0, 29)
T9: 78 – 98 (8.0 – 10.0, 58 – 72)
T10: 21 – 28 (2.1 – 2.9, 15 – 21)
T11: 113 – 132 (11.5 – 13.5, 83 – 98)
1 Cap
2 Strut mount
3 Spacer
4 Upper spring seat
5 Rubber seat
6 Dust cover
7 Helper
8 Coil spring
9 Damper strut
10 Plate CP
11 Housing
12 Ball joint
13 Transverse link
14 Bushing
15 Leading rod bracket
16 Plate
17 Leading rod CP
18 Stabilizer plate
19 Bushing
20 Spacer
21 Stabilizer ASSY
22 Stabilizer clamp
23 Stabilizer bushing
24 Jack-up plate
25 Crossmember CP
Tighten further within 60°
*: Self-locking nuts are coated with special wax to provide proper torque setting. Discard old self-locking nut after removal. Replace with a new one.
SB2029500014000X

Fig. 5 Front suspension assembly. Loyale

7. Remove strut mount, upper spring seat and upper rubber seat from strut assembly.
8. Remove coil spring, dust cover and helper spring.
9. Reverse procedure to install, noting the following:
   a. Mount coil spring with flat end towards top side and inclined end towards bottom side.
   b. Ensure upper spring seat is positioned with "Out" mark facing outward.
   c. Install strut rod with new locking nut.
   d. Refer to **Fig. 7** for tightening specifications.

CONTROL ARM

REPLACE

LOWER

SVX

Refer to **Fig. 13** when performing the following procedure.

1. Raise and support vehicle, then remove front wheels.
2. Disconnect ball joint from steering knuckle, then remove rear support. **Do not remove rear support on both sides at once.**
3. Remove lower arm.
4. Reverse procedure to install, tightening bolts to specifications with vehicle weight on suspension.

STABILIZER BAR

REPLACE

EXCEPT SVX

Refer to **Figs. 4 through 7** when performing the following procedure.

1. Raise and support vehicle.
2. Remove left and right stabilizer to transverse link retaining bolts. Separate plates from transverse link.
3. Remove left and right stabilizer clamp to crossmember retaining bolts. Separate clamps from stabilizer.
4. Remove jack-up plate and stabilizer.
5. Reverse procedure to install, noting the following:
   a. Ensure crossmember bushing is positioned in bent portion of shaft.
   b. Tighten retaining bolts with wheels on the ground and vehicle unloaded.
   c. Refer to **Figs. 4 through 7** for tightening specifications.

SVX

Refer to Fig. 14 when performing the following procedure.

1. Raise and support vehicle, then remove front wheels.
2. Remove stabilizer link, right ABS sensor clamp and right brake hose clamp.
3. Scribe an alignment mark on stabilizer and stabilizer lever, then remove both parts.
4. Remove stabilizer bushing, then the stabilizer from right side of vehicle.
5. Reverse procedure to install, aligning paint mark on stabilizer bushing.

CROSSMEMBER

REPLACE

LOYALE

Refer to **Fig. 5** when performing the following procedure.

1. Disconnect battery negative cable.
2. Remove spare tire.
3. Raise and support vehicle.
4. Remove front wheels.
5. Remove air cleaner assembly and pitching stopper rod. **Install a dust cover over carburetor to prevent entry of foreign material.**
6. Remove parking brake cable bracket from transverse link.
7. Remove ball stud cotter pin and castle nut and disconnect tie rod from housing knuckle arm.
8. Remove front exhaust pipe.
9. Remove nut from transverse link bushing and disconnect link from crossmember.
10. Remove engine mount to crossmember retaining link.
11. Remove torque rod to pinion shaft retaining bolts.
12. Raise engine .39 inches (10mm) using a suitable chain hoist or jack.
13. Position a suitable jack under the crossmember.

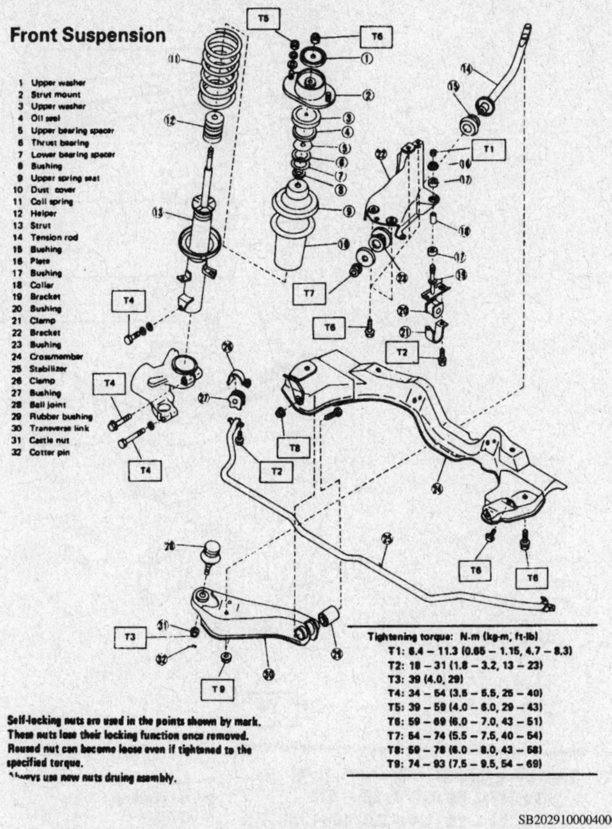
Front Suspension
1 Upper washer
2 Strut mount
3 Upper washer
4 Oil seal
5 Upper bearing spacer
6 Thrust bearing
7 Lower bearing spacer
8 Bushing
9 Upper spring seat
10 Dust cover
11 Coil spring
12 Helper
13 Strut
14 Tension rod
15 Bushing
16 Plate
17 Bushing
18 Collar
19 Bracket
20 Bushing
21 Clamp
22 Bracket
23 Bushing
24 Crossmember
25 Stabilizer
26 Clamp
27 Bushing
28 Ball joint
29 Rubber bushing
30 Transverse link
31 Castle nut
32 Cotter pin
Self-locking nuts are used in the points shown by mark.
These nuts lose their locking function once removed.
Reused nut can become loose even if tightened to the specified torque.
Always use new nuts druing asembly.
Tightening torque: N-m (kg-m, ft-lb)
T1: 6.4 – 11.3 (0.65 – 1.15, 4.7 – 8.3)
T2: 18 – 31 (1.8 – 3.2, 13 – 23)
T3: 39 (4.0, 29)
T4: 34 – 54 (3.5 – 5.5, 25 – 40)
T5: 39 – 59 (4.0 – 6.0, 29 – 43)
T6: 59 – 69 (6.0 – 7.0, 43 – 51)
T7: 54 – 74 (5.5 – 7.5, 40 – 54)
T8: 59 – 78 (6.0 – 8.0, 43 – 58)
T9: 74 – 93 (7.5 – 9.5, 54 – 69)
SB2029100004000X

Fig. 6 Front suspension assembly. Justy

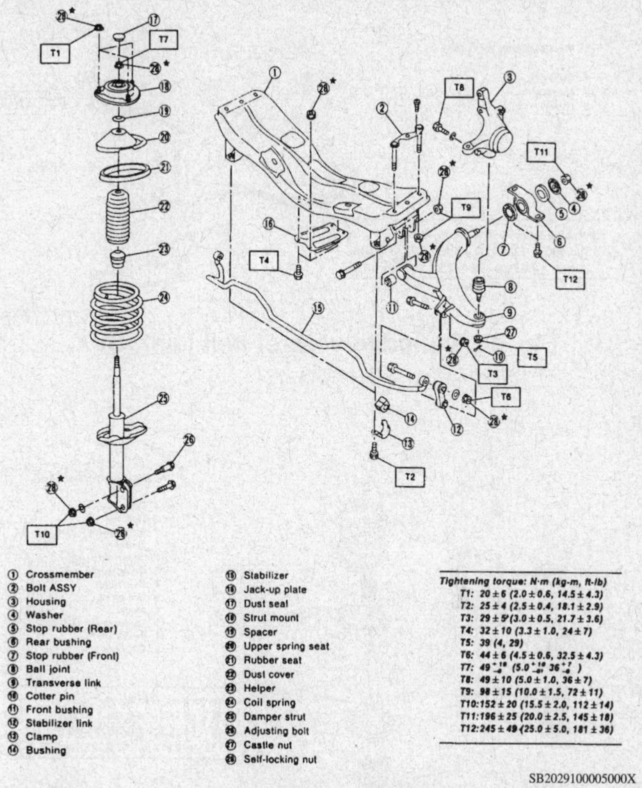
① Crossmember
② Bolt ASSY
③ Housing
④ Washer
⑤ Stop rubber (Rear)
⑥ Rear bushing
⑦ Stop rubber (Front)
⑧ Ball joint
⑨ Transverse link
⑩ Cotter pin
⑪ Front bushing
⑫ Stabilizer link
⑬ Clamp
⑭ Bushing
⑮ Stabilizer
⑯ Jack-up plate
⑰ Dust seal
⑱ Strut mount
⑲ Spacer
⑳ Upper spring seat
㉑ Rubber seat
㉒ Dust cover
㉓ Helper
㉔ Coil spring
㉕ Damper strut
㉖ Adjusting bolt
㉗ Castle nut
㉘ Self-locking nut
Tightening torque: N·m (kg-m, ft-lb)
T1: 20 ± 6 (2.0 ± 0.6, 14.5 ± 4.3)
T2: 25 ± 4 (2.5 ± 0.4, 18.1 ± 2.9)
T3: 29 ± 5 (3.0 ± 0.5, 21.7 ± 3.6)
T4: 32 ± 10 (3.3 ± 1.0, 24 ± 7)
T5: 39 (4, 29)
T6: 44 ± 6 (4.5 ± 0.6, 32.5 ± 4.3)
T7: 49^{+10}_{-4} ($5.0^{+1.0}_{-0.4}$, 36^{+7}_{-3})
T8: 49 ± 10 (5.0 ± 1.0, 36 ± 7)
T9: 98 ± 15 (10.0 ± 1.5, 72 ± 11)
T10: 152 ± 20 (15.5 ± 2.0, 112 ± 14)
T11: 196 ± 25 (20.0 ± 2.5, 145 ± 18)
T12: 245 ± 49 (25.0 ± 5.0, 181 ± 36)
SB2029100005000X

Fig. 7 Front suspension assembly. Impreza

14. Remove crossmember to body retaining nuts and carefully lower crossmember from vehicle.
15. Reverse procedure to install. Refer to **Fig. 5,** for tightening specifications.

JUSTY

Refer to **Fig. 6** when performing the following procedure.

1. Raise and support vehicle.
2. Remove front wheels.
3. Support engine using tool No. 921540000, or equivalent.
4. Remove center undercover.
5. Remove engine mount center member attaching nuts and bolts, then the center member.
6. Remove exhaust system.
7. Remove transverse link to crossmember attaching bolts.
8. Remove engine mount to crossmember attaching nut at crossmember connection.
9. Remove crossmember to body attaching bolt and the crossmember.
10. Reverse procedure to install. Refer to **Fig. 6** for tightening specifications.

IMPREZA & LEGACY

Refer to **Figs. 4 and 7** when performing the following procedure.

1. Raise and support vehicle.
2. Remove stabilizer assembly as outlined under "Stabilizer Bar, Replace."
3. Disconnect tie-rod ends from housing.
4. Remove front exhaust pipe.
5. Remove transverse link to crossmember retaining bolts.
6. Remove engine mount to crossmember retaining nuts.
7. Remove steering torque rod to pinion shaft self-locking nuts.
8. Using a suitable lift, raise engine approximately .39 inch.
9. Support crossmember with a suitable jack, then remove crossmember retaining nuts.
10. Lower crossmember from vehicle.
11. Reverse procedure to install. Refer to **Figs. 4 and 7** for tightening specifications.

POWER STEERING GEAR

REPLACE

EXCEPT SVX

Removal

1. Disconnect battery negative cable.
2. **On Loyale models,** remove spare tire and support, then disconnect thermo sensor electrical connector.
3. **On all models,** raise and support vehicle.
4. Remove front wheels.
5. Remove front exhaust pipe assembly.
6. Disconnect tie-rod ends from steering knuckles.
7. Remove jack-up plate and stabilizer bushing clamp from crossmember.
8. Disconnect fluid lines at center of steering gear. Connect extension tubing and discharge fluid by turning steering wheel from lock to lock.
9. Remove upper and lower universal joint to steering gear and intermediate shaft retaining bolts. Scribe matching marks between shaft, universal joint and steering gear, then disconnect joint from steering gear.
10. Disconnect fluid lines from upper then the lower side of steering gear control valve housing.
11. Remove steering gear clamp bolts, then the steering gear.

Installation

1. Position steering gear on crossmember, then install clamps and retaining bolts.
2. Connect fluid lines to lower port of valve housing and to center ports of gear. Connect the upper line first.
3. Connect fluid lines to upper ports of valve housing. Connect the lower line first.
4. Install steering shaft joint as follows:
   a. Align bolt hole on long end of yoke with notch in steering shaft and push joint onto shaft.
   b. Align bolt hole in short end of yoke with notch in steering gear pinion shaft and engage yoke with pinion shaft.
   c. Align matching marks made during removal.
   d. Install universal yoke retaining bolts. Ensure both bolts are properly engaged in shaft notches, then tighten bolts to specifications.
5. Reverse remaining procedure to complete installation. Tighten bolts and

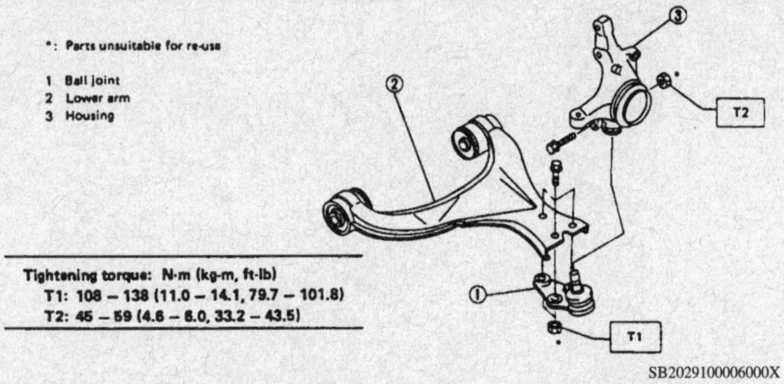
*: Parts unsuitable for re-use
1 Ball joint
2 Lower arm
3 Housing
Tightening torque: N·m (kg-m, ft-lb)
T1: 108 – 138 (11.0 – 14.1, 79.7 – 101.8)
T2: 45 – 59 (4.6 – 6.0, 33.2 – 43.5)
T1
T2
SB2029100006000X

Fig. 8 Exploded view of ball joint. SVX

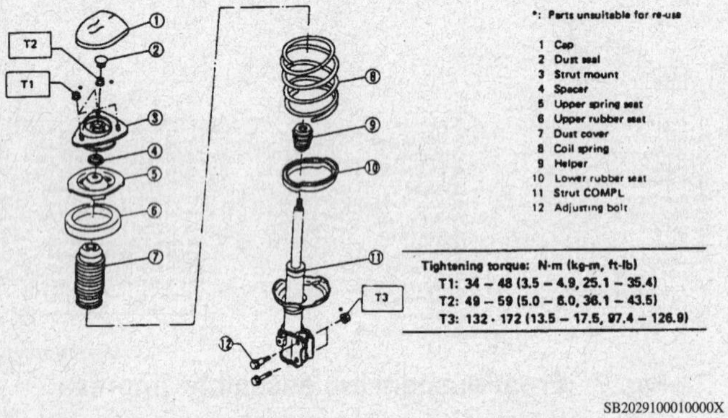
*: Parts unsuitable for re-use
1 Cap
2 Dust seal
3 Strut mount
4 Spacer
5 Upper spring seat
6 Upper rubber seat
7 Dust cover
8 Coil spring
9 Helper
10 Lower rubber seat
11 Strut COMPL
12 Adjusting bolt
Tightening torque: N·m (kg-m, ft-lb)
T1: 34 – 48 (3.5 – 4.9, 25.1 – 35.4)
T2: 49 – 59 (5.0 – 6.0, 36.1 – 43.5)
T3: 132 - 172 (13.5 – 17.5, 97.4 – 126.9)
T1
T2
T3
SB2029100010000X

Fig. 10 Exploded view of strut assembly. SVX

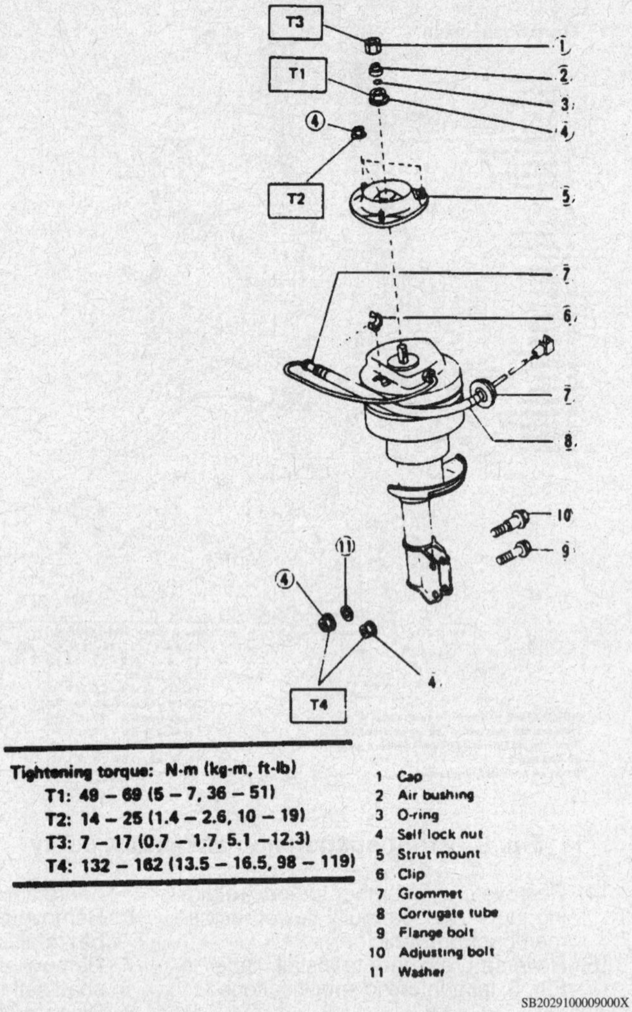
T1
T2
T3
T4
Tightening torque: N·m (kg-m, ft-lb)
T1: 49 – 69 (5 – 7, 36 – 51)
T2: 14 – 25 (1.4 – 2.6, 10 – 19)
T3: 7 – 17 (0.7 – 1.7, 5.1 – 12.3)
T4: 132 – 162 (13.5 – 16.5, 98 – 119)
1 Cap
2 Air bushing
3 O-ring
4 Self lock nut
5 Strut mount
6 Clip
7 Grommet
8 Corrugate tube
9 Flange bolt
10 Adjusting bolt
11 Washer
SB2029100009000X

Fig. 9 Pneumatic suspension components. Legacy

nuts to specifications.

SVX

Refer to **Fig. 15** when performing the following procedure.

1. Disconnect battery ground cable, oxygen sensor and steering harness electrical connector, if equipped.
2. Raise and support vehicle, then remove front wheels.
3. Remove undercover, then disconnect oxygen sensor harness from clip.
4. Remove collector cover and rear catalytic converter protector, then disconnect front exhaust pipe.
5. Using a suitable puller, disconnect tie rod ends from steering knuckles.
6. Remove spring pin securing transaxle spindle to inner CV joint, then remove inner CV joint from transaxle spindle and free from transaxle.
7. Disconnect pipe joint from upper hose, then drain fluid by rotating steering wheel left and right. Also disconnect other pipe and drain fluid.
8. Disconnect performance rod, then the lower arm ball joint from steering knuckle. Cover ball joint with a cloth to prevent damage.
9. Scribe alignment marks on upper and lower part of universal joint, then remove upper and lower universal joint bolts.
10. Remove universal joint in an upward direction, then the bolts securing gearbox to subframe and disconnect gearbox. **Do not turn steering wheel or misalignment of air bag system rollconnector may occur.**
11. Turn gearbox assembly around so that control valve faces rear, then move gearbox assembly full right so that left tie rod end can be removed from subframe.
12. Remove gearbox assembly from vehicle.
13. Reverse procedure to install.

POWER STEERING PUMP

REPLACE

SVX

Refer to **Fig. 15** when performing the following procedure.

1. Disconnect battery ground cable, then remove belt cover.
2. Loosen idler pulley nuts and slider bolt, then remove V-belt.
3. Remove pump pulley, then disconnect pump switch electrical connector.
4. Drain approximately 0.3 qts. of fluid from reservoir, then disconnect hose from reservoir.
5. Disconnect pressure pipe from pump, then remove pump and reservoir assembly.
6. Reverse procedure to install.

IMPREZA & LEGACY

1. Remove battery ground cable, then drain power steering fluid from reservoir.
2. Remove pulley belt cover bracket.
3. Loosen pump pulley nut, then remove alternator mounting bolts.
4. Loosen pulley belt(s), then remove pump pulley nut and pump pulley.
5. Disconnect and plug fluid lines from pump. Disconnect solid line first.
6. Remove 3 front pump mounting bolts, then the pump assembly.
7. Remove bracket mounting bolts, then the bracket.
8. Remove reservoir from pump.
9. Reverse procedure to install.

MANUAL STEERING GEAR

REPLACE

LOYALE & JUSTY

1. Disconnect battery negative cable.
2. Raise and support vehicle.
3. Remove front wheels.

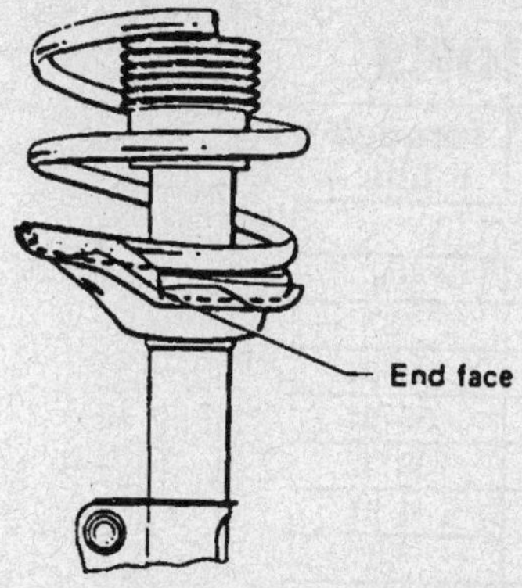
End face
SB2029100011000X

Fig. 11 Aligning coil spring. SVX

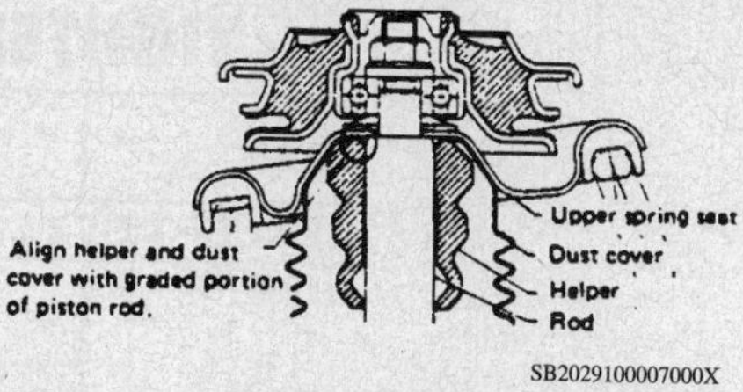
Align helper and dust cover with graded portion of piston rod.
Upper spring seat
Dust cover
Helper
Rod
SB2029100007000X

Fig. 12 Aligning helper & dust cover. SVX

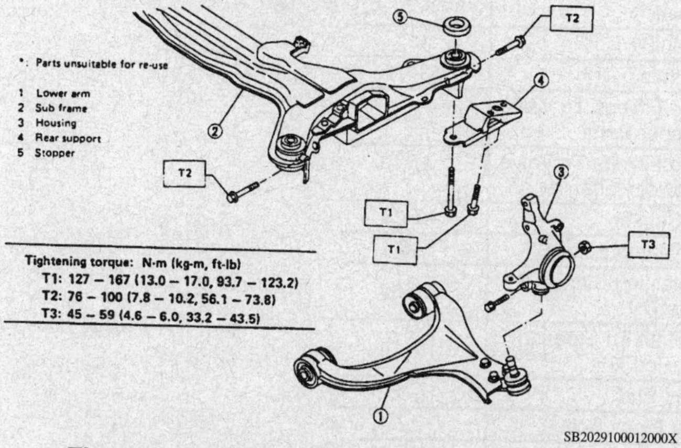
*: Parts unsuitable for re-use
1 Lower arm
2 Sub frame
3 Housing
4 Rear support
5 Stopper
T1
T2
T3
Tightening torque: N·m (kg-m, ft-lb)
T1: 127 – 167 (13.0 – 17.0, 93.7 – 123.2)
T2: 76 – 100 (7.8 – 10.2, 56.1 – 73.8)
T3: 45 – 59 (4.6 – 6.0, 33.2 – 43.5)
SB2029100012000X

Fig. 13 Exploded view of lower arm. SVX

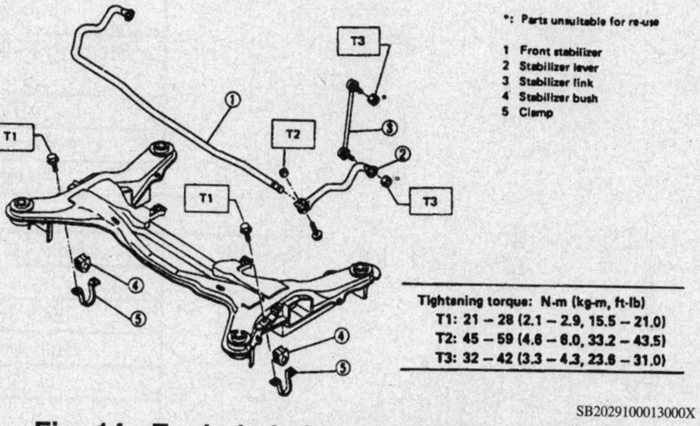
*: Parts unsuitable for re-use
1 Front stabilizer
2 Stabilizer lever
3 Stabilizer link
4 Stabilizer bush
5 Clamp
T1
T2
T3
Tightening torque: N·m (kg-m, ft-lb)
T1: 21 – 28 (2.1 – 2.9, 15.5 – 21.0)
T2: 45 – 59 (4.6 – 6.0, 33.2 – 43.5)
T3: 32 – 42 (3.3 – 4.3, 23.6 – 31.0)
SB2029100013000X

Fig. 14 Exploded view of stabilizer bar. SVX

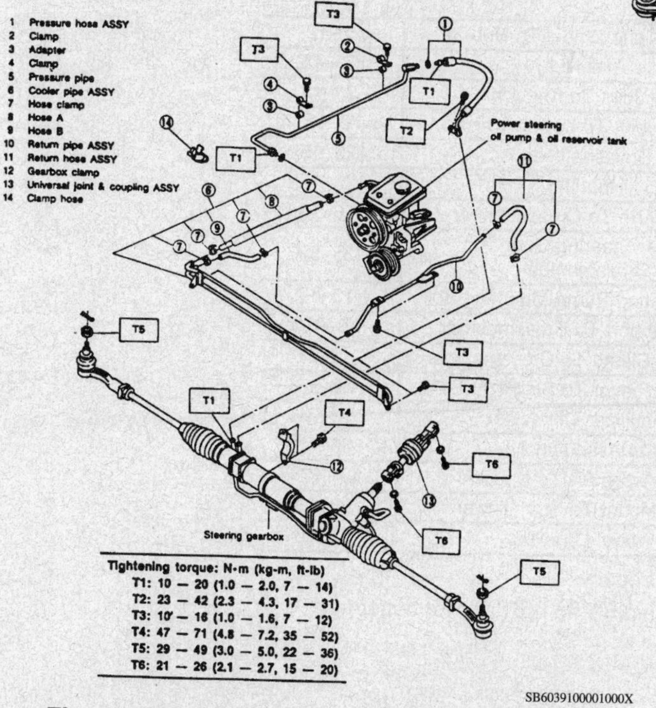
1 Pressure hose ASSY
2 Clamp
3 Adapter
4 Clamp
5 Pressure pipe
6 Cooler pipe ASSY
7 Hose clamp
8 Hose A
9 Hose B
10 Return pipe ASSY
11 Return hose ASSY
12 Gearbox clamp
13 Universal joint & coupling ASSY
14 Clamp hose
Power steering oil pump & oil reservoir tank
Steering gearbox
T1
T2
T3
T4
T5
T6
Tightening torque: N·m (kg-m, ft-lb)
T1: 10 — 20 (1.0 — 2.0, 7 — 14)
T2: 23 — 42 (2.3 — 4.3, 17 — 31)
T3: 10 — 16 (1.0 — 1.6, 7 — 12)
T4: 47 — 71 (4.8 — 7.2, 35 — 52)
T5: 29 — 49 (3.0 — 5.0, 22 — 36)
T6: 21 — 26 (2.1 — 2.7, 15 — 20)
SB6039100001000X

Fig. 15 Power steering gear & pump. SVX

4. Disconnect tie-rod ends from steering knuckles.
5. Remove steering shaft universal joint to steering gear pinch bolt.
6. Disconnect exhaust pipe from manifold.
7. Remove four steering gear mounting bolts.
8. Withdraw steering gear toward pinion side until shaft disengages torque rod universal joint, then rotate steering gear rearward and remove from vehicle.
9. Reverse procedure to install. Tighten bolts and nuts to specifications.

TIGHTENING SPECIFICATIONS

Year	Component	Torque/Ft. Lbs.
EXCEPT SVX		
1993–96	Axle Nut①	②
	Axle Nut③	137
	Brake Caliper③	36–51
	Caliper Mount Bracket①④	36–51
	Caliper Mount Bracket⑤	38–48
	Disc Brake Rotor Splash Shield③	7–13
	Driveshaft Nut①	②
	Driveshaft Nut③	137
	Engine Mount To Crossmember④	14–24
	Hub Nut①	②
	Hub Nut③	137
	Lug Nuts	58–72
1993–96	Power Steering Line Fittings To Valve Housing Upper Ports	7–14
	Power Steering Line Fittings To Valve Housing Lower Ports	7–12
	Speed Sensor	14–29
	Steering Gear Clamp Bolts⑥	48
	Steering Gear Retaining Clamps & Bolts⑦	35–52
	Steering Pinion Shaft To Steering Torque Rod④	10–14
	Tie Rod End	18–22
	Universal Joint Pinch Bolt⑥	17
	Universal Yoke	16–19
SVX		
1993–96	ABS Tone Wheel To Hub	7–12
	Axle Nut	123–152
	Ball Joint To Knuckle	33–43
	Ball Joint To Lower Arm	79–101
	Driveshaft Nut	123–152
	Hub Nut	123–152
	Lower Arm To Crossmember	56–73
	Power Steering Gear To Crossmember	35–52
	Power Steering Pump Mounting Bolts	13–17
	Rear Support To Crossmember	93–123
	Stabilizer Clamp To Crossmember	15–21
	Stabilizer Lever To Stabilizer Bar	33–43
	Stabilizer Link Nuts	23–31
	Strut Assembly Nut	36–43
	Strut Assembly To Knuckle	97–126
	Strut Mount To Strut Tower	25–35
	Wheel Lug Nuts	72–86

① — Except Impreza & Legacy.

② — 145 ft. lbs. and within 30° to next slot for cotter key installation.

③ — Impreza & Legacy.

④ — Except Justy.

⑤ — Justy.

⑥ — Manual Steering Gear.

⑦ — Power Steering Gear.

Wheel Alignment

INDEX

	Page No.
Front Wheel Alignment	39-57
Camber	39-57
Caster	39-57
Toe-In	39-57
Rear Wheel Alignment	39-57
Camber	39-57
Toe-In	39-57
Vehicle Ride Height	39-57
Wheel Alignment Specifications	39-4

FRONT WHEEL ALIGNMENT

CASTER

Caster angles are not adjustable. If caster is not within specifications, inspect suspension components for damage and repair as necessary, then recheck wheel alignment.

CAMBER

Justy & Loyale

Camber angles are not adjustable. If camber is not within specifications, inspect suspension components for damage and repair as necessary, then recheck wheel alignment.

Impreza, Legacy & SVX

Adjust camber angles to specifications by rotating the strut mounting bolt as shown in **Fig. 1**.

TOE-IN

1. Loosen both left and right tie rod locknuts.
2. Turn left and right tie rods an equal amount until toe-in is within specifications.
3. To increase toe-in, turn both tie rods counterclockwise an equal amount.

REAR WHEEL ALIGNMENT

CAMBER

Loyale

1. Raise and support vehicle.
2. Remove rear wheels.
3. Remove lower shock absorber to inner arm attaching bolt, then loosen outer arm mounting bolts, **Fig. 2.**
4. If camber angle is excessive in positive direction, use a piece of wood as a lever and change angle as necessary so that angle formed by inner arm and outer arm center lines increases, **Fig. 3.**
5. If camber angle is excessive in negative direction, use a piece of wood as a lever and change angle as necessary so that angle formed by inner arm and outer arm center lines decreases, **Fig. 3.**
6. Install shock absorber and tighten loosened bolts.

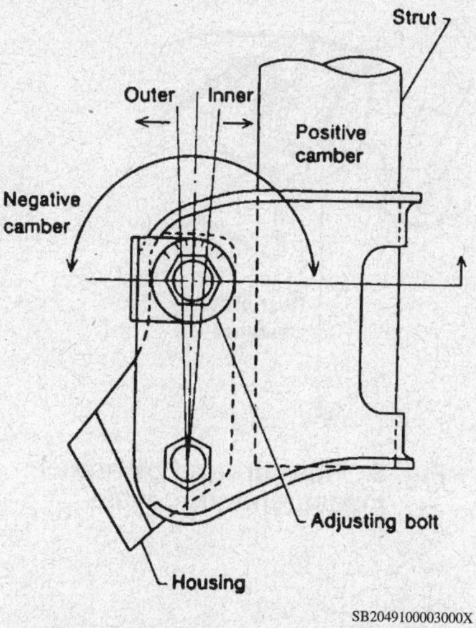

Strut
Outer
Inner
Positive camber
Negative camber
Adjusting bolt
Housing
SB2049100003000X

Fig. 1 Camber adjustment bolt location. Impreza, Legacy & SVX

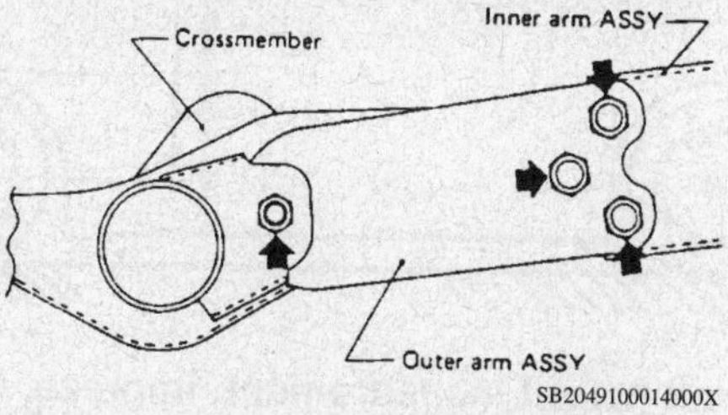

Crossmember
Inner arm ASSY
Outer arm ASSY
SB2049100014000X

Fig. 3 Rear camber adjustment. Loyale

Impreza, Justy, Legacy & SVX

Camber angles cannot be adjusted. If camber is not within specifications, inspect suspension components for damage and replace as necessary, then recheck wheel alignment.

TOE-IN

Loyale

1. Raise and support vehicle.
2. Remove rear wheels.
3. Loosen outer arm mounting bolts, **Fig. 2.**
4. If toe-in is excessive, tighten outer arm mounting bolts while pushing end of spindle towards rear of vehicle.
5. If toe-out is excessive, tighten outer arm mounting bolts while pulling end of spindle toward front of vehicle.

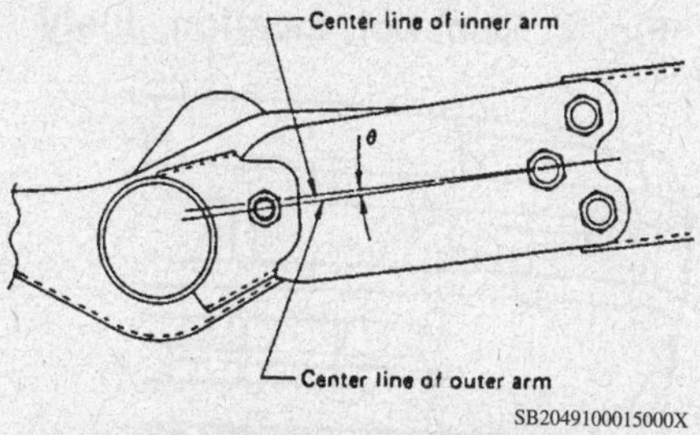

Center line of inner arm
θ
Center line of outer arm
SB2049100015000X

Fig. 2 Outer arm mounting bolts. Loyale

6. Tighten outer arm attaching mounting bolt.

Justy

1. Release parking brake lever.
2. Loosen cam bolt locknut approximately ½ turn, **Fig. 4.**
3. Turn cam bolt in opposite direction of that required to eliminate freeplay, then turn cam bolt as required and adjust toe-in. **Each scale mark on cam represents a .12 inch change in toe-in setting.**
4. After adjustment is completed, tighten locknut.

Impreza, Legacy & SVX

1. **On FWD models,** rotate bolt at lateral link, **Fig. 5,** clockwise while turning adjusting wheel counterclockwise to adjust toe-in. Rotate bolt counterclockwise while turning adjusting wheel clockwise to adjust toe-out.
2. **On SVX, AWD Impreza and Legacy models,** rotate bolt at lateral link, **Fig. 6,** clockwise to adjust toe-in. Rotate bolt counterclockwise to adjust toe-out.

VEHICLE RIDE HEIGHT

1. Park vehicle on a level surface.
2. Ensure tires are properly inflated.
3. **On Justy and Loyale models,** measure clearance as follows:
   a. On front of vehicle, measure between front of transverse link attaching bolt and the ground, **Fig. 7.**
   b. **On Loyale models,** on rear of vehicle measure between lowest point of rear crossmember and the ground, **Fig. 8.**
   c. **On Justy models,** on rear of vehicle measure between trailing link front bushing mount and the ground, **Fig. 9.**

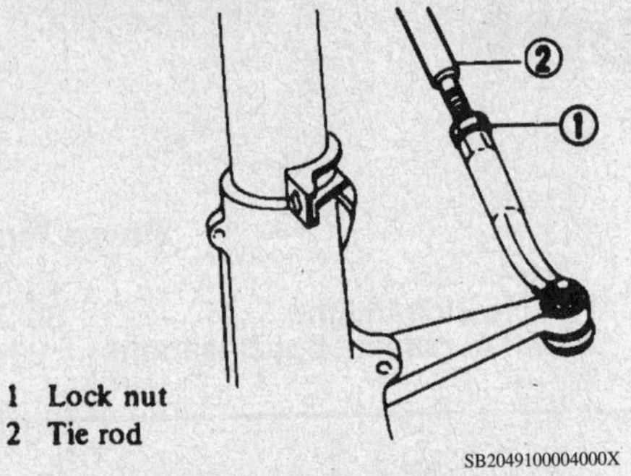
1 Lock nut
2 Tie rod
SB2049100004000X

Fig. 4 Cam bolt location. Justy

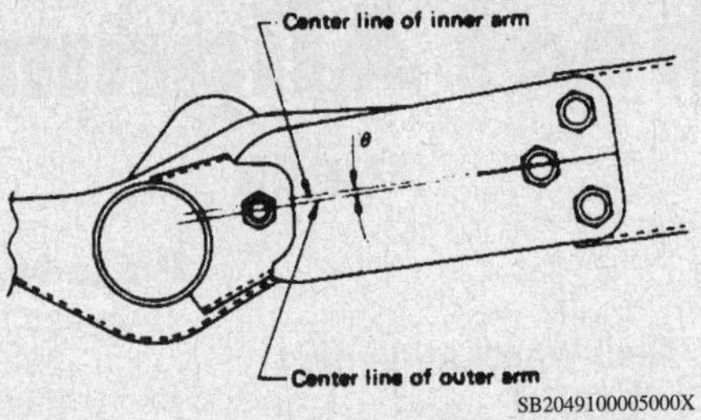
Center line of inner arm
Center line of outer arm
SB2049100005000X

Fig. 5 Rear toe-in adjustment bolt location. FWD Impreza & Legacy

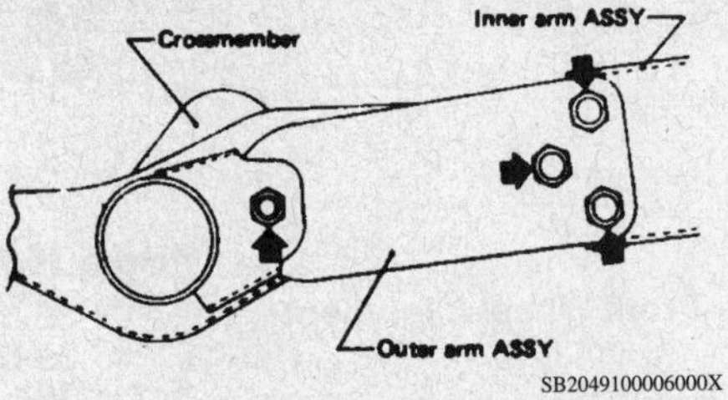
Crossmember
Inner arm ASSY
Outer arm ASSY
SB2049100006000X

Fig. 6 Rear toe-in adjustment bolt location. SVX, AWD Impreza & Legacy

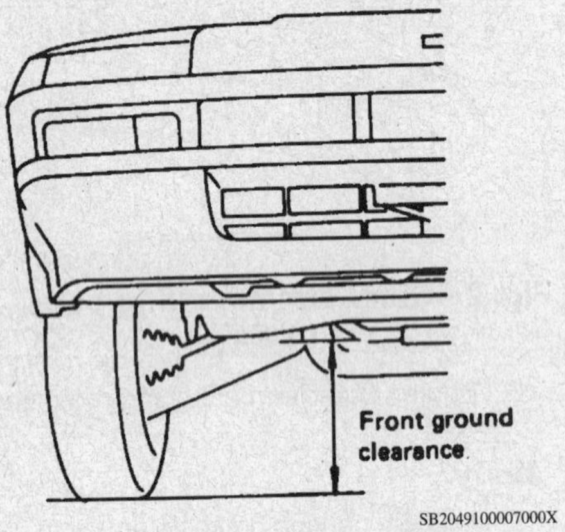
Front ground clearance
SB2049100007000X

Fig. 7 Front ground clearance measurement

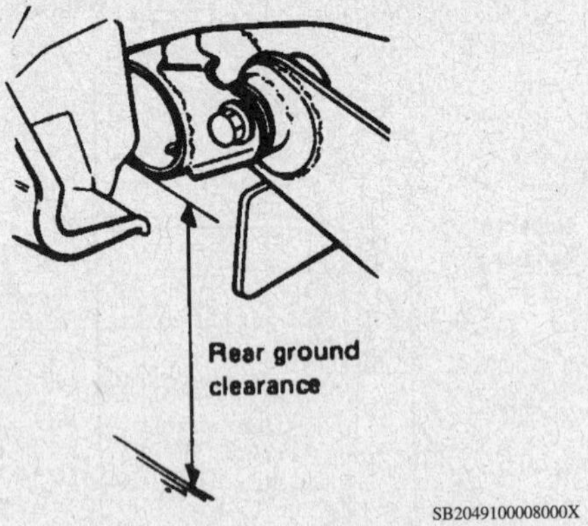
Rear ground clearance
SB2049100008000X

Fig. 8 Rear ground clearance measurement. Loyale

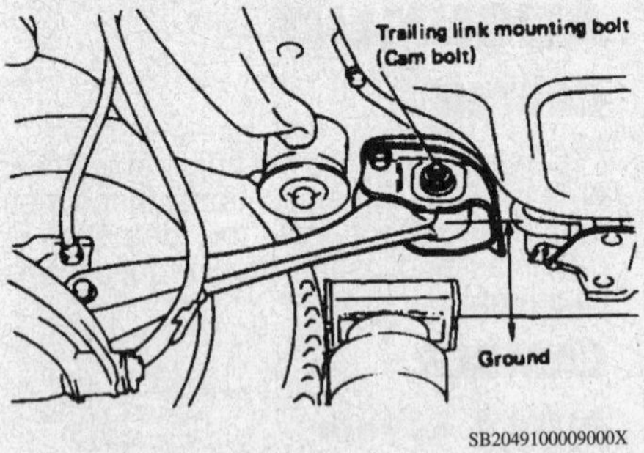
Trailing link mounting bolt (Cam bolt)
Ground
SB2049100009000X

Fig. 9 Rear ground clearance measurement. Justy

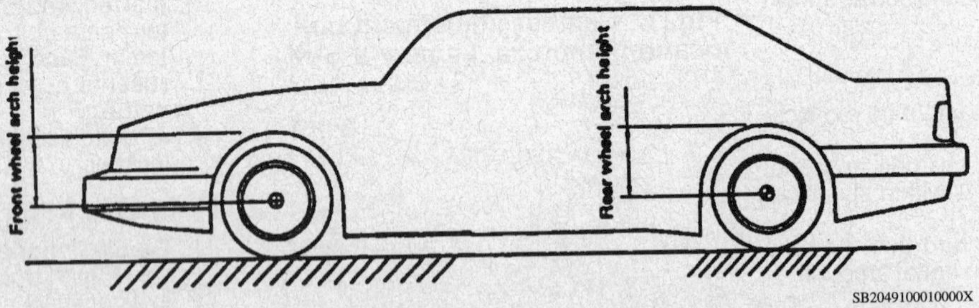
Front wheel arch height
Rear wheel arch height
SB2049100010000X

Fig. 10 Wheel arch height measurement. Impreza, Legacy & SVX

4. **On Impreza, Legacy and SVX models,** take wheel arch height measurements as shown in **Fig. 10.**
5. **On all models,** refer to **Fig. 11.** If clearances are not as specified proceed as follows:
   a. **On conventional suspension,** replace the respective coil springs.
   b. **On pneumatic suspensions,** check for leaking air line or tank fittings, leaking or defective solenoid valves, defective control unit or height sensors. Repair as needed.

Model	Year	Body Style	Ride Height Inch					
			Front			Rear		
			Minimum	Maximum	Preferred	Minimum	Maximum	Preferred
AWD MODELS								
Impreza	1993–94	All	14.45	15.86	15.39	13.98	15.39	14.92
	1995	All	14.45	15.86	15.39	14.53	15.31	14.92
Justy	1993–94	All	9.45	10.63	10.24	10.63	11.81	11.42
Legacy	1993–94	Sedan①	14.49	15.67	15.28	13.74	14.92	14.53
		Sedan②	13.54	14.72	14.33	13.54	14.72	14.33
		Wagon③	14.49	15.67	15.28	14.13	15.31	14.92
		Wagon④	14.49	15.67	15.28	13.74	14.92	14.53
	1995–96	Sedan	14.22	15.63	15.16	13.39	15.00	14.53
		Wagon	14.22	15.63	15.16	13.98	15.39	14.92
Loyale	1993–94	Coupe	9.60	10.94	10.47	9.64	10.82	10.43
		Sedan	9.60	10.94	10.47	9.64	10.82	10.43
		Wagon	9.76	11.1	10.63	10.19	11.37	10.98
SVX	1993–96	All	14.17	15.34	14.95	12.40	13.58	13.19
FWD MODELS								
Impreza	1993–94	All	14.45	15.86	15.39	13.94	15.35	14.88
	1995–96	All	14.45	15.86	15.39	14.49	15.27	14.88
Justy	1993–94	All	9.45	10.63	10.24	10.63	11.81	11.42
Legacy	1993–94	Sedan	14.09	15.27	14.88	13.34	14.52	14.13
		Wagon	14.09	15.27	14.88	13.74	14.92	14.53
	1995–96	Sedan	14.22	15.63	15.16	13.59	15.00	14.53
		Wagon	14.22	15.63	15.16	13.98	15.39	14.92
Loyale	1993–94	Coupe	8.42	9.76	9.29	7.75	8.93	8.54
		Sedan	8.42	9.76	9.29	7.75	8.93	8.54
		Wagon	8.66	10.00	9.53	8.54	9.72	9.33

① — Less turbo.
② — With turbo.
③ — Less air suspension.
④ — With air suspension.

Fig. 11 Vehicle ride height specifications

Air Conditioning

INDEX

Page No.		Page No.		Page No.	
A/C Specifications	39-64	Loyale	39-63	Impreza & SVX	39-60
Belt Tension Data	39-64	SVX	39-63	Legacy & Loyale	39-60
Oil Charge	39-60	**Oil Level Check**	39-63	**Precautions**	39-60
Impreza	39-60	**Performance Test**	39-60	Air Conditioning System	39-60
Legacy	39-63				

PRECAUTIONS

AIR CONDITIONING SYSTEM

1. Do not interchange parts between a R12 system and R134a system.
2. Do not use compressor oil that is not specifically designated for the R134a system.
3. The compressor oil used in R134a systems absorbs water very easily. When any system component is being removed, quickly install a blind plug to prevent contact with the outside air. **Ensure the service container for the compressor oil is tightly closed.**
4. Do not put R12 refrigerant into a R134a system.
5. Do not put R134a refrigerant into a R12 system.
6. Refrigerant boils at approximately -22°F (-30°C), it is cold enough to cause severe frostbite. Always wear goggles and gloves when working on an A/C system.
7. Never expose a container of R134a refrigerant to direct sunlight or to temperatures over 104°F (40°C). Exposure to this kind of heat could cause the pressure inside the container to increase to a dangerous level.
8. When R134a refrigerant is exposed to an open flame or hot metal it forms phosgene, a deadly gas. Never discharge R134a refrigerant directly into the atmosphere.

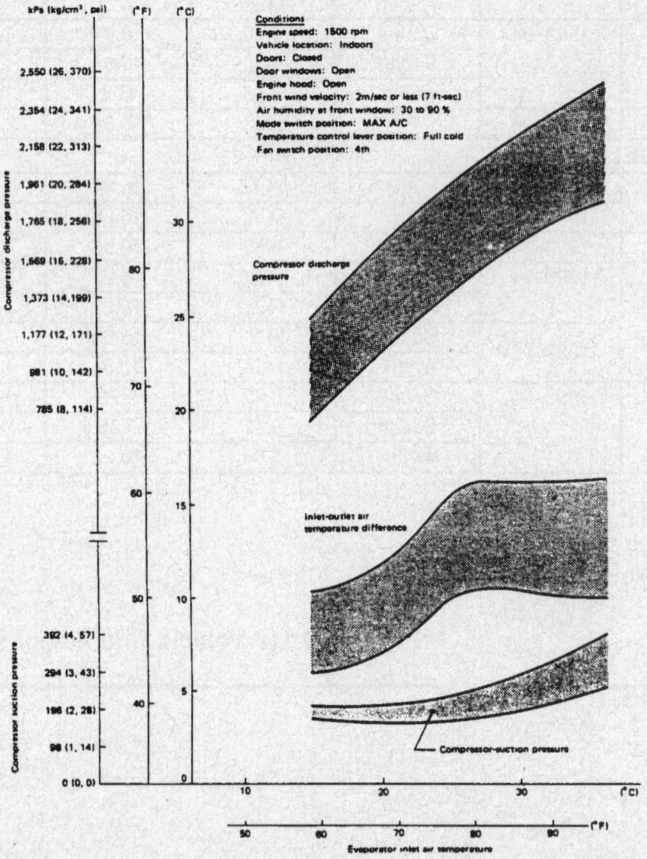

kPa (kg/cm², psi)
(°F)
(°C)
Conditions
Engine speed: 1500 rpm
Vehicle location: Indoors
Doors: Closed
Door windows: Open
Engine hood: Open
Front wind velocity: 2m/sec or less (7 ft-sec)
Air humidity at front window: 30 to 90 %
Mode switch position: MAX A/C
Temperature control lever position: Full cold
Fan switch position: 4th
2,550 (26, 370)
2,354 (24, 341)
2,158 (22, 313)
1,961 (20, 284)
1,765 (18, 256)
1,569 (16, 228)
1,373 (14, 199)
1,177 (12, 171)
981 (10, 142)
785 (8, 114)
Compressor discharge pressure
392 (4, 57)
294 (3, 43)
196 (2, 28)
98 (1, 14)
0 (0, 0)
Compressor suction pressure
80
70
60
50
40
30
25
20
15
10
5
0
Compressor discharge pressure
Inlet-outlet air temperature difference
Compressor-suction pressure
10
20
30
(°C)
50
60
70
80
90
(°F)
Evaporator inlet air temperature

SB7029100024000X

Fig. 1 Air conditioning system performance chart. Legacy w/Calsonic compressor

PERFORMANCE TEST

LEGACY & LOYALE

The cooling performance of the air conditioner changes considerably with changes in surrounding conditions. To check for correct system operation, follow procedure outlined below:

1. Park the vehicle indoors or in the shade.
2. Open all the windows in the vehicle, keeping doors closed.
3. Connect manifold gauge set to high and low side service valves of the system.
4. Set mode switch to A/C MAX position, then air inlet control switch to CIRC.
5. Set temperature lever to COLD position.
6. Start engine and hold speed at 1,500 RPM.
7. After the air conditioner has been operating for 10 minutes, measure system pressures at high pressure (discharge side) and low pressure (suction) side.
8. Measure the temperatures of inlet air to blower and outlet air at the dash panel grilles.
9. Measure the temperature and humidity of the ambient air at a point 3.3 feet from the front of the condenser.
10. Check for any abnormalities by comparing the test results with standard pressure in performance charts **Figs. 1 through 4.**
11. The pressure will change in the following manner with changes in the conditions:
    a. When blower speed is low, discharge pressure will drop.
    b. When the humidity of intake air is low, discharge pressure will drop.
12. The temperature will change in the following manner with changes in conditions:
    a. When ambient air temperature is low, the outlet air temperature will become low.

IMPREZA & SVX

Refer to **Figs. 5 and 6,** for system performance test.

OIL CHARGE

IMPREZA

If compressor is replaced, drain oil from old compressor and measure, then drain

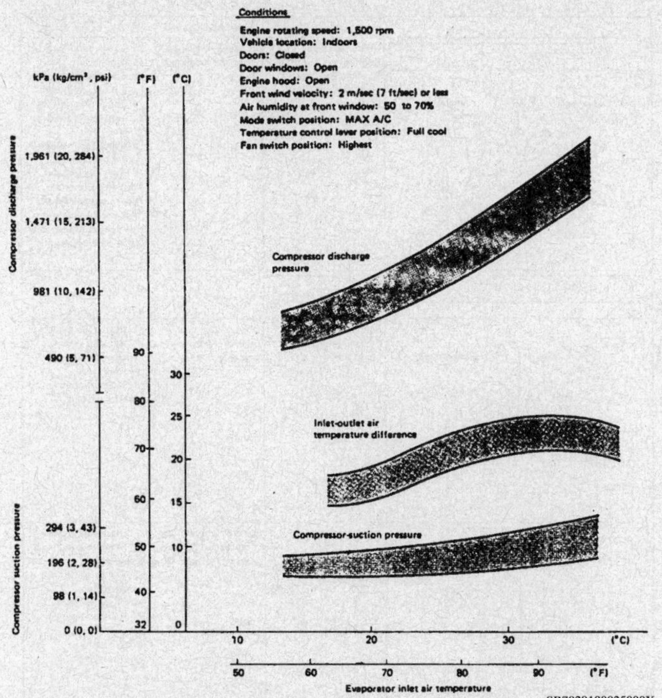
Conditions
Engine rotating speed: 1,500 rpm
Vehicle location: Indoors
Doors: Closed
Door windows: Open
Engine hood: Open
Front wind velocity: 2 m/sec (7 ft/sec) or less
Air humidity at front window: 50 to 70%
Mode switch position: MAX A/C
Temperature control lever position: Full cool
Fan switch position: Highest
kPa (kg/cm², psi)
(°F)
(°C)
Compressor discharge pressure
1,961 (20, 284)
1,471 (15, 213)
981 (10, 142)
490 (5, 71)
Compressor suction pressure
294 (3, 43)
196 (2, 28)
98 (1, 14)
0 (0, 0)
Compressor discharge pressure
Inlet-outlet air temperature difference
Compressor-suction pressure
Evaporator inlet air temperature

SB7029100025000X

Fig. 2 Air conditioning system performance chart. 1993–94 Legacy w/Zexel compressor

PERFORMANCE CHART

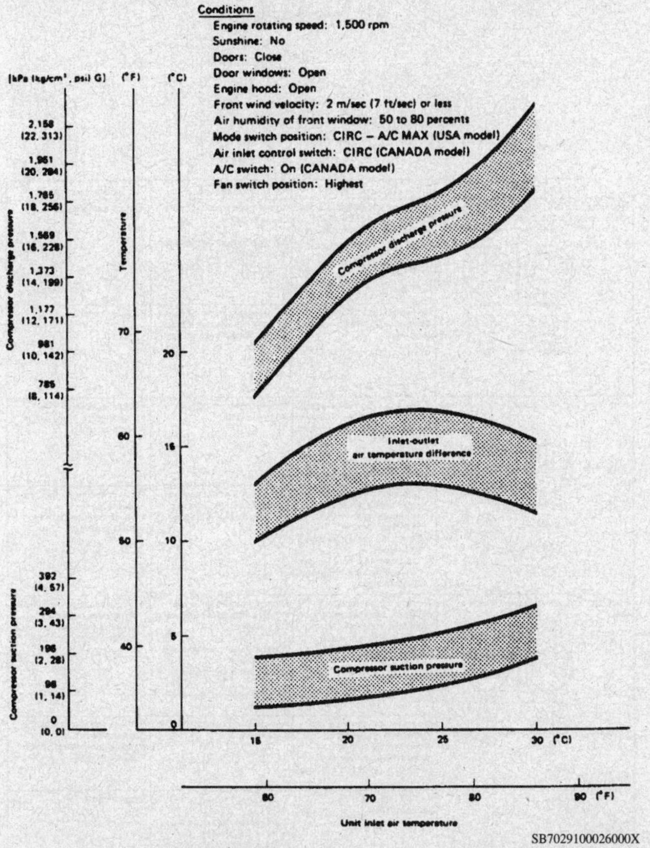
Conditions
Engine rotating speed: 1,500 rpm
Sunshine: No
Doors: Close
Door windows: Open
Engine hood: Open
Front wind velocity: 2 m/sec (7 ft/sec) or less
Air humidity of front window: 50 to 80 percents
Mode switch position: CIRC – A/C MAX (USA model)
Air inlet control switch: CIRC (CANADA model)
A/C switch: On (CANADA model)
Fan switch position: Highest
(kPa (kg/cm², psi) G)
(°F)
(°C)
Compressor discharge pressure
Temperature
Compressor suction pressure
Compressor discharge pressure
Inlet-outlet air temperature difference
Compressor suction pressure
Unit inlet air temperature

SB7029100026000X

Fig. 4 Air conditioning system performance chart. Loyale

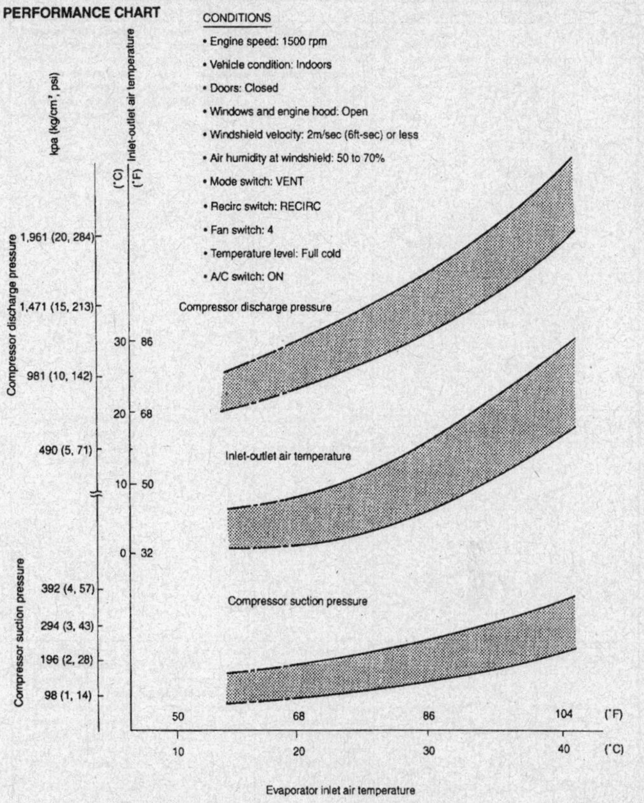
PERFORMANCE CHART
CONDITIONS
• Engine speed: 1500 rpm
• Vehicle condition: Indoors
• Doors: Closed
• Windows and engine hood: Open
• Windshield velocity: 2m/sec (6ft-sec) or less
• Air humidity at windshield: 50 to 70%
• Mode switch: VENT
• Recirc switch: RECIRC
• Fan switch: 4
• Temperature level: Full cold
• A/C switch: ON
kpa (kg/cm², psi)
Inlet-outlet air temperature
Compressor discharge pressure
1,961 (20, 284)
1,471 (15, 213)
981 (10, 142)
490 (5, 71)
Compressor suction pressure
392 (4, 57)
294 (3, 43)
196 (2, 28)
98 (1, 14)
Compressor discharge pressure
Inlet-outlet air temperature
Compressor suction pressure
Evaporator inlet air temperature

SB7029500068000X

Fig. 3 Air conditioning system performance chart. 1995–96 Legacy w/Zexel compressor

Condition		Probable cause	Corrective action
INSUFFICIENT REFRIGERANT CHARGE			
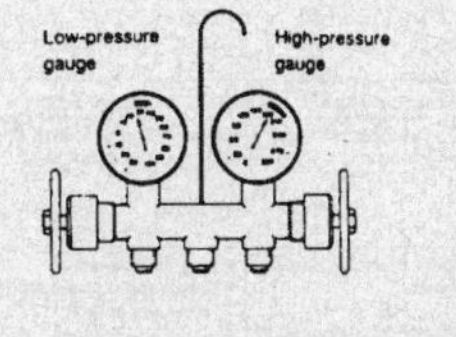 Low-pressure gauge High-pressure gauge	Insufficient cooling. Bubbles appear in sight glass.	Refrigerant is small, or leaking a little.	1. Leak test. 2. Repair leak. 3. Charge system. **Evacuate, as necessary, and recharge system.**
ALMOST NO REFRIGERANT 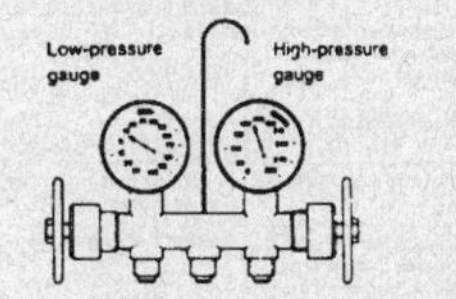 Low-pressure gauge High-pressure gauge	No cooling action. In sight glass appear a lot of bubbles or something like mist.	Serious refrigerant leak.	**Stop compressor immediately.** 1. Leak test. 2. Discharge system. 3. Repair leak(s). 4. Replace receiver drier if necessary. 5. Check oil level. 6. Evacuate and recharge system.
FAULTY EXPANSION VALVE 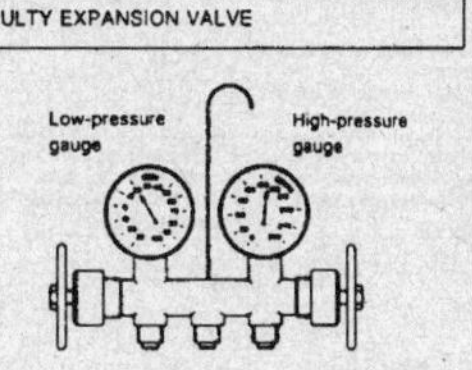 Low-pressure gauge High-pressure gauge	Slight cooling. Sweating or frosted expansion valve inlet.	Expansion valve restricts refrigerant flow. • Expansion valve is clogged. • Expansion valve is inoperative. Valve stuck closed. Thermal bulb has lost charge.	If valve inlet reveals sweat or frost: 1. Discharge system. 2. Remove valve and clean it. Replace it if necessary. 3. Evacuate system. 4. Charge system. If valve does not operate: 1. Discharge system. 2. Replace valve. 3. Evacuate and charge system.

SB7029300069010X

Fig. 5 Manifold gauge pressure readings (Part 1 of 3). Impreza

Condition		Probable cause	Corrective action
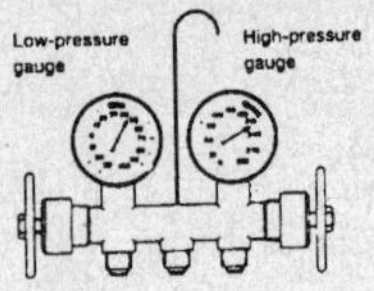Low-pressure gauge High-pressure gauge 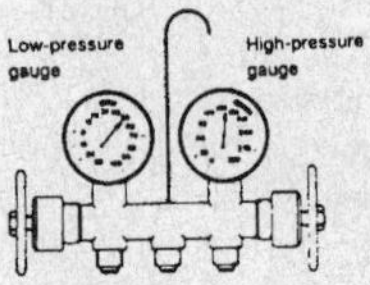Low-pressure gauge High-pressure gauge	Insufficient cooling. Sweated suction line. No cooling. Sweating or frosted suction line.	Expansion valve allows too much refrigerant through evaporator. Faulty seal of O-ring in expansion valve.	Check valve for operation. If suction side does not show a pressure decrease, replace valve. 1. Discharges system. 2. Remove expansion valve and replace O-ring. 3. Evacuate and replace system.
AIR IN SYSTEM 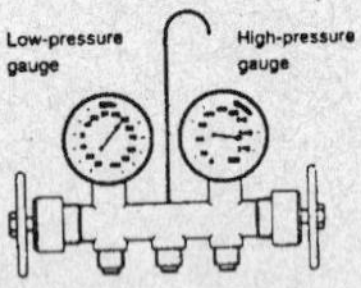Low-pressure gauge High-pressure gauge	Insufficient cooling. Sight glass shows occasional bubbles	Air mixed with refrigerant in system.	1. Discharge system. 2. Replace receiver drier. 3. Evacuate and charge system.
MOISTURE IN SYSTEM 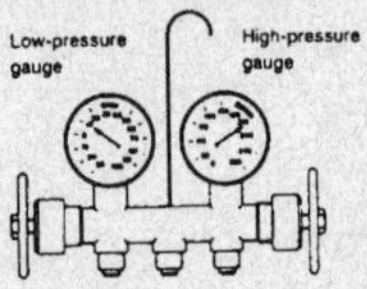Low-pressure gauge High-pressure gauge	After operation for a while, pressure on suction side may show vacuum pressure reading. During this condition, discharge air will be warm. As warning of this, reading shows 39 kPa (0.4 kg/cm², 6 psi) vibration.	Drier is saturated with moisture. Moisture has frozen at expansion valve. Refrigerant flow is restricted.	1. Discharge system. 2. Replace receiver drier (twice if necessary). 3. Evacuate system completely. (Repeat 30-minute evacuating three times.) 4. Recharge system.

SB7029300069020X

Fig. 5 Manifold gauge pressure readings (Part 2 of 3). Impreza

Condition		Probable cause	Corrective action
FAULTY CONDENSER 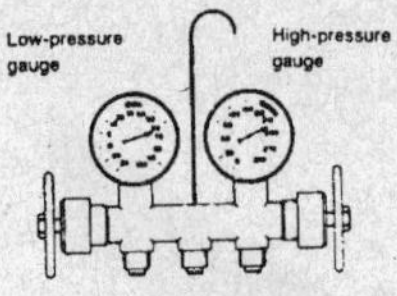Low-pressure gauge High-pressure gauge	No cooling action: Engine may overheat. Bubbles appear in sight glass of drier: Suction line is very hot.	Condenser is often found not functioning well.	• Check condenser cooling fan. • Check condenser for dirt accumulation. • Check engine cooling system for overheat. • Check for refrigerant overcharge. **If pressure remains high in spite of all above actions taken, remove and inspect the condenser for possible oil clogging.**
HIGH-PRESSURE LINE BLOCKED 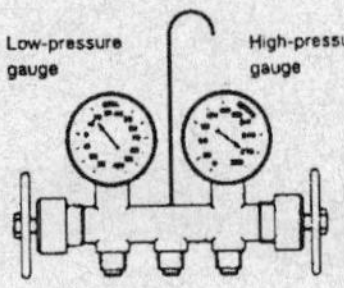Low-pressure gauge High-pressure gauge	Insufficient cooling. Frosted high-pressure liquid line.	Drier clogged, or restriction in high-pressure line.	1. Discharge system. 2. Remove receiver drier or strainer and replace it. 3. Evacuate and charge system.
FAULTY COMPRESSOR 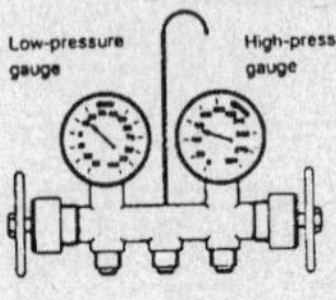Low-pressure gauge High-pressure gauge	Insufficient cooling.	Internal problem in compressor, or damaged gasket and valve.	1. Discharge system. 2. Remove and check compressor. 3. Repair or replace compressor. 4. Check oil level. 5. Replace receiver drier. 6. Evacuate and charge system.

SB7029300069030X

Fig. 5 Manifold gauge pressure readings (Part 3 of 3). Impreza

Gauge indication	Refrigerant cycle	Probable cause	Corrective action
Both high- and low-pressure sides are too high. 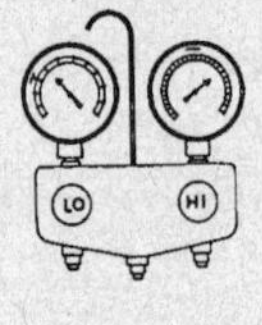LO HI	Pressure is reduced soon after water is splashed on condenser. No air bubbles appear in sight glass when pressure is reduced.	Excessive refrigerant charge in refrigeration cycle	Reduce refrigerant until specified pressure is obtained.
	Air suction by radiator or condenser fan is insufficient.	Insufficient condenser cooling performance ↓ 1) Condenser fin is clogged. 2) Improper rotation of radiator fan or condenser fan	• Clean condenser. • Check and repair cooling fan as necessary.
	• Low-pressure pipe is not cold. • When compressor is stopped, high-pressure value quickly drops by approximately 196 kPa (2 kg/cm², 28 psi). It will then decrease gradually thereafter.	Poor heat exchange in condenser (After compressor operation stops, high pressure decreases too slowly.) ↓ Air in refrigeration cycle	Evacuate repeatedly and recharge system.
	Engine tends to overheat.	Engine cooling systems malfunction.	Check and repair each engine cooling system.
	• Area near low-pressure pipe connection and service valves are considerably cold as compared with area near expansion valve outlet or evaporator. • Parts are sometimes covered with frost.	• Excessive liquid refrigerant on low-pressure side • Excessive refrigerant discharge flow • Expansion valve is open a little compared with the specification. ↓ 1)Improper thermal valve installation 2)Improper expansion valve adjustment	Replace expansion valve.
High-pressure side is too high and low-pressure side is too low. 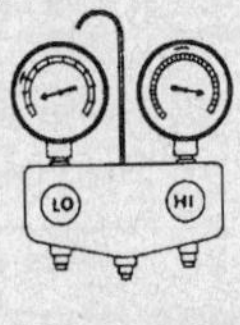LO HI	Upper side of condenser and high-pressure side are hot, however, receiver drier is not so hot.	High-pressure hose or parts located between compressor and condenser are clogged or crushed.	• Check and repair or replace malfunctioning parts. • Check compressor oil for contamination.

SB7029200070010X

Fig. 6 Manifold gauge pressure readings (Part 1 of 3). SVX

Gauge indication	Refrigerant cycle	Probable cause	Corrective action
High-pressure side is too low and low-pressure side is too high. LO HI	High- and low-pressure sides become equal soon after compressor operation stops.	Compressor pressure operation is improper. ↓ Damaged inside packings for compressor	Replace compressor.
	No temperature difference between high and low- pressure sides	Compressor discharge capacity does not change. (Compressor stroke is set at maximum.)	Replace compressor.
Both high- and low-pressure sides are too low. 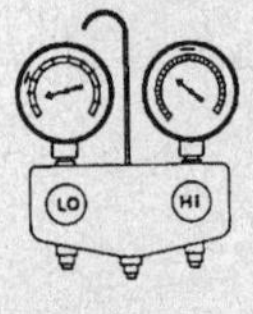LO HI	• There is a big temperature difference between receiver drier outlet and inlet. Outlet temperature is extremely low. • Receiver drier inlet and expansion valve are frosted.	Receiver drier inside is clogged a little.	• Replace receiver drier • Check compressor oil for contamination.
	• Temperature of expansion valve inlet is extremely low as compared with areas near receiver drier. • Expansion valve inlet may be frosted. • Temperature difference occurs somewhere in high-pressure side.	High-pressure pipe located between receiver drier and expansion valve is clogged.	• Check and repair malfunctioning parts. • Check compressor oil for contamination.
Both high and low-pressure sides are too low. LO HI	There is a big temperature difference between expansion valve inlet and outlet while the valve itself is frosted.	Expansion valve becomes closed a little compared with the specification. ↓ 1) Improper expansion valve adjustment 2) Malfunctioning thermal valve 3) Outlet and inlet may be clogged	• Remove foreign particles by using compressed air. • Check compressor oil for contamination.
	Area near low-pressure pipe connection and service valve are extremely cold as compared with area near expansion valve outlet and evaporator.	Low-pressure hose is clogged or crushed.	• Check and repair malfunctioning parts. • Check compressor oil for contamination.
	Air flow volume is not enough or low.	Evaporator is frozen ↓ Compressor discharge capacity does not change. (Compressor stroke is set at maximum length.)	Replace compressur.

SB7029200070020X

Fig. 6 Manifold gauge pressure readings (Part 2 of 3). SVX

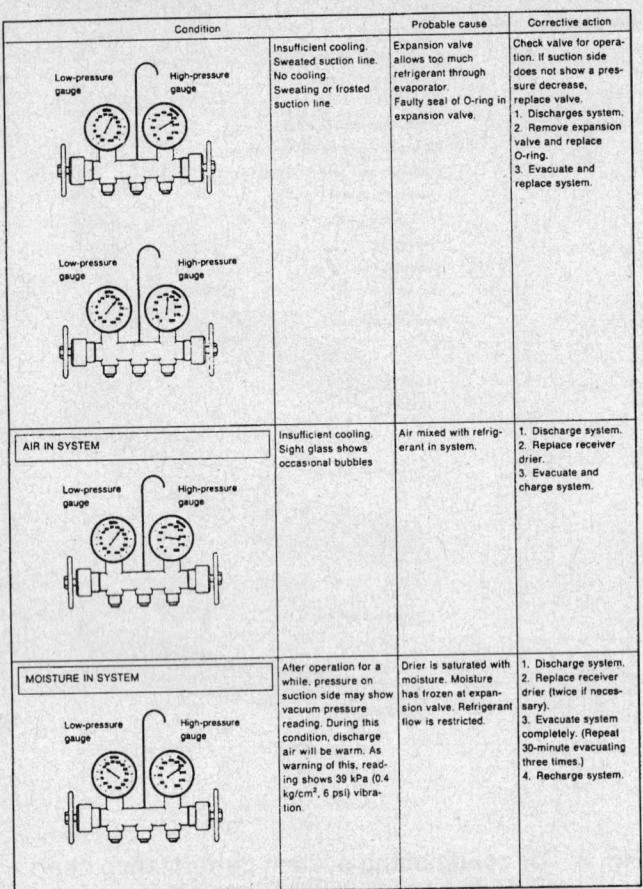

Gauge indication	Refrigerant cycle	Probable cause	Corrective action
Low-pressure side sometimes becomes negative. 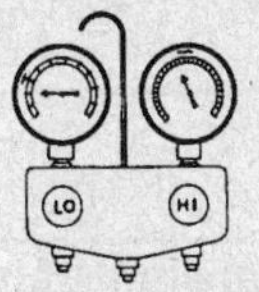 LO HI	• Air conditioning system does not function and does not cyclically cool the compartment air. • The system constantly function for a certain period of time after compressor is stopped and restarted.	Refrigerant does not discharge cyclically. ↓ Moisture is frozen at expansion valve outlet and inlet. ↓ Water is mixed in refrigeration cycle.	• Drain water from refrigerant cycle or replace refrigerant. • Replace receiver drier.
Low-pressure side becomes negative. 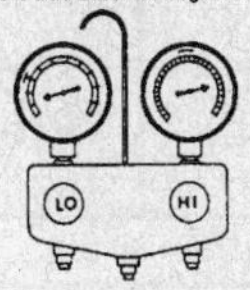 LO HI	Receiver drier or front/rear side of expansion valve's pipe is frosted or dewed.	High-pressure side is closed and refrigerant does not flow. ↓ Expansion valve or receiver drier is frosted.	After the system is left at rest, start again in order to confirm whether or not problem is caused by water or foreign particles. • If the problem is due to water, drain water from refrigeration cycle or replace refrigerant. • If it is due to foreign particles, remove expansion valve and remove it with dry and compressed air. • If either oil the above method cannot correct the problem, replace expansion valve. • Replace receiver drier. • Check compressor oil for contamination.

SB7029200070030X

Fig. 6 Manifold gauge pressure readings (Part 3 of 3). SVX

OIL CHARGE TABLE

Condition		Proper charging method	Amount of oil to be added mℓ (US fl oz, Imp fl oz)	
			HITACHI A/C	PANASONIC A/C
Replacement of compressor		Remove all oil from new compressor* and charge it with amount of oil shown in right column.	70 (2.4, 2.5)	70 (2.4, 2.5)
Replacement of evaporator		Add amount of oil shown in right column.	70 (2.4, 2.5)	60 (2.0, 2.1)
Replacement of receiver drier (liquid tank)		Oil need not be added.	–	–
Replacement of condenser	There is evidence of a large from condenser.	Oil need not be added.	–	–
	There is evidence of a large amount of oil leakage from condenser.	Add amount of oil shown in right column.	50 (1.7, 1.8)	40 (1.4, 1.4)
Replacement of flexible hose or copper tube	There is no sign of oil leakage.	Oil need not be added.	–	–
	There is evidence of a large amount of oil leakage.	Add amount of oil shown in right column.	50 (1.7, 1.8)	40 (1.4, 1.4)
Gas leakage	There is no sign of oil leakage.	Oil need not be added.	–	–
	There is evidence of a large amount of oil leakage.	Add amount of oil shown in right column.	50 (1.7, 1.8)	40 (1.4, 1.4)

SB7029100028000X

Fig. 7 Oil charge table. Loyale

Condition		Proper charging method	Amount of oil to be added mℓ (US fl oz, Imp fl oz)	
			ZEXEL	CALSONIC
Replacement of compressor		Remove all oil from new compressor and charge it with amount of oil shown in right column.	70 (2.4, 2.5)	95 (3.2, 3.3)
Replacement of evaporator		Add amount of oil shown in right column.	70 (2.4, 2.5)	85 (2.9, 3.0)
Replacement of receiver drier (liquid tank)		Oil need not be added.	—	5 (0.2, 0.2)
Replacement of condenser	There is no sign of oil leakage.	Oil need not be added.	—	—
	There is evidence of a large amount of oil leakage from condenser.	Add amount of oil shown in right column.	50 (1.7, 1.8)	85 (2.9, 3.0)
Replacement of flexible hose or aluminum pipe	There is no sign of oil leakage.	Oil need not be added.	—	—
	There is evidence of a large amount of oil leakage.	Add amount of oil shown in right column.	50 (1.7, 1.8)	40 (1.4, 1.4)
Gas leakage	There is no sign of oil leakage.	Oil need not be added.	—	—
	There is evidence of a large amount of oil leakage.	Add amount of oil shown in right column.	50 (1.7, 1.8)	40 (1.4, 1.4)

SB7029200067000X

Fig. 8 Oil charge table. 1993–94 Legacy

Unit: mℓ (US fl oz, Imp fl oz)

Item		Replenishment amount	Remarks
Compressor replacement		70 (2.4, 2.5)	Drain oil completely from new compressor and replenish compressor oil by amount indicated at left.
Evaporator replacement		70 (2.4, 2.5)	
Receiver dryer replacement		—	Replenishment is not necessary.
Condenser replacement	Oil does not appear to leak.	—	Replenishment is not necessary.
	Oil leaks from condenser in large quantities.	50 (1.7, 1.8)	
Flexible hose/pipe replacement	Oil does not appear to leak.	—	Replenishment is not necessary.
	Oil leaks in large quantities.	50 (1.7, 1.8)	
Refrigerant leaks	Oil does not appear to leak.	—	Replenishment is not necessary.
	Oil leaks in large quantities.	50 (1.7, 1.8)	
Every two years			

SB7029100031000X

Fig. 9 Oil charge table. SVX models

new compressor. Refill new compressor with same amount that was drained from old compressor. Refill amount must be a minimum of 3 ounces.

When replacing other system components, add the following quantities of refrigerant oil: Evaporator, 2.8 ounces; Receiver Drier, 2 ounces; Condenser, 1.5 ounces; Hose, 2 ounces.

LOYALE

Refer to oil charge table in **Fig. 7,** when servicing the air conditioning system for oil replacement quantities.

LEGACY

1993–94

Refer to oil charge table in **Fig. 8** when servicing the air conditioning system for oil replacement quantities.

1995–96

If compressor is replaced, drain oil from old compressor and measure, then drain new compressor. Refill new compressor with same amount that was drained from old compressor. Refill amount must be a minimum of 0.70 ounces.

When replacing other system components, add the following quantities of refrigerant oil: Evaporator, 3.90 ounces; Receiver Drier, 0.20 ounces; Condenser, 0.07 ounces; Hose, 0.03 ounces.

SVX

Refer to oil charge table in **Fig. 9,** for oil replacement quantities when servicing the air conditioning system.

OIL LEVEL CHECK

No provision is made for checking oil level on these vehicles and oil is added according to component(s) being replaced. Refer to "Oil Charge."

BELT TENSION DATA

Refer to "Drive Belt Service" in "Engine" section.

A/C SPECIFICATIONS

Compressor Model	Refrigerant Capacity, Lbs.	Refrigerant Types	Refrigerant Oil			Compressor Clutch Air Gap, Inch	Charging Valve Locations	
			Viscosity	Total System Capacity, Ounces	Compressor Oil Level Check, Inches		High Press.	Low Press.
1993								
Impreza	1.43-1.65	R-12	⑤	6.1	⑧	.012-.024	⑨	⑥
Legacy①	1.8-2.0	R-12	⑤	8	⑧	.012-.024	⑨	⑥
Legacy②	1.8-2.0	R-12	⑤	5.1	⑧	.012-.024	⑨	⑥
Loyale	1.76-1.87	R-12	⑦	4.72	⑧	.016-.024	⑨	⑥
SVX	1.43	R-134a	③	5.06	⑧	—	⑨	⑥
1994								
Impreza	1.5	R-134a	④	—	⑧	—	⑨	⑥
Legacy	1.65	R-134a	④	5.3	⑧	—	⑨	⑥
Loyale	1.76-1.87	R-12	⑦	4.72	⑧	.016-.024	⑨	⑥
SVX	1.43	R-134a	③	5.06	⑧	—	⑨	⑥
1995–96								
Impreza	1.3-1.5	R-134a	④	—	⑧	—	⑨	⑥
Legacy	1.3-1.5	R-134a	③	—	⑧	.012-.024	⑨	⑥
SVX	1.43	R-134a	③	5.06	⑧	—	⑨	⑥

① — Models with Calsonic compressor.
② — Models with Zexel compressor.
③ — Type ZXL-100-PG, or equivalent.
④ — Special Polyalkaline Glycol (PAG) lubricant required.
⑤ — Type D-90-PX, or equivalent.
⑥ — On low pressure line.
⑦ — ATMOS S150, or equivalent.
⑧ — Oil level inches cannot be checked.
⑨ — On high pressure line.

Cooling Fans

INDEX

	Page No.		Page No.		Page No.
Component Replacement	39-65	Radiator Fan & Motor	39-65	Condenser Fan	39-65
Condenser Fan & Motor	39-65	**System Diagnosis & Testing**	39-65	Radiator Fan	39-65

SYSTEM DIAGNOSIS & TESTING

RADIATOR FAN

Impreza

Refer to **Fig. 1,** for radiator fan diagnosis.

Legacy

Refer to **Figs. 2 and 3,** for radiator fan diagnosis.

Loyale

Refer to **Fig. 4,** for radiator fan diagnosis.

CONDENSER FAN

Impreza

Refer to **Figs. 5 and 6,** for condenser fan diagnosis.

Legacy

Refer to **Figs. 7 through 10,** for condenser fan diagnosis.

COMPONENT REPLACEMENT

RADIATOR FAN & MOTOR

Removal

1. Disconnect battery negative cable.
2. Disconnect fan motor electrical connector, then the harness from shroud, if necessary.
3. Remove shroud retaining bolts, then the shroud.
4. Remove fan motor mounting nuts, then separate motor from shroud.
5. Remove cooling fan mounting nuts, then separate cooling fan blades fan motor.

Installation

1. Place cooling fan on fan motor, then install mounting nuts. Apply a suitable locking compound to mounting nuts then securely tighten.
2. Place fan motor on shroud and install mounting nuts. **Ensure fan does not contact shroud when installed.**
3. Assemble shroud to radiator.
4. Connect fan motor electrical connector, then secure wiring harness to shroud.
5. Connect negative cable to battery.

CONDENSER FAN & MOTOR

1. Disconnect battery ground cable and fan motor electrical connector.

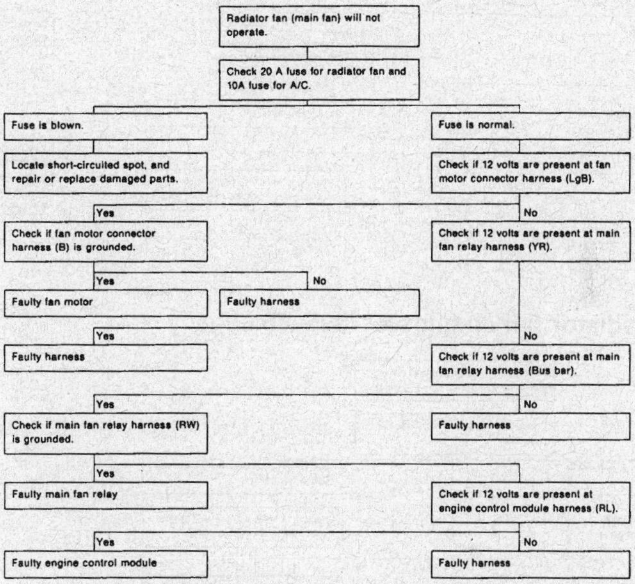

Radiator fan (main fan) will not operate.
Check 20 A fuse for radiator fan and 10A fuse for A/C.
Fuse is blown.
Fuse is normal.
Locate short-circuited spot, and repair or replace damaged parts.
Check if 12 volts are present at fan motor connector harness (LgB).
Yes
No
Check if fan motor connector harness (B) is grounded.
Check if 12 volts are present at main fan relay harness (YR).
Yes
No
Faulty fan motor
Faulty harness
Yes
No
Faulty harness
Check if 12 volts are present at main fan relay harness (Bus bar).
Yes
No
Check if main fan relay harness (RW) is grounded.
Faulty harness
Yes
Faulty main fan relay
Check if 12 volts are present at engine control module harness (RL).
Yes
No
Faulty engine control module
Faulty harness

SB1089100014000X

Fig. 1 Radiator fan diagnosis. Impreza

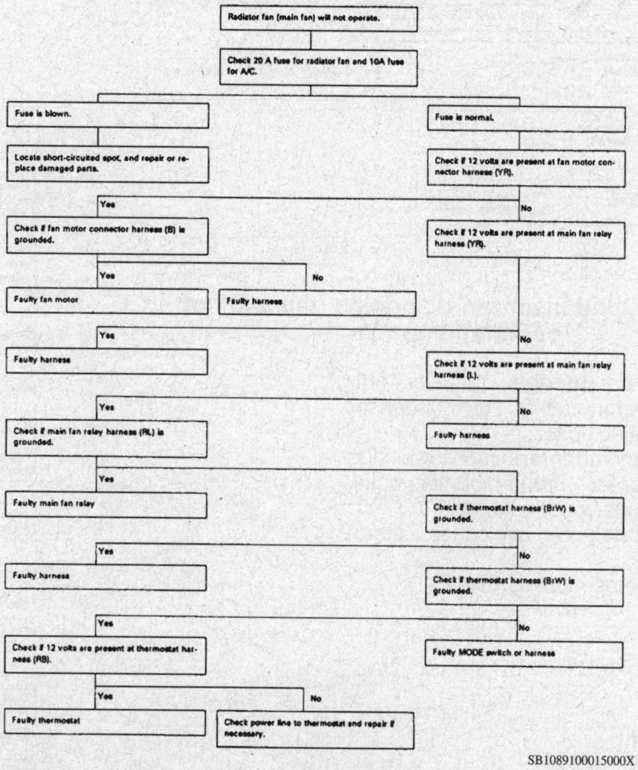

Radiator fan (main fan) will not operate.
Check 20 A fuse for radiator fan and 10A fuse for A/C.
Fuse is blown.
Fuse is normal.
Locate short-circuited spot, and repair or replace damaged parts.
Check if 12 volts are present at fan motor connector harness (YR).
Yes
No
Check if fan motor connector harness (B) is grounded.
Check if 12 volts are present at main fan relay harness (YR).
Yes
No
Faulty fan motor
Faulty harness
Yes
No
Faulty harness
Check if 12 volts are present at main fan relay harness (L).
Yes
No
Check if main fan relay harness (RL) is grounded.
Faulty harness
Yes
Faulty main fan relay
Check if thermostat harness (BrW) is grounded.
Yes
No
Faulty harness
Check if thermostat harness (BrW) is grounded.
Yes
No
Check if 12 volts are present at thermostat harness (RB).
Faulty MODE switch or harness
Yes
No
Faulty thermostat
Check power line to thermostat and repair if necessary.

SB1089100015000X

Fig. 2 Radiator fan diagnosis. 1993–94 Legacy

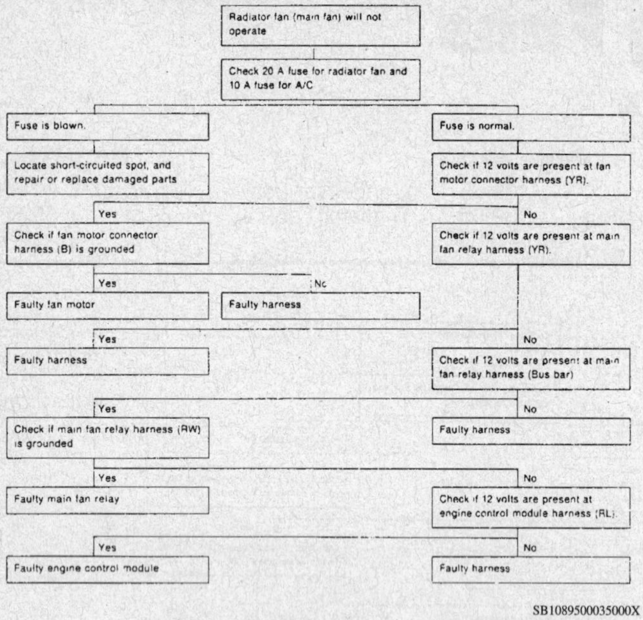
Radiator fan (main fan) will not operate
Check 20 A fuse for radiator fan and 10 A fuse for A/C
Fuse is blown.
Locate short-circuited spot, and repair or replace damaged parts
Fuse is normal.
Check if 12 volts are present at fan motor connector harness (YR).
Yes
Check if fan motor connector harness (B) is grounded
Yes
Faulty fan motor
No
Faulty harness
Yes
Faulty harness
No
Check if 12 volts are present at main fan relay harness (YR).
No
Check if 12 volts are present at main fan relay harness (Bus bar)
Yes
Check if main fan relay harness (RW) is grounded
Yes
Faulty main fan relay
No
Faulty harness
No
Check if 12 volts are present at engine control module harness (RL).
Yes
Faulty engine control module
No
Faulty harness
SB1089500035000X

Fig. 3 Radiator fan diagnosis. 1995–96 Legacy

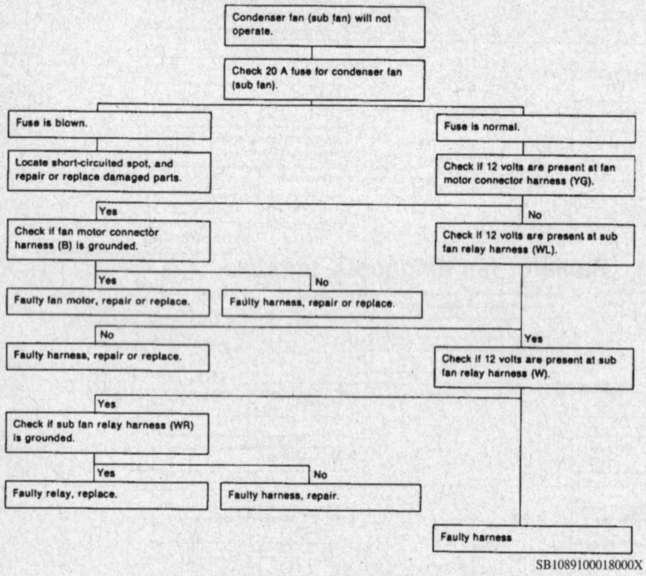
Condenser fan (sub fan) will not operate.
Check 20 A fuse for condenser fan (sub fan).
Fuse is blown.
Locate short-circuited spot, and repair or replace damaged parts.
Fuse is normal.
Check if 12 volts are present at fan motor connector harness (YG).
Yes
Check if fan motor connector harness (B) is grounded.
Yes
Faulty fan motor, repair or replace.
No
Faulty harness, repair or replace.
No
Check if 12 volts are present at sub fan relay harness (WL).
No
Faulty harness, repair or replace.
Yes
Check if 12 volts are present at sub fan relay harness (W).
Yes
Check if sub fan relay harness (WR) is grounded.
Yes
Faulty relay, replace.
No
Faulty harness, repair.
Faulty harness
SB1089100018000X

Fig. 5 Condenser fan diagnosis (fan will not operate). Impreza

2. **On Impreza models,** remove right-hand radiator bracket, then condenser fan mounting bolts.
3. **On Legacy models,** loosen lower side condenser fan shroud mounting bolts, then remove upper side bolts.
4. **On all models,** remove condenser fan assembly.
5. Reverse procedure to install.

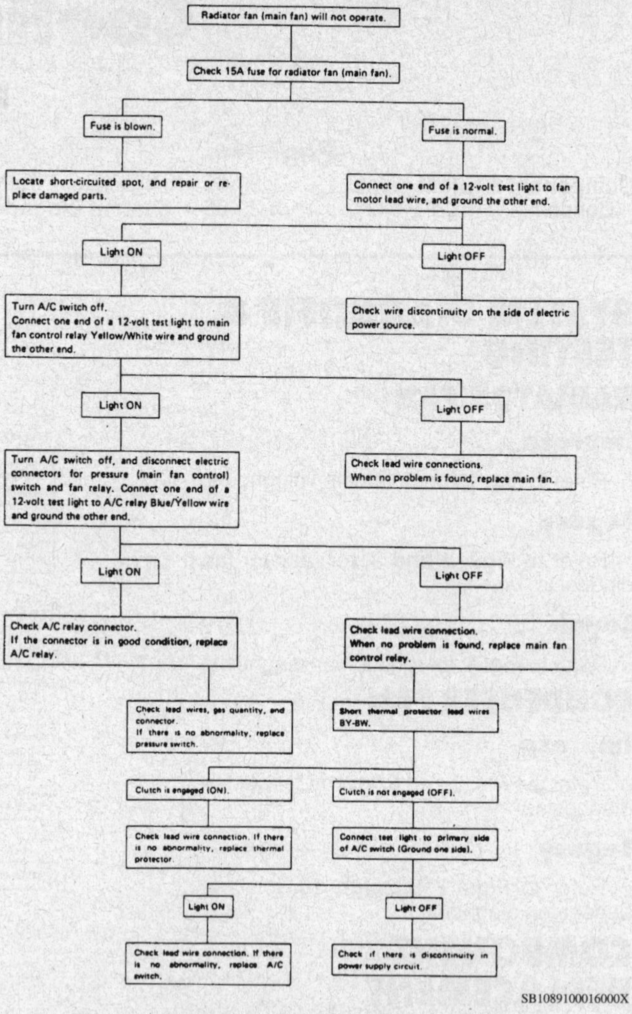
Radiator fan (main fan) will not operate.
Check 15A fuse for radiator fan (main fan).
Fuse is blown.
Locate short-circuited spot, and repair or replace damaged parts.
Fuse is normal.
Connect one end of a 12-volt test light to fan motor lead wire, and ground the other end.
Light ON
Turn A/C switch off. Connect one end of a 12-volt test light to main fan control relay Yellow/White wire and ground the other end.
Light OFF
Check wire discontinuity on the side of electric power source.
Light ON
Turn A/C switch off, and disconnect electric connectors for pressure (main fan control) switch and fan relay. Connect one end of a 12-volt test light to A/C relay Blue/Yellow wire and ground the other end.
Light OFF
Check lead wire connections. When no problem is found, replace main fan.
Light ON
Check A/C relay connector. If the connector is in good condition, replace A/C relay.
Light OFF
Check lead wire connection. When no problem is found, replace main fan control relay.
Check lead wires, gas quantity, and connector. If there is no abnormality, replace pressure switch.
Short thermal protector lead wires BY-BW.
Clutch is engaged (ON).
Check lead wire connection. If there is no abnormality, replace thermal protector.
Clutch is not engaged (OFF).
Connect test light to primary side of A/C switch (Ground one side).
Light ON
Check lead wire connection. If there is no abnormality, replace A/C switch.
Light OFF
Check if there is discontinuity in power supply circuit.
SB1089100016000X

Fig. 4 Radiator fan diagnosis. Loyale

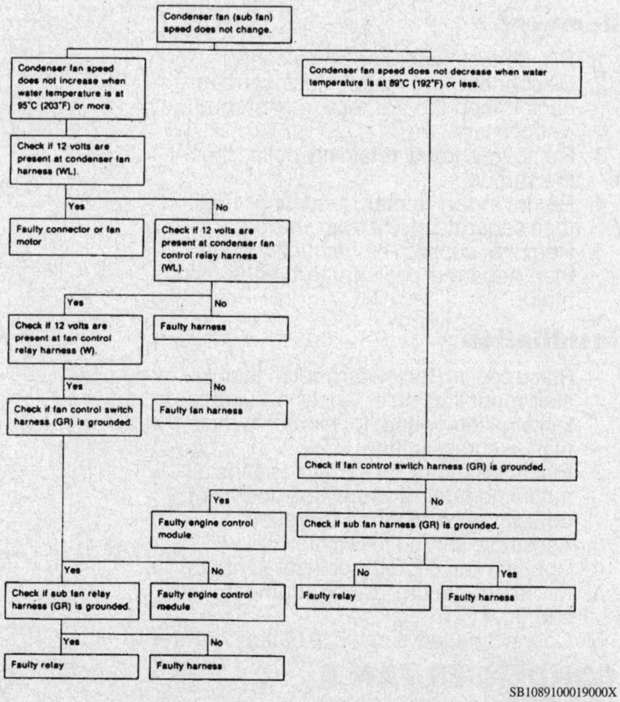
Condenser fan (sub fan) speed does not change.
Condenser fan speed does not increase when water temperature is at 95°C (203°F) or more.
Check if 12 volts are present at condenser fan harness (WL).
Yes
Faulty connector or fan motor
No
Check if 12 volts are present at condenser fan control relay harness (WL).
Yes
Check if 12 volts are present at fan control relay harness (W).
No
Faulty harness
Yes
Check if fan control switch harness (GR) is grounded.
No
Faulty fan harness
Yes
Check if sub fan relay harness (GR) is grounded.
No
Faulty engine control module
Yes
Faulty relay
No
Faulty harness
Condenser fan speed does not decrease when water temperature is at 89°C (192°F) or less.
Check if fan control switch harness (GR) is grounded.
Yes
Faulty engine control module.
No
Check if sub fan harness (GR) is grounded.
No
Faulty relay
Yes
Faulty harness
SB1089100019000X

Fig. 6 Condenser fan diagnosis (fan speed does not change). Impreza

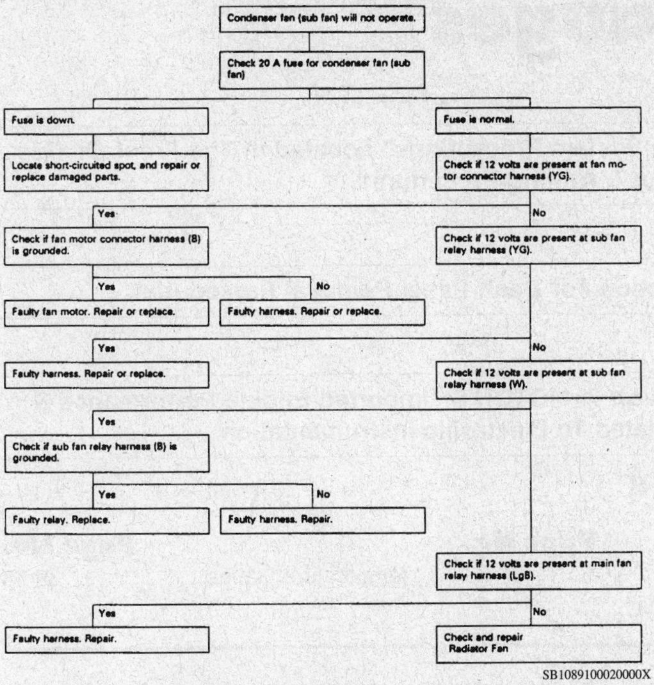
Condenser fan (sub fan) will not operate.
Check 20 A fuse for condenser fan (sub fan)
Fuse is down.
Fuse is normal.
Locate short-circuited spot, and repair or replace damaged parts.
Check if 12 volts are present at fan motor connector harness (YG).
Yes
No
Check if fan motor connector harness (B) is grounded.
Check if 12 volts are present at sub fan relay harness (YG).
Yes
No
Faulty fan motor. Repair or replace.
Faulty harness. Repair or replace.
Yes
No
Faulty harness. Repair or replace.
Check if 12 volts are present at sub fan relay harness (W).
Yes
Check if sub fan relay harness (B) is grounded.
Yes
No
Faulty relay. Replace.
Faulty harness. Repair.
Check if 12 volts are present at main fan relay harness (LgB).
Yes
No
Faulty harness. Repair.
Check and repair Radiator Fan
SB1089100020000X

Fig. 7 Condenser fan diagnosis (fan will not operate). 1993–94 Legacy

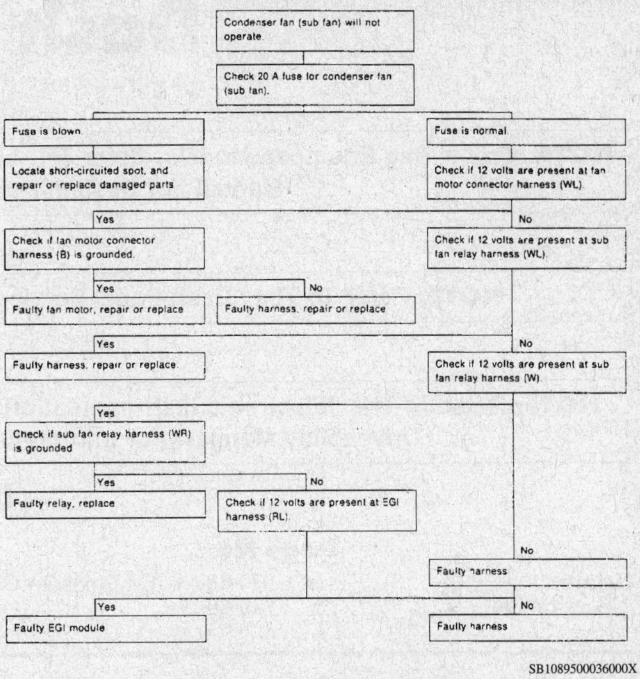
Condenser fan (sub fan) will not operate.
Check 20 A fuse for condenser fan (sub fan).
Fuse is blown
Fuse is normal
Locate short-circuited spot, and repair or replace damaged parts
Check if 12 volts are present at fan motor connector harness (WL).
Yes
No
Check if fan motor connector harness (B) is grounded.
Check if 12 volts are present at sub fan relay harness (WL).
Yes
No
Faulty fan motor, repair or replace
Faulty harness, repair or replace
Yes
No
Faulty harness, repair or replace.
Check if 12 volts are present at sub fan relay harness (W).
Yes
Check if sub fan relay harness (WR) is grounded
Yes
No
Faulty relay, replace
Check if 12 volts are present at EGI harness (RL).
No
Faulty harness
Yes
No
Faulty EGI module
Faulty harness
SB1089500036000X

Fig. 8 Condenser fan diagnosis (fan will not operate). 1995–96 Legacy

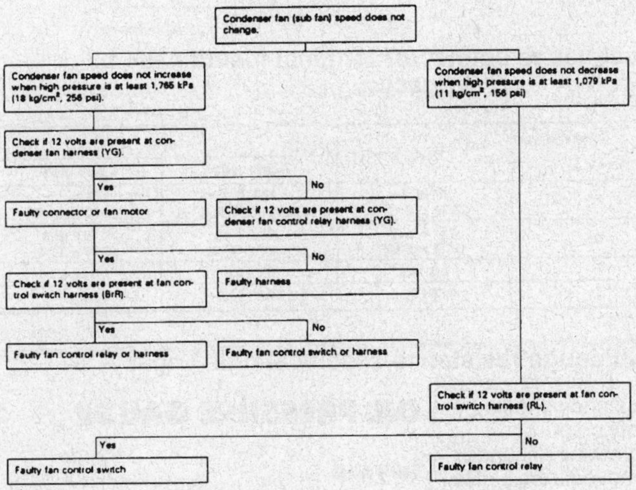
Condenser fan (sub fan) speed does not change.
Condenser fan speed does not increase when high pressure is at least 1,765 kPa (18 kg/cm², 256 psi).
Condenser fan speed does not decrease when high pressure is at least 1,079 kPa (11 kg/cm², 156 psi)
Check if 12 volts are present at condenser fan harness (YG).
Yes
No
Faulty connector or fan motor
Check if 12 volts are present at condenser fan control relay harness (YG).
Yes
No
Check if 12 volts are present at fan control switch harness (BrR).
Faulty harness
Yes
No
Faulty fan control relay or harness
Faulty fan control switch or harness
Check if 12 volts are present at fan control switch harness (RL).
Yes
No
Faulty fan control switch
Faulty fan control relay

SB1089100021000X

Fig. 9 Condenser fan diagnosis (fan speed does not change). 1993–94 Legacy

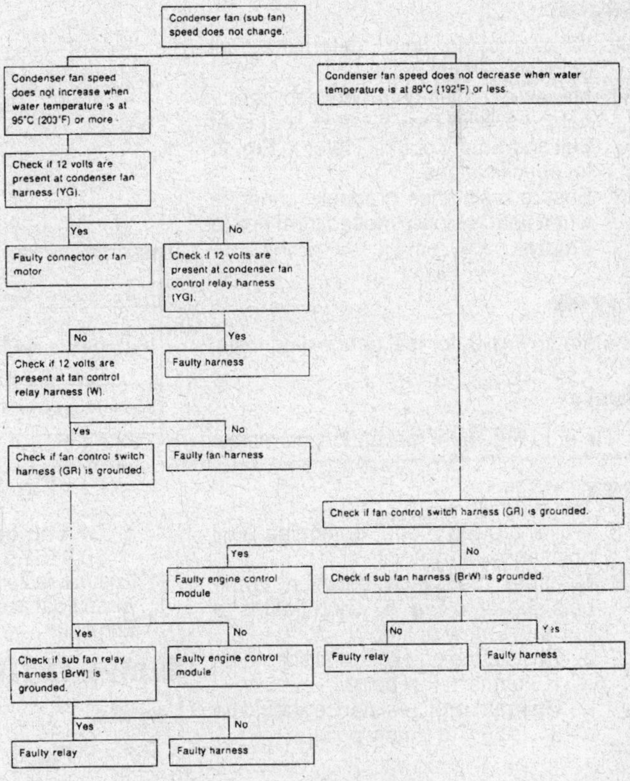
Condenser fan (sub fan) speed does not change.
Condenser fan speed does not increase when water temperature is at 95°C (203°F) or more
Condenser fan speed does not decrease when water temperature is at 89°C (192°F) or less.
Check if 12 volts are present at condenser fan harness (YG).
Yes
No
Faulty connector or fan motor
Check if 12 volts are present at condenser fan control relay harness (YG).
No
Yes
Check if 12 volts are present at fan control relay harness (W).
Faulty harness
Yes
No
Check if fan control switch harness (GR) is grounded.
Faulty fan harness
Check if fan control switch harness (GR) is grounded.
Yes
No
Faulty engine control module
Check if sub fan harness (BrW) is grounded.
Yes
No
No
Yes
Check if sub fan relay harness (BrW) is grounded.
Faulty engine control module
Faulty relay
Faulty harness
Yes
No
Faulty relay
Faulty harness
SB1089500037000X

Fig. 10 Condenser fan diagnosis (fan speed does not change). 1995–96 Legacy

Dash Gauges

NOTE: On Air Bag Equipped Models, Refer To "Air Bag System Precautions" Located In The Front Of This Manual For System Disarming & Arming Procedures.

NOTE: Refer To The "Dash Panel Service" Section For Dash Panel Removal Procedures.

NOTE: Refer To The "Electronic Instrumentation" Section In MOTOR'S "Imported Engine Performance & Driveability Manual" For Information Related To Electronic Instrumentation.

INDEX

	Page No.
Gauges	39-68
Fuel Gauge	39-68
Oil Pressure Gauge	39-68
Temperature Gauge	39-68

GAUGES

FUEL GAUGE

Legacy

1. While moving float, determine Full point and Empty point.
2. Measure resistance between terminals shown in **Fig. 1,** when float is at Full and Empty points. Refer to **Fig. 2,** for specifications.
3. Ensure resistance gradually changes when float is slowly moved from Full to Empty.

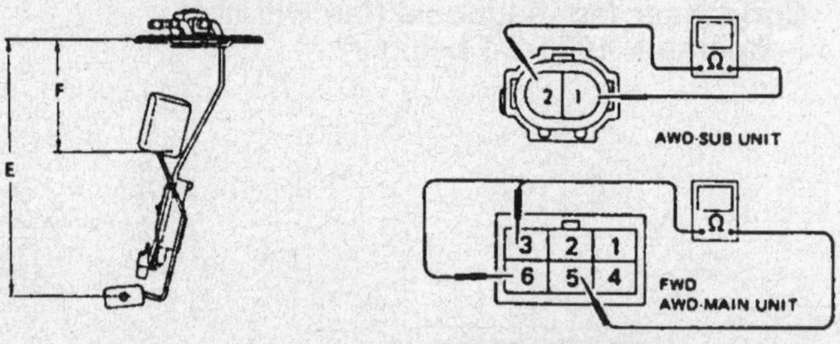

F
E
2 1
AWD-SUB UNIT
3 2 1
6 5 4
FWD
AWD-MAIN UNIT

SB9099200001000X

Fig. 1 Fuel gauge connector terminal identification. Legacy

Float position and resistance \ Vehicle type		FWD	AWD MAIN UNIT	AWD SUB UNIT
Float position mm (in)	F	94 ± 3 (3.70 ± 0.12)	72.1 ± 3 (2.839 ± 0.118)	72.9 ± 3 (2.870 ± 0.118)
	E	230.4 ± 3 (9.07 ± 0.12)	252.0 ± 3 (9.92 ± 0.12)	249.0 ± 3 (9.80 ± 0.12)
Normal resistance (Ω)	F	2.0 - 5.0	0.5 - 2.5	0.5 - 2.5
	E	92.0 - 95.0	50.0 - 52.0	42.0 - 44.0

SB9099200002000X

Fig. 2 Fuel gauge resistance specifications. Legacy

Loyale

Refer to **Fig. 3,** for fuel gauge diagnosis.

Justy

Refer to **Fig. 4,** for fuel gauge diagnosis.

SVX

1. While moving float, determine Full point and Empty point.
2. Measure resistance between terminals shown in **Fig. 5,** when float is at Full and Empty points.
   a. Resistance on either unit should be 1-3 ohms at Full point.
   b. **On main unit,** resistance should be 54.1–56.1 at Empty point.
   c. **On sub unit,** resistance should be 50.9–52.9 at Empty point.
3. Ensure resistance gradually changes when float is slowly moved from Full to Empty.

TEMPERATURE GAUGE

Loyale

Refer to **Fig. 6,** for fuel gauge diagnosis.

OIL PRESSURE GAUGE

Loyale

Refer to **Fig. 7,** for fuel gauge diagnosis.

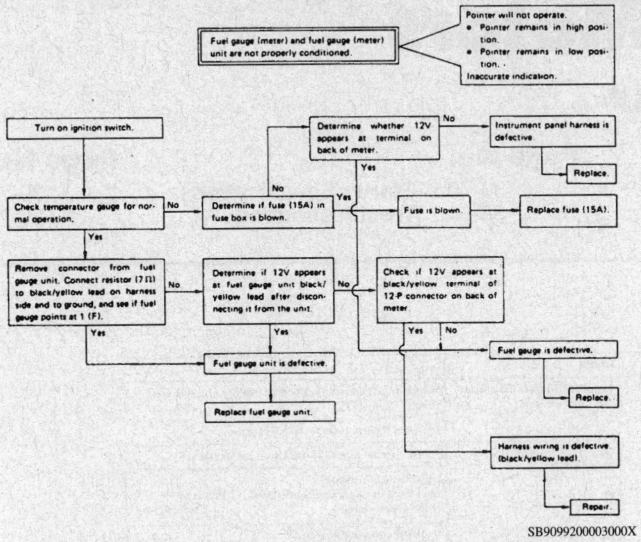
Fuel gauge (meter) and fuel gauge (meter) unit are not properly conditioned.
Pointer will not operate.
Pointer remains in high position.
Pointer remains in low position.
Inaccurate indication.
Turn on ignition switch.
Check temperature gauge for normal operation.
Determine whether 12V appears at terminal on back of meter.
Instrument panel harness is defective.
Replace.
Determine if fuse (15A) in fuse box is blown.
Fuse is blown.
Replace fuse (15A).
Remove connector from fuel gauge unit. Connect resistor (7 Ω) to black/yellow lead on harness side and to ground, and see if fuel gauge points at 1 (F).
Determine if 12V appears at fuel gauge unit black/yellow lead after disconnecting it from the unit.
Check if 12V appears at black/yellow terminal of 12-P connector on back of meter.
Fuel gauge is defective.
Fuel gauge unit is defective.
Replace fuel gauge unit.
Harness wiring is defective. (black/yellow lead).
Repair.
Yes
No
SB9099200003000X

Fig. 3 Fuel gauge troubleshooting. Loyale

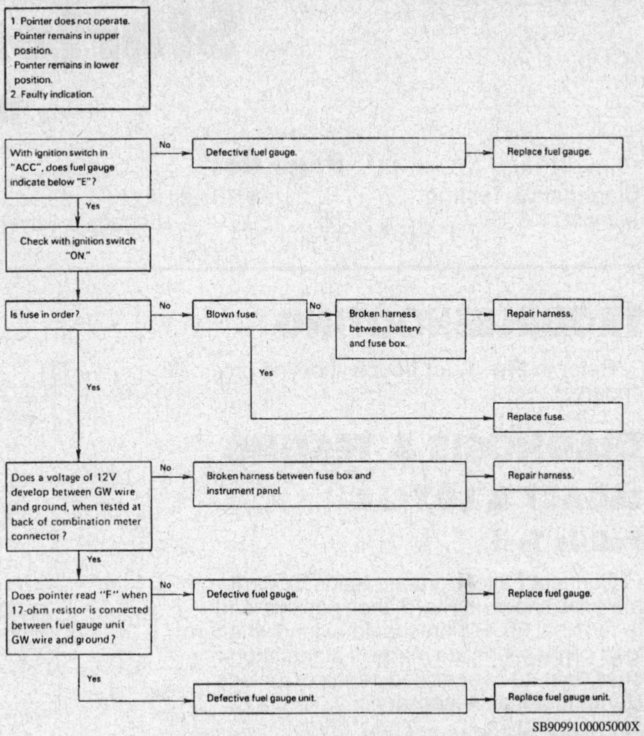
1. Pointer does not operate.
Pointer remains in upper position.
Pointer remains in lower position.
2. Faulty indication.
With ignition switch in "ACC", does fuel gauge indicate below "E"?
Defective fuel gauge.
Replace fuel gauge.
Check with ignition switch "ON"
Is fuse in order?
Blown fuse.
Broken harness between battery and fuse box.
Repair harness.
Replace fuse.
Does a voltage of 12V develop between GW wire and ground, when tested at back of combination meter connector?
Broken harness between fuse box and instrument panel.
Repair harness.
Does pointer read "F" when 17-ohm resistor is connected between fuel gauge unit GW wire and ground?
Defective fuel gauge.
Replace fuel gauge.
Defective fuel gauge unit.
Replace fuel gauge unit.
Yes
No
SB9099100005000X

Fig. 4 Fuel gauge troubleshooting. Justy

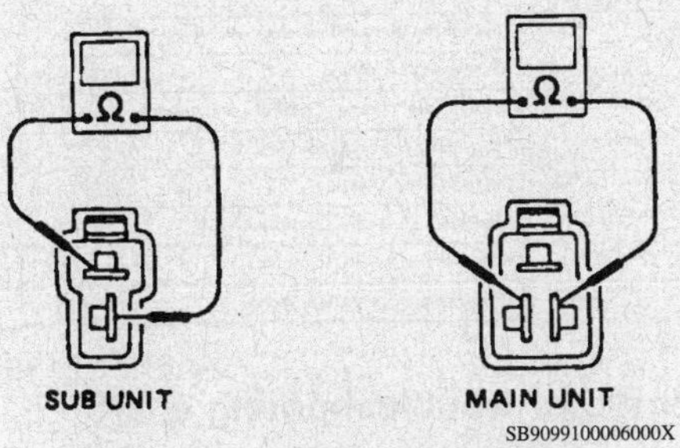
Ω
Ω
SUB UNIT
MAIN UNIT
SB9099100006000X

Fig. 5 Fuel gauge connector terminal identification. SVX

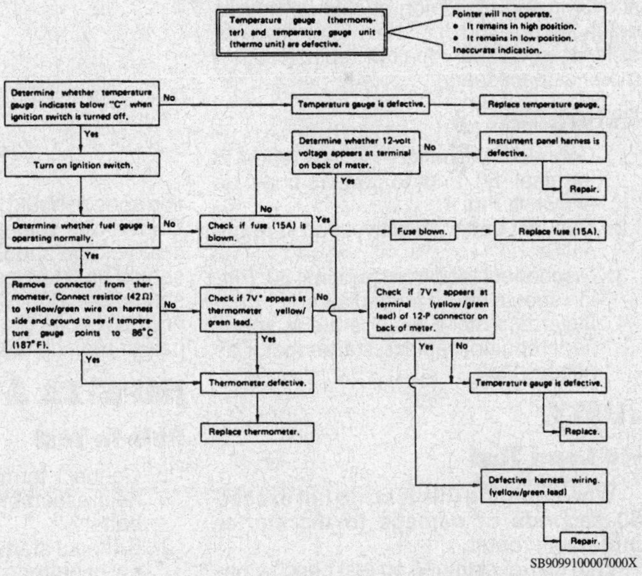
Temperature gauge (thermometer) and temperature gauge unit (thermo unit) are defective.
Pointer will not operate.
It remains in high position.
It remains in low position.
Inaccurate indication.
Determine whether temperature gauge indicates below "C" when ignition switch is turned off.
Temperature gauge is defective.
Replace temperature gauge.
Turn on ignition switch.
Determine whether 12-volt voltage appears at terminal on back of meter.
Instrument panel harness is defective.
Repair.
Determine whether fuel gauge is operating normally.
Check if fuse (15A) is blown.
Fuse blown.
Replace fuse (15A).
Remove connector from thermometer. Connect resistor (42 Ω) to yellow/green wire on harness side and ground to see if temperature gauge points to 86°C (187°F).
Check if 7V* appears at thermometer yellow/green lead.
Check if 7V* appears at terminal (yellow/green lead) of 12-P connector on back of meter.
Thermometer defective.
Replace thermometer.
Temperature gauge is defective.
Replace.
Defective harness wiring. (yellow/green lead)
Repair.
Yes
No
SB9099100007000X

Fig. 6 Temperature gauge troubleshooting. Loyale

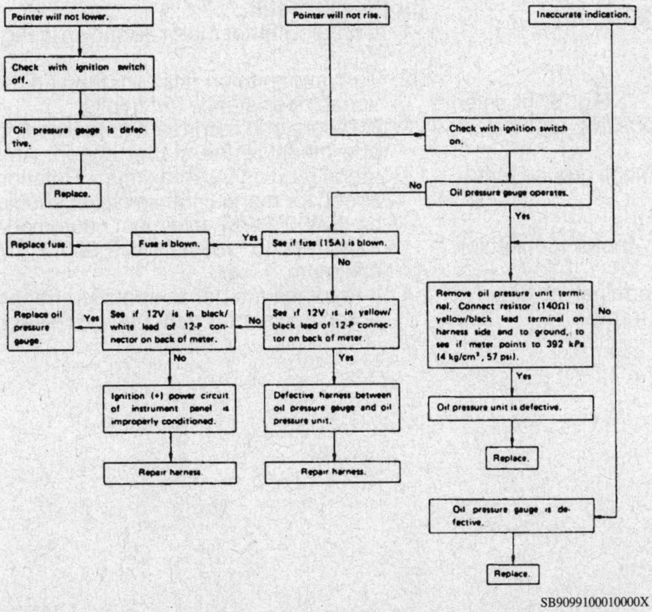
Pointer will not lower.
Check with ignition switch off.
Oil pressure gauge is defective.
Replace.
Pointer will not rise.
Inaccurate indication.
Check with ignition switch on.
Oil pressure gauge operates.
Replace fuse.
Fuse is blown.
See if fuse (15A) is blown.
Replace oil pressure gauge.
See if 12V is in black/white lead of 12-P connector on back of meter.
See if 12V is in yellow/black lead of 12-P connector on back of meter.
Ignition (+) power circuit of instrument panel is improperly conditioned.
Defective harness between oil pressure gauge and oil pressure unit.
Repair harness.
Repair harness.
Remove oil pressure unit terminal. Connect resistor (140Ω) to yellow/black lead terminal on harness side and to ground, to see if meter points to 392 kPa (4 kg/cm², 57 psi).
Oil pressure unit is defective.
Replace.
Oil pressure gauge is defective.
Replace.
Yes
No
SB9099100010000X

Fig. 7 Oil pressure gauge troubleshooting. Loyale

Starter Motors

INDEX

	Page No.
Diagnosis & Testing	39-70
Impreza & SVX	39-70
Justy	39-70
Legacy & Loyale	39-70
Starter Specifications	39-71
Troubleshooting	39-70

TROUBLESHOOTING

Refer to **Fig. 1,** for troubleshooting procedures.

1. Starter

Trouble		Probable cause
Starter does not start.	Magnet switch does not operate (no clicks are heard).	Magnet switch poor contact or discontinuity of pull-in coil circuit
		Improper sliding of magnet switch plunger
	Magnet switch operates (clicks are issued).	Poor contact of magnet switch's main contact point
		Layer short of armature Contaminants on armature commutator High armature mica.
		Improper grounding of yoke field coil
		Insufficient carbon brush length
		Insufficient brush spring pressure
Starter starts but does not crank engine	Failure of pinion gear to engage ring gear	Worn pinion teeth
		Improper sliding of overrunning clutch
		Improper adjustment of stud bolt
	Clutch slippage	Faulty clutch roller spring
Starter starts but engine cranks too slowly.		Poor contact of magnet switch's main contact point
		Layer short of armature
		Discontinuity, burning or wear of armature commutator
		Poor grounding of yoke field coil
		Insufficient brush length
		Insufficient brush spring pressure
		Abnormal brush wear
Starter overruns		Magnet switch coil is a layer short.

SB1129100001000X

Fig. 1 Starter motor troubleshooting chart

DIAGNOSIS & TESTING

LEGACY & LOYALE

Pull-In Test

Connect battery ground leads to starter motor as shown in **Fig. 2,** then positive lead to terminal 50. Pinion should extend when lead connections are made. If starter motor does operate as specified, repair or replace starter motor as necessary.

Hold-In Test

Disconnect lead from terminal C as shown in **Fig. 3.** Pinion should be held in extended position. If starter motor does operate as specified, repair or replace starter motor as necessary.

Return Test

1. Connect two battery ground leads to terminal 50 and to switch body as shown in **Fig. 4.**
2. Connect battery positive lead to terminal C.
3. Disconnect lead from terminal 50. Pinion should return immediately.
4. If starter motor does operate as specified, repair or replace starter motor as necessary.

JUSTY

No Load Test

When running this test, do not exceed 30 seconds or damage to the starter motor will result.

With starter clamped on test bench, connect starter as shown in **Fig. 5.** Measure and record current, voltage and rotation speed. On vehicles equipped with manual transmission voltage should be 11.5. Current draw should be 45 amps or less. Rotation speed should be 5,500 RPM or greater. On vehicles equipped with ECVT transmission voltage should be 11.5. Current draw should be 60 amps or less. Rotation speed should be 6,600 RPM or greater. If the starter motor does not meet specifications, repair or replace starter motor as necessary.

IMPREZA & SVX

Pull-In Test

1. Connect terminal "S", **Fig. 6,** of solenoid assembly to positive terminal of battery.
2. Connect starter frame to ground terminal of battery.
3. Pinion should extend.
4. Disconnect starter motor connector from terminal M.
5. Connect positive terminal of battery, then ground starter frame.
6. Pinion should return.
7. If pinion does not operate as specified, repair or replace starter as necessary.

No Load Test

When running this test, do not exceed 30 seconds or damage to the starter motor will result.

1. Connect starter motor as shown in **Fig. 7.**
2. Turn switch to on position, then adjust variable resistance to 11 volts.
3. Measure and record ammeter reading and measure the starter speed. Ammeter reading 90A maximum. Rotation speed for manual transmission should be 3,000 RPM minimum, automatic transmission should be 2,900 RPM minimum.
4. If readings are not as specified, repair or replace starter motor as necessary.

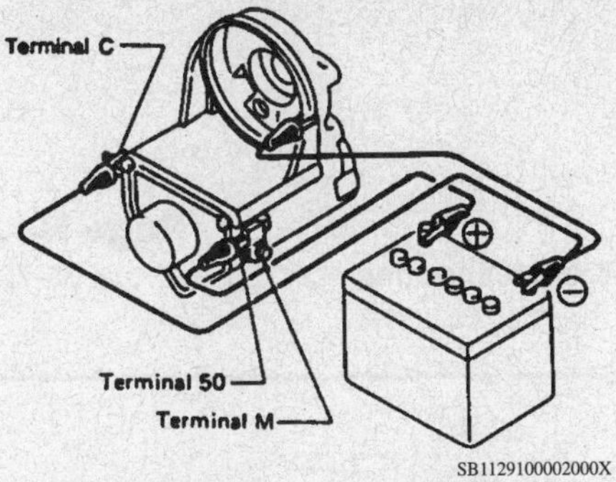
Terminal C
Terminal 50
Terminal M
SB1129100002000X

Fig. 2 Electrical connections for pull-in test. Legacy & Loyale

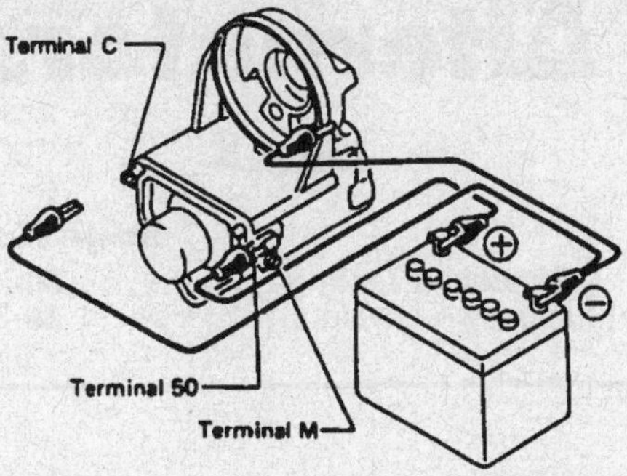
Terminal C
Terminal 50
Terminal M
SB1129100003000X

Fig. 3 Electrical connections for hold-in test. Legacy & Loyale

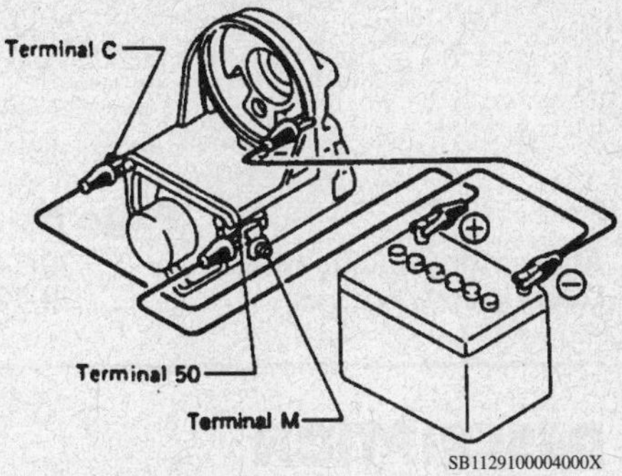
Terminal C
Terminal 50
Terminal M
SB1129100004000X

Fig. 4 Electrical connections for return test. Legacy & Loyale

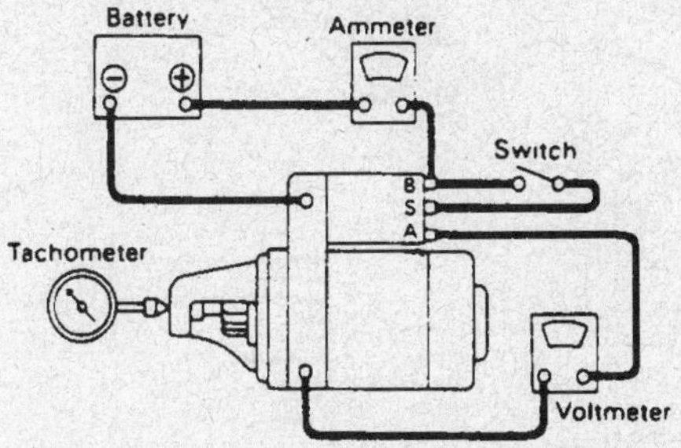
Battery
Ammeter
Switch
B
S
A
Tachometer
Voltmeter
SB1129100005000X

Fig. 5 No load test connections. Justy

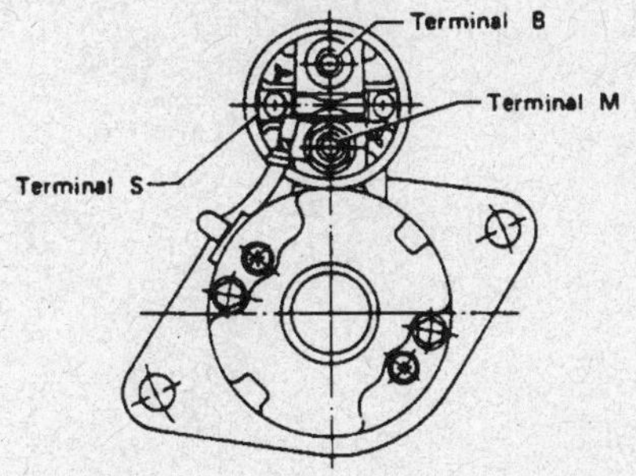
Terminal B
Terminal M
Terminal S
SB1129100006000X

Fig. 6 Starter motor terminal identification. Impreza & SVX

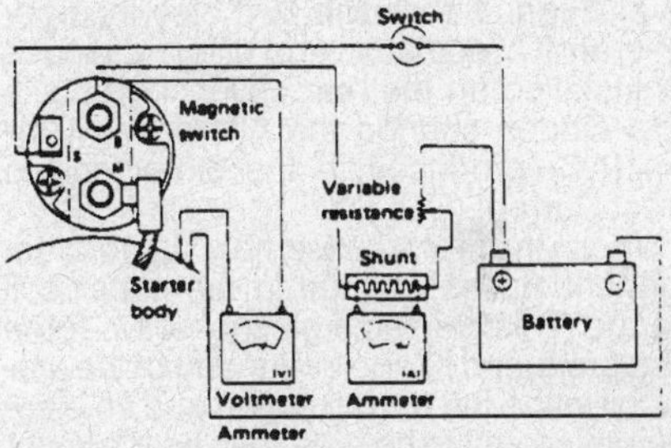
Switch
Magnetic switch
Variable resistance
Shunt
Starter body
Battery
Voltmeter
Ammeter
Ammeter
SB1129100007000X

Fig. 7 No load test connections. Impreza & SVX

STARTER SPECIFICATIONS

Year	Ident. No.	No Load Test			Torque Test		
		Amperes	Volts	RPM	Amperes	Volts	Ft. Lbs.
1993–96	M001T77181	90	11	2900	280	8	6.3
	M1T-75681②	90	11	3000	300	7.7	7
	③④	45	11.5	5500	200	8	3.5
	028000-8581①	90	11.5	3000	230	8	4.7
	028000-9800①	90	11	4000	370	8	10
	③⑤	60	11.5	6600	200	8	3.5
	128000-8321①	90	11	2900	370	8	10.1
	128000-8311①	90	11	3000	280	8	7.2

① — Nippondenso.
② — Mitsubishi.
③ — Justy.
④ — Except ECVT.
⑤ — With ECVT.

Alternators

INDEX

	Page No.
Alternator Specifications	39-74
Description	39-72
Diagnosis & Testing	39-72
Legacy & Loyale	39-72
Troubleshooting	39-72

DESCRIPTION

The alternator is a self ventilating type which consists essentially of a pulley, front cover, rotor with fan blades, stator and rear cover, **Figs. 1 through 6.** It also incorporates an IC regulator, and silicone diodes are installed on the rear cover. These silicone diodes change the Alternating Current (AC) produced in the stator coil to Direct Current (DC).

When the rotor assembly is rotated, magnetic fluxes created in the stator coil change. This causes a electromotive force to be produced on the upper end of the stator coil in the left turn direction and an electromotive force to be produced on the lower end in the right turn direction. When the rotor is turned 180°, then electromotive force changes in its direction, the upper and lower ends of the coil alternate becoming north then south poles, producing an AC voltage in the coil. This AC is rectified to DC by silicone diodes and is then regulated by the IC regulator.

TROUBLESHOOTING

Refer to **Fig. 7,** for alternator troubleshooting procedure.

DIAGNOSIS & TESTING

LEGACY & LOYALE

Mount alternator securely in a suitable test stand prior to testing. Ensure test stand battery is fully charged before conducting any alternator tests.

1. Make appropriate test connections shown in **Figs. 8 and 9,** to test alternator output speed.
2. Open switch SW1 and close switch SW2, then operate alternator test stand.
3. Slowly increase alternator speed while observing alternator output voltage.
4. Output should be 13.5 volts at 900 RPM.
5. Continue raising alternator speed while observing voltmeter. Voltage should remain within 6000 RPM for Legacy, or 5000 RPM for Loyale.
6. Check current output with test connections as shown in **Figs. 8 and 9.** Close switches 1 and 2, then set variable resistor at minimum value.
7. Increase alternator speed, using variable resistor to maintain voltage at 13.5 volts. Current ratings should be as follows:
   a. **On Loyale models,** readings should be at least 18 amps at 1250 RPM; 49 amps at 2500 RPM; and 58 amps at 5000 RPM.
   b. **On Legacy models,** readings should be at least 33 amps at 1500 RPM; 66 amps at 3000 RPM; and 80 amps at 6000 RPM.

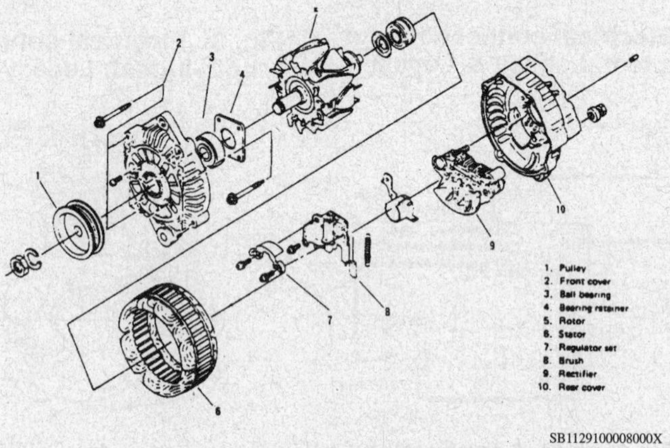

1. Pulley
2. Front cover
3. Ball bearing
4. Bearing retainer
5. Rotor
6. Stator
7. Regulator set
8. Brush
9. Rectifier
10. Rear cover
SB1129100008000X

Fig. 1 Exploded view of alternator assembly. Justy

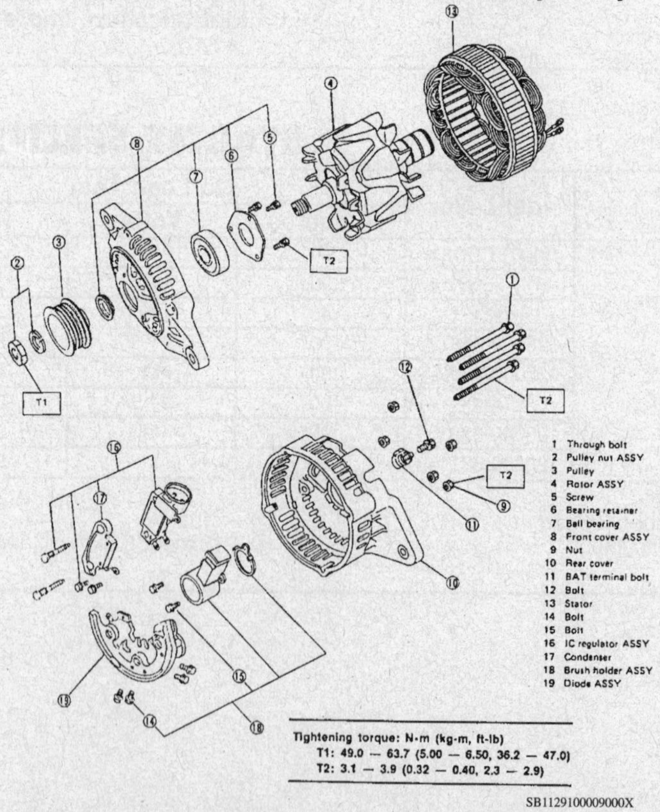

T1
T2
1 Through bolt
2 Pulley nut ASSY
3 Pulley
4 Rotor ASSY
5 Screw
6 Bearing retainer
7 Ball bearing
8 Front cover ASSY
9 Nut
10 Rear cover
11 BAT terminal bolt
12 Bolt
13 Stator
14 Bolt
15 Bolt
16 IC regulator ASSY
17 Condenser
18 Brush holder ASSY
19 Diode ASSY
Tightening torque: N·m (kg-m, ft-lb)
T1: 49.0 — 63.7 (5.00 — 6.50, 36.2 — 47.0)
T2: 3.1 — 3.9 (0.32 — 0.40, 2.3 — 2.9)
SB1129100009000X

Fig. 2 Exploded view of alternator assembly. 1993–94 Legacy

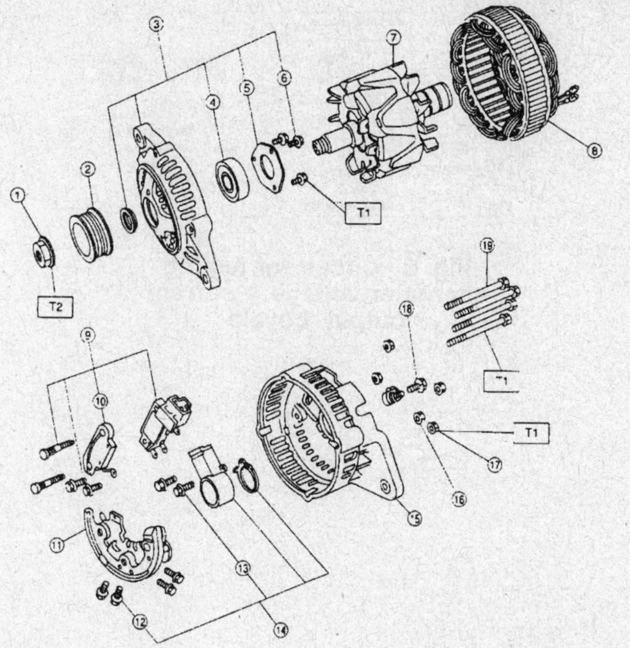
T1
T2
T1
T1

① Pulley nut
② Pulley
③ Front cover ASSY
④ Ball bearing
⑤ Bearing retainer
⑥ Screw
⑦ Rotor
⑧ Stator coil
⑨ IC regulator ASSY
⑩ Condenser
⑪ Diode ASSY
⑫ Bolt
⑬ Bolt
⑭ Brush holder ASSY
⑮ Rear cover
⑯ BAT. terminal
⑰ Nut
⑱ Bolt
⑲ Through bolt

Tightening torque: N·m (kg-m, ft-lb)
T1: 3.1 — 4.4 (0.32 — 0.45, 2.3 — 3.3)
T2: 63.7 — 83.4 (6.5 — 8.5, 47.0 — 61.5)

SB1129500018000X

Fig. 3 Exploded view of alternator assembly. 1995–96 Legacy

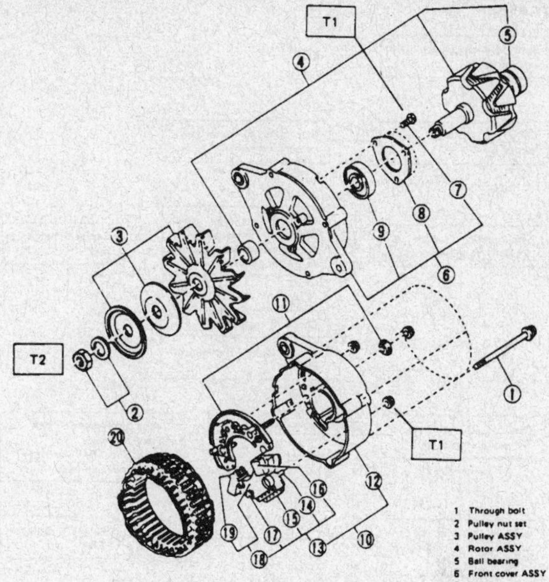
T1
T2
T1

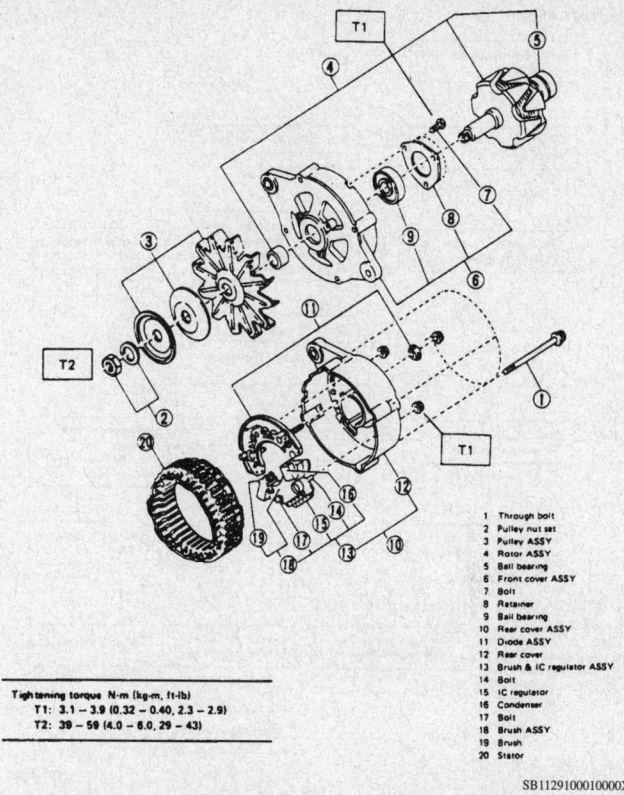

1 Through bolt
2 Pulley nut set
3 Pulley ASSY
4 Rotor ASSY
5 Ball bearing
6 Front cover ASSY
7 Bolt
8 Retainer
9 Ball bearing
10 Rear cover ASSY
11 Diode ASSY
12 Rear cover
13 Brush & IC regulator ASSY
14 Bolt
15 IC regulator
16 Condenser
17 Bolt
18 Brush ASSY
19 Brush
20 Stator

Tightening torque N·m (kg-m, ft-lb)
T1: 3.1 – 3.9 (0.32 – 0.40, 2.3 – 2.9)
T2: 39 – 59 (4.0 – 6.0, 29 – 43)

SB1129100010000X

Fig. 4 Exploded view of alternator assembly. Loyale

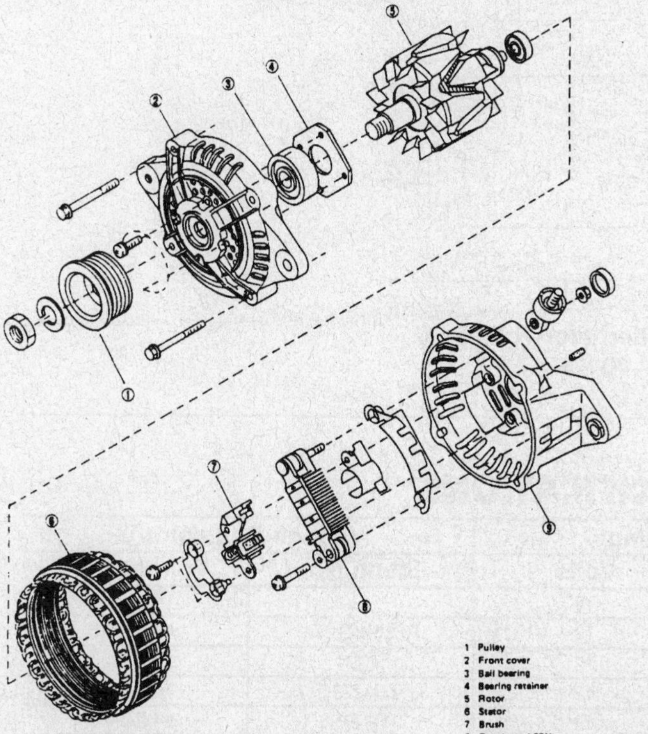

1 Pulley
2 Front cover
3 Ball bearing
4 Bearing retainer
5 Rotor
6 Stator
7 Brush
8 Regulator ASSY
9 Rear cover

SB1129100012000X

Fig. 5 Exploded view of alternator assembly. SVX

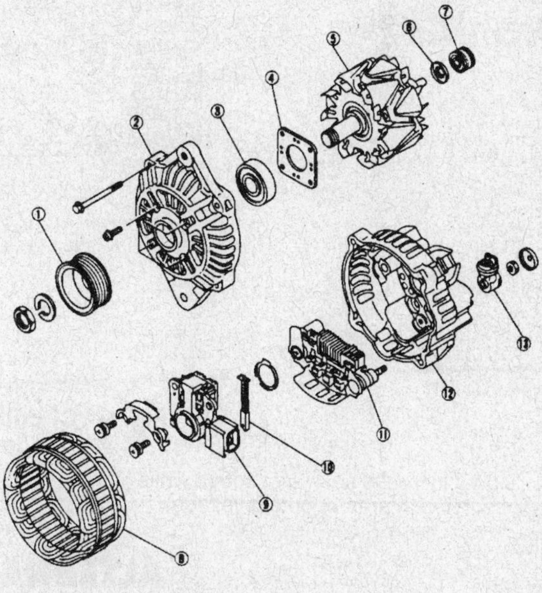

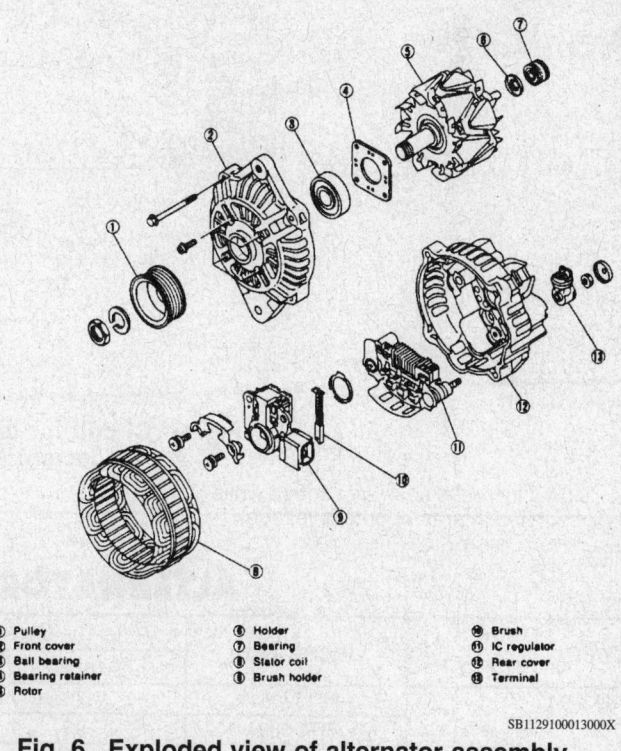

① Pulley
② Front cover
③ Ball bearing
④ Bearing retainer
⑤ Rotor
⑥ Holder
⑦ Bearing
⑧ Stator coil
⑨ Brush holder
⑩ Brush
⑪ IC regulator
⑫ Rear cover
⑬ Terminal

SB1129100013000X

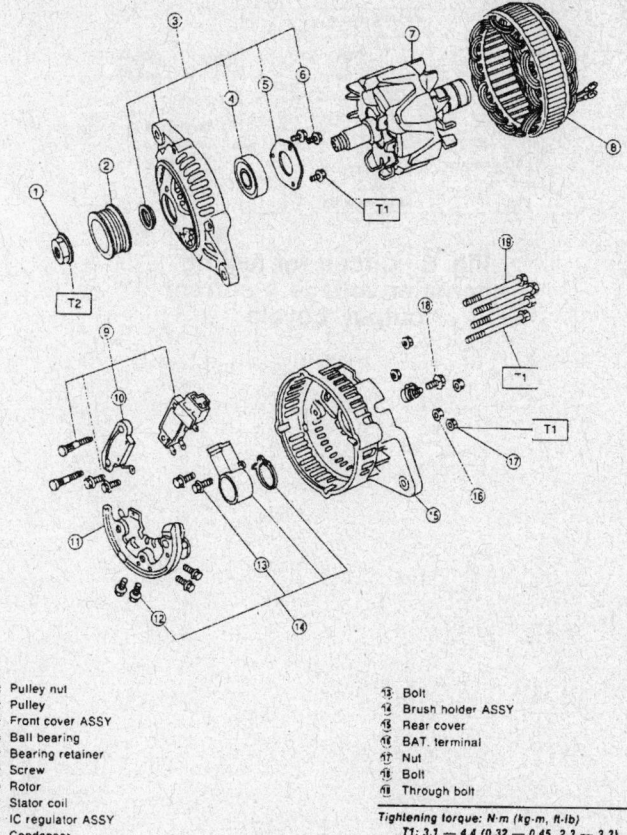

Fig. 6 Exploded view of alternator assembly. Impreza

2. Alternator

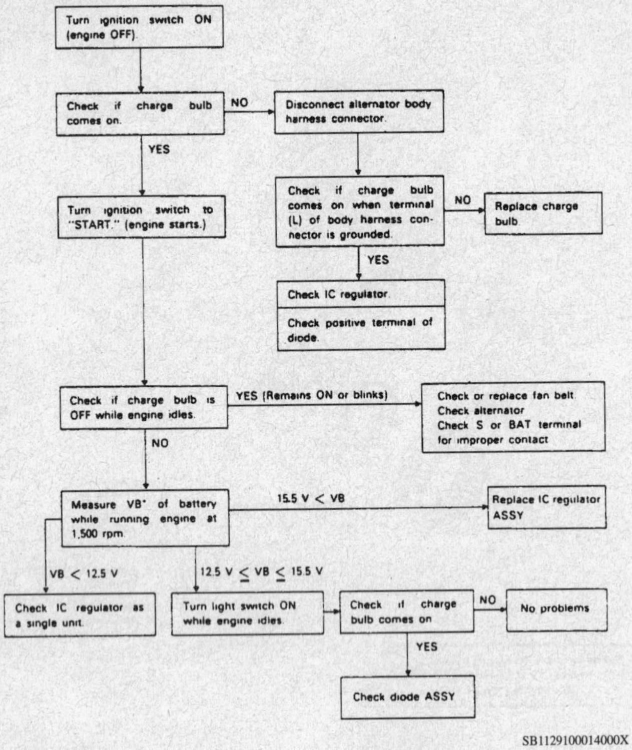
Turn ignition switch ON (engine OFF).
Check if charge bulb comes on.
NO
Disconnect alternator body harness connector.
YES
Check if charge bulb comes on when terminal (L) of body harness connector is grounded.
NO
Replace charge bulb.
Turn ignition switch to "START." (engine starts.)
YES
Check IC regulator.
Check positive terminal of diode.
Check if charge bulb is OFF while engine idles.
YES (Remains ON or blinks)
Check or replace fan belt.
Check alternator.
Check S or BAT terminal for improper contact.
NO
Measure VB* of battery while running engine at 1,500 rpm.
15.5 V < VB
Replace IC regulator ASSY.
VB < 12.5 V
12.5 V ≤ VB ≤ 15.5 V
Check IC regulator as a single unit.
Turn light switch ON while engine idles.
Check if charge bulb comes on
NO
No problems.
YES
Check diode ASSY.
SB1129100014000X

Fig. 7 Alternator troubleshooting chart

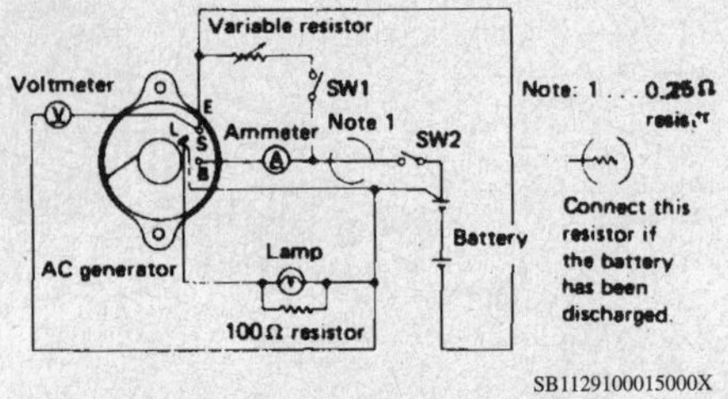
Variable resistor
Voltmeter
SW1
E
L
S
B
Ammeter
Note 1
SW2
Note: 1 . . . 0.25Ω resistor
Connect this resistor if the battery has been discharged.
Battery
AC generator
Lamp
100Ω resistor
SB1129100015000X

Fig. 8 Circuit for testing alternator voltage & current output. Loyale

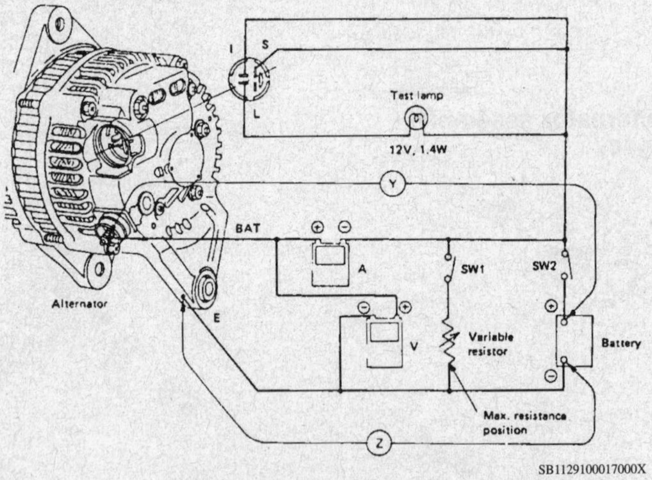
I
S
L
Test lamp
12V, 1.4W
BAT
A
SW1
SW2
Alternator
E
V
Variable resistor
Battery
Max. resistance position
SB1129100017000X

Fig. 9 Circuit for testing alternator voltage & current output. Legacy

ALTERNATOR SPECIFICATIONS

Year	Ident. No.	Current Rating		Voltage Regulator①	
		Amps.②	Volts	Ident. No.	Voltage 68°F
1993–94	A2T39091	76	12	—	14.1-14.8
	A3TO8891	95	12	A866X21271	14.2-14.8
	③	55	12	③	14.2-14.8
	LR160-137	60	12	TR1Z-56	14.2-14.8
	LR160-138	60	12	TR1Z-56	14.2-14.8
	LR170-732C	85	12	TR1Z-102	14.1-14.7

Continued

ALTERNATOR SPECIFICATIONS—Continued

Year	Ident. No.	Current Rating		Voltage Regulator①	
		Amps.②	Volts	Ident. No.	Voltage 68°F
1995–96	A2T39091	76	12	—	14.1-14.8
	A3TO8891	95	12	A866X21271	14.2-14.8
	LR160-137	60	12	TR1Z-56	14.2-14.8
	LR160-138	60	12	TR1Z-56	14.2-14.8
	LR185-701H	85	12	—	14.1-14.8

①— Integral.
②— @ 5000 RPM.
③— Justy.

Speed Control Systems

INDEX

	Page No.
Adjustments	39-76
Speed Control Cable	39-76
Component Diagnosis & Testing	39-77
Control Unit Pin Voltage Test	39-77
Main Switch Test	39-77
Sub Switch Test	39-78
Component Replacement	39-78
Vacuum Pump & Valve	39-78
Description	39-75
Self-Diagnosis System	39-75
Speed Control System	39-75
System Diagnosis & Testing	39-76
Diagnosis Using Select Monitor	39-76
Road Tests	39-77
Troubleshooting	39-75

DESCRIPTION

SPEED CONTROL SYSTEM

The speed control system automatically controls vehicle speed without depressing the accelerator pedal. To achieve this, the speed sensor in the speedometer sends a feedback signal which is compared with the desired speed set in the computer memory. The difference between the sensor and memory speeds is transmitted to the solenoid valves which moves the actuator controlling the throttle and keeps the rate of speed constant.

SELF-DIAGNOSIS SYSTEM

The self-diagnosis function of the cruise control system uses an external select monitor. The self-diagnosis function operates in two categories; cruise cancel conditions diagnosis and real-time diagnosis, which are used depending on type of problems.

This system has built in memory, the select monitor must be connected before beginning diagnosis.

Cruise Cancel Conditions Diagnosis

This category of diagnosis requires actual vehicle driving in order to determine the problem (as when cruise speed is cancelled during driving although no cruise cancel condition is entered).

Real-Time Diagnosis

This category is used to determine whether or not the input of output signal system is in good order, according to signal emitted from switches, sensors.

Vehicle cannot be driven at cruise speeds during this type of diagnosis. Dummy signals are manually entered from the select monitor's keyboard to determine if certain system are operating satisfactory.

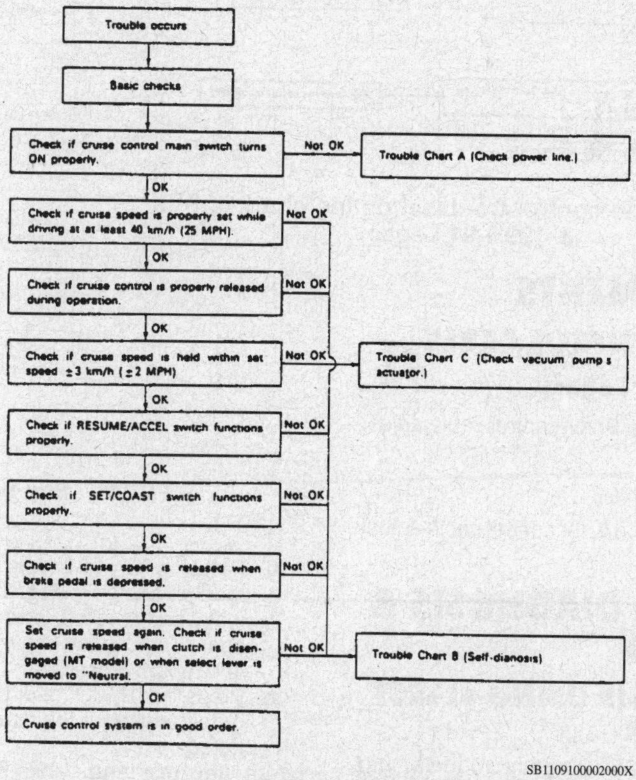
Trouble occurs
Basic checks
Check if cruise control main switch turns ON properly.
Not OK
Trouble Chart A (Check power line.)
OK
Check if cruise speed is properly set while driving at at least 40 km/h (25 MPH).
Not OK
OK
Check if cruise control is properly released during operation.
Not OK
OK
Check if cruise speed is held within set speed ±3 km/h (±2 MPH)
Not OK
Trouble Chart C (Check vacuum pump & actuator.)
OK
Check if RESUME/ACCEL switch functions properly.
Not OK
OK
Check if SET/COAST switch functions properly.
Not OK
OK
Check if cruise speed is released when brake pedal is depressed.
Not OK
OK
Set cruise speed again. Check if cruise speed is released when clutch is disengaged (MT model) or when select lever is moved to "Neutral.
Not OK
Trouble Chart B (Self-dianosis)
OK
Cruise control system is in good order.
SB1109100002000X

Fig. 1 Speed control basic troubleshooting chart. SVX & 1993–94 Legacy

TROUBLESHOOTING

Refer to **Figs. 1 through 8,** for troubleshooting procedures.

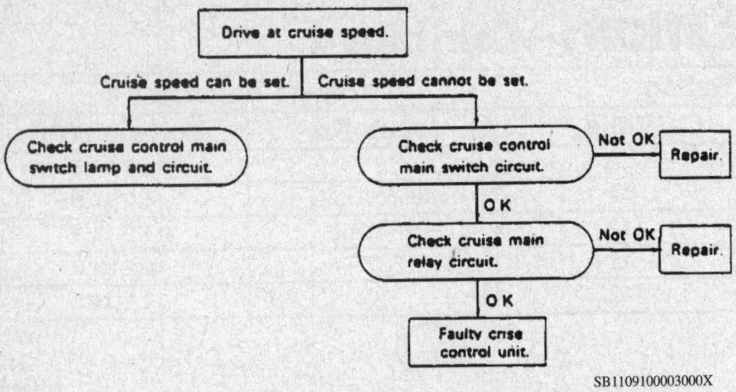
Drive at cruise speed.
Cruise speed can be set.
Cruise speed cannot be set.
Check cruise control main switch lamp and circuit.
Check cruise control main switch circuit.
Not OK
Repair.
OK
Check cruise main relay circuit.
Not OK
Repair.
OK
Faulty crise control unit.
SB1109100003000X

Fig. 2 Speed control troubleshooting chart A. SVX & 1993–94 Legacy

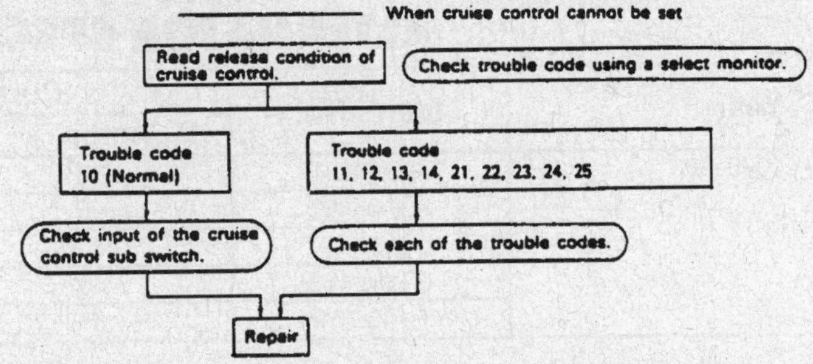
When cruise control cannot be set
Read release condition of cruise control.
Check trouble code using a select monitor.
Trouble code 10 (Normal)
Trouble code 11, 12, 13, 14, 21, 22, 23, 24, 25
Check input of the cruise control sub switch.
Check each of the trouble codes.
Repair

Check trouble code with a select monitor
Check input of cruise control sub switch. (SET/COAST SW, RESUME/ACCEL SW)
Trouble code 11. Stop light switch, brake switch, inhibitor switch and clutch switch
Trouble code 12. Malfunction engine revelusion input signal
Trouble code 13, or 24. Failure in the speed sensor system
Trouble code 14. Simultaneous input signal of SET/SW and RESUME/SW
Trouble code 21, and 22. Malfunction in vacuum pump and vent valve
Trouble code 23. Malfunction in built-in relay of cruise control unit
SB1109100004000X

Fig. 3 Speed control troubleshooting chart B. SVX & 1993–94 Legacy

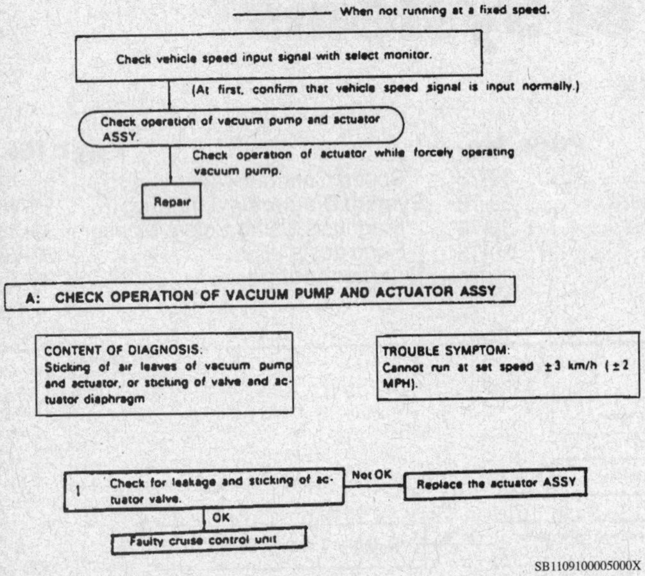
When not running at a fixed speed.
Check vehicle speed input signal with select monitor.
(At first, confirm that vehicle speed signal is input normally.)
Check operation of vacuum pump and actuator ASSY.
Check operation of actuator while forcely operating vacuum pump.
Repair
A: CHECK OPERATION OF VACUUM PUMP AND ACTUATOR ASSY
CONTENT OF DIAGNOSIS: Sticking of air leaves of vacuum pump and actuator, or sticking of valve and actuator diaphragm
TROUBLE SYMPTOM: Cannot run at set speed ±3 km/h (±2 MPH).
1 Check for leakage and sticking of actuator valve.
Not OK
Replace the actuator ASSY
OK
Faulty cruise control unit
SB1109100005000X

Fig. 4 Speed control troubleshooting chart C. SVX & 1993–94 Legacy

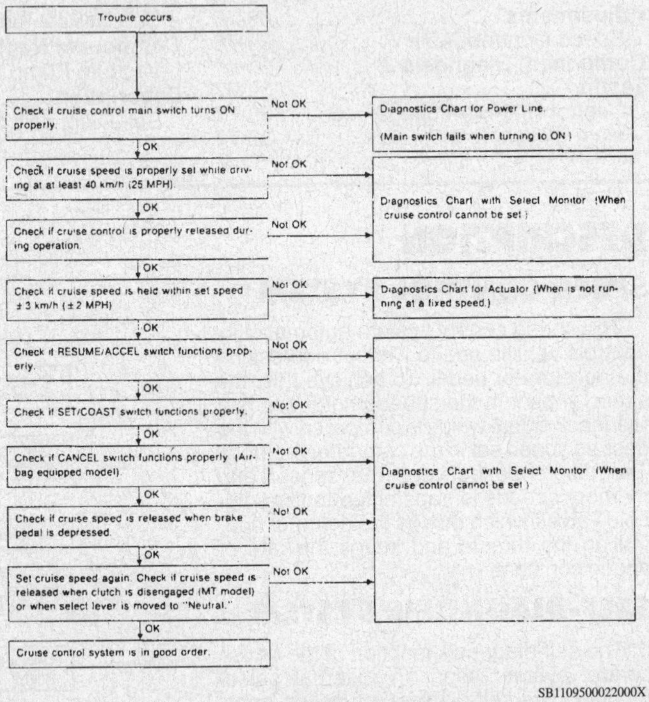
Trouble occurs
Check if cruise control main switch turns ON properly.
Not OK
Diagnostics Chart for Power Line.
(Main switch fails when turning to ON.)
OK
Check if cruise speed is properly set while driving at at least 40 km/h (25 MPH).
Not OK
Diagnostics Chart with Select Monitor (When cruise control cannot be set.)
OK
Check if cruise control is properly released during operation.
Not OK
OK
Check if cruise speed is held within set speed ±3 km/h (±2 MPH)
Not OK
Diagnostics Chart for Actuator (When is not running at a fixed speed.)
OK
Check if RESUME/ACCEL switch functions properly.
Not OK
OK
Check if SET/COAST switch functions properly.
Not OK
OK
Check if CANCEL switch functions properly (Air-bag equipped model).
Not OK
Diagnostics Chart with Select Monitor (When cruise control cannot be set.)
OK
Check if cruise speed is released when brake pedal is depressed.
Not OK
OK
Set cruise speed again. Check if cruise speed is released when clutch is disengaged (MT model) or when select lever is moved to "Neutral."
Not OK
OK
Cruise control system is in good order.
SB1109500022000X

Fig. 5 Speed control basic troubleshooting chart. Impreza & 1995–96 Legacy

ADJUSTMENTS

SPEED CONTROL CABLE

Impreza & Legacy

Refer to **Fig. 9,** for control cable adjustment.

SVX

Refer to **Fig. 10,** for control cable adjustment.

SYSTEM DIAGNOSIS & TESTING

DIAGNOSIS USING SELECT MONITOR

1. **On 1993–94 Legacy models,** proceed as follows:
   a. Connect select monitor to data link connector, located behind lefthand side lower instrument cover.
   b. Turn ignition switch on, then turn cruise main switch to on position.
   c. Turn select monitor on. All LED's will come on. Select monitor display will read as shown in **Fig. 11,** after several seconds.
   d. Pressing "O" will convert display to read as shown in **Fig. 12.** If cruise main switch is off, error 2 will appear. Turn cruise main switch on and repeat procedure.
   e. Press "F," "B," "O" and "ENT" in that order, and enter the desired designated code.
2. **On Impreza and 1995–96 Legacy models,** proceed as follows:
   a. Connect select monitor to data link connector, located behind lefthand side lower instrument cover.
   b. Turn ignition switch on, then turn cruise main switch to on position.
   c. Turn select monitor on. All LED's will come on.
   d. Press "F," "B," "O" and "ENT" in that order, and enter the desired designated code.
3. **On SVX models,** proceed as follows:
   a. Connect select monitor to connector B35.
   b. Turn ignition switch on, then turn cruise main switch to on position.
   c. Turn select monitor on. All LED's will come on. Select monitor display will read as shown in **Fig. 13,** after several seconds.
   d. Press "/" three times. Select monitor display will read as shown in **Fig. 14.**
   e. Press "O" will convert display to read as shown in **Fig. 11.** If cruise main switch is off, error 2 will appear. Turn cruise main switch on and repeat procedure.

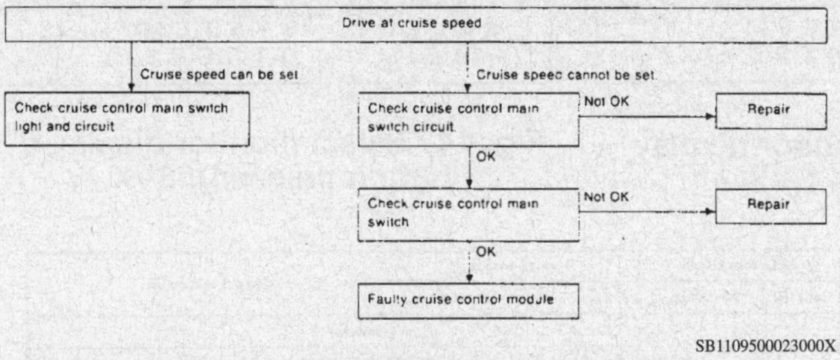
Drive at cruise speed
Cruise speed can be set
Cruise speed cannot be set
Check cruise control main switch light and circuit
Check cruise control main switch circuit
Not OK
Repair
OK
Check cruise control main switch
Not OK
Repair
OK
Faulty cruise control module
SB1109500023000X

Fig. 6 Speed control diagnostics chart for power line. Impreza & 1995–96 Legacy

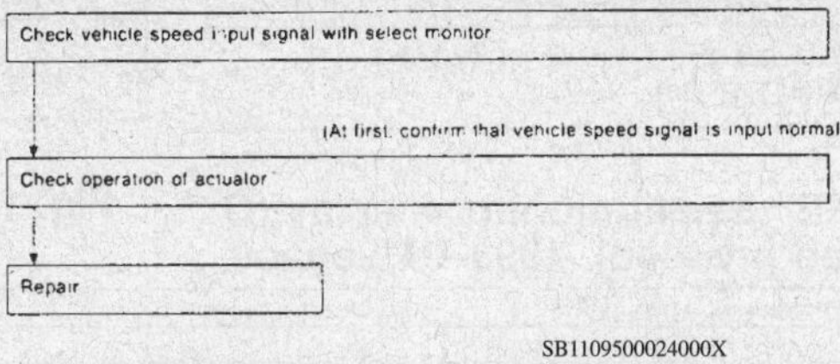
Check vehicle speed input signal with select monitor
(At first, confirm that vehicle speed signal is input normally.)
Check operation of actuator
Repair
SB1109500024000X

Fig. 7 Speed control diagnostics chart for actuator. Impreza & 1995–96 Legacy

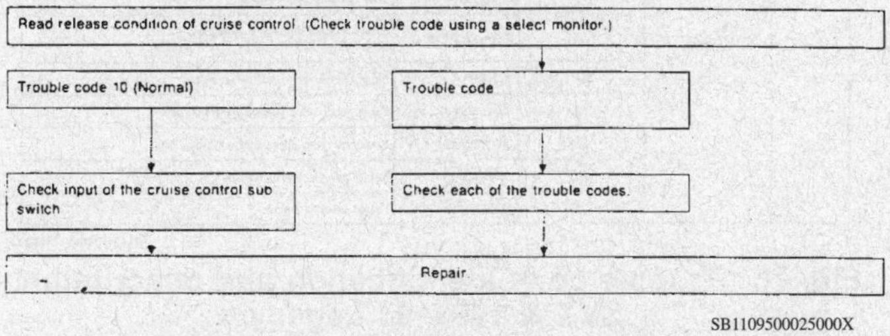
Read release condition of cruise control (Check trouble code using a select monitor.)
Trouble code 10 (Normal)
Trouble code
Check input of the cruise control sub switch
Check each of the trouble codes.
Repair
SB1109500025000X

Fig. 8 Speed control diagnostics chart with select monitor. Impreza & 1995–96 Legacy

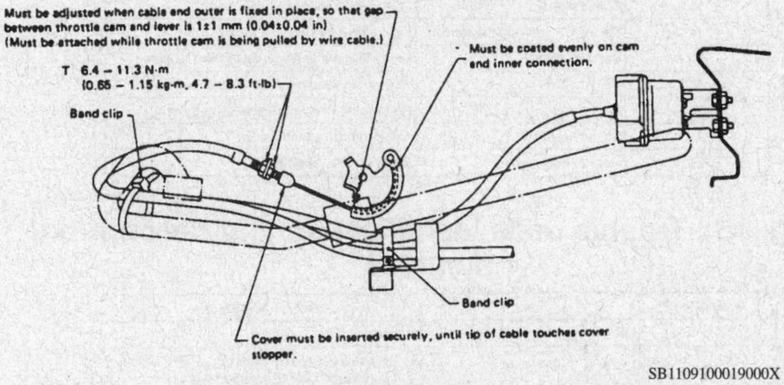
Must be adjusted when cable end outer is fixed in place, so that gap between throttle cam and lever is 1±1 mm (0.04±0.04 in)
(Must be attached while throttle cam is being pulled by wire cable.)
T 6.4 – 11.3 N·m
(0.65 – 1.15 kg-m, 4.7 – 8.3 ft-lb)
Band clip
Must be coated evenly on cam end inner connection.
Band clip
Cover must be inserted securely, until tip of cable touches cover stopper.
SB1109100019000X

Fig. 9 Control cable adjustment. Legacy

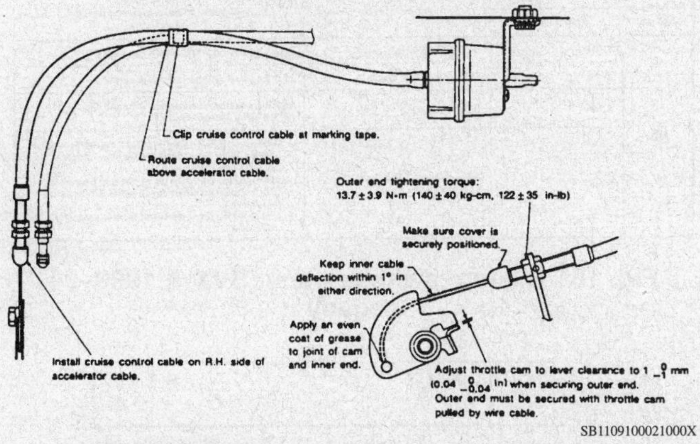
Clip cruise control cable at marking tape.
Route cruise control cable above accelerator cable.
Outer end tightening torque:
13.7±3.9 N·m (140±40 kg-cm, 122±35 in-lb)
Make sure cover is securely positioned.
Keep inner cable deflection within 1° in either direction.
Apply an even coat of grease to joint of cam and inner end.
Install cruise control cable on R.H. side of accelerator cable.
Outer end must be secured with throttle cam pulled by wire cable.
SB1109100021000X

Fig. 10 Control cable adjustment. SVX

CRUISE (/)
YES:0,OTHERS :/
SB1109100007000X

Fig. 11 Select monitor display (Power On). 1993–94 Legacy

f. Press "F," "B," "O" and "ENT" in that order, and enter the desired designated code.

Diagnosis Of Cruise Cancel Conditions

1. Connect select monitor.
2. Turn ignition and cruise main switch on, and set select monitor in "FBO" mode.
3. Start engine and drive vehicle at least 25 mph with cruise speed set.
4. If cruise speed is cancelled itself (without doing any cancel operations), a trouble code will appear on select monitor display.
5. Trouble code will be cleared by turning ignition or cruise main switch off. Refer to **Figs. 15 through 17.**

Real-Time Diagnosis

1. Inspect system switches as follows:
   a. Connect select monitor.
   b. Turn ignition switch and cruise main switch on.
   c. Set select monitor in "FAO" mode.
   d. Ensure normal indication is displayed when switches are operated as shown in **Fig. 18 and 19.**
2. **On SVX and 1993–94 Legacy models,** inspect output systems as follows:
   a. Connect select monitor.
   b. Turn ignition switch and cruise main switch on (engine off).
   c. Set transmission in Drive.
   d. Set select monitor in FB1 mode. The display will read as shown in **Fig. 20,** until input OK is present.
   e. Press "O." Example, pressing "O" in Neutral shows "31 Motor" (which indicates a faulty motor) on display because power supply to vacuum pump motor is disconnected. When this is shown, set select lever to Drive and turn cruise main switch off. Then repeat test procedure. Refer to **Fig. 21,** for output system codes and **Fig. 22,** for select monitor display data.

ROAD TESTS

Acceleration Test

1. Turn main switch on.
2. Set vehicle at speed greater than 25 mph. Ensure vehicle accelerates with switch held in "Resume/Accel" position and optional speed is maintained with switch released.

Constant Speed Test

1. Turn main switch on.
2. Set switch to "Set/Coast" with vehicle speed over 25 mph. Ensure vehicle maintains set speed.

Deceleration Test

1. Turn main switch on.
2. Set vehicle at speed greater than 25 mph. Ensure vehicle decelerates with switch held in "Set/Coast" position and optional speed is maintained with switch released. **During deceleration, cruise control will release when speed reaches 19 mph.**

COMPONENT DIAGNOSIS & TESTING

CONTROL UNIT PIN VOLTAGE TEST

Refer to **Figs. 23 through 26,** for pin voltage test.

MAIN SWITCH TEST

1. Turn ignition switch on.
2. Ensure main switch is not illuminated when in the off position.
3. Ensure main switch is illuminated when in the on position.
4. Leave main switch on.
5. Turn ignition switch off then on. Ensure main switch is not illuminated.

```
CRUISE        (F00)
CONTROL
```

SB1109100008000X

Fig. 12 Select monitor display (O button pressed). 1993–94 Legacy

```
SELECT    SYSTEM
 EG1:0,   OTHERS :/
```

SB1109100009000X

Fig. 13 Select monitor display (Power On). SVX

```
SELECT    SYSTEM
 C/C:0,   OTHERS :/
```

SB1109100010000X

Fig. 14 Select monitor display (/ button pressed). SVX

Trouble code	Item	Contents of diagnosis
10	OK	Normal
11	Brake/switch, Stop light switch	Input signals from brake switch "OFF", stop light switch "ON" (Brake pedal is depressed.)
12	Clutch switch, N position	Input signals from clutch switch "OFF", inhibitor switch "N" (Clutch pedal is depressed, or select lever is set to "N".)
13	Speed limiter	Low-speed control limiter
14	Set switch and resume switch	Input signal from cancel switch "ON"
21	Vacuum valve	Faulty vacuum valve or valve drive system
22	Vent 2 valve	Faulty vent 2 valve or valve drive system
23	Vent 1 valve	Faulty vent 1 valve or valve drive system
24	Speed sensor	Faulty vehicle speed sensor
25	Control module	Faulty control module

SB1109500026000X

Fig. 15 Trouble code identification and description. Impreza

Function code indication		Item to measure		Contents of diagnosis
Code No.	Abbreviation	Trouble code	Abbreviation	
FB0	CANCEL	10	OK	Normal
		11	BR/ST/CL or N	Input signals from brake switch, stop light switch, inhibitor switch (AT)
		12	E/G REV	Engine speed (rpm) limiter
		13	SPEED LIM	Low-speed control limiter
		14	SET+RESUME	Simultaneous entry of two signals (Shorted circuit)
		21	MOTOR	Faulty motor or motor drive system
		22	VENT VALVE	Faulty vent valve and valve drive system
		23	C/U RELAY	Faulty relay built into cruise control unit
		24	SP SENSOR	Faulty vehicle speed sensor
		25	RESUME SW	Faulty resume switch

SB1109100011000X

Fig. 16 Trouble code identification and description. SVX & 1993–94 Legacy

Trouble code	Item	Contents of diagnosis
10	OK	Normal
11	BRAKE/ST/CL or N	• Input signals from brake switch "OFF", stop light switch "ON" (Brake pedal is in depressed condition.) • Input signals from clutch switch "OFF", or inhibitor switch is in "N" position. [Clutch pedal is depressed (MT), or select lever is set to N position (AT).]
12	NOT SET SP	Out of cruise speed range
13	LOW SP LIM	Low-speed control limiter
14	CANCEL SW	Input signal from cancel switch
15	NO MEMORY	No memorized cruise speed
21	SP SENS NG	Faulty vehicle speed sensor 2
22	COM SW NG	Faulty SET/COAST switch or RESUME/ACCEL switch
23	RELAY NG	Faulty safety relay included in cruise control module
24	CPU RAM NG	Faulty CPU RAM included in cruise control module
31	MOTOR NG	Faulty vacuum motor or motor drive system
32	AIR VAL NG	Faulty air valve or valve drive system
33	REL VAL NG	Faulty release valve or valve drive system

SB1109500027000X

Fig. 17 Trouble code identification and description. 1995–96 Legacy

Function code indication		Item to measure	Content of items to be monitored
Code No.	Abbreviation		
FA0	1. SE	SET/COAST switch	LED 1 comes on when switch is turned ON.
	2. RE	RESUME/ACCEL switch	LED 2 comes on when switch is turned ON.
	4. ST	Stop light switch	LED 4 comes on when switch is turned ON. (Brake pedal is depressed.)
	5. BR	Brake switch and clutch switch/inhibitor switch	• Brake switch [Set select lever (AT model) to any position other than "P" or "N"/depress clutch pedal (MT model)]. LED 5 comes on when brake pedal is depressed. • LED 5 comes on when clutch pedal is depressed (MT model). • LED 5 comes on when select lever is set to "N" (AT model).

SB1109100012000X

Fig. 18 System switches test. SVX & 1993–94 Legacy

Function code indication		Item to measure	Content of items to be monitored
Code No	Abbreviation		
FA0	ST	Stop light switch	LED No.1 comes on when switch is turned ON. (Brake pedal is depressed.)
	BR	Brake switch	LED No. 2 comes on when brake pedal is depressed.
	SE	SET/COAST switch	LED No. 3 comes on when switch is turned ON.
	RE	RESUME/ACCEL switch	LED No. 4 comes on when switch is turned ON.
	IH	Clutch switch/inhibitor switch	• LED No. 5 comes on when clutch pedal is depressed (MT model). • LED No. 5 comes on when select lever is set to "N" (AT model).

SB1109500028000X

Fig. 19 System switches test. Impreza & 1995–96 Legacy

```
OUTPUT        (FBI)
ready ?      Yes : 0
```

SB1109100013000X

Fig. 20 Select monitor display (O button pressed, Output systems). SVX & 1993–94 Legacy

SUB SWITCH TEST

1. Ensure switch operation is proper in the "Set/Coast" and "Resume/Accel" positions.
2. Ensure switch returns to original position when released.

COMPONENT REPLACEMENT

VACUUM PUMP & VALVE

Legacy

1. Disconnect battery negative cable.
2. Disconnect vacuum pump electrical connector.
3. Disconnect vacuum hose from body side.
4. Remove vacuum pump retaining nuts.
5. **On 1993–94 Legacy models,** disconnect ABS sensor connector clip from bracket.
6. **On 1995–96 Legacy models,** remove A/C receiver/drier bracket.
7. **On all models,** remove vacuum pump assembly.
8. Reverse procedure to install.

SVX

1. Remove battery.
2. Remove main fuse box mounting bolts, then position fuse box aside.
3. Disconnect vacuum pump wiring harness and hose.
4. Remove vacuum pump attaching bolts, then the pump.
5. Reverse procedure to install.

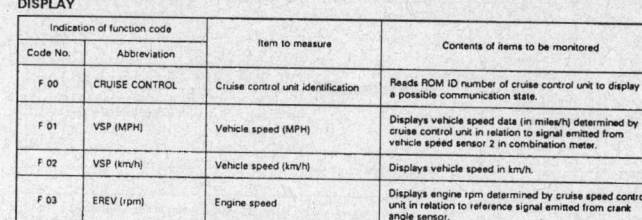

Function code indication		Item to measure		Contents of diagnosis
Code No.	Abbreviation	Trouble code	Abbreviation	
FB1	OUTPUT	10	OK	Normal
		31	MOTOR	Open or shorted vacuum pump motor circuit/harness
		32	VENT VALVE	Open or shorted vent circuit/harness
		33	C/U RELAY	Deposited safety relay built into cruise control unit
		34	C/U VENT V	Faulty vent valve drive circuit of cruise control unit
		35	C/U MOTOR	Faulty vacuum pump motor drive circuit

SB1109100014000X

Fig. 21 Output system codes (Real-time diagnosis) SVX & 1993–94 Legacy

DISPLAY

Indication of function code		Item to measure	Contents of items to be monitored
Code No.	Abbreviation		
F 00	CRUISE CONTROL	Cruise control unit identification	Reads ROM ID number of cruise control unit to display a possible communication state.
F 01	VSP (MPH)	Vehicle speed (MPH)	Displays vehicle speed data (in miles/h) determined by cruise control unit in relation to signal emitted from vehicle speed sensor 2 in combination meter.
F 02	VSP (km/h)	Vehicle speed (km/h)	Displays vehicle speed in km/h.
F 03	EREV (rpm)	Engine speed	Displays engine rpm determined by cruise speed control unit in relation to reference signal emitted from crank angle sensor.

SB1109100015000X

Fig. 22 Select monitor display data. SVX & 1993–94 Legacy

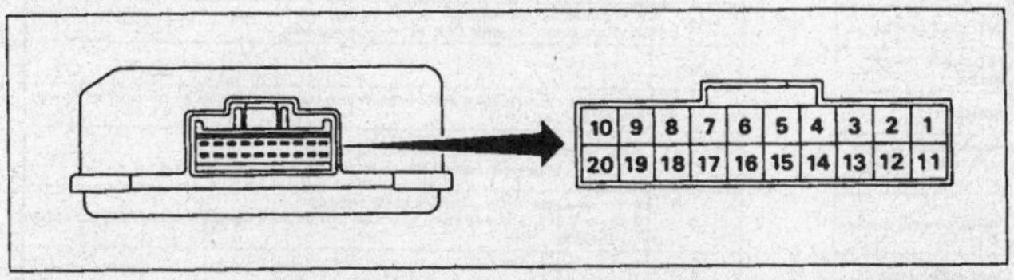
10 9 8 7 6 5 4 3 2 1
20 19 18 17 16 15 14 13 12 11

Content	Terminal No.	Measuring conditions and I/O signals (ignition switch ON and engine idling)
Vent valve	1	• Power supply is ON when vehicle is stopped. • ON-and-OFF (0 and 12 volts) operation is alternately repeated while cruise control is operating.
Safety valve	2	• Power supply is ON when vehicle is stopped. • ON-and-OFF (0 and 12 volts) operation is alternately repeated while cruise control is operating.
Ignition switch	3	• Battery voltage is present when switch is turned on.
Main switch	4	• When main switch is pressed, battery voltage is present. • When main switch is OFF, "0" volt is present.
Power Supply to vacuum valve, vent valve, safety valve and set indicator	5	• When main switch is pressed, battery voltage is present.
SET/COAST switch	6	• When switch is turned ON, battery voltage is present. • When switch is turned OFF, "0" volt is present.
RESUME/ACCEL switch	7	• When switch is turned ON, battery voltage is present. • When switch is turned OFF, "0" volt is present.
Brake switch	8	Set select lever to any position other than "P" or "N" (AT model)/leave clutch released (MT model), with main switch ON. Then check that: • 0 volt is present when brake pedal is depressed. • Battery voltage is present when brake pedal is released, or • 0 volt is present when clutch pedal is depressed (MT model). • Battery voltage is present when clutch pedal is released (MT model). • 0 volt is present when select lever is set to "P" or "N" (AT model). • Battery voltage is present when select lever is in any position other than "P" or "N" (AT model).
Inhibitor switch Clutch switch	9	When switch is turned ON, "0" volt is present.
Vacuum valve	11	• Power supply is ON when vehicle is stopped. • ON-and-OFF (0 and 12 volts) operation is alternately repeated while cruise control is operating.
AT control (Set signal)	12	ECM emits a ground-level signal while driving vehicle at least 40 km/h (25 MPH) with SET switch ON.
GND	13	—
Select monitor (Output)	14	—
Select monitor (Input)	15	—
Vehicle speed sensor	18	• When all four wheels are raised off ground and any wheel is rotated manually, approximately 5 and 0 volt pulse signals are alternately sent to cruise control module.
Stop light switch	19	With ignition switch ON or OFF: • Depress brake pedal to check that battery voltage is present. • "0" volt is present with brake pedal released.
GND	20	—

SB1109100018000X

Fig. 23 Control unit pin voltage test. Impreza

Content	Connector No.	Terminal No.	Measuring conditions and I/O signals (ignition switch ON and engine idling)
Cruise control main switch	B81	1	• When main switch is pressed, battery voltage is present; when it is released, approximately 6.5 volts are present. • When main switch is OFF, "0" volts are present.
Main relay (solenoid)		2	• When main switch is turned ON, indicator comes on and battery voltage is present. • When main switch is turned OFF, "0" volts are present.
Main relay (contacts)		4	↑
Engine speed (rpm) signal	B82	2	When engine starts, a pulse signal is entered (Observe using an oscilloscope.)
Vehicle speed sensor 2		7	When all four wheels are raised off ground and any wheel is rotated manually, approximately 5 and 0 volt pulse signals are alternately sent to cruise control unit.
Brake switch		15	Set select lever to any position other than "P" or "N" (AT model)/leave clutch released (MT model), with main switch ON. Then check that: • 0 volts are present when brake pedal is depressed. • Battery voltage is present when brake pedal is released, or • 0 volts are present when clutch pedal is depressed (MT model). • Battery voltage is present when clutch pedal is released (MT model). • 0 volts are present when select lever is set to "P" or "N" (AT model). • Battery voltage is present when select lever is in any position other than "P" or "N" (AT model).
Stop light switch		20	With ignition switch ON or OFF: • Depress brake pedal to check that battery voltage is present. • "0" volts are present with brake pedal released.
SET/COAST switch		18	• When switch is turned ON, battery voltage is present. • When switch is turned OFF, "0" volts are present.
RESUME/ACCEL switch		19	↑
Set signal		11	ECU emits a ground-level signal while driving vehicle at least 40 km/h (25 MPH) with SET switch ON.
Power supply to vacuum motor, vent valve and safety valve		14	• "0" volts are present when vehicle is stopped. • Battery voltage is present while cruise control system is operating.
Vacuum motor output		8	• Power supply is ON when vehicle is stopped. • ON-and-OFF (0 and 12 volts) operation is alternately repeated while cruise control is operating.
Vent valve output		9	↑

SB1109100016000X

Fig. 24 Control unit pin voltage test. 1993–94 Legacy

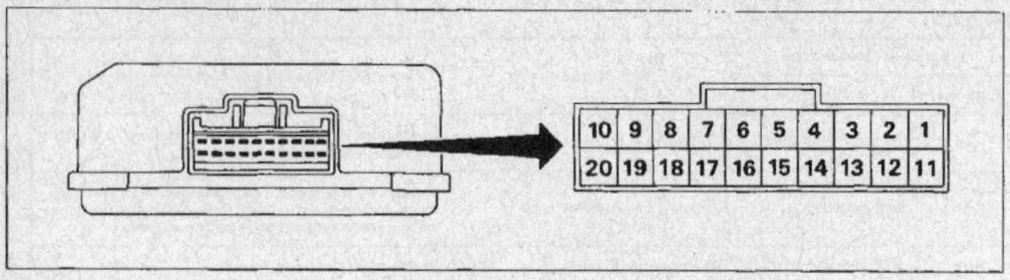
10 9 8 7 6 5 4 3 2 1
20 19 18 17 16 15 14 13 12 11

Content	Terminal No.	Measuring conditions and I/O signals (ignition switch ON and engine idling)
Main power supply	2	• Battery voltage is present when main power is turned ON. • "0" volt is present when main power is turned OFF.
Inhibitor switch (AT) (U.S.A.) N position switch (AT) (CANADA)	4	• "0" volt is present when selector lever is set to P or N position (CANADA: N position only). • Battery voltage is present when selector lever is other than P or N position (CANADA: N position only).
Air valve	5	• "0" volt is present when vehicle is stopped. • ON-and-OFF ("0"-and-battery voltage) operation is alternately repeated while cruise control is operating.
GND	6	—
Vacuum pump motor	7	• "0" volt is present when vehicle is stopped. • ON-and-OFF ("0"-and-battery voltage) operation is alternately repeated while cruise control is operating.
Data link connector	8	—
RESUME/ACCEL switch	9	• Battery voltage is present when switch is turned ON. • "0" volt is present when switch is turned OFF.
SET/COAST switch	10	• Battery voltage is present when switch is turned ON. • "0" volt is present when switch is turned OFF.
Ignition switch	12	• Battery voltage is present when ignition switch is turned ON. • "0" volt is present when ignition switch is turned OFF.
Release valve	13	• "0" volt is present when vehicle is stopped. • ON-and-OFF ("0"-and-battery voltage) operation is alternately repeated while cruise control is operating.
Power supply to vacuum pump motor, air valve, release valve	14	• "0" volt is present when vehicle is stopped. • Battery voltage is present while cruise control is operating.
Cruise main switch	15	• Battery voltage is present during pressing the main switch, and then approx. 6.5 V is present while switch is turned ON. • "0" volt is present when switch is turned OFF.
Brake switch	16	Turn the cruise main switch to ON and leave clutch pedal released (MT). Then check that: • "0" volt is present when brake pedal is depressed. • Battery voltage is present when brake pedal is released. Additionally only in MT vehicle, keep the cruise main switch to ON and leave brake pedal released. Then check that; • "0" volt is present when clutch pedal is depressed. • Battery voltage is present when clutch pedal is released.
Data link connector	17	—
Data link connector	18	—
Vehicle speed sensor 2	19	Lift-up the vehicle until all four wheels are raised off ground, and then rotate any wheel manually. Approx. 5 and 0 volt pulse signals are alternately input to cruise control module.
Stop light switch	20	Turn ignition switch to OFF. Then check that; • Battery voltage is present when brake pedal is depressed. • "0" volt is present when brake pedal is released.

NOTE:
Voltage at terminals 5, 7, 13 and 14 cannot be checked unless vehicle is driving by cruise control operation.

SB1109500029000X

Fig. 25 Control unit pin voltage test. 1995–96 Legacy

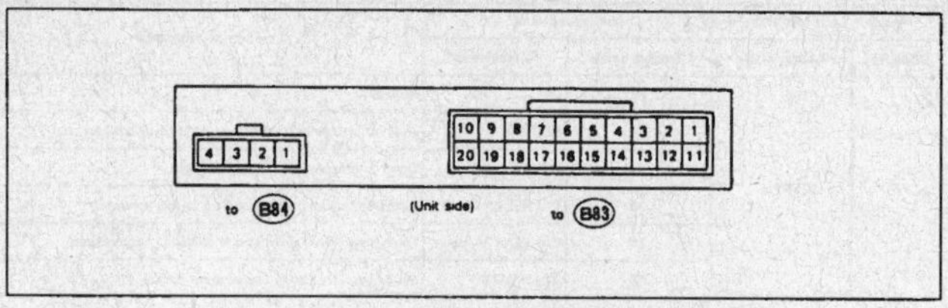
4 3 2 1
10 9 8 7 6 5 4 3 2 1
20 19 18 17 16 15 14 13 12 11
to B84
(Unit side)
to B83

Content	Connector No.	Terminal No.	Measuring conditions and I/O signals (ignition switch ON and engine idling)
Main switch	B84	1	• When main switch is pressed, battery voltage is present; when it is released, approximately 6.5 volts are present. • When main switch is OFF, "0" volts are present.
Main relay (solenoid)	B84	2	• When main switch is turned ON, indicator comes on and battery voltage is present. • When main switch is turned OFF, "0" volts are present.
Main relay (contacts)	B84	4	↑
Engine speed (rpm) signal	B83	2	When engine starts, a pulse signal is entered (Observe using an oscilloscope.)
Vehicle speed sensor	B83	7	When all four wheels are raised off ground and any wheel is rotated manually, approximately 5 and 0 volt pulse signals are alternately sent to cruise control unit.
Brake switch	B83	15	Set select lever to any position other than "P" or "N", with main switch ON. Then check that: • 0 volts are present when brake pedal is depressed. • Battery voltage is present when brake pedal is released, or • 0 volts are present when select lever is set to "P" or "N". • Battery voltage is present when select lever is in any position other than "P" or "N".
Stop light switch	B83	20	With ignition switch ON or OFF: • Depress brake pedal to check that battery voltage is present. • "0" volts are present with brake pedal released.
SET/COAST switch	B83	18	• When switch is turned ON, battery voltage is present. • When switch is turned OFF, "0" volts are present.
RESUME/ACCEL switch	B83	19	↑
Set signal	B83	11	ECU emits a ground-level signal while driving vehicle at at least 40 km/h (25 MPH) with SET switch ON.
Power supply to vacuum motor, vent valve and safety valve	B83	14	• "0" volts are present when vehicle is stopped. • Battery voltage is present while cruise control system is operating.
Vacuum motor output	B83	8	• Power supply is ON when vehicle is stopped. • ON-and-OFF (0 and 12 volts) operation is alternately repeated while cruise control is operating.
Vent valve output	B83	9	↑

SB1109100017000X

Fig. 26 Control unit pin voltage test. SVX

Wiper Systems

INDEX

	Page No.
Component Diagnosis & Testing	39-81
Impreza & Legacy	39-81
Justy	39-81
Loyale	39-81
SVX	39-82
Troubleshooting	39-81
Justy	39-81
Loyale	39-81

TROUBLESHOOTING

LOYALE

Refer to **Fig. 1,** for troubleshooting on front wiper system and **Fig. 2,** for troubleshooting on rear wiper system.

JUSTY

Refer to **Fig. 3,** for troubleshooting on front wiper system.

COMPONENT DIAGNOSIS & TESTING

LOYALE

WIPER SWITCH CONTINUITY TEST

Refer to **Fig. 4,** for continuity test.

JUSTY

WIPER SWITCH CONTINUITY TEST

Refer to **Figs. 5 through 7,** for continuity test.

IMPREZA & LEGACY

WINDSHIELD WIPER SWITCH CONTINUITY TEST

Refer to **Fig. 8,** for connector pin identification and **Fig. 9,** for continuity test.

WINDSHIELD WIPER MOTOR TEST

Impreza & 1993-94 Legacy

1. Inspect wiper motor low speed operation by connecting battery positive lead to terminal 2 of wiper motor connector and negative lead to terminal 4, **Fig. 10.**
2. Inspect wiper motor high speed operation by connecting battery positive lead to terminal 3 of wiper motor connector and negative lead to terminal 4, **Fig. 10.**
3. Inspect wiper motor for proper stoppage as follows:
   a. Connect battery positive lead to terminal 2 of wiper motor connector and negative lead to terminal 4, **Fig. 10.**
   b. After operating motor at low speed, disconnect positive lead from terminal 2.
   c. Reconnect battery positive lead to terminal 5 of wiper motor connector. Ensure wiper motor stops at auto stop after operating at low speed.

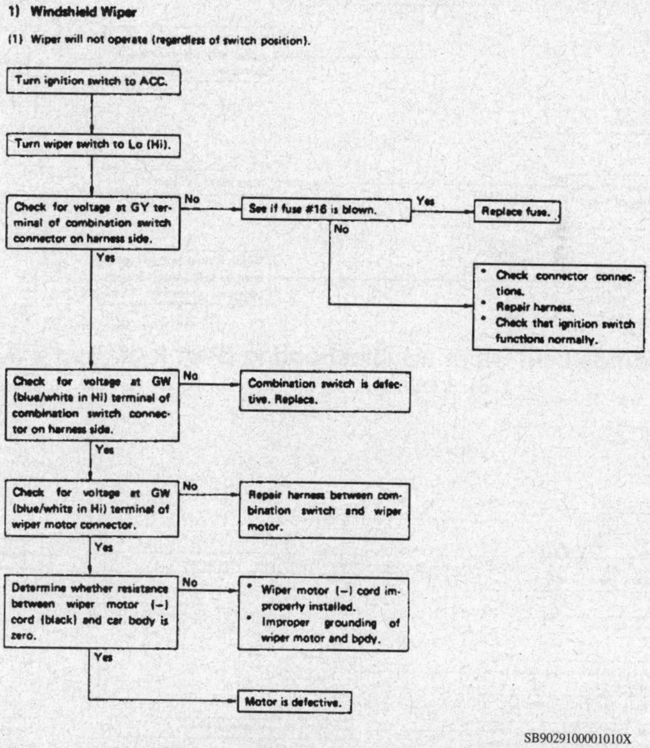

1) Windshield Wiper
(1) Wiper will not operate (regardless of switch position).
Turn ignition switch to ACC.
Turn wiper switch to Lo (Hi).
Check for voltage at GY terminal of combination switch connector on harness side.
No
See if fuse #16 is blown.
Yes
Replace fuse.
No
• Check connector connections.
• Repair harness.
• Check that ignition switch functions normally.
Yes
Check for voltage at GW (blue/white in Hi) terminal of combination switch connector on harness side.
No
Combination switch is defective. Replace.
Yes
Check for voltage at GW (blue/white in Hi) terminal of wiper motor connector.
No
Repair harness between combination switch and wiper motor.
Yes
Determine whether resistance between wiper motor (−) cord (black) and car body is zero.
No
• Wiper motor (−) cord improperly installed.
• Improper grounding of wiper motor and bpdy.
Yes
Motor is defective.
SB9029100001010X

Fig. 1 Windshield wiper troubleshooting (Part 1 of 3). Loyale

1995-96 Legacy

1. Inspect wiper motor low speed operation by connecting battery positive lead to terminal 2 of wiper motor connector and negative lead to terminal 6, **Fig. 11.**
2. Inspect wiper motor high speed operation by connecting battery positive lead to terminal 3 of wiper motor connector and negative lead to terminal 6.
3. Inspect wiper motor for proper stoppage as follows:
   a. Connect battery positive lead to terminal 2 of wiper motor connector and negative lead to terminal 6.
   b. After operating motor at low speed, disconnect positive lead from terminal 2.
   c. Reconnect battery positive lead to terminal 4 of wiper motor connector, then connect a jumper lead between terminal 2 and 5. Ensure wiper motor stops at auto stop after operating at low speed.

REAR WIPER SWITCH CONTINUITY TEST

Refer to **Fig. 8,** for connector pin identification and **Figs. 12 and 13,** for continuity test.

REAR WIPER MOTOR TEST

1. Inspect wiper motor operation by connecting battery positive lead to terminal 2 of wiper motor connector and negative lead to terminal 3, **Fig. 14.**
2. Inspect wiper motor for proper stoppage as follows:
   a. After operating motor as outlined in step 1, disconnect positive lead from terminal 2.
   b. Reconnect battery positive lead to terminal 1 of wiper motor connector, then install a jumper wire between terminals 2 and 4. Ensure

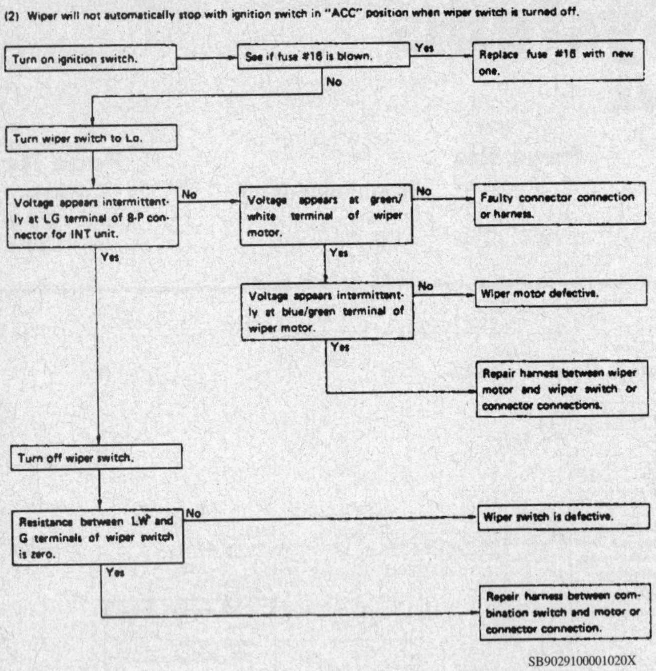
(2) Wiper will not automatically stop with ignition switch in "ACC" position when wiper switch is turned off.
Turn on ignition switch.
See if fuse #16 is blown.
Yes
Replace fuse #16 with new one.
No
Turn wiper switch to Lo.
Voltage appears intermittently at LG terminal of 8-P connector for INT unit.
No
Voltage appears at green/white terminal of wiper motor.
No
Faulty connector connection or harness.
Yes
Yes
Voltage appears intermittently at blue/green terminal of wiper motor.
No
Wiper motor defective.
Yes
Repair harness between wiper motor and wiper switch or connector connections.
Turn off wiper switch.
Resistance between LW and G terminals of wiper switch is zero.
No
Wiper switch is defective.
Yes
Repair harness between combination switch and motor or connector connection.
SB9029100001020X

Fig. 1 Windshield wiper troubleshooting (Part 2 of 3). Loyale

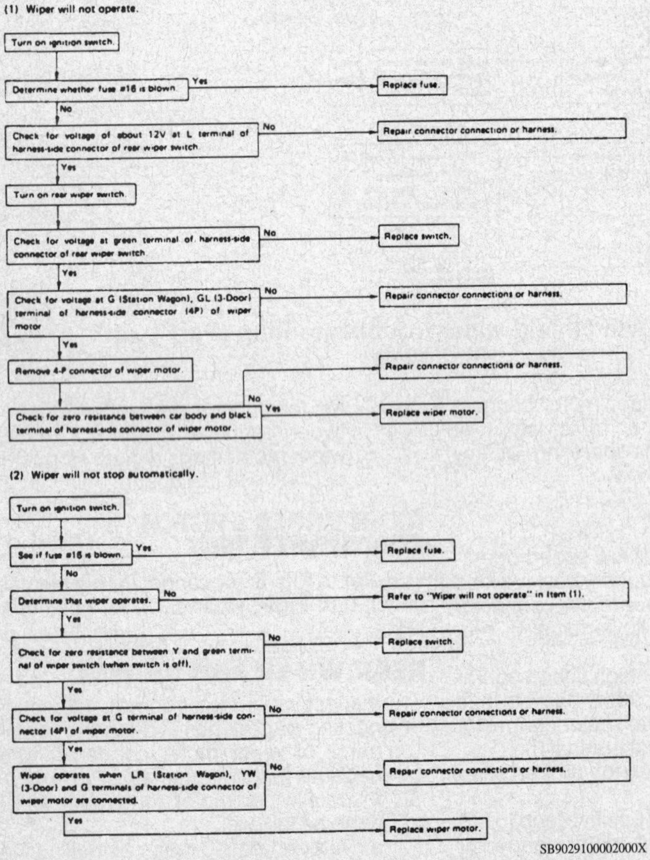
(1) Wiper will not operate.
Turn on ignition switch.
Determine whether fuse #16 is blown.
Yes
Replace fuse.
No
Check for voltage of about 12V at L terminal of harness-side connector of rear wiper switch.
No
Repair connector connection or harness.
Yes
Turn on rear wiper switch.
Check for voltage at green terminal of harness-side connector of rear wiper switch.
No
Replace switch.
Yes
Check for voltage at G (Station Wagon), GL (3-Door) terminal of harness-side connector (4P) of wiper motor
No
Repair connector connections or harness.
Yes
Remove 4-P connector of wiper motor.
Repair connector connections or harness.
No
Check for zero resistance between car body and black terminal of harness-side connector of wiper motor.
Yes
Replace wiper motor.
(2) Wiper will not stop automatically.
Turn on ignition switch.
See if fuse #16 is blown.
Yes
Replace fuse.
No
Determine that wiper operates.
No
Refer to "Wiper will not operate" in Item (1).
Yes
Check for zero resistance between Y and green terminal of wiper switch (when switch is off).
No
Replace switch.
Yes
Check for voltage at G terminal of harness-side connector (4P) of wiper motor.
No
Repair connector connections or harness.
Yes
Wiper operates when LR (Station Wagon), YW (3-Door) and G terminals of harness-side connector of wiper motor are connected.
No
Repair connector connections or harness.
Yes
Replace wiper motor.
SB9029100002000X

Fig. 2 Rear wiper troubleshooting. Loyale

wiper motor stops at auto stop after it has been operated.

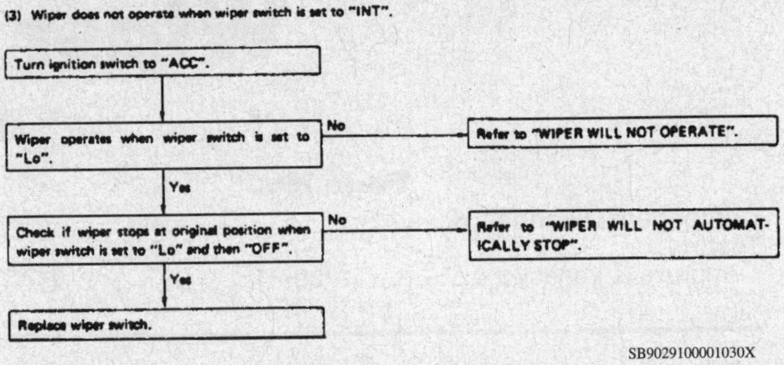
(3) Wiper does not operate when wiper switch is set to "INT".
Turn ignition switch to "ACC".
Wiper operates when wiper switch is set to "Lo".
No
Refer to "WIPER WILL NOT OPERATE".
Yes
Check if wiper stops at original position when wiper switch is set to "Lo" and then "OFF".
No
Refer to "WIPER WILL NOT AUTOMATICALLY STOP".
Yes
Replace wiper switch.
SB9029100001030X

Fig. 1 Windshield wiper troubleshooting (Part 3 of 3). Loyale

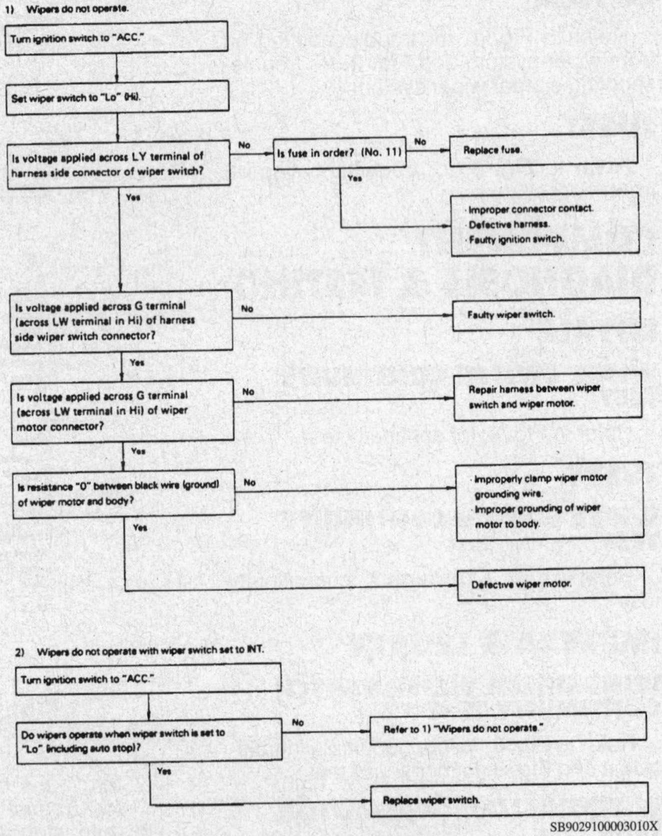
1) Wipers do not operate.
Turn ignition switch to "ACC."
Set wiper switch to "Lo" (Hi).
Is voltage applied across LY terminal of harness side connector of wiper switch?
No
Is fuse in order? (No. 11)
No
Replace fuse.
Yes
·Improper connector contact.
·Defective harness.
·Faulty ignition switch.
Yes
Is voltage applied across G terminal (across LW terminal in Hi) of harness side wiper switch connector?
No
Faulty wiper switch.
Yes
Is voltage applied across G terminal (across LW terminal in Hi) of wiper motor connector?
No
Repair harness between wiper switch and wiper motor.
Yes
Is resistance "0" between black wire (ground) of wiper motor and body?
No
·Improperly clamp wiper motor grounding wire.
·Improper grounding of wiper motor to body.
Yes
Defective wiper motor.
2) Wipers do not operate with wiper switch set to INT.
Turn ignition switch to "ACC."
Do wipers operate when wiper switch is set to "Lo" (including auto stop)?
No
Refer to 1) "Wipers do not operate."
Yes
Replace wiper switch.
SB9029100003010X

Fig. 3 Windshield wiper troubleshooting (Part 1 of 3). Justy

REAR WIPER RELAY CONTINUITY TEST

Refer to **Fig. 15,** for connector pin identification and **Fig. 16,** for continuity test.

SVX

WINDSHIELD WIPER SWITCH CONTINUITY TEST

Refer to **Fig. 17,** for connector pin identification and **Fig. 18,** for continuity test.

REAR WIPER SWITCH CONTINUITY TEST

Refer to **Fig. 17,** for connector pin identification and **Fig. 19,** for continuity test.

3) Wipers operate continuously when wiper switch is set to INT

- Wipers operate continuously when wiper switch is set to INT → Replace intermittent wiper unit.

4) Wipers fail to stop automatically when wiper switch is turned off

• 2-speed model

- Turn ignition switch to "ACC"
- Set wiper switch to "Lo"
- Is voltage applied across LY terminal of wiper motor 4P connector? — No → Repair harness or connector connection between wiper motor and fuse box.
- Yes: Is voltage applied intermittently across Y terminal of wiper 4P connector? — No → Replace wiper motor.
- Yes: Is voltage applied intermittently at Y terminal of wiper switch 17P connector? — No → Repair harness or connector connection between wiper motor and wiper switch.
- Yes → Replace wiper switch.

• 3-speed model

- Turn ignition switch to "ACC"
- Set wiper switch to "Lo"
- Is voltage applied across LY terminal of wiper motor 4P connector? — No → Repair harness or connector connection between wiper motor and fuse box.
- Yes: Is voltage applied intermittently at Y terminal of wiper motor 4P connector? — No → Replace wiper motor.
- Yes → Replace wiper switch.

SB9029100003020X

Fig. 3 Windshield wiper troubleshooting (Part 2 of 3). Justy

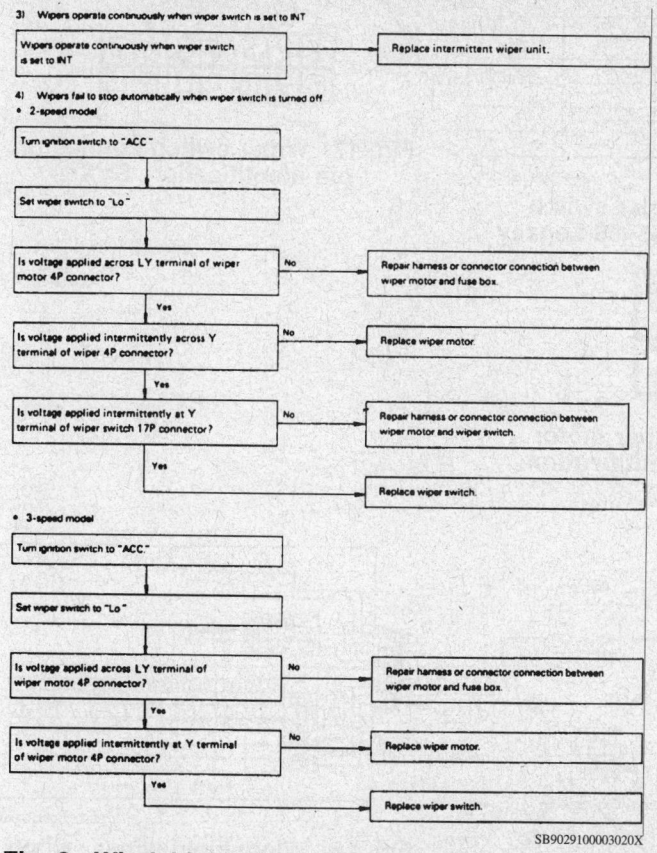

5) Washer fluid does not come out when washer switch is turned on.

- Turn ignition switch to "ACC."
- Is fuse in order? (No. 11) — No → Replace fuse.
- Yes: Is voltage applied across LY terminals of wiper washer switch? — No → Repair harness or connector connection.
- Yes: Is voltage applied across LR terminal of washer switch when washer switch is turned on? — No → Defective washer switch.
- Yes: Is voltage applied across LR terminal of harness end connector of washer pump (when washer switch is turned on)? — No → Repair harness or connector connections.
- Yes: Is resistance "0" between B terminal on harness end connector of washer pump and body? — No → Improper grounding.
- Yes → Defective washer pump.

6) Wipers do not operate when washer switch is turned on (3-speed model only)

- Turn ignition switch to "ACC."
- Do wipers operate properly when wiper is set to "INT"? — No → Refer to 2) and 3).
- Yes: Does washer fluid come out when washer switch is turned on? — No → Refer to 5) "Washer fluid does not come out when washer switch is turned on."
- Yes → Defective intermittent wiper.

SB9029100003030X

Fig. 3 Windshield wiper troubleshooting (Part 3 of 3). Justy

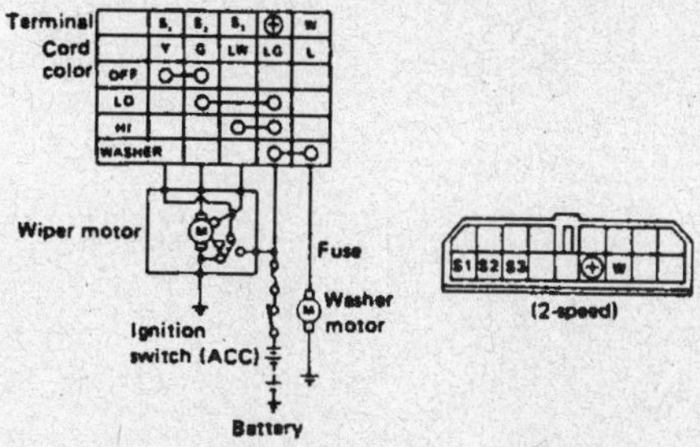
Terminal
Cord color
OFF
LO
HI
WASHER
Wiper motor
Fuse
Washer motor
Ignition switch (ACC)
Battery
(2-speed)

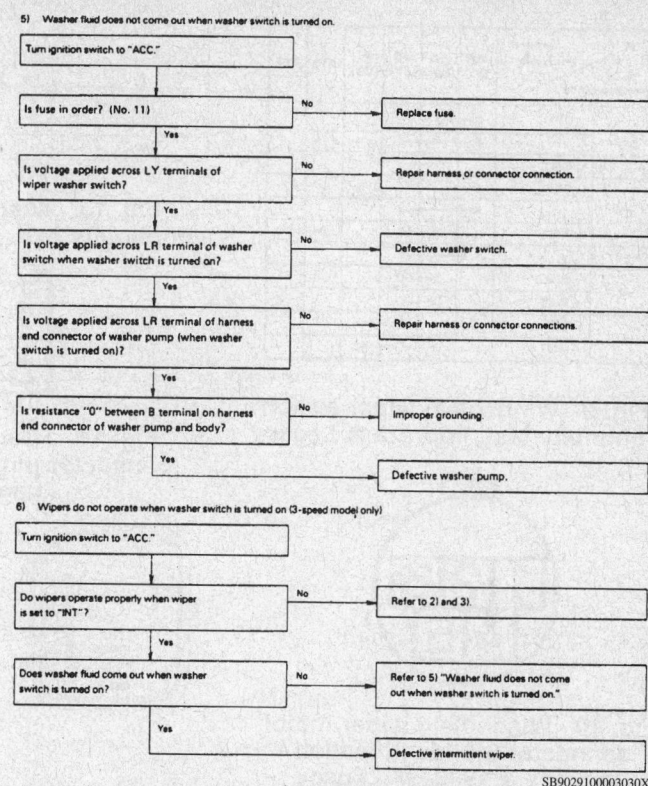

SB9029100004000X

Fig. 4 Wiper switch continuity test. Loyale

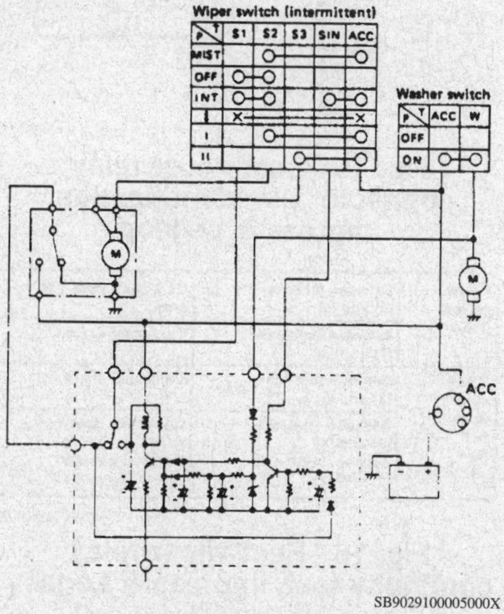
Wiper switch (intermittent)
S1
S2
S3
SIN
ACC
MIST
OFF
INT
Washer switch
ACC
W
OFF
ON
ACC

SB9029100005000X

Fig. 5 Windshield wiper switch continuity test. Justy w/ intermittent wipers

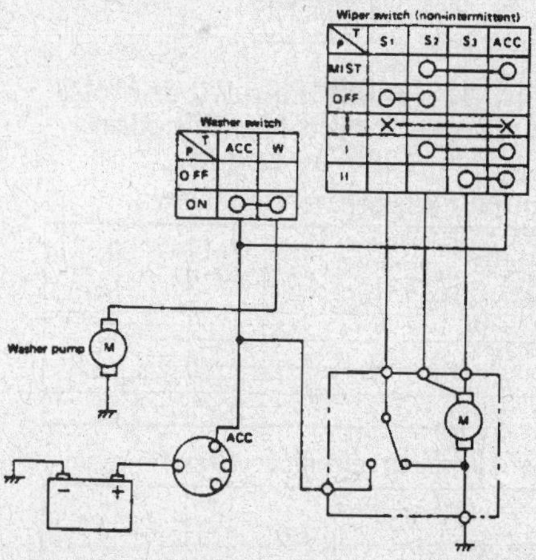
Wiper switch (non-intermittent)
S1
S2
S3
ACC
MIST
OFF
Washer switch
ACC
W
OFF
ON
Washer pump
ACC

SB9029100006000X

Fig. 6 Windshield wiper switch continuity test. Justy w/standard wipers

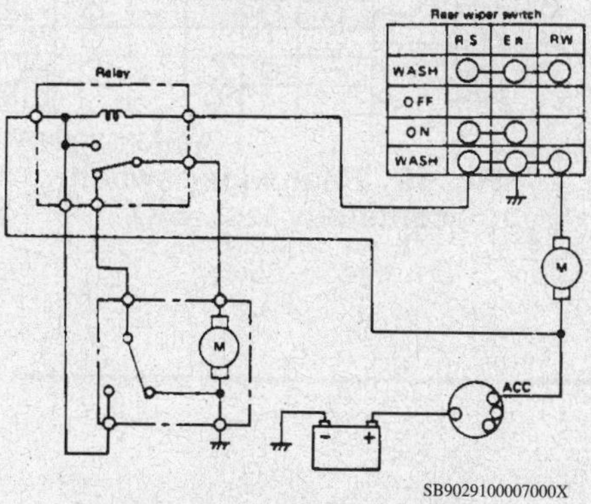
Rear wiper switch
RS
ER
RW
WASH
OFF
ON
WASH
Relay
ACC

SB9029100007000X

Fig. 7 Rear wiper switch continuity test. Justy

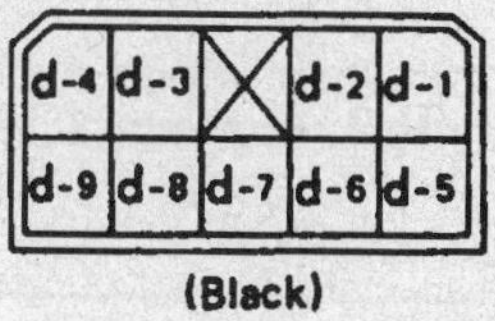
d-4
d-3
d-2
d-1
d-9
d-8
d-7
d-6
d-5
(Black)

SB9029100008000X

Fig. 8 Wiper switch connector pin identification. Impreza & Legacy

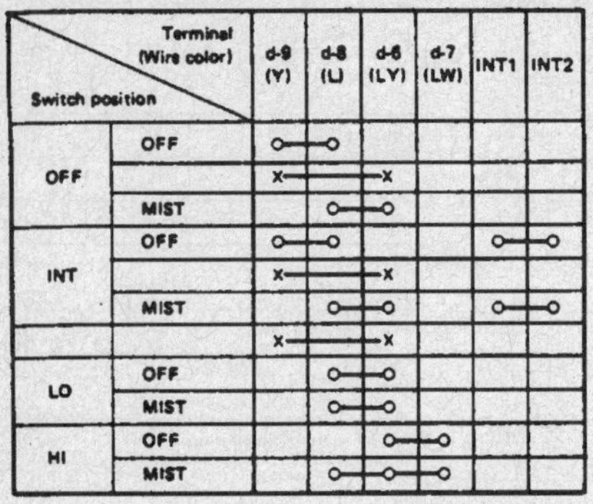
Terminal (Wire color)
Switch position
d-9 (Y)
d-8 (L)
d-6 (LY)
d-7 (LW)
INT1
INT2
OFF
MIST
INT
LO
HI
SB9029100009000X

Fig. 9 Windshield wiper switch continuity test. Impreza & Legacy

1 2 3
4 5
SB9029100010000X

Fig. 10 Windshield wiper motor connector pin identification. Impreza & 1993–94 Legacy

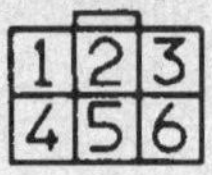
1 2 3
4 5 6
SB9029500020000X

Fig. 11 Windshield wiper motor connector pin identification. 1995–96 Legacy

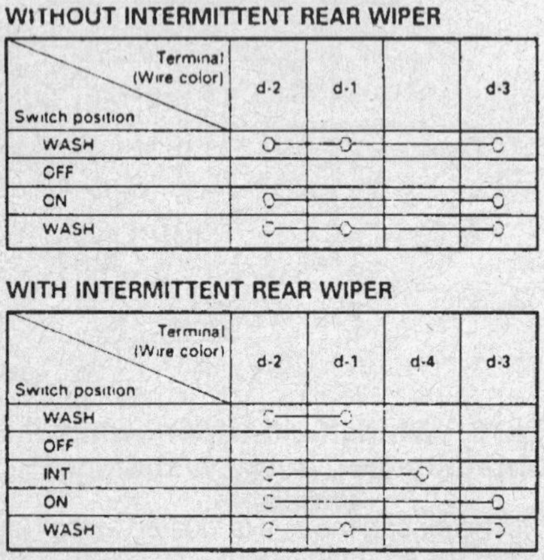
WITHOUT INTERMITTENT REAR WIPER
Terminal (Wire color)
Switch position
d-2
d-1
d-3
WASH
OFF
ON
WASH
WITH INTERMITTENT REAR WIPER
Terminal (Wire color)
Switch position
d-2
d-1
d-4
d-3
WASH
OFF
INT
ON
WASH
SB9029100011000X

Fig. 12 Rear wiper switch continuity test. Impreza & 1993–94 Legacy

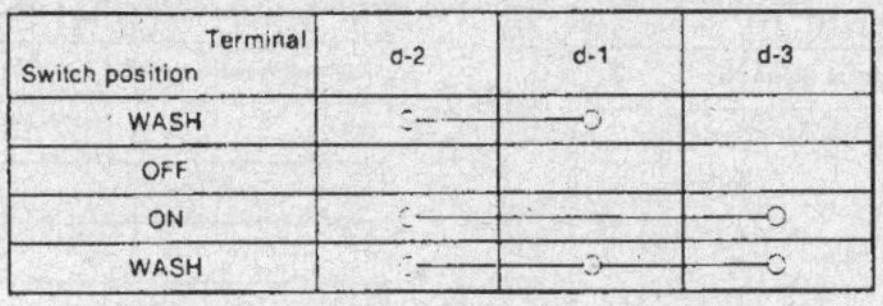
Terminal
Switch position
d-2
d-1
d-3
WASH
OFF
ON
WASH
SB9029500021000X

Fig. 13 Rear wiper switch continuity test. 1995–96 Legacy

1 2
3 4
SB9029100012000X

Fig. 14 Rear wiper motor connector pin identification. Legacy

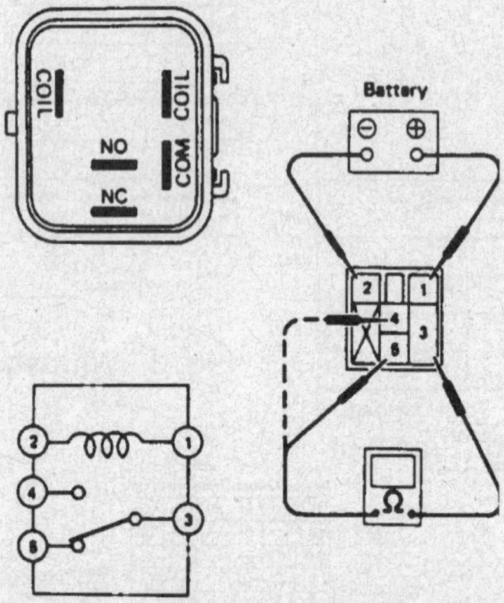
COIL
COIL
NO
COM
NC
Battery
SB9029100013000X

Fig. 15 Rear wiper relay connector pin identification. Impreza & Legacy

When current flows	Between terminals (3) and (5)	Continuity does not exist.
	Between terminals (3) and (4)	Continuity exists.
When current does not flow	Between terminals (3) and (5)	Continuity exists.
	Between terminals (3) and (4) Between terminals (1) and (2)	Continuity does not exist. Continuity exists.

SB9029100014000X

Fig. 16 Rear wiper relay continuity test. Impreza & Legacy

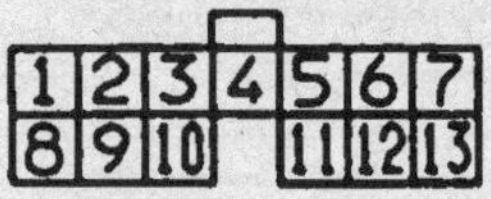
1 2 3 4 5 6 7
8 9 10 11 12 13
SB9029100015000X

Fig. 17 Wiper switch connector pin identification. SVX

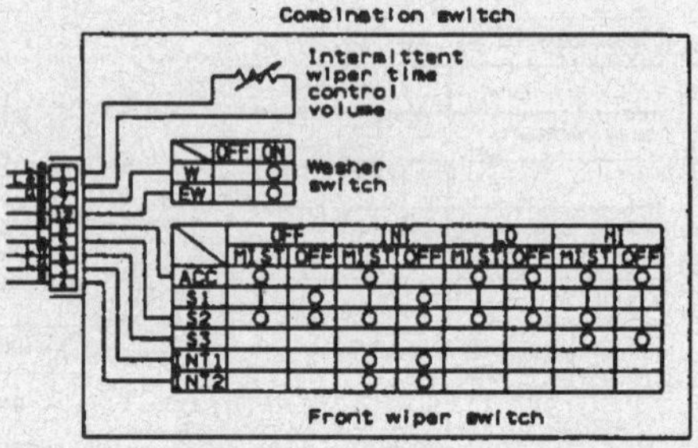
Combination switch
Intermittent wiper time control volume
Washer switch
OFF
ON
W
EW
OFF
INT
LO
HI
MIST
ACC
S1
S2
S3
INT1
INT2
Front wiper switch
SB9029100016000X

Fig. 18 Windshield wiper switch continuity test. SVX

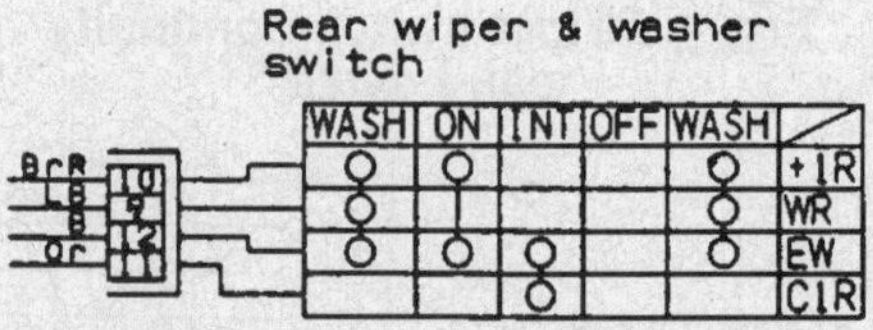
Rear wiper & washer switch
WASH
ON
INT
OFF
WASH
+1R
WR
EW
C1R
SB9029100017000X

Fig. 19 Rear wiper switch continuity test. SVX

Air Bag

INDEX

	Page No.
Air Bag System Disarming & Arming	39-85
Arming	39-85
Disarming	39-85
Collision Inspection	39-95
Component Locations	39-90
Component Service	39-92
Air Bag Assembly Disposal	39-95
Air Bag Control Unit, Replace	39-94
Combination Switch Assembly	39-95
Driver's Air Bag Module, Replace	39-92
Front Sensor, Replace	39-93
Main Harness, Replace	39-93
Passenger's Air Bag Module, Replace	39-92
Description & Operation	39-85
System	39-85
System Components	39-85
Diagnosis & Testing	39-91
Precautions	39-86
Scheduled Maintenance	39-87
Technical Service Bulletins	39-95
Air Bag Lamp Remains Illuminated	39-95
Tightening Specifications	39-96
Wire Harness & Connector Repair	39-90
Wiring Diagrams	39-88

AIR BAG SYSTEM DISARMING & ARMING

Disarming

1. Place ignition switch in the Off position.
2. Disconnect battery negative cable, then battery positive cable.
3. **Wait 20 seconds before beginning repair procedures.**

Arming

1. Ensure no one is inside vehicle.
2. With ignition switch in the Off position, connect battery positive cable, then battery negative cable.
3. Wait at least 20 seconds, then turn ignition On and note air bag warning lamp operation, which should light for approximately eight seconds, then go off. If lamp remains illuminated or fails to light, refer to "Diagnosis and Testing."

DESCRIPTION & OPERATION

SYSTEM

1994 LEGACY

The Supplemental Restraint System (SRS) consists of a control unit, two front sensors, two safety sensor built into the control unit and a driver's air bag module, **Fig. 1.**

The front sensors and the safety sensors are connected in parallel respectively. The front sensors and safety sensor are connected in series, so that the air bag will inflate if at least one front sensor and at least one safety sensor detect an impact at the same time.

SVX, 1994 IMPREZA & 1995-96 LEGACY

The SRS consists of a control unit, two front sensors, a safety sensor built into the control unit and driver's and passenger's air bag modules, **Fig. 2.**

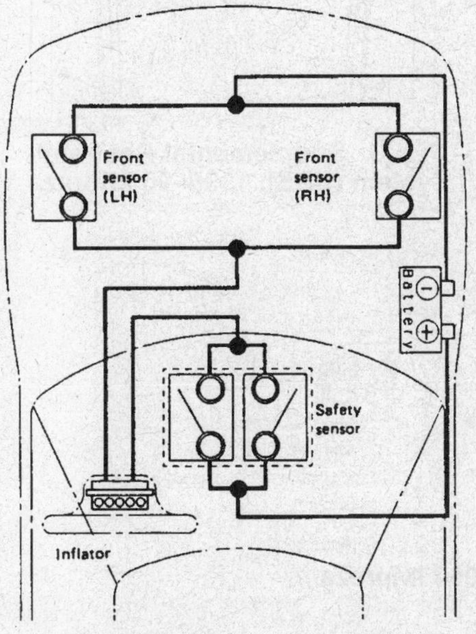

Front sensor (LH)
Front sensor (RH)
Battery
Safety sensor
Inflator
SB8019400032000X

Fig. 1 Supplemental Restraint System (SRS). 1994 Legacy

The front sensors are connected in parallel respectively. The front sensors and safety sensor are connected in series, so that the air bag will inflate if at least one front sensor and the safety sensor detect an impact at the same time.

1995-96 IMPREZA

The SRS consists of a control unit, an electric sensor and a safety sensor which are built into the control unit and driver's and passenger's air bag modules, **Fig. 3.**

The electric sensor and safety sensor are connected in series, so that the air bag will inflate if the two sensors detect an impact at the same time.

SYSTEM COMPONENTS

FRONT SENSOR

Legacy, SVX & 1994 Impreza

Front sensors are installed on either front wheel apron wall. On Impreza, if the rotor type sensor receives a frontal impact exceeding a certain set limit, it rotates to turn the switch on, **Fig. 4.** On Legacy and SVX, if the roller type sensor receives a frontal impact exceeding a certain set limit, it rotates to turn the switch on, **Fig. 5.**

ELECTRIC SENSOR

1995-96 Impreza

The electric sensor is built into the control unit. This sensor is of the semiconductor type and senses deceleration at collision by the change of electrical resistance and the impact sensing circuit, **Fig. 6.**

SAFETY SENSOR

1994 Legacy

Two safety sensors are built into the control unit. These sensors are of the roller type, **Fig. 5.**

1994 Impreza

The safety sensor is built into the control unit. This sensor is of the roller type, **Fig. 5.**

SVX & 1995-96 Legacy

The safety sensor is built into the control unit. A dual pole rotary type safety sensor is used, **Fig. 7.**

1995-96 Impreza

The safety sensor is built into the control unit. A piston type safety sensor is used, **Fig. 8.**

DRIVER'S AIR BAG MODULE

The air bag module is located at the center of the steering wheel, and contains the air bag and inflator, **Fig. 9.** If a collision occurs, the inflator produces a large volume of nitrogen gas to rapidly inflate the air bag.

PASSENGER'S AIR BAG MODULE

The air bag module is located on the passenger side of the instrument panel and contains the air bag and inflator, **Fig. 10.** If a collision occurs, the inflator, produces a large volume of nitrogen gas to rapidly inflate the air bag.

STEERING ROLL CONNECTOR

The steering roll connector is located between the steering column and steering

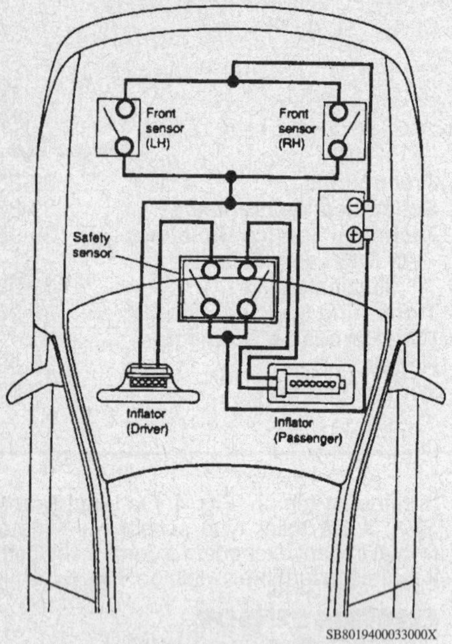
Front sensor (LH)
Front sensor (RH)
Safety sensor
Inflator (Driver)
Inflator (Passenger)
SB8019400033000X

Fig. 2 Supplemental Restraint System (SRS). SVX, 1994 Impreza & 1995–96 Legacy

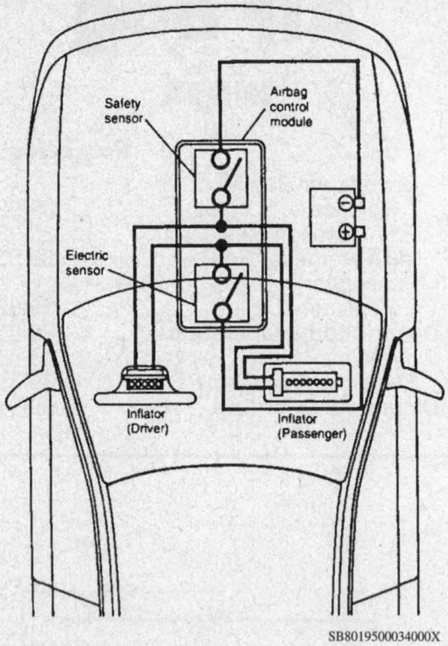
Safety sensor
Airbag control module
Electric sensor
Inflator (Driver)
Inflator (Passenger)
SB8019500034000X

Fig. 3 Supplemental Restraint System (SRS). 1995–96 Impreza

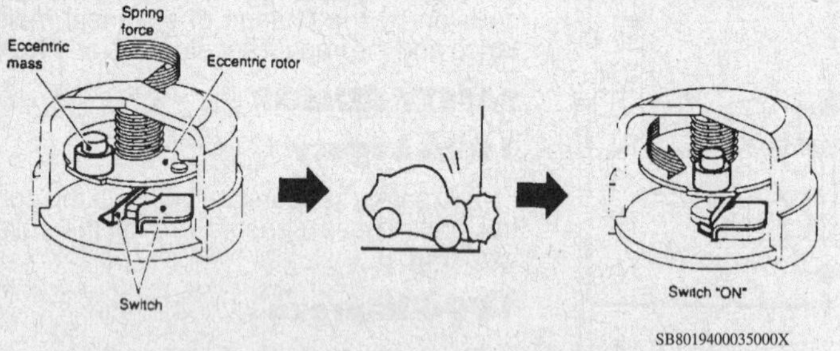
Spring force
Eccentric mass
Eccentric rotor
Switch
Switch "ON"
SB8019400035000X

Fig. 4 Rotor type front sensor. 1994 Impreza

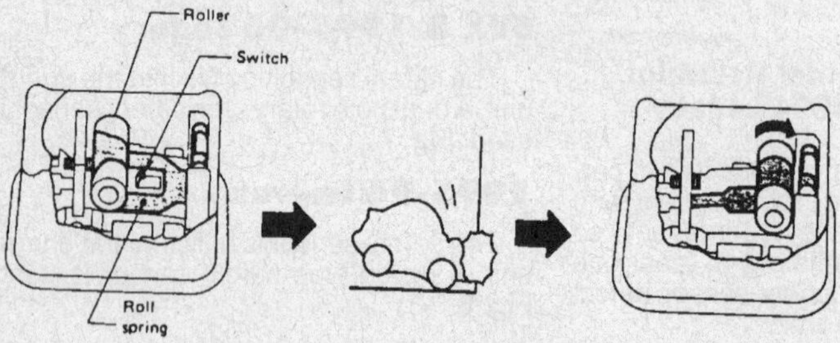
Roller
Switch
Roll spring
SB8019400036000X

Fig. 5 Roller type sensor

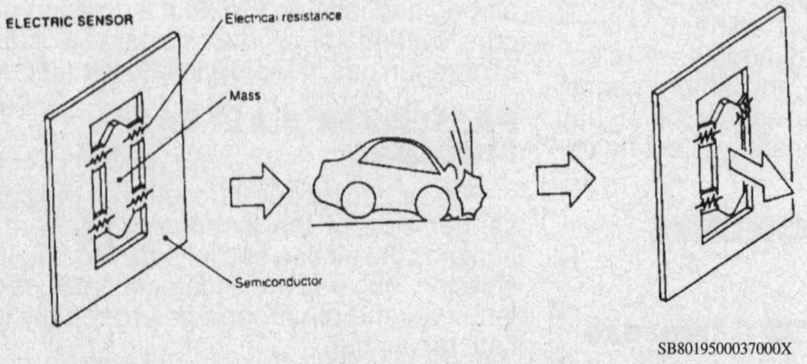
ELECTRIC SENSOR
Electrical resistance
Mass
Semiconductor
SB8019500037000X

Fig. 6 Electric sensor. 1995–96 Impreza

wheel, **Fig. 11.** A flat cable stored in a spiral form transmits the control unit electrical signal to the steering wheel from the body harness.

AIR BAG CONNECTOR

The air bag control unit uses a connector with double lock and coupling error detection mechanisms. If coupling is incomplete, the air bag warning lamp will light.

1. To disconnect the air bag control unit connector, proceed as follows:
   a. Press wire one of the control unit as shown in **Fig. 12,** until green lever two tilts upward. This unlocks the double lock. Pull off connector while pressing connector lock.
2. To connect the air bag control unit connector, proceed as follows:
   a. Insert connector until a click is heard, then push in green lever to apply the double lock.
3. To disconnect connector between harnesses, proceed as follows:
   a. Press lever one, **Fig. 13,** to pop green lever two out. This unlocks the double lock system. Separate the connector by pulling both sides while holding connector sections and pressing in lever one.
4. To connect the connector between harnesses, proceed as follows:
   a. Insert both connectors until a click is heard, then push in green lever until it clicks.

AIR BAG WARNING LAMP

The air bag warning lamp is located on the instrument cluster. It lights if a poor connection is present, or if the air bag control unit detects an SRS problem or condition. When the SRS is functioning normally, the lamp will go off approximately eight seconds after the ignition is turned On.

WIRING HARNESS

The SRS wiring harness is entirely covered with a yellow protective conduit, and can easily be distinguished from harnesses of other systems.

PRECAUTIONS

1. The electrical circuit necessary for SRS deployment is powered directly from the battery and backup power supply. To avoid unwanted deployment and possible personal injury, the SRS must be disarmed prior to performing service procedures. Refer to "Air Bag System Disarming and Arming."
2. Wait 20 seconds before beginning any service procedures.
3. When inspecting the SRS, use a digital circuit tester. **Using an analog circuit tester may cause unwanted deployment.**
4. Do not apply tester probe directly to any SRS connector terminal. Use a test harness when inspecting.
5. Do not inspect air bag module continuity with air bag removed from vehicle.
6. When storing a removed air bag module, place it parallel with floor with pad

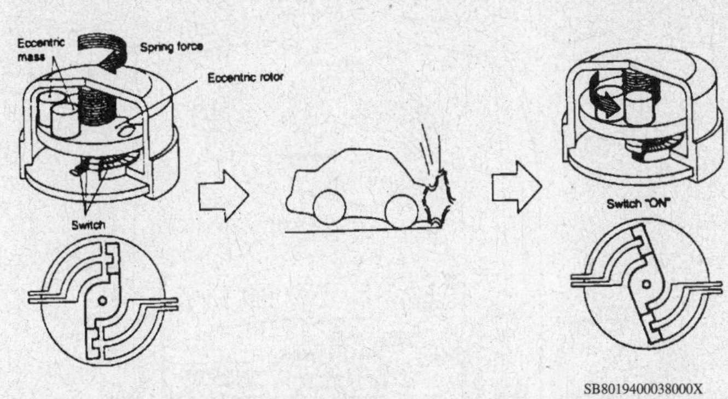
Eccentric mass
Spring force
Eccentric rotor
Switch
Switch "ON"
SB8019400038000X

Fig. 7 Rotor type safety sensor. SVX & 1995–96 Legacy

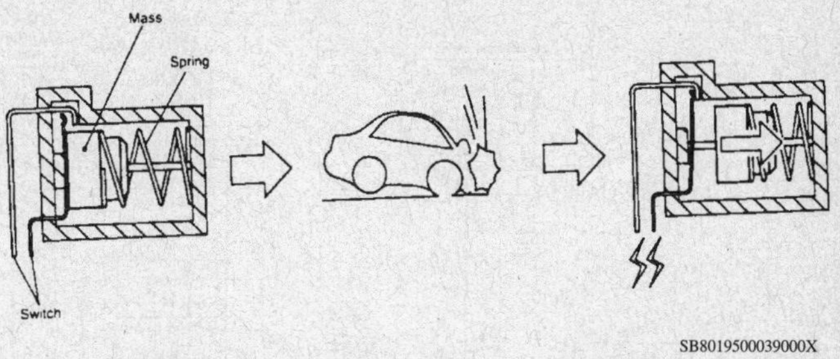
Mass
Spring
Switch
SB8019500039000X

Fig. 8 Piston type safety sensor. 1995–96 Impreza

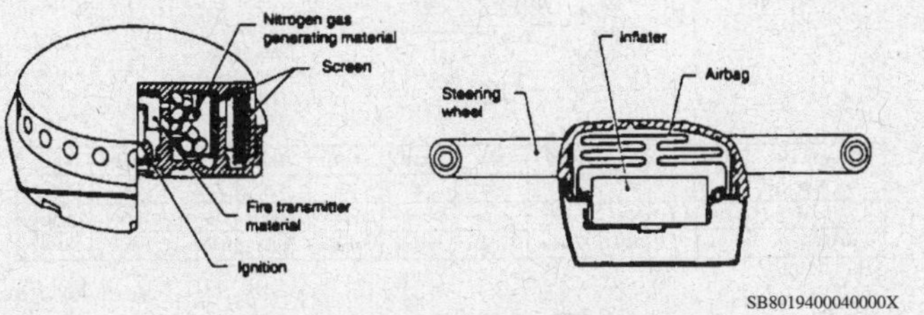
Nitrogen gas generating material
Screen
Fire transmitter material
Ignition
Inflater
Steering wheel
Airbag
SB8019400040000X

Fig. 9 Driver's air bag & inflator

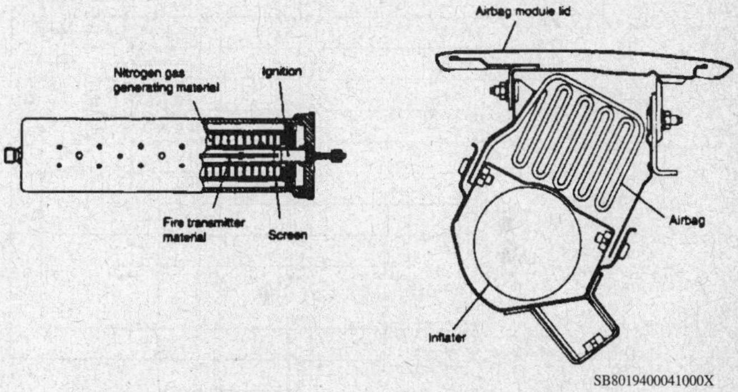
Airbag module lid
Nitrogen gas generating material
Ignition
Fire transmitter material
Screen
Airbag
Inflater
SB8019400041000X

Fig. 10 Passenger's air bag & inflator

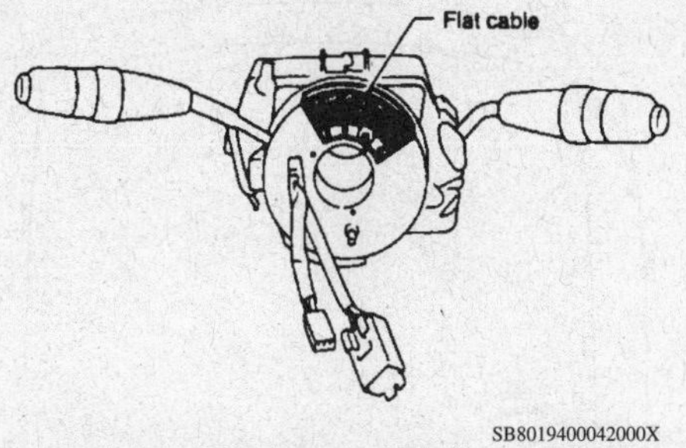
Flat cable
SB8019400042000X

Fig. 11 Steering roll connector

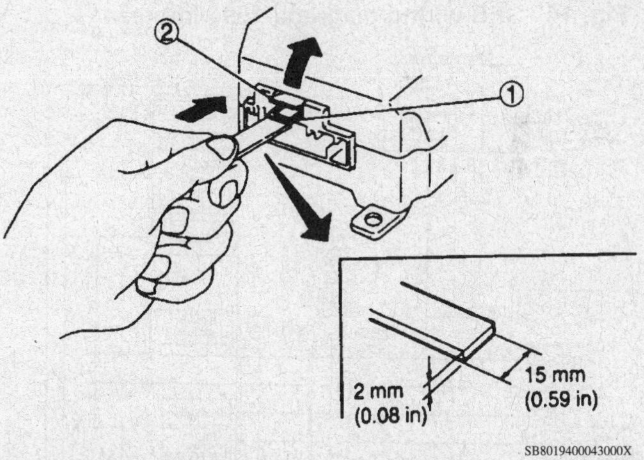
②
①
2 mm
(0.08 in)
15 mm
(0.59 in)
SB8019400043000X

Fig. 12 Air bag control unit double lock connector

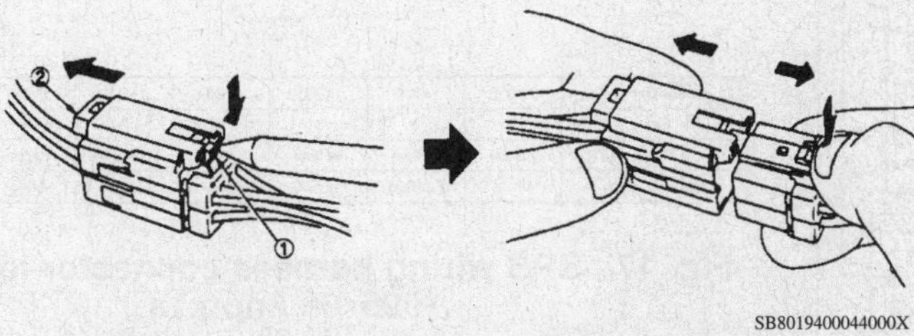
②
①
SB8019400044000X

Fig. 13 Harness double lock connector

facing upward. Do not place module against a wall, or place anything on the pad.

7. After removal, air bag module should be kept away from heat and light sources.
8. Use care not drop SRS components.
9. Do not subject SRS components to temperatures over 194°F.
10. Do not apply oil, grease or water to air bag unit.
11. Air bag module must not be disassembled.
12. Do not paint air bag to correct cosmetic flaws. It must be replaced.
13. If any damage or open circuits are found in SRS wiring harness, do not attempt to repair. Replace the defective harness.
14. Ensure grounding terminal is free from contamination before connecting SRS to ground.

SCHEDULED MAINTENANCE

The SRS must be inspected at 10 year intervals from the date the vehicle was manufactured. Inspect system for diagnostic trouble codes (DTCs) and proper warning lamp operation. Refer to "Diagnosis and Testing." Inspect air bag module for scratches and cracks and other damage. Inspect sensors, control unit and their mounting brackets for damage and proper mounting. Inspect system wiring harnesses and electrical connectors for damage,

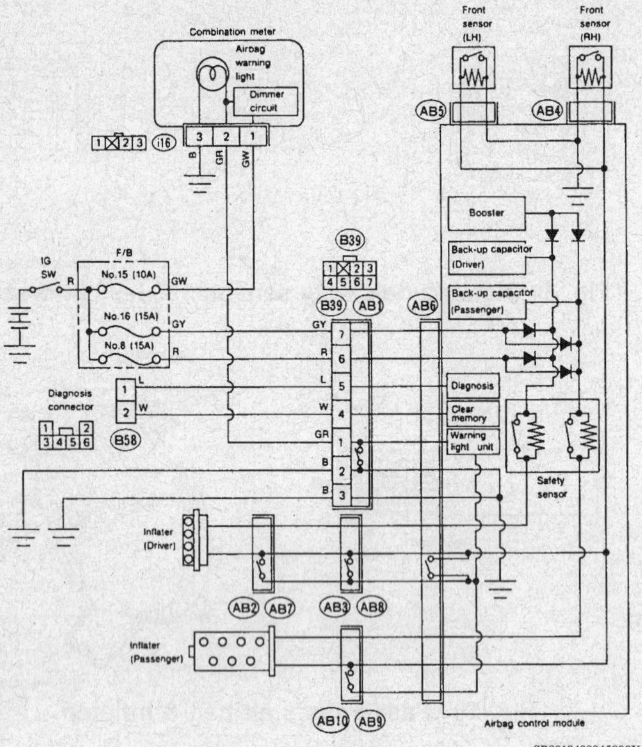
Combination meter
Airbag warning light
Dimmer circuit
Front sensor (LH)
Front sensor (RH)
AB5
AB4
Booster
Back-up capacitor (Driver)
Back-up capacitor (Passenger)
IG SW
F/B
No.15 (10A)
No.16 (15A)
No.8 (15A)
B39
AB1
AB6
Diagnosis connector
B58
i16
Diagnosis
Clear memory
Warning light unit
Safety sensor
Inflater (Driver)
AB2
AB7
AB3
AB8
Inflater (Passenger)
AB10
AB9
Airbag control module

SB8019400045000X

Fig. 14 SRS wiring diagram. 1994 Impreza

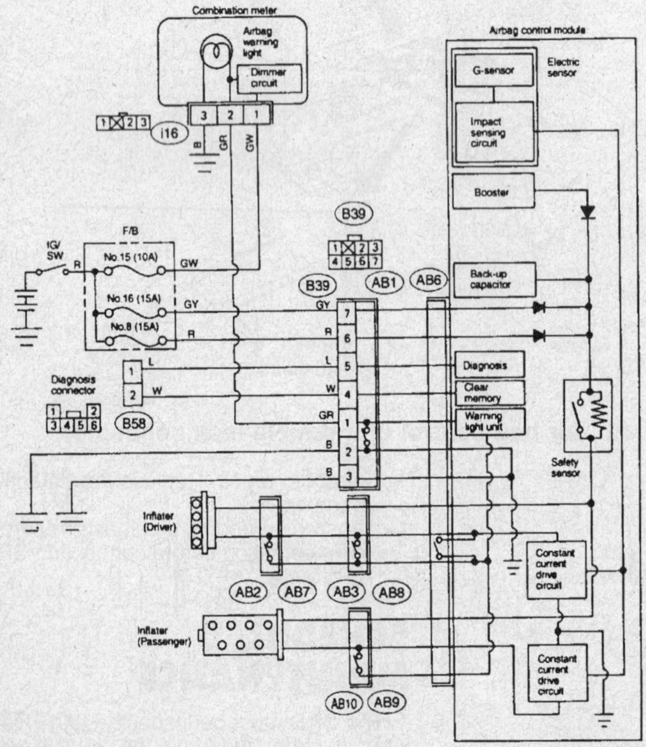
Combination meter
Airbag warning light
Dimmer circuit
i16
Airbag control module
G-sensor
Electric sensor
Impact sensing circuit
Booster
B39
IG/ SW
F/B
No.15 (10A)
No.16 (15A)
No.8 (15A)
AB1
AB6
Back-up capacitor
Diagnosis connector
B58
Diagnosis
Clear memory
Warning light unit
Safety sensor
Inflater (Driver)
Constant current drive circuit
AB2
AB7
AB3
AB8
Inflater (Passenger)
AB10
AB9

SB8019500047000X

Fig. 16 SRS wiring diagram. 1995–96 Impreza

chafing and proper connection. Any components that shown signs of wear or damage should be replaced.

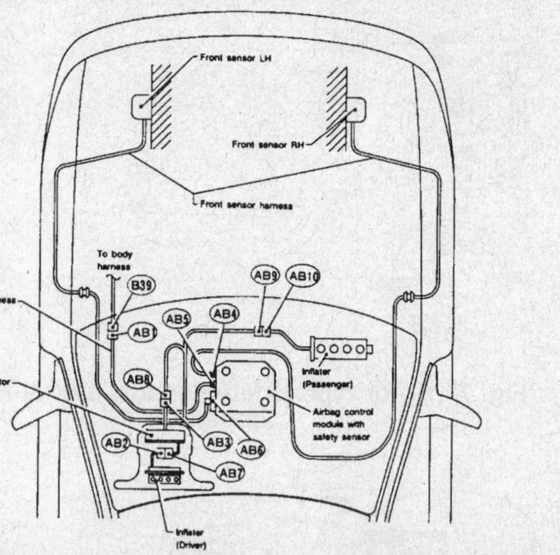
Front sensor LH
Front sensor RH
Front sensor harness
To body harness
Airbag main harness
B39
AB9
AB10
AB5
AB4
AB1
Roll connector
AB8
Inflater (Passenger)
Airbag control module with safety sensor
AB2
AB3
AB6
AB7
Inflater (Driver)

Connector No.	(AB1)	(AB2)	(AB3)	(AB4)	(AB5)	(AB6)	(AB7)	(AB8)	(AB9)	(AB10)
Pole	7	3	3	2	2	12	3	3	3	3
Color	Yellow	Yellow	Yellow	Blue	Orange	Yellow	Yellow	Yellow	Yellow	Yellow
Male/Female	Male	Female	Female	Female	Female	Female	Male	Male	Male	Female

SB8019400046000X

Fig. 15 SRS wiring harness connector locations. 1994 Impreza

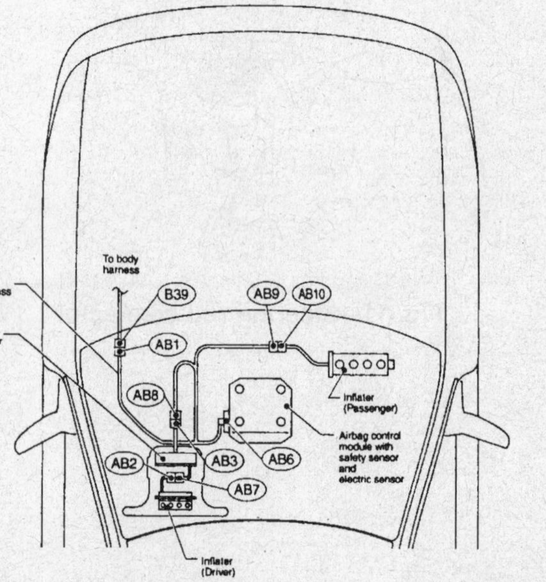
To body harness
Airbag main harness
B39
AB9
AB10
Roll connector
AB1
AB8
Inflater (Passenger)
Airbag control module with safety sensor and electric sensor
AB2
AB3
AB6
AB7
Inflater (Driver)

Connector No.	(AB1)	(AB2)	(AB3)	(AB6)	(AB7)	(AB8)	(AB9)	(AB10)
Pole	7	3	3	12	3	3	3	3
Color	Yellow	Yellow	Yellow	Yellow	Yellow	Yellow	Yellow	Yellow
Male/Female	Male	Female	Female	Female	Male	Male	Male	Female

SB8019500048000X

Fig. 17 SRS wiring harness connector locations. 1995–96 Impreza

WIRING DIAGRAMS

Refer to **Figs. 14 through 23** for system wiring diagrams and connector locations.

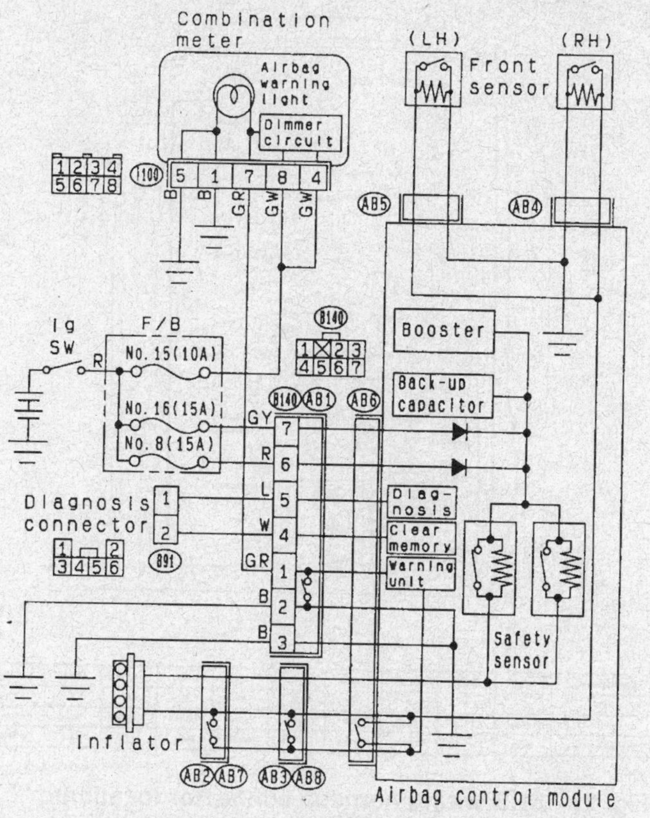
Combination meter
Airbag warning light
Dimmer circuit
(LH)
(RH)
Front sensor
I100
AB5
AB4
Booster
Back-up capacitor
Ig SW
F/B
No.15(10A)
No.16(15A)
No.8(15A)
B140
AB1
AB6
Diagnosis connector
B91
Diag-nosis
Clear memory
Warning unit
Safety sensor
Inflator
AB2
AB7
AB3
AB8
Airbag control module

SB8019400049000X

Fig. 18 SRS wiring diagram. 1994 Legacy

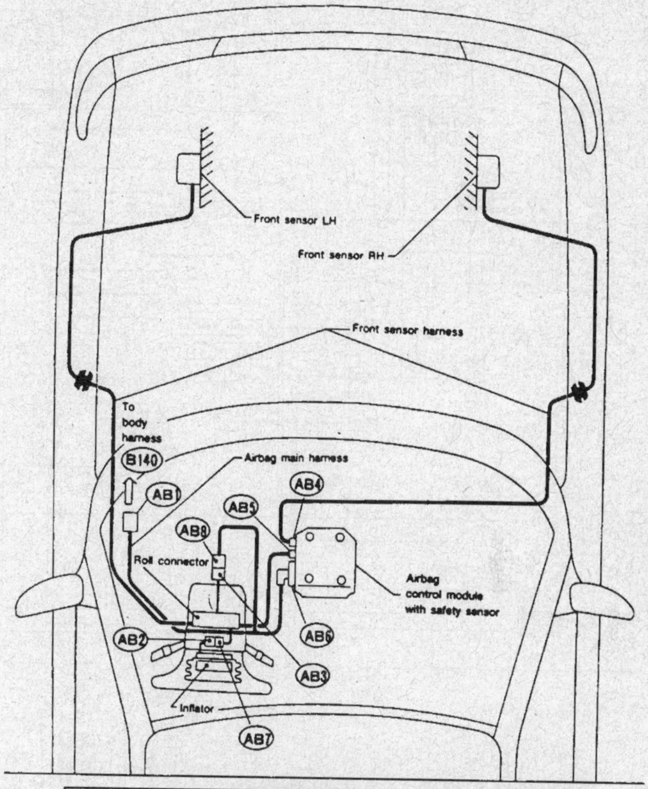
Front sensor LH
Front sensor RH
Front sensor harness
To body harness
B140
Airbag main harness
AB1
AB5
AB4
AB8
Roll connector
Airbag control module with safety sensor
AB2
AB6
AB3
Inflator
AB7

Connector No.	AB1	AB2	AB3	AB4	AB5	AB6	AB7	AB8
Pole	7	3	3	2	2	12	3	3
Color	Yellow	Yellow	Yellow	Blue	Orange	Yellow	Yellow	Yellow
	male	female	female	female	female	female	male	male

SB8019400050000X

Fig. 19 SRS wiring harness connector locations. 1994 Legacy

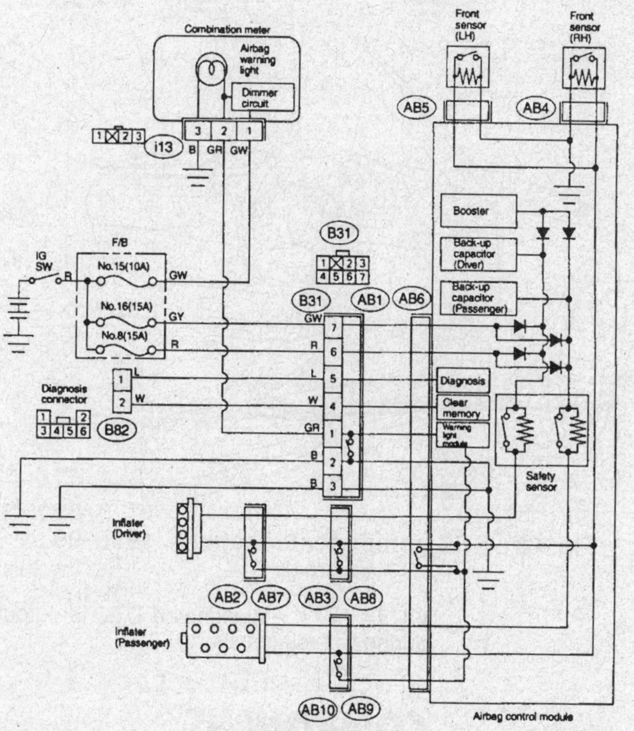
Combination meter
Airbag warning light
Dimmer circuit
Front sensor (LH)
Front sensor (RH)
AB5
AB4
i13
Booster
Back-up capacitor (Driver)
Back-up capacitor (Passenger)
B31
IG SW
F/B
No.15(10A)
No.16(15A)
No.8(15A)
AB1
AB6
Diagnosis connector
B82
Diagnosis
Clear memory
Warning light module
Safety sensor
Inflater (Driver)
AB2
AB7
AB3
AB8
Inflater (Passenger)
AB10
AB9
Airbag control module

SB8019500051000X

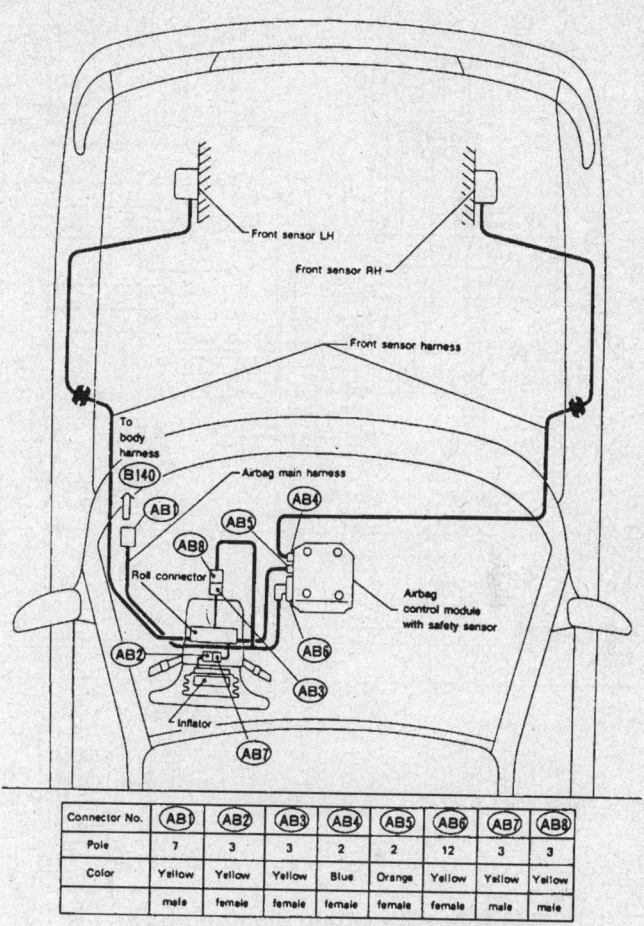

Fig. 20 SRS wiring diagram. 1995–96 Legacy

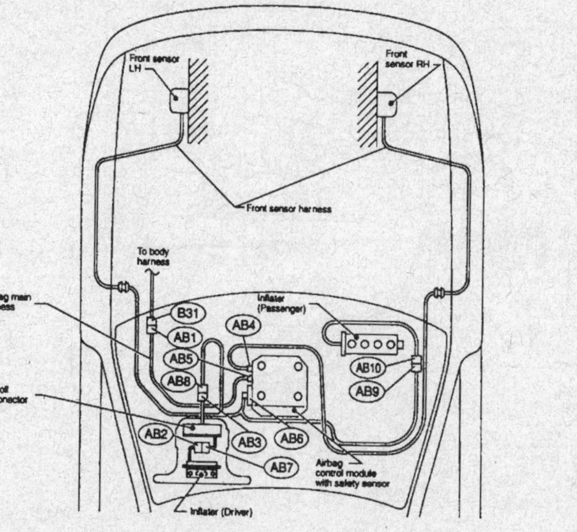
Front sensor LH
Front sensor RH
Front sensor harness
To body harness
Airbag main harness
Inflater (Passenger)
B31
AB4
AB1
AB5
AB8
AB10
AB9
Roll conector
AB2
AB3
AB6
AB7
Airbag control module with safety sensor
Inflater (Driver)

Connector No.	(AB1)	(AB2)	(AB3)	(AB4)	(AB5)	(AB6)	(AB7)	(AB8)	(AB9)	(AB10)
Pole	7	3	3	2	2	12	3	3	3	3
Color	Yellow	Yellow	Yellow	Blue	Orange	Yellow	Yellow	Yellow	Yellow	Yellow
Male/Female	Male	Female	Female	Female	Female	Female	Male	Male	Male	Female

SB8019500052000X

Fig. 21 SRS wiring harness connector locations. 1995–96 Legacy

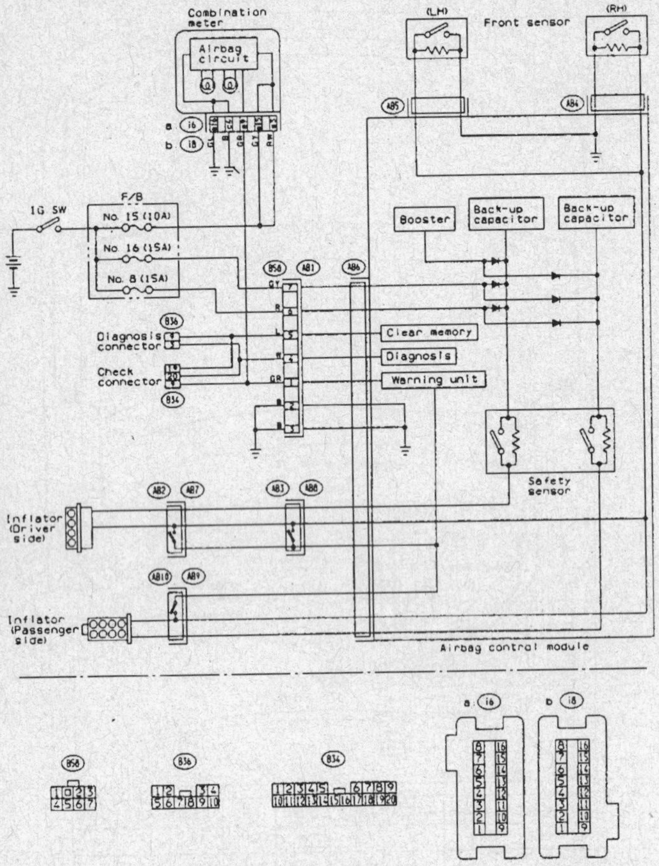
Combination meter
Airbag circuit
Front sensor
(LH)
(RH)
IG SW
F/B
No. 15 (10A)
No. 16 (15A)
No. 8 (15A)
Booster
Back-up capacitor
Back-up capacitor
Diagnosis connector
Check connector
Clear memory
Diagnosis
Warning unit
Safety sensor
Inflator (Driver side)
Inflator (Passenger side)
Airbag control module

SB8019400053000X

Fig. 22 SRS wiring diagram. SVX

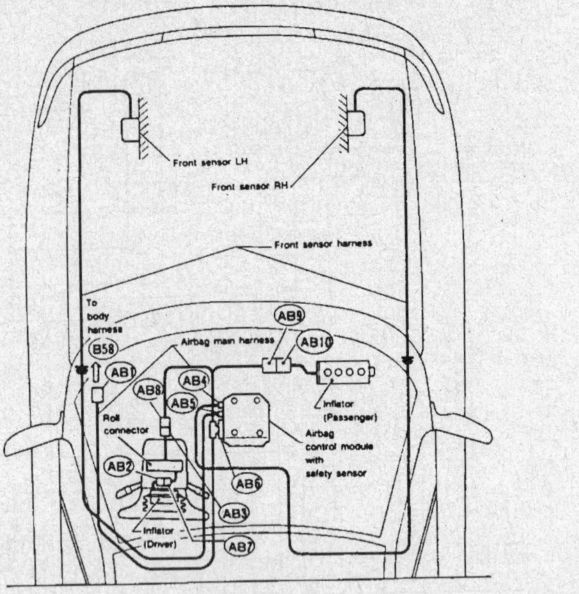
Front sensor LH
Front sensor RH
Front sensor harness
To body harness
Airbag main harness
AB9
AB10
B58
AB1
AB8
AB4
AB5
Roll connector
Inflator (Passenger)
Airbag control module with safety sensor
AB2
AB6
AB3
Inflator (Driver)
AB7

Connector No.	(AB1)	(AB2)	(AB3)	(AB4)	(AB5)	(AB6)	(AB7)	(AB8)	(AB9)	(AB10)
Pole	7	3	3	2	2	12	3	3	3	3
Color	Yellow	Yellow	Yellow	Blue	Orange	Yellow	Yellow	Yellow	Yellow	Yellow
Male/Female	Male	Female	Female	Female	Female	Female	Male	Male	Male	Female

SB8019400054000X

Fig. 23 SRS wiring harness connector locations. SVX

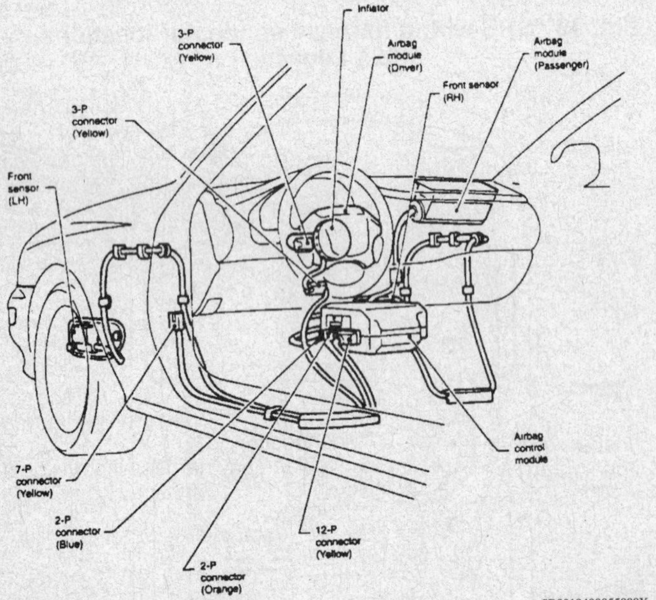
Inflator
3-P connector (Yellow)
Airbag module (Driver)
Airbag module (Passenger)
Front sensor (RH)
3-P connector (Yellow)
Front sensor (LH)
Airbag control module
7-P connector (Yellow)
2-P connector (Blue)
12-P connector (Yellow)
2-P connector (Orange)

SB8019400055000X

Fig. 24 SRS component locations. 1994 Impreza

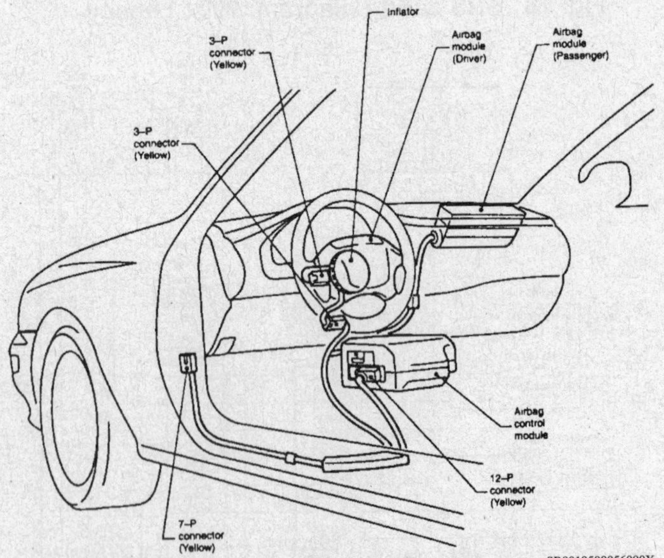
Inflator
3-P connector (Yellow)
Airbag module (Driver)
Airbag module (Passenger)
3-P connector (Yellow)
Airbag control module
12-P connector (Yellow)
7-P connector (Yellow)

SB8019500056000X

Fig. 25 SRS component locations. 1995–96 Impreza

WIRE HARNESS & CONNECTOR REPAIR

The SRS wiring harness is entirely covered with a yellow protective conduit, and can easily be distinguished from harnesses of other systems. Do not attempt to repair SRS wiring harness or electrical connectors. Replace the harness if connectors or harness are found to be damaged or opened, or if a designated DTC is output during self–diagnosis.

COMPONENT LOCATIONS

Refer to **Figs. 24 through 28** for SRS component locations.

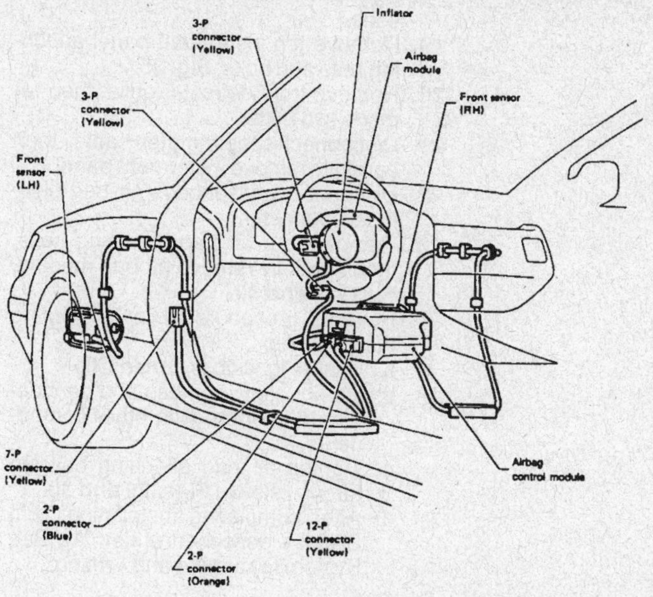
3-P
connector
(Yellow)
Inflator
Airbag
module
3-P
connector
(Yellow)
Front sensor
(RH)
Front
sensor
(LH)
7-P
connector
(Yellow)
Airbag
control module
2-P
connector
(Blue)
12-P
connector
(Yellow)
2-P
connector
(Orange)

SB8019400057000X

Fig. 26 SRS component locations. 1994 Legacy

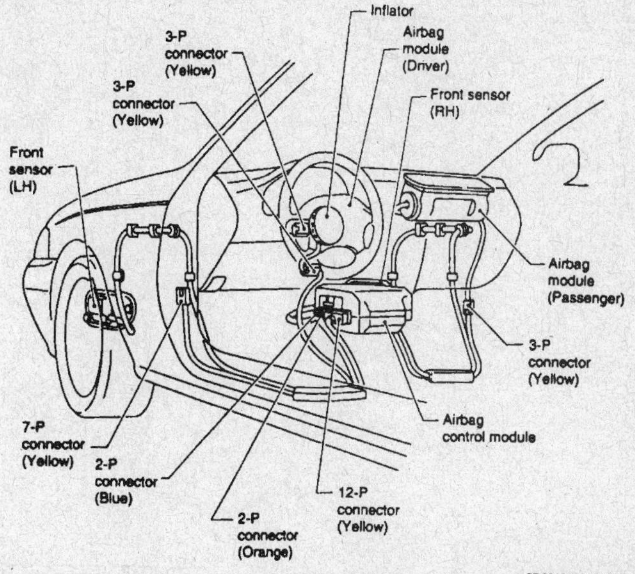
Inflator
3-P
connector
(Yellow)
Airbag
module
(Driver)
3-P
connector
(Yellow)
Front sensor
(RH)
Front
sensor
(LH)
Airbag
module
(Passenger)
3-P
connector
(Yellow)
Airbag
control module
7-P
connector
(Yellow)
2-P
connector
(Blue)
12-P
connector
(Yellow)
2-P
connector
(Orange)

SB8019500058000X

Fig. 27 SRS component locations. 1995–96 Legacy

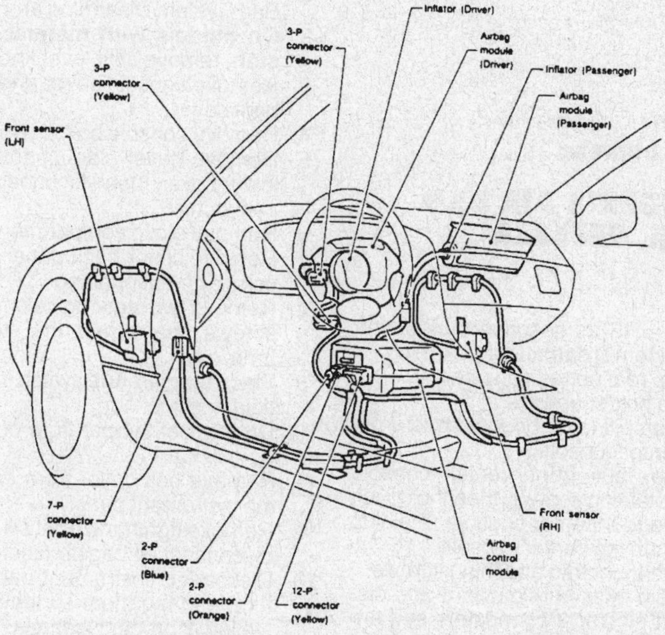
Inflator (Driver)
3-P
connector
(Yellow)
Airbag
module
(Driver)
3-P
connector
(Yellow)
Inflator (Passenger)
Airbag
module
(Passenger)
Front sensor
(LH)
7-P
connector
(Yellow)
2-P
connector
(Blue)
2-P
connector
(Orange)
12-P
connector
(Yellow)
Front sensor
(RH)
Airbag
control
module

SB8019400059000X

Fig. 28 SRS component locations. SVX

DIAGNOSIS & TESTING

Refer to MOTOR'S Air Bag Manual for system diagnosis and testing.

COLLISION INSPECTION

On vehicles which have experienced an air bag system deployment, certain SRS components must be replaced. To determine which components require replacement, refer to the "General Information" section located at the front of this manual.

The SRS must be inspected if the vehicle was involved in a collision even if deployment did not take place. Inspect system for DTCs and proper warning lamp operation. Refer to "Diagnosis and Testing." If deployment has taken place, the air bag module and front sensors must be replaced. Any components which have been diagnosed as faulty should also be replaced. The following inspection should be performed:

1. Inspect the air bag module as follows:
   a. Inspect module pad and side surface for scratches and cracks, and if any are present, replace air bag module.
   b. Inspect module wiring harness and electrical connectors for damage and replace as necessary. Also ensure harness connectors are securely installed.
   c. Inspect air bag to steering wheel mounting for damage. Replace damaged components.
   d. Inspect air bag surfaces for contamination, such as oil or grease on surface. If contaminated, replace air bag module.
2. Inspect front sensors as follows:
   a. Inspect front sensor housing and mounting bracket for cracks and damage, and if any are present, replace front sensor.
   b. Inspect manufacturer identification label on sensor and if missing, replace the sensor.
   c. Inspect front sensor wiring harness and electrical connectors for damage, and replace harness if damage is discovered. Also ensure harness connectors are properly connected.
3. The main wiring harness should be inspected as follows:
   a. If any wiring is open or exposed, that harness should be replaced.
   b. If any electrical connector or conduit is damaged, that harness should be replaced. Also inspect electrical connectors for proper connection.
   c. Replace any harness if a designated DTC is output during self–diagnosis.
4. The air bag control unit should be inspected as follows:
   a. Replace control unit if it is dented or its case is deformed.
   b. If control unit bracket is cracked, bent or damaged, replace as necessary.
   c. Inspect control unit electrical connector for damage and replace if needed.
5. Inspect combination switch and roll connector for cracks and other damage and replace as necessary.
6. Inspect steering wheel and column for

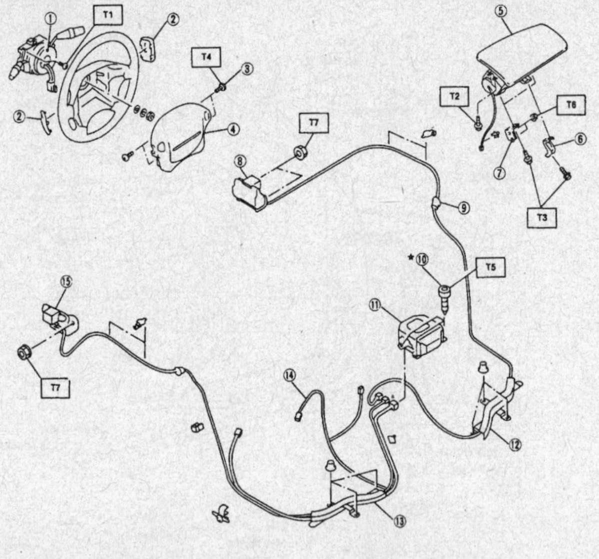
T1
T2
T3
T4
T5
T7

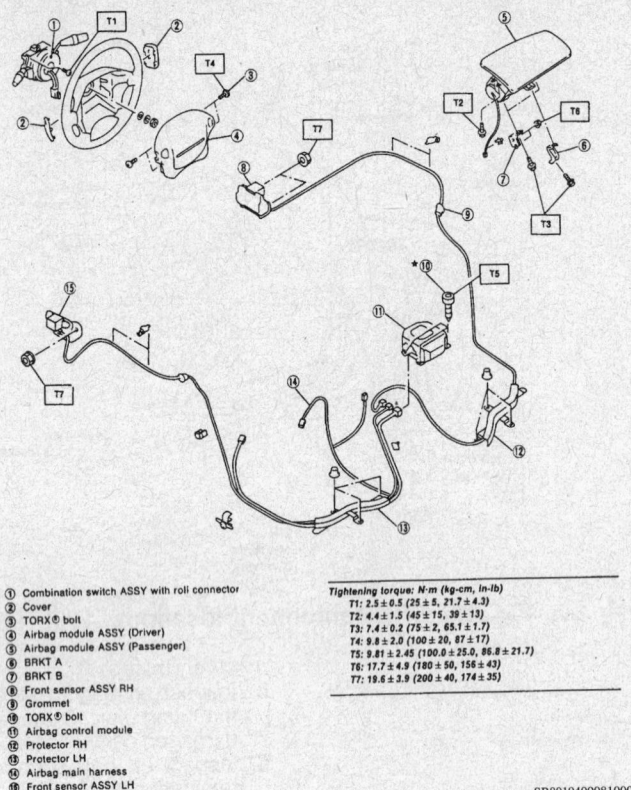

① Combination switch ASSY with roll connector
② Cover
③ TORX® bolt
④ Airbag module ASSY (Driver)
⑤ Airbag module ASSY (Passenger)
⑥ BRKT A
⑦ BRKT B
⑧ Front sensor ASSY RH
⑨ Grommet
⑩ TORX® bolt
⑪ Airbag control module
⑫ Protector RH
⑬ Protector LH
⑭ Airbag main harness
⑮ Front sensor ASSY LH

Tightening torque: N·m (kg-cm, in-lb)
T1: 2.5 ± 0.5 (25 ± 5, 21.7 ± 4.3)
T2: 4.4 ± 1.5 (45 ± 15, 39 ± 13)
T3: 7.4 ± 0.2 (75 ± 2, 65.1 ± 1.7)
T4: 9.8 ± 2.0 (100 ± 20, 87 ± 17)
T5: 9.81 ± 2.45 (100.0 ± 25.0, 86.8 ± 21.7)
T6: 17.7 ± 4.9 (180 ± 50, 156 ± 43)
T7: 19.6 ± 3.9 (200 ± 40, 174 ± 35)

SB8019400081000X

Fig. 29 SRS components. 1994 Impreza

damage and replace if needed.

COMPONENT SERVICE

The deployment electrical circuit is powered directly from the battery and backup power supply. To avoid unwanted deployment and possible personal injury, the SRS must be disarmed. Refer to "Air Bag System Disarming and Arming." Wait 20 seconds prior to starting any service.

DRIVER'S AIR BAG MODULE, REPLACE

1. Set front wheels in straight–ahead position.
2. Disarm SRS as described under "Air Bag System Disarming and Arming."
3. Remove covers from both sides of steering wheel, if equipped, then using T30 Torx bit, remove Torx bolts.
4. Disconnect air bag and horn electrical connectors, then remove air bag unit, **Figs. 29 through 33.**
5. Reverse procedure to install, noting the following:
   a. Ensure ignition is turned Off.
   b. Do not allow harness and connectors to interfere with other components.
   c. Install new Torx bolts and tighten to specifications.
   d. After completing installation, arm SRS as described under "Air Bag System Disarming and Arming."

PASSENGER'S AIR BAG MODULE, REPLACE

Impreza

1. Disarm SRS as described under "Air Bag System Disarming and Arming."
2. Remove rear center console.
3. Pull cup holder upward.
4. Remove shift lever boot or cover from front center console.
5. Remove four front center console cover retaining screws, then the cover.
6. Remove four center console retaining bolts, then the center console.
7. Remove four radio attaching screws.
8. Pull radio assembly outward and disconnect electrical connectors and antenna lead.
9. Remove radio assembly.
10. Remove instrument panel driver side lower cover.
11. Disconnect seat belt timer electrical connector.
12. Remove glove compartment, then the pocket back panel.
13. Remove instrument panel console.
14. Remove steering column retaining bolts, then lower the steering column.
15. Remove retaining screw, then detach hood opening lever from instrument panel.
16. Place temperature switch in maximum cold position and mode switch to defrost position.
17. Disconnect temperature control and mode cables from links.
18. Disconnect instrument panel electrical connectors, **Fig. 34,** and tag them so they can be installed at proper locations.
19. Remove ten instrument panel attaching nuts and bolts, **Fig. 35.**
20. Remove front defroster grille, then remove two bolts.
21. Disconnect speedometer cable, then carefully remove instrument panel.
22. Disconnect passenger's air bag electrical connector.
23. Remove four air bag attaching bolts, then carefully remove air bag module, **Figs. 29 and 30.**
24. Reverse procedure to install, noting the following:
   a. Ensure ignition is turned Off.
   b. Do not allow harness and connectors to interfere with other components.
   c. Tighten air bag attaching bolts to torque listed in **Figs. 29 and 30.**
   d. After completing installation, arm SRS as described under "Air Bag System Disarming and Arming."

Legacy

1. Disarm SRS as described under "Air Bag System Disarming and Arming."
2. **On models with manual transmission,** remove shift lever knob.
3. Remove console cover and shift lever boot cover.
4. Remove console box.
5. Remove driver side instrument panel lower cover, then disconnect electrical connector.
6. Remove glove compartment.
7. Remove cover back panel from glove compartment opening.
8. Remove two steering column retaining screws, then lower the steering column.
9. Place temperature switch in maximum cold position.
10. Disconnect temperature control cable from link.
11. Remove bolt cover from each side of the instrument panel.
12. Remove righthand front sill cover, then disconnect air bag connector.
13. Disconnect instrument panel connectors, and tag them so they can be installed at proper locations.
14. Remove instrument panel attaching bolts.
15. Remove front defroster grille, then two instrument panel attaching bolts.
16. Disconnect speedometer cable, then carefully remove instrument panel.
17. Remove four passenger's air bag attaching bolts, then carefully remove air bag module, **Fig. 32.**
18. Reverse procedure to install, noting the following:
   a. Ensure ignition is turned Off.
   b. Do not allow harness and connectors to interfere with other components.
   c. Tighten air bag attaching bolts to torque listed in **Fig. 32.**
   d. After completing installation, arm SRS as described under "Air Bag System Disarming and Arming."

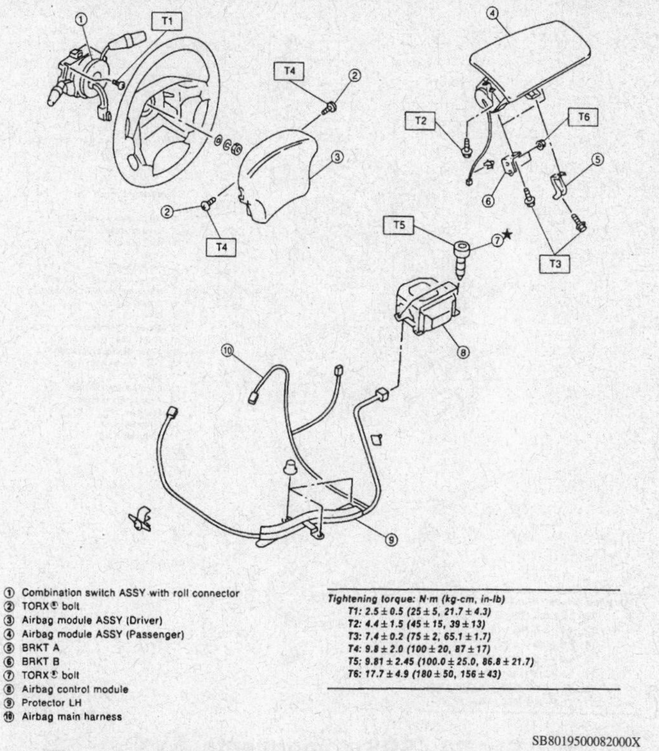
T1
T2
T3
T4
T5
T6
① Combination switch ASSY with roll connector
② TORX® bolt
③ Airbag module ASSY (Driver)
④ Airbag module ASSY (Passenger)
⑤ BRKT A
⑥ BRKT B
⑦ TORX® bolt
⑧ Airbag control module
⑨ Protector LH
⑩ Airbag main harness
Tightening torque: N·m (kg-cm, in-lb)
T1: 2.5 ± 0.5 (25 ± 5, 21.7 ± 4.3)
T2: 4.4 ± 1.5 (45 ± 15, 39 ± 13)
T3: 7.4 ± 0.2 (75 ± 2, 65.1 ± 1.7)
T4: 9.8 ± 2.0 (100 ± 20, 87 ± 17)
T5: 9.81 ± 2.45 (100.0 ± 25.0, 86.8 ± 21.7)
T6: 17.7 ± 4.9 (180 ± 50, 156 ± 43)
SB8019500082000X

Fig. 30 SRS components. 1995–96 Impreza

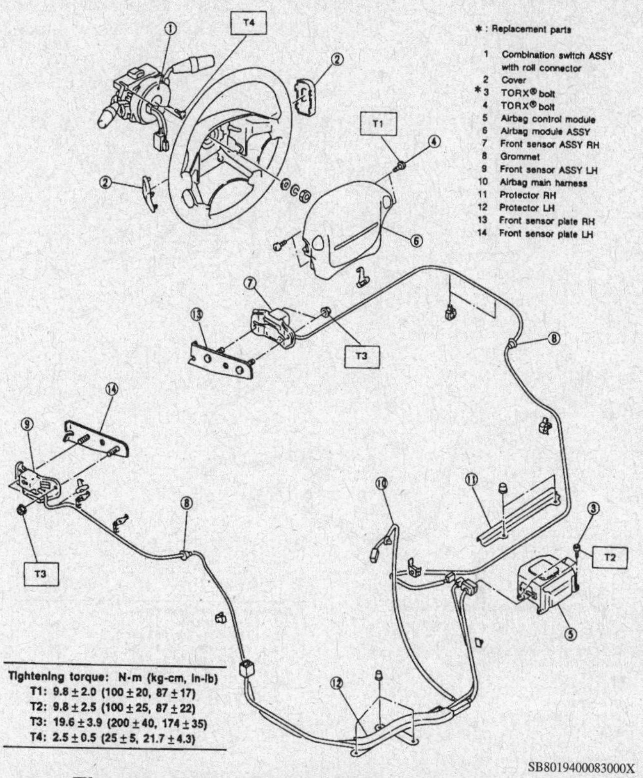
T1
T2
T3
T4
*: Replacement parts
1 Combination switch ASSY with roll connector
2 Cover
*3 TORX® bolt
4 TORX® bolt
5 Airbag control module
6 Airbag module ASSY
7 Front sensor ASSY RH
8 Grommet
9 Front sensor ASSY LH
10 Airbag main harness
11 Protector RH
12 Protector LH
13 Front sensor plate RH
14 Front sensor plate LH
Tightening torque: N·m (kg-cm, in-lb)
T1: 9.8 ± 2.0 (100 ± 20, 87 ± 17)
T2: 9.8 ± 2.5 (100 ± 25, 87 ± 22)
T3: 19.6 ± 3.9 (200 ± 40, 174 ± 35)
T4: 2.5 ± 0.5 (25 ± 5, 21.7 ± 4.3)
SB8019400083000X

Fig. 31 SRS components. 1994 Legacy

SVX

1. Disarm SRS as described under "Air Bag System Disarming and Arming."
2. Remove glove compartment.
3. Remove three bolts from steering support beam, **Fig. 36.**
4. Loosen nut retaining bracket to passenger's air bag module, **Fig. 33.**
5. Remove securing air bag module bracket to steering support beam, then the bracket.
6. Disconnect air bag electrical connector.
7. Remove four air bag retaining screws, then the module.
8. Reverse procedure to install, noting the following:
   a. Ensure ignition is turned Off.
   b. Do not allow harness and connectors to interfere with other components.
   c. Tighten air bag attaching bolts to torque listed in **Fig. 33.**
   d. After completing installation, arm SRS as described under "Air Bag System Disarming and Arming."

FRONT SENSOR, REPLACE

1994 Impreza & 1994–96 Legacy

1. Disarm SRS as described under "Air Bag System Disarming and Arming."
2. Remove lower instrument cover and cover panel, then disconnect air bag connectors AB3 and AB8 below steering column. **Do not connect these again until front sensors are securely installed.**
3. Remove front console box.
4. Disconnect two–pin blue electrical connector (righthand side sensor) and two–pin orange electrical connector (lefthand side sensor) from air bag control unit.
5. Roll up floor mat and side sill cover, then remove front sensor harness from clip and protector.
6. Remove front wheels, then front mud shield.
7. Remove wiring harness clips securing front sensor harness.
8. Remove grommet, then the front sensor unit, **Figs. 29, 31 and 32.**
9. Reverse procedure to install, noting the following:
   a. Tighten front sensor attaching nuts to specifications.
   b. After completing installation, arm SRS as described under "Air Bag System Disarming and Arming."

SVX

1. Disarm SRS as described under "Air Bag System Disarming and Arming."
2. Remove instrument panel lower cover and lower cover panel, then disconnect air bag electrical connector at harness spool. **Do not connect this connector again until front sensors are securely installed.**
3. Remove console panel and base on driver seat side.
4. Disconnect two–pin blue electrical connector (righthand front sensor) and two–pin orange electrical connector (lefthand front sensor) from air bag control unit.
5. Roll up floor mat and remove side sill lower cover, then remove front sensor wiring harness from clip and protector.
6. Remove front wheels, then the front mud shield.
7. Remove wiring harness bracket, then pry off four clips securing front sensor harness.
8. Remove grommet, then the front sensor unit, **Fig. 33.**
9. Reverse procedure to install, noting the following:
   a. On models equipped with sunroof, route drain hose through grommet during grommet installation.
   b. Tighten front sensor attaching bolts to specifications.
   c. After completing installation, arm SRS as described under "Air Bag System Disarming and Arming."

MAIN HARNESS, REPLACE

Impreza & Legacy

1. Disarm SRS as described under "Air Bag System Disarming and Arming."
2. Remove lower cover and lower cover panel, then disconnect air bag connectors AB3 and AB8 below steering column. **Do not connect these connectors again until main harness is securely installed.**
3. Remove front console box.
4. Disconnect 12–pin yellow connector from air bag control unit, then body harness connector from connector AB1.
5. Roll up floor mat and lefthand side sill cover.
6. Remove main harness, **Figs. 29 through 32,** from clip and protector.
7. Reverse procedure to install. After completing installation, arm SRS as

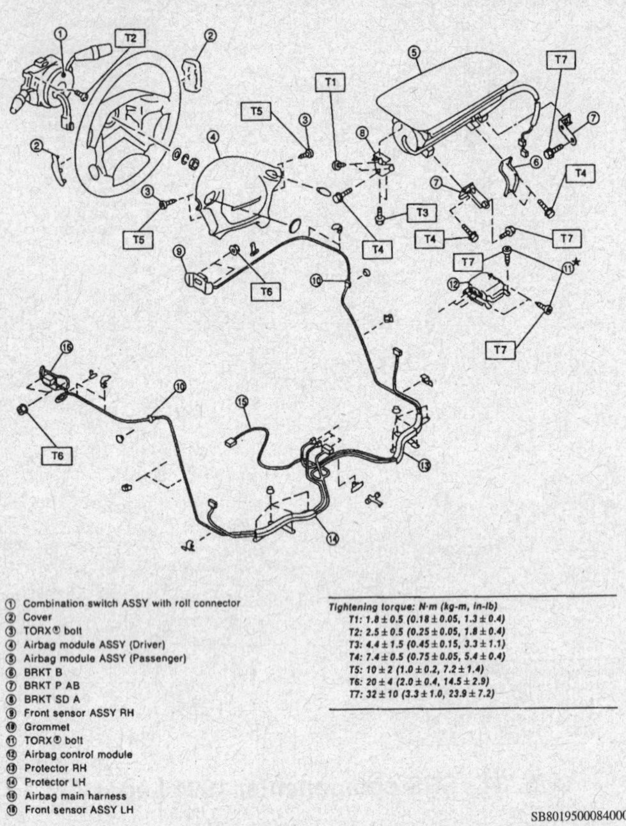
① Combination switch ASSY with roll connector
② Cover
③ TORX® bolt
④ Airbag module ASSY (Driver)
⑤ Airbag module ASSY (Passenger)
⑥ BRKT B
⑦ BRKT P AB
⑧ BRKT SD A
⑨ Front sensor ASSY RH
⑩ Grommet
⑪ TORX® bolt
⑫ Airbag control module
⑬ Protector RH
⑭ Protector LH
⑮ Airbag main harness
⑯ Front sensor ASSY LH
Tightening torque: N·m (kg-m, in-lb)
T1: 1.8 ± 0.5 (0.18 ± 0.05, 1.3 ± 0.4)
T2: 2.5 ± 0.5 (0.25 ± 0.05, 1.8 ± 0.4)
T3: 4.4 ± 1.5 (0.45 ± 0.15, 3.3 ± 1.1)
T4: 7.4 ± 0.5 (0.75 ± 0.05, 5.4 ± 0.4)
T5: 10 ± 2 (1.0 ± 0.2, 7.2 ± 1.4)
T6: 20 ± 4 (2.0 ± 0.4, 14.5 ± 2.9)
T7: 32 ± 10 (3.3 ± 1.0, 23.9 ± 7.2)
SB8019500084000X

Fig. 32 SRS components. 1995–96 Legacy

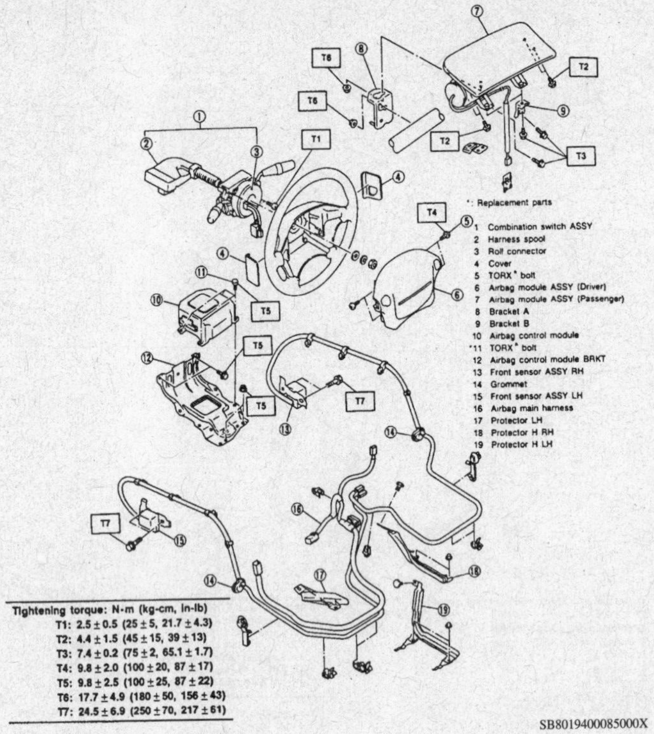
*: Replacement parts
1 Combination switch ASSY
2 Harness spool
3 Roll connector
4 Cover
5 TORX* bolt
6 Airbag module ASSY (Driver)
7 Airbag module ASSY (Passenger)
8 Bracket A
9 Bracket B
10 Airbag control module
11 TORX bolt
12 Airbag control module BRKT
13 Front sensor ASSY RH
14 Grommet
15 Front sensor ASSY LH
16 Airbag main harness
17 Protector LH
18 Protector H RH
19 Protector H LH
Tightening torque: N·m (kg-cm, in-lb)
T1: 2.5 ± 0.5 (25 ± 5, 21.7 ± 4.3)
T2: 4.4 ± 1.5 (45 ± 15, 39 ± 13)
T3: 7.4 ± 0.2 (75 ± 2, 65.1 ± 1.7)
T4: 9.8 ± 2.0 (100 ± 20, 87 ± 17)
T5: 9.8 ± 2.5 (100 ± 25, 87 ± 22)
T6: 17.7 ± 4.9 (180 ± 50, 156 ± 43)
T7: 24.5 ± 6.9 (250 ± 70, 217 ± 61)
SB8019400085000X

Fig. 33 SRS components. SVX

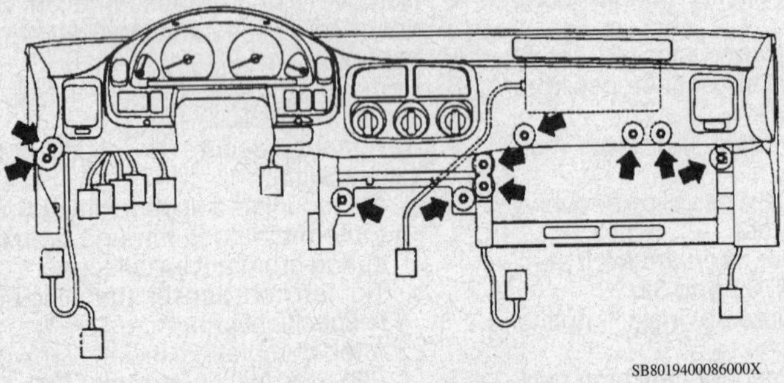
SB8019400086000X

Fig. 34 Instrument panel attaching nut & bolt locations. Impreza

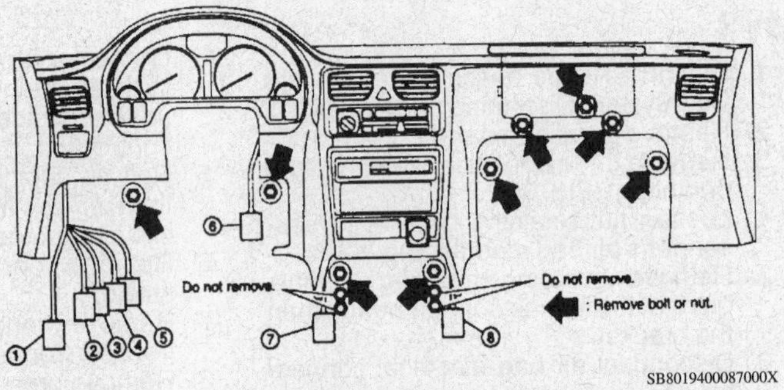
Do not remove.
Do not remove.
: Remove bolt or nut.
SB8019400087000X

Fig. 35 Instrument panel attaching nut & bolt locations. Legacy

described under "Air Bag System Disarming and Arming."

SVX

1. Disarm SRS as described under "Air Bag System Disarming and Arming."
2. Remove lower cover and lower cover panel, then disconnect air bag connector at harness spool. **Do not connect this connector again until main harness is securely installed.**
3. Remove console panel and base on driver seat side.
4. Disconnect 12–pin yellow electrical connector from air bag control unit, then body harness connector B58 from connector AB1.
5. Roll up floor mat and remove lefthand side sill lower cover.
6. Remove main harness, **Fig. 33,** from clip and protector.
7. Reverse procedure to install. After completing installation, arm SRS as described under "Air Bag System Disarming and Arming."

AIR BAG CONTROL UNIT, REPLACE

Impreza & Legacy

1. Disarm SRS as described under "Air Bag System Disarming and Arming."
2. Remove lower cover and lower cover panel, then disconnect air bag connectors AB3 and AB8 below steering column. **Do not connect these connectors again until air bag control unit is securely installed.**
3. Remove front console box.
4. Disconnect 12–pin yellow, two–pin blue and two–pin orange connectors from air bag control unit.
5. Using Torx bit, remove control unit bolts, then control unit, **Figs. 27 and 28.**
6. Reverse procedure to install, noting the following:
   a. Install new Torx bolts, then tighten to specifications.
   b. After completing installation, arm SRS as described under "Air Bag System Disarming and Arming."

SVX

1. Disarm SRS as described under "Air Bag System Disarming and Arming."
2. Remove lower cover and lower cover panel, then disconnect air bag connector at harness spool. **Do not connect this connector again until control unit is securely installed.**
3. Remove console panel and base on driver seat side, then the audio equipment.
4. Disconnect 12–pin yellow, two–pin blue and two–pin orange connectors from control unit.

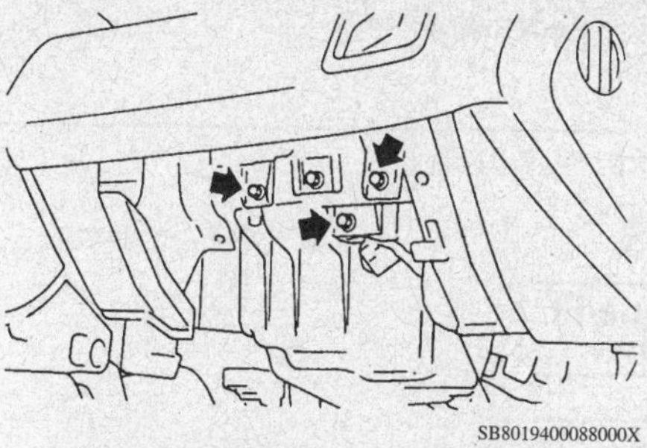
SB8019400088000X

Fig. 36 Removing nuts from steering support beam. SVX

5. Remove two nuts and bolts securing control unit bracket, then control unit and bracket as an assembly.
6. Using T30 Torx bit, remove control unit from bracket.
7. Reverse procedure to install, noting the following:
   a. Install new Torx bolts, then tighten to specifications.
   b. After completing installation, arm SRS as described under "Air Bag System Disarming and Arming."

COMBINATION SWITCH ASSEMBLY

1. Place front wheels in straight–ahead position.
2. Disarm SRS as described under "Air Bag System Disarming and Arming."
3. Remove instrument panel lower cover from lefthand side of instrument panel.
4. Disconnect air bag connector below steering column.
5. Disconnect combination switch connector from wiring harness.
6. Remove air bag module as described under "Air Bag Module, Replace."
7. Remove steering wheel retaining nut, then place alignment marks on wheel hub and shaft for use during installation.
8. Using a suitable puller, remove wheel from shaft.
9. Remove steering column covers.
10. Remove combination switch attaching screws, then remove combination switch with roll connector, **Figs 29 through 33.**
11. Reverse procedure to install, noting the following:
    a. Prior to installation, ensure front wheels are in straight–ahead position and combination switch is in Off position.
    b. Tighten combination switch/roll connector attaching screws to specifications.
    c. After installing combination switch/roll connector, center the roll connector by turning connector pin clockwise until it stops. Turn pin approximately 2.65 turns counterclockwise, aligning marks as shown in **Figs. 37 and 38.**
    d. After completing installation, arm SRS as described under "Air Bag System Disarming and Arming."

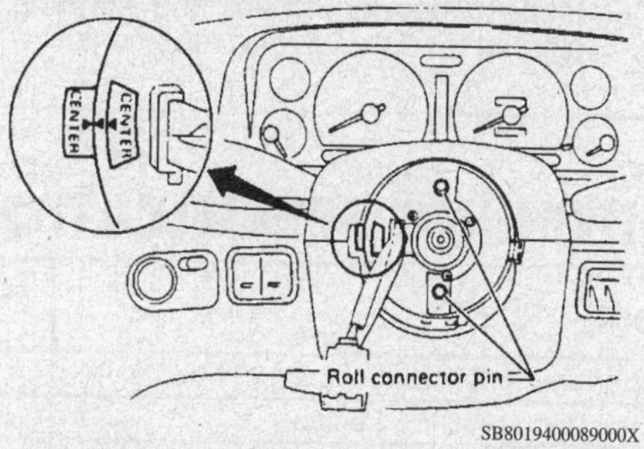
CENTER
Roll connector pin
SB8019400089000X

Fig. 37 Centering roll connector. Legacy, SVX & 1994 Impreza

AIR BAG ASSEMBLY DISPOSAL

When handling a deployed air bag assembly, a face shield and rubber gloves should be worn. Vehicle interior and HVAC ducts should be vacuumed. If sinus or throat irritation is encountered during air bag removal, exit vehicle and breathe fresh air. If skin irritation is encountered, flush affected area with cool water. If sinus, throat, skin or any other type of irritation continues, consult a physician. Wash hands and rinse thoroughly with water after handling a deployed air bag assembly.

A deployed air bag should be removed as described under "Driver's Air Bag Module, Replace" or "Passenger's Air Bag Module, Replace." Place tape over air bag exhaust vents prior to removal. After unit has been removed, it should be placed in a heavy duty plastic bag, sealed securely, then placed with automotive scrap.

TECHNICAL SERVICE BULLETINS

AIR BAG LAMP REMAINS ILLUMINATED

1993 Legacy

If the air bag warning lamp remains illuminated at all times, inspect the double lock connectors (AB2 and AB7) behind the air bag module in the steering wheel. If connectors are properly locked, the SRS control unit memory may not indicate any stored DTCs, but the warning lamp will be illuminated.

COLLISION INSPECTION

The air bag system must be inspected if the vehicle was involved in a collision even if deployment did not take place. Check system for trouble codes and proper warning lamp operation. If deployment has taken place, the air bag module and front sensors must be replaced. Any components which have been diagnosed as faulty should also be replaced. The following inspection should be performed:

1. If deployment did take place, replace the air bag module, If deployment did

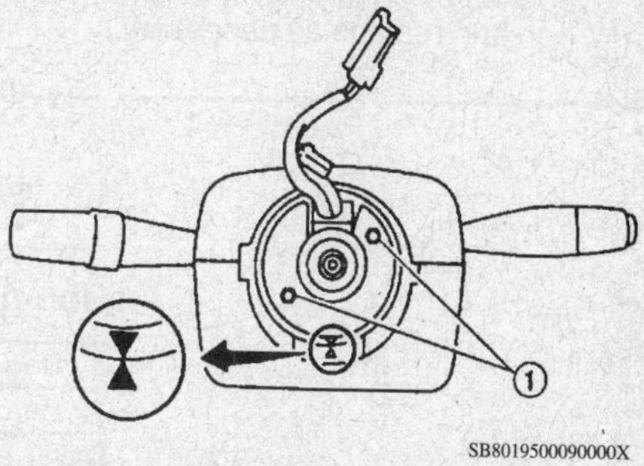
1
SB8019500090000X

Fig. 38 Centering roll connector. 1995–96 Impreza

not take place, inspect the air bag module as follows:
   a. Check air bag module pad and side surface for scratches and cracks. If cracks or scratches are present, replace the air bag module.
   b. Check air bag module wiring harness and electrical connectors for damage and replace as necessary. Also ensure wiring harness electrical connectors are properly connected.
   c. Check air bag to steering wheel mounting for damage. Replace damaged components.
   d. Check air bag surfaces for contamination, such as oil, grease on surface. If surface is contaminated, replace the air bag module.
2. If deployment has taken place, replace the front sensors. If deployment did not take place, inspect the front sensors as follows:
   a. Check front sensor housing for cracks and damage. If cracks and damage are present, replace the front sensor.
   b. Check the sensor mounting bracket for damage and replace as necessary.
   c. Check manufacturer identification label on sensor and replace as necessary.
   d. Check front sensor wiring harness and electrical connectors for damage. If wiring or electrical connectors are damage, replace the wiring harness. Also ensure wiring harness electrical connectors are properly connected.
3. The main wiring harness should be inspected for the follows:
   a. If any wiring is open or exposed the wiring harness should be replaced.
   b. If any electrical connector or conduit is damaged, the wiring harness should be replaced. Also check electrical connectors for proper connection.
4. The air bag control unit should be inspected for the following
   a. If control is dented or case is deformed, replace the control unit.
   b. If control unit bracket is cracked, bent or damaged, replace as necessary.
   c. If control unit electrical connector is damaged, replace as necessary.
5. Inspect combination switch and roll

connector for cracks and other damage and replace as necessary.

6. Inspect steering wheel and steering column for damage and replace as necessary.

TIGHTENING SPECIFICATIONS

Component	Torque/Ft. Lbs.
Air Bag Control Unit (Impreza, SVX & 1994 Legacy)	7
Air Bag Control Unit (1995–96 Legacy)	24②
Driver Air Bag Module To Steering Wheel Screws (Impreza, SVX & 1994 Legacy)	7
Driver Air Bag Module To Steering Wheel Screws (1995–96 Legacy)	12②
Combination Switch W/Roll Connector (Impreza, 1994 Legacy & SVX)	19②
Combination Switch W/Roll Connector (1995–96 Legacy	19②
Front Sensor (1994 Impreza & Legacy)	14
Front Sensor (1995–96 Legacy)	14
Front Sensor (SVX)	18
Passenger Air Bag Module Bracket Nuts (SVX)	13
Passenger Air Bag Module Bolts/Screws	①
Steering Wheel Nut	25

①— Refer to "Passenger's Air Bag Module, Replace" procedure under "Component Service" section.
②— Inch lbs.

Dash Panel Service

NOTE: On Air Bag Equipped Models, Refer To "Air Bag System Precautions" Located In The Front Of This Manual For System Disarming & Arming Procedures.

NOTE: Refer To The "Dash Gauges" Section For Related Information.

INDEX

	Page No.
Dash Panel, Replace	39-96
Impreza	39-99
Justy	39-96
Legacy	39-97
Loyale	39-96
SVX	39-99
Precautions	39-96
Air Bag Systems	39-96

PRECAUTIONS

AIR BAG SYSTEMS

Refer to "Air Bag System Precautions" in the front of this manual for system disarming and arming procedures.

DASH PANEL

REPLACE

JUSTY

Refer to **Figs. 1 through 6** when removing and installing the dash panel.

1. Disconnect battery ground cable, then remove the steering wheel from steering column.
2. Remove glove compartment, then defroster duct.
3. Disconnect heater control cable from inside/outside air selector rod from heater unit.
4. Disconnect speedometer cable, then electrical connectors.
5. Remove instrument panel retaining bolt covers.
6. Remove retaining bolts, then instrument panel from vehicle.
7. Reverse procedure to install.

LOYALE

Refer to **Fig. 7**, during removal and installation of the instrument panel.

1. Disconnect battery ground cable, then remove trim panel (D) from instrument panel shown in **Fig. 8**.
2. Remove three lower instrument panel retaining screws.
3. Remove clip from steering column shaft while lowering cover, if equipped.
4. Disconnect ventilation duct combined with trim panel (D) from heater.
5. Remove three fuse panel retaining bolts, **Fig. 9**.
6. Disconnect ram pressure ventilation cable on driver's side of instrument panel, then from lever rod **Fig. 10**.
7. Disconnect heater control cable from the left side of heater unit, then remove control cable from clamp.
8. Disconnect upper end of cable from select lever rod.

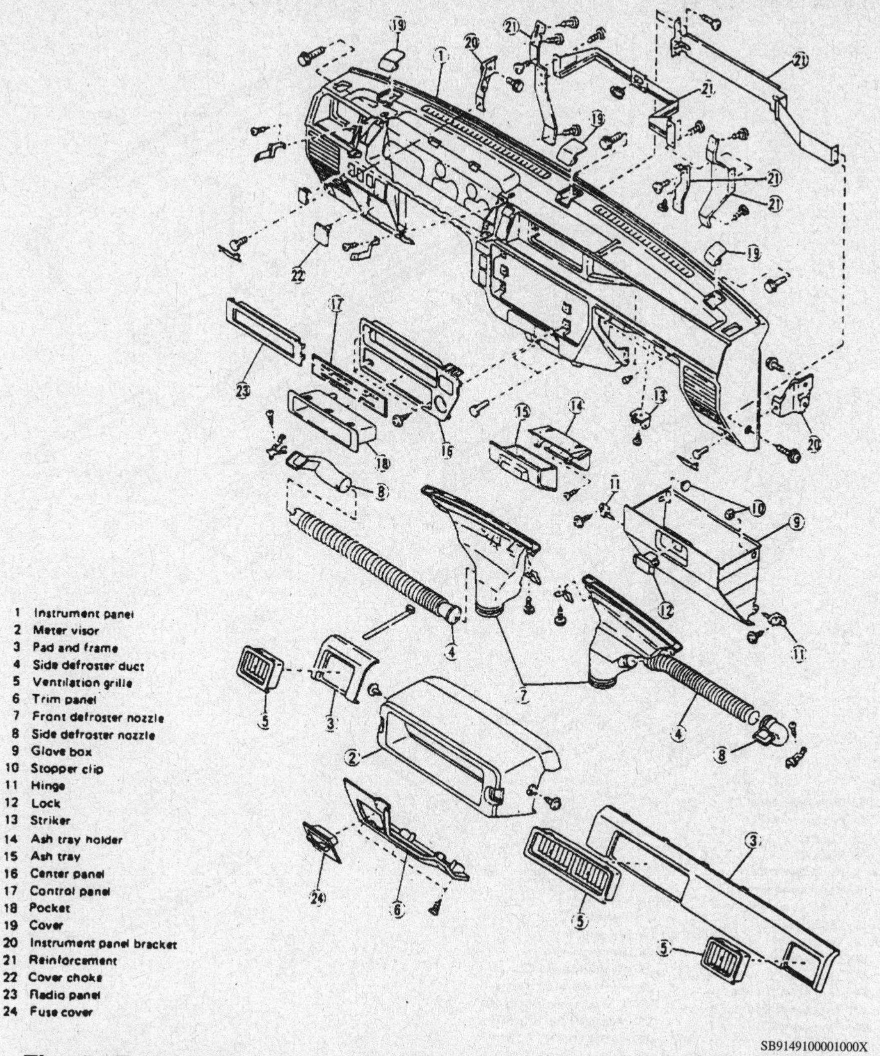
1 Instrument panel
2 Meter visor
3 Pad and frame
4 Side defroster duct
5 Ventilation grille
6 Trim panel
7 Front defroster nozzle
8 Side defroster nozzle
9 Glove box
10 Stopper clip
11 Hinge
12 Lock
13 Striker
14 Ash tray holder
15 Ash tray
16 Center panel
17 Control panel
18 Pocket
19 Cover
20 Instrument panel bracket
21 Reinforcement
22 Cover choke
23 Radio panel
24 Fuse cover
SB9149100001000X

Fig. 1 Exploded view of instrument panel & related components. Justy

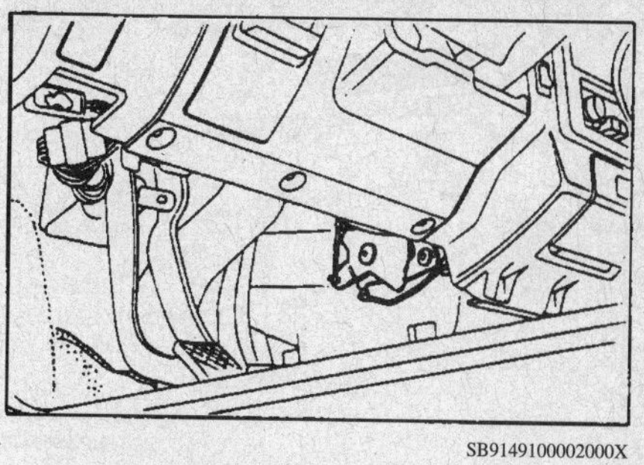
SB9149100002000X

Fig. 2 Selector rod locations. Justy

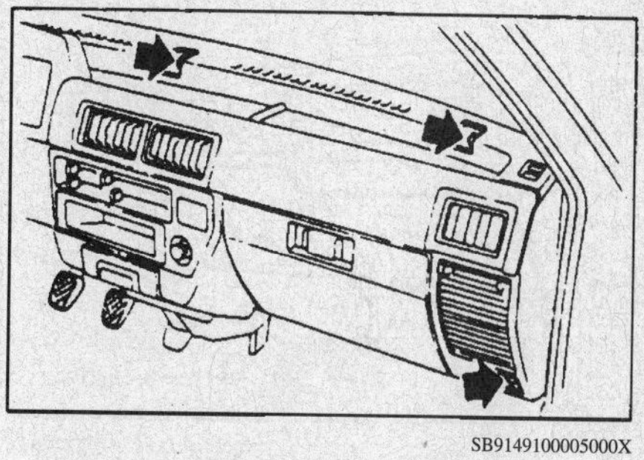
SB9149100005000X

Fig. 5 Righthand instrument panel retaining bolt cover locations. Justy

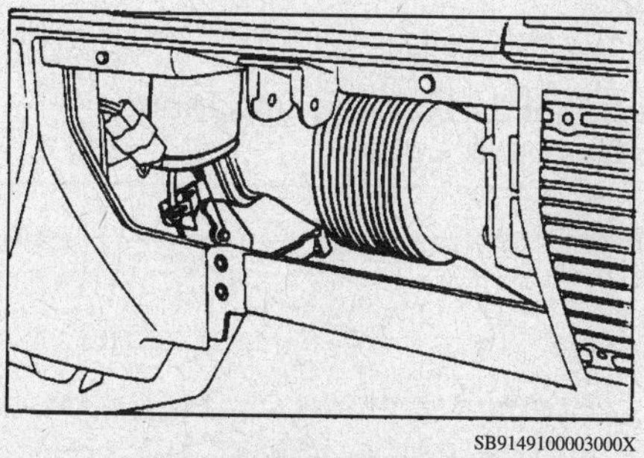
SB9149100003000X

Fig. 3 Heater control cable locations. Justy

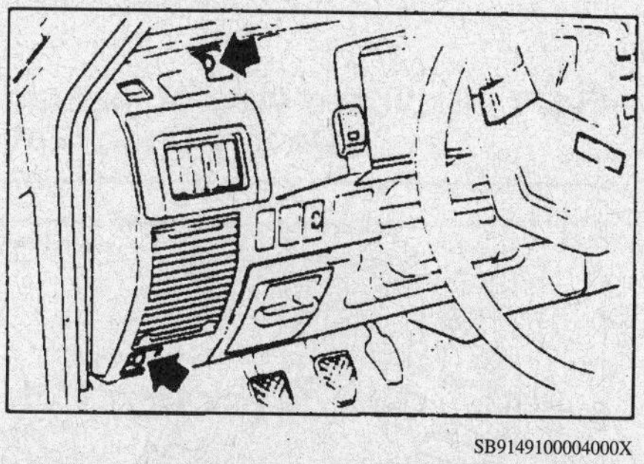
SB9149100004000X

Fig. 4 Lefthand instrument panel retaining bolt cover locations. Justy

9. Disconnect vacuum hoses, **Fig. 11.**
10. Disconnect lefthand side instrument panel and body electrical connectors.
11. Remove steering wheel, then steering column from vehicle.
12. Disconnect speedometer cable.
13. Remove three center tray/console box retaining screws, then center tray/ console box.
14. Remove passenger side lower instrument panel trim cover, then glove compartment hinge retaining screws.
15. Working through glove compartment opening, disconnect blower motor vacuum hose.
16. Disconnect electrical connectors from righthand side of instrument panel.
17. Remove retaining bolt trim covers from instrument panel assembly, **Fig. 12.**
18. Remove instrument panel retaining bolts, then disconnect radio antenna lead.
19. Lower instrument panel, then remove from vehicle.
20. Reverse procedure to install, noting the following:
    a. To set instrument panel into position, attach forward lower center section of instrument panel on cowl bracket flange as shown in **Fig. 13.**
    b. Ensure placement of instrument panel is above windshield cowl weatherstrip as shown in **Fig. 14.**

LEGACY

1993–94

Refer to **Fig. 15,** during removal and installation of the instrument panel.

1. Disconnect battery ground cable, then remove center console box.
2. Using a screwdriver, remove instrument panel retaining bolt covers as shown in **Fig. 16.**
3. Remove lower "A" pillar trim panel from body.
4. Disconnect and remove engine hood release cable from vehicle.
5. Disconnect instrument panel electrical connectors, then speedometer cable.
6. Disconnect ventilation cable from heater unit, then antenna cable from radio.
7. Disconnect temperature control cable from heater unit.
8. Disconnect fuse panel from electrical connector, then remove lower lefthand trim panel.
9. Remove steering column to instrument panel retaining bolts, then instrument panel retaining bolts.
10. Disconnect blower motor vacuum hose , then remove instrument panel from vehicle.

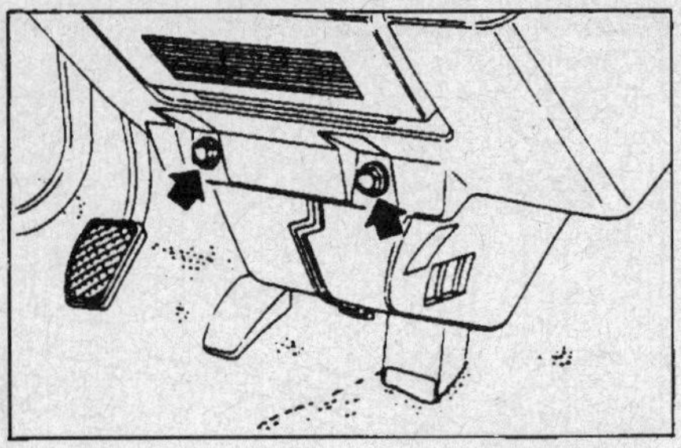

SB9149100006000X

Fig. 6 Lower instrument panel retaining bolt locations. Justy

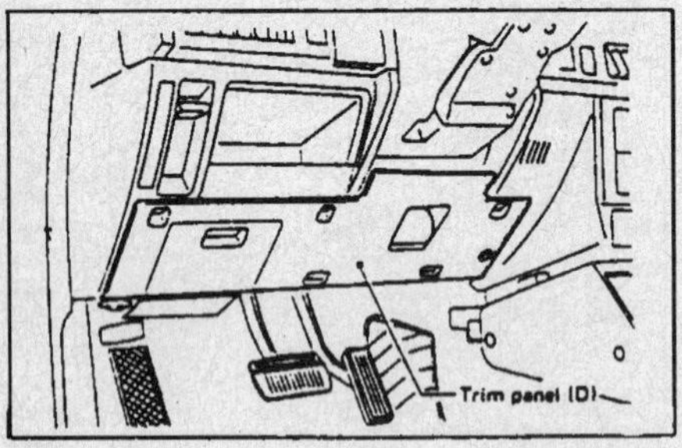
Trim panel (D)

SB9149100008000X

Fig. 8 Trim panel (D) location. 3 Door, 4 Door, Station Wagon & Loyale

11. Reverse procedure to install, noting the following:
    a. To set instrument panel into position, attach forward lower center section of instrument panel on cowl bracket flange as shown in **Fig. 13.**
    b. Ensure placement of instrument panel is above windshield cowl weatherstrip as shown in **Fig. 14.**

1995–96

Refer to **Fig. 17,** during removal and installation of the instrument panel.

1. Disconnect battery ground cable, then remove center console box.
2. Remove lower cover and disconnect connector.
3. Remove glove compartment, then remove glove compartment back panel.
4. Remove two bolts and lower steering column.
5. Set temperature control lever to MAX cold position, then disconnect temperature control cable from heater module link.
6. Remove bolt cover and bolt from both side of instrument panel.
7. Remove front RH side sill cover, then disconnect air bag electrical connectors.
8. Disconnect all instrument panel electrical connections **Fig. 18. Mark connections for installation reference.**
9. Remove front defroster grille, then instrument panel mounting bolts and instrument panel.
10. Reverse procedure to install, noting the following:
    a. When setting instrument panel into position, push two pins into grommet on body panel.
    b. Set clips located at both inside ends of instrument panel onto body side.

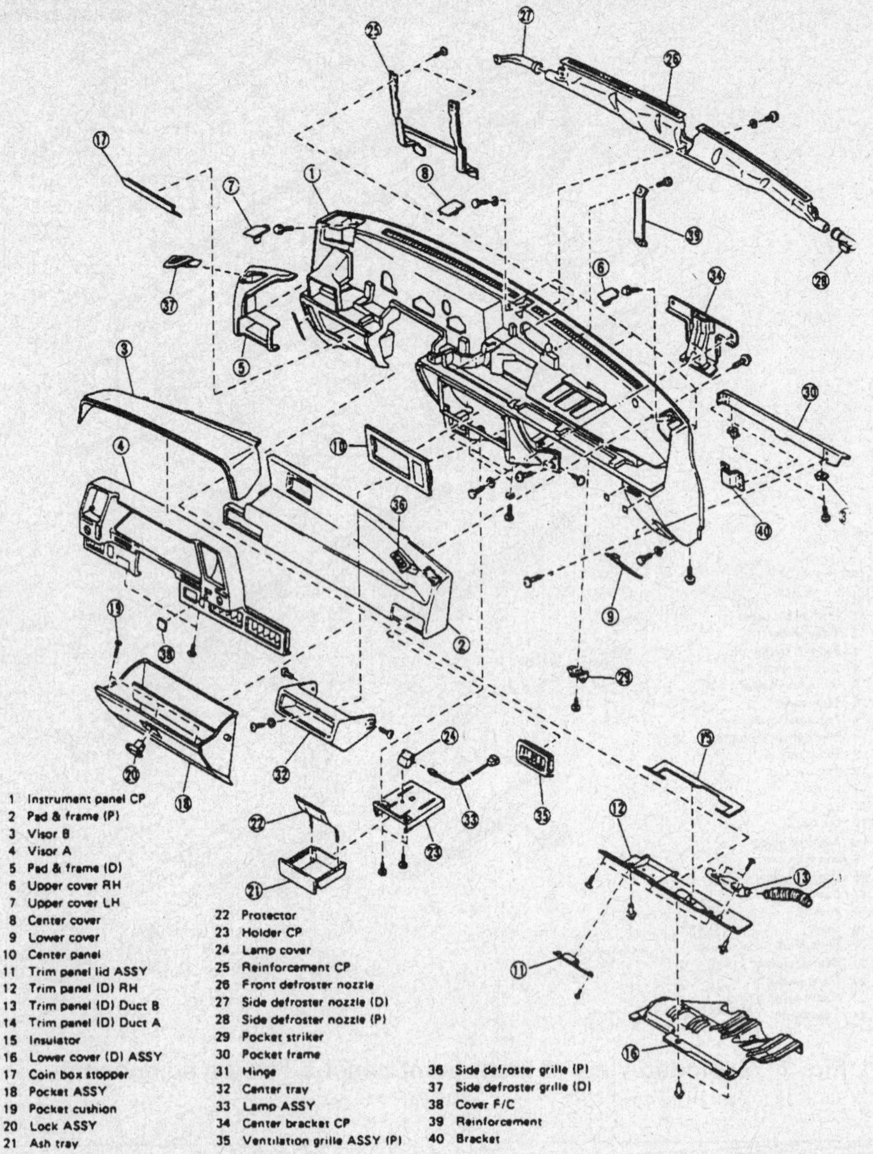
1 Instrument panel CP
2 Pad & frame (P)
3 Visor B
4 Visor A
5 Pad & frame (D)
6 Upper cover RH
7 Upper cover LH
8 Center cover
9 Lower cover
10 Center panel
11 Trim panel lid ASSY
12 Trim panel (D) RH
13 Trim panel (D) Duct B
14 Trim panel (D) Duct A
15 Insulator
16 Lower cover (D) ASSY
17 Coin box stopper
18 Pocket ASSY
19 Pocket cushion
20 Lock ASSY
21 Ash tray
22 Protector
23 Holder CP
24 Lamp cover
25 Reinforcement CP
26 Front defroster nozzle
27 Side defroster nozzle (D)
28 Side defroster nozzle (P)
29 Pocket striker
30 Pocket frame
31 Hinge
32 Center tray
33 Lamp ASSY
34 Center bracket CP
35 Ventilation grille ASSY (P)
36 Side defroster grille (P)
37 Side defroster grille (D)
38 Cover F/C
39 Reinforcement
40 Bracket

SB9149100007000X

Fig. 7 Exploded view of instrument panel & related components. 3 Door, 4 Door, Station Wagon & Loyale

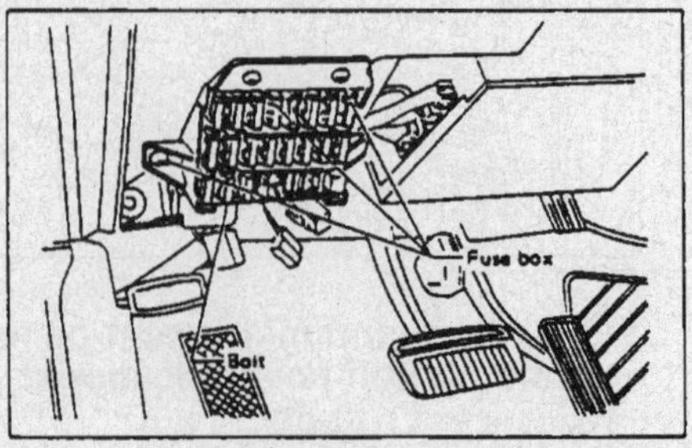
Fuse box
Bolt

SB9149100009000X

Fig. 9 Fuse panel retaining bolt locations. 3 Door, 4 Door, Station Wagon & Loyale

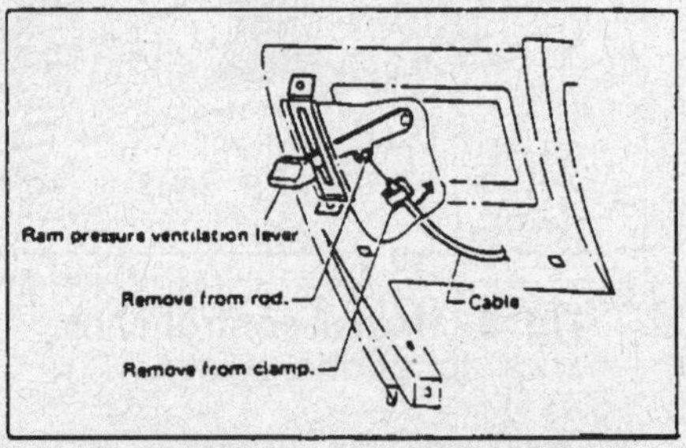
Ram pressure ventilation lever
Remove from rod.
Cable
Remove from clamp.

SB9149100010000X

Fig. 10 Ram pressure ventilation cable location. 3 Door, 4 Door, Station Wagon & Loyale

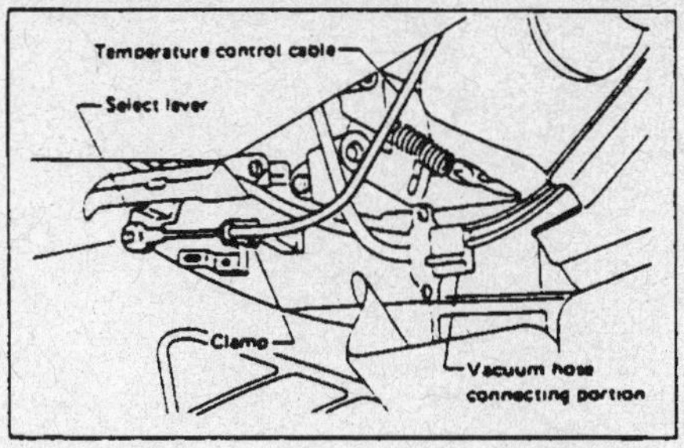
Temperature control cable
Select lever
Clamp
Vacuum hose connecting portion
SB9149100011000X

Fig. 11 Temperature control cable & vacuum hose locations. 3 Door, 4 Door, Station Wagon & Loyale

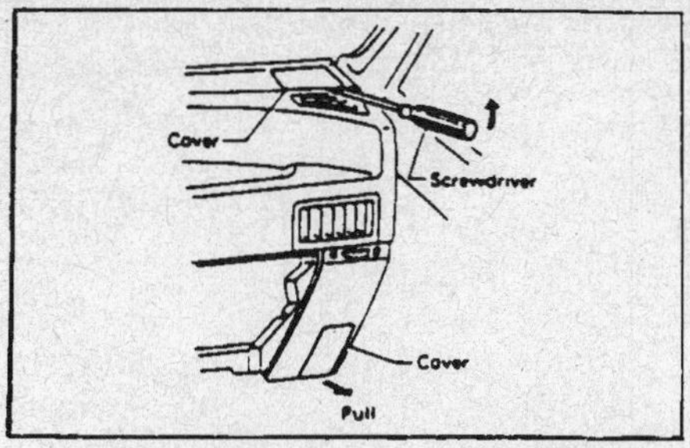
Cover
Screwdriver
Cover
Pull
SB9149100012000X

Fig. 12 Righthand instrument panel retaining bolt cover locations. 3 Door, 4 Door, Station Wagon & Loyale

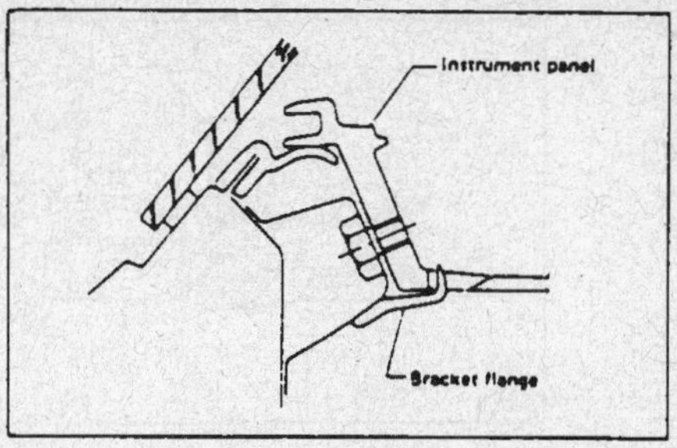
Instrument panel
Bracket flange
SB9149100013000X

Fig. 13 Installation of instrument panel. Except Justy & SVX

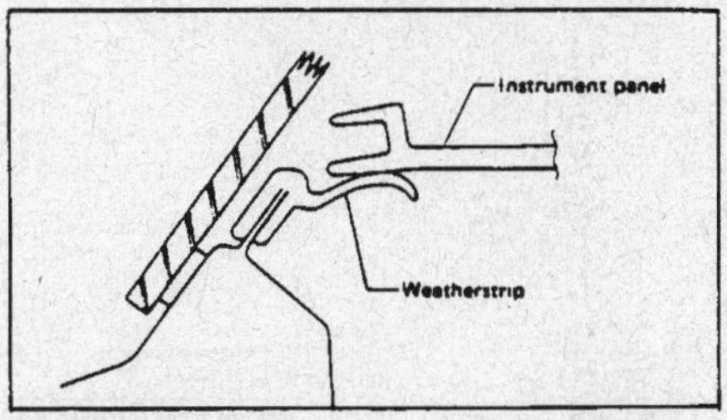
Instrument panel
Weatherstrip
SB9149100014000X

Fig. 14 Correct installation of instrument panel on windshield weatherstrip. Except Justy & SVX

SVX

Refer to **Fig. 19,** during removal and installation of the instrument panel.

1. Remove console box, then the front pillar upper trim panel.
2. Remove radio ground wire, then the remote controlled rear view mirror switch.
3. Remove screw rivet located on lower side of lower cover.
4. Remove lower cover by removing six clips and three connectors.
5. Remove instrument panel lower cover, then disconnect air bag connector at harness spool.
6. Remove two screws from both left and right sides, **Fig. 20,** then lower steering column.
7. Remove caps from both ends of instrument panel, then remove bolts.
8. Remove two instrument panel switch assemblies by pressing forward, then disconnect switch connectors.
9. Remove visor, then disconnect clock connector.
10. Remove instrument cluster, then the meter visor, **Fig. 21,** and glove compartment.
11. Disconnect instrument and body harnesses, then the antenna lead.
12. Cover transmission select lever, then remove instrument panel by pulling forward.
13. Reverse procedure to install, noting the following:
    a. Push instrument panel into position by aligning five pins at end of instrument panel with grommets on body side.
    b. Set clips located at both inside end of instrument panel onto body side.

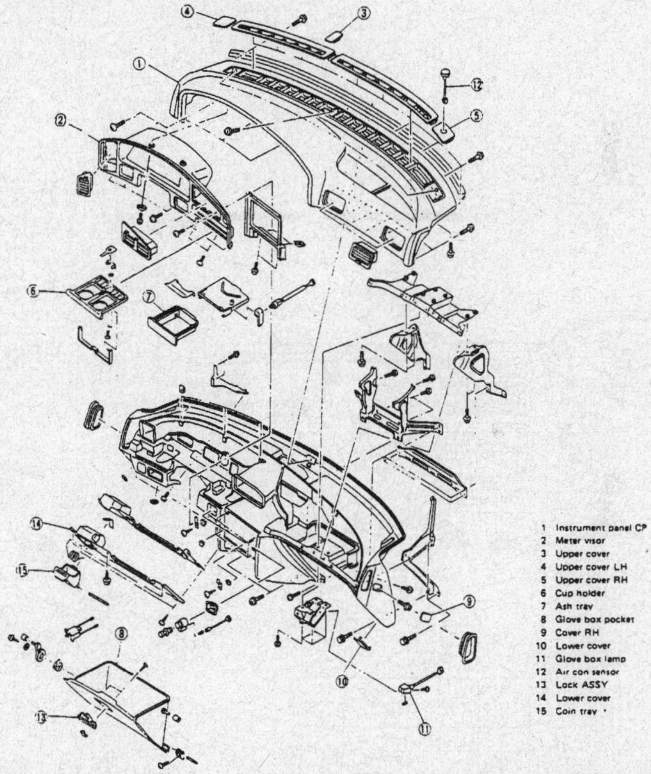
1 Instrument panel CP
2 Meter visor
3 Upper cover
4 Upper cover LH
5 Upper cover RH
6 Cup holder
7 Ash tray
8 Glove box pocket
9 Cover RH
10 Lower cover
11 Glove box lamp
12 Air con sensor
13 Lock ASSY
14 Lower cover
15 Coin tray
SB9149100015000X

Fig. 15 Exploded view of instrument panel & related components. Legacy

IMPREZA

1. Remove rear console box, then the cup holder.
2. **On manual transmission models,** turn over shift lever boot of front end.
3. **On automatic transmission models,** remove select lever cover.
4. **On all models,** remove center console and radio assembly.
5. Remove lower cover, then disconnect seat belt timer connector.
6. Remove data link connector from lower cover.
7. Remove glove compartment, then the center console.
8. Remove two steering column mounting bolts, then lower steering column. Remove hood opener lever.
9. Set temperature control switch to Max. Cold and mode selector switch to defroster position.
10. Disconnect temperature and mode control cables from link.
11. Disconnect harnesses and remove bolts/nuts shown in **Fig. 22.**
12. Remove front defroster grille and two bolts shown in **Fig. 23.**
13. Remove instrument panel assembly. Disconnect speedometer cable from back of instrument cluster.
14. Reverse procedure to install. When setting instrument panel into position, push three pins into grommets on body panel, **Fig. 24.**

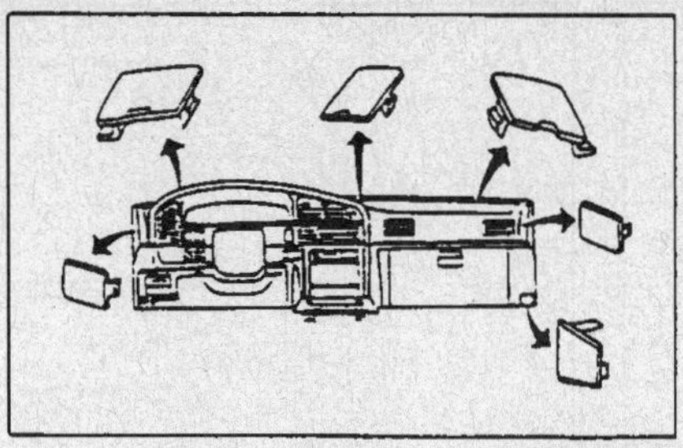

SB9149100016000X

Fig. 16 Instrument panel retaining bolt cover locations. Legacy

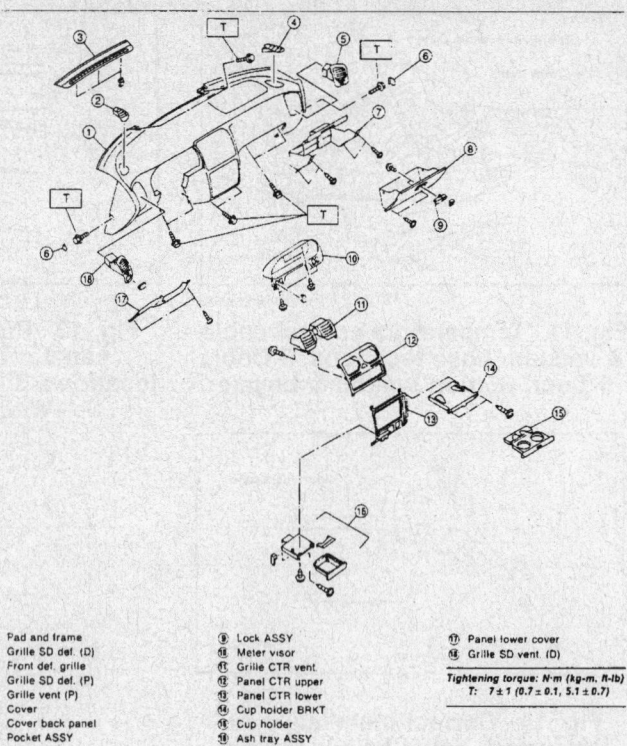

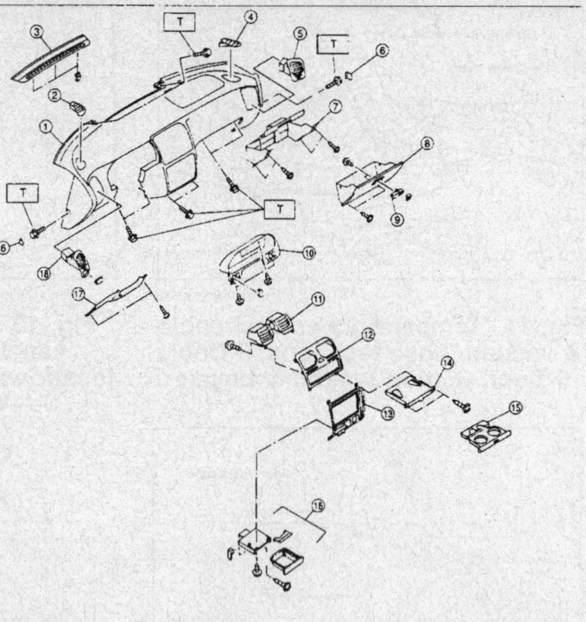
T
T
T
T

1. Pad and frame
2. Grille SD def. (D)
3. Front def. grille
4. Grille SD def. (P)
5. Grille vent (P)
6. Cover
7. Cover back panel
8. Pocket ASSY
9. Lock ASSY
10. Meter visor
11. Grille CTR vent.
12. Panel CTR upper
13. Panel CTR lower
14. Cup holder BRKT
15. Cup holder
16. Ash tray ASSY
17. Panel lower cover
18. Grille SD vent. (D)

Tightening torque: N·m (kg-m, ft-lb)
T: 7 ± 1 (0.7 ± 0.1, 5.1 ± 0.7)

SB9149500024000X

Fig. 17 Exploded view of instrument panel & related components. 1995–96 Legacy

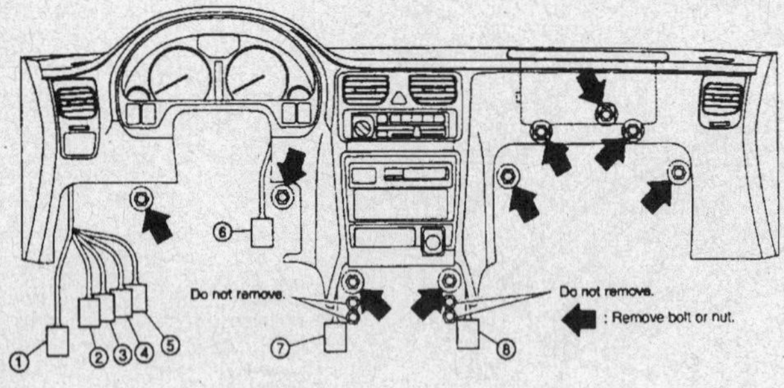
Do not remove.
Do not remove.
: Remove bolt or nut.

①	15P/Gray
②	22P/Brown
③	22P/White
④	20P/Blue
⑤	22P/Black
⑥	4P/Sky blue
⑦	1P/Black
⑧	1P/Black

SB9149500025000X

Fig. 18 Instrument panel electrical connector & bolt locations. 1995–96 Legacy

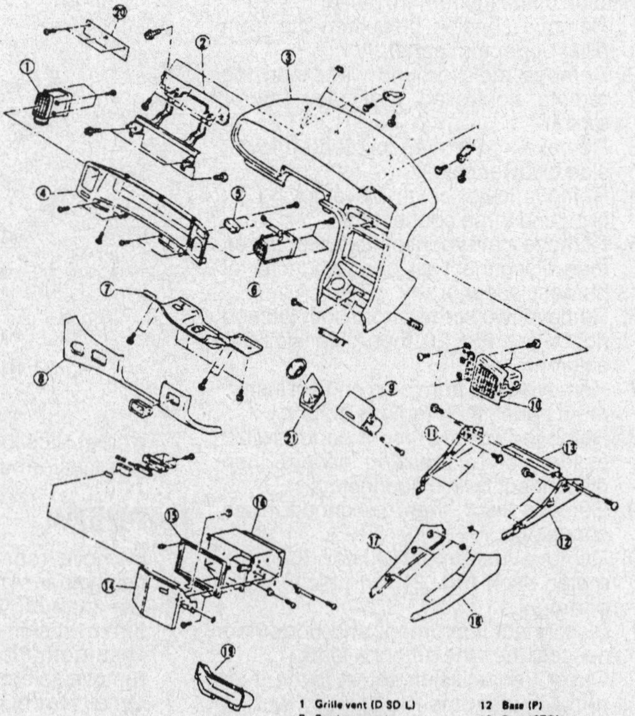

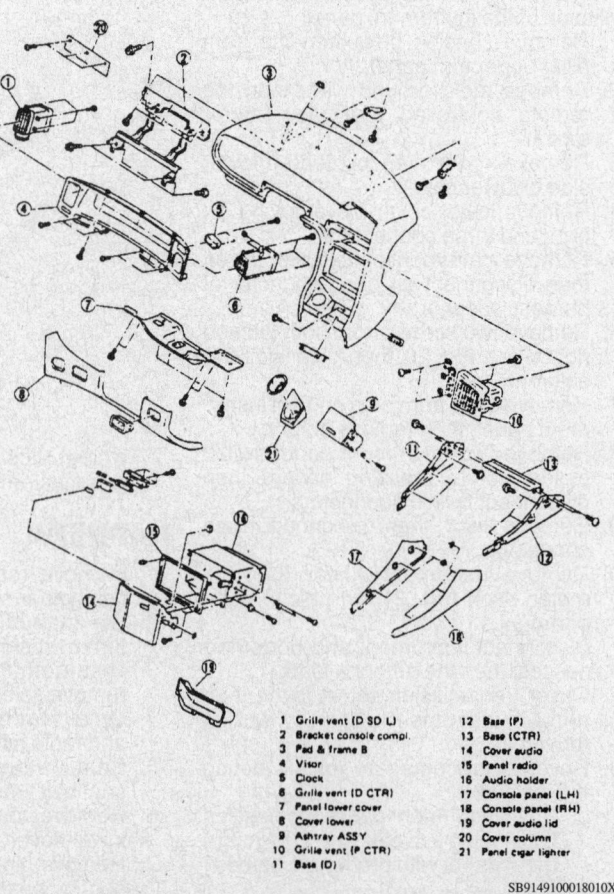

1 Grille vent (D SD L)
2 Bracket console compl.
3 Pad & frame B
4 Visor
5 Clock
6 Grille vent (D CTR)
7 Panel lower cover
8 Cover lower
9 Ashtray ASSY
10 Grille vent (P CTR)
11 Base (D)
12 Base (P)
13 Base (CTR)
14 Cover audio
15 Panel radio
16 Audio holder
17 Console panel (LH)
18 Console panel (RH)
19 Cover audio lid
20 Cover column
21 Panel cigar lighter

SB9149100018010X

Fig. 19 Exploded view of instrument panel & related components (Part 1 of 2). SVX

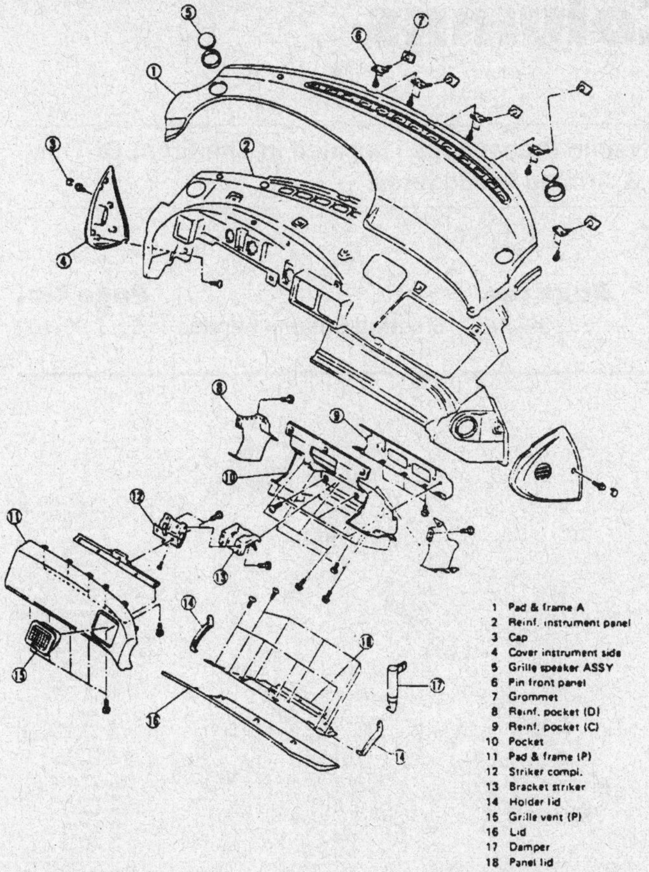
1 Pad & frame A
2 Reinf. instrument panel
3 Cap
4 Cover instrument side
5 Grille speaker ASSY
6 Pin front panel
7 Grommet
8 Reinf. pocket (D)
9 Reinf. pocket (C)
10 Pocket
11 Pad & frame (P)
12 Striker compl.
13 Bracket striker
14 Holder lid
15 Grille vent (P)
16 Lid
17 Damper
18 Panel lid

SB9149100018020X

Fig. 19 Exploded view of instrument panel & related components (Part 2 of 2). SVX

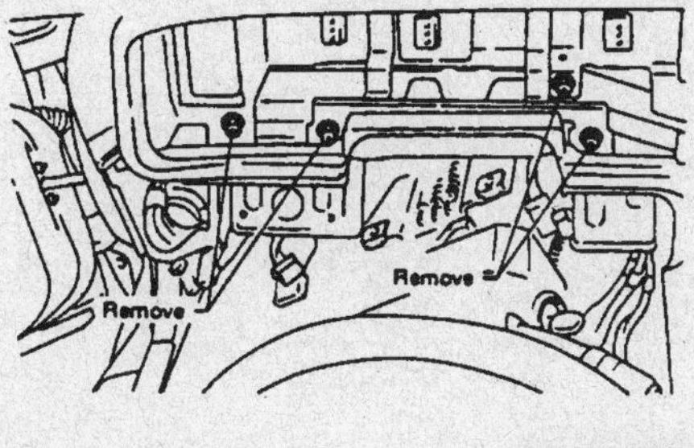
Remove
Remove

SB9149100020000X

Fig. 21 Meter visor removal. SVX

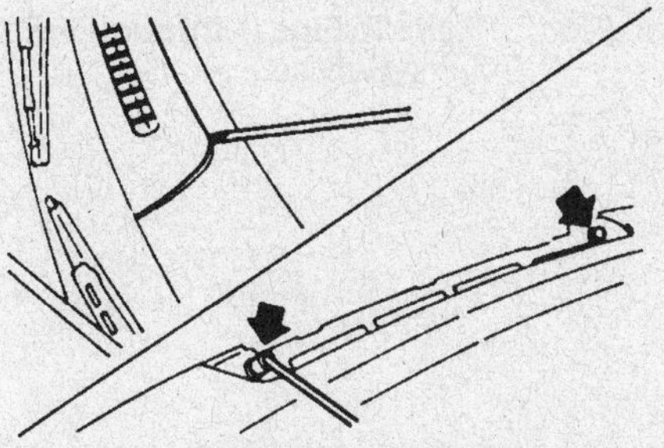

SB9149100022000X

Fig. 23 Defroster grille & bolt removal. Impreza

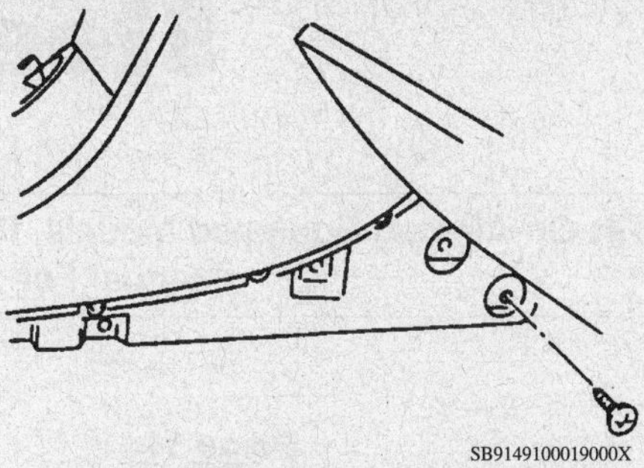

SB9149100019000X

Fig. 20 Instrument panel lower screw removal. SVX

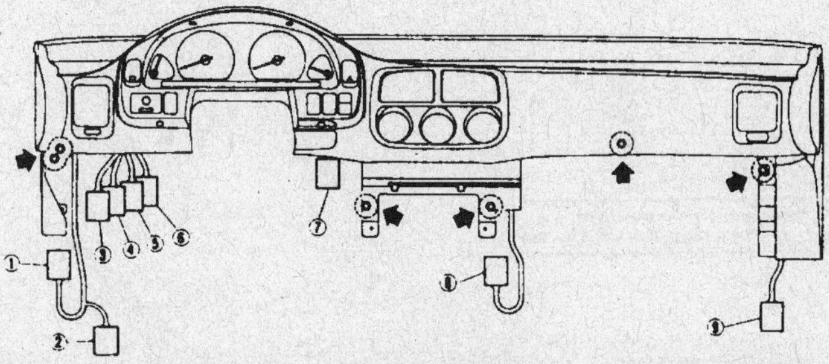

SB9149100021000X

Fig. 22 Instrument panel mounting bolt locations. Impreza

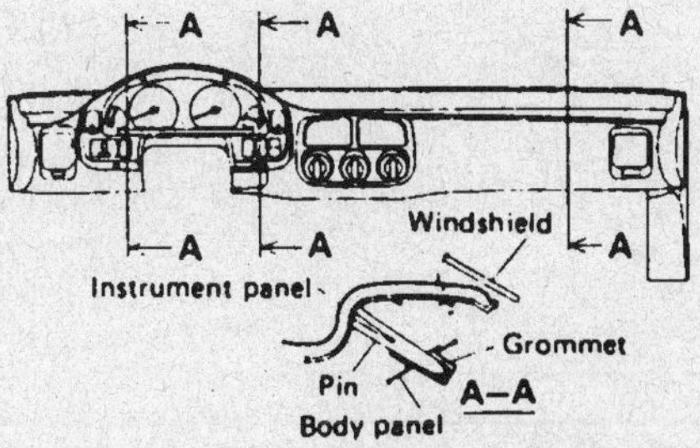
A
A
A
A
A
A
Windshield
Instrument panel
Grommet
Pin
A—A
Body panel

SB9149100023000X

Fig. 24 Instrument panel installation. Impreza

Steering Columns

NOTE: On Air Bag Equipped Models, Refer To "Air Bag System Precautions" Located In The Front Of This Manual For System Disarming & Arming Procedures.

INDEX

	Page No.
Precautions	39-102
Air Bag Systems	39-102
Steering Column Service	39-102

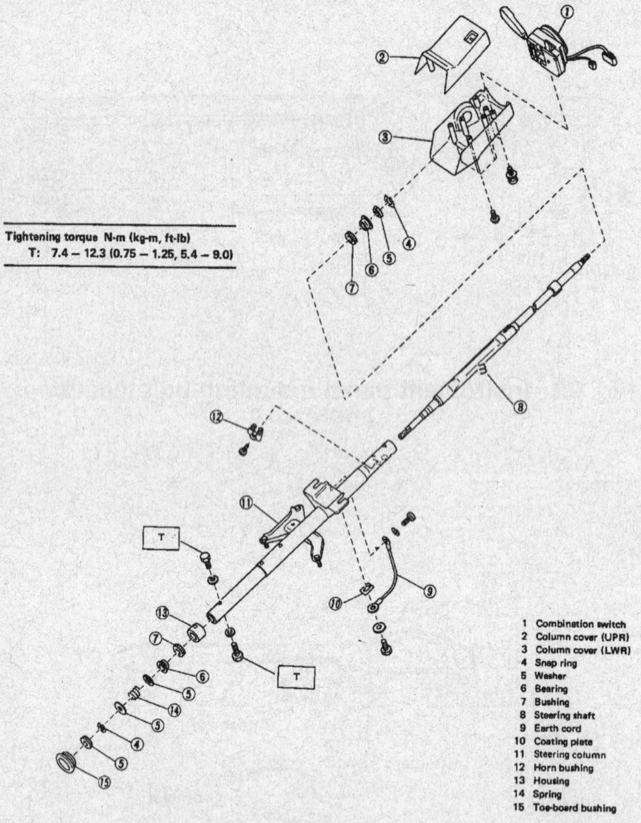

Tightening torque N·m (kg-m, ft-lb)
T: 7.4 – 12.3 (0.75 – 1.25, 5.4 – 9.0)
T
T
1 Combination switch
2 Column cover (UPR)
3 Column cover (LWR)
4 Snap ring
5 Washer
6 Bearing
7 Bushing
8 Steering shaft
9 Earth cord
10 Coating plate
11 Steering column
12 Horn bushing
13 Housing
14 Spring
15 Toe-board bushing
SB6049100001000X

Fig. 1 Exploded view of rigid steering column. Loyale

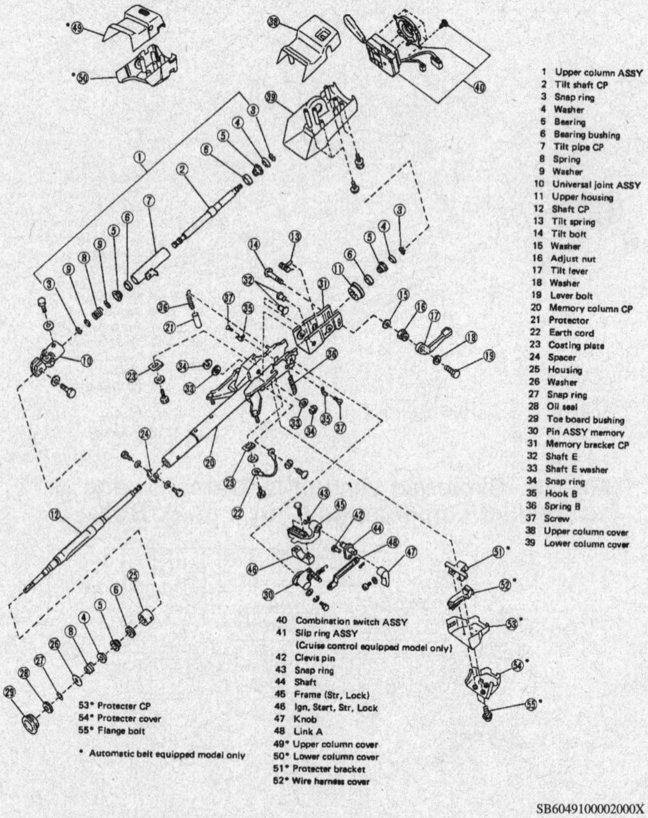

1 Upper column ASSY
2 Tilt shaft CP
3 Snap ring
4 Washer
5 Bearing
6 Bearing bushing
7 Tilt pipe CP
8 Spring
9 Washer
10 Universal joint ASSY
11 Upper housing
12 Shaft CP
13 Tilt spring
14 Tilt bolt
15 Washer
16 Adjust nut
17 Tilt lever
18 Washer
19 Lever bolt
20 Memory column CP
21 Protector
22 Earth cord
23 Coating plate
24 Spacer
25 Housing
26 Washer
27 Snap ring
28 Oil seal
29 Toe board bushing
30 Pin ASSY memory
31 Memory bracket CP
32 Shaft E
33 Shaft E washer
34 Snap ring
35 Hook B
36 Spring B
37 Screw
38 Upper column cover
39 Lower column cover
40 Combination switch ASSY
41 Slip ring ASSY
(Cruise control equipped model only)
42 Clevis pin
43 Snap ring
44 Shaft
45 Frame (Str, Lock)
46 Ign, Start, Str, Lock
47 Knob
48 Link A
49* Upper column cover
50* Lower column cover
51* Protecter bracket
52* Wire harness cover
53* Protecter CP
54* Protecter cover
55* Flange bolt
* Automatic belt equipped model only
SB6049100002000X

Fig. 2 Exploded view of tilt steering column. Loyale

PRECAUTIONS

AIR BAG SYSTEMS

Refer to "Air Bag System Precautions" in the front of this manual for system disarming and arming procedures.

STEERING COLUMN SERVICE

Refer To **Figs. 1 through 7,** For Steering Column Service.

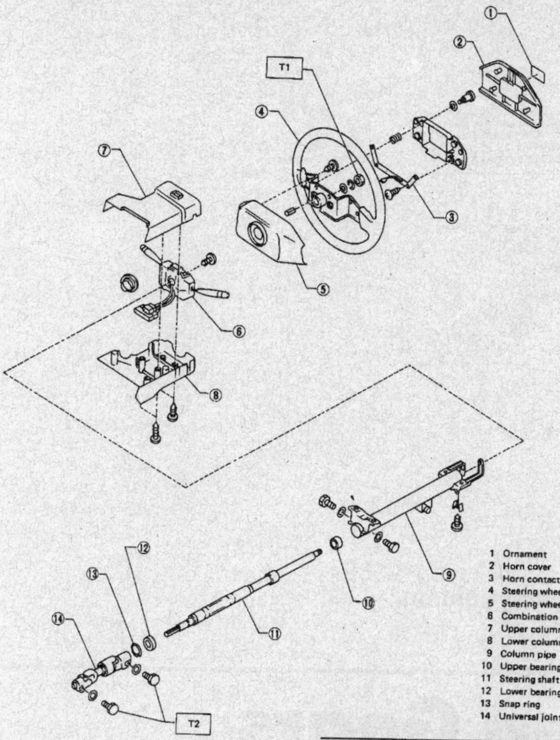

1 Ornament
2 Horn cover
3 Horn contact
4 Steering wheel
5 Steering wheel lower cover
6 Combination switch
7 Upper column cover
8 Lower column cover
9 Column pipe
10 Upper bearing
11 Steering shaft
12 Lower bearing
13 Snap ring
14 Universal joint

Tightening torque: N·m (kg-m, ft-lb)
T1: 49 – 59 (5.0 – 6.0, 36 – 43)
T2: 22 – 25 (2.2 – 2.6, 16 – 19)

SB6049100003000X

Fig. 3 Exploded view of steering column. Justy

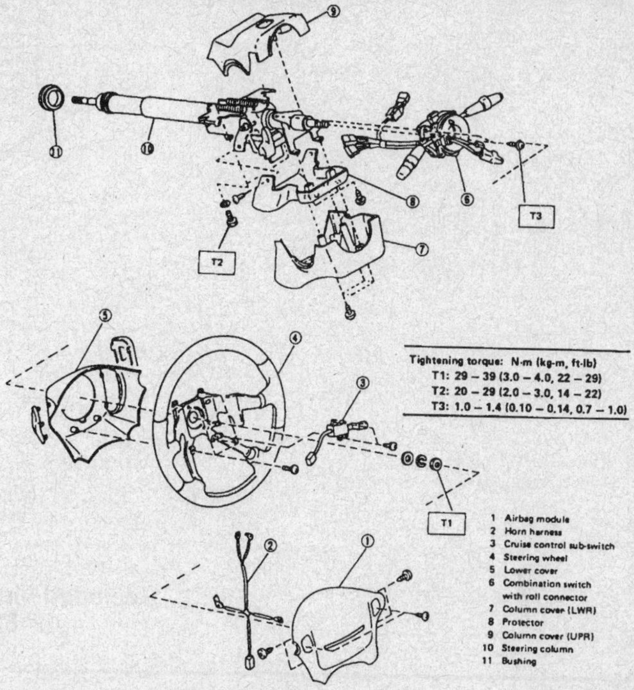

Tightening torque: N·m (kg-m, ft-lb)
T1: 29 – 39 (3.0 – 4.0, 22 – 29)
T2: 20 – 29 (2.0 – 3.0, 14 – 22)
T3: 1.0 – 1.4 (0.10 – 0.14, 0.7 – 1.0)

1 Airbag module
2 Horn harness
3 Cruise control sub-switch
4 Steering wheel
5 Lower cover
6 Combination switch with roll connector
7 Column cover (LWR)
8 Protector
9 Column cover (UPR)
10 Steering column
11 Bushing

SB6049100007000X

Fig. 4 Exploded view of tilt steering column. 1993–94 Legacy

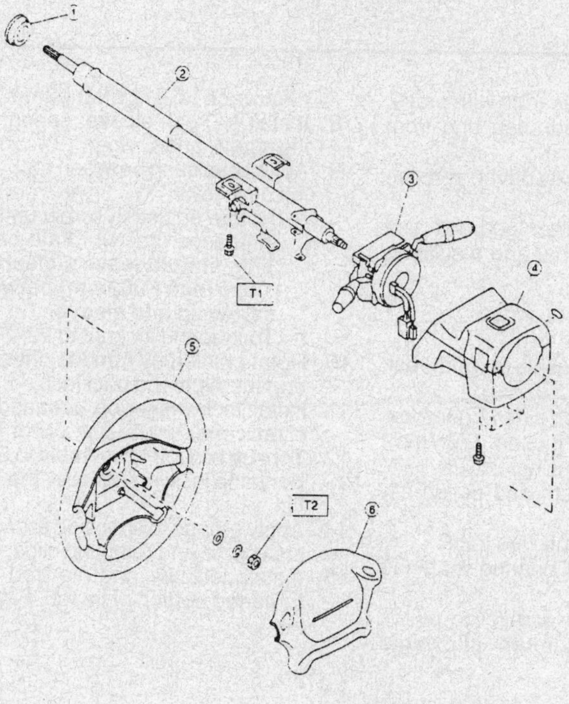

1 Bushing
2 Column shaft
3 Steering roll connector
4 Column cover
5 Steering wheel
6 Airbag module

Tightening torque: N·m (kg-m, ft-lb)
T1: 25 ± 5 (2.5 ± 0.5, 18.1 ± 3.6)
T2: 34 ± 5 (3.5 ± 0.5, 25.3 ± 3.6)

SB6049500011000X

Fig. 5 Exploded view of tilt steering column. 1995–96 Legacy

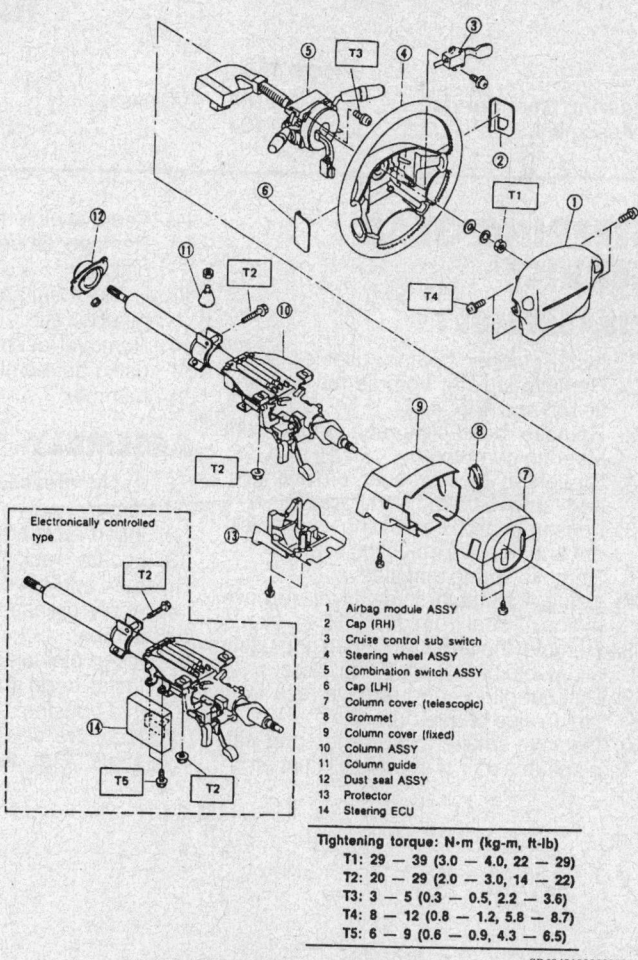

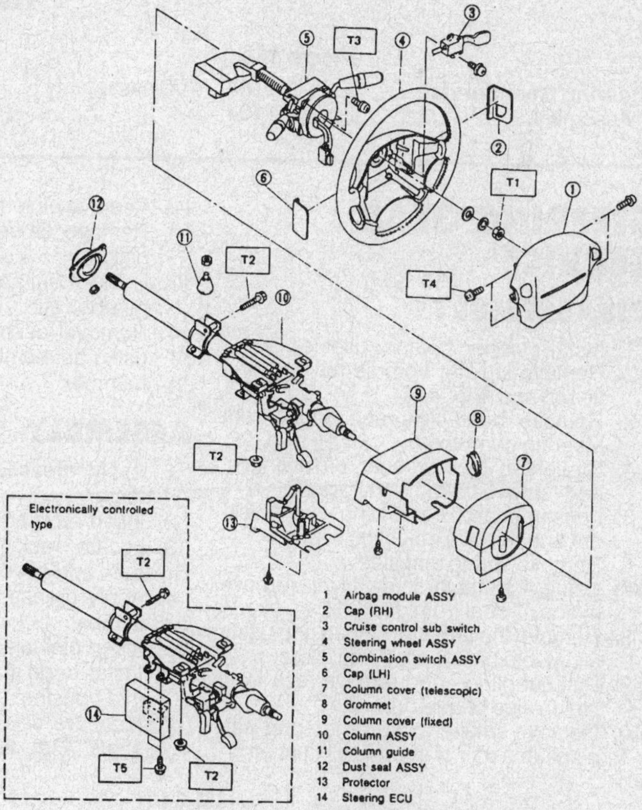
Electronically controlled type

1 Airbag module ASSY
2 Cap (RH)
3 Cruise control sub switch
4 Steering wheel ASSY
5 Combination switch ASSY
6 Cap (LH)
7 Column cover (telescopic)
8 Grommet
9 Column cover (fixed)
10 Column ASSY
11 Column guide
12 Dust seal ASSY
13 Protector
14 Steering ECU

Tightening torque: N·m (kg-m, ft-lb)
T1: 29 — 39 (3.0 — 4.0, 22 — 29)
T2: 20 — 29 (2.0 — 3.0, 14 — 22)
T3: 3 — 5 (0.3 — 0.5, 2.2 — 3.6)
T4: 8 — 12 (0.8 — 1.2, 5.8 — 8.7)
T5: 6 — 9 (0.6 — 0.9, 4.3 — 6.5)

SB6049100008000X

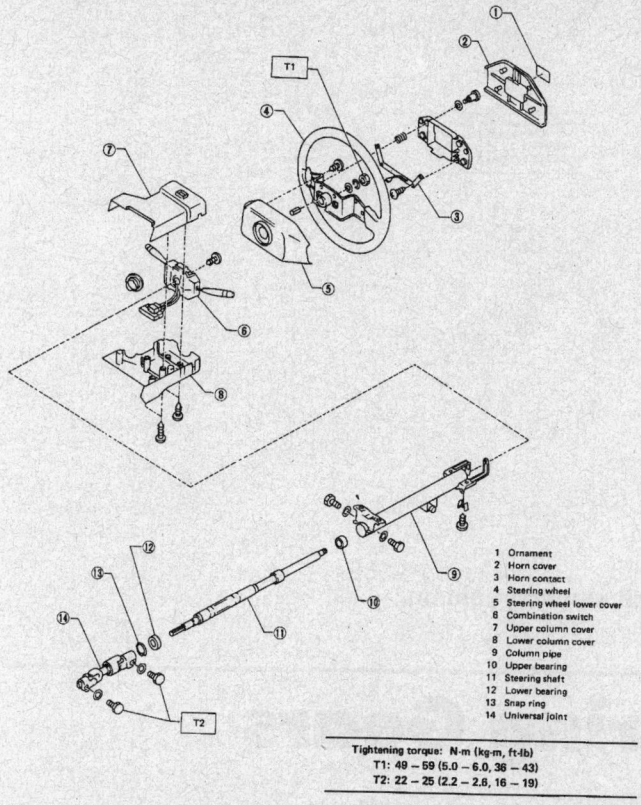

Fig. 6 Exploded view of tilt & telescopic steering column. SVX

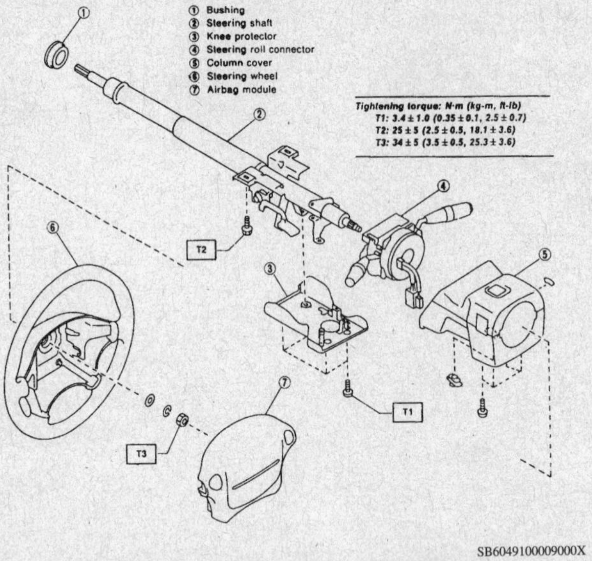
① Bushing
② Steering shaft
③ Knee protector
④ Steering roll connector
⑤ Column cover
⑥ Steering wheel
⑦ Airbag module
Tightening torque: N·m (kg-m, ft-lb)
T1: 3.4 ± 1.0 (0.35 ± 0.1, 2.5 ± 0.7)
T2: 25 ± 5 (2.5 ± 0.5, 18.1 ± 3.6)
T3: 34 ± 5 (3.5 ± 0.5, 25.3 ± 3.6)
T1
T2
T3
SB6049100009000X

Fig. 7 Exploded view of tilt steering column. Impreza

Manual Steering Gears

INDEX

	Page No.
Steering Gear Service	39-104
Assembly	39-104
Disassembly	39-104
Tightening Specifications	39-105

STEERING GEAR SERVICE

DISASSEMBLY

1. Install steering gear in suitable vise.
2. Remove locknut from tie rod end and tie rod end, **Fig. 1.**
3. Remove boot clips and boots from steering gearbox.
4. Straighten lock washer on ball joint and remove tie rod from rack.
5. Loosen gearbox adjusting screw locknut and remove adjusting screw.
6. Remove spring and sleeve.
7. Using a suitable screwdriver, remove pinion oil seal from gearbox.
8. Remove the large rack snap ring using a suitable pair of snap ring pliers.
9. Pull out pinion and remove rack from pinion side of gearbox.
10. Remove smaller pinion snap ring with a suitable pair of snap ring pliers.
11. Remove pinion ball bearing with press.
12. Remove oil seal and snap ring from pinion.
13. Using a suitable screwdriver, remove gearbox clip.
14. Remove bushing from gearbox unit using an aluminum bar and a suitable hammer.

ASSEMBLY

1. Apply grease to bushings and rack teeth.
2. Insert rack into pinion side of gearbox.
3. Locate rack 3.02 inches (76.7mm) from end of gear housing.
4. Apply grease to teeth and pinion assembly.
5. Insert pinion assembly into rack.
6. Install large size ball bearing snap ring into housing.
7. Measure clearance parallel to pinion shaft, **Fig. 2. Maximum allowable clearance is .012 inch (.3mm).**
8. Install oil seal, sleeve, spring, adjusting screw, and O-ring.
9. Adjust backlash between rack and pinion as follows:
   a. Rotate adjusting screw until torque increases greatly, rotate back 15°. **This should leave a clearance of .0025 inch (.063mm) between the screw tip and sleeve.**
   b. **Torque** the locknut to 22–36 ft. lbs.
10. Rotate pinion by hand to check pinion engagement and backlash.
11. Install lockwasher on threaded portion of rack end.
12. **Torque** ball joint assembly to 58 ft. lbs.
13. Bend the lockwasher over the ball joint flat.
14. Apply grease to specified areas and install boots and retaining clips.
15. Install locknut and tie rod end to threaded portion of tie rod, **Fig. 3.**

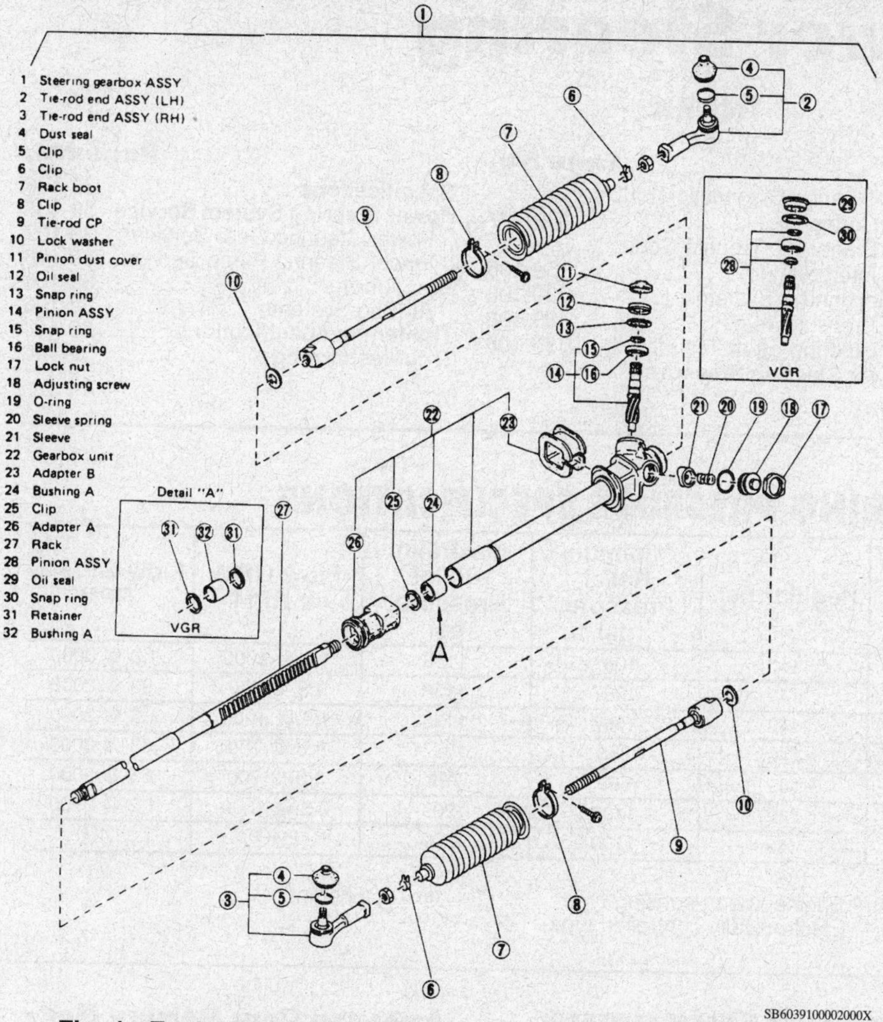
1 Steering gearbox ASSY
2 Tie-rod end ASSY (LH)
3 Tie-rod end ASSY (RH)
4 Dust seal
5 Clip
6 Clip
7 Rack boot
8 Clip
9 Tie-rod CP
10 Lock washer
11 Pinion dust cover
12 Oil seal
13 Snap ring
14 Pinion ASSY
15 Snap ring
16 Ball bearing
17 Lock nut
18 Adjusting screw
19 O-ring
20 Sleeve spring
21 Sleeve
22 Gearbox unit
23 Adapter B
24 Bushing A
25 Clip
26 Adapter A
27 Rack
28 Pinion ASSY
29 Oil seal
30 Snap ring
31 Retainer
32 Bushing A
Detail "A"
VGR
VGR
A
SB6039100002000X

Fig. 1 Exploded view of manual rack & pinion steering gear

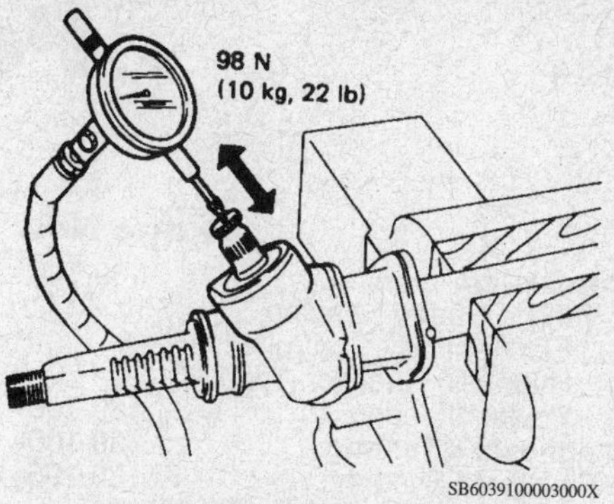
98 N
(10 kg, 22 lb)
SB6039100003000X

Fig. 2 Measuring pinion shaft clearance. Manual steering gear

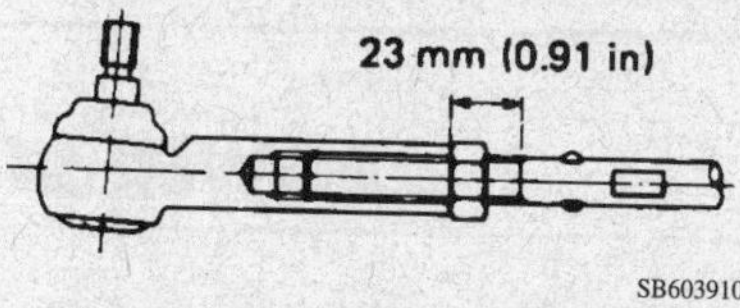
23 mm (0.91 in)
SB6039100004000X

Fig. 3 Positioning tie rod end. Manual steering gear

TIGHTENING SPECIFICATIONS

Model	Component	Torque/Ft. Lbs.
Justy	Adjusting Screw Locknut	36–47
	Lug Nuts	58–72
	Steering Column Upper Retaining Bolt	14–22
	Steering Rack Retaining Clamp Bolts	33–43
	Steering Shaft Pinch Bolts	16–19
	Tie Rod End Locknut	36–47
	Tie Rod End To Steering Knuckle	18–22①
Loyale	Adjust Screw Locknut	36–47
	Inner Tie Rod To Rack	58
	Lug Nuts	58–72
	Steering Rack Retaining Clamp Bolts	35–52
	Steering Shaft Pinch Bolts	15–20
	Tie Rod End Locknut	51–65
	Tie Rod End To Steering Knuckle	18–22①

① — Castle nut may be tightened an additional 60° to align cotter pin.

Power Steering

INDEX

	Page No.
Description	39-106
Vehicle Speed Sensing, Electronically Controlled, Hydraulic Reaction Type Power Steering	39-106
Diagnosis & Testing	39-106
Electronic System	39-106
Accessing Diagnostic Trouble Codes	39-106
Clearing Diagnostic Trouble Codes	39-107
Diagnostic Trouble Code Interpretation	39-106
Mechanical System	39-108
Pressure Tests	39-108
Steering Effort Tests	39-108
Power Steering Pressure	
Specifications	39-106
Power Steering System Service	39-108
Power Steering Gear Service	39-109
Power Steering Pump Service	39-108
Precautions	39-106
Air Bag Systems	39-106
Tightening Specifications	39-114
Troubleshooting	39-106

POWER STEERING PRESSURE SPECIFICATIONS

Vehicle	Year	Engine	Regular psi.	Minimum Relief Pressure, psi	Maximum Relief Pressure, psi	Flow GPM @ RPM	Flow GPM @ RPM
Impreza	1993–96	1.8L	142	1067	1138	1.9 @ 1000	1.3 @ 3000
Legacy	1993–94	2.2L	142	1067	1138	1.9 @ 700	.93 @ 3000
	1995–96	2.2L	142	1067	1138	1.9 @ 1000	1.3 @ 3000
Loyale	1993–94	1.8L①	142	853	1067	1.3 @ 700	.63 @ 3000
	1993–94	1.8L②	142	569	782	1.3 @ 700	.63 @ 3000
SVX③	1993–96	3.3L	142	1109	1209	2.3 @ 1000	1.2 @ 3500
SVX④	1993–96	3.3L	142	1109	1209	2.4⑤	2.4⑤

① — Turbocharged engine.
② — Non Turbocharged engine.
③ — Engine speed sensing type.
④ — Electronically controlled type.
⑤ — Constant.

PRECAUTIONS

AIR BAG SYSTEMS

Refer to "Air Bag System Precautions" in the front of this manual for system disarming and arming procedures.

DESCRIPTION

VEHICLE SPEED SENSING, ELECTRONICALLY CONTROLLED, HYDRAULIC REACTION TYPE POWER STEERING

A hydraulic reaction mechanism is installed between the pinion shaft and input shaft to vary the oil pressure according to the vehicle speed. This permits the driver to use less steering effort during low speed driving and to have a firm, rigid response during high speed driving.

The Electronic Control Unit (ECU), receives input signals from vehicle speed and engine speed sensors, then sends signals to the control valve to control reaction pressure through the reaction control valve.

A built-in fail-safe function enables the system to maintain the same steering characteristic as a conventional steering system even when a problem occurs in various electrical components.

TROUBLESHOOTING

Refer to **Figs. 1 and 2,** for basic troubleshooting procedures.

DIAGNOSIS & TESTING

Electronic System

ACCESSING DIAGNOSTIC TROUBLE CODES

Refer to **Fig. 3,** for proper diagnostic sequence.

Accessing Read Memory Mode

1. Turn ignition switch to off position.
2. Connect male terminal to diagnosis connector terminal 6, **Fig. 4.**
3. Start engine. Read trouble codes.
4. Disconnect male terminal from diagnosis connector terminal 6.

Accessing D Check Mode

1. Turn ignition switch to off position.
2. Connect male terminal to diagnosis connector terminal 5, **Fig. 4.**
3. Start and drive vehicle at least 33 ft.
4. Read trouble codes.
5. Disconnect male terminal from diagnosis connector terminal 5.

Accessing Clear Memory Mode

1. Turn ignition switch to off position.
2. Connect male terminals to diagnosis connector terminals 5 and 6, **Fig. 4.**
3. Start engine.
4. Disconnect male terminals from diagnosis connector terminals 5 and 6.
5. Ensure memory is cleared in read memory mode.

DIAGNOSTIC TROUBLE CODE INTERPRETATION

Refer to **Fig. 5,** for trouble code interpretation, identification and description.

TROUBLE CODE DIAGNOSIS

Refer to wiring diagram **Fig. 6,** when performing the following diagnosis.

Trouble Code "VF" Power Supply System Or Lamp Wiring Is Faulty

1. Check warning lamp wiring negative side as follows:
   a. Turn ignition switch to off position, then disconnect ECU from connector.
   b. Disconnect connector i1, then check continuity between ECU connector terminal No. 1 and ground. Resistance should be 1 meg ohm minimum.

c. Remove combination meter assembly, then disconnect connector i7 from meter.
d. Check continuity between connector i7 terminal 9 and ground. Resistance should be 1 meg ohm minimum.

2. Inspect ECU power supply as follows:
a. Turn ignition switch to off position, then disconnect ECU from connector.
b. Turn ignition switch to on position.
c. Measure voltage between ECU connector terminal 16 and ground. Voltage should be 10 volts minimum.
d. Check continuity between ECU connector terminal 13 and ground. Resistance should be 1 ohm minimum.

3. Inspect wiring harness between ECU and fuse block as follows:
a. Disconnect ECU connector, then turn ignition switch on.
b. Measure voltage across connector B44 terminal 4 and ground. Voltage should be 10 volts minimum.

Trouble Code "WF" Faulty Warning Lamp Or Harness

1. Inspect D-Check and Read-Memory harness as follows:
a. Turn ignition switch off, then disconnect ECU from connector.
b. Check continuity between ECU connector terminal 5 and connector B36 terminal 6. Resistance should be 1 ohm maximum.
c. Check continuity between ECU connector terminal 6 and connector B36 terminal 5. Resistance should be 1 ohm maximum.
d. Check continuity between ECU connector terminal 13 and ground. Resistance should be 1 ohm maximum.

2. Inspect warning lamp system as follows:
a. Disconnect connector i1, then turn ignition switch on.
b. Measure voltage across connector B40 terminal 18 and ground. Voltage should be 10 volts minimum. If reading is not as specified, check for open circuit between connector B40 and ECU terminals, If reading is as specified, proceed to step c.
c. Turn ignition off, then remove steering warning lamp (including combination meter).
d. Apply 12 volts across warning lamp terminals. Ensure lamp illuminates. If lamp does not light, replace lamp. If lamp lights, proceed to step e.
e. Disconnect connector i6 and i7.
f. Check continuity between connector I1 terminal I8 and connector I7 terminal 9. Resistance should be 1 ohm maximum.
g. Turn ignition on.
h. Measure voltage across connector i6 terminal 3 and ground. Voltage should be 10 volts minimum. If voltage is not as specified, check for open circuit between fuse block and combination meter. If voltage is as specified, replace ECU.

Trouble Code "1" Shorted Solenoid

1. Inspect solenoid unit as follows:
a. Turn ignition switch off, then disconnect connector B17.
b. Measure resistance between terminals of B17 connector. Resistance should be 5–9 ohms.

2. Inspect harness between ECU and solenoid as follows:
a. Disconnect ECU from connector, then connect connector B17.
b. Measure resistance between ECU connector terminal 9 and terminal 11. Resistance should be 5–9 ohms.
c. Measure resistance between ECU connector terminal 9 and ground. Resistance should be 1 meg ohm.

3. Inspect harness as follows:
a. Turn ignition switch off, then disconnect ECU from connector B17.
b. Measure voltage across connector B17 terminals 2 and ground. There should be no voltage

4. When battery voltage is produced, line between power supply harness and solenoid positive terminal is shorted to set solenoid in full assist state.

Trouble Code "2" Open In Solenoid Circuit

1. Inspect solenoid unit as follows:
a. Turn ignition switch off, then disconnect connector B17.
b. Measure resistance between terminals of B17 connector. Resistance should be 5–9 ohms.

2. Inspect harness between ECU and solenoid as follows:
a. Disconnect ECU from connector, then connect B17.
b. Measure resistance between connector B53 terminals 9 and 11. Resistance should be 5–9 ohms.
c. Check for continuity between connector B53 terminal 9 and ground. Resistance should be 1 meg ohm minimum.

Trouble Code "3" Faulty Vehicle Speed Sensor 2

1. Inspect vehicle speed sensor 2 input signal at ECU as follows:
a. Connect suitable oscilloscope between ECU and ground.
b. Raise and support vehicle, then slowly rotate wheels.
c. Measure voltage across connector B53 terminal 4 and ground. Voltage should be 0–5 volts.

2. Inspect vehicle speed sensor 2 and harness as follows:
a. Inspect harness routing outside instrument panel.
b. Measure resistance between connector B9 terminal 1 and ECU connector terminal 4. Resistance should be 1 ohm maximum.
c. Measure resistance between ECU connector terminal 4 and ground. Resistance should be 1 meg ohm minimum.
d. Inspect harness routing inside instrument panel.
e. Remove combination meter assembly and instrument panel, then disconnect connector B9.
f. Measure resistance between connector B9 terminal 2 and connector B7 terminal 11. Resistance should be 1 ohm maximum.
g. Measure resistance between connector B7 terminal 11 and ground. Resistance should be 1 meg ohm minimum.
h. Check continuity between connector B9 terminals 2 and ground. Resistance should be 1 meg ohm maximum.

Trouble Code "4" Faulty Back-Up Power Supply

1. Inspect ECU back-up power supply as follows:
a. Disconnect connector from ECU.
b. Measure voltage across ECU connector terminal 15 and ground. Voltage should be 10 volts minimum. If fuse No. 25 is blown, it can be identified by shorted circuit between fuse block and ECU.

2. Inspect back-up power supply harness as follows:
a. Measure voltage across connector F16 terminal 2 and ground. Voltage should be 10 volts minimum. If voltage is not as specified, check for open circuit between connectors F17 and F16. If voltage is as specified, check for open circuit between M/B and ECU (including SMJ).

Trouble Code "5" Faulty Engine Speed Signal

1. Inspect engine speed input signal at ECU as follows:
a. Connect suitable oscilloscope between ECU and ground.
b. Turn ignition switch on, then start engine.
c. Observe wave form pattern shown on oscilloscope screen. Voltage should be 0–10 volts.

2. Inspect engine speed signal harness as follows:
a. Turn ignition off, then disconnect ECU from connectors.
b. Disconnect MPFI ECU from connectors.
c. Measure resistance between ECU connector terminal 3 and MPFI ECU connector terminal 16. Resistance should be 1 ohm maximum.
d. Measure resistance between ECU connector terminal 3 and ground. Resistance should be 1 meg ohm minimum.

CLEARING DIAGNOSTIC TROUBLE CODES

Refer to "Accessing Diagnostic Trouble Codes" in this section.

Mechanical System

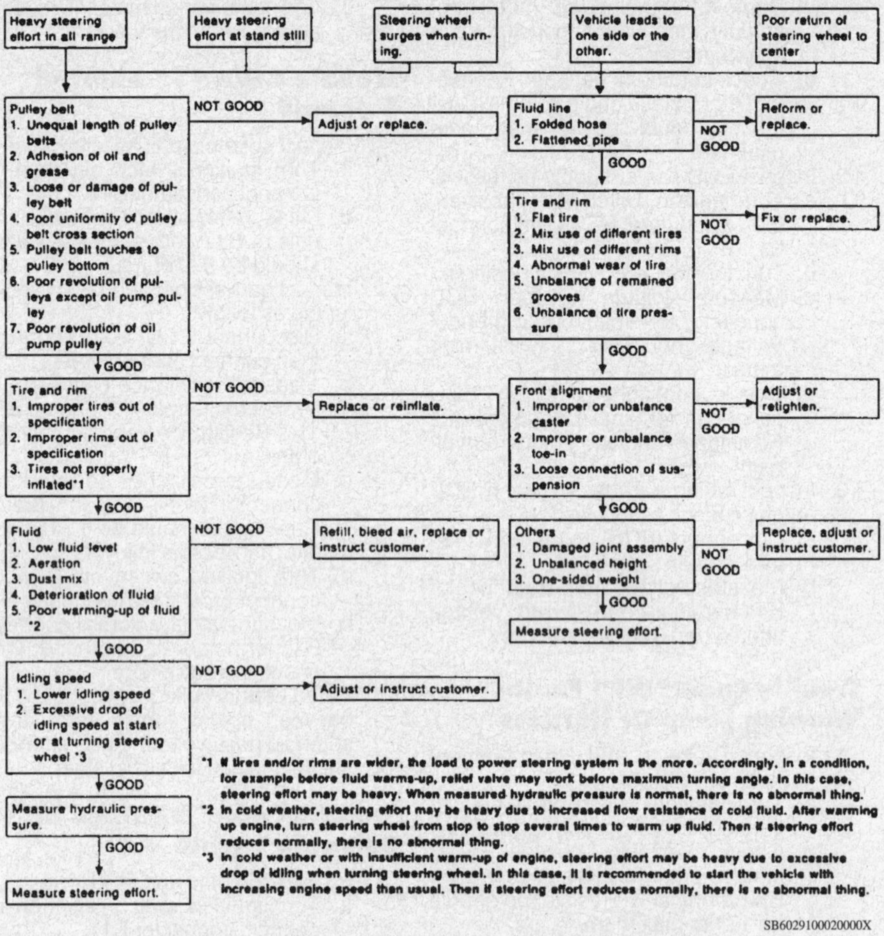

Heavy steering effort in all range
Heavy steering effort at stand still
Steering wheel surges when turning.
Vehicle leads to one side or the other.
Poor return of steering wheel to center
Pulley belt
1. Unequal length of pulley belts
2. Adhesion of oil and grease
3. Loose or damage of pulley belt
4. Poor uniformity of pulley belt cross section
5. Pulley belt touches to pulley bottom
6. Poor revolution of pulleys except oil pump pulley
7. Poor revolution of oil pump pulley
NOT GOOD
Adjust or replace.
GOOD
Tire and rim
1. Improper tires out of specification
2. Improper rims out of specification
3. Tires not properly inflated*1
NOT GOOD
Replace or reinflate.
GOOD
Fluid
1. Low fluid level
2. Aeration
3. Dust mix
4. Deterioration of fluid
5. Poor warming-up of fluid *2
NOT GOOD
Refill, bleed air, replace or instruct customer.
GOOD
Idling speed
1. Lower idling speed
2. Excessive drop of idling speed at start or at turning steering wheel *3
NOT GOOD
Adjust or instruct customer.
GOOD
Measure hydraulic pressure.
GOOD
Measure steering effort.
Fluid line
1. Folded hose
2. Flattened pipe
NOT GOOD
Reform or replace.
GOOD
Tire and rim
1. Flat tire
2. Mix use of different tires
3. Mix use of different rims
4. Abnormal wear of tire
5. Unbalance of remained grooves
6. Unbalance of tire pressure
NOT GOOD
Fix or replace.
GOOD
Front alignment
1. Improper or unbalance caster
2. Improper or unbalance toe-in
3. Loose connection of suspension
NOT GOOD
Adjust or retighten.
GOOD
Others
1. Damaged joint assembly
2. Unbalanced height
3. One-sided weight
NOT GOOD
Replace, adjust or instruct customer.
GOOD
Measure steering effort.
*1 If tires and/or rims are wider, the load to power steering system is the more. Accordingly, in a condition, for example before fluid warms-up, relief valve may work before maximum turning angle. In this case, steering effort may be heavy. When measured hydraulic pressure is normal, there is no abnormal thing.
*2 In cold weather, steering effort may be heavy due to increased flow resistance of cold fluid. After warming up engine, turn steering wheel from stop to stop several times to warm up fluid. Then if steering effort reduces normally, there is no abnormal thing.
*3 In cold weather or with insufficient warm-up of engine, steering effort may be heavy due to excessive drop of idling when turning steering wheel. In this case, it is recommended to start the vehicle with increasing engine speed than usual. Then if steering effort reduces normally, there is no abnormal thing.
SB6029100020000X

Fig. 1 Troubleshooting (steering condition)

PRESSURE TESTS

Refer to "Power Steering Pressure Specifications," for test pressures.

Do not leave valve of pressure gauge closed or hold steering wheel at stop end for 5 seconds or more, as oil pump may be damaged.

1. Connect test equipment as shown in **Fig. 7.**
2. Measure regular pressure at idling with valve open. If regular pressure is not as specified check the following:
   a. Flattened pipes or hoses.
   b. Leakage of fluid lines.
   c. Restricted fluid line.
3. Measure relief pressure at idling with valve closed. If relief pressure is not as specified check the following:
   a. Fluid leakage inside oil pump assembly.
   b. Excessive wear of vane pump mechanism.
   c. Incorrectly operating relief valve.
4. Measure working pressure of control valve at idling with valve opened, turning steering wheel from stop to stop. If pressure is unsatisfactory, check operation of control valve.

STEERING EFFORT TESTS

EXCEPT SVX

1. Measure steering effort in stand still with engine idling on concrete road. Steering effort should be 6.6 lbs. or less in both directions. If effort is not as specified, adjust backlash.
2. Measure steering effort in stand still with engine stalled on concrete road. Steering effort should be as follows:
   a. **On models except Impreza and Legacy,** 20.9 lbs. or less in both directions.
   b. **On Impreza and Legacy models,** 66.2 lbs. or less in both directions.
   c. **On all models,** if effort is not as specified, adjust backlash.
3. Remove joint assembly.
4. Measure steering wheel effort. Steering wheel effort should be .51 lbs. or less in both directions. Variation should be .24 lbs. or less.
5. Measure folding torque of joint assembly. Folding torque should be 1.23 lbs. or less for long yoke or 1.90 lbs. or less for short yoke. If folding torque is not as specified, replace joint assembly.
6. Inspect front wheels for unsteady revolution or rattling and brake for dragging.
7. Remove and inspect tie rod ends.
8. Measure rotating resistance of gearbox assembly. Rotating resistance should be 2.51 lbs. or less in straight ahead position and in all positions as follows:
   a. **On models except Impreza and Legacy,** 2.90 lbs.
   b. **On Impreza and Legacy models,** 3.55 lbs.
   c. **On all models,** variation should not exceed 20 percent difference between clockwise and counterclockwise.
   d. If rotating resistance is not as specified, adjust backlash.
9. Measure sliding resistance of gearbox assembly. Sliding resistance should be 68 lbs. Variation should not exceed 20 percent between left and right directions. If sliding resistance is not as specified, adjust backlash.

SVX

1. Measure steering effort in stand still with engine idling on concrete road. Steering effort should be as follows:
   a. **On engine RPM sensing type,** 6.8 lbs.
   b. **On vehicle speed sensing, electronically controlled type,** 5.1 lbs. or less in both directions.
   c. **On all models,** if effort is not as specified, adjust backlash.
2. Measure steering effort with vehicle stopped and engine off. Ensure wheels are off the ground during measurement. Steering effort should be 3.7 lbs. or less in both directions. If effort is not as specified, adjust backlash.
3. Remove joint assembly.
4. Measure steering wheel effort. Steering wheel effort should be .51 lbs. or less in both directions. Variation should be .24 lbs. or less.
5. Measure folding torque of joint assembly. Folding torque should be 1.23 lbs. or less for long yoke or 1.90 lbs. or less for short yoke. If folding torque is not as specified, replace joint assembly.
6. Inspect front wheels for unsteady revolution or rattling and brake for dragging.
7. Remove and inspect tie rod ends.
8. Measure rotating resistance of gearbox assembly. Rotating resistance should be 2.36 lbs. or less in straight ahead position and in all positions 2.6 lbs. or less. Variation should not exceed 20 percent difference between clockwise and counterclockwise. If rotating resistance is not as specified, adjust backlash.
9. Measure sliding resistance of gearbox assembly. Sliding resistance should be 60 lbs. or less. Variation should not exceed 20 percent between left and right directions. If sliding resistance is not as specified, adjust backlash.

POWER STEERING SYSTEM SERVICE

POWER STEERING PUMP SERVICE

Disassemble

1. Place pump bracket (with pump installed) in soft jawed vise.

Symptom	Cause	Condition	Remedy
Hiss noise (continuous) While engine is running with maximum turning angle.	Relief valve sound *6	Generates at max. turning angle.	Normal (Don't keep this condition over 5 seconds.)
		Generates without steering operation.	Defective Replace oil pump.
Rattling noise (intermittent) While engine is running	Interference with adjacent parts		Check clearance. Correct if necessary.
	Loosened installation of oil pump, oil tank, pump bracket, gearbox or crossmember.		Retighten.
	Loosened installation of oil pump pulley or other pulley(s).		Retighten.
	Loosened linkage or play of steering or suspension. Loosened tightening of joint or steering column.		Retighten or replace.
	Sound generates from the inside of gearbox or oil pump.		Replace the gearbox or oil pump.
Knocking When turning steering wheel in both direction with small angle repeatedly at engine ON or OFF.	Excessive backlash Loosened Lock nut for adjusting backlash.		Adjust and retighten.
	Loosened tightening or play of Tie-rod, Tie-rod end.		Retighten or replace.

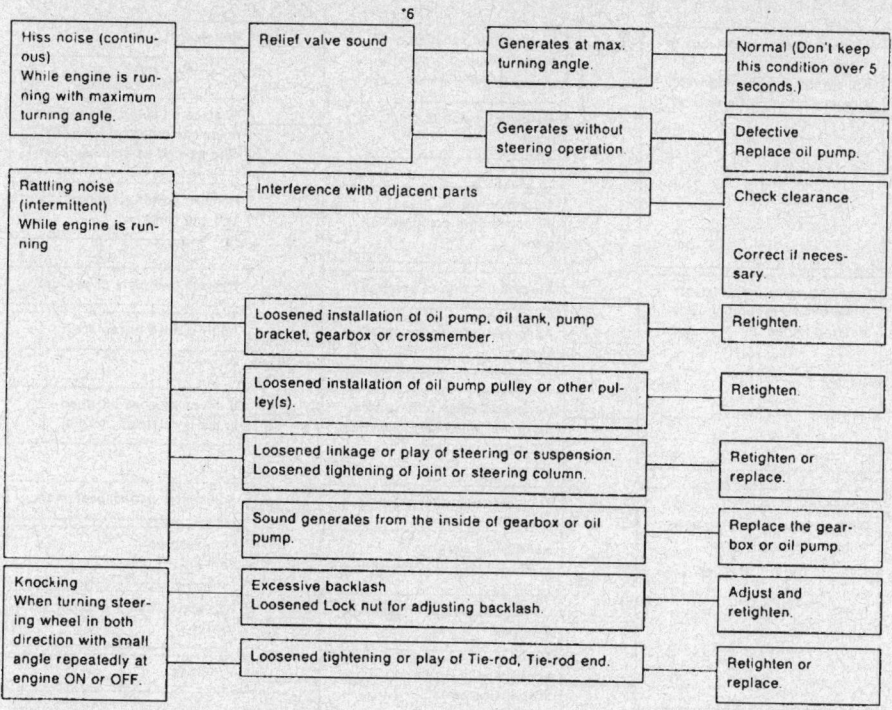

*6 **Don't keep the relief valve operated over 5 sec. at any time or inner parts of the oil pump may be damaged due to rapid increase of fluid temperature.**

SB6029100021010X

Fig. 2 Troubleshooting (noise & vibration, Part 1 of 3)

Symptom	Cause	Remedy
Grinding noise (continuous) While engine is running. *7	Vane pump aeration	Inspect and retighten fluid line connection. Refill fluid and vent air.
	Vane pump seizing	Replace oil pump.
	Pulley bearing seizing of oil pump	
	Folded hose, flat pipe	Replace.
Squeal, squeak. (intermittent or continuous) While engine is running.	Maladjustment of pulley belt Damaged or charged pulley belt Unequal length of pulley belts	Adjust or replace (Replace two belts as a set.)
	Run out or soilage of V-groove surface of oil pump pulley	Clean or replace.
Sizzling noise (continuous) While engine is running.	Fluid aeration	Fix wrong part causing aeration. Replace fluid and vent air.
	Damaged pipe of gearbox	Replace pipe.
	Abnormal inside of hose or pipe. Flat hose or pipe	Rectify or replace.
	Abnormal inside of oil tank	Replace.
	Removed oil tank cap	Install cap.
Whistle (continuous) While engine is running.	Abnormal pipe of gearbox or abnormal inside of hose	Replace bad parts of gearbox or hose.

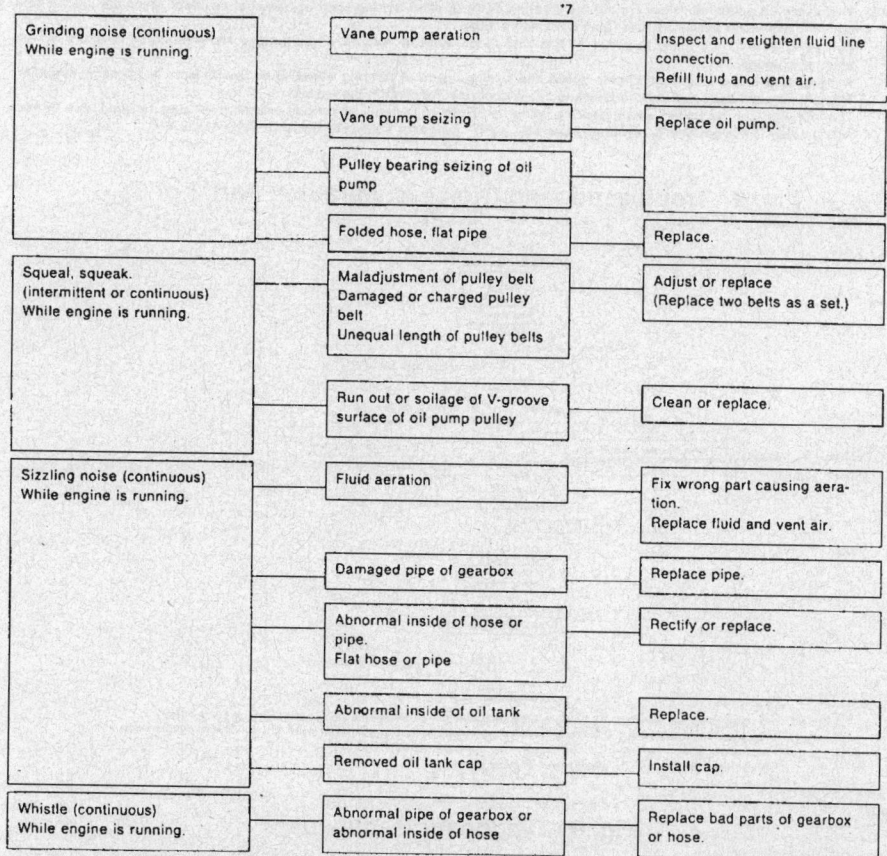

*7 **Grinding noise may be heard immediately after the engine start in extremely cold condition. In this case, if the noise goes off during warm-up there is no abnormal function in the system. This is due to the fluid characteristic in extremely cold condition.**

SB6029100021020X

Fig. 2 Troubleshooting (noise & vibration, Part 2 of 3)

2. **If equipped,** disconnect oil pump switch electrical connector, then remove oil pump switch.
3. Remove valve assembly and spring.
4. Loosen rear body mounting bolts, then remove pump from bracket.
5. Place pump in soft jawed vise.
6. Remove rear body mounting bolts, rear body and gasket.
7. Remove cartridge assembly, pressure plate and pin from front body as a unit. Cartridge assembly consists of a rotor ten vanes and a cam.
8. Remove two types of O-rings by hand.
9. Disassemble front body as follows:
   a. Pry off retaining ring from groove of front body at pulley location.
   b. Using a hand press, remove driveshaft (on cartridge side) and ball bearing out of driveshaft.
   c. Remove oil seal by attaching it to a hooked end plate placed in vise.

Assemble

1. Apply coat of lithium grease to oil seal, then using seal installer No. 926970000, or equivalent, hand press seal into front body.
2. Using guide No. 926980000, or equivalent, hand press drive bearing onto shaft.
3. Install retaining ring on oil seal.
4. Using guide No. 926980000, or equivalent, press shaft and bearing assembly into front body.
5. Lock driveshaft using retaining ring, then place front body in vise with pulley side facing down.
6. Position two O-rings and pressure plate in front body.
7. Install cartridge as follows:
   a. Apply coat of automatic transmission fluid (DEXRON II) to vane.
   b. Install cam, rotor and vane, then insert pin into holes in cam and pressure plate. Ensure vane is installed with "R" side facing cam.
8. Install rear body using new gasket, then hand tighten mounting bolts. Ensure pin hole of rear body aligns with pin in pump.
9. Remove pump from vise.
10. Place pump bracket in vise, then install pump on bracket.
11. **Torque** rear body mounting bolts in a criss-cross pattern to 11–14 ft. lbs.
12. **Torque** rear body mounting bolts in a criss-cross pattern to 22–29 ft. lbs.
13. Position spring and valve assembly in front body.
14. Install oil pump switch with O-ring, then connect electrical connector, if equipped.

POWER STEERING GEAR SERVICE

Except SVX

Refer to **Figs. 8 and 9,** when performing the following procedure.

1. Place attachment tool No. 926200000, or equivalent, in suitable vise, then attach steering gear to tool.
2. Remove clip from boot, then push boot toward tie rod end.

3. Remove boot, big band and medium clips, then push rack fully into gearbox.
4. Straighten tie rod lock washer, using care not to strike rack.
5. **On models except Impreza and Legacy,** loosen locknut, then tighten adjusting screw until it bottoms.
6. **On all models,** remove tie rod from rack.
7. Using spanner wrench No. 9262300000, or equivalent, loosen locknut, then remove adjusting screw.
8. Remove spring and sleeve, then remove dust seal of dust cover, if equipped.
9. Loosen two bolts securing valve assembly, then draw out input shaft and remove valve assembly.
10. **On models except Impreza and Legacy,** using pipe 1.65–1.73 inches ID and press, remove pinion and valve from valve housing.
11. **On Impreza and Legacy models,** using pipe 1.73–1.81 inches ID and press, remove pinion and valve from valve housing.
12. **On all models,** slide mounting rubber to expose slit.
13. Using wrench No. 926340000, or equivalent, rotate rack stopper in clockwise direction until end of circlip comes out of stopper, then rotate rack in counterclockwise direction and pull out circlip.
14. Pull rack assembly from cylinder side. Draw out rack bushing and rack stopper with rack assembly. Do not contact inner wall of cylinder.
15. Remove rack bushing and rack stopper from rack assembly.
16. Replace valve housing oil seal as follows:
    a. Using flathead screwdriver, pry off dust cover, then remove snap ring.
    b. Using flathead screwdriver, pry off oil seal.
    c. Using press and oil seal installer No. 926350000, or equivalent, press oil seal into valve housing.
    d. Install snap ring and dust seal.
17. Replace valve assembly low pressure seal as follows:
    a. Remove and discard snap ring.
    b. **On models except Impreza and Legacy,** press out and discard bearing and backing washer using a 1.46–150 inch ID pipe as a support.
    c. **On Impreza and Legacy models,** press out and discard bearing and backing washer using a 1.52–155 inch ID pipe as a support.
    d. **On all models,** remove oil seal.
    e. Install pinion and valve into valve housing. Apply lubricant to outer diameter surface of input shaft and outer surface of valve body seal ring.
    f. Put installer No. 926360000 over pinion, and insert oil seal, the press fit oil seal into housing using installer No. 926360000 and installer 926370000, or equivalents.
    g. Remove installer No. 926360000, then install backing washer.
    h. Using installer 926370000, or equivalent, press in ball bearing.
    i. Install snap ring.
18. Replace rack housing oil seal and back-up washer as follows:
    a. **On models except Impreza and Legacy,** using hammer and seal remover No. 926410001, or equivalent, drive out oil seal and back-up washer from pinion housing side of rack.

Whine or growl (continuous or intermittent) While engine is running with/without steering turned.	Loosened installation of Oil pump, oil pump bracket	Retighten.
	Abnormal inside of oil pump, hose *8	Replace oil pump, hose, if the noise can be heard when running as well as stand still.
	Torque converter growl air conditioner compression growl	Remove power steering pulley belt and confirm.
Creaking noise (intermittent) While engine is running with steering turned.	Abnormal inside of gearbox.	Replace bad parts of gearbox
	Abnormal bearing for steering shaft	Apply grease or replace.
	Generates when turning steering wheel with brake (service or parking) applied *9	If the noise goes off when brake is released, normal.
Vibration *10 While engine is running with/without steering turned.	Tool low engine speed at start	Adjust and instruct customers.
	Vane pump aeration	Fix wrong part. Vent air.
	Damaged valve in oil pump, Gearbox'	Replace oil pump, bad parts of gearbox.
	Looseness of play of steering, suspension parts	Retighten.

*8 Oil pump makes whine or growl noise slightly due to its mechanism. Even if the noise can be heard when steering wheel is turned at standstill there is no abnormal function in the system provided that the noise eliminates when the car is running.

*9 When stopping with service brake and/or parking brake applied, power steering can be operated easily due to its light steering effort. If doing so, the disk rotates slightly and makes creaking noise. The noise is generated by creaking between the disk and pads. If the noise goes off when the brake is released, there is no abnormal function in the system.

*10 There may be a little vibration around the steering devices when turning steering wheel at standstill, even though the component parts are properly adjusted and have no defects.
Hydraulic systems are likely to generate this kind of vibration as well as working noise and fluid noise because of combined conditions, i.e.,
Road surface and tire surface, Engine speed and turning speed of steering wheel, Fluid temperature and braking condition.
This phenomena does not indicate there is some abnormal function in the system.
The vibration can be known when steering wheel is turned repeatedly at various speeds from slow to rapid step by step with parking brake applied on concrete road and in "D" range for automatic transmission vehicle.

SB6029100021030X

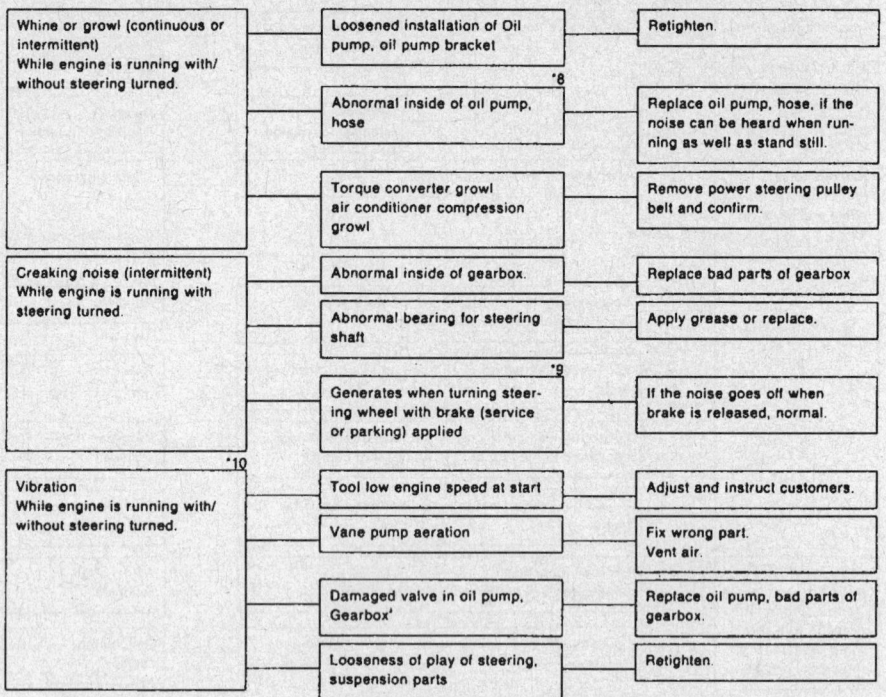

Fig. 2 Troubleshooting (Noise & vibration, Part 3 of 3)

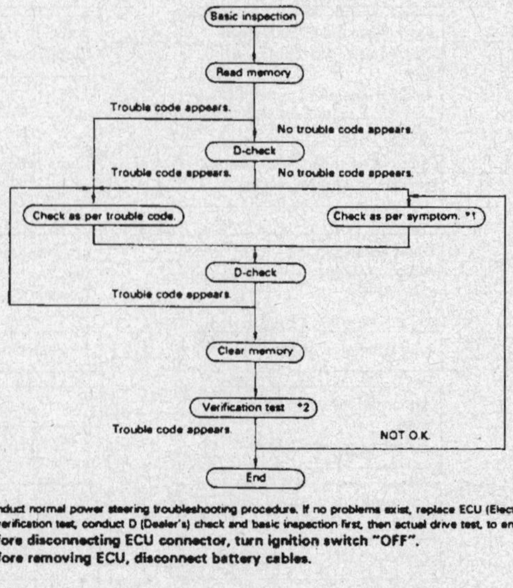
Basic inspection
Read memory
Trouble code appears.
No trouble code appears.
D-check
Trouble code appears.
No trouble code appears.
Check as per trouble code.
Check as per symptom. *1
D-check
Trouble code appears.
Clear memory
Verification test *2
Trouble code appears.
NOT O.K.
End

*1: Conduct normal power steering troubleshooting procedure. If no problems exist, replace ECU (Electronic Control Unit).
*2: In verification test, conduct D (Dealer's) check and basic inspection first, then actual drive test, to ensure that no problems exist.
a. Before disconnecting ECU connector, turn ignition switch "OFF".
b. Before removing ECU, disconnect battery cables.

SB6029100016000X

Fig. 3 Diagnostic sequence

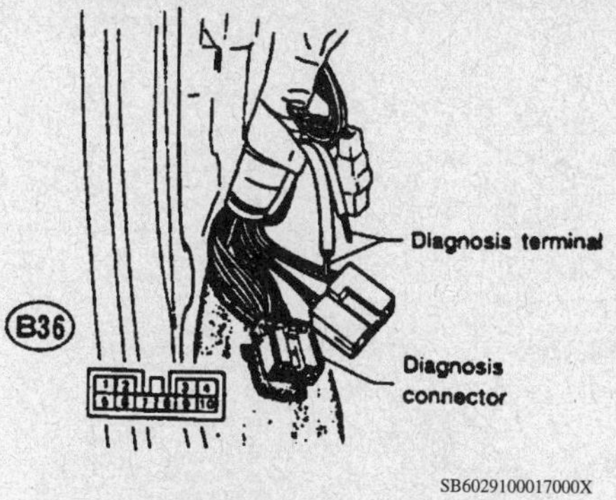
Diagnosis terminal
B36
Diagnosis connector
SB6029100017000X

Fig. 4 Accessing diagnostic modes

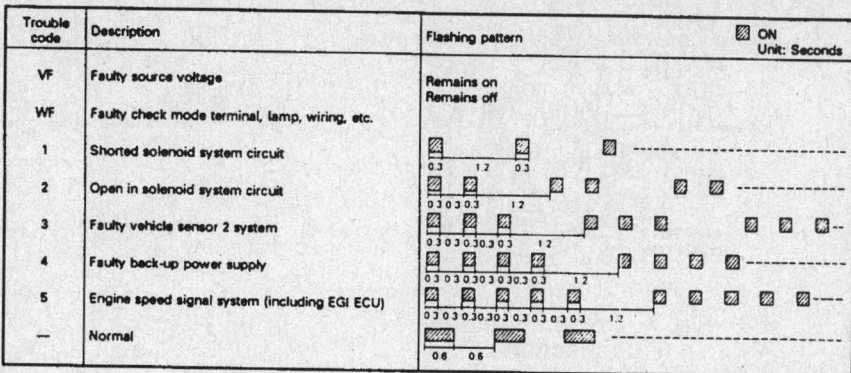

Trouble code	Description	Flashing pattern (▨ ON, Unit: Seconds)
VF	Faulty source voltage	Remains on
WF	Faulty check mode terminal, lamp, wiring, etc.	Remains off
1	Shorted solenoid system circuit	0.3 1.2 0.3
2	Open in solenoid system circuit	0.3 0.3 0.3 1.2
3	Faulty vehicle sensor 2 system	0.3 0.3 0.3 0.3 0.3 0.3 1.2
4	Faulty back-up power supply	0.3 0.3 0.3 0.3 0.3 0.3 0.3 1.2
5	Engine speed signal system (including EGI ECU)	0.3 0.3 0.3 0.3 0.3 0.3 0.3 0.3 0.3 1.2
—	Normal	0.6 0.6

SB6029100018000X

Fig. 5 Trouble code identification

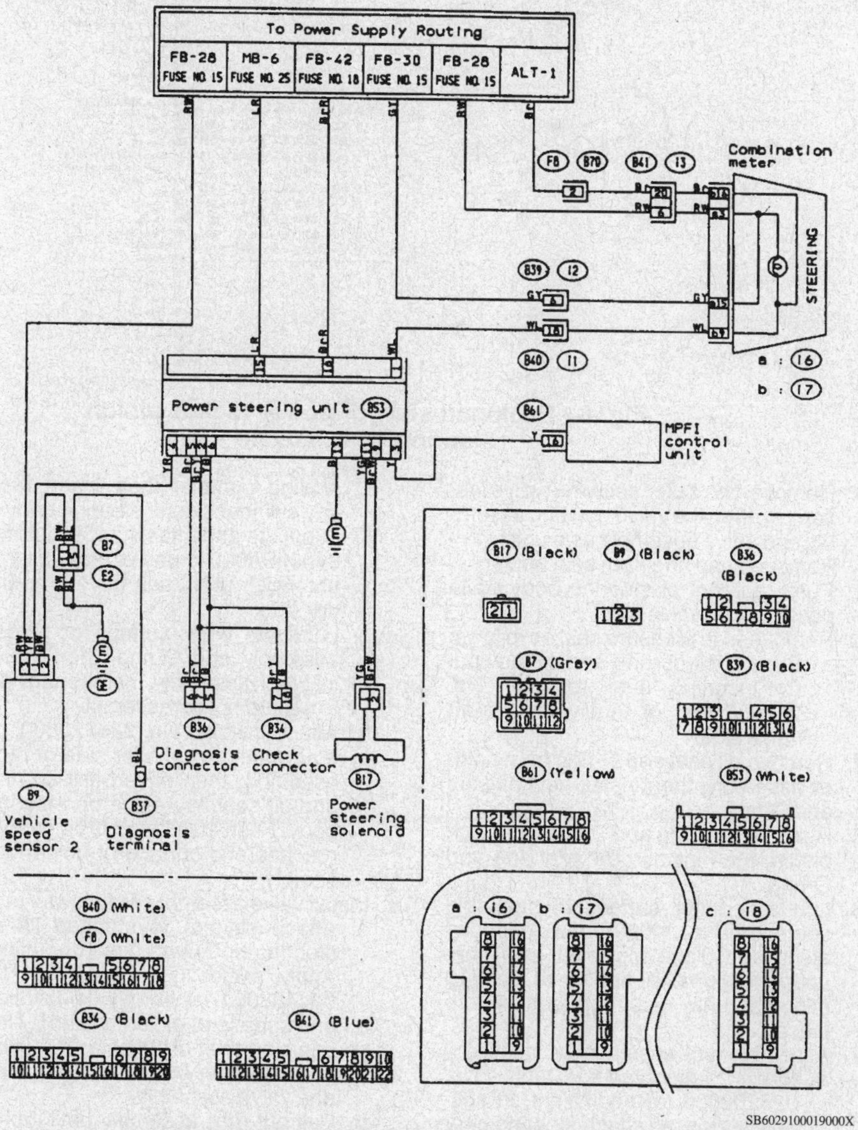
To Power Supply Routing
FB-28 FUSE NO. 15
MB-6 FUSE NO. 25
FB-42 FUSE NO. 18
FB-30 FUSE NO. 15
FB-28 FUSE NO. 15
ALT-1
Combination meter
STEERING
Power steering unit (B53)
MPFI control unit
Diagnosis connector
Check connector
Power steering solenoid
Vehicle speed sensor 2
Diagnosis terminal
SB6029100019000X

Fig. 6 Wiring diagram. Vehicle speed sensing, electronically controlled, hydraulic reaction type power steering

b. **On Impreza and Legacy models,** using hammer and 1.02–1.06 inch diameter round rod, drive out oil seal and back-up washer from pinion housing side of rack.

c. **On all models,** using seal installer No. 926380000, or equivalent, press in oil seal.

19. Install rack housing in stand No. 926200000, or equivalent, then grease teeth of rack assembly. Do not block air passage with grease.
20. Install cover No. 926390001, or equivalent, over toothed portion of rack assembly. Ensure air passage is clear of grease.
21. Insert rack assembly into rack housing from cylinder side. Remove cover after it has passed completely through oil seal.
22. Install guide No. 926400000, or equivalent, over end of rack, then install rack bushing assembly.
23. Insert rack stopper into rack housing, then using wrench No. 926340000, or equivalent, wrap circlip. Rotate wrench another 90°–180° after end of circlip has been wrapped in.
24. Install rubber mounting onto rack housing.
25. Install valve assembly as follows:
    a. Apply grease to pinion gear and bearing of valve.
    b. Center rack shaft to rack housing. If centered correctly, the distance from rack housing to end face of rack will be 2.99 inches.
    c. With rack shaft teeth facing pinion side, insert packing and valve assembly in rack housing. When inserting valve assembly, face cutout portion of input shaft serration toward adjusting screw hole.
    d. **Torque** bolts alternately to 14–22 ft. lbs.
26. Apply a suitable lubricant to sleeve insertion hole and dust seal or dust cover, if equipped.
27. Press fit dust seal into gearbox housing until distance between gearbox and dust seal is .08 inch or less.
28. Apply a suitable lubricant to sliding surface of sleeve and spring seat, then insert sleeve into pinion housing assembly.
29. Insert spring into sleeve screw, then

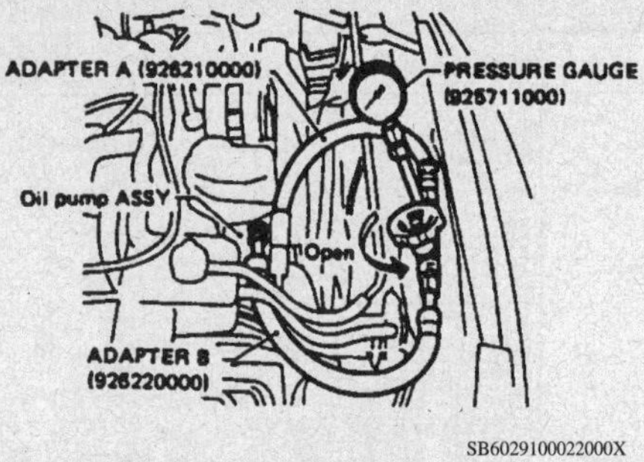
ADAPTER A (926210000)
PRESSURE GAUGE (925711000)
Oil pump ASSY
Open
ADAPTER B (926220000)
SB6029100022000X

Fig. 7 Pressure gauge connection

pack screw with a suitable grease and install.

30. Install tie rods as follows:
    a. Rotate input shaft until rack protrudes approximately 1.57 inch above end surface of gear.
    b. Hold rack in this position, then tighten adjusting screw until it bottoms.
    c. Install tie rods onto rack. Bend lock washer in two place.
31. Adjust rack and pinion backlash as follows:
    a. **Torque** adjusting screw to 3.6 ft. lbs. to seat sleeve against rack, then loosen screw. Repeat this step twice.
    b. **Torque** adjusting screw to 3.6 ft. lbs., then back off 30°
    c. While holding adjusting screw in place, **torque** locknut to 22–36 ft. lbs.
32. Apply a suitable grease to groove of tie rod, then ensure boot is positioned without unusual inflation or deflation.
33. Install clips on boot, then assemble boot to gearbox while retaining gear flange. Fold back boot flange until large clip cannot be seen.
34. Install small boot end clip. Ensure boot end is positioned in groove on tie rod.
35. Screw in tie rod end locknut and tie rod end onto tie rod, then tighten locknut .59 inch from back of nut to threaded portion.

SVX

Refer to **Fig. 10,** when performing the following procedure.

1. Place attachment tool No. 926200000, or equivalent, in suitable vise, then attach steering gear to tool.
2. Disconnect pipes from steering body and control valve housing.
3. Remove tie rod end and locknut.
4. Pry off clip from small end of boot, and slide it toward tie-rod end.
5. Remove lock wire from large end of boot, then cut and remove boot. Boot must be replace whenever it is removed.
6. Set rack so it protrudes about 1.57 inches, then straighten tie rod lock washer, using care not to strike rack.
7. Using wrench tool No. 34099PA100, or equivalent, loosen locknut, then tighten adjusting screw until it bottoms.
8. Remove tie rod from rack, then the adjusting screw.
9. Remove spring and sleeve.

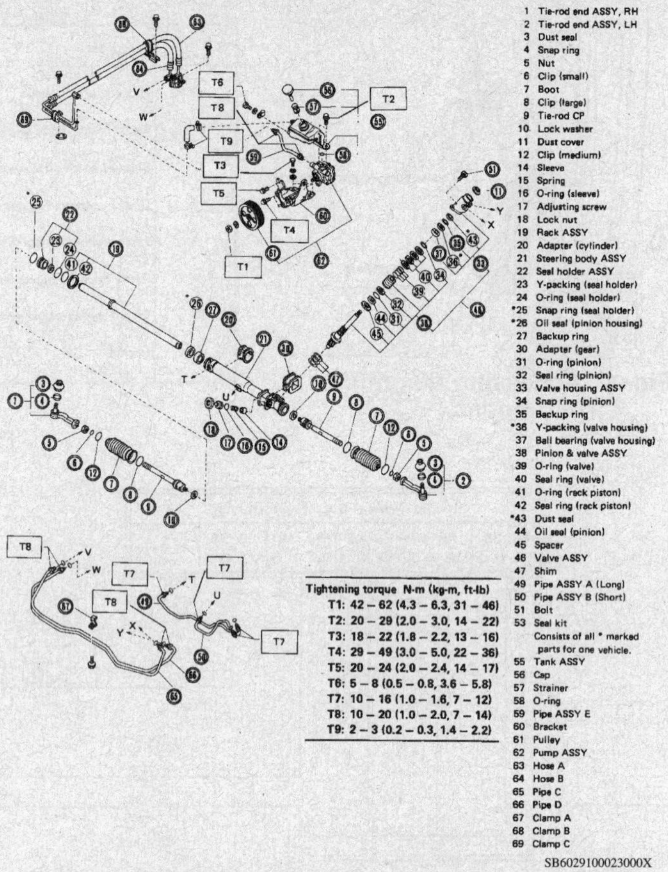
T1
T2
T3
T4
T5
T6
T7
T8
T9
V
W
X
Y
U
T
Tightening torque N-m (kg-m, ft-lb)
T1: 42 – 62 (4.3 – 6.3, 31 – 46)
T2: 20 – 29 (2.0 – 3.0, 14 – 22)
T3: 18 – 22 (1.8 – 2.2, 13 – 16)
T4: 29 – 49 (3.0 – 5.0, 22 – 36)
T5: 20 – 24 (2.0 – 2.4, 14 – 17)
T6: 5 – 8 (0.5 – 0.8, 3.6 – 5.8)
T7: 10 – 16 (1.0 – 1.6, 7 – 12)
T8: 10 – 20 (1.0 – 2.0, 7 – 14)
T9: 2 – 3 (0.2 – 0.3, 1.4 – 2.2)
1 Tie-rod end ASSY, RH
2 Tie-rod end ASSY, LH
3 Dust seal
4 Snap ring
5 Nut
6 Clip (small)
7 Boot
8 Clip (large)
9 Tie-rod CP
10 Lock washer
11 Dust cover
12 Clip (medium)
14 Sleeve
15 Spring
16 O-ring (sleeve)
17 Adjusting screw
18 Lock nut
19 Rack ASSY
20 Adapter (cylinder)
21 Steering body ASSY
22 Seal holder ASSY
23 Y-packing (seal holder)
24 O-ring (seal holder)
*25 Snap ring (seal holder)
*26 Oil seal (pinion housing)
27 Backup ring
30 Adapter (gear)
31 O-ring (pinion)
32 Seal ring (pinion)
33 Valve housing ASSY
34 Snap ring (pinion)
35 Backup ring
*36 Y-packing (valve housing)
37 Ball bearing (valve housing)
38 Pinion & valve ASSY
39 O-ring (valve)
40 Seal ring (valve)
41 O-ring (rack piston)
42 Seal ring (rack piston)
*43 Dust seal
44 Oil seal (pinion)
45 Spacer
46 Valve ASSY
47 Shim
49 Pipe ASSY A (Long)
50 Pipe ASSY B (Short)
51 Bolt
53 Seal kit
Consists of all * marked parts for one vehicle.
55 Tank ASSY
56 Cap
57 Strainer
58 O-ring
59 Pipe ASSY E
60 Bracket
61 Pulley
62 Pump ASSY
63 Hose A
64 Hose B
65 Pipe C
66 Pipe D
67 Clamp A
68 Clamp B
69 Clamp C
SB6029100023000X

Fig. 8 Exploded view of power rack & pinion steering gear. Loyale

10. Remove two bolts securing valve assembly, then the valve housing assembly and valve assembly as a unit.
11. Remove snap ring from seal holder.
12. Push rack out of steering body while pushing it on valve side.
13. Remove high pressure seal as follows:
    a. Push back-up ring and oil seal out by inserting seal remover No. 927580000, or equivalent, from valve side.
14. Remove oil seal and O-ring from holder assembly, then install new oil seal and O-ring.
15. Remove seal ring and O-ring from rack piston, then install new seal ring and O-ring.
16. Lubricate inner surface of seal ring seater tool No. 34099PA000, or equivalent, and place tool over seal ring. Leave tool on seal ring for at least 10 minutes, until seal ring settles into place.
17. Assemble rack assembly as follows:
    a. Place attachment tool No. 926200000, or equivalent, in suitable vise, then attach steering gear to tool.
    b. Lubricate needle bearing.
    c. Using tools shown in **Fig. 11,** install oil seal. Oil seal should be installed to near piston.
    d. Install back-up ring to rack from gear side.
    e. Apply grease to rack teeth grooves, sleeve's sliding portion and piston's sealing surface, then insert rack into cylinder side of steering body.
    f. Lubricate and attach guide tool No. 34099PA020 to part of rack assembly which protrudes beyond cylinder side.
    g. Lubricate inner surface of holder assembly and O-ring, then insert into rack assembly. Install snap ring to secure holder assembly.
    h. Attach installer No. 926320000, or equivalent, to cylinder side of rack assembly, then drive back-up ring and oil seal into place on steering body. Push installer until its groove reaches end surface of holder assembly.
18. Install valve assembly as follows:
    a. Attach shim(s) to stepped lip of steering body and pinion housing. Apply sealer (Fuji Bond C: No. 004403004) uniformly to lip side end surface of pinion housing. Use same number of shims as removed from steering body, valve housing and valve assembly.
    b. Pull out rack assembly until it protrudes 2.99 inches beyond housing end face of pinion side.
    c. Lubricate pinion gear teeth grooves and ball bearing.
    d. Center rack shaft to rack housing. If centered correctly, the distance from rack housing to end face of rack will be 2.99 inches.
    e. Position input shaft so that cutout

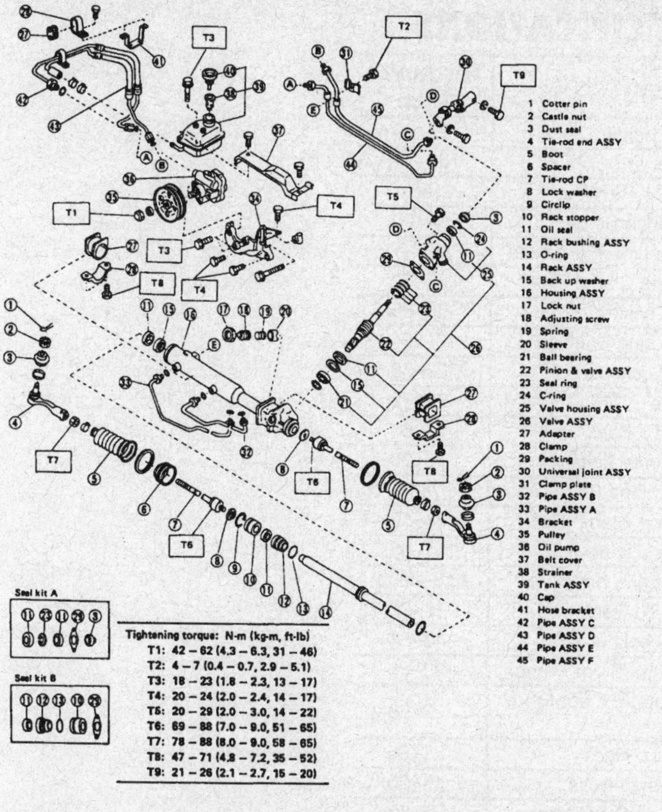
1 Cotter pin
2 Castle nut
3 Dust seal
4 Tie-rod end ASSY
5 Boot
6 Spacer
7 Tie-rod CP
8 Lock washer
9 Circlip
10 Rack stopper
11 Oil seal
12 Rack bushing ASSY
13 O-ring
14 Rack ASSY
15 Back up washer
16 Housing ASSY
17 Lock nut
18 Adjusting screw
19 Spring
20 Sleeve
21 Ball bearing
22 Pinion & valve ASSY
23 Seal ring
24 C-ring
25 Valve housing ASSY
26 Valve ASSY
27 Adapter
28 Clamp
29 Packing
30 Universal joint ASSY
31 Clamp plate
32 Pipe ASSY B
33 Pipe ASSY A
34 Bracket
35 Pulley
36 Oil pump
37 Belt cover
38 Strainer
39 Tank ASSY
40 Cap
41 Hose bracket
42 Pipe ASSY C
43 Pipe ASSY D
44 Pipe ASSY E
45 Pipe ASSY F
Seal kit A
Seal kit B
Tightening torque: N-m (kg-m, ft-lb)
T1: 42 – 62 (4.3 – 6.3, 31 – 46)
T2: 4 – 7 (0.4 – 0.7, 2.9 – 5.1)
T3: 18 – 23 (1.8 – 2.3, 13 – 17)
T4: 20 – 24 (2.0 – 2.4, 14 – 17)
T5: 20 – 29 (2.0 – 3.0, 14 – 22)
T6: 69 – 88 (7.0 – 9.0, 51 – 65)
T7: 78 – 88 (8.0 – 9.0, 58 – 65)
T8: 47 – 71 (4.8 – 7.2, 35 – 52)
T9: 21 – 26 (2.1 – 2.7, 15 – 20)
SB6029100024000X

Fig. 9 Exploded view of power rack & pinion steering gear. Impreza & Legacy

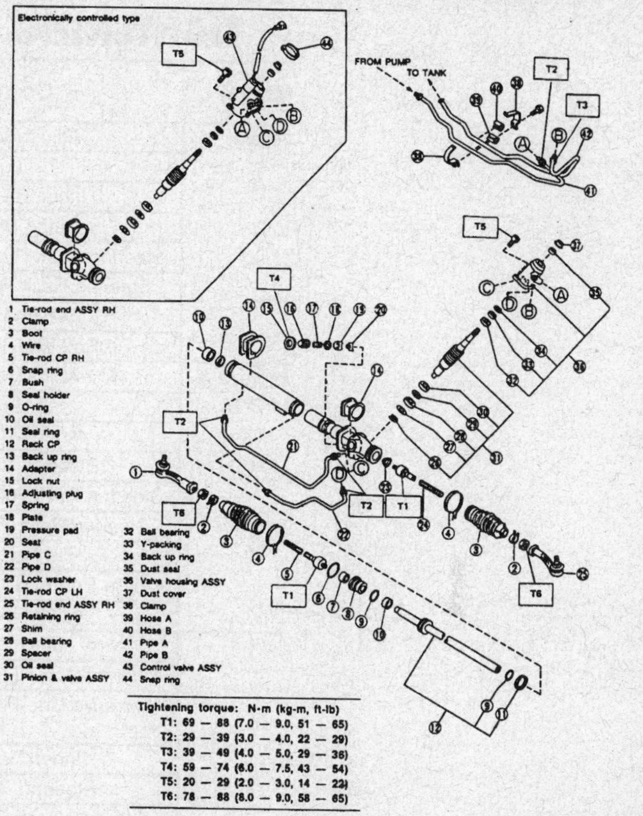
Electronically controlled type
FROM PUMP
TO TANK
1 Tie-rod end ASSY RH
2 Clamp
3 Boot
4 Wire
5 Tie-rod CP RH
6 Snap ring
7 Bush
8 Seal holder
9 O-ring
10 Oil seal
11 Seal ring
12 Rack CP
13 Back up ring
14 Adapter
15 Lock nut
16 Adjusting plug
17 Spring
18 Plate
19 Pressure pad
20 Seat
21 Pipe C
22 Pipe D
23 Lock washer
24 Tie-rod CP LH
25 Tie-rod end ASSY RH
26 Retaining ring
27 Shim
28 Ball bearing
29 Spacer
30 Oil seal
31 Pinion & valve ASSY
32 Ball bearing
33 Y-packing
34 Back up ring
35 Dust seal
36 Valve housing ASSY
37 Dust cover
38 Clamp
39 Hose A
40 Hose B
41 Pipe A
42 Pipe B
43 Control valve ASSY
44 Snap ring
Tightening torque: N·m (kg-m, ft-lb)
T1: 69 — 88 (7.0 — 9.0, 51 — 65)
T2: 29 — 39 (3.0 — 4.0, 22 — 29)
T3: 39 — 49 (4.0 — 5.0, 29 — 36)
T4: 59 — 74 (6.0 — 7.5, 43 — 54)
T5: 20 — 29 (2.0 — 3.0, 14 — 22)
T6: 78 — 88 (8.0 — 9.0, 58 — 65)
SB6029100028000X

Fig. 10 Exploded view of power rack & pinion steering gear. SVX

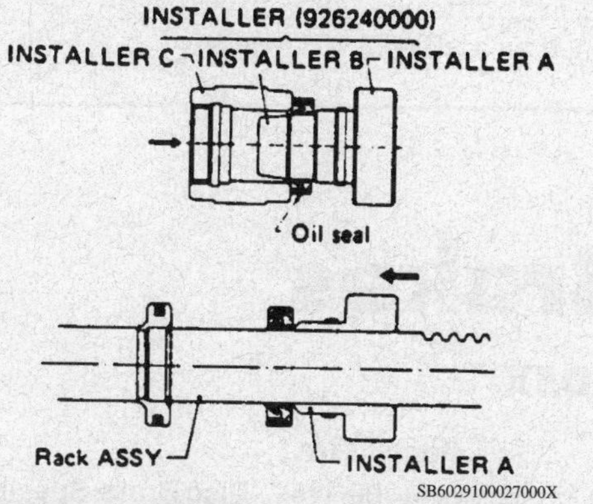
INSTALLER (926240000)
INSTALLER C
INSTALLER B
INSTALLER A
Oil seal
Rack ASSY
INSTALLER A
SB6029100027000X

Fig. 11 Rack oil seal installation

section faces toward sleeve boss.

f. Push in valve assembly.
g. Center rack assembly as outlined in step d, then gradually **torque** socket bolts alternately 14–22 ft. lbs.

19. Apply a suitable lubricant to sliding surface of sleeve and spring seat, then insert sleeve into pinion housing assembly.
20. Insert spring into sleeve screw, then pack screw with a suitable grease and install.
21. Install tie rods as follows:
    a. Rotate input shaft until rack protrudes approximately 1.57 inch above end surface of gear.
    b. Hold rack in this position, then tighten adjusting screw until it bottoms.
    c. Install tie rods onto rack.
22. Adjust rack and pinion backlash as follows:
    a. **Torque** adjusting screw to 14 ft. lbs. to seat sleeve against rack, then loosen screw.
    b. **Torque** adjusting screw to 3.6 ft. lbs., then loosen screw.
    c. **Torque** adjusting screw to 3.6 ft. lbs., then back off 25°.
    d. While holding adjusting screw in place, **torque** locknut to 43–54 ft. lbs.
23. Apply a suitable grease to groove of tie rod, then ensure boot is positioned without unusual inflation or deflation.
24. Wind two complete turns of lock wire on large end of boot, twist wire while pulling it upward with a force of 11 lbs. bend wire end along boot.
25. Install small boot end clip. Ensure boot end is positioned in groove on tie rod.
26. Screw in tie rod end locknut and tie rod end onto tie rod, then tighten locknut 1.00 inch from back of nut to threaded portion.

TIGHTENING SPECIFICATIONS

Model	Component	Torque/Ft. Lbs.
Loyale	Adjust Screw Locknut	22–36
	Lug Nuts	58–72
	Inner Tie Rod To Rack	58
	Steering Shaft Pinch Bolts	15–20
	Steering Rack Hydraulic Line Flare Nuts	7–12
	Steering Rack Retaining Clamp Bolts	35–52
	Tie Rod End Locknut	58–65
	Tie Rod End To Steering Knuckle	18–22①
Impreza & Legacy	Adjust Screw Locknut	22–36
	Lug Nuts	58–72
	Inner Tie Rod To Rack	51–65
	Steering Shaft Pinch Bolts	15–20
	Steering Rack Hydraulic Line Flare Nuts	7–12
	Steering Rack Retaining Clamp Bolts	35–52
	Tie Rod End Locknut	51–65
	Tie Rod End To Steering Knuckle	18–22①
	Valve Housing To Rack	14–22
SVX	Adjust Screw Locknut	43–54
	Hydraulic Line Flare Nuts (From Pump)	29–36
	Hydraulic Line Flare Nuts (Except From Pump)	22–29
	Inner Tie Rod To Rack	51–65
	Steering Shaft Pinch Bolts	15–20
	Steering Rack Retaining Clamp Bolts	35–52
	Tie Rod End Outer Locknut	58–65
	Tie Rod End To Steering Knuckle	22–36
	Valve Housing To Rack	14–22

① — Castle nut may be tightened an additional 60° to align cotter pin.

Disc Brakes

INDEX

	Page No.
Brake Pad Service	39-114
Front	39-114
Rear	39-115
Caliper Service	39-115
Overhaul	39-115
Replacement	39-115
Disc Brake Specifications	39-118
Hill Holder Service	39-117
Tightening Specifications	39-119

BRAKE PAD SERVICE

FRONT

Refer to **Figs. 1 through 7,** when performing the following procedure.

1. Raise and support vehicle.
2. Remove front wheels.
3. **On Loyale models,** remove outer parking brake cable clip and disconnect cable.
4. **On Legacy Turbo and SVX models,** disconnect brake hose from strut.
5. **On all except Justy with 12 inch wheels,** remove caliper lockpin, then rotate caliper on guide pin.
6. **On Justy with 12 inch wheels,** remove caliper-to-support retaining bolts, then the boot protector and caliper.
7. **On all models,** remove brake pads from support.
8. Reverse procedure to install noting the following:
   a. **On all except Justy, Legacy and SVX,** using wrench tool No. 925590000 and spacer tool No. 926440000, or equivalents, slowly rotate caliper piston until seated into caliper bore. **Ensure notch in piston face is aligned with tab on brake pad backing plate.**
   b. **On Justy, Legacy and SVX,** push piston into caliper body. When piston is difficult to insert, loosen the air bleeder, then push into place.
   c. **On all models,** refer to **Figs. 1 through 6,** for tightening values.
   d. After completing installation, depress brake pedal several times to seat brake pads against rotor. If pedal stroke is excessive, bleed hydraulic system as needed.

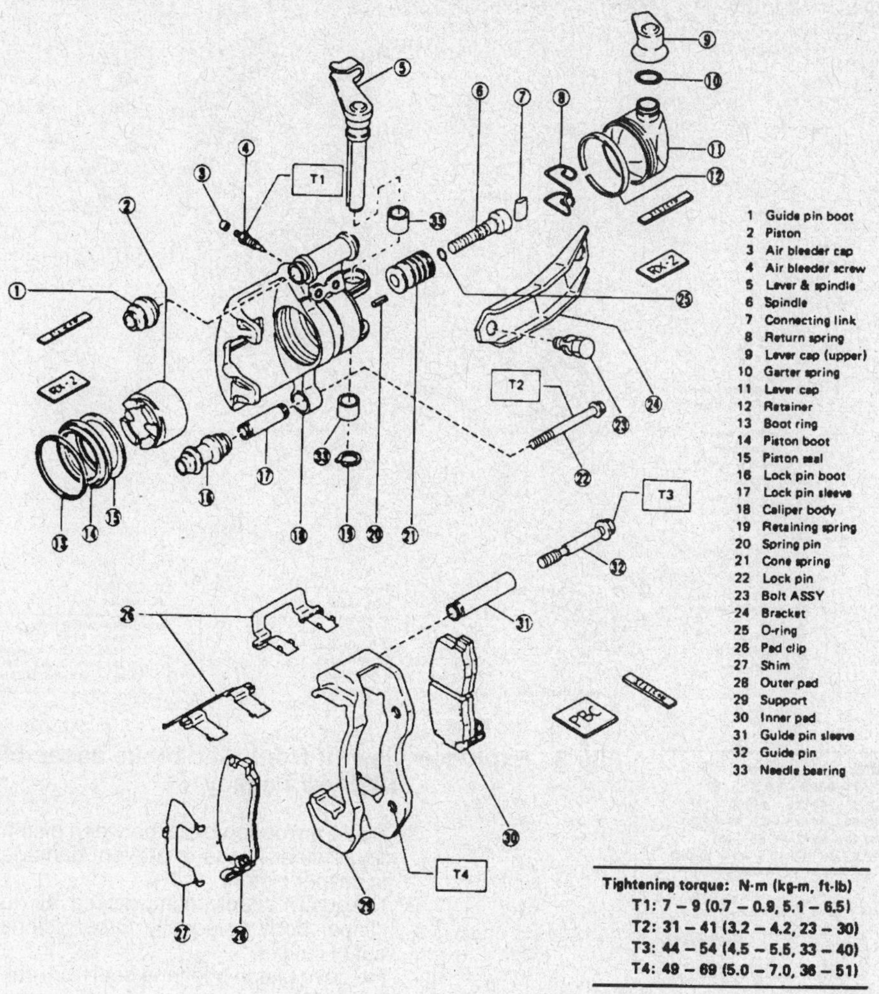

T1
T2
T3
T4
1 Guide pin boot
2 Piston
3 Air bleeder cap
4 Air bleeder screw
5 Lever & spindle
6 Spindle
7 Connecting link
8 Return spring
9 Lever cap (upper)
10 Garter spring
11 Lever cap
12 Retainer
13 Boot ring
14 Piston boot
15 Piston seal
16 Lock pin boot
17 Lock pin sleeve
18 Caliper body
19 Retaining spring
20 Spring pin
21 Cone spring
22 Lock pin
23 Bolt ASSY
24 Bracket
25 O-ring
26 Pad clip
27 Shim
28 Outer pad
29 Support
30 Inner pad
31 Guide pin sleeve
32 Guide pin
33 Needle bearing
Tightening torque: N·m (kg-m, ft-lb)
T1: 7 – 9 (0.7 – 0.9, 5.1 – 6.5)
T2: 31 – 41 (3.2 – 4.2, 23 – 30)
T3: 44 – 54 (4.5 – 5.5, 33 – 40)
T4: 49 – 69 (5.0 – 7.0, 36 – 51)
SB4079100001000X

Fig. 1 Exploded view of front disc brake assembly. Loyale

REAR

Refer to **Figs. 8 through 11,** when performing the following procedure.

1. Raise and support vehicle.
2. Remove rear wheels.
3. Remove lower caliper retaining bolt, then pivot caliper upward.
4. Remove brake pads and springs from support. **Note position of springs for proper installation.**
5. Reverse procedure to install noting the following:
   a. Press piston into caliper body using a suitable clamp.
   b. Refer to **Figs. 8 through 11,** for tightening values.
   c. After completing installation, depress brake pedal several times to seat brake pads against rotor. If pedal stroke is excessive, bleed hydraulic system as needed.

CALIPER SERVICE

REPLACEMENT

FRONT

Refer to **Figs. 1 through 7,** when performing the following procedure.

1. Raise and support vehicle.
2. Remove front wheels.
3. Disconnect brake hose from caliper. Plug hose to prevent fluid leakage.
4. **On Loyale models,** remove outer parking brake cable clip and disconnect cable.
5. **On all except Justy with 12 inch wheels,** remove caliper lockpin, rotate caliper on guide pin, then remove caliper.
6. **On Justy with 12 inch wheels,** remove caliper to support retaining bolts, then the boot protector and caliper.
7. **On all models,** reverse procedure to install noting the following:
   a. Refer to **Figs. 1 through 7,** for tightening values.
   b. After completing installation, bleed hydraulic system.

REAR

Refer to **Figs. 8 through 11,** when performing the following procedure.

1. Raise and support vehicle.
2. Remove rear wheels.
3. Disconnect brake hose from caliper. Plug brake to prevent fluid leakage.
4. Remove caliper retaining bolts and the caliper.
5. Reverse procedure to install noting the following:
   a. Refer to **Figs. 8 through 11,** for tightening values.
   b. After completing installation, bleed hydraulic system.

OVERHAUL

FRONT

Loyale

Refer to **Fig. 1,** when performing the following procedure.

1. Remove caliper as outlined.
2. Remove sleeve and the lockpin boot.
3. Remove boot ring and piston boot.
4. Position a block of wood between piston bore and caliper ears, then remove piston from piston bore by gradually applying compressed air to brake fluid inlet port.
5. Remove piston seal. Use caution not to damage inner wall of cylinder.
6. Remove guide pin boot from caliper.
7. Remove retainer and lever cap, then the retaining spring and spindle.
8. Compress spring washer using puller tool No. 925471000, or equivalent, then remove lever and spindle.
9. Remove puller tool, then the connecting link and return spring.
10. Reverse procedure to install noting the following:
    a. To seat piston in piston bore, slowly rotate piston using wrench tool No. 925590000 and spacer tool No. 926440000, or equivalents. **Ensure notch in piston face is aligned with tab on brake pad backing plate.**

Legacy Except Turbo

Refer to **Fig. 2,** when performing the following procedure.

1. Remove caliper as outlined.
2. Remove sleeve and the lockpin boot.
3. Remove boot ring and piston boot.
4. Position a block of wood between piston bore and caliper ears, then remove piston from piston bore by gradually applying compressed air to brake fluid inlet port.
5. Remove piston seal. Use caution not to damage inner wall of cylinder.
6. Remove guide pin boot from caliper.
7. Reverse procedure to install.

Justy

Refer to **Figs. 4 and 5,** when performing the following procedure.

1. Remove caliper as outlined.
2. Remove piston inner shim.
3. Position a block of wood between piston bore and caliper ears, then remove piston from piston bore by gradually applying compressed air to brake fluid inlet port.
4. Remove piston boot and seal.
5. Reverse procedure to install.

Legacy Turbo & SVX

Refer to **Fig. 6,** when performing the following procedure.

1. Remove caliper assembly as outlined.

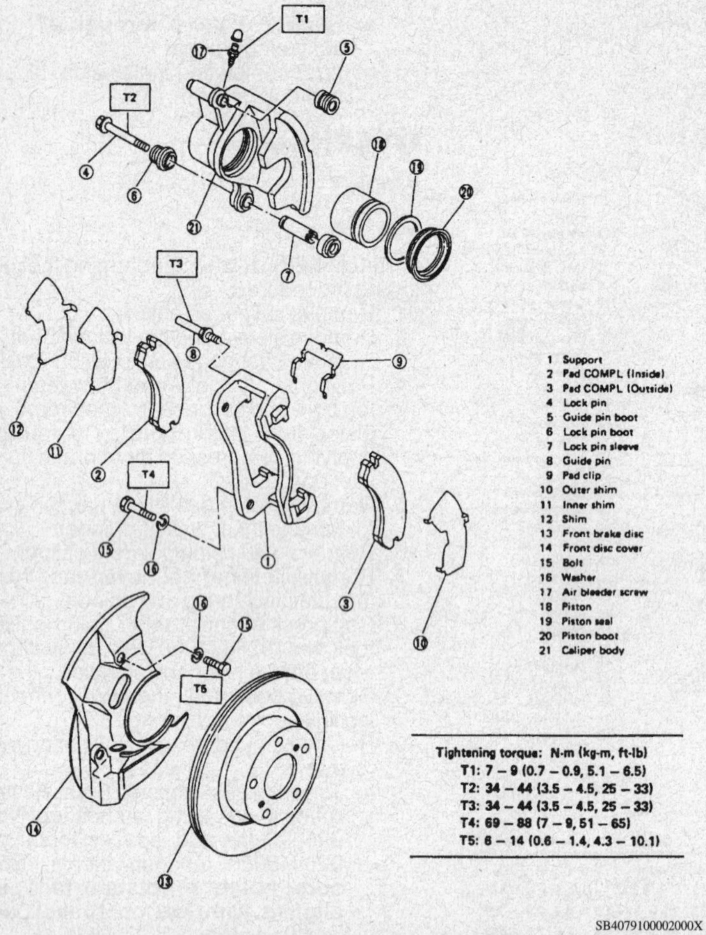
T1
T2
T3
T4
T5
1 Support
2 Pad COMPL (Inside)
3 Pad COMPL (Outside)
4 Lock pin
5 Guide pin boot
6 Lock pin boot
7 Lock pin sleeve
8 Guide pin
9 Pad clip
10 Outer shim
11 Inner shim
12 Shim
13 Front brake disc
14 Front disc cover
15 Bolt
16 Washer
17 Air bleeder screw
18 Piston
19 Piston seal
20 Piston boot
21 Caliper body
Tightening torque: N-m (kg-m, ft-lb)
T1: 7 – 9 (0.7 – 0.9, 5.1 – 6.5)
T2: 34 – 44 (3.5 – 4.5, 25 – 33)
T3: 34 – 44 (3.5 – 4.5, 25 – 33)
T4: 69 – 88 (7 – 9, 51 – 65)
T5: 6 – 14 (0.6 – 1.4, 4.3 – 10.1)
SB4079100002000X

Fig. 2 Exploded view of front disc brake assembly. 1993–94 Legacy non-turbo

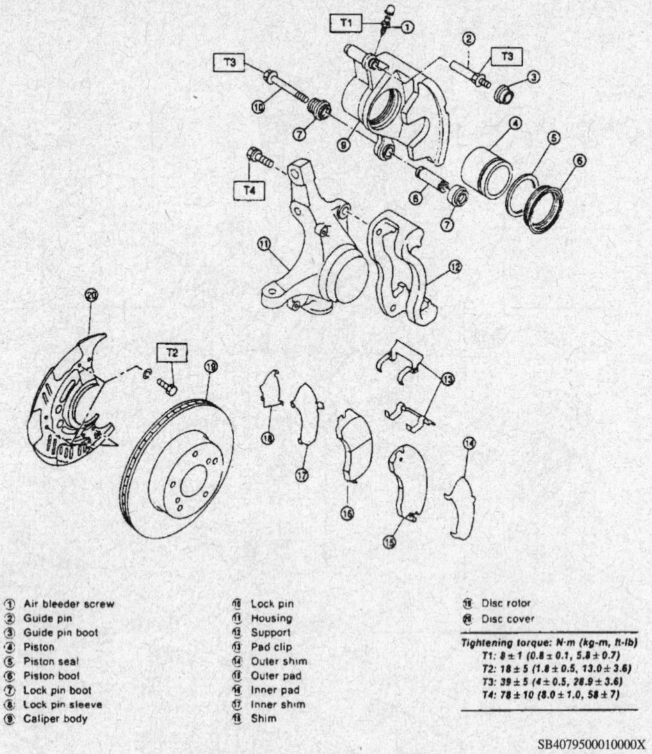
T1
T2
T3
T4
1 Air bleeder screw
2 Guide pin
3 Guide pin boot
4 Piston
5 Piston seal
6 Piston boot
7 Lock pin boot
8 Lock pin sleeve
9 Caliper body
10 Lock pin
11 Housing
12 Support
13 Pad clip
14 Outer shim
15 Outer pad
16 Inner pad
17 Inner shim
18 Shim
19 Disc rotor
20 Disc cover
Tightening torque: N·m (kg-m, ft-lb)
T1: 8 ± 1 (0.8 ± 0.1, 5.8 ± 0.7)
T2: 18 ± 5 (1.8 ± 0.5, 13.0 ± 3.6)
T3: 39 ± 5 (4 ± 0.5, 28.9 ± 3.6)
T4: 78 ± 10 (8.0 ± 1.0, 58 ± 7)
SB4079500010000X

Fig. 3 Exploded view of front disc brake assembly. 1995–96 Legacy

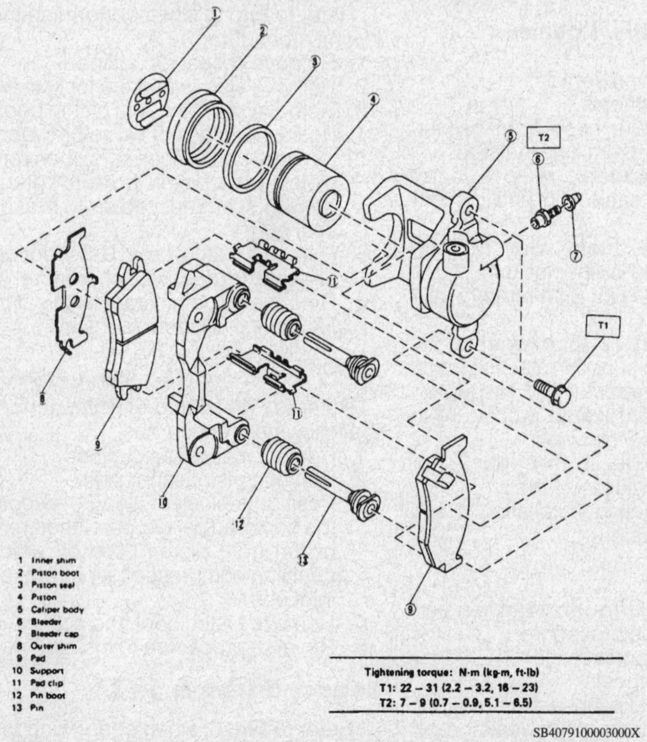
T1
T2
1 Inner shim
2 Piston boot
3 Piston seal
4 Piston
5 Caliper body
6 Bleeder
7 Bleeder cap
8 Outer shim
9 Pad
10 Support
11 Pad clip
12 Pin boot
13 Pin
Tightening torque: N·m (kg-m, ft-lb)
T1: 22 – 31 (2.2 – 3.2, 16 – 23)
T2: 7 – 9 (0.7 – 0.9, 5.1 – 6.5)
SB4079100003000X

Fig. 4 Exploded view of front disc brake assembly. Justy w/12 inch wheel

2. Place a wooden block between piston and caliper flange to prevent damage to caliper piston.
3. Gradually supply compressed air to caliper body to equally force pistons out of caliper.
4. Remove piston boot and seal from caliper body.
5. Remove lockpin sleeve and boot then guide pin boot from caliper body.
6. Reverse procedure to install, coating piston seal and inner surface of cylinder with brake fluid.

Impreza

Refer to **Fig. 7,** when performing the following procedure.

1. Remove caliper assembly as outlined.
2. Using a flathead screwdriver, remove boot ring from piston.
3. Place a wooden block between piston and caliper flange to prevent damage to caliper piston.
4. Gradually supply compressed air to caliper body to equally force pistons out of caliper.
5. Remove piston seal from caliper body.
6. Remove lockpin sleeve and boot, then the guide pin boot from caliper body.
7. Reverse procedure to install, coating piston seal and inner surface of cylinder with brake fluid.

REAR

Refer to **Figs. 8 through 11,** when performing the following procedure.

1. Remove caliper as outlined under "Caliper, Replace."
2. Position a block of wood between piston bore and caliper ears, then remove

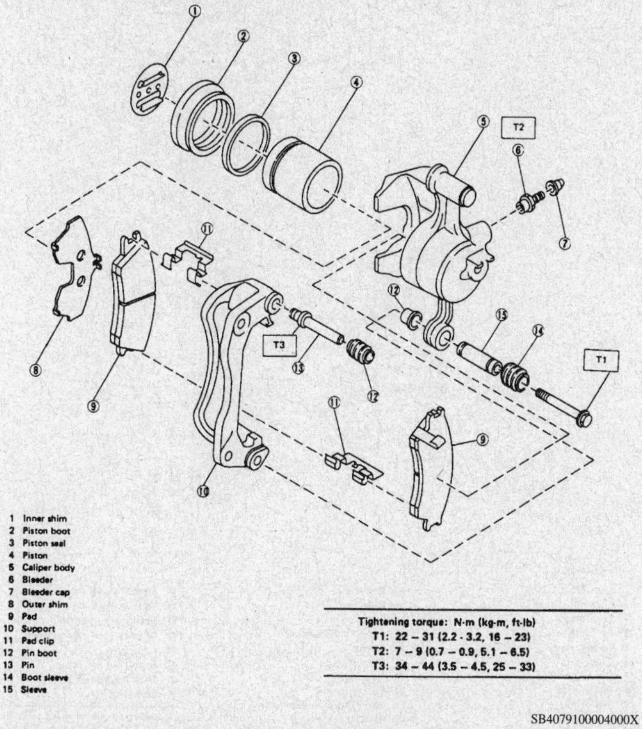

T1
T2
T3
1 Inner shim
2 Piston boot
3 Piston seal
4 Piston
5 Caliper body
6 Bleeder
7 Bleeder cap
8 Outer shim
9 Pad
10 Support
11 Pad clip
12 Pin boot
13 Pin
14 Boot sleeve
15 Sleeve
Tightening torque: N·m (kg-m, ft-lb)
T1: 22 – 31 (2.2 - 3.2, 16 – 23)
T2: 7 – 9 (0.7 – 0.9, 5.1 – 6.5)
T3: 34 – 44 (3.5 – 4.5, 25 – 33)
SB4079100004000X

Fig. 5 Exploded view of front disc brake assembly. Justy w/13 inch wheel

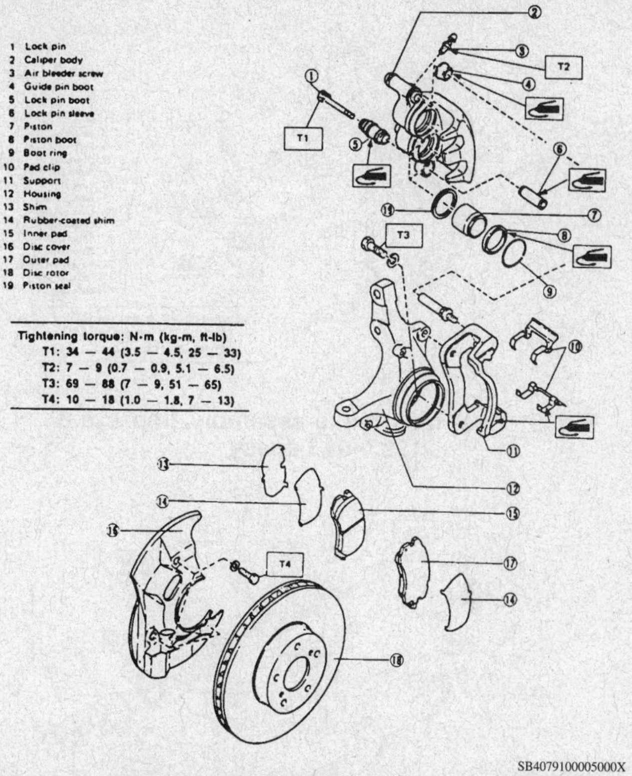

1 Lock pin
2 Caliper body
3 Air bleeder screw
4 Guide pin boot
5 Lock pin boot
6 Lock pin sleeve
7 Piston
8 Piston boot
9 Boot ring
10 Pad clip
11 Support
12 Housing
13 Shim
14 Rubber-coated shim
15 Inner pad
16 Disc cover
17 Outer pad
18 Disc rotor
19 Piston seal
Tightening torque: N·m (kg-m, ft-lb)
T1: 34 — 44 (3.5 — 4.5, 25 — 33)
T2: 7 — 9 (0.7 — 0.9, 5.1 — 6.5)
T3: 69 — 88 (7 — 9, 51 — 65)
T4: 10 — 18 (1.0 — 1.8, 7 — 13)
T1
T2
T3
T4
SB4079100005000X

Fig. 6 Exploded view of front disc brake assembly. SVX & 1993–94 Legacy w/turbo

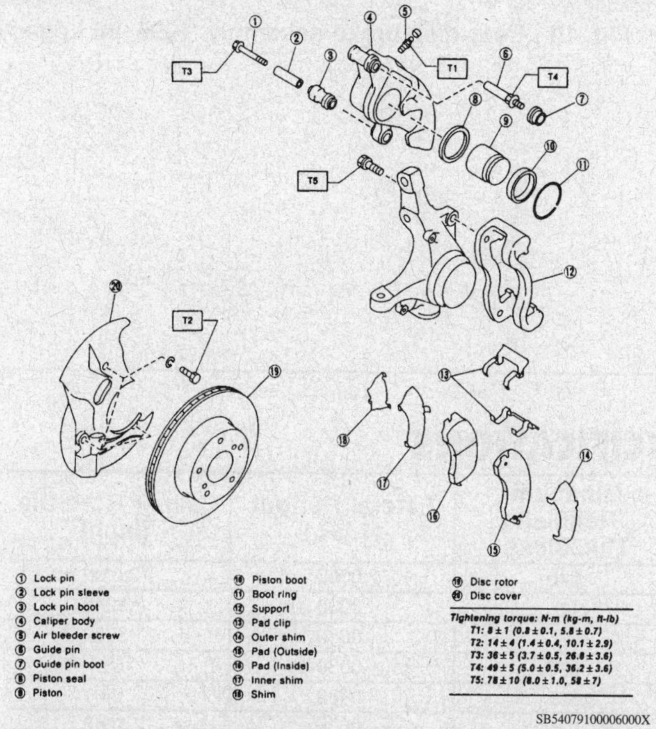

T1
T2
T3
T4
T5
① Lock pin
② Lock pin sleeve
③ Lock pin boot
④ Caliper body
⑤ Air bleeder screw
⑥ Guide pin
⑦ Guide pin boot
⑧ Piston seal
⑨ Piston
⑩ Piston boot
⑪ Boot ring
⑫ Support
⑬ Pad clip
⑭ Outer shim
⑮ Pad (Outside)
⑯ Pad (Inside)
⑰ Inner shim
⑱ Shim
⑲ Disc rotor
⑳ Disc cover
Tightening torque: N·m (kg-m, ft-lb)
T1: 8 ± 1 (0.8 ± 0.1, 5.8 ± 0.7)
T2: 14 ± 4 (1.4 ± 0.4, 10.1 ± 2.9)
T3: 36 ± 5 (3.7 ± 0.5, 26.8 ± 3.6)
T4: 49 ± 5 (5.0 ± 0.5, 36.2 ± 3.6)
T5: 78 ± 10 (8.0 ± 1.0, 58 ± 7)
SB54079100006000X

Fig. 7 Exploded view of front disc brake assembly. Impreza

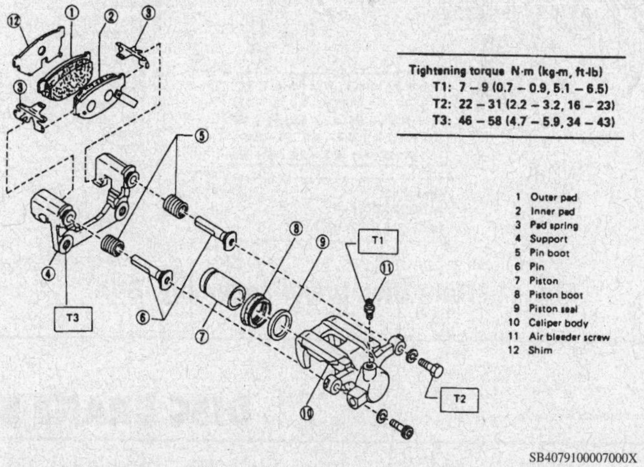

Tightening torque N·m (kg-m, ft-lb)
T1: 7 – 9 (0.7 – 0.9, 5.1 – 6.5)
T2: 22 – 31 (2.2 – 3.2, 16 – 23)
T3: 46 – 58 (4.7 – 5.9, 34 – 43)
1 Outer pad
2 Inner pad
3 Pad spring
4 Support
5 Pin boot
6 Pin
7 Piston
8 Piston boot
9 Piston seal
10 Caliper body
11 Air bleeder screw
12 Shim
T1
T2
T3
SB4079100007000X

Fig. 8 Exploded view of rear disc brake assembly. Loyale

piston from piston bore by gradually applying compressed air to brake fluid inlet port.

3. Remove piston boot and seal.
4. Reverse procedure to install.

HILL HOLDER SERVICE

Refer to "Rear Axle & Suspension" section in this chapter for Hill Holder service information.

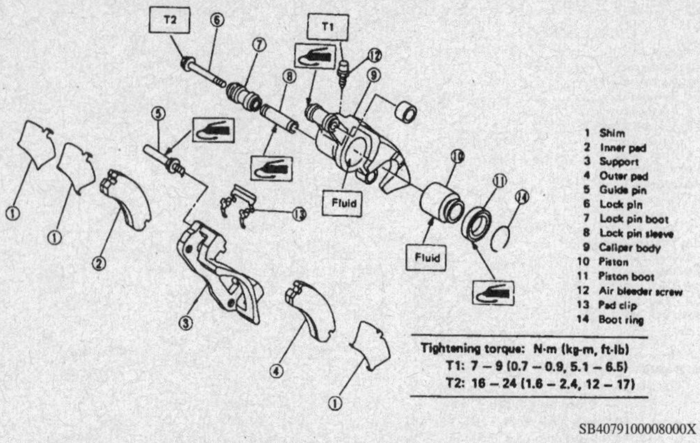
T1
T2
Fluid
1 Shim
2 Inner pad
3 Support
4 Outer pad
5 Guide pin
6 Lock pin
7 Lock pin boot
8 Lock pin sleeve
9 Caliper body
10 Piston
11 Piston boot
12 Air bleeder screw
13 Pad clip
14 Boot ring
Tightening torque: N·m (kg-m, ft-lb)
T1: 7 – 9 (0.7 – 0.9, 5.1 – 6.5)
T2: 16 – 24 (1.6 – 2.4, 12 – 17)
SB4079100008000X

Fig. 9 Rear disc brake assembly. Impreza & 1993–94 Legacy

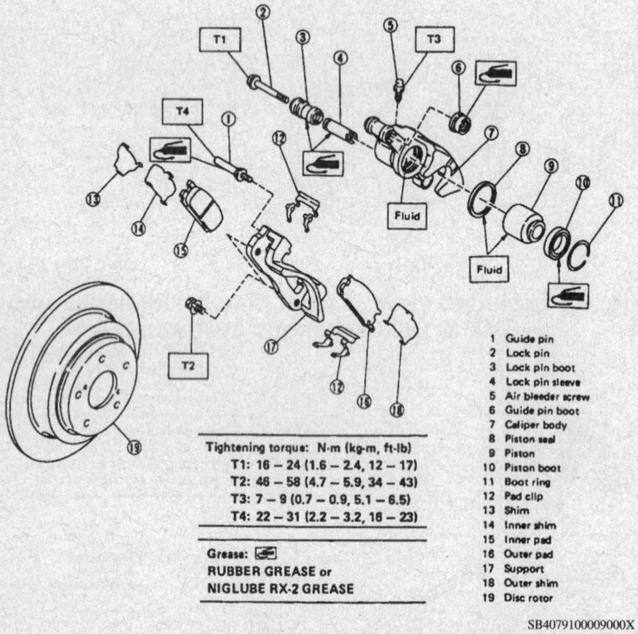
T1
T2
T3
T4
Fluid
1 Guide pin
2 Lock pin
3 Lock pin boot
4 Lock pin sleeve
5 Air bleeder screw
6 Guide pin boot
7 Caliper body
8 Piston seal
9 Piston
10 Piston boot
11 Boot ring
12 Pad clip
13 Shim
14 Inner shim
15 Inner pad
16 Outer pad
17 Support
18 Outer shim
19 Disc rotor
Tightening torque: N·m (kg-m, ft-lb)
T1: 16 – 24 (1.6 – 2.4, 12 – 17)
T2: 46 – 58 (4.7 – 5.9, 34 – 43)
T3: 7 – 9 (0.7 – 0.9, 5.1 – 6.5)
T4: 22 – 31 (2.2 – 3.2, 16 – 23)
Grease:
RUBBER GREASE or
NIGLUBE RX-2 GREASE
SB4079100009000X

Fig. 11 Rear disc brake assembly. SVX

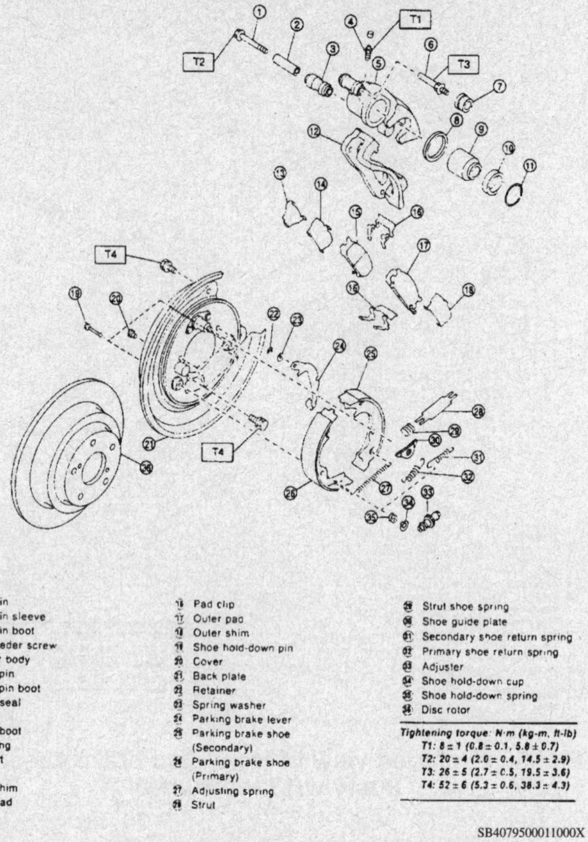
T1
T2
T3
T4
1 Lock pin
2 Lock pin sleeve
3 Lock pin boot
4 Air bleeder screw
5 Caliper body
6 Guide pin
7 Guide pin boot
8 Piston seal
9 Piston
10 Piston boot
11 Boot ring
12 Support
13 Shim
14 Inner shim
15 Inner pad
16 Pad clip
17 Outer pad
18 Outer shim
19 Shoe hold-down pin
20 Cover
21 Back plate
22 Retainer
23 Spring washer
24 Parking brake lever
25 Parking brake shoe (Secondary)
26 Parking brake shoe (Primary)
27 Adjusting spring
28 Strut
29 Strut shoe spring
30 Shoe guide plate
31 Secondary shoe return spring
32 Primary shoe return spring
33 Adjuster
34 Shoe hold-down cup
35 Shoe hold-down spring
36 Disc rotor
Tightening torque: N·m (kg-m, ft-lb)
T1: 8 ± 1 (0.8 ± 0.1, 5.8 ± 0.7)
T2: 20 ± 4 (2.0 ± 0.4, 14.5 ± 2.9)
T3: 26 ± 5 (2.7 ± 0.5, 19.5 ± 3.6)
T4: 52 ± 6 (5.3 ± 0.6, 38.3 ± 4.3)
SB4079500011000X

Fig. 10 Rear disc brake assembly. 1995–96 Legacy

DISC BRAKE SPECIFICATIONS

Model	Year	Nominal Thickness	Minimum Refinish Thickness	Lateral Runout (T.I.R.)	Caliper Bore Dia. (Inch)
Justy	1993–94	.710	.610	.0059	2.012
Impreza①	1993–96	②	③	.0030	2.1248
Impreza④	1993–96	.39	.335	.0039	1.3752
Legacy①	1993–96	.940	.870	.0039	⑤
Legacy④	1993–96	.390	.335	.0039	⑥
Loyale①	1993–94	.710	.630	.0039	2.1248
SVX①	1993–96	1.10	1.02	.0039	—
SVX④	1993–96	.390	.335	.0039	—

① — Front disc.
② — FWD models, .71 inch; AWD models, .94 inch.
③ — FWD models, .63 inch; AWD models, .87 inch.
④ — Rear disc.
⑤ — Non-turbo sedan & station wagon, 2.252; Turbo sedan, .976 inch.
⑥ — Non-turbo sedan & station wagon, 1.500; Turbo sedan, 1.374 inch.

TIGHTENING SPECIFICATIONS

Component	Torque/Ft. Lbs.
Front	
Air Bleeder Screw	5–6
Caliper Body Retaining Bolts	16–23②
Caliper Lockpin	25–30①
Caliper Support To Steering Knuckle	51–65①
Front Disc Cover	4–10①
Guide Pin	33–40①
Guide Pin	25–33②
Wheel Lug Nuts	58–72
Rear	
Air Bleeder Screws	5–6
Caliper Body Retaining Bolts	③
Caliper Support	34–43
Guide Pin	16–23④
Wheel Lug Nuts	58–72

① — Except Justy models.
② — Justy models.
③ — Except Legacy models; 16–23 ft. lbs., Legacy models; 12–17 ft. lbs.
④ — Legacy and SVX models.

Drum Brakes

INDEX

	Page No.
Adjustments	39-119
Drum Brake	39-119
Parking Brake	39-119
Brake Service	39-119
Impreza & Legacy	39-119
Justy	39-119
Loyale	39-119
Drum Brake Specifications	39-121
Tightening Specifications	39-121

BRAKE SERVICE

LOYALE

1. Raise and support vehicle, then remove rear wheels.
2. Remove brake drum, then disconnect brake line from back plate.
3. Using suitable pliers, remove shoe hold-down springs, **Figs. 1 and 2.**
4. Remove shoes.
5. Reverse procedure to install. Refer to **Fig. 2,** for tightening specifications.

IMPREZA & LEGACY

1. Raise and support vehicle, then remove rear wheels.
2. Remove brake drum. If difficult to remove brake drum, remove adjusting hole cover from back plate, then turn adjusting screw until shoe separate from drum.
3. Remove hold-down pin and cup.
4. Disconnect lower shoe return spring from shoes.
5. Remove shoes one by one from back plate with adjuster.
6. Reverse procedure to install. Refer to **Fig. 3,** for tightening specifications.

JUSTY

1. Raise and support vehicle.
2. Remove rear wheels.
3. Remove hub cap, cotter pin, castle nut, conical spring and center piece.
4. Loosen adjusting nut at rear end of parking brake rod to slacken cable tension.
5. Remove brake drum, then insert screwdriver through access hole in backing plate and allow strut assembly adjuster lever to pivot on strut, thereby placing it in initial position.
6. Using suitable pliers, remove shoe hold-down springs, **Fig. 4.**
7. Remove shoes, then disconnect parking brake cable from lever.
8. Reverse procedure to install.

ADJUSTMENTS

PARKING BRAKE

1. **On models except Impreza,** pull parking brake lever three to five times. Mechanism should click six to seven times when a force of 55 lbs. is exerted on the lever.
2. **On Impreza,** pull parking brake lever three to five times. Mechanism should click six times when a force of 44 lbs. is exerted on the lever.
3. **On Loyale,** if lever operation is not as specified, rotate the equalizer cable adjustment nut until play at "A" in **Fig. 5,** is set at 0–.02 inch (0–.5mm).
4. **On Justy,** if lever operation is not as specified, adjust lever stroke at parking brake rod until wheels drag slightly.
5. **On Impreza,** if lever operation is not as specified, adjust lever stroke by turning adjuster nut, **Fig. 6,** until parking brake lever stroke is set to specifications.
6. **On all models,** tighten adjuster locknut. Refer to "Rear Axle, Suspension & Brakes Tightening Specifications " for tightening specifications.

DRUM BRAKE

On Impreza and Justy, brake shoe clearances are automatically adjusted by pumping brake pedal several times as required.

On Loyale, loosen locknut of wedge adjuster and tighten wedge adjuster until wheel can no longer be rotated, then back off adjuster 180° to provide a clearance of .004–.006 inch between brake shoe and drum and retighten adjuster locknut, **Fig. 7.**

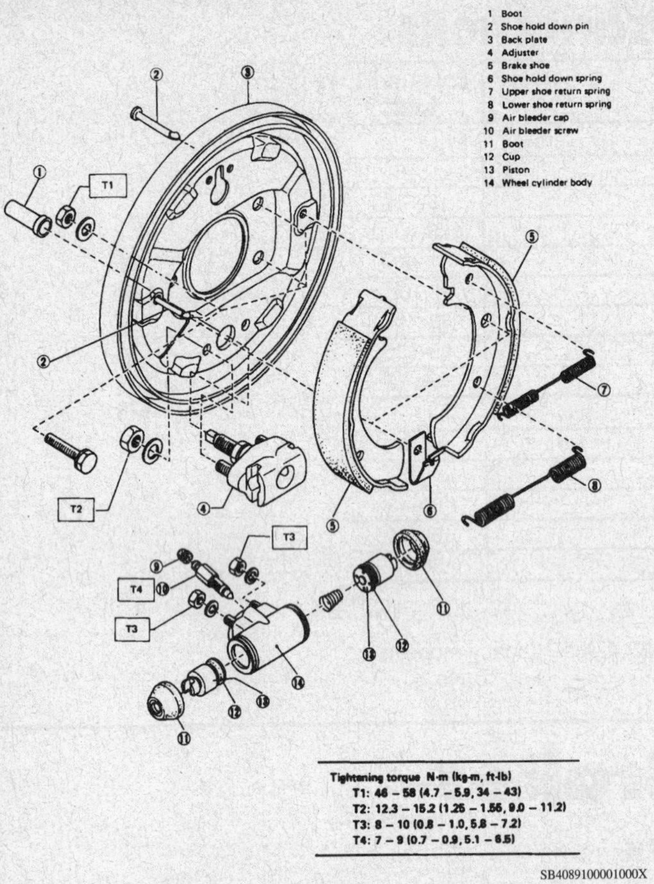
1 Boot
2 Shoe hold down pin
3 Back plate
4 Adjuster
5 Brake shoe
6 Shoe hold down spring
7 Upper shoe return spring
8 Lower shoe return spring
9 Air bleeder cap
10 Air bleeder screw
11 Boot
12 Cup
13 Piston
14 Wheel cylinder body
T1
T2
T3
T4
Tightening torque N·m (kg-m, ft-lb)
T1: 46 – 58 (4.7 – 5.9, 34 – 43)
T2: 12.3 – 15.2 (1.25 – 1.55, 9.0 – 11.2)
T3: 8 – 10 (0.8 – 1.0, 5.8 – 7.2)
T4: 7 – 9 (0.7 – 0.9, 5.1 – 6.5)
SB4089100001000X

Fig. 1 Exploded view of drum brake assembly. FWD Loyale

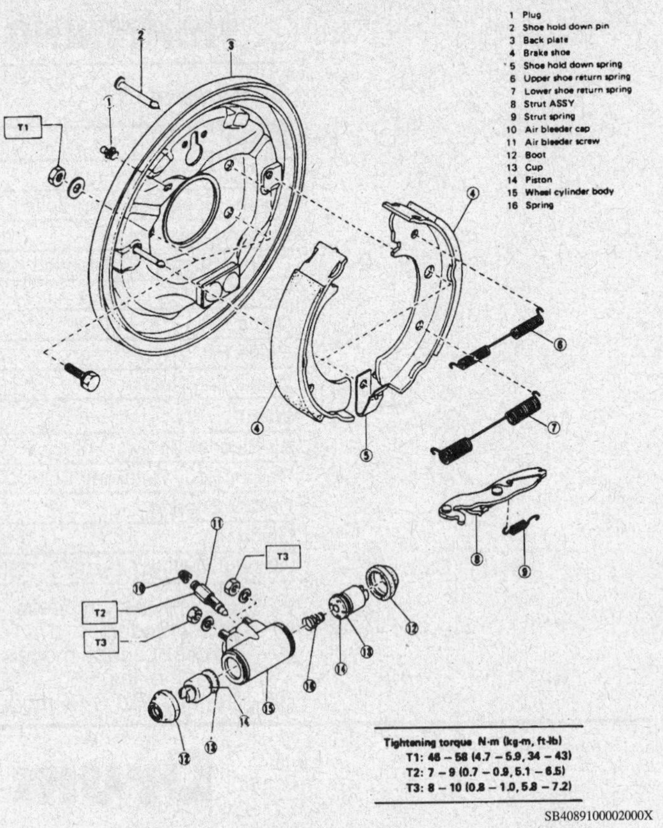
1 Plug
2 Shoe hold down pin
3 Back plate
4 Brake shoe
5 Shoe hold down spring
6 Upper shoe return spring
7 Lower shoe return spring
8 Strut ASSY
9 Strut spring
10 Air bleeder cap
11 Air bleeder screw
12 Boot
13 Cup
14 Piston
15 Wheel cylinder body
16 Spring
T1
T2
T3
Tightening torque N·m (kg-m, ft-lb)
T1: 46 – 58 (4.7 – 5.9, 34 – 43)
T2: 7 – 9 (0.7 – 0.9, 5.1 – 6.5)
T3: 8 – 10 (0.8 – 1.0, 5.8 – 7.2)
SB4089100002000X

Fig. 2 Exploded view of drum brake assembly. AWD Loyale

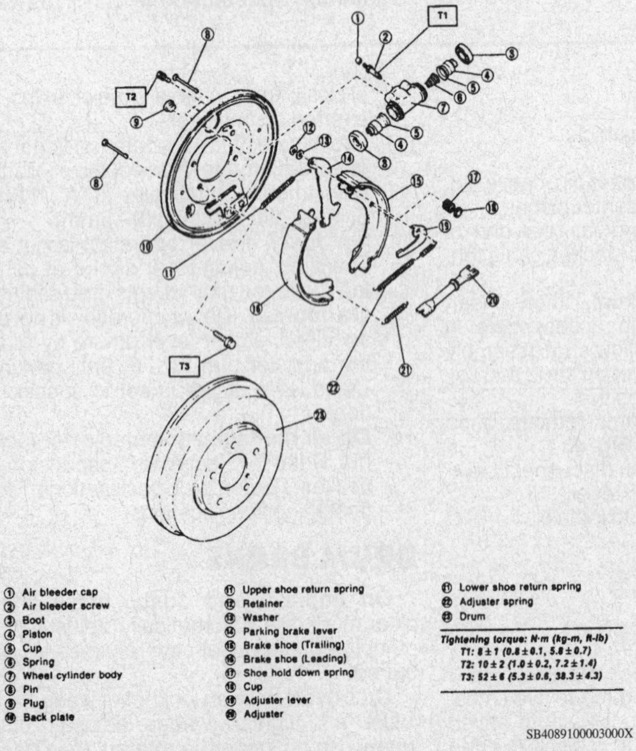
T1
T2
T3
① Air bleeder cap
② Air bleeder screw
③ Boot
④ Piston
⑤ Cup
⑥ Spring
⑦ Wheel cylinder body
⑧ Pin
⑨ Plug
⑩ Back plate
⑪ Upper shoe return spring
⑫ Retainer
⑬ Washer
⑭ Parking brake lever
⑮ Brake shoe (Trailing)
⑯ Brake shoe (Leading)
⑰ Shoe hold down spring
⑱ Cup
⑲ Adjuster lever
⑳ Adjuster
㉑ Lower shoe return spring
㉒ Adjuster spring
㉓ Drum
Tightening torque: N·m (kg-m, ft-lb)
T1: 8 ± 1 (0.8 ± 0.1, 5.8 ± 0.7)
T2: 10 ± 2 (1.0 ± 0.2, 7.2 ± 1.4)
T3: 52 ± 6 (5.3 ± 0.6, 38.3 ± 4.3)
SB4089100003000X

Fig. 3 Exploded view of drum brake assembly. Impreza & Legacy

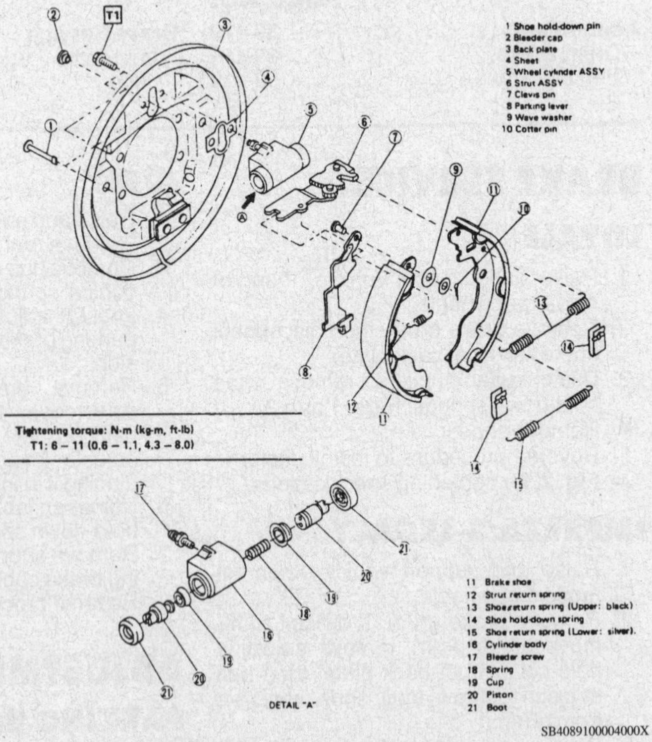
T1
1 Shoe hold-down pin
2 Bleeder cap
3 Back plate
4 Sheet
5 Wheel cylinder ASSY
6 Strut ASSY
7 Clevis pin
8 Parking lever
9 Wave washer
10 Cotter pin
A
Tightening torque: N·m (kg-m, ft-lb)
T1: 6 – 11 (0.6 – 1.1, 4.3 – 8.0)
11 Brake shoe
12 Strut return spring
13 Shoe return spring (Upper: black)
14 Shoe hold-down spring
15 Shoe return spring (Lower: silver).
16 Cylinder body
17 Bleeder screw
18 Spring
19 Cup
20 Piston
21 Boot
DETAIL "A"
SB4089100004000X

Fig. 4 Exploded view of drum brake assembly. Justy

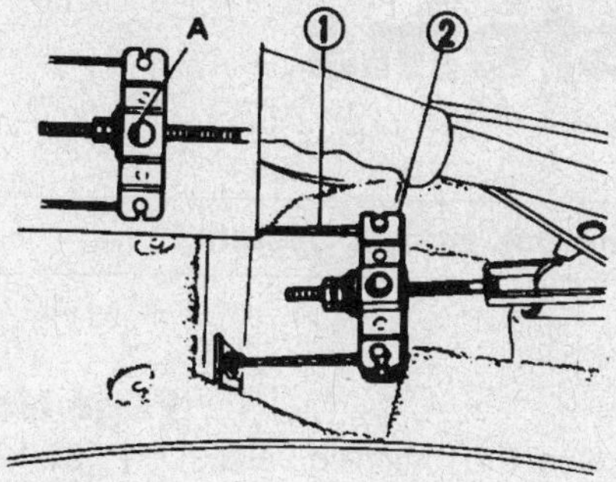
A
1
2

1 Cable
2 Equalizer

SB4089100005000X

Fig. 5 Parking brake adjustment. Loyale

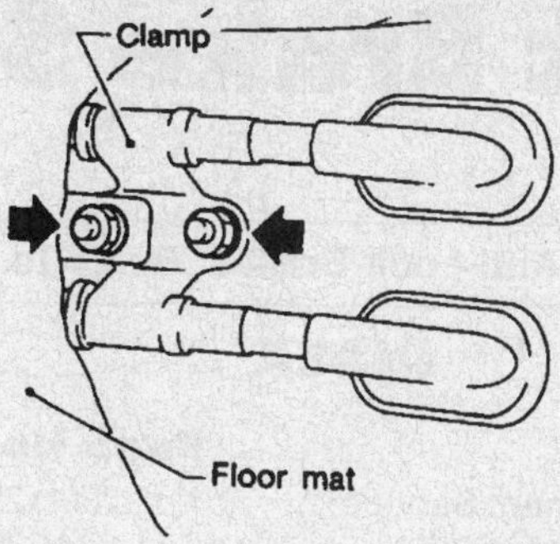
Clamp
Floor mat

SB4089100006000X

Fig. 6 Parking brake adjustment. Impreza

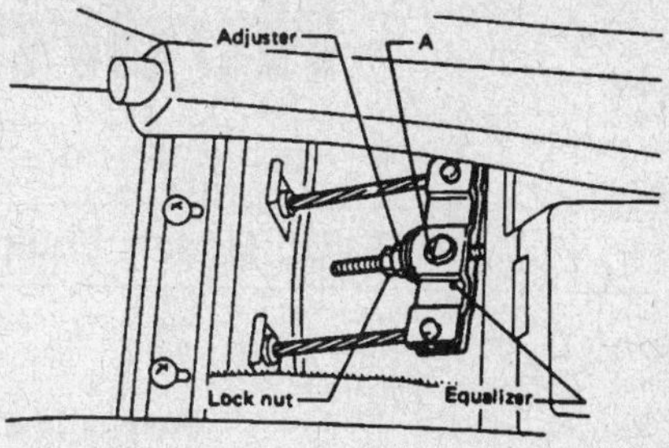
Adjuster
A
Lock nut
Equalizer

SB4089100007000X

Fig. 7 Brake adjustment. Loyale

DRUM BRAKE SPECIFICATIONS

Year	Model	Brake Drum Inside Dia. Inch	Maximum Refinish Dia. Inch
1993–94	Justy & Loyale	7.09	7.17
1993–96	Impreza & Legacy	9.0	9.079

TIGHTENING SPECIFICATIONS

Year	Component	Torque/Ft. Lbs.
IMPREZA & LEGACY		
1993–96	Air Bleeder Screw	5–6
	Adjuster Nut	9-11
	Backing Plate Nuts	34-41
	Wheel Cylinder Nuts	6-9
	Wheel Lug Nuts	58–72
JUSTY		
1993–94	Air Bleeder Screw	5-7
	Adjuster Nut	9-11
	Backing Plate Nuts	14-22
	Wheel Cylinder Nuts	5-8
	Wheel Lug Nuts	58–72
LOYALE		
1993–94	Air Bleeder Screw	5–6
	Adjuster Nut	9-11
	Backing Plate Nuts	33-43
	Wheel Cylinder Nuts	6-7
	Wheel Lug Nuts	58–72

Hydraulic Brake Systems

NOTE: On Models Equipped With Anti-Lock Brakes, Refer To "Anti-Lock Brakes System."

INDEX

	Page No.
Brake System Bleed	39-123
Component Replacement	39-122
Dual Proportioning Valve	39-122
Master Cylinder	39-122
Component Service	39-122
Master Cylinder	39-122
Description	39-122
Dual Proportioning Valve (DPV)	39-122
Master Cylinder	39-122
Troubleshooting	39-122

DESCRIPTION

MASTER CYLINDER

The master cylinder is of the tandem type design and incorporates a fast fill valve in order to improve the feeling on braking. It has a dual design which consists of a primary and a secondary brake system. If one brake system becomes inoperative, the other line will provide braking action. The master cylinder is designed into a "pierce" form so that the rear section is inserted into the brake booster.

DUAL PROPORTIONING VALVE (DPV)

The dual proportioning valve is incorporated as a rear wheel hydraulic pressure control system for the diagonal braking configuration. During hard braking, the DPV prevents rear wheel locking by lowering the fluid pressure in the rear wheel cylinder lower than that of the in the front cylinder.

TROUBLESHOOTING

Refer to **Fig. 1,** when troubleshooting the hydraulic braking system.

Trouble and possible cause	Corrective action
1 Insufficient braking	
(1) Oil leakage from the hydraulic mechanism	Repair or replace (cup, piston, cylinder, pipe or hose)
(2) Entry of air into the hydraulic mechanism	Bleed
(3) Excessively wide shoe clearance	Adjust the clearance
(4) Wear, deteriorated surface material, adhering water or oil on the lining	Replace, grind or clean
(5) Improper operation of master cylinder, wheel cylinder, disc caliper, brake booster or check valve	Correct or replace
2 Unstable or uneven braking	
(1) Oil on the lining drum or rotor	Eliminate cause of oil leakage, clean, or replace
(2) Drum or rotor eccentricity	Correct or replace the drum or rotor
(3) Worn brake drum, or damage to the drum caused by sand	Correct by grinding, or replace
(4) Improper lining contact, deteriorated surface material, improper interior material, or wear	Correct by grinding, or replace.
(5) Deformed backing plate	Correct or replace
(6) Improper tire inflation	Inflate to correct pressure
(7) Disordered wheel alignment	Adjust alignment
(8) Loosened backing plate or support installing bolts	Retighten
(9) Loosened rear wheel bearing	Retighten to normal tightening torque or replace
(10) Trouble in the hydraulic system	Replace the cylinder, brake pipe or hose.
(11) Uneven effect of the hand brake	Check, adjust, or replace the rear brake and cable system
3 Excessive pedal stroke	
(1) Entry of air into the hydraulic mechanism	Bleed
(2) Excessive play in the master cylinder push rod	Adjust
(3) Oil leakage from the hydraulic mechanism	Repair or replace (cup, piston, cylinder, pipe or hose).
(4) Improperly adjusted shoe clearance	Adjust
(5) Improper lining contact or worn lining	Correct or replace
4 Brake dragging or improper brake return	
(1) Insufficient pedal play	Adjust play
(2) Improper master cylinder push rod return	Clean or replace the cylinder
(3) Clogged hydraulic system	Replace
(4) Improper return or adjustment of hand brake	Correct or adjust
(5) Weakened spring tension or breakage of shoe return spring	Replace the spring
(6) Excessively narrow shoe clearance	Adjust the clearance
(7) Improper wheel cylinder operation	Correct or replace

SB4099100001010X

Fig. 1 Hydraulic brake system troubleshooting chart (Part 1 of 2)

COMPONENT REPLACEMENT

MASTER CYLINDER

1. Disconnect brake lines from master cylinder and plug the ends.
2. If applicable, disconnect fluid warning switch electrical connector.
3. Remove master cylinder retaining nuts and the master cylinder.
4. Reverse procedure to install.
5. Bleed hydraulic system after completing installation.

DUAL PROPORTIONING VALVE

Inspect brake line connections at DPV for fluid leakage. If leakage is found tighten lines or replace DPV.

1. Disconnect brake line flare nuts at all connections from DPV.
2. Remove retaining bolt, then DPV from vehicle. **Do not disassemble or adjust valve. The valve must be replaced as a unit.**
3. Reverse procedure to install, noting the following:
   a. **Torque** retaining bolt to 3–5 ft. lbs.
   b. **Torque** flare nuts to 11–14 ft. lbs.

COMPONENT SERVICE

MASTER CYLINDER

1. Remove master cylinder from vehicle.
2. Remove secondary piston stopper screw with screwdriver as shown in **Fig. 2.**
3. Push piston inward, then remove snap ring.
4. Apply pressure to piston assembly while Inserting a small screwdriver into window of piston retainer and raise piston retainer latch as shown in **Fig. 3.**
5. Remove primary and secondary piston assemblies. **Do not disassemble pistons. if disassembled, the spring settings will change.**
6. Inspect master cylinder inside diameter to piston clearance, Service limit is not to exceed 0.043 inch.
7. Clean all parts with clean brake fluid, **do not use part cleaning fluid or seals will swell.**
8. Coat master cylinder inner walls with clean brake fluid, then install secondary piston assembly from repair kit No. 725771240.
9. Install primary piston, then press piston into bore approximately 0.39 inch.
10. Install piston stopper screw and gasket assembly, then **torque** to 5–6.5 ft. lbs.
11. Apply pressure to primary piston, then install snap ring.
12. Install retainer **Fig. 3.** Ensure retainer

Trouble and possible cause	Corrective action
5. Brake noise (1) (creak sound)	
(1) Hardened or deteriorated lining	Replace the shoe ASSY or pad.
(2) Worn lining	Replace the shoe ASSY or pad.
(3) Loosened backing plate or support installing bolts	Retighten.
(4) Loose rear wheel bearing	Retighten to normal tightening torque.
(5) Dirty drum or rotor	Clean the drum or rotor, or clean and replace the brake ASSY
6. Brake noise (2) (hissing sound)	
(1) Worn lining	Replace the shoe ASSY or pad.
(2) Improperly installed shoe or pad	Correct or replace the shoe ASSY or pad
(3) Loose or bent drum or rotor	Retighten or replace.
7. Brake noise (3) (click sound)	
In the case of the front brake	
(1) Excessively worn pad or support	Replace the pad or the support.
In the case of the rear brake	
(1) Excessively worn shoe ridge	Replace the backing plate.
(2) Excessively worn wheel cylinder piston	Replace the wheel cylinder ASSY
(3) Lack of oil on the shoe ridge surface anchor	Add more grease.

SB4099100001020X

Fig. 1 Hydraulic brake system troubleshooting chart (Part 2 of 2)

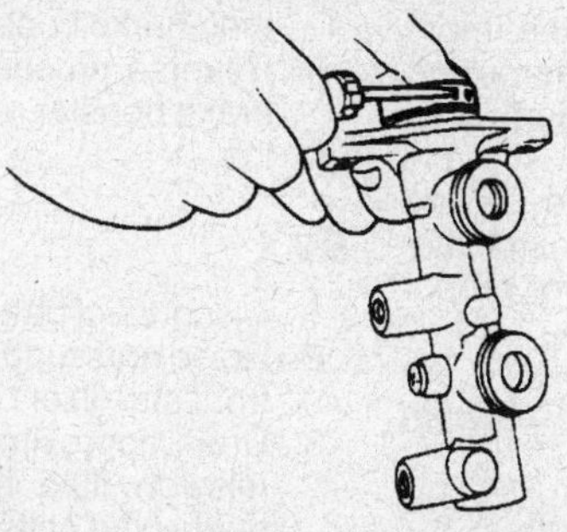

SB4099100003000X

Fig. 3 Removal of piston retainer

latch is securely engaged with master cylinder groove.

13. Install master cylinder in vehicle, then bleed brake system.

BRAKE SYSTEM BLEED

1. Ensure there are no fluid leaks from

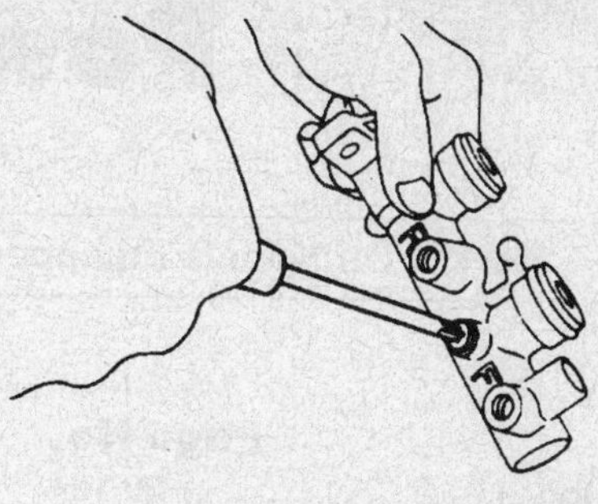

SB4099100002000X

Fig. 2 Secondary piston stopper screw location

joints or connections.

2. When bleeding brakes, bleed brakes connected to the secondary chamber of the master cylinder, then bleed brakes connected to the primary chamber of the master cylinder.
3. Fit one end of vinyl tube into air bleeder and put the other end into a brake fluid container.
4. Slowly depress brake pedal and keep it depressed, then slowly open air bleeder to discharge air together with brake fluid. Keep brake bleeder open for approximately 1 to 2 seconds.
5. Close bleeder and slowly release brake pedal.
6. Repeat steps 4 and 5 until there are no more air bubbles in the vinyl tube.
7. Repeat steps 3, 4 and 5 at each wheel.

Power Brake Units

NOTE: On Models Equipped With Anti-Lock Brakes, Refer To "Anti-Lock Brakes" Section.

INDEX

	Page No.
Description	39-124
Diagnosis & Testing	39-124
Power Brake Unit Service	39-124
Brake Booster, Replace	39-124
Overhaul	39-124

DESCRIPTION

The brake booster is located inline between the master cylinder and the brake pedal. It serves to mechanically boost the force pushing the pistons of the master cylinder.

The brake booster consists of a power cylinder section and a power piston section. The power cylinder is made up of a front shell, rear shell and a diaphragm. The front and rear shells are connected with the diaphragm placed in between the two. The power cylinder chamber is closed to the atmosphere and the left and right chambers of the diaphragm are kept sealed.

The power piston is guided by a tube which slides along the rear shell. A pushrod, which is used to move the primary piston of the master cylinder, is attached to the left of the power piston. The right end of the pushrod closely contacts the rubber reaction disc built into the power piston.

The valve plunger is clinched by the operating pushrod and is pushed against the right wall of the power piston chamber by the valve return spring. The check valve maintains a constant level of vacuum pressure within the brake booster that utilizes the intake manifold vacuum pressure for power.

DIAGNOSIS & TESTING

Perform this procedure with the parking brakes applied.

1. Start engine, then stop after one or two minutes of running time.
2. Depress brake pedal several times with normal force.
3. If pedal travel decreases the more times the brake pedal is depressed, the brake booster and vacuum lines are functioning correctly.
4. If pedal travel does not decrease and remains firm, check brake booster vacuum hose and check valve for proper operation.
5. If vacuum hose and check valve are functioning properly, replace vacuum booster assembly.

POWER BRAKE UNIT SERVICE

BRAKE BOOSTER, REPLACE

Except SVX

1. Disconnect brake fluid level indicator connector, if equipped.
2. Remove master cylinder assembly.
3. Disconnect vacuum hose from brake booster.
4. Working from inside the passenger compartment, remove snap pin and operating rod clevis pin from brake pedal assembly.
5. Remove brake booster retaining nuts, then brake booster from vehicle.
6. Reverse procedure to install. **Torque** brake booster retaining nuts to 9–17 ft. lbs.

SVX

1. Disconnect battery ground cable.
2. Raise and support vehicle and remove front stabilizer bar.
3. Drain approximately 1 quart of transmission fluid and loosen ATF level guide pipe bolts.
4. Remove cruise control actuator.
5. Disconnect positive terminal from starter motor.
6. Disconnect low-pressure AC pipe.
7. Disconnect vacuum hose from booster and remove master cylinder as outlined in "Hydraulic Brake System."
8. Remove snap pin, clevis pin and four brake booster to pedal bracket nuts, then the booster.
9. Reverse procedure to install.

OVERHAUL

The brake booster is not serviceable and must be replaced as an assembly.

Anti-Lock Brakes

TABLE OF CONTENTS

	Page No.
IMPREZA & 1995 LEGACY LESS TCS	39-135
SVX & 1993-94 LEGACY	39-125
1995 LEGACY w/TCS	39-144
1996 LEGACY w/Bosch 5.3	39-153

SVX & 1993-94 Legacy

NOTE: On Air Bag Equipped Models, Refer To "Air Bag System Precautions" Located In The Front Of This Manual For System Disarming & Arming Procedures.

NOTE: Wire Code Identification And Symbol Identification Located In The Front Of This Manual Can Be Used As An Aid When Using Wiring Circuits Found In This Section.

INDEX

	Page No.
Description	39-125
Diagnosis & Testing	39-125
Component	39-129
Speed Sensors	39-129
System	39-125
Trouble Code Diagnosis	39-125
Precautions	39-125
Air Bag Systems	39-125
System Service	39-129
Brake System Bleed	39-129
Legacy	39-129
SVX	39-129
Component Replacement	39-130
ABS Hydraulic Unit	39-130
Electronic Control Unit	39-131
Front Sensors	39-130
Rear Sensors	39-130
Troubleshooting	39-125

PRECAUTIONS

AIR BAG SYSTEMS

Refer to "Air Bag System Precautions" in the front of this manual for system disarming and arming procedures.

DESCRIPTION

The Anti-lock brake system (ABS) electrically controls brake fluid pressure to prevent wheel lock during braking on slippery road surfaces, improving steering stability and shortening the braking distance. If the ABS becomes inoperative, a fail-safe system activates to ensure conventional brake system operation.

The front and rear wheels utilize a four sensor, four channel control design. The front wheels have an independent design which controls fluid pressure to the left and right wheels. The rear wheels have a select low design, which provides the same pressure for the two rear wheels if either starts to lock.

The ABS consists of four tone wheels, four speed sensors, electronic control unit, a G sensor, and a warning lamp. Refer to **Figs. 1 through 4,** for ABS component location and function.

TROUBLESHOOTING

Refer to **Figs. 5 through 10,** for ABS troubleshooting procedures. The ABS control unit receives and sends signals that control system functions. It is important that these input/output signals be consistent. Refer to **Fig. 11,** for control unit and sensor voltage and resistance specifications and **Fig. 12,** for input/output wiring circuit.

DIAGNOSIS & TESTING

System

Both warning light and LED remain on unless the ignition is turned off. Only one trouble code is displayed at a time. If multiple problems occur, only the first problem detected is displayed, that problem must be repaired first in order to check for further trouble codes. If the LED does not activate even though the warning lamp is on, the power supply may be inoperative.

To perform self diagnosis, drive vehicle at a speed greater than 20 mph for at least one minute. If system is malfunctioning, a warning lamp on the dash panel will come on. Approximately ten seconds after the light comes on, an LED located on the ABS control unit displays a trouble code. This trouble code is determined by the number of flashes the LED emits. To read codes, vehicle must remain running. Read LED codes as shown in **Fig. 13.**

Refer to **Fig. 13,** for trouble code identification and **Figs. 14 and 15,** for ABS system wiring circuit.

TROUBLE CODE DIAGNOSIS

TROUBLE CODE 0

1. Turn ignition switch to off position, then disconnect connector from ABS control unit.
2. Disassemble connector as follows:
   a. While pushing 1, disconnect connector, **Fig. 16.**
   b. Remove screw from portion 2, the move rubber boot 3 toward harness.
   c. Slide cover 4 in direction shown by arrow and remove.
3. Turn ignition switch to on position, then measure voltage between control unit connector terminal 1 and ground. Voltage should be 10-12 volts.
4. Start engine, then measure voltage between control unit connector terminal 15 and ground. Voltage should be 13.5 volts.
5. Turn ignition switch to off position, then connect connector to ABS control unit.
6. Turn ignition switch to on position, then measure voltage between control unit connector terminal 20 and ground. Voltage should be 0 volt.
7. **On Legacy models,** turn ignition switch to off position, then disconnect connector from ABS control unit.
8. Measure resistance between control unit connector terminal 29 and ground. Resistance should be 1 Mohm.

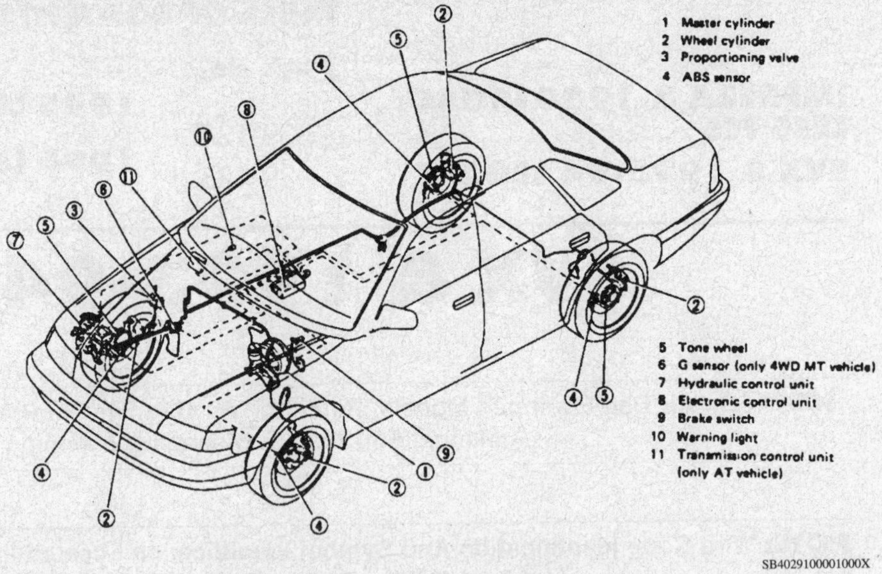
1 Master cylinder
2 Wheel cylinder
3 Proportioning valve
4 ABS sensor
5 Tone wheel
6 G sensor (only 4WD MT vehicle)
7 Hydraulic control unit
8 Electronic control unit
9 Brake switch
10 Warning light
11 Transmission control unit (only AT vehicle)
SB4029100001000X

Fig. 1 ABS component locations

TROUBLE CODE 1-4

Turn ignition switch on, then ground check-connector terminals, and check solenoid valve for operation. Each time solenoid activates, system circuit is interrupted. To check again, first turn ignition switch off then on.

1. **On Legacy models, proceed as follows:**
   a. If trouble code 1 is present, connect jumper wire between terminal 3 of check connector and ground. Listen for operation.
   b. If trouble code 2 is present, connect jumper wire between terminal 12 of check connector and ground. Listen for operation.
   c. If trouble code 3 is present, connect jumper wire between terminal 13 of check connector and ground. Listen for operation.
   d. If trouble code 4 is present, connect jumper wire between terminal 2 of check connector and ground. Listen for operation.
2. **On SVX models, proceed as follows:**
   a. If trouble code 1 is present, connect jumper wire between terminal 2 of check connector and ground. Listen for operation.
   b. If trouble code 2 is present, connect jumper wire between terminal 11 of check connector and ground. Listen for operation.
   c. If trouble code 3 is present, connect jumper wire between terminal 12 of check connector and ground. Listen for operation.
   d. If trouble code 4 is present, connect jumper wire between terminal 3 of check connector and ground. Listen for operation.
3. **On all models,** turn ignition switch to on position.
4. If trouble code 1 is present, measure voltage between control unit connector terminal 2 and ground. Voltage should be 0 volt with solenoid in operation.
5. If trouble code 2 is present, measure voltage between control unit connector terminal 35 and ground. Voltage should be 0 volt with solenoid in operation.
6. If trouble code 3 is present, measure voltage between control unit connector terminal 19 and ground. Voltage should be 0 volt with solenoid in operation.
7. If trouble code 4 is present, measure voltage between control unit connector terminal 18 and ground. Voltage should be 0 volt with solenoid in operation.

TROUBLE CODE 5 & 6

Use a digital circuit tester for this diagnostic procedure.

1. Disconnect connector from ABS control unit, then raise and support vehicle.
2. If trouble code 5 is present, measure voltage between ABS control unit connector terminals 4 and 5 on FWD Legacy models or terminals 4 and 22 on SVX and AWD Legacy models. Voltage should be 200-300 mVolts. At a creep speed on automatic transmission models.
3. If trouble code 6 is present, measure voltage between ABS control unit connector terminals 11 and 21. Voltage should be 200-300 mVolts. At a creep speed on automatic transmission models.
4. Disconnect ABS control unit connector.
5. If trouble code 5 is present, measure resistance between control unit connector terminal 5 on FWD Legacy models or terminal 22 on SVX and AWD Legacy models and ground. Resistance should be 1 Mohm minimum.
6. If trouble code 6 is present, measure resistance between control unit connector terminal 21 and ground. Resistance should be 1 Mohm minimum.
7. Disconnect sensor connector.
8. If trouble code 5 is present, measure resistance between lefthand sensor terminals. Resistance should be 800–1300 ohms.
9. If trouble code 6 is present, measure resistance between righthand sensor terminals. Resistance should be 800–1300 ohms.
10. Measure resistance between left or right sensor terminal 1 and ground. Resistance should be 1 Mohm minimum.

TROUBLE CODE 7 & 8

Use a digital circuit tester for this diagnostic procedure.

1. Disconnect connector from ABS control unit, then raise and support vehicle.
2. If trouble code 7 is present, measure voltage between ABS control unit connector terminals 24 and 26. Voltage should be 200-300 mVolts. At a creep speed on automatic transmission models.
3. If trouble code 8 is present, measure voltage between ABS control unit connector terminals 7 and 9. Voltage should be 200-300 mVolts. At a creep speed on automatic transmission models.
4. Disconnect ABS control unit connector.
5. If trouble code 7 is present, measure resistance between control unit connector terminal 26 and ground. Resistance should be 1 Mohm minimum.
6. If trouble code 8 is present, measure resistance between control unit connector terminal 9 and ground. Resistance should be 1 Mohm minimum.
7. Disconnect sensor connector.
8. If trouble code 7 is present, measure resistance between righthand sensor terminals. Resistance should be 800–1300 ohms.
9. If trouble code 8 is present, measure resistance between lefthand sensor terminals. Resistance should be 800–1300 ohms.
10. Measure resistance between left or right sensor terminal 1 and ground. Resistance should be 1 Mohm minimum.

TROUBLE CODE 9

Legacy

1. Turn ignition switch to off position, then disconnect ABS control unit connector.
2. Disassemble ABS control unit connector, then measure resistance between control unit connector terminals 17 and 28. Resistance should be 45-55 ohms.
3. Disconnect connectors from hydraulic unit.
4. Measure resistance between hydraulic unit connector F8 terminal 2 and connector F9 terminal 4. Resistance should be 1 Mohm minimum.
5. Remove motor relay, then attach tester probes as shown in **Fig. 17.** Resistance should be 0 ohms when 12 volts are applied or 1 Mohms when no voltage is applied.

Item	Function
Tone wheel	Attached to each wheel hub and rotates at the same speed as the hub.
Speed sensor	Emits a wheel speed signal during tone wheel rotation.
Electronic control unit	Receives wheel-speed signals from speed sensors and sends a control signal to hydraulic unit so that fluid pressure is optimally controlled.
Hydraulic control unit	Receives a control signal from electronic control unit and controls respective wheel cylinder fluid pressure.
G sensor (4WD manual transmission model)	Detects vehicle deceleration.
Warning lamp	Comes on when ABS becomes inoperative.

SB4029100002000X

Fig. 2 ABS components

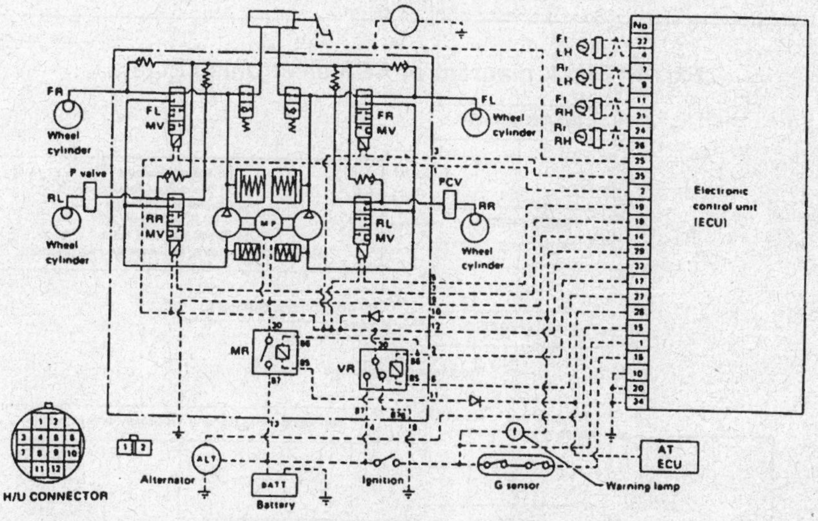

FR
FL
RL
RR
Wheel cylinder
P valve
PCV
MR
VR
Electronic control unit (ECU)
AT ECU
H/U CONNECTOR
Alternator
Battery
Ignition
G sensor
Warning lamp

SB4029100003000X

Fig. 3 ABS system diagram

6. Disconnect connector from hydraulic unit.
7. Measure resistance between hydraulic unit terminals 5 and 6. Resistance should be 45-55 ohms.
   a. When resistance checks out unsatisfactory, check relay as a single unit. If resistance checks out satisfactory, replace hydraulic unit. If resistance checks out unsatisfactory, repair harness connector between ABS control unit and hydraulic unit.
8. Disconnect connectors from ABS control unit and hydraulic unit.
9. Measure resistance between hydraulic unit connector F9 terminal 6 and control unit connector terminal 28. Resistance should be 0 ohm.
10. Measure resistance between hydraulic unit connector F9 terminal 5 and control unit connector terminal 17. Resistance should be 0 ohm.
11. Measure resistance between hydraulic unit connector F9 terminal 6 and ground. Resistance should be 1 Mohm minimum.
12. Measure resistance between hydraulic unit connector F9 terminal 4 and ground. Resistance should be 1 Mohm minimum.
13. Turn ignition switch to on position, then measure voltage between hydraulic unit connector F8 terminal 2 and ground. Voltage should be 10-12 volts.

SVX

1. Turn ignition switch to off position, then disconnect ABS control unit connector.
2. Disassemble ABS control unit connector, then measure resistance between control unit connector terminals 17 and 28. Resistance should be 45-55 ohms.
3. Disconnect connectors from hydraulic unit.
4. Measure resistance between hydraulic unit connector F43 terminal 2 and connector R1 terminal 4. Resistance should be 1 Mohm minimum.
5. Remove motor relay, then attach tester probes as shown in **Fig. 17.** Resistance should be 0 ohms when 12 volts are applied or 1 Mohms when no voltage is applied.
6. Disconnect connector from hydraulic unit.
7. Measure resistance between hydraulic unit terminals 5 and 6. Resistance should be 45-55 ohms.
   a. When resistance checks out unsatisfactory, check relay as a single unit. If resistance checks out satisfactory, replace hydraulic unit. If resistance checks out unsatisfactory, repair harness connector between ABS control unit and hydraulic unit.
8. Disconnect connectors from ABS control unit and hydraulic unit.
9. Measure resistance between hydraulic unit connector R1 terminal 5 and control unit connector terminal 28. Resistance should be 0 ohm.
10. Measure resistance between hydraulic unit connector R1 terminal 6 and control unit connector terminal 17. Resistance should be 0 ohm.
11. Measure resistance between hydraulic unit connector R1 terminal 5 and ground. Resistance should be 1 Mohm minimum.
12. Measure resistance between hydraulic unit connector R1 terminal 7 and ground. Resistance should be 1 Mohm minimum.
13. Turn ignition switch to on position, then measure voltage between hydraulic unit connector F43 terminal 2 and ground. Voltage should be 10-12 volts.

TROUBLE CODE 10

Legacy

1. Turn ignition switch to off position, then disconnect ABS control unit connector.
2. Disassemble ABS control unit connector, then measure resistance between control unit connector terminals 17 and 27. Resistance should be 93-113 ohms.
3. Disconnect connectors from hydraulic unit.
4. Measure resistance between hydraulic unit connector F8 terminal 1 and connector F9 terminal 8. Resistance should be 1 Mohm minimum.
5. Remove valve relay, then attach tester probes as shown in **Fig. 18.**
   a. With terminals 30 and 87 connected. Resistance should be 0 ohms when 12 volts are applied or 1 Mohms when no voltage is applied.
   b. With terminals 30 and 87a connected. Resistance should be 1 Mohm when 12 volts are applied or 0 ohms when no voltage is applied.
6. Disconnect connector from hydraulic unit.
7. Measure resistance between hydraulic unit terminals 5 and 7. Resistance should be 72-88 ohms. When resistance checks out unsatisfactory, check relay as a single unit.
8. Disconnect connectors from ABS control unit and hydraulic unit, then measure as follows:
   a. Measure resistance between hydraulic unit connector F9 terminal 5 and control unit connector terminal 17. Resistance should be 0 ohm.

b. Measure resistance between hydraulic unit connector F9 terminal 7 and control unit connector terminal 27. Resistance should be 0 ohm.
c. Measure resistance between hydraulic unit connector F9 terminal 5 and ground. Resistance should be 1 Mohm minimum.
d. Measure resistance between hydraulic unit connector F9 terminal 7 and ground. Resistance should be 1 Mohm minimum.
e. If the above resistances are satisfactory, replace hydraulic unit. If the above resistance are unsatisfactory, repair harness/connector between ABS control unit and hydraulic unit.

9. Turn ignition switch to on position, then measure voltage between hydraulic unit connector F8 terminal 1 and ground. Voltage should be 10-12 volts.

SVX

1. Turn ignition switch to off position, then disconnect ABS control unit connector.
2. Disassemble ABS control unit connector, then measure resistance between control unit connector terminals 17 and 27. Resistance should be 80-90 ohms.
3. Disconnect connectors from hydraulic unit.
4. Measure resistance between hydraulic unit connector F43 terminal 1 and connector R1 terminal 11. Resistance should be 1 Mohm minimum.
5. Remove valve relay, then attach tester probes as shown in **Fig. 18.**
   a. With terminals 30 and 87 connected. Resistance should be 0 ohms when 12 volts are applied or 1 Mohms when no voltage is applied.
   b. With terminals 30 and 87a connected. Resistance should be 1 Mohm when 12 volts are applied or 0 ohms when no voltage is applied.
6. Disconnect connector from hydraulic unit.
7. Measure resistance between hydraulic unit terminals 6 and 12. Resistance should be 80-90 ohms. When resistance checks out unsatisfactory, check relay as a single unit.
8. Disconnect connectors from ABS control unit and hydraulic unit, then measure as follows:
   a. Measure resistance between hydraulic unit connector R1 terminal 6 and control unit connector terminal 17. Resistance should be 0 ohm.
   b. Measure resistance between hydraulic unit connector R1 terminal 12 and control unit connector terminal 27. Resistance should be 0 ohm.
   c. Measure resistance between hydraulic unit connector R1 terminal 6 and ground. Resistance should be 1 Mohm minimum.
   d. Measure resistance between hydraulic unit connector R1 terminal 12 and ground. Resistance should be 1 Mohm minimum.
   e. If the above resistances are satisfactory, replace hydraulic unit. If the above resistance are unsatisfactory, repair harness/connector between ABS control unit and hydraulic unit.
9. Turn ignition switch to on position, then measure voltage between hydraulic unit connector F43 terminal 1 and ground. Voltage should be 10-12 volts.

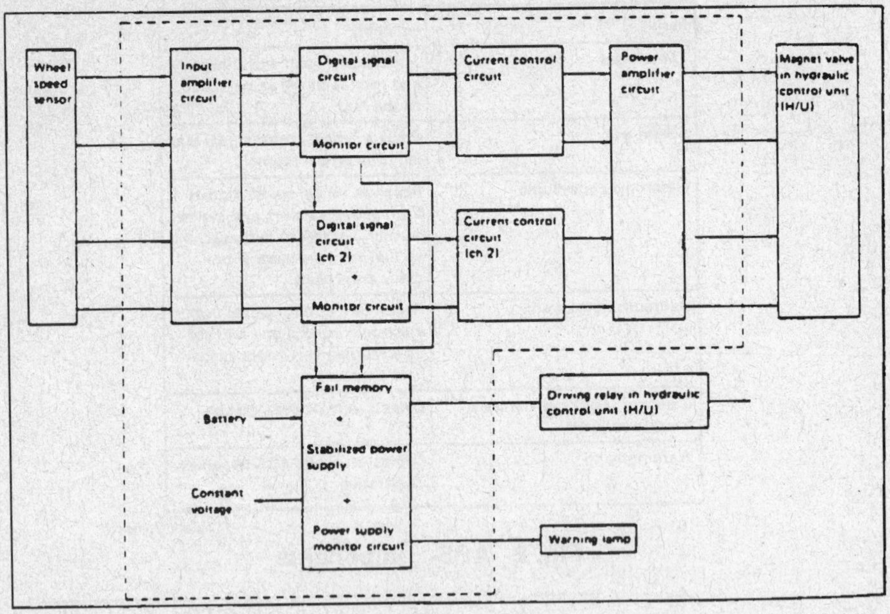
Wheel speed sensor
Input amplifier circuit
Digital signal circuit
Monitor circuit
Current control circuit
Power amplifier circuit
Magnet valve in hydraulic control unit (H/U)
Digital signal circuit (ch 2)
Current control circuit (ch 2)
Monitor circuit
Fail memory
Battery
Stabilized power supply
Constant voltage
Power supply monitor circuit
Driving relay in hydraulic control unit (H/U)
Warning lamp

SB4029100004000X

Fig. 4 Block diagram of ABS electronic circuits

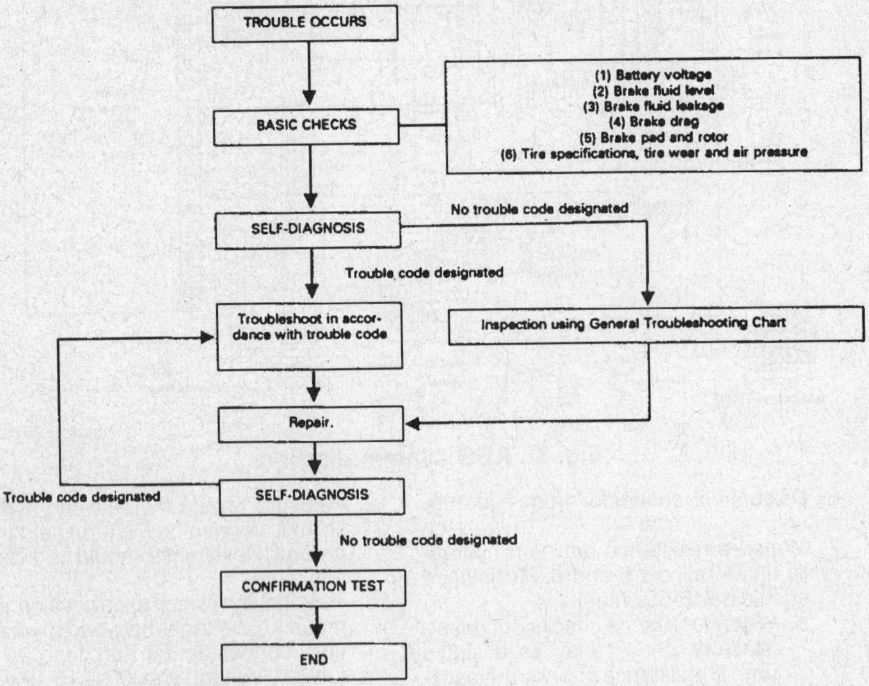
TROUBLE OCCURS
BASIC CHECKS
(1) Battery voltage
(2) Brake fluid level
(3) Brake fluid leakage
(4) Brake drag
(5) Brake pad and rotor
(6) Tire specifications, tire wear and air pressure
SELF-DIAGNOSIS
No trouble code designated
Trouble code designated
Troubleshoot in accordance with trouble code
Inspection using General Troubleshooting Chart
Repair.
Trouble code designated
SELF-DIAGNOSIS
No trouble code designated
CONFIRMATION TEST
END

SB4029100005000X

Fig. 5 Troubleshooting chart (basic)

TROUBLE CODE 16

Legacy

1. Position vehicle on a flat surface, then disconnect ABS control unit connector.
2. Disassemble ABS control unit connector, then measure resistance between control unit connector terminals 1 and 16. Resistance should be 550-670 ohms.
3. Disconnect G sensor connector, then measure resistance between G sensor terminals. Resistance should be 550-670 ohms. Ensure sensor is horizontal during measurement.
4. Turn ignition switch to on position, then connect G sensor connector.
   a. Measure voltage between sensor connector terminal 2 and ground. Voltage should be 10-12 volts.
   b. Measure voltage between control unit connector terminal 16 and

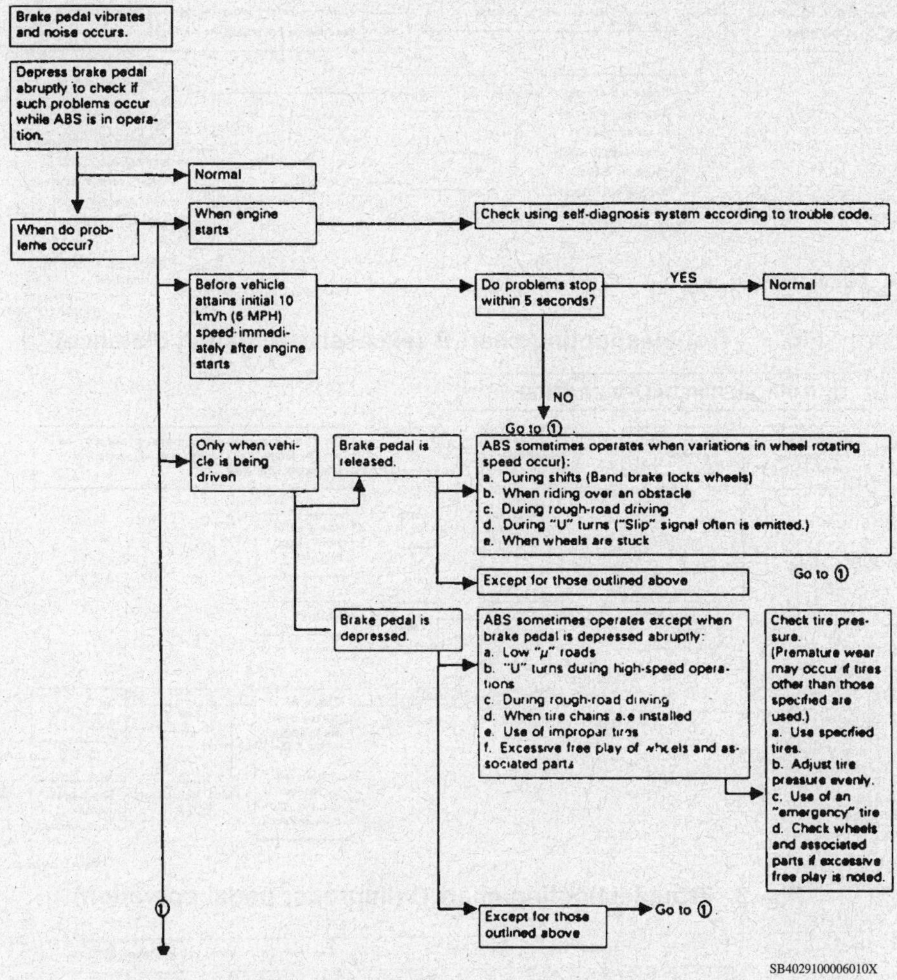
Brake pedal vibrates and noise occurs.
Depress brake pedal abruptly to check if such problems occur while ABS is in operation.
Normal
When do problems occur?
When engine starts
Check using self-diagnosis system according to trouble code.
Before vehicle attains initial 10 km/h (6 MPH) speed immediately after engine starts
Do problems stop within 5 seconds?
YES
Normal
NO
Go to ①
Only when vehicle is being driven
Brake pedal is released.
ABS sometimes operates when variations in wheel rotating speed occur):
a. During shifts (Band brake locks wheels)
b. When riding over an obstacle
c. During rough-road driving
d. During "U" turns ("Slip" signal often is emitted.)
e. When wheels are stuck
Except for those outlined above
Go to ①
Brake pedal is depressed.
ABS sometimes operates except when brake pedal is depressed abruptly:
a. Low "μ" roads
b. "U" turns during high-speed operations
c. During rough-road driving
d. When tire chains are installed
e. Use of improper tires
f. Excessive free play of wheels and associated parts
Check tire pressure. (Premature wear may occur if tires other than those specified are used.)
a. Use specified tires.
b. Adjust tire pressure evenly.
c. Use of an "emergency" tire
d. Check wheels and associated parts if excessive free play is noted.
Except for those outlined above
Go to ①
①
SB4029100006010X

Fig. 6 Troubleshooting chart A (Part 1 of 2). Vibrating pedal & noise

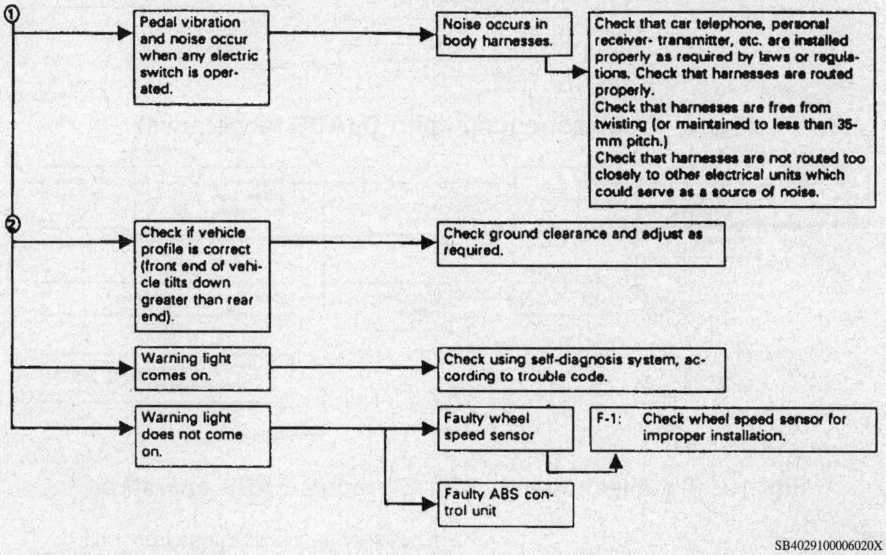
①
Pedal vibration and noise occur when any electric switch is operated.
Noise occurs in body harnesses.
Check that car telephone, personal receiver- transmitter, etc. are installed properly as required by laws or regulations. Check that harnesses are routed properly.
Check that harnesses are free from twisting (or maintained to less than 35-mm pitch.)
Check that harnesses are not routed too closely to other electrical units which could serve as a source of noise.
②
Check if vehicle profile is correct (front end of vehicle tilts down greater than rear end).
Check ground clearance and adjust as required.
Warning light comes on.
Check using self-diagnosis system, according to trouble code.
Warning light does not come on.
Faulty wheel speed sensor
F-1: Check wheel speed sensor for improper installation.
Faulty ABS control unit
SB4029100006020X

Fig. 6 Troubleshooting chart A (Part 2 of 2). Vibrating pedal & noise

ground. Voltage should be 10-12 volts.

c. When resistance is satisfactory, replace ABS control unit.

SVX

1. To check power supply to ABS control unit, refer to "Trouble Code 0."
2. To check ABS sensor, refer to "Trouble Code 5 and 6" and "Trouble Code 7 and 8."

Component

SPEED SENSORS

1. Check pole piece of speed sensor for damage or foreign materials. Clean or replace as needed.
2. Measure resistance between speed sensor terminals. Refer to **Fig. 19,** for specifications. If resistance is not within specifications replace wheel sensor or adjust gap between sensor and tone wheel.
3. Check tone wheels teeth for cracks or dents. Replace if needed.
4. Clearances should be measured one at a time to ensure tone wheel and speed sensor are installed properly. Clearances are as follow:
   a. On except SVX models, front .039–.059 inch. On SVX models, .028–.039 inch
   b. On except SVX models, rear .031–.051 inch. On SVX models, .020–.039 inch.
5. If clearance is narrow, adjust by using spacer part No. 26755AA000. If clearance is to wide check output voltage, replace speed sensor or tone wheel if output voltage is not within specifications. Refer to **Fig. 20.**
6. Output voltage can be checked by installing resistor and condenser as shown in **Fig. 21,** then rotating wheel at 1.7 mph.

SYSTEM SERVICE

Brake System Bleed

LEGACY

1. Bleed air from primary circuit between unit and master cylinder using secondary air bleeder on top of hydraulic unit, **Fig. 22. Torque** bleeder screws to 5–6.5 ft. lbs.
2. Bleed air from primary line between unit and wheel cylinder using bleeder on front RH wheel cylinder.
3. Bleed air from air bleeder on rear LH wheel cylinder.
4. Bleed air from secondary circuit between unit and master cylinder using primary air bleeder on top of hydraulic unit.
5. Bleed air from secondary line between hydraulic unit and wheel cylinder using air bleeder on front LH wheel cylinder.
6. Bleed air from air bleeder on rear RH wheel cylinder.

SVX

Follow sequence in **Figs. 23 and 24. Torque** bleeder screws to 5–6.5 ft. lbs.

Component Replacement

FRONT SENSORS

1. Disconnect front speed sensor located in engine compartment, then remove bolts which secure harness to bracket. **Do not do damage pole piece located at tip of sensor during removal.**
2. Remove disc brake caliper and rotor from housing.
3. Remove front driveshaft, housing, then hub assembly.
4. Remove tone wheel while removing hub from housing and assembly. Refer to **Fig. 25.**
5. Reverse procedure to install, noting the following:
   a. Place a feeler gauge between speed sensors pole piece and tone wheels tooth face, on except SVX models, adjust clearance between .039–.059 inch. On SVX models, adjust clearance between .028–.039 inch.
   b. After clearance is obtained tighten speed sensor to housing.

REAR SENSORS

1. Remove rear seat, disconnect rear speed sensor and remove sensor harness bracket from rear trailing link.
2. Remove backing plate from speed sensor, then remove tone wheel from housing and hub assembly. **Do not damage pole piece of sensor and teeth of tone wheel during removal.**
3. Reverse procedures to install, noting the following:
   a. Place a feeler gauge between speed sensors pole piece and tone wheels tooth face, adjust clearance on except SVX models to .031–.051 inch or .020–.039 inch on SVX models.
   b. After clearance is obtained tighten speed sensor to backing plate.

ABS HYDRAULIC UNIT

REPLACEMENT

Legacy

1. Remove canister from engine compartment, then disconnect lines from hydraulic unit, and plug open ports to prevent foreign particles from entering unit. **Fig. 26 and 27.**
2. Remove relay box cover, **Fig. 28,** then bolts which secure hydraulic unit to bracket, then remove unit from vehicle noting the following precautions:
   a. Hydraulic unit cannot be disassembled. Do not attempt to loosen nuts and bolts.
   b. Do not drop or bump hydraulic unit.
   c. Do not turn hydraulic unit upside down or place it on is side.
   d. Be careful to prevent foreign particles from getting into hydraulic unit.
3. Reverse procedure to install. **Torque** hydraulic unit attaching bolts to 17–31 ft. lbs.

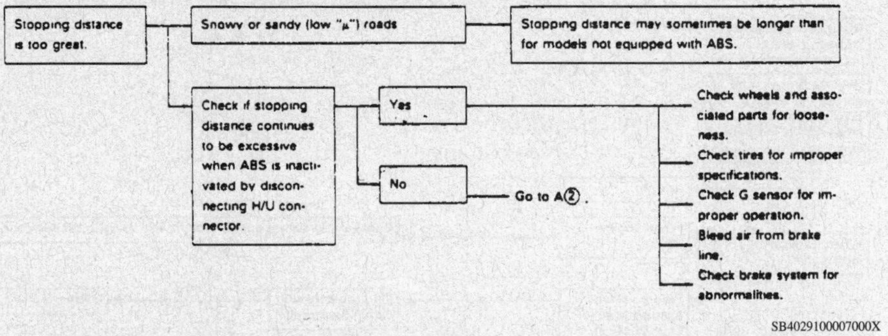

Stopping distance is too great.
Snowy or sandy (low "μ") roads
Stopping distance may sometimes be longer than for models not equipped with ABS.
Check if stopping distance continues to be excessive when ABS is inactivated by disconnecting H/U connector.
Yes
No
Go to A②.
Check wheels and associated parts for looseness.
Check tires for improper specifications.
Check G sensor for improper operation.
Bleed air from brake line.
Check brake system for abnormalities.
SB4029100007000X

Fig. 7 Troubleshooting chart B (excessive stopping distance)

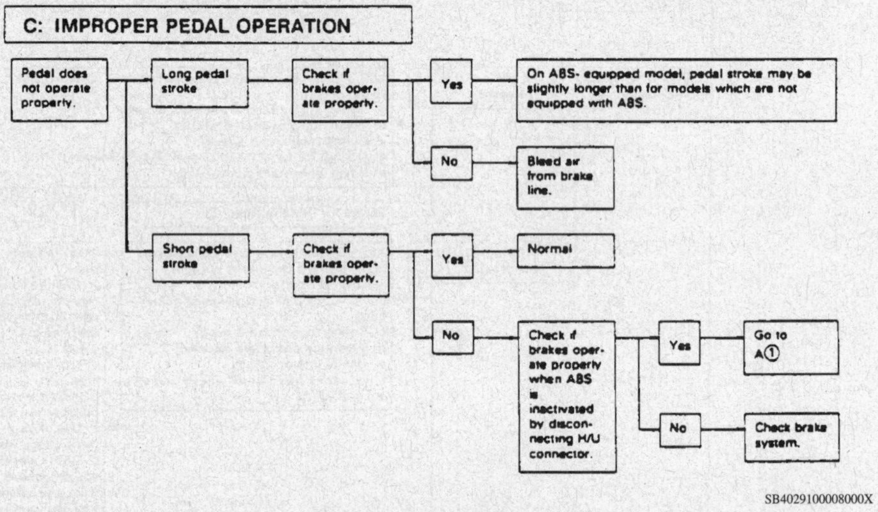

C: IMPROPER PEDAL OPERATION
Pedal does not operate properly.
Long pedal stroke
Check if brakes operate properly.
Yes
On ABS-equipped model, pedal stroke may be slightly longer than for models which are not equipped with ABS.
No
Bleed air from brake line.
Short pedal stroke
Check if brakes operate properly.
Yes
Normal
No
Check if brakes operate properly when ABS is inactivated by disconnecting H/U connector.
Yes
Go to A①
No
Check brake system.
SB4029100008000X

Fig. 8 Troubleshooting chart C (improper pedal operation)

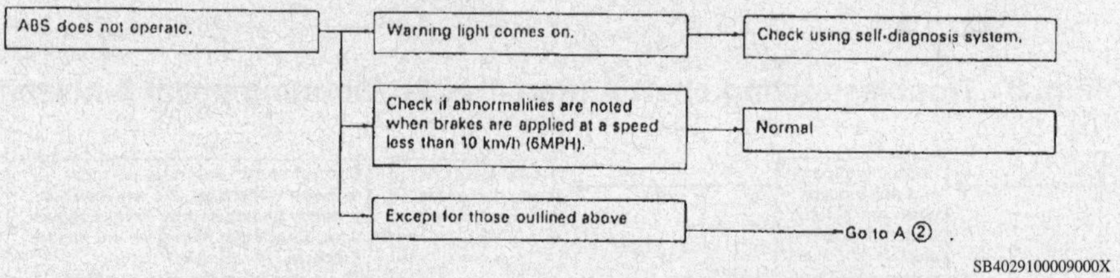

ABS does not operate.
Warning light comes on.
Check using self-diagnosis system.
Check if abnormalities are noted when brakes are applied at a speed less than 10 km/h (6MPH).
Normal
Except for those outlined above
Go to A ②.
SB4029100009000X

Fig. 9 Troubleshooting chart D (ABS inoperative)

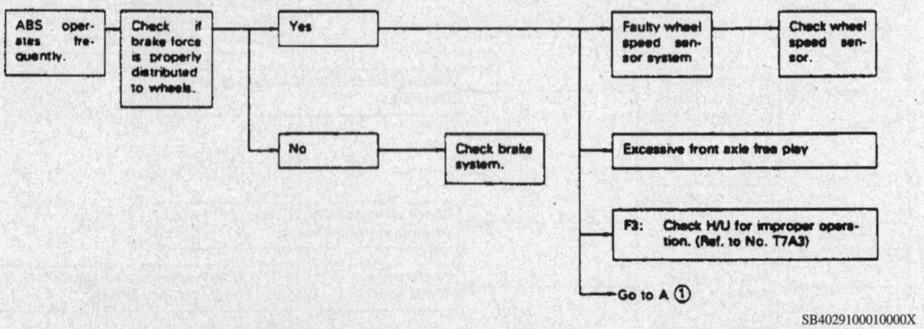

ABS operates frequently.
Check if brake force is properly distributed to wheels.
Yes
No
Check brake system.
Faulty wheel speed sensor system
Check wheel speed sensor.
Excessive front axle free play
F3: Check H/U for improper operation. (Ref. to No. T7A3)
Go to A ①
SB4029100010000X

Fig. 10 Troubleshooting chart E (frequent ABS operation)

SVX

1. Disconnect battery ground cable.
2. Disconnect hydraulic unit electrical connector.
3. Disconnect air flow meter connector.
4. Remove upper and lower air cleaner cover.
5. Disconnect brake lines from unit.
6. Remove hydraulic unit noting the following:
   a. Hydraulic unit cannot be disassembled. Do not attempt to loosen nuts and bolts.
   b. Do not drop or bump hydraulic unit.
   c. Do not turn hydraulic unit upside

Contents			Terminal No.	With engine idling	Input/output signals	
					Measured value	Measuring conditions
Wheel speed sensors	Left front wheel GND		22 4	0 V	200 – 300 mV	• No. 22 – No. 4 • Vehicle speed 2.75 km/h (1.7 MPH)
	Right front wheel GND		11 21	0 V	200 – 300 mV	• No. 11 – No. 21 • Vehicle speed 2.75 km/h (1.7 MPH)
	Left rear wheel GND		7 9	0 V	200 – 300 mV	• No. 7 – No. 9 • Vehicle speed 2.75 km/h (1.7 MPH)
	Right rear wheel GND		24 26	0 V	200 – 300 mV	• No. 24 – No. 26 • Vehicle speed 2.75 km/h (1.7 MPH)
G senor			16	13 – 14 V	0 V	
Stop light switch			25	0 V	13 – 14 V	When brake pedal is depressed.
Motor monitoring			14	0 V	13 – 14 V	When motor operates.
Valve power-supply monitoring			32	13 – 14 V	13 – 14 V	–
Hydraulic unit	Solenoid	Left front wheel	2	13 – 14 V	0 V	When solenoid is energized to produce output.
		Right front wheel	35	13 – 14 V	0 V	
		Left rear wheel	18	13 – 14 V	0 V	
		Right rear wheel	19	13 – 14 V	0 V	
	Valve relay coil		27	0 V	0 V	–
	Motor relay coil		28	13 – 14 V	0 V	When motor operates to produce output
Warning light			29	70 mV	0 V	When warning activates to produce output or when valve relay is OFF
Power supply	Alternator		15	13 – 14 V	1.7 V	Ignition switch ON (Engine OFF)
	Battery		1	13 – 14 V	13 – 14 V	–
	Relay coil (valve, motor, etc)		17	13 – 14 V	13 – 14 V	–

SB4029100011000X

Fig. 11 ABS control unit I/O signal

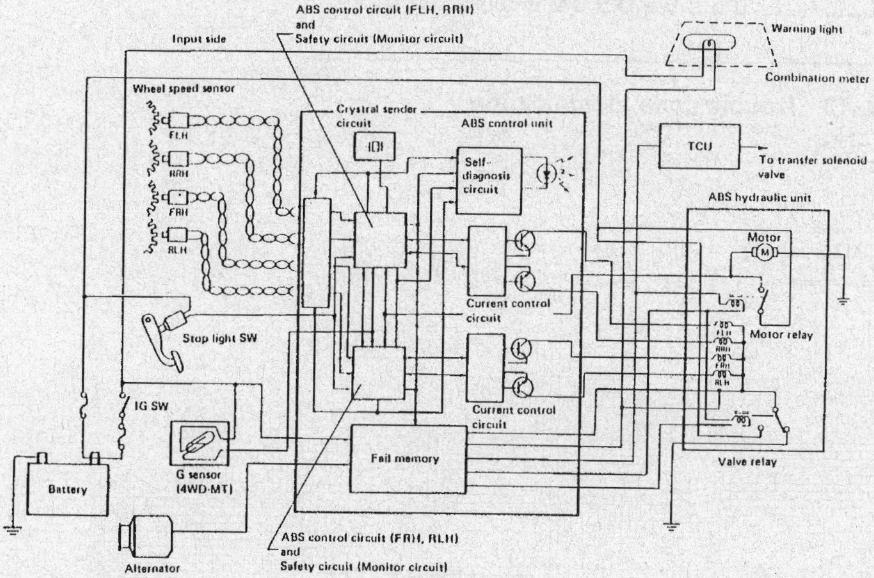
ABS control circuit (FLH, RRH)
and
Safety circuit (Monitor circuit)
Input side
Warning light
Combination meter
Wheel speed sensor
FLH
RRH
FRH
RLH
Crystal sender circuit
ABS control unit
Self-diagnosis circuit
TCU
To transfer solenoid valve
ABS hydraulic unit
Motor
M
Motor relay
Current control circuit
Current control circuit
Stop light SW
IG SW
G sensor
(4WD-MT)
Battery
Fail memory
Valve relay
Alternator
ABS control circuit (FRH, RLH)
and
Safety circuit (Monitor circuit)

SB4029100012000X

Fig. 12 I/O signal diagram

down or place it on is side.

d. Ensure care is taken to prevent foreign particles from getting into hydraulic unit.

7. Reverse procedure to install. **Torque hydraulic unit attaching bolts to 17–31 ft. lbs.**

INSPECTION

Legacy

1. Check bracket on vehicle, then all connectors.
2. Open hydraulic unit relay box and check for open or shorted circuits, **Fig. 29.**

SVX

1. Check bracket on vehicle, then all connectors.
2. Open hydraulic unit relay box and check for open or shorted circuits, **Fig. 30.**

ELECTRONIC CONTROL UNIT

1. Remove floor mat located under lower right side of front seat, then bolts that secure control unit, **Fig. 31.**
2. Remove screws that secure connector to unit, disconnect connector, then remove control unit.
3. Reverse procedure to install, checking that all connectors are connected properly.

Trouble code	Contents of diagnosis	
0 (LED OFF)	Improper power line voltage or faulty harness	
1	Broken or shorted solenoid valve circuit(s) in hydraulic unit	Left front wheel
2		Right front wheel
3		Right rear wheel
4		Left rear wheel
5	Faulty wheel speed sensor	Left front wheel
6		Right front wheel
7		Right rear wheel
8		Left rear wheel
9	Faulty motor and/or motor relay or broken or shorted harness circuit	
10	Faulty valve relay or broken or shorted harness circuit	
16	Faulty ABS control unit or G sensor or broken or shorted harness circuit	

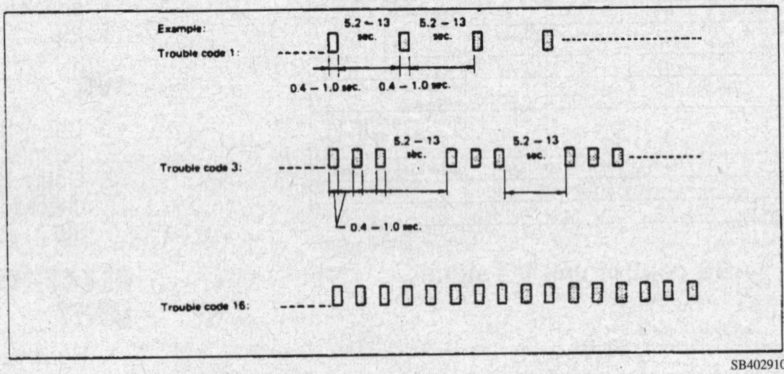
Example:
Trouble code 1:
5.2 – 13 sec.
0.4 – 1.0 sec.
Trouble code 3:
Trouble code 16:

SB4029100013000X

Fig. 13 Trouble code identification

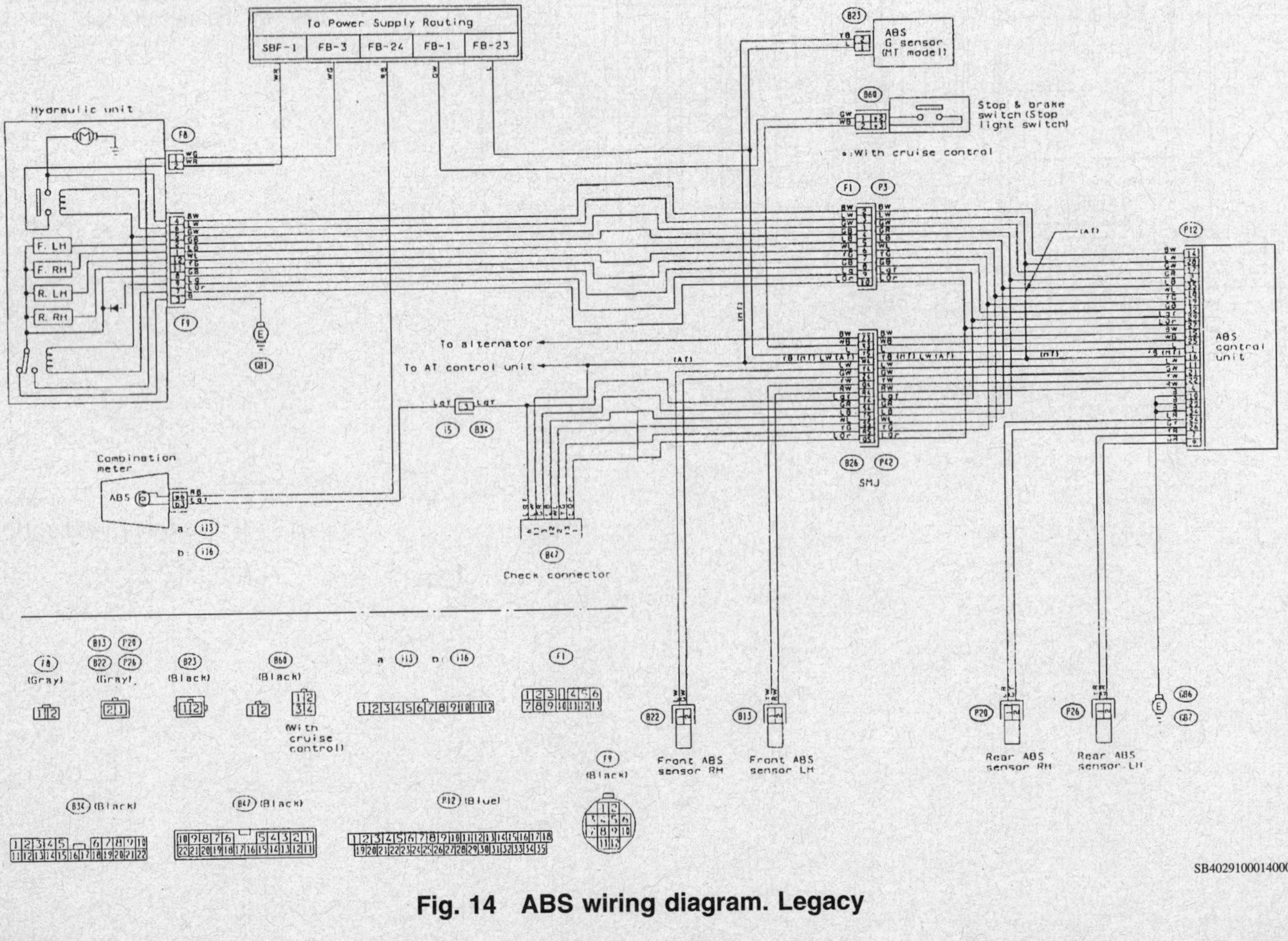
To Power Supply Routing
SBF-1
FB-3
FB-24
FB-1
FB-23
Hydraulic unit
F. LH
F. RH
R. LH
R. RH
ABS G sensor (MT model)
Stop & brake switch (Stop light switch)
*:With cruise control
To alternator
To AT control unit
ABS control unit
SMJ
Combination meter
ABS
Check connector
Front ABS sensor RH
Front ABS sensor LH
Rear ABS sensor RH
Rear ABS sensor LH

SB4029100014000X

Fig. 14 ABS wiring diagram. Legacy

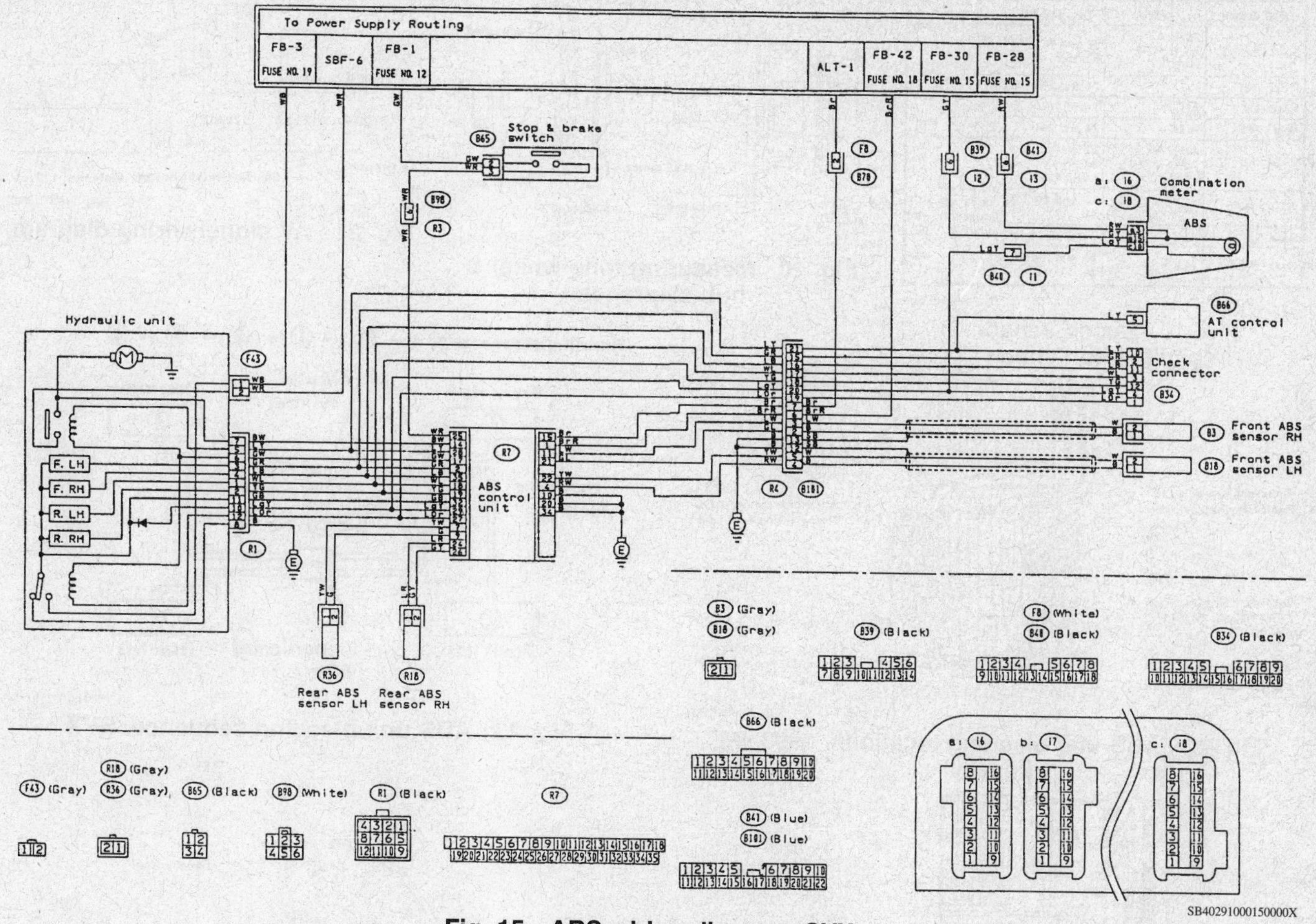
To Power Supply Routing
FB-3
FUSE NO. 19
SBF-6
FB-1
FUSE NO. 12
ALT-1
FB-42
FUSE NO. 18
FB-30
FUSE NO. 15
FB-28
FUSE NO. 15
Stop & brake switch
Combination meter
ABS
AT control unit
Check connector
Front ABS sensor RH
Front ABS sensor LH
Hydraulic unit
F. LH
F. RH
R. LH
R. RH
ABS control unit
Rear ABS sensor LH
Rear ABS sensor RH
(Gray)
(Black)
(White)
(Blue)
SB40291000150000X

Fig. 15 ABS wiring diagram. SVX

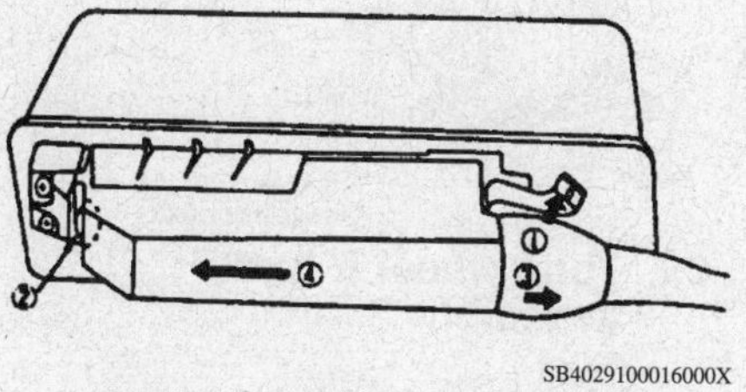
SB4029100016000X

Fig. 16 ABS control unit connector disassembly

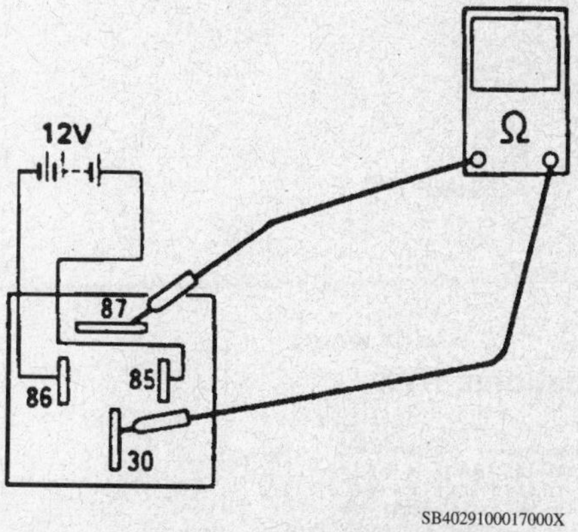
12V
Ω
87
86
85
30
SB4029100017000X

Fig. 17 Motor relay inspection

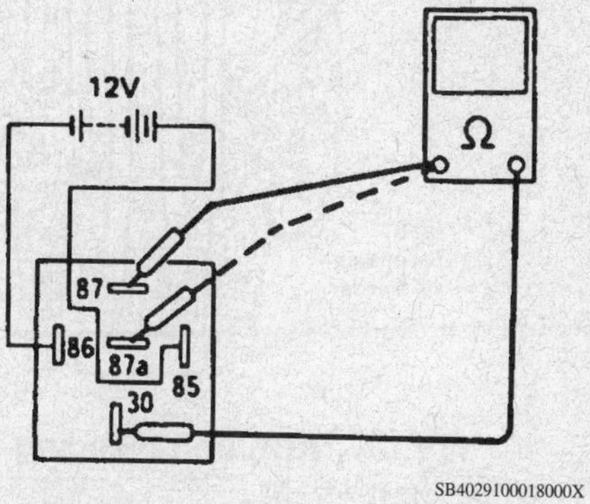
12V
Ω
87
86
87a
85
30
SB4029100018000X

Fig. 18 Valve relay inspection

ABS sensor	Model	Terminal No.	Standard
Front - LH	AWD AT AWD MT FWD	22 and 4 5 and 4	1.0± 0.2 kΩ
Front - RH	ALL	11 and 21	
Rear - LH	ALL	7 and 9	
Rear - RH	ALL	24 and 26	
Front - LH	AWD AT AWD MT FWD	22 and 10, 20, 34 5 and 4	More than 1 x 10^3 kΩ (Insulation resistance)
Front - RH	ALL	11 and 10, 20, 34	
Rear - LH	ALL	7 and 10, 20, 34	
Rear - RH	ALL	24 and 10, 20, 34	

SB4029100019000X

Fig. 19 Speed sensor specification chart

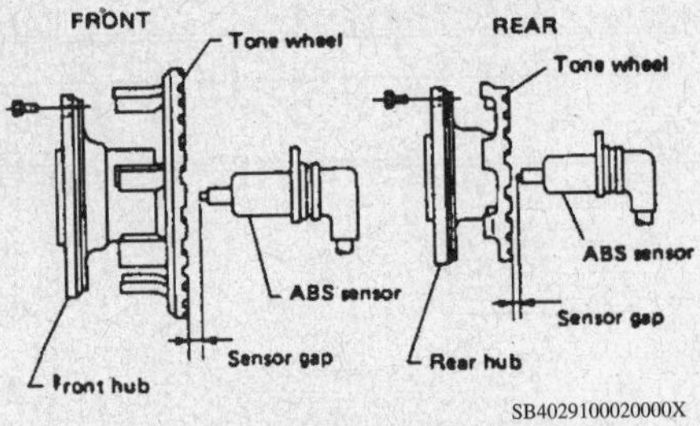

FRONT
Tone wheel
ABS sensor
Sensor gap
Front hub
REAR
Tone wheel
ABS sensor
Sensor gap
Rear hub
SB4029100020000X

Fig. 20 Measuring tone wheel & hub clearance

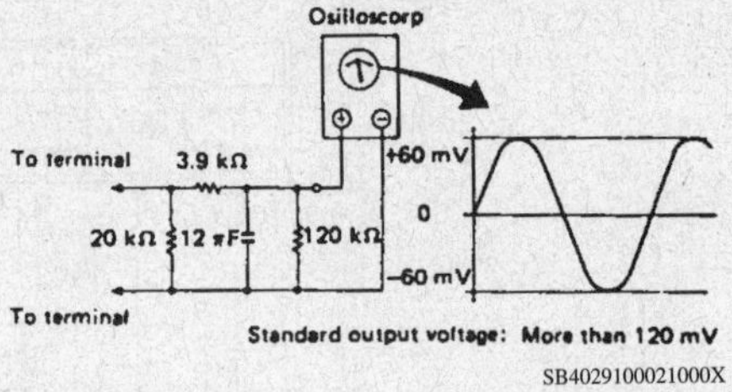

Osilloscorp
To terminal
3.9 kΩ
20 kΩ
12 πF
120 kΩ
To terminal
+60 mV
0
−60 mV
Standard output voltage: More than 120 mV
SB4029100021000X

Fig. 21 AV signal wiring diagram

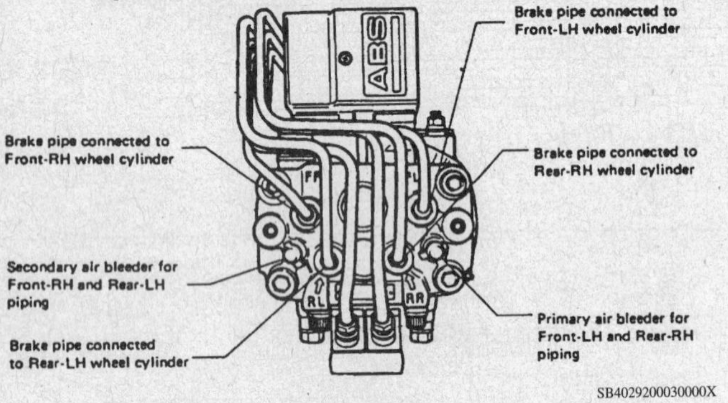

Brake pipe connected to Front-LH wheel cylinder
Brake pipe connected to Front-RH wheel cylinder
Brake pipe connected to Rear-RH wheel cylinder
Secondary air bleeder for Front-RH and Rear-LH piping
Primary air bleeder for Front-LH and Rear-RH piping
Brake pipe connected to Rear-LH wheel cylinder
ABS
FR
FL
RL
RR
SB4029200030000X

Fig. 22 ABS unit bleeding locations. 1993–94 Legacy

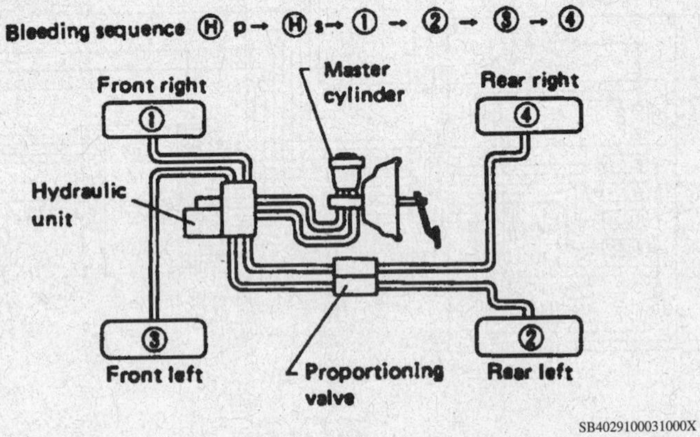

Bleeding sequence Ⓗ p→ Ⓗ s→ ① → ② → ③ → ④
Front right
Master cylinder
Rear right
Hydraulic unit
Front left
Proportioning valve
Rear left
SB4029100031000X

Fig. 23 ABS unit bleeding sequence. SVX

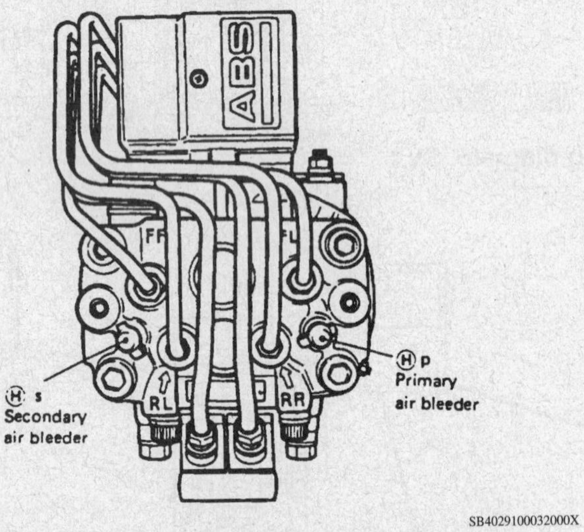

ABS
FR
FL
RL
RR
Ⓗ p
Primary air bleeder
Ⓗ s
Secondary air bleeder
SB4029100032000X

Fig. 24 ABS unit bleeding locations. SVX

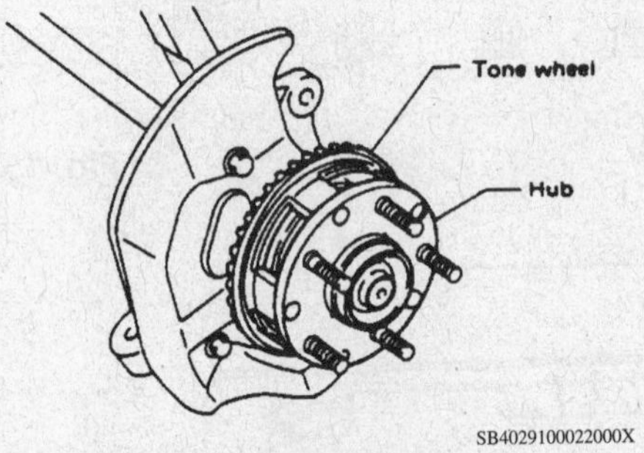

Tone wheel
Hub
SB4029100022000X

Fig. 25 Tone wheel & hub assembly

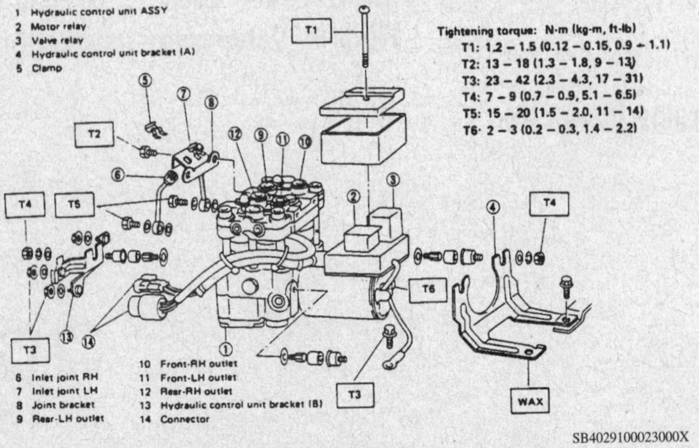

1 Hydraulic control unit ASSY
2 Motor relay
3 Valve relay
4 Hydraulic control unit bracket (A)
5 Clamp
Tightening torque: N-m (kg-m, ft-lb)
T1: 1.2 – 1.5 (0.12 – 0.15, 0.9 – 1.1)
T2: 13 – 18 (1.3 – 1.8, 9 – 13)
T3: 23 – 42 (2.3 – 4.3, 17 – 31)
T4: 7 – 9 (0.7 – 0.9, 5.1 – 6.5)
T5: 15 – 20 (1.5 – 2.0, 11 – 14)
T6· 2 – 3 (0.2 – 0.3, 1.4 – 2.2)
6 Inlet joint RH
7 Inlet joint LH
8 Joint bracket
9 Rear-LH outlet
10 Front-RH outlet
11 Front-LH outlet
12 Rear-RH outlet
13 Hydraulic control unit bracket (B)
14 Connector
WAX
SB4029100023000X

Fig. 26 ABS hydraulic unit. Nippon

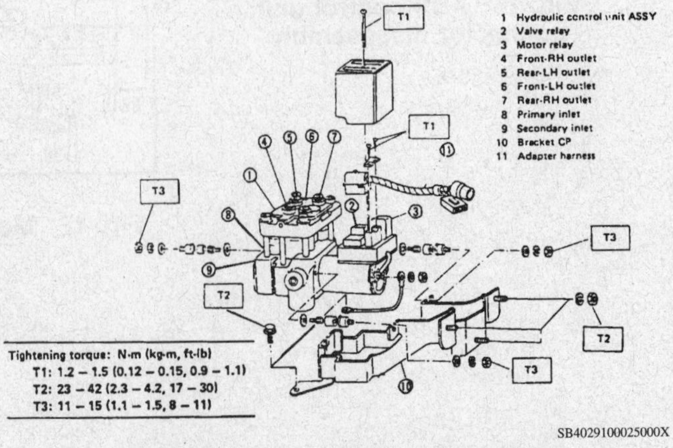

1 Hydraulic control unit ASSY
2 Valve relay
3 Motor relay
4 Front-RH outlet
5 Rear-LH outlet
6 Front-LH outlet
7 Rear-RH outlet
8 Primary inlet
9 Secondary inlet
10 Bracket CP
11 Adapter harness
Tightening torque: N-m (kg-m, ft-lb)
T1: 1.2 – 1.5 (0.12 – 0.15, 0.9 – 1.1)
T2: 23 – 42 (2.3 – 4.2, 17 – 30)
T3: 11 – 15 (1.1 – 1.5, 8 – 11)
SB4029100025000X

Fig. 27 ABS hydraulic unit. Bosch

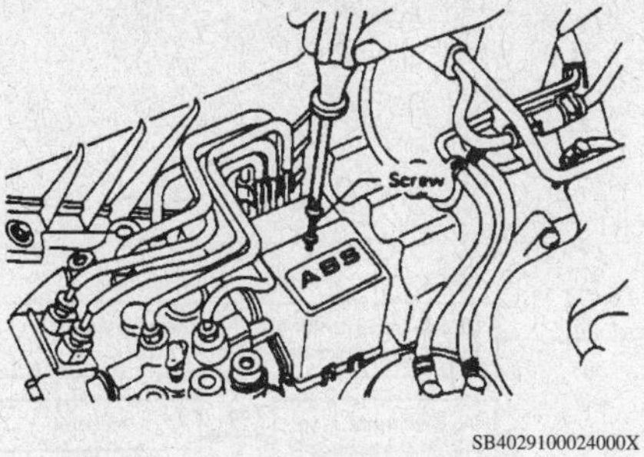
Screw
ABS

SB4029100024000X

Fig. 28 Hydraulic relay unit

	Condition	Terminal number	Standard	Diagram	Terminal location
Valve relay	Turning off electricity.	85 — 86	93 — 113 Ω	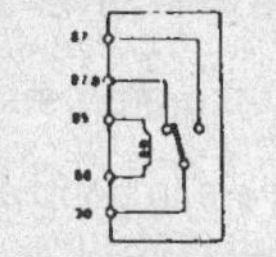	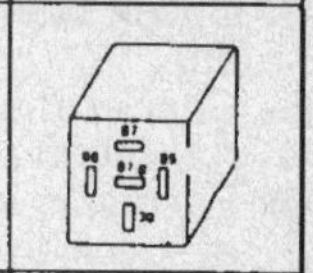
		30 — 87a	0 Ω		
		30 — 87	∞		
	Turning on electricity between 85 and 86. (DC 12 V)	30 — 87a	0 Ω		
		30 — 87	0 Ω		
			—		
Motor relay	Turning off electricity.	85 — 86	72 — 88 Ω	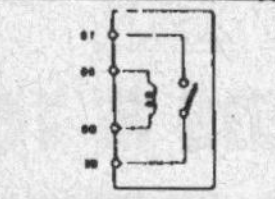	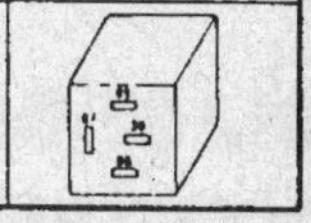
		30 — 87	∞		
	Turning on electricity between 85 and86. (DC 12 V)	30 — 87	0 Ω		

SB4029100026000X

Fig. 29 Hydraulic relay box specification chart. Legacy

	Condition	Terminal number	Standard	Diagram	Terminal location
Valve relay	Turning off electricity.	85 — 86	93 — 113 Ω	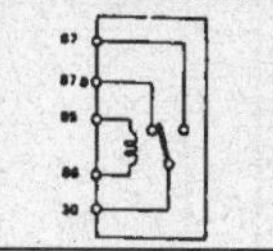	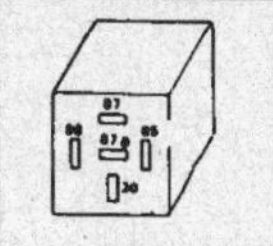
		30 — 87a	0 Ω		
		30 — 87	∞		
	Turning on electricity between 85 and 86. (DC 12 V)	30 — 87a	0Ω		
		30 — 87	0Ω		
			—		
Motor relay	Turning off electricity.	85 — 86	72 — 88 Ω	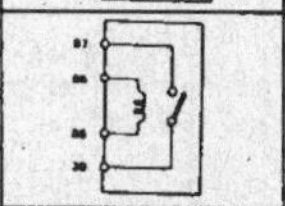	
		30 — 87	∞		
	Turning on electricity between 85 and 86. (DC 12 V)	30 — 87	0 Ω		

SB4029100027000X

Fig. 30 Hydraulic relay box specification chart. SVX

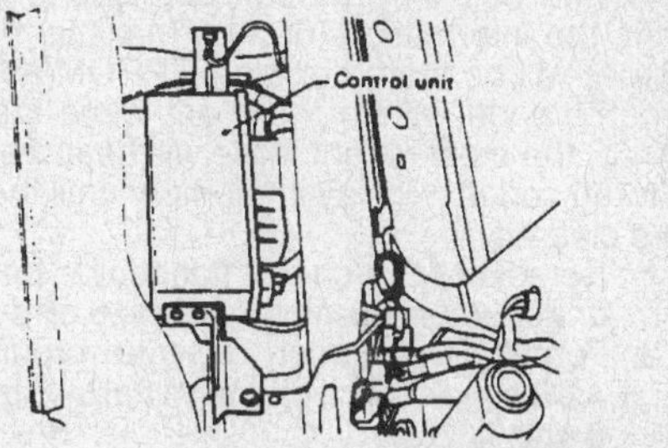
Control unit

SB4029100028000X

Fig. 31 Electronic control unit

Impreza & 1995 Legacy Less TCS

NOTE: On Air Bag Equipped Models, Refer To "Air Bag System Precautions" Located In The Front Of This Manual For System Disarming & Arming Procedures.

NOTE: Wire Code Identification And Symbol Identification Located In The Front Of This Manual Can Be Used As An Aid When Using Wiring Circuits Found In This Section.

INDEX

Page No.

Description 39-135
Diagnosis & Testing 39-136
Accessing Trouble Codes 39-136
Clearing Memory (Erasing Trouble Codes) 39-136
Component Testing 39-141
Diagnostic Procedure 39-136
Trouble Code Diagnosis 39-136
Trouble Code Interpretation 39-136
Precautions 39-135
Air Bag Systems 39-135
System Service 39-142
Brake System Bleed 39-142
Component Replacement 39-143
ABS Control Module 39-144
ABS Hydraulic Unit 39-143
Front Sensor 39-143
G Sensor 39-144
Rear Sensor 39-143
Troubleshooting 39-135
Preliminary Inspection 39-135

PRECAUTIONS

AIR BAG SYSTEMS

Refer to "Air Bag System Precautions" in the front of this manual for system disarming and arming procedures.

DESCRIPTION

The Anti-lock brake system (ABS) electrically controls brake fluid pressure to prevent wheel lock during braking on slippery road surfaces, improving steering stability and shortening the braking distance. If the ABS becomes inoperative, a fail-safe system activates to ensure conventional brake system operation.

The ABS consists of four tone wheels, four speed sensors, electronic control unit, a G sensor, and a warning lamp.

The electronic control unit has the capability of on-board diagnosis. The on-board diagnosis system is designed to detect problems after the vehicle has been driven at 6 mph or more for at least 20 seconds. If a problem is found, the ABS warning light will illuminate to inform the driver of the occurrence of a problem. When the warning light is on, the ABS system will be inactive and the normal braking function will work.

TROUBLESHOOTING

Refer to **Figs. 1 through 5,** for troubleshooting procedures.

PRELIMINARY INSPECTION

1. Ensure battery voltage is 12 volts or more.
2. Ensure specific gravity of battery is 1.260.
3. Check condition of main and other

fuses, harnesses and connector. Also check for proper grounding.

4. Check brake fluid level and for leakage.
5. Check for brake drag, brake pad and rotor condition.
6. Ensure tires are in good condition and at specified air pressure.

DIAGNOSIS & TESTING

ACCESSING TROUBLE CODES

When the control module detects a problem, the information (up to a maximum of three) will be stored in the EEPROM as a trouble code. When there are more than three, the most recent three will be stored. Stored codes will stay in memory until they are cleared.

1. Remove ABS check connector from under steering column, **Figs. 6 and 7.**
2. Turn ignition switch off, then ground ABS check connector terminal L, **Figs. 6 and 7.**
3. Turn ignition switch to on position. The ABS warning light is now in the diagnostic mode and blinks to identify trouble codes.
4. After start code (11) is shown, the trouble code(s) will be shown in order of the last information first. The code(s) will repeat for a maximum of 5 minutes. When there are no trouble codes in memory, only the start code (11) is shown.

TROUBLE CODE INTERPRETATION

Refer to **Fig. 8,** for trouble code interpretation and **Fig. 9,** for trouble code identification and description.

CLEARING MEMORY (ERASING TROUBLE CODES)

After completing necessary repairs, clear trouble code memory as follows:

1. After calling up a trouble code, disconnect ABS check connector terminal L from ground.
2. Repeat connecting and disconnecting terminal L from ground 3 times within approximately 12 seconds. Leave terminal L disconnected for at least ½ second each time.

DIAGNOSTIC PROCEDURE

Refer to **Fig. 10,** for proper diagnostic sequence.

TROUBLE CODE DIAGNOSIS

Refer to wiring diagram, **Figs. 11 and 12,** when performing the following procedures.

Warning Light Does Not Illuminate

1. Turn ignition switch to off position, then disconnect combination meter.
2. Check ABS warning light valve, then turn ignition switch to on position.

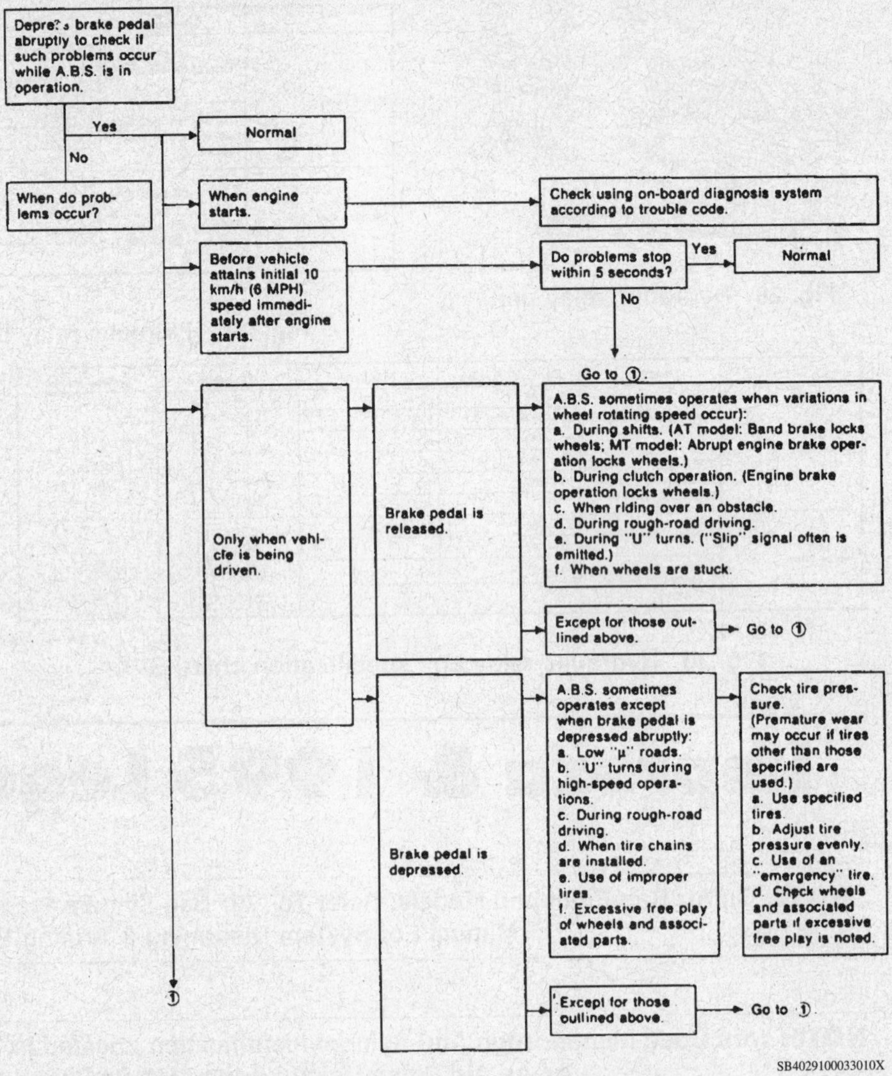

Depre?s brake pedal abruptly to check if such problems occur while A.B.S. is in operation.
Yes
Normal
No
When do problems occur?
When engine starts.
Check using on-board diagnosis system according to trouble code.
Before vehicle attains initial 10 km/h (6 MPH) speed immediately after engine starts.
Do problems stop within 5 seconds?
Yes
Normal
No
Go to ①.
Only when vehicle is being driven.
Brake pedal is released.
A.B.S. sometimes operates when variations in wheel rotating speed occur:
a. During shifts. (AT model: Band brake locks wheels; MT model: Abrupt engine brake operation locks wheels.)
b. During clutch operation. (Engine brake operation locks wheels.)
c. When riding over an obstacle.
d. During rough-road driving.
e. During "U" turns. ("Slip" signal often is emitted.)
f. When wheels are stuck.
Except for those outlined above.
Go to ①
Brake pedal is depressed.
A.B.S. sometimes operates except when brake pedal is depressed abruptly:
a. Low "μ" roads.
b. "U" turns during high-speed operations.
c. During rough-road driving.
d. When tire chains are installed.
e. Use of improper tires
f. Excessive free play of wheels and associated parts.
Check tire pressure. (Premature wear may occur if tires other than those specified are used.)
a. Use specified tires.
b. Adjust tire pressure evenly.
c. Use of an "emergency" tire.
d. Check wheels and associated parts if excessive free play is noted.
①
Except for those outlined above.
Go to ①.
SB4029100033010X

Fig. 1 Troubleshooting chart (vibrating pedal & noise, Part 1 of 2)

3. Measure voltage between combination meter connector i18 terminal 13 and ground on Impreza models and combination meter connector i14 terminal 11 and ground on legacy models. Voltage should be 10-12 volts.
4. Turn ignition switch off, then remove combination meter.
5. Disconnect connectors from ABS control module and hydraulic unit, then turn ignition switch to on position. Measure as follows:
   a. Measure voltage between control module connector terminal 29 and ground. Voltage should be 10-12 volts.
   b. Measure voltage between hydraulic unit connector terminal 10 and ground. Voltage should be 10-12 volts.
   c. Measure resistance between control module connector terminal 10 and ground. Resistance should be 0 ohms.
   d. Measure resistance between control module connector terminal 20 and ground. Resistance should be 0 ohms.
   e. Measure resistance between control module connector terminal 34 and ground. Resistance should be 0 ohms.
   f. Measure resistance between hydraulic unite connector terminal 8 and ground. Resistance should be 0 ohms.
6. Remove valve relay, then attach tester probes as shown in **Fig. 13.**
   a. With terminals 30 and 87 connected. Resistance should be 0 ohms when 12 volts are applied or 1 Mohm when no voltage is applied.
   b. With terminals 30 and 87a connected. Resistance should be 1 Mohm when 12 volts are applied or 0 ohms when no voltage is applied.

Warning Light Remains ON

1. Turn ignition switch to off position, then disconnect control module connector.
2. Turn ignition switch to on position, then measure voltage between control module connector terminal 29 and

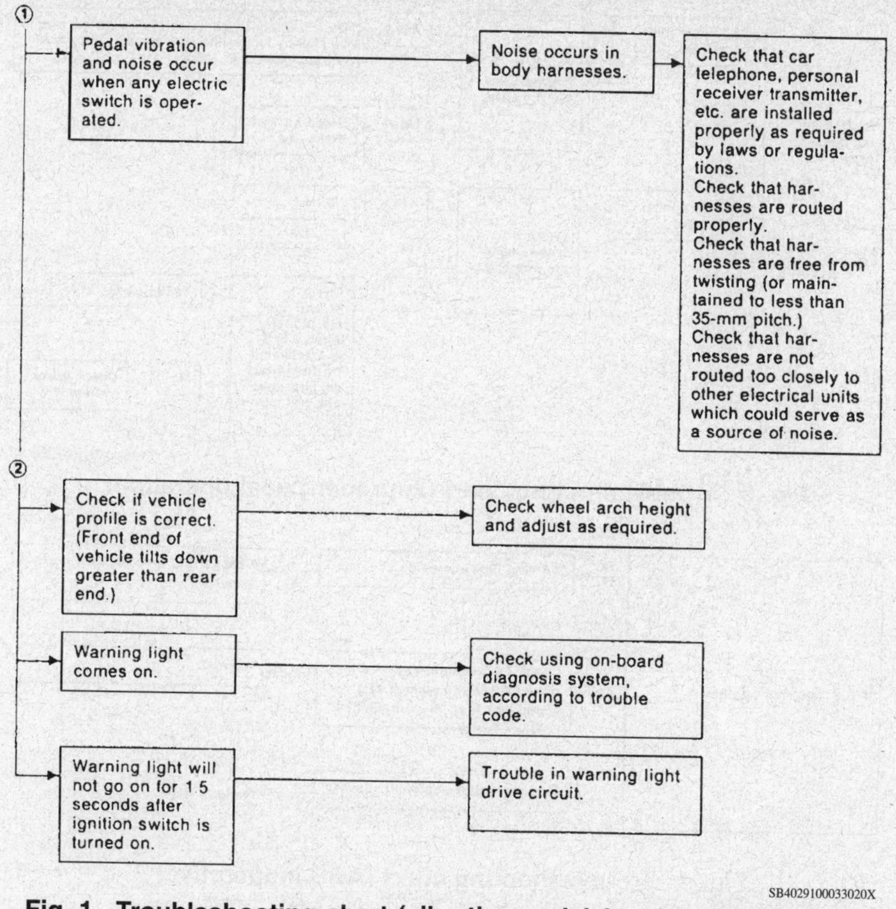
①
Pedal vibration and noise occur when any electric switch is operated.
Noise occurs in body harnesses.
Check that car telephone, personal receiver transmitter, etc. are installed properly as required by laws or regulations.
Check that harnesses are routed properly.
Check that harnesses are free from twisting (or maintained to less than 35-mm pitch.)
Check that harnesses are not routed too closely to other electrical units which could serve as a source of noise.
②
Check if vehicle profile is correct. (Front end of vehicle tilts down greater than rear end.)
Check wheel arch height and adjust as required.
Warning light comes on.
Check using on-board diagnosis system, according to trouble code.
Warning light will not go on for 1.5 seconds after ignition switch is turned on.
Trouble in warning light drive circuit.
SB4029100033020X

Fig. 1 Troubleshooting chart (vibrating pedal & noise, Part 2 of 2)

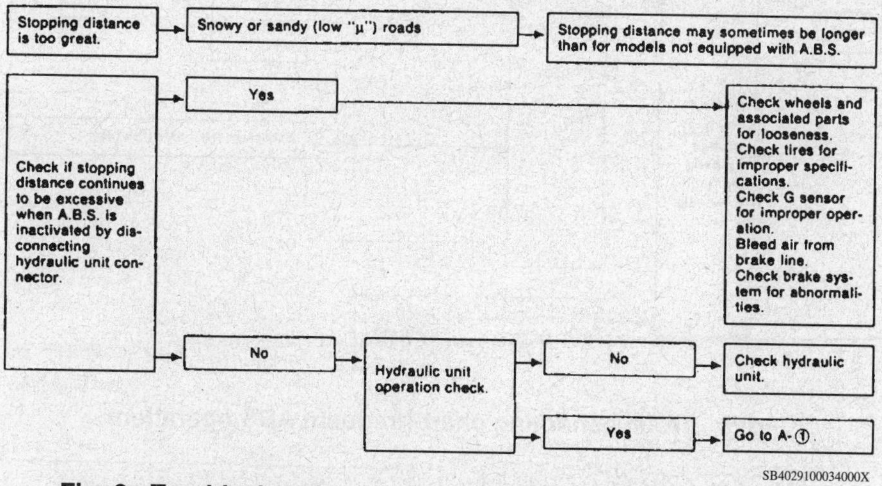
Stopping distance is too great.
Snowy or sandy (low "μ") roads
Stopping distance may sometimes be longer than for models not equipped with A.B.S.
Check if stopping distance continues to be excessive when A.B.S. is inactivated by disconnecting hydraulic unit connector.
Yes
Check wheels and associated parts for looseness.
Check tires for improper specifications.
Check G sensor for improper operation.
Bleed air from brake line.
Check brake system for abnormalities.
No
Hydraulic unit operation check.
No
Check hydraulic unit.
Yes
Go to A-①.
SB4029100034000X

Fig. 2 Troubleshooting chart (excessive stopping distance)

ground. Voltage should be 10-12 volts.

3. Turn ignition switch to on position, then measure voltage between control module connector terminal 1 and ground. Voltage should be 10-12 volts.
4. Measure resistance between control module connector terminal 10 and ground. Resistance should be 0 ohms.
5. Measure resistance between control module connector terminal 20 and ground. Resistance should be 0 ohms.
6. Measure resistance between control module connector terminal 34 and ground. Resistance should be 0 ohms.

Trouble Codes 21, 23, 25 & 27

1. Turn ignition switch to off position, then disconnect control module connector.
2. Measure resistance between control module connector terminals as follows:
   a. If trouble code 21 is present, measure between terminals 23 and 21. Resistance should be 800-1300 ohms on Impreza models and 800–1200 ohms on Legacy models.
   b. If trouble code 23 is present, measure between terminals 22 and 4 on Legacy models and AWD Impreza models or terminals 5 and 4 on FWD Impreza models. Resistance should be 800-1300 ohms on Impreza models and 800–1200 ohms on Legacy models.
   c. If trouble code 25 is present, measure between terminals 24 and 26. Resistance should be 800-1300 ohms on Impreza models and 800–1200 ohms on Legacy models.
   d. If trouble code 27 is present, measure between terminals 8 and 9. Resistance should be 800-1300 ohms on Impreza models and 800–1200 ohms on Legacy models.
3. Measure resistance between control module connector and ground as follows:
   a. If trouble code 21 is present, measure between terminals 23 and ground. Resistance should be 0 ohms.
   b. If trouble code 23 is present, measure between terminals 4 and ground on Impreza models and between terminals 22 and ground on legacy models. Resistance should be 0 ohms.
   c. If trouble code 25 is present, measure between terminals 24 and ground. Resistance should be 0 ohms.
   d. If trouble code 27 is present, measure between terminals 8 and ground. Resistance should be 0 ohms.
4. Turn ignition switch to on position.
5. Measure voltage between control module connector and ground as follows:
   a. If trouble code 21 is present, measure between terminals 23 and ground. Voltage should be 0 ohms.
   b. If trouble code 23 is present, measure between terminals 4 and ground on Impreza models and between terminals 22 and ground on legacy models. Voltage should be 0 ohms.
   c. If trouble code 25 is present, measure between terminals 24 and ground. Voltage should be 0 ohms.
   d. If trouble code 27 is present, measure between terminals 8 and ground. Voltage should be 0 ohms.
6. Turn ignition switch to off position, then raise and support vehicle.
7. Disconnect connector from control module, then remove connector cover as follows:
   a. Remove screw from portion 1, **Fig. 14,** then move rubber boot 2 back (toward harness).
   b. Slide cover 3 in direction shown in **Fig. 14,** and remove.
8. Connect connector back into control module, then connect an oscilloscope to the control module connector as outlined in step 10.
9. Turn ignition switch to on position.
10. Rotate wheels and measure voltage at

a frequency of 10 Hz. Measure voltage as follows:

a. If trouble code 21 is present, measure voltage between terminals 23 and 21. Voltage should be .12–1.0 volt at 10 Hz.
b. If trouble code 23 is present, measure voltage between terminals 22 and 4 on Legacy models and AWD Impreza models or terminals 5 and 4 on FWD Impreza models. Voltage should be .12–1.0 volt at 10 Hz.
c. If trouble code 25 is present, measure voltage between terminals 24 and 26. Voltage should be .12–1.0 volt at 10 Hz.
d. If trouble code 27 is present, measure voltage between terminals 8 and 9. Voltage should be .12–1.0 volt at 10 Hz.
e. When this inspection is completed, the control module could store trouble code 29.

11. Remove brake assembly to gain access to ABS sensor and tone wheel.
12. Check pole piece and tone wheel for accumulation of foreign particles. Clean as necessary.
13. Check tone wheel teeth for cracks or deformities. Replace as necessary.
14. **Torque** tone wheel to 7–12 ft. lbs.
15. Measure tone wheel to pole piece gap over entire perimeter of wheel. Gap for front wheel must be .035–.055 inch. Gap for rear wheel must be .028–.047 inch. If necessary, adjust gap using spacers part No. 26755AA000.
16. Check hub runout. Runout should be .0020 inch.
17. Turn ignition switch off, then disconnect ABS sensor connector.
18. Measure resistance between sensor terminals as follows:
    a. If trouble code 21 is present, measure between front righthand sensor terminals. Resistance should be 800-1300 ohms on Impreza models and 800–1200 ohms on Legacy models.
    b. If trouble code 23 is present, measure between front lefthand sensor terminals. Resistance should be 800-1300 ohms on Impreza models and 800–1200 ohms on Legacy models.
    c. If trouble code 25 is present, measure between rear righthand sensor terminals. Resistance should be 800-1300 ohms on Impreza models and 800–1200 ohms on Legacy models.
    d. If trouble code 27 is present, measure between rear lefthand sensor terminals. Resistance should be 800-1300 ohms on Impreza models and 800–1200 ohms on Legacy models.

Trouble Codes 22, 24, 26 & 28

1. Turn ignition switch to off position, then raise and support vehicle.
2. Disconnect connector from control module, then remove connector cover as follows:

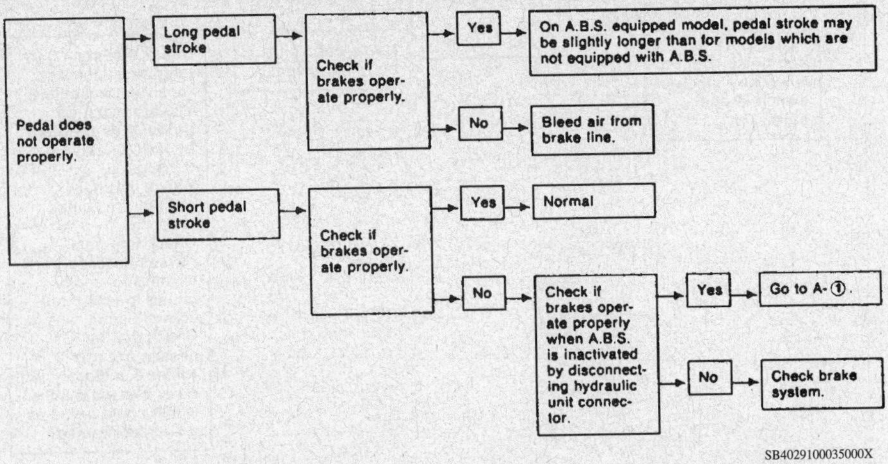

Pedal does not operate properly.
Long pedal stroke
Check if brakes operate properly.
Yes
On A.B.S. equipped model, pedal stroke may be slightly longer than for models which are not equipped with A.B.S.
No
Bleed air from brake line.
Short pedal stroke
Check if brakes operate properly.
Yes
Normal
No
Check if brakes operate properly when A.B.S. is inactivated by disconnecting hydraulic unit connector.
Yes
Go to A-①.
No
Check brake system.
SB4029100035000X

Fig. 3 Troubleshooting chart (improper pedal operation)

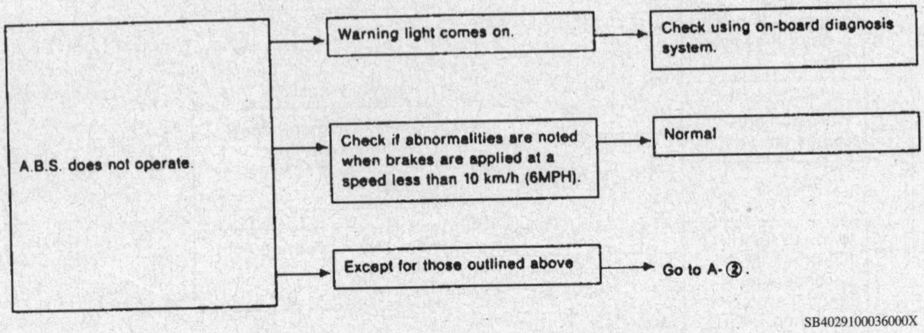

A.B.S. does not operate.
Warning light comes on.
Check using on-board diagnosis system.
Check if abnormalities are noted when brakes are applied at a speed less than 10 km/h (6MPH).
Normal
Except for those outlined above
Go to A-②.
SB4029100036000X

Fig. 4 Troubleshooting chart (ABS inoperative)

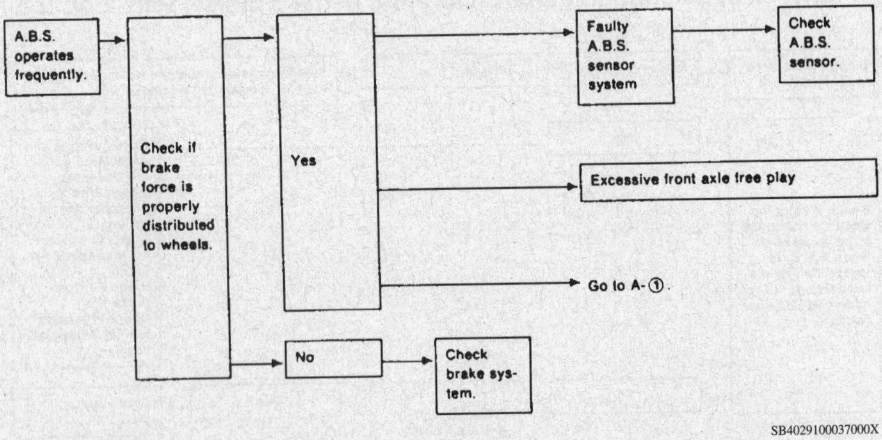

A.B.S. operates frequently.
Check if brake force is properly distributed to wheels.
Yes
Faulty A.B.S. sensor system
Check A.B.S. sensor.
Excessive front axle free play
Go to A-①.
No
Check brake system.
SB4029100037000X

Fig. 5 Troubleshooting chart (frequent ABS operation)

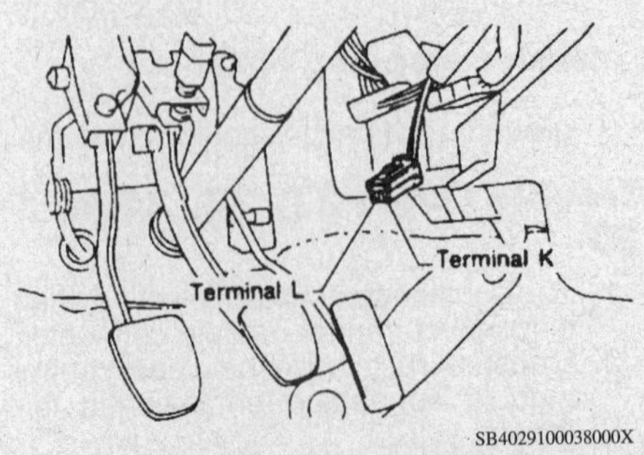

Terminal K
Terminal L
SB4029100038000X

Fig. 6 Check connector terminal identification. Impreza

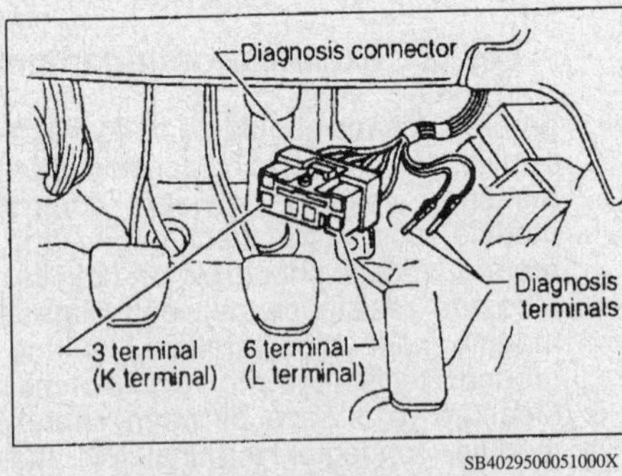

Diagnosis connector
Diagnosis terminals
3 terminal (K terminal)
6 terminal (L terminal)
SB4029500051000X

Fig. 7 Check connector terminal identification. Legacy

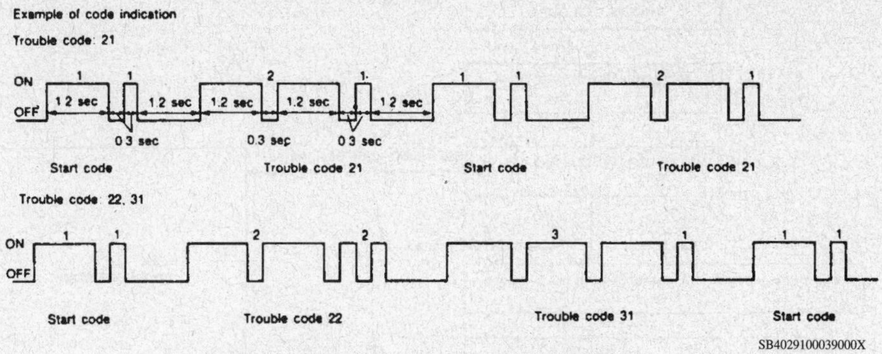
Example of code indication
Trouble code: 21
ON
OFF
1.2 sec
0.3 sec
Start code
Trouble code 21
Trouble code: 22, 31
Start code
Trouble code 22
Trouble code 31
SB4029100039000X

Fig. 8 Trouble code interpretation

Trouble code	Contents of diagnosis	
NONE: A [Warning light OFF]	Trouble in warning light drive circuit (Warning light is not on for 1.5 seconds after ignition switch is on.)	
NONE: B [Warning light ON] or [Abnormal trouble code output]	Trouble in warning light drive circuit	
11	Start code: • Trouble code is shown after start code. • Only start code is shown in normal condition.	
21	Faulty A.B.S. sensor (Open circuit or input voltage excessive)	Front right wheel sensor
23		Front left wheel sensor
25		Rear right wheel sensor
27		Rear left wheel sensor
22	Faulty A.B.S. sensor (When there is no open circuit or speed signal input.)	Front right wheel sensor
24		Front left wheel sensor
26		Rear right wheel sensor
28		Rear left wheel sensor
29	Faulty tone wheel, etc.	
31	Faulty solenoid valve circuit(s) in hydraulic unit	Front right wheel control
33		Front left wheel control
39		Rear wheels control
41	Faulty A.B.S. control module	
42	Source voltage is low.	
51	Faulty valve relay	
52	Faulty hydraulic motor and/or motor relay	
54	Faulty stop light circuit	
56	Use of improper A.B.S. control module specification, or faulty G sensor	

SB4029100040000X

Fig. 9 Trouble code description

a. Remove screw from portion 1, **Fig. 14,** then move rubber boot 2 back (toward harness).
b. Slide cover 3 in direction shown in **Fig. 14,** and remove.

3. Connect connector back into control module, then connect an oscilloscope to the control module connector as outlined in step 5.
4. Turn ignition switch to on position.
5. Rotate wheels and measure voltage at a frequency of 10 Hz. Measure voltage as follows:
   a. If trouble code 22 is present, measure voltage between terminals 23 and 21. Voltage should be .12–1.0 volt at 10 Hz.
   b. If trouble code 24 is present, measure voltage between terminals 22 and 4 on Legacy models and AWD Impreza models or terminals 5 and 4 on FWD Impreza models. Voltage should be .12–1.0 volt at 10 Hz.
   c. If trouble code 26 is present, measure voltage between terminals 24 and 26. Voltage should be .12–1.0 volt at 10 Hz.
   d. If trouble code 28 is present, measure voltage between terminals 8 and 9. Voltage should be .12–1.0 volt at 10 Hz.
   e. When this inspection is completed, the control module could store trouble code 29.
6. Measure resistance between sensor terminals as follows:
   a. If trouble code 22 is present, measure between front righthand sensor terminals. Resistance should be 800-1300 ohms on Impreza models and 800–1200 ohms on Legacy models.
   b. If trouble code 24 is present, measure between front lefthand sensor terminals. Resistance should be 800-1300 ohms on Impreza models and 800–1200 ohms on Legacy models.
   c. If trouble code 26 is present, measure between rear righthand sensor terminals. Resistance should be 800-1300 ohms on Impreza models and 800–1200 ohms on Legacy models.
   d. If trouble code 28 is present, measure between rear lefthand sensor terminals. Resistance should be 800-1300 ohms on Impreza models and 800–1200 ohms on Legacy models.
7. Remove brake assembly to gain access to ABS sensor and tone wheel.
8. Check pole piece and tone wheel for accumulation of foreign particles. Clean as necessary.
9. Check tone wheel teeth for cracks or deformities. Replace as necessary.
10. **Torque** tone wheel to 7–12 ft. lbs.
11. Measure tone wheel to pole piece gap over entire perimeter of wheel. Gap for front wheel must be .035–.055 inch. Gap for rear wheel must be .028–.047 inch. If necessary, adjust gap using spacers part No. 26755AA000.
12. Check hub runout. Runout should be .0020 inch.

Trouble Code 29

1. Turn ignition switch to off position, then raise and support vehicle.
2. Disconnect connector from control module, then remove connector cover as follows:
   a. Remove screw from portion 1, **Fig. 14,** then move rubber boot 2 back (toward harness).
   b. Slide cover 3 in direction shown in **Fig. 14,** and remove.
3. Connect connector back into control module, then connect an oscilloscope to the control module connector as outlined in step 5.
4. Turn ignition switch to on position.
5. Rotate wheels and measure voltage at a frequency of 10 Hz. Measure voltage as follows:
   a. If trouble code 21 is present, measure voltage between terminals 23 and 21. Voltage should be .12–1.0 volt at 10 Hz.
   b. If trouble code 23 is present, measure voltage between terminals 22 and 4 on Legacy models and AWD Impreza models or terminals 5 and 4 on FWD Impreza models. Voltage should be .12–1.0 volt at 10 Hz.
   c. If trouble code 25 is present, measure voltage between terminals 24 and 26. Voltage should be .12–1.0 volt at 10 Hz.
   d. If trouble code 27 is present, measure voltage between terminals 8 and 9. Voltage should be .12–1.0 volt at 10 Hz.
   e. When this inspection is completed, the control module could store trouble code 29.
6. Measure resistance between sensor terminals as follows:
   a. If trouble code 21 is present, measure between front righthand sensor terminals. Resistance should be 800-1300 ohms on Impreza models and 800–1200 ohms on

b. If trouble code 23 is present, measure between front lefthand sensor terminals. Resistance should be 800-1300 ohms on Impreza models and 800–1200 ohms on Legacy models.
c. If trouble code 25 is present, measure between rear righthand sensor terminals. Resistance should be 800-1300 ohms on Impreza models and 800–1200 ohms on Legacy models.
d. If trouble code 27 is present, measure between rear lefthand sensor terminals. Resistance should be 800-1300 ohms on Impreza models and 800–1200 ohms on Legacy models.

7. Remove brake assembly to gain access to ABS sensor and tone wheel.
8. Check pole piece and tone wheel for accumulation of foreign particles. Clean as necessary.
9. Check tone wheel teeth for cracks or deformities. Replace as necessary.
10. **Torque** tone wheel to 7–12 ft. lbs.
11. Measure tone wheel to pole piece gap over entire perimeter of wheel. Gap for front wheel must be .035–.055 inch. Gap for rear wheel must be .028–.047 inch. If necessary, adjust gap using spacers part No. 26755AA000.
12. Check hub runout. Runout should be .0020 inch.

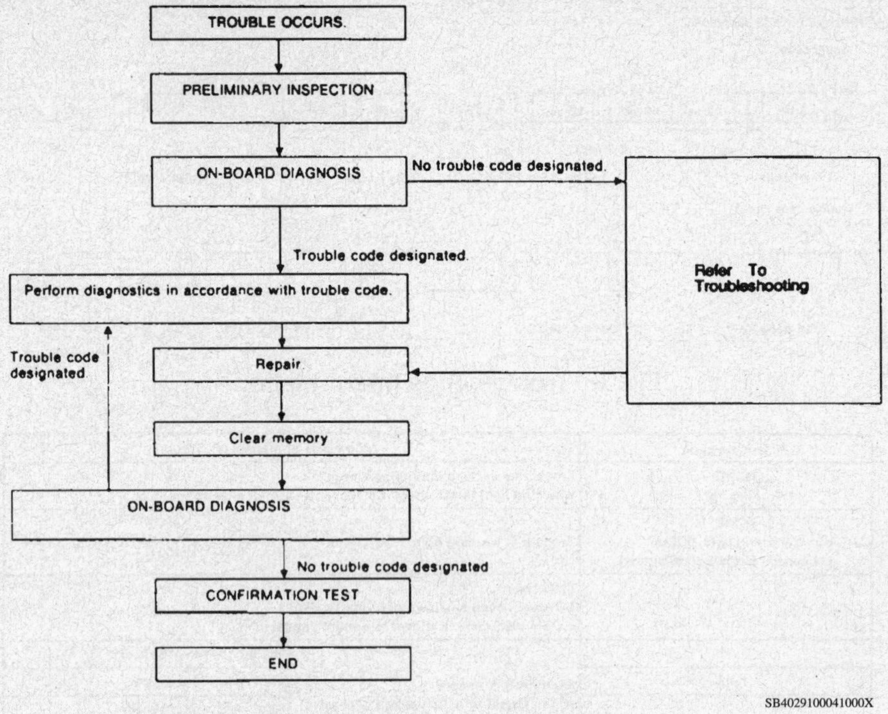

TROUBLE OCCURS.
PRELIMINARY INSPECTION
ON-BOARD DIAGNOSIS
No trouble code designated.
Refer To Troubleshooting
Trouble code designated.
Perform diagnostics in accordance with trouble code.
Trouble code designated.
Repair.
Clear memory
ON-BOARD DIAGNOSIS
No trouble code designated
CONFIRMATION TEST
END
SB4029100041000X

Fig. 10 Diagnostic sequence

Trouble Codes 31, 33 & 39

1. Turn ignition switch to off position.
2. Disconnect connector from control module, then measure resistance between control module connector terminals as follows:
   a. If code 31 is present, measure between terminals 35 and 32. Resistance should be approximately 1 ohm.
   b. If code 33 is present, measure between terminals 2 and 32. Resistance should be approximately 1 ohm.
   c. If code 39 is present, measure between terminals 18 and 32. Resistance should be approximately 1 ohm.
3. Turn ignition switch to off position, then disconnect valve relay from hydraulic unit.
4. Turn ignition switch to on position, then measure voltage between control module connector terminals as follows:
   a. If code 31 is present, measure between terminals 35 and 20. Voltage should be 0 volts.
   b. If code 33 is present, measure between terminals 2 and 20. Voltage should be 0 volts.
   c. If code 39 is present, measure between terminals 18 and 20. Voltage should be 0 volts.
5. Turn ignition switch to off position, then disconnect hydraulic unit.
6. Turn ignition switch to on position, then measure voltage between control module connector terminals as follows:
   a. If code 31 is present, measure between terminals 35 and 20. Voltage should be 0 volts.
   b. If code 33 is present, measure between terminals 2 and 20. Voltage should be 0 volts.
   c. If code 39 is present, measure between terminals 18 and 20. Voltage should be 0 volts.
7. Turn ignition switch to off position, then disconnect connector from hydraulic unit.
8. Measure resistance between hydraulic unit terminals as follows:
   a. If code 31 is present, measure between terminals 4 and 11. Resistance should be approximately 1 ohm.
   b. If code 33 is present, measure between terminals 3 and 11. Resistance should be approximately 1 ohm.
   c. If code 39 is present, measure between terminals 1 and 11. Resistance should be approximately 1 ohm.

Trouble Code 41

Replace control module.

Trouble Code 42

1. Turn ignition switch to off position.
2. Disconnect connector from control module, then remove connector cover as follows:
   a. Remove screw from portion 1, **Fig. 14,** then move rubber boot 2 back (toward harness).
   b. Slide cover 3 in direction shown in **Fig. 14,** and remove.
3. Connect connector back into control module, then turn ignition switch to on position.
4. Measure input voltage between control module connector terminal 32 and ground. Voltage should be 9.2–12 volt on Impreza models and 10–12 volt on Legacy models.
5. Turn ignition switch to off position, then disconnect hydraulic unit connector.
6. Turn ignition switch to on position, then measure input voltage between hydraulic unit connector terminal 1 and ground. Voltage should be 10-12 volts.
7. Turn ignition switch to off position, then disconnect connectors from control module and hydraulic unit.
8. Measure resistance between control module connector terminal 32 and hydraulic unit connector terminal 1 on Impreza models and between control module connector terminal 32 and hydraulic unit connector terminal 11 on Legacy models. Resistance should be 0 ohms.
9. Remove valve relay, then attach tester probes as shown in **Fig. 13.**
   a. With terminals 30 and 87 connected. Resistance should be 0 ohms when 12 volts are applied or 1 Mohm when no voltage is applied.
   b. With terminals 30 and 87a connected. Resistance should be 1 Mohm when 12 volts are applied or 0 ohms when no voltage is applied.

Trouble Code 51

1. Turn ignition switch to off position, then disconnect connector from control module.
2. Turn ignition switch to on position, then measure voltage between control module connector terminals 1 and 20. Voltage should be 10-12 volts.
3. Turn ignition switch to off position, then disconnect control module connector.

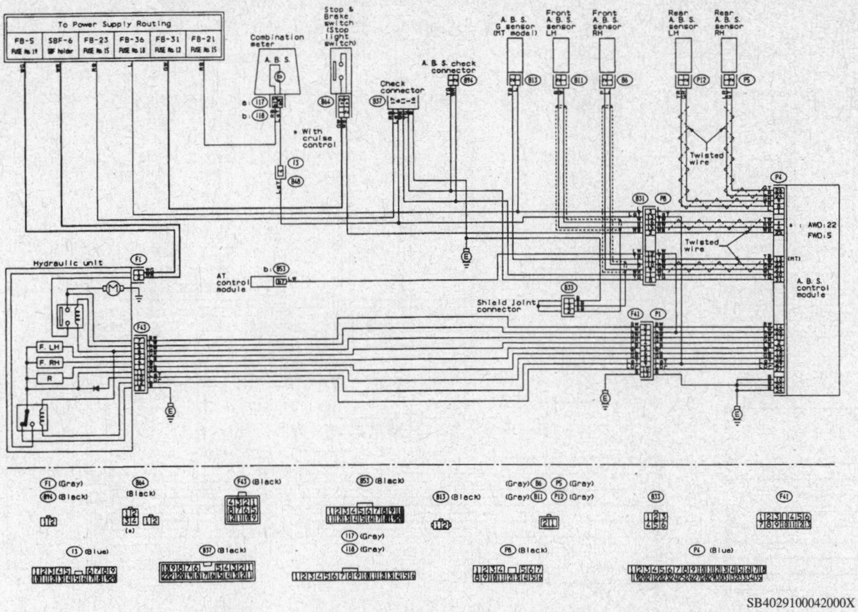
SB4029100042000X

Fig. 11 ABS wiring circuit. Impreza

4. Remove connector cover, then connect connector back into control module.
5. Turn ignition switch to on position, then measure voltage between control module connector terminals 17 and 20. Voltage should be 10-12 volts.
6. Turn ignition switch to on position, then measure voltage between control module connector terminals 32 and 20. Voltage should be 10-12 volts.
7. Turn ignition switch to off position, then disconnect connectors from control module and hydraulic unit. Measure resistance as follows:
   a. Measure resistance between control module connector terminal 17 and hydraulic unit connector terminal 6. Resistance should be 0 ohms.
   b. Measure resistance between control module connector terminal 32 and hydraulic unit connector terminal 11. Resistance should be 0 ohms.
   c. Measure resistance between control module connector terminal 27 and hydraulic unit connector terminal 12. Resistance should be 0 ohms.
8. Turn ignition switch to off position, then disconnect hydraulic unit connector.
9. Turn ignition switch to on position, then measure voltage between hydraulic unit connector terminal 1 and ground. Voltage should be 10-12 volts.
10. Remove valve relay, then attach tester probes as shown in **Fig. 13.**
    a. With terminals 30 and 87 connected. Resistance should be 0 ohms when 12 volts are applied or 1 Mohm when no voltage is applied.
    b. With terminals 30 and 87a connected. Resistance should be 1 Mohm when 12 volts are applied or 0 ohms when no voltage is applied.

Trouble Code 52

1. Turn ignition switch to off position, then disconnect connector from control module.
2. Turn ignition switch to on position, then measure voltage between control module connector terminals 1 and 20. Voltage should be 10-12 volts.
3. Turn ignition switch to off position, then disconnect control module connector.
4. Remove connector cover, then connect connector back into control module.
5. Turn ignition switch to on position, then measure voltage between control module connector terminals 17 and 20. Voltage should be 10-12 volts.
6. Turn ignition switch to off position, then disconnect connectors from control module and hydraulic unit. Measure resistance as follows:
   a. Measure resistance between control module connector terminal 17 and hydraulic unit connector terminal 6. Resistance should be 0 ohms.
   b. Measure resistance between control module connector terminal 28 and hydraulic unit connector terminal 5. Resistance should be 0 ohms.
   c. Measure resistance between control module connector terminal 14 and hydraulic unit connector terminal 7. Resistance should be 0 ohms.
7. Turn ignition switch to off position, then disconnect hydraulic unit connector.
8. Measure voltage between hydraulic unit connector terminal 2 and ground. Voltage should be 10–12 volts.
9. Remove motor relay, then attach tester probes as shown in **Fig. 15.** Resistance should be 0 ohms when 12 volts are applied or 1 Mohm when no voltage is applied.

Trouble Code 54

1. Turn ignition switch to off position, then disconnect control module connector.
2. Measure voltage between control module connector terminals 25 and 10. Voltage should be more than 4 volts when brake pedal is depressed.

Trouble Code 56

1. Position vehicle on a flat surface, then disconnect control module connector.
2. Remove cover from connector, then measure resistance between control module connector terminals 1 and 13. Resistance should be 550-670 ohms.
3. Disconnect G sensor connector, then measure resistance between G sensor terminals. Ensure sensor is horizontal during measurement. Resistance should be 550-670 ohms.
4. Turn ignition switch to on position, then connect G sensor.
5. Measure voltage between control module connector terminal 13 and ground. Voltage should be 10-12 volts.
6. Measure voltage between G sensor connector terminal 1 and ground. Voltage should be 10-12 volts.

COMPONENT TESTING

Speed Sensors

1. Check pole piece of speed sensor for damage or foreign materials. Clean or replace as needed.
2. Measure resistance between control module terminals. Refer to **Fig. 16,** for terminal identification and resistance specifications. If resistance is not within specifications replace wheel sensor or adjust gap between sensor and tone wheel.
3. Check tone wheels teeth for cracks or dents. Replace if needed.
4. Clearances, **Fig. 17,** (sensor gaps) should be measured one at a time to ensure tone wheel and speed sensor are installed properly. Clearances should be as follows:
   a. Front, .039–.059 inch.
   b. Rear, .031–.051 inch.
5. If clearance is narrow, adjust by using spacer part No. 26755AA000.
6. If clearance is wide, check outputted voltage as outlined in step 7. If outputted is not within specifications, replace sensor or tone wheel.
7. Output voltage can be checked by installing resistor and condenser as shown in **Fig. 18,** then rotating wheel at 1.7 mph.

ABS Hydraulic Unit

1. Check bracket on vehicle, then all connectors.
2. Open hydraulic unit relay box and check for open or shorted circuits, **Fig. 19.**

ABS Control Module

Refer to **Fig. 20,** for control module input/output voltage signals.

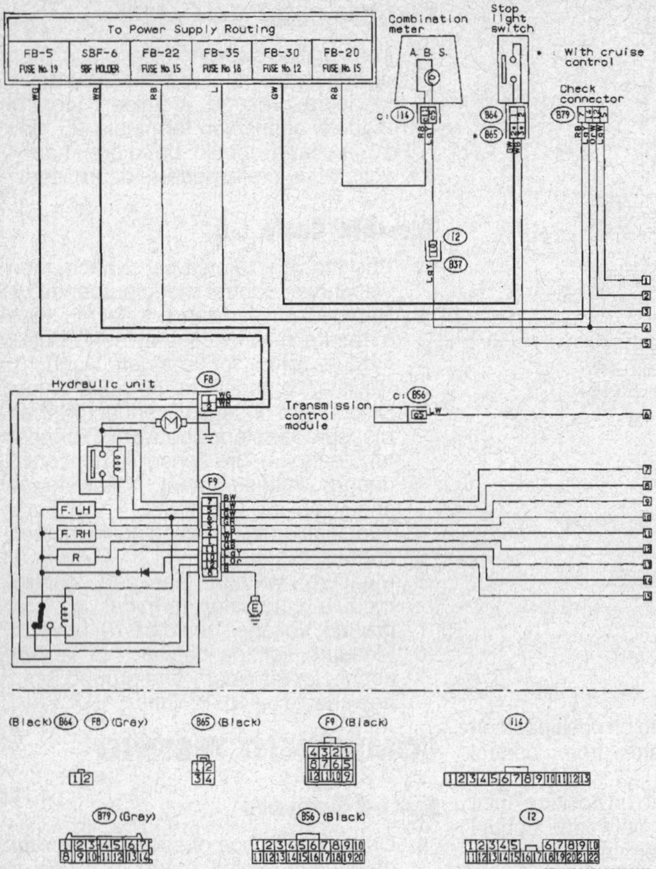
To Power Supply Routing
FB-5
SBF-6
FB-22
FB-35
FB-30
FB-20
Combination meter
Stop light switch
A. B. S.
With cruise control
Check connector
Hydraulic unit
Transmission control module
F. LH
F. RH
R
(Black)
(Gray)
(Black)
(Black)
(Gray)
(Black)

SB4029500052010X

Fig. 12 ABS system wiring diagram (Part 1 of 2). Legacy

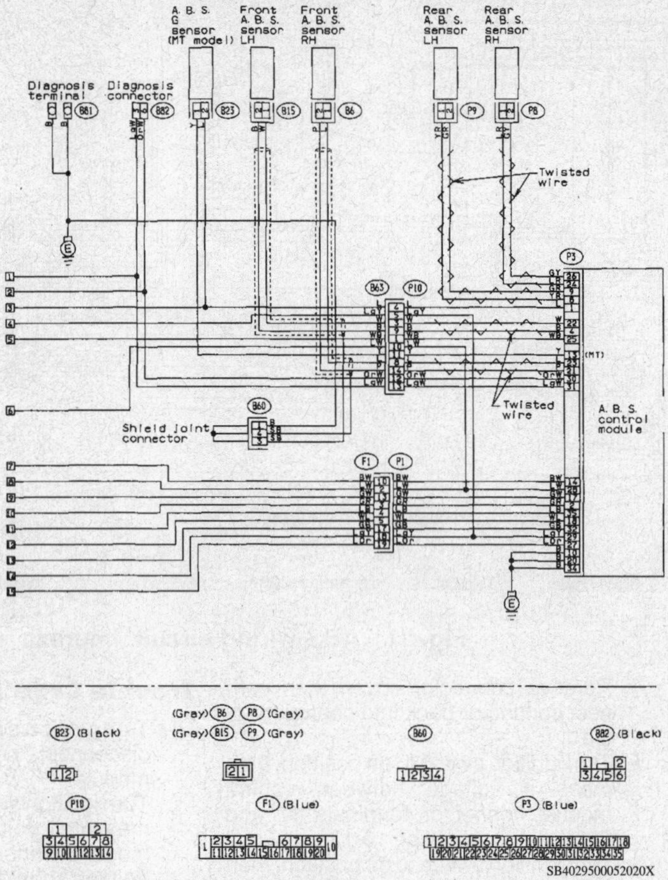
A. B. S. G sensor (MT model)
Front A. B. S. sensor LH
Front A. B. S. sensor RH
Rear A. B. S. sensor LH
Rear A. B. S. sensor RH
Diagnosis terminal
Diagnosis connector
Twisted wire
Twisted wire
Shield joint connector
A. B. S. control module
(MT)
(Black)
(Gray)
(Gray)
(Gray)
(Gray)
(Black)
(Blue)
(Blue)

SB4029500052020X

Fig. 12 ABS system wiring diagram (Part 2 of 2). Legacy

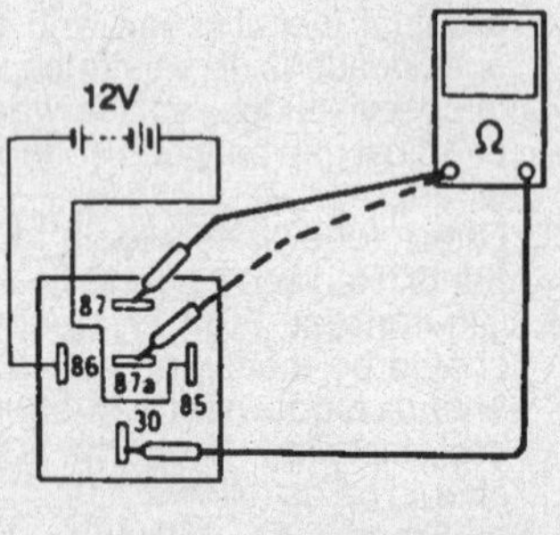
12V
Ω
87
86
87a
85
30

SB4029100043000X

Fig. 13 Valve relay terminal identification

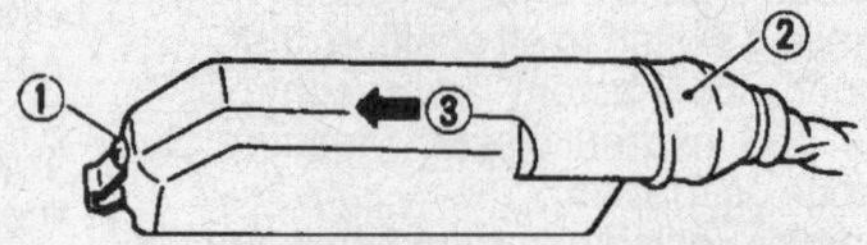
1
2
3

SB4029100044000X

Fig. 14 Connector cover removal

G Sensor

1. Disconnect sensor connector and measure contact resistance between terminals as follows:
   a. With sensor on flat surface, resistance should be 550-670 ohms.
   b. Sensor should turn off from on (610 ohms to more than 100,000 ohms) when it is tilted in a range from 14°–21.3°.

SYSTEM SERVICE

Brake System Bleed

Two technicians are required to bleed the brake system. Brake pedal operation must be very slow. Keep brake fluid reserve tank topped off to prevent entry of air into brake system during bleeding procedure. Check entire brake system for fluid leaks.

1. Start with brakes connected to secondary chamber of master cylinder first.
2. Fit one end of a vinyl tube onto air bleeder and place other end of tube into a container of brake fluid.
3. Slowly depress brake pedal and keep it depressed, then open air bleeder for 1 to 2 seconds.
4. Close air bleeder and slowly release brake pedal.
5. Repeat steps "3" and "4 " until no more air comes out. **Allow 3 to 4 seconds between brake pedal operation.**
6. After bleeding brakes connected to secondary chamber of the master cylinder, repeat steps 2 through 5 on brakes connected to primary chamber of the master cylinder.
7. Fully depress brake pedal for 20 seconds and check entire system for leaks.
8. Turn ignition switch to off position.
9. With engine at idle, inspect brake pedal stroke as follows:
   a. Depress brake pedal with 110 lbs. of force, then measure distance between brake pedal and steering wheel.
   b. Release brake pedal, then measure distance between brake pedal and steering wheel again.
   c. The difference between both measurements should be 3.74 inch. **If measurement is not as specified it is possible that air is still in brake system.**
10. Turn ignition switch to off position, then top off brake fluid level.

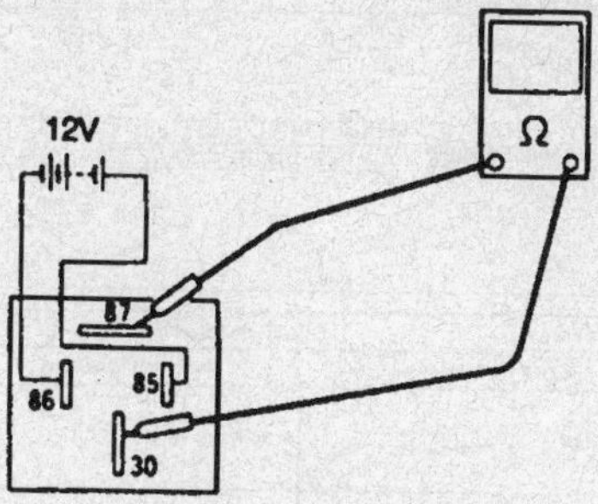

12V
Ω
87
86
85
30

SB4029100045000X

Fig. 15 Motor relay terminal identification

A.B.S. sensor	Model	Terminal No.	Standard
Front - LH	AWD AT FWD AT	22 and 4 5 and 4	1.0 ± 0.2 kΩ
Front - RH	ALL AT	23 and 21	
Rear - LH	ALL AT	8 and 9	
Rear - RH	ALL AT	24 and 26	
Front - LH	AWD AT FWD AT	22 and 10, 20, 34 5 and 10, 20, 34	More than 1 x 10^3 kΩ (Insulation resistance)
Front - RH	ALL AT	23 and 10, 20, 34	
Rear - LH	ALL AT	8 and 10, 20, 34	
Rear - RH	ALL AT	24 and 10, 20, 34	

SB4029100046000X

Fig. 16 Speed sensor specification chart

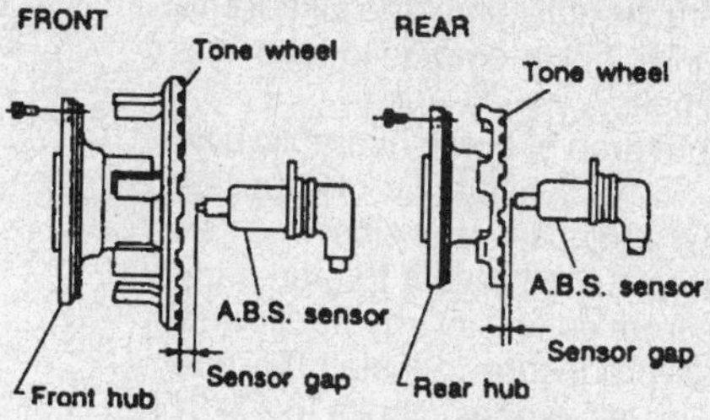

FRONT
Tone wheel
REAR
Tone wheel
A.B.S. sensor
A.B.S. sensor
Sensor gap
Sensor gap
Front hub
Rear hub

SB4029100047000X

Fig. 17 Tone wheel & hub clearance measurement

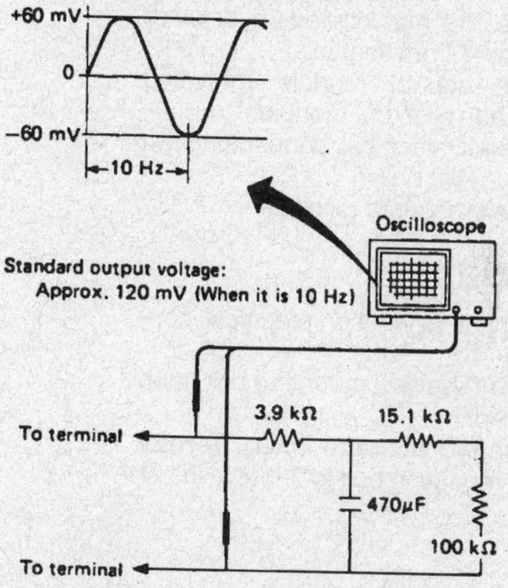

+60 mV
0
–60 mV
10 Hz
Oscilloscope
Standard output voltage:
Approx. 120 mV (When it is 10 Hz)
3.9 kΩ
15.1 kΩ
To terminal
470μF
100 kΩ
To terminal

SB4029100048000X

Fig. 18 Output voltage connection & specification

	Condition	Terminal number	Standard	Diagram	Terminal location
Valve relay	Turning off electricity.	85 — 86	93 — 113 Ω	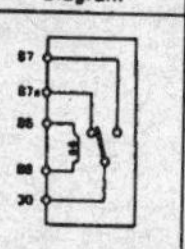	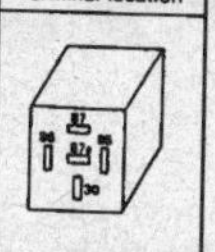
		30 — 87a	0 Ω		
		30 — 87	∞		
	Turning on electricity between 85 and 86. (DC 12 V)	30 — 87a	∞		
		30 — 87	0 Ω		
Motor relay	Turning off electricity.	85 — 86	72 — 88 Ω	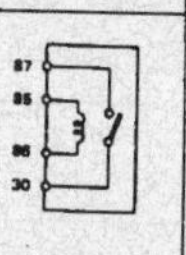	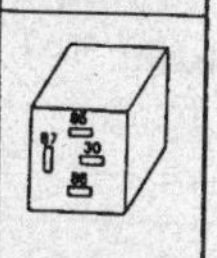
		30 — 87	∞		
	Turning on electricity between 85 and 86. (DC 12 V)	30 — 87	0 Ω		

SB4029100049000X

Fig. 19 Hydraulic relay box specification chart

11. Test drive vehicle at low speed and ensure proper brake operation.

Component Replacement

FRONT SENSOR

1. Disconnect sensor, located in engine compartment.
2. Remove sensor harness to bracket bolts, then sensor to housing bolts.
3. Remove brake caliper, brake rotor, driveshaft, knuckle and hub assemblies.
4. Remove tone wheel while removing hub from knuckle. Ensure teeth faces of tone wheel are not damaged during removal.
5. Reverse procedure to install, noting the following:
   a. Place a thickness gauge between sensor's pole piece and tone wheel's tooth face. After standard clearance is obtained over entire perimeter, tight sensor on housing to 17-31 ft. lbs.

REAR SENSOR

1. Remove rear seat and disconnect sensor connector.
2. Remove sensor harness bracket from trailing link, then sensor from rear back plate.
3. Remove rear tone wheel while removing hub from housing assembly. Ensure teeth faces of tone wheel are not damaged during removal.
4. Reverse procedure to install, noting the following:
   a. Place a thickness gauge between sensor's pole piece and tone wheel's tooth face. After standard clearance is obtained over entire perimeter, tight sensor on housing to 17-31 ft. lbs.

ABS HYDRAULIC UNIT

1. Remove canister from engine compartment, then disconnect lines from hydraulic unit, and plug open ports to prevent foreign particles from entering unit.
2. Remove bolts which secure hydraulic unit to bracket, then remove unit from vehicle noting the following precautions:

a. Hydraulic unit cannot be disassembled. Do not attempt to loosen nuts and bolts.
b. Do not drop or bump hydraulic unit.
c. Do not turn hydraulic unit upside down or place it on is side.
d. Be careful to prevent foreign particles from getting into hydraulic unit.

3. Reverse procedure to install. **Torque** hydraulic unit attaching bolts to 17–31 ft. lbs.

ABS CONTROL MODULE

1. Remove floor mat located under lower right side of front seat.
2. Remove control module mounting screw, then slide out module.
3. Disconnect electrical connector from module.
4. Reverse procedure to install.

G SENSOR

1. Disconnect G sensor electrical connector.
2. Remove G sensor mounting bolt, then the sensor.
3. Reverse procedure to install. **Torque** sensor mounting bolt to 3–6.8 ft. lbs.

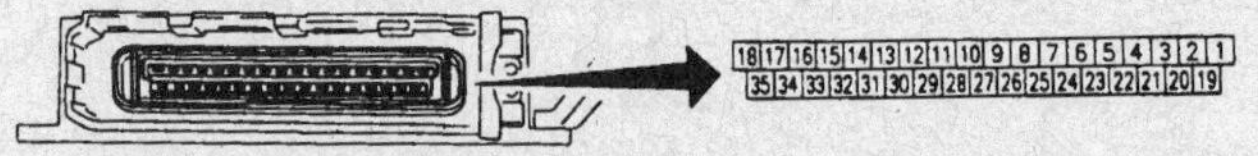
18 17 16 15 14 13 12 11 10 9 8 7 6 5 4 3 2 1
35 34 33 32 31 30 29 28 27 26 25 24 23 22 21 20 19

Contents			Terminal No.	Ignition switch ON, engine OFF	Input/output signals	
					Measured value	Measuring conditions
A.B.S. sensor	Front left wheel		FWD 5 / AWD 22	0V	0.12 — 1V (When it is 10 Hz)	• No. 22 or No. 5 — No. 4
	GND		4			
	Front right wheel		23	0V	0.12 — 1V (When it is 10 Hz)	• No. 23 — No. 21
	GND		21			
	Rear left wheel		8	0V	0.12 — 1V (When it is 10 Hz)	• No. 8 — No. 9
	GND		9			
	Rear right wheel		24	0V	0.12 — 1V (When it is 10 Hz)	• No. 24 — No. 26
	GND		26			
G sensor (AWD MT model)			13	10 — 12V	0V	When slanting about 14° — 21.3° (0)
Check connector			30	—	—	—
			31			
Stop light switch			25	0V	5 — 10V	When brake pedal is depressed.
Motor monitoring			14	0V	10 — 12V	When motor operates.
Valve power supply monitoring			32	10 — 12V	10 — 12V	—
Hydraulic unit	Solenoid	Front left wheel	2	10 — 12V	0V	When solenoid is energized to produce output.
		Front right wheel	35	10 — 12V	0V	
		Rear wheel	18	10 — 12V	0V	
	Valve relay coil		27	0V	0V	—
	Motor relay coil		28	10 — 12V	0V	When motor operates to produce output.
Warning light			29	0V	10 — 12V	Ignition switch ON (Engine OFF)
Power supply	Battery		1	10 — 12V	10 — 12V	—
	Relay coil (valve, motor, etc.)		17	10 — 12V	10 — 12V	—
Grounding line			10	0V	0V	—
			20	0V	0V	—
			34	0V	0V	—

SB4029100050000X

Fig. 20 ABS control module pin voltage specifications

1995 Legacy w/TCS

NOTE: On Air Bag Equipped Models, Refer To "Air Bag System Precautions" Located In The Front Of This Manual For System Disarming & Arming Procedures.

NOTE: Wire Code Identification And Symbol Identification Located In The Front Of This Manual Can Be Used As An Aid When Using Wiring Circuits Found In This Section.

INDEX

Page No.
Description 39-144
Diagnosis & Testing 39-145
Accessing Trouble Codes 39-145
Clearing Memory (Erasing Trouble Codes) 39-145
Component Testing 39-152
Trouble Code Diagnosis 39-145
Trouble Code Interpretation 39-145
Precautions 39-144
Air Bag Systems 39-144
System Service 39-153
Brake System Bleed 39-153
Component Replacement 39-153
Troubleshooting 39-145
Inspection Mode 39-145
Preliminary Inspection 39-145

PRECAUTIONS

AIR BAG SYSTEMS

Refer to "Air Bag System Precautions" in the front of this manual for system disarming and arming procedures.

DESCRIPTION

The ABS/TCS is a system into which both the functions of the anti-lock brake system (ABS) and the traction control system (TCS) are integrated.

The Anti-lock brake system (ABS) electrically controls brake fluid pressure to prevent wheel lock during braking on slippery road surfaces, improving steering stability and shortening the braking distance. If the ABS becomes inoperative, a fail-safe system activates to ensure conventional brake system operation.

The traction control system (TCS) is activated when any of the driving wheels is slipping, that is, when the control module finds the wheel speeds of the driving wheels as compared to the speeds of the non-driving wheels exceed the threshold value. There are kinds of values, one is for engine control and the other is for brake control. When two driving wheels slip the system regards it as caused by the over output of the engine torque and controls engine output by reducing fuel injected into the cylinders in addition to brake control to decrease excess torque.

TROUBLESHOOTING

Refer to **Figs. 1 and 2,** for troubleshooting procedures.

PRELIMINARY INSPECTION

1. Ensure battery voltage is 12 volts or more.
2. Ensure specific gravity of battery is 1.260.
3. Check condition of main and other fuses, harnesses and connector. Also check for proper grounding.
4. Check brake fluid level and for leakage.
5. Check for brake drag, brake pad and rotor condition.
6. Ensure tires are in good condition and at specified air pressure.

INSPECTION MODE

The on board diagnosis system is designed to detect problems after the vehicle has been driven at 6 MPH for more than 20 seconds. If a problem is found, the ABS/TCS warning lamp will illuminate to inform the drive of the occurrence of a problem. When the lamp is on the ABS/TCS system will be inactive and normal braking function will work. Problems will be stored in memory as trouble codes up to a maximum of three.

DIAGNOSIS & TESTING

ACCESSING TROUBLE CODES

When the control module detects a problem, the information (up to a maximum of three) will be stored in the EEPROM as a trouble code. When there are more than three, the most recent three will be stored. Stored codes will stay in memory until they are cleared.

1. Take out ABS check connector from under side of drivers side heater unit, **Fig. 3.**
2. Turn ignition switch off, then ground ABS check connector terminal 4.
3. Turn ignition switch to On position. The ABS/TCS warning light is now in the diagnostic mode and blinks to identify trouble codes.
4. After start code (11) is shown, the trouble code(s) will be shown in order of the last information first. The code(s) will repeat for a maximum of 5 minutes.

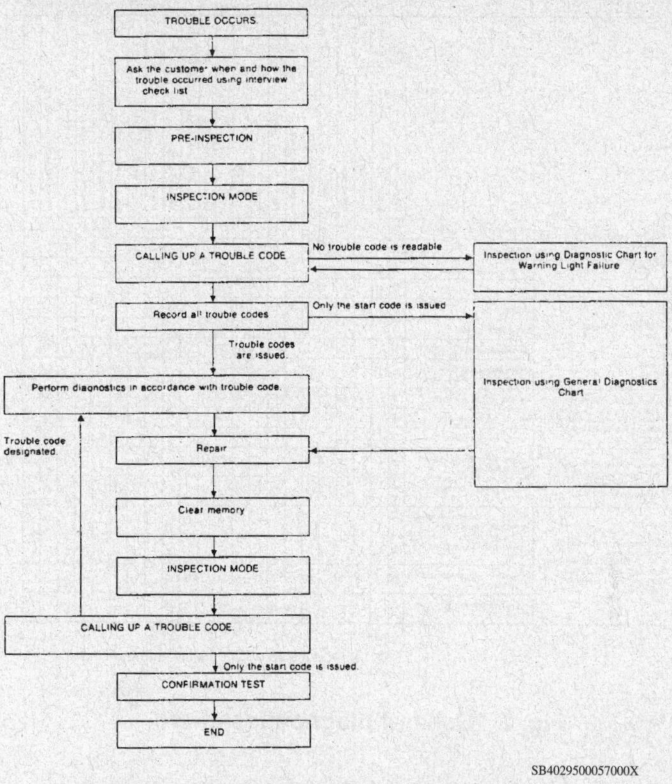
TROUBLE OCCURS.
Ask the customer when and how the trouble occurred using interview check list
PRE-INSPECTION
INSPECTION MODE
CALLING UP A TROUBLE CODE
No trouble code is readable
Inspection using Diagnostic Chart for Warning Light Failure
Record all trouble codes
Only the start code is issued
Trouble codes are issued.
Perform diagnostics in accordance with trouble code.
Inspection using General Diagnostics Chart
Trouble code designated.
Repair
Clear memory
INSPECTION MODE
CALLING UP A TROUBLE CODE.
Only the start code is issued.
CONFIRMATION TEST
END
SB4029500057000X

Fig. 1 Basic troubleshooting chart

When there are no trouble codes in memory, only the start code (11) is shown.

TROUBLE CODE INTERPRETATION

Refer to **Fig. 4,** for trouble code interpretation and **Fig. 5,** for trouble code identification and description.

CLEARING MEMORY (ERASING TROUBLE CODES)

After completing necessary repairs, clear trouble code memory as follows:

1. After calling up a trouble code, disconnect ABS check connector terminal 4 from ground.
2. Repeat connecting and disconnecting terminal 4 from ground 3 times within approximately 12 seconds. Leave terminal 4 disconnected for at least ½ second each time.

TROUBLE CODE DIAGNOSIS

Refer to wiring diagram, **Fig. 6,** when performing the following procedures.

TCS Sequence Control

1. Connect diagnosis terminals to terminal 4 of diagnosis connector beside driver seat heater unit.
2. Set speed of all wheels to at 6 mph or less, then turn ignition switch to off position.
3. Within 0.5 seconds after ABS and TCS warning lamp go out Press TCS OFF switch. With in 1.0 second thereafter, release and press switch again. then keep switch pressed. **When TCS sequence control is on, brake pedal must not be depressed. Engine must operate. When TCS OFF switch is not pressed within 0.5 seconds after ABS and TCS warning lights go off, trouble code mode comes on.**
4. After completion of TCS sequence control, turn ignition switch to off position.

TCS Warning Lamp Remains On

1. Turn ignition switch to off position, then disconnect connectors from ABS/TCS control module.
2. Measure resistance between ABS/TCS control module connector P6 terminal 3 and ground. Resistance should be should be 1 ohm.
3. Turn ignition switch off, then measure resistance between diagnosis terminal connector B81 and ground. Resistance should be should be 0 ohm.
4. Measure resistance between ABS/TCS control module connector B82 terminal 4 and ground. Resistance should be should be 0 ohm.

ABS & TCS Warning Lamps Remain On

1. Inspect brake fluid for proper level, then turn ignition switch to off position.
2. Disconnect connector from brake fluid level sensor.
3. Measure resistance between connector B16 terminals 1 and 2. Resistance should be 0 ohm when float is up and 1 ohm when pushing float down.

◎: Primary expected causes ○: Secondary expected causes

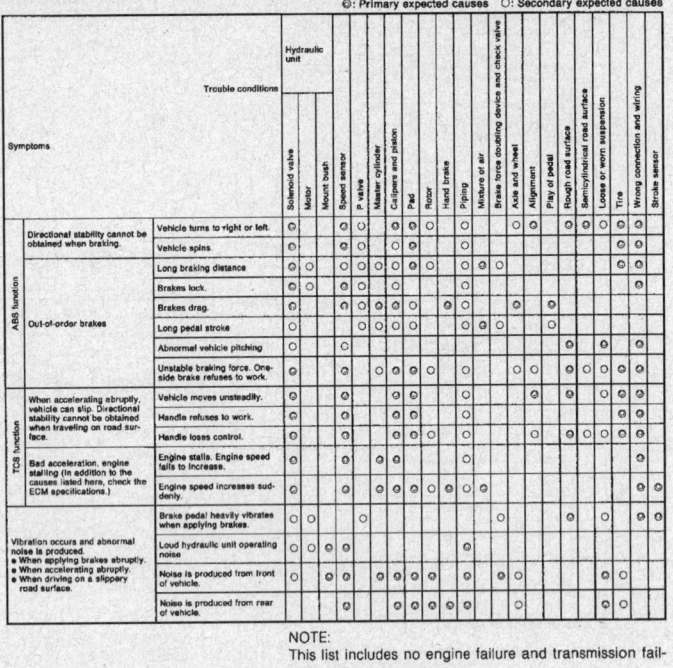

Symptoms		Trouble conditions	Hydraulic unit																				
			Solenoid valve	Motor	Mount bush	Speed sensor	P valve	Master cylinder	Calipers and piston	Pad	Rotor	Hand brake	Piping	Mixture of air	Brake force doubling device and check valve	Axle and wheel	Alignment	Play of pedal	Rough road surface	Semicylindrical road surface	Loose or worn suspension	Tire	Wrong connection and wiring	Stroke sensor
ABS function	Directional stability cannot be obtained when braking.	Vehicle turns to right or left.	◎			◎	○		◎	◎	○		○			○	◎		◎	◎	○	◎	◎	
		Vehicle spins.	◎			◎	○		○	◎			○									◎	◎	
	Out-of-order brakes	Long braking distance	◎	○		○	○	○	○	◎	○		○	◎	○							◎	◎	
		Brakes lock.	◎	○		◎	○		○				○										◎	
		Brakes drag.	◎			◎	○	◎	◎	○		◎	○			◎		◎						
		Long pedal stroke	○				○	○	○	○			○	◎	○			○						
		Abnormal vehicle pitching	○			○													◎		◎		◎	
		Unstable braking force. One-side brake refuses to work.	◎			◎		○	◎	◎	○		○			○	○		◎	○	○	◎	◎	
TCS function	When accelerating abruptly, vehicle can slip. Directional stability cannot be obtained when traveling on road surface.	Vehicle moves unsteadily.	◎			◎			◎	◎			○				◎		◎		○	◎	◎	
		Handle refuses to work.	◎			◎			◎	◎			○									◎	◎	
		Handle loses control.	◎			◎			◎	◎	○		○				○		◎	○	○	◎	◎	
	Bad acceleration, engine stalling (In addition to the causes listed here, check the ECM specifications.)	Engine stalls. Engine speed fails to increase.	◎			◎		◎	◎				○										◎	
		Engine speed increases suddenly.	◎			◎		◎	◎	◎	○	◎	○	◎									◎	◎
Vibration occurs and abnormal noise is produced. • When applying brakes abruptly. • When accelerating abruptly. • When driving on a slippery road surface.		Brake pedal heavily vibrates when applying brakes.	○	○			○								○				◎		○		◎	◎
		Loud hydraulic unit operating noise	○	○	◎	◎							◎											
		Noise is produced from front of vehicle.	○		◎	◎		◎	◎	◎	◎		◎		◎	○					◎	○		
		Noise is produced from rear of vehicle.				◎			◎	◎	◎	◎	◎			○					◎	○		

NOTE:
This list includes no engine failure and transmission failure.

SB4029500053000X

Fig. 2 General diagnostics chart

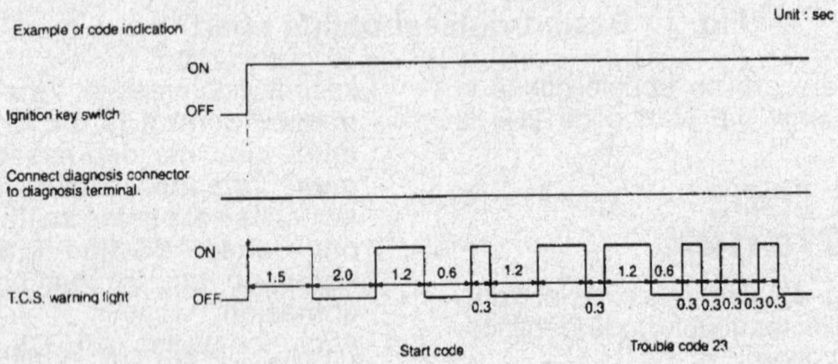

Example of code indication
Unit : sec
ON
Ignition key switch
OFF
Connect diagnosis connector to diagnosis terminal.
ON
T.C.S. warning light
OFF
1.5
2.0
1.2
0.6
1.2
1.2
0.6
0.3
0.3
0.3 0.3 0.3 0.3 0.3
Start code
Trouble code 23

SB4029500055000X

Fig. 4 Trouble code interpretation

4. Connect connector to brake fluid sensor, then disconnect connector P7 from ABS/TCS control module.
5. Measure resistance between ABS/TCS control module connector P7 terminal 20 and ground. Resistance should be 0 ohms with engine off and 1 Mohm with engine on.

ABS Warning Lamp Remains On And TCS Warning Lamp Functions Properly

1. Turn ignition switch to off position, then disconnect connector P6 from ABS/TCS control module and TCS valve relay.
2. Measure resistance between ABS/TCS control module connector P6 terminal 2 and ground. Resistance should be 1 Mohm.

ABS Warning Lamp Remains On and TCS Warning Lamp Does Not Illuminate At All

1. Turn ignition switch to off position, then disconnect connector P5 from ABS/TCS control module and TCS valve relay.
2. Turn ignition switch to on position.
3. Measure voltage between ABS/TCS control module connector P5 terminal 1 and ground. Voltage should be 10–12 volt. **When ABS/TCS control module is defective, same condition occurs.**

TCS Off Indicator Lamp Remains On

1. Turn ignition switch to off position, then disconnect connector P6 from ABS/TCS control module and TCS valve relay.
2. Measure resistance between ABS/TCS control module connector P6 terminal 10 and ground. Resistance should be 1 Mohm.

TCS Operating Indicator Lamp Remains On

1. Turn ignition switch to off position, then disconnect connector P6 from ABS/TCS control module and TCS valve relay.

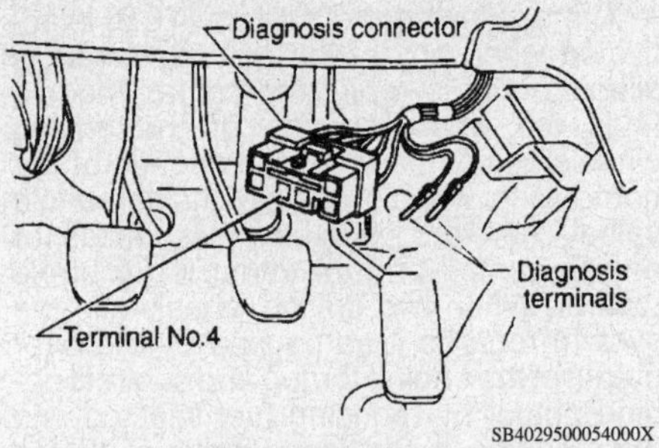

Diagnosis connector
Diagnosis terminals
Terminal No.4

SB4029500054000X

Fig. 3 Check connector terminal identification

2. Measure resistance between ABS/TCS control module connector P6 terminal 11 and ground. Resistance should be 1 Mohm.

TCS Off Switch Does Not Function

1. Turn ignition switch to off position, then disconnect connector i9 from TCS OFF switch.
2. Measure resistance between TCS OFF switch connector i9 terminals 5 and 3. Resistance should be 0 ohm when switch is pressed (On) and 1 Mohm When switch is released (Off).
3. Disconnect connector P7 from ABS/TCS control module.
4. Measure resistance between ABS/TCS control module connector P7 terminal 16 and ground. Resistance should be 0 ohm when switch is pressed (On) and 1 Mohm When switch is released (Off).

ABS Warning, TCS Warning, TCS Operating Indicator And/Or TCS Off Indicator Lamps Do Not Illuminate

1. Turn ignition switch to off position, then disconnect combination meter.
2. Check ABS warning light valve, then turn ignition switch to on position.
3. Measure voltage between combination meter connector i14 terminal 11 and ground. Voltage should be 10–12 volts.
4. Turn ignition switch off, then remove combination meter.
5. Disconnect connectors from ABS/TCS control module, then turn ignition switch to on position. Measure as follows:
   a. Measure voltage between ABS/TCS control module connector P6 terminal 2 and ground. Voltage should be 10–12 volts.
   b. Measure voltage between ABS/TCS control module connector P6 terminal 3 and ground. Voltage should be 10–12 volts.
   c. Measure voltage between ABS/TCS control module connector P6 terminal 11 and ground. Voltage should be 10–12 volts.
   d. Measure voltage between ABS/TCS control module connector P6 terminal 10 and ground. Voltage should be 10–12 volts.

Trouble code	Contents of diagnosis	
*1	Start code • Trouble code is shown after start code. • Only start code is shown in normal condition.	
21	Faulty ABS sensor (Open circuit or short circuit)	Front right wheel speed sensor
23		Front left wheel speed sensor
25		Rear right wheel speed sensor
27		Rear left wheel speed sensor
22	Faulty ABS sensor (Faulty ABS sensor signal)	Front right wheel speed sensor
24		Front left wheel speed sensor
26		Rear right wheel speed sensor
28		Rear left wheel speed sensor
31	Faulty solenoid valve circuit(s) in hydraulic unit	Front right inlet valve
32		Front right outlet valve
33		Front left inlet valve
34		Front left outlet valve
35		Rear right inlet valve
36		Rear right outlet valve
37		Rear left inlet valve
38		Rear left outlet valve
41	Faulty ABS/TCS control module	
42	Source voltage is high.	
43	Faulty engine control module communication cables	
51	Faulty valve relay	
52	Faulty motor, motor sensor and/or motor relay	
54	Faulty stroke sensor and/or stop light switch	
57	Faulty fluid level sensor	
58	Faulty pressure switch	
61	Faulty solenoid valve circuit(s) in hydraulic unit	TCS 1 valve
62		TCS 2 valve

SB4029500056000X

Fig. 5 Trouble code description

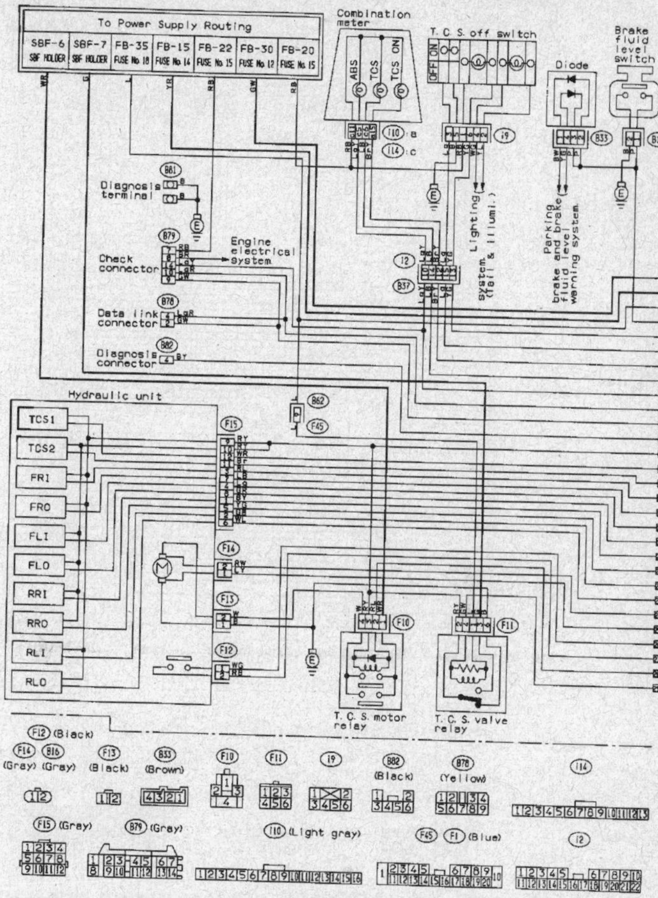
To Power Supply Routing
Combination meter
T. C. S. off switch
Brake fluid level switch
Diode
Diagnosis terminal
Check connector
Engine electrical system
Data link connector
Diagnosis connector
Hydraulic unit
TCS1
TCS2
FRI
FRO
FLI
FLO
RRI
RRO
RLI
RLO
T. C. S. motor relay
T. C. S. valve relay

SB4029500058010X

Fig. 6 ABS/TCS system wiring diagram (Part 1 of 2)

e. Measure resistance between ABS/TCS control module connector P4 terminal 6 and ground. Resistance should be 0 ohms.
f. Measure resistance between ABS/TCS control module connector P5 terminal 5 and ground. Resistance should be 0 ohms.
g. Measure resistance between ABS/TCS control module connector P7 terminal 15 and ground. Resistance should be 0 ohms.

Trouble Codes 21, 23, 25 & 27

1. Turn ignition switch to off position, then disconnect ABS sensor connector.
2. Measure resistance between ABS sensor connector terminals as follows:
   a. If trouble code 21 is present, measure between terminals 1 and 2. Resistance should be 800–1200 ohms.
   b. If trouble code 23 is present, measure between terminals 1 and 2. Resistance should be 800–1200 ohms.
   c. If trouble code 25 is present, measure between terminals 1 and 2. Resistance should be 800–1200 ohms.
   d. If trouble code 27 is present, measure between terminals 1 and 2. Resistance should be 800–1200 ohms.
3. Measure resistance between ABS sensor connector and ground as follows:
   a. If trouble code 21 is present, measure between terminal 1 and ground, then between terminal 2 and ground. Resistance should be 1 Mohms.
   b. If trouble code 23 is present, measure between terminal 1 and ground, then between terminal 2 and ground. Resistance should be 1 Mohms.
   c. If trouble code 25 is present, measure between terminal 1 and ground, then between terminal 2 and ground. Resistance should be 1 Mohms.
   d. If trouble code 27 is present, measure between terminal 1 and ground, then between terminal 2 and ground. Resistance should be 1 Mohms.
4. Reconnect ABS sensor connector, then disconnect ABS/TCS control module connectors.
5. Measure resistance between ABS/TCS control module connector terminals as follows:
   a. If trouble code 21 is present, measure between connector P6 terminals 8 and 16. Resistance should be 800–1200 ohms.
   b. If trouble code 23 is present, measure between connector P7 terminals 1 and 11. Resistance should be 800–1200 ohms.
   c. If trouble code 25 is present, measure between connector P7 terminals 2 and 12. Resistance should be 800–1200 ohms.
   d. If trouble code 27 is present, measure between connector P6 terminals 7 and 15. Resistance should be 800–1200 ohms.
6. Measure resistance between ABS/TCS control module terminals and ground as follows:
   a. If trouble code 21 is present, measure between connector P6 terminal 8 and ground, then terminal 16 and ground. Resistance should be 1 Mohms.
   b. If trouble code 23 is present, measure between connector P6 terminal 1 and ground, then terminal 11 and ground. Resistance should be 1 Mohms.
   c. If trouble code 25 is present, measure between connector P6 terminal 2 and ground, then terminal 12 and ground. Resistance should be 1 Mohms.
   d. If trouble code 27 is present, measure between connector P6 terminal 7 and ground, then terminal 15 and ground. Resistance should be 1 Mohms.

Trouble Codes 22, 24, 26 & 28

1. Remove brake assembly to gain access to ABS sensor and tone wheel.

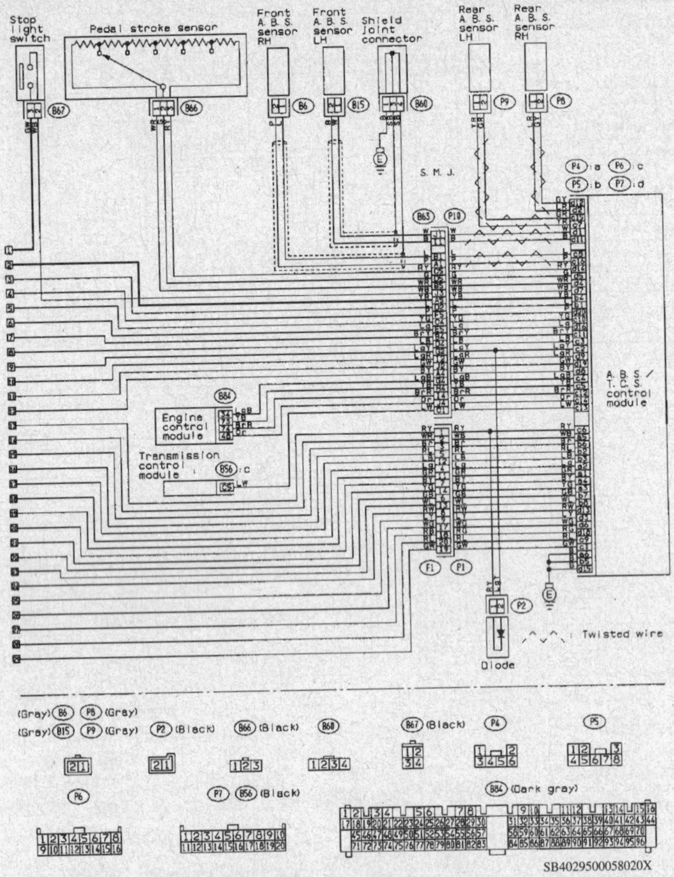
Stop light switch
Pedal stroke sensor
Front A.B.S. sensor RH
Front A.B.S. sensor LH
Shield joint connector
Rear A.B.S. sensor LH
Rear A.B.S. sensor RH
S. M. J.
Engine control module
Transmission control module
A.B.S./T.C.S. control module
Diode
Twisted wire
(Gray) B6
P8 (Gray)
(Gray) B15
P9 (Gray)
P2 (Black)
B66 (Black)
B68
B67 (Black)
P4
P5
P6
P7
B56 (Black)
B84 (Dark gray)
SB4029500058020X

Fig. 6 ABS/TCS system wiring diagram (Part 2 of 2)

2. Check pole piece and tone wheel for accumulation of foreign particles. Clean as necessary.
3. Check tone wheel teeth for cracks or deformities. Replace as necessary.
4. **Torque** tone wheel to 7–12 ft. lbs.
5. Measure tone wheel to pole piece gap over entire perimeter of wheel. Gap for front wheel must be .035–.055 inch. Gap for rear wheel must be .028–.047 inch. If necessary, adjust gap using spacers part No. 26755AA000.
6. Check hub runout. Runout should be .0020 inch.
7. Turn ignition switch to off position, then raise and support vehicle.
8. Connect connector to ABS control module, then connect an oscilloscope to the ABS control module connector as outlined in step 5.
9. Turn ignition switch to on position.
10. Rotate wheels and measure voltage at a frequency of 10 Hz. Measure voltage as follows:
    a. If trouble code 22 is present, measure voltage between connector P6 terminals 8 and 16. Voltage should be .12–1.0 volt at 10 Hz.
    b. If trouble code 24 is present, measure voltage between connector P7 terminals 1 and 11. Voltage should be .12–1.0 volt at 10 Hz.
    c. If trouble code 26 is present, measure voltage between connector P7 terminals 2 and 12. Voltage should be .12–1.0 volt at 10 Hz.
    d. If trouble code 28 is present, measure voltage between connector P6 terminals 7 and 15. Voltage should be .12–1.0 volt at 10 Hz.
    e. When this inspection is completed, the control module could stores the trouble code.
11. Turn ignition switch to off position, then disconnect connectors from ABS/TCS control module.
12. Measure resistance between ABS/TCS control module connectors and ground as follows:
    a. Measure resistance between ABS/TCS control module connector P4 terminal 6 and ground. Resistance should be 0 ohms.
    b. Measure resistance between ABS/TCS control module connector P5 terminal 5 and ground. Resistance should be 0 ohms.
    c. Measure resistance between ABS/TCS control module connector P7 terminal 15 and ground. Resistance should be 0 ohms.
13. Turn ignition switch to off position, then disconnect ABS sensor connector.
14. Measure resistance between ABS sensor connector terminals as follows:
    a. If trouble code 22 is present, measure between terminals 1 and 2. Resistance should be 800–1200 ohms.
    b. If trouble code 24 is present, measure between terminals 1 and 2. Resistance should be 800–1200 ohms.
    c. If trouble code 26 is present, measure between terminals 1 and 2. Resistance should be 800–1200 ohms.
    d. If trouble code 28 is present, measure between terminals 1 and 2. Resistance should be 800–1200 ohms.
15. Reconnect ABS sensor connector, then disconnect ABS/TCS control module connectors.
16. Measure resistance between ABS/TCS control module connector terminals as follows:
    a. If trouble code 21 is present, measure between connector P6 terminals 8 and 16. Resistance should be 800–1200 ohms.
    b. If trouble code 23 is present, measure between connector P7 terminals 1 and 11. Resistance should be 800–1200 ohms.
    c. If trouble code 25 is present, measure between connector P7 terminals 2 and 12. Resistance should be 800–1200 ohms.
    d. If trouble code 27 is present, measure between connector P6 terminals 7 and 15. Resistance should be 800–1200 ohms.

Trouble Codes 31, 33, 35, 37, 61 & 62

1. Turn ignition switch to off position.
2. Disconnect connector from hydraulic unit, then measure resistance between hydraulic unit connector F15 terminals as follows:
    a. If code 31 is present, measure between terminals 3 and 9. Resistance should be approximately 5.5–6.5 ohm.
    b. If code 33 is present, measure between terminals 4 and 10. Resistance should be approximately 5.5–6.5 ohm.
    c. If code 35 is present, measure between terminals 1 and 10. Resistance should be approximately 5.5–6.5 ohm.
    d. If code 37 is present, measure between terminals 2 and 9. Resistance should be approximately 5.5–6.5 ohm.
    e. If code 61 is present, measure between terminals 12 and 9. Resistance should be approximately 5.5–6.5 ohm.
    f. If code 62 is present, measure between terminals 11 and 10. Resistance should be approximately 5.5–6.5 ohm.
3. Measure resistance between hydraulic unit connector F15 terminals and ground as follows:
    a. If code 31 is present, measure between terminal 3 and ground, then between terminal 9 and ground. Resistance should be approximately 1 Mohm.
    b. If code 33 is present, measure between terminal 4 and ground, then between terminal 10 and ground.

Resistance should be approximately 1 Mohm.

c. If code 35 is present, measure between terminal 1 and ground, then between terminal 10 and ground. Resistance should be approximately 1 Mohm.
d. If code 37 is present, measure between terminal 2 and ground, then between terminal 9 and ground. Resistance should be approximately 1 Mohm.
e. If code 61 is present, measure between terminal 12 and ground, then between terminal 9 and ground. Resistance should be approximately 1 Mohm.
f. If code 62 is present, measure between terminal 11 and ground, then between terminal 10 and ground. Resistance should be approximately 1 Mohm.

4. Disconnect connectors from ABS/TCS control module.
5. Measure resistance between ABS/TCS control module connector terminals and ground as follows:
   a. If code 31 is present, measure between connector P5 terminal 2 and ground. Resistance should be approximately 1 Mohm.
   b. If code 33 is present, measure between connector P4 terminal 2 and ground. Resistance should be approximately 1 Mohm.
   c. If code 35 is present, measure between connector P4 terminal 4 and ground. Resistance should be approximately 1 Mohm.
   d. If code 37 is present, measure between connector P5 terminal 7 and ground. Resistance should be approximately 1 Mohm.
   e. If code 61 is present, measure between connector P4 terminal 5 and ground. Resistance should be approximately 1 Mohm.
   f. If code 62 is present, measure between connector P5 terminal 6 and ground. Resistance should be approximately 1 Mohm.
6. Connect connector from hydraulic unit.
7. Measure resistance between ABS/TCS control module connector terminals as follows:
   a. If code 31 is present, measure between connector P5 terminal 2 and connector P6 terminal 6. Resistance should be approximately 5.5–6.5 ohm.
   b. If code 33 is present, measure between connector P4 terminal 2 and connector P6 terminal 6. Resistance should be approximately 5.5–6.5 ohm.
   c. If code 35 is present, measure between connector P4 terminal 4 and connector P6 terminal 6. Resistance should be approximately 5.5–6.5 ohm.
   d. If code 37 is present, measure between connector P5 terminal 7 and connector P6 terminal 6. Resistance should be approximately 5.5–6.5 ohm.
   e. If code 61 is present, measure between connector P4 terminal 5 and connector P6 terminal 6. Resistance should be approximately 5.5–6.5 ohm.
   f. If code 62 is present, measure between connector P5 terminal 6 and connector P6 terminal 6. Resistance should be approximately 5.5–6.5 ohm.

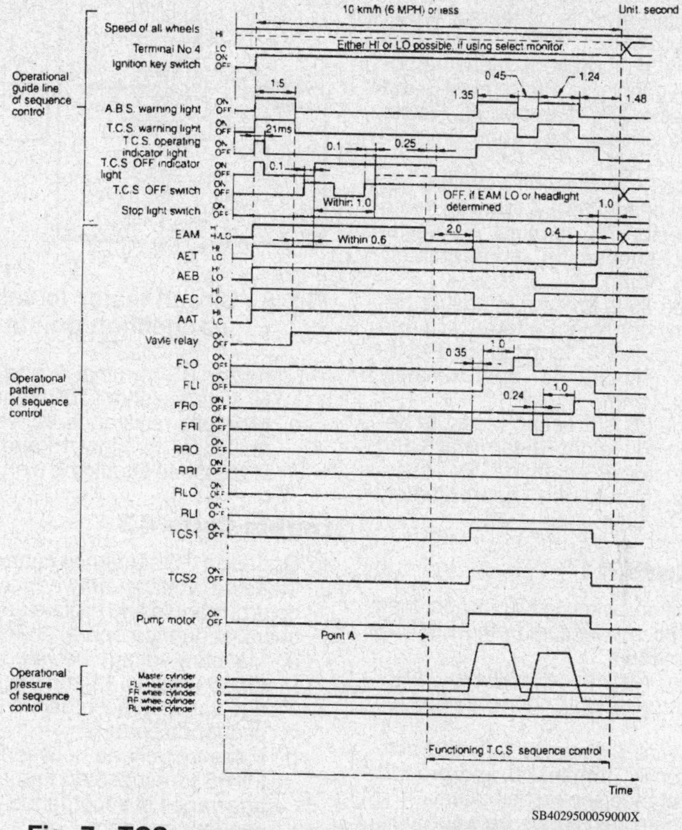
10 km/h (6 MPH) or less
Unit: second
Speed of all wheels
Terminal No 4
Ignition key switch
Either HI or LO possible, if using select monitor.
Operational guide line of sequence control
A.B.S. warning light
T.C.S. warning light
T.C.S. operating indicator light
T.C.S. OFF indicator light
T.C.S. OFF switch
Stop light switch
1.5
0.45
1.24
1.35
1.48
21ms
0.1
0.25
Within 1.0
OFF, if EAM LO or headlight determined
1.0
EAM
AET
AEB
AEC
AAT
Within 0.6
2.0
0.4
Valve relay
0.35
0.24
FLO
FLI
FRO
FRI
RRO
RRI
RLO
RLI
TCS1
TCS2
Pump motor
Operational pattern of sequence control
Point A
Operational pressure of sequence control
Master cylinder
Functioning T.C.S. sequence control
Time
SB4029500059000X

Fig. 7 TCS sequence control operation pattern

Trouble Codes 32, 34, 36 & 38

1. Turn ignition switch to off position.
2. Disconnect connector from hydraulic unit, then measure resistance between hydraulic unit connector F15 terminals as follows:
   a. If code 32 is present, measure between terminals 7 and 9. Resistance should be approximately 3–4 ohm.
   b. If code 34 is present, measure between terminals 8 and 10. Resistance should be approximately 3–4 ohm.
   c. If code 36 is present, measure between terminals 5 and 10. Resistance should be approximately 3–4 ohm.
   d. If code 38 is present, measure between terminals 6 and 9. Resistance should be approximately 3–4 ohm.
3. Measure resistance between hydraulic unit connector F15 terminals and ground as follows:
   a. If code 32 is present, measure between terminal 7 and ground. Resistance should be approximately 1 Mohm.
   b. If code 34 is present, measure between terminal 8 and ground. Resistance should be approximately 1 Mohm.
   c. If code 36 is present, measure between terminal 5 and ground. Resistance should be approximately 1 Mohm.
   d. If code 38 is present, measure between terminal 6 and ground. Resistance should be approximately 1 Mohm.
4. Disconnect connectors from ABS/TCS control module.
5. Measure resistance between ABS/TCS control module connector terminals and ground as follows:
   a. If code 32 is present, measure between connector P5 terminal 3 and ground. Resistance should be approximately 1 Mohm.
   b. If code 34 is present, measure between connector P4 terminal 1 and ground. Resistance should be approximately 1 Mohm.
   c. If code 36 is present, measure between connector P4 terminal 3 and ground. Resistance should be approximately 1 Mohm.
   d. If code 38 is present, measure between connector P5 terminal 8 and ground. Resistance should be approximately 1 Mohm.
6. Connect connector from hydraulic unit.

7. Measure resistance between ABS/TCS control module connector terminals as follows:
   a. If code 32 is present, measure between connector P5 terminal 3 and connector P6 terminal 6. Resistance should be approximately 3.2–4.2 ohm.
   b. If code 34 is present, measure between connector P4 terminal 1 and connector P6 terminal 6. Resistance should be approximately 3.2–4.2 ohm.
   c. If code 36 is present, measure between connector P4 terminal 3 and connector P6 terminal 6. Resistance should be approximately 3.2–4.2 ohm.
   d. If code 38 is present, measure between connector P5 terminal 8 and connector P6 terminal 6. Resistance should be approximately 3.2–4.2 ohm.

Trouble Code 41

1. Turn ignition switch to off position, then disconnect connectors from ABS/TCS control module.
2. Measure resistance between ABS/TCS control module connectors as follows:
   a. Measure resistance between connector P4 terminal 6 and ground. Resistance should be 0 ohms.
   b. Measure resistance between connector P5 terminal 5 and ground. Resistance should be 0 ohms.
   c. Measure resistance between connector P7 terminal 15 and ground. Resistance should be 0 ohms.
3. Turn ignition switch to on position.
4. Measure voltage between ABS/TCS control module connectors as follows:
   a. Measure voltage between connector P5 terminal 1 and ground. Voltage should be 10–12 volt.
   b. Measure voltage between connector P5 terminal 4 and ground. Voltage should be 10–12 volt.

Trouble Code 42

1. Run engine at idle, then measure voltage between alternator B terminal and ground. Voltage should be 14.2–14.8 volt.
2. Ensure battery positive and negative cables are firmly affixed to post.
3. Turn ignition switch to off position, then disconnect ABS/TCS control module connector P5.
4. Run engine at idle.
5. Measure voltage between ABS/TCS control module connector P5 terminal 1 and ground. Voltage should be 14.2–14.8 volt.
6. Turn ignition switch to off position, then disconnect ABS/TCS control module connectors P4 and P7.
7. Measure resistance between ABS/TCS control module connectors as follows:
   a. Measure resistance between connector P4 terminal 6 and ground. Resistance should be 0 ohms.
   b. Measure resistance between connector P5 terminal 5 and ground. Resistance should be 0 ohms.
   c. Measure resistance between connector P7 terminal 15 and ground. Resistance should be 0 ohms.

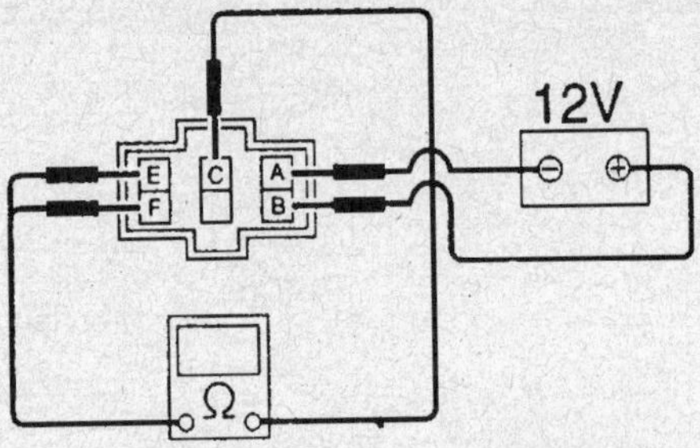
12V
E
F
C
A
B
Ω
SB4029500060000X

Fig. 8 Circuit tester to valve relay connection points

Trouble Code 43

1. Operate TCS sequence control.
2. Measure voltage between ABS/TCS control module and ground during TCS check sequence operation as follows:
   a. Measure voltage between connector P6 terminal 12 and ground. Voltage varies in accordance with TCS sequence pattern.
   b. Measure voltage between connector P6 terminal 5 and ground. Voltage varies in accordance with TCS sequence pattern.
   c. Measure voltage between connector P6 terminal 14 and ground. Voltage varies in accordance with TCS sequence pattern.
   d. Refer to **Fig. 7,** for sequence pattern.
3. Turn ignition switch to off position, then disconnect engine control module and ABS/TCS control module.
4. Measure voltage between ABS/TCS control module connector and ground as follows:
   a. Measure voltage between connector P6 terminal 12 and ground. Voltage should be 0 volt.
   b. Measure voltage between connector P6 terminal 5 and ground. Voltage should be 0 volt.
   c. Measure voltage between connector P6 terminal 14 and ground. Voltage should be 0 volt.
5. Turn ignition switch to on position, then measure voltage between ABS/TCS control module connector and ground as follows:
   a. Measure voltage between connector P6 terminal 12 and ground. Voltage should be 0 volt.
   b. Measure voltage between connector P6 terminal 5 and ground. Voltage should be 0 volt.
   c. Measure voltage between connector P6 terminal 14 and ground. Voltage should be 0 volt.
6. Turn ignition switch to off position, then connect ABS/TCS control module.
7. Measure voltage between ABS/TCS control module connector and ground as follows:
   a. Measure voltage between connector P6 terminal 12 and ground. Voltage should be 0 volt.
   b. Measure voltage between connector P6 terminal 5 and ground. Voltage should be 0 volt.
   c. Measure voltage between connector P6 terminal 14 and ground. Voltage should be 0 volt.
8. Turn ignition switch to on position, then measure voltage between ABS/TCS control module connector and ground as follows:
   a. Measure voltage between connector P6 terminal 12 and ground. Voltage should be 0 volt.
   b. Measure voltage between connector P6 terminal 5 and ground. Voltage should be 0 volt.
   c. Measure voltage between connector P6 terminal 14 and ground. Voltage should be 0 volt.
9. Turn ignition switch to off position, then connect engine control module.
10. Turn ignition switch to on position, then measure voltage between engine control module connector and ground as follows:
    a. Measure voltage between connector B84 terminal 74 and ground. Voltage should be 5 volt.
    b. Measure voltage between connector B84 terminal 73 and ground. Voltage should be 5 volt.
    c. Measure voltage between connector B84 terminal 48 and ground. Voltage should be 5 volt.
11. Turn ignition switch to off position, then disconnect engine control module and ABS/TCS control module.
12. Measure resistance between ABS/TCS control module connector and ground as follows:
    a. Measure resistance between connector P6 terminal 12 and ground. Resistance should be 1 Mohm.
    b. Measure resistance between connector P6 terminal 5 and ground. Resistance should be 1 Mohm.
    c. Measure resistance between connector P6 terminal 14 and ground. Resistance should be 1 Mohm.
13. Measure resistance between ABS/TCS control module connector and engine control module connector as follows:
    a. Measure resistance between connector P6 terminal 12 and connector B84 terminal 74. Resistance should be 0 ohm.
    b. Measure resistance between connector P6 terminal 5 and connector B84 terminal 73. Resistance should be 0 ohm.
    c. Measure resistance between connector P6 terminal 14 and connector B84 terminal 48. Resistance should be 0 ohm.

Trouble Code 51

1. Turn ignition switch to off position, then remove valve relay.
2. Measure resistance between valve relay terminals A and B. Resistance should be 90 ohm.
3. Attach circuit test probes to relay as

Terminal:
No. 3 — No. 2

Stroke Unit: mm (in)	Specified resistance
0 — 3.1 ± 0.5 (0 — 0 122 ± 0.020)	95 — 105 Ω
3.1 — 5.5 ± 0.5 (0.122 — 0.217 ± 0.020)	190 — 210 Ω
5.5 — 7.9 ± 0.5 (0.217 — 0.311 ± 0.020)	285 — 315 Ω
7.9 — 10.3 ± 0.5 (0.311 — 0.406 ± 0.020)	380 — 420 Ω
10.3 — 18 ± 0.5 (0 406 — 0.709 ± 0.020)	475 — 525 Ω

NOTE:
Stroke = 0 when the stroke sensor rod is completely drawn into the sensor unit.

SB4029500061000X

Fig. 9 Stroke sensor resistance. Connector B66

show in **Fig. 8,** then measure resistance between valve relay terminals as follows:
   a. Measure resistance between terminals C and E. Resistance should be 0 ohm with 12 volt applied and 1 Mohm when no voltage is applied.
   b. Measure resistance between terminals C and F. Resistance should be 1 Mohm with 12 volt applied and O ohm when no voltage is applied.
4. Measure resistance between valve relay terminals B and F. Resistance should be 1 Mohm.
5. Measure voltage between valve relay connector F11 and ground as follows:
   a. Measure voltage between terminal 1 and ground. Voltage should be 0 volt.
   b. Measure voltage between terminal 3 and ground. Voltage should be 12 volt.
6. Turn ignition switch to on position, then measure voltage between valve relay connector F11 and ground as follows:
   a. Measure voltage between terminal 1 and ground. Voltage should be 12 volt.
   b. Measure voltage between terminal 3 and ground. Voltage should be 12 volt.
7. Turn ignition switch to off position, then disconnect ABS/TCS control module.
8. Measure resistance between ABS/TCS control module connector F11 terminal 6 and ground. Resistance should be 0 ohm.
9. Measure resistance between ABS/TCS control module connector P6 terminal 6 and ground. Resistance should be 1 Mohm.
10. Connect valve relay, then measure resistance between ABS/TCS control module connector P6 terminal 6 And ground. Resistance should be 0 ohm.
11. Measure resistance between ABS/TCS control module connector P6 terminal 1 and connector P5 terminal 1. Resistance should be 90 ohm.
12. Measure resistance between ABS/TCS control module connector P6 terminal 1 and ground. Resistance should be 1 Mohm.

Trouble Code 52

1. Turn ignition switch to off position, then remove motor relay.
2. Measure resistance between motor relay terminals A and B. Resistance should be 57 ohm.
3. Disconnect motor relay connector, then measure voltage between motor relay connector F10 and ground as follows:
   a. Measure voltage between terminal 1 and ground. Voltage should be 12 volt.
   b. Measure voltage between terminal 3 and ground. Voltage should be 0 volt.
4. Turn ignition switch to on position, then measure voltage between motor relay connector F10 and ground as follows:
   a. Measure voltage between terminal 1 and ground. Voltage should be 12 volt.
   b. Measure voltage between terminal 3 and ground. Voltage should be 12 volt.
5. Turn ignition switch to off position, then disconnect ABS/TCS control module.
6. Measure resistance between ABS/TCS control module connector P6 terminal 9 and ground. Resistance should be 1 Mohm.
7. Connect motor relay connector, then measure resistance between ABS/TCS control module connector P6 terminal 9 and ground. Resistance should be 57 ohm.
8. Operate TCS sequence check, then listen for motor operation.
9. Disconnect motor sensor connector F14, then measure resistance between motor sensor connector terminals 1 and 2. Resistance should be 85 ohm.
10. Measure resistance between motor sensor connector terminals and ground as follows:
   a. Measure resistance between terminal 1 and ground. Resistance should be 1 Mohm.
   b. Measure resistance between terminal 2 and ground. Resistance should be 1 Mohm.
11. Connect motor sensor connector, then measure resistance between ABS/TCS control module connector P7 terminals 3 and 13. Resistance should be 85 ohm.
12. Measure resistance between ABS/TCS control module connector P7 terminals and ground as follows:
   a. Measure resistance between terminal 3 and ground. Resistance should be 1 Mohm.
   b. Measure resistance between terminal 13 and ground. Resistance should be 1 Mohm.
13. Operate TCS sequence check, then measure voltage between motor relay connector F10 terminal 4 and ground. Voltage should be 13.5 volts while TCS operating indicator is on.
14. Turn ignition switch to off position, then disconnect motor connector.
15. Measure resistance between motor connector F13 terminal 2 and motor relay connector F10 terminal 4. Resistance should be 0 ohms.
16. Measure resistance between motor connector F13 terminal 2 and ground. Resistance should be 1 Mohms.
17. Measure resistance between motor connector F13 terminal 1 and ground.

Terminal:
No. 3 — No. 2

Stroke Unit: mm (in)	Specified resistance
0 — 3.1 ± 0.5 (0 — 0 122 ± 0.020)	95 — 105 Ω
3.1 — 5.5 ± 0.5 (0.122 — 0.217 ± 0.020)	190 — 210 Ω
5.5 — 7.9 ± 0.5 (0.217 — 0.311 ± 0.020)	285 — 315 Ω
7.9 — 10.3 ± 0.5 (0.311 — 0.406 ± 0.020)	380 — 420 Ω
10.3 — 18 ± 0.5 (0 406 — 0.709 ± 0.020)	475 — 525 Ω

NOTE:
Stroke = 0 when the stroke sensor rod is completely drawn into the sensor unit.

SB4029500061000X

Fig. 10 Stroke sensor resistance. Connector B67

Resistance should be 1 Mohms.

Trouble Code 54

1. Inspect that stroke sensor has no free play, then ensure stop lamp does not remain illuminated.
2. Turn ignition switch to off position, then disconnect stroke sensor connectors.
3. Measure resistance between stroke sensor connector B66 terminals 1 and 3. Resistance should be 570–630 ohm.
4. Remove stroke sensor, then measure resistance between stroke sensor connector B66 terminals 3 and 2 against rod stroke. Resistance should be as in **Fig. 9.**
5. Measure resistance between stroke sensor connector B66 terminals and stroke sensor threads as follows:
   a. Measure resistance between terminal 1 and stroke sensor threads. Resistance should be 1 Mohm.
   b. Measure resistance between terminal 2 and stroke sensor threads. Resistance should be 1 Mohm.
   c. Measure resistance between terminal 3 and stroke sensor threads. Resistance should be 1 Mohm.
6. Measure resistance between stroke sensor connector B67 terminals 2 and 3 against rod stroke. Resistance should be as in **Fig. 10.**
7. Measure resistance between stroke sensor connector B67 terminals and stroke sensor threads as follows:
   a. Measure resistance between terminal 2 and stroke sensor threads. Resistance should be 1 Mohm.
   b. Measure resistance between terminal 3 and stroke sensor threads. Resistance should be 1 Mohm.
8. Measure voltage between stroke sensor connector B67 terminal 3 and ground. Voltage should be 10–12 volt.
9. Install stoke sensor and connect stroke sensor connector, then disconnect ABS/TCS control module connector P7.
10. Measure voltage between ABS/TCS control module connector P7 terminal 7 and ground. Voltage should be 10–12 volt with brake pedal depressed and 0 volts without brake pedal depressed.
11. Connect ABS/TCS control module connector, then depress brake pedal and ensure stop lamp illuminates.
12. Disconnect ABS/TCS control module

Contents			Connector No.	Terminal No.	Input/Output signals: Measured value and measuring conditions
ABS sensor (Wheel speed sensor)	Front left wheel		P7	1—11	0.12 — 1 V (When it is 10 Hz.)
	Front right wheel		P6	8—16	0.12 — 1 V (When it is 10 Hz.)
	Rear left wheel		P6	7—15	0.12 — 1 V (When it is 10 Hz.)
	Rear right wheel		P7	2—12	0.12 — 1 V (When it is 10 Hz.)
Hydraulic unit	Solenoid valve	Front left outlet	P4	1—GND	About 12 V when the valve is OFF. Less than 1.5 V when the valve is ON.
		Front right outlet	P5	3—GND	
		Rear left outlet	P5	8—GND	
		Rear right outlet	P4	3—GND	
		Front left inlet	P4	2—GND	About 12 V when the valve is OFF. Less than 1.0 V when the valve is ON.
		Front right inlet	P5	2—GND	
		Rear left inlet	P5	7—GND	
		Rear right inlet	P4	4—GND	
		TCS 1	P4	5—GND	About 12 V when the valve is OFF. Less than 1.0 V when the valve is ON.
		TCS 2	P5	6—GND	
	Valve power supply		P6	6—GND	Ignition switch ON, 12 V
	Valve relay power supply		P6	1—GND	Less than 1.2 V when IGN is ON. About 12 V when the system is down.
	Motor relay power supply		P6	9—GND	Less than 1.0 V when the motor is ON. About 12 V when the motor is OFF.
	Motor sensor signals		P7	3—GND	Cyclic waveform of more than 180 Hz when the motor across terminals is ON. About 0 V when the motor is OFF.
			P7	13—GND	
	Pressure switch		P7	6—GND	H/L toggle signal with the brake pedal off (Cycle 14 mS, H: about 12 V, L: less than 0.7 V). About 12 V with the brake pedal depressed.
Pedal stroke sensor	Output signals		P7	5—GND	0.7 — 0.9 V with the brake pedal off
	Power supply		P7	4—GND	5 V
	Ground		P7	14—body	0.01 Ω or less
Stop light switch	Switch		P7	7—GND	0 V when the stop light is off. 12 V when the stop light is on.
	Switch test signal		P7	18—GND	H/L toggle signal with the brake pedal off (Cycle 14 mS, H: about 12 V, L: less than 0.7 V). About 0 V with the brake pedal depressed.
TCS OFF switch			P7	16—GND	Less than 2.0 V with the switch pressed and 12 V with it released.
Indicator light	TCS OFF		P6	10—GND	0 V when the light is on and 12 V when it is off.
	TCS operation		P6	11—GND	
	TCS warning		P6	3—GND	
	ABS warning		P6	2—GND	

SB4029500063010X

Fig. 11 ABS/TCS control module pin voltage specifications (Part 1 of 2)

Contents		Connector No.	Terminal No.	Input/Output signals: Measured value and measuring conditions
TCS control unit ECM communication	TCS → ECM communication (torque command)	P6	14—GND	Less than 0.7 V when the vehicle stands still.
	TCS → ECM communication (torque command)	P6	5—GND	Less than 5 V when the vehicle stands still.
	TCS → ECM communication (TCS operates)	P6	12—GND	5 V when TCS controls no operations. Less than 0.7 V when it controls operations
	ECM → TCS communication (engine control)	P6	4—GND	H/L toggle signal with the accelerator pedal off (Cycle 20 mS, H: about 12 V, L: less than 0.7 V). About 2.0 V with the accelerator pedal depressed. Also when TCS OFF indicator light comes on by TCS OFF switch.
ABS operation signal		P6	13—GND	12 V when the ABS control does not operate still and less than 0.7 V when ABS operates.
Fluid level sensor		P7	20—GND	Less than 2 V when IGN is ON and 12 V when idling.
Select monitor	Data is received	P7	9—GND	5 V when no data is received.
	Data is sent.	P7	19—GND	5 V when no data is sent.
Diagnosis connector		P7	8—GND	12 V when IGN is ON.
Power supply	Ignition	P5	1—GND	12 V when IGN is ON.
	Battery	P5	4—GND	12 V
Grounding line	Power	P5	5—body	0.01 Ω or less
	Digital	P7	15—body	0.01 Ω or less
	Power	P4	6—body	0.01 Ω or less

SB4029500063020X

Fig. 11 ABS/TCS control module pin voltage specifications (Part 2 of 2)

connector P7, then measure resistance between ABS/TCS control module connector P7 terminals as follows:
   a. Measure resistance between terminals 4 and 14. Resistance should be 570–630 ohm.
   b. Measure resistance between terminals 5 and 14. Resistance should be 95–105 ohm.
13. Measure resistance between ABS/TCS control module connector P7 terminals and ground as follows:
   a. Measure resistance between terminal 4 and ground. Resistance should be 1 Mohm.
   b. Measure resistance between terminal 5 and ground. Resistance should be 1 Mohm.
   c. Measure resistance between terminal 14 and ground. Resistance should be 1 Mohm.
14. Connect ABS/TCS control module connector, then operate TCS sequence control and ensure brake fluid pressure increases and decreases correctly.

Trouble Code 57

1. Turn ignition to off position and ensure charge warning lamp is not illuminated.
2. Turn ignition to on position and ensure charge warning lamp is illuminated.
3. With engine at idle ensure charge warning lamp goes off after a few moments.
4. Turn ignition to off position, then disconnect ABS/TCS control module connector P7.
5. Measure voltage between ABS/TCS control module connector P7 terminal 20 and ground. Voltage should be 0 volts with engine off and 13 volts with engine idling.

Trouble Code 58

1. Turn ignition to off position and disconnect hydraulic unit connector F12.
2. Measure resistance between hydraulic unit connector F12 and terminals 1 and 2. Resistance should be 1 Mohm with brake pedal depressed and 0 ohm without brake pedal depressed.
3. Measure resistance between hydraulic unit connector and ground as follows:
   a. Measure resistance between terminal 1 and ground. Resistance should be 1 Mohm.
   b. Measure resistance between terminal 2 and ground. Resistance should be 1 Mohm.
4. Connect hydraulic unit connector F12, then disconnect ABS/TCS control module connector P7.
5. Measure resistance between ABS/TCS control module connector P7 terminal 6 and 18. Resistance should be 1 Mohm with brake pedal depressed and 0 ohm without brake pedal depressed.
6. Measure resistance between ABS/TCS control module connector P7 and ground as follows:
   a. Measure resistance between terminal 6 and ground. Resistance should be 1 Mohm.
   b. Measure resistance between terminal 18 and ground. Resistance should be 1 Mohm.
7. Disconnect stroke sensor connectors, then remove stroke sensor.
8. Measure resistance between stroke sensor connector B67 terminals 2 and 3 against rod stroke. Resistance should be as in **Fig. 10.**
9. Measure resistance between stroke sensor connector B67 terminals and stroke sensor threads as follows:
   a. Measure resistance between terminal 2 and stroke sensor threads. Resistance should be 1 Mohm.
   b. Measure resistance between terminal 3 and stroke sensor threads. Resistance should be 1 Mohm.
10. Measure voltage between stroke sensor connector B67 terminal 3 and ground. Voltage should be 10–12 volt.
11. Install stoke sensor and connect stroke sensor connector, then disconnect ABS/TCS control module connector P7.
12. Measure voltage between ABS/TCS control module connector P7 terminal 7 and ground. Voltage should be 10–12 volt with brake pedal depressed and 0 volts without brake pedal depressed.

COMPONENT TESTING

Speed Sensors

Refer to "Impreza and 1995 Legacy Less TCS" in this section, for test procedure.

ABS Hydraulic Unit

Refer to "Impreza and 1995 Legacy Less TCS" in this section, for test procedure.

ABS Control Module

Refer to **Fig. 11,** for control module input/output voltage signals.

G Sensor

Refer to "Impreza and 1995 Legacy Less TCS" in this section, for test procedure.

SYSTEM SERVICE

Brake System Bleed

Two technicians are required to bleed the brake system. Brake pedal operation must be very slow. Keep brake fluid reserve tank topped off to prevent entry of air into brake system during bleeding procedure. Check entire brake system for fluid leaks.

1. Connect diagnosis terminals to terminal 4 of diagnosis connector beside driver side seat heater unit.
2. Start engine while depressing TCS OFF switch. **Keep switch depressed even after engine has started.**
3. After ABS and TCS warning lamps go out, depress brake pedal within 0.5 seconds.
4. After ensuring TCS ON indicator illuminates, release TCS OFF switch.
5. Ensure there are no leaks from joints and connections of brake system.
6. Bleed air through front righthand caliper as follows:
   a. Fit one end of a vinyl tube onto air bleeder and other end into a container of brake fluid.
   b. Slowly depress brake pedal and keep it depressed, then open air bleeder for 1 to 2 seconds.
   c. With air bleeder closed slowly release brake pedal.
   d. Repeat steps a through c until no more air comes out. **Allow 3 to 4 seconds between brake pedal operations.**
7. Bleed air from suction pipe through front right caliper as follows:
   a. Open air bleeder.
   b. Depress TCS off switch for 20 seconds or more. **Ensure no more air comes out from air bleeder.**
   c. Close air bleeder.
8. Repeat steps 6 and 7 for front left caliper and suction pipe.
9. Repeat step 6 for rear right caliper.
10. Repeat step 6 for rear left caliper.
11. Tighten air bleeders securely when bubbles are visible.
12. Operate front right outlet and rear left outlet valves to bleed air from hydraulic unit outlet circuit as follows:
    a. Press TCS OFF switch while depressing brake pedal.
    b. Ensure ABS warning lamp illuminates.
    c. Repeatedly depress and release brake pedal 10 times or more while pressing TCS OFF switch.
    d. Repeat procedure until no more air escapes the reservoir tank.
13. Repeat step 12 for front left outlet and rear right outlet valves.
14. Fully depress brake pedal for 20 seconds and ensure there are no leaks in brake system.
15. Turn ignition switch to off position.
16. Perform TCS sequence control.
17. With engine at idle, inspect brake pedal stroke as follows:
    a. Depress brake pedal with 110 lbs. of force, then measure distance between brake pedal and steering wheel.
    b. Release brake pedal, then measure distance between brake pedal and steering wheel again.
    c. The difference between both measurements should be 3.74 inch. **If measurement is not as specified it is possible that air is still in brake system.**
18. Turn ignition switch to off position, then top off brake fluid level.
19. Test drive vehicle at low speed and ensure proper brake operation.

Component Replacement

Refer to "Impreza and 1995 Legacy Less TCS" in this section, for replacement procedure.

1996 Legacy w/Bosch 5.3

NOTE: On Air Bag Equipped Models, Refer To "Air Bag System Precautions" Located In The Front Of This Manual For System Disarming & Arming Procedures.

NOTE: Wire Code Identification And Symbol Identification Located In The Front Of This Manual Can Be Used As An Aid When Using Wiring Circuits Found In This Section.

INDEX

	Page No.
Description	39-153
Diagnosis & Testing	39-154
Accessing Trouble Codes	39-154
Clearing Trouble Codes	39-154
Component Testing	39-154
Trouble Code Interpretation	39-154
Precautions	39-153
Air Bag Systems	39-153
System Service	39-154
Brake System Bleed	39-154
Component Replacement	39-155
ABS Control Module	39-157
ABS Hydraulic Unit	39-156
ABS Relay Box	39-156
Front Sensor	39-155
G Sensor	39-157
Rear Sensor	39-155
Troubleshooting	39-154
Inspection Mode	39-154
Preliminary Inspection	39-154

PRECAUTIONS

AIR BAG SYSTEMS

Refer to "Air Bag System Precautions" in the front of this manual for system disarming and arming procedures.

DESCRIPTION

The Anti-lock Brake System (ABS) electrically controls brake fluid pressure to prevent wheel lock during braking on slippery road surfaces, which improves directional steering stability as well as shortening the braking distance.

If ABS becomes inoperative, the fail-safe system activates to ensure it acts as a conventional brake system. The warning light also comes on to indicate that the ABS is malfunctioning.

The front and rear wheels utilize a four sensor, four channel control design. The front wheels have an independent control design, which independently controls fluid pressure to left and right front wheels. The rear wheels have a select low control design, which provides the same pressure control for the two rear wheels if either wheel starts to lock.

Refer to **Figs. 1 and 2** for system component location, description and operation.

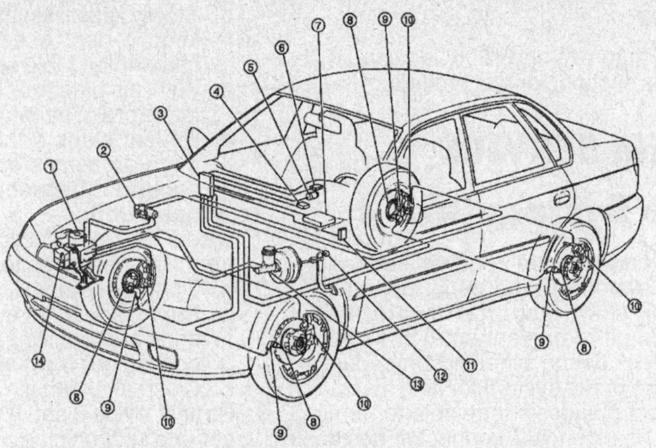

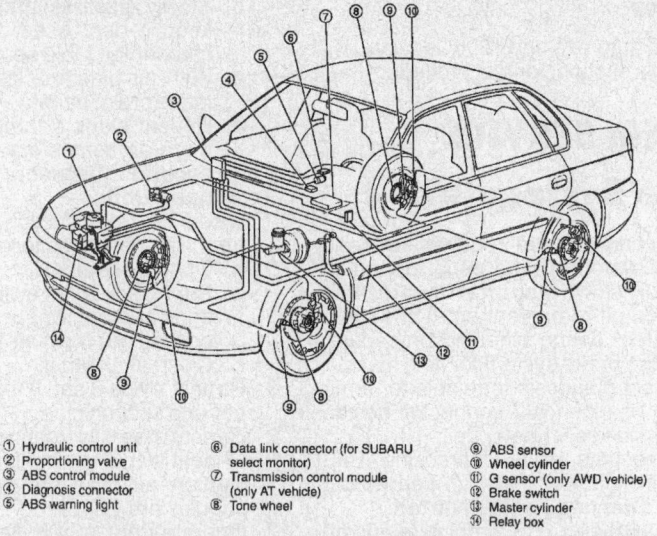

① Hydraulic control unit
② Proportioning valve
③ ABS control module
④ Diagnosis connector
⑤ ABS warning light
⑥ Data link connector (for SUBARU select monitor)
⑦ Transmission control module (only AT vehicle)
⑧ Tone wheel
⑨ ABS sensor
⑩ Wheel cylinder
⑪ G sensor (only AWD vehicle)
⑫ Brake switch
⑬ Master cylinder
⑭ Relay box

SB4029600064000X

Fig. 1 ABS component locations

TROUBLESHOOTING

Refer to **Figs. 3 and 4,** for troubleshooting procedure and **Fig. 5** for wiring diagram.

PRELIMINARY INSPECTION

1. Ensure battery voltage is 12 volts or more.
2. Ensure specific gravity of battery is 1.260.
3. Check condition of main and other fuses, harnesses and connector. Also check for proper grounding.
4. Check brake fluid level and for leakage.
5. Check for brake drag, brake pad and rotor condition.
6. Ensure tires are in good condition and at specified air pressure.

INSPECTION MODE

The on board diagnosis system is designed to detect problems after the vehicle has been driven at 6 MPH for more than 20 seconds. If a problem is found, the ABS warning lamp will illuminate to inform the drive of the occurrence of a problem. When the lamp is on the ABS system will be inactive and normal braking function will work. Problems will be stored in memory as trouble codes. Up to three codes can be stored in memory at one time.

DIAGNOSIS & TESTING

ACCESSING TROUBLE CODES

When the control module detects a problem, the information (up to a maximum of three) will be stored in the EEPROM as a trouble code. When there are more than three, the most recent three will be stored. Stored codes will stay in memory until they are cleared.

1. Remove ABS check connector from under side of drivers side heater unit, **Fig. 6.**
2. Turn ignition switch off, then ground ABS check connector terminal No. 6 to diagnosis terminal.
3. Turn ignition switch to the On position. ABS warning light is now in the diagnostic mode and will blink to identify trouble codes.
4. After start code (11) is shown, the trouble code(s) will be shown in order of the last information first. The code(s) will repeat for a maximum of 5 minutes. When there are no trouble codes in memory, only the start code (11) is shown.

TROUBLE CODE INTERPRETATION

Refer to **Fig. 7,** for trouble code interpretation and **Fig. 8,** for trouble code identification and description.

CLEARING TROUBLE CODES

After completing necessary repairs, clear trouble code memory as follows:

1. After calling up a trouble code, disconnect ABS check connector terminal No. 6 from diagnosis terminal, **Fig. 6.**
2. Repeat connecting and disconnecting terminal No. 6 from diagnosis terminal three times within approximately 12 seconds. Leave terminal No. 6 disconnected for at least ½ second each time.

COMPONENT TESTING

Refer to **Fig. 9** when testing ABS component voltages.

SYSTEM SERVICE

Brake System Bleed

Two technicians are needed to bleed the brake system. Brake pedal operation must be very slow. Keep brake fluid reserve tank full to prevent air from entering the system during the bleeding procedure.

1. Connect ABS check connector diagnosis terminal to terminal No. 6. Connector is located beside driver side seat heater unit.
2. Start engine, then after ABS warning lamp goes out, depress brake pedal within 0.5 seconds.
3. Check entire brake system for fluid leaks.
4. Bleed air from right front caliper as follows:
   a. Fit one end of a vinyl tube onto air bleeder, place other end of tube into a container of brake fluid.
   b. Slowly depress brake pedal and keep it depressed, then open air bleeder for 1 to 2 seconds.
   c. Close air bleeder and slowly release brake pedal.
   d. Repeat steps "a" through "c" until no more air comes out. **Allow 3 to 4 seconds between brake pedal operations.**
5. Bleed air from right front caliper suction pipe as follows:
   a. Open air bleeder.
   b. Depress TCS off switch for 20 seconds or more. **Ensure no more air comes out from air bleeder.**
   c. Close air bleeder.
6. Repeat steps 4 and 5 for left front caliper and suction pipe.
7. Repeat step 4 for right rear caliper.
8. Repeat step 4 for left rear caliper.
9. Tighten air bleeders securely when bubbles are visible.
10. Operate front right outlet and rear left outlet valves to bleed air from hydraulic unit outlet circuit as follows:
    a. Press TCS OFF switch while depressing brake pedal.
    b. Ensure ABS warning lamp illuminates.
    c. Depress and release brake pedal 10 times or more while pressing TCS OFF switch.
    d. Repeat procedure until no more air escapes the reservoir tank.
11. Repeat step 10 for front left and rear right outlet valves.
12. Fully depress brake pedal for 20 seconds and ensure there are no leaks in brake system.
13. Turn ignition switch to off position and perform TCS sequence control.
14. With engine at idle, inspect brake pedal stroke as follows:
    a. Depress brake pedal with 110 lbs. of force, then measure distance between brake pedal and steering wheel.
    b. Release brake pedal, then measure distance between brake pedal and steering wheel again.
    c. The difference between both measurements should be 3.74 inch. **If measurement is not as specified it is possible that air is still in brake system.**
15. Turn ignition switch to off position, then

Name	Function
ABS control module (ABSCM)	• Calculates and determine the conditions of the wheels and body from the wheel speeds and makes a proper decision suitable for the current situation to control the hydraulic unit. • In the ABS operation mode, the module outputs a cooperative control signal to the AT control module. (AT vehicles only) • Whenever the ignition switch is placed at ON, the module makes a self diagnosis. When anything wrong is detected, the module cuts off the system. • Communicates with the Subaru select monitor.
Hydraulic unit (H/U)	In the ABS operation mode, the H/U changes fluid passages to control the fluid pressure of the wheel cylinders in response to an instruction from the ABSCM. The H/U also constitutes the brake fluid passage from the master cylinder to the wheel cylinders together with pipings.
Wheel speed sensor (ABS sensor)	Detects the wheel speed in terms of a change in the magnetic flux density passing through the sensor, converts it into an electrical signal, and outputs the electrical signal to the ABSCM.
Tone wheel	Gives a change in the magnetic flux density by the teeth around the tone wheel to let the ABS sensor generate an electrical signal.
G sensor (AWD vehicle only)	Detects a change in G in the longitudinal direction of the vehicle and outputs it to the ABSCM in terms of a change in voltage.
Relay box	Accommodates the valve relay and motor relay.
Valve relay	Serves as a power switch for the solenoid valve and motor relay coil in response to an instruction from the ABSCM. The valve relay also constitutes one of the duplicated ABS warning light drive circuits.
Motor relay	Serves as a power switch for the pump motor in response to an instruction from the ABSCM.
Stop light switch	Transmits the information on whether the brake pedal is depressed or not to the ABSCM for use as a condition in determining ABS operation.
ABS warning light	Alerts the driver to an ABS fault. When the diagnosis connector and diagnosis terminal are connected, the light flashes to indicate a trouble codes in response to an instruction from the ABSCM.
AT control module (TCM) (AT vehicles only)	Provides shift controls (fixing the speed at 3rd or changing front and rear wheel transmission characteristics on AWD vehicle) in response to an instruction from the ABSCM.

SB4029600065000X

Fig. 2 ABS components

Symptom		Probable faulty units/parts
Vehicle instability during braking	Vehicle pulls to either side.	• Hydraulic unit (solenoid valve) • ABS sensor • Brake (caliper & piston, pads) • Wheel alignment • Tire specifications, tire wear and air pressures • Incorrect wiring or piping connections • Road surface (uneven, camber)
	Vehicle spins.	• Hydraulic unit (solenoid valve) • ABS sensor • Brake (pads) • Tire specifications, tire wear and air pressures • Incorrect wiring or piping connections
Poor braking	Long braking/stopping distance	• Hydraulic unit (solenoid valve) • Brake (pads) • Air in brake line • Tire specifications, tire wear and air pressures • Incorrect wiring or piping connections
	Wheel locks.	• Hydraulic unit (solenoid valve, motor) • ABS sensor • Incorrect wiring or piping connections
	Brake dragging	• Hydraulic unit (solenoid valve) • ABS sensor • Master cylinder • Brake (caliper & piston) • Parking brake • Axle & wheels • Brake pedal play
	Long brake pedal stroke	• Air in brake line • Brake pedal play
	Vehicle pitching	• Suspension play or fatigue (reduced damping) • Incorrect wiring or piping connections • Road surface (uneven)
	Unstable or uneven braking	• Hydraulic unit (solenoid valve) • ABS sensor • Brake (caliper & piston, pads) • Tire specifications, tire wear and air pressures • Incorrect wiring or piping connections • Road surface (uneven)
Vibration and/or noise (while driving on slippery roads)	Excessive pedal vibration	• Incorrect wiring or piping connections • Road surface (uneven)
	Noise from hydraulic unit	• Hydraulic unit (mount bushing) • ABS sensor • Brake piping
	Noise from front of vehicle	• Hydraulic unit (mount bushing) • ABS sensor • Master cylinder • Brake (caliper & piston, pads, rotor) • Brake piping • Brake booster & check valve • Suspension play or fatigue
	Noise from rear of vehicle	• ABS sensor • Brake (caliper & piston, pads, rotor) • Parking brake • Brake piping • Suspension play or fatigue

SB4029600067000X

Fig. 4 General diagnostics chart

top off brake fluid level.

16. Test drive vehicle at low speed and ensure proper brake operation.

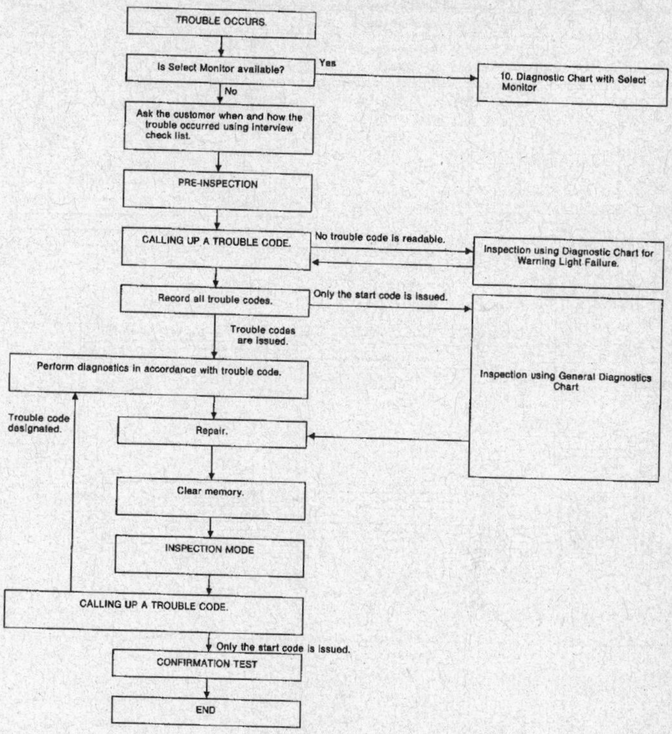

TROUBLE OCCURS.
Is Select Monitor available?
Yes
10. Diagnostic Chart with Select Monitor
No
Ask the customer when and how the trouble occurred using interview check list.
PRE-INSPECTION
CALLING UP A TROUBLE CODE.
No trouble code is readable.
Inspection using Diagnostic Chart for Warning Light Failure.
Record all trouble codes.
Only the start code is issued.
Trouble codes are issued.
Inspection using General Diagnostics Chart
Perform diagnostics in accordance with trouble code.
Trouble code designated.
Repair.
Clear memory.
INSPECTION MODE
CALLING UP A TROUBLE CODE.
Only the start code is issued.
CONFIRMATION TEST
END

NOTE:
- To check harness for broken wires or short circuits, shake it while holding it or the connector.
- When ABS warning light illuminates, read and record trouble code indicated by ABS warning light.

SB4029600066000X

Fig. 3 Basic troubleshooting chart

Component Replacement

FRONT SENSOR

1. Disconnect sensor, located in engine compartment.
2. Remove sensor harness to bracket bolts, then the sensor to housing bolts.
3. Remove brake caliper, brake rotor, driveshaft, knuckle and hub assemblies.
4. Remove tone wheel while removing hub from knuckle. Ensure teeth faces of tone wheel are not damaged during removal.
5. Reverse procedure to install, noting the following:
   a. Place a thickness gauge between sensor's pole piece and tone wheel's tooth face.
   b. After standard clearance is obtained over entire perimeter, **torque** sensor to housing bolts to 17-31 ft. lbs.

REAR SENSOR

1. Remove rear seat and disconnect sensor connector.

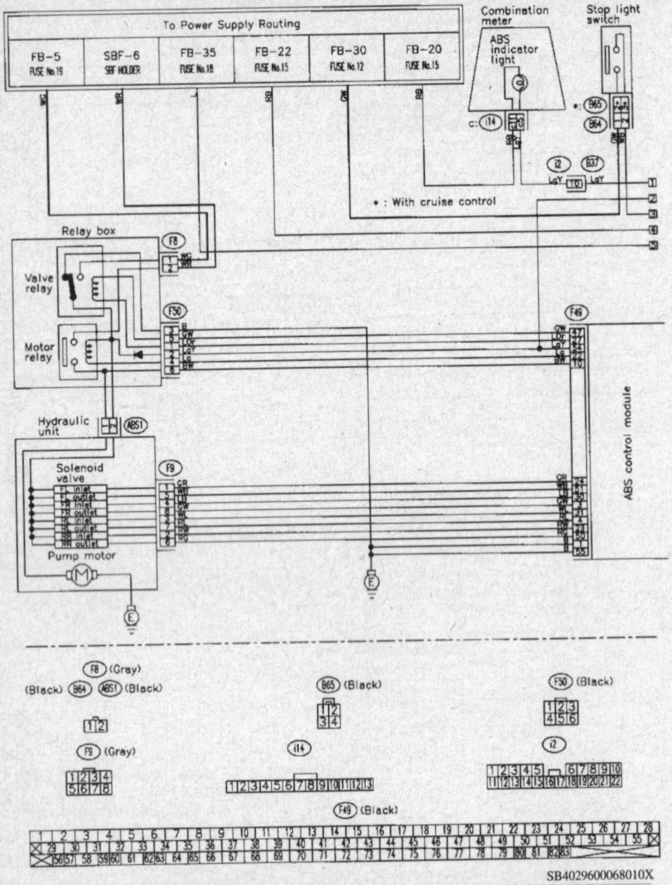
To Power Supply Routing
FB-5 FUSE No.19
SBF-6 SBF HOLDER
FB-35 FUSE No.18
FB-22 FUSE No.15
FB-30 FUSE No.12
FB-20 FUSE No.15
Combination meter
ABS indicator light
Stop light switch
* : With cruise control
Relay box
Valve relay
Motor relay
Hydraulic unit
Solenoid valve
Pump motor
ABS control module
(Gray)
(Black)
(Black)
(Black)
(Gray)
(Black)
(Black)
SB4029600068010X

Fig. 5 ABS wiring diagram (Part 1 of 2)

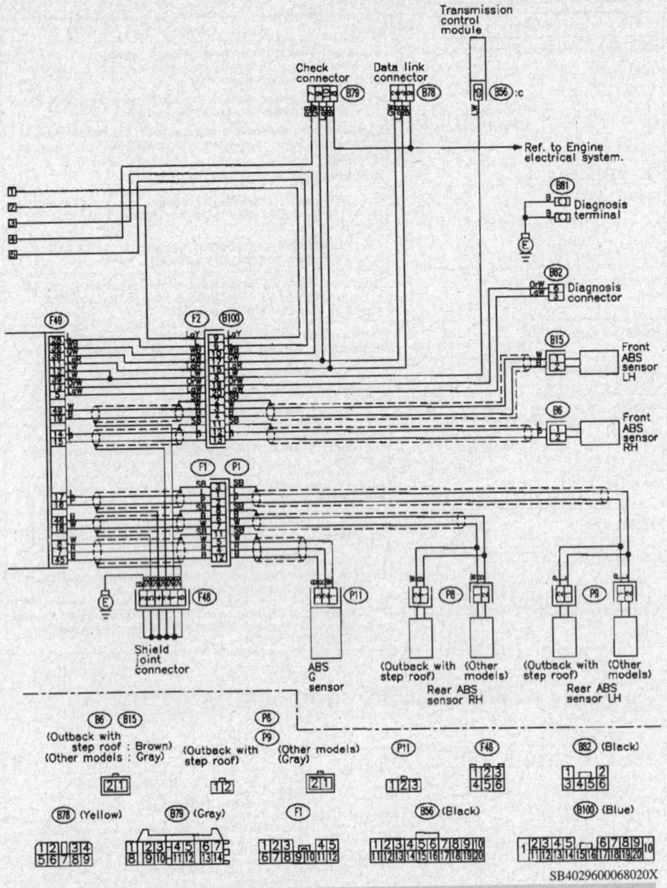
Transmission control module
Check connector
Data link connector
Ref. to Engine electrical system.
Diagnosis terminal
Diagnosis connector
Front ABS sensor LH
Front ABS sensor RH
Shield joint connector
ABS G sensor
(Outback with step roof)
(Other models)
Rear ABS sensor RH
Rear ABS sensor LH
(Outback with step roof : Brown)
(Other models : Gray)
(Other models) (Gray)
(Black)
(Yellow)
(Gray)
(Black)
(Blue)
SB4029600068020X

Fig. 5 ABS wiring diagram (Part 2 of 2)

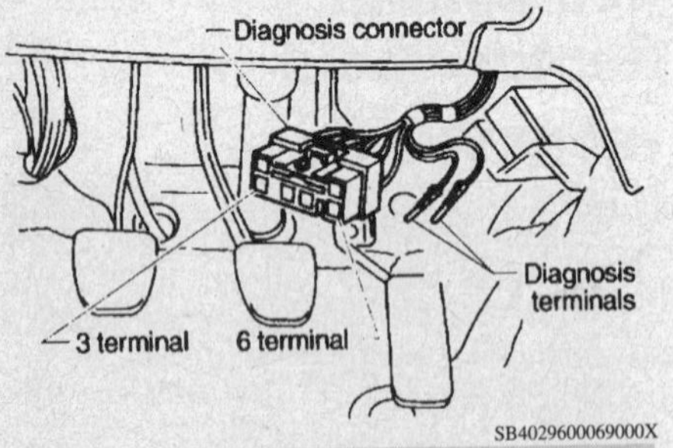
Diagnosis connector
Diagnosis terminals
3 terminal
6 terminal
SB4029600069000X

Fig. 6 Check connector terminal identification

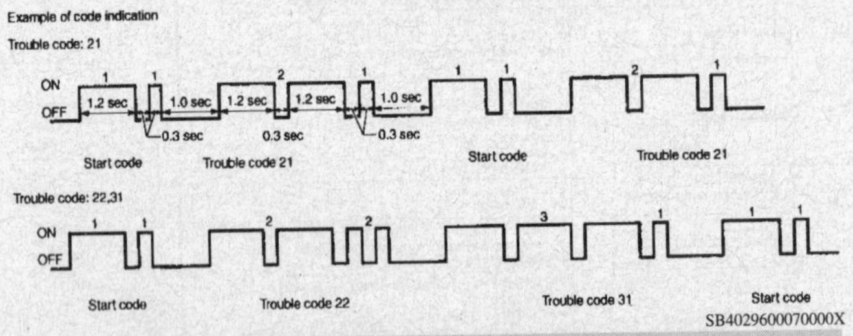
Example of code indication
Trouble code: 21
ON
OFF
1.2 sec
1.0 sec
0.3 sec
Start code
Trouble code 21
Trouble code: 22,31
Trouble code 22
Trouble code 31
SB4029600070000X

Fig. 7 Trouble code interpretation

2. Remove sensor harness bracket from trailing link, then the sensor from rear back plate.
3. Remove rear tone wheel while removing hub from housing assembly. Ensure teeth faces of tone wheel are not damaged during removal.
4. Reverse procedure to install, noting the following:
   a. Place a thickness gauge between sensor's pole piece and tone wheel's tooth face.
   b. After standard clearance is obtained over entire perimeter, **torque** sensor to housing bolts to 17-31 ft. lbs.

ABS HYDRAULIC UNIT

1. Disconnect battery ground cable.
2. Remove air intake duct and canister from engine compartment.
3. Disconnect hydraulic unit electrical connector, then unlock cable clip.
4. Disconnect brake lines from hydraulic unit, and plug open ports to prevent foreign particles from entering unit.
5. Remove hydraulic unit to bracket nuts and bolts, then the unit from the vehicle, noting the following precautions:
   a. Hydraulic unit cannot be disassembled. Do not attempt to loosen nuts and bolts.
   b. Do not drop or bump hydraulic unit.
   c. Do not turn hydraulic unit upside down or place it on is side.
   d. Be careful to prevent foreign particles from getting into hydraulic unit.
6. Reverse procedure to install. **Torque** hydraulic unit attaching bolts to 17–31 ft. lbs.

ABS RELAY BOX

1. Disconnect battery ground cable.
2. Remove air intake duct and canister from engine compartment
3. Disconnect connector from relay box.
4. Unlock cable clip.
5. Remove nuts which secure relay box to bracket, then the relay box and connector bracket from vehicle.
6. Reverse procedure to install.

Trouble code	Contents of diagnosis	
11	Start code • Trouble code is shown after start code. • Only start code is shown in normal condition.	
21	Abnormal ABS sensor (Open circuit or input voltage too high)	Front right ABS sensor
23		Front left ABS sensor
25		Rear right ABS sensor
27		Rear left ABS sensor
22	Abnormal ABS sensor (Abnormal ABS sensor signal)	Front right ABS sensor
24		Front left ABS sensor
26		Rear right ABS sensor
28		Rear left ABS sensor
29		Any one of four
31	Abnormal solenoid valve circuit(s) in hydraulic unit	Front right inlet valve
32		Front right outlet valve
33		Front left inlet valve
34		Front left outlet valve
35		Rear right inlet valve
36		Rear right outlet valve
37		Rear left inlet valve
38		Rear left outlet valve
41	Abnormal ABS control module	
42	Source voltage is low.	
44	A combination of AT control abnormals	
46	Abnormal G sensor power supply voltage	
51	Abnormal valve relay	
52	Abnormal motor and/or motor relay	
54	Abnormal stop light switch	
56	Abnormal G sensor output voltage	

SB4029600071000X

Fig. 8 Trouble code description

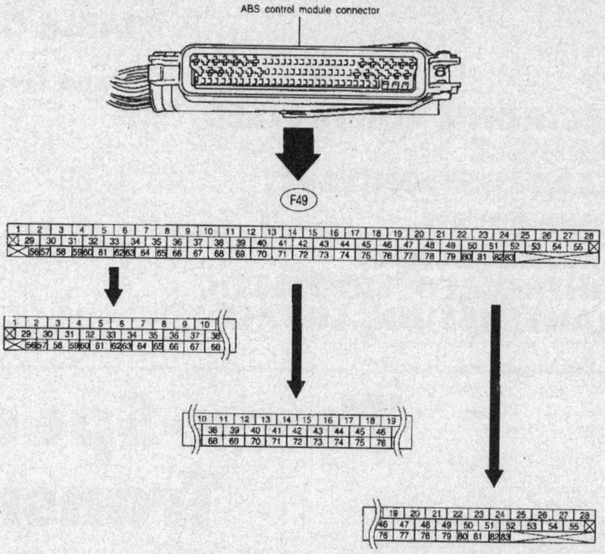
ABS control module connector
F49

SB4029600072010X

Fig. 9 ABS control module I/O signal (Part 1 of 2)

Contents			Terminal No.	Input/Output signal — Measured value and measuring conditions
ABS sensor (Wheel speed sensor)	Front left wheel		49—19	0.12 — 1 V (When it is 20 Hz.)
	Front right wheel		14—15	
	Rear left wheel		18—17	
	Rear right wheel		18—46	
Hydraulic control unit	Solenoid valve	Front left outlet	51—1	10 — 13 V when the valve is OFF and less than 1.5 V when the valve is ON.
		Front right outlet	3—1	
		Rear left outlet	4—1	
		Rear right outlet	50—1	
		Front left inlet	24—1	
		Front right inlet	30—1	
		Rear left inlet	31—1	
		Rear right inlet	23—1	
Relay box	Valve relay power supply		27—1	10 — 13 V when ignition switch is ON.
	Valve relay coil		47—1	Less than 1.5 V when ignition switch is ON.
	Motor relay coil		22—1	More than 10 V when the ABS control does not operate still and less than 1.5 V when ABS operates.
	Motor monitoring		10—1	Less than 1.5 V when the ABS control does not operate still and more than 10 V when ABS operates.
G sensor (AWD model only)	power supply		8—45	4.75 — 5.25 V
	ground		45	—
	output		7—45	2.3±0.2 V when vehicle is in horizontal position.
Stop light switch			36—1	Less than 1.5 V when the stop light is OFF and more than 4.5 V when the stop light is ON.
ABS warning light			54—1	Less than 1.5 V during 1.5 seconds when ignition switch is ON, and 10 — 14 V after 1.5 seconds.
AT ABS signal (AT model only)			12—1	Less than 1.5 V when the ABS control does not operate still and more than 5.5 V when ABS operates.
ABS operation signal monitor			39—1	Less than 1.5 V when the ABS control does not operate still and more than 5.5 V when ABS operates.
Select monitor	Data is received.		11—1	Less than 1.5 V when no data is received.
	Data is sent.		38—1	4.75 — 5.25 V when no data is sent.
Diagnosis connector	Terminal No. 3		5—1	10 — 14 V when ignition switch is ON.
	Terminal No. 6		13—1	10 — 14 V when ignition switch is ON.
Power supply			28—1	10 — 14 V when ignition switch is ON.
Grounding line			1	—
Grounding line			55	—

SB4029600072020X

Fig. 9 ABS control module I/O signal (Part 2 of 2)

ABS CONTROL MODULE

1. Turn ignition switch to off position.
2. Remove lower trim from front pillar.
3. Remove glove box and bracket.
4. Remove pocket back panel.
5. Remove bolt from bracket.
6. Remove bolt cover and bolt.
7. Remove control module upper mounting bolt.
8. Pull lower part of instrument panel rearward approximately two inches. **Do not pull panel more than 2.4 inches rearward or panel will be deformed.**
9. Remove instrument panel securing clips.
10. Remove control module lower mounting bolts.
11. While holding lower part of instrument panel rearward approximately two inches, remove control module.
12. Disconnect electrical connector from module.
13. Reverse procedure to install.

G SENSOR

1. Turn ignition switch to off position.
2. Remove console box.
3. Disconnect G sensor electrical connector.
4. Remove G sensor mounting bolt, then the sensor.
5. Reverse procedure to install. **Torque** sensor mounting bolt to 3–7 ft. lbs.

Automatic Transmissions

TABLE OF CONTENTS

	Page No.
ELECTRONIC CONTROLLED VARIABLE TRANSMISSION(ECVT)	39-172
FOUR-SPEED ELECTRONICALLY CONTROLLED AUTOMATIC TRANSMISSION, LOYALE	39-162
FOUR-SPEED ELECTRONICALLY CONTROLLED AUTOMATIC TRANXMISSION, EXCEPT LOYALE	39-166
THREE-SPEED AUTOMATIC TRANSMISSIONS	39-158

Three-Speed Automatic Transmissions

NOTE: On Air Bag Equipped Models, Refer To "Air Bag System Precautions" Located In The Front Of This Manual For System Disarming & Arming Procedures.

INDEX

	Page No.
Adjustments	39-161
Band	39-161
Manual Linkage	39-161
Description	39-158
Identification	39-158
Maintenance	39-161
Fluid Change	39-161
Fluid Check	39-161
Tightening Specifications	39-162
Transmission, Replace	39-161
Troubleshooting	39-158
Automatic Transmission Fluid Contaminated w/Differential Gear Oil	39-161
Creeping In P	39-160
Differential Gear Oil Is Contaminated w/Automatic Transmission Fluid	39-161
Downshift At Speed Above Kickdown Limit	39-160
Downshifting 2–1 Or Upshifting 2–3 When Selector Lever Is Placed In 2	39-160
Drags When Shifted From 1–2	39-160
Drags When Shifted From 2–3	39-160
Drags When Shifted To R	39-159
Engine Does Not Start In N Or P	39-158
Engine Starts In Every Position Except N Or P	39-158
Excessive Chatter In N Or P	39-160
Excessive Creeping	39-159
Harsh 1–2 Shift	39-159
Harsh 2–1 Downshift When Selector Is Placed In 1	39-160
Harsh 2–3 Shift	39-159
Harsh Engagement When Shifted From N To D	39-159
Loud Noise In R, 2 Or 1	39-161
Loud Noise When Driven In AWD 3	39-161
Loud Noise When Running In 3	39-161
Maximum Speed Too Low Or Insufficient Acceleration	39-159
NO 3–2 Forced Downshift	39-160
No 1–2 Shift In D	39-159
No 2–1 Or 3–1 Shift	39-160
No 2–1 Shift When Selector Lever Is Placed In 1	39-160
No 2–3 Shift In D	39-159
No 3–2 Downshift When Selector Lever Is Placed In 1	39-160
No 3–2 Downshift Within Kickdown Limits	39-160
No 3–2 Shift	39-160
No Drive In Any Selector Position	39-159
No Drive In D Only	39-159
No Drive In D, 1, 2; Slips Easily Or Is Difficult To Accelerate	39-159
No Drive In R; Slips Easily Or Is Hard To Accelerate	39-159
No Engine Braking In 1	39-160
Shifts From 1–3	39-159
Shock Due To Speed Shifting Felt When Accelerator Pedal Is Released	39-160
Slip When Starting In AWD	39-161
Slips 3–2 Downshift	39-160
Total Absence Of Creeping	39-159
Transmission Overheated	39-160
Unusual Oil Smell From Supply Pipe	39-160
Upshifting From 1–2 Or 2–3 When Selector Lever Is Placed In 1	39-160
Vehicle Exhaust Emits White Smoke Or Fluid Spurts Out While Running	39-160
Vehicle Moves In N	39-159
Vehicle Moves Sluggishly	39-159
1–2 Or 2–3 Shift Speed Too High	39-159
1–2 Slips	39-159
2–3 Slips	39-159
3–2 Or 2–1 Shift Speed Too High	39-160

IDENTIFICATION

Refer to **Fig. 1,** for transmission identification number location.

DESCRIPTION

These transmissions are a 3 speed, multiple planetary gear type transmission using a symmetric, 3 element single stage, 2 phase torque converter.

TROUBLESHOOTING

ENGINE DOES NOT START IN N OR P

1. Manual linkage adjustment.
2. Inhibitor switch and wiring.
3. Ignition switch and starter motor.

ENGINE STARTS IN EVERY POSITION EXCEPT N OR P

1. Manual linkage adjustment.
2. Inhibitor switch or wiring.

HARSH ENGAGEMENT WHEN SHIFTED FROM N TO D

1. Engine idle speed high.
2. Vacuum diaphragm or line.
3. Check control pressure.
4. Valve body.
5. Forward clutch.
6. Fluid contamination.

NO DRIVE IN D ONLY

1. Manual linkage adjustment.
2. Check control pressure.
3. Valve body.
4. One-way clutch.
5. Fluid contamination.

NO DRIVE IN D, 1, 2; SLIPS EASILY OR IS DIFFICULT TO ACCELERATE

1. Manual linkage adjustment.
2. Check control pressure.
3. Valve body.
4. Defective gasket between transmission case and differential and reduction case or between differential and reduction case and converter housing.
5. Check fluid level.
6. Forward clutch.
7. Leakage in hydraulic system.
8. Reverse clutch.

NO DRIVE IN R; SLIPS EASILY OR IS HARD TO ACCELERATE

1. Manual linkage adjustment.
2. Check control pressure.
3. Valve body.
4. Low and reverse brake.
5. Reverse clutch.
6. Forward clutch.
7. Leakage in hydraulic system.
8. Reverse clutch check ball.
9. Check fluid level.
10. Fluid contamination.

NO DRIVE IN ANY SELECTOR POSITION

1. Check fluid level.
2. Manual linkage adjustment.
3. Check control pressure.
4. Valve body.
5. Oil pump.
6. Leakage in hydraulic system.
7. Parking linkage.
8. Fluid contamination.

VEHICLE MOVES SLUGGISHLY

1. Check fluid level.
2. Manual linkage adjustment.
3. Check control pressure.
4. Valve body.
5. Oil pump.
6. Leakage in hydraulic system.
7. One-way clutch.
8. Fluid contamination.

VEHICLE MOVES IN N

1. Manual linkage adjustment.
2. Valve body.

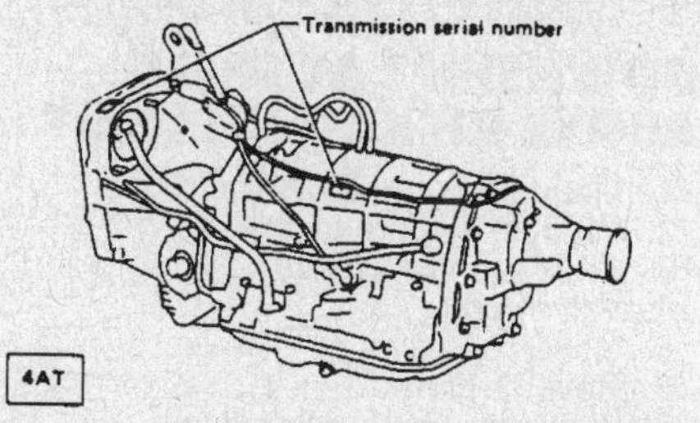
Transmission serial number
4AT
SB5028900075000X

Fig. 1 Transmission identification

3. Forward clutch.
4. Reverse clutch.

MAXIMUM SPEED TOO LOW OR INSUFFICIENT ACCELERATION

1. Check fluid level.
2. Manual linkage adjustment.
3. Check control pressure.
4. Check stall speed.
5. Band adjustment.
6. Valve body.
7. Defective brake band and band servo.
8. Low-reverse brake.
9. Forward clutch.
10. Reverse clutch.
11. Oil pump.
12. Fluid contamination.
13. Torque converter one way clutch.

DRAGS WHEN SHIFTED TO R

1. Band adjustment.
2. Forward clutch.
3. Defective brake band and band servo.
4. Parking linkage.
5. Fluid contamination.

EXCESSIVE CREEPING

Engine idle speed high.

TOTAL ABSENCE OF CREEPING

1. Check fluid level.
2. Manual linkage adjustment.
3. Incorrect engine idle speed.
4. Valve body.
5. Oil pump.
6. Leakage in hydraulic system.
7. Forward clutch.
8. Reverse clutch.
9. Fluid contamination.

NO 1-2 SHIFT IN D

1. Manual linkage adjustment.
2. Vacuum diaphragm or line.
3. Valve body.
4. Governor valve.
5. Band adjustment.
6. Servo pipe.
7. Defective brake band and band servo.
8. Leakage in hydraulic system.
9. Fluid contamination.
10. Governor gear.

NO 2-3 SHIFT IN D

1. Manual linkage adjustment.
2. Vacuum diaphragm or line.
3. Valve body.
4. Governor valve.
5. Band adjustment.
6. Servo pipe.
7. Reverse clutch.
8. Leakage in hydraulic system.
9. Reverse clutch check ball.
10. Check control pressure.
11. Fluid contamination.

1-2 OR 2-3 SHIFT SPEED TOO HIGH

1. Vacuum diaphragm or line.
2. Downshift solenoid, kickdown switch and wiring.
3. Check control pressure.
4. Valve body.
5. Governor valve.
6. Leakage in hydraulic system.
7. Fluid contamination.

SHIFTS FROM 1-3

1. Valve body.
2. Governor valve.
3. Band adjustment.
4. Leakage in hydraulic system.
5. Check control pressure.
6. Fluid contamination.
7. Servo pipe.
8. Defective brake band and band servo.

HARSH 1-2 SHIFT

1. Vacuum diaphragm or line.
2. Check stall speed.
3. Valve body.
4. Band adjustment.
5. Defective brake band and band servo.
6. Check control pressure.
7. Fluid contamination.

HARSH 2-3 SHIFT

1. Vacuum diaphragm or line.
2. Check control pressure.
3. Valve body.
4. Band adjustment.
5. Reverse clutch.
6. Fluid contamination.
7. Servo pipe.
8. Defective brake band and band servo.

1-2 SLIPS

1. Check fluid level.
2. Manual linkage adjustment.
3. Vacuum diaphragm or line.
4. Check control pressure.
5. Valve body.
6. Band adjustment.
7. Servo pipe.
8. Fluid contamination.
9. Defective brake band and band servo.
10. Leakage in hydraulic system.

2-3 SLIPS

1. Check fluid level.
2. Manual linkage adjustment.
3. Vacuum diaphragm or line.
4. Check control pressure.
5. Valve body.
6. Band adjustment.
7. Servo pipe.
8. Reverse clutch.
9. Leakage in hydraulic system.
10. Reverse clutch check ball.
11. Fluid contamination.

DRAGS WHEN SHIFTED FROM 1-2

1. Valve body.
2. Low and reverse band.
3. Reverse clutch.
4. One-way clutch.
5. Fluid contamination.

DRAGS WHEN SHIFTED FROM 2-3

1. Band adjustment.
2. Fluid contamination.
3. Valve body.
4. Brake band and band servo.

NO 3-2 SHIFT

1. Vacuum diaphragm or line.
2. Valve body.
3. Governor valve.
4. Band adjustment.
5. Servo pipe.
6. Reverse clutch.
7. Defective brake band and band servo.
8. Leakage in hydraulic system.
9. Check control pressure.
10. Fluid contamination.

NO 2-1 OR 3-1 SHIFT

1. Vacuum diaphragm or line.
2. Valve body.
3. Governor valve.
4. Band adjustment.
5. Defective brake band and band servo.
6. One-way clutch.
7. Fluid contamination.

SHOCK DUE TO SPEED SHIFTING FELT WHEN ACCELERATOR PEDAL IS RELEASED

1. Manual linkage adjustment.
2. Vacuum diaphragm or line.
3. Downshift solenoid, kickdown switch and wiring.
4. Check control pressure.
5. Valve body.
6. Governor valve.
7. Leakage in hydraulic system.
8. Fluid contamination.

3-2 OR 2-1 SHIFT SPEED TOO HIGH

1. Manual linkage adjustment.
2. Vacuum diaphragm or line.
3. Downshift solenoid, kickdown switch and wiring.
4. Check control pressure.
5. Valve body.
6. Governor valve.
7. Leakage in hydraulic system.
8. Fluid contamination.

NO 3-2 DOWNSHIFT WITHIN KICKDOWN LIMITS

1. Downshift solenoid, kickdown switch and wiring.
2. Vacuum diaphragm or line.
3. Valve body.
4. Governor valve.
5. Servo pipe.
6. Defective brake band and band servo.
7. Fluid contamination.
8. Leakage in hydraulic system.

DOWNSHIFT AT SPEED ABOVE KICKDOWN LIMIT

1. Manual linkage adjustment.
2. Vacuum diaphragm or line.
3. Check control pressure.
4. Valve body.
5. Governor valve.
6. Reverse clutch.
7. Leakage in hydraulic system.
8. Fluid contamination.

SLIPS 3-2 DOWNSHIFT

1. Vacuum diaphragm or line.
2. Check control pressure.
3. Valve body.
4. Band adjustment.
5. Servo pipe.
6. Reverse clutch.
7. Defective brake band and band servo.
8. Leakage in hydraulic system.
9. Reverse clutch check ball.
10. Fluid contamination.

NO 3-2 FORCED DOWNSHIFT

1. Manual linkage adjustment.
2. Check control pressure.
3. Valve body.
4. Band adjustment.
5. Defective brake band and band servo.
6. Leakage in hydraulic system.
7. Fluid contamination.

DOWNSHIFTING 2-1 OR UPSHIFTING 2-3 WHEN SELECTOR LEVER IS PLACED IN 2

1. Manual linkage adjustment.
2. Check control pressure.
3. Valve body.
4. Fluid contamination.

NO 3-2 DOWNSHIFT WHEN SELECTOR LEVER IS PLACED IN 1

1. Manual linkage adjustment.
2. Check control pressure.
3. Valve body.
4. Governor valve.
5. Band adjustment.
6. Reverse clutch.
7. Defective brake band and band servo.
8. Leakage in hydraulic system.
9. Fluid contamination.

NO ENGINE BRAKING IN 1

1. Manual linkage adjustment.
2. Check control pressure.
3. Valve body.
4. Low and reverse band.
5. Leakage in hydraulic system.
6. Fluid contamination.

UPSHIFTING FROM 1-2 OR 2-3 WHEN SELECTOR LEVER IS PLACED IN 1

1. Manual linkage adjustment.
2. Valve body.
3. Leakage in hydraulic system.
4. Fluid contamination.

NO 2-1 SHIFT WHEN SELECTOR LEVER IS PLACED IN 1

1. Check fluid level.
2. Manual linkage adjustment.
3. Valve body.
4. Governor valve.
5. Band adjustment.
6. Low and reverse band.
7. Leakage in hydraulic system.
8. Fluid contamination.

HARSH 2-1 DOWNSHIFT WHEN SELECTOR IS PLACED IN 1

1. Vacuum diaphragm or line.
2. Check stall speed.
3. Valve body.
4. Low and reverse band.
5. Fluid contamination.

TRANSMISSION OVERHEATED

1. Check fluid level.
2. Check control pressure.
3. Check stall speed.
4. Valve body.
5. Band adjustment.
6. Reverse clutch.
7. Defective brake band and band servo.
8. Low and reverse band.
9. Oil pump.
10. Leakage in hydraulic system.
11. Planetary gear.
12. Fluid contamination.

EXCESSIVE CHATTER IN N OR P

1. Check fluid level.
2. Check control pressure.
3. Valve body.
4. Fluid contamination.

CREEPING IN P

1. Parking linkage.

VEHICLE EXHAUST EMITS WHITE SMOKE OR FLUID SPURTS OUT WHILE RUNNING

1. Check fluid level.
2. Vacuum diaphragm or line.
3. Check stall speed.
4. Check control pressure.
5. Reverse clutch.
6. Brake band and band servo.
7. Low and reverse brake.
8. One-way clutch.
9. Forward clutch.

UNUSUAL OIL SMELL FROM SUPPLY PIPE

1. Check fluid level.
2. Fluid contamination.
3. Forward clutch.
4. Reverse clutch.
5. Brake band and band servo.
6. Low and reverse brake.

LOUD NOISE IN R, 2 OR 1

1. Oil pump.
2. One-way clutch.
3. Transfer gear.

SLIP WHEN STARTING IN AWD

Transfer valve, transfer pipe, rear driveshaft seal ring.

DIFFERENTIAL GEAR OIL IS CONTAMINATED w/AUTOMATIC TRANSMISSION FLUID

1. Leak in hydraulic system.
2. Drive pinion rear oil seal.
3. Governor shaft oil seal.
4. Stator shaft and reduction gear oil seal and O-rings.

AUTOMATIC TRANSMISSION FLUID CONTAMINATED w/DIFFERENTIAL GEAR OIL

1. Drive pinion rear oil seal.
2. Governor shaft oil seal.
3. Stator shaft and reduction gear oil seal and O-ring.

LOUD NOISE WHEN RUNNING IN 3

1. Hypoid gear.
2. Reduction gear.

LOUD NOISE WHEN DRIVEN IN AWD 3

Transfer gear.

MAINTENANCE

FLUID CHECK

1. With transmission fluid at operating temperature (140° to 176°F. Driving approximately 3–6 miles or 10 minute warm-up time), park vehicle on a level surface.
2. With engine idling and service and parking brake applied, move selector lever through all ranges and return to Park.
3. Allow engine to idle 1–2 minutes.
4. With engine idling, remove dipstick and check fluid level. Fluid level should be between the Add and Full marks.
5. Add Dexron II type automatic transmission fluid as necessary to bring level within limits.

FLUID CHANGE

Transmission fluid should be changed at 30 month or 30,000 mile intervals.

1. Remove transmission oil pan drain plug and allow transmission to drain.
2. Install transmission oil pan drain plug and gasket and **torque** to 18 ft. lbs.
3. Add approximately 2.6–3.2 quarts of Dexron II automatic transmission fluid through transmission dipstick filler tube.
4. Check transmission fluid level as described previously.

ADJUSTMENTS

MANUAL LINKAGE

1. Move selector lever from P to 1. Lever should come to a set position with a click, which indicates manual valve has gone into its detent position. If lever is not in alignment with proper mark on dial when lever is released, an adjustment is necessary.
2. Move lever to N, loosen locknuts on linkage arm at transmission lever and turn as necessary for transmission lever to click into detent position when selector lever is in N.
3. If necessary for selector lever alignment with console marks, loosen four screws holding the indicator and reposition as necessary.

BAND

If engine speed increases abruptly on 2–3 shift or if there is a delay of more than .7 second on a 3–2 kickdown, excessive clearance between the reverse clutch drum and band may exist and the adjusting screw should be rotated clockwise. If there is a braking action on 2–3 shift or if shock on a 1–2 shift is unusually light, excessive small brake band clearance may exist and the adjusting screw should be rotated counterclockwise. Adjust brake band as follows.

1. Using socket tool No. 398603610, or equivalent, to hold adjusting screw in place, loosen locknut.
2. Loosen or tighten the adjusting screw within ¾ turn, as necessary to properly adjust the band, then **torque** locknut to 19–21 ft. lbs.

If slipping occurs on a 2–3 shift, excessive small brake band clearance may exist. If transmission shifts directly from 1st to 3rd, excessive large brake band clearance may exist. Adjust brake band as follows.

1. Using socket tool No. 398603610, or equivalent, to hold adjusting screw in place, loosen locknut.
2. **Torque** adjusting screw to 6.5 ft. lbs., then back off adjusting screw 2 turns. **Torque** locknut to 19–21 ft. lbs.

TRANSMISSION

REPLACE

1. Raise and support hood, then remove spare tire and support.
2. Disconnect battery negative cable.
3. Disconnect the following electrical connectors and vacuum hoses: oxygen sensor, ATF temperature switch, kickdown solenoid valve, AWD solenoid valve, diaphragm vacuum hose and AWD vacuum hose, if equipped.
4. Remove clip band retaining the air breather hose to pitching stopper.
5. Remove pitching stopper rod, then install engine support assembly 926610000, or equivalent, to pitching stopper rod bracket.
6. Remove starter motor attaching bolts, then the starter motor.
7. Remove timing hole plug, then the four torque converter attaching bolts.
8. Remove right side engine to transmission attaching nut and bolt.
9. **On turbocharged models,** remove exhaust system as follows:
   a. Remove turbo upper heat shield, and accelerator cable cover.
   b. Raise and support vehicle.
   c. Loosen two front exhaust pipe attaching bolts.
   d. Lower vehicle, then remove turbo lower heat shield.
   e. Separate center exhaust pipe from turbocharger.
   f. Raise and support vehicle.
   g. Separate center exhaust pipe from rear pipe.
   h. Disconnect center exhaust pipe from transmission by removing hanger bolt.
10. **On models less turbocharger,** remove exhaust system as follows:
   a. Raise and support vehicle.
   b. Remove front exhaust pipe to engine retaining nuts. Leave one nut attached to temporarily support exhaust pipe.
   c. Separate front exhaust pipe from rear pipe.
   d. Disconnect front exhaust pipe from transmission, by removing hanger bolt.
   e. Remove remaining exhaust pipe to engine retaining nut, then exhaust pipe.
11. **On all models,** remove oil pan drain plug and drain transmission fluid into a suitable container.
12. **On AWD models,** remove propeller shaft and disconnect select rod from transfer rail.
13. **On all models,** disconnect linkage rod from select lever.
14. Disconnect stabilizer from transverse link by loosening nut and bolt on lower side of plate.
15. Remove hand brake cable bracket from transverse link.
16. Remove transverse link nut and bolt, then lower transverse link.
17. Remove spring pin using a suitable tool, then separate axle shaft from driveshaft on each side by pushing rear of tire outward.
18. Remove engine to transmission attaching nuts.
19. Disconnect oil cooler hoses.
20. Support transmission using a suitable jack, then remove rear rubber cushion attaching nuts.
21. Remove rear crossmember, then lower transmission from vehicle.
22. Reverse procedure to install.

TIGHTENING SPECIFICATIONS

Component	Torque/Ft. Lbs.
Drain Plug	30–34
Driveplate To Flywheel	17–20
Engine To Transmission (Lower Nuts)	34–40
Engine To Transmission (Right Side Bolt)	34–40
Exhaust System Brackets	18–25
Front Exhaust Pipe To Engine	19–23
Lug Nuts	58–72
Propeller Shaft To Center Bearing	25–33
Propeller Shaft To Rear Differential	13–20
Rear Crossmember To Body	39–49
Rear Transmission Mount To Rear Crossmember	①
Starter Motor (Lower Nut)	22–27
Starter Motor (Upper Bolt)	34–40
Transverse Link To Front Crossmember	43–51
Transverse Link To Stabilizer	14–22

① — Front wheel drive only; 9–17 ft. lbs., AWD models; 20–35 ft. lbs.

Four-Speed Electronically Controlled Automatic Transmission, Loyale

INDEX

Page No.

Adjustments 39-165
Brake Band 39-165
Inhibitor Switch 39-165
Shift Lever Cable 39-165
Description 39-162
Identification 39-162
Maintenance 39-165
Tightening Specifications 39-166
Transmission, Replace 39-165
Troubleshooting 39-163
Engine Stalls In D, 2 Or 3 39-163
Engine Stalls In R 39-163
Engine Stalls When Shifting, Any Gear 39-163
Engine Stalls, Any Gear 39-163
Erratic Shift Points 39-164
Fluid Overflow 39-164
Front Tires Slip On Start 39-165
Harsh Shifting From N To D 39-163
No 1–2 Shift 39-163
No 2–3 Shift 39-163
No 3–4 Shift 39-163
No Engine Braking In 1, 2 Or 3 39-163
No Engine Braking In 1 39-164
No Engine Braking In 3 39-163
No Kickdown 39-163
No Lock-Up Operation 39-164
No Power Mode In D 39-164
Noise In D1, D2 Or D4 39-163
Noise In D3 39-163
Noise In N Or P 39-163
Odor From Oil Supply Pipe 39-164
Parking Brake Failure 39-164
Poor Acceleration 39-163
Power Mode Not Released In D 39-164
Select Force Too Hard 39-164
Select Force Too Light 39-164
Select Lever Slips Out Of Detents On Rough Roads Or During Acceleration 39-165
Shifting Abnormal 39-164
Shifting Delayed From N To D 39-163
Shock Felt When Accelerator Pedal Is Released At Or Above Medium Speed 39-165
Shudder Noise When Vehicle Is Started 39-163
Starter Runs In D, R, Or 2 But Not In N Or P 39-163
Unusual Changes In Differential Fluid Level 39-164
Vehicle Does Not Move In D Or 3, Engine Revs-Up 39-163
Vehicle Does Not Move In D, 2 Or 3, Engine Revs-Up 39-163
Vehicle Does Not Move In R, Engine Revs-Up 39-163
Vehicle Moves In N & Stalls In P 39-163
Vehicle Will Not Move In Any Gear, Engine Revs-Up 39-163
Vibration On Hard Turns 39-165
Vibration When Driving Straight Ahead 39-165
Will Not Shift To FWD 39-165

IDENTIFICATION

Refer to "Three Speed Automatic Transmission," for transmission identification number location.

DESCRIPTION

This transmission is a 4 speed double row planetary gear type using an electronic/hydraulic control system consisting of various sensors and switches, a transmission control unit and the hydraulic controller including solenoid valves. The system controls the transmission including the shifting, lock-up, overrunning clutch,

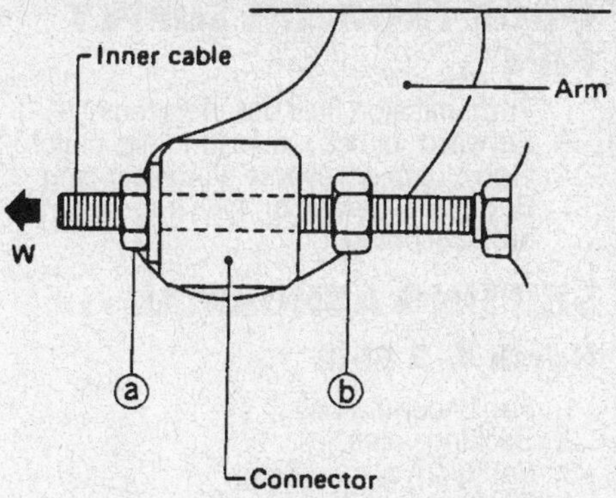
Inner cable
Arm
W
a
b
Connector
SB5028900090000X

Fig. 1 Shift lever cable adjustment

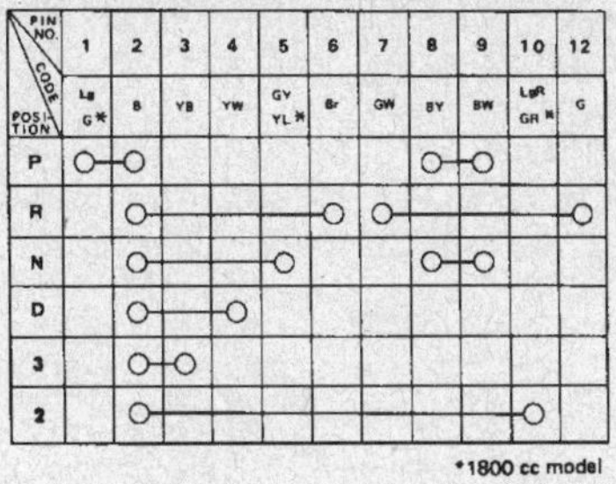
*1800 cc model
SB5028900091000X

Fig. 2 Inhibitor switch continuity inspection

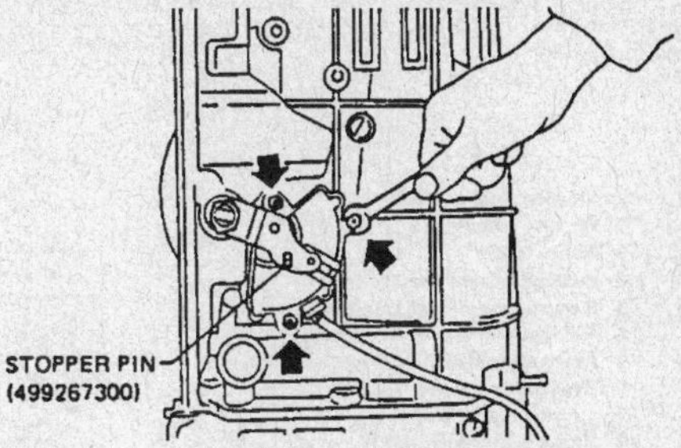
STOPPER PIN
(499267300)
SB5028900092000X

Fig. 3 Inhibitor switch adjustment

line pressure, auto pattern select, shift timing and AWD transfer clutch.

TROUBLESHOOTING

STARTER RUNS IN D, R, OR 2 BUT NOT IN N OR P

1. Inhibitor switch faulty or needs adjustment.
2. Faulty select lever or select cable needs adjustment.
3. Faulty starter motor or harness.

NOISE IN N OR P

1. Transmission fluid low.
2. Drive plate installation improper.
3. Duty solenoid C noisy.
4. Oil pump contaminated, broken or seized.

SHUDDER NOISE WHEN VEHICLE IS STARTED

1. Transmission fluid low.
2. Strainer seal faulty.

NOISE IN D1, D2 OR D4

1. Differential oil low.
2. Final, planetary or reduction gear contact improper.

NOISE IN D3

1. Differential oil low.
2. Final or reduction gear contact improper.

ENGINE STALLS WHEN SHIFTING, ANY GEAR

1. Sticking valve.
2. Engine performance poor.
3. Lock-up clutch seized.

VEHICLE MOVES IN N & STALLS IN P

1. Forward clutch seized.

HARSH SHIFTING FROM N TO D

1. Transmission fluid deteriorated.
2. N-D accumulator faulty.
3. Sticking valve.
4. Control unit faulty.

SHIFTING DELAYED FROM N TO D

1. Sticking valve.
2. Low and reverse brake slipping.
3. Forward clutch slipping.

VEHICLE WILL NOT MOVE IN ANY GEAR, ENGINE REVS-UP

1. Transmission fluid low.
2. Filter clogged.
3. Sticking valve.
4. Drive plate faulty or installation improper.
5. Input shaft or reduction driveshaft broken.
6. Axle shaft, crown gear, differential gear or drive pinion broken.
7. Planetary gear contact improper.
8. Oil pump contaminated, broken or seized.

ENGINE STALLS, ANY GEAR

Parking brake mechanism faulty.

VEHICLE DOES NOT MOVE IN R, ENGINE REVS-UP

1. Sticking valve.
2. Low and reverse brake slipping.
3. Reverse clutch slipping.

ENGINE STALLS IN R

1. Forward clutch seized.
2. Band seized.

VEHICLE DOES NOT MOVE IN D OR 3, ENGINE REVS-UP

1. Faulty one-way clutch (1–2) or one-way clutch (3–4).

VEHICLE DOES NOT MOVE IN D, 2 OR 3, ENGINE REVS-UP

1. Forward clutch slipping.
2. Faulty forward or overrunning clutch relief ball.
3. Sticking valve.
4. Control unit faulty.
5. Faulty one-way clutch (3–4).

ENGINE STALLS IN D, 2 OR 3

Reverse clutch seized.

POOR ACCELERATION

High Stall RPM

1. Transmission fluid low.
2. Sticking valve.
3. Forward or Reverse clutch slipping.

Low Stall RPM

1. Engine performance poor.
2. One-way clutch or torque converter burned or broken.
3. Oil pump Contaminated, broken or seized.

Proper Stall RPM, Poor Acceleration In D, 2 Or 3

1. Control unit faulty.
2. Sticking valve.
3. High clutch or band seized.

Proper Stall RPM, Poor Acceleration In R

1. Sticking valve.
2. Band, high clutch or overrunning clutch seized.

NO 1-2 SHIFT

1. Control unit faulty.
2. Sticking valve.
3. Band or servo slipping.

NO 2-3 SHIFT

1. Control unit faulty.
2. Sticking valve.
3. High clutch slipping.

NO 3-4 SHIFT

1. Control unit faulty.
2. Sticking valve.
3. Transmission fluid temperature sensor faulty.
4. Band or servo slipping.

NO KICKDOWN

1. Control unit faulty.
2. Throttle sensor faulty.

NO ENGINE BRAKING IN 3

1. Control unit faulty.
2. Sticking valve.
3. Throttle sensor faulty.

NO ENGINE BRAKING IN 1, 2 OR 3

1. Forward clutch relief ball faulty.
2. Overrunning clutch slipping.

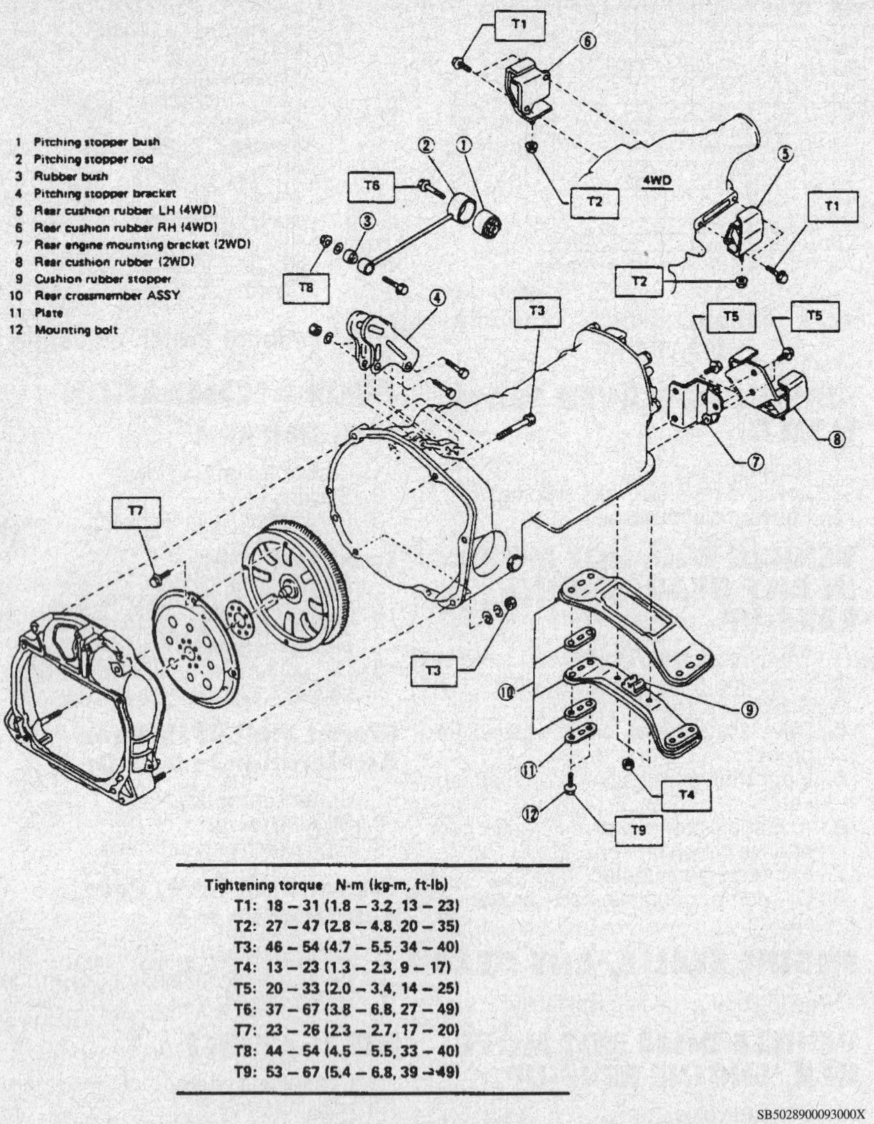

1 Pitching stopper bush
2 Pitching stopper rod
3 Rubber bush
4 Pitching stopper bracket
5 Rear cushion rubber LH (4WD)
6 Rear cushion rubber RH (4WD)
7 Rear engine mounting bracket (2WD)
8 Rear cushion rubber (2WD)
9 Cushion rubber stopper
10 Rear crossmember ASSY
11 Plate
12 Mounting bolt
T1
T2
T3
T4
T5
T6
T7
T8
T9
4WD
Tightening torque N-m (kg-m, ft-lb)
T1: 18 – 31 (1.8 – 3.2, 13 – 23)
T2: 27 – 47 (2.8 – 4.8, 20 – 35)
T3: 46 – 54 (4.7 – 5.5, 34 – 40)
T4: 13 – 23 (1.3 – 2.3, 9 – 17)
T5: 20 – 33 (2.0 – 3.4, 14 – 25)
T6: 37 – 67 (3.8 – 6.8, 27 – 49)
T7: 23 – 26 (2.3 – 2.7, 17 – 20)
T8: 44 – 54 (4.5 – 5.5, 33 – 40)
T9: 53 – 67 (5.4 – 6.8, 39 – 49)
SB5028900093000X

Fig. 4 Exploded view of transmission mounting assembly

NO ENGINE BRAKING IN 1

1. Control unit faulty.
2. Sticking valve.
3. Low and reverse brake slipping.

ERRATIC SHIFT POINTS

1. Control unit faulty.
2. Sticking valve.
3. Throttle sensor faulty.
4. Band and servo slipping.

NO LOCK-UP OPERATION

1. Control unit faulty.
2. Sticking valve.
3. Transmission fluid temperature sensor faulty.
4. Throttle sensor faulty.
5. Lock-up facing worn.

NO POWER MODE IN D

1. Control valve faulty.
2. Throttle sensor faulty.

POWER MODE NOT RELEASED IN D

1. Control valve faulty.
2. Throttle sensor faulty.

PARKING BRAKE FAILURE

1. Faulty select lever or select cable needs adjustment.
2. Parking brake mechanism faulty.

SELECT FORCE TOO HARD

1. Select lever, detent spring or manual plate faulty.

SELECT FORCE TOO LIGHT

1. Detent spring or manual plate faulty.

FLUID OVERFLOW

1. Fluid level too high.

UNUSUAL CHANGES IN DIFFERENTIAL FLUID LEVEL

1. Seal pipe or double oil seal faulty.

ODOR FROM OIL SUPPLY PIPE

1. Transmission fluid deteriorated.
2. Forward clutch, overrunning clutch, high clutch or reverse clutch slipping.
3. Band and servo or low and reverse brake slipping.

SHIFTING ABNORMAL

Harsh 1-2 Shift

1. Faulty control unit.
2. Sticking valve.
3. Faulty 2A accumulator.
4. Faulty throttle sensor.
5. Transmission fluid deteriorated.
6. Engine performance poor.

Slipping 1-2 Shift

1. Faulty control unit.
2. Sticking valve.
3. Faulty 2A accumulator.
4. Faulty throttle sensor.
5. Band and servo slipping.

Harsh 2-3 Shift

1. Faulty control unit.
2. Sticking valve.
3. Faulty throttle sensor.
4. Transmission fluid deteriorated.
5. Band and servo slipping.
6. High clutch slipping.
7. Faulty 3R accumulator.
8. Engine performance poor.

Slipping 2-3 Shift

1. Faulty control unit.
2. Sticking valve.
3. Faulty 3R accumulator.
4. Faulty throttle sensor.
5. Band and servo slipping.
6. High clutch slipping.

Harsh 3-4 Shift

1. Faulty control unit.
2. Sticking valve.
3. Faulty throttle sensor.
4. Transmission fluid deteriorated.
5. Overrunning clutch slipping.
6. Faulty 4A accumulator.
7. Engine performance poor.

Slipping 3-4 Shift

1. Faulty control unit.
2. Sticking valve.
3. Faulty 4A accumulator.
4. Faulty Throttle sensor.
5. Band and servo slipping.

Harsh 3-2 Shift

1. Faulty control unit.
2. Sticking valve.
3. Faulty throttle sensor.
4. Transmission fluid deteriorated.
5. Overrunning clutch slipping.
6. Band and servo slipping.

Harsh D-3 Shift

1. Faulty control unit.
2. Sticking valve.
3. Faulty throttle sensor.
4. Transmission fluid deteriorated.

5. Overrunning clutch slipping.

Harsh 2-1 Shift

1. Faulty control unit.
2. Sticking valve.
3. Faulty throttle sensor.
4. Transmission fluid deteriorated.
5. Overrunning clutch slipping.
6. Low and reverse brake slipping.

SHOCK FELT WHEN ACCELERATOR PEDAL IS RELEASED AT OR ABOVE MEDIUM SPEED

1. Faulty control unit.
2. Sticking valve.
3. Faulty throttle sensor.
4. Poor engine performance.
5. Faulty lock-up damper.
6. Lock-up clutch seized.

VIBRATION WHEN DRIVING STRAIGHT AHEAD

1. Faulty control unit.
2. Faulty lock-up damper.
3. Lock-up clutch seized.

SELECT LEVER SLIPS OUT OF DETENTS ON ROUGH ROADS OR DURING ACCELERATION

1. Select cable adjustment.
2. Faulty detent spring or manual plate.

VIBRATION ON HARD TURNS

AWD Models

1. Faulty car revolution sensor.
2. Transmission fluid deteriorated.
3. Faulty throttle sensor.
4. Faulty control unit.
5. Faulty 1st hold switch.
6. Faulty transfer pipe.
7. Faulty transfer clutch.
8. Sticking transfer valve.
9. Sticking transfer pilot valve.
10. Faulty duty solenoid C.

FRONT TIRES SLIP ON START

1. Faulty car revolution sensor 2.
2. Faulty throttle sensor.
3. Faulty control unit.
4. Faulty 1st hold switch.
5. Faulty transfer pipe.
6. Faulty transfer clutch.
7. Sticking transfer valve.
8. Sticking transfer pilot valve.
9. Faulty duty solenoid C.

WILL NOT SHIFT TO FWD

1. Faulty control unit.
2. Faulty throttle sensor.
3. FWD fuse remains installed.
4. Faulty transfer pipe.
5. Faulty transfer clutch.
6. Sticking transfer valve.
7. Sticking transfer pilot valve.
8. Faulty duty solenoid C.

MAINTENANCE

Refer to the "Four-Speed Electronic Controlled Automatic Transmission, Except Loyale" section for maintenance procedures for this model.

ADJUSTMENTS

BRAKE BAND

Refer to the "Four-Speed Electronic Controlled Automatic Transmission, Except Loyale" section for brake band adjustment procedures for this model.

SHIFT LEVER CABLE

1. To adjust inner cable length, gently push shift lever arm in the (W) position as shown **Fig. 1,** until nut (A) contacts the connector.
2. Using a suitable wrench hold nut (A) while **torquing** nut (B) to 9–17 ft. lbs.

INHIBITOR SWITCH

Before performing this procedure, ensure shift linkage is functioning properly. If shift linkage operation is acceptable, detach cable from select lever, then check for continuity at inhibitor switch electrical connector terminals. Readings should be as specified in **Fig. 2.**

Check for continuity, when the select lever is turned 1.5° in both directions, from the N position. If there is continuity in one direction only, or continuity at unequal points, adjust inhibitor switch as follows.

1. Ensure select lever cable is detached, and lever is in the N position.
2. Loosen inhibitor switch retaining bolts.
3. Insert stopper pin tool No. 499267300, or equivalent, **Fig. 3,** vertically into inhibitor switch lever and switch body.
4. **Torque** retaining bolts to 2.2–2.9 ft. lbs. then remove stopper pin.
5. Repeat test procedures to ensure proper operation. If readings are not as specified, replace as described under "Inhibitor Switch, Replace."

TRANSMISSION

REPLACE

Note the orientation of all parts as they are removed, so they can be properly installed. Refer to **Fig. 4,** when performing the following procedure.

1. Raise and support hood, then remove spare tire and support.
2. Disconnect battery ground cable.
3. Disconnect the following electrical connectors and vacuum hoses: Oxygen sensor; transmission harness; inhibitor switch; revolution sensor; AWD vacuum hose, as equipped. **Disconnect front exhaust pipe before removing speedometer cable.**
4. Remove clip band, retaining air breather hose to pitching stopper.
5. Remove pitching stopper rod, then install engine support assembly tool No. 926610000, or equivalent, to pitching stopper rod brackets.
6. Remove starter motor attaching bolts, then starter motor.
7. Remove timing hole plug, then four torque converter attaching bolts.
8. Remove right side engine to transmission attaching nut and bolt.
9. **On turbocharged models,** remove exhaust system as follows:
   a. Remove turbo upper heat shield, and accelerator cable cover.
   b. Raise and support vehicle, then loosen two front exhaust pipe attaching bolts.
   c. Lower vehicle, then remove turbo lower heat shield.
   d. Separate center exhaust pipe from turbocharger.
   e. Raise and support vehicle, then separate center exhaust pipe from rear pipe.
   f. Disconnect center exhaust pipe from transmission, by removing hanger bolt.
10. **On models less turbocharger,** remove exhaust system as follows:
    a. Raise and support vehicle.
    b. Remove front exhaust pipe to engine retaining nuts. Leave one nut attached to temporarily support the exhaust pipe.
    c. Separate front exhaust pipe from rear pipe.
    d. Disconnect front exhaust pipe from transmission, by removing hanger bolt.
    e. Remove remaining exhaust pipe to engine retaining nut, then exhaust pipe.
11. **On all models,** drain transmission fluid into a suitable container, by removing oil pan drain plug.
12. **On AWD models,** remove propeller shaft.
13. **On AWD models,** disconnect select rod from transfer rail.
14. **On all models,** disconnect cable from select lever. Loosen cable to bracket attaching nut, then separate cable from bracket.
15. Disconnect stabilizer from transverse link, by loosening nut and bolt on lower side of plate.
16. Remove hand brake cable bracket from transverse link.
17. Remove transverse link nut and bolt, then lower transverse link.
18. Remove spring pin using a suitable tool, then separate axle shaft from driveshaft on each side by pushing rear of tire outward.
19. Remove engine to transmission attaching nuts.
20. Disconnect oil cooler hoses.
21. Support transmission using a suitable jack, then remove rear rubber cushion attaching nuts.
22. Remove rear crossmember, then lower transmission from vehicle.
23. Reverse procedure to install.

TIGHTENING SPECIFICATIONS

Component	Torque/Ft. Lbs.
Driveplate To Flywheel	17–20
Drain Plug	30–34
Engine To Transmission (Lower Nuts)	34–40
Engine To Transmission (Right Side Bolt)	34–40
Exhaust System Brackets	18–25
Front Exhaust Pipe To Engine	19–23
Lug Nuts	58–72
Propeller Shaft To Rear Differential	13–20
Propeller Shaft To Center Bearing	25–33
Rear Crossmember To Body	39–49
Rear Transmission Mount To Rear Crossmember	①
Starter Motor (Lower Nut)	22–27
Starter Motor (Upper Bolt)	34–40
Transverse Link To Front Crossmember	43–51
Transverse Link To Stabilizer	14–22

① — Front wheel drive only; 9–17 ft. lbs., AWD models; 20–35 ft. lbs.

Four-Speed Electronically Controlled Automatic Transmission, Except Loyale

INDEX

	Page No.
Adjustments	39-166
Brake Band	39-166
Inhibitor Switch	39-167
Description	39-166
Identification	39-166
Maintenance	39-166
Fluid Change	39-166
Fluid Level Inspection	39-166
Shift Lock System	39-168
Tightening Specifications	39-172
Transmission, Replace	39-167
Impreza & Legacy	39-167
SVX	39-167
Troubleshooting	39-166

IDENTIFICATION

Refer to **Fig. 1,** for transmission identification number location.

DESCRIPTION

These transmissions are a 4 speed double row planetary gear type using a symmetric, 3 element single stage, 2 phase torque converter. This system uses a microcomputer for accurate control of the vehicle speed, engine brake and lock-up operations and gear shift timing. This system is also provided with an automatic drive pattern selecting function which selects between the "normal" and "power"drive patterns. The AWD models use an electronically controlled full-time version on the FWD transmission.

TROUBLESHOOTING

Problems in the electronic controlled automatic transmission may be caused by failure of the engine, the electronic control system, transmission components or by any combination of these. Troubleshooting should be started with simple and easy operations then proceeding to complicated and more difficult operations. When troubleshooting the transmission system, refer to **Fig. 2,** for the general troubleshooting chart.

MAINTENANCE

FLUID LEVEL INSPECTION

1. With transmission fluid at operating temperature (140–176°F. Driving approximately 3–6 miles or 10 minute warm-up time), park vehicle on a level surface.
2. With engine idling, service and parking brake applied, move selector lever through all ranges and return to Park.
3. Allow engine to idle 1–2 minutes.
4. With engine idling, remove dipstick and check fluid level. Fluid level should be between the add and full marks.
5. Add Dexron II type automatic transmission fluid as necessary to bring level within limits.

FLUID CHANGE

Transmission fluid should be changed at 30 months or 30,000 mile intervals.

1. Remove transmission oil pan drain plug, and allow fluid to drain.
2. Install drain plug with gasket, and **torque** to 16.7–19.5 ft. lbs.
3. Add approximately 2.6–3.2 quarts, except AWD models add 6.9–7.4 quarts, of Dexron II automatic transmission fluid through transmission dipstick filler tube.
4. Check transmission fluid level as described previously.

ADJUSTMENTS

BRAKE BAND

If engine speed increases abruptly on 2–3 shift, or if there is a delay of more than 1 second on a 3–2 kickdown, excessive clearance between reverse clutch drum and band may exist, adjusting screw should be rotated clockwise. If there is a braking action on 2–3 shift, excessive small brake band clearance may exist and adjusting screw should be rotated counterclockwise. Adjust brake band as follows:

1. Using socket tool No. 398603610, or equivalent, to hold adjusting screw in place, loosen locknut.
2. Loosen or tighten adjusting screw within 3/4 turn, to properly adjust band, then **torque** to 19–21 ft. lbs.

If slipping occurs on a 2–3 shift, excessive small brake band clearance may exist. If transmission shifts directly from 1st to 3rd, excessive large brake band clearance may exist. Adjust brake band as follows.

1. Using socket 398603610, to hold adjusting screw in place, loosen locknut.
2. **Torque** adjusting screw to 6.5 ft. lbs., then back off adjusting screw 2 turns. **Torque** locknut to 19–21 ft. lbs.

INHIBITOR SWITCH

1. Disconnect cable end from select lever.
2. Disconnect inhibitor switch connector.
3. Check continuity in inhibitor switch circuits with select lever in each position, **Fig. 3.**
4. Ensure continuity does not exists in ignition circuit when select lever is in R, 3,2 and 1 position.
5. Ensure continuity exists at equal points when select lever is turned 1.5° in both directions from the N position. If not continuity exists in one direction but not in the other direction or if there is continuity at unequal points, adjust inhibitor switch as follows:
   a. Loosen three inhibitor switch mounting bolts.
   b. Shift select lever to N range.
   c. Insert stopper pin tool No. 499267300, or equivalent, as vertical as possible into holes in inhibitor switch lever and switch body, **Fig. 4.**
   d. **Torque** inhibitor screws to 2.2–2.9 ft. lbs.
   e. Repeat checks steps 1 through 5. Replace inhibitor switch if it is determined to be faulty.

TRANSMISSION

REPLACE

IMPREZA & LEGACY

1. Raise and support hood, then disconnect battery ground cable.
2. **On non-turbo models,** remove manifold cover and air intake duct.
3. **On turbo models,** remove resonator chamber, then air inlet and outlet ducts, turbocharger cooling duct.
4. **On all models,** disconnect oxygen sensor, transmission harness and ground connectors.
5. Disconnect speedometer cable.
6. Remove starter, then the pitching stopper and bracket.

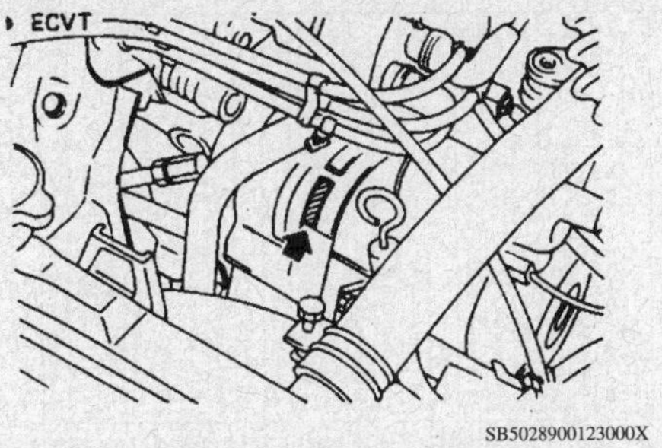
ECVT
SB5028900123000X

Fig. 1 Transmission identification

7. Remove service hole plug from torque converter cover.
8. Remove torque converter to drive plate attaching bolts. Do not drop bolts into torque converter.
9. While rotating engine, remove other bolts.
10. Remove front differential oil level gauge, then the transmission connector bracket.
11. Install engine support fixture tool No. 41099AA000, or equivalent, then remove right upper side of transmission to engine bolts.
12. Remove exhaust system as follows:
    a. **On turbo models,** separate center exhaust pipe from turbocharger.
    b. **On all models,** raise and support vehicle.
    c. **On non-turbo models,** remove front exhaust pipe.
    d. **On turbo models,** remove turbocharger lower cover, then center exhaust pipe.
    e. **On AWD models,** remove rear exhaust pipe.
13. Drain transmission fluid, then disconnect transmission lines from side of transmission.
14. **On AWD models,** remove propeller shaft as follows:
    a. Remove front cover of rear differential mount, then separate propeller shaft from rear differential.
    b. Remove bolts holding center bearing onto body, then the propeller shaft.
15. Remove gear selector cable from selector lever and cable bracket.
16. Remove stabilizer clamp to crossmember bolts.
17. Remove front driveshaft from transmission as follows:
    a. Remove and lower transverse link from housing.
    b. Remove spring pin and separate front driveshaft from each side of transmission.
18. Remove lower side transmission to engine nuts.
19. Place suitable transmission jack stand under transmission.
20. Remove transmission rear crossmember.
21. Remove transmission from vehicle. Move transmission and torque converter as a unit away from engine
22. Reverse procedure to install.

SVX

1. Position vehicle on hoist. Do not lift.
2. Disconnect hood damper, then open hood fully.
3. Disconnect battery ground cable, then remove throttle body cover.
4. Remove air intake boot, then engine hook under throttle body.
5. Remove pitching stopper and bracket. Disconnect transmission air vent hoses from bracket.
6. Disconnect the following electrical connectors:
   a. Transmission harness.
   b. Oxygen sensors.
   c. Vehicle speed sensor 2.
   d. Transmission ground.
7. Disconnect PCV hose, then blow-by hose from crankcase to collector.
8. Raise and support vehicle, then remove lower starter mounting bolts.
9. Lower vehicle, then disconnect power supply terminal and magnet coil connector.
10. Remove upper starter mounting bolts, then the starter.
11. Remove torque converter cover hole plug, then remove torque converter to drive plate attaching bolts. Separate torque converter from drive plate.
12. Install engine support fixture No. 927670000, or equivalent, then remove upper right side transmission to engine bolts.
13. Remove fluid level gauge from transmission and front differential, then raise and support vehicle.
14. Remove under cover, then oxygen sensor harness from clip.
15. remove front exhaust pipes and rear catalyst converter, then the front exhaust cover.
16. Remove propeller shaft to companion flange attaching bolts, then the center bearing to body bolts. Remove propeller shaft from transmission.
17. Remove selector cable from selector lever assembly, then the selector cable bracket from body.
18. Remove performance rod.
19. Remove front axle from transmission as follows:
    a. Remove ball joint from knuckle arm of housing.
    b. Remove stabilizer link from bracket, then the brake hose and ABS sensor harness from start bracket.
    c. Remove spring pin holding axle shaft into front differential drive shaft.
    d. Remove axle shaft from transmission.
20. Disconnect transmission hoses from side of transmission, then remove lower side transmission to engine attaching bolts.
21. Place transmission jack under transmission, then remove rear crossmember to body bolts.
22. Remove transmission from vehicle. Move transmission and torque converter as a unit away from engine
23. Reverse procedure to install.

Symptom \ Problem parts	1 Inhibitor switch	2 Control unit	3 Vehicle speed sensor 1	4 Vehicle speed sensor 2	5 Select cable	6 Select lever	7 FWD switch	8 Starter motor and harness	9 Throttle sensor	10 Manual switch	11 Accumulator ("N" – "D")	12 Accumulator (2A)	13 Accumulator (4A)	14 Accumulator (3R)	15 ATF temperature sensor	16 Strainer	17 Duty solenoid A	18 Duty solenoid B	19 Shift solenoid 1	20 Shift solenoid 2	21 Shift solenoid 3	22 Control valve	23 Detent spring	24 Manual plate	25 Transfer clutch	26 Transfer valve	27 Transfer pipe	28 Duty solenoid C	29 Forward clutch
Starter does not rotate when select lever is in "P" or "N."; starter rotates when select lever is "R", "D", "3" or "2."	X				X	X		X																					
Abnormal noise when select lever is in "P" or "N."																X												X	
Hissing noise occurs during standing starts.																X													
Noise occurs while driving in "D_1" range.																													
Noise occurs while driving in "D_2" range.																													
Noise occurs while driving in "D_3" range.																													
Noise occurs while driving in "D_4" range.																													
Engine stalls while shifting from one range to anther.																						X							
Vehicle moves when select lever is in "N."																													X
Shock occurs when select lever is moved from "N" to "D."		X									X											X							
Excessive time lag occurs when select lever is moved from "N" to "D."																						X							X
Shock occurs when select lever is moved from "N" to "R."		X											X									X							
Excessive time lag occurs when select lever is moved from "N" to "R."																						X							
Vehicle does not start in any shift range (engine revving up).																X						X							
Vehicle does not start in any shift range (engine stall).																													
Vehicle does not start in "R" range only (engine revving up).					X	X																X							
Vehicle does not start in "R" range only (engine stall).																													X
Vehicle does not start in "D" or "3" range (engine revving up).																													X
Vehicle does not start in "D", "3" or "2" range (engine revving up).																													X
Vehicle does not start in "D", "3" or "2" range (engine stall).																													
Vehicle starts in "R" range only (engine revving up).																						X							
Acceleration during standing starts is poor (high stall rpm).																						X							X
Acceleration during standing starts is poor (low stall rpm).																													
Acceleration is poor when select lever is in "D", "3" or "2" range (normal stall rpm).		X																				X							
Acceleration is poor when select lever is in "R" (normal stall rpm).																						X							
No shift occurs from 1st to 2nd gear.		X	X	X					X										X	X		X							
No shift occurs from 2nd to 3rd gear.		X																				X							
No shift occurs from 3rd to 4th gear.		X												X	X						X	X							
No "kickdown" shifts occur.		X							X																				
Engine brake is not effected when select lever is in "3" range.	X	X							X													X							

Symptom \ Problem parts	30 Overrunning clutch	31 Drive pinion	32 Crown gear	33 Axle shaft	34 Differential gear	35 Final gear	36 Seal pipe	37 Oil pump	38 High clutch	39 Band brake	40 Low & reverse clutch	41 Reverse clutch	42 One-way clutch (1-2)	43 One-way clutch (3-4)	44 Double oil seal	45 Input shaft	46 Output shaft	47 Planetary gear	48 Reduction gear	49 Drive plate	50 Torque converter one-way clutch	51 Lock-up facing	52 Lock-up damper	53 ATF deterioration	54 ATF level too high or too low	55 Differential gear oil level too high or too low	56 Engine performance	57 Engine revolution signal	58 Parking brake mechanism
Starter does not rotate when select lever is in "P" or "N."; starter rotates when select lever is "R", "D", "3" or "2."																													
Abnormal noise when select lever is in "P" or "N."								X												X					X				
Hissing noise occurs during standing starts.																									X				
Noise occurs while driving in "D_1" range.						X												X	X							X			
Noise occurs while driving in "D_2" range.						X												X	X							X			
Noise occurs while driving in "D_3" range.						X													X							X			
Noise occurs while driving in "D_4" range.						X												X	X							X			
Engine stalls while shifting from one range to anther.																							X				X		
Vehicle moves when select lever is in "N."																													
Shock occurs when select lever is moved from "N" to "D."																								X					
Excessive time lag occurs when select lever is moved from "N" to "D."																													
Shock occurs when select lever is moved from "N" to "R."																								X					
Excessive time lag occurs when select lever is moved from "N" to "R."											X	X																	
Vehicle does not start in any shift range (engine revving up).		X	X	X	X			X								X	X	X		X					X				
Vehicle does not start in any shift range (engine stall).																													X
Vehicle does not start in "R" range only (engine revving up).											X	X																	
Vehicle does not start in "R" range only (engine stall).										X								X											
Vehicle does not start in "D" or "3" range (engine revving up).													X																
Vehicle does not start in "D", "3" or "2" range (engine revving up).																													
Vehicle does not start in "D", "3" or "2" range (engine stall).												X																	
Vehicle starts in "R" range only (engine revving up).																													
Acceleration during standing starts is poor (high stall rpm).												X														X			
Acceleration during standing starts is poor (low stall rpm).								X													X						X		
Acceleration is poor when select lever is in "D", "3" or "2" range (normal stall rpm).									X	X								X											
Acceleration is poor when select lever is in "R" (normal stall rpm).	X								X	X								X											
No shift occurs from 1st to 2nd gear.										X																			
No shift occurs from 2nd to 3rd gear.									X					X															
No shift occurs from 3rd to 4th gear.										X																			
No "kickdown" shifts occur.																													
Engine brake is not effected when select lever is in "3" range.																													

SB5028900124010X

Fig. 2 General troubleshooting chart (Part 1 of 2)

SHIFT LOCK SYSTEM

Refer to **Figs. 5 through 8,** for shift lock system wiring diagrams and to **Fig. 9,** for diagnosis of the shift lock system.

Symptom / Problem parts	1 Inhibitor switch	2 Control unit	3 Vehicle speed sensor 1	4 Vehicle speed sensor 2	5 Select cable	6 Select lever	7 FWD switch	8 Starter motor and harness	9 Throttle sensor	10 Manual switch	11 Accumulator ("N" – "D")	12 Accumulator (2A)	13 Accumulator (4A)	14 Accumulator (3R)	15 ATF temperature sensor	16 Strainer	17 Duty solenoid A	18 Duty solenoid B	19 Shift solenoid 1	20 Shift solenoid 2	21 Shift solenoid 3	22 Control valve	23 Detent spring	24 Manual plate	25 Transfer clutch	26 Transfer valve	27 Transfer pipe	28 Duty solenoid C	29 Forward clutch	30 Overrunning clutch	31 Drive pinion	32 Crown gear	33 Axle shaft	34 Differential gear	35 Final gear	36 Seal pipe	37 Oil pump	38 High clutch	39 Band brake	40 Low & reverse clutch	41 Reverse clutch	42 One-way clutch (1-2)	43 One-way clutch (3-4)	44 Double oil seal	45 Input shaft	46 Output shaft	47 Planetary gear	48 Reduction gear	49 Drive plate	50 Torque converter one-way clutch	51 Lock-up facing	52 Lock-up damper	53 ATF deterioration	54 ATF level too high or too low	55 Differential gear oil level too high or too low	56 Engine performance	57 Engine revolution signal	58 Parking brake mechanism
Engine brake is not effected when select lever is in "3" or "2" range.																														X																												
Engine brake is not effected when select lever is in "1" range.																						X																		X																		
Shift characteristics are erroneous.	X	X	X	X					X													X																																				
No lockup occurs.		X							X						X							X																													X						X	
Vehicle cannot be set in "D" range power mode.		X							X																																																	
"D" range power mode cannot be released.		X							X						X																																											
Parking brake is not effected.					X	X																																																				X
Shift lever cannot be moved or is hard to move from "P" range.					X	X																																																				X
Select lever is hard to move.					X	X																	X	X																																		
Select lever is too light to move (unreasonable resistance).																							X	X																																		
ATF spurts out.																																																						X				
Differential oil spurts out.																																																							X			
Differential oil level changes excessively.																																				X								X														
Odor is produced from oil supply pipe.																									X				X	X								X	X	X	X										X		X					
Shock occurs when select lever is moved from "1" to "2" range.		X							X			X			X		X					X																	X														X			X		
Slippage occurs when select lever is moved from "1" to "2" range.		X							X			X			X		X					X																	X														X					
Shock occurs when select lever is moved from "2" to "3" range.		X							X					X	X		X					X																X	X														X			X		
Slippage occurs when select lever is moved from "2" to "3" range.		X							X					X	X		X					X																X	X																			
Shock occurs when select lever is moved from "3" to "4" range.		X							X				X		X		X					X								X									X														X			X		
Slippage occurs when select lever is moved from "3" to "4" range.		X							X				X		X		X					X																	X																			
Shock occurs when select lever is moved from "3" to "2" range.		X							X						X		X					X								X									X														X					
Shock occurs when select lever is moved from "D" to "1" range.		X							X						X		X					X																															X					
Shock occurs when select lever is moved from "2" to "1" range.		X							X						X		X					X																		X													X					
Shock occurs when accelerator pedal is released at medium speeds.		X							X						X		X					X																														X				X		
Vibration occurs during straight-forward operation.		X																X																																	X	X						
Select lever slips out of position during acceleration or while driving on rough terrain.					X	X																	X	X																																		
Vibration occurs during turns tight corner "braking" phenomenon).		X	X	X					X	X					X										X	X		X																									X					
Front wheel slippage occurs during standing starts.		X		X			X		X	X					X							X			X	X	X	X																														
Vehicle is not set in FWD mode.		X					X																		X	X		X																														
	1	2	3	4	5	6	7	8	9	10	11	12	13	14	15	16	17	18	19	20	21	22	23	24	25	26	27	28	29	30	31	32	33	34	35	36	37	38	39	40	41	42	43	44	45	46	47	48	49	50	51	52	53	54	55	56	57	58

SB5028900124020X

Fig. 2 General troubleshooting chart (Part 2 of 2)

Pin No.	4	3	2	1	8	7	6	5	12	11	10	9
Lead color / Position	B	YL	Br	YG	YW	YB	R	GW	BY	BW	B W	GB
P	O	O							O	O		
R	O	—	O								O	O
N	O	—	—	O					O	O		
D	O	—	—	—	O							
3	O	—	—	—	—	O						
2	O	—	—	—	—	—	O					
1	O	—	—	—	—	—	—	O				
	Signal sent to AT control unit								Ignition circuit		Back-up light circuit	

SB5028900170000X

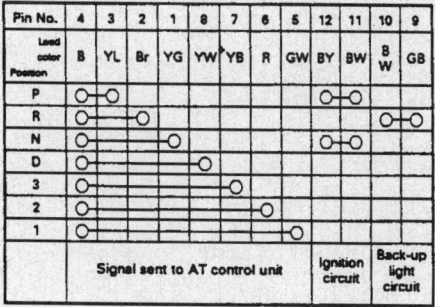

Fig. 3 Inhibitor switch continuity inspection

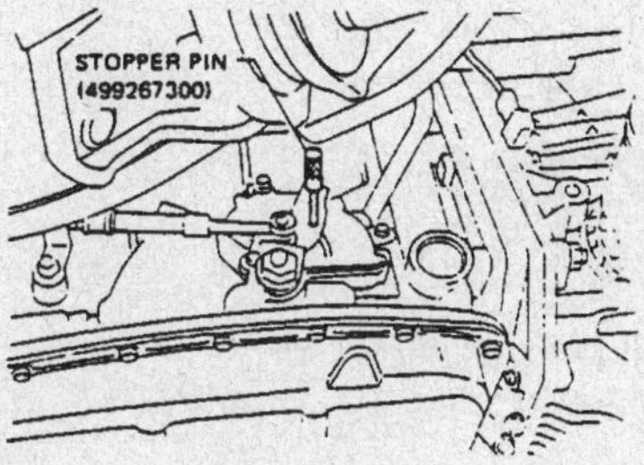
STOPPER PIN
(499267300)

SB5028900171000X

Fig. 4 Inhibitor switch adjustment

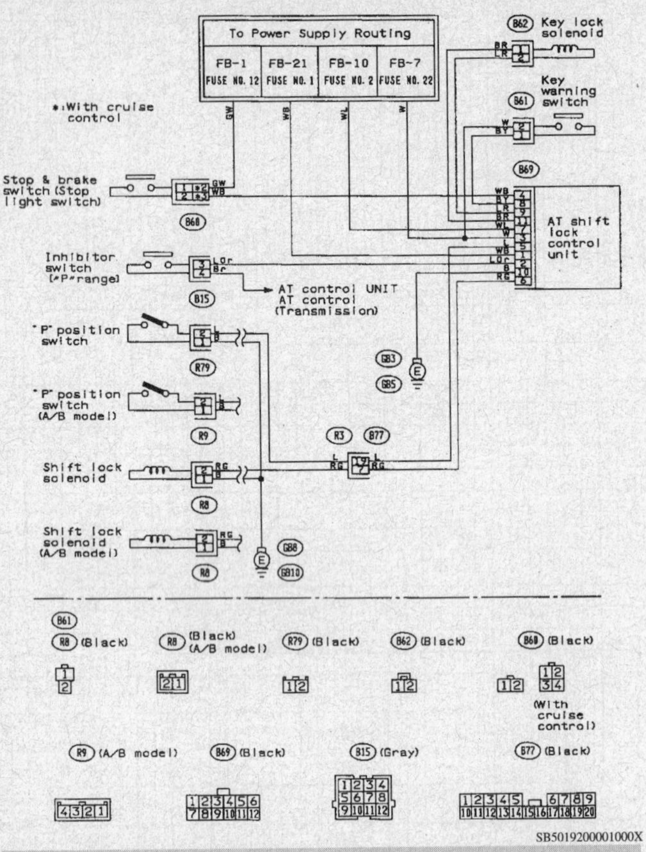
To Power Supply Routing
FB-1 FUSE NO. 12
FB-21 FUSE NO. 1
FB-10 FUSE NO. 2
FB-7 FUSE NO. 22
Key lock solenoid
Key warning switch
*: With cruise control
Stop & brake switch (Stop light switch)
AT shift lock control unit
Inhibitor switch ["P" range]
AT control UNIT
AT control (Transmission)
"P" position switch
"P" position switch (A/B model)
Shift lock solenoid
Shift lock solenoid (A/B model)
SB5019200001000X

Fig. 5 Shift lock system wiring diagram. Legacy

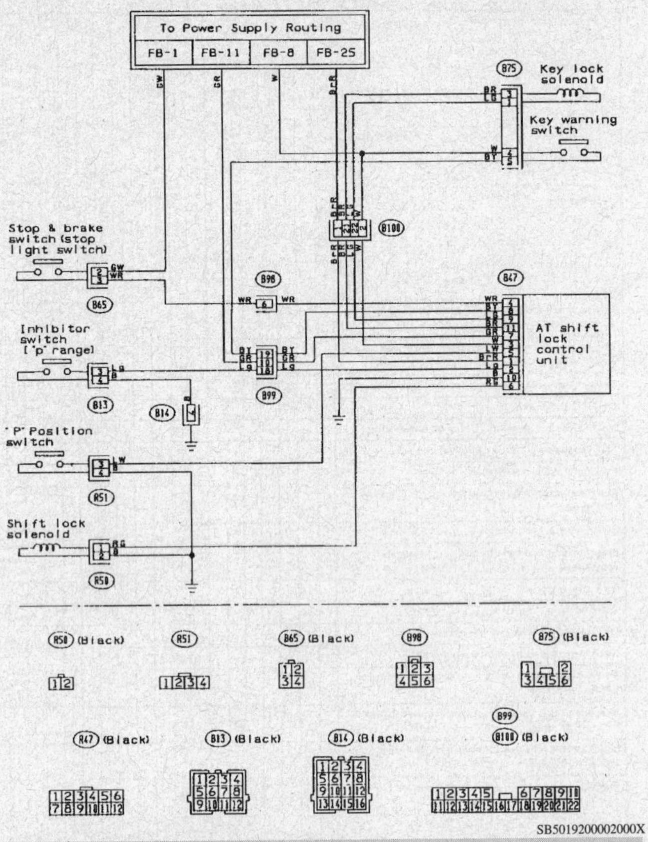
To Power Supply Routing
FB-1
FB-11
FB-8
FB-25
Key lock solenoid
Key warning switch
Stop & brake switch (stop light switch)
Inhibitor switch ["p" range]
AT shift lock control unit
"P" Position switch
Shift lock solenoid
SB5019200002000X

Fig. 6 Shift lock system wiring diagram. 1993 SVX

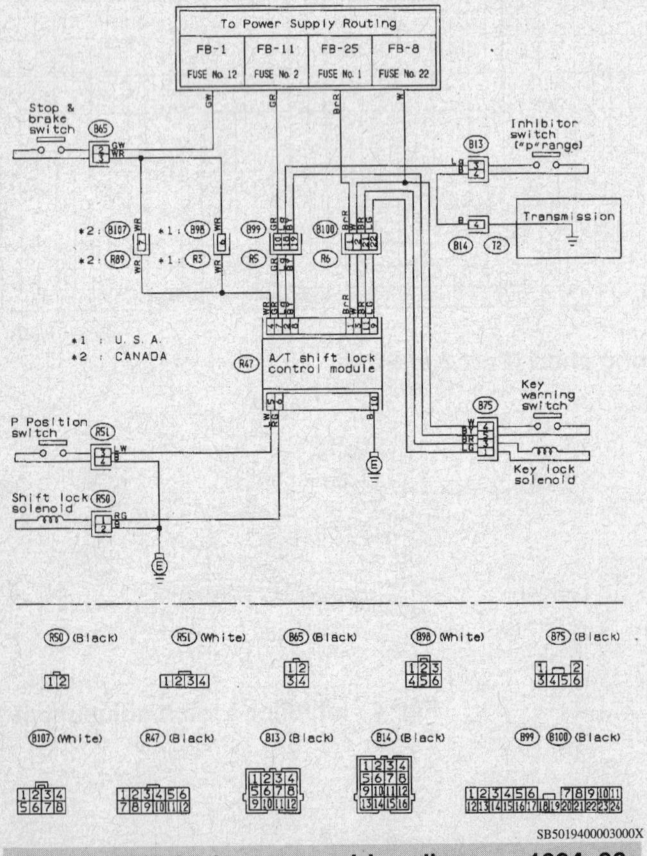
To Power Supply Routing
FB-1 FUSE No. 12
FB-11 FUSE No. 2
FB-25 FUSE No. 1
FB-8 FUSE No. 22
Stop & brake switch
Inhibitor switch ["P" range]
Transmission
*1 : U. S. A.
*2 : CANADA
A/T shift lock control module
Key warning switch
Key lock solenoid
P Position switch
Shift lock solenoid
SB5019400003000X

Fig. 7 Shift lock system wiring diagram. 1994–96 SVX

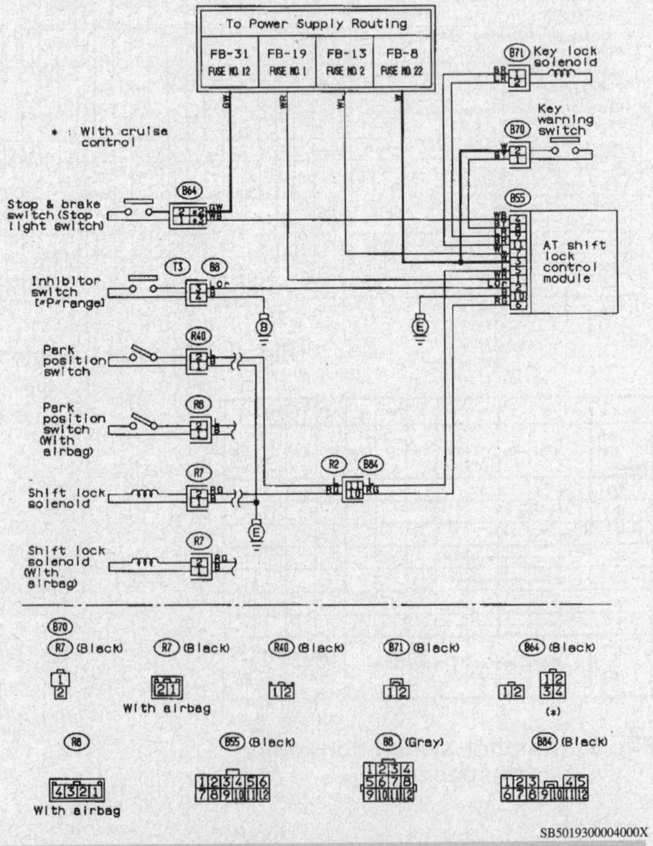
To Power Supply Routing
FB-31 FUSE NO. 12
FB-19 FUSE NO. 1
FB-13 FUSE NO. 2
FB-8 FUSE NO. 22
Key lock solenoid
Key warning switch
* : With cruise control
Stop & brake switch (Stop light switch)
AT shift lock control module
Inhibitor switch ["P" range]
Park position switch
Park position switch (With airbag)
Shift lock solenoid
Shift lock solenoid (With airbag)
With airbag
SB5019300004000X

Fig. 8 Shift lock system wiring diagram. Impreza

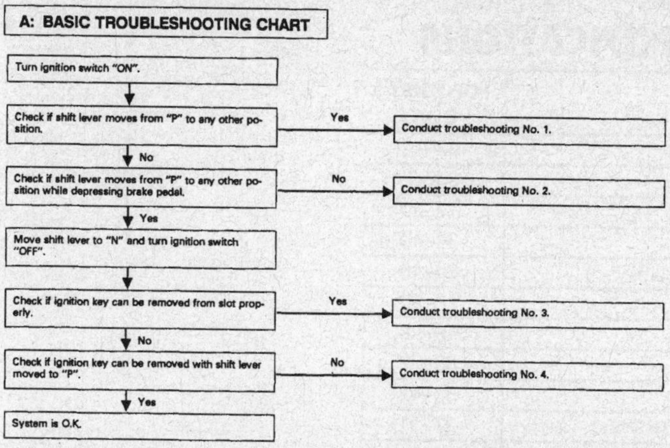
A: BASIC TROUBLESHOOTING CHART
Turn ignition switch "ON".
Check if shift lever moves from "P" to any other position.
Yes
Conduct troubleshooting No. 1.
No
Check if shift lever moves from "P" to any other position while depressing brake pedal.
No
Conduct troubleshooting No. 2.
Yes
Move shift lever to "N" and turn ignition switch "OFF".
Check if ignition key can be removed from slot properly.
Yes
Conduct troubleshooting No. 3.
No
Check if ignition key can be removed with shift lever moved to "P".
No
Conduct troubleshooting No. 4.
Yes
System is O.K.

SB5019200005010X

Fig. 9 Shift lock system diagnosis (Part 1 of 5)

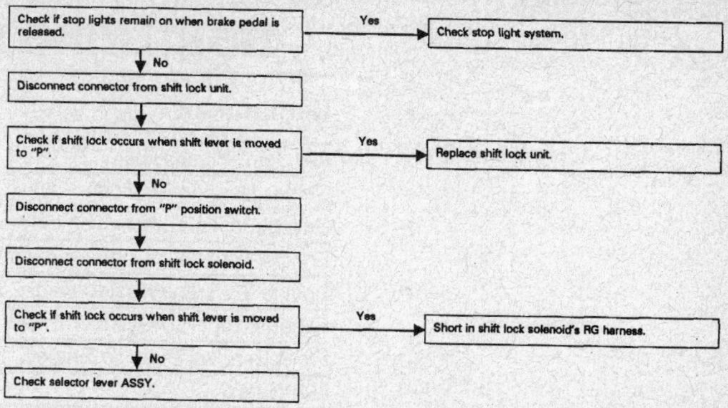
Check if stop lights remain on when brake pedal is released.
Yes
Check stop light system.
No
Disconnect connector from shift lock unit.
Check if shift lock occurs when shift lever is moved to "P".
Yes
Replace shift lock unit.
No
Disconnect connector from "P" position switch.
Disconnect connector from shift lock solenoid.
Check if shift lock occurs when shift lever is moved to "P".
Yes
Short in shift lock solenoid's RG harness.
No
Check selector lever ASSY.

SB5019200005020X

Fig. 9 Shift lock system diagnosis (Part 2 of 5)

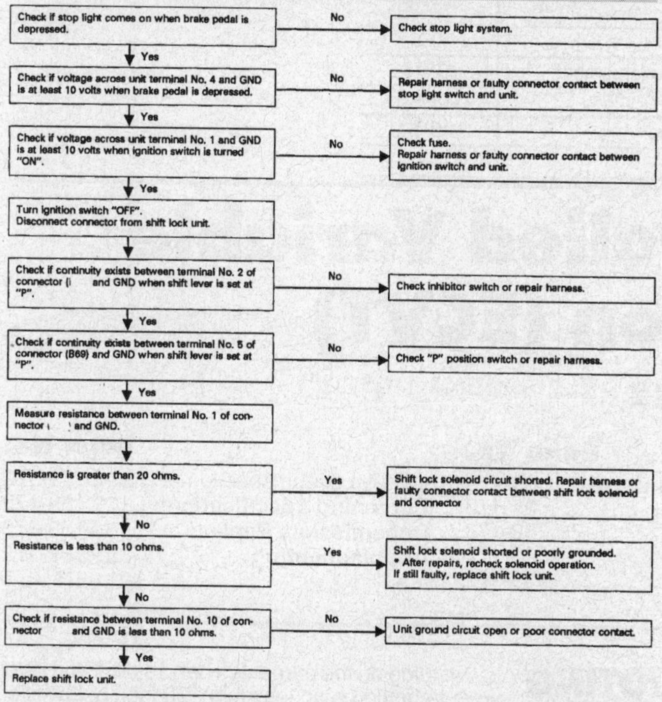
Check if stop light comes on when brake pedal is depressed.
No
Check stop light system.
Yes
Check if voltage across unit terminal No. 4 and GND is at least 10 volts when brake pedal is depressed.
No
Repair harness or faulty connector contact between stop light switch and unit.
Yes
Check if voltage across unit terminal No. 1 and GND is at least 10 volts when ignition switch is turned "ON".
No
Check fuse.
Repair harness or faulty connector contact between ignition switch and unit.
Yes
Turn ignition switch "OFF".
Disconnect connector from shift lock unit.
Check if continuity exists between terminal No. 2 of connector (i and GND when shift lever is set at "P".
No
Check inhibitor switch or repair harness.
Yes
Check if continuity exists between terminal No. 5 of connector (B69) and GND when shift lever is set at "P".
No
Check "P" position switch or repair harness.
Yes
Measure resistance between terminal No. 1 of connector and GND.
Resistance is greater than 20 ohms.
Yes
Shift lock solenoid circuit shorted. Repair harness or faulty connector contact between shift lock solenoid and connector
No
Resistance is less than 10 ohms.
Yes
Shift lock solenoid shorted or poorly grounded.
* After repairs, recheck solenoid operation.
If still faulty, replace shift lock unit.
No
Check if resistance between terminal No. 10 of connector and GND is less than 10 ohms.
No
Unit ground circuit open or poor connector contact.
Yes
Replace shift lock unit.

SB5019200005030X

Fig. 9 Shift lock system diagnosis (Part 3 of 5)

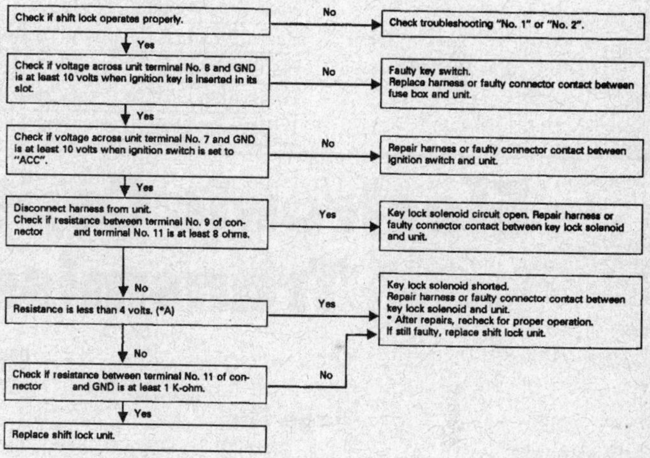
Check if shift lock operates properly.
No
Check troubleshooting "No. 1" or "No. 2".
Yes
Check if voltage across unit terminal No. 8 and GND is at least 10 volts when ignition key is inserted in its slot.
No
Faulty key switch.
Replace harness or faulty connector contact between fuse box and unit.
Yes
Check if voltage across unit terminal No. 7 and GND is at least 10 volts when ignition switch is set to "ACC".
No
Repair harness or faulty connector contact between ignition switch and unit.
Yes
Disconnect harness from unit.
Check if resistance between terminal No. 9 of connector and terminal No. 11 is at least 8 ohms.
Yes
Key lock solenoid circuit open. Repair harness or faulty connector contact between key lock solenoid and unit.
No
Resistance is less than 4 volts. (*A)
Yes
Key lock solenoid shorted.
Repair harness or faulty connector contact between key lock solenoid and unit.
* After repairs, recheck for proper operation.
If still faulty, replace shift lock unit.
No
Check if resistance between terminal No. 11 of connector and GND is at least 1 K-ohm.
No
Yes
Replace shift lock unit.

***A: When conducting operational checks of the key lock solenoid, do not apply 12 volts to solenoid for more than one second, since this may break solenoid circuit.**

SB5019200005040X

Fig. 9 Shift lock system diagnosis (Part 4 of 5)

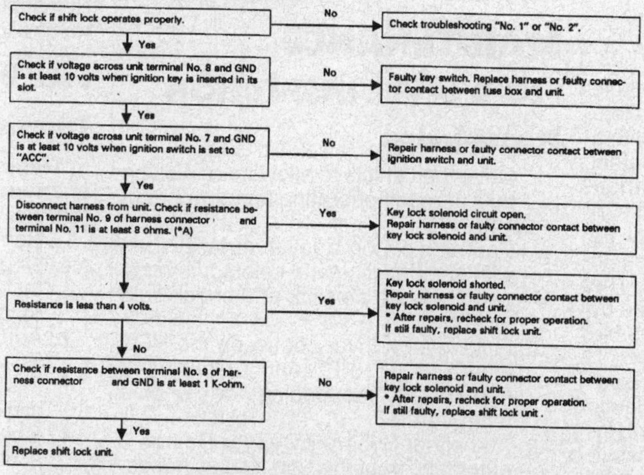
Check if shift lock operates properly.
No
Check troubleshooting "No. 1" or "No. 2".
Yes
Check if voltage across unit terminal No. 8 and GND is at least 10 volts when ignition key is inserted in its slot.
No
Faulty key switch. Replace harness or faulty connector contact between fuse box and unit.
Yes
Check if voltage across unit terminal No. 7 and GND is at least 10 volts when ignition switch is set to "ACC".
No
Repair harness or faulty connector contact between ignition switch and unit.
Yes
Disconnect harness from unit. Check if resistance between terminal No. 9 of harness connector and terminal No. 11 is at least 8 ohms. (*A)
Yes
Key lock solenoid circuit open.
Repair harness or faulty connector contact between key lock solenoid and unit.
Resistance is less than 4 volts.
Yes
Key lock solenoid shorted.
Repair harness or faulty connector contact between key lock solenoid and unit.
* After repairs, recheck for proper operation.
If still faulty, replace shift lock unit.
No
Check if resistance between terminal No. 9 of harness connector and GND is at least 1 K-ohm.
No
Repair harness or faulty connector contact between key lock solenoid and unit.
* After repairs, recheck for proper operation.
If still faulty, replace shift lock unit .
Yes
Replace shift lock unit.

***A: When conducting operational checks of the key lock solenoid, do not apply 12 volts to solenoid for more than one second, since this may break solenoid circuit.**

SB5019200005050X

Fig. 9 Shift lock system diagnosis (Part 5 of 5)

TIGHTENING SPECIFICATIONS

Component	Torque/Ft. Lbs.
Ball Joint Pinch Bolt	33–42
Center Bearing To Body	35–42
Driveplate To Torque Converter	17–20
Engine To Transmission (Lower Nuts)	34–40
Engine To Transmission (Right Side Bolt)	34–40
Exhaust Pipe To Cylinder Head	18–25
Front Exhaust Pipe To Engine	19–23
Lug Nuts	58–72
Performance Rod	33–42
Pitching Stopper Bracket	27–31
Pitching Stopper (Body Side)	35–39
Pitching Stopper (Bracket Side)	25–40
Propeller Shaft To Companion Flange	17–29
Rear Crossmember To Body	40–61
Rear Transmission Mount To Rear Crossmember	9–17
Starter Motor	34–40
Transverse Link To Front Crossmember	43–51
Transverse Link To Stabilizer	14–22

Electronic Controlled Variable Transmission (ECVT)

INDEX

Page No.

Adjustments 39-173
Accelerator Switch & Throttle-Position Switch 39-173
Inhibitor Switch 39-173
Selector Cable Neutral Position . 39-173
Transmission Control Cable 39-173
Description 39-172
Identification 39-172
Maintenance 39-172
Fluid Change 39-172
Fluid Level Inspection 39-172
Tightening Specifications 39-178
Transmission, Replace 39-173
Troubleshooting 39-172

IDENTIFICATION

Refer to **Fig. 1,** for transmission identification number location.

DESCRIPTION

The Electronic Controlled Variable Transmission (ECVT) combines an electronically controlled magnetic clutch with a variable transmission that is driven by steel belt pulleys to provide high running performance, low fuel consumption and ease of control. Hydraulic line pressure can be changed from high to low or vice versa, in response to engine load and output. The ECU and clutch are optimally controlled by a microcomputer to enhance high transmitting efficiency and excellent driveability.

Rationalization of the system is accomplished by controlling the electromagnetic clutch through coolant temperature and ignition advance signals which are transmitted from the ECU while line pressure is regulated through a torque signal.

The AWD model is equipped with a hydraulically operated selective transfer unit at the rear of the front differential.

TROUBLESHOOTING

Refer to **Figs. 2 through 18,** when troubleshooting the transmission system.

MAINTENANCE

FLUID LEVEL INSPECTION

Transmission

1. Drive the vehicle to allow transmission fluid to reach operating temperature of 140–176°F.
2. Park vehicle on a level surface, then with engine idling and selector lever in park, remove dipstick and check fluid level.
3. Fluid level will vary between the HOT mark (140–176°F), and COOL mark (68–104°F), depending on engine temperature.
4. Add either Subaru ECVT, or Dexron II automatic transmission fluid as necessary to bring level within limits.

Differential

Check differential fluid by removing filler plug on the carrier left hand side. Fluid level should be no less than .20 inch below filler plug hole. Add SAE 80W, 85W or 90W gear oil as necessary to bring fluid within limits. Reinstall drain plug with gasket, and **torque** to 22–28 ft. lbs.

FLUID CHANGE

Transmission

Transmission fluid should be changed at 30 month or 30,000 mile intervals.

1. Remove transmission oil pan drain plug, and allow the fluid to drain.
2. Install drain plug with gasket, and **torque** to 18 ft. lbs.
3. Add approximately 2 quarts of Subaru ECVT, or Dexron II automatic transmission fluid through transmission dipstick filler tube.
4. Check transmission fluid level as described previously.

Differential

Differential gear oil should be changed at intervals of 30 months or 30,000 miles.

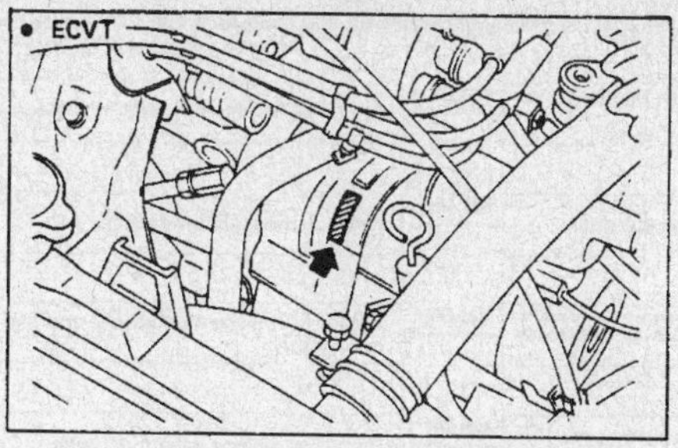
ECVT

SB5058900001000X

Fig. 1 Transmission identification

1. Remove differential drain plug, and allow gear oil to drain.
2. Install differential drain plug with gasket, and **torque** to 22–28 ft. lbs.
3. Remove differential filler plug and add approximately 1.6 pts. of SAE 80W, 85W, or 90W gear oil to differential. Fluid level should be no less than .20 inch below filler plug hole.
4. Reinstall filler plug with gasket, and **torque** to 22–28 ft. lbs.

Symptom	Probable cause		Part to check
Stalling	Brake light switch circuit Vehicle speed switch circuit		Check and repair defective parts.
Clutch temperature warning buzzer sounds (4WD)	Slip ring dirty, causing overheating of the clutch. Intermittent noise may occur (excessive friction in the clutch system).		If intermittent noise occurs, the clutch system is defective.
Poor acceleration	Perform the stall test.	If the stall speed is too high, the clutch torque is too low.	Check and repair the clutch.
		If the stall speed is normal, the ECVT pulley is sticking on the overdrive side.	Check and repair the control valve.
		If the stall speed is too low, the engine torque is too low or clutch torque is too high.	Check the engine. Check and replace the clutch.
Clutch does not disengage	Short between the negative terminal of the clutch circuit and body ground.		Check the clutch circuit.
Irregular engine speed above 30km/h (19 mile/h).	Clutch torque is too low. Defective vehicle speed switch or speedometer cable.		Check the clutch. Check the vehicle speed switch and the speedometer cable.
Clunking noise when accelerating after coasting at speeds between 10 and 20km/h (6 and 13 mile/h).	Lowest speed line does not correspond to specifications.		Repair or replace the control valve.
Clutch disengages slowly after deceleration.	Defective vehicle speed switch.		Check the vehicle speed switch signal circuit.
Clutch disengages when the accelerator pedal is released at speeds above 20km/h (13 mile/h).	Defective brake light switch.		Check the brake light switch.
Switching between FWD and 4WD is not possible.	Defective line pressure solenoid system. Defective 4WD selector switch. Defective 4WD switch. Defective hydraulic circuit.		Check and repair defective parts.

SB5059000096000X

Fig. 2 Troubleshooting inspection chart 1

ADJUSTMENTS

TRANSMISSION CONTROL CABLE

1. Loosen locknuts 1 and 2, **Fig. 19.**
2. Pull inner cable with throttle valve, to the fully open position so there is zero freeplay.
3. Tighten locknuts 1 and 2.
4. Loosen locknut 1, one and one half revolutions, then tighten locknut 2.
5. Fully open carburetor throttle valve, and lightly pull transmission control cable. freeplay should be .020–.059 inch.
6. Install rubber boot.

SELECTOR CABLE NEUTRAL POSITION

1. Position select lever to N range.
2. Push nut (A) toward the lever end **Fig. 20,** then adjust inner cable with nut (B).
3. Check for proper operation.

INHIBITOR SWITCH

Ensure select lever is relative to the shift cams and inhibitor switch positions. Also ensure vehicle starts and back-up lamp illuminates when select lever is properly positioned. Check for continuity at inhibitor switch electrical connector terminals by following the continuity inspection chart **Fig. 21.**

1. Position select lever to N range, then loosen inhibitor switch retaining bolts.
2. While holding pressure against select lever toward P range, match the locator to bracket hole and the moving plate pin to arm hole, then tighten inhibitor switch retaining bolts.
3. Check for proper operation.

ACCELERATOR SWITCH & THROTTLE-POSITION SWITCH

Refer to **Fig. 22,** when checking accelerator switch or throttle-position switch adjustment.

The accelerator switch should turn ON .04–.20 inch from the accelerator pedal released position. The throttle position switch should turn ON .63–.79 inch from the accelerator pedal released position.

TRANSMISSION

REPLACE

Note position of all parts as they are removed, so they can be properly installed. Always remove ECVT transmission with the engine, or the oil shaft may be damaged. Refer to **Fig. 23,** when performing the following procedure.

1. Open hood, wider than normal, and support with stay.
2. Relieve fuel system pressure as follows:
   a. Remove rear seat assembly.
   b. Remove fuel pump cover and disconnect fuel pump connector.
   c. Run engine until it stalls.
   d. Crank starter for 5–10 seconds to relieve remaining fuel pressure. Turn ignition switch to off position.
   e. After fuel system service, connect fuel pump connector and install fuel pump cover and rear seat assembly.
3. Disconnect battery then remove battery and tray assembly.
4. Drain cooling system and disconnect radiator electrical connectors, then remove the radiator.
5. Disconnect hood release cable, then remove upper radiator member.
6. Disconnect horn.
7. Disconnect air clearer hoses and cables, then remove the air cleaner. **Cover carburetor to prevent contamination.**
8. Disconnect all carburetor, heater and brake booster hoses.
9. Disconnect clutch cable and carburetor linkages.
10. Disconnect speedometer cable from transmission.
11. Disconnect ignition coil to distributor electrical cable.
12. Mark and disconnect AWD/FWD change over hoses.
13. Position select lever to N range, then remove attaching clip and detach selector cable from bracket.
14. Remove snap and clevis pins, then separate selector cable from transmission.
15. Disconnect pitching stopper from bracket.
16. Disconnect starter cable positive electrical connector.
17. Disconnect two engine wiring harness electrical connectors.
18. Disconnect engine and transmission ground lead connectors.
19. Disconnect brush holder harness connector.
20. Remove rear transmission hanger, then raise and support vehicle.
21. Remove under covers.
22. Remove air suction pipe, then the front and rear exhaust pipe.
23. Remove propeller shaft, then the transverse link.

The encircled numbers represent the sequence of inspection for this component.

Shift lever position	Symptom \ Possible cause	On-vehicle inspection: Manual linkage	Transmission control cable	Brush holder	Vehicle speed sensor circuit	Accelerator switch and throttle position switch	Range switches for P, R, N, D and Ds	Control unit	ECVT fluid	Line pressure control solenoid valve	4WD solenoid valve	Off-vehicle inspection: Electromagnetic clutch	Forward and reverse selector and park lock mechanism	Pulleys and steel belt	Oil pump	Control valve	Final reduction gear	Pitot pressure system	FWD-4WD selector actuator
D or R	Starter can be activated.	①					②												
D or R	Vehicle does not start.	②	③	④		①	⑥	⑦				⑤	⑨	⑩	⑧	⑪	⑫		
D or R	Stalls soon after starting.							②				①							
D or R	Clutch engages too early.			②		①		④				③							
D or R	Excessive clunking noise when starting.					②			①	⑦		③		④	⑥	⑤			
D or R	Creeping			②		①		④				③							
D or R	Transmission remains in low gear.								①					③		②			
D or R	Engine cannot be increased with the kick-down switch (remains in OD).		①												③	②		④	
D or R	Stall speed is too low.			①								②							
D or R	Stall speed is too high.			①								②							
D or R	Engine speed increases abruptly while driving.	②		④		①	③					⑤			⑥	⑧		⑦	
D or R	Gear noise when shifting from N to P or N to R.	②		④		①	③					⑤	⑥						
D or R	Impossible to shift from N to D or N to R.											①	②						
D or R	Clutch cannot be disengaged below 20km/h (13 mile/h).				②	①		④				③							
Ds	Starter rotates.	①					②												
Ds	Engine brake does not work while shifting from D to Ds.	①														②			
Ds	Excessive clunking noise while shifting from D to Ds.					①	②							③					
Ds	Engine surges while shifting from D to Ds.	①					②												
Ds	Impossible to shift from D to Ds.	①											②						
P	Starter does not rotate.	①					②												
P	Vehicle does not come to a complete stop.	①											②						
P	Impossible to shift between P and R.	①											②						
P	Stuck in any other range.												①						
General	Vehicle speed too low. Poor acceleration.		①					②				③			⑥	④		⑤	
General	Impossible to shift between FWD and 4WD (4WD vehicles).							③		②	①					⑤			④

SB5059000097000X

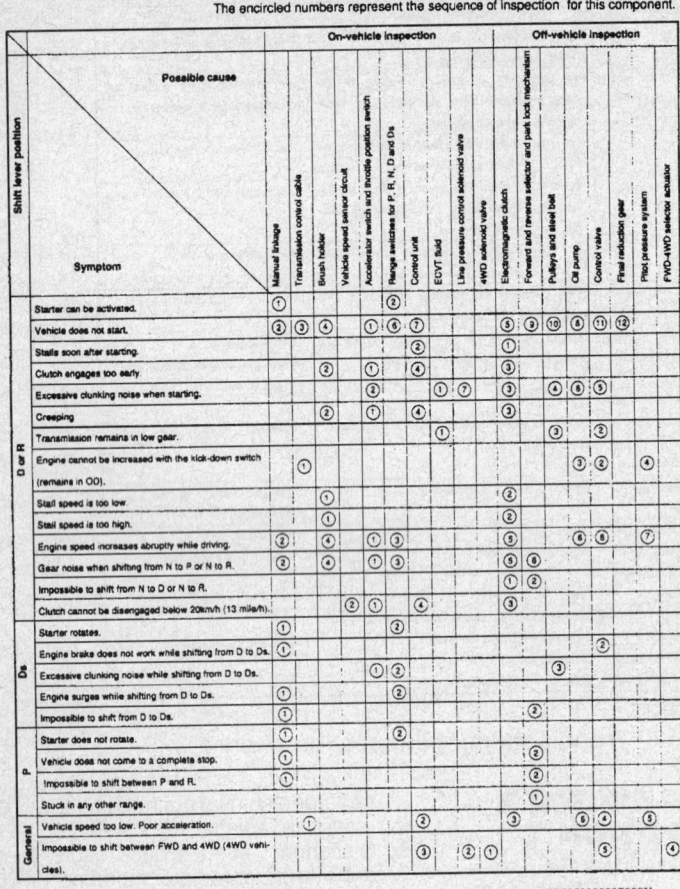

Fig. 3 Troubleshooting inspection chart 2

- Check the power supply to the ECU. (Does the check lamp light up when the ignition switch is turned to ON?) — Not OK → Check the harness. If it is OK, replace the ECU.
- OK ↓ Check the accelerator switch circuit. — Not OK → Adjust or replace the accelerator and throttle position switches.
- OK ↓ Check the adjustment of the selector linkage. — Not OK → Adjust or replace the selector linkage or the selector cable.
- OK ↓ Does the check lamp go out after the engine starts? — Not OK → Check and repair harness and connector of the ignition signal circuit.
- OK ↓ Check the R, D and Ds range circuits. — Not OK → Check and repair the inhibitor switch, harness and connector.
- OK ↓ Check the electromagnetic clutch circuit. — Not OK → Check and replace the electromagnetic clutch and the brush holder.
- OK ↓ Replace the ECU.
- ↓ Start the vehicle. — Not OK, Cannot be started. → Check the transmission components.
- OK, Can be started. ↓ End

SB5059000099000X

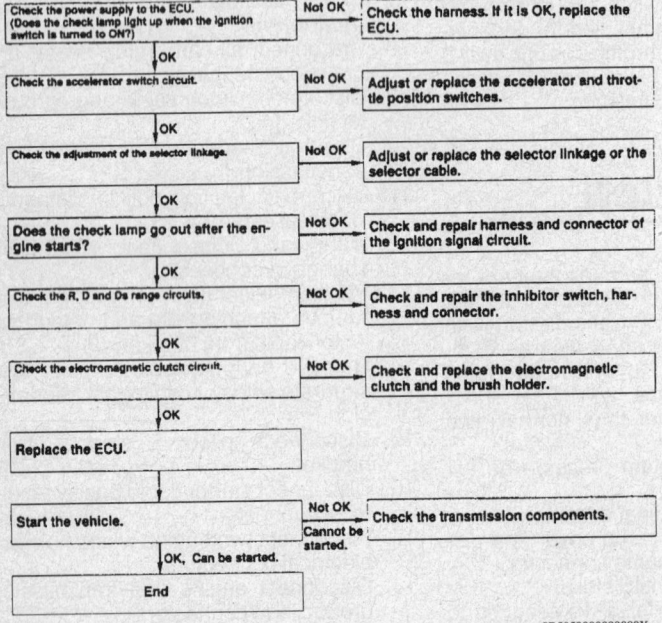

Fig. 5 Vehicle will not start

24. Remove spring pin, then separate the front axle shaft.
25. Remove right hand mounting bracket to engine retaining bolts.
26. Remove left hand mounting bracket to left hand bracket B retaining bolts.
27. Using a suitable engine lift, raise engine slightly.

First check the voltage and the specific gravity of the battery and make sure that they are as specified.

- Check the adjustment of the selector linkage. — Not OK → Adjust or replace the selector linkage.
- OK ↓ Check the N and P range circuits. — Not OK → Replace the inhibitor switch.
- OK ↓ Check the connection between the ignition switch and the starter, as well as between the battery and the starter. — Not OK → Repair or replace the harness and the connector.
- OK ↓ Check the ignition switch and the starter. — Not OK → Repair or replace defective parts.
- OK ↓ End

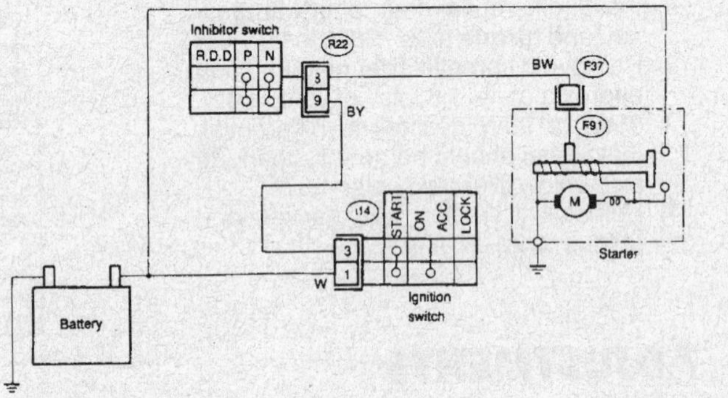
Inhibitor switch
R.D.D
P
N
R22
3
9
BY
BW
F37
F91
M
Starter
i14
START
ON
ACC
LOCK
3
1
W
Ignition switch
Battery

SB5059000098000X

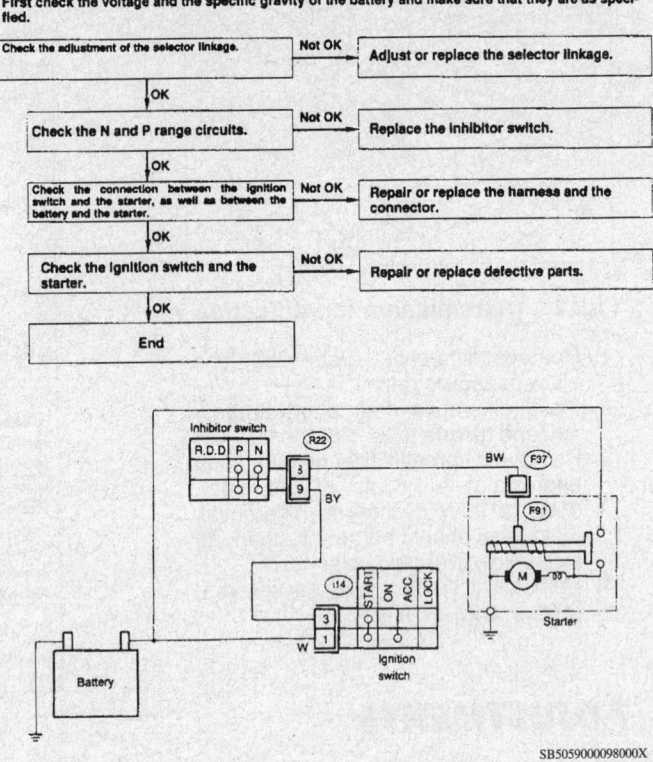

Fig. 4 Vehicle will not start in N or P range

- Check the accelerator switch circuit.
  - OK → • Incorrect installation position of the accelerator switch or the throttle position switch. • Replace the ECU. • Defective electromagnetic clutch. ↓ Repair or replace.
  - Not OK ↓ • Defective accelerator switch. • Open wire in harness, defective connector. • Short in accelerator switch. • Short in throttle position switch. ↓ Repair or replace.

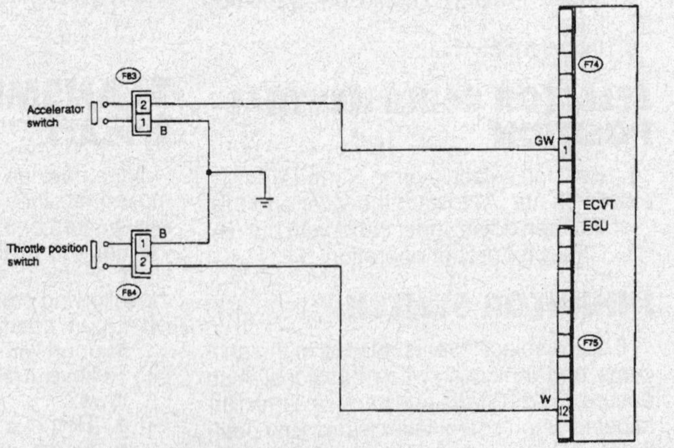
F83
Accelerator switch
2
1
B
Throttle position switch
1
2
B
F84
F74
GW
1
ECVT ECU
F75
W
12

SB5059000100000X

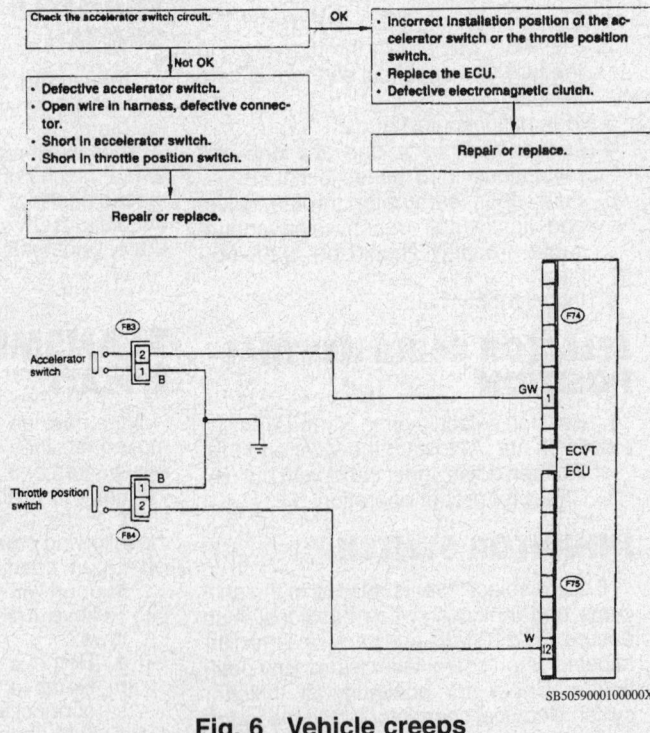

Fig. 6 Vehicle creeps

28. Remove the center member and crossmember.
29. Remove engine with transmission from vehicle.
30. Reverse procedure to install.

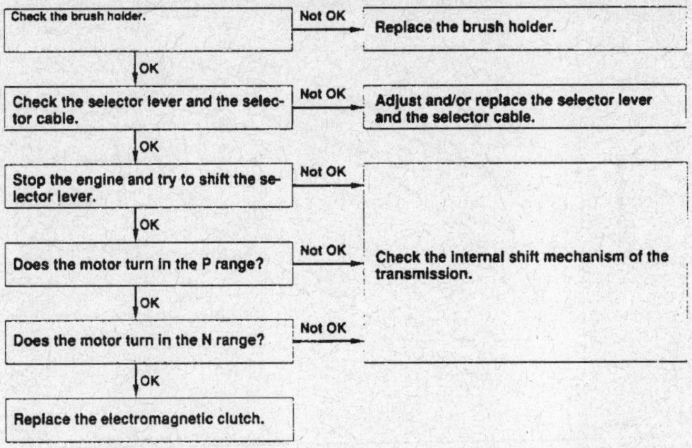
Check the brush holder.
Not OK
Replace the brush holder.
OK
Check the selector lever and the selector cable.
Not OK
Adjust and/or replace the selector lever and the selector cable.
OK
Stop the engine and try to shift the selector lever.
Not OK
OK
Does the motor turn in the P range?
Not OK
Check the internal shift mechanism of the transmission.
OK
Does the motor turn in the N range?
Not OK
OK
Replace the electromagnetic clutch.

SB5059000101000X

Fig. 7 Selector lever is hard to shift

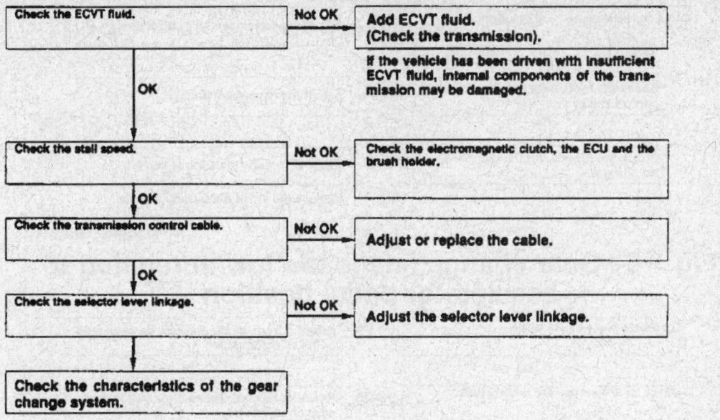
Check the ECVT fluid.
Not OK
Add ECVT fluid.
(Check the transmission).
If the vehicle has been driven with insufficient ECVT fluid, internal components of the transmission may be damaged.
OK
Check the stall speed.
Not OK
Check the electromagnetic clutch, the ECU and the brush holder.
OK
Check the transmission control cable.
Not OK
Adjust or replace the cable.
OK
Check the selector lever linkage.
Not OK
Adjust the selector lever linkage.
Check the characteristics of the gear change system.

SB5059000102000X

Fig. 8 Gear change system rough

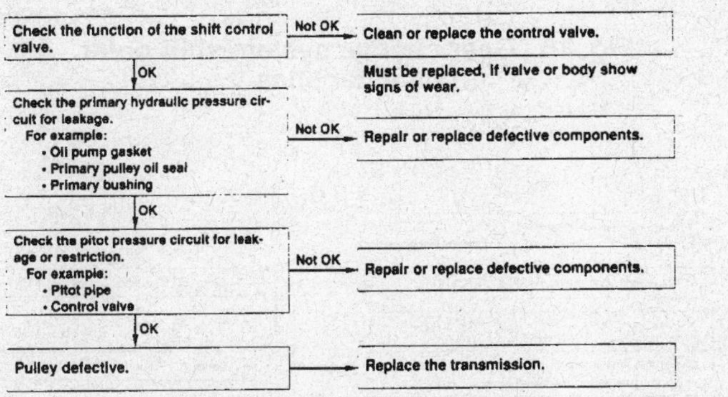
Check the function of the shift control valve.
Not OK
Clean or replace the control valve.
Must be replaced, if valve or body show signs of wear.
OK
Check the primary hydraulic pressure circuit for leakage.
For example:
• Oil pump gasket
• Primary pulley oil seal
• Primary bushing
Not OK
Repair or replace defective components.
OK
Check the pitot pressure circuit for leakage or restriction.
For example:
• Pitot pipe
• Control valve
Not OK
Repair or replace defective components.
OK
Pulley defective.
Replace the transmission.

SB5059000103000X

Fig. 9 Vehicle remains in LOW

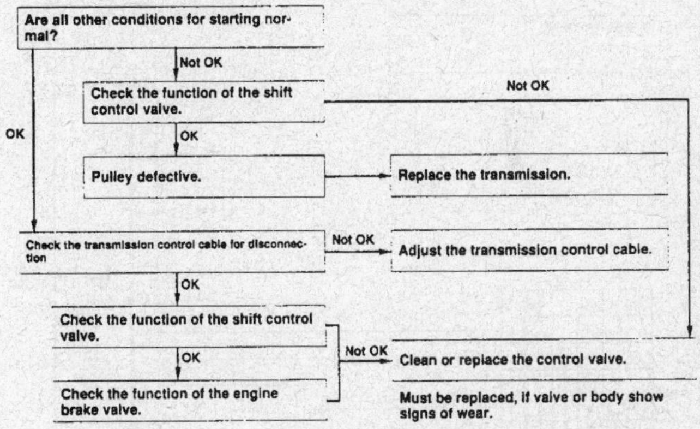
Are all other conditions for starting normal?
Not OK
Check the function of the shift control valve.
Not OK
OK
OK
Pulley defective.
Replace the transmission.
Check the transmission control cable for disconnection
Not OK
Adjust the transmission control cable.
OK
Check the function of the shift control valve.
OK
Check the function of the engine brake valve.
Not OK
Clean or replace the control valve.
Must be replaced, if valve or body show signs of wear.

SB5059000104000X

Fig. 10 Vehicle remains in OD

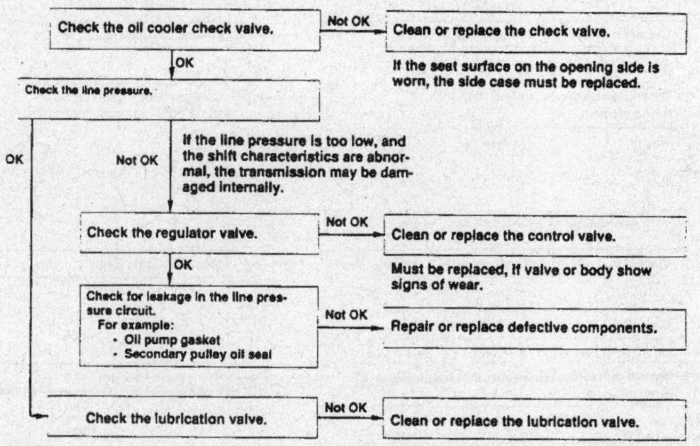
Check the oil cooler check valve.
Not OK
Clean or replace the check valve.
If the seat surface on the opening side is worn, the side case must be replaced.
OK
Check the line pressure.
OK
Not OK
If the line pressure is too low, and the shift characteristics are abnormal, the transmission may be damaged internally.
Check the regulator valve.
Not OK
Clean or replace the control valve.
Must be replaced, if valve or body show signs of wear.
OK
Check for leakage in the line pressure circuit.
For example:
• Oil pump gasket
• Secondary pulley oil seal
Not OK
Repair or replace defective components.
Check the lubrication valve.
Not OK
Clean or replace the lubrication valve.

SB5059000105000X

Fig. 11 Engine brake is suddenly activated while driving in D

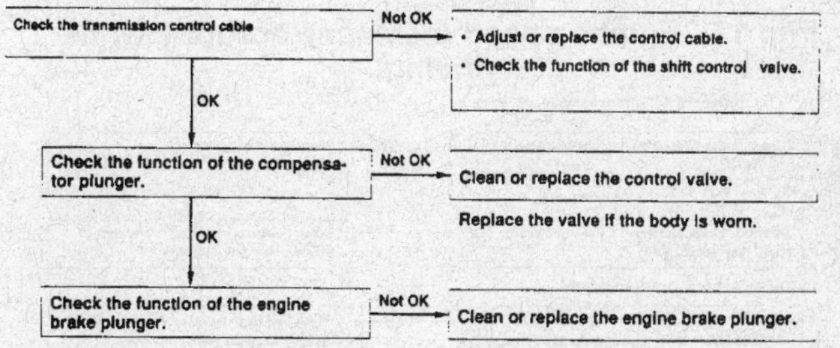
Check the transmission control cable
Not OK
• Adjust or replace the control cable.
• Check the function of the shift control valve.
OK
Check the function of the compensator plunger.
Not OK
Clean or replace the control valve.
Replace the valve if the body is worn.
OK
Check the function of the engine brake plunger.
Not OK
Clean or replace the engine brake plunger.

SB5059000106000X

Fig. 12 Engine brake is too effective in D

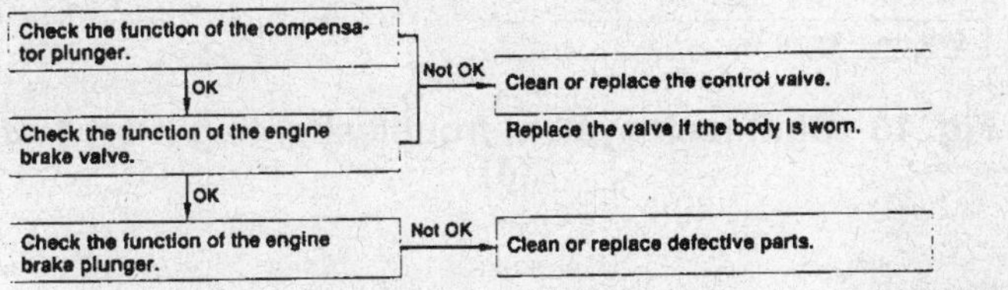
Check the function of the compensator plunger.
OK
Check the function of the engine brake valve.
Not OK
Clean or replace the control valve.
Replace the valve if the body is worn.
OK
Check the function of the engine brake plunger.
Not OK
Clean or replace defective parts.

SB5059000107000X

Fig. 13 Engine brake does not work in D

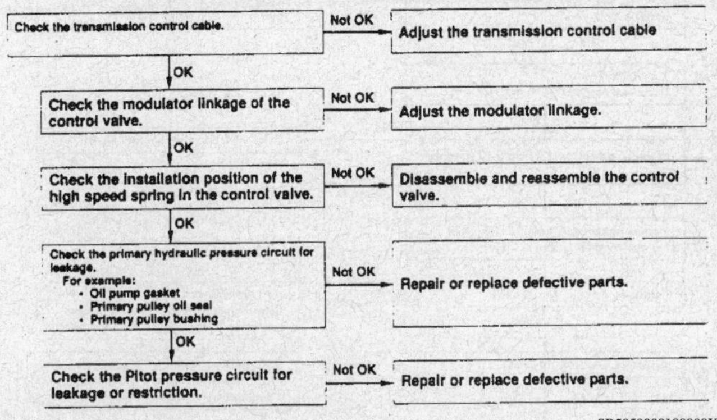
Check the transmission control cable.
Not OK
Adjust the transmission control cable
OK
Check the modulator linkage of the control valve.
Not OK
Adjust the modulator linkage.
OK
Check the installation position of the high speed spring in the control valve.
Not OK
Disassemble and reassemble the control valve.
OK
Check the primary hydraulic pressure circuit for leakage.
For example:
• Oil pump gasket
• Primary pulley oil seal
• Primary pulley bushing
Not OK
Repair or replace defective parts.
OK
Check the Pitot pressure circuit for leakage or restriction.
Not OK
Repair or replace defective parts.

SB5059000108000X

Fig. 14 Gear change line is too high in relation to accelerator pedal position

- Check the transmission control cable. — Not OK → Adjust the transmission control cable
- OK ↓
- Check the modulator linkage of the control valve. — Not OK → Adjust the modulator linkage.
- OK ↓
- Check the function of the compensator plunger. — Not OK → Clean or replace the control valve. Replace the valve if the body is worn.

SB5059000109000X

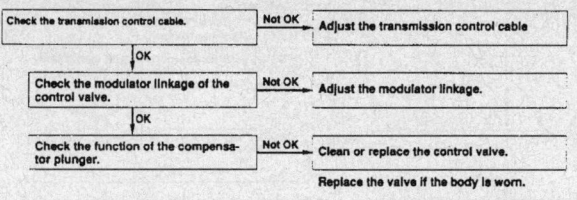

Fig. 15 Gear change line is too low in relation to accelerator pedal position

- Check the selector lever linkage. — Not OK → Adjust or replace the selector lever linkage or the selector cable.
- OK ↓
- Check the R, D and Ds range switch circuits. — Not OK → Repair or replace the inhibitor switch, harness or connector.
- OK ↓
- Check the electromagnetic clutch circuit. — Not OK → Repair or replace the electromagnetic clutch or the slip ring.
- OK ↓
- Incorrect gear change.

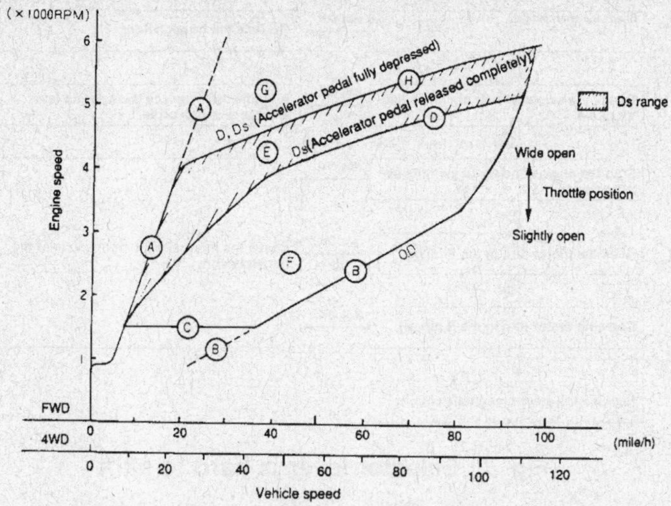

(×1000RPM)
Engine speed
D, Ds (Accelerator pedal fully depressed)
Ds (Accelerator pedal released completely)
Ds range
Wide open
Throttle position
Slightly open
O/D
A
B
C
D
E
F
G
H
FWD
4WD
Vehicle speed
(mile/h)

SB5059000110000X

Fig. 16 Gear change system shift point characteristics

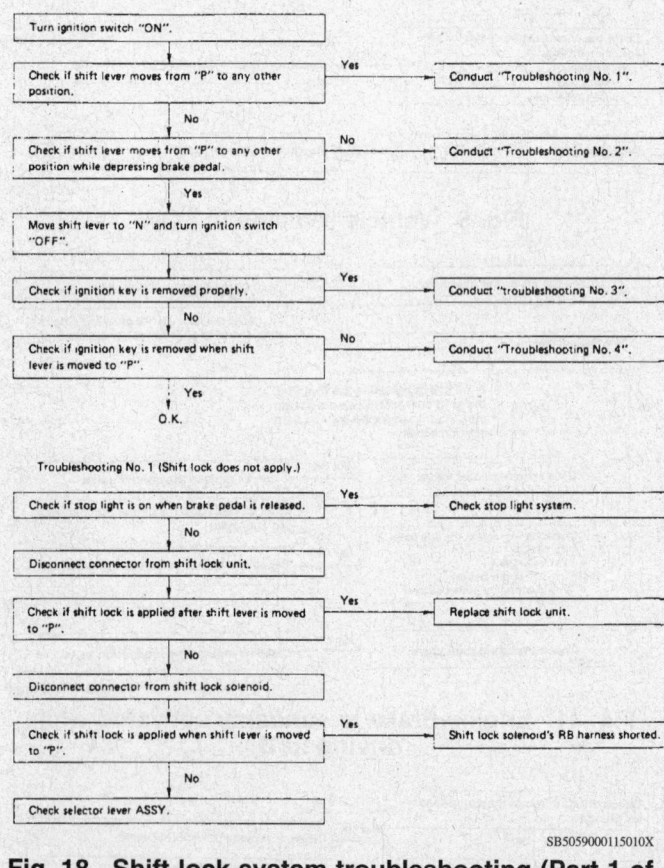

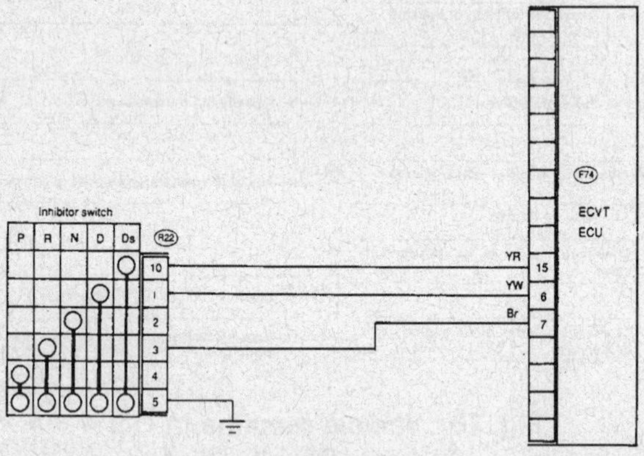

Inhibitor switch
P R N D Ds
R22
F74
ECVT
ECU
YR
YW
Br
15
6
7
10
1
2
3
4
5

SB5059000111000X

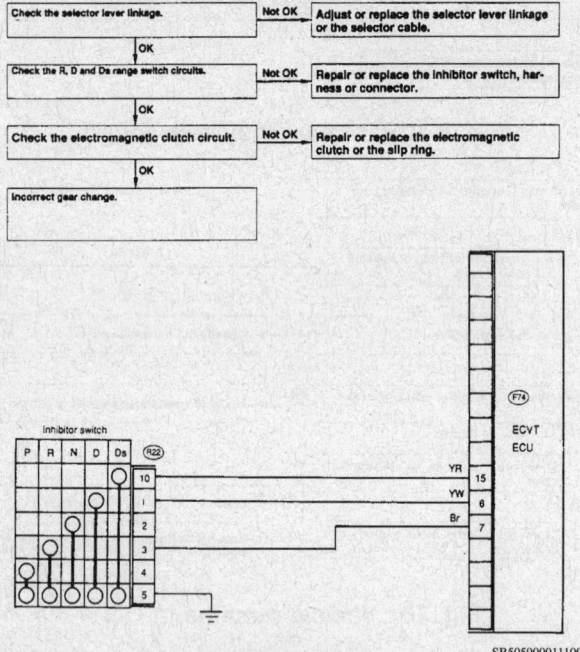

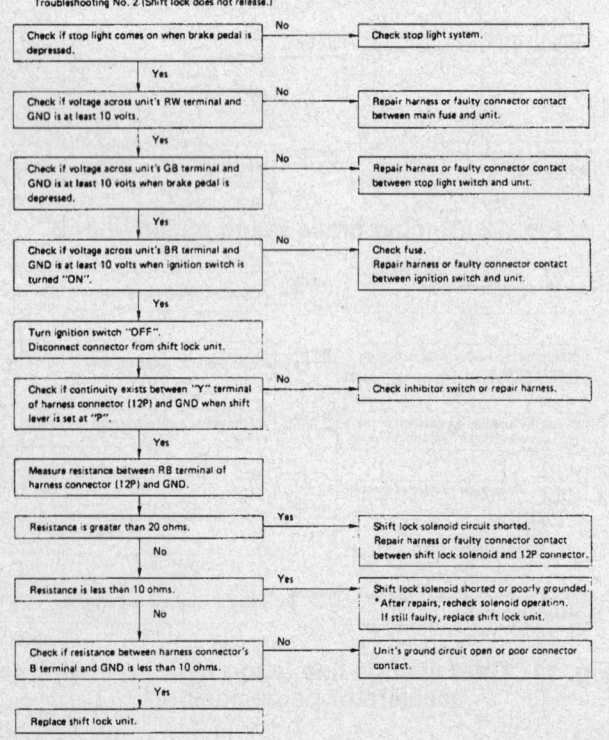

Fig. 17 Engine speed increases abruptly while driving

- Turn ignition switch "ON".
- Check if shift lever moves from "P" to any other position. — Yes → Conduct "Troubleshooting No. 1".
- No ↓
- Check if shift lever moves from "P" to any other position while depressing brake pedal. — No → Conduct "Troubleshooting No. 2".
- Yes ↓
- Move shift lever to "N" and turn ignition switch "OFF".
- Check if ignition key is removed properly. — Yes → Conduct "troubleshooting No. 3".
- No ↓
- Check if ignition key is removed when shift lever is moved to "P". — No → Conduct "Troubleshooting No. 4".
- Yes ↓
- O.K.

Troubleshooting No. 1 (Shift lock does not apply.)

- Check if stop light is on when brake pedal is released. — Yes → Check stop light system.
- No ↓
- Disconnect connector from shift lock unit.
- Check if shift lock is applied after shift lever is moved to "P". — Yes → Replace shift lock unit.
- No ↓
- Disconnect connector from shift lock solenoid.
- Check if shift lock is applied when shift lever is moved to "P". — Yes → Shift lock solenoid's RB harness shorted.
- No ↓
- Check selector lever ASSY.

SB5059000115010X

Fig. 18 Shift lock system troubleshooting (Part 1 of 4)

Troubleshooting No. 2 (Shift lock does not release.)

- Check if stop light comes on when brake pedal is depressed. — No → Check stop light system.
- Yes ↓
- Check if voltage across unit's RW terminal and GND is at least 10 volts. — No → Repair harness or faulty connector contact between main fuse and unit.
- Yes ↓
- Check if voltage across unit's GB terminal and GND is at least 10 volts when brake pedal is depressed. — No → Repair harness or faulty connector contact between stop light switch and unit.
- Yes ↓
- Check if voltage across unit's BR terminal and GND is at least 10 volts when ignition switch is turned "ON". — No → Check fuse. Repair harness or faulty connector contact between ignition switch and unit.
- Yes ↓
- Turn ignition switch "OFF". Disconnect connector from shift lock unit.
- Check if continuity exists between "Y" terminal of harness connector (12P) and GND when shift lever is set at "P". — No → Check inhibitor switch or repair harness.
- Yes ↓
- Measure resistance between RB terminal of harness connector (12P) and GND.
- Resistance is greater than 20 ohms. — Yes → Shift lock solenoid circuit shorted. Repair harness or faulty connector contact between shift lock solenoid and 12P connector.
- No ↓
- Resistance is less than 10 ohms. — Yes → Shift lock solenoid shorted or poorly grounded. *After repairs, recheck solenoid operation. If still faulty, replace shift lock unit.
- No ↓
- Check if resistance between harness connector's B terminal and GND is less than 10 ohms. — No → Unit's ground circuit open or poor connector contact.
- Yes ↓
- Replace shift lock unit.

SB5059000115020X

Fig. 18 Shift lock system troubleshooting (Part 2 of 4)

3) Troubleshooting No. 3 (Key interlock does not operate.)

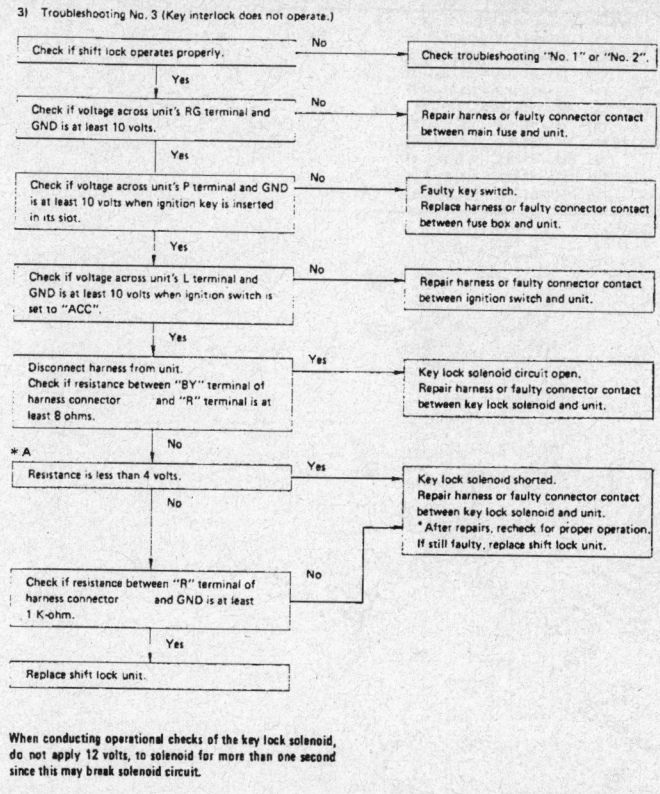

- Check if shift lock operates properly.
  - No → Check troubleshooting "No. 1" or "No. 2".
  - Yes ↓
- Check if voltage across unit's RG terminal and GND is at least 10 volts.
  - No → Repair harness or faulty connector contact between main fuse and unit.
  - Yes ↓
- Check if voltage across unit's P terminal and GND is at least 10 volts when ignition key is inserted in its slot.
  - No → Faulty key switch. Replace harness or faulty connector contact between fuse box and unit.
  - Yes ↓
- Check if voltage across unit's L terminal and GND is at least 10 volts when ignition switch is set to "ACC".
  - No → Repair harness or faulty connector contact between ignition switch and unit.
  - Yes ↓
- Disconnect harness from unit. Check if resistance between "BY" terminal of harness connector and "R" terminal is at least 8 ohms.
  - Yes → Key lock solenoid circuit open. Repair harness or faulty connector contact between key lock solenoid and unit.
  - No ↓
- * A Resistance is less than 4 volts.
  - Yes → Key lock solenoid shorted. Repair harness or faulty connector contact between key lock solenoid and unit. * After repairs, recheck for proper operation. If still faulty, replace shift lock unit.
  - No ↓
- Check if resistance between "R" terminal of harness connector and GND is at least 1 K-ohm.
  - No → Key lock solenoid shorted. Repair harness or faulty connector contact between key lock solenoid and unit. * After repairs, recheck for proper operation. If still faulty, replace shift lock unit.
  - Yes ↓
- Replace shift lock unit.

When conducting operational checks of the key lock solenoid, do not apply 12 volts, to solenoid for more than one second since this may break solenoid circuit.

SB5059000115030X

Fig. 18 Shift lock system troubleshooting (Part 3 of 4)

4) Troubleshooting No. 4 (Key interlock does not release.)

(Use the same procedures as those indicated under "Troubleshooting No. 3", as far as steps marked with "* A".)

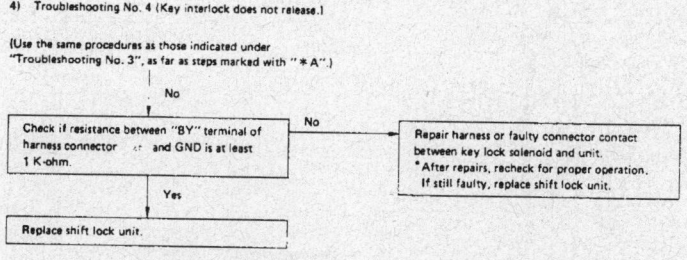

- No ↓
- Check if resistance between "BY" terminal of harness connector and GND is at least 1 K-ohm.
  - No → Repair harness or faulty connector contact between key lock solenoid and unit. * After repairs, recheck for proper operation. If still faulty, replace shift lock unit.
  - Yes ↓
- Replace shift lock unit.

SB5059000115040X

Fig. 18 Shift lock system troubleshooting (Part 4 of 4)

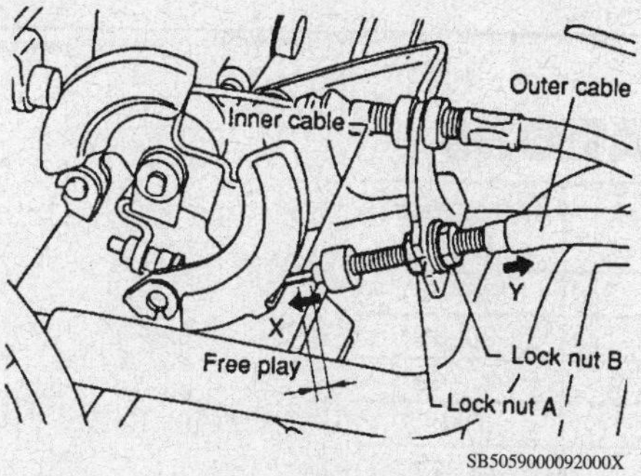
Outer cable
Inner cable
Y
X
Free play
Lock nut B
Lock nut A

SB5059000092000X

Fig. 19 Transmission control cable adjustment

Tightening torque	13 – 23N·m (1.3 – 2.3kg-m, 9.4 – 16.6ft-lb)

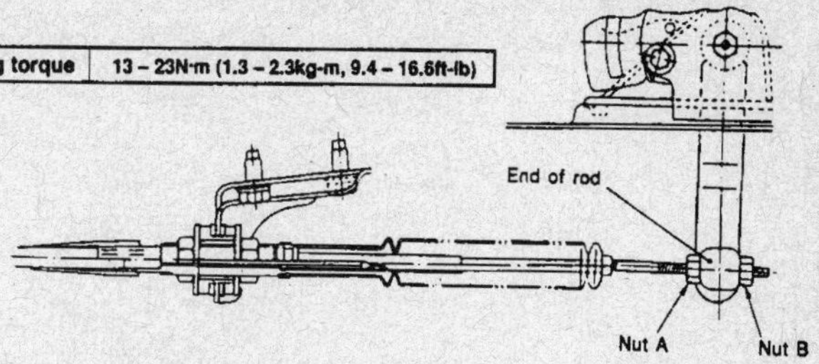
End of rod
Nut A
Nut B

SB5059000094000X

Fig. 20 Selector cable neutral position adjustment

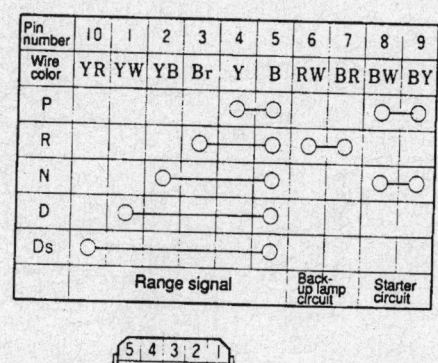

Pin number	10	1	2	3	4	5	6	7	8	9
Wire color	YR	YW	YB	Br	Y	B	RW	BR	BW	BY
P					O	O			O	O
R				O		O	O	O		
N			O			O			O	O
D		O				O				
Ds	O					O				
	Range signal						Back-up lamp circuit		Starter circuit	

5	4	3	2	1
10	9	8	7	6

SB5059000095000X

Fig. 21 Inhibitor switch continuity inspection chart

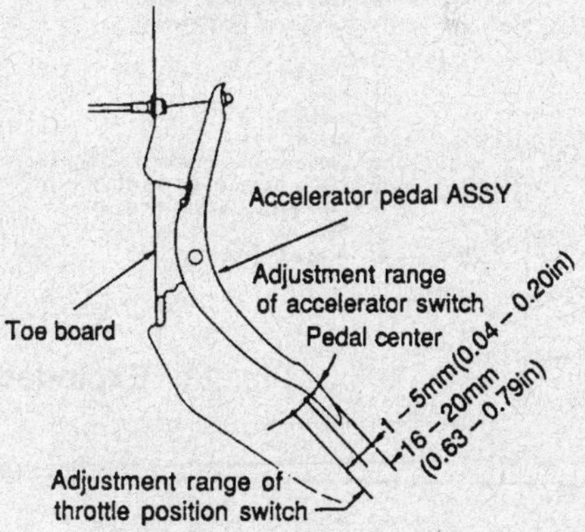
Accelerator pedal ASSY
Adjustment range of accelerator switch
Toe board
Pedal center
1 – 5mm(0.04 – 0.20in)
16 – 20mm (0.63 – 0.79in)
Adjustment range of throttle position switch

SB5059000093000X

Fig. 22 Accelerator & throttle-position switch adjustment

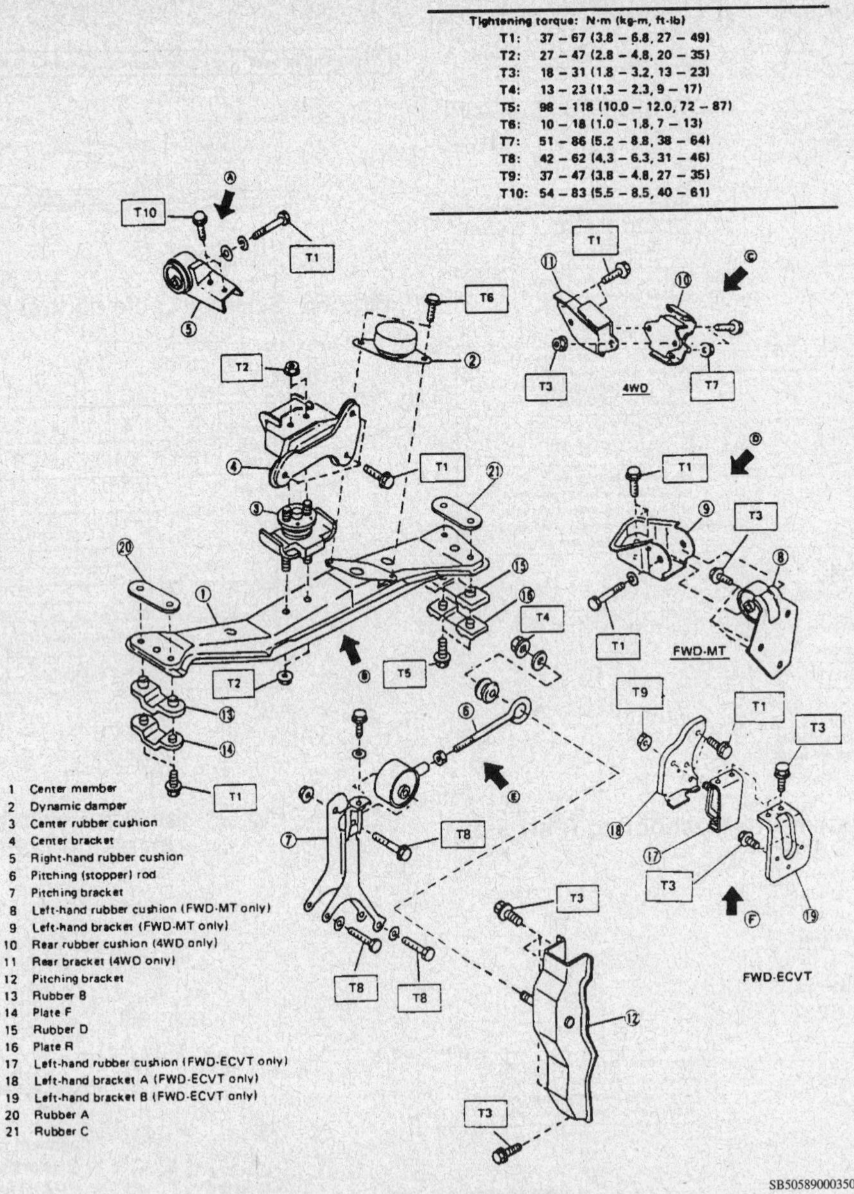
Tightening torque: N·m (kg-m, ft-lb)
T1: 37 – 67 (3.8 – 6.8, 27 – 49)
T2: 27 – 47 (2.8 – 4.8, 20 – 35)
T3: 18 – 31 (1.8 – 3.2, 13 – 23)
T4: 13 – 23 (1.3 – 2.3, 9 – 17)
T5: 98 – 118 (10.0 – 12.0, 72 – 87)
T6: 10 – 18 (1.0 – 1.8, 7 – 13)
T7: 51 – 86 (5.2 – 8.8, 38 – 64)
T8: 42 – 62 (4.3 – 6.3, 31 – 46)
T9: 37 – 47 (3.8 – 4.8, 27 – 35)
T10: 54 – 83 (5.5 – 8.5, 40 – 61)
4WD
FWD-MT
FWD-ECVT
1 Center member
2 Dynamic damper
3 Center rubber cushion
4 Center bracket
5 Right-hand rubber cushion
6 Pitching (stopper) rod
7 Pitching bracket
8 Left-hand rubber cushion (FWD-MT only)
9 Left-hand bracket (FWD-MT only)
10 Rear rubber cushion (4WD only)
11 Rear bracket (4WD only)
12 Pitching bracket
13 Rubber B
14 Plate F
15 Rubber D
16 Plate R
17 Left-hand rubber cushion (FWD-ECVT only)
18 Left-hand bracket A (FWD-ECVT only)
19 Left-hand bracket B (FWD-ECVT only)
20 Rubber A
21 Rubber C
SB5058900035000X

Fig. 23 Exploded view of transmission & engine mounting components

TIGHTENING SPECIFICATIONS

Component	Torque/Ft. Lbs.
Center Rubber Cushion To Center Bracket	20–35
Center Rubber Cushion To Crossmember	20–35
Crossmember To Body	27–49
Dynamic Damper	7–13
Righthand Rubber Cushion	27–49
Pitching Rod To Body	9–17
Pitching Rod To Engine	31–46

① — Front wheel drive only; 9–17 ft. lbs., AWD models; 20–35 ft. lbs.

Front Wheel Drive Axles

NOTE: The Following Abbreviations Are Used In This Section, DOJ For Double Offset Joint And CVJ For Constant Velocity Joint.

INDEX

	Page No.
Driveshaft, Replace	39-179
Impreza & Legacy	39-179
Justy & Loyale	39-179
SVX	39-179
Driveshaft Service	39-179
Assembly	39-179
Disassembly	39-179
Inspection	39-179

DRIVESHAFT

REPLACE

JUSTY & LOYALE

1. Raise and support vehicle.
2. Remove front wheels.
3. Remove parking brake cable bracket from transverse link and disconnect cable from disc brake caliper.
4. Using a drift and hammer, remove and discard driveshaft spring pin, **Fig. 1.**
5. Remove caliper support retaining bolts and the disc brake assembly. Suspend assembly from strut.
6. Disconnect tie-rod end, transverse link and damper strut from axle housing.
7. Remove axle shaft with housing from differential.
8. Separate axle shaft from housing using a suitable puller. **Check axle housing bearing for wear or damage and replace oil seals, Fig. 2.**
9. Reverse procedure to install.

IMPREZA & LEGACY

1. Raise and support vehicle.
2. Remove front wheels.
3. Remove and discard axle nut.
4. Remove stabilizer and transverse link from crossmember.
5. Using a drift and hammer, remove and discard DOJ spring pin, **Fig. 3.**
6. Remove DOJ from transmission spindle.
7. Remove driveshaft assembly. If necessary, use puller tool No. 926470000, or equivalent.
8. Inspect all parts for wear, damage or corrosion and replace as necessary.
9. Reverse procedure to install noting the following:
   a. When replacing axle shaft, install new inner oil seal.
   b. Seat under cut free joint into hub using axle shaft installer tool No. 922431000 and extension tool No. 927130000, or equivalents.
   c. Install axle shaft to hub with new axle nut. Refer to **Fig. 3,** for tightening specifications.

SVX

1. Raise and support vehicle.
2. Remove tire and wheel assembly.

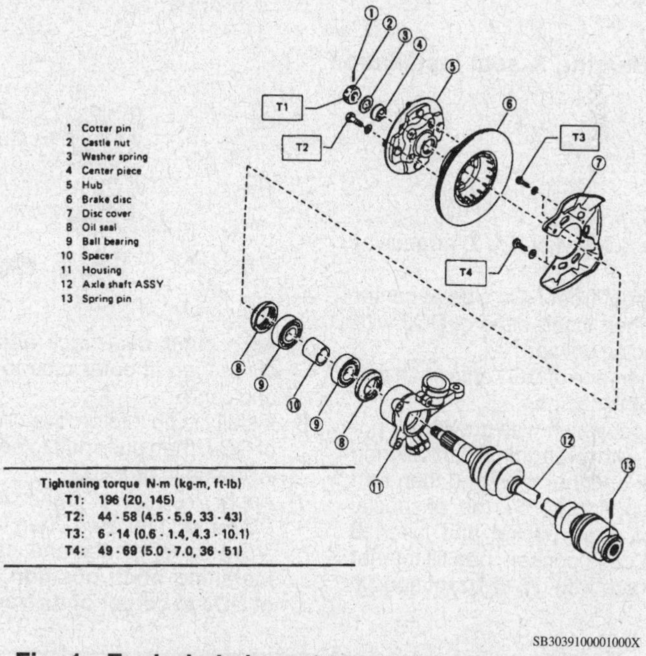

1 Cotter pin
2 Castle nut
3 Washer spring
4 Center piece
5 Hub
6 Brake disc
7 Disc cover
8 Oil seal
9 Ball bearing
10 Spacer
11 Housing
12 Axle shaft ASSY
13 Spring pin
T1
T2
T3
T4
Tightening torque N·m (kg-m, ft-lb)
T1: 196 (20, 145)
T2: 44 - 58 (4.5 - 5.9, 33 - 43)
T3: 6 - 14 (0.6 - 1.4, 4.3 - 10.1)
T4: 49 - 69 (5.0 - 7.0, 36 - 51)
SB3039100001000X

Fig. 1 Exploded view of front drive axle. Justy & Loyale

3. Depress brake pedal and remove axle nut.
4. Remove stabilizer link and disconnect anti-lock brake sensor harness and brake hose clamps from strut.
5. Scribe alignment marks on stabilizer and stabilizer lever. **If removing right-hand driveshaft,** loosen stabilizer clamp.
6. Remove spring pin at tripod joint, then CV joint from knuckle (remover and plate tool Nos. 92647000 and 28099PA110, or equivalent, may be required to separate joint and knuckle).
7. Reverse procedure to install.

DRIVESHAFT SERVICE

DISASSEMBLY

1. Remove axle shaft as described previously.
2. Straighten bent claw of large end of boot on DOJ side of axle shaft, then loosen boot band.
3. Remove boot band on small end of DOJ side in same manner, then slide boot away from joint.
4. Remove round circlip at neck of outer race on DOJ side with screwdriver.
5. Remove outer race on DOJ side from shaft assembly.
6. Remove balls and move cage to boot side, then turn cage by ½ pitch to track groove of inner race and remove snap ring, inner race, cage and boot. **The CVJ is not to be disassembled.**

INSPECTION

1. Check DOJ and CVJ for seizure, corrosion, damage, or excessive wear.
2. Check shaft for bending, twisting, damage and wear.
3. Check boot for wear, warping and cracking.

ASSEMBLY

1. Install boot on CVJ side and fill with 2–2.5 oz. of special constant velocity

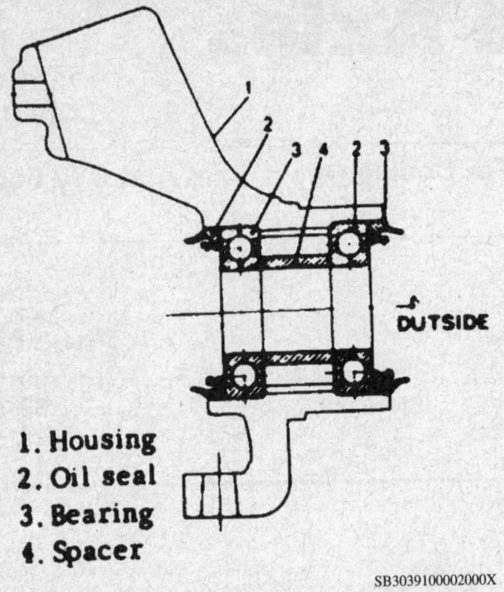
1
2
3 4 2 3
OUTSIDE
1. Housing
2. Oil seal
3. Bearing
4. Spacer
SB3039100002000X

Fig. 2 Bearing & seal installation

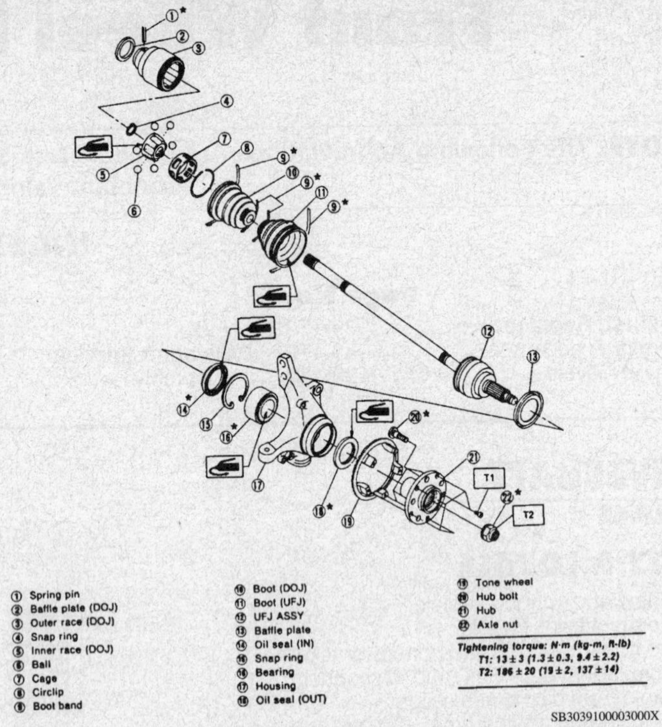
T1
T2
① Spring pin
② Baffle plate (DOJ)
③ Outer race (DOJ)
④ Snap ring
⑤ Inner race (DOJ)
⑥ Ball
⑦ Cage
⑧ Circlip
⑨ Boot band
⑩ Boot (DOJ)
⑪ Boot (UFJ)
⑫ UFJ ASSY
⑬ Baffle plate
⑭ Oil seal (IN)
⑮ Snap ring
⑯ Bearing
⑰ Housing
⑱ Oil seal (OUT)
⑲ Tone wheel
⑳ Hub bolt
㉑ Hub
㉒ Axle nut
Tightening torque: N·m (kg-m, ft-lb)
T1: 13 ± 3 (1.3 ± 0.3, 9.4 ± 2.2)
T2: 186 ± 20 (19 ± 2, 137 ± 14)
SB3039100003000X

Fig. 3 Exploded view of front drive axle. Impreza, Legacy (SVX similar)

joint grease Molylex No. 2, or equivalent.

2. Position boot from DOJ side at center of shaft, then insert cage of DOJ with recess facing outward.
3. Install inner race of DOJ onto shaft and secure with snap ring.
4. Install cage, which was previously positioned, with protruding part aligned with track on inner race and then turn by ½ pitch. Apply .75–1 oz. of special grease to cage pocket and insert 6 balls into cage pocket, then fill interior of outer race with .75–1 oz. of special grease.
5. Align outer race track and ball positions, then fit outer race to inner race and cage.
6. Install circlip into groove on outer race of DOJ, then pull shaft to ensure circlip is seated in groove.
7. Apply .75–1 oz. of grease to interior of DOJ and shaft area, then fill boot with .75–1 oz. of grease and install. **When installing boot, position outer race of DOJ at center of its travel.**
8. Install new boot bands using suitable tool and tighten until it cannot be moved by hand. **While tightening band, be sure there is enough air within boot.**
9. Tap on clip of band with suitable punch at end of tightening tool and cut off excess band at about .4 inch (10mm) from clip, then bend band over clip.
10. Fill CVJ boot and CVJ with special grease and install in same manner as DOJ boot.

All-Wheel Drive Systems

INDEX

	Page No.
Description	39-180
Impreza, Legacy & SVX	39-180
Transfer Case, Replace	39-181
Impreza & Legacy	39-182
Justy	39-182
Loyale	39-181

DESCRIPTION

IMPREZA, LEGACY & SVX

The electronically controlled multi-plate transfer type AWD system consist of a transfer hydraulic pressure control unit incorporating a vehicle speed sensor, control unit, and duty solenoid and a transfer clutch.

The control unit stores optimum transfer clutch torque data for a variety of driving conditions. When actual driving conditions are detected by the sensors, the control unit selects a duty ratio most suitable to the given condition from the memory. It then controls the operation of the transfer clutch by means of the hydraulic pressure which controls the duty solenoid and provides optimum rear torque distribution.

Various sensors and the control unit also serve as gear shift control, lock-up control and hydraulic pressure control.

The AWD transfer system is housed in the extension case together with the bearing and rear drive shaft.M

TRANSFER CASE

REPLACE

LOYALE

Refer to **Figs. 1 and 2,** when performing the following procedure.

Removal

1. Install transmission in a suitable holding fixture.
2. Remove two clutch sleeve clips from front of transmission, then the clutch release bearing.
3. Remove release dust cover, then the release lever retainer spring, from release lever, by pushing release lever from outside of main case. **Use caution not to damage clutch sleeve clips and release lever retainer spring.**
4. Remove release lever.
5. Using a suitable tool, drive out transfer shifter shaft and transfer shifter lever spring pin from right side of transfer case.
6. Remove transfer shifter lever from transfer shifter shaft.
7. Remove snap pin and 8mm clevis pin, then the cable from transfer shifter lever.
8. Remove five 8mm bolts from actuator and cable, then the actuator and cable assembly.
9. Remove transfer cover attaching bolts, then the transfer cover.
10. Remove straight pin from transfer shifter fork using a suitable tool.
11. Turn transfer shifter rod 180°, then remove rod.
12. Move reverse checking sleeve .08–.12 inch (2–3mm) toward outside, then remove transfer shifter fork, transfer case check ball and check ball spring.
13. Remove seven extension attaching bolts.
14. Remove extension and transfer gear assembly.
15. Remove transfer shifter shaft from right side of transfer case.
16. Remove transfer case filler with gasket, then the reverse accent spring and ball.
17. Remove reverse check sleeve assembly attaching bolts, then move sleeve until it rotates freely.
18. Remove shifter fork screw from selector arm.
19. Remove transfer case and shifter assembly attaching bolts, then the transfer case and shifter assembly from transmission case by tapping with plastic hammer.

Installation

1. Install transfer case and shifter assembly and eight attaching bolts. **Torque** attaching bolts to 18 ft. lbs. **Ensure gasket is installed in rear of case.**
2. Install selector arm to shifter arm and secure with shifter fork screw. **Torque** fork screw to 7 ft. lbs.
3. Install ball, reverse accent spring, gasket and plug. **Torque** plug to 7 ft. lbs.
4. Shift transmission into 3rd gear position, then ensure shifter arm turns lightly toward 1st/2nd gear side but heavily toward reverse gear side.
5. Adjust neutral position as necessary by removing bolts holding reverse check sleeve assembly to case, move sleeve assembly outward, and place adjustment shims between sleeve assembly and case to adjust clearance, **Fig. 3.** When shim is removed, neutral position will move closer to reverse. When shim is added, neutral position will move closer to 1st gear. **Use caution not to break O-ring when replacing shim. Also, if shims cannot adjust clearance, replace accent shaft and repeat step 4.**
6. Shift shifter arm to 5th and then to reverse to see if reverse check mechanism operates properly, then check to see if arm returns to neutral when released from reverse position. If arm does not return satisfactorily, replace reverse check plate, **Figs. 4 and 5.**
7. Install extension with transfer gasket, then the extension attaching bolts. **Torque** bolts to 25–30 ft. lbs. **Ensure transfer drive and driven gears engage each other.**
8. Apply suitable oil to nylon pawl of fork, then install transfer shifter fork to coupling sleeve, aligning cutout section of fork with arm of transfer shifter shaft.
9. Install check ball spring and ball to transfer case. **Use caution not to drop ball and spring into transfer case.**
10. Apply suitable oil to transfer shifter rod, then install transfer shifter rod and rod spring pin. **Ensure spring pin protrudes slightly beyond holes.**
11. Connect end of cable and shifter lever with clevis pin and snap pin.
12. Install actuator and three actuator attaching bolts to left side of transmission case. **Torque** attaching bolts to 12 ft. lbs.
13. Install cable plate, two cable plate attaching bolts and washers on transfer case. **Torque** attaching bolts to 12 ft. lbs.
14. Connect transfer shifter lever to transfer shifter shaft.
15. Align hole in transfer shifter lever with hole in shifter shaft, then install spring pin using suitable tools.
16. Connect a hose to pipe on outside of actuator, then apply vacuum, using a suitable vacuum pump, to the actuator until cable is shortened as much as possible.
17. While applying vacuum pressure, turn turnbuckle in direction that shortens cable until it no longer turns, then back off turnbuckle 180° and **torque** two locknuts to 3.6 ft. lbs.
18. Operate actuator to ensure shifting from front wheel drive to AWD is satisfactory.
19. Install transfer cover, gasket and gasket attaching bolts. **Torque** attaching bolts to 13–16 ft. lbs.
20. Install retaining spring on release lever.
21. Install release lever pivot to lefthand transmission case attaching bolts.

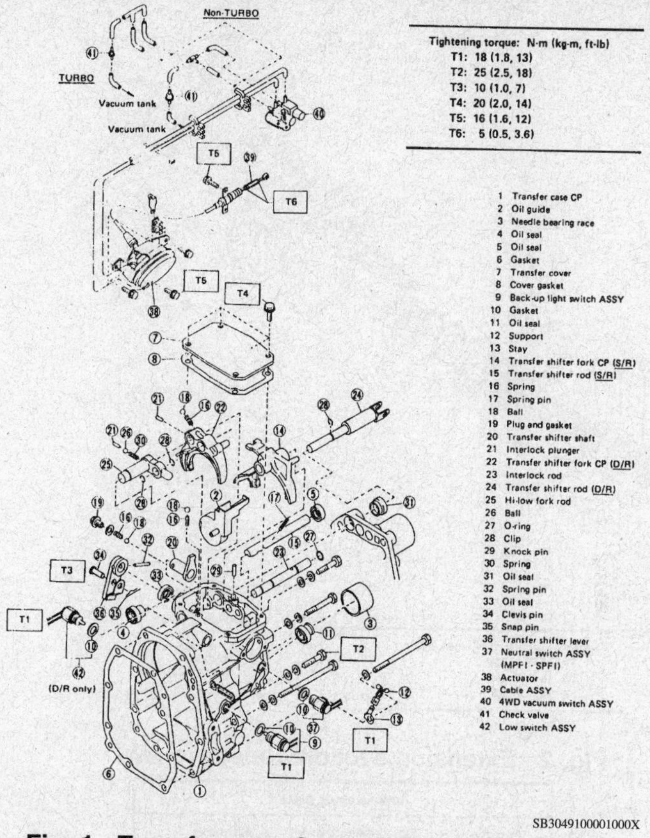

Non-TURBO
TURBO
Vacuum tank
Vacuum tank
T1
T2
T3
T4
T5
T6
(D/R only)
Tightening torque: N·m (kg-m, ft-lb)
T1: 18 (1.8, 13)
T2: 25 (2.5, 18)
T3: 10 (1.0, 7)
T4: 20 (2.0, 14)
T5: 16 (1.6, 12)
T6: 5 (0.5, 3.6)
1 Transfer case CP
2 Oil guide
3 Needle bearing race
4 Oil seal
5 Oil seal
6 Gasket
7 Transfer cover
8 Cover gasket
9 Back-up light switch ASSY
10 Gasket
11 Oil seal
12 Support
13 Stay
14 Transfer shifter fork CP (S/R)
15 Transfer shifter rod (S/R)
16 Spring
17 Spring pin
18 Ball
19 Plug and gasket
20 Transfer shifter shaft
21 Interlock plunger
22 Transfer shifter fork CP (D/R)
23 Interlock rod
24 Transfer shifter rod (D/R)
25 Hi-low fork rod
26 Ball
27 O-ring
28 Clip
29 Knock pin
30 Spring
31 Oil seal
32 Spring pin
33 Oil seal
34 Clevis pin
35 Snap pin
36 Transfer shifter lever
37 Neutral switch ASSY (MPFI · SPFI)
38 Actuator
39 Cable ASSY
40 4WD vacuum switch ASSY
41 Check valve
42 Low switch ASSY
SB3049100001000X

Fig. 1 Transfer case & transfer control system. Selective AWD

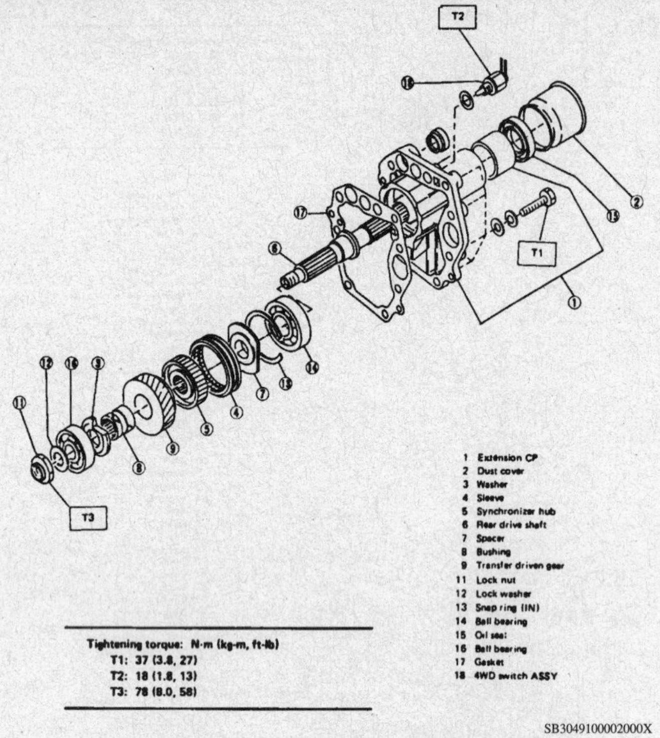
T2
T1
T3
1 Extension CP
2 Dust cover
3 Washer
4 Sleeve
5 Synchronizer hub
6 Rear drive shaft
7 Spacer
8 Bushing
9 Transfer driven gear
11 Lock nut
12 Lock washer
13 Snap ring (IN)
14 Ball bearing
15 Oil seal
16 Ball bearing
17 Gasket
18 4WD switch ASSY
Tightening torque: N·m (kg-m, ft-lb)
T1: 37 (3.8, 27)
T2: 18 (1.8, 13)
T3: 78 (8.0, 58)
SB3049100002000X

Fig. 2 Extension section. Selective AWD

Reverse check plate			
Part No.	No.	Angle θ	Remarks
32189AA000	0	28°	Arm stops closer to "5th".
32189AA010	1	31°	Arm stops closer to "5th".
32189AA020	2	34°	Standard
32189AA030	3	37°	Arm stops closer to reverse.
32189AA040	4	40°	Arm stops closer to reverse.

SB3049100004000X

Fig. 4 Reverse check plate chart

Torque attaching bolts to 12 ft. lbs.

22. Push release lever against pivot, then with lever held in position, twist it to left and right so that retaining spring moves into the stepped surface on rear of pivot. **Ensure proper positioning of retainer spring through access window on case.**
23. Install release bearing sleeve assembly and secure with two clutch sleeve clips.
24. Install dust release cover to case.

JUSTY

Refer to **Figs. 6 and 7,** when performing the following procedure.

Removal

1. Remove transmission as outlined previously.
2. Remove side cover and main case.
3. Remove attaching bolts, then separate extension case and transfer bearing case from clutch housing.
4. Remove attaching bolts, then the transfer cover and gasket from transfer case side cover.
5. Remove circlip from shifter shaft, then remove washer and shifter lever.
6. Remove side cover attaching bolts, then the diaphragm cover and diaphragm.
7. Remove side cover attaching bolts, then the side cover and gasket.
8. Remove shifter rail spring plug, spring and ball from housing.
9. Remove shifter rail, together with synchronizer, through case side.
10. Tap transfer shaft assembly from case using suitable mallet.

Installation

1. Install transfer shaft assembly, together with drive pinion shim and O-ring into case. **Torque** attaching bolts to 13–16 ft. lbs.
2. Install bearing case and height shim, then **torque** bearing case attaching bolts to 20–24 ft. lbs. Ensure backlash is between .0039–.0059 inch. Adjust backlash by changing shim as required.

Reverse accent shaft		
Part No.	Mark	Remarks
32188AA020	A	Neutral position is closer to 1st gear.
32188AA002	B	Standard
32188AA030	C	Neutral position is closer to reverse gear.

SB3049100003000X

Fig. 3 Reverse accent shaft chart

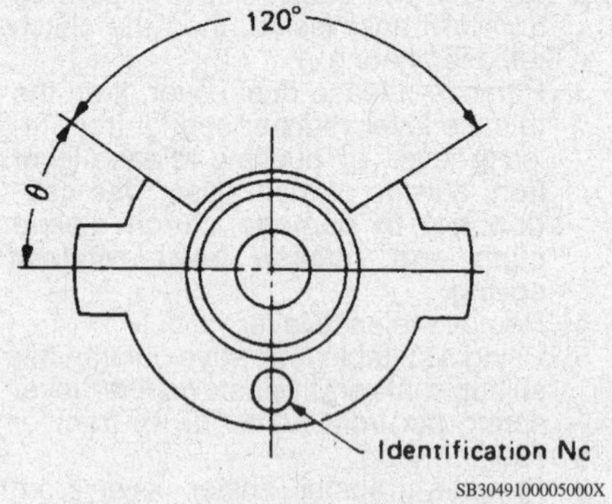
120°
θ
Identification Nc
SB3049100005000X

Fig. 5 Reverse check plate adjustment

3. Press new seal into extension case using suitable tool.
4. Install extension case using new gasket, then **torque** attaching bolts to 17–20 ft. lbs.
5. Press oil seal and knock pipe into side case, then install shifter shaft into side cover.
6. Attach seal to knock pipe, then align knock pipe with transfer rail hole in clutch housing.
7. Install side cover, adjusting shim, transfer shaft bearing and gasket, then **torque** attaching bolts to 13–16 ft. lbs.
8. Install shifter rail and synchronizer into side cover from main case side.
9. Install diaphragm, then assemble shifter lever and washer to shifter shaft and retain with clip.
10. Install diaphragm cover to side cover.
11. Install transfer cover and gasket to clutch housing, then **torque** attaching bolts to 7 ft. lbs.
12. Install ball, spring and shifter rail spring plug into clutch housing and **torque** plug to 14 ft. lbs.

IMPREZA & LEGACY

Refer to **Fig. 8** when performing the following procedure.

Removal

1. Install transmission in a suitable holding stand.
2. Disconnect harness electrical connectors.
3. Remove transfer cover.
4. Remove shifter fork screw retaining the selector arm to shifter arm.
5. Remove transfer case and extension assembly.

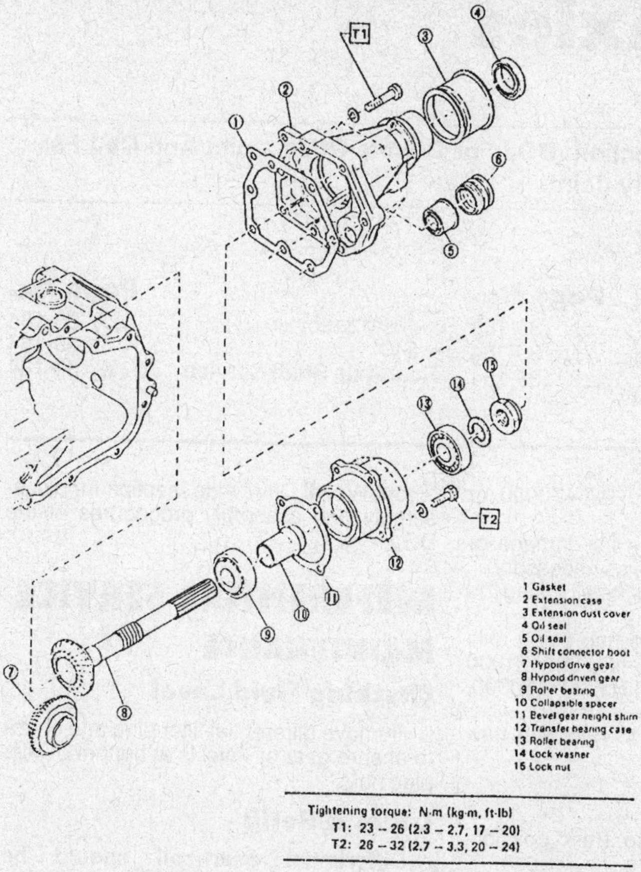
T1
T2
1 Gasket
2 Extension case
3 Extension dust cover
4 Oil seal
5 Oil seal
6 Shift connector boot
7 Hypoid drive gear
8 Hypoid driven gear
9 Roller bearing
10 Collapsible spacer
11 Bevel gear height shim
12 Transfer bearing case
13 Roller bearing
14 Lock washer
15 Lock nut
Tightening torque: N·m (kg-m, ft-lb)
T1: 23 – 26 (2.3 – 2.7, 17 – 20)
T2: 26 – 32 (2.7 – 3.3, 20 – 24)
SB3049100008000X

Fig. 6 Extension case & components. Justy

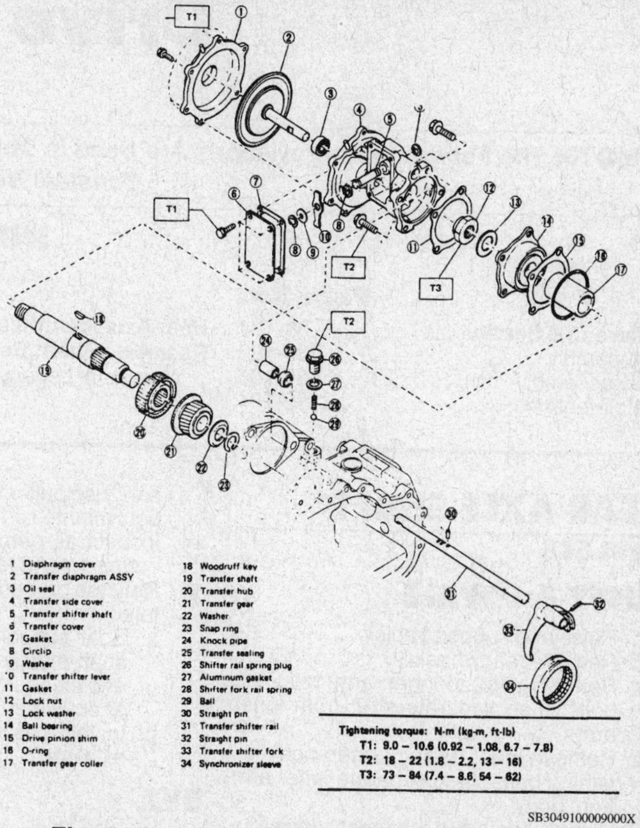
T1
T2
T3
1 Diaphragm cover
2 Transfer diaphragm ASSY
3 Oil seal
4 Transfer side cover
5 Transfer shifter shaft
6 Transfer cover
7 Gasket
8 Circlip
9 Washer
10 Transfer shifter lever
11 Gasket
12 Lock nut
13 Lock washer
14 Ball bearing
15 Drive pinion shim
16 O-ring
17 Transfer gear collar
18 Woodruff key
19 Transfer shaft
20 Transfer hub
21 Transfer gear
22 Washer
23 Snap ring
24 Knock pipe
25 Transfer sealing
26 Shifter rail spring plug
27 Aluminum gasket
28 Shifter fork rail spring
29 Ball
30 Straight pin
31 Transfer shifter rail
32 Straight pin
33 Transfer shifter fork
34 Synchronizer sleeve
Tightening torque: N·m (kg-m, ft-lb)
T1: 9.0 – 10.6 (0.92 – 1.08, 6.7 – 7.8)
T2: 18 – 22 (1.8 – 2.2, 13 – 16)
T3: 73 – 84 (7.4 – 8.6, 54 – 62)
SB3049100009000X

Fig. 7 Transfer case & components. Justy

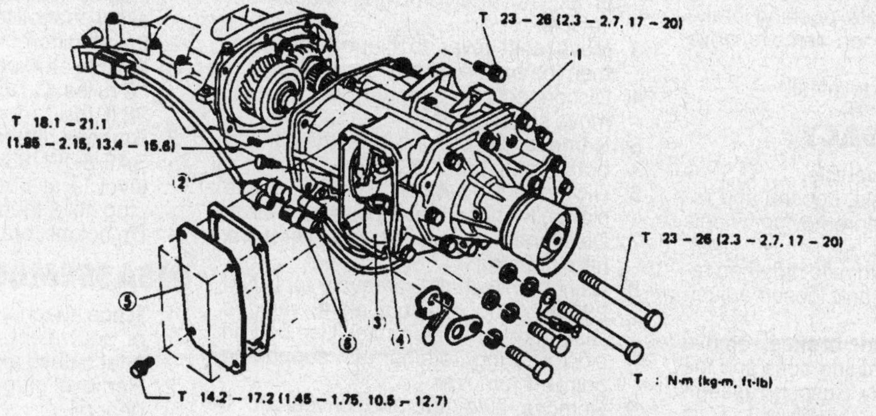
T 23 – 26 (2.3 – 2.7, 17 – 20)
T 18.1 – 21.1
(1.85 – 2.15, 13.4 – 15.6)
T 23 – 26 (2.3 – 2.7, 17 – 20)
T : N·m (kg-m, ft-lb)
T 14.2 – 17.2 (1.45 – 1.75, 10.5 – 12.7)
SB3049100010000X

Fig. 8 Transfer case & extension assembly. Impreza & Legacy

Installation

1. Install transfer case and extension assembly.
2. Install selector arm to shifter arm and secure with shifter fork screw. **Ensure shifter arm is caught by pawl of rod and selector arm is engaged with reverse check sleeve assembly.**
3. Adjust neutral position as necessary by removing bolts holding reverse check sleeve assembly to case, move sleeve assembly outward and place adjustment shims between sleeve assembly and case to adjust clearance. When shim is removed, neutral position will move closer to reverse. When shim is added, neutral position will move closer to 1st gear. **Use caution not to break O-ring when replacing shim. Also, if shims cannot adjust clearance, replace accent shaft and repeat adjustment.**
4. Shift shifter arm to 5th and then to reverse to see if reverse check mechanism operates properly, then check to see if arm returns to neutral when released from reverse position. If arm does not return satisfactorily, replace reverse check plate.
5. Install transfer cover with gasket.
6. Connect harness electrical connectors.

Drive Axles

NOTE: The Following Abbreviations Are Used In This Section: DOJ For Double Offset Joint And CVJ For Constant Velocity Joint.

INDEX

	Page No.
Differential Service	39-184
Assembly	39-185
Disassembly	39-184
Maintenance	39-184
Rear Axle Identification	39-188
Rear Axle Shaft, Replace	39-184
Impreza & Legacy	39-184
Justy & Loyale	39-184
SVX	39-184
Rear Axle Shaft Service	39-184

REAR AXLE SHAFT

REPLACE

JUSTY & LOYALE

1. Raise and support vehicle.
2. Remove rear wheels.
3. Remove strut-to-inner arm retaining bolts, then separate strut from inner arm.
4. Remove inner trailing arm-to-body retaining bolts, then separate inner arm from body.
5. Using a drift and hammer, drive out spring pins at both ends of drive axle, **Fig. 1.**
6. Separate outer DOJ from rear axle spindle by pushing inner DOJ toward rear differential while pushing brake drum downward, then remove drive axle.
7. Reverse procedure to install.

IMPREZA & LEGACY

1. Raise and support vehicle.
2. Remove rear wheels. Loosen and retighten axle nut after removing wheels from vehicle.
3. Remove and discard axle nut, then return parking brake and loosen adjuster.
4. **On models with disc brakes,** remove caliper support retaining bolts and the disc brake assembly. Suspend assembly from strut.
5. Remove disc brake rotor, then disconnect end of parking brake cable.
6. **On models with drum brakes,** remove brake drum from hub. **If brake drum is difficult to remove drive it out by installing an 8 mm bolt into brake drum bolt hole.**
7. **On all models,** disconnect brake pipe from wheel cylinder, then disconnect end of parking brake cable.
8. Remove stabilizer clamp.
9. If equipped, remove speed sensor from backing plate.
10. Remove lateral link and trailing link-to-housing retaining bolts.
11. Using a drift and hammer, remove DOJ spring pin.
12. Remove DOJ from differential spindle.
13. Remove driveshaft assembly. If necessary, use puller tool No. 926470000, or equivalent.
14. Inspect all parts for wear damage or corrosion and replace as necessary.
15. Reverse procedure to install noting the following:
    a. Seat bell joint into hub using axle shaft installer tool No. 922431000 and extension tool No. 927130000, or equivalents.
    b. Install axle shaft to hub with new axle nut.

SVX

1. Move select lever to Park position, then set parking brake.
2. Raise and support vehicle, then remove rear wheels. Loosen and retighten axle nut after removing wheels from vehicle.
3. Move shift lever to Neutral position, then the parking brake lever forward.
4. Disconnect rear exhaust pipe, then remove stabilizer link.
5. Remove ABS clamps, then the parking brake cable bracket.
6. Disconnect parking brake cable clamp, then the brake hose from strut.
7. Disconnect trailing link and lateral link from housing.
8. Using driveshaft remover tool No. 28099PA100, or equivalent, remove DOJ from rear differential. Use bolt on side bearing retainer as supporting point for remover.
9. Remove axle nut and driveshaft. If driveshaft is hard to remove, use remover tool No. 926470000 and plate tool No. 28099PA110, or equivalents.
10. Reverse procedure to install, noting the following:
    a. Seat bell joint into hub using axle shaft installer tool No. 922431000 and adapter tool No. 927390000, or equivalents.
    b. Install axle shaft to hub with new axle nut.
    c. Using side oil seal protector tool No. 28099PA090, or equivalent, install DOJ.

REAR AXLE SHAFT SERVICE

Refer to "Front Axle Shaft Service" in the "Front Wheel Drive Axle" section for disassembly and assembly procedures of the DOJ, **Fig. 1.**

DIFFERENTIAL SERVICE

MAINTENANCE

Checking Fluid Level

Remove differential filler plug and check to ensure gear oil level is at bottom of filler plug hole.

Drain & Refill

Differential gear oil should be changed at intervals of 30 months or 30,000 miles.

1. Remove differential drain plug and allow gear oil to drain.
2. Install differential drain plug with gasket. On all except Justy, **torque** plug to 18 ft. lbs. On Justy, **torque** plug to 22–28 ft. lbs.
3. Remove differential filler plug and add SAE 80W, 85W, or 90W gear oil to oil level is at bottom of differential filler plug hole, then install filler plug.
4. Do not mix brands or weights of oil.

DISASSEMBLY

1. Place attachment tool No. 398217700, or equivalent, in a suitable vise, then attach drive axle assembly to tool.
2. Remove plug, then drain differential gear oil.
3. Loosen attaching bolts, then remove spindles, using a suitable tool.
4. Mark position of left and right side retainers to facilitate installation, then attach tool No. 398457700, or equivalent, to differential case and remove retainers, using a suitable puller, **Fig. 2.**
5. Remove differential carrier. Ensure teeth do not contact case. **When replacing side bearing, pull bearing cup from side bearing retainer.**
6. Remove bearing cone from differential carrier, using puller tool No. 399527700, or equivalent.
7. Remove drive gear by straightening lock plates and removing retaining bolts.
8. Drive out pinion shaft lockpin using a

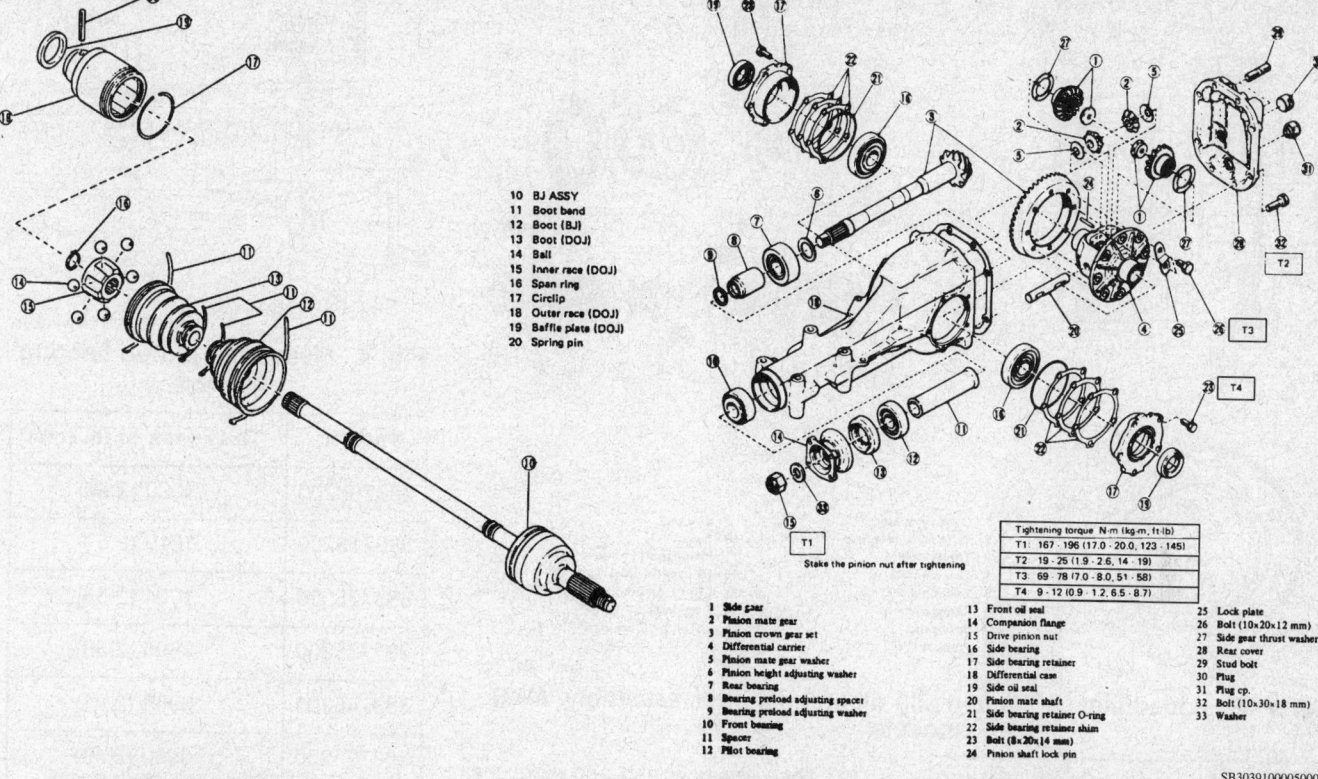

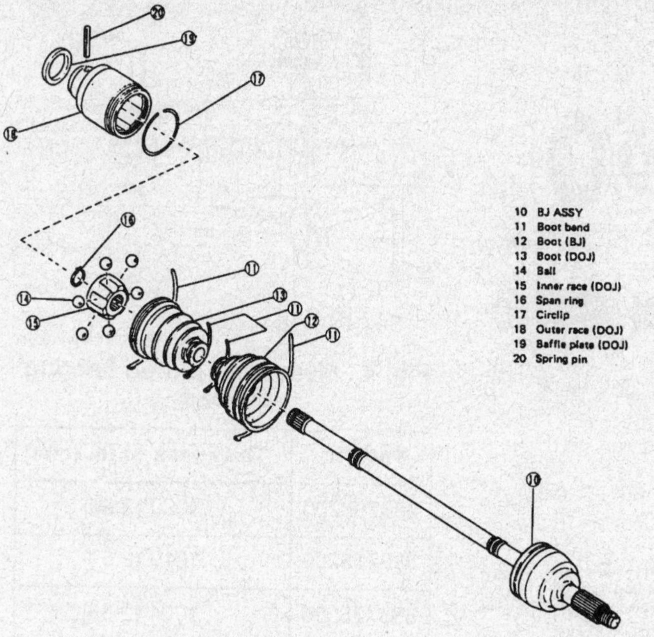
10 BJ ASSY
11 Boot bend
12 Boot (BJ)
13 Boot (DOJ)
14 Ball
15 Inner race (DOJ)
16 Span ring
17 Circlip
18 Outer race (DOJ)
19 Baffle plate (DOJ)
20 Spring pin

Tightening torque: N-m (kg-m, ft-lb)
T1: 167 – 206 (17 – 21, 123 – 152)
T2: 10 – 16 (1.0 – 1.6, 7 – 12)

SB3039100004000X

Fig. 1 Exploded view of rear drive axle

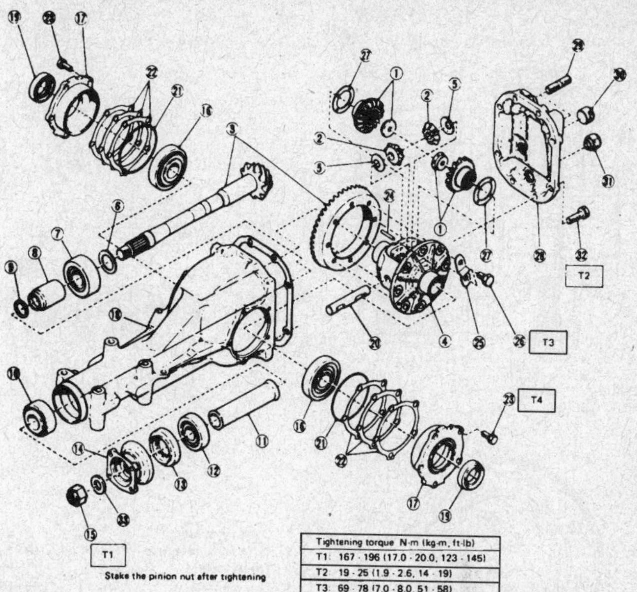
T1
T2
T3
T4
Stake the pinion nut after tightening

Tightening torque N·m (kg-m, ft-lb)
T1: 167 - 196 (17.0 - 20.0, 123 - 145)
T2: 19 - 25 (1.9 - 2.6, 14 - 19)
T3: 69 - 78 (7.0 - 8.0, 51 - 58)
T4: 9 - 12 (0.9 - 1.2, 6.5 - 8.7)

1 Side gear
2 Pinion mate gear
3 Pinion crown gear set
4 Differential carrier
5 Pinion mate gear washer
6 Pinion height adjusting washer
7 Rear bearing
8 Bearing preload adjusting spacer
9 Bearing preload adjusting washer
10 Front bearing
11 Spacer
12 Pilot bearing
13 Front oil seal
14 Companion flange
15 Drive pinion nut
16 Side bearing
17 Side bearing retainer
18 Differential case
19 Side oil seal
20 Pinion mate shaft
21 Side bearing retainer O-ring
22 Side bearing retainer shim
23 Bolt (8x20x14 mm)
24 Pinion shaft lock pin
25 Lock plate
26 Bolt (10x20x12 mm)
27 Side gear thrust washer
28 Rear cover
29 Stud bolt
30 Plug
31 Plug cp.
32 Bolt (10x30x18 mm)
33 Washer

SB3039100005000X

Fig. 2 Exploded view of drive axle assembly. AWD models

suitable punch. **Lockpin is staked to the differential case, do not drive out before unstaking.**

9. Remove pinion shaft, pinion gears, side gears and thrust washers. **On models with limited slip differential, replacement differential case components, Fig. 3, are not available, therefore disassembly is not recommended.**
10. Hold companion flange using tool No. 398427700, or equivalent, then remove drive pinion nut.
11. Remove companion flange using a suitable puller.
12. Using a suitable drift, press end of pinion shaft and remove with bearing inner race, spacer and washer.
13. Press rear bearing inner race from drive pinion by supporting inner race with tool No. 398517700, or equivalent.
14. Remove oil seal from differential carrier.
15. Remove pilot bearing with front bearing inner race using a suitable drift.
16. When replacing pinion bearings, tap front bearing outer race and rear bearing outer race using a brass drift.

ASSEMBLY

1. Reverse procedure to assemble, **Fig. 2.**
   a. Apply gear oil when installing bearings and thrust washers.
   b. Ensure left and righthand races of bearings are installed in correct positions.
2. Adjust pinion bearing preload as follows:
   a. Adjust pinion bearing preload with a spacer and washer between front and rear bearings. The adjustment must be carried out without the oil seal.
   b. Press front and rear bearing outer races into differential carrier using a suitable drift.
   c. Insert dummy pinion shaft No. 398507702 with pinion height adjusting washer and rear bearing inner race into carrier.
   d. Install preload adjusting spacer and washer, front bearing inner race, dummy collar No. 398507703 and companion flange.
   e. Rotate drive pinion by hand to seat bearings and tighten pinion nut while measuring preload, **Fig. 4.** Select the adjusting washer and spacer so that specified preload is obtained when nut is **torqued** to 123–145 ft. lbs., **Figs. 5 and 6.**
3. Adjust drive pinion height as follows:
   a. Adjust pinion height with a washer installed between rear bearing inner race and back of pinion gear.
   b. Install dummy shaft, collar and gauge, tool set No. 398501600 equivalent, and apply specified preload on bearings, **Fig. 7.**
   c. Measure clearance between end of gauge and end surface of dummy shaft by using a feeler gauge.
   d. Obtain thickness of pinion height adjusting washer, **Fig. 8,** to be installed from the following formula: T = To + N – (H X .01) – .20mm when T = thickness of pinion height adjusting washer in mm, To = thickness of washer temporarily inserted in mm, N = reading of thickness gauge in mm and H = figure marked on drive piston head.
   e. Install selected pinion height washer on drive pinion and press rear bearing inner race into position using tool No. 398177700, or equivalent.
   f. Insert drive pinion into gear carrier, installed previously, selected preload adjusting spacer, washer, oil seal, companion flange and tighten with pinion nut. **Torque** pinion nut to 123–145 ft. lbs.
4. Assemble differential case as follows:
   a. Install side gears and pinion gears with thrust washers and pinion shaft into differential case. **Apply gear oil on both sides of thrust washers and side gears before installing.**
   b. Measure clearance between differential case and back of side gear.
   c. Adjust clearance as specified by selecting the side gear thrust washer. Side gear back clearance should be .004–.008 inch, **Fig. 9.**
   d. Check condition of rotation after applying oil to gear tooth surfaces and thrust surfaces.

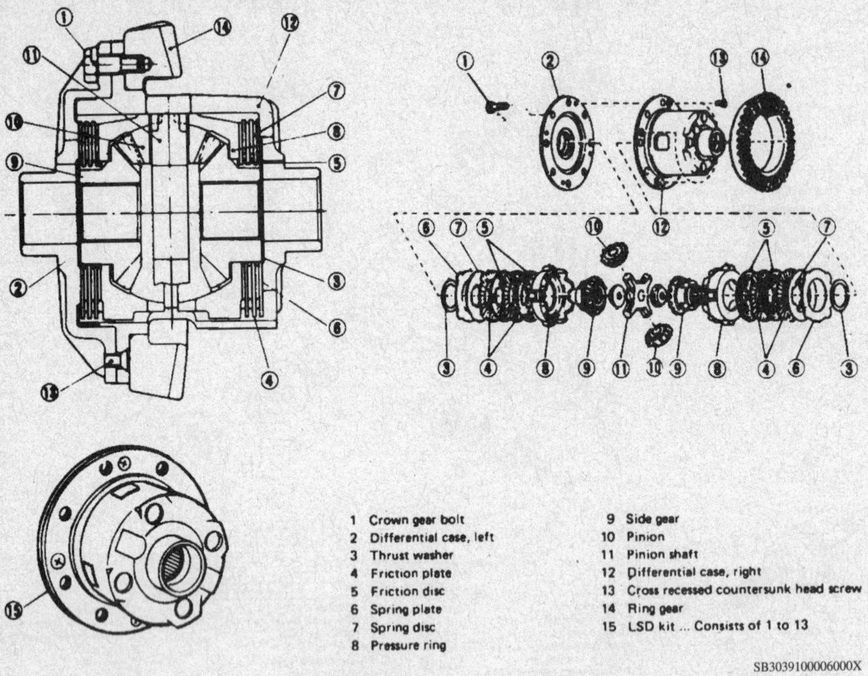
1 Crown gear bolt
2 Differential case, left
3 Thrust washer
4 Friction plate
5 Friction disc
6 Spring plate
7 Spring disc
8 Pressure ring
9 Side gear
10 Pinion
11 Pinion shaft
12 Differential case, right
13 Cross recessed countersunk head screw
14 Ring gear
15 LSD kit ... Consists of 1 to 13
SB3039100006000X

Fig. 3 Exploded view of limited slip differential case assembly. AWD models

Part No.	Length In In. (mm)
383695201	2.213 (56.2)
383695202	2.220 (56.4)
383695203	2.228 (56.6)
383695204	2.236 (56.8)
383695205	2.244 (57.0)
383695206	2.252 (57.2)

SB3039100008000X

Fig. 5 Pinion bearing preload adjusting spacer identification chart

e. After driving in pinion shaft lockpin, stake both sides of hole to prevent pin from falling out.
f. Install drive gear on differential case. **Torque** attaching bolts to 51–58 ft. lbs., then lock washer. **Tighten diagonally while tapping bolt heads.**

5. Measure width of side bearing as follows:
   a. Before installing side bearings, measure bearing width by using a weight block of about 5.5 lbs., **Fig. 10.** Standard bearing width is .787 inch.
   b. Press side bearing inner race onto differential case using a suitable drift and tool No. 398497701 included in puller set No. 399527700, or equivalents, **Fig. 11.**
6. Adjust side gear preload as follows:
   a. The gear backlash and side gear preload can be determined by side retainer shim thickness.
   b. When replacing differential carrier, differential case, side bearing and side retainer, **Fig. 12,** obtain left and right retainer shim thicknesses, **Fig. 13,** by the following formula: T1 (left) = (A + C + G – D – E + H) X .01 + .76mm; T2 (right) = (B + D + G – F – H) X .01 + .76mm. when T1 & T2 = thickness of left and right retainer adjusting shims in mm, A & B = figure mark on differential carrier, C & D = figure mark on differential case, E & F = difference of width of left and right side bearings from standard width 20mm expressed in a unit of 1⁄100mm, G = figure marked on side retainer and H = figure marked on drive gear. **If figure is not marked, regard as zero.**
   c. Use several shims to obtain calculated thickness.
   d. Reverse disassembly procedure to install differential case to differential carrier.
   e. Install selected shim and O-ring on side retainer, then install retainer on carrier with arrow on retainer facing as shown in **Fig. 14. Torque** to 7–9 ft. lbs.
   f. Measure drive gear to drive pinion backlash. Backlash should be .004–.008 inch. If reading is not within limits, correct by decreasing shim thickness on one side and increasing shim thickness on the other side by the same amount. Total shim thickness must be the same to maintain proper preload.
   g. At the same time measure rotating

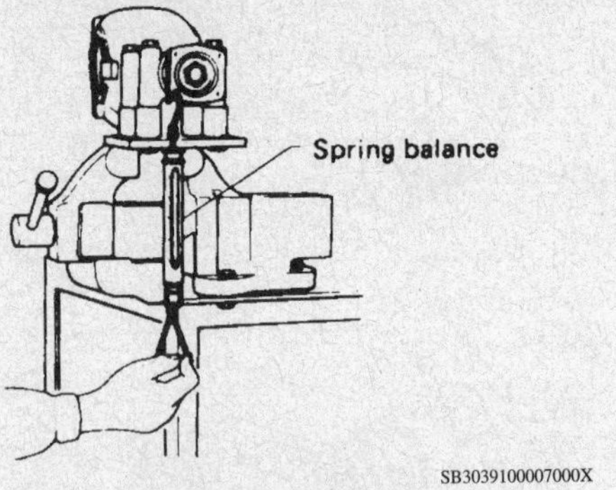
Spring balance
SB3039100007000X

Fig. 4 Measuring pinion bearing preload

Part No.	Thickness In In. (mm)
383705200	.1020 (2.59)
383715200	.1012 (2.57)
383725200	.1004 (2.55)
383735200	.0996 (2.53)
383745200	.0988 (2.51)
383755200	.0980 (2.49)
383765200	.0972 (2.47)
383775200	.0965 (2.45)
383785200	.0957 (2.43)
383795200	.0949 (2.41)
383805200	.0941 (2.39)
383815200	.0933 (2.37)
383825200	.0925 (2.35)
383835200	.0917 (2.33)
383845200	.0909 (2.31)

SB3039100009000X

Fig. 6 Pinion bearing preload adjusting washer identification chart

resistance of drive pinion. Compare with resistance when differential case was not installed, if the increase in resistance is not within .07–.43 ft. lbs., readjust side retainer shim.
   h. Recheck backlash between drive gear and pinion after readjusting shims, **Fig. 15.**
   i. Check drive gear runout and pinion and drive gear rotation for smoothness, **Fig. 16.**
7. Check and adjust tooth contact of drive gear, proceed as follows:

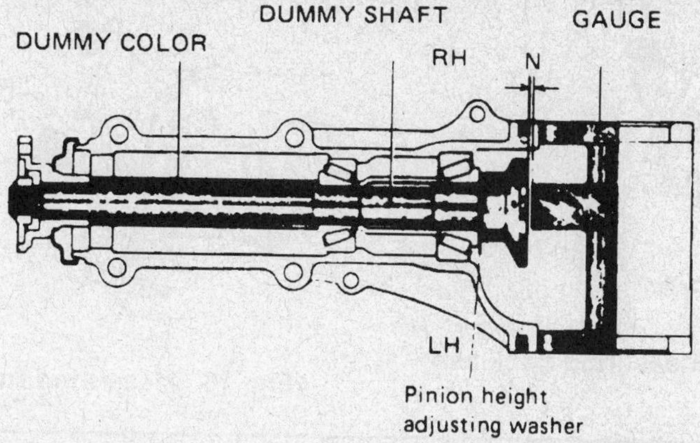
DUMMY COLOR
DUMMY SHAFT
GAUGE
RH
N
LH
Pinion height
adjusting washer

SB3039100010000X

Fig. 7 Installation position of tools for adjusting drive pinion height

Part No.	Thickness In In. (mm)
383445201	.0295-.0315 (.75-.80)
383445202	.0315-.0335 (.80-.85)
383445203	.0335-.0354 (.85-.90)

SB3039100012000X

Fig. 9 Side gear thrust washer identification chart

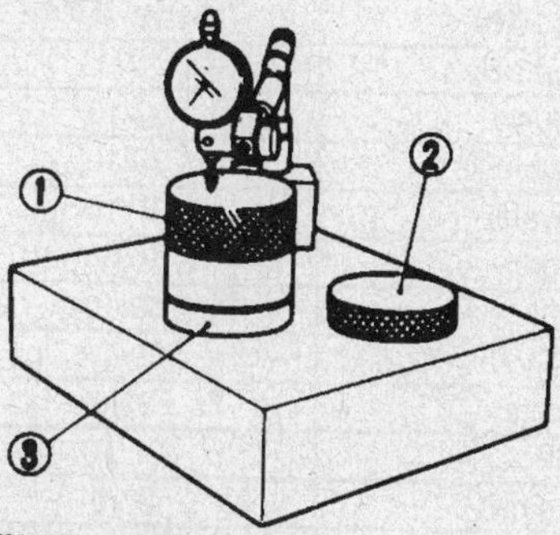
1
2
3

1 **Weight (398227700)**
2 **Gauge (398237700)**
3 **Side bearing**

SB3039100013000X

Fig. 10 Measuring side bearing width

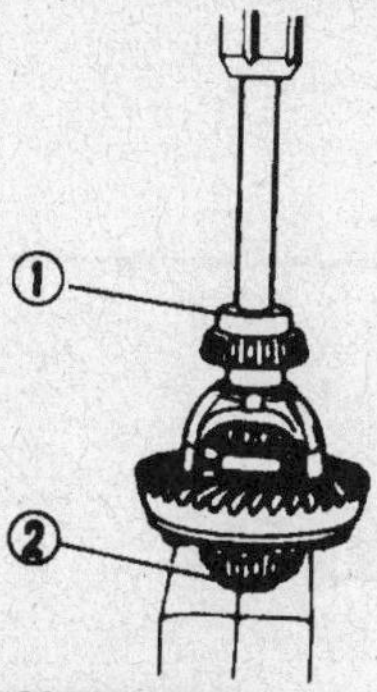
1
2

1 **Drift (398487700)**
2 **Adapter (398497701)**

SB3039100014000X

Fig. 11 Installing side bearing

a. Apply red lead to both sides of three of four drive gear teeth.
b. Check the contact pattern after rotating drive gear several times. **Ensure red lead is completely removed after inspection.**

8. Using a suitable drift install oil seal and rear cover. **Apply chassis grease to seal lips before installation.**
9. After installation in vehicle, fill differential as described under "Maintenance." **Torque** differential assembly nut to 51–58 ft. lbs., propeller shaft flange yoke to companion flange to 13–18 ft. lbs. and spindle retaining bolt to 23.1–27 ft. lbs.

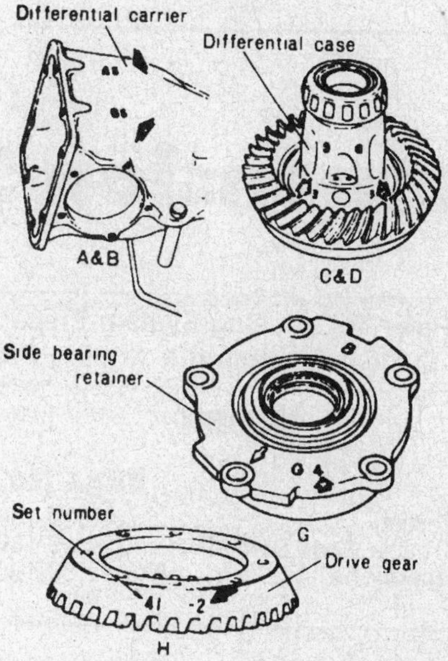
Differential carrier
Differential case
A&B
C&D
Side bearing
retainer
Set number
G
Drive gear
H

SB3039100015000X

Fig. 12 Differential markings positions

Part No.	Thickness In In. (mm)
383495200	.1217 (3.09)
383505200	.1228 (3.12)
383515200	.1240 (3.15)
383525200	.1252 (3.18)
383535200	.1264 (3.21)
383545200	.1276 (3.24)
383555200	.1287 (3.27)
383565200	.1299 (3.30)
383575200	.1311 (3.33)
383585200	.1323 (3.36)
383595200	.1335 (3.39)
383605200	.1346 (3.42)
383615200	.1358 (3.45)
383625200	.1370 (3.48)
383635200	.1382 (3.51)
383645200	.1394 (3.54)
383655200	.1406 (3.57)
383665200	.1417 (3.60)
383675200	.1429 (3.63)
383685200	.1441 (3.66)

SB3039100011000X

Fig. 8 Pinion height adjusting washer identification chart

Part No.	Thickness In In. (mm)
383475201	.0079 (.20)
383475202	.0098 (.25)
383475203	.0118 (.30)
383475204	.0158 (.40)
383475205	.0197 (.50)

SB3039100016000X

Fig. 13 Side retainer adjusting shim identification chart

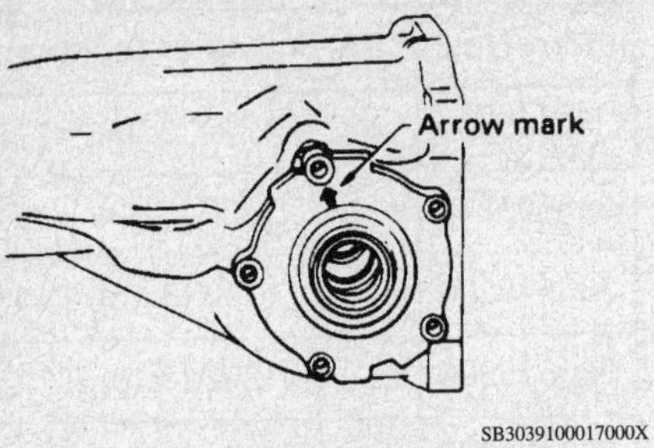
Arrow mark
SB3039100017000X

Fig. 14 Side bearing retainer position

SB3039100018000X

Fig. 15 Measuring backlash

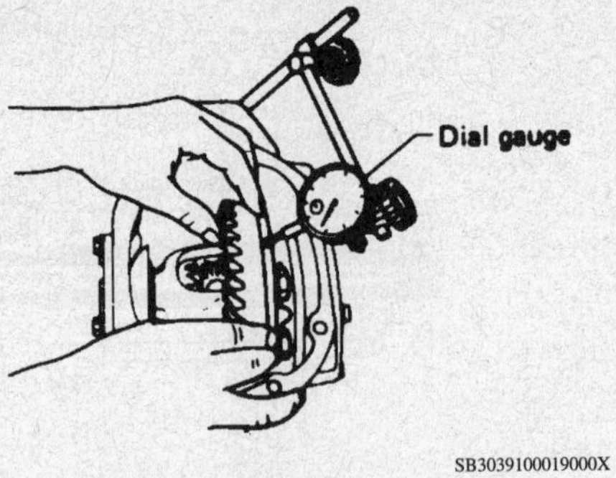
Dial gauge
SB3039100019000X

Fig. 16 Measuring runout

REAR AXLE IDENTIFICATION

Year	Model	Axle ID①	Gear Ratio
1993–94	Impreza	37/9	4.1
	Justy	37/10	3.7
	Loyale②	39/10	3.9
	Loyale③	37/10	3.7
	Legacy②	37/9	4.1
	Legacy③	39/10	3.9
	SVX	39/11	3.5
1995–96	Impreza④	37/9	4.1
	Impreza⑤	39/10	3.9
	Legacy④	37/9	4.1
	Legacy⑤	39/10	3.9
	SVX	39/11	3.5

① — Number of gear teeth.
② — Except turbocharged.
③ — Turbocharged.
④ — M/T
⑤ — A/T

Active Suspension Systems

NOTE: On Air Bag Equipped Models, Refer To "Air Bag System Precautions" Located In The Front Of This Manual For System Disarming & Arming Procedures.

INDEX

	Page No.
Description	39-189
Diagnosis & Testing	39-189
Inspection	39-189
Testing	39-189
Trouble Code Diagnosis	39-189
Precautions	39-188
Active Suspension	39-188
Air Bag Systems	39-188

PRECAUTIONS

AIR BAG SYSTEMS

Refer to "Air Bag System Precautions" in the front of this manual for system disarming and arming procedures.

ACTIVE SUSPENSION

1. Prior to system inspection, check battery voltage.
2. Prior to raising vehicle for service, place height control in Normal position and height control switch in off position. Ensure indicator lamp is off.
3. Disconnect battery negative cable prior to servicing vehicle or troubleshooting system for problems other than electrical.
4. Do not apply under coating or rust protection to air bags or air compressor.

DESCRIPTION

This system consists of various components to regulate the riding height of the vehicle, **Fig. 1.**

When the height control switch is in the normal position, vehicle remains at its normal riding height at all times. When the height control switch is moved to the Hi position, the vehicle is raised to provide ground clearance. At speeds over approximately 55 mph, the vehicle automatically lowers to its normal riding height.

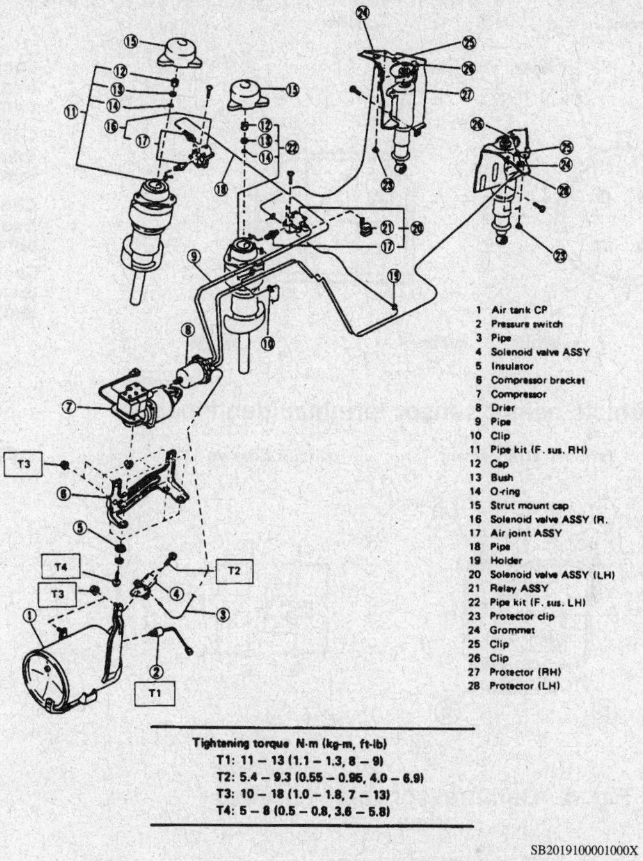
T1
T2
T3
T4
1 Air tank CP
2 Pressure switch
3 Pipe
4 Solenoid valve ASSY
5 Insulator
6 Compressor bracket
7 Compressor
8 Drier
9 Pipe
10 Clip
11 Pipe kit (F. sus. RH)
12 Cap
13 Bush
14 O-ring
15 Strut mount cap
16 Solenoid valve ASSY (R.
17 Air joint ASSY
18 Pipe
19 Holder
20 Solenoid valve ASSY (LH)
21 Relay ASSY
22 Pipe kit (F. sus. LH)
23 Protector clip
24 Grommet
25 Clip
26 Clip
27 Protector (RH)
28 Protector (LH)
Tightening torque N·m (kg-m, ft-lb)
T1: 11 – 13 (1.1 – 1.3, 8 – 9)
T2: 5.4 – 9.3 (0.55 – 0.95, 4.0 – 6.9)
T3: 10 – 18 (1.0 – 1.8, 7 – 13)
T4: 5 – 8 (0.5 – 0.8, 3.6 – 5.8)
SB2019100001000X

Fig. 1 Automatic level control system

DIAGNOSIS & TESTING

INSPECTION

When performing system inspection, ensure vehicle is unloaded, and do not enter or exit the vehicle.

1. Start the engine, then adjust vehicle to its normal height by setting the height control switch to the Normal position.
2. Take time measurements as follows:
   a. Time from High to Normal position, when air suspension solenoid valve closes, should be 10–20 seconds.
   b. Running time of compressor, after height control switch is pushed, should be 80–150 seconds.
   c. Time from Normal to High position, when rear air suspension solenoid valve closes, should be 10–30 seconds.

TESTING

A1-Air Line Leakage Above Strut Mount

Inspect lines and joints for air leak, using a soap and water solution. Ensure soap solution does not enter bearings on strut mount.

A2-Air Line Leak

Check air tubes and joints in air line for leakage. Check compressor assembly and air discharge solenoid valve seat for leakage.

A3-Pressure Switch

Check pressure switch for proper operating pressure. Pressure should be 137 psi with switch off or 109 psi with switch on.

A-4 Air Leakage At Suspension Assembly

Remove front or rear suspension assembly, then apply air pressure. Place suspension assembly into water, then check for air leaks. **Do not allow water to enter strut mount bearing. After checking for leakage, remove excess water from assembly using compressed air.**

A5-Air Tank Leakage

Remove air tank assembly, then apply compressed air to tank by connecting suitable a 12 volt source to tank solenoid valve and compressor relay. Place tank assembly in water, then check for leakage.

A6-Vehicle Height Sensor

Compress and extend from or rear suspension assembly, then check for continuity between suspension assembly harness terminals, **Fig. 2.** Continuity should be as described, **Fig. 3.**

A7-Leakage Solenoid Valve

With compressed air applied to front or rear suspension system, disconnect air line from air joint furthest from suspension assembly, using tool No. 926520000, or equivalent, then check for leakage at assembly and solenoid valve.

A8-Break In Solenoid Valve

Connect a suitable 12 volt source to coupler, then check for operating noise or for continuity between terminals.

A9-Clogged Air Line

Check for foreign material or twisted lines and repair as necessary.

A10-Compressor Relay

Connect a suitable 12 volt source to solenoid valve, then apply compressed air and check that air passes through solenoid. If air does not pass through valve, replace.

A11-Compressor Malfunction

Connect a suitable 12 volt source to compressor and check for proper operation. If circuit breaker is tripped due to high temperatures, allow compressor to cool, then operation should return to normal.

A12-Compressor Relay

Connect a suitable 12 volt source to terminal A, and ground terminal B, **Fig. 4.** Check that continuity exists between terminals C and D. Disconnect 12 volt source and check that no continuity exists between terminals C and D. Replace relay if continuity checks are not as specified.

A13-Electrical Circuit

When checking circuit, disconnect component from circuit and check for continuity. Also, check for proper grounding.

TROUBLE CODE DIAGNOSIS

Accessing Diagnostic Codes

1. Jumper the check connector terminals, as shown in **Fig. 5.**
2. Perform the following steps within one minute:
   a. Turn ignition switch off, turn height selector switch on, then turn the ignition switch on.
   b. Turn ignition switch off, turn height selector switch off, then turn the ignition switch on.
   c. Turn ignition switch off, turn height selector switch on, then turn the ignition switch on. The self diagnosis system is activated.
3. The diagnostic code(s) can be read by the number of blinks of the vehicle height indicator, **Fig. 6.**

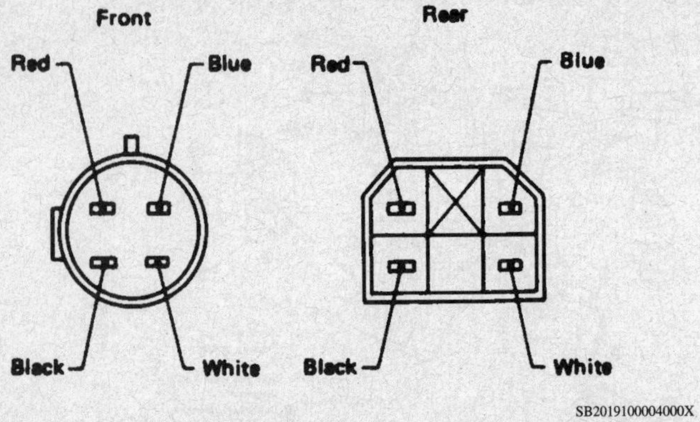
Front
Rear
Red
Blue
Red
Blue
Black
White
Black
White
SB2019100004000X

Fig. 2 Vehicle height sensor terminal identification

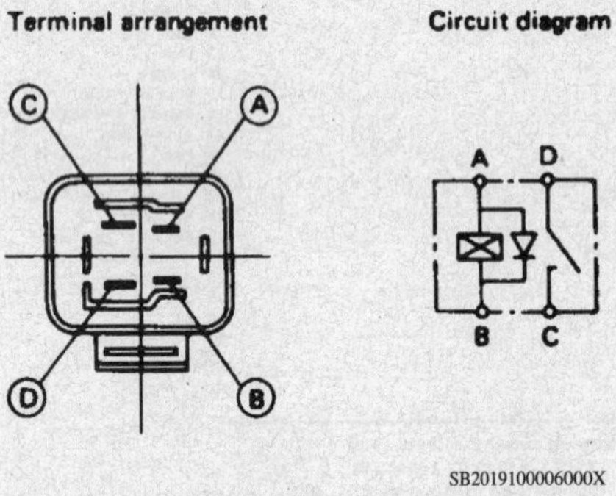
Terminal arrangement
Circuit diagram
C
A
D
B
A
D
B
C
SB2019100006000X

Fig. 4 Compressor relay terminal view

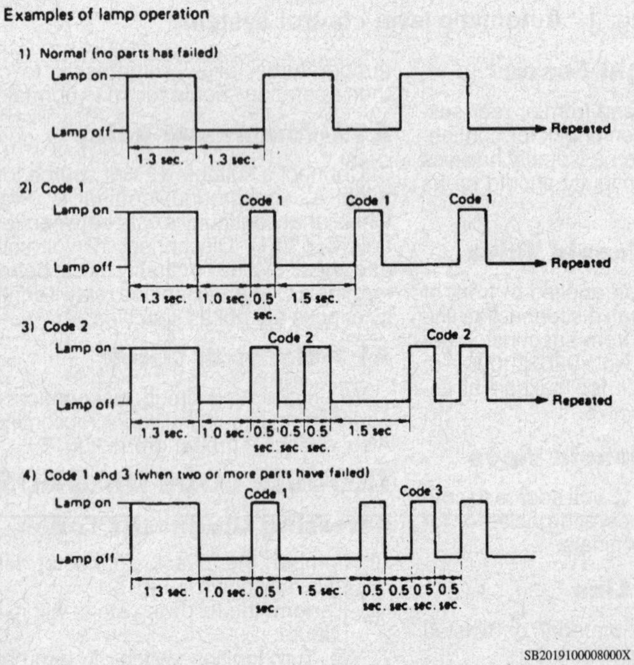
Examples of lamp operation
1) Normal (no parts has failed)
Lamp on
Lamp off
Repeated
1.3 sec.
1.3 sec.
2) Code 1
Lamp on
Code 1
Code 1
Code 1
Lamp off
Repeated
1.3 sec.
1.0 sec.
0.5 sec.
1.5 sec.
3) Code 2
Lamp on
Code 2
Code 2
Lamp off
Repeated
1.3 sec.
1.0 sec.
0.5 sec.
0.5 sec.
0.5 sec.
1.5 sec
4) Code 1 and 3 (when two or more parts have failed)
Lamp on
Code 1
Code 3
Lamp off
1.3 sec.
1.0 sec.
0.5 sec.
1.5 sec.
0.5 sec.
0.5 sec.
0.5 sec.
0.5 sec.
SB2019100008000X

Fig. 6 Reading diagnostic trouble codes

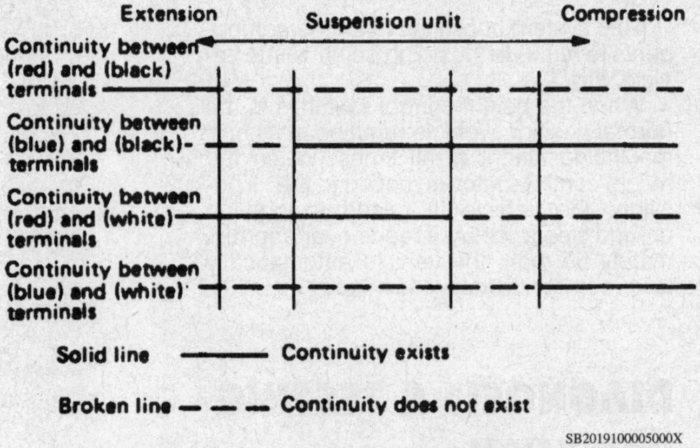
Extension
Suspension unit
Compression
Continuity between (red) and (black) terminals
Continuity between (blue) and (black) terminals
Continuity between (red) and (white) terminals
Continuity between (blue) and (white) terminals
Solid line — Continuity exists
Broken line — Continuity does not exist
SB2019100005000X

Fig. 3 Vehicle height sensor continuity chart

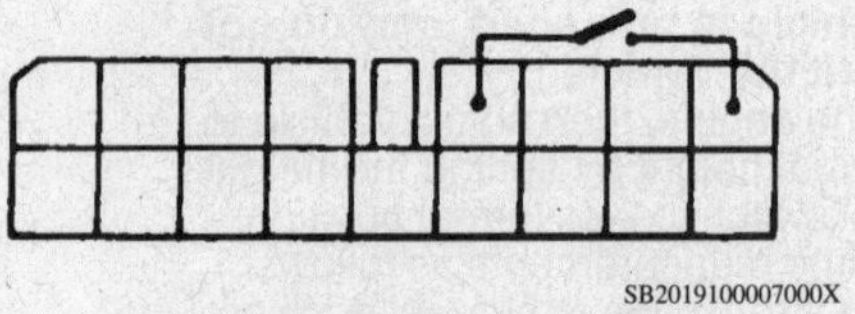
SB2019100007000X

Fig. 5 Check connector

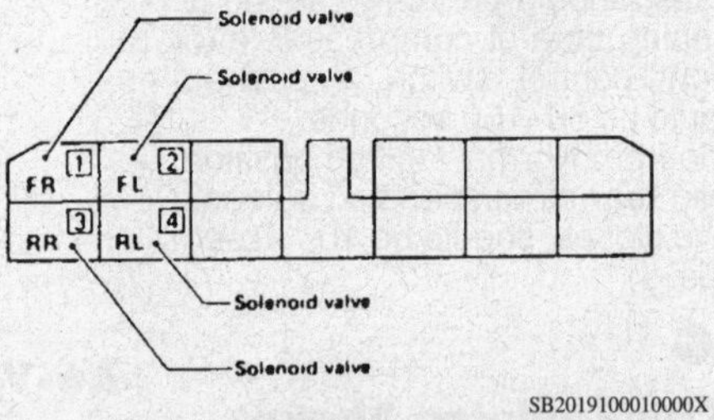
Solenoid valve
Solenoid valve
1
FR
2
FL
3
RR
4
RL
Solenoid valve
Solenoid valve
SB2019100010000X

Fig. 7 Solenoid valve check. Except 4-speed automatic transmission

4. Make corrections as specified under "Diagnostic Code Troubleshooting."
5. Return diagnostic system to the normal mode by turning the ignition switch off, and then on. If fault is not eliminated, the vehicle indicator will illuminate.
6. Reset memory by disconnecting battery negative cable.
7. Remove check connector jumper wire.

Diagnostic Code Troubleshooting

Refer to **Figs. 7 through 10,** for diagnostic code troubleshooting procedures.

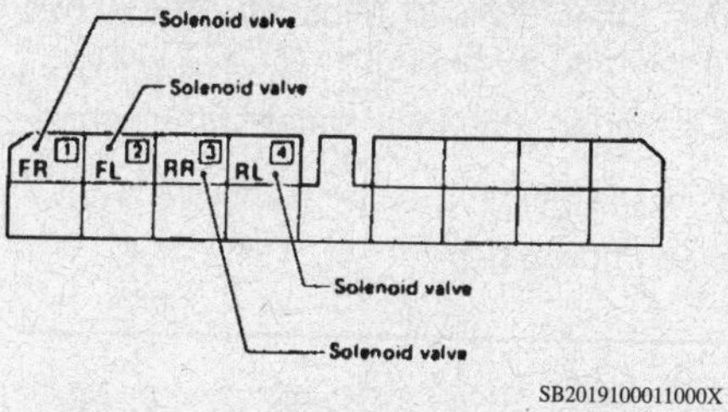
Solenoid valve
Solenoid valve
FR 1
FL 2
RR 3
RL 4
Solenoid valve
Solenoid valve
SB2019100011000X

Fig. 8 Solenoid valve check. 4-speed automatic transmission

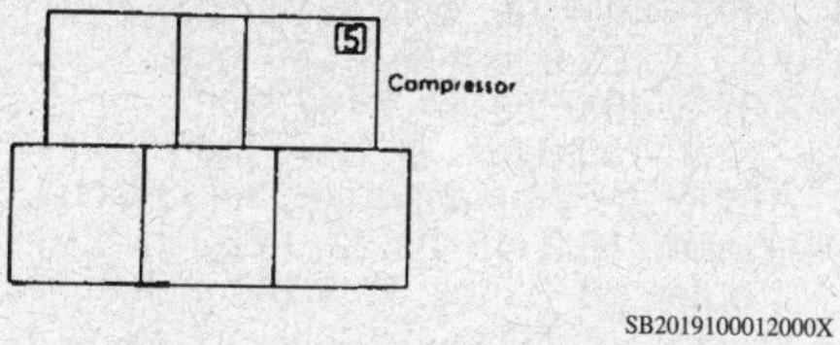
5
Compressor
SB2019100012000X

Fig. 9 Compressor check

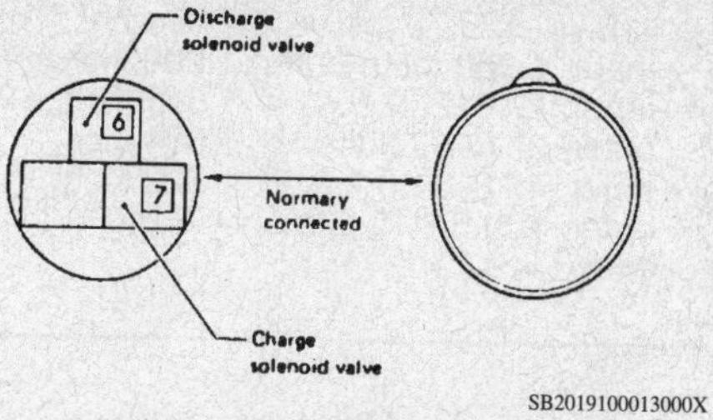
Discharge solenoid valve
6
7
Normary connected
Charge solenoid valve
SB2019100013000X

Fig. 10 Charge & discharge solenoid valve check

Engine Rebuilding Specifications

INDEX

	Page No.
Camshaft	39-192
Crankshaft, Bearings & Rods	39-193
Cylinder Block	39-194
Cylinder Head, Valve Guide & Valve Seats	39-191
Oil Pump	39-194
Pistons, Pins & Rings	39-193
Valve Springs	39-191
Valves	39-191

CYLINDER HEAD, VALVE GUIDE & VALVE SEATS

All measurements given in inches, unless otherwise specified.

Engine Liter	Year	Cylinder Head: Warpage Limit	Cylinder Head: Grinding Limit	Cylinder Head: Standard Height	Valve Guides: Standard Inside Diameter	Valve Guides: Protrusion Above Head	Valve Guides: Stem To Guide Clearance Intake	Valve Guides: Stem To Guide Clearance Exhaust	Valve Seats: Seat Angle Degrees	Valve Seats: Seat Width Intake	Valve Seats: Seat Width Exhaust	Valve Seats: Runout
1.2L	1993–94	.0020	.008	4.39	.2756-.2762	.807	.0008-.0020	.0016-.0028	45	.039	.051	—
1.8L①	1993–94	.0020	.012	3.567	.2756-.2762	.689-.728	.0014-.0026	.0016-.0028	45	.047-.071	.059-.079	.020
1.8L②	1993–94	.0020	.004	3.870	.2362-.2367	.689-.709	.0014-.0024	.0016-.0026	45	.028-.055	.039-.071	—
1.8L②	1995–96	.0020	.004	3.870	.2362-.2367	.689-.709	.0014-.0024	.0016-.0026	45	.028-.055	.055-.071	—
2.2L	1993–94	.0020	.004	3.870	.2362-.2367	.689-.709	.0014-.0024	.0016-.0026	45	.028-.055	.039-.071	—
2.2L	1995–96	.0020	.004	3.870	.2362-.2367	.689-.709	.0014-.0024	.0016-.0026	45	.028-.055	.055-.071	—
3.3L	1993–96	.0020	.0118	5.020	.2362-.2367	.335	.0012-.0022	.0016-.0026	45	.039-.067	.059-.087	—

① — Loyale.
② — Impreza.

VALVE SPRINGS

All measurements given in inches, unless otherwise specified.

Engine Liter	Year	Free Length	Seated Pressure Pounds @ Inches	Compressed Pressure Pounds @ Inches	Out Of Square Limit
1.2L	1993–94	1.8311	—	①	—
1.8L⑬	1993–94	②	③	④	.087
1.8L⑭	1993–96	1.8173	⑤	⑥	.079
2.2L	1993–94	1.8173	⑤	⑥	.079
2.2L	1995–96	1.7342	⑦	⑧	.075
3.3L	1993–96	⑨	⑩	⑪	⑫

① — 112.79–129.76 lbs. @ 1.248 inch.
② — Inner, 1.980 inch; outer, 1.996 inch.
③ — Inner, 19.8–22.7 lbs. @ 1.516 inch; outer, 39.9–45.9 lbs. @ 1.634 inch.
④ — Inner, 45.2–51.8 lbs. @ 1.122 inch; outer, 100.5–115.5 lbs. @ 1.240 inch.
⑤ — 42.8–49.4 lbs. @ 1.457 inch.
⑥ — 90.2–103.9 lbs. @ 1.150 inch.
⑦ — 39.2–45.0 lbs. @ 1.147 inch.
⑧ — 91.1–103.0 lbs. @ 1.110 inch.
⑨ — Inner, 1.374 inch; outer, 1.433 inch.
⑩ — Inner, 13.2–15 lbs. @ 1.083 inch; outer, 28–32 lbs. @ 1.140 inch.
⑪ — Inner, 33.1–37.9 lbs. @ .772 inch; outer, 69.5–80 lbs. @ .831 inch.
⑫ — Inner, .059 inch; outer, .063 inch.
⑬ — Loyale.
⑭ — Impreza.

VALVES

All measurements given in inches, unless otherwise specified.

Engine Liter	Year	Stem Diameter		Overall Length	Face Angle Degrees	Margin	Valve Clearance	
		Intake	Exhaust				Intake	Exhaust
1.2L	1993–94	.2742-.2748	.2734-.2740	①	45	.039	.006C	.010C
1.8L⑨	1993–94	.2736-.2742	.2734-.2740	②	45	③	④	④
1.8L⑩	1993–96	.2343-.2348	.2341-.2346	⑤	45	⑥	④	④
2.2L	1993–96	.2343-.2348	.2341-.2346	⑤	45	⑥	④	④
3.3L	1993–96	.2344-.2350	.2341-.2346	⑦	45	⑧	④	④

① — Intake, 4.26 inch; exhaust, 4.27 inch.
② — Turbo models intake, 4.235 inch; turbo models exhaust, 4.256 inch; non-turbo models, intake & exhaust 4.235 inch.
③ — Turbo models intake, .051 inch; turbo models exhaust, .071 inch; non-turbo models, intake & exhaust .051 inch.
④ — Equipped with hydraulic valve lash adjusters.
⑤ — Intake, 3.976 inch; exhaust, 3.984 inch.
⑥ — Intake, .039 inch; Exhaust, .047 inch.
⑦ — Intake, 3.5433 inch; exhaust, 3.5768 inch.
⑧ — Intake, .031 inch; exhaust, .039 inch.
⑨ — Loyale.
⑩ — Impreza.

CAMSHAFT

All measurements given in inches, unless otherwise specified.

Engine Liter	Year	Camshaft Journal Diameter	Bend Limit	Camshaft Bearing Clearance	Thrust Clearance	Cam Lobe Height	Valve Lash Adjuster		
							O.D.	Cylinder Head Adjuster Hole I.D.	Adjuster To Hole Clearance
1.2L	1993–94	—	—	—	.0012-.0150	1.4520-1.4528	①	—	—
1.8L⑪	1993–94	②	.0010	.0008-.0021	.0012-.0102	1.5650-1.5689	.8417-.8422	.8430-.8453	.0008-.0035
1.8L⑫	1993–94	③	.0010	.0022-.0035	.0012-.0102	1.2742-1.2781	④	—	—
1.8L⑫	1995–96	③	.0010	.0022-.0035	.0012-.0102	1.2742-1.2781	⑤	—	—
2.2L	1993–94	③	.0010	.0022-.0035	.0012-.0102	⑥	④	—	—
2.2L	1995–96	③	.0010	.0022-.0035	.0012-.0102	⑦	⑤	—	—
3.3L	1993–96	⑧	.0008	.0015-.0028	⑨	⑩	1.2978-1.2982	1.2996-1.3004	.0011-.0031

① — Valve rocker clearance between arm & shaft, .0006–.0020 inch.
② — Front, 1.4946–1.4953 inch; Rear, 1.8883–1.8890 inch; center, 1.9080–1.9087 inch; lefthand distributor, 1.5340–1.5346 inch.
③ — Front, 1.2573–1.2579 inch; center, 1.4738–1.4744 inch; rear, 1.4935–1.4941 inch.
④ — Valve rocker clearance between arm & shaft, .0008–.0032 inch.
⑤ — Valve rocker clearance between arm & shaft, .0008–.0021 inch.
⑥ — Non-Turbo, 1.2742–1.2781 inch; turbo, 1.2711–1.2750 inch.
⑦ — Intake, 1.2596–1.2635 inch; exhaust, 1.2844–1.2883 inch.
⑧ — No. 1, 1.2577–1.2584 inch; Nos. 2, 3 & 4, 1.1002–1.1009 inch.
⑨ — Intake, .0012–.0035 inch; exhaust, .0008–.0031 inch.
⑩ — Intake, 1.5374–1.5413 inch; exhaust, 1.5689–1.5728 inch.
⑪ — Loyale.
⑫ — Impreza.

CRANKSHAFT, BEARINGS & RODS

All measurements given in inches, unless otherwise specified.

Engine Liter	Year	Crankshaft				Bearing Clearance			Connecting Rods	
		Standard Diameter		Out Of Round All	Taper All	Main Bearings	Connecting Rod Bearings	Thrust Bearing Clearance	Pin Bore Diameter	Side Clearance
		Main Bearing	Crank Pin							
1.2L	1993–94	1.6525-1.6529	1.6531-1.6535	.0012	.008	.0006-.0018	.0008-.0021	.0031-.0070	—	—
1.8L⑤	1993–94	①	1.7715-1.7720	.0012	.0028	②	.0004-.0021	.0004-.0037	1.8898-1.8905	.0028-.0130
1.8L⑥	1993–94	2.3616-2.3622	2.0466-2.0472	.0012	—	.0004-.0012	.0006-.0017	.0012-.0045	—	.0028-.0130
1.8L⑥	1995–96	2.3616-2.3625	2.0466-2.0472	.0012	—	.0004-.0012	.0006-.0018	.0012-.0045	—	.0028-.0130
2.2L	1993–94	2.3616-2.3622	2.0466-2.0472	.0012	.0028	.0004-.0012	③	.0012-.0045	—	.0028-.0130
2.2L	1995–96	2.3616-2.3625	2.0466-2.0472	.0012	—	.0004-.0012	.0006-.0018	.0012-.0045	—	.0028-.0130
3.3L	1993–96	2.3619-2.3625	2.0466-2.0472	.0012	.0028	④	.0008-.0018	.0012-.0045	—	.0028-.0130

① — Front, 2.1637–2.1642 inch; center, 2.1635–2.1642 inch; rear, 2.1624–2.1630 inch.
② — Center, .0003–.0011 inch; front & rear, .0001–.0014 inch.
③ — Non-turbo models, .0006–.0017; turbo models, .0010–.0021.
④ — No. 1-3-7, .0002–.0014; No. 2-4-6, .0005–.0015; No. 5, .0005–.0013.
⑤ — Loyale.
⑥ — Impreza.

PISTONS, PINS & RINGS

All measurements given in inches, unless otherwise specified.

Engine Liter	Year	Piston Std. Diameter	Piston Clearance	Piston Pin Diameter	Piston Pin To Piston Clearance	Piston Ring End Gap		Piston Ring Side Clearance	
						Comp.	Oil	Comp.	Oil
1.2L	1993–94	3.0690-3.0694	.0015-.0028	.7084-.7087	.0002-.0003	.0079-.0138	.012-.035	①	0
1.8L⑫	1993–94	②	③	.8265-.8268	.00004-.00059	.0079-.0138	.012-.035	④	0
1.8L⑬	1993–94	⑤	.0004-.0012	.9053-.9055	.0002-.0003	⑥	.0079-.0276	⑦	—
1.8L⑬	1995–96	⑤	.0004-.0012	—	.0002-.0004	.0079-.0138	.0079-.0276	⑦	—
2.2L	1993–94	⑧	.0004-.0012	.9053-.9055	.0002-.0003	⑨	.0079-.0276	⑦	—
2.2L	1995–96	⑧	.0004-.0012	—	.0002-.0004	.0079-.0138	.0079-.0276	⑦	—
3.3L	1993–96	⑧	.0004-.0012	—	.0002-.0003	⑩	.0079-.0236	⑪	—

① — Top ring, .0014–.0030 inch; second ring .0010–.0026 inch.
② — Non-turbo models, 3.6209–3.6213 inch. Turbo models, 3.6211–3.6214 inch.
③ — Non-turbo models, .0006–.0014 inch. Turbo models, .0004–.0012 inch.
④ — Top ring, .0016–.0031 inch; second ring, .0012–.0028 inch.
⑤ — Grade size symbol A, 3.4600–3.4604 inch; symbol B, 3.4596–3.4600 inch; symbol C, 3.4592–3.4596 inch.
⑥ — Top ring, .0079–.0138 inch; 2nd ring, .0146–.0205 inch.
⑦ — Top ring, .0016–.0031 inch; second ring, .0012–.0028 inch.
⑧ — Grade size symbol A, 3.8144–3.8148 inch; symbol B, 3.8140–3.8144 inch; symbol C, 3.8136–3.8140 inch.
⑨ — Top ring, non-turbo .0079–.0138 inch, turbo .0079–.0098 inch; 2nd ring, .0146–.0205 inch.
⑩ — Top ring, .0079–.0118 inch; 2nd ring, .0146–.0205 inch.
⑪ — Top ring, .0016–.0035 inch; second ring, .0012–.0028 inch.
⑫ — Loyale.
⑬ — Impreza.

CYLINDER BLOCK

All measurements given in inches, unless otherwise specified.

Engine Liter	Year	Bore Diameter	Cylinder Bore Taper Max.	Cylinder Bore Out Of Round Max.
1.2L	1993–94	3.07	.0020	.0020
1.8L	1993–94	3.62	.0020	.0020
1.8L	1993–96	②	.0020	.0020
2.2L	1993–96	①	.0020	.0020
3.3L	1993–96	①	.0020	.0020

① — Bore size symbol A, 3.8151–3.8155 inch; symbol B, 3.8148–3.8151 inch; symbol C, 3.8144–3.8148 inch.
② — Bore size symbol A, 3.4608–3.4612 inch; symbol B, 3.4604–3.4608 inch; symbol C, 3.4600–3.4604 inch.

OIL PUMP

All measurements given in inches, unless otherwise specified.

Engine Liter	Year	Rotor				Height Of Oil Pump Case Protrusion, Inch	Side Clearance Between Rotor & Crankcase, Inch	Case Clearance Between Rotor & Crankcase, Inch	Relief Valve Spring, Inch
		Inner Rotor O.D.	Outer Rotor O.D.	Height	Housing Depth				
1.2L	1993–94	1.1693-1.1709	1.5957-1.5968	—	—	—	—	—	①
1.8L	1993–94	1.4035-1.4055	1.9665-1.9685	②	.8646-.8677	.3138-.3150	.0020-.0063	.0039-.0071	③
1.8L	1993–96	—	3.07	—	—	—	.0008-.0028	.0039-.0069	—
2.2L	1993–96	—	3.07	—	—	—	.0008-.0028	.0039-.0069	—
3.3L	1993–96	—	3.07	—	—	—	.0008-.0028	.0039-.0069	④

① — Free length, 1.843 inch.
② — Stamp making A, .5468–.5476 inch; B, .5472–.5480 inch; C, .5476–.5484 inch.
③ — Free length, 1.854 inch; installed length, 1.319; load when installed, 8.56–9.44 lbs.
④ — Free length, 2.902 inch; installed length, 2.154 inch; load when installed, 20.9 lbs.

Page No.

SUZUKI 40-1

TOYOTA:

VEHICLE SERVICE:

Corolla 41-1

Avalon & Camry 42-1

Celica & Supra 43-1

MR2 44-1

Previa 45-1

Paseo & Tercel 46-1

Land Cruiser, Pickups, RAV4

& 4Runner 47-1

UNIT REPAIR 48-1

VOLKSWAGEN 49-1

VOLVO 50-1

GENERAL INFORMATION

Manual Information Locator, Inside Rear Cover

Vehicle Identification 0-1

Air Bag System Precautions 0-8

Service Reminder & Warning Lamp Reset Procedures 0-10

Vehicle Lift Points 0-34

Vehicle Maintenance Schedules 0-69

Electrical Symbol & Wire Color Code Identification 0-139

Page No.

SUZUKI 40-1

TOYOTA:

VEHICLE SERVICE:

Corolla 41-1

Avalon & Camry 42-1

Celica & Supra 43-1

MR2 44-1

Previa 45-1

Paseo & Tercel 46-1

Land Cruiser, Pickups, RAV4

& 4Runner 47-1

UNIT REPAIR 48-1

VOLKSWAGEN 49-1

VOLVO 50-1

GENERAL INFORMATION

Manual Information Locator, Inside Rear Cover

Vehicle Identification 0-1

Air Bag System Precautions 0-8

Service Reminder & Warning Lamp Reset Procedures 0-10

Vehicle Lift Points 0-34

Vehicle Maintenance Schedules 0-69

Electrical Symbol & Wire Color Code Identification 0-139

SUZUKI

INDEX OF SERVICE OPERATIONS

	Page No.
AIR BAG SYSTEM PRECAUTIONS	0-8
AUTOMATIC TRANSMISSIONS/ TRANSAXLES	40-145
BRAKES	
Anti-Lock Brakes	40-131
Disc Brakes	40-116
Drum Brakes	40-122
Hydraulic Brake Systems	40-127
Power Brake Units	40-129
CLUTCH & MANUAL TRANSMISSION	
Adjustments	40-55
Clutch, Replace	40-55
Tightening Specifications	40-57
Transmission, Replace	40-55
Drive Axles	40-159
ELECTRICAL	
Air Bags	40-97
Air Conditioning	40-76
Alternators	40-84
Blower Motor, Replace	40-6
Combination Switch, Replace	40-6
Cooling Fans	40-78
Cruise Control	40-86
Dash Gauges	40-79
Dash Panels	40-103
Distributor, Replace	40-5
Evaporator Core, Replace	40-8
Fuel Pump Relay Location	40-5
Fuse Panel & Flasher Location	40-5
Heater Core, Replace	40-7
Ignition Coils, Replace	40-6
Ignition Lock, Replace	40-6
Ignition Switch, Replace	40-6
Instrument Cluster, Replace	40-6
Passive Restraints	40-97
Precautions	40-5
Speed Controls	40-86
Starter Motors	40-81
Starter, Replace	40-5
Steering Columns	40-104
Steering Wheel, Replace	40-6
Wiper Motor, Replace	40-6
Wiper Systems	40-94
ELECTRICAL SYMBOL IDENTIFICATION	0-139
FRONT SUSPENSION & STEERING	
Axle Shaft Joint, Replace	40-67
Ball Joint Inspection	40-67
Ball Joint, Replace	40-68
Coil Spring & Strut Service	40-68
Coil Spring, Replace	40-68
Hub & Bearing Outside Inner Race, Replace	40-67
Hub & Bearing, Replace	40-66
Leaf Spring, Replace	40-68
Manual Steering Gears	40-110
Power Steering	40-112
Power Steering Pump, Replace	40-72
Shock Absorber, Replace	40-68
Stabilizer Bar, Replace	40-69
Steering Gear, Replace	40-71
Steering Knuckle & Bearing, Replace	40-69
Steering Knuckle, Replace	40-68
Strut, Replace	40-68
Suspension Arm, Replace	40-70
Suspension Control Arm, Ball Joint & Bushings, Replace	40-70
Tightening Specifications	40-73
Wheel Bearing, Adjust	40-66
FRONT WHEEL DRIVE AXLES	40-155
REAR AXLE & SUSPENSION	
Coil Spring & Suspension Arm, Replace	40-62
Coil Spring, Replace	40-61
Control Rod, Replace	40-62
Hub & Knuckle, Replace	40-60
Leaf Spring, Replace	40-61
Rear Axle Shaft Service	40-59
Shock Absorber, Replace	40-61
Stabilizer Bar, Replace	40-63
Strut, Replace	40-60
Tightening Specifications	40-64
Trailing Rod, Replace	40-62
Upper Arm, Replace	40-62
Wheel Bearing, Replace	40-60
SERVICE REMINDER & WARNING LAMP RESET PROCEDURES	0-139
SPECIFICATIONS	
Fluid Capacities & Cooling System Data	40-4
Front Wheel Alignment Specifications	40-4
General Engine Specifications	40-2
Lubricant Data	40-4
Rear Wheel Alignment Specifications	40-4
Tune Up Specifications	40-3
TRANSFER CASE	40-65
VEHICLE IDENTIFICATION	0-1
VEHICLE LIFT POINTS	0-34
VEHICLE MAINTENANCE SCHEDULES	0-69
WHEEL ALIGNMENT	
Front Wheel Alignment	40-75
Rear Wheel Alignment	40-75
Vehicle Ride Height	40-75
Wheel Alignment Specifications	40-4
WIRE COLOR CODE IDENTIFICATION	0-144
1.0L ENGINE	
Belt Tension Data	40-14
Camshaft, Replace	40-12
Compression Pressure	40-9
Cooling System Bleed	40-14
Crankshaft Rear Oil Seal, Replace	40-13
Cylinder Head, Replace	40-10
Engine Mount, Replace	40-9
Engine Rebuilding Specifications	40-165
Engine, Replace	40-9
Exhaust Manifold, Replace	40-10
Fuel Filter, Replace	40-15
Fuel Pump, Replace	40-14
Hydraulic Valve Lash Adjuster Service	40-11
Intake Manifold, Replace	40-10
Main & Rod Bearings	40-13
Oil Pan, Replace	40-13
Oil Pump, Replace	40-13
Oil Pump Service	40-13
Piston & Rod Assembly	40-13
Pistons, Pins & Rings	40-13
Precautions	40-9
Radiator, Replace	40-14
Thermostat, Replace	40-14
Tightening Specifications	40-15
Timing Belt, Replace	40-11
Valve Adjustment	40-11
Valve Arrangement	40-11
Valve Guides	40-11
Water Pump, Replace	40-14
1.3L ENGINE (SAMURAI)	
Belt Tension Data	40-21
Component Service	40-17
Compression Pressure	40-16
Cooling System Bleed	40-21
Engine Assemble	40-18
Engine Disassemble	40-16
Engine Rebuilding Specifications	40-165
Engine, Replace	40-16
Fuel Filter, Replace	40-22
Fuel Pump, Replace	40-21
Precautions	40-16
Radiator, Replace	40-21
Thermostat, Replace	40-21
Tightening Specifications	40-23
Timing Belt, Replace	40-20
Valve Adjustment	40-20
Valve Clearance Specifications	40-20
Water Pump, Replace	40-21
1.3L ENGINE (SWIFT)	
Belt Tension Data	40-35
Camshaft, Replace	40-30
Compression Pressure	40-24
Cooling System Bleed	40-35
Cylinder Head, Replace	40-26
Engine Rebuilding Specifications	40-165
Engine, Replace	40-24
Exhaust Manifold, Replace	40-26
Fuel Filter, Replace	40-36
Fuel Pump, Replace	40-36
Intake Manifold, Replace	40-25
Main & Rod Bearings	40-33
Oil Pump Service	40-34
Piston & Rod Assembly	40-32
Precautions	40-24
Radiator, Replace	40-36
Rocker Arms	40-29
Rocker Arms, Replace	40-29
Thermostat, Replace	40-35
Tightening Specifications	40-36
Timing Belt, Replace	40-29
Valve Adjustment	40-28
Valve Clearance Specifications	40-28
Valve Lifters	40-28
Water Pump, Replace	40-35
1.6L ENGINE	
Belt Tension Data	40-47
Camshaft, Replace	40-44
Compression Pressure	40-38

Page No.

Cooling System Bleed 40-47
Crankshaft Rear Oil Seal, Replace 40-46
Cylinder Head, Replace....... 40-40
Engine Mount, Replace 40-38
Engine Rebuilding Specifications.................40-165
Engine, Replace 40-38
Exhaust Manifold, Replace.... 40-40
Fuel Filter, Replace 40-48
Fuel Pump, Replace 40-47
Intake Manifold, Replace...... 40-39
Main & Rod Bearings 40-45
Oil Pan, Replace.............. 40-46
Oil Pump, Replace............ 40-46
Piston & Rod Assembly....... 40-45
Precautions................... 40-38
Radiator, Replace............. 40-47
Rocker Arms, Replace 40-41
Thermostat, Replace.......... 40-47
Tightening Specifications...... 40-48
Timing Belt, Replace.......... 40-44
Valve & Valve Springs, Replace 40-43
Valve Adjustment 40-40
Valve Clearance Specifications................. 40-40
Water Pump, Replace 40-47

1.8L ENGINE

Belt Tension Data............. 40-53
Camshaft, Replace 40-51
Compression Pressure........ 40-50
Cooling System Bleed 40-53
Cylinder Head, Replace....... 40-51
Engine Rebuilding Specifications.................40-165
Engine, Replace 40-50
Exhaust Manifold, Replace.... 40-51
Fuel Filter, Replace 40-53
Fuel Pump, Replace 40-53
Intake Manifold, Replace...... 40-50
Oil Pan, Replace.............. 40-52
Oil Pump, Replace............ 40-53
Piston & Rod Assembly....... 40-52
Precautions................... 40-50
Radiator, Replace............. 40-53
Thermostat, Replace.......... 40-53
Tightening Specifications...... 40-54
Timing Chain, Replace........ 40-51
Valve Clearance Specifications................. 40-51

Specifications

GENERAL ENGINE SPECIFICATIONS

Year	Engine Liters	Fuel System	Bore & Stroke Inch (mm)	Compression Ratio	Maximum Brake HP @ RPM	Maximum Torque Ft. Lbs. @ RPM	Normal Oil Pressure, psi @ 4000 RPM
1993	1.3L①	TBI	2.91 X 2.97 (74 X 75.5)	9.5	66 @ 6000	76 @ 3500	47–61
	1.3L③	MPI	2.91 X 2.97 (74 X 75.5)	10	100 @ 6500	83 @ 5000	54–68
	1.6L①	TBI	2.95 X 3.54 (75 X 90)	8.9	80 @ 5400	94 @ 3000	47–61
	1.6L②	MPI	2.95 X 3.54 (75 X 90)	9.5	95 @ 5600	98 @ 4000	47–61
1994	1.3L①	TBI	2.91 X 2.97 (74 X 75.5)	9.5	66 @ 6000	76 @ 3500	47–61
	1.3L③	MPI	2.91 X 2.97 (74 X 75.5)	10	100 @ 6500	83 @ 5000	54–68
	1.6L①	TBI	2.95 X 3.54 (75 X 90)	8.9	80 @ 5400	94 @ 3000	47–61
	1.6L②	MPI	2.95 X 3.54 (75 X 90)	9.5	95 @ 5600	98 @ 4000	47–61
1995	1.3L	TBI	2.91 X 2.97 (74 X 75.5)	9.5	66 @ 6000	76 @ 3500	47-61
	1.6L①	TBI	2.95 X 3.54 (75 X 90)	8.9	80 @ 5400	94 @ 3000	47–61
	1.6L②	MPI	2.95 X 3.54 (75 X 90)	9.5	95 @ 5600	98 @ 4000	47–61
1996	1.3L	TBI	2.91 X 2.97 (74 X 75.5)	9.5	70 @ 5500	74 @ 3000	47-61
	1.6L	MPI	2.95 X 3.54 (75 X 90)	9.5	95 @ 5600	98 @ 4000	47–61
	1.8L	MPI	3.31 X 3.27 (84 X 83)	9.8	120 @ 6500	114 @ 3500	55-67

①–SOHC w/2 valves per cylinder.
②–SOHC w/4 valves per cylinder.
③–DOHC.

TUNE UP SPECIFICATIONS

Year & Engine	Spark Plug Gap Inch	Ignition Timing: Firing Order Fig.②	Ignition Timing: Timing ° BTDC	Ignition Timing: Timing Mark	Curb Idle Speed③: Man. Trans.	Curb Idle Speed③: Auto. Trans.	Fast Idle Speed	Fuel Pressure psi	Valve Lash⑨: Intake	Valve Lash⑨: Exhaust
1993–94										
1.3L Samurai	.029	1-3-4-2	8⑥	A	800-950	—	⑦	34-40	.0090-.0110	.0102-.0118
1.3L Swift①	.041	1-3-4-2	5⑥	A	700-950	800-950	⑦	34–40	.0090-.0110	.0102-.0118
1.3L Swift GT④	.029	1-3-4-2 ⑧	6⑥	A	750	850N	⑦	23–30	⑩	⑩
1.6L Sidekick①	.029	1-3-4-2	5⑪	E	750-850	750-850	⑦	35–38	.0090-.0110	.0100-.0110
1.6L Sidekick⑤	.029	1-3-4-2	5⑪	E	750-850	800-1050	⑦	36-42	.0070-.0080	.0070-.0080
1995–96										
1.3L Samurai	.029	1-3-4-2	8⑥	A	800-950	—	⑦	34-40	.0090-.0110	.0102-.0118
1.3L Swift①	.041	1-3-4-2	5⑥	A	700-950	800-950	⑦	34–40	.0090-.0110	.0102-.0118
1.3L Swift GT④	.029	1-3-4-2 ⑧	6⑥	A	750	850N	⑦	23–30	⑩	⑩
1.6L Esteem	.029	1-3-4-2	5⑫	D	700-800	750-850	⑦	38-44	.0050-.0070	.0070-.0080
1.6L Sidekick①	.029	1-3-4-2	5⑪	E	750-850	750-850	⑦	35–38	.0090-.0110	.0100-.0110
1.6L Sidekick⑤	.029	1-3-4-2	5⑪	E	750-850	800-1050	⑦	36-42	.0070-.0080	.0070-.0080
1.6L X-90	.029	1-3-4-2	5⑪	E	800-1000	800-1000	⑦	34-39	.0070-.0080	.0070-.0080
1.8L Sidekick	.029	1-3-4-2	5⑬	C	800/1000	800-1000	⑦	34–39	⑩	⑩

BTDC — Before Top Dead Center

① — SOHC w/2 valves per cylinder.

② — Before disconnecting spark plug wires from distributor cap, determine location of number 1 wire in cap, as distributor position may have been altered from that shown.

③ — Highest idle speeds listed are with idle-up actuator energized. When adjusting idle speed, set parking brake & chock drive wheels.

④ — DOHC.

⑤ — SOHC w/4 valves per cylinder.

⑥ — Remove cap from monitor coupler & connect jumper wire between terminals C & D of connector. The monitor coupler is located in the engine compartment, next to the ignition coil.

⑦ — Controlled by idle air control valve.

⑧ — Refer to Fig. B for spark plug wire connections at distributor cap.

⑨ — Measure valve lash with engine at operation temperature.

⑩ — Equipped with hydraulic lash adjusters, no adjustment is necessary.

⑪ — Remove cap from monitor coupler & connect jumper wire between terminals D & E of connector. The monitor coupler is located in the engine compartment, next to the battery.

⑫ — Connect jumper wire between terminals D & E of diagnostic connector No. 1. The diagnostic connector is located on the lefthand side of the engine compartment, in the engine compartment relay box.

⑬ — Remove cap from monitor coupler & connect jumper wire between terminals 3 & 4 of connector. The monitor coupler is located on the lefthand side of the engine compartment.

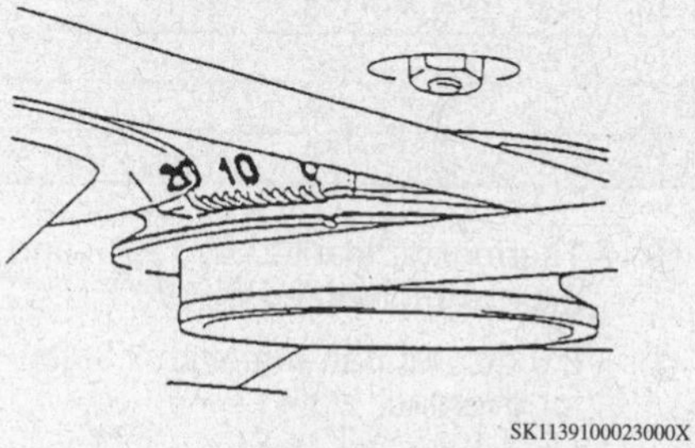
SK1139100023000X

Fig. A

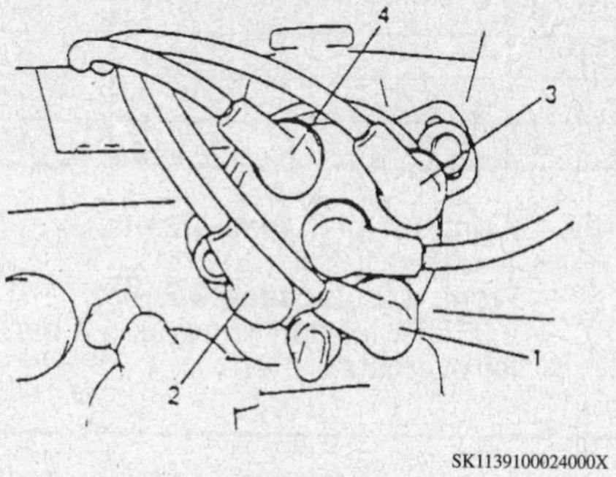
4
3
2
1
SK1139100024000X

Fig. B

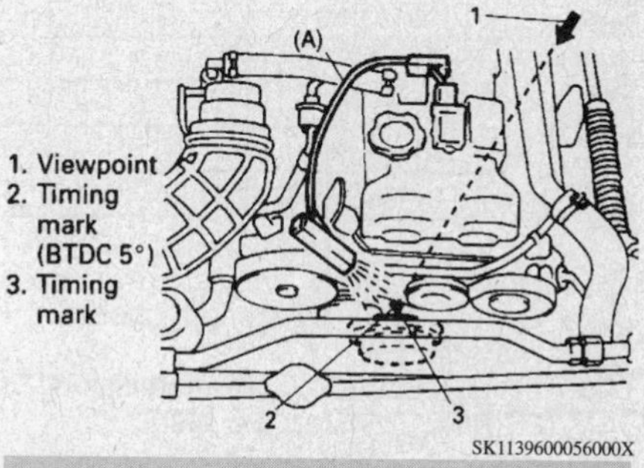
1
(A)
1. Viewpoint
2. Timing mark (BTDC 5°)
3. Timing mark
2
3
SK1139600056000X

Fig. C

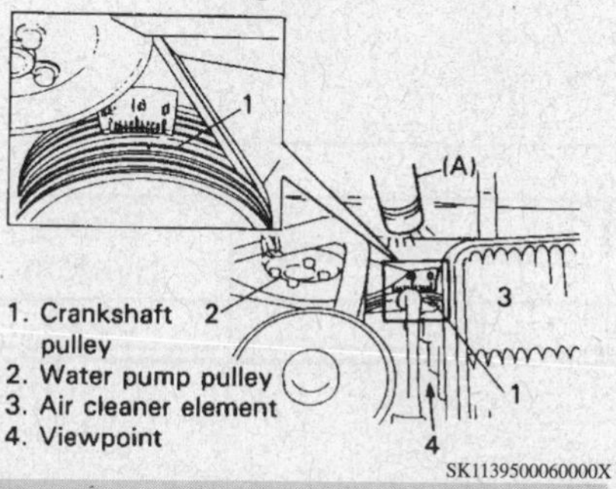
1
(A)
2
3
1
4
1. Crankshaft pulley
2. Water pump pulley
3. Air cleaner element
4. Viewpoint
SK1139500060000X

Fig. D

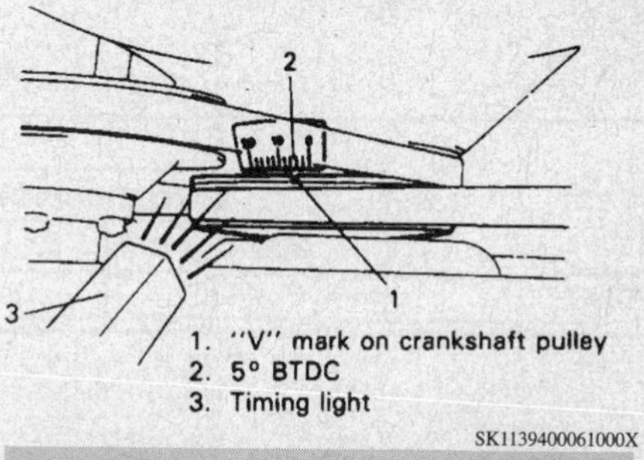
2
1
3
1. "V" mark on crankshaft pulley
2. 5° BTDC
3. Timing light
SK1139400061000X

Fig. E

FRONT WHEEL ALIGNMENT SPECIFICATIONS

Year	Model	Caster Angle, Degrees		Camber Angles, Degrees		Toe, Inch①	Kingpin Inclination, Degrees		Ball Joint Wear
		Limits	Desired	Limits	Desired		Limits	Desired	
1993–96	Samurai	—	+3 ½	—	+1	.08 to .24	—	9	②
	Sidekick	+ ½ to +2 ½	+1 ½	– ½ to +1 ½	+ ½	+.08 to +.24	—	—	②
	Swift	+1 to +5	+3	–1 to +1	0	–.079 to +.079	9 11⁄12 to 15 11⁄12	12 11⁄12	②
1995–96	Esteem	+1 to +5	+3	-1 to +1	0	–.079 to +.079	9 7⁄12 to 15 7⁄12	12 7⁄12	②
1996	X-90	+ ½ to +2 ½	+1 ½	- ½ to +1 ½	+ ½	+.08 to +.24	—	—	②

① — Toe-in (+); toe-out (-).
② — Refer to "Ball Joint Inspection" in "Front Suspension & Steering" section.

REAR WHEEL ALIGNMENT SPECIFICATIONS

Year	Model	Toe, Inch①
1993–96	Swift	0 to +.158
1995–96	Esteem	-.079 to +.079

① — Toe-in (+); toe-out (-).

FLUID CAPACITIES & COOLING SYSTEM DATA

Year	Model	Coolant System Capacity Qts.	Radiator Cap Relief Pressure psi	Thermo. Open Temp. Deg. F	Fuel Tank Gals.	Engine Oil Qts.①	Transmission		Differential
							Man. Trans. Pts.	Auto. Trans. Refill Qts.②	
1993–94	Samurai	5	12.8	⑧	10.6	3.7	2.7⑤	—	⑥
	Sidekick	5.5	12.8	179	11.1	4.4	③	⑦	④
	Swift	4.9	12.8	190	10.6	3.5	5.1	5.2	—
	Swift GT	4.9	12.8	179	10.6	3.5	4.7	5.4	—
1995–96	Esteem	4.8	12.8	190	13.5	3.3	5	5.7	—
	Samurai	5	12.8	⑧	10.6	3.7	2.7⑤	—	⑥
	Sidekick	5.5	12.8	179	14.5	4.4	③	⑨	④
	Sidekick Sport	6.9	12.8	179	18.5	5.3	③	6.5	④
	Swift	4.9	12.8	190	10.6	3.5	5	5.2	—
	Swift GT	4.9	12.8	179	10.6	3.5	4.7	5.4	—
	X-90	5.3	12.8	190	14.5	4.3	③	⑨	④

① — Includes filter.
② — Approximate, make final check with dipstick.
③ — 2WD, 4 pts.; 4WD, transmission, 3.2 pts., transfer, 3.6 pts.
④ — Front, 2.1 pts.; rear, 4.6 pts.
⑤ — Transfer, 1.7 pts.
⑥ — Front, 4.2 pts.; rear, 3.2 pts.
⑦ — 2.95 qts. for pan removal; 5.4 qts. for overhaul.
⑧ — Thermostat marked A, 179°F and thermostat marked B, 190°F.
⑨ — 2.6 qts. for pan removal; 7.3 qts. for overhaul.

LUBRICANT DATA

Year	Lubricant Type					
	Transmission		Transfer Case	Rear Axle	Power Steering	Brake System
	Manual	Automatic				
1993–96	75W-90	Dexron III	75W-90	75W-90	Dexron III	DOT 3

Electrical

NOTE: On Air Bag Equipped Models, Refer To "Air Bag System Precautions" Located In The Front Of This Manual For System Disarming & Arming Procedures.

INDEX

	Page No.
Air Bags	40-97
Air Conditioning	40-76
Alternators	40-84
Blower Motor, Replace	40-6
Esteem	40-7
Samurai	40-6
Sidekick, Swift & X-90	40-7
Combination Switch, Replace	40-6
Cooling Fans	40-78
Cruise Control	40-86
Dash Gauges	40-79
Dash Panels	40-103
Distributor, Replace	40-5
Esteem	40-6
Samurai & Sidekick w/1.6L 8 Valve Engine	40-5
Sidekick w/1.6L 16 Valve Engine & X-90	40-5
Swift	40-5
Evaporator Core, Replace	40-8
Esteem	40-8
Sidekick, Swift & X-90	40-8
Fuel Pump Relay Location	40-5
Esteem	40-5
Samurai	40-5
Swift	40-5
1993–95 Sidekick	40-5
1996 Sidekick & X-90	40-5
Fuse Panel & Flasher Location	40-5
Heater Core, Replace	40-7
Esteem	40-8
Samurai	40-7
Sidekick & X-90	40-7
Swift	40-8
Ignition Coils, Replace	40-6
1.8L Engine	40-6
Ignition Lock, Replace	40-6
Ignition Switch, Replace	40-6
Instrument Cluster, Replace	40-6
Passive Restraints	40-97
Precautions	40-5
Air Bag Systems	40-5
Speed Controls	40-86
Starter Motors	40-81
Starter, Replace	40-5
Steering Columns	40-104
Steering Wheel, Replace	40-6
Wiper Motor, Replace	40-6
Front	40-6
Rear	40-6
Wiper Systems	40-94

PRECAUTIONS

AIR BAG SYSTEMS

Refer to "Air Bag System Precautions" in the front of this manual for system disarming and arming procedures.

FUEL PUMP RELAY LOCATION

ESTEEM

The fuel pump relay is located in the relay box on the lefthand side of the engine compartment.

SAMURAI

The fuel pump relay is located behind the righthand side of the instrument panel, near the Engine Control Module (ECM).

SWIFT

The fuel pump relay is located on the lefthand side of the engine compartment.

1993–95 SIDEKICK

The fuel pump relay is located behind the lefthand side of the instrument panel, near the Engine Control Module (ECM).

1996 SIDEKICK & X-90

The fuel pump relay is located behind the center of the instrument panel, on the heater unit.

FUSE PANEL & FLASHER LOCATION

The fuse panel and flasher are located under the lefthand side of the instrument panel.

STARTER

REPLACE

1. Disconnect battery ground cable.
2. Disconnect solenoid electrical connector and battery cable from starter terminals.
3. Remove two starter motor attaching bolts, then the starter.
4. Reverse procedure to install.

DISTRIBUTOR

REPLACE

SAMURAI & SIDEKICK w/1.6L 8 VALVE ENGINE

1. Disconnect battery ground cable, then the vacuum hoses, if equipped.
2. Disconnect electrical connectors, then remove distributor cap.
3. Remove hold-down bolts, then the distributor.
4. Reverse procedure to install, noting the following:
   a. Turn crankshaft clockwise as viewed from crankshaft pulley until "V" mark on pulley aligns with timing mark "0" on timing tab.
   b. Turn crankshaft clockwise as viewed from crankshaft pulley until "V" mark on pulley aligns with timing mark "0" on timing tab.
   c. Remove cylinder head cover and visually confirm rocker arms are not riding on camshaft cams of No. 1 cylinder. If arms are riding on cams, turn over crankshaft one full turn aligning two marks again.
   d. Align center of rotor with cap bolt hole center, then install distributor.

When installing distributor, rotor will slightly turn counterclockwise on Sidekick models or clockwise on Samurai models.

SIDEKICK w/1.6L 16 VALVE ENGINE & X-90

1. Disconnect battery ground cable, then the distributor electrical connector.
2. Remove distributor cap, then turn crankshaft clockwise until rotor is positioned at No. 1 terminal of cap.
3. Remove distributor flange bolt, then the distributor assembly.
4. Apply engine oil to distributor O-ring, then align punch mark on gear with "V" mark on housing.
5. Insert distributor into case ensuring center of distributor flange coincides with flange bolt hole provided in gear case. When inserting distributor completely, rotor should be in one o'clock position.
6. Install distributor cap, then connect distributor electrical connector and battery ground cable.

SWIFT

1. Disconnect battery ground cable, then the vacuum hoses, if equipped.
2. Disconnect electrical connectors, then remove distributor cap.
3. Remove hold-down bolts, then the distributor.
4. Reverse procedure to install, noting the following:
   a. Fit dogs of distributor coupling into slots of camshaft.
   b. If dogs cannot be fit into slots, turn distributor shaft 180°.

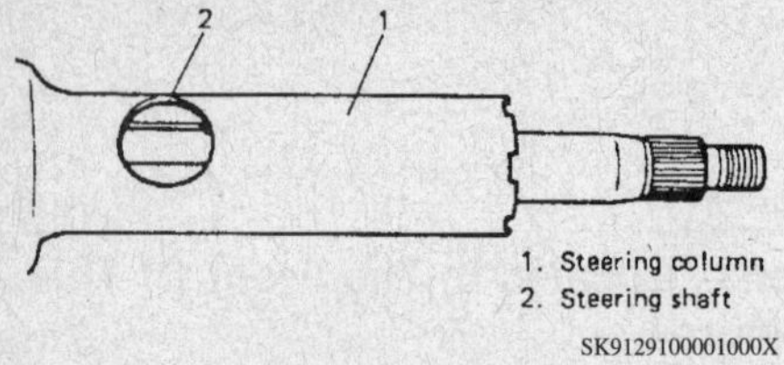
2
1
1. Steering column
2. Steering shaft
SK9129100001000X

Fig. 1 Ignition lock/switch Installation

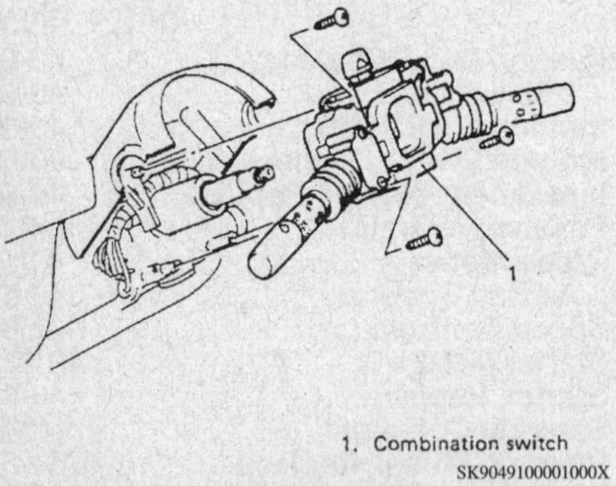
1
1. Combination switch
SK9049100001000X

Fig. 2 Combination switch replacement

ESTEEM

1. Disconnect battery ground cable.
2. Disconnect electrical connectors, then remove distributor cap.
3. Remove flange bolts, then the distributor.
4. Reverse procedure to install, noting the following:
    a. Fit cogs of distributor coupling into slots of camshaft.
    b. If cogs cannot be fit into slots, turn distributor shaft 180°.
    c. Check and adjust ignition timing.

IGNITION COILS

REPLACE

1.8L ENGINE

Each cylinder is equipped with an ignition coil.

1. Disconnect battery ground cable.
2. Remove ignition coil cover.
3. Remove ignition coil retaining bolt, then the coil from spark plug.
4. Reverse procedure to install.

IGNITION LOCK

REPLACE

Refer to "Ignition Switch, Replace" for replacement procedure.

IGNITION SWITCH

REPLACE

1. Remove steering wheel as outlined under "Steering Wheel, Replace."
2. Remove combination switch as outlined under "Combination Switch, Replace."
3. Remove steering column from vehicle as follows:

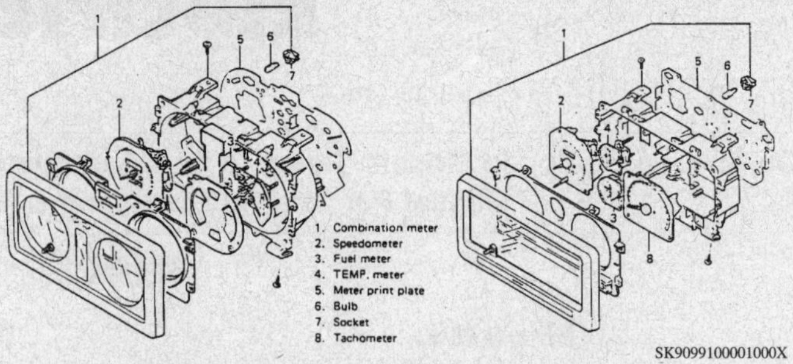
1. Combination meter
2. Speedometer
3. Fuel meter
4. TEMP. meter
5. Meter print plate
6. Bulb
7. Socket
8. Tachometer
SK9099100001000X

Fig. 3 Instrument cluster removal

    a. Disconnect all electrical connectors from steering column.
    b. **On Swift models,** remove steering shaft joint cover.
    c. **On all models,** disconnect steering joint by removing joint bolt.
    d. Remove steering column mounting bolts.
    e. **On Swift models with automatic transmission,** remove back drive cable from column assembly.
    f. **On all models,** remove steering column from vehicle.
4. Using center punch, remove steering lock/switch mounting bolts. Use care not to damage aluminum part of steering lock/switch body.
5. Turn ignition key to ACC or ON position, then remove lock/switch assembly from steering column.
6. Install ignition lock/switch to steering column as follows:
    a. Position oblong hole of steering shaft in center of hole in column, **Fig. 1.**
    b. Turn ignition key to ACC or ON position, then install lock/switch assembly onto column.
    c. Turn ignition key to LOCK position, then remove key.
    d. Align hub on lock/switch with oblong hole of steering shaft. Ensure steering shaft is locked.
    e. Tighten bolts until heads of bolts twist off.
    f. Using ignition key, ensure smooth operation of steering shaft.
7. Reverse steps 1 through 3 to complete assembly.

COMBINATION SWITCH

REPLACE

1. Remove steering wheel as outlined under "Steering Wheel, Replace."
2. Remove steering column covers.
3. Disconnect lead wire at coupler from combination switch.
4. Remove combination switch attaching bolts, then the switch **Fig. 2.**
5. Reverse procedure to install.

STEERING WHEEL

REPLACE

1. Disconnect battery ground cable.
2. **On models with air bag,** disarm and remove air bag module from steering wheel as outlined under "Precautions."
3. **On models less air bag,** remove horn pad from steering wheel.
4. **On all models,** remove steering wheel shaft nut.
5. Scribe alignment marks on steering wheel and shaft for installation reference.
6. Remove steering wheel with suitable puller.
7. Reverse procedure to install, noting the following:
    a. Align marks on shaft and steering wheel.
    b. **Torque** shaft nut to 25 ft. lbs.

INSTRUMENT CLUSTER

REPLACE

1. Disconnect battery ground cable.
2. Remove steering wheel trim panels.
3. Lower steering column.
4. Remove instrument panel cluster bezel attaching screws and bezel, **Fig. 3.**
5. Disconnect speedometer cable and wire harness electrical connector, then remove instrument cluster.
6. Reverse procedure to install.

WIPER MOTOR

REPLACE

FRONT

1. Disconnect linkage assembly from wiper motor shaft.
2. Disconnect electrical connectors from wiper motor.
3. Remove wiper motor attaching bolts, then the wiper motor.

REAR

1. Remove wiper blade and arm assembly.
2. Remove access panel on back door.
3. Disconnect linkage assembly from wiper motor shaft.
4. Disconnect electrical connectors from wiper motor.
5. Remove wiper motor attaching bolts, then the wiper motor.

BLOWER MOTOR

REPLACE

SAMURAI

1. Disconnect battery ground cable, then drain coolant system into appropriate container.

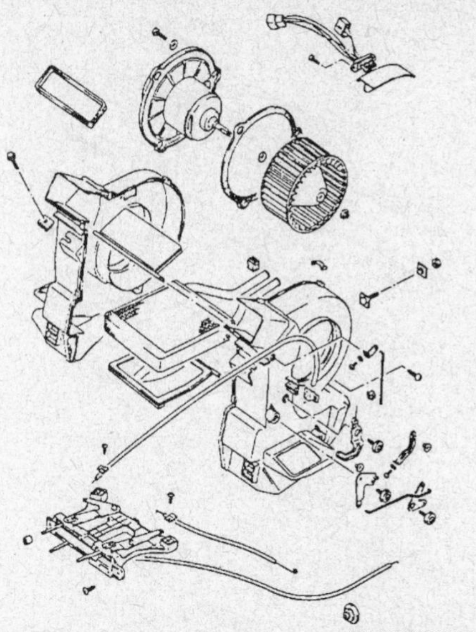

SK7029100016000X

Fig. 4 Exploded view of heater & blower motor assembly. Samurai

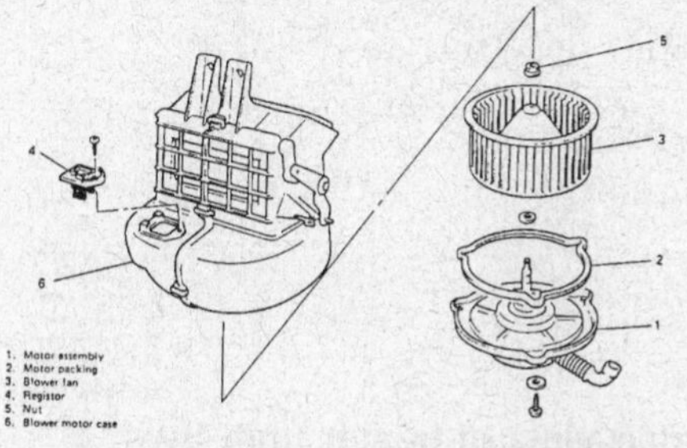

SK7029100017000X

Fig. 5 Exploded view of blower motor assembly. Sidekick, Swift & X-90

2. Disconnect heater inlet and outlet hoses from heater unit pipes.
3. Remove instrument panel assembly as follows:
   a. Remove horn pad, then steering wheel using a suitable puller.
   b. Remove radio case stay screws and pull out radio case with radio and cigarette lighter, then disconnect radio and cigarette lighter electrical connectors.
   c. Remove ashtray, then the ashtray plate attaching screws.
   d. Disconnect front hood opening cable from lock assembly.
   e. Loosen glove compartment stay screw and hood opening cable locknut from backside of glove compartment cover.
   f. Disconnect electrical connectors and control cables from heater control panel, **Fig. 4.**
   g. Pull out heater control knobs and plate, then loosen heater lever case screws.
   h. Disconnect electrical connectors from speedometer and instrument panel.
   i. Disconnect speedometer cable.
   j. Release wire harness clamps installed to instrument panel.

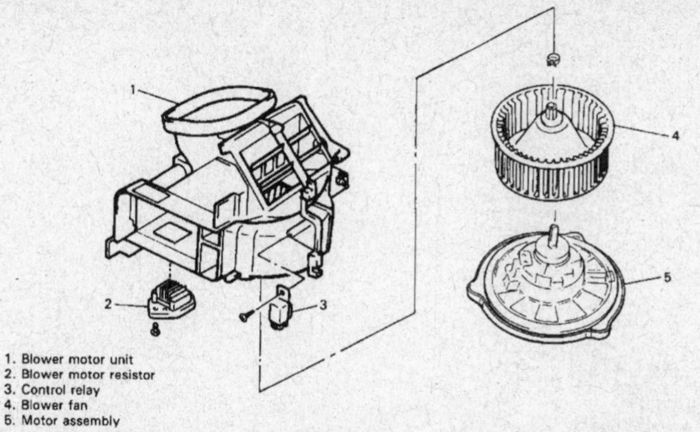
1
2
3
4
5
1. Blower motor unit
2. Blower motor resistor
3. Control relay
4. Blower fan
5. Motor assembly

SK7029600044000X

Fig. 6 Exploded view of blower motor assembly. Esteem

   k. Loosen screws securing instrument panel, then remove instrument panel.
4. Loosen front door stopper screws, then remove steering column holder.
5. Disconnect blower motor and resistor electrical connectors.
6. Loosen heater case securing nut from inside engine compartment, then remove heater assembly, **Fig. 4.**
7. Remove blower motor, **Fig. 4.**
8. Separate heater unit case halves, then remove heater core from heater unit.
9. Reverse procedure to install.

SIDEKICK, SWIFT & X-90

1. Disconnect battery ground cable.
2. **On models with air bag,** disarm and remove air bag module from steering wheel as outlined under "Precautions."
3. **On all models,** remove glove compartment and holder stay.
4. Disconnect all electrical connectors from blower motor.
5. Disconnect fresh air control cable from blower motor case.
6. Remove blower motor attaching bolts, then the blower motor **Fig. 5.**
7. Reverse procedure to install.

ESTEEM

1. Disconnect battery ground cable.
2. **On models with air bag,** disarm and remove air bag modules as outlined under "Precautions."
3. **On all models,** remove glove compartment and holder stay.
4. Remove engine control module (ECM) and instrument panel lower member.
5. Disconnect all electrical connectors from blower motor.
6. Disconnect fresh air control cable from blower motor case.
7. Remove blower motor attaching bolts, then the blower motor, **Fig. 6.**
8. Reverse procedure to install.

HEATER CORE

REPLACE

SAMURAI

Refer to "Blower Motor, Replace," for heater core replacement procedure.

SIDEKICK & X-90

1. Drain radiator into appropriate container and disconnect water hoses from heater core.
2. Remove instrument panel assembly as follows:
   a. Disconnect battery ground cable.
   b. **On models with air bag,** disarm and remove air bag modules as outlined under "Precautions."
   c. **On all models,** remove screws from front of console, then back lockpins from rear of console.
   d. Holding shifter boot inward, remove housing and console.
   e. Remove steering column covers.
   f. Remove attaching screws from instrument cluster front shroud, then the shroud.
   g. Remove instrument cluster attaching screws and pull cluster rearward.
   h. Remove speedometer, then disconnect cluster wiring harness and remove cluster.
   i. Remove inspection screw covers, then the upper housing attaching bolts.
   j. Remove lower housing attaching bolts located on the driver's side of the instrument panel.
   k. Remove center support dash mount.
   l. Open glove compartment and remove two glove compartment lockpins, then lift glove compartment out of the instrument panel.
   m. Remove instrument panel attaching screws from lower righthand side of the instrument panel.
   n. Remove handle bar from right side of the instrument panel.
   o. Remove hood release lever attaching bolt.
   p. Disconnect center mounting bracket from the radio and ashtray.
   q. Disconnect dash panel wiring harness and remove dash panel.
3. Remove heater case attaching bolts.
4. Remove heater core from heater unit, **Fig. 7.**
5. Reverse procedure to install.

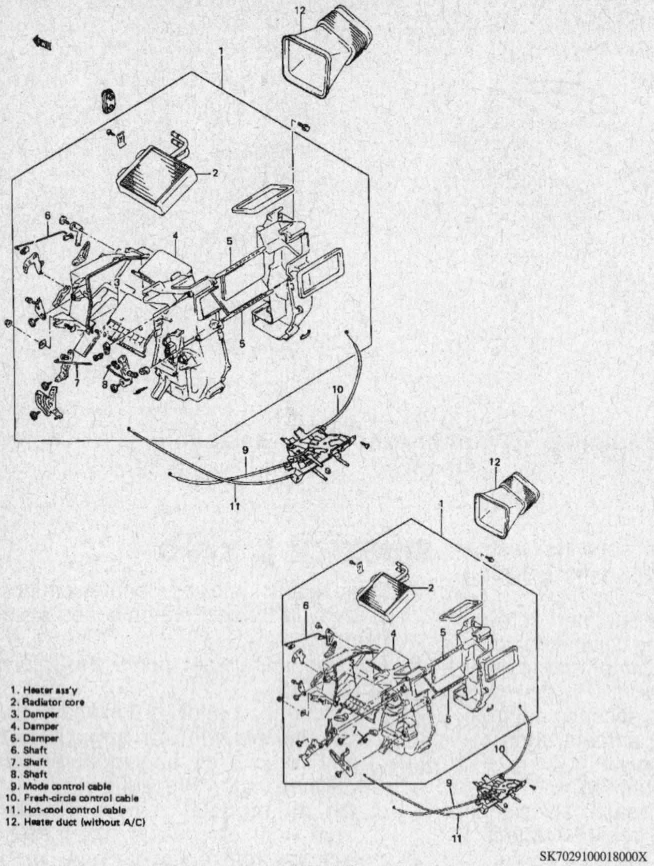
1. Heater ass'y
2. Radiator core
3. Damper
4. Damper
5. Damper
6. Shaft
7. Shaft
8. Shaft
9. Mode control cable
10. Fresh-circle control cable
11. Hot-cool control cable
12. Heater duct (without A/C)
SK7029100018000X

Fig. 7 Exploded view of heater unit. Sidekick & X-90

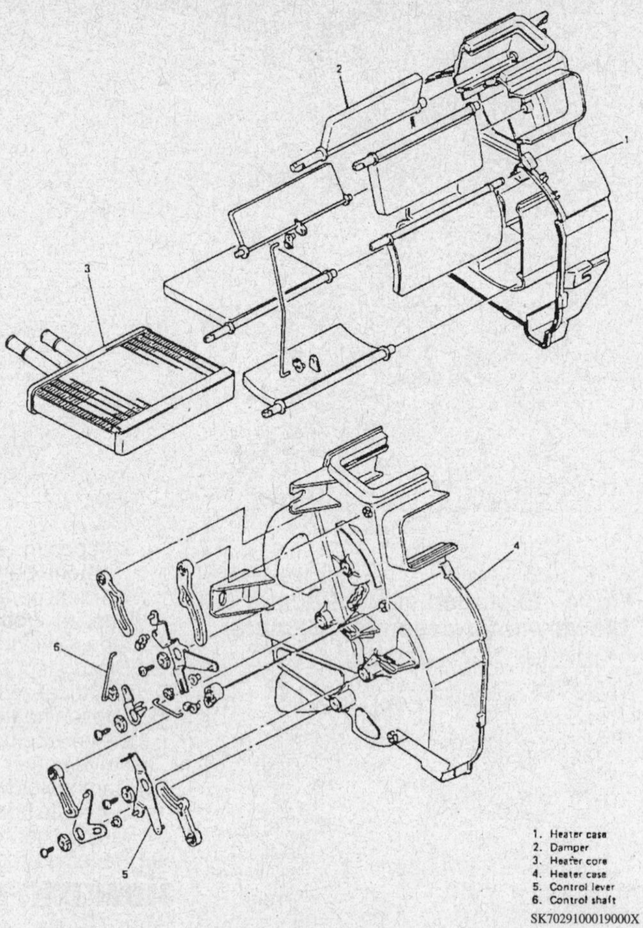
1. Heater case
2. Damper
3. Heater core
4. Heater case
5. Control lever
6. Control shaft
SK7029100019000X

Fig. 8 Exploded view of heater unit. Swift & Esteem

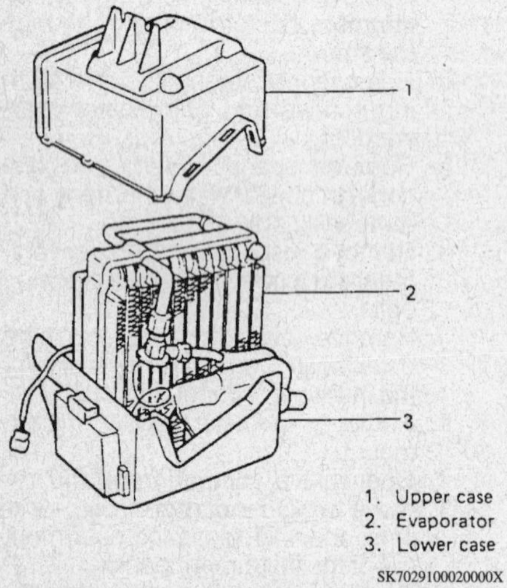
1. Upper case
2. Evaporator
3. Lower case
SK7029100020000X

Fig. 9 Evaporator case separation. Sidekick, X-90 & Swift

SWIFT

1. Disconnect battery ground cable.
2. Drain radiator into appropriate container and disconnect water hoses from heater core.
3. Disconnect all wires and cables from heater and blower units.
4. Remove steering wheel and steering column as outlined under "Ignition Switch & Lock Assembly, Replace."
5. Disconnect speedometer cable, then remove speedometer assembly.
6. Remove both front speaker garnishes and center cover.
7. Remove instrument panel member mounting bolts.
8. Remove instrument panel and panel member as an assembly.
9. Remove heater unit, **Fig. 8.**
10. Remove heater unit clips and screws, then separate heater unit.
11. Remove heater core from heater unit.
12. Reverse procedure to install.

ESTEEM

Refer to "Blower Motor, Replace," for heater core replacement procedure.

EVAPORATOR CORE

REPLACE

SIDEKICK, SWIFT & X-90

1. Disconnect battery ground cable.
2. **On models with air bag,** disarm and remove air bag modules as outlined under "Precautions."
3. **On all models,** recover refrigerant from A/C system. **Care should be taken to avoid excess compressor oil discharge with refrigerant.**
4. Remove all electrical connectors and fresh air control cable from blower motor.
5. Remove glove compartment, blower motor and heater to evaporator connecting band.
6. **On Swift models,** disconnect A/C amplifier connector.
7. **On all models,** disconnect thermistor wire connector.
8. Disconnect compressor suction hose and receiver/dryer outlet hose from cooling unit fittings. **Cap all opened fittings to prevent moisture from entering A/C system.**
9. Remove evaporator case attaching bracket, then the evaporator unit.
10. Remove case clamps, then separate evaporator case halves, **Fig. 9.**
11. Remove evaporator core attaching screws, then the evaporator core.
12. Reverse procedure to install.

ESTEEM

1. Disconnect battery ground cable.
2. **On models with air bag,** disarm and remove air bag module from steering wheel and passenger side as outlined under "Precautions."
3. **On all models,** recover refrigerant from A/C system. **Care should be taken to avoid excess compressor oil discharge with refrigerant.**

4. Remove blower motor unit as outlined in "Blower Motor, Replace".
5. Disconnect A/C amplifier and thermistor wire connectors.
6. Disconnect compressor suction hose and receiver/dryer outlet hose from cooling unit fittings. **Cap all opened fittings to prevent moisture from entering A/C system.**
7. Remove evaporator case, then the evaporator unit.
8. Remove case clamps, then separate evaporator case halves, **Fig. 10.**
9. Remove evaporator core attaching screws, then the evaporator core.
10. Reverse procedure to install.

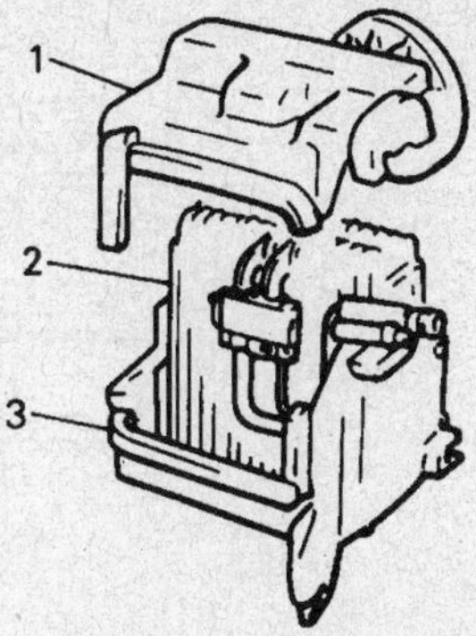
1
2
3
1. Upper case
2. Evaporator
3. Lower case
SK7029600045000X

Fig. 10 Evaporator case separation. Esteem

1.0L Engine

NOTE: On Air Bag Equipped Models, Refer To "Air Bag System Precautions" Located In The Front Of This Manual For System Disarming & Arming Procedures.

INDEX

	Page No.
Belt Tension Data	40-14
Camshaft, Replace	40-12
Installation	40-12
Removal	40-12
Compression Pressure	40-9
Cooling System Bleed	40-14
Crankshaft Rear Oil Seal, Replace	40-13
Cylinder Head, Replace	40-10
Engine Mount, Replace	40-9
Front	40-9
Rear	40-9
Engine Rebuilding Specifications	40-165
Engine, Replace	40-9
Exhaust Manifold, Replace	40-10
Fuel Filter, Replace	40-15
Fuel Pump, Replace	40-14
Hydraulic Valve Lash Adjuster Service	40-11
Intake Manifold, Replace	40-10
Main & Rod Bearings	40-13
Oil Pan, Replace	40-13
Oil Pump, Replace	40-13
Installation	40-13
Removal	40-13
Oil Pump Service	40-13
Piston & Rod Assembly	40-13
Pistons, Pins & Rings	40-13
Precautions	40-9
Air Bag Systems	40-9
Fuel System Pressure Relief	40-9
Radiator, Replace	40-14
Swift	40-14
Thermostat, Replace	40-14
Tightening Specifications	40-15
Timing Belt, Replace	40-11
Inspection	40-11
Installation	40-12
Removal	40-11
Valve Adjustment	40-11
Valve Arrangement	40-11
Front To Rear	40-11
Valve Guides	40-11
Water Pump, Replace	40-14

PRECAUTIONS

AIR BAG SYSTEMS

Refer to "Air Bag System Precautions" in the front of this manual for system disarming and arming procedures.

FUEL SYSTEM PRESSURE RELIEF

1. Loosen fuel filler cap to relieve fuel tank pressure
2. Remove fuel pump relay from relay box located at the lefthand front of the engine compartment, next to the battery, **Fig. 1.**
3. Crank engine and allow to stall. Crank engine for several seconds more to ensure relief of any remaining fuel.
4. Remove battery ground cable.

COMPRESSION PRESSURE

Standard compression pressure is 199 psi with a minimum of 154 psi. Maximum allowable difference between cylinders is 14.2 psi.

ENGINE MOUNT

REPLACE

FRONT

1. Disconnect battery ground cable.
2. Remove engine mount nut, then raise and support vehicle.
3. Support engine using an engine support fixture.
4. Remove engine mount and frame bracket, then remove mount from bracket.
5. Reverse procedure to install.

REAR

1. Disconnect battery ground cable.
2. Remove engine mount nut, then raise and support vehicle.
3. Remove nut retaining mount to body bracket.
4. Support engine using an engine support fixture.
5. Remove frame bracket, then remove mount.
6. Reverse procedure to install.

ENGINE

REPLACE

1. Relieve fuel system pressure as outlined under "Precautions".
2. Disconnect battery ground cable.

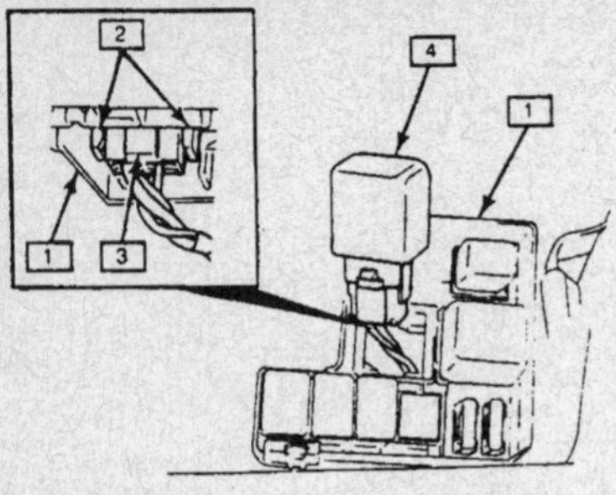
2
4
1
1
3

1 MAIN FUSE BOX
2 LOCK TABS
3 FUEL PUMP RELAY ELECTRICAL CONNECTOR
4 FUEL PUMP RELAY

GC1029102746000X

Fig. 1 Fuel pump relay location

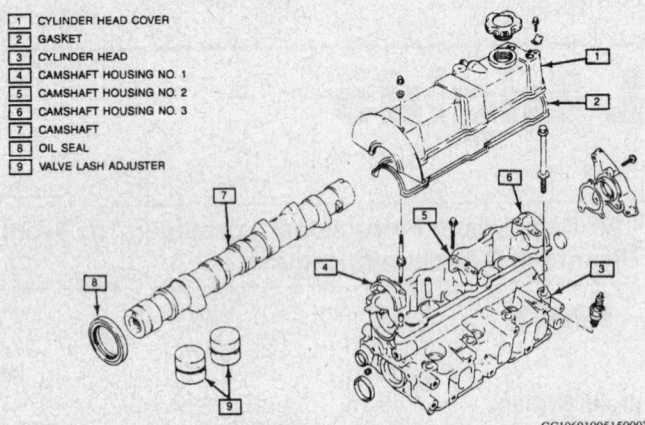

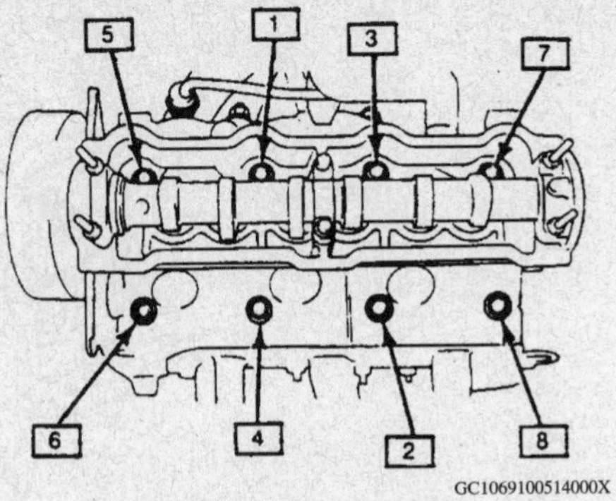
5
1
3
7
6
4
2
8
GC1069100514000X

Fig. 2 Cylinder head bolt tightening sequence

1 CYLINDER HEAD COVER
2 GASKET
3 CYLINDER HEAD
4 CAMSHAFT HOUSING NO. 1
5 CAMSHAFT HOUSING NO. 2
6 CAMSHAFT HOUSING NO. 3
7 CAMSHAFT
8 OIL SEAL
9 VALVE LASH ADJUSTER

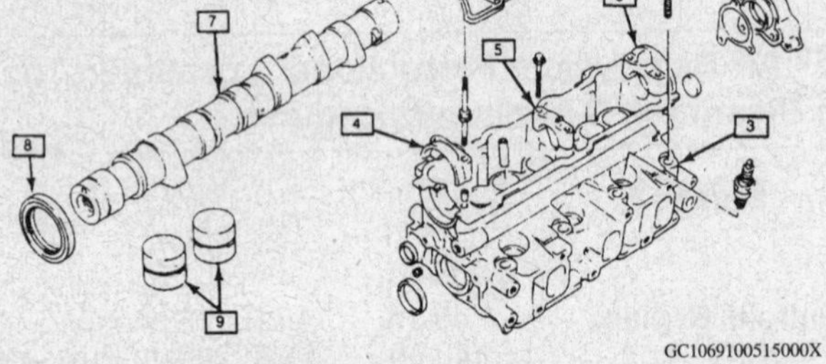
1
2
6
7
5
4
3
8
9
GC1069100515000X

Fig. 3 Camshaft & hydraulic valve lash adjuster replacement

3. Disconnect windshield washer hose, then remove hood.
4. Remove air cleaner assembly.
5. Drain cooling system, then remove radiator and engine cooling fan.
6. Disconnect high tension lead from ignition coil.
7. Disconnect electrical connector from distributor.
8. Disconnect electrical connectors from coolant temperature sender, engine coolant temperature sensor, engine cooling fan switch and engine oil pressure sender.
9. Disconnect electrical connector from EGR vacuum switching valve.
10. Disconnect electrical connectors from idle speed control valve, throttle position switch, fuel injector and pressure sensor.
11. Disconnect electrical connectors and wiring from alternator and starter motor.
12. Disconnect electrical connector from oxygen sensor.
13. Disconnect battery ground cable from transaxle.
14. **On models with manual transaxle,** disconnect electrical connector from back-up lamp switch.
15. **On models with automatic transaxle,** disconnect electrical connectors from neutral safety switch, speed sensor and direct clutch and second brake solenoids.
16. **On all models,** disconnect intake manifold to power brake unit vacuum hose.
17. Disconnect evaporative emission canister hoses from intake manifold and tube connections.
18. Disconnect fuel hoses from throttle body.
19. Disconnect heater hoses from engine.
20. Disconnect accelerator cable from throttle body.
21. **On models with manual transaxle,** disconnect clutch cable from fork and housing.
22. **On models with automatic transaxle,** disconnect shift control and fluid pressure control cables from transaxle.
23. **On all models,** disconnect speedometer cable from transaxle.
24. Raise and support vehicle, then disconnect exhaust pipe from exhaust manifold.
25. Drain engine crankcase, then drain fluid from transaxle.
26. **On models with manual transaxle,** disconnect control shaft and extension rod from transaxle.
27. **On all models,** separate drive axles from transaxle. Support drive axles from chassis using wire.
28. **On models with automatic transaxle,** remove engine torque rod bracket from transaxle.
29. Lower vehicle and install an engine lifting fixture.
30. Remove engine and transaxle mounting bolts, then remove engine and transaxle assembly from vehicle.
31. Reverse procedure to install.

INTAKE MANIFOLD

REPLACE

1. Relieve fuel system pressure as outlined under "Precautions".
2. Disconnect battery ground cable.
3. Drain cooling system, then remove air cleaner assembly.
4. Disconnect electrical connectors from coolant temperature sender, engine and coolant temperature sensor.
5. Disconnect electrical connector from EGR vacuum switching valve.
6. Disconnect electrical connectors from idle speed control valve, throttle position switch and fuel injector.
7. Disconnect ground wires from intake manifold.
8. Disconnect fuel hoses from throttle body.
9. Disconnect coolant hoses from intake manifold.
10. Disconnect MAP sensor hose from intake manifold.
11. Disconnect evaporative emission hoses from intake manifold and tube.
12. Disconnect power brake unit vacuum hose from intake manifold.
13. Disconnect PCV valve hose from cylinder head cover.
14. Disconnect accelerator cable from throttle body.
15. Disconnect all other electrical connectors and hoses to permit intake manifold and throttle body removal.
16. Remove intake manifold to cylinder head attaching nuts and bolts, then remove intake manifold and throttle body as an assembly.
17. Reverse procedure to Install.

EXHAUST MANIFOLD

REPLACE

1. Disconnect battery ground cable.
2. Disconnect oxygen sensor electrical connector, then release wiring harness from clamps.
3. Disconnect exhaust pipe from exhaust manifold.
4. Remove exhaust manifold attaching bolts and nuts, then remove exhaust manifold from cylinder head.
5. Reverse procedure to install.

CYLINDER HEAD

REPLACE

1. Relieve fuel system pressure as outlined under "Precautions".
2. Disconnect battery ground cable.
3. Drain cooling system, then remove air cleaner assembly.
4. Disconnect coil wire from distributor cap.
5. Disconnect electrical connector from distributor.
6. Disconnect electrical connectors from

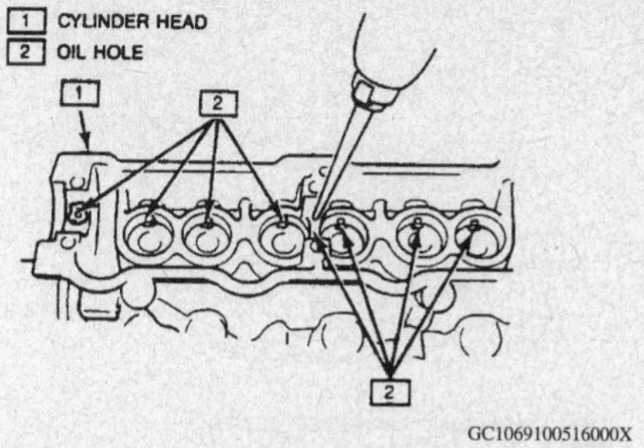

1 CYLINDER HEAD
2 OIL HOLE
1
2
2
GC1069100516000X

Fig. 4 Application of engine oil to camshaft

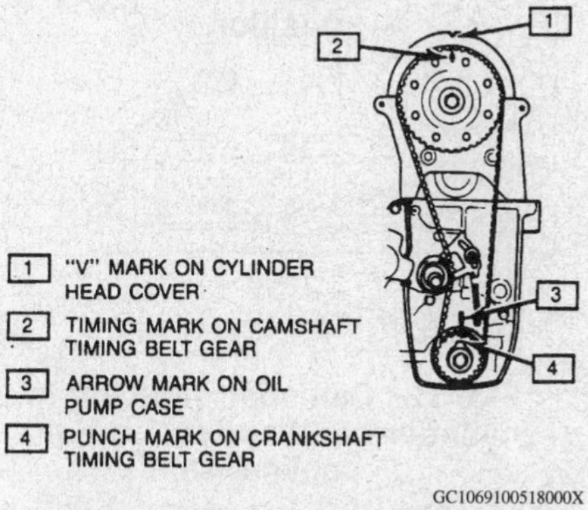

1 "V" MARK ON CYLINDER HEAD COVER
2 TIMING MARK ON CAMSHAFT TIMING BELT GEAR
3 ARROW MARK ON OIL PUMP CASE
4 PUNCH MARK ON CRANKSHAFT TIMING BELT GEAR
1
2
3
4
GC1069100518000X

Fig. 6 Camshaft & crankshaft sprocket timing mark alignment

coolant temperature sender, engine coolant temperature sensor and engine cooling fan switch.

7. Disconnect electrical connector from EGR vacuum switching valve.
8. Disconnect electrical connectors from idle speed control valve, throttle position switch and fuel injector.
9. Disconnect oxygen sensor electrical connector, then detach wiring harness from clamps.
10. Disconnect ground wires from intake manifold.
11. Disconnect heater hose from intake manifold and radiator hose from thermostat housing.
12. Disconnect fuel hoses from throttle body.
13. Disconnect MAP sensor hose from intake manifold.
14. Disconnect evaporative emission hoses from intake manifold and tube.
15. Disconnect power brake unit vacuum hose from intake manifold.
16. Disconnect accelerator cable from throttle body.
17. Raise and support vehicle, then disconnect exhaust pipe from exhaust manifold.
18. Lower vehicle, then remove cylinder head cover.
19. Remove cylinder head attaching bolts, then remove cylinder head.
20. Reverse procedure to install. Tighten cylinder head bolts to specification, in sequence, **Fig. 2.**

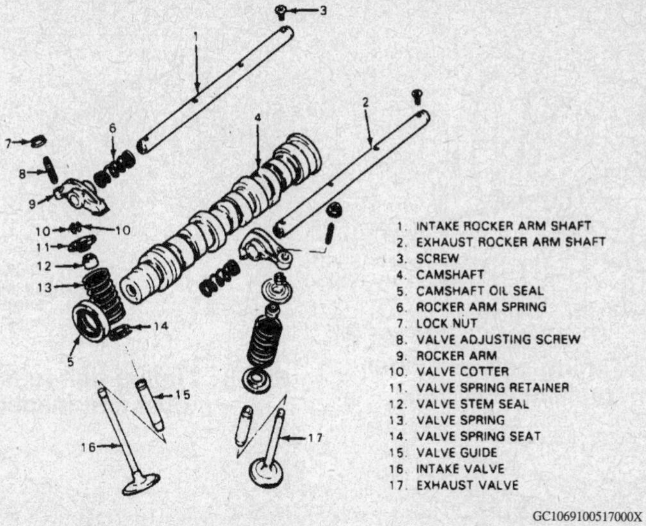

1. INTAKE ROCKER ARM SHAFT
2. EXHAUST ROCKER ARM SHAFT
3. SCREW
4. CAMSHAFT
5. CAMSHAFT OIL SEAL
6. ROCKER ARM SPRING
7. LOCK NUT
8. VALVE ADJUSTING SCREW
9. ROCKER ARM
10. VALVE COTTER
11. VALVE SPRING RETAINER
12. VALVE STEM SEAL
13. VALVE SPRING
14. VALVE SPRING SEAT
15. VALVE GUIDE
16. INTAKE VALVE
17. EXHAUST VALVE
GC1069100517000X

Fig. 5 Timing belt & cover replacement

VALVE ARRANGEMENT

FRONT TO REAR

1.0L...I-E-I-E-I-E

VALVE ADJUSTMENT

These engines are equipped with hydraulic valve lash adjusters and no adjustment is required.

VALVE GUIDES

Valves and valve guides are available in standard size only. The valve guide can be driven from cylinder bore using valve guide remover tool No. J-37968-1, or equivalent. The valve guide should be driven from the combustion chamber side of the cylinder head out through the valve spring side.

The cylinder head valve guide bore should be reamed with an 11mm reamer prior to valve guide Installation. Heat cylinder head to 176 to 212°F, then drive valve guide into cylinder head bore using valve guide remover tool No. J-37968-1 and valve guide installer tool No. J-37968-2, or equivalent. Valve guide should be driven in until tool contacts cylinder head. Valve guide protrusion should be .45 inch from cylinder head surface. After Installation, ream valve guide with a 5.5 mm reamer.

HYDRAULIC VALVE LASH ADJUSTER SERVICE

Hydraulic valve lash adjusters should not be disassembled.

1. Remove camshaft as outlined under "Camshaft, Replace."
2. Remove hydraulic valve lash adjusters from cylinder head, **Fig. 3.**
3. Check hydraulic valve lash adjusters for wear and damage and replace as necessary.
4. Using a micrometer, measure outside diameter of hydraulic valve lash adjuster. Outside diameter should be 1.2188 to 1.2194 inches.
5. Measure hydraulic valve lash adjuster bore in cylinder head. Bore diameter should be 1.2205 to 1.2214 inches.
6. To determine hydraulic valve lash adjuster to cylinder head bore clearance, subtract adjuster outside diameter from cylinder head adjuster bore diameter. Adjuster to bore clearance should be .0010 to .0025 inch. If clearance is greater than .0059 inch, replace adjuster or cylinder head as necessary.
7. Place valve lash adjuster in clean engine oil prior to Installation. Also pour engine oil through camshaft journal oil holes, until oil is emitted from hydraulic valve lash adjuster oil holes, **Fig. 4.**
8. Apply engine oil to valve lash adjuster, then position adjuster in cylinder head bore and install camshaft.

TIMING BELT

REPLACE

REMOVAL

1. Disconnect battery ground cable, then raise and support vehicle.
2. Remove fender apron extension from right hand side of vehicle.
3. Remove water pump drive belt, then remove water pump pulley.
4. Remove four attaching bolts and crankshaft pulley.
5. Remove outer timing belt cover, **Fig. 5.**
6. Align camshaft and crankshaft timing marks, **Fig. 6.**
7. Remove timing belt tensioner, tensioner plate, spring and damper.
8. Remove timing belt.

INSPECTION

Check timing belt for wear and cracks and replace as necessary. Check timing

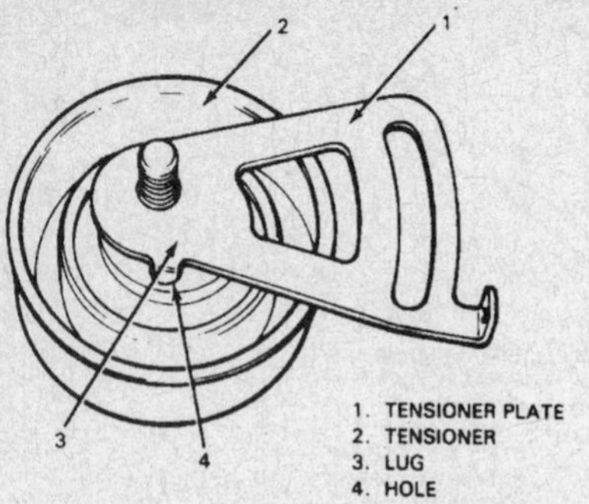
1. TENSIONER PLATE
2. TENSIONER
3. LUG
4. HOLE

GC1069100519000X

Fig. 7 Timing belt tensioner replacement

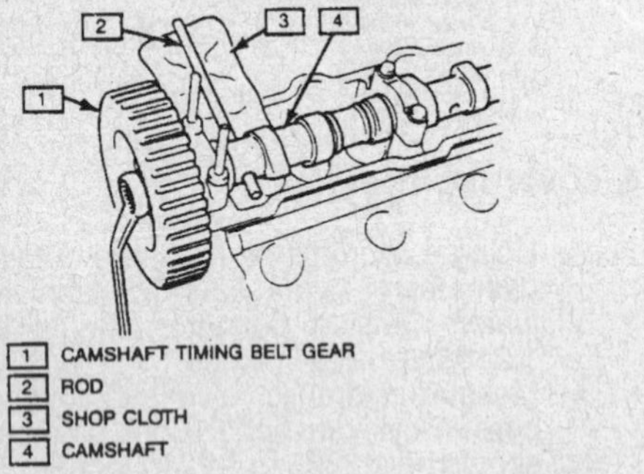
CAMSHAFT TIMING BELT GEAR
ROD
SHOP CLOTH
CAMSHAFT

GC1069100522000X

Fig. 10 Camshaft sprocket bolt replacement

belt tensioner for smoothness of rotation and replace as necessary.

INSTALLATION

1. Position lug on tensioner plate to hole in tensioner, **Fig. 7.**
2. Position tensioner and tensioner plate to engine, then install and hand tighten attaching bolt. Ensure tensioner and tensioner plate move in the same direction, **Fig. 8.** If movement is not as indicated, remove tensioner and reinsert tensioner plate lug into tensioner.
3. Ensure camshaft and crankshaft timing marks are aligned, **Fig. 6.**
4. With tensioner plate pushed upward, install timing belt over camshaft and crankshaft pulleys. **Arrow on timing belt should face toward direction of crankshaft rotation. When installing timing belt, keep drive side of belt free of slack.**
5. Install tensioner spring and damper, then hand tighten tensioner stud.
6. Rotate crankshaft two revolutions clockwise direction to remove slack from belt. **Ensure slack is removed from drive belt and that camshaft and crankshaft timing marks are aligned.**
7. Tighten tensioner stud and bolt to specification.
8. Install timing belt outer cover and crankshaft pulley. **Ensure seal is between oil pump housing and water pump.**
9. Install water pump pulley and drive belt.
10. Install right hand side fender apron extension, then lower vehicle and connect battery ground cable.

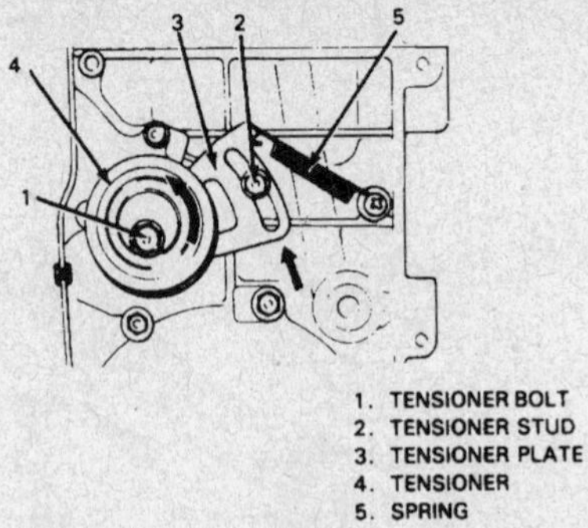
1. TENSIONER BOLT
2. TENSIONER STUD
3. TENSIONER PLATE
4. TENSIONER
5. SPRING

GC1069100520000X

Fig. 8 Timing belt tensioner plate movement inspection

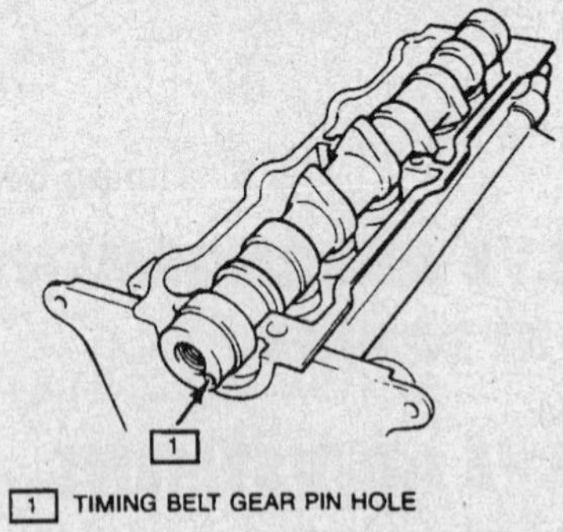
TIMING BELT GEAR PIN HOLE

GC1069100523000X

Fig. 11 Camshaft sprocket pin hole position

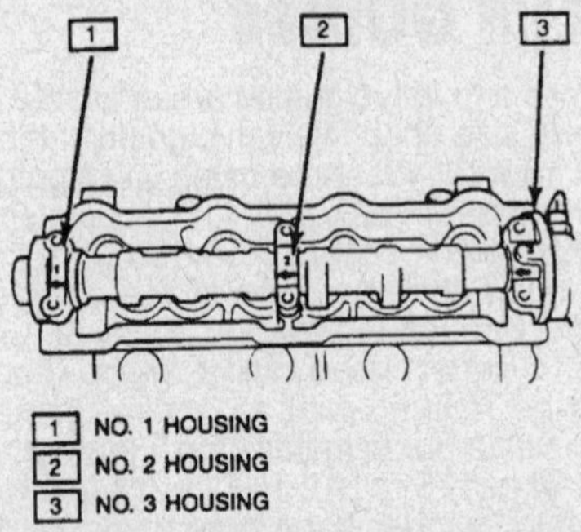
NO. 1 HOUSING
NO. 2 HOUSING
NO. 3 HOUSING

GC1069100525000X

Fig. 13 Camshaft housing locations

CAMSHAFT

REPLACE

REMOVAL

1. Disconnect battery ground cable.
2. Remove air cleaner assembly, then remove cylinder head cover.
3. Remove distributor from cylinder head.
4. Remove timing belt as outlined under "Timing Belt, Replace."
5. After timing belt has been removed, position crankshaft sprocket key, **Fig. 9.**
6. Hold camshaft in position by inserting a rod into .39 inch hole in camshaft, then remove camshaft sprocket retaining bolt, **Fig. 10.** Place shop cloth under rod to prevent damage to cylinder head surface.
7. Remove camshaft housings to cylinder head attaching bolts and studs, **Fig. 3.**
8. Remove camshaft from cylinder head. **Hydraulic valve lash adjusters should also be removed and placed in engine oil until Installation.**

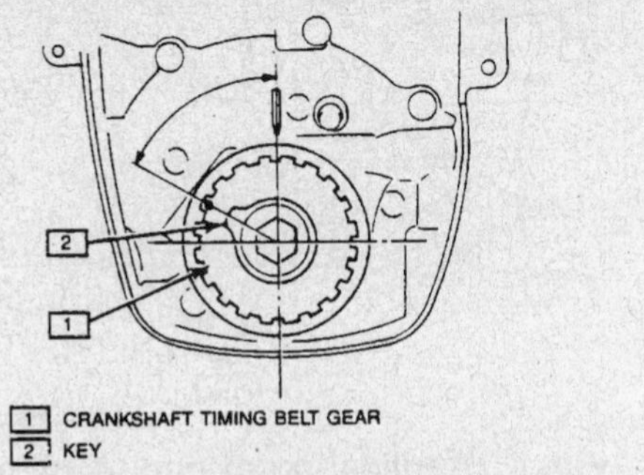
CRANKSHAFT TIMING BELT GEAR
KEY

GC1069100521000X

Fig. 9 Crankshaft sprocket key position

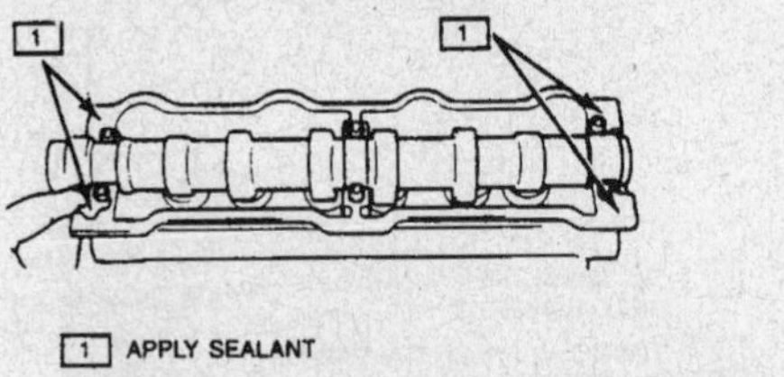
APPLY SEALANT

GC1069100524000X

Fig. 12 Camshaft housing to cylinder head surface sealant application

INSTALLATION

1. Pour engine oil into camshaft journal oil holes until oil is emitted from hydraulic valve lash adjuster holes, **Fig. 4.**
2. Lubricate valve lash adjusters with engine oil and install on cylinder head.
3. Lubricate camshaft with engine oil, then position on cylinder head with sprocket pin hole positioned, **Fig. 11.**
4. Lubricate camshaft journal bores in camshaft housing with engine oil.
5. Apply sealant to cylinder head mating surface of camshaft housings No. 1 and No. 3, **Fig. 12.**
6. Position camshaft housings over camshaft and onto cylinder head mating surface. **Arrow on camshaft housing should face camshaft sprocket side of cylinder head.** Camshaft housings are numbered from 1 to 3. The housings are positioned on the cylinder head in numerical order, starting with No. 1 at camshaft sprocket side of cylinder head, **Fig. 13.**
7. Apply engine oil to camshaft housing attaching bolts and studs, then loosely install bolts and studs. Tighten bolts and studs in sequence to specification, **Fig. 14.**
8. Apply engine oil to camshaft oil seal lip, then install seal. Seal surface should be flush with housing surface.
9. Hold camshaft in position by inserting

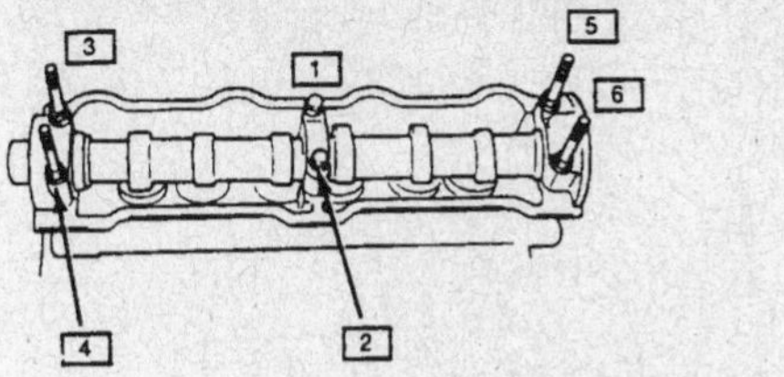
3
1
5
6
4
2

GC1069100526000X

Fig. 14 Camshaft housing bolt tightening sequence

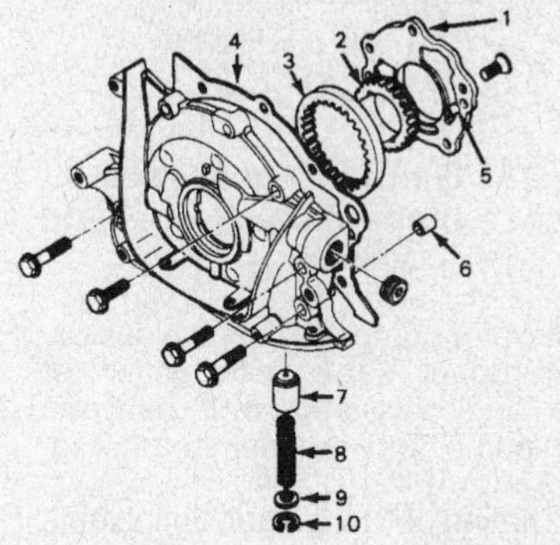
1. GEAR PLATE
2. INNER GEAR
3. OUTER GEAR
4. GASKET
5. PIN
6. PIN
7. RELIEF VALVE
8. SPRING
9. RETAINER
10. RETAINER RING

GC1099100087000X

Fig. 17 Rotor type (Trochoid) oil pump replacement

a rod into .39 inch hole in camshaft, then install and tighten camshaft sprocket retaining bolt, **Fig. 10** to specification. Place shop cloth under rod to prevent damage to cylinder head surface.
10. Install cylinder head cover.
11. Install timing belt as outlined under "Timing Belt, Replace."
12. Install ignition distributor, then install air cleaner assembly.
13. Connect battery ground cable, then adjust ignition timing.

PISTON & ROD ASSEMBLY

Refer to **Fig. 15** when assembling piston and connecting rod. When installing piston and connecting rod, arrow on piston head should face front of engine and oil hole in connecting rod should face intake manifold. When installing connecting rod cap, arrow on cap should face front of engine.

Measure rod bearing side clearance using a feeler gauge. Connecting rod bearing side clearance should be .0039 to .0078 inch.

PISTONS, PINS & RINGS

Pistons and rings are available in standard size and oversizes of .010 and .020 inch. Piston pins are supplied with pistons in matched sets.

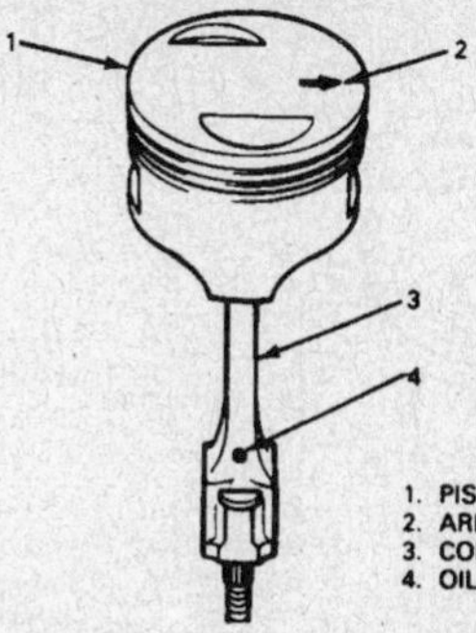
1. PISTON
2. ARROW MARK
3. CONNECTING ROD
4. OIL HOLE

GC1069100527000X

Fig. 15 Piston & connecting rod replacement

MAIN & ROD BEARINGS

Main and rod bearings are available in standard size and under size of .010 inch. Crankshaft thrust bearings are available in standard size and under size of .005 inch.

CRANKSHAFT REAR OIL SEAL

REPLACE

1. Remove transaxle as outlined under "Transaxle, Replace " in the "Automatic Transaxle" or "Clutch & Manual Transaxle" sections.
2. **On models with manual transaxle,** remove pressure plate and clutch disc.
3. **On all models,** remove flywheel.
4. Remove seal retainer, then remove seal from retainer.
5. Reverse procedure to install.

OIL PAN

REPLACE

1. Disconnect battery ground cable.
2. Raise and support vehicle.
3. Drain oil pan.
4. Remove flywheel dust cover.
5. Disconnect exhaust pipe at manifold.
6. Remove oil pan bolts and pan, **Fig. 16.**
7. Remove oil pump screen.
8. Reverse procedure to install. Apply continuous bead of silicon type sealer to oil pan flange inside bolt holes. When tightening oil pan attaching bolts, start at center and working outward. Tighten bolts to specifications.

OIL PUMP

REPLACE

REMOVAL

1. Refer to "Timing Belt, Replace" procedure to remove timing belt.
2. Refer to "Oil Pan, Replace" procedure to remove oil pan.
3. Remove crankshaft timing belt sprocket.
4. Remove alternator mounting bracket, if necessary.
5. **On models with A/C,** remove compressor mounting bracket.

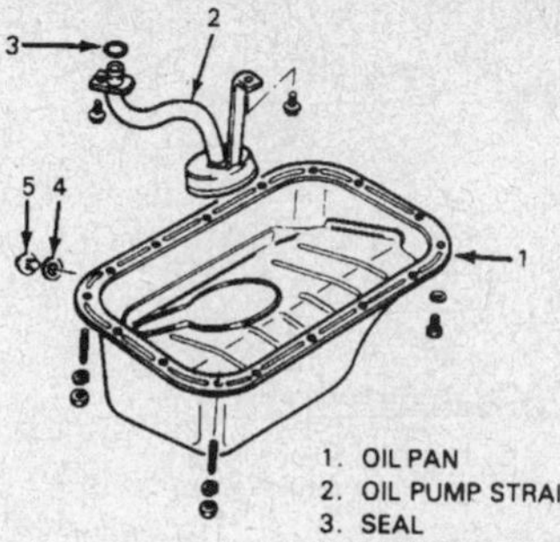
1. OIL PAN
2. OIL PUMP STRAINER
3. SEAL
4. DRAIN PLUG GASKET
5. DRAIN PLUG

GC1099100086000X

Fig. 16 Oil pan & pick-up tube replacement

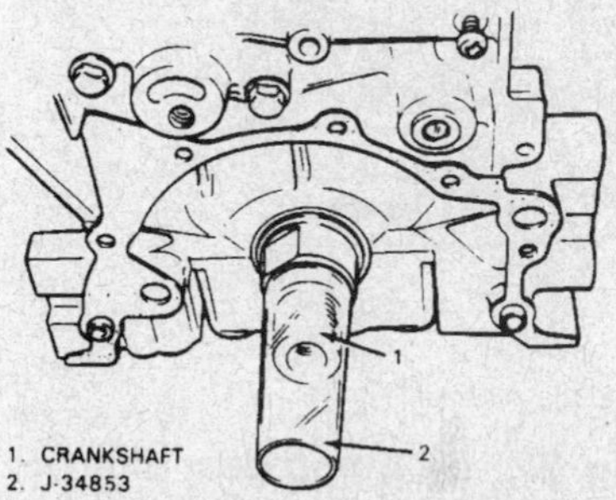
1. CRANKSHAFT
2. J-34853

GC1099100088000X

Fig. 18 Crankshaft oil seal guide tool Installation

6. **On all models,** remove alternator adjusting bolt and upper cover bolt, if necessary.
7. Remove oil pump bolts and pump, **Fig. 17.**

INSTALLATION

1. Install oil pump pins and gasket on engine block.
2. Install oil seal guide tool No. J-34853, or equivalent, onto crankshaft to prevent damage to oil seal lip, **Fig. 18.** Apply engine oil to Installation tool.
3. Install oil pump onto crankshaft and engine block. Note location of mounting bolts, **Fig. 19.** No. 1 bolts are shorter then No. 2 bolts in length. Install bolts, **Fig. 19,** then tighten to specifications.
4. After installing oil pump, check that oil seal lip is not twisted, then remove tool.
5. Install rubber seal between oil pump and water pump, **Fig. 20.**
6. If necessary, trim edges of oil pump seal flush with oil pan mating surface.
7. Install timing belt guide, key and crankshaft timing sprocket. Note that timing belt guide must be installed so that curved side faces oil pump.
8. Install timing belt and tensioner components.
9. Adjust water pump belt tension.
10. Fill crankcase.
11. Connect battery ground cable.
12. Run engine to ensure oil pressure is correct.

OIL PUMP SERVICE

1. Remove dipstick tube from oil pump.

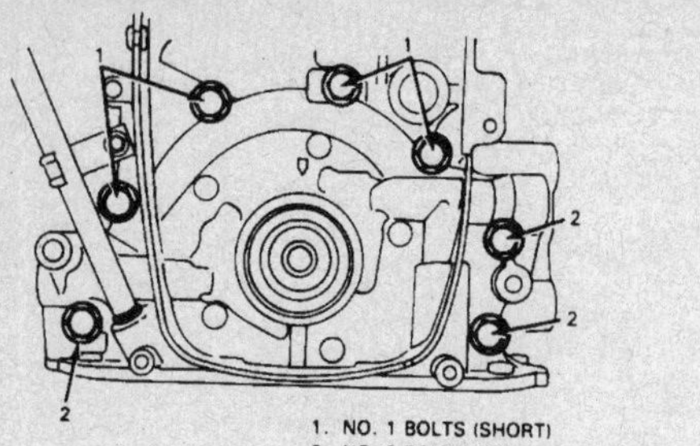
1. NO. 1 BOLTS (SHORT)
2. NO. 2 BOLTS (LONG)
GC1099100089000X

Fig. 19 Oil pump bolt location

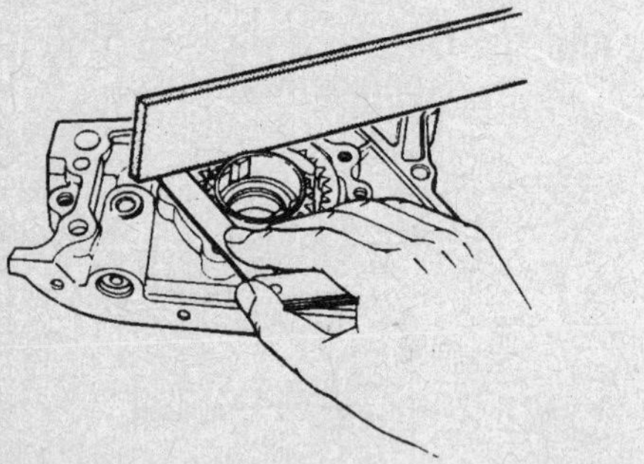
GC1099100092000X

Fig. 22 Oil pump gear side clearance inspection. Rotor type similar

2. Remove gear/rotor plate screws and gear plate.
3. Remove outer and inner gears/rotors.
4. Inspect oil seal lip for damage and replace as necessary.
5. Inspect outer and inner gears/rotors, gear/rotor plate, and oil pump case for excessive wear or damage.
6. Using feeler gauge, check radial clearance between outer gear/rotor and crescent, **Fig. 21.** If clearance exceeds .0122 inch, replace outer gear/rotor.
7. Using straightedge and feeler gauge, measure side clearance which should not exceed .0059 inch, **Fig. 22.**
8. Wash, clean and dry all oil pump parts.
9. Apply light coat of engine oil to inner and outer gears/rotors, oil seal lip portion, and inside surfaces of oil pump case and plate.
10. Install outer and inner gears/rotors in pump case.
11. Install gear/rotor plate and tighten screws securely. Check that gears turn smoothly by hand.
12. Install O-ring in pump case, then dipstick tube.

BELT TENSION DATA

Belt & Year	Belt Deflection Inch①
A/C Compressor	
1993–95	.20–.25
Alternator & Water Pump	
1993–95 New	.20–.27
1993–95 Used	.24–.31

① — With 22 lbs. pressure applied.

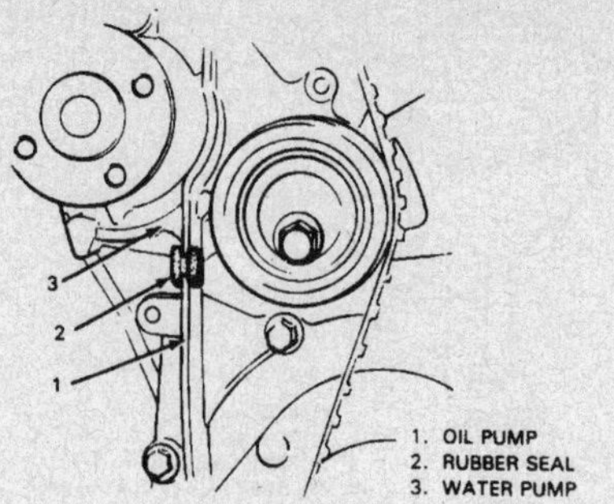
1. OIL PUMP
2. RUBBER SEAL
3. WATER PUMP
GC1099100090000X

Fig. 20 Rubber seal Installation

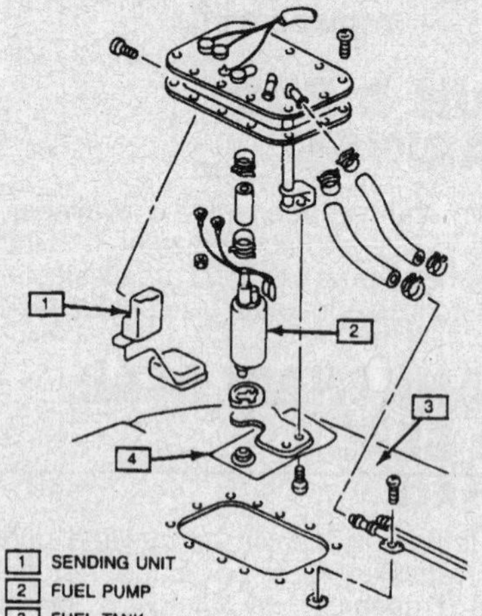
1 SENDING UNIT
2 FUEL PUMP
3 FUEL TANK
4 FUEL FILTER
GC1029102747000X

Fig. 24 Electric fuel pump & sending unit replacement

COOLING SYSTEM BLEED

These engines do not require a specified bleed procedure. After filling cooling system, run engine to operating temperature with radiator/pressure cap off. Air will then be automatically bled through cap opening.

THERMOSTAT

REPLACE

1. Disconnect battery ground cable.
2. Drain cooling system.
3. Remove radiator inlet hose at thermostat housing.
4. Remove thermostat housing and thermostat.
5. Clean both gasket surfaces thoroughly.
6. Reverse procedure to install.

WATER PUMP

REPLACE

1. Disconnect battery ground cable.
2. Drain cooling system.
3. Remove drive belt, water pump pulley, crankshaft pulley, timing belt outside cover, timing belt and timing belt tensioner.
4. Remove water pump mounting bolts and nuts, and water pump.

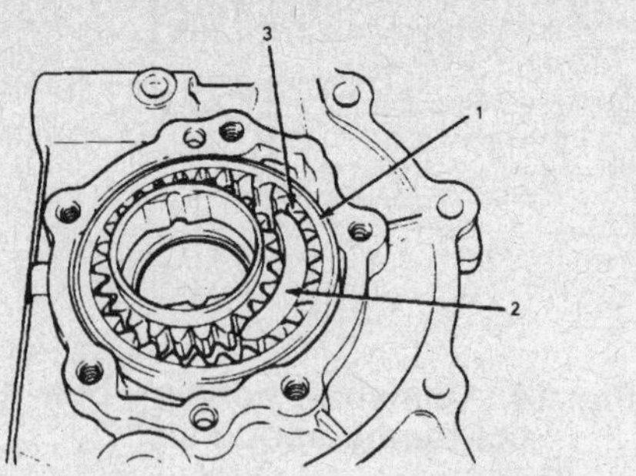
1. OUTER GAUGE
2. CRESCENT
3. CLEARANCE
GC1099100091000X

Fig. 21 Oil pump gear radial clearance inspection. Rotor type similar

5. Install water pump on engine block.
6. Install rubber seals between water pump and oil pump, and between water pump and cylinder head, **Fig. 23.**
7. Install timing belt tensioner, timing belt, timing belt outside cover, crankshaft pulley, water pump pulley and drive belt.
8. Tighten drive belt so it deflects .25–.35 inch on span between water pump pulley and crankshaft pulley.
9. Install valve cover and air cleaner.
10. Fill cooling system.
11. Connect battery ground cable.

RADIATOR

REPLACE

SWIFT

1. Disconnect battery ground cable.
2. Drain cooling system.
3. Remove upper, lower, and overflow hoses from radiator.
4. Disconnect cooling fan electrical connector.
5. **On models with automatic transaxle,** disconnect transaxle cooling lines from bottom of radiator.
6. **On all models,** remove upper radiator/fan mounting bolts, then remove radiator/fan assembly from vehicle.
7. Reverse procedure to install.

FUEL PUMP

REPLACE

1. Relieve fuel system pressure as follows:
   a. Remove fuel pump relay from main fuse panel located in engine compartment, **Fig. 1.**
   b. Operate engine until it stalls, then crank engine several times in three second intervals.
   c. Remove fuel tank filler cap to release vapor pressure, then reinstall cap.
   d. Place ignition switch in off position, then install fuel pump relay.
2. Disconnect battery ground cable.
3. Remove rear seat cushion, then disconnect fuel pump and sending unit

electrical connectors, then push harness through floor pan grommet.
4. Drain fuel tank, then disconnect inlet hose from fuel filter.
5. Disconnect fuel filler hose from fuel tank.
6. Disconnect vapor hoses and fuel feed and return hoses at fuel tank and pump.
7. Remove fuel tank mounting bolts, then lower fuel tank from vehicle.
8. Remove fuel pump to fuel tank attaching bolts, then remove fuel pump, **Fig. 24.**
9. Separate fuel pump from motor and sending unit as necessary.
10. Reverse procedure to install.

FUEL FILTER

REPLACE

The fuel filter is located at the lefthand front corner of the fuel tank assembly.

1. Relieve fuel system pressure as follows:
   a. Remove fuel pump relay from main fuse panel located in engine compartment, **Fig. 1.**
   b. Start engine and allow to run until it stalls, then crank engine several times in three second intervals.
   c. Remove fuel tank filler cap to release vapor pressure, then reinstall cap.
   d. Place ignition switch in off position, then install fuel pump relay.
2. Disconnect battery ground cable.
3. Raise and support vehicle, then place approved fuel holding container under fuel filter.
4. Disconnect fuel filter inlet hose clamp and hose from filter. **A small amount of fuel may be released after the fuel hose is disconnected. In order to reduce the chance of personal injury, cover the fittings with a shop towel.**
5. Disconnect fuel filter outlet hose clamp and hose from filter.
6. Remove mounting bracket and filter as an assembly.

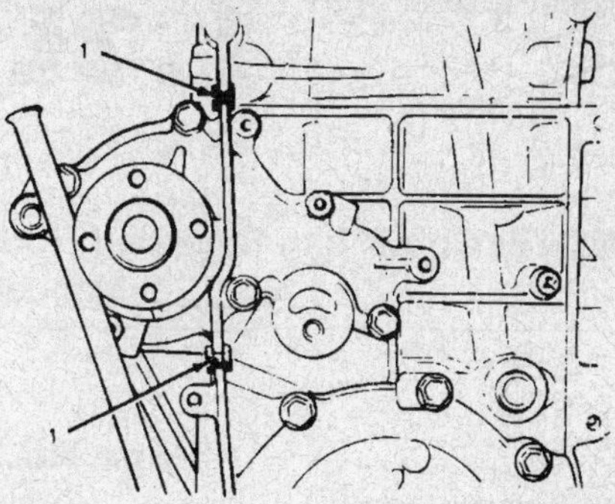
1
1
1. RUBBER SEAL
GC1099100093000X

Fig. 23 Water pump rubber seal replacement

7. Reverse procedure to install.

TIGHTENING SPECIFICATIONS

Tightening specifications are for clean and lightly lubricated threads only. Dry or dirty threads produce increased friction which prevents accurate measurement of tightness.

Component	Torque/Ft. Lbs.
Alternator Mounting Bolts & Nuts	17
Camshaft Housing To Cylinder Head	8
Camshaft Sprocket Bolt	44
Connecting Rod Cap Bolts	26
Crankshaft Pulley Bolts	8
Crankshaft Sprocket Bolt	81
Cylinder Head Bolts	54
Cylinder Head Cover	4
Exhaust Manifold To Cylinder Head	17
Flywheel To Crankshaft	45
Ignition Distributor To Cylinder Head	10
Intake Manifold To Cylinder Head	17
Main Bearing Cap Bolts	40
Oil Pan Drain Plug	26
Oil Pan To Engine	8
Oil Pressure Switch	10
Oil Pump Pickup Tube Bolts	8
Oil Pump Rotor Plate Screws	8
Oil Pump To Engine	8
Spark Plug	18
Starter Mounting Bolts	17
Timing Belt Cover Nuts & Bolts	8
Timing Belt Tensioner Bolt	20
Timing Belt Tensioner Stud	8
Water Pump To Engine	8–9

1.3L Engine (Samurai)

NOTE: On Air Bag Equipped Models, Refer To "Air Bag System Precautions" Located In The Front Of This Manual For System Disarming & Arming Procedures.

INDEX

	Page No.
Belt Tension Data	40-21
Component Service	40-17
Connecting Rod Bearings	40-17
Main Bearings	40-17
Oil Pump	40-18
Pistons & Connecting Rods	40-17
Rocker Arm & Shafts	40-17
Valve Guides	40-17
Compression Pressure	40-16
Cooling System Bleed	40-21
Engine Assemble	40-18
Engine Disassemble	40-16
Engine Rebuilding Specifications	40-165
Engine, Replace	40-16
Fuel Filter, Replace	40-22
Fuel Pump, Replace	40-21
Precautions	40-16
Air Bag Systems	40-16
Fuel System Pressure Relief	40-16
Radiator, Replace	40-21
Thermostat, Replace	40-21
Tightening Specifications	40-23
Timing Belt, Replace	40-20
Valve Adjustment	40-20
Valve Clearance Specifications	40-20
Water Pump, Replace	40-21

PRECAUTIONS

AIR BAG SYSTEMS

Refer to "Air Bag System Precautions" in the front of this manual for system disarming and arming procedures.

FUEL SYSTEM PRESSURE RELIEF

1. Place manual transmission models in Neutral or automatic transmission models in Park, then set parking brake and block drive wheels.
2. Disconnect coupler from fuel pump relay, **Fig. 1.**
3. Remove fuel filler cap to release fuel vapor pressure in tank, then install cap.
4. Start and run engine until it stalls. Repeat cranking engine three times for three seconds each time, to dissipate fuel pressure in fuel lines.

COMPRESSION PRESSURE

Standard compression pressure is 199 psi with a minimum of 170 psi. Maximum allowable difference between cylinders is 14.2 psi.

ENGINE

REPLACE

1. Relieve fuel system pressure as outlined under "Precautions."
2. Disconnect battery cables.
3. Disconnect electrical connectors from starter.
4. Disconnect electrical connectors from alternator.
5. Disconnect water temperature gauge and thermal switch electrical connectors from intake manifold, then the ground wire.
6. Disconnect carburetor fuel cut solenoid valve, vent solenoid valve and mixture control solenoid valve, then the TWSV (Three Way Solenoid Valve) and VSV (Vacuum Switching Valve).
7. Remove breather hoses from air cleaner case.
8. Remove air intake case from carburetor body, then the air inlet hose.
9. Disconnect accelerator cable from carburetor.
10. Disconnect vacuum hoses from Thermostatically Controlled Air Cleaner (TCAC) and canister from intake manifold.
11. Remove fuel tank filler cap to release fuel pressure, then disconnect fuel feed and return hoses from fuel pump.
12. Disconnect electrical connector from oil pressure sending unit and oxygen sensor.
13. Disconnect electrical connectors from transmission.
14. Disconnect electrical connector from distributor, then remove high tension cable from ignition coil.
15. Drain coolant system into appropriate container and disconnect radiator hoses from engine.
16. Remove fan shroud and cooling fan, then the radiator.
17. Disconnect brake booster vacuum hose from pipe.
18. Disconnect electrical connector from distributor gear case.
19. Remove bolts attaching gear shift lever boot and slide boot upward.
20. Slide inner gear shift lever dust boot upwards, then remove gear shift lever attaching bolts and gear shift lever.
21. Raise and support vehicle.
22. Disconnect exhaust pipe from manifold.
23. Disconnect clutch cable from engine mounting bracket and clutch release lever.
24. Drain transmission oil into appropriate container.
25. Disconnect propeller shafts from transmission and transfer case.
26. Install a suitable engine lifting device to prevent engine from dropping.
27. Remove catalytic converter bracket mounting bolts.
28. Remove transmission crossmember attaching bolts, then the crossmember.
29. Lower vehicle, then remove bolts securing engine mounts.
30. Remove engine and transmission as an assembly. **Before removing engine, ensure all hoses, cables and electrical connectors are disconnected.**
31. Remove clutch lower plate and separate transmission from engine.
32. Reverse procedure to install.

ENGINE DISASSEMBLE

1. Drain engine oil into appropriate container.
2. Using flywheel holder tool, No. 09924-17810, or equivalent, remove clutch cover attaching bolts, then the clutch cover and disc.
3. Disconnect spark plug wires and vacuum hoses noting direction for Installation, then remove distributor assembly.
4. Remove fuel pump attaching bolts, then the fuel pump and rod.
5. Remove crankshaft pulley attaching bolts, then the crankshaft pulley, **Fig. 2. It is not necessary to remove crankshaft pulley center bolt.**
6. Remove timing belt cover attaching bolts, then the timing belt cover.
7. Loosen tensioner bolt and stud, then remove timing belt from crankshaft timing belt pulley by pushing upward on tensioner with finger, **Fig. 3.**
8. Remove timing belt tensioner, tensioner plate and spring.
9. Using camshaft holder tool, No. 09917-68210, or equivalent, remove camshaft timing belt pulley.
10. Using flywheel holder tool, No. 09924-17810, or equivalent, so that crankshaft will not rotate, remove crankshaft timing belt pulley bolt, pulley and belt guide, **Figs. 4 and 5.**
11. Remove crankshaft timing belt pulley key from crankshaft.

12. Remove water pump attaching bolts, then the water pump.
13. Remove exhaust manifold shield attaching bolts, then the shield.
14. Remove exhaust manifold attaching bolts, then the exhaust manifold.
15. Remove oil filter.
16. Remove hoses from water pump inlet pipe.
17. Disconnect positive PCV hose from valve cover.
18. Remove intake manifold attaching bolts, then the intake and carburetor as an assembly.
19. Remove water pump inlet pipe attaching bolts, then the inlet pipe.
20. Remove valve cover attaching bolts, then the valve cover.
21. Loosen all valve adjusting screws and rocker arm shaft bolts, then pull out rocker arm shaft while separating rocker arms and springs.
22. Remove camshaft from rear of engine.
23. Remove cylinder head attaching bolts, then the cylinder head.
24. Using a suitable spring compressor, compress valve springs and remove valve locks, then the spring and valve.
25. Using a suitable screwdriver, remove valve stem oil seals from valve guides, then the valve spring seats. **Do not reuse oil seals after removal.**
26. Using flywheel holder tool, No. 09924-17810, or equivalent, remove flywheel attaching bolts, then the flywheel.
27. Remove oil dipstick attaching bolt, then the oil dipstick.
28. Remove oil pan attaching bolts, then the oil pan.
29. Remove oil pump strainer attaching bolts, then the oil pump strainer.
30. Remove connecting rod bearing cap bolts, then the bearing caps noting direction for Installation.
31. Remove carbon top of each cylinder bore, before removing pistons from cylinder.
32. Remove piston and connecting rod assemblies out through top of cylinder bore. **Before removing pistons, scribe cylinder number on top of pistons and ensure each bearing cap matches rod and piston assemblies for Installation.**
33. Remove oil pump attaching bolts, then the oil pump and pump rotor plate.
34. Remove oil seal housing attaching bolts, then the oil seal housing.
35. Remove crankshaft bearing cap bolts, then the bearing caps noting direction for Installation.
36. Remove crankshaft from cylinder block.

COMPONENT SERVICE

ROCKER ARM & SHAFTS

1. Using a suitable micrometer and a bore gauge, measure rocker shaft diameter and rocker arm inside diameter. Note readings.
2. Rocker shaft diameter should be 0.628–0.629 inch (15.973–15.988 mm). If diameter is not as specified, replace shaft.

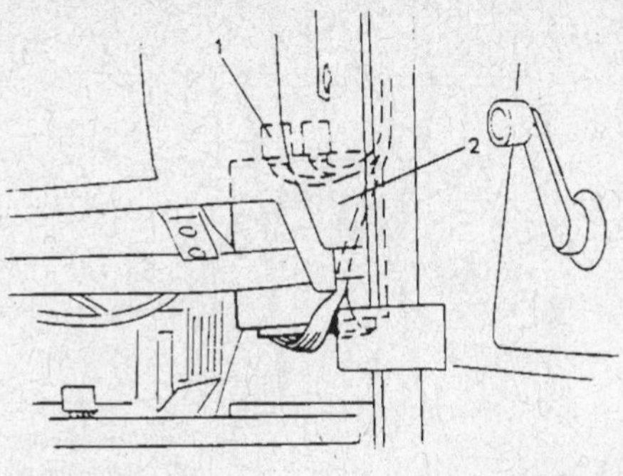
1
2

1. Fuel pump relay
2. ECM
SK8019100001000X

Fig. 1 Fuel system relay location

3. Rocker arm inside diameter should be 0.629–0.630 inch (16.000–16.018 mm). If diameter is not as specified, replace arm.
4. Take readings obtained in steps 2 and 3, and the difference between the two readings is arm to shaft clearance. Arm to shaft clearance should be 0.0005–0.0017 inch (0.012–0.045 mm). If clearance is not as specified, replace shaft or arm as necessary.
5. Using "V" blocks and a suitable dial indicator, check runout of rocker arm shaft. Runout should not exceed 0.004 inch (0.12 mm).

VALVE GUIDES

1. Using valve guide removal tool, No. 09916-44511, or equivalent, remove valve guides, **Fig. 6. Do not reuse valve guides after removal.**
2. Using a suitable micrometer and bore gauge, measure diameter of valve stem and valve guide inside diameter, to determine stem clearance in guide.
3. Clearances should be as follows:
   a. Intake valve stem diameter should be 0.2742–0.2748 inch (6.965–6.980 mm) and exhaust valve stem diameter 0.2737–0.2742 inch (6.950–6.965 mm).
   b. Valve guide inside diameter should be 0.2756–0.2761 inch (7.000–7.015 mm).
   c. Intake stem to guide clearance should be 0.0008–0.0019 inch (0.020–0.050 mm) and exhaust stem to guide 0.0014–0.0025 inch (0.035–0.065 mm).
4. If bore gauge is not available, check valve stem end deflection using a suitable dial indicator, **Fig. 7.** Move stem end back and forth, **Fig. 7.** and measure valve stem end deflection.
5. Valve stem end deflection should be as follows:
   a. Intake - 0.005 inch (0.14 mm).
   b. Exhaust - 0.007 inch (0.18 mm).
6. If specifications are not as specified, replace valve and guide as necessary.

PISTONS & CONNECTING RODS

Using a suitable piston ring expander, remove rings from pistons then position piston in an arbor press, and using a suitable drift, remove piston pins from pistons.

Each piston top is stamped with a No. 1 or 2, depending on its outer diameter. A No. 1 stamped piston, outer diameter should be 2.9121–2.9130 inches (73.98–73.88 mm) and a No. 2 stamped piston, outer diameter should be 2.9122–2.9126 inches (73.97–73.98 mm).

When installing piston and connecting rod assemblies, ensure number on piston top matches cylinder number stamped in block, **Fig. 8,** and arrows on top of pistons are facing front of engine, crankshaft pulley side, **Fig. 9.**

Pistons are available in standard sizes and oversizes of 0.0098 inch (0.25 mm) and 0.0196 inch (0.50 mm).

CONNECTING ROD BEARINGS

Two types of rod bearings are available, standard and 0.0098 inch (0.25 mm) undersize bearings. To distinguish then apart, the 0.0098 inch (0.25 mm) bearing has a stamped number (US025) on its back and the standard size bearing has no markings.

MAIN BEARINGS

Two types of main bearings are available, standard and 0.0098 inch (0.25 mm) undersize, and each of them has five kinds of bearings differing in tolerance. Each main bearing cap is stamped with a number and an arrow. When installing bearing cap, arrow must point towards crankshaft pulley side, **Fig. 10.** Check main bearing clearance as follows:

1. Clean bearings and crankshaft main journals using a suitable solvent.
2. Place a piece of Plastigage the full width of the bearing (parallel to crankshaft) on journal, avoiding oil passage hole.
3. Install bearing cap and tighten cap bolts to specification. **Do not rotate crankshaft while Plastigage is installed.**
4. Remove bearing cap, and using Plastigage scale, measure width at widest point, **Fig. 11.**
5. Bearing clearance should be 0.0008–0.0016 inch (0.020–0.040 mm) and must not exceed 0.0023 inch (0.060 mm). **A new standard bearing may produce proper clearance, if not, it will be necessary to regrind crankshaft journal for use of 0.0098 inch (0.25 mm) undersize bearing. After selecting appropriate bearing, recheck clearance.**

Standard Bearing Selection

1. Using a suitable micrometer, measure journal diameter. Crank webs of No. 2 and No. 3 cylinders have five stamped numbers, **Fig. 12.** These numbers represent the following journal diameters:
   a. No. 1 - 1.7714–1.7716 inches (44.994–45.000 mm).
   b. No. 2 - 1.7712–1.7714 inches (44.988–44.994 mm).
   c. No. 3 - 1.7710–1.7712 inches (44.982–44.988 mm).
2. The first, second, third, fourth and fifth (left to right) stamped numbers on

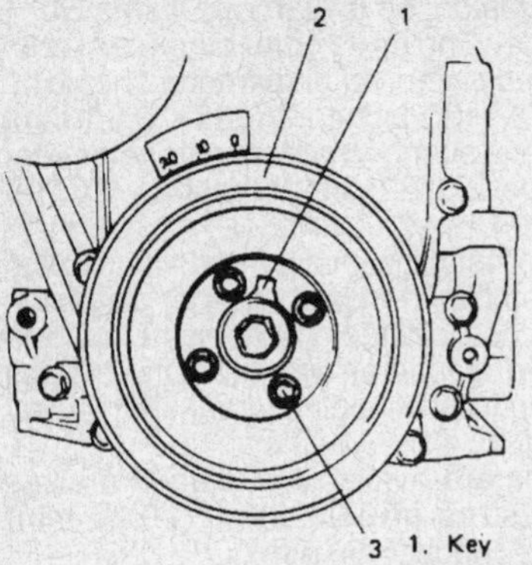
1. Key
2. Crankshaft pulley
3. Pulley bolt
SK1069100001000X

Fig. 2 Crankshaft pulley replacement

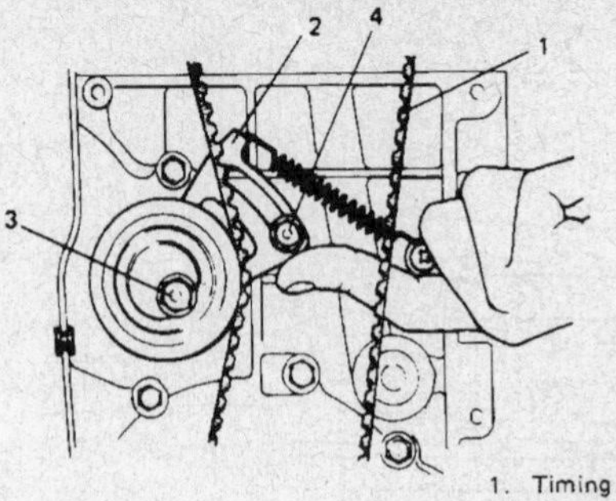
1. Timing belt
2. Tensioner plate
3. Tensioner bolt
4. Tensioner stud
SK1069100008000X

Fig. 3 Timing belt replacement

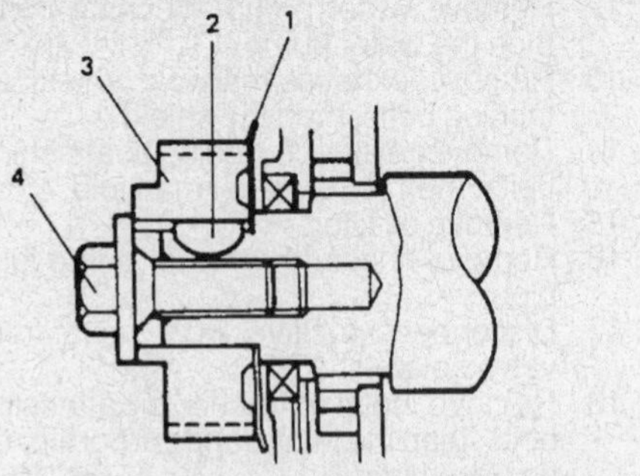
1. Timing belt guide
2. Key
3. Crankshaft timing belt pulley
4. Pulley bolt
SK1069100009000X

Fig. 4 Crankshaft timing pulley bolt removal

crank webs of No. 2 and No. 3 cylinders, **Fig. 12,** indicate journal diameters at bearing caps 1, 2, 3, 4 and 5. For example, the first No. 3 indicates that journal diameter at bearing No. 1 is within 1.7710–1.7712 (44.982–44.988 mm), and second No. 1 indicates that journal diameter at bearing cap No. 2 is within 1.7714–1.7716 inches (44.994–45.000 mm).

3. Using a suitable micrometer, check bearing cap bore without bearing. There are five letters stamped on mating surface of cylinder block, **Fig. 13.** These letters represents cap bore diameters as follows:
   a. "A" - 1.9292–1.9294 inches (49.000–49.006 mm).
   b. "B" - 1.9294–1.9296 inches (49.006–49.012 mm).
   c. "C" - 1.9296–1.9298 inches (49.012–49.018 mm).
4. The first, second, third, fourth and fifth (left to right) stamped letters indicate cap bore diameter of bearing caps 1, 2, 3, 4 and 5, **Fig. 13.** For example, the first letter "B" indicates that cap bore diameter of bearing cap No. 1 is within 1.9294–1.9296 inches (49.006–49.012 mm), and the fifth letter "A" indicates that cap bore diameter of cap No. 5 is within 1.9292–1.9294 inches (49.000–49.006 mm).
5. There are five types of standard bearings differing in thickness. Each bearing has a painted identification color on it. Each color indicates thickness at center of bearing as follows:
   a. Green - 0.0786–0.0787 inch (1.996–2.000 mm).
   b. Black - 0.0787–0.0788 inch (1.999–2.003 mm).
   c. Colorless (no paint) - 0.0788–0.0789 inch (2.002–2.006 mm).
   d. Yellow - 0.0789–0.0790 inch (2.005–2.009 mm).
   e. Blue - 0.0790–0.0791 inch (2.008–2.012 mm).
6. From the number stamped on crank webs of No. 2 and No. 3 cylinders, **Fig. 12,** and the letters stamped on surface of cylinder block, **Fig. 13,** determine new standard bearing to be installed to journal, by referring to table, **Fig. 14.**

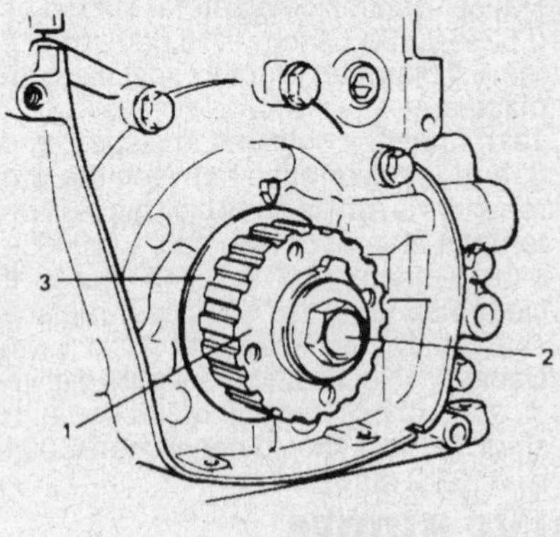
1. Crankshaft timing belt pulley
2. Pulley bolt
3. Timing belt guide
SK1069100010000X

Fig. 5 Crankshaft timing belt pulley removal

For example, if number stamped on crank web is "1" and letter stamped on cylinder block is "B," install new standard bearing with a "Black" painted identification mark.

7. Using Plastigage, check bearing clearance with new standard bearing selected. If clearance exceeds limits, use next thicker bearing and recheck clearance.
8. If replacing crankshaft or cylinder block, select new standard bearings by numbers stamped on new crankshaft or letters stamped on cylinder surface.

Undersize Bearing Selection

1. The 0.0098 inch (0.25 mm) undersize bearing is available in five different thicknesses. To distinguish them, each bearing has a painted identification color on it. Each color indicates thickness at center of bearing as follows:
   a. Green and red: 0.0835–0.0836 inch (2.121–2.125 mm).
   b. Black and red: 0.0836–0.0837 inch (2.124–2.128 mm).
   c. Red: 0.0837–0.0838 inch (2.127–2.131 mm).
   d. Yellow and red: 0.0838–0.0839 inch (2.130–2.134 mm).
   e. Blue and red: 0.0839–0.0840 inch (2.133–2.137 mm).
2. If crankshaft has to be re-ground to undersize, grind journal and select undersize bearing to be used as follows:
   a. Grind journal to obtain a finished diameter of 1.7612–1.7618 inches (44.732–44.750 mm).
   b. Using a suitable micrometer, measure re-ground journal diameter. Measurement should be made in two directions perpendicular to each other in order to check for out of round condition.
   c. From journal diameter measured above and letters stamped on cylinder block, select appropriate undersize bearing to be installed referring to **Fig. 15.**
   d. Check bearing clearance with undersize bearing selected.

OIL PUMP

1. Inspect oil seal lip for damage, and replace as necessary.
2. Inspect outer and inner rotors for excessive wear or damage.
3. Using a suitable feeler gauge, measure radial clearance between outer rotor and case, **Fig. 16.** Clearance should be 0.0122 inch (0.310 mm). If clearance is not as specified, replace outer rotor or case.
4. Using a straightedge and a suitable feeler gauge, measure oil pump side clearance, **Fig. 17.** Clearance should be 0.0059 inch (0.15 mm). If clearance is not as specified, replace outer or inner rotors as necessary.

ENGINE ASSEMBLE

1. Install selected main bearings into cylinder block, then lubricate bearings with oil. **Ensure bearing half with oil hole passage is installed into cylinder block and other half without oil groove to bearing cap. Also ensure both halves are painted with same color.**
2. Install thrust washer to cylinder block between No. 2 and No. 3 cylinders. **Ensure oil groove sides face crank webs.**
3. Install crankshaft into cylinder block, then lubricate journals with oil.
4. Install bearing caps onto journals. Ensure arrow on each cap is pointing towards crankshaft pulley. Tighten cap bolts to specifications, starting from

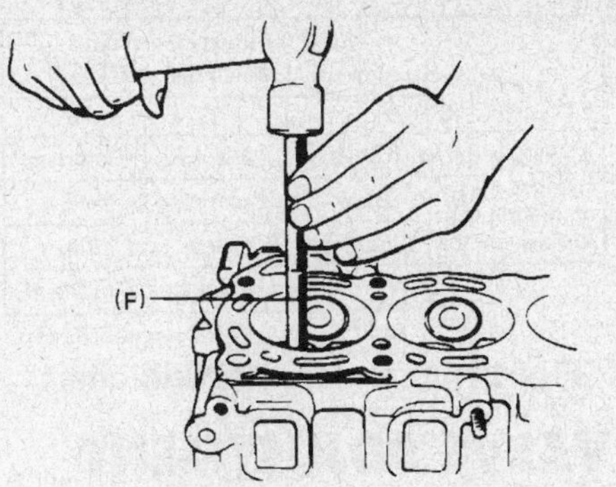
(F)

(F) Valve guide remover (Special tool 09916-44511

SK1069100011000X

Fig. 6 Valve guide removal

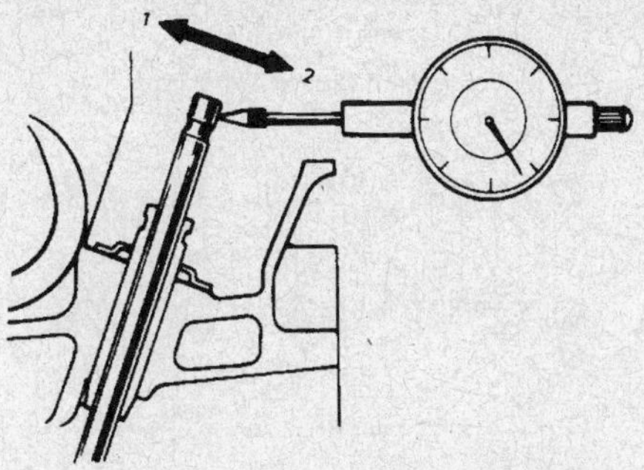
1
2

SK1069100012000X

Fig. 7 Valve stem end deflection inspection

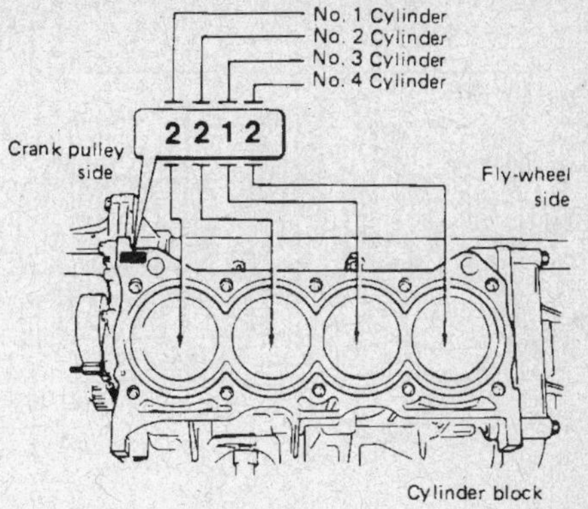
No. 1 Cylinder
No. 2 Cylinder
No. 3 Cylinder
No. 4 Cylinder
2 2 1 2
Crank pulley side
Fly-wheel side
Cylinder block

SK1069100013000X

Fig. 8 Engine block stamping location

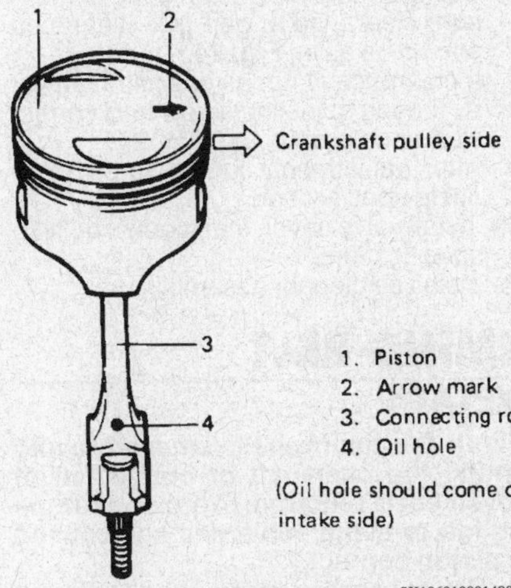
1
2
Crankshaft pulley side
3
4

1. Piston
2. Arrow mark
3. Connecting rod
4. Oil hole

(Oil hole should come on intake side)

SK1069100014000X

Fig. 9 Piston replacement

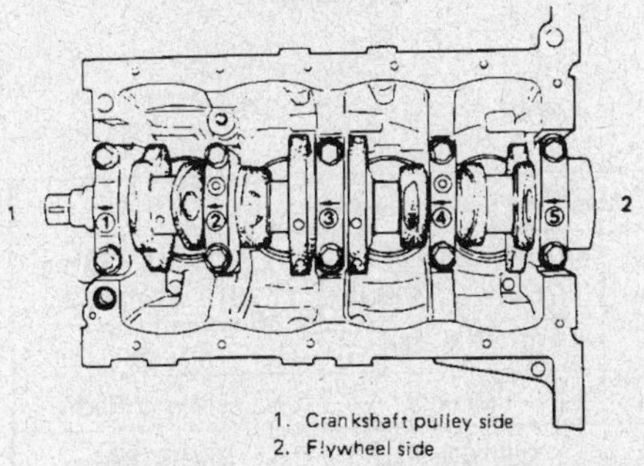
1
2
1. Crankshaft pulley side
2. Flywheel side

SK1069100015000X

Fig. 10 Main bearing cap replacement

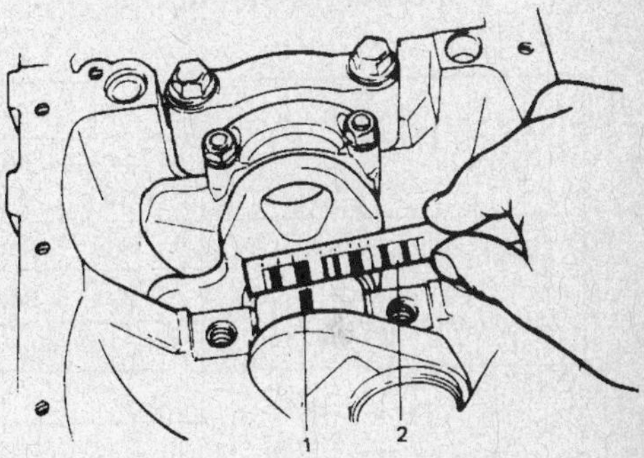
1
2

1. Gaging plastic
2. Scale

SK1069100016000X

Fig. 11 Plastigage measurement

crankshaft pulley side, No. 1. **After tightening cap bolts, ensure crankshaft rotates smoothly when turned by hand.**

5. Install oil seal housing and a new gasket. Apply oil to oil seal lip before installing. Tighten bolts to specification.
6. If oil pump was disassembled, assemble as follows:
   a. Clean all components using a suitable solvent.
   b. Lubricate inner and outer rotors, oil seal lip and inside surfaces of oil pump case and plate with engine oil.
   c. Install outer and inner rotors into pump case.
   d. Install gear plate. **After installing gear plate, ensure gears rotate smoothly by hand.**
7. Install two oil pump pins and a new gasket onto cylinder block.
8. Install oil guide tool, No. 09926-18210, or equivalent, onto crankshaft to prevent oil seal lip damage when installing oil pump assembly.
9. Install oil pump No. 1 and No. 2 bolt and tighten to specification.
10. Install piston rings onto piston as follows:
    a. Apply engine oil to piston pin bores in piston and rod and fit connect rod to piston, **Fig. 9.**
    b. Place piston on tool, No. 09910-38210, or equivalent, so arrow mark on piston head faces up. Press piston pin into piston and connecting rod, **Fig. 18.**
    c. Install piston second ring so marked side of second ring faces top of piston, **Fig. 19.** Note shape of ring 2. The first ring has been modified. The stamp marking has been eliminated, therefore there is no longer a specified up or down direction.
    d. Install oil ring spacer first, then the two rails.
    e. Align ring end gaps, **Fig. 20.** Pistons and connecting rod assemblies must be installed in block so arrows on pistons face front (pulley end) of engine, **Fig. 9.**
11. Install connecting rod bearing caps. Tighten cap nuts to specification. **Ensure arrow (marked on each bearing cap) points towards crankshaft pulley side.**
12. Using a suitable feeler gauge, measure side clearance of connecting rod big end, **Fig. 21.** Big end side clearance should be 0.0039–0.0078 inch (0.10–0.20 mm), and must not exceed 0.0137 inch (0.35 mm). If clearance exceeds limit, replace connecting rod.
13. Install oil pump strainer. Tighten bolts to specification.
14. Apply suitable sealant to oil pan, then install oil pan. Tighten bolts, starting at center, to specification.
15. Install gasket on drain plug, then drain plug into oil pan. Tighten drain plug to specification.
16. Install guide seal into oil pump case, then the oil dipstick.
17. Install flywheel to crankshaft, then the flywheel holder tool, No. 09924-17810, or equivalent. Tighten flywheel attaching bolts to specification.
18. Install valve guides into cylinder head as follows:
    a. Ream guide hole using a 12 mm reamer, to remove any burrs. Ensure guide hole diameter is 0.4736–0.4743 inch (12.030–12.048 mm) after reaming.
    b. Heat cylinder head to approximately 176–212°F (80–100°C), then using tools, No. 09917-88210 and 09916-57321, or equivalent, drive in new valve guide until valve guide protrudes 0.55 inch (14 mm) from cylinder head.
    c. Using a 7 mm reamer, ream valve guide bore. After reaming, clean bore.
19. Install valve spring seat to cylinder head, then the valve stem seal to valve guide.
20. Lubricate stem seal, valve guide bore and valve stem, then install valve into valve guide.
21. Install valve springs, then the retainers using a suitable valve spring compressor. **Ensure to install springs with bottom end (small pitch end) down to valve spring seat.**
22. Install new head gasket, then the cylinder head onto cylinder block. Using sequence shown in **Fig. 22, torque** cylinder head bolts in two or three

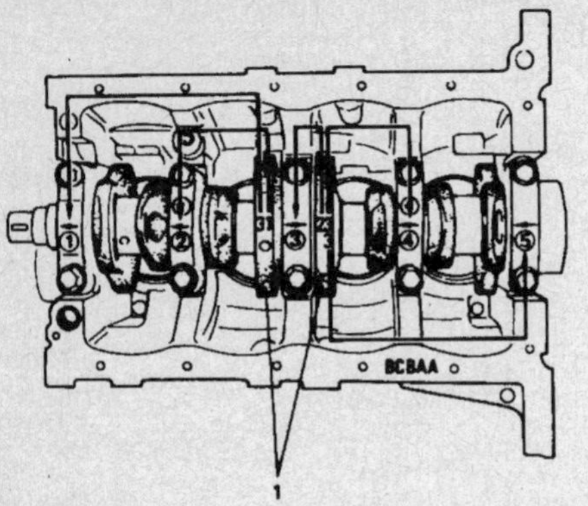
BCBAA
1

1. Crank webs of No. 2 and 3 cylinder

SK1069100017000X

Fig. 12 Crankshaft journal diameter selection

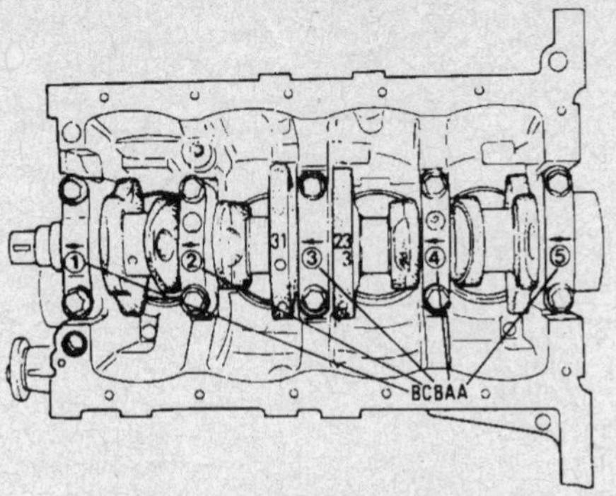
BCBAA

SK1069100018000X

Fig. 13 Cap bore diameter selection

		Numerals stamped on crank webs (Journals diameter)		
		1	2	3
Alphabets stamped on mating surface	A	Green	Black	Colorless
	B	Black	Colorless	Yellow
	C	Colorless	Yellow	Blue
		New standard bearing to be installed.		

SK1069100019000X

Fig. 14 Standard bearing chart

		Measured journal diameter		
		44.744 – 44.750 mm (1.7616 – 1.7618 in.)	44.738 – 44.744 mm (1.7614 – 1.7616 in.)	44.732 – 44.738 mm (1.7612 – 1.7614 in.)
Alphabets stamped on mating surface of cylinder block	A	Green & Red	Black & Red	Red only
	B	Black & Red	Red only	Yellow & Red
	C	Red only	Yellow & Red	Blue & Red
		Undersize bearing to be installed.		

SK1069100020000X

Fig. 15 Undersize bearing chart

passes to 51–54 ft. lbs.

23. Apply engine oil onto camshaft, then install camshaft from transmission case side.
24. Lubricate rocker arms and rocker arm shafts, then install rocker arms, springs and rocker shafts. **Rocker arm shafts are not identical. Dimensions of their stepped ends differ, Fig. 23. Install intake rocker arm shaft, facing stepped end to camshaft pulley side and exhaust rocker arm shaft, facing its stepped end to distributor side (rear side).**
25. Tighten rocker arms shaft screws to specification.
26. Install water inlet pipe to cylinder block. Install new O-ring to inlet pipe before installing.
27. Install intake manifold with carburetor using a new gasket. Tighten bolts to specification.
28. Connect water hoses to water inlet pipe, and secure hoses with clamps.
29. Install oil filter.
30. Install exhaust manifold using a new gasket, and tighten bolts to specification.
31. Install water pump and new gasket. Tighten bolts to specification.
32. Install two rubber seats, one between oil pump and water pump and the other between water pump and cylinder head.
33. Install timing belt inside cover, then the crankshaft timing belt guide, key and pulley. Tighten timing belt pulley bolt to specification.
34. Install camshaft timing belt pulley key, then the pulley. Tighten pulley bolt to specification.
35. Install timing belt tensioner, tensioner plate and spring.
36. Install timing belt, refer to "Timing Belt, Replace" as outlined.
37. Install crankshaft pulley key, then the crankshaft pulley. Tighten pulley bolts to specification.
38. Install alternator.
39. Install distributor case 0-ring to cylinder block, then the distributor case. Tighten bolts to specification. **After tightening distributor case, fill distributor case with approximately 1 ounce of engine oil.**
40. Install fuel pump rod, gasket and fuel pump onto cylinder head. Lubricate rod with engine oil before installing.
41. Install clutch disc and cover using alignment tool, No. 09923-38220, or equivalent, and tighten bolts to specification.
42. Install transmission assembly onto engine. Tighten bolts to specification.
43. Install distributor assembly into distributor case, then connect spark plug wires.
44. Adjust valve clearance, refer to "Valve Adjustment" as outlined.
45. Install valve cover. Tighten bolts to specification and check ignition timing.

VALVE CLEARANCE SPECIFICATIONS

Refer to **Fig. 24** for proper valve clearance.

VALVE ADJUSTMENT

1. Remove air cleaner assembly, then the valve cover.
2. Rotate crankshaft to position cam lobe and rocker arm, **Fig. 25.**
3. Using a suitable feeler gauge, measure clearance at gap (A). Clearance should be as in, **Fig. 24.**
4. If clearance is not as specified, adjust by turning adjusting screw until correct clearance is obtained, **Fig. 25.**
5. After adjustment, tighten screw locknut to specification.
6. Install valve cover, then tighten bolts to specification.
7. Install air cleaner assembly.

TIMING BELT

REPLACE

With the timing belt removed, avoid turning the camshaft or crankshaft. If movement is required, exercise extreme caution to avoid valve damage caused by piston contact.

1. Disconnect battery ground cable.
2. Loosen fan drive belt and remove bolts securing radiator fan shroud and cooling fan, then the shroud and fan.
3. Remove water pump belt and pump pulley.
4. Remove crankshaft pulley attaching bolts and the pulley, **Fig. 2.** It is not necessary to remove crankshaft pulley center bolt.
5. Remove timing belt cover attaching bolts, then the timing belt cover.
6. Loosen tensioner nut and bolt, **Fig. 26,** and remove timing belt.
7. Remove valve cover, then loosen all valve adjusting screws enough to allow free rotation of camshaft.
8. Rotate camshaft pulley clockwise and align timing mark on camshaft pulley with "V" mark on belt inside cover, **Fig. 27.**
9. Rotate crankshaft clockwise using a 17 mm wrench on crankshaft timing belt pulley bolt, **Fig. 28,** and align punch mark on timing belt pulley with arrow mark on oil pump, **Fig. 28.**
10. With all timing marks aligned, install timing belt ensuring drive side of belt is free from any slack with tensioner plate pushed up by finger, **Fig. 26. When installing timing belt, match arrow on timing belt with rotating direction of crankshaft.**
11. Rotate crankshaft two complete revolutions to allow belt to be free of any slack, then tighten tensioner and tensioner bolt to specification, **Fig. 29.**

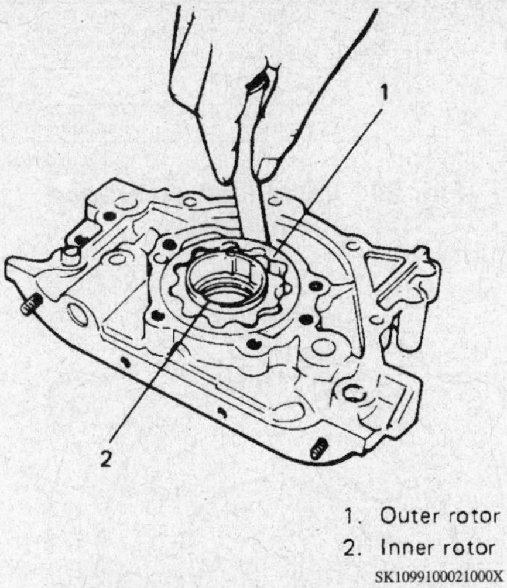
1
2
1. Outer rotor
2. Inner rotor
SK1099100021000X

Fig. 16 Oil pump gear radial clearance inspection

SK1099100022000X

Fig. 17 Oil pump gear side clearance inspection

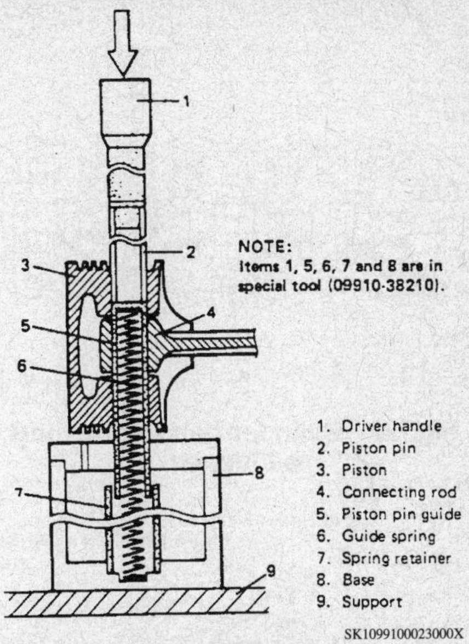
NOTE:
Items 1, 5, 6, 7 and 8 are in special tool (09910-38210).
1. Driver handle
2. Piston pin
3. Piston
4. Connecting rod
5. Piston pin guide
6. Guide spring
7. Spring retainer
8. Base
9. Support
SK1099100023000X

Fig. 18 Piston pin replacement

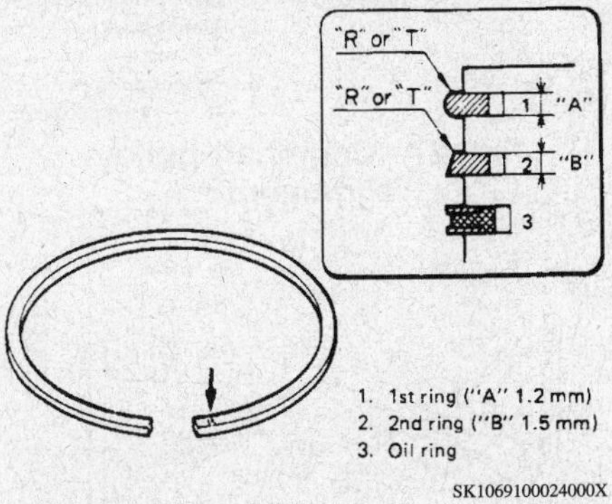
"R" or "T"
"R" or "T"
"A"
"B"
1. 1st ring ("A" 1.2 mm)
2. 2nd ring ("B" 1.5 mm)
3. Oil ring
SK1069100024000X

Fig. 19 Piston ring replacement

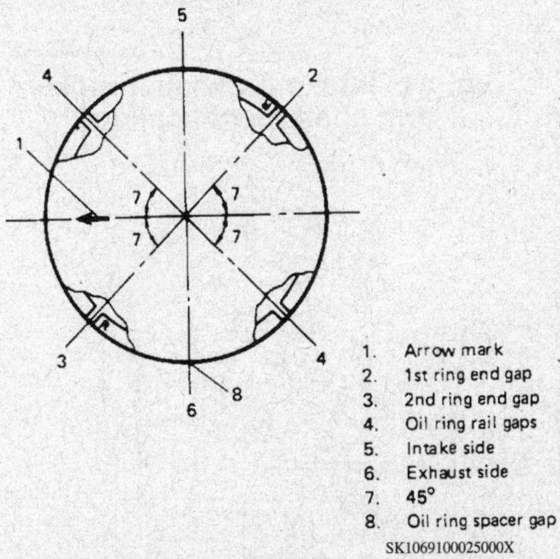
1. Arrow mark
2. 1st ring end gap
3. 2nd ring end gap
4. Oil ring rail gaps
5. Intake side
6. Exhaust side
7. 45°
8. Oil ring spacer gap
SK1069100025000X

Fig. 20 Ring end gap alignment

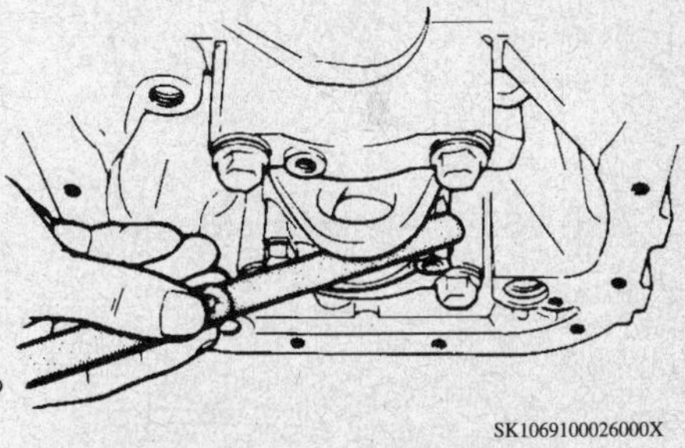
SK1069100026000X

Fig. 21 Rod bearing side clearance measurement

12. Install timing belt cover. Tighten bolts to specification.
13. Install water pump belt and pulley.
14. Install crankshaft pulley bolts and tighten to specification, **Fig. 2.**
15. Refer to "Valve Adjustment" as outlined to adjust valve clearance.

BELT TENSION DATA

Year	Belt	Belt Deflection Inch①
1993–95	Alternator & Water Pump	.24–.35

① — With 22 lbs. pressure applied.

COOLING SYSTEM BLEED

This engine does not require a specific bleed procedure. After filling coolant system, run engine to operating temperature with radiator/pressure cap off. Air will then be automatically bled through cap opening.

THERMOSTAT

REPLACE

1. Drain coolant system into appropriate container, then remove thermostat cap from intake manifold.
2. Remove thermostat.
3. Install thermostat, ensuring air breather valve is positioned to front side of engine.
4. Install gasket and thermostat cap to intake manifold, then fill and bleed coolant system.

WATER PUMP

REPLACE

1. Drain coolant system into appropriate container.
2. Remove radiator shroud attaching bolts and cooling fan assembly attaching bolts, then the radiator shroud and cooling fan as an assembly.
3. Loosen water pump drive belt tensioner, then remove water pump pulley and drive belt.
4. Remove four crankshaft pulley attaching bolts, **Fig. 2,** then the crankshaft pulley. **It is not necessary to loosen crankshaft pulley center bolt.**
5. Loosen tensioner bolt and stud, **Fig. 3,** then push up on tensioner plate and remove belt from crankshaft timing belt pulley and camshaft pulley.
6. Remove timing belt tensioner, plate and spring.
7. Remove water pump attaching bolts, then the water pump, **Fig. 30.**
8. Reverse procedure to install noting the following:
   a. Tighten water pump bolts to specification.
   b. Refer to "Timing Belt, Replace" to ensure timing belt is correctly installed.

RADIATOR, REPLACE

1. Disconnect battery ground cable.
2. Drain cooling system.
3. **On models equipped with automatic transmission,** disconnect transmission cooler lines at radiator.
4. **On all models,** remove cooling fan/clutch and radiator shroud.
5. Disconnect radiator inlet and outlet hoses, and reservoir tank hose.
6. Remove radiator and cooling fan motor.
7. Reverse procedure to install

FUEL PUMP

REPLACE

1. Relieve fuel system pressure as outlined under "Precautions."
2. Disconnect battery ground cable and level gauge lead wire.
3. Raise and support vehicle, then drain fuel tank into appropriate container.
4. Disconnect filler hose, fuel hoses and fuel pipe from fuel tank.

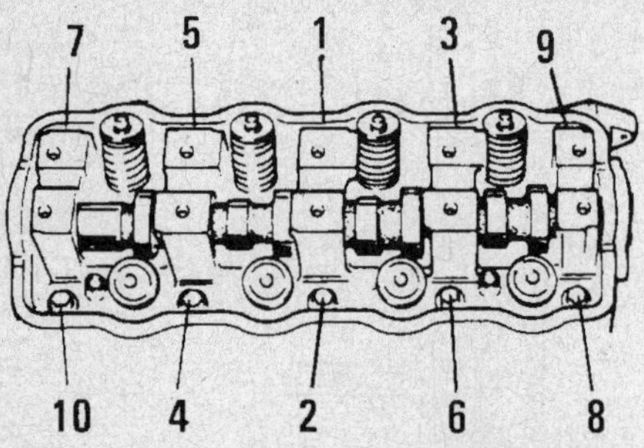
7
5
1
3
9
10
4
2
6
8

SK1069100027000X

Fig. 22 Cylinder head tightening sequence

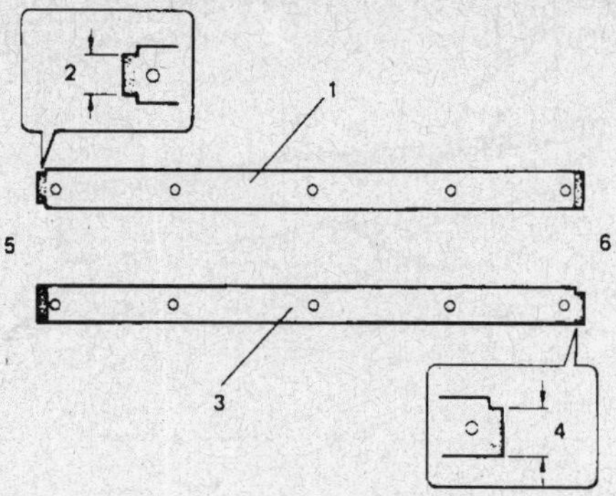
2
1
5
6
3
4

1. Intake rocker arm shaft
2. 14 mm (0.55 in)
3. Exhaust rocker arm shaft
4. 15 mm (0.59 in)
5. Camshaft pulley side
6. Distributor side

SK1069100028000X

Fig. 23 Intake & exhaust rocker arm shaft identification

		When cold (Coolant temperature is 15 – 25°C or 59 – 77°F)	When hot (Coolant temperature is 60 – 68°C or 140 – 154°F)
Valve lash (gap A) specification	Intake	0.13 - 0.17 mm (0.0051 - 0.0067 in)	0.23 - 0.27 mm (0.009 - 0.011 in)
	Exhaust	0.16 - 0.20 mm (0.0063 - 0.0079 in)	0.26 - 0.30 mm (0.0102 - 0.0118 in)

SK1069100007000X

Fig. 24 Valve lash clearance specification

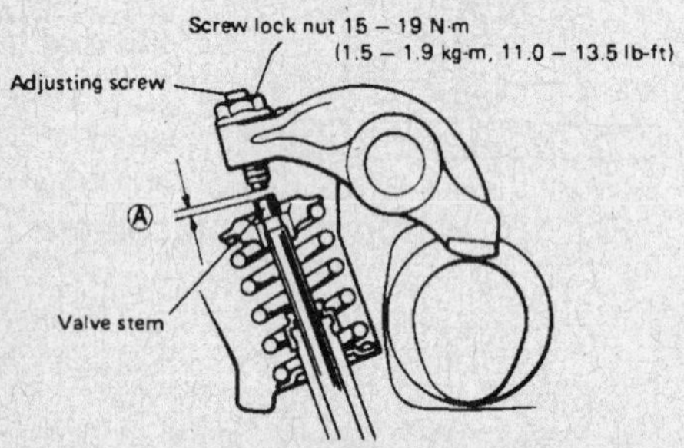
Screw lock nut 15 – 19 N·m
(1.5 – 1.9 kg-m, 11.0 – 13.5 lb-ft)
Adjusting screw
Ⓐ
Valve stem

SK1069100006000X

Fig. 25 Valve lash adjustment

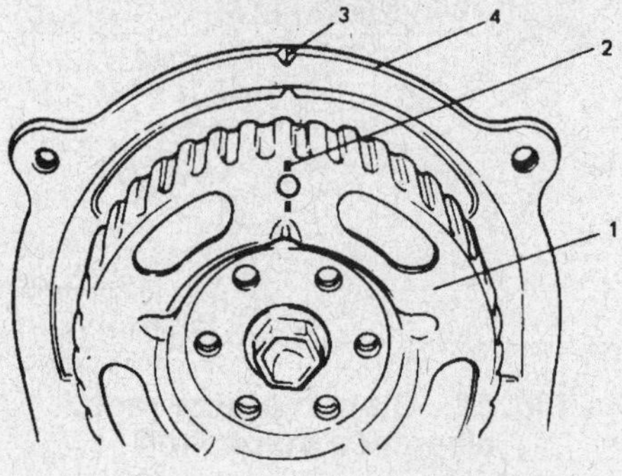
3
4
2
1

1. Camshaft timing pulley
2. Timing mark
3. "V" mark
4. Belt inside cover

SK1069100003000X

Fig. 27 Camshaft pulley alignment

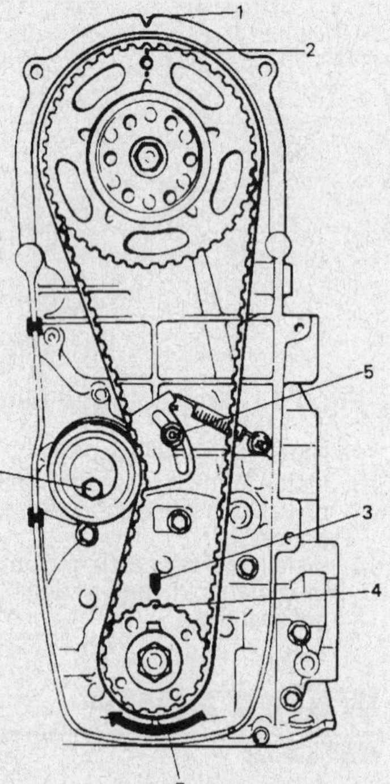
1
2
5
6
3
4
7

1. "V" mark
2. Timing mark
3. Arrow mark
4. Punch mark
5. Tensioner nut
6. Tensioner bolt
7. Turning direction

SK1069100002000X

Fig. 26 Timing belt replacement

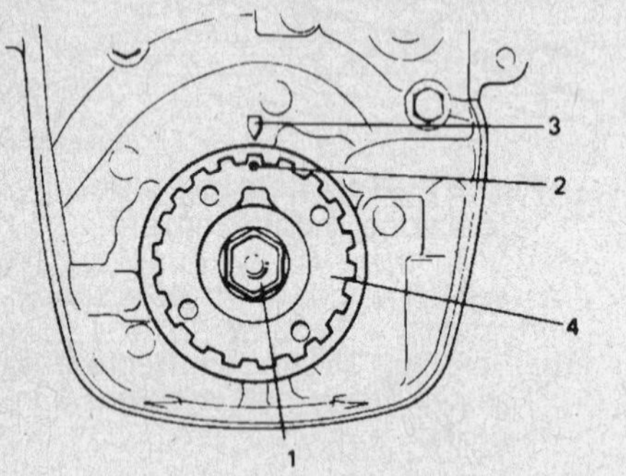
3
2
4
1

1. Crankshaft timing belt pulley bolt
2. Punch mark
3. Arrow mark
4. Crankshaft timing belt pulley

SK1069100004000X

Fig. 28 Timing belt pulley alignment

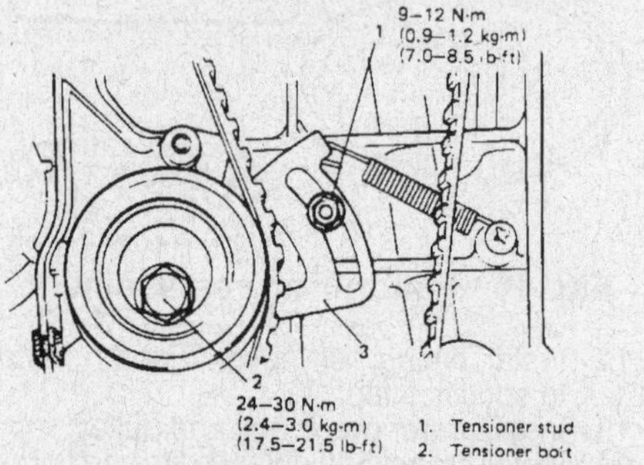
9–12 N·m
(0.9–1.2 kg-m)
(7.0–8.5 lb-ft)
1
2
3
24–30 N·m
(2.4–3.0 kg-m)
(17.5–21.5 lb-ft)

1. Tensioner stud
2. Tensioner bolt
3. Tensioner plate

SK1069100005000X

Fig. 29 Timing belt tension alignment

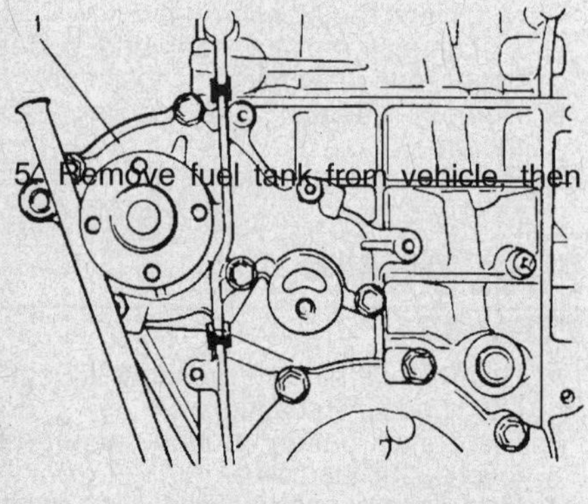
1

1. Water pump

SK1089100001000X

Fig. 30 Water pump replacement

5. Remove fuel tank from vehicle, then the fuel pump from fuel tank.
6. Reverse procedure to install.

FUEL FILTER

REPLACE

1. Relieve fuel system pressure as outlined under "Precautions."
2. Disconnect battery ground cable.
3. The fuel filter is located in the front part of the fuel tank, inside the righthand side of chassis. **Replacement must be performed in a well ventilated area and away from any open flames or gas hot water heaters.**
4. Hoist vehicle, then place fuel container under fuel filter.
5. Remove inlet and outlet pipes from fuel filter by using two wrenches, **Fig. 31.**
6. Remove fuel filter from chassis frame.
7. Reverse procedure to install, noting the following
   a. Using new gaskets, ensure gasket surfaces are free from any damage.
   b. Inlet and outlet pipes should come into recess of plate, **Fig. 32.**

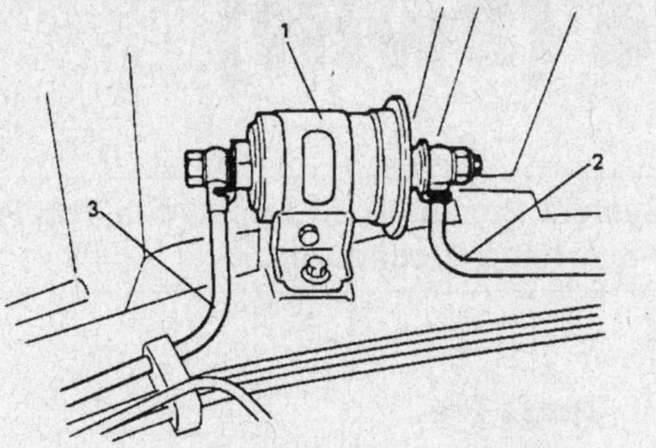
1
2
3
1. Fuel filter
2. Inlet pipe
3. Outlet pipe
SK1029100001000X

Fig. 31 Fuel filter location

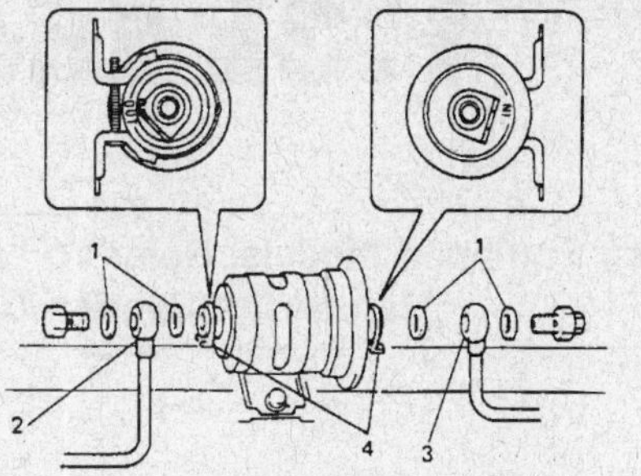
1
1
2
4
3
1. Gasket
2. Outlet pipe
3. Inlet pipe
4. Recess
SK1029100002000X

Fig. 32 Fuel filter replacement

TIGHTENING SPECIFICATIONS

Year	Component	Torque/Ft. Lbs.
1993–95	Air Temperature Sensor	26-39
	Camshaft Timing Belt Pulley Bolt	41-46
	Clutch Cover Bolt	14-20
	Connecting Rod Bearing Cap Nut	24-26
	Cooling Fan Nut	7
	Crankshaft Pulley Bolt	9
	Crankshaft Timing Belt Pulley Bolt	76-83
	Cylinder Head Bolt	①
	Cylinder Head Cover Bolt	3.5
	Distributor Case Bolt	6-8
	Exhaust Manifold Bolt	14-20
	Flywheel Attaching Bolt	42-47
	Injector Cover Screw	2
	Intake Manifold Bolt	14-20
	Main Bearing Cap Bolt	37-41
	Mechanical Fuel Pump Bolt	7-11
	Oil Filter Stand	14-18
	Oil Drain Plug	22-28
	Oil Pan Bolt	8
	Oil Pressure Switch	10
	Oil Pump Attaching Pump Bolt	8
	Oil Pump Rotor Plate Screw	8
	Oil Pump Strainer Bolt	8
	Oil Seal Housing Bolt	9
	Oxygen Sensor	33-39
	Rocker Arms Shaft Screw	8
	Spark Plugs	15-21
	Tensioner Bolt	18-21
	Tensioner Stud	8
	Throttle Body Mounting Bolt	14-20
	Throttle Position Sensor Bolt	3
	Timing Belt Cover Bolt	8
	Transmission To Engine Attaching Bolt	16-25
	Valve Adjusting Screw Locknut	11–13
	Water Pump Bolt	8
	Water Temperature Sensor	26-39

① — Refer to "Cylinder Head, Replace" for tightening procedure.

1.3L Engine (Swift)

NOTE: On Air Bag Equipped Models, Refer To "Air Bag System Precautions" Located In The Front Of This Manual For System Disarming & Arming Procedures.

INDEX

	Page No.
Belt Tension Data	40-35
Camshaft, Replace	40-30
DOHC	40-31
SOHC	40-30
Compression Pressure	40-24
Cooling System Bleed	40-35
Cylinder Head, Replace	40-26
Assembly	40-27
Disassembly	40-26
Inspection	40-27
Installation	40-28
Removal	40-26
Engine Rebuilding Specifications	40-165
Engine, Replace	40-24
Exhaust Manifold, Replace	40-26
Fuel Filter, Replace	40-36
Fuel Pump, Replace	40-36
Intake Manifold, Replace	40-25
DOHC	40-25
SOHC	40-25
Main & Rod Bearings	40-33
Connecting Rod Bearing	40-34
Main Bearings	40-33
Oil Pump Service	40-34
Assembly	40-35
Disassembly	40-34
Inspection	40-34
Installation	40-35
Removal	40-34
Piston & Rod Assembly	40-32
Precautions	40-24
Air Bag Systems	40-24
Fuel System Pressure Relief	40-24
Radiator, Replace	40-36
Rocker Arms, Replace	40-29
Rocker Arms	40-29
Thermostat, Replace	40-35
DOHC	40-35
SOHC	40-35
Tightening Specifications	40-36
DOHC Engine	40-36
SOHC Engine	40-37
Timing Belt, Replace	40-29
DOHC	40-29
SOHC	40-30
Valve Adjustment	40-28
SOHC	40-28
Valve Clearance Specifications	40-28
Valve Lifters	40-28
Water Pump, Replace	40-35

PRECAUTIONS

AIR BAG SYSTEMS

Refer to "Air Bag System Precautions" in the front of this manual for system disarming and arming procedures.

FUEL SYSTEM PRESSURE RELIEF

1. Place manual transmission models in Neutral or automatic transmission models in Park, then set parking brake and block drive wheels.
2. Remove main fuse box cover and engine cooling water reservoir.
3. Detach main fuse box from body and disconnect coupler from fuel pump relay, **Fig. 1.**
4. Remove fuel filler cap to release fuel vapor pressure in tank, then install cap.
5. Start and run engine until it stalls. Repeat cranking engine three times for three seconds each time to dissipate fuel pressure in fuel lines.

COMPRESSION PRESSURE

Standard compression pressure is 199 psi with a minimum of 154 psi. Maximum allowable difference between cylinders is 14.2 psi.

ENGINE

REPLACE

1. Relieve fuel system pressure as outlined under "Precautions."

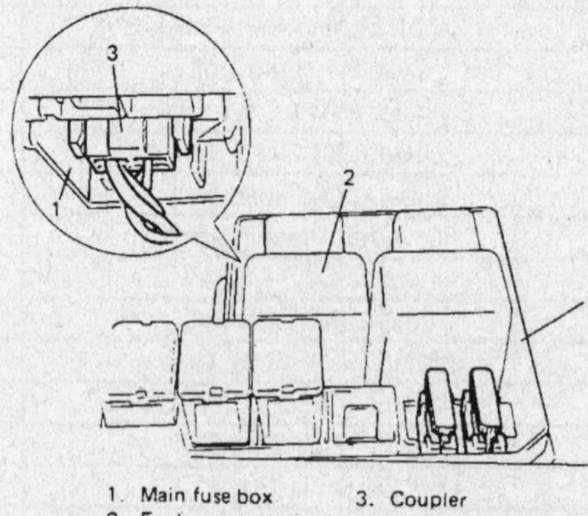

3
2
1
1
1. Main fuse box
2. Fuel pump relay
3. Coupler
SK8019100002000X

Fig. 1 Fuel pump relay coupler location

2. Remove battery and tray, then the engine hood.
3. Drain coolant system into appropriate container.
4. Remove air cleaner assembly with Air Flow Meter (AFM) outlet hose.
5. Remove radiator cooling fan, then the battery ground cable from transmission.
6. Disconnect following electrical wires:
   a. **On models with automatic transmissions,** disconnect direct clutch and second brake connectors.
   b. Disconnect shift switch and speed sensor connectors.
   c. **On models with manual transmissions,** disconnect back-up light switch connector.
   d. **On all models,** disconnect noise filter ground wire, then the Idle Speed Control (ISC) valve connector.
   e. Disconnect high tension cable from ignition coil, then the distributor Crank Angle Sensor (CAS) connector.
   f. **On California models,** disconnect Recirculated Exhaust Gas Temperature Sensor (REGTS) and Exhaust Gas Recirculation Vacuum Switching Valve (EGR VSV) connectors.
   g. **On all models,** disconnect Water Temperature Sensor (WTS) and oxygen sensor connectors.
   h. Disconnect canister purge VSV connector, then the ground wire from intake manifold.
   i. Disconnect Throttle Position Sensor (TPS) and fuel injector connectors.
   j. Disconnect all electrical wires from alternator and starter.
   k. Disconnect oil pressure gauge connector.
   l. Ensure all wires are free of clamps on engine.
7. Disconnect following cables:
   a. Disconnect accelerator cable from throttle lever and bracket.
   b. **On models with manual transmission,** disconnect clutch cable.
   c. **On models with automatic transmission,** disconnect gear select and oil pressure control cables.
   d. **On all models,** disconnect speed meter cable from transmission.
8. Disconnect brake booster and canister purge hoses.
9. **On California models,** disconnect A/C VSV hose.

10. **On all models,** disconnect fuel feed and return hoses.
11. Disconnect heater inlet and outlet hoses, then remove charcoal canister from body.
12. Raise and support vehicle, then remove exhaust pipe from manifold.
13. **On models with manual transmission,** remove gear shift control shaft and extension rod.
14. **On all models,** drain engine and transmission oil into appropriate container.
15. Remove lefthand driveshaft joint from differential gear of transmission. Remove righthand driveshaft joint from center bearing support.
16. **On models with automatic transmission,** remove rear torque rod bracket from transmission case.
17. **On all models,** lower vehicle, then install engine lifting device.
18. **On models with manual transmission,** remove rear mounting from body. On automatic transmission, remove rear mounting nut, **Figs. 2 and 3.**
19. **On all models,** remove lefthand side engine mounting bracket bolts and mounting bolt.
20. Remove righthand side engine mounting from bracket.
21. **Ensure all hoses, electric wires and cable are disconnected from engine and transmission.**
22. Remove engine and transmission from vehicle.
23. Remove torque convertor housing lower plate.
24. Remove driveplate bolts. Use flat head screwdriver to lock driveplate and driveplate gear.
25. Remove engine to transmission attaching bolts, then separate engine from transmission.
26. Reverse procedure to install, tighten all bolts and nuts to specification.

INTAKE MANIFOLD

REPLACE

DOHC

1. Disconnect battery ground cable, then drain coolant system into appropriate container.
2. Disconnect following hoses:
   a. Disconnect AFM and PCV hoses.
   b. Disconnect cylinder head breather and brake booster hoses.
   c. **On California models,** disconnect A/C VSV, EGR modulator and EGR vacuum valve hoses.
   d. **On all models,** disconnect canister purge hose from canister, then the vacuum hose from fuel pressure regulator.
3. Disconnect following wires:
   a. Disconnect ISC solenoid valve and canister purge VSV connectors.
   b. **On California models,** disconnect REGTS and EGR VSV connectors.
   c. **On all models,** disconnect TPS connector, then the ground wires from intake manifold.
4. Remove accelerator cable from throttle valve lever and bracket.

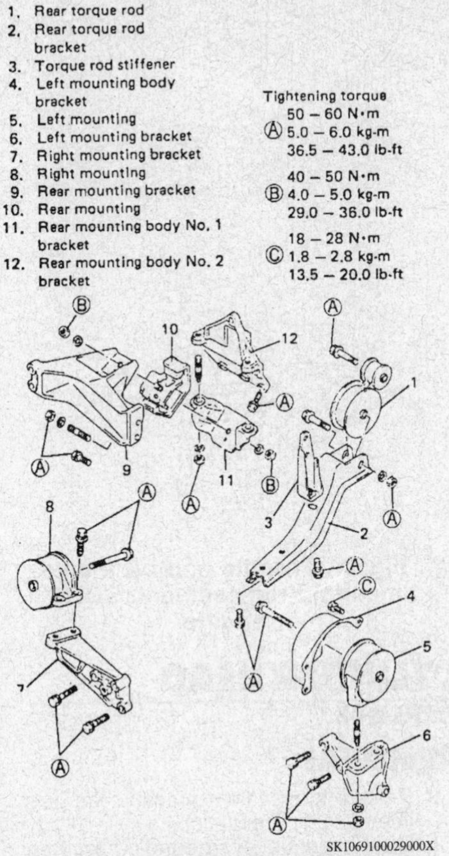
1. Rear torque rod
2. Rear torque rod bracket
3. Torque rod stiffener
4. Left mounting body bracket
5. Left mounting
6. Left mounting bracket
7. Right mounting bracket
8. Right mounting
9. Rear mounting bracket
10. Rear mounting
11. Rear mounting body No. 1 bracket
12. Rear mounting body No. 2 bracket
Tightening torque
50 – 60 N·m
Ⓐ 5.0 – 6.0 kg-m
36.5 – 43.0 lb-ft
40 – 50 N·m
Ⓑ 4.0 – 5.0 kg-m
29.0 – 36.0 lb-ft
18 – 28 N·m
Ⓒ 1.8 – 2.8 kg-m
13.5 – 20.0 lb-ft
SK1069100029000X

Fig. 2 Exploded view of engine mounting. Automatic transmission

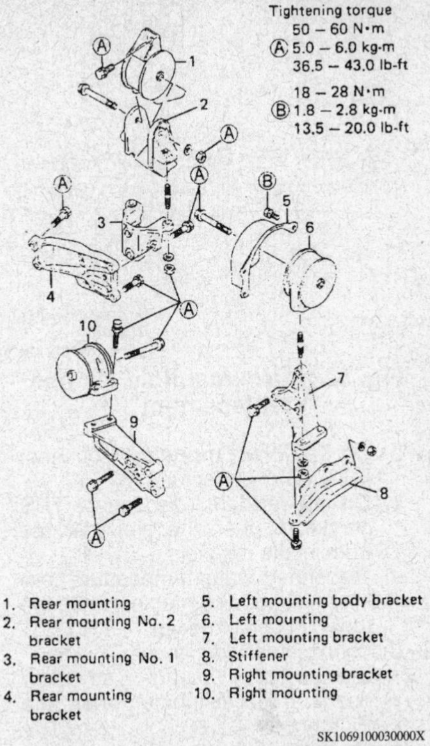
Tightening torque
50 – 60 N·m
Ⓐ 5.0 – 6.0 kg-m
36.5 – 43.0 lb-ft
18 – 28 N·m
Ⓑ 1.8 – 2.8 kg-m
13.5 – 20.0 lb-ft
1. Rear mounting
2. Rear mounting No. 2 bracket
3. Rear mounting No. 1 bracket
4. Rear mounting bracket
5. Left mounting body bracket
6. Left mounting
7. Left mounting bracket
8. Stiffener
9. Right mounting bracket
10. Right mounting
SK1069100030000X

Fig. 3 Exploded view of engine mounting. Manual transmission

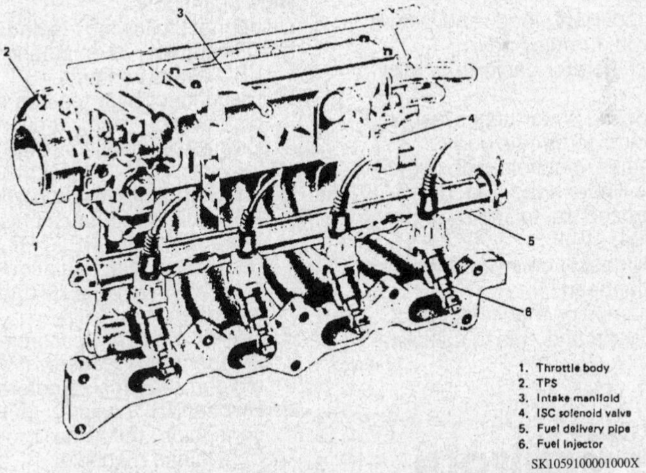
1. Throttle body
2. TPS
3. Intake manifold
4. ISC solenoid valve
5. Fuel delivery pipe
6. Fuel injector
SK1059100001000X

Fig. 4 Throttle body & intake manifold replacement. DOHC engine

5. Remove cooling water hoses from air valve and throttle body.
6. Remove alternator adjusting arm stiffener.
7. Remove intake manifold bracket, then the intake manifold with throttle body from cylinder head, **Fig. 4.**
8. Reverse procedure to install, noting the following:
   a. Use new gasket on intake manifold to cylinder head.
   b. Install clamps on manifold, **Fig. 5.**
   c. Tighten bolts and nuts to specification.

SOHC

1. Disconnect battery ground cable, then drain coolant system into appropriate container.
2. Remove air cleaner.
3. Disconnect following wires:
   a. Disconnect ISC solenoid valve and radiator cooling fan thermo switch connectors.

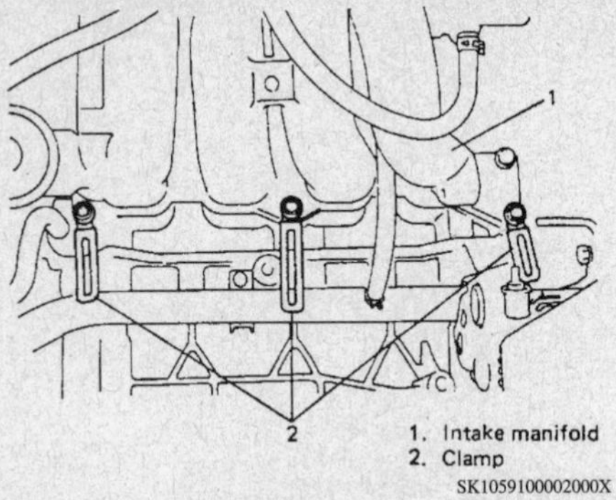
1
2
1. Intake manifold
2. Clamp
SK1059100002000X

Fig. 5 Intake manifold clamps replacement

   b. **On California models,** disconnect EGR VSV connectors.
   c. **On all models,** disconnect TPS connector, then the ground wires from intake manifold.
   d. Disconnect water temperature sensor and gauge connectors, then the fuel injector connector.
4. Disconnect following hoses:
   a. Disconnect vacuum advancer hoses from distributor, then the PCV hose.
   b. Disconnect power steering hose and brake booster hose from intake manifold.
   c. **On California models,** disconnect EGR modulator and EGR VSV hoses.
   d. **On all models,** disconnect canister purge hose from intake manifold and pipe.
   e. Disconnect fuel feed and return hoses from throttle body.
5. Remove accelerator cable from throttle body.
6. Remove cooling water hoses from intake manifold and throttle body.
7. Remove intake manifold with throttle body from cylinder head, **Fig. 6.**
8. Reverse procedure to install, noting the following:
   a. Use new gasket on intake manifold to cylinder head.
   b. Install clamps on manifold, **Fig. 5.**
   c. Tighten bolts and nuts to specification.

EXHAUST MANIFOLD

REPLACE

1. Disconnect battery ground cable.
2. Disconnect oxygen sensor coupler, then release sensor wire from clamps.
3. Remove exhaust manifold cover and manifold stiffener bolt.
4. Remove exhaust pipe from manifold.
5. Remove exhaust manifold and gasket from cylinder head, **Fig. 7.**
6. Reverse procedure to install, noting the following:
   a. Inspect gasket for deterioration or damage, replace as necessary.
   b. Tighten bolts and nuts to specification.

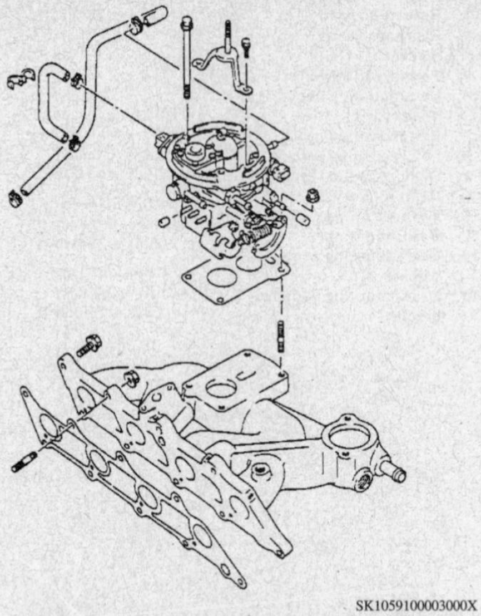
SK1059100003000X

Fig. 6 Throttle body & intake manifold replacement. SOHC engine

CYLINDER HEAD

REPLACE

REMOVAL

1. Relieve fuel system pressure as outlined under "Precautions"
2. Disconnect battery ground cable, then drain coolant system into appropriate container.
3. Remove air cleaner assembly with AFM outlet hose.
4. Disconnect following electrical wires:
   a. Disconnect Idle Speed Control (ISC) valve connector.
   b. Disconnect high tension cord from distributor, then the distributor Crank Angle Sensor (CAS) connector.
   c. **On California models,** disconnect Recirculated Exhaust Gas Temperature Sensor (REGTS) and Exhaust Gas Recirculation Vacuum Switching Valve (EGR VSV) connectors.
   d. **On all models,** disconnect Water Temperature Sensor (WTS) and oxygen sensor connectors.
   e. Disconnect canister purge VSV connector, then the ground wire from intake manifold.
   f. Disconnect Throttle Position Sensor (TPS) and fuel injector connectors.
   g. Disconnect Water Temperature Gauge (WTG) and radiator fan thermo switch.
   h. Ensure all wires are free of clamps on engine.
5. Disconnect vacuum hoses from brake booster and canister purge.
6. Remove accelerator cable from throttle lever and bracket.
7. Remove radiator hose from thermostat housing, heater hose from cylinder head and throttle body hose from throttle body.
8. Remove fuel feed and return hoses

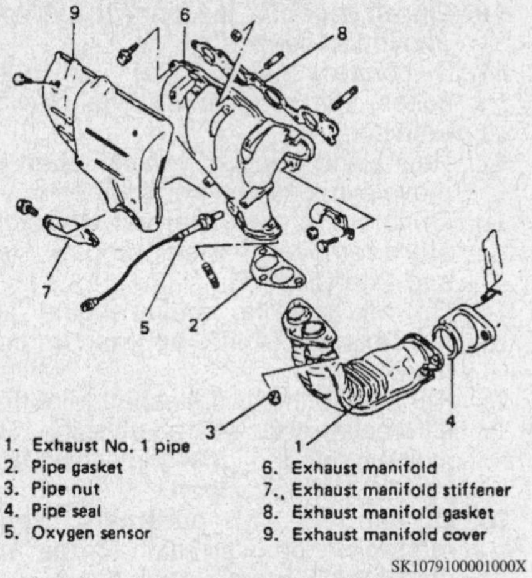
9
6
8
7
5
2
3
1
4
1. Exhaust No. 1 pipe
2. Pipe gasket
3. Pipe nut
4. Pipe seal
5. Oxygen sensor
6. Exhaust manifold
7. Exhaust manifold stiffener
8. Exhaust manifold gasket
9. Exhaust manifold cover
SK1079100001000X

Fig. 7 Exploded view of exhaust manifold

from delivery pipe.

9. Remove timing belt as outlined under "Timing Belt & Tensioner, Replace."
10. **On DOHC models,** remove timing belt inside cover, then the exhaust pipe from manifold.
11. **On SOHC models,** remove alternator adjusting arm stiffener, then the intake manifold bracket.
12. **On all models,** remove cylinder head cover.
13. Using 18 mm hexagon socket, remove cylinder head bolts.
14. Remove cylinder head, intake manifold, exhaust manifold, distributor, fuel delivery pipe and injectors as an assembly. **Do not place assembly on flat surface as one valve is in the open position.**

DISASSEMBLY

DOHC

1. Remove delivery pipe with injectors, intake manifold with throttle body, exhaust manifold and distributor from cylinder head.
2. Remove camshaft timing belt pulleys, camshafts and valve lash adjusters as outlined under "Camshafts & Hydraulic Valve Lash Adjuster, Replace."
3. Using valve lifter tools, No. 09916-14510 and No. 09916-48910, or equivalent, compress valve springs, then using forceps remove valve cotters **Fig. 8.**
4. Release tool and remove spring retainer and valve spring.
5. Remove valve from cylinder head.
6. Remove valve stem seal from valve guide, then the valve spring seat.
7. Using valve guide remover tool, No. 09916-44910, or equivalent, drive valve guide out from combustion chamber side to valve spring side.

SOHC

1. Remove intake manifold with throttle body, exhaust manifold and distributor from cylinder head.
2. Remove rocker arm shafts, rocker arms, springs and camshaft as outlined under "Rocker Arms, Rocker Arm

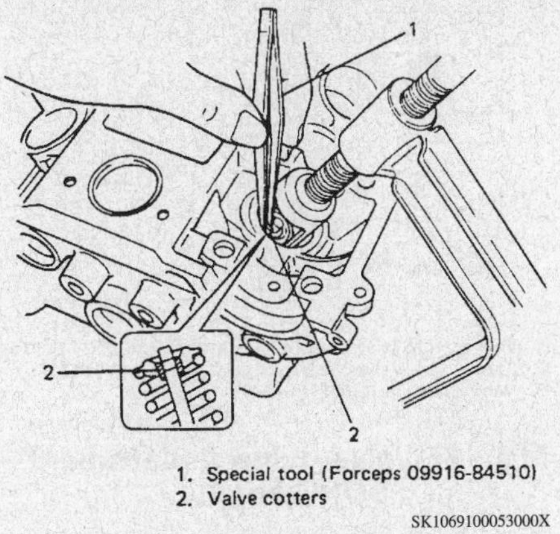
1
2
2
1. Special tool (Forceps 09916-84510)
2. Valve cotters
SK1069100053000X

Fig. 8 Valve cotters replacement

SK1069100056000X

Fig. 11 Valve radial runout measurement

Shafts & Camshaft, Replace."

3. Using valve lifter tools, No. 09916-14510 and No. 09916-48210, or equivalent, compress valve springs, then using forceps remove valve cotters **Fig. 8.**
4. Release tool and remove spring retainer and valve spring.
5. Remove valve from cylinder head.
6. Remove valve stem seal from valve guide, then the valve spring seat.
7. Using valve guide remover tool, No. 09916-46010, or equivalent, drive valve guide out from combustion chamber side to valve spring side.

INSPECTION

Valve Guides

Using micrometer and bore gauge, take diameter readings on valve stems and guides to check stem to guide clearance. Take reading at more than one place along length of each stem and guide.

If clearance exceeds 0.0027 inch for intake stems or 0.0035 inch for exhaust stems, replace valve and valve guide.

Valves

1. Remove all carbon from valves.
2. Inspect each valve for wear, burn or distortion, replace as necessary.
3. Measure thickness of valve head **Fig. 9.** If measured thickness exceeds 0.023 inch for intake valves or 0.027 inch for exhaust valves, replace valve.
4. Inspect valve stem end face for pitting and wear. If pitting or wear of stem end face is present, valve stem may be resurfaced, providing that its length will not be reduced to less than 0.14 inch. If

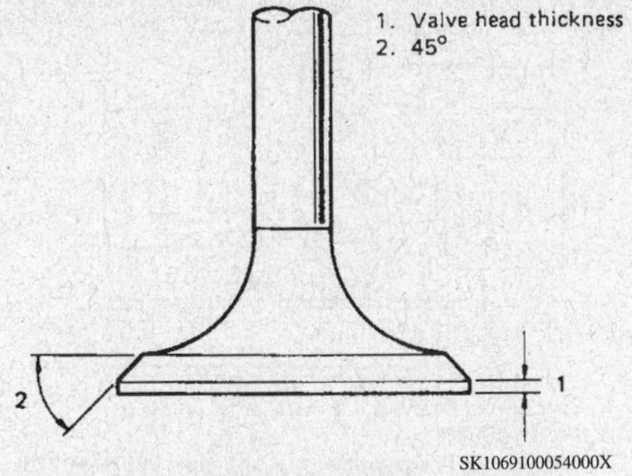
1. Valve head thickness
2. 45°
1
2
SK1069100054000X

Fig. 9 Valve head thickness measurement

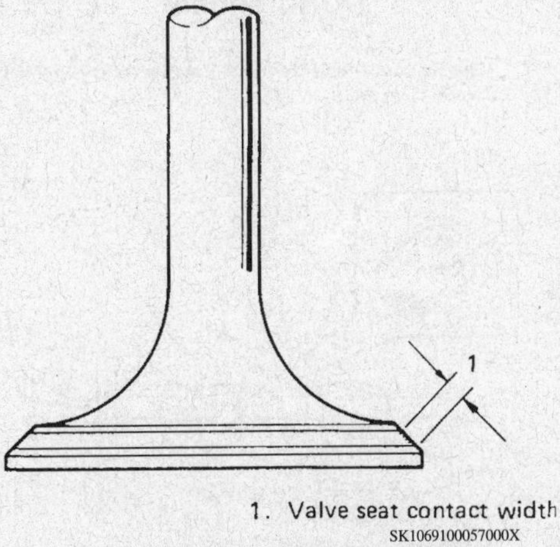
1
1. Valve seat contact width
SK1069100057000X

Fig. 12 Valve seating contact width measurement

length becomes less that specified, valve must be replaced **Fig. 10.**

5. Using dial gauge, check each valve for radial runout **Fig. 11.** If measure runout exceeds 0.003 inch, replace valve.
6. Inspect seating contact width on each valve as follows:
   a. Apply a uniform coat of red-lead paste to valve seat.
   b. Tap each seat to valve head. Valve lapping tool must be used.
   c. Pattern produced on seating face of each valve must be a continuous ring without any break, width of pattern must be within 0.0512–0.0590 inch, **Fig. 12.** Any valve seat not producing uniform contact or showing seating contact that is off the specified width must be repaired.

Cylinder Head

1. Inspect cylinder head for cracks in intake and exhaust ports, combustion chambers and head surface.
2. Using straightedge and thickness gauge, check gasket surface at six locations **Fig. 13.** If distortion limit of 0.002 inch is exceeded, correct gasket surface with a surface plate and abrasive paper. If abrasive paper fails to reduce thickness gauge readings to within specification, replace cylinder head.
3. Inspect manifold seating faces in same manner as step two. If distortion limit of

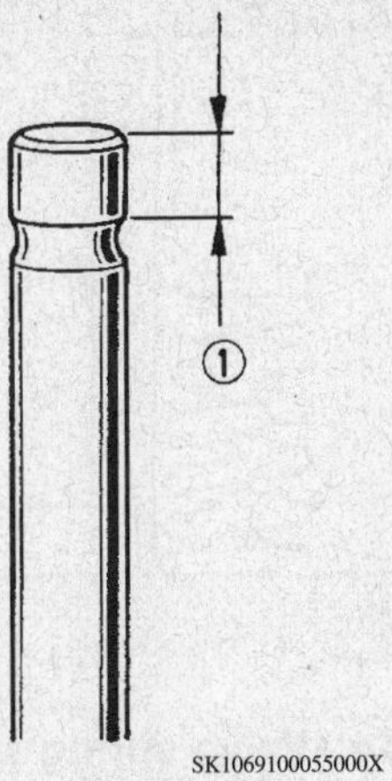
①
SK1069100055000X

Fig. 10 Valve stem end face measurement

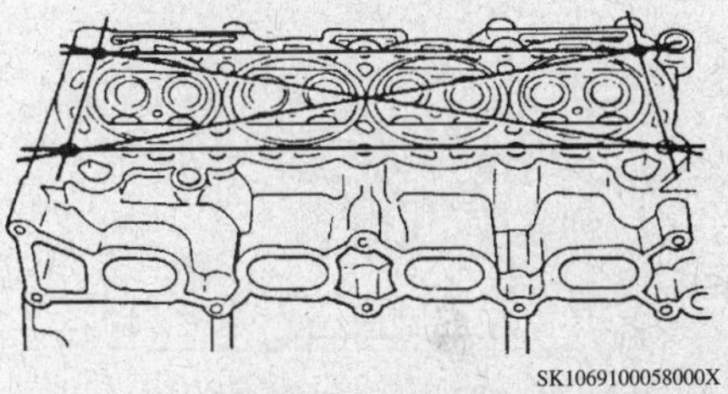
SK1069100058000X

Fig. 13 Cylinder head distortion measurement

0.004 inch is exceeded, correct in same manner as step two. If thickness gauge readings are not within specification, replace cylinder head.

Valve Springs

1. Ensure valve spring free length and preload are within specification.
2. Using square and surface plate, check each spring for squareness, **Fig. 14.** Springs that exceed 0.079 inch out of square must be replaced.

ASSEMBLY

1. Ream guide holes using 11 mm for DOHC or 12 mm for SOHC reamer to remove burrs.
2. Heat cylinder head uniformly to a temperature of 176–212°F, then drive new oversize valve guide into hole using tools, **Figs. 15 and 16.** Drive new valve guide until valve guide installer contact cylinder head. Ensure valve guide protrudes by 0.91 inch for DOHC or 0.55 inch for SOHC from cylinder head.
3. Ream valve guide bore using 5.5 mm for DOHC or 7 mm for SOHC reamer. Clean bore after reaming.
4. Install valve spring seat on cylinder head.
5. Lubricate and install new valve stem seal to valve guide, **Figs. 17 and 18.** Install seal to guide by pushing tool by hand.
6. Lubricate and install valves, then valve spring and spring retainer. Each valve spring has top end (large pitch end) and bottom end (small pitch end). Small pitch end must be facing bottom (spring seat side) **Fig. 19.**

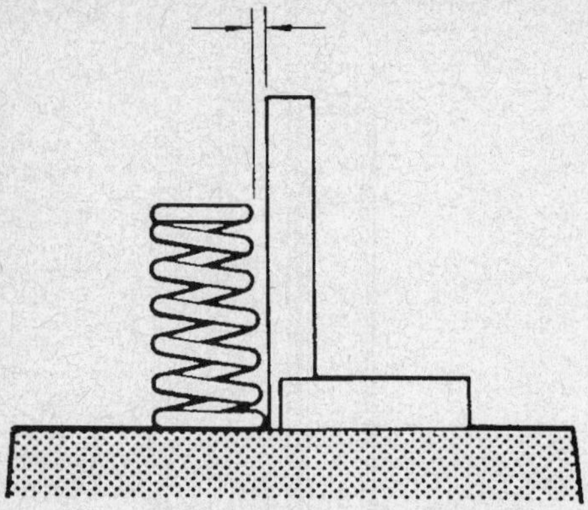

SK1069100059000X

Fig. 14 Valve spring squareness measurement

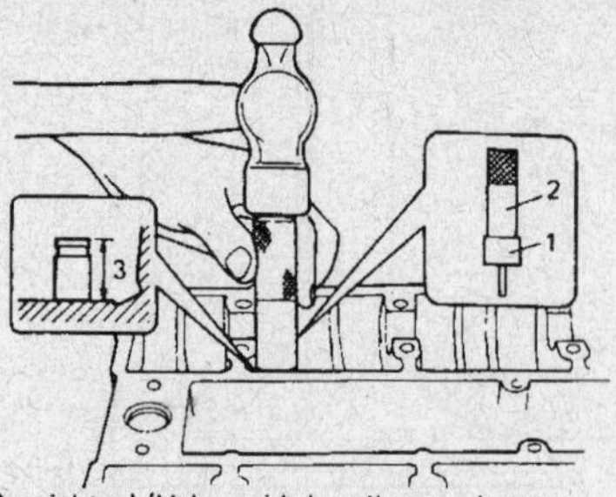
3
2
1

1. Special tool (Valve guide installer attachment 09916-56020)
2. Special tool (Valve guide installer handle 09916-58210)
3. Valve guide protrusion (23 mm, 0.91 in.)

SK1069100060000X

Fig. 15 Valve guide replacement. DOHC engine

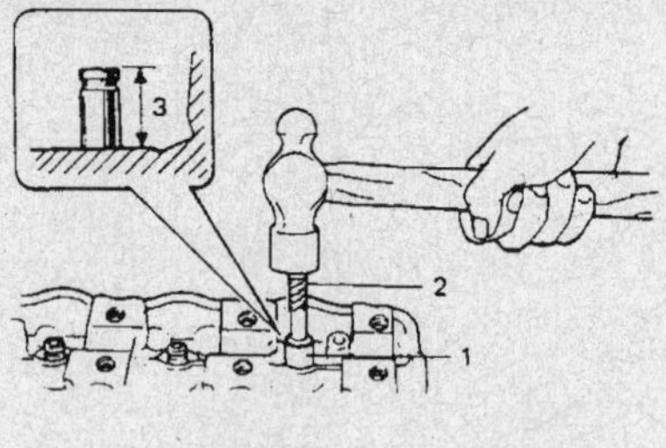
3
2
1

1. Special tool (Valve guide installer attachment 09917-88210)
2. Special tool (Valve guide installer handle 09916-57321)
3. Valve guide protrusion (14mm)

SK1069100061000X

Fig. 16 Valve guide replacement. SOHC engine

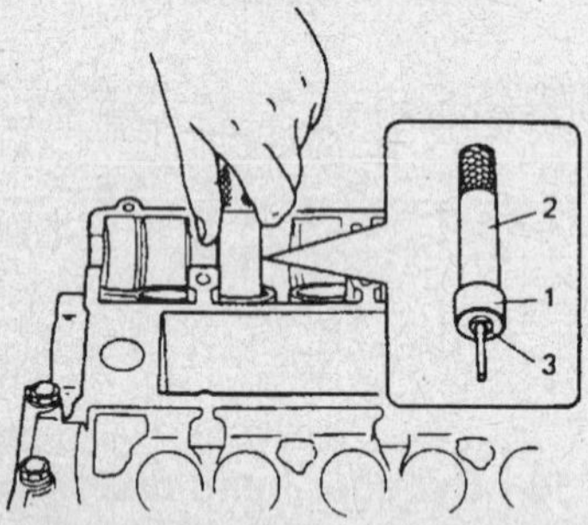
2
1
3

1. Special tool (Valve stem seal installer 09917-98220)
2. Special tool (Valve guide installer handle)
3. Valve stem seal

SK1069100062000X

Fig. 17 Valve stem seal replacement. DOHC engine

1. Special tool (Valve stem seal installer 09917-98210)
2. Valve stem seal

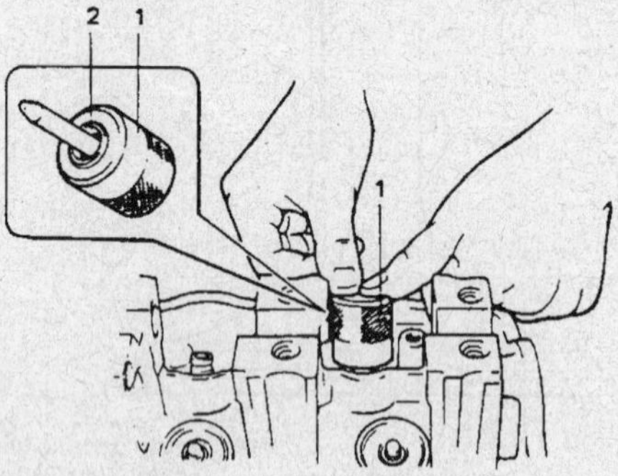
2 1
1

SK1069100063000X

Fig. 18 Valve stem seal replacement. SOHC engine

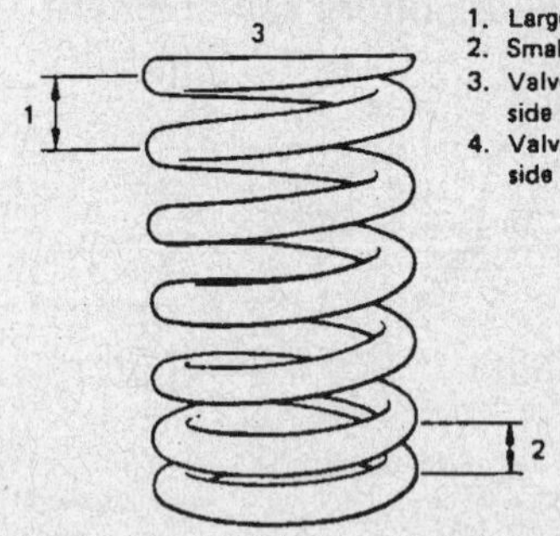
3
1
2
4

1. Larger pitch
2. Smaller pitch
3. Valve spring retainer side
4. Valve spring seat side

SK1069100064000X

Fig. 19 Valve spring replacement

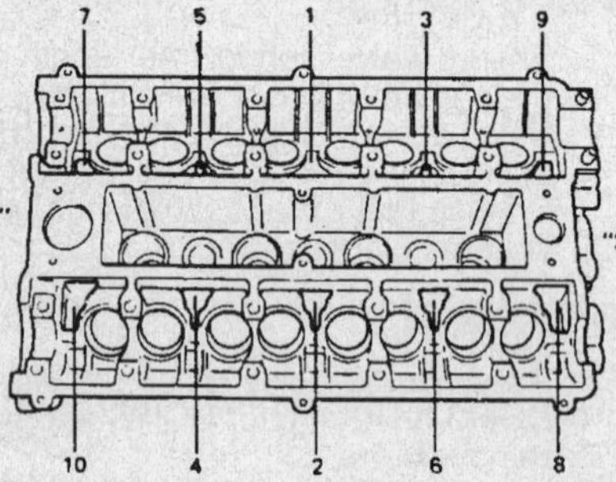
7 5 1 3 9
"1"
"2"
10 4 2 6 8

"1" Camshaft pulley side
"2" Distributor side

SK1069100065000X

Fig. 20 Cylinder head tightening sequence

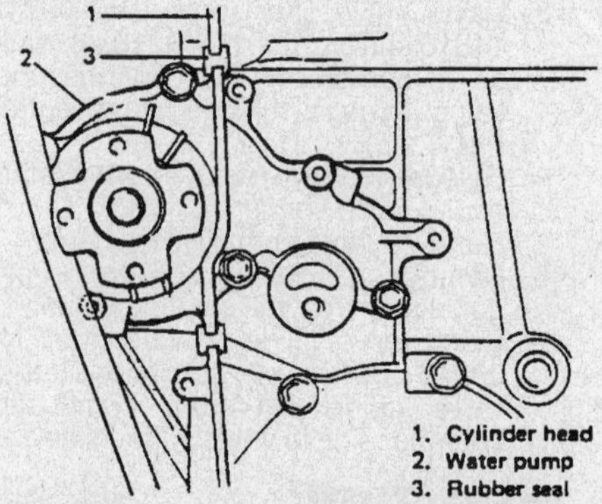
1
2
3

1. Cylinder head
2. Water pump
3. Rubber seal

SK1069100066000X

Fig. 21 Water pump rubber seal Installation

7. Compress valve spring and fit two valve cotters into groove provided on valve stem.
8. Install intake manifold with throttle body, exhaust manifold and delivery pipe with injectors to cylinder head.

INSTALLATION

1. Install new head gasket with TOP mark on gasket on top and facing crankshaft pulley side.
2. Install cylinder head, then using sequence shown in **Fig. 20, torque** cylinder head bolts in two or three steps to 48–54 ft. lbs.
3. **On DOHC models,** install valve lash adjuster, camshafts and camshaft timing belt pulleys as outlined under "Camshafts & Hydraulic Valve Lash Adjuster, Replace."
4. **On SOHC models,** install rocker arm shafts, rocker arms, springs and camshaft as outlined under "Rocker Arms, Rocker Arm Shafts & Camshaft, Replace."
5. Install cylinder head cover, then the timing belt inside covers. Ensure rubber seal is installed between water pump and cylinder head, **Fig. 21.**
6. Install distributor to cylinder head.
7. **On SOHC models,** adjust valve lash as outlined under "Valve Adjustment."
8. Reverse procedure to install.

VALVE LIFTERS

Replace valve lifters as outlined under "Cylinder Head, Replace."

VALVE CLEARANCE SPECIFICATIONS

Refer to **Fig. 22** for proper valve clearance.

VALVE ADJUSTMENT

SOHC

1. Disconnect battery ground cable, then remove cylinder head cover.
2. Raise and support vehicle, then remove right side fender apron extension.
3. Using 17 mm socket, turn crankshaft pulley clockwise until "V" mark on pulley aligns with "0" mark on timing belt cover.
4. Remove distributor cap, then check if rotor is positioned, **Fig. 23.** If rotor is out of place, turn crankshaft clockwise one full turn.
5. Check valve lash at valves 1, 2, 5 and 7, **Fig. 24.**
6. Using a suitable feeler gauge, measure clearance at gap (A), **Fig. 25.** Clearance should be as specified, **Fig. 22.**
7. If clearance is not as specified, adjust by turning adjusting screw until correct clearance is obtained, **Fig. 25.**

		When cold (Coolant temperature is 15 – 25°C or 59 – 77°F)	When hot (Coolant temperature is 60 – 68°C or 140 – 154°F)
Valve lash (gap A) specification	Intake	0.13 – 0.17 mm (0.0051 – 0.0067 in)	0.23 – 0.27 mm (0.009 – 0.011 in)
	Exhaust	0.16 – 0.20 mm (0.0063 – 0.0079 in)	0.26 – 0.30 mm (0.0102 – 0.0118 in)

SK1069100041000X

Fig. 22 Valve lash specification. SOHC engine

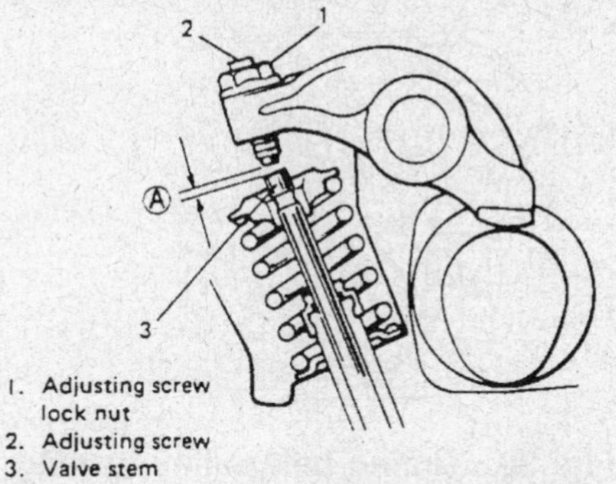
2
1
Ⓐ
3
1. Adjusting screw lock nut
2. Adjusting screw
3. Valve stem
SK1069100040000X

Fig. 25 Valve lash measurement. SOHC engine

8. After adjustment, tighten screw locknut to specification while holding adjusting screw with screwdriver.
9. Rotate crankshaft one full turn.
10. Check valve lash at valves 3, 4, 6, and 8 in same manner.
11. Install valve cover and distributor cap. Tighten bolts to specification.
12. Install air cleaner assembly.

ROCKER ARMS

For rocker arm replacement procedure, refer to "Camshaft, Replace," found in this section.

ROCKER ARMS

REPLACE

For rocker arm shaft replacement procedure, refer to "Camshaft, Replace," found in this section.

TIMING BELT

REPLACE

DOHC

With the timing belt removed, avoid turning the camshaft or crankshaft. If movement is required, exercise extreme caution to avoid valve damage caused by piston contact.

Removal

1. Disconnect battery ground cable.
2. Remove air cleaner assembly with AFM and AFM outlet hose, then the air cleaner bracket.
3. Raise and support vehicle.
4. Remove righthand side fender apron extension. Do not push center pin in too far as it may fall into fender.
5. Remove alternator/water pump belt and water pump pulley.

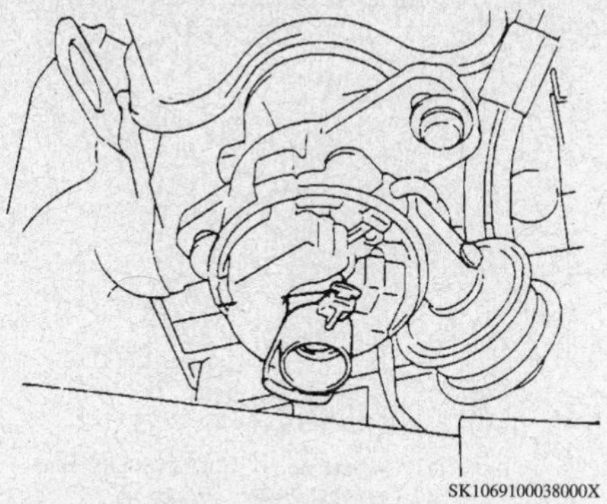
SK1069100038000X

Fig. 23 Rotor position inspection. SOHC engine

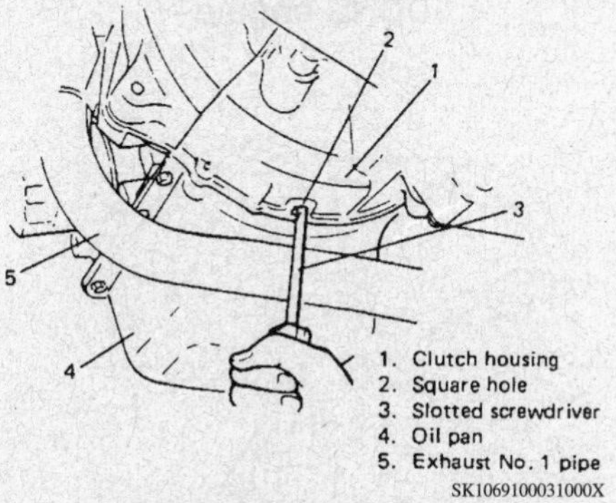
2
1
3
5
4
1. Clutch housing
2. Square hole
3. Slotted screwdriver
4. Oil pan
5. Exhaust No. 1 pipe
SK1069100031000X

Fig. 26 Crankshaft position lock. Manual transmission

6. Remove crankshaft pulley as follows:
   a. Lock crankshaft to loosen crankshaft timing belt pulley bolt and crankshaft pulley bolts, **Figs. 26 and 27.** If engine is in vehicle, it is necessary to remove crankshaft timing belt pulley bolt. If engine is removed from vehicle, crankshaft timing belt pulley bolt need not be removed.
   b. Remove crankshaft pulley bolts using 5 mm hexagon socket.
   c. Remove crankshaft timing belt pulley bolt using 17 mm socket.
7. Remove timing belt upper and lower outside covers.
8. For Installation of timing belt, set camshaft timing belt pulley and crankshaft timing belt pulley, **Fig. 28,** by turning crankshaft.
9. Remove timing belt as follows:
   a. Remove tensioner stud and loosen tensioner bolt, **Fig. 29.**
   b. Remove tensioner spring and damper, then the timing belt. **Once timing belt is removed, never turn camshafts or crankshaft independently more than shown, Fig. 30,** or internal engine damage may occur.
10. Remove tensioner and tensioner plate.

Inspection

1. Inspect timing belt for wear or cracks, replace as necessary.
2. Ensure tensioner rotates smoothly.

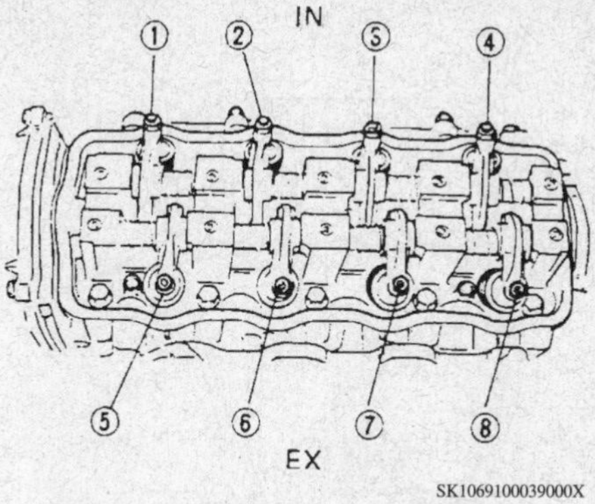
IN
①
②
⑤
④
⑤
⑥
⑦
⑧
EX
SK1069100039000X

Fig. 24 Valve identification. SOHC engine

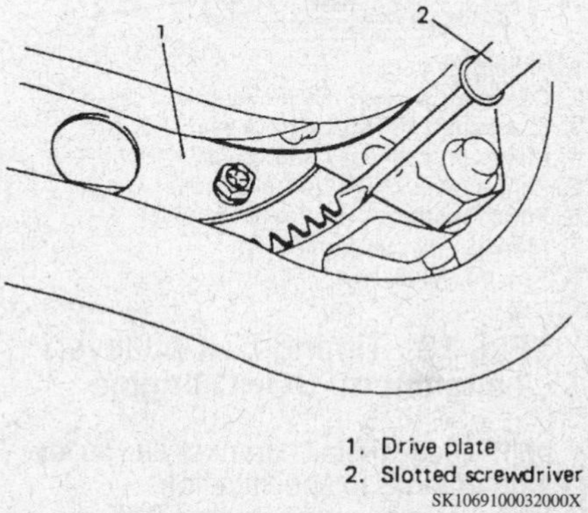
1
2
1. Drive plate
2. Slotted screwdriver
SK1069100032000X

Fig. 27 Crankshaft position lock. Automatic transmission

Installation

1. Install tensioner plate on tensioner. Lug of tensioner plate must fit in hole of tensioner.
2. Install tensioner assembly. Hand tighten tensioner bolt only at this time. Plate movement in upward direction should cause tensioner to move in same direction. If not, repeat step one.
3. Turn camshaft timing belt pulleys until punch mark on pulleys aligns with marks on cylinder head. **Do not turn each pulley beyond range specified in Fig. 30. If pulleys do not stop in place due to counter force of valve spring, hold pulleys in place using bolts shown, Fig. 31.**
4. Turn crankshaft timing belt pulley until punch mark on pulley aligns with arrow mark on oil pump case. **Do not turn pulley beyond range specified in Fig. 30.**
5. Install timing belt on pulleys with drive side of belt free from any slack. **Match arrow mark on timing belt with rotating direction of crankshaft (clockwise).**
6. Install tensioner spring and spring damper. Hand tighten tensioner stud.
7. Turn crankshaft two rotations clockwise after installing belt to take up slack of belt. Ensure marks on all pulleys are aligned.
8. Ensure seal is between water pump and oil pump case, then install timing belt outside covers.
9. Remove crankshaft timing belts pulley

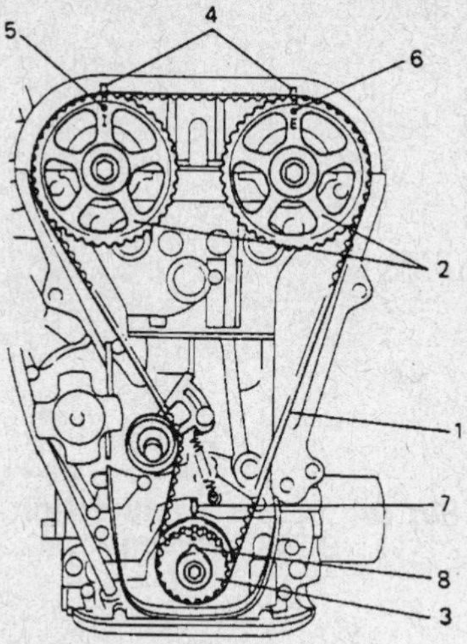
4
5
6
2
1
7
8
3

1. Timing belt
2. Camshaft timing belt pulleys
3. Crankshaft timing belt pulleys
4. Marks on cylinder head cover
5. Punch mark by "I" (intake side)
6. Punch mark by "E" (exhaust side)
7. Mark on oil pump case
8. Key on crankshaft

SK1069100033000X

Fig. 28 Timing belt pulleys alignment. DOHC engine

bolt, then install crankshaft pulley. Tighten bolts to specification.

10. Install water pump pulley and drive belt.
11. Install air cleaner bracket, then the air cleaner assembly.
12. Install right side fender apron extension, then connect battery ground cable.

SOHC

Removal

1. Disconnect battery ground cable, then raise and support vehicle.
2. Remove right side fender apron extension. Do not push center pin in too far as it may fall into fender.
3. Remove alternator/water pump belt and water pump pulley.
4. Remove crankshaft pulley as follows:
   a. Lock crankshaft to loosen crankshaft timing belt pulley bolt and crankshaft pulley bolts, **Figs. 26 and 27.** If engine is in vehicle, it is necessary to remove crankshaft timing belt pulley bolt. If engine is removed from vehicle, crankshaft timing belt pulley bolt need not be removed.
   b. Using 17mm socket remove crankshaft pulley bolts and timing belt pulley bolt.
5. Remove timing outside cover.
6. Loosen tensioner bolt and stud, then push tensioner plate fully upward and remove timing belt from pulleys.

Inspection

1. Inspect timing belt for wear or cracks, replace as necessary.
2. Ensure tensioner rotates smoothly.

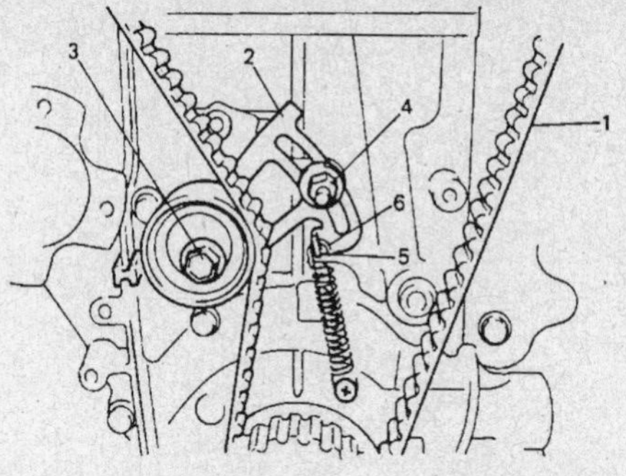
3
2
4
1
6
5

1. Timing belt
2. Tensioner plate
3. Tensioner bolt
4. Tensioner stud
5. Spring
6. Spring damper

SK1069100034000X

Fig. 29 Timing belt replacement. DOHC engine

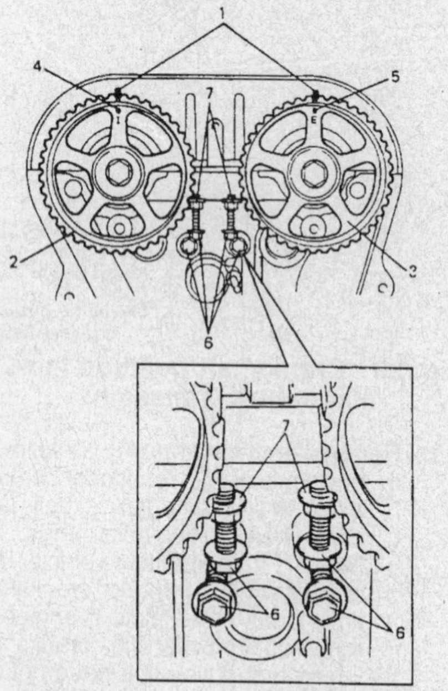
1
4
5
7
2
3
6
7
6
6

1. Mark on cylinder head cover
2. Intake side camshaft timing belt pulley
3. Exhaust side camshaft timing belt pulley
4. Punch mark at "I" mark
5. Punch mark at "E" mark
6. Bolts (M8)
7. Flanged nuts (M8)

SK1069100036000X

Fig. 31 Camshaft pulley timing mark alignment. DOHC engine

Installation

1. Install tensioner plate on tensioner. Lug of tensioner plate must fit in hole of tensioner.
2. Install tensioner assembly. Hand tighten tensioner bolt only at this time. Plate movement in upward direction should cause tensioner to move in same direction. If not, repeat step one.
3. Remove cylinder head cover, then completely loosen all Valve adjusting screws and locknuts on intake and exhaust rocker arms.
4. Turn camshaft pulley clockwise until timing mark on pulley aligns with "V" mark on belt inside cover, **Fig. 32.**
5. Turn crankshaft timing belt pulley bolt clockwise until punch mark on pulley aligns with arrow mark on oil pump

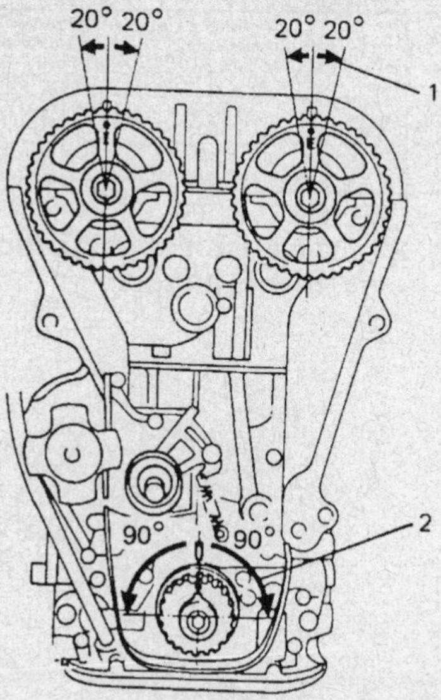
20° 20°
20° 20°
1
90°
90°
2

SK1069100035000X

Fig. 30 Timing belt pulley turning range measurement. DOHC engine

case, **Fig. 32.**

6. Install timing belt on pulleys with drive side of belt free from any slack and with tensioner plate pushed up by finger. **Match arrow mark on timing belt with rotating direction of crankshaft (clockwise). In this position, No. 4 piston is at top dead center (TDC) of compression stroke.**
7. Turn crankshaft two rotations clockwise after installing belt to take up slack of belt. Ensure marks on all pulleys are aligned.
8. Tighten tensioner stud, then the tensioner bolt.
9. Ensure seal is between water pump and oil pump case, then install timing belt outside cover.
10. Remove crankshaft timing belts pulley bolt, then install crankshaft pulley. Tighten bolts to specification.
11. Adjust valves as outlined under "Valve Adjustment."
12. Install water pump pulley and drive belt.
13. Install cylinder head cover, then the air cleaner assembly.
14. Install right side fender apron extension, then connect battery ground cable.

CAMSHAFT

REPLACE

SOHC

REMOVAL

1. Disconnect battery ground cable, then remove cylinder head cover.
2. Remove distributor from cylinder head.
3. Loosen all valve adjusting screw locknuts, then turn adjusting screws back completely.
4. Remove rocker arm shaft screws, then pull out both rocker arm shafts.
5. Remove rocker arms and springs.

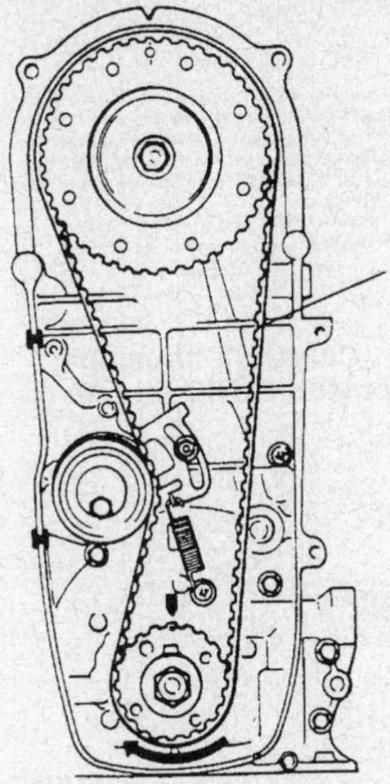
1
Direction of crankshaft
1. Drive side of belt
SK1069100037000X

Fig. 32 Timing belt pulley alignment. SOHC engine

6. Remove timing belt as outlined under "Timing Belt & Tensioner, Replace."
7. Insert rod into hole of camshaft, then remove camshaft pulley bolt.
8. Remove distributor case and camshaft from cylinder head.

INSPECTION

Rocker Arm & Shaft

1. Using a suitable micrometer and a bore gauge, measure rocker shaft diameter and rocker arm inside diameter. Note readings.
2. Rocker shaft diameter should be 0.628–0.629 inch. If diameter is not as specified, replace shaft.
3. Rocker arm inside diameter should be 0.629–0.630 inch. If diameter is not as specified, replace arm.
4. Take readings obtained in steps 2 and 3, and the difference between the two readings is arm to shaft clearance. Arm to shaft clearance should be 0.0005–0.0017 inch. If clearance is not as specified, replace shaft or arm as necessary.
5. Using "V" blocks and a suitable dial indicator, check runout of rocker arm shaft. Runout should not exceed 0.004 inch.

Camshaft Lobe Height & Runout

1. Using a micrometer, measure cam lobe height. If measured height is below 1.4975 inches for intake or exhaust cam, replace camshaft.
2. Using dial gauge, measure camshaft runout. If measured runout exceeds 0.0039 inch, replace camshaft.

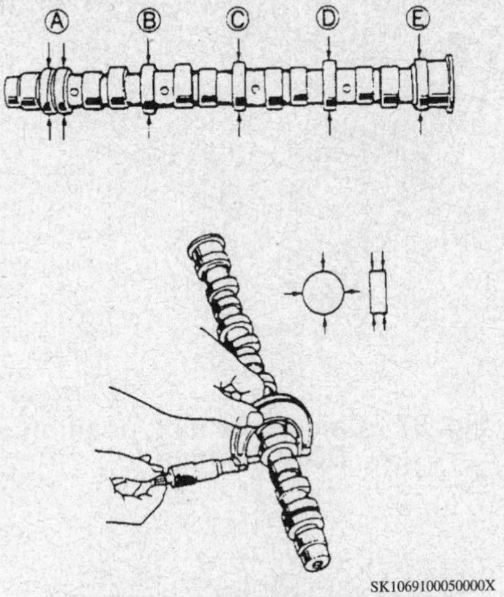
Ⓐ
Ⓑ
Ⓒ
Ⓓ
Ⓔ
SK1069100050000X

Fig. 33 Camshaft journal measurement. SOHC engine

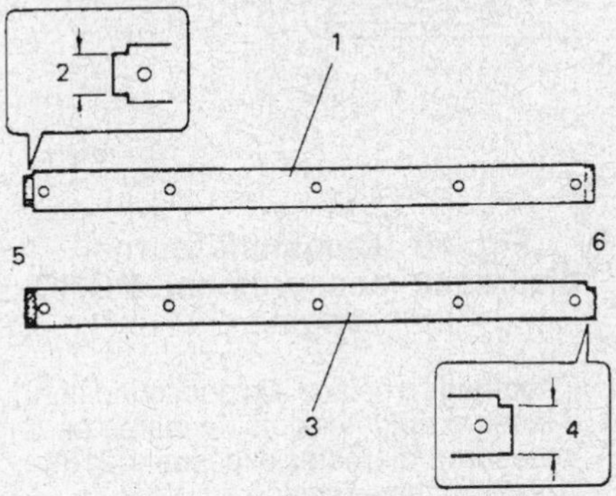
1
2
5
6
3
4
1. Intake rocker arm shaft
2. 14mm (0.55 in)
3. Exhaust rocker arm shaft
4. 15mm (0.59 in)
5. Camshaft pulley side
6. Distributor side
SK1069100052000X

Fig. 35 Rocker arm shaft replacement. SOHC engine

Camshaft Journal Wear

1. Measure journal diameter at four places on each journal, **Fig. 33.** Journal diameter should be as specified, **Fig. 34.**
2. Using bore gauge, measure journal bores in cylinder head. Journal bore diameter should be as specified, **Fig. 34.**
3. Subtract journal diameter measurement from journal bore measurement to determine journal clearance. Journal clearance should not exceed 0.0059 inch.
4. If journal clearance exceeds specification, replace camshaft and/or cylinder head.

INSTALLATION

Reverse removal procedure to install, noting the following:

1. Install camshaft to cylinder head from transmission case side.
2. Install rocker arm shafts as specified, **Fig. 35.**

	Camshaft journal dia.	Journal bore dia.
Ⓐ	44.125 – 44.150 mm (1.7372 – 1.7381 in.)	44.200 – 44.216 mm (1.7402 – 1.7407 in.)
Ⓑ	44.325 – 44.350 mm (1.7451 – 1.7460 in.)	44.400 – 44.416 mm (1.7480 – 1.7486 in.)
Ⓒ	44.525 – 44.550 mm (1.7530 – 1.7539 in.)	44.600 – 44.616 mm (1.7560 – 1.7565 in.)
Ⓓ	44.725 – 44.750 mm (1.7609 – 1.7618 in.)	44.800 – 44.816 mm (1.7638 – 1.7644 in.)
Ⓔ	44.925 – 44.950 mm (1.7687 – 1.7697 in.)	45.000 – 45.016 mm (1.7716 – 1.7723 in.)

SK1069100051000X

Fig. 34 Camshaft journal & journal bore specifications. SOHC engine

3. Adjust valve lash as outlined under "Valves Adjustment."

DOHC

REMOVAL

1. Disconnect battery ground cable.
2. Remove timing belt as outlined under "Timing Belt & Tensioner, Replace."
3. Set key on crankshaft in position, **Fig. 36,** to prevent interference between valve and piston.
4. Remove cylinder head cover, then the distributor assembly.
5. Lock camshaft, **Fig. 37,** then remove camshaft timing belt pulleys.
6. Remove camshaft housing and camshafts from cylinder head.
7. Remove valve lash adjusters from cylinder head. **Do not disassemble hydraulic adjusters. Immerse adjusters in clean engine oil.**

INSPECTION

Camshaft Lobe Height & Runout

1. Using a micrometer, measure cam lobe height. If measured height is below 1.5880 inches for intake cam or 1.5877 inches for exhaust cam, replace camshaft.
2. Using dial gauge, measure camshaft runout. If measured runout exceeds 0.0039 inch, replace camshaft.

Camshaft Journal Wear

1. Inspect camshaft journals and camshaft housings for pitting, scratches, wear or damage. If a problem condition is found, replace camshaft or cylinder head with housing. Never replace cylinder head without replacing housings.
2. Using gaging plastic, check clearance as follows:
   a. Clean housings and camshaft journals.
   b. With all valve lash adjusters removed, install camshaft to cylinder head.
   c. Place a piece of gaging plastic the full width of journal.
   d. Install housings **Fig. 38,** then tighten in sequence **Fig. 39.** Housings must be tightened to specification

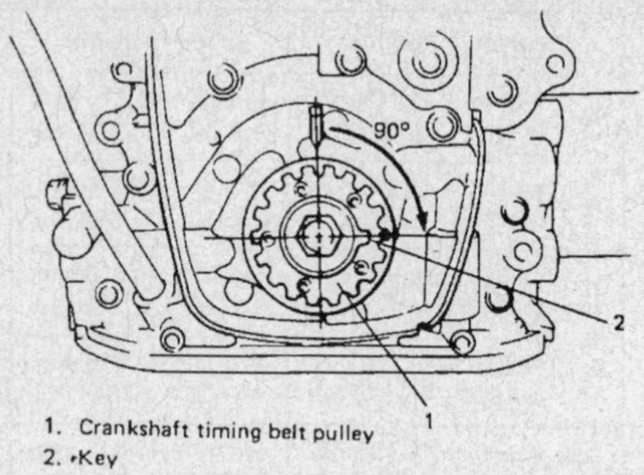
90°
1
2
1. Crankshaft timing belt pulley
2. Key

SK1069100042000X

Fig. 36 Crankshaft key replacement. DOHC engine

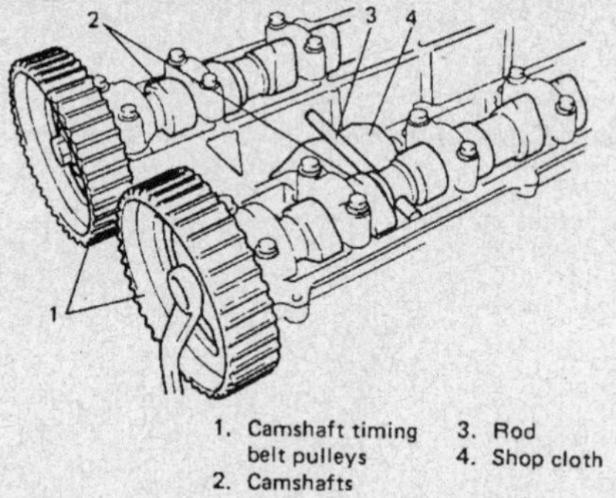
2
3
4
1
1. Camshaft timing belt pulleys
2. Camshafts
3. Rod
4. Shop cloth

SK1069100043000X

Fig. 37 Camshafts lock position. DOHC engine

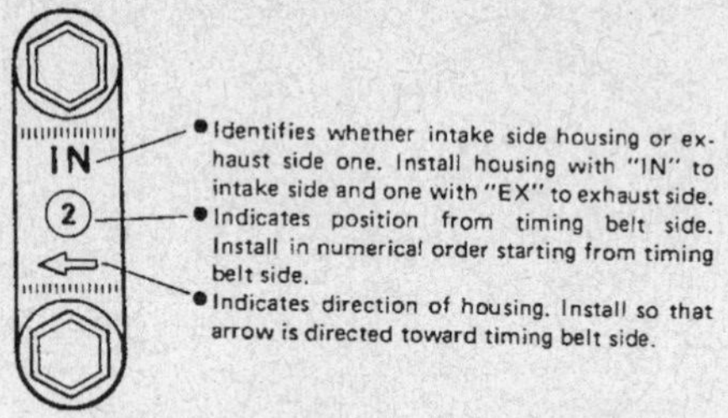
IN
2
• Identifies whether intake side housing or exhaust side one. Install housing with "IN" to intake side and one with "EX" to exhaust side.
• Indicates position from timing belt side. Install in numerical order starting from timing belt side.
• Indicates direction of housing. Install so that arrow is directed toward timing belt side.

SK1069100044000X

Fig. 38 Camshaft housings replacement. DOHC engine

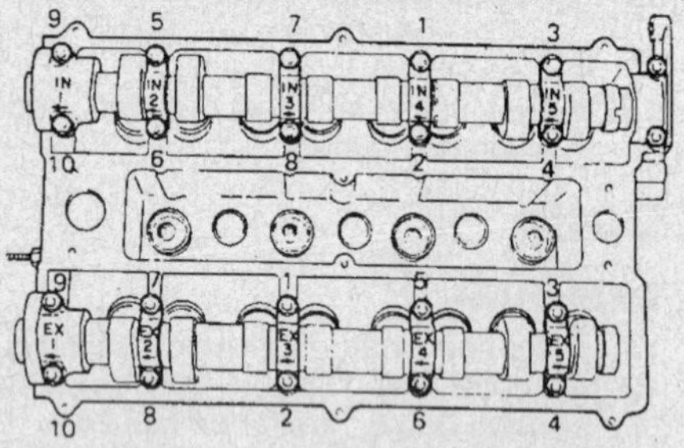
9
5
7
1
3
IN
10
6
8
2
4
EX
9
7
1
5
3
10
8
2
6
4

SK1069100045000X

Fig. 39 Camshaft tightening sequence. DOHC engine

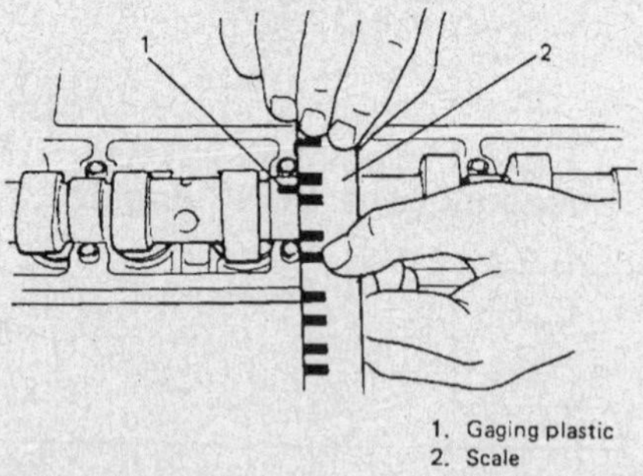
1
2
1. Gaging plastic
2. Scale

SK1069100046000X

Fig. 40 Camshaft journal clearance measurement. DOHC engine

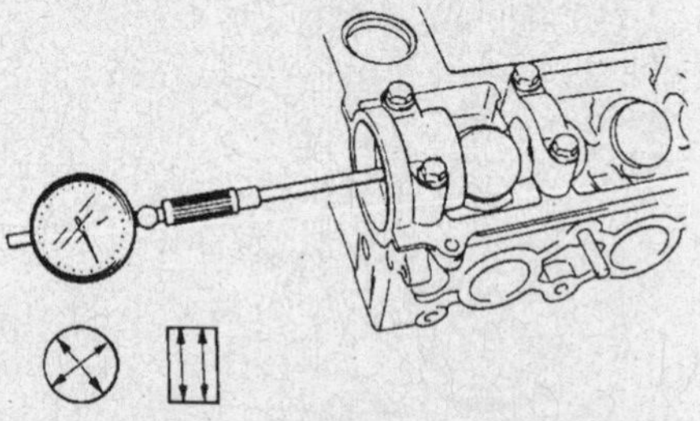

SK1069100047000X

Fig. 41 Camshaft journal bore measurement. DOHC engine

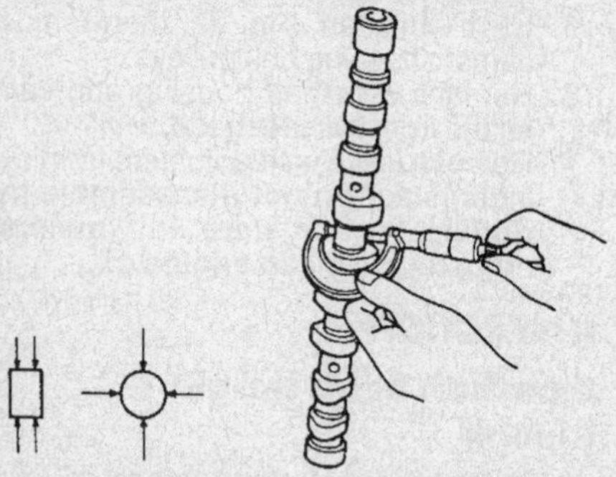

SK1069100048000X

Fig. 42 Camshaft journal diameter measurement. DOHC engine

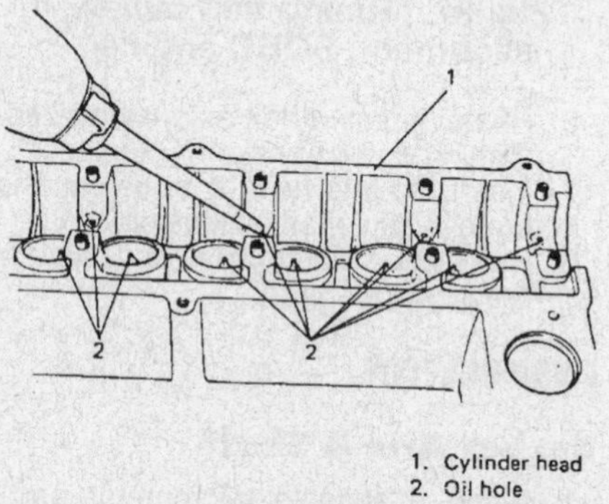
1
2
2
1. Cylinder head
2. Oil hole

SK1069100049000X

Fig. 43 Oil passages inspection. DOHC engine

to ensure proper reading of camshaft journal clearance. **Do not rotate camshaft while gaging plastic is installed.**

e. Remove housings. Using scale on gaging plastic envelop, measure gaging plastic width at widest point **Fig. 40.** If measured camshaft journal clearance exceeds 0.0047 inch, measure journal housing bore **Fig. 41,** and outside diameter of camshaft journal **Fig. 42.** If journal housing bore is not within 1.1024–1.1032 inches, replace cylinder head assembly. If outside diameter of camshaft journal is not within 1.1007–1.1015 inches, replace camshaft.

Hydraulic Valve Lash Adjuster Wear

1. Inspect adjuster for pitting, scratches or damage, replace if in poor condition.
2. Measure adjuster outside diameter. If measured diameter exceeds 1.2188–1.2194 inches, replace adjuster.
3. Measure cylinder adjuster bore. If measured bore diameter exceeds 1.2205–1.2214 inches, replace cylinder head.

INSTALLATION

1. Pour engine oil through camshaft journal oil holes. Ensure oil comes out of oil holes in valve lash adjuster bores, **Fig. 43.**
2. Lubricate and install valve lash adjusters.
3. Lubricate and install camshafts. **Camshaft pulley pin hole must be at bottom center position.**
4. Install camshaft housings as follows:
   a. Lubricate sliding surfaces of each housings.
   b. Apply sealant No. 99000-31110, or equivalent, to mating surface of intake 1 and exhaust 1 housings and cylinder head.
   c. Install housings on correct journals, **Fig. 38.** Camshaft housing intake 1 or exhaust 1 retains camshaft in proper position as to thrust direction. Securely fit these housings to respective No. 1 journals first.
   d. Tighten housing bolts evenly in a four step procedure in sequence shown, **Fig. 39,** until specified torque is reached.
5. Lubricate and press fit camshaft oil seal until oil seal surface becomes flush with housing surface.
6. Install pins to each camshaft, then install camshaft timing belt pulleys. Pin for intake pulley must be in slot marked "I." Pin for exhaust pulley must be in slot marked "E."
7. Reverse procedure to install, noting the following:
   a. Tighten all bolts to specification.
   b. Do not turn camshafts or start engine for 30 minutes after reinstalling hydraulic valve lash adjusters and camshafts.
   c. If air is trapped in valve lash adjuster, valve may make tapping sound when engine is operated. In such cases, run engine for 30 minutes at 2,000 RPM, this will purge air from adjuster. If tapping is still present, a possible defective adjuster is present, replace defective adjuster.

PISTON & ROD ASSEMBLY

Before replacing the piston and connecting rods, remove carbon from top of cylinder bore. When installing first and second

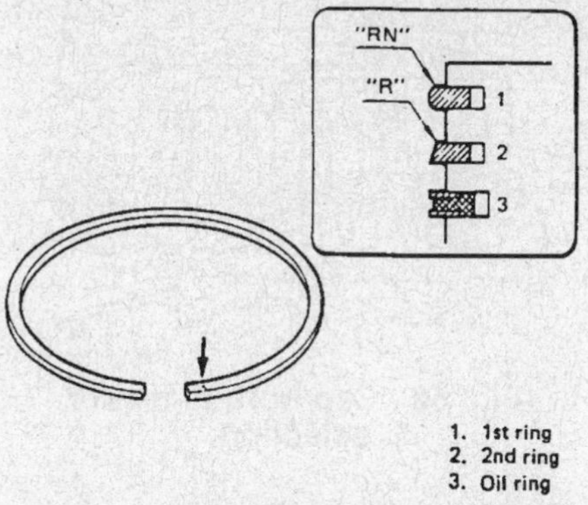
"RN"
"R"
1
2
3
1. 1st ring
2. 2nd ring
3. Oil ring
SK1069100067000X

Fig. 44 Piston ring replacement

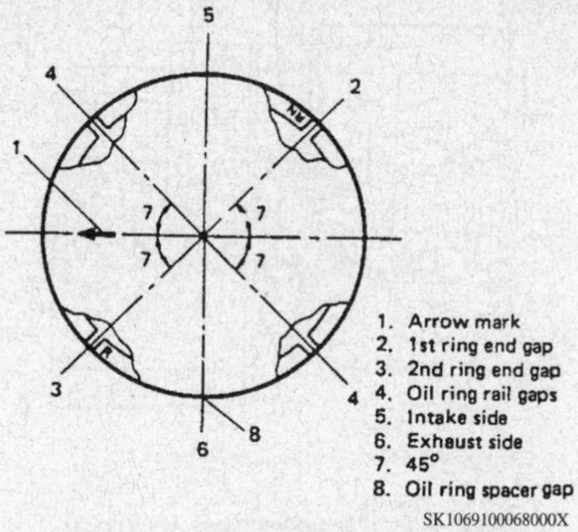
1. Arrow mark
2. 1st ring end gap
3. 2nd ring end gap
4. Oil ring rail gaps
5. Intake side
6. Exhaust side
7. 45°
8. Oil ring spacer gap
SK1069100068000X

Fig. 45 Piston ring end gap locations

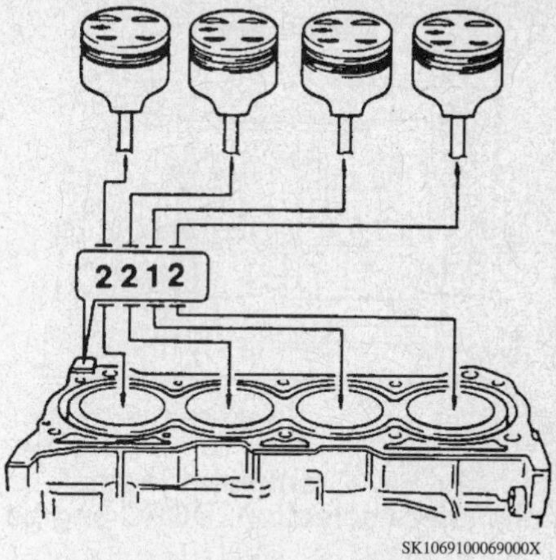
2212
SK1069100069000X

Fig. 46 Piston to cylinder Installation position

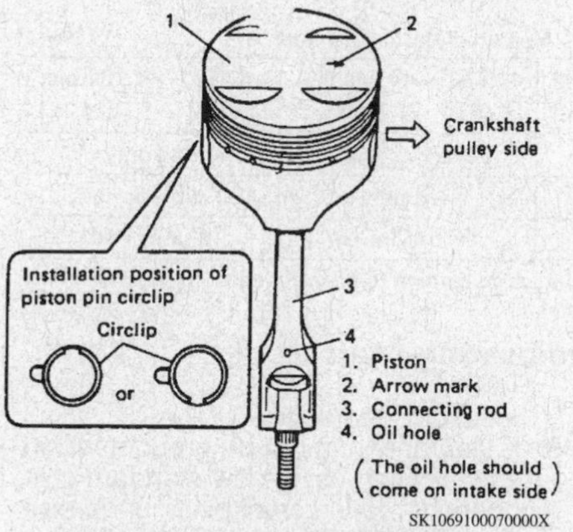
Crankshaft pulley side
Installation position of piston pin circlip
Circlip
or
1. Piston
2. Arrow mark
3. Connecting rod
4. Oil hole
(The oil hole should come on intake side)
SK1069100070000X

Fig. 47 Piston Installation

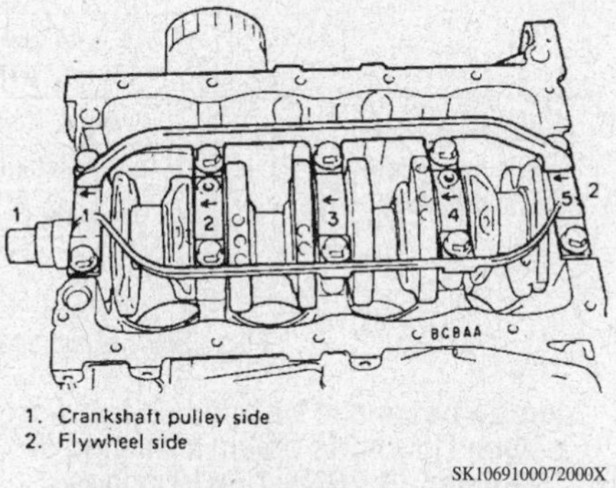
1. Crankshaft pulley side
2. Flywheel side
SK1069100072000X

Fig. 48 Main bearing caps Installation

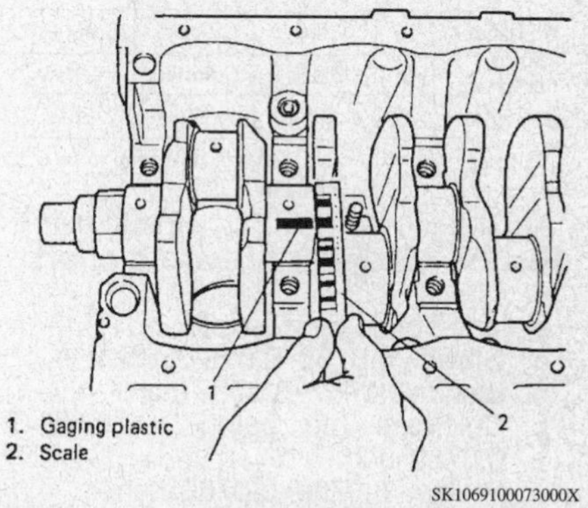
1. Gaging plastic
2. Scale
SK1069100073000X

Fig. 49 Main bearing clearance measurement

rings, direct marked side of each ring toward top of piston, **Fig. 44.** The compression ring gap should be staggered and not inline with the oil ring gap, **Fig. 45.**

Each piston top is stamped with a No. 1 or 2, depending on its outer diameter. A No. 1 stamped piston, outer diameter should be 2.9126–2.9130 inches and a No. 2 stamped piston, outer diameter should be 2.9122–2.9126 inches.

When installing piston and connecting rod assemblies, ensure number on piston top matches cylinder number stamped in block, **Fig. 46,** and arrows on top of pistons are facing front of engine, crankshaft pulley side, **Fig. 47.**

Pistons are available in standard sizes and oversizes of 0.0098 inch and 0.0196 inch.

MAIN & ROD BEARINGS

MAIN BEARINGS

Two types of main bearings are available, standard and 0.0098 inch (0.25 mm) undersize, and each of them has five kinds of bearings differing in tolerance. Each main bearing cap is stamped with a number and an arrow. When installing bearing cap, arrow must point towards crankshaft pulley side, **Fig. 48.** Check main bearing clearance as follows:

1. Clean bearings and crankshaft main journals using a suitable solvent.
2. Place a piece of gaging plastic the full width of the bearing (parallel to crankshaft) on journal, avoiding oil passage hole.
3. Install bearing cap and tighten cap bolts to specification. **Do not rotate crankshaft while gaging plastic is installed.**
4. Remove bearing cap. Using scale on gaging plastic envelope, measure gaging plastic width at widest point, **Fig. 49.**
5. If clearance exceeds 0.0023 inch, replace bearing. Always replace both upper and lower inserts as a unit. **A new standard bearing may produce proper clearance, if not, it will be necessary to regrind crankshaft journal for use of 0.0098 inch undersize bearing. After selecting appropriate bearing, recheck clearance.**

Standard Bearing Selection

If bearing is in poor condition, or bearing clearance is out of specification, select a new standard bearing according to the following procedure.

1. Using a suitable micrometer, measure journal diameter. On DOHC models, crank web of No. 1 cylinder has five stamped numbers, **Fig. 50.** On SOHC models, crank webs of No. 2 and No. 3 cylinder has five stamped numbers, **Fig. 51.** The numbers represent the following journal diameters:
   a. No. 1 - 1.7714–1.7716 inches.
   b. No. 2 - 1.7712–1.7714 inches.
   c. No. 3 - 1.7710–1.7712 inches.
2. The first, second, third, fourth and fifth (intake manifold side to exhaust manifold side on DOHC or left to right on SOHC) stamped numbers on crank web, indicate journal diameters at bearing caps 1, 2, 3, 4 and 5 respectively. For example, the first No. 3 indicates that journal diameter at bearing No. 1 is within 1.7710–1.7712 inches, and second No. 1 indicates that journal diameter at bearing cap No. 2 is within 1.7714–1.7716 inches.
3. Using a suitable micrometer, check bearing cap bore without bearing. There are five letters stamped on mating surface of cylinder block, **Fig. 52.** These letters represent cap bore diameters as follows:
   a. "A" - 1.9292–1.9294 inches.
   b. "B" - 1.9294–1.9296 inches.
   c. "C" - 1.9296–1.9298 inches.
4. The first, second, third, fourth and fifth (left to right) stamped letters indicate cap bore diameter of bearing caps 1, 2, 3, 4 and 5 respectively, **Fig. 52.** For example, the "B" indicates that cap bore diameter of bearing cap No. 1 is within 1.9294–1.9296 inches, and the fifth letter "A" indicates that cap bore diameter of cap No. 5 is within 1.9292–1.9294 inches.
5. There are five types of standard bearings differing in thickness. Each bearing has a painted identification color on its side. Each color indicates thickness

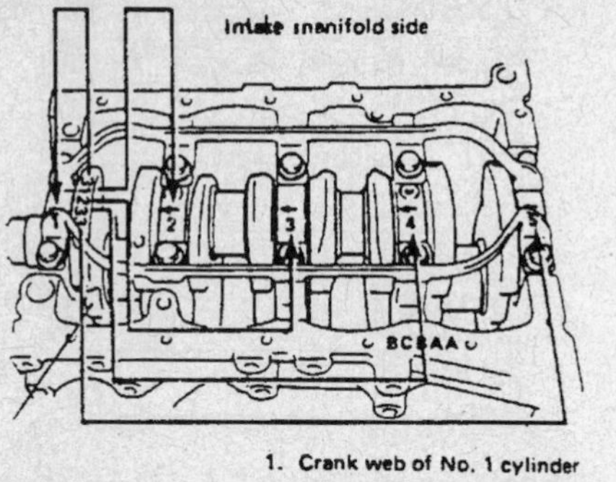
Intake manifold side
BCBAA

1. Crank web of No. 1 cylinder

SK1069100074000X

Fig. 50 Crankshaft journal diameters selection. DOHC engine

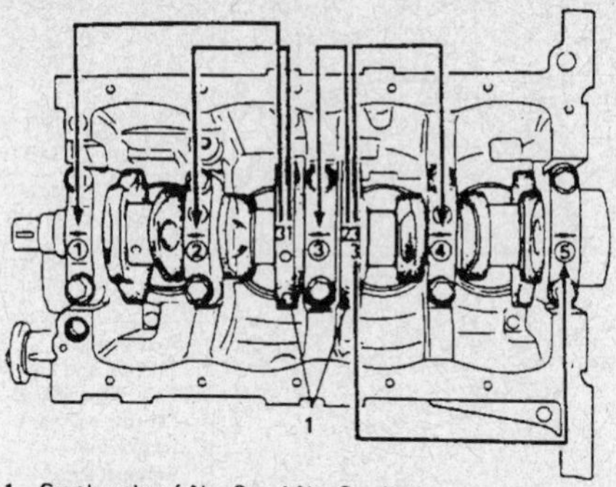
1

1. Crank webs of No. 2 and No. 3 cylinders

SK1069100075000X

Fig. 51 Crankshaft journal diameters selection. SOHC engine

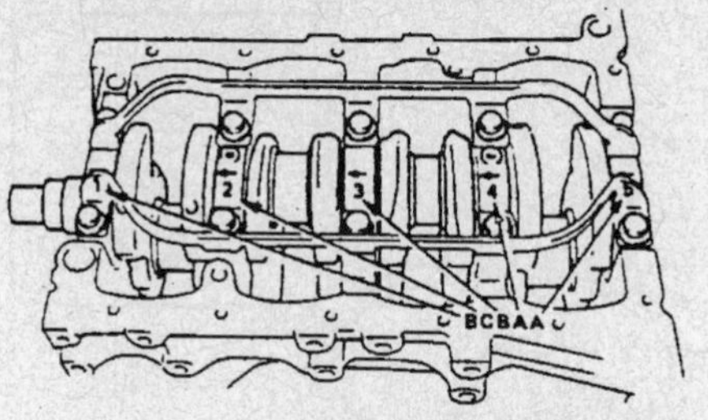
BCBAA

SK1069100076000X

Fig. 52 Cap bore diameter selection

		Numeral stamped on crank web (Journal diameter)		
		1	2	3
Alphabet stamped on mating surface	A	Green	Black	Colorless
	B	Black	Colorless	Yellow
	C	Colorless	Yellow	Blue
		New standard bearing to be installed.		

SK1069100077000X

Fig. 53 Standard bearing chart

		Measured journal diameter		
		44.744 – 44.750 mm (1.7616 – 1.7618 in.)	44.738 – 44.744 mm (1.7614 – 1.7616 in.)	44.732 – 44.738 mm (1.7612 – 1.7614 in.)
Alphabets stamped on mating surface of cylinder block	A	Green & Red	Black & Red	Red only
	B	Black & Red	Red only	Yellow & Red
	C	Red only	Yellow & Red	Blue & Red
		Undersize beraing to be installed.		

SK1069100078000X

Fig. 54 Undersize bearing chart

at center of bearing as follows:

a. Green - 0.0786–0.0787 inch.
b. Black - 0.0787–0.0788 inch.
c. Colorless (no paint) - 0.0788–0.0789 inch.
d. Yellow - 0.0789–0.0790 inch.
e. Blue - 0.0790–0.0791 inch.

6. From the number stamped on crank web, **Fig. 50 and 51,** and the letters stamped on surface of cylinder block, **Fig. 52,** determine new standard bearing to be installed to journal, by referring to table, **Fig. 53.** For example, if number stamped on crank web is 3 and letter stamped on cylinder block is B, install new standard bearing with a yellow painted identification mark.
7. Using gaging plastic, check bearing clearance with new standard bearing selected. If clearance exceeds limits, use next thicker bearing and recheck clearance.
8. If replacing crankshaft or cylinder block, select new standard bearings by numbers stamped on new crankshaft or letters stamped on cylinder surface.

Undersize Bearing Selection

1. The 0.0098 inch undersize bearing is available in five different thicknesses. To distinguish them, each bearing has a painted identification color on its side. Each color indicates thickness at center of bearing as follows:
   a. Green and red - 0.0835–0.0836 inch.
   b. Black and red - 0.0836–0.0837 inch.
   c. Red - 0.0837–0.0838 inch.
   d. Yellow and red - 0.0838–0.0839 inch.
   e. Blue and red - 0.0839–0.0840 inch.
2. If crankshaft has to be re-ground to undersize, grind journal and select undersize bearing to be used as follows:
   a. Grind journal to obtain a finished diameter a 1.7612–1.7618 inches.
   b. Using a suitable micrometer, measure re-ground journal diameter. Measurement should be made in two directions perpendicular to each other in order to check for out of round condition.
   c. From journal diameter measured above and letters stamped on cylinder block, select appropriate undersize bearing to be installed referring to **Fig. 54.**
   d. Check bearing clearance with undersize bearing selected.

CONNECTING ROD BEARING

Two types of rod bearings are available, standard and a 0.0098 inch undersize bearing, To distinguish them, the undersize bearing has the stamped number US025 on its back and the standard size bearing has no markings. Check rod bearing clearance as follows:

1. Clean bearings and crankshaft pin using a suitable solvent.
2. Place a piece of gaging plastic the full width of the crankpin as contacted by bearing (parallel to crankshaft), avoiding oil passage hole.
3. Install rod bearing cap and tighten cap bolts to specification. Ensure arrow mark on cap is pointed toward crankshaft pulley. **Do not rotate crankshaft while gaging plastic is installed.**
4. Remove rod bearing cap. Using scale on gaging plastic envelope, measure gaging plastic width at widest point, **Fig. 55.**
5. If clearance exceeds 0.0031 inch, use a new standard size bearing and remeasure clearance.
6. If clearance cannot be brought within specification using new standard size bearing, regrind crankpin to undersize and use 0.0098 inch undersize bearing.

OIL PUMP SERVICE

REMOVAL

1. Disconnect battery ground cable.
2. Raise and support vehicle.
3. Drain engine oil into appropriate container.
4. Remove water pump belt, pulley, alternator and bracket.
5. Remove timing belt as outlined under "Timing Belt & Tensioner, Replace."
6. Remove engine oil level gauge and its guide bolt.
7. Remove crankshaft timing belt pulley and timing belt guide.
8. Remove oil pan and oil pump strainer.
9. Remove oil pump attaching bolts, then the oil pump.

DISASSEMBLY

1. Remove oil level gauge guide from pump.
2. Remove rotor plate, then the inner and outer rotors.

INSPECTION

1. Inspect oil seal lip for damage, replace as necessary.
2. Inspect inner and outer rotors, rotor plate and oil pump case for excessive wear or damage.
3. Using thickness gauge, measure radial clearance between outer rotor and case, **Fig. 56.** If clearance exceeds 0.0122 inch, replace outer rotor or case.

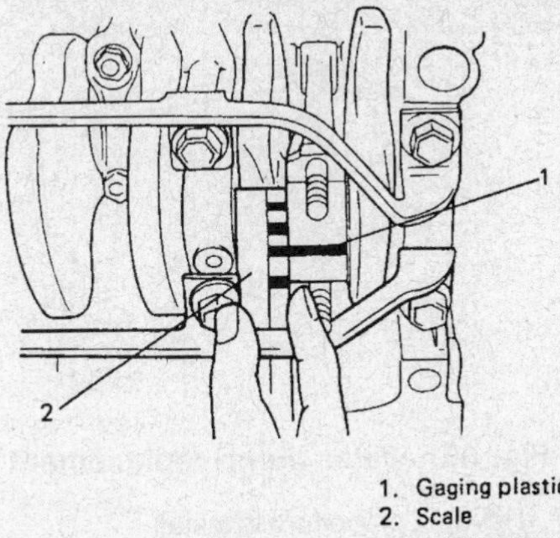
1
2
1. Gaging plastic
2. Scale
SK1069100071000X

Fig. 55 Rod bearing clearance measurement

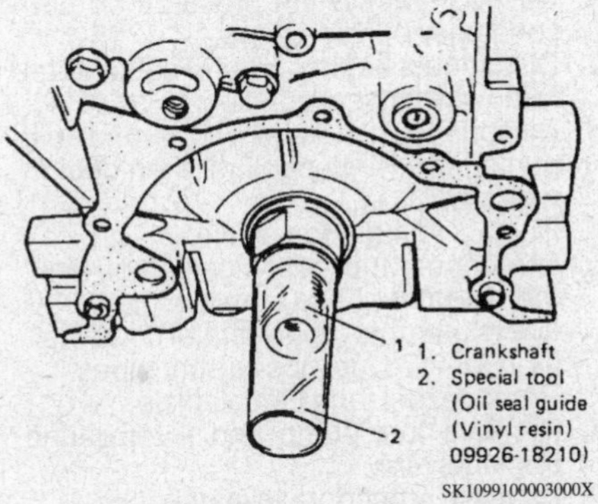
1
2
1. Crankshaft
2. Special tool (Oil seal guide (Vinyl resin) 09926-18210)
SK1099100003000X

Fig. 58 Oil pump replacement

4. Using straightedge and thickness gauge, measure side clearance, **Fig. 57.** Clearance should not exceed 0.0059 inch.

ASSEMBLY

1. Clean and dry all disassembled parts.
2. Apply thin coat of engine oil to inner and outer rotors, oil seal lip portion and inside surfaces of oil pump case and plate.
3. Install inner and outer rotors to case.
4. Install rotor plate. Tighten screws securely. **Ensure gears turn smoothly by hand.**
5. Install guide seal to pump case, then the oil level gauge guide.

INSTALLATION

1. Install two oil pump pins and new oil pump gasket to cylinder block.
2. Install oil pump to crankshaft, using tool shown, **Fig. 58.**
3. Install oil pump attaching bolts, **Fig. 59,** tighten bolts to specification. Ensure oil seal lip is not upturned, then remove tool.
4. Install rubber seal between oil pump and water pump, **Fig. 60.**
5. If edge of pump gasket bulges out, cut bulge off with sharp knife. Gasket edge must be smooth and flush with end faces of pump case and cylinder block.
6. Install timing belt guide, key and crankshaft timing belt pulley, **Fig. 61.** Timing belt guide must be installed with concave side facing oil pump.
7. Install timing belt as outlined under "Timing Belt & Tensioner, Replace."

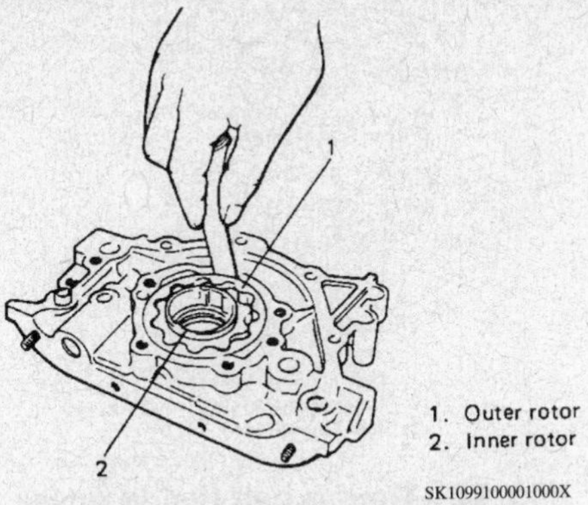
1
2
1. Outer rotor
2. Inner rotor
SK1099100001000X

Fig. 56 Oil pump gear radial clearance measurement

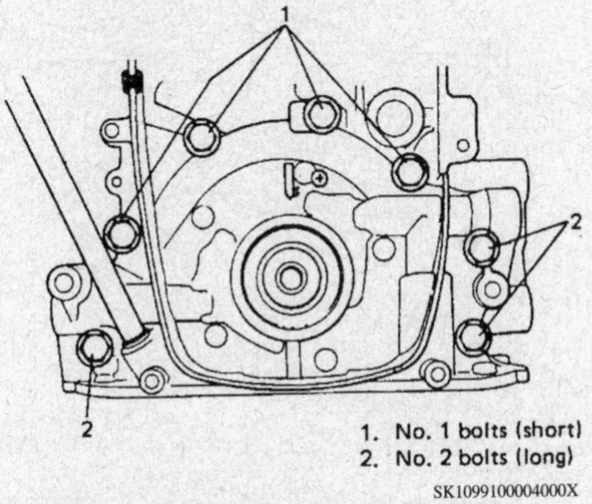
1
2
2
1. No. 1 bolts (short)
2. No. 2 bolts (long)
SK1099100004000X

Fig. 59 Oil pump bolt location

BELT TENSION DATA

Belt & Year	Belt Deflection Inch①
A/C Compressor	
1993–96	.20-.25
A/C Compressor & Power Steering	
1993–96	.31-.39
Alternator & Water Pump	
1993–96	②

① — With 22 lbs. pressure applied.
② — New, .20–.27; used, .24–.31.

COOLING SYSTEM BLEED

This engine does not require a specific bleed procedure. After filling coolant system, run engine to operating temperature with radiator/pressure cap off. Air will then be automatically bled through cap opening.

THERMOSTAT

REPLACE

SOHC

1. Drain coolant system into appropriate container, then remove thermostat cap from intake manifold.
2. Remove thermostat.
3. Install thermostat, ensuring air breather valve is positioned to front side of engine.
4. Install gasket and thermostat cap to intake manifold, then fill and bleed coolant system.

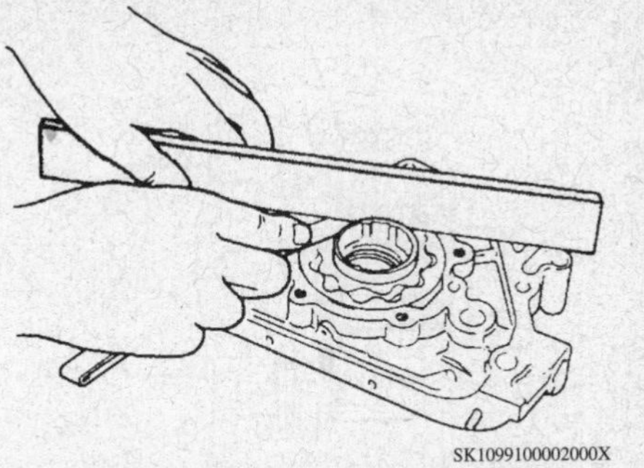
SK1099100002000X

Fig. 57 Oil pump gear side clearance measurement

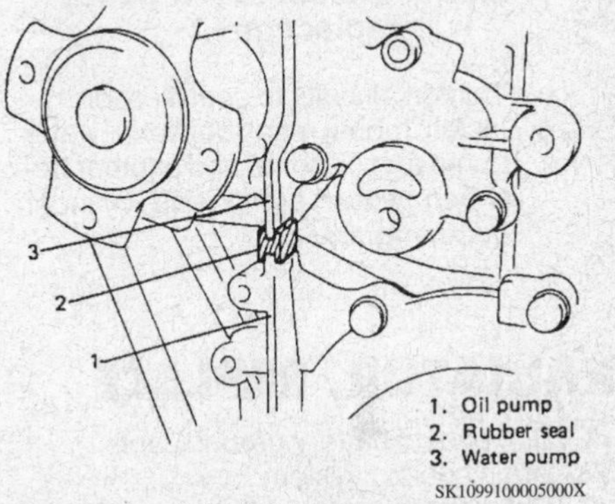
3
2
1
1. Oil pump
2. Rubber seal
3. Water pump
SK1099100005000X

Fig. 60 Water pump rubber seal replacement

DOHC

1. Drain coolant system into appropriate container, then remove thermostat cap from thermostat case.
2. Remove thermostat.
3. Install thermostat, ensuring air bleed valve is positioned upwards.
4. Install gasket and thermostat cap to thermostat case, aligning arrow marks on cap and case, then fill and bleed coolant system.

WATER PUMP

REPLACE

1. Disconnect battery ground cable, then drain coolant system into appropriate container.
2. Remove timing belt as outlined under "Timing Belt & Tensioner, Replace."
3. **On DOHC models,** remove timing belt inside cover (rear side) and water pump belt adjusting arm, **Fig. 62.**
4. **On all models,** remove water pump assembly, **Fig. 63.**
5. Reverse procedure to install, noting the following:
   a. Use new gasket for water pump to cylinder block.

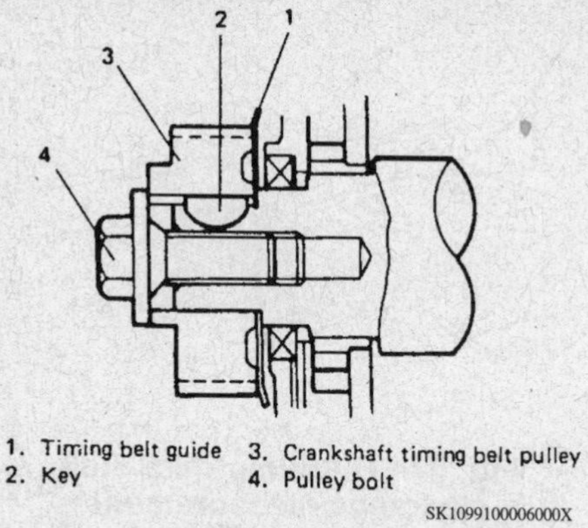
1. Timing belt guide
2. Key
3. Crankshaft timing belt pulley
4. Pulley bolt
SK1099100006000X

Fig. 61 Guide, key & pulley replacement

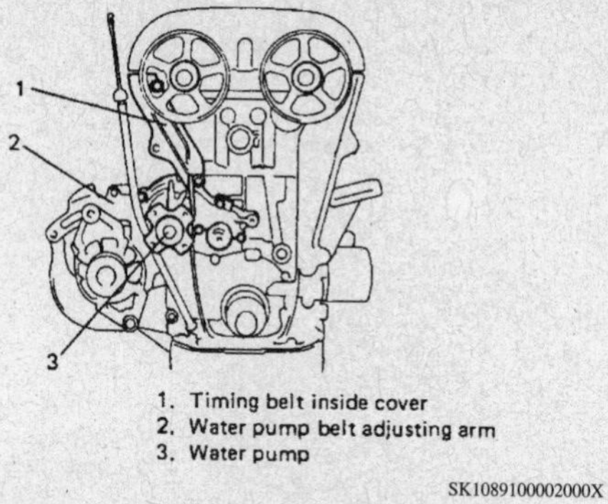
1. Timing belt inside cover
2. Water pump belt adjusting arm
3. Water pump
SK1089100002000X

Fig. 62 Timing belt inside cover replacement

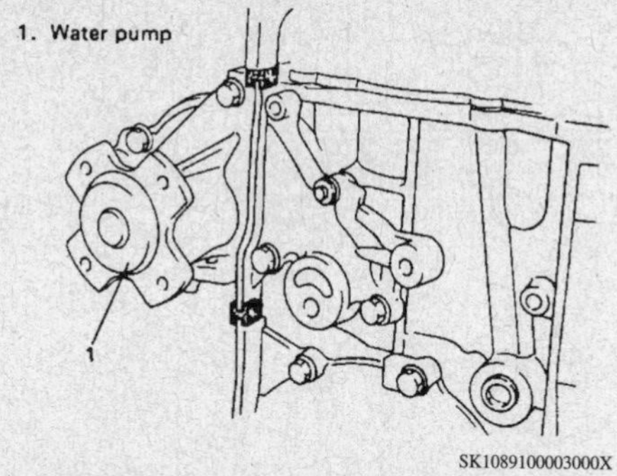
1. Water pump
SK1089100003000X

Fig. 63 Water pump replacement

b. Tighten all bolts to specification.
c. Install rubber seal between water pump and oil pump and another between water pump and cylinder head, **Fig. 63.**

7. Reverse procedure to install

RADIATOR, REPLACE

1. Disconnect battery ground cable.
2. Drain cooling system.
3. Disconnect cooling fan electrical connector.
4. Disconnect radiator inlet and outlet hoses, and reservoir tank hose.
5. **On models equipped with automatic transmission,** disconnect transmission cooler lines at radiator.
6. **On all models,** remove radiator and cooling fan motor.

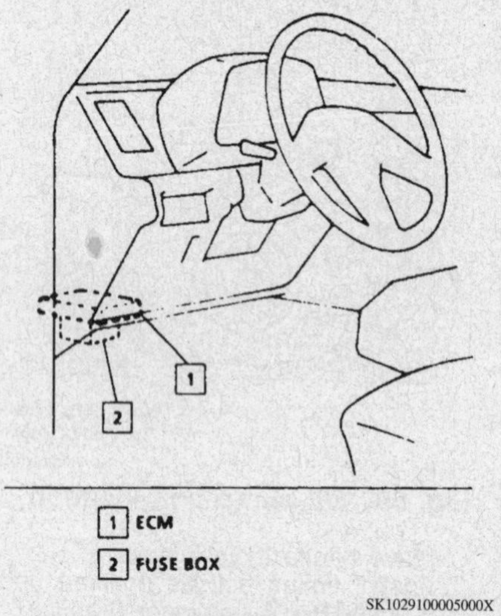
1 ECM
2 FUSE BOX
SK1029100005000X

Fig. 64 Fuel filter replacement

FUEL PUMP

REPLACE

1. Relieve fuel system pressure as outlined under "Precautions."
2. Disconnect battery ground cable, then remove rear seat cushion.
3. Disconnect fuel level gauge and fuel pump lead wire couplers, then detach wire tape.
4. Raise and support vehicle.
5. Disconnect fuel filler hose from tank, then breather hose from filler neck.
6. Drain fuel into appropriate container, then remove fuel hoses from pipes.
7. Remove fuel tank from vehicle.
8. Remove fuel pump and level gauge from fuel tank.
9. Reverse procedure to install.

FUEL FILTER

REPLACE

The fuel filter is located in front of the fuel tank and filters the fuel sent under pressure from the fuel pump. The fuel filter cannot be disassembled, it must replaced as an assembly, **Fig. 64.**

TIGHTENING SPECIFICATIONS

DOHC ENGINE

Year	Component	Torque/Ft. Lbs.
1993–95	Alternator Adjusting Arm Stiffener	14-20
	Camshaft Housing Bolt	8
	Camshaft Timing Belt Pulley Bolt	41-46
	Connecting Rod Bearing Cap Nut	24-26
	Crankshaft Main Bearing Cap Nut	37-41
	Crankshaft Pulley Bolt	11-13
	Crankshaft Timing Belt Pulley Bolt	76-83
	Cylinder Head Bolt	①
	Cylinder Head Cover Bolt	5
	Exhaust Manifold Bolt/Nut	14-20
	Exhaust Manifold Stiffener Bolt	29-43
	Exhaust Pipe Nut	29-43
	Flywheel Bolt	42-47
	Fuel Delivery Pipe Bolt	14-20
	Intake Manifold Bolt/Nut	14-20

Continued

TIGHTENING SPECIFICATIONS

DOHC ENGINE—Continued

1993–95	Intake Manifold Bracket Bolt/Nut	29-43
	Oil Drain Plug	22-28
	Oil Filter Stand	15-18
	Oil Pan Bolt/Nut	8
	Oil Pressure Switch	10
	Oil Pump Case Bolt	8
	Oil Pump Rotor Plate Screw	6-9
	Oil Pump Strainer Bolt	8
	Oxygen Sensor	33-39
	Rear Oil Seal Housing	9
	Throttle Position Sensor Screw	3
	Timing Belt Outside Cover	8
	Timing Belt Tensioner Bolt	18-22
	Timing Belt Tensioner Stud	8
	Water Pump Bolt	9
	Water Pump Pulley Bolt	8
	Water Temperature Sensor	4-10

① — Refer to "Cylinder Head, Replace" for tightening procedure.

TIGHTENING SPECIFICATIONS

SOHC ENGINE

Year	Component	Torque/Ft. Lbs.
1993–94	Camshaft Timing Belt Pulley Bolt	41-46
	Connecting Rod Bearing Cap Nut	25
	Crankshaft Main Bering Cap Bolt	37-41
	Crankshaft Pulley Bolt	11-13
	Crankshaft Timing Belt Pulley Bolt	76-83
	Cylinder Head Bolt	①
	Cylinder Head Cover Bolt	3
	Exhaust Manifold Bolt	14-20
	Flywheel Bolt	49-52
	Intake Manifold Bolt	14-20
	Oil Drain Plug	22-28
	Oil Pan Bolt/Nut	8
	Oil Pressure Switch	10
	Oil Pump Case Bolt	8
	Oil Pump Strainer Bolt	8
	Oil Pump Rotor Plate Screw	6-9
	Timing Belt Cover Bolt	8
	Timing Belt Tensioner Bolt	18-21
	Timing Belt Tensioner Stud	8
	Valve Adjusting Screw Locknut	12

① — Refer to "Cylinder Head, Replace" for tightening procedure.

1.6L Engine

NOTE: On Air Bag Equipped Models, Refer To "Air Bag System Precautions" Located In The Front Of This Manual For System Disarming & Arming Procedures.

INDEX

	Page No.
Belt Tension Data	40-47
Camshaft, Replace	40-44
8 Valve Engine	40-44
Compression Pressure	40-38
Cooling System Bleed	40-47
Crankshaft Rear Oil Seal, Replace	40-46
Cylinder Head, Replace	40-40
8 Valve Engine	40-40
16 Valve Engine	40-40
Engine Rebuilding Specifications	40-165
Engine Mount, Replace	40-38
Lefthand Mount	40-38
Righthand Mount	40-38
Engine, Replace	40-38
8 Valve Engine	40-38
16 Valve Engine	40-39
Exhaust Manifold, Replace	40-40
Fuel Filter, Replace	40-48
Fuel Pump, Replace	40-47
Intake Manifold, Replace	40-39
8 Valve Engine	40-39
16 Valve Engine	40-39
Main & Rod Bearings	40-45
Oil Pan, Replace	40-46
Oil Pump, Replace	40-46
Piston & Rod Assembly	40-45
Precautions	40-38
Air Bag Systems	40-38
Fuel System Pressure Relief	40-38
Radiator, Replace	40-47
Rocker Arms, Replace	40-41
8 Valve Engine	40-41
16 Valve Engine	40-41
Thermostat, Replace	40-47
Tightening Specifications	40-48
8 Valve Engine	40-48
16 Valve Engine	40-49
Timing Belt, Replace	40-44
8 Valve Engine	40-44
16 Valve Engine	40-44
Valve & Valve Springs, Replace	40-43
8 Valve Engine	40-43
16 Valve Engine	40-43
Valve Adjustment	40-40
Valve Clearance Specifications	40-40
8 Valve Engine	40-40
16 Valve Engine	40-40
Water Pump, Replace	40-47

PRECAUTIONS

AIR BAG SYSTEMS

Refer to "Air Bag System Precautions" in the front of this manual for system disarming and arming procedures.

FUEL SYSTEM PRESSURE RELIEF

1. Place manual transmission models in Neutral or automatic transmission models in Park, then set parking brake and block drive wheels.
2. Disconnect fuel pump relay, **Figs. 1 and 2.**
3. Remove fuel filler cap to release fuel vapor pressure in tank, then install cap.
4. Start and run engine until it stalls. Repeat cranking engine three times for three seconds each time to dissipate fuel pressure in fuel lines.

COMPRESSION PRESSURE

Standard compression pressure is 199 psi with a minimum of 170 psi. Maximum allowable difference between cylinders is 14.2 psi.

ENGINE MOUNT

REPLACE

LEFTHAND MOUNT

1. Disconnect battery ground cable, then remove radiator shroud.
2. Raise and support vehicle.
3. Remove skid pan from under vehicle, then the exhaust pipe to bracket nut.
4. Remove engine mount to engine bolts, **Fig. 3.**
5. Lower vehicle and support engine.
6. Remove exhaust bracket bolts and bracket, then the engine mount to frame bracket bolts.
7. Raise engine slightly and remove engine mount assembly.
8. Remove mount from mount to frame bracket.
9. Reverse procedure to install.

RIGHTHAND MOUNT

1. Disconnect battery ground cable.
2. Remove radiator shroud.
3. Raise and support vehicle.
4. Remove skid pan from under vehicle, then lower and support engine.
5. Disconnect electrical connections from starter.
6. Remove engine mount to frame bracket bolts, **Fig. 3.**
7. Remove engine mount to engine bracket bolts.
8. Raise engine slightly and remove engine mount assembly.
9. Remove mount from mount to frame bracket.
10. Reverse procedure to install.

ENGINE

REPLACE

8 VALVE ENGINE

1. Disconnect battery cable.
2. Mark position and remove hood.
3. Drain coolant system into appropriate container.
4. Remove radiator reservoir fan, shroud and radiator. On models equipped with A/C, remove A/C condenser.
5. Disconnect air cleaner outlet hose.
6. Disconnect accelerator cable and automatic transmission kickdown cable from throttle body.
7. Disconnect all engine electrical connectors, marking for assembly reference.
8. Remove starter motor.
9. Relieve fuel system pressure as outlined under "Precautions."
10. Disconnect all engine vacuum, fuel and coolant hoses, marking for assembly reference.
11. Raise and support vehicle.
12. Drain engine oil into appropriate container.
13. Remove exhaust center pipe from exhaust manifold.
14. **On models with manual transmission,** disconnect clutch cable and clutch housing lower plate.
15. **On models with automatic transmission,** disconnect transmission fluid hoses, torque converter housing lower plate and torque converter bolts using driveplate locking tool, No. J3571, or equivalent.
16. **On all models,** lower vehicle.
17. Remove engine to transmission bolts.
18. Support transmission using a suitable stand or jack. **Do not support automatic transmission under oil pan.**
19. Install engine lifting device, **Fig. 4.**
20. Disconnect engine mounts as outlined under "Engine Mounts, Replace."
21. Remove engine assembly by sliding engine toward the front side of engine compartment, then hoist engine assembly from vehicle. **Before lifting engine, ensure all electrical wires,**

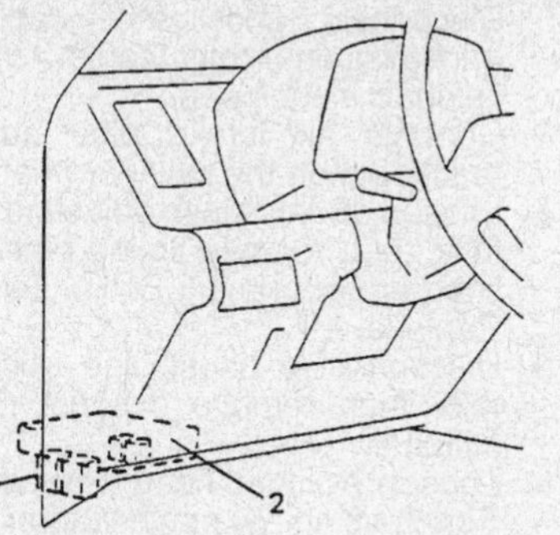
1
2
1. Fuel pump relay (Relay with Pink wire)
2. ECM
SK1069100079000X

Fig. 1 Fuel pump relay. 1993–95

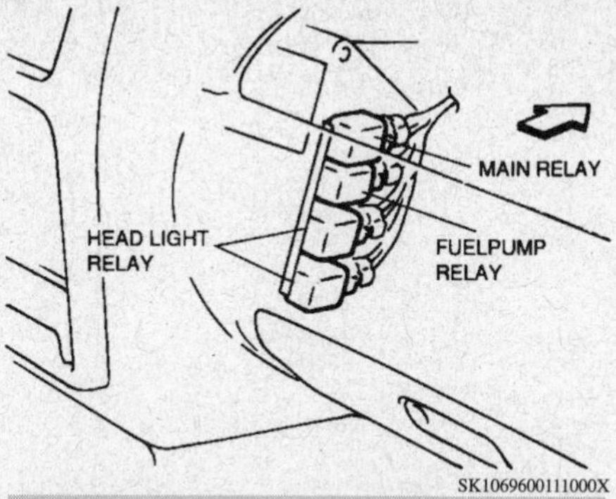
MAIN RELAY
HEAD LIGHT
RELAY
FUELPUMP
RELAY
SK1069600111000X

Fig. 2 Fuel pump relay. 1996

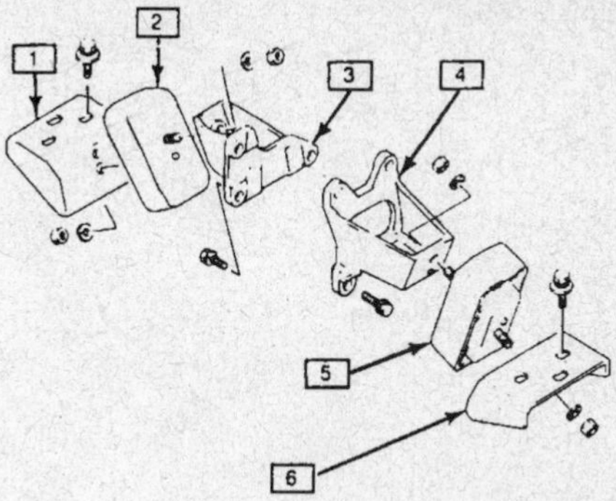
1
2
3
4
5
6
1 CHASSIS SIDE MOUNTING BRACKET (LEFT SIDE)
2 MOUNTING (LEFT SIDE)
3 ENGINE SIDE MOUNTING BRACKET (LEFT SIDE)
4 ENGINE SIDE MOUNTING BRACKET (RIGHT SIDE)
5 MOUNTING (RIGHT SIDE)
6 CHASSIS SIDE MOUNTING BRACKET (RIGHT SIDE)
SK1069100080000X

Fig. 3 Exploded view of engine mount

hoses and cables are marked and disconnected.

22. Reverse procedure to install, noting the following:
    a. Adjust clutch pedal free travel. Refer to procedure "Clutch Pedal, Adjust" in the "Clutch & Manual Transmission" section.
    b. Adjust accelerator cable and kick-down cable.
    c. Refill all fluid levels.
    d. **On models with A/C,** evacuate and charge A/C system.

16 VALVE ENGINE

1. Relieve fuel system pressure as outlined under "Precautions."
2. Disconnect and remove battery, then mark hood for reference and remove hood.
3. Drain coolant system into appropriate container, then remove radiator fan and fan shroud.
4. Remove air intake pipe with hoses, then disconnect accelerator cable and transmission throttle cable from throttle body, if equipped.
5. Remove intake manifold stiffener, then electrical harnesses from clamps.
6. Remove starter motor, then disconnect electrical connectors, ground wires and hoses as necessary.
7. Loosen bolts securing engine to transmission, then raise and support vehicle.
8. Drain engine oil into appropriate container, then disconnect fuel feed and return hoses from pipes.
9. Remove righthand transmission stiffener and transmission fluid hose clamp bolt, if equipped.
10. Remove exhaust pipes, lefthand transmission stiffener, then the clutch or torque converter housing lower plate.
11. **On models with automatic transmission,** remove torque converter bolts, using gear stopper tool, No. 09927-56010, or equivalent, to secure flywheel.
12. **On models equipped with power steering,** disconnect power steering pump with hoses attached and position aside.
13. **On models equipped with A/C,** disconnect A/C compressor with bracket attached and position aside.

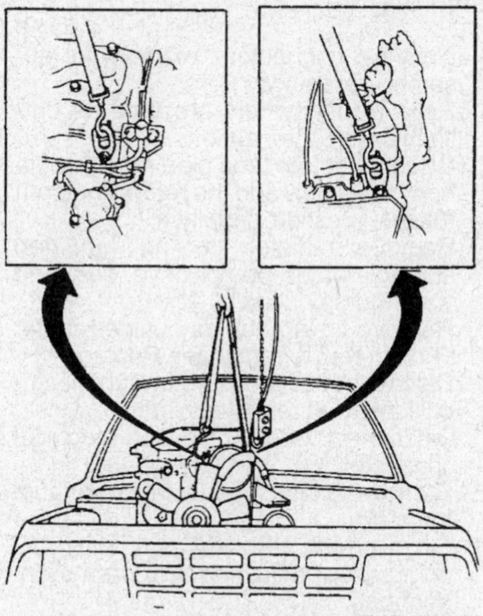
SK1069100081000X

Fig. 4 Engine lifting point location

14. **On all models,** remove nuts securing engine to transmission, then lower vehicle and support transmission with a suitable jack. **Do not lift, or support automatic transmission by oil pan.**
15. Install a suitable lifting device, **Fig. 4**, then remove right and left engine mounting bracket bolts.
16. Remove engine assembly from chassis and transmission by sliding towards front, then carefully hoisting from vehicle.
17. Reverse procedure to install, noting the following:
    a. Tighten nuts and bolts to specification.
    b. Adjust water pump, power steering pump and A/C compressor drive belt tension.
    c. Adjust accelerator and transmission throttle cable play.
    d. Ensure there are no fuel, water or exhaust gas leakages.

INTAKE MANIFOLD

REPLACE

8 VALVE ENGINE

1. Disconnect battery ground cable, then drain coolant system into appropriate container.
2. Remove air intake case.
3. **On models equipped with automatic transmission,** disconnect accelerator cable and kick-down cable from throttle body.
4. **On all models,** disconnect injector, throttle position sensor, ISC control solenoid valve and EGR sensor connectors.
5. Disconnect vacuum hoses from throttle body and throttle opener.
6. Disconnect water hose from ISC solenoid valve, then the ISC air hose.
7. With throttle valve lever held at full open, disconnect fuel feed pipe from throttle body and intake manifold.
8. Disconnect fuel return hose from pressure regulator.
9. Remove throttle body from intake manifold, then disconnect PCV hose from valve.
10. Disconnect pressure sensor and brake booster hoses from intake manifold.
11. **On models equipped with automatic transmission,** disconnect vacuum hose for transmission from intake manifold.
12. **On all models,** disconnect VSV hoses from intake manifold.
13. Disconnect water hose from thermostat cap, heater inlet hose and water bypass hose from intake manifold.
14. Disconnect EGR hose from valve, then the ground wires from intake manifold.
15. Disconnect all necessary electrical connectors.
16. Release wire harness from clamps.
17. Remove intake manifold from cylinder head.
18. Reverse procedure to install.

16 VALVE ENGINE

Refer to **Fig. 5** when performing the following procedure.

1. Relieve fuel system pressure as outlined under "Precautions."
2. Disconnect battery ground cable, then

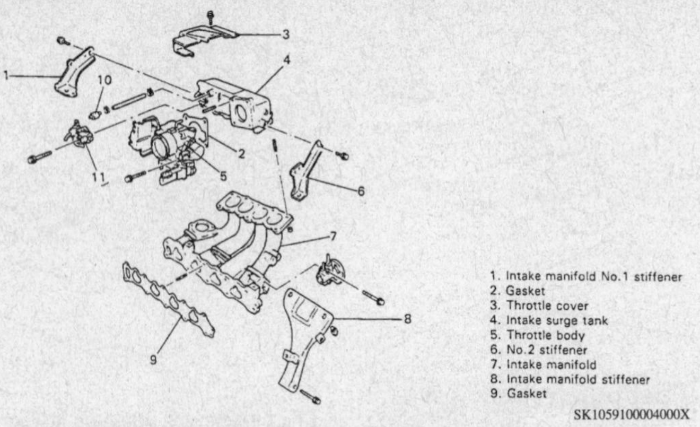
1
2
3
4
5
6
7
8
9
10
11
1. Intake manifold No.1 stiffener
2. Gasket
3. Throttle cover
4. Intake surge tank
5. Throttle body
6. No.2 stiffener
7. Intake manifold
8. Intake manifold stiffener
9. Gasket
SK1059100004000X

Fig. 5 Exploded view of throttle body & intake manifold. 16 valve engine

drain coolant system.

3. Remove air intake pipe, then disconnect accelerator cable and transmission throttle cable from throttle body, if equipped.
4. Disconnect electrical connectors, ground wires and hoses as necessary.
5. Disconnect fuel feed hose joint, using a back-up wrench while loosening flare nut, then remove fuel return hose from pipe.
6. Remove generator adjustment arm stiffener, intake manifold stiffener, Nos. 1 and 2 stiffener with EGR modulator.
7. Remove intake manifold with surge tank and throttle body from cylinder head.
8. Reverse procedure to install, noting the following:
   a. Adjust accelerator and transmission throttle cable play.
   b. Ensure there are no fuel, water or exhaust gas leakages.

EXHAUST MANIFOLD

REPLACE

1. Disconnect battery ground cable, then remove air intake pipe with bracket and air cleaner outlet hose.
2. Disconnect oxygen sensor electrical connector, then remove manifold stiffener.
3. Remove manifold upper cover, then the exhaust pipe from manifold.
4. Remove manifold mounting bolts and nut, then the manifold.
5. Reverse procedure to install.

CYLINDER HEAD

REPLACE

8 VALVE ENGINE

1. Disconnect battery ground cable.
2. Drain engine coolant system into appropriate container.
3. Disconnect accelerator cable and kickdown cable, if equipped, from throttle body.
4. Disconnect all engine cylinder head vacuum, fuel and coolant hoses, marking for assembly reference.
5. Disconnect all engine cylinder head electrical connectors, marking for assembly reference.
6. Relieve fuel system pressure as outlined under "Precautions."
7. Disconnect fuel feed pipe from throttle body assembly and the return line from the fuel pressure regulator.
8. Remove radiator cooling fan, fan shroud, water pump drive belt and water pump pulley.
9. Remove timing belt as outlined under "Timing Belt & Tensioner, Replace."
10. Disconnect oil pressure switch electrical lead from retaining clamp.
11. Disconnect oxygen sensor electrical connector.
12. Remove exhaust pipe from exhaust manifold.
13. **On models with A/C,** remove A/C compressor adjusting arm from cylinder head.
14. **On all models,** remove cylinder head cover.
15. Remove cylinder head bolts.
16. Using an appropriate lifting device, remove cylinder head with distributor, exhaust manifold, intake manifold and carburetor assembly from cylinder block.
17. Reverse procedure to install, noting the following:
   a. Install new cylinder head gasket with the side marked TOP facing upward toward the crankshaft pulley.
   b. Lightly oil cylinder head bolts, then using sequence shown in **Fig. 6, torque** bolts in two or three steps to 54 ft. lbs.
   c. Ensure there are no fuel, coolant or exhaust leakages.
   d. **On models with A/C,** evacuate and charge A/C system.

16 VALVE ENGINE

1. Relieve fuel system pressure as outlined under "Precautions," then disconnect battery ground cable.
2. Drain coolant system into appropriate container, then remove intake manifold stiffener.
3. Disconnect electrical connectors, ground wires, vacuum hoses and coolant hoses as necessary.
4. Disconnect fuel feed and return lines, then remove throttle cover.
5. Disconnect accelerator cable and transmission throttle cable from throttle body, if equipped.
6. Remove air intake pipe and pipe bracket, then the cylinder head cover.
7. Loosen all valve lash adjusting screws fully, then remove timing belt as outlined under "Timing Belt & Tensioner, Replace. "
8. Disconnect exhaust pipe from manifold, then remove exhaust manifold stiffener.
9. Loosen cylinder head bolts in order, **Fig. 7,** using a 8 mm hexagon wrench bit tool, No. 09900-00415 and hexagon wrench socket tool, No. 09900-00411, or equivalent.
10. Remove components that may interfere with removal, then the cylinder head with intake and exhaust manifolds and distributor using a suitable lifting device.
11. Reverse procedure to install, noting the following:
   a. Install new cylinder head gasket with side marked TOP facing upward toward the crankshaft pulley side.
   b. Ensure oil jet (venturi plug) is installed and not plugged.
   c. Apply engine oil to cylinder head bolts, then using sequence shown in **Fig. 8, torque** bolts in three steps; first step to 25 ft. lbs., second step to 40 ft. lbs., third step to 48–51 ft. lbs.
   d. Adjust accessory belt tensions, valve clearance, accelerator cable and transmission throttle cable play, and ignition timing.
   e. Ensure there are no fuel, coolant or exhaust leakages at all connections.

VALVE CLEARANCE SPECIFICATIONS

8 VALVE ENGINE

Valve clearance for intake valves should be 0.0051–0.0067 inch (cold) or 0.009–0.011 inch (hot).

Valve clearance for exhaust valves should be 0.0063–0.0075 inch (cold) or 0.0102–0.0108 inch (hot).

16 VALVE ENGINE

Valve clearance for intake and exhaust valves should be 0.0031–0.0047 inch (cold) or 0.0047–0.0063 inch (hot).

VALVE ADJUSTMENT

1. Disconnect battery ground cable, then remove cylinder head cover.
2. Rotate crankshaft clockwise using a 17mm socket until "V" mark on pulley aligns with "0" calibration on timing belt cover.
3. Remove distributor cap and check rotor position. If rotor is pointing to No. 1 cylinder on distributor cap, check valve lash at valves 1, 2, 5 and 7, **Figs. 9 and 10.** If rotor is pointing to No. 4

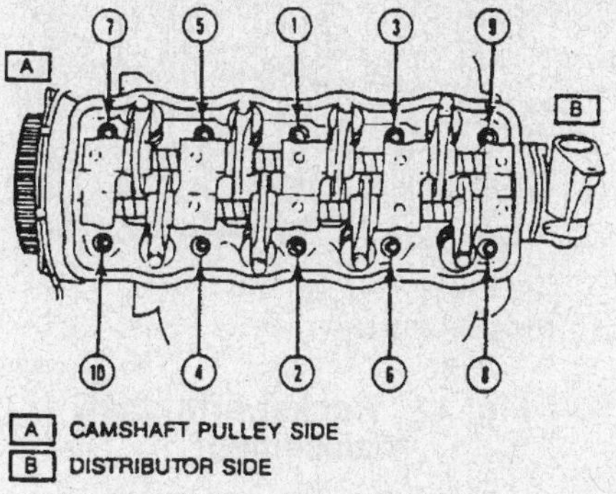
A
B
A CAMSHAFT PULLEY SIDE
B DISTRIBUTOR SIDE
SK1069100082000X

Fig. 6 Cylinder head bolt tightening sequence

cylinder on distributor cap, check valve lash at valves 3, 4, 6 and 8, **Figs. 9 and 10.**

4. If valve lash is out of specification, adjust as necessary. Use tappet adjuster wrench tool, No. 09917-18210, or equivalent, for 16 valve engines.
5. Install cylinder head cover, then connect battery ground cable.

ROCKER ARMS

REPLACE

8 VALVE ENGINE

1. Disconnect battery ground cable, then remove hood.
2. Remove front grille, then hood lock from front upper member.
3. Drain coolant system into appropriate container, then remove cooling fan and shroud.
4. Remove flexible A/C compressor suction hose from pipe, if equipped.
5. Remove radiator, then the water pump drive belt and pump pulley.
6. Remove timing belt and tensioner as outlined under "Timing Belt & Tensioner, Replace."
7. Remove air intake case and cylinder head cover.
8. Remove camshaft timing belt pulley and timing belt inside cover by inserting a 0.35 inch rod into hole in camshaft to lock camshaft, **Fig. 11.**
9. Loosen all valve lash adjusting screw locknuts and completely back off all adjusting screws.
10. Remove rocker arm shaft screws.
11. Remove intake and exhaust rocker arm shafts, rocker arms and springs, **Fig. 12.**
12. Inspect rocker arm as follows:
    a. Replace adjusting screw if tip is badly worn.
    b. Replace rocker arm if cam riding surface is badly worn.
13. Measure rocker arm shaft runout as follows:
    a. Using "V" blocks and dial indicator, measure shaft runout. Shaft runout should be less than 0.0004 inch.
    b. Measure rocker arm shaft outer diameter and rocker arm inner diameter using a micrometer and a bore gauge.

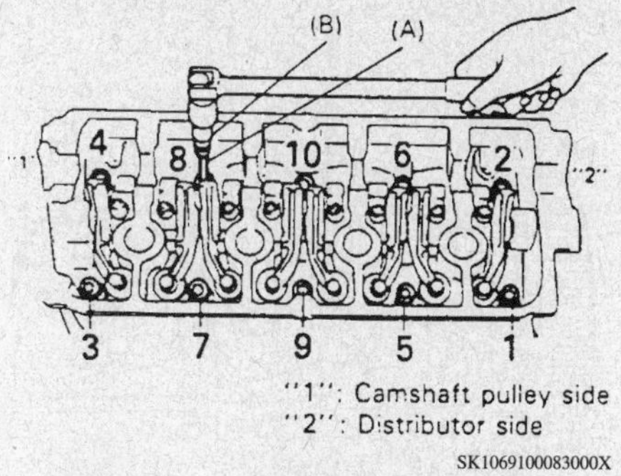
(B)
(A)
"1"
"2"
4
8
10
6
2
3
7
9
5
1
"1": Camshaft pulley side
"2": Distributor side
SK1069100083000X

Fig. 7 Cylinder head bolt loosening sequence. 16 valve engine

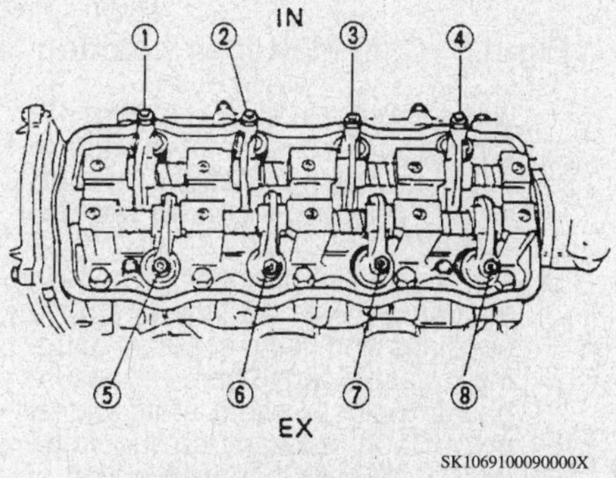
IN
EX
SK1069100090000X

Fig. 9 Valve identification. 8 valve engine

    c. Rocker arm shaft outer diameter should be 0.628–0.629 inch.
    d. Rocker arm inner diameter should be 0.629–0.630 inch.
    e. Rocker arm to shaft clearance should be 0.0005–0.00017 inch.
14. Reverse procedure to install, noting the following:
    a. Apply a thin coat of engine oil to the rocker arms and shafts.
    b. When installing the rocker arm shafts, ensure the correct shaft is used for both intake and exhaust rocker arms, **Fig. 13.**
    c. Install intake rocker arm shaft with the stepped side toward the camshaft pulley while the exhaust rocker arm shaft is toward the distributor gear case.
    d. Adjust valve lash as outlined under "Valve Adjustment."
    e. **On models with A/C,** evacuate and charge A/C system.

16 VALVE ENGINE

Removal

1. Disconnect battery ground cable, then remove front grille, **Fig. 14.**
2. Remove hood lock from front upper member, then disconnect horn electrical connector and remove front upper member from body, **Fig. 15.**
3. Drain coolant system into appropriate container, then place a drain pan under radiator and disconnect transmission hoses from radiator, if equipped.
4. Remove cooling fan/clutch and radiator shroud, then disconnect reservoir

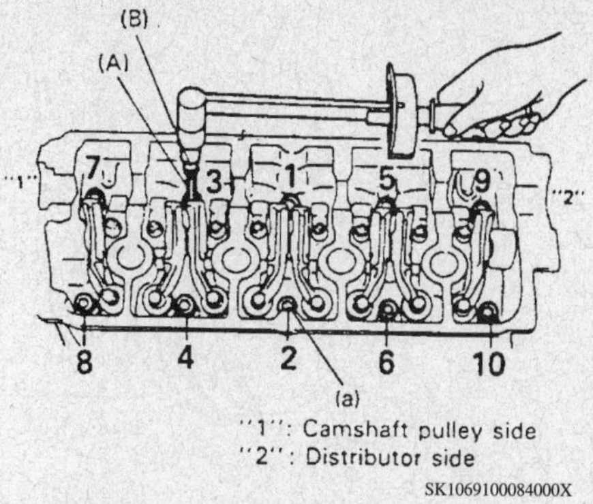
(B)
(A)
"1"
"2"
7
3
1
5
9
8
4
2
6
10
(a)
"1": Camshaft pulley side
"2": Distributor side
SK1069100084000X

Fig. 8 Cylinder head bolt tightening sequence. 16 valve engine

tank and hoses from radiator.

5. Remove radiator, then the timing belt as outlined under "Timing Belt, Replace."
6. Remove camshaft timing belt pulley using camshaft pulley holder tool, No. 09917-68220, or equivalent, then remove cylinder head cover.
7. Remove distributor as outlined in the "Electrical" section, then the distributor case from cylinder head. **Place a rag or container under case to catch oil after removal of case.**
8. Loosen all valve lash adjusting screws all the way to allow rocker arms to move freely.
9. Loosen camshaft housing bolts in sequence, **Fig. 16,** then remove camshaft housing and camshaft.
10. Remove rocker arm shaft plug and timing belt inner cover, then the intake rocker arm with clip from rocker arm shaft.
11. Remove rocker arm shaft bolts, then push off rocker arm shaft end to distributor side and remove O-ring from shaft.
12. Remove exhaust rocker arms and wave washer by pulling rocker arm shaft to front side.

Inspection

1. Inspect rocker arm cam face and adjusting screw tip for excessive wear. Replace if necessary.
2. Using "V" blocks and a dial gauge, check rocker arm shaft runout. If runout exceeds 0.008 inch, replace rocker arm shaft.
3. Check rocker arm to rocker arm shaft clearance using a micrometer and bore gauge. Measure rocker arm inner diameter (ID) and rocker arm shaft outer diameter (OD), difference between two readings is arm to shaft clearance. Rocker arm ID should be 0.629–0.630 inch, rocker arm shaft OD should be 0.6287–0.6293 inch and arm to shaft clearance should be 0.0001–0.0014 inch with a limit of 0.0035 inch. If limit is exceeded, replace shaft or arm as necessary.
4. Check camshaft wear using a micrometer. Height of intake lobes should be 1.4551–1.4557 inches with a limit of 1.4512 inches, exhaust lobes should be 1.4328–1.4334 inches with

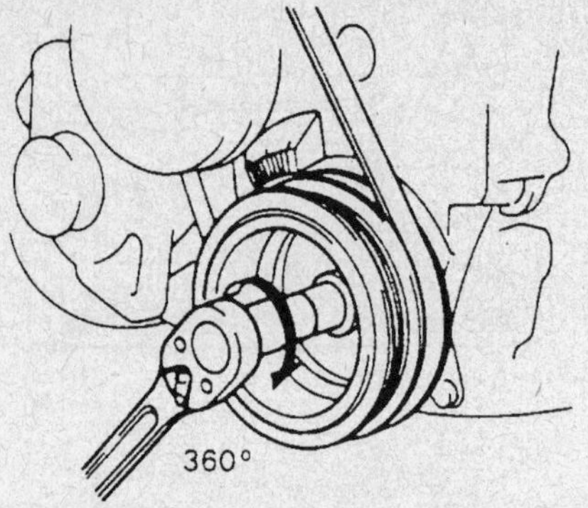
360°

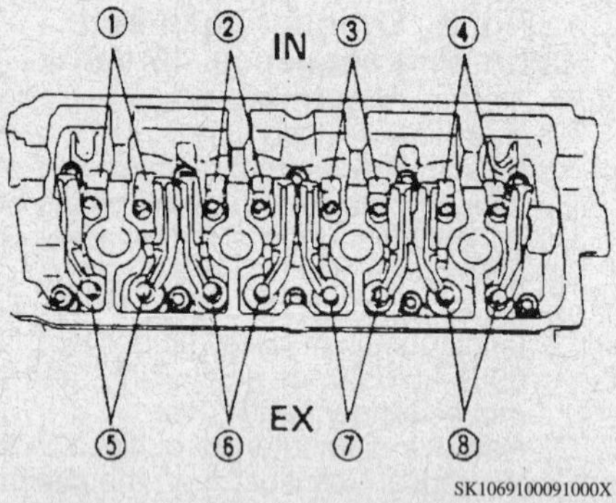
① ② IN ③ ④
EX
⑤ ⑥ ⑦ ⑧
SK1069100091000X

Fig. 10 Valve identification. 16 valve engine

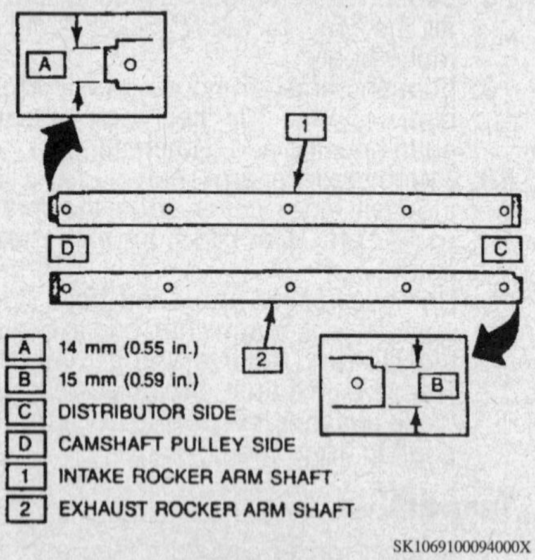
A
1
D
C
2
B
A 14 mm (0.55 in.)
B 15 mm (0.59 in.)
C DISTRIBUTOR SIDE
D CAMSHAFT PULLEY SIDE
1 INTAKE ROCKER ARM SHAFT
2 EXHAUST ROCKER ARM SHAFT
SK1069100094000X

Fig. 13 Rocker arm shaft replacement

a limit of 1.4289 inches. If measured height is below limit, replace camshaft.

5. Using "V" blocks and a dial gauge, check camshaft runout. If runout exceeds 0.0039 inch, replace camshaft.
6. Inspect camshaft journals and camshaft housings for pitting, scratches, wear or damage. Do not replace cylinder head without replacing housing.
7. Check camshaft journal clearance using a suitable gauging plastic as follows:
   a. Clean camshaft housings and journals, then install camshaft on cylinder head.
   b. Place pieces of gauging plastic the full width of camshaft journal onto camshaft journals parallel to camshaft.
   c. Install camshaft housings, then using sequence shown in **Fig. 17, torque** bolts in two or three steps to 7–9 ft. lbs. **Do not rotate camshaft while gauging plastic is installed.**
   d. Loosen camshaft housings bolts in sequence, **Fig. 16,** then remove housings and using scale on gauging plastic envelope, measure gauging plastic width at its widest point. Journal clearance should be 0.0016–0.0032 inch with a limit of 0.0047 inch.
8. If camshaft journal clearances exceed limit, measure journal housing bores and outer diameter of camshaft journals. Camshaft journal bore diameter should be 1.1024–1.1031 inches and camshaft journal OD should be 1.1000–1.1008 inches. Replace camshaft or cylinder head assembly, whichever difference from specification is greater.

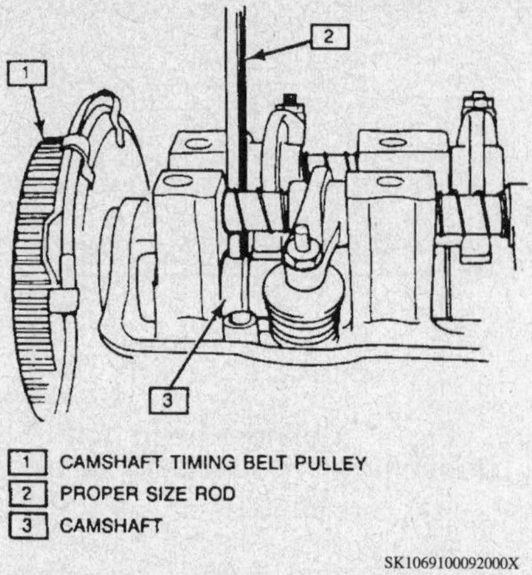
1
2
3
1 CAMSHAFT TIMING BELT PULLEY
2 PROPER SIZE ROD
3 CAMSHAFT
SK1069100092000X

Fig. 11 Camshaft lock position

Installation

1. Apply engine oil to rocker arm shaft and rocker arms, then install rocker arm shaft, exhaust side rocker arms and wave washer.
2. Install rocker arm shaft O-ring, then set rocker arm shaft so that cut part faces down and is parallel with head cover mating surface.
3. Install rocker arm shaft bolts and tighten to specification.
4. Fill arm pivot holding portions of rocker arm shaft with small amounts of engine oil, then install intake rocker arms with clips to rocker arm shaft.
5. Apply engine oil to lobes and journals on camshaft and journals on cylinder head, install camshaft to cylinder head.
6. Apply engine oil to camshaft housings journal surfaces, and Suzuki bond No. 1215 sealant No. 99000-31110, or equivalent, to surface of No. 6 camshaft housing which will mate with cylinder head.
7. Apply engine oil to housing bolts, then using sequence shown in **Fig. 17, torque** bolts in three or four steps to 7–9 ft. lbs.
8. Apply engine oil to camshaft oil seal lip, then press-fit oil seal until it becomes flush with housing surface.
9. Install rocker arm shaft plug and timing belt inner cover, then tighten rocker arm shaft plug to specification.
10. Install camshaft timing belt pulley to camshaft while fitting pin on camshaft into slot at "E" mark, **Fig. 18.**
11. Tighten camshaft timing belt pulley bolt to specification using camshaft pulley holder tool, No. 09917-68220, or equivalent.
12. Install timing belt as outlined under "Timing Belt, Replace."
13. Apply Suzuki bond No. 1215 sealant, No. 99000-31110, or equivalent, to part "A," **Fig. 19,** then install distributor case to cylinder head and tighten to specification.
14. Install distributor assembly as outlined in the "Electrical" section.
15. Adjust valve clearance as outlined under "Valve Adjustment," then install cylinder head cover and air intake pipe.
16. Install radiator and fill coolant system.
17. Install hood lock to front upper member, connect horn electrical connector,

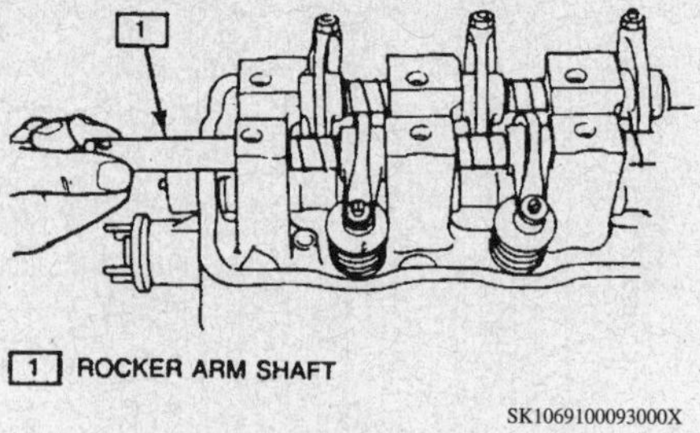
1
1 ROCKER ARM SHAFT
SK1069100093000X

Fig. 12 Rocker arm shaft replacement

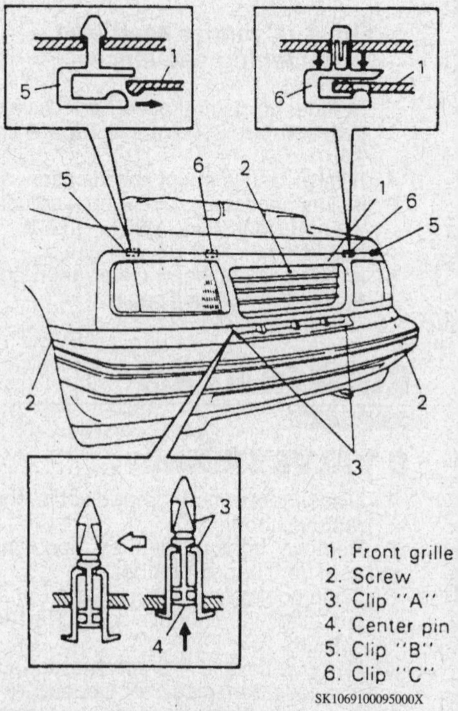
1. Front grille
2. Screw
3. Clip "A"
4. Center pin
5. Clip "B"
6. Clip "C"
SK1069100095000X

Fig. 14 Front grille replacement. 16 valve engine

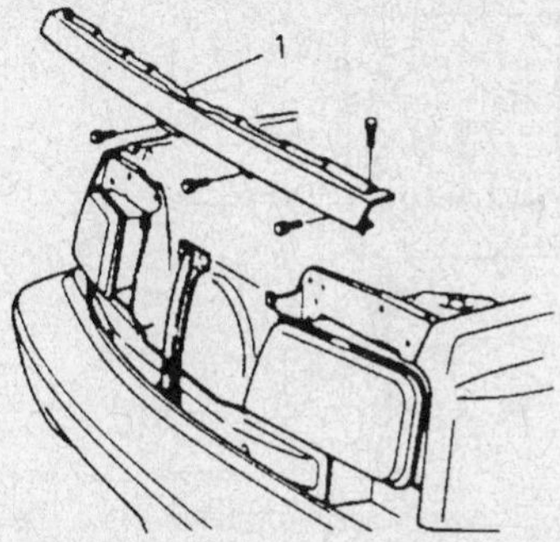
1
1. Front upper member
SK1069100096000X

Fig. 15 Front upper member replacement. 16 valve engine

then install front upper member to body.
18. Remove clip "C," **Fig. 14,** from front grille and install to body, then install front grille.
19. Connect battery ground cable. Ensure there are no water or oil leaks.
20. Adjust ignition timing.

VALVE & VALVE SPRINGS

REPLACE

8 VALVE ENGINE

1. Remove cylinder head assembly as outlined under "Cylinder Head, Replace."
2. Using valve spring compressor tool, No. J8062, or equivalent, compress valve springs, then remove valve cotters, **Fig. 20.**
3. Release valve lifter tool and remove valve spring retainers and valve springs.
4. Remove valves from cylinder head. **Before removing valves from head, ensure there are no burrs on valve stem from spring removal procedure.**
5. Using valve guide oil seal removal tool, No. J37281-A or J37755, or equivalent, remove valve stem oil seals and valve spring seats.
6. Reverse procedure to install, noting the following:
   a. Install new valve guides by driving out valve guides using valve guide removal tool, No. J34833, or equivalent, toward the valve spring side.
   b. Ream valve guide holes using valve guide reamer tool, No. J34832, or equivalent, to remove any burrs and to ensure the hole is perfectly round.
   c. Install valve guides by heating cylinder head uniformly at a temperature of 176–212°F to prevent head distortion. Using valve guide Installation tool No. J34834, or equivalent, drive valve guide into cylinder head leaving a 0.55 inch protrusion above the cylinder head, **Fig. 21.**
   d. Ream valve guide bore after Installation into the cylinder head using valve guide reamer tool, No. J34831, or equivalent.
   e. Install new valve stem oil seals using oil seal Installation tool, No. J34835, or equivalent.
   f. Install valve springs with small pitch end on the valve seat side, **Fig. 22.**

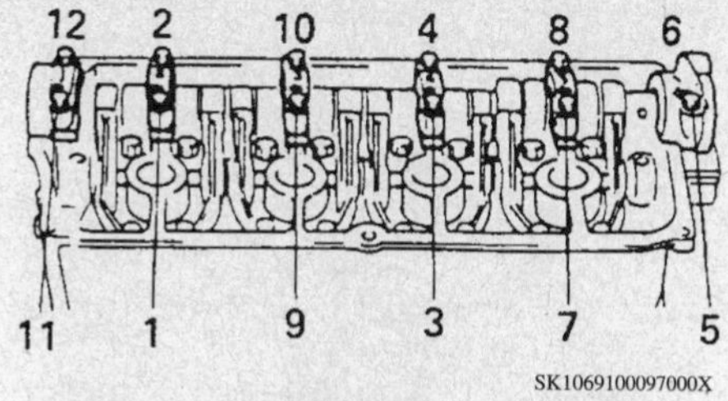
12 2 10 4 8 6
11 1 9 3 7 5
SK1069100097000X

Fig. 16 Camshaft housing bolt loosening sequence. 16 valve engine

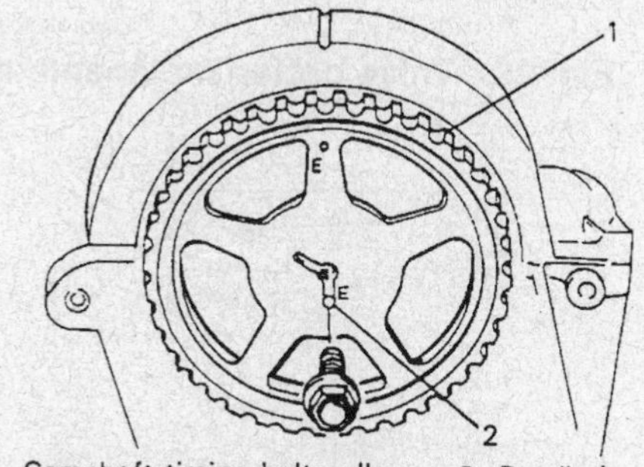
1
E
E
2
1. Camshaft timing belt pulley
2. Dwell pin
SK1069100099000X

Fig. 18 Camshaft pulley to camshaft position, slot "E." 16 valve engine

16 VALVE ENGINE

Disassembly

1. Remove cylinder head assembly as outlined under "Cylinder Head, Replace," then the distributor gear case, intake manifold with throttle body and exhaust manifold from cylinder head.
2. Remove rocker arms, rocker arm shaft and camshaft as outlined under "Rocker Arms, Replace" & "Camshaft, Replace."
3. Compress valve springs using valve lifter tool, No. 09916-14510 and valve lifter attachment tool, No. 09916-14910, or equivalent, then remove valve cotters using forceps tool, No. 09916-84510, or equivalent.
4. Remove valve lifter and valve lifter attachment, then spring retainers and valve springs.
5. Remove valves from cylinder head. **Prior to removing valves from head, ensure there are no burrs on valve stems.**
6. Remove valve stem oil seals from valve guides, then the spring seats.
7. Drive valve guides out from combustion chamber side to valve spring side using valve guide remover tool, No. 09916-44910, or equivalent.
8. Place disassembled components in order so they can be installed in their original positions. **Do not reuse valve stem seals or valve guides.**
9. Inspect all components for wear, burn, distortion and proper clearances and replace as necessary.

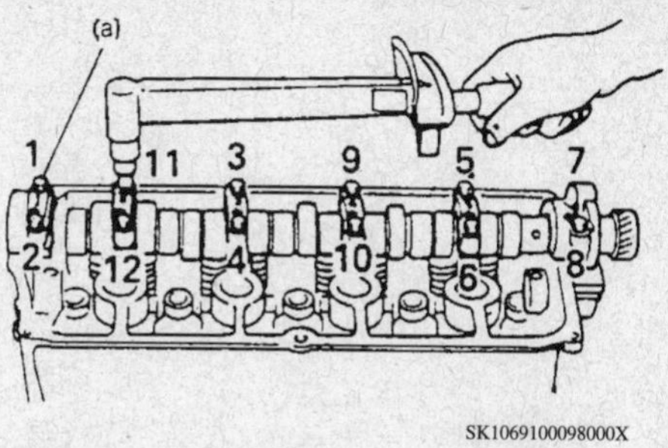
(a)
1 11 3 9 5 7
2 12 4 10 6 8
SK1069100098000X

Fig. 17 Camshaft housing bolt tightening sequence. 16 valve engine

Assembly

1. Ream valve guide bores using 11mm reamer tool, No. 09916-38210 and reamer handle tool, No. 09916-34541, or equivalent, to remove burrs and true bores.
2. Heat cylinder head uniformly to a temperature of 176–212°F so head will not be distorted, then drive new valve guides into bores using valve guide installer handle tool, No. 09916-58210 and valve guide installer attachment tool, No. 09916-56011, or equivalent. Drive valve guides in until valve guide installer contacts cylinder head. After Installation, ensure guides protrude by 0.045 inch from cylinder head.
3. Ream valve guides using 5.5 mm reamer tool, No. 09916-34550 and reamer handle tool, No. 09916-34541, or equivalent, then install valve seats to cylinder head.
4. Apply engine oil to new stem seals and spindle of valve stem seal installer tool, No. 09917-98221, or equivalent, fit oil seal to spindle. Install seals to valve guides by hand, using valve guide installer handle tool, No. 09916-58210, or equivalent.
5. Apply engine oil to valve stem seals, valve stems and valve guides, then install valves into guides.
6. Install valve springs and spring retainers, **Fig. 22.**
7. Compress valve springs using valve lifter tool, No. 09916-14510 and valve lifter attachment tool, No. 09916-14910, or equivalent, then fit two valve cotters into groove in valve stems using forceps tool, No. 09916-84510, or equivalent.
8. Install rocker arms, rocker arm shaft and camshaft as outlined under "Rocker Arms, Replace" & "Camshaft, Replace."
9. Install distributor gear case, intake

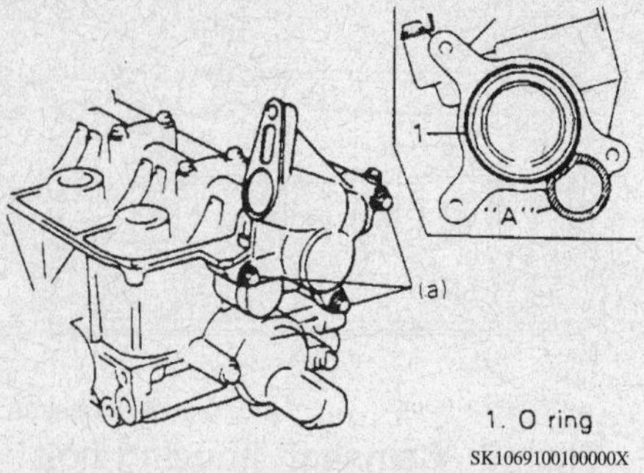
(a)
1. O ring
SK1069100100000X

Fig. 19 Sealant application part "A." 16 valve engine

manifold with throttle body and exhaust manifold to cylinder head, then the cylinder head assembly as outlined under "Cylinder Head, Replace."

TIMING BELT

REPLACE

With the timing belt removed, avoid turning the camshaft or crankshaft. If movement is required, exercise extreme caution to avoid valve damage caused by piston contact.

8 VALVE ENGINE

Removal

1. Disconnect battery ground cable, then remove coolant reservoir tank, cooling fan and fan shroud.
2. **On models with A/C,** discharge A/C system and remove compressor flexible suction hose from suction pipe.
3. **On all models,** remove engine accessory drive belts.
4. Remove water pump and crankshaft pulleys, then the timing belt outer cover.
5. Remove timing belt tensioner spring and stud, then loosen the tensioner bolt, **Fig. 23.**
6. Remove timing belt by pushing up tensioner pulley by hand.
7. Remove tensioner and tensioner plate.

Installation

1. Insert lock tab of tensioner plate into the lock tab slot of the tensioner.
2. Install tensioner assembly. Hand tighten tensioner bolt only at this time. Plate movement in upward direction should cause tensioner to move in same direction. If not, repeat step one.
3. Remove cylinder head cover, then loosen all valve lash adjusting screws and locknuts.
4. Turn crankshaft pulley clockwise and align timing mark on camshaft pulley with the "V" mark on the inner belt cover, **Fig. 24.**
5. Turn crankshaft clockwise and align punch mark on crankshaft with arrow on oil pump, **Fig. 24.**
6. Install timing belt so there is no slack on the drive side of the belt.
7. Hook tensioner spring to tensioner plate and bolt, then hand tighten tensioner stud.

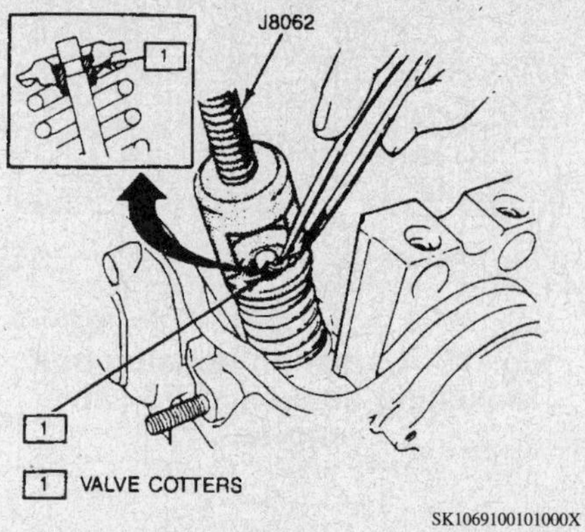
J8062
1
1 VALVE COTTERS
SK1069100101000X

Fig. 20 Valve cotter replacement

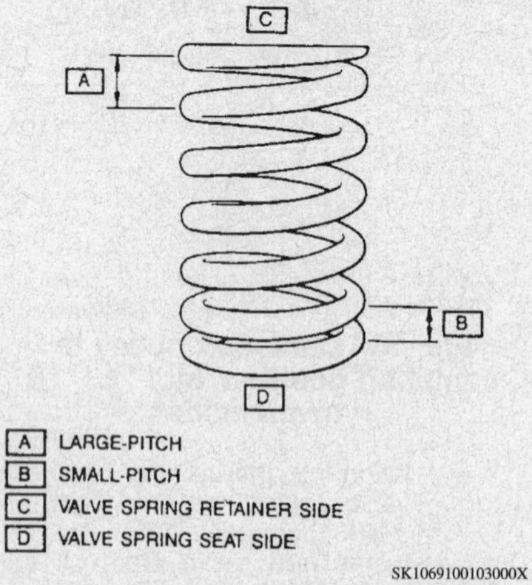
C
A
B
D
A LARGE-PITCH
B SMALL-PITCH
C VALVE SPRING RETAINER SIDE
D VALVE SPRING SEAT SIDE
SK1069100103000X

Fig. 22 Valve spring replacement

8. Turn crankshaft two full rotations clockwise after belt Installation.
9. Tighten tensioner stud and nut to specification.
10. Install timing belt outer cover.
11. Install crankshaft pulley and tighten to specification.
12. Install radiator shroud, water pump pulley, radiator cooling fan and A/C compressor flexible suction hose.
13. Install compressor and water pump drive belts and adjust tension.
14. Adjust valve lash. Refer to "Valve Adjustment" for procedure.
15. Install cylinder head cover and connect battery ground cable.
16. **On models with A/C,** evacuate and charge A/C system.

16 VALVE ENGINE

Removal

1. Disconnect battery ground cable, then remove power steering or A/C compressor belt, if equipped.
2. Remove radiator cooling fan, water pump pulley, water pump drive belt and fan shroud. **If it is difficult to remove fan shroud, drain coolant into appropriate container, then disconnect radiator inlet hose from radiator.**
3. Remove crankshaft pulley, then the timing belt outer cover.
4. Turn crankshaft to align timing marks,

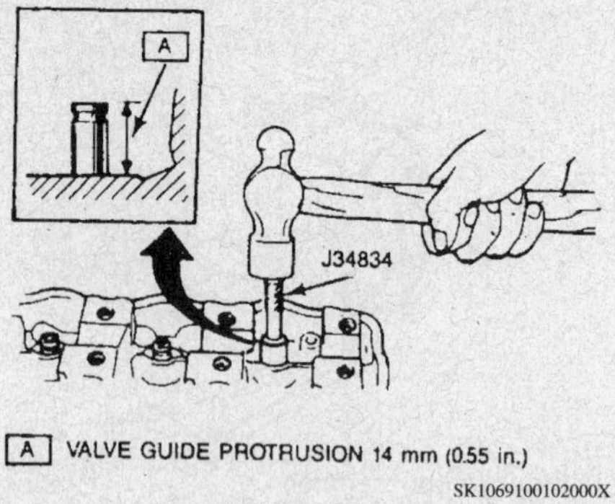
A
J34834
A VALVE GUIDE PROTRUSION 14 mm (0.55 in.)
SK1069100102000X

Fig. 21 Valve guide replacement

Fig. 25, then remove timing belt tensioner, tensioner plate, tensioner spring and timing belt, **Fig. 26. Do not rotate camshaft or crankshaft more than 90° clockwise or counterclockwise after timing belt is removed, or damage to pistons or valves may result.**

Installation

1. Install tensioner plate to tensioner, inserting lug of tensioner plate into hole in tensioner.
2. Install tensioner and tensioner plate, then hand tighten tensioner bolt.
3. Ensure timing mark on camshaft timing belt pulley is aligned with "V" mark on cylinder head cover, and punch mark on crankshaft timing belt pulley is aligned with arrow mark on oil pump case. **Do not rotate camshaft or crankshaft more than 90° clockwise or counterclockwise while timing belt is removed, or damage to pistons or valves may result.**
4. With timing marks aligned and tensioner pushed upwards, install timing belt on two pulleys so that drive side of belt is free of slack. **When installing belt, match arrow mark on belt with rotational direction of crankshaft.**
5. Install tensioner spring, **Fig. 27,** then hand tighten tensioner stud.
6. Take up slack of timing belt by turning crankshaft two rotations clockwise. Tighten tensioner stud, then the tensioner bolt to specification and ensure timing marks are properly aligned.
7. Install timing belt outer cover, ensuring seal is between water pump and oil pump case.
8. Install crankshaft pulley, tighten bolts to specification.
9. Install radiator fan shroud, water pump pulley, cooling fan and water pump drive belt.
10. Install power steering or A/C compressor belts, if equipped.
11. Ensure all nuts and bolts are tightened to specification.

CAMSHAFT

REPLACE

8 VALVE ENGINE

1. Remove cylinder head assembly as outlined under "Cylinder Head, Replace."

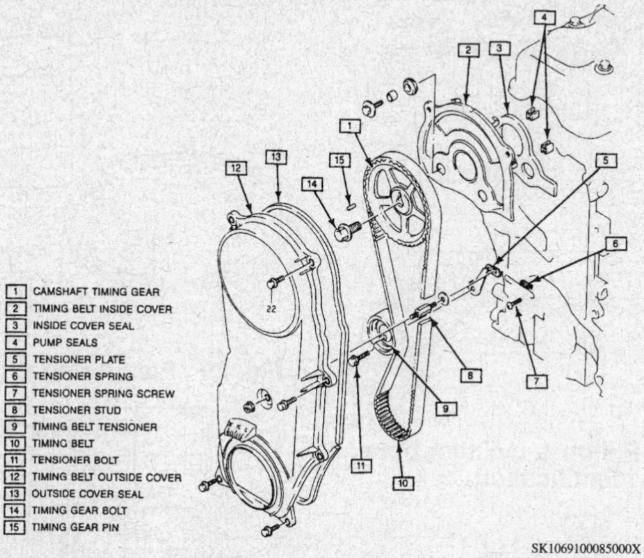
1 CAMSHAFT TIMING GEAR
2 TIMING BELT INSIDE COVER
3 INSIDE COVER SEAL
4 PUMP SEALS
5 TENSIONER PLATE
6 TENSIONER SPRING
7 TENSIONER SPRING SCREW
8 TENSIONER STUD
9 TIMING BELT TENSIONER
10 TIMING BELT
11 TENSIONER BOLT
12 TIMING BELT OUTSIDE COVER
13 OUTSIDE COVER SEAL
14 TIMING GEAR BOLT
15 TIMING GEAR PIN
SK1069100085000X

Fig. 23 Exploded view of timing belt & tensioner. 8 valve engine

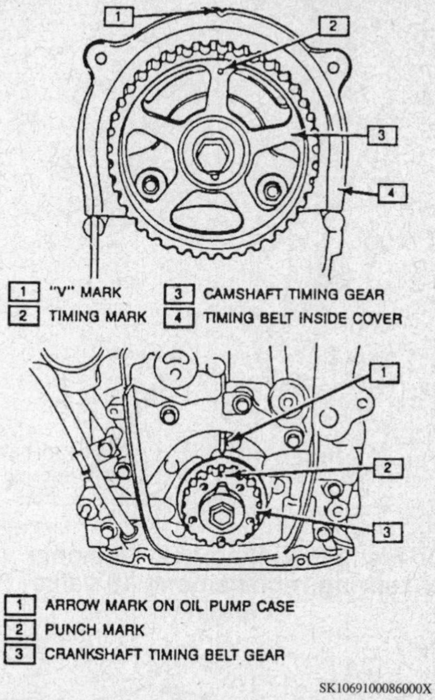
1 "V" MARK
2 TIMING MARK
3 CAMSHAFT TIMING GEAR
4 TIMING BELT INSIDE COVER
1 ARROW MARK ON OIL PUMP CASE
2 PUNCH MARK
3 CRANKSHAFT TIMING BELT GEAR
SK1069100086000X

Fig. 24 Timing belt pulley mark location. 8 valve engine

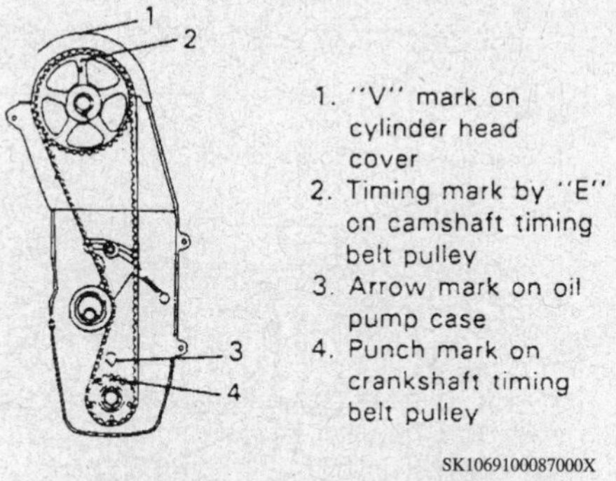
1. "V" mark on cylinder head cover
2. Timing mark by "E" on camshaft timing belt pulley
3. Arrow mark on oil pump case
4. Punch mark on crankshaft timing belt pulley
SK1069100087000X

Fig. 25 Timing belt pulley mark location. 16 valve engine

2. Remove distributor gear case, intake and exhaust manifold from cylinder head.
3. Remove camshaft timing belt pulley and timing belt inside cover.
4. Remove rocker arms, springs and rocker arm shafts as outlined under "Rocker Arm, Replace."
5. Remove camshaft from cylinder head.
6. Reverse procedure to install, noting the following:
   a. Apply engine oil to lobes and journals.
   b. Install a new camshaft end seal.

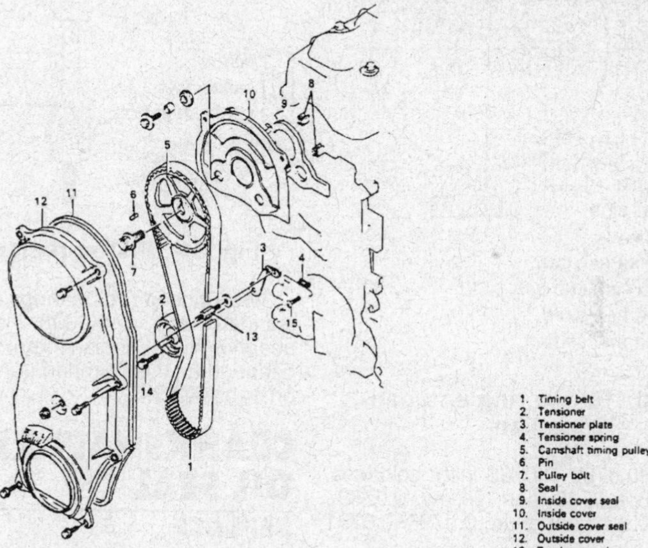
1. Timing belt
2. Tensioner
3. Tensioner plate
4. Tensioner spring
5. Camshaft timing pulley
6. Pin
7. Pulley bolt
8. Seal
9. Inside cover seal
10. Inside cover
11. Outside cover seal
12. Outside cover
13. Tensioner stud
14. Tensioner bolt
15. Tensioner spring bolt
SK1069100088000X

Fig. 26 Exploded view of timing belt & tensioner. 16 valve engine

PISTON & ROD ASSEMBLY

Each standard size piston has a No. 1 or No. 2 stamped on it representing outer diameter. There are also numbers stamped on cylinder block machined surface representing inner diameters of cylinders, **Fig. 28.** Stamped numbers on pistons and stamped numbers on cylinder block should correspond.

Before replacing the piston and connecting rods, decarbonize the top of the cylinder bore. When installing first and second rings, marked side of each ring should be toward top of piston, **Fig. 29.** The compression ring gap should be staggered and not inline with the oil ring gap, **Fig. 30.** Install piston, **Fig. 31.**

MAIN & ROD BEARINGS

Select new standard size main bearings as follows:

1. Crank webs of No. 2 and No. 3 cylinders have 5 stamped numbers on them, **Fig. 32.** These numbers represent journal diameters at bearing caps 1, 2, 3, 4 and 5 respectively. These numbers, 1, 2 and 3, represent the following diameters: No. 1, 2.0470–2.0472 inches; No. 2, 2.0468–2.0470 inches and No. 3, 2.0465–2.0468 inches.
2. Mating surface of cylinder block has 5 letters stamped on it, **Fig. 32.** These letters represent main bearing cap bore diameters at bearing caps 1, 2, 3, 4 and 5 respectively. These letters, A, B and C, represent the following diameters: A, 2.2047–2.2050 inches; B, 2.2050–2.2052 inches and C, 2.2052–2.2054 inches.
3. There are 5 standard bearing thicknesses, distinguished by paint marks as follows: green, 0.0786–0.0787 inch;

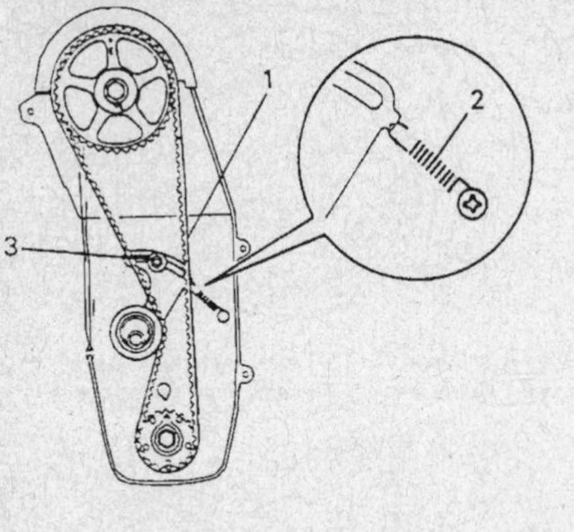
1
2
3

1. Drive side of belt
2. Tensioner spring
3. Tensioner stud

SK1069100089000X

Fig. 27 Timing belt tensioner spring replacement. 16 valve engine

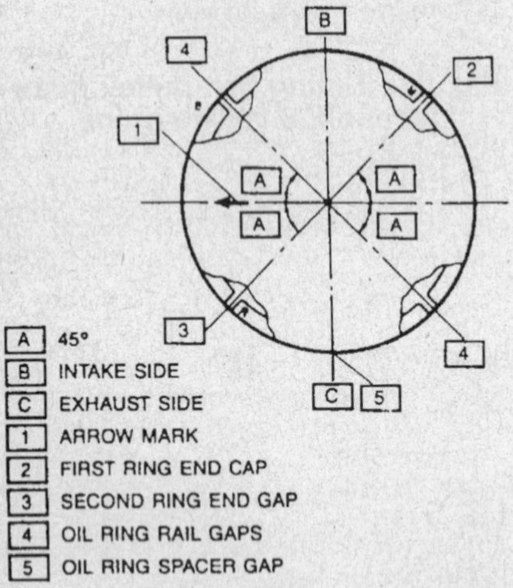
B
4
2
1
A
A
A
A
3
4
C
5
A 45°
B INTAKE SIDE
C EXHAUST SIDE
1 ARROW MARK
2 FIRST RING END CAP
3 SECOND RING END GAP
4 OIL RING RAIL GAPS
5 OIL RING SPACER GAP

SK1069100106000X

Fig. 30 Piston ring end gap position

black, 0.0787–0.0788 inch; colorless, 0.0788–0.0789 inch; yellow, 0.0789–0.0790 inch and blue, 0.0790–0.0791 inch.

4. Using numbers stamped on No. 2 and No. 3 crank webs and letters stamped on mating surface of cylinder block, determine new bearing to be installed using chart shown, **Fig. 33.**

Main bearings also come in 0.25 mm undersize, available in five thicknesses distinguished by paint marks as follows: green and red, 0.0835–0.0836 inch; black and red, 0.0836–0.0837 inch; red, 0.0837–0.0838 inch; yellow and red, 0.0838–0.0839 inch and blue and red, 0.0939–0.0840 inch.

When necessary to install undersize bearings, regrind journal to 2.0367–2.0373 inches diameter, measure re-ground journal diameter in two perpendicular directions, then using journal diameter measured and letters stamped on cylinder block, select the proper bearing using the chart shown, **Fig. 34.**

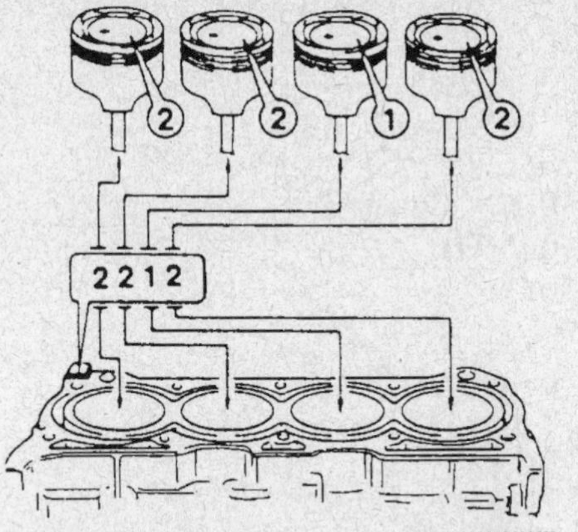
2
2
1
2
2 2 1 2

SK1069100104000X

Fig. 28 Piston & cylinder bore identification

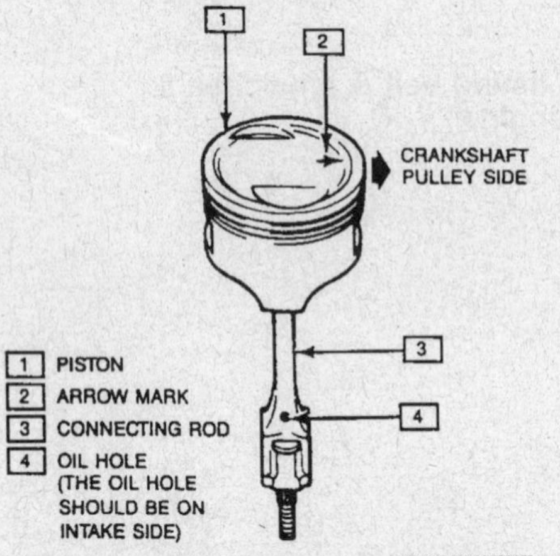
1
2
CRANKSHAFT PULLEY SIDE
3
4
1 PISTON
2 ARROW MARK
3 CONNECTING ROD
4 OIL HOLE (THE OIL HOLE SHOULD BE ON INTAKE SIDE)

SK1069100107000X

Fig. 31 Piston replacement

Two kinds of rod bearings are available, standard and a 0.0098 inch undersize bearing. To distinguish them, the undersize bearing has the stamped number "US025" on its backside.

CRANKSHAFT REAR OIL SEAL

REPLACE

1. Remove transmission and transfer case.
2. **On models with manual transmission,** remove clutch cover and clutch disc.
3. **On all models,** remove flywheel.
4. Remove rear main oil seal using a universal seal puller.
5. Reverse procedure to install.

OIL PAN

REPLACE

1. Raise and support vehicle.
2. Remove front differential assembly from chassis. Refer to "Drive Axles" for removal procedure.
3. Drain engine oil into appropriate container.
4. Remove clutch or torque converter housing lower plate.

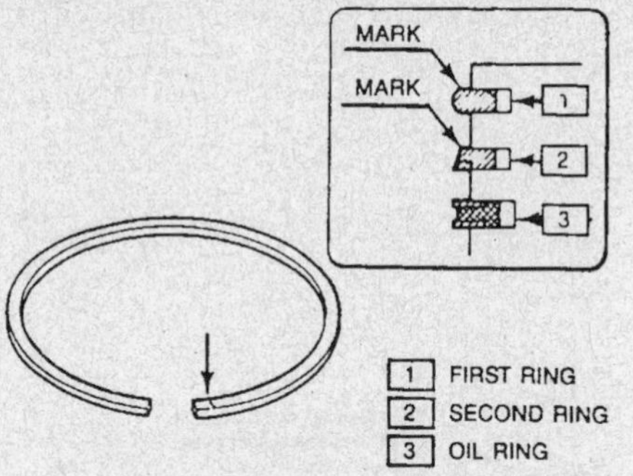
MARK
MARK
1
2
3
1 FIRST RING
2 SECOND RING
3 OIL RING

SK1069100105000X

Fig. 29 Piston ring replacement

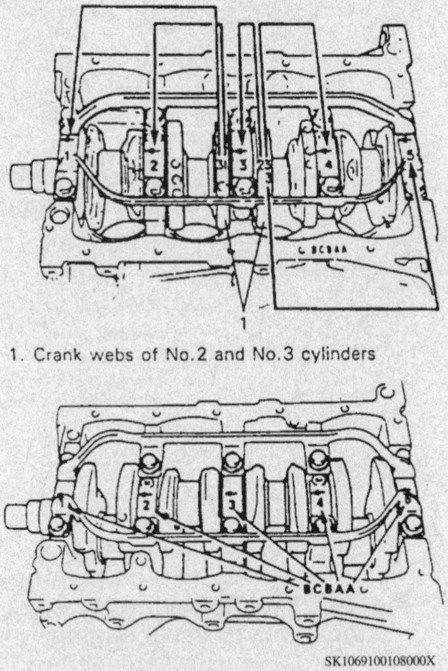
1
1. Crank webs of No.2 and No.3 cylinders

SK1069100108000X

Fig. 32 Crank web numbers & main bearing cap bore letters locations

5. Remove oil pan.
6. Reverse procedure to install.

OIL PUMP

REPLACE

1. Disconnect battery ground cable.
2. Remove timing belt and tensioner as outlined under "Timing Belt, Replace."
3. Remove generator and mounting brackets, then the power steering pump bracket or A/C compressor bracket, if equipped.
4. Lock crankshaft using gear stopper tool, No. 09927-56010, or equivalent, on flywheel, then remove crankshaft timing belt pulley.
5. Remove oil pan as outlined under "Oil Pan, Replace."
6. Remove oil pump mounting bolts, then the oil pump.
7. Inspect oil pump as follows:
   a. Inspect oil lip seal for wear or damage.
   b. Inspect oil pump outer and inner

		Numeral stamped on crank web (Journal diameter)		
		1	2	3
Alphabet stamped on mating surface (Bearing cap bore dia.)	A	Green	Black	Colorless
	B	Black	Colorless	Yellow
	C	Colorless	Yellow	Blue
		New standard bearing to be installed.		

SK1069100109000X

Fig. 33 Standard size main bearing selection chart

		Measured journal diameter		
		51.744–51.750 mm (2.0371–2.0373 in.)	51.738–51.744 mm (2.0369–2.0371 in.)	51.732–51.738 mm (2.0367–2.0369 in.)
Alphabets stamped on mating surface of cylinder block	A	Green & Red	Black & Red	Red only
	B	Black & Red	Red only	Yellow & Red
	C	Red only	Yellow & Red	Blue & Red
		Undersize bearing to be installed		

SK1069100110000X

Fig. 34 Undersize main bearing selection chart

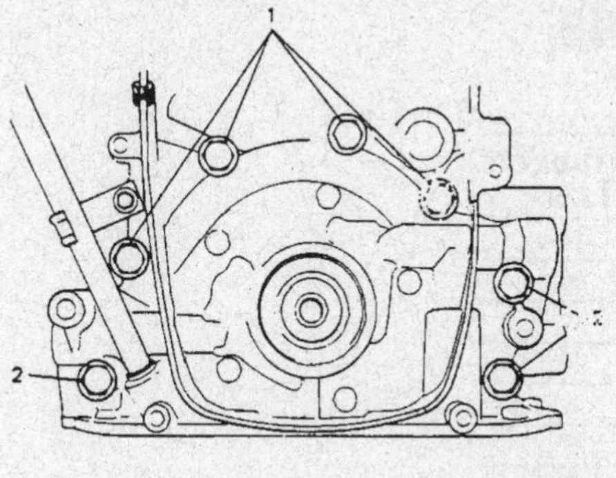
1
2

1. No. 1 bolts (short)
2. No. 2 bolts (long)

SK1099100007000X

Fig. 35 Oil pump bolt location

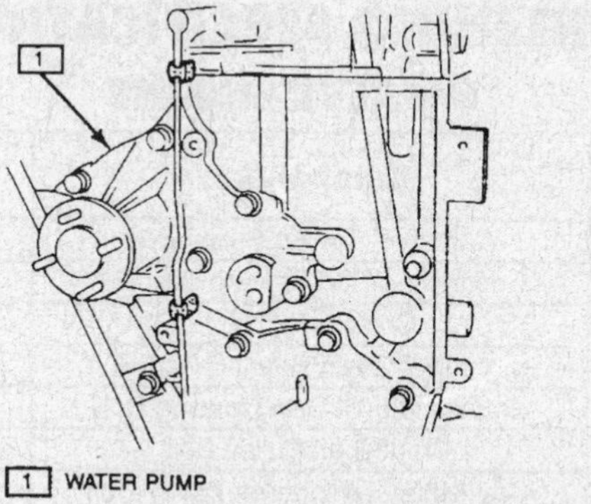
1
1 WATER PUMP

SK1089100004000X

Fig. 36 Water pump front cover seal replacement

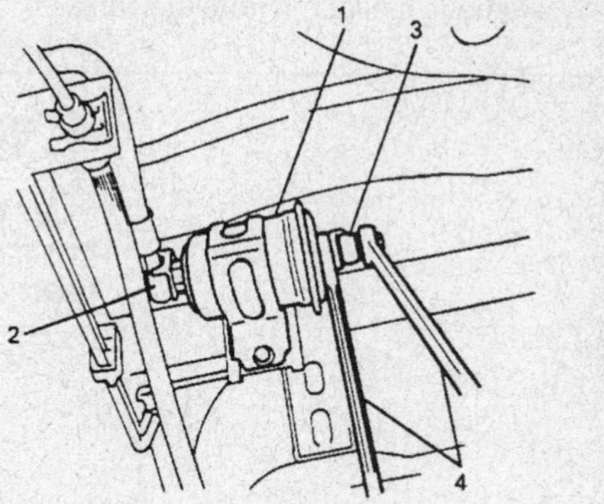
1
3
2
4

1. Fuel filter
2. Outlet pipe
3. Inlet pipe
4. Wrenches

SK1029100003000X

Fig. 37 Fuel filter removal

gears, gear plates and oil pump housing for excessive wear or damage.

c. Using thickness gauge, check radial clearance between outer rotor and case. Radial clearance should be 0.0122 inch. If clearance exceeds specifications, replace outer rotor or case.

d. Using straightedge, check side clearance of oil pump. Side clearance should be 0.0059 inch.

8. Reverse procedure to install, noting the following:
   a. Use oil seal guide tool, No. J34853, or equivalent, during Installation.
   b. Install bolts, **Fig. 35.**
   c. Install rubber seals between oil pump and water pump.

BELT TENSION DATA

Belt & Year	Belt Deflection Inch①
A/C Compressor	
1993–96	②
Alternator & Water Pump	
1993–96	.24–.31

①— With 22 lbs. pressure applied.
②— On Sidekick and X-90 models, .24–.36; on Esteem models, .30–.40.

COOLING SYSTEM BLEED

This engine does not require a specific bleed procedure. After filling coolant system, run engine to operating temperature with radiator/pressure cap off. Air will then be automatically bled through cap opening.

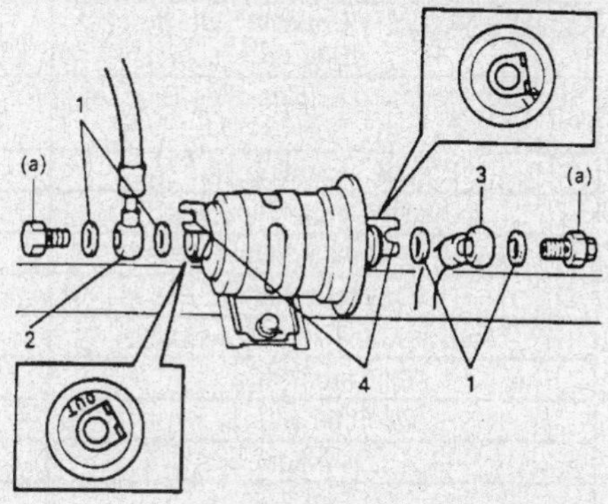
1
(a)
3
(a)
2
4
1

1. Gasket
2. Outlet pipe
3. Inlet pipe
4. Recess

SK1029100004000X

Fig. 38 Fuel filter Installation

THERMOSTAT

REPLACE

1. Drain coolant system into appropriate container, then remove thermostat cap from intake manifold.
2. Remove thermostat.
3. Install thermostat, ensuring air breather valve is positioned to front side of engine.
4. Install gasket and thermostat cap to intake manifold, then fill and bleed coolant system.

WATER PUMP

REPLACE

1. Disconnect battery ground cable, then drain coolant system into appropriate container.
2. Remove timing belt and tensioner as outlined under "Timing Belt, Replace."
3. Remove seal between oil pump and water pump, then the dipstick tube with dipstick.
4. Remove alternator adjusting arm, then the water pump.
5. Reverse procedure to install, using new gasket and rubber seals, **Fig. 36.**

RADIATOR, REPLACE

1. Disconnect battery ground cable.
2. Drain cooling system.
3. Disconnect cooling fan electrical connector.
4. **On models equipped with automatic transmission,** disconnect transmission cooler lines at radiator.
5. Remove cooling fan clutch and radiator shroud.
6. Disconnect radiator inlet and outlet hoses, and reservoir tank hose.
7. Remove radiator.
8. Reverse procedure to install.

FUEL PUMP

REPLACE

1. Relieve fuel system pressure as outlined under "Precautions."

2. Disconnect battery ground cable, then remove rear bumper cover.
3. Disconnect level gauge and fuel pump lead wire couplers.
4. Remove fuel tank filler hose and inlet valve, then drain fuel tank into appropriate container.
5. Remove fuel filter inlet pipe from filter, then the vapor and return hoses.
6. Remove tank protector, then the fuel tank.
7. Remove fuel pump from fuel tank.
8. Reverse procedure to install.

FUEL FILTER

REPLACE

1. Relieve fuel system pressure as outlined under "Precautions."
2. Disconnect battery ground cable and raise vehicle.
3. Disconnect inlet and outlet pipes from fuel filter using two wrenches, **Fig. 37.**
4. Remove fuel filter from chassis frame.
5. Reverse procedure to install, noting the following:
   a. Ensure gasket surfaces are free from damage.
   b. Ensure inlet and outlet pipes come into recess, **Fig. 38.**
   c. **Torque** union bolts to 22–28.5 lb. ft.
   d. Ensure there are no fuel leaks at each connection.

TIGHTENING SPECIFICATIONS

8 VALVE ENGINE

Year	Component	Torque/Ft. Lbs.
1993–95	Camshaft Timing Pulley Bolt	44
	Connecting Rod Bearing Cap Nut	26
	Cooling Fan Nut	8
	Crankshaft Main Bearing Cap Bolt	40
	Crankshaft Oil Seal Housing Bolt	8
	Crankshaft Pulley Bolt	8
	Crankshaft Timing Belt Pulley Bolt	52
	Cylinder Head Bolts	③
	Cylinder Head Cover Bolt	3.7
	Driveplate②	58
	Engine Mounting Chassis Side Bracket Bolt	41
	Engine Mounting Engine Side Bracket Bolt	41
	Engine Mounting Nut	33
	Exhaust Center Pipe Nut	37
	Exhaust Manifold Nut & Bolt	17
	Flywheel Bolt①	58
	Intake Manifold Nut & Bolt	17
	Oil Drain Plug	26
1993–95	Oil Filter Stand	17
	Oil Filter	10
	Oil Pan Bolt	8
	Oil Pressure Switch	10
	Oil Pump Case Bolt	8
	Oil Pump Rotor Plate Screw	8
	Oil Pump Strainer	8
	Rocker Arm Shaft Screw	8
	Spark Plugs	18
	Throttle Body Bolt	17
	Timing Belt Cover Bolt	8
	Timing Belt Tensioner Bolt	20
	Timing Belt Tensioner Stud	8
	Torque Converter Bolt	41
	Valve Adjusting Screw Locknut	13
	Water Pump Bolt	8

① — Manual transmission.
② — Automatic transmission.
③ — Refer to "Cylinder Head, Replace" for tightening procedure.

TIGHTENING SPECIFICATIONS

16 VALVE ENGINE

Year	Component	Torque/Ft. Lbs.
1993–96	Camshaft Housing Bolts	④
	Camshaft Timing Pulley Bolt	41–46
	Connecting Rod Bearing Cap Nut	24–27
	Cooling Fan Nut	7–9
	Crankshaft Main Bearing Cap Bolt	37–41
	Crankshaft Pulley Bolt	11–13
	Crankshaft Timing Belt Pulley Bolt	76–83
	Cylinder Head Bolts	③
	Cylinder Head Cover Bolt	7–9
	Cylinder Head Venturi Plug	3–4
	Driveplate②	55–58
	Engine Mounting Chassis Side Bracket Bolt	29–43
	Engine Mounting Engine Side Bracket Bolt	29–43
	Engine Mounting Nut	29–36
	Exhaust Pipe Nuts & Bolts	29–43
	Exhaust Manifold Nut & Bolt	14–20
	Exhaust Manifold Stiffener Nut	29–43
	Flywheel Bolt①	55–58
	Fuel Feed Pipe Flare Nut	29–36
	Intake Manifold Nuts & Bolts	14–20
	Intake Manifold Stiffener Bolts	29–43
	Oil Pan Drain Plug	22–29
	Oil Pan Nuts & Bolts	7–9
1993–96	Oil Pressure Switch	9–11
	Oil Pump Case Bolts	7–9
	Oil Pump Rotor Plate Screw	7–9
	Oil Pump Stay Bolt	7–9
	Oil Pump Strainer Bolt	7–9
	Rocker Arm Shaft Bolts	7–9
	Rocker Arm Shaft Plug	22–25
	Thermostat Case Bolts	8–12
	Throttle Body Bolt	14–20
	Timing Belt Cover Nuts & Bolts	7–9
	Timing Belt Tensioner Bolt	16–20
	Timing Belt Tensioner Stud	7-9
	Torque Converter Bolts	44–51
	Transmission Stiffener Bolts	29–43
	Transmission To Engine Bolts	51–72
	Valve Adjusting Screw Locknut	8–9
	Water Pump Bolt	8–9

① — Manual transmission.
② — Automatic transmission.
③ — Refer to "Cylinder Head, Replace" for tightening procedure.
④ — Refer to "Rocker Arms, Replace" for tightening procedure.

1.8L Engine

NOTE: On Air Bag Equipped Models, Refer To "Air Bag System Precautions" Located In The Front Of This Manual For System Disarming & Arming Procedures.

INDEX

	Page No.
Belt Tension Data	40-53
Camshaft, Replace	40-51
Compression Pressure	40-50
Cooling System Bleed	40-53
Cylinder Head, Replace	40-51
Engine Rebuilding Specifications	40-165
Engine, Replace	40-50
Exhaust Manifold, Replace	40-51
Fuel Filter, Replace	40-53
Fuel Pump, Replace	40-53
Intake Manifold, Replace	40-50
Oil Pan, Replace	40-52
Oil Pump, Replace	40-53
Piston & Rod Assembly	40-52
Precautions	40-50
Air Bag Systems	40-50
Fuel System Pressure Relief	40-50
Radiator, Replace	40-53
Thermostat, Replace	40-53
Tightening Specifications	40-54
Timing Chain, Replace	40-51
Valve Clearance Specifications	40-51

PRECAUTIONS

AIR BAG SYSTEMS

Refer to "Air Bag System Precautions" in the front of this manual for system disarming and arming procedures.

FUEL SYSTEM PRESSURE RELIEF

1. Place manual transmission models in Neutral or automatic transmission models in Park, then set parking brake and block drive wheels.
2. Disconnect fuel pump relay, **Fig. 1.**
3. Remove fuel filler cap to release fuel vapor pressure in tank, then install cap.
4. Start and run engine until it stalls. Repeat cranking engine three times for three seconds each time to dissipate fuel pressure in fuel lines.

COMPRESSION PRESSURE

Standard compression pressure is 199 psi with a minimum of 170 psi. Maximum allowable difference between cylinders is 14.2 psi.

ENGINE

REPLACE

1. Relieve fuel system pressure as outlined under "Precautions."
2. Disconnect and remove battery, then mark hood for reference and remove hood.
3. Drain engine oil and coolant.
4. Remove radiator fan, fan shroud and cooling fan.
5. Disconnect accelerator cable.
6. **On models with automatic transmission,** disconnect throttle cable.
7. **On all models,** remove strut tower bar.
8. Remove air intake pipe with hoses, then disconnect accelerator cable and transmission throttle cable from throttle body.
9. Remove electrical harness connectors.
10. Remove fuel feed and return lines.
11. Remove heater hoses from heater core.
12. Remove EVAP canister hose and brake booster vacuum hose.
13. Remove MAP sensor hose.
14. **On models with power steering,** disconnect power steering pump with hoses attached and position aside.
15. **On models with A/C,** disconnect A/C compressor with bracket attached and position aside.
16. **On all models,** raise and support vehicle.
17. Remove transfer case as outlined in "Transfer Case " section.
18. Remove exhaust pipe.
19. Remove righthand transmission stiffener and transmission fluid hose clamp bolt, if equipped.
20. Remove clutch housing lower plate.
21. **On models with automatic transmission,** remove torque converter bolts.
22. **On all models,** lower vehicle and remove starter motor.
23. Raise and support vehicle, then support transmission using a suitable jack.
24. Loosen bolts securing engine to transmission.
25. Install a suitable lifting device, then remove right and left engine mounting bracket bolts.
26. Remove engine assembly from chassis and transmission by sliding towards front, then carefully hoisting from vehicle.
27. Reverse procedure to install, noting the following:
    a. Tighten nuts and bolts to specification.
    b. Adjust water pump, power steering pump and A/C compressor drive belt tension.
    c. Adjust accelerator and transmission throttle cable play.

INTAKE MANIFOLD

REPLACE

1. Relieve fuel system pressure as outlined under "Precautions."
2. Disconnect battery ground cable, then drain engine coolant.
3. Remove strut tower bar and air temperature sensor.
4. Remove air cleaner upper case and outlet hose as a unit.
5. Remove throttle cover, then disconnect accelerator cable.
6. **On models with automatic transmission,** disconnect throttle cable.
7. **On all models,** disconnect the following electrical connectors:
    a. Exhaust gas recirculation (EGR) valve.
    b. Idle air control (IAC) valve.
    c. Throttle position (TP) sensor.
    d. Manifold absolute pressure (MAP) sensor.
    e. Evaporative emissions (EVAP) solenoid purge valve.
    f. Ground terminal from intake manifold.
8. Disconnect hoses as necessary.
9. Remove throttle body, **Fig. 2.**
10. Remove intake manifold front and rear stiffeners.
11. Disconnect water pipe from intake manifold.
12. Remove intake manifold and gasket from cylinder head.
13. Reverse procedure to install, noting the following:
    a. Install new intake manifold gasket.
    b. Tighten to specifications.
    c. Adjust accelerator and transmission throttle cable play.
    d. Ensure there are no fuel, water or exhaust gas leakages.

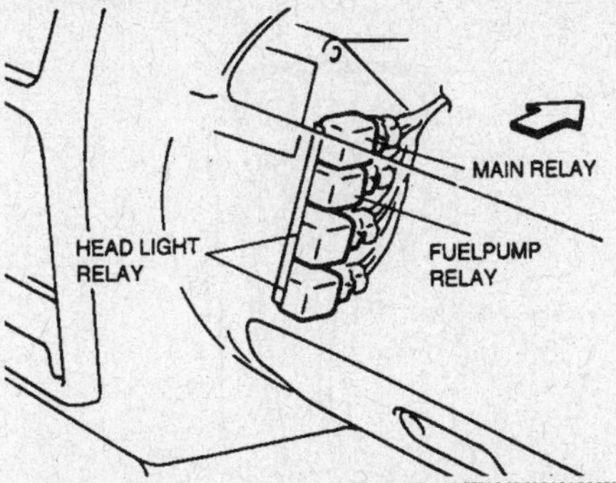
MAIN RELAY
HEAD LIGHT RELAY
FUELPUMP RELAY
SK1069600121000X

Fig. 1 Fuel pump relay

EXHAUST MANIFOLD

REPLACE

1. Disconnect battery ground cable, then remove strut tower bar.
2. Disconnect heated oxygen sensor electrical connector, then remove manifold upper cover.
3. Remove manifold stiffener, then the exhaust pipe from manifold.
4. Remove manifold mounting bolts and nut, then the manifold and gasket.
5. Reverse procedure to install.

CYLINDER HEAD

REPLACE

1. Relieve fuel system pressure as outlined under "Precautions," then disconnect battery ground cable.
2. Drain engine oil and coolant, then remove strut tower bar.
3. Remove air cleaner outlet hose.
4. Disconnect accelerator cable.
5. **On models with automatic transmission,** disconnect throttle cable.
6. **On all models,** remove 1st timing chain as outlined in "Timing Chain, Replace".
7. Disconnect the following electrical connectors:
   a. Exhaust gas recirculation (EGR) valve.
   b. Idle air control (IAC) valve.
   c. Throttle position (TP) sensor.
   d. Manifold absolute pressure (MAP) sensor.
   e. Evaporative emissions (EVAP) solenoid purge valve.
   f. Heated oxygen sensor (H2OS).
   g. Coolant temperature switch.
   h. Engine coolant temperature (ECT) sensor.
   i. Injector wire harness.
   j. Ground terminal from intake manifold.
8. Disconnect hoses and lines, as necessary.
9. Remove intake manifold front stiffener.
10. Disconnect water pipe from intake manifold.
11. Remove exhaust pipe and exhaust manifold stiffener.
12. Loosen cylinder head bolts in sequence, **Fig. 3. Remove M6 bolt.**

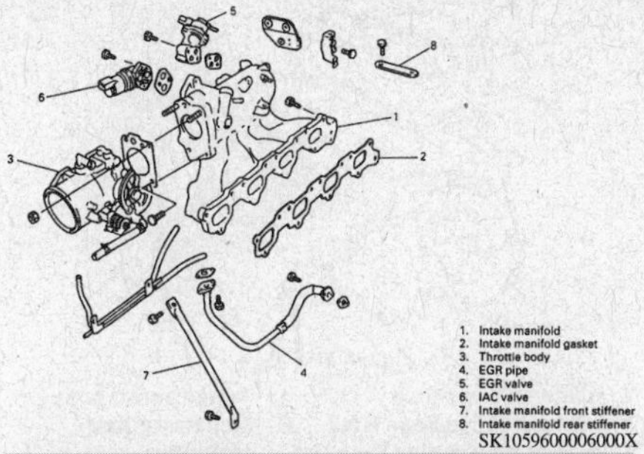
1. Intake manifold
2. Intake manifold gasket
3. Throttle body
4. EGR pipe
5. EGR valve
6. IAC valve
7. Intake manifold front stiffener
8. Intake manifold rear stiffener
SK1059600006000X

Fig. 2 Exploded view of throttle body & intake manifold

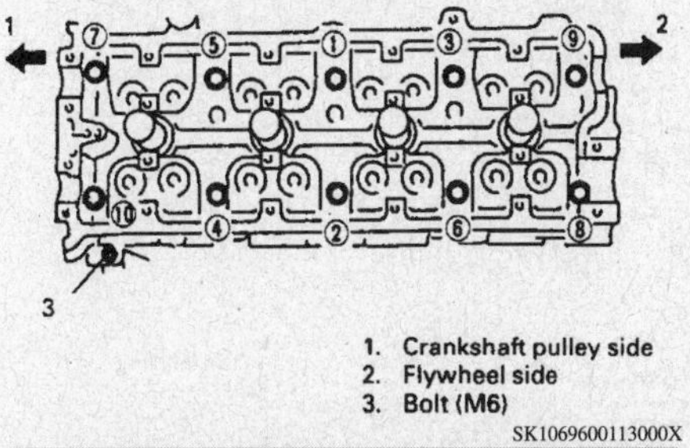
1. Crankshaft pulley side
2. Flywheel side
3. Bolt (M6)
SK1069600113000X

Fig. 4 Cylinder head bolt tightening sequence.

13. Using a suitable lifting device, remove cylinder head with intake and exhaust manifolds.
14. Reverse procedure to install. Apply engine oil to cylinder head bolts, then using sequence shown in **Fig. 4,** tighten bolts as follows:
    a. **Torque** bolts to 39 ft. lbs.
    b. **Torque** bolts to 61 ft. lbs.
    c. Loosen bolts completely using sequence shown in **Fig. 3.**
    d. **Torque** bolts to 76 ft. lbs.
    e. **Torque** M6 bolt to 8 ft. lbs. after securing head bolts.

VALVE CLEARANCE SPECIFICATIONS

The 1.8L engine is equipped with hydraulic lash adjusters and valve clearance is not adjustable.

TIMING CHAIN

REPLACE

1. Disconnect battery ground cable.
2. Drain engine oil and engine coolant.
3. Remove oil pan as outlined in "Oil Pan, Replace." Remove oil strainer, **Fig. 5.**
4. Remove cylinder head cover.
5. Remove water bypass and bypass hose No. 2, **Fig. 6.**
6. Remove cooling fan, fan pulley and fan belt.
7. Turn drive belt tensioner center bolt in a clockwise direction and remove alternator belt.
8. Remove water pump pulley, belt tensioner and idler pulley.
9. Disconnect radiator outlet hose from thermostat housing.

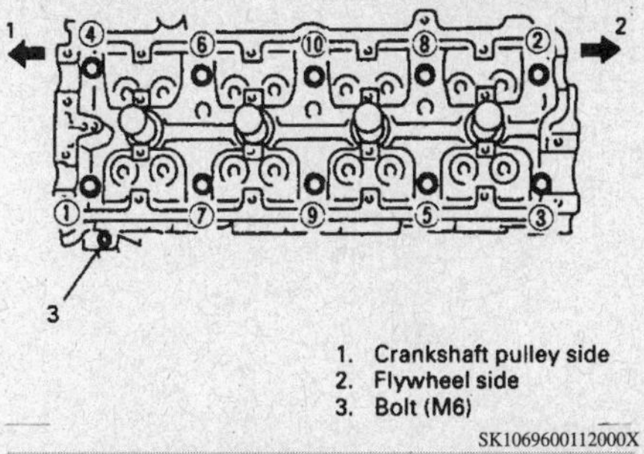
1. Crankshaft pulley side
2. Flywheel side
3. Bolt (M6)
SK1069600112000X

Fig. 3 Cylinder head bolt loosening sequence

10. Remove A/C compressor from bracket and position aside.
11. Remove crankshaft pulley using puller tool No. 09044036011 and attachment No. 09926–58010, or equivalents.
12. Remove timing case cover.
13. Rotate crankshaft until key on crankshaft points straight up, arrow mark on idler sprocket points straight up and marks on sprockets match with marks on cylinder head, **Fig. 7.**
14. Remove timing chain tensioner No. 2 by turning intake camshaft counterclockwise a little while pushing back pad, **Fig. 8.**
15. Remove camshaft sprockets and timing chain.
16. Remove timing chain guide No. 1, then adjuster No. 1 and tensioner, **Fig. 9.**
17. Remove idler sprocket and 1st timing chain. Remove crankshaft timing sprocket, if necessary.
18. Reverse procedure to install, noting the following:
    a. Install 1st timing chain by aligning dark blue plate of chain with match mark on idler sprocket, **Fig. 10,** then ensure yellow plate chain aligns with match mark on crankshaft timing sprocket, **Fig. 11.**
    b. Apply sealant No. 99000–31150, or equivalent, to timing case cover.
    c. Tighten to specification.

CAMSHAFT

REPLACE

1. Disconnect battery ground cable.
2. Drain engine oil and coolant.
3. Remove oil pan as outlined in "Oil Pan, Replace."
4. Remove cylinder head cover.
5. Remove timing chain cover, 2nd timing chain and chain tensioner as outlined in "Timing Chain, Replace".
6. Remove camshaft position sensor (CMP), **Fig. 12.**
7. Rotate crankshaft to position key as shown, **Fig. 13.**
8. Loosen, then remove camshaft housing bolts in sequence, **Fig. 14.** Note and mark location of camshaft housings.
9. Remove camshafts.
10. Reverse procedure to install, noting the following:
    a. Match key on crankshaft to timing mark, **Fig. 15.**

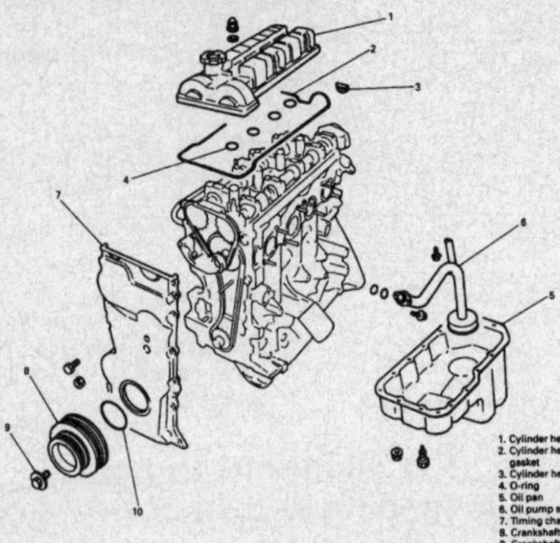

1. Cylinder head cover
2. Cylinder head cover gasket
3. Cylinder head side seal
4. O-ring
5. Oil pan
6. Oil pump strainer
7. Timing chain cover
8. Crankshaft pulley
9. Crankshaft pulley bolt
10. Oil seal

SK1069600114000X

Fig. 5 Timing chain cover removal

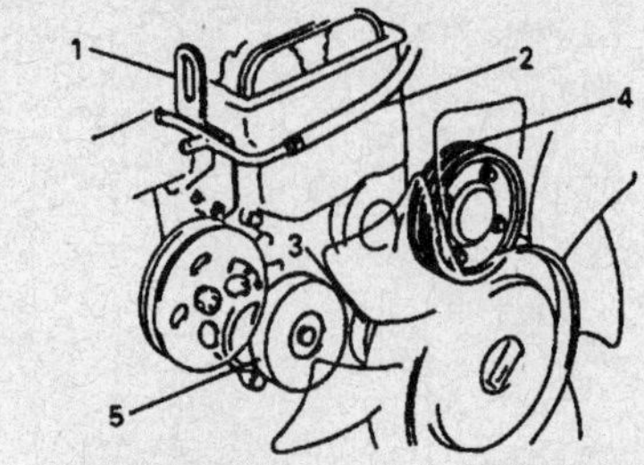

1. Water bypass pipe
2. Water bypass hose No.2
3. Cooling fan pulley
4. Water pump pulley
5. Generator belt tensioner

SK1069600115000X

Fig. 6 Water bypass & bypass hose No. 2 removal

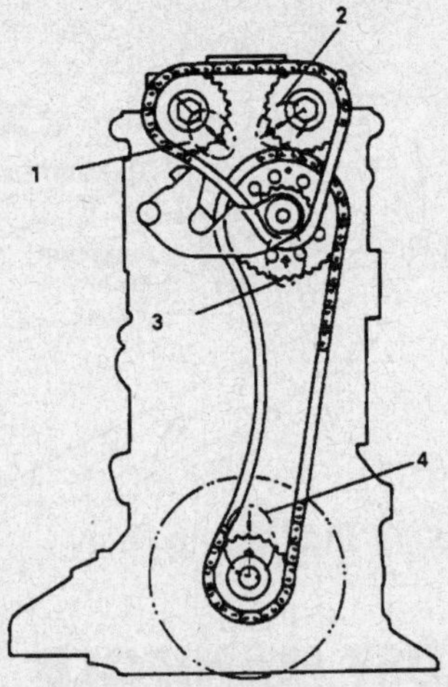

1. Timing marks of intake camshaft timing sprocket
2. Timing marks of exhaust camshaft timing sprocket
3. Arrow mark on idler sprocket
4. Timing marks of crankshaft timing sprocket

SK1069600116000X

Fig. 7 Timing chain marks

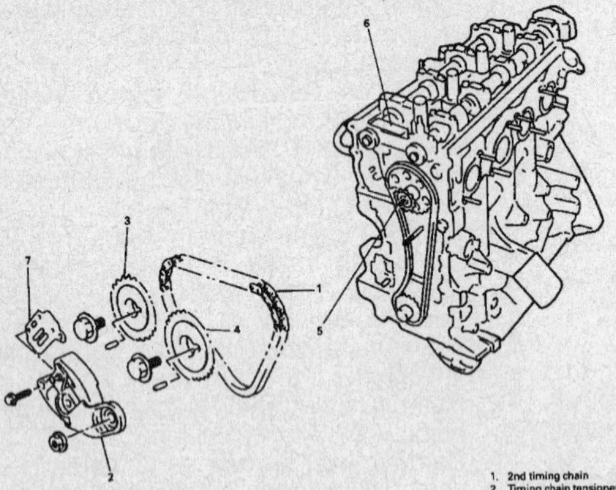

1. 2nd timing chain
2. Timing chain tensioner adjuster No.2
3. Intake camshaft timing sprocket
4. Exhaust camshaft timing sprocket
5. Idler sprocket
6. Timing chain guide No.2
7. Tensioner adjuster No.2 gasket

SK106960117000X

Fig. 8 Timing chain tensioner adjuster No. 2 removal

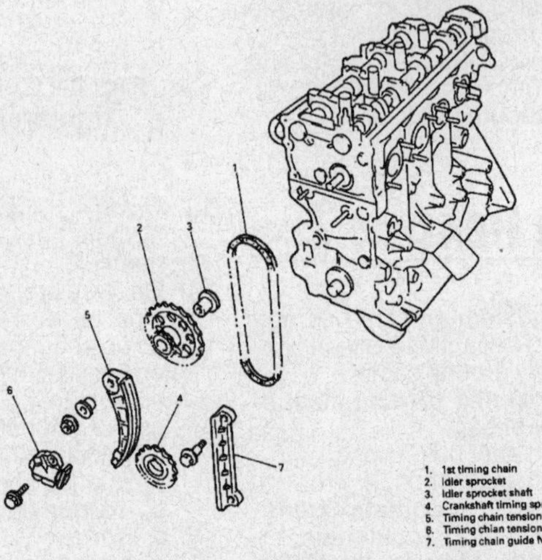

1. 1st timing chain
2. Idler sprocket
3. Idler sprocket shaft
4. Crankshaft timing sprocket
5. Timing chain tensioner
6. Timing chian tensioner adjuster No.1
7. Timing chain guide No.1

SK1069600118000X

Fig. 9 1st timing chain removal

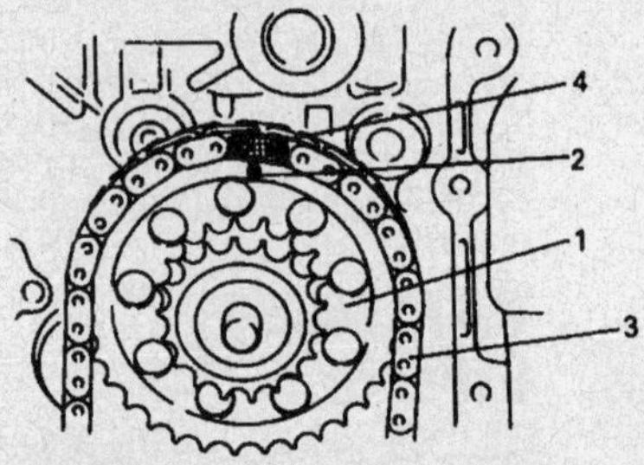

1. Idler sprocket
2. Match mark on idler sprocket
3. 1st timing chain
4. Dark blue plate

SK1069600119000X

Fig. 10 Idler sprocket & 1st timing chain blue plate alignment

b. Apply engine oil to lobes and journals.
c. Align marks on cylinder head and camshafts, **Fig. 16.**
d. Replace camshaft housings in original positions.
e. Using sequence shown in **Fig. 17, torque** camshaft housing bolts to 8 ft. lbs.
f. Tighten all nuts and bolts to specification.

PISTON & ROD ASSEMBLY

Each standard size piston has a No. 1 or No. 2 stamped on it representing outer diameter. There are also red or blue colors painted on cylinder block surface representing inner diameters of cylinders **Fig. 18.** Stamped numbers on pistons and painted colors on cylinder block should correspond, **Fig. 19.**

OIL PAN

REPLACE

1. Raise and support vehicle.
2. Remove oil level gauge.
3. Remove front differential assembly from chassis. Refer to "Drive Axles" for removal procedure.
4. Remove tie rod, center link and idler arm.
5. Drain engine oil.
6. Remove oil pan and lower pan to crossmember bolts.
7. Insert wrench into oil pan and remove oil strainer bolts.
8. Remove oil pan.
9. Reverse procedure to install, noting the following:

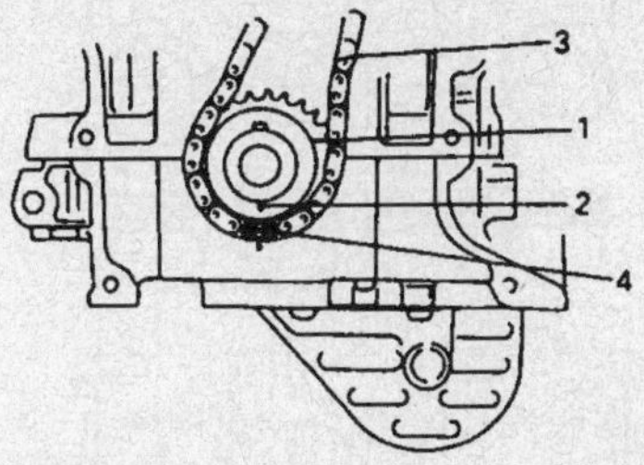

1. Crankshaft timing sprocket
2. Match mark
3. 1st timing chain
4. Yellow plate

SK1069600120000X

Fig. 11 crankshaft sprocket & 1st timing chain yellow plate alignment

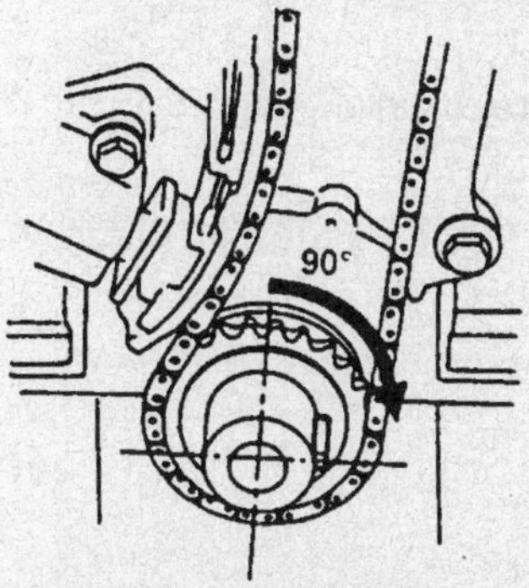

90°

SK1069600123000X

Fig. 13 Crankshaft key position for camshaft removal

a. Clean mating surface of oil pan and crankcase.
b. Apply sealant No. 99000–31150, or equivalent, to mating surface of oil pan.
c. Tighten to specification.

OIL PUMP

REPLACE

1. Disconnect battery ground cable.
2. Remove oil pan as outlined under "Oil Pan, Replace."
3. Remove oil pump sprocket cover.
4. Remove oil pump mounting bolts, then the oil pump.
5. Inspect oil pump as follows:
   a. Inspect oil lip seal for wear or damage.
   b. Inspect pump outer and inner rotors, pump housing and relief valve for excessive wear or damage.
   c. Measure free length of relief spring. Free length should be 2.5 inches.
   d. Using thickness gauge, check radial clearance between outer rotor and case. Radial clearance should be 0.0059 inch. If clearance exceeds specifications, replace outer rotor, or case.
   e. Using straightedge, check oil pump side clearance. Side clearance should be 0.0043 inch.
6. Reverse procedure to install. Tighten to specifications.

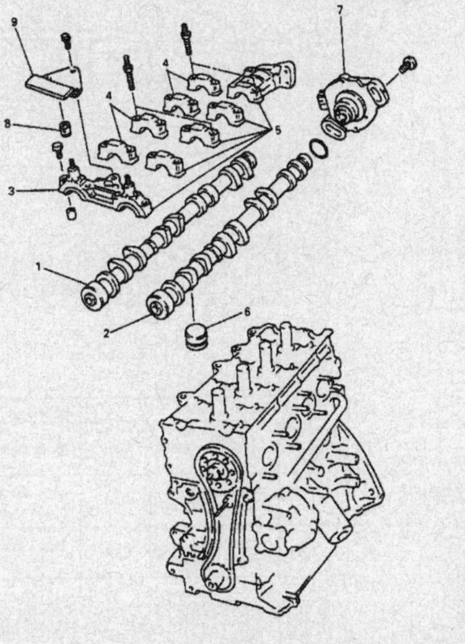

1. Intake camshaft
2. Exhaust camshaft
3. Camshaft housing
4. Intake camshaft housing
5. Exhaust camshaft housing
6. Valve lash adjuster
7. CMP sensor
8. Oil relief valve
9. Timing chain guide No.2

SK1069600122000X

Fig. 12 Exploded view of camshaft components

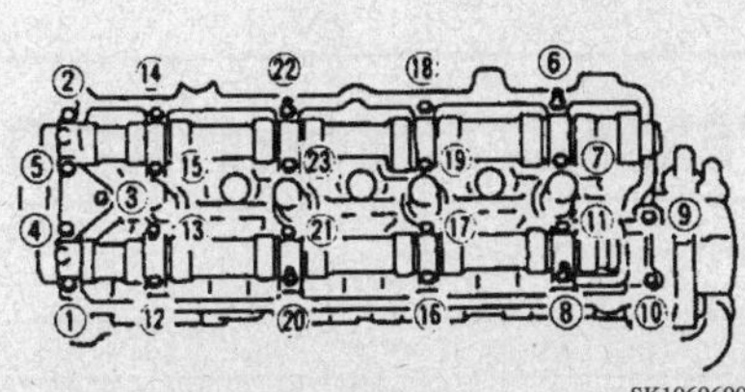

SK1069600124000X

Fig. 14 Camshaft housing bolt removal sequence

BELT TENSION DATA

Year	Belt Deflection Inch①	
	New	Used
1996	.16–.20	.20-.27

① — With 22 lbs. pressure applied between fan pulley and crankshaft pulley.

COOLING SYSTEM BLEED

This engine does not require a specific bleed procedure. After filling coolant system, run engine to operating temperature with radiator/pressure cap off. Air will then be automatically bled through cap opening.

THERMOSTAT

REPLACE

1. Drain coolant system into appropriate container.

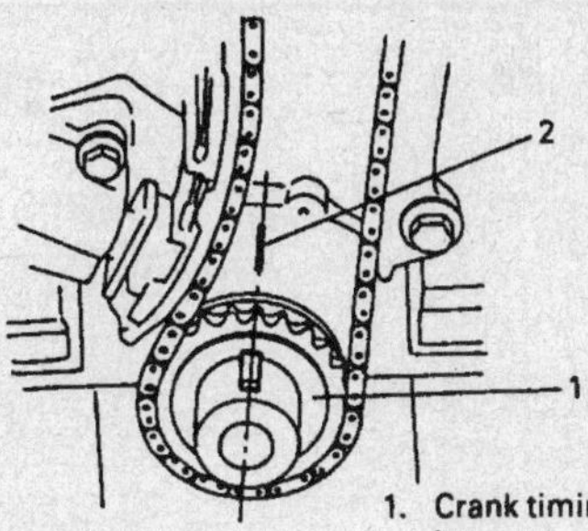

1. Crank timing sprocket key
2. Timing mark

SK1069600125000X

Fig. 15 Crankshaft key alignment

2. Remove radiator outlet hose at thermostat housing, then the housing.
3. Remove thermostat.
4. Reverse procedure to install noting the following:
   a. Ensure air breather valve is positioned to front side of engine.
   b. Fill and bleed coolant system.

RADIATOR, REPLACE

Refer to "1.6L Engine."

FUEL PUMP

REPLACE

Refer to "1.6L Engine."

FUEL FILTER

REPLACE

Refer to "1.6L Engine."

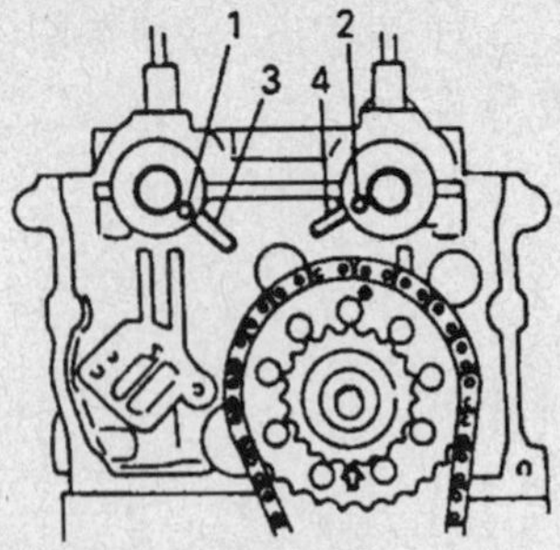
1
2
3
4

1. Knock pin of intake camshaft
2. Knock pin of exhaust camshaft
3. Match mark of intake camshaft
4. Match mark of exhaust camshaft

SK1069600126000X

Fig. 16 Camshafts & cylinder head alignment

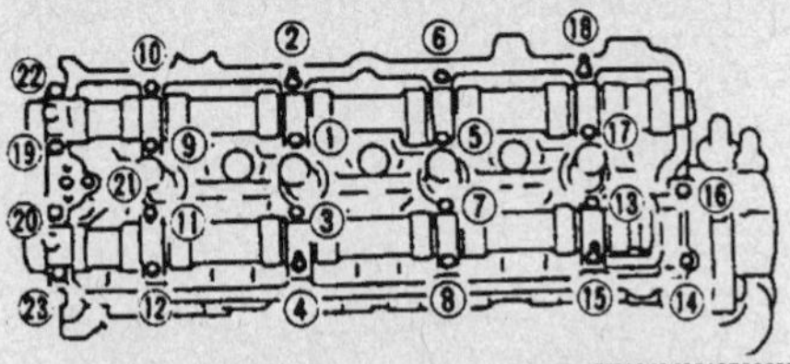

SK1069600127000X

Fig. 17 Camshaft housing bolt tightening sequence

Piston		Cylinder		Piston-to-cylinder clearance
Number at the top (mark)	Outer diameter	Mark	Bore diameter	
1	83.98 – 83.99 mm (3.3063 – 3.3066 in.)	Red	84.01 – 84.02 mm (3.3075 – 3.3078 in.)	0.02 – 0.04 mm (0.0008 – 0.0015 in.)
2	83.97 – 83.98 mm (3.3059 – 3.3062 in.)	Blue	84.00 – 84.01 mm (3.3071 – 3.3074 in.)	0.02 – 0.04 mm (0.0008 – 0.0015 in.)

SK1069600129000X

Fig. 19 Piston & cylinder chart

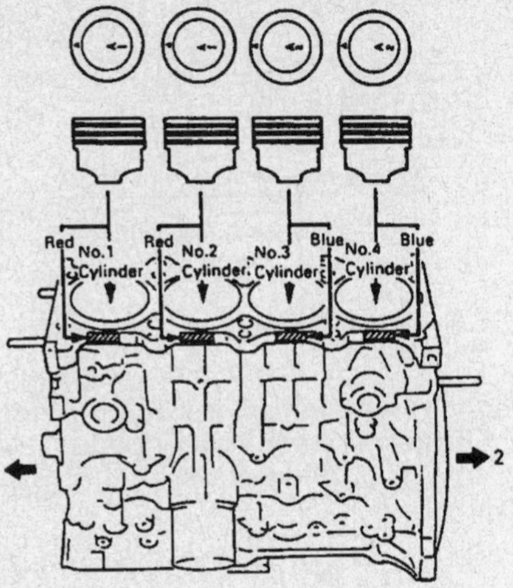
Red
No.1 Cylinder
Red
No.2 Cylinder
Blue
No.3 Cylinder
Blue
No.4 Cylinder
2

1. Crankshaft pulley side
2. Flywheel side

SK1069600128000X

Fig. 18 Piston & cylinder diagram

TIGHTENING SPECIFICATIONS

Year	Component	Torque/Ft. Lbs.
1996	A/C Compressor Bracket	40
	Alternator Belt Tensioner	18
	Alternator Idler Pulley	33
	Bypass Pipe	17
	Camshaft Timing Pulley Bolt	44
	Camshaft Housing Bolts	②
	Connecting Rod Bearing Cap Nut	33
	Crankshaft Pulley Bolt	108
	Cylinder Head Bolts	①
	Cylinder Head Cover Bolt	8
	Engine Mounting Bracket Bolt	37
	Engine Mounting Engine Side Bracket Bolt	37
	Engine Mounting Nut	37
	Exhaust Manifold Nut & Bolt	17
	Exhaust Manifold Stiffener	37
	Exhaust Pipe	37
	Flywheel Bolt	51
	Intake Manifold Nut & Bolt	17
	Intake Manifold Front Stiffener	36
	Intake Manifold Rear Stiffener	18
	Oil Drain Plug	26
	Oil Pan Bolt	8
	Oil Pump Case Bolt	9
	Oil Pump Mounting	15
	Oil Pump Relief Valve Retainer	21
	Oil Pump Sprocket Cover	8
	Oil Pump Strainer Bracket Bolt	8
	Oil Pump Strainer Bolts	8
	Spark Plugs	18
	Strut Tower Bar	65
	Throttle Body Bolt	9.5

Continued

TIGHTENING SPECIFICATIONS—Continued

Year	Component	Torque/Ft. Lbs.
1996	Timing Chain Cover Bolt	8
	Timing Chain Guide No. 1	8
	Timing Chain Tensioner No. 1	19
	Timing Chain Tensioner Adjuster No. 1	8
	Timing Chain No. 2 Tensioner Bolt	8
	Timing Chain No. 2 Tensioner Stud	33
	Torque Converter Bolt	47
	Transmission To Engine	58
	Transmission Stiffener	37
	Water Pump Bolt	18

① — Refer to "Cylinder Head, Replace" for tightening procedure.
② — Refer to "Camshaft, Replace" for tightening procedure.

Clutch & Manual Transmission

INDEX

	Page No.
Adjustments	40-55
Clutch Pedal Free Travel	40-55
Clutch Pedal Height	40-55
Clutch, Replace	40-55
Tightening Specifications	40-57
Esteem	40-58
Samurai	40-57
Sidekick & X-90	40-58
Swift	40-58
Transmission, Replace	40-55
Esteem	40-57
Samurai	40-55
Sidekick & X-90	40-56
Swift	40-56

ADJUSTMENTS

CLUTCH PEDAL HEIGHT

1. Loosen clutch cable locknut and turn adjusting nut as necessary until clutch pedal height is as follows:
   a. **On Samurai models,** ensure clutch pedal height (dimension A) is 5.83–6.06 inches, **Fig. 1.**
   b. If clutch pedal height is not as specified, adjust by loosening locknut and turning pedal stopper bolt.
   c. **On Sidekick and X-90 models,** clutch pedal should be 5 mm higher than brake pedal, **Fig. 2.**
   d. **On Swift models,** clutch pedal should be 8mm higher than brake pedal, **Fig. 3.**
   e. **On Esteem models,** clutch pedal height (dimension A) should be 15 mm higher than brake pedal, **Fig. 4.**
2. **On all models,** Tighten locknut after adjustment is completed.

CLUTCH PEDAL FREE TRAVEL

1. Depress clutch pedal until resistance is felt, then measure distance traveled, **Fig. 5.** Free travel should measure as follows:
   a. **On Samurai models,** clutch pedal free travel should be 0.8–1.1 inches.
   b. **On Sidekick and X-90 models,** clutch pedal free travel should be 0.6–1.1 inches.
   c. **On Swift and Esteem models,** clutch pedal free travel should be 0.6–0.8 inch.
2. **On all models,** if clutch pedal free travel is not within specification, adjust free travel as follows:
   a. **On Samurai models,** turn clutch cable outer nuts as necessary, **Fig. 6.**
   b. **On Sidekick and X-90 models,** turn joint nut as necessary, **Fig. 7.** Ensure cable outer nuts are tightened to specification.
   c. **On Swift and Esteem models,** turn joint nut as necessary, **Fig. 8.**
3. **On all models,** after adjustment check clutch function with engine running.

CLUTCH

REPLACE

1. Remove transmission from vehicle as outlined under "Transmission, Replace."
2. Loosen pressure plate attaching bolts one turn at a time, then remove bolts, pressure plate and clutch disc.
3. Install new clutch disc and pressure plate assembly. Tighten attaching bolts one turn at a time while ensuring disc and plate are properly aligned.
4. Install transmission and adjust clutch as outlined under "Clutch Pedal, Adjust."

TRANSMISSION

REPLACE

SAMURAI

1. Remove battery ground cable.
2. Remove four bolts fastening outer gear shift lever boot and slide boot toward shift knob.
3. Remove three gear shift lever case bolts, then the gear shift lever.
4. Disconnect back-up light and fifth gear switch electrical connectors from transmission.
5. Disconnect wiring from starter, then remove starter.
6. Remove fuel hose clamp from transmission case.
7. Raise and support vehicle.
8. Remove transmission drain plug and drain oil into appropriate container.
9. Disconnect clutch wire from clutch release lever.
10. Remove propeller shaft from transmission to transfer case.
11. Remove propeller shaft from transfer case to front differential.
12. Remove clutch housing lower plate from transmission case.
13. Support transmission with a suitable jack, then remove bolts securing transmission to engine.
14. Remove support pipe and exhaust center pipe.
15. Remove transmission rear mounting bracket from chassis and transmission.

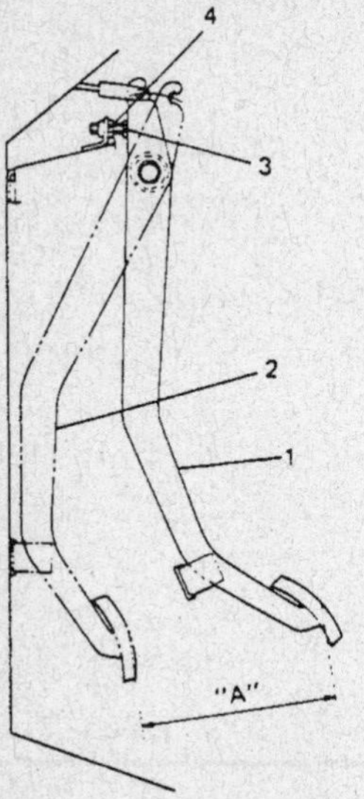

1. Clutch pedal free position
2. Fully depressed position
3. Clutch pedal stopper bolt
4. Lock nut
A: Clutch pedal height

SK5049100008000X

Fig. 1 Clutch pedal height adjustment. Samurai

1. Adjust bolt
2. Lock nut
3. Pedal bracket
4. Clutch pedal
5. Brake pedal
6. Measure

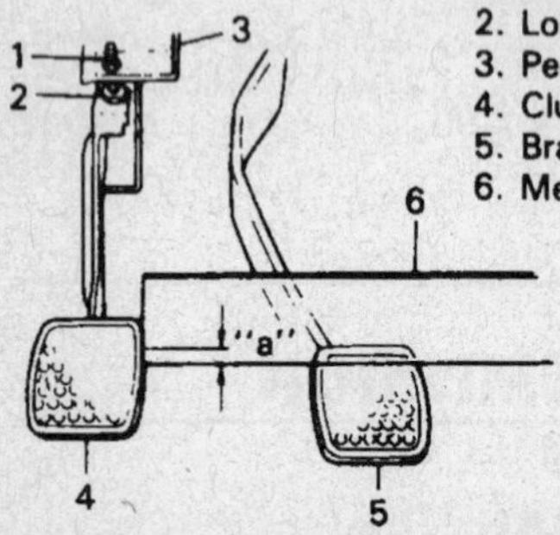

SK5049500015000X

Fig. 4 Clutch pedal height adjustment. Esteem

16. Ensure all connectors are unfastened from transmission, then carefully lower transmission from vehicle.
17. Reverse procedure to install.

SIDEKICK & X-90

1. Remove console box attaching screws, then the console box and bracket.
2. Lift up boot cover and boot No. 2.
3. Remove boot clamp, then boot No. 1 from transmission shift lever case.
4. Press down on shift control case cover and turn counterclockwise, then remove shift control lever.
5. **On 4WD models,** remove transfer case shift control lever knob.
6. **On 2WD models,** remove extension case.
7. **On all models,** disconnect battery ground cable, then the transmission breather hose from rear of cylinder head.
8. Remove wiring harness clamp from rear end of intake manifold.
9. Remove starter motor, then the transmission to engine attaching bolts.

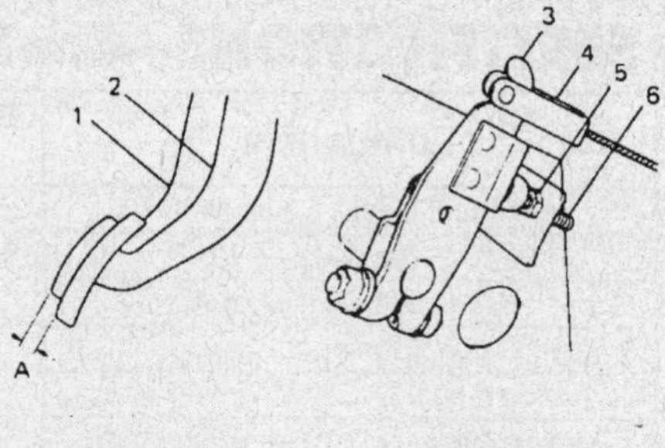

1. Clutch pedal
2. Brake pedal
3. Clutch pedal shaft arm
4. Clutch cable assembly
5. Lock nut
6. Adjust bolt
A: Height difference 5 mm/0.2 in.

SK5049100009000X

Fig. 2 Clutch pedal height adjustment. Sidekick & X-90

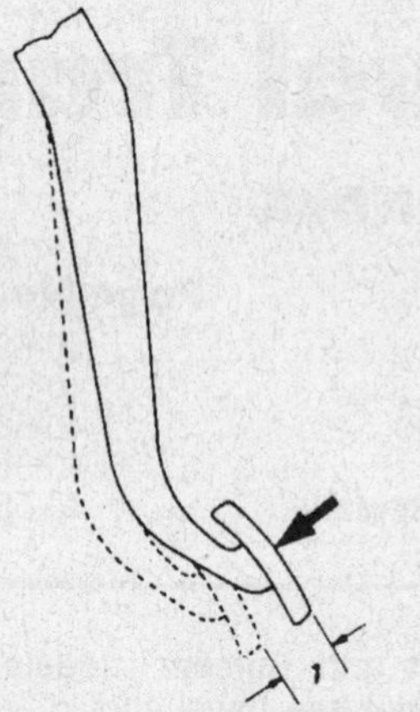

1. Clutch pedal free travel

SK5049100011000X

Fig. 5 Clutch pedal free travel measurement

10. Drain oil from transmission and transfer case into appropriate container.
11. Remove front and rear propeller shafts.
12. Disconnect clutch cable from transmission housing.
13. Remove clutch housing lower plate, then the exhaust center pipe.
14. Remove nuts retaining speedometer cable and disengage cable to transfer case.
15. Install a suitable jack under transmission and transfer case.
16. Remove engine rear mounting crossmember attaching bolts, then the crossmember.
17. Move transmission rearward and lower from vehicle.
18. Remove transmission wiring harness from transmission.
19. **On 4WD models,** remove gear shift lever case and transfer case from transmission assembly.
20. **On 2WD models,** remove gear shift lever case and extension case from transmission assembly.
21. **On all models,** reverse procedure to install.

SWIFT

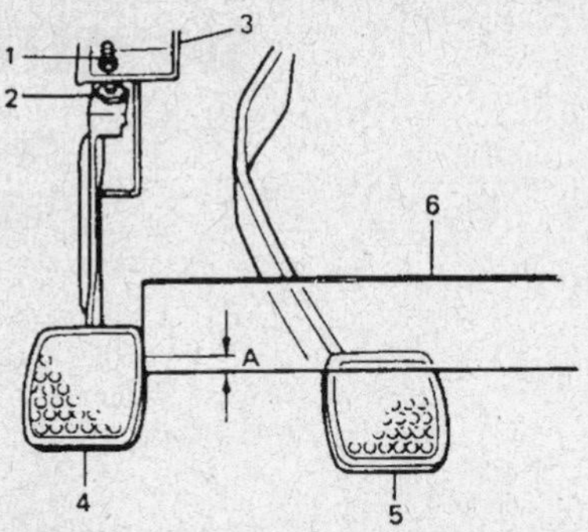

1. Adjust bolt
2. Lock nut
3. Pedal bracket
4. Clutch pedal
5. Brake pedal
6. Measure
A: Height difference 8 mm/0.3 in.

SK5049100010000X

Fig. 3 Clutch pedal height adjustment. Swift

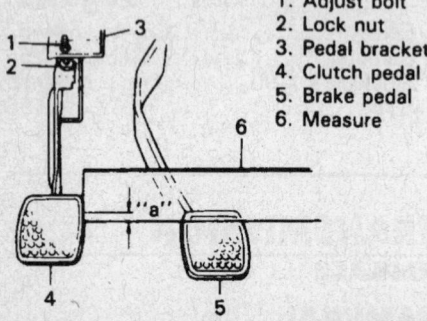

1. Disconnect battery ground cable, then remove battery and tray.
2. Remove clutch cable joint nut, joint pin from cable and cable from bracket.
3. Disconnect wiring harness clamps and couplers.
4. Remove speedometer cable from case, then disconnect radiator outlet pipe from transmission side cover.
5. Remove transmission upper attaching bolts, then the starter motor.
6. Raise and support vehicle, then drain transmission oil into appropriate container.
7. Remove lefthand side fender apron extension, then the exhaust pipe from manifold.
8. Disconnect control shaft from gear shift shaft, then remove extension rod with washers.
9. Remove clutch housing lower plate, then disconnect lower suspension (control) arm from steering knuckle.
10. Disconnect lefthand side driveshaft joint from differential gear of transmission.
11. Remove center bearing support bolts and pull out center driveshaft from differential gear.
12. Remove transmission stiffener, then the transmission to engine attaching bolt.
13. Remove engine rear mounting bracket and bolts.
14. Lower vehicle as necessary and support engine and transmission with suitable jacks.
15. Remove engine mounting lefthand bracket and stiffener, then remove any parts still attached to transmission.
16. Pull transmission rearward to disconnect input shaft from clutch disc.
17. Lower and remove transmission from vehicle.
18. Reverse procedure to install, noting the following:
    a. Apply Suzuki No. 1215 sealant, or equivalent, to threads of engine rear mounting bracket upper bolt.
    b. Push in lefthand side driveshaft joint fully. Ensure snap ring of shaft engages with differential gear.
    c. Apply grease to gear shift control shaft bushing. Do not lubricate extension rod bushing.

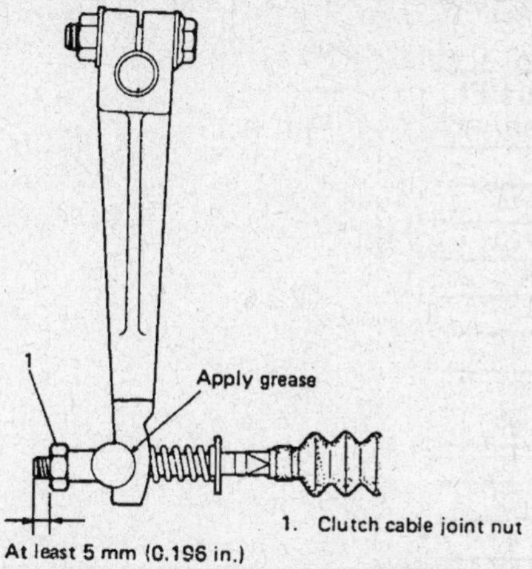

1
Apply grease
1. Clutch cable joint nut
At least 5 mm (0.196 in.)

SK5049100012000X

Fig. 6 Clutch pedal free travel adjustment. Samurai

d. Adjust clutch cable as outlined under "Clutch Pedal, Adjust."

ESTEEM

1. Disconnect battery ground cable.
2. Remove clutch cable joint nut, joint pin from cable, then cable from bracket.
3. Disconnect wiring harness clamps and connectors.
4. Remove starter and starter plate.
5. Remove exhaust manifold cover and loosen nuts on exhaust No. 1 pipe.
6. Raise and support vehicle.
7. Drain transmission oil.
8. Remove left side engine cover and exhaust No. 1 pipe.

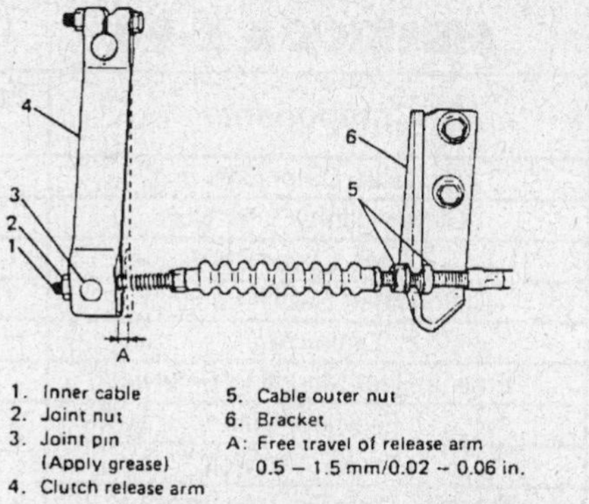

1. Inner cable
2. Joint nut
3. Joint pin (Apply grease)
4. Clutch release arm
5. Cable outer nut
6. Bracket
A: Free travel of release arm 0.5 – 1.5 mm/0.02 – 0.06 in.

SK5049100013000X

Fig. 7 Clutch pedal free travel adjustment. Sidekick & X-90

9. Remove gear shift control shaft bolt and nut, then detach control shaft from gear shift shaft.
10. Remove extension rod nut, then the rod and washers.
11. Remove clutch housing lower plate and disconnect stabilizer joint from suspension arm.
12. Remove ball stud from right and left knuckles, then disconnect each suspension arm.
13. Using suitable large screwdrivers, pry away shaft joints at differential side to access and remove snap ring for left-hand drive shaft.
14. Remove center bearing support bolts and pull out center drive shaft from differential gear.

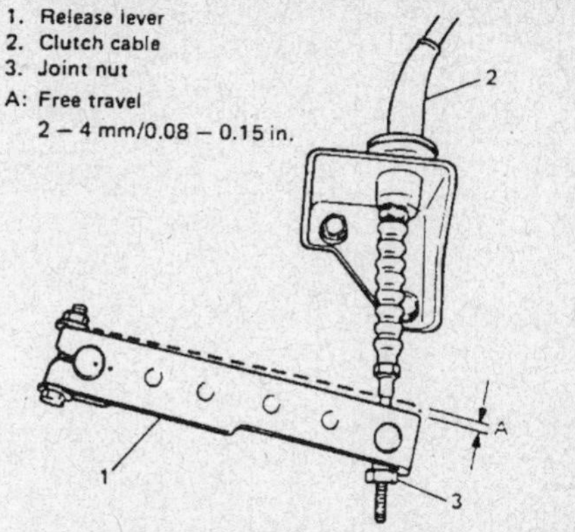

1. Release lever
2. Clutch cable
3. Joint nut
A: Free travel
2 – 4 mm/0.08 – 0.15 in.

SK5049100014000X

Fig. 8 Clutch pedal free travel adjustment. Swift

15. Remove transmission stiffener.
16. Support transmission using suitable jack.
17. Remove transmission to engine bolt and nut.
18. Remove engine rear mounting bracket bolts.
19. Lower vehicle and remove No. 1 left-hand engine mounting bracket.
20. Remove any remaining parts connected to transmission.
21. Remove transmission while disconnecting input shaft from clutch disc, then lower transmission out of vehicle.
22. Reverse procedure to install. Tighten to specification.

TIGHTENING SPECIFICATIONS

SAMURAI

Year	Component	Torque/Ft. Lbs.
1993–95	Clutch Cover Bolts	14-20
	Clutch Release Arm Bolt/Nut	8-11
	Drain Plug	14-20
	Extension Case Bolt	14-20
	Flywheel Bolts	42-47
	Gear Shift Lever Case Bolt	14-20
	Input Shaft Bearing Retainer Bolt	14-20
	Transmission Case Bolt	14-20
	Transmission Oil Level Plug	8-11

SIDEKICK & X-90

Year	Component	Torque/Ft. Lbs.
1993–96	Cable Outer Bolt	4
	Clutch Cable Outer Nut	11-14
	Clutch Cover Bolt	14-20
	Clutch Start Switch Locknut	9
	Drain plug	14-20
	Engine Rear Mounting Bolt/Nut	29-43
	Flywheel Bolt	56
	Release Arm Bolt	14-20
	Transfer Case To Transmission	14-20
	Transmission To Engine Bolt/Nut	51-72
	Universal Joint Flange Bolt	37-43

SWIFT

Year	Component	Torque/Ft. Lbs.
1993–96	Cable Bracket Bolt	14-20
	Clutch Cable Outer Bolt	4
	Clutch Cover Bolt	14-20
	Drain Plug	14-16
	Engine Mounting LH Bracket Bolt	29-43
	Engine Mounting LH Bracket Nut	37-43
	Engine Rear Mounting Bracket Bolt	29-43
	Extension Rod Nut	19-28
	Extension Rod Stud Bolt	11-14
	Flywheel Bolt	42-47
	Gear Shift Housing to Boot Cover	4
	Release Arm Bolt	8-11
	Speedometer Gear to Case Bolt	4
	Transmission Case Bolt	11-15

ESTEEM

Year	Component	Torque/Ft. Lbs.
1995–96	Ball Stud Bolt	44
	Center Bearing Support	37
	Drain Plug	16
	Engine Mounting LH Bracket Bolt	37
	Engine Rear Mounting Bracket Bolt	37
	Exhaust Pipe	37
	Extension Rod Nut	24
	Gear Shift Control Shaft	13
	Stabilizer Bar Link	21
	Speedometer Gear to Case Bolt	4
	Transmission Case Bolt	65
	Transmission Case Lower Stiffener	37

Rear Axle & Suspension

INDEX

	Page No.
Coil Spring & Suspension Arm, Replace	40-62
Swift	40-62
Coil Spring, Replace	40-61
Sidekick & X-90	40-61
Control Rod, Replace	40-62
Esteem	40-62
Swift	40-62
Hub & Knuckle, Replace	40-60
Esteem	40-60
Swift	40-60
Leaf Spring, Replace	40-61
Samurai	40-61
Rear Axle Shaft Service	40-59
Samurai	40-59
Sidekick & X-90	40-59
Shock Absorber, Replace	40-61
Samurai	40-61
Sidekick & X-90	40-61
Stabilizer Bar, Replace	40-63
Swift	40-63
Strut, Replace	40-60
Esteem	40-61
Swift	40-60
Tightening Specifications	40-64
Esteem	40-65
Samurai	40-64
Sidekick & X-90	40-64
Swift	40-64
Trailing Rod, Replace	40-62
Esteem	40-62
Sidekick & X-90	40-62
Upper Arm, Replace	40-62
Sidekick & X-90	40-62
Wheel Bearing, Replace	40-60
Esteem	40-60
Swift	40-60

REAR AXLE SHAFT SERVICE

SAMURAI

Rear Wheel Bearing Check

1. Check wheel bearing thrust play by attaching a suitable dial indicator to drum center, **Fig. 1.**
2. Wheel bearing thrust play must not exceed 0.03 inch (0.8 mm). If measurement exceeds limit, replace bearing as outlined under "Axle Shaft Removal."

Axle Shaft Removal

1. Raise and support vehicle.
2. Remove wheel center cap, then the wheel assembly.
3. Using slide hammer tool, No. 09942-15510 and brake drum remover tool, No. 09943-35511, or equivalent, remove drum.
4. Remove axle housing drain plug, then drain oil from axle housing into appropriate container.
5. Disconnect brake line from wheel cylinder. Plug openings.
6. Remove four brake backing plate attaching bolts.
7. Using rear axle remover tool, No. 09922-66010 and slide hammer tool, No. 09942-15510, or equivalent, remove axle shaft with brake backing plate.
8. Pry seal from axle housing taking care not to damage housing.
9. Remove retaining ring from shaft by grinding two parts of bearing retainer ring until it becomes thin, **Fig. 2.**
10. Using a hammer and chisel, break retainer ring.
11. Using pulley tools, No. 09927-18410 and 09926-57810, or equivalent, remove bearing from shaft, then the backing plate.

Axle Shaft Installation

1. Install oil seal ensuring side with spring faces differential side. Grease seal lip before installing.
2. Install new bearing and spacer on shaft, ensuring wheel bearing spacer is installed with tapered side of inner diameter facing towards brake drum side.
3. Reverse steps 1 through 10 of removal procedure to complete Installation. Tighten backing plate bolts to specifications.
4. When mounting hub bolts into rear axle shaft, ensure to fit head securely in stepped part of axle shaft.
5. Tighten hub bolt nuts to specification.

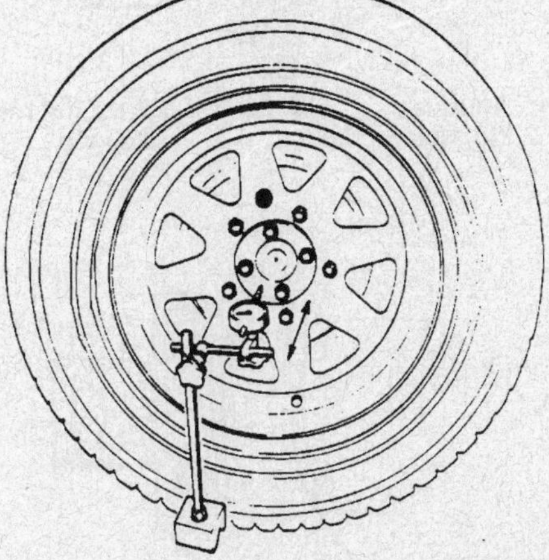

SK3039100001000X

Fig. 1 Wheel bearing thrust play inspection. Samurai

SIDEKICK & X-90

Axle Shaft & Bearings, Replace

1. Drain differential gear oil into appropriate container.
2. Raise and support vehicle. Remove wheel and brake drum, then the rear wheel bearing retainer nuts from axle housing.
3. If there is no clearance between rear wheel bearing retainer and parking shoe, loosen parking cable adjusting nut and pull down brake shoe hold pin stopper plate.
4. Using axle shaft tool, No. J37781 and puller tool, No. J2619-01, or equivalent, remove axle shaft.
5. Remove retainer ring from axle shaft using a grinder to flatten two parts of bearing retainer ring, **Fig. 2.**
6. With a chisel remove retainer ring, then using a suitable press remove bearing from axle shaft.
7. Reverse procedure to install. Apply Suzuki Bond No. 1215, or equivalent, to mating surface of bearing retainer to brake backing plate. Tighten to specification.

Rear Axle Housing, Replace

1. Drain differential gear oil into appropriate container.
2. Remove brake drums, then the brake lines from rear wheel cylinders.
3. Remove rear wheel bearing retainer nuts from rear axle housing.
4. If there is no clearance between rear wheel bearing retainer and parking shoe, loosen parking cable adjusting nut and pull down brake shoe hold pin stopper plate.
5. Using axle shaft tool, No. J37781 and puller tool, No. J2619-01, or equivalent, remove axle shaft.
6. Remove brake line and breather hose from rear axle.
7. Remove propeller shaft from differential and secure to one side.
8. Support rear axle beneath the differential with a suitable jack, then remove ball joint bracket from differential carrier, then the differential carrier assembly.
9. Remove rear trailing rod to axle housing retaining nut, but do not remove bolt.
10. Remove lower shock absorber to axle housing retaining bolt.
11. Lower axle enough to increase coil spring tension, then remove trailing rod from axle housing. Lower and remove axle.
12. Reverse procedure to install.

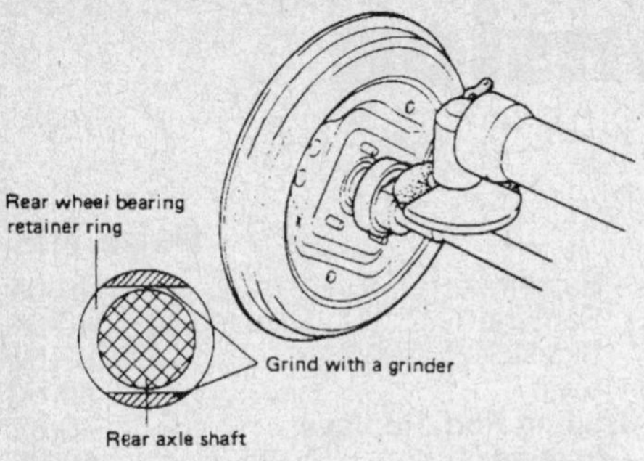
Rear wheel bearing retainer ring
Grind with a grinder
Rear axle shaft
SK3039100002000X

Fig. 2 Retaining ring replacement

HUB & KNUCKLE

REPLACE

SWIFT

GT Models

1. Raise and support vehicle, then remove rear wheels.
2. Remove rear caliper and disc as outlined in the "Disc Brakes" section.
3. Remove spindle cap, then the spindle nut and washer.
4. Pull wheel hub off using tools, **Fig. 3.**
5. Disconnect brake hose bracket from knuckle.
6. Remove brake disc dust cover and caliper carrier from knuckle.
7. Support suspension arm with suitable jack.
8. Confirm rear toe setting, **Fig. 4.** Remove nut and washer from inside of control arm.
9. Remove control arm outside nut from knuckle stud bolt.
10. Remove strut and knuckle lower mounting bolts.
11. Disconnect knuckle from suspension arm, then remove knuckle from strut.
12. Reverse procedure to install.

Except GT Models

1. Raise and support vehicle, then remove rear wheels.
2. Remove rear brake drum.
3. Disconnect brake line from wheel cylinder.
4. Remove brake backing plate from knuckle.
5. Support suspension arm with suitable jack.
6. Confirm rear toe setting, **Fig. 4.** Remove nut and washer from inside of control arm.
7. Remove control arm outside nut from knuckle stud bolt.
8. Remove strut and knuckle lower mounting bolts.
9. Disconnect knuckle from suspension arm, then remove knuckle from strut.
10. Reverse procedure to install.

ESTEEM

1. Raise and support vehicle.
2. Remove brake drum and spindle cap.
3. Remove spindle nut and washer, then pull off wheel hub using puller tools No. 09943–17912 and No. 09942–15510, or equivalents.
4. Disconnect and plug brake hose to wheel cylinder.
5. **On models with ABS,** remove wheel speed sensor.
6. **On all models,** remove brake backing plate from knuckle.
7. Loosen control rod outer bolts, trailing rod rear bolt and strut bracket nuts.
8. Disconnect control rods from knuckle.
9. Disconnect trailing rod from knuckle, then remove knuckle from strut, **Fig. 5.**
10. Reverse procedure to install, noting the following:
    a. Apply sealant No. 99000–31090, or equivalent, to mating surfaces of brake back plate and knuckle.
    b. Install new spindle nut.
    c. Tighten to specification.
    d. Bleed brake system.

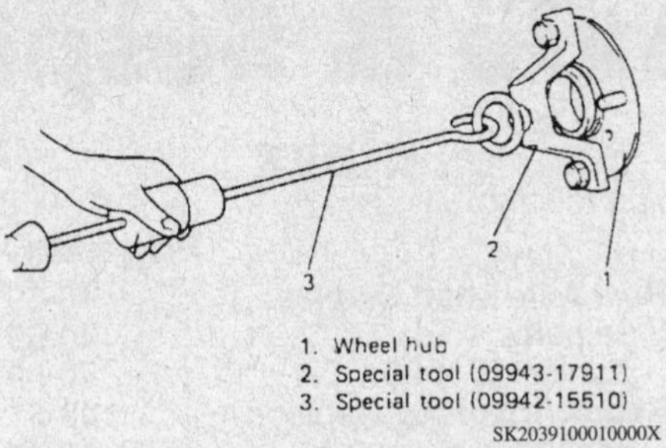
1
2
3
1. Wheel hub
2. Special tool (09943-17911)
3. Special tool (09942-15510)
SK2039100010000X

Fig. 3 Wheel hub replacement. Swift

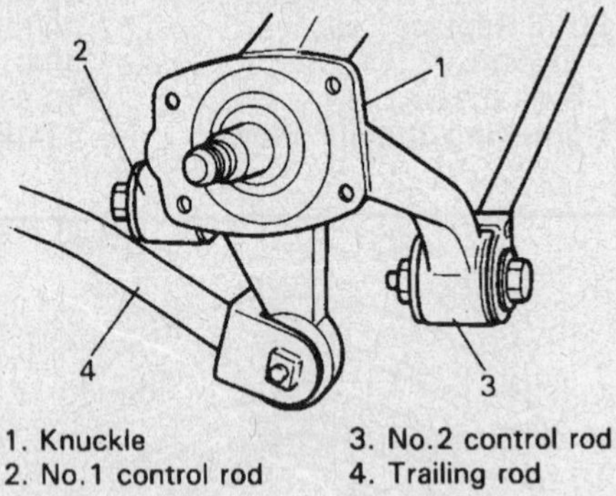
1
2
3
4
1. Knuckle
2. No.1 control rod
3. No.2 control rod
4. Trailing rod

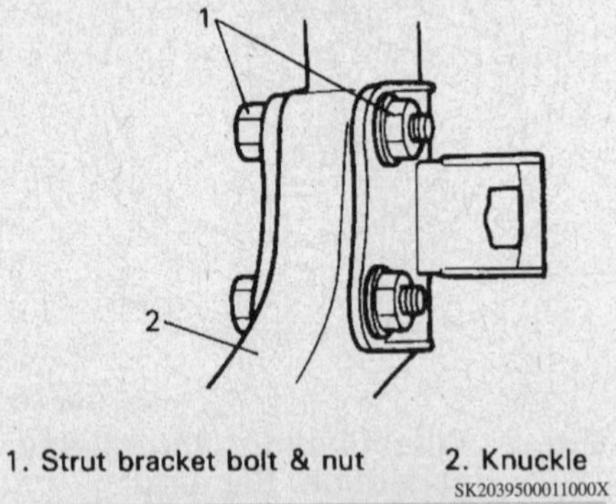
1
2
1. Strut bracket bolt & nut
2. Knuckle
SK2039500011000X

Fig. 5 Rear suspension components. Esteem

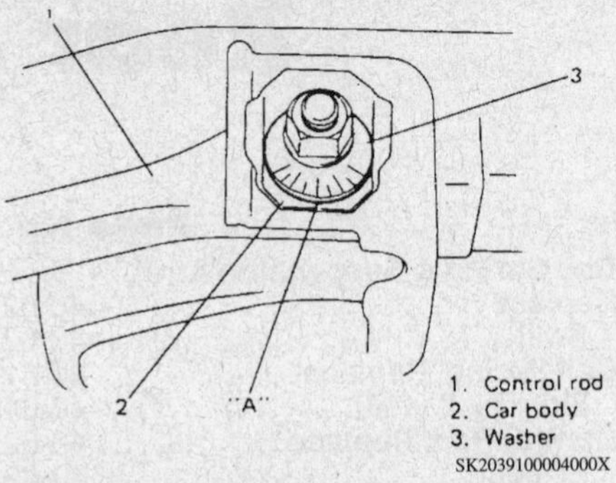
1
2
3
"A"
1. Control rod
2. Car body
3. Washer
SK2039100004000X

Fig. 4 Rear toe measurement. Swift

WHEEL BEARING

REPLACE

SWIFT

Except GT Models

1. Remove brake drum.
2. Remove wheel bearings from brake drum.
3. Reverse procedure to install, noting the following:
    a. Install both bearings with sealed side outward.
    b. Fill 40 percent of bearing cavity with bearing lubricant.

GT Models

Wheel bearing and hub form a solid unit. If wheel bearing is defective, replace hub as an assembly.

ESTEEM

Wheel bearing and hub form a solid unit. If wheel bearing is defective, replace hub as an assembly.

STRUT

REPLACE

SWIFT

1. Raise and support vehicle, then remove rear wheels.
2. Using suitable jack, support rear axle housing to prevent it from lowering.
3. Remove strut support nuts, then push strut fully downward to compress strut.
4. Remove strut lower mount bolt.
5. Lower jack slightly to facilitate strut removal.
6. Remove strut from knuckle by pulling it upward, **Fig. 6.** If strut is hard to remove, open slit of knuckle using wedge.
7. Reverse procedure to install, noting the following:
    a. Align projection of strut with slit of knuckle. Push strut into knuckle until upper end of knuckle contacts projection of strut.

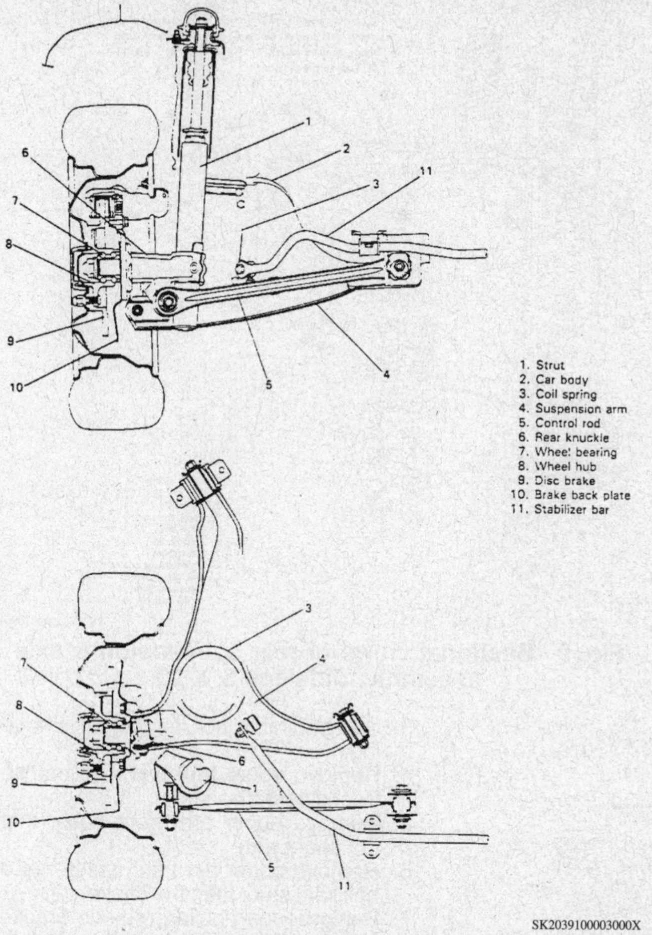
1. Strut
2. Car body
3. Coil spring
4. Suspension arm
5. Control rod
6. Rear knuckle
7. Wheel bearing
8. Wheel hub
9. Disc brake
10. Brake back plate
11. Stabilizer bar
SK2039100003000X

Fig. 6 Sectional views of rear suspension. Swift

b. Tighten all bolts and nuts to specification.

ESTEEM

1. Raise and support vehicle, allowing rear suspension to hang free.
2. Remove rear wheel.
3. Remove E-ring securing brake hose.
4. Disconnect brake pipe from wheel cylinder and install bleeder plug cap to prevent fluid loss.
5. Remove strut bracket bolts and nuts, then the brake hose from strut.
6. Remove strut, **Fig. 7.**
7. Reverse procedure to install, noting the following:
   a. Tighten all bolts and nuts to specification.
   b. Bleed and test brake system.

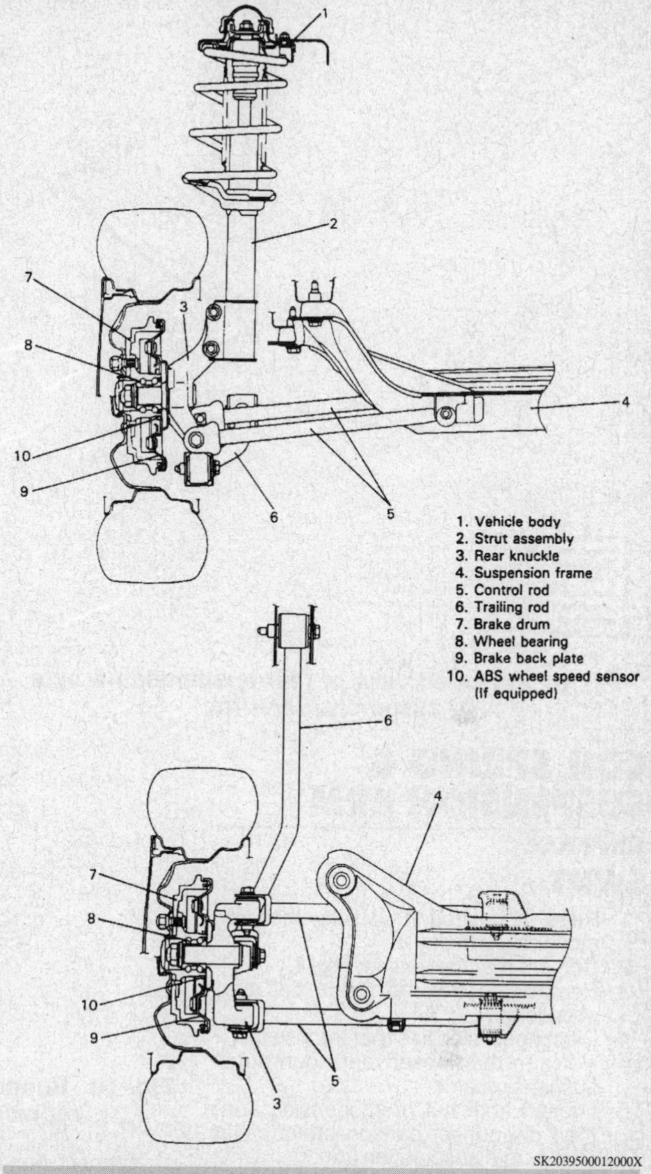
1. Vehicle body
2. Strut assembly
3. Rear knuckle
4. Suspension frame
5. Control rod
6. Trailing rod
7. Brake drum
8. Wheel bearing
9. Brake back plate
10. ABS wheel speed sensor (If equipped)
SK2039500012000X

Fig. 7 Sectional views of rear suspension. Esteem

SHOCK ABSORBER

REPLACE

SAMURAI

1. Raise and support vehicle.
2. Remove upper and lower nuts, **Fig. 8,** and remove shock.
3. Reverse procedure to install.

SIDEKICK & X-90

1. Raise and support vehicle.
2. Using suitable jack, support rear axle housing to prevent it from lowering.
3. Remove upper and lower attaching bolt, **Fig. 9,** then remove shock absorber.
4. Reverse procedure to install.

COIL SPRING

REPLACE

SIDEKICK & X-90

1. Raise and support vehicle, then remove rear wheels.
2. Using suitable jack, support rear axle housing.
3. Disconnect parking brake cable hangers from trailing rod and chassis body.
4. Remove shock absorber lower mounting bolt, **Fig. 9.**
5. Lower rear axle housing gradually until coil spring can be removed. Remove coil spring.
6. Reverse procedure to install.

LEAF SPRING

REPLACE

SAMURAI

1. Raise and support vehicle. Position suitable jack stands under rear axle assembly.
2. Remove rear wheel assembly.
3. Remove U-bolts and nuts.
4. Remove shackle nuts, then the leaf spring nuts, **Fig. 8.**
5. Pull out leaf spring bolt, then remove leaf spring from shackle pin.
6. Reverse procedure to install.

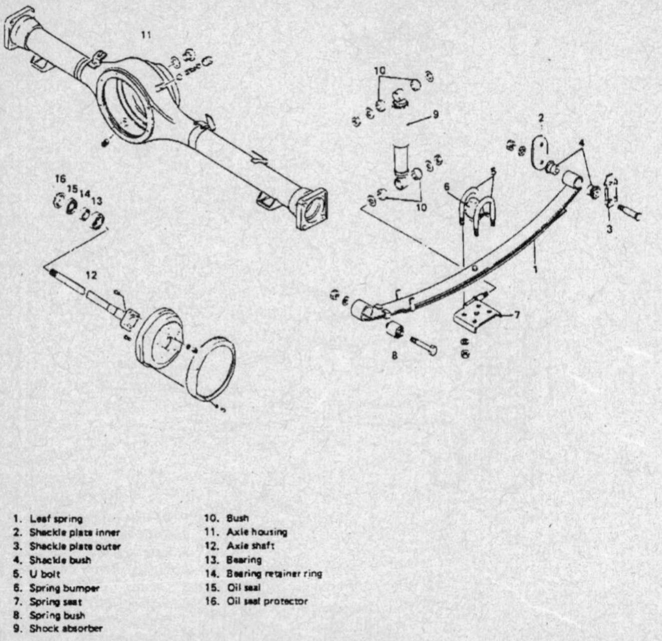
1. Leaf spring
2. Shackle plate inner
3. Shackle plate outer
4. Shackle bush
5. U bolt
6. Spring bumper
7. Spring seat
8. Spring bush
9. Shock absorber
10. Bush
11. Axle housing
12. Axle shaft
13. Bearing
14. Bearing retainer ring
15. Oil seal
16. Oil seal protector
SK2039100001000X

Fig. 8 Exploded view of rear suspension & axle assembly. Samurai

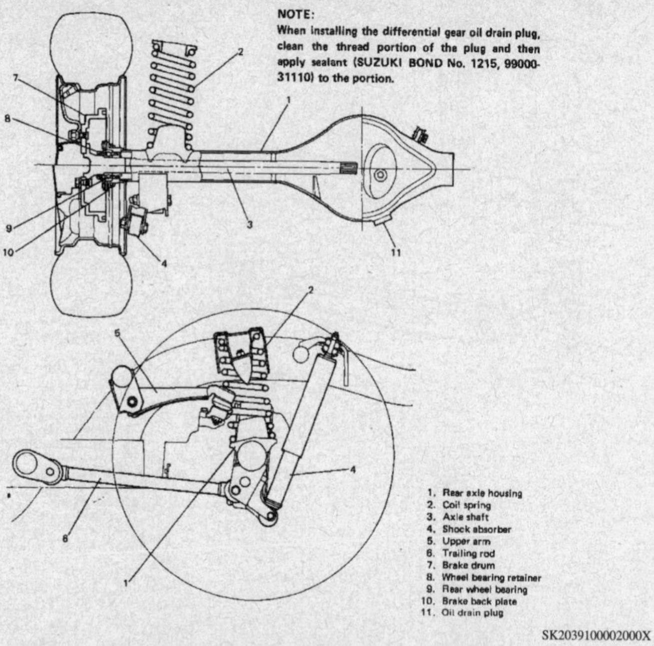
NOTE:
When installing the differential gear oil drain plug, clean the thread portion of the plug and then apply sealant (SUZUKI BOND No. 1215, 99000-31110) to the portion.
1. Rear axle housing
2. Coil spring
3. Axle shaft
4. Shock absorber
5. Upper arm
6. Trailing rod
7. Brake drum
8. Wheel bearing retainer
9. Rear wheel bearing
10. Brake back plate
11. Oil drain plug
SK2039100002000X

Fig. 9 Sectional views of rear suspension & axle assembly. Sidekick & X-90

COIL SPRING & SUSPENSION ARM

REPLACE

SWIFT

1. Raise and support vehicle, then remove rear wheels.
2. Confirm rear toe setting, **Fig. 4.**
3. Remove control rod inside bolt and outside nut.
4. Disconnect stabilizer bar from suspension arm, then loosen rear mount nut of suspension arm.
5. Loosen front nut of suspension arm, then disconnect parking brake cable clamp from suspension arm.
6. Place suitable jack under suspension arm, then remove lower mount nut of knuckle.
7. Separate lower mount of knuckle from suspension arm by pulling brake assembly to outside of vehicle.
8. Lower jack gradually and remove coil spring.
9. Remove suspension arm front bracket attaching bolts, then the suspension arm.
10. Reverse procedure to install, noting the following:
    a. Install suspension arm with slit "A" facing outside of body. Ensure bushing is installed properly in regard to its vertical direction, **Fig. 10.**
    b. Tighten all bolts and nuts to specification.
    c. Set rear toe adjustment as confirmed before removal.

TRAILING ROD

REPLACE

SIDEKICK & X-90

1. Raise and support vehicle, then disconnect parking brake cable hanger from trailing rod.
2. Using suitable jack, support rear axle housing.
3. Remove trailing rod rear mounting bolts, then the trailing arm.
4. Remove trailing rod bushings using press and tools, **Fig. 11.**
5. Reverse procedure to install.

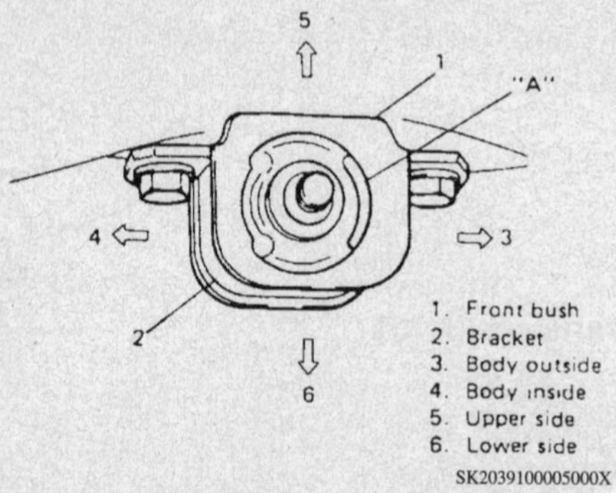
5
1
"A"
4
3
2
6
1. Front bush
2. Bracket
3. Body outside
4. Body inside
5. Upper side
6. Lower side
SK2039100005000X

Fig. 10 Suspension arm bushing replacement. Swift

ESTEEM

1. Raise and support vehicle, then disconnect parking brake cable hanger from trailing rod, **Fig. 7.**
2. Remove trailing rod rear mounting bolts, then the trailing arm.
3. Reverse procedure to install.

UPPER ARM

REPLACE

SIDEKICK & X-90

1. Raise and support vehicle.
2. Remove bracket from upper arm, **Fig. 12.**
3. Using suitable jack, support axle housing.
4. Remove upper arm ball joint bracket from differential carrier.
5. Remove upper arm front bolts, then the upper arm.
6. Remove cotter pin from castle nut of ball joint stud, then the castle nut.
7. Using bearing puller, remove bracket from ball joint stud.
8. Remove ball joint boot set ring and boot.
9. To replace upper arm front bushing, cut off rubber flange, **Fig. 13,** then using tools, **Fig. 14,** press out bushing.
10. Reverse procedure to install.

CONTROL ROD

REPLACE

SWIFT

1. Raise and support vehicle.
2. Disconnect brake flexible hose from control rod. Confirm rear toe setting, **Fig. 4.**
3. Remove control rod outside and inside nuts, then the control rod.
4. Reverse procedure to install, noting the following:
    a. Install control rod inside bolt with cam facing downward.
    b. Tighten all bolts and nuts to specification.
    c. Set rear toe adjustment as confirmed before removal.

ESTEEM

1. Raise and support vehicle.
2. **On models with ABS,** remove ABS speed sensor pipe from No. 2 control arm.
3. **On all models,** place match marks on washer and frame for adjustment reference, **Fig. 15.**

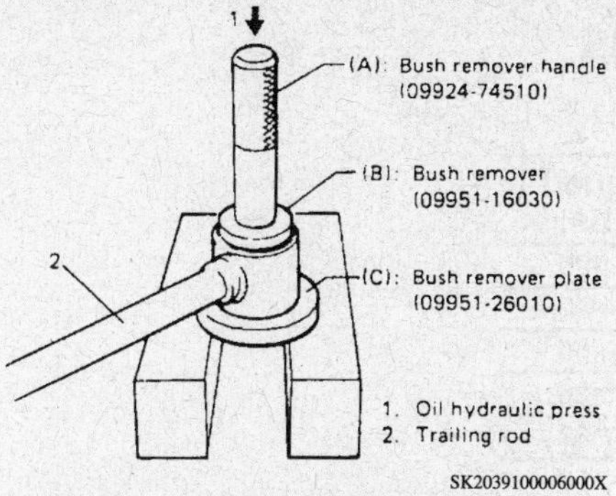
1
(A): Bush remover handle (09924-74510)
(B): Bush remover (09951-16030)
(C): Bush remover plate (09951-26010)
2
1. Oil hydraulic press
2. Trailing rod
SK2039100006000X

Fig. 11 Trailing arm bushing replacement. Sidekick & X-90

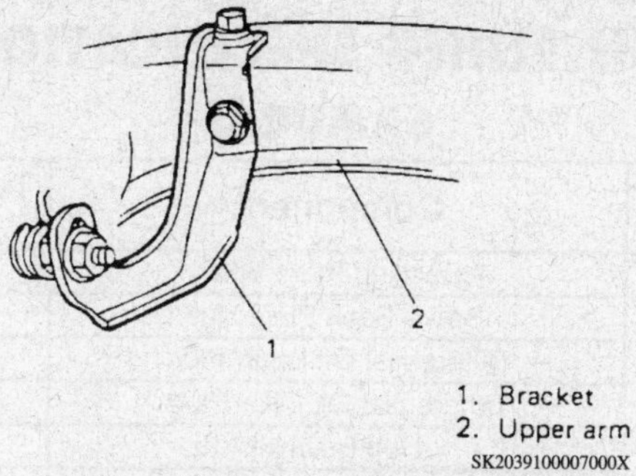
1
2
1. Bracket
2. Upper arm
SK2039100007000X

Fig. 12 Upper arm bracket replacement. Sidekick & X-90

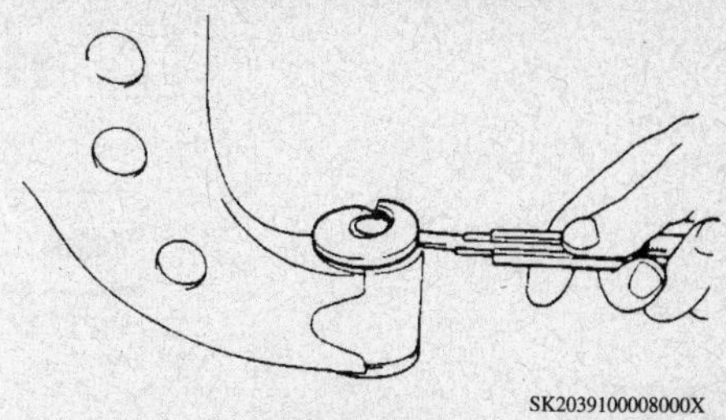
SK2039100008000X

Fig. 13 Upper arm bushing flange removal. Sidekick & X-90

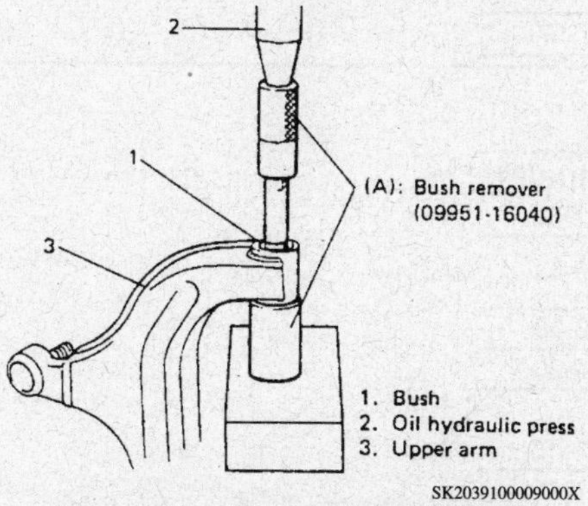
2
1
3
(A): Bush remover (09951-16040)
1. Bush
2. Oil hydraulic press
3. Upper arm
SK2039100009000X

Fig. 14 Upper arm bushing replacement. Sidekick & X-90

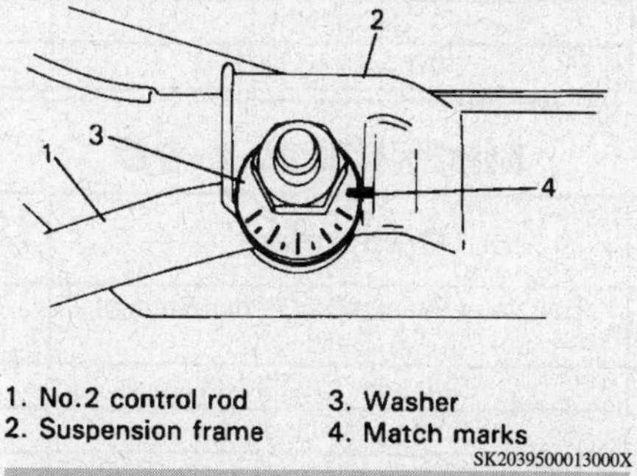
2
3
1
4
1. No.2 control rod
2. Suspension frame
3. Washer
4. Match marks
SK2039500013000X

Fig. 15 Toe adjustment. Esteem

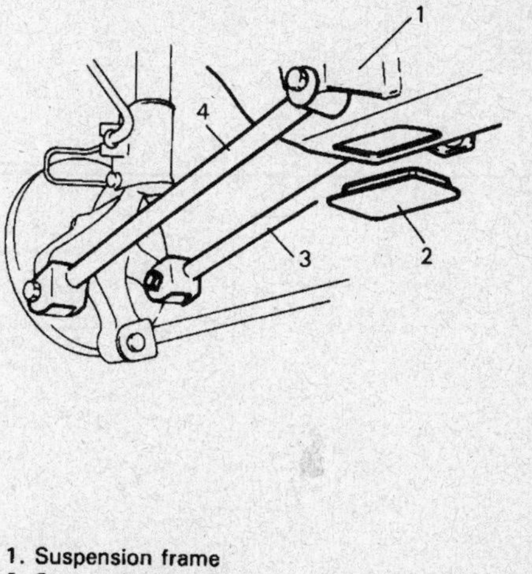
1
4
3
2
1. Suspension frame
2. Suspension frame cap
3. No.1 control rod
4. No.2 control rod
SK2039500014000X

Fig. 16 Control rods. Esteem

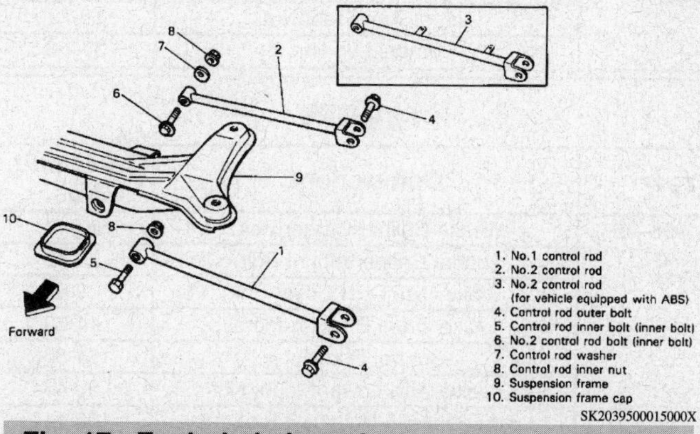
Forward
1. No.1 control rod
2. No.2 control rod
3. No.2 control rod (for vehicle equipped with ABS)
4. Control rod outer bolt
5. Control rod inner bolt (inner bolt)
6. No.2 control rod bolt (inner bolt)
7. Control rod washer
8. Control rod inner nut
9. Suspension frame
10. Suspension frame cap
SK2039500015000X

Fig. 17 Exploded view of control rods assembly. Esteem

4. Remove suspension frame cap.
5. Remove No. 2 control rod from frame and knuckle, **Fig. 16.**
6. Remove No. 1 control rod from frame and knuckle.
7. Reverse procedure to install, noting the following:
   a. Install No. 1 control rod with welded nut toward rear, **Fig. 17.**
   b. Insert inner and outer bolts from vehicle front and tighten temporarily by hand.
   c. Install No. 2 control rod with welded nut toward front.
   d. Insert No. 2 control rod bolt from vehicle front and outer bolt from rear. Tighten temporarily by hand.
   e. Set rear toe adjustment.
   f. Tighten all bolts and nuts to specification.

STABILIZER BAR

REPLACE

SWIFT

1. Raise and support vehicle.
2. Remove stabilizer bar left and right end nuts.
3. Remove stabilizer bar brackets, then the stabilizer bar.
4. Reverse procedure to install, noting the following:
   a. Ensure paint on stabilizer bar aligns with mounting bushing.
   b. Tighten bolts and nuts to specification.

TIGHTENING SPECIFICATIONS

SAMURAI

Year	Component	Torque/Ft. Lbs.
1993–95	Backing Plate Bolt	14-20
	Brake Back Plate Nut	14-20
	Differential Oil Drain Plug	29-50
	Differential Oil Filler Plug	26-36
	Hub Bolt/Nut	37-57
	Leaf Spring Nut	33-50
	Shackle Pin Bolt	22-39
	Shock Absorber Bolts	23-39
	U-Bolt Nut	44-57
	Wheel Lug Nut	37-57

SIDEKICK & X-90

Year	Component	Torque/Ft. Lbs.
1993–96	Ball Joint Bracket to Carrier Bracket Bolts	29-43
	Ball Joint Castle Nut	33-50
	Bearing Retainer Nut	14-20
	Brake Drum Nut	37-57
	Brake Line Flare Nuts	11–15
	Carrier Bolts	14–20
	Propeller Shaft Nuts	29-43
	Shaft Bearing Nuts	14-20
	Shock Absorber Nuts	58-72
	Trailing Rod Nuts	58-72
	Upper Arm Front Nut	58-72
	Wheel Lug Nut	37–58

SWIFT

Year	Component	Torque/Ft. Lbs.
1993–95	Brake Caliper Carrier Bolt	29-43
	Brake Caliper Mount Bolt	29-43
	Brake Disc Dust Cover Bolt	29-43
	Brake Drum Backing Plate	14-20
	Control Rod Nut	51-65
	Knuckle Arm Lower Mount Nut	29-43
	Rear Spindle Nut (Disc Brake)	108-144
	Rear Spindle Nut (Drum Brake)	58-86
	Strut Lower Mount Bolt	36-50
	Strut Support Nut	20-27
	Strut Upper Nut	29-43
	Suspension Arm Front Nut	36-50
	Suspension Arm Mounting Bracket Bolt	25-39
	Suspension Arm Rear Nut	29-43
	Wheel Lug Nut	36-50

ESTEEM

Year	Component	Torque/Ft. Lbs.
1995–96	Axle Nut	127
	Brake Back Plate Bolts	17
	Brake Line To Brake Back Plate	12
	Control Rod Bolts	65
	Hub Nut	127
	Rear Spindle Nut	127
	Strut Bracket	65
	Strut Lower Mount Bolt	65
	Strut Upper Nut	40
	Strut Upper Mount Nut	21
	Suspension Frame Bolt	65
	Trailing Rod Bolts	65
	Wheel Lug Nut	62
	Wheel Speed Sensor Bolt	17

Transfer Case

INDEX

Page No.	Page No.	Page No.
Transfer Case, Replace 40-65	Samurai 40-65	Sidekick & X-90................ 40-65

TRANSFER CASE

REPLACE

SAMURAI

4WD Models

1. Raise and support vehicle.
2. Remove three securing bolts from each of three universal joints from transfer case.
3. Remove clamp and boot from transfer case.
4. Remove control lever from transfer case by depressing lever guide and turning counterclockwise.
5. Drain oil from transfer case into appropriate container by removing drain plug.
6. Disconnect speedometer cable from transfer case.
7. Disconnect 4WD switch electrical connector from transfer case.
8. Remove transfer case-to-chassis attaching nuts and carefully lower transfer case assembly from vehicle.
9. Reverse procedure to install. **Torque** transfer case attaching nuts to 18.5–25.0 ft. lbs.

2WD Models

1. Raise and support vehicle, then disconnect propeller shafts from transfer case.
2. Remove drain plug and drain extension case into appropriate container.
3. Disconnect speedometer drive cable from case, then support transfer case with suitable jack.
4. Remove transfer case mounting nuts, then the transfer case.
5. Reverse procedure to install.

SIDEKICK & X-90

1. Disconnect battery ground cable.
2. Remove distributor assembly, then install a suitable block of wood to prevent engine from hanging down when rear crossmember is removed.
3. Remove console assembly, then the transmission and transfer case shift levers.
4. Raise and support vehicle.
5. Drain transfer case into appropriate container.
6. Remove front and rear propeller shafts.
7. Remove exhaust center pipe, then disconnect speedometer cable.
8. Support transmission using suitable jack, then remove rear crossmember.
9. Lower transmission slowly and check that wood block acts as a stopper for the engine.
10. Remove transmission jack, then lower vehicle.
11. Remove gear shift lever case attaching bolts.
12. Remove breather hose.
13. Remove gear shift lever case, then the transfer case center bolt.
14. Raise and support vehicle.
15. Remove transfer case mounting attaching bolts.
16. Support transfer case using suitable jack.
17. Disconnect 4WD switch electrical connector.
18. Remove front case attaching bolts.
19. Slide transfer case rearward and remove.
20. Reverse procedure to install.

Front Suspension & Steering

NOTE: For Front Axle Service Procedures Not Covered In This Section, Refer To The "Front Wheel Drive Axles" Section.

INDEX

	Page No.
Axle Shaft Joint, Replace	40-67
Samurai	40-67
Ball Joint, Replace	40-68
Esteem & Swift	40-68
Sidekick & X-90	40-68
Ball Joint Inspection	40-67
Coil Spring, Replace	40-68
Sidekick & X-90	40-68
Coil Spring & Strut Service	40-68
Swift	40-68
Hub & Bearing, Replace	40-66
Samurai	40-66
Sidekick & X-90	40-66
Hub & Bearing Outside Inner Race, Replace	40-67
Esteem	40-67
Swift	40-67
Leaf Spring, Replace	40-68
Samurai	40-68
Manual Steering Gears	40-110
Power Steering	40-112
Power Steering Pump, Replace	40-72
Esteem	40-72
Sidekick & X-90	40-72
Shock Absorber, Replace	40-68
Samurai	40-68
Stabilizer Bar, Replace	40-69
Esteem	40-70
Samurai	40-69
Sidekick, X-90 & Swift	40-69
Steering Gear, Replace	40-71
Esteem	40-72
Samurai	40-71
Sidekick & X-90	40-71
Swift	40-71
Steering Knuckle & Bearing, Replace	40-69
Swift	40-69
Steering Knuckle, Replace	40-68
Samurai	40-68
Sidekick & X-90	40-69
Strut, Replace	40-68
Esteem	40-68
Sidekick & X-90	40-68
Suspension Arm, Replace	40-70
Esteem	40-70
Swift	40-70
Suspension Control Arm, Ball Joint & Bushings, Replace	40-70
Sidekick & X-90	40-70
Tightening Specifications	40-73
Esteem	40-74
Samurai	40-73
Sidekick & X-90	40-73
Swift	40-74
Wheel Bearing, Adjust	40-66
Samurai	40-66
Sidekick, X-90 & Swift	40-66

WHEEL BEARING

ADJUST

SAMURAI

1. Remove wheel, drive flange or free wheeling hub (if equipped), caliper and holder as outlined previously.
2. Using a suitable spring scale, measure wheel bearing preload, **Fig. 1.**
3. Preload should be 2.2–6.6 ft. lbs.
4. If preload is not as specified, adjust as follows:
   a. Remove wheel bearing locknut and lock washer, then **torque** bearing nut, **Fig. 2,** to 57.5 ft. lbs., while spinning hub by hand.
   b. Loosen bearing nut until torque becomes 0, then **torque** nut to 7.5–10.5 ft. lbs. obtaining a preload of 2.2–6.6 ft. lbs.
   c. After adjustment, install lock washer and tighten locknut, **Fig. 2,** to specification.
   d. Recheck bearing preload.
5. Install axle shaft drive flange or free wheeling hub (if equipped), circlip, disc brake, caliper and holder and wheel assembly as outlined previously.

SIDEKICK, X-90 & SWIFT

The cassette type double taper roller bearing is so designed as to provide proper preload as long as it is tightened to specified torque.

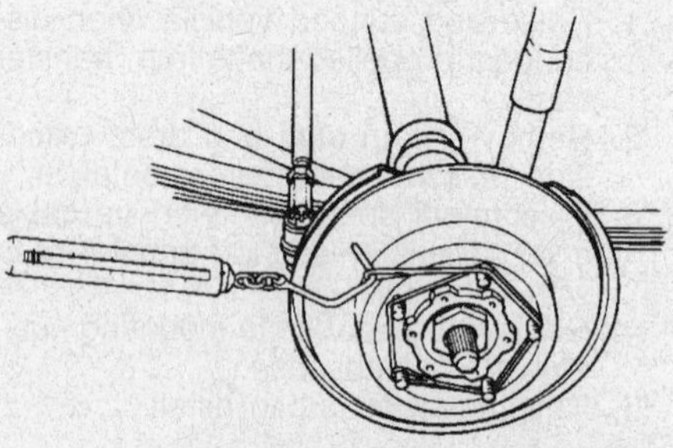
SK2049100011000X

Fig. 1 Wheel bearing preload measurement. Samurai

HUB & BEARING

REPLACE

SAMURAI

1. Loosen wheel lug nuts, then raise and support vehicle. Position jack stands under axle housing.
2. Remove lug nuts, then the wheel assembly.
3. Remove caliper carrier bolts, then the support caliper with wire.
4. Remove brake disc. **If brake disc cannot be removed by hand, install two 8 mm bolts in holes provided, then tighten to remove disc.**
5. **On models with free wheeling hubs,** proceed as follows:
   a. Remove free wheeling hub cover attaching screws, then the cover.
   b. Using needlenose pliers, remove free wheeling hub circlip, then free wheeling hub body.
6. **On models less free wheeling hub,** proceed as follows:
   a. Remove front axle shaft cap.
   b. Using needlenose pliers, remove circlip retaining the front axle shaft drive flange from the front driveshaft.
   c. Remove front axle shaft drive flange attaching bolts, then the drive flange.
7. **On all models,** bend up lock washer tab and remove wheel bearing locknut using tool, No. 09941-10, or equivalent.
8. Using tool, No. 09941-10, or equivalent, remove nut from front wheel spindle, then the washer.
9. Remove hub.
10. Remove oil seal and bearings from hub. If necessary, using a suitable hammer and drift, remove inner and outer bearing races from hub.
11. Reverse procedure to install, noting the following:
    a. Refer to "Wheel Bearings, Adjust," and adjust wheel bearing preload as outlined.
    b. Tighten front axle shaft drive flange bolts to specification.

SIDEKICK & X-90

Removal

1. Raise vehicle and remove wheel.
2. Remove locking hub assembly.
3. Remove brake caliper assembly, then

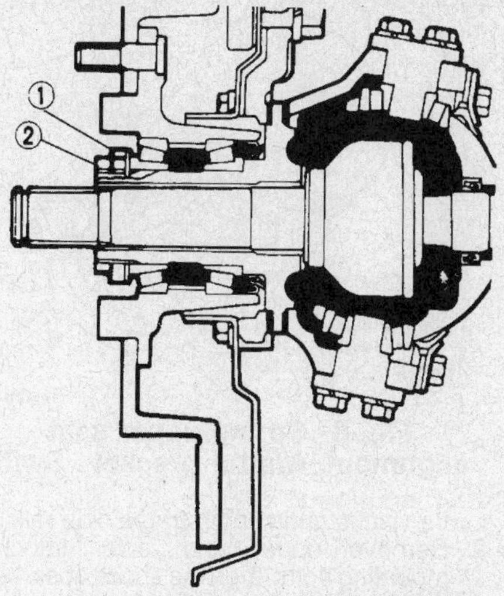
①
②

SK2049100012000X

Fig. 2 Wheel bearing nut & locknut location. Samurai

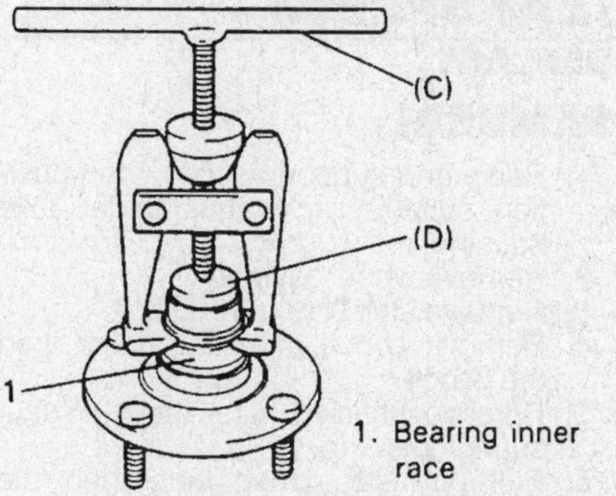
(C)
(D)
1
1. Bearing inner race

SK2049100003000X

Fig. 5 Wheel bearing inner race replacement. Swift

suspend out of way.

4. Remove brake disc, then the bearing lock plate retaining screws and lock plate.
5. Using bearing tool, No. J37763, or equivalent, remove wheel bearing locknut and washer.
6. Remove entire wheel hub assembly. If assembly cannot be removed by hand use tools, **Fig. 3,** to remove.
7. Remove wheel bearing oil seal, then the bearing circlip.
8. Remove bearing outer race using bearing installer handle tool, No. J8092 and front wheel hub bearing remover tool, No. J37772, or equivalent, by tapping out with hammer.

Installation

1. Using bearing installer handle tool, No. J8092 and front wheel hub bearing installer tool, No. J37777, or equivalent, press fit bearing outer race until firmly seated in wheel hub.
2. Pack bearing with Suzuki Super Grease, No. 99000-25010, or equivalent.
3. Install bearing circlip, then the bearing oil seal using front wheel hub and bearing oil seal installer tool, No. J37774, or equivalent.
4. Fill oil seal recess and cover oil seal lip

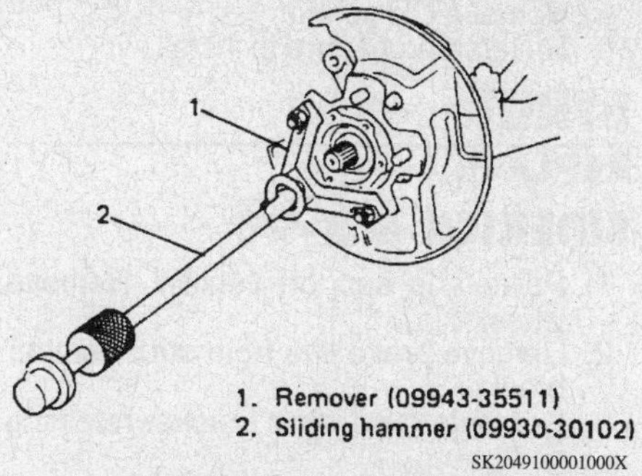
1
2
1. Remover (09943-35511)
2. Sliding hammer (09930-30102)

SK2049100001000X

Fig. 3 Wheel hub replacement. Sidekick & X-90

with Suzuki Super Grease No. 99000-25010, or equivalent.

5. Install wheel hub assembly onto front wheel spindle, then the spindle thrust washer.
6. Using wheel bearing tightening tool, No. J37763, or equivalent, install wheel bearing nut, then tighten to specification.
7. Install brake disc and caliper assembly, then tighten caliper bolt to specification.
8. Install wheel, then the locking hub assembly.

HUB & BEARING OUTSIDE INNER RACE

REPLACE

SWIFT

1. Raise and support vehicle, then remove front wheels.
2. Remove driveshaft nut while depressing brake pedal.
3. Remove caliper carrier bolts, then the carrier with caliper.
4. Remove brake disc screws, then the disc using 8 mm bolts.
5. Remove wheel hub using tools, **Fig. 4.**
6. Remove hub studs, then the wheel bearing inner race using tools, **Fig. 5.**
7. Reverse procedure to install, noting the following:
   a. Install outside inner race, **Fig. 6.**
   b. Apply Suzuki grease, No. 99000-25010, or equivalent, to outside bearing, outside inner race and oil seal lip.
   c. Tighten all bolts and nuts to specification.
   d. Install and secure new driveshaft nut.

ESTEEM

1. Raise and support vehicle, then remove front wheels.
2. Remove driveshaft nut while depressing brake pedal.
3. Remove caliper carrier and caliper. Position caliper aside to prevent bending or twisting of brake hose.
4. Remove brake disc screws, then the disc using by two 8 mm bolts screwed into disc face.
5. Remove wheel hub using puller tools

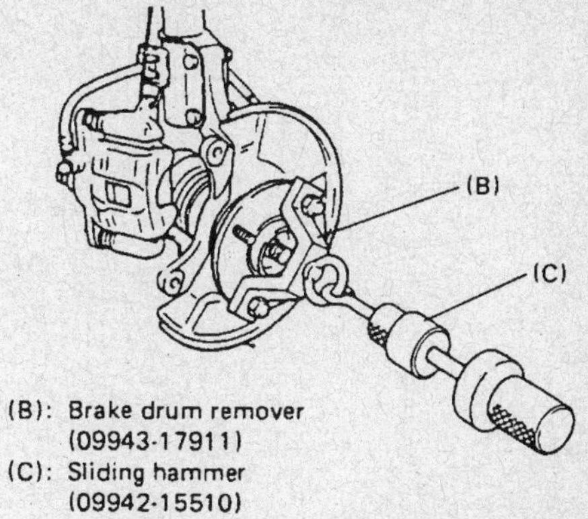
(B)
(C)
(B): Brake drum remover (09943-17911)
(C): Sliding hammer (09942-15510)

SK2049100002000X

Fig. 4 Wheel hub replacement. Swift

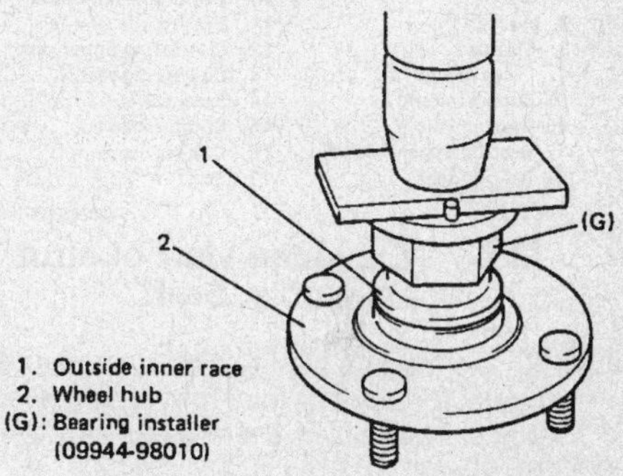
1
2
(G)
1. Outside inner race
2. Wheel hub
(G): Bearing installer (09944-98010)

SK2049100004000X

Fig. 6 Outside inner race replacement. Swift

No. 09943–17912 and 09942–15510, or equivalents.

6. Remove hub studs, then the wheel bearing inner race using tools No. 09913–65810 and No. 09913–85230, or equivalents.
7. Reverse procedure to install, noting the following:
   a. Install outside inner race, using suitable shop press.
   b. Apply Suzuki grease, No. 99000-25010, or equivalent, to outside bearing, outside inner race and oil seal lip.
   c. Install and secure new driveshaft nut.
   d. Tighten all bolts and nuts to specification.

AXLE SHAFT JOINT

REPLACE

SAMURAI

1. Repeat steps 1 through 7 as outlined under "Steering Knuckle, Replace."
2. Drain oil from differential housing into appropriate container.
3. Remove axle shaft joint from axle housing.
4. Reverse procedure to install.

BALL JOINT INSPECTION

1. Raise and support vehicle.
2. Grasp tire at top and bottom.

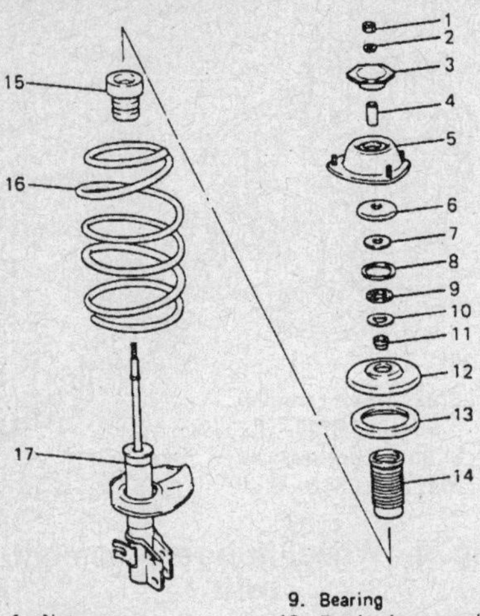
1
2
3
4
5
6
7
8
9
10
11
12
13
14
15
16
17

1. Nut
2. Washer
3. Stopper
4. Inner spacer
5. Support comp.
6. Bearing seat
7. Bearing upper washer
8. Bearing seal
9. Bearing
10. Bearing lower washer
11. Bearing spacer
12. Coil spring upper seat
13. Coil spring seat
14. Strut cover
15. Bump stopper
16. Coil spring
17. Strut

SK2029100002000X

Fig. 7 Exploded view of strut assembly. Swift

3. Shake tire in a side to side motion and check for any ball joint movement. Replace ball joint if there is any movement.
4. Check ball stud and ball joint dust cover for damage. Replace ball joint if any damage is present.

BALL JOINT

REPLACE

ESTEEM & SWIFT

Ball joint and suspension arm cannot be separated, refer to "Suspension Arm, Replace" for ball joint replacement.

SIDEKICK & X-90

Refer to "Suspension Control Arm, Ball Joint & Bushings, Replace" for ball joint replacement.

COIL SPRING

REPLACE

SIDEKICK & X-90

1. Raise and support vehicle. Remove wheels.
2. Remove locking hub, then the front axle shaft circlip and washer.
3. Remove brake caliper assembly, then suspend out of way.
4. Remove brake disc, then the stabilizer ball joint.
5. Using tie rod end remover tool, No. J21687-02, or equivalent, remove tie rod end.
6. Using a suitable jack, support the suspension arm, then remove the lower strut bracket from the suspension arm.
7. Remove ball stud castle nut from ball stud
8. Lower jack, then remove steering knuckle and wheel hub assembly.
9. Remove coil spring.
10. Reverse procedure to install.

STRUT

REPLACE

SIDEKICK & X-90

1. Raise and support vehicle. Remove wheels.
2. Remove brake line from strut damper bracket.
3. Remove lower strut bracket retaining bolts.
4. Supporting the strut, remove the upper strut retaining bolts, then the strut.
5. Reverse procedure to install.

ESTEEM

1. Raise and support vehicle.
2. Remove wheels, allowing front suspension to hang free.
3. Remove brake hose from strut bracket.
4. **On models with ABS,** remove ABS wheel speed sensor
5. **On all models,** remove lower strut bracket retaining bolts.
6. Supporting strut, then remove upper strut retaining bolts and strut.
7. Reverse procedure to install. Tighten to specification.

COIL SPRING & STRUT SERVICE

SWIFT

Removal

1. Raise and support vehicle. Allow front suspension to hang free.
2. Remove wheels, then disconnect brake hose clip from strut bracket.
3. Remove strut lower attaching bolts, then the upper support nuts.
4. Remove strut from vehicle.

Disassemble

1. Using spring compressor, compress spring until tension is released from upper spring seat. Tension is released when strut turns lightly with spring held stationary.
2. Remove strut nut, then disassemble strut, **Fig. 7.**

Assemble

1. Spring should be compressed to a length of nine inches (230 mm).
2. Mate spring end with stepped part of lower spring seat.
3. Assemble strut in reverse numbered sequence, **Fig. 7,** noting the following:
   a. Align spring upper seat with strut bracket, **Fig. 8.**
   b. Tighten bolts and nuts to specification.
4. Reverse procedure to install.

SHOCK ABSORBER

REPLACE

SAMURAI

1. Raise and support vehicle, then position jackstands under frame side rails.
2. Remove upper and lower shock mounting bolts, then the shock absorber, **Fig. 9.**
3. Reverse procedure to install.

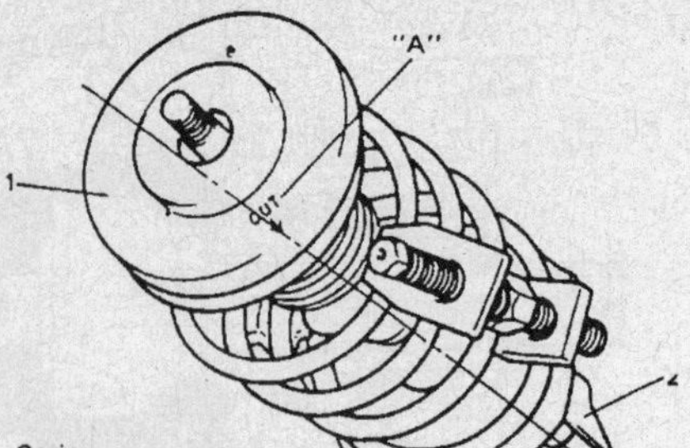
"A"
1
2
OUT

1. Spring upper seat
2. Strut bracket
A: Mark (out)

SK2029100003000X

Fig. 8 Spring upper seat alignment, w/strut bracket . Swift

LEAF SPRING

REPLACE

SAMURAI

1. Raise and support vehicle, then position suitable jackstands under axle housing.
2. Remove wheel assembly.
3. Remove stabilizer nut and bolt.
4. Remove U-bolt attaching bolts, then the U-bolt.
5. Remove shackle nuts, then the leaf spring nuts, **Fig. 9.**
6. Pull out leaf spring bolt, then the shackle pin and remove leaf spring.
7. Reverse procedure to install.

STEERING KNUCKLE

REPLACE

SAMURAI

1. Repeat steps 1 through 9 as outlined under "Hub & Bearing, Replace."
2. Loosen bolts securing upper and lower kingpins, **Fig. 9. Do not remove kingpins.**
3. Remove disc dust cover attaching bolts, then the disc dust cover, caliper holder and wheel spindle.
4. Remove tie rod end castle nut, then using tie rod remover **Fig. 10,** disconnect tie rod from steering knuckle.
5. Remove joint seal attaching bolts, then the oil seal cover, pad, oil seal and retainer from knuckle.
6. Remove upper and lower kingpins. **When removing kingpins, mark with identification marks for Installation. Also, check number of shims used for each side.**
7. Pull off steering knuckle. **When removing steering knuckle, kingpin lower bearing may fall out. Mark upper and lower kingpin bearings for Installation.**
8. Reverse procedure to install, noting the following:
   a. Tighten joint seal bolts and upper and lower kingpin bolts to specification.

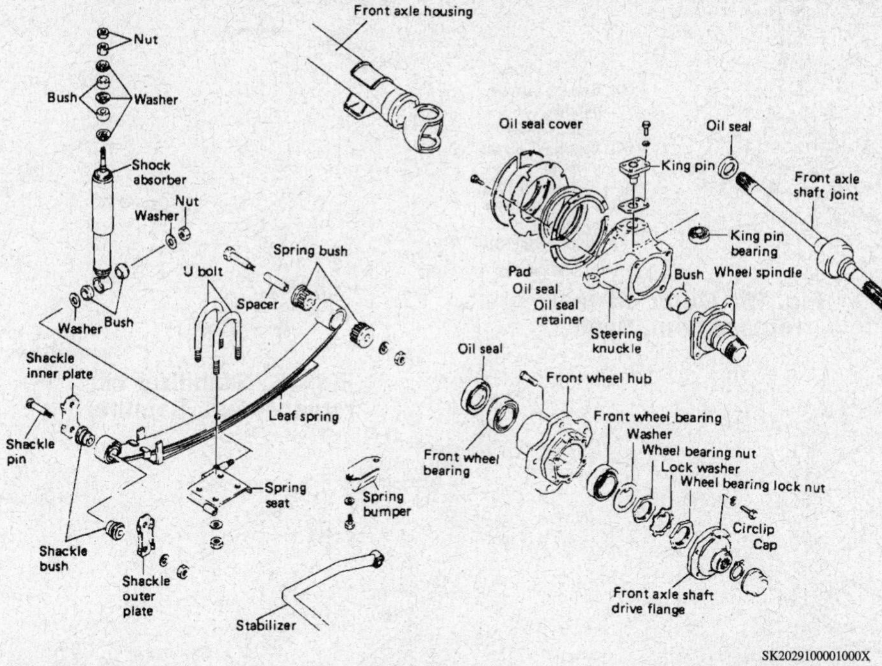
Front axle housing
Nut
Bush
Washer
Shock absorber
Nut
Washer
Spring bush
U bolt
Spacer
Washer
Bush
Shackle inner plate
Shackle pin
Leaf spring
Spring seat
Spring bumper
Shackle bush
Shackle outer plate
Stabilizer
Oil seal cover
Oil seal
King pin
Front axle shaft joint
King pin bearing
Pad
Oil seal
Oil seal retainer
Bush
Wheel spindle
Steering knuckle
Oil seal
Front wheel hub
Front wheel bearing
Washer
Wheel bearing nut
Lock washer
Wheel bearing lock nut
Front wheel bearing
Circlip
Cap
Front axle shaft drive flange
SK2029100001000X

Fig. 9 Exploded view of front suspension & axle assembly. Samurai

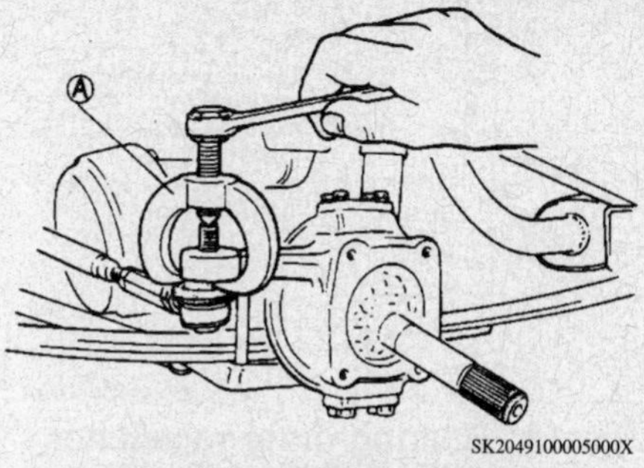
A
SK2049100005000X

Fig. 10 Tie rod from steering knuckle separation

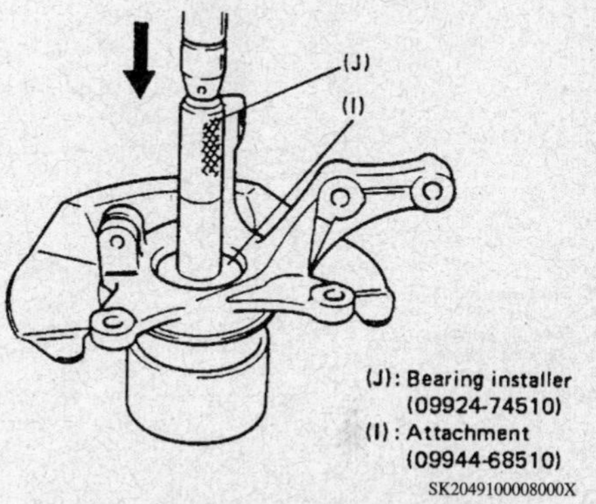
(J)
(I)
(J): Bearing installer (09924-74510)
(I): Attachment (09944-68510)
SK2049100008000X

Fig. 13 Bearing outer race/inner bearing removal. Swift

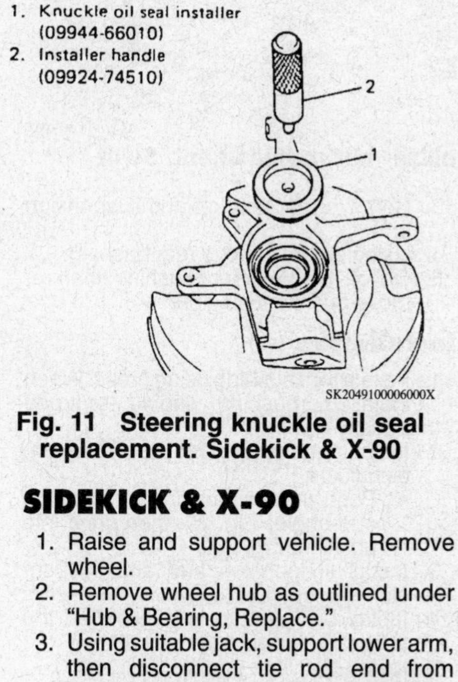
1. Knuckle oil seal installer (09944-66010)
2. Installer handle (09924-74510)
2
1
SK2049100006000X

Fig. 11 Steering knuckle oil seal replacement. Sidekick & X-90

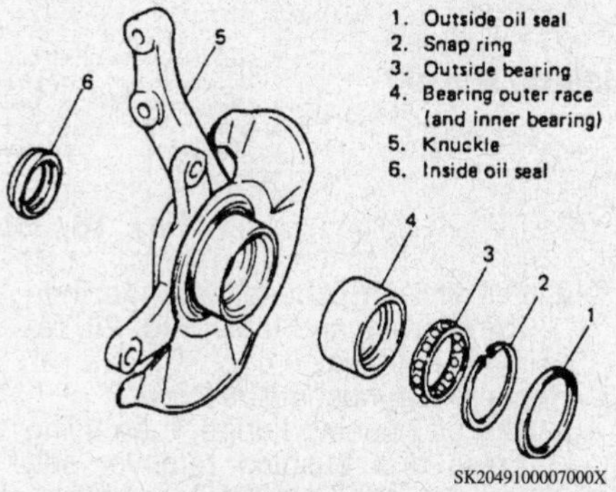
1. Outside oil seal
2. Snap ring
3. Outside bearing
4. Bearing outer race (and inner bearing)
5. Knuckle
6. Inside oil seal
5
6
4
3
2
1
SK2049100007000X

Fig. 12 Exploded view of steering knuckle & bearing. Swift

SIDEKICK & X-90

1. Raise and support vehicle. Remove wheel.
2. Remove wheel hub as outlined under "Hub & Bearing, Replace."
3. Using suitable jack, support lower arm, then disconnect tie rod end from knuckle using tie rod remover, **Fig. 10.**
4. Remove ball stud nut, then the strut bracket bolts from strut bracket.
5. Remove steering knuckle from ball stud by tapping with hammer.
6. While lowering jack, remove knuckle and wheel spindle assembly.
7. Remove oil seal, dust cover and wheel spindle from steering knuckle.
8. Reverse procedure to install, noting the following:
   a. Coat mating surface of wheel spindle and steering knuckle with Suzuki Bond No. 1215, or equivalent.
   b. Fill in spindle recess and knuckle seal recess with Suzuki lithium grease No. 99000-25010, or equivalent.
   c. Drive in knuckle oil seal until its end contacts stepped surface of knuckle using tools, **Fig. 11.**

STEERING KNUCKLE & BEARING

REPLACE

SWIFT

Removal

1. Raise and support vehicle.
2. Remove wheel hub as outlined under "Wheel Hub & Bearing Outside Inner Race, Replace."
3. Disconnect tie rod end from knuckle using tie rod remover **Fig. 10.**
4. Remove strut bracket bolts from strut bracket, then the ball stud bolt.
5. Remove knuckle.

Disassembly

1. Remove outside oil seal, snap ring, outside bearing, inside oil seal and inside bearing, **Fig. 12.**
2. Remove bearing outer race/inner bearing using press and tools, **Fig. 13.**

Assembly

Once bearing outer race is removed, bearing set (outer race, bearings and inner races) should be replaced.

1. Press fit bearing outer race/inner bearing using tools, **Fig. 14.**
2. Lubricate and install bearing outer race, bearings and oil seals.
3. Drive in inside oil seal until flush with stopped surface of knuckle.
4. Drive in outside oil seal until its end contacts snap ring using tools, **Fig. 15.**

Installation

1. Reverse removal procedure to install.

STABILIZER BAR

REPLACE

SAMURAI

1. Raise and support vehicle.
2. Remove stabilizer bar attaching bolts, then the stabilizer bar, **Fig. 16.**
3. Reverse procedure to install.

SIDEKICK, X-90 & SWIFT

1. Raise and support vehicle.
2. Disconnect stabilizer ball joint from front suspension arms, **Figs. 17 and 18.**
3. Remove stabilizer bar mount bushing bracket bolts, then the stabilizer bar.

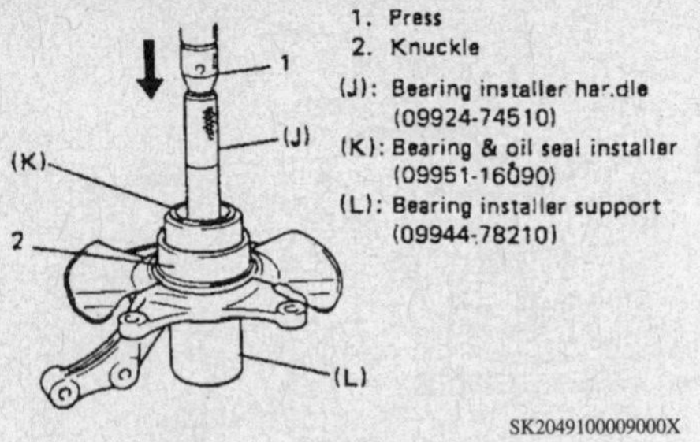
1. Press
2. Knuckle
(J): Bearing installer handle (09924-74510)
(K): Bearing & oil seal installer (09951-16090)
(L): Bearing installer support (09944-78210)
1
2
(J)
(K)
(L)
SK2049100009000X

Fig. 14 Bearing outer race/inner bearing installation. Swift

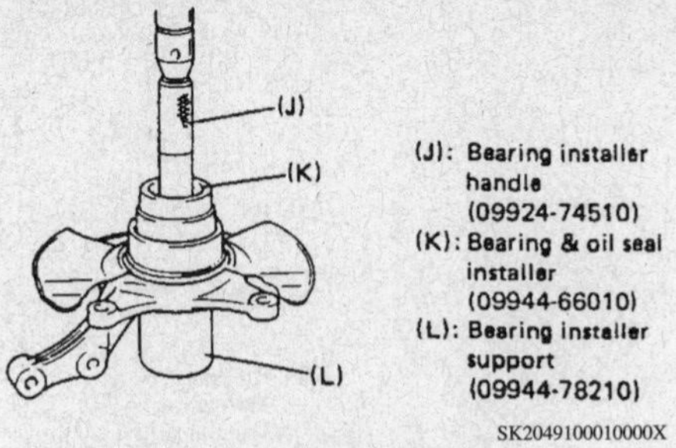
(J)
(K)
(L)
(J): Bearing installer handle (09924-74510)
(K): Bearing & oil seal installer (09944-66010)
(L): Bearing installer support (09944-78210)
SK2049100010000X

Fig. 15 Outer oil seal replacement. Swift

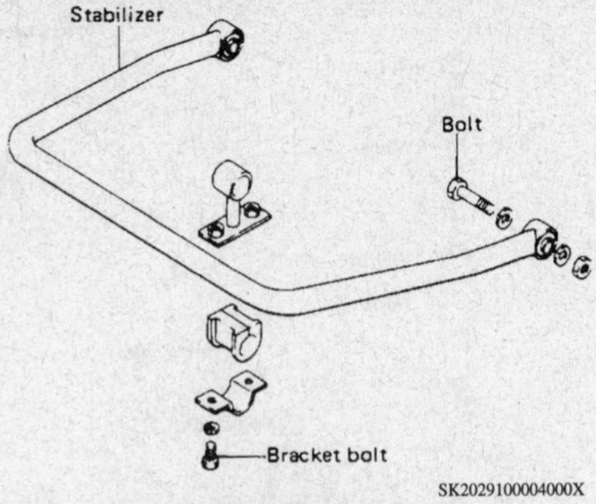
Stabilizer
Bolt
Bracket bolt
SK2029100004000X

Fig. 16 Stabilizer bar replacement. Samurai

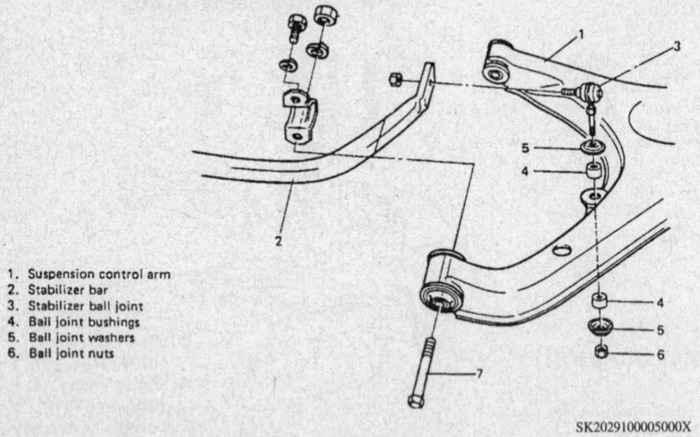
1. Suspension control arm
2. Stabilizer bar
3. Stabilizer ball joint
4. Ball joint bushings
5. Ball joint washers
6. Ball joint nuts
SK2029100005000X

Fig. 17 Stabilizer bar replacement. Sidekick & X-90

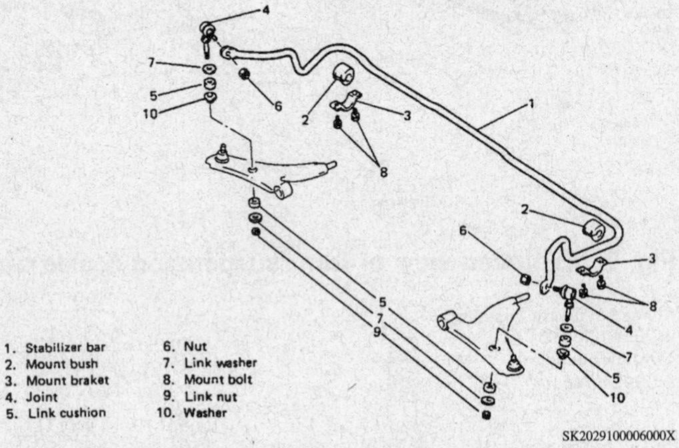
1. Stabilizer bar
2. Mount bush
3. Mount braket
4. Joint
5. Link cushion
6. Nut
7. Link washer
8. Mount bolt
9. Link nut
10. Washer
SK2029100006000X

Fig. 18 Stabilizer bar replacement. Swift

4. Reverse procedure to install, noting the following:
   a. Ensure paint on stabilizer bar aligns with mount bushings for correct side to side Installation.
   b. Tighten all bolts and nuts to specification.

ESTEEM

1. Raise and support vehicle.
2. Remove stabilizer link nuts, washers and cushions, **Fig. 19.**
3. Remove stabilizer mount brackets, then the stabilizer bar.
4. Reverse procedure to install, noting the following:
   a. Ensure paint on stabilizer bar aligns with mount bushings for correct side to side Installation.
   b. Tighten all bolts and nuts to specification.

SUSPENSION CONTROL ARM, BALL JOINT & BUSHINGS

REPLACE

SIDEKICK & X-90

Removal

1. Remove coil spring as outlined under "Coil Spring, Replace."
2. Remove lower arm bracket bolts, then the lower arm.
3. Remove ball joint assembly attaching bolts, then the ball joint.
4. Remove front bushing as follows:
   a. Cut off 5 mm of bushing flange, then using press and tools, **Fig. 20,** remove bushing.
5. Remove rear bushing as follows:
   a. Cut off bushing flange, then using press and bushing remover set, tool No. 09951-16040, or equivalent, remove bushing.

Installation

1. Press fit front bushing until its flange contacts housing edge of lower arm. Set bushing in arm aligning hollow areas, **Fig. 21.**
2. Press fit rear bushing ensuring lower arm housing is held between its flanges.
3. Install ball joint to lower arm. Tighten bolts to specification.
4. Install lower arm to chassis.
5. Refer to "Coil Spring, Replace" to complete Installation procedure.

SUSPENSION ARM

REPLACE

SWIFT

Removal

1. Raise and support vehicle, then remove stabilizer links.
2. Remove ball stud bolt, then the suspension arm bracket bolts.
3. Remove rear bracket and suspension arm.
4. Using press, remove rear bushing.
5. Cut off flange of front bushing, then remove bushing using press.

Installation

1. Install front bushing using press. When installed, bushing should protrude equally on both sides.
2. Install rear bushing to suspension arm as follows:
   a. Push in rear bushing in direction and angle, **Fig. 22,** then drive into position, **Fig. 23.**
3. Install suspension arm and suspension arm bracket.
4. Install ball stud to knuckle, then the suspension arm rear bracket.
5. Install stabilizer links.
6. Tighten all bolts and nuts to specification.
7. Install wheels, then lower vehicle.
8. Check toe setting and adjust as required.

ESTEEM

Removal

1. Raise and support vehicle, then remove stabilizer links.
2. Remove ball stud bolt, then the suspension arm bracket bolts.
3. Remove rear bracket and suspension arm.

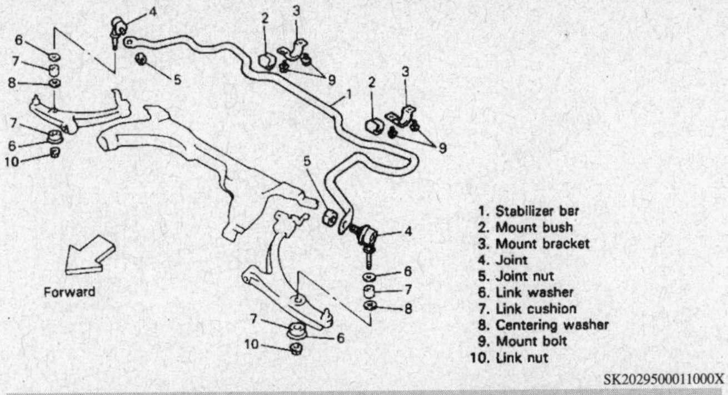
Forward
1. Stabilizer bar
2. Mount bush
3. Mount bracket
4. Joint
5. Joint nut
6. Link washer
7. Link cushion
8. Centering washer
9. Mount bolt
10. Link nut
SK2029500011000X

Fig. 19 Stabilizer bar replacement. Esteem

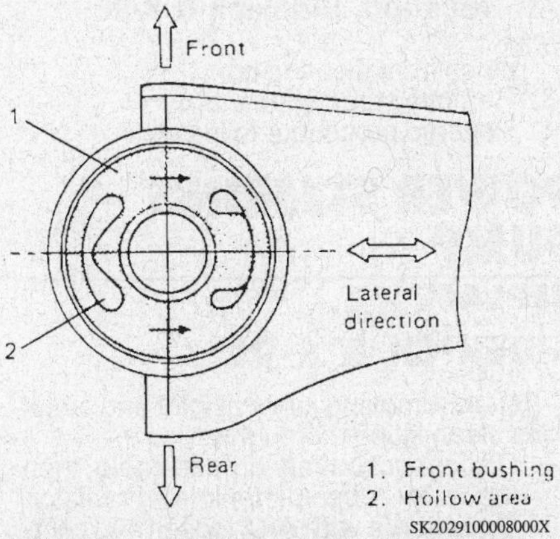
Front
Lateral direction
Rear
1. Front bushing
2. Hollow area
SK2029100008000X

Fig. 21 Suspension control arm front bushing alignment. Sidekick & X-90

4. Using press, remove rear bushing.
5. Cut off flange of front bushing, then remove bushing using press.

Installation

1. Install front bushing using press. When installed, bushing should protrude equally on both sides.
2. Install rear bushing to suspension arm as follows:
   a. Push in rear bushing in direction and angle, **Fig. 24,** then drive into position.
3. Install suspension arm and suspension arm bracket.
4. Install ball stud to knuckle, then the suspension arm rear bracket.
5. Install stabilizer links.
6. Tighten all bolts and nuts to specification.
7. Install wheels, then lower vehicle.
8. Check toe setting.

STEERING GEAR

REPLACE

SAMURAI

1. Remove steering column shaft to steering gear coupling bolt.
2. Remove radiator undercover.
3. Using tie rod remover, or equivalent, **Fig. 10,** disconnect ball stud of drag rod and steering damper from pitman arm.

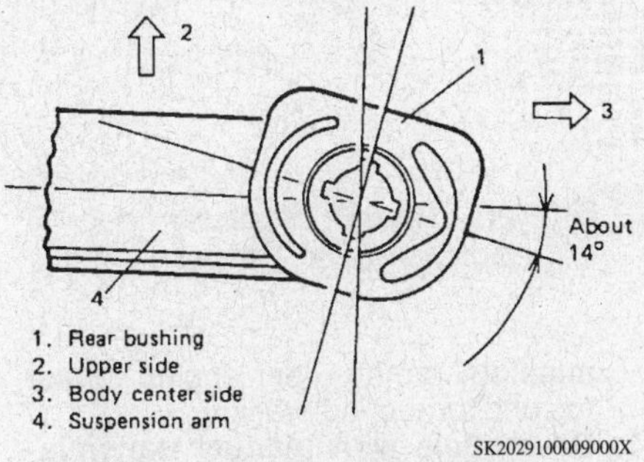
About 14°
1. Rear bushing
2. Upper side
3. Body center side
4. Suspension arm
SK2029100009000X

Fig. 22 Direction & angle of suspension arm rear bushing. Swift

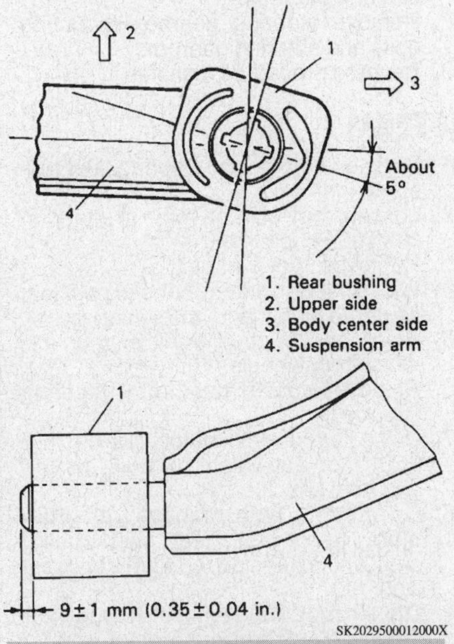
About 5°
1. Rear bushing
2. Upper side
3. Body center side
4. Suspension arm
9±1 mm (0.35±0.04 in.)
SK2029500012000X

Fig. 24 Suspension arm rear bushing replacement. Esteem

4. Remove steering gear attaching bolts, then the steering gear.
5. Reverse procedure to install.

SIDEKICK & X-90

1. **On models with power steering,** disconnect coolant reservoir tank from radiator.
2. **On all models,** remove steering lower

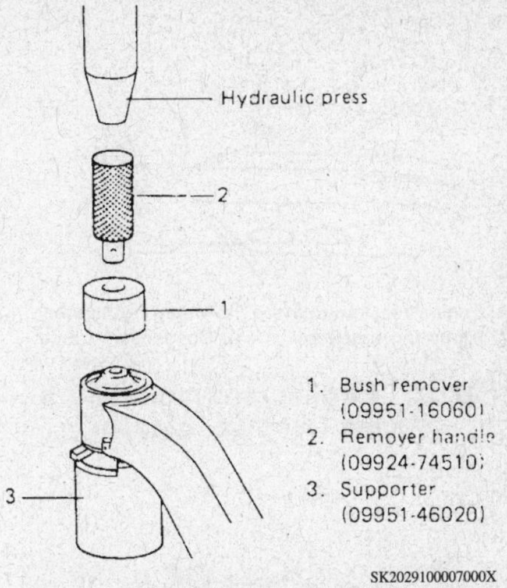
Hydraulic press
1. Bush remover (09951-16060)
2. Remover handle (09924-74510)
3. Supporter (09951-46020)
SK2029100007000X

Fig. 20 Suspension control arm front bushing replacement. Sidekick & X-90

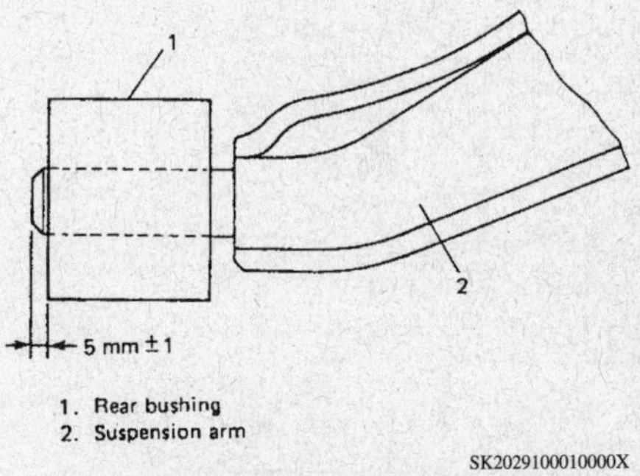
5 mm ±1
1. Rear bushing
2. Suspension arm
SK2029100010000X

Fig. 23 Suspension arm rear bushing replacement. Swift

shaft attaching bolt, then the center link end from pitman arm.
3. **On models with power steering,** disconnect pressure hose from gearbox.
4. Disconnect return hose from oil tank. Place container under tank to receive fluid.
5. **On all models,** remove three steering gearbox attaching bolts.
6. Remove steering gearbox, disconnecting steering lower shaft joint.
7. **On models with power steering,** remove pitman arm from gearbox.
8. Reverse procedure to install.

SWIFT

Manual Steering

1. Slide drivers seat back as far as possible.
2. Remove front part of drivers floor mat, then the steering shaft joint cover.
3. Loosen steering shaft upper joint bolt but do not remove.
4. Remove steering shaft lower joint bolt, then disconnect lower joint from pinion.
5. Raise and support vehicle, remove front wheels.
6. Disconnect tie rods ends from knuckles using tie rod remover, **Fig. 10.**
7. Remove steering gear case mounting bolts, case bracket and steering gear.

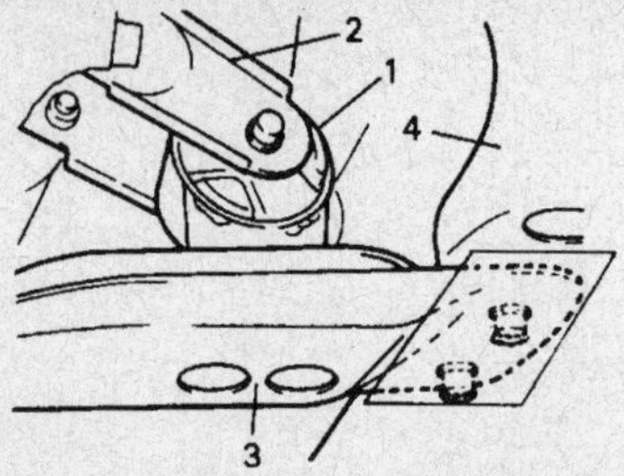

1. Engine rear mounting 3. Mounting member
2. Mounting bracket 4. Suspension frame

SK2029500013000X

Fig. 25 Engine rear mounting & bracket removal. Esteem

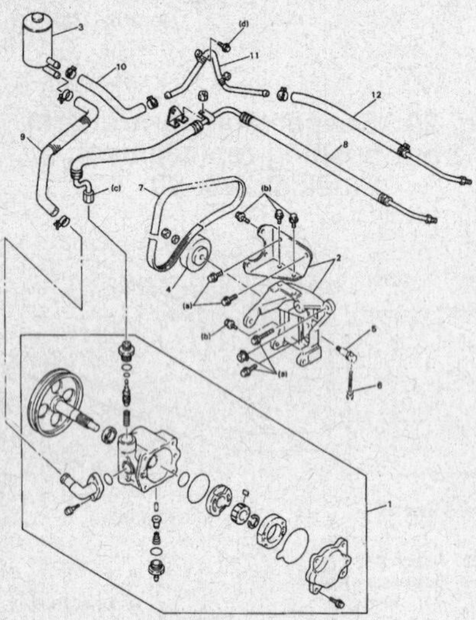

1. Power steering pump assembly
2. Bracket
3. Power steering oil tank
4. Belt tension pulley
5. Belt tension pulley bolt
6. Belt tension bolt
7. Power steering belt
8. High pressure hose & pipe
9. Suction hose
10. Low pressure return hose (Tank side)
11. Low pressure return pipe
12. Low pressure return hose & pipe (Gear box side)

SK6029500008000X

Fig. 28 Power steering pump components. Esteem

8. Reverse procedure to install, noting the following:
   a. Ensure steering wheel and brake discs are in straight ahead position.
   b. Tighten lower steering shaft joint bolt first, then the upper bolt.

Power Steering

1. Loosen steering shaft upper joint bolt, but do not remove, then remove lower joint bolt and separate pinion and lower joint.
2. Raise and support vehicle, then remove front wheels.
3. Disconnect tie rods from steering knuckles using tie rod end remover tool, No. 09913-65210, or equivalent, then remove exhaust pipe.
4. **On models with automatic transmission,** remove rear engine torque rod and torque rod bracket.
5. **On models with manual transmission,** disconnect transmission side of gear shift control shaft and extension rod.
6. **On all models,** disconnect piping from steering gearbox.
7. Remove steering gearbox mounting bolts and steering gearbox.
8. Reverse procedure to install.

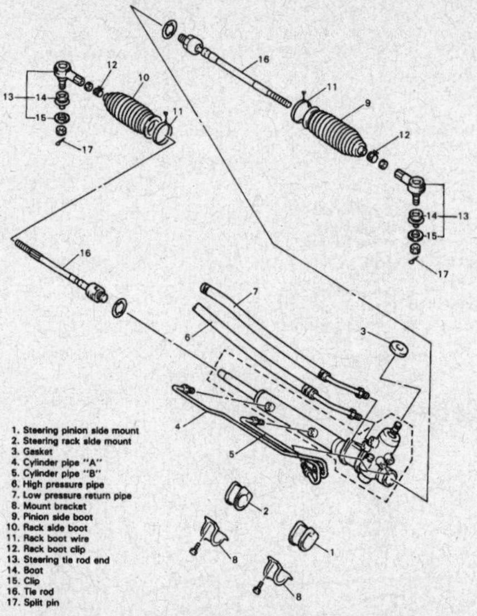

1. Steering pinion side mount
2. Steering rack side mount
3. Gasket
4. Cylinder pipe "A"
5. Cylinder pipe "B"
6. High pressure pipe
7. Low pressure return pipe
8. Mount bracket
9. Pinion side boot
10. Rack side boot
11. Rack boot wire
12. Rack boot clip
13. Steering tie rod end
14. Boot
15. Clip
16. Tie rod
17. Split pin

SK2029500014000X

Fig. 26 Power steering box components. Esteem

ESTEEM

1. Drain oil from power steering fluid reservoir.
2. Loosen, but do not remove steering shaft upper joint bolt.
3. Remove lower joint bolt.
4. With wheels in straight-ahead position, separate pinion and lower joint.
5. Raise and support vehicle, then remove front wheels.
6. Remove castle nut from steering knuckle.
7. Using tie rod removal tool No. 09913–65210, or equivalent, remove tie rod end from knuckle.
8. **On models with manual transmission,** disconnect gear shift control shaft and extension rod form transmission.
9. **On all models,** remove engine rear mounting and bracket, **Fig. 25.**
10. Detach mounting member from suspension frame.
11. Remove cylinder pipes "A" and "B" from steering gear box, **Fig. 26.**
12. Disconnect high and low pressure pipes from steering box.
13. Remove steering gear box.
14. Reverse procedure to install.

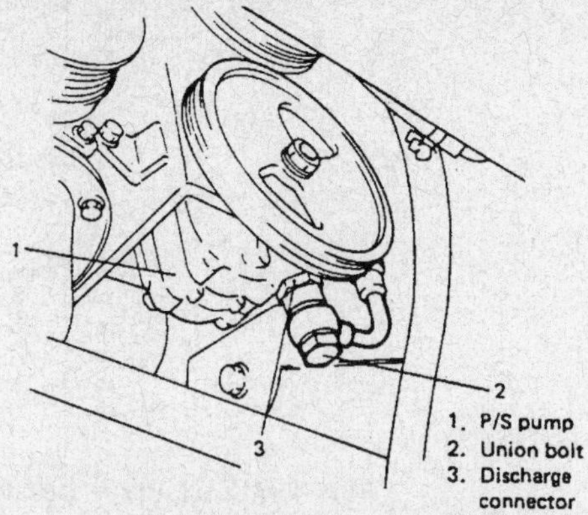
1
2
3

1. P/S pump
2. Union bolt
3. Discharge connector

SK6039100001000X

Fig. 27 Discharge connector location. Sidekick & X-90

POWER STEERING PUMP

REPLACE

SIDEKICK & X-90

Before removing joints at inlet and outlet ports clean fitting thoroughly.

1. Disconnect battery ground cable, then the water reservoir tank from radiator.
2. **On models with A/C,** loosen A/C compressor adjusting bolt and pivot bolts.
3. **On models less A/C,** loosen power steering pump adjusting and mounting bolts.
4. Remove power steering belt.
5. Remove union bolt. Hold discharge connector with wrench to prevent fluid from draining, **Fig. 27.**
6. Disconnect pump suction hose from oil tank, then the pump pressure switch lead wire at switch terminal.
7. Remove engine oil filter, then the pump adjusting and mounting bolts.
8. Remove power steering pump. **Plug ports to prevent any foreign matter from entering.**
9. Reverse procedure to install.

ESTEEM

1. Remove engine right side undercover, then loosen belt tension pulley to remove power steering belt, **Fig. 28.**
2. Disconnect high pressure hose and suction hose from pump.
3. Disconnect pressure switch lead harness.
4. **On models with A/C,** remove compressor and position aside.
5. **On all models,** remove power steering pump and bracket.
6. Reverse procedure to install. Tighten to specification.

TIGHTENING SPECIFICATIONS

SAMURAI

Year	Component	Torque/Ft. Lbs.
1993–95	Bearing Locknut (2)	44-65
	Drag Rod Nut	22-50
	Front Axle Shaft Drive Flange Bolt	14-21
	Joint Seal Bolts	6-8
	Leaf Spring Nut	33-50
	Shackle Pin Nut	22-39
	Shock lower mounting bolt	26-39
	Shock upper mounting bolt	16-25
	Stabilizer Bracket Bolt	51-65
	Stabilizer Nuts	16-25
	Steering Damper Nut	26-39
	Steering Gear Attaching Bolts	51-65
	Tie Rod Castle Nut	22-39
	U-Bolt Nuts	44-57
	Upper And Lower Kingpin Bolts	15-21
	Wheel Lug Nut	37-57

SIDEKICK & X-90

Year	Component	Torque/Ft. Lbs.
1993–96	A/C Compressor Adjusting Bolt	18-22
	A/C Compressor Pivot Bolt	18-22
	Ball Joint Bolt	51-75
	Ball Joint Stud Castle Nut	33-50
	Bump Stopper	29-43
	Caliper Bolt	51-75
	Center Link Castle Nut	22-50
	Control Arm Front Nut	51-75
	Control Arm Rear Nut	65-101
	Locking Hub Bolt	15-22
	Locking Hub Cover Bolt	6-8
	Power Steering Gearbox Union Bolt	22-28
	Power Steering Pump Adjusting Bolt	15-21
	Power Steering Pump Mounting Bolt	15-21
	Power Steering Pump Union Bolt	37-50
	Stabilizer Bar Ball Joint Nut	29-43
	Steering Gearbox Bolt	51-72
	Steering Lower Shaft Bolt	15-21
	Strut Bracket Nut	58-75
	Strut Nut	50-75
	Strut Support Nut	15-22
	Tie Rod End Castle Nut	22-39
	Wheel Bearing Locknut	89-140
	Wheel Lug Nut	37-58

SWIFT

Year	Component	Torque/Ft. Lbs.
1993–96	Axle Nut	109-144
	Ball Stud Nut	37-50
	Bracket Nut	72-108
	Driveshaft Nut	109-144
	Hub Nut	109-144
	Stabilizer Bracket Bolt	14-20
	Stabilizer Joint Nut	29-43
	Stabilizer Link Nut	14-20
	Steering Gear Case Bolt	15-21
	Steering Shaft Joint Bolt	15-21
	Strut Bracket Nut	50-65
	Strut Nut	29-43
	Strut Support Nut	16-23
	Suspension Arm Bracket Bolt	61-72
	Suspension Arm Rear Bracket Bolt	22-39
	Tie Rod End Castle Nut	22-39
	Tie Rod End Locknut	25-39
	Wheel Lug Nut	37-50

ESTEEM

Year	Component	Torque/Ft. Lbs.
1995–96	ABS Wheel Speed Sensor	17
	Axle Nut	127
	Ball Stud Nut	44
	Brake Disc Mount	4
	Caliper Carrier Bolt	62
	Driveshaft Nut	127
	Hub Nut	127
	Power Steering Cylinder Pipes A & B	15
	Power Steering High & Low Pressure Pipes	24
	Power Steering Gear Mounting Brackets	40
	Power Steering Pump Mounting Bracket	48
	Stabilizer Bracket Bolt	17
	Stabilizer Joint Nut	37
	Stabilizer Link Nut	21
	Steering Knuckle Castle Nut	26-40
	Steering Shaft Joint Bolt	19
	Strut Bracket Nut	65
	Strut Nut	40
	Strut Support Nut	21
	Suspension Arm Front Bushing Bolt	65
	Suspension Arm Rear Bracket Bolt	27
	Tie Rod End Castle Nut	33
	Wheel Lug Nut	62

Wheel Alignment

INDEX

Page No.		Page No.		Page No.	
Front Wheel Alignment	40-75	Preliminary Inspection	40-75	**Vehicle Ride Height**	40-76
Adjustment	40-75	**Rear Wheel Alignment**	40-75	**Wheel Alignment Specifications**	40-4
Description	40-75	Swift & Esteem	40-75		

FRONT WHEEL ALIGNMENT

DESCRIPTION

Front wheel alignment is the angular relationship between the front wheels, front suspension attaching parts and the ground. The only adjustment required for front end alignment is toe setting. Camber and caster cannot be adjusted. Should camber or caster be out of specification due to damage caused by hazardous road conditions, collision, whether the damage is in the body or in the suspension should be determined. If the body is damaged, it should be repaired and if the suspension is damaged, it should be replaced.

Camber is the tilting of front wheels from the vertical, when viewed from front of vehicle, **Fig. 1.** When the wheels tilt outward at the top, camber is positive. When wheels tilt inward at the top, camber is negative. Amount of tilt is measured in degrees.

Toe is the turning in or out of the front wheels, **Fig. 2.** The purpose of toe is to ensure parallel rolling of the front wheels. Excessive toe-in or toe-out may increase tire wear. Amount of toe can be obtained by subtracting "A" from "B,"**Fig. 2,** and is given in inches or millimeters.

PRELIMINARY INSPECTION

Steering and vibration complaints are not always the result of improper alignment. An additional item to be checked is the possibility of tire lead. Lead is the deviation of the vehicle from a straight path on a level road without hand pressure on the steering wheel.

Before making any adjustment affecting toe setting, the following checks and inspections should be made to ensure correctness of alignment readings and adjustments.

1. Check all tires for proper inflation pressures and approximately same tread wear.
2. Check suspension parts for excessive looseness, replace as needed.
3. Check runout of wheels and tires.
4. Check vehicle ride height; if out of limits and a correction is to be made, it must be made before adjusting toe.
5. Consideration must be given to excess loads, such as tool boxes. If this excess load is normally carried in vehicle, it should remain in vehicle during alignment checks.
6. Vehicle must be on a level surface both front and rear and side to side.

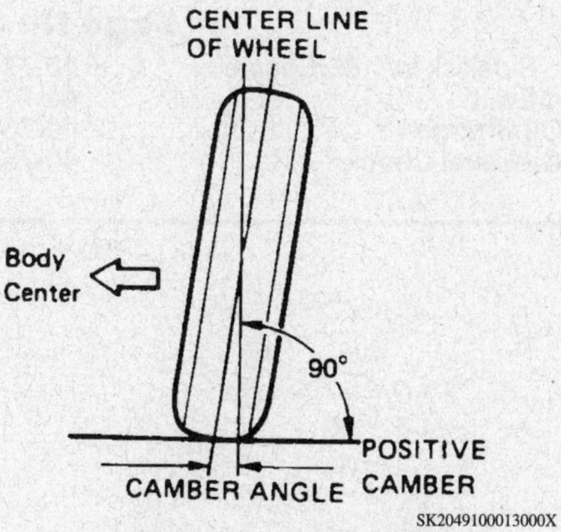
CENTER LINE
OF WHEEL
Body
Center
90°
POSITIVE
CAMBER
CAMBER ANGLE
SK2049100013000X

Fig. 1 Camber angle

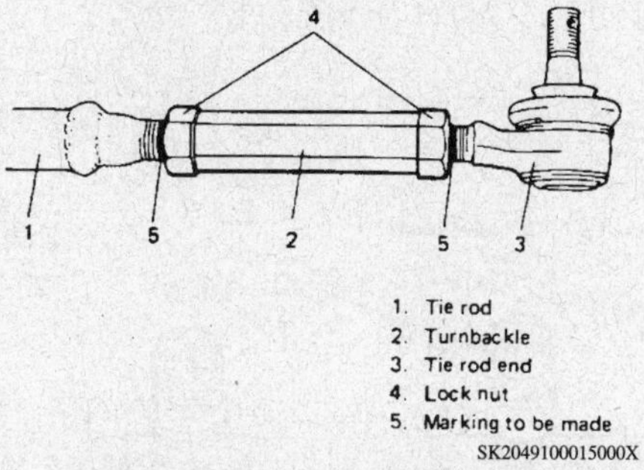
4
1
5
2
5
3
1. Tie rod
2. Turnbuckle
3. Tie rod end
4. Lock nut
5. Marking to be made
SK2049100015000X

Fig. 3 Toe-in adjustment

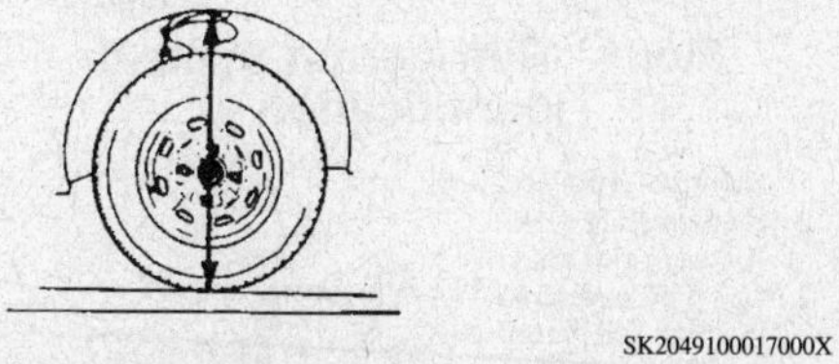
SK2049100017000X

Fig. 5 Ride height measurement

ADJUSTMENT

Camber & Caster

Should camber or caster be out of specifications when inspecting, locate its cause. If cause is damaged, loose, bent, dented or worn suspension parts, they should be replaced. If it is chassis frame (body), repair it. To prevent incorrect reading of camber or caster, vehicle front end must be moved up and down several times before inspection.

Toe-In

Toe-In is adjusted by changing tie rod length.

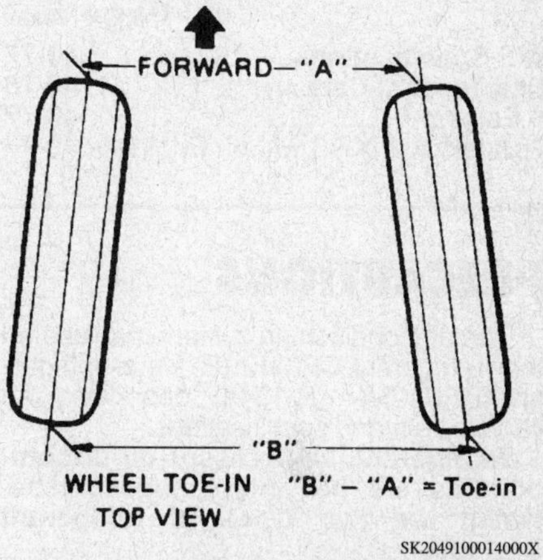
FORWARD—"A"
"B"
WHEEL TOE-IN
TOP VIEW
"B" – "A" = Toe-in
SK2049100014000X

Fig. 2 Toe-in measurement

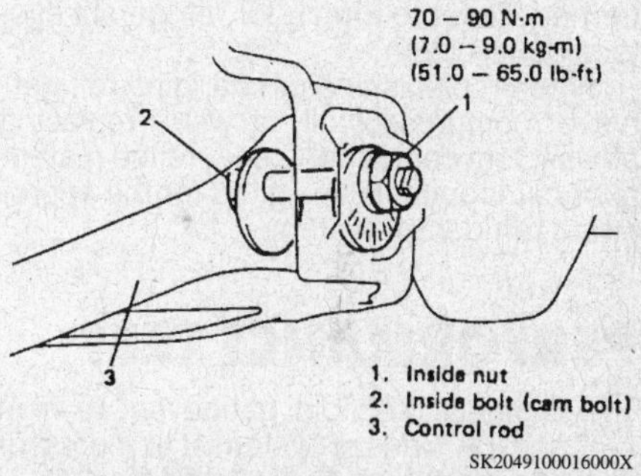
70 – 90 N·m
(7.0 – 9.0 kg-m)
(51.0 – 65.0 lb-ft)
1
2
3
1. Inside nut
2. Inside bolt (cam bolt)
3. Control rod
SK2049100016000X

Fig. 4 Rear toe adjustment. Swift

1. Loosen right and left tie rod end locknuts, **Fig. 3.**
2. Rotate turnbuckle and adjust toe-in to specification. **Ensure rack boots do not twist during this procedure.**
3. Thread lengths, **Fig. 3,** should be equal lengths. **Torque** locknuts to 51–72 ft. lbs.

REAR WHEEL ALIGNMENT

SWIFT & ESTEEM

Rear wheel toe is the only adjustable angle. If camber is not within specifications, inspect for worn or damaged rear suspension components.

Toe Adjustment

1. Loosen right and left control rod inside nuts, **Fig. 4.**
2. Adjust toe to specification by turning

right and left control rod inside bolts by the same amount.

3. After adjustment, **torque** right and left inside nuts to 51–65 ft. lbs., while holding cam bolt with another wrench to prevent it from turning.

VEHICLE RIDE HEIGHT

Right to left ride height difference should be within .6 inch (15 mm) with curb weight, **Fig. 5.**

Air Conditioning

INDEX

	Page No.
A/C Specifications	40-77
Belt Tension Data	40-76
Esteem	40-77
Sidekick & X-90 w/1.6L Engine	40-77
Sidekick w/1.8L Engine	40-77
Swift	40-77
Oil Charge	40-76
Oil Level Check	40-76
Performance Test	40-76
Precautions	40-76
Refrigerant Recovery Procedure	40-77

PRECAUTIONS

The air conditioning system may use either refrigerant CFC-12 (R-12) or refrigerant HFC-134a (R-134a) depending on vehicle year and specifications.

Refrigerant, compressor oil or components are not interchangeable between the two types of refrigerant systems.

Ensure to check which refrigerant is used before any system service is performed. Refer to **Fig. 1,** for refrigerant system identification.

When replenishing or changing refrigerant or compressor oil, or when replacing any system component, ensure the material or component is designed for the appropriate refrigerant system.

PERFORMANCE TEST

1. Connect manifold gauge set to high and low sides of system at compressor service valves, **Figs. 2 and 3.**
2. Start engine and allow to run at approximately 2000 RPM, then activate air conditioner.
3. Set blower switch to HI position and temperature lever to COOL position.
4. Open all windows and doors, then position dry bulb thermometer in cool air outlet and psychrometer (combination dry/wet bulb thermometer) near to evaporator inlet.
5. Check that high pressure gauge reading is between 200-220 psi. **If high pressure gauge reading is above specified range, pour water on condenser until specified range is reached. If gauge reading is below specified range, cover condenser front surface area.**
6. Ensure dry bulb portion of psychrometer is 77–95°F, then operate system until all gauges and thermometers have stabilized.
7. Compare temperatures of dry and wet bulb portions of psychrometer, then determine relative humidity using graph, **Fig. 4.** Record reading.
8. Measure the difference in dry bulb temperatures at cool air outlet and evaporator inlet. Record reading.
9. Using information gathered in steps 8 and 9, determine if system is operating properly by using graph, **Fig. 5.** Intersection of the two points should be within the diagonal lines as shown.

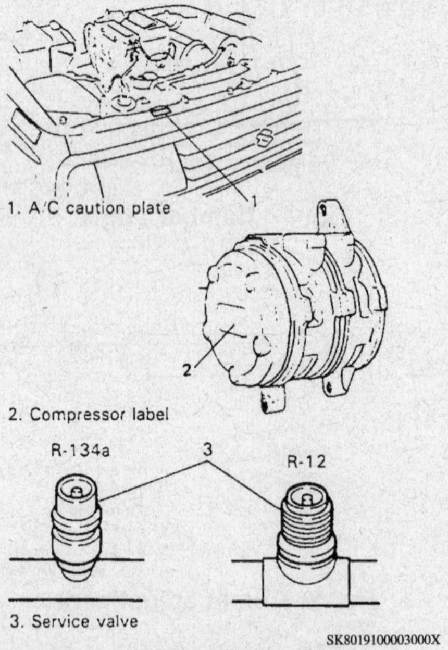
1. A/C caution plate
2. Compressor label
R-134a
R-12
3. Service valve
SK8019100003000X

Fig. 1 Refrigerant system identification

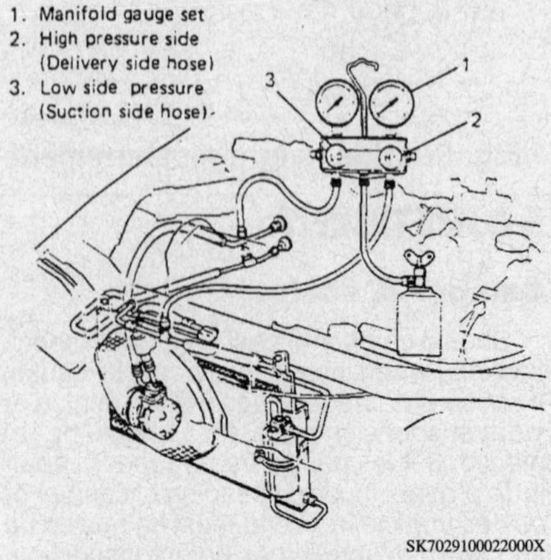
1. Manifold gauge set
2. High pressure side
(Delivery side hose)
3. Low side pressure
(Suction side hose)
SK7029100022000X

Fig. 3 Manifold gauge set connections. Esteem & Swift

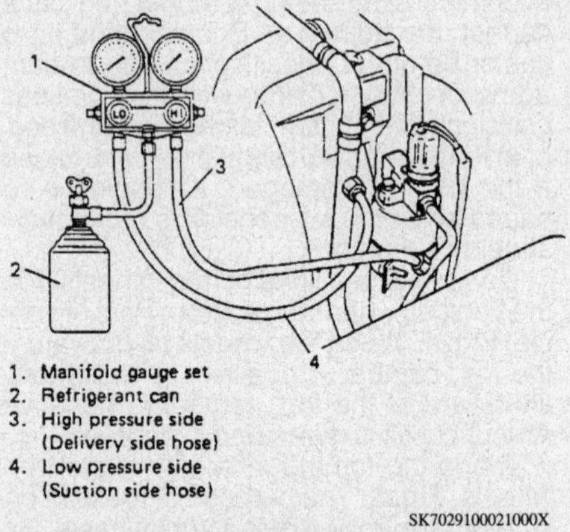
1. Manifold gauge set
2. Refrigerant can
3. High pressure side
(Delivery side hose)
4. Low pressure side
(Suction side hose)
SK7029100021000X

Fig. 2 Manifold gauge set connections. Sidekick & X-90

OIL CHARGE

When replacing compressor, drain 1.4 ounces from replacement compressor prior to installation. When replacing other components, add the following amounts of oil to system: Condenser, 1 ounce; Receiver/Drier, 0.33 ounce.

OIL LEVEL CHECK

No provision is made for checking oil level on these vehicles and oil is added according to component(s) being replaced. Refer to "Oil Charge" as outlined.

BELT TENSION DATA

When checking drive belt deflection, apply 22 lbs. of pressure between compressor clutch pulley and crankshaft pulley.

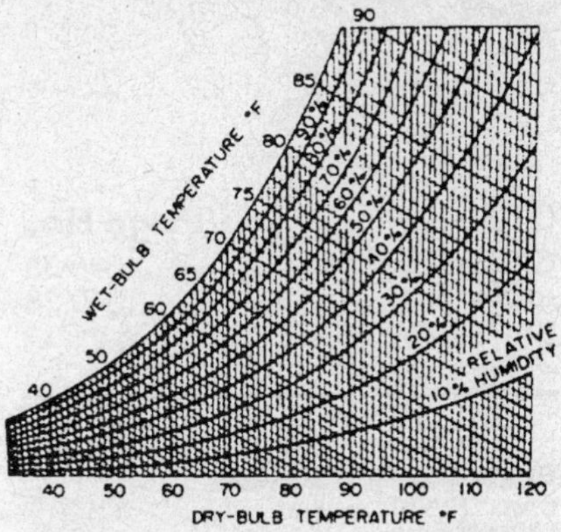
WET-BULB TEMPERATURE °F
DRY-BULB TEMPERATURE °F
40
50
60
70
80
90
100
110
120
RELATIVE HUMIDITY (%)
10%
20%
30%
40%
50%
60%
70%
80%
90%
SK7029100023000X

Fig. 4 Relative humidity graph

SWIFT

1993-94

Adjust belt until deflection is within 0.20–0.25 inch.

1995-96

Adjust belt until deflection is within 0.30–0.40 inch.

ESTEEM

Adjust belt until deflection is within 0.30–0.40 inch.

SIDEKICK & X-90 w/1.6L ENGINE

Adjust belt until deflection is within 0.24–0.35 inch.

SIDEKICK w/1.8L ENGINE

A tensioner controls the belt tension on this engine.

REFRIGERANT RECOVERY PROCEDURE

The use of refrigerant recovery and recycling stations allows the recovery and reuse of refrigerant after contaminants and moisture have been removed.

When using a recovery or recycling station, follow the manufacturer's operating instructions, noting the following:

1. **Use extreme caution and observe all safety and service precautions related to use of refrigerants.**
2. Connect refrigerant recycling station hoses to vehicle A/C service ports and recovery station inlet fitting. Hoses should have shutoff devices or check valve within 12 inches of hose ends to minimize introduction of air into recycling station and to minimize amount of refrigerant release when hoses are disconnected.
3. Turn recycling station ON to start recovery process. Allow recycling station to pump refrigerant from A/C system until station pressure gauge indicates vacuum.
4. After vehicle A/C system has been evacuated, close station inlet valve, if equipped.

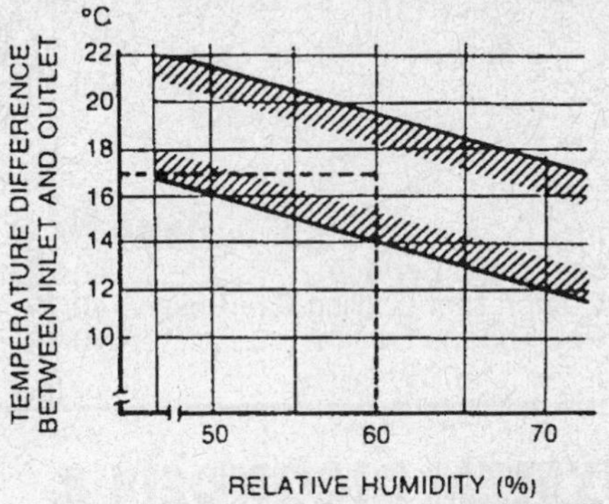
°C
TEMPERATURE DIFFERENCE BETWEEN INLET AND OUTLET
22
20
18
16
14
12
10
50
60
70
RELATIVE HUMIDITY (%)
SK7029100024000X

Fig. 5 Temperature humidity chart

5. Turn station OFF. On some stations the pump will automatically be turned Off by a low pressure switch.
6. Allow vehicle A/C system to remain closed for approximately two minutes. Observe vacuum level indicated on gauge. If pressure does not rise, disconnect recycling station hoses.
7. If system pressure rises, repeat steps 3 through 6 until vacuum level remains stable for two minutes.
8. Service A/C system as necessary, then evacuate and recharge A/C system.

A/C SPECIFICATIONS

Year	Model	Refrigerant		Refrigerant Oil			Compressor Clutch Air Gap, Inches
		Capacity, Lbs.	Type	Viscosity	Total System Capacity, Ounces	Compressor Oil Level Check, Inches	
1993	Sidekick	1.3	R-12	—	2.7	①	.016–.028
	Swift	1.1	R-12	—	2.7	①	.016–.028
1994	Sidekick	1.3	R-134a	②	2.7	①	016–.028
	Swift	1.1	R-134a	②	2.7	①	016–.028
1995	Esteem	1.4	R-134a	②	5	①	.012-.020
	Sidekick	1.3	R-134a	②	2.7	①	.016–.028
	Swift	1.1	R-134a	②	2.7	①	.016–.028
1996	Esteem	1.4	R-134a	②	5	①	.012-.020
	Sidekick	1.4	R-134a	②	③	①	④
	Swift	1.1	R-134a	②	2.7	①	.016-.028
	X-90	1.4	R-134a	②	③	①	④

① — Oil level cannot be checked. Refer to "Oil Charge" for compressor oil level adjustment.
② — Use only the proper compressor oil designated for use with R-134a.
③ — Nippondenso compressor, 3.3 oz.; Sanden compressor, 3.0 oz.
④ — Nippondenso compressor, .016–.028; Sanden compressor, .014–.025

Cooling Fans

INDEX

	Page No.
Component Service	40-78
Compressor/Cooling Fan Relay	40-79
Fan Thermo Switch	40-78
Water Temperature Switch	40-78
System Diagnosis & Testing	40-78
A/C Condenser Fan	40-78
Radiator Fan	40-78

SYSTEM DIAGNOSIS & TESTING

RADIATOR FAN

Refer to **Fig. 1,** for proper procedures.

A/C CONDENSER FAN

Refer to **Fig. 2,** for proper procedures.

COMPONENT SERVICE

FAN THERMO SWITCH

Replacement

1. Disconnect battery ground cable.
2. Drain coolant system into appropriate container.
3. Disconnect thermo switch connector from thermo switch.
4. Remove thermo switch from thermostat case.
5. Reverse procedure to install.

Inspection

1. Immerse switch in water up to suitable level, then connect suitable ohmmeter.
2. Heat water gradually, noting if there is no continuity (switch Off) when water temperature is under 190°F and continuity (switch On) when temperature is above 199°F.
3. If not within specifications, replace fan thermo switch.

WATER TEMPERATURE SWITCH

Replacement

1. Disconnect battery ground cable.
2. Disconnect thermo switch connector from thermo switch.
3. Remove switch from vehicle.
4. Reverse procedure to install.

Inspection

1. Immerse switch in silicon oil or glycerin up to level shown, **Fig. 3,** then connect suitable ohmmeter.
2. **On Sidekick models,** check for continuity (switch open) with temperature of liquid above 235°F.
3. **On Swift models,** check for continuity (switch open) with temperature of liquid above 226°F.
4. **On all models,** if continuity is not within specification, replace water temperature switch.

	TEST	RESULT	ACTION
A1.	Start and run engine. Make certain that engine coolant temperature is below 93° C (199° F).	RADIATOR FAN MOTOR operates.	GO TO A2.
		RADIATOR FAN MOTOR does not operate.	GO TO A3.
A2.	Disconnect RADIATOR FAN SWITCH connector.	RADIATOR FAN MOTOR continues to operate.	Repair short to voltage in BLU wire between RADIATOR FAN SWITCH and RADIATOR FAN MOTOR.
		RADIATOR FAN MOTOR stops running.	Replace RADIATOR FAN SWITCH.
A3.	Run engine until engine coolant temperature is above 98° C (208° F).	RADIATOR FAN MOTOR operates.	All systems diagnosed in this cell are functioning normally.
		RADIATOR FAN MOTOR does not operate.	GO TO A4.
A4.	Disconnect RADIATOR FAN SWITCH connector. Connect a fused jumper between RADIATOR FAN SWITCH connector cavities 1 and 2.	RADIATOR FAN operates.	Replace RADIATOR FAN SWITCH.
		RADIATOR FAN does not operate.	GO TO A5.
A5.	Turn ignition switch to "OFF." Backprobe RADIATOR FAN MOTOR connector with a digital multimeter from cavity 1 to chassis ground. Measure resistance.	More than 0.3 ohms.	Repair BLK ground wire between RADIATOR FAN MOTOR and G101.
		Less than 0.3 ohms.	GO TO A6.
A6.	Backprobe RADIATOR FAN MOTOR connector with a test lamp from cavity 2 to chassis ground.	Test lamp lights.	Replace RADIATOR FAN MOTOR.
		Test lamp does not light.	GO TO A7.
A7.	Connect a test lamp from RADIATOR FAN SWITCH connector cavity 1 to chassis ground.	Test lamp lights.	Repair open in BLU wire between RADIATOR FAN SWITCH and RADIATOR FAN MOTOR.
		Test lamp does not light.	Repair open in BLK/WHT wire between RADIATOR FAN SWITCH and JUNCTION BLOCK.

SK1089100005000X

Fig. 1 Coolant fan diagnostic chart. Swift

	TEST	RESULT	ACTION
B1.	Turn ignition switch to "ON." Press A/C switch.	A/C CONDENSER FAN operates.	All systems diagnosed in this cell are functioning normally.
		A/C CONDENSER FAN does not operate.	GO TO B2.
B2.	Backprobe A/C CONDENSER FAN connector with a test lamp from cavity 2 to chassis ground.	Test lamp lights.	GO TO B3.
		Test lamp does not light.	GO TO B4.
B3.	Disconnect A/C CONDENSER FAN connector. Connect a digital multimeter from cavity 1 to chassis ground. Measure resistance.	More than 0.3 ohms.	Repair BLK ground wire between A/C CONDENSER FAN and G104.
		Less than 0.3 ohms.	Replace A/C CONDENSER FAN.
B4.	Backprobe A/C CONDENSER FAN RELAY connector with a test lamp from cavity 4 to chassis ground.	Test lamp lights.	Repair open in BLU/BLK wire between A/C CONDENSER FAN and A/C CONDENSER FAN RELAY.
		Test lamp does not light.	GO TO B5.
B5.	Backprobe A/C CONDENSER FAN RELAY connector with a test lamp from cavity 2 to chassis ground.	Test lamp does not light.	GO TO B6.
		Test lamp lights.	GO TO B7.
B6.	Backprobe A/C CLUTCH RELAY connector with a test lamp from cavity 2 to chassis ground.	Test lamp lights.	Repair open in RED wire between A/C CLUTCH RELAY and A/C CONDENSER FAN RELAY.
		Test lamp does not light.	Repair open in RED wire between A/C CLUTCH RELAY and FUSIBLE LINK BOX.
B7.	Backprobe A/C CONDENSER FAN RELAY connector with a test lamp from cavity 1 to chassis ground.	Test lamp lights.	GO TO B8.
		Test lamp does not light.	GO TO B9.
B8.	Disconnect A/C CONDENSER FAN RELAY connector. Connect a digital multimeter from cavity 3 to chassis ground. Measure resistance.	More than 0.3 ohms.	Repair BLK ground wire between A/C CONDENSER FAN RELAY and G104.
		Less than 0.3 ohms.	Replace A/C CONDENSER FAN RELAY.
B9.	Backprobe A/C CLUTCH RELAY connector with a test lamp from cavity 4 to chassis ground.	Test lamp lights.	Repair open in BLK/WHT wire between A/C CLUTCH RELAY and A/C CONDENSER FAN RELAY.
		Test lamp does not light.	GO TO B10.
B10.	Backprobe A/C CLUTCH RELAY connector with a test lamp from cavity 1 to chassis ground.	Test lamp lights.	GO TO B11
		Test lamp does not light.	GO TO B13.
B11.	Disconnect A/C AMPLIFIER connector. Connect a jumper from A/C AMPLIFIER connector cavity 7 to chassis ground. Backprobe A/C CLUTCH RELAY with a test lamp from cavity 4 to chassis ground.	Test lamp does not light.	GO TO B12.
		Test lamp lights.	A/C AMPLIFIER diagnosis.
B12.	Remove jumper. Disconnect A/C CLUTCH RELAY connector. Connect a digital multimeter from A/C CLUTCH RELAY connector cavity 3 to A/C AMPLIFIER connector cavity 7. Measure resistance.	More than 0.3 ohms.	Repair open in PNK wire between A/C CLUTCH RELAY and A/C AMPLIFIER.
		Less than 0.3 ohms.	Replace A/C CLUTCH RELAY.
B13.	Backprobe DUAL PRESSURE SWITCH connector with a test lamp from cavity 1 to chassis ground.	Test lamp lights.	Repair open in YEL wire between DUAL PRESSURE SWITCH and A/C CLUTCH RELAY.
		Test lamo does not light.	GO TO B14.
B14.	Backprobe DUAL PRESSURE SWITCH connector with a test lamp from cavity 2 to chassis ground.	Test lamp lights.	Replace DUAL PRESSURE SWITCH.
		Test lamp does not light.	GO TO B15.
B15.	Backprobe connector C111 with a test lamp from cavity 3 to chassis ground.	Test lamp lights.	Repair open in LT GRN wire between connector C111 and DUAL PRESSURE SWITCH.
		Test lamp does not light.	Repair open in BLK/WHT wire between connector C111 and JUNCTION BLOCK.

SK1089100006000X

Fig. 2 A/C condenser fan diagnostic chart. Swift

COMPRESSOR/COOLING FAN RELAY

Replacement

1. Disconnect battery ground cable.
2. Disconnect relay connector from relay.
3. Remove relay from vehicle.
4. Reverse procedure to install.

Inspection

1. Using suitable ohmmeter, connect to relay as shown, **Fig. 4.**
2. If open continuity is found between terminals 3 and 4, replace relay.

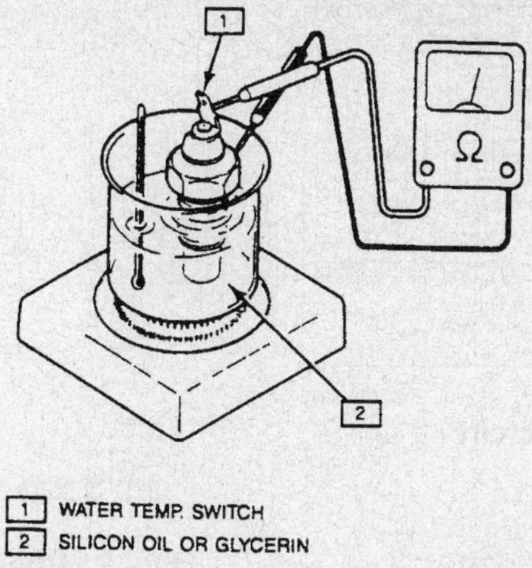
1
2
Ω
1 WATER TEMP. SWITCH
2 SILICON OIL OR GLYCERIN
SK1089100008000X

Fig. 3 Water temperature switch inspection

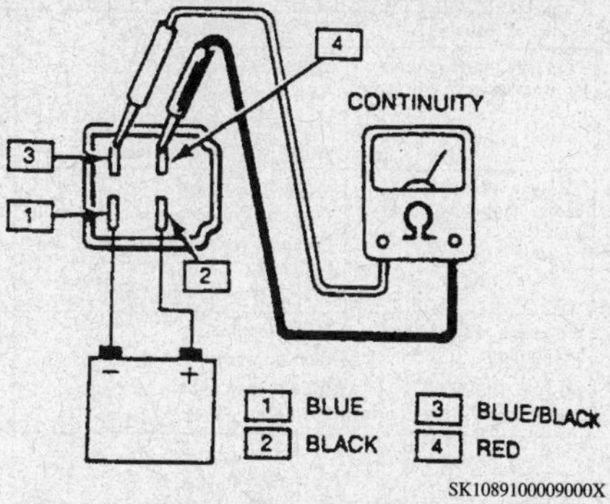
CONTINUITY
3
1
4
2
Ω
−
+
1 BLUE
2 BLACK
3 BLUE/BLACK
4 RED
SK1089100009000X

Fig. 4 Compressor/cooling fan relay inspection

Dash Gauges

NOTE: On Air Bag Equipped Models, Refer To "Air Bag System Precautions" Located In The Front Of This Manual For System Disarming & Arming Procedures.

NOTE: Refer To The "Dash Panel Service" Section For Dash Panel Removal Procedures.

NOTE: Refer To The "Electronic Instrumentation" Section In MOTOR'S "Imported Engine Performance & Driveability Manual" For Information Related To Electronic Instrumentation.

INDEX

	Page No.
Diagnosis & Testing	40-79
Coolant (Water) Temperature Meter & Gauge Unit	40-80
Fuel Level Meter & Gauge Unit	40-80
Oil Pressure Light	40-80
Gauges	40-79
Coolant Temperature	40-79
Fuel Gauges	40-79
Oil Pressure Light	40-79
Precautions	40-79
Air Bag Systems	40-79
Troubleshooting	40-79

PRECAUTIONS

AIR BAG SYSTEMS

Refer to "Air Bag System Precautions" in the front of this manual for system disarming and arming procedures.

GAUGES

COOLANT TEMPERATURE

This temperature indicating system consists of a sending unit, located on the cylinder head, and an electrical temperature gauge. As engine temperature increases or decreases, the resistance of the sending unit changes, in turn controlling current flow through the gauge. When engine temperature is low sending unit resistance is high, current flow through the gauge is restricted, and the gauge pointer remains against the stop or moves very little. As engine temperature increases sending unit resistance decreases and current flow through the gauge increases, resulting in increased pointer movement.

FUEL GAUGES

The fuel gauge system consists of a sending unit, and an electric fuel gauge. The sending unit is a variable resistor that is controlled by a float. Corresponding to actual fuel level, the float will rise or fall. When the ignition is turned to the On position, voltage is applied to the gauge, completing the gauge ground circuit through the sending unit.

OIL PRESSURE LIGHT

This oil pressure indicating system incorporates an oil pressure switch installed in the cylinder block and oil pressure light in the combination meter. When the engine is started the oil pressure acts upon the switch in such a way that it turns the switch "OFF."

TROUBLESHOOTING

Refer to troubleshooting chart, **Fig. 1.**

DIAGNOSIS & TESTING

Trouble	Possible cause	Correction
Fuel level meter shows no operation.	Meter fuse blown	Replace fuse to check for short.
	Fuel meter faulty	Check meter.
	Fuel level gauge unit faulty	Check gauge unit.
	Wiring or grounding faulty	Repair.
Coolant (Water) temp. meter shows no operation.	Meter fuse blown	Replace fuse to check for short.
	Coolant (Water) temp. meter faulty	Check meter.
	Coolant (Water) temp. gauge unit faulty	Check gauge unit.
	Wiring or grounding faulty	Repair.
Oil pressure light shows no lighting.	Light fuse blown	Replace fuse to check for short.
	Bulb burnt out	Replace bulb.
	Oil pressure switch faulty	Check switch.
	Wiring or grounding faulty	Repair.

SK9099100002000X

Fig. 1 Troubleshooting chart

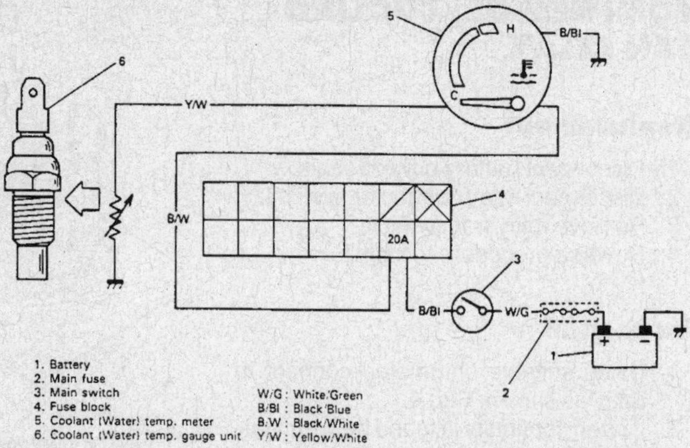

B/Bl
Y/W
B/W
20A
B/Bl
W/G
1. Battery
2. Main fuse
3. Main switch
4. Fuse block
5. Coolant (Water) temp. meter
6. Coolant (Water) temp. gauge unit
W/G : White/Green
B/Bl : Black/Blue
B/W : Black/White
Y/W : Yellow/White

SK9099100003000X

Fig. 2 Coolant temperature meter & gauge unit wiring

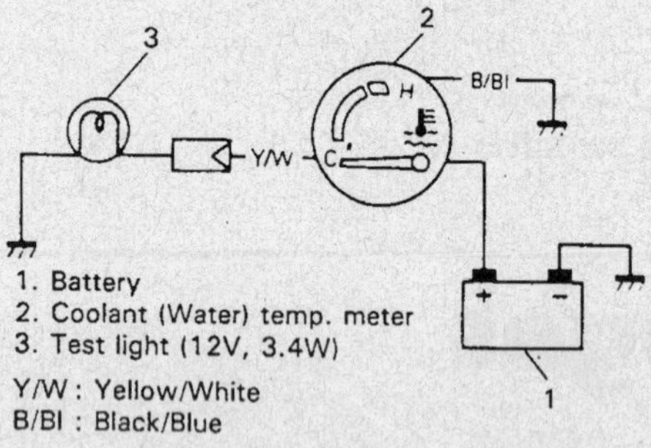

B/Bl
Y/W
1. Battery
2. Coolant (Water) temp. meter
3. Test light (12V, 3.4W)
Y/W : Yellow/White
B/Bl : Black/Blue

SK9099100004000X

Fig. 3 Coolant temperature meter inspection

Temperature	Resistance
50°C (122°F)	133.9–178.9 Ω
80°C (176°F)	47.5– 56.8 Ω
100°C (212°F)	26.2– 29.3 Ω

SK9099100005000X

Fig. 4 Gauge unit temperature resistance chart. 1993

Temperature	Resistance
50°C (122°F)	189.4–259.6 Ω
115°C (239°F)	24.2–28.1 Ω

SK9099500014000X

Fig. 5 Gauge unit temperature resistance chart. 1994-96

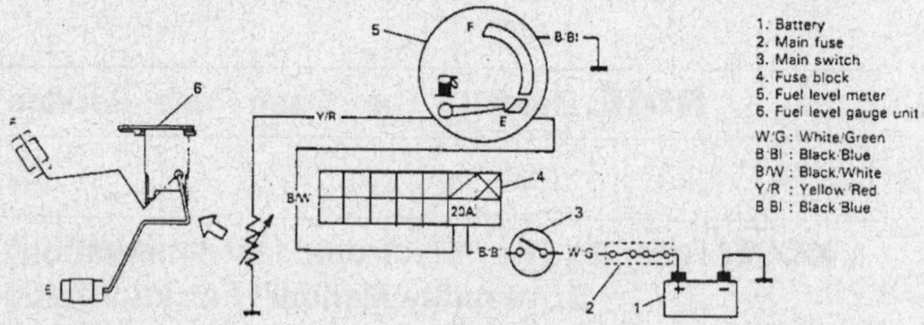

1. Battery
2. Main fuse
3. Main switch
4. Fuse block
5. Fuel level meter
6. Fuel level gauge unit
W/G : White/Green
B/Bl : Black/Blue
B/W : Black/White
Y/R : Yellow/Red
B/Bl : Black/Blue

SK9099100006000X

Fig. 6 Fuel level meter & gauge unit wiring

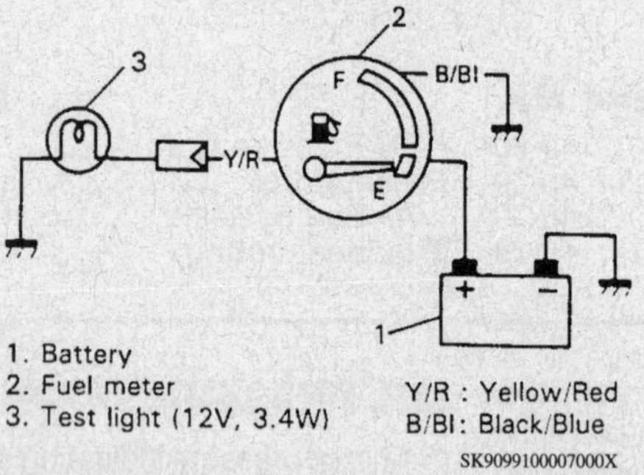

B/Bl
Y/R
1. Battery
2. Fuel meter
3. Test light (12V, 3.4W)
Y/R : Yellow/Red
B/Bl: Black/Blue

SK9099100007000X

Fig. 7 Fuel level meter inspection

Position	Resistance
E	120±8 Ω
F	3±2 Ω
1/2	32.5±4 Ω

SK9099100008000X

Fig. 8 Gauge unit float position-to-resistance chart

COOLANT (WATER) TEMPERATURE METER & GAUGE UNIT

1. Disconnect Yellow/White lead wire going to gauge unit installed on intake manifold, **Fig. 2.**
2. Using a 12 volt (3.4 W) bulb, ground wire as shown, **Fig. 3.**
3. Turn ignition On. Ensure bulb is lighted with meter pointer wavering several seconds after.
4. If meter is faulty, replace as necessary.
5. After warming up gauge unit, ensure resistance decreases with the increase of temperature as shown, **Figs. 4 and 5**

FUEL LEVEL METER & GAUGE UNIT

1. Remove rear seat, then disconnect Yellow/Red lead wire going to gauge unit, **Fig. 6.**
2. Using a 12 volt (3.4 W) bulb, ground lead wire as shown, **Fig. 7.**
3. Turn ignition switch On. Ensure bulb is lighted with meter pointer wavering several seconds after.
4. If meter is faulty, replace as necessary.
5. Using an ohmmeter, ensure resistance of level gauge unit changes with a change of float position, **Fig. 7.**

OIL PRESSURE LIGHT

1. Using a suitable ohmmeter, disconnect Yellow/Black and Black/White lead wires from oil pressure switch. Measure switch continuity, **Fig. 9.**
2. With engine running, there should be no continuity.
3. With engine stopped, there should be continuity.

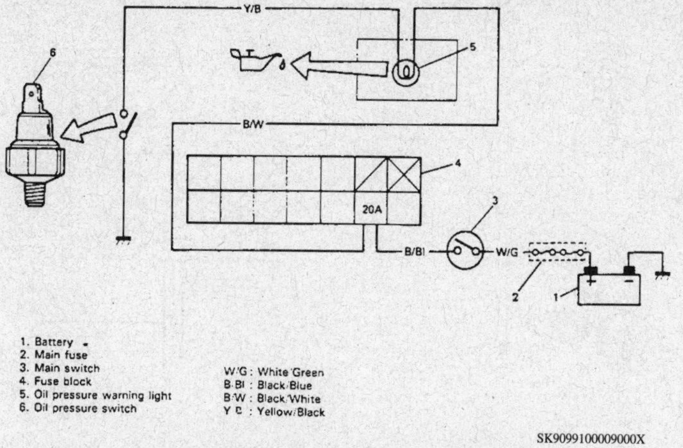

Y/B
B/W
20A
B/Bl
W/G
1. Battery
2. Main fuse
3. Main switch
4. Fuse block
5. Oil pressure warning light
6. Oil pressure switch
W/G : White/Green
B/Bl : Black/Blue
B/W : Black/White
Y/B : Yellow/Black
SK9099100009000X

Fig. 9 Oil pressure light wiring

Starter Motors

INDEX

	Page No.
Description	40-81
Conventional Type	40-81
Diagnosis & Testing	40-81
Performance Test	40-81
Starter Specifications	40-84
Troubleshooting	40-81

DESCRIPTION

CONVENTIONAL TYPE

A conventional type starter uses four individually wound magnets to produce a strong magnetic field, which in turn forces the armature to turn against these fields. Because these magnetic fields are constantly opposing themselves, the starter engages until power is lost to the plunger. This starter is used on the Suzuki vehicles, **Figs. 1 through 5.**

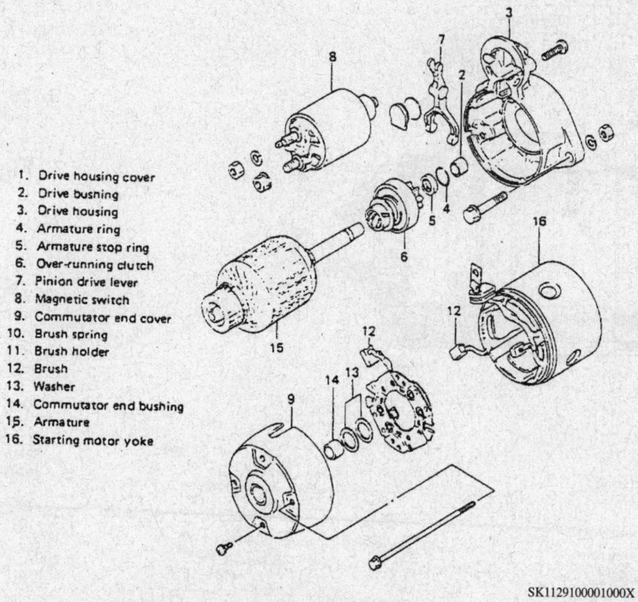

1. Drive housing cover
2. Drive bushing
3. Drive housing
4. Armature ring
5. Armature stop ring
6. Over-running clutch
7. Pinion drive lever
8. Magnetic switch
9. Commutator end cover
10. Brush spring
11. Brush holder
12. Brush
13. Washer
14. Commutator end bushing
15. Armature
16. Starting motor yoke
SK1129100001000X

Fig. 1 Exploded view of starter motor. Samurai

TROUBLESHOOTING

Refer to **Fig. 6,** for troubleshooting charts.

DIAGNOSIS & TESTING

PERFORMANCE TEST

Each test must be performed within 3–5 seconds to avoid damage to coil from burning.

Pull-In Test

1. Disconnect field coil from terminal "M."
2. Connect test leads as shown, **Fig. 7.**
3. Ensure pinion (overrunning clutch) jumps out.
4. If pinion is not as specified, replace magnetic switch.

Hold-In Test

1. Perform "Pull-In Test," then disconnect negative lead from terminal "M," **Fig. 8.**
2. Ensure pinion remains outside. If pinion retracts, replace magnetic switch.

Pinion Return Test

1. Perform "Hold-In Test," then disconnect negative lead from body, **Fig. 9.**
2. Ensure pinion retracts quickly. If pinion remains out, replace magnetic switch.

No-Load Performance Test

1. Connect test leads as shown, **Fig. 10.**
2. Ensure pinion moves out and motor runs without stopping.
3. Measure ammeter current. Refer to "Starter Motor Specifications" for correct specification.

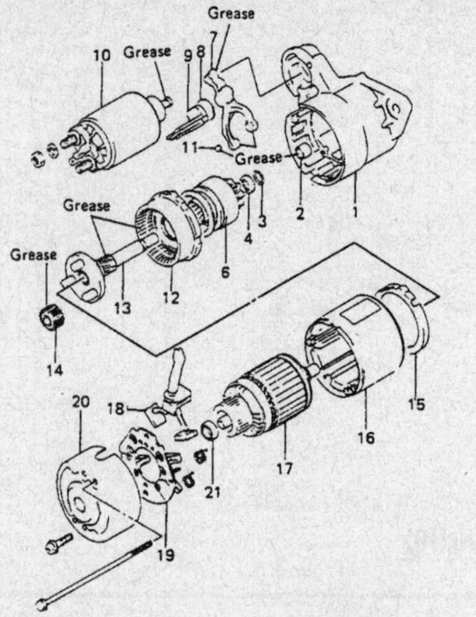
Grease
Grease
Grease
Grease
Grease

1. Front housing
2. Bush
3. Ring
4. Stop ring
5. Pinion gear
6. Over-running clutch
7. Lever
8. Plate
9. Seal rubber
10. Magnetic switch
11. Ball
12. Internal gear
13. Gear shaft ass'y
14. Idle gear
15. Packing
16. Yoke
17. Armature
18. Brush
19. Brush holder
20. Rear bracket
21. Bearing
22. Spring washer

SK1129100002000X

Fig. 2 Exploded view of starter motor. Sidekick & X-90

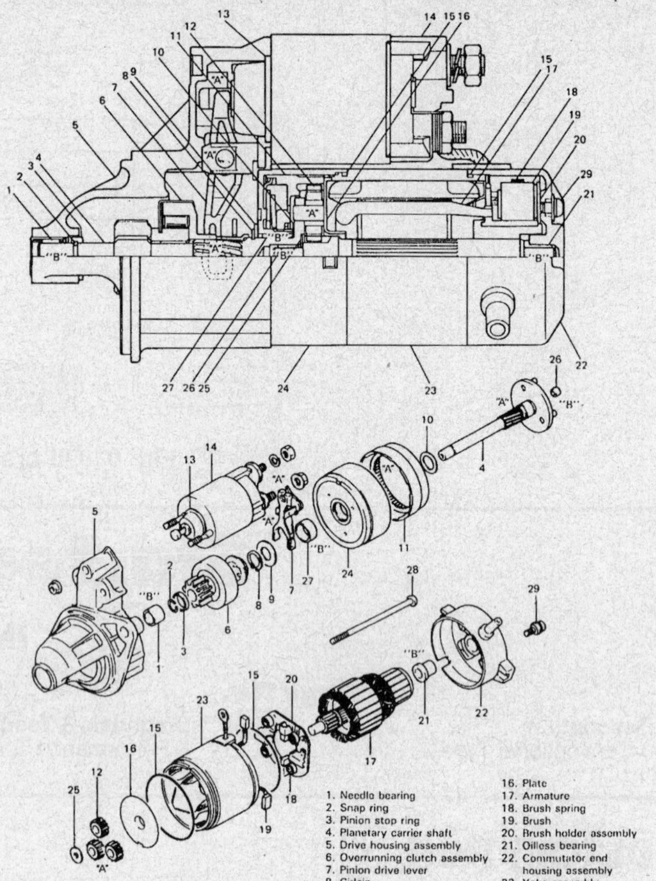

1. Needle bearing
2. Snap ring
3. Pinion stop ring
4. Planetary carrier shaft
5. Drive housing assembly
6. Overrunning clutch assembly
7. Pinion drive lever
8. Cirlcip
9. Washer
10. Washer
11. Internal gear
12. Planetary gear
13. Boot
14. Magnetic switch
15. O ring
16. Plate
17. Armature
18. Brush spring
19. Brush
20. Brush holder assembly
21. Oilless bearing
22. Commutator end housing assembly
23. Yoke assembly
24. Center bearing & shock absorber assembly
25. Washer
26. Oilless bearing
27. Oilless bearing
28. Housing bolt
29. Screw with O ring

"A": Apply grease
"B": DO NOT wash nor lubricate. Spare parts have been lubricated.

SK1129300004000X

Fig. 3 Exploded view of starter motor. 1993-94 Swift

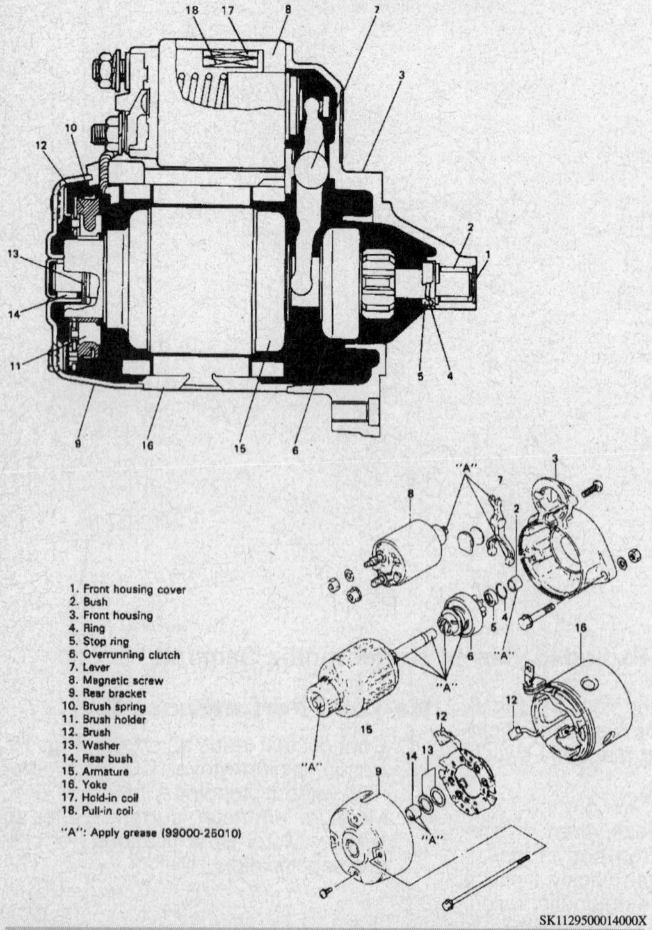

1. Front housing cover
2. Bush
3. Front housing
4. Ring
5. Stop ring
6. Overrunning clutch
7. Lever
8. Magnetic screw
9. Rear bracket
10. Brush spring
11. Brush holder
12. Brush
13. Washer
14. Rear bush
15. Armature
16. Yoke
17. Hold-in coil
18. Pull-in coil

"A": Apply grease (99000-25010)

SK1129500014000X

Fig. 4 Exploded view of starter motor. 1995–96 Swift w/manual transmission

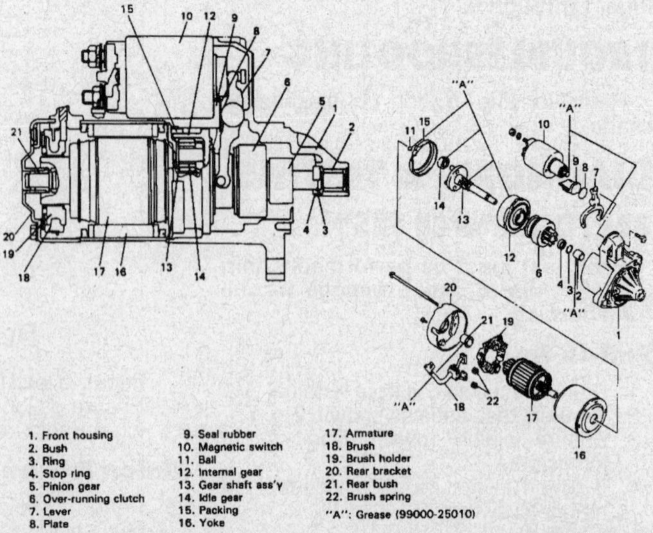

1. Front housing
2. Bush
3. Ring
4. Stop ring
5. Pinion gear
6. Over-running clutch
7. Lever
8. Plate
9. Seal rubber
10. Magnetic switch
11. Ball
12. Internal gear
13. Gear shaft ass'y
14. Idle gear
15. Packing
16. Yoke
17. Armature
18. Brush
19. Brush holder
20. Rear bracket
21. Rear bush
22. Brush spring

"A": Grease (99000-25010)

SK1129500015000X

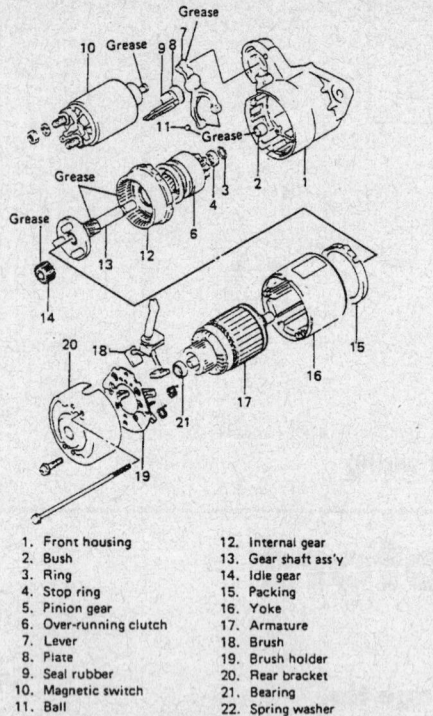

Fig. 5 Exploded view of starter motor. Esteem & 1995–96 Swift w/automatic transmission

Condition	Possible Cause	Correction
Motor not running	No operating sound of magnetic switch	
	1. Clutch pedal is not depressed fully or clutch start switch is not adjusted (M/T)	Depress clutch pedal or adjust clutch start switch
	2. Shift lever switch is not in P or N, or not adjusted (A/T)	Shift in P or N, or adjust switch
	3. Battery run down	Recharge battery
	4. Battery voltage too low due to battery deterioration	Replace battery
	5. Poor contact in battery terminal connection	Retighten or replace
	6. Loose grounding cable connection	Retighten
	7. Fuse set loose or blown off	Tighten or replace
	8. Poor contacting action of ignition switch	Replace
	9. Lead wire coupler loose in place	Retighten
	10. Open-circuit between ignition switch and magnetic switch	Repair
	11. Open-circuit in pull-in coil	Replace magnetic switch
	12. Poor sliding of plunger	Replace
Motor not running	Operating sound of magnetic switch heard	
	1. Battery run down	Recharge battery
	2. Battery voltage too low due to battery deterioration	Replace battery
	3. Loose battery cable connections	Retighten
	4. Burnt main contact point, or poor contacting action of magnetic switch	Replace magnetic switch
	5. Brushes are seating poorly or worn down	Repair or replace
	6. Weakened brush spring	Replace
	7. Burnt commutator	Replace
	8. Poor grounding of field coil	Repair
	9. Layer short-circuit of armature	Replace
	10. Crankshaft rotation obstructed	Repair

SK1129100005010X

Fig. 6 Troubleshooting chart (Part 1 of 2)

Condition	Possible Cause	Correction
Starting motor running but too slow (small torque)	If battery and wiring are satisfactory, inspect starting motor	
	1. Insufficient contact of magnetic switch main contacts	Replace
	2. Layer short-circuit of armature	Replace
	3. Disconnected, burnt or worn commutator	Repair or replace
	4. Poor grounding of field coil	Repair
	5. Worn brushes	Replace
	6. Weakened brush springs	Replace spring
	7. Burnt or abnormally worn end bushings	Replace
Starting motor running, but not cranking engine	1. Worn pinion tip	Replace over-running clutch
	2. Poor sliding of over-running clutch	Replace
	3. Over-running clutch slipping	Replace
	4. Worn teeth of ring gear	Replace flywheel
	5. Shock absorber slipping (Reduction type)	Replace
Noise	1. Abnormally worn bush	Replace
	2. Worn pinion or worn teeth of ring gear	Replace pinion or flywheel
	3. Poor sliding of pinion (failure in return movement)	Repair or replace
Starting motor does not stop running	1. Fused contact points of magnetic switch	Replace
	2. Short-circuit between turns of magnetic switch coil (layer short-circuit)	Replace
	3. Failure of returning action in ignition switch	Replace

SK1129100005020X

Fig. 6 Troubleshooting chart (Part 2 of 2)

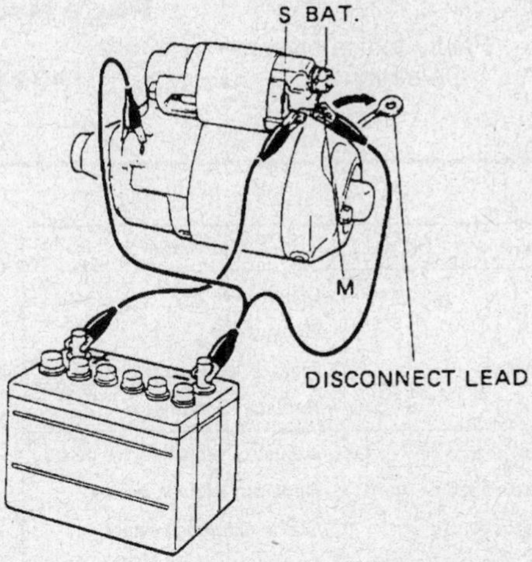
S BAT.
M
DISCONNECT LEAD

SK1129100006000X

Fig. 7 Pull-in test lead connections

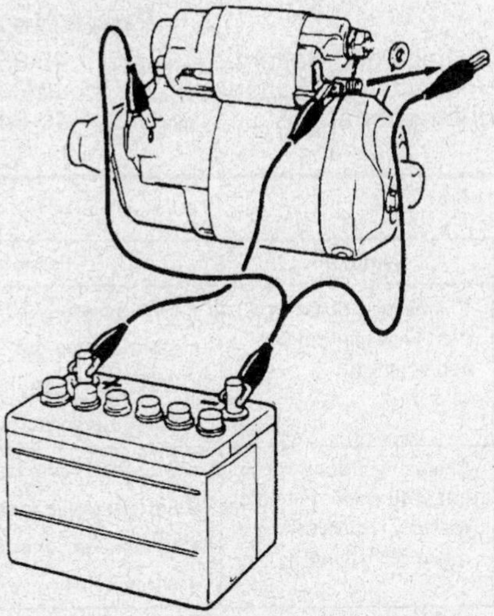

SK1129100007000X

Fig. 8 Hold-in test lead connections

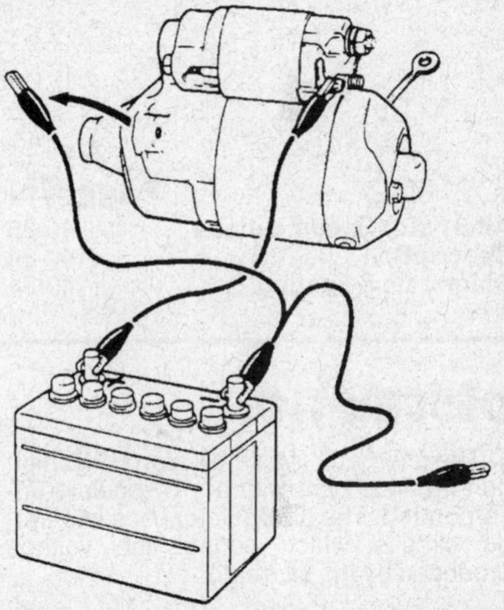

SK1129100008000X

Fig. 9 Pinion return test lead connections

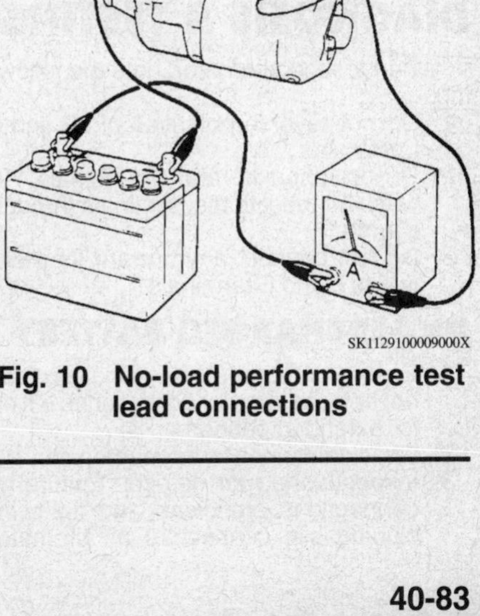
A

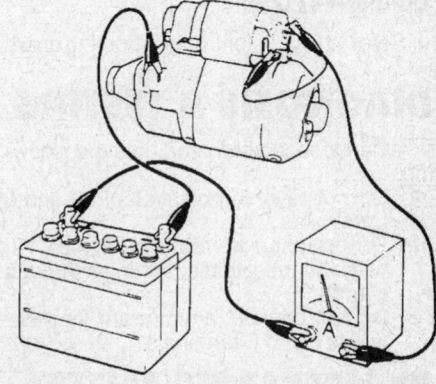

SK1129100009000X

Fig. 10 No-load performance test lead connections

STARTER SPECIFICATIONS

Year	Model	Volts	Output, kW	Direction of Rotation	Brush Length, Inch	No. of Pinion Teeth	No Load Test		
							Amps	Volts	RPM②
1993–95	Samurai	12	0.9	CW	0.67	8	60	11.5	6600
	Sidekick	12	①	CW	0.69	9	90	11.0	3000
	Swift	12	④	CW	⑤	8	⑥	⑦	③
	Esteem	12	①	CW	⑧	8	90	11	3000
1996	Esteem	12	①	CW	⑧	8	90	11	3000
	Sidekick & X-90	12	①	CW	0.69	9	90	11	3000
	Swift	12	④	CW	⑤	8	⑥	⑦	③

①— Automatic transmission, 1.4; manual transaxle, 1.2.
②— Minimum.
③— Automatic transmission 3000–4000 RPM; manual transaxle 6600 RPM.
④— Automatic transmission, 1.2 kW; manual transaxle, 0.9 kW.
⑤— Automatic transmission, 0.69 inch; manual transaxle, 0.67 inch.
⑥— Automatic transmission, 50–75 amps; manual transaxle, 60 amps.
⑦— Automatic transmission, 11 volts; manual transaxle, 11.5 volts.
⑧— Automatic transmission, 0.65 inch; manual transaxle, 0.69 inch.

Alternators

INDEX

	Page No.
Alternator Specifications	40-85
Description	40-84
Diagnosis & Testing	40-84
Overcharged Battery	40-85
Undercharged Battery	40-84
Troubleshooting	40-84
Faulty Indicator Lamp Operation	40-84

DESCRIPTION

The alternator is a small, high RPM, high performance type with an IC regulator incorporated. The IC regulator uses integrated circuits which control the voltage produced by the alternator.

TROUBLESHOOTING

FAULTY INDICATOR LAMP OPERATION

Refer to **Fig. 1**, for troubleshooting chart.

Symptom	Possible cause	Correction
Charge light does not light with ignition ON and engine off	• Fuse blown	Check fuse
	• Light burned out	Replace light
	• Wiring connection loose	Tighten loose connections
	• IC regulator faulty	Replace IC regulator
Charge light does not go out with engine running (battery requires frequent recharging)	• Drive belt loose or worn	Adjust or replace drive belt
	• Battery cables loose, corroded or worn	Repair or replace cables
	• IC regulator or alternator faulty	Check charging system
	• Wiring faulty	Repair wiring

SK1129100010000X

Fig. 1 Indicator lamp troubleshooting chart

DIAGNOSIS & TESTING

When testing alternator, note the following:

1. Do not reverse polarities of IG and L terminals.
2. Do not short IG and L terminals. Always connect these terminals through a lamp.
3. Do not connect any current load between L and E terminals.

UNDERCHARGED BATTERY

1. Ensure undercharged condition has not been caused by accessories left on for extended periods.
2. Check drive belt for proper tension.
3. Inspect wiring for defects. Ensure all connections are clean and tight, including slip connectors at alternator and bulkhead. Also, check battery cable connections at battery, starter and ignition ground cable.

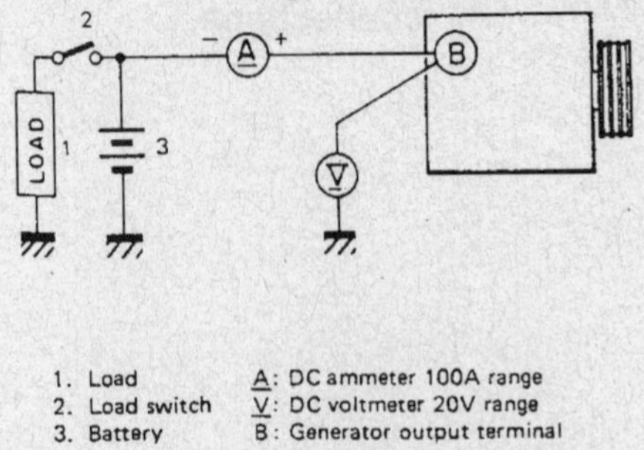

2
A
B
V
LOAD
1
3
1. Load
2. Load switch
3. Battery
A: DC ammeter 100A range
V: DC voltmeter 20V range
B: Generator output terminal

SK1129100011000X

Fig. 2 Alternator output measurement

4. Connect a suitable voltmeter and ammeter as shown, **Fig. 2.** Connect voltmeter between alternator B terminal and ground. Connect ammeter between alternator B terminal and battery positive terminal.
5. Perform no-load check as follows:
   a. Increase engine speed from idle to 2000 RPM and note readings. Voltage readings will vary with regulator case temperature.
   b. **On Sidekick models,** if voltage is higher than 14.4–15.0 volts at 68°F, check ground of brush. If brush ground is satisfactory, replace IC regulator.
   c. **On Samurai and Swift models,** if voltage is higher than 14.2–14.8 volts at 77°F, replace IC regulator.

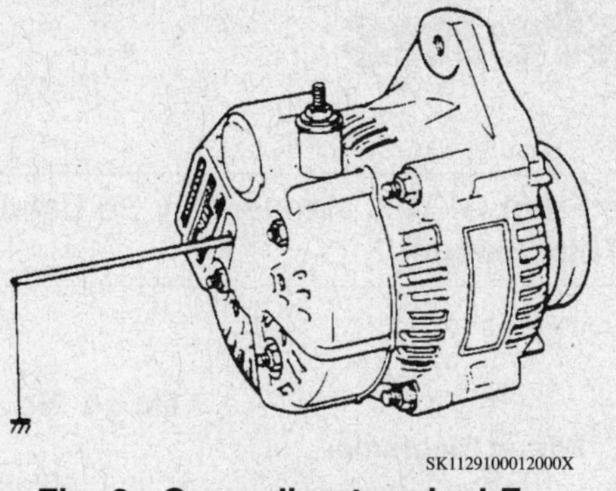

Fig. 3 Grounding terminal F. Samurai

d. **On Samurai and Swift models,** if voltage is below specification, check IC regulator and alternator by measuring voltage at B terminal while grounding F terminal, **Figs. 3 and 4.** If voltage is above specification, replace IC regulator.

e. **On all models,** if voltage is below specification, perform load check.

6. Perform load check as follows:
   a. Run engine at 2000 RPM and switch on headlights and heater blower motor.
   b. Ensure current is at least 20 amps, if less, alternator is defective.

OVERCHARGED BATTERY

If an overcharging condition exists, such as spewing of electrolyte, check field windings for grounds and shorts. If defective, replace rotor and test regulator using a suitable tester.

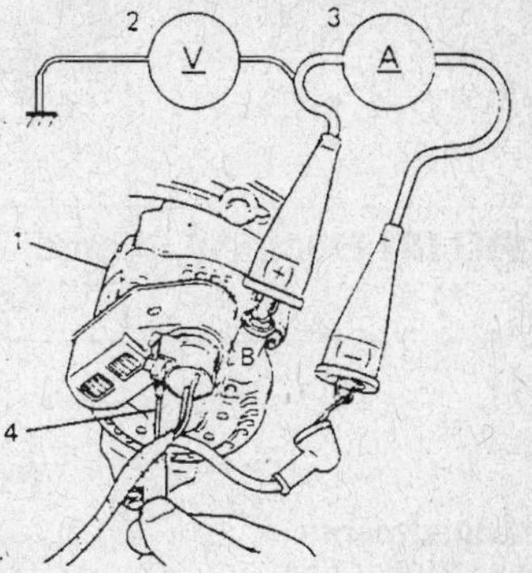

1
2
3
4
V
A
B

1. Generator
2. Voltmeter
3. Ammeter
4. Small screwdriver to ground F (NEVER contact it with magnetic switch terminal of starting motor)

Fig. 4 Grounding terminal F. Swift

ALTERNATOR SPECIFICATIONS

Year	Model	Current Rating		Voltage Regulator	
		Amps	Volts	Voltage	RPM
1993	Samurai	50	12	14.2-14.8	—
	Sidekick	55	12	14.4-15.0	—
	Swift	50	13.5	14.2 -14.8	5000 ①
1994	Samurai	50	12	14.2-14.8	—
	Sidekick	55	12	14.4-15.0	—
	Swift	50	13.5	14.2-14.8	5000①
1995	Esteem	70	12	13.6-14.4	—
	Samurai	50	12	14.2–14.8	—
	Sidekick	55	12	14.4–15.0	—
	Swift	55	12	14.4-15.0	—
1996	Esteem	70	12	13.6–14.4	—
	Sidekick	55	12	14.4-15.0	—
	Swift	55	12	14.4–15.0	—
	X-90	55	12	14.4–15.0	—

① — Minimum.

Speed Control Systems

NOTE: Electrical Symbol & Wire Color Code Identification Located In The Front Of This Manual May Be Used As An Aid When Using Wiring Circuits Found In This Section.

INDEX

	Page No.
Adjustments	40-86
Actuator Cable	40-86
Brake Light Switch	40-86
Shift Selector Switch	40-86
Component Diagnosis & Testing	40-89
1993	40-89
1994–96	40-90
Description	40-86
Precautions	40-86
Air Bag Systems	40-86
System Diagnosis & Testing	40-86
1993	40-86
1994–96	40-87
Troubleshooting	40-86
Preliminary Checks	40-86
Wiring Diagrams:	
1993	40-89
1994-95:	
Esteem	40-90
Except Esteem	40-89
1996:	
Sidekick & X-90	40-90

DESCRIPTION

This cruise control system is a device which maintains a preset vehicle speed during high speed vehicle operation. The system will maintain any desired constant speed between 25 and 75 mph without depressing the accelerator pedal. Other cruise control system functions include:
SET COAST and ACCEL RESUME switches, to change vehicle speed without using accelerator pedal.
CANCEL switch, to end cruise control operation.
ACCEL RESUME switch, to resume speed stored in memory automatically after cruise control is cancelled.

The main components of the cruise control system are vehicle speed sensor, control unit, actuator, SET COAST switch, ACCEL RESUME switch, and CANCEL switch, **Figs. 1 through 3.**

PRECAUTIONS

AIR BAG SYSTEMS

Refer to "Air Bag System Precautions" in the front of this manual for system disarming and arming procedures.

TROUBLESHOOTING

PRELIMINARY CHECKS

When performing preliminary checks refer to function test, **Figs. 4 and 5**

ADJUSTMENTS

ACTUATOR CABLE

1. Disconnect battery ground cable.
2. Remove actuator cover, loosen lock nuts.
3. Adjust cable to obtain .04–.08 of an inch play, **Fig. 6,** with actuator lever fully closed.
4. **Torque** locknuts to 4 ft. lbs.

BRAKE LIGHT SWITCH

1. Start engine.
2. Depress brake pedal a few times.
3. Apply approximately 66 lbs. of pressure to brake pedal and hold, then measure pedal height. Pedal height should be greater than 5.12 inches.
4. Adjust brake light switch as required.

SHIFT SELECTOR SWITCH

1. Shift select lever to "N" range.
2. Ensure engine starts in "N" and "P" ranges but does not start in "D," "2," "L" or "R" range.
3. Check back-up lamps light in "R" range.

SYSTEM DIAGNOSIS & TESTING

When performing system diagnosis and testing refer to wiring diagrams,**Figs. 7 through 10**, and control unit electrical connector terminal identification diagram, **Figs. 11 and 12.**

1993

Indicator Light Circuit

1. With main switch in the On position, check voltage between terminal 8 of control unit connector and ground, **Fig. 11**
2. Circuit is good if within 10–14 volts.
3. If not test lead wires, connectors, fuses, if good replace indicator light bulb.

Shift Switch Circuit

1. Check resistance between terminal 12 of control unit electrical connector and ground, **Fig. 11** with shift lever set in "P" or "N" range and main switch On.
2. If zero ohms exist, then shift switch is in good condition.
3. If not check lead wires, grounds and electrical connectors.
4. If these items are in good condition, then check shift switch for continuity, refer to "Component Diagnosis & Testing" as outlined in this section.

Set Coast/Accel/Resume/ Cancel Switch Circuit

1. Check continuity between the following terminals:
   With "ACCEL/RESUME" switch in the On position, terminal 2 of control unit electrical connector and ground, **Fig. 11.**
   With "COAST" switch in the On position, terminal 3 and ground.
   With "CANCEL" switch in the On position, terminal 9 and ground.
2. If no continuity exist, then check wires and electrical connectors. If circuit is good, then test switch, refer to "Component Diagnosis & Testing" as outlined in this section.

Vehicle Speed Sensor Circuit

1. Check continuity between terminal 10, **Fig. 11,** of control unit electrical connector and ground while proceeding as follows:
   a. Raise and support rear of vehicle.
   b. Turn rear left tire slowly with right rear tire locked.
   c. Check ohmmeter for deflection between infinity and omega, 2–3 pulses for each tire revolution.
2. If continuity occurs as outlined above, then speed sensor circuit is good.
3. If not test wires and electrical connectors. If they are good test speed sensor, refer to "Component Diagnosis & Testing" as outlined in this section.

Cruise Main Switch Circuit

1. With cruise and main switch in the On position, check voltage between terminal 11 of control unit electrical connector and ground, **Fig. 11.**
2. If within 10–14 volts, then switch circuit is good.
3. If not check wires, grounds and electrical connectors.
4. If good, check cruise main switch, refer to "Component Diagnosis & Testing"

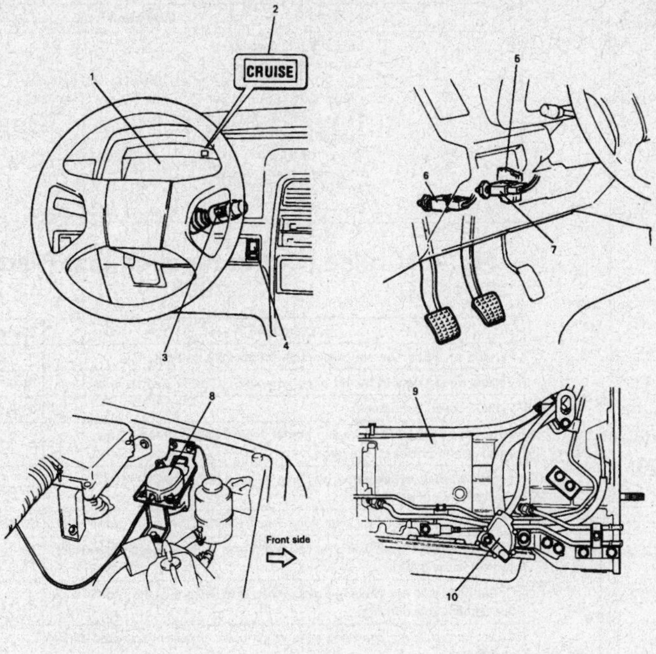
CRUISE
Front side

1. Vehicle speed sensor (Reed switch within combination meter)
2. Indicator light
3. SET COAST/ACCEL RESUME/CANCEL switch
4. Cruise main switch
5. Cruise control unit (right side of steering column)
6. Clutch pedal position switch (For M/T vehicle)
7. Stop light switch
8. Cruise control actuator
9. Automatic transmission
10. Shift switch (For A/T vehicle)

SK1109300001000X

Fig. 1 Cruise control system components. Manual transmission

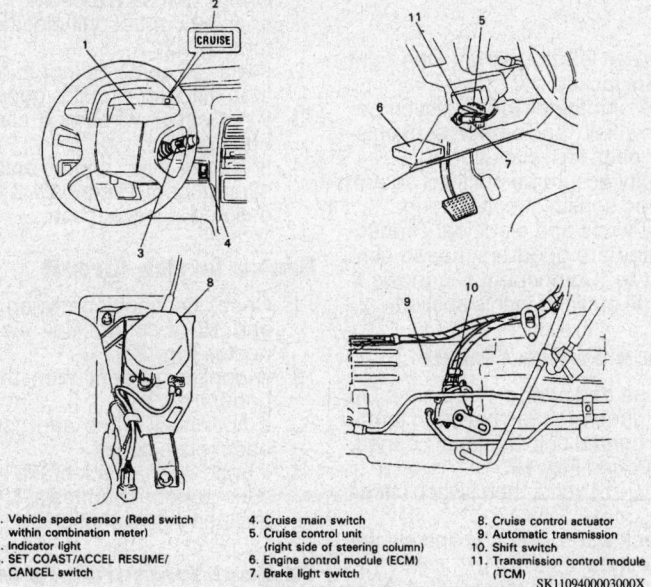

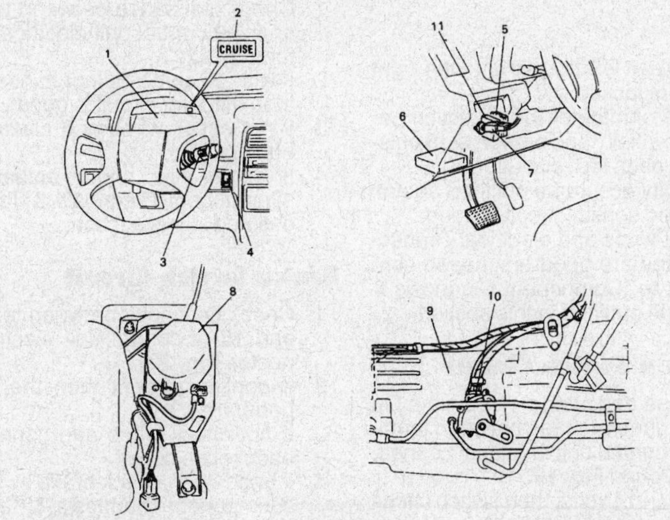
CRUISE

1. Vehicle speed sensor (Reed switch within combination meter)
2. Indicator light
3. SET COAST/ACCEL RESUME/CANCEL switch
4. Cruise main switch
5. Cruise control unit (right side of steering column)
6. Engine control module (ECM)
7. Brake light switch
8. Cruise control actuator
9. Automatic transmission
10. Shift switch
11. Transmission control module (TCM)

SK1109400003000X

Fig. 3 Cruise control components. Automatic transmission

as outlined in this section.

Brake Light Switch Circuit

1. With brake pedal depressed check voltage between terminal 7 of control unit electrical connector, **Fig. 11.**
2. If within 10–14 volts, brake light switch circuit is good.
3. If not check wires, connectors and fuses.
4. If good, then check brake light switch, refer to "Component Diagnosis & Testing" as outlined in this section.

Actuator Circuit

1. With main switch and cruise main switch in the On position, check voltage between terminal 5 of control unit electrical connector and ground, **Fig. 11.**
2. If within 10–14 volts, actuator circuit is good.

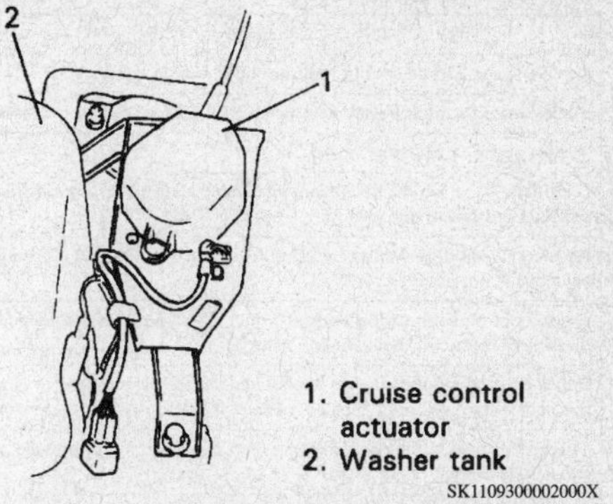
1. Cruise control actuator
2. Washer tank

SK1109300002000X

Fig. 2 Cruise control actuator. Manual transmission

3. If not check wires and electrical connectors.
4. If good, then check actuator, refer "Component Diagnosis & Testing" as outlined in this section.

Clutch Pedal Position (CPP) Switch Circuit

1. With main and CPP switch in the On position, clutch pedal depressed, check voltage between terminal 4 of control unit connector and ground, **Fig. 11.**
2. If 10–14 volts then circuit is good.
3. If not check wires and electrical connectors.
4. If good, then check CPP switch, refer to "Component Diagnosis & Testing" as outlined in this section.

Cruise Control Unit Circuit

1. Disconnect cruise control unit connector from control unit and complete test, **Fig. 13.**
2. If all items within system are in good condition and cruise control system fails to operate properly, then replace control unit.

1994–96

Indicator Light Circuit

1. With ignition switch in the On position, check voltage between terminal 17 of control unit connector and ground, **Fig. 12.**
2. Circuit is good if within 10–14 volts.
3. If not test lead wires, connectors, fuses, if good replace indicator light bulb.

Shift Switch Circuit

1. Check resistance between terminal 14 of control unit electrical connector and ground, **Fig. 12,** with shift lever set in "P" or "N" range and main switch On.
2. If continuity exist, then shift switch is in good condition.
3. If not check lead wires, grounds and electrical connectors.
4. If these items are in good condition, then check shift switch for continuity, refer to "Component Diagnosis & Testing" as outlined in this section.

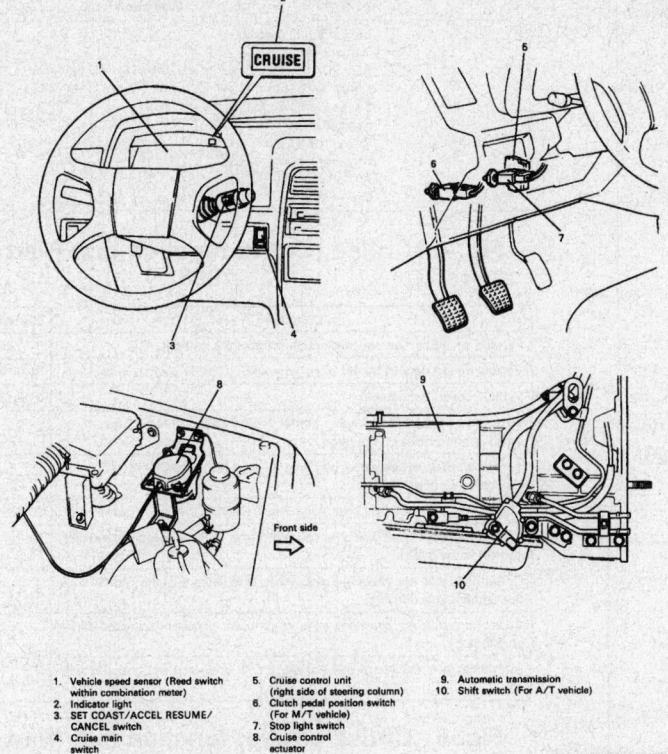

Condition	Inspection item number
Vehicle speed can be set but indicator light fails to light.	1, 10
Vehicle speed cannot be set even when SET COAST switch is pressed.	3, 4, 5, 6, 7, 8, 9, 10
Vehicle speed is unstable.	2, 9, 10
Difference (± α km/h) between actual vehicle speed during constant cruising and preset one is large.	2, 10
Acceleration or deceleration by using ACCEL RESUME/SET COAST switches is not attained.	3, 10
Cruise control is not cancelled even when clutch pedal is depressed during constant cruising. (For MT vehicle)	4, 10
Cruise control is not cancelled even when shift lever is shifted to N range during constant cruising. (For AT vehicle)	5, 10
Cruise control is not cancelled even when brake pedal is depressed during constant cruising.	8, 10
Cruise control is not cancelled even when CANCEL switch is turned ON.	3, 10
ACCEL RESUME switch fails to resume preset vehicle speed after cruise control is cancelled.	3, 10

SK1109300004010X

Fig. 4 Cruise control function test (Part 1 of 2). 1993

	Inspection item
1	Indicator light circuit
2	Actuator cable play
3	SET COAST/ACCEL RESUME CANCEL switch circuit
4	Clutch pedal position switch circuit (For M/T vehicle)
5	Shift switch circuit (For AT vehicle)
6	Vehicle speed sensor circuit
7	Cruise main switch circuit
8	Stop light switch circuit
9	Actuator circuit
10	Cruise control unit circuit

SK1109300004020X

Fig. 4 Cruise control function test (Part 2 of 2). 1993

Condition	Inspection item number
Vehicle speed can be set but indicator light fails to light.	1, 12
Vehicle speed cannot be set even when SET COAST switch is pressed.	3, 4, 5, 6, 7, 8, 9, 12
Vehicle speed is unstable.	2, 8, 9, 10, 11, 12
Difference (± α km/h) between actual vehicle speed during constant cruising and preset one is large.	2, 10, 11, 12
Acceleration or deceleration by using ACCEL RESUME/SET COAST switches is not attained.	3, 12
Cruise control is not cancelled even when CANCEL switch is turned ON.	3, 12
ACCEL RESUME switch fails to resume preset vehicle speed after cruise control is cancelled.	3, 12
Cruise control is not cancelled even when shift lever is shifted to N range during constant cruising.	4, 12
Cruise control is not cancelled even when brake pedal is depressed during constant cruising.	7, 12
Automatic transmission is not shifted to O/D gear or is not occured lock-up.	10, 11, 12

SK1109400019010X

Fig. 5 Cruise control function test (Part 1 of 2). 1994–96

	Inspection item
1	Indicator light circuit
2	Actuator cable play
3	SET COAST/ACCEL RESUME/CANCEL switch circuit
4	Shift switch circuit
5	Vehicle speed sensor circuit
6	Cruise main switch circuit
7	Stop light switch circuit
8	Actuator circuit
9	Brake switch circuit
10	Coolant temp. switch signal circuit
11	Throttle valve opening signal circuit
12	Cruise control unit and its circuit

SK1109400019020X

Fig. 5 Cruise control function test (Part 2 of 2). 1994–96

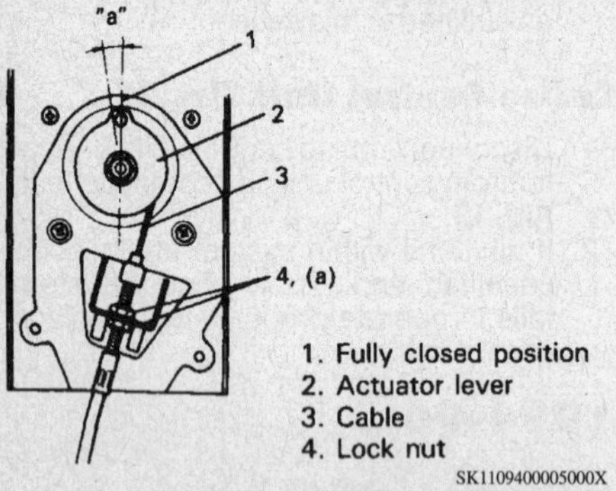
"a"
1
2
3
4, (a)
1. Fully closed position
2. Actuator lever
3. Cable
4. Lock nut
SK1109400005000X

Fig. 6 Actuator cable adjustment

Set Coast/Accel/Resume/Cancel Switch Circuit

1. Check continuity between the following terminals:
   a. With "ACCEL/RESUME" switch in the On position, terminal 12 of control unit electrical connector and ground, **Fig. 12.**
2. If no continuity exist, then check wires and electrical connectors. If circuit is good, then test switch, refer to "Component Diagnosis & Testing" as outlined in this section.

Vehicle Speed Sensor Circuit

1. Check continuity between terminal 11 of control unit electrical connector and ground, **Fig. 12,** while proceeding as follows:
   a. Raise and support rear of vehicle.
   b. Turn rear left tire slowly with right rear tire locked.
   c. Check ohmmeter for deflection between infinity and omega, 2–3 pulses for each tire revolution.
2. If continuity occurs as outlined above, then speed sensor circuit is good.
3. If not test wires and electrical connectors. If they are good test speed sensor, refer to "Component Diagnosis & Testing" as outlined in this section.

Cruise Main Switch Circuit

1. With cruise and main switch in the On position, check voltage between terminal 16 of control unit electrical connector and ground **Fig. 12.**
2. If within 10–14 volts, then switch circuit is good.
3. If not check wires, grounds and electrical connectors.
4. If good, check cruise main switch, refer to "Component Diagnosis & Testing" as outlined in this section.

Brake Light Switch Circuit

1. With brake pedal depressed check voltage between terminal 4 of control unit electrical connector.
2. If within 10–14 volts, brake light switch circuit is good.
3. If not check wires, connectors and fuses.
4. If good, then check brake light switch, refer to "Component Diagnosis & Testing" as outlined in this section.

Actuator Circuit

1. Check resistance between terminal 3 and 7 of control unit electrical connector, **Fig. 12.**
2. If with 15 ohms plus or minus 3 ohms, then actuator circuit is good.
3. If not check wires and electrical connectors.
4. If good, then check actuator, refer "Component Diagnosis & Testing" as outlined in this section.

Brake Switch Circuit

1. Check continuity between terminals 3 and 15 of control unit electrical connector, **Fig. 12.**
2. If continuity exist then the circuit is good.
3. If not check wires and connectors of each relate circuit.
4. If good, then check brake switch, refer "Component Diagnosis & Testing" as outlined in this section.

Coolant Temperature Switch Circuit

1. With ignition switch in the On position, check voltage between terminal 10 and ground, **Fig. 12.**
2. With engine temperature below 77°F voltage should read 0–1 volt.
3. With engine temperature above 86°F voltage should read 10–14 volt.

Throttle Valve Opening Circuit

1. Check voltage between terminal 2 and body ground, **Fig. 12.**
2. If duty signal appears, **Fig. 14,** then throttle valve opening signal is good.

3. If not then check wires, fuses, electrical connectors and ECM.

Cruise Control Unit Circuit

1. Disconnect cruise control unit connector from control unit, then perform voltage test, **Fig. 15,** and resistance test, **Fig. 16.**
2. If all items within system are in good condition and cruise control system fails to operate properly, then replace control unit.

COMPONENT DIAGNOSIS & TESTING

1993

Shift Switch

Refer to "Automatic Transmissions" for shift switch replacement procedure.

Vehicle Speed Sensor

1. Disconnect battery ground cable.
2. Remove combination meter from instrument panel.
3. Check continuity between speed sensor and ground, **Fig. 17.**
4. Four pulses should occur within one complete revolution of flat on speedometer cable.
5. If defective replace speed sensor.

Cruise Main Switch

1. Connect 12 volts battery positive power to terminal 3 of cruise main switch and negative to terminal 5, **Fig. 18.**
2. Connect positive terminal of circuit tester to terminal 1 and negative to terminal 5.
3. Turn cruise switch, circuit tester should read 10–14 volts.
4. Push switch Off, voltage should read zero volts.
5. If not replace cruise main switch.

Brake Light Switch

1. Disconnect brake light switch electrical connector, then remove switch from pedal bracket.
2. Using an ohmmeter check switch for continuity, **Fig. 19,** if defective then replace switch.
3. After installing brake switch, refer to "Adjustments " for adjustment procedure.

Actuator

1. With engine in the Off position, pull wiring harness terminals from connector by unlocking terminal lock in connector, **Fig. 20.**
2. Disconnect cruise control actuator electrical connector.
3. Check for continuity between terminals 1 and 3, **Fig. 20.**
4. Resistance of clutch coil should read 15 ohms plus or minus 3 ohms.
5. Connect terminals 2 and 3 to battery positive and terminals 1 and 4 to ground, **Fig. 21.**

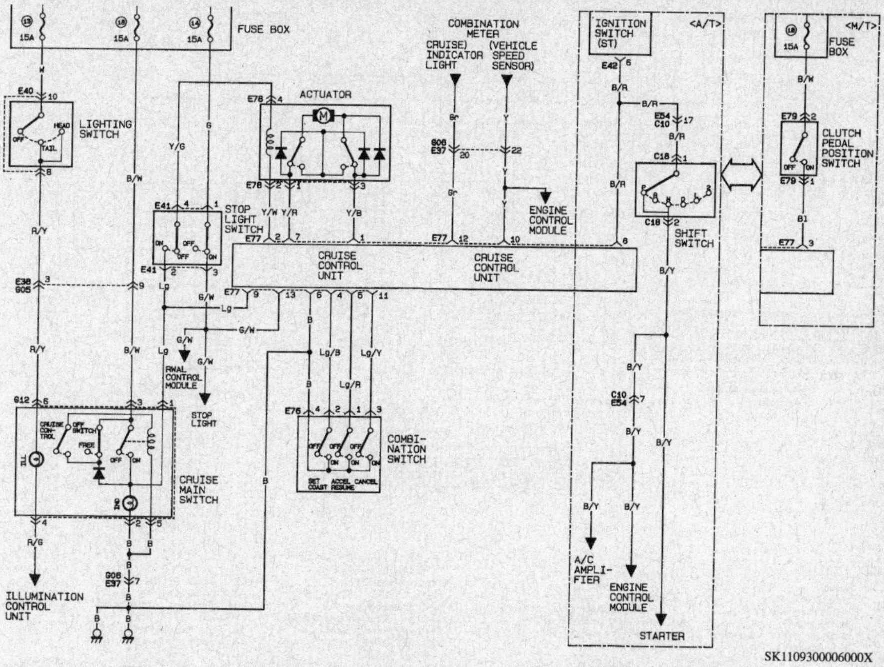
FUSE BOX
LIGHTING SWITCH
ACTUATOR
COMBINATION METER
CRUISE) INDICATOR LIGHT
(VEHICLE SPEED SENSOR)
IGNITION SWITCH (ST)
<A/T>
<M/T>
CLUTCH PEDAL POSITION SWITCH
STOP LIGHT SWITCH
ENGINE CONTROL MODULE
SHIFT SWITCH
CRUISE CONTROL UNIT
RWAL CONTROL MODULE
STOP LIGHT
COMBI-NATION SWITCH
CRUISE MAIN SWITCH
ILLUMINATION CONTROL UNIT
A/C AMPLI-FIER
STARTER
SK1109300006000X

Fig. 7 Cruise control system wiring diagram. 1993

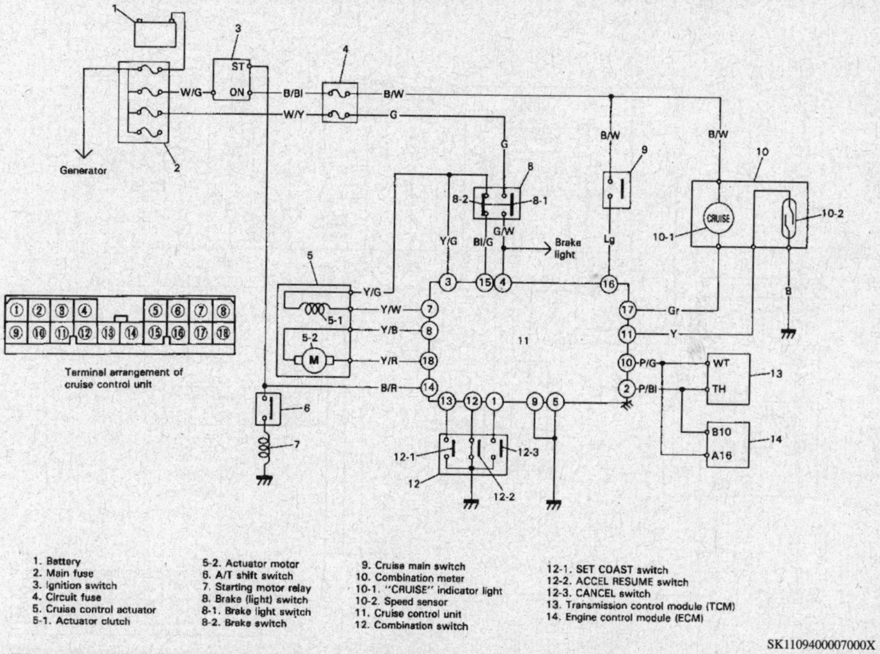
Generator
ST
ON
W/G
B/Bl
B/W
W/Y
G
Y/G
Bl/G
G/W
Brake light
Lg
Gr
Y
P/G
P/Bl
WT
TH
B10
A16
Y/W
Y/B
Y/R
B/R
CRUISE
Terminal arrangement of cruise control unit
1. Battery
2. Main fuse
3. Ignition switch
4. Circuit fuse
5. Cruise control actuator
5-1. Actuator clutch
5-2. Actuator motor
6. A/T shift switch
7. Starting motor relay
8. Brake (light) switch
8-1. Brake light switch
8-2. Brake switch
9. Cruise main switch
10. Combination meter
10-1. "CRUISE" indicator light
10-2. Speed sensor
11. Cruise control unit
12. Combination switch
12-1. SET COAST switch
12-2. ACCEL RESUME switch
12-3. CANCEL switch
13. Transmission control module (TCM)
14. Engine control module (ECM)
SK1109400007000X

Fig. 8 Cruise control system wiring diagram. 1994–95 except Esteem

6. Ensure motor pulls cable actuating lever to the fully open position, **Fig. 21.**
7. Disconnect probe from terminal 3 ensuring cable returns quickly, allowing actuator lever to return to the fully closed position.
8. Connect battery positive to terminal 3 and battery ground to terminal 1.
9. Ensure clutch operation maintains actuator cable position at this time.
10. With actuator lever pulled by hand to its fully open position, connect terminal 3 and 4 to battery positive and terminals 1 and 2 to battery ground.
11. Ensure cable is released by motor and actuator lever returns to fully closed position, **Fig. 22.**
12. If any of the preceding test failed, replace actuator.
13. Ensure terminals are properly secured in connector.

Set Coast/Accel Resume/Cancel Switch

1. Remove turn signal/dimmer switch assembly.
2. Using a suitable circuit tester, check continuity between terminals, **Fig. 23,** at each switch position, **Fig. 24.**

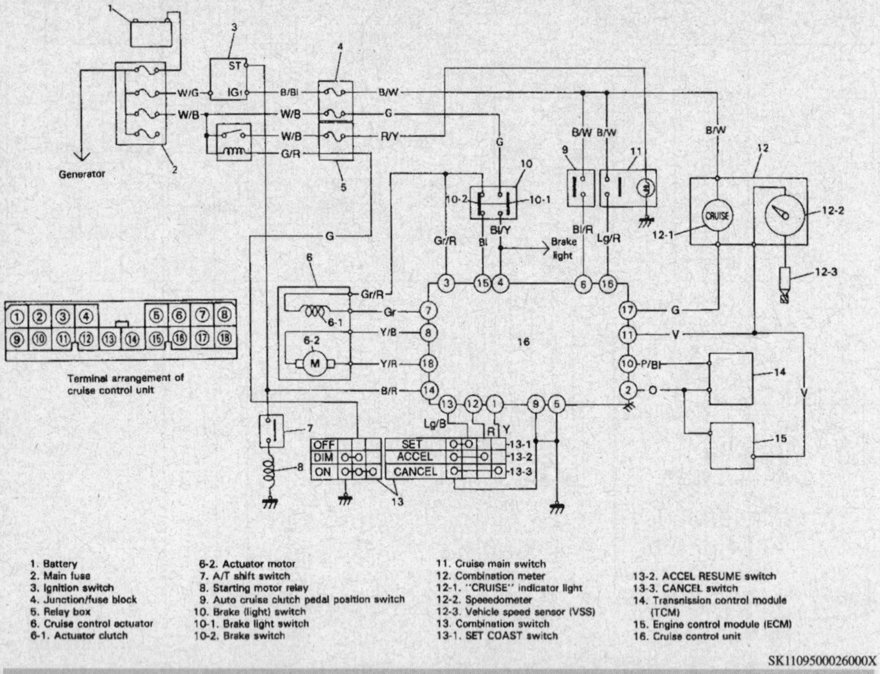
Generator
Terminal arrangement of cruise control unit
1. Battery
2. Main fuse
3. Ignition switch
4. Junction/fuse block
5. Relay box
6. Cruise control actuator
6-1. Actuator clutch
6-2. Actuator motor
7. A/T shift switch
8. Starting motor relay
9. Auto cruise clutch pedal position switch
10. Brake (light) switch
10-1. Brake light switch
10-2. Brake switch
11. Cruise main switch
12. Combination meter
12-1. "CRUISE" indicator light
12-2. Speedometer
12-3. Vehicle speed sensor (VSS)
13. Combination switch
13-1. SET COAST switch
13-2. ACCEL RESUME switch
13-3. CANCEL switch
14. Transmission control module (TCM)
15. Engine control module (ECM)
16. Cruise control unit
SK1109500026000X

Fig. 9 Cruise control system wiring diagram. Esteem

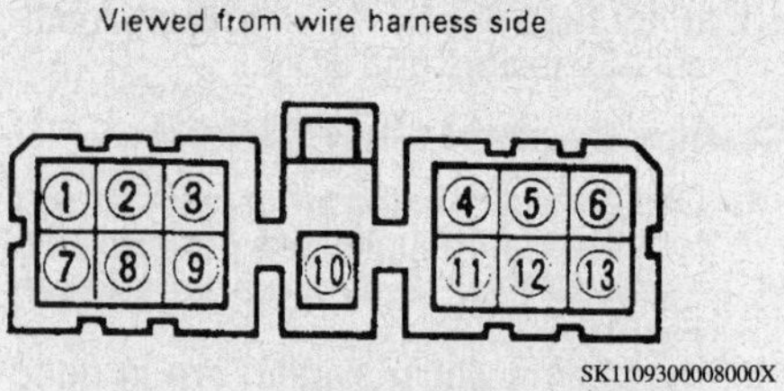
Viewed from wire harness side
SK1109300008000X

Fig. 11 Control unit electrical connector terminal identification. 1993

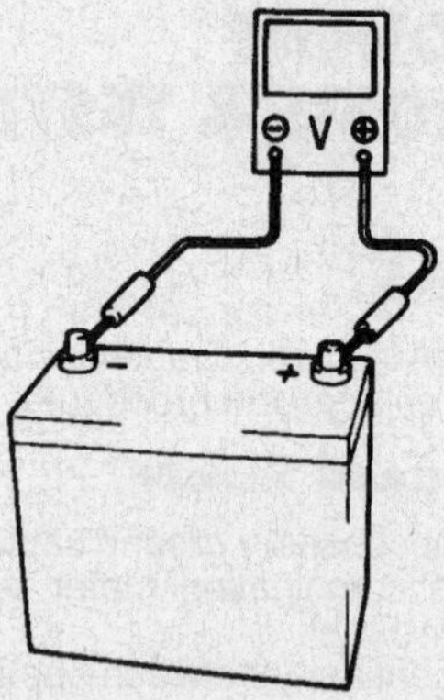

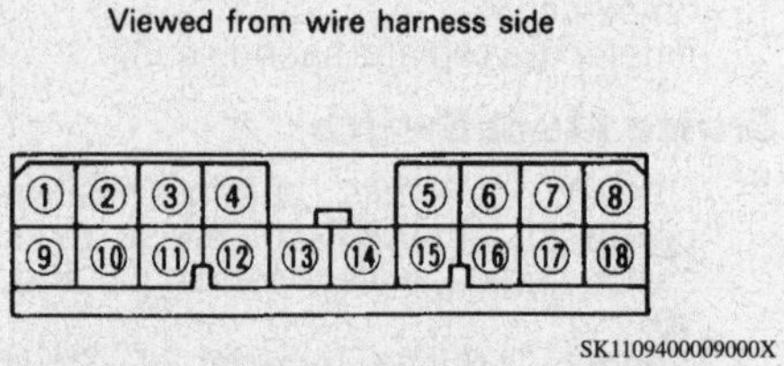
Viewed from wire harness side
SK1109400009000X

Fig. 12 Control unit electrical connector terminal identification. 1994–96

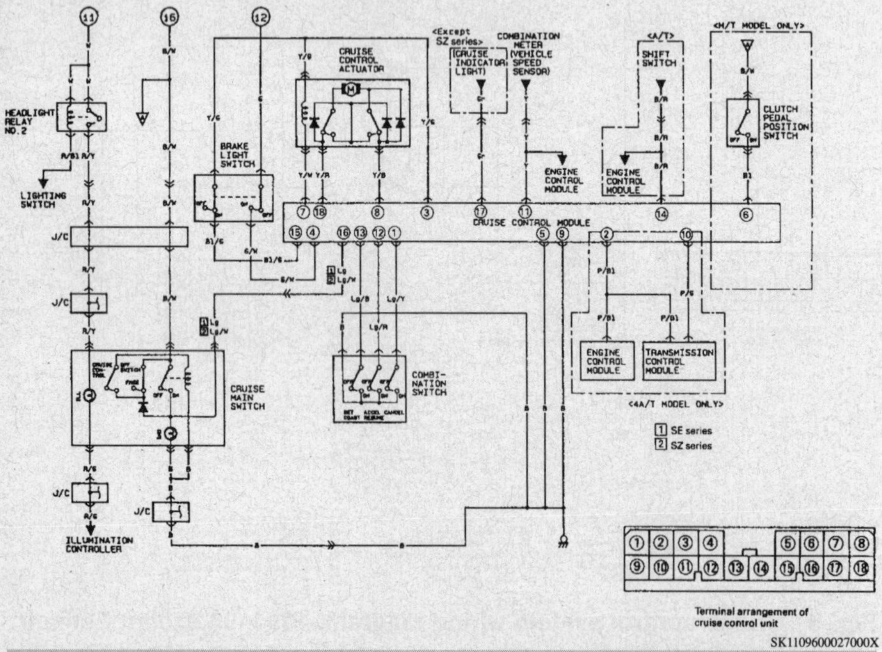
HEADLIGHT RELAY NO.2
LIGHTING SWITCH
BRAKE LIGHT SWITCH
CRUISE CONTROL ACTUATOR
COMBINATION METER
SHIFT SWITCH
CLUTCH PEDAL POSITION SWITCH
ENGINE CONTROL MODULE
CRUISE CONTROL MODULE
TRANSMISSION CONTROL MODULE
CRUISE MAIN SWITCH
COMBINATION SWITCH
ILLUMINATION CONTROLLER
SE series
SZ series
Terminal arrangement of cruise control unit
SK1109600027000X

Fig. 10 Cruise control system wiring diagram. 1996 Sidekick & X-90

3. If any test result is not good, then replace turn signal/dimmer switch assembly.

Clutch Pedal Position (CPP) Switch Circuit

1. Disconnect CPP switch connector, then remove switch from pedal bracket.
2. Check continuity across switch terminals.
3. When switch is pushed in continuity should not exist.
4. When released switch should have continuity.

1994–96

Indicator Light

1. With ignition switch in the On position, check voltage between terminal 17 of control unit connector and ground, **Fig. 12.**
2. Circuit is good if within 10–14 volts.
3. If not test lead wires, connectors, fuses, if good replace indicator light bulb.

Shift Switch

Refer to "Automatic Transmissions" for shift switch replacement procedure.

Vehicle Speed Sensor

1. Disconnect battery ground cable.
2. Remove combination meter from instrument panel.
3. Check continuity between speed sensor and ground, **Fig. 25.**
4. Four pulses should occur within one complete revolution of flat on speedometer cable.
5. If not good replace speed sensor.

Cruise Main Switch

1. Connect 12 volts battery positive power to terminal 3 of cruise main switch and negative to terminal 5, **Fig. 18.**
2. Connect positive terminal of circuit tester to terminal 1 and negative to terminal 5.
3. Turn cruise switch, circuit tester should read 10–14 volts.
4. Push switch Off, voltage should read 0–1 volt.
5. If not replace cruise main switch.

Terminal	Connection of measure item	Tester connection	Condition		Result
①	Body ground	① - Body ground	——		Continuity
②	ACCEL RESUME switch	② - Body ground	ACCEL RESUME switch OFF		No continuity
			ACCEL RESUME switch ON		Continuity
③	SET COAST switch	③ - Body ground	SET COAST switch OFF		No continuity
			SET COAST switch ON		Continuity
④	Clutch pedal position switch	④ - Body ground	Main switch ON	Clutch pedal released	0 V
				Clutch pedal depressed	10 - 14 V
⑤	Actuator	⑤ - Body ground	Main switch ON and Cruise main switch ON	Brake pedal released	10 - 14 V
				Brake pedal depressed	0 V
⑥	Actuator	⑥ - ⑬	Place actuator lever (cable) at about intermidiate position between fully closed and fully open positions.		Continuity
⑦	Stop light switch	⑦ - Body ground	Brake pedal released		0 V
			Brake pedal depressed		10 - 14 V
⑧	Indicator light	⑧ - Body ground	Main switch OFF		0 V
			Main switch ON		10 - 14 V
⑨	CANCEL switch	⑨ - Body ground	CANCEL switch OFF		No continuity
			CANCEL switch ON		Continuity
⑩	Speed sensor	⑩ - Body ground	Hoist rear end of vehicle. Turn rear left tire slowly with rear right one locked.		2 - 3 pulses (continuity) each one tire-revolution.
⑪	Cruise main switch	⑪ - Body ground	Main switch ON	Cruise main switch OFF	0 V
				Cruise main switch ON	10 - 14 V
⑫	Shift switch	⑫ - Body ground	Shift into P or N range		Approx. 0 Ω

SK1109300016000X

Fig. 13 Cruise control circuit test. 1993

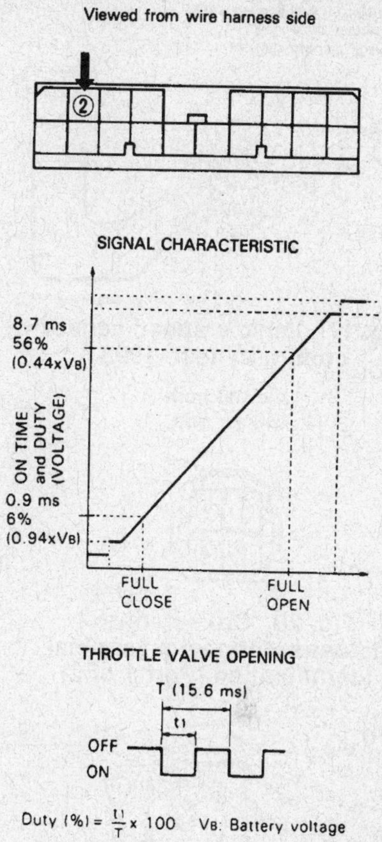
Viewed from wire harness side
②
SIGNAL CHARACTERISTIC
8.7 ms
56%
(0.44xVB)
ON TIME and DUTY (VOLTAGE)
0.9 ms
6%
(0.94xVB)
FULL CLOSE
FULL OPEN
THROTTLE VALVE OPENING
T (15.6 ms)
t1
OFF
ON
Duty (%) = t1/T x 100   VB: Battery voltage

SK1059400005000X

Fig. 14 Throttle valve opening signal circuit test. 1994–96

TER-MINAL	CIRCUIT	CONDITION	NORMAL VOLTAGE
①	CANCEL switch	Ignition switch ON, CANCEL switch OFF	10–14 V
		Ignition switch ON, CANCEL switch ON	0 V
②	Throttle valve opening signal from ECM	Ignition switch ON. Voltage varies as specified at graph in previous page while throttle valve is opened gradually.	
③	Brake switch	Ignition switch and cruise main switch ON, and brake pedal released.	About 9 V
		Ignition switch and cruise main switch ON, and brake pedal depressed	0–1 V
④	Brake light switch	Brake pedal released	0–1 V
		Brake pedal depressed	10–14 V
⑤	Ground	——	——
⑦	Actuator clutch	Ignition switch and cruise main switch ON, and brake pedal released	About 9 V
⑧	Actuator motor	Ignition and cruise main switch ON	10–14 V
⑨	Ground	——	——
⑩	Coolant temp. switch signal	Ignition switch ON Engine coolant temp. is below 25°C (77°F)	0–1 V
		Ignition switch ON Engine coolant temp. is above 30°C (86°F)	10–14 V
⑪	Vehicle speed sensor	Igniton switch and cruise main switch ON. Hoist rear end of vehicle. Turn rear left tire slowly with rear right tire locked	Indicator deflection repeated between 0–1V and 3–5V
⑫	ACCEL RESUME switch	Ignition and cruise main switch ON ACCEL RESUME switch OFF	10–14 V
		Ignition and cruise main switch ON ACCEL RESUME switch ON	0–1 V
⑬	SET COAST switch	Ignition and cruise main switch ON SET COAST switch OFF	10–14 V
		Ignition and cruise main switch ON SET COAST switch ON	0–1 V
⑭	Shift switch	Ignition and cruise main switch ON Selector lever in "P" or "N" range	0–1 V
		Ignition and cruise main switch ON Selector lever in "R", "D", "2" or "L" range	10–14 V
⑮	Actuator clutch power supply	Ignition switch ON Cruise main switch ON	About 9 V
⑯	Cruise main switch	Ignition and cruise main switch ON	10–14 V
		Ignition switch ON. Cruise main switch OFF	0–1 V
⑰	CRUISE indicator light	Ignition switch ON	10–14 V
⑱	Actuator motor	Ignition and cruise main switch ON	10–14 V

KS1109400017000X

Fig. 15 Cruise control unit voltage test. 1994–96

TERMINALS	CIRCUIT	CONDITION	NORMAL RESISTANCE
①–Body ground	CANCEL switch	CANCEL switch OFF	No continuity
		CANCEL switch ON	Continuity
③–⑦	Actuator clutch	——	12–18Ω
③–⑮	Brake switch	Brake pedal released	Continuity
		Brake pedal depressed	No continuity
⑤–Body ground	Ground	——	Continuity
⑨–Body ground	Ground	——	Continuity
⑪–Body ground	Vehicle speed sensor	Hoist rear end of vehicle. Turn rear left tire slowly with rear right tire locked	Ohmmeter indicator deflect between continuity and ∞
⑫–Body ground	ACCEL RESUME switch	ACCEL RESUME switch OFF	No continuity
		ACCEL RESUME switch ON	Continuity
⑬–Body ground	SET COAST switch	SET COAST switch OFF	No continuity
		SET COAST switch ON	Continuity
⑭–Body ground	Shift switch	Selector lever in "P" or "N" range	Continuity
		Selector lever in "R", "D", "2" or "L" range	No continuity

SK1109400018000X

Fig. 16 Cruise control unit resistance test. 1994–96

Brake Light Switch

1. Disconnect brake light switch electrical connector, then remove switch from pedal bracket.
2. Using an ohmmeter check switch for continuity, **Fig. 26,** if defective then replace switch.
3. After installing brake switch, refer to "Adjustments " for adjustment procedure.

Actuator

1. With engine in the Off position, pull wiring harness terminals from connector, **Fig. 20,** by unlocking terminal lock in connector.
2. Disconnect cruise control actuator electrical connector.
3. Check for continuity between terminals 1 and 3, **Fig. 20.**
4. Resistance of clutch coil should read 15 ohms plus or minus 3 ohms.
5. Connect terminals 2 and 3 to battery positive and terminals 1 and 4 to ground, **Fig. 21.**
6. Ensure motor pulls cable actuating lever to the fully open position.
7. Disconnect probe from terminal 3 ensuring cable returns quickly, allowing actuator lever to return to the fully closed position.
8. Connect battery positive to terminal 3 and battery ground to terminal 1.
9. Ensure clutch operation maintains actuator cable position at this time.
10. With actuator lever pulled by hand to its fully open position, **Fig. 22,** connect

1. Dent part for speedometer cable
2. For ground
3. For vehicle speed sensor (indicated "R.S")

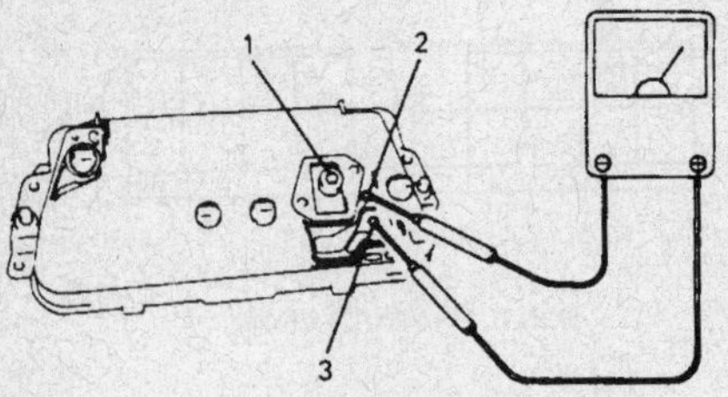
1
2
3

SK1109300010000X

Fig. 17 Vehicle speed sensor continuity test. 1993

Viewed from coupler side

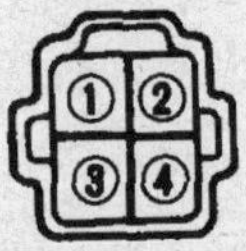
1
2
3
4

SK1109300013010X

Fig. 20 Cruise control actuator connector terminal identification (Part 1 of 2)

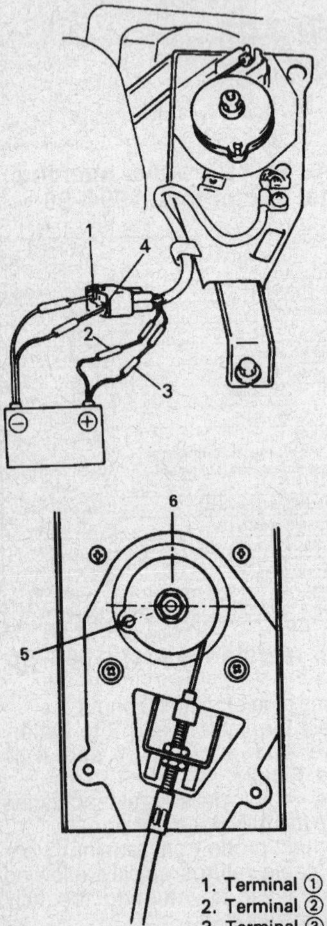
1
4
2
3
6
5

1. Terminal ①
2. Terminal ②
3. Terminal ③
4. Terminal ④
5. Fully open position
6. Fully closed position

SK1109300014000X

Fig. 21 Actuator terminals 1, 2, 3 & 4 location

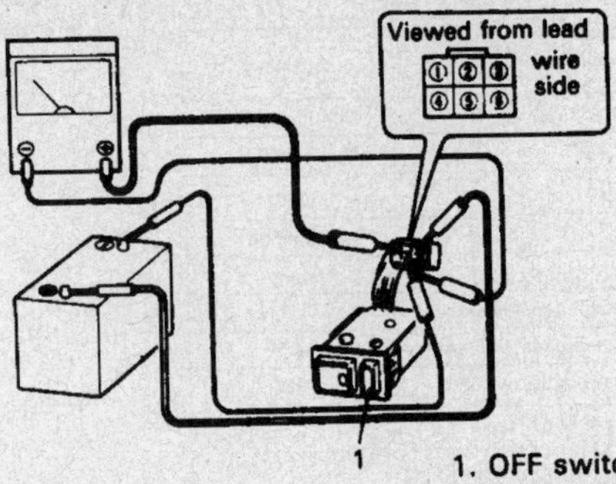
Viewed from lead wire side
1
2
3
4
5
6
1

1. OFF switch

SK1109300012000X

Fig. 18 Cruise main switch voltage test

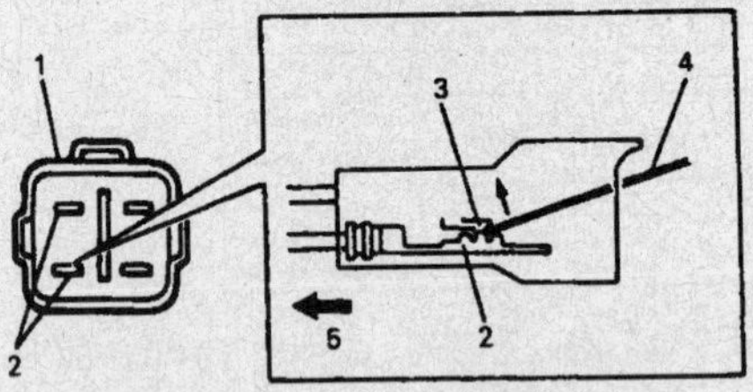
1
2
3
4
5
2

1. Coupler
2. Actuator terminals
3. Terminal lock
4. Thin wire
5. Pull out while unlocking

SK1109300013020X

Fig. 20 Cruise control actuator connector terminal identification (Part 2 of 2)

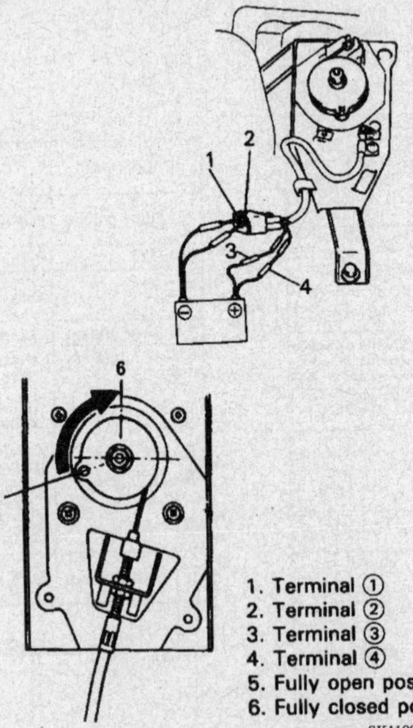
2
1
3
4
6
5

1. Terminal ①
2. Terminal ②
3. Terminal ③
4. Terminal ④
5. Fully open position
6. Fully closed position

SK1109300015000X

Fig. 22 Cruise control actuator fully closed position

terminal 3 and 4 to battery positive and terminals 1 and 2 to battery ground.

11. Ensure cable is released by motor and actuator lever returns to fully closed position.
12. If any of the preceding test failed, replace actuator.
13. Ensure terminals are properly secured in connector.

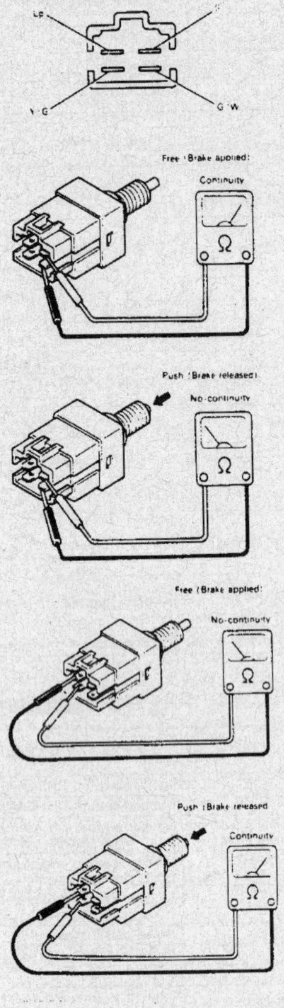
Free (Brake applied)
Continuity
Push (Brake released)
No-continuity
Free (Brake applied)
No-continuity
Push (Brake released)
Continuity

SK1049300001000X

Fig. 19 Brake switch test. 1993

Viewed from coupler side

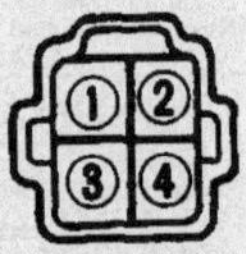
1
2
3
4

SK1109300020000X

Fig. 23 Set Coast, Accel Resume & Cancel switch continuity test

Set Coast/Accel Resume/ Cancel Switch

1. Remove turn signal/dimmer switch assembly.
2. Using a suitable circuit tester, check continuity between terminals, **Fig. 23**, at each switch position, **Fig. 24**.
3. If check result is not good then replace turn signal/dimmer switch assembly.

Terminal	③	①	②	④
OFF				
SET COAST (ON)	○	○		
ACCEL RESUME (ON)	○		○	
CANCEL (ON)	○			○

SK1109300021000X

Fig. 24 Set Coast, Accel Resume & Cancel switch position test

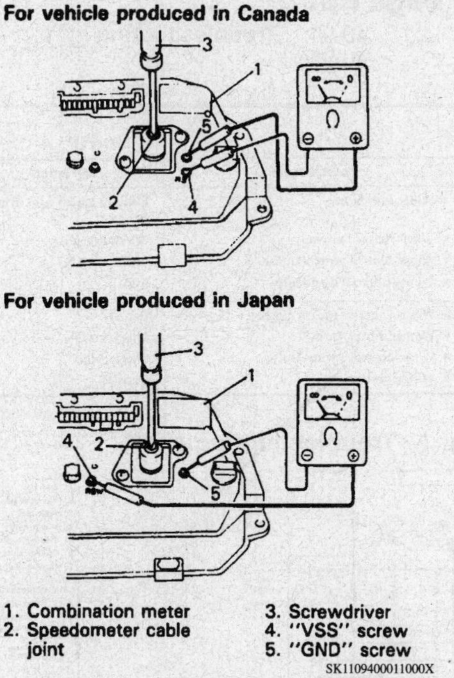

For vehicle produced in Canada
For vehicle produced in Japan
1. Combination meter
2. Speedometer cable joint
3. Screwdriver
4. "VSS" screw
5. "GND" screw
SK1109400011000X

Fig. 25 Vehicle speed sensor. 1994–96

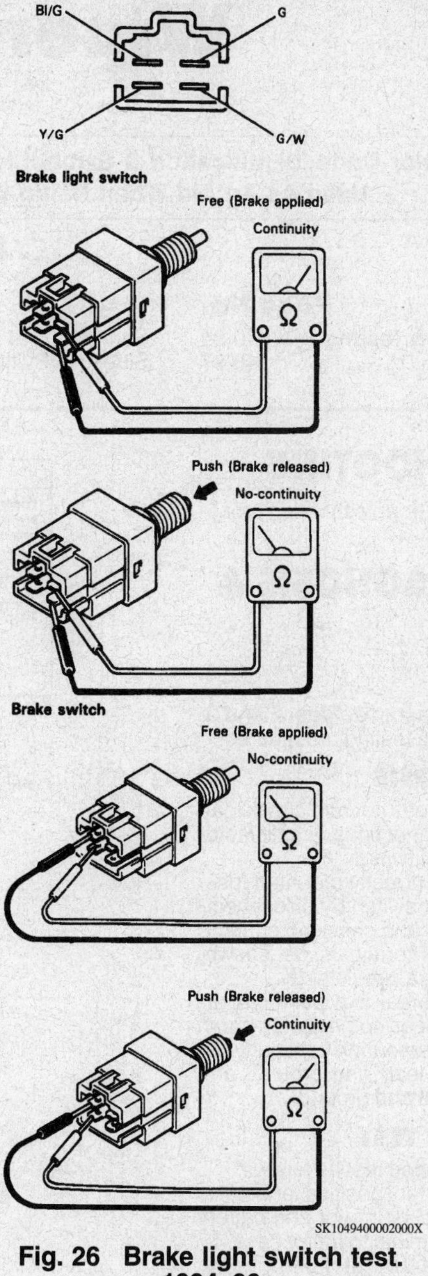

Bl/G
G
Y/G
G/W
Brake light switch
Free (Brake applied)
Continuity
Push (Brake released)
No-continuity
Brake switch
Free (Brake applied)
No-continuity
Push (Brake released)
Continuity
SK1049400002000X

Fig. 26 Brake light switch test. 1994–96

Wiper Systems

NOTE: Wire Color Code Identification & Symbol Identification Located In The Front Of This Manual May Be Used As An Aid When Using Wiring Circuits Found In This Section.

INDEX

	Page No.		Page No.		Page No.
System Diagnosis & Testing	40-94	Samurai	40-94	**Troubleshooting**	40-94
Esteem	40-97	Sidekick, Swift & X-90	40-95		

TROUBLESHOOTING

Refer to **Fig. 1** for troubleshooting procedures.

Trouble	Possible cause	Correction
Wiper malfunctions or does not return to original position.	• Wiper fuse blown	Replace blown fuse to check for short.
	• Wiper motor faulty	Check motor.
	• Wiper control switch faulty	Check switch.
	• Wiring or grounding faulty	Repair.
Washer malfunctions.	• Washer hose or nozzle clogged	Repair.
	• Washer motor faulty	Check motor.
	• Wiper control switch faulty	Check switch.
	• Wiring faulty	Repair.

SK9029100001000X

Fig. 1 Troubleshooting chart

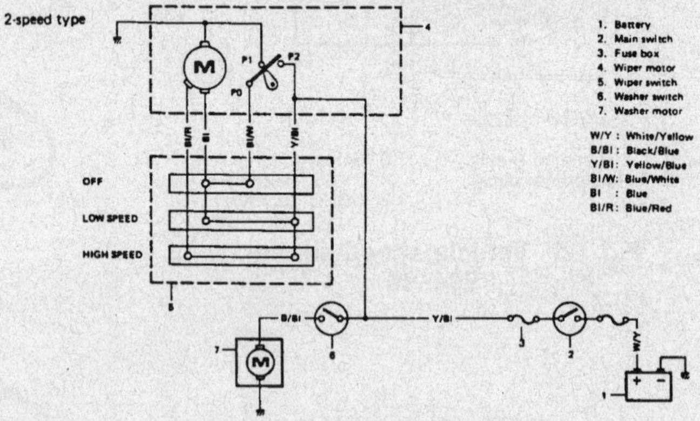

2-speed type
M
P1
P2
P0
Bl/R
Bl
Bl/W
Y/Bl
OFF
LOW SPEED
HIGH SPEED
B/Bl
Y/Bl
W/Y
1. Battery
2. Main switch
3. Fuse box
4. Wiper motor
5. Wiper switch
6. Washer switch
7. Washer motor
W/Y : White/Yellow
B/Bl : Black/Blue
Y/Bl : Yellow/Blue
Bl/W: Blue/White
Bl : Blue
Bl/R: Blue/Red

SK

Fig. 2 Wiper/washer system wiring. Samurai w/2-speed wipers

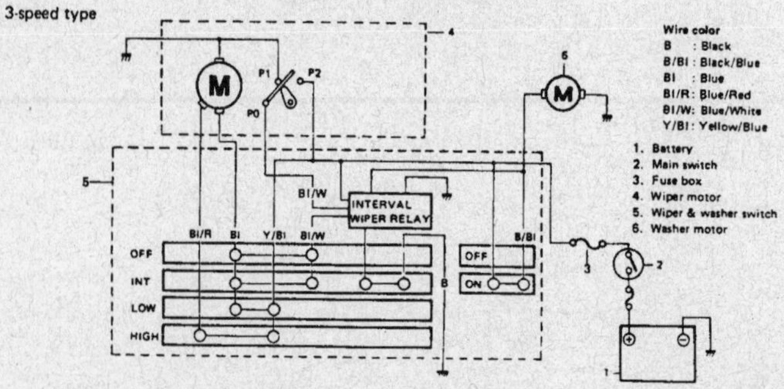

3-speed type
M
P1
P2
P0
INTERVAL WIPER RELAY
Bl/W
Bl/R
Bl
Y/Bl
B/Bl
OFF
INT
LOW
HIGH
ON
B
Wire color
B : Black
B/Bl : Black/Blue
Bl : Blue
Bl/R: Blue/Red
Bl/W: Blue/White
Y/Bl: Yellow/Blue
1. Battery
2. Main switch
3. Fuse box
4. Wiper motor
5. Wiper & washer switch
6. Washer motor

SK9029100002000X

Fig. 3 Wiper/washer system wiring. Samurai w/3-speed wipers

SYSTEM DIAGNOSIS & TESTING

SAMURAI

Refer to wiring diagrams, **Figs. 2 and 3,** during diagnosis and testing procedures.

WIPER DIAGNOSIS

1. If wiper motor does not run, check lead and coupler connections. If satisfactory, check the following:
   a. Blown or incorrectly mounted fuse.
   b. Check wiper switch by disconnecting couplers and checking continuity between terminals as shown, **Fig. 4,** using a circuit tester.
   c. Check for a break in wiper motor armature or poor commutator brush contact by measuring continuity between blue lead and ground, and blue/red wire and ground.

NO-LOAD RUN TEST

1. Perform low-speed test as follows:
   a. Connect battery positive terminal to blue terminal on motor and battery negative terminal to motor case.
   b. If motor rotates at 45–57 RPM, motor is operating properly.
   c. If not, motor is defective, replace motor.
2. Perform high-speed test as follows:
   a. Connect battery positive terminal to blue/red terminal on motor and battery negative terminal to motor case.
   b. If motor rotates at 67–81 RPM, motor is operating properly.
   c. If not, motor is defective, replace motor.

AUTOMATIC STOP ACTION TEST

1. Connect battery positive terminal to yellow terminal of motor and battery negative terminal to motor case, then connect a jumper between blue/white and blue/black terminals of motor.
2. Motor output shaft should come to a halt at a certain angular position, corresponding to starting position of wiper blade.
3. Stop motor a number of times, and ensure motor stops in same position each time.

INTERNAL WIPER RELAY TEST

1. Disconnect wiper and washer switch electrical connector, then turn wiper switch to INT position.
2. Connect battery positive terminal to yellow/white terminal and battery negative terminal to black terminal.
3. If an operating sound is emitted, relay

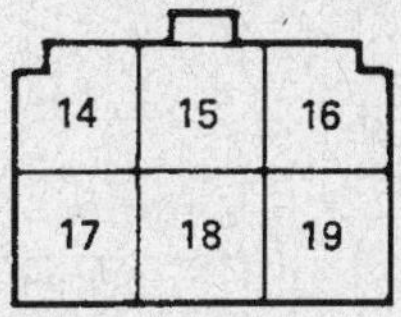

14. Yellow/White
15. Blue
16. Blue/Red
17. Blue/Black
18. Black
19. Blue/White

2-speed type

	Yellow/white	Blue	Blue/red	Blue/white
High speed	●		●	
Low speed	●	●		
OFF		●		●

Wiper switch

3-speed type

	Yellow/white	Blue/white	Blue	Blue/red	To replay	Black
OFF		●	●			
Interval		●	●		●	●
Low speed	●		●			
High speed	●			●		

Wiper switch

SK9029100003000X

Fig. 4 Wiper/washer switch continuity. Samurai

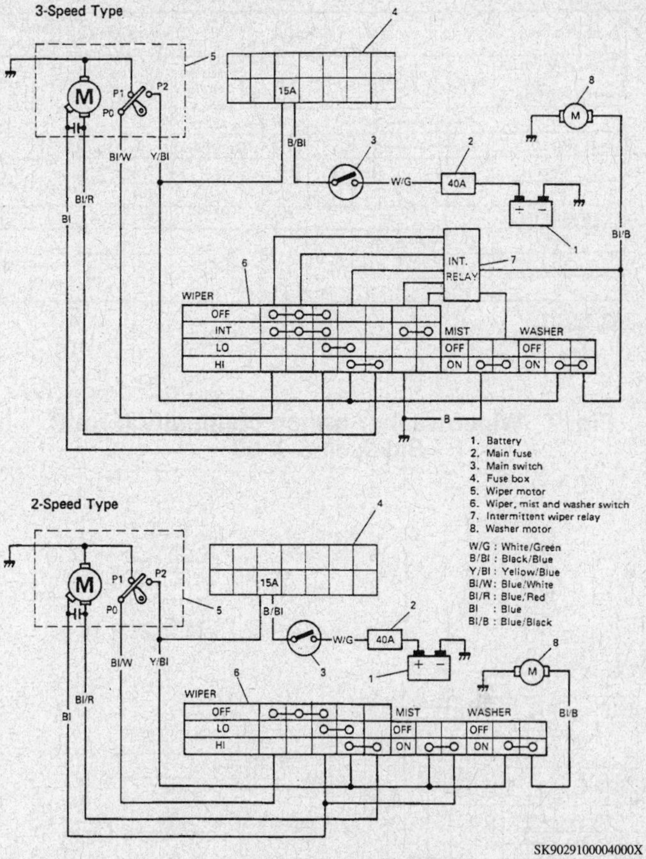
3-Speed Type
2-Speed Type
1. Battery
2. Main fuse
3. Main switch
4. Fuse box
5. Wiper motor
6. Wiper, mist and washer switch
7. Intermittent wiper relay
8. Washer motor
W/G : White/Green
B/Bl : Black/Blue
Y/Bl : Yellow/Blue
Bl/W : Blue/White
Bl/R : Blue/Red
Bl : Blue
Bl/B : Blue/Black
SK9029100004000X

Fig. 5 Wiper/washer system wiring (Front). Sidekick & X-90

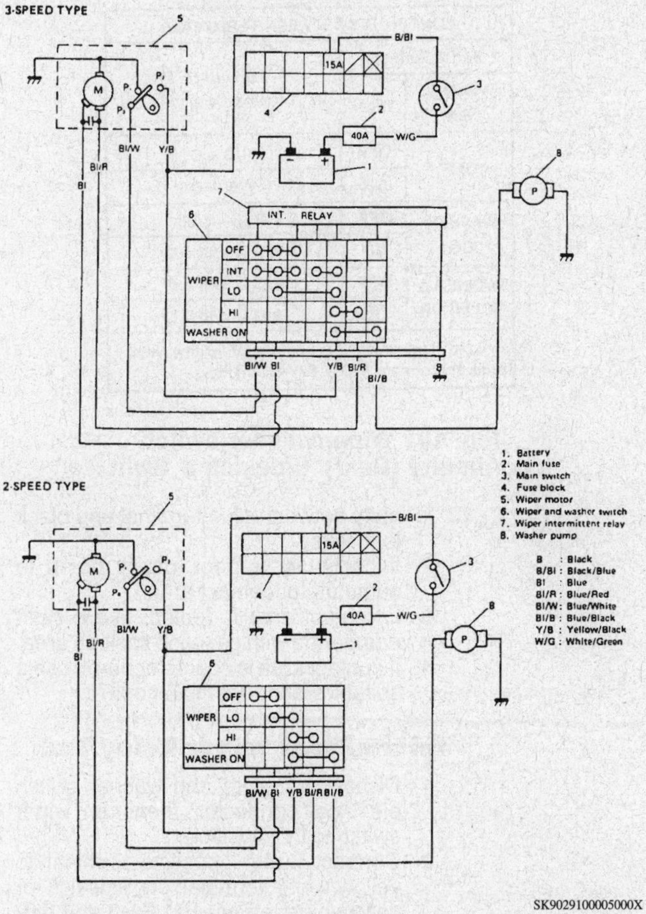
3-SPEED TYPE
2-SPEED TYPE
1. Battery
2. Main fuse
3. Main switch
4. Fuse block
5. Wiper motor
6. Wiper and washer switch
7. Wiper intermittent relay
8. Washer pump
B : Black
B/Bl : Black/Blue
Bl : Blue
Bl/R : Blue/Red
Bl/W : Blue/White
Bl/B : Blue/Black
Y/B : Yellow/Black
W/G : White/Green
SK9029100005000X

Fig. 6 Wiper/washer system wiring (Front). Swift

is operating properly.

SIDEKICK, SWIFT & X-90

FRONT

Refer to wiring diagrams, **Figs. 5 and 6,** during diagnosis and testing procedures.

Wiper/Washer Switch Test

Refer to **Figs. 7 and 8,** while using a circuit tester to measure switch for terminal to terminal continuity.

No-Load Run Test

1. Perform low-speed test as follows:
   a. Connect battery positive terminal to blue terminal on motor and battery negative terminal to black lead wire on motor.
   b. If motor rotates at 45–55 RPM, motor is operating properly.
   c. If not, motor is defective, replace motor.
2. Perform high-speed test as follows:
   a. Connect battery positive terminal to blue/red terminal on motor and battery negative terminal to black lead wire on motor.
   b. If motor rotates at 68–78 RPM, motor is operating properly. If not, replace motor.

Automatic Stop Action Test

1. Connect battery positive terminal to yellow/blue terminal of motor on Sidekick or yellow/black terminal of motor on Swift and battery negative terminal to black lead wire on motor, then connect a jumper between blue/white and blue terminals of motor.
2. Motor output shaft should come to a halt at a certain angular position, corresponding to starting position of wiper blade.

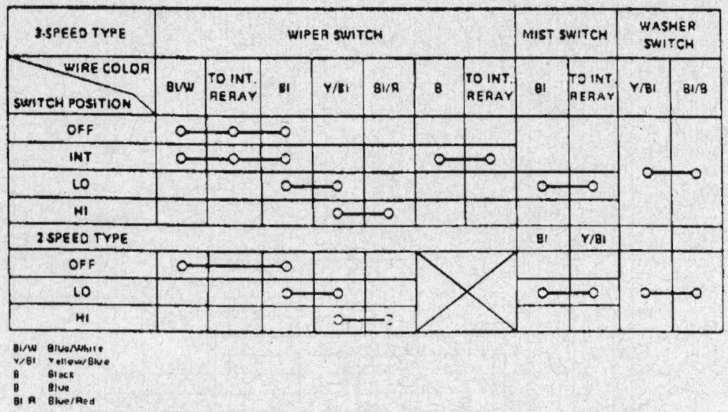
3-SPEED TYPE
WIPER SWITCH
MIST SWITCH
WASHER SWITCH
WIRE COLOR
SWITCH POSITION
Bl/W
TO INT. RERAY
Bl
Y/Bl
Bl/R
B
OFF
INT
LO
HI
2 SPEED TYPE
Bl/W Blue/White
Y/Bl Yellow/Blue
B Black
Bl Blue
Bl/R Blue/Red

SK9029100006000X

Fig. 7 Wiper/washer switch continuity (Front). Sidekick & X-90

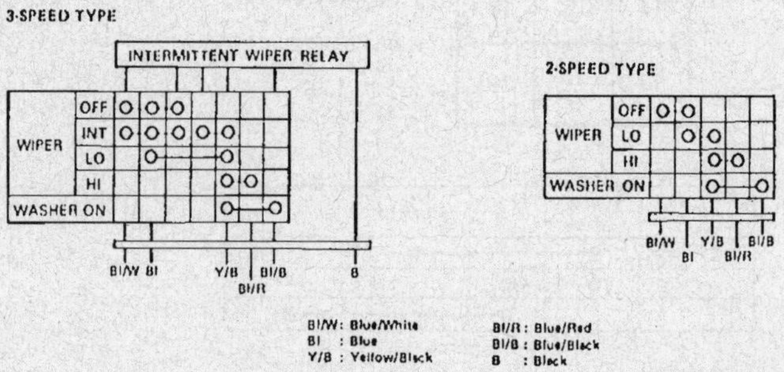
3-SPEED TYPE
INTERMITTENT WIPER RELAY
WIPER
OFF
INT
LO
HI
WASHER ON
2-SPEED TYPE
Bl/W: Blue/White
Bl : Blue
Y/B : Yellow/Black
Bl/R : Blue/Red
Bl/B : Blue/Black
B : Black

SK9029100007000X

Fig. 8 Wiper/washer switch continuity (Front). Swift

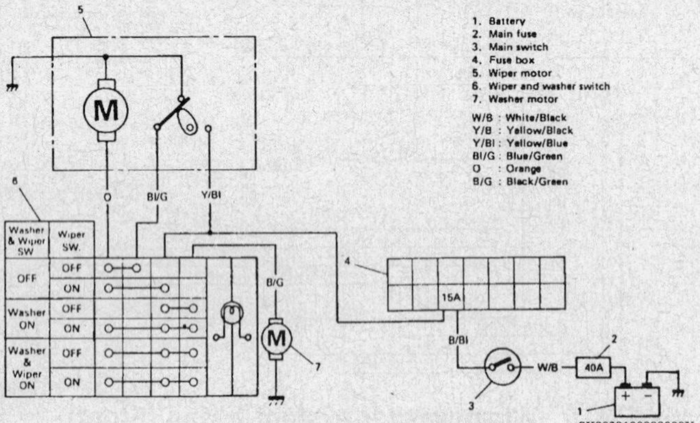
1. Battery
2. Main fuse
3. Main switch
4. Fuse box
5. Wiper motor
6. Wiper and washer switch
7. Washer motor
W/B : White/Black
Y/B : Yellow/Black
Y/Bl : Yellow/Blue
Bl/G : Blue/Green
O : Orange
B/G : Black/Green
15A
40A

SK9029100008000X

Fig. 9 Wiper/washer system wiring (Rear). Sidekick & Swift

REAR WIPER & WASHER SWITCH CONTINUITY			
O			B/G
R/Y	Y/Bl	R/G	Bl/G

B/G : Black/Green
Y/Bl : Yellow/Blue
O : Orange
R/G : Red/Green
R/Y : Red/Yellow
Bl/G : Blue/Green

CONTINUITY BETWEEN TERMINALS		
Switch Position		Terminal-to-Terminal Continuity
Washer & Wiper	Wiper	
OFF	OFF	Bl/G – O
	ON	Y/Bl – O
WASHER ON	OFF	B/G – Y/Bl
	ON	B/G – Y/Bl – O
WASHER & WIPER ON	OFF	B/G – Y/Bl – O
	ON	B/G – Y/Bl – O

R/G, an illumination light lead wire of lighting switch, produces constant R/G – R/Y continuity.

SK9029100009000X

Fig. 10 Wiper/washer switch continuity (Rear). Sidekick & Swift

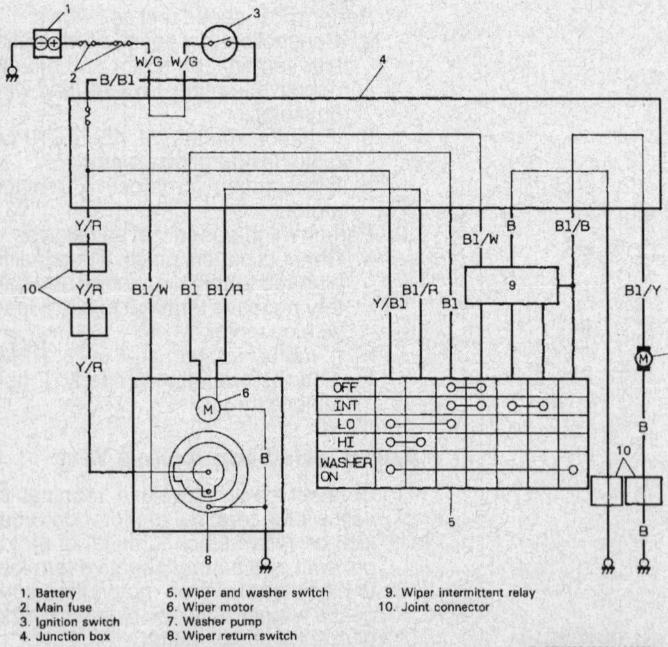
W/G
B/Bl
Y/R
Bl/W
Bl
Bl/R
Y/Bl
B
Bl/B
Bl/Y
OFF
INT
LO
HI
WASHER ON
1. Battery
2. Main fuse
3. Ignition switch
4. Junction box
5. Wiper and washer switch
6. Wiper motor
7. Washer pump
8. Wiper return switch
9. Wiper intermittent relay
10. Joint connector

SK9029500011000X

Fig. 11 Wiper/washer switch test. Esteem

3. Stop motor a number of times, and ensure motor stops in same position each time.

Brush & Commutator Test

1. Using a circuit tester, measure continuity between blue terminal and black lead wire.
2. If continuity is poor, check brush to commutator contact area.
3. If contact area is fouled, use a cloth dampened with gasoline to clean area.
4. If contact area is coarse or burnt, use a suitable sandpaper to smooth it.

Intermittent Wiper Relay Test

1. Disconnect wiper and washer switch electrical connector, then turn wiper switch to INT position.
2. Connect battery positive terminal to yellow/white terminal on Sidekick or yellow/blue terminal on Swift and battery negative terminal to black terminal.
3. If an operating sound is emitted, relay is operating properly.

REAR

Refer to wiring diagrams, **Fig. 9,** during diagnosis and testing procedures.

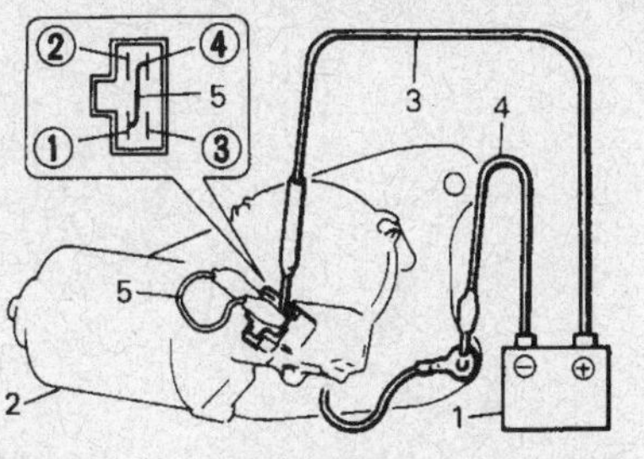
1
2
3
4
5
5

1. Battery 3. ⊕-Red lead 5. Jumper
2. Wiper motor 4. ⊖-Black lead

SK9029500012000X

Fig. 12 Automatic stop action test. Esteem

Wiper/Washer Switch Test

Refer to **Fig. 10,** while using a circuit tester to measure switch for terminal to terminal continuity.

No-Load Run Test

1. Connect battery positive terminal to orange terminal on motor and battery negative terminal to black lead wire on motor.
2. If motor rotates at 38–46 RPM, motor is operating properly. If not, replace motor.

Automatic Stop Action Test

1. Connect battery positive terminal to yellow/blue terminal of motor and battery negative terminal to black lead wire on motor, then connect a jumper between orange and blue/green terminals of motor.
2. Motor output shaft should come to a halt at a certain angular position, corresponding to starting position of wiper blade.
3. Stop motor a number of times, and ensure motor stops in same position each time.

Brush & Commutator Test

1. Using a circuit tester, measure continuity between orange terminal and black lead wire.
2. If continuity is poor, check brush to commutator contact area.
3. If contact area is fouled, use a cloth dampened with gasoline to clean area.
4. If contact area is coarse or burnt, use a suitable sandpaper to smooth it.

ESTEEM

WIPER/WASHER SWITCH TEST

Refer to **Fig. 11** while using a circuit tester to measure switch for terminal to terminal continuity.

AUTOMATIC STOP ACTION TEST

1. Connect battery positive terminal to No. 3 terminal of motor and battery negative terminal to black lead wire on motor, then connect a jumper between No. 1 and No. 4 terminals of motor, **Fig. 12.**
2. Motor output shaft should come to a halt at a certain angular position, corresponding to starting position of wiper blade.
3. Stop motor a number of times, and ensure motor stops in same position each time.

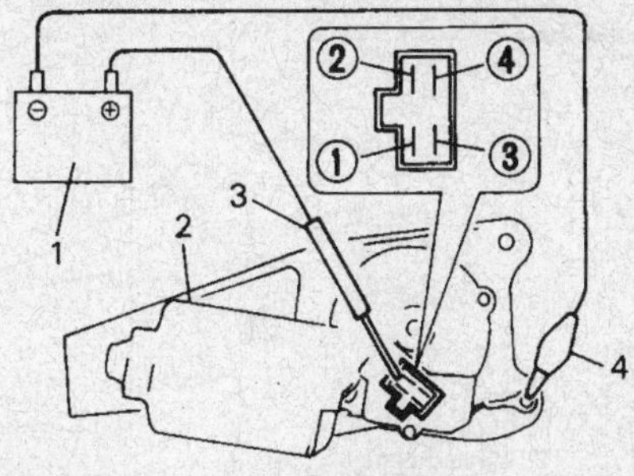
1
2
3
4

1. Battery 3. ⊕-Red lead
2. Wiper motor 4. ⊖-Black lead

SK9029500013000X

Fig. 13 Wiper motor speed test. Esteem

WIPER MOTOR SPEED TEST

1. Connect battery positive terminal to No. 1 terminal of motor and battery negative terminal to black lead wire on motor, **Fig. 13.** Ensure motor rotates at low speed of 47–57 RPM.
2. Connect battery positive terminal to No. 2 terminal of motor and battery negative terminal to black lead wire on motor. Ensure motor rotates at high speed of 70–84 RPM.

Air Bag System

INDEX

	Page No.
Air Bag System Disarming & Arming	40-97
Arming	40-97
Disarming	40-97
Collision Inspection	40-98
Component Service	40-100
Air Bag Module Disposal	40-101
Air Bag Module, Replace	40-100
Contact Coil, Replace	40-100
Forward Sensor, Replace	40-100
Sensing & Diagnostic Module (SDM), Replace	40-101
Description & Operation	40-97
System Components	40-98
Diagnosis & Testing	40-98
Precautions	40-98
Tightening Specifications	40-103

AIR BAG SYSTEM DISARMING & ARMING

Disarming

1. Ensure front wheels are pointed straight ahead, then turn ignition switch to Lock position.
2. Remove IGN and CIG & RADIO fuse from junction block No. 1.
3. Remove Connector Position Assurance (CPA) and disconnect lower steering column (yellow two-cavity) connector at base of steering column.
4. **On models with passenger air bag,** open glove box door and gently pry off passenger inflator module connector retainer.
5. Remove CPA and disconnect yellow 2-way connector from passenger inflator module.

Arming

1. Turn ignition switch to Lock position.
2. **On models with passenger air bag,** connect passenger inflator module 2-way connector and secure with CPA.
3. **On all models,** connect lower steering column yellow two-cavity connector and secure with CPA.
4. Install IGN and CIG & RADIO fuses.
5. Turn ignition switch to ACC or On positions and verify that the air bag indicator illuminates steady for approximately six seconds and then turns off.

DESCRIPTION & OPERATION

The Supplemental Restraint System (SRS) offers driver and front passenger protection in addition to seat belts by deploying steering wheel and instrument panel air bags if the vehicle is in a frontal collision of sufficient force up to 30 degrees off vehicle centerline.

System components include: Sensing and Diagnostic Module (SDM), driver's and passenger's air bag modules, contact coil assembly, SRS wiring harness and air bag

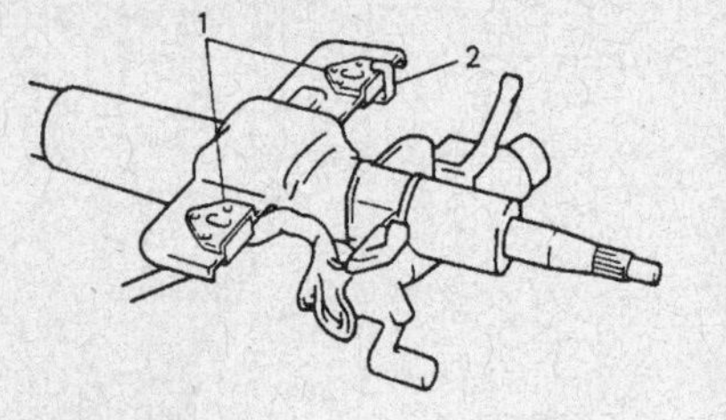
1
2
1. Capsules
2. Ripping plate
SK8019400033000X

Fig. 1 Steering column capsule & ripping plate inspection

warning lamp, and on Swift models, forward discriminating sensor.

SYSTEM COMPONENTS

SENSING & DIAGNOSTIC MODULE (SDM)

The SDM sensing device converts vehicle velocity changes into electrical signals. These signals are processed and compared to memory values. If a signal exceeds the specified value stored, an additional signal processing is performed and compared to the memory value. When two of the generated signals exceed the stored value or when one of the generated signals exceeds the stored value and the forward discriminating sensor closes, current is supplied to deploy the air bag modules.

The SDM also monitors SRS components and stores Diagnostic Trouble Codes (DTCs) if a system condition is encountered. Once a DTC has been stored, the SDM will light the air bag warning lamp.

AIR BAG MODULE

Driver's

Located in the steering wheel, the driver's air bag module consists of an inflatable bag and inflator (a canister of gas generating material and initiating device). Current passing from the SDM through the initiator ignites the inflator material, producing a gas that rapidly inflates the bag.

Passenger's

Located in the instrument panel, the passenger's air bag module consists of an inflatable bag, an inflator (a canister of gas and initiating device) and a pressure sensing device. Current passing from the SDM through the initiator generates pressure, depressing a plunger and releasing the stored gas that rapidly inflates the bag. The pressure sensing devices ensures there is adequate pressure to inflate the bag.

CONTACT COIL

Combined with the combination switch assembly on the steering column, the contact coil assembly has two deployment loop coils and a horn circuit coil. This allows steering wheel rotation while maintaining continuous deployment loop contact.

FORWARD DISCRIMINATING SENSOR

Located in the front of the vehicle, the forward discriminating sensor consists of a sensing element, open switch contacts and diagnostic resistor. If there is a severe vehicle velocity change warranting air bag deployment, the sensing element closes the contacts. Connected in parallel with the switch, the diagnostic resistor will causes a voltage drop in conjunction with the SDM resistors, allowing the SDM to monitor the forward discriminating sensor and associated circuitry.

PRECAUTIONS

1. To avoid unwanted deployment and possible personal injury, always disarm the Supplemental Restraint System (SRS) prior to performing service procedures. Refer to "Air Bag System Disarming & Arming." The Sensing and Diagnostic Module (SDM) can maintain sufficient deployment voltage for up to 10 seconds after ignition has been turned Off, air bag fuse removed or battery disconnected. Performing service before the minimum 10 second lapse may cause unwanted deployment and possible injury.
2. When handling a deployed air bag assembly, a face shield and rubber gloves should be worn. Vehicle interior and HVAC ducts should be vacuumed. If sinus or throat irritation is encountered during air bag removal, exit vehicle and breathe fresh air. If skin irritation is encountered, flush affected area with cool water. If any type of irritation continues, consult a physician. Wash hands and rinse thoroughly with water after handling a deployed air bag assembly.
3. A deployed air bag unit should be placed in a heavy duty plastic bag, sealed securely, then placed with automotive scrap.
4. **Do not use electrical test equipment such as battery or A/C powered voltmeters, Ohmmeters or any type of electrical equipment other than specified,** when troubleshooting the SRS. Do not use any non-powered probe type testers.
5. Use digital multimeter with a maximum test current of 10 mA or less at the minimum range of resistance measurement, only.
6. Do not attempt to measure air bag module resistance.
7. Discriminating sensor must always be installed with arrow mark facing vehicle front.
8. Inspect sensors for cracks, deformities or rust prior to installation and replace as necessary.
9. When handling or storing an air bag module, always position it with pad side facing upward.
10. Carry air bag module with pad facing away from body.
11. Keep air bag assembly free of oil, grease, detergents and water.

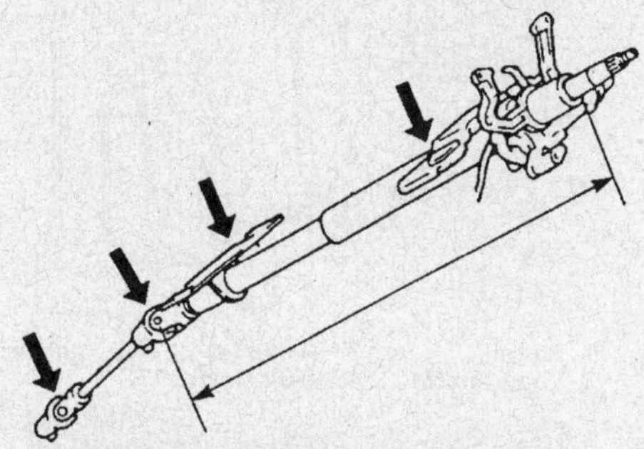
SK8019400034000X

Fig. 2 Steering column inspection

12. Do not expose air bag assembly to temperatures that exceed 200° F.
13. Do not use air bag system components from another vehicle. Always install new replacement components.
14. Inspect all components prior to installation. Do not install any that appear to have been improperly handled or stored, or that show any signs of damage.
15. When performing service procedures, do not expose sensors, wiring or other air bag system components to heat guns, welding or spray guns.
16. Do not modify steering wheel, instrument panel or any SRS component, as system performance may be hampered.
17. Do not paint air bag module to correct cosmetic flaws. It must be replaced.
18. If SRS and another vehicle system are both in need of repair, service SRS prior to any other system.
19. Always follow caution/warning label instructions on labels attached to SRS components.
20. Do not dispose of undeployed air bag modules. Modules must be deployed before being scraped.
21. Immediately after deployment, air bag modules are very hot. Wait at least 30 minutes before handling deployed modules.
22. Do not strike or jar SDM. Do not apply power to SRS when SDM is not rigidly attached to vehicle with all mounting bracket fasteners carefully tightened to specifications.
23. Do not apply power to SRS unless all components are connected or diagnostic chart specifies.
24. When using electric welding equipment, disarming SRS as outlined under "Air Bag System Disarming & Arming."

DIAGNOSIS & TESTING

Refer to MOTOR'S "Air Bag Manual" for diagnosis and testing.

COLLISION INSPECTION

On vehicles which have experienced an SRS deployment, certain air bag

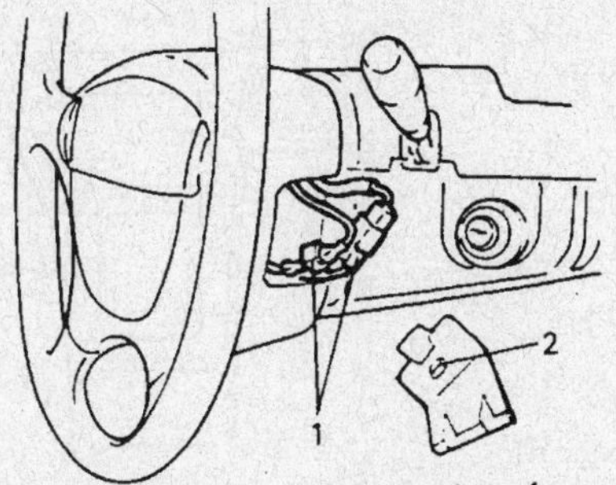
2
1
1. Horn connectors
2. Projection of cap
SK8019400035000X

Fig. 3 Steering wheel cap removal & horn disconnection

components must be replaced. To determine which components require replacement, refer to the "General Information " section located at the front of this manual.

All system components should be inspected for dents, cracks, exposure to excessive heat and other damage, even if deployment did not take place. To ensure proper SRS operation, the vehicle structure must be returned to its original configuration. When repairing the vehicle, the SRS must be disarmed as outlined under "Air Bag System Disarming & Arming." Also, when performing service procedures, do not expose components or wiring to heat guns, welding or spray guns. To ensure proper system operation on a vehicle involved in a collision, perform procedures as outlined under "Diagnosis and Testing."

The following components should be inspected whether air bag deployment has occurred or not:

1. Inspect steering column and steering shaft joints for damage as follows:
   a. Ensure the two capsules are securely attached to steering column bracket. Also inspect ripping plate (2), **Fig. 1,** for cracks. Inspect components for looseness and other damage. Replace column if any damage is discovered.
   b. Measure steering column assembly length, **Fig. 2.** Replace column if length is less than 20.79 inches.
   c. Inspect steering shaft joints for looseness, cracks and other damage and replace as necessary.
   d. Inspect steering shaft for smoothness of rotation. If, rotation is not smooth, replace steering column.
   e. Ensure steering column and shaft are not bent or cracked, or they must be replaced.
2. Inspect driver's air bag module and steering wheel as follows:
   a. If air bag has not deployment, inspect module trim cover for cracks and other damage. Also inspect air bag module for proper mounting to steering wheel. Replace air bag module or steering wheel if needed.
   b. Inspect steering wheel for cracks and damage, then replace as necessary.

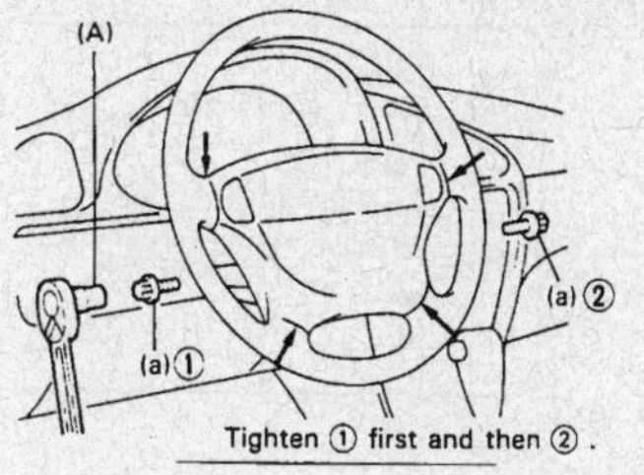
(A)
(a)①
(a)②
Tighten ① first and then ②.
SK8019400036000X

Fig. 4 Driver's air bag module replacement

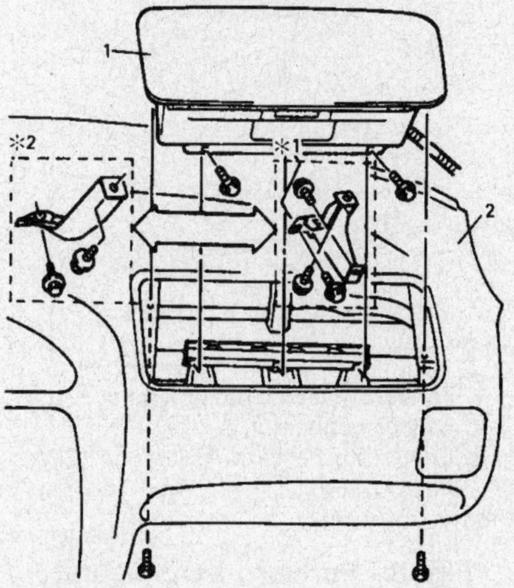
1
2
※2
※1
※1: SE series
※2: SZ series
1. Passenger air bag (inflator) module
2. Instrument panel
SK8019600050000X

Fig. 6 Passenger's air bag module replacement. Sidekick & X-90

   c. Inspect wiring harness for proper connection and damage, or replace harness in case of damage.
3. Inspect passenger's air bag and instrument panel, knee bolster and reinforcement as follows:
   a. If air bag has not deployed, inspect module trim cover for cracks, dents and other damage. Replace air bag module as necessary. Also inspect air bag module for proper mounting to instrument panel.
   b. Inspect instrument panel, knee bolster and reinforcement for distortion, cracking, bending and other damage. Repair or replace faulty components.
   c. Inspect wiring harness for proper connection and damage. If damage is present, replace wiring harness.
4. Inspect forward sensor and mounting bracket as follows:
   a. If forward sensor is in area of accident damage (an area which is bent, crushed or damaged), it should be replaced.
   b. Sensor wiring harness and connectors should be inspected for chafing and interference with other components.
   c. Inspect sensor mounting bracket

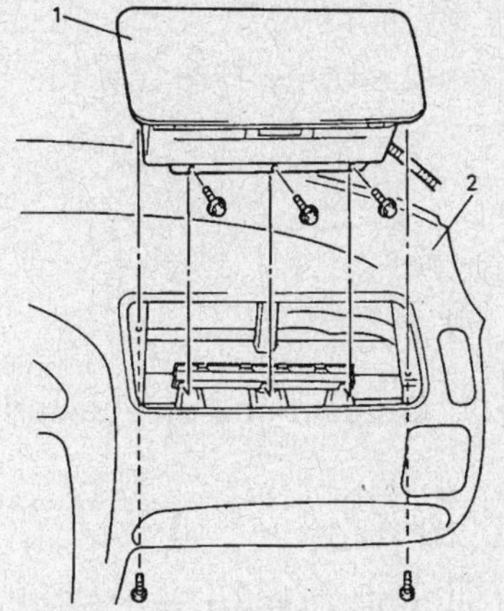
1
2
1. Passenger air bag (inflator) module
2. Instrument panel
SK8019400037000X

Fig. 5 Passenger's air bag module replacement. Swift

   for damage or rust and replace as necessary.
   d. To ensure proper forward sensor operation, the vehicle structure must be returned to its original configuration.
5. Inspect SDM and mounting bracket as follows:
   a. If SDM is in area of accident damage (an area which is bent, crushed or damaged), it should be replaced.
   b. SDM wiring harness and connectors should be inspected for chafing and interference with other components. Also inspect SDM connector and terminals for tightness.
   c. Inspect SDM and mounting bracket for dents, cracks and other damage, then replace if necessary.
   d. To ensure proper SDM operation, the vehicle structure must be returned to its original configuration.
6. Inspect contact coil and combination switch as follows:
   a. Inspect contact coil and combination switch case for damage and replace if damage is found.
   b. Inspect wiring harness and connectors for damage and tightness.
7. Inspect air bag system wiring harness as follows:
   a. Inspect harness and connectors for damage, tightness and proper routing.
   b. Inspect harness for proper mounting to harness clamps.
   c. Inspect harness grommets for proper installation and proper routing through grommets.
   d. Wiring harness and connectors should be inspected for chafing and interference with other components.
   e. Inspect wiring harness for heat damage.
   f. If wiring harness is found to be faulty, it should be replaced.
8. Inspect seat belts and mountings for

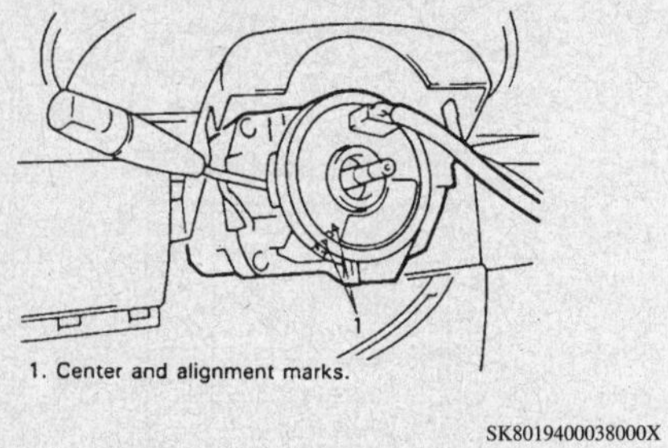
1. Center and alignment marks.
SK8019400038000X

Fig. 7 Contact coil unit centering

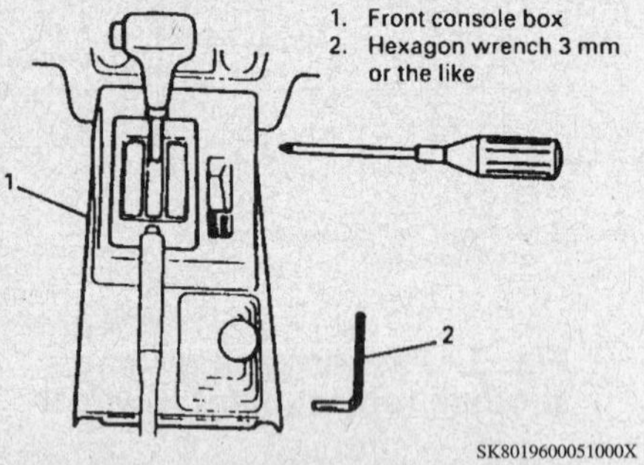
1. Front console box
2. Hexagon wrench 3 mm or the like
1
2
SK8019600051000X

Fig. 10 Rear & front console box replacement. Sidekick & X-90

damage, then repair or replace as needed.

COMPONENT SERVICE

When servicing the vehicle, the SRS should be disarmed as outlined under "Air Bag System Disarming & Arming." Also, when performing service procedures, do not expose components or wiring to heat guns, welding or spray guns.

AIR BAG MODULE, REPLACE

DRIVER'S

Removal

1. Disarm SRS as outlined under "Air Bag System Disarming & Arming."
2. Remove cap from righthand side of steering wheel, then disconnect horn connector, **Fig. 3.**
3. Using suitable Torx wrench and socket, remove bolts attaching air bag unit to steering wheel, **Fig. 4.**
4. Tilt air bag module forward and disconnect electrical connector, then remove module. Handle with cover facing away from body.

Installation

1. Position air bag module to steering wheel, then connect electrical connector. **Ensure connector properly engages module, wiring is properly routed and not caught between module and wheel. Support air bag in position: Do not allow it to hang from wiring or connector.**
2. Install attaching bolts and tighten to specifications: lefthand bolt first, then righthand bolt. Ensure clearance be-

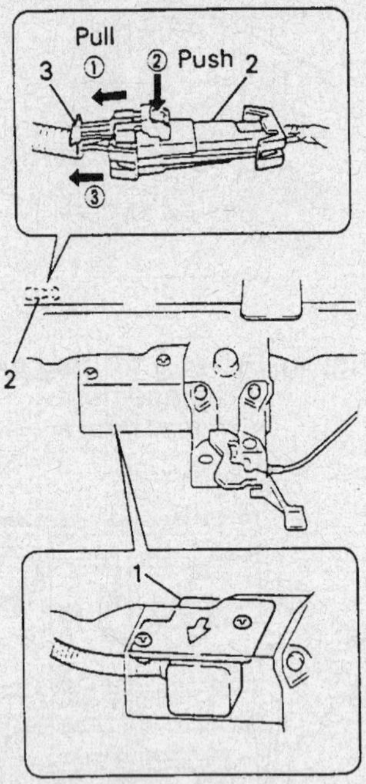
Pull
3
①
② Push
2
③
2
1

1. Forward (discriminating) sensor
2. Sensor connector
3. Connector Position Assurance (CPA)

SK8019400039000X

Fig. 8 Forward sensor unit replacement

tween air bag module and steering wheel is uniform
3. Connect horn connector and secure connector to cap projection, then install cap to steering wheel lower cover.
4. Arm SRS as outlined under "Air Bag System Disarming & Arming."

PASSENGER'S

1. Disarm SRS as outlined under "Air Bag System Disarming & Arming."
2. Remove passenger's air bag module attaching screws, then air bag module, **Figs. 5 and 6.**
3. Reverse procedure to install, tighten attaching screws to specifications and arm SRS as outlined under "Air Bag System Disarming & Arming."

CONTACT COIL, REPLACE

REMOVAL

1. Disarm SRS as outlined under "Air Bag System Disarming & Arming."
2. Place front wheels in straight–ahead position, then turn ignition to Lock and remove key.
3. Remove driver's air bag module as outlined under "Air Bag Module, Replace."
4. Remove steering wheel retaining nut.
5. Place alignment marks on wheel hub and steering shaft for assembly reference.
6. Using suitable steering wheel puller, remove wheel from column shaft.
7. Remove steering column hole cover and knee protector, then steering col-

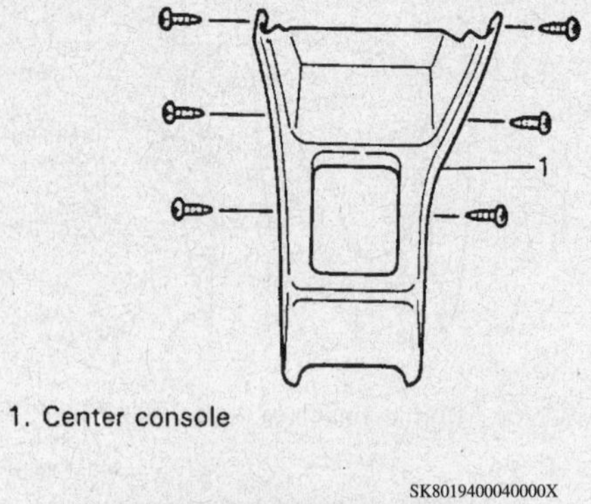
1
1. Center console
SK8019400040000X

Fig. 9 Center console replacement. Swift

umn upper and lower covers. If upper cover is difficult to remove, loosen steering shaft upper joint bolt, then steering column mounting bolts.
8. Loosen contact coil and combination switch assembly wiring harness clamps and bands, then disconnect connectors.
9. Remove contact coil and combination switch attaching screws, then remove coil and switch assembly. **Contact coil is part of the combination switch. Do not attempt to remove coil from switch.**

INSTALLATION

1. Ensure front wheels are in straight–ahead position and ignition is turned to Lock.
2. Slowly rotate contact coil counterclockwise with light force until it stops. Rotate in a clockwise direction approximately two and one half turns, aligning the centering marks, **Fig. 7.** New coil assemblies are locked in center position by a pin.
3. Position contact coil assembly and combination switch to steering column, then install attaching screws and connect all except yellow electrical connectors. On new coil assemblies, remove centering pin.
4. Install steering column upper and lower covers, then hole cover and knee protector.
5. Align steering wheel hub and shaft marks made during disassembly. Install wheel and tighten retaining nut to specifications.
6. Install driver's air bag module as outlined under "Air Bag Module, Replace."
7. Arm SRS as outlined under "Air Bag System Disarming & Arming."

FORWARD SENSOR, REPLACE

1. Disarm SRS as outlined under "Air Bag System Disarming & Arming."
2. Disconnect forward sensor electrical connector, **Fig. 8.**
3. Remove sensor attaching screws, then sensor.
4. Reverse procedure to install, noting following:
   a. Apply thread locking compound

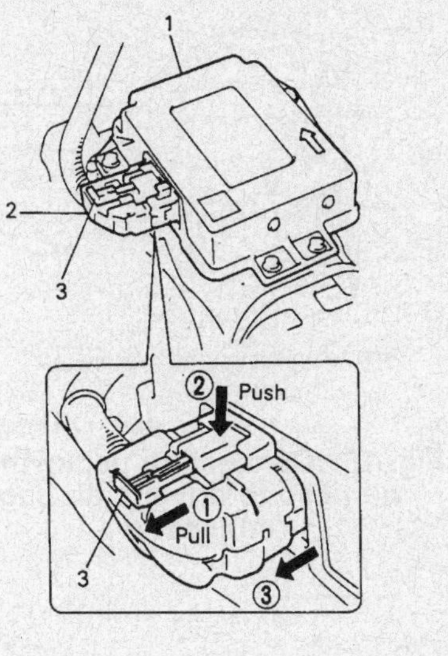
1
2
3
② Push
① Pull
③
3

1. SDM
2. SDM connector
3. Connector Position Assurance (CPA)

SK8019400041000X

Fig. 11 SDM electrical connector removal. Swift

No. 99000-32050 or equivalent, to screw threads prior to installing sensor.

b. When installing forward sensor, ensure arrow stamped on sensor faces toward vehicle front.
c. Tighten attaching screws to specifications.
d. Ensure sensor connector is properly installed and connector position assurance (CAP) is properly engaged.
e. Arm SRS as outlined under "Air Bag System Disarming & Arming."

SENSING & DIAGNOSTIC MODULE (SDM), REPLACE

Use care not to strike or jar SDM. Improper handling could result in improper SRS operation. Never connect SRS power source when the SDM is not rigidly attached to vehicle with all mounting bracket fasteners carefully tightened to specifications.

1. Disarm air bag as outlined under "Air Bag System Disarming & Arming."
2. **On Swift models,** remove center console attaching screws, then center console, **Fig. 9.**
3. **On Sidekick and X-90 models,** remove rear then front console boxes, **Fig. 10.**
4. **On all models,** remove SDM electrical connector, **Figs. 11 and 12.**
5. Remove SDM attaching screws, then SDM, **Fig. 13.**
6. Reverse procedure to install, noting following:

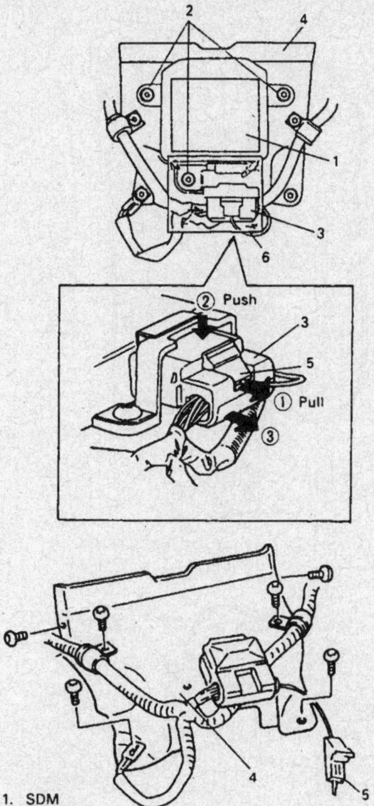
2
4
1
3
6
② Push
3
5
① Pull
③
4
5

1. SDM
2. SDM bolt
3. SDM connector
4. SDM bracket
5. Connector Position Assurance (CPA)
6. SDM cover

SK8019600052000X

Fig. 12 SDM replacement. Sidekick & X-90

a. Position SDM to mounting with arrow facing toward vehicle front
b. Apply suitable thread lock cement and tighten attaching screws to specifications.
c. Ensure SDM electrical connector properly engages, then push lock tab down. Also ensure wiring is properly routed.
d. Arm SRS as outlined under "Air Bag System Disarming & Arming."

AIR BAG MODULE DISPOSAL

When handling a deployed air bag assembly, safety glasses and rubber gloves should be worn. Vehicle interior and HVAC ducts should be vacuumed. If sinus or throat irritation is encountered during air bag removal, exit vehicle and breathe fresh air. If skin irritation is encountered, flush affected area with cool water. If sinus, throat, skin or any other type of irritation continues, consult a physician. Wash hands and rinse thoroughly with water after handling a deployed air bag assembly.

A deployed air bag unit should be removed as outlined under "Air Bag Module, Replace." After unit has been removed, it should be placed in a heavy duty plastic bag and sealed securely, then placed with automotive scrap.

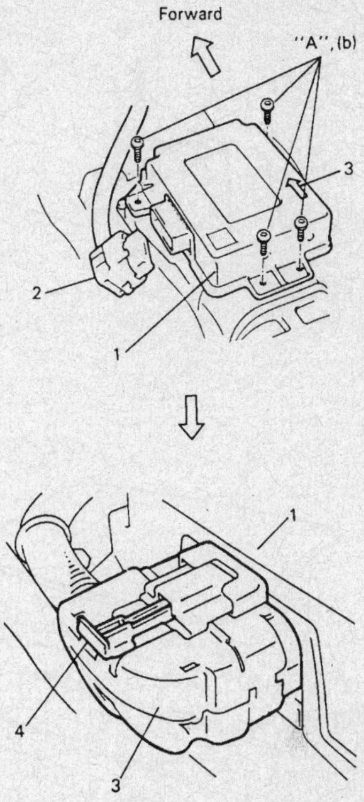
Forward
"A", (b)
3
2
1
1
4
3

1. SDM
2. SDM connector
3. Arrow
4. CPA

SK8019400042000X

Fig. 13 SDM replacement. Swift

All undeployed air bag units must be deployed prior to disposal.

OUTSIDE VEHICLE DEPLOYMENT

1. Disarm SRS as outlined under "Air Bag System Disarming & Arming."
2. Remove air bag module(s) as outlined under "Air Bag Module, Replace."
3. Connect special air bag deployment harness tool No. 09932-75030, or equivalent. Plug harness leads together.
4. If deploying a driver's air bag module, place air bag with cover side facing upward, in a clear, well ventilated outdoor location free of flammable objects. Area should be clear for at least six feet in all directions.
5. If deploying a passengers air bag module, proceed as follows:
   a. Install air bag to special deployment adapter tool No. 09932-75040, or equivalent, with cover side facing upward, **Fig. 14.**
   b. Position air bag and adapter on ground. This area should be clear and well ventilated for at least six feet in all directions, and free of people, animals and any flammable objects.
   c. Fill deployment adapter plastic reservoir with water.
   d. Ensure air bag unit is securely mounted to adapter.
6. Stretch deployment harness from

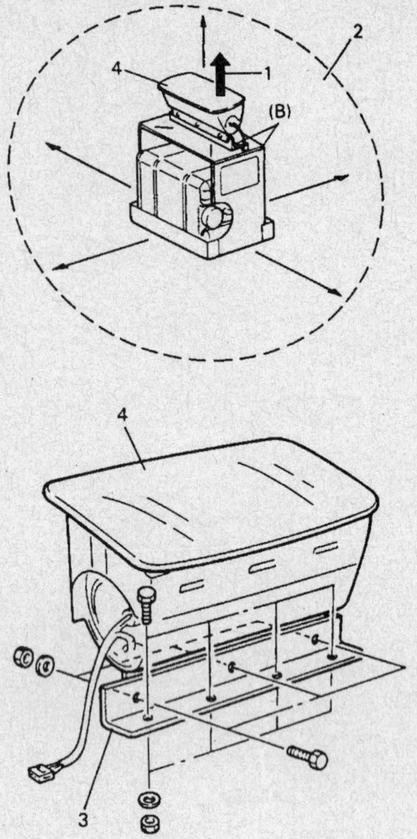

1
2
4
(B)
4
3

1. Trim cover must face up
2. 185 cm (6 feet) of clearance
3. Mounting attachment
4. Bag opening side

SK8019400043000X

Fig. 14 Mounting passenger's air bag unit to deployment adapter

module out to its full length, approximately 33 ft.

7. Position a fully charged 12 volt battery near end of harness opposite air bag unit. **Do not connect battery to deployment harness at this time.**
8. Connect deployment harness to air bag module electrical connector.
9. Ensure no people, animals or objects are in area of air bag unit.
10. Contact one plug lead to battery positive terminal and other lead to negative terminal, then air bag module should deploy, **Fig. 15.** Module will jump approximately one foot into air.
11. No poisonous gas is produced upon deployment. However, do not inhale gas since it could irritate throat and can cause choking.
12. Allow at least 30 minutes after deployment for air bag components to cool.
13. Do not attempt to disassemble air bag: it cannot be used again.
14. If air bag did not deploy, consult Suzuki for disposal procedures.

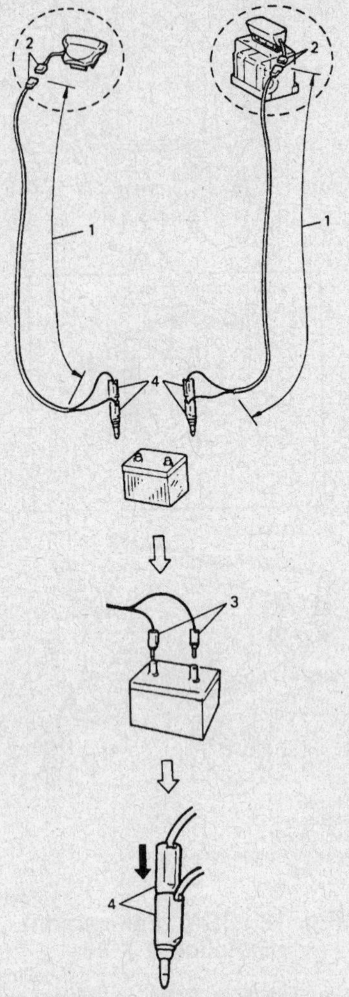

2
2
1
1
4
3
4

1. Stretch deployment harness to full length 10 m (33 ft).
2. Connect connectors.
3. Connect one banana plug to positive terminal of 12V vehicle battery and then the other to negative terminal to immediately deploy.
4. Short the two deployment harness leads.

SK8019400044000X

Fig. 15 Air bag unit deployment outside vehicle

IN VEHICLE DEPLOYMENT

Before scrapping a vehicle equipped with air bag(s), air bag module(s) must be deployed.

1. Turn ignition to Lock position and disconnect battery ground cable.
2. Remove all objects from seats and instrument panel, then open vehicle windows.
3. If deploying driver's air bag module, remove cap from lefthand side of steering wheel and disconnect electrical connector.
4. If deploying passenger's air bag module, open glove compartment, push inward on lefthand and righthand side stoppers and remove compartment, then disconnect electrical connector.
5. Ensure air bag modules are firmly

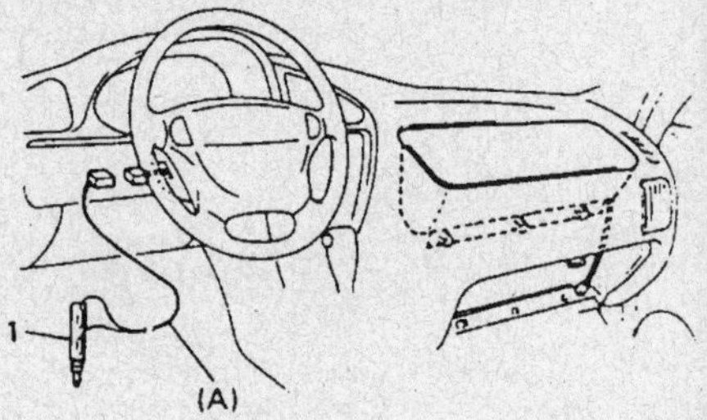

1
(A)

1. Short deployment harness leads

SK8019400045000X

Fig. 16 Connecting deployment harness to driver's air bag connector

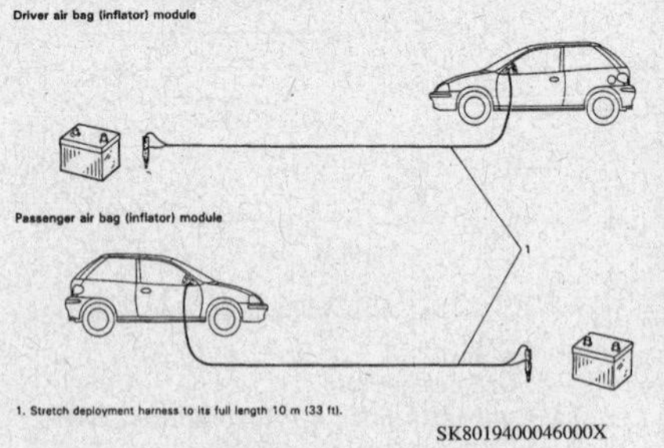

Driver air bag (inflator) module
Passenger air bag (inflator) module
1
1. Stretch deployment harness to its full length 10 m (33 ft).

SK8019400046000X

Fig. 17 In vehicle air bag module deployment

mounted to vehicle.

6. Connect special air bag deployment harness tool No. 09932-75030, or equivalent, and plug harness leads together.
7. Stretch deployment harness from air bag module out full length, approximately 33 ft.
8. Position a fully charged 12 volt battery near end of harness opposite air bag module. **Do not connect battery to deployment harness at this time.**
9. Connect deployment harness to air bag module electrical connector, **Fig. 16.**
10. Cover windshield and front window openings with drop cloth, then ensure no people, animals or objects are in area of vehicle.
11. Separate two deployment harness plug leads.
12. Deploy air bag module by contacting one plug lead to battery positive terminal and other lead to negative terminal, **Fig. 17.**
13. **When deploying air bag, ensure area is clear.** No poisonous gas is produced upon deployment. However, do not inhale gas since it could irritate throat and can cause choking.
14. Allow at least 30 minutes after deployment for air bag components to cool.
15. Do not attempt to disassemble air bags: they cannot be used again.
16. If air bags did not deploy, consult Suzuki for disposal procedures.

TIGHTENING SPECIFICATIONS

Component	Torque/Ft. Lbs.
SWIFT	
Air Bag Module Mounting Bolts, Driver's	13.5-20①
Air Bag Module Mounting Lower Bolts, Passenger's	36-60②
Air Bag Module Mounting Upper Bolts, Passenger's	13.5-19.5
Forward Sensor Attaching Screws	36-60②
SDM Bolts	36-60②
Steering Wheel Nut	18.5-28.5
SIDEKICK & X-90	
Air Bag Module Mounting Bolts, Driver's	17①
Air Bag Module Mounting Lower Bolts, Passenger's	48②
Air Bag Module Mounting Upper Bolts, Passenger's	16.5
SDM Bolts	48②
Steering Wheel Nut	23.5

① — Tighten lefthand first, then righthand.
② — Inch lbs.

Dash Panel Service

NOTE: Refer To "Dash Gauges" Section For Related Information.

INDEX

Page No.	Page No.	Page No.
Dash Panel, Replace 40-103	Samurai 40-103	Swift 40-104
Esteem 40-104	Sidekick & X-90 40-103	

DASH PANEL

REPLACE

SAMURAI

1. Remove horn pad, then the steering wheel using a suitable puller.
2. Remove radio case stay screws and pull out radio case with radio and cigarette lighter, then disconnect radio and cigarette lighter electrical connectors.
3. Remove ashtray, then the ashtray plate attaching screws.
4. Disconnect front hood opening cable from lock assembly.
5. Loosen glove compartment stay screw and hood opening cable locknut from backside of glove compartment cover.
6. Disconnect electrical connectors and control cables from heater control panel.
7. Pull out heater control knobs and plate, then loosen heater lever case screws.
8. Disconnect electrical connectors from speedometer and instrument panel.
9. Disconnect speedometer cable.
10. Release wire harness clamps installed to instrument panel.
11. Loosen screws securing instrument panel, then remove instrument panel.
12. Reverse procedure to install.

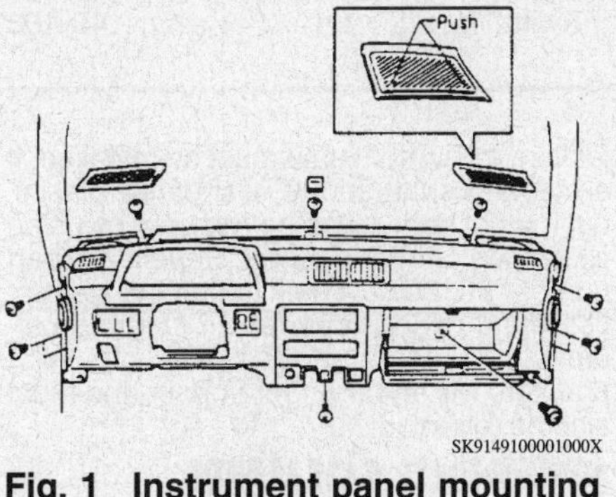

Push
SK9149100001000X

Fig. 1 Instrument panel mounting bolts. Swift

SIDEKICK & X-90

1. Disconnect battery ground cable.
2. Remove two screws from front of console, then two back lockpins from rear of console.
3. Holding shifter boot inward, remove housing and console.
4. Remove steering column covers.
5. Remove four attaching screws from instrument cluster front shroud, then the shroud.
6. Remove instrument cluster attaching screws and pull cluster rearward.
7. Remove speedometer, then disconnect cluster wiring harness and remove cluster.
8. Remove three inspection screw covers, then the three upper housing attaching bolts.
9. Remove three lower housing attaching bolts located on the driver's side of the instrument panel.
10. Remove center support dash mount.
11. Open glove compartment and remove two glove compartment lockpins, then lift glove compartment out of the instrument panel.
12. Remove three instrument panel attaching screws from lower RH side of the instrument panel.
13. Remove handle bar from RH side of the instrument panel.
14. Remove hood release lever attaching bolt.
15. Disconnect center mounting bracket from the radio and ashtray.
16. Disconnect dash panel wiring harness

and remove instrument panel.
17. Reverse procedure to install.

SWIFT

1. Disconnect battery ground cable, then remove console box.
2. Disconnect all wires and cables from heater and blower units.
3. Remove steering wheel, steering column and steering joint upper bolt.
4. Disconnect speedometer cable, then remove speedometer assembly.
5. Remove both front speaker garnishes and center cover.
6. Remove instrument panel member mounting bolts, **Fig. 1.**
7. Remove instrument panel and panel member as an assembly.
8. Reverse procedure to install.

ESTEEM

1. Disconnect battery ground cable, then remove console box and front extension.

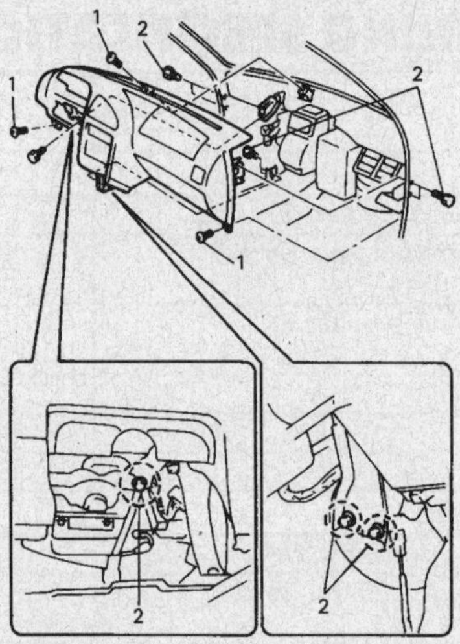
1
2
2
1
1
2
2

1. Mounting screw
2. Mounting bolt

SK9149500002000X

Fig. 2 Instrument panel mounting bolts. Esteem

2. Disconnect all wires and cables from heater and blower units.
3. Remove steering wheel, steering column and steering joint upper bolt.
4. Remove engine control module (ECM).
5. Remove engine hood opener.
6. Remove front pillar trim on both sides.
7. Remove all electrical connectors to dash panel.
8. Remove body ground at center of floor.
9. Remove instrument panel mounting bolts, **Fig. 2,** then instrument panel.
10. Reverse procedure to install.

Steering Columns

NOTE: On Air Bag Equipped Models, Refer To "Air Bag System Precautions" Located In The Front Of This Manual For System Disarming & Arming Procedures.

INDEX

Page No.

Precautions 40-104
Air Bag Systems 40-104
Service 40-104
Steering Column Damage 40-104
Steering Column, Replace 40-104
Esteem 40-105
Samurai 40-104
Sidekick & X-90 40-105
Swift 40-105
Swift 40-105
Steering Column Service 40-106
SIR Coil & Turn Signal & Dimmer Switch 40-106
Steering Column Lock 40-106

PRECAUTIONS

AIR BAG SYSTEMS

Refer to "Air Bag System Precautions" in the front of this manual for system disarming and arming procedures.

SERVICE

It is important that only the specified screws, bolts and nuts be used during the mandatory assembling sequence and torqued to specifications to ensure proper breakaway action of column under impact. Avoid using excessively long bolts as they may prevent a portion of the steering column from collapsing under impact.

When removing or installing, steering wheel, ignition switch or lock, turn signal switch, adjusting transmission linkage, or installing and adjusting neutral-start or back-up light switch, refer to appropriate car chapter.

If a shift tube shows a sheared plastic injection, a new shift tube must be installed. If a steering shaft shows a sheared plastic, but it is not bent, it can be repaired by using a Service Steering Shaft Repair Kit part number 7810077. The kit contains instructions and dimensions for all steering columns. On some models, the attaching brackets will shear under impact and must also be replaced.

STEERING COLUMN DAMAGE

When the steering column is removed from the vehicle, it is extremely susceptible to damage. Dropping the steering column assembly on its end could collapse the steering shaft assembly or loosen plastic injections that keep the steering column assembly rigid. Leaning on the steering column assembly could cause the jacket to bend or deform. Any of these conditions could impair the steering column assembly's collapsible design. If the steering wheel must be removed, use only the specified steering wheel puller and steering wheel puller bolts. Never hammer on the end of the shaft.

STEERING COLUMN

REPLACE

SAMURAI

1. Remove steering wheel, then the lower steering cover, **Fig. 1.**
2. Remove instrument lower panel, then loosen steering column mounting screws and nuts.
3. Remove upper cover.
4. Remove combination switch electrical connectors, then the combination switch.
5. Remove bolt joining steering shafts in engine compartment.
6. Remove steering column assembly.
7. Reverse procedure to install.

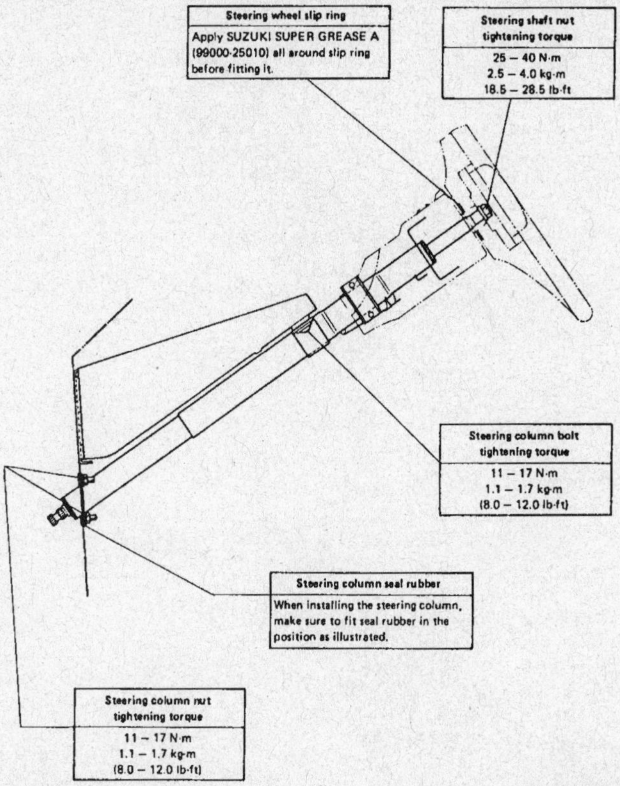
Steering wheel slip ring
Apply SUZUKI SUPER GREASE A (99000-25010) all around slip ring before fitting it.
Steering shaft nut tightening torque
25 – 40 N·m
2.5 – 4.0 kg-m
18.5 – 28.5 lb-ft
Steering column bolt tightening torque
11 – 17 N·m
1.1 – 1.7 kg-m
(8.0 – 12.0 lb-ft)
Steering column seal rubber
When installing the steering column, make sure to fit seal rubber in the position as illustrated.
Steering column nut tightening torque
11 – 17 N·m
1.1 – 1.7 kg-m
(8.0 – 12.0 lb-ft)

SK6049100001000X

Fig. 1 Exploded view of steering column. Samurai

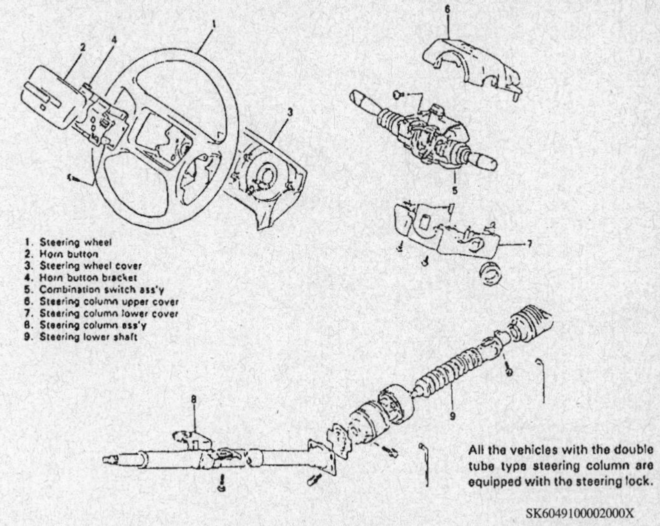
1. Steering wheel
2. Horn button
3. Steering wheel cover
4. Horn button bracket
5. Combination switch ass'y
6. Steering column upper cover
7. Steering column lower cover
8. Steering column ass'y
9. Steering lower shaft
All the vehicles with the double tube type steering column are equipped with the steering lock.

SK6049100002000X

Fig. 2 Exploded view of steering column. 1993–95 Sidekick less SIR

SIDEKICK & X-90

1993-95

1. Disconnect battery ground cable, then remove steering wheel, **Fig. 2.**
2. Remove turn signal/dimmer switch, then disconnect ignition switch electrical connectors.
3. **On automatic transmission models,** disconnect brake interlock cable from ignition switch assembly and clamp.
4. **On all models,** disconnect steering joint by removing joint bolt.
5. Remove steering column mounting bolts, then the steering column assembly.
6. Reverse procedure to install.

1996

1. Disconnect battery ground cable, then, ensure SIR/air bag system is disarmed.
2. Remove steering wheel and contact coil, **Fig. 3.**
3. Remove hole cover and knee bolster panel.
4. Disconnect electrical connectors for ignition switch, contact coil and combination switch.
5. Disconnect steering joint bolt and steering column bolts.
6. **On models with automatic transmission,** disconnect shift interlock cable from ignition switch assembly and clamp.
7. **On all models,** remove steering column assembly.
8. Reverse procedure to install, noting the following:
   a. **Torque** interlock cable screw to 19 inch lbs.
   b. **Torque** steering column lower mounting nuts, then upper mounting nuts to 17 ft. lbs.
   c. **Torque** steering shaft upper joint to 18 ft. lbs.

SWIFT

1. Disconnect battery ground cable, then remove steering wheel, **Fig. 4.**
2. Remove combination switch, then disconnect ignition switch electrical connectors.
3. Remove floor mat at foot of steering shaft, then the steering joint cover.
4. **On automatic transmission models,** remove back drive cable from steering column assembly.
5. **On all models,** disconnect steering joint by removing joint bolt.
6. Remove steering column mounting bolts, then the steering column assembly.
7. Reverse procedure to install.

SWIFT

Less SIR

Refer to **Figs. 5 through 8** for removal and installation procedures.

With SIR

Wheels must be in a straight forward position and the key must be in the Lock position when removing or installing column to ensure proper alignment of components during installation.

Care must be taken when handling column with a live inflator module. Never point bag deploy surface toward you, and never stand column on steering wheel. Accidental deployment in these positions may cause injury. Always face bag deploy surface toward open space to allow for unrestricted expansion.

1. Remove steering wheel as follows:
   a. Remove four screw from rear of steering wheel, then remove inflator module from steering wheel.
   b. Remove steering attaching nut.
   c. Attach wheel puller tool Nos. J 8433-1 and J 8433-3, or equivalents, **Fig. 9,** then remove steering wheel.
2. Remove steering shaft trim panel.
3. Remove lower column steering trim panel attaching screws, then trim panel.
4. Remove lower column reinforcement plate attaching screws, then plate.
5. Disconnect steering column electrical connectors.
6. **On models with automatic transmissions,** remove transaxle shift interlock cable from ignition switch.
7. **On all models,** remove column to steering shaft joint pinch bolt, **Fig. 10.**
8. Remove two upper and lower column attaching bolts, then column.
9. Measure column as shown in **Fig. 11.** If measurement is less than 20.96 inches, replace column.
10. Reverse procedure to install, noting the following:
    a. **Torque** upper and lower steering column attaching bolts to 124 inch lbs.
    b. **Torque** steering column to steering shaft pinch bolt to 18 ft. lbs.

ESTEEM

1. Disconnect battery ground cable, then, ensure SIR/air bag system is disarmed.
2. Remove steering wheel, contact coil and combination switch, **Fig. 12.**

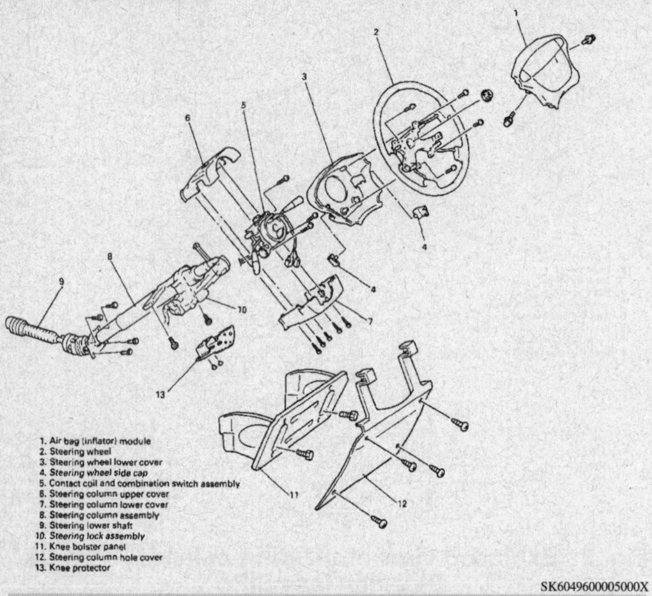
1. Air bag (inflator) module
2. Steering wheel
3. Steering wheel lower cover
4. Steering wheel side cap
5. Contact coil and combination switch assembly
6. Steering column upper cover
7. Steering column lower cover
8. Steering column assembly
9. Steering lower shaft
10. Steering lock assembly
11. Knee bolster panel
12. Steering column hole cover
13. Knee protector
SK6049600005000X

Fig. 3 Exploded view of steering column. 1996 Sidekick & X-90 w/SIR

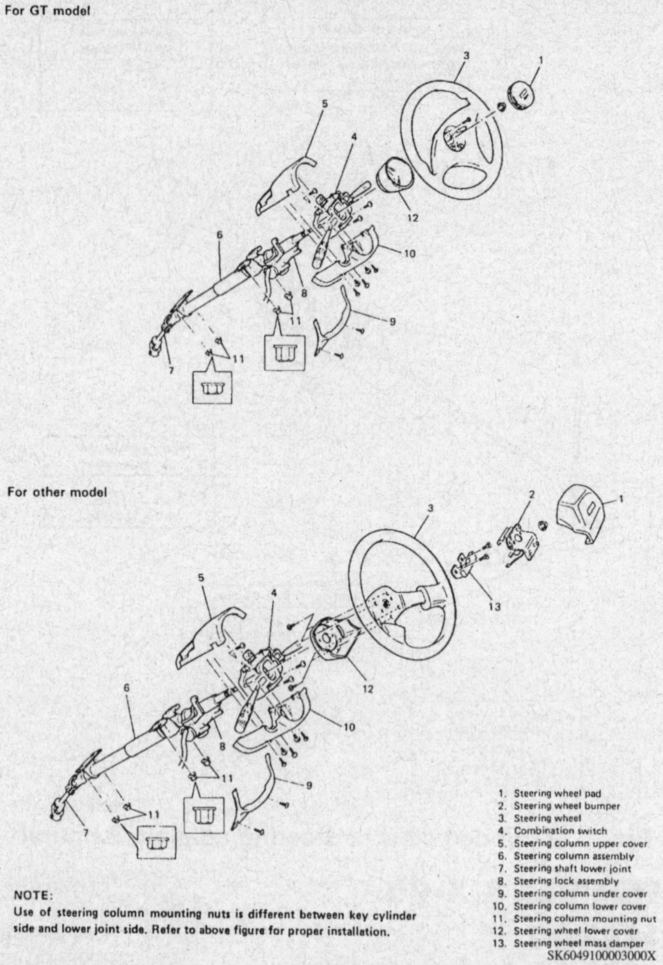
For GT model
For other model
NOTE:
Use of steering column mounting nuts is different between key cylinder side and lower joint side. Refer to above figure for proper installation.
1. Steering wheel pad
2. Steering wheel bumper
3. Steering wheel
4. Combination switch
5. Steering column upper cover
6. Steering column assembly
7. Steering shaft lower joint
8. Steering lock assembly
9. Steering column under cover
10. Steering column lower cover
11. Steering column mounting nut
12. Steering wheel lower cover
13. Steering wheel mass damper
SK6049100003000X

Fig. 4 Exploded view of steering column. Swift

3. Remove hole cover and knee bolster panel.
4. Remove steering column harness from column.
5. Disconnect electrical connectors
6. Remove steering joint upper cover, then upper joint bolt.
7. Remove steering column mounting nuts.
8. **On models with automatic transmission,** disconnect shift interlock cable from ignition switch with switch positioned at ACC. After disconnecting, turn lock switch to LOCK position.
9. **On all models,** remove steering column.
10. Reverse procedure to install, noting the following:
    a. **Torque** steering column upper mounting nuts, then lower mounting nuts to 10.5 ft. lbs.
    b. **Torque** steering shaft upper joint to 18 ft. lbs.

STEERING COLUMN SERVICE

SIR COIL & TURN SIGNAL & DIMMER SWITCH

Remove steering wheel as outlined in "Steering Column, Replace" in this section.

1. Remove six screws retaining upper and lower steering column covers, then remove column covers.
2. Remove two electrical connectors from fuse box, one from the SIR harness, and one from the main wiring harness, **Fig. 13.**
3. Remove SIR coil and turn signal/ dimmer switch attaching screws, then switch assembly.
4. Reverse procedure to install, noting the following:
    a. Ensure SIR coil is centered. If not position wheels of vehicle in the straightforward position.
    b. Check position of SIR coil, **Fig. 14.**
    c. If Neutral mark is at the alignment mark the coil is centered and no adjustment is necessary.
    d. If R1 mark is close to the alignment mark coil is one rotation off to the right from its center state and needs to be adjusted on turn counterclockwise. The R2 mark indicates that the coil is two rotations off.
    e. If L1 mark is close to the alignment mark coil is one rotation off to the left from its center state and needs to be adjusted on turn clockwise. The L2 mark indicates that the coil is two rotations off.
    f. To adjust remove SIR coil, hold coil lead at its base and turn in the direction specified in steps d and e. Then replace SIR coil.

STEERING COLUMN LOCK

Remove steering wheel as outlined in "Steering Column, Replace" in this section.

1. Remove ignition switch attaching screw, then switch.
2. Remove ignition key warning switch attaching screws, then switch.
3. Loosen and remove two steering column lock retaining bolts using a center punch, **Fig. 15. When using center punch do not damage aluminum parts of lock assembly.**
4. Turn ignition key to On or ACC position, then remove lock assembly from steering column.
5. Reverse procedure to install.

NOTICE:
Once the steering column is removed from the car, the column is extremely susceptible to damage. Dropping the column assembly on its end could collapse the steering shaft or loosen the plastic injections which maintain column length. Leaning on the column assembly could cause the jacket to bend or deform. Any of the above damage could impair the column's collapsible design. If it is necessary to remove the steering wheel, use standard wheel puller. Under no condition should the end of the shaft be hammered upon as hammering could loosen the plastic injections which maintain column length.

REMOVAL

1) Disconnect negative battery cable.
2) Remove steering wheel.
3) Remove turn signal/dimmer switch.
4) Disconnect lead wires from ignition and ignition key warning switch electrical connector at junction/fusebox
5) Pull off floor mat at the foot of steering shaft and remove steering joint cover.

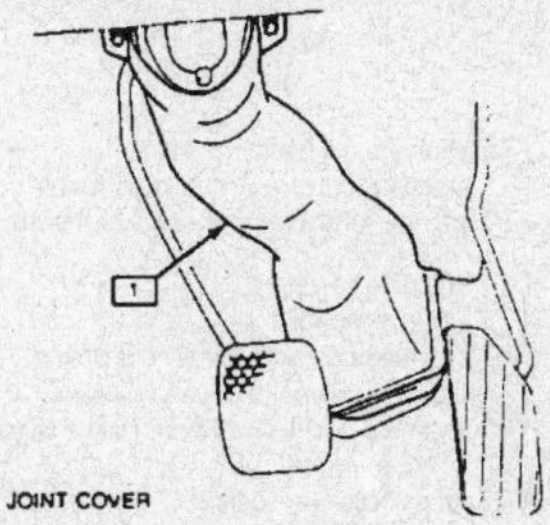
1
1 JOINT COVER

6) Remove steering shaft joint upper side bolt.

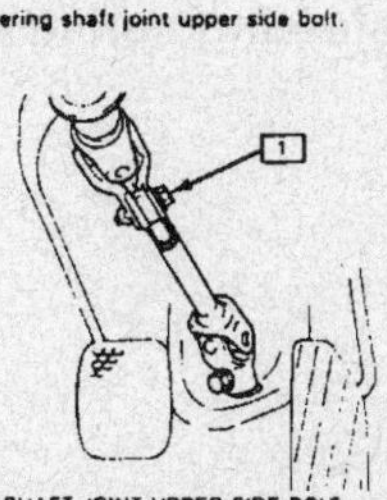
1
1 STEERING SHAFT JOINT UPPER SIDE BOLT

7) Remove steering column mount nuts.

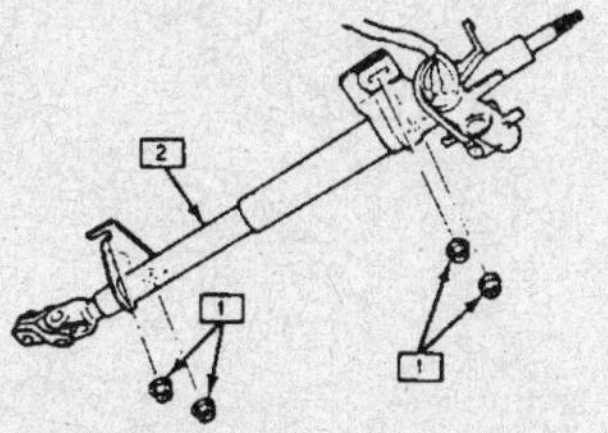
2
1
1
1 STEERING COLUMN MOUNTING NUTS
2 STEERING COLUMN

8) Remove steering column assembly.

NOTICE: Do not disassemble steering column assembly into column and shaft. If steering column or shaft is found defective, replace as an assembly.

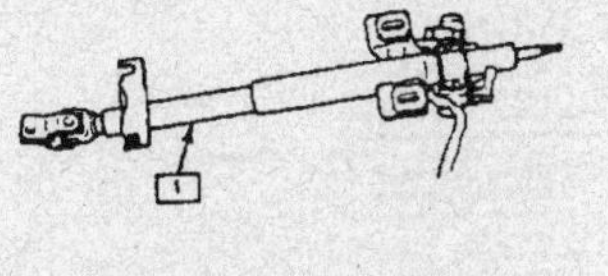
1
1 STEERING COLUMN ASSEMBLY

GC6049100058000X

Fig. 5 Steering column removal. Swift less SIR

INSTALLATION

1) Align flat part "A" of lower joint shaft with bolt hole "B" of upper side joint as shown. Then insert upper side joint into lower joint shaft.

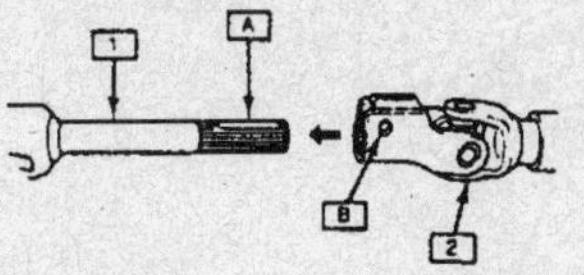
1
A
B
2
1 LOWER JOINT
2 UPPER JOINT

2) Install steering column assembly to lower and upper brackets. Torque steering column nuts to specifications as given below:
   - Tighten nuts (a) to 14 N·m (10 lb.ft.).
   - Tighten nuts (b) to 14 N·m (10 lb.ft.).

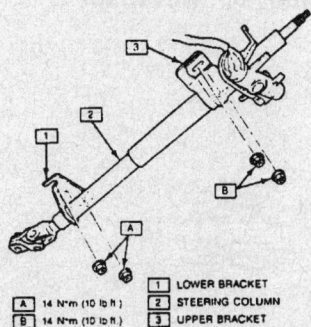

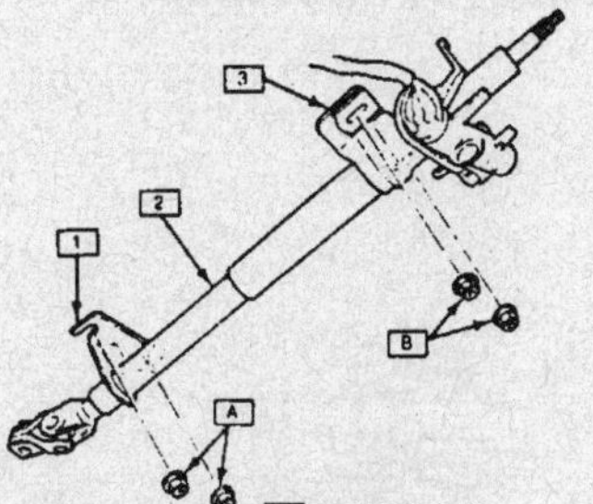
3
2
1
B
A
A 14 N·m (10 lb ft)
B 14 N·m (10 lb ft)
1 LOWER BRACKET
2 STEERING COLUMN
3 UPPER BRACKET

3) Install bolt to steering shaft upper joint and tighten to specified torque.

NOTICE: After tightening column nuts, steering shaft joint upper side bolt should be tightened.

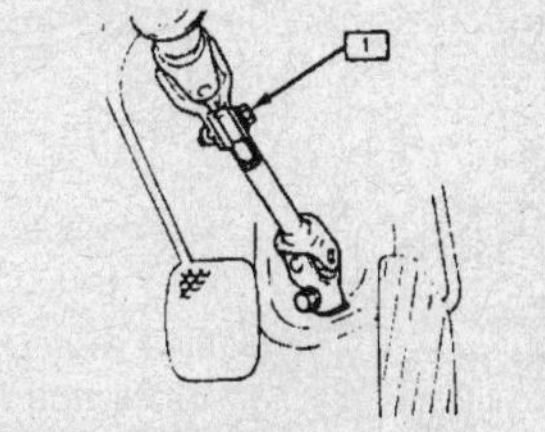
1
1 STEERING SHAFT JOINT UPPER SIDE BOLT
25 N·m (18 lb ft)

4) Install steering joint cover and put floor mat back as it was originally.
5) Connect lead wires from ignition switch and ignition key warning switch at connector.
6) Install turn signal/dimmer switch. Refer to steps 1 through 4 under TURN SIGNAL/DIMMER SWITCH INSTALLATION.
7) Install steering wheel and steering pad. Refer to STEERING WHEEL INSTALLATION.

GC6049100059000X

Fig. 6 Steering column installation. Swift less SIR

REMOVAL

1) Disconnect negative battery cable.
2) Pull steering pad off and disconnect ground wire from inside of steering pad.
3) Remove steering wheel damper attaching screws and then steering wheel damper.
4) Remove steering shaft nut.
5) Scribe a line on the steering wheel and shaft to use as guide during reinstallation.
6) Remove steering wheel with special tool (A).

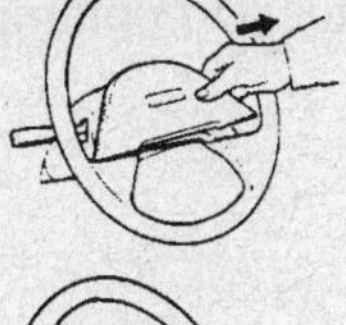

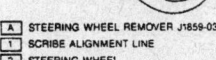

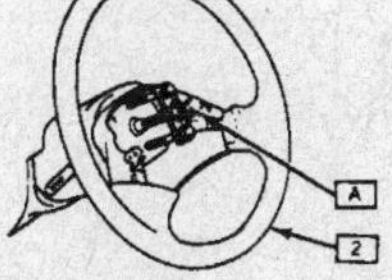
A
2
A STEERING WHEEL REMOVER J1859-03
1 SCRIBE ALIGNMENT LINE
2 STEERING WHEEL

INSTALLATION

1) Install steering wheel onto shaft, using the alignment marks.
2) Install steering shaft nut and torque to 33 N·m (24.0 lb.ft.) as shown below.
3) Install steering wheel damper and damper attaching screws.

NOTICE: When installing steering wheel damper, be sure ground wire runs through center of damper and is not pinched underneath it.

4) Connect ground wire to inside of steering pad and press steering pad on.
5) Connect negative battery cable.

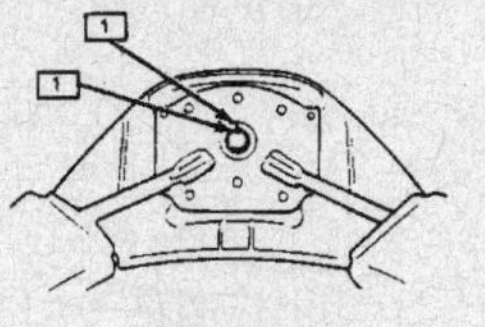
1
1

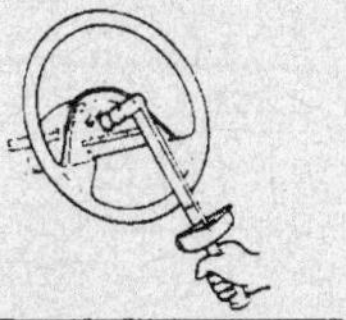

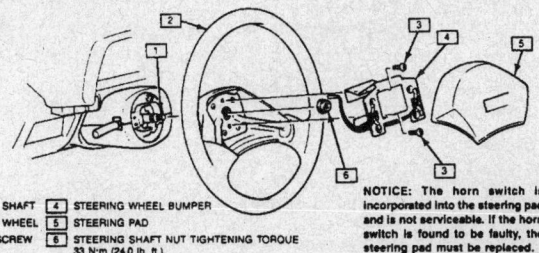

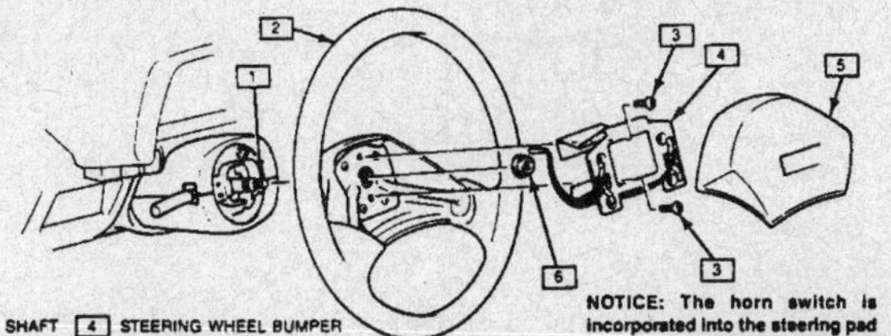
2
1
3
4
5
6
3
1 STEERING SHAFT
2 STEERING WHEEL
3 BUMPER SCREW
4 STEERING WHEEL BUMPER
5 STEERING PAD
6 STEERING SHAFT NUT TIGHTENING TORQUE 33 N·m (24.0 lb. ft.)

NOTICE: The horn switch is incorporated into the steering pad and is not serviceable. If the horn switch is found to be faulty, the steering pad must be replaced.

GC6049100060000X

Fig. 7 Steering wheel replacement. Swift less SIR

REMOVAL

1) Disconnect negative battery cable.
2) Before removing this switch, remove steering wheel. Refer to STEERING WHEEL REMOVAL.
3) Remove column covers (under and lower).

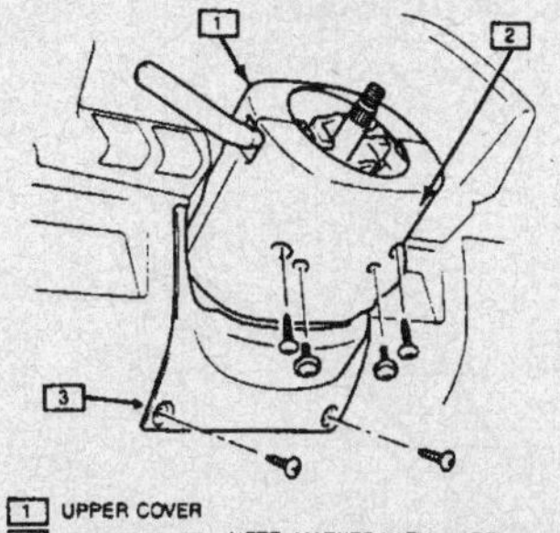
1
2
3
1 UPPER COVER
2 LOWER COVER
3 UNDER COVER
NOTE: MARKED WITH * ARE STANDARD SCREWS. ALL OTHERS ARE TAPPING SCREWS.

4) Disconnect lead wire from turn signal/dimmer switch electrical connector.
5) Loosen wire bands.
6) Remove three turn signal/dimmer switch attaching screws and the switch from the steering column shaft.

INSTALLATION

1) Install turn signal/dimmer switch and three attaching screws to the steering column shaft.
2) Connect lead wire to turn signal/dimmer switch electrical connector.
3) Tighten wire bands.
4) Install column lower and under covers.
5) Install steering wheel and steering pad. Refer to STEERING WHEEL INSTALLATION.

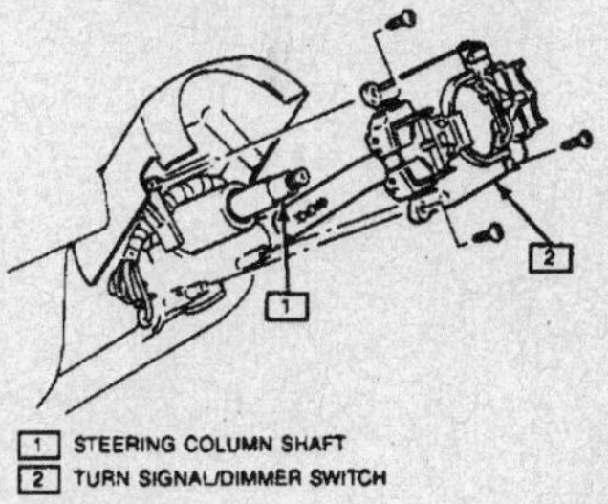
2
1
1 STEERING COLUMN SHAFT
2 TURN SIGNAL/DIMMER SWITCH

GC6049100061000X

Fig. 8 Turn signal/dimmer switch replacement. Swift less SIR

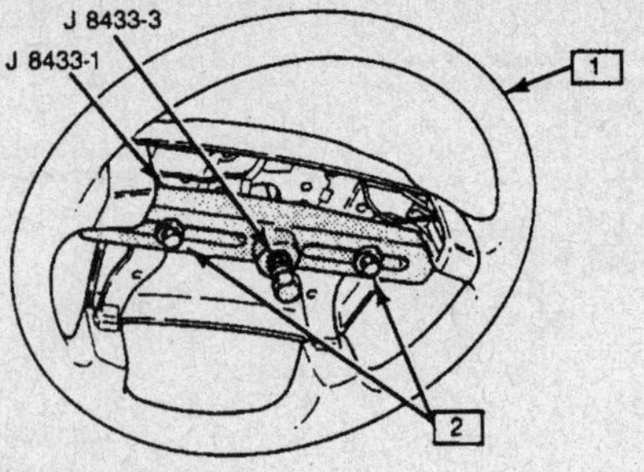
J 8433-3
J 8433-1
1
2

1 STEERING WHEEL
2 TWO 1/4 X 2-INCH THROUGH BOLTS AND NUTS

GC6049100062000X

Fig. 9 Steering wheel removal. Swift w/SIR

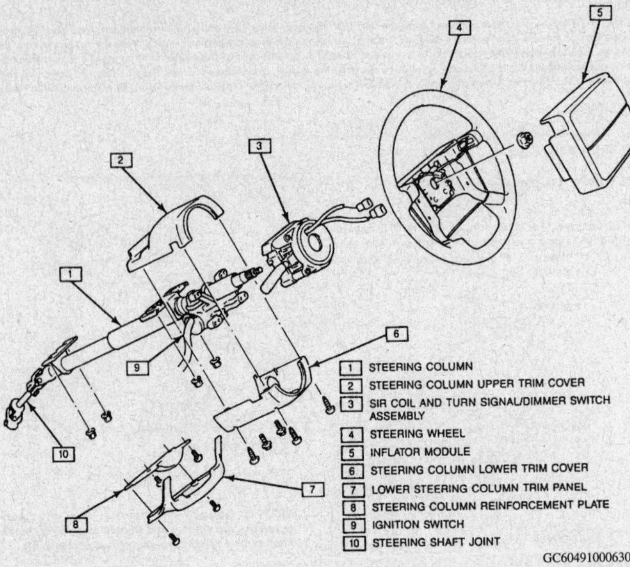
1
2
3
4
5
6
7
8
9
10

1 STEERING COLUMN
2 STEERING COLUMN UPPER TRIM COVER
3 SIR COIL AND TURN SIGNAL/DIMMER SWITCH ASSEMBLY
4 STEERING WHEEL
5 INFLATOR MODULE
6 STEERING COLUMN LOWER TRIM COVER
7 LOWER STEERING COLUMN TRIM PANEL
8 STEERING COLUMN REINFORCEMENT PLATE
9 IGNITION SWITCH
10 STEERING SHAFT JOINT

GC6049100063000X

Fig. 10 Exploded view of steering column. Swift w/SIR

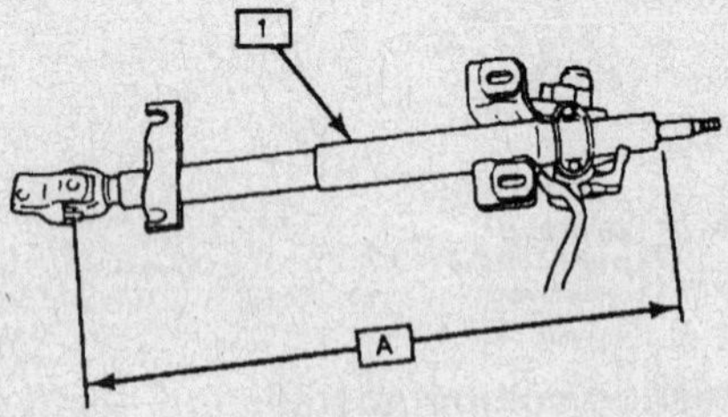
1
A

A 532.5 mm (20.96 INCHES)
1 STEERING COLUMN

GC6049100064000X

Fig. 11 Steering column measurement. Swift w/SIR

1. Air bag (inflator) module
2. Steering wheel
3. Steering wheel lower cover
4. Steering wheel side cap
5. Contact coil and combination switch assembly
6. Steering column upper cover
7. Steering column lower cover
8. Steering column assembly
9. Lower joint
10. Steering lock assembly
11. Knee bolster panel
12. Steering column hole cover
13. Knee protector
14. Steering column mounting nut

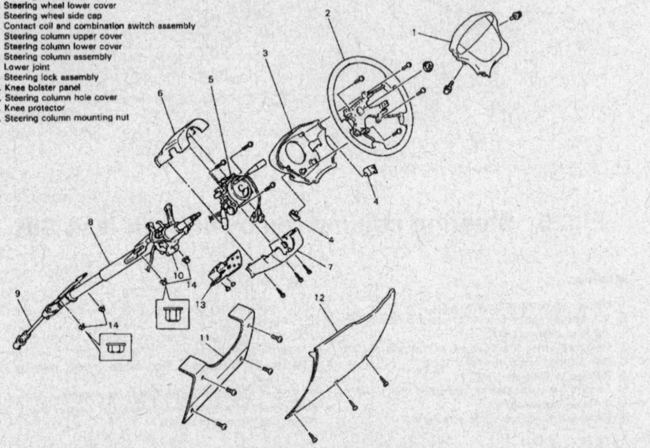

SK6049500004000X

Fig. 12 Exploded view of steering column. Esteem

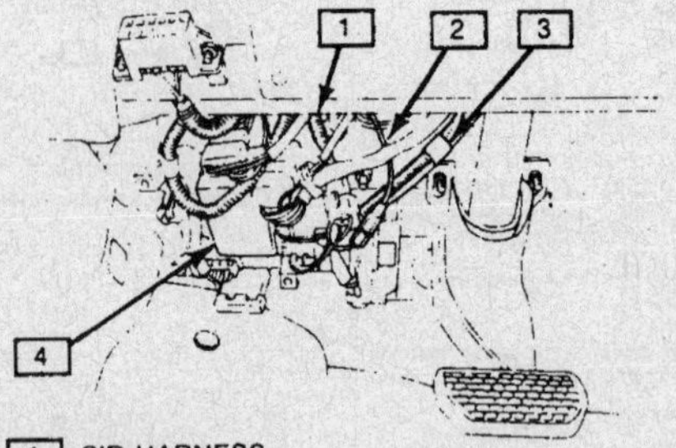
1
2
3
4

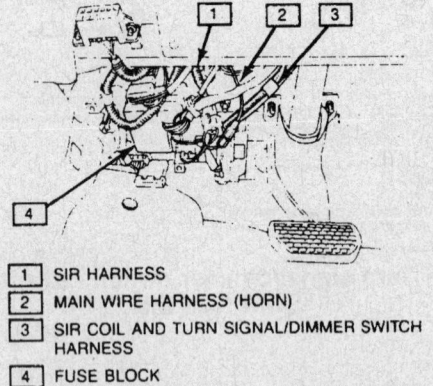

1 SIR HARNESS
2 MAIN WIRE HARNESS (HORN)
3 SIR COIL AND TURN SIGNAL/DIMMER SWITCH HARNESS
4 FUSE BLOCK

GC6049100122000X

Fig. 13 Electrical connector locations. Swift w/SIR

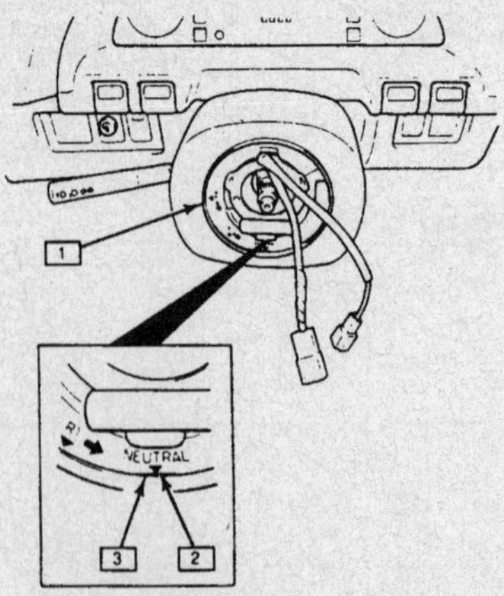
1
NEUTRAL
3
2

1 SIR COIL
2 NEUTRAL MARK
3 ALIGNMENT MARK

GC6049100123000X

Fig. 14 Checking position of SIR coil. Swift w/SIR

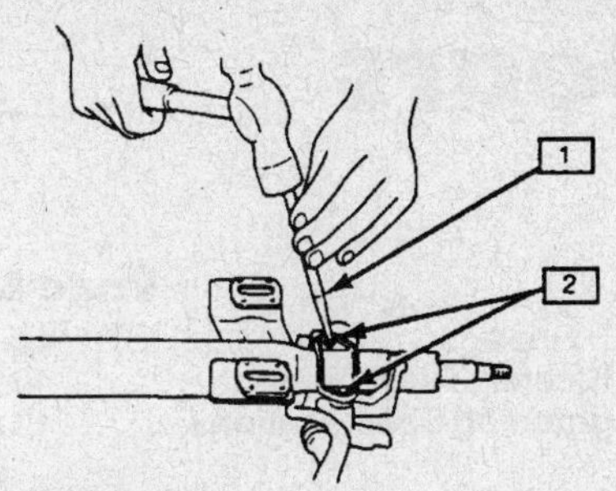
1
2

1 CENTER PUNCH
2 STEERING COLUMN LOCK BOLTS

GC6049100124000X

Fig. 15 Steering column lock bolts removal. Swift w/SIR

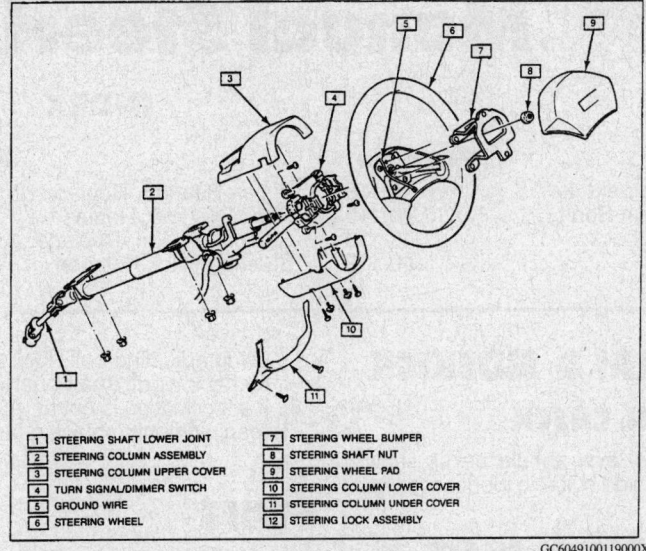

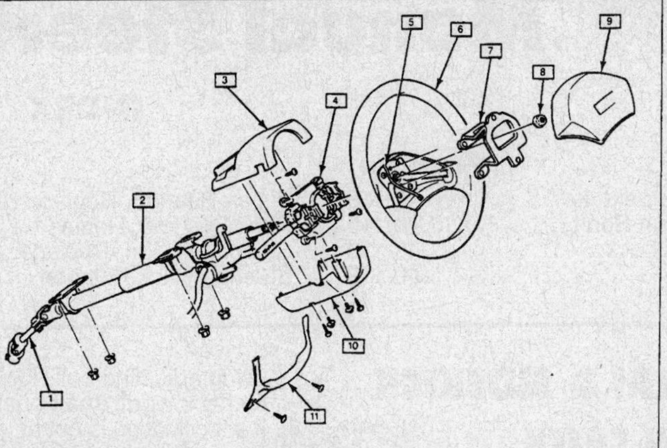
1
2
3
4
5
6
7
8
9
10
11

1 STEERING SHAFT LOWER JOINT
2 STEERING COLUMN ASSEMBLY
3 STEERING COLUMN UPPER COVER
4 TURN SIGNAL/DIMMER SWITCH
5 GROUND WIRE
6 STEERING WHEEL
7 STEERING WHEEL BUMPER
8 STEERING SHAFT NUT
9 STEERING WHEEL PAD
10 STEERING COLUMN LOWER COVER
11 STEERING COLUMN UNDER COVER
12 STEERING LOCK ASSEMBLY

GC6049100119000X

Fig. 16 Exploded view of steering column. Swift less SIR

REMOVAL

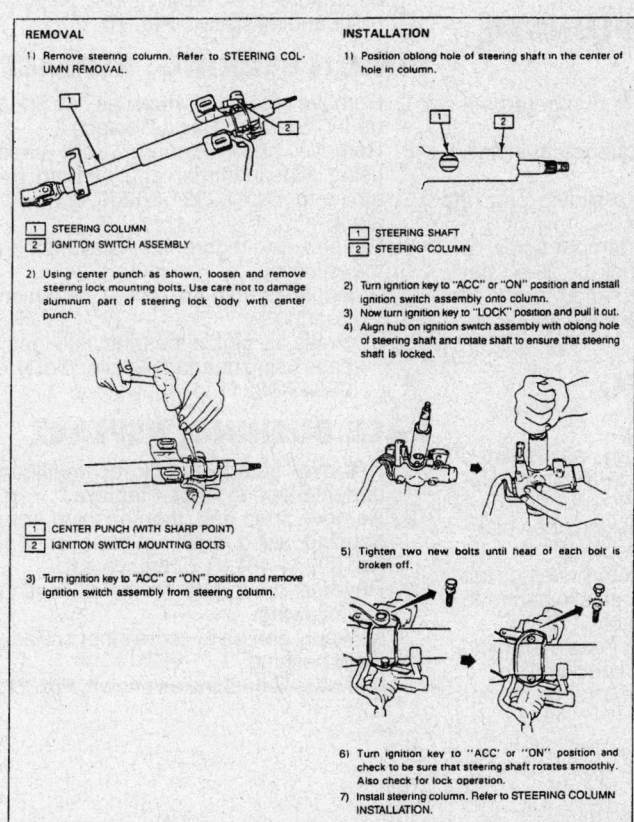

1) Remove steering column. Refer to STEERING COLUMN REMOVAL.

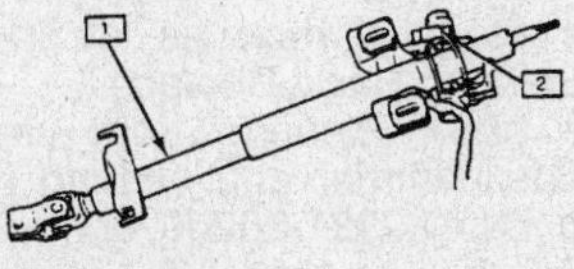
1
2

1 STEERING COLUMN
2 IGNITION SWITCH ASSEMBLY

2) Using center punch as shown, loosen and remove steering lock mounting bolts. Use care not to damage aluminum part of steering lock body with center punch.

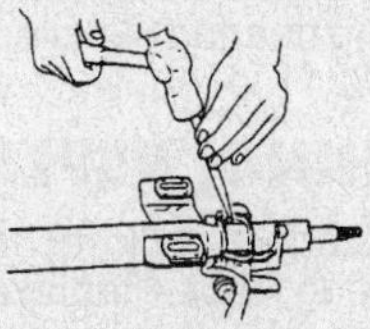

1 CENTER PUNCH (WITH SHARP POINT)
2 IGNITION SWITCH MOUNTING BOLTS

3) Turn ignition key to "ACC" or "ON" position and remove ignition switch assembly from steering column.

INSTALLATION

1) Position oblong hole of steering shaft in the center of hole in column.

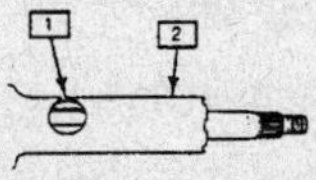
1
2

1 STEERING SHAFT
2 STEERING COLUMN

2) Turn ignition key to "ACC" or "ON" position and install ignition switch assembly onto column.
3) Now turn ignition key to "LOCK" position and pull it out.
4) Align hub on ignition switch assembly with oblong hole of steering shaft and rotate shaft to ensure that steering shaft is locked.

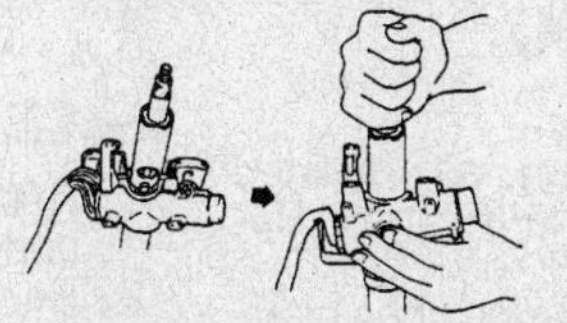

5) Tighten two new bolts until head of each bolt is broken off.

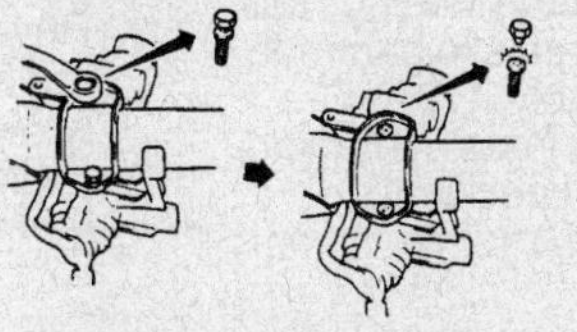

6) Turn ignition key to "ACC" or "ON" position and check to be sure that steering shaft rotates smoothly. Also check for lock operation.
7) Install steering column. Refer to STEERING COLUMN INSTALLATION.

GC6049100120000X

Fig. 17 Steering lock replacement. Swift less SIR

REMOVAL

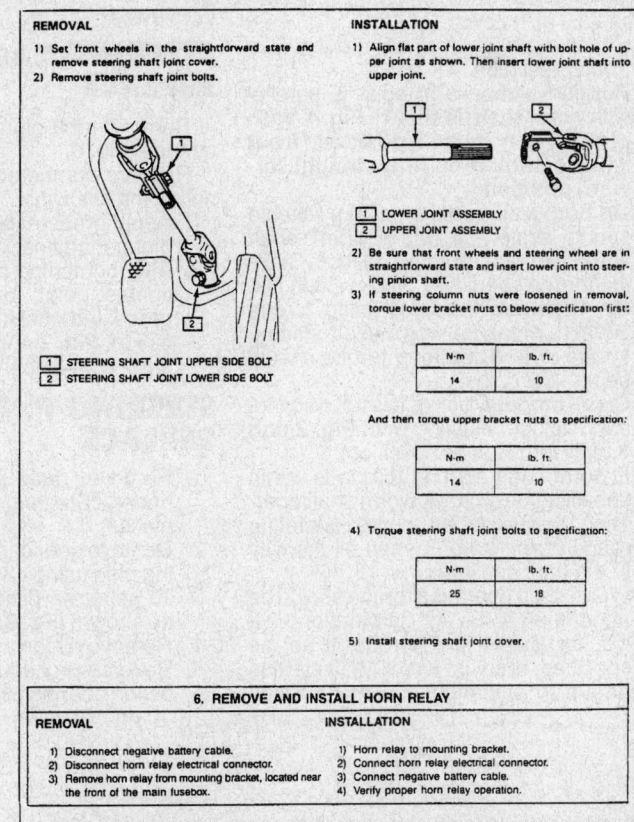

1) Set front wheels in the straightforward state and remove steering shaft joint cover.
2) Remove steering shaft joint bolts.

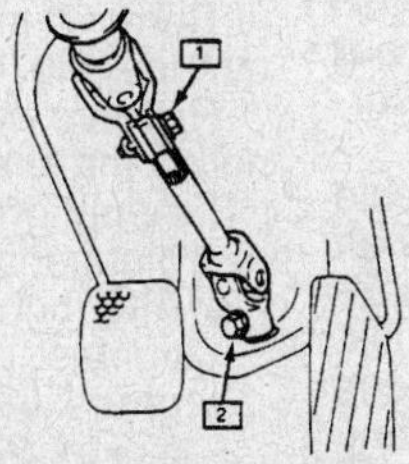
1
2

1 STEERING SHAFT JOINT UPPER SIDE BOLT
2 STEERING SHAFT JOINT LOWER SIDE BOLT

INSTALLATION

1) Align flat part of lower joint shaft with bolt hole of upper joint as shown. Then insert lower joint shaft into upper joint.

1
2

1 LOWER JOINT ASSEMBLY
2 UPPER JOINT ASSEMBLY

2) Be sure that front wheels and steering wheel are in straightforward state and insert lower joint into steering pinion shaft.
3) If steering column nuts were loosened in removal, torque lower bracket nuts to below specification first:

N·m	lb. ft.
14	10

And then torque upper bracket nuts to specification:

N·m	lb. ft.
14	10

4) Torque steering shaft joint bolts to specification:

N·m	lb. ft.
25	18

5) Install steering shaft joint cover.

6. REMOVE AND INSTALL HORN RELAY

REMOVAL

1) Disconnect negative battery cable.
2) Disconnect horn relay electrical connector.
3) Remove horn relay from mounting bracket, located near the front of the main fusebox.

INSTALLATION

1) Horn relay to mounting bracket.
2) Connect horn relay electrical connector.
3) Connect negative battery cable.
4) Verify proper horn relay operation.

GC6049100121000X

Fig. 18 Steering shaft lower joint & horn relay replacement. Swift less SIR

Manual Steering Gears

INDEX

	Page No.
Samurai & Sidekick	40-110
Adjust Worm Shaft	40-110
Oil Level Check	40-110
Swift	40-110
Pinion Bearing, Replace	40-110
Rack Bushing, Replace	40-110
Steering Pinion, Replace	40-110
Steering Rack Plunger, Replace	40-110
Steering Rack, Replace	40-110
Tightening Specifications	40-112

SAMURAI & SIDEKICK

OIL LEVEL CHECK

Oil surface level should be as shown, **Fig. 1.** If not, add suitable lubricant as necessary.

ADJUST WORM SHAFT

The steering gearbox is provided with an adjusting bolt, **Figs. 2 and 3,** which provides preload to selector shaft. If necessary, adjust as follows:

1. Check worm shaft to ensure it is free from thrust play.
2. Position pitman arm so it is parallel with worm shaft as shown, **Fig. 4. With pitman arm in this position, front wheels should be in a straight forward position.**
3. **On Samurai models,** using a suitable spring scale, measure worm shaft starting torque as shown, **Fig. 5.** Starting torque should be 3.48–5.80 ft. lbs.
4. **On Sidekick models,** using torque wrench, measure worm shaft starting torque, **Fig. 3.** Starting torque should be 0.4–0.7 ft. lbs.
5. **On all models,** if torque is not as specified, adjust adjusting bolt, **Fig. 2 and 3,** until torque is as specified.
6. If worm shaft starting torque is within specifications, check worm shaft operating torque in its entire operating range (turning worm shaft all the way to the right and left).
7. Worm shaft operating torque should be under 6.96 ft. lbs. for Samurai or 0.9 ft lbs. for Sidekick. If torque is not as specified, readjust worm shaft starting torque in a straight forward position using adjusting bolt, **Fig. 2 or 3,** then recheck worm shaft operating torque.
8. If specification is not as specified after readjustment, replace gearbox.

SWIFT

For the following procedures remove steering gear case from vehicle as outlined under "Steering Gear, Replace" in the "Front Suspension & Steering" section of this chapter.

STEERING RACK PLUNGER, REPLACE

Remove rack plunger in numbered sequence, **Fig. 6.**

Reverse numbered sequence to install, noting the following:

1. Apply grease lightly to sliding part of plunger against rack.
2. After tightening rack damper screw to tightest point, turn back by 0–90 degrees and check for rotation torque of pinion, **Fig. 7.** Pinion torque should be 0.58–0.94 ft. lbs.

STEERING PINION, REPLACE

1. Remove rack plunger as outlined under "Steering Rack Plunger, Replace."
2. Remove gear case packing, then bearing plug using 43 mm socket.
3. To separate pinion from housing, tap as shown, **Fig. 8,** with plastic hammer.
4. Remove pinion assembly.
5. Reverse procedure to install, torquing pinion bearing plug to specification.

STEERING RACK, REPLACE

1. Move both boots toward tie rod ends, then remove tie rods from steering rack.
2. Remove steering pinion as outlined under "Steering Pinion, Replace."
3. Remove rack from case as shown, **Fig. 9.**
4. Reverse procedure to install, noting the following:
   a. Apply grease to entire teeth surface of rack.
   b. Ensure rack side mount is positioned as shown, **Fig. 10.**

PINION BEARING, REPLACE

1. Remove steering rack as outlined under "Steering Rack, Replace."
2. Remove pinion bearing from case using slide hammer and bearing remover tool No. 09921-20200, or equivalent.
3. Reverse procedure to install, noting the following:
   a. Apply grease to rollers of pinion bearing.
   b. Press fit pinion bearing into gear case using bearing installer tool No. 09943-88211, or equivalent.

RACK BUSHING, REPLACE

1. Remove steering rack as outlined under "Steering Rack, Replace."
2. Remove snap ring, then bushing from housing using bushing remover tool No. 09944-48210, or equivalent.
3. Reverse procedure to install, noting the following:
   a. Apply grease to entire inner surface of bushing.
   b. Press fit bushing as shown, **Fig. 11.**

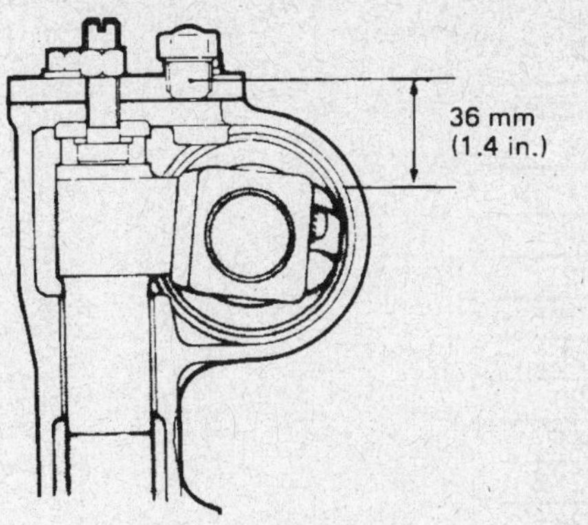
36 mm
(1.4 in.)
SK6039100002000X

Fig. 1 Oil level check

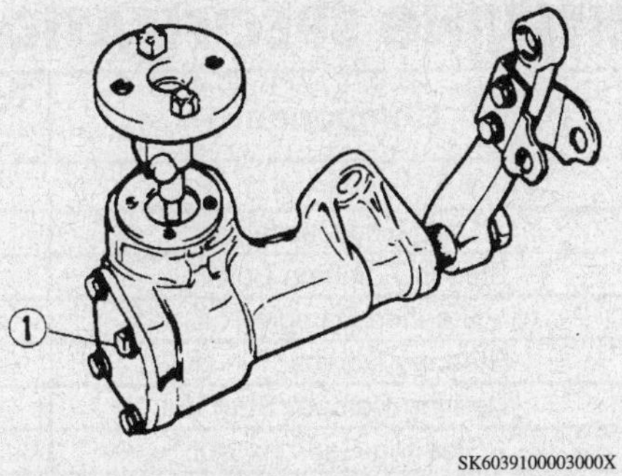
①
SK6039100003000X

Fig. 2 Steering gearbox adjusting bolt. Samurai

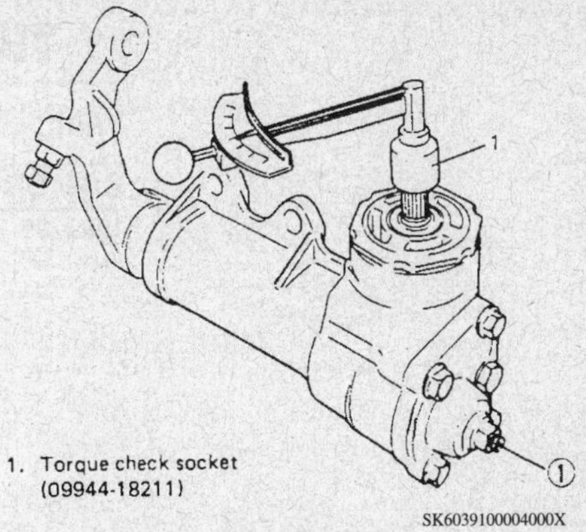
1
①
1. Torque check socket
(09944-18211)
SK6039100004000X

Fig. 3 Steering gearbox adjusting bolt. Sidekick

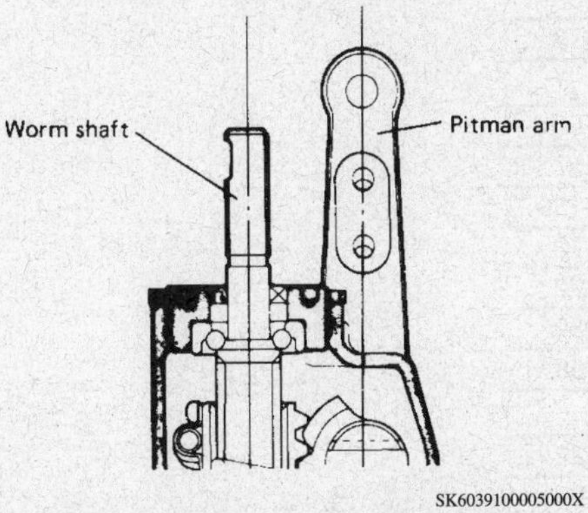
Worm shaft
Pitman arm
SK6039100005000X

Fig. 4 Pitman arm installation

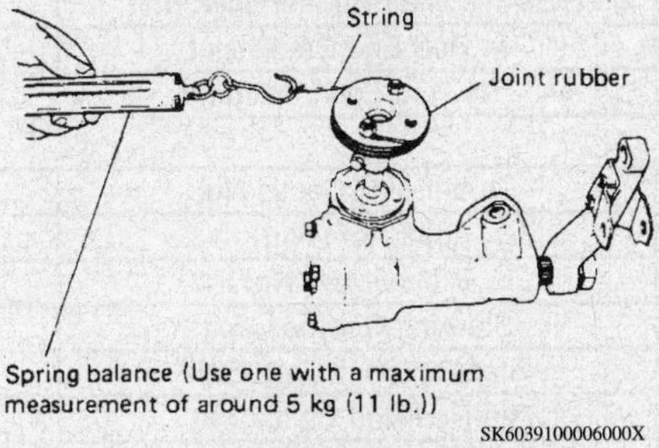
String
Joint rubber
Spring balance (Use one with a maximum measurement of around 5 kg (11 lb.))
SK6039100006000X

Fig. 5 Worm shaft torque measurement

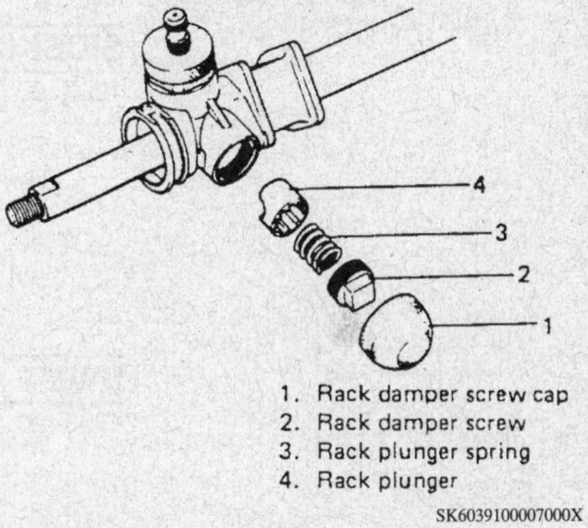
4
3
2
1
1. Rack damper screw cap
2. Rack damper screw
3. Rack plunger spring
4. Rack plunger
SK6039100007000X

Fig. 6 Rack plunger replacement. Swift

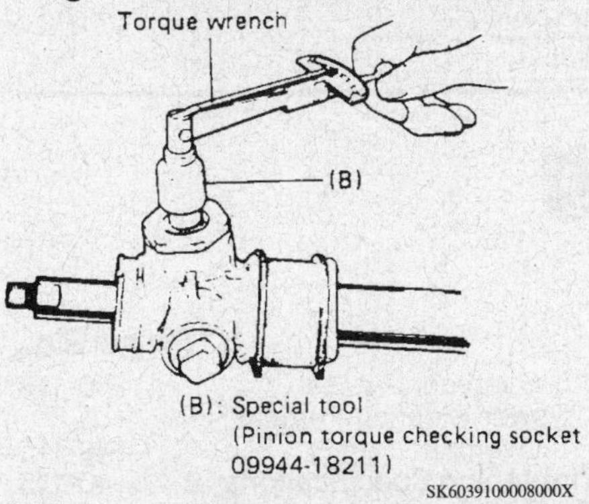
Torque wrench
(B)
(B): Special tool
(Pinion torque checking socket
09944-18211)
SK6039100008000X

Fig. 7 Rotation torque of pinion inspection. Swift

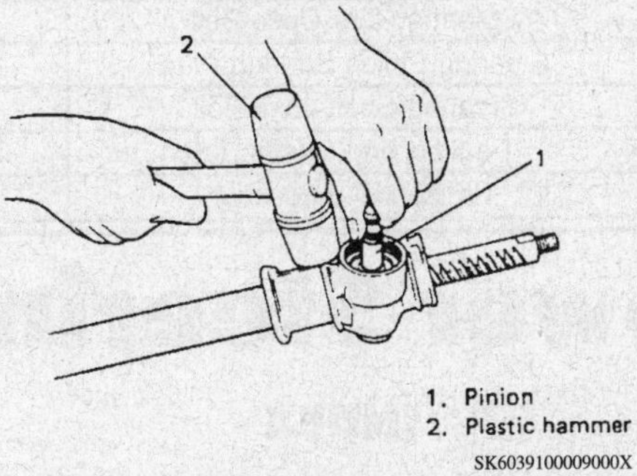
2
1
1. Pinion
2. Plastic hammer
SK6039100009000X

Fig. 8 Steering pinion removal. Swift

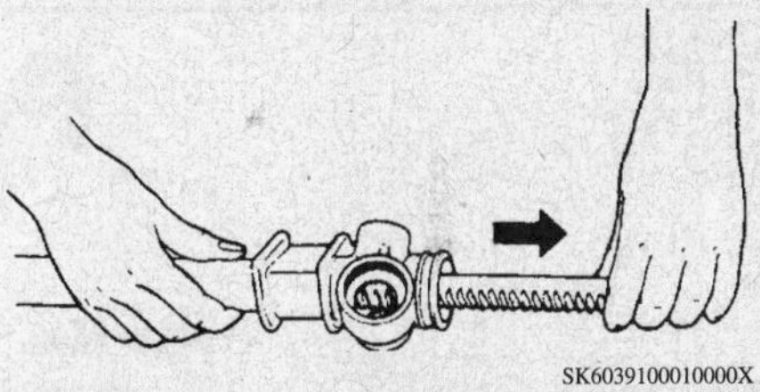
SK6039100010000X

Fig. 9 Steering rack removal. Swift

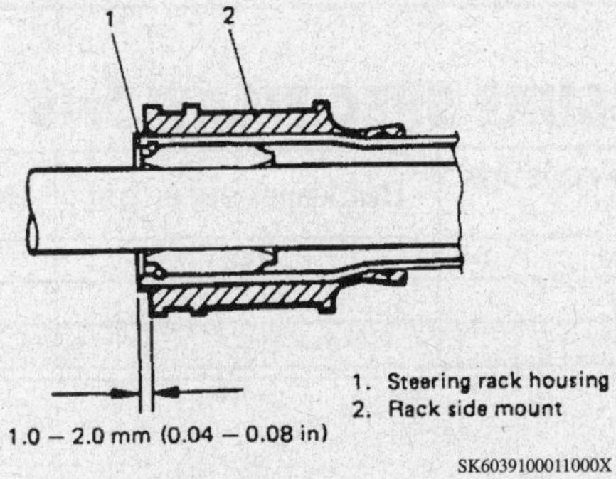
1
2
1. Steering rack housing
2. Rack side mount
1.0 – 2.0 mm (0.04 – 0.08 in)
SK6039100011000X

Fig. 10 Rack side mount installation. Swift

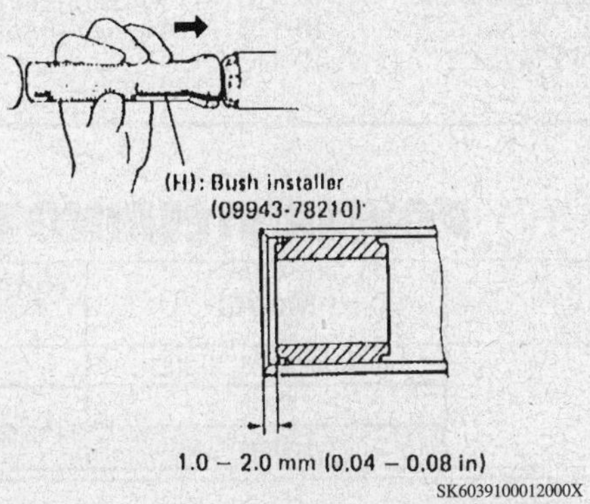
(H): Bush installer
(09943-78210)
1.0 – 2.0 mm (0.04 – 0.08 in)
SK6039100012000X

Fig. 11 Rack bushing installation. Swift

TIGHTENING SPECIFICATIONS

Year	Component	Torque/Ft. Lbs.
SAMURAI		
1993–95	Drag Rod Castle Nut	22-50
	Steering Column Bolt/Nut	8-12
	Steering Damper Nut	25.5-39.5
	Steering Damper Pin Nut	16-25
	Steering Damper Stay Nut	14-20
	Steering Gearbox Nut	51-65
	Steering Shaft Joint Flange Bolt	14.5-21.5
	Steering Shaft Nut	18.5-28.5
	Steering Shaft Rubber Joint Bolt	11-18
	Tie Rod End Castle Nut	22-39
	Tie Rod End Locknut	51-72
SIDEKICK		
1993–95	Center Link Castle Nut	22-50
	Idler Arm Nut	50-57
	Pitman Arm Nut	101-129
	Steering Gearbox Bolt	50-72
	Steering Shaft Joint Bolt	14-22
	Tie Rod End Castle Nut	22-39
	Tie Rod End Locknut	36-58
SWIFT		
1993–96	Steering Gear Case Bolt	15-22
	Steering Pinion Bearing Plug	58-80
	Steering Shaft Joint Bolt	15-22
	Tie Rod End Castle Nut	22-39
	Tie Rod End Locknut	26-39

Power Steering

INDEX

Page No.

Diagnosis & Testing 40-113
Hydraulic Pressure In Circuit.... 40-113
Idle Up System 40-113
Power Steering Belt Tension 40-113
Steering Force.................. 40-113
Steering Wheel Play 40-113
Power Steering Pressure Specifications 40-112
Power Steering System Service . 40-114
Air Bleeding 40-114
Power Steering Gearbox, Overhaul 40-115
Power Steering Pump, Overhaul 40-115
Tightening Specifications 40-115
Troubleshooting 40-113

POWER STEERING PRESSURE SPECIFICATIONS

Year	Model	Hydraulic Pressure, psi	Backpressure, psi	Relief Pressure, psi
1993–96	Sidekick & X-90	1000	142	850–1140
	Swift	711	142	640–924
	Esteem	1137	142	1109-1208

Condition	Possible Cause	Correction
Steering wheel feels heavy (at low speed)	1. Fluid deteriorated, low viscocity, different type of fluid mixed	Replace fluid.
	2. Pipes or hoses deformed, air entering through joint	Replace defective part.
	3. Insufficient air purging from P/S circuit	Purge air.
	4. P/S belt worn, lacking in tension	Adjust belt tension or replace belt as necessary.
	5. Tire inflation pressure excessively low	Inflate tire.
	6. Front end alignment maladjusted	Check and adjust front end alignment.
	7. Steering wheel installed improperly (twisted)	Install steering wheel correctly.
	8. Bind in tie rod or tie rod end ball joint	Replace defective part.
	9. P/S pump hydraulic pressure fails to increase	Replace P/S pump.
	10. P/S pump hydraulic pressure increases but slowly	Replace P/S pump.
	NOTE: Make sure to warm up engine fully before measuring hydraulic pressure from pump.	
Steering wheel feels heavy momentarily when turning it to the left (right)	1. Air drawn in due to insufficient amount of fluid	Add fluid and purge air.
	2. Slipping P/S belt	Adjust belt tension or replace belt as necessary.
	3. Refer to check items 9 and 10 in above section	
No idle-up	1. P/S pump pressure switch defective	Replace P/S pump.
Poor recovery from turns	NOTE: To check steering wheel for recovery, with car running at 22 mile/h (35 km/h), turn it 90° and let it free. It should return more than 60°.	
	1. Deformed pipes or hoses	Replace defective part.
	2. Steering column installed improperly	Install steering column correctly.
	3. Front end alignment maladjusted	Check and adjust front end alignment.
	4. Ball joints binding	Replace defective part.
	5. Refer to items 9 and 10 in above section	

SK6029100001010X

Fig. 1 Troubleshooting chart (Part 1 of 2)

Condition	Possible Cause	Correction
Vehicle pulls to one side during straight driving	1. Low or uneven tire inflation pressure	Inflate tires to proper pressure or adjust right & left tires inflation pressure.
	2. Front end alignment maladjusted	Check and adjust front end alignment.
	3. Malfunction of control valve in gear box	Replace gear box.
	4. Refer to check items 9 and 10 in previous page	
Steering wheel play is large and vehicle wanders	1. Loose steering shaft nut	Retighten.
	2. Loose linkage or joints	Retighten.
	3. Loose gear box fastening bolt	Retighten.
	4. Front wheel bearing worn	Replace wheel bearing.
Oil leakage	1. Loose joints of (hydraulic pressure) pipes and hoses	Retighten.
	2. Deformed or damaged pipes or hoses	Replace defective part.
Abnormal noise	NOTE: Some sound may be heard through steering column when turning steering wheel with vehicle at a stop but it is not an abnormal noise but operating sound of valve in gear box.	
	1. Air drawn in due to insufficient amount of fluid	Add fluid and purge air.
	2. Air mixed into fluid from pipes or hoses	Replace pipes or hoses.
	3. Slipping (loose) P/S belt	Adjust belt tension.
	4. Worn P/S belt	Replace belt.
	5. Loose gear box fastening bolt	Retighten bolts.
	6. Loose pitman arm nut	Retighten nut.
	7. Loose linkage or joints	Retighten.
	8. Pipes or hoses in contact with part of vehicle body	Install pipes and hoses correctly.
	9. Vanes of P/S pump defective	Replace pump.
	10. Malfunction of control valve in gear box	Replace gear box.
	11. Bearing of P/S pump shaft defective	Replace pump.

SK6029100001020X

Fig. 1 Troubleshooting chart (Part 2 of 2)

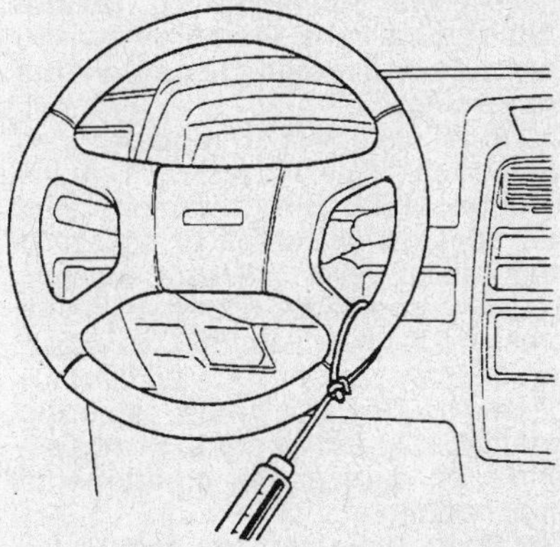

SK6029100002000X

Fig. 2 Steering force inspection

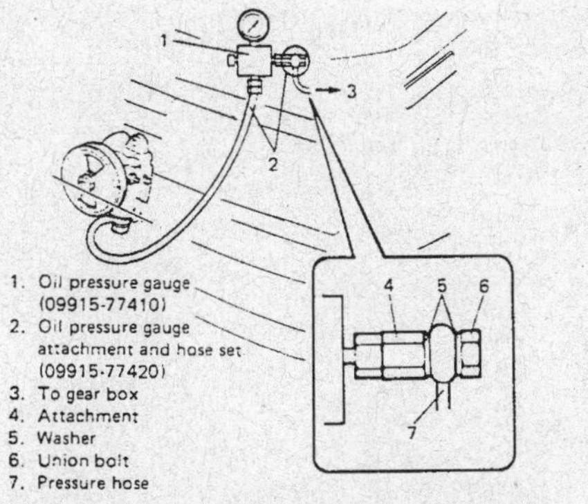
1
2
3
4
5
6
7
1. Oil pressure gauge (09915-77410)
2. Oil pressure gauge attachment and hose set (09915-77420)
3. To gear box
4. Attachment
5. Washer
6. Union bolt
7. Pressure hose

SK6029100003000X

Fig. 3 Oil pressure gauge installation. Sidekick & X-90

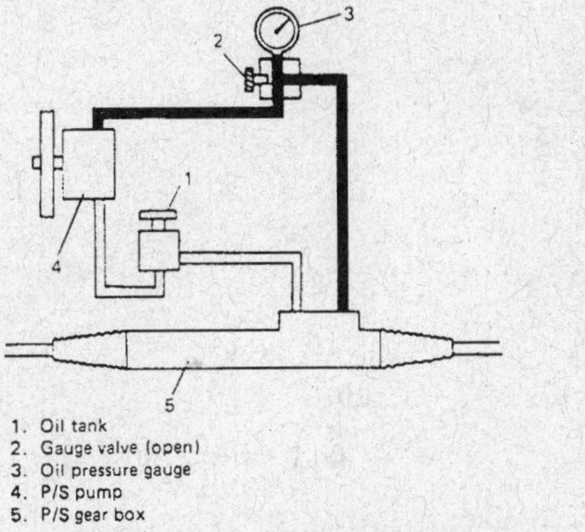
1
2
3
4
5
1. Oil tank
2. Gauge valve (open)
3. Oil pressure gauge
4. P/S pump
5. P/S gear box

SK6029100004000X

Fig. 4 Oil pressure gauge installation. Swift

TROUBLESHOOTING

Refer to **Fig. 1** for troubleshooting procedures.

DIAGNOSIS & TESTING

STEERING WHEEL PLAY

With engine Off, move steering wheel lightly in both directions without turning wheels, and measure distance along its circumference. Distance measured should be less than 1.2 inch.

STEERING FORCE

1. Place vehicle on a level surface and set steering wheel to straight ahead position.
2. Ensure tire pressure is proper, then start engine and warm power steering fluid to 122–140°F.
3. With engine idling, measure steering force using a spring balancer hooked to steering wheel, **Fig. 2.**
4. Steering force should be less than 11 lbs. on Sidekick and X-90 and less than 8.8 lbs. on Swift and Esteem.

POWER STEERING BELT TENSION

1. Ensure belt is free of damage and fits properly in pulley groove.
2. Check belt deflection at midway point between power steering pulley and crankshaft pulley using about 22 lbs. of force.
3. Belt deflection should be 0.24–0.35 inch on Sidekick, X-90 and Esteem and 0.31–0.39 inch on Swift.

IDLE UP SYSTEM

With A/C turned Off, if equipped, turn steering wheel and ensure engine idling speed is not slowed down even when load is applied by power steering pump.

HYDRAULIC PRESSURE IN CIRCUIT

1. **On Sidekick and X-90 models,** thoroughly clean hose connections, then disconnect pressure hose from pump and connect oil pressure gauge tool No. 09915-77410 and attachment hose set tool No. 09915-77420, or equivalents, as shown, **Fig. 3. When connecting gauge, route hose so that it does not contact power steering belt, or hinder movement of center link.**
2. **On Swift and Esteem models,** thoroughly clean hose connections, then disconnect pressure hose and connect

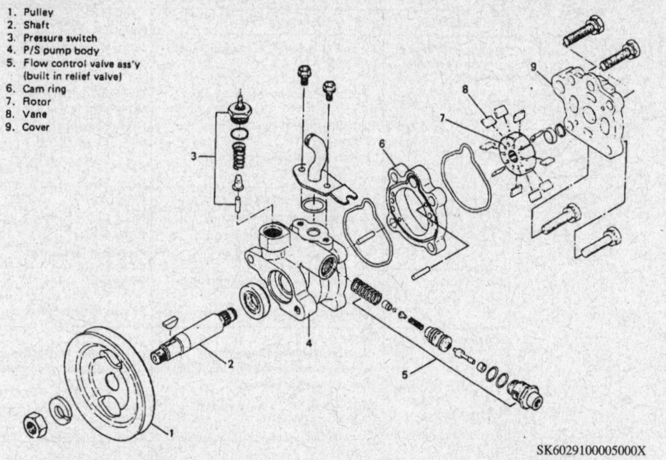
1. Pulley
2. Shaft
3. Pressure switch
4. P/S pump body
5. Flow control valve ass'y (built in relief valve)
6. Cam ring
7. Rotor
8. Vane
9. Cover
SK6029100005000X

Fig. 5 Exploded view of power steering pump

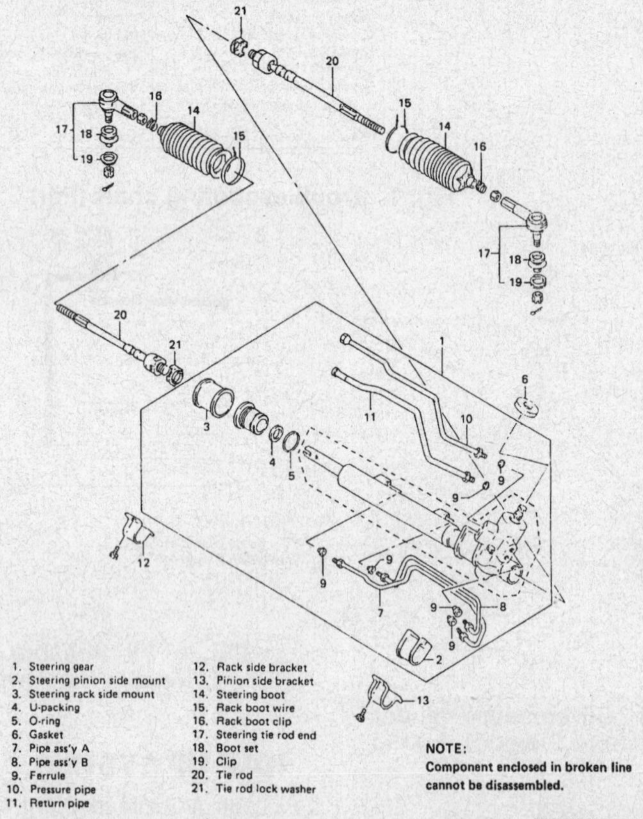
1. Steering gear
2. Steering pinion side mount
3. Steering rack side mount
4. U-packing
5. O-ring
6. Gasket
7. Pipe ass'y A
8. Pipe ass'y B
9. Ferrule
10. Pressure pipe
11. Return pipe
12. Rack side bracket
13. Pinion side bracket
14. Steering boot
15. Rack boot wire
16. Rack boot clip
17. Steering tie rod end
18. Boot set
19. Clip
20. Tie rod
21. Tie rod lock washer
NOTE:
Component enclosed in broken line cannot be disassembled.
SK6029100006000X

Fig. 6 Exploded view of power gearbox. Swift

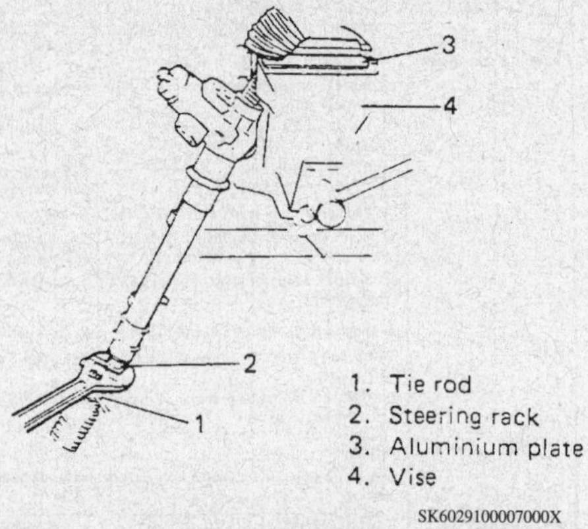
1. Tie rod
2. Steering rack
3. Aluminium plate
4. Vise
SK6029100007000X

Fig. 7 Tie rod end from gearbox removal. Swift

oil pressure gauge tool No. 09915-77410, or equivalent, between high pressure hose and high pressure pipe as shown, **Fig. 4**.

3. **On all models,** fill power steering fluid reservoir and bleed system of air, refer to "Air Bleeding" procedure as outlined.
4. With engine idling, turn steering wheel to right and left stops to warm fluid in reservoir to 122–140°F. **Do not hold steering against stop for longer than 10 seconds or damage to components may occur.**
5. With wheels straight forward and engine running at idle, check backpressure on gauge, pressure should be lower than 142 psi. If pressure is higher than 142 psi, check control valve and pipes for obstruction.
6. **On Sidekick and X-90 models,** increase engine speed to 1500 RPM minimum, then close gauge valve gradually while observing pressure increase and record relief pressure, which should be 850–1140 psi. If pressure is higher than 1140 psi, relief valve may have malfunctioned, replace power steering pump. If lower than 850 psi, power steering pump may have failed or relief valve spring setting is incorrect, replace power steering pump. **Do not close gauge valve for longer than 10 seconds or damage to components may occur.**
7. **On Swift and Esteem models,** increase engine speed to 1500 RPM minimum, then close gauge valve gradually while observing pressure increase and record relief pressure, which should be 640–924 psi. If pressure is higher than 924 psi, relief valve may have malfunctioned, replace steering gearbox components. If pressure is lower than 640 psi, power steering pump may have failed or relief valve spring setting is incorrect, replace power steering pump. **Do not close gauge valve for longer than 10 seconds or damage to components may occur.**
8. **On Sidekick and X-90 models,** open gauge valve fully and increase engine speed to 1500 RPM minimum, then turn steering wheel left or right stop and record relief pressure reading, pressure should be 850–1140 psi. If pressure is lower than 850 psi, steering gearbox may have failed, replace gearbox. **Do not hold steering against stop for longer than 10 seconds or damage to components may occur.**
9. **On Swift & Esteem models,** open gauge valve fully and increase engine speed to 1500 RPM minimum, then turn steering wheel left or right stop and record relief pressure reading, pressure should be 640–924 psi. If pressure is lower than 640 psi, steering gearbox may have failed, replace gearbox. **Do not hold steering against stop for longer than 10 seconds or damage to components may occur.**

POWER STEERING SYSTEM SERVICE

AIR BLEEDING

1. Raise and support front of vehicle.
2. Fill oil tank with fluid to specified level, then turn steering wheel left or right three or four times.
3. After running engine at idling speed for three to five seconds, stop engine and add fluid to meet specification.

4. With engine stopped, turn steering wheel to right and left as far as possible, then repeat a few times and add fluid to specified level.
5. With engine idling, repeat stop-to-stop turn of steering wheel until all foam in oil tank is gone.
6. **Bleed air completely. If air remains in fluid, power steering pump may make humming noise or steering wheel may feel heavy.**
7. Ensure fluid is filled to specified level.

POWER STEERING PUMP, OVERHAUL

1. Remove power steering pump as outlined under "Power Steering Pump, Replace" in "Front Suspension & Steering" section.
2. Using transfer flange lock holder tool No. 09930-40113, or equivalent, remove pump pulley.
3. Remove suction connector bolts, then the pressure switch and flow control assembly, **Fig. 5.**
4. Remove pump cover bolts, then the cam ring.
5. Remove snap ring and pull out rotor. When pulling rotor out of shaft, be careful not to lose vanes.
6. Remove shaft and oil seal.
7. Reverse procedure to install, ensuring rotor is installed to shaft with splined part chamfered side facing cover.

POWER STEERING GEAR, OVERHAUL

Esteem, Sidekick & X-90

Gearbox on these models cannot be overhauled.

Swift

Refer to **Fig. 6** when overhauling gearbox.

1. Remove gearbox as outlined under "Power Steering Gear, Replace" in "Front Suspension & Steering " section.
2. Move boot ensuring joint section of tie rod and steering rack is exposed, then remove tie rod with tie rod end as shown, **Fig. 7.**
3. Using ring nut wrench tool No. 09917-23610, or equivalent, remove adjustment cover, then the O-ring and or U-packing.
4. Reverse procedure to assemble, noting the following:
   a. Apply Suzuki super grease to O-ring and U-packing of adjustment cover and install in groove of adjustment cover.
   b. Tighten adjustment cover and tie rod to specification.
   c. Use new tie rod lockwasher and caulk after installation.

TIGHTENING SPECIFICATIONS

Year	Component	Torque/Ft. Lbs.
SIDEKICK		
1993–95	Discharge Connector Bolts	29-43
	Pressure Switch	18.5-21.5
	Pump Cover Bolts	13.5-15.5
	Suction Connector Bolt	4.5-7
SIDEKICK & X-90		
1996	Castle Nut	36.5
	Gear Box Mounting Bolt	61.5
	Gear Box Union Bolt	25.5
	Lower Shaft Bolt	18
	Pitman Arm To Sector Shaft	101.5
	Pump Adjusting Bolt	18
	Pump Union Bolt	43.5
SWIFT		
1993–95	Discharge Connector Bolts	29-43
	Gearbox Adjusting Cover	29-36
	Pipe Assembly A & B Flare Nut	14.5-21.5
	Pressure Pipe Flare Nut	22-28.5
	Pressure Switch	18.5-21.5
	Pump Cover Bolts	13.5-15.5
	Return Pipe Flare Nut	29-36
	Suction Connector Bolt	4.5-7
	Tie Rod	43.5-57.5

Continued

TIGHTENING SPECIFICATIONS—Continued

Year	Component	Torque/Ft. Lbs.
ESTEEM		
1996	Belt Tension Pulley Nut	32.5
	Compressor Bracket Bolt	47.5
	Discharge Connector Bolts	43.5
	Gear Box Cylinder Pipe Flare Nuts	14.5
	Gear Box High & Low Pressure Pipe Flare Nuts	24
	Gear Box Mounting Bolts	40
	Pipe Clamp Bolt	7.5
	Pipe To Pump Flare Nut	32
	Pressure Switch	13.5
	Pump Cover Bolts	17.5
1996	Pump Mounting Bracket Bolts	25.5
	Suction Connector Bolt	7.5
	Tie Rod Ball Nut	65.5
	Tie Rod End Castle Nut	25.5-39.5
	Tie Rod End Lock Nut	32.5

Disc Brakes

INDEX

Page No.

Brake Pad Service 40-116
Front 40-116
Rear 40-117
Caliper Service 40-118
Caliper Assembly 40-118
Caliper Disassembly 40-118
Caliper Installation 40-118
Caliper Removal 40-118
Disc Brake Specifications 40-120
Tightening Specifications 40-121

BRAKE PAD SERVICE

FRONT

SAMURAI

Pads, Replace

1. Raise and support vehicle, then remove wheel assembly.
2. Remove caliper anti-rattle clip, **Figs. 1 and 2.**
3. Remove caliper guide pin caps.
4. Using a 6 mm Allen wrench, remove caliper guide pins.
5. Remove pad protectors, then the caliper cylinder.
6. Remove brake pads.
7. Reverse procedure to install, noting the following:
   a. Tighten caliper bolts to specification.
   b. Install wheel assemblies.
   c. Lower vehicle and perform brake test.

Caliper Service

1. Raise and support vehicle.
2. Disconnect brake hose from caliper.
3. Remove caliper guide pin caps.
4. Using a 6 mm Allen wrench, remove caliper guide pins, then the caliper.
5. Clean caliper with brake fluid.
6. Using compressed air, remove piston from caliper. Keep fingers away from piston.
7. Using a suitable screwdriver, remove piston seal from caliper. **Take care not to damage bore of cylinder.**
8. Install new piston seal in cylinder.
9. Install new boot on piston as shown, **Fig. 3.**
10. Install piston into cylinder by hand. Ensure boot fits in groove in piston.
11. Install caliper, then the brake pads.
12. Tighten caliper bolts and brake hose to specification.
13. Install wheel assembly, then lower vehicle and test brakes.

Disc, Replace

1. Raise and support vehicle, then remove wheels.
2. Remove caliper assembly by loosening carrier bolts. **During removal, be careful not to damage brake flexible hose or depress brake pedal.**
3. **On Swift models,** remove brake disc screws.
4. **On all models,** remove disc by using two 8 mm bolts, **Fig. 4.**
5. Reverse procedure to install.

ESTEEM, SIDEKICK, SWIFT & X-90

Pads, Replace

1. Raise and support vehicle, then remove wheels.
2. Remove caliper pin bolts, **Figs. 5 through 7.**
3. Remove caliper from caliper carrier. Hang removed caliper with wire hook to prevent damage to brake hose.
4. Remove brake pads.
5. Reverse procedure to install.

Caliper, Replace

1. Raise and support vehicle.
2. Remove brake hose mounting bolt from caliper. Drain any brake fluid into suitable container.
3. Remove caliper pin bolts, then the caliper.
4. Reverse procedure to install, noting the following:
   a. Tighten caliper pin and brake hose mounting bolts to specification.

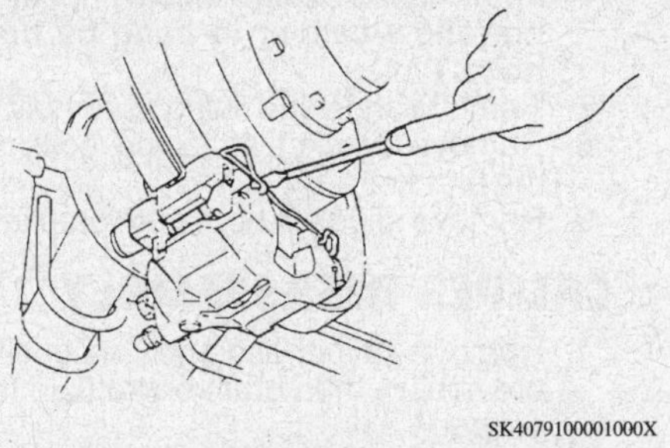
SK4079100001000X

Fig. 1 Caliper anti-rattle clip removal. Samurai

b. Bleed brake system.

Disc, Replace

1. Raise and support vehicle, then remove wheels.
2. Remove caliper assembly by loosening carrier bolts. **During removal, be careful not to damage brake flexible hose or depress brake pedal.**
3. **On Swift and Esteem models,** remove brake disc screws.
4. **On all models,** remove disc by using two 8 mm bolts, **Fig. 4.**
5. Reverse procedure to install.

Caliper Overhaul

1. Remove caliper as outlined under "Caliper, Replace, " then clean caliper with brake fluid.
2. Using compressed air, remove piston from cylinder. Keep fingers away from piston. Piston should be taken out gradually.
3. Remove piston seal using a suitable thin blade. **Use caution not to damage inside of cylinder.**
4. Reverse procedure to install, noting the following:
   a. Before installing piston into cylinder, install boot to piston as shown, **Fig. 3.**

REAR

SWIFT

Pads, Replace

1. Raise and support vehicle, then remove wheels.
2. Remove caliper pin bolts, then release parking brake lever.
3. Remove caliper from caliper carrier. Hang removed caliper with wire hook to prevent damage to brake hose.
4. Remove brake pads.
5. Reverse procedure to install, noting the following:
   a. Using tool No. 09945-16030, or equivalent, **Fig. 8,** turn caliper piston clockwise to obtain clearance between disc and pad.
   b. **Torque** caliper pin bolts to 16–23 lb. ft.
   c. Depress brake pedal five times to obtain proper disc to pad clearance.

Caliper, Replace

1. Raise and support vehicle, then remove wheels.

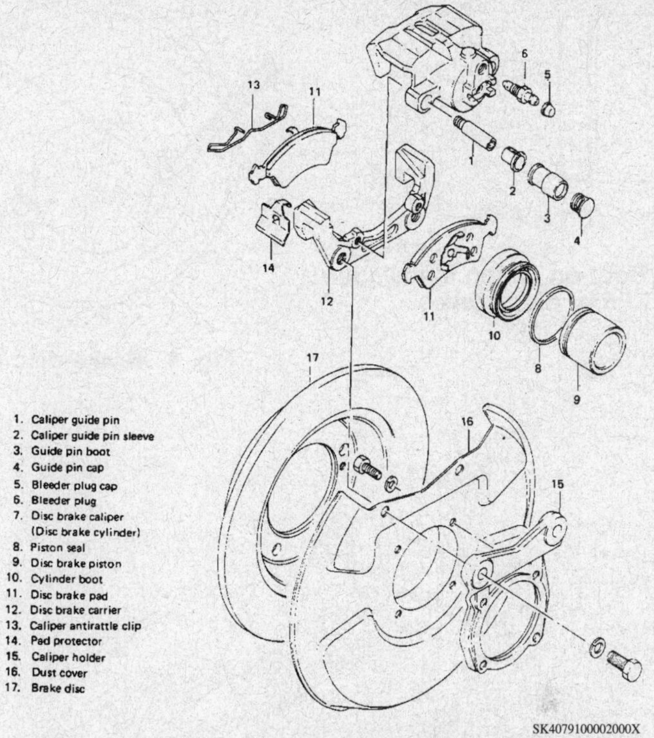
1. Caliper guide pin
2. Caliper guide pin sleeve
3. Guide pin boot
4. Guide pin cap
5. Bleeder plug cap
6. Bleeder plug
7. Disc brake caliper (Disc brake cylinder)
8. Piston seal
9. Disc brake piston
10. Cylinder boot
11. Disc brake pad
12. Disc brake carrier
13. Caliper antirattle clip
14. Pad protector
15. Caliper holder
16. Dust cover
17. Brake disc
SK4079100002000X

Fig. 2 Exploded view of front brake assembly. Samurai

2. Remove brake hose mounting bolt from caliper. Drain brake fluid into appropriate container.
3. Release parking brake lever and remove caliper pin bolts.
4. Remove caliper from carrier, then the parking brake cable retaining clip.
5. Disconnect parking brake cable from camshaft lever on caliper, then remove cover.
6. Reverse procedure to install.

Disc, Replace

1. Raise and support vehicle, then remove wheels.
2. Remove disc screws, then release parking brake lever.
3. Remove caliper assembly by loosening carrier bolts.
4. Remove disc by using two 8 mm bolts, **Fig. 4.**
5. Reverse procedure to install, noting the following:
   a. **Torque** caliper carrier bolts to 29–43 lb. ft.
   b. Depress brake pedal five times to obtain proper disc to pad clearance.

Caliper Overhaul

Refer to **Fig. 9,** during overhaul procedure.

1. Remove caliper as outlined under "Caliper, Replace, " then clean caliper with brake fluid.
2. Release parking brake lever and remove caliper pins, **Fig. 8.**
3. Remove parking brake cable E-ring.
4. Disconnect parking brake cable from lever on caliper.
5. Remove cover.
6. Reverse procedure to install, noting the following:
   a. Install cover to caliper.
   b. Connect parking brake cable to camshaft lever and cable bracket, then the clip and E-ring to bracket side.
   c. Install caliper to carrier and tighten caliper pin bolts to specification.
   d. Install brake flexible hose to caliper and **torque** to 14.5–18 lb. ft.
   e. Fill reservoir tank with specified fluid and bleed brake system.

Seal, Piston Dust Boot & Parking Brake Cam, Replace

1. Clean caliper with brake fluid, then remove piston and boot by turning piston counterclockwise with piston installer tool No. 09945-16030, or equivalent.
2. Remove piston seal. **Be careful not to damage inside (bore side) of cylinder.**
3. Using snap ring pliers (closing type) tool No. 09945-16010, or equivalent, remove snap ring.
4. Remove spring seat No. 2, coil spring and seat No. 1.
5. Using snap ring pliers, remove key plate snap ring, then the key plate, pushrod and rod.
6. Remove return spring, **Fig. 10,** then the lever, camshaft and camshaft boot.
7. Reverse procedure to install, noting the following:
   a. Position camshaft bearing as shown, **Fig. 11.**
   b. Determine camshaft position in the cylinder as shown, **Fig. 12.**

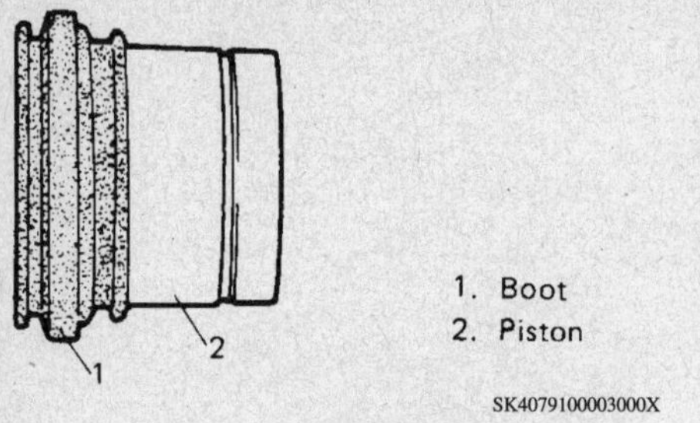
1. Boot
2. Piston
1
2
SK4079100003000X

Fig. 3 Boot on piston installation. Front disc brakes

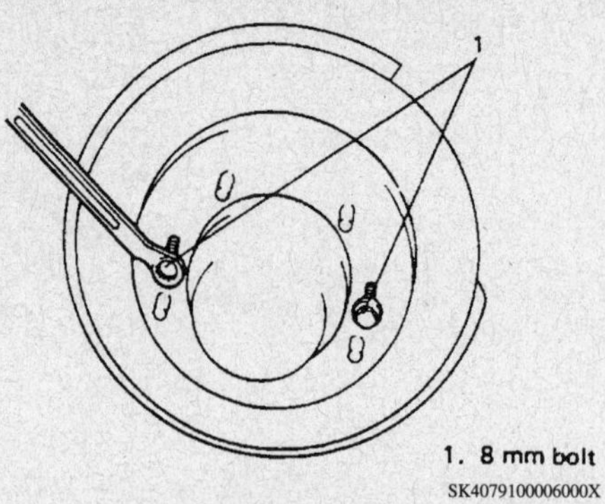
1
1. 8 mm bolt
SK4079100006000X

Fig. 4 Brake disc removal

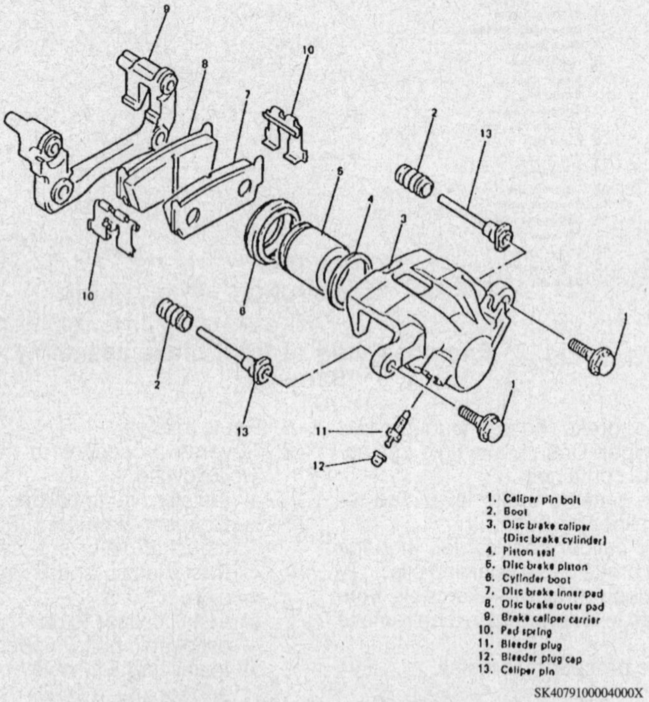
1. Caliper pin bolt
2. Boot
3. Disc brake caliper (Disc brake cylinder)
4. Piston seal
5. Disc brake piston
6. Cylinder boot
7. Disc brake inner pad
8. Disc brake outer pad
9. Brake caliper carrier
10. Pad spring
11. Bleeder plug
12. Bleeder plug cap
13. Caliper pin
SK4079100004000X

Fig. 5 Exploded view of front caliper assembly. Sidekick & X-90

c. Assemble rod, seal ring and key plate onto pushrod, then install as an assembly. Ensure pin A of key plate fits into hole B in cylinder when installing, **Fig. 13.**
d. Turn camshaft while pressing screw part of pushrod by hand. Ensure pushrod moves about 0.039 inch (1 mm) up and down, **Fig. 14.**
e. After installation of seat No. 1, coil spring and spring seat No. 2, tighten with spring installer tool No. 09945-16040, or equivalent, **Fig. 15,** until spring seat No. 2 lightly contacts snap ring fixing key plate. Install snap ring and remove tool.
f. **Torque** camshaft lever nut to 18.5–21.5 lb. ft.

Parking Brake, Adjust

Parking brake lever should be adjusted so lever comes up 4–9 notches with 44 lbs. of pull applied, **Fig. 16.**

Adjust travel by loosening self locking nut, **Fig. 17.**

CALIPER SERVICE

CALIPER REMOVAL

1. Disconnect negative battery cable.
2. Remove approximately ⅔ of brake fluid from master cylinder.
3. Raise and support vehicle.
4. Mark relationship between front wheel and axle, then remove wheel and tire assembly.
5. If caliper assembly is to be serviced, remove inlet fitting attaching bolt, copper washer, and inlet fitting from caliper housing. Plug opening in inlet fitting to prevent fluid loss and contamination. **Do not crimp brake hose, as this may damage internal structure of hose. If only shoe and lining assemblies are to be replaced, do not disconnect brake line fitting from caliper.**
6. Remove caliper slide pins and the caliper. If only shoe and lining assemblies are to be replaced, suspend caliper from chassis using suitable hanger. **Do not allow caliper to hang by brake hose.**
7. Remove shoe and lining assembly.
8. Remove bracket attaching bolts and the bracket.
9. Remove slide pin boot from bracket.

CALIPER DISASSEMBLY

1. Remove caliper assembly as outlined previously, then drain brake fluid from caliper.
2. Use clean shop towels to pad interior of caliper assembly, then remove piston by directing compressed air into caliper brake hose inlet hole, **Fig. 18. Use just enough air pressure to ease piston out of bore. Do not place fingers in front of piston for any reason when applying compressed air. This could result in serious personal injury.**
3. Remove dust boot from piston.
4. Using a small piece of wood or plastic, remove piston seal from bore. **Do not use a metal tool of any kind to remove seal as it may damage bore.**
5. Remove bleeder valve.
6. Inspect piston for scoring, nicks, corrosion, and wear and replace as needed.
7. Inspect caliper housing and seal groove for corrosion, nicks, scoring and excessive wear, and use crocus cloth to polish away corrosion from housing bore. Replace caliper housing if corrosion in and around seal groove will not clean up with crocus cloth.
8. Clean all parts with denatured alcohol. Dry with unlubricated compressed air. Blow out all passages in housing and bleeder valve.

CALIPER ASSEMBLY

1. Apply suitable grease to piston seal and cylinder wall, then install the seal. Check to ensure piston seal is not twisted.
2. Apply suitable grease to sliding portion of piston and install dust boot.
3. Insert edge of dust boot into boot groove, then slowly force piston fully into cylinder.
4. Install bleeder valve.

CALIPER INSTALLATION

1. Apply suitable grease to inner face of slide pin boot.
2. Install slide pin boot to bracket.
3. Install bracket and attaching bolts.
4. Install shoe and lining assembly, ensure wear indicators are located on trailing edge of shoe assemblies during forward wheel rotation.
5. Install caliper assembly to bracket. Tighten attaching bolts to specifications.
6. Attach hose to caliper.
7. Install wheel and tire assembly, then lower vehicle.
8. Fill master cylinder to proper level and bleed brakes. **Before moving vehicle, pump brake pedal several times to be sure it is firm. Do not move vehicle until a firm pedal is obtained.**

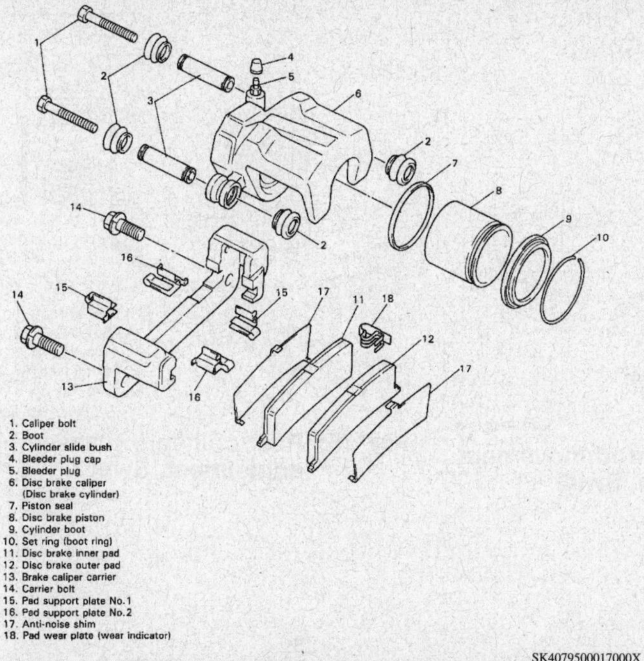
1. Caliper bolt
2. Boot
3. Cylinder slide bush
4. Bleeder plug cap
5. Bleeder plug
6. Disc brake caliper (Disc brake cylinder)
7. Piston seal
8. Disc brake piston
9. Cylinder boot
10. Set ring (boot ring)
11. Disc brake inner pad
12. Disc brake outer pad
13. Brake caliper carrier
14. Carrier bolt
15. Pad support plate No.1
16. Pad support plate No.2
17. Anti-noise shim
18. Pad wear plate (wear indicator)
SK4079500017000X

Fig. 6 Exploded view of front caliper assembly. Esteem

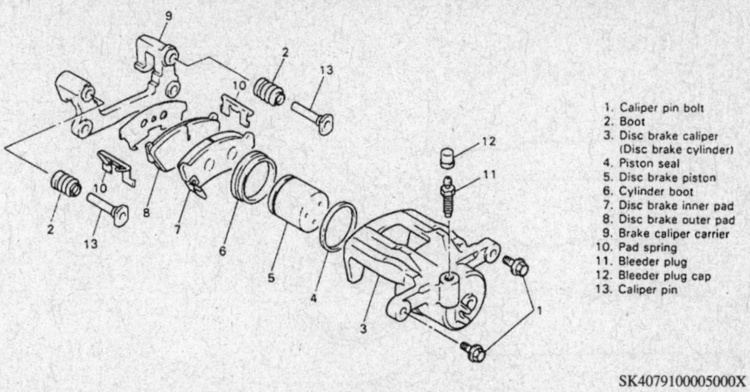
1. Caliper pin bolt
2. Boot
3. Disc brake caliper (Disc brake cylinder)
4. Piston seal
5. Disc brake piston
6. Cylinder boot
7. Disc brake inner pad
8. Disc brake outer pad
9. Brake caliper carrier
10. Pad spring
11. Bleeder plug
12. Bleeder plug cap
13. Caliper pin
SK4079100005000X

Fig. 7 Exploded view of front caliper assembly. Swift

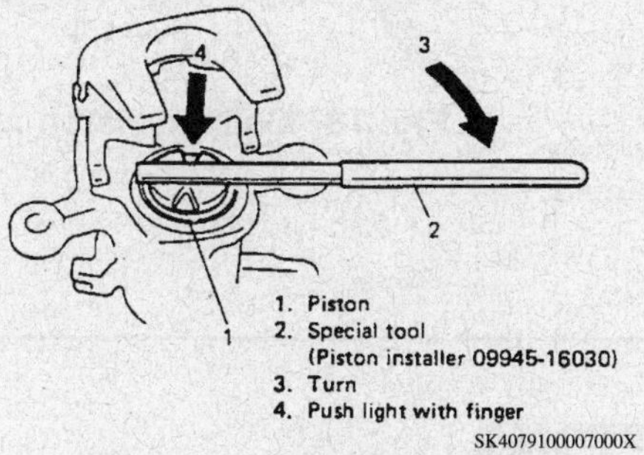
1. Piston
2. Special tool (Piston installer 09945-16030)
3. Turn
4. Push light with finger
SK4079100007000X

Fig. 8 Rear caliper piston adjustment. Swift

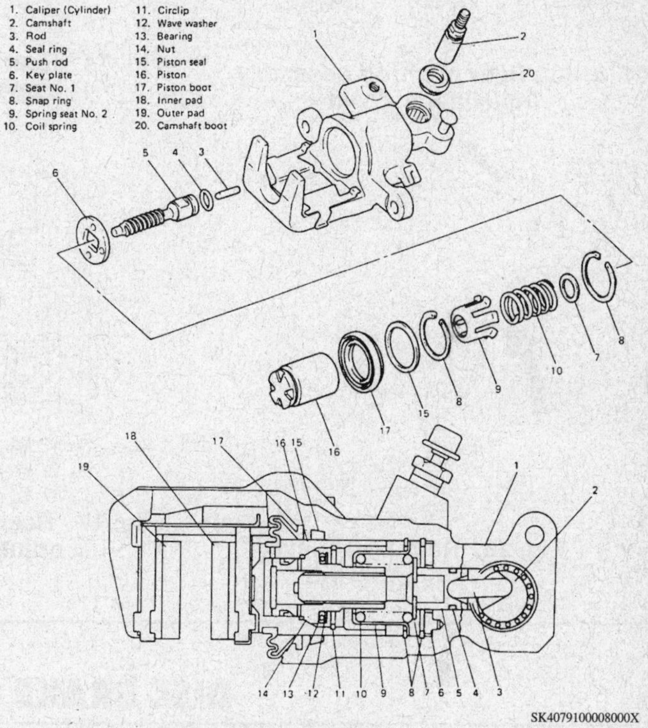
1. Caliper (Cylinder)
2. Camshaft
3. Rod
4. Seal ring
5. Push rod
6. Key plate
7. Seat No. 1
8. Snap ring
9. Spring seat No. 2
10. Coil spring
11. Circlip
12. Wave washer
13. Bearing
14. Nut
15. Piston seal
16. Piston
17. Piston boot
18. Inner pad
19. Outer pad
20. Camshaft boot
SK4079100008000X

Fig. 9 Exploded view of rear caliper. Swift

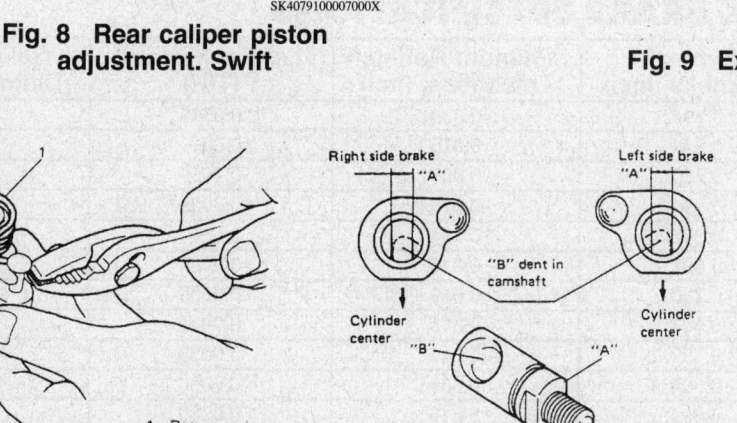

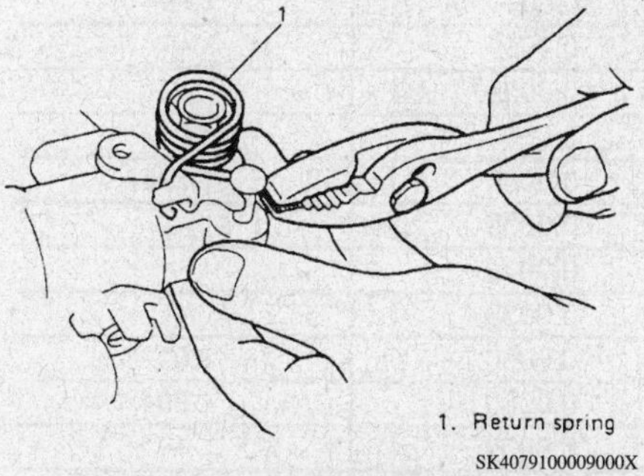
1. Return spring
SK4079100009000X

Fig. 10 Rear return spring removal. Swift

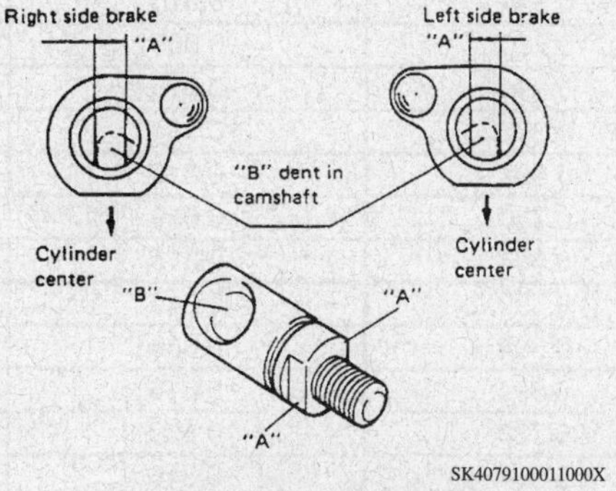
Right side brake
"A"
Left side brake
"A"
"B" dent in camshaft
Cylinder center
Cylinder center
"B"
"A"
"A"
SK4079100011000X

Fig. 12 Rear camshaft installation. Swift

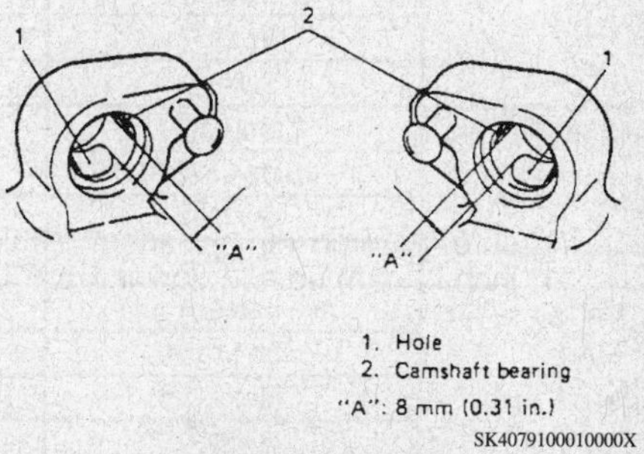
"A"
"A"
1. Hole
2. Camshaft bearing
"A": 8 mm (0.31 in.)
SK4079100010000X

Fig. 11 Rear camshaft bearing installation. Swift

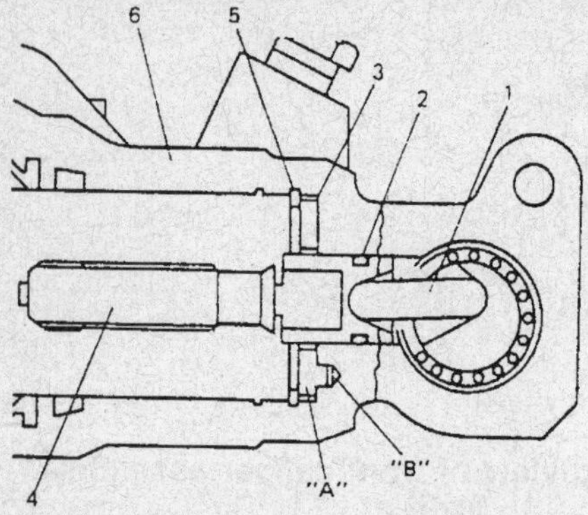
6
5
3
2
1
4
"A"
"B"
1. Rod
2. Seal ring
3. Key plate
4. Push rod
5. Snap ring
6. Cylinder (Caliper)
SK4079100012000X

Fig. 13 Rear pushrod assembly installation. Swift

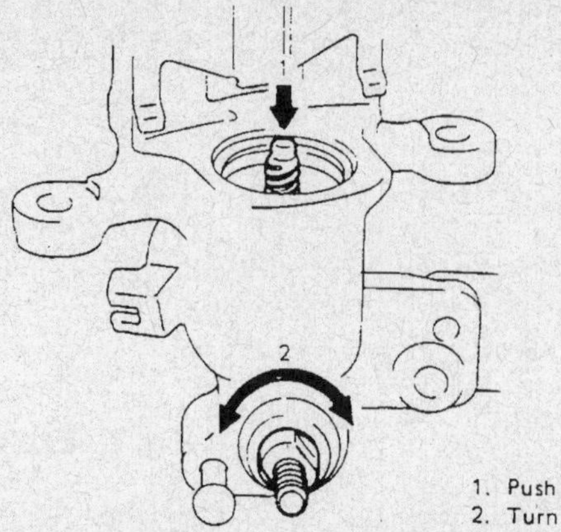
1
2
1. Push
2. Turn
SK4079100013000X

Fig. 14 Rear pushrod movement inspection. Swift

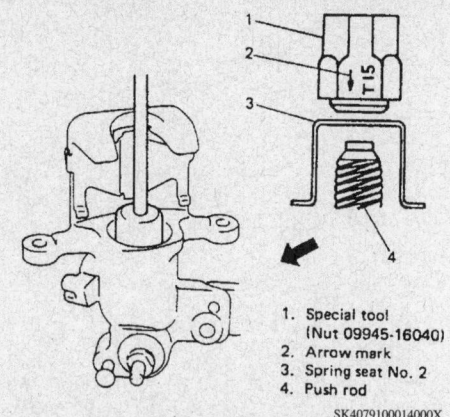

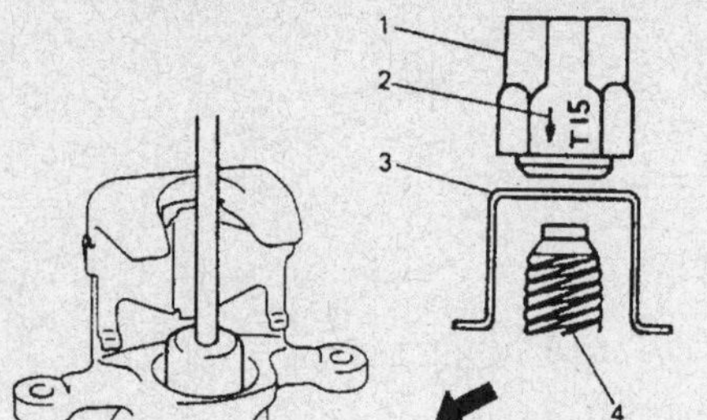
1
2
3
4
T15
1. Special tool (Nut 09945-16040)
2. Arrow mark
3. Spring seat No. 2
4. Push rod
SK4079100014000X

Fig. 15 Rear coil spring assembly adjustment. Swift

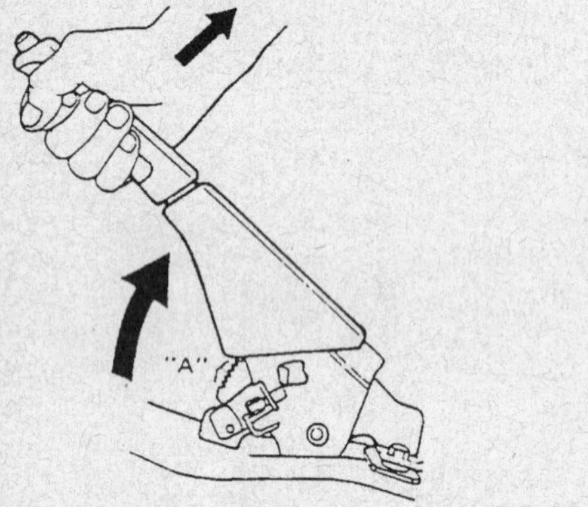
"A"
SK4079100015000X

Fig. 16 Rear brake lever adjustment. Swift

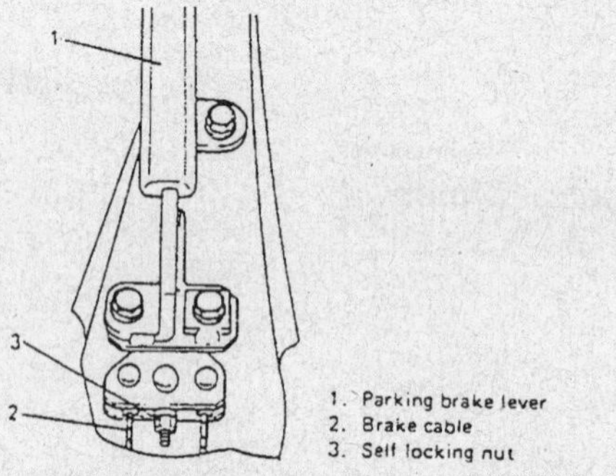
1
2
3
1. Parking brake lever
2. Brake cable
3. Self locking nut
SK4079100016000X

Fig. 17 Rear parking brake lever adjustment. Swift

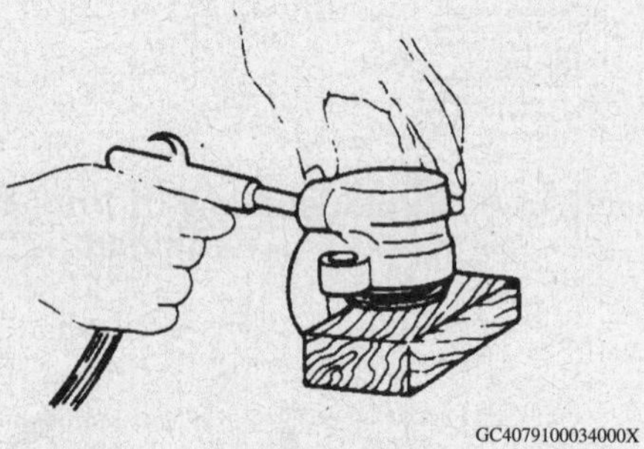
GC4079100034000X

Fig. 18 Caliper piston removal

DISC BRAKE SPECIFICATIONS

Year	Model	Nominal Thickness, Inch	Minimum Refinish Thickness, Inch	Lateral Runout (TIR)	Caliper Bore Diameter, Inch
1993	Samurai①	0.394	0.334	0.0060	2.012
	Sidekick①	0.394	0.315	0.0060	1.894
	Swift①	0.730	0.650	0.0039	—
	Swift②	0.394	0.315	0.0039	—
1994	Samurai①	0.394	0.334	0.0060	2.012
	Sidekick①	0.394	0.315	0.0060	1.894
	Swift①	0.730	0.650	0.0039	—
	Swift②	0.394	0.315	0.0039	—
1995	Esteem	0.590	0.240	0.0039	—
	Samurai①	0.394	0.334	0.0060	2.012
	Sidekick①	0.394	0.315	0.0060	1.894
	Swift①	0.730	0.650	0.0039	—
	Swift②	0.394	0.315	0.0039	—
1996	Esteem	0.590	0.240	0.0039	—
	Sidekick①	③	④	0.0060	1.894
	Swift①	0.730	0.650	0.0039	—
	Swift②	0.394	0.315	0.0039	—
	X-90①	③	④	0.0060	1.894

① — Front Brake.
② — Rear Brake.
③ — 2-door models, 0.394 inch; 4-door models, 0.670 inch.
④ — 2-door models, 0.315 inch; 4-door models, 0.590 inch.

TIGHTENING SPECIFICATIONS

Year	Component	Torque/ Ft. Lbs.
SAMURAI & SIDEKICK		
1993-95	Bleeder Screw	7-9
	Brake Pipe Flare Nut	11-13
	Brake Hose Bolt (Samurai)	15-28
	Brake Hose Bolt (Sidekick)	15-18
	Caliper Carrier Bolt	51-72
	Caliper Guide Pin	19-21
	Caliper Holder Bolt	29-43
	Master Cylinder Nut	8-11
SIDEKICK & X-90		
1996	Bleeder Screw	6.5
	Brake Pipe Flare Nut	11.5
	Brake Hose Bolt	17
	Caliper Carrier Bolt	61.5
	Caliper Guide Pin	19.5
	Master Cylinder Nut	9.5
	Wheel Lug Nut	69
SWIFT		
1993-96	Caliper Carrier Bolts	29-43
	Caliper Hose	15-18
	Caliper Mounting Bolts	16-23
	Front Drive Shaft Nut	109-146
	Wheel Lug Nuts	37-58
ESTEEM		
1995–96	Brake Pipe Flare Nut	11.5
	Caliper Carrier Bolts	61.5
	Caliper Pin Bolt	19.5
	Flexible Hose Bolt	17
	Wheel Lug Nuts	69

Drum Brakes

INDEX

	Page No.
Adjustments	40-125
Service Brake	40-125
Brake Service	40-122
Brake Drum, Replace	40-122
Brake Shoe, Replace	40-123
Wheel Cylinder, Replace	40-123
Drum Brake Specifications	40-125
Parking Brake Service	40-124
Adjustment	40-124
Tightening Specifications	40-126

BRAKE SERVICE

BRAKE DRUM, REPLACE

Samurai

1. Raise and support vehicle
2. Remove wheel center cap.
3. Remove rear wheel assembly. **Ensure parking brake lever is not pulled up.**
4. Increase the clearance between brake shoe and drum by removing parking brake shoe lever return spring, then disconnect parking brake cable joint from parking brake shoe lever, **Fig. 1.**
5. Remove parking brake shoe lever stopper plate, **Fig. 2.**
6. Remove drum to axle hub attaching bolts, then using slide hammer tool No. 09942-15510, or equivalent, and brake drum remover tool No. 09943-35511, or equivalent, pull off brake drum.
7. Reverse procedure to install, noting the following:
   a. Before installing drum, maximize brake shoe to drum clearance by pushing down on ratchet using a screwdriver as shown, **Fig. 3.**
   b. Install brake drum, drum to axle hub nuts and wheel assembly.
   c. Install center cap.
   d. Depress brake pedal several times to obtain proper drum to shoe clearance and adjust parking brake. Ensure brake drum does not drag.
   e. Lower vehicle and test brake operation.

Sidekick & X-90

1. Engage parking brake, then raise and support vehicle.
2. Remove wheels and brake drum nuts, then release parking brake lever.
3. Loosen parking brake cable locking nut, then lift rear part of brake lever cover to access brake cable.
4. **On 1993–95 Sidekick models,** to increase clearance between shoe and drum, proceed as follows:
   a. Remove backing plate plug.
   b. Insert screwdriver into plug hole till its tip contacts shoe hold-down spring, then push hold-down spring as shown, **Fig. 4.**
5. **On 1993–95 Sidekick models,** pull brake drum off using sliding hammer tool No. 09942-15510 and brake drum remover tool No. 09943-35511, or equivalents, as shown, **Fig. 5.**
6. **On 1996 Sidekick and X-90 models,**

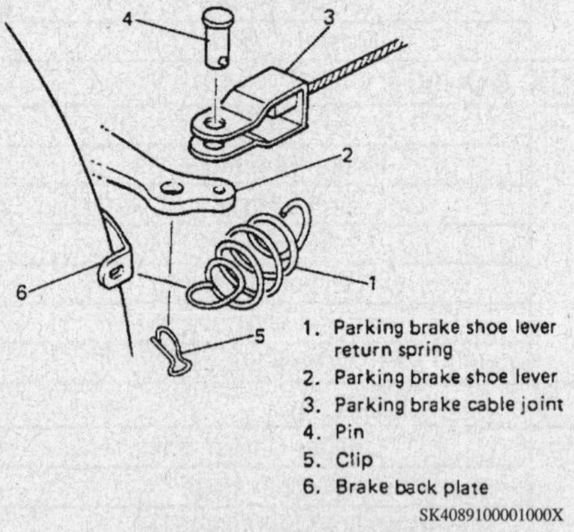
1. Parking brake shoe lever return spring
2. Parking brake shoe lever
3. Parking brake cable joint
4. Pin
5. Clip
6. Brake back plate
SK4089100001000X

Fig. 1 Parking brake cable joint removal. Samurai

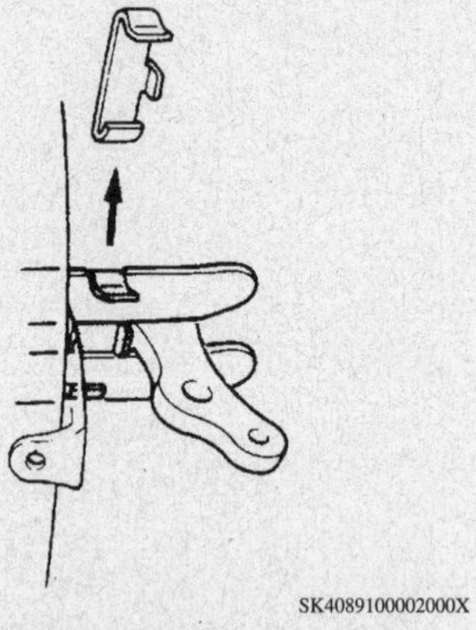
SK4089100002000X

Fig. 2 Stopper plate removal. Samurai

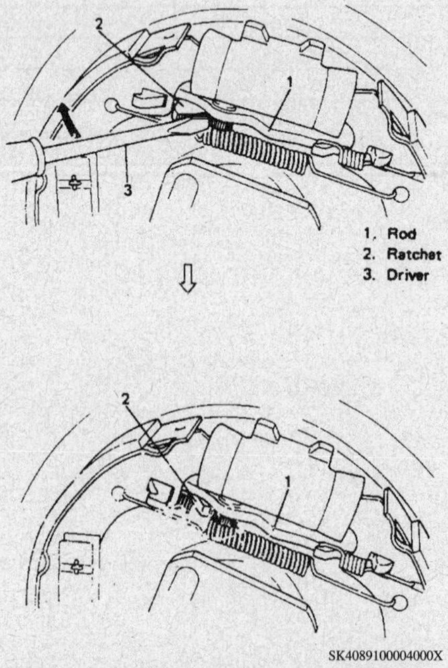
1. Rod
2. Ratchet
3. Driver
SK4089100004000X

Fig. 3 Retracting brake shoes

7. Remove brake drum by fitting two 8mm bolts into holes on drum and extracting drum off wheel hub.
8. **On all Models,** reverse procedure to install, noting the following:
   a. **On 1993–95 Sidekick models,** before installing drum, maximize brake shoe to drum clearance by pushing down on ratchet using a screwdriver as shown, **Fig. 3.**
   b. **On all models,** tighten drum nuts to specification.
   c. Depress brake pedal five times to obtain proper drum to shoe clearance.
   d. Adjust parking brake cable as outlined under "Parking Brake, Adjust."

Swift

1. Raise and support vehicle, then remove wheel and spindle cap.
2. **On sedan models,** remove drum screws.
3. **On all models,** unstake and remove spindle nut and washer, then release parking brake lever.
4. Remove parking brake lever cover, then loosen parking brake cable locknut.
5. To increase clearance between shoe and drum, proceed as follows:
   a. Remove backing plate plug.
   b. Insert screwdriver into plug hole till its tip contacts shoe hold-down spring, then push hold-down spring as shown, **Fig. 6.**
6. Using slide hammer and drum remover tools, pull off brake drum.
7. Reverse procedure to install, noting the following:
   a. Before installing drum, maximize brake shoe to drum clearance by pushing down on ratchet using a screwdriver as shown, **Fig. 3.**
   b. Put brake shoe hold-down spring back to its original position, **Fig. 7.**
   c. Tighten spindle nut to specification. Caulk spindle nut after tightening.
   d. Depress brake pedal five times to obtain proper drum to shoe clearance.

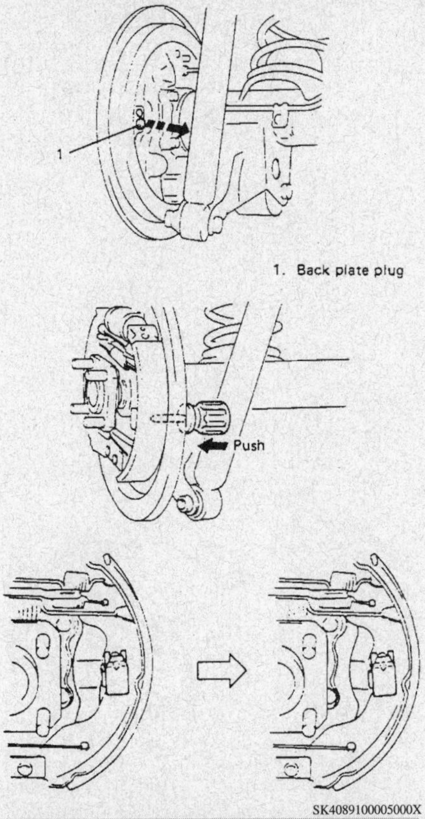
1
1. Back plate plug
Push
SK4089100005000X

Fig. 4 Brake shoe clearance adjustment. 1993–95 Sidekick

e. Adjust parking brake cable as outlined under "Parking Brake, Adjust."

Esteem

1. Raise and support vehicle, then remove wheel.
2. Remove drum screws.
3. Release parking brake lever.
4. Remove parking brake lever cover, then loosen parking brake cable locking nut.
5. To increase clearance between shoe and drum, proceed as follows:
   a. Remove backing plate plug.
   b. Insert screwdriver into plug hole till its tip contacts shoe hold-down spring, then push hold-down spring as shown, **Fig. 6.**
6. Remove brake drum by fitting two 8mm bolts into holes on drum and extracting drum off wheel hub.
7. Reverse procedure to install, noting the following:
   a. Before installing drum, maximize brake shoe to drum clearance by pushing down on ratchet using a screwdriver as shown, **Fig. 3.**
   b. Put brake shoe hold-down spring back to its original position, **Fig. 7.**
   c. Tighten spindle nut to specification.
   d. Depress brake pedal five times to obtain proper drum to shoe clearance.
   e. Adjust parking brake cable as outlined under "Parking Brake, Adjust."

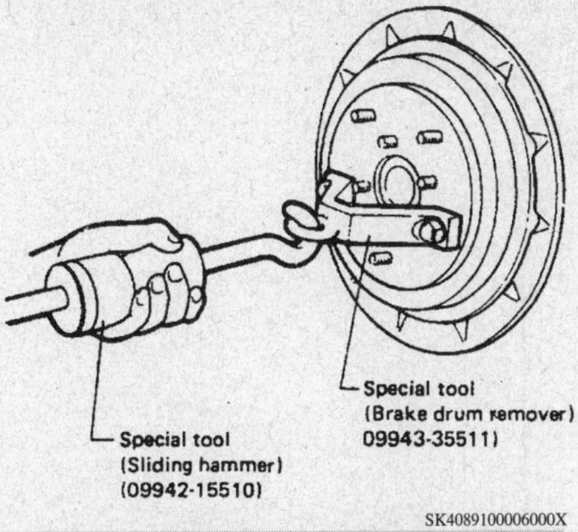
Special tool
(Brake drum remover)
09943-35511)
Special tool
(Sliding hammer)
(09942-15510)
SK4089100006000X

Fig. 5 Brake drum removal. 1993–95 Sidekick

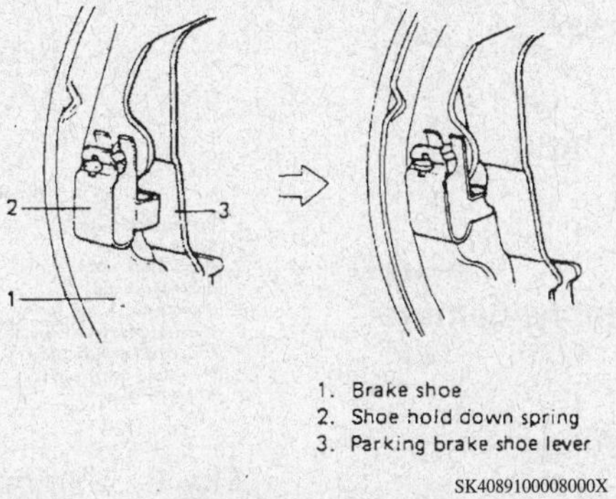
1
2
3
1. Brake shoe
2. Shoe hold down spring
3. Parking brake shoe lever
SK4089100008000X

Fig. 7 Hold-down spring location. Esteem & Swift

BRAKE SHOE, REPLACE

Samurai

1. Remove brake shoe hold-down springs by turning shoe hold-down pins, then remove brake shoes and brake shoe strut.
2. Disconnect brake line and remove wheel cylinder attaching bolts, then the wheel cylinder. Inspect wheel cylinder for leaks. If leakage is found, replace wheel cylinder inner components.
3. Reverse procedure to install, noting the following:
   a. Install wheel cylinder to backing plate and tighten bolts to specification.
   b. Install brake line and tighten flare nut to specification.
   c. Assemble brake shoes, levers and springs, **Fig. 8.**
   d. Push shoe hold-down springs into place, then turn hold-down pins to engage springs.
   e. Install parking brake shoe lever stopper plate, **Fig. 2.**
   f. Connect brake cable joint to parking brake shoe lever, **Fig. 1,** then parking brake shoe lever return spring.

Sidekick & X-90

Refer to **Fig. 9,** during replacement procedure.

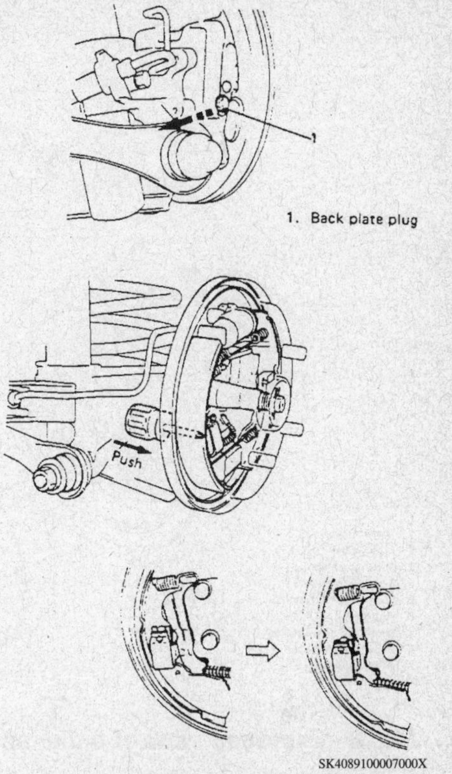
1
1. Back plate plug
Push
SK4089100007000X

Fig. 6 Brake shoe clearance adjustment. Esteem & Swift

1. Remove drum as outlined under "Brake Drum, Replace."
2. Remove shoe hold-down springs, then disconnect parking brake cable from parking brake shoe lever.
3. Remove brake shoe assembly.
4. Remove brake strut rod and spring from brake shoes.
5. Remove parking brake shoe lever from shoe rim.
6. Reverse procedure to install.

Esteem & Swift

Refer to **Fig. 10,** during replacement procedure.

1. Remove drum as outlined under "Brake Drum, Replace. "
2. Remove shoe hold-down springs, then disconnect parking brake cable from parking brake shoe lever.
3. Remove brake shoe assembly.
4. Remove brake strut rod and spring from brake shoes.
5. Remove parking brake shoe lever from shoe rim.
6. Reverse procedure to install.

WHEEL CYLINDER, REPLACE

Sidekick & X-90

1. Remove drum as outlined under "Brake Drum, Replace."
2. Remove brake shoes as outlined under "Brake Shoe, Replace."
3. Loosen brake pipe flare nut. **Fluid should not leak out of pipe or cylinder.**
4. Remove wheel cylinder mounting

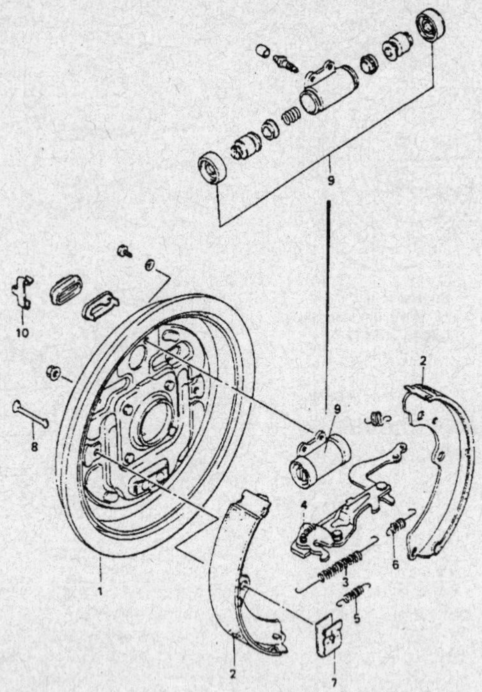
1. Brake back plate
2. Brake shoe
3. Shoe return spring (A)
4. Brake strut rod
5. Shoe return spring (B)
6. Rod spring
7. Shoe hold down spring
8. Shoe hold down pin
9. Wheel cylinder
10. Stopper plate
SK4089100003000X

Fig. 8 Exploded view of brake assembly. Samurai

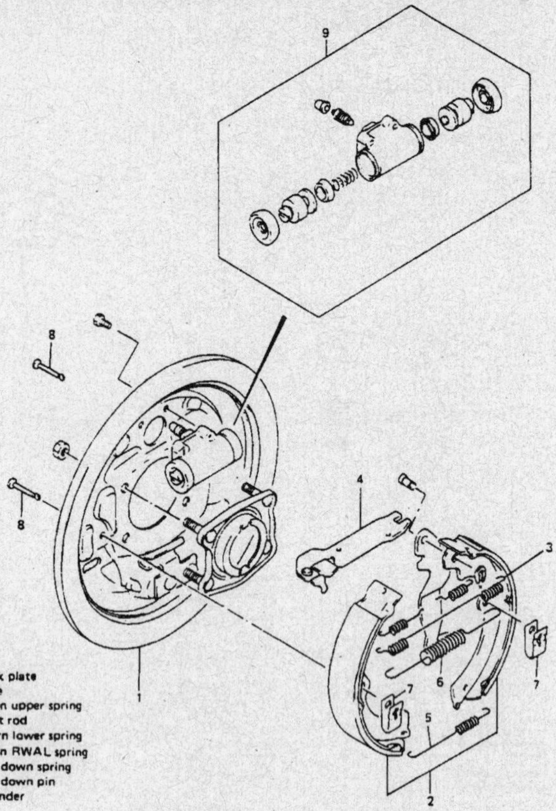
1. Brake back plate
2. Brake shoe
3. Shoe return upper spring
4. Brake strut rod
5. Shoe return lower spring
6. Shoe return RWAL spring
7. Shoe hold down spring
8. Shoe hold down pin
9. Wheel cylinder
SK4089100009000X

Fig. 9 Exploded view of brake assembly. Sidekick & X-90

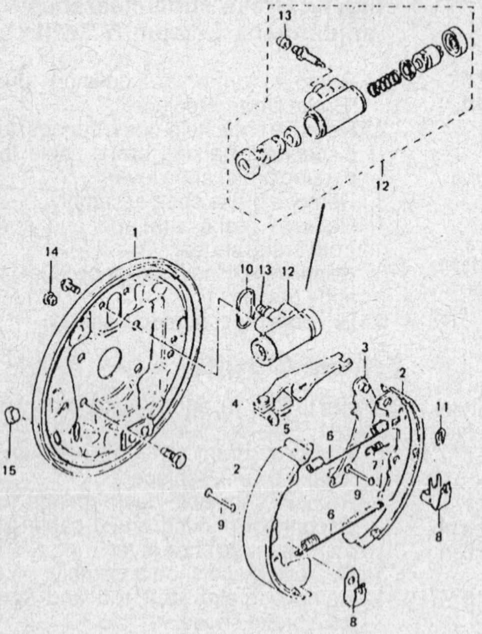
1. Brake back plate
2. Brake shoe
3. Parking brake shoe lever
4. Brake strut
5. Quadrant spring
6. Shoe return spring
7. Antirattle spring
8. Shoe hold down spring
9. Shoe hold down pin
10. Packing
11. Parking lever retainer
12. Wheel cylinder
13. Bleeder plug cap
14. Rubber plug
15. Rubber plug
SK4089100010000X

Fig. 10 Exploded view of brake assembly. Esteem & Swift

bolts, then disconnect brake pipe from wheel cylinder.

5. Reverse procedure to install, noting the following:
   a. Apply water tight sealant to wheel cylinder and backing plate mating surface.
   b. Tighten wheel cylinder mounting bolts and brake pipe flare nut to specification.
   c. Bleed brake system.

Esteem & Swift

1. Remove drum as outlined under "Brake Drum, Replace."
2. Remove brake shoes as outlined under "Brake Shoe, Replace."
3. Loosen brake pipe flare nut. **Fluid should not leak out of pipe or cylinder.**
4. Remove wheel cylinder mounting bolts, then disconnect brake pipe from wheel cylinder.
5. Reverse procedure to install, noting the following:
   a. Tighten wheel cylinder mounting bolts and brake pipe to specification.
   b. Bleed brake system.

PARKING BRAKE SERVICE

ADJUSTMENT

1. Parking brake lever should be adjusted as follows:
   a. **On Samurai models,** 3–8 notches.
   b. **On Sidekick and X-90 models,** 6–8 notches.
   c. **On Swift models,** 4–9 notches.
   d. **On Esteem models,** 3–5 notches.
2. **On all models,** lever should be adjusted with 44 lbs. of pull applied, **Fig. 11.**

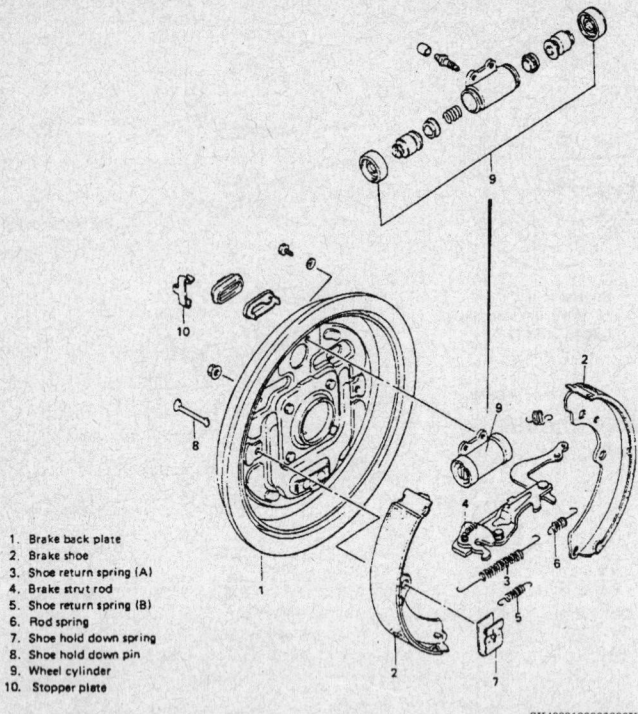

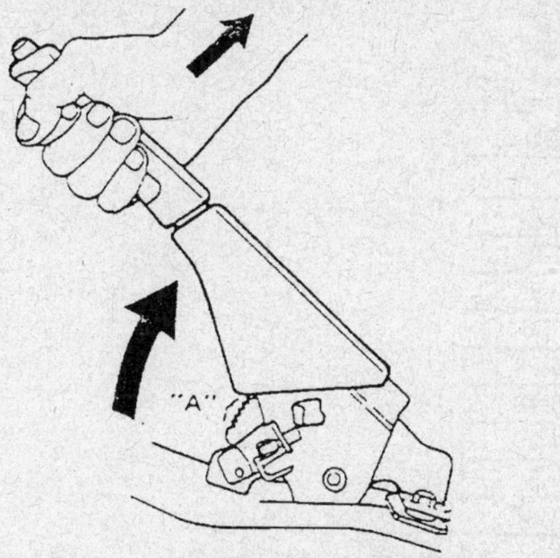
"A"

SK4089100011000X

Fig. 11 Parking brake lever adjustment

3. Adjust travel by loosening adjustment nuts, **Fig. 12,** or self locking nut, **Fig. 13.**

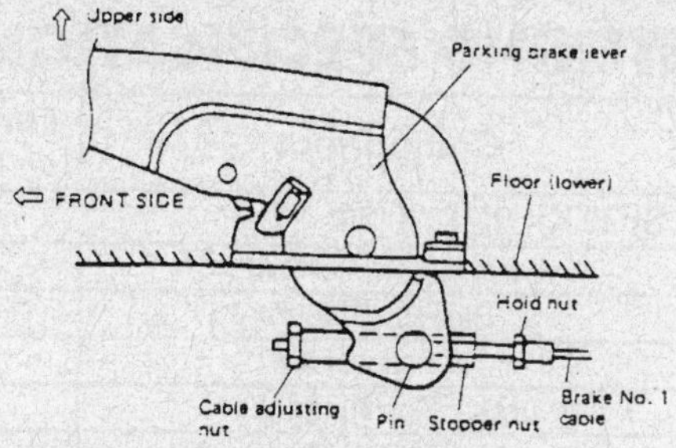
Upper side
Parking brake lever
FRONT SIDE
Floor (lower)
Hold nut
Cable adjusting nut
Pin
Stopper nut
Brake No. 1 cable

SK4089100012000X

Fig. 12 Parking brake lever adjustment. Samurai

ADJUSTMENTS

SERVICE BRAKE

These brakes are self-adjusting, but do require adjustment for proper drum to shoe clearance when brake shoe has been replaced or brake drum has been removed.

Adjustment is automatically accomplished by depressing brake pedal 5 times with approximately 66 lbs. force on brake pedal.

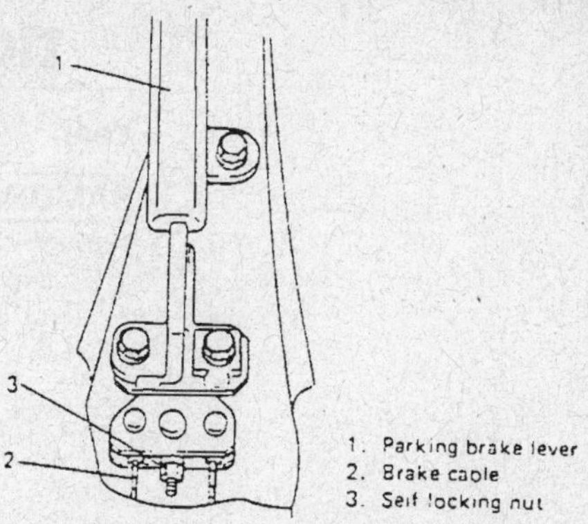
1
2
3
1. Parking brake lever
2. Brake cable
3. Self locking nut

SK4089100013000X

Fig. 13 Parking brake lever adjustment. Esteem, Sidekick, Swift & X-90

DRUM BRAKE SPECIFICATIONS

Year	Model	Brake Drum Inside Diameter, Inches	Maximum Refinish Diameter, Inches
1993	Samurai	8.66	8.74
	Sidekick	③	④
	Swift①	7.09	7.16
	Swift②	7.87	7.95
1994	Samurai	8.66	8.74
	Sidekick	③	④
	Swift①	7.09	7.16
	Swift②	7.87	7.95
1995	Esteem	7.87	7.95
	Samurai	8.66	8.74
	Sidekick	③	④
	Swift①	7.09	7.16
	Swift②	7.87	7.95
1996	Esteem	7.87	7.95
	Sidekick	③	④
	Swift①	7.09	7.16
	Swift②	7.87	7.95
	X-90	8.66	8.74

①–Hatchback model.

②–Sedan model.

③ — 2-door models, 8.66 inches; 4-door models, 10.00 inches.

④ — 2-door models, 8.74 inches; 4-door models, 10.07 inches.

TIGHTENING SPECIFICATIONS

Year	Component	Torque/Ft. Lbs.
SAMURAI, SIDEKICK & X-90		
1993–96	Backing Plate Nut	17
	Bleeder Screw	7-9
	Booster Nut	9.5
	Brake Pipe Flare Nut	11.5
	Brake Hose Bolt (Samurai)	15-28
	Brake Hose Bolt (Sidekick & X-90)	15-18
	Brake Pedal Shaft Nut	14-20
	Master Cylinder Nut	9.5
	Rear Drum Nut	37-57
	Wheel Cylinder Mounting Bolt	9-12
	Wheel Lug Nut	69
SWIFT		
1993–96	Backing Plate Mounting Bolt (Drum)	14-20
	Bleeder Screw	6-7
	Booster Nut	9-11
	Brake Hose Bolt	15-18
	Brake Pedal Shaft Nut	14-20
	Front Driveshaft Nut	109-144
	Master Cylinder Bolt	9-11
	Rear Spindle Nut	109-144
	Wheel Cylinder Mounting Bolt	8-9
ESTEEM		
1995-96	Backing Plate Mounting Bolt (Drum)	17
	Bleeder Screw	6
	Booster Nut	9.5
	Brake Hose Bolt	17
	Brake Pedal Shaft Nut	17
	Master Cylinder Nut	9.5
	Wheel Cylinder Mounting Bolt	9
	Wheel Lug Nut	61.5

Hydraulic Brake Systems

INDEX

	Page No.
Adjustments	40-127
Brake Pedal Height	40-127
Brake Pedal Travel Check	40-127
Brake System Bleed	40-128
Master Cylinder Bleeding	40-129
System Bleeding	40-128
Component Replacement	40-128
Master Cylinder, Replace	40-128
Component Service	40-128
Master Cylinder Overhaul	40-128
Description	40-127
Diagnosis & Testing	40-127
Brake Fluid Leakage Inspection	40-127
Road Test	40-127
Substandard Or Contaminated Brake Fluid	40-127
Troubleshooting	40-127
Brake Pull	40-127
Brake Warning Light On Or Flashing, After Engine Start	40-127
Brake Warning Light On, w/Brake Pedal Applied	40-127
Dragging Brakes	40-127
Excessive Pedal Travel	40-127
Low Braking Force	40-127

DESCRIPTION

When the brake pedal is depressed, a vacuum builds up in the booster which amplifies the pedal force, pressing on the piston in the master cylinder. The piston raises the hydraulic pressure in the cylinder. This hydraulic pressure is then applied to each respective brake caliper and wheel cylinder, and acts to press the brake pads and shoes against the rotating discs and drums. The resulting friction converts the rotational energy to thermal energy, stopping the vehicle.

TROUBLESHOOTING

LOW BRAKING FORCE

1. Fluid leakage from brake lines and/or hoses.
2. Air in brake system.
3. Malfunctioning wheel cylinder and/or caliper assembly.

BRAKE PULL

1. Malfunctioning wheel cylinder and/or caliper assembly.
2. Loose calipers.
3. Restricted brake line or hose.

EXCESSIVE PEDAL TRAVEL

1. Partial brake system failure.
2. Insufficient fluid in master cylinder reservoirs.
3. Air in system.

DRAGGING BRAKES

1. Master cylinder pistons not returning correctly.
2. Restricted brake line or hose.
3. Wheel cylinder or caliper piston sticking.

BRAKE WARNING LIGHT ON OR FLASHING, AFTER ENGINE START

1. Insufficient fluid in master cylinder reservoirs.
2. Fluid leakage from brake lines and/or hoses.

BRAKE WARNING LIGHT ON, W/BRAKE PEDAL APPLIED

1. Insufficient fluid in master cylinder reservoirs.
2. Fluid leakage from brake lines and/or hoses.

DIAGNOSIS & TESTING

ROAD TEST

Brakes should be tested on dry, clean, smooth and reasonable level roadway which is not crowned. Road test brakes by making brake applications with both light and heavy pedal forces at various speeds to determine if car stops evenly and effectively.

Also road test vehicle to see if it pulls to one side without brake application. If it does, check tire pressure, front end alignment and front suspension attachments for looseness.

BRAKE FLUID LEAKAGE INSPECTION

Check master cylinder fluid levels. While a slight drop in reservoir level does result from normal lining wear, an abnormally low level indicates a leak in the system. In such a case, check the entire brake system for leakage. If even a slight evidence of leakage is noted, the cause should be corrected or defective parts should be replaced.

SUBSTANDARD OR CONTAMINATED BRAKE FLUID

Improper brake fluid, mineral oil or water in the fluid may cause the brake fluid to boil or the rubber components in the hydraulic system to deteriorate.

If deterioration of rubber is evident, disassemble all hydraulic parts and wash with alcohol. Dry these parts with compressed air before assembly to keep alcohol out of the system. Replace all rubber parts in the system, including hoses. Also, when working on the brake mechanisms, check for fluid on linings. If excessive fluid is found, replace pads/shoes.

If master cylinder piston seals are satisfactory, check for leakage or excessive heat conditions. If condition is not found, drain fluid, flush with brake fluid, refill and bleed system.

The system must be flushed if there is any doubt as to the grade of fluid in the system or if fluid has been used which contained parts that have been subjected to contaminated fluid.

ADJUSTMENTS

BRAKE PEDAL HEIGHT

The brake pedal should be at the same height as clutch pedal. Ensure distance between brake booster mounting surface (with gasket) and pushrod clevis pin hole is as follows:

1. **On Samurai models,** 4.94–4.98 inches (125.5–126.5 mm)
2. **On 1993–95 Sidekick models,** 6.60–6.64 inches (167.6–168.6 mm)
3. **On Swift models,** 4.51–4.54 inches (114.5–115.5 mm).

BRAKE PEDAL TRAVEL CHECK

1. Start engine, then depress brake pedal a few times.
2. Apply approximately 66 lbs. load to brake pedal, and measure pedal arm to wall clearance, "B," **Fig. 1.**
3. Clearance should not exceed the following:
   a. **On Samurai models,** 2.95 inches (75 mm).
   b. **On 1993–95 Sidekick models,** 5.12 inches (130 mm).
   c. **On 1996 Sidekick and X-90 models,** 3.15 inches (80 mm).
   d. **On Esteem models,** 3.54 inches (90 mm).
   e. **On Swift models,** 2.36 inches (60 mm).
4. **On all models,** possible causes for a low pedal are:
   a. Worn rear brake shoes.
   b. Brake lines need bleeding.

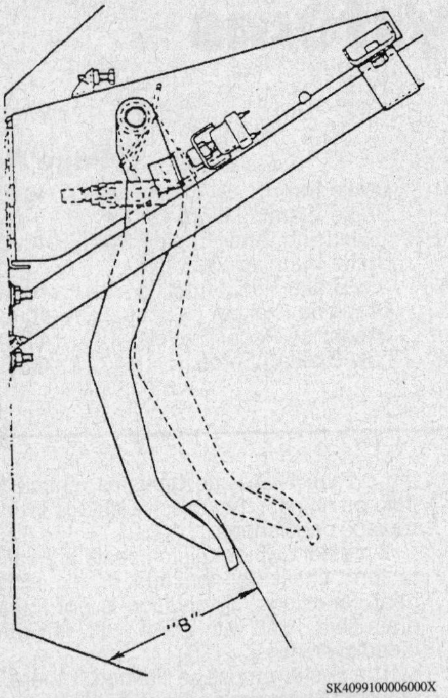
"B"
SK4099100006000X

Fig. 1 Pedal arm to wall clearance measurement

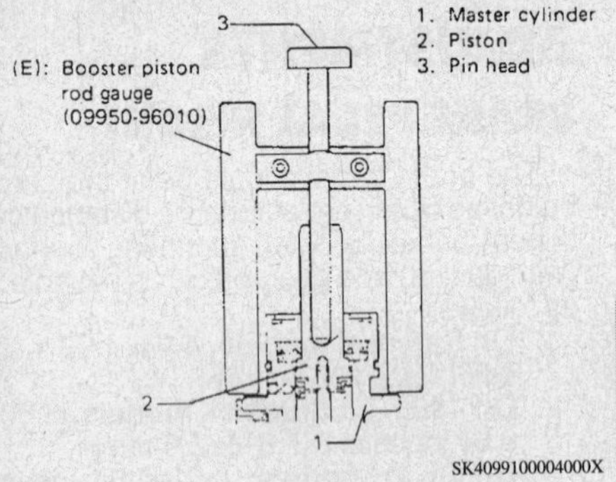
1. Master cylinder
2. Piston
3. Pin head
(E): Booster piston rod gauge (09950-96010)
SK4099100004000X

Fig. 3 Piston installation

c. Booster pushrod out of alignment.
d. Rear brake shoes malfunctioning.

COMPONENT REPLACEMENT

MASTER CYLINDER, REPLACE

1. Clean any dirt from around reservoir cap. Remove cap, then drain brake fluid into appropriate container.
2. Remove reservoir connector screw, **Fig. 2,** then the reservoir.
3. Disconnect brake lines from master cylinder. **Do not allow brake fluid to get on painted surfaces.**
4. Remove master cylinder attaching bolts, then the master cylinder.
5. Adjust clearance of booster piston rod to master cylinder piston as follows:
   a. Push piston rod several times to ensure reaction disc is in place.
   b. Measure with gasket in place on master cylinder and booster at atmospheric pressure.
   c. Set measuring tool No. 09950-98210, or equivalent, on master cylinder and push pin until it contacts piston, **Fig. 3.**
   d. Turn tool upside down and place on booster, **Fig. 4.** Adjust booster piston rod length until rod end contacts piston head.
6. When adjusted, if negative pressure is applied to booster with engine at idle, piston to piston rod clearance should be as follows:
   a. **On Samurai models,** 0.004–0.020 inch (0.1–0.5 mm)
   b. **On Sidekick and X-90 models less ABS,** 0.010–0.020 inch (0.25–0.50 mm)
   c. **On Sidekick and X-90 models with ABS,** 0.006–0.014 inch (0.14–0.35 mm)
   d. **On Swift models,** 0.004–0.013 inch (0.10–0.35 mm).
   e. **On Esteem models less ABS,** 0.010–0.020 inch (0.25–0.50 mm)
   f. **On Esteem models with ABS,** 0 inch (0 mm)
7. **On all models,** install reservoir on master cylinder, then the reservoir connector screw.
8. Install master cylinder on studs, then the mounting nuts.
9. Connect hydraulic lines.
10. Fill reservoir with brake fluid.
11. Check brake pedal height and pedal travel as outlined under "Adjustments."

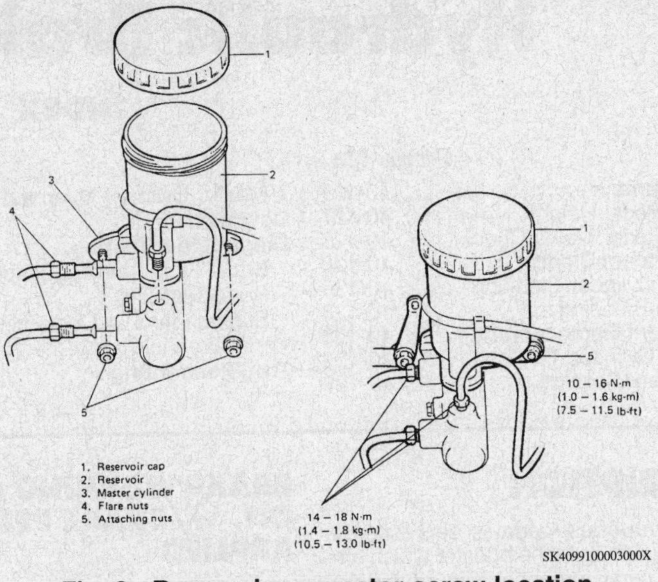
1. Reservoir cap
2. Reservoir
3. Master cylinder
4. Flare nuts
5. Attaching nuts
10 – 16 N·m
(1.0 – 1.6 kg-m)
(7.5 – 11.5 lb-ft)
14 – 18 N·m
(1.4 – 1.8 kg-m)
(10.5 – 13.0 lb-ft)
SK4099100003000X

Fig. 2 Reservoir connector screw location

COMPONENT SERVICE

MASTER CYLINDER OVERHAUL

1. Remove master cylinder as outlined under "Master Cylinder, Replace."
2. Remove circlip, then the primary piston.
3. Remove piston stopper bolt, then using compressed air, remove secondary piston. Blow compressed air into hole where stopper bolt was removed.
4. Reverse procedure to assemble.

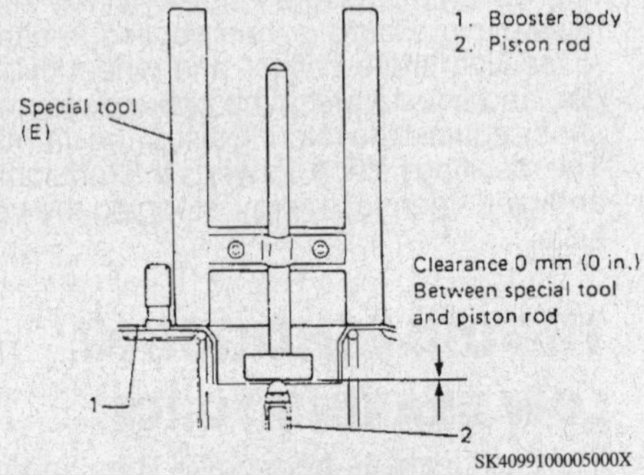
1. Booster body
2. Piston rod
Special tool (E)
Clearance 0 mm (0 in.) Between special tool and piston rod
SK4099100005000X

Fig. 4 Piston rod length adjustment

BRAKE SYSTEM BLEED

Brake fluid is extremely damaging to paint. If fluid should accidentally touch painted surface, immediately wipe fluid from paint and clean painted surface.

SYSTEM BLEEDING

Samurai, Sidekick & X-90

On Samurai models, bleeding is required at four places; both front wheels, P & B valve and left rear wheel cylinder, **Fig. 5.**

On Sidekick and X-90 models, bleeding is required at four places; both front wheels, pressure limit valve and left rear wheel cylinder, **Fig. 6.**

Esteem & Swift

The hydraulic lines of the brake system are based on a diagonal split system. When a brake line or hose is disconnected, bleeding operation must be performed at both ends of the line disconnected.

1. Fill master cylinder reservoir. Reservoir should be kept at least half full during bleeding operation.

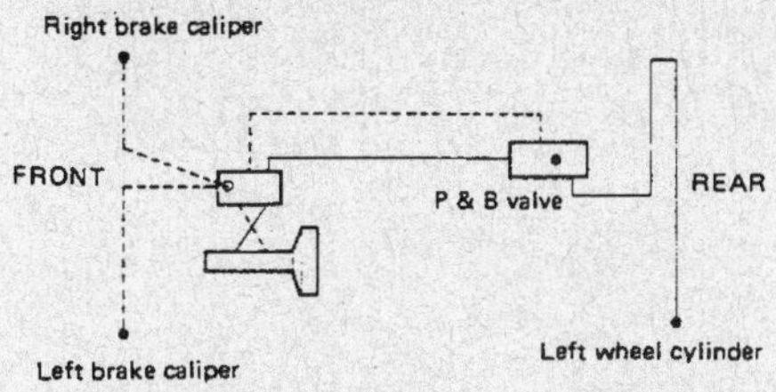
Right brake caliper
FRONT
P & B valve
REAR
Left wheel cylinder
Left brake caliper
SK4099100001000X

Fig. 5 Brake system bleed points. Samurai

2. Remove bleeder plug cap, then attach vinyl tube to bleeder plug of component to be bled. Insert other end of tube into suitable container.
3. Depress brake pedal several times, then while holding pedal depressed, loosen bleeder plug ½ turn.
4. When fluid pressure in cylinder is almost depleted, retighten bleeder plug.
5. Repeat steps 3 and 4, until there are no more air bubbles in hydraulic line.
6. When bubbles stop, depress and hold brake pedal, then tighten bleeder plug.
7. Attach bleeder cap.
8. After completing bleeding operation, apply fluid pressure to hydraulic system and check for leakage.
9. Fill master cylinder reservoir up to specified level.
10. Check brake pedal for sponginess. If pedal is spongy, repeat entire procedure.

MASTER CYLINDER BLEEDING

On Sidekick and X–90 models, when the master cylinder hydraulic system has been opened in any way, the master cylinder must be bled before system bleeding can be done.

1. Fill master cylinder reservoir with brake fluid. Wait for at least 1 minute before proceeding.
2. Disconnect brake line from primary (rear brakes) side.
3. With discharge port opened, depress brake pedal gradually. With discharge port closed with finger, release brake pedal gradually and keep it closed for about 5 seconds before depressing brake pedal again. **Do not lift finger off port while releasing brake pedal as air will be drawn into master cylinder.**

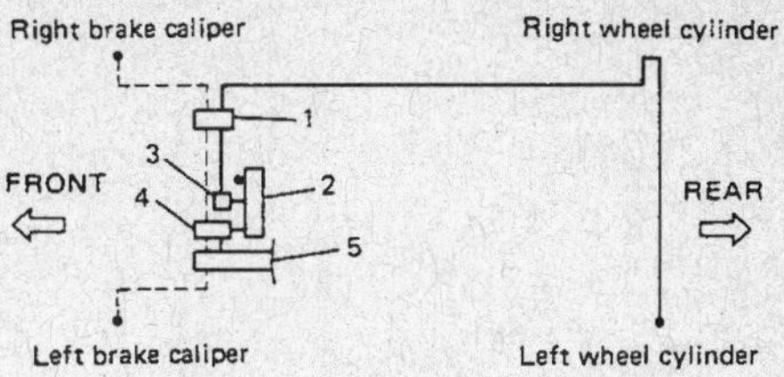
Right brake caliper
Right wheel cylinder
FRONT
REAR
1
2
3
4
5
Left brake caliper
Left wheel cylinder

1. 4-way joint
2. Pressure limit valve
3. 2-way joint
4. P & Differential valve
5. Master cylinder
: air bleeding point

SK4099100002000X

Fig. 6 Brake system bleed points. Sidekick & X-90

4. Repeat step 3 until liquid comes out of discharge port. Repeat step 3 at least four more times, then connect primary side brake pipe.
5. Disconnect two brake lines from secondary (front brakes) side.
6. Repeat steps 3 and 4 keeping fingers over both open ports.
7. Connect brake lines to secondary side.

Power Brake Units

INDEX

	Page No.
Description	40-129
Power Brake Unit Service	40-129
Brake Booster Overhaul	40-129
Power Brake Unit, Replace	40-129

DESCRIPTION

When the brake pedal is depressed, a vacuum builds up in the booster which amplifies the pedal force, pressing on the piston in the master cylinder. The piston raises the hydraulic pressure in the cylinder. This hydraulic pressure is then applied to each respective brake cylinder, and acts to press the brake pads and shoes against the rotating rotor discs and rotors. The resulting friction converts the rotational energy to thermal energy, stopping the vehicle.

POWER BRAKE UNIT SERVICE

POWER BRAKE UNIT, REPLACE

1. Remove master cylinder from booster as outlined under "Master Cylinder, Replace," in the "Hydraulic Brakes " section.
2. Disconnect pushrod clevis from brake pedal arm.
3. Disconnect vacuum hose from booster.
4. Remove booster attaching nuts, then the booster assembly.
5. Reverse procedure to install, then ensure brake pedal height and pedal travel is correct as outlined under "Brake Pedal Height, Adjust," and "Brake Pedal Travel Check" in the "Hydraulic Brakes" section.

BRAKE BOOSTER OVERHAUL

Samurai, Swift & 1993-95 Sidekick

Refer to **Figs. 1 through 3,** when performing this procedure.

1. Remove piston rod from booster, then the pushrod clevis and nut.
2. Set booster in booster overhaul set, No. 09950-88210 or equivalent, **Fig. 4.**
3. Tighten tool bolt clockwise until No. 1 body projecting part and No. 2 body depressed part fit each other, **Fig. 5.** Mark both body parts.
4. Remove booster from tool, then separate No. 1 and No. 2 bodies. **Hold both bodies carefully to prevent either body from jumping off by spring force.**
5. Remove piston return spring.
6. From No. 2 body, remove boot, air cleaner elements and air cleaner separator.
7. **On 1993–95 Sidekick models,** remove valve stopper key cushion from stopper key.
8. **On Samurai models,** using camshaft pulley holder tool No. 09917-68210, or equivalent, remove booster piston.
9. **On all models,** while compressing air valve spring, remove valve stopper key, then the booster air valve assembly. **Air valve assembly cannot be disassembled.**
10. **On 1993–95 Sidekick models,** remove diaphragm circular ring from booster piston.
11. **On Samurai models,** remove diaphragm from pressure plate.
12. **On 1993–95 Sidekick and Swift models,** remove diaphragm from booster piston.
13. **On all models,** remove reaction disc from booster piston.
14. **On Samurai models,** using oil seal replacers, No. 09951-08210 and No. 09951-18210 or equivalent, remove oil seal from No. 2 body.
15. **On 1993–95 Sidekick and Swift models,** using oil seal replacers, No. 09951-16020 and No. 09951-18210 or equivalent, remove oil seal from No. 2 body.
16. **On all models,** reverse procedure to assemble. Ensure brake pedal height and pedal travel are correct as outlined

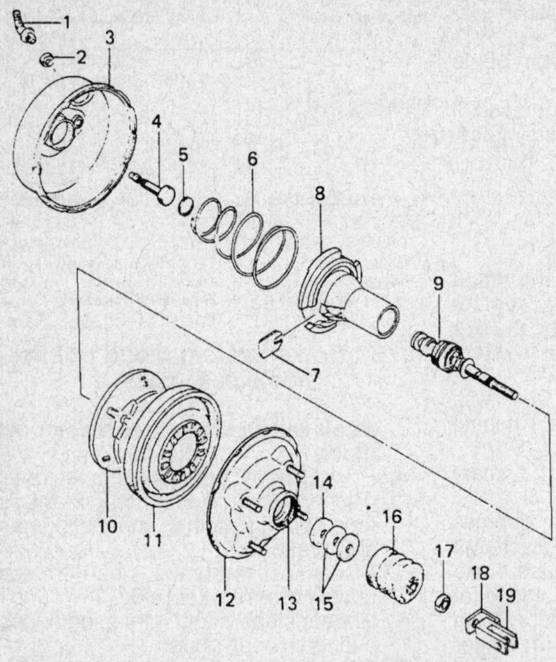

1. Vacuum check valve
2. Grommet
3. Booster No. 1 body
4. Piston rod
5. Reaction disc
6. Booster piston return spring
7. Valve stopper key
8. Booster piston
9. Booster air valve assembly
10. Pressure plate
11. Diaphragm
12. Booster No. 2 body
13. No. 2 body oil seal
14. Air cleaner separator
15. Air cleaner element
16. Body boot
17. Nut
18. Bracket
19. Push rod clevis

SK4039100001000X

Fig. 1 Exploded view of booster assembly. Samurai

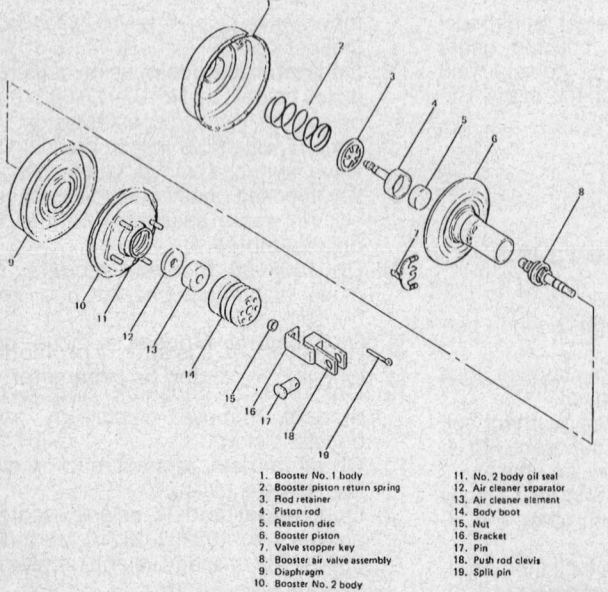

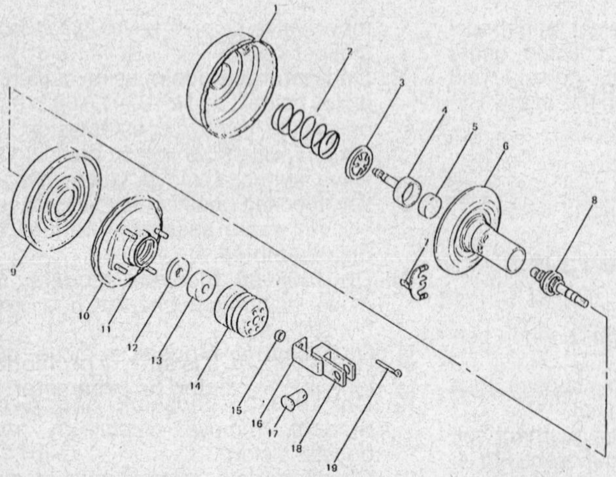

1. Booster No. 1 body
2. Booster piston return spring
3. Rod retainer
4. Piston rod
5. Reaction disc
6. Booster piston
7. Valve stopper key
8. Booster air valve assembly
9. Diaphragm
10. Booster No. 2 body
11. No. 2 body oil seal
12. Air cleaner separator
13. Air cleaner element
14. Body boot
15. Nut
16. Bracket
17. Pin
18. Push rod clevis
19. Split pin

SK4039100003000X

Fig. 3 Exploded view of booster assembly. Swift

under "Brake Pedal Height, Adjust," and "Brake Pedal Travel Check" in the "Hydraulic Brakes" section.

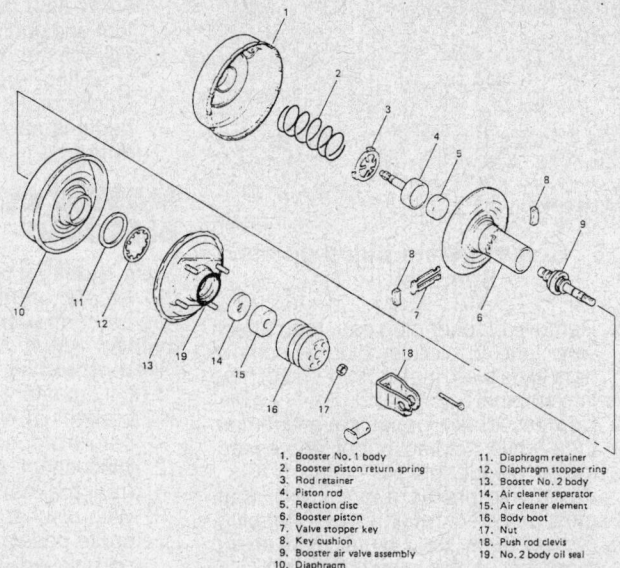

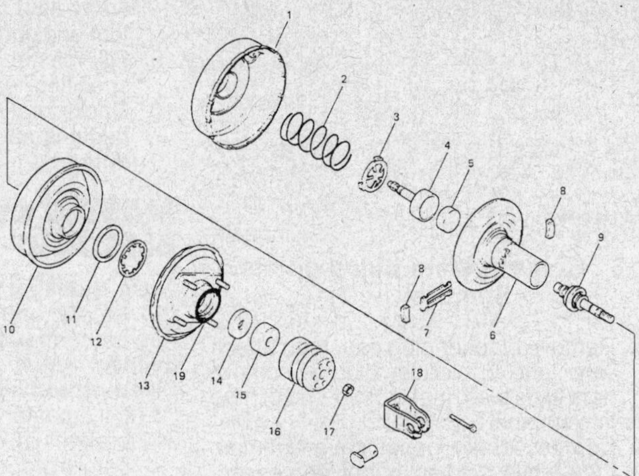

1. Booster No. 1 body
2. Booster piston return spring
3. Rod retainer
4. Piston rod
5. Reaction disc
6. Booster piston
7. Valve stopper key
8. Key cushion
9. Booster air valve assembly
10. Diaphragm
11. Diaphragm retainer
12. Diaphragm stopper ring
13. Booster No. 2 body
14. Air cleaner separator
15. Air cleaner element
16. Body boot
17. Nut
18. Push rod clevis
19. No. 2 body oil seal

SK4039100002000X

Fig. 2 Exploded view of booster assembly. 1993–95 Sidekick

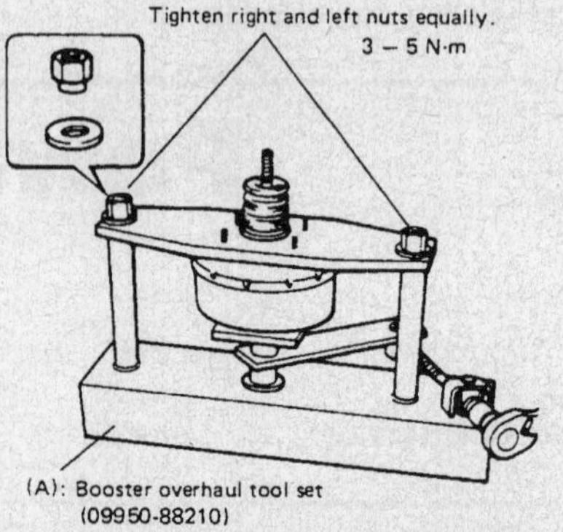
Tighten right and left nuts equally.
3 – 5 N·m
(A): Booster overhaul tool set
(09950-88210)

SK4039100004000X

Fig. 4 Positioning booster in booster overhaul set. Samurai, Swift & 1993–95 Sidekick

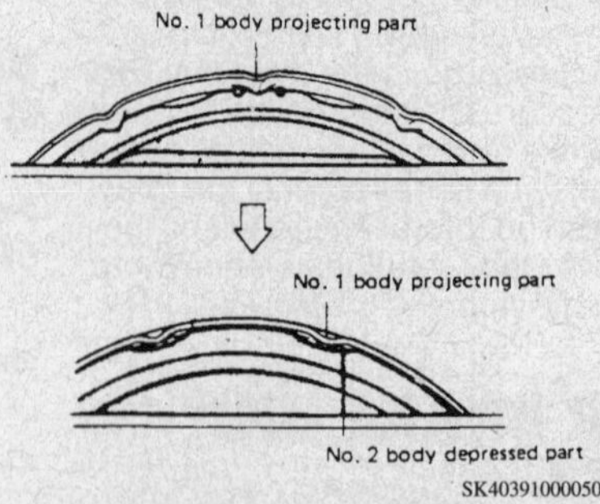
No. 1 body projecting part
No. 1 body projecting part
No. 2 body depressed part

SK4039100005000X

Fig. 5 Booster body depression alignment. Samurai, Swift & 1993–95 Sidekick

Esteem & 1996 Sidekick & X-90

The booster unit is not serviceable and should be replaced as a unit.

Anti-Lock Brakes

NOTE: Wire Code Identification & Symbol Identification Located In The Front Of This Manual May Be Used As An Aid When Using Wiring Circuits Found In This Section.

NOTE: On Air Bag Equipped Models, Refer To "Air Bag System Precautions" Located In The Front Of This Manual For System Disarming & Arming Procedures.

INDEX

Page No.
ABS-VI 40-139
Rear Wheel Anti-Lock 40-131

Rear Wheel Anti-Lock

INDEX

Page No.
Description 40-131
Diagnosis & Testing 40-131
Accessing Diagnostic Trouble Codes 40-131
Component Testing 40-131
Diagnostic Trouble Code Interpretation 40-131
Diagnostic Chart Index 40-135
Precautions 40-131
Air Bag Systems 40-131
System Service 40-133
Brake System Bleed 40-133
Sidekick 40-133
Component Replacement 40-133
4WD Switch 40-133
RWAL Control Module 40-133
Wheel Speed Sensor 40-133
Service Precautions 40-133
Troubleshooting 40-131
Wiring Diagram 40-132

PRECAUTIONS

AIR BAG SYSTEMS

Refer to "Air Bag System Precautions" in the front of this manual for system disarming and arming procedures.

DESCRIPTION

On Sidekick models, the Rear Wheel Anti-Lock (RWAL) system is controlled by the rear hydraulic brake line pressure which is regulated by a pressure limit valve. The pressure limit valve is located under the master cylinder and consists of two valves. One is a dump valve which releases pressure into an accumulator and the other is an isolation valve which holds rear brake pressure. The valve is controlled by a microcomputer which is a part of the RWAL control module. The RWAL control module is installed near the fuse box located under the LH side of the instrument panel.

The RWAL control module operates by receiving signals from the speed sensor in the rear differential and the stop light switch. It is designed to make the pressure limit valve (dump/isolation valve) operate when the brake pedal is depressed for hard braking.

The RWAL control module conducts system check and self-check at engine start and during normal driving. The main components are monitored and when any faulty condition is detected, the RWAL operation is stopped and the brake fluid warning light illuminates.

TROUBLESHOOTING

Refer to **Fig. 1,** for troubleshooting flow charts, **Fig. 2,** for wiring diagram and **Fig. 3,** for connector pin identification.

DIAGNOSIS & TESTING

ACCESSING DIAGNOSTIC TROUBLE CODES

Release parking brake. Momentarily jump terminal 5 of monitor coupler to terminal 3, **Fig. 4.** Connect jumper for longer than 2 seconds. Brake warning light should start flashing.

DIAGNOSTIC TROUBLE CODE INTERPRETATION

Each code consists of short flashes and a final long flash. Flashing is repeated until ignition key is turned Off.

If engine is turned Off before code is read, the code will be lost. There may be cases where the code will reappear when the engine is restarted. But in other cases it may be necessary to drive the vehicle to reproduce the same problem.

Even when more than one system fault exists, only the smallest diagnostic code is flashed out.

Refer to **Fig. 5,** for diagnostic code table and **Figs. 6 through 16,** for diagnostic code flow charts.

COMPONENT TESTING

RWAL System Electric Circuit Check

The electrical circuit of the RWAL system can be checked by measuring voltage of the RWAL control module connector terminals. **RWAL control module cannot be checked by itself. It is strictly prohibited to connect voltmeter or ohmmeter to RWAL control module with harness connector disconnected from it.**

Battery must be fully charged to perform this test as terminal voltage will be directly affected by battery voltage.

1. Remove RWAL control module from body.
2. Connect RWAL control module harness coupler to RWAL ECM.
3. Ensure voltage at each terminal of coupler connection is as specified, **Fig. 17.**

Wheel Speed Sensor

1. Raise and support vehicle, then remove sensor cover.
2. Disconnect coupler.

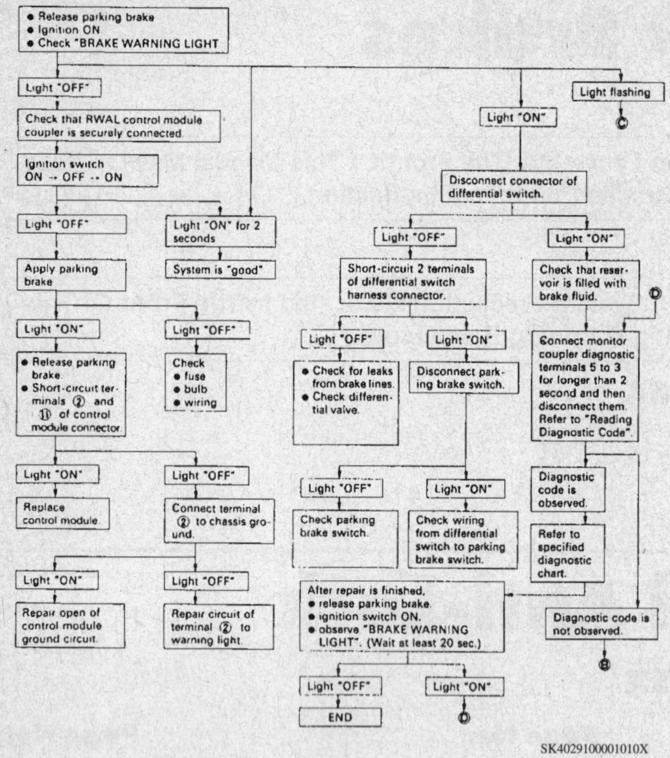

• Release parking brake
• Ignition ON
• Check "BRAKE WARNING LIGHT
Light "OFF"
Check that RWAL control module coupler is securely connected.
Ignition switch ON → OFF → ON
Light "OFF"
Light "ON" for 2 seconds
Apply parking brake
System is "good"
Light "ON"
Light "OFF"
• Release parking brake.
• Short-circuit terminals ② and ⑪ of control module connector.
Check
• fuse
• bulb
• wiring
Light "ON"
Light "OFF"
Replace control module.
Connect terminal ② to chassis ground.
Light "ON"
Light "OFF"
Repair open of control module ground circuit.
Repair circuit of terminal ② to warning light.
Light flashing
Light "ON"
Disconnect connector of differential switch.
Light "OFF"
Light "ON"
Short-circuit 2 terminals of differential switch harness connector.
Check that reservoir is filled with brake fluid.
Light "OFF"
Light "ON"
• Check for leaks from brake lines.
• Check differential valve.
Disconnect parking brake switch.
Connect monitor coupler diagnostic terminals 5 to 3 for longer than 2 second and then disconnect them. Refer to "Reading Diagnostic Code".
Light "OFF"
Light "ON"
Diagnostic code is observed.
Check parking brake switch.
Check wiring from differential switch to parking brake switch.
Refer to specified diagnostic chart.
After repair is finished,
• release parking brake.
• ignition switch ON.
• observe "BRAKE WARNING LIGHT". (Wait at least 20 sec.)
Diagnostic code is not observed.
Light "OFF"
Light "ON"
END
SK4029100001010X

Fig. 1 Troubleshooting chart (Part 1 of 3)

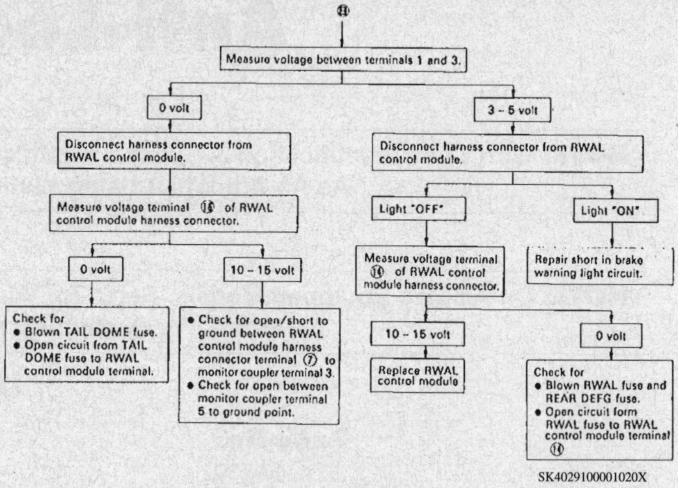

Measure voltage between terminals 1 and 3.
0 volt
3 – 5 volt
Disconnect harness connector from RWAL control module.
Disconnect harness connector from RWAL control module.
Measure voltage terminal ⑮ of RWAL control module harness connector.
Light "OFF"
Light "ON"
0 volt
10 – 15 volt
Measure voltage terminal ⑭ of RWAL control module harness connector.
Repair short in brake warning light circuit.
Check for
• Blown TAIL DOME fuse.
• Open circuit from TAIL DOME fuse to RWAL control module terminal.
• Check for open/short to ground between RWAL control module harness connector terminal ⑦ to monitor coupler terminal 3.
• Check for open between monitor coupler terminal 5 to ground point.
10 – 15 volt
0 volt
Replace RWAL control module
Check for
• Blown RWAL fuse and REAR DEFG fuse.
• Open circuit form RWAL fuse to RWAL control module terminal ⑭
SK4029100001020X

Fig. 1 Troubleshooting chart (Part 2 of 3)

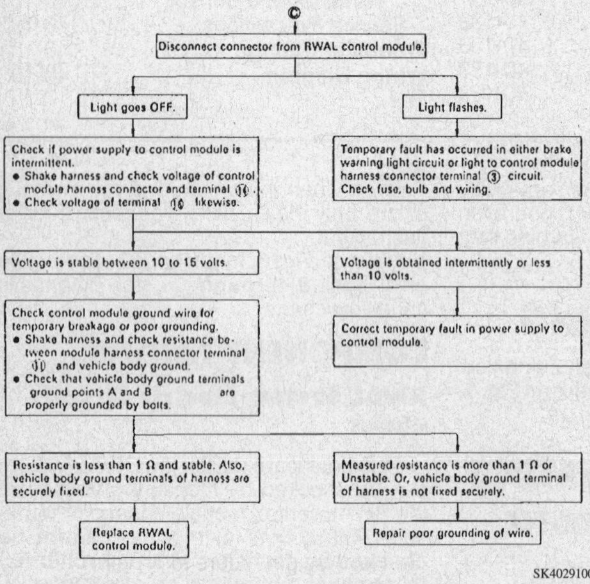

Disconnect connector from RWAL control module.
Light goes OFF.
Light flashes.
Check if power supply to control module is intermittent.
• Shake harness and check voltage of control module harness connector and terminal ⑭ .
• Check voltage of terminal ⑮ likewise.
Temporary fault has occurred in either brake warning light circuit or light to control module harness connector terminal ③ circuit. Check fuse, bulb and wiring.
Voltage is stable between 10 to 15 volts.
Voltage is obtained intermittently or less than 10 volts.
Check control module ground wire for temporary breakage or poor grounding.
• Shake harness and check resistance between module harness connector terminal ⑪ and vehicle body ground.
• Check that vehicle body ground terminals ground points A and B are properly grounded by bolts.
Correct temporary fault in power supply to control module.
Resistance is less than 1 Ω and stable. Also, vehicle body ground terminals of harness are securely fixed.
Measured resistance is more than 1 Ω or Unstable. Or, vehicle body ground terminal of harness is not fixed securely.
Replace RWAL control module.
Repair poor grounding of wire.
SK4029100001030X

Fig. 1 Troubleshooting chart (Part 3 of 3)

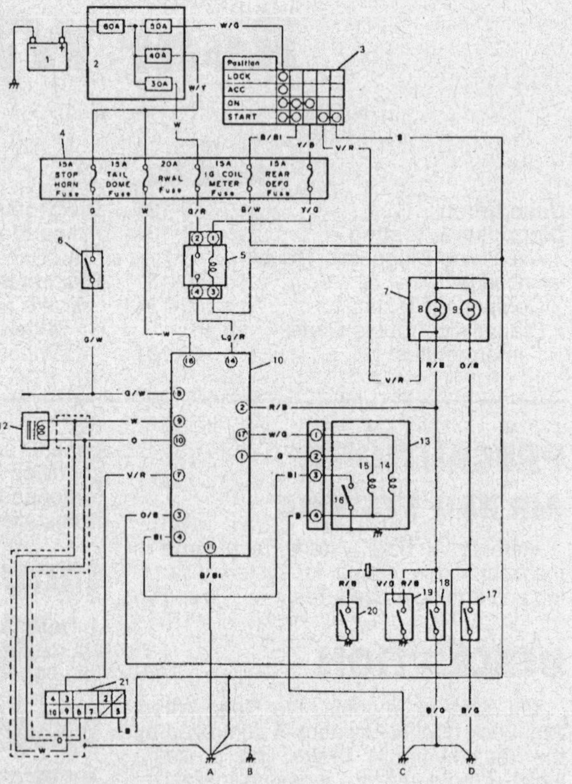

1. Battery	8 Brake warning light	15. Isolation solenoid	Ground points
2 Main fuse box	9. 4WD light (4WD model only)	16. Valve reset switch	A Below left front pillar
3. Ignition switch	10. RWAL control module	17. 4WD switch (4WD model only)	B Below right front pillar
4. Fuse box	11. To stop lights	18. Brake fluid level switch	C Beside of ignition coil
5 RWAL relay	12 Rear wheel speed sensor	19 Differential switch	D: Distributor case
6 Stop light switch	13 Pressure limit valve	20. Parking brake switch	
7 Combination meter	14. Dump solenoid	21 Monitor coupler	

SK4029100002000X

Fig. 2 RWAL wiring diagram

3. Using an ohmmeter, measure resistance between sensor terminals, and between terminal and sensor body.
   a. Resistance between terminals should be 1282.5—1567.5 ohms at 77°F.
   b. Resistance between terminal and sensor body should be 100,000 ohms.
4. Replace wheel sensor if resistance is not as specified.

4WD Switch

1. Turn ignition switch Off, then raise and support vehicle.
2. Disconnect 4WD switch connector, then connect ohmmeter to connector terminals.
3. Ensure 4WD switch turns On at only 4WD (4H and 4L) position.
4. Replace 4WD switch if not as specified.

Stop Light Switch

1. Disconnect coupler from stop light switch.
2. Connect ohmmeter to switch terminals, then check for continuity, **Fig. 18.**
3. With brake pedal released no continuity should exist.
4. With brake pedal applied continuity should exist.
5. Replace switch if not as specified.

RWAL Relay

1. Disconnect battery ground cable, then remove monitor coupler bracket.

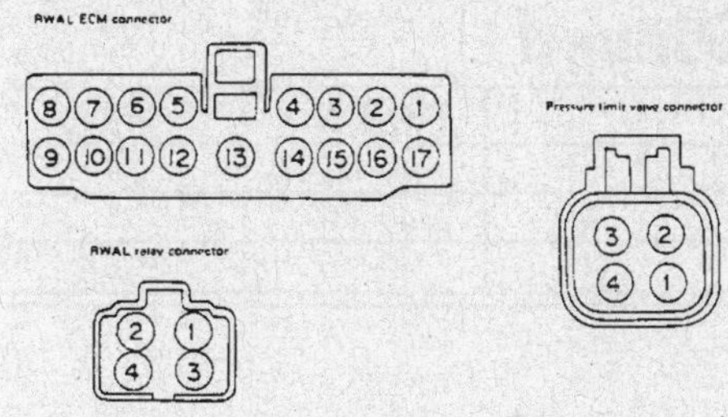
RWAL ECM connector
Pressure limit valve connector
RWAL relay connector
SK4029100003000X

Fig. 3 Connector pin identification

2. Disconnect yellow coupler from RWAL relay, then remove RWAL relay from its bracket.
3. Measure resistance between terminals A and B, then terminals C and D, **Fig. 19.**
4. Resistance between terminals A and B should be infinity.
5. Resistance between terminals C and D should be 90–110 ohms.
6. If resistance is as specified, proceed to step 7. If resistance is not as specified, replace relay.
7. Measure continuity between terminals A and B when battery is connected to terminals C and D, **Fig. 20.**
8. Replace relay if not as specified.

Pressure Limit (Isolation/ Dump) Valve

The pressure limit valve is not serviceable. It must be replaced as an assembly if test results are not satisfactory.

1. Turn ignition switch Off, then disconnect coupler from pressure limit valve.
2. Measure resistance between terminals as shown, **Figs. 21 and 22.**
3. Resistance should be as shown, **Fig. 21.**
4. If resistance is not as specified, replace valve.

SYSTEM SERVICE

SERVICE PRECAUTIONS

Before performing any repairs on the ABS system, note the following precautions:

1. If any welding work is to be done on the vehicle using and arc welder, the EBCM and hydraulic modulator connectors should be disconnected.
2. Hydraulic modulator and EBCM connectors should never be disconnected when the ignition switch is on.
3. Do not use a fast charger to charge battery when battery is connected. Always disconnect battery from system before using a fast charger. **Never disconnect battery from system with engine running.**
4. Always note routing, position and mounting of electrical components, wiring and connectors of the ABS system.
5. Many components of the ABS system are non-serviceable and must be replaced as assemblies. **Do not disassemble any component which is designated non-serviceable.**
6. After any component of the ABS system has been replaced it will be necessary to check the system. Refer to "Diagnosis & Testing."

Brake System Bleed

SIDEKICK

Bleed brakes as outlined in "Hydraulic Brake System."

Component Replacement

RWAL CONTROL MODULE

1. Disconnect battery ground cable, then remove left side radio speaker from instrument panel.
2. Remove engine ECM with cover, bracket and fuse box from steering column holder.
3. Disconnect coupler from RWAL control module, then remove RWAL control module from dash panel.
4. Reverse procedure to install.

WHEEL SPEED SENSOR

1. Turn ignition switch Off, then remove sensor cover.
2. Disconnect coupler from sensor, then remove sensor from differential carrier.
3. Reverse procedure to install, noting the following:
   a. Check O-ring for damage, replace as necessary.
   b. Ensure sensor tooth is free from any metal particles.
   c. Coat O-ring with thin film of differential oil.

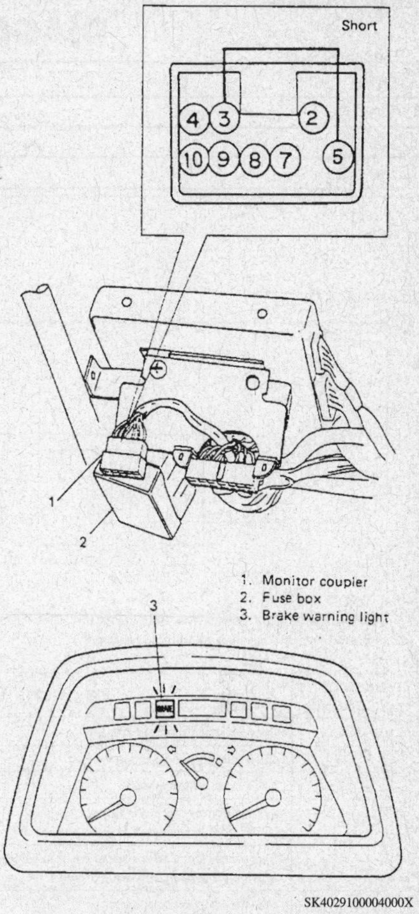
Short
1. Monitor coupler
2. Fuse box
3. Brake warning light
SK4029100004000X

Fig. 4 Accessing diagnostic trouble code

4WD SWITCH

1. Turn ignition switch Off, then raise and support vehicle.
2. Unclamp 4WD switch wiring, then disconnect switch coupler.
3. Lower vehicle, then remove boot cover of transfer gear shift lever from floor panel.
4. Remove 4WD switch.
5. Reverse procedure to install.

DIAGNOSTIC CHART INDEX

Code	Description	Page No.	Fig. No.
—	Diagnostic Code Table	40-134	5
Code 3	Open Dump Solenoid Circuit	40-135	7
Code 4	Valve Rest Switch Closed	40-135	8
Code 5	System Dumps Too Many Times	40-135	9
Code 6	Rear Speed Sensor Signal Change Rapidly	40-136	10
Code 7	Shorted Isolation Solenoid Circuit	40-136	11
Code 8	Shorted Dump Solenoid Circuit	40-136	12
Code 9	Open Rear Wheel Speed Circuit	40-137	13

Continued

DIAGNOSTIC CHART INDEX—Continued

Code	Description	Page No.	Fig. No.
Code 10	Stop Light Switch Remains On	40-137	14
Code 11	Shorted Rear Wheel Speed Sensor Circuit	40-137	15
Code 13	RWAL ECM Malfunction	40-137	16

EXAMPLE: Code 4

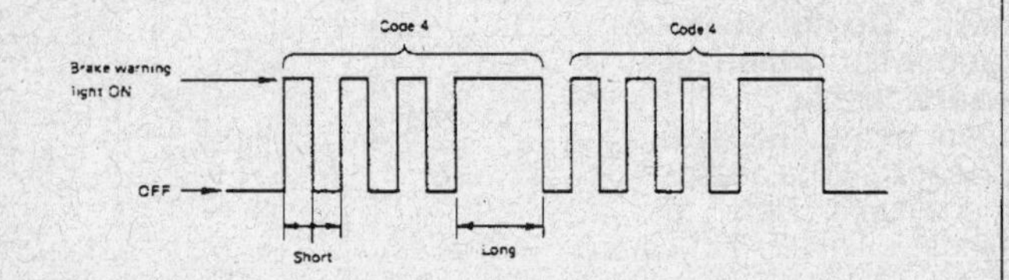
Code 4
Code 4
Brake warning light ON
OFF
Short
Long

NOTE:
When RWAL ECM detects two or more of the following conditions, only the smallest one among their corresponding codes is indicated repeatedly.

DIAGNOSTIC CODE NO.	CONDITION	ACTION TO TAKE
2	Open isolation solenoid circuit	Diagnose according to diagnosis procedure for each code.
3	Open dump solenoid circuit	
4	Valve reset switch closed	
5	System dumps too many times (Condition occurs when brake is applied during driving.)	
6	Rear wheel speed sensor signal changed rapidly (Condition only occurs while driving.)	
7	Shorted isolation solenoid circuit	
8	Shorted dump solenoid circuit	
9	Open rear wheel speed sensor circuit	
10	Stop light switch remains ON	
11	Shorted rear wheel speed sensor circuit	
13	RWAL ECM malfunction	

SK4029100005000X

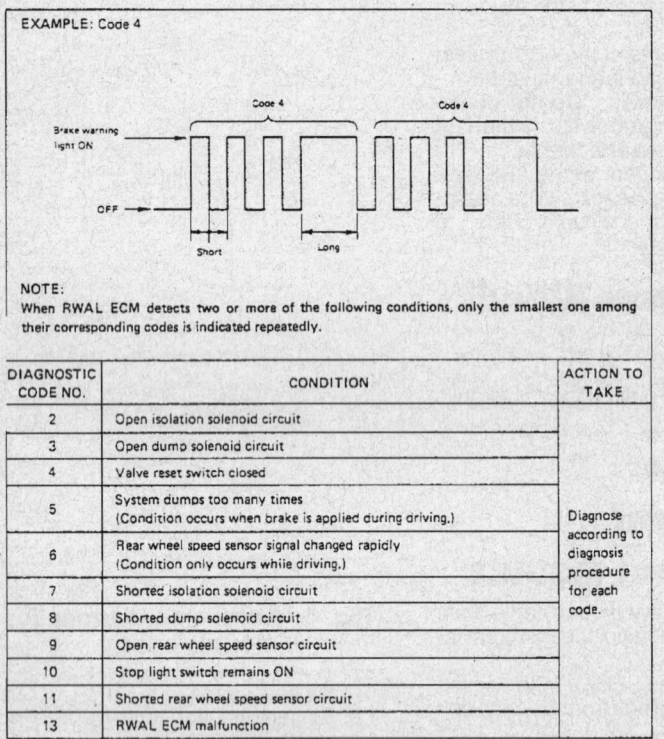

Fig. 5 Diagnostic trouble code table

DIAGNOSTIC CODE 2
Open isolation solenoid circuit

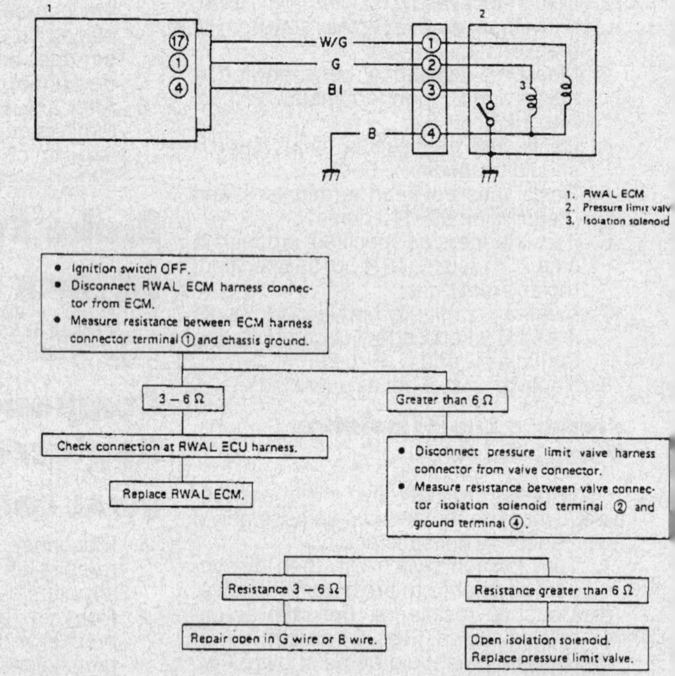
1
2
3
17
1
4
W/G
G
Bl
B
1. RWAL ECM
2. Pressure limit valv
3. Isolation solenoid
• Ignition switch OFF.
• Disconnect RWAL ECM harness connector from ECM.
• Measure resistance between ECM harness connector terminal ① and chassis ground.
3 – 6 Ω
Greater than 6 Ω
Check connection at RWAL ECU harness.
Replace RWAL ECM.
• Disconnect pressure limit valve harness connector from valve connector.
• Measure resistance between valve connector isolation solenoid terminal ② and ground terminal ④.
Resistance 3 – 6 Ω
Resistance greater than 6 Ω
Repair open in G wire or B wire.
Open isolation solenoid. Replace pressure limit valve.

SK4029100006000X

Fig. 6 Code 2: Open Isolation Solenoid Circuit

DIAGNOSTIC CODE 3

Open dump solenoid circuit

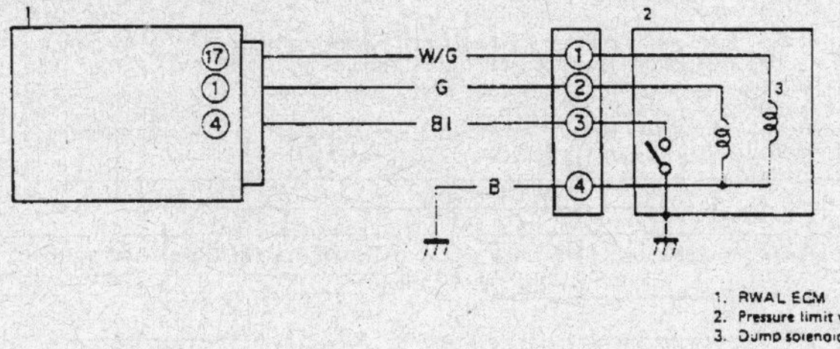
1
2
17
1
4
W/G
G
Bl
B
1
2
3
4
3
1. RWAL ECM
2. Pressure limit valve
3. Dump solenoid

- Ignition switch OFF.
- Disconnect RWAL ECM harness connector from ECM.
- Measure resistance between ECM harness connector terminal ⑰ and chassis ground.

Resistance 1 – 3 Ω

Check connection at RWAL ECM harness.

Replace RWAL ECM.

Resistance greater than 3 Ω

- Disconnect pressure limit valve harness connector from valve connector.
- Measure resistance between valve connector dump solenoid terminal ① and ground terminal ④.

Resistance 1 – 3 Ω

Repair open in W/G wire or B wire.

Resistance greater than 3 Ω

Open dump solenoid.
Repaice pressure limit valve.

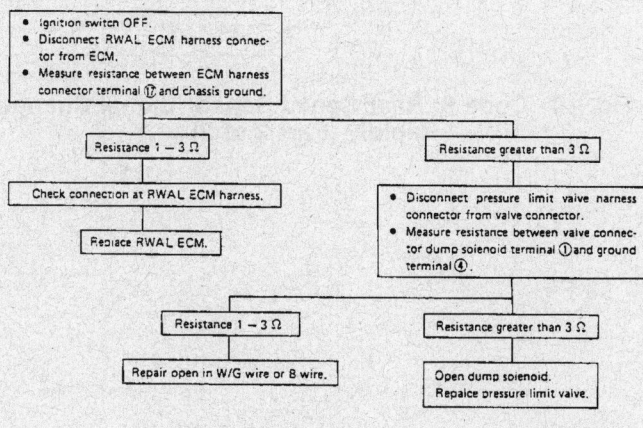

SK4029100007000X

Fig. 7 Code 3: Open Dump Solenoid Circuit

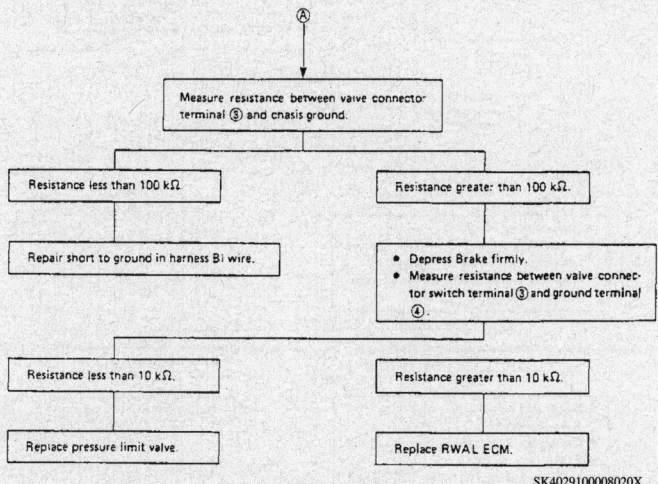

DIAGNOSTIC CODE 4

Valve reset switch closed

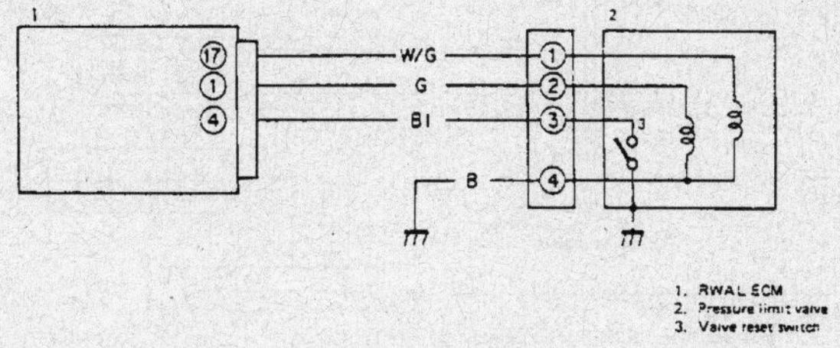
1
2
17
1
4
W/G
G
Bl
B
1
2
3
4
3
1. RWAL ECM
2. Pressure limit valve
3. Valve reset switch

NOTE:
This code remains in memory as long as +12V battery power is supplied to RWAL ECM. Therefore, to erase this code, disconnect negative cable from battery for at least 5 seconds.

- Ignition switch OFF.
- Disconnect RWAL ECM harness connector from ECM.
- Measure resistance between ECM harness connector terminal ④ and chassis ground.

Resistance greater than 10 kΩ

Check connection at RWAL ECM harness.

Replace RWAL ECM.

Resistance less than 10 kΩ

- Disconnect pressure limit valve connector from valve harness connector.
- Measure resistance between valve connector valve reset switch terminal ③ and ground terminal ④.

Resistance greater than 10 kΩ

→ Ⓐ

Resistance less than 10 kΩ

Vavle reset switch malfunction.
Replace pressure limit valve.

SK4029100008010X

Fig. 8 Code 4: Valve Rest Switch Closed (Part 1 of 2)

Ⓐ

Measure resistance between valve connector terminal ③ and chasis ground.

Resistance less than 100 kΩ.

Repair short to ground in harness Bl wire.

Resistance greater than 100 kΩ.

- Depress Brake firmly.
- Measure resistance between valve connector switch terminal ③ and ground terminal ④.

Resistance less than 10 kΩ.

Replace pressure limit valve.

Resistance greater than 10 kΩ.

Replace RWAL ECM.

SK4029100008020X

Fig. 8 Code 4: Valve Rest Switch Closed (Part 2 of 2)

DIAGNOSTIC CODE 5

System dumps too many times. It is possible that this condition arises only when brake is applied during driving.

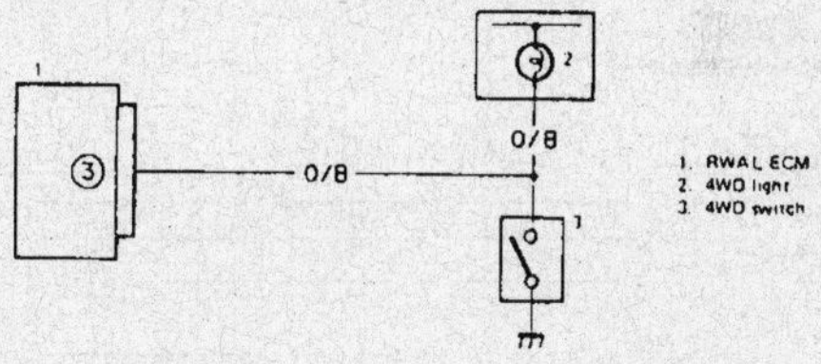
1
3
O/B
O/B
2
3
1. RWAL ECM
2. 4WD light
3. 4WD switch

NOTE:
This code remains in memory as long as +12V battery power is supplied to RWAL ECM. Therefore, to erase this code, disconnect negative cable from battery for at least 5 seconds.

Check if rear wheel brake drags.

No dragging occurs.

Check whether vehicle is 4WD model or 2WD model.

4WD model

- Disconnect RWAL ECM harness connector from ECM.
- Shift to 4WD setting.
- Turn ignition switch ON.
- Check voltage of RWAL ECM harness connector ③.

Less than 1 volt

- Replace pressure limit valve.
- Erase diagnostic code.
- Drive in 2WD setting.
- In safe area, apply hard brake and check that rear wheels do not lock.

Greater than 1 volt

Repair 4WD switch or open circuit of its wiring.

2WD model

→ (go to: Replace pressure limit valve, Erase diagnostic code, Drive in 2WD setting, check rear wheels do not lock)

Dragging occurs.

Correct to eliminate rear wheel brake dragging.

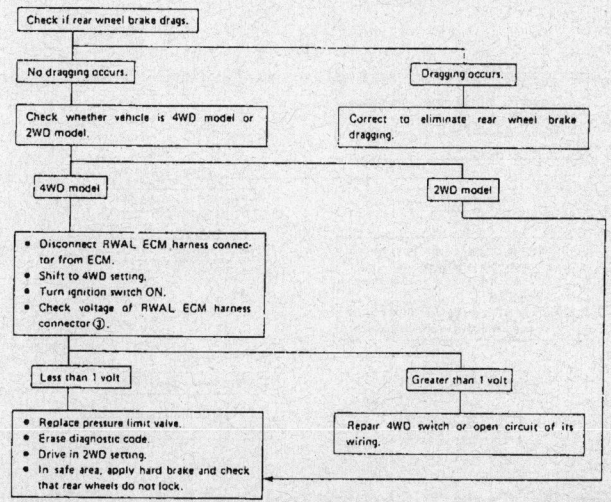

SK4029100009000X

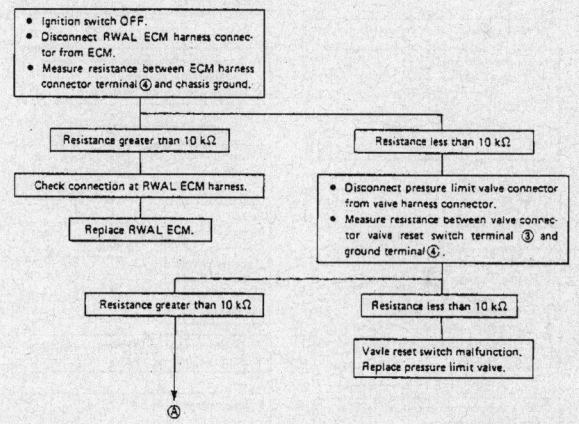

Fig. 9 Code 5: System Dumps Too Many Times

DIAGNOSTIC CODE 6

Rear wheel speed sensor signal changed rapidly. This condition is detected only while driving at higher than 35 mph.

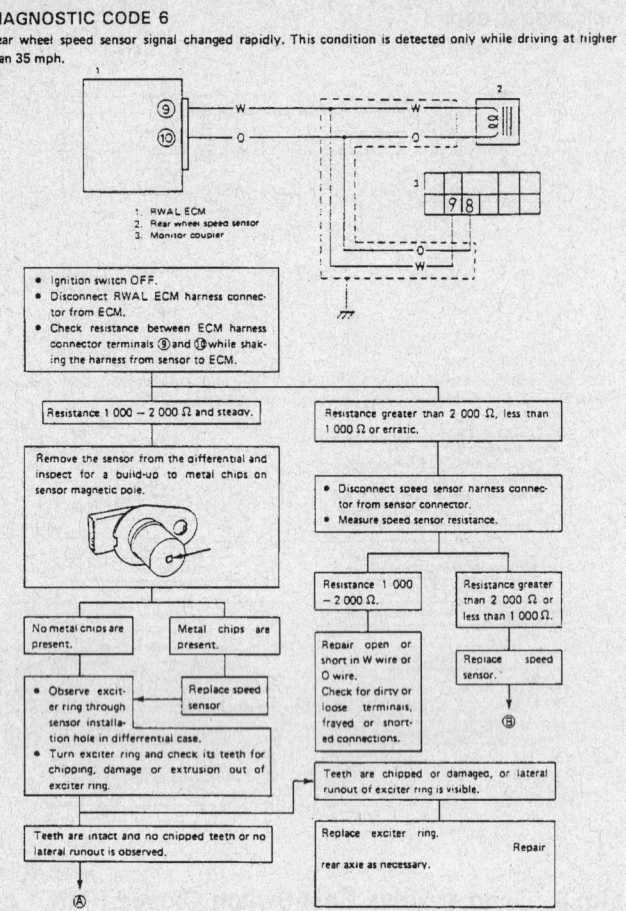

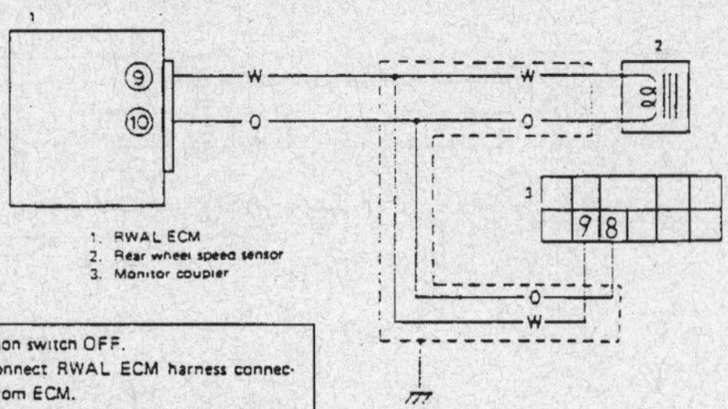
1
2
3
9
10
W
O
9 8
1. RWAL ECM
2. Rear wheel speed sensor
3. Monitor coupler

- Ignition switch OFF.
- Disconnect RWAL ECM harness connector from ECM.
- Check resistance between ECM harness connector terminals ⑨ and ⑩ while shaking the harness from sensor to ECM.

Resistance 1 000 – 2 000 Ω and steady.

Remove the sensor from the differential and inspect for a build-up to metal chips on sensor magnetic pole.

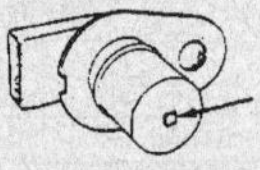

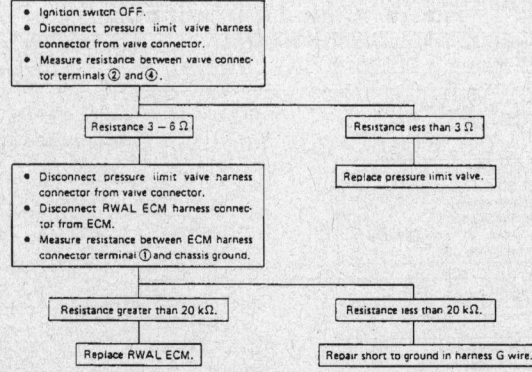

- No metal chips are present.
  - Observe exciter ring through sensor installation hole in differential case.
  - Turn exciter ring and check its teeth for chipping, damage or extrusion out of exciter ring.
- Metal chips are present.
  - Replace speed sensor (then observe exciter ring as above).

Teeth are intact and no chipped teeth or no lateral runout is observed. → Ⓐ

Teeth are chipped or damaged, or lateral runout of exciter ring is visible.
→ Replace exciter ring. Repair rear axle as necessary.

Resistance greater than 2 000 Ω, less than 1 000 Ω or erratic.

- Disconnect speed sensor harness connector from sensor connector.
- Measure speed sensor resistance.

Resistance 1 000 – 2 000 Ω.
→ Repair open or short in W wire or O wire. Check for dirty or loose terminals, frayed or shorted connections.

Resistance greater than 2 000 Ω or less than 1 000 Ω.
→ Replace speed sensor. → Ⓑ

SK4029100010010X

Fig. 10 Code 6: Rear Speed Sensor Signal Change Rapidly (Part 1 of 2)

DIAGNOSTIC CODE 7

Shorted isolation solenoid circuit

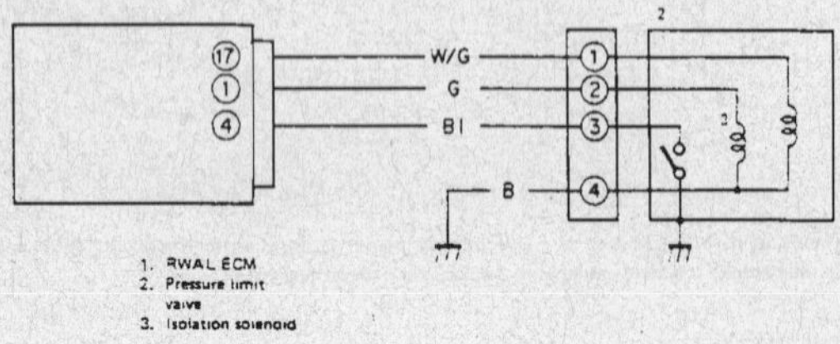
2
17
1
4
W/G
G
Bl
B
1
2
3
4
3
1. RWAL ECM
2. Pressure limit valve
3. Isolation solenoid

- Ignition switch OFF.
- Disconnect pressure limit valve harness connector from valve connector.
- Measure resistance between valve connector terminals ② and ④.

Resistance 3 – 6 Ω

- Disconnect pressure limit valve harness connector from valve connector.
- Disconnect RWAL ECM harness connector from ECM.
- Measure resistance between ECM harness connector terminal ① and chassis ground.

Resistance greater than 20 kΩ. → Replace RWAL ECM.

Resistance less than 20 kΩ. → Repair short to ground in harness G wire.

Resistance less than 3 Ω → Replace pressure limit valve.

SK4029100011000X

Fig. 11 Code 7: Shorted Isolation Solenoid Circuit

Ⓐ

Measuring method 1
- Reinstall speed sensor and connect speed sensor harness connector.
- Connect RWAL ECM harness connector to ECM connector.
- Position vehicle on a hoist and raise rear wheels to clear floor.
- Start engine and turn wheels at 20 mph.
- Measure AC voltage between RWAL ECM terminals ⑨ and ⑩ using AC voltmeter (input resistance greater than 1MΩ).

Voltage greater than 650 mV RMS and steady. → Replace RWAL ECM.

Voltage less than 650 mV RMS or erratic. → Replace speed sensor.

Ⓑ → Check to make sure that speed sensor output voltage is greater than 650 mV RMS.

SK4029100010020X

Fig. 10 Code 6: Rear Speed Sensor Signal Change Rapidly (Part 2 of 2)

DIAGNOSTIC CODE 8

Shorted dump solenoid circuit

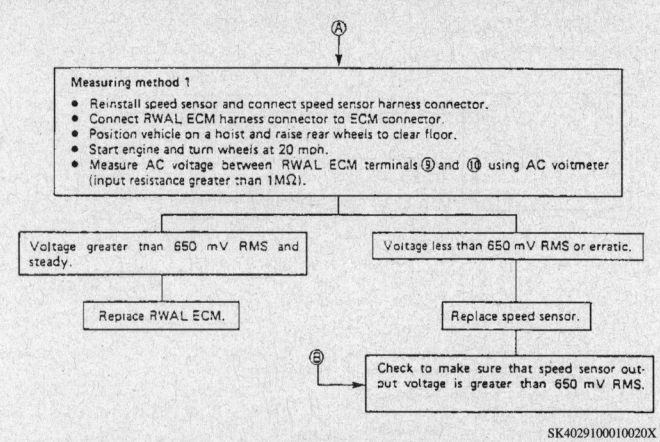

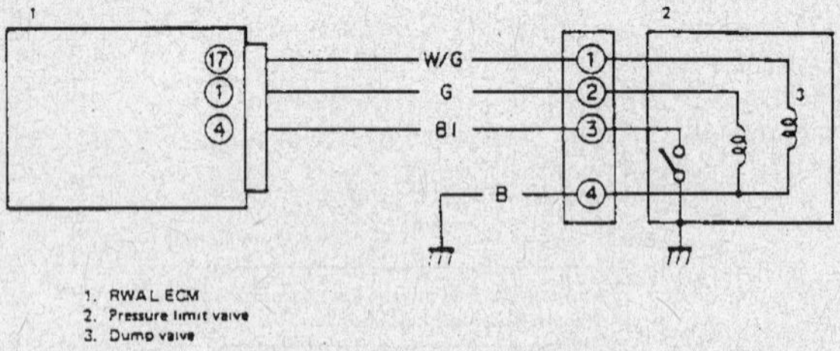
1
2
3
17
1
4
W/G
G
Bl
B
1
2
3
4
1. RWAL ECM
2. Pressure limit valve
3. Dump valve

- Ignition switch OFF.
- Disconnect pressure limit valve harness connector from valve connector.
- Measure resistance between valve connector terminals ① and ④.

Resistance 1 – 3 Ω

- Disconnect valve harness connector from valve connector.
- Disconnect ECM harness connector from ECM.
- Measure resistance between ECM harness connector terminal ⑰ and chassis ground.

Resistance greater than 20 kΩ. → Replace RWAL ECM.

Resistance less than 20 kΩ. → Repair short to ground in harness W/G wire.

Resistance les than 1 Ω. → Replace pressure limit valve.

SK4029100012000X

Fig. 12 Code 8: Shorted Dump Solenoid Circuit

DIAGNOSTIC CODE 9

Open rear wheel speed sensor circuit

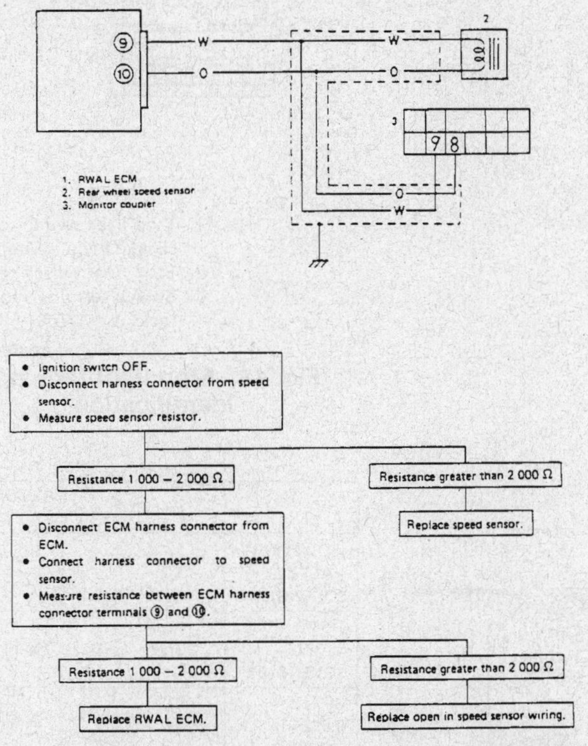

9
10
W
O
W
O
2
3
9 8
O
W
1. RWAL ECM
2. Rear wheel speed sensor
3. Monitor coupler
• Ignition switch OFF.
• Disconnect harness connector from speed sensor.
• Measure speed sensor resistor.
Resistance 1 000 – 2 000 Ω
Resistance greater than 2 000 Ω
Replace speed sensor.
• Disconnect ECM harness connector from ECM.
• Connect harness connector to speed sensor.
• Measure resistance between ECM harness connector terminals ⑨ and ⑩.
Resistance 1 000 – 2 000 Ω
Resistance greater than 2 000 Ω
Replace RWAL ECM.
Replace open in speed sensor wiring.

PK4029100013000X

Fig. 13 Code 9: Open Rear Wheel Speed Circuit

DIAGNOSTIC CODE 10

Stop light switch remains ON. This condition is detected only while driving at higher than 37.5 mph.

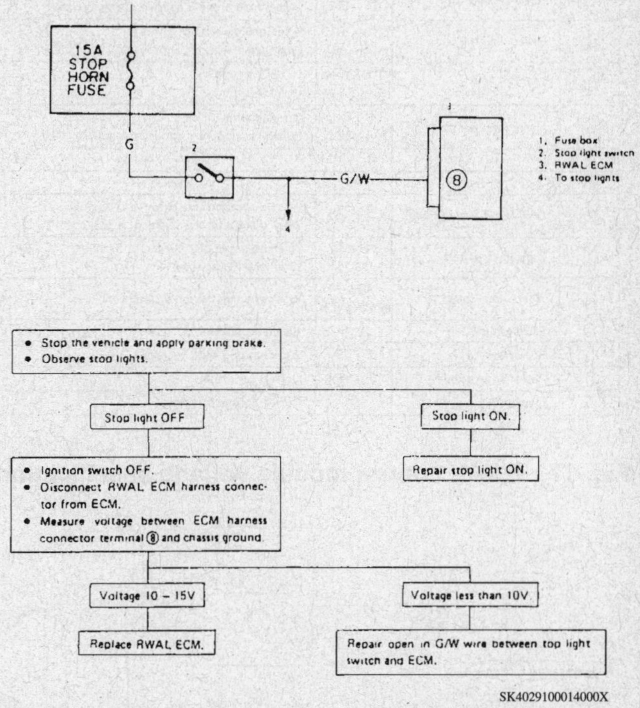

15A
STOP
HORN
FUSE
G
2
G/W
3
8
4
1. Fuse box
2. Stop light switch
3. RWAL ECM
4. To stop lights
• Stop the vehicle and apply parking brake.
• Observe stop lights.
Stop light OFF
Stop light ON.
Repair stop light ON.
• Ignition switch OFF.
• Disconnect RWAL ECM harness connector from ECM.
• Measure voltage between ECM harness connector terminal ⑧ and chassis ground.
Voltage 10 – 15V
Voltage less than 10V
Replace RWAL ECM.
Repair open in G/W wire between top light switch and ECM.

SK4029100014000X

Fig. 14 Code 10: Stop Light Switch Remains On

DIAGNOSTIC CODE 11

Shorted rear wheel speed sensor circuit

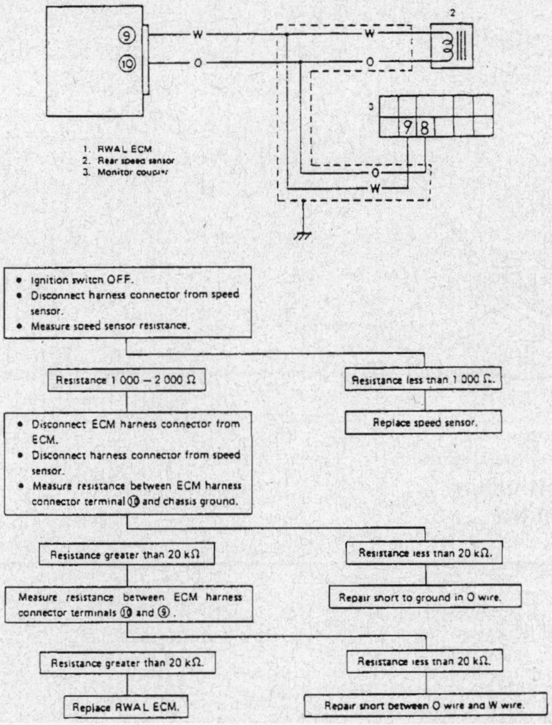

9
10
W
O
W
O
2
3
9 8
O
W
1. RWAL ECM
2. Rear speed sensor
3. Monitor coupler
• Ignition switch OFF.
• Disconnect harness connector from speed sensor.
• Measure speed sensor resistance.
Resistance 1 000 – 2 000 Ω
Resistance less than 1 000 Ω.
Replace speed sensor.
• Disconnect ECM harness connector from ECM.
• Disconnect harness connector from speed sensor.
• Measure resistance between ECM harness connector terminal ⑩ and chassis ground.
Resistance greater than 20 kΩ
Resistance less than 20 kΩ.
Measure resistance between ECM harness connector terminals ⑩ and ⑨.
Repair short to ground in O wire.
Resistance greater than 20 kΩ.
Resistance less than 20 kΩ.
Replace RWAL ECM.
Repair short between O wire and W wire.

SK4029100015000X

Fig. 15 Code 11: Shorted Rear Wheel Speed Sensor Circuit

DIAGNOSTIC CODE 13

RWAL ECM malfunction

Replace RWAL ECM.

SK4029100016000X

Fig. 16 Code 13: RWAL ECM Malfunction

TERMINAL	CIRCUIT	NORMAL VOLTAGE	CONDITION
①	Isolation solenoid	0V (10 – 15V)	During normal driving (When hard brake is applied during driving)
②	Brake warning light	10 – 15V 0 – 3V	When brake warning light is OFF When brake warning light is ON
③	4WD signal	10 – 15V 0 – 0.5V	In 2WD setting In 4WD setting
④	Valve reset switch	4 – 5V (0 – 0.5V)	During normal driving (When hard brake is applied during driving)
⑤	———	——	———
⑥	———	——	———
⑦	Diagnostic test terminal	3 – 5V 0 – 0.5V	When diagnostic test terminal is open When diagnostic test terminal is grounded
⑧	Stop light switch	0 – 0.5V 10 – 15V	When no brake is applied When brake is applied
⑨ – ⑩	Rear wheel speed sensor	About 3.5V (AC)	When driving at about 20 mph
⑪	ECM ground	0V	Normal condition
⑭	Power source (ignition)	10 – 15V	When ignition switch is ON
⑮	Power source (battery)	10 – 15V	Normal condition
⑰	Dump solenoid	0V	During normal driving

SK4029100017000X

Fig. 17 RWAL control module voltage specification

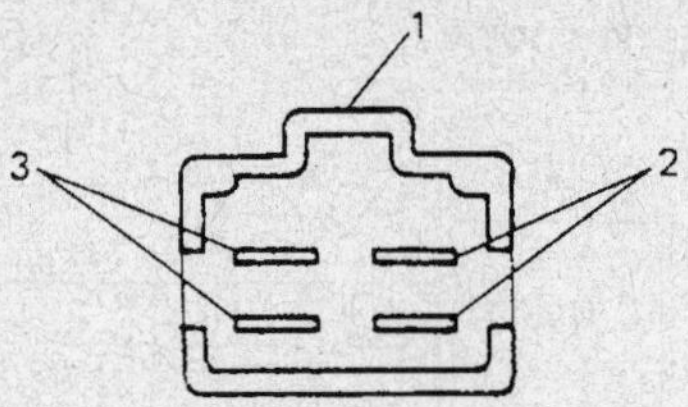
1
2
3

1. Stop light switch (Brake pedal switch)
2. Stop light switch terminals
3. Switch terminals for A/T lock-up system

SK4029100018000X

Fig. 18 Stop light terminal identification

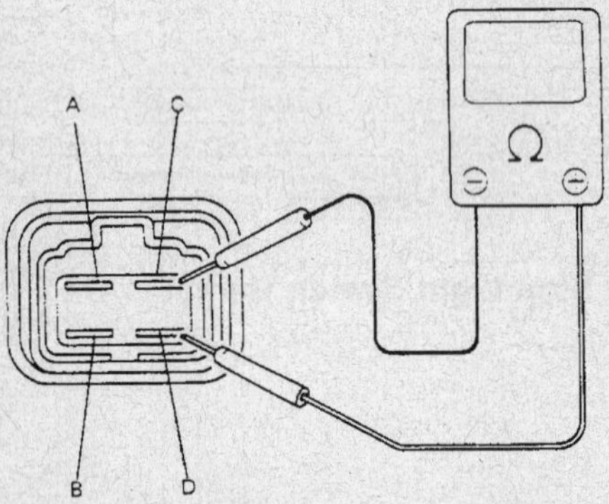
A
C
B
D
Ω

SK4029100019000X

Fig. 19 RWAL relay resistance inspection

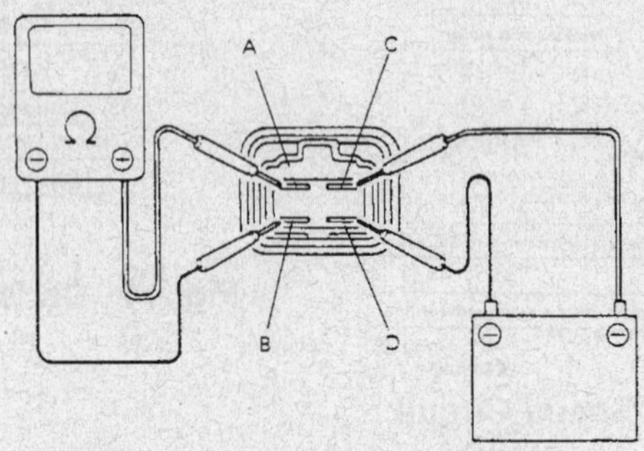
A
C
B
D
Ω

SK4029100020000X

Fig. 20 RWAL relay continuity inspection

	TERMINALS	RESISTANCE at 20°C (68°F)
ISOLATION VALVE SOLENOID	ISO – GND	3 – 6 ohms
DUMP VALVE SOLENOID	DUMP – GND	1 – 3 ohms
BRAKE RESET SWITCH	RESET – VALVE BODY	∞ (infinity)

SK4029100021000X

Fig. 21 Pressure limit valve resistance specification

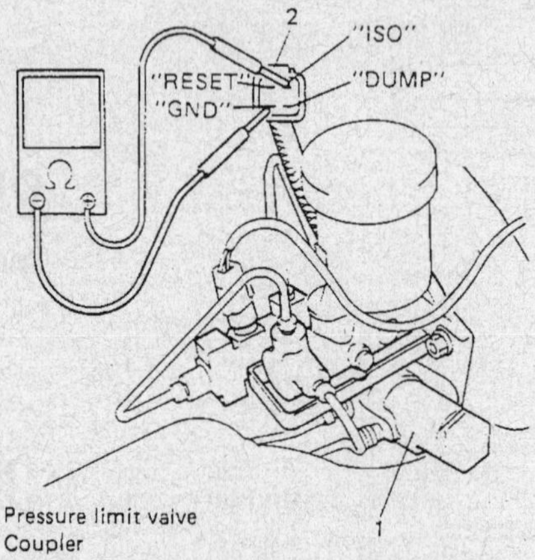
2
"ISO"
"RESET"
"DUMP"
"GND"
Ω
1

1. Pressure limit valve
2. Coupler

SK4029100022000X

Fig. 22 Pressure limit valve terminal identification

ABS-VI

NOTE: Electrical Symbol & Wire Color Code Identification Located In The Front Of This Manual May Be Used As An Aid When Using Wiring Circuits Found In This Section.

NOTE: On Air Bag Equipped Models, Refer To "Air Bag System Precautions" Located In The Front Of This Manual For System Disarming & Arming Procedures.

INDEX

	Page No.
Diagnosis & Testing	40-139
Accessing Diagnostic Trouble Codes	40-139
Enhanced Diagnostics	40-139
On Board Diagnostics	40-139
Clearing Diagnostic Trouble Codes	40-139
Diagnostic Trouble Code Interpretation	40-139
Diagnostic Chart Index	40-142
Precautions	40-139
Air Bag Systems	40-139
System Service	40-139
Adjustments	40-142
Brake System Bleed	40-139
Inspection	40-139
Manual Bleeding	40-140
Pressure Bleeding	40-140
Wheel Bleed Sequence	40-140
Component Replacement	40-140
ABS Hydraulic Modulator & Master Cylinder Assembly	40-142
ABS Hydraulic Modulator Gears	40-142
ABS Hydraulic Modulator Solenoid Assembly	40-141
ABS Lamp Driver Module	40-140
Electronic Brake Control Module (EBCM)	40-141
Enable Relay	40-140
Front Wheel Speed Sensor	40-141
Rear Wheel Speed Sensor	40-141
Troubleshooting	40-139
Wiring Diagrams:	
1995-96 Swift	40-141
1996 Sidekick & X-90	40-141

PRECAUTIONS

AIR BAG SYSTEMS

Avoid contact with brake fluid when servicing ABS system. If skin contact occurs, wash with soap and water. If brake fluid gets in eyes, rinse thoroughly with water.

Refer to "Air Bag System Precautions" in the front of this manual for system disarming and arming procedures.

TROUBLESHOOTING

Refer to "Diagnosis & Testing" for troubleshooting procedures.

DIAGNOSIS & TESTING

Accessing Diagnostic Trouble Codes

ON BOARD DIAGNOSTICS

This system has a sophisticated diagnosis system, that when accessed with a bi-directional "Scan" tool, is designed to identify any system fault as specifically as possible, including intermittent faults. Each input and output to the system can be monitored by using a suitable bi-directional "Scan" tool, monitoring inputs and outputs allows for fault confirmation and repair verification. The "Scan" tool can also be used to manually control components and perform functional tests. Connect "Scan" tool to data link connector located in lower left-hand instrument panel to the left of steering column.

When using the following diagnostic procedure refer to **Fig. 1** for "Scan" tool functions, **Figs. 2 through 6** for system wiring diagram and connectors.

ABS diagnostic trouble codes (DTC) may be accessed using a tool No. 09931–76011 Tech-1 diagnostic scan tool with tool No. 09932–65020 ABS-Air Bag cartridge, or equivalents.

1. Connect tool No. 09931–76011 Tech-1 diagnostic scan tool with tool No. 09932–65020 ABS-Air Bag cartridge, or equivalents.

ENHANCED DIAGNOSTICS

This information is found in the "CODE HISTORY" function of the "Scan" tool, and is used to provide specific fault occurrence information. This data is stored for each of the first five and the very last fault code, the data stored identifies the specific trouble code, the number of times the fault occurred and the number of drive cycles since the failure first and last occurred (a drive cycle occurs when the ignition is cycled "ON" and the vehicle is driven faster than 10 mph). If a fault is present, the drive cycle will increment by turning the ignition "ON" and "OFF." The order that the first five fault codes occurred can be useful in determining if a previous fault is linked to a more recent fault. This data can also be used to determine how often and under what circumstances the fault occurs.

Diagnostic Trouble Code Interpretation

Refer to Fig.7 for diagnostic trouble code interpretation.

Clearing Diagnostic Trouble Codes

The diagnostic trouble codes (DTC) stored in EBCM memory can be erased in either of the two ways as follows:

1. Method 1, using a Tech-1 diagnostic scan tool or equivalent, select F2 for "Trouble Codes-DTC."
2. After DTC have been reviewed, Tech-1 will prompt, "Clear Codes," with question mark, then press "Yes," and DTCs will be cleared.
3. Method 2, using ignition cycle default.
4. If no DTC occurs for 100 drive cycles, ignition switch is cycled to the On position and vehicle driven at speed greater than 10 mph, any existing DTCs will be cleared. "This is not an acceptable method of clearing ABS DTCs. Use Method 1 to properly clear ABS DTC codes."

SYSTEM SERVICE

Brake System Bleed

INSPECTION

The hydraulic lines of this brake system are based on a diagonal split system. When a brake line or hose is disconnected, bleeding operation must be performed at both ends of the line disconnected.

Prior to bleeding brakes, both front and rear displacement cylinder pistons must be returned to the top-most or home position. Motor re-home cannot be performed if current diagnostic trouble codes (DTC) are present. If DTC's are present, vehicle must be repaired and DTC's cleared before performing the motor rehome function. Perform this procedure as follows:

Raise and suitably support front end of vehicle so that drive wheels are off of the ground.

Start engine, engage transaxle and run vehicle above 3 mph for at least ten seconds. Observe ABS indicator. Ensure indicator goes out after three seconds.

If ABS indicator remains illuminated, a Tech-1 or equivalent must be used to diagnose malfunction.

If ABS indicator goes out and stays off, stop engine and repeat, previous three steps

Using Tech-1 or equivalent, enter manual control function and apply the front and rear motors.

1. Fill master cylinder reservoir. Reservoir should be kept at least half full during bleeding operation.
2. Remove bleeder screw cap, then attach vinyl tube to bleeder screw "A," **Fig. 62,** or component to be bled. Insert other end of tube into suitable container.
3. Depress brake pedal several times, then while holding pedal depressed, loosen bleeder screw ½ turn.
4. When fluid pressure in cylinder is almost depleted, retighten bleeder screw.
5. Repeat steps 3 and 4, until there are no more air bubbles in hydraulic line.
6. When bubbles stop, depress and hold brake pedal, then tighten bleeder screw to specification.
7. Attach bleeder cap.
8. Repeat steps 1 through 6 for bleeder plug "B," **Fig. 8.**
9. Bleed brake calipers and wheel cylinders as shown, **Fig. 9.**
10. Start with wheel cylinder or caliper farthest from master cylinder, then bleed front caliper of same brake line.
11. After completing bleeding operation, apply fluid pressure to hydraulic system and check for leakage.
12. Fill master cylinder reservoir up to specified level.
13. Check brake pedal for sponginess. If pedal is spongy, repeat entire procedure.

WHEEL BLEED SEQUENCE

Refer to **Figs. 9 and 10,** as outlined in "Brake System Bleeding," found in this section.

PRESSURE BLEEDING

1. Remove master cylinder cover, ensure reservoir is properly filled.
2. Connect bleeder adapter tool No. J 35589, or equivalent, to master cylinder reservoir.
3. Connect bleeder adapter to pressure bleeding equipment.
4. Connect a clear plastic bleeder hose to modulator assembly rearward bleeder valve, submerge other end of hose into clean container partially filled with brake fluid.
5. Adjust pressure bleeding equipment to 5–10 psi, then wait for approximately

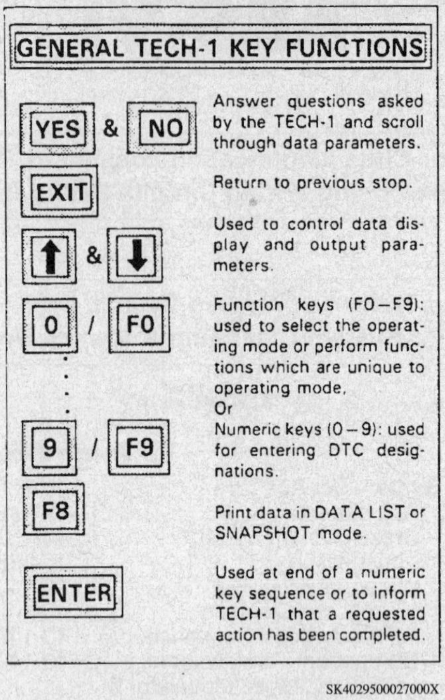
GENERAL TECH-1 KEY FUNCTIONS
YES & NO
Answer questions asked by the TECH-1 and scroll through data parameters.
EXIT
Return to previous stop.
↑ & ↓
Used to control data display and output parameters.
0 / F0
Function keys (F0–F9): used to select the operating mode or perform functions which are unique to operating mode.
Or
Numeric keys (0–9): used for entering DTC designations.
9 / F9
F8
Print data in DATA LIST or SNAPSHOT mode.
ENTER
Used at end of a numeric key sequence or to inform TECH-1 that a requested action has been completed.
SK4029500027000X

Fig. 1 Tech 1 scan tool key function

30 seconds to ensure there is no leakage.

6. Adjust pressure bleed equipment to 30–35 psi.
7. To bleed ABS hydraulic modulator and master cylinder, proceed as follows:
   a. Slowly open rearward bleeder valve and allow fluid to flow until no air is seen in fluid, then **torque** valve to 65 inch lbs.
   b. Attach bleeder hose to modulator assembly forward bleeder hose.
   c. Slowly open forward bleeder valve and allow fluid to flow until no air is seen in fluid, then **torque** valve to 65 inch lbs.
8. To bleed brake pipe to modulator assembly connections, proceed as follows:
   a. Place a shop cloth between brake pipe connections and the top of the motor pack assembly.
   b. Loosen forward most brake pipe nut and check for air escaping in fluid.
   c. When air flow ceases, **torque** brake pipe nut to 24 ft. lbs.
   d. Repeat steps b and c for remaining three brake pipe connections, moving from front to rear.
9. To bleed wheel brakes, proceed as follows:
   a. Raise and support vehicle.
   b. Attach bleeder hose to bleeder valve of right rear wheel, submerge other end of hose into clean container partially filled with brake fluid.
   c. Loosen bleeder valve and allow fluid to flow, close valve when fluid begins to flow without any air bubbles.
   d. Repeat steps b and c, first for left rear wheel, then the right front caliper, then the left front caliper.
10. Road test vehicle, to verify brake performance.

MANUAL BLEEDING

1. Ensure brake fluid reservoir is properly filled.
2. Attach bleeder hose to modulator assembly rearward bleed valve, submerge other end of hose into clean container partially filled with brake fluid.
3. Pump brake pedal several times, then slowly open bleeder valve ½ to ¾ turns.
4. Depress brake pedal and hold until fluid begins to flow.
5. Close valve and repeat steps 3 and 4 on forward valve. Once fluid is seen to flow from both the forward and rearward valves, modulator valve and master cylinder are filled sufficiently filled with fluid. However, modulator and master cylinder assemblies may not be purged of air. At this point, bleed the wheel brakes.
6. Raise and support vehicle.
7. Attach bleeder hose to bleeder valve of right rear wheel, submerge other end of hose into clean container partially filled with brake fluid.
8. Open bleeder valve and slowly depress brake pedal, close valve and slowly release brake pedal, wait five seconds.
9. Repeat step 8, until brake pedal feels firm and no air bubbles are observed in bleeder hose.
10. Repeat steps 7, 8 and 9, first for left rear wheel, then the right front caliper, then the left front caliper.
11. Lower vehicle and attach bleeder hose to rearward bleeder valve.
12. Depress brake pedal using moderate pressure, then slowly open bleeder valve ½ to ¾ turns and allow fluid to flow.
13. Close valve and release brake pedal, wait five seconds.
14. Repeat steps 12 and 13, until all air is purged from system.
15. Repeat steps 11, 12, 13 and 14, on forward bleeder valve.
16. Road test vehicle, to verify brake performance.

Component Replacement

ENABLE RELAY

1. Disconnect battery ground cable.
2. Remove enable relay cover, **Fig. 11.**
3. Disconnect relay from electrical connector.
4. Reverse procedure to install.

ABS LAMP DRIVER MODULE

1. Disconnect battery ground cable.
2. Remove fasteners on lower sound insulator panel under steering column.
3. Disconnect lamp driver module from instrument panel harness on left side

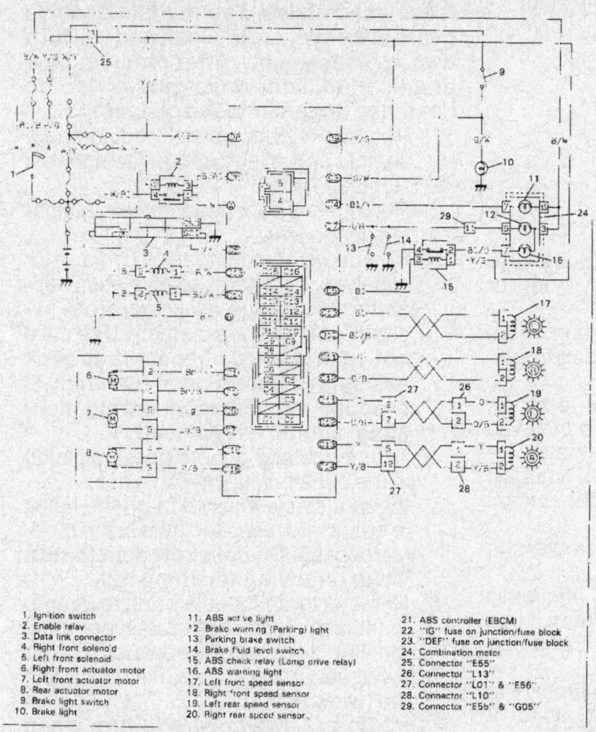
1. Ignition switch
2. Enable relay
3. Data link connector
4. Right front solenoid
5. Left front solenoid
6. Right front actuator motor
7. Left front actuator motor
8. Rear actuator motor
9. Brake light switch
10. Brake light
11. ABS active light
12. Brake warning (Parking) light
13. Parking brake switch
14. Brake fluid level switch
15. ABS check relay (Lamp drive relay)
16. ABS warning light
17. Left front speed sensor
18. Right front speed sensor
19. Left rear speed sensor
20. Right rear speed sensor
21. ABS controller (EBCM)
22. "IG" fuse on junction/fuse block
23. "DEF" fuse on junction/fuse block
24. Combination meter
25. Connector "E55"
26. Connector "L13"
27. Connector "L01" & "E56"
28. Connector "L10"
29. Connector "E55" & "G05"
SK4029500028000X

Fig. 2 ABS-VI system wiring circuit. 1995–96 Swift

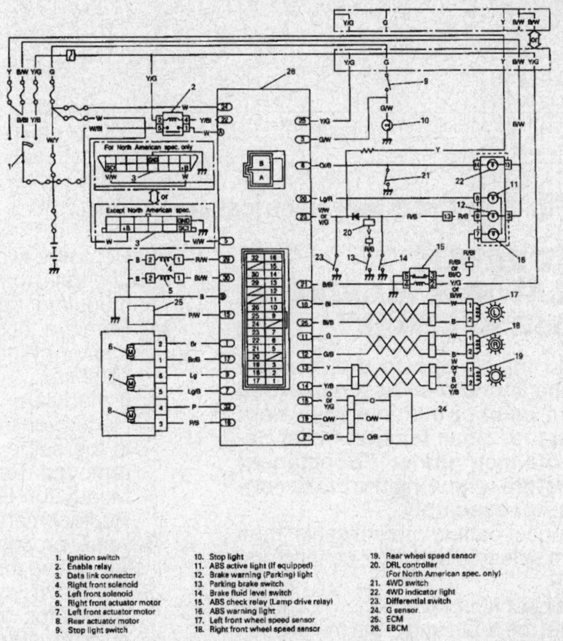
1. Ignition switch
2. Enable relay
3. Data link connector
4. Right front solenoid
5. Left front solenoid
6. Right front actuator motor
7. Left front actuator motor
8. Rear actuator motor
9. Stop light switch
10. Stop light
11. ABS active light (If equipped)
12. Brake warning (Parking) light
13. Parking brake switch
14. Brake fluid level switch
15. ABS check relay (Lamp drive relay)
16. ABS warning light
17. Left front wheel speed sensor
18. Right front wheel speed sensor
19. Rear wheel speed sensor
20. DRL controller (For North American spec. only)
21. 4WD switch
22. 4WD indicator light
23. Differential switch
24. G sensor
25. ECM
26. EBCM
SK4029600094000X

Fig. 3 ABS-VI system wiring circuit. 1996 Sidekick & X-90

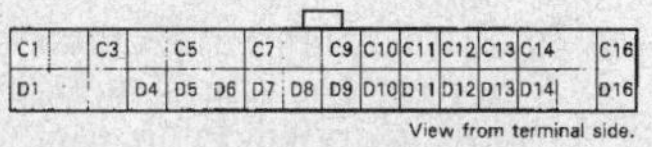
C1
C3
C5
C7
C9
C10
C11
C12
C13
C14
C16
D1
D4
D5
D6
D7
D8
D9
D10
D11
D12
D13
D14
D16
View from terminal side.

TERMINAL	CIRCUIT	TERMINAL	CIRCUIT
C1	Right front motor high	D1	Right front motor low
—	—	—	—
C3	Stop light switch (Brake switch terminal)	—	—
—	—	D4	ABS active light
C5	Serial data	D5	ABS warning light relay
—	—	D6	Enable relay
C7	Left front motor low	D7	Brake warning light
—	—	D8	Backup power supply
C9	Left front motor high	D9	Ignition power supply
C10	Left front wheel speed sensor (high)	D10	Left front wheel speed sensor (low)
C11	Right front wheel speed sensor (high)	D11	Left rear wheel speed sensor (high)
C12	Right front wheel speed sensor (low)	D12	Left rear wheel speed sensor (low)
C13	Right rear wheel speed senosr (high)	D13	Right front solenoid
C14	Right rear wheel speed sensor (low)	D14	Left front solenoid
—	—	—	—
C16	Rear motor low	D16	Rear motor high

SK4029500029000X

Fig. 4 EBCM 32 way electrical connector. 1995–96 Swift

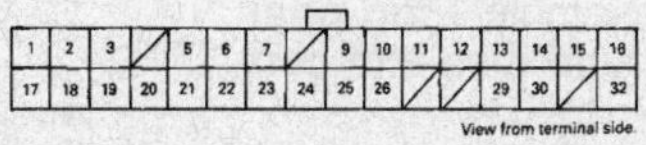
1 2 3 5 6 7 9 10 11 12 13 14 15 16
17 18 19 20 21 22 23 24 25 26 29 30 32
View from terminal side.

TERMINAL	CIRCUIT	TERMINAL	CIRCUIT
1	Right front motor high	17	Right front motor low
2	G sensor	18	G sensor
3	Stop light switch (Brake switch terminal)	19	G sensor
		20	ABS active light
—	—	21	ABS warning light relay
5	Serial data	22	Enable relay
6	4WD switch	23	Brake warning light
7	Left front motor low	24	Backup power supply
—	—	25	Ignition power supply
9	Left front motor high	26	Left front wheel speed sensor (low)
10	Left front wheel speed sensor (high)	—	—
11	Right front wheel speed sensor (high)	—	—
12	Right front wheel speed sensor (low)	29	Right front solenoid
13	Rear wheel speed sensor (high)	30	Left front solenoid
14	Rear wheel speed sensor (low)	—	—
15	Engine control module (ECM)	32	Rear motor high
16	Rear motor low		

SK4029600095000X

Fig. 5 EBCM 32 way electrical connector. 1996 Sidekick & X-90

near parking brake.

4. Reverse procedure to install.

ABS HYDRAULIC MODULATOR SOLENOID ASSEMBLY

1. Disconnect battery ground cable.
2. Disconnect solenoid electrical connector. Remove Torx head bolts, then the solenoid assembly.
3. Reverse procedure to install, **torque** ABS modulator assembly Torx head bolts, "A" to 3 ft lbs. and "B" to 3.5 ft. lbs., **Fig. 12.**

ELECTRONIC BRAKE CONTROL MODULE (EBCM)

1. Disconnect battery ground cable.
2. Remove fasteners on lower sound insulator panel under steering column.
3. Remove EBCM, to dash panel attaching screws, **Fig. 13.**
4. Disconnect EBCM electrical connectors, then remove EBCM, **Fig. 14.**
5. Reverse procedure to install.

FRONT WHEEL SPEED SENSOR

1. Disconnect battery ground cable.
2. Raise and support vehicle, then remove wheel and tire assembly.
3. Disconnect wheel sensor connector.
4. Remove speed sensor from steering knuckle.
5. Reverse procedure to install, noting the following:
   a. Check O-ring for damage replace as required.
   b. Install front wheel speed sensor to steering knuckle, **torque** sensor bolt 6–8 ft. lbs.

REAR WHEEL SPEED SENSOR

1. Disconnect battery ground cable, then raise and support vehicle.
2. Remove rear wheel and tire assembly.
3. Disconnect sensor electrical connector, remove sensor assembly from backing plate.
4. Reverse procedure to install, **torque**-sensor assembly attaching bolt to 6–8 ft. lbs.

A B
View from terminal side

TERMINAL	CIRCUIT	TERMINAL	CIRCUIT
A	Battery power supply	B	Ground

SK4029500030000X

Fig. 6 EBCM 2 way electrical connector

ABS HYDRAULIC MODULATOR & MASTER CYLINDER ASSEMBLY

To avoid injury, due to the retained load on the modulator assembly. Use the TECH 1 scan or suitable equivalent to perform the "Gear Tension Relief Sequence" outlined under "Component Testing" before removing the brake control and motor assembly.

1. Disconnect battery ground cable, then the two solenoid electrical connectors, **Fig. 15.**
2. Disconnect fluid level sensor connector, then the 6-pin and 3-pin motor pack electrical connectors.
3. Drain brake fluid from master cylinder
4. Place a shop cloth between brake pipe connections and the top of the motor pack assembly, then disconnect brake pipes from the assembly. **Plug open lines to prevent fluid loss and contamination.**
5. Remove two ABS hydraulic modulator assembly attaching nuts.
6. Remove modulator assembly from vehicle.
7. To separate hydraulic modulator from master cylinder, proceed as follows:
   a. Remove six Torx head screws that attach gear the gear cover.
   b. Remove four Torx head screws that attach the motor pack assembly.
   c. Remove two modulator assembly to master cylinder through bolts, then separate master cylinder from modulator assembly.
   d. Remove two transfer tubes with O-rings from master cylinder or modulator assembly.
   e. Remove through bolt O-rings from master cylinder and modulator assemblies.
   f. If modulator assembly is to be replaced, ensure gears are installed in the same position as they were removed. Refer to "ABS Hydraulic Modulator Gears" in "Component Replacement " section.
8. Reverse procedure to assemble and install, noting the following:
   a. If master cylinder and hydraulic modulator were separated, use new transfer tube assemblies and new O-rings.
   b. **Torque** modulator assembly to master cylinder through bolts to 12 ft. lbs.
   c. **Torque** modulator assembly to vacuum booster nuts to 20 ft. lbs.
   d. Bleed hydraulic system as outlined in "ABS System Bleeding."
   e. **Torque** modulator assembly, **Fig. 16,** mounting nuts to 6–8 ft. lbs.
   f. **Torque** hydraulic brake pipe fittings to 11–13 ft. lbs.
   g. Bleed hydraulic system as outlined in "ABS System Bleeding."

ABS HYDRAULIC MODULATOR GEARS

Do not attempt to repair defective motor packs or modulator assemblies. Modulator drive gear replacement is the only service that can be performed on these assemblies. The modulator drive gears are under spring load and will turn during disassembly. After removing hydraulic modulator drive gear cover, do not place fingers into the gear set.

1. Remove ABS hydraulic modulator assembly as outlined under "Component Replacement."
2. Remove six Torx head screws attaching gear cover.
3. Remove four motor pack to modulator assembly Torx head screws, then separate motor pack assembly from hydraulic modulator assembly. **Use care not to drop or damage motor pack assembly. If motor pack assembly is dropped or damaged during handling, it must be replaced.**
4. Turn modulator gear to position piston in the center of its travel.
5. Place a screwdriver through the holes in gears into recessed hole in the modulator base. **Do not allow gear to turn while removing retaining nut.**
6. Remove three modulator drive gear to modulator driveshaft retaining nuts, then the gears from modulator.
7. Reverse procedure to install, noting the following:
   a. **Do not allow gears to turn when tightening retaining nuts.**
   b. **Torque** retaining nuts to 75 inch lbs.
   c. Rotate each modulator gear counterclockwise until movement stops, before positioning motor pack assembly onto hydraulic modulator.
   d. **Torque** motor pack assembly to hydraulic modulator assembly Torx head screws to 40 inch lbs.
   e. **Torque** gear cover Torx screws to 27 inch lbs.

Adjustments

When performing adjustments refer to "System Service" found in this section.

Code	Description
Code 14	ABS Enable Relay Contact Circuit Open
Code 15	ABS Enable Relay Circuit Shorted To Battery Or Always Closed
Code 16	ABS Enable Relay Coil Circuit Open
Code 17	ABS Enable Relay Coil Circuit Shorted To Ground
Code 18	ABS Enable Relay Coil Shorted To Battery
Code 21	Left Front Wheel Speed, Zero Or Unreasonable
Code 22	Right Front Wheel Speed, Zero Or Unreasonable
Code 23	Left Rear Wheel Speed, Zero Or Unreasonable
Code 24	Right Rear Wheel Speed, Zero Or Unreasonable
Code 25	Left Front Excessive Wheel Speed Variation
Code 26	Right Front Excessive Wheel Speed Variation
Code 27	Left Rear Excessive Wheel Speed Variation
Code 28	Right Rear Excessive Wheel Speed Variation
Code 36	Low System Voltage
Code 37	High System Voltage

Fig. 7 Diagnostic code interpretation (Part 1 of 2).

Code	Description
Code 38	Left Front ESB Will Not Hold Motor
Code 41	Right Front ESB Will Not Hold Motor
Code 42	Rear ESB Will Not Hold Motor
Code 44	Left Front Channel Will Not Move
Code 45	Right Front Channel Will Not Move
Code 46	Rear Channel Will Not Move
Code 47	Left Front Motor Free Spins
Code 48	Right Front Motor Free Spins
Code 51	Rear Motor Free Spins
Code 52	Left Front Channel In Release Too Long
Code 53	Right Front Channel In Release Too Long
Code 54	Rear Channel In Release Too Long
Code 55	EBCM Malfunction
Code 56	Left Front Motor Circuit Open
Code 57	Left Front Motor Circuit Shorted To Ground
Code 58	Left Front Motor Circuit Shorted To Battery
Code 61	Right Front Motor Circuit Open
Code 62	Right Front Motor Circuit Shorted To Ground
Code 63	Right Front Motor Circuit Shorted To Battery
Code 64	Rear Motor Circuit Open
Code 65	Rear Motor Circuit Shorted To Ground
Code 66	Rear Motor Circuit Shorted To Battery
Code 76	Left Front Solenoid Circuit Open Or Shorted To Battery
Code 77	Left Front Solenoid Circuit Shorted To Ground
Code 78	Right Front Solenoid Circuit Open Or Shorted To Battery
Code 81	Right Front Solenoid Circuit Shorted To Ground
Code 82	Calibration Malfunction
Code 86	EBCM Turned On Red Brake Warning Light
Code 87	Brake Warning Light Circuit Open
Code 88	Brake Warning Light Circuit Shorted To Battery
Code 91	Open Brake Switch During Deceleration
Code 92	Open Brake Switch When ABS Was Required
Code 93	Code 91 Or 92 Set In Current Or Previous Ignition Cycle
Code 94	Brake Switch Contacts Always Closed
Code 95	Brake Switch Circuit Open

Fig. 7 Diagnostic code interpretation (Part 2 of 2).

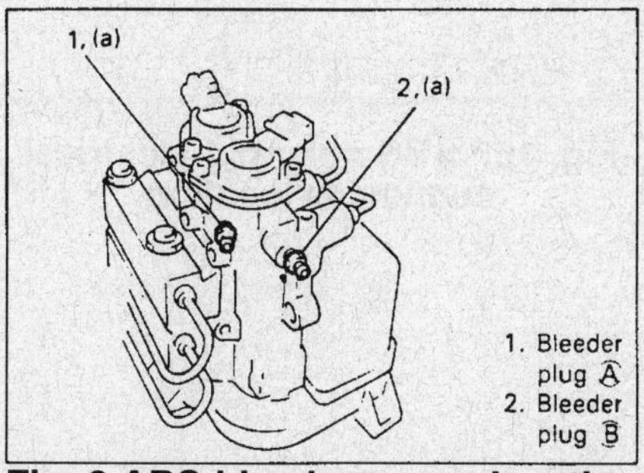
1,(a)
2,(a)
1. Bleeder plug Ⓐ
2. Bleeder plug Ⓑ

Fig. 8 ABS bleeder screw location

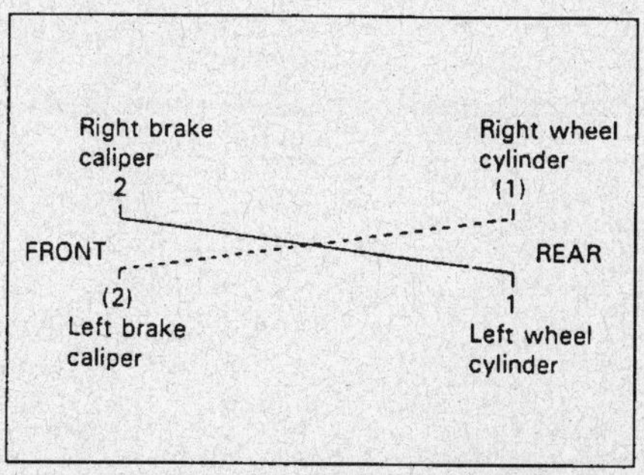
Right brake caliper
2
Right wheel cylinder
(1)
FRONT
REAR
(2)
Left brake caliper
1
Left wheel cylinder

SK4019500024000X

Fig. 9 Wheel bleed sequence. 1995–96 Swift

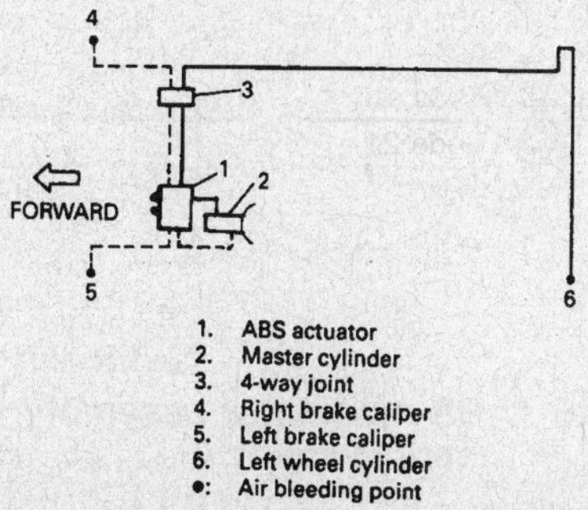
4
3
1
2
FORWARD
5
6
1. ABS actuator
2. Master cylinder
3. 4-way joint
4. Right brake caliper
5. Left brake caliper
6. Left wheel cylinder
●: Air bleeding point

SK4019600026000X

Fig. 10 Wheel bleed sequence. 1996 Sidekick & X-90

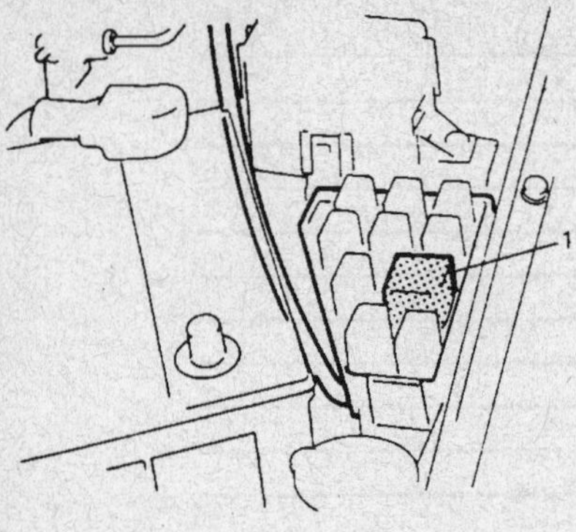
1
1. ABS enable relay

SK4029500087000X

Fig. 11 ABS enable relay location

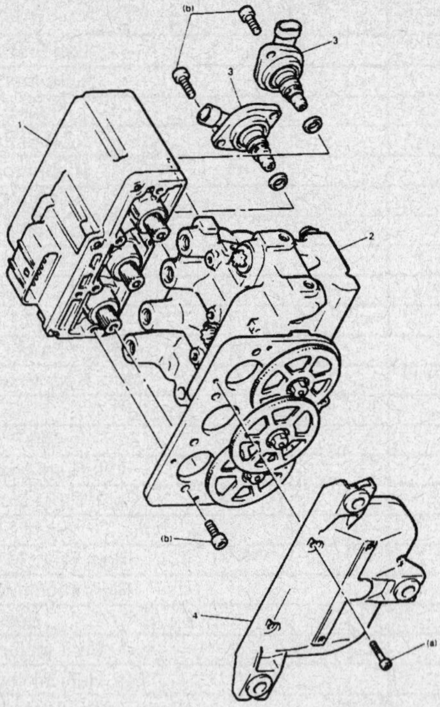
(b)
3
1
3
2
(b)
4
(a)
1. Motor pack
2. ABS actuator
(Hydraulic modulator)
3. Solenoid
4. Under cover
Tightening Torque
(a): 4 N·m (0.4 kg-m, 3.0 lb-ft)
(b): 4.5 N·m (0.45 kg-m, 3.5 lb-ft)

SK4029500088000X

Fig. 12 Exploded view of ABS modulator assembly

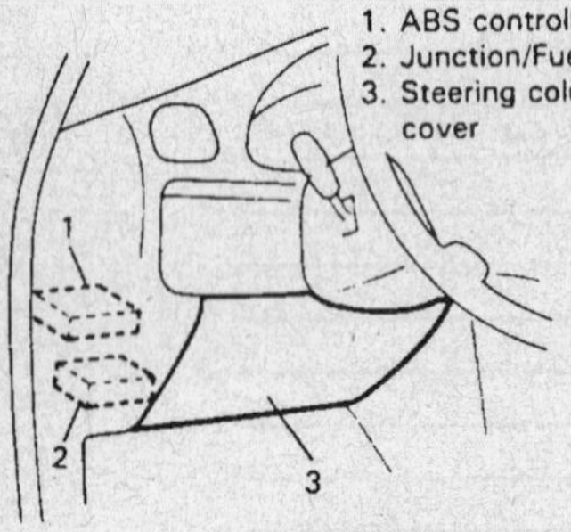
1. ABS controller ass'y
2. Junction/Fuel block
3. Steering column hole cover
1
2
3

SK4029500089000X

Fig. 13 Lower dash panel replacement

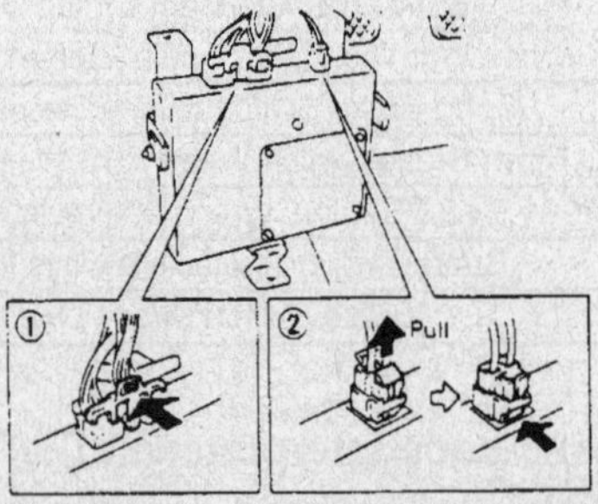
①
②
Pull

SK4029500090000X

Fig. 14 ABS electronic brake control module replacement

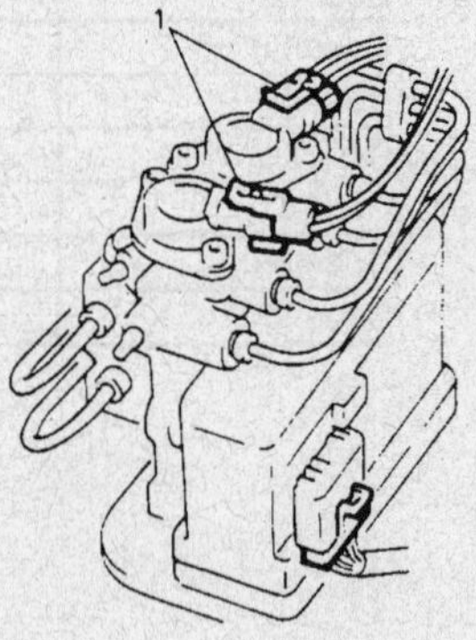
1
1. Solenoid couplers

SK4029500091000X

Fig. 15 ABS solenoid electrical connector location

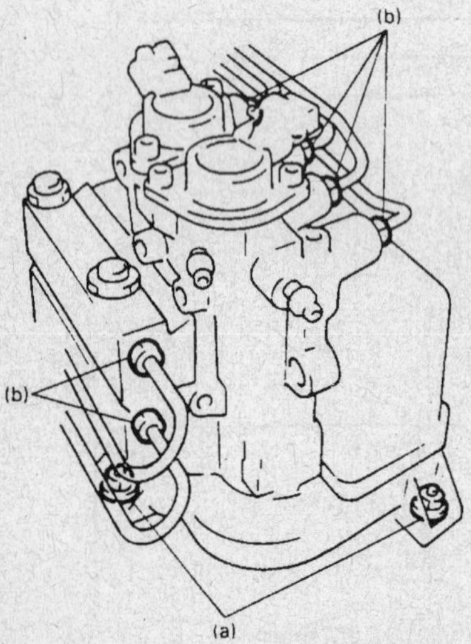
(b)
(b)
(a)

SK4029500092000X

Fig. 16 ABS modulator assembly replacement

Automatic Transmissions/ Transaxles

INDEX

	Page No.		Page No.		Page No.
Esteem Automatic Transaxle	40-154	2-Door Sidekick Automatic Transmission (THM-3L30)	40-145	4-Door Sidekick & X-90 Automatic Transmission	40-148
Swift Automatic Transaxle	40-150				

2-Door Sidekick Automatic Transmission (THM-3L30)

INDEX

	Page No.		Page No.		Page No.
Adjustments	40-146	Kickdown Cable, Replace	40-147	**Maintenance**	40-145
Brake Interlock Cable	40-146	Rear Extension Oil Seal, Replace	40-147	Fluid Change	40-145
Kickdown Cable	40-146	Select Cable, Replace	40-147	Fluid Check	40-145
Select Cable	40-146	Speedometer Driven Gear, Replace	40-146	**Precautions**	40-145
Description	40-145	Vacuum Modulator, Replace	40-147	Fuel System Pressure Release	40-145
Identification	40-145			**Tightening Specifications**	40-148
In-Vehicle Repairs	40-146			**Transmission, Replace**	40-147
Brake Interlock Cable, Replace	40-147				

PRECAUTIONS

FUEL SYSTEM PRESSURE RELEASE

1. Disconnect fuel pump harness connector at the fuel tank rear side. **Cover fuel pipe line with rag after relieving pressure as certain pressure may still remain.**
2. Start engine and let idle until engine stops by itself, then turn ignition switch to Off. **Failure to relieve fuel system pressure prior to disconnecting fuel system components may cause fire or personal injury.**
3. Disconnect battery ground cable.
4. Connect fuel pump harness connector.
5. After repairs have been completed, connect positive battery terminal to fuel pump drive terminal and the negative terminal to the chassis. Ensure fuel pump operates at this time.

IDENTIFICATION

Refer to **Fig. 1,** for proper transmission identification.

DESCRIPTION

The THM-180C transmission is a fully automatic unit which can provide three forward speeds and reverse. The units primary components include a four-element hydraulic torque converter and a compound planetary gear set, **Fig. 2.**

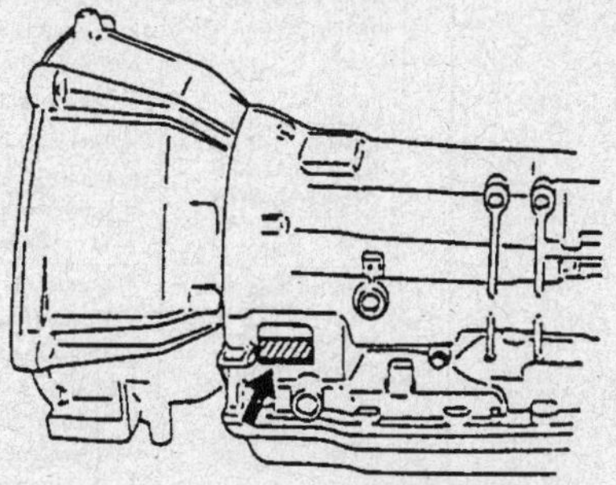

Copyrighted Material Reprinted with Permission from Hydra-Matic Div., GM Corp.

TH5029100006000X

Fig. 1 Transmission identification

Three multiple disc clutches, a roller clutch and a band provide the friction elements required to obtain the desired function of the compound planetary gear set.

Oil pressure and shift points of the transmission are controlled by a vacuum modulator that senses engine torque as a relation to engine vacuum.

MAINTENANCE

FLUID CHECK

To check fluid, drive vehicle for at least 15 minutes to bring fluid to operating temperature (200°F). With vehicle on a level surface and engine idling in Park and parking brake applied, move the selector lever through each gear range. Check the level on the dipstick, it should be at the "Full Hot" mark. To bring the fluid level from the ADD mark to the FULL HOT mark requires one pint of fluid. If vehicle cannot be driven sufficiently to bring fluid to operating temperature, the level on the dipstick should be between the two dimples on the dipstick with fluid temperature at 70°F.

If additional fluid is required, use only Dexron II automatic transmission fluid.

When adding fluid, do not overfill, as foaming and loss of fluid through the vent may occur as the fluid heats up. Also, if fluid level is too low, complete loss of drive may occur especially when cold, which can cause transmission failure. The oil should be drained, the oil pan removed, the screen cleaned and fresh fluid added every 100,000 miles. For vehicles subjected to more severe use such as heavy city traffic especially in hot weather, prolonged periods of idling or towing, this maintenance should be performed every 15,000 miles.

FLUID CHANGE

1. Raise and support vehicle.
2. Remove lower propeller shaft universal joint flange and position aside to the right.
3. Place suitable container under oil pan, then remove oil pan attaching bolts except for the three rear bolts.
4. Loosen three rear oil pan bolts, then drain fluid from front side of oil pan.
5. Remove three remaining attaching bolts, then the oil pan and gasket.

6. Check the strainer screen and clean or replace as necessary.
7. Install oil pan and new gasket. Tighten oil pan attaching bolts to specifications.
8. Connect propeller shaft to differential flange. Tighten bolts to specification.
9. Lower vehicle and add proper amount of Dexron II or equivalent.

ADJUSTMENTS

SELECT CABLE

1. Shift selector to Neutral position.
2. Move manual select lever to Low position, which is the lowest position of switch, then set cable to cable bracket with E-ring.
3. While installing cable end through manual select lever, shift manual select lever back to Neutral position and fix position by tightening adjusting nut and locknut, **Fig. 4. Cable adjustment must be made so there is no clearance between lever and adjust nut.** Tighten locknut to specification.
4. Ensure proper operation of all ranges.

BRAKE INTERLOCK CABLE

1. Shift select lever to P range, then turn key to lock position.
2. Pull manual release knob and hold, then shift select lever to R range. Ensure inner cable is not bent, then loosen locknuts and pull cable out in F direction **Fig. 5,** until free of slack.
3. Secure cable with nuts A and B.

KICKDOWN CABLE

1. Ensure accelerator cable play is within 0.04–0.06 inch (10–15 mm). If needed adjust cable.
2. Loosen kickdown cable locknut and adjusting nut, **Fig. 6.**
3. With accelerator pedal depressed fully and kickdown cable pulled in A direction, **Fig. 6,** adjust locknut to bracket clearance to 0–0.039 inch (0–1 mm) by turning locknut. **When adjusting clearance, ensure adjusting nut does not contact bracket.**
4. Release accelerator pedal and adjust locknut to bracket clearance to 0–0.039 inch (0–1 mm) by tightening adjusting nut. Use care to keep locknut in place.
5. When turning adjusting nut, position nut as shown, **Fig. 7.** When adjusting nut position is determined, fit adjusting nut to bracket as shown, **Fig. 7.**
6. Tighten locknut securely.

IN-VEHICLE REPAIRS

SPEEDOMETER DRIVEN GEAR, REPLACE

1. Remove bolt securing driven gear housing retainer, then the retainer.
2. Pull speedometer driven gear from housing.
3. Install speedometer driven gear into housing, then the retainer into slot of

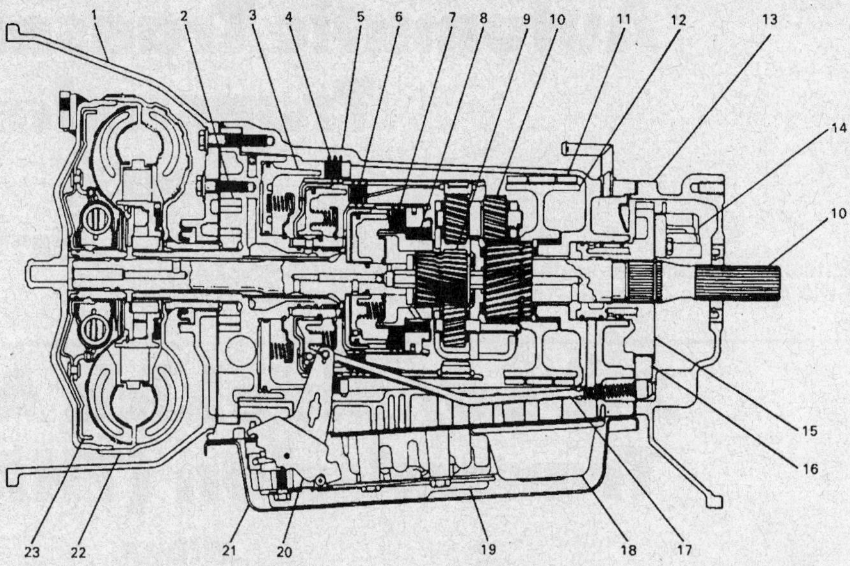

1. Torque converter housing
2. Oil pump
3. Reverse clutch piston
4. Reverse clutch plate
5. Transmission case
6. 2nd clutch
7. 3rd clutch
8. Sprag assembly (one-way clutch)
9. Planetary input sun gear
10. Planetary gear carrier
11. Low brake band
12. Planetary rear sun gear
13. Adapter case
14. Governor assembly
15. Governor hub
16. Parking lock pawl
17. Parking lock actuator
18. Servo piston cover
19. Valve body assembly
20. Select shaft inner lever
21. Oil pan
22. Torque converter
23. Torque converter clutch

TH5029100007000X

Fig. 2 Cross-sectional view of THM 3L30 transmission

	Condition	Possible cause	Correction
CONCERNS TRANSMISSION FLUID	**Low fluid level.**	• Fluid coming out of oil filler tube. • External fluid leak. • Failed vacuum modulator.	Adjust fluid level. Repair leak. Replace modulator.
	Fluid coming out of oil filler tube.	• Fluid level too high. • Coolant in transmission fluid. • Breather hose pinched. • Leak in oil pump suction circuit.	Adjust level. Replace radiator. Correct piping. Overhaul.
	External fluid leaks in the area of torque converter housing.	• Leaking torque converter. • Converter housing oil seal. • Converter housing to case seal. • Loose fastening bolts.	Replace torque converter. Replace oil seal. Replace seal. Tighten bolts.
	External fluid leaks in the area of transmission case and transfer adapter case.	• Manual select shaft seal. • Adapter case seal. • Oil pan gasket. • Adapter case gasket. • Vacuum modulator O ring. • Cooler line fittings. • Oil filler tube O ring. • Kick-down cable O ring. • Line pressure gauge connection. • Electrical connector O ring.	Replace oil seal. Replace oil seal. Replace gasket. Replace gasket. Replace O ring. Tighten fastenings. Replace O ring. Replace cable. Tighten plug. Replace O ring.
	Low fluid pressure.	• Low fluid level. • Clogged oil pump screen. • Leak in oil pump suction circuit. • Leak in oil pressure circuit. • Pressure regulator valve malfunction. • Sealing ball (plug) in valve body dropped out.	Adjust fluid level. Wash screen. Overhaul. Overhaul. Overhaul oil pump. Replace valve body.
	High fluid pressure.	• Modulator vacuum line leaky or interrupted. • Failed vacuum modulator. • Leak in any part of engine or accessory vacuum system. • Pressure regulator valve malfunction.	Repair line. Replace modulator. Repair leak. Overhaul oil pump.
	Excessive smoke coming from exhaust.	Failed vacuum modulator.	Replace modulator.

TH5029100008010X

Fig. 3 Troubleshooting chart (Part 1 of 5)

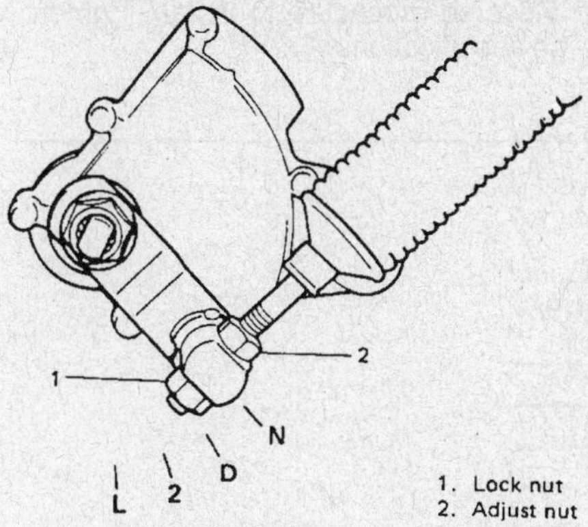
1
2
N
D
L
2
1. Lock nut
2. Adjust nut

TH5029100009000X

Fig. 3 Select cable adjustment

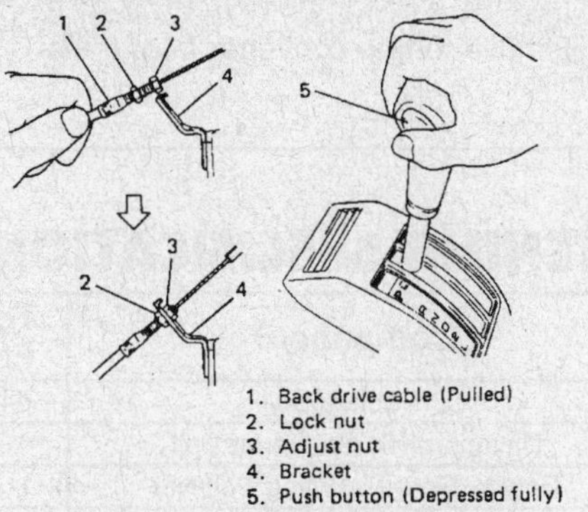
1 2 3
4
5
3
2
4
1. Back drive cable (Pulled)
2. Lock nut
3. Adjust nut
4. Bracket
5. Push button (Depressed fully)

TH5029100010000X

Fig. 4 Backdrive cable adjustment

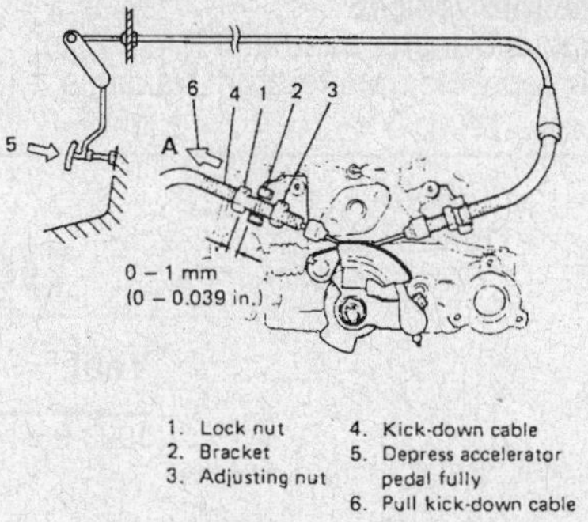
6 4 1 2 3
5
A
0 – 1 mm
(0 – 0.039 in.)
1. Lock nut
2. Bracket
3. Adjusting nut
4. Kick-down cable
5. Depress accelerator pedal fully
6. Pull kick-down cable

TH5029100011000X

Fig. 5 Kickdown cable adjustment

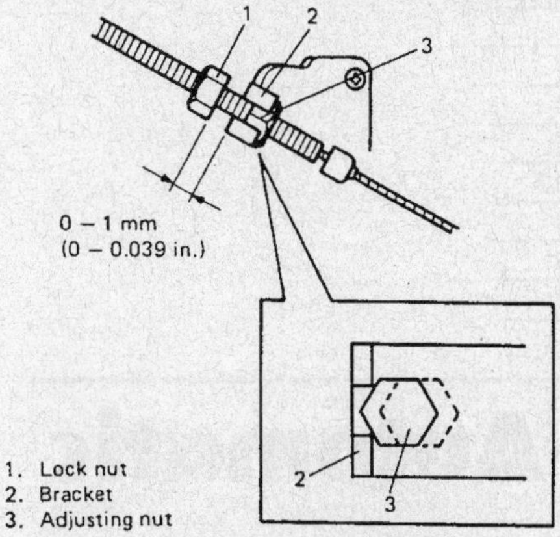
1 2
3
0 – 1 mm
(0 – 0.039 in.)
2
3
1. Lock nut
2. Bracket
3. Adjusting nut

TH5029100012000X

Fig. 6 Kickdown cable nut adjustment

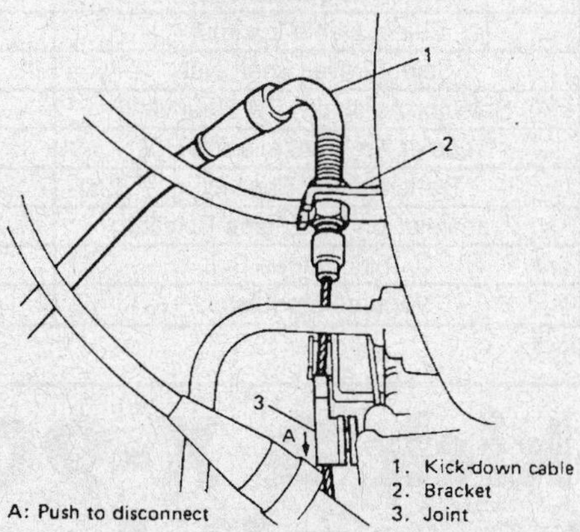
1
2
3
A
A: Push to disconnect
1. Kick-down cable
2. Bracket
3. Joint

TH5029100013000X

Fig. 7 Kickdown cable plastic joint removal

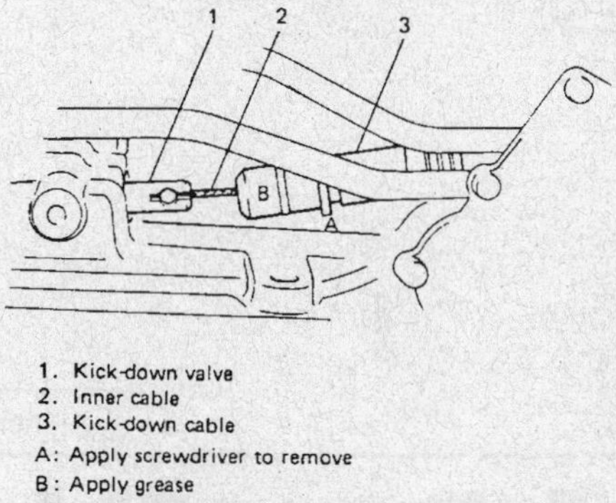
1 2 3
B
A
1. Kick-down valve
2. Inner cable
3. Kick-down cable
A: Apply screwdriver to remove
B: Apply grease

TH5029100014000X

Fig. 8 Kickdown cable removal

driven gear housing.
4. Install retainer attaching bolt.

REAR EXTENSION OIL SEAL, REPLACE

1. Remove propeller shaft.
2. Remove oil seal using suitable tool.
3. Lubricate new seal lip with transmission fluid and install seal into extension housing with seal installation tool No. J-21426, or equivalent.
4. Install propeller shaft.

VACUUM MODULATOR, REPLACE

1. Disconnect vacuum hose from modulator stem.
2. Using wrench tool No. 09920-36020/J-23100, or equivalent, remove modulator assembly from transmission.
3. Reverse procedure to install using new O-ring seal. Tighten modulator to specification.
4. Check and adjust fluid level.

SELECT CABLE, REPLACE

1. Remove console box. Push in center pin first, then remove rear clips.
2. Remove four bolts and raise manual selector assembly.
3. Remove cable clip, washer and outer cable E-ring, then disconnect cable from selector.
4. Raise and support vehicle.
5. Remove locknut from cable end at transmission.
6. Pull down manual select lever and disconnect cable and lever.
7. Remove cable and E-ring.
8. Reverse procedure to install.

BRAKE INTERLOCK CABLE, REPLACE

1. Remove meter hood and steering cover.
2. Remove back drive cable clamp screw, then disconnect cable eye end.
3. Remove console box, then disconnect cable by loosening locknut and cable end clip in manual selector assembly.
4. Reverse procedure to install.

KICKDOWN CABLE, REPLACE

1. Pushing cable toward "A," remove plastic joint at end of cable, **Fig. 7.**
2. Loosen nut at bracket and disconnect cable, then remove cable bracket.
3. Pull cable out, then apply screwdriver at flange "A" and disconnect inner cable end connected to valve, **Fig. 8.**
4. Reverse procedure to install.

TRANSMISSION

REPLACE

1. Relieve fuel system pressure as outlined under "Precautions."
2. Disconnect battery ground cable, then remove the following components from engine compartment:
   a. Wiring harness couplers, breather hose clamp, kickdown cable, vacuum hose, transmission to engine bolts and starter.
3. Raise and support vehicle.
4. Drain transfer oil into appropriate container.
5. Remove front and rear propeller shafts.
6. Release select cable by removing nut from end of cable and E-ring from bracket.
7. Remove select cable bracket, then disconnect oil cooler hoses from pipes.
8. Remove torque converter housing lower plate.
9. Holding driveplate stationary using gear stopper tool No. 09927-56010, or equivalent, remove plate attaching bolts.
10. Remove exhaust center pipe, then engine to transmission nuts.
11. Remove meter cable end nut and disconnect cable.
12. Support transmission using suitable jack, then remove rear mounting member bolts and member.
13. Remove transmission and transfer

case from vehicle.
14. Remove transfer case attaching bolts, then separate transfer from transmission.
15. Remove torque converter from transmission.
16. Reverse procedure to install. Tighten to specifications.

TIGHTENING SPECIFICATIONS

Year	Component	Torque/ Ft. Lbs.
1993-96	Driveplate Bolt	54.5-57.5
	Driveplate To Converter Bolt	40
	Engine Rear Mounting Bolt/Nut	36
	Kick-Down Cable Bracket Bolt	8
	Oil Cooler Hose Clamp	12①
	Oil Pan Bolt	9
	Propeller Shaft To Differential	37
	Select Cable Bracket Bolt	17
	Select Cable Locknut	5
	Select Lever Shaft Nut	14
	Selector Assembly To Floor Bolt	13
	Transfer To Transmission Bolt	17
	Transmission Case Plug	11-13
	Transmission To Engine Bolt/Nut	62
	U-Joint Flange Bolt	40
	Vacuum Modulator	38

① — Inch lbs.

4-Door Sidekick & X-90 Automatic Transmission

INDEX

	Page No.
Adjustments	40-149
A/T Throttle Cable	40-149
Select Cable	40-149
Shift Switch	40-149
Description	40-148
Identification	40-148
Maintenance	40-148
Changing Fluid	40-149
Fluid Level Check	40-148
Precautions	40-148
Fuel System Pressure Release	40-148
Tightening Specifications	40-150
Transmission, Replace	40-149
Troubleshooting	40-148

PRECAUTIONS

FUEL SYSTEM PRESSURE RELEASE

1. Disconnect fuel pump harness connector at the fuel tank rear side. **Cover fuel pipe line with rag after relieving pressure as certain pressure may still remain.**
2. Start engine and let idle until engine stops by itself, then turn ignition switch to Off. **Failure to relieve fuel system pressure prior to disconnecting fuel system components may cause fire or personal injury.**
3. Disconnect battery ground cable.
4. Connect fuel pump harness connector.
5. After repairs have been completed, connect positive battery terminal to fuel pump drive terminal and the negative terminal to the chassis. Ensure fuel pump operates at this time.

IDENTIFICATION

Refer to **Fig. 1,** for transmission identification.

DESCRIPTION

This unit is a fully automatic, electronically controlled, transmission which can provide four forward speeds and reverse. The units primary components include a three-element hydraulic torque converter and a compound planetary gear set.

TROUBLESHOOTING

In conjunction with the prerequisites noted below, refer to charts, **Figs. 2 through 4,** when troubleshooting this transmission:

1. Engine coolant is at normal operating temperature.
2. Engine idle speed is 750–850 RPM with A/C Off.
3. Transmission fluid level is correct and at normal operating temperature.
4. Throttle and select cables are properly adjusted.
5. Gear shift control system wiring is in good condition.

MAINTENANCE

FLUID LEVEL CHECK

1. Drive vehicle for approximately 15 minutes to bring fluid up to normal operating temperature.
2. With vehicle on level surface, apply parking brake and block drive wheels.
3. With selector lever in Park position, start engine, then move selector lever through each range and return to Park.
4. Remove dipstick and check fluid level.

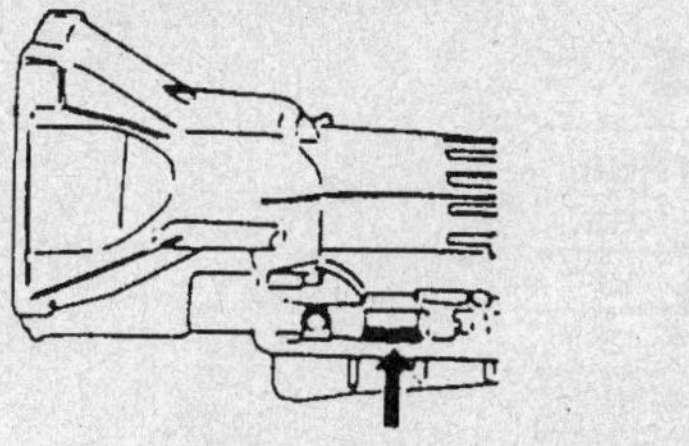
A/T

SK5029100001000X

Fig. 1 Transmission identification

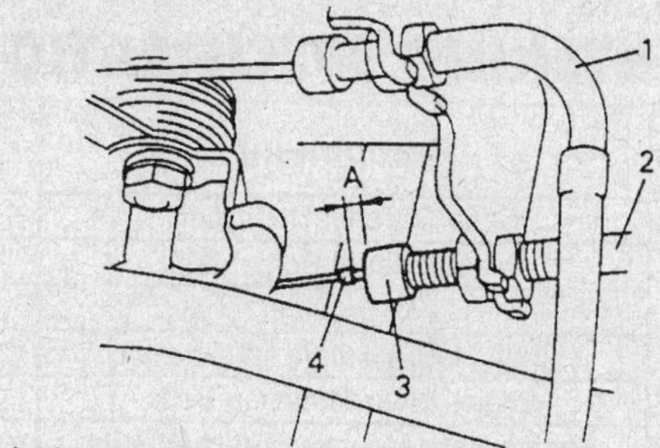
A
1
2
3
4

1. Accelerator wire
2. A/T throttle cable
3. Boot
4. Adjustment mark

SK5029100005000X

Fig. 2 Throttle cable adjustment

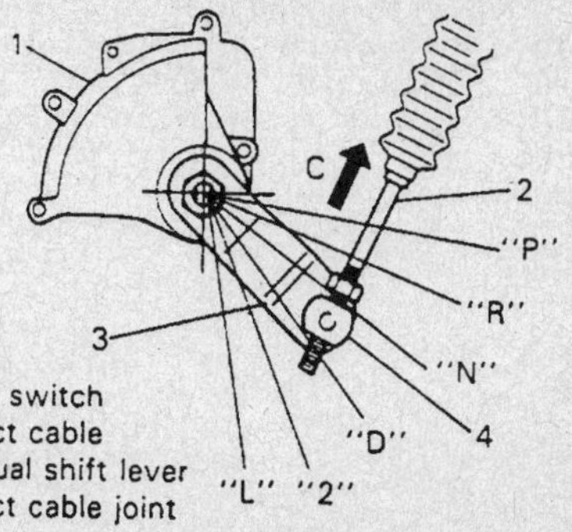
1
2
3
4
C
"P"
"R"
"N"
"D"
"L"
"2"

1. Shift switch
2. Select cable
3. Manual shift lever
4. Select cable joint

SK5029100006000X

Fig. 3 Shift switch range locations

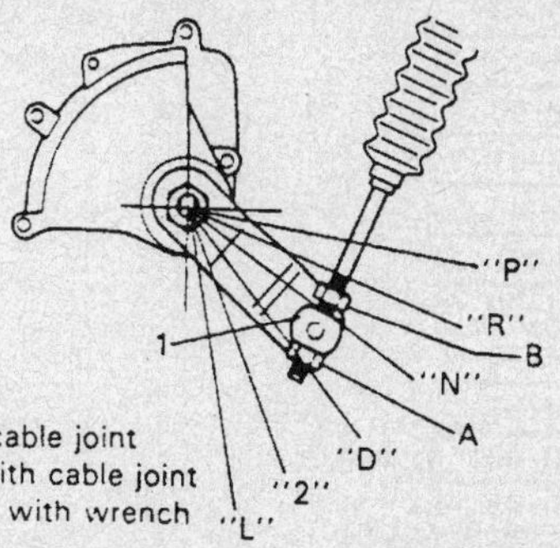
"P"
"R"
B
"N"
A
"D"
"2"
"L"
1

1. Select cable joint
A: Align with cable joint
B: Tighten with wrench

SK5029100007000X

Fig. 4 Select cable adjustment

5. Fluid level should be between HOT marks on dipstick.
6. Add fluid as required to bring fluid to specified level. When adding fluid use only Dexron II type transmission fluid or equivalent.

CHANGING FLUID

Under normal driving conditions, transmission fluid should be changed every 100,000 miles. To service, proceed as follows:

1. Raise and support vehicle.
2. With engine cool, remove drain plug and drain fluid from oil pan.
3. Install drain plug and tighten to specification.
4. Lower vehicle and fill transmission with 2.6 quarts of Dexron II or equivalent.
5. Check fluid as outlined under "Fluid Level Check."

ADJUSTMENTS

A/T THROTTLE CABLE

Ensure distance "A" in **Fig. 2,** is 0.031-0.059 inch. Adjust as necessary.

SELECT CABLE

1. Loosen cable end nut, then shift select lever and manual shift lever to Neutral position, **Fig. 3.** Ensure nut and cable joint sufficient clearance. If select cable has been removed, push cable in direction as shown, **Fig. 3.**
2. Hand tighten nut "A," **Fig. 4,** until it contacts manual select cable joint, then tighten nut "B" with wrench.

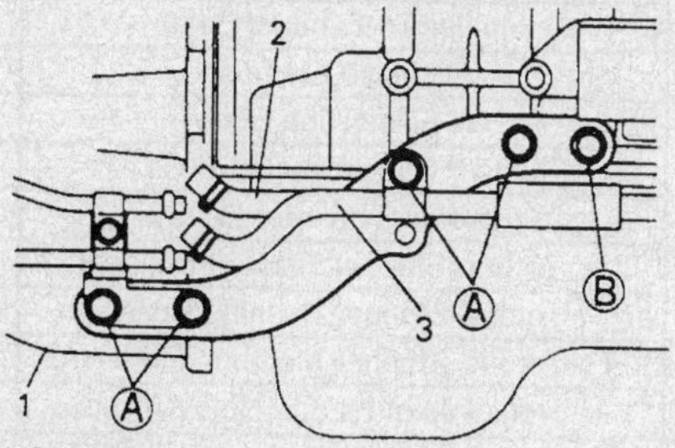
1
2
3
A
B

1. Converter housing
2. Outlet hose
3. Inlet hose

SK5029100008000X

Fig. 5 Case right stiffener mounting bolts

3. Confirm proper operation of select cable.

SHIFT SWITCH

1. Shift select lever to Neutral position.
2. Align groove in switch with match marks on shaft.
3. Ensure engine only starts in Neutral and Park ranges and back-up lamps illuminate in Reverse range.

TRANSMISSION

REPLACE

1. Relieve fuel system pressure as outlined under "Precautions."
2. Remove clips at rear of console box, then the console box mounting screws at front and retaining clips at rear and console box.
3. Remove shift lever boot cover, then the No. 2 boot.
4. Remove transfer gear shift lever boot clamp, then the transfer gear shift boot.
5. To remove shift control lever, push down gear shift control case cover with fingers and turn it counterclockwise.
6. To remove transfer shift control lever, push down gear shift control case cover with fingers and turn it counterclockwise.
7. Remove battery, dipstick and oil filler tube.
8. Disconnect A/T throttle cable from throttle cam and bracket.
9. Disconnect wiring harness couplers, then remove starter. Do not disconnect starter wiring harness.
10. Remove upper transmission to engine bolts. Right side bolt is longer.
11. Drain transfer oil into appropriate container. If transmission is to be overhauled, drain transmission fluid into appropriate container.
12. Place match marks on joint flanges and propeller shafts, then remove both propeller shafts.
13. Remove nut from end of select cable and E-ring from bracket. Position cable aside.
14. Remove select cable bracket, then remove front exhaust pipes.
15. Remove case left stiffener, then disconnect oil cooler hoses from pipes. Plug all open fittings.
16. On right stiffener, remove bolt "A" and loosen bolt "B," **Fig. 5.**
17. Install driveplate holding tool, part No. 09927-56010 or equivalent, then remove torque converter mounting bolts.
18. Remove lower engine to transmission nuts, then disconnect speedometer cable.
19. Install suitable transmission jack, then remove rear mounting member, torque stopper member and torque stopper bushing.
20. Remove transmission, transfer case and torque converter as an assembly. **Keep transmission/transfer assembly horizontal. If assembly is tilted, torque converter may fall off causing personal injury.**
21. Remove wiring harness and breather hoses.
22. Remove transfer case mounting bolts, then separate transfer case from transmission.
23. Reverse procedure to install. Tighten to specifications.

TIGHTENING SPECIFICATIONS

Year	Component	Torque/ Ft. Lbs.
1993–96	Case Stiffener Bolts, Left	29–43
	Case Stiffener Bolts, Right	29–43
	Drain Plug	14-20
	Driveplate To Converter Bolts	44-50
	Engine Rear Mounting Bolts	29–43
	Engine Rear Mounting Bracket Bolts	29–43
	Engine Rear Mounting Member Bolts	29–43
	Engine To Transmission Nuts	51–72
	Exhaust Pipe Bracket Bolts	29–43
	Exhaust Pipe To Manifold Nuts	37–51
	Muffler To Exhaust Bolts	29–43
	Oil Hose Clamps	12①
	Oil Filler Tube Bolts	14–20
	Select Cable Bracket Bolts	14–20
	Torque Converter Bolts	44–51
	Torque Stopper Bracket Bolts	29–43
	Torque Stopper Bushing Bolts	29–43
	Torque Stopper Member Bolts	29–43
	Universal Joint Flange Nuts & Bolts	37–43

① — Inch lbs.

Swift Automatic Transaxle

INDEX

Page No.

Adjustments 40-151
Interlock Cable.................... 40-151
Oil Pressure Control Cable...... 40-151
Description 40-150
Identification..................... 40-150
In-Vehicle Repairs 40-151
Direct Clutch & Second Brake Solenoids, Replace 40-151
Interlock Cable, Replace........ 40-152
Oil Pressure Control Cable, Replace 40-151
Shift Lever Switch, Replace..... 40-152
Shift Lock Solenoid, Replace ... 40-152
Speed Sensor, Replace......... 40-152
Transaxle Selector Cable, Replace 40-151
Transaxle Selector Lever, Replace 40-151
Maintenance 40-150
Fluid Change 40-150
Fluid Check......................... 40-150
Precautions........................ 40-150
Fuel System Pressure Release . 40-150
Tightening Specifications 40-153
Transaxle, Replace 40-153

PRECAUTIONS

FUEL SYSTEM PRESSURE RELEASE

1. Disconnect fuel pump harness connector at the fuel tank rear side. **Cover fuel pipe line with rag after relieving pressure as certain pressure may still remain.**
2. Start engine and let idle until engine stops by itself, then turn ignition switch to Off. **Failure to relieve fuel system pressure prior to disconnecting fuel system components may cause fire or personal injury.**
3. Disconnect battery ground cable.
4. Connect fuel pump harness connector.
5. After repairs have been completed, connect positive battery terminal to fuel pump drive terminal and the negative terminal to the chassis. Ensure fuel pump operates at this time.

IDENTIFICATION

Refer to **Fig. 1,** for proper transmission identification.

DESCRIPTION

This automatic transmission is an electronically controlled three speed automatic transmission, utilizing a hydraulic torque converter, countershaft and differential.

The transmission uses two planetary gears, two disc clutches, one band brake, one disc brake and one one-way clutch. .

MAINTENANCE

FLUID CHECK

1. Drive vehicle for approximately 15 minutes to bring fluid up to normal operating temperature.
2. With vehicle on level surface, apply parking brake and block drive wheels.
3. With selector lever in Park position, start engine, then move selector lever through each range and return to Park.
4. Remove dipstick and check fluid level.
5. Fluid level should be between HOT marks on dipstick.
6. Add fluid as required to bring fluid to specified level. When adding fluid use only Dexron II type transaxle fluid or equivalent.

FLUID CHANGE

Under normal driving conditions, fluid level should be changed and oil strainer cleaned every 100,000 miles. To service, proceed as follows:

1. Raise and support front of vehicle.
2. Remove drain plug and drain fluid from oil pan into appropriate container.
3. Remove oil pan attaching bolts and the oil pan.
4. Remove oil strainer-to-valve body attaching bolts, then the oil strainer.
5. Clean strainer and oil pan in suitable

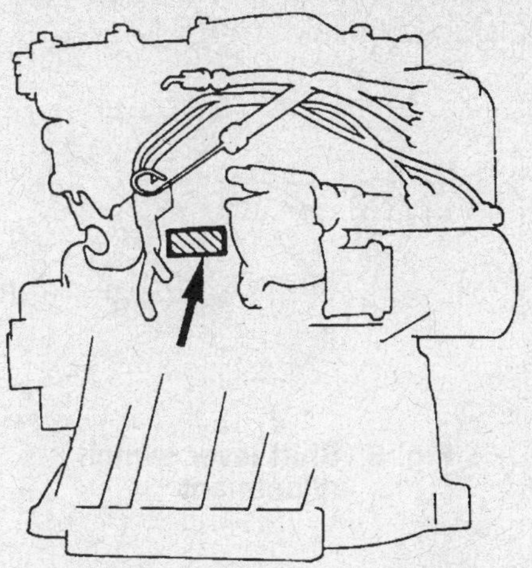

SK5029100009000X

Fig. 1 Transaxle identification

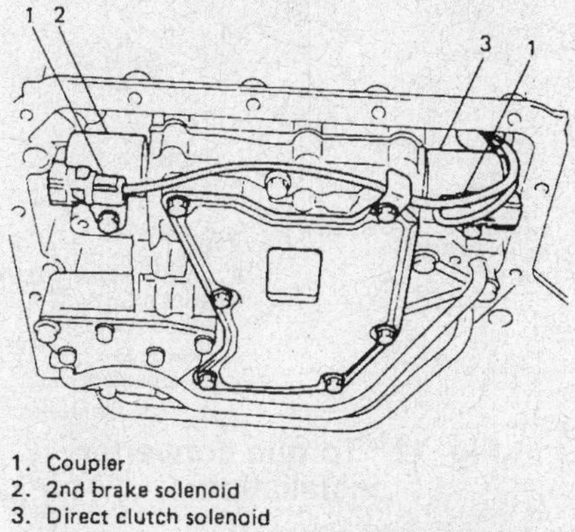
1 2
3 1
1. Coupler
2. 2nd brake solenoid
3. Direct clutch solenoid

SK5029100016000X

Fig. 4 Direct clutch & second brake solenoid replacement

solvent. Engine magnet in oil pan is positioned directly below oil strainer.

6. Install oil strainer and attaching bolts. Tighten to specification.
7. Install oil pan using new gasket. Tighten to specification. **Two of the oil pan attaching bolts have crossed grooves on the bolt head. When installing these two bolts, coat threads with suitable sealant and install in positions shown, Fig. 5.**
8. Lower vehicle and refill oil pan with approximately 1.5 quarts of Dexron II type transaxle fluid or equivalent.
9. Check fluid level as previously described and adjust as necessary.

ADJUSTMENTS

INTERLOCK CABLE

1. Loosen cable nuts "A" and "B" as shown, **Fig. 2.**
2. Shift selector lever to Park position.
3. While pulling outer cable as far as possible in direction of arrow "C," **Fig. 2,** align nut "B" with bracket and tighten locknut "A." When outer cable is pulled in "C" direction, release shaft spring in steering lock should be depressed fully.
4. After adjustment is complete, ensure the following:

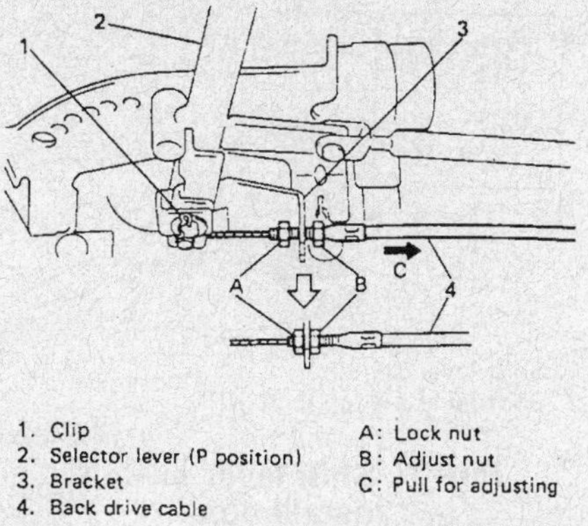
2
1
3
A
B
C
4
1. Clip
2. Selector lever (P position)
3. Bracket
4. Back drive cable
A: Lock nut
B: Adjust nut
C: Pull for adjusting

SK5029100014000X

Fig. 2 Interlock cable adjustment

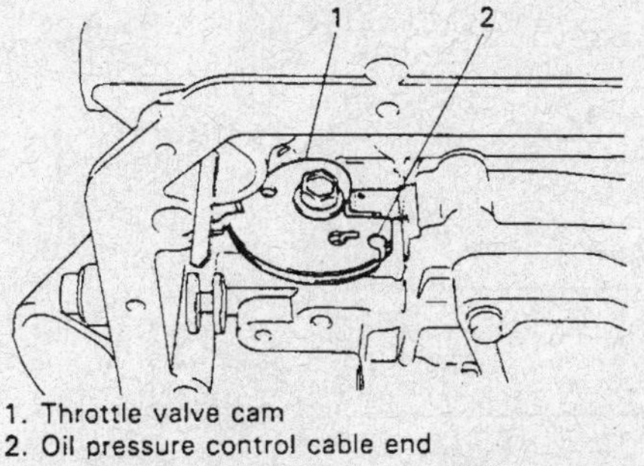
1
2
1. Throttle valve cam
2. Oil pressure control cable end

SK5029100017000X

Fig. 5 Oil pressure control cable replacement

a. With selector lever in Park position, ensure ignition key can be turned from "ACC" to "LOCK" position and removed from ignition switch.
b. Ensure ignition key cannot be turned to Lock position when selector lever is in any other range than Park.

OIL PRESSURE CONTROL CABLE

1. Check and, if necessary, adjust accelerator cable.
2. Start engine and allow to reach normal operating temperature.
3. Remove control cable cover and ensure boot to inner cable stopper clearance is 0–0.020 inch as shown, **Fig. 3.**
4. If clearance is not as specified, loosen, then tighten adjusting nuts "A" until specified clearance is obtained. If clearance is still not within specifications, turn adjusting nuts "B" and repeat procedure outlined above.

IN-VEHICLE REPAIRS

DIRECT CLUTCH & SECOND BRAKE SOLENOIDS, REPLACE

1. Disconnect battery ground cable.
2. Drain transaxle fluid into appropriate container and remove oil pan.
3. Disconnect electrical connectors from direct clutch and second brake solenoids, then remove solenoids, **Fig. 4.**

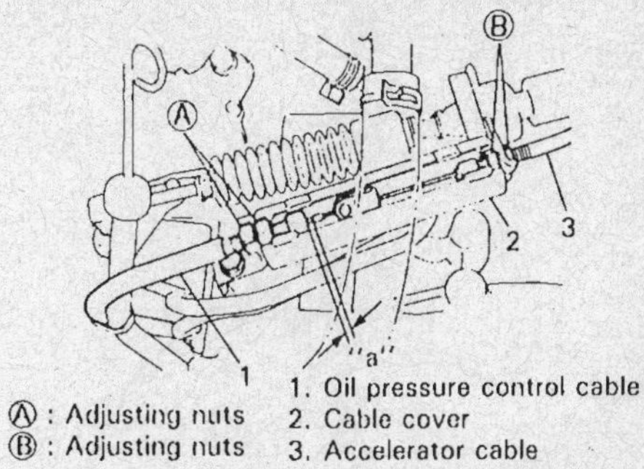
Ⓑ
Ⓐ
1
2
3
"a"
Ⓐ : Adjusting nuts
Ⓑ : Adjusting nuts
1. Oil pressure control cable
2. Cable cover
3. Accelerator cable

SK5029100015000X

Fig. 3 Oil pressure control cable adjustment

4. Remove solenoid wire harness with grommet from upper side.
5. Reverse procedure to install.

OIL PRESSURE CONTROL CABLE, REPLACE

1. Remove cable cover, then disconnect oil pressure control cable from accelerator cable.
2. Drain transaxle fluid into appropriate container and remove oil pan.
3. Disconnect oil pressure control cable from throttle valve cam, then remove cable from transaxle case, **Fig. 5.**
4. Reverse procedure to install.

TRANSAXLE SELECTOR LEVER, REPLACE

1. Disconnect battery ground cable.
2. Remove selector lever knob, then the console assembly.
3. Remove selector indicator assembly, then disconnect cable from selector lever.
4. Disconnect interlock cable and the shift lock solenoid electrical connector.
5. Raise and support vehicle.
6. Remove housing attaching nuts, then the housing seat and housing with selector lever.
7. Reverse procedure to install.

TRANSAXLE SELECTOR CABLE, REPLACE

Removal

1. Remove console assembly, then the selector indicator assembly.
2. Disconnect selector cable from selector lever, floor and transaxle.
3. Raise and support vehicle.
4. Remove selector cable from front panel.

Installation

1. Raise and support vehicle.
2. Position selector cable in front panel, then lower vehicle.
3. Apply suitable grease to selector cable pin, then connect cable to lever.
4. Install selector indicator, then the console assembly.
5. Connect cable to bracket on transaxle, then slide cable into manual select joint hole and position manual shift lever in Neutral range.

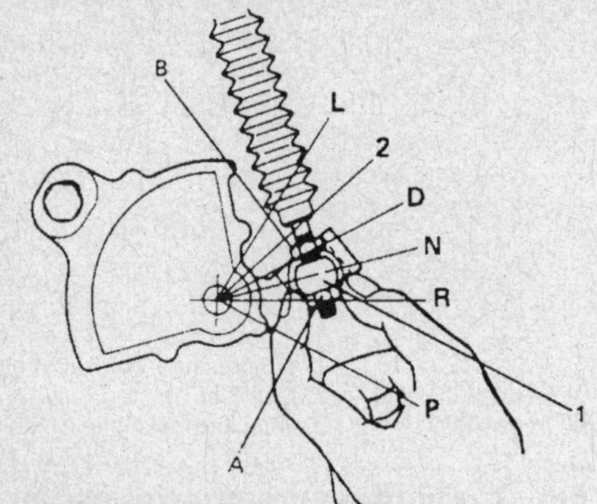
B
L
2
D
N
R
P
1
A

1. Manual select cable joint
A: Align with cable joint
B: Tighten with wrench

SK5029100018000X

Fig. 6 Transaxle selector cable installation

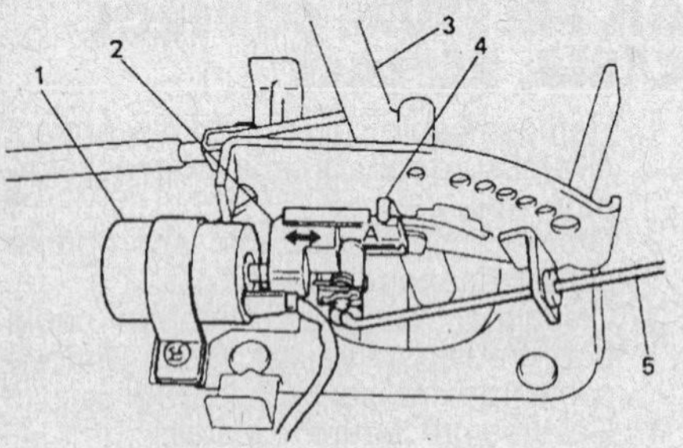
1
2
3
4
5

1. Back drive solenoid assembly
2. Lock plate
3. Selector lever (in P)
4. Detent pin
5. Manual release rod
A: Apply grease

SK5029100021000X

Fig. 9 Shift lock solenoid replacement

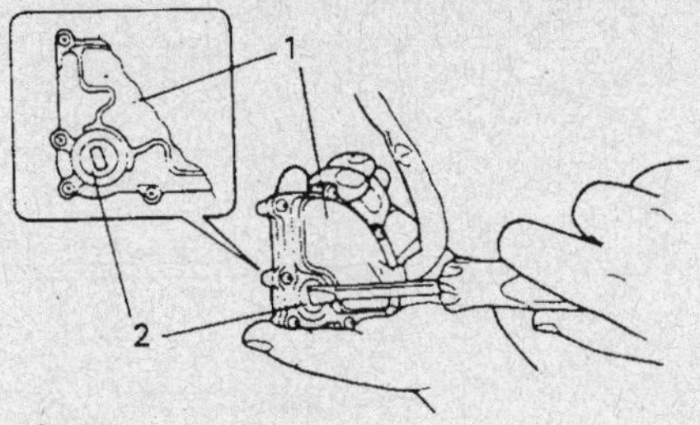
1
2

1. Shift lever switch
2. Shift lever switch joint

SK5029100019000X

Fig. 7 Shift lever switch installation

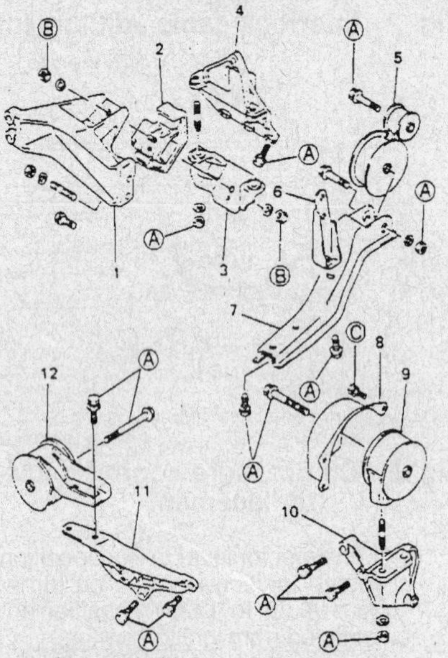
B
4
A
2
5
6
1
3
7
C
8
9
12
11
10

1. Rear mounting bracket
2. Rear mounting
3. Rear mounting body No. 1 bracket
4. Rear mounting body No. 2 bracket
5. Rear torque rod
6. Rear torque rod stiffener
7. Rear torque rod bracket
8. Left mounting body bracket
9. Left mounting
10. Left mounting bracket
11. Right mounting bracket
12. Right mounting

Tightening torque	
Ⓐ	50 – 60 N·m 5.0 – 6.0 kg-m 36.5 – 43.0 lb-ft
Ⓑ	40 – 50 N·m 4.0 – 5.0 kg-m 29.0 – 36.0 lb-ft
Ⓒ	18 – 28 N·m 1.8 – 2.8 kg-m 13.5 – 20.0 lb-ft

SK5029100022000X

Fig. 10 Engine mounting

1. Shift lever switch

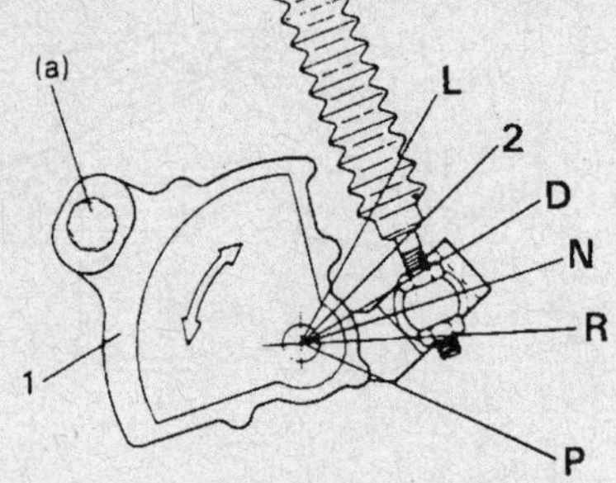
(a)
L
2
D
N
R
1
P

SK5029100020000X

Fig. 8 Shift lever switch adjustment

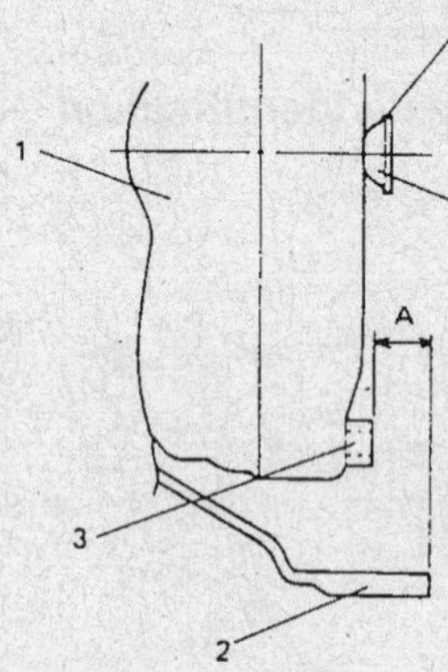
5
1
4
A
3
2

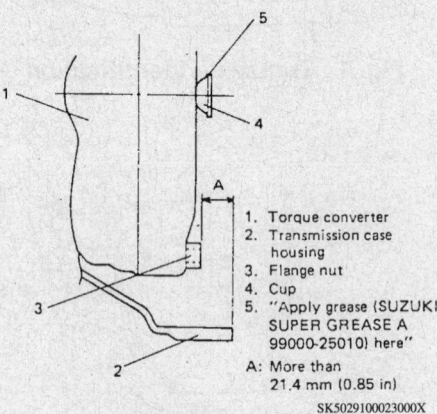

1. Torque converter
2. Transmission case housing
3. Flange nut
4. Cup
5. "Apply grease (SUZUKI SUPER GREASE A 99000-25010) here"

A: More than 21.4 mm (0.85 in)

SK5029100023000X

Fig. 11 Torque converter installation

6. Turn nut "A," **Fig. 6,** by hand until it contacts manual select cable joint, then tighten nut "B" with wrench.
7. After tightening cable nuts, check the following:
   a. With selector lever in Park position, vehicle cannot move when pushed.
   b. With selector lever in Neutral position, vehicle cannot be driven.
   c. With selector in Drive, Second or Low ranges, vehicle can be driven.
   d. With selector lever in Reverse range, vehicle can be backed up.

SHIFT LEVER SWITCH, REPLACE

Removal

1. Disconnect battery ground cable.
2. Disconnect electrical connectors from shift lever switch.
3. Remove shift lever switch from manual shift shaft.

Installation

1. Shift manual shift lever to Manual range.
2. Using a suitable screwdriver, turn shift lever switch to the position as shown, **Fig. 7,** and ensure a click is heard from joint at this position.
3. Install switch to manual shift shaft, then move the shaft in direction of arrow, **Fig. 8,** until a click is heard. Stop at this position and tighten to specification.
4. Connect electrical connectors to switch, then install clamp.
5. Apply parking brake and block wheels, then check the following:
   a. With selector lever in Park position and ignition switch On, ensure starter motor operates.
   b. With selector lever in Neutral position and ignition switch On, ensure starter motor operates.
   c. After moving selector lever from Neutral to Low position, then back to Neutral position, ensure starter motor operates with ignition switch On.
   d. With selector lever in Park position and ignition switch On, ensure starter motor operates.
   e. In any range other than Park or Neutral positions, ensure starter motor cannot be operated.
   f. With selector lever in Reverse position and ignition switch On, (engine not running), ensure back-up lamps light.

INTERLOCK CABLE, REPLACE

1. Remove steering column cover and column hole cover.
2. Remove interlock cable clamp screw, located at steering lock.
3. Push in release shaft "A" fully, then disconnect cable end. **Do not remove release shaft E-ring.**
4. Remove console box and parking brake lever cover.
5. Remove cable by loosening nut and removing clip in manual selector.
6. Reverse procedure to install.

SPEED SENSOR, REPLACE

1. Disconnect wiring harness clamp, then the speed sensor coupler.
2. Remove speed sensor bolt.
3. Remove sensor by gripping sensor body.
4. Reverse procedure to install.

SHIFT LOCK SOLENOID, REPLACE

1. Shift selector lever to Low position, then remove console box, parking brake lever cover, shift control lever cover and select indicator.

2. Remove shift lock solenoid attaching screw, then the solenoid, **Fig. 9.**
3. Reverse procedure to install, noting the following:
   a. Ensure detent pin is locked at Park position by lock plate.
   b. Ensure lock plate is pulled in when ignition key is turned On.

TRANSAXLE

REPLACE

The engine and transaxle must be removed as an assembly.

1. Relieve fuel system pressure as outlined under "Precautions."
2. Remove battery and tray, then the engine hood.
3. Drain coolant system into appropriate container.
4. Remove air cleaner assembly with Air Flow Meter (AFM) outlet hose.
5. Remove radiator cooling fan, then the battery ground cable from transmission.
6. Disconnect the following electrical wires:
   a. Disconnect direct clutch and second brake connectors.
   b. Disconnect shift switch and speed sensor connectors.
   c. Disconnect noise filter ground wire, then the Idle Speed Control (ISC) valve connector.
   d. Disconnect high tension cable from ignition coil, then the Distributor Crank Angle Sensor (CAS) connector.
   e. **On California models,** disconnect the Recirculated Exhaust Gas Temperature Sensor (REGTS) and the Exhaust Gas Recirculation Vacuum Switching Valve (EGR VSV) connectors.
   f. **On all models,** disconnect the Water Temperature Sensor (WTS) and oxygen sensor connectors.
   g. Disconnect canister purge VSV connector, then the ground wire from intake manifold.
   h. Disconnect Throttle Position Sensor (TPS) and fuel injector connectors.
   i. Disconnect all electrical wires from alternator and starter.
   j. Disconnect oil pressure gauge connector.
   k. Ensure all wires are free of clamps on engine.
7. Disconnect the following cables:
   a. Disconnect accelerator cable from throttle lever and bracket.
   b. Disconnect gear select and oil pressure control cables.
   c. Disconnect speedometer cable from transmission.
8. Disconnect brake booster and canister purge hoses.
9. **On California models,** disconnect A/C VSV hose.
10. **On all models,** disconnect fuel feed and return hoses.
11. Disconnect heater inlet and outlet hoses, then remove charcoal canister from body.
12. Raise and support vehicle, then remove exhaust pipe from manifold.
13. Drain engine and transmission oil into appropriate container.
14. Remove LH side driveshaft joint from differential gear of transmission. Remove RH side driveshaft joint from center bearing support.
15. Remove rear torque rod bracket from transmission case.
16. Lower vehicle, then install engine lifting device.
17. Remove rear mounting nut, **Fig. 10.**
18. Remove left side engine mounting bracket bolts and mounting bolt.
19. Remove right side engine mounting from bracket.
20. **Ensure all hoses, electric wires and cable are disconnected from engine and transmission.**
21. Remove engine and transmission from vehicle.
22. Remove torque convertor housing lower plate.
23. Remove driveplate bolts. Use flat head screwdriver to lock driveplate and driveplate gear.
24. Remove starter motor, then the transmission stiffener.
25. Remove engine to transmission attaching bolts, then separate engine from transmission.
26. Reverse procedure to install, noting the following:
   a. Apply grease around cup at center of torque converter, **Fig. 11.**
   b. Measure distance "A," **Fig. 11.** This distance should exceed 0.85 inch. If distance is less than specified, the torque converter is improperly installed.
   c. Tighten to specification.

TIGHTENING SPECIFICATIONS

Year	Component	Torque/ Ft. Lbs.
1993–96	Drain Plug	14-17
	Driveplate To Converter Bolt	13-14
	Engine Rear Mounting Bolt	36–43
	Oil Cooler Hose Clamp	12①
	Oil Pan Bolt	36-48①
	Oil Strainer Bolt	48①
	Selector Housing Nut	8-12
	Selector Lever Shaft Nut	13-16
	Shift Lever Switch Bolt	10-17
	Shift Solenoid Bolt	6-7
	Speed Sensor Bolt	6-7
	Transmission Case Plug	5-7
	Transmission To Engine Bolt/Nut	29-43

①— Inch lbs.

Esteem Automatic Transaxle

INDEX

	Page No.
Description	40-154
Identification	40-154
Maintenance	40-154
Fluid Change	40-154
Fluid Check	40-154
Precautions	40-154
Fuel System Pressure Release	40-154
Tightening Specifications	40-155
Transaxle, Replace	40-154

PRECAUTIONS

FUEL SYSTEM PRESSURE RELEASE

1. Remove fuel pump relay from relay box located in left rear of engine compartment.
2. Remove fuel filler cap to release vapor pressure in fuel tank, then replace cap.
3. Start engine and let idle until engine stops for lack of fuel.
4. Crank engine for 3 seconds and repeat 2–3 times to release fuel pressure in fuel lines.
5. Disconnect battery ground cable.
6. After repairs have been completed, connect negative terminal to the battery and replace fuel pump relay.

IDENTIFICATION

Refer to **Fig. 1** for proper transmission identification.

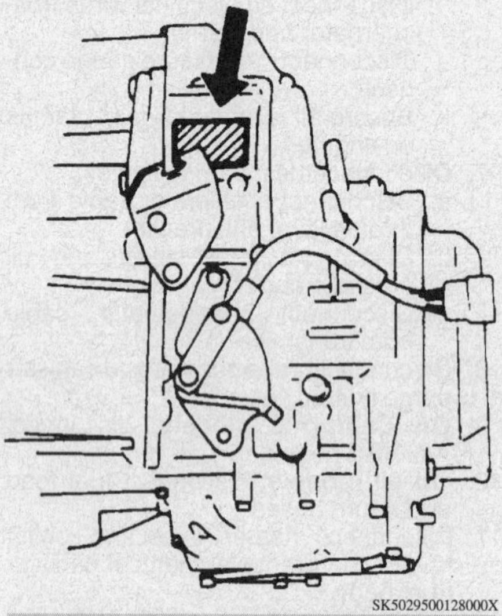
SK5029500128000X

Fig. 1 Transaxle identification

DESCRIPTION

This automatic transmission is an electronically controlled 3–speed automatic transmission with overdrive (OD). The torque converter is a 3–element, 1–step and 2–phase type and is equipped with an electronically controlled lock-up mechanism.

The gear shift device consists of 2 sets of planetary gear units, 4 disc clutches, a disc brake, a band brake, and 2 one-way clutches.

MAINTENANCE

FLUID CHECK

1. Drive vehicle to bring fluid up to normal operating temperature.
2. With vehicle on level surface, apply parking brake and block drive wheels.
3. With selector lever in Park position, start engine.
4. While idling, shift selector slowly to L (Low) and back to P (Park)
5. Remove dipstick and check fluid level.
6. Fluid level should be between FULL HOT and LOW HOT marks on dipstick.
7. Add fluid as required to bring fluid to specified level. When adding fluid use only Dexron III type transaxle fluid or equivalent.

FLUID CHANGE

Under normal driving conditions, fluid level should be changed and oil strainer cleaned every 100,000 miles. To service, proceed as follows:

1. Raise and support front of vehicle.
2. Remove drain plug and drain fluid from oil pan into appropriate container.
3. Lower vehicle and refill oil pan with approximately 2.6 quarts of Dexron II type transaxle fluid or equivalent.
4. Check fluid level as previously described and adjust as necessary.

TRANSAXLE

REPLACE

1. Relieve fuel system pressure as outlined under "Precautions."
2. Disconnect battery ground cable and transmission ground cable.
3. Disconnect electrical connectors from transmission.
4. Remove gear select cable from transmission.
5. Drain cooling system and remove water intake pipe.
6. Remove upper transmission to engine bolts.
7. Remove starter motor and plate.
8. Remove exhaust manifold cover, then manifold to pipe No. 1 nuts.
9. Properly support engine and remove or disconnect any components necessary to remove transmission.
10. Raise and support vehicle while still supporting engine.
11. Drain transmission fluid.
12. Remove engine under covers.
13. Disconnect oil cooler hoses.
14. Remove mounting member, exhaust pipe and stiffener.
15. Remove transmission housing lower plate.
16. While holding drive plate with suitable large screwdriver, remove drive plate bolts, **Fig. 2.**
17. Using two suitable large screwdrivers, pry against drive shaft joints at differential side to release snap ring fitting, **Fig. 3.**
18. Disconnect stabilizer joints from suspension arms on both sides
19. Remove ball stud bolts and nuts from knuckles and detach suspension arms, then pull out both drive shaft joints from differential.

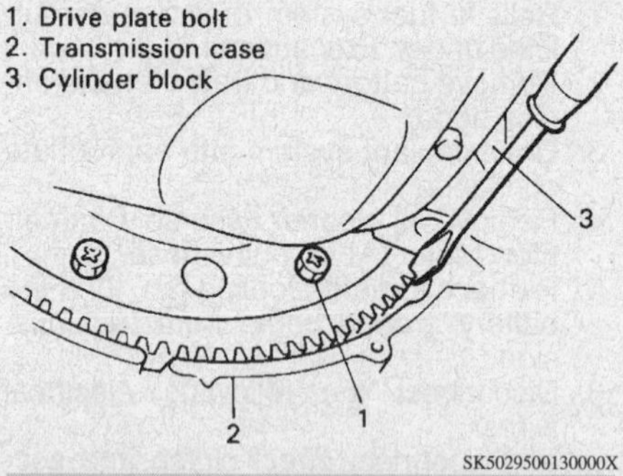
1. Drive plate bolt
2. Transmission case
3. Cylinder block
1
2
3
SK5029500130000X

Fig. 2 Drive plate bolt removal

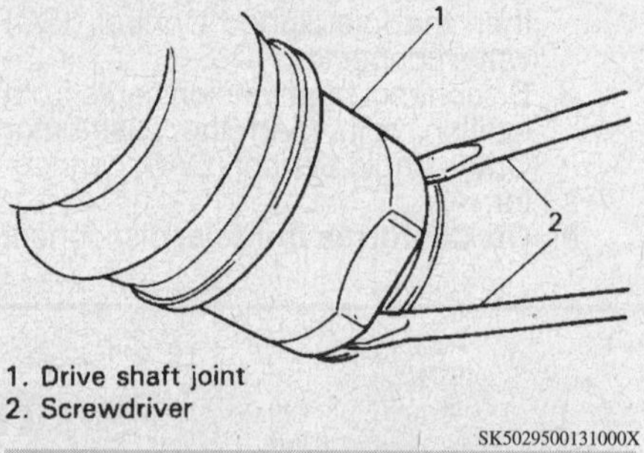
1
2
1. Drive shaft joint
2. Screwdriver
SK5029500131000X

Fig. 3 Snap ring fitting removal

20. Remove engine rear mounting and bracket.
21. Remove lower engine to transmission bolt and nut. Ensure transmission is still suitably supported.
22. Remove bolts from lefthand engine mounting.
23. Remove transmission and torque converter from engine compartment.
24. Reverse procedure to install, noting the following:
    a. Ensure each drive shaft joint is fully seated and snap ring is in place.
    b. Adjust select cable.
    c. Tighten to specification.

TIGHTENING SPECIFICATIONS

Year	Component	Torque/ Ft. Lbs.
1995–96	Drain Plug	29
	Driveplate Bolts	14
	Engine Mounting Nuts	33
	Engine Mounting Member Bolts & Nuts	40
	Exhaust Manifold To Pipes	36
	Oil Cooler Hose Clamp	12①
	Oil Pump Bolts	9
	Shift Lever Switch Bolt	5
	Stabilizer Link Nuts	20
	Steering Knuckle Ball Stud	43
	Transmission Case Bolt	22
	Transmission Rear Cover Bolts	18
	Transmission To Engine Bolt/Nut	65

① — Inch lbs.

Front Wheel Drive Axles

INDEX

Page No.

Driveshaft, Replace 40-155
Esteem & Swift 40-155
Double Offset Joint (DOJ) Type 40-155
Tripod Joint Type 40-156
Samurai 40-155
Installation 40-155
Removal 40-155
Sidekick & X-90 40-155
Installation 40-155
Removal 40-155
Driveshaft Service 40-156
Esteem & Swift 40-157
Double Offset Joint (DOJ) Type 40-157
Tripod Joint Type 40-158
Samurai 40-156
Sidekick & X-90 40-156
Assemble 40-157
Disassemble 40-156

DRIVESHAFT

REPLACE

Samurai

REMOVAL

1. Remove front hub and bearing, as outlined in "Front Suspension & Steering" section.
2. Remove steering knuckle as outlined in the "Steering" section.
3. Drain oil from differential housing.
4. Pull axle shaft from front axle housing.

INSTALLATION

1. Reverse removal procedure to install, noting the following:
    a. Tighten all bolts to specification.
    b. Refill differential housing with Hypoid gear oil SAE 80W-90.

Sidekick & X-90

REMOVAL

1. Raise and support vehicle, then drain transaxle oil into appropriate container.
2. Remove locking hub, then the driveshaft circlip.
3. Remove stabilizer ball joint nut, then the tie rod castle nut.
4. Remove caliper bolt, then the caliper from disc.
5. Remove knuckle ball joint stud nut, then support lower arm with suitable jack.
6. Remove strut bracket bolts.
7. Remove knuckle and wheel hub assembly, by lowering jack.
8. **On RH side,** to detach snap ring fitted on spline of differential side joint from differential side gear, pull inboard joint using a tire lever, **Fig. 1.** Remove driveshaft from differential assembly.
9. **On LH side,** disconnect driveshaft bolts, then remove driveshaft from differential assembly.

INSTALLATION

Reverse removal procedure to install.

Esteem & Swift

DOUBLE OFFSET JOINT (DOJ) TYPE

This type of front driveshaft is used for manual transmission models.

REMOVAL

LH Side Shaft

1. Remove caulking and driveshaft nut and washer.
2. Drain transmission oil into appropriate container.
3. Using large size screwdrivers, pull out driveshaft joint. This will release snap

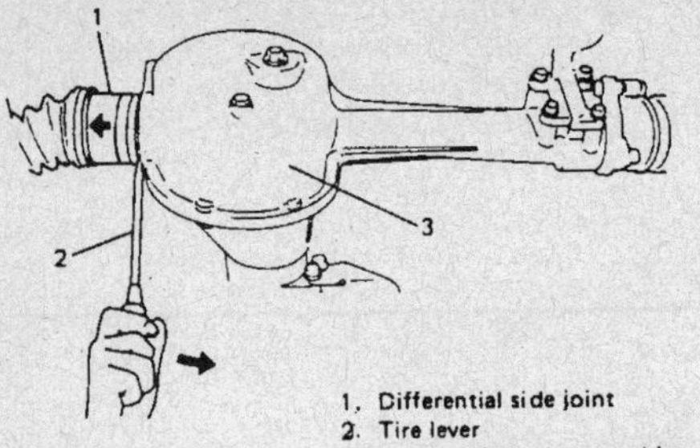
1. Differential side joint
2. Tire lever
3. Front differential assembly
SK3039100003000X

Fig. 1 Snap ring from differential side gear removal. Sidekick & X-90

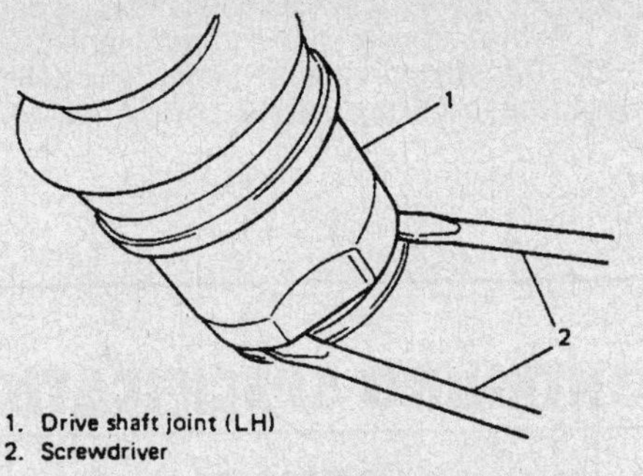
1. Drive shaft joint (LH)
2. Screwdriver
SK3039100008000X

Fig. 2 Snap ring from differential removal. Esteem & Swift

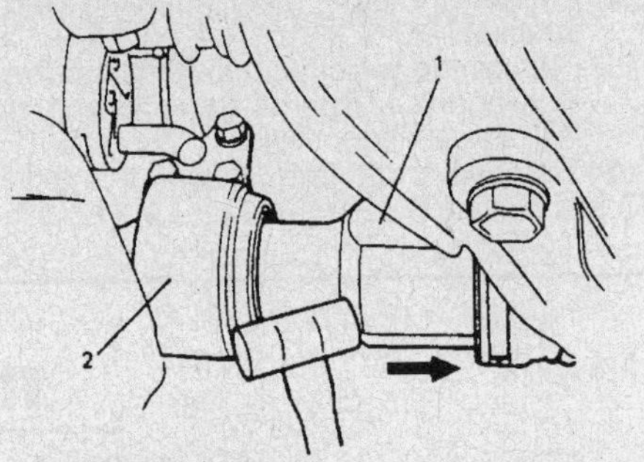
1. Drive shaft joint
2. Center bearing support
SK3039100009000X

Fig. 3 Driveshaft from center bearing support removal. Esteem & Swift

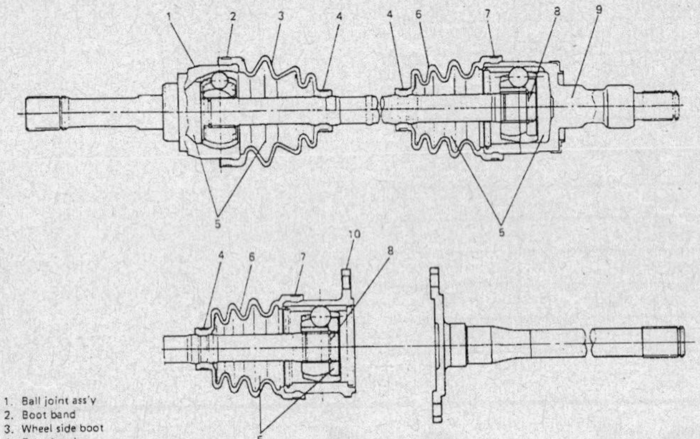
1. Ball joint ass'y
2. Boot band
3. Wheel side boot
4. Boot band
5. Grease (about 90 gram)
6. Diff. side boot
7. Boot band
8. Circlip
9. Double off-set joint ass'y (RH side)
10. Double off-set joint ass'y (LH side)
SK3039100004000X

Fig. 4 Cross-sectional view of driveshaft assembly. Sidekick & X-90

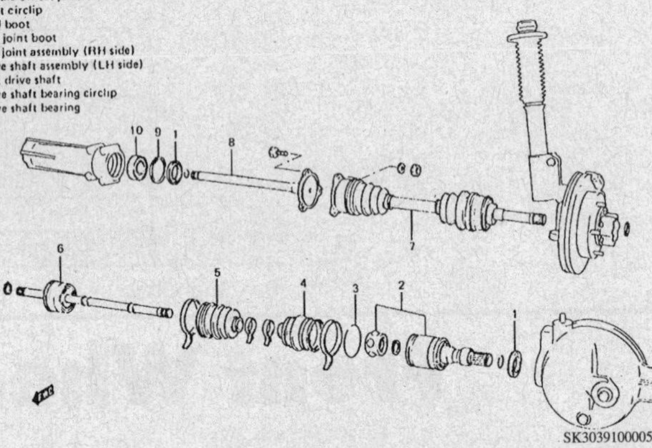
1. Drive shaft oil seal
2. Double off-set joint (DOJ)
3. Joint circlip
4. DOJ boot
5. Ball joint boot
6. Ball joint assembly (RH side)
7. Drive shaft assembly (LH side)
8. Left drive shaft
9. Drive shaft bearing circlip
10. Drive shaft bearing
SK3039100005000X

Fig. 5 Exploded view of front axle assembly. Sidekick & X-90

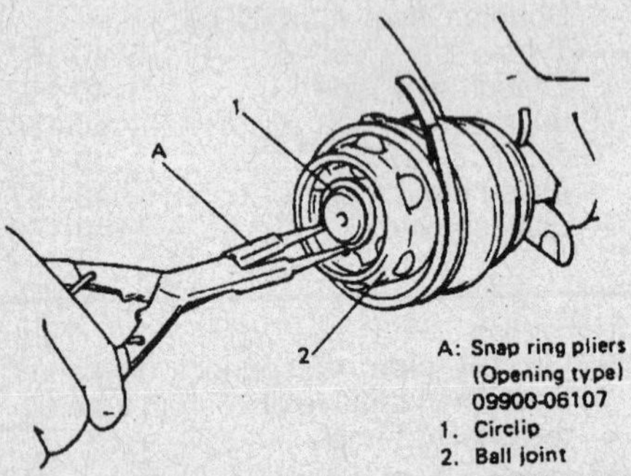
A: Snap ring pliers
(Opening type)
09900-06107
1. Circlip
2. Ball joint
SK3039100006000X

Fig. 6 Circlip from ball joint removal. Sidekick & X-90

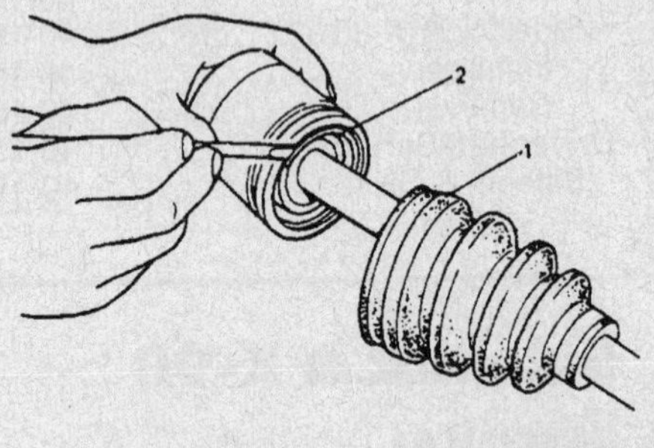
1. Boot
2. Snap ring
SK3039100010000X

Fig. 7 Snap ring from outer race removal. Esteem & Swift

ring fitting of joint spline at differential side, **Fig. 2.**

4. Disconnect stabilizer joint from suspension arm.
5. Remove ball stud bolt and nut, then separate suspension arm from knuckle.
6. Remove driveshaft assembly.

RH Side Shaft

1. Remove caulking and driveshaft nut and washer.
2. Using plastic hammer, drive out driveshaft joint. This will release snap ring fitting of joint spline at center shaft, **Fig. 3.**
3. Disconnect stabilizer joint from suspension arm.
4. Remove ball stud bolt and nut, then separate suspension arm from knuckle.
5. Remove driveshaft assembly.
6. Drain transmission oil into appropriate container.
7. Loosen center bearing support bolts, then remove center shaft from differential side gear.

INSTALLATION

Reverse removal procedure to install LH and RH driveshafts, noting the following:

1. Install wheel side joint to steering knuckle first and DOJ to differential side.

TRIPOD JOINT TYPE

This type of front driveshaft is used for automatic transmission models.

Refer to "Double Offset Joint (DOJ) Type" for service procedures.

DRIVESHAFT SERVICE

Samurai

This front axle is equipped with a Barfield Joint type axle. Check driveshaft for axial play by using a push-pull motion while holding axle in both hands. If play exceeds service limit, .06 of an inch, then the axle must be replaced.

Sidekick & X-90

DISASSEMBLE

Only the double off-set joints are serviceable, **Fig. 4. Do not disassemble wheel**

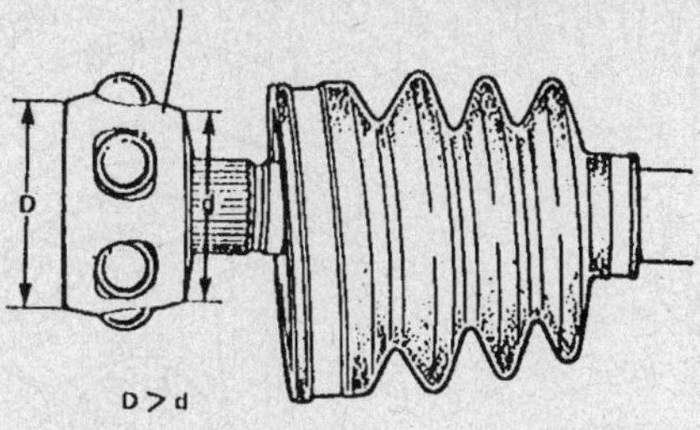
D
d
D > d
1. Cage
SK3039100011000X

Fig. 8 Bearing cage installation. Esteem & Swift w/double offset joint type driveshaft.

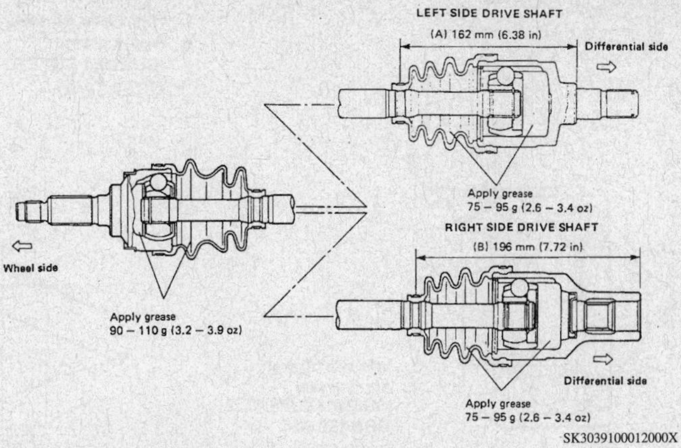
LEFT SIDE DRIVE SHAFT
(A) 162 mm (6.38 in)
Differential side
Apply grease
75 – 95 g (2.6 – 3.4 oz)
RIGHT SIDE DRIVE SHAFT
(B) 196 mm (7.72 in)
Wheel side
Apply grease
90 – 110 g (3.2 – 3.9 oz)
Differential side
Apply grease
75 – 95 g (2.6 – 3.4 oz)
SK3039100012000X

Fig. 9 Boot length measurement. Swift GT

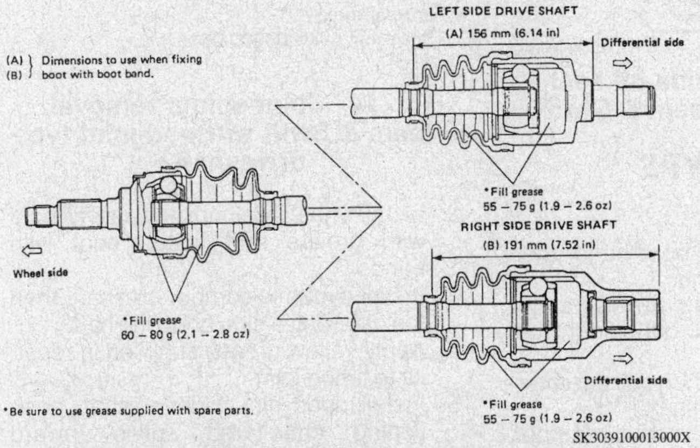
(A) } Dimensions to use when fixing
(B) } boot with boot band.
LEFT SIDE DRIVE SHAFT
(A) 156 mm (6.14 in)
Differential side
*Fill grease
55 – 75 g (1.9 – 2.6 oz)
RIGHT SIDE DRIVE SHAFT
(B) 191 mm (7.52 in)
Wheel side
*Fill grease
60 – 80 g (2.1 – 2.8 oz)
Differential side
*Be sure to use grease supplied with spare parts.
*Fill grease
55 – 75 g (1.9 – 2.6 oz)
SK3039100013000X

Fig. 10 Boot length measurement. Swift.

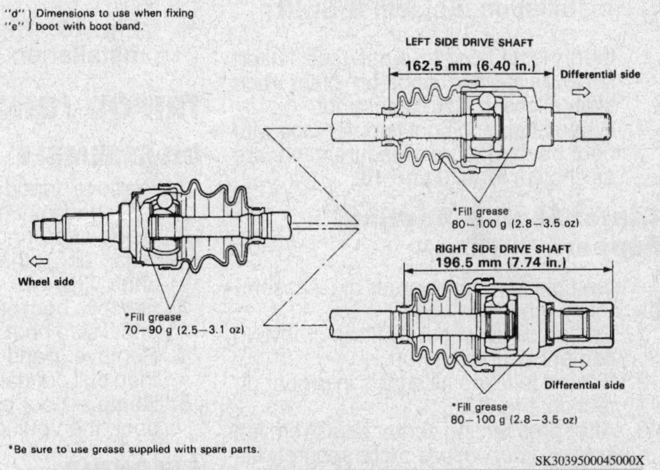
"d" } Dimensions to use when fixing
"e" } boot with boot band.
LEFT SIDE DRIVE SHAFT
162.5 mm (6.40 in.)
Differential side
*Fill grease
80–100 g (2.8–3.5 oz)
RIGHT SIDE DRIVE SHAFT
196.5 mm (7.74 in.)
Wheel side
*Fill grease
70–90 g (2.5–3.1 oz)
Differential side
*Fill grease
80–100 g (2.8–3.5 oz)
*Be sure to use grease supplied with spare parts.
SK3039500045000X

Fig. 11 Boot length measurement. Esteem

side joint or ball joint of differential side joint, Fig. 5. If any problem exists, replace these joints as an assembly.

1. Remove boot band from differential side joint.
2. Remove circlip, then the housing of differential side joint.
3. Remove circlip (snap ring), then the ball joint, **Fig. 6.**
4. Remove inside and outside boots from shaft.

ASSEMBLE

1. Apply joint grease, supplied in repair kit, to wheel side joint.
2. Fit wheel side boot on shaft. Fill inside of boot with joint grease, then install boot bands.
3. Fit differential side boot on shaft. Apply joint grease, supplied in repair kit, to differential side joint.
4. Install differential side ball joint on shaft. Position flush side of joint to wheel side joint. Fit snap ring in groove of shaft.
5. Fill inside of differential side boot with joint grease, then install housing.
6. Attach boot to housing using boot band. When clamping boot band, bend its end in reverse direction against driveshaft rotating direction.

Esteem & Swift

DOUBLE OFFSET JOINT (DOJ) TYPE

DISASSEMBLE

Driveshaft

Do not disassemble wheel side joint. If any problem is found, replace as an assembly.

1. Remove boot band of differential side joint.
2. Slide boot toward center of shaft. Remove snap ring from outer race, then take shaft out of outer race, **Fig. 7.**
3. Using snap ring pliers, remove circlip (snap ring) used to attach bearing cage.
4. Remove bearing cage and boot from shaft.

Center Shaft & Bearing Support

1. Remove right side oil seal from center bearing support, then circlip.
2. Using press, draw out center shaft from center bearing.
3. Remove left side oil seal from center bearing support.
4. Remove bearing support circlip.
5. Remove center bearing from center bearing support.

ASSEMBLE

Driveshaft

1. Install boot onto driveshaft until small diameter side fits into shaft groove. Attach boot band.
2. Install bearing cage. Smaller outside diameter should be installed to shaft end, **Fig. 8.**
3. Using snap ring pliers, install circlip (snap ring).
4. Apply grease, supplied in repair kit, to entire surface of bearing cage.
5. Insert bearing cage into outer race, then attach snap ring into groove of outer race. Ensure opening of snap ring is not in alignment with a ball (bearing).
6. Apply grease to inside of outer race,

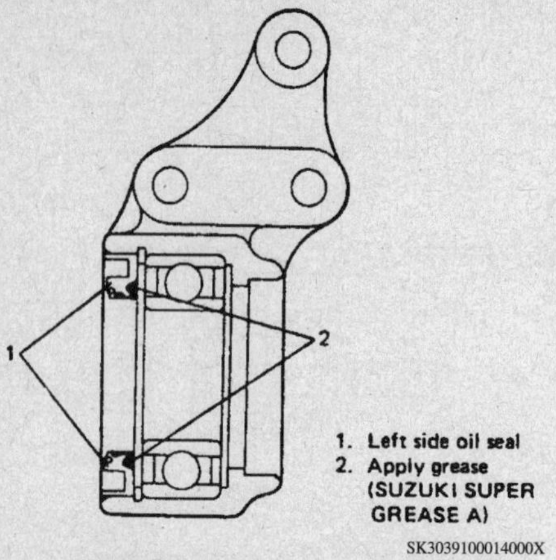
1
2
1. Left side oil seal
2. Apply grease
(SUZUKI SUPER
GREASE A)
SK3039100014000X

Fig. 12 Left side oil seal installation. Esteem & Swift

then install boot to outer race. Insert screwdriver into boot on outer race side, allowing air to enter boot.

7. When attaching boot to outer race with boot band, ensure measurements are as shown, **Figs. 9 and 10.**

Center Shaft & Bearing Support

Assemble in reverse order of disassembly, noting the following:

1. Ensure circlip securely fits in groove in center bearing support.
2. Ensure left side oil seal is in proper direction, **Fig. 12.**
3. After press-fitting center shaft from left side oil side, ensure circlip securely fits in groove in shaft.
4. Ensure right side oil seal is in proper direction, **Fig. 13.**

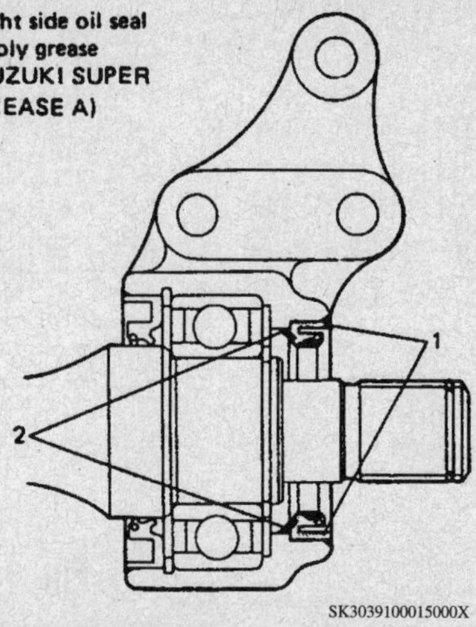
1. Right side oil seal
2. Apply grease
(SUZUKI SUPER
GREASE A)
1
2
SK3039100015000X

Fig. 13 Right side oil seal installation. Esteem & Swift

TRIPOD JOINT TYPE

DISASSEMBLE

1. Remove tripod joint boot band, then the tripod joint housing.
2. Using snap ring pliers, remove circlip (snap ring), then pull out spider from shaft, **Fig. 14.**
3. Remove boot band, then pull out differential side boot from shaft.
4. Remove band of dynamic damper, then pull out damper through shaft.
5. Remove boot band of wheel side joint boot, then pull out boot through shaft.

ASSEMBLE

1. Apply black grease supplied in repair kit to wheel side joint.

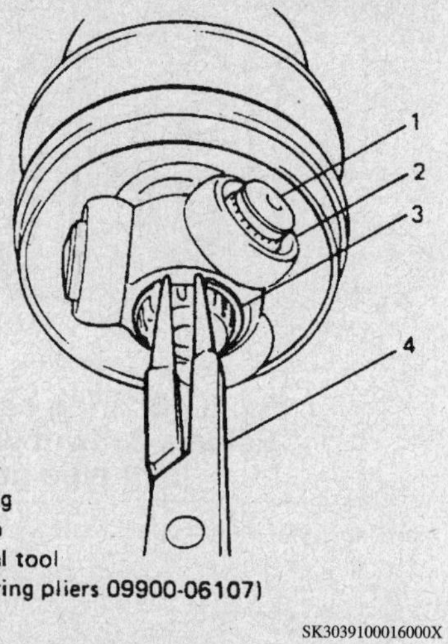
1
2
3
4
1. Spider
2. Bearing
3. Circlip
4. Special tool
Snap ring pliers 09900-06107)
SK3039100016000X

Fig. 14 Joint spider removal. Esteem & Swift w/tripod joint type driveshaft

2. Install wheel side boot on shaft, fill boot with grease and fasten boot with bands.
3. Install dynamic damper on shaft, then the differential side boot on shaft.
4. Apply yellow grease supplied in repair kit to tripod joint.
5. Install tripod joint spider on shaft, positioning chamfered spline inward (wheel side), then fasten with circlip (snap ring).
6. Fill differential side boot with grease, then install housing.
7. Attach boot band. Bend each boot band against forward rotation of driveshaft.

Drive Axles

INDEX

	Page No.		Page No.		Page No.
Description	40-159	Sidekick & X-90	40-159	Samurai	40-160
Differential, Replace	40-159	**Differential Service**	40-160	Sidekick & X-90	40-164
Samurai	40-159				

DESCRIPTION

On Samurai models, the front and rear axles are identical as far as the designs of pinion and gear and differential gearing are concerned. The major difference is the shape of the housing. The bevel gear drive is of hypoid design, pinion and gear have hypoid gear teeth. It is the meshing of these teeth that causes the hypoid gear oil to be used for the differential. A total of 8 gears are mounted on the differential carrier case bolted to the housing, **Fig. 1.**

On Sidekick and X-90 models, the differential assemblies installed to the front and rear axles use a hypoid bevel pinion and gear. The rear differential is set in an axle housing while the front differential is set in an aluminum housing mounted under the chassis frame. The reduction ratio for manual transmission equipped vehicles is different from automatic transmission equipped vehicles, **Figs. 2 and 3.**

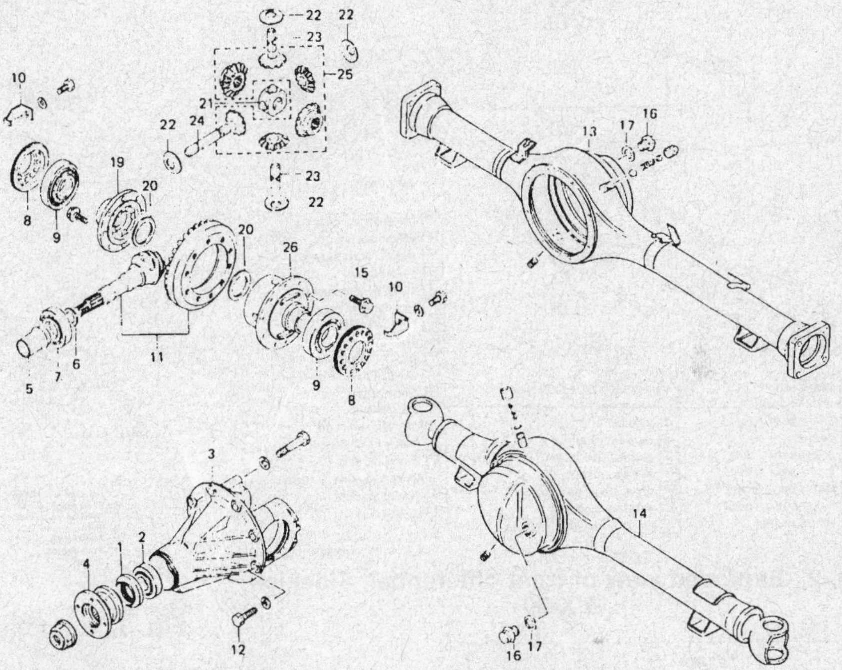

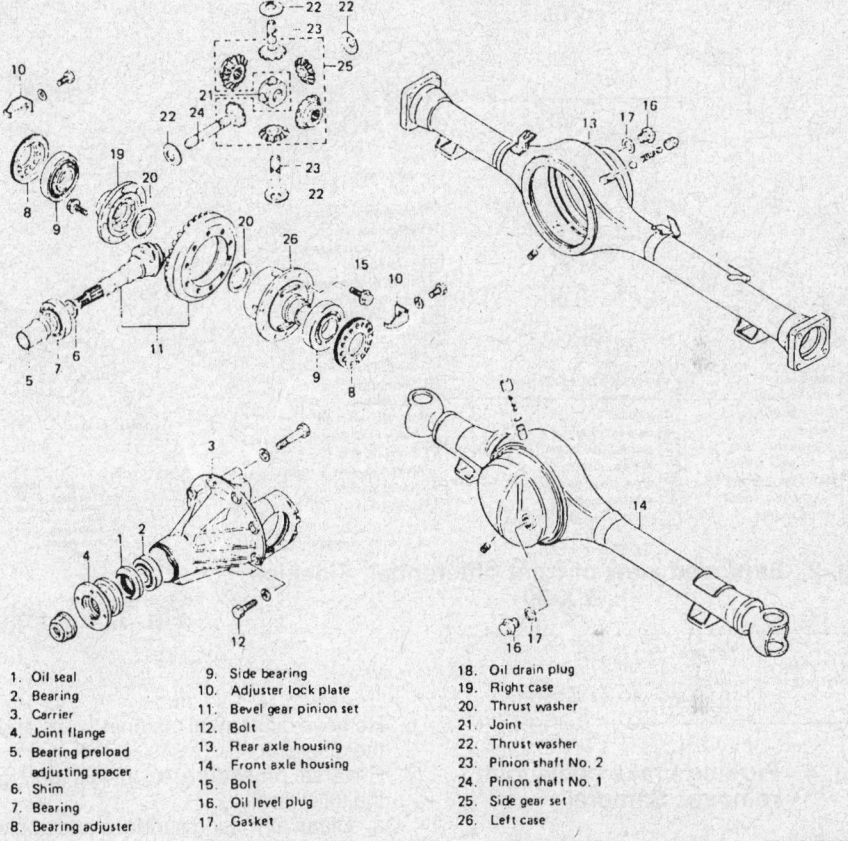

1. Oil seal
2. Bearing
3. Carrier
4. Joint flange
5. Bearing preload adjusting spacer
6. Shim
7. Bearing
8. Bearing adjuster
9. Side bearing
10. Adjuster lock plate
11. Bevel gear pinion set
12. Bolt
13. Rear axle housing
14. Front axle housing
15. Bolt
16. Oil level plug
17. Gasket
18. Oil drain plug
19. Right case
20. Thrust washer
21. Joint
22. Thrust washer
23. Pinion shaft No. 2
24. Pinion shaft No. 1
25. Side gear set
26. Left case

SK3039100017000X

Fig. 1 Exploded view of differential. Samurai

DIFFERENTIAL

REPLACE

SAMURAI

REMOVAL

Rear

1. Remove rear wheels.
2. Using slide hammer tool No. 09942-15510 and brake drum remover tool No. 09943-35511, or equivalents, remove drum. **Before removing drum, increase the clearance between brake shoe and brake drum by removing parking brake shoe lever return spring, disconnecting parking brake cable joint from parking brake shoe lever, Fig. 4, then remove parking brake shoe lever stopper plate.**
3. Disconnect brake pipe from wheel cylinder, then plug all openings.
4. Remove brake backing plate attaching bolts, then slide hammer tool and rear axle remover tool No. 09922-66010, or equivalent, remove axle shaft with brake backing plate.
5. Disconnect propeller shaft, then remove differential case attaching bolts, then the differential.

Front

1. Raise and support vehicle, then remove front wheels.
2. Remove disc brake caliper and carrier. Hang caliper with wire hook.
3. Remove tie rods from steering knuckles.
4. Remove oil seal cover attaching bolts, then the cover, felt pad, oil seal and seal retainer from steering knuckle.
5. Remove top and bottom kingpins from steering knuckle. Mark kingpins for proper assembly.
6. Draw out axle shaft from axle housing. Remove lower kingpin bearing while pulling off knuckle.
7. Disconnect propeller shaft, then remove differential carrier to housing attaching bolts.
8. Remove differential carrier from housing.

INSTALLATION

1. Reverse removal procedure to install, noting the following:
   a. Clean surfaces of differential carrier and housing, then apply suitable sealant.
   b. **On rear differential,** if brake line was disconnected from wheel cylinder, ensure to bleed brake system. Check that joint seam of brake line is not leaking.
   c. **On all models,** tighten all bolts to specification, **Fig. 5.**

SIDEKICK & X-90

FRONT

1. Raise and support vehicle, then drain oil.
2. Disconnect breather hose.
3. Disconnect and support propeller shaft.
4. Remove left mounting bracket bolts and driveshaft flange bolts, **Fig. 6.**
5. Support differential and remove bolts from crossmember and right end of housing.
6. Disconnect RH side driveshaft joint and remove housing assembly using

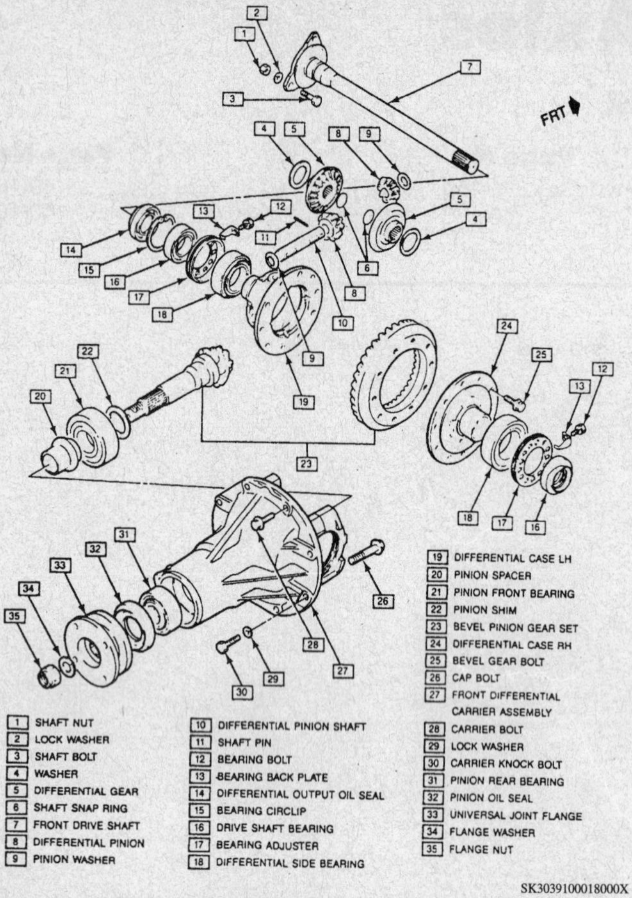
FRT
1 SHAFT NUT
2 LOCK WASHER
3 SHAFT BOLT
4 WASHER
5 DIFFERENTIAL GEAR
6 SHAFT SNAP RING
7 FRONT DRIVE SHAFT
8 DIFFERENTIAL PINION
9 PINION WASHER
10 DIFFERENTIAL PINION SHAFT
11 SHAFT PIN
12 BEARING BOLT
13 BEARING BACK PLATE
14 DIFFERENTIAL OUTPUT OIL SEAL
15 BEARING CIRCLIP
16 DRIVE SHAFT BEARING
17 BEARING ADJUSTER
18 DIFFERENTIAL SIDE BEARING
19 DIFFERENTIAL CASE LH
20 PINION SPACER
21 PINION FRONT BEARING
22 PINION SHIM
23 BEVEL PINION GEAR SET
24 DIFFERENTIAL CASE RH
25 BEVEL GEAR BOLT
26 CAP BOLT
27 FRONT DIFFERENTIAL CARRIER ASSEMBLY
28 CARRIER BOLT
29 LOCK WASHER
30 CARRIER KNOCK BOLT
31 PINION REAR BEARING
32 PINION OIL SEAL
33 UNIVERSAL JOINT FLANGE
34 FLANGE WASHER
35 FLANGE NUT
SK3039100018000X

Fig. 2 Exploded view of front differential. Sidekick & X-90

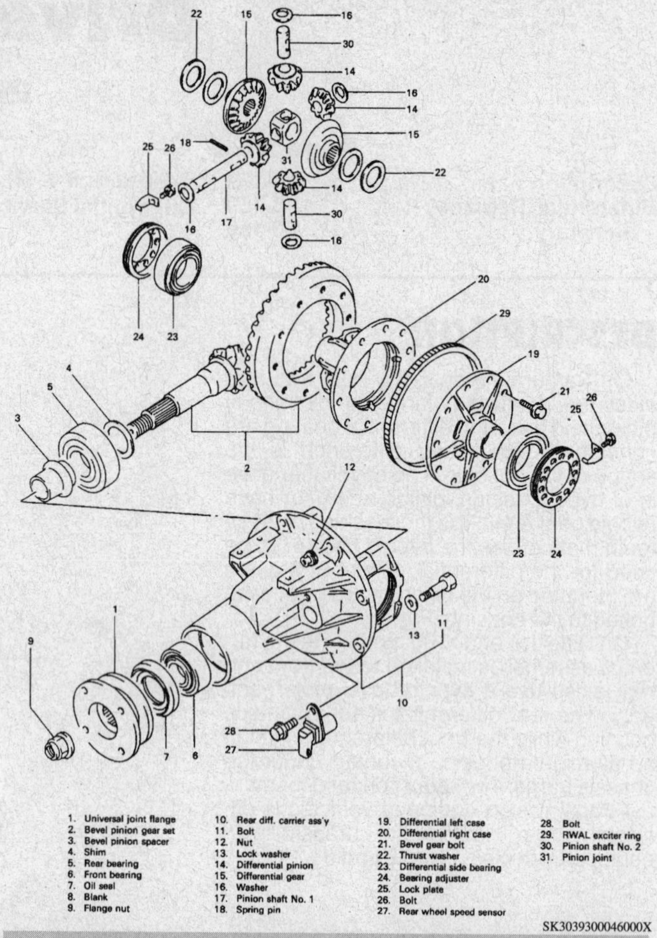
1. Universal joint flange
2. Bevel pinion gear set
3. Bevel pinion spacer
4. Shim
5. Rear bearing
6. Front bearing
7. Oil seal
8. Blank
9. Flange nut
10. Rear diff. carrier ass'y
11. Bolt
12. Nut
13. Lock washer
14. Differential pinion
15. Differential gear
16. Washer
17. Pinion shaft No. 1
18. Spring pin
19. Differential left case
20. Differential right case
21. Bevel gear bolt
22. Thrust washer
23. Differential side bearing
24. Bearing adjuster
25. Lock plate
26. Bolt
27. Rear wheel speed sensor
28. Bolt
29. RWAL exciter ring
30. Pinion shaft No. 2
31. Pinion joint
SK3039300046000X

Fig. 3 Exploded view of rear differential. Sidekick & X-90

Sizes of shims for bevel pinion	1.00, 1.03, 1.06, 1.09, 1.12, 1.15, 1.18, 1.21, 1.24, 1.27, 1.30 & 0.3 mm (0.039, 0.041, 0.042, 0.043, 0.044, 0.045, 0.046, 0.047, 0.048, 0.049, 0.050 & 0.012 in.

SK3039100019000X

Fig. 4 Parking brake cable joint removal. Samurai

suitable pry bars.

7. Reverse procedure to install, noting the following:
   a. **Torque** mounting bracket bolts to 37 ft. lbs.
   b. **Torque** front driveshaft flange bolts to 36.5–43 ft. lbs.
   c. **Torque** propeller shaft flange bolts to 36.5–43 ft. lbs.

REAR

1. Raise and support vehicle.
2. Remove right and left axle shafts.
3. Remove propeller shaft bolts and shaft.
4. **On models with rear anti-lock brakes,** remove rear wheel speed sensor cover, then disconnect sensor electrical connector.
5. **On all models,** support axle assembly and remove upper arm mounting bolts and lower axle. **Rear shock absorbers must remain installed during this process. Without them, axle may fall and cause personal injury.**
6. Remove differential fastening nuts and the differential.
7. Reverse procedure to install, noting the following:
   a. Clean all mating surfaces and apply Suzuki bond sealant, No. 1215.
   b. **Torque** rear differential carrier nuts to 36.5–43 ft. lbs.
   c. **Torque** upper arm bolts to 29–43 ft. lbs.
   d. **Torque** propeller shaft flange bolts to 36.5–43 ft. lbs.
   e. Fill axle with SAE 75W-90 hypoid gear oil and **torque** fill plug to 32 ft. lbs.

DIFFERENTIAL SERVICE

SAMURAI

DISASSEMBLY

1. Using holder tool No. 09930-40113, or equivalent, **Fig. 7**, remove nut from end of bevel pinion shank.
2. Scribe identification marks on each cap bolted to the saddle portion of carrier case and the caps holding down the side bearings.
3. On each side, loosen bolts on bearing adjuster stopper and remove bearing cap attaching bolts, then bearing cap.
4. Remove differential case assembly from carrier.
5. Remove ten bolts attaching bevel gear to differential case, then separate gear from case.
6. Using holder tool, **Fig. 8,** remove bolts securing the two differential case halves, then separate case halves.
7. Remove side gears, differential pinions and thrust washers.
8. Using puller tool No. 09913-60910 and adapter tool No. 09913-85230, or equivalents, **Fig. 9,** remove side bearing from each differential case half.
9. Using a suitable puller and an arbor press, remove inner race of bevel pinion bearing.

ADJUSTMENT & INSPECTION

Side Gear Backlash

1. Assemble differential gearing and

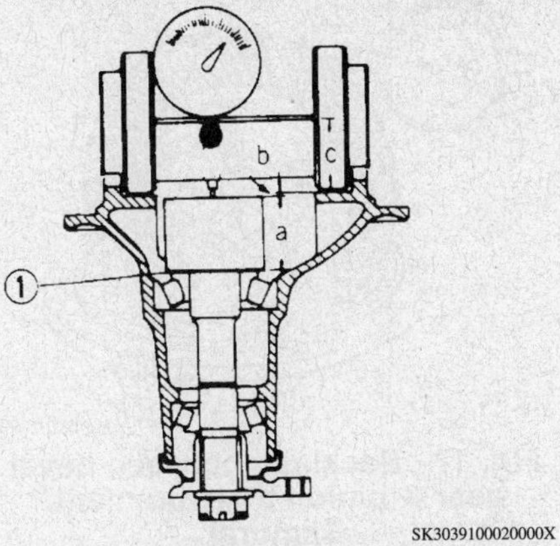
b
c
a
1
SK3039100020000X

Fig. 5 Tightening specification chart. Samurai

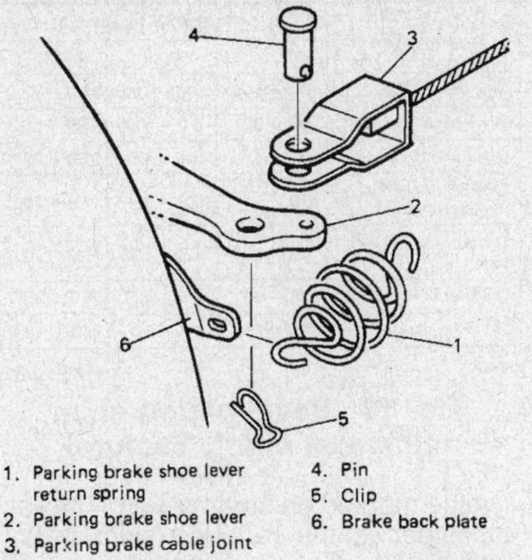
1. Parking brake shoe lever return spring
2. Parking brake shoe lever
3. Parking brake cable joint
4. Pin
5. Clip
6. Brake back plate
SK3039100021000X

Fig. 6 Mounting bracket removal. Sidekick & X-90

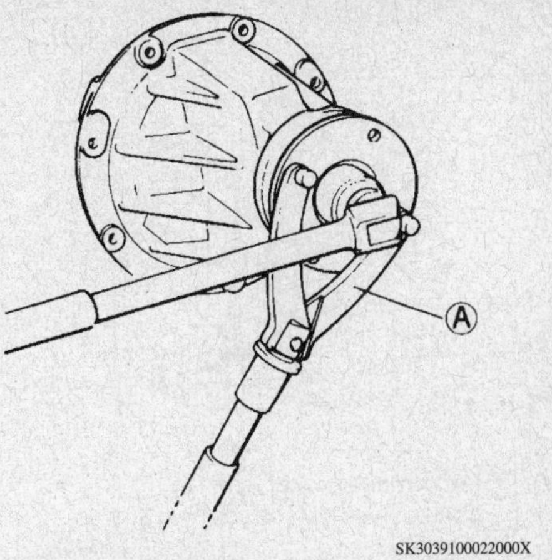
A
SK3039100022000X

Fig. 7 Nut from bevel pinion shank removal. Samurai

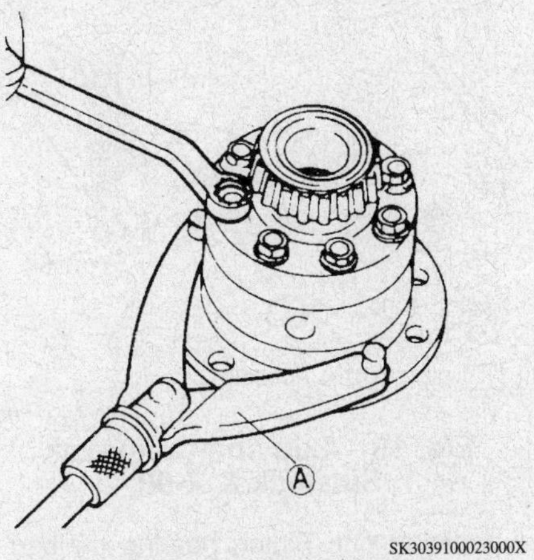
A
SK3039100023000X

Fig. 8 Differential case halves separation. Samurai

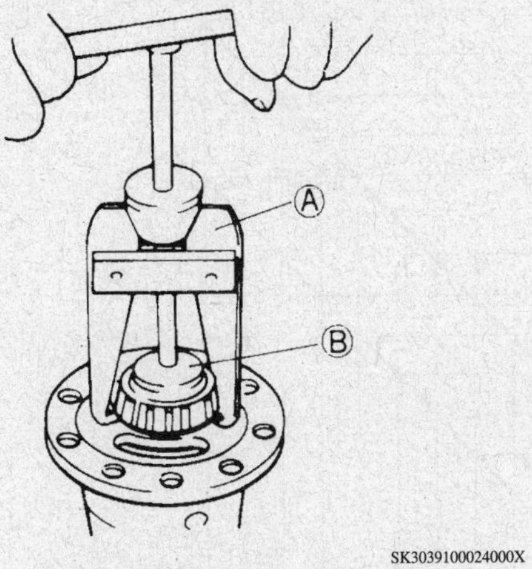
A
B
SK3039100024000X

Fig. 9 Side bearing from differential case half removal. Samurai

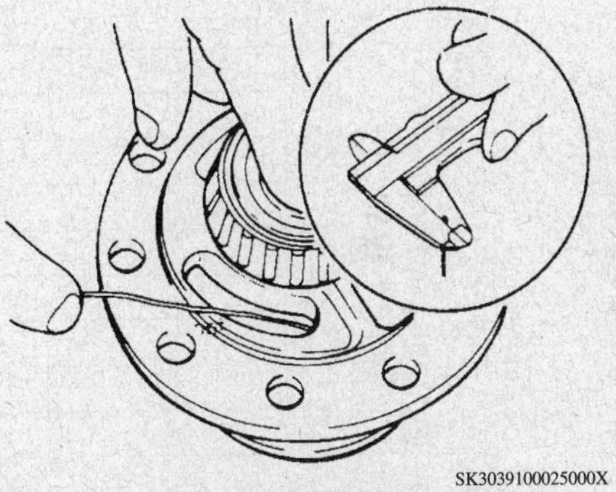
SK3039100025000X

Fig. 10 Side gear backlash measurement. Samurai

Available thrust washer sizes (thickness)	0.9, 1.0, 1.1 & 1.2 mm (0.035, 0.039, 0.043 & 0.047 in.)

SK3039100026000X

Fig. 11 Side gear thrust washer chart. Samurai

case as shown, **Fig. 10. Torque** case half bolts to 27–32.5 ft. lbs.

2. Using a suitable vernier caliper and a piece of solder as shown, **Fig. 10,** measure side gear backlash. Backlash should be 0.002–0.006 inch (0.05–0.15 mm).
3. Using a suitable dial indicator, measure side gear thrust play. Thrust play should be 0.005–0.014 inch (0.12–0.37 mm).
4. If measurements are not within specifications, increase or decrease thickness of thrust washers on inner side of each case half with appropriate thrust washer as shown, **Fig. 11.**

Bevel Pinion Shim Thickness

Thickness of shims to be used on bevel pinion varies from one vehicle to another due to machining during assembly. Therefore, for each vehicle, the thickness of shims necessary for locating pinion in correct (producing proper backlash between pinion and gear) must be determined when reassembling.

To facilitate this determination, a two piece dummy tool is available. The following procedure is based on the use with the dummy tool set in the carrier, without any shims as follows:

1. Install a suitable dial indicator on dummy pinion, allowing indicator spindle to protrude 5–6 mm from bottom of pinion dummy as shown, **Fig. 12.**
2. Rest dummy on surface plate, then set dial indicator to zero, **Fig. 13.**
3. Install dummy pinion with bearings into carrier, then the joint flange.
4. Tighten bevel pinion by hand, then install differential gear preload adjuster tool No. 09922-75221, or equivalent, **Fig. 14,** on universal joint flange.

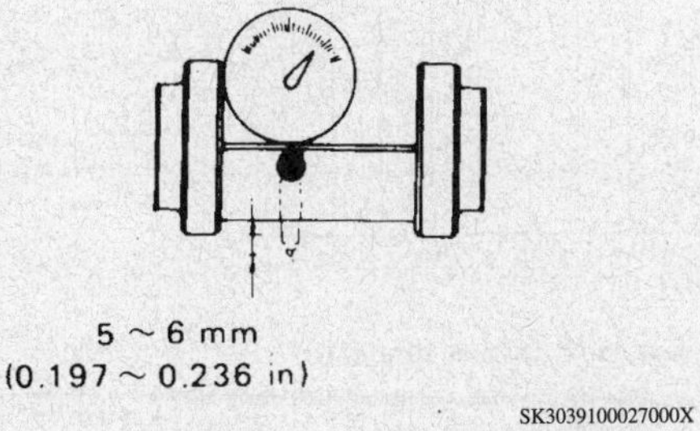
5 ~ 6 mm
(0.197 ~ 0.236 in)
SK3039100027000X

Fig. 12 Dial indicator on dummy pinion installation. Samurai

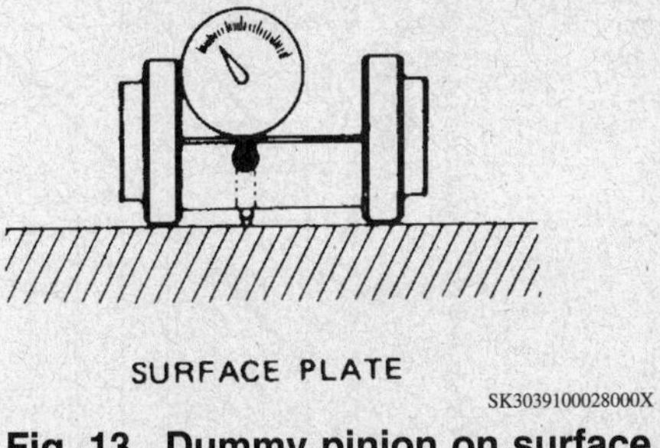
SURFACE PLATE
SK3039100028000X

Fig. 13 Dummy pinion on surface plate installation. Samurai

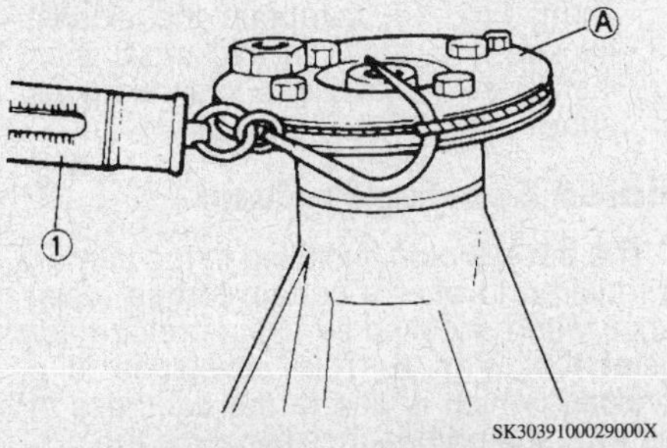
A
1
SK3039100029000X

Fig. 14 Pinion starting torque measurement. Samurai

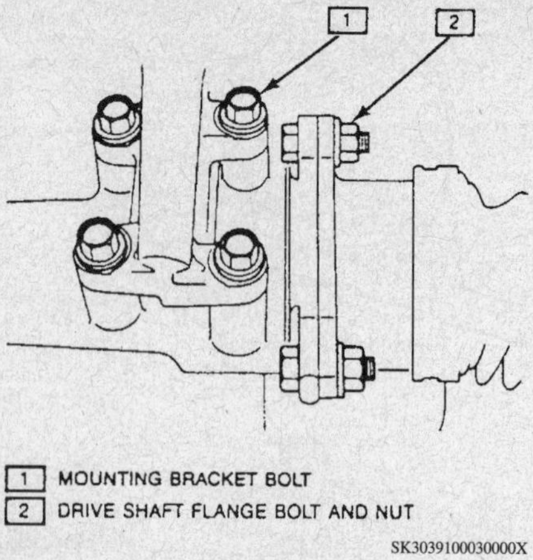

1
2
1 MOUNTING BRACKET BOLT
2 DRIVE SHAFT FLANGE BOLT AND NUT
SK3039100030000X

Fig. 15 Shim thickness selection. Samurai

Fastening parts	Tightening torque		
	N·m	kg·m	lb-ft
Side bearing cap bolt	70 – 100	7.0 – 10.0	51.0 – 72.0
Drive bevel gear bolt	80 – 90	8.0 – 9.0	58.0 – 65.0
Differential case bolt	37 – 45	3.7 – 4.5	27.0 – 32.5
Side bearing adjuster lock bolt	9 – 14	0.9 – 1.4	7.0 – 10.0
Differential carrier bolt	18 – 28	1.8 – 2.8	13.5 – 20.0
Oil level & filler plug	35 – 50	3.5 – 5.0	25.5 – 36.0
Oil drain plug	18 – 25	1.8 – 2.5	13.5 – 18.0

SK3039100031000X

Fig. 16 Bevel pinion shim thickness chart. Samurai

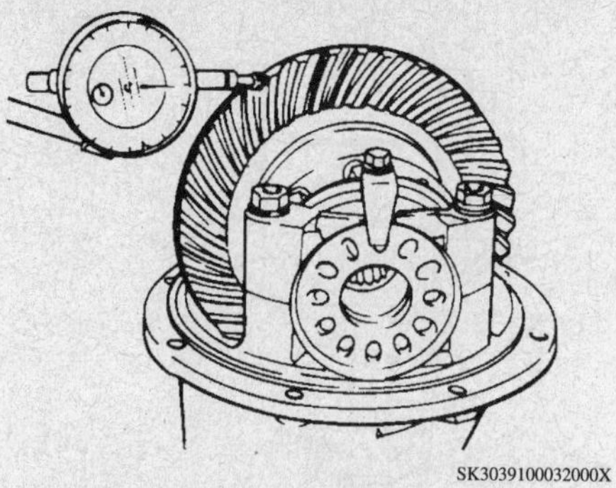

SK3039100032000X

Fig. 17 Backlash between bevel gear & pinion measurement. Samurai

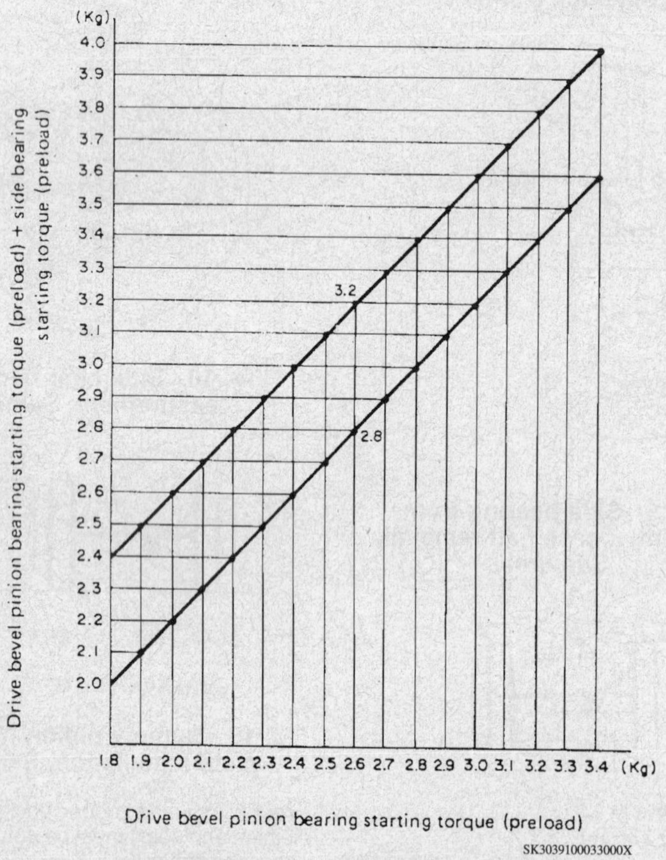

(Kg)
4.0
3.9
3.8
3.7
3.6
3.5
3.4
3.3
3.2
3.1
3.0
2.9
2.8
2.7
2.6
2.5
2.4
2.3
2.2
2.1
2.0
3.2
2.8
Drive bevel pinion bearing starting torque (preload) + side bearing starting torque (preload)
1.8 1.9 2.0 2.1 2.2 2.3 2.4 2.5 2.6 2.7 2.8 2.9 3.0 3.1 3.2 3.3 3.4 (Kg)
Drive bevel pinion bearing starting torque (preload)
SK3039100033000X

Fig. 18 Drive bevel pinion graphic chart. Samurai

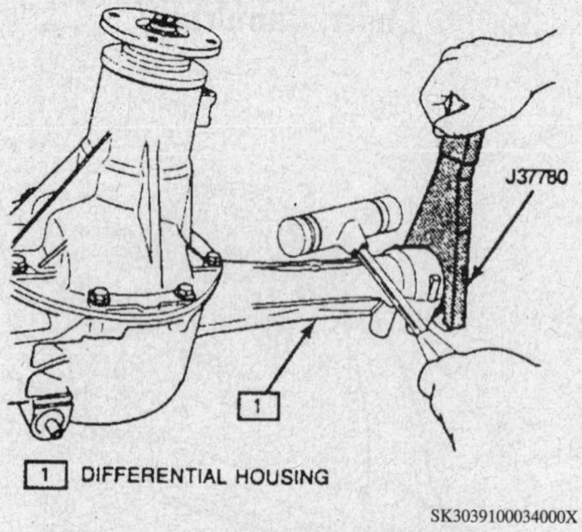

J37780
1
1 DIFFERENTIAL HOUSING
SK3039100034000X

Fig. 19 Axle shaft removal. Sidekick & X-90

5. Using a suitable spring scale, turn pinion several times, then tighten pinion nut gradually until pinion starting **torque** reaches 4.0–7.5 lbs., **Fig. 14.**
6. Refer to **Fig. 15,** noting the three dimensions, a, b and c. The value of "b" is unknown at this time. The values of "a" and "c" are given. The sum "a + c," is 94 mm, which is indicated on the dummy tool.
7. With dummy tool installed, the dial indicator pointer may have deflected from "0" mark to a certain value, note value, that value is now "b." Add this value to 94 mm and from the total, subtract value marked on bevel pinion. The remainder is the required shim thickness.
8. There are 12 selective shim thicknesses. Select one or two shim(s) from chart, **Fig. 16,** to obtain the closest thickness to required thickness, then install shim piece into clearance as shown, **Fig. 15.**

Pinion Bearing Preload

The bevel pinion, installed in the carrier, is required to offer a certain torque resistance when checked by using preload adjuster tool, **Fig. 6.** This resistance is a "preload" which is due to the tightness of the two tapered bearings by which the pinion is held in carrier. This tightness is determined primarily by tightening torque of bevel pinion nut. Pinion bearing preload should be 7.8–14.7 inch lbs. Adjust preload of bevel pinion bearings, as follows:

1. Install pinion bearings, spacer, bevel pinion, oil seal and universal joint flange to differential carrier. **Apply gear oil to bearings and grease oil seal lip.**
2. Tighten bevel pinion nut by hand, then install preload adjuster tool to universal joint flange.
3. Turn pinion several times, then tighten pinion nut gradually while checking pinion starting torque, using a suitable spring scale, **Fig. 6.** Starting **torque** should be 4.0–7.5 lbs.
4. Stake bevel pinion nut to prevent it from loosening. **Pinion bearing preload is adjusted by tightening bevel pinion nut to compress spacer. Use a new spacer for adjustment. If specification exceeds limit, replace spacer and repeat preload adjustment procedure.**

Bevel Gear Backlash

Backlash between bevel gear and pinion is checked using a suitable dial indicator as shown, **Fig. 17.** The differential case assembly is mounted in the normal manner and fastened down by tightening side bearing cap bolts to 7.7–14 ft. lbs. Screw in each adjuster until it contacts bearing outer race so that outer race is prevented from inclining. The dial indicator spindle is pointed squarely to "heel" on drive side (convex side) of gear tooth. Hold bevel pinion, then

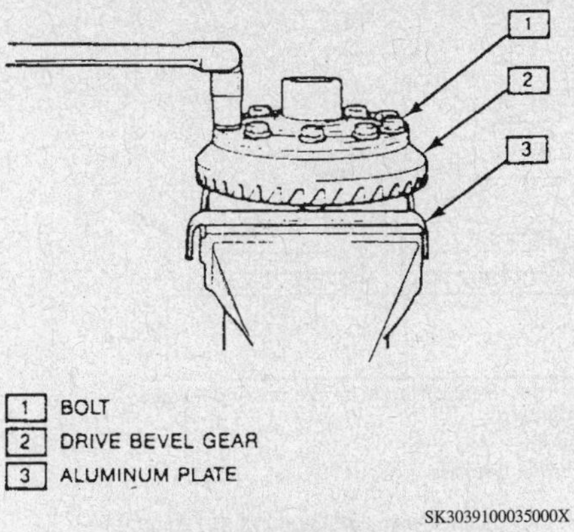
1
2
3
1 BOLT
2 DRIVE BEVEL GEAR
3 ALUMINUM PLATE
SK3039100035000X

Fig. 20 Bevel gear removal. Sidekick & X-90

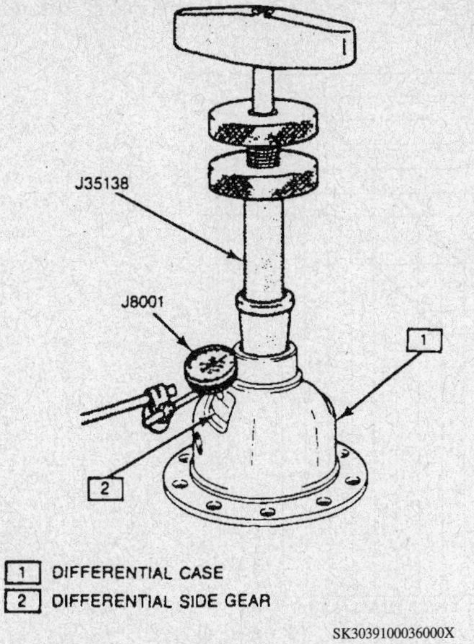
J35138
J8001
1
2
1 DIFFERENTIAL CASE
2 DIFFERENTIAL SIDE GEAR
SK3039100036000X

Fig. 21 Side gear thrust measurement. Sidekick & X-90

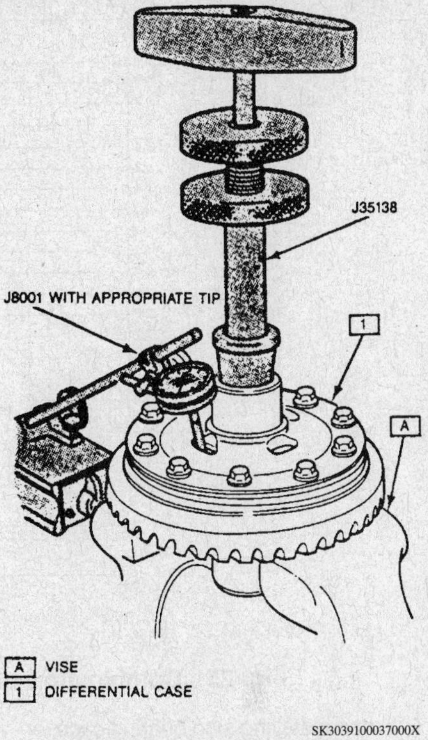
J35138
J8001 WITH APPROPRIATE TIP
1
A
A VISE
1 DIFFERENTIAL CASE
SK3039100037000X

Fig. 22 Bearing preload adjustment. Sidekick & X-90

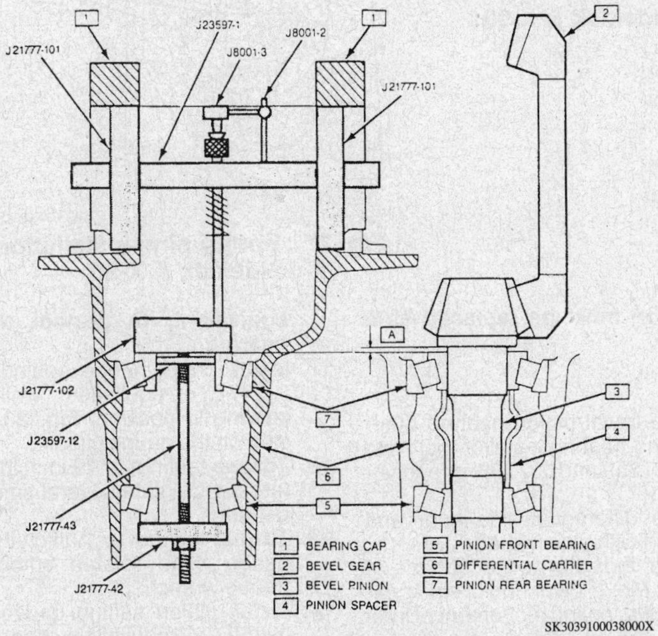
1
J23597-1
J8001-2
J21777-101
J8001-3
1
2
J21777-101
A
J21777-102
3
7
J23597-12
4
6
5
J21777-43
J21777-42
1 BEARING CAP
2 BEVEL GEAR
3 BEVEL PINION
4 PINION SPACER
5 PINION FRONT BEARING
6 DIFFERENTIAL CARRIER
7 PINION REAR BEARING
SK3039100038000X

Fig. 23 Bevel pinion mounting distance. Sidekick & X-90

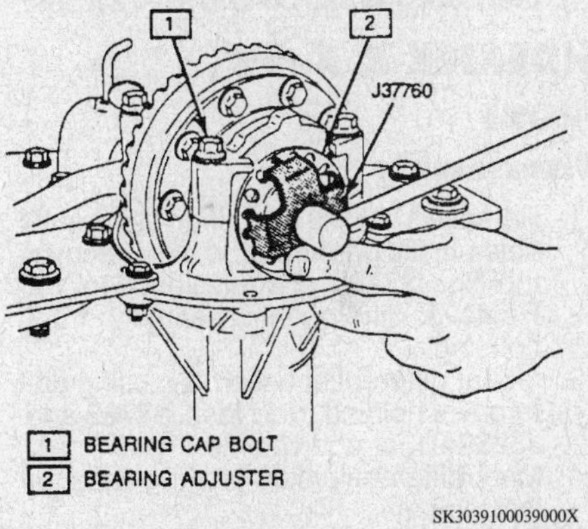
1
2
J37760
1 BEARING CAP BOLT
2 BEARING ADJUSTER
SK3039100039000X

Fig. 24 Side bearing adjustment. Sidekick & X-90

turn gear back and forth. Bevel gear backlash should be 0.004–0.006 inch (0.10–0.15 mm).

To increase or decrease backlash, displace bevel gear toward or away from pinion by turning in one adjuster and turning out the other by equal amounts. Turning adjuster one notch changes backlash approximately 0.002 inch (0.05 mm). **Adjust preload on side bearing during backlash adjustment using a suitable spring scale and mounting preload adjuster tool as shown, Fig. 14.** If reading at bevel gear starts moving within range given, **Fig. 18,** side bearing preload is acceptable. Referring to **Fig. 18,** for example, when drive bevel pinion bearing preload measures 5.73 lbs., drive bevel pinion bearing preload + bevel gear side bearing preload should be 6.17–7.05 lbs. After adjustment, **torque** bearing cap bolts to 51–72 ft. lbs.

ASSEMBLY

Reverse disassembly procedure to reassemble, noting the following:

1. The bevel pinion and bevel gear are replaced as a set. Even when only the bevel pinion or bevel gear replacement is necessary, ensure to replace both as a set.
2. When installing differential pinion shaft into differential case, ensure to install longer end of shaft first into pinion joint.
3. The bolts securing bevel gear to differential case are subject to shear stress, since drive is transmitted by these bolts from gear to case. These are special bolts made from chrome steel and must never be replaced by common bolts. Apply Loctite to threads of bolts before installing them.
4. Using bearing installer tool No. 09940-53111, or equivalent, and a press, install differential side bearings into differential case.
5. A press must be used to install two tapered roller bearings on bevel pinion. Outer races are press fitted into the differential carrier and inner races onto the pinion.
6. After installing bevel pinion, spacer, bearings and universal joint flange to carrier, and completing bevel pinion bearing preload adjustment, stake bevel pinion nut to prevent it from loosening.

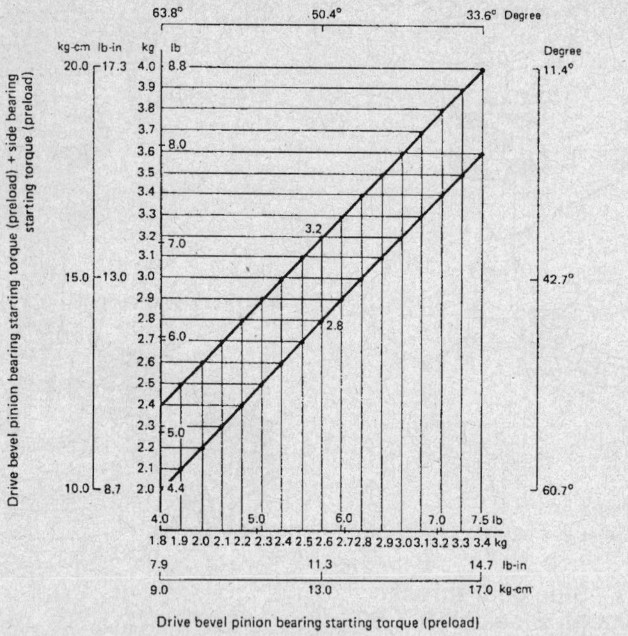
63.8°
50.4°
33.6° Degree
kg-cm lb-in kg lb
Degree
11.4°
42.7°
60.7°
Drive bevel pinion bearing starting torque (preload) + side bearing starting torque (preload)
Drive bevel pinion bearing starting torque (preload)
SK3039100040000X

Fig. 25 Combination of preloads. Sidekick & X-90

7. When installing side bearing caps, ensure match marks scribed at the time of disassembly align, then after completing bevel gear backlash adjustment, **torque** cap bolts to 51–72 ft. lbs.

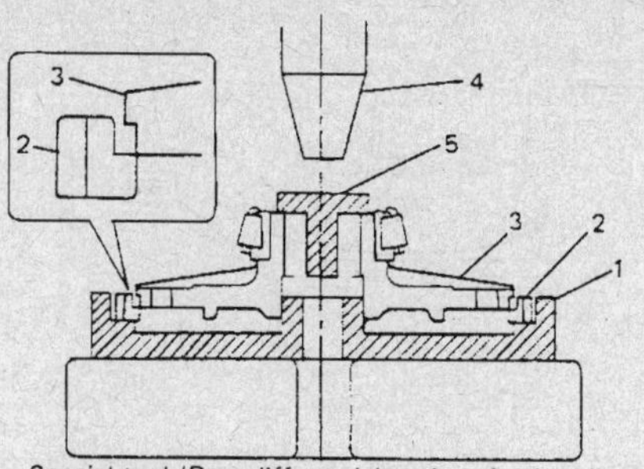

1. Special tool (Rear differential exciter ring installer 09928-26010)
2. Exciter ring
3. Differential left case
4. Press
5. Special tool (Bearing installer jig 09913-85230-002)

SK3039100041000X

Fig. 26 Exciter ring installation. Sidekick & X-90 w/rear anti-lock brakes

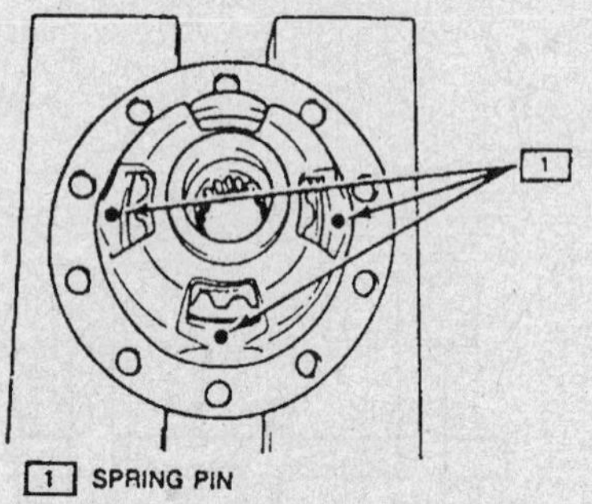
1 SPRING PIN

SK3039100042000X

Fig. 27 Spring pins installation. Sidekick & X-90

SIDEKICK & X-90

FRONT

Disassembly

1. Remove front RH driveshaft using suitable plastic hammer and axle removal tool No. J37780, or equivalent, **Fig. 19.**
2. Remove differential assembly from housing.
3. Mount differential assembly, using differential holding tool Nos. J37769 and J3289-01, or equivalents.
4. Mark differential side bearing caps for installation.
5. Remove side bearing lock plate, caps, adjusters, outer races and bevel pinion and gear assembly.
6. Rotate differential assembly using flange holding tool No. J8614-01, or equivalent.
7. Remove universal joint flange nut, bevel pinion, flange and oil seal using seal removal tool Nos. J8614-01 and J26941, or equivalents.
8. Remove differential side bearing using bearing removal tool Nos. J22888 and J8107-4, or equivalents.
9. Remove bevel gear attaching bolts, then the gear, **Fig. 20. When mounting differential in a vise, use aluminum plates to avoid damage.**
10. Drive out spring pin. Disassemble differential side gears, pinions, washers and shaft in differential case.
11. Press out bevel pinion gear using side bearing remover tool No. J22912-01, or equivalent.
12. Drive out bevel pinion bearing outer race using suitable tools. **Bevel gear and pinion must be replaced as a set.**

Assembly

1. Assemble bevel pinion bearing outer races using bearing installer tool Nos. J8092, J37759 and J37758, or equivalents.
2. Assemble differential side gear and side pinion with pinion shaft.
3. Mount dial indicator to top surface of side gear. Move lower end of side gear up and down, noting movement of indicator, **Fig. 21.**
4. Install a 0.043 inch thrust washer and ensure a 0.005–0.014 inch side gear thrust play is obtained.
5. Drive spring pin in until it is flush with the differential case surface.
6. Install bevel gear to differential case and **torque** bolts to 70 ft. lbs.
7. Mount dial indicator tool to back of side gear, **Fig. 22.**
8. Install a 0.043 inch thrust washer and side thrust gear installation tool No. J35138, or equivalent, onto differential side gear.
9. Move tool up and down in a straight forward manner and ensure a side gear thrust play of 0.005–0.014 inch is obtained.
10. Install side bearings using bearing installation tool No. J8092 and J24433, or equivalents. **Be sure to use side bearing removal tool No. J8107-4, or equivalent, to protect the lower bearing.**
11. Install depth gauge setting tool No. J21777, or equivalent, while holding bearing in position, **Fig. 23.** Use low step on the gauge plate.
12. **Torque** tool nut to 19 inch lbs. and rotate gauge plate several times to seat bearings.
13. **Torque** tool nut to 19 inch lbs. or until gauge plate rotates smoothly with torque wrench.
14. Install pinion setting gauge tool No. J23597, or equivalent, and assemble the gauge shaft in the carrier so that the dial indicator rod is centered on the gauging area of the gauge block.
15. Install side bearing caps and **torque** bolts to 63 ft. lbs.
16. Adjust dial indicator until a zero reading is obtained.
17. Adjust the position of gauge shaft mounting post so contact button touches the indicator pad.
18. Push the dial indicator downward into the gauge plate until the needle rotates ¾ of a turn then tighten in this position.
19. Slowly rotate the gauge shaft back and forth. At the point of greatest deflection, reset the dial indicator to zero. Repeat and ensure zero reading.
20. Rotate the gauge shaft until the dial indicator rod no longer touches the gauge plate.
21. Read movement on the dial indicator.

Total movement on the dial indicator indicates thickness of shim required.
22. Assemble pinion rear bearing, pinion shim and bevel pinion assembly.
23. Install front bearing to differential carrier with new spacer inserted.
24. Install oil seal into differential carrier until seal is flush with carrier end. Apply grease to lip of seal.
25. Install pinion washer and nut. Hold pinion flange and rotate pinion to seat bearing. Tighten pinion flange nut until endplay is taken up. **Preload specification is reached when endplay is no longer detectable. No further tightening should be attempted until preload has been checked.**
26. Using an inch lb. torque wrench, adjust bearing preload **torque** to 11 inch lbs.
27. Install bevel gear and differential case assembly, side bearing outer races, bearing adjusters and bearing caps, noting alignment mark.
28. **Torque** bearing caps bolts to 63 ft. lbs.
29. Turn bearing adjuster to push side bearing lightly so that outer races are in contact with inner races, **Fig. 24.**
30. Measure preload of pinion with an inch lb. torque wrench.
31. Adjust side bearing until gear backlash and bearing preload are within specification, **Fig. 25.**
32. Install bearing lock plates.
33. Clean mating surfaces of housing and carrier and apply Suzuki Bond No. 1215 (part No. 99000-31110).
34. Position differential assembly in housing with two reamer bolts, then install six bolts, **torquing** to 17 ft. lbs.

REAR

Use front differential procedure with the exception of the following:

1. **On models with rear anti-lock brakes,** an exciter ring is attached to the left case. To remove exciter ring, tap along ring rim evenly with copper hammer. To install exciter ring, press fit ring as shown, **Fig. 26.** Ensure end face of left case is flush with or higher than end face of exciter ring.
2. **On all models,** rear differential side bearing installation requires the use of bearing installer tool No. J37758, or equivalent, in place of tool No. J24433, or equivalent.
3. Rear differential is a four pinion type. After installing pinions, align pinion shaft hole position with differential case and drive in three spring pins until they are flush with the end surface of case, **Fig. 27.**
4. Use the high step on pinion setting gauge tool No. J21777-102, or equivalent gauge plate when setting pinion depth in rear differential, **Fig. 23.**

Engine Rebuilding Specifications

INDEX

	Page No.
Camshaft	40-167
Crankshaft, Bearings & Rods	40-167
Cylinder Block	40-169
Cylinder Head, Valve Guide & Valve Seats	40-165
Oil Pump	40-170
Pistons, Pins & Rings	40-168
Valve Springs	40-166
Valves	40-166

CYLINDER HEAD, VALVE GUIDE & VALVE SEATS

All Specifications Given In Inches, Unless Otherwise Specified.

Year	Engine Liter	Cylinder Head Warpage Limit	Valve Guides			Valve Seats		
			Inner Diameter	Stem To Guide Clearance		Seat Angle, Degrees	Seat Width	
				Intake	Exhaust		Intake	Exhaust
1993	1.3L①	.002	.2756-.2761	.0008-.0019	.0014-.0025	45	.0512-.0590	.0512-.0590
	1.3L②	.002	.2165-.2170	.0008-.0018	.0018-.0028	45	.0512-.0590	.0512-.0590
	1.6L④	.002	.2756-.2761	.0008-.0019	.0014-.0025	45	.0512-.0590	.0512-.0590
	1.6L③	.002	.2166-.2170	.0008-.0018	.0018-.0028	45	.0433-.0512	.0433-.0512
1994	1.3L①	.002	.2756-.2761	.0008-.0019	.0014-.0025	45	.0512-.0590	.0512-.0590
	1.3L②	.002	.2165-.2170	.0008-.0018	.0018-.0028	45	.0512-.0590	.0512-.0590
	1.6L④	.002	.2756-.2761	.0008-.0019	.0014-.0025	45	.0512-.0590	.0512-.0590
	1.6L③	.002	.2166-.2170	.0008-.0018	.0018-.0028	45	.0433-.0512	.0433-.0512
1995	1.3L①	.002	.2756-.2761	.0008-.0019	.0014-.0025	45	.0512-.0590	.0512-.0590
	1.6L④	.002	.2756-.2761	.0008-.0019	.0014-.0025	45	.0512-.0590	.0512-.0590
	1.6L③	.002	.2166-.2170	.0008-.0018	.0018-.0028	45	.0433-.0512	.0433-.0512
1996	1.3L①	.002	.2756-.2761	.0008-.0019	.0014-.0025	45	.0512-.0590	.0512-.0590
	1.6L③	.002	.2166-.2170	.0008-.0018	.0018-.0028	45	.0433-.0512	.0433-.0512
	1.8L	.002	.2362-.2366	.0008-.0018	.0018-.0028	45	.0433-.0512	.0433-.0512

①–Single overhead camshaft.
②–Double overhead camshaft w/4 valves per cylinder.
③–Single overhead camshaft w/4 valves per cylinder.
④–Single overhead camshaft w/2 valves per cylinder.

VALVE SPRINGS

All Specifications Given In Inches, Unless Otherwise Specified.

Year	Engine Liter	Free Length	Installed Height	Seated Pressure Pounds @ Inches	Comp. Pressure Pounds @ Inches	Out Of Square Limit
1993	1.3L ③	1.8937	—	54.7-64.3 @ 1.63	50.2 @ 1.63	.079
	1.3L ②	1.9409	—	54.7–64.3 @ 1.63	50.2 @ 1.63	.079
	1.3L ④	1.9567	—	60.6-73.8 @ 1.67	56.6 @ 1.67	.079
	1.6L ⑤	1.9094	—	54.7-64.3 @ 1.63	50.2 @ 1.63	.079
	1.6L ①	1.4043	—	23.6-27.5 @ 1.24	20.5 @ 1.24	.079
1994	1.3L ③	1.8937	—	54.7-64.3 @ 1.63	50.2 @ 1.63	.079
	1.3L ②	1.9409	—	54.7–64.3 @ 1.63	50.2 @ 1.63	.079
	1.3L ④	1.9567	—	60.6-73.8 @ 1.67	56.6 @ 1.67	.079
	1.6L ⑤	1.9094	—	54.7-64.3 @ 1.63	50.2 @ 1.63	.079
	1.6L ①	1.4043	—	23.6-27.5 @ 1.24	20.5 @ 1.24	.079
1995	1.3L ③	1.8937	—	54.7-64.3 @ 1.63	50.2 @ 1.63	.079
	1.3L ②	1.9409	—	54.7–64.3 @ 1.63	50.2 @ 1.63	.079
	1.3L ④	1.9567	—	60.6-73.8 @ 1.67	56.6 @ 1.67	.079
	1.6L ⑤	1.9094	—	54.7-64.3 @ 1.63	50.2 @ 1.63	.079
	1.6L ①	1.4043	—	23.6-27.5 @ 1.24	20.5 @ 1.24	.079
1996	1.3L ③	1.8937	—	54.7-64.3 @ 1.63	50.2 @ 1.63	.079
	1.3L ④	1.9567	—	60.6-73.8 @ 1.67	56.6 @ 1.67	.079
	1.6L ①	1.4043	—	23.6-27.5 @ 1.24	20.5 @ 1.24	.079
	1.8L	1.6339	—	49.2-56.7 @ 1.28	46.7 @ 1.28	.079

① — Single overhead camshaft w/4 valves per cylinder.
② — Samurai.
③ — Single overhead camshaft.
④ — Double overhead camshaft w/4 valves per cylinder.
⑤ — Single overhead camshaft w/2 valves per cylinder.

VALVES

All Specifications Given In Inches, Unless Otherwise Specified.

Year	Engine Liter	Valves					
		Stem Diameter		Face Angle, °	Min. Margin Intake/Exhaust	Clearance	
		Intake	Exhaust			Intake	Exhaust
1993	1.3L③	.2742-.2748	.2737-.2742	45	.023–.027	①	②
	1.3L④	.2152-.2157	.2142–.2148	45	.023–.027	—	—
	1.6L	.2152-.2157	.2142-.2148	45	.024–.027	⑤	⑤
1994	1.3L③	.2742-.2748	.2737-.2742	45	.023–.027	①	②
	1.3L④	.2152–.2157	.2142–.2148	45	.023–.027	—	—
	1.6L	.2152-.2157	.2142-.2148	45	.024–.027	⑤	⑤
1995	1.3L③	.2742-.2748	.2737-.2742	45	.023–.027	①	②
	1.6L	.2152-.2157	.2142-.2148	45	.024–.027	⑤	⑤
1996	1.3L③	.2742-.2748	.2737-.2742	45	.023–.027	①	②
	1.6L	.2152-.2157	.2142-.2148	45	.024–.027	⑤	⑤
	1.8L	.2348-.2354	.2239-.2344	45	—	—	—

① — Cold (coolant temperature at 59–77°F), .0051–.0067 inch; hot (coolant temperature at 140–154°F), .009–.011 inch.
② — Cold (coolant temperature at 59–77°F), .0063–.0079 inch; hot (coolant temperature at 140–154°F), .0102–.0118 inch.
③ — Single overhead camshaft.
④ — Double overhead camshaft w/4 valves per cylinder.
⑤ — Cold (coolant temperature at 59–77°F), .0031–.0047 inch; hot (coolant temperature at 140–154°F), .0047–.0063 inch
⑥ — Single overhead camshaft w/4 valves per cylinder.

CAMSHAFT

All Specifications Given In Inches, Unless Otherwise Specified.

Year	Engine Liter	Camshaft Journal Diameter	Maximum Journal Runout	Camshaft Journal Clearance
1993	1.3L②	①	.0039	.0020-.0036
	1.3L③	1.1007–1.1015④	.0039	.0008-.0024
	1.6L⑤	①	.0039	.0020-.0036
	1.6L⑥	1.1000–1.1008	.0039	.0016-.0032
1994	1.3L②	①	.0039	.0020-.0036
	1.3L③	1.1007–1.1015④	.0039	.0008-.0024
	1.6L⑤	①	.0039	.0020-.0036
	1.6L⑥	1.1000–1.1008	.0039	.0016-.0032
1995	1.3L②	①	.0039	.0020-.0036
	1.6L⑤	①	.0039	.0020-.0036
	1.6L⑥	1.1000–1.1008	.0039	.0016-.0032
1996	1.3L②	①	.0039	.0020-.0036
	1.6L⑥	1.1000–1.1008	.0039	.0016-.0032
	1.8L	⑦	.0039	.0008-.0029

① — Starting from front of cam, measure No. 1 journal, 1.7372–1.7381 inches, No. 2 journal, 1.7451–1.7460 inches, No. 3 journal, 1.7530–1.7539 inches, No. 4 journal, 1.7609–1.7618 inches & No. 5 journal, 1.7687–1.7697 inches.
② — Single overhead camshaft.
③ — Double overhead camshaft w/4 valves per cylinder.
④ — Intake & exhaust camshafts.
⑤ — Single overhead camshaft w/2 valves per cylinder.
⑥ — Single overhead camshaft w/4 valves per cylinder.
⑦ — Journal No. 1, 1.0220–1.0228; journal No. 2 & 3, 1.1795–1.1803.

CRANKSHAFT BEARINGS & RODS

All Specifications Given In Inches, Unless Otherwise Specified.

Year	Engine Liter	Crankshaft				Bearing Clearance			Connecting Rods	
		Main Bearing Journal Diameter	Connecting Rod Journal Diameter	Max. Out Of Round All	Max. Taper All	Main Bearings	Connecting Rod Bearings	Crankshaft Endplay	Pin Bore Diameter	Side Clearance
1993	1.3L②	⑦	1.6529–1.6535	.0004	.0004	.0008–.0016	.0008-.0019	.0044–.0122	.6680–.6684	.0039–.0078
	1.3L③	⑦	1.6529–1.6535	.0004	.0004	.0008–.0016	.0008–.0019	.0044–.0122	.7481–.7484	.0039–.0078
	1.6L⑤	④	1.7316–1.7323	.0004	.0004	.0008–.0016	.0008–.0019	.0044–.0122	—	.0039–.0078
	1.6L⑥	④	1.7316–1.7322	.0004	.0004	.0008–.0016	.0008–.0019	.0044–.0122	.7482–.7486	.0039–.0078
1994	1.3L②	⑦	1.6529–1.6535	.0004	.0004	.0008–.0016	.0008-.0019	.0044–.0122	.6680-.6684	.0039–.0078
	1.3L③	⑦	1.6529–1.6535	.0004	.0004	.0008–.0016	.0008–.0019	.0044–.0122	.7481–.7484	.0039–.0078
	1.6L⑤	④	1.7316–1.7323	.0004	.0004	.0008–.0016	.0008–.0019	.0044–.0122	—	.0039–.0078
	1.6L⑥	④	1.7316–1.7322	.0004	.0004	.0008–.0016	.0008–.0019	.0044–.0122	.7482–.7486	.0039–.0078

Continued

CRANKSHAFT BEARINGS & RODS—Continued

All Specifications Given In Inches, Unless Otherwise Specified.

Year	Engine Liter	Crankshaft				Bearing Clearance			Connecting Rods	
		Main Bearing Journal Diameter	Connecting Rod Journal Diameter	Max. Out Of Round All	Max. Taper All	Main Bearings	Connecting Rod Bearings	Crankshaft Endplay	Pin Bore Diameter	Side Clearance
1995	1.3L ②	⑦	1.6529–1.6535	.0004	.0004	.0008–.0016	.0008-.0019	.0044–.0122	.6680–.6684	.0039–.0078
	1.6L ⑤	④	1.7316–1.7323	.0004	.0004	.0008–.0016	.0008-.0019	.0044–.0122	—	.0039–.0078
	1.6L ⑥	④	1.7316–1.7322	.0004	.0004	.0008–.0016	.0008-.0019	.0044–.0122	.7482–.7486	.0039–.0078
1996	1.3L ②	⑦	1.6529–1.6535	.0004	.0004	.0008–.0016	.0008-.0019	.0044–.0122	.6680–.6684	.0039–.0078
	1.6L ⑥	④	1.7316–1.7322	.0004	.0004	.0008–.0016	.0008–.0019	.0044–.0122	.7482–.7486	.0039–.0078
	1.8L	①	1.9678-1.9685	.0004	.0004	.0010-.0018	.0018-.0024	.0039-.0138	.8269-.8272	.0099-.0150

① — Journal stamped No. 1, 2.2832–2.2834 inches; journal stamped No. 2, 2.2830–2.2832 inches; journal stamped No. 3, 2.2828–2.2829 inches.
② — Single overhead camshaft.
③ — Double overhead camshaft w/4 valves per cylinder.
④ — Journal stamped No. 1, 2.0470–2.0472 inches; journal stamped No. 2, 2.0468–2.0470 inches; journal stamped No. 3, 2.0465–2.0468 inches; refer to text for identification.
⑤ — Single overhead camshaft w/2 valves per cylinder.
⑥ — Single overhead camshaft w/4 valves per cylinder.
⑦ — The counter weights of No. 1 cylinder have four stamped numbers, they indicate the journal diameters at bearing caps respectively. No. 1, 1.7714–17716 inch; No. 2, 1.7712–1.7714 inch & No. 3, 1.7710–1.7712 inch

PISTONS, PINS & RINGS

All Specifications Given In Inches, Unless Otherwise Specified.

Year	Engine Liter	Piston Dia.	Piston Clearance	Piston Pin Diameter	Piston Ring End Gap			Piston Ring Side Clearance	
					Top	Second	Oil	Top	Second
1993	1.3L②	①	.0008-.0015	.6691-.6693	.0079-.0118	.0079-.0118	.0079-.0275	.0012–.0027	.0008–.0023
	1.3L③	①	.0008-.0015	.7478-.7480	.0079–.0118	.0079–.0118	.0079–.0236	.0012–.0027	.0008–.0023
	1.6L⑤	④	.0008-.0015	.7479–.7489	.0079-.0137	.0079-.0137	.0079-.0275	.0012–.0027	.0008–.0023
1994	1.3L②	①	.0008-.0015	.6691-.6693	.0079-.0118	.0079-.0118	.0079-.0275	.0012–.0027	.0008–.0023
	1.3L③	①	.0008-.0015	.7478-.7480	.0079–.0118	.0079–.0118	.0079–.0236	.0012–.0027	.0008–.0023
	1.6L⑤	④	.0008-.0015	.7479–.7489	.0079-.0137	.0079-.0137	.0079-.0275	.0012–.0027	.0008–.0023
1995	1.3L②	①	.0008-.0015	.6691-.6693	.0079-.0118	.0079-.0118	.0079-.0275	.0012–.0027	.0008–.0023
	1.6L⑤	④	.0008-.0015	.7479–.7489	.0079-.0137	.0079-.0137	.0079-.0275	.0012–.0027	.0008–.0023
1996	1.3L②	①	.0008-.0015	.6691-.6693	.0079-.0118	.0079-.0118	.0079-.0275	.0012–.0027	.0008–.0023
	1.6L	2.9516-2.9523	.0008-.0015	.7479-.7480	.0079-.0137	.0079-.0137	.0079-.0275	.0012–.0027	.0008–.0023
	1.8L	3.3059-3.3066	.0008-.0015	.8267-.8270	.0079-.0137	.0138-.0196	.0079-.0275	.0008–.0015	.0008–.0015

① — Piston stamped No. 1, 2.9126–2.9130 inches; piston stamped No. 2, 2.9122–2.9126 inches; refer to text for identification.
② — Single overhead camshaft.
③ — Double overhead camshaft w/4 valves per cylinder.
④ — Piston stamped No. 1, 2.9520–2.9524 inches; piston stamped No. 2, 2.9516–2.9520 inches; refer to text for identification.
⑤ — Single overhead camshaft w/4 valves per cylinder.

CYLINDER BLOCK

All Specifications Given In Inches, Unless Otherwise Specified.

Year	Engine Liter	Cylinder Bore Diameter (Std.)	Cylinder Bore Taper Max.	Cylinder Bore Out Of Round Max.
1993	1.3L②	①	0.0039	0.0039
	1.3L③	①	0.0039	0.0039
	1.6L⑤	④	0.0039	0.0039
	1.6L	2.9586	0.0039	0.0039
1994	1.3L②	①	0.0039	0.0039
	1.3L③	①	0.0039	0.0039
	1.6L⑤	④	0.0039	0.0039
	1.6L	2.9586	0.0039	0.0039
1995	1.3L②	①	0.0039	0.0039
	1.6L⑤	④	0.0039	0.0039
	1.6L	2.9586	0.0039	0.0039
1996	1.3L②	①	0.0039	0.0039
	1.6L	2.9586	0.0039	0.0039
	1.8L	3.3090	0.004	0.004

① — Cylinder stamped No. 1, 2.9138–2.9142 inches; cylinder stamped No. 2, 2.9134–2.9138 inches; refer to text for identification.
② — Single overhead camshaft.
③ — Double overhead camshaft w/4 valves per cylinder.
④ — Cylinder stamped No. 1, 2.9531–2.9535 inches; cylinder stamped No. 2, 2.9528–2.531 inches; refer to text for identification.
⑤ — Single overhead camshaft w/4 valves per cylinder

OIL PUMP

All Specifications Given In Inches, Unless Otherwise Specified.

Year	Engine Liter	Side Clearance	Gear To Body Clearance
1993	1.3L ①	.0059	.0122
	1.3L ②	.0059	.0122
	1.6L	.0059	.0122
1994	1.3L ①	.0059	.0122
	1.3L ②	.0059	.0122
	1.6L	.0059	.0122
1995	1.3L ①	.0059	.0122
	1.6L	.0059	.0122
1996	1.3L ①	.0059	.0122
	1.6L	.0059	.0122
	1.8L	.0043	.0059

① — Single overhead camshaft.
② — Double overhead camshaft w/4 valves per cylinder.

TOYOTA COROLLA

INDEX OF SERVICE OPERATIONS

Page No.

AIR BAG SYSTEM PRECAUTIONS 0-8
AUTOMATIC TRANSMISSION/ TRANSAXLES 48-1
BRAKES
Anti-Lock Brakes 48-1
Disc Brakes 48-1
Drum Brakes ....
Hydraulic Brake Systems 48-1
Power Brake Units 48-1
CLUTCH & MANUAL TRANSAXLE
Adjustments 41-15
Clutch, Replace 41-16
Hydraulic System Service 41-15
Precautions 41-15
Tightening Specifications 41-17
Transaxle, Replace 41-16
ELECTRICAL
Air Bags 48-1
Air Conditioning 48-1
Alternators 48-1
Blower Motor, Replace 41-6
Combination Switch, Replace . 41-5
Cooling Fans 48-1
Cruise Control 48-1
Dash Gauges 48-1
Dash Panels 48-1
Distributor, Replace 41-4
Evaporator Core, Replace 41-6
Fuel Pump Relay Location 41-4
Fuse Panel & Flasher Location 41-4
Heater Core, Replace 41-6
Ignition Lock, Replace 41-5
Ignition Switch, Replace 41-5
Instrument Cluster, Replace ... 41-5
Neutral Safety Switch, Adjust . 41-5
Passive Restraints 48-1
Precautions 41-4
Radio, Replace 41-6
Relay Center Location 41-4
Speed Controls 48-1
Starter Motors 48-1
Starter, Replace 41-4
Steering Columns 48-1
Steering Wheel, Replace 41-5
Stop Light Switch, Replace ... 41-5
Wiper Motor, Replace 41-6
Wiper Switch, Replace 41-6
Wiper Systems 48-1
ELECTRICAL SYMBOL IDENTIFICATION 0-139
FRONT SUSPENSION & STEERING
Ball Joint Inspection 41-22
Coil Spring, Replace 41-22
Lower Suspension Arm, Replace 41-22
Manual Steering Gears 48-1
Power Steering 48-1
Power Steering Gear, Replace 41-23
Power Steering Pump, Replace 41-24
Power Steering System Bleed 41-24
Precautions 41-21
Shock Absorber, Replace 41-22
Stabilizer Bar, Replace 41-23
Strut, Replace 41-22
Tightening Specifications 41-25
Wheel Bearing, Adjust 41-21
Wheel Hub & Steering Knuckle, Replace 41-21
FRONT WHEEL DRIVE AXLES 48-1
REAR AXLE & SUSPENSION
Coil Spring, Replace 41-19
Hub & Bearing, Replace 41-18
Lower Suspension Arm & Strut Rod, Replace 41-19
Rear Axle Carrier, Replace 41-18
Shock Absorber, Replace 41-19
Stabilizer Bar, Replace 41-19
Strut, Replace 41-18
Strut Rod, Replace 41-18
Suspension Arm, Replace 41-19
Tightening Specifications 41-20
SERVICE REMINDER & WARNING LAMP RESET PROCEDURES 0-10
SPECIFICATIONS
Fluid Capacities & Cooling System Data 41-3
Front Wheel Alignment Specifications 41-3
General Engine Specifications 41-2
Lubricant Data 41-3
Rear Wheel Alignment Specifications 41-3
Tune Up Specifications 41-2
VEHICLE IDENTIFICATION . 0-1
VEHICLE LIFT POINTS 0-34
VEHICLE MAINTENANCE SCHEDULES 0-69
WHEEL ALIGNMENT
Front Wheel Alignment 41-26
Preliminary Inspection 41-26
Rear Wheel Alignment 41-26
Vehicle Ride Height 41-26
Wheel Alignment Specifications 41-3
WHEEL COLOR CODE IDENTIFICATION 0-144
4A-FE 1.6L & 7A-FE 1.8L ENGINES
Belt Tension Data 41-11
Camshaft, Replace 41-11
Compression Pressure 41-7
Cooling System Bleed 41-11
Cylinder Head, Replace 41-8
Engine Rebuilding Specifications 48-1
Engine, Replace 41-8
Exhaust Manifold, Replace 41-8
Fuel Filter, Replace 41-13
Fuel Pump, Replace 41-13
Hydraulic Lifters, Replace 41-10
Intake Manifold, Replace 41-8
Main & Rod Bearings 41-11
Oil Pan, Replace 41-11
Oil Pump, Replace 41-11
Oil Pump Service 41-11
Piston & Rod Assembly 41-11
Precautions 41-7
Radiator, Replace 41-13
Thermostat, Replace 41-11
Tightening Specifications 41-14
Timing Belt, Replace 41-10
Valve Adjustment 41-9
Valve Clearance Specifications 41-9
Valve Guides 41-9
Water Pump, Replace 41-12

Specifications

GENERAL ENGINE SPECIFICATIONS

Year	Engine	Fuel System	Bore & Stroke, Inches	Compression Ratio	Maximum Brake H.P. @ RPM	Maximum Torques Ft. Lbs. @ RPM	Normal Oil Pressure, psi
1993	1.6L 4A-FE	MFI	3.19 x 3.03	9.5	③	100 @ 4800	①
	1.8L 7A-FE	MFI	3.19 x 3.37	9.5	④	②	①
1994	1.6L 4A-FE	MFI	3.19 x 3.03	9.5	③	100 @ 4800	①
	1.8L 7A-FE	MFI	3.19 x 3.37	9.5	④	115 @ 2800	①
1995	1.6L 4A-FE	MFI	3.19 x 3.03	9.5	③	100 @ 4800	①
	1.8L 7A-FE	MFI	3.19 x 3.37	9.5	105 @ 5200	117 @ 2800	①
1996	1.6L 4A-FE	SFI	3.19 x 3.03	9.5	③	100 @ 4800	①
	1.8L 7A-FE	SFI	3.19 x 3.37	9.5	105 @ 5800	117 @ 2800	①

① — At idle, 4.3 psi or more; @ 3000 RPM, 36–71 psi.
② — California, 125 @ 5400; federal, 115 @ 2800.
③ — California, 100 @ 5800; federal, 105 @ 5800.
④ — California, 110 @ 5600; federal, 115 @ 5600.

TUNE UP SPECIFICATIONS

The following specifications are published from the latest information available. This data should be used only in the absence of a decal affixed in the engine compartment.

When checking ignition timing, it may be necessary to disconnect certain hoses and/or electrical connectors. Refer to vehicle emission control label for specific instructions.

Before disconnecting spark plug wires from distributor cap, determine location of No. 1 wire in cap, as distributor position may have been altered from that shown.

Year	Engine	Spark Plug Gap, Inch	Ignition			Curb Idle Speed, RPM①		Fuel Pump Pressure, psi	Valve Clearance, Inch	
			Firing Order	Timing, ° BTDC②	Timing Mark, Fig.	Man. Trans.	Auto. Trans.		Int.	Exh.
1993	1.6L 4A-FE	.031	1-3-4-2	10	A	700N	700N	38–44	.006–.010	.010–.014
	1.8L 7A-FE	.031	1-3-4-2	10	A	700N	700N	38–44	.006–.010	.010–.014
1994–96	1.6L 4A-FE	.031	1-3-4-2	10	A	700N	700N	38–44	.006–.010	.010–.014
	1.8L 7A-FE	.031	1-3-4-2	10	A	700N	700N	38–44	.006–.010	.010–.014

BTDC — Before Top Dead Center.
N — Neutral.
① — Controlled by idle air controller.
② — With check terminal TE1 and E1 connected.

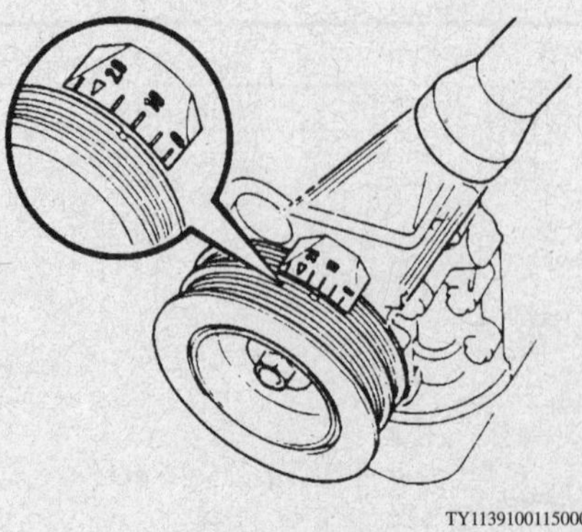

TY1139100115000X

Fig. A

FRONT WHEEL ALIGNMENT SPECIFICATIONS

The specifications listed below are for unloaded vehicles

Year	Model	Caster Angle, Degrees		Camber Angle, Degrees		Toe-In, Inch	Toe-Out on Turns, Deg.		Steering Axis Inclination, Deg.	Ball Joint Wear
		Limits	Desired	Limits	Desired		Outer Wheel	Inner Wheel		
1993–96	All	$+\frac{7}{12}$ to $+2\frac{1}{12}$	$+1\frac{1}{3}$	$-\frac{11}{12}$ to $+\frac{7}{12}$	$-\frac{1}{6}$	.04	39	33	$+12\frac{7}{12}$	①

① — Refer to "Ball Joint Inspection" under "Front Suspension & Steering."

REAR WHEEL ALIGNMENT SPECIFICATIONS

The specifications listed below are for unloaded vehicles

Year	Camber Angle, Degrees		Toe-In, Inch
	Limits	Desired	
1993	$-1\frac{1}{2}$ to $-\frac{1}{6}$	$-\frac{11}{12}$	.12±.08
1994–96	$-1\frac{2}{3}$ to $-\frac{1}{6}$	$-\frac{11}{12}$	.12±.08

FLUID CAPACITIES & COOLING SYSTEM DATA

Year	Engine	Coolant Capacity, Qts.		Radiator Cap Relief Pressure, Lbs.	Thermo. Opening Temp., °F	Fuel Tank, Gals.	Engine Oil Refill, Qts.①	Transmission/ Transaxle Oil		Axle Oil, Pints
		Less A/C	With A/C					5 Speed, Pints	Auto. Trans, Qts.	
1993–94	1.6L 4A-FE	6.3	6.310	13	176–183	13.2	3.5	5.4	5.8	2.2
	1.8L 7A-FE	③	③	13	180	13.2	3.9	5.4	8	—
1995–96	1.6L 4A-FE	②	②	13	180	13.2	3.2	5.2	5.8	2.2
	1.8L 7A-FE	④	④	13	180	13.2	3.9	5.2	8	—

① — With filter change.
② — With Nippondenso radiator, man. trans., 5.6 qts.; auto. trans., 6.2 qts. With Harrison radiator, man. trans., 6.3 qts.; auto. trans., 6.2qts. With Toyo radiator, 5.5 qts.
③ — Auto. trans. 6.4 qts.; man. trans., 6.6 qts..
④ — With Nippondenso radiator, man. trans., 5.8 qts.; auto. trans., 6.6 qts. w/Harrison radiator, man. trans., 6.6 qts.; auto. trans., 6.4 qts.

LUBRICANT DATA

Year	Lubricant Type					
	Transaxle		Transfer Case	Rear Axle	Power Steering	Brake System
	Manual	Automatic				
1993–94	API GL3, GL4, GL5, SAE 75W-90	ATF Dexron II	Transaxle Oil E50, API GL5, SAE 75W-90	API GL5①	ATF Dexron II	DOT 3
1995–96	75W-90 GL4/5	Dexron II/IIE/III	—	—	Dexron II/IIE/III	DOT 3

① — Below 0°F, SAE 80W-90; above 0°F, SAE 90.

Electrical

NOTE: On Air Bag Equipped Models, Refer To "Air Bag System Precautions" Located In The Front Of This Manual For System Disarming & Arming Procedures.

INDEX

	Page No.
Air Bags	48-1
Air Conditioning	48-1
Alternators	48-1
Blower Motor, Replace	41-6
Combination Switch, Replace	41-5
Cooling Fans	48-1
Cruise Control	48-1
Dash Gauges	48-1
Dash Panels	48-1
Distributor, Replace	41-4
Evaporator Core, Replace	41-6
1993–94	41-6
1995–96	41-6
Fuel Pump Relay Location	41-4
Fuse Panel & Flasher Location	41-4
Heater Core, Replace	41-6
Ignition Lock, Replace	41-5
Ignition Switch, Replace	41-5
Instrument Cluster, Replace	41-5
Neutral Safety Switch, Adjust	41-5
Passive Restraints	48-1
Precautions	41-4
Air Bag System	41-4
Audio Coded Anti-Theft System	41-4
Radio, Replace	41-6
Relay Center Location	41-4
Speed Controls	48-1
Starter Motors	48-1
Starter, Replace	41-4
Steering Columns	48-1
Steering Wheel, Replace	41-5
Less Air Bag	41-5
With Air Bag	41-5
Stop Light Switch, Replace	41-5
Wiper Motor, Replace	41-6
Front	41-6
Rear	41-6
Wiper Switch, Replace	41-6
Wiper Systems	48-1

PRECAUTIONS

AIR BAG SYSTEM

Refer to "Air Bag System Precautions" in the front of this manual for system disarming and arming procedures.

AUDIO CODED ANTI-THEFT SYSTEM

Some models are equipped with an audio coded anti-theft system that will disable the radio when the battery cable is disconnected. The system can be identified by the words "ANTI-THEFT SYSTEM" on the cassette tape lid. Obtain three digit customer code for input. Reset system after service as follows:

1. Obtain three digit audio anti-theft code.
2. Depress 1 (PROG) while depressing righthand side of TUNE SEEK button, - - - will appear in tape operation display.
3. To enter first digit, depress 1 (PROG) button repeatedly until the number of times depressed equals the first digit beginning with zero (depress the 1 button six times if the first digit is five).
4. To enter second digit, depress 2 (APS) button repeatedly until the number of times depressed equals the second digit beginning with zero.
5. To enter third digit, depress 3 (RPT) button repeatedly until the number of times depressed equals the third digit beginning with zero.
6. If - - - is displayed during code input, repeat procedure.
7. When code appears in display, depress and hold SCAN button until SEC appears.
8. When SEC disappears audio system should be operative.
9. If Err is displayed, repeat procedure. **Attempting to input code more than nine times may permanently disable audio system.**

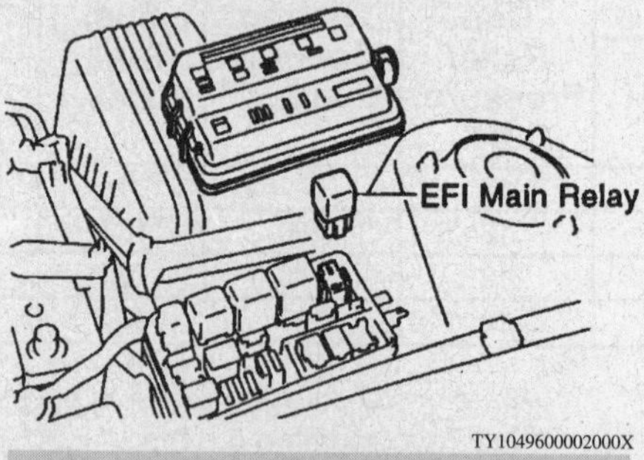

EFI Main Relay
TY1049600002000X

Fig. 1 Fuel pump relay location

FUSE PANEL & FLASHER LOCATION

There are two fuse blocks; the first is on the left front kick panel and the second is behind the battery. The turn signal/hazard flasher is under the dash, left of the steering column.

FUEL PUMP RELAY LOCATION

The fuel pump relay is located in the engine compartment relay center, on the lefthand side of the engine compartment, **Fig. 1.**

RELAY CENTER LOCATION

There are three relay centers. One is located below the righthand side of the instrument panel, another behind the upper center of the instrument cluster and the third is at the righthand side of the engine compartment.

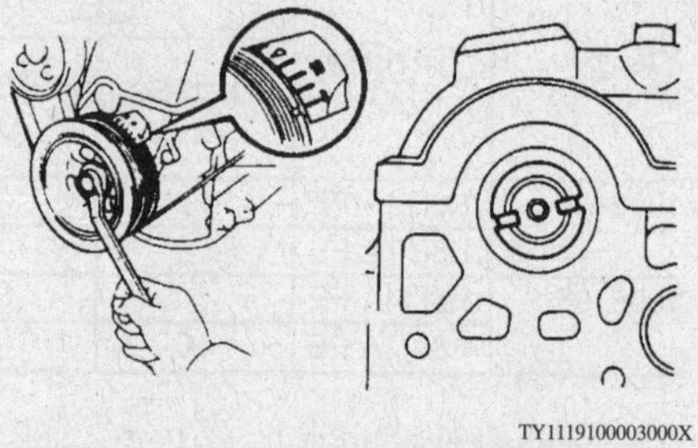

TY1119100003000X

Fig. 2 Setting No. 1 cylinder to TDC. 4A-FE engine

STARTER

REPLACE

1. **On models with audio coded anti-theft system,** obtain three digit anti-theft code.
2. **On all models,** disconnect battery ground cable.
3. Remove air cleaner assembly.
4. Disconnect electrical connectors from starter motor.
5. Remove starter motor attaching bolts, heat shield (if equipped), then the starter motor.
6. Reverse procedure to install. Reset audio anti-theft system, if equipped, as outlined under "Precautions."

DISTRIBUTOR

REPLACE

1. **On models with audio coded anti-theft system,** obtain three digit anti-theft code.
2. **On all models,** disconnect battery ground cable.
3. Disconnect electrical connectors, then mark and remove spark plug wires.
4. Remove distributor bolts, then distributor and O-ring.

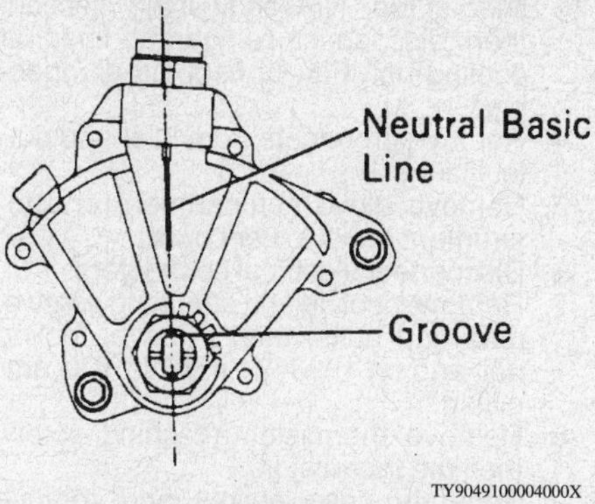
Neutral Basic Line
Groove
TY9049100004000X

Fig. 3 Neutral start switch adjustment

5. Reverse procedure to install, noting the following:
   a. Set No. 1 cylinder to TDC by turning crankshaft clockwise. Position slit of camshaft on righthand head, **Fig. 2.**
   b. Install new O-ring, then align cutout of coupling with mark on housing.
   c. Install distributor aligning center of flange with bolt hole on cylinder head.
   d. Adjust ignition timing. **Torque** hold-down bolt to 15 ft. lbs.
   e. Reset audio anti-theft system, if equipped, as outlined under "Precautions."

IGNITION LOCK

REPLACE

1. **On models with audio coded anti-theft system,**obtain three digit anti-theft code.
2. **On all models,** disconnect battery ground cable.
3. Turn ignition switch to ACC position.
4. Insert a small diameter rod into hole located on side of lock cylinder, then while holding down pin, remove lock cylinder.
5. Reverse procedure to install. Ensure lock cylinder is in ACC position. Reset audio anti-theft system, if equipped, as outlined under "Precautions."

IGNITION SWITCH

REPLACE

1. **On models with audio coded anti-theft system,**obtain three digit anti-theft code.
2. **On all models,** disconnect battery ground cable.
3. Remove steering wheel, if necessary, steering column garnish, if equipped, upper and lower covers.
4. Disconnect electrical connectors from ignition switch.
5. Turn ignition key to ACC position and remove ignition key cylinder.
6. Remove screw and ignition switch.
7. Reverse procedure to install. Reset audio anti-theft system, if equipped, as outlined under "Precautions."

NEUTRAL SAFETY SWITCH

ADJUST

1. Raise and support vehicle.
2. Disconnect shift control cable from shift lever, then loosen neutral safety switch bracket bolt.
3. Position transmission shift lever into Neutral.
4. Align switch shaft groove with neutral base line, then retighten switch bracket bolt, **Fig. 3.**
5. Connect electrical connector to switch.

STOP LIGHT SWITCH

REPLACE

1. Remove brake pedal tension spring.
2. Disconnect switch wire connector.
3. Remove switch mounting nut, then slide switch from mounting bracket.
4. Reverse procedure to install.

COMBINATION SWITCH

REPLACE

1. **On models with audio coded anti-theft system,** obtain three digit anti-theft code.
2. **On all models,** disconnect battery ground cable.
3. Remove steering wheel as outlined under "Steering Wheel, Replace."
4. Remove steering column upper and lower covers.
5. Remove combination switch with spiral cable assembly.
6. Reverse procedure to install. Reset audio anti-theft system, if equipped, as outlined under "Precautions."

STEERING WHEEL

REPLACE

LESS AIR BAG

1. Disconnect battery ground cable.
2. Remove trim cover from center of steering wheel.
3. Place alignment marks on steering wheel and mainshaft for assembly reference.
4. Remove nut attaching steering wheel to steering shaft.
5. Using a suitable puller, remove steering wheel. On some models, a steering wheel puller may not be necessary.
6. Reverse procedure to install.

WITH AIR BAG

1. **On models with audio coded anti-theft system,**obtain three digit anti-theft code.
2. **On all models,** position front wheels straight ahead.
3. Remove No. 2 and 3 steering wheel pad covers, then loosen steering wheel pad Torx screws until screw circumference groove catches on screw case.
4. Carefully pull steering wheel pad rearward, then disconnect air bag electrical connector. **Do not pull air bag wiring harness. Store air bag assembly with upper surface of pad facing upward.**

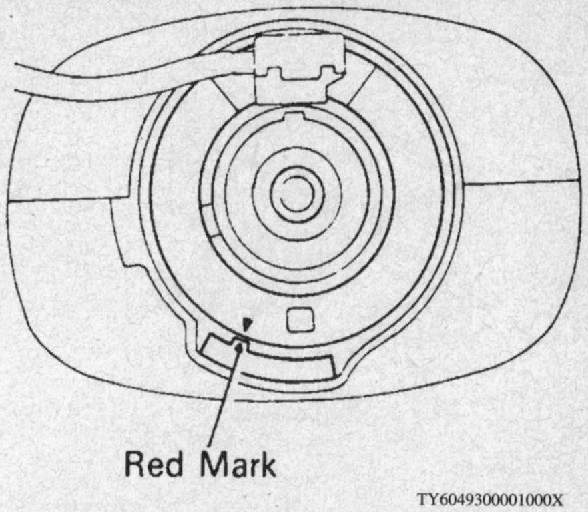
Red Mark
TY6049300001000X

Fig. 4 Spiral cable installation alignment

5. Disconnect steering wheel electrical connector, then remove set nut.
6. Place installation alignment marks on steering wheel and main shaft.
7. Using suitable steering wheel puller, remove steering wheel.
8. Reverse procedure to install, noting the following:
   a. If spiral cable was removed, ensure front wheels are straight ahead, the turn spiral cable counterclockwise by hand until becomes harder to turn cable, then rotate cable clockwise three turn to align red mark, **Fig. 4.**
   b. **Torque** steering wheel attaching bolt to 26 ft. lbs.
   c. **Torque** steering wheel pad attaching Torx screws to 78 inch lbs.
   d. Reset audio anti-theft system, if equipped, as outlined under "Precautions."

INSTRUMENT CLUSTER

REPLACE

1. **On models with audio coded anti-theft system,**obtain three digit anti-theft code.
2. **On all models,** disconnect battery ground cable.
3. Remove steering wheel.
4. Remove following parts:
   a. Steering column cover.
   b. Shifting hole bezel.
   c. Rear console box.
   d. Engine hood release lever.
   e. Lower finish panel.
   f. Combination switch.
   g. Lower panel.
5. Remove center cluster lower finish panel, then disconnect connector.
6. Remove center cluster finish panel and combination meter.
7. Remove following parts:
   a. Lower center finish panel.
   b. Cluster finish panel sub-assembly.
   c. Heater to register duct No. 2.
   d. Side defroster nozzle No. 2.
8. Disconnect connectors, then remove five bolts, then two bolts and junction block Nos. 1 and 4.
9. Remove instrument panel.

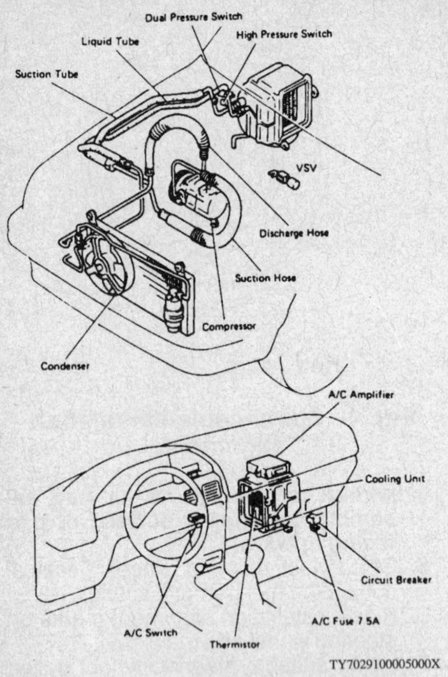
Dual Pressure Switch
Liquid Tube
High Pressure Switch
Suction Tube
VSV
Discharge Hose
Suction Hose
Compressor
Condenser
A/C Amplifier
Cooling Unit
Circuit Breaker
A/C Fuse 7.5A
A/C Switch
Thermistor
TY7029100005000X

Fig. 5 A/C system components. 1993–94

10. Reverse procedure to install. Reset audio anti-theft system, if equipped, as outlined under "Precautions."

RADIO

REPLACE

1. **On models with audio coded anti-theft system,** obtain three digit anti-theft code.
2. **On all models,** disconnect battery ground cable.
3. Remove instrument panel center finish panel.
4. Remove radio attaching screws, then pull rearward.
5. Disconnect electrical connectors and antenna lead, then remove radio.
6. Reverse procedure to install. Reset audio anti-theft system, if equipped, as outlined under "Precautions."

WIPER MOTOR

REPLACE

FRONT

1. **On models with audio coded anti-theft system,**obtain three digit anti-theft code.
2. **On all models,** disconnect battery ground cable.
3. Disconnect wiper motor wire connector, then remove wiper motor service cover, if equipped.
4. Remove wiper motor attaching bolts.
5. Using a screwdriver disconnect wiper link from wiper motor and remove wiper motor.
6. Reverse procedure to install. Reset audio anti-theft system, if equipped, as outlined under "Precautions."

REAR

1. Disconnect battery ground cable.
2. Remove wiper arm and rear door trim cover.
3. Disconnect wiper motor wire connector.
4. Remove wiper motor bracket attaching bolts and wiper motor and bracket.
5. Reverse procedure to install.

WIPER SWITCH

REPLACE

Refer to "Combination Switch, Replace" procedure.

BLOWER MOTOR

REPLACE

1. Disconnect battery ground cable.
2. Remove glove compartment assembly, then disconnect blower motor electrical connector.
3. Remove blower motor attaching screws, then the blower motor.
4. Reverse procedure to install.

HEATER CORE

REPLACE

1. Remove cooling unit as described under "Evaporator Core, Replace."
2. Drain engine coolant from radiator.
3. Disconnect water hoses from heater core pipes.
4. Remove pipe grommets.
5. Remove instrument panel as described under "Dash Panel Service."
6. Remove instrument panel reinforcement No. 1 brace.
7. Remove instrument panel reinforcement No. 2 brace.
8. Remove duct heater to register No. 3.
9. Remove front defroster nozzle.
10. Remove heater unit.
11. Reverse procedure to install.

EVAPORATOR CORE

REPLACE

1993–94

1. **On models with audio coded anti-theft system,**obtain three digit anti-theft code.
2. **On all models,** disconnect battery ground cable.
3. Discharge system refrigerant as outlined in the "Air Conditioning" section, then disconnect refrigerant lines at cooling unit **Fig. 5,** capping all openings.
4. Remove grommets from inlet and outlet fittings.
5. Remove glove compartment and instrument panel lower cover.
6. Disconnect electrical connectors.
7. Remove cooling unit attaching screws, nuts and bolts, then remove cooling unit and on 1993–94 models, A/C amplifier .
8. Remove thermistor attaching screw, then the thermistor.
9. Separate case halves and remove evaporator, **Fig. 6.**
10. Remove packing and clamp from evaporator outlet tube.
11. Disconnect liquid line tube from inlet fitting of expansion valve.
12. Disconnect expansion valve from inlet fitting of evaporator.
13. Reverse procedure to install, then evacuate and recharge system and check for leaks. If evaporator is replaced, add 1.4–1.7 oz. of new refrigerant oil to compressor. Reset audio anti-theft system, if equipped, as outlined under "Precautions."

1995–96

1. **On models with audio coded anti-theft system,**obtain three digit anti-theft code.
2. **On all models,** disconnect battery ground cable.
3. Discharge system refrigerant as outlined in "Air Conditioning" section, then disconnect refrigerant lines at cooling unit, capping all openings.
4. Remove front door scuff plate.
5. Remove glove compartment.
6. Disconnect blower resistor connector, **Fig. 7.**
7. Disconnect A/C amplifier connector.
8. Remove cooling unit and A/C amplifier.
9. Disconnect A/C harness from thermistor.
10. Remove thermistor connector from upper case.
11. Separate upper and lower evaporator case.
12. Remove evaporator core from cooling unit.
13. Remove blower motor resistor from upper case.
14. Remove thermistor from evaporator.
15. Remove expansion valve, liquid and suction tube from evaporator.
16. Reverse procedure to install, then evacuate and recharge system and check for leaks. If evaporator is replaced, add 1.4–1.7 oz. of new refrigerant oil to compressor. Reset audio anti-theft system, if equipped, as outlined under "Precautions."

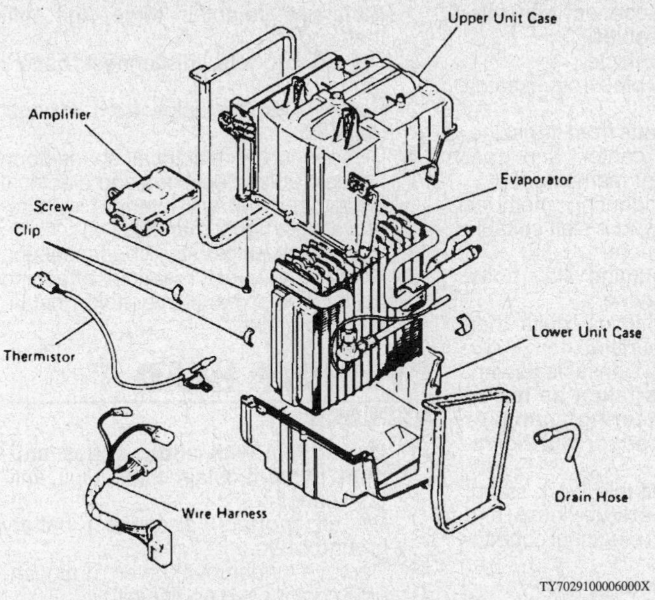
Upper Unit Case
Amplifier
Screw
Clip
Evaporator
Thermistor
Lower Unit Case
Drain Hose
Wire Harness
TY7029100006000X

Fig. 6 Exploded view of cooling unit. 1993–94

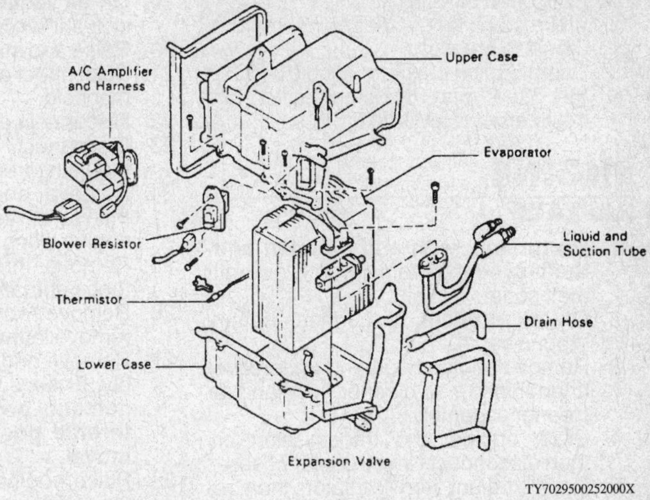
A/C Amplifier and Harness
Upper Case
Evaporator
Blower Resistor
Liquid and Suction Tube
Thermistor
Drain Hose
Lower Case
Expansion Valve
TY7029500252000X

Fig. 7 Exploded view of cooling unit. 1995–96

4A-FE 1.6L & 7A-FE 1.8L Engines

NOTE: On Air Bag Equipped Models, Refer To "Air Bag System Precautions" Located In The Front Of This Manual For System Disarming & Arming Procedures.

INDEX

	Page No.
Belt Tension Data	41-11
Camshaft, Replace	41-11
Compression Pressure	41-7
Cooling System Bleed	41-11
Cylinder Head, Replace	41-8
Engine Rebuilding Specifications	48-1
Engine, Replace	41-8
Exhaust Manifold, Replace	41-8
Fuel Filter, Replace	41-13
Fuel Pump, Replace	41-13
Hydraulic Lifters, Replace	41-10
Intake Manifold, Replace	41-8
Main & Rod Bearings	41-11
Oil Pan, Replace	41-11
Oil Pump, Replace	41-11
Oil Pump Service	41-11
Piston & Rod Assembly	41-11
Precautions	41-7
Air Bag Systems	41-7
Audio Coded Anti-Theft System	41-7
Radiator, Replace	41-13
Thermostat, Replace	41-11
Tightening Specifications	41-14
Timing Belt, Replace	41-10
Installation	41-10
Removal	41-10
Valve Adjustment	41-9
Valve Clearance Specifications	41-9
Valve Guides	41-9
Water Pump, Replace	41-12

PRECAUTIONS

AIR BAG SYSTEMS

Refer to "Air Bag System Precautions" in the front of this manual for system disarming and arming procedures.

AUDIO CODED ANTI-THEFT SYSTEM

Some models are equipped with an audio coded anti-theft system that will disable the radio when the battery cable is disconnected. The system can be identified by the words "ANTI-THEFT SYSTEM" on the cassette tape lid. Obtain three digit customer code for input. Reset system after service as follows:

1. Obtain three digit audio anti-theft code.
2. Depress 1 (PROG) while depressing righthand side of TUNE SEEK button, - - - will appear in tape operation display.
3. To enter the first digit, depress 1 (PROG) button repeatedly until the number of times depressed equals the first digit beginning with zero (depress the 1 button six times if the first digit is five).
4. To enter second digit, depress 2 (APS) button repeatedly until the number of times depressed equals the second digit beginning with zero.
5. To enter third digit, depress 3 (RPT) button repeatedly until the number of times depressed equals the third digit beginning with zero.
6. If - - - is displayed during code input, repeat procedure.
7. When code appears in display, depress and hold SCAN button until SEC appears.
8. When SEC disappears audio system should be operative.
9. If Err is displayed, repeat procedure. **Attempting to input code more than nine times may permanently disable audio system.**

COMPRESSION PRESSURE

1. Start engine and warm to normal operating temperature, then turn engine off.
2. Disconnect distributor connectors.
3. Disconnect spark plug wires.
4. Remove spark plugs.
5. Insert compression gauge into spark plug hole.

6. Fully open throttle.
7. While cranking engine, measure compression pressure.
8. Compression pressure should be 142–191 psi or more. Maximum difference between each cylinder is 14 psi.

ENGINE

REPLACE

1. **On models with audio coded anti-theft system,** obtain three digit anti-theft code.
2. **On all models,** disconnect battery ground cable.
3. Remove engine hood and undercover (if equipped), air cleaner hose and air cleaner assembly.
4. Drain engine and transmission oil, then disconnect two oil cooler hoses.
5. Drain coolant from radiator, then remove two heater hoses.
6. Disconnect coolant reservoir hose, then remove coolant reservoir.
7. Remove radiator attaching bolts, then the radiator and cooling fan as an assembly.
8. Disconnect throttle cables from carburetor, then all necessary electrical connectors.
9. Disconnect brake booster, power steering, MAP hose from gas filter, A/C actuator connector and A/C and EBCV vacuum hoses.
10. **On models with cruise control,** remove cruise control actuator.
11. Disconnect engine wire as follows:
    a. Remove lefthand front door scuff plate, lower finish panel and righthand front door scuff plate.
    b. Remove lower panel with glove compartment door.
    c. Remove radio, center cluster finish panel and rear console box.
    d. **On models with manual transmissions,** remove shift lever knob.
    e. **On models with automatic transmissions,** remove shifting hole bezel.
    f. **On all models,** remove finish lower center panel and floor carpet bracket.
    g. Disconnect three ECM connectors and cowl wire connector.
    h. Pull out engine wire from cowl panel.
12. Remove charcoal canister.
13. **On all models,** disconnect heater water hoses.
14. Disconnect fuel hoses from fuel pump.
15. **On models with power steering,** remove power steering pump and bracket and position aside. **Do not disconnect power steering pump hoses.**
16. **On models with A/C,** remove A/C compressor and bracket and position aside. **Do not disconnect refrigerant lines.**
17. **On all models,** disconnect speedometer cable from transaxle.
18. **On models with manual transmissions,** remove clutch release cylinder from transaxle and position aside. **Do not disconnect fluid line from release cylinder.**
19. **On all models,** disconnect transmission shifter control cables.
20. Raise and support vehicle.
21. Disconnect exhaust pipe from exhaust manifold.
22. Disconnect driveshafts from transaxle.
23. Disconnect front, center and rear mounting from center member.
24. Remove engine mounting member, then lower vehicle and install suitable engine lifting equipment.
25. Remove three mounting stay bolts, then righthand mounting.
26. Remove two mounting stay bolts, then remove lefthand mounting.
27. Remove engine and transaxle assembly. **Ensure care is taken as not to damage power steering pump or throttle position sensor during removal.**
28. Place engine in suitable work stand, then disconnect back-up lamp and neutral safety switch electrical connectors.
29. Remove rear end plate.
30. **On models with automatic transmission,** remove six torque convertor mounting bolts.
31. **On all models,** remove starter, then transaxle from engine.
32. Reverse procedure to install. Tighten attaching nuts and bolts to specifications. Reset audio anti-theft system, if equipped, as outlined under "Precautions."

INTAKE MANIFOLD

REPLACE

1. **On models with audio coded anti-theft system,** obtain three digit anti-theft code.
2. **On all models,** disconnect battery ground cable.
3. Remove air cleaner assembly.
4. Disconnect all electrical connectors, hoses, cables, fuel lines and electrical equipment that will interfere with removal of and intake manifold. Ensure following are removed:
    a. Ground strap.
    b. ISC valve connector.
    c. Cold start injector connector.
    d. Throttle position sensor connector.
    e. If equipped. EGR VSV and gas temperature sensor connectors.
    f. Vacuum sensor connector.
    g. Disconnect wire clamp from vacuum pipe and remove engine wire from manifold.
    h. Vacuum sensor hose from gas filter.
    i. Fuel return hose from air pipe.
5. Remove manifold stay, then water bypass hose from air pipe.
6. Remove intake retaining bolts, ground strap, intake manifold and gasket.
7. Reverse procedure to install. Tighten to specifications. Reset audio anti-theft system, if equipped, as outlined under "Precautions."

EXHAUST MANIFOLD

REPLACE

1. **On models with audio coded anti-theft system,** obtain three digit anti-theft code.
2. **On all models,** disconnect battery ground cable.
3. Remove exhaust pipe from exhaust manifold.
4. Disconnect all electrical connectors, hoses, cables, fuel lines and electrical equipment that will interfere with removal of exhaust manifold.
5. Remove manifold stay, then insulator.
6. Remove exhaust manifold attaching bolts, then exhaust manifold, insulators and gasket.

CYLINDER HEAD

REPLACE

1. **On models with audio coded anti-theft system,** obtain three digit anti-theft code.
2. **On all models,** disconnect battery ground cable.
3. Remove undercover, then drain engine coolant and engine oil.
4. Disconnect exhaust pipe from exhaust manifold.
5. Remove air cleaner assembly.
6. Remove distributor and alternator.
7. Disconnect accelerator cable and throttle cable, if equipped.
8. Remove cruise control actuator cable.
9. Disconnect all necessary electrical connectors.
10. Disconnect necessary vacuum lines.
11. Disconnect radiator hoses from engine.
12. Disconnect heater hoses, then remove water outlet.
13. Remove exhaust manifold upper shield, then the manifold.
14. Disconnect hoses from water inlet housing and remove housing.
15. **On models with 4A-FE engine,** remove fuel delivery pipe with fuel injectors as an assembly.
16. **On models with 7A-FE engine,** remove engine hanger nut, then engine hanger.
17. **On models with 7A-FE engine,** disconnect following hoses and connectors:
    a. Ground strap connector and MAP connector.
    b. A/C pressure switch.
    c. Engine wire from righthand fender apron.
    d. MAP sensor hose from gas filter.
    e. Brake booster vacuum hose.
    f. **On models with A/C,** A/C vacuum hose from actuator, then A/C actuator connector.
    g. **On models with power steering,** air hose from air pipe.
18. Disconnect engine wire clamp, then remove intake manifold stay and air pipe.
19. **On all models,** remove cold start injector pipe.
20. Remove EGR vacuum modulator.
21. Disconnect PCV and water hoses from intake manifold, then remove the manifold.
22. **On models with 7A-FE engine,** remove righthand engine mounting insulator.

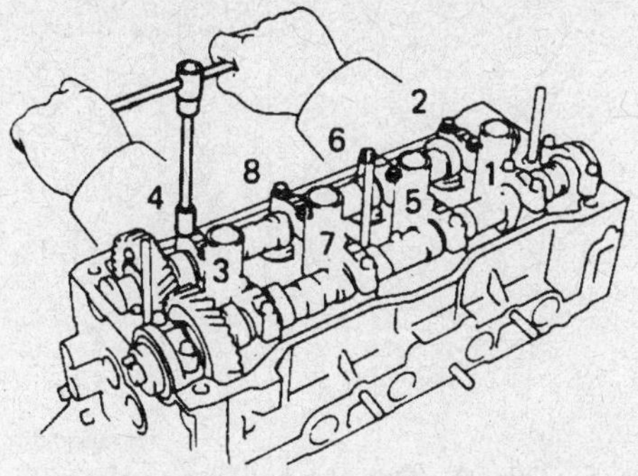

TY1069100085000X

Fig. 1 Intake camshaft bearing cap bolt removal

TY1069100086000X

Fig. 2 Exhaust camshaft bearing cap bolt removal. 4A-FE & 7A-FE engines

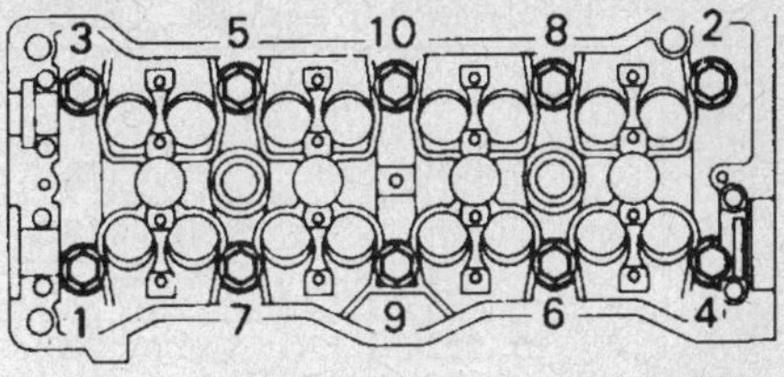

TY1069100087000X

Fig. 3 Cylinder head bolt removal sequence

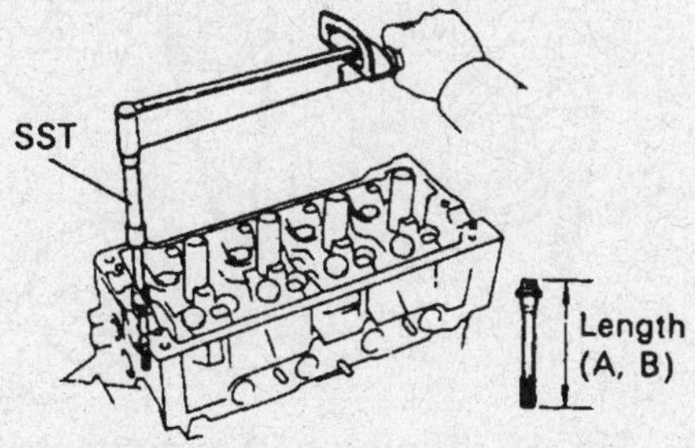

SST
Length
(A, B)

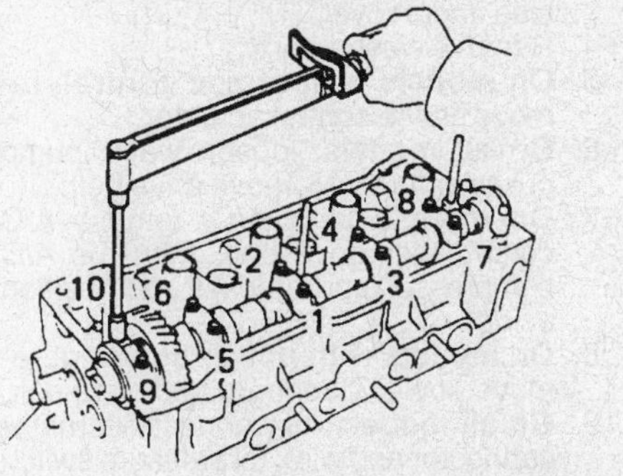

TY1069100090000X

Fig. 5 Exhaust camshaft bearing cap bolt tightening sequence

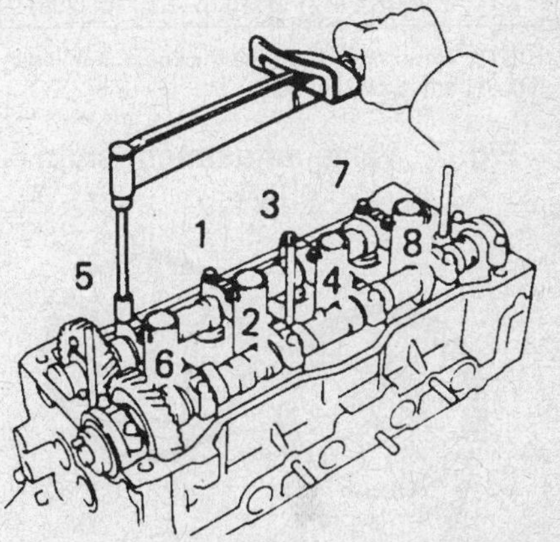

TY1069100091000X

Fig. 6 Intake camshaft bearing cap bolt tightening sequence

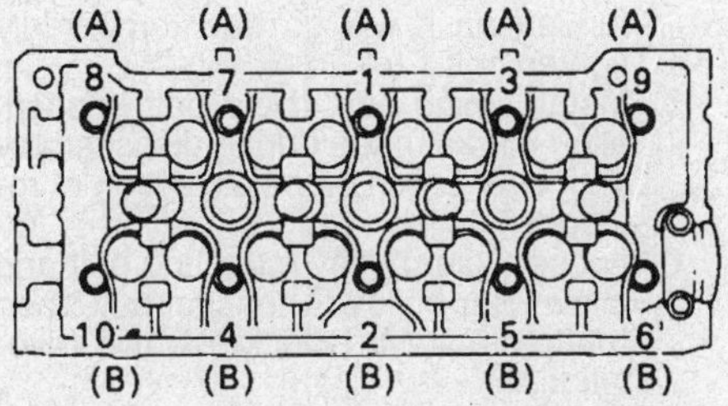

(A)
(A)
(A)
(A)
(A)
(B)
(B)
(B)
(B)
(B)

TY1069300089000X

Fig. 4 Cylinder head bolt tightening sequence

23. **On models with 4A-FE engine,** remove water pump pulley, then the drive belt.
24. **On all models,** remove power steering pump stay if equipped, then the spark plugs.
25. Remove cylinder head cover and gasket.
26. Remove No. 3 and No. 2 timing belt covers.
27. If timing belt is to be replaced, refer to "Timing Belt, Replace" for procedure. If timing belt is to be reused, proceed as follows:
    a. Turn crankshaft pulley and align groove with "0"mark on the No. 1 timing belt cover. **Ensure all valve lifters on the No. 1 cylinder are loose. If not, turn crankshaft pulley one complete revolution.**
    b. Place alignment marks on the camshaft timing pulley and belt.
    c. Loosen idler pulley bolt, then push idler pulley as far left as possible and temporarily tighten it.
    d. Remove timing belt from camshaft timing pulleys. **Support timing belt so meshing of crankshaft timing pulley and timing belt does not shift.**
    e. Remove camshaft timing pulley.
28. **On models with 7A-FE engine,** remove engine hanger, alternator bracket, oil dipstick guide and dipstick and water inlet No. 2.
29. Measure camshaft thrust clearance. If clearance is greater than .0043 inch, replace camshaft and/or cylinder head.
30. Loosen No. 1 intake and exhaust bearing cap bolts gradually, then remove bearing caps.
31. Secure intake camshaft sub-gear to main gear, using a suitable 6 mm bolt.
32. Loosen bearing cap bolts gradually in sequence shown in **Figs. 1 and 2,** then remove the bearing caps.
33. Remove intake and exhaust camshafts. **Do not pry on camshafts or cylinder head.**
34. Remove semi-circular plugs.
35. **On all models,** loosen and remove cylinder head attaching bolts gradually in sequence shown in **Fig. 3, Head warpage or cracking could result from removing cylinder head bolts in incorrect order.**
36. Remove cylinder head.
37. Reverse procedure to install. **Torque** cylinder head attaching bolts in several passes to 22 ft. lbs. in sequence shown, **Fig. 4.** Cylinder head bolts are in lengths of 3.54 inch (90 mm) and 4.25 inch (108 mm). Install bolts labeled "A" in righthand side and bolts labeled "B" in exhaust manifold side, **Fig. 4.**
38. **Torque** bearing cap attaching bolts gradually in three steps in sequence **Figs. 5 and 6,** to 9 ft. lbs.
39. Reset audio anti-theft system, if equipped, as outlined under "Precautions."

VALVE CLEARANCE SPECIFICATIONS

Clearance should be .006–.010 inch on intake valves and .010–.014 inch on exhaust valves.

VALVE ADJUSTMENT

Valve adjustment is accomplished by installing shims to achieve the proper valve clearance. Shims are available in .0020 inch (.050 mm) increments, **Fig. 7.**

1. With No. 1 piston at TDC on compression stroke, adjust following valves to specification: No. 1 intake and exhaust, No. 2 intake and No. 3 exhaust.
2. Turn crankshaft in normal direction of rotation one full revolution (360°) and adjust following cylinders valves to specification: No. 2 exhaust, No. 3 intake and No. 4 intake and exhaust.

VALVE GUIDES

1. Using a suitable tool and hammer, strike valve guide bushing to break it off at cylinder head casting.
2. Heat cylinder head to 176–212°F (80–100°C).

New shim thickness mm (in.)

Shim No.	Thickness	Shim No.	Thickness
1	2.55 (0.1004)	9	2.95 (0.1161)
2	2.60 (0.1024)	10	3.00 (0.1181)
3	2.65 (0.1043)	11	3.05 (0.1201)
4	2.70 (0.1063)	12	3.10 (0.1220)
5	2.75 (0.1083)	13	3.15 (0.1240)
6	2.80 (0.1102)	14	3.20 (0.1260)
7	2.85 (0.1122)	15	3.25 (0.1280)
8	2.90 (0.1142)	16	3.30 (0.1299)

HINT: New shims have the thickness in millimeters imprinted on the face.

TY1069300093000X

Fig. 7 Valve adjustment shim chart

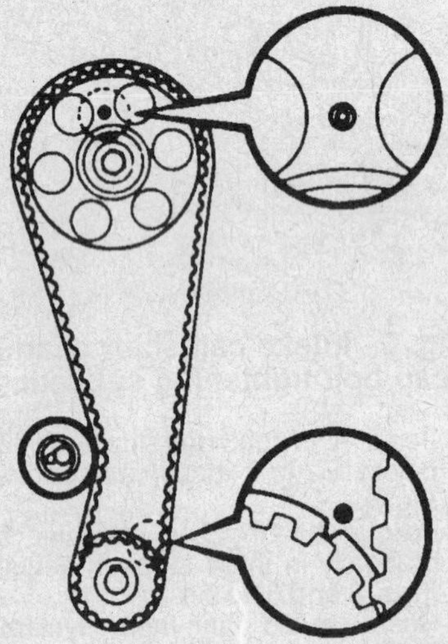

TY1069100099000X

Fig. 10 Timing belt alignment check. 4A-FE engine

3. Using suitable valve guide removal tool, tap out bushing.
4. Install snap ring on new valve guide, then install new valve guide using tool as described above, drive in from opposite side of removal.
5. Ream new valve guide, if necessary. Refer to "Valve Specifications" for stem clearances.

HYDRAULIC LIFTERS

REPLACE

Check lifters for excessive wear and/or damage. Replace worn or damaged valve lifters as required. Lubricate hydraulic valve lifter before installation.

TIMING BELT

REPLACE

REMOVAL

1. **On models with audio coded anti-theft system,**obtain three digit anti-theft code.
2. **On all models,** disconnect battery ground cable.

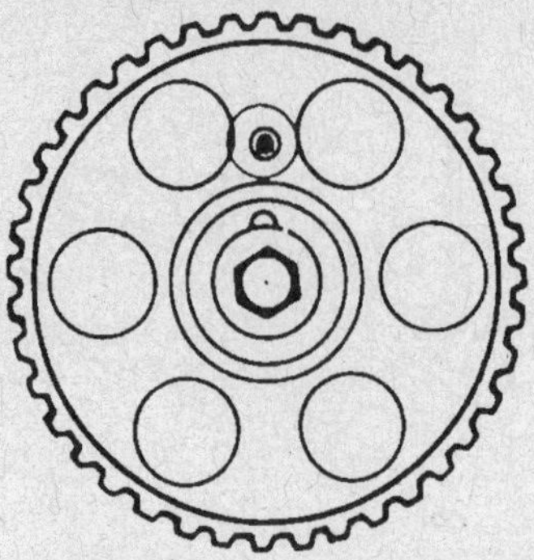

TY1069100097000X

Fig. 8 Camshaft sprocket alignment

3. Remove right front wheel, then right side undercover.
4. Remove washer tank.
5. **On models with cruise control,** remove cruise control actuator.
6. **On all models,** loosen water pump pulley bolts and remove drive belt.
7. **On models with A/C,** remove A/C compressor drive belt, then the A/C compressor and bracket and position aside.
8. **On models with power steering,** remove power steering pump drive belt.
9. **On all models,** disconnect alternator connector and wire, oil pressure switch connector and equipped with A/C, compressor connector. Remove bolt(s) with engine wire cover and disconnect engine wire from cylinder head.
10. Remove spark plugs, cylinder head cover and gasket.
11. Set cylinder No. 1 to TDC of compression stroke by rotating crankshaft pulley as necessary to align pulley groove with "0"timing mark. Ensure valve lifters on No. 1 cylinder are loose. If not rotate crankshaft pulley one complete revolution.
12. Remove righthand mounting insulator, then the water pump pulley.
13. Remove crankshaft pulley using a suitable puller.
14. Remove timing belt covers, then the timing belt guide from crankshaft.
15. Remove timing belt and idler pulley. **If belt is to be reused, place reference marks on belt and pulleys, then place a mark on belt noting direction of rotation.**
16. Remove crankshaft timing pulley.
17. Remove camshaft timing pulley.
18. Inspect idler pulley for smooth operation.
19. Measure tension spring free length, free length should be 1.512 inches (38.4 mm).
20. Check tension spring tension, tension should be 8.4 lbs. at 1.976 inch.

INSTALLATION

1. Install camshaft timing pulley, then tighten attaching bolt to specification.
2. Align hole in camshaft pulley with mark on bearing cap **Fig. 8.**
3. Install crankshaft timing pulley, then align timing marks as shown in **Fig. 9.**

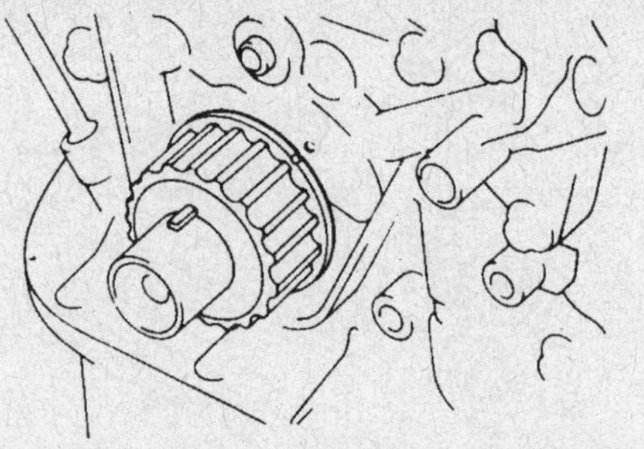

TY1069100098000X

Fig. 9 Crankshaft sprocket alignment

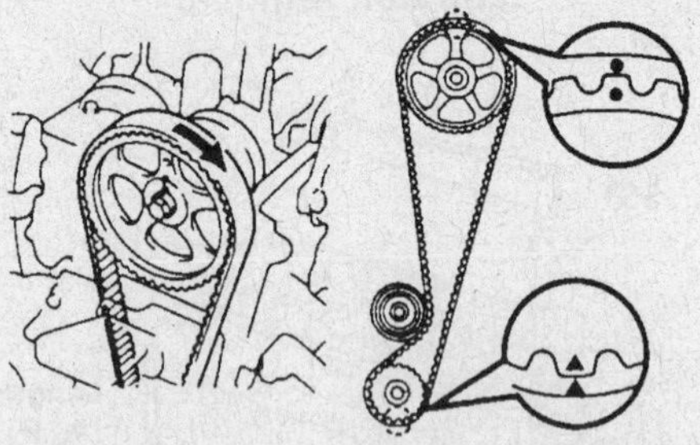

TY1069100100000X

Fig. 11 Timing belt alignment check. 7A-FE engine

4. Install timing belt idler pulley, then the tension spring. Position idler pulley as far left as it will go and temporarily tighten bolt.
5. Install timing belt. If old belt is used, align marks made during disassembly an install belt in proper direction of rotation.
6. Loosen idler pulley mounting bolt and allow idler pulley to tension belt, then rotate crankshaft clockwise two revolutions.
7. Check timing marks to ensure proper alignment as shown in **Figs. 10 and 11.**
8. Tighten idler pulley mounting bolt to specification.
9. Check timing belt deflection. Deflection should be .020–.024 inch (5–6 mm) at 4.4 lbs.
10. Install timing belt guide on crankshaft. **Cup side of guide should face outward.**
11. Install timing belt covers.
12. Install crankshaft pulley, then pulley attaching bolt and tighten to specification.
13. Install water pump pulley temporarily.
14. **On 1993–94 models,** install ground connector to ground wire on righthand side fender apron.
15. **On all models,** install righthand engine mount insulator.
16. Install righthand mounting stay.
17. Install cylinder head cover and gasket.
18. Install spark plugs.
19. Install power steering drive belt.
20. Install A/C compressor and bracket, then the drive belt.
21. Install alternator drive belt. Adjust drive belts to specifications as outlined under "Belt Tension Data."
22. Tighten water pump pulley bolts, then

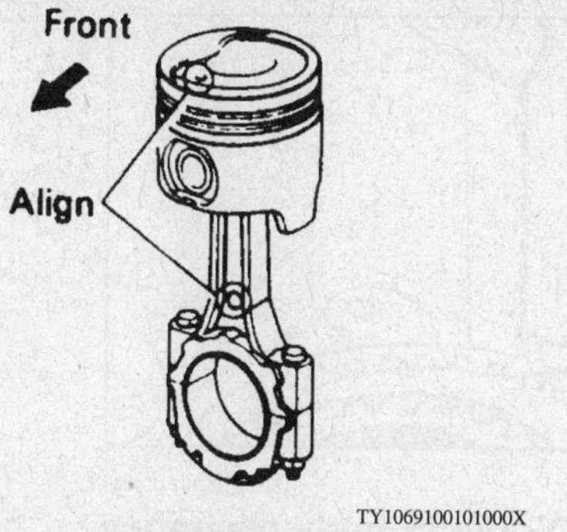
Front
Align
TY1069100101000X

Fig. 12 Piston & connecting rod assembly

install air cleaner assembly.

23. Install righthand undercover, then the right front wheel.
24. Reset audio anti-theft system, if equipped, as outlined under "Precautions."

CAMSHAFT

REPLACE

Refer to "Cylinder Head, Replace" for camshaft removal procedure.

PISTON & ROD ASSEMBLY

Pistons are available in standard and oversize of .050 inch. If piston bore is not within specifications, replace piston and/or cylinder block. When assembling piston onto connecting rod, ensure mark on top of piston and mark on connecting rod are on same side, **Fig. 12.** When installing piston and connecting rod assembly, ensure mark on top of piston is facing toward front of engine.

MAIN & ROD BEARINGS

Main and connecting rod bearings are available in standard and undersizes of .010 inch (.25mm).

OIL PAN

REPLACE

1. **On models with audio coded anti-theft system,**obtain three digit anti-theft code.
2. **On all models,** disconnect battery ground cable.
3. Scribe hood installation alignment marks, then remove hood and engine undercovers.
4. Drain engine oil.
5. Remove timing belt as outlined.
6. Remove oil dipstick and dipstick guide.
7. Remove front exhaust pipe.
8. Remove center mount and stiffening plate.
9. Disconnect oil cooler hose and union from oil pan.
10. Remove oil pan attaching nuts and bolts, then remove pan.
11. Remove oil strainer.

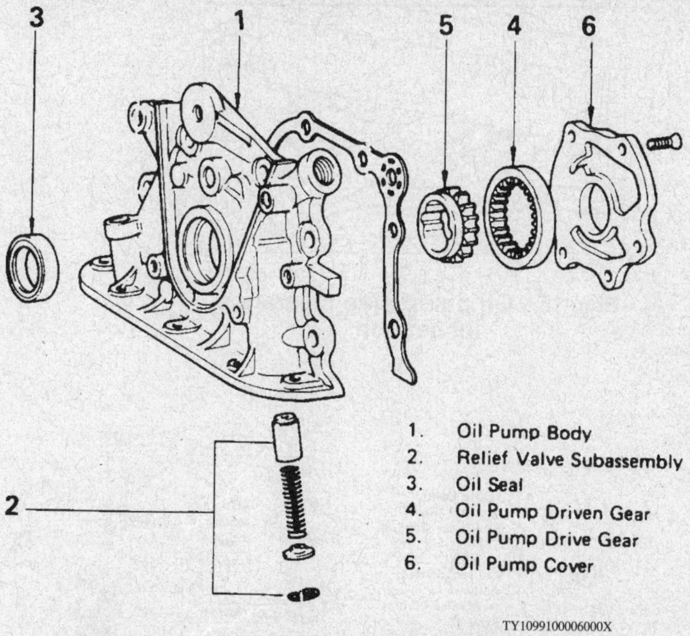
3
1
5
4
6
2
1. Oil Pump Body
2. Relief Valve Subassembly
3. Oil Seal
4. Oil Pump Driven Gear
5. Oil Pump Drive Gear
6. Oil Pump Cover
TY1099100006000X

Fig. 13 Exploded view of oil pump

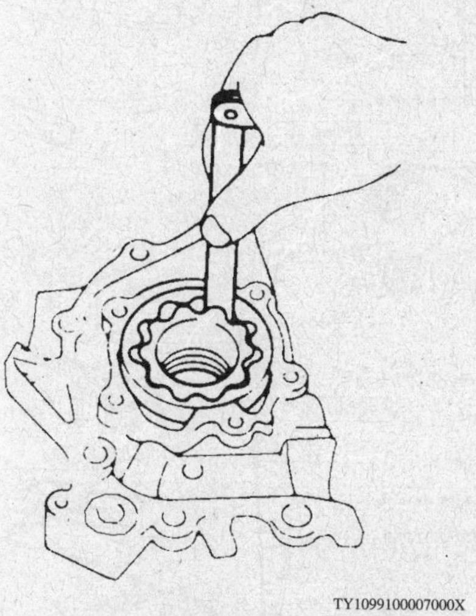
TY1099100007000X

Fig. 14 Oil pump tip clearance inspection

12. Remove oil baffle plate.
13. Remove oil pump attaching bolts, then oil pump.
14. Reverse procedure to install. Reset audio anti-theft system, if equipped, as outlined under "Precautions."

OIL PUMP

REPLACE

Refer to "Oil Pan, Replace" for procedure.

OIL PUMP SERVICE

1. Remove oil pump cover, drive gear and driven gear, **Fig. 13.**
2. Remove oil seal and relief valve subassembly.
3. Check contact surfaces of oil seal and drive gear for damage and wear.
4. Using suitable feeler gauge, measure clearance between rotor tips, **Fig. 14.** If clearance is greater than .0138 inch (.35 mm), replace rotor set.
5. Measure side clearance between rotor and cover, **Fig. 15.** If clearance exceeds .0039 inch (.10 mm), replace rotor or pump body as necessary.
6. Measure body clearance between driven rotor and pump body, **Fig. 16.** If clearance is greater than .0079 inch (.20 mm), replace rotor or pump body as necessary.

BELT TENSION DATA

Belt tension is as follows using a belt tension gauge. A new belt is considered used after five minutes of use.

Engine	Belt	New Lbs.	Used Lbs.
4A-FE	Air Cond.	140–180	80–120
	Alternator	140–180	110–150
	Power Steer.	100–150	60–100
7A-FE	Air Cond.	140–180	80–120
	Alternator	170–180	95–135
	Power Steer.	100–150	60–100

COOLING SYSTEM BLEED

These engines do not require a specified bleed procedure. After filling cooling system, run engine to operating temperature with radiator/pressure cap off. Air will then be automatically bled through cap opening.

THERMOSTAT

REPLACE

On 1993–94 models, complete removal of the thermostat without reinstalling may have an adverse affect by lowering

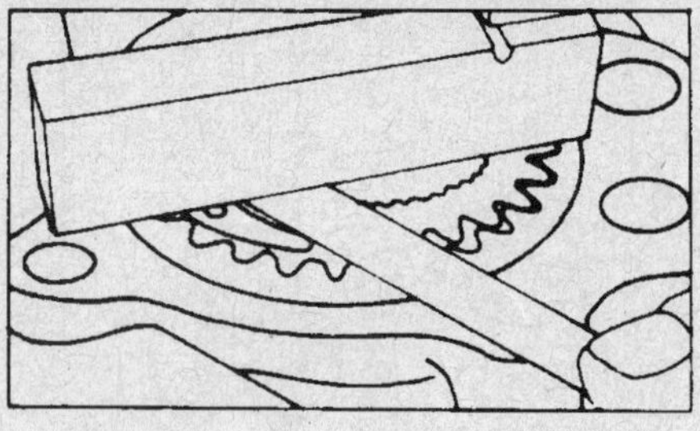

TY1099100008000X

Fig. 15 Oil pump side clearance inspection

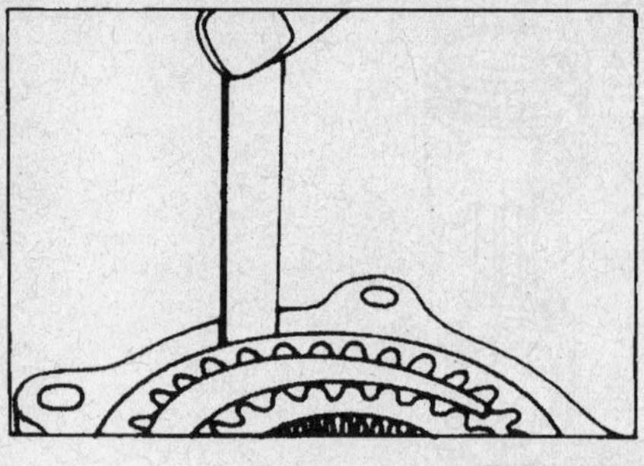

TY1099100009000X

Fig. 16 Oil pump body clearance inspection

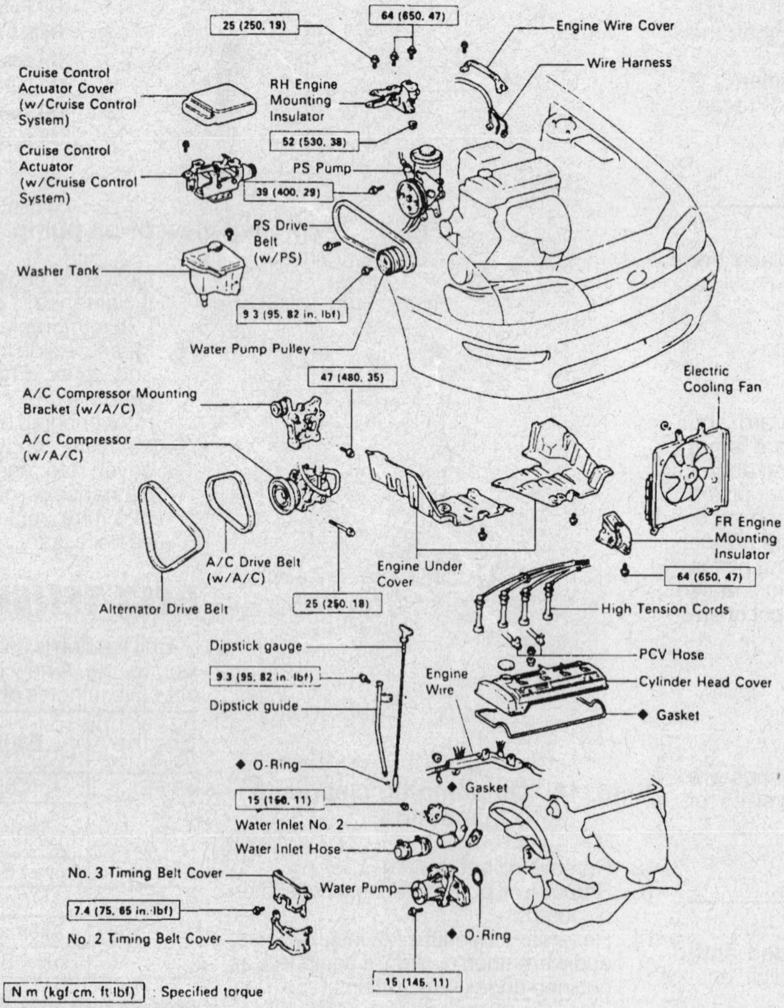
25 (250, 19)
64 (650, 47)
Engine Wire Cover
Wire Harness
Cruise Control Actuator Cover (w/Cruise Control System)
RH Engine Mounting Insulator
52 (530, 38)
Cruise Control Actuator (w/Cruise Control System)
PS Pump
39 (400, 29)
PS Drive Belt (w/PS)
Washer Tank
9.3 (95, 82 in. lbf)
Water Pump Pulley
Electric Cooling Fan
47 (480, 35)
A/C Compressor Mounting Bracket (w/A/C)
A/C Compressor (w/A/C)
FR Engine Mounting Insulator
A/C Drive Belt (w/A/C)
Engine Under Cover
64 (650, 47)
Alternator Drive Belt
25 (250, 18)
High Tension Cords
Dipstick gauge
PCV Hose
9.3 (95, 82 in. lbf)
Engine Wire
Cylinder Head Cover
Dipstick guide
◆ Gasket
◆ O-Ring
◆ Gasket
15 (150, 11)
Water Inlet No. 2
Water Inlet Hose
No. 3 Timing Belt Cover
Water Pump
7.4 (75, 65 in.·lbf)
No. 2 Timing Belt Cover
◆ O-Ring
15 (145, 11)
N·m (kgf·cm, ft·lbf) : Specified torque
◆ Non-reusable part

Fig. 17 Water inlet & bypass hoses

the engine's cooling efficiency. Do not remove the thermostat even if the engine tends to overheat.

1. **On models with audio coded anti-theft system,**obtain three digit anti-theft code.
2. **On all models,** disconnect battery ground cable.
3. Drain engine coolant.
4. Disconnect ECT switch connector.
5. **On all models,** remove water inlet housing attaching nuts, then remove water housing.
6. Remove thermostat and gasket.
7. Reverse procedure to install. Reset audio anti-theft system, if equipped, as outlined under "Precautions."

WATER PUMP

REPLACE

1. **On models with audio coded anti-theft system,**obtain three digit anti-theft code.
2. **On all models,** disconnect battery ground cable.
3. Drain coolant.
4. Remove righthand engine mount.
5. Remove No. 2 and 3 timing belt covers.
6. **On models with power steering,** remove front mount hole cover, remove mount attaching nut and through bolt, then remove mount.
7. **On models with power steering,** remove electric cooling fan.

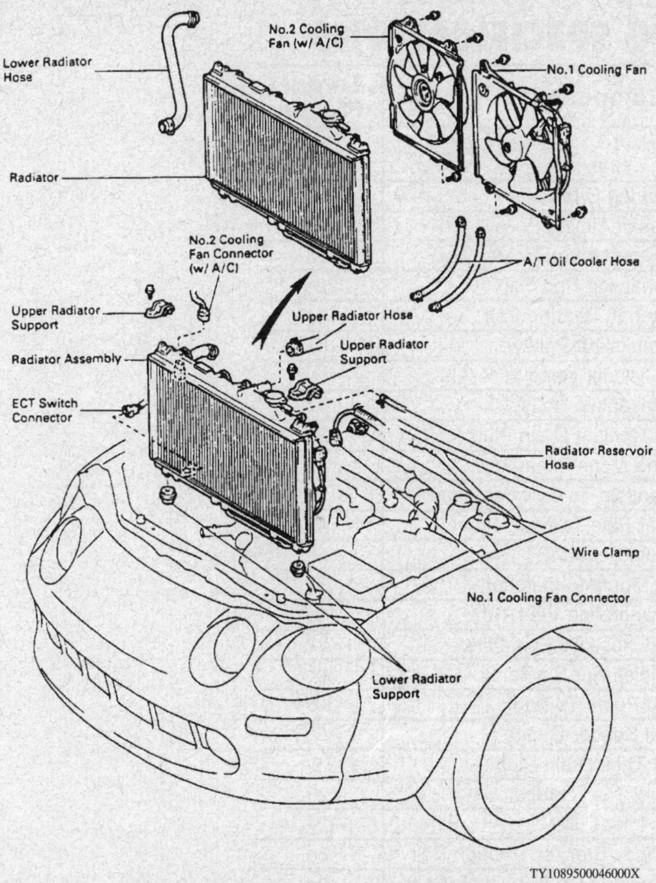
Lower Radiator Hose
No.2 Cooling Fan (w/ A/C)
No.1 Cooling Fan
Radiator
No.2 Cooling Fan Connector (w/ A/C)
A/T Oil Cooler Hose
Upper Radiator Support
Upper Radiator Hose
Upper Radiator Support
Radiator Assembly
ECT Switch Connector
Radiator Reservoir Hose
Wire Clamp
No.1 Cooling Fan Connector
Lower Radiator Support
TY1089500046000X

Fig. 18 Radiator replacement

8. **On all models,** disconnect engine wire.
9. Disconnect water inlet and water by-pass hoses from inlet pipe, **Fig. 17.**
10. Disconnect heater water hose from inlet pipe.
11. Remove water inlet pipe attaching nuts and clamp bolts, then remove inlet pipe and O-ring.
12. Remove water pump and water pump pulley. **Do not get coolant on timing belt.**
13. Reverse procedure to install. Reset audio anti-theft system, if equipped, as outlined under "Precautions."

RADIATOR

REPLACE

1. Disconnect battery ground cable.
2. Drain engine coolant.
3. Disconnect cooling fan electrical connector, **Fig. 18.**
4. Disconnect radiator hoses.
5. Disconnect coolant reservoir hose.

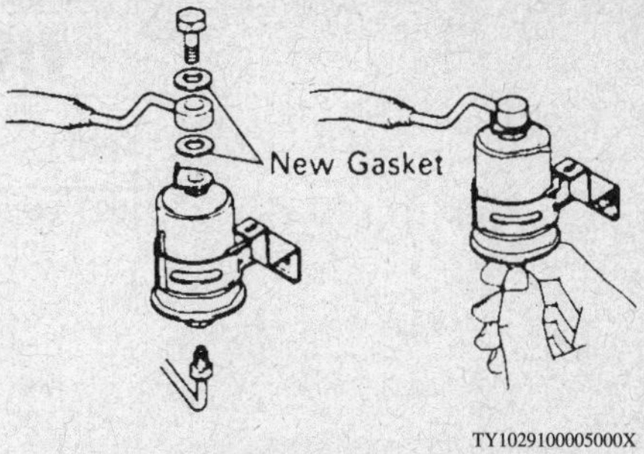
New Gasket
TY1029100005000X

Fig. 19 Fuel filter replacement

6. **On models with automatic transaxle,** disconnect oil cooler hoses.
7. **On all models,** remove radiator supports, radiator and electric cooling fan.
8. Remove electric cooling fan from radiator.
9. Reverse procedure to install.

FUEL PUMP

REPLACE

1. **On models with audio coded anti-theft system,**obtain three digit anti-theft code.
2. **On all models,** disconnect battery ground cable.
3. Remove rear seat cushion.
4. Disconnect fuel pump connector, then remove five screws and service hole cover.
5. Remove fuel pump lead wire, then disconnect fuel line from fuel pump bracket. **Remove fuel filter cap to prevent fuel from flowing out.**
6. Remove fuel pump bracket assembly, gasket and pull pump out.
7. Reverse procedure to install. Reset audio anti-theft system, if equipped, as outlined under "Precautions."

FUEL FILTER

REPLACE

Refer to **Fig. 19**for replacement procedure.

TIGHTENING SPECIFICATIONS

Year	Component	Torque/ Ft. Lbs.
1993–96	A/C Compressor To A/C Compressor Bracket	18
	Bearing Cap Bolts	①
	Camshaft Timing Pulley	43
	Center & Rear Mount To Member	38
	Connecting Rod Cap	22③
	Crankshaft Bearing Cap	44
	Crankshaft Pulley	87
	Cylinder Head	①
	Driveplate (A/T)	47
	Engine Coolant Drain Plug	25
	Engine Mount Member	45
	Exhaust Manifold To Cylinder Head	25
	Exhaust Pipe-To-Manifold	46
	Flywheel (M/T)	58
	Front Mount to Member	35
	Fuel Evaporation Vent Tube	16②
	Fuel Inlet Hose To Fuel Filter	22
	Fuel Inlet Pipe To Tank	30②
	Fuel Pump To Tank	30②
	Fuel Sender Gauge	30②
	Fuel Tank Drain Plug	9
	Fuel Tank Straps	29
	Idler Pulley	27
	Insulator To Body Bracket Through Bolt	64
	Insulator To Engine Mount Bracket (Bolt)	29
	Insulator To Engine Mount Bracket (Nut)	38
	Intake Manifold To Cylinder Head	29
	LH Mounting Insulator To Bracket (Bolt)	47
	LH Mounting Insulator To Bracket (Nut)	38
	LH Mount Insulator To Transaxle Case	35
	LH Mount Stay	15
	LH Mount Through Bolt	64
	Oil Cooler Pipe	25
	Oil Dipstick Guide	7
	Oil Pan	43②
	Oil Pump	16③
	Oil Strainer	7
	Power Steering Pump Bracket	29
	RH Mounting Insulator To Bracket Bolt	47
	RH Mounting Insulator To Bracket Nut	38
	RH Mount Stay	31
	RH Mount Through Bolt	64
	Spark Plug	13
	Thermostat Water Inlet	7
	Water Pump	11

① — Refer to "Cylinder Head, Replace."
② — Inch lbs.
③ — Tighten an additional 90°.

Clutch & Manual Transaxle

NOTE: On Air Bag Equipped Models, Refer To "Air Bag System Precautions" Located In The Front Of This Manual For System Disarming & Arming Procedures.

INDEX

	Page No.
Adjustments	41-15
Clutch Pedal Height	41-15
Clutch, Replace	41-16
Hydraulic System Service	41-15
Clutch Release Cylinder, Replace	41-15
Clutch Slave Cylinder, Replace	41-15
Clutch System Bleed	41-15
Precautions	41-15
Air Bag Systems	41-15
Audio Coded Anti-Theft System	41-15
Tightening Specifications	41-17
Transaxle, Replace	41-16
C50 & C52 Transaxle	41-16

PRECAUTIONS

AIR BAG SYSTEMS

Refer to "Air Bag System Precautions" in the front of this manual for system disarming and arming procedures.

AUDIO CODED ANTI-THEFT SYSTEM

Some models are equipped with an audio coded anti-theft system that will disable the radio when the battery cable is disconnected. The system can be identified by the words "ANTI-THEFT SYSTEM" on the cassette tape lid. Obtain three digit customer code for input. Reset system after service as follows:

1. Obtain three digit audio anti-theft code.
2. Depress 1 (PROG) while depressing righthand side of TUNE SEEK button, - - - will appear in tape operation display.
3. To enter the first digit, depress 1 (PROG) button repeatedly until the number of times depressed equals the first digit beginning with zero (depress the 1 button six times if the first digit is five).
4. To enter second digit, depress 2 (APS) button repeatedly until the number of times depressed equals the second digit beginning with zero.
5. To enter third digit, depress 3 (RPT) button repeatedly until the number of times depressed equals the third digit beginning with zero.
6. If - - - is displayed during code input, repeat procedure.
7. When code appears in display, depress and hold SCAN button until SEC appears.
8. When SEC disappears audio system should be operative.
9. If Err is displayed, repeat procedure. **Attempting to input code more than nine times may permanently disable audio system.**

ADJUSTMENTS

CLUTCH PEDAL HEIGHT

1. Measure clutch pedal height as shown, **Fig. 1.**
2. Clutch pedal height should be 5.61–6.00 inches.

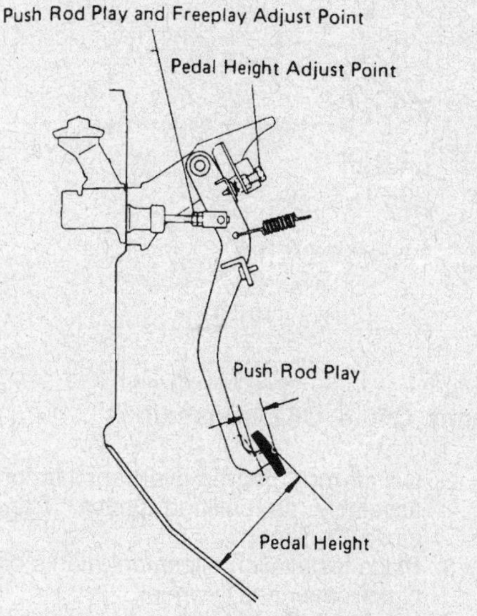

Push Rod Play and Freeplay Adjust Point
Pedal Height Adjust Point
Push Rod Play
Pedal Height
TY5049100013000X

Fig. 1 Clutch pedal height

3. If clutch pedal height is not as specified, remove lower instrument panel finish panel and air duct.
4. Loosen clutch pedal locknut, then rotate stopper bolt until specified height is achieved.
5. Tighten locknut.
6. Check clutch pedal freeplay by depressing clutch pedal until resistance is felt. Freeplay should be .197–.591 inch. pushrod play at top of pedal should be .039–.197 inch.
7. If necessary to adjust freeplay, loosen locknut and rotate pushrod until freeplay is as specified.
8. Tighten locknut.
9. Ensure clutch pedal height and freeplay are as specified, then reinstall air duct and finish panel.

HYDRAULIC SYSTEM SERVICE

CLUTCH SLAVE CYLINDER, REPLACE

1. **On models with audio coded anti-theft system,** obtain three digit anti-theft code.
2. Remove brake booster.
3. Remove clutch tube from clutch hose.
4. Remove clip, clevis pin and return spring.
5. Remove clutch slave cylinder, then if necessary clutch tube from cylinder.
6. Reverse procedure to install. Tighten to specifications, then bleed and adjust system. Reset audio anti-theft system, if equipped, as outlined under "Precautions."

CLUTCH RELEASE CYLINDER, REPLACE

1. Using suitable tool, disconnect clutch line tube, using suitable container to catch fluid.
2. Remove release cylinder attaching bolts, then remove cylinder.
3. Reverse procedure to install. Tighten attaching bolts to specifications, then bleed clutch system as outlined under "Clutch System Bleed."

CLUTCH SYSTEM BLEED

If any service is performed on the clutch system or air is suspected in the clutch lines, bleed the system.

1. Fill clutch reservoir with suitable brake fluid. **Do not allow fluid to come in contact with painted surfaces.**
2. Check reservoir frequently, add fluid as required.
3. Connect vinyl tube to bleeder plug, then insert other tube end in half full container of brake fluid.
4. Slowly pump clutch pedal several times.
5. While depressing, pedal, loosen bleeder plug until fluid runs out, then close bleeder plug.
6. Repeat procedure until air bubbles are no longer evident in fluid. **Do not reuse fluid.**

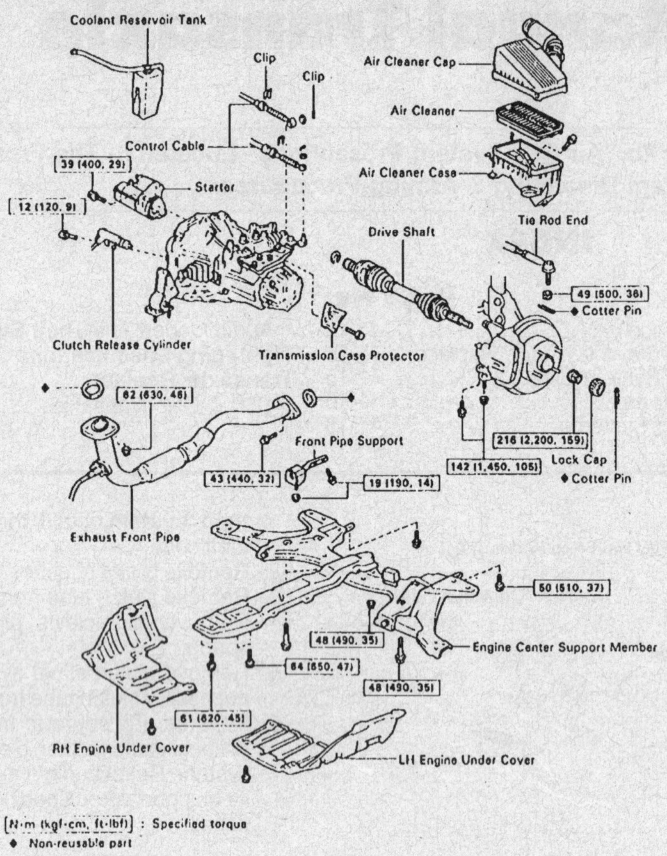
Coolant Reservoir Tank
Clip
Clip
Air Cleaner Cap
Air Cleaner
Control Cable
39 (400, 29)
Starter
12 (120, 9)
Air Cleaner Case
Drive Shaft
Tie Rod End
49 (500, 36)
Cotter Pin
Clutch Release Cylinder
Transmission Case Protector
62 (630, 46)
Front Pipe Support
216 (2,200, 159)
142 (1,450, 105)
Lock Cap
Cotter Pin
43 (440, 32)
19 (190, 14)
Exhaust Front Pipe
50 (510, 37)
48 (490, 35)
Engine Center Support Member
64 (650, 47)
48 (490, 35)
61 (620, 45)
RH Engine Under Cover
LH Engine Under Cover
N·m (kgf·cm, ft·lbf) : Specified torque
Non-reusable part

TY5039300189000X

Fig. 2 Transaxle replacement. C50 & C52 transaxle

CLUTCH

REPLACE

1. **On models with audio coded anti-theft system,**obtain three digit anti-theft code.
2. **On all models,** remove transmission assembly as outlined under "Transaxle, Replace."
3. Place installation alignment marks on clutch cover and flywheel.
4. Loosen each set bolt one turn at a time until spring tension is released.
5. Remove clutch cover attaching bolts, then remove cover and disc.
6. Remove release bearing, fork and boot.
7. Using suitable calipers, measure clutch disc rivet head depth. Minimum rivet depth should be .012 inch. If not as indicated, replace clutch disc.
8. Using suitable dial indicator, measure flywheel runout. Maximum runout should be .004 inch. If not as indicated, replace flywheel.
9. Measure clutch disc runout, maximum runout is .031 inch. If not as indicated, replace disc.
10. Reverse to install, noting the following:
    a. Using suitable tool, install clutch disc.
    b. Match clutch cover and flywheel alignment marks, then **torque** cover bolts to 14 ft. lbs. one turn at a time in a criss-cross pattern, ensuring clutch disc and pressure plate remain aligned.
    c. Reset audio anti-theft system, if equipped, as outlined under "Precautions."

TRANSAXLE

REPLACE

The transaxle and engine must be removed from the vehicle as an assembly.

C50 & C52 TRANSAXLE

Refer to **Fig. 2,** for transaxle replacement procedure.

TIGHTENING SPECIFICATIONS

Year	Component	Torque/ Ft. Lbs.
1993–96	Back-Up Lamp Switch	30
	Bleeder Plug	8
	Bond Cable To Body	14
	Clutch Accumulator	15
	Clutch Cover	14
	Clutch Line Union	11
	Clutch Master Cylinder	9
	Control Shaft Cover	14
	Drain Plug	29
	Driveshaft To Side Gear Shaft	27
	Exhaust Pipe Clamp Bolt	14
	Exhaust Pipe To Converter	32
	Exhaust Pipe To Manifold	46
	Filler Plug	29
	Front Bearing Retainer	8
	Front Engine Mount	58
	Lock Ball Assembly	29
	Lower Ball Joint	47
	Master Cylinder Reservoir Tank	18
	Output Shaft Bearing Lock Plate	8
	Release Cylinder To Transaxle	9
	Shift Fork To Set Bolt	12
	Speedometer Driven Gear Lock Plate	8
	Transaxle Case Protector	9
	Transaxle Case To Case Cover	13
	Transaxle Case To Transaxle Case	22
	Transaxle To Engine (8mm)	8
	Transaxle To Engine (10mm)	17
	Transaxle To Engine (10mm)	34
	Transaxle To Engine (12mm)	47
	Transaxle To Starter	29

Rear Axle & Suspension

INDEX

	Page No.
Coil Spring, Replace	41-19
Hub & Bearing, Replace	41-18
Lower Suspension Arm & Strut Rod, Replace	41-19
Rear Axle Carrier, Replace	41-18
Shock Absorber, Replace	41-19
Stabilizer Bar, Replace	41-19
Strut, Replace	41-18
Strut Rod, Replace	41-18
Suspension Arm, Replace	41-19
Tightening Specifications	41-20

HUB & BEARING

REPLACE

1. Remove brake drum or rotor and check bearing axial play. Play should not exceed .002 inch.
2. **On models with anti-lock brakes,** remove ABS speed sensor.
3. **On models with drum brakes,** disconnect brake line from wheel cylinder, **Fig. 1.**
4. **On all models,** remove 4 bolts holding axle hub to axle carrier and remove axle hub and rear brake assembly.
5. Remove O-ring.
6. Place hub in suitable vise. Using hammer and chisel, loosen stake part of nut and remove nut.
7. Using axle shaft remover tool No. 09550-20014, or equivalent, push axle shaft off axle hub.
8. Remove inside portion of bearing inner race.
9. Using puller tool No. 09950-20014, or equivalent, pull outside portion of bearing inner race from axle shaft.
10. Remove oil seal.
11. To replace wheel bearing, place old inner race (outside) on bearing, then using bearing remover tools Nos. 09228-22020 and 09636-20010, or equivalents, press out bearing.
12. Apply MP grease around bearing outer race and replacer pipe tool No. 09316-60010, or equivalent, press new bearing into axle hub.
13. Using countershaft bearing replacer tool No. 09310-35010, or equivalent, drive new oil seal into axle hub.
14. Apply MP grease to oil seal lip.
15. Place inside portion of bearing inner race on bearing.
16. Using installer tool Nos. 09636-20010 and 09228-22020, or equivalents, press inner race with axle hub onto axle shaft.
17. Tighten axle hub nut to specification.
18. **On models with anti-lock brakes,** install ABS speed sensor.
19. Place new O-ring on axle carrier.
20. Install axle hub and rear brake assembly with four bolts. Tighten bolts to specifications.
21. **On models with drum brakes,** connect brake line to wheel cylinder, then install brake drum and bleed brakes.
22. **On models with disc brakes,** install rotor and caliper assembly.

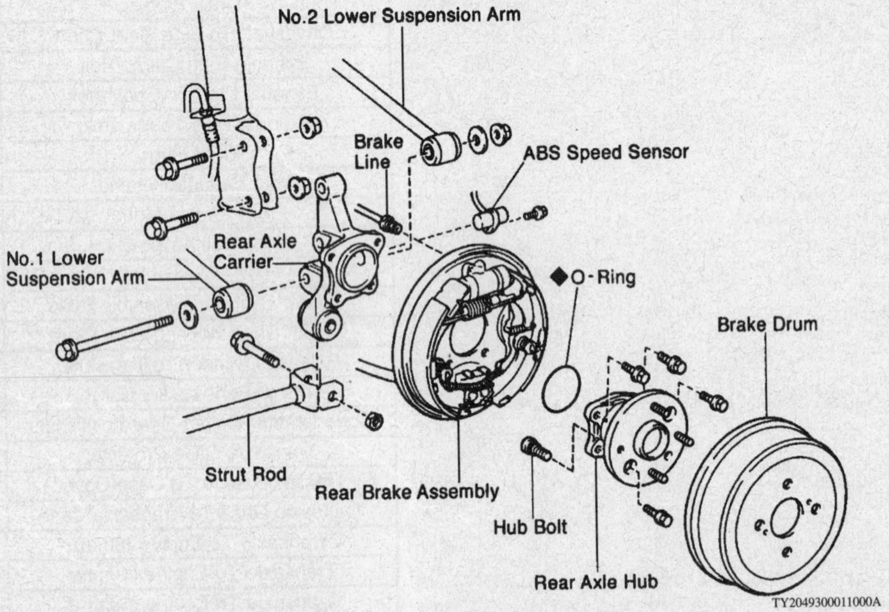

No.2 Lower Suspension Arm
Brake Line
ABS Speed Sensor
Rear Axle Carrier
No.1 Lower Suspension Arm
◆O-Ring
Brake Drum
Strut Rod
Rear Brake Assembly
Hub Bolt
Rear Axle Hub
TY2049300011000A

Fig. 1 Rear wheel bearing replacement

REAR AXLE CARRIER

REPLACE

1. Remove rear axle hub as outlined.
2. Remove brake hose from strut assembly, then backing plate from rear axle carrier.
3. Loosen three nuts but do not remove bolts.
4. Remove strut rod to rear axle carrier bolt and nut and disconnect strut rod from carrier.
5. Remove three nuts, bolts and carrier.
6. Reverse procedure to install. Tighten nuts and bolts to specifications.

STRUT

REPLACE

1. Remove rear seat cushion and seatback.
2. Remove rear wheel.
3. **On models with ABS,** disconnect ABS speed sensor wire harness clamp from strut, **Fig. 2.**
4. **On all models,** remove brake hose retaining clip from strut and disconnect brake line using tool No. 09023-00100, or equivalent.
5. Disconnect stabilizer bar link from strut.
6. Loosen (do not remove) lower strut retaining nuts.
7. Support rear axle carrier with suitable jack.
8. Remove cap from suspension support.
9. Loosen (do not remove) center nut at shock tower in engine compartment, then remove remaining three upper strut retaining nuts. **Center nut should only be loosened if strut is to be disassembled.**
10. Lower rear axle carrier and remove two lower strut retaining bolts.
11. Remove strut assembly.
12. Reverse procedure to install. Tighten to specifications.

STRUT ROD

REPLACE

1. Raise and support rear of vehicle.
2. Remove nut and bolt securing strut rod to axle carrier.
3. Remove nut and bolt securing strut rod to body, then remove strut rod.
4. Reverse procedure to install. Prior to tightening attaching nuts and bolts, lower vehicle to ground and bounce vehicle up and down several times to stabilize suspension, then tighten attaching nuts and bolts to specification with vehicle weight on suspension.

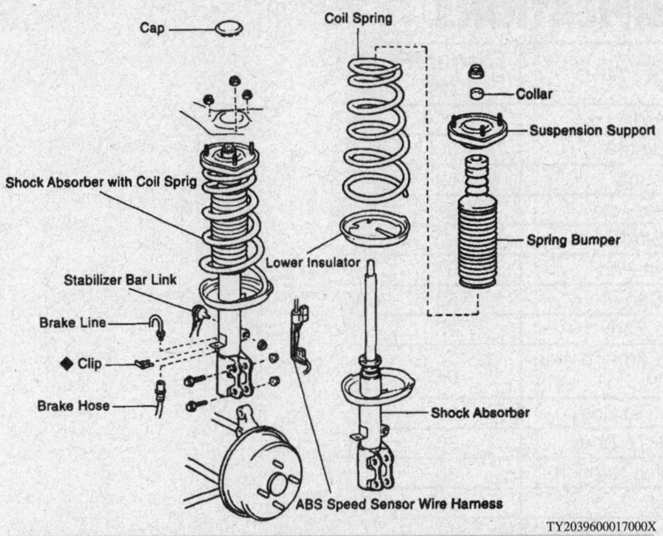
Cap
Coil Spring
Collar
Suspension Support
Shock Absorber with Coil Sprig
Spring Bumper
Lower Insulator
Stabilizer Bar Link
Brake Line
◆ Clip
Brake Hose
Shock Absorber
ABS Speed Sensor Wire Harness
TY2039600017000X

Fig. 2 Rear suspension strut assembly

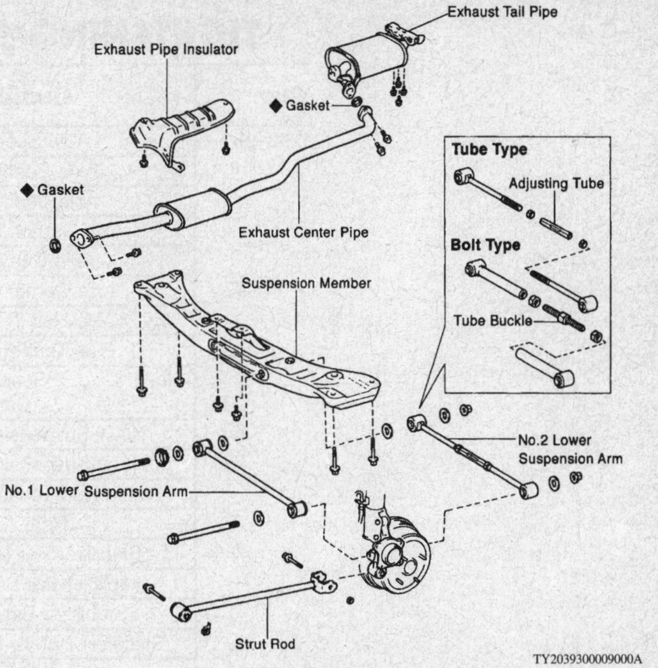
Exhaust Tail Pipe
Exhaust Pipe Insulator
◆ Gasket
Tube Type
Adjusting Tube
◆ Gasket
Exhaust Center Pipe
Bolt Type
Suspension Member
Tube Buckle
No.2 Lower Suspension Arm
No.1 Lower Suspension Arm
Strut Rod
TY2039300009000A

Fig. 3 Rear suspension

SHOCK ABSORBER

REPLACE

Refer to "Strut, Replace" for procedure.

COIL SPRING

REPLACE

1. Remove strut assembly as described under "Strut, Replace."
2. Install strut assembly lower bracket bolts and nuts, then place strut assembly in vise so vise grips lower bracket at bolts.
3. Using spring compression tool No. 09727–30020, or equivalent, compress coil spring.
4. Remove collar and upper strut suspension support retaining nut, **Fig. 2.**
5. Remove coil spring.
6. Reverse procedure to assemble.

STABILIZER BAR

REPLACE

1. Raise and support rear of vehicle, then remove rear wheels.
2. Remove both stabilizer bar links and bushings.
3. Remove exhaust center pipe and tail pipe.
4. Remove exhaust pipe insulator and right fuel tank band. **Do not remove left fuel tank band.**
5. Support suspension member with a jack, remove six bolts and lower suspension member.
6. Remove stabilizer bar. Reverse procedure to install, tighten bolts to specifications.

SUSPENSION ARM

REPLACE

Refer to "Lower Suspension Arm & Strut Rod, Replace " for procedure.

LOWER SUSPENSION ARM & STRUT ROD

REPLACE

1. Raise and support vehicle, then remove rear tires.
2. Remove strut rods two attaching nuts and bolts, then strut rod, **Fig. 3.**
3. **On models with ABS,** disconnect LSPV spring from lower arm.
4. **On all models,** remove No. 2 lower suspension arm attaching nuts, then suspension arm.
5. Remove stabilizer bar bushing retainer, then exhaust center and tail pipe.
6. Support suspension member with a suitable jack, remove six nuts, then left and right suspension member lower stopper.
7. Lower suspension member, remove No. 1 lower suspension arm attaching bolts, then suspension arm.
8. Reverse procedure to install, tighten nuts and bolts to specifications.

TIGHTENING SPECIFICATIONS

Year	Component	Torque/Ft. Lbs.
1993–96	ABS Speed Sensor	69①
	Axle Bearing Locknut	90
	Axle Bearing Set Bolt	59
	Axle Carrier To Lower Arm	87
	Axle Carrier To Strut	105
	Axle Carrier To Strut Rod	67
	Axle Hub To Axle Carrier	59
	Fuel Tank Band To Body	29
	No. 1 & No. 2 Suspension Arm To Axle Carrier	65
	No. 1 Suspension Arm To Body	65
	No. 2 Suspension Arm To Body	80
	Piston Rod To Suspension Support	36
	Rear Axle Hub	59
	Stabilizer Bar Bracket To Body	14
	Stabilizer Bar Bushing Retainers	14
	Stabilizer Bar Link Set Nuts	33
	Stabilizer Bar To Stabilizer Bar Link	26
	Strut Rod To Body	65
	Strut Rod To Rear Axle Carrier Nuts	67
	Strut Assembly Suspension Support Retaining Nut	34
	Strut Lower Retaining Bolts	105
	Strut Upper Retaining Nuts	29
	Suspension Arm Locknut	41
	Suspension Member To Body	55
	Suspension Upper Support To Body	29
	Suspension Upper Support To Piston Rod	36
	Wheel Lug Nut	76

① — Inch lbs.

Front Suspension & Steering

NOTE: On Air Bag Equipped Models, Refer To "Air Bag System Precautions" Located In The Front Of This Manual For System Disarming & Arming Procedures.

INDEX

	Page No.
Ball Joint Inspection	41-22
Coil Spring, Replace	41-22
Lower Suspension Arm, Replace	41-22
Manual Steering Gears	48-1
Power Steering	48-1
Power Steering Gear, Replace	41-23
Power Steering Pump, Replace	41-24
Power Steering System Bleed	41-24
Precautions	41-21
Air Bag Systems	41-21
Audio Coded Anti-Theft System	41-21
Shock Absorber, Replace	41-22
Stabilizer Bar, Replace	41-23
Strut, Replace	41-22
Tightening Specifications	41-25
Wheel Bearing, Adjust	41-21
Wheel Hub & Steering Knuckle, Replace	41-21

PRECAUTIONS

AIR BAG SYSTEMS

Refer to "Air Bag System Precautions" in the front of this manual for system disarming and arming procedures.

AUDIO CODED ANTI-THEFT SYSTEM

Some models are equipped with an audio coded anti-theft system that will disable the radio when the battery cable is disconnected. The system can be identified by the words "ANTI-THEFT SYSTEM" on the cassette tape lid. Obtain three digit customer code for input. Reset system after service as follows:

1. Obtain three digit audio anti-theft code.
2. Depress 1 (PROG) while depressing righthand side of TUNE SEEK button, - - - will appear in tape operation display.
3. To enter the first digit, depress 1 (PROG) button repeatedly until the number of times depressed equals the first digit beginning with zero (depress the 1 button six times if the first digit is five).
4. To enter second digit, depress 2 (APS) button repeatedly until the number of times depressed equals the second digit beginning with zero.
5. To enter third digit, depress 3 (RPT) button repeatedly until the number of times depressed equals the third digit beginning with zero.
6. If - - - is displayed during code input, repeat procedure.
7. When code appears in display, depress and hold SCAN button until SEC appears.
8. When SEC disappears audio system should be operative.
9. If Err is displayed, repeat procedure. **Attempting to input code more than nine times may permanently disable audio system.**

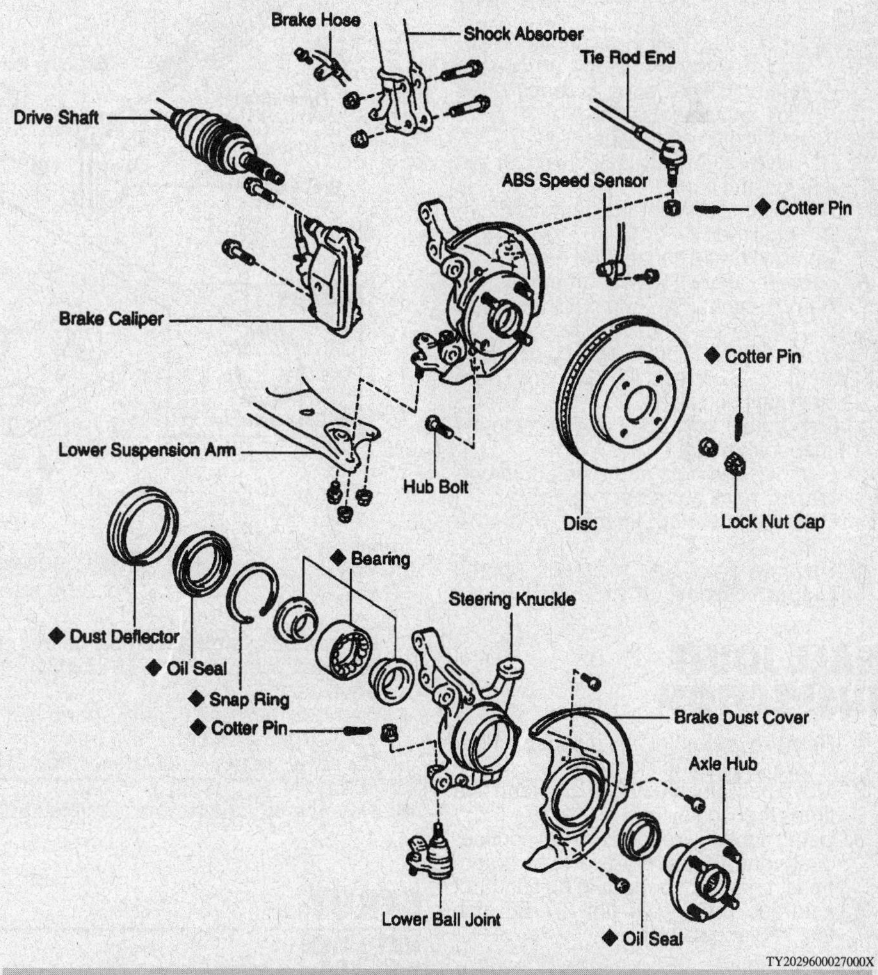

Brake Hose
Shock Absorber
Tie Rod End
Drive Shaft
ABS Speed Sensor
◆ Cotter Pin
Brake Caliper
◆ Cotter Pin
Lower Suspension Arm
Hub Bolt
Disc
Lock Nut Cap
◆ Bearing
Steering Knuckle
◆ Dust Deflector
◆ Oil Seal
◆ Snap Ring
◆ Cotter Pin
Brake Dust Cover
Axle Hub
Lower Ball Joint
◆ Oil Seal
TY2029600027000X

Fig. 1 Front axle hub & steering knuckle replacement

WHEEL BEARING

ADJUST

Corolla models incorporate lubed for life, sealed front wheel bearings with no provision for adjustment.

WHEEL HUB & STEERING KNUCKLE

REPLACE

1. Remove front wheel.
2. Remove ABS speed sensor, **Fig. 1.**
3. Disconnect brake hose from shock absorber.
4. Check for bearing backlash and axle hub deviation as follows:
   a. Remove brake caliper and disc. Support caliper securely.
   b. Place dial indicator near center of axle hub and check backlash in bearing shaft direction. If backlash measurement exceeds .0020 inch, replace bearing.
   c. Using dial indicator, check deviation at surface of axle hub outside hub bolt. If deviation exceeds .0028 inch, replace axle hub.
   d. Install disc and caliper.
5. Remove driveshaft locknut cotter pin and locknut cap.
6. While depressing brake, remove driveshaft locknut.
7. Remove brake caliper and disc.
8. Loosen lower shock absorber nuts.
9. Remove cotter pin and nut from lower ball joint at steering knuckle.
10. Using tool No. 09628–62011, or equivalent, disconnect tie rod end from steering knuckle.
11. Disconnect lower ball joint from lower suspension arm.
12. Remove two nuts and a bolt from bottom of shock absorber.
13. Remove steering knuckle with axle hub.
14. Reverse procedure to install. Tighten to specifications.

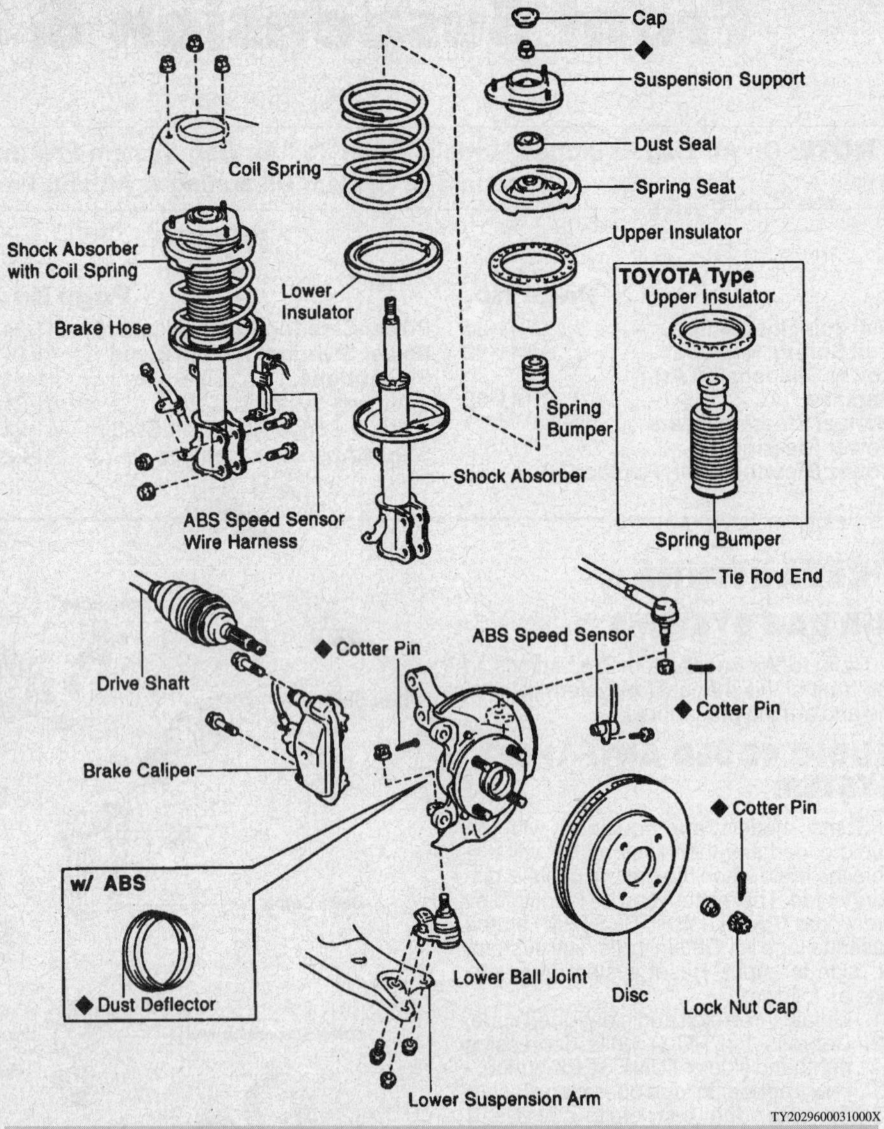

Cap
◆
Suspension Support
Dust Seal
Coil Spring
Spring Seat
Upper Insulator
Shock Absorber with Coil Spring
Lower Insulator
TOYOTA Type
Upper Insulator
Brake Hose
Spring Bumper
Shock Absorber
ABS Speed Sensor Wire Harness
Spring Bumper
Tie Rod End
ABS Speed Sensor
◆ Cotter Pin
Drive Shaft
◆ Cotter Pin
Brake Caliper
◆ Cotter Pin
w/ ABS
◆ Dust Deflector
Lower Ball Joint
Disc
Lock Nut Cap
Lower Suspension Arm
TY2029600031000X

Fig. 2 Front suspension strut assembly

BALL JOINT INSPECTION

1. Remove ball joint as outlined under "Lower Ball Joint, Replace."
2. Move ball joint stud back and forth five times then install nut.
3. Using tighten wrench, turn nut continuously one turn every two to four seconds, take torque reading on fifth turn.
4. If torque reading is not 8.7–26 inch lbs., replace ball joint.

COIL SPRING

REPLACE

1. Remove strut assembly, **Fig. 2,** as described under "Strut, Replace."
2. Place strut assembly in vise, then using spring compressor tool No. 09727–30020, or equivalent, compress coil spring.
3. Remove upper cap and suspension support from strut assembly using nut removal tool No. 09729–22031, or equivalent.
4. Remove dust seal and spring seat from strut assembly.
5. Remove upper insulator and coil spring.
6. Reverse procedure to assemble strut.

STRUT

REPLACE

1. Remove front wheel and disconnect ABS wire harness clamp.
2. Disconnect brake hose from shock absorber, **Fig. 2.**
3. Remove three nuts on upper side of strut in engine compartment.
4. Remove two nuts and bolts from lower side of strut assembly.
5. Remove strut assembly.
6. Reverse procedure to install. Tighten to specifications.

SHOCK ABSORBER

REPLACE

Refer to "Strut, Replace" for procedure.

LOWER SUSPENSION ARM

REPLACE

1. Raise and support vehicle, then remove front wheel.
2. Remove stabilizer bar, **Fig. 3,** as described under "Stabilizer Bar, Replace."
3. Disconnect lower suspension arm from lower ball joint.
4. Disconnect righthand side of lower suspension arm.
5. Disconnect lefthand side of lower suspension arm and remove front suspension crossmember with lower suspension arm.

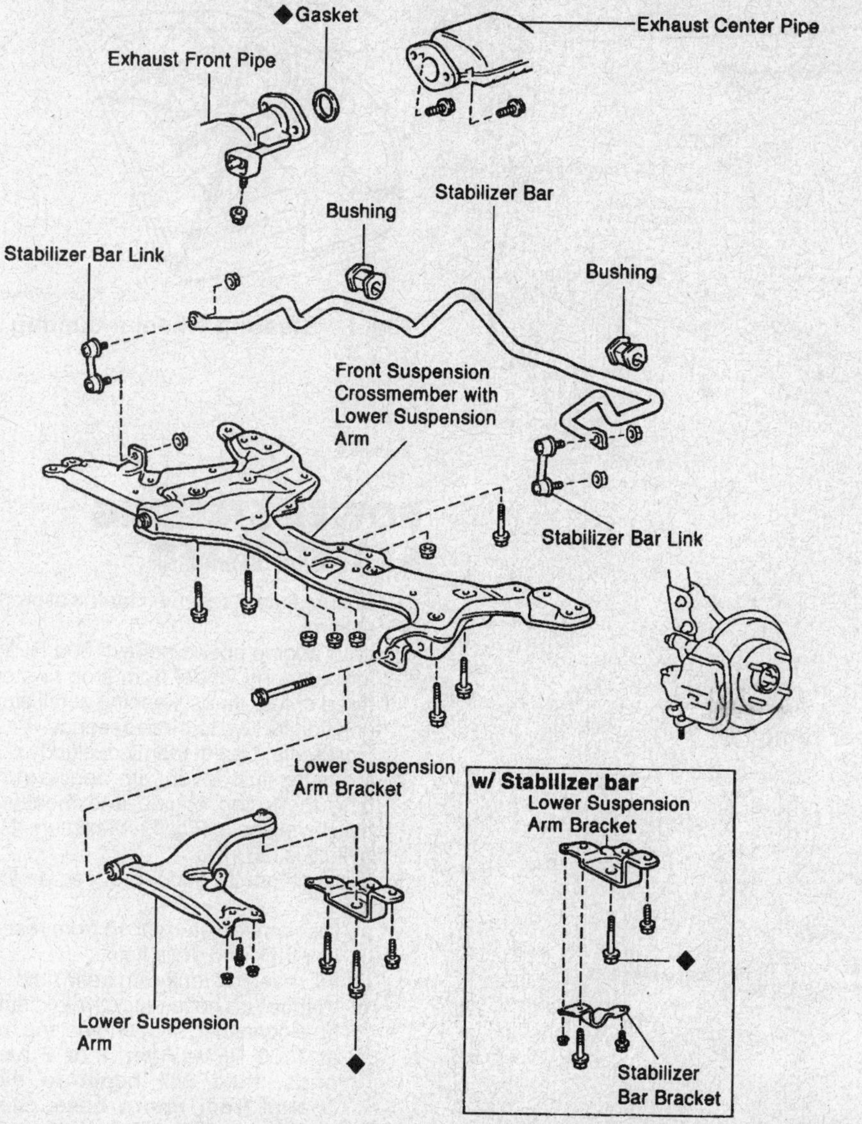
◆Gasket
Exhaust Front Pipe
Exhaust Center Pipe
Stabilizer Bar
Bushing
Stabilizer Bar Link
Bushing
Front Suspension
Crossmember with
Lower Suspension
Arm
Stabilizer Bar Link
Lower Suspension
Arm Bracket
w/ Stabilizer bar
Lower Suspension
Arm Bracket
Lower Suspension
Arm
Stabilizer
Bar Bracket

TY2029300007000A

Fig. 3 Front suspension components

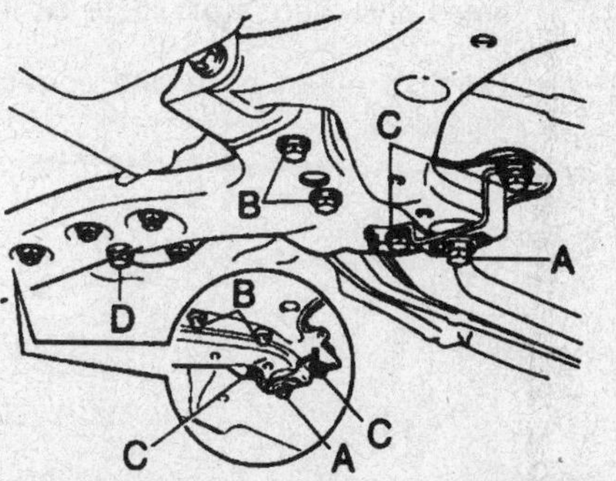
C
B
A
D
B
C
C
A

TY2029600030000X

Fig. 5 Crossmember & lefthand side lower suspension arm bolts

6. Remove lower suspension arm from suspension crossmember.
7. Reverse procedure to install, noting the following:
   a. Referring to **Fig. 4, torque** "A" bolt to 161 ft. lbs., "B" bolt to 129 ft. lbs. and "C" bolts to 109 ft. lbs.
   b. Referring to **Fig. 5, torque** "A" bolt to 129 ft. lbs., "B" bolt to 167 ft. lbs. and "C" bolts to 109 ft. lbs. **Torque** nut to 45 ft. lbs.

STABILIZER BAR

REPLACE

1. Remove front wheels.
2. Disconnect exhaust pipe.
3. Disconnect left and right stabilizer bar links, **Fig. 3.** If ball joint turns together with nut, use a hexagon wrench to hold stud.
4. Remove left and right stabilizer bar brackets and bushing.
5. Remove stabilizer bar.
6. Reverse procedure to install. Referring to **Fig. 6, torque** stabilizer bar bracket "A" bolt to 109 ft. lbs., "B" bolt to 37 ft. lbs. and nut to 14 ft. lbs. Tighten remaining fasteners to specifications.

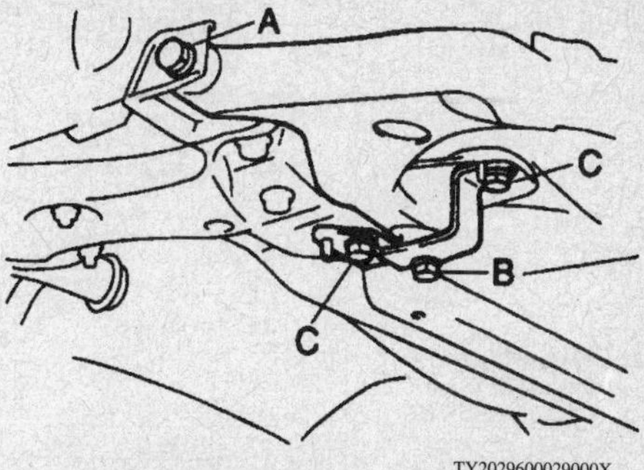
A
C
B
C

TY2029600029000X

Fig. 4 Righthand side lower suspension arm bolts

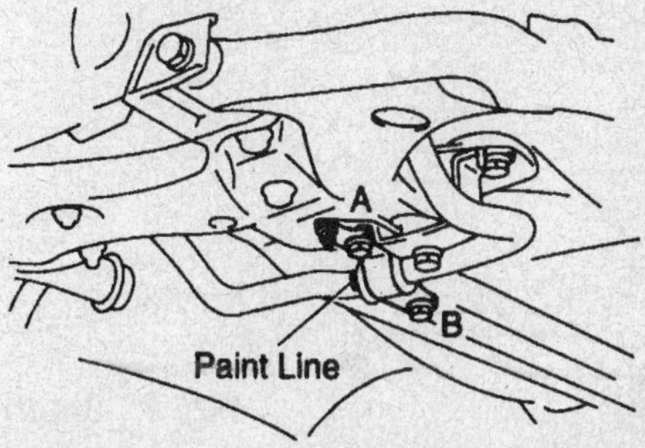
A
B
Paint Line

TY2029600028000X

Fig. 6 Stabilizer bar bracket bolts & nut

POWER STEERING GEAR

REPLACE

Refer to **Fig. 7** when replacing power steering gear, noting the following:

1. **On models with audio coded anti-theft system,** obtain three digit anti-theft code.
2. **On all models,** disconnect universal joint as follows:
   a. Position front wheels facing straight ahead.
   b. Using seat belt of driver's seat, fix steering wheel so that it does not turn, **Fig. 8.**
   c. Place alignment marks on universal joint and control valve shaft.
   d. Loosen upper universal joint bolt and remove lower universal joint bolt, then disconnect universal joint.
3. Disconnect tie rod ends using ball joint puller tool No. 09628-62011, or equivalent.
4. Disconnect and connect pressure and return tubes using power steering hose nut wrench set tool No. 09631-22020, or equivalent.
5. Slide gear assembly to righthand side to remove.
6. When connecting universal joint, set gear housing so that it matches dimensions shown in **Fig. 9,** with gear housing at center point.
7. Align marks made during removal and connect universal joint.

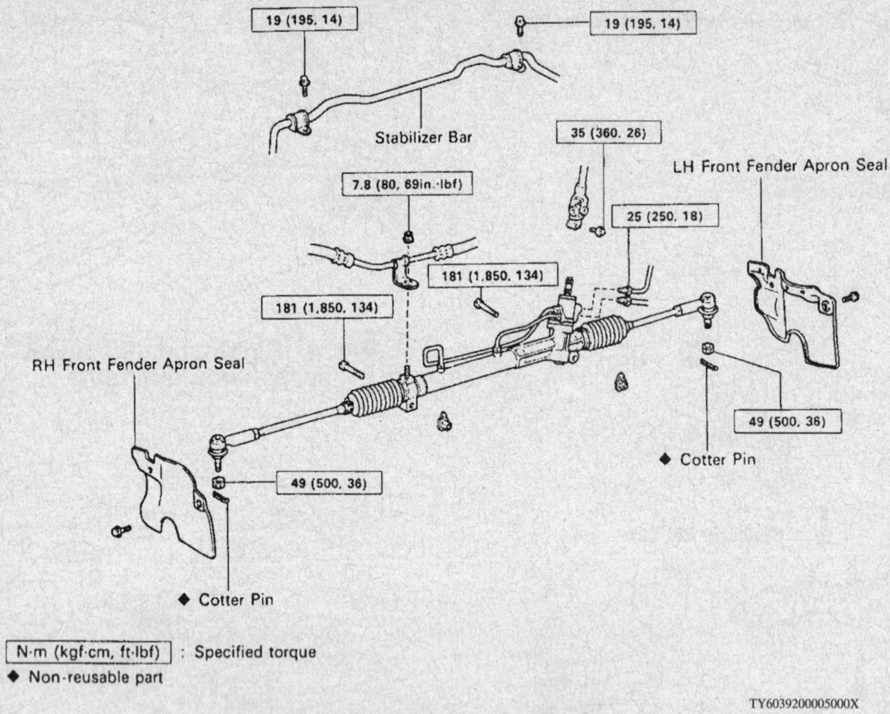
19 (195, 14)
19 (195, 14)
Stabilizer Bar
35 (360, 26)
LH Front Fender Apron Seal
7.8 (80, 69in.·lbf)
25 (250, 18)
181 (1,850, 134)
181 (1,850, 134)
RH Front Fender Apron Seal
49 (500, 36)
◆ Cotter Pin
49 (500, 36)
◆ Cotter Pin
N·m (kgf·cm, ft·lbf) : Specified torque
◆ Non-reusable part
TY6039200005000X

Fig. 7 Steering gear removal

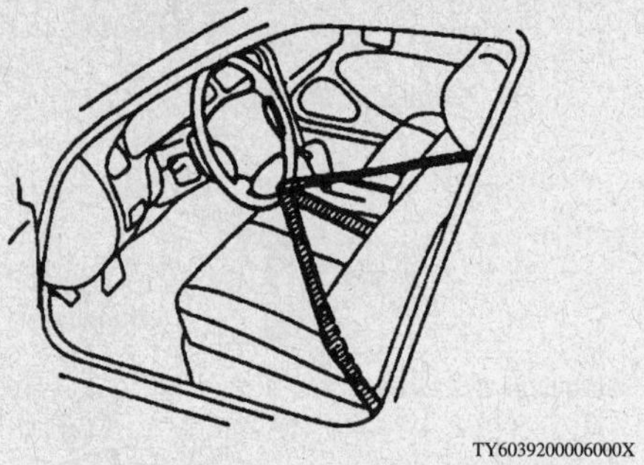
TY6039200006000X

Fig. 8 Steering wheel mounting

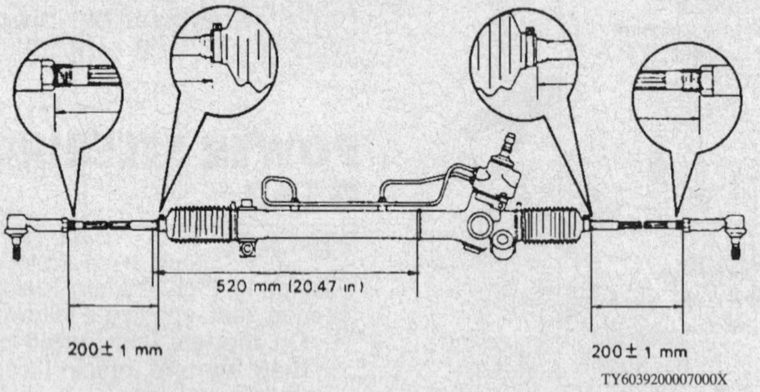
520 mm (20.47 in)
200± 1 mm
200± 1 mm
TY6039200007000X

Fig. 9 Steering gear installation

POWER STEERING PUMP

REPLACE

Refer to **Fig. 10** when replacing power steering pump, noting the following:

1. Disconnect and connect pressure line using power steering hose nut wrench set tool No. 09631-22020, or equivalent.
2. **On all models,** bleed power steering system after installation.

POWER STEERING SYSTEM BLEED

1. Ensure fluid in reservoir tank is at proper level.
2. With engine speed below 1000 RPM, turn steering wheel from stop to stop three or four times, keeping at full stop position for two to three seconds.
3. Ensure fluid is not foamy or cloudy.
4. Measure fluid lever with engine running then stop engine and measure fluid level again, **Fig. 11.** Maximum rise of fluid is .20 inch.
5. If a problem is found, proceed as follows:
   a. Disconnect return hose from reservoir tank and drain fluid.
   b. Fill reservoir tank with fresh fluid.
   c. With return hose placed into a suitable container, start engine and run at 1000 RPM. **After 1 or 2 seconds, fluid will begin to discharge from return hose. Stop engine immediately at this time. Ensure some fluid remains in reservoir tank.**
   d. Repeat steps b and c four or five times until there is no more air in fluid.
   e. Connect return hose and correct fluid level.

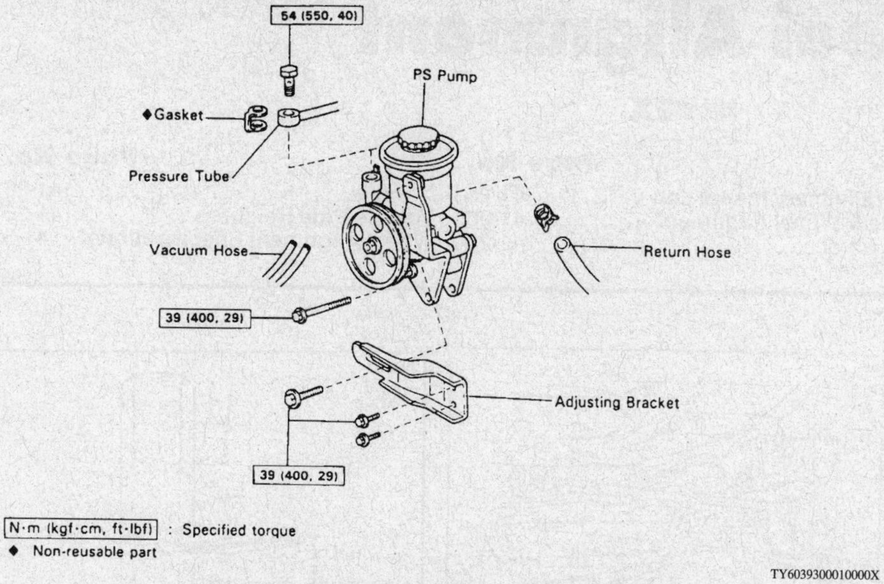
54 (550, 40)
PS Pump
◆Gasket
Pressure Tube
Vacuum Hose
Return Hose
39 (400, 29)
Adjusting Bracket
39 (400, 29)
N·m (kgf·cm, ft·lbf) : Specified torque
◆ Non-reusable part
TY6039300010000X

Fig. 10 Power steering pump removal

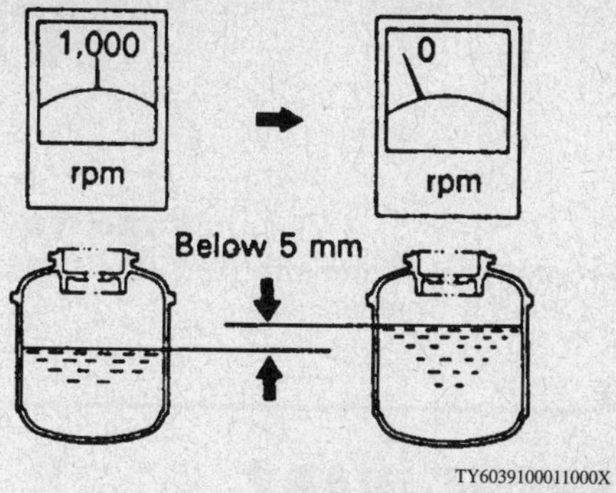
1,000
rpm
0
rpm
Below 5 mm
TY6039100011000X

Fig. 11 Power steering system bleed

TIGHTENING SPECIFICATIONS

Year	Component	Torque/Ft. Lbs.
1993–96	ABS Speed Sensor	6
	ABS Wire Harness To Shock Absorber	48①
	Axle Hub Nut	159
	Ball Joint To Lower Arm	105
	Ball Joint To Steering Knuckle	87
	Brake Hose To Shock Absorber	22
	Driveshaft Locknut	159
	Engine Mount Bracket To Suspension Crossmember	35
	Front Exhaust Pipe Bracket To Suspension Center Member	14
	Front Exhaust Pipe To Center Exhaust Pipe	32
	Lower Ball Joint To Lower Suspension Arm	105
	Lower Shock Absorber Nuts	203
	Lower Suspension Arm	③
	Stabilizer Bar Brackets	②
	Stabilizer Bar Link Set Nut	33
	Steering Knuckle To Brake Cylinder	65
	Steering Knuckle To Shock Absorber	203
	Steering Knuckle To Tie Rod End	36
	Suspension Crossmember To Body	152
	Suspension Crossmember To Suspension Center Member	45
	Suspension Upper Support To Body	29
	Suspension Upper Support To Piston Rod	34
	Tie Rod End Locknut	41
	Wheel Lug Nuts	76

① — Inch lbs.
② — Refer to "Stabilizer Bar, Replace."
③ — Refer to "Lower Suspension Arm, Replace."

Wheel Alignment

INDEX

	Page No.
Front Wheel Alignment	41-26
Caster & Camber	41-26
Toe-In	41-26
Preliminary Inspection	41-26
Rear Wheel Alignment	41-26
Camber	41-26
Toe-In	41-26
Vehicle Ride Height	41-26
Wheel Alignment Specifications	41-3

PRELIMINARY INSPECTION

Inspect the following prior to adjusting wheel alignment.

1. Check tires for wear and proper inflation.
2. Check wheel runout, .039 (1 mm) inch should be indicated.
3. Check front wheel bearings, front suspension, steering linkage and ball joints for wear or looseness.
4. Ensure front shock absorbers are functioning properly.

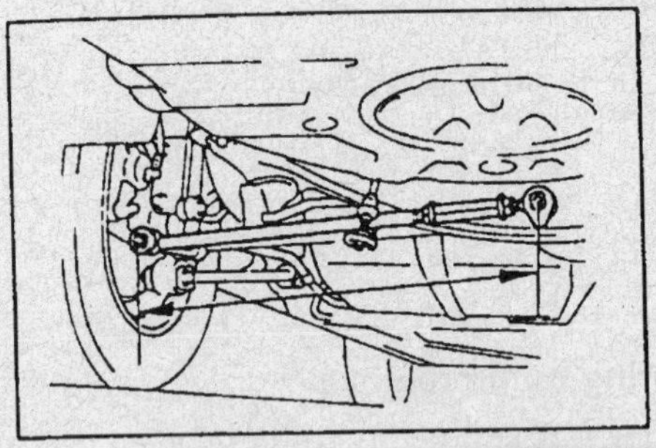

TY2049300016000X

Fig. 1 Rear toe-in adjustment

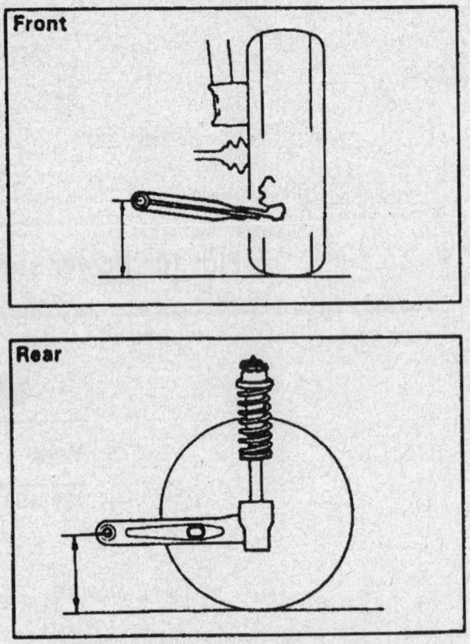
Front
Rear

TY2049100017000X

Fig. 2 Vehicle ride height measurement

FRONT WHEEL ALIGNMENT

CASTER & CAMBER

Camber and caster is not adjustable on these models. If camber and caster angle is not within limits, check for worn or damaged suspension parts and replace as necessary.

TOE-IN

1. Remove clamps from steering gear boots.
2. Loosen tie rod end locknuts.
3. Turn left and right tie rod ends an equal amount to adjust toe-in.
4. Ensure length of both tie rods are equal following adjustment.
5. Following adjustment, install steering gear boot clamps and **torque** tie rod locknuts to 41 ft. lbs.

Tire size	Front	Rear
P175/65R14 81S 175/65R14 82S	185 mm (7.28 in.)	245 mm (9.65 in.)
P185/65R14 85S 185/65R14 85S	190 mm (7.48 in.)	250 mm (9.84 in.)

TY2049300020000X

Fig. 3 Vehicle ride height specifications

REAR WHEEL ALIGNMENT

CAMBER

Camber angle is preset and not adjustable. If camber angle is not to specification, inspect and/or replace suspension components as required.

TOE-IN

1. Measure length of left and right No. 2 lower suspension arms, **Fig. 1.**
2. Adjust length of lower suspension arms if difference in length is greater than .04 inch.
3. Loosen locknuts and turn left and right adjusting tubes an equal distance to adjust toe-in.
4. One turn of adjusting tube will adjust toe-in approximately .43 inch.
5. Following adjustment, **torque** locknuts to 41 ft. lbs.

VEHICLE RIDE HEIGHT

Refer to **Figs. 2 and 3,** for ride height measurements and trim height specifications.

TOYOTA AVALON & CAMRY

INDEX OF SERVICE OPERATIONS

Page No.

AIR BAG SYSTEM PRECAUTIONS 0-8
AUTOMATIC TRANSMISSIONS/ TRANSAXLES 48-1
BRAKES 48-1
- Anti-Lock Brakes 48-1
- Disc Brakes 48-1
- Drum Brakes 48-1
- Hydraulic Brake Systems 48-1
- Power Brake Units 48-1

CLUTCH & MANUAL TRANSAXLE
- Adjustments 42-36
- Clutch, Replace 42-37
- Hydraulic System Service 42-37
- Precautions 42-36
- Tightening Specifications 42-38
- Transaxle, Replace 42-38

ELECTRICAL
- Air Bags 48-1
- Air Conditioning 48-1
- Alternators 48-1
- Alternator, Replace 42-5
- Blower Motor, Replace 42-9
- Coil Pack, Replace 42-6
- Combination Switch, Replace 42-7
- Cooling Fans 48-1
- Cruise Control 48-1
- Dash Gauges 48-1
- Dash Panels 48-1
- Distributor, Replace 42-6
- Evaporator Core, Replace 42-10
- Fuel Pump Relay Location 42-5
- Fuse Panel & Flasher Location 42-5
- Headlamp Switch, Replace 42-7
- Heater Core, Replace 42-9
- Ignition Lock, Replace 42-6
- Ignition Switch, Replace 42-6
- Instrument Cluster, Replace 42-8
- Neutral Safety Switch, Replace 42-7
- Passive Restraints 48-1
- Precautions 42-4
- Radio, Replace 42-9
- Relay Center Location 42-5
- Speed Controls 48-1
- Starter, Replace 42-5
- Starter Motors 48-1
- Steering C olumns 48-1
- Steering Wheel, Replace 42-8
- Stop Light Switch, Replace 42-7
- Turn Signal Switch, Replace 42-7
- Wiper Motor, Replace 42-9
- Wiper Systems 48-1
- Wiper Switch, Replace 42-9

ELECTRICAL SYMBOL IDENTIFICATION 0-139
FRONT SUSPENSION & STEERING
- Ball Joint, Replace 42-43
- Ball Joint Inspection 42-43
- Coil Spring, Replace 42-44
- Hub & Steering Knuckle, Replace 42-43
- Lower Suspension Arm, Replace 42-44
- Manual Steering Gears 48-1
- Power Steering 48-1
- Power Steering Gear, Replace 42-45
- Power Steering Pump, Replace 42-46
- Power Steering System Bleed 42-46
- Precautions 42-43
- Stabilizer Bar, Replace 42-45
- Strut, Replace 42-44
- Tightening Specifications 42-47
- Wheel Bearing, Adjust 42-43

FRONT WHEEL DRIVE AXLES 48-1
REAR AXLE & SUSPENSION
- Coil Spring, Replace 42-41
- Hub & Bearing, Replace 42-40
- Lower Suspension Arm & Strut Rod, Replace 42-41
- Precautions 42-40
- Rear Axle Carrier, Replace 42-40
- Stabilizer Bar, Replace 42-41
- Suspension Arm, Replace 42-41
- Tightening Specifications 42-42

SERVICE REMINDER & WARNING LAMP RESET PROCEDURES 0-10
SPECIFICATIONS
- Fluid Capacities & Cooling System Data 42-3
- Front Wheel Alignment Specifications 42-3
- General Engine Specifications 42-2
- Lubricant Data 42-4
- Rear Wheel Alignment Specifications 42-3
- Tune Up Specifications 42-2

VEHICLE IDENTIFICATION 0-1
VEHICLE LIFT POINTS 0-34
VEHICLE MAINTENANCE SCHEDULES 0-69
WHEEL ALIGNMENT
- Front Wheel Alignment 42-48
- Preliminary Inspection 42-48
- Rear Wheel Alignment 42-48
- Vehicle Ride Height 42-48
- Wheel Alignment Specifications 42-3

WIRE COLOR CODE IDENTIFICATION 0-144
1MZ-FE 3.0L & 3VZ-FE 3.0L ENGINES
- Belt Tension Data 42-31
- Camshaft, Replace 42-30
- Compression Pressure 42-19
- Cooling System Bleed 42-31
- Cylinder Head, Replace 42-22
- Engine, Replace 42-19
- Engine Rebuilding Specifications 48-1
- Exhaust Manifold, Replace 42-22
- Fuel Filter, Replace 42-32
- Fuel Pump, Replace 42-32
- Hydraulic Lifters, Replace 42-29
- Intake Manifold, Replace 42-22
- Main & Rod Bearings 42-30
- Oil Pan, Replace 42-30
- Oil Pump, Replace 42-31
- Oil Pump Service 42-31
- Piston & Rod Assembly 42-30
- Precautions 42-19
- Radiator, Replace 42-32
- Thermostat, Replace 42-31
- Tightening Specifications 42-33
- Timing Belt, Replace 42-29
- Valve Adjustment 42-28
- Valve Clearance Specifications 42-25
- Valve Guides 42-29
- Water Pump, Replace 42-32

5S-FE 2.2L ENGINE
- Belt Tension Data 42-17
- Camshaft, Replace 42-17
- Compression Pressure 42-11
- Cooling System Bleed 42-17
- Cylinder Head, Replace 42-13
- Engine, Replace 42-11
- Engine Rebuilding Specifications 48-1
- Exhaust Manifold, Replace 42-13
- Fuel Filter, Replace 42-18
- Fuel Pump, Replace 42-18
- Hydraulic Lifters, Replace 42-16
- Intake Manifold, Replace 42-12
- Main & Rod Bearings 42-17
- Oil Pan, Replace 42-17
- Oil Pump, Replace 42-17
- Oil Pump Service 42-17
- Piston & Rod Assembly 42-17
- Precautions 42-11
- Radiator, Replace 42-17
- Thermostat, Replace 42-17
- Tightening Specifications 42-18
- Timing Belt, Replace 42-16
- Valve Adjustment 42-16
- Valve Clearance Specifications 42-16
- Valve Guides 42-16
- Water Pump, Replace 42-17

Specifications

GENERAL ENGINE SPECIFICATIONS

Year	Model	Engine, Liter	Fuel System	Bore & Stroke	Compression Ratio	Maximum Brake H.P. @ RPM	Maximum Torque Ft. Lbs. @ RPM	Normal Oil Pressure, psi
1993	Camry	2.2L	Fuel Inj.	3.43 x 3.58	9.5	130 @ 5400	145 @ 4400	①
		3.0L ③	Fuel Inj.	3.44 x 3.23	9.6	185 @ 5200	195 @ 4400	②
1994	Camry	2.2L	Fuel Inj.	3.43 x 3.58	9.5	125 @ 5400	145 @ 4400	①
		3.0L④	Fuel Inj.	3.44 x 3.27	10.5	188 @ 5200	203 @ 4400	②
1995	Avalon	3.0L④	Fuel Inj.	3.44 x 3.27	10.5	188 @ 5200	203 @ 4400	②
	Camry	2.2L	Fuel Inj.	3.43 x 3.58	9.5	125 @ 5400	145 @ 4400	①
		3.0L④	Fuel Inj.	3.44 x 3.27	10.5	188 @ 5200	203 @ 4400	②
1996	Avalon	3.0L④	Fuel Inj.	3.44 x 3.27	10.5	192 @ 5200	210 @ 4400	②
	Camry	2.2L	Fuel Inj.	3.43 x 3.58	9.5	125 @ 5400	145 @ 4400	①
		3.0L	Fuel Inj.	3.44 x 3.27	10.5	188 @ 5200	203 @ 4400	②

① — At idle, 4.3 psi or more; at 3000 RPM, 36–71 psi.
② — At idle, 4.3 psi or more; at 3000 RPM, 43–78 psi.
③ — 3VZ-FE engine.
④ — 1MZ-FE engine.

TUNE UP SPECIFICATIONS

Year, Model & Engine Code	Spark Plug Gap Inch	Ignition			Curb Idle Speed①		Fuel Pump Pressure, psi	Valve Clearance, Inch	
		Firing Order Fig.②	Timing BTDC④	Timing Mark Fig.	Man. Trans.	Auto. Trans.		Int.	Exh.
1993									
Camry 5S-FE	.043	⑥	10	A	750	750N	38–44	.007–.011	.011–.015
Camry 3VZ-FE	.043	⑤	10	B	700	700N	38–44	.005–.009	.011–.015
1994									
Camry 5S-FE	.043	⑥	10	A	750	750N	38–44	.007–.011	.011–.015
Camry 1MZ-FE	.043	③	10	B	700	700N	38–44	.006–.010	.010–014
1995–96									
Avalon 1MZ-FE	.043	③	10	C	700	700N	38–44	.006–.010	.010–.014
Camry 5S-FE	.043	⑥	10	A	750	750N	38–44	.007–.011	.011–.015
Camry 1MZ-FE	.043	③	10	B	700	700N	38–44	.006–.010	.010–.014

N — Neutral.
BTDC — Before Top Dead Center.
① — Controlled by idle air control valve.
② — Before disconnecting spark plug wires from distributor cap, determine location of number 1 wire in cap, as distributor position may have been altered from that shown.
③ — Firing order, 1-2-3-4-5-6.
④ — With jumper wire connected between check connector (DLC1) terminals TE1 & E1.
⑤ — Cylinder numbering from front of engine to rear, right bank, 1-3-5; left bank, 2-4-6. Firing order, 1-2-3-4-5-6.
⑥ — No. 1 cylinder located at front of engine, cylinder numbering 1-2-3-4; firing order 1-3-4-2.

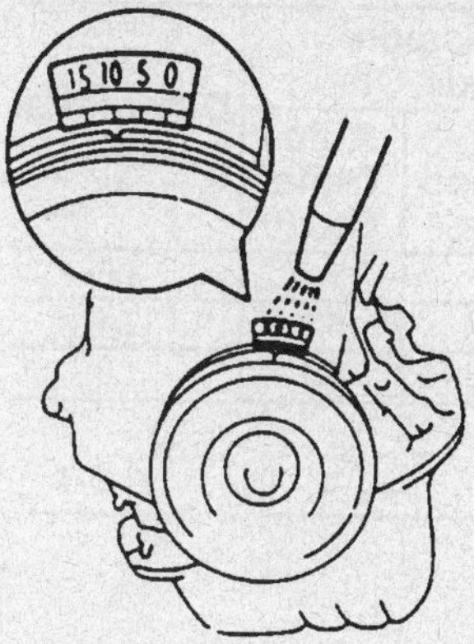
15 10 5 0

TY1138800042000X

Fig. A

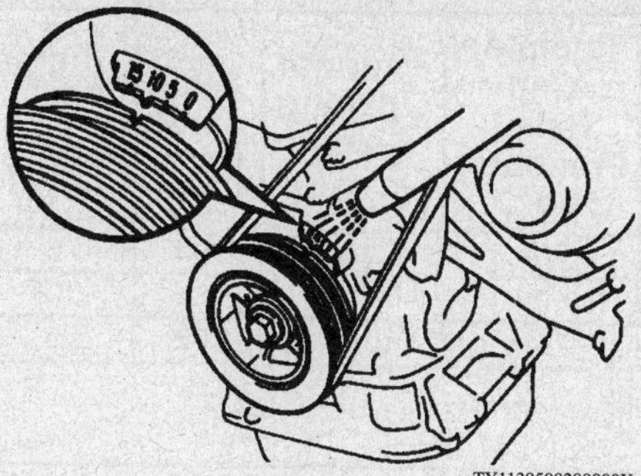
15 10 5 0

TY1139500280000X

Fig. B

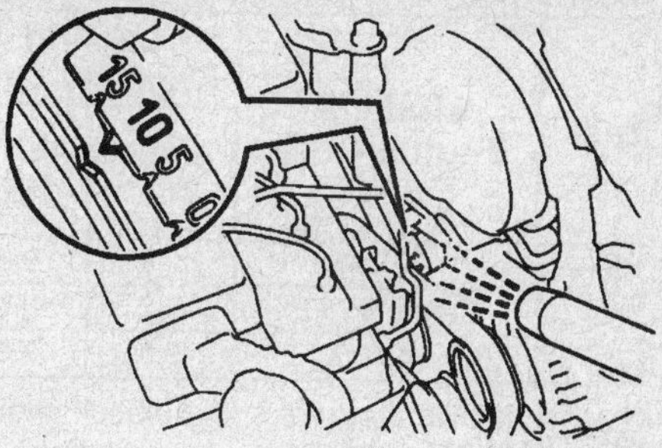
15 10 5 0

TY1139600281000X

Fig. C

FRONT WHEEL ALIGNMENT SPECIFICATIONS

Year	Model	Caster Angle, Degrees		Camber Angle, Degrees		Toe, Inch③	Toe-Out on Turns, Deg.		Steering Axis Inclination, Deg.	Ball Joint Wear
		Limits	Desired	Limits	Desired		Inner Wheel	Outer Wheel		
1993	Camry	+5⁄12 to +1 11⁄12	+1 1⁄6	–1 1⁄3 to + 1⁄6	– 7⁄12	–.08 to +.08	②	①	13 1⁄12	④
1994–96	Camry	+5⁄12 to +1 11⁄12	+1 1⁄6	–1 1⁄3 to + 1⁄6	– 7⁄12	–.08 to +.08	②	①	13 1⁄12	④
1995–96	Avalon	+5⁄12 to +1 11⁄12	+1 1⁄6	-1 1⁄3 to +1⁄6	-7⁄12	-.08 to +.08	36	31 1⁄4	13 1⁄12	④

① — With P195/70R14 tires, 32 1/6; w/P205/65R15 tires, 31 1/3.
② — With P195/70R14 tires, 37 1/3; w/P205/65R15 tires, 36.
③ — Toe-in (+); toe-out (-).
④ — Refer to "Ball Joint Inspection" under "Front Suspension & Steering."

REAR WHEEL ALIGNMENT SPECIFICATIONS

Year	Model	Camber Angle, Degrees		Toe, Inch①
		Limits	Desired	
1993–94	Camry	–1 1⁄4 to + 1⁄4	–1⁄2	+.08 to +.24
1995–96	Avalon	-1 1⁄2 to 0	-3⁄4	+.08 to +.24
	Camry ②	-1 1⁄6 to +1⁄3	-7⁄12	+.08 to +.24
	Camry ③	-1 to +1⁄2	-1⁄4	+.08 to +.24

① — Toe-in (+); toe-out (-).
② — Coupe & sedan.
③ — Wagon.

FLUID CAPACITIES & COOLING SYSTEM DATA

Year	Model & Engine Code	Cooling Capacity Qts.		Radiator Cap Relief Pressure, Lbs.	Thermo. Opening Temp. °F	Fuel Tank Gals.	Engine Oil Refill Qts.②	Transmission/ Transaxle Oil			Differential Oil Pts.
		Less A/C	With A/C					4 Speed Pts.	5 Speed Pts.	Auto. Trans. Qts.①	
1993	Camry 5S-FE	6.7	6.7	13	180	18.5	3.8	—	5.4	5.9	3.4
	Camry 3VZ-FE	8.9	8.9	13.2	180	18.5	4.5	—	8.8	7.7	1.6
1994	Camry 5S-FE	6.7	6.7	14	180	18.5	3.8	—	5.4	5.9	3.4
	Camry 1MZ-FE	9.2	9.2	14	180	18.5	5	—	5.4	7.1	1.6

Continued

Year	Model & Engine Code	Cooling Capacity Qts.		Radiator Cap Relief Pressure, Lbs.	Thermo. Opening Temp. °F	Fuel Tank Gals.	Engine Oil Refill Qts.②	Transmission/ Transaxle Oil			Differential Oil Pts.
		Less A/C	With A/C					4 Speed Pts.	5 Speed Pts.	Auto. Trans. Qts.①	
1995–96	Avalon	9.8	9.8	14	180	18.5	5	—	—	7.1	1.8
	Camry 5S-FE	6.7	6.7	13	180	18.5	3.8	—	5.4	5.9	3.4
	Camry 1MZ-FE	9.8	9.8	14	180	18.5	5	—	—	7.1	1.8

①— Approximate, make final check w/dipstick.
②— With filter change.

LUBRICANT DATA

Year	Model	Lubricant Type				
		Transmission		Rear Axle	Power Steering	Brake System
		Manual	Automatic			
1993–96	All	75W-90 GL-5	Dexron II/IIE/III	—	Dexron II/IIE/III	DOT 3

Electrical

NOTE: On Air Bag Equipped Models, Refer To "Air Bag System Precautions" Located In The Front Of This Manual For System Disarming & Arming Procedures.

INDEX

	Page No.
Air Bags	48-1
Air Conditioning	48-1
Alternators	48-1
Alternator, Replace	42-5
Avalon & Camry w/1MZ-FE Engine	42-5
Camry w/5S-FE Engine	42-6
Blower Motor, Replace	42-9
Coil Pack, Replace	42-6
1MZ-FE Engine	42-6
Combination Switch, Replace	42-7
Camry	42-7
Cooling Fans	48-1
Cruise Control	48-1
Dash Gauges	48-1
Dash Panels	48-1
Distributor, Replace	42-6
Camry	42-6
Evaporator Core, Replace	42-10
Avalon	42-10
Camry	42-10
Fuel Pump Relay Location	42-5
Fuse Panel & Flasher Location	42-5
Avalon	42-5
Camry	42-5
Headlamp Switch, Replace	42-7
Avalon	42-7
Camry	42-7
Heater Core, Replace	42-9
Avalon	42-9
Camry	42-9
Ignition Lock, Replace	42-6
Ignition Switch, Replace	42-6
Avalon	42-6
Camry	42-6
Instrument Cluster, Replace	42-8
Avalon	42-8
Camry	42-8
Neutral Safety Switch, Replace	42-7
Adjustment	42-7
Installation	42-7
Removal	42-7
Passive Restraints	48-1
Precautions	42-4
Air Bag Systems	42-4
Audio Coded Anti-Theft System	42-4
Radio, Replace	42-9
Relay Center Location	42-5
Avalon	42-5
Camry	42-5
Speed Controls	48-1
Starter, Replace	42-5
Avalon	42-5
Camry	42-5
Starter Motors	48-1
Steering Columns	48-1
Steering Wheel, Replace	42-8
Stop Light Switch, Replace	42-7
Avalon	42-7
Camry	42-7
Turn Signal Switch, Replace	42-7
Avalon	42-7
Camry	42-7
Wiper Motor, Replace	42-9
Avalon	42-9
Camry	42-9
Wiper Switch, Replace	42-9
Avalon	42-9
Camry	42-9
Wiper Systems	48-1

PRECAUTIONS

AIR BAG SYSTEMS

Refer to "Air Bag System Precautions" in the front of this manual for system disarming and arming procedures.

AUDIO CODED ANTI-THEFT SYSTEM

Some models are equipped with an audio coded anti-theft system that will disable the radio when battery power is removed from the radio. The system can be identified by the "ANTI-THEFT SYSTEM" on the cassette tape lid. Obtain the three digit code from the customer for input before disconnecting battery power to the audio unit. Reset system after service as follows:

1. Obtain three digit code from customer.
2. Depress No. 1 (PROG) button while depressing righthand side of TUNE SEEK button, - - - will appear in tape operation display.
3. Enter code as follows:
   a. To enter first digit, press No. 1 (PROG) button a sufficient number of times, starting with zero, to enter digit (if first digit of code is five press button six times).
   b. To enter second digit, press No. 2 (APS) button a sufficient number of

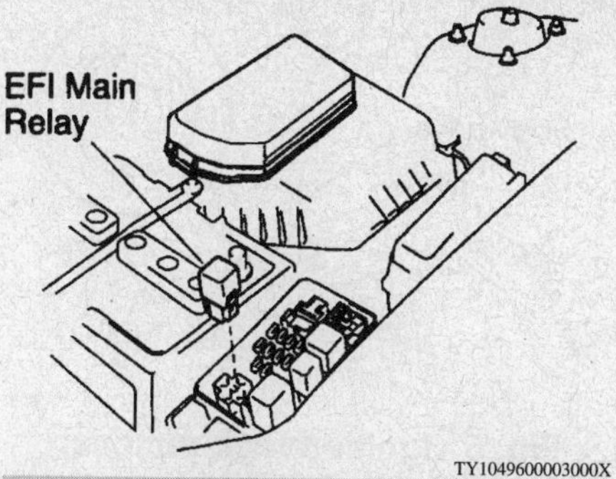
EFI Main Relay
TY1049600003000X

Fig. 1 Fuel pump relay location

times, starting with zero, to enter digit.

c. To enter third digit press, No. 3 (RPT) button a sufficient number of times, starting with zero, to enter digit.

4. If three dashes (- - -) appear in tape operation display during input of digits, restart procedure from beginning.
5. When code digits are correctly input and displayed, press and hold SCAN button until SEC appears in tape operation display.
6. When SEC disappears from display audio unit should be operative.
7. If unit is not operative or Err is displayed, repeat procedure. **Attempting to input code more than nine times may permanently disable audio unit.**

FUSE PANEL & FLASHER LOCATION

AVALON

Main Fuse Panel

The main fuse/relay panel is located under the lefthand lower end of the instrument panel.

Engine Compartment Fuse Panel

The engine compartment fuse/relay panel is located on the lefthand front corner of the engine compartment.

Fusible Link Panel

The fusible link/relay panel is located on the lefthand side of the engine compartment, next to the air filter box.

Flasher

The flasher unit is located behind the lefthand side of the instrument panel, behind the instrument cluster.

CAMRY

The passenger compartment fuse block is located behind the driver side kick panel. The engine compartment fuse/relay panel is located behind the battery. The turn signal/hazard flasher is located behind the lefthand side of the instrument panel, left of the steering column.

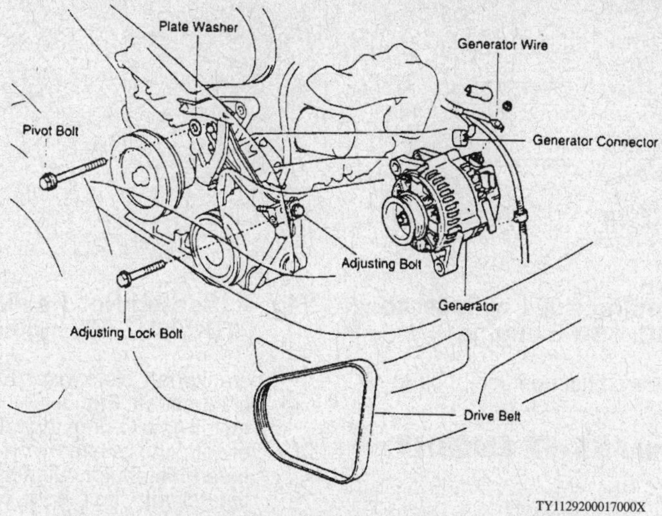
Plate Washer
Generator Wire
Pivot Bolt
Generator Connector
Adjusting Bolt
Generator
Adjusting Lock Bolt
Drive Belt
TY1129200017000X

Fig. 2 Alternator removal. Avalon & Camry w/1MZ-FE engine

FUEL PUMP RELAY LOCATION

The fuel pump relay is located in the engine compartment relay box, **Fig. 1.**

RELAY CENTER LOCATION

AVALON

The main relay/fuse panel is located under the lefthand lower end of the instrument panel. The engine compartment relay/fuse panel is located on the front lefthand corner of the engine compartment. The relay/fusible link panel is located on the lefthand side of the engine compartment, next to the air filter box. Relay block No. 8 (A/C clutch and radiator fans) is located on the lefthand side of the engine compartment, on the shock tower.

CAMRY

There are three relay centers. One is located below the righthand side of the instrument panel, another behind the upper center of the instrument cluster and the third is on the righthand side of the engine compartment.

STARTER

REPLACE

AVALON

1. **On models with coded audio anti-theft systems,** refer to "Precautions" for code procedures.
2. **On all models,** remove battery and tray.
3. **On models with cruise control,** remove cruise control actuator as follows:
   a. Remove bolt, clip and actuator cover.
   b. Disconnect actuator connector and clamp.
   c. Remove three bolts, and disconnect actuator with bracket.
4. **On all models,** disconnect starter connector and starter to battery cable.
5. Remove two bolts, then the starter.
6. Reverse procedure to install, noting the following:
   a. **Torque** starter mounting bolts to 29 ft. lbs.
   b. Reset audio anti-theft system, if necessary, as outlined under "Precautions."

CAMRY

1. **On models with coded audio anti-theft systems,** refer to "Precautions" for code procedures.
2. **On all models,** disconnect battery ground cable.
3. **On models equipped with cruise control,** remove battery and cruise control actuator.
4. **On all models,** disconnect electrical connectors from starter motor.
5. Remove starter motor attaching bolts, heat shield (if equipped), then the starter motor.
6. Reverse procedure to install.

ALTERNATOR

REPLACE

AVALON & CAMRY w/1MZ-FE ENGINE

1. Loosen alternator pivot bolt, adjusting lock bolt, and adjusting bolt, then remove drive belt, **Fig. 2.**
2. Disconnect alternator connector.
3. Disconnect alternator to battery cable.
4. Disconnect wire harness from clip.
5. Remove pivot bolt, plate washer, adjusting lock bolt and alternator.
6. Reverse procedure to install, noting the following:
   a. Tension drive belt as outlined under "Belt Tension Data" in the "1MZ-FE Engine" section.
   b. **Torque** pivot bolt to 41 ft. lbs.

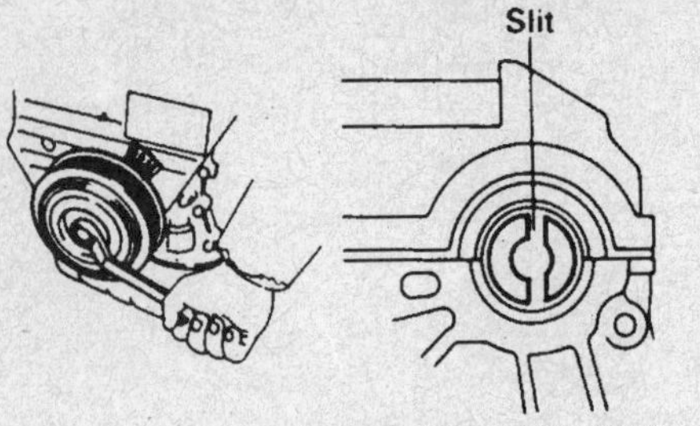
Slit
TY1119100001000X

Fig. 3 Setting No. 1 cylinder to TDC. 5S-FE engine

c. **Torque** adjustment lock bolt to 13 ft. lbs.

CAMRY w/5S-FE ENGINE

With A/C

1. Disconnect wire routing clamps and wiring connectors from alternator.
2. Loosen adjuster lock bolt, pivot bolt and adjusting bolt, then remove drive belt.
3. Remove adjuster lock bolt, pivot bolt and adjusting bolt, then the alternator.
4. Reverse procedure to install, noting the following:
   a. Tension drive belt as outlined under "Belt Tension Data" in the "5S-FE Engine" section.
   b. **Torque** pivot bolt to 38 ft. lbs.
   c. **Torque** adjustment lock bolt to 13 ft. lbs.

Less A/C

1. Disconnect wire routing clamps and wiring connectors from alternator.
2. Loosen pivot bolt and adjustment lock bolt, then remove drive belt.
3. Remove pivot bolt and adjustment lock bolt, then the alternator.
4. Reverse procedure to install, noting the following:
   a. Tension drive belt as outlined under "5S-FE engine."
   b. **Torque** pivot bolt to 38 ft. lbs.
   c. **Torque** adjustment lock bolt to 13 ft. lbs.

DISTRIBUTOR

REPLACE

CAMRY

5S-FE Engine

1. **On models with coded audio anti-theft systems,**refer to "Precautions" for code procedures.
2. **On all models,** disconnect battery ground cable.
3. Disconnect accelerator linkage from throttle linkage, then remove air cleaner cover, resonator and hose.
4. Disconnect electrical connectors, then mark and remove spark plug wires.
5. Remove distributor bolts, then distributor and O-ring.
6. Reverse procedure to install, noting the following:
   a. Set No. 1 cylinder to TDC by turning crankshaft clockwise. Position slit of camshaft, **Fig. 3.**
   b. Install new O-ring, then align cutout of coupling with mark on housing.
   c. Insert distributor, aligning center of flange with bolt hole on cylinder head, then tighten hold-down bolts.
   d. Reverse remaining installation procedure, then adjust ignition timing.
   e. **Torque** hold-down bolt to 14 ft. lbs.
   f. Reset audio anti-theft system, if necessary, as outlined under "Precautions."

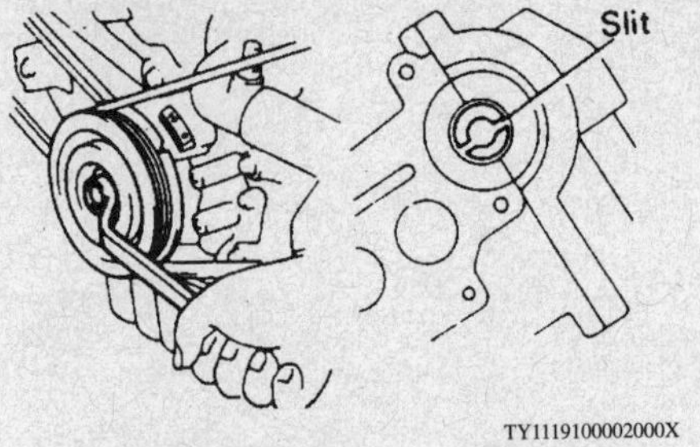
Slit
TY1119100002000X

Fig. 4 Setting No. 1 cylinder to TDC. 3VZ-FE engine

3VZ-FE Engine

1. **On models with coded audio anti-theft systems,**refer to "Precautions" for code procedures.
2. **On all models,** disconnect battery ground cable.
3. Remove air cleaner cover, hose and air meter.
4. Disconnect connectors, then mark and remove spark plug wires.
5. Remove distributor bolts, then distributor and O-ring.
6. Reverse procedure to install, noting the following:
   a. Set No. 1 cylinder to TDC by turning crankshaft clockwise. Position slit of camshaft on righthand head, **Fig. 4.**
   b. Install new O-ring, then align cutout of coupling with mark on housing.
   c. Install distributor, aligning mark on housing with notch on distributor attachment bearing cap.
   d. Adjust ignition timing. **Torque** hold-down bolt to 13 ft. lbs.
   e. Reset audio anti-theft system, if necessary, as outlined under "Precautions."

COIL PACK

REPLACE

1MZ-FE ENGINE

1. **On models with coded audio anti-theft systems,**refer to "Precautions" for code procedures.
2. **On all models,** disconnect battery ground cable.
3. Disconnect high-tension cords from ignition coils.
4. Disconnect ignition coil connectors and remove ignition coils from lefthand cylinder head.
5. Reverse procedure to install.

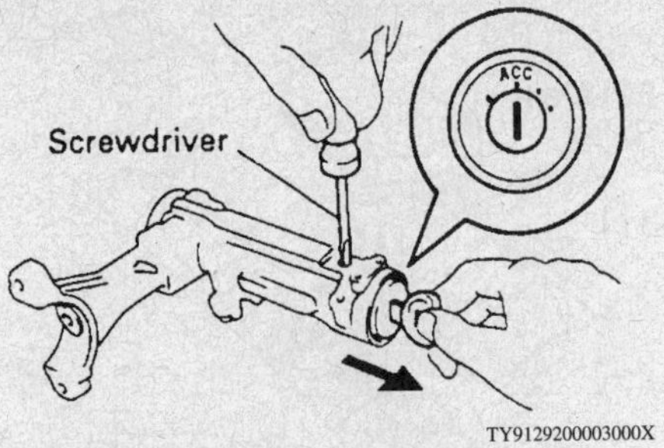
ACC
Screwdriver
TY9129200003000X

Fig. 5 Ignition lock removal

IGNITION LOCK

REPLACE

1. **On models with coded audio anti-theft systems,**refer to "Precautions" for code procedures.
2. **On all models,** remove upper and lower steering column covers.
3. Place ignition lock in ACC position.
4. Using a suitable thin rod or screwdriver, press down on lockpin through hole in lock body, **Fig. 5.**
5. Place new ignition lock in ACC position, then slide into lock body.
6. Ensure lockpin is engaged and lock turns freely.
7. Reset audio anti-theft system, if necessary, as outlined under "Precautions."

IGNITION SWITCH

REPLACE

AVALON

1. **On models with coded audio anti-theft systems,**refer to "Precautions" for code procedures.
2. **On all models,** remove upper and lower steering column covers.
3. Place ignition switch in OFF position, then disconnect ignition switch connector.
4. Remove four retaining screws and ignition switch. If necessary, remove lower steering column.
5. Reverse procedure to install. Reset audio anti-theft system, if necessary, as outlined under "Precautions."

CAMRY

1. **On models with coded audio anti-theft systems,**refer to "Precautions" for code procedures.
2. **On all models,** disconnect battery ground cable.
3. Remove steering wheel, if necessary, steering column garnish, if equipped, upper and lower covers.
4. Disconnect electrical connectors from ignition switch.
5. Turn ignition key to ACC position and remove ignition key cylinder.
6. Remove screw and ignition switch.
7. Reverse procedure to install. Reset audio anti-theft system, if necessary, as outlined under "Precautions."

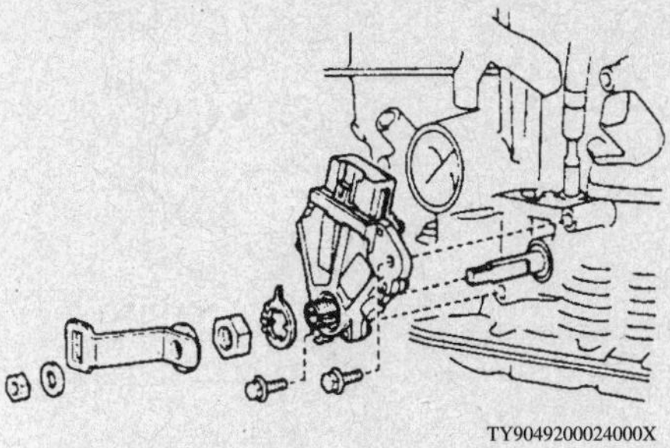
TY9049200024000X
Fig. 6 Neutral safety switch removal

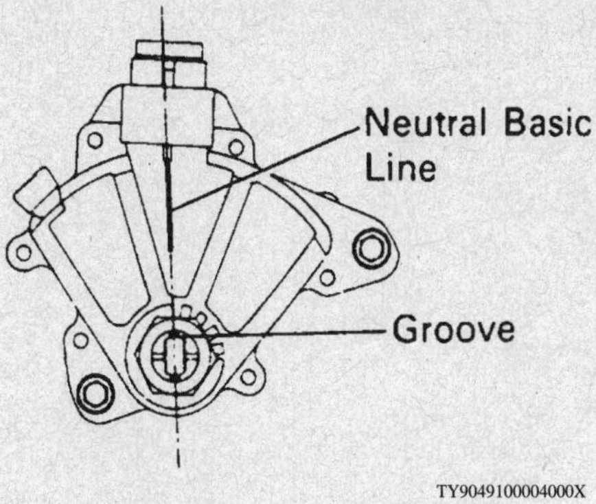
Neutral Basic Line
Groove
TY9049100004000X
Fig. 7 Neutral start switch adjustment. Camry

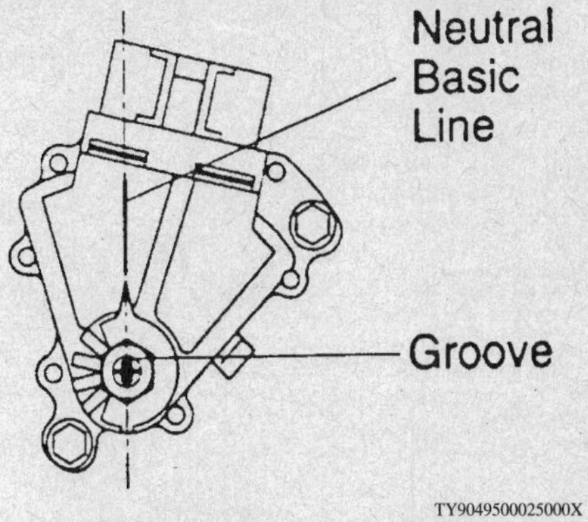
Neutral Basic Line
Groove
TY9049500025000X
Fig. 8 Neutral start switch adjustment. Avalon

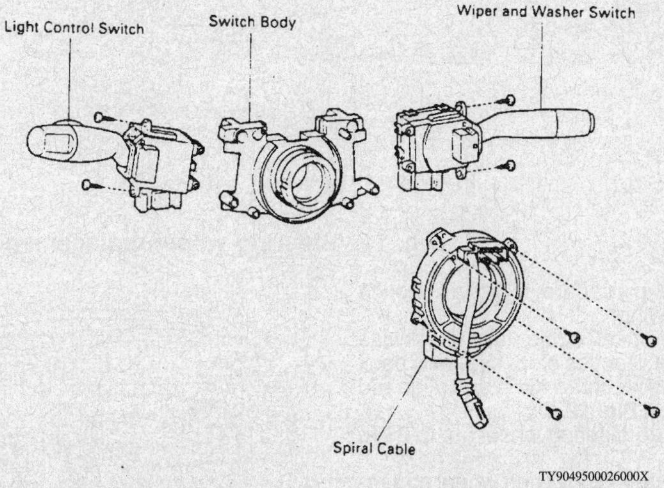
Light Control Switch
Switch Body
Wiper and Washer Switch
Spiral Cable
TY9049500026000X
Fig. 9 Light control & wiper switch. Avalon

NEUTRAL SAFETY SWITCH

REPLACE

REMOVAL

1. Remove air cleaner assembly, then disconnect electrical connector from neutral safety switch.
2. Disconnect shift control cable.
3. Remove shift control lever retaining nut, then remove lever, **Fig. 6.**
4. Straighten shaft nut locktab, then remove shaft nut.
5. Remove retaining bolts, then neutral safety switch.

INSTALLATION

1. Place switch onto shaft, then install retaining bolts hand tight.
2. Install shaft nut and locktab washer, tighten nut and stake locktab.
3. Install shift arm and nut.
4. Adjust switch as outlined under "Adjustment."

ADJUSTMENT

1. Disconnect shift control cable from shift lever, then loosen neutral safety switch bracket bolt.
2. Position transmission shift lever into Neutral.
3. Align switch shaft groove with neutral base line, then tighten switch bracket bolt, **Figs. 7 and 8.**
4. Connect electrical connector to switch.

HEADLAMP SWITCH

REPLACE

AVALON

1. **On models with coded audio anti-theft systems,**refer to "Precautions" for code procedures.
2. **On all models,** remove upper and lower steering column covers.
3. Disconnect headlamp switch electrical connector.
4. Remove retaining screws and switch, **Fig. 9.**
5. Reverse procedure to install, reset audio anti-theft system, if necessary, as outlined under "Precautions."

CAMRY

Refer to "Combination Switch, Replace."

STOP LIGHT SWITCH

REPLACE

AVALON

1. Remove panel from lower lefthand side of instrument panel.
2. Disconnect stop lamp switch connector.
3. Loosen jam nut, then unscrew switch from pedal bracket.
4. Reverse procedure to install. Adjust switch by threading switch in or out of bracket, then tighten locknut.

CAMRY

1. Remove brake pedal tension spring.
2. Disconnect switch wire connector.
3. Remove switch mounting nut, then slide switch from mounting bracket.
4. Reverse procedure to install.

COMBINATION SWITCH

REPLACE

CAMRY

1. **On models with coded audio anti-theft systems,**refer to "Precautions" for code procedures.
2. **On all models,** disconnect battery ground cable.
3. Remove steering wheel as outlined under "Steering Wheel, Replace."
4. Remove steering column upper and lower covers.
5. Remove combination switch, **Fig. 10.**
6. Reverse procedure to install. Reset audio anti-theft system, if necessary, as outlined under "Precautions."

TURN SIGNAL SWITCH

REPLACE

AVALON

1. **On models with coded audio anti-theft systems,**refer to "Precautions" for code procedures.
2. **On all models,** remove upper and lower steering column covers.
3. Disconnect turn signal switch electrical connector.
4. Remove retaining screws, then remove switch, **Fig. 9.**
5. Reverse procedure to install. Reset audio anti-theft system, if necessary, as outlined under "Precautions."

CAMRY

Refer to "Combination Switch, Replace" for procedure.

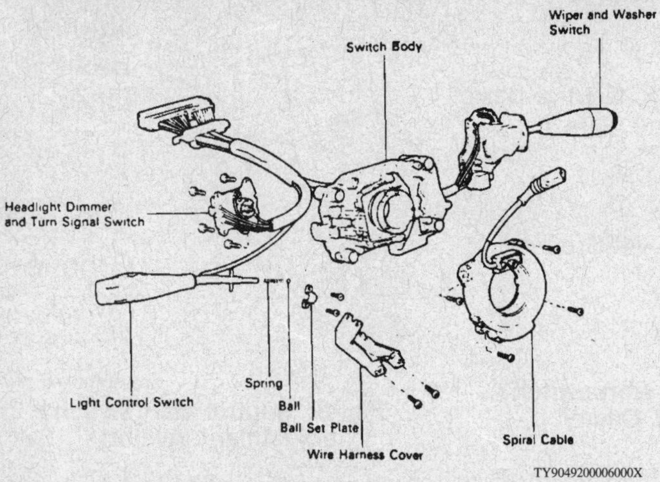
Wiper and Washer Switch
Switch Body
Headlight Dimmer and Turn Signal Switch
Light Control Switch
Spring
Ball
Ball Set Plate
Wire Harness Cover
Spiral Cable
TY9049200006000X

Fig. 10 Combination switch assembly. Camry

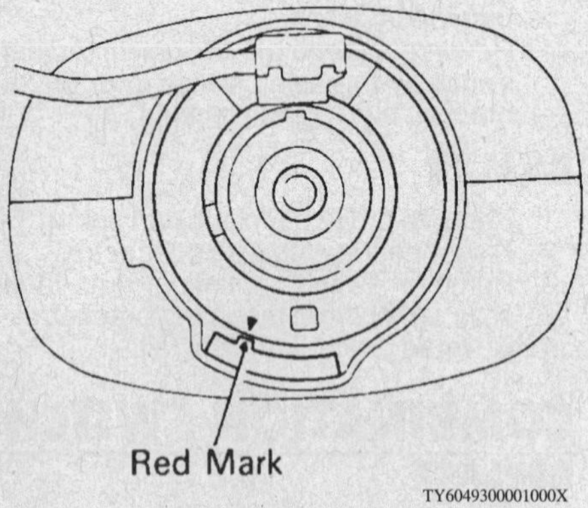
Red Mark
TY6049300001000X

Fig. 12 Spiral cable installation alignment

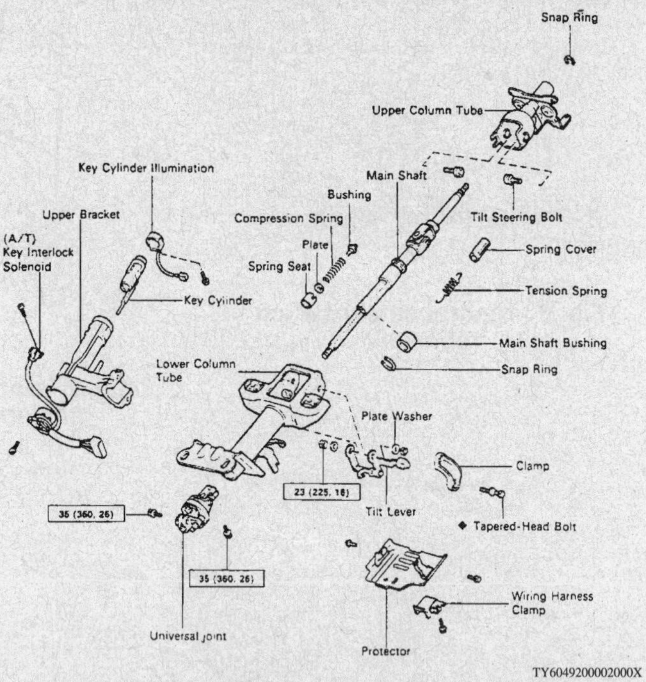
Snap Ring
Upper Column Tube
Key Cylinder Illumination
Main Shaft
Bushing
Upper Bracket
Compression Spring
Tilt Steering Bolt
(A/T) Key Interlock Solenoid
Plate
Spring Seat
Spring Cover
Tension Spring
Key Cylinder
Main Shaft Bushing
Lower Column Tube
Snap Ring
Plate Washer
Clamp
23 (225, 16)
35 (360, 26)
Tilt Lever
Tapered-Head Bolt
35 (360, 26)
Wiring Harness Clamp
Universal joint
Protector
TY6049200002000X

Fig. 11 Steering wheel replacement

7. Reverse procedure to install, noting the following:
   a. Turn spiral cable fully clockwise until it reaches stop, then turn back clockwise three turns and align red marks, **Fig. 12.**
   b. **Torque** steering wheel nut to 26 ft. lbs.
   c. **Torque** torx steering wheel pad retaining screws to 7 ft. lbs.

STEERING WHEEL

REPLACE

During the following procedures do not store air bag pad face down. If air bag module is dropped, dented or otherwise damaged, replace with a new part. It is recommended that only new parts be used for replacement.

Ensure ignition switch is in OFF position during air bag module removal. Disconnecting the module with switch in ON or ACC position will cause an error code to be stored in air bag system ECU.

1. Place front wheels in a straight ahead position.
2. Remove blind hole plugs on back of steering wheel to access Torx mounting screws.
3. Using a suitable driver, back out Torx screws evenly. They are retained in pad by a cage, **Fig. 11.**
4. Without pulling on or placing a strain on connector wire, disconnect lead from pad.
5. Remove retaining nut, then place match marks on steering wheel and column shaft.
6. Install steering wheel puller tool No. 09950–50010, or equivalent, and press wheel from shaft. **Do not strike shaft or puller.**

INSTRUMENT CLUSTER

REPLACE

AVALON

1. **On models with coded audio anti-theft systems,**refer to “Precautions” for code procedures.
2. **On all models,** remove steering wheel as outlined under “Steering Wheel, Replace.”
3. Remove upper and lower steering column cover.
4. Remove trim panels around instrument cluster, **Fig. 13,** then remove instrument cluster.
5. Reverse procedure to install. Reset audio anti-theft system, if necessary, as outlined under “Precautions.”

CAMRY

1. **On models with coded audio anti-theft systems,**refer to “Precautions” for code procedures.
2. **On all models,** disconnect battery ground cable.
3. Pull front door inside scuff plate to remove.
4. Pull front door opening cover rearward to remove.
5. Remove hood lock release lever attaching screws, then pull rearward to remove.

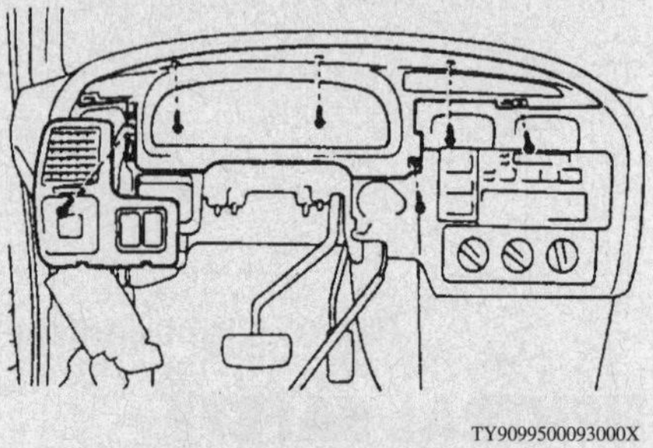
TY9099500093000X

Fig. 13 Instrument cluster replacement. Avalon

6. Remove cowl side trim panel clip, then pull rearward to remove.
7. Remove steering wheel as outlined under “Steering Wheel, Replace.”
8. Remove steering column cover.
9. Remove console upper panel.
10. Remove two rear console box attaching bolts and screws, then remove box.
11. Depress coin box sides, then pull box rearward to remove.
12. Remove coin box bezel attaching screws, then the coin box bezel.
13. Remove four instrument panel lower pad attaching bolts and screw, then the lower pad.
14. Disconnect combination switch electrical connectors.
15. Remove combination switch attaching screws, then the switch.
16. Pull undercover No. 2 rearward to remove.
17. Remove instrument panel lower panel attaching screws, then pull panel rearward to remove.
18. Remove front console box clips, then the two attaching screws and box.
19. Remove glove compartment attaching screws, then the glove compartment.

20. Using suitable taped screwdriver, remove center cluster finish panel.
21. Remove four cluster finish panel attaching screws.
22. Using suitable taped screwdriver, remove cluster finish panel and disconnect electrical connectors.
23. Remove four instrument cluster attaching screws, pull cluster rearward, disconnect electrical connectors, then remove cluster.
24. Reverse procedure to instal. Reset audio anti-theft system, if necessary, as outlined under "Precautions."

RADIO

REPLACE

1. **On models with coded audio anti-theft systems,**refer to "Precautions" for code procedures.
2. **On all models,** remove center upper trim panel.
3. Remove retaining screws. Slide out and disconnect electrical connectors and antenna lead from audio unit.
4. Reverse procedure to install, reset audio anti-theft system, if necessary, as outlined under "Precautions."

WIPER MOTOR

REPLACE

AVALON

1. **On models with coded audio anti-theft systems,**refer to "Precautions" for code procedures.
2. **On all models,** remove wiper arms, **Fig. 14.**
3. Carefully lift weather strip away from cowl trim.
4. Remove clips, then slide cowl trims forward.
5. Disconnect wiper linkage from wiper motor
6. Remove wiper motor mounting bolts, then the wiper motor.
7. Reverse procedure to install. Reset audio anti-theft system, if necessary, as outlined under "Precautions."

CAMRY

Front

1. **On models with coded audio anti-theft systems,**refer to "Precautions" for code procedures.
2. **On all models,** disconnect battery ground cable.
3. Disconnect wiper motor wire connector, then remove wiper motor service cover, if equipped.
4. Remove wiper motor attaching bolts.
5. Using a screwdriver, disconnect wiper link from wiper motor and remove wiper motor.
6. Reverse procedure to install. Reset audio anti-theft system, if necessary, as outlined under "Precautions."

Rear

1. **On models with coded audio anti-theft systems,**refer to "Precautions" for code procedures.
2. **On all models,** disconnect battery ground cable.
3. Remove wiper arm and rear door trim cover.
4. Disconnect wiper motor wire connector.
5. Remove wiper motor bracket attaching bolt, then the wiper motor and bracket.
6. Reverse procedure to install. Reset audio anti-theft system, if necessary, as outlined under "Precautions."

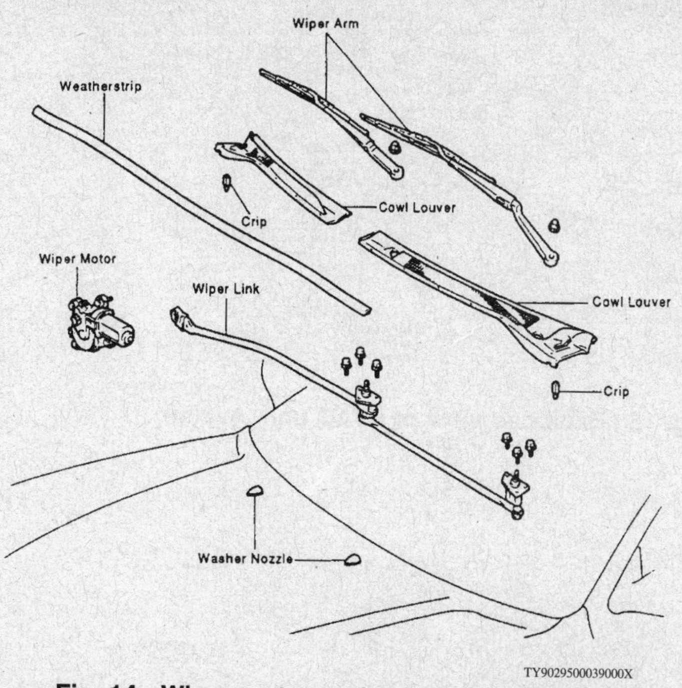
Wiper Arm
Weatherstrip
Cowl Louver
Crip
Wiper Motor
Wiper Link
Cowl Louver
Crip
Washer Nozzle
TY9029500039000X

Fig. 14 Wiper motor replacement. Avalon

WIPER SWITCH

REPLACE

AVALON

1. **On models with coded audio anti-theft systems,**refer to "Precautions" for code procedures.
2. **On all models,** remove upper and lower steering column covers.
3. Disconnect wiper switch electrical connector.
4. Remove retaining screws, then the switch, **Fig. 9.**
5. Reverse procedure to install. Reset audio anti-theft system, if necessary, as outlined under "Precautions."

CAMRY

Refer to "Combination Switch, Replace" for procedure.

BLOWER MOTOR

REPLACE

1. **On models with coded audio anti-theft systems,**refer to "Precautions" for code procedures.
2. **On all models,** disconnect battery ground cable.
3. Remove instrument panel lower panel and undercover No. 2.
4. Disconnect connector bracket electrical connector.
5. Remove blower motor attaching screws, then the blower motor.
6. Reverse procedure to install. Reset audio anti-theft system, if necessary, as outlined under "Precautions."

HEATER CORE

REPLACE

AVALON

1. Drain engine coolant.
2. Remove instrument panel as outlined under "Instrument Panel, Replace."
3. Remove water valve control cable guide, **Fig. 15.**
4. Remove three heater core clamps.
5. Pull heater core to the left and remove from vehicle
6. Reverse procedure to install.

CAMRY

1. **On models with coded audio anti-theft systems,**refer to "Precautions" for code procedures.
2. **On all models,** disconnect battery ground cable.
3. Recover A/C refrigerant as outlined under "Air Conditioning " and drain coolant.
4. Disconnect water inlet control cable from water valve.
5. Disconnect water hoses from heater core pipes.
6. Remove instrument panel and reinforcements as outlined under "Dash Panel Service."

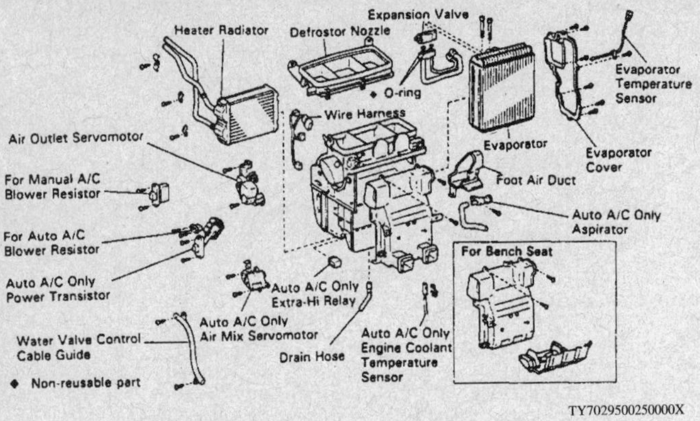
Expansion Valve
Heater Radiator
Defrostor Nozzle
O-ring
Evaporator Temperature Sensor
Wire Harness
Air Outlet Servomotor
Evaporator
Evaporator Cover
For Manual A/C Blower Resistor
Foot Air Duct
Auto A/C Only Aspirator
For Auto A/C Blower Resistor
For Bench Seat
Auto A/C Only Power Transistor
Auto A/C Only Extra-Hi Relay
Auto A/C Only Air Mix Servomotor
Water Valve Control Cable Guide
Drain Hose
Auto A/C Only Engine Coolant Temperature Sensor
◆ Non-reusable part
TY7029500250000X

Fig. 15 Exploded view of HVAC unit. Avalon

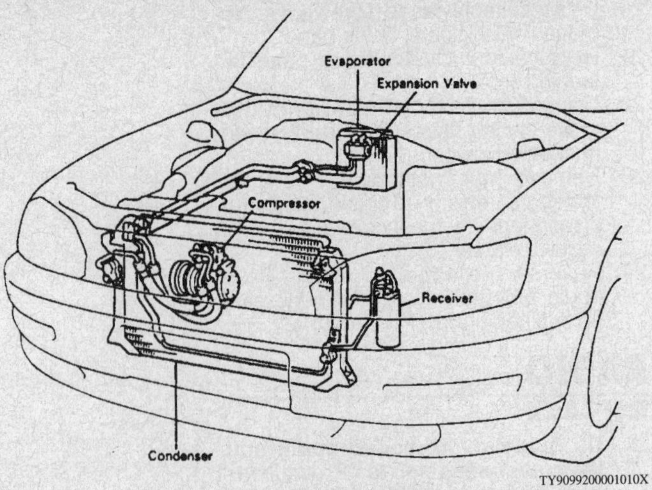
Evaporator
Expansion Valve
Compressor
Receiver
Condenser
TY9099200001010X

Fig. 16 A/C system components (Part 1 of 2). Camry

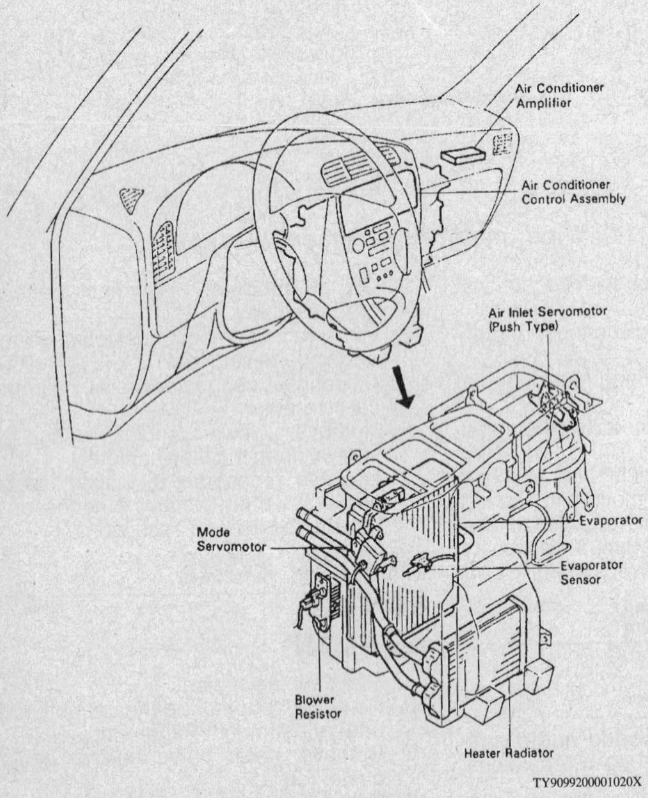
Air Conditioner Amplifier
Air Conditioner Control Assembly
Air Inlet Servomotor (Push Type)
Mode Servomotor
Evaporator
Evaporator Sensor
Blower Resistor
Heater Radiator
TY9099200001020X

Fig. 16 A/C system components (Part 2 of 2). Camry

TY7029500251000X

Fig. 17 Blower & housing unit removal. Avalon

7. Remove blower unit, as follows:
   a. Disconnect ECU electrical connector, then remove ECU and bracket.
   b. Disconnect connector bracket electrical connector, then remove connector bracket.
   c. Disconnect blower unit electrical connector.
   d. Disconnect air inlet damper control cable.
   e. Remove three blower unit attaching screws and nut, then the blower unit.
8. Disconnect and cap liquid and suction tube from block joint, **Fig. 16.**
9. Remove heater protector attaching clips, then the protector.
10. Remove three heater core attaching screws and clamps.
11. Disconnect and cap heater pipes, then remove heater core.
12. Reverse procedure to install. Reset audio anti-theft system, if necessary, as outlined under "Precautions."

EVAPORATOR CORE

REPLACE

AVALON

1. **On models with coded audio anti-theft systems,**refer to "Precautions" for code procedures.
2. **On all models,** disconnect battery.
3. Remove glove compartment, then the righthand instrument panel undercover.
4. Remove ECM, ECU and bracket.
5. Remove blower and housing unit, **Fig. 17.**
6. Discharge and recover A/C system refrigerant.
7. Disconnect liquid tube and suction tube.
8. Remove thermister from evaporator.
9. Remove evaporator cover, **Fig. 15.**
10. Pull out evaporator.
11. Reverse procedure to install, noting the following:
    a. Evacuate and recharge system and check for leaks.
    b. If evaporator is replaced, add 1.4 oz. of suitable refrigerant oil to compressor.
    c. Reset audio anti-theft system, if necessary, as outlined under "Precautions."

CAMRY

1. **On models with coded audio anti-theft systems,**refer to "Precautions" for code procedures.
2. **On all models,** disconnect battery ground cable.
3. Recover refrigerant as outlined in "Air Conditioning " section.
4. Remove blower unit, as follows:
   a. Remove glove compartment.
   b. Disconnect ECU electrical connector, then remove ECU and bracket.
   c. Disconnect connector bracket electrical connector, then remove connector bracket.

d. Disconnect blower unit electrical connector.
e. Disconnect air inlet damper control cable.
f. Remove three blower unit attaching screws and nut, then the blower unit.

5. Disconnect and cap evaporator liquid and suction tubes.
6. Remove evaporator cover.
7. Remove evaporator assembly, then separate evaporator and expansion tube.
8. Reverse procedure to install. Reset audio anti-theft system, if necessary, as outlined under "Precautions."

5S-FE 2.2L Engine

NOTE: On Air Bag Equipped Models, Refer To "Air Bag System Precautions" Located In The Front Of This Manual For System Disarming & Arming Procedures.

NOTE: For Procedures Not Found In This Section, Refer to Celica & Supra 5S-FE Engine Section.

INDEX

	Page No.
Belt Tension Data	42-17
Camshaft, Replace	42-17
Compression Pressure	42-11
Cooling System Bleed	42-17
Cylinder Head, Replace	42-13
Installation	42-15
Removal	42-13
Engine Rebuilding Specifications	48-1
Engine, Replace	42-11
Exhaust Manifold, Replace	42-13
Fuel Filter, Replace	42-18
Fuel Pump, Replace	42-18
Hydraulic Lifters, Replace	42-16
Intake Manifold, Replace	42-12
Main & Rod Bearings	42-17
Oil Pan, Replace	42-17
Oil Pump, Replace	42-17
Oil Pump Service	42-17
Piston & Rod Assembly	42-17
Precautions	42-11
Air Bag Systems	42-11
Audio Coded Anti-Theft System	42-11
Radiator, Replace	42-17
Thermostat, Replace	42-17
Tightening Specifications	42-18
Timing Belt, Replace	42-16
Installation	42-16
Removal	42-16
Valve Adjustment	42-16
Valve Clearance Specifications	42-16
Valve Guides	42-16
Water Pump, Replace	42-17

PRECAUTIONS

AIR BAG SYSTEMS

Refer to "Air Bag System Precautions" in the front of this manual for system disarming and arming procedures.

AUDIO CODED ANTI-THEFT SYSTEM

Some models are equipped with an audio coded anti-theft system that will disable the radio when the battery cable is disconnected. The system can be identified by the words "ANTI-THEFT SYSTEM" on the cassette tape lid. Obtain three digit customer code for input. Reset system after service as follows:

1. Obtain three digit audio anti-theft code.
2. Depress 1 (PROG) button while depressing righthand side of TUNE SEEK button, - - - will appear in tape operation display.
3. To enter first digit, depress 1 (PROG) button repeatedly until number of times depressed equals first digit beginning with zero (depress 1 button six times if first digit is five).
4. To enter second digit, depress 2 (APS) button repeatedly until the number of times depressed equals the second digit beginning with zero.
5. To enter third digit, depress 3 (RPT) button repeatedly until the number of times depressed equals the third digit beginning with zero.
6. If - - - is displayed during code input, repeat procedure.
7. When code appears in display, depress and hold SCAN button until SEC appears.
8. When SEC disappears audio system should be operative.
9. If Err is displayed, repeat procedure. **Attempting to input code more than nine times may permanently disable audio system.**

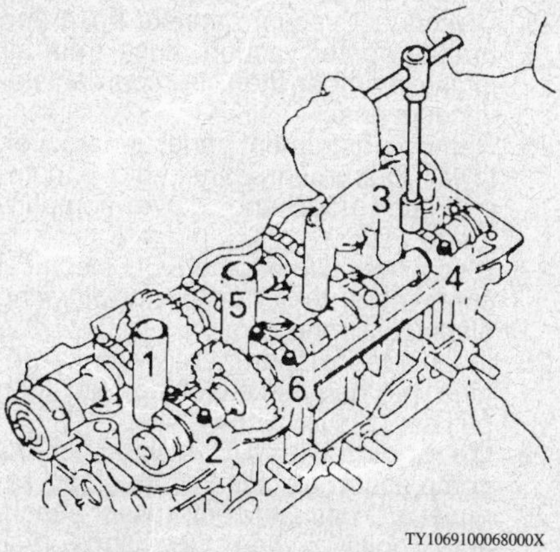

3
4
5
1
6
2
TY1069100068000X

Fig. 1 Exhaust camshaft bearing cap bolt loosening sequence

COMPRESSION PRESSURE

1. Start engine and warm to normal operating temperature.
2. Disconnect distributor electrical connector.
3. Disconnect spark plug wires.
4. Insert compression gauge into spark plug hole.
5. Fully open throttle.
6. While cranking engine, measure compression pressure.
7. Compression pressure should be 142–178 psi.
8. Maximum pressure difference between cylinders should not exceed 14 psi.

ENGINE

REPLACE

1. **On models with coded audio anti-theft systems,** refer to "Precautions" for code procedures.
2. **On all models,** disconnect battery ground cable.
3. Remove battery and tray.
4. Scribe hood installation alignment marks, then remove hood.
5. Remove engine undercover.
6. Drain engine coolant and oil.

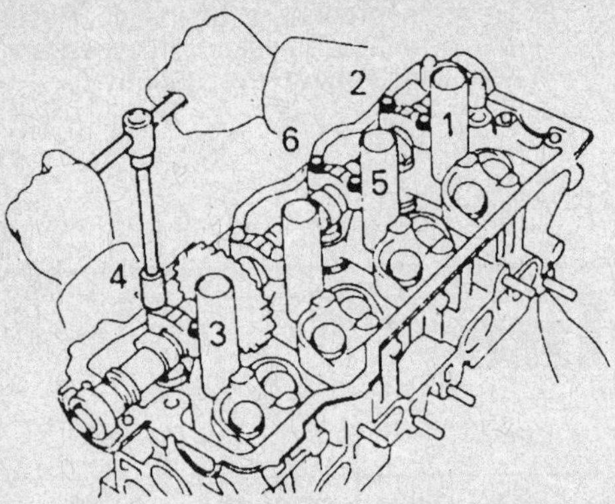
2
6
1
5
4
3

TY1069100069000X

Fig. 2 Intake camshaft bearing cap bolt loosening sequence

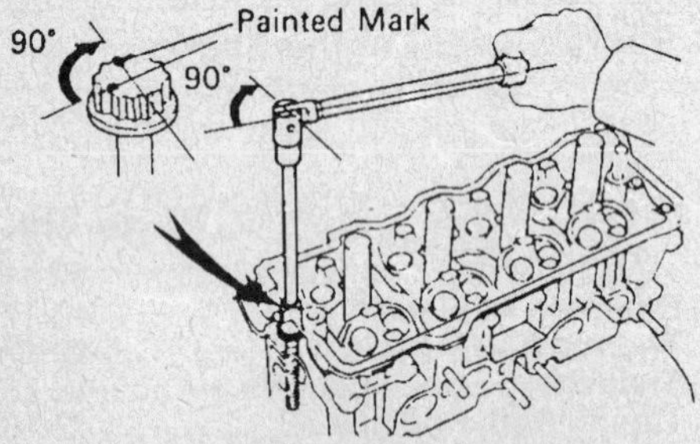
Painted Mark
90°
90°

TY1069100072000X

Fig. 5 Cylinder head bolt tightening sequence (Step 2)

7. Disconnect accelerator cable from throttle body.
8. **On models with automatic transaxle,** disconnect throttle cable from throttle body.
9. **On all models,** disconnect air intake temperature sensor electrical connector.
10. Disconnect cruise control actuator cable from clamp on resonator and air cleaner.
11. Loosen air cleaner hose clamp bolt, then remove air cleaner cap clips.
12. Disconnect air cleaner hose from throttle body, then remove air cleaner cap with resonator and hose assembly.
13. Remove air cleaner case attaching bolts, then remove cleaner case.
14. **On models with cruise control,** remove cruise control actuator.
15. **On all models,** disconnect ground strap from battery carrier.
16. Remove radiator, then disconnect coolant reservoir hose.
17. Disconnect washer tank electrical connector and hose, then remove washer tank assembly.
18. Disconnect engine relay box electrical connectors, then remove relay box.
19. Disconnect the following:
    a. Two connectors on lefthand fender apron.
    b. Igniter connector.
    c. Noise filter connector.
    d. Check connector.
    e. A/C magnet switch connector.
    f. Vacuum sensor connector.
    g. Back-up lamp connector.

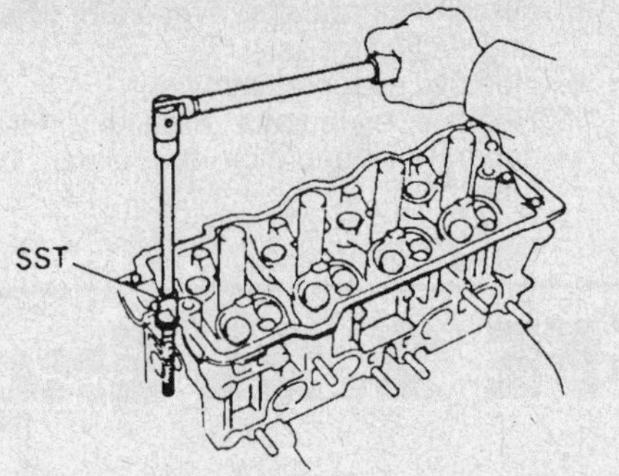
SST

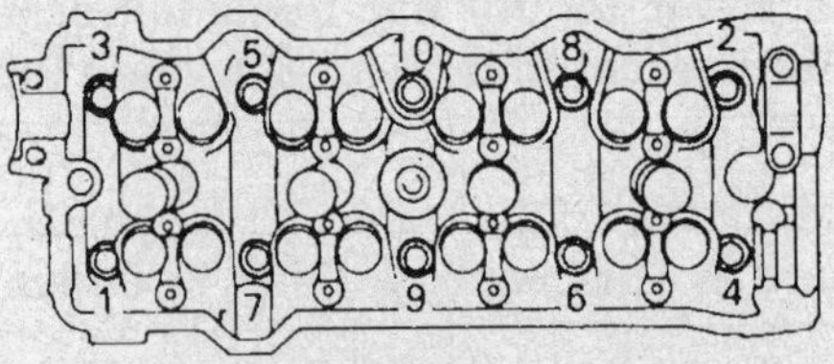
3
5
10
8
2
1
7
9
6
4

TY1069100070000X

Fig. 3 Cylinder head bolt loosening sequence

    h. Righthand fender apron ground strap.
    i. Speed sensor connector.
20. Disconnect heater hoses.
21. Place suitable container below fuel return hose, then disconnect hose.
22. Place suitable container below fuel inlet hose, then disconnect hose.
23. **On models with manual transaxle,** remove starter, then clutch release cylinder. **Do not disconnect clutch release cylinder tube.**
24. **On all models,** disconnect transaxle control cables.
25. Disconnect vacuum sensor hose and brake booster vacuum hose from air intake chamber, then charcoal canister vacuum hose.
26. Remove instrument panel undercover, lower instrument panel, glove compartment door and glove compartment.
27. Disconnect two engine ECU electrical connectors, then the four cowl wiring electrical connectors.
28. In engine compartment, remove engine wire harness attaching nuts, then pull harness from cowl.
29. **On models with A/C,** disconnect A/C compressor electrical connector, remove A/C belt and compressor attaching bolts, then position A/C compressor assembly aside. **Do not disconnect compressor tubes.**
30. **On all models,** disconnect front exhaust pipe, then remove driveshafts.
31. **On models with power steering,** disconnect power steering pump electrical connector, remove belt and pump attaching bolts, then position power steering pump assembly aside. **Do not disconnect pump hoses.**
32. **On all models,** remove lefthand engine mount attaching bolts, then disconnect mount.
33. Remove righthand rear engine mount hole plugs, then remove attaching nuts and disconnect mount.

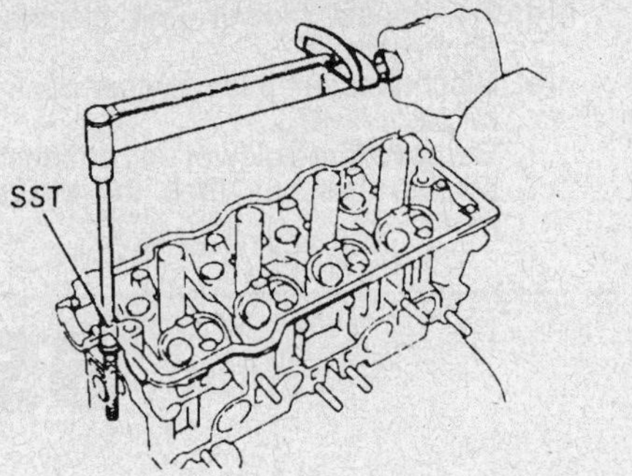
SST

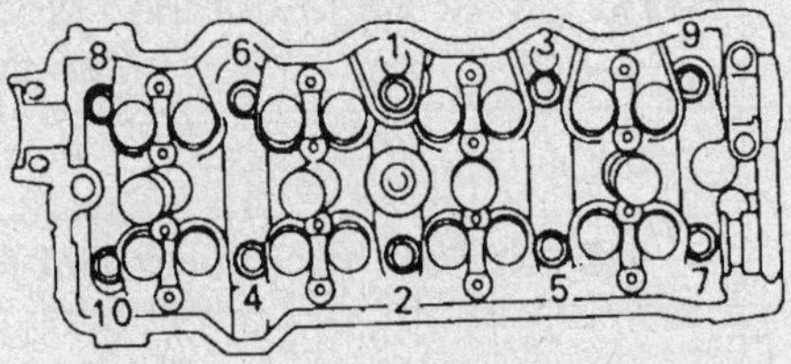
8
6
1
3
9
10
4
2
5
7

TY1069100071000X

Fig. 4 Cylinder head bolt tightening sequence (Step 1)

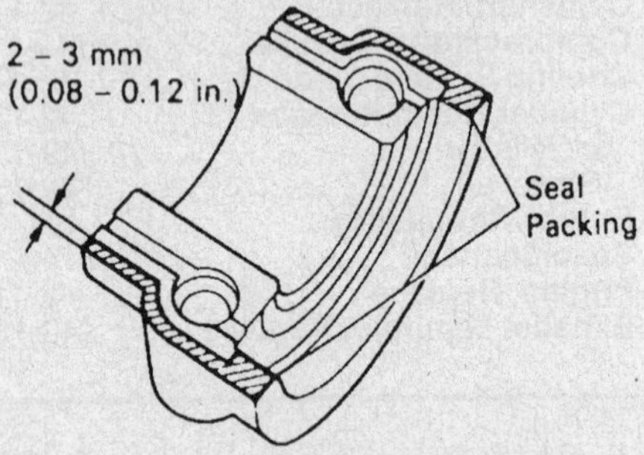
2 – 3 mm
(0.08 – 0.12 in.)
Seal
Packing

TY1069100073000X

Fig. 6 No. 1 bearing cap seal packing

34. Remove righthand front engine mount attaching bolts, then disconnect mount.
35. Install suitable engine lifting equipment.
36. Remove engine moving control rod.
37. Remove engine and transaxle assembly.
38. **On models with automatic transaxle,** remove starter assembly.
39. **On all models,** separate engine and transaxle.
40. Remove No. 2 righthand engine mount bracket.
41. Remove front righthand engine mount.
42. Remove rear righthand engine mount.
43. Reverse procedure to install, noting the following:
    a. Tighten attaching nuts and bolts to specifications.
    b. Reset audio anti-theft system, if necessary, as outlined under "Precautions."

INTAKE MANIFOLD

REPLACE

1. **On models with coded audio anti-theft systems,**refer to "Precautions" for code procedures.

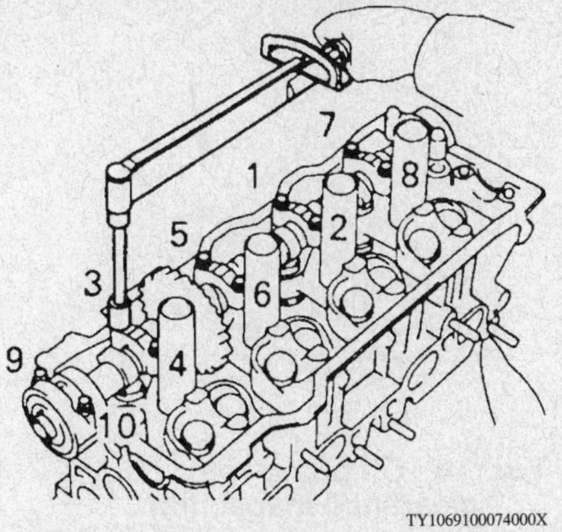
7
1
8
5
2
6
3
6
9
4
10
TY1069100074000X

Fig. 7 Intake camshaft bearing cap bolt tightening sequence

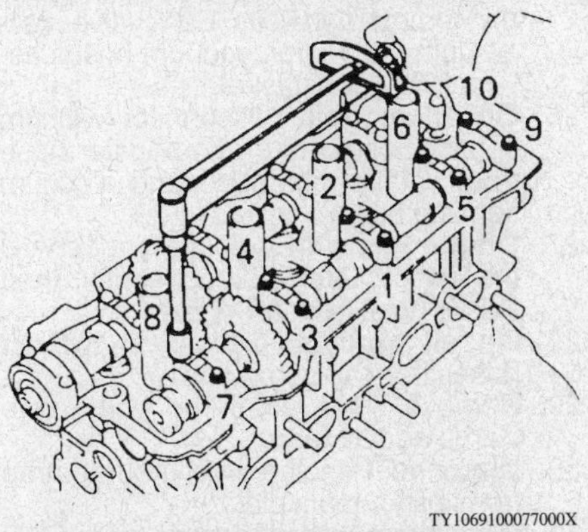
10
9
6
2
5
4
1
8
3
7
TY1069100077000X

Fig. 10 Exhaust camshaft bearing cap bolt tightening sequence

2. **On all models,** disconnect battery ground cable.
3. **On models with automatic transmission,** remove throttle cable bracket from cylinder head cover.
4. **On all models,** remove accelerator and actuator cable bracket from cylinder head cover.
5. Disconnect all electrical connectors, hoses, cables, fuel lines and electrical equipment that will interfere with removal of intake manifold.
6. Remove air tube, and if equipped, power steering air hoses.
7. Remove manifold stay.
8. Remove intake manifold attaching bolts, then the intake manifold and gasket.
9. Reverse procedure to install, noting the following:
   a. Tighten to specifications.
   b. Reset audio anti-theft system, if necessary, as outlined under "Precautions."

EXHAUST MANIFOLD

REPLACE

1. **On models with coded audio anti-theft systems,** refer to "Precautions" for code procedures.
2. **On all models,** disconnect battery ground cable.
3. Remove exhaust pipe from exhaust manifold.

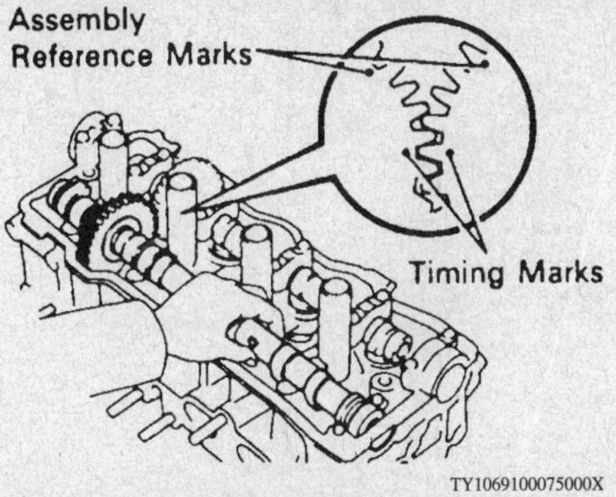
Assembly
Reference Marks
Timing Marks
TY1069100075000X

Fig. 8 Camshaft gear timing mark location

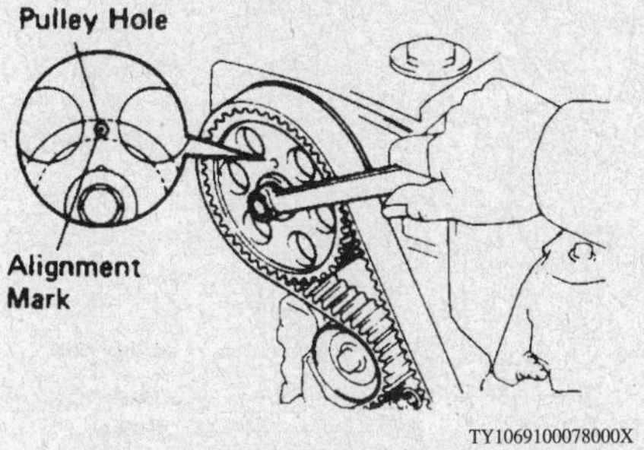
Pulley Hole
Alignment
Mark
TY1069100078000X

Fig. 11 Camshaft sprocket alignment

4. Disconnect all electrical connectors, hoses, cables, fuel lines and electrical equipment that will interfere with removal of exhaust manifold.
5. Remove lower insulators, and if necessary, catalytic converter.
6. Remove exhaust manifold attaching bolts, then exhaust manifold and gasket.
7. Reverse procedure to install, noting the following:
   a. Tighten fasteners to specifications.
   b. Reset audio anti-theft system, if necessary, as outlined under "Precautions."

CYLINDER HEAD

REPLACE

REMOVAL

1. **On models with coded audio anti-theft systems,** refer to "Precautions" for code procedures.
2. **On models with automatic transmission,** disconnect throttle cable from throttle body.
3. **On all models,** drain coolant into a suitable container.
4. Disconnect accelerator cable from throttle body.
5. Disconnect the following:
   a. Air intake connector.
   b. Cruise control actuator cable from clamp on resonator and air cleaner cap.
   c. Loosen air cleaner hose clamp bolt, then disconnect four air cleaner cap clips.
   d. Air cleaner hose from throttle body. Remove air cleaner cap together with resonator and air cleaner hose.

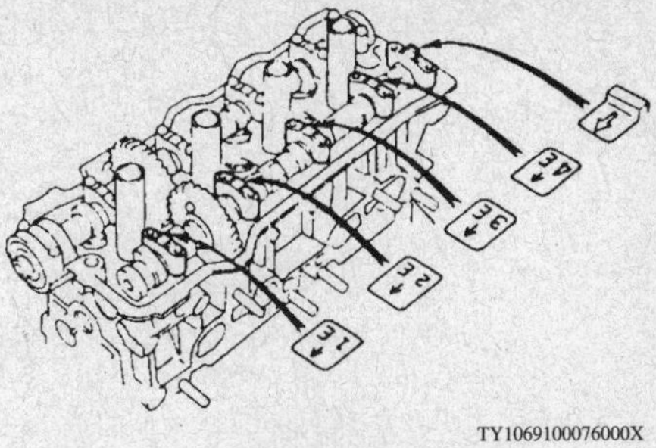
TY1069100076000X

Fig. 9 Exhaust bearing cap location

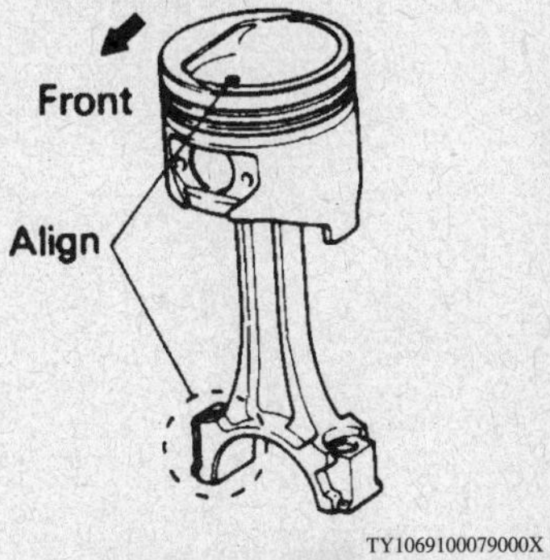
Front
Align
TY1069100079000X

Fig. 12 Piston & connecting rod assembly

6. Remove alternator drive belt, then disconnect alternator connector and wire. Remove alternator.
7. Remove distributor as outlined under "Distributor, Replace."
8. Disconnect front exhaust pipe.
9. **On Federal models,** disconnect oxygen sensor connector, then remove six bolts and manifold upper heat insulator.
10. **On California models,** disconnect main and sub-oxygen sensor connectors, then remove six bolts and manifold upper heat insulator.
11. **On all models,** remove bolt, nut and manifold No. 1 stay.
12. Remove bolt, nut and manifold stay.
13. **On Federal models,** remove six nuts and exhaust manifold, then four bolts and lower heat insulator.
14. **On California models,** remove the following parts:
    a. Six nuts, exhaust manifold and catalytic converter.
    b. Three bolts.
    c. Manifold lower heat insulator.
    d. Eight bolts.
    e. Two catalytic converter heat insulators
    f. Three bolts and two nuts.
    g. Exhaust manifold, gasket, retainer and cushion.
    h. Catalytic converter.
15. **On all models,** disconnect oil pressure switch connector and engine wire (for oxygen sensor(s)) from engine hanger.
16. Disconnect following connectors:
    a. Water temperature sender gauge connector.
    b. Water temperature sensor connector.

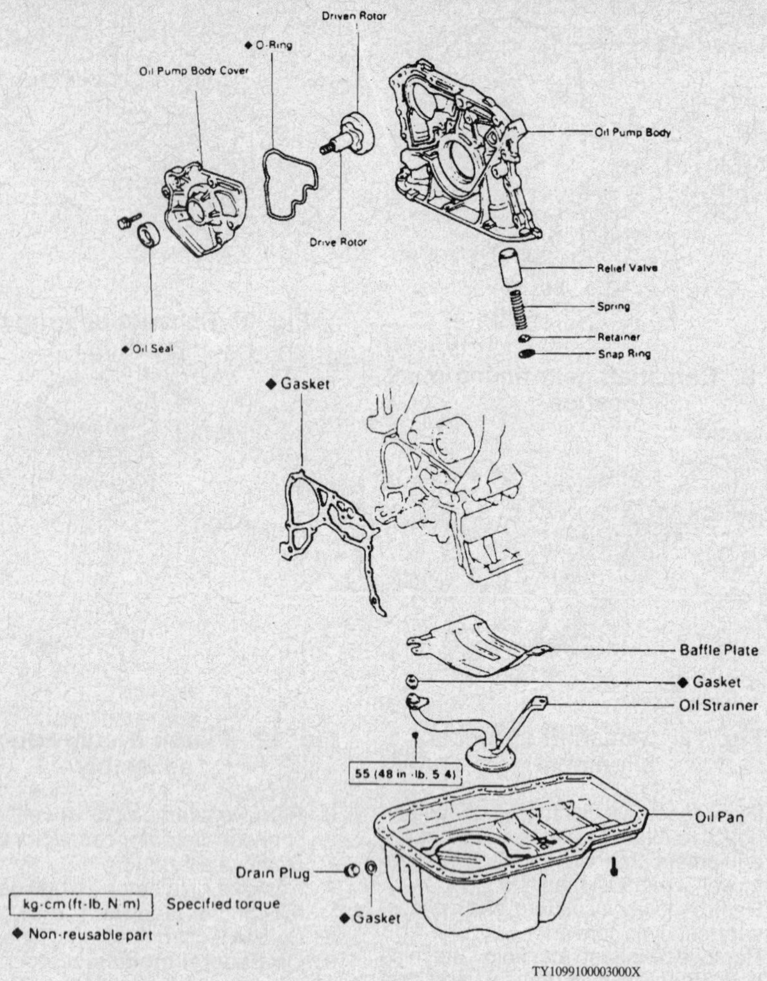
Driven Rotor
◆ O-Ring
Oil Pump Body Cover
Oil Pump Body
Drive Rotor
Relief Valve
Spring
Retainer
Snap Ring
◆ Oil Seal
◆ Gasket
Baffle Plate
◆ Gasket
Oil Strainer
55 (48 in.-lb, 5.4)
Oil Pan
Drain Plug
◆ Gasket
kg-cm (ft-lb, N·m) Specified torque
◆ Non-reusable part
TY1099100003000X

Fig. 13 Oil pump & components

17. Disconnect following hoses from water outlet:
    a. Upper radiator hose.
    b. Water bypass pipe hose.
    c. Heater water hose.
    d. ISC water bypass hose.
    e. Two EVAP BVSV vacuum hoses.
18. Remove two bolts, gasket and water outlet.
19. Disconnect following hoses from water bypass pipe:
    a. ISC water bypass hose.
    b. Heater water hose.
    c. **On models with oil cooler,** two oil cooler water bypass hoses.
20. **On all models,** remove two bolts, two nuts, water bypass pipe, gasket and O-ring.
21. Disconnect following connectors from throttle body:
    a. Throttle position sensor connector.
    b. ISC valve connector.
22. Disconnect following hoses from top end of throttle body:
    a. PCV hose.
    b. Two vacuum hoses from EGR vacuum modulator.
    c. Vacuum hose from EVAP VSV.
23. Remove four throttle body mounting bolts.
24. Disconnect following hoses from bottom end of throttle body:

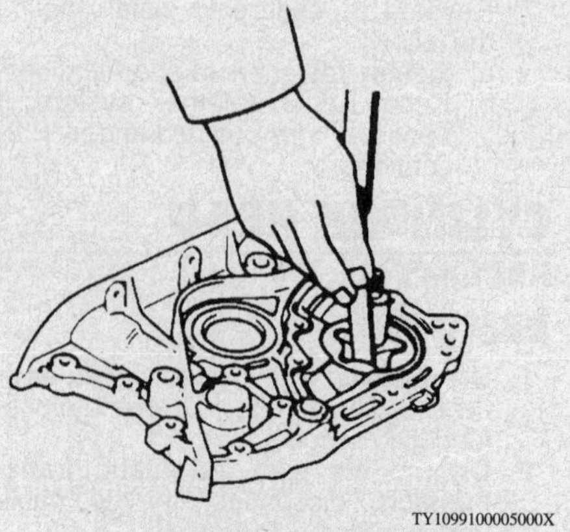
TY1099100005000X

Fig. 15 Oil pump rotor body clearance inspection

    a. Water bypass hose from water outlet.
    b. Water bypass hose from water bypass pipe.
    c. Air hose from air tube.
25. **On California models,** disconnect and remove the following EGR system components:
    a. EGR gas temperature sensor connector.
    b. Remove two vacuum hoses from EGR VSV and vacuum hose from

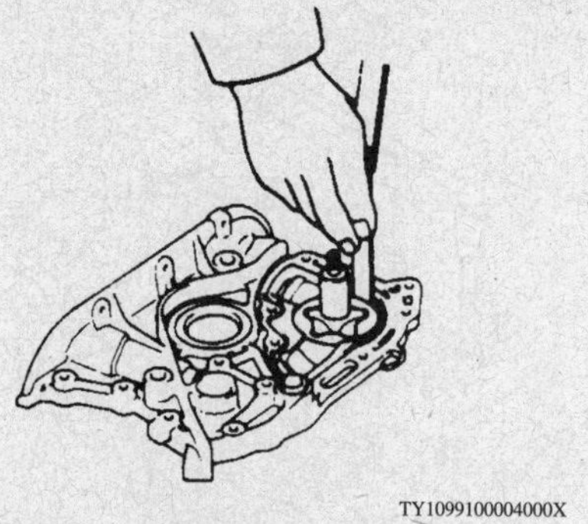
TY1099100004000X

Fig. 14 Oil pump rotor body clearance inspection

charcoal canister.
    c. Disconnect vacuum hose clamp, then loosen union nut of EGR pipe.
    d. Remove two bolts, EGR valve, vacuum modulator, vacuum hoses assembly and gasket.
26. **On all models,** disconnect vacuum sensor hose and brake booster hose from intake chamber and vacuum sensing hose.
27. **On models with A/C,** disconnect A/C magnetic clutch VSV connector, then the air hose from A/C VSV.
28. **On all models,** disconnect two air hoses from air pump.
29. Remove three air pump bolts, wire clamp and air tube.
30. Disconnect engine wire ground strap from intake manifold.
31. Disconnect knock sensor and EGR VSV connectors.
32. Remove intake manifold as follows:
    a. Remove four bolts, No. 1 air intake chamber and manifold stays.
    b. **On California models,** remove wire bracket.
    c. **On all models,** remove six bolts, two nuts, intake manifold and gasket.
    d. Disconnect two wire clamps from wire bracket on intake manifold.
33. Remove delivery pipe and injectors as follows:
    a. Disconnect injector connectors.
    b. Loosen pulsation damper, then disconnect fuel inlet hose.
    c. Disconnect fuel return hose.
    d. Remove two bolts and delivery pipe together with four injectors. **Do not drop injectors when removing delivery pipe.**
    e. Remove four insulators and two spacers from cylinder head.
    f. Pull out four injectors from delivery pipe.
    g. Remove O-ring and grommet from each injector.
34. Remove camshaft timing pulley as outlined under "Timing Belt, Replace."
35. Remove No. 1 idler pulley and tension spring.
36. Remove No. 3 timing belt cover. **Support timing belt so that meshing of crankshaft timing pulley and timing belt does not shift. Do not allow dust, oil or water to come in contact with timing belt.**
37. Remove engine hangers, alternator

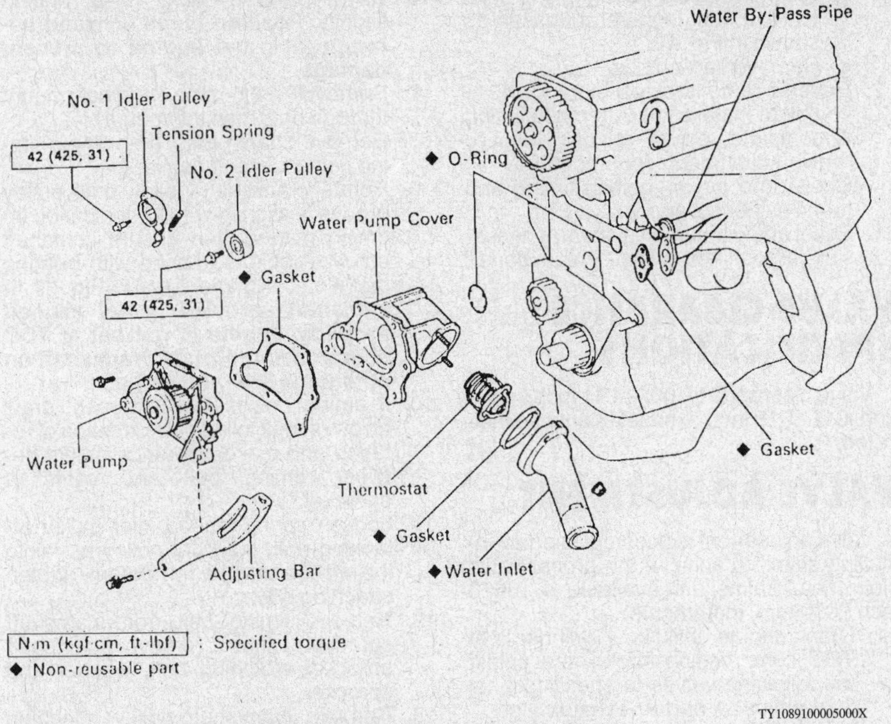
Water By-Pass Pipe
No. 1 Idler Pulley
Tension Spring
42 (425, 31)
No. 2 Idler Pulley
◆ O-Ring
Water Pump Cover
◆ Gasket
42 (425, 31)
Water Pump
◆ Gasket
Thermostat
◆ Gasket
Adjusting Bar
◆ Water Inlet
N·m (kgf·cm, ft·lbf) : Specified torque
◆ Non-reusable part
TY1089100005000X

Fig. 16 Water pump removal

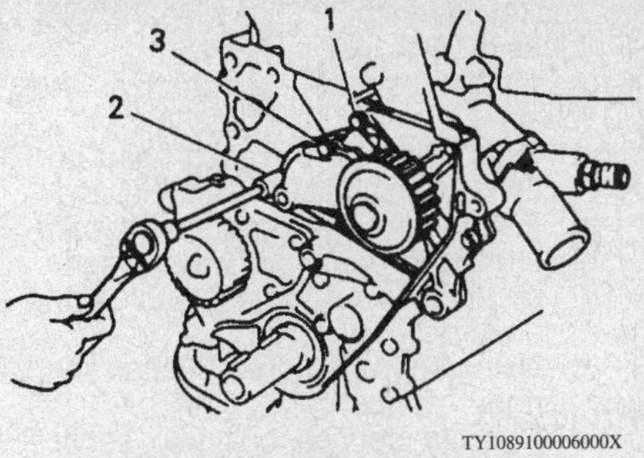
1
2
3
TY1089100006000X

Fig. 17 Water pump bolt tightening sequence

bracket and oil pressure switch.

38. Remove cylinder head cover and gasket. Arrange grommets in correct order so they can be installed in original position.
39. Remove high-tension cord, clamp and PCV valve.
40. Remove camshafts. **Since clearance of camshafts is small, camshaft must be level when removed. If camshaft is not kept level, shaft thrust may crack or damage camshaft.**
41. Remove exhaust camshaft as follows:
    a. Set knock pin of intake camshaft at 10–45° BTDC of camshaft angle. The above angle allows No. 2 and No. 4 cylinder cam lobes of exhaust camshaft to push their valve lifters evenly.
    b. Secure exhaust camshaft sub-gear to drive gear with a service bolt. Recommended service bolt is .63–.79 inch (16–20 mm) long and has a .2362 inch (6 mm) thread diameter and a .0393 inch (1 mm) thread pitch. When removing camshaft, ensure torsional spring force of sub-gear has been eliminated by above operation.
    c. Remove two bolts and bearing cap.
    d. Uniformly loosen and remove six bolts on No. 1, No. 2 and No. 4 bearing caps in several passes in sequence shown, **Fig. 1.** Remove No. 1, No. 2 and No. 4 bearing caps.
    e. Alternately loosen and remove two bolts on No. 3 bearing cap. As the two No. 3 bearing cap bolts are loosened. Ensure camshaft is lifted out evenly. If camshaft is not being lifted out evenly, retighten two No. 3 bearing cap bolts, then reverse order of Steps e through a and reset knock pin of intake camshaft 10–45° BTDC and repeat Steps b through e.
    f. Remove No. 3 bearing cap and exhaust camshaft.

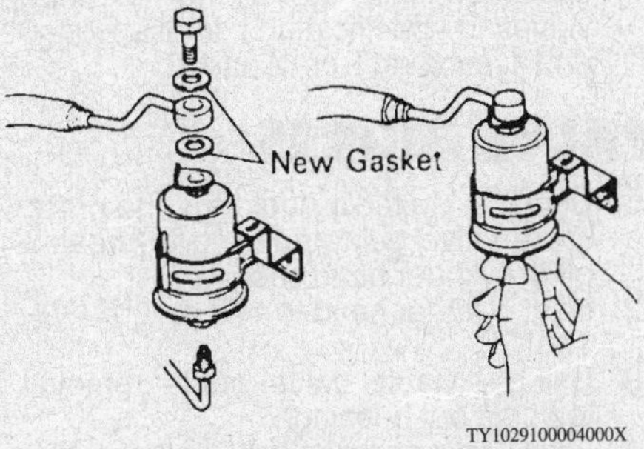
New Gasket
TY1029100004000X

Fig. 18 Fuel filter replacement

42. Remove intake camshaft as follows:
    a. Set knock pin of intake camshaft at 80–115° BTDC of camshaft angle. The above angle allows No. 1 and No. 3 cylinder cam lobes of intake camshaft to push their valve lifters evenly.
    b. Remove two bolts, front bearing cap and oil seal.
    c. Uniformly loosen and remove six bolts on No. 1, No. 3 and No. 4 bearing caps in several passes in sequence shown, **Fig. 2.** Do not remove No. 2 bearing cap bolts at this time. Remove No. 1, No. 3 and No. 4 bearing caps.
    d. Alternately loosen and remove two bolts on No. 2 bearing cap. As two No. 2 bearing cap bolts are loosened, ensure camshaft is lifted out evenly after breaking adhesion on front bearing cap. If camshaft is not being lifted out evenly, retighten two No. 2 bearing cap bolts, then reverse order of Steps d through a and reset knock pin of intake camshaft 80–115° BTDC and repeat Steps b through d.
    e. Remove No. 2 bearing cap and exhaust camshaft.
43. Disassemble exhaust camshaft as follows:
    a. Mount hexagon wrench portion of camshaft in a suitable vise. **Do not damage camshaft.**
    b. Insert a service bolt into service hole of camshaft sub-gear, then using a screwdriver, turn sub-gear clockwise and remove service bolt. **Do not damage camshaft.**
    c. Using snap ring pliers, remove snap ring.
    d. Remove wave washer, camshaft sub-gear and camshaft gear spring.
44. Remove cylinder head as follows:
    a. Using a 12–point 12 mm socket, tool No. 09011-38121, or equivalent, uniformly loosen and remove cylinder head bolts in several passes as shown, **Fig. 3. Cylinder head warpage or cracking may occur from removing bolts in incorrect order.**
    b. Lift cylinder head from dowels on cylinder block and place cylinder head on wooden blocks on a bench.

INSTALLATION

1. Install new gasket on engine block, then place cylinder head on cylinder block.
2. Coat cylinder head bolt threads and under bolt head with clean engine oil, then install cylinder head bolts.
3. Using a 12–point 12 mm socket, tool No. 09011-38121, or equivalent, uniformly tighten cylinder head bolts in several passes as shown, **Fig. 4. Torque** bolts to 36 ft. lbs.
4. Mark front of cylinder head bolt with paint, then retighten bolts 90° in numerical order shown in **Fig. 4.** Ensure painted mark is 90° to front, **Fig. 5.**
5. Screw threads of spark plug tube coated with adhesive into cylinder head. Using spark plug tube nut and 30 mm

socket wrench, tighten spark plug tubes to 29 ft. lbs.

6. Assemble exhaust camshaft as follows:
   a. Mount hexagon wrench head portion of camshaft in a suitable vise.
   b. Install camshaft gear spring, camshaft sub-gear and wave washer. Align pins on gears with spring ends.
   c. Using snap ring pliers, install snap ring.
   d. Insert a service bolt into service hole of camshaft sub-gear, then using a screwdriver, align holes of camshaft main and sub-gear by turning camshaft sub-gear clockwise and install a service bolt.
7. Install intake camshaft as follows:
   a. **Since clearance of camshafts is small, camshaft must be level when installed. If camshaft is not kept level, shaft thrust may crack or damage camshaft.**
   b. Apply multi-purpose grease to thrust portion of camshaft.
   c. Place camshaft at 80–115° BTDC of camshaft angle on cylinder head. This angle allows No. 1 and No. 3 cylinder cam lobes of intake camshaft to push their valve lifters evenly.
   d. Apply seal packing to No. 1 bearing cap as shown in **Fig. 6.** Install bearing caps in their proper locations.
   e. Apply a thin coat of clean engine oil on threads and under bolt head of bearing cap bolts. Install and uniformly **torque**bolts to 14 ft. lbs. in several passes, **Fig. 7.**
   f. Apply suitable grease to new oil seal lip, then using crankshaft front oil seal replacer tool No. 09223-46011, or equivalent, tap in seal.
8. Install exhaust camshaft as follows:
   a. Set knock pin of intake camshaft to 10–45° BTDC of camshaft angle. This angle allows No. 2 and No. 4 cylinder cam lobes of exhaust camshaft to push their valve lifters evenly.
   b. Apply suitable grease to thrust portions of camshaft. Engage exhaust camshaft gear to intake camshaft gear by matching timing marks on each gear.
   c. Roll down exhaust camshaft onto bearing journals while engaging gears with each other. **There are also assembly reference marks on each gear as shown in Fig. 8. Do not use these marks.**
   d. Turn intake camshaft clockwise or counterclockwise little by little until exhaust camshaft sits in bearing journals evenly without rocking camshaft on bearing journals. **It is very important to place camshaft in bearing journals evenly while tightening bearing caps as shown in Fig. 9.**
   e. Install bearing caps in their proper locations.
   f. Apply a light coat of clean engine oil on threads and under bolt head of bearing cap bolts. Install and uniformly **torque**ten bearing cap bolts to 14 ft. lbs. in several passes as shown in **Fig. 10.**
   g. Remove service bolt.
9. Reverse removal steps 1 through 42 to complete installation. After installation is complete, adjust valves. Refer to "Valve Adjustment" for procedure.
10. Check and adjust ignition timing and toe-in as necessary.
11. Reset audio anti-theft system, if necessary, as outlined under "Precautions."

VALVE CLEARANCE SPECIFICATIONS

Valve clearance of .007–.011 inch intake and .011–.015 inch exhaust should be indicated.

VALVE ADJUSTMENT

Valve adjustment is accomplished by installing shims to achieve the proper valve clearance. Shims are available in .0020 inch (.050 mm) increments.

1. Crank engine until No. 1 cylinder is at TDC compression stroke and adjust the following valves to specifications: intake Nos. 1 and 2, exhaust Nos. 1 and 3.
2. Rotate engine one complete revolution clockwise and adjust the following valves to specifications: intake Nos. 3 and 4, exhaust Nos. 2 and 4.

VALVE GUIDES

1. Using a suitable tool and hammer, strike valve guide bushing to break it off at cylinder head casting.
2. Heat cylinder head to 176–212°F (80–100°C).
3. Using suitable valve guide removal tool, tap out bushing.
4. Install snap ring on new valve guide, then install new valve guide using tool as outlined above and driving in from reverse side of removal.
5. Ream new valve guide, if necessary.

HYDRAULIC LIFTERS

REPLACE

Inspect lifters for excessive wear and/or damage. Replace worn or damaged valve lifters as required. Lubricate hydraulic valve lifter before installation.

TIMING BELT

REPLACE

REMOVAL

1. **On models with coded audio anti-theft systems,**refer to "Precautions" for code procedures.
2. **On all models,** disconnect battery ground cable.
3. Remove right front wheel and undercover.
4. Remove cruise control actuator and bracket (if equipped).
5. Remove accessory drive belts, then alternator and alternator bracket.
6. Using suitable jack, raise engine slightly. **Position block of wood between jack and engine to prevent damage.**
7. Remove right side engine mount through bolt, then the mount.
8. Remove spark plugs, then upper timing belt cover and gasket.
9. Rotate crankshaft pulley until pulley groove is aligned with "0" indication on timing marks, then ensure camshaft sprocket hole is aligned with bearing cap No. 1 alignment mark, **Fig. 11. If camshaft sprocket is not aligned properly, engine is not set at TDC compression. Rotate crankshaft an additional 360° and recheck.**
10. If timing belt is to be reused, draw arrow on belt to indicate direction of rotation and make reference marks between timing belt and camshaft sprocket.
11. Loosen spring loaded idler pulley attaching bolt, then pry pulley as far to the left as possible. Temporarily tighten attaching bolt.
12. Remove timing belt from camshaft sprocket, then remove camshaft sprocket attaching bolt, washer and sprocket.
13. Remove crankshaft pulley attaching bolt, then using suitable puller, remove crankshaft pulley.
14. Remove lower timing belt cover and gasket.
15. If timing belt is to be reused, make reference marks between timing belt and crankshaft sprocket, then remove belt and belt guide.
16. Remove spring loaded idler pulley attaching bolt, then the pulley and tension spring.
17. Remove fixed idler pulley attaching bolt, then the idler pulley.
18. Pry off crankshaft sprocket with two screwdrivers.
19. While holding oil pump sprocket with suitable tool, remove oil pump nut and sprocket.

INSTALLATION

1. Install oil pump sprocket. Tighten attaching nut to specification.
2. Install crankshaft sprocket, then the fixed idler pulley. Tighten idler pulley attaching bolt to specification.
3. Install spring loaded idler pulley and loosely install attaching bolt. Install spring, then pry pulley as far to the left as possible and tighten attaching bolt.
4. Temporarily install timing belt on crankshaft sprocket, oil pump sprocket, fixed idler pulley and water pump sprocket. If belt is being reused, install in proper direction and align reference mark on crankshaft sprocket made during removal procedures. **The engine should be cold during belt installation.**
5. Install timing belt guide, cup side up on crankshaft sprocket, then the lower timing cover.
6. Install crankshaft pulley. Tighten attaching bolt to specification. Ensure crankshaft pulley groove is still aligned with "0" timing mark, indicating No. 1

cylinder is at TDC of compression stroke.
7. Install camshaft sprocket, washer and attaching bolt. Tighten attaching bolt to specification. Rotate camshaft by turning sprocket attaching bolt to align bearing cap mark and camshaft sprocket, **Fig. 11.**
8. Install timing belt on camshaft sprocket. If timing belt is being reused, align reference marks made during removal procedures.
9. Ensure belt has tension between crankshaft sprocket, water pump sprocket and camshaft sprocket.
10. Loosen spring loaded idler pulley attaching bolt just enough to allow pulley to move by itself under spring tension. Allow pulley to take up belt tension.
11. Rotate crankshaft clockwise two complete revolutions, from TDC compression stroke to TDC compression stroke, then tighten spring loaded idler pulley to specification. **Ensure timing belt has tension between water pump sprocket and camshaft sprocket.**
12. Install upper timing belt cover and spark plugs.
13. Install right side engine mount, then lower engine.
14. Install alternator bracket, alternator and accessory drive belts.
15. Install cruise control actuator and bracket.
16. Install engine undercover and right front wheel, then battery ground cable.
17. Reset audio anti-theft system, if necessary, as outlined under "Precautions."

CAMSHAFT

REPLACE

Refer to "Cylinder Head, Replace" for camshaft removal procedures.

PISTON & ROD ASSEMBLY

Only standard pistons are available, if piston bore is not within specifications, replace piston and/or cylinder block. When assembling piston onto connecting rod, ensure mark on top of piston and mark on connecting rod are on same side, **Fig. 12.** When installing piston and connecting rod assembly, ensure mark on top of piston is facing toward front of engine.

MAIN & ROD BEARINGS

Only standard bearings are available. If crankshaft journals or crankpins are worn or scored, the crankshaft must be replaced.

OIL PAN

REPLACE

1. **On models with coded audio anti-theft systems,**refer to "Precautions" for code procedures.
2. **On all models,** disconnect battery ground cable.
3. Remove engine hood.
4. Raise and support vehicle.
5. Remove engine undercovers, then drain engine oil.
6. Disconnect exhaust pipe from catalytic converter.
7. Remove suspension lower crossmember, then the engine mount center member.
8. Remove stiffener plate, then the oil dipstick.
9. Remove oil pan attaching bolts, then the oil pan. **Use caution not to damage oil pan flange.**
10. Remove two attaching bolts, nuts, oil pan baffle plate, then the oil strainer with gasket, **Fig. 13.**
11. Attach a suitable hoist to engine, then lift and suspend engine with hoist.
12. Remove timing belt and pulleys. Refer to "Timing Belt, Replace" for procedure.
13. Remove oil pump attaching bolts, then the oil pump.
14. Reverse procedure to install, noting the following:
    a. Use new gaskets and O-ring seals as applicable.
    b. Tighten fasteners to specifications.
    c. Reset audio anti-theft system, if necessary, as outlined under "Precautions."

OIL PUMP

REPLACE

Refer to "Oil Pan, Replace" for procedure.

OIL PUMP SERVICE

1. Using a suitable feeler gauge, measure clearance between driven rotor and pump case, **Fig. 14.**
2. Clearance should be .0039–.0067 inch. If feeler gauge clearance obtained exceeds .0079 inch, replace oil pump rotor set and/or pump case.
3. Using a feeler gauge, measure clearance between both rotor tips, **Fig. 15.** Clearance should be .0016–.0067 inch. If feeler gauge clearance obtained exceeds .0079 inch, replace oil pump rotor set.

BELT TENSION DATA

Belt tension is as follows using a belt tension gauge. A new belt is considered used after five minutes of use.

Belt	New, Lbs.	Used, Lbs.
Alternator w/A/C	170–180	120–140
Alternator Less A/C	100–150	75–115
Power Steer.	100–150	60–100

COOLING SYSTEM BLEED

These engines do not require a specified bleed procedure. After filling cooling system, run engine to operating temperature with radiator/pressure cap off. Air will then be automatically bled through cap opening.

THERMOSTAT

REPLACE

1. **On models with coded audio anti-theft systems,**refer to "Precautions" for code procedures.
2. **On all models,** disconnect battery ground cable.
3. Drain coolant.
4. Disconnect radiator from water inlet housing.
5. Remove water inlet housing attaching nuts from water pump, then remove inlet housing.
6. Remove thermostat and gasket.
7. Reverse procedure to install. Reset audio anti-theft system, if necessary, as outlined under "Precautions."

WATER PUMP

REPLACE

1. **On models with coded audio anti-theft systems,**refer to "Precautions" for code procedures.
2. **On all models,** disconnect battery ground cable.
3. Disconnect lower radiator hose from coolant inlet housing, then the coolant temperature switch connector.
4. Remove timing belt and sprockets. Refer to "Timing Belt, Replace" for procedure.
5. Remove alternator belt adjusting bar.
6. Remove water bypass tubes to water pump cover attaching bolts, then the three water pump attaching bolts, **Fig. 16.**
7. Remove water pump and pump cover as an assembly, then remove two O-rings and gasket.
8. Remove water pump to water pump cover attaching bolts, then remove water pump.
9. Reverse procedure to install, noting the following:
    a. Tighten water pump bolts to specifications in sequence shown, **Fig. 17.**
    b. Reset audio anti-theft system, if necessary, as outlined under "Precautions."

RADIATOR

REPLACE

1. **On models with coded audio anti-theft systems,**refer to "Precautions" for code procedures.
2. **On all models,** disconnect battery ground cable, then raise and support vehicle.
3. Drain coolant from engine and radiator.
4. Remove cruise control actuator cover.
5. Disconnect upper radiator and coolant reservoir hoses from radiator.
6. Disconnect lower radiator hose at engine, then transaxle oil cooler extension lines.
7. Disconnect electric cooling fan and

temperature sensor connectors, then cruise control cable from holder on fan shroud.

8. Remove upper radiator mounts, then lift out radiator and cooling fans as a unit.
9. Remove transaxle cooler extension lines and lower radiator from radiator.
10. Remove securing bolts, then the electric cooling fans and shrouds.
11. Remove lower radiator mounts.
12. Reverse procedure to install. Reset audio anti-theft system, if necessary, as outlined under "Precautions."

FUEL PUMP

REPLACE

1. **On models with coded audio anti-theft systems,** refer to "Precautions" for code procedures.
2. **On all models,** remove rear seat cushion.
3. Disconnect fuel pump connector, then remove five screws and service hole cover.
4. Remove fuel pump lead wire, then disconnect fuel line from fuel pump bracket. **Remove fuel filter cap to prevent fuel from flowing out.**
5. Remove fuel pump bracket assembly, gasket and pull pump out.
6. Reverse procedure to install. Reset audio anti-theft system, if necessary, as outlined under "Precautions."

FUEL FILTER

REPLACE

Refer to **Fig. 18** for replacement procedure.

TIGHTENING SPECIFICATIONS

Year	Component	Torque/Ft. Lbs.
1993–96	A/C Compressor	20
	Alternator Bracket To Cylinder Head	31
	Camshaft Timing Pulley To Camshaft	40
	Catalytic Converter To Exhaust Manifold	22
	Cylinder Head Bolts To Cylinder Block	①
	Cylinder Head Cover To Cylinder Head	17
	Engine Moving Control Rod	47
	Exhaust Manifold To Cylinder Head	36
	Front Engine Mount	59
	Front Engine Mount Bracket	57
	Front Exhaust Pipe	46
	Front Exhaust Pipe To Exhaust Manifold	46
	Front Exhaust Pipe To Main Catalytic Converter	46
	Fuel Inlet Hose	22
	Intake Manifold To Cylinder Head	14
	LH Engine Mount	47
	Manifold Stay	31
	No. 2 Engine Mount Bracket	38
	No. 2 Idler Pulley To Cylinder Block	31
	Oil Pan Bolts	48②
	Oil Pump Bolts	7
	Oil Pump Pulley To Oil Pump Driveshaft	21
	Oil Strainer	48②
	Power Steering Pump	31
	Rear Engine Mount Bracket	47
	Rear Engine Mount	48
	Spark Plug Tube To Cylinder Head	29
	Stiffener Plate	27
	Throttle Body To Cylinder Head	13
	Water Pump Bolts	7

① — Torque to 36 ft. lbs., then an additional 90°.

② — Inch lbs.

1MZ-FE 3.0L & 3VZ-FE 3.0L Engines

NOTE: On Air Bag Equipped Models, Refer To "Air Bag System Precautions" Located In The Front Of This Manual For System Disarming & Arming Procedures.

INDEX

	Page No.
Belt Tension Data	42-31
Camshaft, Replace	42-30
Compression Pressure	42-19
Cooling System Bleed	42-31
Cylinder Head, Replace	42-22
1MZ-FE Engine	42-22
3VZ-FE Engine	42-25
Engine Rebuilding Specifications	48-1
Engine, Replace	42-19
1MZ-FE Engine	42-19
3VZ-FE Engine	42-21
Exhaust Manifold, Replace	42-22
Fuel Filter, Replace	42-32
Fuel Pump, Replace	42-32
Hydraulic Lifters, Replace	42-29
Intake Manifold, Replace	42-22
Main & Rod Bearings	42-30
Oil Pan, Replace	42-30
1MZ-FE Engine	42-30
3VZ-FE Engine	42-31
Oil Pump, Replace	42-31
Oil Pump Service	42-31
Piston & Rod Assembly	42-30
Precautions	42-19
Air Bag Systems	42-19
Audio Coded Anti-Theft System	42-19
Radiator, Replace	42-32
1993–94 Camry	42-32
Avalon & 1995–96 Camry	42-32
Thermostat, Replace	42-31
1MZ-FE Engine	42-31
3VZ-FE Engines	42-31
Tightening Specifications	42-33
1MZ-FE Engine	42-33
3VZ-FE Engine	42-35
Timing Belt, Replace	42-29
Installation	42-30
Removal	42-29
Valve Adjustment	42-28
Valve Clearance Specifications	42-25
1MZ-FE Engine	42-28
3VZ-FE Engine	42-28
Valve Guides	42-29
Water Pump, Replace	42-32
1MZ-FE Engine	42-32
3VZ-FE Engine	42-32

PRECAUTIONS

AIR BAG SYSTEMS

Refer to "Air Bag System Precautions" in the front of this manual for system disarming and arming procedures.

AUDIO CODED ANTI-THEFT SYSTEM

Some models are with an audio coded anti-theft system that will disable the radio when battery power is removed from the radio. The system can be identified by the words "ANTI-THEFT SYSTEM" on the cassette tape lid. Obtain the code from the customer for input before disconnecting battery power to the audio unit. Reset system after service as follows:

1. Obtain three digit code from customer.
2. Depress No. 1 (PROG) button while depressing righthand side of TUNE SEEK button, - - - will appear in tape operation display.
3. Enter code as follows:
   a. To enter first digit press No. 1 (PROG) button a sufficient number of times, starting with zero, to enter digit (if first digit of code is five press button six times).
   b. To enter second digit press No. 2 (APS) button a sufficient number of times, starting with zero, to enter digit.
   c. To enter third digit press No. 3 (RPT) button a sufficient number of times, starting with zero, to enter digit.
4. If three dashes (- - -) appear in tape operation display during input of digits, restart procedure from beginning.
5. When code digits are correctly input and displayed, press and hold SCAN button until SEC appears in tape operation display.
6. When SEC disappears from display audio unit should be operative.
7. If unit is not operative or Err is displayed, repeat procedure. **Attempting to input code more than nine times may permanently disable audio unit.**

COMPRESSION PRESSURE

1. Start and run engine until it reaches normal operating temperature.
2. Remove ignition coils as outlined under "Coil Pack, Replace."
3. Insert compression gauge into spark plug hole.
4. Fully open throttle.
5. While cranking engine, measure compression pressure.
6. Compression pressure should be 145–218 psi.
7. Maximum allowable difference between cylinders is 15 psi.

ENGINE

REPLACE

1MZ-FE ENGINE

Camry

1. **On models with coded audio anti-theft systems,** refer to "Precautions" for code procedures.
2. **On all models,** remove battery and tray, then the hood.
3. Raise and support vehicle, then drain engine oil and coolant.
4. Disconnect accelerator and throttle cables.
5. Remove air cleaner cap, volume air flow meter and air cleaner hose, as follows:
   a. Disconnect volume air flow meter connector, wire clamp and accelerator cable clamp.
   b. Disconnect PCV hose and loosen air cleaner hose clamp bolt.
   c. Disconnect four air cleaner cap clips, then remove air cleaner cap and volume air flow meter together with air cleaner hose.
   d. Remove air cleaner element and three bolts, then the air cleaner case.
6. **On models with cruise control,** remove cruise control actuator.
7. **On all models,** remove radiator, then disconnect engine wiring as follows:
   a. Two bolts to engine relay box.
   b. Five connectors from relay box.
   c. Two igniter connectors and noise filter connector.
   d. Connector from lefthand fender apron and two ground straps.
8. Disconnect engine attaching vacuum hoses and heater hoses.
9. Place suitable container below fuel lines, then disconnect lines.
10. Disconnect transaxle control cable from transaxle.
11. Disconnect passenger compartment

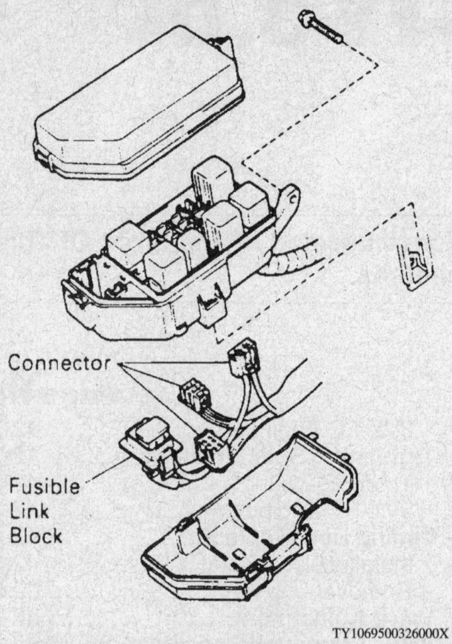
Connector
Fusible Link Block
TY1069500326000X

Fig. 1 Relay box removal. Avalon

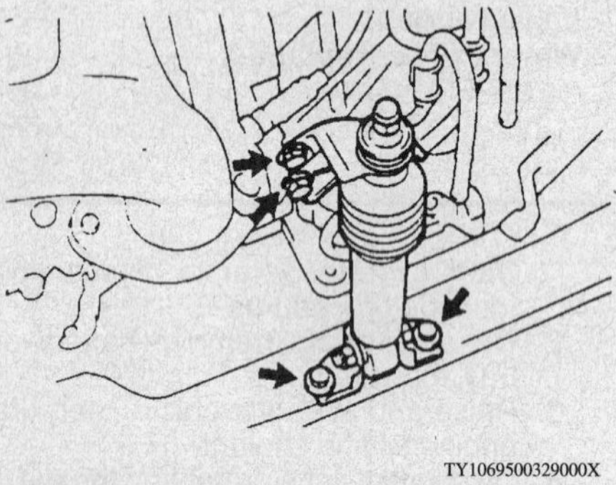
TY1069500329000X

Fig. 4 Engine mount absorber removal. Avalon

engine control wiring electrical connectors as follows:

a. Three ECM connectors.
b. Five cowl connectors.
c. Cooling fan ECU connector.
d. Wire clamp, then remove two nuts and pull engine wire from cowl panel.

12. Remove A/C compressor leaving pressure hoses connected. Position compressor and hoses aside.
13. Remove front exhaust pipe.
14. Remove both drive axles, then the power steering pressure tube.
15. Disconnect hydraulic cooling fan pressure hose.
16. Remove power steering pump, do not disconnect hoses and position aside.
17. Remove four left engine mount attaching bolts, then disconnect mount.
18. Remove two right rear engine mount hole plugs, then the four bolts and mount.
19. Remove four engine mounting shock absorber attaching bolts.
20. Remove three front right engine mount attaching bolts, then the mount.
21. Install suitable engine lifting equipment, then remove coolant reservoir tank.

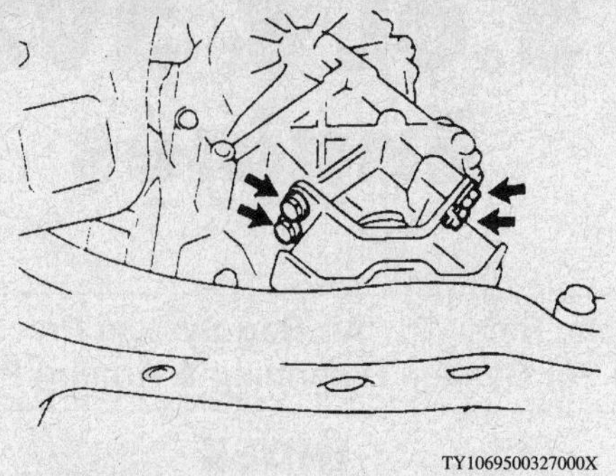
TY1069500327000X

Fig. 2 Transaxle mount. Avalon

22. Disconnect all ground straps, then remove No. 1 righthand engine mount three attaching bolts and mount.
23. Remove engine moving control rod and No. 2 right engine mount.
24. Remove engine and transaxle assembly, then the starter.
25. Separate engine/transaxle assembly.
26. Reverse procedure to install. Reset audio anti-theft system, if necessary, as outlined under "Precautions."

Avalon

1. **On models with coded audio anti-theft systems,** refer to "Precautions" for code procedures.
2. **On all models,** remove battery, battery tray and hood.
3. Remove engine undercover, then remove engine fender apron seals.
4. Drain engine coolant and engine oil.
5. Disconnect accelerator cable.
6. Remove air cleaner cap assembly and air cleaner case.
7. Remove cruise control actuator.
8. Remove radiator as outlined under "Radiator Replace."
9. Remove front exhaust pipe and catalytic converter as an assembly.
10. Disconnect engine wire harness from engine compartment relay box as follows:
    a. Remove bolt, and disconnect relay box from bracket, **Fig. 1.**
    b. Remove upper and lower covers.
    c. Disconnect three connectors and fusible link block from relay box.
11. Disconnect the following connectors, cables, clamps and hoses:
    a. Windshield wiper motor connector.
    b. Two igniter connectors and one noise filter connector on lefthand fender apron.
    c. Ground strap connectors from lefthand and righthand fender apron.
    d. Engine compartment main wire harness connectors on lefthand fender apron.
    e. Ground cable from battery to body bracket.
    f. Engine wire protector clamp from battery to body bracket.
    g. Engine wiring clamps from fuel filter and bracket on righthand fender apron.
    h. Brake booster vacuum hose from air intake chamber.
    i. Radiator and heater hoses.

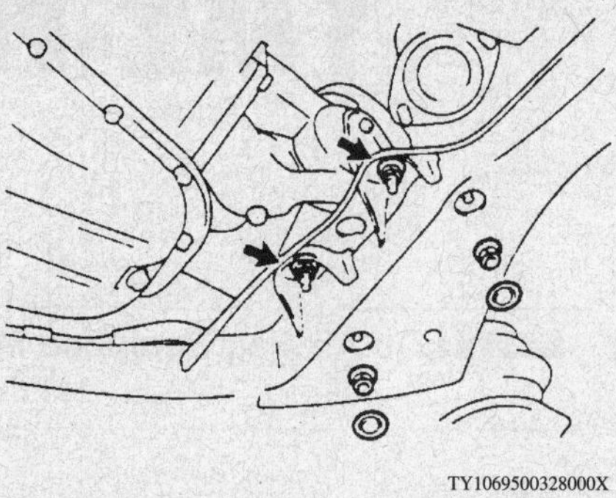
TY1069500328000X

Fig. 3 Rear engine mount. Avalon

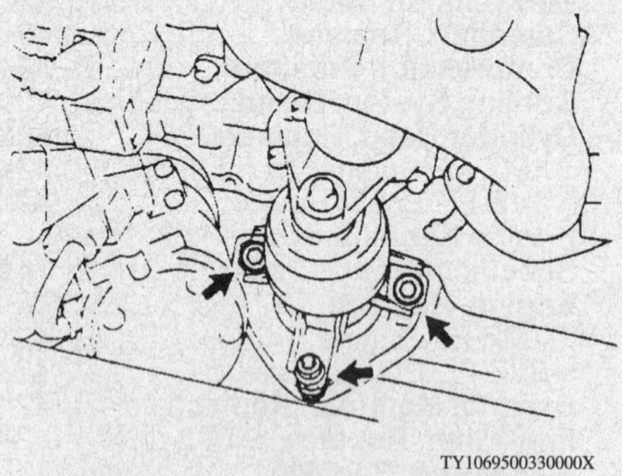
TY1069500330000X

Fig. 5 Front engine mount. Avalon

    j. Fuel hoses from fuel filter and return pipe.
    k. **On California models,** EVAP hose from pipe on emission control valve set.
    l. **Except California models,** EVAP hose from charcoal canister.
    m. **On all models,** two vacuum hoses from vacuum tank for ACIS.
12. Disconnect engine wire harness connectors from ECM under dash as follows.
    a. Remove under dash cover.
    b. Disconnect three ECM connectors and three cowl wire connectors.
    c. Disconnect grommet from cowl panel, then pull engine wire harness through cowl.
13. Remove driveshafts as outlined in "Drive Axles" section.
14. Without discharging system, disconnect A/C compressor from engine and secure aside.
15. Disconnect transaxle control cable from transaxle.
16. Without disconnecting hoses, remove power steering pump from engine and secure aside.
17. Remove four bolts holding transaxle to mounting insulator, **Fig. 2.**
18. Remove two hole plugs in subframe, then disconnect rear engine mounting bracket from subframe, **Fig. 3.**
19. Remove engine mounting absorber, **Fig. 4.**
20. Disconnect front engine mounting by removing three bolts holding mounting insulator to subframe, **Fig. 5.**
21. Attach a suitable engine lifting device to engine as follows:
    a. Install No. 2 engine hanger, tool No.

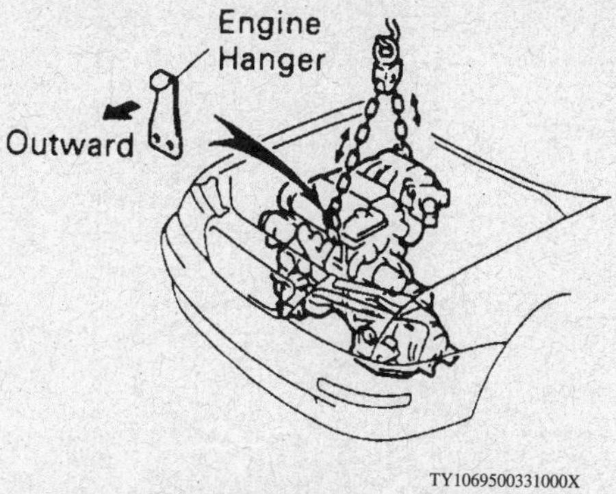
Engine
Hanger
Outward
TY1069500331000X

Fig. 6 Engine hanger installation. Avalon

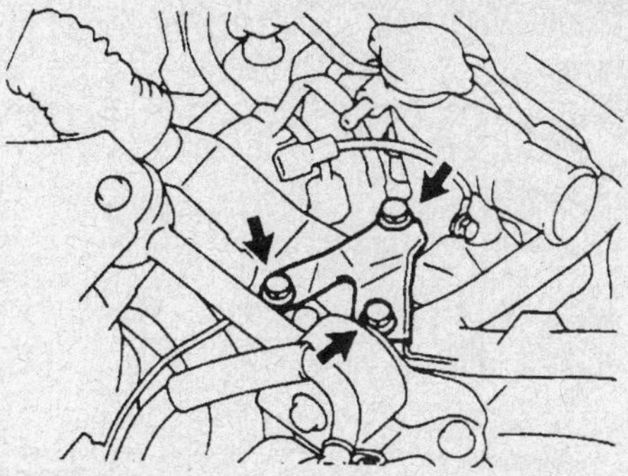
TY1069500332000X

Fig. 7 Righthand engine mount stay removal. Avalon

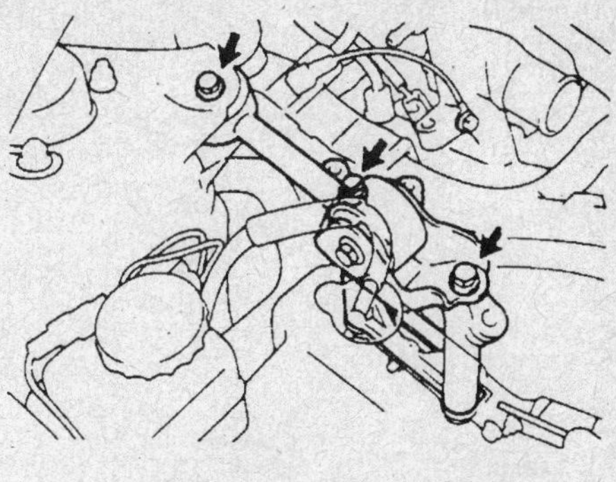
TY1069500333000X

Fig. 8 Movement control rod & No. 2 Righthand engine mount removal. Avalon

12282–20020, or equivalent, with two bolts to engine. Ensure correct location, **Fig. 6. Torque** bolts to 14 ft. lbs.

b. Attach engine lifting device to engine hangers. **Do not attempt to lift engine by hooking chain to any other part.**

22. Remove three bolts and ground strap, then the righthand engine mounting stay, **Fig. 7.**
23. Remove three bolts, then remove engine control rod and No. 2 righthand engine mounting bracket, **Fig. 8.**
24. Remove engine and transaxle assembly from vehicle. Ensure sufficient clearance for transmission Park/Neutral position switch during removal.
25. Place engine and transaxle assembly onto a suitable stand.
26. Remove four bolts and front engine mounting insulator from engine.
27. Remove four bolts, then the rear engine mounting insulator and bracket assembly.
28. Separate transaxle from engine as follows:
    a. Disconnect throttle cable from throttle body, then remove starter.
    b. Disconnect engine wire harness from transaxle.
    c. Remove two bolts and flywheel housing cover.
    d. Turn crankshaft pulley bolt to gain access to all six torque converter bolts.
    e. Hold crankshaft pulley bolt with a wrench, and remove bolts.
    f. Remove lefthand and righthand exhaust manifold stays
    g. Remove transaxle to engine bolts and ground strap.
    h. Remove transaxle together with torque converter from engine.
    i. Remove eight bolts, rear plate, drive plate and front spacer.
29. Reverse procedure to install, noting the following:
    a. Use suitable thread loctite on torque converter drive plate and torque converter mounting bolts.
    b. Tighten bolts to specifications.
    c. Use caution during engine installation not to damage PNP switch.
    d. Use new gaskets and manifold nuts when installing exhaust pipe.
    e. Reset audio anti-theft system, if necessary, as outlined under "Precautions."

3VZ-FE ENGINE

1. **On models with coded audio anti-theft systems,**refer to "Precautions" for code procedures.
2. **On all models,** remove battery and tray.
3. Scribe hood installation alignment marks, then remove hood.
4. Remove engine undercover.
5. Drain engine coolant and oil.
6. Disconnect accelerator cable from throttle body.
7. **On models with automatic transaxle,** disconnect throttle cable from throttle body.
8. **On all models,** disconnect air flow meter electrical connector, then PCV and ISC valve hoses.
9. Loosen air cleaner hose clamp bolt, then disconnect air cleaner cap clips.
10. Disconnect air cleaner hose from throttle body, then remove air cleaner cap with air flow meter and hose assembly.
11. Remove air cleaner element, air cleaner case attaching bolts, and air cleaner case.
12. **On models with cruise control,** remove cruise control actuator.
13. **On all models,** disconnect ground strap from battery carrier.
14. Remove radiator, then disconnect coolant reservoir hose.
15. Disconnect washer tank electrical connector and hose, then remove washer tank assembly.
16. Remove coolant reservoir tank.
17. Disconnect engine relay box electrical connectors, then remove relay box.
18. Disconnect the following:
    a. Two connectors on lefthand fender apron.
    b. Igniter connector.
    c. Ignition coil connector.
    d. High-tension cord from ignition coil.
    e. Noise filter connector.
    f. Check connector.
    g. Back-up lamp connector.
    h. Righthand fender apron ground strap.
    i. Speed sensor connector.
19. Disconnect heater hoses.
20. Place suitable container below fuel return hose, then disconnect hose.
21. Place suitable container below fuel inlet hose, then disconnect hose.
22. **On models with manual transaxle,** remove starter, then clutch release cylinder. **Do not disconnect clutch release cylinder tube.**
23. **On all models,** disconnect transaxle control cables.
24. Disconnect vacuum hoses from brake booster air intake chamber, charcoal canister and IACV vacuum tank.
25. Remove instrument panel undercover, lower instrument panel, glove compartment door and glove compartment.
26. Disconnect three engine ECU electrical connectors, five cowl wiring electrical connectors, then cooling ECU electrical connector.
27. In engine compartment, remove engine wire harness attaching nuts, then pull harness from cowl.
28. **On models with A/C,** disconnect A/C compressor electrical connector, remove A/C belt and compressor attaching bolts, then position A/C compressor assembly aside. **Do not disconnect compressor tubes.**
29. **On all models,** disconnect front exhaust pipe and gasket, then remove driveshafts.
30. **On models with power steering,** disconnect two power steering air hoses, then remove attaching nuts and disconnect power steering air control valve (PS ACV).
31. **On all models,** using suitable tool, disconnect hydraulic cooling fan pressure hose.
32. Disconnect power steering pump electrical connector, remove belt and pump attaching bolts, then position power steering pump assembly aside. **Do not disconnect pump hoses.**
33. Remove lefthand engine mount attaching bolts, then disconnect mount.
34. Remove righthand rear engine mount hole plugs, then remove attaching nuts and disconnect mount.
35. Remove engine mount absorber.
36. Remove righthand front engine mount attaching bolts, then disconnect mount.
37. Install suitable engine lifting equipment.

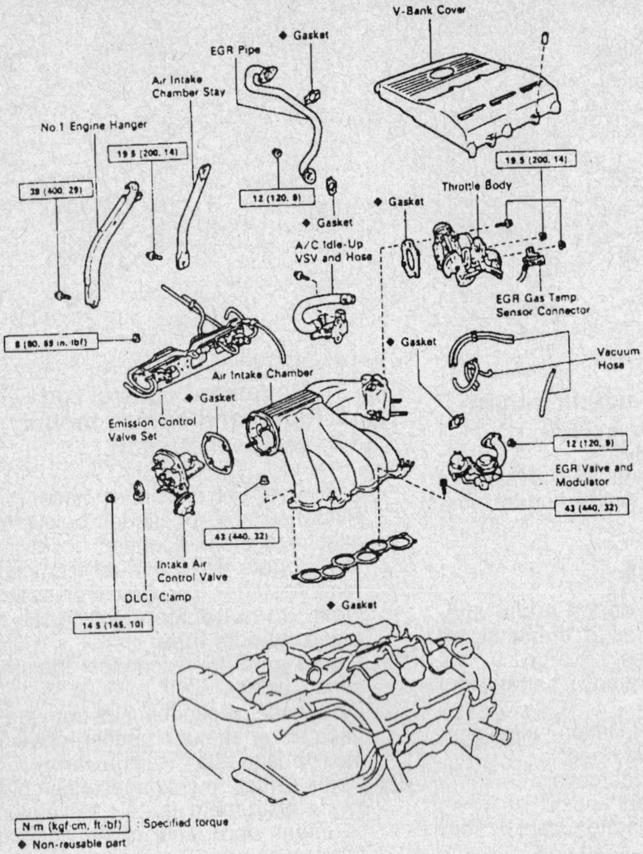
V-Bank Cover
◆ Gasket
EGR Pipe
Air Intake Chamber Stay
No.1 Engine Hanger
19.5 (200, 14)
38 (400, 29)
12 (120, 9)
◆ Gasket
Throttle Body
19.5 (200, 14)
◆ Gasket
A/C Idle-Up VSV and Hose
EGR Gas Temp Sensor Connector
8 (80, 69 in.·lbf)
◆ Gasket
Vacuum Hose
Air Intake Chamber
◆ Gasket
Emission Control Valve Set
12 (120, 9)
EGR Valve and Modulator
43 (440, 32)
43 (440, 32)
Intake Air Control Valve
DLC1 Clamp
◆ Gasket
14.5 (145, 10)
N·m (kgf·cm, ft·lbf) : Specified torque
◆ Non-reusable part

TY1069100102010X

Fig. 9 Cylinder head replacement (Part 1 of 5). 1MZ-FE

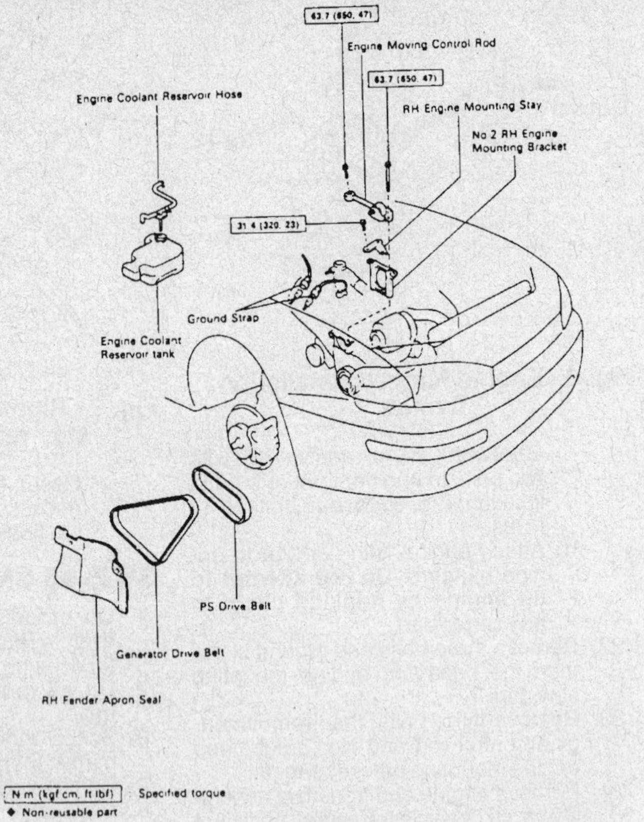
63.7 (650, 47)
Engine Moving Control Rod
63.7 (650, 47)
RH Engine Mounting Stay
Engine Coolant Reservoir Hose
No.2 RH Engine Mounting Bracket
31.4 (320, 23)
Ground Strap
Engine Coolant Reservoir tank
PS Drive Belt
Generator Drive Belt
RH Fender Apron Seal
N·m (kgf·cm, ft·lbf) : Specified torque
◆ Non-reusable part

TY1069100102020X

Fig. 9 Cylinder head replacement (Part 2 of 5). 1MZ-FE

38. Remove engine moving control rod.
39. Remove engine and transaxle assembly.
40. **On models with automatic transaxle,** remove starter assembly.
41. **On all models,** separate engine and transaxle.
42. Remove No. 2 righthand engine mount bracket.
43. Remove front righthand engine mount.
44. Remove rear righthand engine mount.
45. Reverse procedure to install, noting the following:
    a. Tighten fasteners to specifications
    b. Reset audio anti-theft system, if necessary, as outlined under "Precautions."

INTAKE MANIFOLD

REPLACE

Refer to "Cylinder Head, Replace" for procedure.

EXHAUST MANIFOLD

REPLACE

Refer to "Cylinder Head, Replace" for procedure.

CYLINDER HEAD

REPLACE

1MZ-FE ENGINE

1. **On models with coded audio anti-theft systems,**refer to "Precautions" for code procedures.
2. **On all models,** remove battery tray and cruise control module.
3. Raise and support vehicle, drain coolant, then remove air cleaner case, volume air flow meter and air cleaner hose, **Fig. 9.**
4. Disconnect ground straps and remove righthand engine mount.
5. Disconnect radiator and heater hoses.
6. Disconnect fuel lines, then the hydraulic motor pressure hose.
7. Remove valve cover, then the emission control valve set as follows:
    a. Disconnect vacuum hoses from fuel pressure control vacuum switching valve (VSV), fuel pressure regulator, cylinder head from rear plate, intake air control valve VSV, EGR vacuum modulator and EGR valve.
    b. Disconnect air control valve, fuel pressure and EGR VSV connectors.
    c. Remove two nuts, then emission control valve set.
8. Remove air intake chamber as follows:
    a. Remove all vacuum hoses, then data link connector No. 1 and No. 2 ground straps.
    b. Remove hydraulic motor pressure hose from air intake chamber, then the ground strap.
    c. Disconnect righthand oxygen sensor connector clamp from power steering pressure tube, then the tube.
    d. Disconnect power steering air hoses.
9. Remove No. 1 engine hanger, then the air chamber stay.
10. Remove EGR pipe, then disconnect the following connectors:
    a. Throttle position sensor.
    b. IAC valve.
    c. EGR gas temperature sensor.
    d. A/C idle-up valve.
    e. Camshaft position sensor.
11. Disconnect all vacuum, two water bypass and air assist hoses.
12. Remove air intake chamber and gasket.
13. Remove intake air control valve from air intake chamber.
14. Remove A/C idle-up VSV from air intake chamber.
15. Remove throttle body from air intake chamber.
16. Disconnect EGR valve and vacuum modulator from air intake chamber, then engine wire from engine lefthand side as follows:
    a. Three injector connectors.
    b. Three ignition coil connectors.
17. Disconnect wiring from timing belt cover, engine rear and righthand rear side, then remove ignition coils and spark plugs.
18. Remove front exhaust pipe then the timing belts following procedure outlined under "Timing Belt, Replace."

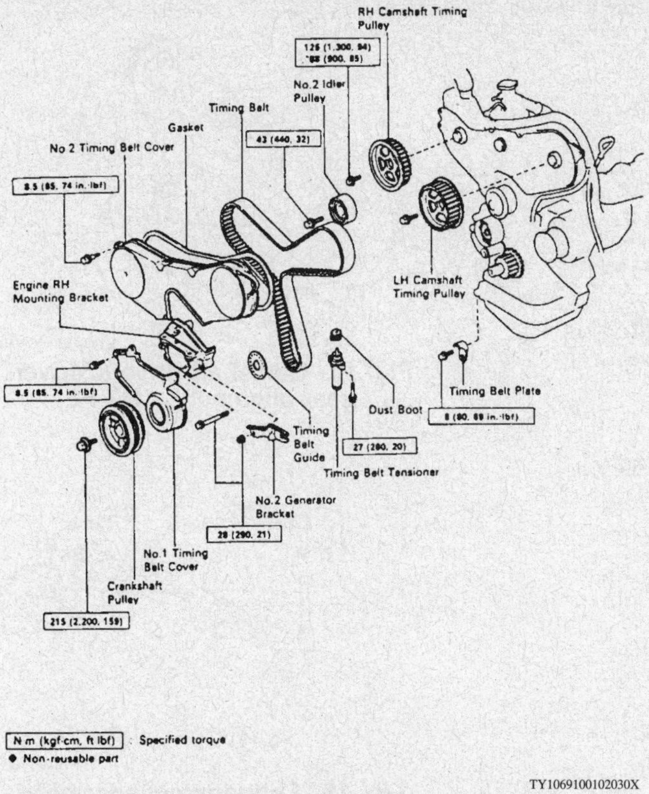

RH Camshaft Timing Pulley
125 (1,300, 94)
88 (900, 65)
No.2 Idler Pulley
Timing Belt
Gasket
No 2 Timing Belt Cover
43 (440, 32)
8.5 (85, 74 in.·lbf)
Engine RH Mounting Bracket
LH Camshaft Timing Pulley
8.5 (85, 74 in.·lbf)
Timing Belt Plate
Dust Boot
8 (80, 69 in.·lbf)
Timing Belt Guide
27 (280, 20)
Timing Belt Tensioner
No.2 Generator Bracket
28 (290, 21)
No.1 Timing Belt Cover
Crankshaft Pulley
215 (2,200, 159)
N·m (kgf·cm, ft·lbf) : Specified torque
◆ Non-reusable part
TY1069100102030X

Fig. 9 Cylinder head replacement (Part 3 of 5). 1MZ-FE

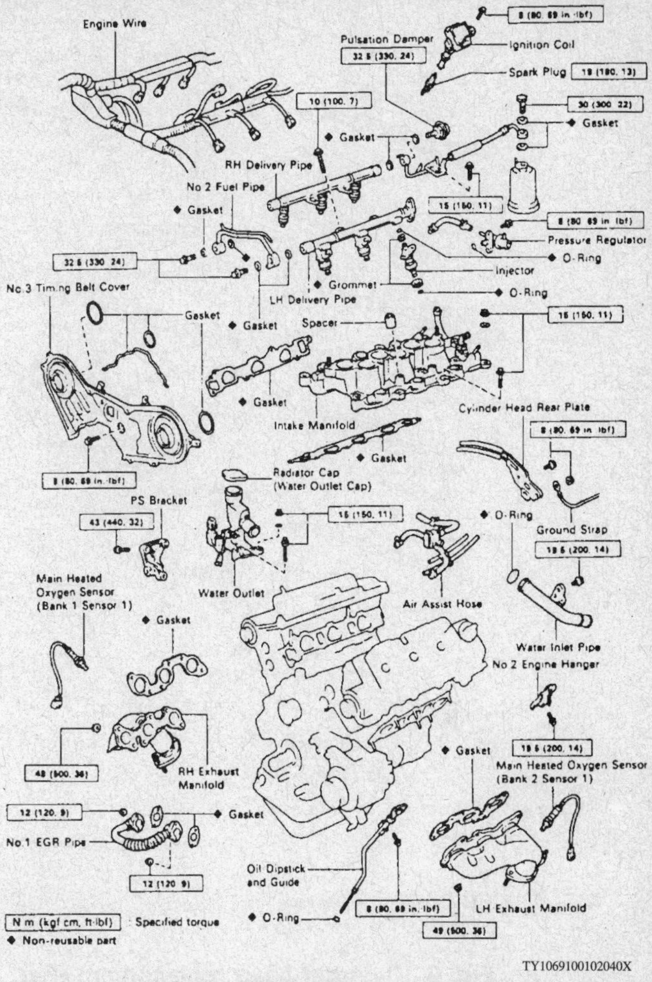

Engine Wire
8 (80, 69 in.·lbf)
Pulsation Damper
32.5 (330, 24)
Ignition Coil
Spark Plug
18 (180, 13)
10 (100, 7)
30 (300, 22)
◆ Gasket
RH Delivery Pipe
No 2 Fuel Pipe
15 (150, 11)
8 (80, 69 in.·lbf)
Pressure Regulator
◆ O-Ring
32.5 (330, 24)
Injector
No.3 Timing Belt Cover
◆ Grommet
LH Delivery Pipe
◆ O-Ring
Gasket
Spacer
15 (150, 11)
◆ Gasket
Cylinder Head Rear Plate
Intake Manifold
8 (80, 69 in.·lbf)
8 (80, 69 in.·lbf)
Radiator Cap (Water Outlet Cap)
PS Bracket
15 (150, 11)
◆ O-Ring
43 (440, 32)
Ground Strap
19.5 (200, 14)
Main Heated Oxygen Sensor (Bank 1 Sensor 1)
Water Outlet
Air Assist Hose
◆ Gasket
Water Inlet Pipe
No 2 Engine Hanger
◆ Gasket
19.5 (200, 14)
Main Heated Oxygen Sensor (Bank 2 Sensor 1)
49 (500, 36)
RH Exhaust Manifold
12 (120, 9)
◆ Gasket
No.1 EGR Pipe
Oil Dipstick and Guide
12 (120, 9)
8 (80, 69 in.·lbf)
LH Exhaust Manifold
N·m (kgf·cm, ft·lbf) : Specified torque
◆ Non-reusable part
◆ O-Ring
49 (500, 36)
TY1069100102040X

Fig. 9 Cylinder head replacement (Part 4 of 5). 1MZ-FE

19. Remove camshaft timing pulleys and No. 2 idler pulley.
20. Remove No. 3 timing belt cover, then the cylinder head rear plate.
21. Remove water inlet pipe and air assist and vacuum hoses.
22. Remove intake manifold deliver pipes and injectors, then the fuel pressure regulator from lefthand delivery pipe.
23. Remove thermal vacuum valve (TVV) from intake manifold.
24. Remove fuel pulsation damper and No. 1 and No. 2 fuel pipes.
25. Remove delivery pipes and injectors, than the water outlet.
26. Remove engine hangers, then the lefthand exhaust manifold.
27. Remove oil dipstick and tube, then the power steering bracket.
28. Remove EGR pipe, then the righthand exhaust manifold.
29. Remove valve covers, then the camshafts, as follows:
    a. **Camshaft thrust clearance is small. To remove, hold camshaft level and pull upward.**
    b. Remove righthand cylinder head intake camshaft. Align timing marks on camshaft drive and driven gears by turning camshaft with a suitable wrench, **Fig. 10.**
    c. Install suitable bolt to secure intake camshaft sub-gear to driven gear.
    d. Uniformly loosen and remove ten bearing cap attaching bolts in several passes, in sequence shown, **Fig. 11,** then the five bearing caps and intake camshaft assembly.
    e. Remove righthand cylinder head intake camshaft.
    f. Using sequence shown in **Fig. 12,** remove ten bearing cap bolts in several passes.
    g. Remove five bearing caps, oil seal and intake camshaft.
    h. Align lefthand cylinder head camshaft drive and driven gears by turning camshaft, **Fig. 10.**
    i. Install suitable bolt to secure lefthand cylinder head intake camshaft sub-gear to driven gear.
    j. Uniformly loosen and remove ten lefthand cylinder head intake camshaft bearing cap attaching bolts in several passes, then remove five bearing caps and intake camshaft, **Fig. 13.**
    k. Using sequence shown in **Fig. 14,** remove ten bearing cap attaching bolts in several passes.
    l. Remove five bearing caps, oil seal and intake camshaft assembly. Arrange bearing caps in correct order.
30. Remove cylinder head assemblies as follows:
    a. Using a suitable tool, remove two 8 mm recessed cylinder head bolts.
    b. Using sequence shown in **Fig. 15,** loosen and remove cylinder head attaching bolts in several passes,
    c. Lift cylinder head(s) from cylinder block dowels and position cylinder head on suitable work area. If cylinder head is difficult to remove, use suitable wedge to separate cylinder head from block. **Do not damage cylinder head to engine block mating surface.**
31. Reverse procedure to install, noting the following:
    a. Place cylinder head(s) onto block. Place a new cylinder head gasket in position on block as shown in **Fig. 16.**
    b. Apply a light coat of clean engine oil onto bolt threads and under bolt heads, then install 12–sided cylinder head attaching bolts.
    c. Using sequence shown in **Fig. 17, torque** bolts in several passes to 25 ft. lbs.
    d. Place a dab of paint or scribe a mark on front of each bolt head, then tighten bolts in correct sequence an additional 90°.
    e. Tighten bolts another 90° in sequence.
    f. Install two recessed head bolts and **torque** to 13 ft. lbs.
32. Install camshaft assemblies as follows:

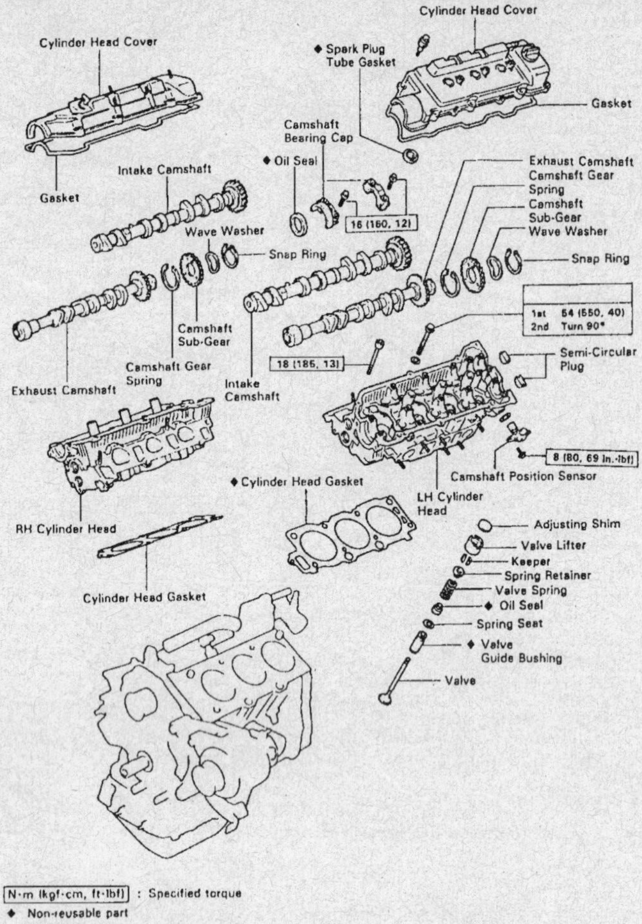

Cylinder Head Cover
Cylinder Head Cover
◆ Spark Plug Tube Gasket
Gasket
Camshaft Bearing Cap
Gasket
Intake Camshaft
◆ Oil Seal
Exhaust Camshaft
Camshaft Gear
Spring
Camshaft Sub-Gear
Wave Washer
Wave Washer
16 (160, 12)
Snap Ring
Snap Ring
Camshaft Sub-Gear
1st 54 (550, 40)
2nd Turn 90°
Camshaft Gear Spring
Exhaust Camshaft
Intake Camshaft
18 (185, 13)
Semi-Circular Plug
8 (80, 69 in.·lbf)
Camshaft Position Sensor
◆ Cylinder Head Gasket
LH Cylinder Head
RH Cylinder Head
Adjusting Shim
Valve Lifter
Keeper
Spring Retainer
Valve Spring
◆ Oil Seal
Cylinder Head Gasket
Spring Seat
◆ Valve Guide Bushing
Valve
N·m (kgf·cm, ft·lbf) : Specified torque
◆ Non-reusable part

TY1069100102050X

Fig. 9 Cylinder head replacement (Part 5 of 5). 1MZ-FE

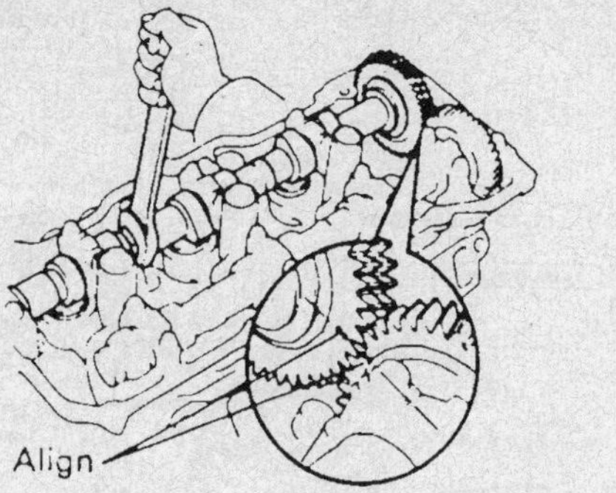

Align

TY1069100103000X

Fig. 10 Camshaft drive & driven gear alignment. 1MZ-FE

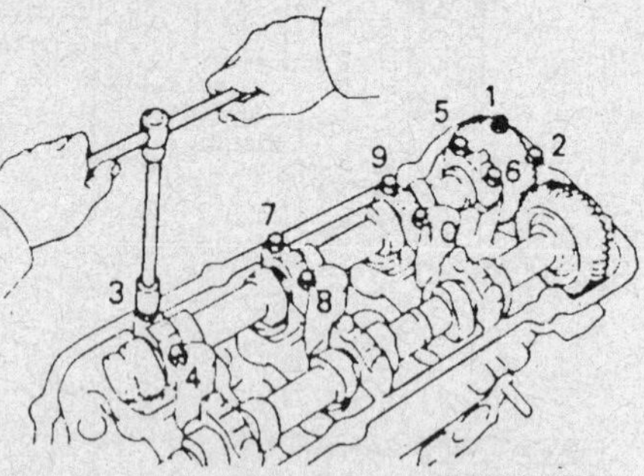

1
2
3
4
5
6
7
8
9

TY1069100106000X

Fig. 13 Lefthand cylinder head intake camshaft bearing cap bolt loosening sequence. 1MZ-FE

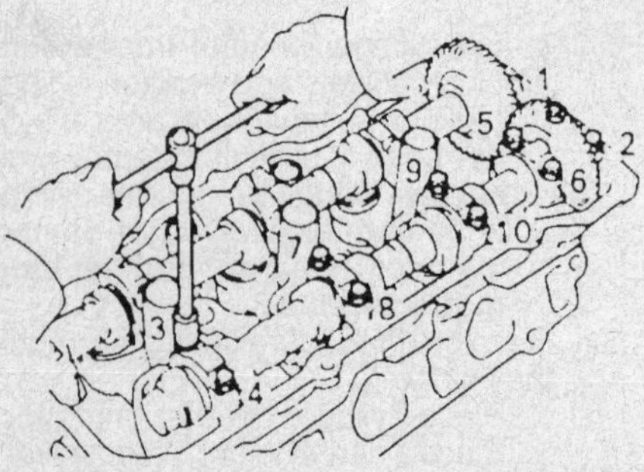

1
2
3
4
5
6
7
8
9
10

TY1069100104000X

Fig. 11 Righthand cylinder head intake camshaft bearing cap bolt loosening sequence. 1MZ-FE

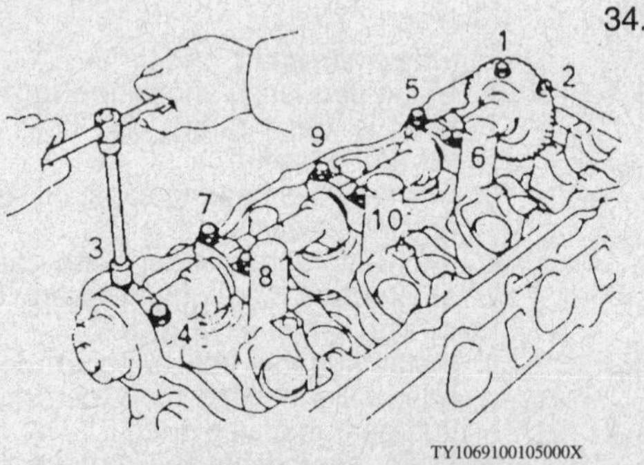

1
2
3
4
5
6
7
8
9
10

TY1069100105000X

Fig. 12 Righthand cylinder head exhaust camshaft bearing cap bolt loosening sequence. 1MZ-FE

a. To install exhaust camshaft of righthand cylinder head, apply new engine oil to thrust portion and journal of camshaft.
b. Place exhaust camshaft at a 90° angle of timing mark, then apply suitable grease to oil seal lip.
c. Install oil seal to camshaft, then apply seal packing part No. 08826-00080, or equivalent, to No. 1 bearing cap.
d. Install five bearing caps in their proper locations, **Fig. 18.**
e. Apply light coat of engine oil on threads and under heads of bearing cap bolts, then install uniformly, tighten ten bearing caps bolts in several passes to specification as shown in **Fig. 19.**

33. To install intake camshaft of righthand cylinder head, proceed as follows:
    a. Apply new engine oil to thrust portion and journal of camshaft.
    b. Place intake camshaft at a 90° angle of timing mark.
    c. Install five bearing caps in their proper locations, **Fig. 20.**
    d. Apply light coat of engine oil on threads and under heads of bearing cap bolts, then install and tighten ten bearing caps bolts in several passes to specification as shown in **Fig. 21.**
    e. Remove service bolt.
34. To install lefthand cylinder head exhaust camshaft, proceed as follows:
    a. Apply suitable grease to thrust portion of camshaft, then to new oil seal.
    b. Apply seal packing material part No. 08826-00080, or equivalent, to bearing No. 1, then install five bearing caps in their proper locations, **Fig. 22.**
    c. Apply light coat of engine oil on threads and under heads of bearing cap bolts, then install and tighten ten bearing caps bolts in several passes to specification, **Fig. 23.**
35. To install lefthand cylinder head intake camshaft, proceed as follows:
    a. Apply suitable grease to thrust portion of camshaft, then to new oil seal.
    b. Align timing marks of camshaft drive and driven gears, **Fig. 10.**
    c. Place intake camshaft on cylinder head, then install five bearing caps in proper locations, **Fig. 24.**
    d. Apply light coat of engine oil on threads and under heads of bearing cap bolts, then install and tighten ten bearing caps bolts in several passes to specification, **Fig. 25.**
    e. Remove service bolt.
36. Reverse remaining procedure to install, noting the following:

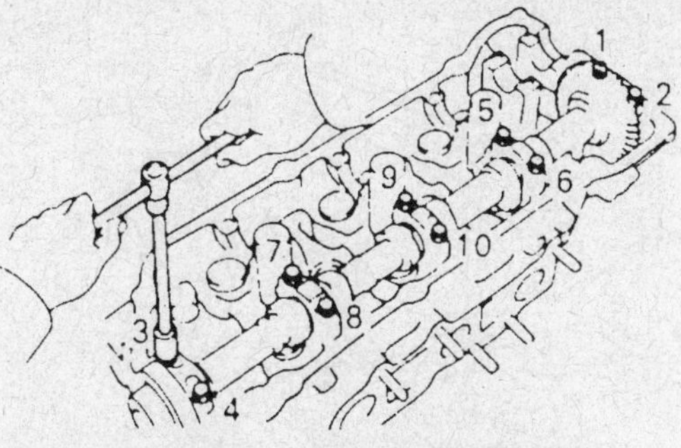
1
2
5
9
6
7
10
8
3
4
TY1069100107000X

Fig. 14 Lefthand cylinder head exhaust camshaft bearing cap bolt loosening sequence. 1MZ-FE

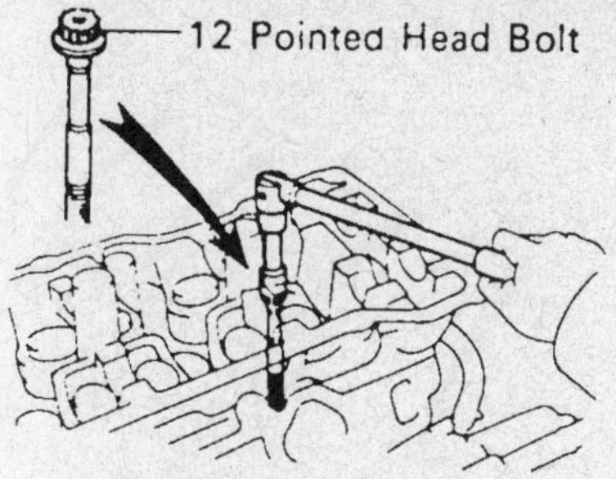
12 Pointed Head Bolt

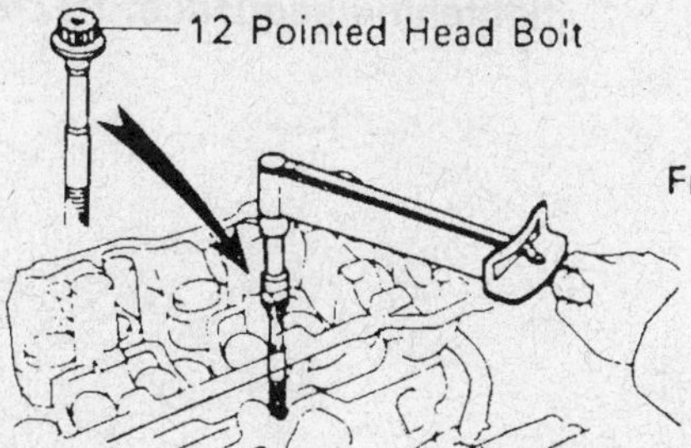
12 Pointed Head Bolt

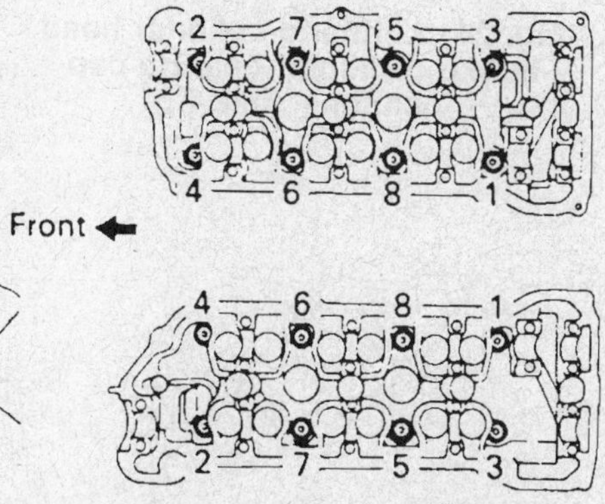
2 7 5 3
4 6 8 1
Front
4 6 8 1
2 7 5 3
TY1069100108000X

Fig. 15 Cylinder head bolt loosening sequence. 1MZ-FE

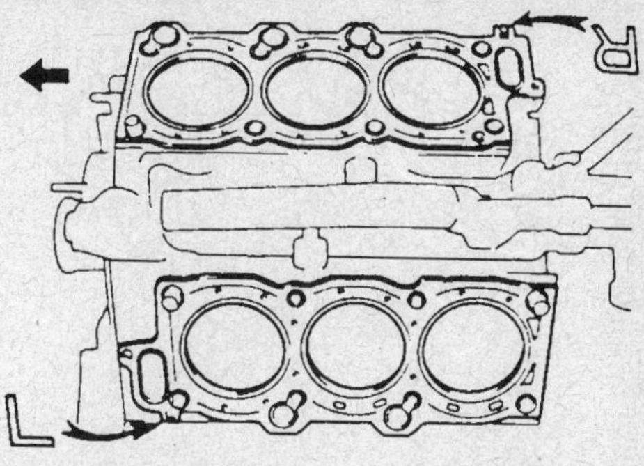
R
L
TY1069100109000X

Fig. 16 Cylinder head gasket identification. 1MZ-FE

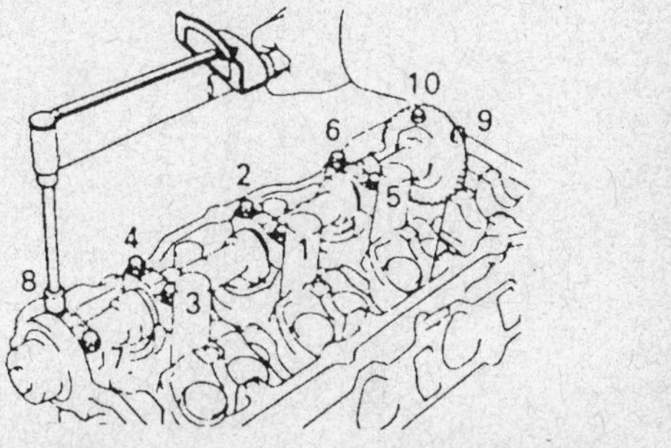
10
9
6
2
5
4
1
8
3
7
TY1069100112000X

Fig. 19 Righthand cylinder head exhaust camshaft bearing cap bolt tightening sequence. 1MZ-FE

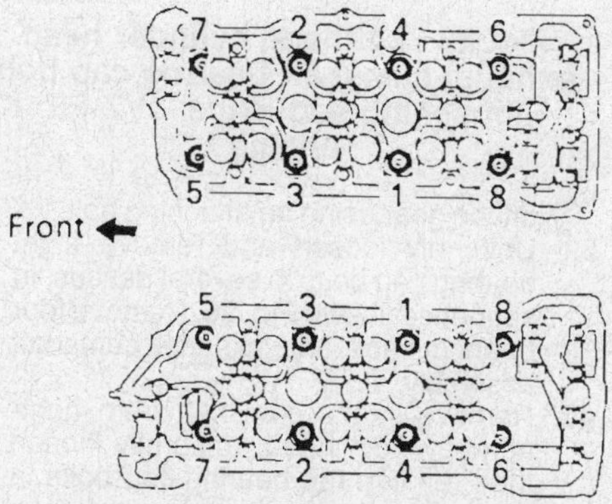
7 2 4 6
5 3 1 8
Front
5 3 1 8
7 2 4 6
TY1069100110000X

Fig. 17 Cylinder head bolt tightening sequence. 1MZ-FE

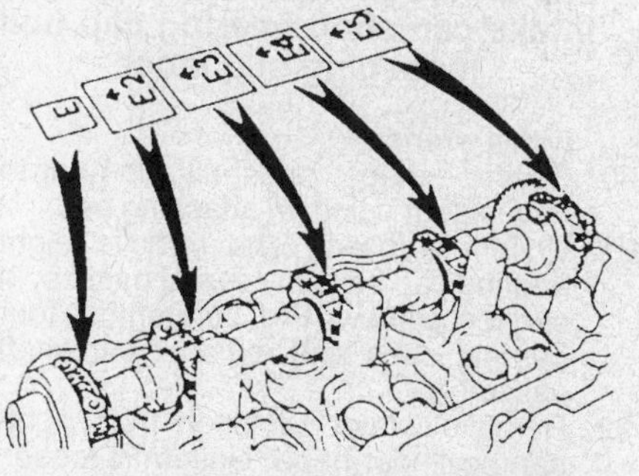
E
E2
E3
E4
E5
TY1069100111000X

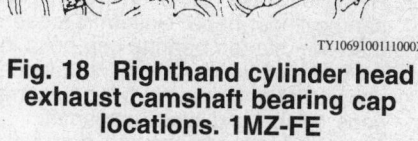

Fig. 18 Righthand cylinder head exhaust camshaft bearing cap locations. 1MZ-FE

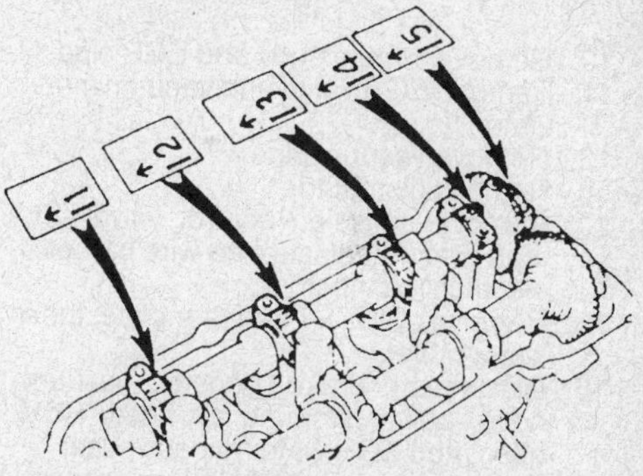
I1
I2
I3
I4
I5
TY1069100115000X

Fig. 22 Lefthand cylinder head exhaust camshaft bearing cap locations. 1MZ-FE

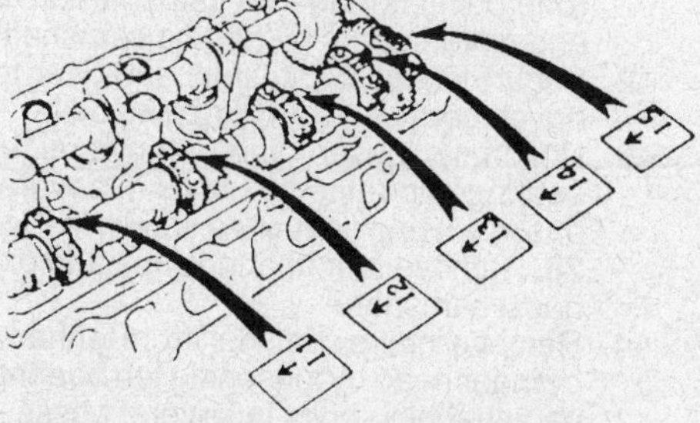
I5
I4
I3
I2
I1
TY1069100113000X

Fig. 20 Righthand cylinder head intake camshaft bearing cap locations. 1MZ-FE

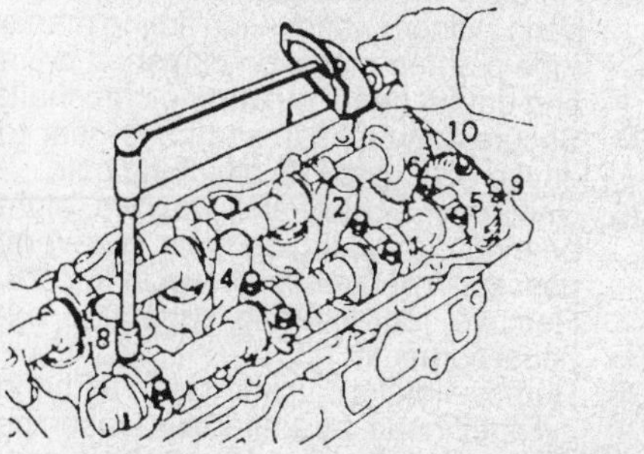
10
9
6
2
5
4
1
8
3
7
TY1069100114000X

Fig. 21 Righthand cylinder head intake camshaft bearing cap bolt tightening sequence. 1MZ-FE

a. Tighten fasteners to specifications.
b. Adjust valves following procedure outlined under "Valve Adjustment."
c. Reset audio anti-theft system, if necessary, as outlined under "Precautions."

3VZ-FE ENGINE

1. **On models with coded audio anti-theft systems,** refer to "Precautions" for code procedures.
2. **On all models,** disconnect battery ground cable.
3. Drain oil and coolant from engine.
4. Disconnect throttle cable from throttle body, if equipped.
5. Disconnect accelerator cable from throttle body.
6. Remove front exhaust pipe.
7. Remove alternator.
8. Remove V-bank cover.
9. Remove ISC or IAC valve.

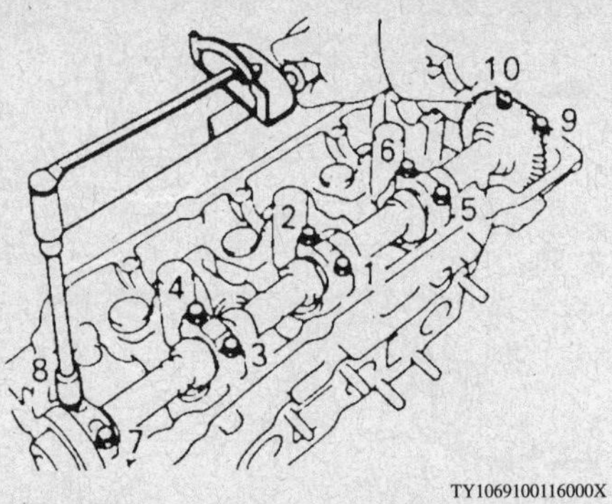

10
9
6
2
5
4
1
8
3
7
TY1069100116000X

Fig. 23 Lefthand cylinder head exhaust camshaft bearing cap bolt tightening sequence. 1MZ-FE

1
2
3
4
5
TY1069100282000X

Fig. 24 Lefthand cylinder head intake camshaft bearing cap locations. 1MZ-FE

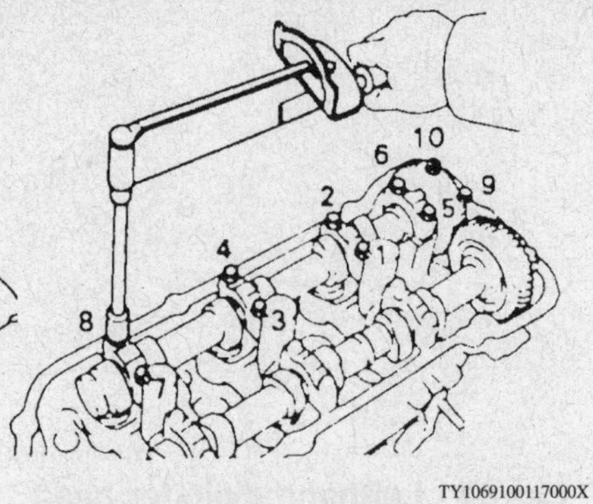

10
6
9
2
5
4
8
3
TY1069100117000X

Fig. 25 Lefthand cylinder head intake camshaft bearing cap bolt tightening sequence. 1MZ-FE

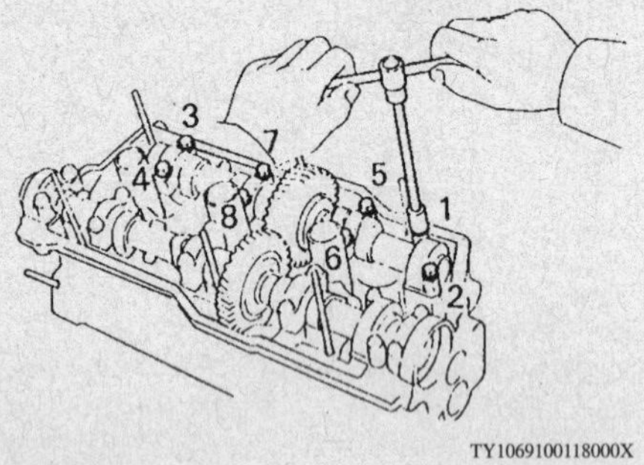

3
7
4
5
8
1
6
2
TY1069100118000X

Fig. 26 Righthand cylinder head exhaust camshaft bearing cap bolt loosening sequence. 3VZ-FE engine

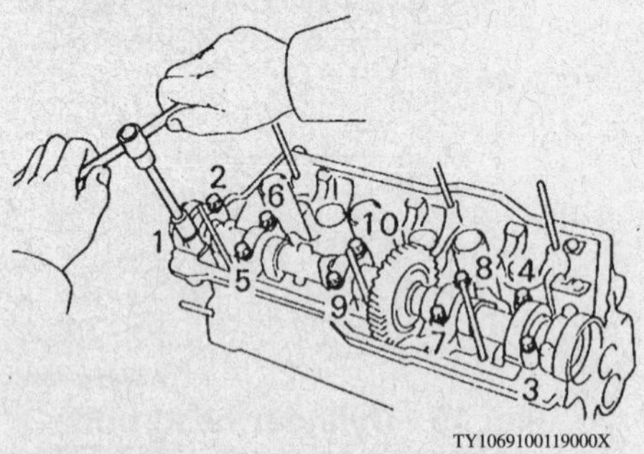

2
6
10
1
5
8
4
9
7
3
TY1069100119000X

Fig. 27 Righthand cylinder head intake camshaft bearing cap bolt loosening sequence

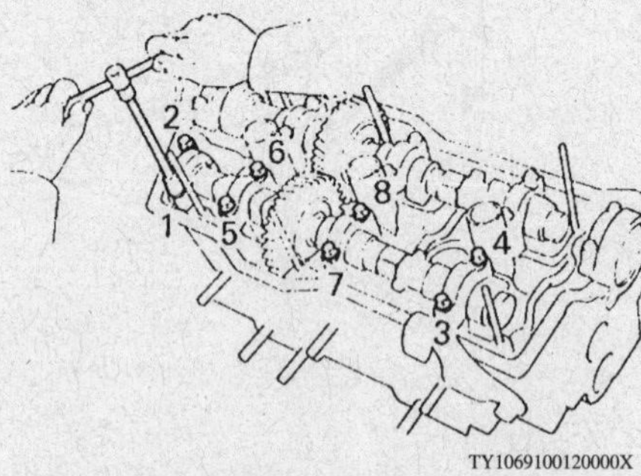

2
6
8
1
5
4
7
3
TY1069100120000X

Fig. 28 Lefthand cylinder head exhaust camshaft bearing cap bolt loosening sequence. 3VZ-FE engine

10. Remove throttle body and EGR pipe.
11. Remove EGR valve and vacuum modulator.
12. Remove vacuum pipe.
13. Remove distributor.
14. Remove emission control valve set, then disconnect lefthand wire harness electrical connectors.
15. Remove cylinder head rear plate, then water outlet.
16. Disconnect brake booster vacuum hose, power steering air hose, PCV hose, and EGR water bypass hose.
17. Disconnect cold start injector connector.
18. Remove air intake chamber.
19. Remove fuel delivery pipes and injectors.
20. Remove No. 1 cooler, then disconnect and remove righthand engine wire harness.
21. Remove water bypass outlet.
22. Remove intake manifold.
23. Remove righthand rear exhaust manifold.
24. Remove lefthand exhaust manifold.
25. Remove oil dipstick assembly and spark plugs.
26. Remove timing belt, camshaft timing pulleys (sprockets) and No. 2 idler pulley (sprocket) as outlined under "Timing Belt, Replace."
27. Remove No. 3 timing belt cover.
28. Remove cylinder head covers.
29. Remove exhaust camshaft from righthand cylinder head. Align timing marks (two pointed marks) on camshaft drive and driven gears by turning camshaft with a wrench.
30. Secure exhaust camshaft sub-gear to driven gear using an attaching bolt.
31. Uniformly loosen and remove eight bearing cap bolts in several passes, in sequence shown **Fig. 26.** Remove four bearing caps and exhaust camshaft assembly.
32. Remove intake camshaft from righthand cylinder head. Uniformly loosen then remove ten bearing cap bolts in several passes, using sequence shown in **Fig. 27.** Remove five bearing caps, oil seal and intake camshaft.
33. Remove exhaust camshaft from lefthand cylinder head. Align timing marks (one pointed mark) on camshaft drive and driven gears by turning camshaft.
34. Secure exhaust camshaft sub-gear to driven gear using an attaching bolt.
35. Uniformly loosen and remove eight bearing cap attaching bolts in several passes, in sequence shown in **Fig. 28.** Remove four bearing caps and exhaust camshaft.
36. Remove intake camshaft from lefthand cylinder head by uniformly loosening ten bearing cap attaching bolts in several passes, in sequence shown in **Fig. 29.** Remove five bearing caps, oil seal and intake camshaft assembly. Arrange bearing caps in correct order.
37. Remove exhaust camshaft from righthand cylinder head. Align timing marks (two pointed marks) on camshaft drive and driven gears by turning camshaft with a wrench.
38. Secure exhaust camshaft sub-gear to driven gear using an attaching bolt.
39. Uniformly loosen and remove eight bearing cap bolts in several passes, in sequence shown **Fig. 26.** Remove four bearing caps and exhaust camshaft assembly.
40. Remove intake camshaft from righthand cylinder head. Uniformly loosen then remove ten bearing cap bolts in several passes, using sequence shown in **Fig. 27.** Remove five bearing caps, oil seal and intake camshaft.
41. Remove exhaust camshaft from lefthand cylinder head. Align timing marks (one pointed mark) on camshaft drive and driven gears by turning camshaft.
42. Secure exhaust camshaft sub-gear to driven gear using an attaching bolt.
43. Uniformly loosen and remove eight bearing cap attaching bolts in several passes, using sequence shown in **Fig. 28.** Remove four bearing caps and exhaust camshaft.
44. Remove intake camshaft from lefthand cylinder head by loosening ten bearing cap attaching bolts in several passes, using sequence shown in **Fig. 29.** Remove five bearing caps, oil seal and intake camshaft assembly. Arrange bearing caps in correct order.
45. Remove power steering pump bracket.
46. Remove lefthand engine hanger.
47. Remove cylinder head assemblies as follows:
    a. Using a suitable tool, remove two 8

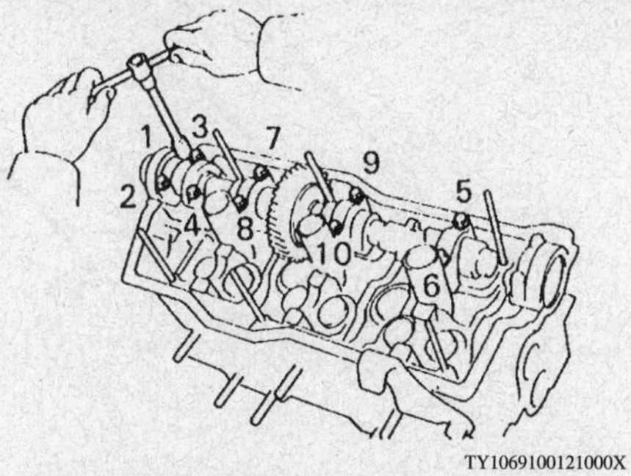
1
3
7
9
2
4
8
10
5
6
TY1069100121000X

Fig. 29 Lefthand cylinder head intake camshaft bearing cap bolt loosening sequence. 3VZ-FE engine

90°
TY1069100124000X

Fig. 32 Cylinder head bolt tightening sequence. 3VZ-FE engine

mm recessed cylinder head bolts.

b. Loosen and remove cylinder head attaching bolts in several passes, using sequence shown in **Fig. 30.**

c. Lift cylinder head(s) from dowels on cylinder block and place cylinder head on a suitable workbench. If cylinder head is difficult to remove, use a suitable screwdriver to pry off. **Do not damage cylinder head to engine block mating surface.**

48. Reverse procedure to install cylinder head assemblies, noting the following:

a. Place cylinder head(s) onto block. Place a new cylinder head gasket in position on block as shown in **Fig. 31.**

b. Install 12 sided cylinder head attaching bolts. Apply a light coat of clean engine oil onto bolt threads and under bolt heads. Using sequence shown in **Fig. 32, torque** bolts in several passes to 25 ft. lbs.

c. Put a dab of paint or scribe a mark on front of each bolt head. Tighten bolts in correct sequence an additional 90°. Tighten bolts another 90° in sequence.

d. Install two recessed head bolts and **torque** to 13 ft. lbs.

49. During installation of camshaft assemblies, proceed as follows:

a. Install intake camshaft onto righthand cylinder head. Apply suitable grease to thrust portion of camshaft. Place intake camshaft at approximately a 90° angle of timing mark (two pointed marks on cylinder head), **Fig. 33.** Apply seal packing (part No. 08826-00080 or equivalent) to No. 1 bearing cap.

b. Install five bearing caps in their proper locations as shown in **Fig. 34.** Apply a light coat of clean engine oil onto bolt threads and under bolt heads. Install and tighten ten bearing cap bolts in several passes, using sequence shown in **Fig. 35. Torque** bolts to 12 ft. lbs.

c. Install exhaust camshaft onto righthand cylinder head. Apply suitable grease to thrust portion of camshaft. Align timing marks (two pointed marks) of camshaft drive and driven gears as shown in **Fig. 36.**

d. Place intake camshaft onto cylinder head. Install four bearing caps in their proper locations as shown in **Fig. 37.**

e. Apply a light coat of clean engine oil onto bolt threads and under bolt heads. Install and tighten eight bearing cap bolts in several passes, using sequence shown in **Fig. 38. Torque** bolts to 12 ft. lbs. and remove service bolt (B).

f. Install intake camshaft onto lefthand cylinder head. Apply suitable grease onto thrust portion of camshaft.

g. Place intake camshaft at a 90° angle of timing mark (one pointed mark) on cylinder head as shown in **Fig. 39.**

h. Apply seal packing part No. 08826-00080, or equivalent, to No. 1 bearing cap, then install five bearing caps in their proper locations as shown in **Fig. 40.**

i. Apply a light coat of clean engine oil on bolt threads and under bolt heads. Install and tighten ten bearing cap bolts in several passes, using sequence shown in **Fig. 41. Torque** bolts to 12 ft. lbs.

j. Install exhaust camshaft onto lefthand cylinder head. Apply suitable grease to thrust portion of camshaft.

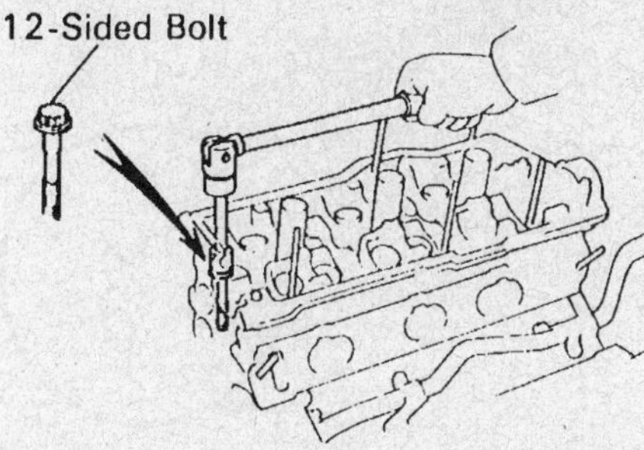
12-Sided Bolt

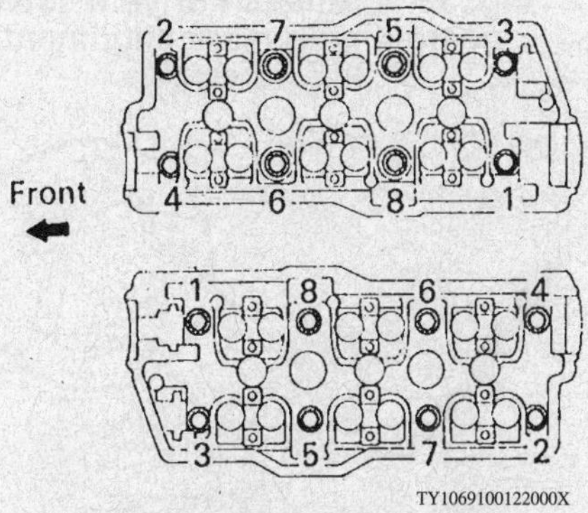
Front
2 7 5 3
4 6 8 1
1 8 6 4
3 5 7 2
TY1069100122000X

Fig. 30 Cylinder head bolt loosening sequence. 3VZ-FE engine

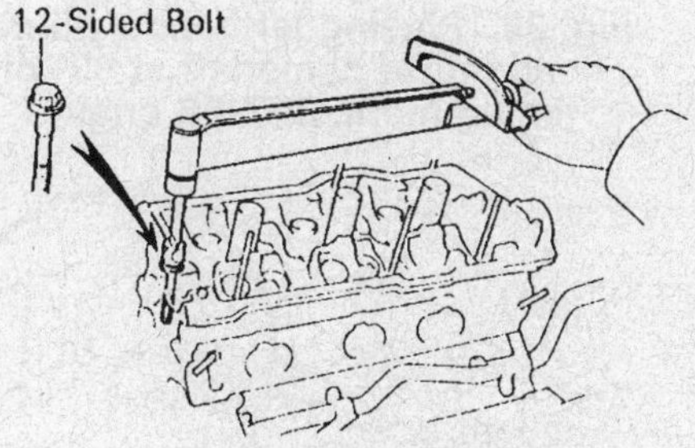
12-Sided Bolt

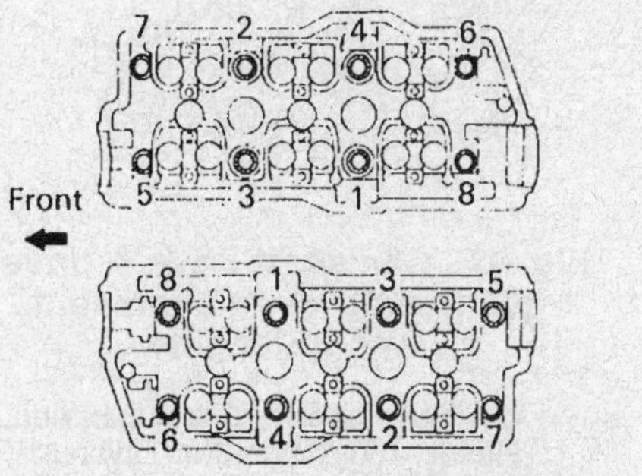
Front
7 2 4 6
5 3 1 8
8 1 3 5
6 4 2 7
TY1069100125000X

Fig. 33 Placing righthand cylinder head intake camshaft at 90° of timing mark. 3VZ-FE engine

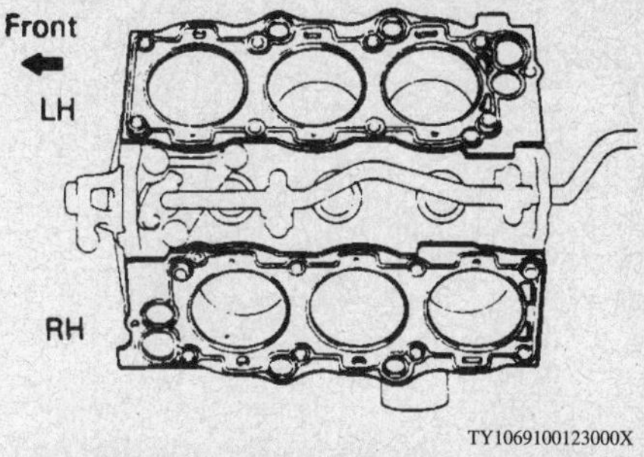
Front
LH
RH
TY1069100123000X

Fig. 31 Cylinder head gasket identification. 3VZ-FE engine

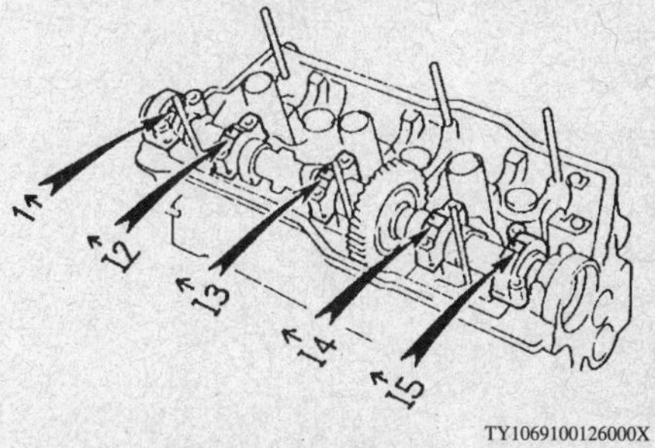
11
12
13
14
15
TY1069100126000X

Fig. 34 Bearing caps to righthand cylinder head intake camshaft installation. 3VZ-FE engine

TY1069100127000X

Fig. 35 Righthand cylinder head intake camshaft bearing cap bolt tightening sequence. 3VZ-FE engine

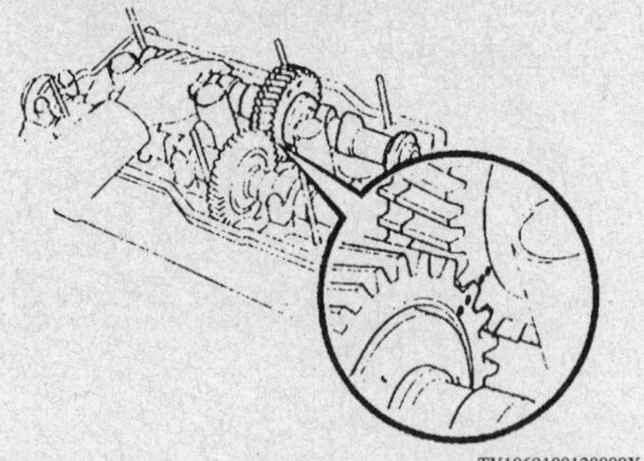
TY1069100128000X

Fig. 36 Camshaft drive & driven gears timing mark alignment. 3VZ-FE engine

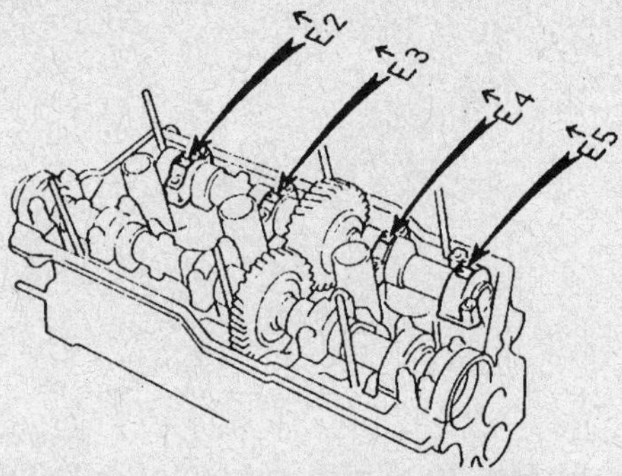
E2
E3
E4
E5
TY1069100129000X

Fig. 37 Bearing caps to righthand cylinder head exhaust camshaft installation. 3VZ-FE engine

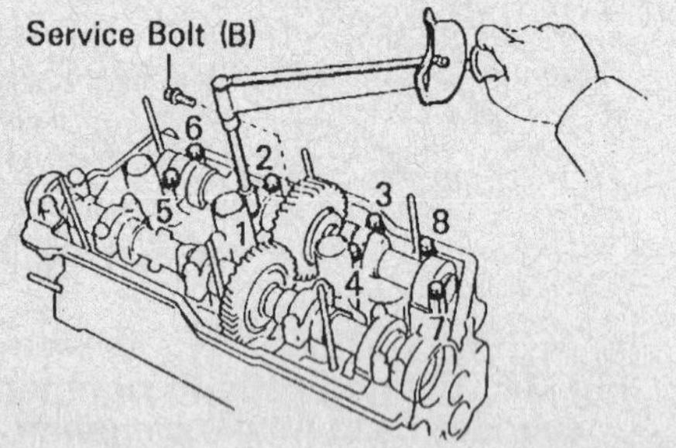
Service Bolt (B)
TY1069100130000X

Fig. 38 Righthand cylinder head exhaust camshaft bearing cap bolt tightening sequence. 3VZ-FE engine

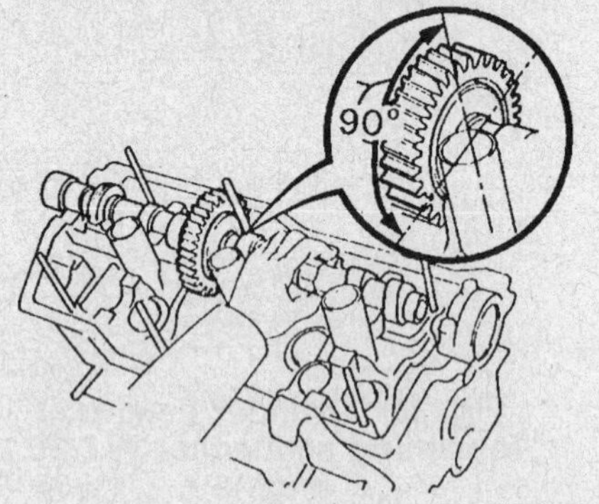
90°
TY1069100131000X

Fig. 39 Placing lefthand cylinder head intake camshaft at 90° of timing mark. 3VZ-FE engine

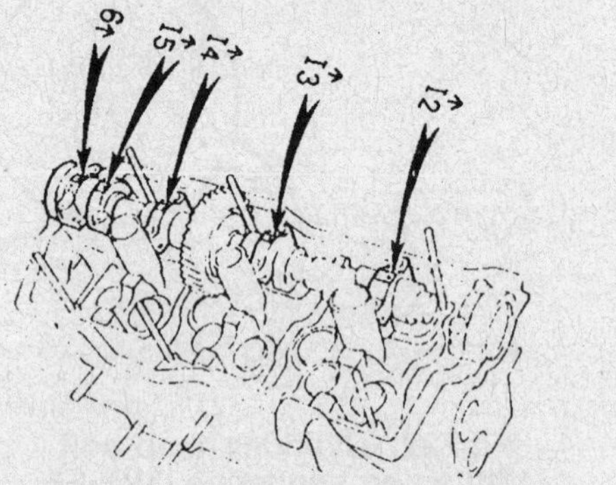
I6
I5
I4
I3
I2
TY1069100132000X

Fig. 40 Lefthand cylinder head intake camshaft bearing cap locations. 3VZ-FE engine

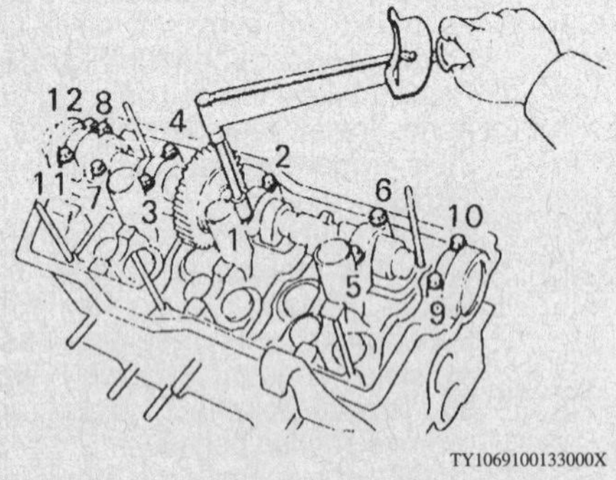
TY1069100133000X

Fig. 41 Lefthand cylinder head intake camshaft bearing cap bolt tightening sequence. 3VZ-FE engine

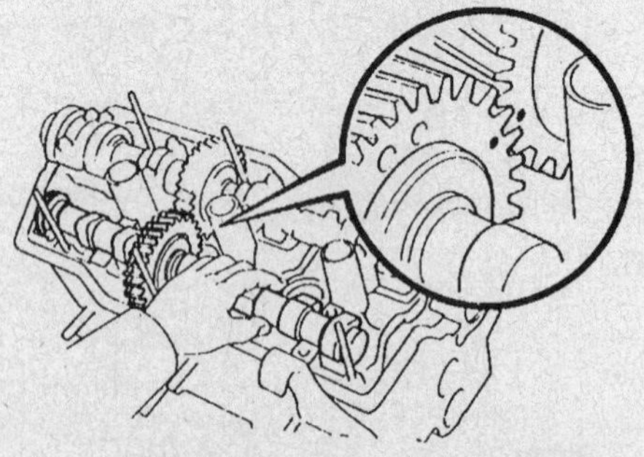
TY1069100134000X

Fig. 42 Camshaft drive & driven gear timing mark alignment. 3VZ-FE engine

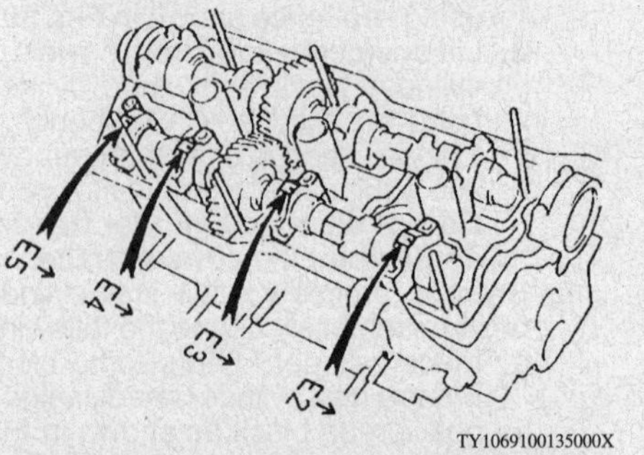
E5
E4
E3
E2
TY1069100135000X

Fig. 43 Lefthand cylinder head exhaust camshaft bearing cap locations. 3VZ-FE engine

k. Align timing marks (one pointed mark) of camshaft drive and driven gears as shown in **Fig. 42.**

l. Place intake camshaft onto cylinder head. Install four bearing caps in their proper locations as shown in **Fig. 43.**

m. Apply a light coat of clean engine oil to bolt threads and under bolt heads. Install and tighten eight bearing cap bolts in several passes, using sequence shown in **Fig. 44. Torque** bolts to 12 ft. lbs. and remove service bolt (B).

50. Reverse remaining procedures to install, noting the following:

a. Tighten fasteners to specifications.

b. Adjust valves following procedure outlined under "Valve Adjustment."

c. Reset audio anti-theft system, if necessary, as outlined under "Precautions."

VALVE CLEARANCE SPECIFICATIONS

1MZ-FE ENGINE

On 1MZ-FE engine, valve clearance on cold engines should be .006–.010 inch, intake and .010–.014 inch exhaust.

3VZ-FE ENGINE

On 3VZ-FE engines, valve clearance on cold engines should be .005–.009 inch, intake and .011–.015 inch exhaust.

VALVE ADJUSTMENT

Valve clearance is adjusted through the use of shims. Shims are available in increments of .0020 inch.

1. With engine cold, turn crankshaft pulley and align its groove with timing mark "0" of No. 1 timing belt cover. In this position No. 1 cylinder is at TDC of compression stroke.
2. Ensure intake valves on No. 1 cylinder are loose and exhaust valves on No. 1 cylinder are tight. If not turn crankshaft one complete revolution (360°) and align the timing marks.
3. Using a feeler gauge, measure clearance between valve lifter and camshaft. Record valve clearance

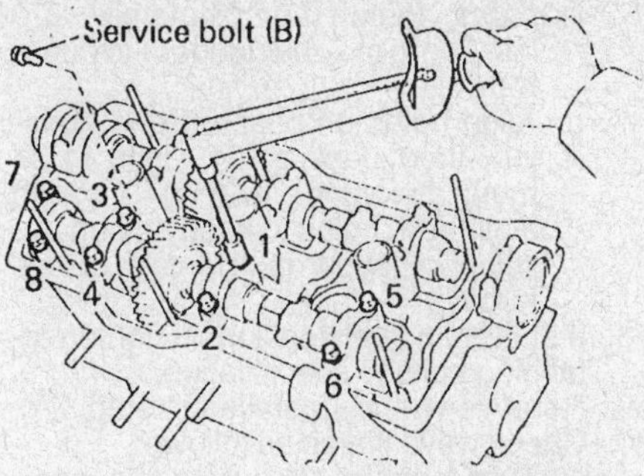
Service bolt (B)
1
2
3
4
5
6
7
8

TY1069100136000X

Fig. 44 Lefthand cylinder head exhaust camshaft bearing cap bolt tightening sequence. 3VZ-FE engine

measurements that are not to specification.

4. With engine set to No. 1 cylinder at TDC compression stroke, check the following valves:
   a. Both intake valves on righthand intake camshaft No. 1 cylinder.
   b. Both exhaust valves on lefthand exhaust camshaft No. 2 cylinder.
   c. Both exhaust valves on righthand exhaust camshaft No. 3 cylinder.
   d. Both intake valves on lefthand intake camshaft No. 6 cylinder.
5. Turn crankshaft ⅔ of a revolution (240°) and check the following valves:
   a. Both intake valves on lefthand intake camshaft No. 2 cylinder.
   b. Both intake valves on righthand intake camshaft No. 3 cylinder.
   c. Both exhaust valves on lefthand exhaust camshaft No. 4 cylinder.
   d. Both exhaust valves on righthand exhaust camshaft No. 5 cylinder.
6. Turn crankshaft another ⅔ of a revolution (240°) and check the following valve:
   a. Both exhaust valves on righthand exhaust camshaft No. 1 cylinder.
   b. Both intake valves on lefthand intake camshaft No. 4 cylinder.
   c. Both intake valves on righthand intake camshaft No. 5 cylinder.
   d. Both exhaust valves on lefthand exhaust camshaft No. 6 cylinder.
7. Turn crankshaft so that cam lobe for valve that is to be adjusted faces up, then using suitable tools, depress valve lifter between camshaft and valve lifter. **Before depressing valve lifter, position notch toward spark plug.**
8. Remove adjusting shim with suitable small screwdriver and magnetic finger.
9. Determine replacement shim size as follows:
   a. Using suitable micrometer, measure thickness of removed shim.
   b. New shim thickness should equal measured valve clearance less clearance specification plus thickness of used shim.
   c. Select new shim with thickness as close as possible to value calculated in step b, **Fig. 45.**
10. Install new shim, then recheck valve clearance.

VALVE GUIDES

1. Using a suitable tool and hammer, strike valve guide bushing to break it off at cylinder head casting.
2. Heat cylinder head to 176–212°F.
3. Using suitable valve guide removal tool, tap out bushing.
4. Install snap ring on new valve guide, then install new valve guide using tool as outlined above and driving in from reverse side of removal.
5. Ream new valve guide, if necessary. Refer to "Valve Specifications" for stem clearances.

HYDRAULIC LIFTERS

REPLACE

Check lifters for excessive wear and/or damage. Replace worn or damaged valve lifters as required. Lubricate hydraulic valve lifter before installation.

TIMING BELT

REPLACE

REMOVAL

1. **On 3VZ-FE engine,** proceed as follows:
   a. **On models with coded audio anti-theft systems,**refer to "Precautions" for code procedures.
   b. **On all models,** disconnect coolant reservoir hose.
   c. Remove washer tank and coolant reservoir tank.
   d. Remove No. 2 and No. 3 righthand engine mount stays.
   e. Remove alternator drive belt.
   f. Remove righthand front wheel, tire assembly and fender apron seal.
   g. Remove power steering drive belt and disconnect ground straps.
   h. Using suitable jack, raise engine slightly to take weight from righthand side engine mount, then remove engine moving control rod.
   i. Disconnect ground wire connector on righthand fender apron.
   j. Remove righthand engine mount stay and No. 2 righthand engine mount bracket.
   k. Remove power steering oil reservoir tank. **Do not disconnect hoses.**
   l. Remove timing belt cover and gasket.
   m. If original timing belt will be used, ensure there are four alignment (installation) marks on timing belt by turning crankshaft pulley. The four marks should be as follows; R-CAM (indicating righthand camshaft), L-CAM (indicating lefthand camshaft), CR (indicating crankshaft) and dots across timing belt located between idler pulley and crankshaft sprocket. If original timing marks have disappeared, place new installation marks before removing timing belt, **Fig. 46.**
   n. Remove righthand engine mount bracket.

mm (in.)

Shim No.	Thickness	Shim No.	Thickness
1	2.50 (0.0984)	10	2.95 (0.1161)
2	2.55 (0.1004)	11	3.00 (0.1181)
3	2.60 (0.1024)	12	3.05 (0.1201)
4	2.65 (0.1043)	13	3.10 (0.1220)
5	2.70 (0.1063)	14	3.15 (0.1240)
6	2.75 (0.1083)	15	3.20 (0.1260)
7	2.80 (0.1102)	16	3.25 (0.1280)
8	2.85 (0.1122)	17	3.30 (0.1299)
9	2.90 (0.1142)		

TY1069100137000X

Fig. 45 Valve clearance shim chart

2. **On 1MZ-FE engine,** proceed as follows:
   a. **On models with coded audio anti-theft systems,**refer to "Precautions" for code procedures.
   b. **On all models,** disconnect coolant reservoir hose.
   c. Remove coolant reservoir tank.
   d. Remove alternator drive belt.
   e. Remove righthand front wheel and fender apron seal.
   f. Remove power steering drive belt and disconnect ground straps.
   g. Remove righthand engine mount stay.
   h. Remove engine movement control and No. 2 righthand engine mount bracket.
   i. Loosen alternator pivot bolt, then remove alternator No. 2 bracket.
   j. Using crankshaft pulley bolt tool Nos. 09213-54015 and 09330-00021, or equivalents, remove crankshaft pulley bolt.
   k. Using crankshaft pulley puller tool No. 0213-00060, or equivalent, remove crankshaft pulley.
   l. Remove No. 1 timing belt cover.
   m. Remove engine wiring to No. 3 timing belt cover attaching bolt, then disconnect engine wiring from clamp.
   n. Remove No. 2 timing belt cover.
   o. Remove righthand engine mount bracket.
   p. Remove timing belt guide.
3. If original timing belt will be used, ensure there are four alignment (installation) marks on timing belt by turning crankshaft pulley. The four marks should be as follows; R-CAM (indicating righthand camshaft), L-CAM (indicating lefthand camshaft), CR (indicating crankshaft) and dots across timing belt located between idler pulley and crankshaft sprocket. If original timing marks have disappeared, place new installation marks before removing timing belt, **Fig. 46.**
4. Place No. 1 cylinder at TDC of compression stroke by turning crankshaft pulley and aligning pulley groove (v notch) with No. 1 timing belt cover timing mark "0." Ensure timing marks on camshaft timing sprockets and No. 3

timing belt cover are properly aligned. If not, turn crankshaft sprocket 360° (one complete revolution) and align marks.
5. Remove timing belt tensioner.
6. Remove timing belt from camshaft timing sprocket as follows:
   a. If installation marks have disappeared, before removing timing belt, place new installation marks on timing belt to match timing marks on camshaft timing sprockets.
   b. Loosen tension between lefthand and righthand camshaft timing sprockets by slightly turning righthand camshaft timing sprocket clockwise.
   c. Remove timing belt from camshaft timing sprocket.
   d. If installation marks have disappeared, after removing timing belt from camshaft sprockets, place a new installation mark on timing belt to match end of No. 1 timing belt cover.
7. Remove sprockets, No. 2 idler pulley and crankshaft pulley. When crankshaft pulley bolt is loosened, position of timing mark on crankshaft pulley and installation mark may slip. Check and align marks as necessary.
8. Remove No. 1 timing belt cover and timing belt guide.
9. Remove timing belt. If installation marks have disappeared, place new installation marks on timing belt to match drilled mark on crankshaft timing sprocket.

INSTALLATION

1. Install crankshaft timing sprocket and No. 1 idler pulley, if removed. Tighten idler pulley attaching bolt to specification.
2. With engine cold, temporarily install timing belt. Remove any oil or water from crankshaft timing sprocket, No. 1 idler and water pump pulley. Align installation mark on timing belt with drilled mark on crankshaft timing sprocket.
3. Install timing belt onto crankshaft timing sprocket, No. 1 idler and water pump pulley.
4. Install timing belt guide.
5. Install No. 1 timing belt cover.
6. Install crankshaft pulley and tighten attaching bolt to specification.
7. Install No. 2 idler pulley and tighten attaching bolt to specification.
8. Install lefthand camshaft timing sprocket, slide sprocket with flange side facing outward. Align knock pin hole on camshaft with knock pin groove on timing sprocket and install knock pin. Tighten attaching bolt to specification.
9. To correctly obtain crankshaft positioning, proceed as follows:
   a. Place No. 1 cylinder at TDC of compression stroke.
   b. To accomplish this, turn crankshaft pulley and align groove on pulley with "0" mark on No. 1 timing cover.
10. To correctly obtain righthand camshaft

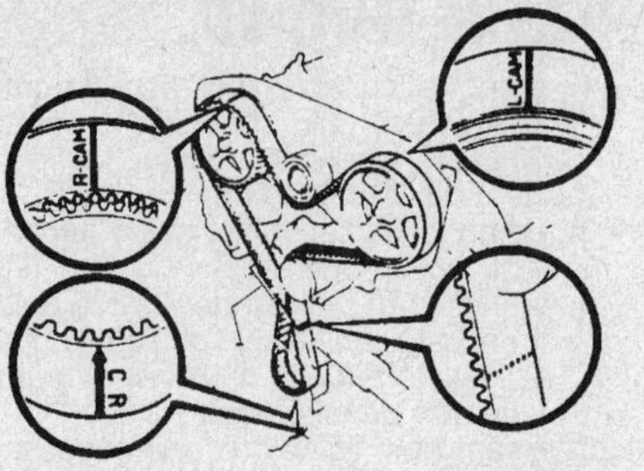
R-CAM
L-CAM
C.R
TY1069100138000X

Fig. 46 Placing timing marks on sprockets & timing belt

timing sprocket position, proceed as follows:
   a. Turn camshaft and align knock pin hole on camshaft with timing mark on No. 3 timing belt cover.
   b. In this position, righthand camshaft is correctly aligned.
11. To correctly obtain lefthand camshaft timing sprocket position, proceed as follows:
   a. Turn camshaft timing sprocket and align timing marks on camshaft timing sprocket and No. 3 timing belt cover.
   b. In this position, lefthand camshaft is correctly aligned.
12. Install timing belt onto lefthand camshaft timing sprocket. Ensure installation mark on timing belt matches end of No. 1 timing belt cover. If installation marks do not align properly, shift meshing of timing belt and crankshaft timing sprocket until they align. Do not over shift timing belt meshing.
13. Remove any water, oil or dirt from lefthand camshaft timing sprocket.
14. Using a suitable tool, slightly turn lefthand camshaft timing sprocket clockwise. Align installation mark on timing belt with timing mark on camshaft timing sprocket and hang timing belt on lefthand camshaft timing sprocket. Using a suitable tool, align timing marks on lefthand camshaft sprocket and No. 3 timing belt cover. Ensure timing belt has tension between crankshaft timing sprocket and lefthand camshaft sprocket.
15. Install righthand camshaft timing sprocket and timing belt on sprocket. Remove any water, oil or dirt from righthand camshaft sprocket and No. 2 idler pulley. Hang timing belt on righthand camshaft timing sprocket. Align timing marks on righthand camshaft timing sprocket and No. 3 timing belt cover. Slide righthand camshaft timing sprocket onto camshaft assembly. Using a suitable tool, align knock pin hole on camshaft with knock pin groove on sprocket, then install pin.
16. Using a suitable tool, install and tighten attaching bolt to specification.
17. Correctly set timing belt tensioner as follows:
   a. Place a plate washer between tensioner and a press tool block.
   b. Using a suitable press, slowly apply press force (approximately 220 lbs., more may be needed) to pushrod.
   c. Align holes on pushrod and housing, then pass a .049 inch (1.27 mm) hexagon wrench through alignment holes to keep setting position of pushrod. Release press force.
18. Install timing belt tensioner. Tighten attaching bolts to specification.
19. Remove wrench installed in step 17c.
20. Check valve timing as follows:
   a. Turn crankshaft pulley two complete revolutions from TDC to TDC. Turn crankshaft clockwise.
   b. Ensure each pulley/sprocket aligns with timing marks, **Fig. 47.**
   c. If timing marks do not align, remove timing belt and correctly install it.
21. Reverse removal procedure to complete installation. Reset audio antitheft system, if necessary, as outlined under "Precautions."

CAMSHAFT

REPLACE

Refer to "Cylinder Head, Replace" for camshaft removal procedures.

PISTON & ROD ASSEMBLY

Pistons are available in standard and oversizes of .020 inch (.50 mm). When assembling piston onto connecting rod, ensure mark on top of piston and mark on connecting rod are on same side, **Fig. 48.** When installing piston and connecting rod assembly, ensure mark on top of piston is facing toward front of engine.

MAIN & ROD BEARINGS

Main and connecting rod bearings are available in standard and undersizes of .010 inch (.25 mm).

OIL PAN

REPLACE

1MZ-FE ENGINE

1. **On models with coded audio antitheft systems,**refer to "Precautions" for code procedures.
2. **On all models** drain engine oil and remove oil dipstick.
3. Remove timing belt and pulleys as outlined under "Timing Belt, Replace."
4. Disconnect crankshaft position sensor electrical connector, engine wiring from clamp and alternator electrical connector.
5. Remove alternator wire attaching nut and disconnect, then the engine wire from three clamps.
6. Remove six No. 3 timing belt cover attaching bolts, then the cover.
7. Remove alternator and crankshaft position sensor.
8. Remove four oil hole cover plates.

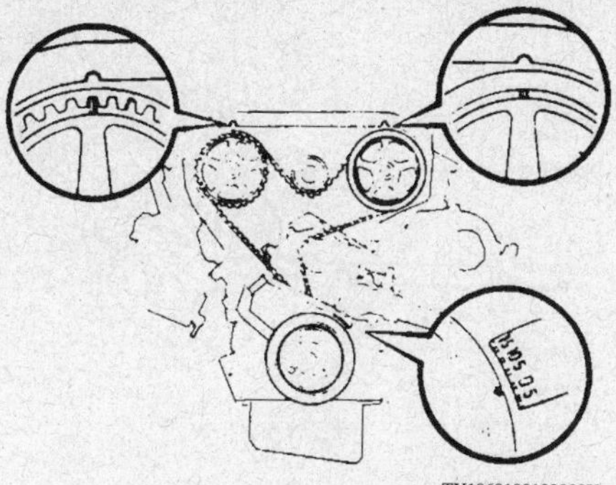

TY1069100139000X

Fig. 47 Timing mark check

9. Remove A/C compressor drive belt. Disconnect electrical connector. Remove compressor, do not disconnect hoses, then position assembly aside.
10. Remove A/C compressor housing bracket.
11. Remove front exhaust pipe and bracket.
12. Remove flywheel housing undercover.
13. Remove two No. 1 oil pan to transaxle attaching bolts.
14. Remove No. 2 oil pan attaching bolt, then using suitable blade between No. 1 and No. 2 oil pans, cut off sealer and remove No. 2 oil pan.
15. Remove oil strainer.
16. Remove remaining No. 1 oil pan attaching bolts, then using suitable screwdriver pry downward on oil pan to remove.
17. Remove oil baffle plate, then the oil pump with O-ring.
18. Reverse procedure to install. Reset audio anti-theft system, if necessary, as outlined under "Precautions."

3VZ-FE ENGINE

1. **On models with coded audio anti-theft systems,**refer to "Precautions" for code procedures.
2. **On all models,** scribe hood installation alignment hinge locations and remove hood.
3. Drain engine coolant and oil, then remove front exhaust pipe and stiffener plate.
4. Remove oil dipstick, then the oil pan attaching nuts and bolts.
5. Install tool No. SST 09302-00100, or equivalent, between cylinder block and oil pan, then cut off sealer and remove oil pan. **Do not damage oil pan and baffle plate flanges.**
6. Remove oil strainer and oil baffle plate.
7. Remove washer tank.
8. **On models with A/C,** remove alternator.
9. **On all models,** disconnect lower radiator hose.
10. **On models with A/C,** disconnect A/C compressor electrical connector, remove drive belt, belt adjusting bar, compressor attaching bolts, then position compressor assembly aside. **Do not disconnect compressor hoses.**
11. **On models with A/C,** remove water inlet pipe, alternator bracket and A/C compressor bracket.
12. **On all models,** install suitable engine lifting equipment.
13. Remove timing belt as outlined under "Timing Belt, Replace."
14. Remove No. 1 idler pulley, plate washer and crankshaft timing pulley.
15. Remove oil pump attaching bolts.
16. Position suitable screwdriver between oil pump and main bearing cap, then pry oil pump rearward. Remove oil pump and O-ring.
17. Reverse procedure to install. Reset audio anti-theft system, if necessary, as outlined under "Precautions."

OIL PUMP

REPLACE

Refer to "Oil Pan, Replace" for procedure.

OIL PUMP SERVICE

1. Remove driven and drive rotor, then the relief valve.
2. Inspect relief valve. Replace if worn or damaged.
3. Using a suitable feeler gauge, measure clearance between driven rotor and pump body. Clearance obtained should be .0039–.0069 inch and should not exceed .0118 inch. If not, replace oil pump rotor set and/or pump body.
4. Using a feeler gauge, measure clearance between both rotor tips. Clearance obtained should be .0043–.0094 inch and should not exceed .0138 inch. If not, replace oil pump rotor set.
5. Using a suitable feeler gauge and a flat block, measure side clearance by placing flat block (square edge) across pump body and measuring (using feeler gauge) between flat edge and top of rotor assembly. Clearance obtained should be .0012–.0035 inch and should not exceed .0059 inch. If not, replace oil pump rotor set and/or pump body assembly.

BELT TENSION DATA

Belt tension is as follows using a belt tension gauge. A new belt is considered used after five minutes of use.

Belt	New Lbs.	Used Lbs.
Alternator	170–180	95–135
Power Steer.	150–185	95–135

COOLING SYSTEM BLEED

1. Remove radiator cap, then drain coolant from engine and radiator drain cocks. Engine drain cocks are located at front center and rear right of cylinder block.
2. Close drain cocks and tighten to specification.
3. To release air from system, loosen union bolt of water outlet five revolutions.
4. Slowly refill system with coolant, then tighten union bolt to specification.

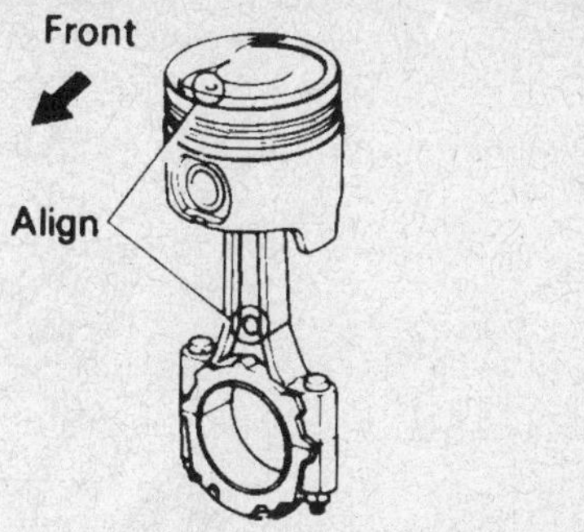
Front
Align

TY1069100140000X

Fig. 48 Piston & connecting rod assembly

5. Install radiator cap, then start engine and check for leaks.
6. Check coolant level and fill as necessary.

THERMOSTAT

REPLACE

1MZ-FE ENGINE

1. **On models with coded audio anti-theft systems,**refer to "Precautions" for code procedures.
2. **On all models,** drain engine coolant.
3. Remove air cleaner cap, volume air flow meter and air cleaner hose, as follows:
   a. Disconnect volume air flow meter electrical connector and wire clamp.
   b. Disconnect accelerator cable clamp and PCV hose.
   c. Loosen air cleaner hose clamp bolt.
   d. Disconnect four air cleaner air cap clips.
   e. Remove air cleaner cap, volume air meter and air cleaner hose as an assembly.
4. Disconnect heater hose and hydraulic motor pressure hose.
5. Remove two water inlet to cylinder head engine wiring attaching nuts, then disconnect wiring.
6. Disconnect engine coolant temperature sensor (ECT) electrical connector.
7. Remove water inlet pipe and O-ring.
8. Remove water inlet, then the thermostat and gasket.
9. Reverse procedure to install. Reset audio anti-theft system, if necessary, as outlined under "Precautions."

3VZ-FE ENGINES

1. **On models with coded audio anti-theft systems,**refer to "Precautions" for code procedures.
2. **On all models,** drain engine coolant.
3. Remove water inlet pipe to alternator adjusting bar attaching bolts, then remove water inlet pipe and O-ring.
4. Disconnect water temperature sensor electrical connector.
5. Remove water inlet from water pump, then thermostat and gasket.
6. Reverse procedure to install. Reset audio anti-theft system, if necessary, as outlined under "Precautions."

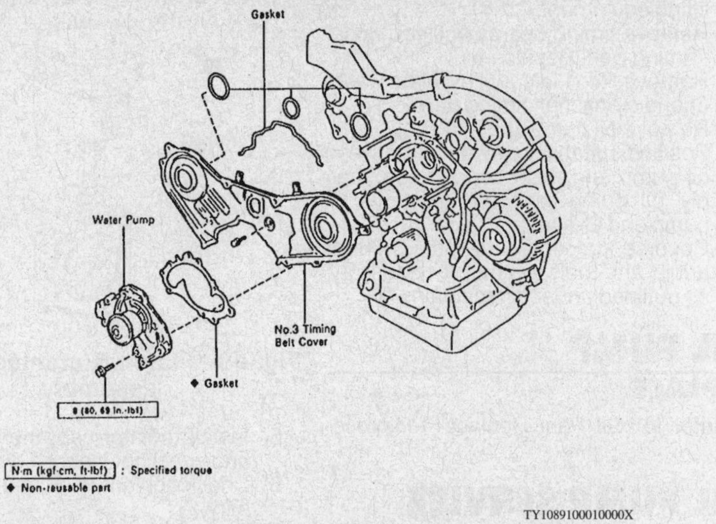
Gasket
Water Pump
No.3 Timing Belt Cover
◆ Gasket
8 (80, 69 in.-lbf)
N·m (kgf·cm, ft·lbf) : Specified torque
◆ Non-reusable part
TY1089100010000X

Fig. 49 Water pump assembly. 1MZ-FE engine

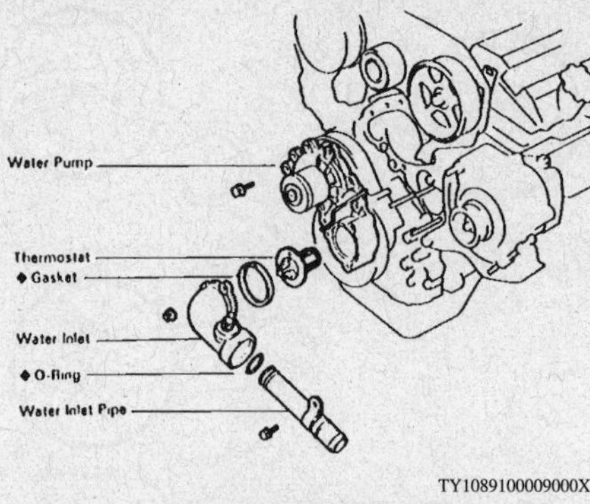
Water Pump
Thermostat
◆ Gasket
Water Inlet
◆ O-Ring
Water Inlet Pipe
TY1089100009000X

Fig. 50 Water pump assembly. 3VZ-FE engine

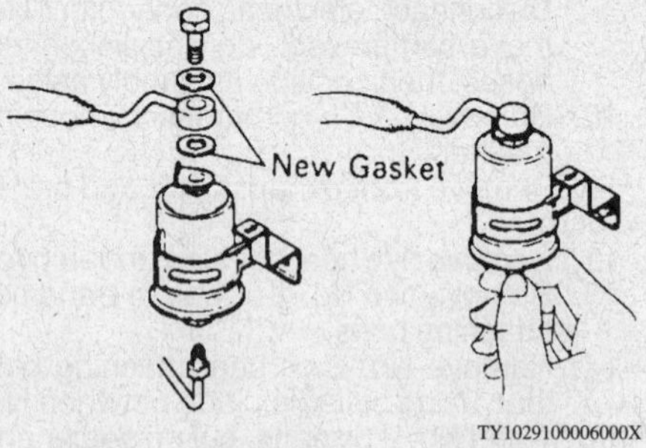
New Gasket
TY1029100006000X

Fig. 51 Fuel filter replacement

WATER PUMP

REPLACE

1MZ-FE ENGINE

1. **On models with coded audio anti-theft systems,**refer to "Precautions" for code procedures.
2. **On all models** drain engine coolant.
3. Remove time belt and pulleys as outlined under "Timing, Belt, Replace."
4. Remove No. 2 idler pulley, **Fig. 49.**
5. Disconnect engine wiring from No. 3 timing belt cover, then remove cover.
6. Remove water pump attaching bolts, then the water pump.
7. Reverse procedure to install. Reset audio anti-theft system, if necessary, as outlined under "Precautions."

3VZ-FE ENGINE

1. **On models with coded audio anti-theft systems,**refer to "Precautions" for code procedures.
2. **On all models,** disconnect battery ground cable.
3. Drain coolant from engine.
4. Disconnect radiator lower hose from water inlet pipe, **Fig. 50.**
5. Disconnect timing belt from water pump pulley.
6. Remove water inlet and thermostat, then water pump.
7. Reverse procedure to install. Reset audio anti-theft system, if necessary, as outlined under "Precautions."

RADIATOR

REPLACE

1993–94 CAMRY

1. **On models with coded audio anti-theft systems,**refer to "Precautions" for code procedures.
2. **On all models,** disconnect battery ground cable, then raise and support vehicle.
3. Drain coolant from engine and radiator.
4. Remove cruise control actuator cover.
5. Place a suitable catch basin or shop towel under line connections for hydraulic cooling fan drive, then disconnect pressure hose.
6. Disconnect upper radiator and coolant reservoir hoses from radiator.
7. Disconnect hydraulic cooling fan drive return hose.
8. Disconnect lower radiator hose at engine and transaxle oil cooler extension lines.
9. Remove upper radiator mounts, then lift out radiator and cooling fan as a unit.
10. Remove transaxle cooler extension lines and lower radiator from radiator.
11. Remove hydraulic cooling fan and shroud.
12. Remove lower radiator mounts.
13. Reverse procedure to install. Reset audio anti-theft system, if necessary, as outlined under "Precautions."

AVALON & 1995–96 CAMRY

1. **On models with coded audio anti-theft systems,**refer to "Precautions" for code procedures.
2. **On all models,** disconnect battery ground cable, then raise and support vehicle.
3. Drain coolant from engine and radiator.
4. Remove battery and tray, then disconnect cruise control actuator and mounting from body.
5. Disconnect upper radiator and coolant reservoir hoses from radiator.
6. Disconnect lower radiator hose at engine, then transaxle oil cooler extension lines.
7. Disconnect electric cooling fan connectors, then cruise control cable from holder on fan shroud.
8. Remove upper radiator mounts, then lift out radiator and cooling fans as a unit.
9. Remove transaxle cooler extension lines and lower radiator from radiator.
10. Remove electric cooling fans and shrouds.
11. Remove lower radiator mounts.
12. Reverse procedure to install. Reset audio anti-theft system, if necessary, as outlined under "Precautions."

FUEL PUMP

REPLACE

1. **On models with coded audio anti-theft systems,**refer to "Precautions" for code procedures.
2. **On all models,** remove rear seat cushion, then floor service hole cover.
3. Remove fuel pump lead wire.
4. Using suitable tool, disconnect fuel pipe and hose from fuel pump bracket.
5. Remove fuel pump bracket and gasket from fuel tank.
6. Remove fuel pump from fuel pump bracket.
7. Reverse procedure to install. Reset audio anti-theft system, if necessary, as outlined under "Precautions."

FUEL FILTER

REPLACE

Refer to **Fig. 51** for replacement procedure.

TIGHTENING SPECIFICATIONS

1 MZ-FE ENGINE

Year	Component	Torque/ Ft. Lbs.
1994–96	A/C Compressor To Alternator Bracket	18
	A/C Compressor To Cylinder Block	18
	Air Intake Chamber Stay To Air Intake Chamber	14
	Air Intake Chamber Stay To Cylinder Head	14
	Air Intake Chamber To Intake Manifold	32
	Camshaft Bearing Cap To Cylinder Head	12
	Camshaft Timing Pulley	⑤
	Connecting Rod Cap	④
	Coolant Drain Cock To Cylinder Block	29
	Crankshaft Position Sensor	6
	Crankshaft Pulley	159
	Cylinder Head	②
	Cylinder Head Cover	6
	Delivery Pipe To Intake Chamber	7
	Drain Hose Clamp To Cylinder Block	14
	Driveplate	61
	EGR Pipe To Righthand Exhaust Manifold	9
	Emission Control Valve Set To Air Intake Chamber	6
	Engine Mounting Absorber To Transaxle	35
	Engine Moving Control Rod To No. 2 RH Engine Mount Bracket	47
	Engine RH Mount Bracket To Cylinder Block	21
	Exhaust Manifold	36
	Flywheel	61
	Front Exhaust Pipe To Exhaust Manifold	46
	Front RH Engine Mount To Cylinder Block	47
	Front RH Engine Mount To Front Suspension Member	59
	Fuel Inlet Hose To Fuel Filter	22
	Fuel Pipe To Fuel Pump Bracket	22
	Fuel Pump Bracket To Fuel Tank	35①
	Hydraulic Pressure Pipe To Air Intake Chamber	14
	Intake Manifold	11
	Knock Sensor	29
	LH Engine Mount To Transaxle	47
	Main Bearing Caps	③
	No. 1 Idler Pulley To Oil Pump	25
	No. 1 Oil Pan To Cylinder Block	14
	No. 1 Oil Pan To Oil Pump	6
	No. 1 Oil Pan To Rear Oil Seal Retainer	6
	No. 2 Oil Pan To No. 1 Oil Pan	6
	No. 2 Idler Pulley	32
	No. 3 Timing Belt Cover	7
	Oil Drain Plug	27
	Oil Hole Cover Plate	6
	Oil Pan Baffle Plate	6
	Oil Pressure Switch	9
	Oil Pump (10 mm Bolt)	6
	Oil Pump (12 mm Bolt)	14 6

Continued

TIGHTENING SPECIFICATIONS

1 MZ-FE ENGINE—Continued

1994–96	Oil Strainer	6
	Power Steering Pump	31
	Power Steering Pump Bracket	32
	Rear End Plate To Cylinder Block	6
	Rear Oil Seal Retainer	6
	RH Engine Mount Stay To Intake Manifold	21
	RH Engine Mount Stay To No. 2 RH Engine Mount Bracket	21
	RH Rear Engine Mount To Cylinder Block	57
	RH Rear Engine Mount To Front Suspension Member	59
	Spark Plug	13
	Throttle Body	14
	Timing Belt Tensioner	20
	Water Bypass Pipe To Cylinder Block	74
	Water Inlet To Housing	6
	Water Pump	6

① — Inch lbs.

② — 12 pointed head bolts, torque to 40 ft. lbs. in sequence, then turn an additional 90°; recessed head bolt, torque to 18 ft. lbs.

③ — First torque to 45 ft. lbs., then tighten an additional 90°.

④ — First torque to 18 ft. lbs., then tighten an additional 90°.

⑤ — With tool No. SST 09960-10010 (09962-01000), or equivalent, to 65 ft. lbs.; less tool No. SST 09960-10010 (09962-01000), or equivalent, to 94 ft. lbs.

3VZ-FE ENGINE

Year	Component	Torque/Ft. Lbs.
1993	A/C Compressor To Alternator Bracket	20
	A/C Compressor To Cylinder Block	20
	Air Intake Chamber Stay To Air Intake Chamber	29
	Air Intake Chamber Stay To Cylinder Head	29
	Air Intake Chamber To Intake Manifold	32
	Air Pipe To Intake Manifold	7
	Camshaft Bearing Cap To Cylinder Head	12
	Camshaft Timing Pulley To Camshaft	80
	Camshaft Timing Pulley To Camshaft (SST)	55
	Center Exhaust Pipe To Tail Pipe	32
	Cold Start Injector Pipe To Cold Start Injector	11
	Connecting Rod Cap To Connecting Rod	④
	Coolant Drain Cock To Cylinder Block	29
	Crankshaft Pulley To Crankshaft	181
	Cylinder Head Cover To Cylinder Head	52①
	Cylinder Head To Cylinder Block	②
	Cylinder Head To Cylinder Block (Recessed Head Bolt)	②
	Delivery Pipe To Intake Chamber	13
	Drain Hose Clamp To Cylinder Block	14
	Driveplate To Crankshaft (A/T)	61

Continued

3VZ-FE ENGINE—Continued

1993	EGR Pipe To Exhaust Manifold	58
	EGR Valve To Air Intake Chamber	13
	Emission Control Valve Set To Air Intake Chamber	7
	Engine Mounting Absorber To Transaxle	35
	Engine Moving Control Rod To No. 2 RH Engine Mounting Bracket	47
	Engine RH Mounting Bracket To Cylinder Block	30
	Exhaust Manifold To Cylinder Head	29
	Flywheel To Crankshaft (M/T)	61
	Front Engine Mounting Insulator To Cylinder Block	57
	Front Engine Mounting Insulator To Front Suspension Member	59
	Front Exhaust Manifold To Catalytic Converter	32
	Front Exhaust Pipe To Exhaust Manifold	46
	Fuel Inlet Hose To Fuel Filter	22
	Fuel Pipe To Fuel Pump Bracket	22
	Fuel Pump Bracket To Fuel Tank	35①
	Hydraulic Pressure Pipe To Air Intake Chamber	14
	Intake Manifold To Cylinder Head	13
	Knock Sensor To Cylinder Block	33
	LH Engine Hanger To LH Cylinder Head	29
	LH Engine Mounting Insulator To Transaxle	47
	Main Bearing Cap To Cylinder Block	③
	No. 1 EGR Cooler To Air Intake Chamber	13
	No. 1 Engine Hanger To Air Intake Chamber	29
	No. 1 Engine Hanger To Cylinder Head	29
	No. 1 Idler Pulley To Oil Pump	25
	No. 2 Idler Pulley Bracket Stay To Intake Manifold	13
	No. 2 Idler Pulley Bracket Stay To No. 2 Idler Pulley Bracket	13
	No. 2 Idler Pulley Bracket To Cylinder Block	27
	No. 2 Idler Pulley To No. 2 Idler Pulley Bracket	29
	No. 2 RH Engine Mounting Stay (Bolt)	55
	No. 2 RH Engine Mounting Stay (Nut)	46
	No. 3 RH Engine Mounting Stay (Bolt)	54
	No. 3 Timing Belt Cover To Cylinder Block	6
	No. 3 Timing Belt Cover To Cylinder Head	6
	PS Pump Bracket To RH Cylinder Head	32
	PS Pump To PS Pump Bracket	31
	Rear End Plate To Cylinder Block	7
	Rear Oil Seal Retainer To Cylinder Block	6
	RH Engine Mounting Stay To Intake Manifold	23

Continued

3VZ-FE ENGINE—Continued

1993	RH Engine Mounting Stay To No. 2 righthand Engine Mounting Bracket	23
	RH Rear Engine Mounting Insulator To Cylinder Block	57
	RH Rear Engine Mounting Insulator To Front Suspension Member	59
	Spark Plug To Cylinder Head	13
	Throttle Body To Air Intake Chamber	9
	Timing Belt Tension To Oil Pump	20
	Water Bypass Outlet To Intake Manifold	7
	Water Bypass Pipe To Cylinder Block	74
	Water Inlet	14
	Water Outlet To Intake Manifold	7
	Water Pump	14

① — Inch lbs.
② — Refer to "Cylinder Head, Replace."
③ — First torque to 45 ft. lbs., then tighten an additional 90°.
④ — First torque to 18 ft. lbs., then tighten an additional 90°.

Clutch & Manual Transaxle

NOTE: On Air Bag Equipped Models, Refer To "Air Bag System Precautions" Located In The Front Of This Manual For System Disarming & Arming Procedures.

INDEX

	Page No.
Adjustments	42-36
Clutch Pedal Height	42-36
Clutch, Replace	42-37
Hydraulic System Service	42-37
Clutch Release Cylinder, Replace	42-37
Clutch Slave Cylinder, Replace	42-37
Clutch System Bleed	42-37
Precautions	42-36
Air Bag Systems	42-36
Audio Coded Anti-Theft System	42-36
Tightening Specifications	42-38
Transaxle, Replace	42-38

PRECAUTIONS

AIR BAG SYSTEMS

Refer to "Air Bag System Precautions" in the front of this manual for system disarming and arming procedures.

AUDIO CODED ANTI-THEFT SYSTEM

Some models are with an audio coded anti-theft system that will disable the radio when the battery cable is disconnected. The system can be identified by the words "ANTI-THEFT SYSTEM" on the cassette tape lid. Obtain three digit customer code for input. Reset system after service as follows:

1. Obtain three digit audio anti-theft code.
2. Depress 1 (PROG) while depressing righthand side of TUNE SEEK button, - - - will appear in tape operation display.
3. To enter the first digit, depress 1 (PROG) button repeatedly until the number of times depressed equals the first digit beginning with zero (depress the 1 button six times if the first digit is five).
4. To enter second digit, depress 2 (APS) button repeatedly until the number of times depressed equals the second digit beginning with zero.
5. To enter third digit, depress 3 (RPT) button repeatedly until the number of times depressed equals the third digit beginning with zero.
6. If - - - is displayed during code input, repeat procedure.
7. When code appears in display, depress and hold SCAN button until SEC appears.
8. When SEC disappears audio system should be operative.
9. If Err is displayed, repeat procedure. **Attempting to input code more than nine times may permanently disable audio system.**

ADJUSTMENTS

CLUTCH PEDAL HEIGHT

1. Measure clutch pedal height as shown, **Fig. 1.**
2. **On 1993 models with 3VZ-FE engine,** clutch pedal height should be 6.48–6.88 inches.
3. **On 1993 models with 5SFE engine and all 1994–96 models,** clutch pedal height should be 6.33–6.72 inches.
4. **On all models,** if clutch pedal height is not as specified, remove lower instrument panel finish panel and air duct.
5. Loosen clutch pedal locknut, then rotate stopper bolt until specified height is achieved.
6. Tighten locknut.
7. Check clutch pedal freeplay by depressing clutch pedal until resistance is felt. Freeplay should be .197–.591 inch. Pushrod play at top of pedal

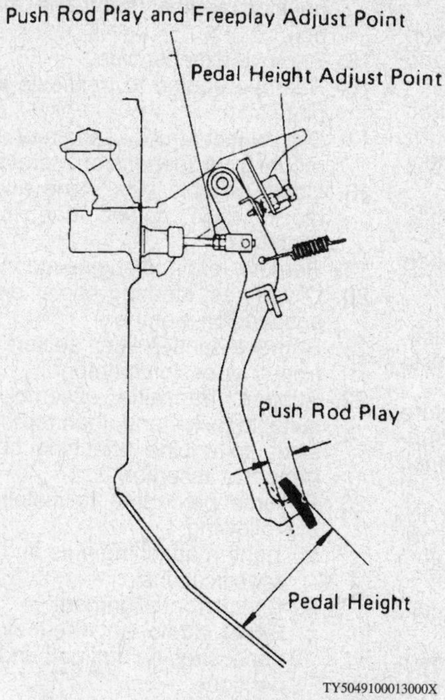

Push Rod Play and Freeplay Adjust Point
Pedal Height Adjust Point
Push Rod Play
Pedal Height
TY5049100013000X

Fig. 1 Clutch pedal height

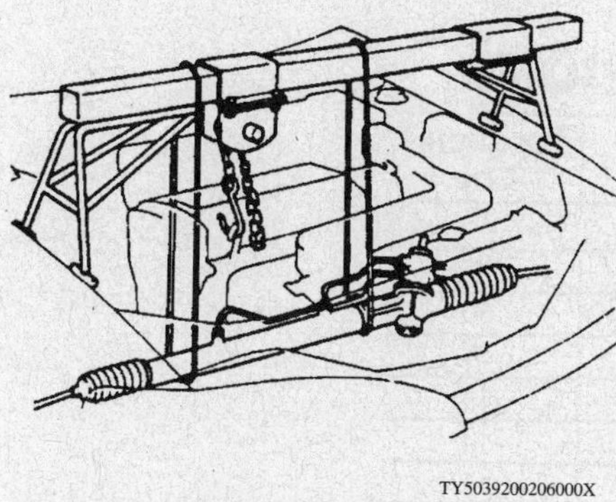

TY5039200206000X

Fig. 3 Engine & steering gear support

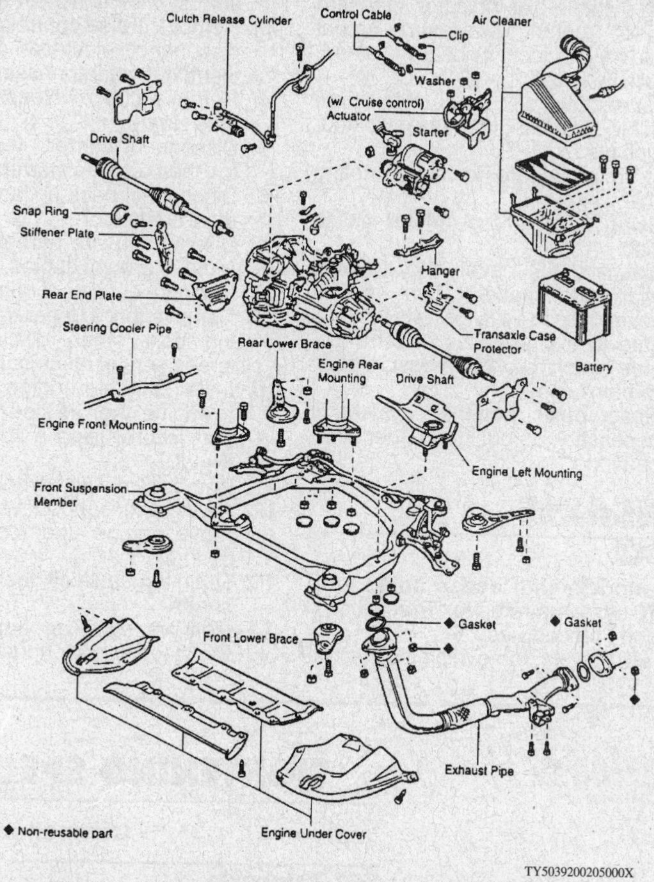

Clutch Release Cylinder
Control Cable
Clip
Air Cleaner
Washer
(w/ Cruise control) Actuator
Drive Shaft
Starter
Snap Ring
Stiffener Plate
Hanger
Rear End Plate
Steering Cooler Pipe
Transaxle Case Protector
Rear Lower Brace
Engine Rear Mounting
Drive Shaft
Battery
Engine Front Mounting
Engine Left Mounting
Front Suspension Member
Gasket
Gasket
Front Lower Brace
Exhaust Pipe
◆ Non-reusable part
Engine Under Cover
TY5039200205000X

Fig. 2 Transaxle components replacement

should be .039–.197 inch.

8. If necessary to adjust freeplay, loosen locknut and rotate pushrod until freeplay is as specified.
9. Tighten locknut.
10. Ensure clutch pedal height and freeplay are as specified, then reinstall air duct and finish panel.

HYDRAULIC SYSTEM SERVICE

CLUTCH SLAVE CYLINDER, REPLACE

1. **On models with coded audio anti-theft systems,**refer to "Precautions" for code procedures.
2. **On all models,** remove fluid using syringe, then disconnect clutch line tube.
3. Remove clevis pin and clip with spring washer.
4. Remove clutch slave cylinder.
5. Reverse procedure to install, noting the following:
   a. Tighten fasteners to specifications.
   b. Bleed and adjust system as outlined under "Clutch System Bleed" and "Adjustments."
   c. Reset audio anti-theft system, if necessary, as outlined under "Precautions."

CLUTCH RELEASE CYLINDER, REPLACE

1. Using suitable tool, disconnect clutch line tube. Use suitable container to catch fluid.
2. Remove release cylinder attaching bolts, then remove cylinder.
3. Reverse procedure to install. Tighten attaching bolts to specifications, then bleed clutch system as outlined under "Clutch System Bleed."

CLUTCH SYSTEM BLEED

If any service is performed on the clutch system or air is suspected in the clutch lines, bleed the system as follows:

1. Fill clutch reservoir with suitable brake fluid. **Do not allow fluid to come in contact with painted surfaces.**
2. Check reservoir frequently, add fluid as required.
3. Connect vinyl tube to bleeder plug, then insert other tube end in half full container of brake fluid.
4. Slowly pump clutch pedal several times.
5. While depressing pedal, loosen bleeder plug until fluid runs out. Close bleeder plug.
6. Repeat procedure until air bubbles are not evident in the fluid. **Do not reuse the fluid that was bled.**

CLUTCH

REPLACE

1. **On models with coded audio anti-theft systems,**refer to "Precautions" for code procedures.
2. **On all models,** remove transmission assembly as outlined under "Transaxle, Replace."
3. Place installation alignment marks on clutch cover and flywheel.
4. Loosen each set bolt one turn at a time until spring tension is released.
5. Remove clutch cover attaching bolts, then remove cover and disc.
6. Remove release bearing, fork and boot.
7. Using suitable calipers, measure clutch disc rivet head depth. Minimum rivet depth should be .012 inch. If not as indicated, replace clutch disc.

8. Using suitable dial indicator, measure flywheel runout. Maximum runout should be .004 inch. If not as indicated, replace flywheel.
9. Measure clutch disc runout. Maximum runout is .031 inch. If not as indicated, replace disc.
10. Reverse procedure to install, noting the following:
    a. Using suitable tool, install clutch disc.
    b. Match clutch cover and flywheel alignment marks, then **torque** cover bolts to 14 ft. lbs. one turn at a time in a criss-cross pattern. Ensure clutch disc and pressure plate remain aligned.
    c. Reset audio anti-theft system, if necessary, as outlined under "Precautions."

TRANSAXLE

REPLACE

1. **On models with coded audio anti-theft systems,**refer to "Precautions" for code procedures.
2. **On all models,** remove air cleaner assembly with air hose, **Fig. 2.**
3. Remove cruise control actuator cover, disconnect electrical connector and dismount actuator assembly.
4. Remove clutch release cylinder and tube clamp.
5. Disconnect starter electrical connector, then remove starter.
6. Disconnect back-up lamp switch electrical connector.
7. Disconnect wire harness clamp, then remove ground cables.
8. Disconnect shifter control cables.
9. Remove three upper transaxle attaching bolts, then disconnect vehicle speed sensor electrical connector.
10. Install suitable engine support fixture to engine, then tie steering gear to support fixture using a suitable material, **Fig. 3.**
11. Remove front wheel and tire assembly.
12. Raise and support vehicle, then remove engine undercovers and side covers.
13. Drain transaxle oil, then remove driveshafts.
14. Remove stabilizer bar bracket, then the steering gear housing to front suspension member (subframe) attaching bolt.
15. Remove exhaust pipe.
16. Remove engine to transaxle stiffener plate.
17. Disconnect front and rear engine mount from suspension member.
18. Using suitable jack stand and wood block, raise engine and transaxle slightly.
19. Remove lefthand engine mount.
20. Disconnect steering cooler pipe from suspension member.
21. Remove fender liner setscrews and front suspension member.
22. Support transaxle assembly using suitable jack stand, then remove transaxle to engine attaching bolts and transaxle assembly.
23. Reverse procedure to install, noting the following:
    a. Tighten attaching nuts and bolts to specifications.
    b. Check front alignment.
    c. Reset audio anti-theft system, if necessary, as outlined under "Precautions."

TIGHTENING SPECIFICATIONS

Year	Component	Torque/Ft. Lbs.
E53 Transaxle		
1993–96	Axle Hub Nut	217
	Back-Up Light Switch	30
	Bleeder Plug	7
	Clutch Accumulator	14
	Clutch Cover	14
	Clutch Line Union	11
	Clutch Release Cylinder To Transaxle	9
	Drain Plug	36
	Driveshaft To Pinion Shaft	48
	Driveshaft Center Bearing Lock Bolt	24
	Engine Absorber Lock Bolt	35
	Engine Mount To Suspension Member	59
	Filler Plug	36
	Front Exhaust Pipe To Converter	32
	Front Exhaust Pipe To Manifold	46
	Front Lower Brace To Body	27
	Front Suspension Member To Body	134
	Rear Lower Brace To Body (Bolt)	24
	Rear Lower Brace To Body (Nut)	27
	Selecting Bellcrank Lock Bolt	14
	Shift Lever Lock Bolt	36
	Shift & Select Lever Lock Bolt	14
	Speed Sensor Lock Bolt	6
	Stabilizer Bar Bracket	14
	Steering Gear Housing To Suspension Member	134
	Stiffener Plate To Engine	13

Continued

TIGHTENING SPECIFICATIONS—Continued

Year	Component	Torque/Ft. Lbs.
E53 Transaxle		
1993–96	Stiffener Plate To Transaxle	27
	Transaxle To Engine (10 mm Bolt)	34
	Transaxle To Engine (12 mm Bolt)	47
	Transaxle To Starter	29
S51Transaxle		
1993–96	Axle Hub Nut	137
	Back-Up Lamp Switch	33
	Clutch Release Cylinder To Housing	9
	Clutch Release Bearing Retainer	5
	Control Shaft Cover	27
	Drain Plug	36
	Driveshaft Center Bearing Lock Bolt	24
	Engine Mount To Sub Frame	59
	Filler Plug	36
	Front Exhaust Pipe To Center Pipe	32
	Front Exhaust Pipe To Converter	46
	Input Shaft Oil Receiver	5
	Output Shaft Front Bearing Lock Plate	13
	Reverse Shift Arm Bracket	13
	Side Bearing Retainer	13
	Starter To Clutch Housing	29
	Stiffener Plate To Clutch Housing	27
	Straight Screw Plug (Reverse Restrict Pin)	9
	Straight Screw Plug (Shift Fork Shaft)	9
	Sub Frame To Body	134
	Transaxle Case	22
	Transaxle Case Protector	13
	Transaxle To Engine (8 mm)	8
	Transaxle To Engine (10 mm)	34
	Transaxle To Engine (12 mm)	47
	Transaxle To Starter	29

Rear Axle & Suspension

NOTE: On Air Bag Equipped Models, Refer To "Air Bag System Precautions" Located In The Front Of This Manual For System Disarming & Arming Procedures.

INDEX

	Page No.
Coil Spring, Replace	42-41
Hub & Bearing, Replace	42-40
Lower Suspension Arm & Strut Rod, Replace	42-41
Precautions	42-40
Air Bag Systems	42-40
Audio Coded Anti-Theft System	42-40
Rear Axle Carrier, Replace	42-40
Stabilizer Bar, Replace	42-41
Suspension Arm, Replace	42-41
Tightening Specifications	42-42

PRECAUTIONS

AIR BAG SYSTEMS

Refer to "Air Bag System Precautions" in the front of this manual for system disarming and arming procedures.

AUDIO CODED ANTI-THEFT SYSTEM

Some models are with an audio coded anti-theft system that will disable the radio when the battery cable is disconnected. The system can be identified by the words "ANTI-THEFT SYSTEM" on the cassette tape lid. Obtain three digit customer code for input. Reset system after service as follows:

1. Obtain three digit audio anti-theft code.
2. Depress 1 (PROG) while depressing righthand side of TUNE SEEK button, - - - will appear in tape operation display.
3. To enter the first digit, depress 1 (PROG) button repeatedly until the number of times depressed equals the first digit beginning with zero (depress the 1 button six times if the first digit if five).
4. To enter second digit, depress 2 (APS) button repeatedly until the number of times depressed equals the second digit beginning with zero.
5. To enter third digit, depress 3 (RPT) button repeatedly until the number of times depressed equals the third digit beginning with zero.
6. If - - - is displayed during code input, repeat procedure.
7. When code appears in display, depress and hold SCAN button until SEC appears.
8. When SEC disappears audio system should be operative.
9. If Err is displayed, repeat procedure. **Attempting to input code more than nine times may permanently disable audio system.**

HUB & BEARING

REPLACE

1. **On models with drum brakes,** remove brake drum, **Fig. 1.**

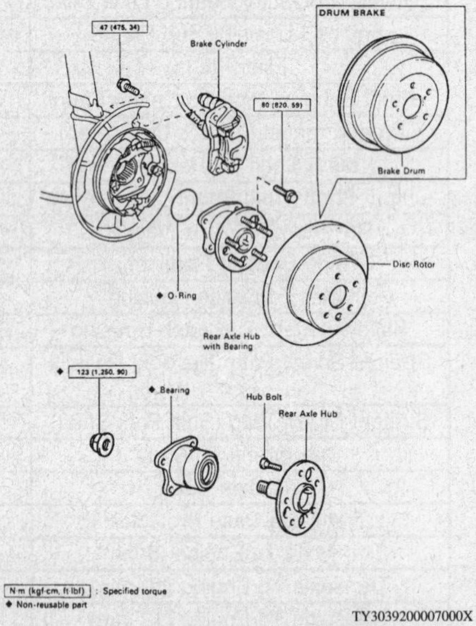
DRUM BRAKE
Brake Cylinder
Brake Drum
Disc Rotor
O-Ring
Rear Axle Hub with Bearing
Bearing
Hub Bolt
Rear Axle Hub
N·m (kgf·cm, ft·lbf) : Specified torque
Non-reusable part
TY3039200007000X

Fig. 1 Rear axle hub replacement

2. **On models with disc brakes,** remove brake caliper and position aside using suitable wire, then remove brake rotor.
3. **On all models,** using suitable dial indicator, measure bearing play in axial direction. Maximum of .0020 inch should be indicated. If not as indicated, replace bearing.
4. Using suitable dial indicator, measure deviation at surface of axle hub outside hub bolt. Maximum of .0028 inch should be indicated. If not as indicated, replace axle shaft and bearing.
5. Remove four rear axle hub attaching bolts, then the axle hub and O-ring.
6. **On models with anti-lock brakes,** do not disassemble rear axle shaft and bearing.
7. **On models less anti-lock brakes,** using suitable hammer and chisel, unstake and remove locknut.
8. **On all models,** using suitable tool, remove axle shaft from axle hub.
9. Remove bearing inner race (outside).

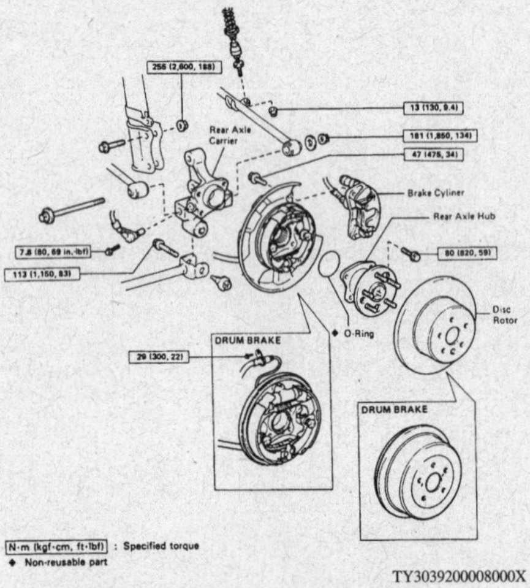
Rear Axle Carrier
Brake Cyliner
Rear Axle Hub
Disc Rotor
O-Ring
DRUM BRAKE
N·m (kgf·cm, ft·lbf) : Specified torque
Non-reusable part
TY3039200008000X

Fig. 2 Rear axle carrier replacement

10. Reverse procedure to install.

REAR AXLE CARRIER

REPLACE

1. Remove rear axle hub as outlined under "Hub & Bearing, Replace."
2. Remove brake hose from shock absorber.
3. Remove backing plate from rear axle carrier and position aside using suitable wire.
4. **On models with anti-lock brakes,** remove ABS speed sensor from axle carrier and disconnect Load Sensing Proportioning Valve (LSPV) spring from lower arm.
5. **On all models,** loosen but do not remove three axle carrier attaching nuts, **Fig. 2.**
6. Disconnect strut rod from axle carrier.
7. Remove axle carrier three attaching nuts and bolts, then remove axle carrier.
8. Reverse procedure to install.

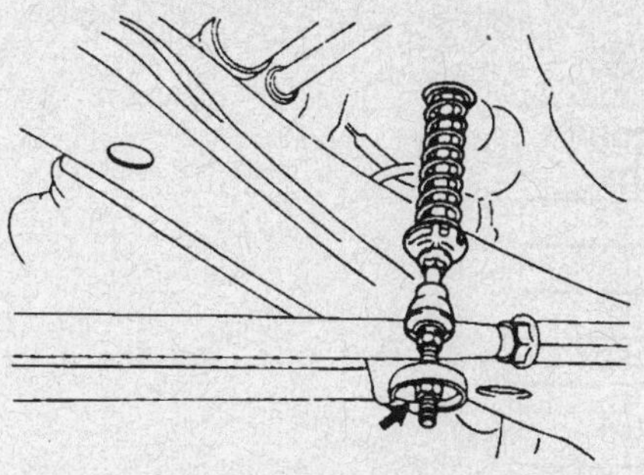

TY2039200005000X

Fig. 3 Load Sensing Proportioning Valve (LSPV) spring removal

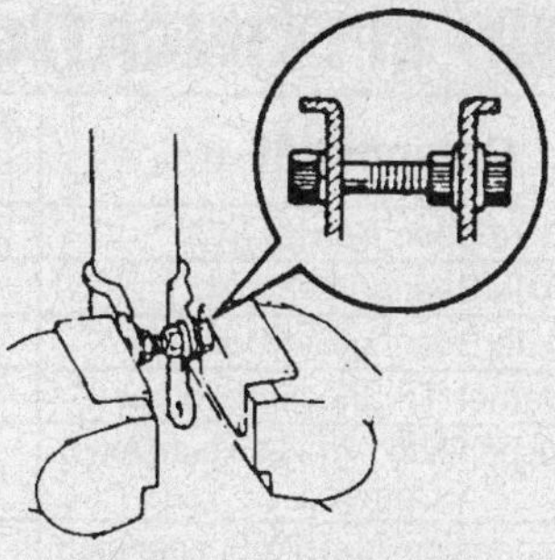

TY2039200006000X

Fig. 4 Shock absorber installation

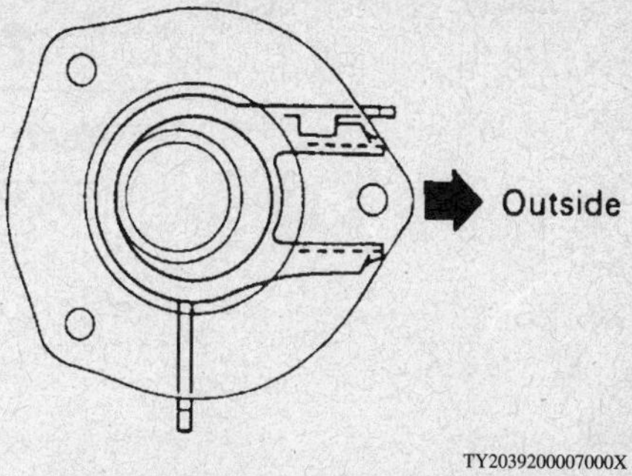
Outside

TY2039200007000X

Fig. 5 Upper support position

COIL SPRING

REPLACE

1. Remove rear seat, then package tray trim.
2. Raise and support vehicle, then remove rear wheels.
3. **On models with ABS,** disconnect Load Sensing Proportioning Valve (LSPV) spring from lower arm, **Fig. 3.**
4. Disconnect ABS speed sensor wire, then brake hose from shock absorber.
5. **On all models,** disconnect stabilizer bar link from shock absorber.
6. Support rear axle carrier with a suitable jack, loosen two lower shock attaching nuts, then remove three upper support attaching nuts.
7. Lower rear axle carrier, remove two lower attaching bolts, then remove shock absorber from vehicle.
8. Remove cap, attach spring compress tool No. SST 09727-30020, or equivalent, then compress spring.
9. Install a bolt and two nuts to bracket at lower portion of shock absorber, then place in vice, **Fig. 4.**
10. Using spring compress to hold upper support, remove shock absorber attaching nut, then the coil spring.
11. Reverse procedure to install, noting the following:
    a. When replacing upper support, use a new attaching nut.
    b. Rotate upper support and set in direction as shown in **Fig. 5.**

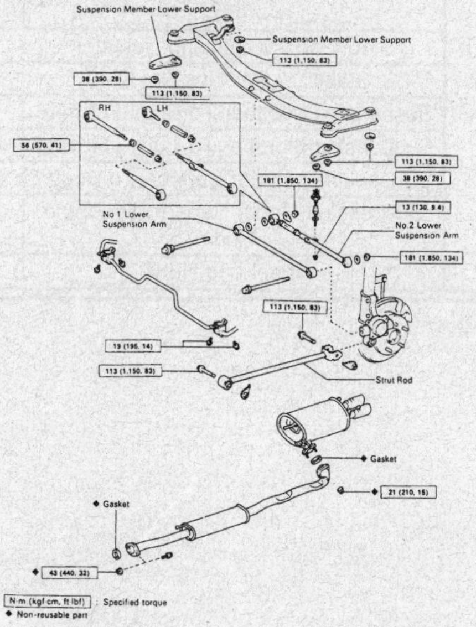
Suspension Member Lower Support
Suspension Member Lower Support
RH
LH
No.1 Lower Suspension Arm
No.2 Lower Suspension Arm
Strut Rod
Gasket
Gasket
N·m (kgf·cm, ft·lbf) : Specified torque
◆ Non-reusable part

TY2039200009000X

Fig. 6 Rear suspension

    c. Tighten all nuts and bolts to specifications.

STABILIZER BAR

REPLACE

1. Raise and support rear of vehicle, then remove rear wheels.
2. Disconnect bolts securing stabilizer bar to link brackets and axle housing.
3. Disconnect bolts securing stabilizer bar to frame, then remove stabilizer bar.
4. Reverse procedure to install. Tighten to specifications.

SUSPENSION ARM

REPLACE

Refer to "Lower Suspension Arm & Strut Rod, Replace" for procedure.

LOWER SUSPENSION ARM & STRUT ROD

REPLACE

1. Raise and support vehicle, then remove rear tires.
2. Remove two strut rod attaching nuts and bolts, then the strut rod, **Fig. 6.**
3. **On models with ABS,** disconnect Load Sensing Proportioning Valve (LSPV) spring from lower arm, **Fig. 3.**
4. **On all models,** remove No. 2 lower suspension arm attaching nuts, then suspension arm.
5. Remove stabilizer bar bushing retainer, then exhaust center and tail pipe.
6. Support suspension member with a suitable jack. Remove six nuts, then left and right suspension member lower stopper.
7. Lower suspension member. Remove No. 1 lower suspension arm attaching bolts, then suspension arm.
8. Reverse procedure to install. Tighten nuts and bolts to specifications.

TIGHTENING SPECIFICATIONS

Year	Component	Torque/Ft. Lbs.
1993–96	ABS Speed Sensor Bolt	6
	Axle Bearing Locknut	90
	Axle Bearing Set Bolt	90
	Axle Carrier To Shock Absorber	188
	Lower Suspension Arm To Rear Axle Carrier	134
	Lower Suspension Arm To Suspension Member	134
	Load Sensing Proportioning Valve (LSPV) Spring To Lower Suspension Arm	9
	Stabilizer Bar Bushing Retainer	14
	Stabilizer Bar Link Set Nut	47
	Suspension Member To Body (17 mm)	83
	Suspension Member To Body (14 mm)	28
	Suspension Upper Support To Body	29
	Suspension Upper Support To Piston Rod	36
	Wheel Lug Nuts	76

Front Suspension & Steering

NOTE: On Air Bag Equipped Models, Refer To "Air Bag System Precautions" Located In The Front Of This Manual For System Disarming & Arming Procedures.

INDEX

	Page No.
Ball Joint, Replace	42-43
Ball Joint Inspection	42-43
Coil Spring, Replace	42-44
Hub & Steering Knuckle, Replace	42-43
Lower Suspension Arm, Replace	42-44
Manual Steering Gears	48-1
Power Steering	48-1
Power Steering Gear, Replace	42-45
Power Steering Pump, Replace	42-46
Power Steering System Bleed	42-46
Precautions	42-43
Air Bag Systems	42-43
Audio Coded Anti-Theft System	42-43
Stabilizer Bar, Replace	42-45
Strut, Replace	42-44
Tightening Specifications	42-47
Wheel Bearing, Adjust	42-43

PRECAUTIONS

AIR BAG SYSTEMS

Refer to "Air Bag System Precautions" in the front of this manual for system disarming and arming procedures.

AUDIO CODED ANTI-THEFT SYSTEM

Some models are with an audio coded anti-theft system that will disable the radio when the battery cable is disconnected. The system can be identified by the word "ANTI-THEFT SYSTEM" on the cassette tape lid. Obtain three digit customer code for input. Reset system after service as follows:

1. Obtain three digit audio anti-theft code.
2. Depress 1 (PROG) while depressing righthand side of TUNE SEEK button, - - - will appear in tape operation display.
3. To enter first digit, depress 1 (PROG) button repeatedly until number of times depressed equals first digit beginning with zero (depress 1 button six times if first digit is five).
4. To enter second digit, depress 2 (APS) button repeatedly until number of times depressed equals the second digit beginning with zero.
5. To enter third digit, depress 3 (RPT) button repeatedly until number of times depressed equals third digit beginning with zero.
6. If - - - is displayed during code input, repeat procedure.
7. When code appears in display, depress and hold SCAN button until SEC appears.
8. When SEC disappears audio system should be operative.
9. If Err is displayed, repeat procedure. **Attempting to input code more than nine times may permanently disable audio system.**

WHEEL BEARING

ADJUST

These models incorporate lubed for life, sealed front wheel bearings with no provision for adjustment.

HUB & STEERING KNUCKLE

REPLACE

1. Raise and support vehicle, then remove front wheels.
2. Remove brake caliper and support with wire, then the rotor, **Fig. 1.**
3. Place a dial indicator near center ofaxle hub and check backlash in bearing shaft direction, **Fig. 2.** If backlash is greater than .002 inch, replace bearing.
4. Place a dial indicator at surface of axle hub outside hub bolt and check hub runout, **Fig. 3.**If runout is greater than .002 inch, replace axle hub.
5. Install rotor and brake caliper, then remove driveshaft locknut while applying brakes.
6. Remove brake caliper and support with wire. Remove rotor.
7. Remove ABS speed sensor from steering knuckle, then loosen nuts on lower side of shock absorber. **Do not remove bolts at this time.**
8. Disconnect tie rod end from steering knuckle using ball joint puller tool No. 09628-62011, or equivalent, then the lower ball joint from lower suspension arm.
9. Remove bolts on lower side of shock absorber, then the steering knuckle and hub.
10. Using a suitable screwdriver, remove dust deflector.
11. Remove lower ball joint using ball joint puller tool No. 09628-62011, or equivalent, then the hub using rear axle shaft puller tool No. 09520-00031, or equivalent.
12. Remove inner race hub using bearing remover tool No. 09950-00020, or equivalent, and a suitable press.
13. Remove dust cover, then the bearing snap ring from steering knuckle.
14. Place inner race on outside of bearing, then using countershaft bearing replacer tool No. 09310-35010, or equivalent, and a hammer, remove bearing.
15. Reverse procedure to install, noting the following:
    a. Press new bearing into steering knuckle using steering knuckle oil seal replacer tool No. 09608-32010, or equivalent.
    b. Press hub into steering knuckle using countershaft bearing replacer tool No. 09310-35010 and steering knuckle oil seal replacer tool No. 09608-32010, or equivalents.
    c. Install a new dust deflector using transmission and transfer bearing replacer tool No. 09316-60010, or equivalent, and a hammer. **Align holes for ABS speed sensor in dust deflector and steering knuckle.**

BALL JOINT INSPECTION

1. Remove ball joint as outlined under "Ball Joint, Replace."
2. Move ball joint stud back and forth five times, then install nut.
3. Using torque wrench, turn nut continuously one turn every 2–4 seconds and take torque reading on fifth turn.
4. If torque reading is not 9–29 inch lbs., replace ball joint.

BALL JOINT

REPLACE

1. Raise and support vehicle, then remove front wheels.
2. Remove steering knuckle and hub as outlined under "Hub & Steering Knuckle, Replace."
3. Using a suitable screwdriver, remove driveshaft dust deflector from steering knuckle.
4. Remove lower ball joint using ball joint puller tool No. 09628-62011, or equivalent.
5. Inspect ball joint as outlined under "Ball Joint Inspection."

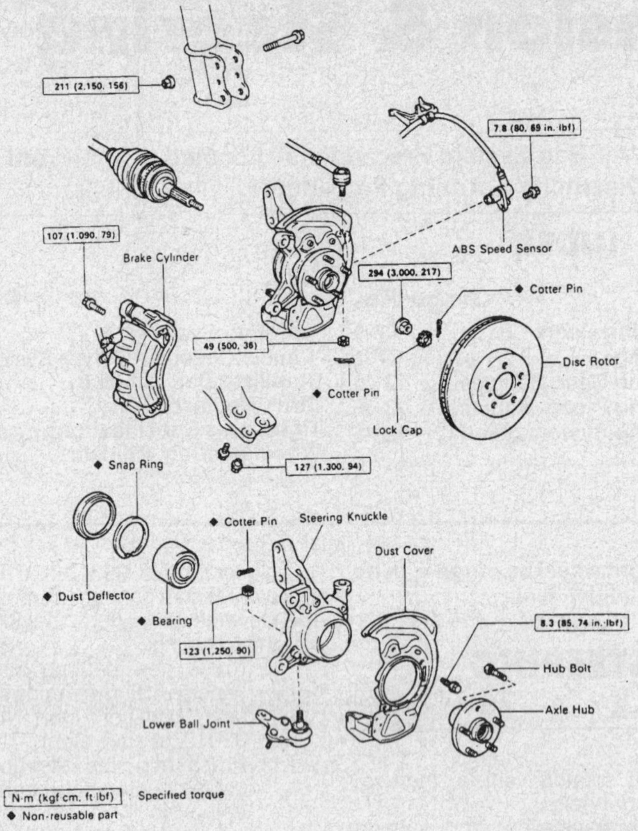
211 (2,150, 156)
7.8 (80, 69 in.·lbf)
107 (1,090, 79)
Brake Cylinder
ABS Speed Sensor
294 (3,000, 217)
◆ Cotter Pin
49 (500, 36)
Disc Rotor
◆ Cotter Pin
Lock Cap
127 (1,300, 94)
◆ Snap Ring
◆ Cotter Pin
Steering Knuckle
Dust Cover
◆ Dust Deflector
◆ Bearing
8.3 (85, 74 in.·lbf)
123 (1,250, 90)
Hub Bolt
Axle Hub
Lower Ball Joint
N·m (kgf·cm, ft·lbf) : Specified torque
◆ Non-reusable part

TY2049200013000X

Fig. 1 Exploded view of knuckle, hub & bearing

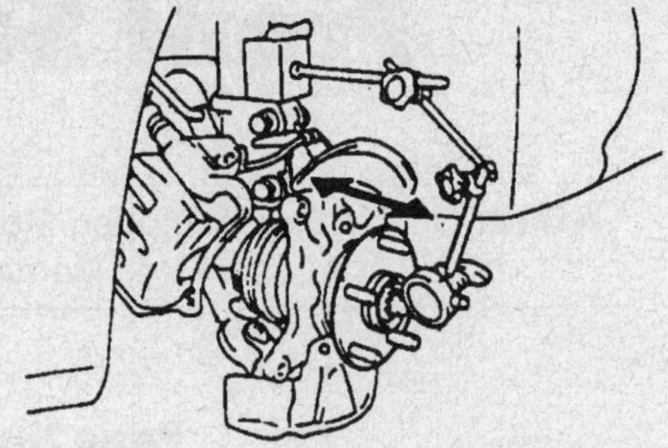

TY2049200014000X

Fig. 2 Bearing backlash measurement

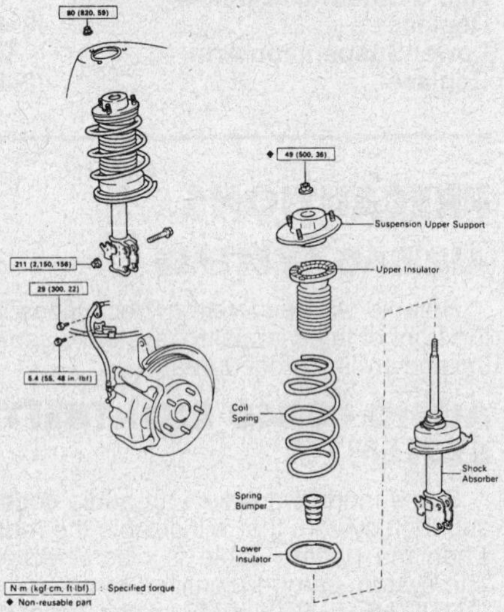
80 (820, 59)
◆ 49 (500, 36)
Suspension Upper Support
Upper Insulator
211 (2,150, 156)
29 (300, 22)
5.4 (55, 48 in.·lbf)
Coil Spring
Shock Absorber
Spring Bumper
Lower Insulator
N·m (kgf·cm, ft·lbf) : Specified torque
◆ Non-reusable part

TY2029200005000X

Fig. 4 Exploded view of strut assembly. 1993–94 Camry

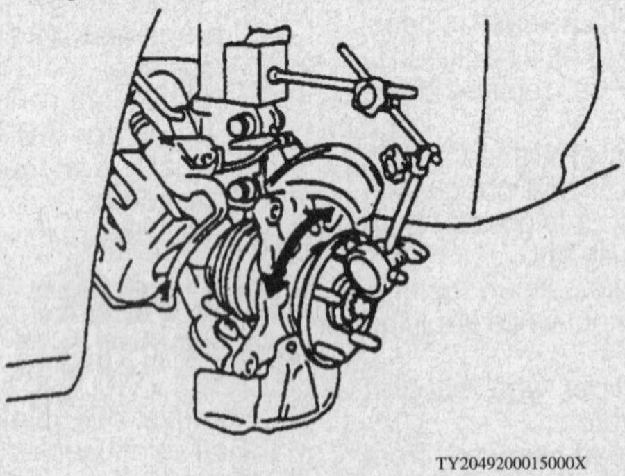

TY2049200015000X

Fig. 3 Hub runout measurement

6. Reverse procedure to install, noting the following:
   a. Install a new dust deflector using transmission and transfer bearing replacer tool No. 09316-60010, or equivalent.

COIL SPRING

REPLACE

1. Raise and support vehicle, then remove front wheels.
2. Disconnect brake hose and anti-lock brake system speed sensor wire from shock absorber.
3. Remove lower strut attaching nuts and bolts, **Figs. 4 and 5.**
4. Remove three nuts holding top of suspension support.
5. Remove strut from body. **Cover driveshaft boot to prevent damage during removal.**
6. Using coil spring compressor tool No. 09727-00045, 09727-30020, or equivalent, compress coil spring.
7. Install a bolt and two nuts to lower portion of strut shell and secure in vise.
8. Using spring seat holding tool No. 09729-22031, or equivalent, remove nut, suspension upper support, upper insulator, coil spring, spring bumper and lower insulator. **Do not disassemble spring lower seat.**
9. Reverse procedure to install, noting the following:
   a. Fit lower end of coil spring into gap of lower seat.
   b. Prior to installation of nut, rotate upper support until lowest bolt on support is aligned with projection part of spring lower seat.
   c. Tighten all attaching nuts and bolts to specifications.

STRUT

REPLACE

Refer to "Coil Spring, Replace" for procedure.

LOWER SUSPENSION ARM

REPLACE

1. Raise and support vehicle, then remove front wheels.
2. Remove driveshaft locknut, then disconnect tie rod end from steering knuckle using ball joint puller tool No. 09628-62011, or equivalent.
3. Remove left and right stabilizer end brackets from lower suspension arm, **Fig. 6.**
4. Disconnect lower suspension arm from lower ball joint.
5. Remove driveshaft from axle hub and support with wire. **Use care not to damage driveshaft boot and ABS sensor rotor.**
6. Remove two bolts on front side of lower suspension arm, nut and bolt on rear side, then the lower suspension arm.
7. Reverse procedure to install.

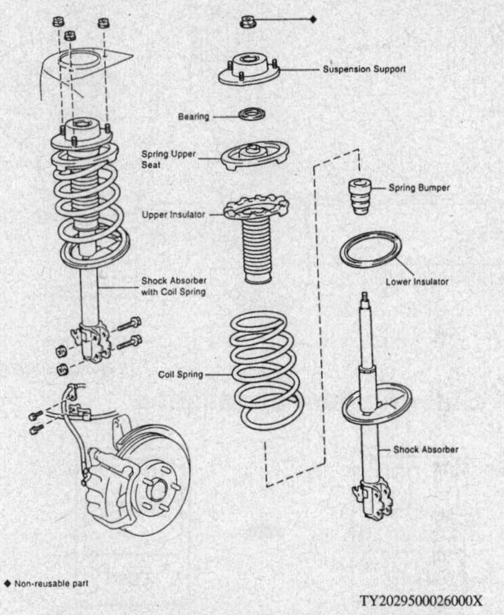
Suspension Support
Bearing
Spring Upper Seat
Spring Bumper
Upper Insulator
Lower Insulator
Shock Absorber with Coil Spring
Coil Spring
Shock Absorber
◆ Non-reusable part
TY2029500026000X

Fig. 5 Exploded view of strut assembly. Avalon & 1995–96 Camry

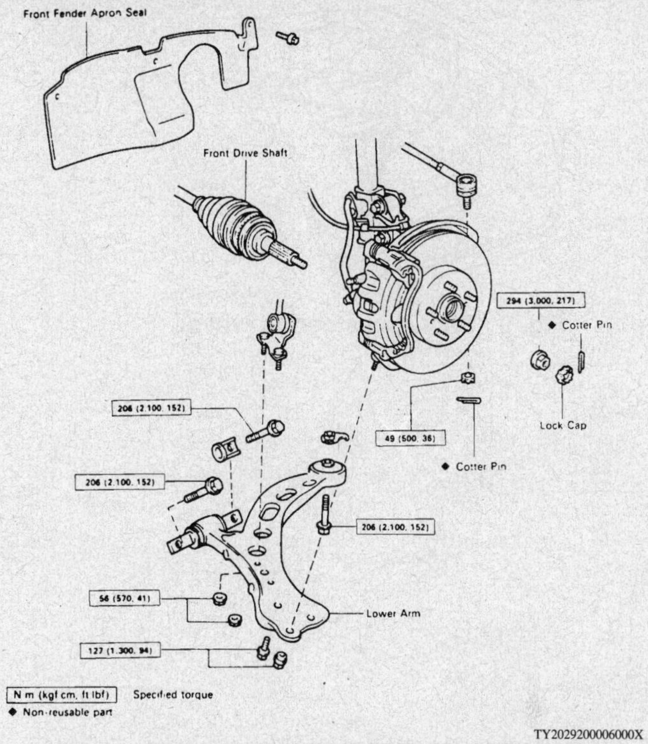
Front Fender Apron Seal
Front Drive Shaft
294 (3,000, 217)
◆ Cotter Pin
Lock Cap
206 (2,100, 152)
49 (500, 36)
◆ Cotter Pin
206 (2,100, 152)
206 (2,100, 152)
56 (570, 41)
Lower Arm
127 (1,300, 94)
N·m (kgf·cm, ft·lbf) : Specified torque
◆ Non-reusable part
TY2029200006000X

Fig. 6 Exploded view of lower suspension arm

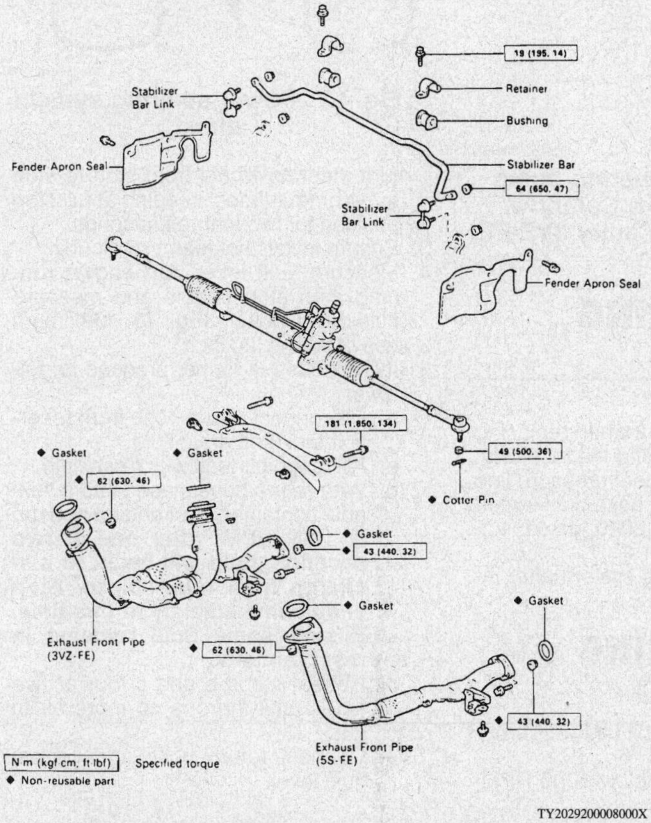
19 (195, 14)
Stabilizer Bar Link
Retainer
Bushing
Fender Apron Seal
Stabilizer Bar
64 (650, 47)
Stabilizer Bar Link
Fender Apron Seal
181 (1,850, 134)
◆ Gasket
◆ Gasket
◆ 62 (630, 46)
49 (500, 36)
◆ Cotter Pin
◆ Gasket
◆ 43 (440, 32)
◆ Gasket
◆ Gasket
Exhaust Front Pipe (3VZ-FE)
◆ 62 (630, 46)
◆ 43 (440, 32)
Exhaust Front Pipe (5S-FE)
N·m (kgf·cm, ft·lbf) : Specified torque
◆ Non-reusable part
TY2029200008000X

Fig. 7 Exploded view of stabilizer bar

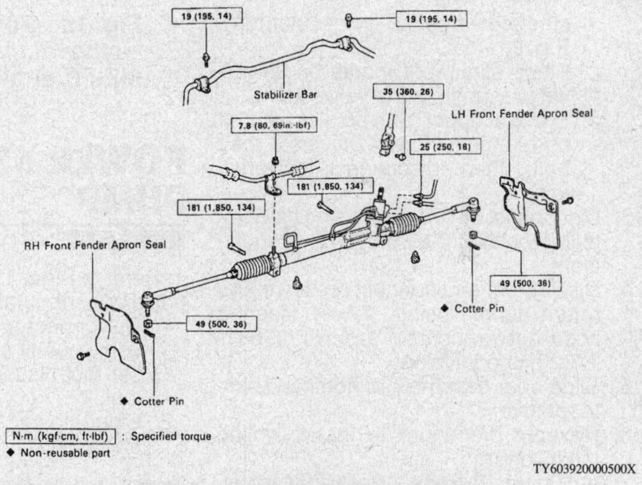
19 (195, 14)
19 (195, 14)
Stabilizer Bar
35 (360, 26)
LH Front Fender Apron Seal
7.8 (80, 69in.·lbf)
25 (250, 18)
181 (1,850, 134)
181 (1,850, 134)
RH Front Fender Apron Seal
49 (500, 36)
◆ Cotter Pin
49 (500, 36)
◆ Cotter Pin
N·m (kgf·cm, ft·lbf) : Specified torque
◆ Non-reusable part
TY603920000500X

Fig. 8 Steering gear removal

STABILIZER BAR

REPLACE

1. Raise and support vehicle, then remove front wheels.
2. Remove left and right fender apron seals, then disconnect left and right tie rod ends from steering knuckles using ball joint puller tool No. 09628-62011, or equivalent.
3. Remove left and right stabilizer bar links, left and right bushing retainers and left and right bushings, **Fig. 7.**
4. Remove front exhaust pipe, then the steering gear mounting nuts and bolts.
5. Lift steering gear up, then remove stabilizer bar.
6. Reverse procedure to install.

POWER STEERING GEAR

REPLACE

Refer to **Fig. 8** when replacing power steering gear, noting the following:

1. **On models with audio coded anti-theft system,**obtain three digit anti-theft code.
2. **On all models,** disconnect universal joint as follows:
   a. Position front wheels facing straight ahead.
   b. Using seat belt of drivers seat, fix

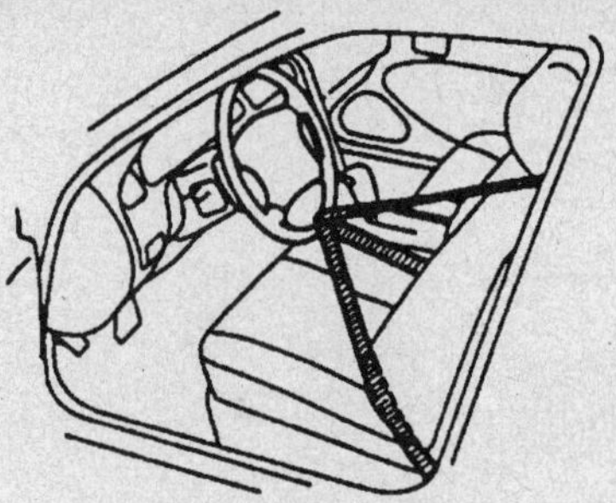

TY6039200006000X

Fig. 9 Securing steering wheel

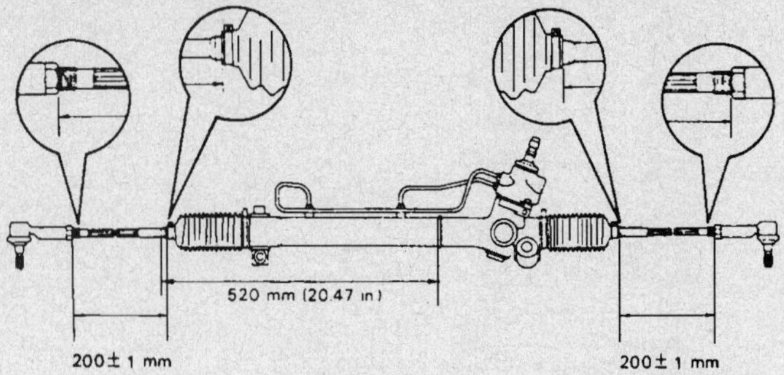
520 mm (20.47 in)
200± 1 mm
200± 1 mm

TY6039200007000X

Fig. 10 Steering gear installation

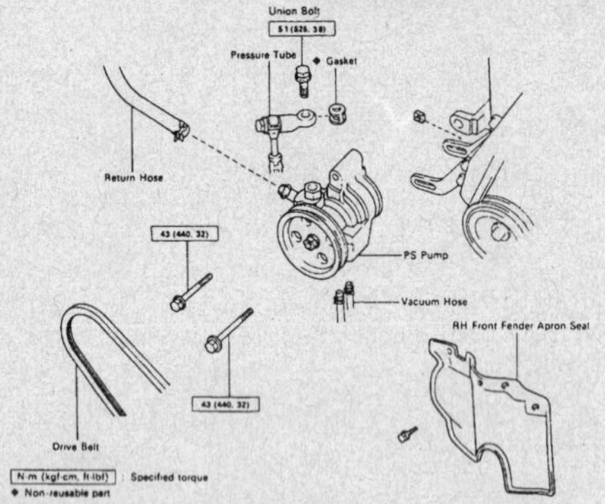
Union Bolt
Pressure Tube
Gasket
Return Hose
PS Pump
Vacuum Hose
RH Front Fender Apron Seal
Drive Belt
Specified torque
Non-reusable part

TY6039200008000X

Fig. 11 Power steering pump removal. Camry w/5S-FE engine

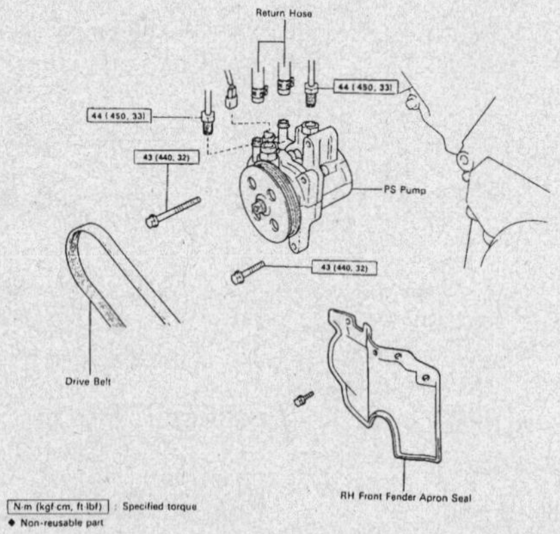
Return Hose
PS Pump
Drive Belt
RH Front Fender Apron Seal
Specified torque
Non-reusable part

TY6039200009000X

Fig. 12 Power steering pump removal. Avalon & Camry w/ 1MZ-FE engine & Camry 3VZ-FE engine

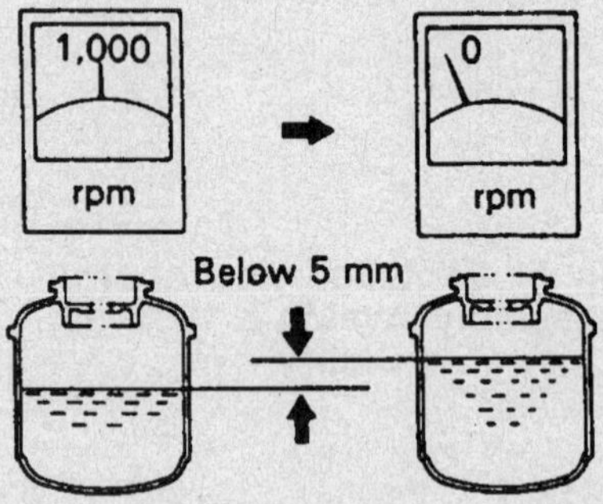
1,000
rpm
0
rpm
Below 5 mm

TY6039100011000X

Fig. 13 Power steering system bleed

steering wheel so it does not turn, **Fig. 9.**

c. Place alignment marks on universal joint and control valve shaft.
d. Loosen upper universal joint bolt and remove lower universal joint bolt, then disconnect universal joint.

3. Disconnect tie rod ends using ball joint puller tool No. 09628-62011, or equivalent.
4. Disconnect and connect pressure and return tubes using power steering hose nut wrench set tool No. 09631-22020, or equivalent.
5. Slide gear assembly to righthand side to remove.
6. Reverse procedure to install, noting the following:
   a. Tighten fasteners to specifications.
   b. When connecting universal joint, set gear housing so it matches dimensions shown in **Fig. 10,** with gear housing at center point.
   c. Align marks made during removal and connect universal joint.

POWER STEERING PUMP

REPLACE

Refer to **Figs. 11 and 12** when replacing power steering pump, noting the following:

1. Disconnect and connect pressure line using power steering hose nut wrench set tool No. 09631-22020, or equivalent.
2. Bleed power steering system after installation.

POWER STEERING SYSTEM BLEED

1. Ensure fluid in reservoir tank is at proper level.
2. With engine speed below 1000 RPM, turn steering wheel from stop to stop three or four times, keeping at full stop position for two to three seconds.
3. Ensure fluid is not foamy or cloudy.
4. Measure fluid lever with engine running then stop engine and measure fluid level again, **Fig. 13.** Maximum rise of fluid is .20 inch.
5. If a problem is found, proceed as follows:
   a. Disconnect return hose from reservoir tank and drain fluid.
   b. Fill reservoir tank with fresh fluid.
   c. With return hose placed into a suitable container, start engine and run at 1000 RPM. **After one or two seconds, fluid will begin to discharge from return hose. Stop engine immediately at this time. Ensure some fluid remains in reservoir tank.**
   d. Repeat steps b and c four or five times until there is no more air in fluid.
   e. Connect return hose and correct fluid level.

TIGHTENING SPECIFICATIONS

Year	Component	Torque/Ft. Lbs.
1993–96	ABS Speed Sensor To Steering Knuckle	6
	ABS Speed Sensor Wire To Strut Bolt	48①
	Ball Joint To Lower Suspension Arm	94
	Ball Joint To Steering Knuckle	90
	Brake Caliper Bolts	79
	Brake Hose To Strut Bolt	22
	Driveshaft To Axle Hub Locknut	217
	Dust Cover To Steering Knuckle	6
	Front Exhaust Pipe To Converter Nuts	32
	Front Exhaust Pipe To Manifold Nuts	46
	Lower Suspension Arm Mounting Bolts	152
	Power Steering Pump Mounting Bolts	32
	Power Steering Pump Pressure Tubes	33
	Strut Nut	36
	Strut To Steering Knuckle	156
	Strut To Strut Tower	59
	Stabilizer Bar End Bracket To Lower Suspension Arm	41
	Stabilizer Bar Link Nuts	47
	Stabilizer Bar Retainer Bracket Bolts	14
	Steering Rack Line Clamp Nut	6
	Steering Rack Mounting Bolts	134
	Steering Rack Pressure & Return Tubes	18
	Steering Rack Universal Joint Bolt	26
	Tie Rod End To Steering Knuckle	36
	Wheel Lug Nut	76

① — Inch lbs.

Wheel Alignment

INDEX

	Page No.
Front Wheel Alignment	42-48
Caster & Camber	42-48
Toe-In	42-48
Preliminary Inspection	42-48
Rear Wheel Alignment	42-48
Camber	42-48
Toe-In	42-48
Vehicle Ride Height	42-48
Wheel Alignment Specifications	42-3

PRELIMINARY INSPECTION

Inspect the following prior to adjusting wheel alignment.

1. Check tires for wear and proper inflation.
2. Check wheel runout, .039 (1 mm) inch should be indicated.
3. Check front wheel bearings, front suspension, steering linkage and ball joints for wear or looseness.
4. Ensure front shock absorbers are functioning properly.

FRONT WHEEL ALIGNMENT

CASTER & CAMBER

Camry

Camber and caster are not adjustable on these models. If camber and caster angle is not within limits, check for worn or damaged suspension parts and replace as necessary.

TOE-IN

1. Remove clamps from steering gear boots.
2. Loosen tie rod end locknuts.
3. Turn left and right tie rod ends an equal amount to adjust toe-in.
4. Ensure length of both tie rods are equal following adjustment.
5. Following adjustment, install steering gear boot clamps and **torque** tie rod locknuts to 54 ft. lbs.

REAR WHEEL ALIGNMENT

CAMBER

Camber angle is preset and not adjustable. If camber angle is not to specification, inspect and/or replace suspension components as required.

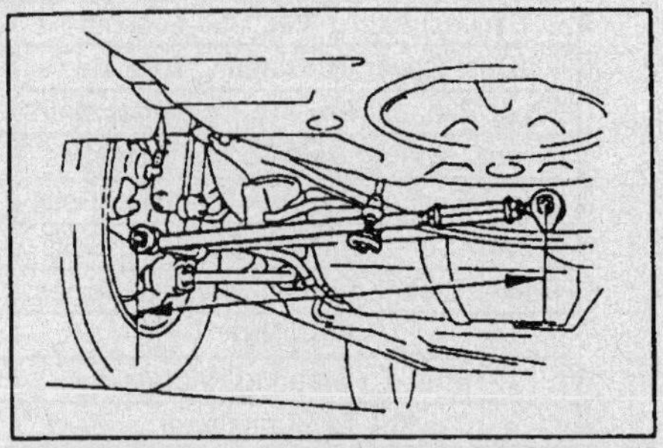

TY2049300016000X

Fig. 1 Rear toe-in adjustment. Camry

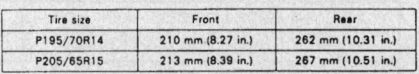

Tire size	Front	Rear
P195/70R14	210 mm (8.27 in.)	262 mm (10.31 in.)
P205/65R15	213 mm (8.39 in.)	267 mm (10.51 in.)

TY2049300022000X

Fig. 3 Vehicle ride height specifications. Avalon & Camry sedan/coupe

TOE-IN

Camry

1. Measure length of left and right No. 2 lower suspension arms, **Fig. 1.**
2. Adjust length of lower suspension arms if difference in length is greater than .04 inch.
3. Loosen locknuts and turn left and right adjusting tubes an equal distance to adjust toe-in.
4. One turn of adjusting tube will adjust toe-in approximately .264 inch.
5. Following adjustment, **torque** locknuts to 41 ft. lbs.

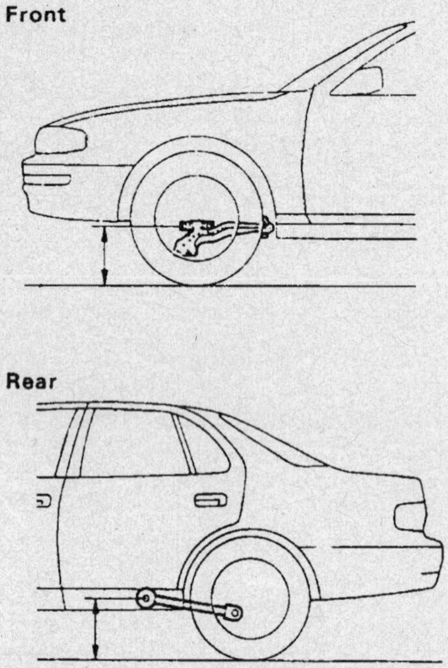
Front
Rear

TY2049200018000X

Fig. 2 Vehicle ride height measurement

Tire size	Front
P195/70R14	210 mm (8.27 in.)
P205/65R15	214 mm (8.43 in.)
	Rear
P195/70R14	272 mm (10.71 in.)
P205/65R15	277 mm (10.91 in.)

TY2049400051000X

Fig. 4 Vehicle ride height specifications. Camry wagon

VEHICLE RIDE HEIGHT

Refer to **Figs. 2 through 4** for ride height measurements and trim height specifications.

TOYOTA CELICA & SUPRA

INDEX OF SERVICE OPERATIONS

Page No.

AIR BAG SYSTEM PRECAUTIONS 0-8
AUTOMATIC TRANSMISSIONS/ TRANSAXLES 48-1
BRAKES
Anti-Lock Brakes 48-1
Disc Brakes 48-1
Drum Brakes 48-1
Hydraulic Brake Systems 48-1
Power Brake Units 48-1
CLUTCH & MANUAL TRANSAXLE/ TRANSMISSION
Adjustments 43-39
Clutch, Replace 43-39
Hydraulic System Service 43-39
Precautions 43-39
Tightening Specifications 43-42
Transaxle, Replace 43-40
Transmission, Replace 43-41
ELECTRICAL
Air Bags 48-1
Air Conditioning 48-1
Alternators 48-1
Blower Motor, Replace 43-9
Coil Pack, Replace 43-6
Combination Switch, Replace 43-7
Cooling Fans 48-1
Cruise Control 48-1
Dash Gauges 48-1
Dash Panels 48-1
Distributor, Replace 43-6
Evaporator Core, Replace 43-9
Fuel Pump Relay Location 43-5
Fuse Panel & Flasher Location 43-5
Heater Core, Replace 43-9
Ignition Lock, Replace 43-6
Ignition Switch, Replace 43-6
Instrument Cluster, Replace 43-7
Neutral Safety Switch, Replace 43-6
Passive Restraints 48-1
Precautions 43-5
Radio, Replace 43-8
Relay Center Location 43-5
Speed Controls 48-1
Starter Motors 48-1
Starter, Replace 43-5
Steering Columns 48-1
Steering Wheel, Replace 43-7
Stop Light Switch, Replace 43-7
Wiper Motor, Replace 43-9
Wiper Switch, Replace 43-9
Wiper Systems 48-1
ELECTRICAL SYMBOL IDENTIFICATION 0-139
FRONT SUSPENSION & STEERING
Ball Joint Inspection 43-50
Coil Spring, Replace 43-50
Control Arm, Replace 43-51
Hub & Bearing, Replace 43-49
Manual Steering Gears 48-1
Power Steering 48-1
Power Steering Gear, Replace 43-51
Precautions 43-49
Stabilizer Bar, Replace 43-51

Page No.

Steering Knuckle, Replace 43-51
Strut, Replace 43-51
Tightening Specifications 43-53
Wheel Bearing, Adjust 43-49
FRONT WHEEL DRIVE AXLES 48-1
REAR AXLE & SUSPENSION
Axle Hub, Replace 43-45
Coil Spring, Replace 43-46
Control Arm, Replace 43-47
Hub & Bearing, Replace 43-44
Rear Axle Shaft, Replace 43-44
Shock Absorber, Replace 43-46
Stabilizer Bar, Replace 43-47
Strut Rod, Replace 43-45
Suspension Arm, Replace 43-47
Tightening Specifications 43-48
SERVICE REMINDER & WARNING LAMP RESET PROCEDURES 0-10
SPECIFICATIONS
Engine Identification 43-2
Fluid Capacities & Cooling System Data 43-4
Front Wheel Alignment Specifications 43-3
General Engine Specifications 43-2
Lubricant Data 43-4
Rear Wheel Alignment Specifications 43-3
Tune Up Specifications 43-2
VEHICLE IDENTIFICATION 0-1
VEHICLE LIFT POINTS 0-34
VEHICLE MAINTENANCE SCHEDULES 0-69
WHEEL ALIGNMENT
Front Wheel Alignment 43-54
Preliminary Inspection 43-54
Rear Wheel Alignment 43-55
Vehicle Ride Height 43-55
Wheel Alignment Specifications 43-3
WIRE COLOR CODE IDENTIFICATION 0-144
2JZ-GE & 2JZ-GTE 3.0L ENGINES
Belt Tension Data 43-35
Camshaft, Replace 43-34
Compression Pressure 43-32
Cooling System Bleed 43-35
Cylinder Head, Replace 43-33
Engine Rebuilding Specifications 48-1
Engine, Replace 43-32
Exhaust Manifold, Replace 43-33
Fuel Filter, Replace 43-36
Fuel Pump, Replace 43-36
Intake Manifold, Replace 43-33
Main & Rod Bearings 43-34
Oil Pan, Replace 43-34
Oil Pump, Replace 43-34
Oil Pump Service 43-35
Piston & Rod Assembly 43-34
Precautions 43-32
Radiator, Replace 43-36
Thermostat, Replace 43-35
Tightening Specifications 43-38
Timing Belt, Replace 43-34

Page No.

Valve Adjustment 43-33
Valve Clearance Specifications 43-33
Valve Guides 43-34
Water Pump, Replace 43-35
3S-GTE 2.0L ENGINE
Belt Tension Data 43-15
Camshaft, Replace 43-14
Compression Pressure 43-11
Cooling System Bleed 43-15
Cylinder Head, Replace 43-12
Engine Rebuilding Specifications 48-1
Engine, Replace 43-11
Fuel Filter, Replace 43-16
Fuel Pump, Replace 43-16
Hydraulic Lifters, Replace 43-13
Main & Rod Bearings 43-15
Oil Pan, Replace 43-15
Oil Pump, Replace 43-15
Oil Pump Service 43-15
Piston & Rod Assembly 43-15
Precautions 43-11
Radiator, Replace 43-16
Thermostat, Replace 43-15
Tightening Specifications 43-17
Timing Belt, Replace 43-14
Valve Adjustment 43-13
Valve Clearance Specifications 43-13
Valve Guides 43-13
Water Pump, Replace 43-15
4A-FE 1.6L & 7A-FE 1.8L ENGINES
Compression Pressure 43-18
Engine Rebuilding Specifications 48-1
Engine, Replace 43-18
Precautions 43-18
Radiator, Replace 43-19
Tightening Specifications 43-20
5S-FE 2.2L ENGINE
Belt Tension Data 43-29
Camshaft, Replace 43-29
Compression Pressure 43-22
Cooling System Bleed 43-29
Cylinder Head, Replace 43-23
Engine Rebuilding Specifications 48-1
Engine, Replace 43-22
Exhaust Manifold, Replace 43-23
Fuel Filter, Replace 43-31
Fuel Pump, Replace 43-31
Hydraulic Lifters, Replace 43-27
Intake Manifold, Replace 43-23
Main & Rod Bearings 43-29
Oil Pan, Replace 43-29
Oil Pump, Replace 43-29
Oil Pump Service 43-29
Piston & Rod Assembly 43-29
Precautions 43-22
Radiator, Replace 43-31
Thermostat, Replace 43-29
Tightening Specifications 43-32
Timing Belt, Replace 43-28
Valve Adjustment 43-27
Valve Clearance Specifications 43-27
Valve Guides 43-27
Water Pump, Replace 43-30

Specifications

ENGINE IDENTIFICATION

Model	Year	Engine Code	Engine, Liter
Celica	1993	4A-FE	1.6L
		3S-GTE	2.0L
		5S-FE	2.2L
	1994–96	7A-FE	1.8L
		5S-FE	2.2L
Supra	1993–96	2JZ-GE	3.0L
		2JZ-GTE	3.0L

GENERAL ENGINE SPECIFICATIONS

Year	Engine	Fuel System	Bore & Stroke	Compression Ratio	Maximum Brake, H.P. @ RPM	Maximum Torque, Ft. Lbs. @ RPM	Normal Oil Pressure, psi @ RPM
1993	1.6L 4A-FE	Fuel Inj.	3.19 X 3.10	9.5	103 @ 6000	102 @ 3200	36–71 @ 3000
	2.0L 3S-GTE	Fuel Inj.	3.39 x 3.39	8.8	200 @ 6000	200 @ 3200	36–71 @ 3000
	2.2L 5S-FE	Fuel Inj.	3.43 x 3.58	9.5	130 @ 5400	140 @ 4400	36–71 @ 3000
	3.0L 2JZ-GE①	Fuel Inj.	3.39 x 3.39	10.0	220 @ 5800	210 @ 4800	47–84 @ 4000
	3.0L 2JZ-GTE②	Fuel Inj.	3.39 x 3.39	8.5	320 @ 5600	315 @ 4000	47–84 @ 4000
1994–95	1.8L 7A-FE	Fuel Inj.	3.19 x 3.37	9.5	110 @ 5600	115 @ 2800	36–71 @ 3000
	2.2L 5S-FE	Fuel Inj.	3.43 x 3.58	9.5	130 @ 5400	140 @ 4400	36–71 @ 3000
	3.0L 2JZ-GE①	Fuel Inj.	3.39 x 3.39	10.0	220 @ 5800	210 @ 4800	47–84 @ 4000
	3.0L 2JZ-GTE②	Fuel Inj.	3.39 x 3.39	8.5	320 @ 5600	315 @ 4000	47–84 @ 4000
1996	1.8L 7A-FE	Fuel Inj.	3.19 x 3.37	9.5	105 @ 5200	117 @ 2800	36–71 @ 3000
	2.2L 5S-FE	Fuel Inj.	3.43 x 3.58	9.5	130 @ 5400	145 @ 4400	36–71 @ 3000
	3.0L 2JZ-GE①	Fuel Inj.	3.39 x 3.39	10.0	220 @ 5800	210 @ 4800	47–84 @ 4000
	3.0L 2JZ-GTE②	Fuel Inj.	3.39 x 3.39	8.5	320 @ 5600	315 @ 4000	47–84 @ 4000

① — Non-turbo engine.
② — Turbo engine.

TUNE UP SPECIFICATIONS

The following specifications are published from the latest information available. This data should be used only in the absence of a decal affixed in the engine compartment.

When checking ignition timing, it may be necessary to disconnect certain hoses and/or electrical connectors. Refer to vehicle emission control label for specific instructions.

Before disconnecting spark plug wires from distributor cap, determine location of No. 1 wire in cap, as distributor position may have been altered from that shown.

Year	Engine	Spark Plug Gap, Inch	Ignition Timing			Curb Idle Speed, RPM		Fuel Pump Pressure, psi	Valve Clearance, Inch	
			Firing Order	Timing, °BTDC	Timing Mark Fig.	Man. Trans.	Auto. Trans.		Int.	Exh.
1993	1.6L 4A-FE	.031	1-3-4-2	10①	B	800	800	38–44	.006–.010	.010–.014
	2.0L 3S-GTE	.031	1-3-4-2	10①	A	800	800	33–38	.006–.010	.011–.015
	2.2L 5S-FE	.043	1-3-4-2	10①	B	700	700	38–44	.007–.011	.011–.015
	3.0L 2JZ-GE	.043	1-5-3-6-2-4	10②	A	700	700N	38–44	.006–.010	.010–.014
	3.0L 2JZ-GTE	.043	1-5-3-6-2-4	10②	A	650	650N	38–44	.006–.010	.010–.014
1994–96	1.8L 7A-FE	.031	1-3-4-2	10②	B	700	700N	38–44	.006–.010	.010–.014
	2.2L 5S-FE	.043	1-3-4-2	10①	B	750	750N	38–44	.007–.011	.011–.015
	3.0L 2JZ-GE	.043	1-5-3-6-2-4	10②	A	700	700N	38–44	.006–.010	.010–.014
	3.0L 2JZ-GTE	.043	1-5-3-6-2-4	10②	A	650	650N	38–44	.006–.010	.010–.014

BTDC — Before Top Dead Center.
N — Neutral.

① — With check connector terminals T & E shorted.

② — With terminals TE1 and E1 connected of DCL1.

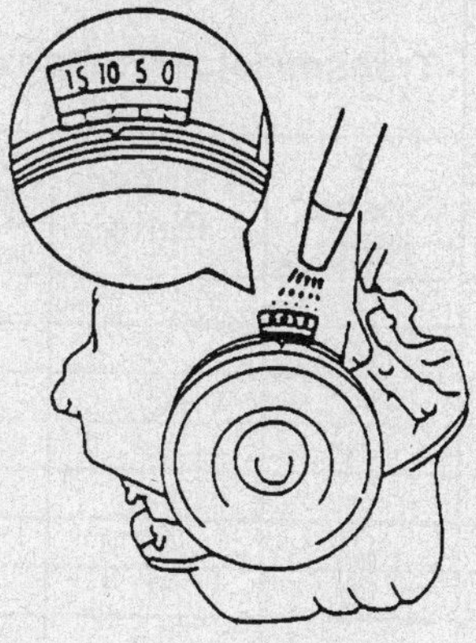
15 10 5 0

TY1139100110000X

Fig. A

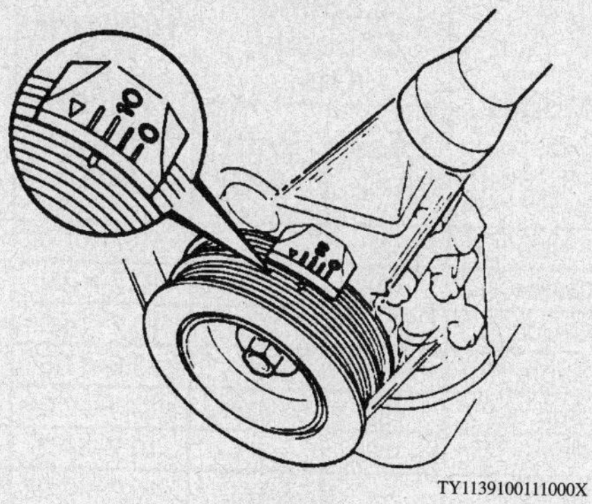

TY1139100111000X

Fig. B

FRONT WHEEL ALIGNMENT SPECIFICATIONS

The specifications listed below are for unloaded vehicles.

Year	Model	Caster Angle, Degrees		Camber Angle, Degrees		Toe-In, Inch	Toe-Out On Turns, Deg.		Ball Joint Wear
		Limits	Desired	Limits	Desired		Outer Wheel	Inner Wheel	
1993	Celica	①	②	−11/12 to +7/12	−1/6	.08	29 1/2	33 1/2	⑦
	Supra	+6 5/6 to +8 1/3	+7 7/12	−11/12 to +7/12	−1/6	0	31 3/4	32 1/2–36	⑦
1994	Celica③	+1 5/12 to +2 5/6	+2 1/12	−1 31/60 to −1/60	−23/30	0	30 11/15	36 9/10	⑦
	Celica④	+1 11/30 to +2 13/15	+2 7/60	−1 3/5 to −1/10	−51/60	0	30 19/30	36 3/5	⑦
	Supra⑤	2 3/4 to 4 1/4	+3 1/2	−1 1/12 to + 5/12	−1/3	0	30 3/4	35	⑦
	Supra⑥	2 3/40 to 4 1/4	+3 1/2	−1 1/4 to +1/4	−1/2	0	30 7/12	34 11/12	⑦
1995–96	Celica③	+1 1/3 to +2 5/6	+2 1/12	-1 1/2 to 0	-3/4	-.08 to +.08	36 9/10	30 11/15	⑦
	Celica④	+1 1/3 to +2 5/6	+2 1/12	-1 7/12 to -5/12	-5/6	-.08 to +.08	36 3/4	30 3/5	⑦
	Supra⑤	2 3/4 to 4 1/4	+3 1/2	−1 1/12 to +5/12	−1/3	0	30 3/4	35	⑦
	Supra⑥	2 3/40 to 4 1/4	+3 1/2	−1 1/4 to +1/4	−1/2	0	30 7/12	34 11/12	⑦

① — 2WD, +1/6 to +1 1/2; 4WD, +1/12 to +1 7/12.
② — 2WD, +11/12, 4WD, +5/6.
③ — 5S-FE engine.
④ — 7A-FE engine.
⑤ — 2JZ-GE engine.
⑥ — 2JZ-GTE engine.
⑦ — Refer to "Ball Joint Inspection" under "Front Suspension & Steering."

REAR WHEEL ALIGNMENT SPECIFICATIONS

The specifications listed below are for unloaded vehicles

Year	Model	Camber Angle, Degrees		Toe-In, Inch
		Limits	Desired	
1993	Celica	−2 to −1/2	−1 1/4	.20 ± .08
	Supra	−2 1/3 to 1/3	−1	0.12 ± .08
1994	Celica②	−1 11/12 to −5/12	−1 1/6	0.14 ± .08
	Celica①	−2 1/60 to −31/60	−1 4/15	0.14 ± .08
	Supra	−2 1/3 to 1/3	-1	+.04 to +.20
1995–96	Celica	-2 to -1/2	-1 1/4	+.06 to +.22
	Supra	−2 1/3 to 1/3	-1	+.04 to +.20

① — 7A-FE engine.
② — 5S-FE engine.

FLUID CAPACITIES & COOLING SYSTEM DATA

Year	Model	Cooling Capacity, Qts.		Radiator Cap Relief Pressure, Lbs.	Thermo. Opening Temp., °F	Fuel Tank, Gals.	Engine Oil Refill, Qts.①	Transmission/Transaxle Oil			Axle Oil, Pints
		Less A/C	With A/C					4 Speed, Pints	5 Speed, Pints	Auto. Trans., Qts.	
1993	Celica⑩	⑨	⑨	10.7–14.9	180	15.9	3.2	⑦	⑦	⑧	2.4
	Celica⑫	⑬	⑬	10.7–14.9	180	15.9	3.2	⑦	⑦	⑧	2.4
	Celica⑤	6.9	6.9	10.7–14.9	180	15.9	⑭	⑦	⑦	⑧	2.4
	Supra⑰	④	④	13.5–17.8	180	18.5	5.5	—	5.4	7.6	2.8
	Supra⑥	⑮	⑪	13.5–17.8	180	18.5	5.3	—	5.4	8.7	2.8
1994	Celica⑫	⑬	⑬	10.7–14.9	180	15.9	3.2	⑦	⑦	⑧	2.4
	Celica⑯	—	—	10.7–14.9	180	15.9	4.7	⑦	⑦	⑨	2.7
	Supra⑰	④	④	13.5–17.8	180	18.5	5.5	—	5.4	7.6	2.8
	Supra⑥	⑮	⑪	13.5–17.8	180	18.5	5.3	—	5.4	8.7	2.8
1995–96	Celica⑯	②	②	13	180	15.9	4.0	—	5.4	8	—
	Celica⑫	③	③	13	180	15.9	4.0	—	5.4	5.9	3.4
	Supra⑰	④	④	16	180	18.5	5.6	—	5.4	7.6	2.86
	Supra⑥	10	10	16	180	18.5	5.3	—	3.8	8.7	2.86

① — With oil filter change.
② — Man. trans., 8.6; auto. trans., 7.
③ — Man. trans., 7.1; auto. trans., 7.5.
④ — Automatic transaxle, 8.8; manual transaxle, 7.7.
⑤ — 3S-GTE engine.
⑥ — 2JZ-GTE engine.
⑦ — C52 & S53, 2.7; E150F, 5.5.
⑧ — A241E & A241L, 8.5; A243L, 8.1.
⑨ — Automatic transaxle, 5.9; manual transaxle, 5.5.
⑩ — 4A-FE engine.
⑪ — Automatic transaxle, 9.9; manual transaxle, 10.0.
⑫ — 5S-FE engine.
⑬ — Automatic transaxle, 6.4; manual transaxle, 6.6.
⑭ — With oil cooler, 4.4, less oil cooler, 4.3.
⑮ — Automatic transaxle, 8.8; manual transaxle, 7.7.
⑯ — 7A-FE engine.
⑰ — 2JZ-GE engine.

LUBRICANT DATA

Year	Model	Lubricant Type				
		Transaxle		Rear Axle	Power Steering	Brake System
		Manual	Automatic			
1993–94	Celica	①	Dexron II	GL-5	Dexron II	DOT 3
	Supra	GL-4,5	Dexron II	GL-5②	Dexron II	DOT 3
1995–96	Celica	75W-90 GL-3/4/5	Dexron II/IIE/III	—	Dexron II/IIE/III	DOT 3
	Supra	75W-90 GL-5	Dexron II/IIE/III	80W-90 GL-5	Dexron II/IIE/III	DOT 3

① — 2WD, GL-3; 4WD, GL-5.
② — With limited slip differential use LSD fluid only.

Electrical

NOTE: On Air Bag Equipped Models, Refer To "Air Bag System Precautions" Located In The Front Of This Manual For System Disarming & Arming Procedures.

INDEX

	Page No.
Air Bags	48-1
Air Conditioning	48-1
Alternators	48-1
Blower Motor, Replace	43-9
Celica	43-9
Supra	43-9
Coil Pack, Replace	43-6
Supra w/2JZ-GTE Engine	43-6
Combination Switch, Replace	43-7
Replacement	43-7
Service	43-7
Cooling Fans	48-1
Cruise Control	48-1
Dash Gauges	48-1
Dash Panels	48-1
Distributor, Replace	43-6
Celica	43-6
Supra w/2JZ-GE Engine	43-6
Evaporator Core, Replace	43-9
Celica	43-9
Supra	43-9
Fuel Pump Relay Location	43-5
Fuse Panel & Flasher Location	43-5
Heater Core, Replace	43-9
Celica	43-9
Supra	43-9
Ignition Lock, Replace	43-6
Ignition Switch, Replace	43-6
Instrument Cluster, Replace	43-7
Celica	43-7
Supra	43-8
Neutral Safety Switch, Replace	43-6
Passive Restraints	48-1
Precautions	43-5
Air Bag Systems	43-5
Audio Coded Anti-Theft System	43-5
Radio, Replace	43-8
Celica	43-8
Supra	43-8
Relay Center Location	43-5
Speed Controls	48-1
Starter Motors	48-1
Starter, Replace	43-5
Celica	43-5
Supra	43-5
Steering Columns	48-1
Steering Wheel, Replace	43-7
Stop Light Switch, Replace	43-7
Wiper Motor, Replace	43-9
Front	43-9
Rear	43-9
Wiper Switch, Replace	43-9
Wiper Systems	48-1

PRECAUTIONS

AIR BAG SYSTEMS

Refer to "Air Bag System Precautions" in the front of this manual for system disarming and arming procedures.

AUDIO CODED ANTI-THEFT SYSTEM

Some models are equipped with an audio coded anti-theft system that will disable the radio when the battery cable is disconnected. The system can be identified by the "ANTI-THEFT SYSTEM" on the cassette tape lid. Obtain 3 digit customer code for input. Reset system after service as follows:

1. Obtain 3 digit audio anti-theft code.
2. Depress 1 (PROG) while depressing righthand side of TUNE SEEK button, - - - will appear in tape operation display.
3. To enter the first digit, depress 1 (PROG) button repeatedly until the number of times depressed equals the first digit beginning with zero (depress the 1 button six times if the first digit if five).
4. To enter second digit, depress 2 (APS) button repeatedly until the number of times depressed equals the second digit beginning with zero.
5. To enter third digit, depress 3 (RPT) button repeatedly until the number of times depressed equals the second digit beginning with zero.
6. If - - - is displayed during code input, repeat procedure.
7. When code appears in display, depress and hold SCAN button until SEC appears.

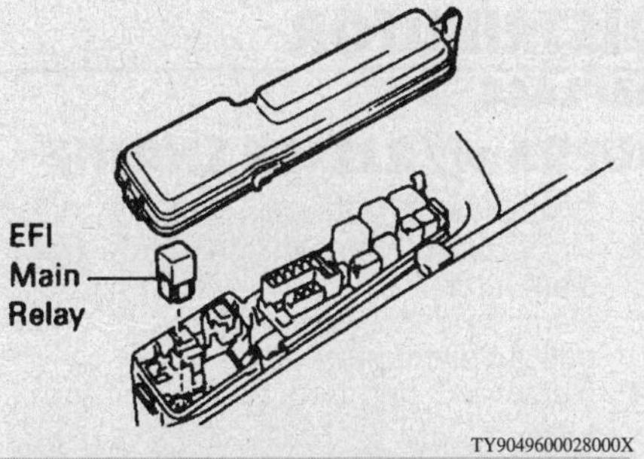
EFI
Main
Relay
TY9049600028000X

Fig. 1 Fuel pump relay. Celica

8. When SEC disappears audio system should be operative.
9. If Err is displayed, repeat procedure. **Attempting to input code more than nine times may permanently disable audio system.**

FUSE PANEL & FLASHER LOCATION

There are three fuse blocks; the first is located on the left front kick panel, the second is on the right front kick panel and the third is next to the battery. On models with ABS brakes, an additional fuse block is located in the engine compartment. The turn signal/hazard flasher is on the left front kick panel fuse block.

FUEL PUMP RELAY LOCATION

The fuel pump relay is located in the engine compartment relay center, **Figs. 1 and 2.**

RELAY CENTER LOCATION

The relay center is located at the left-hand front of the engine compartment on the fender apron.

STARTER

REPLACE

SUPRA

1. Obtain audio anti-theft code, if equipped, as outlined in "Precautions."
2. Disconnect electrical connectors from starter motor.
3. Remove starter attaching bolts, then remove.
4. Reverse to install. Reset audio coded anti-theft, if equipped, as outlined in "Precautions."

CELICA

4A-FE Engine

1. Obtain audio anti-theft code, if equipped, as outlined in "Precautions."
2. Raise and support vehicle.
3. Remove lower suspension crossmember retaining bolts and nuts, then lower crossmember.
4. Remove air cleaner cap as follows:
   a. Disconnect intake air temperature sensor connector.
   b. Disconnect accelerator cable from bracket on air cleaner cap.

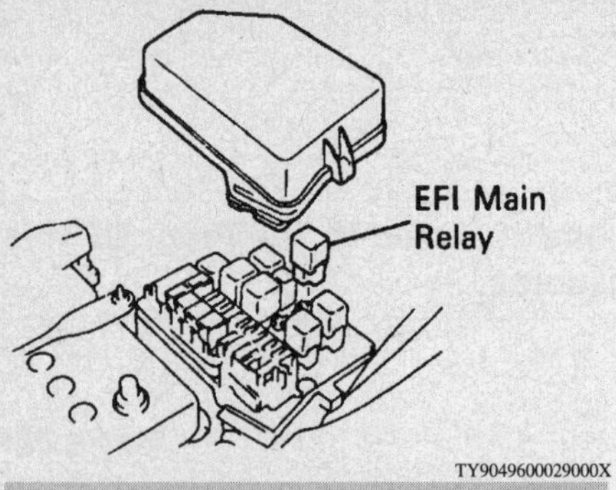
EFI Main
Relay
TY9049600029000X

Fig. 2 Fuel pump relay. Supra

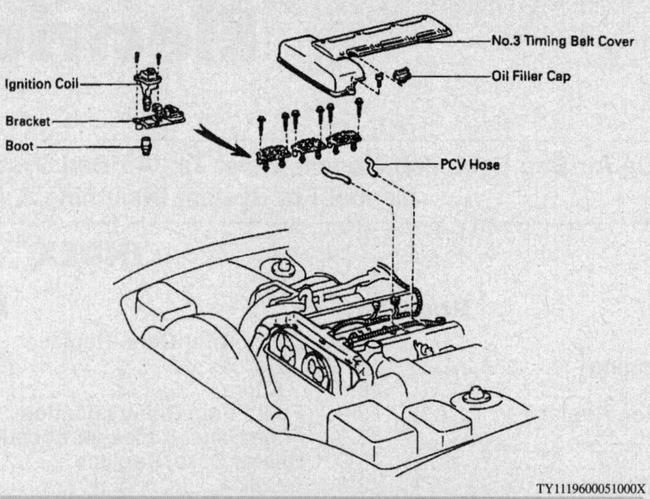
No.3 Timing Belt Cover
Ignition Coil
Oil Filler Cap
Bracket
Boot
PCV Hose
TY1119600051000X

Fig. 3 Ignition coil replacement

   c. Disconnect four air cleaner cap clips, then air hose from air pipe.
   d. Disconnect air cleaner hose from throttle body and remove air cleaner cap and filter element.
5. Remove two starter to transaxle retaining bolts.
6. Disconnect starter electrical connector, starter wire and remove starter.
7. Reverse procedure to install, **torque** starter retaining bolts to 29 ft. lbs.
8. Reset audio coded anti-theft, if equipped, as outlined in "Precautions."

5S-FE Engine

1. Obtain audio anti-theft code, if equipped, as outlined in "Precautions."
2. Remove air cleaner case assembly as follows:
   a. Disconnect air intake temperature sensor connector.
   b. Disconnect four air cleaner cap clips.
   c. Disconnect air cleaner hose from throttle body and remove air cleaner cap and filter element.
   d. Remove three air cleaner case retaining bolts, then the case.
3. Remove engine compartment relay box as follows:
   a. Remove two relay box retaining nuts and disconnect relay box from the battery.
   b. Remove lower cover from relay box.
   c. Disconnect fusible link cassette and two connectors of the engine wire from relay box.
4. **On models with cruise control and anti-lock brakes,** disconnect cruise control actuator connector, then remove four actuator retaining bolts and remove actuator.
5. **On all models,** disconnect starter electrical connector and starter wire.
6. Remove two starter retaining bolts, then the starter.
7. Reverse procedure to install, **torque** starter retaining bolts to 29 ft. lbs.
8. Reset audio coded anti-theft, if equipped, as outlined in "Precautions."

7A-FE Engine

1. Obtain audio anti-theft code, if equipped, as outlined under "Precautions."
2. Remove air cleaner assembly, then disconnect the following:
   a. IAT sensor connector.
   b. Accelerator cable and cruise control actuator cable.
   c. Vacuum hose from throttle body at air cleaner assembly hose.
3. Disconnect engine wire clamp from transaxle.
4. Remove starter motor attaching bolts and the starter motor.
5. Reverse procedure to install.

DISTRIBUTOR

REPLACE

SUPRA w/2JZ-GE ENGINE

1. Disconnect distributor connector.
2. Disconnect high tension cords from distributor.
3. Remove distributor retaining nut and pull out distributor.
4. Remove O-ring from distributor housing.
5. Reverse procedure to install.

CELICA

1. Obtain audio anti-theft code, if equipped, as outlined in "Precautions."
2. **On 5S-FE models,** remove air cleaner hose.
3. **On 3S-GTE models,** remove intercooler.
4. **On all models,** disconnect distributor electrical connector.
5. Disconnect spark plug wires from plugs and ignition coil.
6. Remove distributor attaching bolts, then remove.
7. Reverse to install. Reset audio coded anti-theft, if equipped, as outlined in "Precautions."

COIL PACK

REPLACE

SUPRA w/2JZ-GTE ENGINE

1. Remove No. 3 timing belt cover, **Fig. 3.**
2. Remove PCV hoses.
3. Disconnect ignition coil connectors.
4. Remove two bolts and twin ignition coil assembly.
5. Remove rubber boot from ignition coil.
6. Remove two screws and ignition coil from assembly.
7. Reverse procedure to install.

IGNITION LOCK

REPLACE

1. Obtain audio anti-theft code, if equipped, as outlined in "Precautions."
2. Turn ignition switch to ACC position.
3. Insert a small diameter rod into hole located on side of lock cylinder, then while holding down pin, remove lock cylinder.
4. Reverse procedure to install. Ensure lock cylinder is in ACC position.
5. Reset audio coded anti-theft, if equipped, as outlined in "Precautions."

IGNITION SWITCH

REPLACE

1. Obtain audio anti-theft code, if equipped, as outlined in "Precautions."
2. Remove steering wheel as outlined under "Steering Wheel, Replace."
3. Disconnect electrical connectors from ignition switch.
4. Turn ignition key to ACC position and remove ignition key cylinder.
5. Remove screw and ignition switch.
6. Reverse procedure to install. Reset audio coded anti-theft, if equipped, as outlined in "Precautions."

NEUTRAL SAFETY SWITCH

REPLACE

1. Raise and support vehicle.
2. Loosen neutral safety switch bracket bolt.
3. Position transmission shift lever into Neutral.
4. Align switch shaft groove with neutral base line, **Fig. 4,** then retighten switch bracket bolt.

5. Connect electrical connector to switch.

STOP LIGHT SWITCH

REPLACE

1. Remove brake pedal tension spring.
2. Disconnect switch wire connector.
3. Remove switch mounting nut, then slide switch from mounting bracket.
4. Reverse procedure to install.

COMBINATION SWITCH

REPLACE

REPLACEMENT

1. Obtain audio anti-theft code, if equipped, as outlined in "Precautions."
2. **On models equipped with air bag,** pull wheel pad out from steering wheel and disconnect air bag connector. **When removing wheel pad, take care not to pull air bag wire harness. When storing wheel pad, keep upper surface of the pad facing upward. Never disassemble wheel pad.**
3. **On all models,** remove horn button screws and horn button.
4. Scribe alignment marks on steering wheel and steering shaft.
5. Remove steering wheel nut.
6. Using a steering wheel puller, remove steering wheel.
7. Remove steering column upper and lower covers.
8. Remove combination switch.
9. Reverse procedure to install. Reset audio coded anti-theft, if equipped, as outlined in "Precautions."

SERVICE

Headlight & Dimmer Switch

1. Obtain audio anti-theft code, if equipped, as outlined in "Precautions."
2. **On models equipped with air bag,** pull wheel pad out from steering wheel and disconnect air bag connector. **When removing wheel pad, take care not to pull air bag wire harness. When storing wheel pad, keep upper surface of the pad facing upward. Never disassemble wheel pad.**
3. **On all models,** remove steering wheel, then upper and lower steering column covers.
4. Disconnect combination switch connector, then using a small screwdriver, disengage headlight and dimmer switch wiring from combination switch connector. **Note position of wires.**
5. **On models with cruise control, removal of slip ring may be necessary.** Remove screws, headlight and dimmer switch, then ball and spring assembly, **Fig. 5.**
6. **On all models,** install headlight and dimmer switch onto combination switch.
7. Insert spring into headlight and dimmer lever, than install lever and screw onto combination switch.
8. Position ball on the spring, **Fig. 6,** and

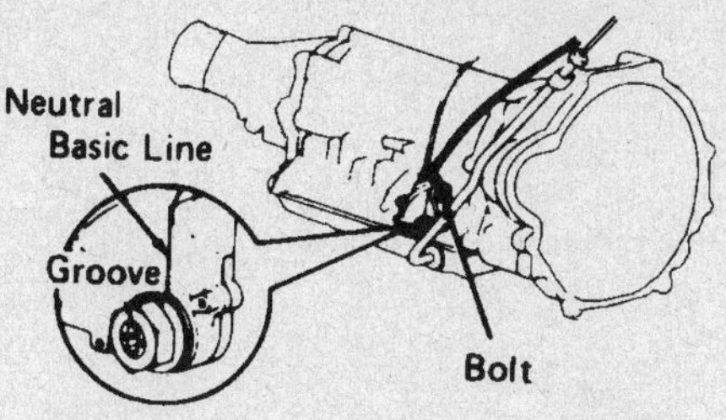
Neutral
Basic Line
Groove
Bolt
TY9049100001000X

Fig. 4 Neutral safety switch adjustment

place headlight and dimmer switch lever into HI position. Install screws and clamp, **Fig. 6.**
9. Ensure switch operates smoothly in each position.
10. Install electrical terminals into combination switch connector in the same position as they were removed.
11. Install combination switch connector, then the steering column upper and lower covers and steering wheel.
12. Connect battery ground cable. Reset audio coded anti-theft, if equipped, as outlined in "Precautions."

Hazard & Turn Signal Switch

1. Obtain audio anti-theft code, if equipped, as outlined in "Precautions."
2. **On models equipped with air bag,** pull wheel pad out from steering wheel and disconnect air bag connector. **When removing wheel pad, take care not to pull air bag wire harness. When storing wheel pad, keep upper surface of the pad facing upward. Never disassemble wheel pad.**
3. **On all models,** remove steering wheel, then upper and lower steering column covers.
4. Disconnect hazard and turn signal switch connector, then using a small screwdriver, disengage hazard and turn signal switch wiring from combination switch connector. **Note position of wires.**
5. Remove screws, clamp, hazard and turn signal switch assembly from combination switch.
6. Reverse procedure to install. Reset audio coded anti-theft, if equipped, as outlined in "Precautions."

Windshield Wiper/Washer Switch

1. Obtain audio anti-theft code, if equipped, as outlined in "Precautions."
2. **On models equipped with air bag,** pull wheel pad out from steering wheel and disconnect air bag connector. **When removing wheel pad, take care not to pull air bag wire harness. When storing wheel pad, keep upper surface of the pad facing upward. Never disassemble wheel pad.**
3. **On all models,** remove steering wheel, then upper and lower steering column covers.
4. Disconnect battery ground cable, then remove steering wheel and upper and lower steering column covers.
5. Disconnect wire terminal from horn contact.
6. Disconnect battery ground cable. **Allow at least 20 seconds after ignition switch is turned to the "Lock" position and battery is disconnected before beginning work.**
7. Disconnect windshield wiper/washer switch connector, then using a small screwdriver, disengage windshield wiper/washer switch wiring from combination switch connector. **Note position of wires.**
8. Remove screw, clamp and windshield wiper/washer switch assembly.
9. Reverse procedure to install. Reset audio coded anti-theft, if equipped, as outlined in "Precautions."

STEERING WHEEL

REPLACE

1. Obtain audio anti-theft code, if equipped, as outlined in "Precautions."
2. **On models equipped with air bag,** pull wheel pad out from steering wheel and disconnect air bag connector. **When removing wheel pad, take care not to pull air bag wire harness. When storing wheel pad, keep upper surface of the pad facing upward. Never disassemble wheel pad.**
3. **On all models,** remove steering wheel pad.
4. Place alignment marks on steering wheel and mainshaft for assembly reference.
5. Remove nut attaching steering wheel to steering shaft.
6. Using a suitable puller, remove steering wheel.
7. Reverse procedure to install. Reset audio coded anti-theft, if equipped, as outlined in "Precautions."

INSTRUMENT CLUSTER

REPLACE

CELICA

1. Obtain audio anti-theft code, if equipped, as outlined under "Precautions."
2. **On models equipped with air bag,** pull wheel pad out from steering wheel and disconnect air bag connector. **When removing wheel pad, take care not to pull air bag wire harness. When storing wheel pad, keep upper surface of the pad facing upward. Never disassemble wheel pad.**
3. **On all models,** remove steering wheel, then upper and lower steering column covers.
4. Remove engine hood release lever from lower part of instrument panel.
5. Remove scuff plate, then the six left side I/P lower finish panel attaching screws, then remove finish panels.

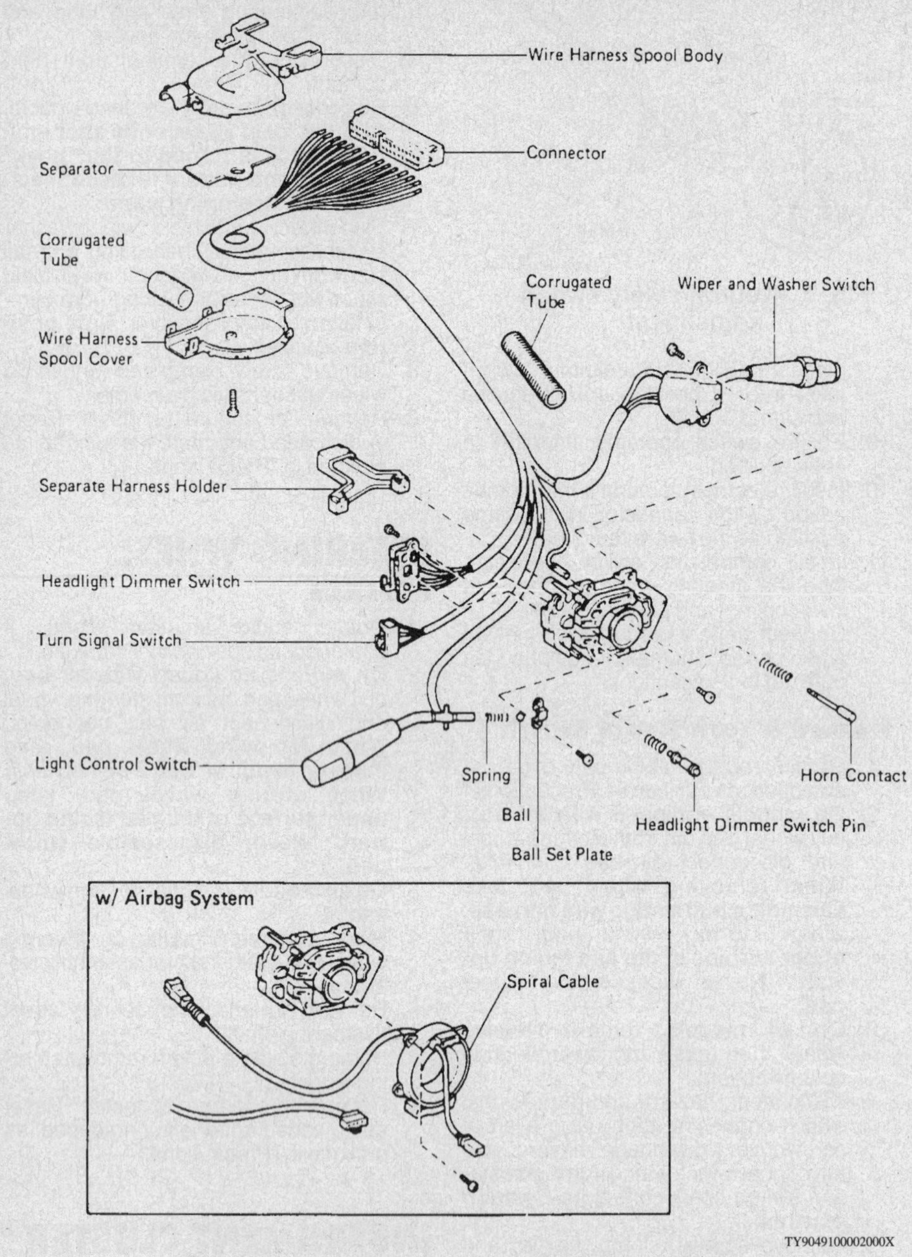
Wire Harness Spool Body
Connector
Separator
Corrugated Tube
Wire Harness Spool Cover
Corrugated Tube
Wiper and Washer Switch
Separate Harness Holder
Headlight Dimmer Switch
Turn Signal Switch
Light Control Switch
Spring
Ball
Ball Set Plate
Headlight Dimmer Switch Pin
Horn Contact
w/ Airbag System
Spiral Cable
TY9049100002000X

Fig. 5 Exploded view of combination switch

6. Using a screwdriver, remove screw caps from lower instrument cluster finish panel.
7. Remove five instrument cluster finish panel attaching screws, then the panel.
8. Remove four combination meter attaching screws.
9. Disconnect electrical connectors from rear of combination meter and remove meter.
10. Remove speedometer cable by pushing on pawls on right and left sides of the meter bracket.
11. Reverse to install. Reset audio coded anti-theft, if equipped, as outlined under "Precautions."

SUPRA

1. Obtain audio anti-theft code, if equipped, as outlined under "Precautions."
2. Remove steering wheel as outlined in "Steering Wheel, Replace."
3. Remove steering column cover.
4. Remove hood release lever attaching bolts, then remove.
5. Remove instrument panel hole cover.
6. Remove I/P left lower panel.
7. Pull lower I/P finish panel rearward, disconnect switch electrical connectors, then remove panel.
8. Remove ash tray assembly, then remove ash tray panel and disconnect electrical connectors.
9. **On models equipped with manual transmission,**remove shift lever knob.
10. **On all models,** remove instrument cluster finish panel attaching screws.
11. Remove instrument cluster attaching screws, then remove.
12. Reverse to install. Reset audio coded anti-theft, if equipped, as outlined under "Precautions."

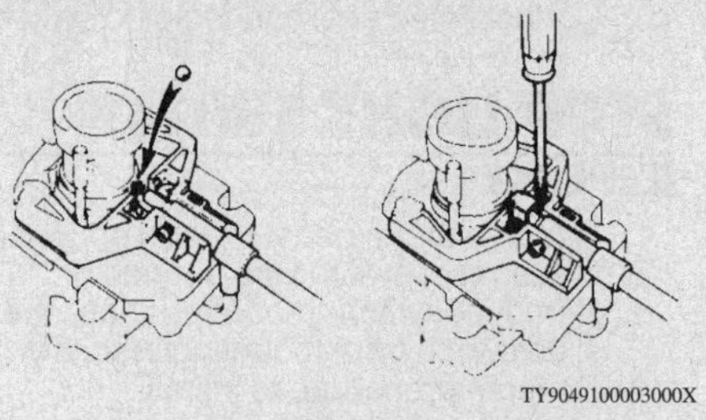
TY9049100003000X

Fig. 6 Positioning ball onto spring

RADIO

REPLACE

CELICA

1. Obtain audio anti-theft code, if equipped, as outlined under "Precautions."
2. **On models equipped with air bag,** pull wheel pad out from steering wheel and disconnect air bag connector. **When removing wheel pad, take care not to pull air bag wire harness. When storing wheel pad, keep upper surface of the pad facing upward. Never disassemble wheel pad.**
3. **On all models,** remove steering wheel, then upper and lower steering column covers.
4. Remove console upper panel, then using a screwdriver remove four console cap screws.
5. Remove four screws and two bolts that attach console box to floor.
6. Disconnect all electrical connectors, then remove console box.
7. Remove two center cluster finish panel attaching screws, then using a screwdriver remove center cluster finish panel and disconnect electrical connector.
8. Remove four radio attaching screws, then disconnect antenna lead, speaker and electrical connectors and remove radio.
9. Reverse to install. Reset audio coded anti-theft, if equipped, as outlined under "Precautions."

SUPRA

1. Obtain audio anti-theft code, if equipped, as outlined under "Precautions."
2. **On models equipped with air bag,** pull wheel pad out from steering wheel and disconnect air bag connector. **When removing wheel pad, take care not to pull air bag wire harness. When storing wheel pad, keep upper surface of the pad facing upward. Never disassemble wheel pad.**
3. **On all models,** remove steering wheel, then upper and lower steering column covers.

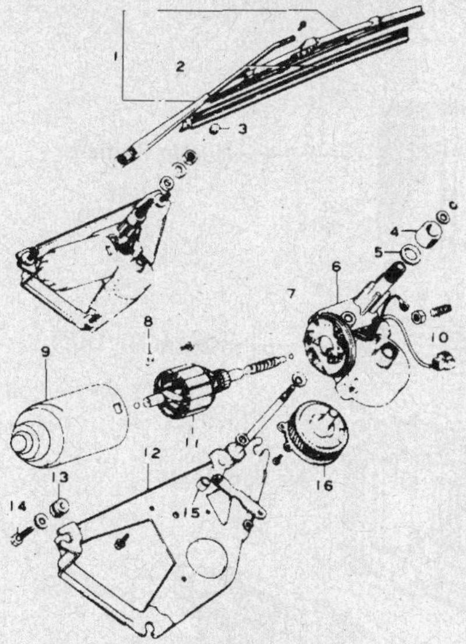
1
2
3
4
5
6
7
8
9
10
11
12
13
14
15
16

1. Windshield Wiper Arm And Blade
2. Windshield Wiper Blade
3. Cap Nut
4. Wiper Link Packing
5. Wiper Link Washer
6. Gear Housing
7. Boll
8. Nut
9. Wiper Motor Stator
10. Stop Screw
11. Wiper Motor Armature
12. Wiper Bracket
13. Bush
14. Bolt
15. Stopper
16. Wiper Motor Gear

TY9029100001000X

Fig. 7 Exploded view of rear wiper motor

4. Remove ashtray and ashtray retainer.
5. **On models equipped with manual transmission,**remove shift lever knob.
6. **On all models,** remove three instrument center cluster finish panel attaching screws, then disconnect the panel electrical connectors and remove the panel.
7. Remove four radio attaching screws, then disconnect electrical connectors and antenna lead and remove radio.
8. Reverse procedure to install. Reset audio coded anti-theft, if equipped, as outlined under "Precautions."

WIPER MOTOR

REPLACE

FRONT

1. Disconnect battery ground cable.
2. Disconnect wiper motor wire connector, then remove wiper motor service cover, if equipped.
3. Remove wiper motor attaching bolts.
4. Using a screwdriver disconnect wiper link from wiper motor and remove wiper motor.
5. Reverse procedure to install.

REAR

1. Disconnect battery ground cable.
2. Remove wiper arm and rear door trim cover.
3. Disconnect wiper motor wire connector.
4. Remove wiper motor bracket attaching bolts and wiper motor and bracket, **Fig. 7.**

WIPER SWITCH

REPLACE

Refer to "Combination Switch, Replace" procedure.

BLOWER MOTOR

REPLACE

CELICA

1. Remove cooling unit as outlined under "Evaporator Core, Replace."
2. Disconnect blower motor connector.
3. Disconnect electrical connector from air inlet damper control servomotor.
4. Remove wire harness.
5. Remove blower unit retaining nuts and the blower unit.
6. Remove wire harness clamp from blower unit.
7. Remove three blower motor screws and pull blower motor with fan from bottom of blower unit, **Fig. 8.**
8. Reverse procedure to install.

SUPRA

Remove A/C unit as outlined under "Evaporator Core, Replace," then refer to **Fig. 9** to remove blower motor.

HEATER CORE

REPLACE

CELICA

1. Remove cooling unit as outlined under "Evaporator Core, Replace."
2. Drain engine coolant from radiator.
3. Disconnect water hoses from heater unit.
4. Remove pipe grommets.
5. Disconnect heater unit connector and remove wire harness.
6. Remove four retaining nuts and the heater unit, **Fig. 10.**
7. Remove heater air duct from heater unit.
8. Remove heater core pipe clamps and pull out heater core with return pipe.
9. Reverse procedure to install.

SUPRA

Remove A/C unit as outlined under "Evaporator Core, Replace," then refer to **Fig. 8** to remove heater core.

EVAPORATOR CORE

REPLACE

CELICA

1. Obtain audio anti-theft code, if equipped, as outlined under "Precautions."

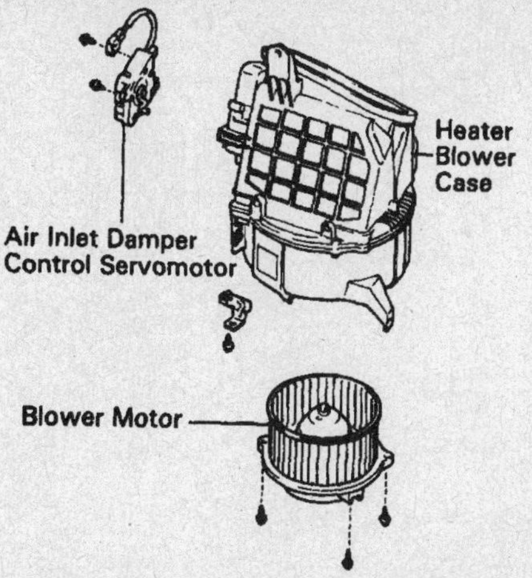
Heater
Blower
Case
Air Inlet Damper
Control Servomotor
Blower Motor

TY7029600254000X

Fig. 8 Blower motor removal. Celica

2. Discharge and recover A/C refrigerant, then disconnect suction tube from cooling unit outlet fitting.
3. Disconnect liquid tube from cooling unit inlet fitting **Fig. 11,** then cap open fittings immediately to keep moisture from entering the system.
4. Remove grommets from inlet and outlet fittings.
5. Remove glove box and reinforcement, then disconnect electrical connectors.
6. Remove three nuts and four bolts that attach the cooling unit to the instrument panel and cowl.
7. With cooling unit removed from vehicle, disconnect connectors from upper case unit.
8. Remove four clips and four screws that attach upper case to lower case, **Fig. 12.**
9. Remove thermistor and thermistor holder, then the lower case.
10. Remove packing and heat sensing tube from suction and liquid tubes.
11. Remove expansion valve from evaporator.
12. Reverse procedure to install, noting the following:
    a. **Torque** bolt attaching expansion valve, suction and liquid lines tubes to evaporator core to 48 inch lbs. **Ensure O-rings are properly positioned on the tube fittings.**
    b. **Torque** nut attaching liquid tube to cooling unit inlet fitting to 10 ft. lbs.
    c. **Torque** nut attaching suction tube to cooling unit outlet fitting to 24 ft. lbs.
    d. Add 1.4–1.7 fl. oz. of compressor oil to compressor before recharging system.
    e. Reset audio coded anti-theft, if equipped, as outlined under "Precautions."

SUPRA

1. Obtain audio anti-theft code, if equipped, as outlined under "Precautions," then discharge and recover A/C refrigerant.
2. Drain engine coolant from radiator.

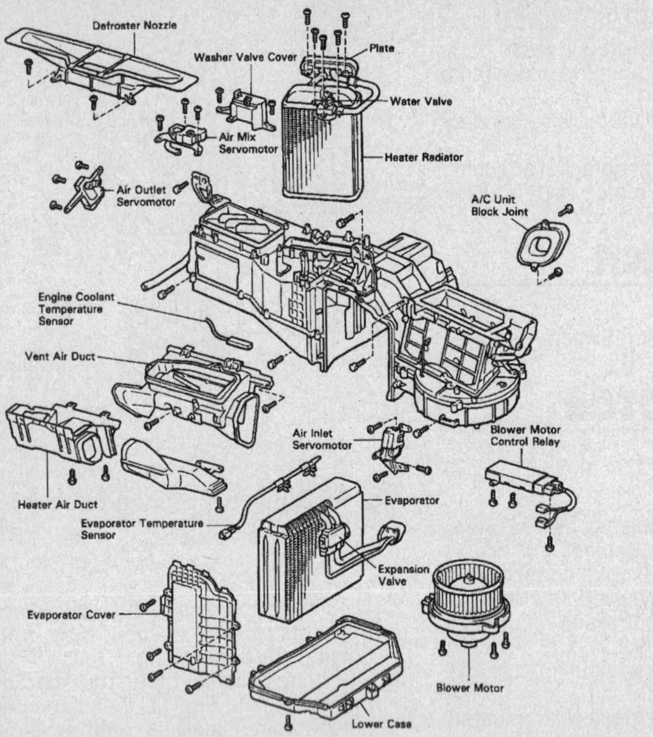
Defroster Nozzle
Washer Valve Cover
Plate
Water Valve
Air Mix Servomotor
Heater Radiator
Air Outlet Servomotor
A/C Unit Block Joint
Engine Coolant Temperature Sensor
Vent Air Duct
Air Inlet Servomotor
Blower Motor Control Relay
Heater Air Duct
Evaporator
Evaporator Temperature Sensor
Expansion Valve
Evaporator Cover
Blower Motor
Lower Case
TY7029600255000X

Fig. 9 Exploded view of A/C unit. Supra

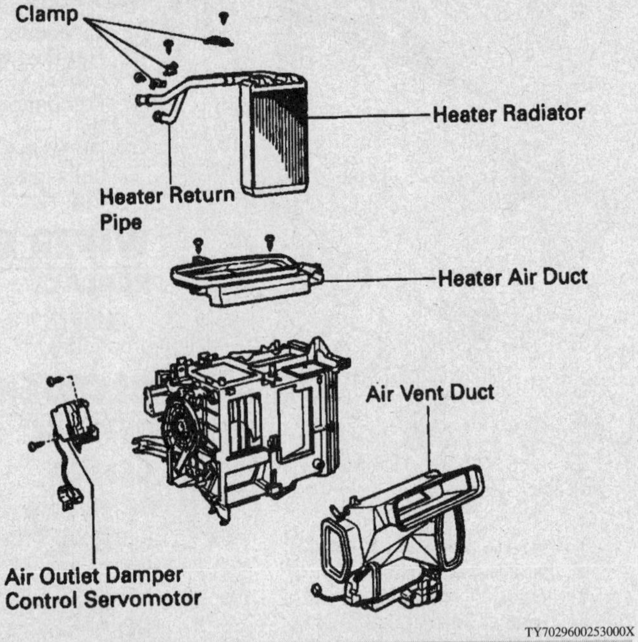
Clamp
Heater Radiator
Heater Return Pipe
Heater Air Duct
Air Vent Duct
Air Outlet Damper Control Servomotor
TY7029600253000X

Fig. 10 Heater core removal. Celica

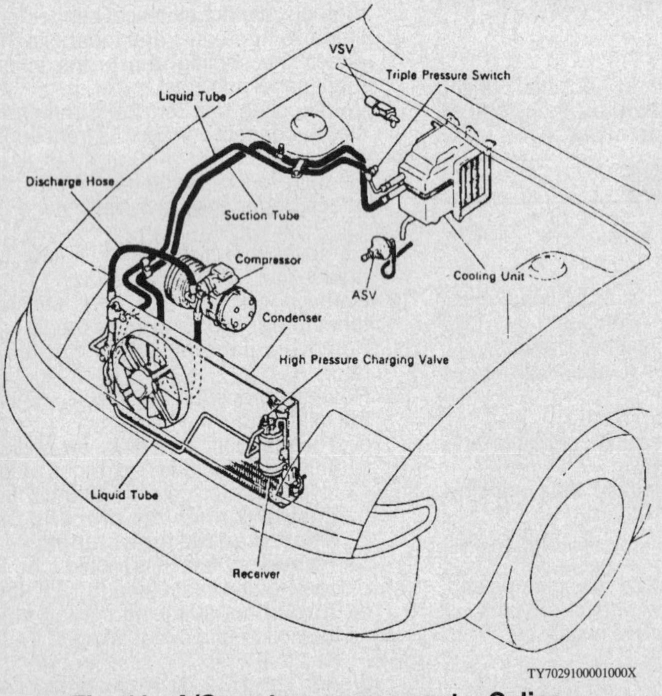
VSV
Triple Pressure Switch
Liquid Tube
Discharge Hose
Suction Tube
Compressor
Cooling Unit
ASV
Condenser
High Pressure Charging Valve
Liquid Tube
Receiver
TY7029100001000X

Fig. 11 A/C system components. Celica

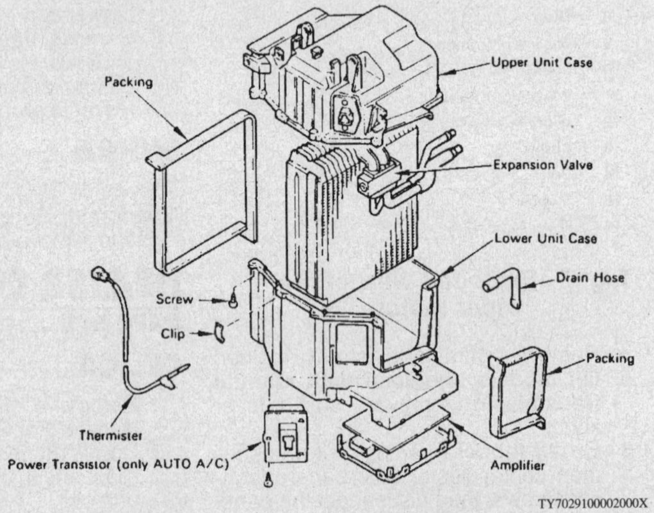
Packing
Upper Unit Case
Expansion Valve
Lower Unit Case
Drain Hose
Screw
Clip
Packing
Thermister
Power Transistor (only AUTO A/C)
Amplifier
TY7029100002000X

Fig. 12 Cooling unit. Celica

3. Remove engine wire harness bracket mounting bolt.
4. Remove brake tube bracket mounting bolts from dash panel.
5. Disconnect water hose from heater core.
6. Remove insulator retainer.
7. Remove ABS actuator, if equipped.
8. Disconnect liquid and suction tubes from A/C unit.
9. Remove plate cover.
10. Remove instrument panel as outlined under "Dash Panel Service."
11. Remove heater to register No. 3 duct.
12. Disconnect A/C unit connectors and remove A/C unit.
13. Disconnect air inlet servomotor control link and remove air inlet servomotor, **Fig. 8.**
14. Remove blower motor.
15. Remove foot air duct and A/C unit block joint.
16. Remove A/C unit lower case cover and evaporator cover.
17. Pull evaporator out of A/C unit case.
18. Reverse procedure to install. If evaporator was replaced, add 1.4 oz. compressor oil to compressor.

3S-GTE 2.0L Engine

NOTE: On Air Bag Equipped Models, Refer To "Air Bag System Precautions" Located In The Front Of This Manual For System Disarming & Arming Procedures.

INDEX

	Page No.
Belt Tension Data	43-15
Camshaft, Replace	43-14
Compression Pressure	43-11
Cooling System Bleed	43-15
Cylinder Head, Replace	43-12
Engine Rebuilding Specifications	48-1
Engine, Replace	43-11
Fuel Filter, Replace	43-16
Fuel Pump, Replace	43-16
Hydraulic Lifters, Replace	43-13
Main & Rod Bearings	43-15
Oil Pan, Replace	43-15
Oil Pump, Replace	43-15
Oil Pump Service	43-15
Piston & Rod Assembly	43-15
Precautions	43-11
Air Bag Systems	43-11
Audio Coded Anti-Theft System	43-11
Radiator, Replace	43-16
Thermostat, Replace	43-15
Tightening Specifications	43-17
Timing Belt, Replace	43-14
Installation	43-14
Removal	43-14
Valve Adjustment	43-13
Valve Clearance Specifications	43-13
Valve Guides	43-13
Water Pump, Replace	43-15

PRECAUTIONS

AIR BAG SYSTEMS

Refer to "Air Bag System Precautions" in the front of this manual for system disarming and arming procedures.

AUDIO CODED ANTI-THEFT SYSTEM

Some models are equipped with an audio coded anti-theft system that will disable the radio when the battery cable is disconnected. The system can be identified by the "ANTI-THEFT SYSTEM" on the cassette tape lid. Obtain 3 digit customer code for input. Reset system after service as follows:

1. Obtain 3 digit audio anti-theft code.
2. Depress 1 (PROG) while depressing righthand side of TUNE SEEK button, - - - will appear in tape operation display.
3. To enter the first digit, depress 1 (PROG) button repeatedly until the number of times depressed equals the first digit beginning with zero (depress the 1 button six times if the first digit if five).
4. To enter second digit, depress 2 (APS) button repeatedly until the number of times depressed equals the second digit beginning with zero.
5. To enter third digit, depress 3 (RPT) button repeatedly until the number of times depressed equals the second digit beginning with zero.
6. If - - - is displayed during code input, repeat procedure.
7. When code appears in display, depress and hold SCAN button until SEC appears.
8. When SEC disappears audio system should be operative.
9. If Err is displayed, repeat procedure. **Attempting to input code more than nine times may permanently disable audio system.**

COMPRESSION PRESSURE

1. Start engine and warm to normal operating temperature.
2. Remove charge air cooler.
3. Disconnect solenoid resistor connector.
4. Disconnect cold start injector connector.
5. Disconnect distributor connectors.
6. Remove spark plugs.
7. Insert compression pressure gauge into spark plug hole.
8. Fully open throttle.
9. Measure compression pressure while cranking engine.
10. Standard compression pressure is 164 psi or more. Minimum pressure should be 128 psi.
11. Compression pressure difference between cylinders should not exceed 14 psi.

ENGINE

REPLACE

1. Obtain audio anti-theft code, if equipped, as outlined in "Precautions."
2. Remove hood and engine undercover.
3. Drain engine coolant, then engine oil.
4. Remove air cleaner assembly as follows:
   a. Disconnect intake air temperature sensor electrical connector.
   b. Disconnect accelerator cable from bracket on air cleaner cap.
   c. Disconnect four air cleaner cap clips, then air hose from air pipe.
   d. Disconnect air cleaner hose from throttle body, then remove air cleaner cap and element.
   e. Remove three air cleaner case retaining bolts, then the case.
5. Disconnect accelerator cable from throttle body.
6. Remove two engine relay box retaining nuts and disconnect relay box from battery.
7. Remove lower cover from relay box, then disconnect fusible link cassette and two connectors of engine wire from relay box.
8. Remove A/C relay box from bracket, then the battery.
9. **On models with cruise control and anti-lock brake system (ABS),** disconnect cruise control actuator electrical connector, remove four actuator attaching bolts, actuator and bracket.
10. **On models with cruise control less anti-lock brake system (ABS),** proceed as follows:
    a. Remove cruise control actuator cover, then disconnect vacuum hose from air intake chamber.
    b. Disconnect actuator connector, then cable from actuator.
    c. Remove three actuator attaching bolts and actuator.
11. **On all models,** disconnect electric cooling fan connector, then remove upper radiator support seal.
12. Disconnect coolant reservoir hose, then remaining radiator hoses.
13. **On models with automatic transmission,** disconnect oil cooler hoses from the radiator.
14. **On all models,** remove two radiator upper support retaining bolts.
15. Lift radiator out of engine compartment, then remove radiator reservoir tank.
16. Disconnect wires and connectors from check connector, igniter connector and vacuum sensor connector.
17. Disconnect ground strap from left fender apron.
18. Disconnect engine wire clamp from wire bracket, then remove bracket retaining bolts and bracket.
19. Disconnect noise filter.
20. Disconnect two vacuum hoses from charcoal canister, then remove canister retaining bolts and canister.
21. Disconnect heater hose from water inlet.

22. Disconnect speedometer cable from transaxle.
23. Disconnect fuel hoses, catching any leaking fluid in a container.
24. Remove three clutch release cylinder retaining bolts, then the clutch release cylinder from the transaxle.
25. Disconnect transaxle control cables from transaxle.
26. Disconnect the following vacuum hoses:
    a. Vacuum sensor hose from gas filter on air intake chamber.
    b. Brake booster hose from air intake chamber.
    c. Three A/C hoses from air switching valve (ASV) on air intake chamber.
    d. A/C hose from air pipe.
27. Remove engine wire clamp from wire bracket on right fender apron, then disconnect two cowl wire connectors.
28. Disconnect electrical connectors shown in **Fig. 1.**
29. Remove two engine wire to cowl panel attaching nuts, then pull wire from panel.
30. Raise and support vehicle.
31. Remove lower crossmember attaching bolts and nuts, then the crossmember.
32. Remove front exhaust pipe as follows:
    a. Disconnect oxygen sensor connector.
    b. Loosen bolt, then disconnect clamp from support bracket.
    c. Remove front exhaust pipe-to-catalytic converter attaching bolts and nuts.
    d. Disconnect support hook on front exhaust pipe from support bracket, then remove front exhaust pipe and gaskets.
33. **On models with automatic transmission,** disconnect transaxle control cable from engine mounting center member.
34. **On all models,** remove front driveshafts as follows:
    a. Remove tire and wheel assemblies.
    b. Remove cotter pin and locknut cap.
    c. Remove bearing locknut while depressing brake pedal.
    d. Drain oil from transaxle.
    e. Remove brake caliper from steering knuckle and suspend it with wire.
    f. Scribe reference marks on hub and rotor disc, then remove rotor disc.
    g. Remove cotter pin and tie rod end nut from steering knuckle, then using tie rod end removal tool No. 09628-62011, or equivalent, separate tie rod end from steering knuckle.
    h. Remove bolt and two nuts attaching lower arm to steering knuckle, then disconnect lower arm from steering knuckle.
    i. Using puller tool No. 09950-20017, or equivalent, disconnect left side driveshaft from steering knuckle. **Cover driveshaft boot shaft with cloth to prevent it from damage.**
    j. Using a hammer and hub nut wrench or an equivalent, remove left side driveshaft from transaxle. **Ensure care is taken not to damage dust cover. Cover hub nut wrench with cloth so transaxle body is not damaged.**
35. Disconnect heater hose from water inlet pipe.
36. **On models equipped with A/C,** proceed as follows:
    a. Disconnect A/C compressor connector, then remove drive belt.
    b. Remove four A/C compressor retaining bolts, pull compressor away from mounting.
    c. Using wire, suspend compressor from radiator support.
37. **On all models,** remove power steering pump drive belt.
38. Remove two power steering pump attaching bolts, then use a wire to suspend pump to cowl.
39. Remove eight engine mounting center member attaching bolts, then the center member.
40. Remove front engine mounting through bolt and mounting insulator.
41. Remove two mounting bracket attaching bolts and bracket.
42. Remove rear engine mounting through bolt and mounting insulator.
43. Remove three mounting bracket attaching bolts and bracket.
44. Remove connector from ground wire on righthand fender apron.
45. Remove three right side engine mounting stay attaching bolts and mounting stay.
46. Remove two left side engine mounting stay attaching bolts and mounting stay.
47. Remove ground strap from transaxle.
48. Attach an engine chain hoist, or equivalent, to engine hangers.
49. Remove through bolt and three lefthand mounting insulator attaching bolts, then the insulator.
50. Remove three lefthand mounting bracket attaching bolts.
51. Remove through bolt and two righthand mounting insulator attaching bolts, then the insulator.
52. Lift engine slowly and carefully out of vehicle. **Be careful not to hit power steering gear housing or neutral start switch.**
53. Reverse procedure to install. Reset audio coded anti-theft, if equipped, as outlined in "Precautions."

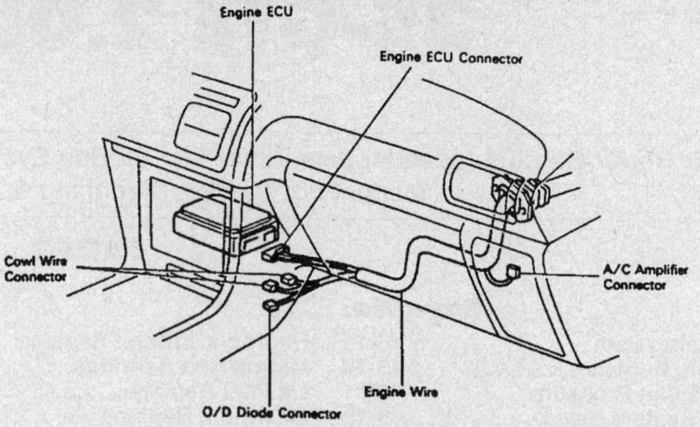
Engine ECU
Engine ECU Connector
Cowl Wire Connector
A/C Amplifier Connector
Engine Wire
O/D Diode Connector
TY1069100001000X

Fig. 1 Electrical connectors

CYLINDER HEAD

REPLACE

1. Obtain audio anti-theft code, if equipped, as outlined in "Precautions."
2. Drain coolant and oil from engine.
3. Drain coolant from intercooler assembly.
4. Remove suspension under brace.
5. Disconnect accelerator cable from throttle body assembly.
6. Remove reservoir tank and air cleaner assembly.
7. Remove alternator.
8. Raise and support vehicle.
9. Remove righthand front wheel.
10. Remove engine undercovers.
11. Remove suspension lower crossmember.
12. Remove front exhaust pipe, then catalytic converter.
13. Remove alternator brackets.
14. Remove turbocharger and exhaust manifold assemblies.
15. Remove distributor.
16. Remove No. 2 air pipe.
17. Remove lefthand engine hanger.
18. Remove oil pressure switch and water outlet.
19. Remove water bypass pipe.
20. Remove throttle body.
21. Disconnect cold start injector connector. Remove EGR valve, vacuum modulator and EGR control VSV.
22. Remove vacuum pipe and intake manifold stays.
23. Remove No. 1 air pipe.
24. Remove fuel pressure VSV.
25. Remove T-VIS, VSV, vacuum tank and turbocharger pressure VSV.
26. Remove intake manifold and air control valve.
27. Remove power steering oil reservoir tank without disconnecting lines.
28. Remove spark plugs.
29. Remove No. 2 timing belt cover.
30. Remove timing belt as follows:
    a. Place No. 1 cylinder to TDC of compression stroke by turning crankshaft pulley (sprocket) and aligning

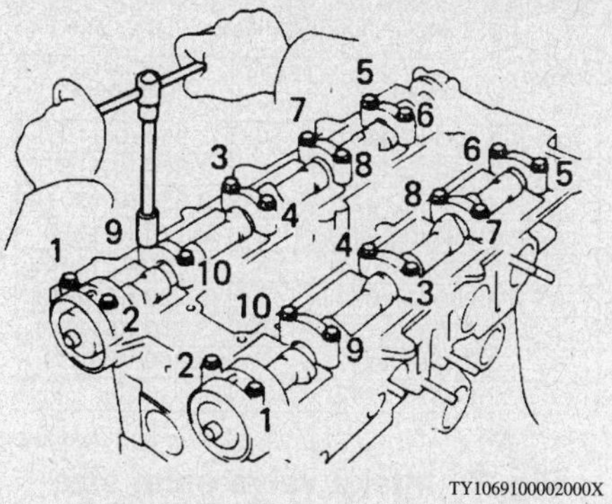
TY1069100002000X

Fig. 2 Intake & exhaust camshaft bearing cap bolt loosening sequence

pulley groove with No. 1 timing belt cover marking "0."
  b. Check that the alignment marks on the camshaft timing pulleys and No. 3 timing belt cover are aligned. If not, turn the crankshaft one revolution (360°).
  c. With timing marks properly aligned, remove timing belt.
31. Remove PCV pipe and cylinder head cover.
32. Remove camshaft timing pulleys (sprockets).
33. Remove No. 1 idler pulley (sprocket) and tension spring.
34. Remove No. 3 timing belt cover.
35. Remove intake and exhaust camshafts as follows:
  a. Uniformly loosen and remove the twenty bearing cap bolts in several passes, in sequence shown, in **Fig. 2.**
  b. Remove the ten bearing cap, two oil seals and two camshaft assemblies. Arrange the intake and exhaust camshaft and components in order removed.
36. Remove righthand rear engine hanger.
37. Remove cylinder head as follows:
  a. Using adapter tool No. 09043-38100, or equivalent, uniformly loosen and remove the ten cylinder head attaching bolts in several passes, in sequence shown in **Fig. 3. Cylinder head warpage or cracking could result from loosening the bolts in incorrect order.**
  b. Lift the cylinder head from the dowels on the cylinder block and place it on a suitable workbench.
38. If cylinder head is difficult to remove, pry cylinder head off using a suitable screwdriver. When doing so, do not damage cylinder head or block surfaces.
39. Reverse procedure to install, noting the following:
  a. The cylinder head bolts are tighten in steps.
  b. If any of the bolts break or deform, replace them.
  c. Apply a light coat of clean engine oil onto bolt threads and under the heads of the bolts.
  d. Using adapter tool No. 09043-

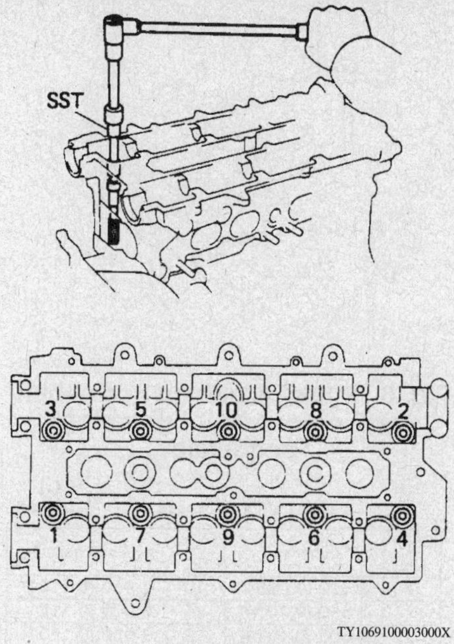
SST
TY1069100003000X

Fig. 3 Cylinder head bolt loosening sequence

38100, or equivalent, install a uniformly tighten cylinder head bolts in several passes, in sequence shown in **Fig. 4.**
  e. **Torque** bolts to 40 ft. lbs. If any of the bolts do not meet the required specification, replace the bolt.
  f. Mark the front of the cylinder head bolt head with paint.
  g. Tighten the ten cylinder head bolts an additional 90° in sequence shown.
  h. Ensure paint mark applied, is now at a 90° angle from the front.
  i. During installation of the intake and exhaust camshafts, place the camshaft onto the cylinder with the No. 1 camshaft lobe facing outward. Apply seal packing to the No. 1 bearing cap.
  j. Install the bearing caps in their correct locations, as shown in **Fig. 5. Each bearing cap has a number and front mark.** Apply a light coat of clean engine oil onto the threads and under the heads of the bearing cap attaching bolts. Install and uniformly tighten the twenty bearing cap bolts in several passes, in sequence shown in **Fig. 6.** Tighten to specification.
  k. Reset audio coded anti-theft, if equipped, as outlined in "Precautions."

VALVE CLEARANCE SPECIFICATIONS

Year	Stem-To-Guide Clearance	
	Intake	Exhaust
1993	.006–.010	.011–.015

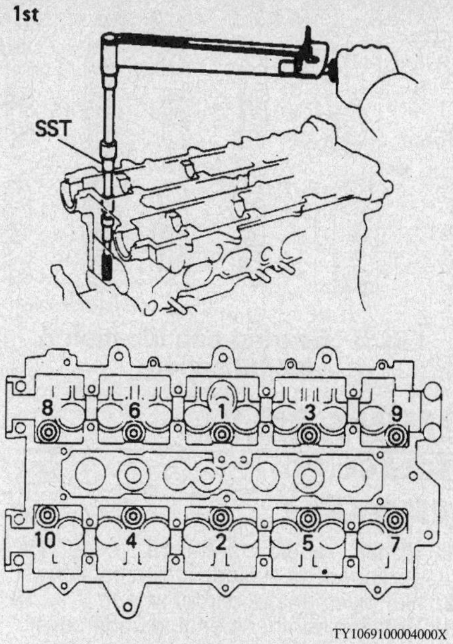
1st
SST
TY1069100004000X

Fig. 4 Cylinder head bolt tightening sequence

VALVE ADJUSTMENT

Valve adjustment is accomplished by installing the proper thickness shim to achieve proper valve clearance. Refer to "Valve Clearance Specifications" for proper specifications. Shims are available in .0020 inch (.050 mm) increments, **Figs. 7 and 8.**

1. Crank engine until No. 1 cylinder is at TDC compression stroke and adjust the following cylinders valves to specifications: intake Nos. 1, 2 and exhaust Nos. 1, 3.
2. Rotate engine one complete revolution clockwise and adjust the following cylinders valves to specifications: intake Nos. 3, 4 and exhaust Nos. 2, 4.

VALVE GUIDES

1. Using a suitable tool and hammer, strike valve guide bushing to break it off at cylinder head casting.
2. Heat cylinder head to 176–212°F (80–100°C).
3. Using suitable valve guide removal tool, tap out bushing.
4. Install snap ring on new valve guide, then install new valve guide using tool as above and driving in from the reverse side of removal.
5. Ream new valve guide, if necessary. Refer to "Valve Specifications" for stem clearances.

HYDRAULIC LIFTERS

REPLACE

Check lifters for excessive wear and/or damage. Replace worn or damaged valve lifters as required. Lubricate hydraulic valve lifter before installation.

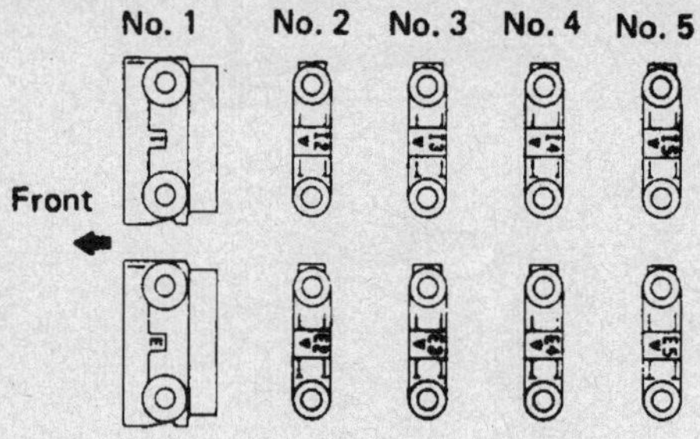
No. 1
No. 2
No. 3
No. 4
No. 5
Front

TY1069100005000X

Fig. 5 Bearing cap location & identification

TIMING BELT

REPLACE

REMOVAL

1. Obtain audio anti-theft code, if equipped, as outlined in "Precautions."
2. Remove righthand front wheel.
3. Remove righthand engine undercover.
4. Remove radiator reservoir tank.
5. Loosen power steering oil reservoir tank.
6. Remove accessory drive belts.
7. Remove alternator and alternator brackets.
8. Raise engine slightly to remove weight from engine mounting on the righthand side.
9. Remove righthand engine mount insulator and bracket.
10. Remove throttle body assembly.
11. Remove No. 2 timing belt cover.
12. Remove spark plugs.
13. Place No. 1 cylinder at TDC of compression stroke by turning the crankshaft pulley to align its groove with the No. 1 timing belt cover "0" mark.
14. Ensure alignment marks on camshaft sprockets and the No. 3 timing belt cover are aligned properly as shown in **Fig. 9.** If not, turn crankshaft one complete revolution (360°) to align marks.
15. Remove timing belt from camshaft timing sprockets. If the original timing belt is going to be used, place alignment marks on the camshaft timing sprockets and the timing belt as shown in **Fig. 10.**
16. Loosen the No.1 idler pulley attaching bolt and shift toward the left as far as possible.
17. Temporarily tighten the pulley attaching bolt, then relieve tension from timing belt.
18. Remove timing belt from the camshaft sprocket. **Support the timing belt so the meshing of the crankshaft sprocket and timing belt does not shift. Do not drop anything inside the timing belt cover. Do not allow dust, oil or water to come into contact with the timing belt.**
19. Remove sprockets, No. 1 timing belt covers, timing belt guide and the timing belt. **If the original timing belt is going to be used, draw a direction arrow on the timing belt (draw the arrow in direction of engine rotation) and place alignment marks on the timing belt and crankshaft timing sprocket.**

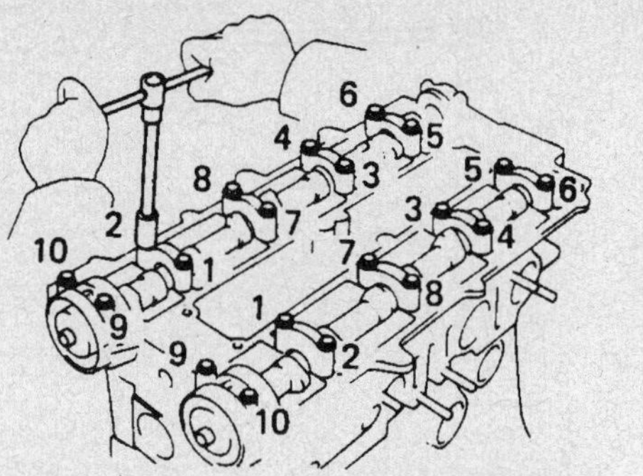

TY1069100006000X

Fig. 6 Intake & exhaust camshaft bearing cap bolt tightening sequence

New shim thickness mm (in.)

Shim No.	Thickness	Shim No.	Thickness
1	2.500 (0.0984)	10	2.950 (0.1161)
2	2.550 (0.1004)	11	3.000 (0.1181)
3	2.600 (0.1024)	12	3.050 (0.1201)
4	2.650 (0.1043)	13	3.100 (0.1220)
5	2.700 (0.1063)	14	3.150 (0.1240)
6	2.750 (0.1083)	15	3.200 (0.1260)
7	2.800 (0.1102)	16	3.250 (0.1280)
8	2.850 (0.1122)	17	3.300 (0.1299)
9	2.900 (0.1142)		

TY1069100008000X

Fig. 8 Exhaust valve shim size chart

INSTALLATION

Before installing the original timing belt onto the engine, ensure belt is in good condition. Carefully check timing belt for discoloration (an indication of fluid contact with the belt) or cracks. Do not install a timing belt showing signs of wear or stress. Installing a worn or damaged belt will result in serious engine damage.

1. Install crankshaft sprocket and No. 2 idler pulley. Tighten pulley bolt to specification.
2. Temporarily install the No. 1 idler pulley and tension spring. Install pulley attaching bolt. Do not tighten bolt. Install the tension spring, then pry toward the left as far as it will go and tighten it. Remove any oil or water on the idler pulley.
3. With engine cold, temporarily install the timing belt. Install belt onto the crankshaft sprocket, oil pump, No. 2 idler pulley and water pump pulley. **If the original timing belt is used, align the marks made during removal and install the belt with the arrow pointing in direction of engine rotation.**
4. Install the timing belt guide.
5. Install the No. 1 timing belt cover and gasket. Tighten cover attaching bolts to specification.
6. Install the crankshaft pulley. Tighten bolt to specification.
7. Install camshaft sprockets. Using a suitable wrench, turn and align the camshaft groove with the drilled out mark of the No. 1 camshaft bearing cap. Slide the timing sprocket onto the camshaft with the "S" mark on the sprocket facing upward. Align the pin holes on the camshaft sprocket and timing pulley, then insert the knock pin. Secure sprocket from rotating, then tighten the attaching bolts. Tighten bolts to specification. Install cylinder head cover.
8. Place No. 1 cylinder at TDC of compression stroke by turning the crankshaft pulley and aligning its groove with the "0" mark on the No. 1 timing belt cover. Turn the camshaft and align the marks on the camshaft sprockets and cylinder head cover.
9. Install timing belt. If the original timing belt is going to be used, first align the marks on the camshaft sprockets and timing belt. Install the timing belt. Ensure the tension between the crankshaft and intake camshaft timing sprockets exists.
10. With timing belt installed, check valve timing as follows:
    a. Loosen the No. 1 idler pulley attaching bolt and stretch timing belt. Do not loosen the pulley bolt further than the point where the idler returns.
    b. Slowly turn the crankshaft pulley two revolutions from TDC to TDC. **Always turn the crankshaft clockwise.**
    c. Ensure the camshaft sprocket timing marks align with the cylinder head cover marks and the crankshaft pulley mark (V notch) aligns with the "0" mark on the timing belt cover (timing tab). **If not, remove timing belt and correctly install it.**
    d. Tighten the No. 1 idler pulley attaching bolt to specification.
    e. Ensure timing belt tension exists between the crankshaft and intake camshaft timing sprockets.
11. Reverse procedure to install to complete installation. Reset audio coded anti-theft, if equipped, as outlined in "Precautions."

New shim thickness mm (in.)

Shim No.	Thickness	Shim No.	Thickness
1	2.500 (0.0984)	10	2.950 (0.1161)
2	2.550 (0.1004)	11	3.000 (0.1181)
3	2.600 (0.1024)	12	3.050 (0.1201)
4	2.650 (0.1043)	13	3.100 (0.1220)
5	2.700 (0.1063)	14	3.150 (0.1240)
6	2.750 (0.1083)	15	3.200 (0.1260)
7	2.800 (0.1102)	16	3.250 (0.1280)
8	2.850 (0.1122)	17	3.300 (0.1299)
9	2.900 (0.1142)		

TY1069100007000X

Fig. 7 Intake valve shim size chart

CAMSHAFT

REPLACE

Refer to "Cylinder Head, Replace" for camshaft removal procedures.

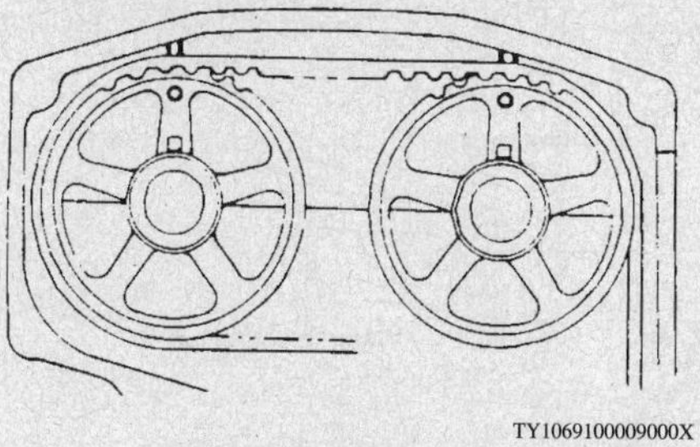
TY1069100009000X

Fig. 9 Camshaft sprocket timing mark alignment

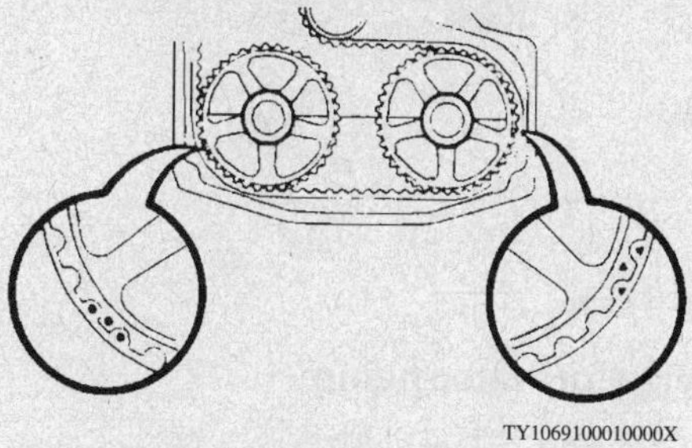
TY1069100010000X

Fig. 10 Sprocket & timing belt alignment

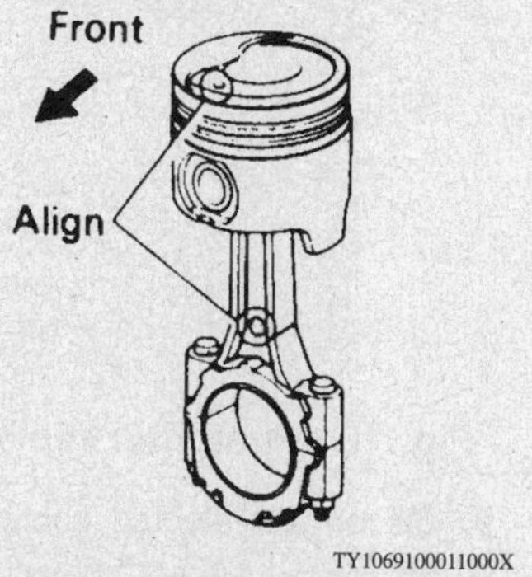
Front
Align
TY1069100011000X

Fig. 11 Piston & connecting rod assembly

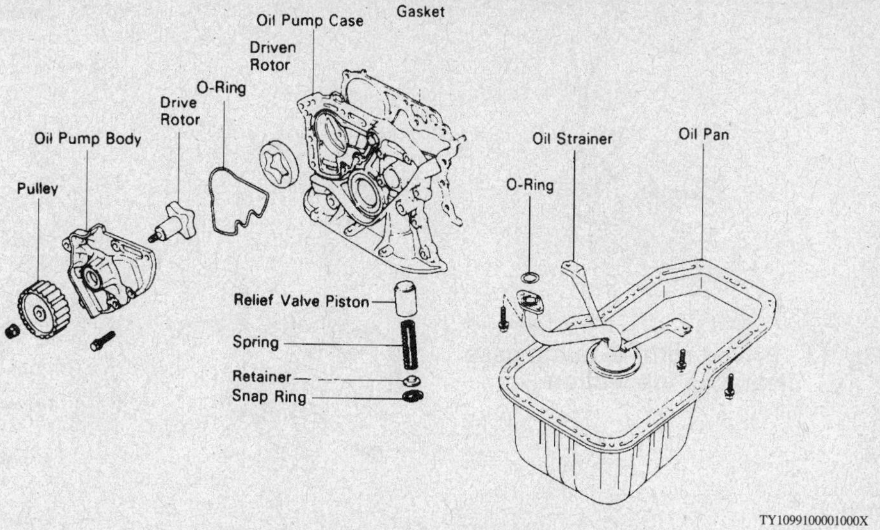
Oil Pump Case
Gasket
Driven Rotor
O-Ring
Drive Rotor
Oil Pump Body
Pulley
Oil Strainer
Oil Pan
O-Ring
Relief Valve Piston
Spring
Retainer
Snap Ring
TY1099100001000X

Fig. 12 Exploded view of oil pump

PISTON & ROD ASSEMBLY

Oversize pistons are not available; if piston bore is not within specifications, replace piston and/or cylinder block. When assembling piston onto connecting rod, ensure mark on top of piston and mark on connecting rod are on same side, **Fig. 11.** When installing piston and connecting rod assembly, ensure mark on top of piston is facing toward front of engine.

MAIN & ROD BEARINGS

Undersize bearings are not available. If crankshaft journals or crankpins are worn or scored, the crankshaft must be replaced.

OIL PAN

REPLACE

1. Obtain audio anti-theft code, if equipped, as outlined in "Precautions."
2. Raise and support vehicle.
3. Remove engine undercovers, then drain engine oil.
4. Disconnect exhaust pipe from exhaust manifold or turbocharger assembly, if equipped.
5. Remove suspension lower crossmember, then the engine mount center member.
6. Remove stiffener plate, then the oil dipstick.
7. Remove oil pan attaching bolts, then the oil pan. **Use caution not to damage oil pan flange.**
8. Remove 2 attaching bolts, nuts, oil pan baffle plate, then the oil strainer with gasket.
9. Attach a suitable hoist to engine, then lift and suspend engine with hoist.
10. Remove timing belt and pulleys. Refer to "Timing Belt, Replace" for procedure.
11. Remove oil pump attaching bolts, then the oil pump.
12. Reverse procedure to install, using new gaskets and O-ring seals as applicable. Reset audio coded anti-theft, if equipped, as outlined in "Precautions."

OIL PUMP

REPLACE

Refer to "Oil Pan, Replace" for procedure.

OIL PUMP SERVICE

1. Using a suitable feeler gauge, measure clearance between driven rotor and pump case, **Figs. 12 and 13.**
2. Clearance should be .0039–.0063 inch. If feeler gauge clearance obtained exceeds specified limits, replace oil pump rotor set and/or pump case.
3. Using a feeler gauge, measure clearance between both rotor tips. Clearance should be .0016–.0063 inch. If feeler gauge clearance obtained exceeds specified limit, replace oil pump rotor set.

BELT TENSION DATA

Belt	New, Lbs.	Used, Lbs.
Alternator	①	②
Power Steer.	100–150	60–100

① — With A/C, new 170–180; used, 95–135.
② — Less A/C, new 125–175; used, 105–155.

COOLING SYSTEM BLEED

These engines do not require a specified bleed procedure. After filling cooling system, run engine to operating temperature with radiator/pressure cap off. Air will then be automatically bled through cap opening.

THERMOSTAT

REPLACE

1. Obtain audio anti-theft code, if equipped, as outlined in "Precautions."
2. Drain engine coolant into suitable container.
3. Remove alternator.
4. Remove lower radiator hose, then water inlet and thermostat.
5. Reverse procedure to install. Ensure jiggle valve is aligned with upper side of inlet stud bolt.

WATER PUMP

REPLACE

1. Obtain audio anti-theft code, if equipped, as outlined in "Precautions."
2. then the coolant temperature switch connector.
3. Disconnect lower radiator hose from coolant inlet housing.

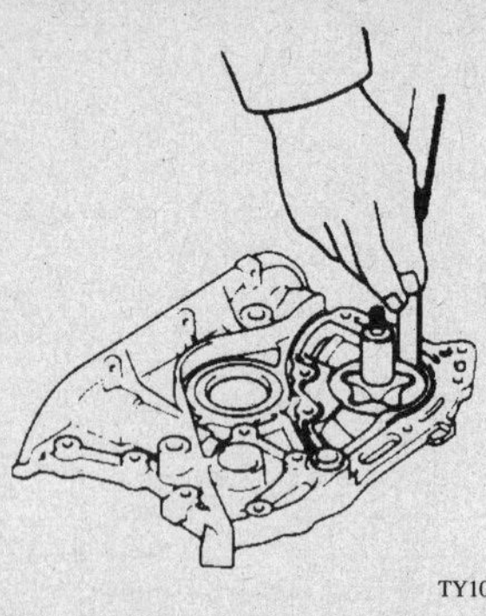
TY1099100002000X

Fig. 13 Driven rotor & pump case clearance inspection

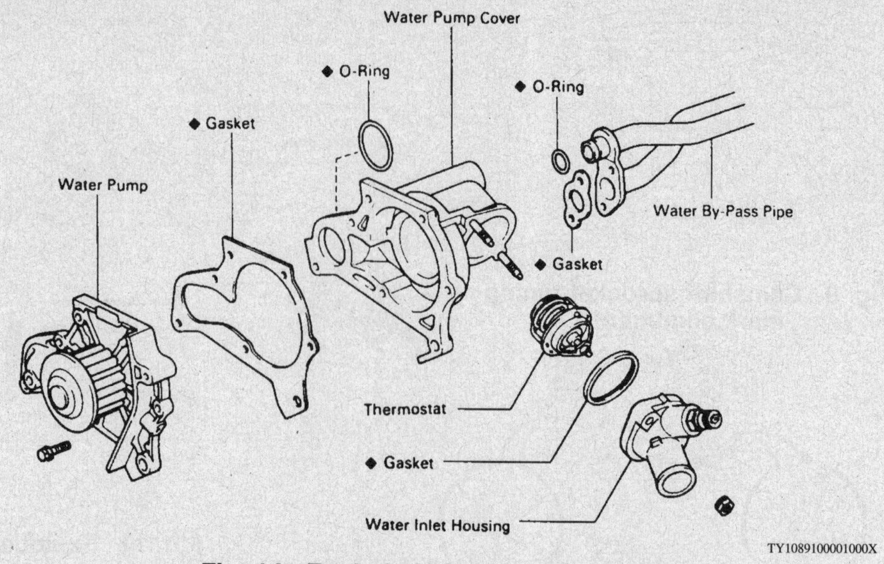
Water Pump Cover
◆ O-Ring
◆ O-Ring
◆ Gasket
Water Pump
Water By-Pass Pipe
◆ Gasket
Thermostat
◆ Gasket
Water Inlet Housing
TY1089100001000X

Fig. 14 Exploded view of water pump

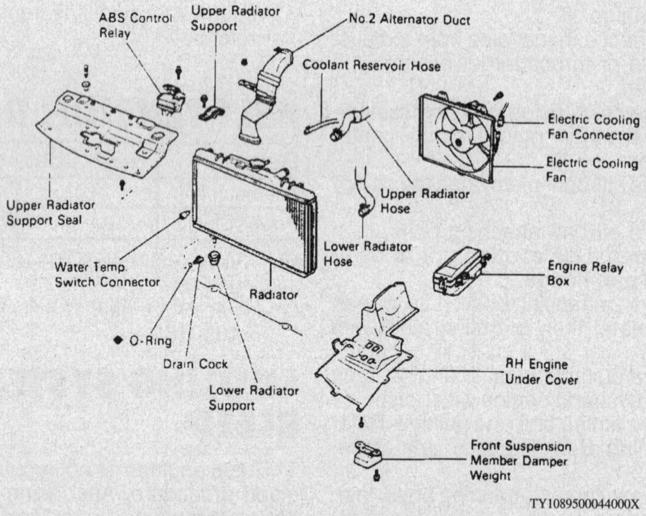
ABS Control Relay
Upper Radiator Support
No.2 Alternator Duct
Coolant Reservoir Hose
Electric Cooling Fan Connector
Electric Cooling Fan
Upper Radiator Support Seal
Upper Radiator Hose
Lower Radiator Hose
Engine Relay Box
Water Temp. Switch Connector
Radiator
◆ O-Ring
Drain Cock
Lower Radiator Support
RH Engine Under Cover
Front Suspension Member Damper Weight
TY1089500044000X

Fig. 15 Radiator replacement

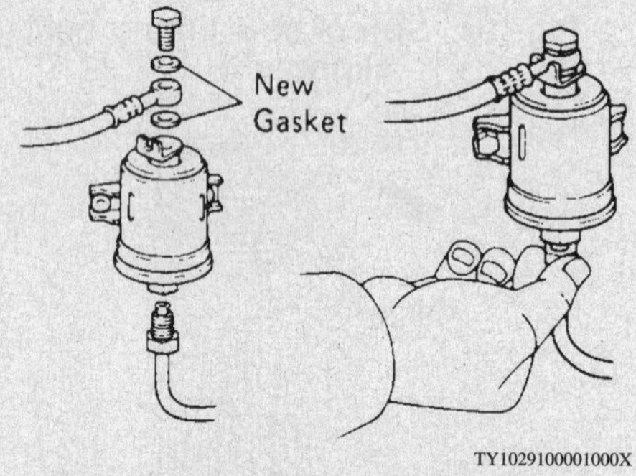
New Gasket
TY1029100001000X

Fig. 16 Fuel filter replacement.

4. Remove timing belt and sprockets. Refer to "Timing Belt, Replace" for procedure.
5. Remove water bypass tubes-to-water pump cover attaching bolts, then the three water pump attaching bolts, **Fig. 14.**
6. Remove water pump and pump cover as an assembly, then remove two O-rings and gasket.
7. Remove water pump-to-water pump cover attaching bolts, then remove water pump.
8. Reverse procedure to install. Reset audio coded anti-theft, if equipped, as outlined in "Precautions."

RADIATOR

REPLACE

1. Disconnect battery ground cable.
2. Remove righthand engine under cover, **Fig. 15.**
3. Drain coolant.
4. Disconnect water temperature switch connector.
5. **On models with ABS,** disconnect ABS control relay from radiator.
6. **On all models, remove No. 2 alternator duct.**
7. Disconnect engine relay box from battery
8. Remove upper radiator support seal.
9. Disconnect electric cooling fan connector.
10. Disconnect coolant reservoir hose.
11. Disconnect radiator hoses.
12. **On models with automatic transmission,** disconnect transmission oil cooler hoses.
13. **On all models,** remove radiator and electric cooling fan.
14. Reverse procedure to install.

FUEL PUMP

REPLACE

1. Drain fuel from tank.
2. Remove fuel tank, then the fuel pump bracket from tank.
3. Remove fuel pump from fuel pump bracket.
4. Remove filter from pump.
5. Reverse procedure to install.

FUEL FILTER

REPLACE

Refer to **Fig. 16** for replacement procedure.

TIGHTENING SPECIFICATIONS

Year	Component	Torque/Ft. Lbs.
1993	A/C Compressor	20
	Alternator Bracket	29
	Bearing Cap Bolts	14
	Camshaft Sprocket	43
	Camshaft Timing Pulley	43
	Catalytic Converter	22
	Catalytic Converter Bracket	43
	Crankshaft Mains	43
	Crankshaft Pulley	80
	Cylinder Head	①
	Cylinder Head Cover	21②
	EGR Valve & Pipe	14
	Exhaust Manifold	38
	Front Engine Mount Bracket	57
	Intake Manifold	14
	Intake Manifold Bracket	19
	Knock Sensor	33
	LH Engine Mount Bolt	47
	LH Engine Mount Stay	54
	LH Engine Mount Through Bolt	64
	No. 1 Idler Pulley	38
	No. 2 Idler Pulley	32
	No. 3 Timing Belt Cover	78②
	Oil Pump Pulley	21
	Power Steering Pump Adjusting Bolt	29
	Power Steering Pump Bracket	32
	Rear End Plate	82
	Rear Oil Seal Retainer	82②
	RH Engine Mount Bracket	38
	RH Engine Mount Nut	38
	RH Engine Mount Stay	54
	RH Engine Mount Through Bolt	64
	Spark Plugs	13
	Spring Loaded Idler Pulley	32
	Suspension Lower Crossmember	112
	Suspension Upper Brace Bolt	15
	Suspension Upper Brace Nut	47
	Timing Belt Tensioner	13
	Timing Cover	78②
	Transaxle Oil Cooler Tube	25
	Water Bypass Pipe	69②
	Water Outlet	29

①— Refer to "Cylinder Head, Replace" for tightening procedure.
②— Inch lbs.

4A-FE 1.6L & 7A-FE 1.8L Engines

NOTE: For Procedures Not Found In This Section, Refer To Toyota Corolla Engine Section.

NOTE: On Air Bag Equipped Models, Refer To "Air Bag System Precautions" Located In The Front Of This Manual For System Disarming & Arming Procedures.

INDEX

	Page No.
Compression Pressure	43-18
Engine Rebuilding Specifications	48-1
Engine, Replace	43-18
Precautions	43-18
Air Bag Systems	43-18
Audio Coded Anti-Theft System	43-18
Radiator, Replace	43-19
4A-FE Engine	43-19
7A-FE Engine	43-19
Tightening Specifications	43-20

PRECAUTIONS

AIR BAG SYSTEMS

Refer to "Air Bag System Precautions" in the front of this manual for system disarming and arming procedures.

AUDIO CODED ANTI-THEFT SYSTEM

Some models are equipped with an audio coded anti-theft system that will disable the radio when the battery cable is disconnected. The system can be identified by the "ANTI-THEFT SYSTEM" on the cassette tape lid. Obtain 3 digit customer code for input. Reset system after service as follows:

1. Obtain 3 digit audio anti-theft code.
2. Depress 1 (PROG) while depressing righthand side of TUNE SEEK button, - - - will appear in tape operation display.
3. To enter the first digit, depress 1 (PROG) button repeatedly until the number of times depressed equals the first digit beginning with zero (depress the 1 button six times if the first digit if five).
4. To enter second digit, depress 2 (APS) button repeatedly until the number of times depressed equals the second digit beginning with zero.
5. To enter third digit, depress 3 (RPT) button repeatedly until the number of times depressed equals the second digit beginning with zero.
6. If - - - is displayed during code input, repeat procedure.
7. When code appears in display, depress and hold SCAN button until SEC appears.
8. When SEC disappears audio system should be operative.
9. If Err is displayed, repeat procedure. **Attempting to input code more than nine times may permanently disable audio system.**

COMPRESSION PRESSURE

1. Start engine and warm to normal operating temperature.
2. Remove charge air cooler.
3. Disconnect solenoid resistor connector.
4. Disconnect cold start injector connector.
5. Disconnect distributor connectors.
6. Remove spark plugs.
7. Insert compression pressure gauge into spark plug hole.
8. Fully open throttle.
9. Measure compression pressure while cranking engine.
10. Standard compression pressure is 191 psi or more. Minimum pressure should be 142 psi.
11. Compression pressure difference between cylinders should not exceed 14 psi.

ENGINE

REPLACE

1. Obtain audio anti-theft code, if equipped, as outlined in "Precautions."
2. Remove hood and engine undercover.
3. Drain engine coolant, then engine oil.
4. Remove air cleaner assembly as follows:
   a. Disconnect intake air temperature sensor electrical connector.
   b. Disconnect accelerator cable from bracket on air cleaner cap.
   c. Disconnect four air cleaner cap clips, then air hose from air pipe.
   d. Disconnect air cleaner hose from throttle body, then remove air cleaner cap and element.
   e. Remove three air cleaner case retaining bolts, then the case.
5. Disconnect accelerator cable from throttle body.
6. Remove two engine relay box retaining nuts and disconnect relay box from battery.
7. Remove lower cover from relay box, then disconnect fusible link cassette and two connectors of engine wire from relay box.
8. Remove A/C relay box from bracket, then the battery.
9. **On models with cruise control and anti-lock brake system (ABS),** disconnect cruise control actuator electrical connector, remove four actuator attaching bolts, actuator and bracket.
10. **On models with cruise control less anti-lock brake system (ABS),** proceed as follows:
    a. Remove cruise control actuator cover, then disconnect vacuum hose from air intake chamber.
    b. Disconnect actuator connector, then cable from actuator.
    c. Remove three actuator attaching bolts and actuator.
11. **On all models,** disconnect electric cooling fan connector, then remove upper radiator support seal.
12. Disconnect coolant reservoir hose, then remaining radiator hoses.
13. **On models with automatic transmission,** disconnect oil cooler hoses from the radiator.
14. **On all models,** remove two radiator upper support retaining bolts.
15. Lift radiator out of engine compartment, then remove radiator reservoir tank.
16. Disconnect wires and connectors from check connector, igniter connector and vacuum sensor connector.
17. Disconnect ground strap from left fender apron.
18. Disconnect engine wire clamp from wire bracket, then remove bracket retaining bolts and bracket.
19. Disconnect noise filter.
20. Disconnect two vacuum hoses from charcoal canister, then remove canister retaining bolts and canister.
21. Disconnect heater hose from water inlet.
22. Disconnect speedometer cable from transaxle.

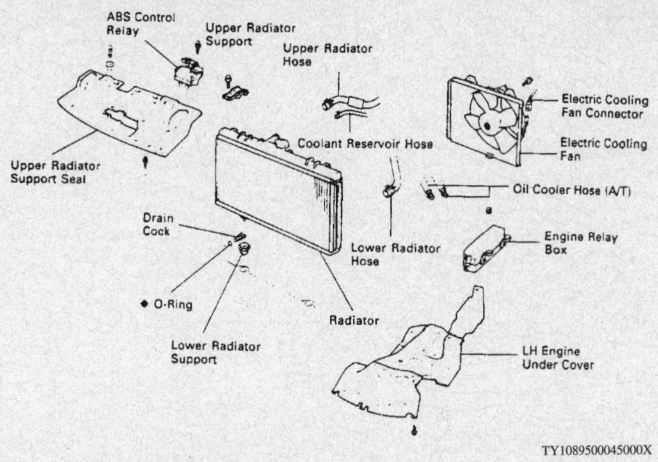
ABS Control Relay
Upper Radiator Support
Upper Radiator Hose
Electric Cooling Fan Connector
Coolant Reservoir Hose
Electric Cooling Fan
Upper Radiator Support Seal
Oil Cooler Hose (A/T)
Drain Cock
Engine Relay Box
Lower Radiator Hose
◆ O-Ring
Radiator
Lower Radiator Support
LH Engine Under Cover
TY1089500045000X

Fig. 1 Radiator replacement. 4A-FE engine

23. Disconnect fuel hoses, catching any leaking fluid in a container.
24. Remove three clutch release cylinder retaining bolts, then the clutch release cylinder from the transaxle.
25. Disconnect transaxle control cables from transaxle.
26. Disconnect the following vacuum hoses:
    a. Vacuum sensor hose from gas filter on air intake chamber.
    b. Brake booster hose from air intake chamber.
    c. Three A/C hoses from air switching valve (ASV) on air intake chamber.
    d. A/C hose from air pipe.
27. Remove engine wire clamp from wire bracket on right fender apron, then disconnect two cowl wire connectors.
28. Disconnect electrical connectors.
29. Remove two engine wire to cowl panel attaching nuts, then pull wire from panel.
30. Raise and support vehicle.
31. Remove lower crossmember attaching bolts and nuts, then the crossmember.
32. Remove front exhaust pipe as follows:
    a. Disconnect oxygen sensor connector.
    b. Loosen bolt, then disconnect clamp from support bracket.
    c. Remove front exhaust pipe-to-catalytic converter attaching bolts and nuts.
    d. Disconnect support hook on front exhaust pipe from support bracket, then remove front exhaust pipe and gaskets.
33. **On models with automatic transmission,** disconnect transaxle control cable from engine mounting center member.
34. **On all models,** remove front driveshafts as follows:
    a. Remove tire and wheel assemblies.
    b. Remove cotter pin and locknut cap.
    c. Remove bearing locknut while depressing brake pedal.
    d. Drain oil from transaxle.
    e. Remove brake caliper from steering knuckle and suspend it with wire.
    f. Scribe reference marks on hub and rotor disc, then remove rotor disc.
    g. Remove cotter pin and tie rod end nut from steering knuckle, then using tie rod end removal tool No. 09628-62011, or equivalent, separate tie rod end from steering knuckle.
    h. Remove bolt and two nuts attaching lower arm to steering knuckle, then disconnect lower arm from steering knuckle.
    i. Using puller tool No. 09950-20017, or equivalent, disconnect left side driveshaft from steering knuckle. **Cover driveshaft boot shaft with cloth to prevent damage.**
    j. Using a hammer and hub nut wrench, remove left side driveshaft from transaxle. **Ensure care is taken to not damage dust cover. Cover hub nut wrench with cloth to prevent damage to transaxle body.**
    k. Use a hammer and brass bar to tap out right side driveshaft.
35. Disconnect heater hose from water inlet pipe.
36. **On models equipped with A/C,** proceed as follows:
    a. Disconnect A/C compressor connector, then remove drive belt.
    b. Remove four A/C compressor retaining bolts, pull compressor away from mounting.
    c. Using wire, suspend compressor from radiator support.
37. **On all models,** remove power steering pump drive belt.
38. Remove two power steering pump attaching bolts, then use a wire to suspend pump from cowl.
39. Remove eight engine mounting center member attaching bolts, then the center member.
40. Remove front engine mounting through bolt and mounting insulator.
41. Remove two mounting bracket attaching bolts and bracket.
42. Remove rear engine mounting through bolt and mounting insulator.
43. Remove three mounting bracket attaching bolts and bracket.
44. Remove connector from ground wire on righthand fender apron.
45. Remove three right side engine mounting stay attaching bolts and mounting stay.
46. Remove two left side engine mounting stay attaching bolts and mounting stay.
47. Remove ground strap from transaxle.
48. Attach an engine chain hoist, or equivalent, to engine hangers.
49. Remove through bolt and three lefthand mounting insulator attaching bolts, then the insulator.
50. Remove three lefthand mounting bracket attaching bolts.
51. Remove through bolt and two righthand mounting insulator attaching bolts, then the insulator.
52. Lift engine slowly and carefully out of vehicle. **Ensure to not hit power steering gear housing or neutral start switch.**
53. Reverse procedure to install. Reset audio coded anti-theft, if equipped, as outlined in "Precautions."

RADIATOR

REPLACE

4A-FE ENGINE

1. Disconnect battery ground cable.
2. Remove lefthand engine under cover, **Fig. 1.**
3. Drain coolant.
4. **On models with ABS,** disconnect ABS control relay from radiator.
5. **On all models,** disconnect engine relay box from battery
6. Remove upper radiator support seal.
7. Disconnect electric cooling fan connector.
8. Disconnect coolant reservoir hose.
9. Disconnect radiator hoses.
10. **On models with automatic transmission,** disconnect transmission oil cooler hoses.
11. **On all models,** remove radiator and electric cooling fan.
12. Reverse procedure to install.

7A-FE ENGINE

1. Disconnect battery ground cable.
2. Drain coolant.
3. Disconnect radiator hoses, **Fig. 2.**
4. Disconnect coolant reservoir hose.
5. Disconnect No. 1 cooling fan connector.
6. **On models with A/C,** disconnect No. 2 cooling fan connector.
7. **On models with automatic transmission,** disconnect transmission oil cooler hoses.
8. **On all models,** remove upper radiator support seal.
9. Reverse procedure to install.

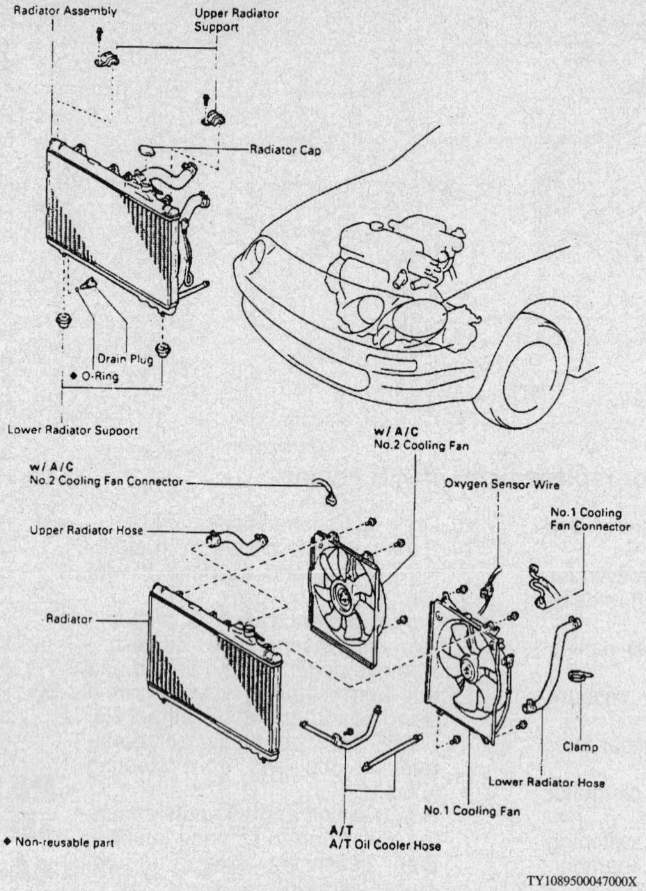
Radiator Assembly
Upper Radiator Support
Radiator Cap
Drain Plug
◆ O-Ring
Lower Radiator Support
w/ A/C
No.2 Cooling Fan
w/ A/C
No.2 Cooling Fan Connector
Oxygen Sensor Wire
No.1 Cooling Fan Connector
Upper Radiator Hose
Radiator
Clamp
Lower Radiator Hose
No.1 Cooling Fan
A/T
A/T Oil Cooler Hose
◆ Non-reusable part
TY1089500047000X

Fig. 2 Radiator replace. 7A-FE engine

TIGHTENING SPECIFICATIONS

Year	Component	Torque/Ft. Lbs.
1993–96	A/C Compressor To A/C Compressor Bracket	18
	Bearing Cap Bolts	①
	Camshaft Timing Pulley	43
	Center & Rear Mount To Member	38
	Connecting Rod Cap	22④
	Crankshaft Bearing Cap	44
	Crankshaft Pulley	87
	Cylinder Head	①
	Driveplate (A/T)	47
	Engine Coolant Drain Plug	25
	Engine Mount Member	45
	Exhaust Manifold To Cylinder Head	25
	Exhaust Pipe-To-Manifold	46
	Flywheel (M/T)	58
	Front Mount to Member	35
	Fuel Evaporation Vent Tube	16②
	Fuel Inlet Hose To Fuel Filter	22
	Fuel Inlet Pipe To Tank	30②
	Fuel Pump To Tank	30②
	Fuel Sender Gauge	30②
	Fuel Tank Drain Plug	9

Continued

TIGHTENING SPECIFICATIONS—Continued

Year	Component	Torque/Ft. Lbs.
1993–96	Fuel Tank Straps	29
	Idler Pulley	27
	Insulator To Body Bracket Through Bolt	64
	Insulator To Engine Mount Bracket (Bolt)	29
	Insulator To Engine Mount Bracket (Nut)	38
	Intake Manifold To Cylinder Head	29
	LH Mounting Insulator To Bracket (Bolt)	47
	LH Mounting Insulator To Bracket (Nut)	38
	LH Mount Insulutor To Transaxle Case	35
	LH Mount Stay	15
	LH Mount Through Bolt	64
	Oil Cooler Pipe	25
	Oil Dipstick Guide	82②
	Oil Pan	43②
	Oil Pump	16③
	Oil Strainer	82②
	Power Steering Pump Bracket	29
	Radiator Support	9
	RH Mounting Insulator To Bracket Bolt	47
	RH Mounting Insulator To Bracket Nut	38
	RH Mount Stay	31
	RH Mount Through Bolt	64
	Spark Plug	13
	Thermostat Water Inlet	82②
	Water Pump	11

①— Refer to “Cylinder Head, Replace” in Toyota Corolla “Engine” section, for tightening procedure.
②— Inch lbs.
③— 4A-FE, 43 inch lbs.; 7A-FE, 12 ft. lbs.
④— Plus an additional 90°.

5S-FE 2.2L Engine

NOTE: On Air Bag Equipped Models, Refer To "Air Bag System Precautions" Located In The Front Of This Manual For System Disarming & Arming Procedures.

INDEX

	Page No.
Belt Tension Data	43-29
Camshaft, Replace	43-29
Compression Pressure	43-22
Cooling System Bleed	43-29
Cylinder Head, Replace	43-23
Engine Rebuilding Specifications	48-1
Engine, Replace	43-22
Exhaust Manifold, Replace	43-23
Fuel Filter, Replace	43-31
Fuel Pump, Replace	43-31
Hydraulic Lifters, Replace	43-27
Intake Manifold, Replace	43-23
Main & Rod Bearings	43-29
Oil Pan, Replace	43-29
Oil Pump, Replace	43-29
Oil Pump Service	43-29
Piston & Rod Assembly	43-29
Precautions	43-22
Air Bag Systems	43-22
Audio Coded Anti-Theft System	43-22
Radiator, Replace	43-31
Thermostat, Replace	43-29
Tightening Specifications	43-31
Timing Belt, Replace	43-28
Installation	43-28
Removal	43-28
Valve Adjustment	43-27
Valve Clearance Specifications	43-27
Valve Guides	43-27
Water Pump, Replace	43-30

PRECAUTIONS

AIR BAG SYSTEMS

Refer to "Air Bag System Precautions" in the front of this manual for system disarming and arming procedures.

AUDIO CODED ANTI-THEFT SYSTEM

Some models are equipped with an audio coded anti-theft system that will disable the radio when the battery cable is disconnected. The system can be identified by the "ANTI-THEFT SYSTEM" on the cassette tape lid. Obtain 3 digit customer code for input. Reset system after service as follows:

1. Obtain 3 digit audio anti-theft code.
2. Depress 1 (PROG) while depressing righthand side of TUNE SEEK button, - - - will appear in tape operation display.
3. To enter the first digit, depress 1 (PROG) button repeatedly until the number of times depressed equals the first digit beginning with zero (depress the 1 button six times if the first digit if five).
4. To enter second digit, depress 2 (APS) button repeatedly until the number of times depressed equals the second digit beginning with zero.
5. To enter third digit, depress 3 (RPT) button repeatedly until the number of times depressed equals the second digit beginning with zero.
6. If - - - is displayed during code input, repeat procedure.
7. When code appears in display, depress and hold SCAN button until SEC appears.
8. When SEC disappears audio system should be operative.
9. If Err is displayed, repeat procedure. **Attempting to input code more than nine times may permanently disable audio system.**

COMPRESSION PRESSURE

1. Start engine and warm to normal operating temperature.
2. Disconnect distributor connectors.
3. Remove spark plugs.
4. Insert compression pressure gauge into spark plug hole.
5. Fully open throttle.
6. Measure compression pressure while cranking engine.
7. Standard compression pressure is 178 psi or more. Minimum pressure should be 142 psi.
8. Compression pressure difference between cylinders should not exceed 14 psi.

ENGINE

REPLACE

1. Obtain audio anti-theft code, if equipped, as outlined in "Precautions."
2. Remove hood and engine undercover.
3. Drain engine coolant, then engine oil.
4. Remove air cleaner assembly as follows:
   a. Disconnect intake air temperature sensor electrical connector.
   b. Disconnect accelerator cable from bracket on air cleaner cap.
   c. Disconnect four air cleaner cap clips, then air hose from air pipe.
   d. Disconnect air cleaner hose from throttle body, then remove air cleaner cap and element.
   e. Remove three air cleaner case retaining bolts, then the case.
5. Disconnect accelerator cable from throttle body.
6. Remove two engine relay box retaining nuts and disconnect relay box from battery.
7. Remove lower cover from relay box, then disconnect fusible link cassette and two connectors of engine wire from relay box.
8. Remove A/C relay box from bracket, then the battery.
9. **On models with cruise control and anti-lock brake system (ABS),** disconnect cruise control actuator electrical connector, remove four actuator attaching bolts, actuator and bracket.
10. **On models with cruise control less anti-lock brake system (ABS),** proceed as follows:
    a. Remove cruise control actuator cover, then disconnect vacuum hose from air intake chamber.
    b. Disconnect actuator connector, then cable from actuator.
    c. Remove three actuator attaching bolts and actuator.
11. **On all models,** disconnect electric cooling fan connector, then remove upper radiator support seal.
12. Disconnect coolant reservoir hose, then remaining radiator hoses.
13. **On models with automatic transmission,** disconnect oil cooler hoses from the radiator.
14. **On all models,** remove two radiator upper support retaining bolts.
15. Lift radiator out of engine compartment, then remove radiator reservoir tank.
16. Remove two wiper arms, then outside lower windshield molding.
17. Remove two bolts and four nuts that attach upper suspension mounting brace to cowl and strut towers.
18. Remove upper suspension mounting brace.
19. Disconnect ignition coil connector and high-tension cord.
20. Remove two ignition coil attaching bolts and ignition coil.
21. Disconnect wires and connectors from check connector, igniter connector and vacuum sensor connector.
22. Disconnect ground strap from left fender apron.

23. Disconnect engine wire clamp from wire bracket, then remove bracket retaining bolts and bracket.
24. Disconnect noise filter.
25. Disconnect two vacuum hoses from charcoal canister, then remove canister retaining bolts and canister.
26. Disconnect heater hose from water inlet.
27. Disconnect speedometer cable from transaxle.
28. Disconnect fuel hoses, catching any leaking fluid in a container.
29. Remove three clutch release cylinder retaining bolts, then the clutch release cylinder from the transaxle.
30. Disconnect transaxle control cables from transaxle.
31. Disconnect the following vacuum hoses:
    a. Vacuum sensor hose from gas filter on air intake chamber.
    b. Brake booster hose from air intake chamber.
    c. Three A/C hoses from air switching valve (ASV) on air intake chamber.
    d. A/C hose from air pipe.
32. Remove engine wire clamp from wire bracket on right fender apron, then disconnect two cowl wire connectors.
33. Disconnect ECU, A/C amplifier, cowl wire and O/D diode electrical connectors.
34. Remove two engine wire to cowl panel attaching nuts, then pull wire from panel.
35. Raise and support vehicle.
36. Remove lower crossmember attaching bolts and nuts, then the crossmember.
37. Remove front exhaust pipe as follows:
    a. Disconnect oxygen sensor connector.
    b. Loosen bolt, then disconnect clamp from support bracket.
    c. Remove front exhaust pipe-to-catalytic converter attaching bolts and nuts.
    d. Disconnect support hook on front exhaust pipe from support bracket, then remove front exhaust pipe and gaskets.
38. **On models with automatic transmission,** disconnect transaxle control cable from engine mounting center member.
39. **On all models,** remove front driveshafts as follows:
    a. Remove tire and wheel assemblies.
    b. Remove cotter pin and locknut cap.
    c. Remove bearing locknut while depressing brake pedal.
    d. Drain oil from transaxle.
    e. Remove brake caliper from steering knuckle and suspend it with wire.
    f. Scribe reference marks on hub and rotor disc, then remove rotor disc.
    g. Remove cotter pin and tie rod end nut from steering knuckle, then using tie rod end removal tool No. 09628-62011, or equivalent, separate tie rod end from steering knuckle.
    h. Remove bolt and two nuts attaching lower arm to steering knuckle, then disconnect lower arm from steering knuckle.

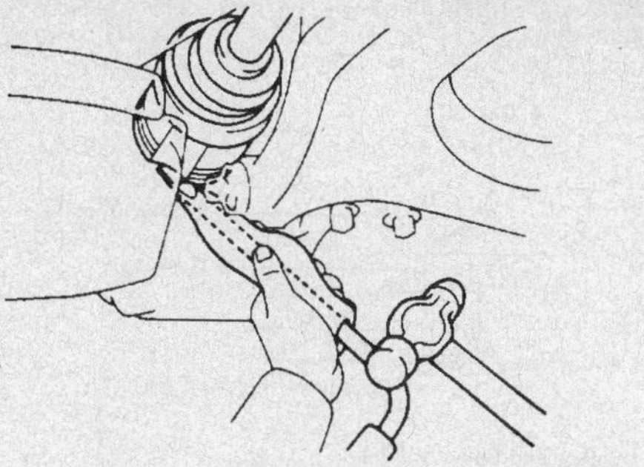
TY1069100012000X

Fig. 1 Left side driveshaft removal

    i. Using puller tool No. 09950-20017, or equivalent, disconnect left side driveshaft from steering knuckle. **Cover driveshaft boot shaft with cloth to prevent it from damage.**
    j. Using a hammer and hub nut wrench or an equivalent, remove left side driveshaft from transaxle, **Fig. 1. Ensure care is taken not to damage dust cover. Cover hub nut wrench with cloth so transaxle body is not damaged.**
    k. Remove two bolts of center bearing bracket and pull out right side driveshaft together with center bearing case and center driveshaft.
40. Disconnect heater hose from water inlet pipe.
41. **On models equipped with A/C,** proceed as follows:
    a. Disconnect A/C compressor connector, then remove drive belt.
    b. Remove four A/C compressor retaining bolts, pull compressor away from mounting.
    c. Using wire, suspend compressor from radiator support.
42. **On all models,** remove power steering pump drive belt.
43. Remove two power steering pump attaching bolts, then use a wire to suspend pump to cowl.
44. Remove eight engine mounting center member attaching bolts, then the center member.
45. Remove front engine mounting through bolt and mounting insulator.
46. Remove two mounting bracket attaching bolts and bracket.
47. Remove rear engine mounting through bolt and mounting insulator.
48. Remove three mounting bracket attaching bolts and bracket.
49. Remove connector from ground wire on righthand fender apron.
50. Remove three right side engine mounting stay attaching bolts and mounting stay.
51. Remove two left side engine mounting stay attaching bolts and mounting stay.
52. Remove ground strap from transaxle.
53. Attach an engine chain hoist, or equivalent, to engine hangers.
54. Remove through bolt and three lefthand mounting insulator attaching bolts, then the insulator.
55. Remove three lefthand mounting bracket attaching bolts.
56. Remove through bolt and two righthand mounting insulator attaching bolts, then the insulator.
57. Lift engine slowly and carefully out of vehicle. **Be careful not to hit power steering gear housing or neutral start switch.**
58. Reverse procedure to install. Reset audio coded anti-theft, if equipped, as outlined in "Precautions."

INTAKE MANIFOLD

REPLACE

Refer to "Cylinder Head, Replace," for intake manifold replacement procedure.

EXHAUST MANIFOLD

REPLACE

Refer to "Cylinder Head, Replace," for exhaust manifold replacement.

CYLINDER HEAD

REPLACE

1. Obtain audio anti-theft code, if equipped, then disable air bag system, then drain engine coolant.
2. **On models with automatic transaxle,** disconnect throttle cable from throttle body.
3. **On all models,** disconnect accelerator cable from throttle body.
4. **On models with cruise control and anti-lock brake system (ABS),** disconnect cruise control actuator electrical connector, remove four actuator attaching bolts, actuator and bracket.
5. **On models with cruise control less anti-lock brake system (ABS),** proceed as follows:
    a. Remove cruise control actuator cover, then disconnect vacuum hose from air intake chamber.
    b. Disconnect actuator connector, then cable from actuator.
    c. Remove three actuator attaching bolts and actuator.
6. **On all models,** remove air cleaner assembly as follows:
    a. Disconnect intake air temperature sensor electrical connector.
    b. Disconnect accelerator cable from bracket on air cleaner cap.
    c. Disconnect four air cleaner cap clips, then air hose from air pipe.
    d. Disconnect air cleaner hose from throttle body, then remove air cleaner cap and element.
    e. Remove three air cleaner case retaining bolts, then the case.
7. Remove alternator, then A/C compressor without disconnecting A/C lines.
8. Disconnect distributor electrical connector, then using a screwdriver separate high tension cord from ignition coil.
9. Disconnect spark plug wires from spark plugs, then remove distributor.
10. Remove engine undercovers.
11. Raise and support vehicle.

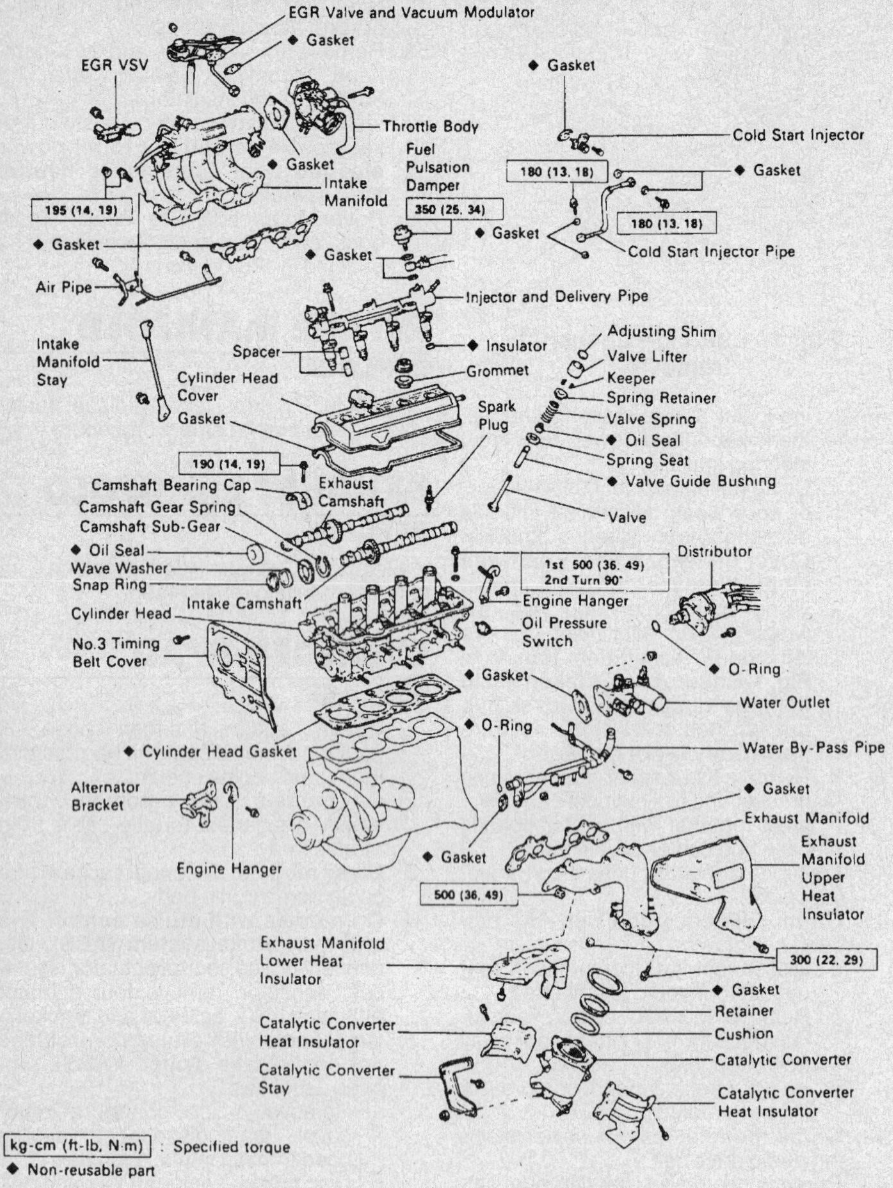
EGR Valve and Vacuum Modulator
◆ Gasket
EGR VSV
◆ Gasket
Throttle Body
Cold Start Injector
◆ Gasket
Fuel Pulsation Damper
Intake Manifold
180 (13, 18)
◆ Gasket
195 (14, 19)
350 (25, 34)
180 (13, 18)
◆ Gasket
◆ Gasket
◆ Gasket
Cold Start Injector Pipe
Air Pipe
Injector and Delivery Pipe
Adjusting Shim
Intake Manifold Stay
Spacer
◆ Insulator
Valve Lifter
Cylinder Head Cover
Grommet
Keeper
Spring Retainer
Gasket
Spark Plug
Valve Spring
◆ Oil Seal
190 (14, 19)
Spring Seat
Camshaft Bearing Cap
Exhaust Camshaft
◆ Valve Guide Bushing
Camshaft Gear Spring
Camshaft Sub-Gear
Valve
◆ Oil Seal
Distributor
Wave Washer
1st 500 (36, 49)
2nd Turn 90°
Snap Ring
Intake Camshaft
Engine Hanger
Cylinder Head
Oil Pressure Switch
No.3 Timing Belt Cover
◆ O-Ring
◆ Gasket
Water Outlet
◆ O-Ring
◆ Cylinder Head Gasket
Water By-Pass Pipe
Alternator Bracket
◆ Gasket
Exhaust Manifold
Engine Hanger
◆ Gasket
Exhaust Manifold Upper Heat Insulator
500 (36, 49)
Exhaust Manifold Lower Heat Insulator
300 (22, 29)
◆ Gasket
Retainer
Catalytic Converter Heat Insulator
Cushion
Catalytic Converter
Catalytic Converter Stay
Catalytic Converter Heat Insulator
kg-cm (ft-lb, N·m) : Specified torque
◆ Non-reusable part
TY1069100013000X

Fig. 2 Cylinder head components

12. Remove lower crossmember attaching bolts and nuts, then the crossmember.
13. Remove front exhaust pipe as follows:
    a. Disconnect oxygen sensor connector.
    b. Loosen bolt, then disconnect clamp from support bracket.
    c. Remove front exhaust pipe-to-catalytic converter attaching bolts and nuts.
    d. Disconnect support hook on front exhaust pipe from support bracket, then remove front exhaust pipe and gaskets.
14. **On California models,** disconnect sub-oxygen sensor connector.
15. **On all models,** disconnect main oxygen sensor connector and lower vehicle.
16. Remove six manifold upper heat insulator attaching bolts and insulator.
17. Remove two bolts and nuts from catalytic converter stay.
18. Remove six exhaust manifold retaining nuts, then exhaust manifold and catalytic converter assembly.
19. Separate exhaust manifold and catalytic converter assembly as shown in **Fig. 2.**
20. Disconnect water temperature sender gauge connector, water temperature sensor connector and cold start injector time switch connector.
21. Disconnect cooling system hoses and vacuum hoses shown in **Fig. 3.**
22. Remove two water outlet attaching bolts, water outlet and gasket.
23. Remove two water bypass pipe attaching bolts and nuts, water bypass pipe and gasket.
24. Remove O-ring from water bypass hose.
25. Disconnect throttle position sensor electrical connector and idle speed control valve connector.

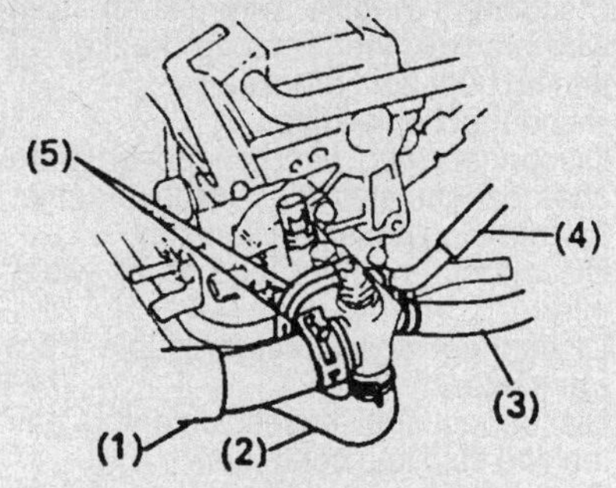
(5)
(4)
(3)
(1)
(2)

(1) Upper radiator hose
(2) Water by-pass pipe hose
(3) Heater water hose
(4) ISC water by-pass hose
(5) Two EVAP BVSV vacuum hoses

TY1069100014000X

Fig. 3 Cooling system & vacuum hoses

26. Disconnect PCV hose, vacuum modulator vacuum hoses and vacuum switching valve vacuum hoses from throttle body.
27. Remove four throttle body attaching bolts, throttle body and gasket.
28. Remove two cold start injector pipe union bolts, four injector gaskets and injector pipe. **When removing union bolts, place a shop towel under injector pipe and slowly loosen union bolt.**
29. Remove two cold start injector bolts, cold start injector and gasket.
30. **On California models,** disconnect EGR gas temperature sensor connector.
31. **On all models,** remove vacuum hoses from EGR vacuum switching valve and vacuum hose from charcoal canister.
32. Loosen union nut from EGR pipe, then two EGR attaching bolts, EGR valve, vacuum modulator, vacuum hoses assembly and gasket.
33. Disconnect vacuum sensor hose and brake booster hoses from air intake chamber.
34. Disconnect two A/C vacuum hoses from air switching valve on air intake chamber.
35. Disconnect air hose from intake manifold, air hose from A/C air switching valve and two air hoses from power steering pump.
36. Disconnect engine wire clamp, then remove two bolts wire bracket and air tube.
37. Disconnect engine wire ground strap from intake manifold, then remove EGR vacuum switching valve.
38. Disconnect two wire clamps from wire brackets on top of intake manifold.
39. Disconnect wire clip from accelerator bracket, then remove two intake manifold stay attaching bolts and stay.
40. Loosen pulsation damper and two bolts holding delivery pipe to cylinder head.
41. Remove pulsation damper and disconnect fuel inlet hose from delivery pipe.

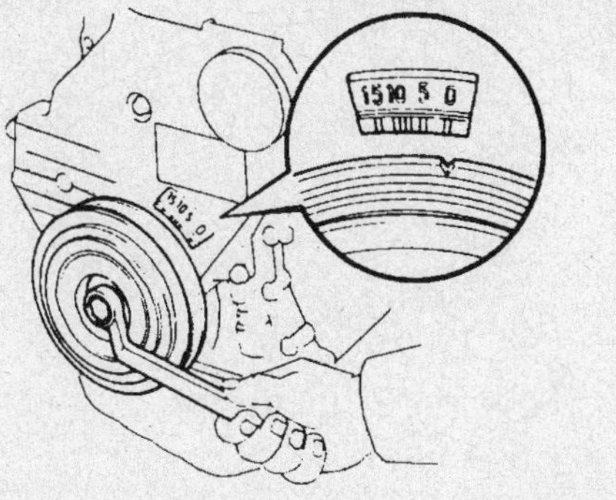

TY1069100015000X

Fig. 4 Crankshaft pulley & timing mark alignment

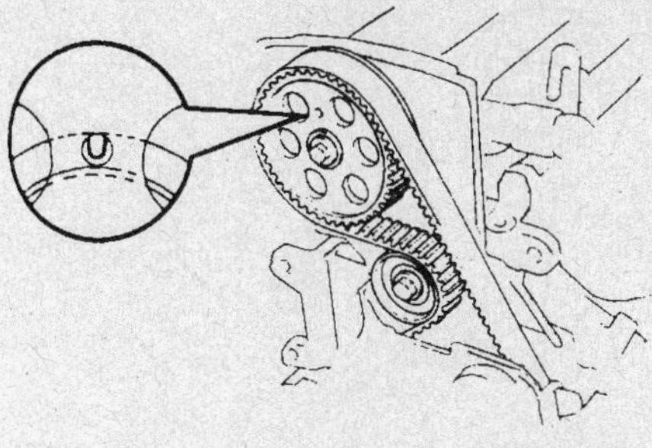

TY1069100016000X

Fig. 5 Bearing cap mark alignment

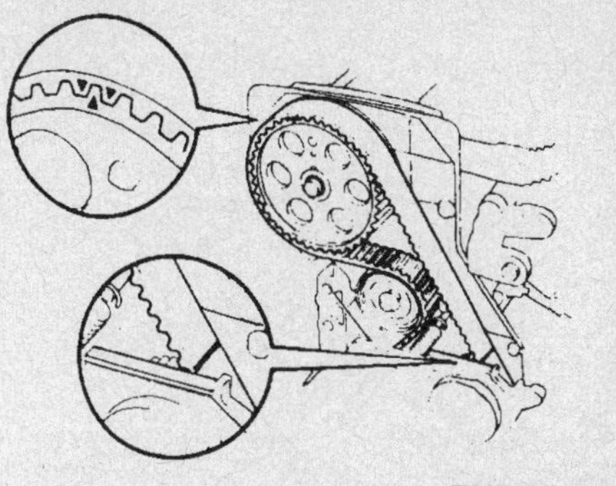

TY1069100017000X

Fig. 6 Timing belt & camshaft pulley matchmarks

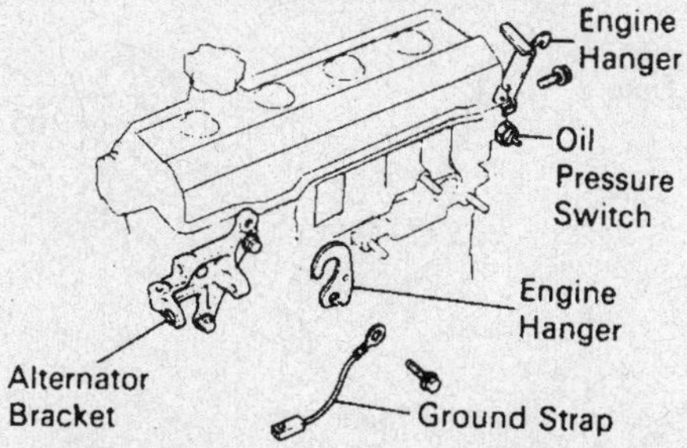
Engine Hanger
Oil Pressure Switch
Engine Hanger
Alternator Bracket
Ground Strap

TY1069100018000X

Fig. 7 Engine hanger removal & disconnecting ground strap

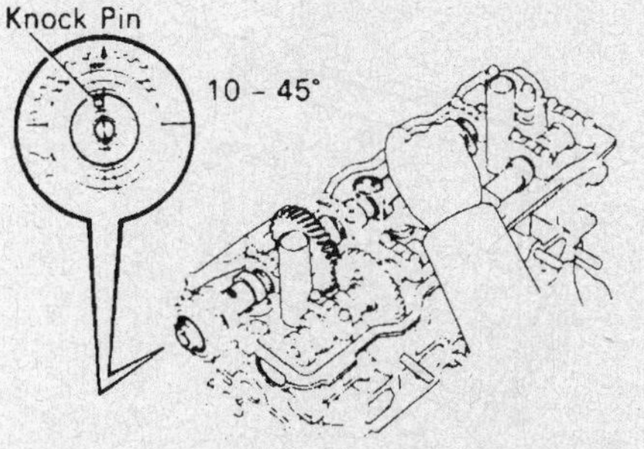
Knock Pin
10 - 45°

TY1069100019000X

Fig. 8 Setting knock pin of intake camshaft to 10–45° BTDC

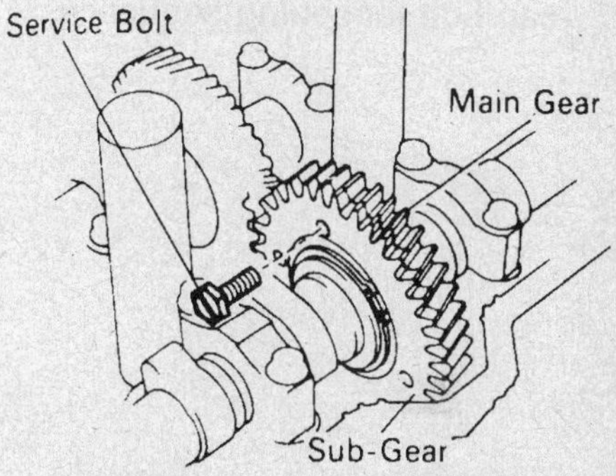
Service Bolt
Main Gear
Sub-Gear

TY1069100020000X

Fig. 9 Securing camshaft sub-gear to drive gear

42. Remove two bolts and delivery pipe together with four injectors. **Be careful not to drop injectors, when removing delivery pipe.**
43. Remove right front wheel assembly, then the power steering drive belt.
44. Slightly raise engine assembly enough to remove weight from right side engine mounting assembly.
45. Disconnect connector from ground wire on right side fender apron.
46. Remove righthand engine mounting stay and disconnect power steering reservoir tank from bracket.
47. Remove right side engine mounting insulator through bolt, two nuts and insulator.
48. Lower engine, then remove three right side engine mounting bracket attaching bolts and bracket.
49. Remove spark plugs.
50. Disconnect engine wire from alternator bracket and adjusting bar.
51. Remove five timing belt cover attaching bolts, cover and two gaskets.
52. Turn crankshaft pulley and align its groove with timing mark "0" of the No. 1 timing belt cover, **Fig. 4.**
53. Check that hole of camshaft timing pulley is aligned with timing mark of bearing cap, **Fig. 5.**If not turn crankshaft 360°.
54. Scribe matchmarks on timing belt and camshaft timing pulley to match end of No. 1 timing belt cover as shown in **Fig. 6.**
55. Remove timing belt from camshaft pulley.
56. Using torque wrench adapter tool No. 09249-63010 and driveshaft holding tool No. 09278-54012, or equivalents, remove camshaft pulley bolt, plate washer and pulley.
57. Remove No. 1 idler pulley and tension spring.
58. Remove four No. 3 timing belt cover attaching bolts and cover. **Support timing belt, so meshing of crankshaft timing pulley and timing belt does not shift. Be careful not to drop anything inside timing belt cover. Do not let belt come in contact with oil, water or dust.**
59. Remove engine hangers attaching bolts, engine hangers and ground strap, **Fig. 7.**
60. Remove three alternator bracket attaching bolts, bracket and oil pressure switch.
61. Remove cylinder head cover attaching nuts, grommets, cover and gasket. **Arrange grommets in correct order, so that they can be installed in their original position. This eliminates any possibility of oil leakage when original gaskets are used.**
62. **Before removing camshafts note that thrust clearance of the camshaft is small and camshaft must be kept level while it is being removed. If camshaft is not kept level, the portion of the cylinder head receiving the shaft thrust may crack or be damaged, causing camshaft to seize or break.**
63. Remove exhaust camshaft as follows:
    a. Set knock pin of intake camshaft at 10–45° BTDC of camshaft angle, **Fig. 8.** This angle allows No. 2 and No. 4 cylinder lobes of the exhaust camshaft to push their valve lifters evenly.
    b. Using a 6mm bolt, secure camshaft sub-gear to drive gear as shown in **Fig. 9.** This will remove torsional spring force of sub-gear.
    c. Remove two rear bearing cap retaining bolts and bearing cap.
    d. Uniformly loosen and remove six bolts on No. 1, No. 2 and No. 4 bearing caps with several passes and in sequence shown in **Fig. 10. Do not remove No. 3 bearing cap bolts at this time.**
    e. Remove No. 1, No. 2 and No. 4 bearing caps.
    f. Alternately loosen and remove No. 3 bearing cap retaining bolts. When removing No. 3 bearing cap bolts, ensure camshaft is being lifted out straight and level. If camshaft is not lifted out straight and level, retighten No. 3 bearing cap bolts. Then reverse order of above steps from step (e) to step (a) and reset knock pin of intake camshaft at 10–45° BTDC, then repeat steps from (b) to (e) once again. **Do not pry on or attempt to force camshaft with a tool or other object.**
    g. Remove No. 3 bearing cap and remove camshaft.
64. Remove intake camshaft as follows:
    a. Set knock pin of intake camshaft at 80–115° BTDC of camshaft angle as shown in **Fig. 11.** This angle allows No. 1 and No. 3 cylinder cam lobes of the intake camshaft to push their lifters evenly.
    b. Remove two front bearing cap and oil seal retaining bolts, then the front bearing cap and oil seal.

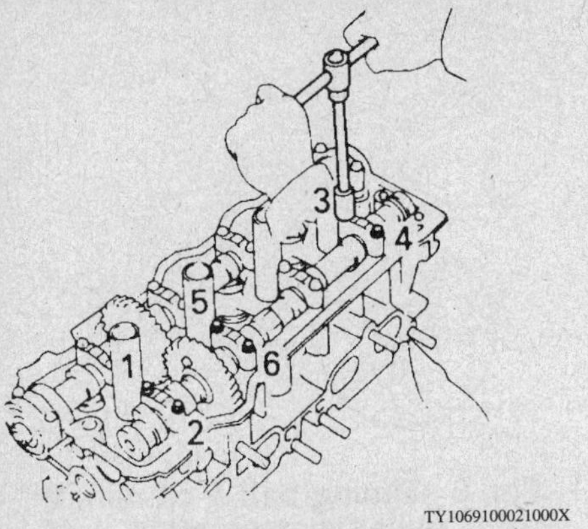
TY1069100021000X

Fig. 10 Exhaust camshaft bearing cap bolt loosening sequence

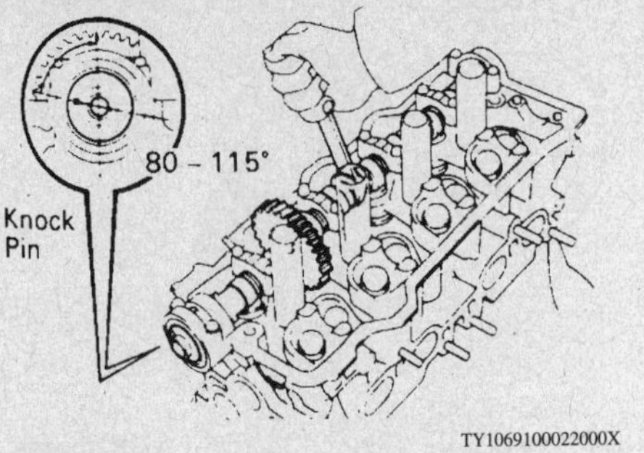
80 – 115°
Knock Pin
TY1069100022000X

Fig. 11 Setting knock pin of intake camshaft to 80–115° BTDC

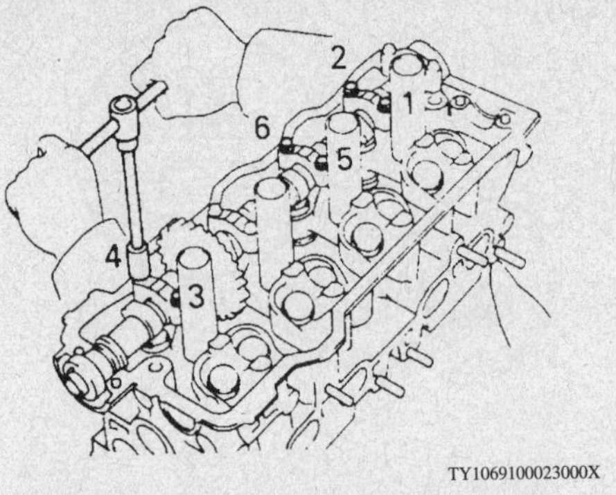
TY1069100023000X

Fig. 12 Intake camshaft bearing cap bolt loosening sequence

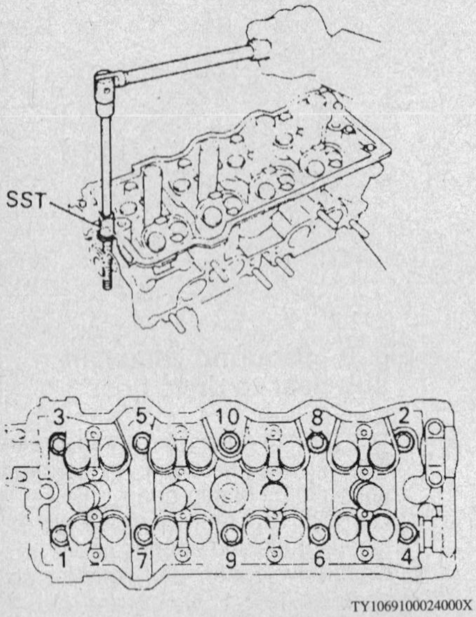
SST
TY1069100024000X

Fig. 13 Cylinder head bolt loosening sequence

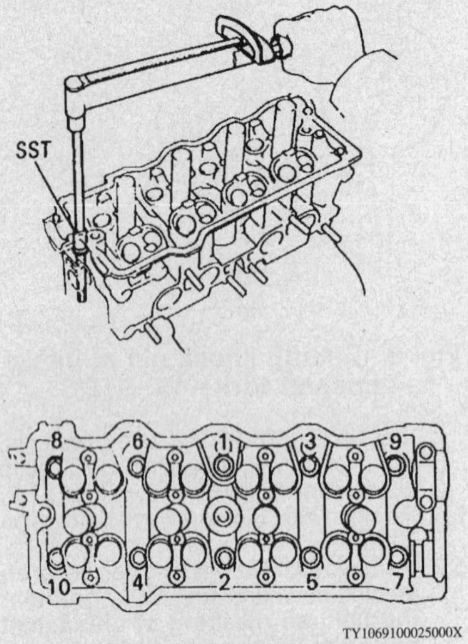
SST
TY1069100025000X

Fig. 14 Cylinder head bolt tightening sequence

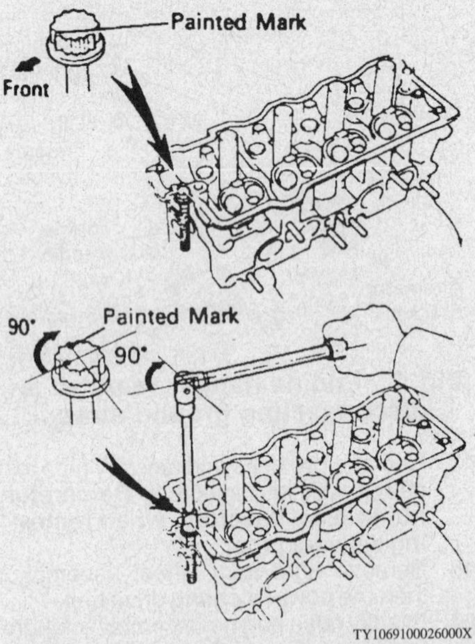
Painted Mark
Front
90°
Painted Mark
90°
TY1069100026000X

Fig. 15 Cylinder head bolt marking

c. Uniformly loosen and remove bolts on No. 1, No. 3 and No. 4 bearing caps in several passes and sequence shown in **Fig. 12.**

d. Alternately loosen and remove No. 2 bearing cap retaining bolts. When removing No. 3 bearing cap bolts, ensure camshaft is being lifted out straight and level. If camshaft is not lifted out straight and level, retighten No. 3 bearing cap bolts. Then reverse order of above steps from step (c) to step (a) and reset knock pin of intake camshaft at 80–115° BTDC, then repeat steps from (b) and (c) once again. **Do not pry on or attempt to force camshaft with a tool or other object.**

e. Remove No. 2 bearing cap and camshaft.

65. Uniformly loosen and remove ten cylinder head retaining bolts in sequence shown in **Fig. 13. Head warpage or cracking could result from removing bolts in the incorrect order.**

66. Lift cylinder head from dowels on the cylinder block.

67. Reverse procedure to install, noting the following:

a. When placing a new gasket in position on cylinder block, ensure direction is correct.

b. Apply a light coat of engine oil to threads of cylinder head bolts. Install and uniformly **torque** cylinder head bolts to 36 ft. lbs. in several passes in sequence shown in **Fig. 14.**

c. Mark cylinder head bolt with paint as shown in **Fig. 15.** Retighten cylinder head bolts an additional 90°. Ensure painted mark is now at a 90° angle to the front.

d. Install spark plug tubes and tighten to specifications.

e. Apply multi-purpose grease to thrust portion of intake camshaft and place camshaft at 80–115° BTDC of camshaft angle on cylinder head.

f. Apply seal packing to No. 1 bearing cap as shown in **Fig. 16,** then install bearing caps in their proper locations. Apply a light coat of engine oil to bearing cap retaining bolts and **torque** to 14 ft. lbs. in several passes in sequence shown in **Fig. 17.**

g. Apply multi-purpose grease to new oil seal lip, then using seal installation tool No. 09223-46011, or equivalent, tap in oil seal.

h. Set knock pin of intake camshaft at 10–45° BTDC of camshaft angle.

i. Apply multi-purpose grease to thrust portion of exhaust camshaft, then engage exhaust camshaft gear to intake camshaft gear by matching timing marks on each gear as shown in **Fig. 18.** Roll down exhaust camshaft onto bearing journals while engaging gears with each other.

j. Turn intake camshaft clockwise or counterclockwise a little at a time until exhaust camshaft sits in bearing journals evenly without rocking camshaft on bearing journals. **It is very important to replace camshaft in bearing journals evenly while tightening bearing caps.**

k. Install bearing caps in their proper position, then apply a light coat of engine oil to bearing cap retaining

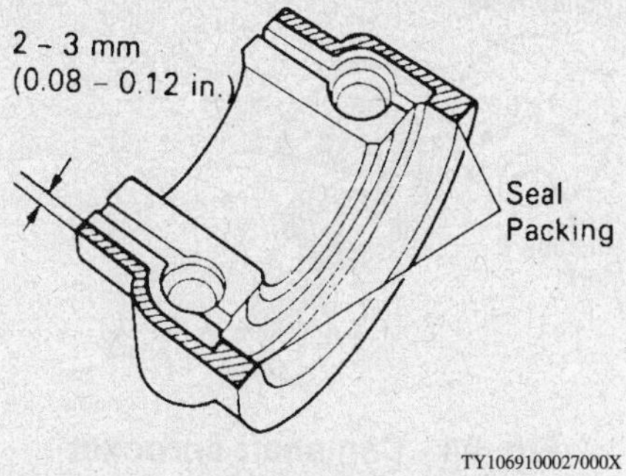
2 - 3 mm
(0.08 - 0.12 in.)
Seal
Packing

TY1069100027000X

Fig. 16 Bearing cap packing

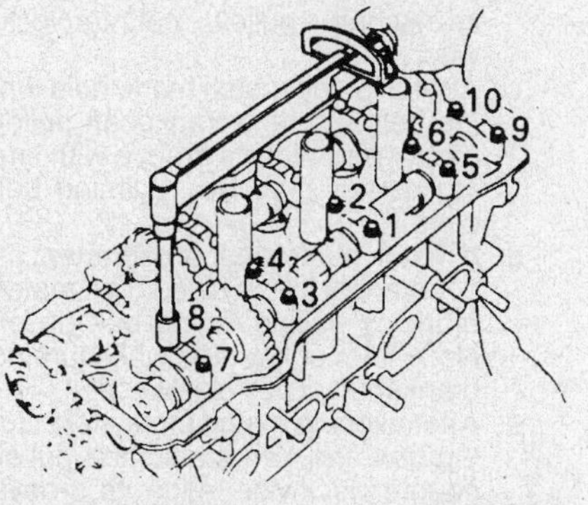

TY1069100030000X

Fig. 19 Exhaust camshaft bearing cap bolt tightening sequence

bolts. Install and uniformly **torque** ten bearing cap bolts to 14 ft. lbs. in several passes, in sequence shown in **Fig. 19.**

l. Remove service bolt holding sub-gear and main gear, then check valve clearance adjust clearance if necessary.
m. Apply seal packing to semi-circular plugs and install them into cylinder head as shown in **Fig. 20.**
n. Reset audio coded anti-theft, if equipped, as outlined in "Precautions."

VALVE CLEARANCE SPECIFICATIONS

Year	Stem-To-Guide Clearance	
	Intake	Exhaust
1993–96	.007–.011	.011–.015

VALVE ADJUSTMENT

On 5S-FE engines, valve adjustment is accomplished by installing the proper thickness shim to achieve proper valve clearance. Shims are available in .0020 inch (.050 mm) increments, **Figs. 21 and 22.**

1. With engine cold, place No. 1 cylinder at TDC of compression stroke by turning the crankshaft pulley and aligning its groove with the timing mark "0" of the timing pointer.
2. Ensure valves on No. 1 cylinder are loose and valve on No. 4 cylinder are tight. If not turn crankshaft 360° (one complete revolution) and align timing marks.
3. With engine in this position check clearance of the following valves:
   a. No. 1 intake and exhaust valves.
   b. No. 2 intake valves.
   c. No. 3 exhaust valves.
4. Turn crankshaft pulley 360° (one complete revolution) and align timing marks as outlined previously and check the following valves:
   a. No. 2 exhaust valves.
   b. No. 3 intake valves.
   c. No. 4 intake and exhaust valves.

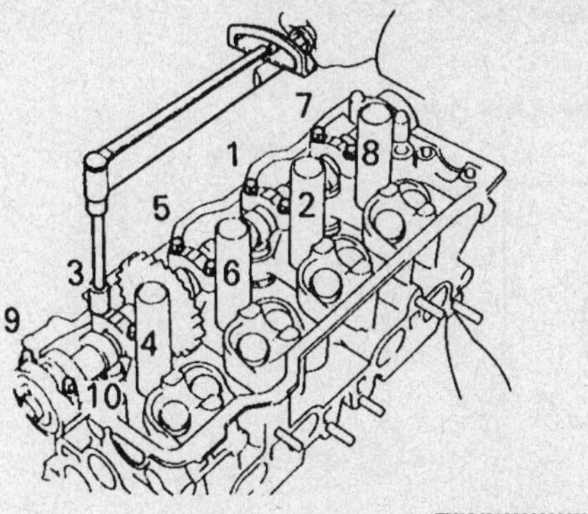

TY1069100028000X

Fig. 17 Intake camshaft bearing cap bolt tightening sequence

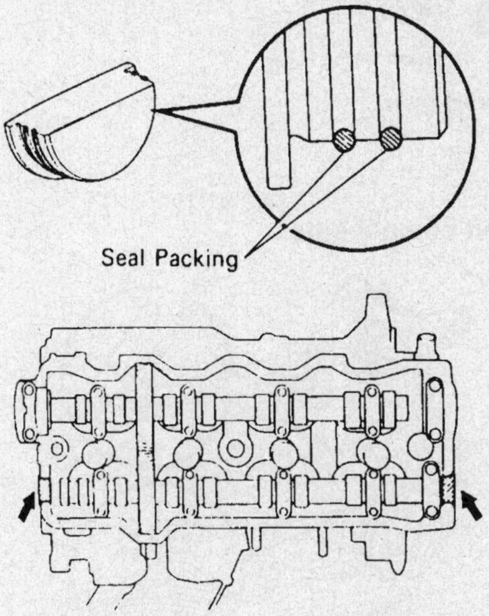
Seal Packing

TY1069100031000X

Fig. 20 Semi-circular plugs to cylinder head installation

New shim thickness mm (in.)

Shim No.	Thickness	Shim No.	Thickness
1	2.500 (0.0984)	10	2.950 (0.1161)
2	2.550 (0.1004)	11	3.000 (0.1181)
3	2.600 (0.1024)	12	3.050 (0.1201)
4	2.650 (0.1043)	13	3.100 (0.1220)
5	2.700 (0.1063)	14	3.150 (0.1240)
6	2.750 (0.1083)	15	3.200 (0.1260)
7	2.800 (0.1102)	16	3.250 (0.1280)
8	2.850 (0.1122)	17	3.300 (0.1299)
9	2.900 (0.1142)		

TY1069100033000X

Fig. 22 Exhaust valve shim size chart

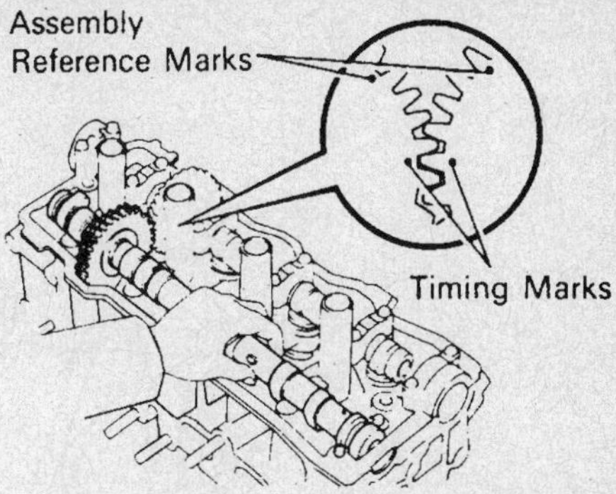
Assembly
Reference Marks
Timing Marks

TY1069100029000X

Fig. 18 Intake & exhaust gear timing mark alignment

New shim thickness mm (in.)

Shim No.	Thickness	Shim No.	Thickness
1	2.500 (0.0984)	10	2.950 (0.1161)
2	2.550 (0.1004)	11	3.000 (0.1181)
3	2.600 (0.1024)	12	3.050 (0.1201)
4	2.650 (0.1043)	13	3.100 (0.1220)
5	2.700 (0.1063)	14	3.150 (0.1240)
6	2.750 (0.1083)	15	3.200 (0.1260)
7	2.800 (0.1102)	16	3.250 (0.1280)
8	2.850 (0.1122)	17	3.300 (0.1299)
9	2.900 (0.1142)		

TY1069100032000X

Fig. 21 Intake valve shim size chart

VALVE GUIDES

1. Using a suitable tool and hammer, strike valve guide bushing to break it off at cylinder head casting.
2. Heat cylinder head to 176–212°F (80–100°C).
3. Using suitable valve guide removal tool, tap out bushing.
4. Install snap ring on new valve guide, then install new valve guide using tool as above and driving in from the reverse side of removal.
5. Ream new valve guide, if necessary. Refer to "Valve Clearance Specifications" for stem clearances.

HYDRAULIC LIFTERS

REPLACE

Check lifters for excessive wear and/or damage. Replace worn or damaged valve lifters as required. Lubricate hydraulic valve lifter before installation.

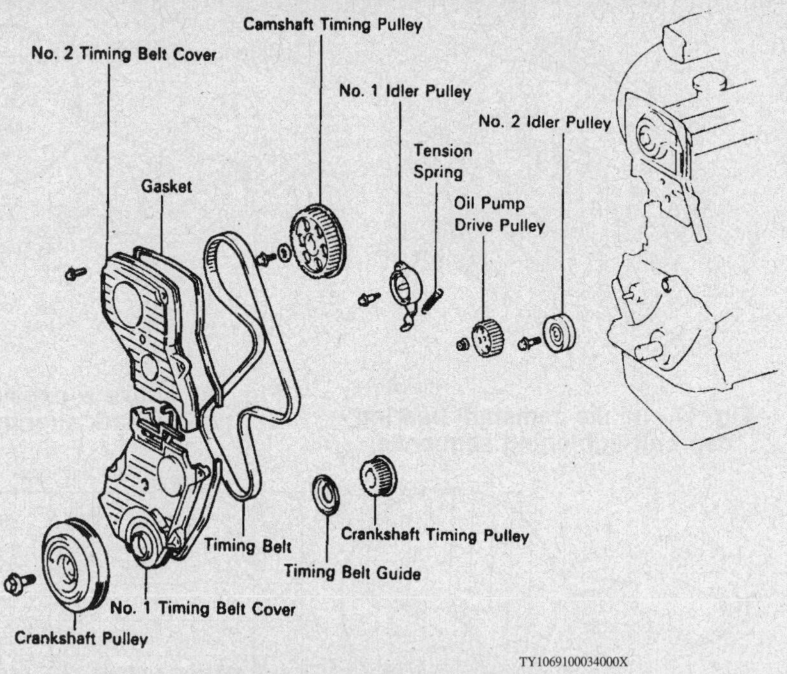
Camshaft Timing Pulley
No. 2 Timing Belt Cover
No. 1 Idler Pulley
No. 2 Idler Pulley
Tension
Spring
Gasket
Oil Pump
Drive Pulley
Crankshaft Timing Pulley
Timing Belt
Timing Belt Guide
No. 1 Timing Belt Cover
Crankshaft Pulley
TY1069100034000X

Fig. 23 Timing belt components

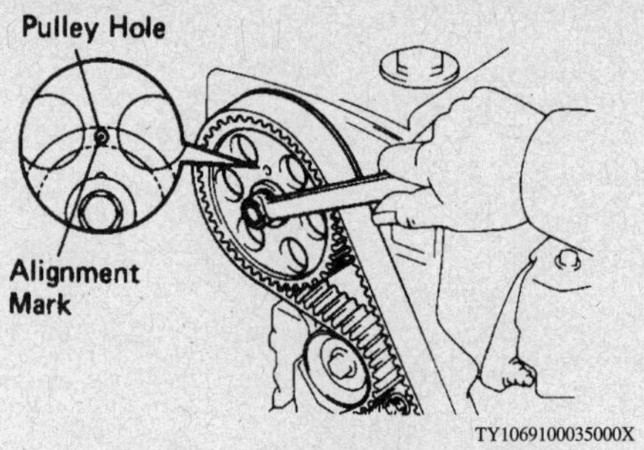
Pulley Hole
Alignment
Mark
TY1069100035000X

Fig. 24 Camshaft sprocket alignment

TIMING BELT

REPLACE

REMOVAL

1. Obtain audio anti-theft code, if equipped, as outlined in "Precautions," then remove right front wheel and engine undercover.
2. Remove cruise control actuator and bracket (if equipped).
3. Remove accessory drive belts, then alternator and alternator bracket.
4. Using suitable jack, raise engine enough to remove weight from right side engine mounting.
5. Disconnect connector from ground wire on right side fender apron.
6. Remove right side engine mounting stay, then disconnect power steering reservoir tank from bracket.
7. Remove right side engine mounting insulator through bolt, two mounting insulator attaching nuts and the insulator.
8. Remove three right side engine mounting bracket attaching bolts and mount, lower jack and perform operation with engine fully down.
9. Remove spark plugs, then disconnect engine wire from alternator bracket and adjusting bar.
10. Remove No. 2 timing belt cover and two gaskets, **Fig. 23.**
11. Rotate crankshaft pulley until pulley groove is aligned with "0" indication on timing marks, then ensure camshaft sprocket hole is aligned bearing cap No. 1 alignment mark, **Fig. 24. If camshaft sprocket is not aligned properly, engine is not set at TDC compression. Rotate crankshaft an additional 360° and recheck.**
12. If timing belt is to be reused, draw arrow on belt to indicate direction of rotation and make reference marks between timing belt and camshaft sprocket.

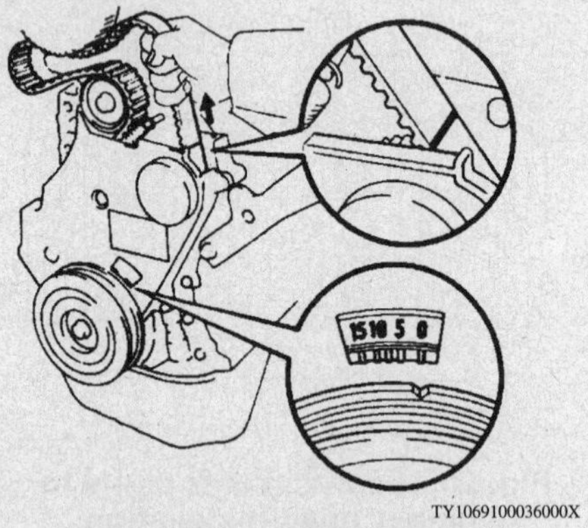
TY1069100036000X

Fig. 25 Timing belt alignment inspection

13. Loosen spring loaded idler pulley attaching bolt, then pry pulley as far to the left as possible. Temporarily tighten attaching bolt.
14. Remove timing belt from camshaft sprocket, then remove camshaft sprocket attaching bolt, washer and sprocket.
15. Remove crankshaft pulley attaching bolt, if timing belt is to be reused, proceed as follows:
    a. After loosening crankshaft pulley bolt, check that timing belt match mark aligns with end of No. 1 timing belt cover when crankshaft pulley groove is aligned with timing mark "0" of No. 1 timing belt cover as shown in **Fig. 25.** If match mark aligns, proceed to step 16. If match mark does not align, proceed to step b.
    b. If match mark is out of alignment on clockwise side, align match mark by pulling timing belt up on washer pump pulley side while turning crankshaft pulley counterclockwise.
    c. After aligning match mark, hold timing belt and turn crankshaft pulley clockwise. Align its groove with timing mark "0" of No. 1 timing belt cove.
    d. If match mark is out of alignment on counterclockwise side, align match mark by pulling timing belt up on No. 1 idler pulley side while turning crankshaft pulley clockwise.
    e. After aligning match mark, hold timing belt and turn crankshaft pulley counterclockwise. Align its groove with timing mark "0 " of No. 1 timing cover.
16. Using puller tool No. 09213-60017, or equivalent, remove crankshaft pulley, when reusing timing belt remove pulley without turning it.
17. Remove No. 1 timing belt cover, gasket timing belt guide.
18. If timing belt is to be reused, draw a direction arrow on the timing belt and make reference marks between timing belt and crankshaft timing pulley, then remove belt.
19. Remove No. 1 idler pulley attaching bolt, then pulley and tension spring.
20. Remove No. 2 idler pulley attaching bolt, then the idler pulley.
21. Pry off crankshaft timing pulley with two screwdrivers.
22. While holding oil pump sprocket with suitable tool, remove oil pump nut and sprocket.

INSTALLATION

1. Install oil pump pulley. Tighten attaching nut to specification.
2. Install crankshaft timing pulley, aligning timing pulley set key with key groove of the pulley. Slide pulley on, facing flange side inward.
3. Install No. 2 idler pulley. Tighten idler pulley attaching bolt to specification. Ensure pulley moves smoothly.
4. Install spring loaded No. 1 idler pulley and loosely install attaching bolt. Install spring, then pry pulley as far to the left as possible and tighten attaching bolt. Ensure pulley moves smoothly.
5. Temporarily install timing belt as follows:
    a. Using crankshaft pulley bolt, turn crankshaft pulley and position key groove of the pulley upward.
    b. Remove any oil or water on the

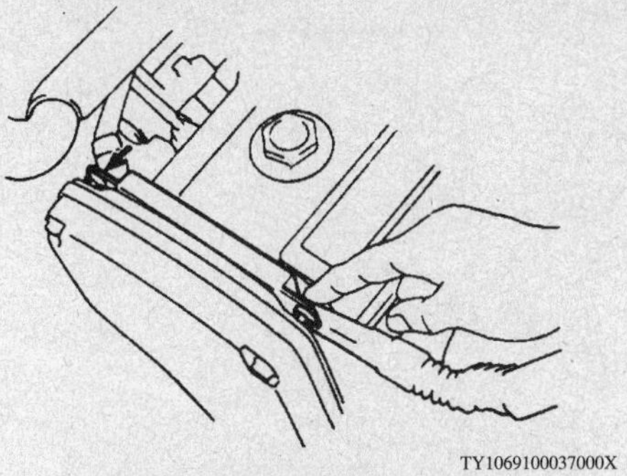
TY1069100037000X

Fig. 26 Engine wire to No. 2 timing belt cover installation

crankshaft, oil pump, water pump, No. 1 and No. 2 idler pulleys.
   c. Install timing belt onto crankshaft pulley, oil pump pulley, No. 1 idler pulley, water pump pulley and No. 2 idler pulley. If belt is being reused, install in proper direction and align reference mark on crankshaft pulley made during removal procedures. **The engine should be cold during belt installation.**
6. Install timing belt guide, cup side outward.
7. Install No. 1 timing belt cover.
8. Install crankshaft pulley. Tighten attaching bolt to specification. Ensure crankshaft pulley groove is still aligned with "0" timing mark, indicating No. 1 cylinder is at TDC of compression stroke.
9. Install camshaft timing pulley, washer and attaching bolt. Tighten attaching bolt to specification. Rotate camshaft by turning sprocket attaching bolt to align bearing cap mark and camshaft timing pulley, **Fig. 24.**
10. Install timing belt on camshaft timing pulley. If timing belt is being reused, align reference marks made during removal procedures.
11. Ensure belt has tension between crankshaft timing pulley and camshaft timing pulley.
12. Loosen No. 1 idler pulley attaching bolt ½ turn, rotate crankshaft clockwise two complete revolutions, from TDC compression stroke to TDC compression stroke, check that each pulley aligns with timing marks. If timing marks do not align, remove timing belt and reinstall. Tighten No. 1 idler pulley to specification.
13. Install No. 2 timing belt cover and install two clamps of engine wire to each bolt, **Fig. 26.**
14. Install engine wire to alternator bracket and adjusting bar.
15. Install spark plugs, then the right side engine mounting bracket.
16. Install right side engine mounting insulator, then power steering reservoir to bracket.
17. Install right side engine mounting stay, then connect ground connector to ground wire on right fender apron.
18. Install power steering belt, pivot bolt and adjusting bolt.
19. Install alternator, then the cruise control actuator and bracket.
20. Install engine undercover and right front wheel, then battery ground cable.

CAMSHAFT

REPLACE

Refer to "Cylinder Head, Replace" for camshaft removal procedures.

PISTON & ROD ASSEMBLY

If piston bore is not within specifications, replace piston and/or cylinder block. When assembling piston onto connecting rod, ensure mark on top of piston and mark on connecting rod are on same side, **Fig. 27.** When installing piston and connecting rod assembly, ensure mark on top of piston is facing toward front of engine.

MAIN & ROD BEARINGS

Undersize bearings are not available. If crankshaft journals or crankpins are worn or scored, the crankshaft must be replaced.

OIL PAN

REPLACE

1. Obtain audio anti-theft code, if equipped, as outlined under "Precautions."
2. Remove hood and engine undercovers, then drain engine oil.
3. Remove suspension lower crossmember attaching nuts and bolts, then the crossmember.
4. Remove front exhaust pipe as outlined in "Engine, Replace."
5. Remove eight engine center member attaching bolts, then center member.
6. Remove two stiffener plate attaching bolts and plate.
7. Remove oil dipstick, oil pan attaching nuts and bolts.
8. Insert blade of tool No. 09032-00100, or equivalent, between cylinder block and oil pan, cut off applied sealer and remove oil pan.
9. Remove oil strainer and baffle plate attaching nuts and bolts, oil strainer, baffle plate and gasket.
10. Suspend engine with engine chain hoist, then remove timing belt, No. 2 idler pulley, crankshaft timing pulley and oil pump pulley as outlined in "Timing Belt, Replace."
11. Remove 12 oil pump attaching bolts, then using a plastic faced hammer remove oil pump by gently tapping on oil pump body.
12. Reverse procedure to install. Reset audio coded anti-theft, if equipped, as outlined under "Precautions."

OIL PUMP

REPLACE

Refer to "Oil Pan, Replace" for procedure.

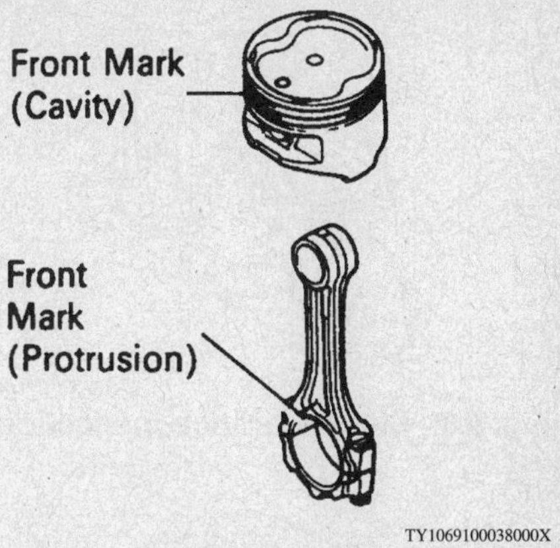
Front Mark
(Cavity)
Front
Mark
(Protrusion)
TY1069100038000X

Fig. 27 Piston & connecting rod assembly

OIL PUMP SERVICE

1. Using snap ring pliers, remove snap ring from oil pump body.
2. Remove retainer, spring and relief valve.
3. Remove two pump body cover bolts, pump body cover, O-ring, drive and driven gears.
4. Coat relief valve with engine oil and check that it falls smoothly into valve hole by its own weight. If it does not, replace valve and if necessary replace oil pump assembly.
5. Using a feeler gauge, measure clearance between driven rotor and body, **Fig. 28.** If clearance is greater than .0079 inch, replace rotors as a set. If necessary replace oil pump.
6. Using a feeler gauge, measure clearance between drive and driven rotors, **Fig. 29.** If tip clearance is greater than .0079 inch, replace rotors as a set.

BELT TENSION DATA

Belt	New, Lbs.	Used, Lbs.
Alt. Less A/C	100–150	75–115
Alt. w/A/C	170–180	120–140
Power Steer.	100–150	60–100

COOLING SYSTEM BLEED

These engines do not require a specified bleed procedure. After filling cooling system, run engine to operating temperature with radiator/pressure cap off. Air will then be automatically bled through cap opening.

THERMOSTAT

REPLACE

1. Obtain audio anti-theft code, if equipped, as outlined in "Precautions."
2. Drain engine coolant into suitable container.
3. Remove lower radiator hose, then water inlet and thermostat.
4. Reverse procedure to install. Ensure jiggle valve is aligned with upper side of inlet stud bolt.

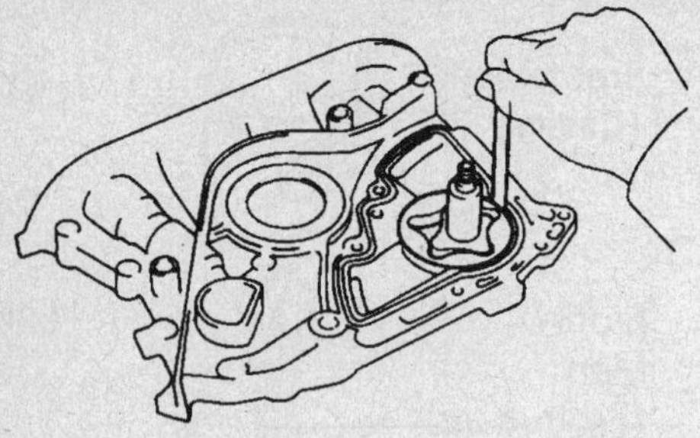
TY1069100039000X

Fig. 28 Side clearance inspection

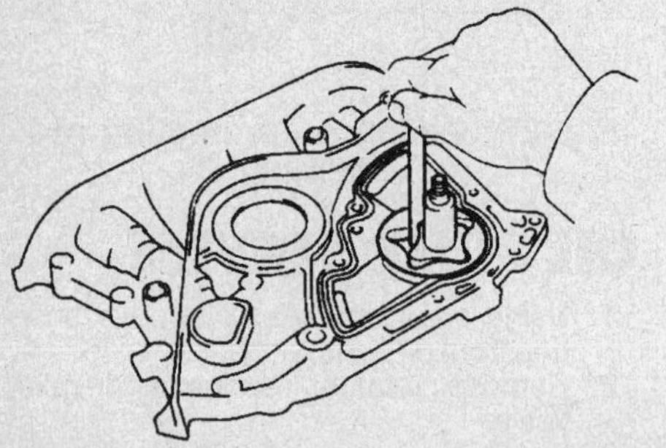
TY1069100040000X

Fig. 29 Rotor tip clearance inspection

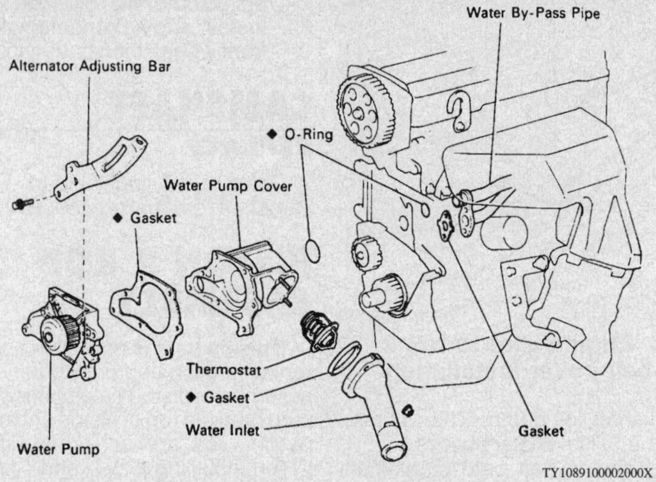
Water By-Pass Pipe
Alternator Adjusting Bar
◆ O-Ring
Water Pump Cover
◆ Gasket
Thermostat
◆ Gasket
Water Inlet
Gasket
Water Pump
TY1089100002000X

Fig. 30 Water pump removal

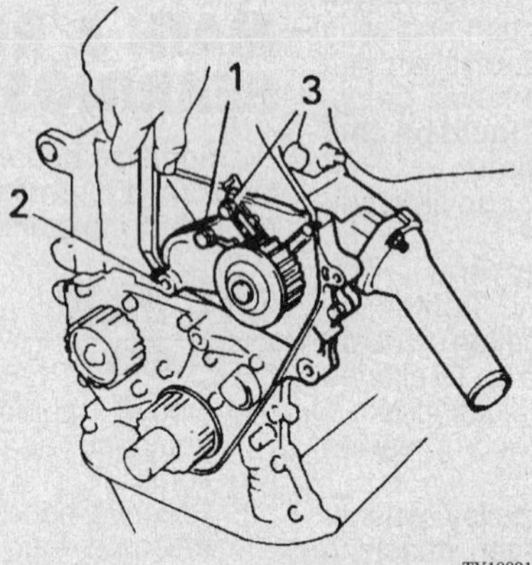
1
3
2
TY1089100003000X

Fig. 31 Water pump bolt removal sequence

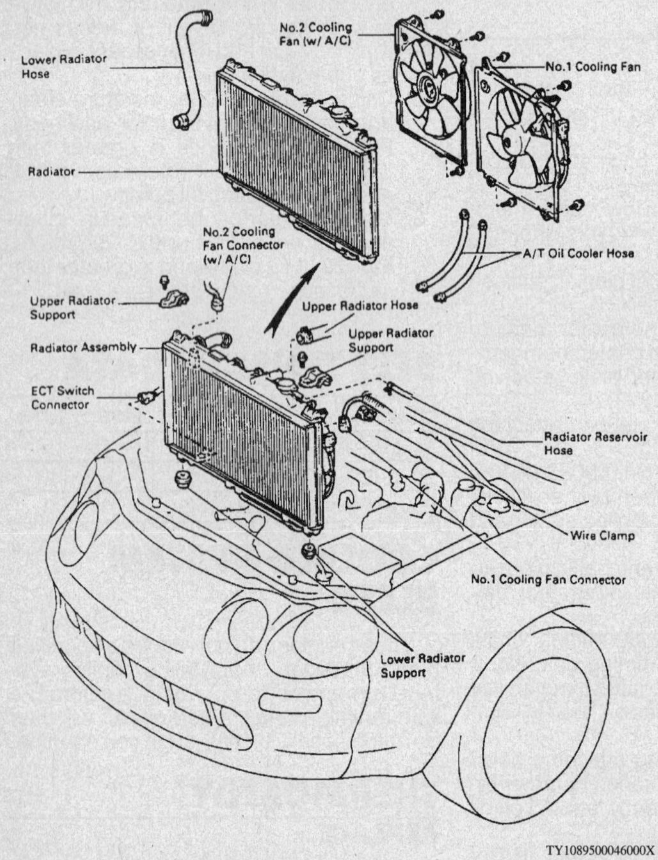
No.2 Cooling Fan (w/ A/C)
Lower Radiator Hose
No.1 Cooling Fan
Radiator
No.2 Cooling Fan Connector (w/ A/C)
A/T Oil Cooler Hose
Upper Radiator Support
Upper Radiator Hose
Radiator Assembly
Upper Radiator Support
ECT Switch Connector
Radiator Reservoir Hose
Wire Clamp
No.1 Cooling Fan Connector
Lower Radiator Support
TY1089500046000X

Fig. 32 Radiator replacement

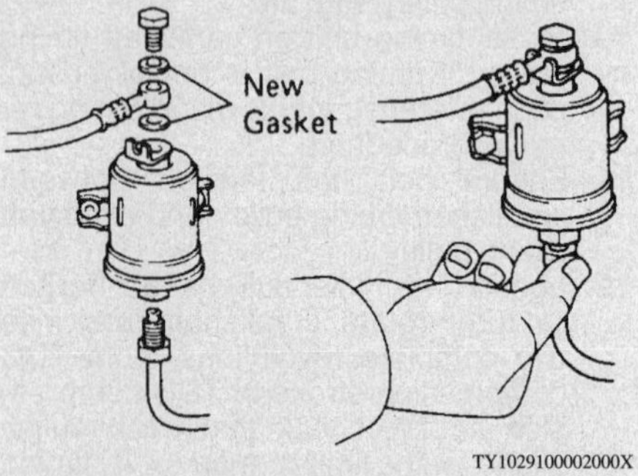
New Gasket
TY1029100002000X

Fig. 33 Fuel filter replacement

WATER PUMP

REPLACE

1. Obtain audio anti-theft code, if equipped, as outlined in "Precautions," then drain engine coolant.
2. Disconnect lower radiator hose from water inlet.
3. Remove timing belt as outlined in "Timing Belt, Replace."
4. Remove idler pulleys and alternator belt adjusting bar.
5. Remove two water pump to water by-pass pipe attaching nuts, **Fig. 30.**
6. Remove three water pump attaching bolts in sequence shown in **Fig. 31.**
7. Pull out water pump and water pump cover, then remove gasket and two O-rings from water pump and water bypass pipe.
8. Separate water pump and water pump cover, then remove water inlet and thermostat from water pump cover.
9. Reverse procedure to install.

RADIATOR

REPLACE

1. Disconnect battery ground cable.
2. Drain coolant.
3. Disconnect No. 1 cooling fan connector, **Fig. 32.**
4. **On models with A/C,** disconnect No. 2 cooling fan connector.
5. **On all models,** disconnect engine coolant temperature switch connector.
6. Disconnect coolant reservoir hose.
7. Disconnect radiator hoses.
8. **On models with automatic transmission,** disconnect transmission oil cooler hoses.
9. **On all models,** remove upper radiator support, then radiator.
10. Reverse procedure to install.

FUEL PUMP

REPLACE

1. Obtain audio anti-theft code, if equipped, as outlined in "Precautions," then drain fuel from tank.
2. Remove fuel tank, then the fuel pump bracket from tank.
3. Remove fuel pump from fuel pump bracket.
4. Remove filter from pump.
5. Reverse procedure to install.

FUEL FILTER

REPLACE

Refer to **Fig. 33** for replacement procedure.

TIGHTENING SPECIFICATIONS

Year	Component	Torque/Ft. Lbs.
1993–96	A/C Compressor	20
	Alternator Bracket	31
	Bearing Cap Bolts	①
	Camshaft Timing Pulley	27
	Center Engine Mount	38
	Center Engine Mount Insulator	54
	Crankshaft Mains	31
	Crankshaft Pulley	80
	Cylinder Head	①
	Cylinder Head Cover	17
	Driveplate	61
	EGR Valve Union Nut	43
	EGR Valve Bolt	9
	Engine Hanger	18
	Exhaust Manifold	31
	Exhaust Pipe To Catalytic Converter	46
	Exhaust Pipe To Center Exhaust	32
	Flywheel	65
	Front Engine Mount Bracket	57
	Front Engine Mount Through Bolt	64
	Fuel Hose Union Bolts	22
	Idler Pulley	31
	Intake Manifold	14
	LH Engine Mount Bracket	38
	LH Engine Mount Nut	38
	LH Engine Mount Stay	15
	LH Engine Mount Through Bolt	64
	Lower Suspension Crossmember	112
	No. 3 Timing Belt Cover	69②
	Oil Pump Pulley	21
	Power Steering Pump Bracket	32
	Power Steering Pump Adjusting Bolt	29
	Rear End Plate	82
	Rear Engine Mount Bracket	57
	Rear Engine Mount Through Bolt	64
	Rear Oil Seal Retainer	82②
	RH Engine Mount Bracket	38
	RH Engine Mount Stay	54
	Spark Plugs	13
	Spark Plug Tubes	29
	Suspension Upper Brace Bolt	15
	Suspension Upper Brace Nut	47

Continued

TIGHTENING SPECIFICATIONS—Continued

Year	Component	Torque/Ft. Lbs.
1993–96	Water Bypass Pipe	82②
	Water Outlet	11

① — Refer to "Cylinder Head, Replace" for tightening procedure.
② — Inch lbs.

2JZ-GE & 2JZ-GTE 3.0L Engines

NOTE: On Air Bag Equipped Models, Refer To "Air Bag System Precautions" Located In The Front Of This Manual For System Disarming & Arming Procedures.

INDEX

	Page No.
Belt Tension Data	43-35
Camshaft, Replace	43-34
Compression Pressure	43-32
Cooling System Bleed	43-35
Cylinder Head, Replace	43-33
Engine Rebuilding Specifications	48-1
Engine, Replace	43-32
Exhaust Manifold, Replace	43-33
Fuel Filter, Replace	43-36
Fuel Pump, Replace	43-36
Intake Manifold, Replace	43-33
Main & Rod Bearings	43-34
Oil Pan, Replace	43-34
Oil Pump, Replace	43-34
Oil Pump Service	43-35
Inspection	43-35
Piston & Rod Assembly	43-34
Precautions	43-32
Air Bag Systems	43-32
Audio Coded Anti-Theft System	43-32
Radiator, Replace	43-36
2JZ-GE Engine	43-36
2JZ-GTE Engine	43-36
Thermostat, Replace	43-35
Tightening Specifications	43-38
Timing Belt, Replace	43-34
Valve Adjustment	43-33
Valve Clearance Specifications	43-33
Valve Guides	43-34
Water Pump, Replace	43-35
2JZ-GE Engine	43-35
2JZ-GTE Engine	43-36

PRECAUTIONS

AIR BAG SYSTEMS

Refer to "Air Bag System Precautions" in the front of this manual for system disarming and arming procedures.

AUDIO CODED ANTI-THEFT SYSTEM

Some models are equipped with an audio coded anti-theft system that will disable the radio when the battery cable is disconnected. The system can be identified by the "ANTI-THEFT SYSTEM" on the cassette tape lid. Obtain 3 digit customer code for input. Reset system after service as follows:

1. Obtain 3 digit audio anti-theft code.
2. Depress 1 (PROG) while depressing righthand side of TUNE SEEK button, - - - will appear in tape operation display.
3. To enter the first digit, depress 1 (PROG) button repeatedly until the number of times depressed equals the first digit beginning with zero (depress the 1 button six times if the first digit if five).
4. To enter second digit, depress 2 (APS) button repeatedly until the number of times depressed equals the second digit beginning with zero.
5. To enter third digit, depress 3 (RPT) button repeatedly until the number of times depressed equals the second digit beginning with zero.
6. If - - - is displayed during code input, repeat procedure.
7. When code appears in display, depress and hold SCAN button until SEC appears.
8. When SEC disappears audio system should be operative.
9. If Err is displayed, repeat procedure. **Attempting to input code more than nine times may permanently disable audio system.**

COMPRESSION PRESSURE

1. Start engine and warm to normal operating temperature.
2. **On 2JZ-GE engine,** proceed as follows:
   a. Disconnect distributor connector.
   b. Disconnect spark plug wires.
3. **On 2JZ-GTE engine,** proceed as follows:
   a. Disconnect camshaft position sensor connectors.
   b. Remove ignition coils as outlined under "Coil Pack, Replace" in "Electrical" section.
4. **On all models,** remove spark plugs.
5. Insert compression gauge into spark plug hole.
6. While cranking engine, measure compression pressure.
7. **On 2JZ-GE engine,** standard compression pressure is 185 psi. Minimum compression pressure is 156 psi.
8. **On 2JZ-GTE engine,** standard compression pressure is 156 psi. Minimum compression pressure is 128 psi.
9. **On all models,** maximum compression pressure difference between cylinders should not exceed 14 psi.

ENGINE

REPLACE

1. Obtain audio coded anti-theft code, if equipped, disarm air bag system as outlined under "Precautions."
2. Remove battery and battery tray, then the hood.
3. Raise and support vehicle, then remove engine undercover, drain coolant, oil and fuel.
4. Lower vehicle and disconnect control cables from throttle body, then remove air cleaner duct.
5. **On turbocharged models,** remove air cleaner assembly, MAF meter and intake air connector pipe assembly.
6. **On all models,** remove air cleaner assembly, VAF meter and intake air connector pipe assembly.
7. **On turbocharged models,** remove No. 1, 2 and 5 air tubes.
8. **On all models,** remove No. 2 fan shroud.
9. Remove lefthand headlight beam angle gauge, then the radiator.

10. **On models with automatic transmission,** disconnect oil cooler hoses from cooler tubes and plug hose ends.
11. **On all models,** remove drive belt, fan, fluid coupling assembly and water pump pulley.
12. Remove charcoal canister, then disconnect heater hoses.
13. Disconnect brake booster vacuum hose and EVAP hose.
14. Disconnect all engine wire connectors.
15. Disconnect fuel inlet and return lines. **Put a suitable container or shop towel under fuel pipe support to soak up any spillage.**
16. Remove engine wire bracket, then disconnect power steering pump without disconnecting the hoses.
17. Position power steering pump assembly aside, then disconnect power steering pressure tube from engine.
18. Disconnect air conditioning compressor without disconnecting any hoses and secure aside. **Handle hoses carefully to avoid kinks or other damage.**
19. Disconnect engine wire from cowl panel and from inside vehicle.
20. **On models with manual transmission,** remove upper console panel, shift lever boots and holding bolts, then disconnect clutch release cylinder and transmission ground strap.
21. **On turbocharged models,** disconnect sub-heated oxygen sensor from exhaust.
22. **On all models,** remove No. 2 exhaust pipe from front exhaust pipe.
23. Remove exhaust heat insulator, then the propeller shaft.
24. Disconnect transmission control rod and shift lever.
25. Remove rear engine support member, then attach engine hoist chain and carefully lift engine/transmission assembly from vehicle.
26. Reverse procedure to install. Reset audio coded anti-theft system, if equipped, as outlined under "Precautions."

INTAKE MANIFOLD

REPLACE

Refer to "Cylinder Head, Replace" for procedure.

EXHAUST MANIFOLD

REPLACE

Refer to "Cylinder Head, Replace" for procedure.

CYLINDER HEAD

REPLACE

1. Obtain audio coded anti-theft code, if equipped, disarm air bag system as outlined under "Precautions."
2. **On models with turbocharger,** remove turbocharger.
3. **On all models,** raise and support vehicle, then remove lower engine cover and drain coolant.
4. **On models less turbocharger,** remove air cleaner duct, air cleaner, VAF meter and intake air pipe assembly.
5. **On all models,** remove drive belt and No. 2 exhaust pipe.
6. Remove exhaust manifold as follows:
   a. Remove manifold heat insulator nuts and the insulator.
   b. Disconnect two main heated oxygen sensor connectors.
   c. **On models with turbocharger,** remove 12 exhaust manifold bolts.
   d. **On models less turbocharger,** remove 8 nuts then No. 1 and 2 exhaust manifolds.
7. Disconnect power steering pump and position aside.
8. Disconnect brake booster vacuum hose and EVAP hose.
9. Remove throttle body and intake air connector assembly.
10. **On models with turbocharger,** disconnect the following connectors:
    a. Six injectors.
    b. Two camshaft position sensors.
    c. Three engine wire clamps from injector holders.
11. Remove starter.
12. **On all models,** remove air intake chamber stays and No. 2 vacuum pipe and VSV assembly.
13. Remove No. 3 timing belt cover and the cylinder head rear cover.
14. Disconnect plug wires from cylinder head covers.
15. Remove distributor and plug wire assembly.
16. Remove spark plugs.
17. Remove timing belt from camshaft timing pulleys.
18. Remove water bypass outlet and No. 1 water bypass pipe
19. Disconnect fuel return lines and plug hose end.
20. Remove engine wire bracket and oil dipstick guide for engine and transmission.
21. Remove air intake chamber and vacuum control valve set.
22. Remove bolt and disconnect engine wire bracket from water pump.
23. **On models less turbocharger**, disconnect 2 ground straps from intake manifold and the following connectors:
    a. 6 injectors.
    b. ECT sensor.
    c. ECT sender gauge.
24. **On all models,** remove water outlet and No. 1 bypass hose assembly.
25. Remove intake manifold stay.
26. Remove fuel pressure pulsation damper and fuel inlet pipe.
27. Remove intake manifold and delivery pipe assembly.
28. **On models with turbocharger**, remove ignition coils assemblies, spark plugs, then Nos. 1 and 2 cylinder head covers.
29. **On models less turbocharger,** remove Nos. 3, 1 and 2 cylinder head covers.
30. **On all models,** remove camshaft timing pulleys, then the No. 4 timing belt cover.
31. Remove camshafts by uniformly loosening and removing bearing cap bolts in sequence shown, **Fig. 1.**
32. Remove cylinder head by uniformly loosening and removing cylinder head bolts in sequence shown, **Fig. 2.**
33. Reverse procedure to install, noting the following:
    a. Check cylinder head for warpage on all contact surfaces. Maximum warpage allowed is .0039 inch.
    b. Using sequence shown in **Fig. 3, torque** cylinder head bolts in three steps; first step to 25 ft. lbs., second step an additional 90°, third step an additional 90°.
    c. Reset audio coded anti-theft system, if equipped, as outlined under "Precautions."

VALVE CLEARANCE SPECIFICATIONS

Year	Stem-To-Guide Clearance	
	Intake	Exhaust
1993-96	.006-.0010	.010-.014

VALVE ADJUSTMENT

Valve clearance is adjusted through the use of shims. Shims are available in increments of .0020 inch.

1. Obtain audio coded anti-theft code, if equipped, disarm air bag system as outlined under "Precautions."
2. **On models less turbocharger,** remove throttle body and intake air connector assembly.
3. **On all models,** remove No. 3 timing belt cover and cylinder head rear cover.
4. Disconnect spark plug wires from cylinder head covers, then remove Nos. 1, 2 and 3 covers.
5. **On models with turbocharger,** remove ignition coils, then disconnect engine wire protector from No. 4 timing belt cover.
6. Disconnect engine wire protector from cowl top panel and remove IAC valve pipe.
7. Remove No. 1 and 2 cylinder head covers.
8. **On all models,** set No. 1 cylinder to TDC by turning the crankshaft and align its groove with timing mark "0" on No. 1 timing belt cover. **Always turn crankshaft clockwise.**
9. Ensure timing marks of crankshaft timing pulleys are aligned with timing marks of No. timing belt cover. If not, turn crankshaft one revolution (360°).
10. **Adjust only those valves shown in Fig. 4.** Using a feeler gauge, measure clearance between valve lift and camshaft. Record valve clearance measurement of those out of specification to use later to determine required replacement adjusting shim.
11. Turn crank pulley 1 revolution (360°) and align groove with timing mark "0" of No. 1 timing belt cover.
12. **Adjust only those valves shown in Fig. 5** and using a feeler gauge, measure clearance between valve lift and

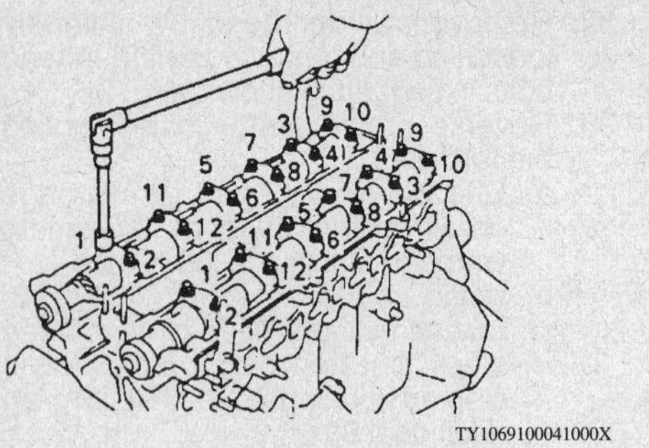
1
2
3
4
5
6
7
8
9
10
11
12
TY1069100041000X

Fig. 1 Cylinder head bolt loosening sequence

camshaft. Record valve clearance measurement of those out of specification to use later to determine required replacement adjusting shim.

13. To remove adjusting shim turn camshaft so that cam lobe for valve to be adjusted is facing up.
14. Turn valve lifter with screwdriver so notches are perpendicular to camshaft, **Fig. 6.**
15. Using shim removal tool No. 09248-05410, or equivalent, hold camshaft as shown in **Fig. 7.**, then press down lifter and place tool between camshaft and valve lifter, **Fig. 8.**
16. Using a screwdriver and magnet, remove adjusting shim.
17. Measure thickness of removed shim, **Fig. 9** and calculate thickness of new shim so valve clearances meet specifications. Refer **Figs. 10 and 11.**
18. Reset audio coded anti-theft system, if equipped, as outlined under "Precautions."

VALVE GUIDES

1. Using a suitable tool, tap out guide bushing from combustion chamber side.
2. Select new guide and tap in new guide to protrusion height of .484–.500 inch on intake valves and .449–.465 inch on exhaust valves.

TIMING BELT

REPLACE

1. Obtain audio coded anti-theft code, if equipped, disarm air bag system as outlined under "Precautions."then remove battery and battery tray.
2. Remove engine undercover.
3. **On models less turbocharger,** remove No. 2 air tube.
4. **On all models,** drain engine coolant and remove air cleaner duct.
5. **On models with turbocharger,** remove No. 5 air hose.
6. **On all models,** remove lefthand headlight beam angle gauge.
7. Remove No. 2 fan shroud, then the radiator.
8. **On turbocharged models with manual transmission,** remove drive belt tensioner damper.
9. **On all models,** remove drive belt, fan fluid coupling assembly and water pump pulley.

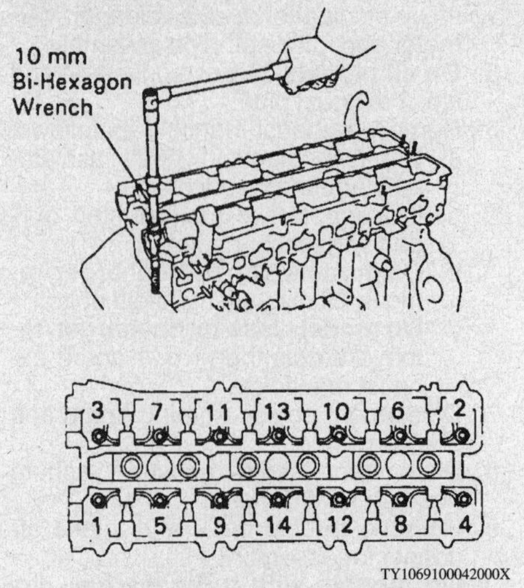
10 mm
Bi-Hexagon
Wrench
3 7 11 13 10 6 2
1 5 9 14 12 8 4
TY1069100042000X

Fig. 2 Cylinder head bolt loosening sequence

10. **On models less turbocharger**, loosen 6 bolts to remove timing belt cover No. 3.
11. **On models with turbocharger,** loosen 10 bolts to remove timing belt cover No. 3.
12. **On all models,** remove timing belt No. 2, then drive belt tensioner.
13. Set No. 1 cylinder to TDC by turning crankshaft and aligning its groove with timing mark "0" on No. 1 timing belt cover.
14. Ensure timing marks of camshaft timing pulley are aligned with timing marks of No. 4 timing belt cover. If not, turn the crankshaft one revolution (360°) clockwise.
15. If re-using old timing belt, place match marks on belt and camshaft as shown in **Fig. 12. Do not install a timing belt showing signs of wear or stress. Installing a worn or damaged belt will result in serious engine damage.**
16. Alternately loosen two bolts **Fig. 13,** then remove bolts tensioner and dust boot.
17. Disconnect timing belt from camshaft timing pulleys.
18. Remove both timing pulley bolts then pulleys.
19. Using a suitable puller, remove crankshaft pulley.
20. **On models less turbocharger,** remove power steering bracket.
21. **On all models,** remove No. 1 timing belt cover.
22. Remove timing belt guide, then the timing belt.
23. Reverse procedure to install, noting the following:
    a. Ensure crankshaft timing pulley set key is with key groove of pulley **Fig. 14.**
    b. When re-using old timing belt, align match marks of crankshaft timing pulley and timing belt, then install belt with arrow pointing in direction of engine rotation.
    c. Reset audio coded anti-theft system, if equipped, as outlined under "Precautions."

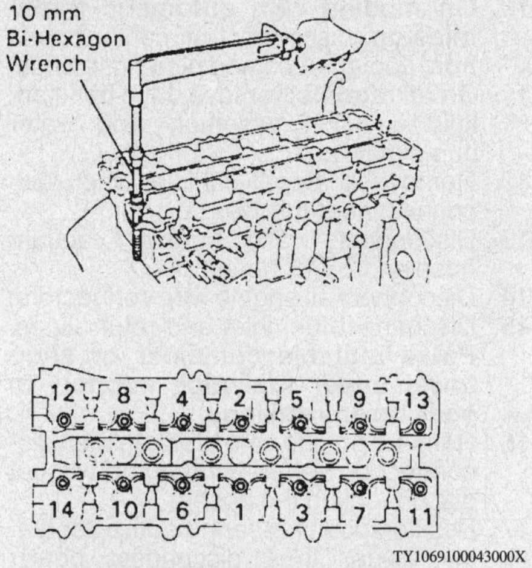
10 mm
Bi-Hexagon
Wrench
12 8 4 2 5 9 13
14 10 6 1 3 7 11
TY1069100043000X

Fig. 3 Cylinder head bolt tightening sequence

CAMSHAFT

REPLACE

Refer to "Cylinder Head, Replace" for camshaft removal procedures.

PISTON & ROD ASSEMBLY

If piston bore is not within specifications, replace piston and/or cylinder block. When assembling piston and rod, ensure mark on top of piston and on connecting rod are the same. Always install in cylinder that assembly originally was removed from.

MAIN & ROD BEARINGS

Undersized rod bearings are available in .0016–.0031 inch. Main bearings are available in .0010–.0024 inch undersizes.

OIL PAN

REPLACE

Refer to "Oil Pump, Replace."

OIL PUMP

REPLACE

1. Obtain audio anti-theft code, if equipped, as outlined under "Precautions," then remove battery and battery tray.
2. Remove engine as outlined under "Engine, Replace. "
3. **On models with turbocharger,** remove crankshaft position sensor and alternator.
4. **On all models,** remove timing belt following procedure outlined under "Timing Belt, Replace,"then the idler pulley.
5. **On models with turbocharger,** remove drive belt tensioner bracket then the timing belt plate and crankshaft timing pulley.
6. **On all models,** remove crankshaft timing pulley, then the oil dipstick and tube assembly.

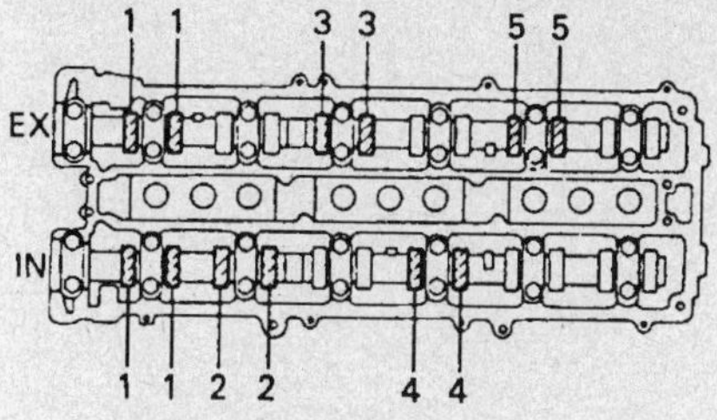
1 1 3 3 5 5
EX
IN
1 1 2 2 4 4

TY1069100044000X

Fig. 4 1st valve adjustment sequence

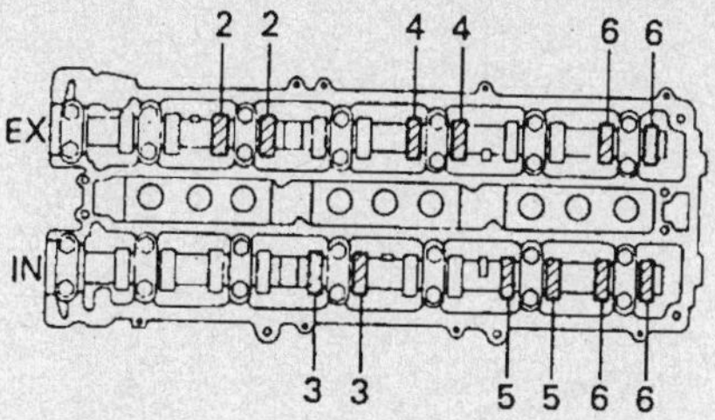
2 2 4 4 6 6
EX
IN
3 3 5 5 6 6

TY1069100045000X

Fig. 5 2nd valve adjustment sequence

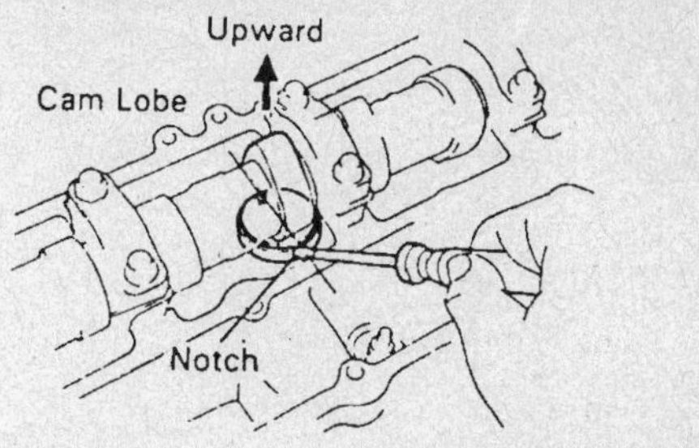
Upward
Cam Lobe
Notch

TY1069100046000X

Fig. 6 Valve adjusting shim notch removal

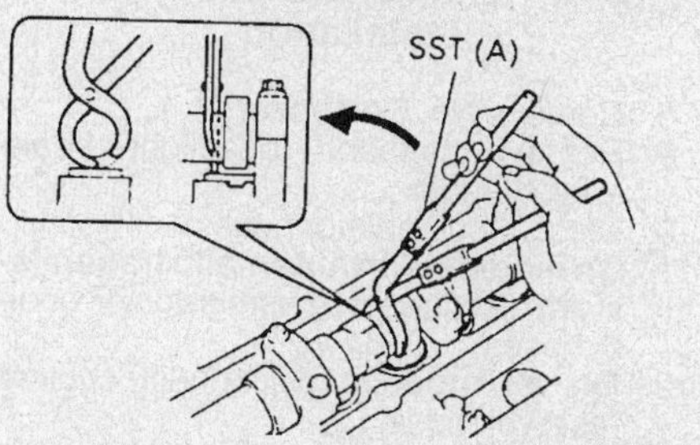
SST (A)

TY1069100047000X

Fig. 7 Valve shim removal tool

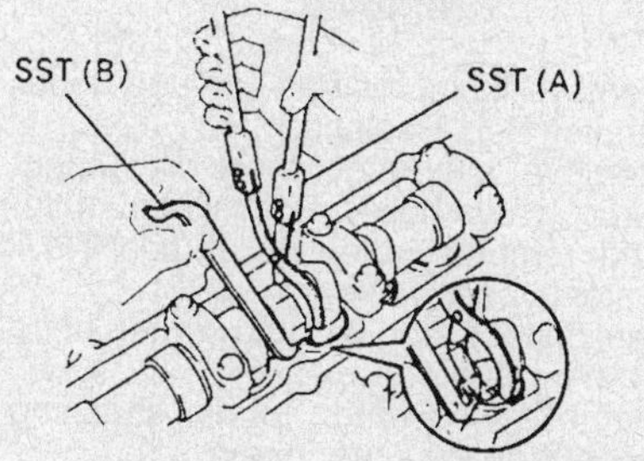
SST (B)
SST (A)

TY1069100048000X

Fig. 8 Valve shim removal

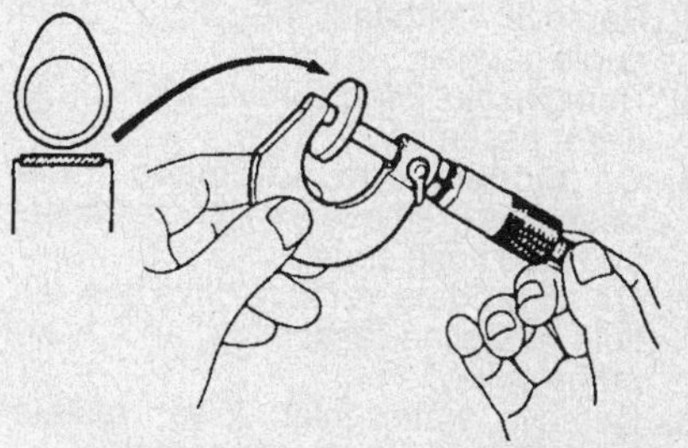

TY1069100049000X

Fig. 9 Valve shim measurement

New shim thickness mm (in.)

Shim No.	Thickness	Shim No.	Thickness
1	2.500 (0.0984)	10	2.950 (0.1161)
2	2.550 (0.1004)	11	3.000 (0.1181)
3	2.600 (0.1024)	12	3.050 (0.1201)
4	2.650 (0.1043)	13	3.100 (0.1220)
5	2.700 (0.1063)	14	3.150 (0.1240)
6	2.750 (0.1083)	15	3.200 (0.1260)
7	2.800 (0.1102)	16	3.250 (0.1280)
8	2.850 (0.1122)	17	3.300 (0.1299)
9	2.900 (0.1142)		

TY1069100050000X

Fig. 10 Intake valve shim size chart

7. Remove oil level sensor, then the No. 2 oil pan.
8. Remove oil strainer, then the oil pan baffle plate.
9. **On models with turbocharger,** remove turbo oil outlet pipe.
10. **On all models,** remove No. 2 oil pan by prying between cylinder block and No. 1 oil pan.
11. Remove crankshaft front oil seal, then the oil pump.
12. Reverse procedure to install. Reset audio coded anti-theft system, if equipped, as outlined under "Precautions."

OIL PUMP SERVICE

INSPECTION

1. Remove oil pump relief valve, then the pump body cover, the drive and driven gears.
2. Coat relief valve with engine oil and ensure it falls smoothly into valve hole under its own weight. If not, replace relief valve.
3. Inspect drive and driven rotors by placing in oil pump body. **The marks on the rotors must face up.**
4. Using a feeler gauge, measure clearance between driven rotor and pump housing. Standard tip clearance is .0039–.0069 inch maximum being .0079 inch for engines less turbocharger and .0031–.0053 inch, maximum being .0063 inch for engines with turbocharger. If the body clearance is greater than maximum, replace rotors as a set. If necessary, replace oil pump assembly.

BELT TENSION DATA

Check that belt tensioner moves downward when drive belt is pressed down at points in **Fig. 15** with approximately 22 ft. lbs.

Check that arrow mark on belt tensioner falls within area A in **Fig. 16.** If new belt is installed, it should be within area B.

COOLING SYSTEM BLEED

These engines do not require a specific bleed procedure. After filling cooling system, run engine to operating temperature with radiator/pressure cap off. Air will then be automatically bled through cap opening.

THERMOSTAT

REPLACE

1. Obtain audio anti-theft code, if equipped, as outlined under "Precautions," then disconnect battery ground cable.
2. Remove engine undercover and drain coolant.

New shim thickness mm (in.)

Shim No.	Thickness	Shim No.	Thickness
1	2.500 (0.0984)	10	2.950 (0.1161)
2	2.550 (0.1004)	11	3.000 (0.1181)
3	2.600 (0.1024)	12	3.050 (0.1201)
4	2.650 (0.1043)	13	3.100 (0.1220)
5	2.700 (0.1063)	14	3.150 (0.1240)
6	2.750 (0.1083)	15	3.200 (0.1260)
7	2.800 (0.1102)	16	3.250 (0.1280)
8	2.850 (0.1122)	17	3.300 (0.1299)
9	2.900 (0.1142)		

TY1069100051000X

Fig. 11 Exhaust valve shim size chart

3. **On models with turbocharger,** disconnect water inlet from water pump and remove thermostat.
4. **On models less turbocharger,** remove water inlet, lower radiator hose assembly, then the thermostat.
5. **On all models,** reverse procedure to install. Reset audio coded anti-theft system, if equipped, as outlined under "Precautions."

WATER PUMP

REPLACE

2JZ-GE ENGINE

1. Obtain audio coded anti-theft code, if equipped, disarm air bag system as outlined under "Precautions."
2. Remove battery and battery tray, then the engine undercover.
3. Drain coolant, then remove air cleaner, VAF meter and intake air connector pipe assembly.

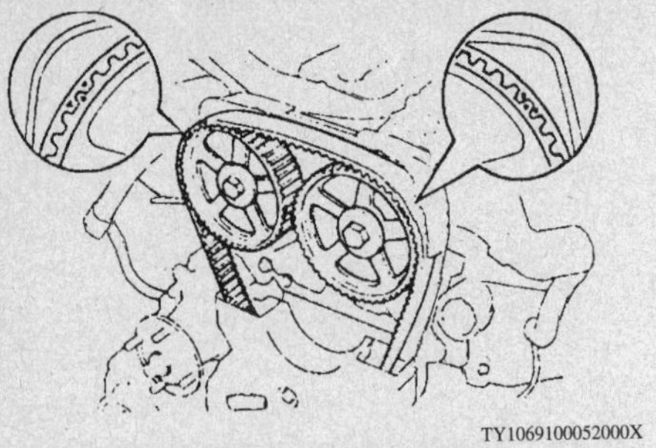
TY1069100052000X

Fig. 12 Timing belt alignment

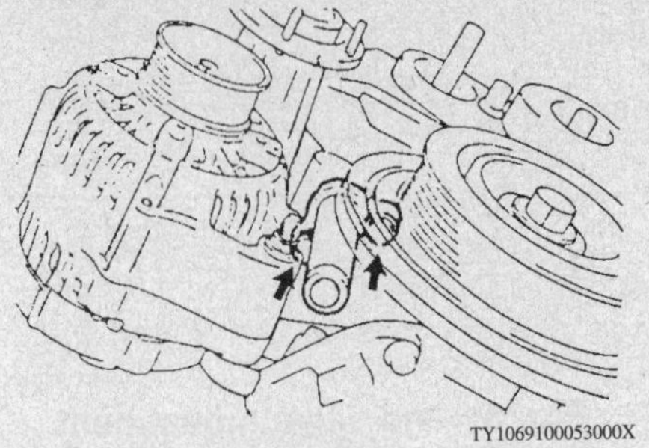
TY1069100053000X

Fig. 13 Timing belt tensioner removal

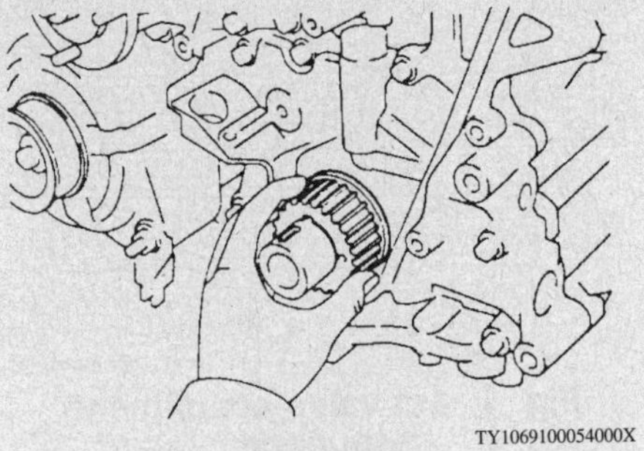
TY1069100054000X

Fig. 14 Crankshaft timing pulley installation

4. Remove lefthand headlight beam angle gauge.
5. Remove No. 2 fan shroud, than the radiator assembly.
6. **On models with automatic transmissions,** remove two cooler hoses and plug hose ends.
7. **On all models,** remove drive belt, fan, fluid coupling assembly and water pump pulley.
8. Remove water inlet, lower radiator hose assembly and thermostat.
9. Remove timing belt as outlined under "Timing Belt, Replace."
10. Remove exhaust manifold heat insulator, then the water bypass outlet and No. 1 water bypass pipe.
11. Remove mounting bolt and disconnect engine wire bracket. Loosen alternator mounting nut and disconnect from water pump.
12. Remove six water pump attaching bolts, then the water pump.
13. Reverse procedure to install. Reset audio coded anti-theft system, if equipped, as outlined under "Precautions."

2JZ-GTE ENGINE

1. Obtain audio coded anti-theft code, if equipped, disarm air bag system as outlined under "Precautions."
2. Remove battery and battery tray, then the engine undercover.
3. Remove No. 1 and No. 2 air tubes, then drain coolant.
4. Remove air cleaner and MAF meter assembly, then the No. 5 air hose.
5. Remove lefthand headlight beam angle gauge.
6. Remove No. 2 fan shroud, than the radiator assembly.
7. **On models with automatic transmissions,** remove two cooler hoses and plug hose ends.
8. **On all models,** remove drive belt tensioner damper.
9. Remove drive belt, fan, fluid coupling assembly and water pump pulley.
10. Remove water inlet, lower radiator hose assembly and thermostat.
11. Remove timing belt as outlined under "Timing Belt, Replace."
12. Remove alternator, then disconnect turbo water hoses from water outlet and remove water outlet and No.1 water bypass valve.
13. Disconnect No. 3 turbo water hose from water pump.
14. Remove six water pump attaching bolts, then the water pump.
15. Reverse procedure to install. Reset audio coded anti-theft system, if equipped, as outlined under "Precautions."

RADIATOR

REPLACE

2JZ-GE ENGINE

1. Disconnect battery ground cable.
2. Remove engine under cover, **Fig. 17.**
3. Remove battery and battery tray.
4. Drain coolant.
5. Remove No. 2 fan shroud.
6. Remove air cleaner duct.
7. Remove lefthand headlight beam angle gauge.
8. Disconnect radiator hoses.
9. **On models with automatic transmission,** disconnect transmission oil cooler hoses.
10. **On all models,** disconnect coolant reservoir hose.
11. Remove upper radiator support, then the radiator with No. 1 shroud attached.
12. Reverse procedure to install.

2JZ-GTE ENGINE

1. Disconnect battery ground cable.
2. Remove engine under cover, **Fig. 18.**
3. Remove battery and battery tray.
4. Drain coolant.
5. Remove No. 2 air tube.
6. Remove No. 2 fan shroud.
7. Remove air cleaner duct.
8. Remove No. 5 air hose.
9. Remove lefthand headlight beam angle gauge.
10. Disconnect radiator hoses.
11. **On models with automatic transmission,** disconnect transmission oil cooler hoses.
12. **On all models,** disconnect coolant reservoir hose.
13. Disconnect electric cooling fan connector and engine coolant temperature switch connector.
14. Remove upper radiator support, then the radiator with No. 1 shroud attached.
15. Reverse procedure to install.

FUEL PUMP

REPLACE

1. Obtain audio anti-theft code, if equipped, then disable air bag as outlined under "Precautions."
2. Remove luggage compartment carpet, then spare wheel and cover.
3. Remove 6 nuts and the service hole cover.
4. Disconnect fuel pump connector, fuel outlet hose, fuel return hose and fuel breather hose.
5. Remove retainer clip, then fuel pump.
6. Reverse procedure to install. Reset audio coded anti-theft system, if equipped, as outlined under "Precautions."

FUEL FILTER

REPLACE

1. Obtain audio anti-theft code, if equipped, as outlined in "Precautions."
2. Remove union bolt and 2 gaskets, **Fig. 19.**
3. Disconnect fuel inlet and outlet hoses.
4. Reverse procedure to install. Install new gaskets. Reset audio coded anti-theft system, if equipped, as outlined under "Precautions."

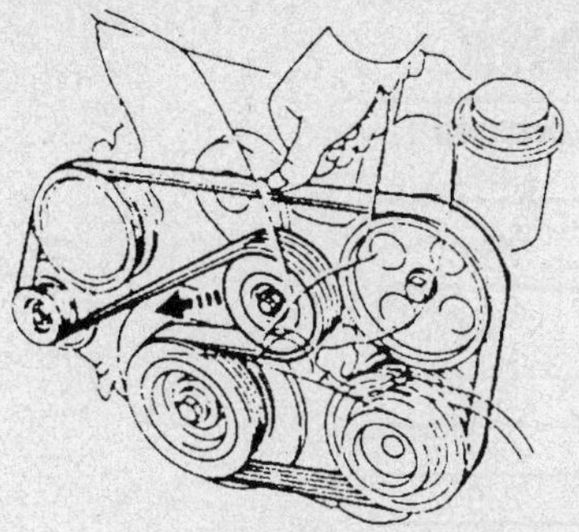

TY1069100055000X

Fig. 15 Drive belt tension inspection

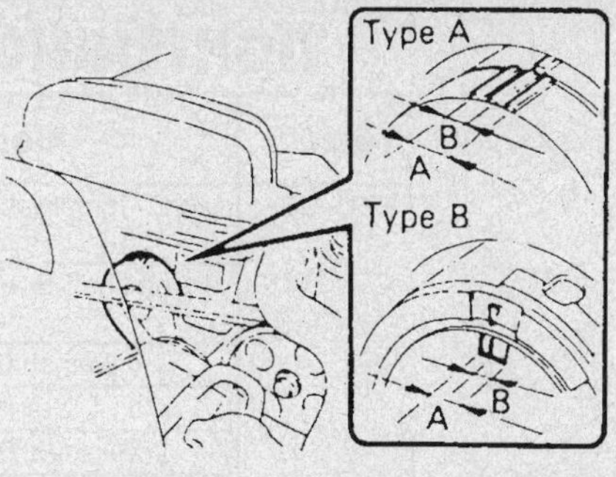

Type A
B
A
Type B
A
B

TY1069100056000X

Fig. 16 Drive belt tension for old or new belt

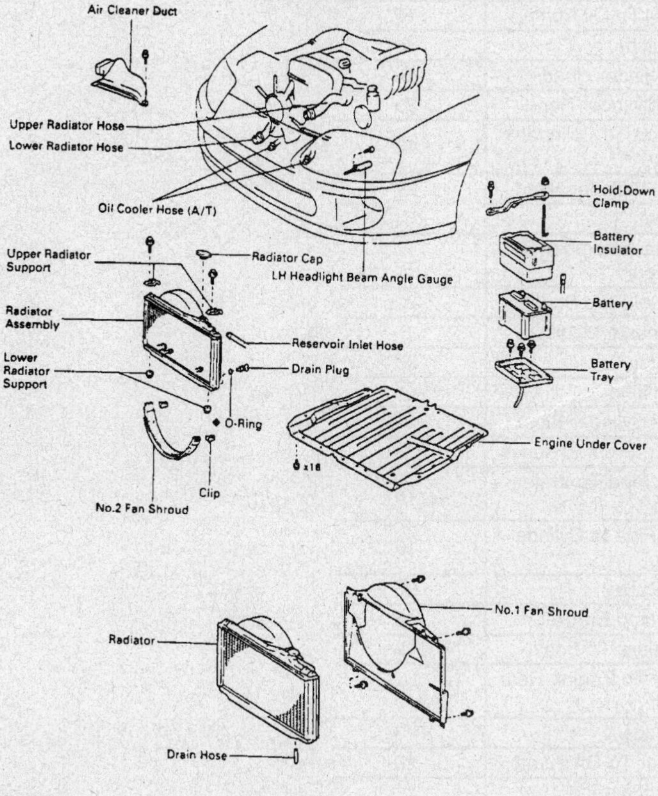

Air Cleaner Duct
Upper Radiator Hose
Lower Radiator Hose
Oil Cooler Hose (A/T)
Hold-Down Clamp
Battery Insulator
Upper Radiator Support
Radiator Cap
LH Headlight Beam Angle Gauge
Radiator Assembly
Battery
Reservoir Inlet Hose
Lower Radiator Support
Drain Plug
Battery Tray
◆ O-Ring
Engine Under Cover
x16
Clip
No.2 Fan Shroud
No.1 Fan Shroud
Radiator
Drain Hose

◆ Non-reusable part

TY1089500042000X

Fig. 17 Radiator replacement. 2JZ-GE engine

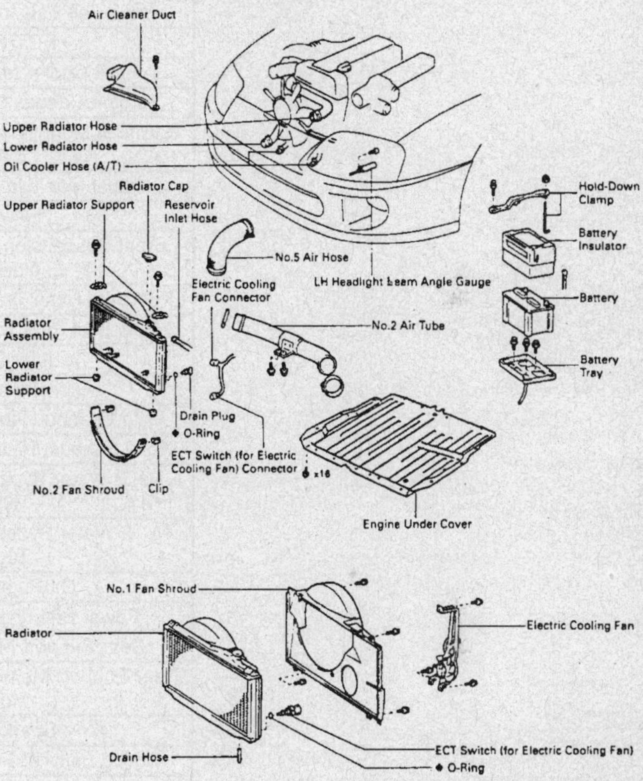

Air Cleaner Duct
Upper Radiator Hose
Lower Radiator Hose
Oil Cooler Hose (A/T)
Radiator Cap
Upper Radiator Support
Reservoir Inlet Hose
Hold-Down Clamp
Battery Insulator
No.5 Air Hose
Electric Cooling Fan Connector
LH Headlight Beam Angle Gauge
Battery
Radiator Assembly
No.2 Air Tube
Lower Radiator Support
Battery Tray
Drain Plug
◆ O-Ring
ECT Switch (for Electric Cooling Fan) Connector
x16
No.2 Fan Shroud
Clip
Engine Under Cover
No.1 Fan Shroud
Radiator
Electric Cooling Fan
Drain Hose
ECT Switch (for Electric Cooling Fan)
◆ O-Ring

◆ Non-reusable part

TY1089500043000X

Fig. 18 Radiator replacement. 2JZ-GTE engine

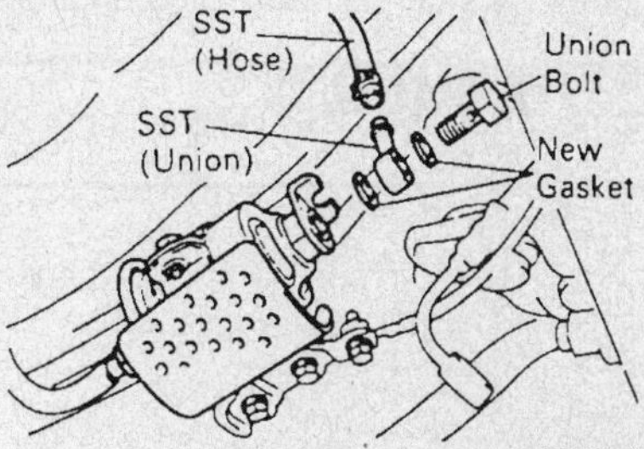

SST (Hose)
Union Bolt
SST (Union)
New Gasket

TY1029100003000X

Fig. 19 Fuel filter replacement

TIGHTENING SPECIFICATIONS

Year	Component	Torque/Ft. Lbs.
1993–96	A/C Compressor To Power Steering Pump Bracket	43
	Camshaft Bearing Cap To Cylinder Head	14
	Camshaft Timing Pulley	59
	Crankshaft Mains	33③
	Crankshaft Pulley To Crankshaft	239
	Cylinder Head To Cylinder Block	①
	Cylinder Head Cover	②
	Driveplate	25
	Drive Belt Tensioner To Oil Pump	15
	ECT Switch	5
	EGR Cooler to Cylinder Head	6
	Engine Hanger To Cylinder Head	29
	Engine Mount Bracket To Cylinder Block	43
	Exhaust Manifold To Cylinder Head	29
	Flywheel	26③
	Front Suspension Crossmember To Engine Mount	43
	Fuel Inlet Hose To Fuel Pipe Support	22
	Fuel Inlet Pipe To Intake Manifold	6
	Idler Pulley	25
	Intake Manifold	④
	Main Bearing Cap to Cylinder Block	33③
	No. 2 Exhaust Pipe To Front Exhaust	43
	No. 2 Water Bypass Pipe To Water Pump	15
	No. 2 Water Bypass Pipe to Cylinder Block	15
	Oil Pump Pulley	25
	Power Steering Pump Bracket	43
	Rear Support Member To Body	19
	Rear Support Member To Engine Rear Mount	10
	Spark Plugs	13
	Timing Belt Tensioner To Oil Pump	20
	Upper Radiator Support	11
	Water Outlet	15

① — Refer to "Cylinder Head, Replace" for tightening procedure.
② — 2JZ-GE engine, 74 inch lbs.; 2JZ-GTE engine, 48 inch lbs.
③ — Then turn bolts an additional 90°.
④ — 2JZ-GE engine, 15 ft. lbs.; 2JZ-GTE engine, 20 ft. lbs.

Clutch & Manual Transaxle/ Transmission

NOTE: On Air Bag Equipped Models, Refer To "Air Bag System Precautions" Located In The Front Of This Manual For System Disarming & Arming Procedures.

INDEX

	Page No.
Adjustments	43-39
Clutch Pedal Height	43-39
Clutch, Replace	43-39
Hydraulic System Service	43-39
Clutch Slave Cylinder, Replace	43-39
Clutch System Bleed	43-39
Precautions	43-39
Air Bag Systems	43-39
Audio Coded Anti-Theft System	43-39
Tightening Specifications	43-42
Transaxle, Replace	43-40
Celica	43-40
Transmission, Replace	43-41
Supra	43-41

PRECAUTIONS

AIR BAG SYSTEMS

Refer to "Air Bag System Precautions" in the front of this manual for system disarming and arming procedures.

AUDIO CODED ANTI-THEFT SYSTEM

Some models are equipped with an audio coded anti-theft system that will disable the radio when the battery cable is disconnected. The system can be identified by the "ANTI-THEFT SYSTEM" on the cassette tape lid. Obtain 3 digit customer code for input. Reset system after service as follows:

1. Obtain 3 digit audio anti-theft code.
2. Depress 1 (PROG) while depressing righthand side of TUNE SEEK button, - - - will appear in tape operation display.
3. To enter the first digit, depress 1 (PROG) button repeatedly until the number of times depressed equals the first digit beginning with zero (depress the 1 button six times if the first digit if five).
4. To enter second digit, depress 2 (APS) button repeatedly until the number of times depressed equals the second digit beginning with zero.
5. To enter third digit, depress 3 (RPT) button repeatedly until the number of times depressed equals the second digit beginning with zero.
6. If - - - is displayed during code input, repeat procedure.
7. When code appears in display, depress and hold SCAN button until SEC appears.
8. When SEC disappears audio system should be operative.
9. If Err is displayed, repeat procedure. **Attempting to input code more than nine times may permanently disable audio system.**

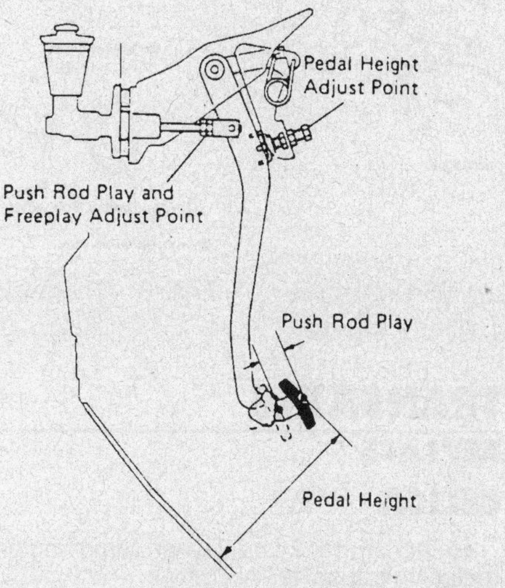

Pedal Height Adjust Point
Push Rod Play and Freeplay Adjust Point
Push Rod Play
Pedal Height
TY5049100012000X

Fig. 1 Clutch pedal adjustment

ADJUSTMENTS

CLUTCH PEDAL HEIGHT

1. Check clutch pedal height, **Fig. 1.**
2. Clutch pedal height should be as follows:
   a. **On Celica models,** 6.41–6.80 inches.
   b. **On Supra models,** 5.76–6.15 inches.
3. **On all models,** if clutch pedal height is not as specified, loosen locknut and turn adjusting bolt until specified clutch pedal height is obtained, then tighten adjusting bolt locknut.
4. Clutch freeplay should be as follows:
   a. **On Supra models,** .197–.591 inch. Pushrod play at pedal should be .039–.197 inch.
   b. **On Celica models,** freeplay should be 0.197–0.591 inch.
5. **On all models,** if clutch pedal freeplay is not as specified, loosen locknut and turn pushrod adjusting screw until specified pedal freeplay is obtained.
6. Tighten locknut, then recheck clutch pedal height.

HYDRAULIC SYSTEM SERVICE

CLUTCH SYSTEM BLEED

If any service is performed on the clutch system or air is suspected in the clutch lines, bleed the system.

1. Fill clutch reservoir with suitable brake fluid. **Do not allow fluid to come in contact with painted surfaces.**
2. Check reservoir frequently, add fluid as required.
3. Connect vinyl tube to bleeder plug, then insert other tube end in half full container of brake fluid.
4. Slowly pump clutch pedal several times.
5. While depressing, pedal, loosen bleeder plug until fluid runs out, then close bleeder plug.
6. Repeat procedure until air bubbles are evident in the fluid. **Do not reuse the fluid that was bled.**

CLUTCH SLAVE CYLINDER, REPLACE

1. Remove clutch slave cylinder hose or tube.
2. Remove slave cylinder.
3. Reverse procedure to install. Tighten bolts to specifications.
4. Bleed clutch system.

CLUTCH

REPLACE

1. Remove transaxle assembly as outlined under "Transaxle, Replace."
2. Place installation alignment on clutch cover and flywheel.
3. Loosen each set bolt one turn at a time until spring tension is released.
4. Remove clutch cover attaching bolts, then cover and disc.

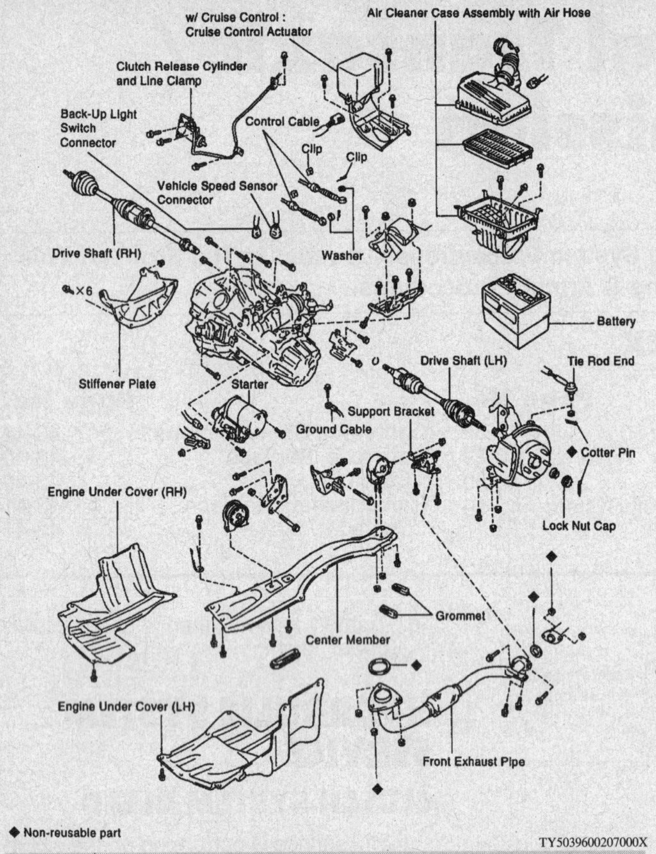
w/ Cruise Control :
Cruise Control Actuator
Air Cleaner Case Assembly with Air Hose
Clutch Release Cylinder and Line Clamp
Back-Up Light Switch Connector
Control Cable
Clip
Clip
Vehicle Speed Sensor Connector
Drive Shaft (RH)
Washer
×6
Battery
Drive Shaft (LH)
Tie Rod End
Stiffener Plate
Starter
Support Bracket
Ground Cable
Cotter Pin
Engine Under Cover (RH)
Lock Nut Cap
Grommet
Center Member
Engine Under Cover (LH)
Front Exhaust Pipe
◆ Non-reusable part
TY5039600207000X

Fig. 2 Transaxle replacement. Celica w/S54 manual transaxle

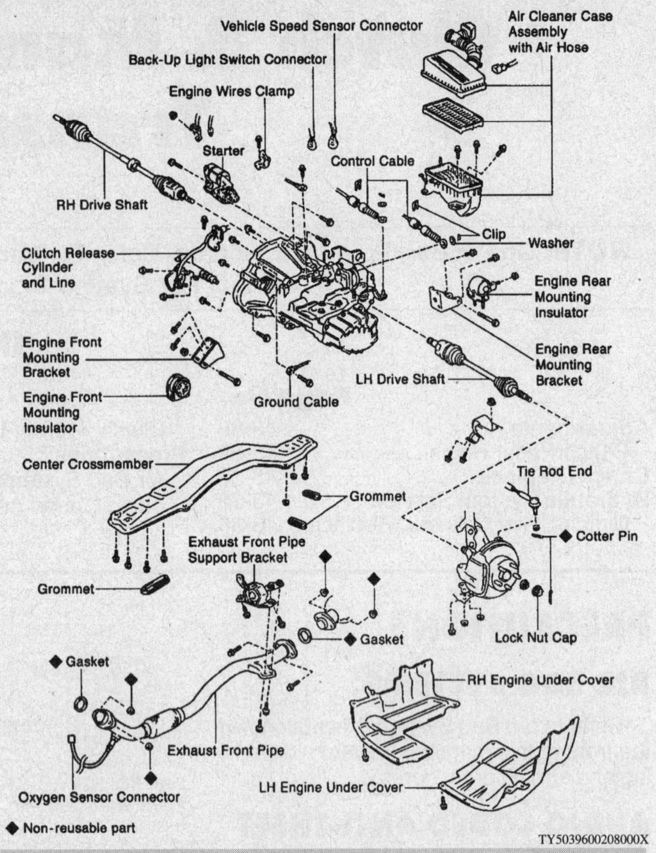
Vehicle Speed Sensor Connector
Air Cleaner Case Assembly with Air Hose
Back-Up Light Switch Connector
Engine Wires Clamp
Starter
Control Cable
RH Drive Shaft
Clip
Washer
Clutch Release Cylinder and Line
Engine Rear Mounting Insulator
Engine Front Mounting Bracket
Engine Rear Mounting Bracket
LH Drive Shaft
Engine Front Mounting Insulator
Ground Cable
Center Crossmember
Tie Rod End
Grommet
Exhaust Front Pipe Support Bracket
Cotter Pin
Grommet
Gasket
Lock Nut Cap
Gasket
RH Engine Under Cover
Exhaust Front Pipe
LH Engine Under Cover
Oxygen Sensor Connector
◆ Non-reusable part
TY5039600208000X

Fig. 3 Transaxle replacement. Celica w/C52 manual transaxle

5. Remove release bearing, fork and boot.
6. Using suitable calipers, measure clutch disc rivet head depth. Minimum rivet depth should be .012 inch. If not as indicated, replace clutch disc.
7. Using suitable dial indicator, measure flywheel runout. Maximum runout should be .004 inch on Celica models and .008 inch on Supra models. If not as indicated, replace flywheel.
8. Measure clutch disc runout, maximum runout is .031 inch. If not as indicated, replace disc.
9. Using suitable calipers, measure diaphragm spring depth and width. Depth should be 0.024 inch and width should be 0.197 inch. If not as indicated, replace clutch cover.
10. Reverse to install, noting the following:
    a. Using clutch guide tool No. 09301–17010 or 093201–20020, or equivalent, install clutch disc.
    b. Match clutch cover and flywheel alignment marks, then tighten cover bolts to specifications, one turn at a time in a criss-cross pattern, ensuring clutch disc and pressure plate remain aligned.
    c. Using suitable dial indicator, check diaphragm spring tip alignment, .020 inch is maximum allowable out of alignment.

TRANSAXLE

REPLACE

CELICA

Refer to **Figs. 2 and 3** when removing or replacing transaxle.

1993

1. Obtain audio anti-theft code, if equipped, as outlined in "Precautions."
2. Remove hood, and engine undercovers.
3. Drain engine coolant, oil and transaxle fluid.
4. Remove air cleaner assembly as follows:
    a. Disconnect air flow meter connector and four air cleaner cap clips.
    b. Disconnect vacuum hose from turbocharger, PCV hose from cylinder head and air hose from air tube.
    c. Remove air cleaner cap, air flow meter assembly and element.
5. Disconnect accelerator cable from throttle body.
6. Remove engine relay box as follows:
    a. Remove relay box retaining nuts, then disconnect relay box from battery.
    b. Remove lower cover from relay box, then disconnect fusible link cassette and two engine to relay box electrical connectors.
7. Remove A/C relay box, then remove battery.
8. Remove injector solenoid resistor and fuel pump resistor.
9. Remove radiator and radiator reservoir tank.
10. **On models equipped with cruise control,** remove cruise control actuator.
11. **On all models,** remove suspension upper brace.
12. Remove ignition coil, then disconnect check connector, igniter connector and ground strap from left fender apron.
13. Remove engine wire bracket.
14. Remove charcoal canister, then disconnect heater hoses and speedometer cable.
15. Disconnect fuel hoses.
16. Remove starter.
17. Remove four clutch release cylinder retaining bolts, then the cylinder and cylinder tube from transaxle.
18. Disconnect transaxle control cables from transaxle.
19. Disconnect oil cooler hoses.
20. Disconnect turbo charging pressure sensor and A/C ASV.
21. Disconnect ECU, cowl and A/C amplifier connectors.
22. Remove suspension lower crossmember.
23. Remove front exhaust pipe.

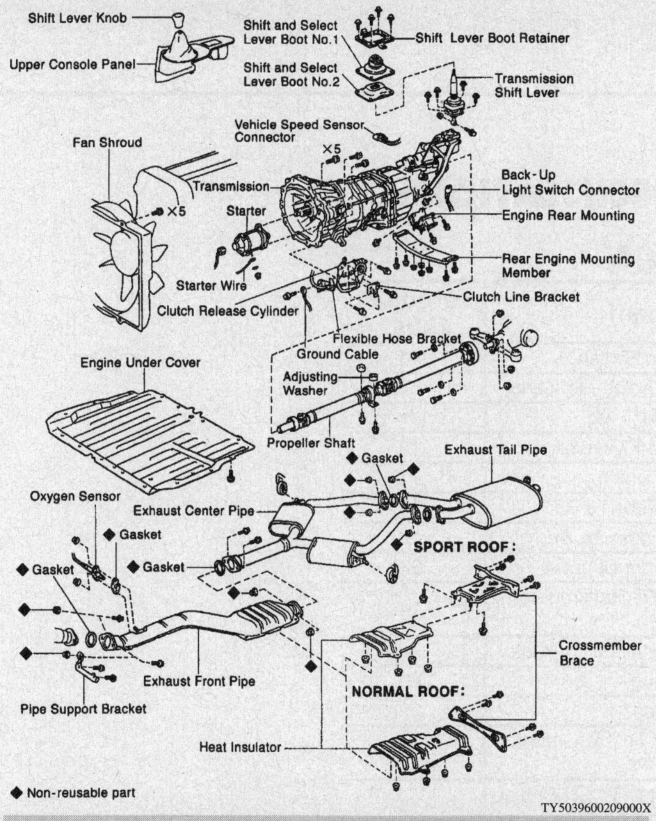
Shift Lever Knob
Shift and Select Lever Boot No.1
Shift Lever Boot Retainer
Upper Console Panel
Shift and Select Lever Boot No.2
Transmission Shift Lever
Vehicle Speed Sensor Connector
Fan Shroud
×5
Transmission
Back-Up Light Switch Connector
×5
Starter
Engine Rear Mounting
Rear Engine Mounting Member
Starter Wire
Clutch Line Bracket
Clutch Release Cylinder
Flexible Hose Bracket
Ground Cable
Engine Under Cover
Adjusting Washer
Propeller Shaft
◆ Gasket
Exhaust Tail Pipe
Oxygen Sensor
Exhaust Center Pipe
◆ Gasket
SPORT ROOF:
◆ Gasket
◆ Gasket
Crossmember Brace
Exhaust Front Pipe
NORMAL ROOF:
Pipe Support Bracket
Heat Insulator
◆ Non-reusable part
TY5039600209000X

Fig. 4 Transmission replacement. Supra w/W58 manual transmission

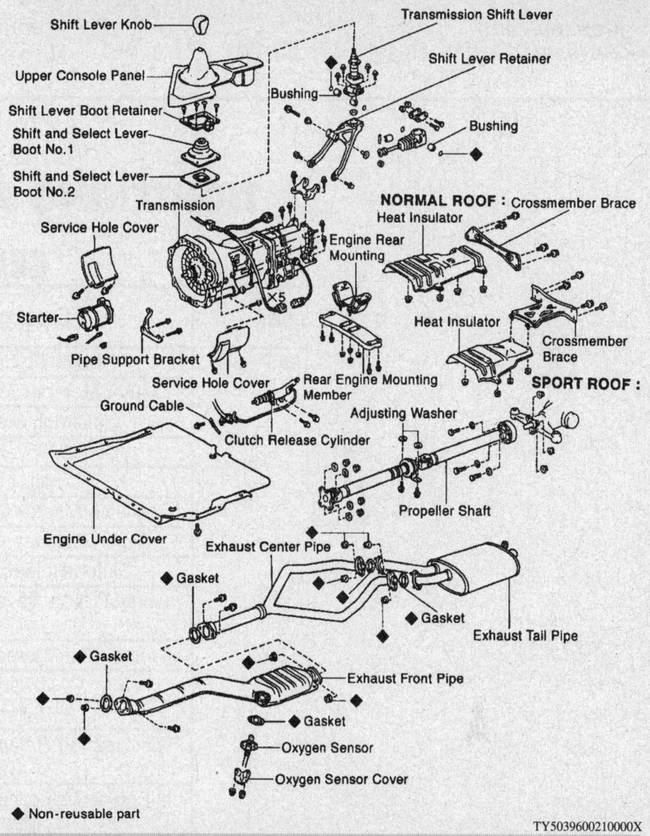
Shift Lever Knob
Transmission Shift Lever
Shift Lever Retainer
Upper Console Panel
Bushing
Shift Lever Boot Retainer
Bushing
Shift and Select Lever Boot No.1
Shift and Select Lever Boot No.2
Transmission
NORMAL ROOF : Crossmember Brace
Heat Insulator
Service Hole Cover
Engine Rear Mounting
×5
Starter
Heat Insulator
Crossmember Brace
Pipe Support Bracket
Service Hole Cover
Rear Engine Mounting Member
SPORT ROOF :
Ground Cable
Adjusting Washer
Clutch Release Cylinder
Propeller Shaft
Engine Under Cover
Exhaust Center Pipe
◆ Gasket
◆ Gasket
Exhaust Tail Pipe
◆ Gasket
Exhaust Front Pipe
◆ Gasket
Oxygen Sensor
Oxygen Sensor Cover
◆ Non-reusable part
TY5039600210000X

Fig. 5 Transmission replacement. Supra w/V160 manual transmission

24. Remove driveshafts and front propeller shaft.
25. Remove deflector from transfer extension housing.
26. Remove damper from transfer extension housing.
27. Remove alternator, idler pulley bracket and A/C compressor. **Do not disconnect A/C hoses from compressor.**
28. Remove power steering pump. **Do not disconnect hoses from pump.**
29. Remove engine front crossmember and engine front mounting insulator and bracket.
30. Remove engine rear mounting insulator and bracket.
31. Remove catalytic converter.
32. Remove engine left and right mounting brackets.
33. Attach engine chain hoist to engine hangers.
34. Remove left and right engine mount bolts and brackets, then remove engine and transaxle assembly from vehicle.
35. Separate transaxle from engine.
36. Reverse procedure to install. Reset audio coded anti-theft, if equipped, as outlined in "Precautions."

1994-96

1. Obtain audio anti-theft code, if equipped, as outlined in "Precautions."
2. Drain engine coolant, oil and transaxle fluid.
3. Remove battery.
4. Remove air cleaner case assembly and air hose.
5. Remove cruise control actuator, if equipped.
6. Disconnect starter connector and remove starter.
7. Remove clutch release cylinder and line clamp.
8. Disconnect transaxle ground cable.
9. Disconnect back-up lamp switch and VSS connector.
10. Disconnect control cable from transaxle.
11. Remove three upper side transaxle mounting bolts.
12. Remove engine upper side left mounting bolt and nut.
13. Install engine support fixture over engine compartment.
14. Remove front wheel.
15. Raise and support vehicle, then remove engine under cover.
16. Remove lefthand and righthand side driveshafts.
17. Remove front exhaust pipe and pipe support bracket.
18. Remove engine front mounting insulator and bracket.
19. Remove engine rear mounting insulator and bracket.
20. Remove engine left lower mounting bolt.
21. Remove center member and stiffener plate.
22. Remove transaxle mounting bolts.
23. Lower engine left side and remove transaxle from engine.
24. Reverse procedure to install. Tighten to specifications.

TRANSMISSION

REPLACE

SUPRA

Refer to **Figs. 4 and 5** when removing or replacing transmission.

1. Obtain audio anti-theft code, if equipped, as outlined in "Precautions."
2. Remove upper console panel.
3. Remove shift lever from inside vehicle.
4. Raise and support vehicle, then drain transmission fluid.
5. Remove engine undercover.
6. Remove crossmember brace.
7. Using extension housing tool No. 09325–20010, or equivalent, remove propeller shaft.
8. Disconnect front exhaust pipe from tail pipe, then remove exhaust pipe.
9. Disconnect back-up light switch electrical connector.
10. **On models equipped with anti-lock brake system,** disconnect rear speed sensor electrical connector.
11. **On all models,** remove clutch release cylinder.
12. Remove starter attaching bolts, then position starter aside.
13. Using suitable transmission jack, raise transmission slightly.
14. Remove rear engine mounting member, then engine mount.
15. Remove transmission attaching bolts and flywheel housing undercover.
16. **Lower engine rear side and remove**

transmission.

17. Reverse to install. Reset audio coded anti-theft, if equipped, as outlined in "Precautions."

TIGHTENING SPECIFICATIONS

CELICA

Year	Component	Torque/Ft. Lbs.
1993–96	Back-Up Lamp Switch	30
	Center Member To Engine Mounting	47
	Clutch Bleeder Plug	6
	Clutch Cover To Flywheel	14
	Clutch Line Union	11
	Clutch Master Cylinder To Body	27
	Clutch Release Cylinder To Body	9
	Clutch Release Fork Support	27
	Control Shaft Cover To Transmission Case	14
	Control Shift Lever Retainer To PLate	9
	Drain Plug	29
	Filler Plug	29
	Front Bearing Retainer To Transmission Case	8
	LH Engine Mounting Stay To LH Engine Mounting	15
	LH Engine Mounting Stay To Transaxle	15
	LH Engine Mounting To Bracket	35
	LH Engine Mounting To Transaxle	38
	Lock Ball Assembly	29
	Mounting Insulator To Bracket	64
	Oil Receiver To Transaxle Case	13
	Oil Receiver To Transmission Case	8
	Output Shaft Front Bearing Lock Plate Bolt	8
	Rear Bearing Retainer To Transmission Case	14
	Reverse Idler Gear Shaft Lock Bolt	22
	Reverse Restrict Pin Holder	14
	Reverse Shift Arm Bracket To Transaxle Case	13
	Ring Gear To Differential Case	71
	Selecting Spring Cover To Control Shift Lever Retainer	43①
	Shift And Select Lever Shaft Lock Bolt	22
	Shift Fork To Fork Shaft	12
	Speedometer Shaft Sleeve Lock Plate Bolt	8
	Straight Screw Plug	18
	Transaxle Case To Transmission Case	22
	Transaxle To Engine (10 mm Bolt)	47
	Transaxle To Engine (12 mm Bolt)	47
	Transaxle To Front Engine Mounting	57
	Transaxle To Rear End Plate (8 mm Bolt)	8
	Transaxle To Rear End Plate (10 mm Bolt)	17
	Transaxle To Rear Engine Mounting	57

Continued

CELICA—Continued

Year	Component	Torque/Ft. Lbs.
1993–96	Transaxle To Starter	29
	Transmission Case Cover To Transmission Case	13
	Transmission Case Protector To Transmission Case	9
	5th Driven Gear Locknut	87

① — Inch lbs.

SUPRA

Component	Torque/Ft. Lbs.
CLUTCH	
Bleeder Plug	8
Clutch Cover To Flywheel Bolts	14
Clutch Line Tube Union	11
Flexible Hose To Release Cylinder	17
Flywheel To Crankshaft Bolts	54
Release Cylinder To Clutch Housing Mounting Bolts	9
Reservoir Mounting Bolts	18
W58 TRANSMISSION	
Back-Up Lamp Switch	30
Center Bearing Retainer To Intermediate Plate	9
Clutch Housing To Engine	29
Clutch Housing To Transmission Case	27
Drain And Filler Plug	30
Engine Rear Mounting Bolts	18
Extension Housing To Intermediate Plate	27
Front Bearing Retainer Set Bolts	18
Restrict Pin	30
Reverse Idler Gear Shaft Stopper Bolt	18
Shift Fork Set Bolt	9
Shift Lever Housing To Shift & Select Lever Shaft	29
Shift Lever Retainer To Extension Housing	13
Stiffener Plate Bolt	27
Straight Screw Plug	18
V160 TRANSMISSION	
Clutch Cover Set Bolt	9
Clutch Release Cylinder	14
Crossmember Brace	9
Exhaust Center Pipe Bolts	14
Exhaust Pipe Support Bracket To Clutch Housing	27
Heat Insulator	48①
Rear Engine Mounting Member Bolt	19
Rear Engine Mounting Member Nut	10
Shift Lever Retaining Bolts	14
Shift Lever Set Bolts	6
Transmission Mounting Bolts	53
Transmission Rear Mounting Bolts	18

① — Inch lbs.

Rear Axle & Suspension

INDEX

	Page No.
Axle Hub, Replace	43-45
Supra	43-45
Coil Spring, Replace	43-46
Celica	43-46
Supra	43-47
Control Arm, Replace	43-47
Supra	43-47
Hub & Bearing, Replace	43-44
Celica 2WD	43-44
Rear Axle Shaft, Replace	43-44
Celica AWD	43-44
Shock Absorber, Replace	43-46
Celica	43-46
Supra	43-46
Stabilizer Bar, Replace	43-47
Celica	43-47
Supra	43-47
Strut Rod, Replace	43-45
Celica	43-45
Supra	43-46
Suspension Arm, Replace	43-47
Celica	43-47
Supra	43-47
Tightening Specifications	43-48
Celica	43-48
Supra	43-48

REAR AXLE SHAFT

REPLACE

CELICA AWD

1. Remove axle shaft from axle hub.
2. Remove bearing inner race (outer) from axle shaft, **Fig. 1.**
3. Remove dust cover, then the inner and outer oil seals.
4. Remove hole snap ring.
5. Remove bearing.
6. Install bearing.
7. Install hole snap ring and outer seal.
8. Install dust cover, axle shaft and inner oil seal.
9. Install axle carrier with axle hub. Install carrier with axle hub. Place rear axle carrier to the shock absorber lower bracket. Install the two attaching bolts and nuts. Tighten nuts to specifications.
10. Temporarily install the No. 2 suspension arm to the axle carrier and the No. 1 suspension arm to the axle carrier.
11. Temporarily install the strut rod to the axle carrier.
12. Install parking brake cable, parking brake assembly and rotor disc. Install brake caliper and tighten attaching bolts to specifications.
13. Install plate washer, bearing locknut, bearing locknut cap and a new cotter pin. Tighten attaching nut to specification.
14. Tighten strut rod to axle carrier mount bolts and suspension arm to axle carrier attaching bolts to specifications.

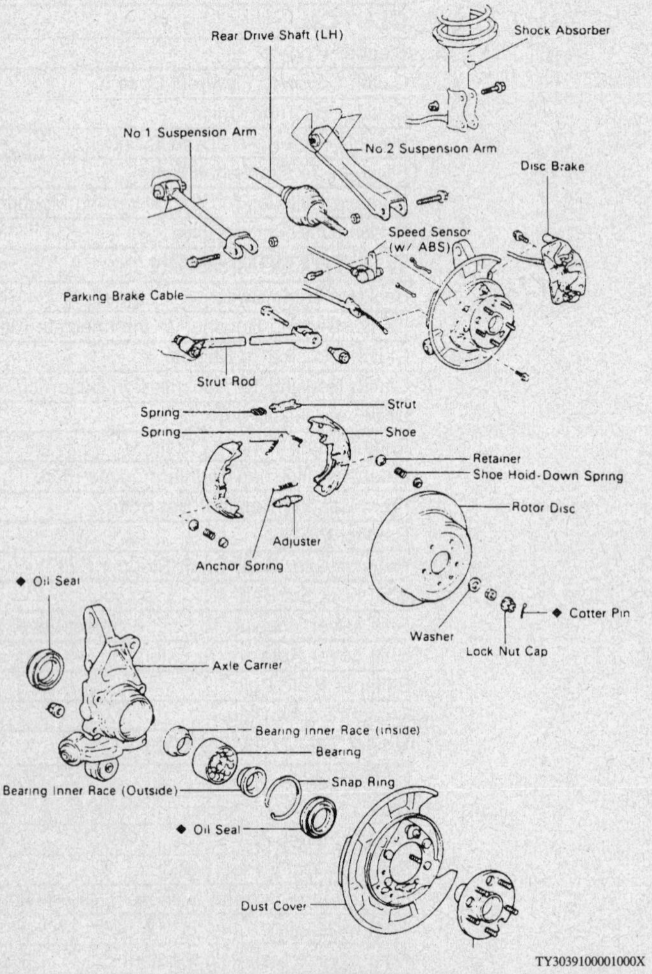

Rear Drive Shaft (LH)
Shock Absorber
No 1 Suspension Arm
No 2 Suspension Arm
Disc Brake
Speed Sensor (w/ ABS)
Parking Brake Cable
Strut Rod
Spring
Spring
Strut
Shoe
Retainer
Shoe Hold-Down Spring
Rotor Disc
Adjuster
Anchor Spring
◆ Oil Seal
◆ Cotter Pin
Washer
Lock Nut Cap
Axle Carrier
Bearing Inner Race (Inside)
Bearing
Snap Ring
Bearing Inner Race (Outside)
◆ Oil Seal
Dust Cover
TY3039100001000X

Fig. 1 Axle shaft bearing & oil seal replace. Celica w/AWD

HUB & BEARING

REPLACE

CELICA 2WD

1. Remove brake drum or rotor and check bearing axial play. Play should not exceed .002 inch.
2. **On models equipped with anti-lock brakes,** remove speed sensor.
3. **On models equipped with drum brakes,** disconnect brake line from wheel cylinder, **Fig. 2.**
4. **On all models,** remove 4 bolts holding axle hub to axle carrier and remove axle hub and rear brake assembly.
5. Remove O-ring.
6. Remove strut rod from axle carrier, then remove No. 1 and 2 suspension arms, then remove axle carrier to shock absorber attaching bolts.
7. Place hub in suitable vise. Using hammer and chisel, loosen stake part of nut and remove nut.
8. Using axle shaft remover tool No. 09550-20017, or equivalent, push axle shaft off axle hub.
9. Remove oil seal, then inside portion of bearing inner race.
10. Using puller tool No. 09950-10010, or equivalent, pull outside portion of bearing inner race from axle shaft.
11. To replace wheel bearing, place old inner race (outside) on bearing, then using bearing remover tools Nos. 09552-10010 and 09555-10010, or equivalent, press out bearing.
12. Apply MP grease around bearing outer race and replacer pipe tool No. 09550-10012, or equivalent, press new bearing into axle hub.

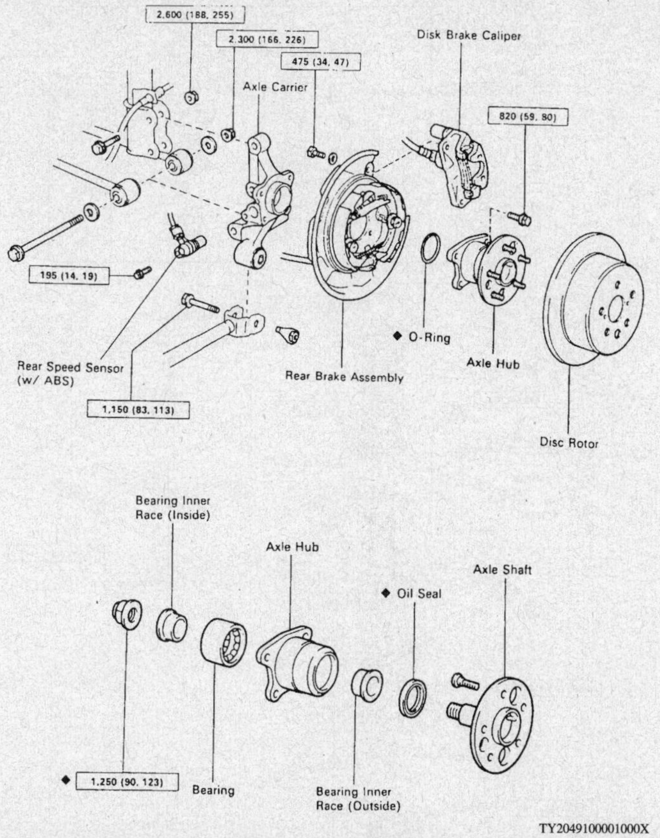
2,600 (188, 255)
2,300 (166, 226)
475 (34, 47)
Disk Brake Caliper
Axle Carrier
820 (59, 80)
195 (14, 19)
◆ O-Ring
Axle Hub
Rear Speed Sensor (w/ ABS)
Rear Brake Assembly
1,150 (83, 113)
Disc Rotor
Bearing Inner Race (Inside)
Axle Hub
Axle Shaft
◆ Oil Seal
◆ 1,250 (90, 123)
Bearing
Bearing Inner Race (Outside)
TY2049100001000X

Fig. 2 Exploded view of rear wheel bearing. Celica less AWD

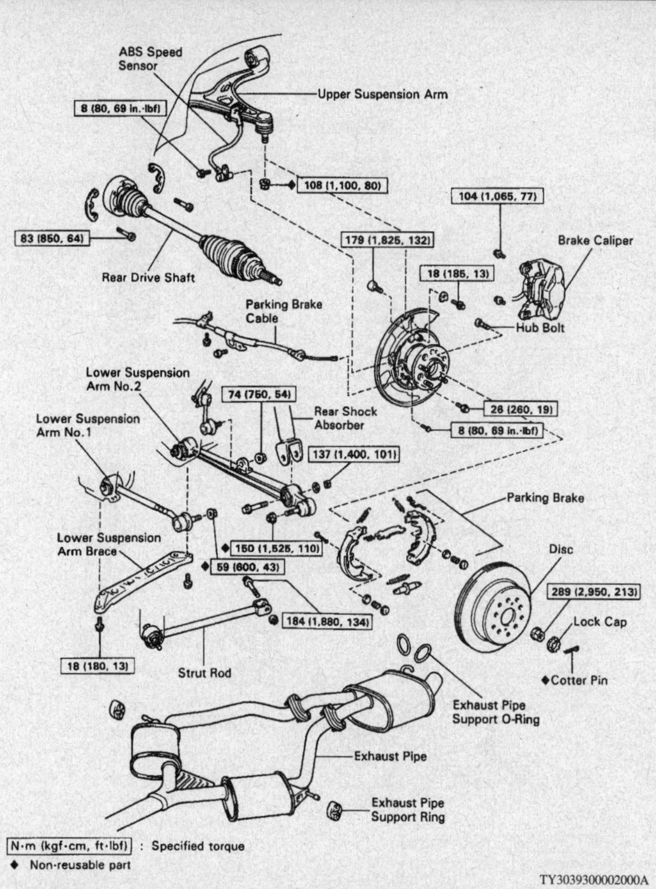
ABS Speed Sensor
8 (80, 69 in.·lbf)
Upper Suspension Arm
108 (1,100, 80)
104 (1,065, 77)
83 (850, 64)
179 (1,825, 132)
Brake Caliper
Rear Drive Shaft
18 (185, 13)
Parking Brake Cable
Hub Bolt
Lower Suspension Arm No.2
74 (750, 54)
Rear Shock Absorber
Lower Suspension Arm No.1
26 (260, 19)
8 (80, 69 in.·lbf)
137 (1,400, 101)
Parking Brake
Lower Suspension Arm Brace
150 (1,525, 110)
59 (600, 43)
Disc
289 (2,950, 213)
184 (1,880, 134)
Lock Cap
18 (180, 13)
Strut Rod
◆Cotter Pin
Exhaust Pipe Support O-Ring
Exhaust Pipe
Exhaust Pipe Support Ring
N·m (kgf·cm, ft·lbf) : Specified torque
◆ Non-reusable part
TY3039300002000A

Fig. 3 Exploded view of rear axle hub. Supra

13. Using countershaft bearing replacer tool No. 09310-35010, or equivalent, drive new oil seal into axle hub.
14. Apply MP grease to oil seal lip.
15. Place inside portion of bearing inner race on bearing.
16. Using installer tool Nos. 09636-20010 and 09228-22020, or equivalents, press inner race with axle hub onto axle shaft.
17. Tighten axle hub nut to specification.
18. Place new O-ring on axle carrier.
19. Install axle hub and rear brake assembly with four bolts. Tighten bolts to specifications.
20. **On models equipped with drum brakes,** connect brake line to wheel cylinder, then install brake drum and bleed brakes.
21. **On models equipped with disc brakes,** install rotor and caliper assembly.
22. **On models equipped with ABS,** install speed sensor.

AXLE HUB

REPLACE

SUPRA

Removal

1. Raise and support rear of vehicle, then remove wheel and tire assembly.
2. Remove brake caliper from axle carrier and suspend with wire.
3. Remove brake disc, then install suitable dial indicator and measure axial hub bearing play. If play is within .002 inch play is satisfactory. If play exceeds .002 inch, disassemble and inspect axle hub.
4. Check axle flange runout. If runout exceeds .002 inch, replace axle shaft.
5. Remove axle shaft.
6. Remove parking brake assembly.
7. **On models with ABS,** disconnect speed sensor.
8. **On all models,** remove No. 1 lower suspension arm attaching nut from axle carrier, then using suitable puller, disconnect suspension arm, **Figs. 3 and 4.**
9. Disconnect No. 2 lower suspension arm and strut rod from axle carrier.
10. Disconnect shock absorber from axle carrier.
11. Disconnect upper control arm from body, then remove axle carrier and upper control arm as an assembly.
12. Remove upper arm-to-axle carrier attaching nut, then separate components.
13. Remove brake backing plate from axle carrier.

Installation

1. Install upper control arm to body. Do not tighten attaching nuts at this time.
2. Install axle carrier on upper control arm and install new nut. Do not tighten at this time.
3. Install No. 1 suspension arm on axle carrier. Tighten attaching nut to specification.
4. Install No. 2 suspension arm on axle carrier. Do not tighten attaching nut at this time.
5. Install strut rod on axle carrier. Do not tighten attaching nut at this time.
6. Tighten upper control arm-to-axle carrier attaching nut to specification.
7. Install shock absorber on axle carrier. Tighten attaching nut to specification.
8. Install parking brake assembly and brake disc.
9. Install axle shaft.
10. Install brake caliper. Tighten attaching bolts to specification.
11. Lower vehicle to ground, then bounce vehicle up and down several times to stabilize suspension.
12. With vehicle weight on suspension, tighten upper control arm-to-body attaching nuts, No. 2 lower suspension arm-to-axle carrier attaching nut and strut rod-to-axle carrier attaching nut to specifications.

STRUT ROD

REPLACE

CELICA

1. Raise and support rear of vehicle.
2. Remove nut and bolt securing strut rod to axle carrier, **Figs. 5 and 6.**
3. Remove nut and bolt securing strut rod to body, then remove strut rod.
4. Reverse procedure to install. Prior to tightening attaching nuts and bolts, lower vehicle to ground and bounce vehicle up and down several times to

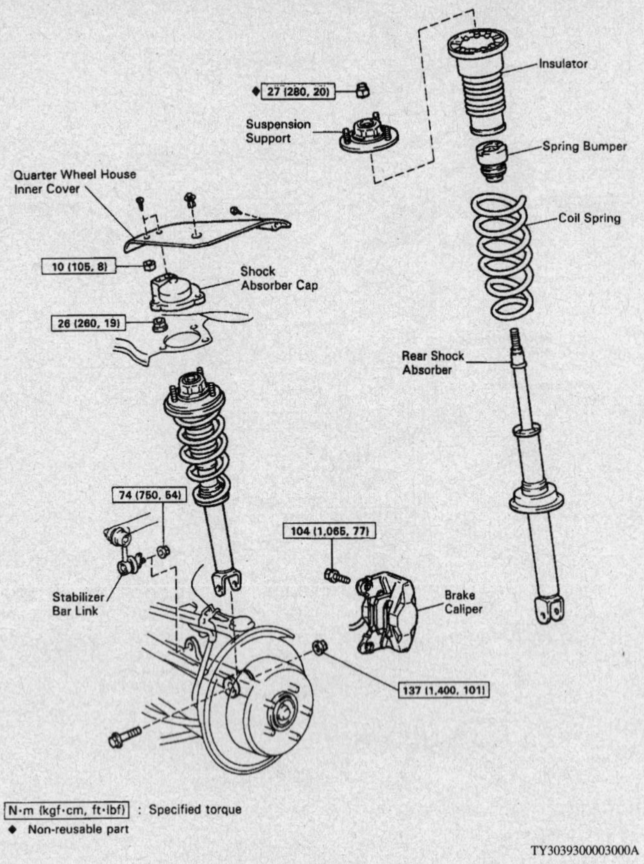

◆ 27 (280, 20)
Insulator
Suspension Support
Spring Bumper
Quarter Wheel House Inner Cover
Coil Spring
10 (105, 8)
Shock Absorber Cap
26 (260, 19)
Rear Shock Absorber
74 (750, 54)
104 (1,065, 77)
Stabilizer Bar Link
Brake Caliper
137 (1,400, 101)
N·m (kgf·cm, ft·lbf) : Specified torque
◆ Non-reusable part
TY3039300003000A

Fig. 4 Exploded view of rear suspension components. Supra

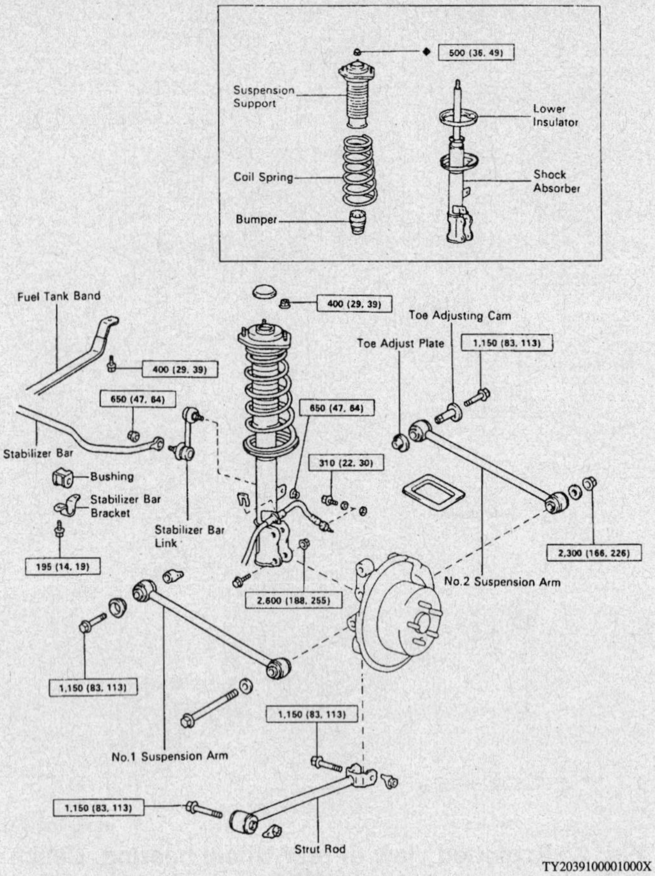

500 (36, 49)
Suspension Support
Lower Insulator
Coil Spring
Shock Absorber
Bumper
Fuel Tank Band
400 (29, 39)
Toe Adjusting Cam
Toe Adjust Plate
1,150 (83, 113)
400 (29, 39)
650 (47, 64)
650 (47, 64)
Stabilizer Bar
310 (22, 30)
Bushing
Stabilizer Bar Bracket
Stabilizer Bar Link
195 (14, 19)
2,300 (166, 226)
2,600 (188, 255)
No.2 Suspension Arm
1,150 (83, 113)
1,150 (83, 113)
No.1 Suspension Arm
1,150 (83, 113)
Strut Rod
TY2039100001000X

Fig. 5 Exploded view of rear suspension. Celica less AWD

stabilize suspension, then tighten attaching nuts and bolts to specification with vehicle weight on suspension.

SUPRA

1. Raise and support rear of vehicle.
2. Remove strut rod-to-axle carrier attaching nut, then the bolt and strut rod.
3. Remove strut rod-to-body attaching bolt, then the strut rod.
4. Reverse procedure to install. Prior to tightening attaching parts, lower vehicle to ground and bounce vehicle several times to stabilize suspension. Tighten strut rod attaching nuts and bolts to specification.

SHOCK ABSORBER

REPLACE

CELICA

Refer to "Coil Spring, Replace" for shock absorber replacement procedures.

SUPRA

1. Raise and support rear of vehicle, then remove wheel and tire assembly.
2. Remove rear brake caliper and secure aside with wire.
3. Disconnect rear stabilizer link from lower suspension arm No. 2, then remove lower shock mounting bolt. Lower vehicle.
4. Remove speaker grille above shock absorber being replaced.
5. **On models equipped with Toyota Electronically Modulated Suspension (TEMS),** remove quarter panel trim.
6. **On all models,** remove shock absorber-to-axle carrier attaching nut and bolt, **Fig. 4.**
7. Working inside vehicle, remove shock absorber cap, then on models equipped with TEMS, the TEMS actuator.
8. Remove three upper shock absorber attaching nuts, then the shock absorber and spring assembly. Install shock absorber and spring assembly in suitable vise, positioning vise jaws at lower shock mount.
9. Remove coil spring as follows:
   a. Using front coil spring compressor tool No. 09727-22032, or equivalent, compress coil spring.
   b. Remove suspension support nut, then the suspension support.
   c. Remove coil spring and bumper.
10. Reverse procedure to install, noting the following:
    a. Install bumper and coil spring on shock absorber.
    b. Align coil spring end with lower seat hollow.
    c. Tighten suspension support nut to specification.
    d. Tighten three upper shock absorber attaching nuts to specification.
    e. Tighten shock absorber-to-axle carrier attaching bolts to specification.

COIL SPRING

REPLACE

CELICA

1. **On coupe models,** remove rear speaker board.
2. **On hatchback models,** remove rear speaker grill.
3. **On models equipped with ABS,** disconnect speed sensor electrical connector from shock absorber.
4. **On all models,** disconnect brake hose from wheel cylinder or caliper, then disconnect brake hose from shock absorber.
5. Working inside vehicle, loosen nut securing suspension support to shock absorber, **Fig. 5. Do not remove nut at this time.**
6. Disconnect stabilizer bar from shock absorber.
7. Remove bolts securing shock absorber to axle carrier, then disconnect shock absorber from carrier.
8. Working inside vehicle, remove nuts securing suspension support to vehicle body, then remove shock absorber, **Fig. 5.**
9. Install a bolt and two nuts in shock absorber lower mounting bracket and

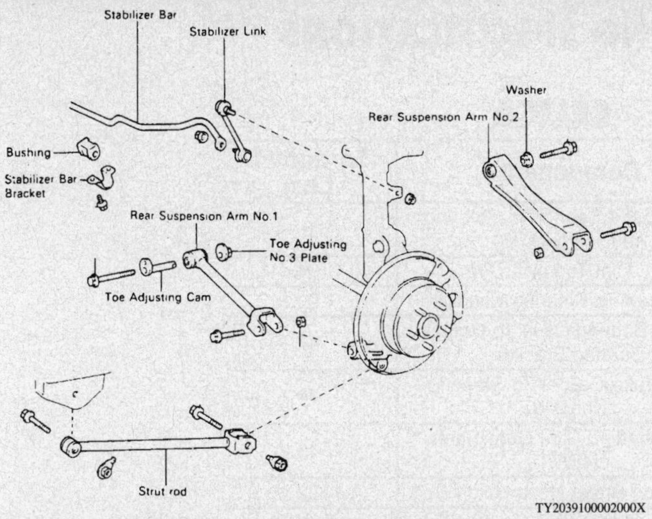
Stabilizer Bar
Stabilizer Link
Washer
Rear Suspension Arm No.2
Bushing
Stabilizer Bar Bracket
Rear Suspension Arm No.1
Toe Adjusting No.3 Plate
Toe Adjusting Cam
Strut rod
TY2039100002000X

Fig. 6 Exploded view of rear suspension. Celica w/AWD

clamp unit in a suitable vise using lower mounting bracket as clamping surface.

10. Using a suitable spring compressor, compress coil spring.
11. Remove nut securing suspension support to shock absorber, then remove suspension support, coil spring, insulator and spring bumper, **Fig. 5. Shock absorber is filled with colorless, odorless and non-poisonous high pressure gas. Upon removal, handle shock absorber with care. Do not score or scratch exposed part of piston rod or allow paint or oil to come in contact with it. Do not rotate piston rod and cylinder assembly with shock absorber fully extended. When discarding shock absorber, drill a small hole in bottom of cylinder to relieve pressure.**
12. Reverse procedure to install.

SUPRA

Refer to "Shock Absorber, Replace" procedure for coil spring replacement procedures.

CONTROL ARM

REPLACE

SUPRA

Removal

Refer to "Rear Axle Hub, Replace" for upper control arm replacement procedures.

Inspection

1. Flip ball joint stud back and forth five times, then install nut.
2. Using torque wrench, turn nut continuously one turn each 2–4 seconds and take torque reading on fifth turn.
3. If turning **torque** is not 9–30 inch lbs., replace upper control arm.

Installation

Refer to "Rear Axle Hub, Replace" for upper control arm installation procedures.

STABILIZER BAR

REPLACE

CELICA

1. Raise and support rear of vehicle, then remove rear wheels.
2. Disconnect bolts securing stabilizer bar to axle housing, **Figs. 5 and 6.**
3. Disconnect bolts securing stabilizer bar to frame, then remove stabilizer bar.
4. Reverse procedure to install.

SUPRA

1. Raise and support rear of vehicle.
2. Disconnect two exhaust support rings and secure exhaust pipe aside with wire.
3. Disconnect both stabilizer bar links, **Fig. 4.**
4. Remove both stabilizer bar bracket attaching bolts, then the stabilizer bar.
5. Remove stabilizer bar links from bar.
6. Reverse procedure to install. Tighten stabilizer bar bracket attaching bolts and stabilizer link-to-No. 1 lower suspension arm attaching bolts to specifications.

SUSPENSION ARM

REPLACE

CELICA

Removal

1. Raise and support vehicle.
2. Remove Nos. 1 and 2 suspension arm-to-steering knuckle attaching nut and bolt, **Figs. 5 and 6.**
3. Scribe reference marks on adjusting cam, then remove No. 2 suspension arm-to-crossmember attaching nut and bolt. Remove suspension arm.
4. Remove No. 1 suspension arm attaching nut, plate and bolt, then remove suspension arm.

Installation

1. Install serrated bushing side of No. 1 suspension arm in crossmember, then install bolt, plate and nut. Do not tighten at this time. **Suspension arms are marked with "L" of "R" for installation identification.**
2. Install serrated bushing side of No. 2 suspension arm in crossmember, then install cam, bolt and nut, but do not tighten. Align cam reference marks made during removal. **Ensure side of suspension arm with spot of white paint is facing outward.**
3. Connect Nos. 1 and 2 suspension arms on steering knuckle, then install attaching bolt and nut. Do not tighten at this time.
4. Lower vehicle to ground, then bounce vehicle up and down several times to stabilize suspension.
5. With vehicle weight on suspension, tighten attaching nuts and bolts to specifications.

SUPRA

Removal

1. Raise and support rear of vehicle, disconnect brake caliper and secure aside with wire.
2. Disconnect ABS speed sensor and wire harness.
3. Remove axle shaft, then the No. 1 suspension arm-to-axle carrier attaching nut.
4. Remove suspension arm No. 1 tie rod end from axle carrier, then disconnect parking brake cable.
5. Scribe reference marks between suspension arm No. 1 adjusting cam and crossmember, then remove arm pivot nut, bolt, cams and arm.
6. Remove suspension arm No. 2 to axle carrier attaching nut and bolt, then disconnect arm from carrier.
7. Scribe reference marks between suspension arm No. 2 adjusting cam and crossmember, then remove arm pivot nut, bolt, cams and arm.

Inspection

1. Flip tie rod end stud back and forth five times, then install nut.
2. Using torque wrench, turn nut continuously one turn each 2–4 seconds and take torque reading on fifth turn.
3. If turning **torque** is not 7–30 inch lbs., replace No. 1 suspension arm.

Installation

Reverse procedure to install. Prior to tightening attaching parts, lower vehicle to ground and bounce vehicle several times to stabilize suspension. Tighten No. 1 suspension arm-to-axle carrier attaching nut, suspension arms-to-crossmember attaching nuts and suspension arm-to-axle carrier attaching nuts to specifications.

TIGHTENING SPECIFICATIONS

CELICA

Year	Component	Torque/Ft. Lbs.
1993–96	ABS Speed Sensor To Steering Knuckle (w/ABS)	6
	Ball Joint To Lower Arm	94
	Ball Joint To Steering Knuckle	93
	Center Bearing Case To Center Bearing Bracket	47
	Disc Brake Caliper To Steering Knuckle	79
	Driveshaft To Side Gear Shaft (4WD)	48
	Front Disc Brake Hose Union Bolt	22
	Front Exhaust Pipe Support To Body	14
	Front Exhaust Pipe To Rear Exhaust Pipe	32
	Hub Bearing Locknut	137
	Lower Arm Damper Plate Bolt	48
	Lower Arm Front Setting Nut	156
	Lower Arm Rear Bracket To Body	72
	Lower Arm Rear Nut	101
	Piston Rod To Suspension Support	34
	Shock Absorber To Steering Knuckle	224
	Stabilizer Bar To Lower Arm	26
	Stabilizer Bracket To Body	13
	Suspension Arm Shaft To Body	112
	Suspension Crossmember To Body	112
	Suspension Support To Body	59
	Tie Rod End Locknut	41
1993–96	Tie Rod End To Steering Knuckle	36
	Transmission Case Protector Bolt (4WD)	13
	Wheel Lug Nut	76

SUPRA

Year	Component	Torque/Ft. Lbs.
1993–96	Axle Hub Locknuts	147
	Brake Hose Bracket To Steering Knuckle	14
	Disc Brake Caliper To Steering Knuckle	77
	Front & Rear Adjusting Cam Bolts	177
	Front Shock Absorber To Body	26
	Front Shock Absorber To Lower Suspension Arm	106
	Lower Ball Joint To Lower Suspension Arm	94
	Lower Ball Joint To Steering Knuckle	92
	Piston Rod Locknut	22
	Speed Sensor Set Bolt	14
	Stabilizer Bar Bracket To Body	13
	Stabilizer Link To Lower Suspension Arm	47
	Stabilizer Link To Stabilizer Bar	47

Continued

Year	Component	Torque/Ft. Lbs.
1993–96	Steering Knuckle To Upper Suspension Arm	76
	Tie Rod End Clamp Bolt	14
	Tie Rod End To Steering Knuckle	36
	Upper Suspension Arm Mounting Nut	121
	Wheel Lug Nut	76

Front Suspension & Steering

NOTE: On Air Bag Equipped Models, Refer To "Air Bag System Precautions" Located In The Front Of This Manual For System Disarming & Arming Procedures.

INDEX

	Page No.
Ball Joint Inspection	43-50
Coil Spring, Replace	43-50
Celica	43-50
Supra	43-51
Control Arm, Replace	43-51
Lower	43-51
Hub & Bearing, Replace	43-49
Celica	43-49
Supra	43-49
Manual Steering Gears	48-1
Power Steering	48-1
Power Steering Gear, Replace	43-51
Celica	43-51
Supra	43-52
Precautions	43-49
Air Bag Systems	43-49
Stabilizer Bar, Replace	43-51
Supra	43-51
Steering Knuckle, Replace	43-51
Celica	43-51
Strut, Replace	43-51
Tightening Specifications	43-53
Celica	43-53
Supra	43-54
Wheel Bearing, Adjust	43-49

PRECAUTIONS

AIR BAG SYSTEMS

Refer to "Air Bag System Precautions" in the front of this manual for system disarming and arming procedures.

WHEEL BEARING

ADJUST

Celica and Supra models incorporate lubed for life, sealed front wheel bearings with no provision for adjustment.

HUB & BEARING

REPLACE

CELICA

1. Raise and support front of vehicle, then remove tire and wheel assembly.
2. Remove cotter pin and bearing locknut cap.
3. With brake pedal depressed, remove bearing locknut, **Fig. 1.**
4. Remove brake caliper from steering knuckle and suspend out of way.
5. Remove disc rotor, then ensure bearing play in axial direction does not exceed .002 inch.
6. **On models equipped with ABS,** remove speed sensor from steering knuckle.
7. **On all models,** remove cotter pin and nut, then, using suitable puller, disconnect tie rod end from steering knuckle.
8. Remove steering knuckle-to-strut lower bracket attaching nuts and bolts.
9. Disconnect steering knuckle from lower suspension arm.
10. Using plastic hammer, tap axle shaft to loosen it while removing steering knuckle and axle hub. Using puller tool No. 09950-20017, or equivalent, remove hub from axle shaft. **Cover driveshaft boot with cloth to prevent damage.**
11. Remove ball joint from steering knuckle.
12. Remove steering knuckle inner seal.
13. Using suitable pliers, remove axle hub snap ring.
14. Remove bolts securing disc brake dust cover to steering knuckle.
15. Using suitable puller, remove hub from steering knuckle.
16. Remove inside bearing inner race from bearing.
17. Using suitable puller, remove outside inner race from axle hub.
18. Using suitable screwdriver, remove oil seal from steering knuckle.
19. Place an outside bearing inner race on bearing and, using suitable tool and hammer, drive out bearing. **Always replace the bearing as an assembly.**
20. Using suitable tool, press new bearing into steering knuckle.
21. Rotate and insert the side lip of a new outer oil seal into seal tool No. 09608-32010, or equivalent, then, using seal installer tool No. 09710-14012, or equivalent, drive oil seal into steering knuckle.
22. Apply suitable grease to oil seal lip.
23. Install disc brake dust cover.
24. Apply suitable grease to oil seal and bearing, then, using suitable tool, press hub into steering knuckle.
25. Install hub snap ring in steering knuckle.
26. Using suitable tool, drive a new oil seal and dust deflector (if equipped) into steering knuckle surface, then apply suitable grease to oil seal lip and axle shaft.
27. If removed, install ball joint.
28. Reverse procedure to install, tighten two strut to steering knuckle attaching nuts and bolts, steering knuckle to lower suspension arm attaching bolts, tie rod end attaching nut and bearing locknut to specifications.

SUPRA

1. Raise and support front of vehicle, then remove tire and wheel assembly.
2. Remove speed sensor and brake hose bracket from steering knuckle, **Fig. 2.**
3. Remove brake caliper from steering knuckle and suspend out of way.
4. Remove rotor disc, then ensure bearing play in axial direction does not exceed .002 inch.
5. Remove cotter pin and nut from steering knuckle, then using suitable tool, disconnect tie rod end from steering gear knuckle.
6. Remove cotter pin and nut, then using suitable tool, disconnect steering knuckle from upper suspension arm.
7. Remove clip and nut, then using suitable tool, remove steering knuckle

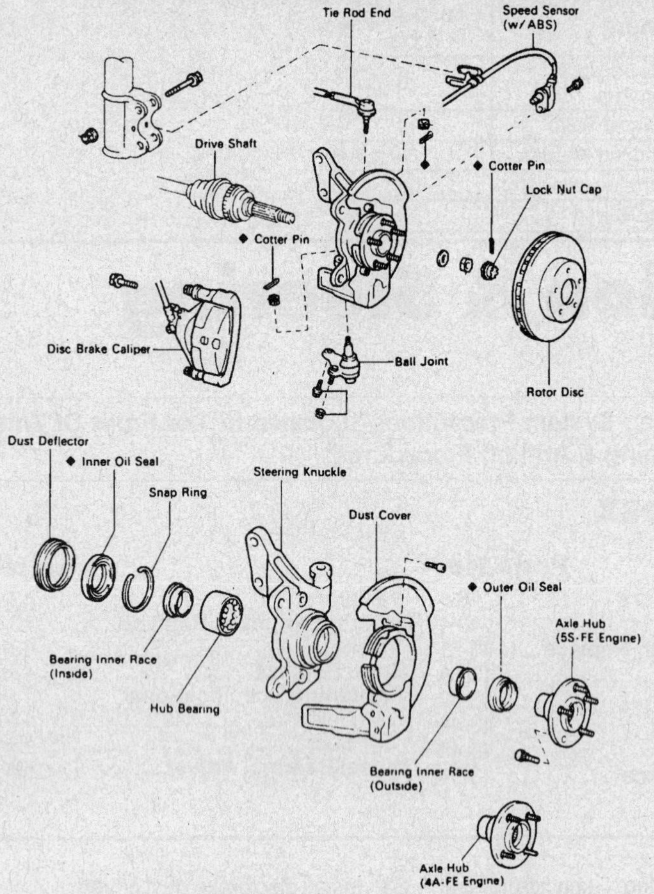

Tie Rod End
Speed Sensor (w/ABS)
Drive Shaft
◆ Cotter Pin
Lock Nut Cap
◆ Cotter Pin
Disc Brake Caliper
Ball Joint
Rotor Disc
Dust Deflector
◆ Inner Oil Seal
Snap Ring
Steering Knuckle
Dust Cover
◆ Outer Oil Seal
Axle Hub (5S-FE Engine)
Bearing Inner Race (Inside)
Hub Bearing
Bearing Inner Race (Outside)
Axle Hub (4A-FE Engine)
TY2049100002000X

Fig. 1 Exploded view of axle hub & steering knuckle. Celica

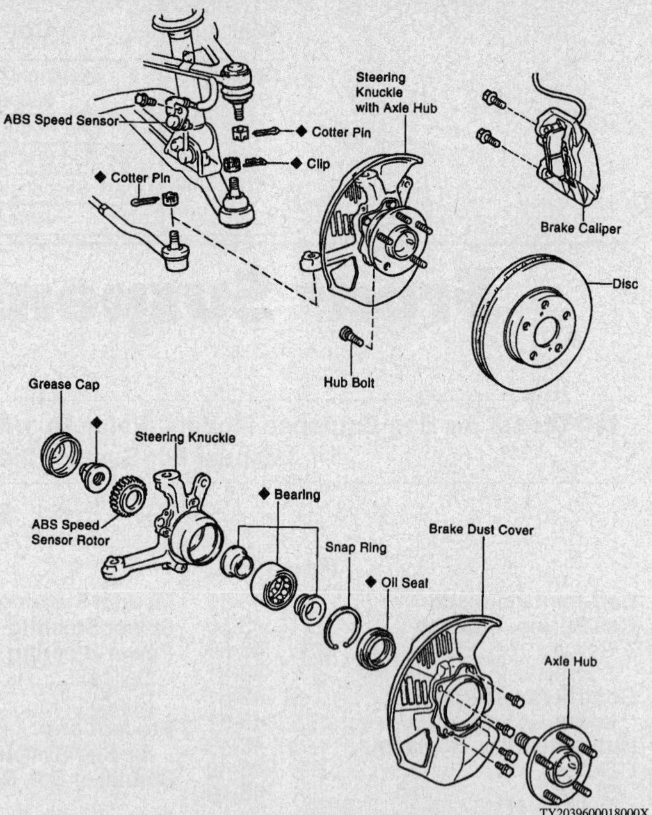

Steering Knuckle with Axle Hub
ABS Speed Sensor
◆ Cotter Pin
◆ Clip
◆ Cotter Pin
Brake Caliper
Disc
Hub Bolt
Grease Cap
Steering Knuckle
◆ Bearing
ABS Speed Sensor Rotor
Snap Ring
Brake Dust Cover
◆ Oil Seal
Axle Hub
TY2039600018000X

Fig. 2 Exploded view of axle hub & steering knuckle. Supra

from the upper suspension arm, then axle hub.

8. Using a suitable tool, remove hub bearing cap.
9. Secure axle hub in vice, then using a hammer and chisel, loosen the staked part of the luck nut, then remove.
10. Using a suitable tool, remove axle hub from axle bearing.
11. Using a suitable tool, remove hub bearing inner race (outside) from axle hub.
12. Remove dust cover retaining bolts, then the dust cover from steering knuckle.
13. Using a screwdriver, remove outer oil seal from steering knuckle.
14. Using snap ring pliers, remove the hole snap rings.
15. Temporarily install hub bearing inner race (outside) to the hub bearing, then using suitable tool and hammer, remove hub bearing from steering knuckle.
16. Using a suitable tool, press new bearing into steering knuckle.
17. Install the hole snap ring, then using steering knuckle seal tool No. 09608–32010, or equivalent, install the hub bearing inner race (outside) to the hub bearing then, using axle hub tool set No. 09608–35014, or equivalent, press the oil seal into the steering knuckle.
18. Install disc brake dust cover.
19. Install hub bearing inner race (inside) to the hub bearing, then using a suitable tool install axle hub to steering knuckle.
20. Install and tighten new axle hub locknut to specification, then using punch and hammer stake the locknut.
21. Install hub bearing cap.
22. Reverse procedure to install. Tighten attaching nuts and bolts to specifications.

BALL JOINT INSPECTION

1. Raise front of vehicle and place a 7–8 inch block under one tire.
2. Lower vehicle until the front springs are about half loaded. Place stands under vehicle.
3. Ensure front wheels are in a straight forward position, then chock front wheels.
4. Using suitable lever, move lower control arm up and down and check ball joint for excessive play. If any ball joint play is observed, replace ball joint.
5. Repeat procedure for opposite ball joint.

COIL SPRING

REPLACE

CELICA

1. Remove union bolt and two washers, then disconnect brake hose from disc caliper.
2. Drain brake fluid into a suitable container, then remove clip from brake hose and separate brake hose from bracket.
3. **On models with anti-lock brake system (ABS),** remove speed sensor wire harness clamp bracket bolt and disconnect wire harness clamp.
4. **On all models,** remove lower strut assembly-to-steering knuckle attaching bolts.
5. Remove three nuts holding top of strut assembly to body, then remove strut assembly. **Cover driveshaft boot with cloth to avoid damage.**
6. Install a bolt and two nuts to assembly bracket as shown in **Fig. 3,** then secure assembly in a vise.
7. Compress coil spring, using spring compression tool No. 09727-30020, or equivalent, then retain seat with tool No. 09729-22031, or equivalent, and remove suspension support nut.
8. Remove suspension support, spring seat, spring, insulators and bumper.
9. Reverse procedure to install, noting the following:
   a. When installing upper spring seat,

face the "OUT" mark of the seat towards outside of vehicle.

b. Tighten three strut assembly-to-body nuts and two strut assembly-to-steering knuckle bolts to specifications.
c. Pack suspension support bearing with suitable multi-purpose grease before installing dust cover.
d. Tighten brake caliper bolts to specification.

SUPRA

1. Raise and support vehicle, then remove wheel.
2. Remove brake caliper from steering knuckle, **Fig. 4.** Suspend caliper aside with suitable wire. **Leave brake hose attached.**
3. **On models equipped with Toyota Electronically Modulated Suspension (TEMS),** remove TEMS actuator cover and actuator from top of strut.
4. **On all models,** loosen piston rod locknut enough that it can be turned by hand.
5. Remove upper suspension arm to vehicle body attaching nuts and bolts, then disconnect suspension arm from body.
6. Remove three strut assembly to vehicle body attaching nuts.
7. Remove strut to lower suspension arm attaching nut and bolt, then the strut.
8. Place strut in suitable holding devise, then compress coil spring with spring compressing tool No. 09727-30020, or equivalent.
9. Remove top strut support center nut, then suspension support, coil spring and spring bumper.
10. Reverse procedure to install. Tighten strut to vehicle attaching nuts and strut to lower suspension arm attaching nut to specifications. Temporarily install upper suspension arm, then lower vehicle and bounce several times to stabilize suspension. With vehicle weight on suspension, tighten upper suspension arm to vehicle body attaching nuts and piston rod locknut specifications.

STRUT

REPLACE

Refer to "Coil Spring, Replace" for procedure.

CONTROL ARM

REPLACE

LOWER

Celica

1. Raise and support vehicle, then remove wheel and tire assembly.
2. Remove steering knuckle to lower suspension arm attaching bolt and two nuts, **Fig. 5.**
3. Remove attaching nut, then disconnect stabilizer link from lower suspension arm.
4. Remove lower suspension arm, except lefthand arm on models with automatic transaxle, as follows:
   a. Remove lower suspension arm front setting nut and washer.
   b. Remove lower suspension arm rear bracket bolts, then the lower suspension arm.
   c. Remove four attaching bolts and two nuts, then the suspension lower crossmember.
   d. Remove attaching bolt and nut, then the lower suspension arm shaft.
5. Remove lefthand lower suspension arm on models with automatic transaxle as follows:
   a. Remove lower suspension arm front setting nut and washer.
   b. Remove four attaching bolts and two nuts, then the lower crossmember.
   c. Remove attaching bolt and nut, then the lower suspension arm and lower arm shaft.
6. Reverse procedure to install. Tighten attaching nuts and bolts to specifications.

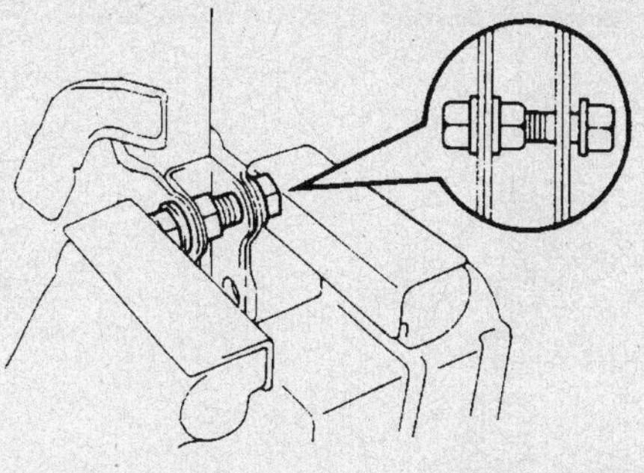
TY2029100003000X

Fig. 3 Setting strut assembly into vise

Supra

1. Raise and support vehicle, remove lower engine cover and brake caliper, then secure caliper aside with wire.
2. Disconnect stabilizer bar link from lower suspension arm, **Fig. 6.**
3. Remove lower ball joint locknut, then using suitable puller, disconnect ball joint from steering knuckle.
4. Remove shock absorber-to-lower suspension arm attaching nut and bolt, then disconnect shock absorber from arm.
5. Make reference marks between lower suspension arm alignment cams and their mounting surfaces, then remove nuts, alignment cams, bolts and suspension arm.
6. Reverse procedure to install, noting the following:
   a. Tighten lower suspension arm-to-ball joint attaching nuts and bolts to specification.
   b. Install lower suspension arm. Do not tighten alignment cams at this time.
   c. When installing ball joint to steering knuckle, install conventional nut first and tighten to specification, then install locking nut and tighten to specification.
   d. Tighten shock absorber lower mounting nut and bolt, stabilizer link attaching nut to specification.
   e. Lower vehicle and allow the weight to rest on suspension. Bounce vehicle several times to settle suspension, then align marks made on cams. Tighten adjusting cam nuts to specification with vehicle weight on suspension.

STEERING KNUCKLE

REPLACE

CELICA

Refer to "Hub & Bearing, Replace" for steering knuckle replacement procedure.

STABILIZER BAR

REPLACE

SUPRA

1. Disconnect stabilizer link from stabilizer bar, **Fig. 6.**
2. Remove stabilizer link from lower suspension arm.
3. Remove stabilizer bar bracket attaching bolts, then the stabilizer bar, cushions and brackets.
4. Reverse procedure to install. Tighten all attaching nuts and bolts to specification.

POWER STEERING GEAR

REPLACE

CELICA

1. Position front wheels facing straight ahead, then using seat belt of the driver's seat, fix steering wheel so that it will not turn.
2. Scribe matchmarks on universal joint and control valve shaft as shown in **Fig. 7.**
3. Loosen bolt on upper side of universal joint, then remove bolt on lower side and disconnect universal joint.
4. Remove cotter pin and nut at tie rod end, then using pressing tool No. 09611-22012, or equivalent, disconnect tie rod end from knuckle arm.
5. Using line removal tool No. 09631-22020, or equivalent, disconnect pressure and return lines from gear housing.
6. **On 4WD model,** proceed as follows:
   a. Mark propeller shaft flange and intermediate shaft flange for installation alignment.
   b. Remove propeller shaft attaching nuts and bolts, then using removal tool No. 09325-20010, or equivalent, remove propeller shaft.
   c. Remove righthand stabilizer bar bracket, then disconnect stabilizer bar from link.
   d. Remove gear housing attaching nuts and bolts.
   e. Remove power steering tube clamp bolt.

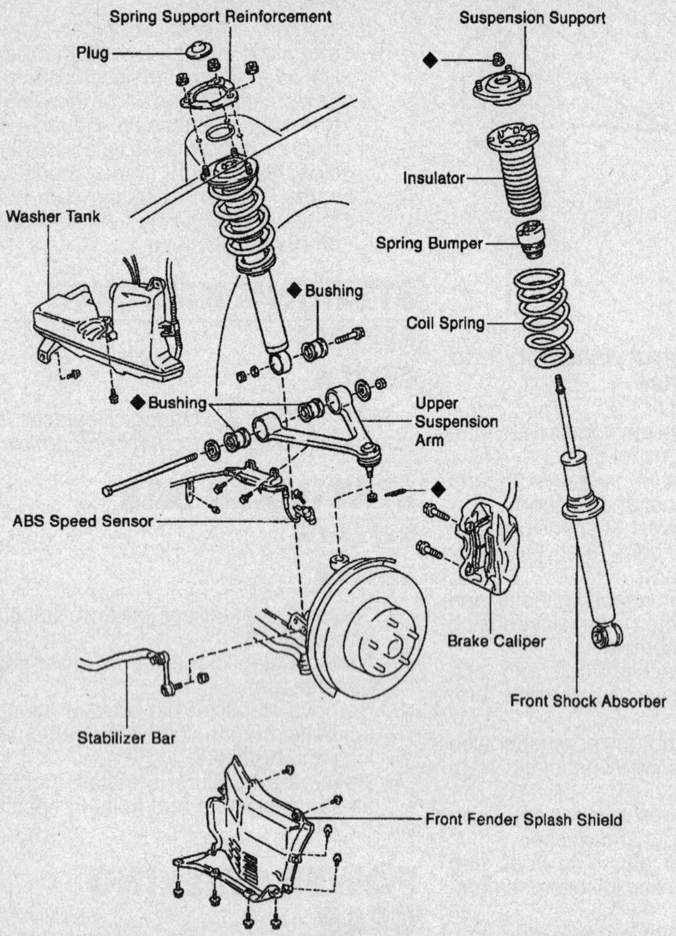
Spring Support Reinforcement
Plug
Suspension Support
Insulator
Washer Tank
Spring Bumper
◆ Bushing
Coil Spring
◆ Bushing
Upper Suspension Arm
ABS Speed Sensor
Brake Caliper
Front Shock Absorber
Stabilizer Bar
Front Fender Splash Shield

TY2029600032000X

Fig. 4 Front suspension strut & coil spring components. Supra

f. Position gear housing to right side of the vehicle, then remove.

7. **On 2WD models,** slide gear housing to the right side of the vehicle, then pull gear housing out through lefthand lower side of vehicle body, **Fig. 8. Do not damage pressure tubes.**
8. **On all models,** reverse procedure to install, noting the following:
   a. Set gear housing so that it matches dimensions shown in **Fig. 9,** with gear housing at center point.
   b. Align matchmarks on universal joint and control valve shaft.
   c. Check steering wheel center point and toe-in.

SUPRA

1. Ensure steering wheel in center and locked into place. Raise and support front of vehicle, then position front wheels straight ahead.
2. Remove engine undercover.
3. Remove steering shaft universal joint bolt on pinion shaft side, then loosen universal joint bolt on main shaft side. Make alignment marks between pinion shaft and universal joint, then pull out universal joint from pinion shaft.
4. Remove power steering pressure and return lines from gear housing.

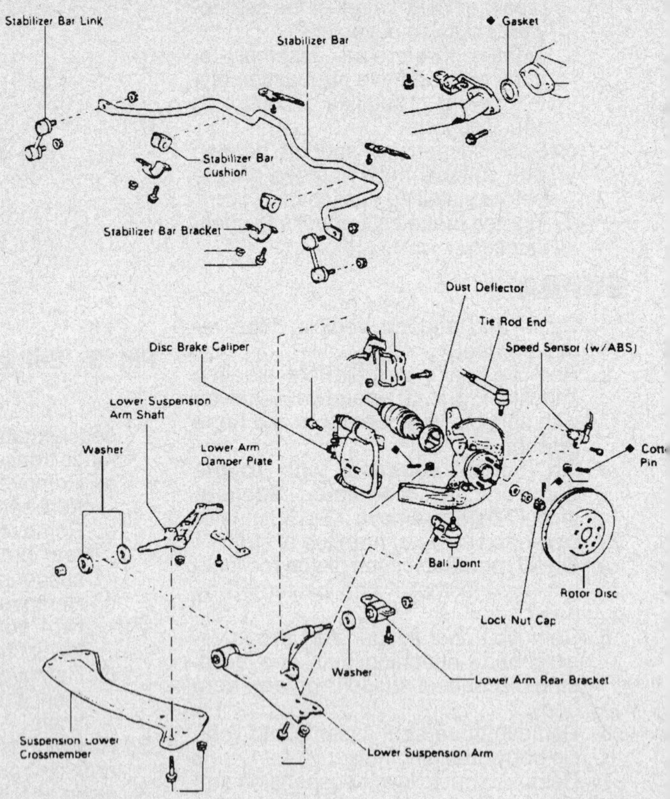
Stabilizer Bar Link
Stabilizer Bar
◆ Gasket
Stabilizer Bar Cushion
Stabilizer Bar Bracket
Dust Deflector
Tie Rod End
Disc Brake Caliper
Speed Sensor (w/ABS)
Lower Suspension Arm Shaft
Washer
Lower Arm Damper Plate
◆ Cott
Pin
Ball Joint
Rotor Disc
Lock Nut Cap
Washer
Lower Arm Rear Bracket
Suspension Lower Crossmember
Lower Suspension Arm

TY2029100001000X

Fig. 5 Exploded view of front suspension. Celica

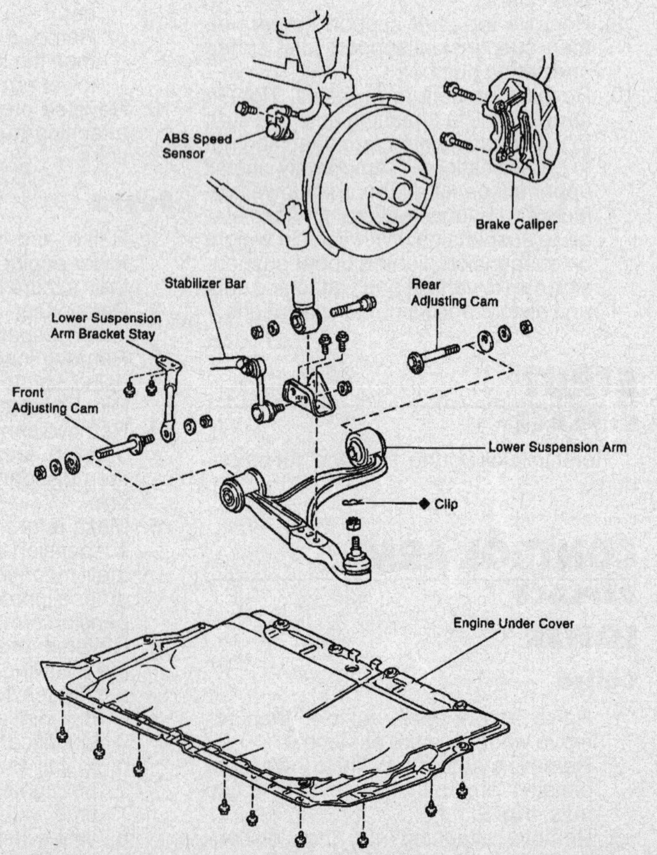
ABS Speed Sensor
Brake Caliper
Stabilizer Bar
Rear Adjusting Cam
Lower Suspension Arm Bracket Stay
Front Adjusting Cam
Lower Suspension Arm
◆ Clip
Engine Under Cover

TY2029600002000A

Fig. 6 Exploded view of front suspension. Supra

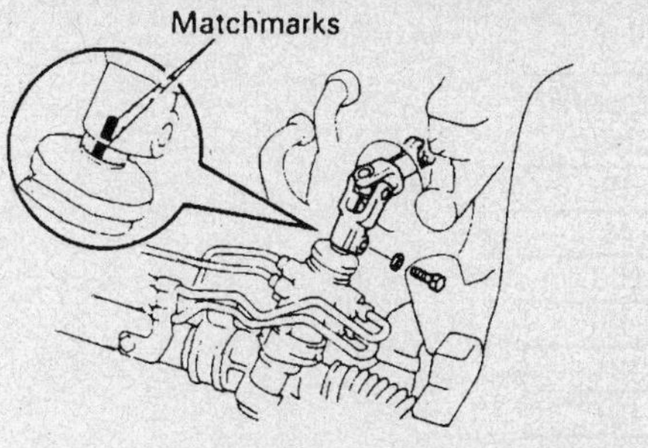
Matchmarks

TY6039100001000X

Fig. 7 Scribing matchmarks on universal joint & control valve shaft

5. Remove cotter pins and nuts from tie rod ends, then using suitable puller, separate tie rod ends from steering knuckles.

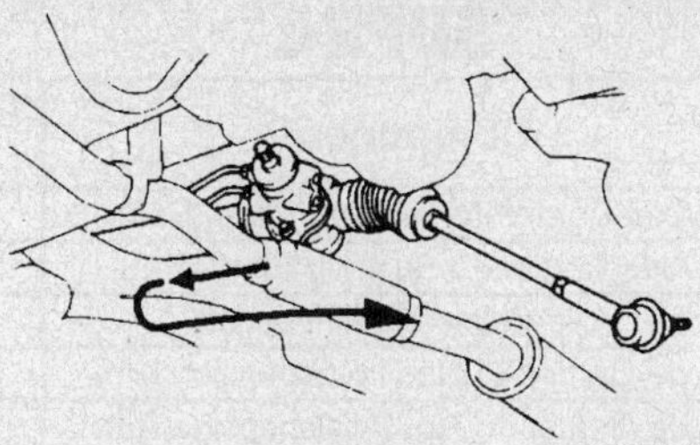

TY6039100002000X

Fig. 8 Steering gear removal

6. Disconnect pressure feed and return tubes.
7. **On turbo models,** remove air intake connector and air hose.
8. **On all models,** remove steering damper attaching bolts, then the damper.
9. Remove power steering hose clamp bolts, then the gear housing bracket attaching bolts.
10. Remove steering gear housing from vehicle.
11. Reverse procedure to install. Tighten attaching nuts and bolts to specifications.

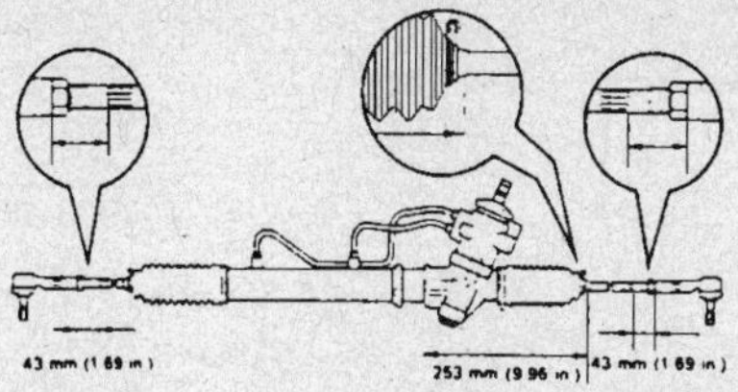

TY6039100003000X

Fig. 9 Steering gear installation dimensions

TIGHTENING SPECIFICATIONS

CELICA

Year	Component	Torque/Ft. Lbs.
1993–96	Axle Carrier To Backing Plate	53
	Axle Hub To Axle Carrier	59
	Axle Shaft To Axle Hub	90
	Brake Tube Flare Nut	11
	Differential To Support Member (Rear Side)	108
	Differential To Support Member (Upper Side)	70
	Drain Plug	36
	Driveshaft To Side Gear Shaft	51
	Filler Plug	29
	Fuel Tank Band To Body	29
	No. 1 & No. 2 Suspension Arm To Axle Carrier	166
	Parking Brake Cable To Backing Plate	6
	Propeller Shaft To Companion Flange	54
	Rear Crossmember To Body	53
	Rear Disc Brake Caliper To Axle Carrier	34
	Rear Disc Brake Hose Union Bolt	22
	Rear Driveshaft To Axle Hub	137
	Rear Shock Absorber To Body	29
	Rear Shock Absorber To Holding Nut	36
	Rear Shock Absorber To Rear Axle Carrier	188
	Rear Shock Absorber To Stabilizer Bar Link	47
	Rear Speed Sensor To Axle Carrier (w/ABS)	14
	Stabilizer Bar Bracket To Body	14
	Stabilizer Bar Link To Stabilizer Bar	47
	Strut Rod To Axle Carrier	83
	Strut Rod To Body	83
	Suspension Arm To Axle Carrier	90
	Suspension Arm To Body	83
	Wheel Lug Nut	76

SUPRA

Year	Component	Torque/Ft. Lbs.
1993–96	Axle Carrier To Backing Plate (Bolt)	19
	Axle Carrier To Backing Plate (Nut)	43
	Axle Carrier To Driveshaft	203
	Axle Carrier To No, 1 Suspension Arm	43
	Axle Carrier To No. 2 Suspension Arm	121
	Axle Carrier To Shock Absorber	101
	Axle Carrier To Strut Rod	121
	Axle Carrier To Torque Plate	34
	Axle Carrier To Upper Arm	80
	Body To Differential (Front Bolts)	122
	Body To Differential (Nuts)	67
	Body To Differential (Rear Bolts)	67
	Body To Differential (Stud Bolts)	58
	Body To No. 1 Suspension Arm	136
	Body To No. 2 Suspension Arm	136
	Body To Stabilizer Bar Bracket	21
	Body To Strut Rod	121
	Body To Suspension Support	10
	Body To Upper Arm	121
	Carrier To Carrier Cover	34
	Companion Flange To Propeller Shaft	54
	Drain Plug	36
	Driveshaft To Differential	51
	Filler Plug	36
	Shock Absorber To Suspension Support	20
	Side Bearing Cap To Carrier	58
	Stabilizer Bar To Link	26
	Wheel Lug Nuts	76

Wheel Alignment

INDEX

	Page No.
Front Wheel Alignment	43-54
AWD Models	43-55
FWD Models	43-54
Preliminary Inspection	43-54
Rear Wheel Alignment	43-55
Celica	43-55
Supra	43-55
Vehicle Ride Height	43-55
Wheel Alignment Specifications	43-3

PRELIMINARY INSPECTION

Inspect the following prior to adjusting wheel alignment.

1. Check tires for wear and proper inflation pressure.
2. Check front wheel bearings, front suspension, steering linkage and ball joints for wear or looseness.
3. Ensure front shock absorbers are functioning properly.

FRONT WHEEL ALIGNMENT

Prior to checking and resetting front wheel alignment, check wheel runout with a dial indicator. Wheel runout should not exceed .055 inch (1.4 mm) on Supra models and .039 inch (1.0 mm) on Celica models.

FWD MODELS

CASTER & CAMBER

1993–95 Celica

Caster and camber are not adjustable. If measurements are not within specifications, inspect suspension components for damage or excessive wear. Replace as necessary.

1996 Celica

Caster is not adjustable. If caster is not within specifications, check for worn or damaged suspension parts and replace are required.

1. Remove front wheels.
2. Remove two nuts from lower side of shock absorber.
3. Coat threads of nuts with engine oil and temporarily install.
4. Adjust camber by pushing or pulling lower side of shock absorber in direction in which camber adjustment is required, **Fig. 1.**
5. Tighten nuts, then check camber.
6. If camber is not within specifications, estimate how much additional camber adjustment is required and select camber adjusting bolt from, **Figs. 2 and 3.**
7. Install selected bolts and adjust camber by pushing or pulling lower side of shock absorber in direction in which camber adjustment is required.
8. **Torque** nuts to 113 ft. lbs.

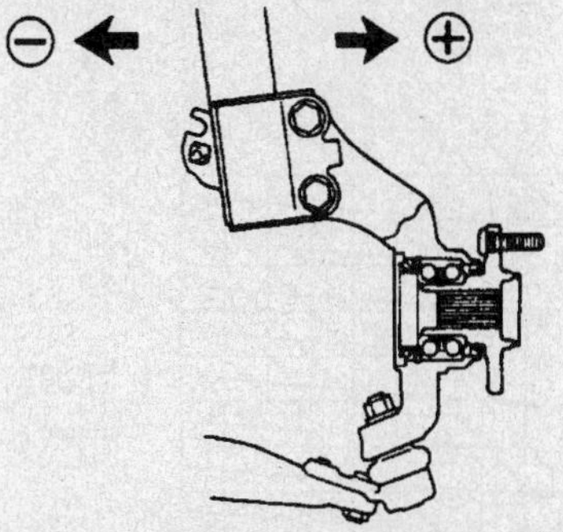
⊖
⊕

TY2049600055000X

Fig. 1 Front camber adjustment

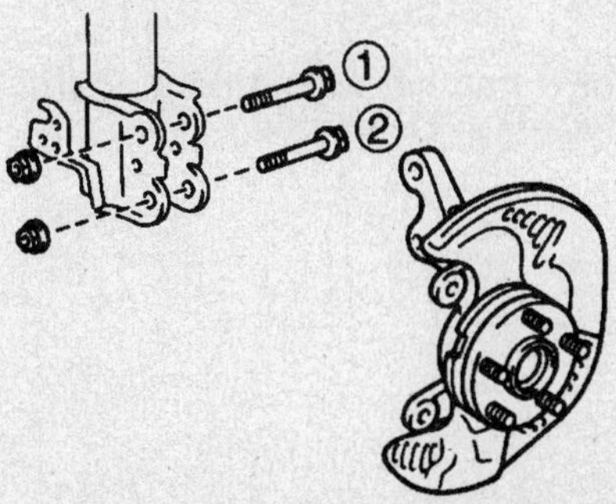
①
②

TY2049600056000X

Fig. 2 Front camber adjustment bolts

Adjusting Value \ Bolt	Set Bolt: Original (11) ①	Set Bolt: Original (11) ②	Adjusting Bolt: OD=13.9 mm, 1 Dot (•11) ①	OD=13.9 mm, 1 Dot ②	Adjusting Bolt: OD=13.3 mm, 2 Dots (•11•) ①	OD=13.3 mm, 2 Dots ②	Adjusting Bolt: OD=12.4 mm, 3 Dots (•11•) ①	OD=12.4 mm, 3 Dots ②
15'	●			●				
30'	●					●		
45'	●							●
1°00'			●					●
1°15'					●			●
1°30'							●	●

TY2049600057000X

Fig. 3 Front camber adjust bolt selection chart

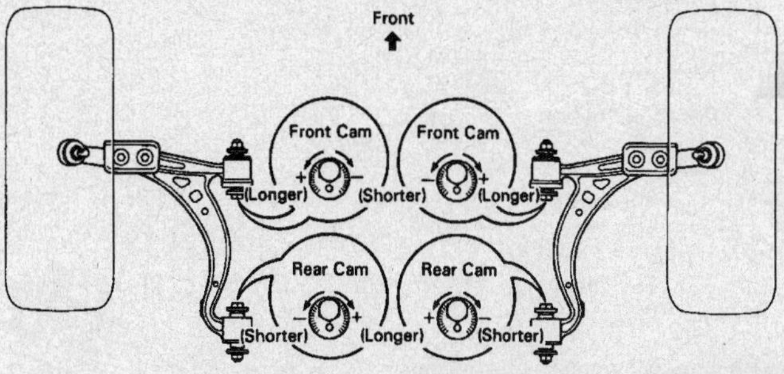
Front
Front Cam
Front Cam
(Longer)
(Shorter)
(Longer)
Rear Cam
Rear Cam
(Shorter)
(Longer)
(Shorter)

TY2049600058000X

Fig. 4 Front camber/caster adjustment cams. Supra

Supra

Caster and camber are adjusted by rotating front and/or rear adjusting cams as shown, **Fig. 4.** Take measurements of vehicle front caster and camber, then plot measurements on adjustment charts, **Figs. 5 and 6,** to obtain the amount that adjusting cams should be turned.

TOE-IN

Measure length of tie rod end on each side and adjust to be equal. Adjust toe-in by turning tubes equal amounts. Clamp adjusting tubes after aligning clamps with tube slots. Lock tie rod ends so that inner and outer ends are at right angles to each other.

AWD MODELS

CAMBER

If camber angle is not to specification, adjust by turning the camber adjusting cam. Loosen the shock absorber set nut and turn cam to obtain correct adjustment. Camber angle changes approximately 20° with each graduation of the adjusting cam. After adjustment, **torque** cam adjusting bolt to 166 ft. lbs.

CASTER

Caster angle is not adjustable. If caster angle is not to specification, check suspension components and replace worn or damaged components as required.

TOE-IN

If toe-in reading obtained is not as specified, remove boot clip and loosen locknut. Turn the left and right rack ends in equal amounts to adjust. Ensure the lengths of the left and right tie rods are the same.

REAR WHEEL ALIGNMENT

CELICA

CAMBER

Measure camber angle with suitable wheel alignment gauge and adjust to specifications. If reading is not within specification, check for worn or damaged bushings, bent or damaged rear suspension components and replace as required.

TOE-IN

1993

1. Measure distance between wheel disc and corner of cam bracket, **Fig. 7.** Distance should be identical for both wheels.
2. If toe-in is not within specification, rotate cam bolt(s) until specification is obtained, **Fig. 8.** Toe-in will change about .06 inch (1.5 mm) with each graduation marked on cam.

1994-96

1. Measure length of lefthand and righthand No. 2 lower suspension arms.
2. If the difference between lefthand and righthand suspension arm length is greater than .04 inch, adjust toe-in by turning adjusting tubes, **Fig. 9.** One turn of each adjusting tube will adjust toe-in about .36 inch.
3. **Torque** lock nuts to 55 ft. lbs.

SUPRA

CAMBER & TOE-IN

1. Measure length of lower suspension arm No. 1 and No. 2 as shown in **Fig. 10.**
2. If (E-F) or (F-E) is greater than 4 mm, length of arms must be adjusted by turning adjusting cam(s).
3. Measure camber and toe-in, then plot measurements on adjustment chart, **Fig. 11.**
4. Read from chart the amounts to turn adjusting cams, **Fig. 12.**

VEHICLE RIDE HEIGHT

Refer to **Figs. 13 through 18,** for trim height and specifications.

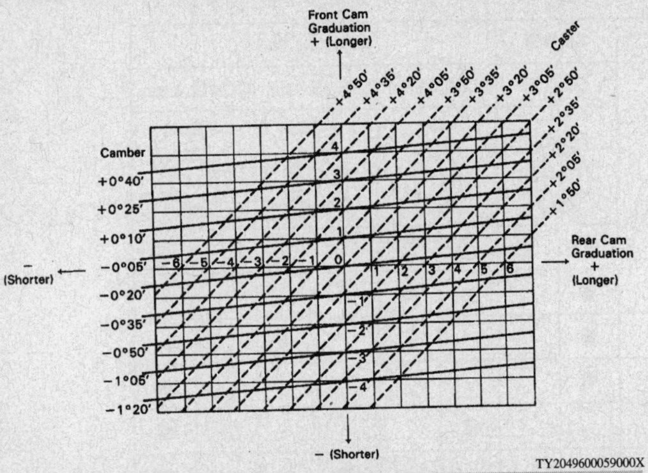
Front Cam
Graduation
+ (Longer)
Caster
+4°50'
+4°35'
+4°20'
+4°05'
+3°50'
+3°35'
+3°20'
+3°05'
+2°50'
+2°35'
+2°20'
+2°05'
+1°50'
Camber
+0°40'
+0°25'
+0°10'
−0°05'
−0°20'
−0°35'
−0°50'
−1°05'
−1°20'
− (Shorter)
Rear Cam
Graduation
+
(Longer)
− (Shorter)
TY2049600059000X

Fig. 5 Front caster & camber adjustment chart. Supra w/2JZ-GE engine

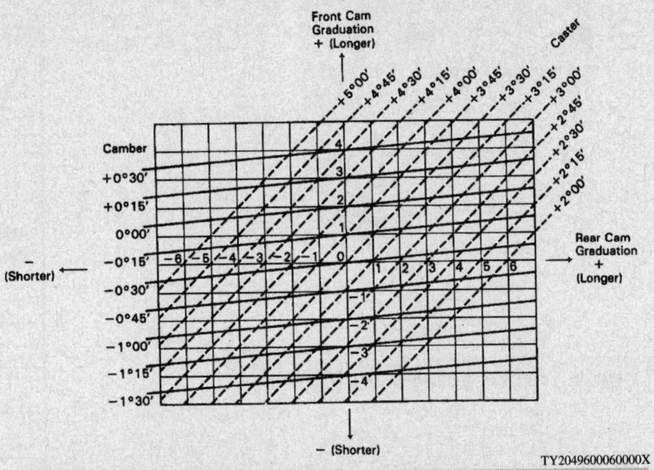
Front Cam
Graduation
+ (Longer)
Caster
+5°00'
+4°45'
+4°30'
+4°15'
+4°00'
+3°45'
+3°30'
+3°15'
+3°00'
+2°45'
+2°30'
+2°15'
+2°00'
Camber
+0°30'
+0°15'
0°00'
−0°15'
−0°30'
−0°45'
−1°00'
−1°15'
−1°30'
− (Shorter)
Rear Cam
Graduation
+
(Longer)
− (Shorter)
TY2049600060000X

Fig. 6 Front caster & camber adjustment chart. Supra w/2JZ-GTE engine

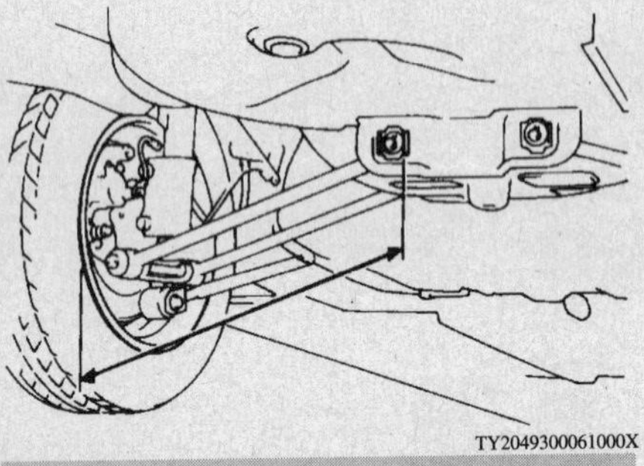
TY2049300061000X

Fig. 7 Rear toe-in measurement. 1993 Celica

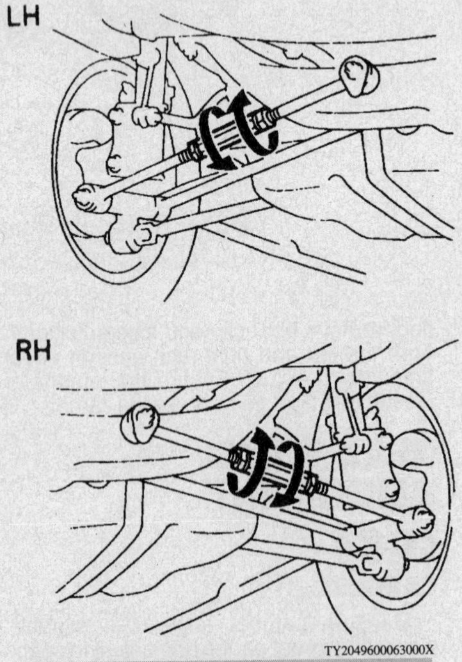
LH
RH
TY2049600063000X

Fig. 9 Rear toe-in adjustment. 1994-96 Celica

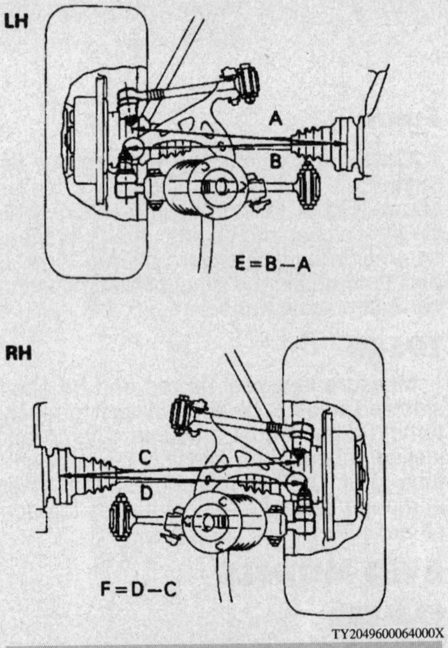
LH
A
B
E=B−A
RH
C
D
F=D−C
TY2049600064000X

Fig. 10 Rear camber & toe-in measurement. Supra

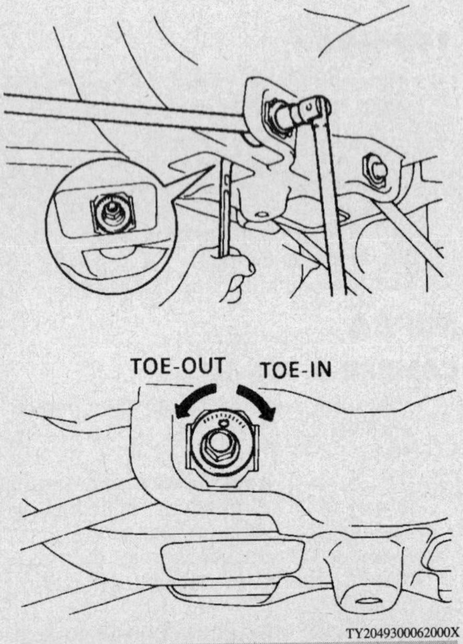
TOE-OUT
TOE-IN
TY2049300062000X

Fig. 8 Rear toe-in adjustment cam. 1993 Celica

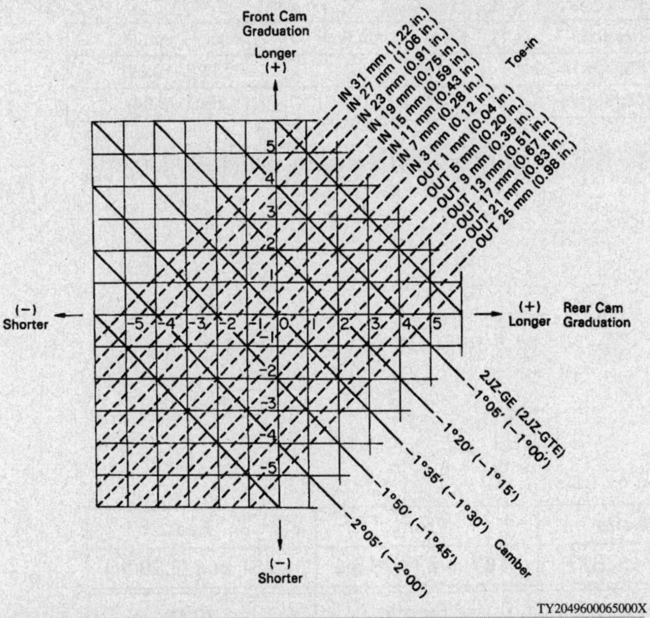
Front Cam
Graduation
Longer
(+)
Toe-in
IN 31 mm (1.22 in.)
IN 27 mm (1.06 in.)
IN 23 mm (0.91 in.)
IN 19 mm (0.75 in.)
IN 15 mm (0.59 in.)
IN 11 mm (0.43 in.)
IN 7 mm (0.28 in.)
IN 3 mm (0.12 in.)
OUT 1 mm (0.04 in.)
OUT 5 mm (0.20 in.)
OUT 9 mm (0.35 in.)
OUT 13 mm (0.51 in.)
OUT 17 mm (0.67 in.)
OUT 21 mm (0.83 in.)
OUT 25 mm (0.98 in.)
(−)
Shorter
(+)
Longer
Rear Cam
Graduation
2JZ-GE (2JZ-GTE)
−1°05′ (−1°00′)
−1°20′ (−1°15′)
−1°35′ (−1°30′)
−1°50′ (−1°45′)
−2°05′ (−2°00′)
Camber
(−)
Shorter

TY2049600065000X

Fig. 11 Rear camber & toe-in adjustment chart. Supra

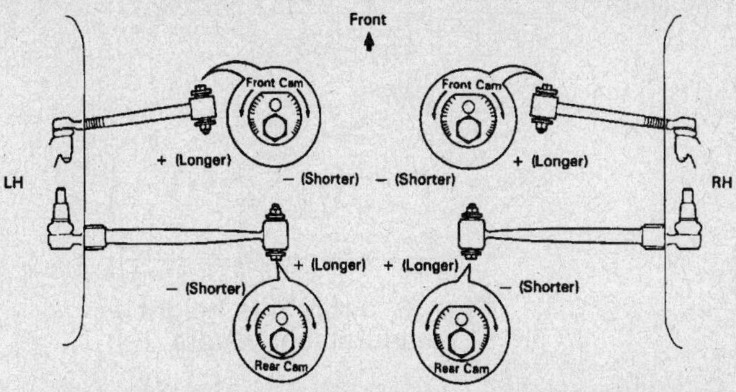
Front
Front Cam
Front Cam
+ (Longer)
− (Shorter)
− (Shorter)
+ (Longer)
LH
RH
+ (Longer)
+ (Longer)
− (Shorter)
− (Shorter)
Rear Cam
Rear Cam

TY2049600066000X

Fig. 12 Rear camber & toe-in adjusting cams. Supra

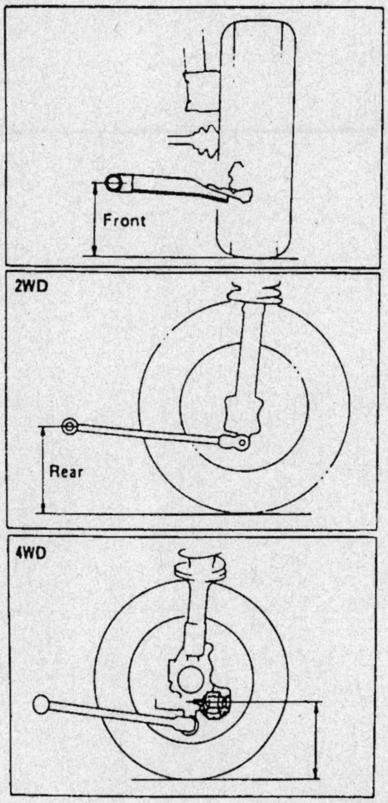
Front
2WD
Rear
4WD

TY2049100005000X

Fig. 13 Ride height measurement. Celica

	2WD	4WD
Front	185.0 mm (7.283 in.)	187.5 mm (7.390 in.)
Rear	251.5 mm (9.902 in.)	237.0 mm (9.323 in.)

TY2049100006000X

Fig. 14 Ride height specifications. 1993 Celica

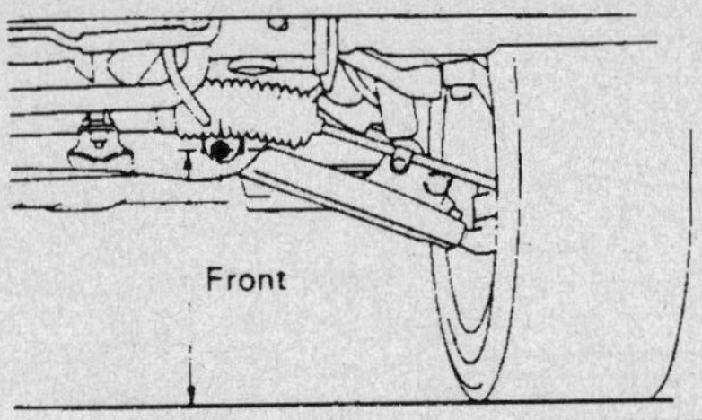
Front

TY2049100007000X

Fig. 16 Front ride height measurement. Supra

Tire size	Front mm (in.)	Rear mm (in.)
P185/70R14	187.6 (7.39)	255.8 (10.07)
P205/55R15	182.6 (7.19)	250.0 (9.84)

TY2049600054000X

Fig. 15 Ride height specifications. 1994–96 Celica

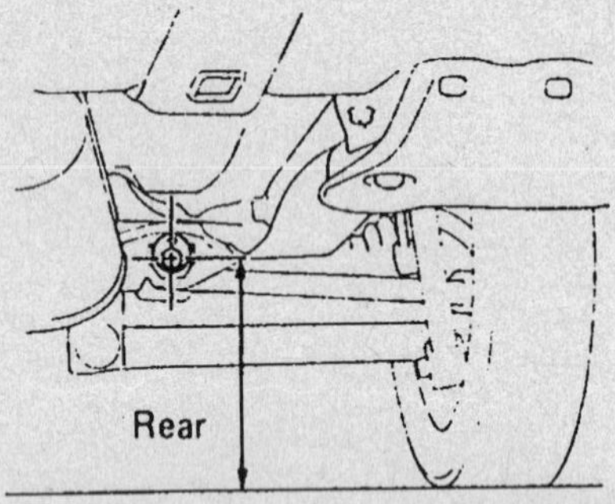
Rear

TY2049100008000X

Fig. 17 Rear ride height measurement. Supra

Tire size	Front	Rear
P235/45ZR17	187 mm (7.36 in.)	251 mm (9.88 in.)
Tire size	Front	Rear
P225/50ZR16	185 mm (7.28 in.)	250 mm (9.84 in.)

TY2049300010000X

Fig. 18 Ride height specifications. Supra

TOYOTA MR2

INDEX OF SERVICE OPERATIONS

	Page No.
AIR BAG SYSTEM PRECAUTIONS	0-8
AUTOMATIC TRANSMISSION/ TRANSAXLES	48-1
BRAKES	
Anti-Lock Brakes	48-1
Disc Brakes	48-1
Drum Brakes	48-1
Hydraulic Brake Systems	48-1
Power Brake Units	48-1
CLUTCH & MANUAL TRANSAXLE	
Adjustments	44-26
Clutch, Replace	44-26
Hydraulic System Service	44-26
Precautions	44-26
Tightening Specifications	44-28
Transaxle, Replace	44-27
ELECTRICAL	
Air Bags	48-1
Air Conditioning	48-1
Alternators	48-1
Blower Motor, Replace	44-7
Combination Switch, Replace	44-6
Combination Switch Service	44-6
Cooling Fans	48-1
Cruise Control	48-1
Dash Gauges	48-1
Dash Panels	48-1
Distributor, Replace	44-5
Evaporator Core, Replace	44-7
Fuel Pump Relay Location	44-5
Fuse Panel & Flasher Location	44-5
Headlamp Switch, Replace	44-6
Ignition Lock, Replace	44-6
Ignition Switch, Replace	44-6
Instrument Cluster, Replace	44-7
Neutral Safety Switch, Adjust	44-6
Passive Restraints	48-1
Precautions	44-4
Radio, Replace	44-7
Relay Center Location	44-5
Speed Controls	48-1
Starter Motors	48-1
Starter, Replace	44-5
Steering Columns	48-1
Steering Wheel, Replace	44-7
Stop Light Switch, Replace	44-6
Turn Signal Switch, Replace	44-7
Wiper Motor, Replace	44-7
Wiper Switch, Replace	44-7
Wiper Systems	48-1
ELECTRICAL SYMBOL IDENTIFICATION	0-139

	Page No.
FRONT SUSPENSION & STEERING	
Ball Joint Inspection	44-33
Coil Spring, Replace	44-33
Lower Suspension Arm, Replace	44-33
Manual Steering Gear, Replace	44-34
Manual Steering Gears	48-1
Power Steering	48-1
Power Steering Gear, Replace	44-34
Power Steering Pump, Replace	44-34
Precautions	44-32
Stabilizer Bar, Replace	44-33
Steering Knuckle, Replace	44-33
Strut, Replace	44-33
Strut Bar, Replace	44-34
Tightening Specifications	44-36
Wheel Bearing, Adjust	44-32
Wheel Bearing, Replace	44-32
FRONT WHEEL DRIVE AXLES	48-1
REAR AXLE & SUSPENSION	
Axle Shaft & Constant Velocity Joint, Replace	44-28
Coil Spring, Replace	44-30
Lower Arm, Replace	44-30
Rear Axle Hub, Replace	44-28
Shock Absorber, Replace	44-29
Stabilizer Bar, Replace	44-30
Strut Rod, Replace	44-29
Suspension Arm, Replace	44-30
Tightening Specifications	44-30
SERVICE REMINDER & WARNING LAMP RESET PROCEDURES	0-10
SPECIFICATIONS	
Fluid Capacities & Cooling System Data	44-3
Front Wheel Alignment Specifications	44-3
General Engine Specifications	44-2
Lubricant Data	44-3
Rear Wheel Alignment Specifications	44-3
Tune Up Specifications	44-2
VEHICLE IDENTIFICATION	0-1
VEHICLE LIFT POINTS	0-34
VEHICLE MAINTENANCE SCHEDULES	0-69

	Page No.
WHEEL ALIGNMENT	
Front Wheel Alignment	44-36
Preliminary Inspection	44-36
Rear Wheel Alignment	44-36
Vehicle Ride Height	44-36
Wheel Alignment Specifications	44-3
WIRE COLOR CODE IDENTIFICATION	0-144
2.0L 3S-GTE ENGINE	
Belt Tension Data	44-13
Camshaft, Replace	44-12
Compression Pressure	44-8
Cooling System Bleed	44-13
Cylinder Head, Replace	44-9
Engine Rebuilding Specifications	48-1
Engine, Replace	44-8
Fuel Filter, Replace	44-16
Fuel Pump, Replace	44-15
Hydraulic Lifters, Replace	44-11
Main & Rod Bearings	44-12
Oil Pan, Replace	44-12
Oil Pump, Replace	44-13
Piston & Rod Assembly	44-12
Precautions	44-8
Radiator, Replace	44-13
Thermostat, Replace	44-13
Tightening Specifications	44-16
Timing Belt, Replace	44-11
Turbocharger, Replace	44-16
Valve Adjustment	44-10
Valve Clearance Specifications	44-10
Water Pump, Replace	44-13
2.2L 5S-FE ENGINE	
Belt Tension Data	44-22
Compression Pressure	44-19
Cooling System Bleed	44-22
Cylinder Head, Replace	44-20
Engine Rebuilding Specifications	48-1
Engine, Replace	44-19
Fuel Filter, Replace	44-23
Fuel Pump, Replace	44-23
Oil Pan, Replace	44-21
Oil Pump, Replace	44-21
Precautions	44-18
Radiator, Replace	44-22
Thermostat, Replace	44-22
Tightening Specifications	44-24
Valve Adjustment	44-20
Valve Clearance Specifications	44-20
Water Pump, Replace	44-22

Specifications

GENERAL ENGINE SPECIFICATIONS

Year	Engine, Liter	Fuel System	Bore & Stroke, Inch	Compression Ratio	Maximum Brake H.P. @ RPM	Maximum Torque Ft. Lbs. @ RPM	Normal Oil Pressure, psi @ 3000 RPM
1993–94	2.0L①	Fuel Inj.	3.39 x 3.39	8.5	190 @ 6000	190 @ 3200	36–71
	2.2L	Fuel Inj.	3.43 x 3.58	9.5	130 @ 5400	140 @ 4400	36–71
1995	2.0L①	Fuel Inj.	3.39 x 3.39	8.8	200 @ 6000	200 @ 3200	36–71
	2.2L	Fuel Inj.	3.43 x 3.58	9.5	130 @ 5400	145 @ 4400	36–71

① — Turbocharged.

TUNE UP SPECIFICATIONS

The following specifications are published from the latest information available. This data should be used only in the absence of a decal affixed in the engine compartment.

When checking ignition timing, it may be necessary to disconnect certain hoses and/or electrical connectors. Refer to vehicle emission control label for specific instructions.

Before disconnecting spark plug wires from distributor cap, determine location of No. 1 wire in cap, as distributor position may have been altered from that shown.

Year	Engine, Liter	Spark Plug Gap, Inch	Ignition Timing			Curb Idle Speed③		Fuel Pump Pressure, psi	Valve Clearance, Inch	
			Firing Order	Timing, °BTDC	Timing Mark, Fig.	Man. Trans.	Auto. Trans.		Int.	Exh.
1993–95	2.0L	.031	②	10①	A	800	800N	33–38	.006–.010	.011–.015
	2.2L	.043	②	10①	A	750	700N	38–44	.007–.011	.011–.015

BTDC — Before Top Dead Center.
N — Neutral.
① — With check connector terminals T & E shorted, Fig B.
② — No. 1 cylinder located at front of engine, cylinder numbering 1-2-3-4, firing order 1-3-4-2.
③ — Controlled by idle air controller.

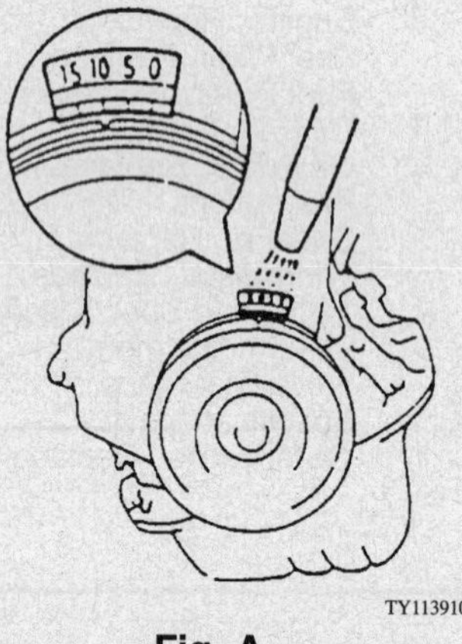
15 10 5 0
TY1139100117000X

Fig. A

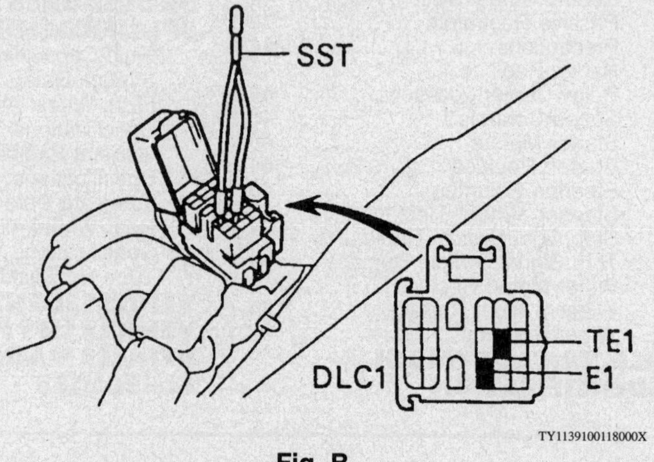
SST
TE1
E1
DLC1
TY1139100118000X

Fig. B

FRONT WHEEL ALIGNMENT SPECIFICATIONS

The following specifications are for unloaded vehicles.

Year	Caster Angle, Degrees		Camber Angle, Degrees		Toe-In, Inch①	Toe-Out On Turns, Degrees		Steering Axis Inclination, Degrees	Ball Joint Wear
	Limits	Desired	Limits	Desired		Outer Wheel	Inner Wheel		
1993	+2 1/12 to +3 7/12	+2 5/6	-1 3/4 to -1/4	-1	-.04 to +.12	32	37	13 5/6	②
1994–95	+2 1/2 to +4	+3 1/4	-1 3/4 to -1/4	-1	-.04 to +.12	32	37	13 5/6	②

① — Toe-in (+), toe-out (-).

② — Refer to "Ball Joint Inspection"under "Front Suspension & Steering" section.

REAR WHEEL ALIGNMENT SPECIFICATIONS

The following specifications are for unloaded vehicles.

Year	Camber Angle, Degrees		Toe-In, Inch①
	Limits	Desired	
1993	-2 1/3 to -5/6	-1 7/12	+.20 to +.28
1994–95	-2 1/3 to -5/6	-1 7/12	+.08 to +.24

① — Toe-in (+), toe-out (-).

FLUID CAPACITIES & COOLING SYSTEM DATA

Year	Engine	Coolant Capacity, Qts.		Radiator Cap Relief Pressure, Lbs.	Thermo. Opening Temp., °F	Fuel Tank, Gals.	Engine Oil Refill, Qts.	Transaxle Oil	
		Less A/C	With A/C					Man. Trans., Pts.	Auto Trans., Qts.
1993–95	3S-GTE	14.4	14.4	13	180	14.3	4.1①	②	8.5
	5S-FE	13.7	13.7	13	180	14.3	4.4①	5.4	8.5

① — With filter change.

② — Standard differential, 8.8 pts. Viscous coupling limited slip differential, 8.2 pts.

LUBRICANT DATA

Year	Model	Lubricant Type			
		Transaxle		Power Steering	Brake System
		Manual	Automatic		
1993–95	All	①	Dexron II	②	DOT 3

① — S54, API GL-3 SAE 75-90w; E153, Transaxle Oil E50.

② — Toyota Power Steering Fluid EH.

Electrical

NOTE: On Air Bag Equipped Models, Refer To "Air Bag System Precautions" Located In The Front Of This Manual For System Disarming & Arming Procedures.

INDEX

	Page No.
Air Bags	48-1
Air Conditioning	48-1
Alternators	48-1
Blower Motor, Replace	44-7
Combination Switch, Replace	44-6
Combination Switch Service	44-6
Internal Switch Replacement	44-6
Cooling Fans	48-1
Cruise Control	48-1
Dash Gauges	48-1
Dash Panels	48-1
Distributor, Replace	44-5
Installation	44-5
Removal	44-5
Evaporator Core, Replace	44-7
Fuel Pump Relay Location	44-5
Fuse Panel & Flasher Location	44-5
Headlamp Switch, Replace	44-6
Ignition Lock, Replace	44-6
Ignition Switch, Replace	44-6
Instrument Cluster, Replace	44-7
Neutral Safety Switch, Adjust	44-6
Passive Restraints	48-1
Precautions	44-4
Air Bag Systems	44-4
Audio Coded Anti-Theft System	44-4
Radio, Replace	44-7
Relay Center Location	44-5
Speed Controls	48-1
Starter Motors	48-1
Starter, Replace	44-5
Steering Columns	48-1
Steering Wheel, Replace	44-7
Stop Light Switch, Replace	44-6
Turn Signal Switch, Replace	44-7
Wiper Motor, Replace	44-7
Wiper Switch, Replace	44-7
Wiper Systems	48-1

PRECAUTIONS

AIR BAG SYSTEMS

Refer to "Air Bag System Precautions" in the front of this manual for system disarming and arming procedures.

AUDIO CODED ANTI-THEFT SYSTEM

Some models are equipped with an audio coded anti-theft system that will disable the radio when battery power is removed from the radio. The system can be identified by the "ANTI-THEFT SYSTEM" on the cassette tape lid. Obtain the three digit code from the customer for input before disconnecting battery power to the audio unit. Reset system after service as follows:

1. Obtain three digit code from customer.
2. Depress No. 1 (PROG) button while depressing righthand side of TUNE SEEK button, - - - will appear in tape operation display.
3. Enter code as follows:
   a. To enter first digit, press No. 1 (PROG) button a sufficient number of times, starting with zero, to enter digit (if first digit of code is five press button six times).
   b. To enter second digit, press No. 2 (APS) button a sufficient number of times, starting with zero, to enter digit.
   c. To enter third digit press, No. 3 (RPT) button a sufficient number of times, starting with zero, to enter digit.
4. If three dashes (- - -) appear in tape operation display during input of digits, restart procedure from beginning.
5. When code digits are correctly input and displayed, press and hold SCAN button until SEC appears in tape operation display.

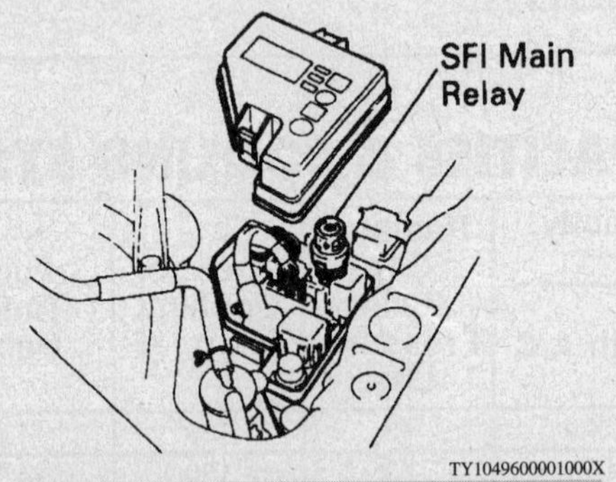

SFI Main Relay
TY1049600001000X

Fig. 1 Fuel pump relay location

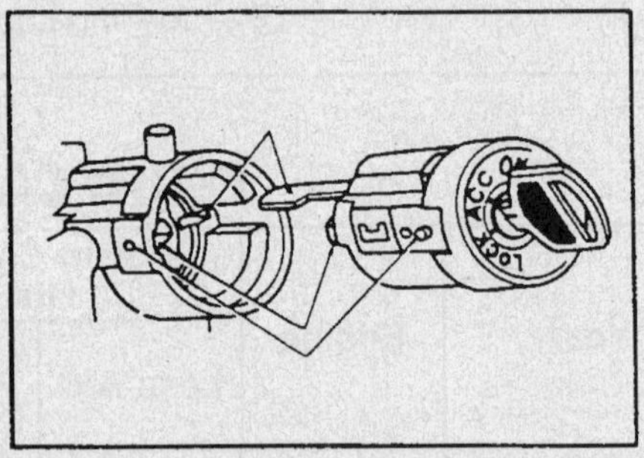

TY9129100001000X

Fig. 2 Ignition lock removal

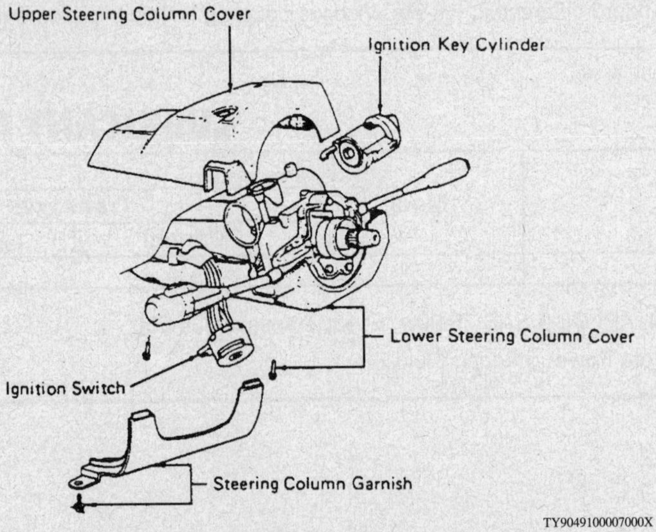

Upper Steering Column Cover
Ignition Key Cylinder
Lower Steering Column Cover
Ignition Switch
Steering Column Garnish
TY9049100007000X

Fig. 3 Exploded view of steering column & ignition switch assembly

6. When SEC disappears from display audio unit should be operative.
7. If unit is not operative or Err is displayed, repeat procedure. **Attempting**

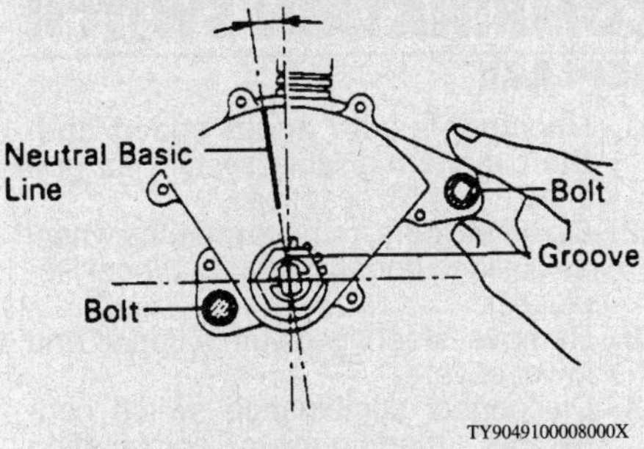
Neutral Basic Line
Bolt
Groove
Bolt
TY9049100008000X

Fig. 4 Neutral safety switch adjustment

to input code more than nine times may permanently disable audio unit.

FUSE PANEL & FLASHER LOCATION

There are three fuse block locations. Fuse block No. 1 is located behind the left-hand kick panel. Fuse block No. 2 is located in the engine compartment. Fuse block No. 5 is located in the front trunk compartment. The flasher is located in fuse block No. 1.

FUEL PUMP RELAY LOCATION

The fuel pump relay is located on the left-hand side of the engine compartment, in relay block No. 2, **Fig. 1.**

RELAY CENTER LOCATION

Relay block No. 1 is located behind the lefthand side kick panel. Relay block No. 2 is located in the front lefthand side of the engine compartment. Relay block No. 5 is located in the righthand side of the luggage compartment.

STARTER

REPLACE

1. **On models with audio coded anti-theft system,**disable system as outlined under "Precautions."
2. **On all models,** remove lefthand hood side panel.
3. Remove battery, battery tray and igniter bracket, if necessary.
4. Remove air cleaner assembly, if necessary.
5. Disconnect electrical connectors from starter motor.
6. Remove starter motor attaching bolts, heat shield (if equipped), then the starter motor.
7. Reverse procedure to install. If audio system was disabled, activate as outlined under "Precautions."

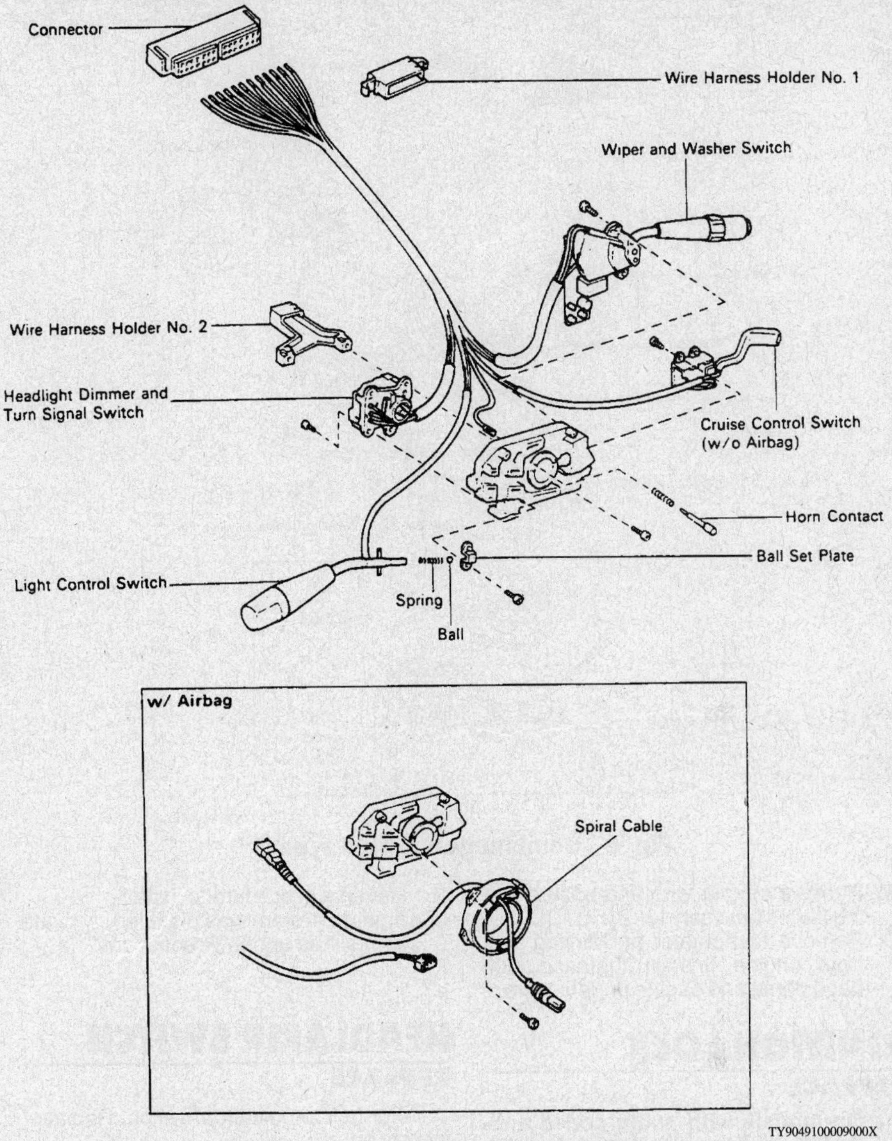
Connector
Wire Harness Holder No. 1
Wiper and Washer Switch
Wire Harness Holder No. 2
Headlight Dimmer and Turn Signal Switch
Cruise Control Switch (w/o Airbag)
Horn Contact
Ball Set Plate
Light Control Switch
Spring
Ball
w/ Airbag
Spiral Cable
TY9049100009000X

Fig. 5 Combination switch type A

DISTRIBUTOR

REPLACE

REMOVAL

1. **On models with audio coded anti-theft system,**disable system as outlined under "Precautions."
2. **On all models,** disconnect distributor connector and remove spark plug wires from ignition coil and spark plugs.
3. Remove hold-down bolts and remove distributor.
4. Replace distributor O-ring.
5. If audio system was disabled, activate as outlined under "Precautions."

INSTALLATION

1. Remove engine undercovers and righthand hood side panels.
2. Set No. 1 cylinder to TDC by aligning groove on crank with 0 mark on timing cover. Ensure slit on end of camshaft is straight up and down. If not, rotate crankshaft one full revolution.
3. Align cutout portion of distributor with groove of distributor housing. Insert distributor, aligning center of flange with bolt hole on cylinder head. Lightly tighten hold-down bolts.
4. Connect spark plug wires to coil and spark plugs: firing order 1-3-4-2.
5. Connect distributor connector.
6. Start engine and allow to warm up.
7. Connect tachometer to terminal IG- of check connector. Connect timing light to engine and install jumper between terminals TE1 and E1 of check connector. The check connector is located on fender apron.
8. Place transmission in Neutral. Ensure ignition timing is 10° BTDC at idle. If not, adjust.

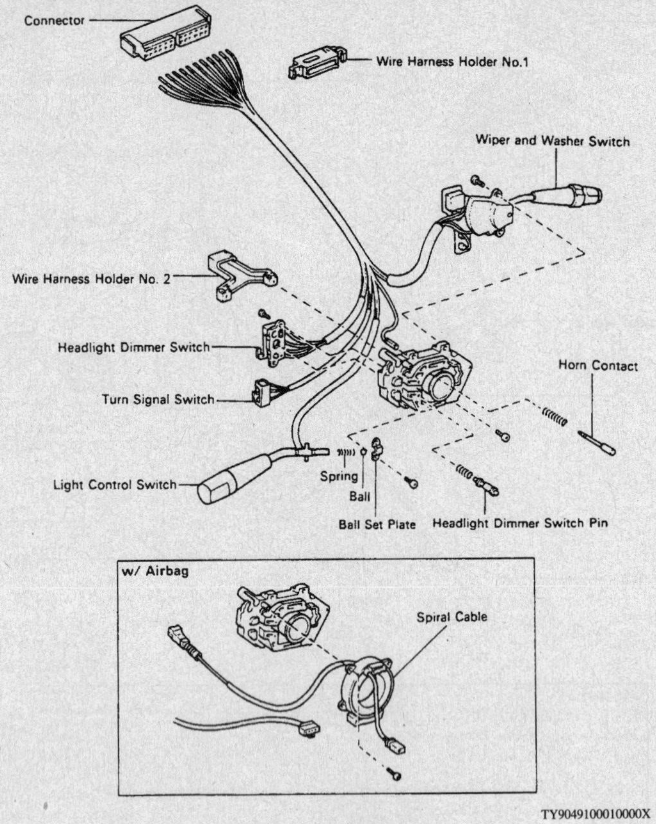
Connector
Wire Harness Holder No.1
Wiper and Washer Switch
Wire Harness Holder No. 2
Headlight Dimmer Switch
Horn Contact
Turn Signal Switch
Light Control Switch
Spring
Ball
Ball Set Plate
Headlight Dimmer Switch Pin
w/ Airbag
Spiral Cable
TY9049100010000X

Fig. 6 Combination switch type B

9. Remove jumper wire and ensure timing varies between 13–21° BTDC.
10. Remove tachometer and timing light from engine. Install righthand side hood panel and engine undercovers.

IGNITION LOCK

REPLACE

1. **On models with audio coded anti-theft system,**disable system as outlined under "Precautions."
2. **On all models,** turn ignition switch to ACC position.
3. Insert a small diameter rod into hole located on side of lock cylinder, then while holding down pin, remove lock cylinder, **Fig. 2.**
4. Reverse procedure to install. Ensure lock cylinder is in ACC position.
5. If audio system was disabled, activate as outlined under "Precautions."

IGNITION SWITCH

REPLACE

1. **On models with audio coded anti-theft system,**disable system as outlined under "Precautions."
2. **On all models,** remove steering wheel, if necessary, steering column garnish, if equipped, upper and lower covers, **Fig. 3.**
3. Disconnect electrical connectors from ignition switch.
4. Turn ignition key to ACC position and remove ignition key cylinder.
5. Remove screw and ignition switch.
6. Reverse procedure to install.
7. If audio system was disabled, activate as outlined under "Precautions."

HEADLAMP SWITCH

REPLACE

Refer to "Combination Switch, Replace" for procedure.

NEUTRAL SAFETY SWITCH

ADJUST

1. Raise and support vehicle.
2. Loosen neutral safety switch bracket bolt.
3. Position transmission shift lever into Neutral.
4. Align switch shaft groove with neutral base line, **Fig. 4,** then tighten switch bracket bolt.
5. Connect electrical connector to switch.

STOP LIGHT SWITCH

REPLACE

1. Remove brake pedal tension spring.
2. Disconnect switch wire connector.
3. Remove switch mounting nut, then slide switch from mounting bracket.
4. Reverse procedure to install.

COMBINATION SWITCH

REPLACE

1. **On models with audio coded anti-theft system,**disable system as outlined under "Precautions."
2. **On all models,** remove steering wheel as outlined under "Steering Wheel Replace."
3. Remove steering column upper and lower covers.
4. Disconnect combination switch connectors, then remove combination switch.
5. Reverse procedure to install. If audio system was disabled, activate as outlined under "Precautions."

COMBINATION SWITCH SERVICE

Refer to **Figs. 5 and 6** for component replacement procedure.

INTERNAL SWITCH REPLACEMENT

1. **On models with audio coded anti-theft system,**disable system as outlined under "Precautions."
2. **On all models,** remove steering wheel, then upper and lower steering column covers.
3. Remove four screws, disconnect connectors and remove spiral cable sub-assembly.
4. Disconnect combination switch connector, then using a small screwdriver, disengage wiring from combination switch connector. **Note position of wires.**
5. **On models with cruise control,** removal of slip ring may be necessary.
6. Remove screws and ball set plate. Remove ball and slide out light control switch assembly with spring.
7. **On models with type A combination switch, Fig. 5 ,** remove headlamp dimmer and turn signal switch by removing four and switch assembly.
8. **On models with type B combination switch, Fig. 6,** remove headlamp dimmer and turn signal switch as follows:
   a. Pry loose two locking lugs and remove turn signal switch.
   b. Remove two screws and dimmer switch.
   c. Remove headlamp dimmer switch pin from switch body with spring.
9. **On all models,** remove two screws and wiper/washer switch, if equipped in column.
10. Remove two screws and cruise control switch. Then remove horn contact.
11. Reverse procedure to install, noting the following:
    a. Ensure light control switch operates correctly before final assembly.
    b. Ensure terminals are seated in connectors completely.
    c. If audio system was disabled, activate as outlined under "Precautions."

TURN SIGNAL SWITCH

REPLACE

Refer to "Combination Switch, Replace" for procedure.

STEERING WHEEL

REPLACE

1. **On models with audio coded anti-theft system,** disable system as outlined under "Precautions."
2. **On all models,** remove wheel pad from steering wheel by loosening screws behind wheel pad using a Torx 30 wrench. Disconnect air bag connector. **When removing wheel pad, take care not to pull air bag wire harness. When storing wheel pad, keep upper surface of the pad facing upward. Never disassemble wheel pad.**
3. **On models with 4 spoke wheel,** remove trim cover from center of steering wheel.
4. **On all models,** place alignment marks on steering wheel and mainshaft for assembly reference.
5. Remove nut attaching steering wheel to steering shaft.
6. Using steering wheel puller tool No. 09213–31021, or equivalent, remove steering wheel. On some models, a steering wheel puller may not be necessary.
7. Reverse procedure to install, noting the following:
   a. **Torque** steering wheel retaining nut to 26 ft. lbs.
   b. If audio system was disabled, activate as outlined under "Precautions."

INSTRUMENT CLUSTER

REPLACE

Refer to "Dash Panel Service" for figure references and removal procedures as necessary.

1. **On models with audio coded anti-theft system,** disable system as outlined under "Precautions."
2. **On all models,** remove steering wheel as outlined under "Steering Wheel, Replace," then remove steering column covers.
3. Remove rheostat knob and rheostat from finish panel. Then remove cluster finish panel and disconnect connector.
4. Remove two screws and upper cluster finish panel screws and panel.
5. Remove cluster screws, disconnect connectors and remove cluster.
6. Reverse procedure to install. If audio system was disabled, activate as outlined under "Precautions."

RADIO

REPLACE

1. **On models with audio coded anti-theft system,** disable system as outlined under "Precautions."
2. **On all models,** remove ashtray receptacle.
3. Remove two screws and pry out center cluster finish panel.
4. Remove four bolts and radio.
5. Reverse procedure to install. If audio system was disabled, activate as outlined under "Precautions."

WIPER MOTOR

REPLACE

1. With wiper arms in Up position and wiper switch on Low, turn ignition switch Off.
2. **On models with audio coded anti-theft system,** disable system as outlined under "Precautions."
3. **On all models,** disconnect wiper motor electrical connector, then remove light retractor relay from wiper bracket.
4. Remove wiper motor attaching bolts. Manually lower wiper arms, then hook wiper link hook to dash panel service hole.
5. Disconnect wiper motor from wiper link.
6. Remove wiper motor.
7. Reverse procedure to install. If audio system was disabled, activate as outlined under "Precautions."

WIPER SWITCH

REPLACE

Replace wiper switch as outlined under "Combination Switch, Replace."

BLOWER MOTOR

REPLACE

1. **On models with audio coded anti-theft system,** disable system as outlined under "Precautions."
2. **On all models,** remove glove compartment and righthand side undercovers.
3. Disconnect connectors and remove blower motor.
4. Reverse procedure to install. If audio system was disabled, activate as outlined under "Precautions."

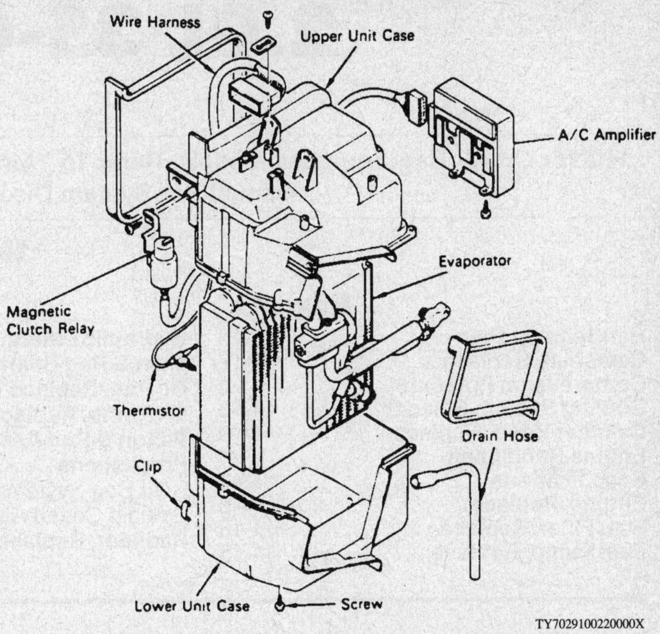

Wire Harness
Upper Unit Case
A/C Amplifier
Evaporator
Magnetic Clutch Relay
Thermistor
Drain Hose
Clip
Lower Unit Case
Screw
TY7029100220000X

Fig. 7 Exploded view of cooling unit

EVAPORATOR CORE

REPLACE

1. **On models with audio coded anti-theft system,** disable system as outlined under "Precautions."
2. **On all models,** discharge and recover system refrigerant.
3. Disconnect refrigerant lines at cooling unit, capping all openings.
4. Remove grommets from inlet and outlet fittings.
5. Remove glove compartment, then the lower instrument panel cover.
6. Disconnect cooling unit electrical connectors.
7. Remove nuts and screws retaining cooling unit, then the cooling unit.
8. Loosen four screws and clamps, then remove upper and lower cases, **Fig. 7.**
9. Remove packing and clamp from evaporator outlet tube, then disconnect refrigerant line from inlet fitting of expansion valve.
10. Disconnect expansion valve from evaporator inlet fitting.
11. Reverse procedure to install, noting the following:
    a. Charge system and check for leaks. If evaporator was replaced, add 1.4 to 1.7 oz. of new refrigerant oil to compressor.
    b. If audio system was disabled, activate as outlined under "Precautions."

2.0L 3S-GTE Engine

NOTE: On Air Bag Equipped Models, Refer To "Air Bag System Precautions" Located In The Front Of This Manual For System Disarming & Arming Procedures.

INDEX

	Page No.
Belt Tension Data	44-13
Camshaft, Replace	44-12
Compression Pressure	44-8
Cooling System Bleed	44-13
Cylinder Head, Replace	44-9
Engine Rebuilding Specifications	48-1
Engine, Replace	44-8
Fuel Filter, Replace	44-16
Fuel Pump, Replace	44-15
Hydraulic Lifters, Replace	44-11
Main & Rod Bearings	44-12
Oil Pan, Replace	44-12
Oil Pump, Replace	44-13
Piston & Rod Assembly	44-12
Precautions	44-8
Air Bag Systems	44-8
Audio Coded Anti-Theft System	44-8
Radiator, Replace	44-13
Thermostat, Replace	44-13
Tightening Specifications	44-16
Timing Belt, Replace	44-11
Installation	44-11
Removal	44-11
Turbocharger, Replace	44-16
Valve Adjustment	44-10
Valve Clearance Specifications	44-10
Water Pump, Replace	44-13

PRECAUTIONS

AIR BAG SYSTEMS

Refer to "Air Bag System Precautions" in the front of this manual for system disarming and arming procedures.

AUDIO CODED ANTI-THEFT SYSTEM

Some models are equipped with an audio coded anti-theft system that will disable the radio when battery power is removed from the radio. The system can be identified by the "ANTI-THEFT SYSTEM" on the cassette tape lid. Obtain the three digit code from the customer for input before disconnecting battery power to the audio unit. Reset system after service as follows:

1. Obtain three digit code from customer.
2. Depress No. 1 (PROG) button while depressing righthand side of TUNE SEEK button, - - - will appear in tape operation display.
3. Enter code as follows:
   a. To enter first digit, press No. 1 (PROG) button a sufficient number of times, starting with zero, to enter digit (if first digit of code is five press button six times).
   b. To enter second digit, press No. 2 (APS) button a sufficient number of times, starting with zero, to enter digit.
   c. To enter third digit press, No. 3 (RPT) button a sufficient number of times, starting with zero, to enter digit.
4. If three dashes (- - -) appear in tape operation display during input of digits, restart procedure from beginning.
5. When code digits are correctly input and displayed, press and hold SCAN button until SEC appears in tape operation display.
6. When SEC disappears from display audio unit should be operative.
7. If unit is not operative or Err is displayed, repeat procedure. **Attempting to input code more than nine times may permanently disable audio unit.**

COMPRESSION PRESSURE

1. Start engine and warm to normal operating temperature.
2. Disconnect distributor electrical connector.
3. Remove No. 1 intake air connector.
4. Disconnect high-tension cords from spark plugs.
5. Remove spark plugs.
6. Insert compression gauge into spark plug hole.
7. Fully open throttle.
8. While cranking engine, measure compression pressure.
9. Standard compression pressure is 164 psi or more. Minimum compression pressure is 128 psi.
10. Maximum difference between each cylinder should be 14 psi.

ENGINE

REPLACE

1. **On models with audio coded anti-theft system,** disable system as outlined under "Precautions."
2. **On all models,** remove hood, hood side panels and undercovers, **Fig. 1.**
3. Drain engine coolant, engine oil and transaxle oil.
4. Remove suspension upper brace, then air cleaner assembly.
5. Remove No. 1 and 2 air intake connectors.
6. Disconnect accelerator cable. Then remove cruise actuator and linkage, if equipped.
7. Disconnect brake booster vacuum hose and engine ground strap connector.
8. Remove check connector and turbocharger pressure sensor.
9. Remove injector solenoid resistor, fuel pump relay, fuel pump resistor and A/C VSV.
10. Remove water filler tube and charcoal canister.
11. Remove engine relay box, ignition coil and igniter. Disconnect engine wire.
12. Disconnect engine wire from luggage compartment. Then disconnect starter cable.
13. Disconnect water inlet hose, fuel inlet hose, fuel return hose and radiator hose from water outlet housing.
14. Disconnect transaxle control cables.
15. Remove tailpipe and front exhaust pipe.
16. Remove engine compartment cooling fan.
17. Remove idler pulley bracket and A/C compressor without disconnecting hoses.
18. Remove intercooler.
19. Remove rear engine mounting insulator. Then disconnect speedometer cable.
20. Remove rear suspension crossmember, then front engine mounting insulator.
21. Remove front engine mounting bracket and clutch release cylinder.
22. Remove righthand and lefthand engine mounting stays.
23. Remove lateral control rod and air cleaner case bracket.
24. Remove engine and transaxle assembly from vehicle.
25. Remove rear engine mounting bracket, lefthand mounting bracket and starter. Then separate engine and transaxle.
26. Reverse procedure to install, noting the following:
    a. Tighten all fasteners to specifications.
    b. If audio system was disabled, activate as outlined under "Precautions."

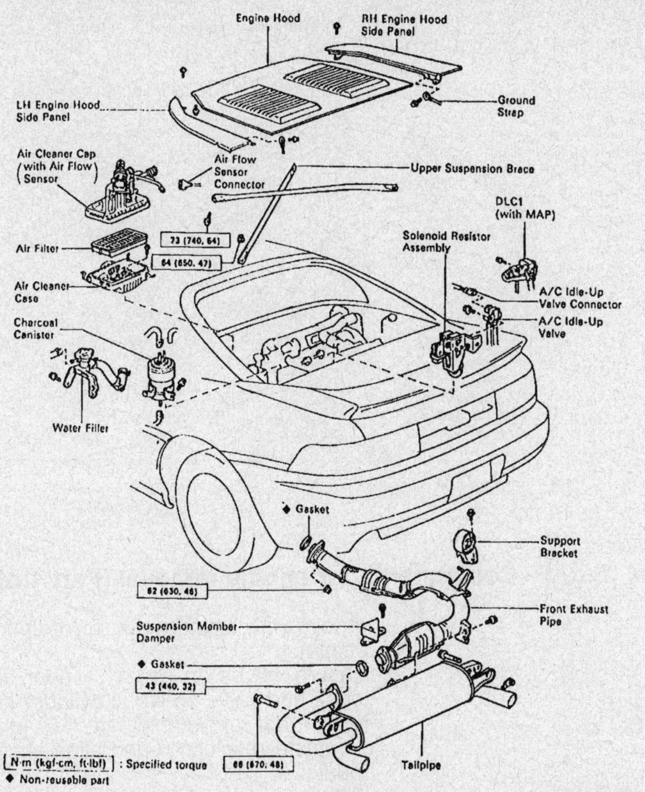
Engine Hood
RH Engine Hood Side Panel
LH Engine Hood Side Panel
Ground Strap
Air Cleaner Cap (with Air Flow Sensor)
Air Flow Sensor Connector
Upper Suspension Brace
DLC1 (with MAP)
Solenoid Resistor Assembly
Air Filter
73 (740, 54)
64 (650, 47)
Air Cleaner Case
A/C Idle-Up Valve Connector
A/C Idle-Up Valve
Charcoal Canister
Water Filler
Gasket
Support Bracket
62 (630, 46)
Front Exhaust Pipe
Suspension Member Damper
Gasket
43 (440, 32)
Tailpipe
N·m (kgf·cm, ft·lbf) : Specified torque
Non-reusable part

TY1069100141010X

Fig. 1 Components for engine removal (Part 1 of 4)

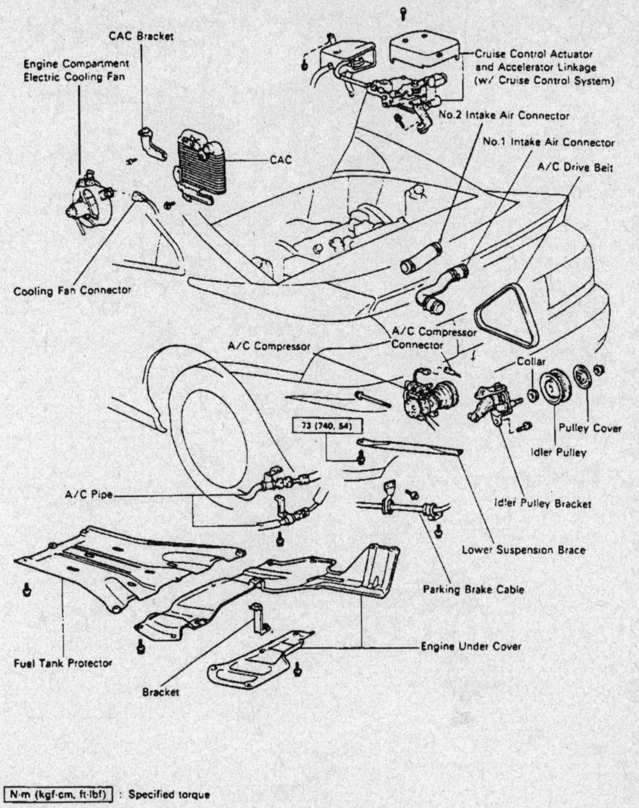
CAC Bracket
Engine Compartment Electric Cooling Fan
Cruise Control Actuator and Accelerator Linkage (w/ Cruise Control System)
No.2 Intake Air Connector
No.1 Intake Air Connector
A/C Drive Belt
CAC
Cooling Fan Connector
A/C Compressor
A/C Compressor Connector
Collar
73 (740, 54)
Pulley Cover
Idler Pulley
A/C Pipe
Idler Pulley Bracket
Lower Suspension Brace
Parking Brake Cable
Engine Under Cover
Fuel Tank Protector
Bracket
N·m (kgf·cm, ft·lbf) : Specified torque

TY1069100141020X

Fig. 1 Components for engine removal (Part 2 of 4)

CYLINDER HEAD

REPLACE

1. Obtain audio anti-theft code, if equipped, as outlined in "Precautions."
2. Drain coolant and oil from engine.
3. Drain coolant from intercooler assembly.
4. Remove suspension under brace.
5. Disconnect accelerator cable from throttle body assembly.
6. Remove reservoir tank and air cleaner assembly.
7. Remove alternator.
8. Raise and support vehicle.
9. Remove righthand front wheel.
10. Remove engine undercovers.
11. Remove suspension lower crossmember.
12. Remove front exhaust pipe, then catalytic converter.
13. Remove alternator brackets.
14. Remove turbocharger and exhaust manifold assemblies.
15. Remove distributor.
16. Remove No. 2 air pipe.
17. Remove lefthand engine hanger.
18. Remove oil pressure switch and water outlet.
19. Remove water bypass pipe.
20. Remove throttle body.
21. Disconnect cold start injector connector. Remove EGR valve, vacuum modulator and EGR control VSV.
22. Remove vacuum pipe and intake manifold stays.
23. Remove No. 1 air pipe.
24. Remove fuel pressure VSV.
25. Remove T-VIS, VSV, vacuum tank and turbocharger pressure VSV.
26. Remove intake manifold and air control valve.
27. Remove power steering oil reservoir tank without disconnecting lines.
28. Remove spark plugs.
29. Remove No. 2 timing belt cover.
30. Remove timing belt as follows:
    a. Place No. 1 cylinder to TDC of compression stroke by turning crankshaft pulley (sprocket) and aligning pulley groove with No. 1 timing belt cover marking "0."
    b. Ensure alignment marks on the camshaft timing pulleys and No. 3 timing belt cover are aligned. If not, turn crankshaft one revolution (360°).
    c. With timing marks properly aligned, remove timing belt.
31. Remove PCV pipe and cylinder head cover.
32. Remove camshaft timing pulleys (sprockets).
33. Remove No. 1 idler pulley (sprocket) and tension spring.
34. Remove No. 3 timing belt cover.
35. Remove intake and exhaust camshafts as follows:
    a. Uniformly loosen and remove 20 bearing cap bolts in several passes, in sequence shown in **Fig. 2.**
    b. Remove ten bearing cap bolts, two oil seals and two camshaft assemblies. Arrange intake and exhaust camshaft and components in order removed.
36. Remove righthand rear engine hanger.
37. Remove cylinder head as follows:
    a. Using adapter tool No. 09043-38100, or equivalent, loosen and remove ten cylinder head attaching bolts in several passes, using sequence shown in **Fig. 3. Cylinder head warpage or cracking could result from loosening bolts in incorrect order.**
    b. Lift cylinder head from dowels on cylinder block and place it on a suitable workbench.
38. If cylinder head is difficult to remove, pry cylinder head off using a suitable screwdriver. When doing so, do not damage cylinder head or block surfaces.
39. Reverse procedure to install, noting the following:
    a. Apply a light coat of clean engine oil onto bolt threads and under bolt heads.
    b. Using adapter tool No. 09043-38100, or equivalent, install and tighten cylinder head bolts in several passes, using sequence shown in **Fig. 4.**
    c. **Torque** bolts to 40 ft. lbs. **Replace any bolts that break, deform, or will not tighten specification.**
    d. Mark front of bolt head with paint.
    e. Tighten ten cylinder head bolts an additional 90° in sequence shown.
    f. Ensure paint mark applied, is now

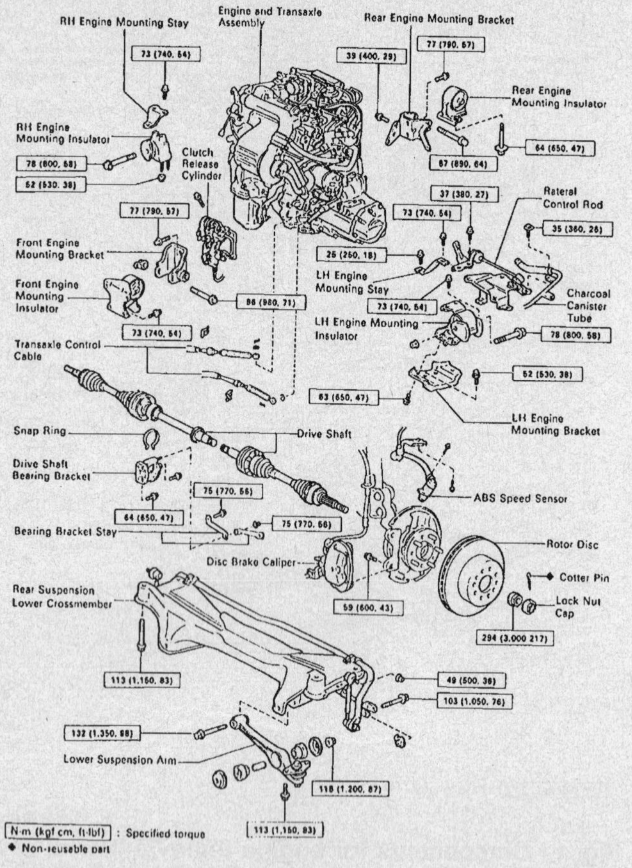
RH Engine Mounting Stay
Engine and Transaxle Assembly
Rear Engine Mounting Bracket
73 (740, 54)
39 (400, 29)
77 (790, 57)
Rear Engine Mounting Insulator
RH Engine Mounting Insulator
Clutch Release Cylinder
78 (800, 58)
52 (530, 38)
64 (650, 47)
87 (890, 64)
37 (380, 27)
Lateral Control Rod
77 (790, 57)
73 (740, 54)
35 (360, 26)
Front Engine Mounting Bracket
25 (250, 18)
LH Engine Mounting Stay
Front Engine Mounting Insulator
96 (980, 71)
73 (740, 54)
Charcoal Canister Tube
LH Engine Mounting Insulator
73 (740, 54)
78 (800, 58)
Transaxle Control Cable
52 (530, 38)
63 (650, 47)
LH Engine Mounting Bracket
Snap Ring
Drive Shaft
Drive Shaft Bearing Bracket
75 (770, 56)
ABS Speed Sensor
64 (650, 47)
75 (770, 56)
Bearing Bracket Stay
Rotor Disc
Disc Brake Caliper
Cotter Pin
Rear Suspension Lower Crossmember
59 (600, 43)
Lock Nut Cap
294 (3,000 217)
113 (1,150, 83)
49 (500, 36)
103 (1,050, 76)
132 (1,350, 98)
Lower Suspension Arm
118 (1,200, 87)
N·m (kgf cm, ft·lbf) : Specified torque
◆ Non-reusable part
113 (1,150, 83)
TY1069100141030X

Fig. 1 Components for engine removal (Part 3 of 4)

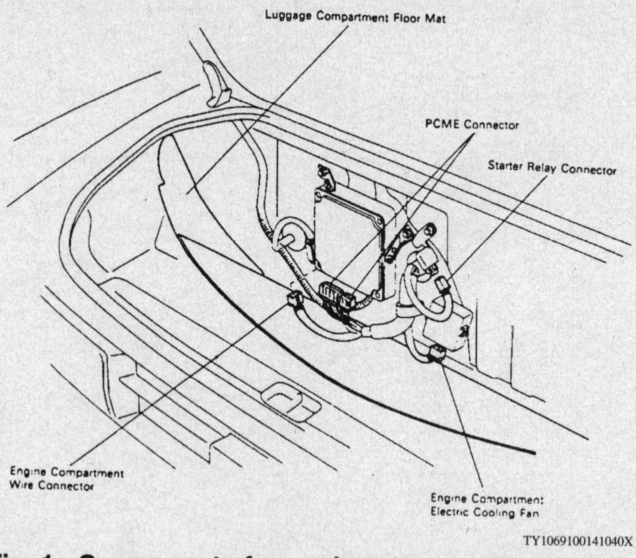
Luggage Compartment Floor Mat
PCME Connector
Starter Relay Connector
Engine Compartment Wire Connector
Engine Compartment Electric Cooling Fan
TY1069100141040X

Fig. 1 Components for engine removal (Part 4 of 4)

at a 90° angle from front.

g. During installation of intake and exhaust camshafts, place camshaft onto cylinder with No. 1 camshaft lobe facing outward. Apply seal packing to No. 1 bearing cap.
h. Install bearing caps in their correct locations, as shown in **Fig. 5. Each bearing cap has a number and front mark.** Apply a light coat of clean engine oil onto threads and under heads of bearing cap attaching bolts. Install and tighten bearing cap bolts to specification in several passes, using sequence shown in **Fig. 6.**
i. Reset audio coded anti-theft system, if equipped, as outlined in "Precautions."

VALVE CLEARANCE SPECIFICATIONS

Shims of various thicknesses are used to achieve the correct valve clearance, **Figs. 7 and 8.** Clearance should be .011–.015 inch.

VALVE ADJUSTMENT

1. **On models with audio coded anti-theft system,** disable system as outlined under "Precautions."
2. **On all models,** disconnect accelerator cable from throttle body, then remove air intake connector and connector stay.

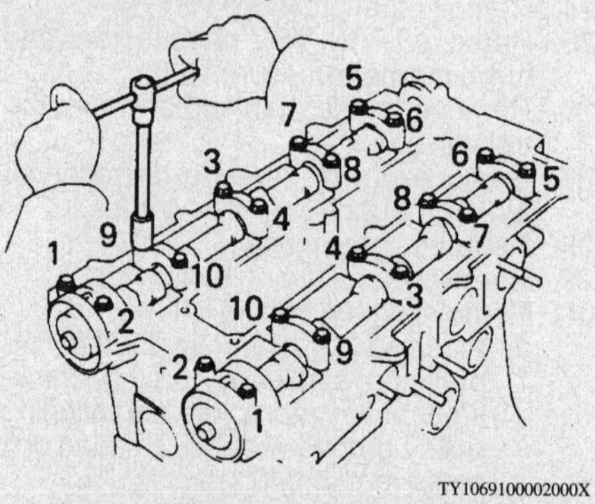
5
7
6
3
6
8
5
8
4
7
1
9
4
10
3
2
10
9
2
1
TY1069100002000X

Fig. 2 Intake & exhaust camshaft bearing cap bolt loosening sequence

3. Drain engine coolant.
4. Disconnect vacuum and water hoses from throttle body, then remove the throttle body.
5. Remove EGR/VSV vacuum modulator.
6. Remove cylinder head cover. Use care when removing spark plug connectors, pull only on connector not on wire.
7. With engine cold, place No. 1 cylinder at TDC of compression stroke by turning crankshaft pulley and aligning its groove with timing mark "0" of timing pointer.
8. Ensure valves on No. 1 cylinder are loose and valve on No. 4 cylinder are tight. If not turn crankshaft 360° (one complete revolution) and align timing marks.
9. With engine in this position check clearance of the following valves and record readings:
   a. No. 1 intake and exhaust valves.
   b. No. 2 intake valves.
   c. No. 3 exhaust valves.
10. If any measurement is not within specifications, remove valve adjustment shim using valve lifter cam wrench set tool No. 09248-55040, or equivalent, to depress lifter and a magnet to remove shim **Figs. 9 and 10.**
11. Using a micrometer measure thickness of removed shim, record this dimension.
12. Determine difference between desired and actual valve clearance measurement, add difference to dimension of measured shim. Refer to shim charts **Figs. 7 through 8** to select a replacement.
13. Install new shim in lifter, then remove lifter tools. Repeat steps 9 through 12 for any other valves found out of adjustment.
14. Rotate crankshaft pulley two full turns, recheck valves as outlined in steps 7 through 9.
15. Turn crankshaft pulley 360° (one complete revolution) and align timing marks as outlined previously and check the following valves:
   a. No. 2 exhaust valves.
   b. No. 3 intake valves.
   c. No. 4 intake and exhaust valves. Repeat steps 10 through 14, if necessary.
   d. Reinstall removed parts, Bleed cooling system as outlined under "Cooling System Bleed." If audio system was disabled, activate as

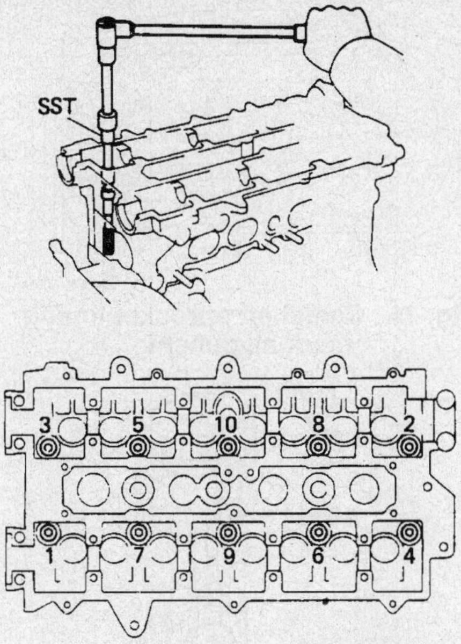
SST
3
5
10
8
2
1
7
9
6
4

Fig. 3 Cylinder head bolt loosening sequence

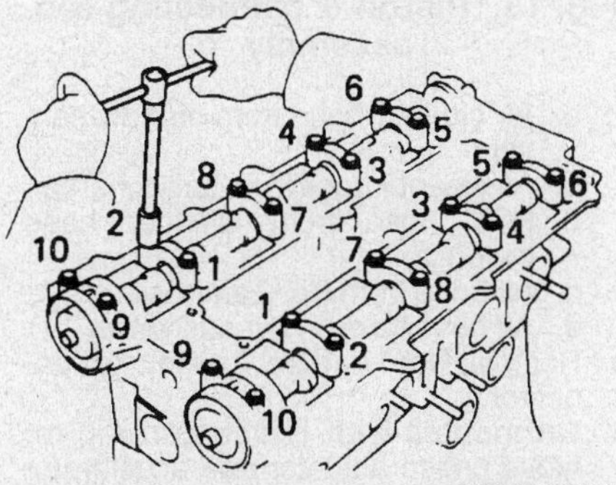
6
4
5
8
3
5
6
2
7
3
4
10
1
7
8
9
1
9
2
10

Fig. 6 Intake & exhaust camshaft bearing cap bolt tightening sequence

outlined under "Precautions."

HYDRAULIC LIFTERS

REPLACE

Check lifters for excessive wear and/or damage. Replace worn or damaged valve lifters as required. Lubricate hydraulic valve lifter before installation.

TIMING BELT

REPLACE

REMOVAL

1. Obtain audio anti-theft code, if equipped, as outlined in "Precautions."
2. Remove righthand front wheel.
3. Remove righthand engine undercover.
4. Remove radiator reservoir tank.
5. Loosen power steering oil reservoir tank.
6. Remove accessory drive belts.
7. Remove alternator and alternator brackets.

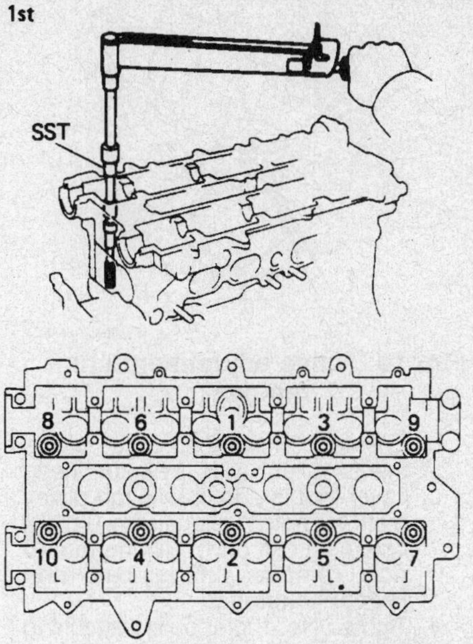
1st
SST
8
6
1
3
9
10
4
2
5
7

Fig. 4 Cylinder head bolt tightening sequence

New shim thickness mm (in.)

Shim No.	Thickness	Shim No.	Thickness
1	2.500 (0.0984)	10	2.950 (0.1161)
2	2.550 (0.1004)	11	3.000 (0.1181)
3	2.600 (0.1024)	12	3.050 (0.1201)
4	2.650 (0.1043)	13	3.100 (0.1220)
5	2.700 (0.1063)	14	3.150 (0.1240)
6	2.750 (0.1083)	15	3.200 (0.1260)
7	2.800 (0.1102)	16	3.250 (0.1280)
8	2.850 (0.1122)	17	3.300 (0.1299)
9	2.900 (0.1142)		

HINT: New shims have the thickness in millimeters imprinted on the face.

Fig. 7 Intake valve shim size chart

8. Raise engine slightly to remove weight from engine mounting on righthand side.
9. Remove righthand engine mount insulator and bracket.
10. Remove throttle body assembly.
11. Remove No. 2 timing belt cover.
12. Remove spark plugs.
13. Place No. 1 cylinder at TDC of compression stroke by turning crankshaft pulley to align its groove with No. 1 timing belt cover 0 mark.
14. Ensure alignment marks on camshaft sprockets and No. 3 timing belt cover are aligned properly as shown in **Fig. 11.** If not, turn crankshaft one complete revolution (360°) to align marks.
15. Remove timing belt from camshaft timing sprockets. If original timing belt is going to be used, place alignment marks on camshaft timing sprockets and timing belt as shown in **Fig. 12.**
16. Loosen No.1 idler pulley attaching bolt and shift toward left side as far as possible.
17. Temporarily tighten pulley attaching bolt, then relieve tension from timing belt.

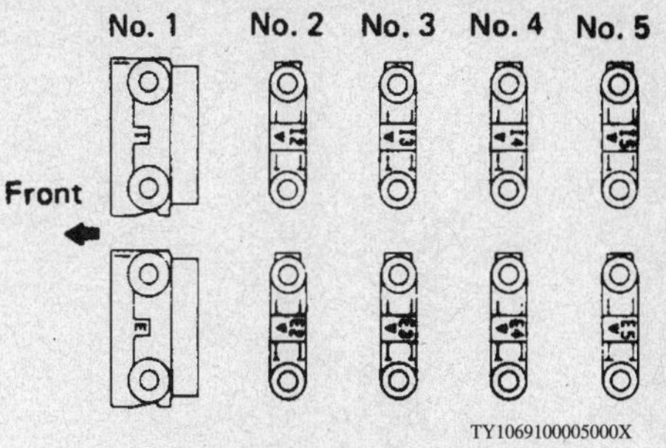
No. 1
No. 2
No. 3
No. 4
No. 5
Front

Fig. 5 Bearing cap location & identification

New shim thickness mm (in.)

Shim No.	Thickness	Shim No.	Thickness
1	2.500 (0.0984)	10	2.950 (0.1161)
2	2.550 (0.1004)	11	3.000 (0.1181)
3	2.600 (0.1024)	12	3.050 (0.1201)
4	2.650 (0.1043)	13	3.100 (0.1220)
5	2.700 (0.1063)	14	3.150 (0.1240)
6	2.750 (0.1083)	15	3.200 (0.1260)
7	2.800 (0.1102)	16	3.250 (0.1280)
8	2.850 (0.1122)	17	3.300 (0.1299)
9	2.900 (0.1142)		

HINT: New shims have the thickness in millimeters imprinted on the face.

Fig. 8 Exhaust valve shim size chart

18. Remove timing belt from camshaft sprocket. **Support timing belt so meshing of crankshaft sprocket and timing belt does not shift. Do not drop anything inside timing belt cover. Do not allow dust, oil or water to come into contact with timing belt.**
19. Remove sprockets, No. 1 timing belt covers, timing belt guide and timing belt. **If original timing belt is going to be used, draw a direction arrow on timing belt (draw arrow in direction of engine rotation) and place alignment marks on timing belt and crankshaft timing sprocket.**

INSTALLATION

Before installing the original timing belt onto the engine, ensure belt is in good condition. Carefully check timing belt for discoloration (an indication of fluid contact with the belt) or cracks. Do not install a timing belt that shows signs of wear or stress. Installing a worn or damaged belt will result in serious engine damage.

1. Install crankshaft sprocket and No. 2 idler pulley. Tighten pulley bolt to specification.
2. Temporarily install No. 1 idler pulley and tension spring. Install pulley attaching bolt. Do not tighten bolt. Install tension spring, then pry toward left as far as it will go and tighten it. Remove any oil or water on idler pulley.
3. With engine cold, temporarily install timing belt. Install belt onto crankshaft sprocket, oil pump, No. 2 idler pulley and water pump pulley. **If original timing belt is used, align marks made**

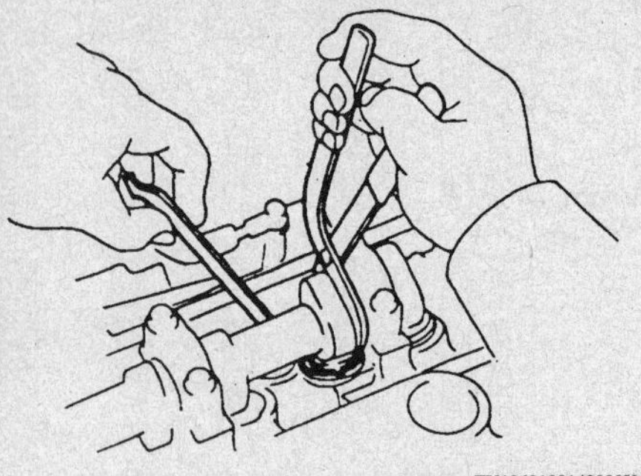
TY1069100142000X

Fig. 9 Valve lifter compression

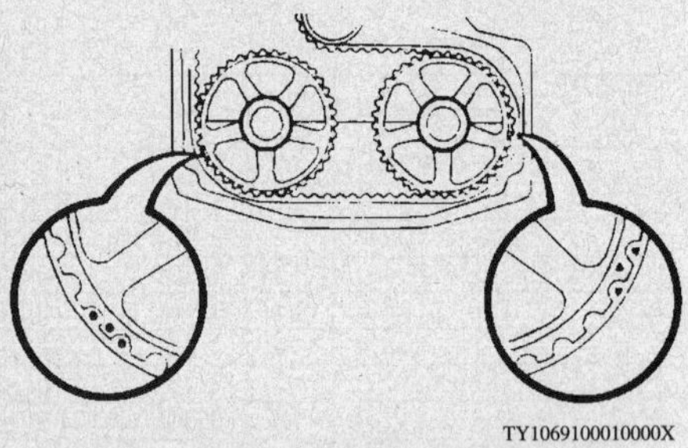
TY1069100010000X

Fig. 12 Sprocket & timing belt alignment

during removal and install belt with arrow pointing in direction of engine rotation.
4. Install timing belt guide.
5. Install No. 1 timing belt cover and gasket. Tighten cover attaching bolts to specification.
6. Install crankshaft pulley. Tighten bolt to specification.
7. Install camshaft sprockets. Using a suitable wrench, turn and align camshaft groove with drilled out mark of No. 1 camshaft bearing cap. Slide timing sprocket onto camshaft with S mark on sprocket facing upward. Align pin holes on camshaft sprocket and timing pulley, then insert knock pin. Secure sprocket from rotating, then tighten attaching bolts. Tighten bolts to specification. Install cylinder head cover.
8. Place No. 1 cylinder at TDC of compression stroke by turning crankshaft pulley and aligning its groove with 0 mark on No. 1 timing belt cover. Turn camshaft and align marks on camshaft sprockets and cylinder head cover.
9. Install timing belt. If original timing belt is going to be used, first align marks on camshaft sprockets and timing belt. Install timing belt. Ensure tension between crankshaft and intake camshaft timing sprockets exists.
10. With timing belt installed, check valve timing as follows:
   a. Loosen No. 1 idler pulley attaching bolt and stretch timing belt. Do not loosen pulley bolt further than point where idler returns.
   b. Slowly turn crankshaft pulley two revolutions from TDC to TDC. **Always turn crankshaft clockwise.**

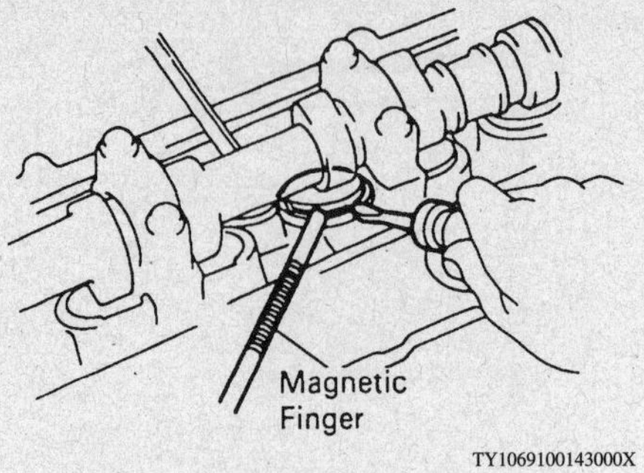
Magnetic
Finger
TY1069100143000X

Fig. 10 Valve adjustment shim removal

   c. Ensure camshaft sprocket timing marks align with cylinder head cover marks and crankshaft pulley mark (V notch) aligns with 0 mark on timing belt cover (timing tab). **If not, remove timing belt and properly install it.**
   d. Tighten No. 1 idler pulley attaching bolt to specification.
   e. Ensure timing belt tension exists between crankshaft and intake camshaft timing sprockets.
11. Reverse procedure to install. Reset audio coded anti-theft, if equipped, as outlined in "Precautions."

CAMSHAFT

REPLACE

Refer to "Cylinder Head, Replace" for camshaft removal procedures.

PISTON & ROD ASSEMBLY

Oversize pistons are not available; if piston bore is not within specifications, replace piston and/or cylinder block. When assembling piston onto connecting rod, ensure mark on top of piston and mark on connecting rod are on same side, **Fig. 13.** When installing piston and connecting rod assembly, ensure mark on top of piston is facing toward front of engine.

MAIN & ROD BEARINGS

Undersize bearings are not available. If crankshaft journals or crankpins are worn or scored, the crankshaft must be replaced.

OIL PAN

REPLACE

1. **On models with audio coded anti-theft system,**disable system as outlined under "Precautions".
2. **On all models,** drain oil and remove undercovers.
3. Remove righthand hood side panel, then the upper suspension brace, **Fig. 14.**
4. Disconnect the following hoses:

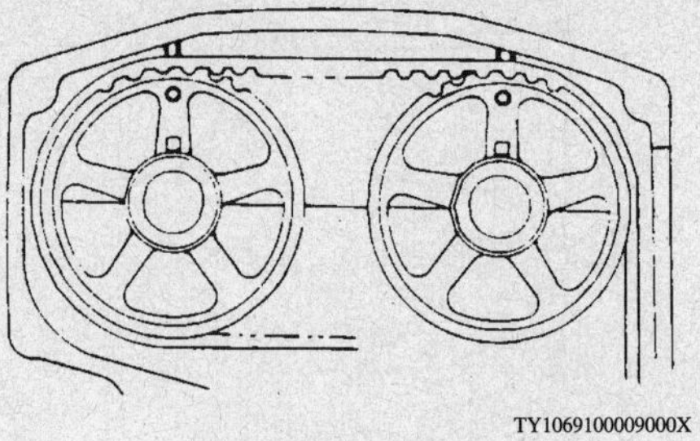
TY1069100009000X

Fig. 11 Camshaft sprocket timing mark alignment

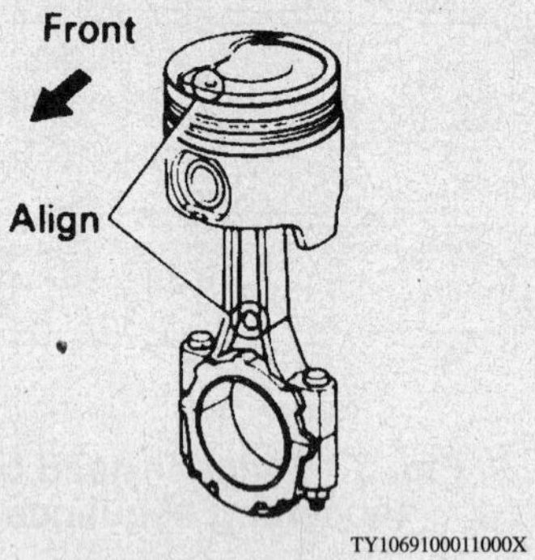
Front
Align
TY1069100011000X

Fig. 13 Piston & connecting rod assembly

   a. Air cleaner hose from air flow sensor.
   b. Air cleaner hose from turbocharger.
   c. PCV hose from cylinder head cover.
   d. Air hose from No. 2 air hose.
   e. Air hose from air bypass valve.
5. Remove No. 1 and No. 2 air intake connectors.
6. **On models with cruise control,** remove cruise actuator and accelerator linkage.
7. **On all models,** remove engine compartment electric cooling fan.
8. Remove A/C compressor without disconnecting hoses.
9. Remove tailpipe.
10. Remove front exhaust pipe.
11. Remove front engine mounting insulator.
12. Remove front engine mounting bracket and clutch release cylinder. Suspend clutch release cylinder from suspension brace with a suitable string or wire.
13. Remove stiffener plate and main three-way catalytic converter.
14. Disconnect oil level sensor connector and turbocharger oil outlet hose from oil pan, then remove dipstick.
15. Remove oil pan, oil strainer and baffle plate.
16. Suspend engine with engine chain hoist, then remove timing belt as outlined under "Timing Belt, Replace."
17. Remove No. 2 idler pulley, crankshaft timing pulley and oil pump pulley.
18. Remove oil pump.
19. Reverse procedure to install, tightening all bolts to specifications. If audio

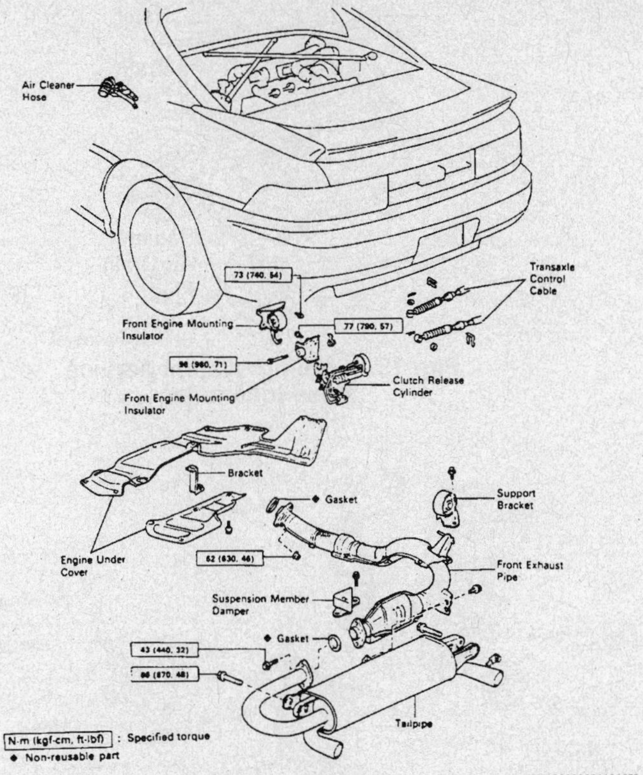
Air Cleaner Hose
Transaxle Control Cable
73 (740, 54)
Front Engine Mounting Insulator
77 (790, 57)
96 (980, 71)
Clutch Release Cylinder
Front Engine Mounting Insulator
Bracket
Gasket
Support Bracket
Engine Under Cover
62 (630, 46)
Front Exhaust Pipe
Suspension Member Damper
Gasket
43 (440, 32)
Tailpipe
N·m (kgf-cm, ft-lbf) : Specified torque
◆ Non-reusable part
TY1099300011010X

Fig. 14 Oil pump removal (Part 1 of 3)

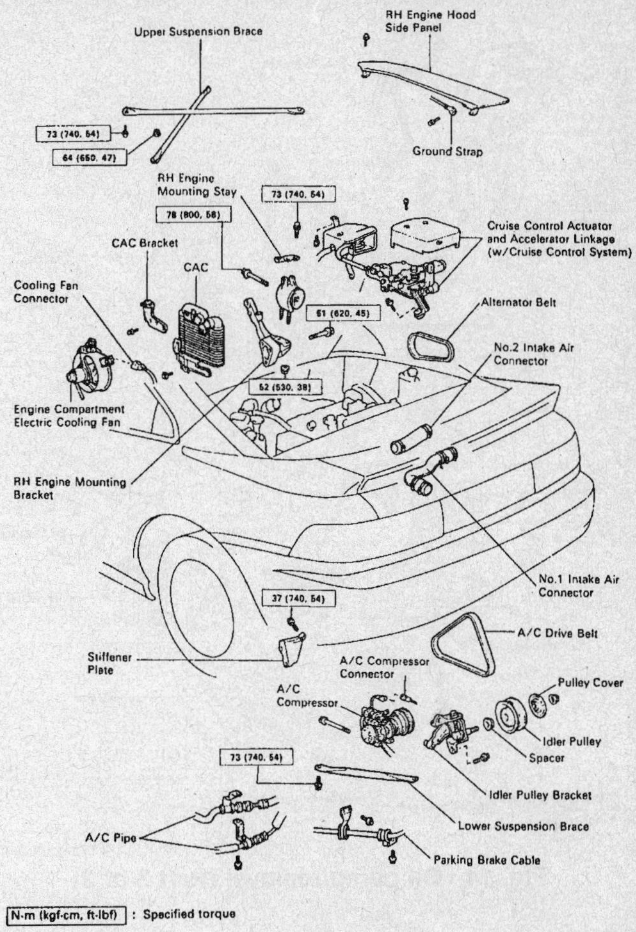
Upper Suspension Brace
RH Engine Hood Side Panel
73 (740, 54)
64 (650, 47)
Ground Strap
RH Engine Mounting Stay
73 (740, 54)
78 (800, 58)
CAC Bracket
CAC
Cruise Control Actuator and Accelerator Linkage (w/Cruise Control System)
Cooling Fan Connector
61 (620, 45)
Alternator Belt
No.2 Intake Air Connector
52 (530, 38)
Engine Compartment Electric Cooling Fan
RH Engine Mounting Bracket
No.1 Intake Air Connector
A/C Drive Belt
Stiffener Plate
A/C Compressor Connector
A/C Compressor
Pulley Cover
Idler Pulley
Spacer
73 (740, 54)
Idler Pulley Bracket
Lower Suspension Brace
A/C Pipe
Parking Brake Cable
N·m (kgf-cm, ft-lbf) : Specified torque
TY1099300011020X

Fig. 14 Oil pump removal (Part 2 of 3)

system was disabled, activate as outlined under "Precautions."

OIL PUMP

REPLACE

Refer to "Oil Pan, Replace" for procedure.

BELT TENSION DATA

Belt	New, Lbs.	Used, Lbs.
A/C	①	80–120
Alternator	100–140	84–124

① — 1993, 140–180 lbs.; 1994–95, 135–185 lbs.

COOLING SYSTEM BLEED

1. Remove spare tire, luggage compartment trim and upper radiator support seal.
2. Connect service hoses to radiator air drain and heater valve. Suspend opposite end of service hose connected to radiator to front hood stay. Suspend opposite end of heater valve service hose to front of hood, **Fig. 15.**
3. Set heater control to Hot. Open radiator and heater air drain plugs three turns. Slowly fill with coolant. Ensure air is absent from air drain plugs while filling water inlet to top with coolant.
4. Ensure level of coolant in drain service hoses is same as in water filler. When coolant level in air drain hoses stops dropping, close air drain plugs of radiator and heater. Close radiator cap to first stopping point.
5. Start engine and run at fast idle for three minutes and stop engine.
6. Add more coolant and repeat steps 5. Ensure coolant level in water filler has not dropped.
7. Completely tighten radiator cap and coolant reservoir to Full mark.
8. Install upper radiator support seal, luggage compartment trim, spare tire, fuel tank protector and luggage compartment undercovers.

THERMOSTAT

REPLACE

1. Disconnect A/C compressor from engine without removing hoses.
2. Drain coolant into suitable container.
3. Disconnect water hose from inlet.
4. Disconnect oil dipstick guide from water inlet.
5. Remove water inlet, then thermostat.
6. Reverse procedure to install, noting the following:
   a. Align protrusion of water inlet.
   b. Tighten inlet attaching bolts to specifications.

WATER PUMP

REPLACE

1. Drain coolant and disconnect radiator hose from water inlet.
2. Remove timing belt as outlined under "Timing Belt, Replace."
3. Remove No. 2 idler pulley, **Fig. 16.**
4. Reverse procedure to install, noting the following:
   a. Tighten fasteners to specifications.
   b. Bleed cooling system.

RADIATOR

REPLACE

1. Remove radiator lower air deflector, **Fig. 17.**
2. Drain engine coolant.
3. Remove upper radiator support seal.
4. **On models with A/C,** disconnect two cooling fan connectors, then remove Nos. 1 and 2 cooling fan mounting bolts and fans.
5. **On models less A/C,** disconnect cooling fan connector and remove No. 1 cooling fan (single fan).
6. **On models with A/C,** disconnect ECT sensor connector.
7. **On models less A/C,** disconnect ECT switch connector.
8. **On all models,** disconnect radiator hoses.

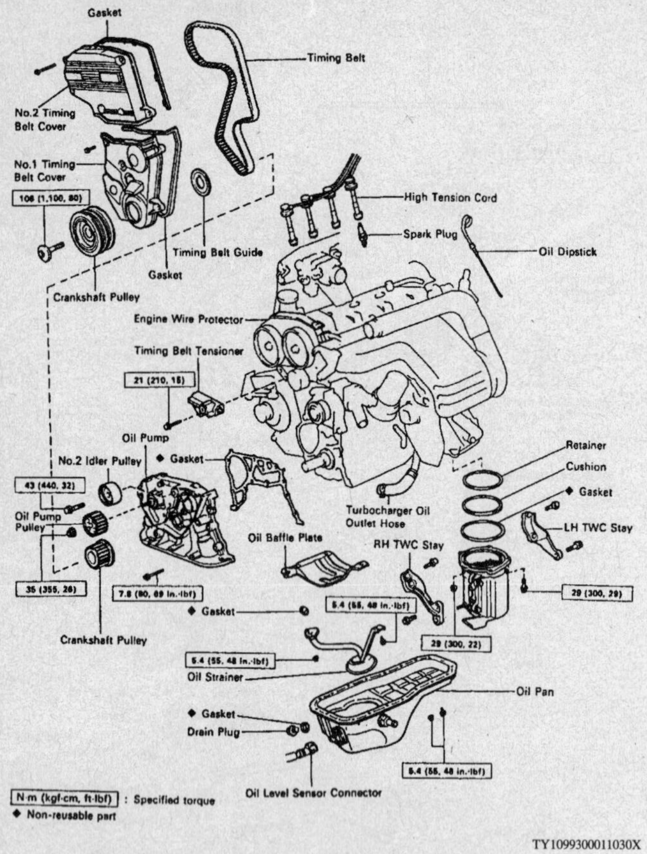
Gasket
Timing Belt
No.2 Timing Belt Cover
No.1 Timing Belt Cover
106 (1,100, 80)
High Tension Cord
Spark Plug
Oil Dipstick
Timing Belt Guide
Gasket
Crankshaft Pulley
Engine Wire Protector
Timing Belt Tensioner
21 (210, 15)
Oil Pump
No.2 Idler Pulley
◆ Gasket
43 (440, 32)
Oil Pump Pulley
Retainer
Cushion
◆ Gasket
Turbocharger Oil Outlet Hose
LH TWC Stay
Oil Baffle Plate
RH TWC Stay
35 (355, 26)
7.8 (80, 69 in.-lbf)
29 (300, 29)
◆ Gasket
5.4 (55, 48 in.-lbf)
Crankshaft Pulley
29 (300, 22)
5.4 (55, 48 in.-lbf)
Oil Strainer
Oil Pan
◆ Gasket
Drain Plug
5.4 (55, 48 in.-lbf)
Oil Level Sensor Connector
N·m (kgf-cm, ft-lbf) : Specified torque
◆ Non-reusable part
TY1099300011030X

Fig. 14 Oil pump removal (Part 3 of 3)

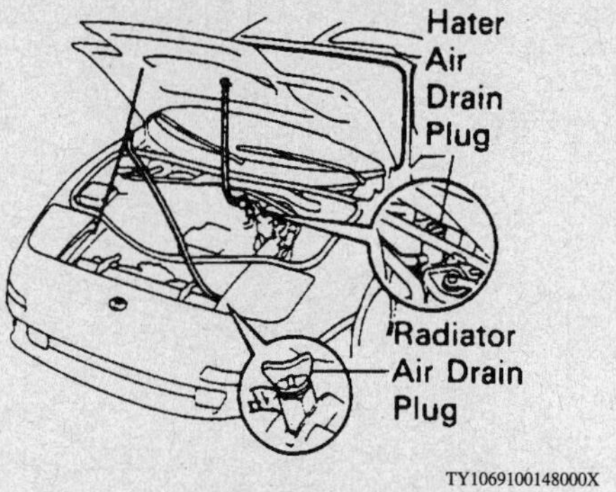
Hater
Air
Drain
Plug
Radiator
Air Drain
Plug
TY1069100148000X

Fig. 15 Cooling system service hose locations

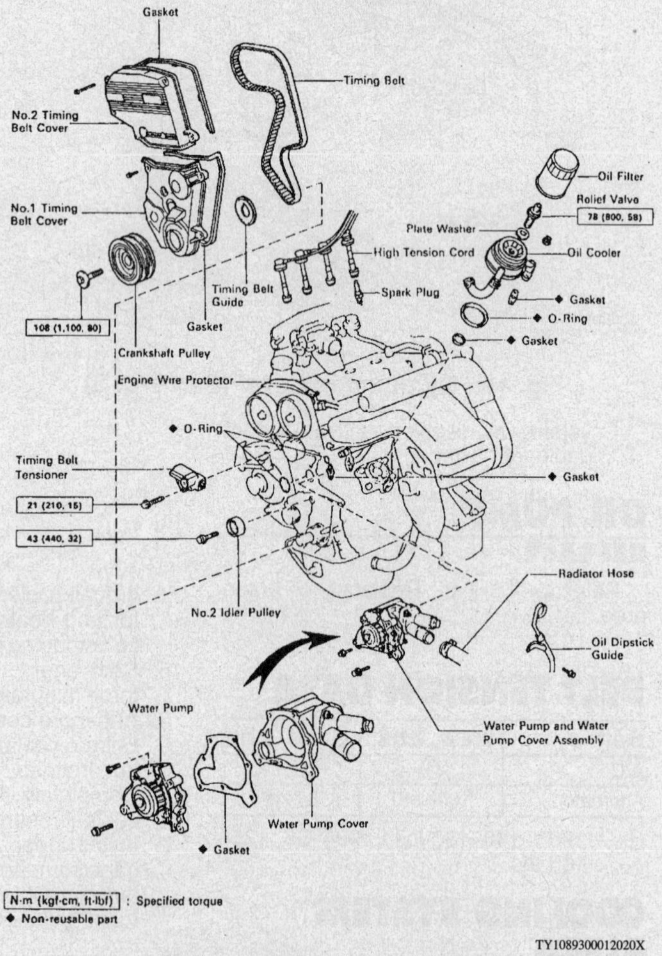
Gasket
Timing Belt
No.2 Timing Belt Cover
Oil Filter
Relief Valve
78 (800, 58)
No.1 Timing Belt Cover
Plate Washer
High Tension Cord
Oil Cooler
Spark Plug
◆ Gasket
◆ O-Ring
◆ Gasket
Timing Belt Guide
106 (1,100, 80)
Gasket
Crankshaft Pulley
Engine Wire Protector
◆ O-Ring
Timing Belt Tensioner
◆ Gasket
21 (210, 15)
43 (440, 32)
Radiator Hose
No.2 Idler Pulley
Oil Dipstick Guide
Water Pump
Water Pump and Water Pump Cover Assembly
Water Pump Cover
◆ Gasket
N·m (kgf-cm, ft-lbf) : Specified torque
◆ Non-reusable part
TY1089300012020X

Fig. 16 Water pump removal (Part 2 of 2)

9. Remove radiator upper support bolts and two radiator upper supports.
10. Remove radiator and two lower supports.
11. **On models with A/C,** remove ECT sensor from radiator.
12. **On models less A/C,** remove ECT switch from radiator.
13. **On all models,** reverse procedure to install. Use new O-rings and tighten bolts to specifications.

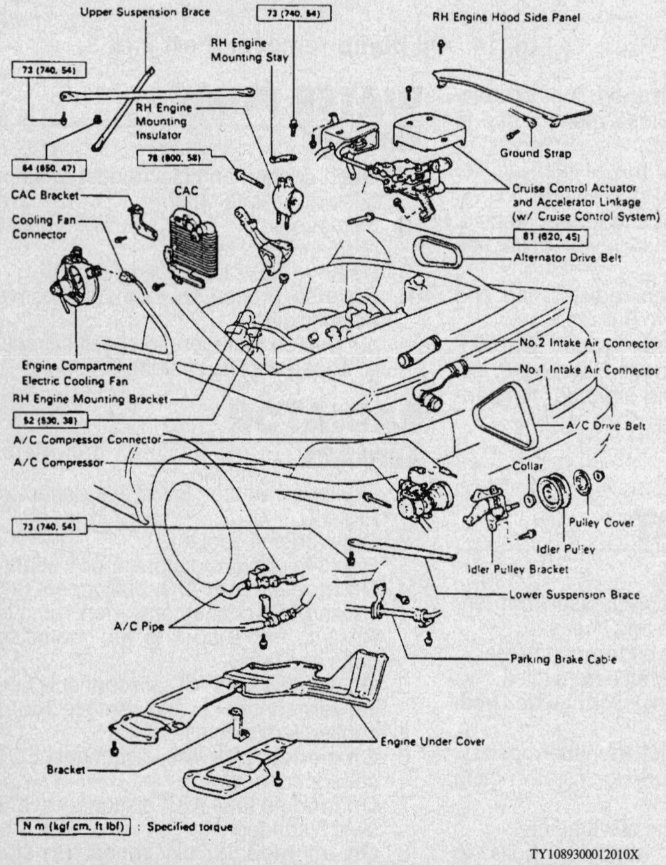
Upper Suspension Brace
73 (740, 54)
RH Engine Hood Side Panel
RH Engine Mounting Stay
73 (740, 54)
RH Engine Mounting Insulator
64 (650, 47)
78 (800, 58)
Ground Strap
CAC Bracket
CAC
Cruise Control Actuator and Accelerator Linkage (w/ Cruise Control System)
Cooling Fan Connector
61 (620, 45)
Alternator Drive Belt
No.2 Intake Air Connector
No.1 Intake Air Connector
Engine Compartment Electric Cooling Fan
RH Engine Mounting Bracket
52 (530, 38)
A/C Drive Belt
A/C Compressor Connector
A/C Compressor
Collar
Pulley Cover
73 (740, 54)
Idler Pulley
Idler Pulley Bracket
Lower Suspension Brace
A/C Pipe
Parking Brake Cable
Engine Under Cover
Bracket
N·m (kgf-cm, ft-lbf) : Specified torque
TY1089300012010X

Fig. 16 Water pump removal (Part 1 of 2)

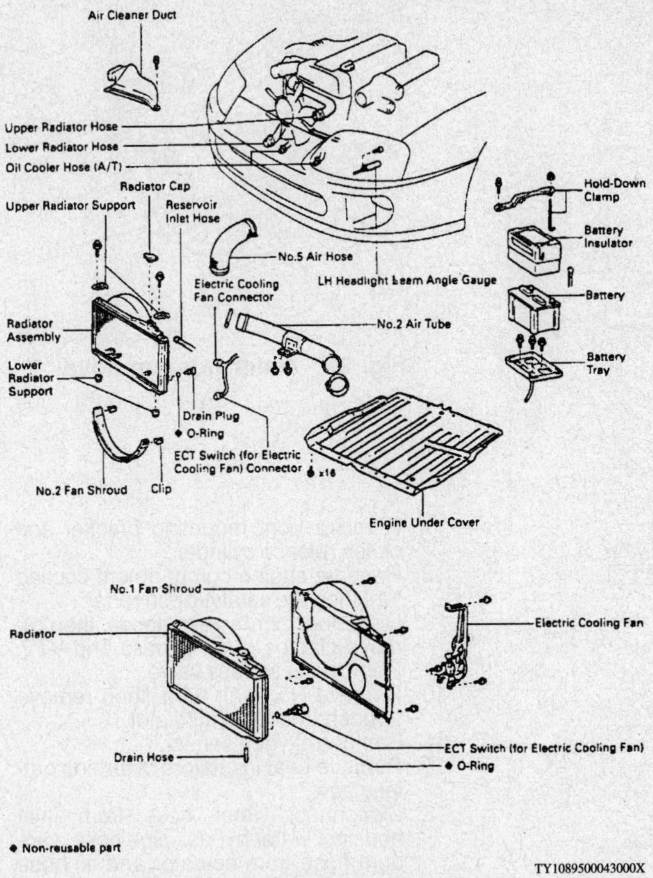
Air Cleaner Duct
Upper Radiator Hose
Lower Radiator Hose
Oil Cooler Hose (A/T)
Radiator Cap
Upper Radiator Support
Reservoir Inlet Hose
Hold-Down Clamp
Battery Insulator
No.5 Air Hose
Electric Cooling Fan Connector
LH Headlight Beam Angle Gauge
Battery
No.2 Air Tube
Radiator Assembly
Lower Radiator Support
Battery Tray
Drain Plug
◆ O-Ring
ECT Switch (for Electric Cooling Fan) Connector
x16
No.2 Fan Shroud
Clip
Engine Under Cover
No.1 Fan Shroud
Electric Cooling Fan
Radiator
ECT Switch (for Electric Cooling Fan)
◆ O-Ring
Drain Hose
◆ Non-reusable part
TY1089500043000X

Fig. 17 Radiator replacement

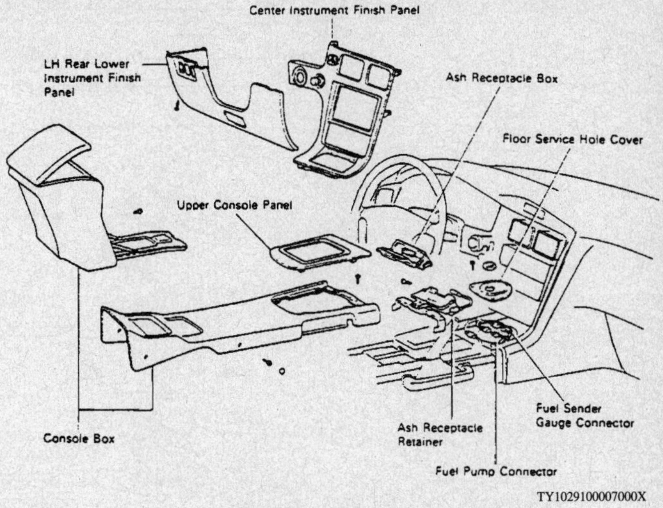
Center Instrument Finish Panel
LH Rear Lower Instrument Finish Panel
Ash Receptacle Box
Floor Service Hole Cover
Upper Console Panel
Console Box
Ash Receptacle Retainer
Fuel Sender Gauge Connector
Fuel Pump Connector
TY1029100007000X

Fig. 18 Exploded view of console

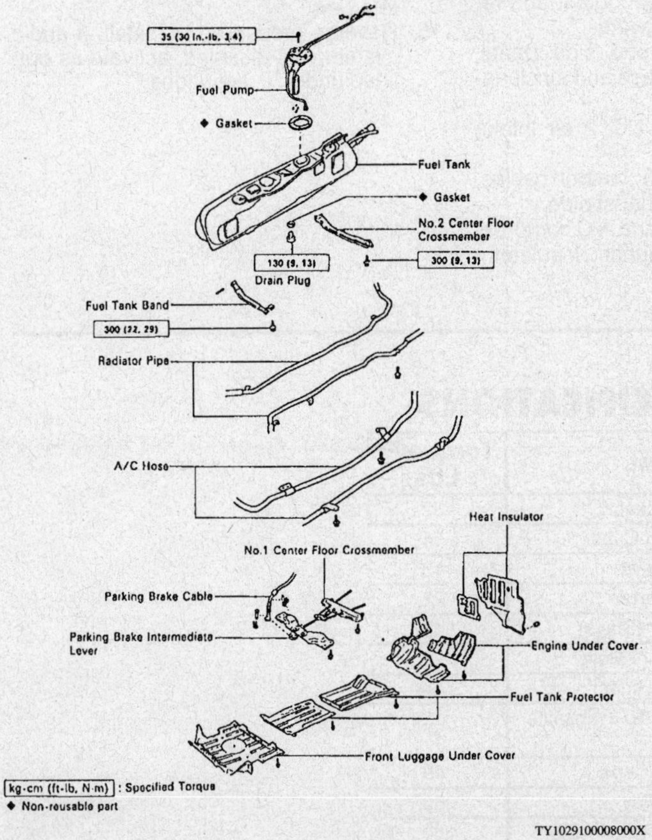
35 (30 in.-lb, 3.4)
Fuel Pump
◆ Gasket
Fuel Tank
◆ Gasket
No.2 Center Floor Crossmember
130 (9, 13)
Drain Plug
300 (9, 13)
Fuel Tank Band
300 (22, 29)
Radiator Pipe
A/C Hose
Heat Insulator
No.1 Center Floor Crossmember
Parking Brake Cable
Parking Brake Intermediate Lever
Engine Under Cover
Fuel Tank Protector
Front Luggage Under Cover
kg-cm (ft-lb, N·m) : Specified Torque
◆ Non-reusable part
TY1029100008000X

Fig. 19 Exploded view of fuel pump components

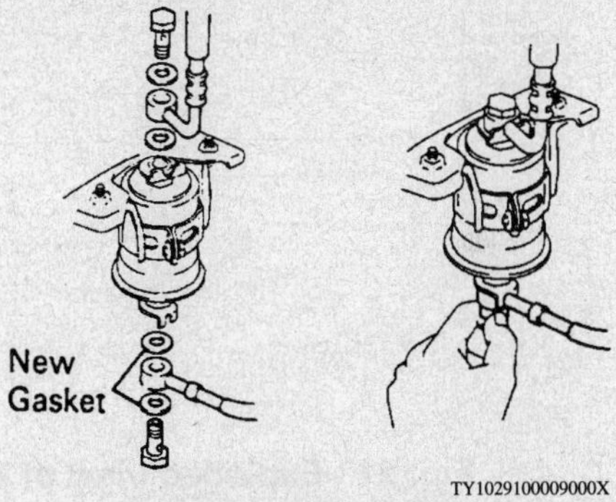
New Gasket
TY1029100009000X

Fig. 20 Fuel filter replacement

FUEL PUMP

REPLACE

1. **On models with audio coded anti-theft system,** disable system as outlined under "Precautions."
2. **On all models,** remove console boxes, **Fig. 18.**
3. Remove lefthand lower instrument finish panel, then the center finish panel.
4. Remove ash receptacle box and retainer.
5. Disconnect fuel pump connector and fuel sender connector.
6. Remove floor service cover.
7. Remove engine undercovers, luggage undercover and fuel tank protectors. Drain fuel tank, **Fig. 19.**
8. Remove parking brake intermediate lever and No. 1 center floor crossmember.
9. Disconnect A/C hoses and radiator pipes from body.
10. Remove fuel tank insulators.
11. Disconnect fuel hoses and tube, then remove fuel tank.
12. Remove fuel pump from tank.
13. Reverse procedure to install. Tighten attaching nuts and bolts to specifications. If audio system was disabled, activate as outlined under "Precautions."

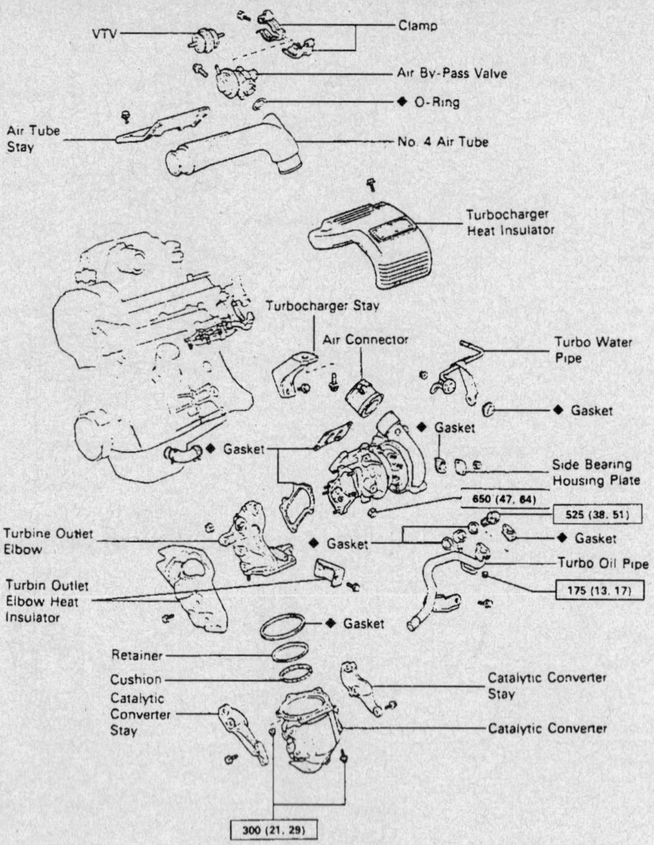
VTV
Clamp
Air By-Pass Valve
◆ O-Ring
Air Tube Stay
No. 4 Air Tube
Turbocharger Heat Insulator
Turbocharger Stay
Air Connector
Turbo Water Pipe
◆ Gasket
◆ Gasket
◆ Gasket
Side Bearing Housing Plate
650 (47, 64)
525 (38, 51)
Turbine Outlet Elbow
◆ Gasket
◆ Gasket
Turbo Oil Pipe
Turbin Outlet Elbow Heat Insulator
175 (13, 17)
◆ Gasket
Retainer
Cushion
Catalytic Converter Stay
Catalytic Converter Stay
Catalytic Converter
300 (21, 29)
TY1059100001000X

Fig. 21 Exploded view of turbocharger

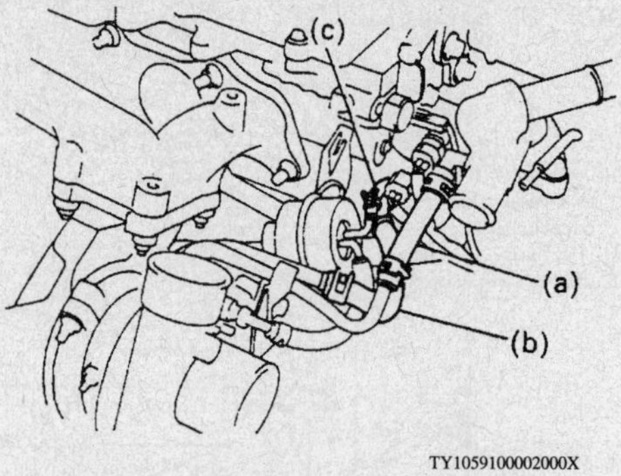
(c)
(a)
(b)
TY1059100002000X

Fig. 22 Water hose removal

FUEL FILTER

REPLACE

Refer to **Fig. 20** for replacement procedure.

TURBOCHARGER

REPLACE

1. **On models with audio coded anti-theft system,** disable system as outlined under "Precautions."
2. **On all models,** drain coolant and remove engine undercovers.
3. Remove lefthand hood side panel, suspension upper brace and air cleaner, **Fig. 21.**
4. Remove No. 1 and No. 2 air intake chamber.
5. Disconnect transaxle control cables, then remove front exhaust pipe.
6. Remove idler pulley and A/C compressor, then the front mounting insulator.
7. Remove front mounting bracket and clutch release cylinder.
8. Remove engine compartment cooling fan, then the catalytic converter.
9. Disconnect air bypass hoses, then remove clamps of air bypass and VTV. Remove air bypass valve.
10. Remove No. 4 air tube, then remove turbocharger heat insulator.
11. Remove oxygen sensor.
12. Remove heat insulators of turbine outlet elbow.
13. Disconnect water hose from inlet housing, water bypass pipe hose, vacuum hose from actuator and oil hose from turbo oil pipe, **Fig. 22.**
14. Remove turbocharger stay and turbocharger.
15. Reverse procedure to install. If audio system was disabled, activate as outlined under "Precautions."

TIGHTENING SPECIFICATIONS

Year	Component	Torque/Ft. Lbs.
1993–95	Alternator Bracket	32
	Camshaft Bearing Caps	14
	Camshaft Pulleys	43
	Catalytic Converter	22
	Catalytic Converter (Stays)	43
	Center Crossmember Bolts	22
	Clutch Release Cylinder	9
	Clutch Release Cylinder To Transaxle Bolts	57
	Connecting Rod Caps	49
	Crankshaft Pulley	80
	Cylinder Head Bolts	②
	Cylinder Head Cover	21①
	Distributor Mounting Bolts	29
	EGR Valve (Head Side)	19

Continued

TIGHTENING SPECIFICATIONS—Continued

Year	Component	Torque/Ft. Lbs.
1993–95	EGR Valve (Intake Side)	14
	Exhaust Manifold	38
	Exhaust Pipe To Catalytic Converter	46
	Flywheel	80
	Front Engine Mounting Bracket	57
	Front Engine Mounting Insulator	54
	Front Engine Mounting Insulator To Body	57
	Front Engine Mounting Insulator To Mounting Bracket	71
	Front Exhaust Pipe	46
	Front Exhaust Pipe Damper	15
	Front Exhaust Pipe Support Bracket	15
	Fuel Inlet Hose To Fuel Filter	22
	Fuel Pump Bracket To Fuel Tank	35①
	Fuel Tank Bolts	22
	Idle Pulley Bracket Bolt (Longest)	18
	Idle Pulley Bracket Bolt (Medium)	20
	Idle Pulley Bracket Bolt (Shortest)	27
	Intake Manifold	14
	Intake Manifold Stays	19
	Knock Sensor	27
	LH Engine Hanger (12mm Bolt)	9
	LH Engine Hanger (14mm Bolt)	14
	LH Engine Mounting Stay (Mounting Insulator Side)	54
	LH Engine Mounting Stay (Transaxle Side)	18
	LH Mounting Bracket	38
	LH Three Way Catalytic Converter Stay	43
	Lower Suspension Brace	54
	Main Bearing Caps	43
	No. 1 Idler Pulley Pivot Bolt	38
	No. 2 Idler Pulley Nut	32
	No. 3 Timing Belt Cover	7
	Oil Cooler Bracket	6
	Oil Nozzles	7
	Oil Pan	48①
	Oil Pan Drain Bolt	29
	Oil Pipe To Turbo	13
	Oil Pump Baffle Plate & Strainer	48①
	Oil Pump Pulley Nut	26
	Oil Pump To Engine	6
	Oxygen Sensor	33
	Rear End Plate	7
	Rear Engine Mounting Bracket (14mm Bolt)	29
	Rear Engine Mounting Bracket (17mm Bolt)	57
	Rear Engine Mounting Insulator To Mounting Bracket	64
	Rear Engine Mounting Insulator	47
	Rear Oil Seal Retainer	7
	Rear Suspension Lower Crossmember	83
	RH Engine Mounting Bracket	45

Continued

TIGHTENING SPECIFICATIONS—Continued

Year	Component	Torque/Ft. Lbs.
1993–95	RH Engine Mounting Insulator Bolt	58
	RH Engine Mounting Insulator Nut	38
	RH Front Engine Hanger To Cylinder Head	29
	RH Front Engine Hanger To Mounting Bracket	45
	RH Mounting Stay	54
	Spark Plugs	13
	Stabilizer Link	36
	Stiffener Plate	27
	Suspension Upper Brace Bolt	54
	Suspension Upper Brace Nut	47
	Timing Belt Tensioner	13
	Timing Cover	7
	Transaxle Oil Cooler Tube	25
	Turbo Stay To Block	43
	Turbo Stay To Turbo	51
	Turbo To Exhaust Manifold	47
	Upper Radiator Support Bolts	9
	Upper Suspension Brace Bolt	54
	Upper Suspension Brace Nut	47
	Water Bypass Pipe	6
	Water Outlet Housing	29
	Water Pump Bolts	6
	Water Pump To Bypass Pipe (12mm Bolt)	9

① — Inch lbs.
② — Torque to 36 ft. lbs., then tighten an additional 90°.

2.2L 5S-FE Engine

NOTE: On Air Bag Equipped Models, Refer To "Air Bag System Precautions" Located In The Front Of This Manual For System Disarming & Arming Procedures.

NOTE: For Procedures Not Found In This Section, Refer To Celica & Supra Engine Section.

INDEX

	Page No.
Belt Tension Data	44-22
Compression Pressure	44-19
Cooling System Bleed	44-22
Cylinder Head, Replace	44-20
Engine Rebuilding Specifications	48-1
Engine, Replace	44-19
Fuel Filter, Replace	44-23
Fuel Pump, Replace	44-23
Oil Pan, Replace	44-21
Oil Pump, Replace	44-21
Precautions	44-18
Air Bag Systems	44-18
Audio Coded Anti-Theft System	44-18
Radiator, Replace	44-22
Thermostat, Replace	44-22
Tightening Specifications	44-24
Valve Adjustment	44-20
Valve Clearance Specifications	44-20
Water Pump, Replace	44-22

PRECAUTIONS

AIR BAG SYSTEMS

Refer to "Air Bag System Precautions" in the front of this manual for system disarming and arming procedures.

AUDIO CODED ANTI-THEFT SYSTEM

Some models are equipped with an audio coded anti-theft system that will disable the radio when battery power is removed from the radio. The system can be identified by the "ANTI-THEFT SYSTEM" on the cassette tape lid. Obtain the three

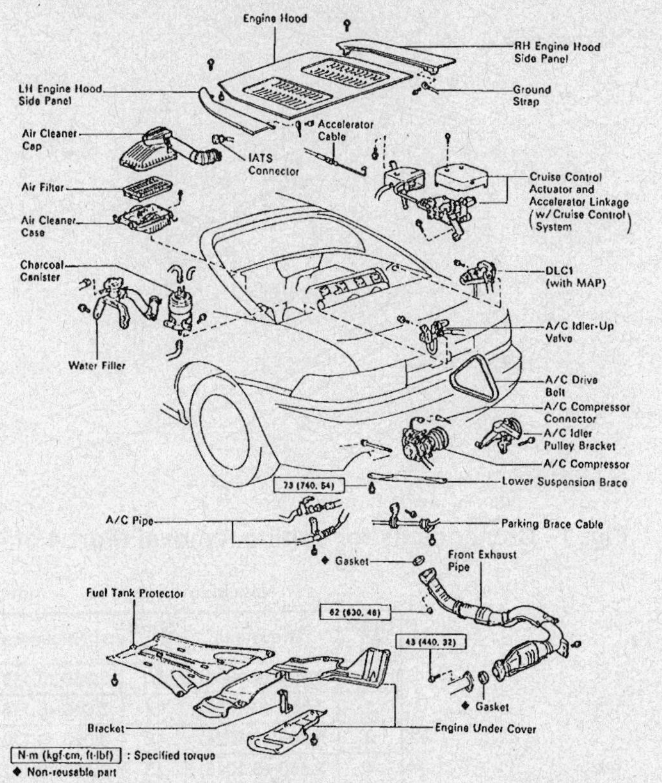
Engine Hood
RH Engine Hood Side Panel
LH Engine Hood Side Panel
Ground Strap
Accelerator Cable
Air Cleaner Cap
IATS Connector
Air Filter
Cruise Control Actuator and Accelerator Linkage (w/ Cruise Control System)
Air Cleaner Case
Charcoal Canister
DLC1 (with MAP)
A/C Idler-Up Valve
Water Filler
A/C Drive Belt
A/C Compressor Connector
A/C Idler Pulley Bracket
A/C Compressor
73 (740, 54)
Lower Suspension Brace
A/C Pipe
Parking Brace Cable
Gasket
Front Exhaust Pipe
Fuel Tank Protector
62 (630, 46)
43 (440, 32)
Gasket
Bracket
Engine Under Cover
N·m (kgf·cm, ft·lbf) : Specified torque
◆ Non-reusable part

TY1069100149010X

Fig. 1 Components for engine removal (Part 1 of 4)

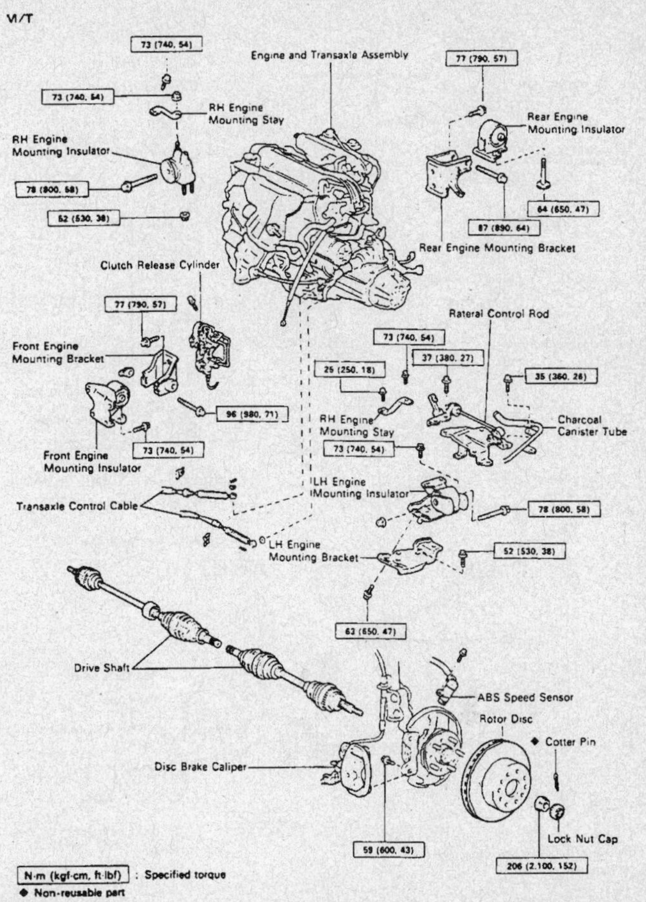
M/T
73 (740, 54)
Engine and Transaxle Assembly
77 (790, 57)
RH Engine Mounting Stay
Rear Engine Mounting Insulator
RH Engine Mounting Insulator
78 (800, 58)
52 (530, 38)
64 (650, 47)
87 (890, 64)
Rear Engine Mounting Bracket
Clutch Release Cylinder
Rateral Control Rod
77 (790, 57)
37 (380, 27)
Front Engine Mounting Bracket
25 (250, 18)
35 (360, 26)
96 (980, 71)
RH Engine Mounting Stay
Charcoal Canister Tube
Front Engine Mounting Insulator
Transaxle Control Cable
LH Engine Mounting Insulator
78 (800, 58)
LH Engine Mounting Bracket
52 (530, 38)
63 (650, 47)
Drive Shaft
ABS Speed Sensor
Rotor Disc
Cotter Pin
Disc Brake Caliper
Lock Nut Cap
59 (600, 43)
206 (2,100, 152)
N·m (kgf·cm, ft·lbf) : Specified torque
◆ Non-reusable part

TY1069100149020X

Fig. 1 Components for engine removal (Part 2 of 4)

digit code from the customer for input before disconnecting battery power to the audio unit. Reset system after service as follows:

1. Obtain three digit code from customer.
2. Depress No. 1 (PROG) button while depressing righthand side of TUNE SEEK button, - - - will appear in tape operation display.
3. Enter code as follows:
   a. To enter first digit, press No. 1 (PROG) button a sufficient number of times, starting with zero, to enter digit (if first digit of code is five press button six times).
   b. To enter second digit, press No. 2 (APS) button a sufficient number of times, starting with zero, to enter digit.
   c. To enter third digit press, No. 3 (RPT) button a sufficient number of times, starting with zero, to enter digit.
4. If three dashes (- - -) appear in tape operation display during input of digits, restart procedure from beginning.
5. When code digits are correctly input and displayed, press and hold SCAN button until SEC appears in tape operation display.
6. When SEC disappears from display audio unit should be operative.
7. If unit is not operative or Err is displayed, repeat procedure. **Attempting to input code more than nine times may permanently disable audio unit.**

COMPRESSION PRESSURE

1. Start engine and warm to normal operating temperature.
2. Disconnect distributor electrical connector.
3. Remove No. 1 intake air connector.
4. Disconnect high-tension cords from spark plugs.
5. Remove spark plugs.
6. Insert compression gauge into spark plug hole.
7. Fully open throttle.
8. While cranking engine, measure compression pressure.
9. Standard compression pressure is 142–178 psi or more. Maximum difference between each cylinder should be 14 psi.

ENGINE

REPLACE

1. **On models with audio coded anti-theft system,**disable system as outlined under "Precautions".
2. **On all models,** remove hood, hood side panels and undercovers.
3. Drain engine coolant, engine oil and transaxle oil.
4. Remove suspension upper brace, **Fig. 1,** then air cleaner assembly.
5. Disconnect accelerator cable, then remove cruise actuator and linkage, if equipped.
6. Disconnect brake booster vacuum hose and engine ground strap connector.
7. Remove check connector and vacuum sensor, then A/C VSV.
8. Remove water filler tube and charcoal canister.
9. Remove engine relay box, ignition coil and igniter. Disconnect engine wire.
10. Disconnect engine wire from luggage compartment. Then disconnect starter cable.
11. Disconnect water inlet hose, fuel inlet hose, fuel return hose and radiator hose from water outlet housing.
12. Disconnect transaxle control cables.
13. **On automatic transmission,** disconnect oil cooler lines.
14. **On all models,** remove front exhaust pipe.
15. Remove driveshaft.
16. Remove idler pulley bracket and A/C compressor without disconnecting hoses.
17. Disconnect speedometer cable. Then remove front and rear engine mounting insulator (remove rear first).
18. **On manual transmission,** remove

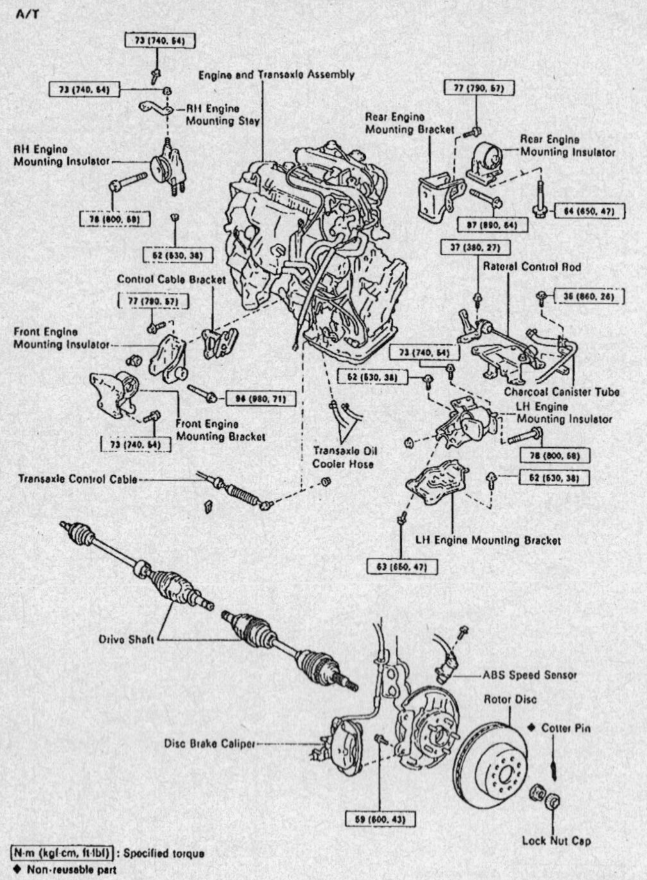
A/T
73 (740, 54)
Engine and Transaxle Assembly
77 (790, 57)
RH Engine Mounting Stay
Rear Engine Mounting Bracket
RH Engine Mounting Insulator
Rear Engine Mounting Insulator
78 (800, 58)
64 (650, 47)
87 (890, 64)
52 (530, 38)
37 (380, 27)
Rateral Control Rod
Control Cable Bracket
77 (790, 57)
35 (360, 26)
Front Engine Mounting Insulator
73 (740, 54)
52 (530, 38)
Charcoal Canister Tube
96 (980, 71)
LH Engine Mounting Insulator
Front Engine Mounting Bracket
73 (740, 54)
Transaxle Oil Cooler Hose
78 (800, 58)
Transaxle Control Cable
52 (530, 38)
LH Engine Mounting Bracket
63 (650, 47)
Drive Shaft
ABS Speed Sensor
Rotor Disc
◆ Cotter Pin
Disc Brake Caliper
59 (600, 43)
Lock Nut Cap
N·m (kgf·cm, ft·lbf) : Specified torque
◆ Non-reusable part

TY1069100149030X

Fig. 1 Components for engine removal (Part 3 of 4)

front engine mounting bracket and re-

New shim thickness mm (in.)

Shim No.	Thickness	Shim No.	Thickness
1	2.500 (0.0984)	10	2.950 (0.1161)
2	2.550 (0.1004)	11	3.000 (0.1181)
3	2.600 (0.1024)	12	3.050 (0.1201)
4	2.650 (0.1043)	13	3.100 (0.1220)
5	2.700 (0.1063)	14	3.150 (0.1240)
6	2.750 (0.1083)	15	3.200 (0.1260)
7	2.800 (0.1102)	16	3.250 (0.1280)
8	2.850 (0.1122)	17	3.300 (0.1299)
9	2.900 (0.1142)		

HINT: New shims have the thickness in millimeters imprinted on the face.

TY1069100153000X

Fig. 2 Intake valve shim size chart

lease cylinder.

19. **On automatic transmission,** disconnect transmission control cables.
20. **On all models,** remove rear engine mounting bracket and righthand engine mounting stay.
21. **On manual transmission,** remove lefthand mounting stay. Then remove lateral control rod.
22. **On all models,** remove air cleaner case bracket.
23. Attach chain and hoist to engine hangers.
24. Remove lefthand mounting insulator and brackets from transaxle. Then remove righthand mounting insulator and bracket from engine assembly.
25. Remove engine and transaxle assembly from vehicle.
26. Reverse procedure to install. If audio system was disabled, activate as outlined under "Precautions."

CYLINDER HEAD

REPLACE

Refer to appropriate engine section of "Celica & Supra" chapter, noting the following:

1. After draining coolant, remove engine undercovers and hood side panels, then the suspension upper brace.
2. It is not necessary to remove alternator and A/C compressor.
3. Remove right rear wheel.

VALVE CLEARANCE SPECIFICATIONS

Shims of various thickness are used to achieve the correct valve clearance, **Figs. 2 and 3.** Clearance should be .007–.011 inch for intake valves and .011–.015 inch for exhaust valves.

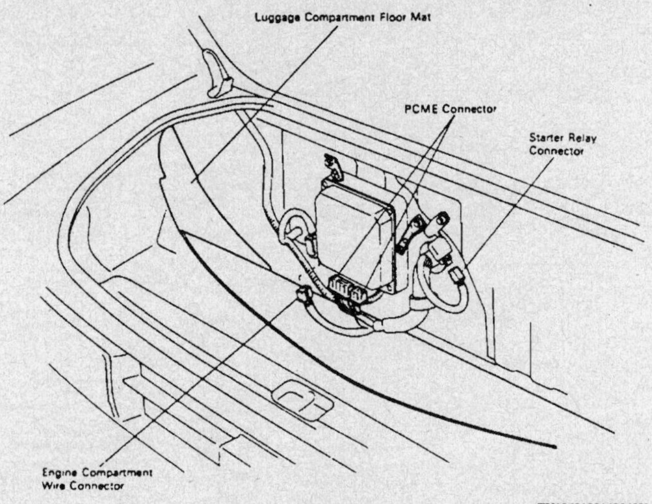
Luggage Compartment Floor Mat
PCME Connector
Starter Relay Connector
Engine Compartment Wire Connector

TY1069100149040X

Fig. 1 Components for engine removal (Part 4 of 4)

New shim thickness mm (in.)

Shim No.	Thickness	Shim No.	Thickness
1	2.500 (0.0984)	10	2.950 (0.1161)
2	2.550 (0.1004)	11	3.000 (0.1181)
3	2.600 (0.1024)	12	3.050 (0.1201)
4	2.650 (0.1043)	13	3.100 (0.1220)
5	2.700 (0.1063)	14	3.150 (0.1240)
6	2.750 (0.1083)	15	3.200 (0.1260)
7	2.800 (0.1102)	16	3.250 (0.1280)
8	2.850 (0.1122)	17	3.300 (0.1299)
9	2.900 (0.1142)		

HINT: New shims have the thickness in millimeters imprinted on the face.

TY1069100155000X

Fig. 3 Exhaust valve shim size chart

VALVE ADJUSTMENT

1. **On models with audio coded anti-theft system,** disable system as outlined under "Precautions".
2. **On all models,** drain engine coolant.
3. Remove air intake, throttle body and cylinder head cover.
4. With engine cold, place No. 1 cylinder at TDC of compression stroke by turning crankshaft pulley and aligning its groove with timing mark "0" of timing pointer.
5. Ensure valves on No. 1 cylinder are loose and valve on No. 4 cylinder are tight. If not turn crankshaft 360° (one complete revolution) and align timing marks.
6. With engine in this position check clearance of the following valves:
   a. No. 1 intake and exhaust valves.
   b. No. 2 intake valves.
   c. No. 3 exhaust valves.
   d. Record readings
7. If any measurement is outside specifications, remove valve adjustment shim using valve lifter cam wrench set tool No. SST 09248-55040, or equivalent, to depress lifter and a magnet to remove shim **Figs. 4 and 5.**

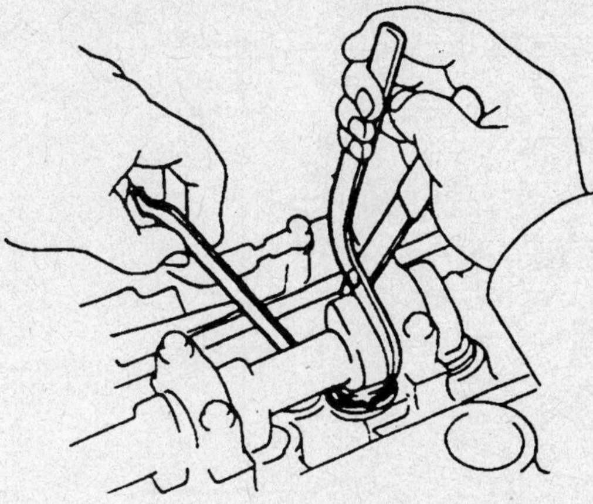

TY1069100150000X

Fig. 4 Valve lifter compression

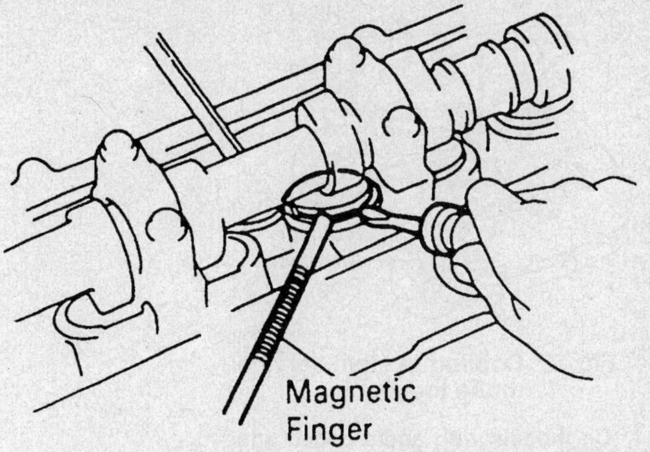
Magnetic
Finger

TY1069100151000X

Fig. 5 Valve adjustment shim removal

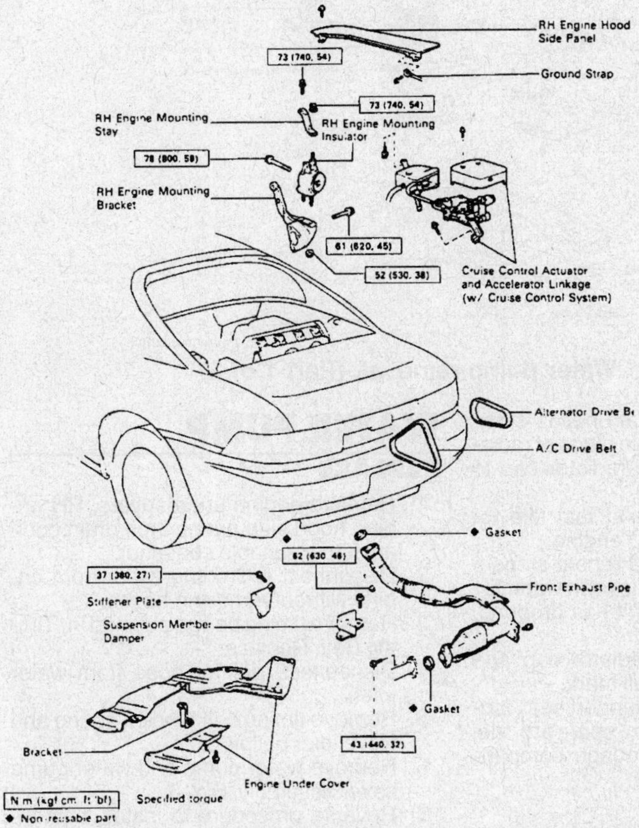
RH Engine Hood Side Panel
73 (740, 54)
Ground Strap
73 (740, 54)
RH Engine Mounting Stay
RH Engine Mounting Insulator
78 (800, 58)
RH Engine Mounting Bracket
61 (620, 45)
52 (530, 38)
Cruise Control Actuator and Accelerator Linkage (w/ Cruise Control System)
Alternator Drive Be
A/C Drive Belt
Gasket
62 (630, 46)
37 (380, 27)
Front Exhaust Pipe
Stiffener Plate
Suspension Member Damper
Gasket
Bracket
43 (440, 32)
Engine Under Cover
N·m (kgf·cm, ft·lbf) Specified torque
◆ Non-reusable part

TY1099100015010X

Fig. 6 Oil pump removal (Part 1 of 2)

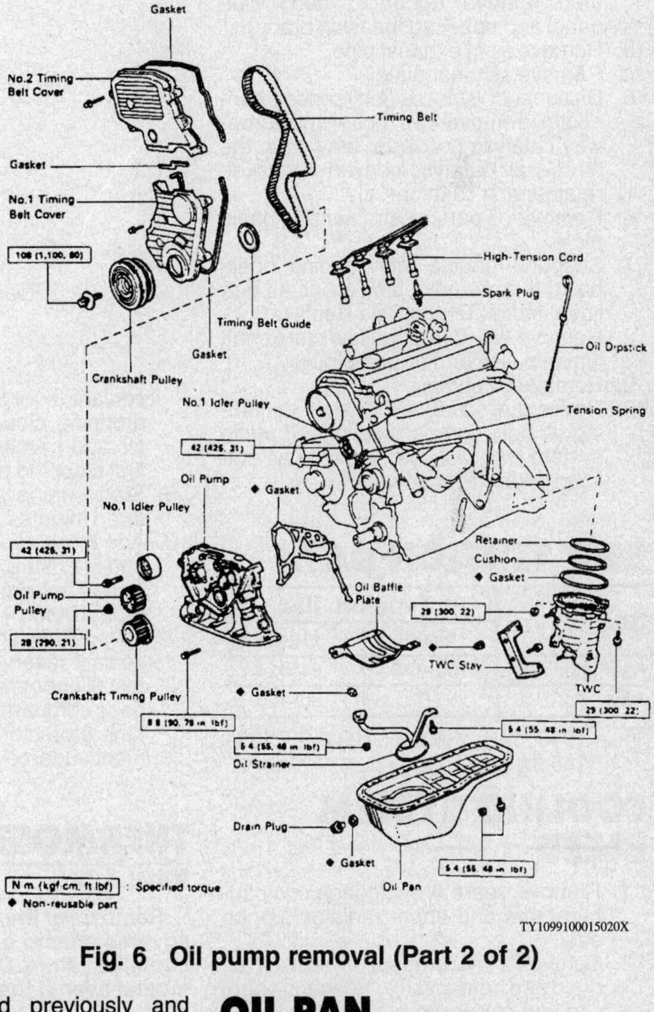
Gasket
No.2 Timing Belt Cover
Timing Belt
Gasket
No.1 Timing Belt Cover
108 (1,100, 80)
High-Tension Cord
Spark Plug
Timing Belt Guide
Gasket
Oil Dipstick
Crankshaft Pulley
No.1 Idler Pulley
Tension Spring
42 (425, 31)
Oil Pump
◆ Gasket
No.1 Idler Pulley
42 (425, 31)
Retainer
Cushion
◆ Gasket
Oil Pump Pulley
Oil Baffle Plate
29 (300, 22)
28 (290, 21)
TWC Stay
TWC
Crankshaft Timing Pulley
◆ Gasket
29 (300, 22)
5.4 (55, 48 in. lbf)
5.4 (55, 48 in. lbf)
Oil Strainer
Drain Plug
◆ Gasket
5.4 (55, 48 in. lbf)
Oil Pan
N·m (kgf·cm, ft·lbf) : Specified torque
◆ Non-reusable part

TY1099100015020X

Fig. 6 Oil pump removal (Part 2 of 2)

8. Using a suitable micrometer measure thickness of removed shim, record dimension.
9. Determine difference between desired and actual valve clearance measurement, add difference to dimension of measured shim, refer to **Figs. 2 through 3**to select a replacement.
10. Install new shim in lifter, then remove lifter tools. Repeat steps 6 through 9 for any valves out of adjustment.
11. Rotate crankshaft pulley two full turns, recheck valves as outlined in steps 4 through 6.
12. Turn crankshaft pulley 360° (one complete revolution) and align timing marks as outlined previously and check the following valves:
    a. No. 2 exhaust valves.
    b. No. 3 intake valves.
    c. No. 4 intake and exhaust valves, repeat steps 6 through 10 if necessary.
    d. Install engine parts, then bleed cooling system as outlined under "Cooling System Bleed." If audio system was disabled, activate as outlined under "Precautions."

OIL PAN

REPLACE

Refer to "Oil Pump, Replace" for procedure.

OIL PUMP

REPLACE

Refer to **Fig. 6** for oil pump removal.

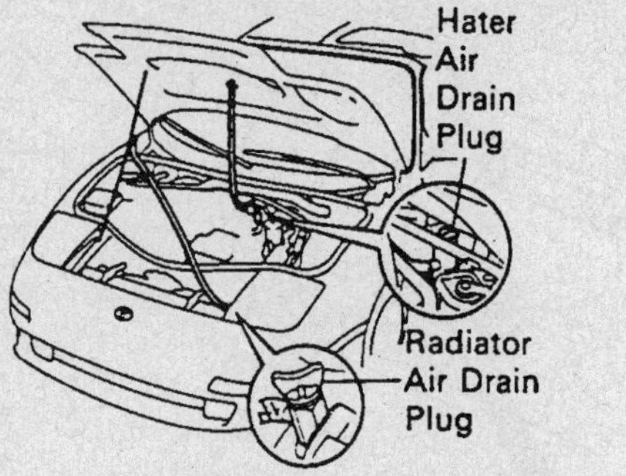
Hater
Air
Drain
Plug
Radiator
Air Drain
Plug

TY1089100013000X

Fig. 7 Cooling system service hose locations

1. **On models with audio coded anti-theft system,** disable system as outlined under "Precautions".
2. Drain oil and remove undercovers, then remove righthand hood side panel and upper suspension brace.
3. Remove front exhaust pipe.
4. Remove stiffener plate.
5. Disconnect sub-oxygen sensor connector, remove two bolts and three-way catalytic converter stay, then the three-way catalytic converter, gasket, retainer and cushion.
6. Remove oil pan, oil strainer and baffle plate.
7. Suspend engine with engine chain hoist, then remove timing belt as outlined under "Timing Belt, Replace."
8. Remove No. 2 idler pulley, crankshaft timing pulley and oil pump pulley.
9. Remove oil pump.
10. Reverse procedure to install, tightening all bolts to specifications. If audio system was disabled, activate as outlined under "Precautions."

BELT TENSION DATA

Belt	Tension, lbs.	
	New	Used
Alternator	100–140	84–124
A/C	①	80–120

① — 1993, 140–180 lbs.; 1994–95, 135–185 lbs.

COOLING SYSTEM BLEED

1. Remove spare tire, luggage compartment trim and upper radiator support seal.
2. Connect service hoses to radiator air drain and heater valve. Suspend opposite end of service hose connected to radiator to front hood stay. Suspend opposite end of heater valve service hose to front of hood, **Fig. 7.**
3. Set heater control to Hot. Open radiator and heater air drain plugs three turns. Slowly fill with coolant. Ensure air drain plugs are absent from air while filling water inlet to top with coolant.
4. Ensure level of coolant in drain service hoses are same as in water filler. When coolant level in air drain hoses stops dropping, close air drain plugs of radiator and heater. Close radiator cap to first stopping point.
5. Start engine and run at fast idle for three minutes and stop engine.
6. Add more coolant and repeat steps 5 and 6. Ensure coolant level in water filler has not dropped. If it has dropped, repeat steps 4 onward.
7. Completely tighten radiator cap and coolant reservoir to Full mark.
8. Install upper radiator support seal, luggage compartment trim, spare tire, fuel tank protector and luggage compartment undercovers.

THERMOSTAT

REPLACE

Removal of the thermostat may cause adverse effects on the efficiency of the cooling system. Do not remove the thermostat even if the engine tends to overheat.

1. Disconnect A/C compressor from engine without removing hoses.
2. Drain coolant into suitable container.
3. Disconnect water hose from inlet.
4. Disconnect oil dipstick guide from water inlet.
5. Remove water inlet, then thermostat.
6. Reverse procedure to install, ensure to align jiggle valve with protrusion of water inlet. Tighten inlet attaching bolts to specifications.

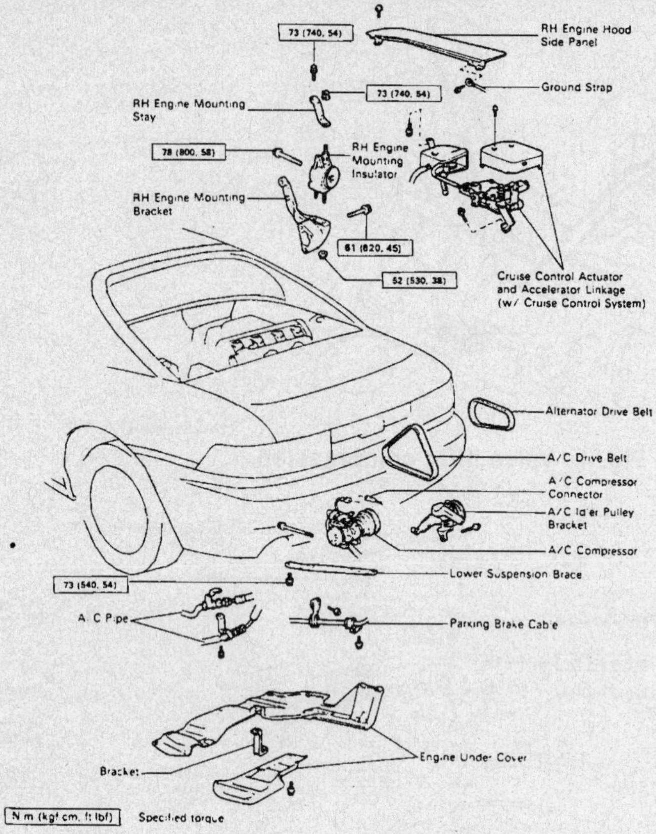
73 (740, 54)
RH Engine Hood Side Panel
73 (740, 54)
Ground Strap
RH Engine Mounting Stay
78 (800, 58)
RH Engine Mounting Insulator
RH Engine Mounting Bracket
61 (620, 45)
52 (530, 38)
Cruise Control Actuator and Accelerator Linkage (w/ Cruise Control System)
Alternator Drive Belt
A/C Drive Belt
A/C Compressor Connector
A/C Idler Pulley Bracket
A/C Compressor
Lower Suspension Brace
73 (540, 54)
A/C Pipe
Parking Brake Cable
Engine Under Cover
Bracket
N·m (kgf·cm, ft·lbf)
Specified torque

TY1089100015010X

Fig. 8 Water pump removal. (Part 1 of 2)

WATER PUMP

REPLACE

1. Remove engine undercovers, RH engine hood side panel, then drain coolant into a suitable container.
2. Disconnect A/C compressor from engine without removing hoses.
3. Remove timing belt as outlined in "Timing Belt, Replace."
4. Disconnect radiator hose from water inlet.
5. Remove timing belt tension spring and No. 2 idler pulley.
6. Remove water pump and water pump cover assembly, **Fig. 8.**
7. Reverse procedure to install, tightening all bolts to specifications.

RADIATOR

REPLACE

1. Remove radiator lower air deflector, **Figs. 9 and 10.**
2. Drain engine coolant.
3. Remove upper radiator support seal.
4. **On models with A/C,** disconnect cooling fan electrical connectors and remove No. 1 and No. 2 cooling fans, **Fig. 10.**
5. **On models less A/C,** disconnect cooling fan electrical connector and remove No. 2 fan shroud and No. 1 cooling fan, **Fig. 9.**
6. **On models with A/C,** disconnect ECT sensor connector.

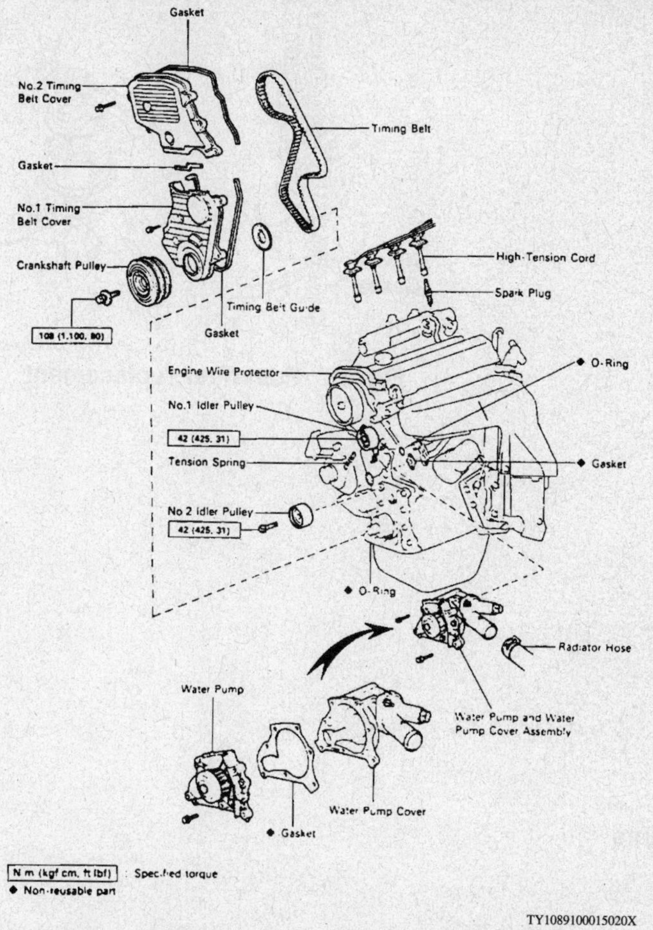
Gasket
No.2 Timing Belt Cover
Timing Belt
Gasket
No.1 Timing Belt Cover
Crankshaft Pulley
High-Tension Cord
Spark Plug
Timing Belt Guide
108 (1,100, 80)
Gasket
Engine Wire Protector
O-Ring
No.1 Idler Pulley
42 (425, 31)
Tension Spring
Gasket
No 2 Idler Pulley
42 (425, 31)
O-Ring
Radiator Hose
Water Pump
Water Pump and Water Pump Cover Assembly
Water Pump Cover
Gasket
N m (kgf cm, ft lbf) : Specified torque
Non-reusable part
TY1089100015020X

Fig. 8 Water pump removal. (Part 2 of 2)

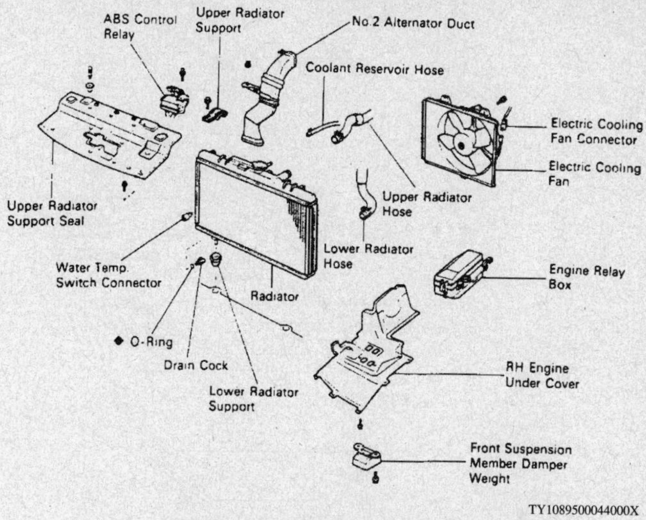
ABS Control Relay
Upper Radiator Support
No.2 Alternator Duct
Coolant Reservoir Hose
Electric Cooling Fan Connector
Electric Cooling Fan
Upper Radiator Support Seal
Upper Radiator Hose
Lower Radiator Hose
Water Temp. Switch Connector
Engine Relay Box
Radiator
O-Ring
Drain Cock
RH Engine Under Cover
Lower Radiator Support
Front Suspension Member Damper Weight
TY1089500044000X

Fig. 9 Radiator replacement. Less A/C

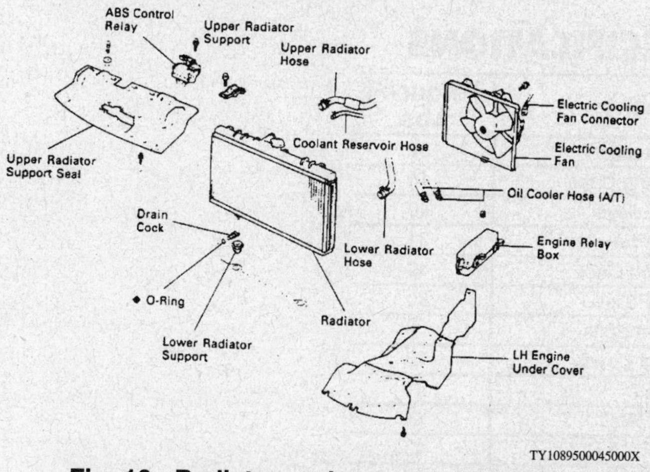
ABS Control Relay
Upper Radiator Support
Upper Radiator Hose
Electric Cooling Fan Connector
Coolant Reservoir Hose
Electric Cooling Fan
Upper Radiator Support Seal
Oil Cooler Hose (A/T)
Drain Cock
Engine Relay Box
Lower Radiator Hose
O-Ring
Radiator
Lower Radiator Support
LH Engine Under Cover
TY1089500045000X

Fig. 10 Radiator replacement. With A/C

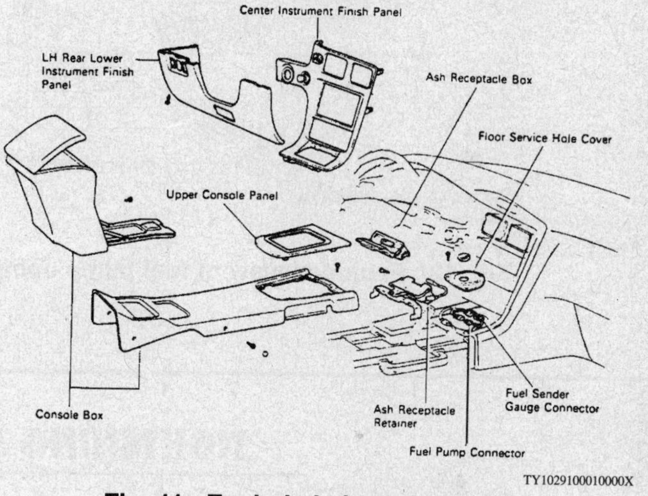
Center Instrument Finish Panel
LH Rear Lower Instrument Finish Panel
Ash Receptacle Box
Floor Service Hole Cover
Upper Console Panel
Fuel Sender Gauge Connector
Console Box
Ash Receptacle Retainer
Fuel Pump Connector
TY1029100010000X

Fig. 11 Exploded view of console

7. **On models less A/C,** disconnect ECT switch connector.
8. **On all models,** disconnect radiator hoses.
9. Remove two radiator upper supports.
10. Remove radiator and radiator lower supports.
11. **On models with A/C,** remove ECT sensor from radiator.
12. **On models less A/C,** remove ECT switch from radiator.
13. **On all models,** reverse procedure to install. Replace O-rings and tighten bolts to specifications.

FUEL PUMP

REPLACE

1. **On models with audio coded anti-theft system,** disable system as outlined under "Precautions."
2. **On all models,** remove components as follows:
   a. Console boxes, **Fig. 11.**
   b. Lefthand lower instrument finish panel.
   c. Center finish panel.
   d. Ash receptacle box and retainer.
   e. Disconnect fuel pump connector and fuel sender connector. Remove floor service cover.
3. Remove engine undercovers, luggage undercover and fuel tank protectors. Drain fuel tank, **Fig. 12.**
4. Remove parking brake intermediate lever and No. 1 center floor crossmember.
5. Disconnect A/C hoses and radiator pipes from body.
6. Remove fuel tank insulators.
7. Disconnect fuel hoses and tube, then remove fuel tank.
8. Remove fuel pump from tank.
9. Reverse procedure to install. Tighten attaching nuts and bolts to specifications. If audio system was disabled, activate as outlined under "Precautions."

FUEL FILTER

REPLACE

Refer to **Fig. 13** for replacement procedure.

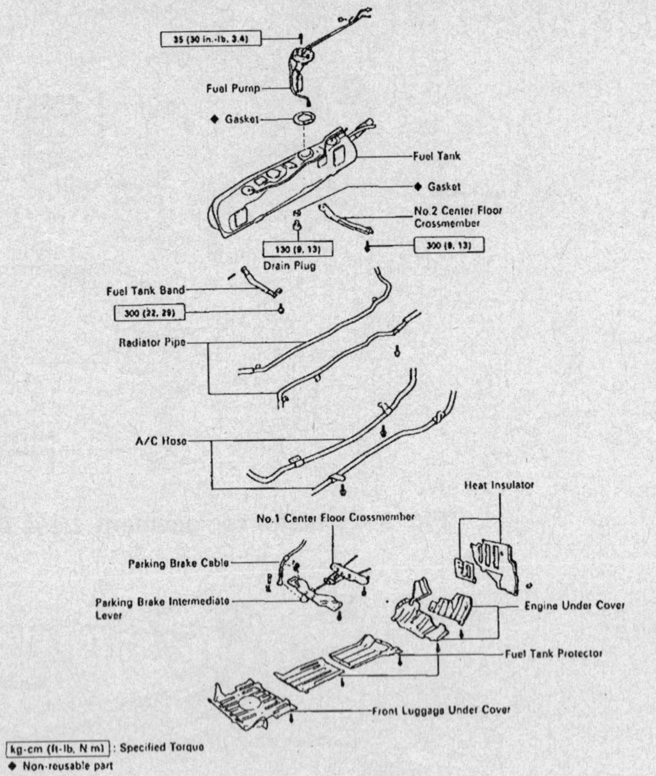
35 (30 in.-lb, 3.4)
Fuel Pump
◆ Gasket
Fuel Tank
◆ Gasket
No.2 Center Floor Crossmember
130 (9, 13)
Drain Plug
300 (9, 13)
Fuel Tank Band
300 (22, 29)
Radiator Pipe
A/C Hose
Heat Insulator
No.1 Center Floor Crossmember
Parking Brake Cable
Parking Brake Intermediate Lever
Engine Under Cover
Fuel Tank Protector
Front Luggage Under Cover
kg-cm (ft-lb, N·m) : Specified Torque
◆ Non-reusable part

TY1029100011000X

Fig. 12 Exploded view of fuel pump components

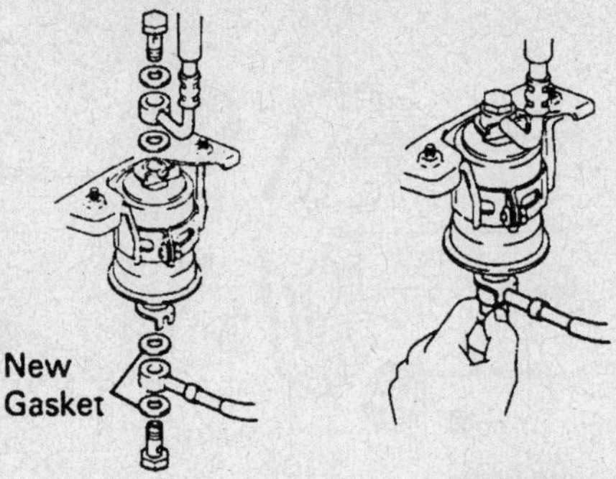
New
Gasket

TY1029100012000X

Fig. 13 Fuel filter replacement

TIGHTENING SPECIFICATIONS

Year	Component	Torque/Ft. Lbs.
1993–95	Alternator Bracket	32
	Camshaft Bearing Caps	14
	Camshaft Pulleys	40
	Catalytic Converter Stay	31
	Connecting Rod Caps	49
	Crankshaft Pulley	80
	Cylinder Head Bolts	②
	Cylinder Head Cover	13
	Driveplate	61
	EGR Valve, Bolt	9
	EGR Valve, Union Nut	43
	Exhaust Manifold To Catalytic Converter	22
	Exhaust Manifold To Cylinder Head	36
	Flywheel	65
	Front Engine Hangers	18
	Front Engine Mounting Insulator	54
	Fuel Inlet Hose To Fuel Filter	22
	Intake Manifold	14
	Intake Manifold Stay, 12mm Bolt	14
	Intake Manifold Stay, 14mm Bolt	31
	LH Engine Mounting Stay, Insulator Side	54

Continued

TIGHTENING SPECIFICATIONS—Continued

Year	Component	Torque/Ft. Lbs.
1993–95	LH Engine Mounting Stay, Transaxle Side	18
	LH Mounting Bracket To Transaxle	38
	Main Bearing Caps	43
	No. 1 Idler Pulley	31
	No. 2 Idler Pulley	31
	No. 3 Timing Belt Cover	69①
	Oil Pan	48①
	Oil Pan Drain Bolt	29
	Oil Pump Baffle Plate & Strainer	48①
	Oil Pump Pulley	26
	Oil Pump To Engine	82①
	Rear End Plate	82
	Rear Engine Mounting Bracket	57
	Rear Engine Mounting Insulator	47
	Rear Oil Seal Retainer	82①
	Release Cylinder To Transaxle	9
	RH Mounting Insulator To Mounting Bracket	38
	RH Engine Mounting Bracket	45
	RH Engine Mounting Insulator, Bolt	58
	RH Engine Mounting Insulator, Nut	38
	RH Engine Mounting Stay	54
	Spark Plug Tubes	29
	Spark Plugs	13
	Stiffener Plate	27
	Suspension Upper Brace, Bolt	54
	Suspension Upper Brace, Nut	47
	Transaxle Control Cable Mounting Bracket	57
	Upper Radiator Support Bolts	9
	Water By-Pass Pipe	82①
	Water Outlet Housing	11
	Water Pump Mounting Bolts	82①
	Water Pump To By-Pass Pipe	82①

① — Inch lbs.

② — Torque to 36 ft. lbs., then tighten an additional 90°.

Clutch & Manual Transaxle

NOTE: On Air Bag Equipped Models, Refer To "Air Bag System Precautions" Located In The Front Of This Manual For System Disarming & Arming Procedures.

INDEX

	Page No.
Adjustments	44-26
Clutch Pedal	44-26
Clutch, Replace	44-26
Hydraulic System Service	44-26
Clutch Master Cylinder, Replace	44-26
Clutch Slave Cylinder, Replace	44-26
Clutch System Bleed	44-26
Precautions	44-26
Air Bag Systems	44-26
Audio Coded Anti-Theft System	44-26
Tightening Specifications	44-28
Transaxle, Replace	44-27

PRECAUTIONS

AIR BAG SYSTEMS

Refer to "Air Bag System Precautions" in the front of this manual for system disarming and arming procedures.

AUDIO CODED ANTI-THEFT SYSTEM

Some models are equipped with an audio coded anti-theft system that will disable the radio when battery power is removed from the radio. The system can be identified by the "ANTI-THEFT SYSTEM" on the cassette tape lid. Obtain the three digit code from the customer for input before disconnecting battery power to the audio unit. Reset system after service as follows:

1. Obtain three digit code from customer.
2. Depress No. 1 (PROG) button while depressing righthand side of TUNE SEEK button, - - - will appear in tape operation display.
3. Enter code as follows:
   a. To enter first digit, press No. 1 (PROG) button a sufficient number of times, starting with zero, to enter digit (if first digit of code is five press button six times).
   b. To enter second digit, press No. 2 (APS) button a sufficient number of times, starting with zero, to enter digit.
   c. To enter third digit press, No. 3 (RPT) button a sufficient number of times, starting with zero, to enter digit.
4. If three dashes (- - -) appear in tape operation display during input of digits, restart procedure from beginning.
5. When code digits are correctly input and displayed, press and hold SCAN button until SEC appears in tape operation display.
6. When SEC disappears from display audio unit should be operative.
7. If unit is not operative or Err is displayed, repeat procedure. **Attempting to input code more than nine times may permanently disable audio unit.**

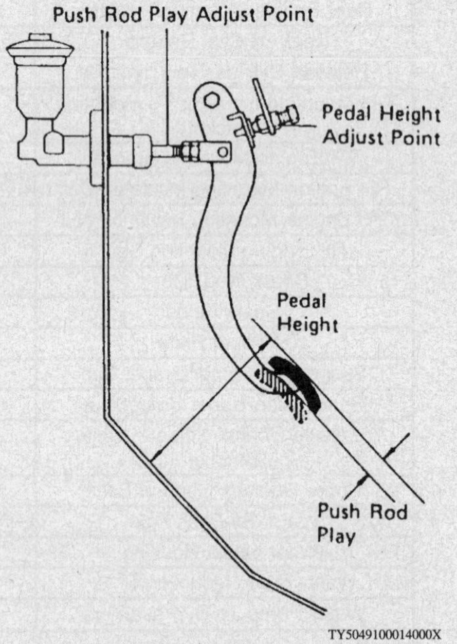

Push Rod Play Adjust Point
Pedal Height Adjust Point
Pedal Height
Push Rod Play
TY5049100014000X

Fig. 1 Clutch pedal adjustments

ADJUSTMENTS

CLUTCH PEDAL

1. Refer to **Fig. 1**and check clutch pedal height, which should measure 6.89–7.28 inches. If specified clutch pedal height cannot be obtained, remove instrument panel lower trim panel and air duct, loosen locknut and turn adjusting bolt until specified clutch pedal height is obtained.
2. After correct clutch pedal height is obtained, tighten locknut.
3. Refer to **Fig. 1**and check pedal freeplay. Depress clutch pedal until clutch resistance is obtained, then check freeplay, which should measure 197–.591 inch.
4. Check clutch cylinder pushrod play at top of pedal. Play should be .039–.197 inch.

HYDRAULIC SYSTEM SERVICE

CLUTCH MASTER CYLINDER, REPLACE

1. Remove pushrod pin and retractor control relay, **Fig. 2.**
2. Disconnect clutch line union using line wrench tool No. 09751–36011, 090123–00100, or equivalents. Remove master cylinder.
3. Reverse procedure to install, bleed clutch system.

CLUTCH SLAVE CYLINDER, REPLACE

1. Remove No. 1 engine undercover, **Fig. 3,** then disconnect transaxle control cables.
2. Disconnect clutch line union using line wrench tool No. 09751–36011, or equivalent.
3. Support engine and transmission with a jackstand and remove front engine mounting bracket set bolts.
4. Remove bolt and pull out release cylinder assembly.
5. Reverse procedure to install, bleed clutch system.

CLUTCH SYSTEM BLEED

1. Fill clutch reservoir with fluid. Check reservoir frequently, add if necessary.
2. Connect vinyl tube to bleeder plug, insert opposite end in container half full of fluid.
3. Pump clutch pedal several times. Hold pedal down and open bleeder plug. Close bleeder plug and repeat this step until no more air bubbles are in fluid.

CLUTCH

REPLACE

1. Remove transaxle as outlined under "Transaxle, Replace."
2. Loosen pressure plate attaching bolts

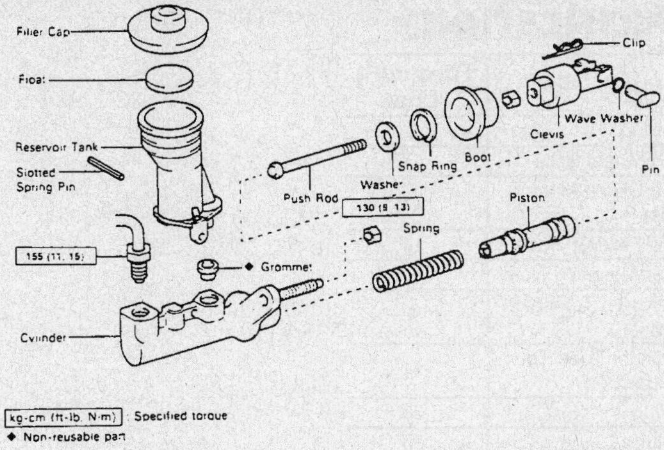

Filler Cap
Float
Reservoir Tank
Slotted Spring Pin
155 (11, 15)
Grommet
Cylinder
Push Rod
Washer
130 (9, 13)
Snap Ring
Boot
Clevis
Wave Washer
Clip
Pin
Piston
Spring
kg-cm (ft-lb, N·m) : Specified torque
◆ Non-reusable part
TY5049100015000X

Fig. 2 Exploded view of clutch master cylinder

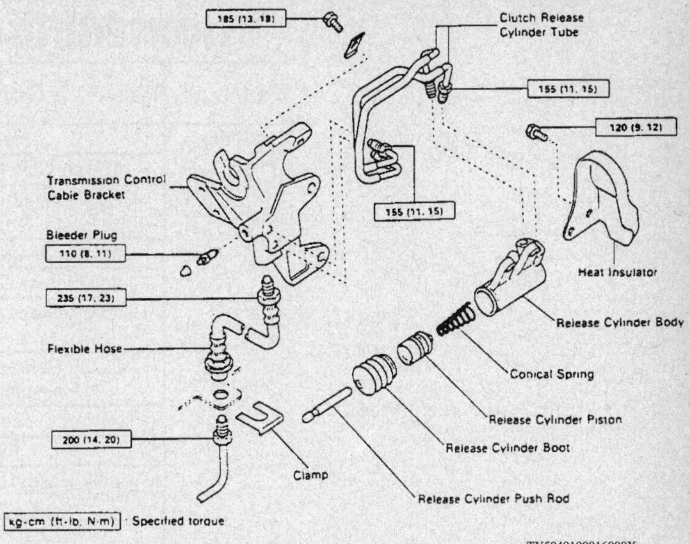

185 (13, 18)
Clutch Release Cylinder Tube
155 (11, 15)
120 (9, 12)
Transmission Control Cable Bracket
155 (11, 15)
Bleeder Plug
110 (8, 11)
Heat Insulator
235 (17, 23)
Release Cylinder Body
Flexible Hose
Conical Spring
Release Cylinder Piston
200 (14, 20)
Release Cylinder Boot
Clamp
Release Cylinder Push Rod
kg-cm (ft-lb, N·m) : Specified torque
TY5049100016000X

Fig. 3 Exploded view of clutch slave cylinder

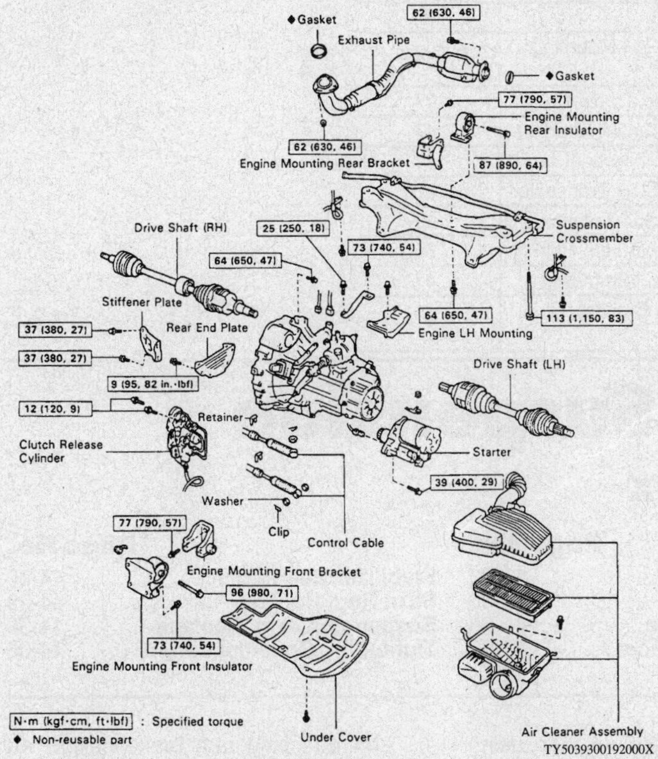

◆Gasket
62 (630, 46)
Exhaust Pipe
◆Gasket
77 (790, 57)
Engine Mounting Rear Insulator
62 (630, 46)
Engine Mounting Rear Bracket
87 (890, 64)
Drive Shaft (RH)
25 (250, 18)
Suspension Crossmember
73 (740, 54)
64 (650, 47)
Stiffener Plate
64 (650, 47)
113 (1,150, 83)
37 (380, 27)
Rear End Plate
Engine LH Mounting
37 (380, 27)
Drive Shaft (LH)
9 (95, 82 in.·lbf)
12 (120, 9)
Retainer
Clutch Release Cylinder
Starter
39 (400, 29)
Washer
Clip
Control Cable
77 (790, 57)
Engine Mounting Front Bracket
96 (980, 71)
73 (740, 54)
Engine Mounting Front Insulator
N·m (kgf·cm, ft·lbf) : Specified torque
◆ Non-reusable part
Under Cover
Air Cleaner Assembly
TY5039300192000X

Fig. 4 Components for transaxle removal

one turn at a time, then remove bolts, pressure plate and clutch disc.

3. Install new clutch disc and pressure plate assembly, ensuring disc and plate are properly aligned. Tighten attaching bolts one turn at a time while ensuring clutch disc and pressure plate remain aligned. Tighten all bolts to specifications.
4. Install transaxle, then bleed system and adjust clutch pedal.

TRANSAXLE

REPLACE

1. **On models with audio coded anti-theft system,** disable system as outlined under "Precautions."
2. **On all models,** remove air cleaner housing and air hose assembly, then left engine mounting stay, **Fig. 4.**
3. Remove starter.
4. Disconnect back-up light switch connector, earth cable and vehicle speed sensor connector.
5. Remove upper transaxle mounting bolts.
6. Remove rear wheels then raise and support vehicle.
7. Remove engine undercover and drain transaxle fluid into suitable container.
8. Remove driveshaft.
9. Disconnect control cables.
10. Remove exhaust pipe.
11. Install suitable engine support fixture.
12. Remove engine front mounting.
13. Remove clutch release cylinder.
14. Remove rear engine mount.
15. Remove suspension arm from rear axle hub, disconnect speed sensor bracket from rear suspension crossmember then remove suspension crossmember.
16. Remove left engine mounting set bolts.
17. Remove stiffener plate and rear end plate.
18. Remove transaxle bolts from engine and remove transaxle.
19. Reverse procedure to install. If audio system was disabled, activate as outlined under "Precautions."

TIGHTENING SPECIFICATIONS

Year	Component	Torque/Ft. Lbs.
1993–95	Bleeder Plug	8
	Clutch Cover To Flywheel Bolts	14
	Clutch Line Union To Clutch Master Cylinder	11
	Clutch Line Union To Flexible Hose	14
	Clutch Master Cylinder Mounting Nuts	9
	Clutch Release Cylinder To Transaxle Case	9
	Clutch Release Cylinder Tube To Release Cylinder Body	11
	Drain Plug	36
	Filler Plug	36
	Flexible Hose To Transmission Control Cable	17
	Flywheel	72
	LH Mounting Stay To LH Mounting Bracket	54
	LH Mounting Stay To Transaxle	27
	LH Mounting To LH Mounting Bracket	47
	Pressure Plate To Flywheel	14
	Starter To Transaxle, E153 Transaxle	27
	Starter To Transaxle, S54 Transaxle	29
	Transaxle To Engine, 10mm Bolt	34
	Transaxle To Engine, 12mm Bolt	47
	Transaxle To Mounting Bracket, Front & Rear	57

Rear Axle & Suspension

INDEX

	Page No.
Axle Shaft & Constant Velocity Joint, Replace	44-28
2.0L Engine	44-29
2.2L Engine	44-29
Coil Spring, Replace	44-30
Lower Arm, Replace	44-30
Rear Axle Hub, Replace	44-28
Shock Absorber, Replace	44-29
Stabilizer Bar, Replace	44-30
Strut Rod, Replace	44-29
Suspension Arm, Replace	44-30
Tightening Specifications	44-30

REAR AXLE HUB

REPLACE

1. Raise and support vehicle and remove tire and wheel assembly.
2. Remove cotter pin and bearing locknut cap, **Fig. 1.**
3. With parking brake set, remove bearing locknut.
4. Remove brake caliper from rear axle carrier and suspend out of way.
5. Remove disc rotor, then ensure bearing play in axial direction does not exceed .002 inch.
6. Disconnect stabilizer link and remove ABS speed sensor, if equipped, then remove bolt and nut, then suspension arm.
7. Remove cotter pin and nut, then, using remover tool No. I09610-20012, or equivalent, disconnect suspension arm from rear axle carrier, then remove bolt, nut and suspension arm.
8. Disconnect rear axle carrier from ball joint and lower arm.
9. Scribe alignment marks on shock absorber lower bracket and camber adjusting cam.
10. Remove two axle carrier set nuts and two bolts with camber adjusting cam.
11. Remove rear axle carrier and axle hub. **Cover driveshaft boot with cloth to prevent damage.**
12. Reverse procedure to install. Tighten two axle carrier nuts, rear axle carrier to lower arm attaching nut, suspension arm attaching nut, brake caliper attaching bolts and bearing locknut to specifications.

AXLE SHAFT & CONSTANT VELOCITY JOINT

REPLACE

The hub bearing may be damaged if it is subjected to vehicle weight, such as when moving the vehicle with the driveshaft removed. Therefore, if it is absolutely necessary to place the vehicle weight on the hub bearing, first support it with hub support tool No. 09608-16041, or equivalent.

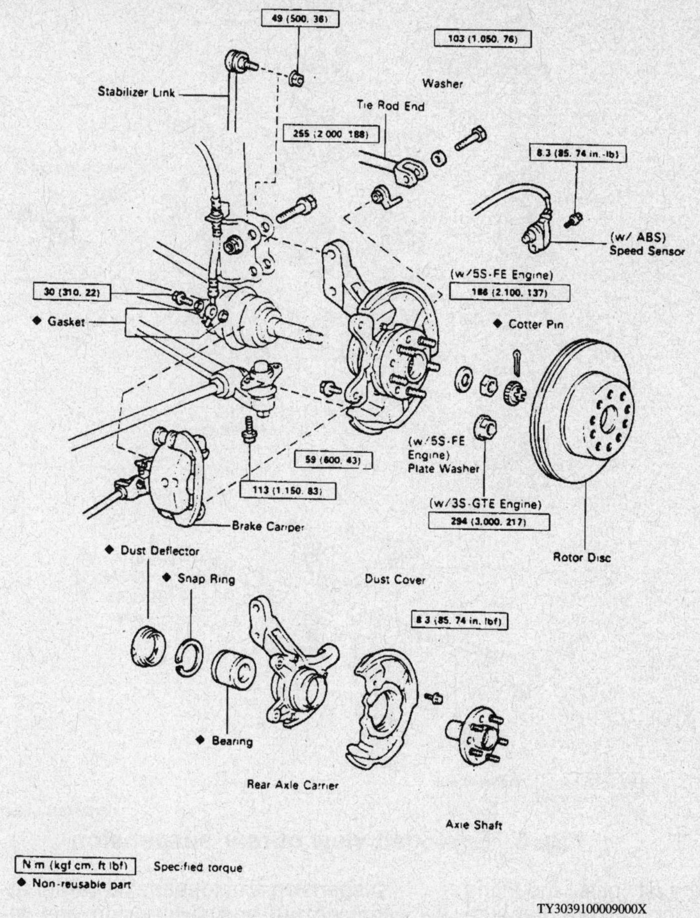

49 (500, 36)
103 (1,050, 76)
Stabilizer Link
Washer
Tie Rod End
255 (2,000 188)
8.3 (85, 74 in.-lb)
(w/ ABS)
Speed Sensor
(w/5S-FE Engine)
186 (2,100, 137)
30 (310, 22)
◆ Gasket
◆ Cotter Pin
(w/5S-FE Engine) Plate Washer
59 (600, 43)
113 (1,150, 83)
(w/3S-GTE Engine)
294 (3,000, 217)
Brake Caliper
◆ Dust Deflector
◆ Snap Ring
Dust Cover
Rotor Disc
8.3 (85, 74 in. lbf)
◆ Bearing
Rear Axle Carrier
Axle Shaft
N·m (kgf·cm, ft·lbf) Specified torque
◆ Non-reusable part
TY3039100009000X

Fig. 1 Rear axle hub

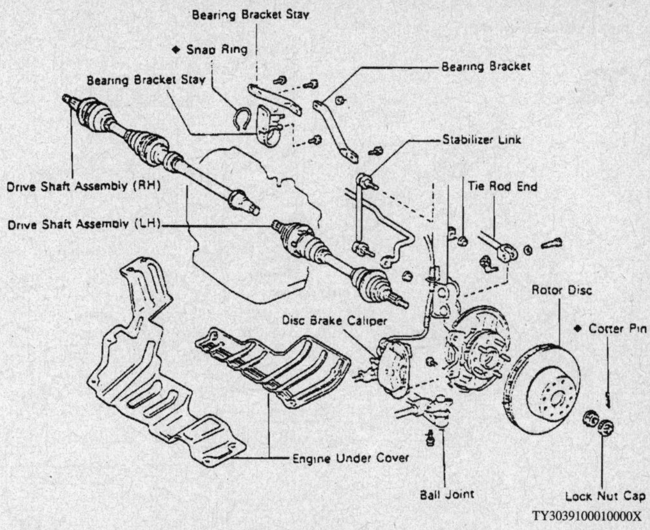

Bearing Bracket Stay
◆ Snap Ring
Bearing Bracket Stay
Bearing Bracket
Stabilizer Link
Drive Shaft Assembly (RH)
Tie Rod End
Drive Shaft Assembly (LH)
Rotor Disc
Disc Brake Caliper
◆ Cotter Pin
Engine Under Cover
Ball Joint
Lock Nut Cap
TY3039100010000X

Fig. 2 Exploded view of rear axle assembly. 2.0L engine

2.0L ENGINE

1. Remove engine undercovers, then drain transaxle oil.
2. Remove cotter pin from axle shaft, then locknut cap.
3. With emergency brake applied, remove axle shaft nut.
4. With brake applied, remove six rear driveshaft to transaxle side gear shaft attaching nuts, then raise and support rear of vehicle.
5. Remove brake caliper and rotor disc, **Fig. 2.**
6. Disconnect stabilizer link and remove ABS speed sensor.
7. Remove lower ball joint-to-rear axle carrier attaching bolts, then disconnect lower arm.
8. Remove suspension arm-to-rear axle carrier attaching nut.
9. Using hub puller tool No. 09950–20017, or equivalent, remove driveshaft from axle carrier, **Fig. 3.**
10. Using hammer and brass bar, tap lefthand axle shaft from axle carrier and remove.
11. Remove snap ring from bearing bracket, remove bolt from bearing bracket and remove righthand driveshaft.
12. Reverse procedure to install, refer to "Tightening Specifications" for torque values.

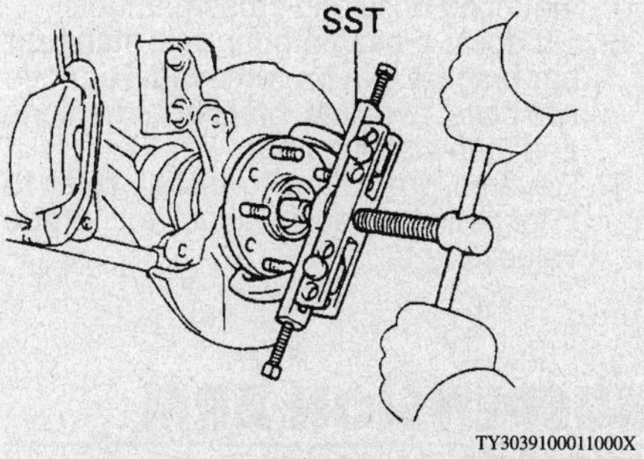

SST
TY3039100011000X

Fig. 3 Driveshaft removal

2.2L ENGINE

1. Remove engine undercovers and drain transaxle oil.
2. With parking brake applied, remove cotter pin, locknut cap and bearing locknut.
3. Remove brake caliper and rotor, **Fig. 4.**
4. Disconnect stabilizer link, then remove ABS sensor.
5. Disconnect lower arm from rear axle, then disconnect tie rod end.
6. Disconnect driveshaft from axle carrier using puller tool No. 09950–20017, or equivalent, **Fig. 3.**
7. Tap out driveshafts with hammer and covered pry bar.
8. Reverse procedure to install, refer to "Tightening Specifications" for torque values.

STRUT ROD

REPLACE

1. Raise and support vehicle.
2. Remove strut rod nut and retainer.
3. Remove strut rod attaching nut and bolt with cushion from body side.
4. Remove cushion collar and retainer from lower arm side of strut rod.
5. Reverse procedure to install. Prior to tightening nuts, lower vehicle to ground and bounce vehicle several times to stabilize suspension. Tighten lower arm side strut rod attaching nut and body side strut rod attaching nut to specifications with suspension loaded.

SHOCK ABSORBER

REPLACE

1. Raise and support vehicle, then remove brake hose attaching clip, **Fig. 5.**
2. Remove union bolt and two gaskets and disconnect brake hose, draining brake fluid into suitable container.
3. Remove clip and brake hose from shock absorber.
4. Disconnect stabilizer link from shock absorber, if equipped.
5. Remove ABS speed sensor, if equipped.
6. Disconnect rear axle carrier as follows:
   a. Scribe alignment marks on shock absorber lower bracket and camber adjustment cam.
   b. Remove two axle carrier set nuts and bolts with camber adjustment cam.
7. Remove engine hood side panel.
8. Remove three upper shock absorber attaching nuts and shock absorber. **Cover driveshaft boot with cloth to prevent damage.**
9. Install bolt and two nuts on bracket at lower portion of shock absorber shell and secure assembly in suitable vise.

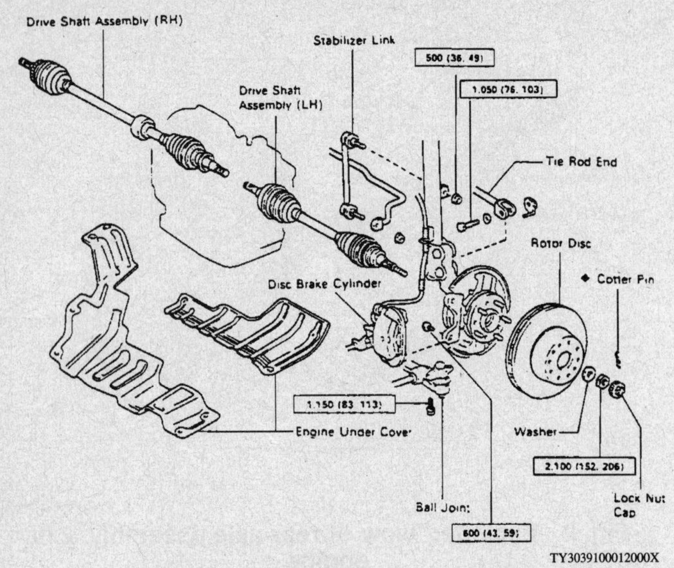
Drive Shaft Assembly (RH)
Stabilizer Link
500 (36, 49)
1,050 (76, 103)
Drive Shaft Assembly (LH)
Tie Rod End
Rotor Disc
◆ Cotter Pin
Disc Brake Cylinder
1,150 (83, 113)
Engine Under Cover
Washer
2,100 (152, 206)
Lock Nut Cap
Ball Joint
600 (43, 59)
TY3039100012000X

Fig. 4 Exploded view of rear axle assembly. 2.2L engine

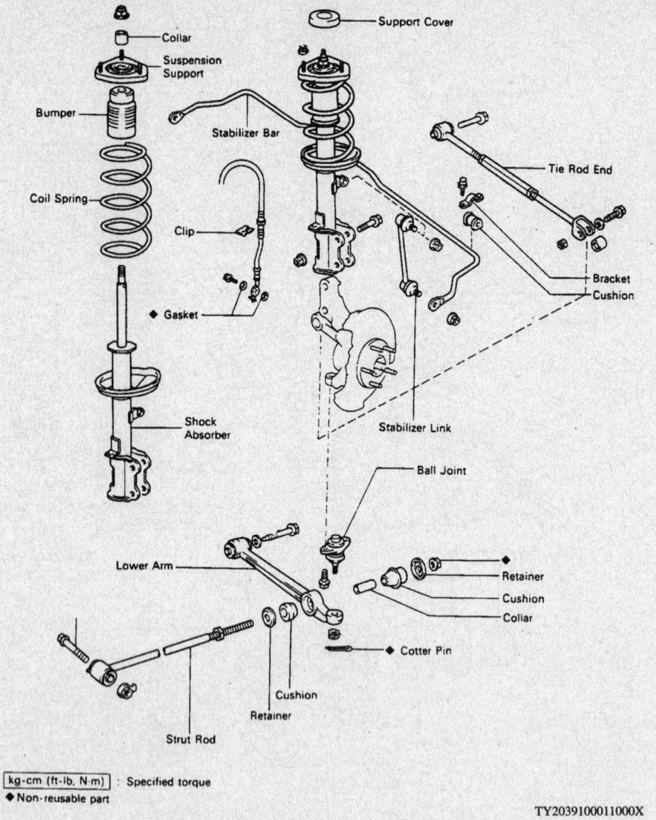
Support Cover
Collar
Suspension Support
Bumper
Stabilizer Bar
Tie Rod End
Coil Spring
Clip
Bracket
Cushion
◆ Gasket
Shock Absorber
Stabilizer Link
Ball Joint
Lower Arm
◆
Retainer
Cushion
Collar
◆ Cotter Pin
Cushion
Retainer
Strut Rod
kg-cm (ft-lb, N·m) : Specified torque
◆ Non-reusable part
TY2039100011000X

Fig. 5 Exploded view of rear suspension

10. Remove coil spring as follows:
    a. Using front coil spring compressor tool No. 09727-22032, or equivalent, compress coil spring.
    b. Hold octagon head of suspension support in vise.
    c. Remove suspension support cover and suspension support nut.
    d. Remove suspension support, coil spring, insulator and bumper.
11. Reverse procedure to install, noting the following:
    a. Align coil spring end with lower seat hollow.
    b. Tighten suspension components to specification.

COIL SPRING

REPLACE

Refer to "Shock Absorber, Replace" for coil spring replacement procedures.

STABILIZER BAR

REPLACE

1. Disconnect stabilizer link from stabilizer bar, **Fig. 5,** then remove stabilizer link from shock absorber.
2. Remove ABS speed sensor bracket.
3. Disconnect rear axle carrier from lower arm. Then disconnect tie rod from rear axle carrier.
4. Disconnect exhaust pipe mounting and rear engine mount from rear suspension crossmember.
5. Remove suspension crossmember mounting bolts and crossmember.
6. Lift down crossmember until stabilizer bar bracket can be removed. Remove two bolts, two nuts, brackets, cushions and then stabilizer bar.
7. Reverse procedure to install, refer to "Tightening Specifications" for torque values.

SUSPENSION ARM

REPLACE

1. Raise and support vehicle.
2. Remove bolt and nut, then remove arm from axle carrier.
3. Remove suspension arm attaching nut and suspension arm.
4. Reverse procedure to install. Tighten suspension arm to rear axle carrier attaching nut and suspension arm attaching nut to specifications.

LOWER ARM

REPLACE

1. Raise and support vehicle.
2. Remove cotter pin and nut and, using puller tool No. 09610-55012, or equivalent, disconnect lower arm from ball joint.
3. Remove stud rod nut and retainer from lower arm.
4. Remove lower arm to body attaching bolt and lower arm.
5. Remove strut rod cushion, collar and retainer from lower arm.
6. Reverse procedure to install. Refer to "Tightening Specifications" for torque values.

TIGHTENING SPECIFICATIONS

Year	Component	Torque/Ft. Lbs.
1993–95	ABS Speed Sensor To Axle Carrier	69①
	Axle Carrier To Ball Joint	83
	Axle Carrier To Lower Arm	83

Continued

TIGHTENING SPECIFICATIONS—Continued

Year	Component	Torque/Ft. Lbs.
1993–95	Axle Carrier To Shock Absorber	127
	Axle Carrier To Tie Rod End	76
	Bearing Bracket Stay To Bearing Bracket	56
	Bearing Bracket Stay To Engine	56
	Bearing Bracket To Driveshaft Center Bearing	24
	Bearing Bracket To Engine	47
	Disc Brake Caliper To Axle Carrier	43
	Driveshaft Inboard Joint Holding Hexagon Bolts	48
	Engine Mount To Suspension Crossmember	57
	Exhaust Pipe To Suspension Crossmember	15
	Hub Bearing Locknut, 2.0L Engine	217
	Hub Bearing Locknut, 2.2L Engine	152
	Lower Arm Holding Nut	98
	Lower Arm To Ball Joint	67
	Piston Rod To Suspension Support	54
	Stabilizer Bar To Body	14
	Stabilizer Bar To Stabilizer Link	36
	Stabilizer Link To Shock Absorber	36
	Strut Rod Nut	66
	Strut Rod To Body	87
	Suspension Arm To Body	76
	Suspension Crossmember To Body	83
	Suspension Support To Body	59
	Tie Rod End	76
	Wheel Lug Nuts	76

① — Inch lbs.

Front Suspension & Steering

NOTE: **On Air Bag Equipped Models, Refer To "Air Bag System Precautions" Located In The Front Of This Manual For System Disarming & Arming Procedures.**

INDEX

Page No.

Ball Joint Inspection 44-33
Coil Spring, Replace 44-33
Lower Suspension Arm, Replace 44-33
Manual Steering Gear, Replace .. 44-34
Manual Steering Gears 48-1
Power Steering 48-1

Page No.

Power Steering Gear, Replace ... 44-34
Power Steering Pump, Replace .. 44-34
Precautions 44-32
Air Bag Systems 44-32
Audio Coded Anti-Theft System . 44-32
Stabilizer Bar, Replace 44-33

Page No.

Steering Knuckle, Replace 44-33
Strut, Replace 44-33
Strut Bar, Replace 44-34
Tightening Specifications 44-35
Wheel Bearing, Adjust 44-32
Wheel Bearing, Replace 44-32

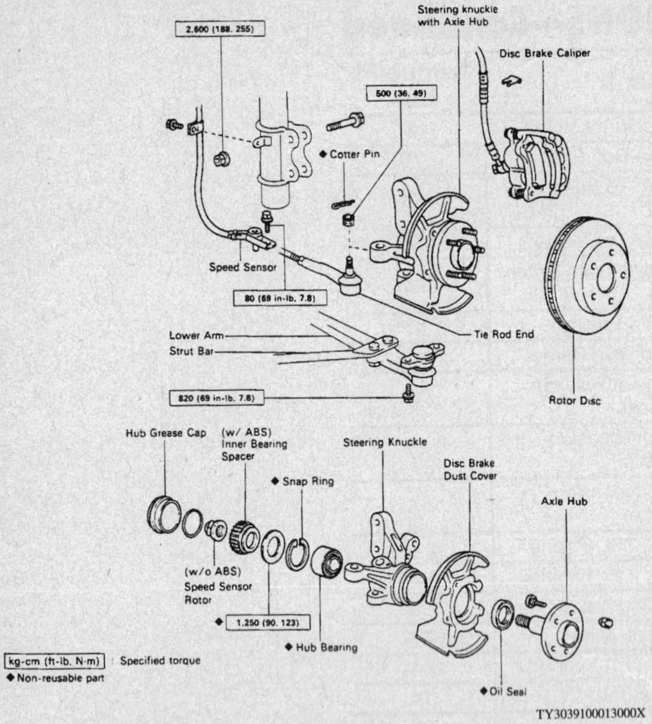

2,600 (188, 255)
Steering knuckle with Axle Hub
Disc Brake Caliper
500 (36, 49)
◆ Cotter Pin
Speed Sensor
80 (69 in-lb, 7.8)
Lower Arm
Strut Bar
Tie Rod End
820 (69 in-lb, 7.8)
Rotor Disc
Hub Grease Cap
(w/ ABS) Inner Bearing Spacer
Steering Knuckle
◆ Snap Ring
Disc Brake Dust Cover
Axle Hub
(w/o ABS) Speed Sensor Rotor
◆ 1,250 (90, 123)
◆ Hub Bearing
kg-cm (ft-lb, N·m) : Specified torque
◆ Non-reusable part
◆ Oil Seal
TY3039100013000X

Fig. 1 Exploded view of front axle hub

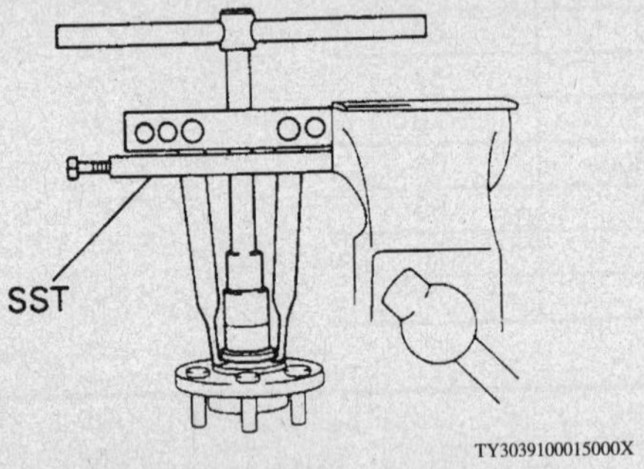

SST
TY3039100015000X

Fig. 3 Inner race removal

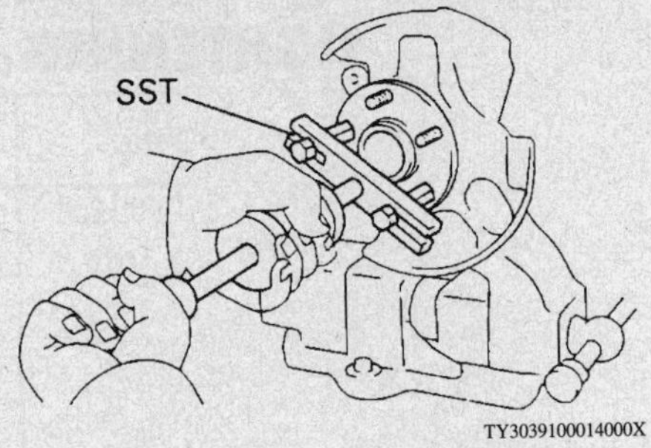

SST
TY3039100014000X

Fig. 2 Axle hub removal

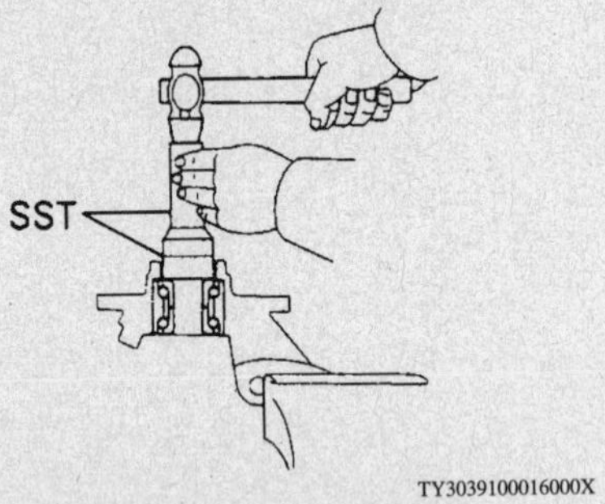

SST
TY3039100016000X

Fig. 4 Outer race removal

PRECAUTIONS

AIR BAG SYSTEMS

Refer to "Air Bag System Precautions" in the front of this manual for system disarming and arming procedures.

AUDIO CODED ANTI-THEFT SYSTEM

Some models are equipped with an audio coded anti-theft system that will disable the radio when battery power is removed from the radio. The system can be identified by the "ANTI-THEFT SYSTEM" on the cassette tape lid. Obtain the three digit code from the customer for input before disconnecting battery power to the audio unit. Reset system after service as follows:

1. Obtain three digit code from customer.
2. Depress No. 1 (PROG) button while depressing righthand side of TUNE SEEK button, - - - will appear in tape operation display.
3. Enter code as follows:
   a. To enter first digit, press No. 1 (PROG) button a sufficient number of times, starting with zero, to enter digit (if first digit of code is five press button six times).
   b. To enter second digit, press No. 2 (APS) button a sufficient number of times, starting with zero, to enter digit.
   c. To enter third digit press, No. 3 (RPT) button a sufficient number of times, starting with zero, to enter digit.
4. If three dashes (- - -) appear in tape operation display during input of digits, restart procedure from beginning.
5. When code digits are correctly input and displayed, press and hold SCAN button until SEC appears in tape operation display.
6. When SEC disappears from display audio unit should be operative.
7. If unit is not operative or Err is displayed, repeat procedure. **Attempting to input code more than nine times may permanently disable audio unit.**

WHEEL BEARING

ADJUST

These models incorporate "lubed for life" sealed front wheel bearings with no provision for adjustment.

WHEEL BEARING

REPLACE

1. Remove front steering knuckle as outlined under "Steering Knuckle, Replace."
2. Clamp steering knuckle in strong vice. Tap out hub bearing cap with hammer and screwdriver.
3. Remove axle hub locknut, **Fig. 1.**
4. **On models with ABS,** remove speed sensor rotor.
5. **On models less ABS,** remove bearing inner spacer.
6. **On all models,** using hub puller tool No. 09520–00031, or equivalent, remove axle hub, **Fig. 2.**
7. Remove snap ring, then remove bearing inner race (outside) using puller tool No. 09950–20017, or equivalent, **Fig. 3.**
8. Remove outer race by placing removed inner race in bearing. Then using removal tool No. 09068–30012, or equivalent, tap bearing from hub, **Fig. 4.**
9. Install bearing with installer tool No. 09068–30012, or equivalent. Then install snap ring.
10. Coat lip seals with suitable grease, then install inner and outer races to hub bearing.
11. Using installer tool No. 09608–30012, or equivalent, install axle hub to steering knuckle.

TY2029100009000X

Fig. 5 Ball joint inspection

12. **On vehicles with ABS,** install speed sensor rotor.
13. **On vehicles less ABS,** install bearing inner spacer.
14. **On all models,** install and **torque** axle hub locknut to 90 ft. lbs. Then stake nut.
15. Using installer tool No. 09608–30012, or equivalent, install hub grease cap.

BALL JOINT INSPECTION

1. Raise front of vehicle and place wooden block with height of 7.09–7.87 inches under one front tire.
2. With wheels in straight ahead position, lower vehicle until coil spring has about half a load on it. **Place jack stands under vehicle for safety, Fig. 5.**
3. Move lower arm up and down and ensure ball joint has no play.

COIL SPRING

REPLACE

1. Raise and support vehicle.
2. Remove union bolt and disconnect brake hose from disc brake caliper, draining brake fluid into suitable container.
3. Remove clip from strut assembly and pull brake hose free of shock absorber, **Fig. 6.**
4. **On models with ABS,** remove speed sensor harness from strut.
5. **On all models,** disconnect stabilizer link strut assembly.
6. Scribe alignment marks on strut lower bracket and camber adjusting cam.
7. Remove attaching nuts and bolts and disconnect steering knuckle and strut.
8. Remove bolts securing top of suspension support and remove strut from body.
9. Install bolt and two nuts to bracket at lower portion of strut and secure assembly in suitable vise.
10. Using strut compressor 09727–00045 and 09727–30020, or equivalent and compress coil spring.
11. Using suitable tool to prevent spring seat from turning, remove top attaching nut.
12. Remove suspension support, dust seal, spring seat, spring, insulator and bumper.
13. Reverse procedure to install, ensuring that OUT mark on spring seat faces toward outside of vehicle. Refer to "Tightening Specifications " for torque values.

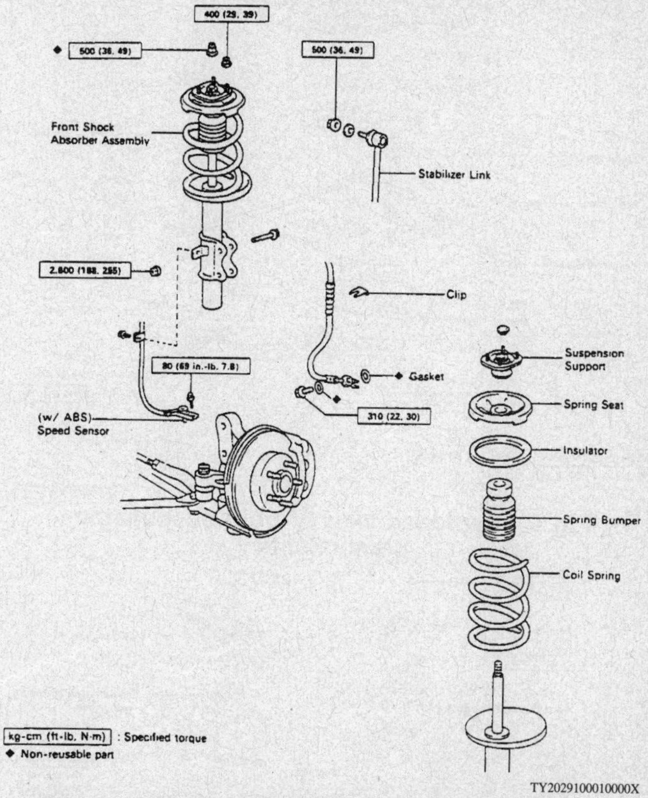
400 (29, 39)
500 (36, 49)
500 (36, 49)
Front Shock Absorber Assembly
Stabilizer Link
2,800 (188, 255)
Clip
80 (69 in.-lb. 7.8)
Gasket
(w/ ABS) Speed Sensor
310 (22, 30)
Suspension Support
Spring Seat
Insulator
Spring Bumper
Coil Spring
kg-cm (ft-lb, N·m) : Specified torque
◆ Non-reusable part
TY2029100010000X

Fig. 6 Exploded view of front strut assembly

STRUT

REPLACE

Refer to "Coil Spring, Replace" for procedure.

LOWER SUSPENSION ARM

REPLACE

1. Raise and support vehicle.
2. Remove cotter pin and castle nut, **Fig. 7.**
3. Using tool No. 09610-20012, or equivalent, disconnect lower arm from ball joint.
4. Remove two nuts and disconnect strut bar from lower arm.
5. Remove bolt and lower arm from body.
6. Reverse procedure to install, noting the following:
   a. Tighten ball joint castle nut and strut bar to lower arm attaching bolts to specifications.
   b. Lower vehicle and allow weight to rest on suspension.
   c. Bounce vehicle several times to settle suspension, then tighten lower arm to body attaching bolt to specification with suspension loaded.

STEERING KNUCKLE

REPLACE

1. Remove brake caliper and rotor disc. Inspect bearing play in axial direction, if more than .0020, replace bearing.
2. Remove ABS sensor, if equipped.
3. Place scribe marks on knuckle and strut for wheel alignment cam locations.
4. Loosen bolts and nuts holding knuckle to strut. Remove nuts and leave bolts in place.
5. Disconnect lower ball joint and tie rod end. Using puller tool No. 09610–20012, or equivalent, remove tie rod end from steering knuckle.
6. Remove two bolts from strut and remove steering knuckle.
7. Reverse procedure to install, refer to "Tightening Specifications" for torque values.

STABILIZER BAR

REPLACE

1. Raise and support vehicle.
2. Remove nut and disconnect stabilizer link from stabilizer bar.
3. Remove stabilizer bar to body attaching bolts, then the stabilizer bar and brackets.
4. Remove stabilizer link from front shock absorber assembly.
5. Remove stabilizer bracket and stabilizer bar cushion.
6. Reverse procedure to install.

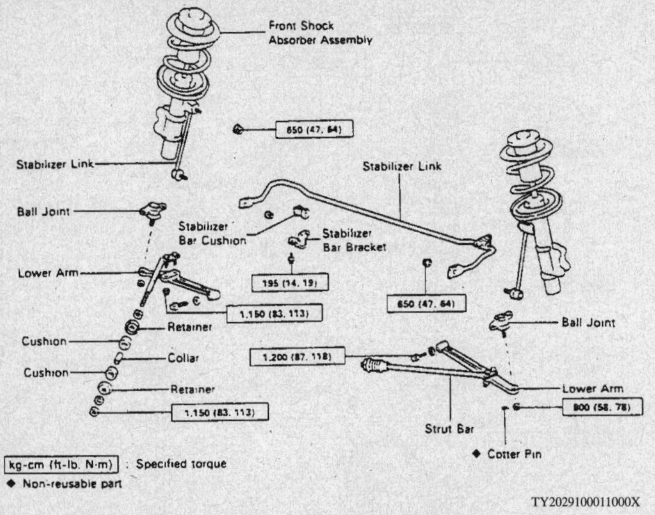
Front Shock Absorber Assembly
650 (47, 64)
Stabilizer Link
Stabilizer Link
Ball Joint
Stabilizer Bar Cushion
Stabilizer Bar Bracket
Lower Arm
195 (14, 19)
650 (47, 64)
1,150 (83, 113)
Retainer
Ball Joint
Cushion
Collar
1,200 (87, 118)
Cushion
Retainer
Lower Arm
800 (58, 78)
1,150 (83, 113)
Strut Bar
◆ Cotter Pin
kg-cm (ft-lb, N·m) : Specified torque
◆ Non-reusable part
TY2029100011000X

Fig. 7 Exploded view of front suspension components

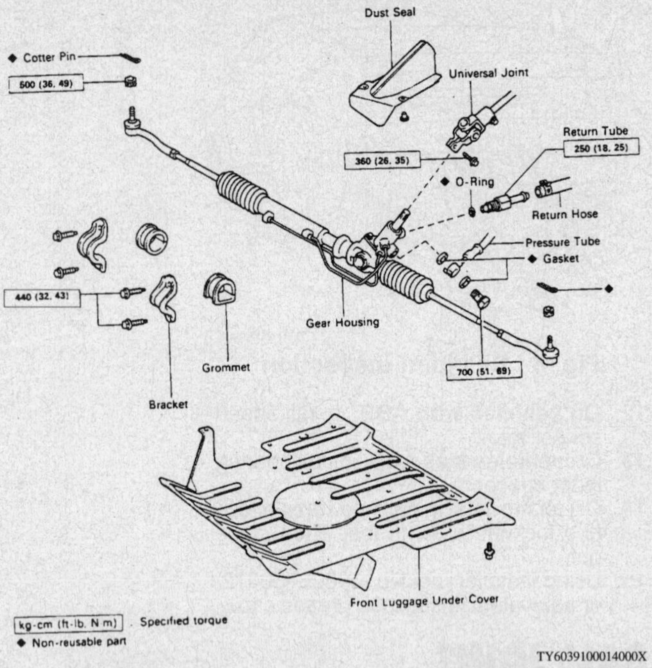
Dust Seal
◆ Cotter Pin
500 (36, 49)
Universal Joint
Return Tube
250 (18, 25)
360 (26, 35)
◆ O-Ring
Return Hose
Pressure Tube
◆ Gasket
440 (32, 43)
Gear Housing
Grommet
700 (51, 69)
Bracket
Front Luggage Under Cover
kg-cm (ft-lb, N·m) : Specified torque
◆ Non-reusable part
TY6039100014000X

Fig. 8 Power steering gear removal

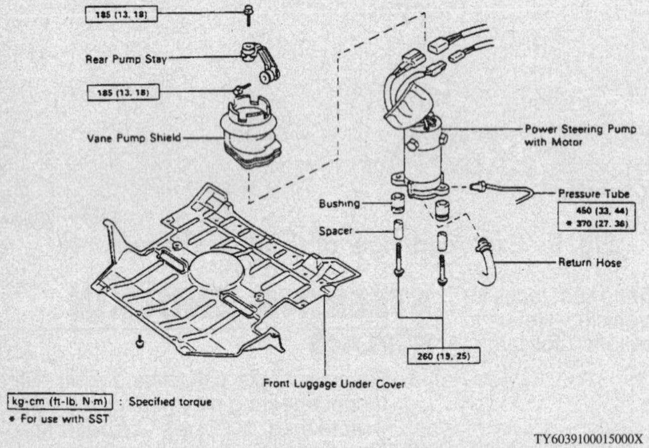
185 (13, 18)
Rear Pump Stay
185 (13, 18)
Vane Pump Shield
Power Steering Pump with Motor
Pressure Tube
450 (33, 44)
* 370 (27, 36)
Bushing
Spacer
Return Hose
260 (19, 25)
Front Luggage Under Cover
kg-cm (ft-lb, N·m) : Specified torque
* For use with SST
TY6039100015000X

Fig. 9 Power steering pump removal

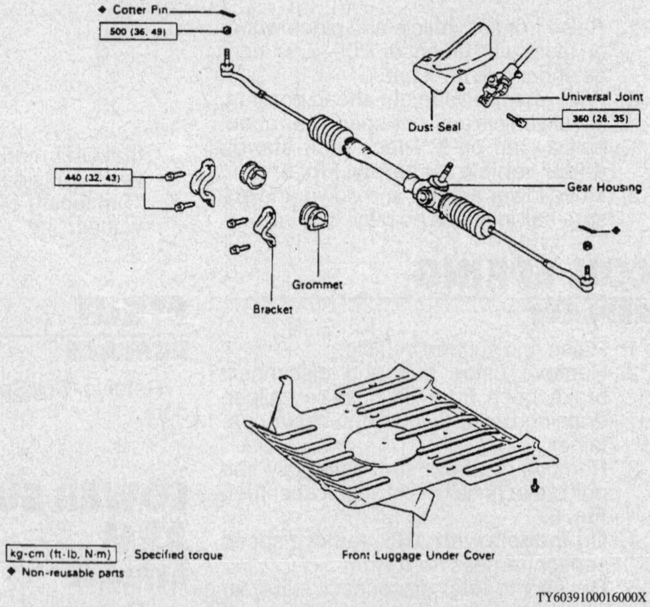
◆ Cotter Pin
500 (36, 49)
Universal Joint
360 (26, 35)
Dust Seal
440 (32, 43)
Gear Housing
Grommet
Bracket
Front Luggage Under Cover
kg-cm (ft-lb, N·m) : Specified torque
◆ Non-reusable parts
TY6039100016000X

Fig. 10 Manual steering gear removal

STRUT BAR

REPLACE

1. Remove strut rod nut and retainer.
2. Remove strut rod holding nut and bolt with cushion from body side.
3. Remove cushion collar and retainer from strut rod on lower control arm side.
4. Reverse procedure to install.

POWER STEERING GEAR

REPLACE

On models with audio coded anti-theft system refer to "Precautions," then remove components as shown in **Fig. 8.** Reverse procedure to install.

POWER STEERING PUMP

REPLACE

Refer to **Fig. 9,** for power steering pump replacement.

MANUAL STEERING GEAR

REPLACE

Refer to **Fig. 10,** for manual steering gear replacement.

TIGHTENING SPECIFICATIONS

Year	Component	Torque/Ft. Lbs.
1993–95	ABS Speed Sensor To Steering Knuckle	69①
	Axle Hub Locknut	90
	Ball Joint To Steering Knuckle	59
	Brake Caliper To Steering Knuckle	43
	Brake Hose To Disc Brake Caliper	22
	Disc Brake Dust Cover To Steering Knuckle	74①
	Hub Nut	76
	Lower Arm To Ball Joint	58
	Lower Arm To Body	87
	P/S Pump To Crossmember	19
	Piston Rod To Suspension Support	36
	Pressure Tube Union Bolt	27
	Rear Pump Stay To Body	13
	Rear Pump Stay To P/S Pump	13
	Stabilizer Bar To Body	14
	Stabilizer Bar To Stabilizer Link	47
	Stabilizer Link To Shock Absorber	47
	Steering Gear Housing To Body	32
	Steering Knuckle To Shock Absorber	127
	Strut Bar To Body	83
	Strut Bar To Lower Arm	83
	Suspension Support To Body	29
	Tie Rod End Locknut	41
	Tie Rod End To Steering Knuckle	36
	Universal Joint Bolt	26
	Wheel Lug Nuts	76

① — Inch lbs.

Wheel Alignment

INDEX

	Page No.
Front Wheel Alignment	44-36
Camber	44-36
Caster	44-36
Toe-in	44-36
Preliminary Inspection	44-36
Rear Wheel Alignment	44-36
Camber	44-36
Toe-In	44-36
Vehicle Ride Height	44-36
Wheel Alignment Specifications	44-3

PRELIMINARY INSPECTION

1. Inspect and correct tire pressure.
2. Inspect front end components, replace as required.
3. Inspect wheel bearings for looseness and correct as necessary.
4. With suitable dial indicator, inspect wheel runout, runout should not exceed .055 inch (1.4mm), if not as indicated repair.

FRONT WHEEL ALIGNMENT

CAMBER

Camber is not adjustable. If camber is not within specifications, inspect and replace bad suspension parts as necessary.

CASTER

Caster is not adjustable. If caster is not within specifications, inspect and replace bad suspension parts as necessary.

TOE-IN

If toe-in is not within specifications, then adjust as follows.

1. Remove boot clips and loosen tie rod end locknuts.
2. Turn left and right tie rod ends equal amounts to adjust within specification. Ensure left and right tie rod end lengths are the same.
3. **Torque** locknuts to 35 ft. lbs. Place boot on seat and install clamp. Ensure boot is not twisted.

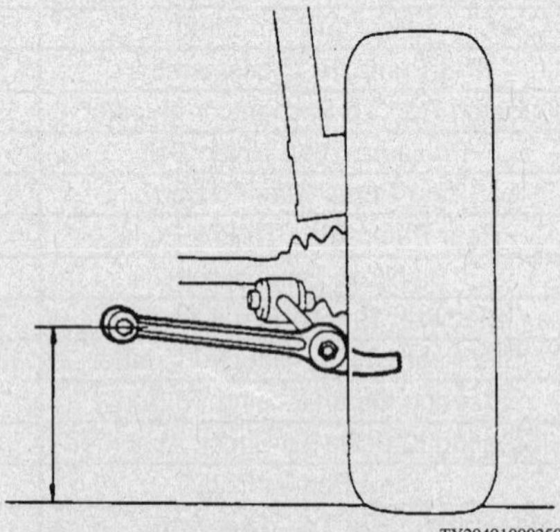
TY2049100025000X

Fig. 1 Vehicle ride height inspection

REAR WHEEL ALIGNMENT

CAMBER

Camber is non-adjustable. If rear camber is not within specification, inspect and replace suspension parts as necessary.

TOE-IN

1. Rock vehicle up and down to stabilize suspension.
2. Move vehicle forward approximately 16.4 ft. with front wheel in straight ahead position on a level surface. **If vehicle was backed up, move it forward same distance.**
3. Mark center of each rear tread and measure distance between marks.
4. Move vehicle forward until marks on rear sides of tires come to measuring heights of gauge on front side. **If tire rolls too far, repeat step 2.**
5. Measure distance between marks on front of tires.
6. If toe-in is not to specification, adjust as follows:
   a. Loosen clamp bolts or locknuts, whichever vehicle is equipped with.
   b. Turn left and right adjusting tubes an equal amount.
   c. Ensure lengths of left and right adjusting tubes are equal.
   d. Tighten clamps and locknuts.

VEHICLE RIDE HEIGHT

Bounce vehicle up and down to settle suspension. Refer to **Fig. 1** for ride height inspection location. Front measurement should be 8.524 inches. Rear measurement should be 7.614 inches. If measurements are not within specification, inspect and replace suspension parts as needed.

TOYOTA PREVIA

INDEX OF SERVICE OPERATIONS

	Page No.
AIR BAG SYSTEM PRECAUTIONS	0-8
CLUTCH & MANUAL TRANSMISSION	
Adjustments	45-18
Clutch, Replace	45-19
Hydraulic System Service	45-19
Precautions	45-18
Tightening Specifications	45-19
Transmission, Replace	45-19
ELECTRICAL	
Air Bags	48-1
Air Conditioning	48-1
Alternators	48-1
Blower Motor, Replace	45-6
Combination Switch, Replace	45-4
Cooling Fans	48-1
Cruise Control	48-1
Dash Gauges	48-1
Dash Panels	48-1
Distributor, Replace	45-4
Evaporator Core, Replace	45-6
Fuel Pump Relay Location	45-3
Fuse Panel & Flasher Location	45-3
Ignition Lock, Replace	45-4
Ignition Switch, Replace	45-4
Instrument Cluster, Replace	45-5
Neutral Safety Switch, Replace	45-4
Passive Restraints	48-1
Precautions	45-3
Radio, Replace	45-5
Relay Center Location	45-3
Speed Controls	48-1
Starter Motors	48-1
Starter, Replace	45-3
Steering Columns	48-1
Steering Wheel, Replace	45-5
Stop Light Switch, Replace	45-4
Wiper Motor, Replace	45-6
Wiper Systems	48-1
ELECTRICAL SYMBOL IDENTIFICATION	0-139
FRONT SUSPENSION & STEERING	
Ball Joint, Replace	45-22
Ball Joint Inspection	45-22
Coil Spring, Replace	45-22
Control Arm, Replace	45-23
Hub, Bearing & Seal, Replace	45-22
Manual Steering Gears	48-1
Power Steering	48-1
Power Steering Gear, Replace	45-24
Power Steering Pump, Replace	45-24
Precautions	45-22
Shock Absorber, Replace	45-22
Stabilizer Bar, Replace	45-24
Steering Knuckle, Replace	45-24
Tightening Specifications	45-24
REAR AXLE & SUSPENSION	
Axle Shaft Bearing & Oil Seal, Replace	45-20
Coil Spring, Replace	45-21
Control Arm, Replace	45-21
Lateral Rod, Replace	45-21
Rear Axle Shaft, Replace	45-20
Shock Absorber, Replace	45-21
Tightening Specifications	45-21
SERVICE REMINDER & WARNING LAMP RESET PROCEDURES	0-10
SPECIFICATIONS	
Fluid Capacities & Cooling System Data	45-3
Front Wheel Alignment Specifications	45-2
General Engine Specifications	45-2
Lubricant Data	45-3
Tune Up Specifications	45-2
VEHICLE IDENTIFICATION	0-1
VEHICLE LIFT POINTS	0-34
VEHICLE MAINTENANCE SCHEDULES	0-69
WHEEL ALIGNMENT	
Front Wheel Alignment	45-26
Preliminary Inspection	45-26
Vehicle Ride Height	45-26
Wheel Alignment Specifications	45-2
WIRE COLOR CODE IDENTIFICATION	0-144
2TZ-FE & 2TZ-FZE 2.4L ENGINES	
Belt Tension Data	45-12
Camshaft, Replace	45-11
Compression Pressure	45-7
Cooling System Bleed	45-14
Cylinder Head, Replace	45-8
Engine Rebuilding Specifications	48-1
Engine, Replace	45-7
Exhaust Manifold, Replace	45-8
Fuel Filter, Replace	45-14
Fuel Pump, Replace	45-14
Hydraulic Lifters, Replace	45-10
Intake Manifold, Replace	45-8
Main & Rod Bearings	45-11
Oil Pump, Replace	45-11
Oil Pump Service	45-11
Piston & Rod Assembly	45-11
Precautions	45-7
Radiator, Replace	45-14
Separated Accessory Drive System	45-12
Supercharger, Replace	45-15
Thermostat, Replace	45-14
Tightening Specifications	45-17
Timing Chain, Replace	45-10
Valve Adjustment	45-9
Valve Clearance Specifications	45-9
Valve Guides	45-10
Water Pump, Replace	45-14

Specifications

GENERAL ENGINE SPECIFICATIONS

Year	Engine	Fuel System	Bore & Stroke	Compression Ratio	Maximum Brake, H.P. @ RPM	Maximum Torque, Ft. Lbs. @ RPM	Normal Oil Pressure, psi①
1993–94	2.4L 2TZ-FE	Fuel Inj.	3.74 x 3.39	9.3	138 @ 5000	90 @ 3000	36
1995	2.4L 2TZ-FE	Fuel Inj.	3.74 x 3.39	9.3	138 @ 5000	154 @ 4000	36
	2.4L 2TZ-FZE②	Fuel Inj.	3.74 x 3.39	8.9	161 @ 5000	201 @ 3600	36
1996	2.4L 2TZ-FZE②	Fuel Inj.	3.74 x 3.39	8.9	161 @ 5000	201 @ 3600	36

① — At 3000 RPM.
② — Supercharged engine.

TUNE UP SPECIFICATIONS

Year	Engine	Spark Plug Gap, Inch	Ignition			Curb Idle Speed, RPM①		Fuel Pump Pressure, psi	Valve Clearance, Inch	
			Firing Order	Timing, °BTDC	Timing Mark, Fig.	Man. Trans.	Auto. Trans.		Int.	Exh.
1993–96	2.4L	.043	1-3-4-2	5	A	750	750N	38–44	.006–.010	.010–.014

BTDC — Before Top Dead Center
N — Neutral
① — Controlled by idle air controller (IAC).

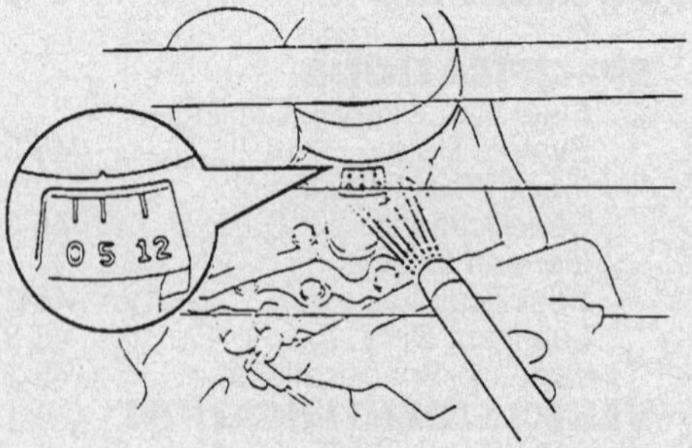
0 5 12

TY1139100120000X

Fig. A

FRONT WHEEL ALIGNMENT SPECIFICATIONS

The following specifications are for unloaded vehicles.

Year	Model	Caster Angle, Degrees		Camber Angle, Degrees		Toe, Inch①	Toe-Out On Turns, Deg.		Steering Axis Inclination, Deg.	Ball Joint Wear
		Limits	Desired	Limits	Desired		Outer Wheel	Inner Wheel		
1993–96	2WD	+4 ¾ to +6 ¼	+5 ½	-⅔ to +⅚	+1/12	.0 to +.16	32 ¾	35 7/12	10 7/12	②
	4WD	+4 7/12 to +6 1/12	+5 ⅓	-½ to 1	+¼	+.04 to +.20	33	35 7/12	10 ⅓	②

① — Toe-in (+); toe-out (-).
② — Refer to "Ball Joint Inspection" under "Front Suspension & Steering."

FLUID CAPACITIES & COOLING SYSTEM DATA

Year	Coolant Capacity, Qts		Radiator Cap Relief Pressure, Lbs.	Thermo. Opening Temp, °F	Fuel Tank, Gals.	Engine Oil Refill, Qts.①	4 Speed, Pints	Transmission Oil		Axle Oil, Pints
	Less A/C	With A/C						5 Speed, Pints	Auto. Trans., Qts.	
1993–94	12.3	12.3	10.7–15	176–183	19.8	5.4	—	②	③	④
1995–96	13	13	13	180	19.8	6.1	—	5.4	③	④

① — With oil filter change.
② — 2WD, 4.6; 4WD, 5.4.
③ — Drain & refill, 2.5 qts.; dry fill, 6 qts.
④ — Front, 2.2 pts.; rear, 3.2 pts.

LUBRICANT DATA

Year	Model	Lubricant Type					
		Transmission		Transfer Case	Rear Axle	Power Steering	Brake System
		Manual	Automatic				
1993–94	All	API GL-4,5	Dexron II	API GL-4,5	API GL-5	Dexron II	DOT 3
1995–96	All	75W-90 GL-4/5	Dexron II/IIE/III	75W-90 GL-4/5	80W-90 GL-5	Dexron II/IIE/III	DOT 3

Electrical

NOTE: On Air Bag Equipped Models, Refer To "Air Bag System Precautions" Located In The Front Of This Manual For System Disarming & Arming Procedures.

INDEX

	Page No.
Air Bags	48-1
Air Conditioning	48-1
Alternators	48-1
Blower Motor, Replace	45-6
Cool/Ice Box	45-6
Front	45-6
Rear	45-6
Combination Switch, Replace	45-4
Replacement	45-4
Service	45-4
Cooling Fans	48-1
Cruise Control	48-1
Dash Gauges	48-1
Dash Panels	48-1
Distributor, Replace	45-4
Evaporator Core, Replace	45-6
Cool/Ice Box	45-7
Front	45-6
Rear	45-6
Fuel Pump Relay Location	45-3
Fuse Panel & Flasher Location	45-3
Ignition Lock, Replace	45-4
Ignition Switch, Replace	45-4
Instrument Cluster, Replace	45-5
Neutral Safety Switch, Replace	45-4
Passive Restraints	48-1
Precautions	45-3
Air Bag Systems	45-3
Radio, Replace	45-5
Relay Center Location	45-3
Speed Controls	48-1
Starter Motors	48-1
Starter, Replace	45-3
Steering Columns	48-1
Steering Wheel, Replace	45-5
Stop Light Switch, Replace	45-4
Wiper Motor, Replace	45-6
Front	45-6
Rear	45-6
Wiper Systems	48-1

PRECAUTIONS

AIR BAG SYSTEMS

Refer to "Air Bag System Precautions" in the front of this manual for system disarming and arming procedures.

FUSE PANEL & FLASHER LOCATION

The junction block/fuse panel is located behind the center of the instrument panel. The turn signal and hazard flasher are located at the junction block behind the center of the instrument panel.

FUEL PUMP RELAY LOCATION

The fuel pump relay is located on the front righthand side of the engine compartment, **Fig. 1.**

RELAY CENTER LOCATION

The relay center is located behind the upper center of the instrument panel.

STARTER

REPLACE

1. Disconnect battery ground cable.
2. **On 4WD models,** remove front propeller shaft.
3. **On models with manual transmission,** disconnect clutch slave cylinder and position aside. **Do not disconnect clutch line.**
4. **On all models,** remove battery cable to starter attaching nut.
5. Remove starter electrical connector.
6. **On 2WD models,** remove starter attaching nuts and bolt, then the starter.

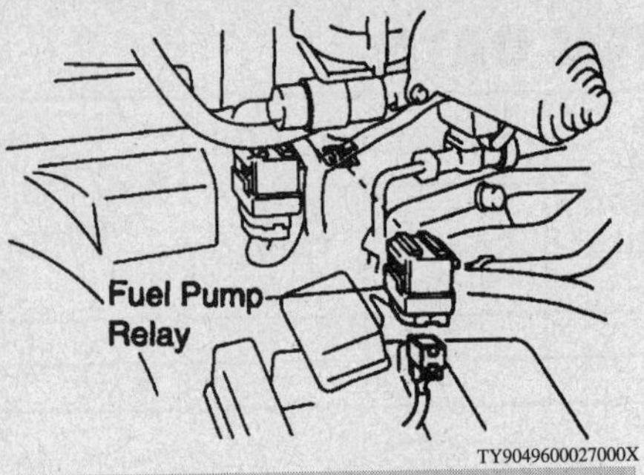
Fuel Pump
Relay
TY9049600027000X

Fig. 1 Fuel pump relay location

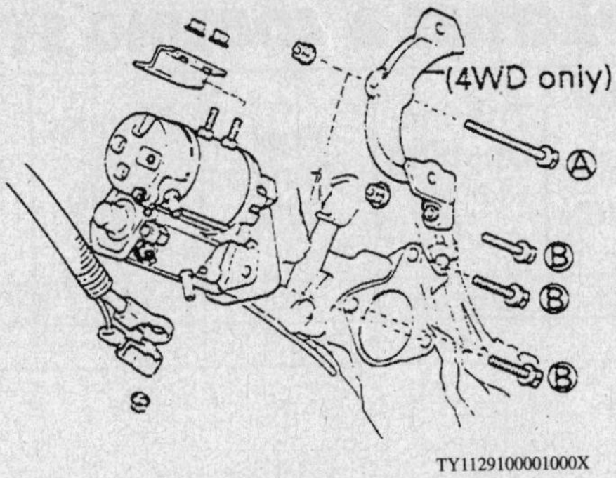
(4WD only)
A
B
B
B
TY1129100001000X

Fig. 2 Starter motor installation

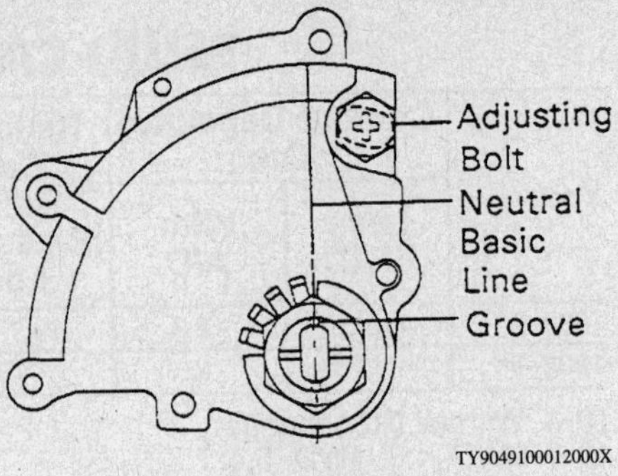
Adjusting
Bolt
Neutral
Basic
Line
Groove
TY9049100012000X

Fig. 3 Neutral start switch adjustment

7. **On 4WD models,** remove center support bracket and starter attaching nuts and bolts, then the starter.
8. **On all models,** reverse procedure to install. **Torque** A starter bolts as shown in **Fig. 2,** to 41 ft. lbs. and B starter bolts to 30 ft. lbs. On 4WD models, **torque** center support bracket to stiffener plate to 43 ft. lbs. and bracket to starter to 12 ft. lbs.
9. Reverse procedure to install.

DISTRIBUTOR

REPLACE

1. Disconnect battery ground cable.
2. Disconnect distributor cap spark plug wires.
3. Disconnect distributor electrical connector.
4. Remove ventilation hoses.
5. Remove distributor cap and packing.
6. Set No. 1 cylinder to TDC, as follows:
   a. Install service nut and bolt to accessory driveshaft.
   b. Turn crankshaft in normal direction until timing mark is aligned with 0 mark on timing chain case.
7. Remove distributor attaching bolts, then the distributor.
8. Reverse procedure to install. **Torque** distributor attaching bolts to 14 ft. lbs.

IGNITION LOCK

REPLACE

1. Disconnect battery ground cable.
2. Turn ignition switch to ACC position.
3. Insert small diameter rod to hole in side of lock cylinder, then holding pin down, remove lock cylinder.
4. Ensure lock cylinder is in ACC position.
5. Reverse procedure to install.

IGNITION SWITCH

REPLACE

1. Disconnect battery ground cable.
2. Remove steering column upper and lower covers.
3. Disconnect ignition switch electrical connectors.
4. Turn ignition key to ACC position, then remove ignition key cylinder.
5. Remove ignition switch attaching screws, then the ignition switch.
6. Reverse procedure to install.

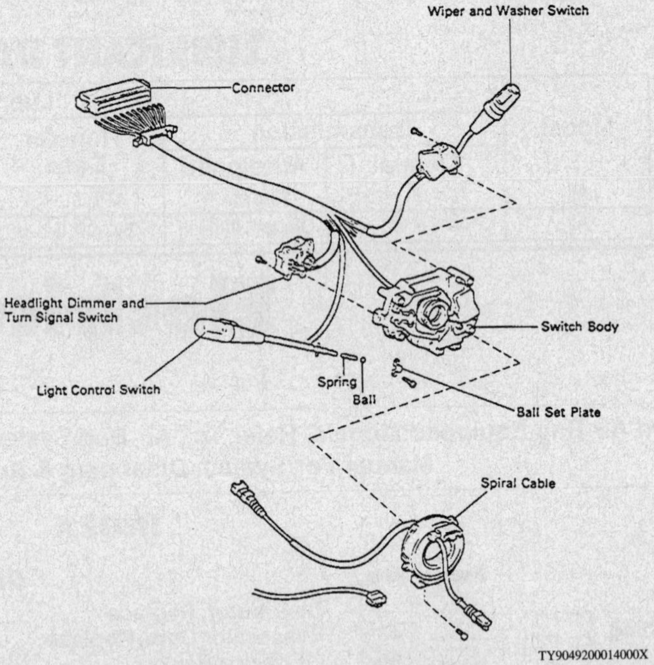
Wiper and Washer Switch
Connector
Headlight Dimmer and
Turn Signal Switch
Switch Body
Light Control Switch
Spring
Ball
Ball Set Plate
Spiral Cable
TY9049200014000X

Fig. 4 Combination switch.

NEUTRAL SAFETY SWITCH

REPLACE

1. Raise and support vehicle.
2. Disconnect switch electrical connector.
3. Loosen neutral start switch adjusting bolt, **Fig. 3.**
4. Position transmission shift lever in Neutral.
5. Align neutral base line and switch groove.
6. **Torque** adjusting bolt to 48 inch lbs.
7. Bend at least two lock washer tabs.

STOP LIGHT SWITCH

REPLACE

1. Remove brake pedal tension spring.
2. Disconnect switch electrical connector.
3. Remove switch attaching nut, then slide switch from bracket.
4. Reverse procedure to install.

COMBINATION SWITCH

REPLACE

REPLACEMENT

1. Disconnect battery ground cable.
2. Remove steering wheel as outlined under "Steering Wheel, Replace."
3. Remove steering column upper and lower covers.
4. Disconnect combination switch and spiral cable electrical connectors, then remove combination switch.
5. Reverse procedure to install.

SERVICE

Spiral Cable

1. Remove combination switch as outlined previously.
2. Remove spiral cable attaching screws.
3. Separate spiral cable from combination switch body, **Fig. 4.**
4. Reverse procedure to install. **Ensure spiral cable is in correct mounting position.**

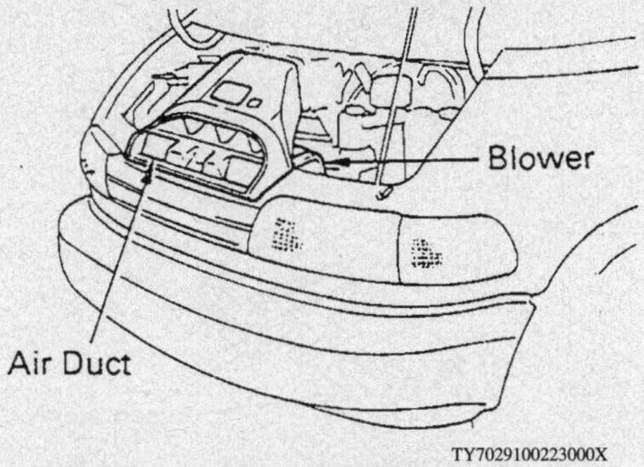
Blower
Air Duct
TY7029100223000X

Fig. 5 Front evaporator core replacement

Headlight Dimmer & Turn Signal Switch

1. Remove combination switch as outlined previously.
2. Using suitable small screwdriver, disengage headlight dimmer and turn signal switch wiring from combination switch connector. **Note position of wires.**
3. Remove switch to switch body attaching screws, **Fig. 4.**
4. Reverse procedure to install, noting the following:
   a. Ensure smooth switch operation in all positions.
   b. Install electrical terminals to combination switch in same position as they were removed.

Windshield Wiper/Washer Switch

1. Remove combination switch as outlined previously.
2. Using suitable small screwdriver, disengage headlight dimmer and turn signal switch wiring from combination switch connector. **Note position of wires.**
3. Remove switch to switch body attaching screws, **Fig. 4.**
4. Reverse procedure to install, noting the following:
   a. Ensure smooth switch operation in all positions.
   b. Install electrical terminals to combination switch in same position as they were removed.

Headlamp Switch

1. Remove combination switch as outlined previously.
2. Using suitable small screwdriver, disengage headlight dimmer and turn signal switch wiring from combination switch connector. **Note position of wires.**
3. Remove headlamp switch attaching screws, **Fig. 4.**
4. Remove switch, then the ball and spring assembly.
5. Reverse procedure to install, noting the following:
   a. Ensure smooth switch operation in all positions.
   b. Install electrical terminals to combination switch in same position as they were removed.

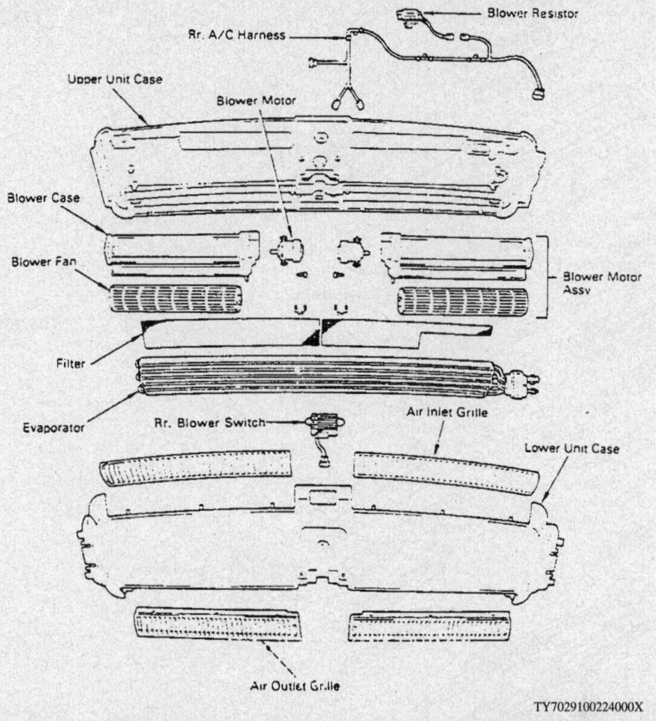
Blower Resistor
Rr. A/C Harness
Upper Unit Case
Blower Motor
Blower Case
Blower Fan
Blower Motor Assy
Filter
Evaporator
Rr. Blower Switch
Air Inlet Grille
Lower Unit Case
Air Outlet Grille
TY7029100224000X

Fig. 6 Exploded view of rear cooling unit. Denso type

STEERING WHEEL

REPLACE

1. Disconnect battery ground cable.
2. **On models with air bag,** remove four wheel pad attaching screws with T30 Torx wrench, then pull pad rearward and disconnect air bag connector.
3. **On models less air bag,** remove steering wheel pad attaching screw, then pull rearward and disconnect electrical connector.
4. Place alignment marks on steering wheel and mainshaft for assembly reference.
5. Remove steering wheel attaching nut.
6. Using steering wheel puller tool No. 09609-20011, or equivalent, remove steering wheel.
7. **Torque** steering wheel attaching bolt to 25 ft. lbs.
8. **On models with air bag, torque** wheel pad attaching screws to 5 ft. lbs. with suitable Torx wrench.
9. Reverse procedure to install.

INSTRUMENT CLUSTER

REPLACE

1. Disconnect battery ground cable.
2. Remove steering wheel as outlined under "Steering Wheel, Replace."
3. Remove steering column upper and lower covers.
4. Remove lefthand kick panel.
5. Remove hood release lever attaching screws, then slide forward to remove.
6. Remove instrument cluster lower finish panel attaching screws.
7. Pull cluster finish panel rearward and disconnect electrical connectors, then remove cluster finish panel.
8. Depress cluster finish center upper panel release lock, then pull panel rearward to unclip.
9. Depress sides of console box while pulling rearward to remove.
10. Remove four ash tray and cup holder unit attaching screws.
11. Pull ash tray and cup holder unit rearward and disconnect electrical connectors, then remove ashtray and cup holder unit.
12. Remove cluster finish center panel and radio attaching screws.
13. Pull panel rearward, disconnect electrical connectors and antenna, then remove radio and finish panel as an assembly.
14. Remove instrument cluster upper finish panel attaching screws, then the cluster upper finish panel.
15. Remove four instrument cluster attaching screws, then pull cluster rearward.
16. **On models with automatic transmission,** disconnect cable from control lever.
17. **On models with manual transmission,** disconnect cable from roller.
18. **On all models,** disconnect instrument cluster electrical connectors and remove cluster.
19. Reverse procedure to install.

RADIO

REPLACE

Refer to "Instrument Cluster, Replace" for radio replacement.

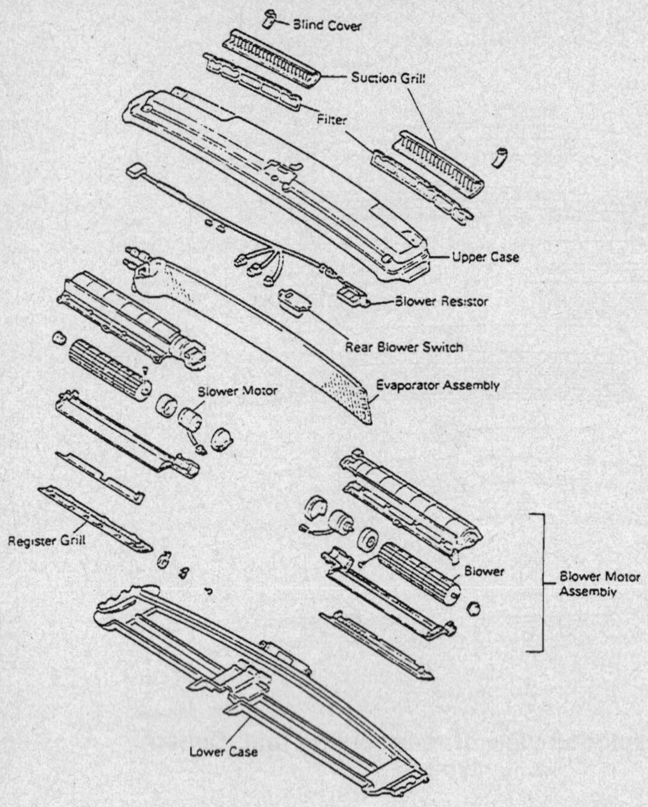
Blind Cover
Suction Grill
Filter
Upper Case
Blower Resistor
Rear Blower Switch
Evaporator Assembly
Blower Motor
Register Grill
Blower
Blower Motor Assembly
Lower Case

TY7029100225000X

Fig. 7 Exploded view of rear cooling unit. Panasonic type

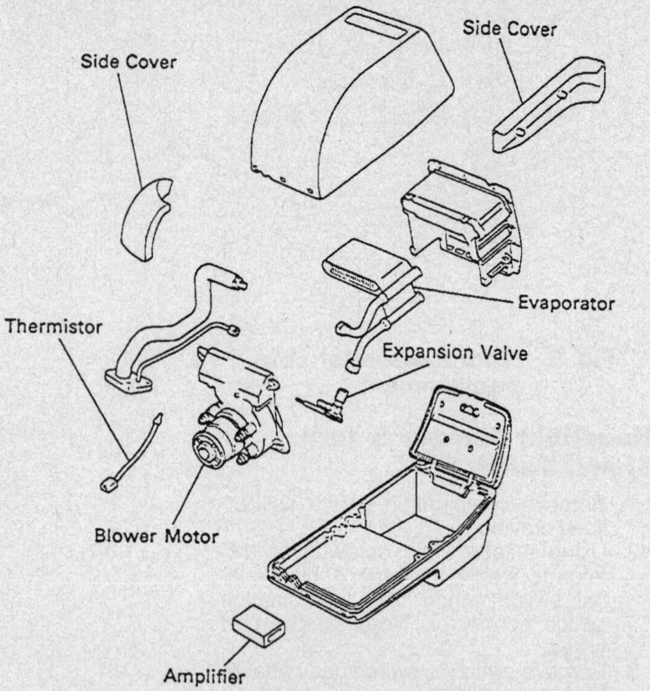
Side Cover
Side Cover
Evaporator
Thermistor
Expansion Valve
Blower Motor
Amplifier

TY7029200227000X

Fig. 8 Exploded view of cool/ice box

WIPER MOTOR

REPLACE

FRONT

1. Disconnect battery ground cable.
2. Disconnect wiper motor electrical connector.
3. Remove wiper motor attaching bolts.
4. Using suitable screwdriver, disconnect wiper link from wiper motor, then remove wiper motor.
5. Reverse procedure to install.

REAR

1. Disconnect battery ground cable.
2. Remove wiper arm and rear door trim cover.
3. Disconnect wiper motor electrical connector.
4. Remove wiper motor bracket attaching bolts, then wiper motor and bracket.
5. Reverse procedure to install.

BLOWER MOTOR

REPLACE

FRONT

1. Disconnect battery ground cable.
2. Remove front air duct, **Fig. 5.**
3. Disconnect blower motor electrical connector.
4. Remove blower motor attaching bolts, then the blower motor.
5. Reverse procedure to install.

REAR

Denso Type

1. Disconnect battery ground cable.
2. Discharge A/C system. Refer to "Air Conditioning" section.
3. Remove right and left air inlet grills and air outlet grills, **Fig. 6.**
4. Remove filter.
5. Remove rear A/C switch.
6. Remove evaporator assembly.
7. Remove right and left blower assemblies.
8. Reverse procedure to install.

Panasonic Type

1. Disconnect battery ground cable.
2. Discharge A/C system. Refer to "Air Conditioning" section.
3. Remove right and left suction grills, register grills and filters, **Fig. 7.**
4. Drain lower case, then remove lower case attaching and separate from upper case.
5. Remove right and left blower motor attaching screws, then disconnect electrical connector.
6. Disengage eight blower motor pawls.
7. Separate upper and lower blower motor case.
8. Remove blower motor attaching screws, then the blower motor with rubber mount.
9. Reverse procedure to install.

COOL/ICE BOX

1. Disconnect battery ground cable.
2. Discharge A/C system as outlined in the "Air Conditioning" section.
3. Remove righthand side kick panels.
4. Disconnect cool/ice box electrical connectors.
5. Disconnect cool/ice box A/C suction and liquid tubes. Refer to "Air Conditioning" section.
6. Remove cool box attaching bolts and the cool box.
7. Separate cool box upper and lower panels, **Fig. 8.**
8. Remove blower motor.
9. Reverse procedure to install.

EVAPORATOR CORE

REPLACE

FRONT

1. Disconnect battery ground cable.
2. Discharge A/C system as described in the "Air Conditioning" section.
3. Remove front air duct, **Fig. 5.**
4. Remove blower motor.
5. Disconnect evaporator core electrical connectors.
6. Disconnect A/C suction and liquid tubes.
7. Remove evaporator cover attaching nuts, then the cover.
8. Remove evaporator attaching nuts and bolt, then the evaporator.
9. Reverse procedure to install. Rearm air bag system as described under "Precautions."

REAR

Denso Type

1. Disconnect battery ground cable.

2. Discharge A/C system. Refer to "Air Conditioning" section.
3. Remove right and left air inlet grills and air outlet grills, **Fig. 6.**
4. Remove filter.
5. Remove rear A/C switch.
6. Remove evaporator assembly.
7. Remove right and left blower motor assemblies.
8. Using suitable wrench, remove expansion valve to evaporator attaching bolts.
9. Reverse procedure to install.

Panasonic Type

1. Disconnect battery ground cable.
2. Discharge A/C system. Refer to "Air Conditioning" section.
3. Remove right and left suction grills, register grills and filters, **Fig. 7.**
4. Drain lower case, then remove lower case attaching and separate from upper case.
5. Remove right and left blower motor attaching screws, then disconnect electrical connector.
6. Disengage and remove eight pawls from blower motor.
7. Remove blower resistor electrical connector, then the attaching screws.
8. Remove rear blower motor switch electrical connector, then the attaching screws.
9. Remove evaporator assembly.
10. Remove heater protective insulators, then liquid line from expansion valve.
11. Separate heat sensing tube from suction tube.
12. Remove expansion valve from evaporator.
13. Reverse procedure to install.

COOL/ICE BOX

1. Disconnect battery ground cable.
2. Discharge A/C system, refer to "Air Conditioning" section.
3. Remove righthand side kick panels.
4. Disconnect cool/ice box electrical connectors.
5. Disconnect cool/ice box A/C suction and liquid tubes.
6. Remove cool/ice box attaching bolts, then the cool/ice box.
7. Separate cool/ice box upper and lower panels, **Fig. 8.**
8. Remove evaporator core.
9. Reverse procedure to install.

2TZ-FE & 2TZ-FZE 2.4L Engines

NOTE: On Air Bag Equipped Models, Refer To "Air Bag System Precautions" Located In The Front Of This Manual For System Disarming & Arming Procedures.

INDEX

	Page No.
Belt Tension Data	45-12
Camshaft, Replace	45-11
Compression Pressure	45-7
Cooling System Bleed	45-14
Cylinder Head, Replace	45-9
Engine Rebuilding Specifications	48-1
Engine, Replace	45-7
Exhaust Manifold, Replace	45-8
Fuel Filter, Replace	45-14
Fuel Pump, Replace	45-14
Hydraulic Lifters, Replace	45-10
Intake Manifold, Replace	45-8
Main & Rod Bearings	45-11
Oil Pump, Replace	45-11
Oil Pump Service	45-11
Piston & Rod Assembly	45-11
Precautions	45-7
Air Bag Systems	45-7
Fuel System Pressure Relief	45-7
Radiator, Replace	45-14
2TZ-FE Engine	45-14
2TZ-FZE Engine	45-14
Separated Accessory Drive System	45-12
Accessory Driveshaft Housing, Replace	45-14
Accessory Driveshaft, Replace	45-12
Description	45-12
Service Precautions	45-12
Supercharger, Replace	45-15
Thermostat, Replace	45-14
Tightening Specifications	45-17
Timing Chain, Replace	45-10
Inspection	45-10
Installation	45-10
Removal	45-10
Valve Adjustment	45-9
1993	45-9
1994–96	45-9
Valve Clearance Specifications	45-9
Valve Guides	45-10
Water Pump, Replace	45-14

PRECAUTIONS

AIR BAG SYSTEMS

Refer to "Air Bag System Precautions" in the front of this manual for system disarming and arming procedures.

FUEL SYSTEM PRESSURE RELIEF

1. Place ignition switch in LOCK position.
2. Disconnect battery ground cable.
3. Wait a minimum of 90 seconds before disconnecting any fuel line or component.

COMPRESSION PRESSURE

1. Start engine and warm to normal operating temperature.
2. Disconnect high tension cord from ignition coil.
3. Disconnect high tension cords from spark plugs.
4. Remove spark plugs.
5. Insert compression pressure gauge into spark plug hole.
6. Fully open throttle.
7. While cranking engine, measure compression pressure.
8. Standard compression pressure is 178 psi. Minimum compression pressure should be at least 128 psi.
9. Maximum difference between compression pressures should be 14 psi.

ENGINE

REPLACE

The engine and transmission are removed as an assembly.

1. Disconnect battery ground cable.
2. Remove engine undercovers.
3. Drain coolant and oil.
4. Paint installation alignment marks on accessory driveshaft rear coupling and crankshaft pulley, then disconnect accessory driveshaft from crankshaft pulley.
5. Remove alternator belt, then A/C belt.
6. Install nut and bolt to front of accessory driveshaft, **Fig. 1.**
7. Rotate accessory driveshaft, **Fig. 1,** then remove three A bolts and washers.
8. Remove B bolts, then disconnect driveshaft from pulley, leave driveshaft in same position.
9. Disconnect radiator hose from water inlet, then radiator from water outlet, then heater hose from water pump and oil auto feed hose from No. 1 return pipe.

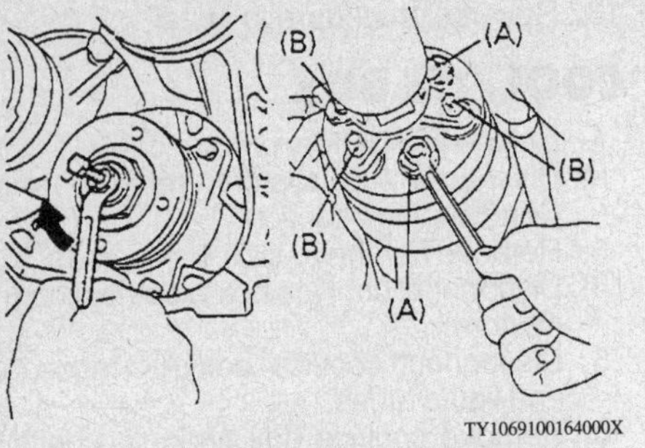
(B)
(A)
(B)
(B)
(A)
TY1069100164000X

Fig. 1 Accessory driveshaft removal

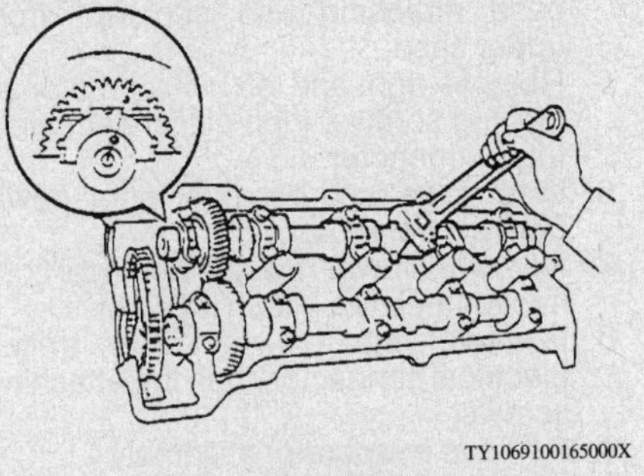
TY1069100165000X

Fig. 2 Setting exhaust camshaft to BTDC

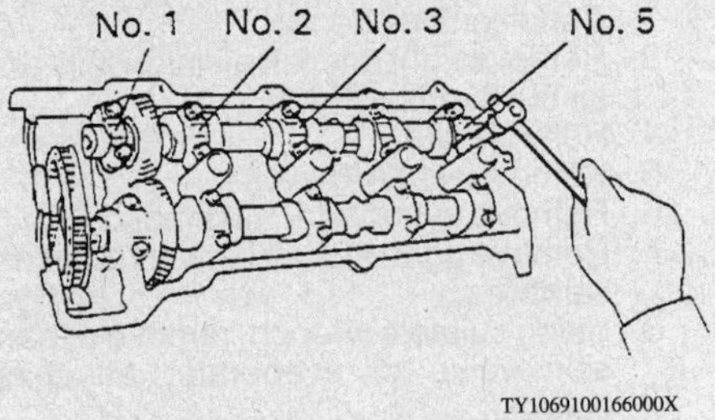
No. 1
No. 2
No. 3
No. 5
TY1069100166000X

Fig. 3 Exhaust bearing cap Nos. 1, 2, 3 & 5 removal

10. Disconnect accelerator wire from throttle body.
11. Disconnect check, ECU, two cowl and igniter electrical connectors.
12. **On 4WD models,** remove propeller shaft assembly.
13. **On all models,** disconnect water bypass hose from floor pipe and brake booster hose from floor pipe.
14. Disconnect lefthand front engine ground strap, starter electrical connectors, then hose from intake manifold union.
15. **On models with manual transmission,** remove clutch release cylinder clamp and attaching bolts, .
16. **On models with automatic transmission,** remove shift cable as follows:
    a. Remove shift cable to transmission lever attaching nut.
    b. Disconnect shift cable from lever.
    c. Disconnect shift cable from dipstick guide.
    d. Remove cable to floor panel attaching nut.
    e. Remove shift cable from vehicle.
17. **On all models,** disconnect VSV hose from A/C, No. 2 ventilation hose from case, distribution ventilation air hose, ISC valve air hose, then disconnect air intake connector electrical connector.
18. Disconnect VSV fuel pressure control hoses from engine and intake manifold.
19. Disconnect EVAP vacuum hose from charcoal canister, then distributor ventilation air hose from intake manifold.
20. Disconnect IAC valve, cold start injector, throttle position sensor, fuel pressure control VSV and A/C VSV electrical connectors.
21. Remove engine wire to floor panel clamps, then disconnect from floor panel.
22. Disconnect fuel inlet and outlet hoses.
23. Disconnect two oxygen sensors, then remove front exhaust pipe.
24. **On models with automatic transmissions,** disconnect oil cooler hoses from oil cooler lines.
25. **On models with manual transmissions,** disconnect shift cables.
26. **On all models,** disconnect ignition coil and condenser electrical connectors.
27. Disconnect ignition coil high tension cord, then transmission to floor panel ground strap.
28. **On models with manual transmission,** disconnect back-up light switch and speedometer speed sensor connectors.
29. **On models with automatic transmissions,** disconnect speed sensor, neutral start switch, solenoid and A/T oil temperature sensor electrical connectors.
30. **On all models,** remove rear propeller shaft assembly.
31. Install suitable engine lifting equipment, ensure all connectors and hoses are disconnected.
32. Lower vehicle slightly while supporting engine and transmission.
33. Remove righthand and lefthand engine mounts, then rear engine mount.
34. Lower engine and transmission assembly.
35. Reverse procedure to install.

INTAKE MANIFOLD

REPLACE

Refer to "Cylinder Head, Replace" for intake manifold replacement procedure.

EXHAUST MANIFOLD

REPLACE

Refer to "Cylinder Head, Replace" for exhaust manifold replacement.

CYLINDER HEAD

REPLACE

1. Disconnect battery ground cable.
2. Remove engine harness cover attaching bolts, then disconnect.
3. Disconnect pressure regulator vacuum hose.
4. Disconnect the following electrical connectors:
    a. Oil pressure switch.
    b. Oil level sensor.
    c. Distributor connector.
    d. Start injector time switch.
    e. **On California models,** EGR gas temperature sensor.
    f. **On all models,** water temperature sensor and sender gauge.
    g. Knock sensor.
    h. Four injector connectors.
5. Remove No. 2 cylinder head cover.
6. Disconnect No. 2 and 3 air hoses, then remove distributor.
7. Remove EGR valve, pipe and gaskets.
8. Remove delivery pipe and cold start injector union bolts and gaskets.
9. Remove pressure regulator and hose, then the fuel pipe.
10. Remove water outlet and No. 2 water bypass pipe and gasket.
11. Remove PCV hose.
12. Remove delivery pipe.
13. Disconnect water pump hose, the remove intake manifold brackets and manifold.
14. Remove righthand engine mount.
15. Remove exhaust manifold attaching nuts, then the exhaust manifold.
16. Remove righthand engine mount.
17. Remove exhaust manifold heat insulator.
18. Remove No. 1 oil return pipe.
19. Remove No. 1 cylinder head cover, then half circular plugs.
20. Place installation alignment marks on camshaft sprocket and chain.
21. Hold camshaft, then remove cam sprocket bolt.
22. Remove chain tensioner and gasket.
23. Remove cam sprocket and chain. **Do not remove slipper and damper.**
24. Remove No. 6 bearing cap bolt.
25. Remove exhaust camshafts as follows:
    a. **Camshaft must be held level during removal or cylinder head damage may result.**
    b. Set exhaust knock pin hole at 5–30° BTDC, **Fig. 2.**
    c. Install service bolt to camshaft subgear and main gear.
    d. Using sequence shown in **Fig. 3,** alternately and uniformly loosen and remove bearing cap Nos. 1, 2, 3 and 5.
    e. Alternately and uniformly loosen No. 4 bearing cap bolt, **Fig. 4.** Ensure camshaft is being lifted straight out, if not, retighten No. 4 cap and reverse camshaft removal procedure. **Do not pry or force camshaft.**
    f. Remove No. 4 bearing cap and exhaust camshaft.
26. Remove intake camshafts as follows:
    a. Set exhaust knock pin hole at 75–100° BTDC, **Fig. 5.**
    b. Install service bolt to camshaft subgear and main gear.
    c. Using sequence shown in **Fig. 6,** loosen and remove Nos. 1, 2, 4 and 5 bearing caps.
    d. Loosen No. 3 bearing cap bolt, **Fig. 7,** ensure camshaft is being lifted straight out, if not retighten No. 3

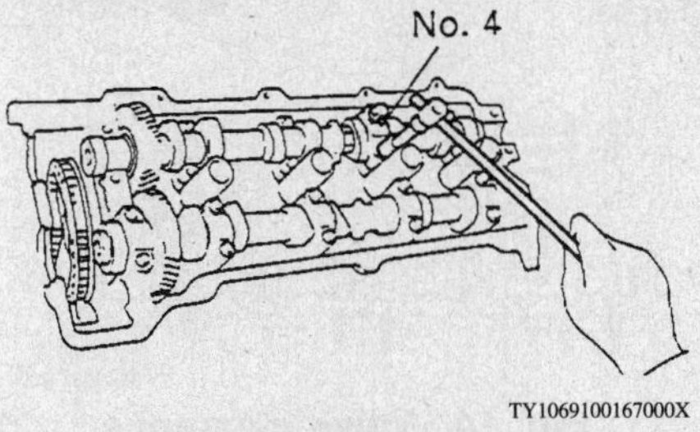
No. 4
TY1069100167000X

Fig. 4 Exhaust bearing cap No. 4 removal

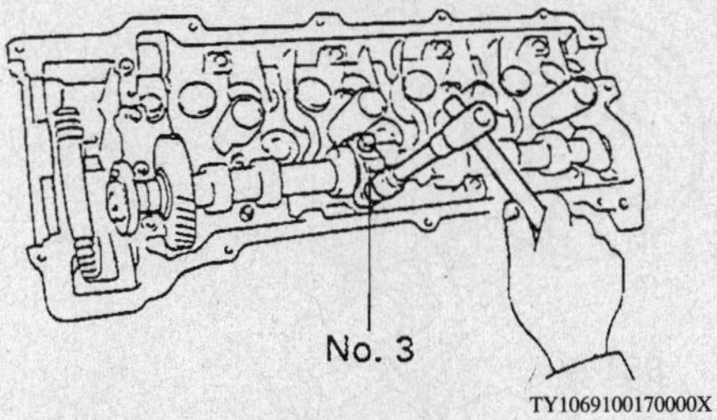
No. 3
TY1069100170000X

Fig. 7 Intake bearing cap No. 3 removal

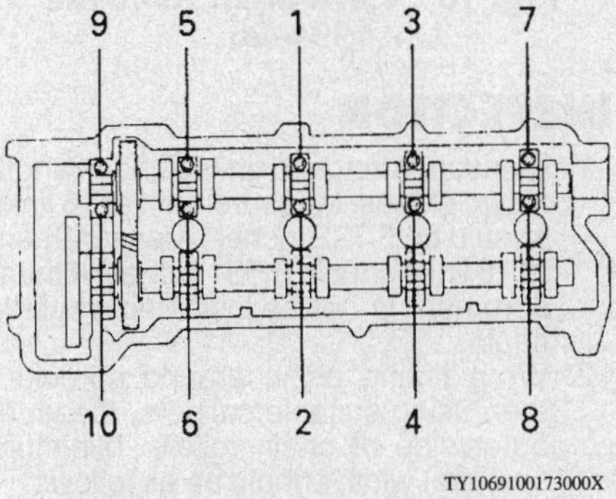
9 5 1 3 7
10 6 2 4 8
TY1069100173000X

Fig. 10 Exhaust camshaft tightening sequence

cap and reverse camshaft removal procedure. **Do not pry or force camshaft.**

e. Remove No. 3 bearing cap and exhaust camshaft.

27. Remove two front cylinder head bolts, then the remaining cylinder head bolts in two or three steps using sequence shown in **Fig. 8.**
28. Reverse procedure to install, noting the following:
    a. **Torque** cylinder head bolts in reverse order of removal sequence, **Fig. 8,** in three steps to 29 ft. lbs. Mark top front side of each bolt, then tighten an additional 90°, ensure alignment mark is facing sideward. Tighten an additional 90°, ensure alignment mark is facing rearward.
    b. **Torque** two front cylinder head bolts to 15 ft. lbs.
    c. Using sequence shown in **Fig. 9, torque** intake bearing caps in three steps to 12 ft. lbs.
    d. Using sequence shown in **Fig. 10, torque** exhaust bearing caps in three steps to 12 ft. lbs.

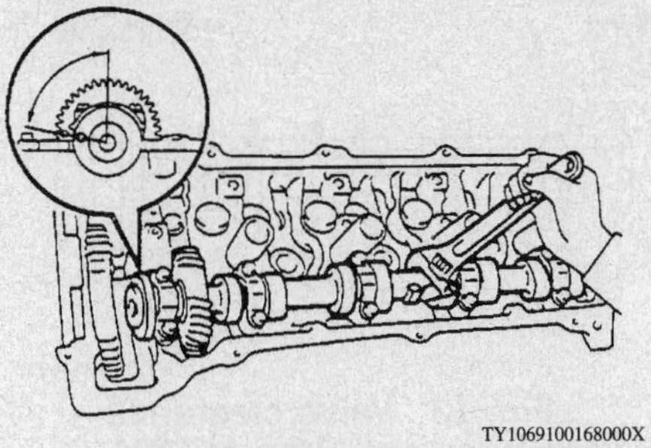
TY1069100168000X

Fig. 5 Setting intake camshaft to BTDC

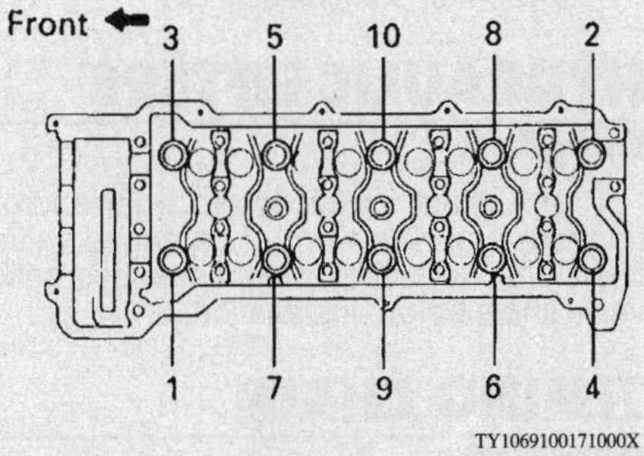
Front
3 5 10 8 2
1 7 9 6 4
TY1069100171000X

Fig. 8 Cylinder head loosening sequence

e. Using sequence shown in **Fig. 11, torque** cylinder head cover bolts to 6 ft. lbs.

VALVE CLEARANCE SPECIFICATIONS

Year	Stem-To-Guide Clearance	
	Intake	Exhaust
1993–96	.006–.010	.010–.014

VALVE ADJUSTMENT

1993

Valve adjustment is accomplished by installing the proper thickness shim to achieve the specified valve clearance. Refer to “Valve Clearance Specifications” for proper clearance. Shims are available in .0020 inch (.050 mm) increments from .0984 inch (2.5 mm) to .1299 inch (3.30 mm).

1. With engine cold, turn accessory driveshaft to TDC alignment mark, then set pulley groove to 0.
2. Ensure Nos. 1 and 4 valve lifters are tight. If not, turn crankshaft 360° (one complete revolution) and align timing marks.
3. With engine in this position check clearance of the following valves:
    a. No. 1 intake and exhaust valves.
    b. No 2 intake valves.
    c. No. 3 exhaust valves.
4. Turn crankshaft pulley 360° (one complete revolution) and align timing marks as outlined previously and check the following valves:

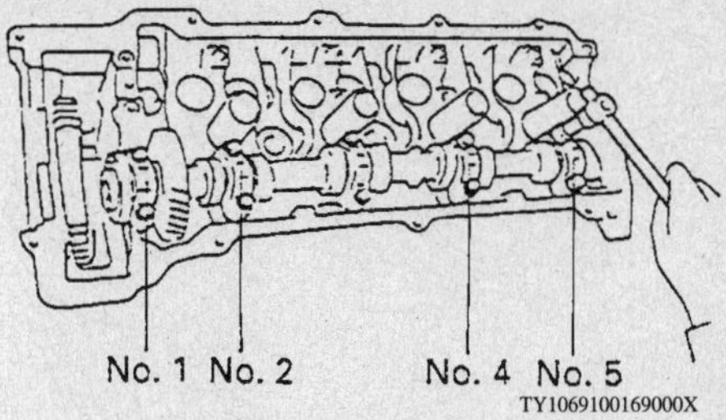
No. 1 No. 2
No. 4 No. 5
TY1069100169000X

Fig. 6 Intake bearing cap Nos. 1, 2, 4 & 5 removal

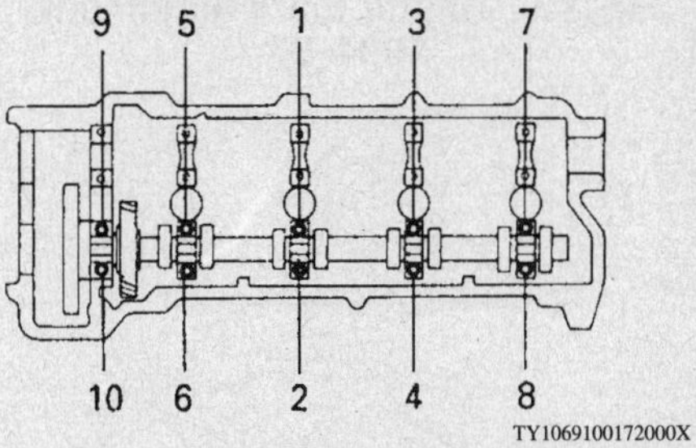
9 5 1 3 7
10 6 2 4 8
TY1069100172000X

Fig. 9 Intake camshaft tightening sequence

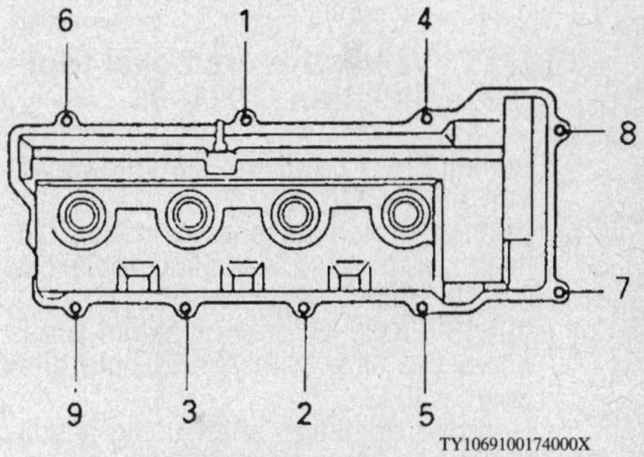
6 1 4
8
7
9 3 2 5
TY1069100174000X

Fig. 11 Cylinder head cover tightening sequence

a. No. 2 exhaust valves.
b. No. 3 exhaust valves.
c. No. 4 intake and exhaust valves.

1994–96

Valve adjustment is accomplished by installing the proper thickness shim to achieve the specified valve clearance. Refer to “Valve Clearance Specifications” for proper clearance. Shims are available in .0020 inch (.050 mm) increments from .0984 inch (2.5 mm) to .1299 inch (3.30 mm).

1. With engine cold, turn accessory driveshaft to TDC alignment mark, then set pulley groove to 0.
2. Ensure No. 1 valve lifters are loose and No. 4 valve lifters are tight. If not, turn crankshaft 360° (one complete revolution) and align timing marks **Fig. 12.**
3. With engine in this position, check clearance of the valves indicated in **Fig. 13.**
4. Check valve clearance and record measurements that are out of specification to determine required replacement shims.
5. Turn equipment driveshaft 360° (one complete revolution), align timing

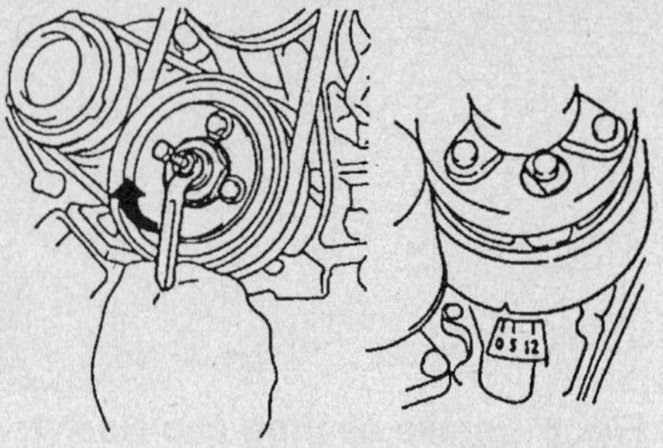
0 5 12

TY1069400175000X

Fig. 12 Timing mark alignment. 1994–96

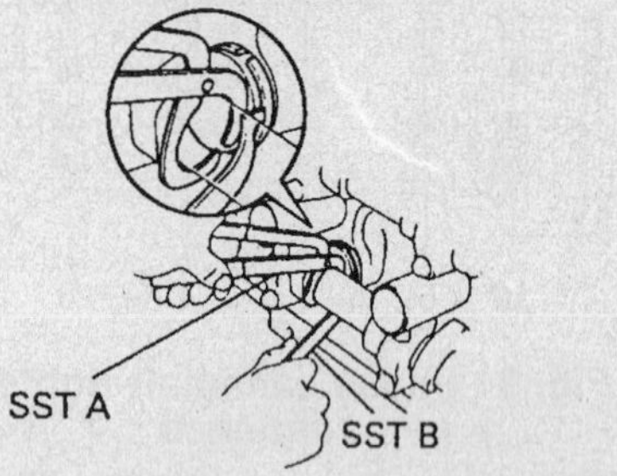
SST A
SST B

TY1069400178000X

Fig. 15 Valve shim removal tool installation. 1994–96

marks, **Fig. 12** and measure the valves indicated in **Fig. 14.**

6. Position notch as shown in **Fig. 15**, then using valve adjusting tools No. 09248-55020 (09248-05011 (A), 09248-05021 (B) or equivalents, press down the lifter with A and hold lifter down with B.
7. Remove adjusting shim using a suitable tool and magnet, **Fig. 16.**
8. To determine replacement shim, proceed as follows:
   a. Using a micrometer, measure removed shim.
   b. Calculate the thickness of the new shim required for specified value, using the variables: T = thickness of used shim, A = measured valve clearance and N = thickness of new shim.
   c. To determine correct intake valve shim, use the formula N = T (A - .008 inch).
   d. To determine correct exhaust valve shim, use the formula N = T (A - .012 inch).
9. Select shim with thickness closest to calculated value.

VALVE GUIDES

1. Using suitable tool and hammer, strike valve guide bushing to break it off cylinder head casting.
2. Heat cylinder head to 176–212°F (80–100°C).
3. Using suitable valve guide removal tool, tap out bushing.
4. Install snap ring on new valve guide, then install new valve guide using toll as above and driving in from the reverse side of removal.
5. Ream valve guide if required. Refer to

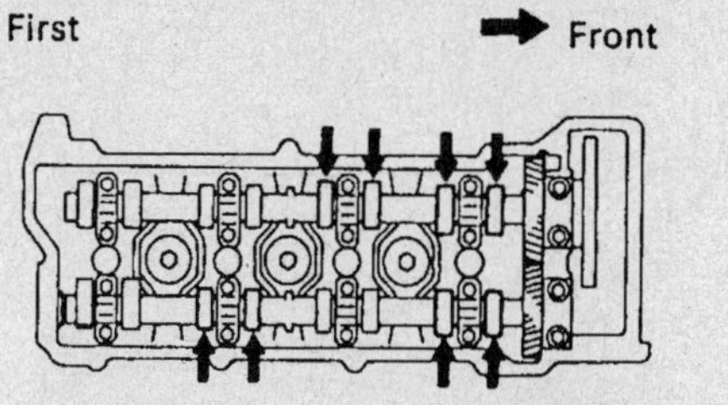
First
Front

TY1069400176000X

Fig. 13 Valve clearance measurement, Step 1. 1994–96

"Engine Rebuilding Specifications" section for stem clearance.

HYDRAULIC LIFTERS

REPLACE

Check lifters for excessive wear and/or damage. Replace worn or damaged valve lifters as required. Lubricate hydraulic valve lifters before installation.

TIMING CHAIN

REPLACE

REMOVAL

1. Remove engine as outlined under "Engine, Replace."
2. Remove cylinder head as outlined under "Cylinder Head, Replace."
3. Using crankshaft pulley holding tool No. 09213-58012 and flange holding tool No. 09330-00021, or equivalents, remove crankshaft pulley bolt.
4. Using puller set tool No. 09950-20012, or equivalent, remove crankshaft pulley.
5. Remove left engine mount and stay.
6. Remove oil pressure switch.
7. Remove crankcase assembly as follows:
   a. Remove engine oil dipstick.
   b. Remove ventilation case with engine hanger and gasket.
   c. Remove oil dipstick tube and gasket.
   d. Remove crankcase attaching nuts and bolts.
   e. Using seal cutter tool No. 09032-00100, or equivalent, and suitable brass bar, separate crankcase from cylinder block. **Do not damage crankcase flange.**
   f. Remove baffle plate attaching nuts, then the baffle plate.
8. Remove oil filter bracket, **Fig. 17.**
9. Remove timing chain case O-ring.
10. Remove 12 timing chain cover attaching bolts and 2 nuts, **Fig. 18.**
11. Using suitable plastic hammer, loosen timing chain cover, then remove case and two gaskets.
12. Remove chain slipper and damper.
13. Remove oil nozzle and gasket.
14. Loosen idler gear bolts, then pushing idler gear chain guide to left side retighten bolt.
15. Remove idler gear bolts, idler gear and chain assembly.
16. Remove crankshaft sprocket as required.

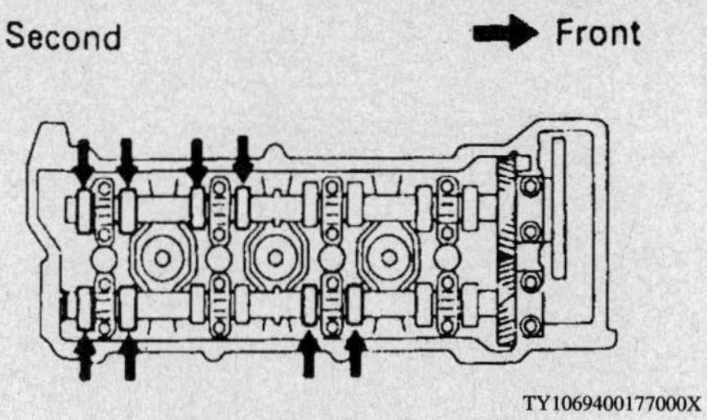
Second
Front

TY1069400177000X

Fig. 14 Valve clearance measurement, Step 2. 1994–96

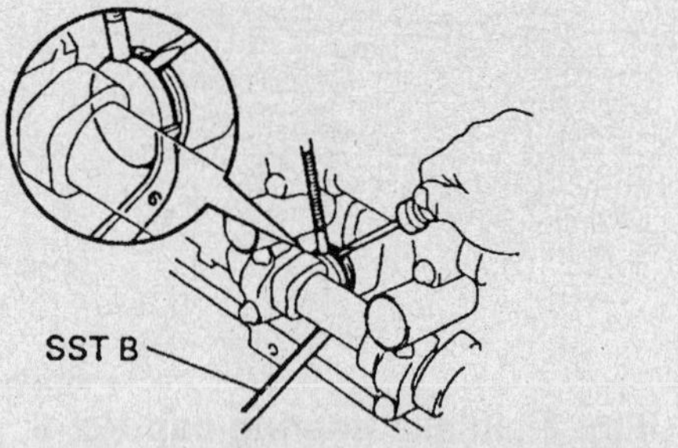
SST B

TY1069400179000X

Fig. 16 Valve shim removal. 1994–96

INSPECTION

1. Measure stretched timing chain length in two places. Measurement at 16 links should be 5.772 inches. Measurement at 18 links should 5.531 inches. If measurement is not as indicated, replace chain.
2. Wrap timing chain around sprocket, then using suitable calipers, measure outer side of chain rollers. Minimum sprocket width should be as follows:
   a. No. 1 crankshaft sprocket, 2.339 inches.
   b. Camshaft sprocket, 4.480 inches.
   c. No. 2 crankshaft sprocket, 2.752 inches.
   d. Idle sprocket, 2.244 inches.
   e. If measurement is less than minimum, replace sprocket.
3. Using a suitable micrometer, measure chain damper and slipper, maximum wear is .039 inch. If wear is more than .039 inch, replace damper and/or slipper.
4. Check idle sprocket for rough operation or noise, replace as necessary.

INSTALLATION

1. Turn crankshaft until shaft key is at top, then slide sprocket on crankshaft.
2. Install No. 2 timing chain on idler sprocket and crankshaft sprocket, then tighten bolts to specifications.
3. Loosen bolt, ensuring chain guide presses against chain.
4. Depress and release chain guide ensuring proper operation, then tighten chain guide to specifications.
5. Install oil nozzle.
6. Install chain damper and slipper.
7. Install No. 1 timing chain to camshaft sprocket, ensuring timing mark is between two bright chain links.
8. Install timing chain to crankshaft sprocket, ensuring timing mark is

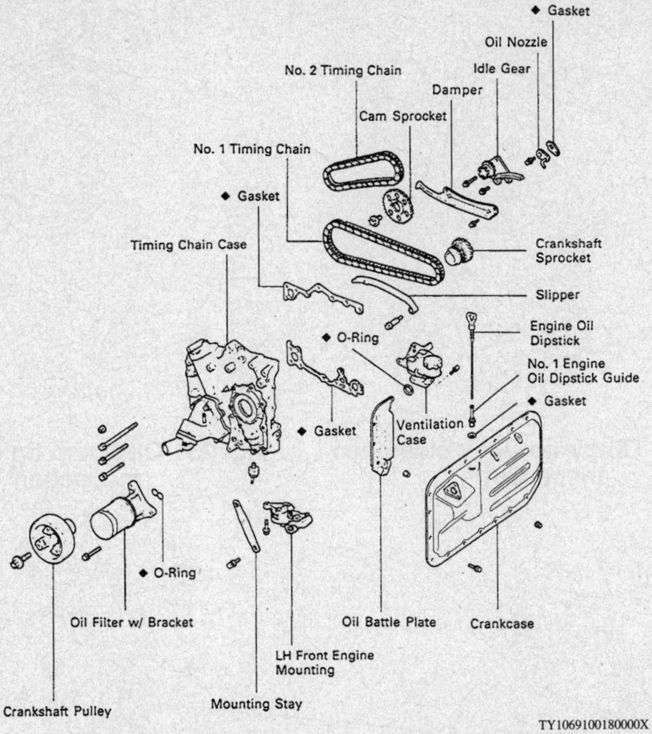
◆ Gasket
Oil Nozzle
No. 2 Timing Chain
Idle Gear
Damper
Cam Sprocket
No. 1 Timing Chain
◆ Gasket
Timing Chain Case
Crankshaft Sprocket
Slipper
◆ O-Ring
Engine Oil Dipstick
No. 1 Engine Oil Dipstick Guide
◆ Gasket
◆ Gasket
Ventilation Case
◆ O-Ring
Oil Filter w/ Bracket
Oil Battle Plate
Crankcase
LH Front Engine Mounting
Crankshaft Pulley
Mounting Stay
TY1069100180000X

Fig. 17 Exploded view of timing chain

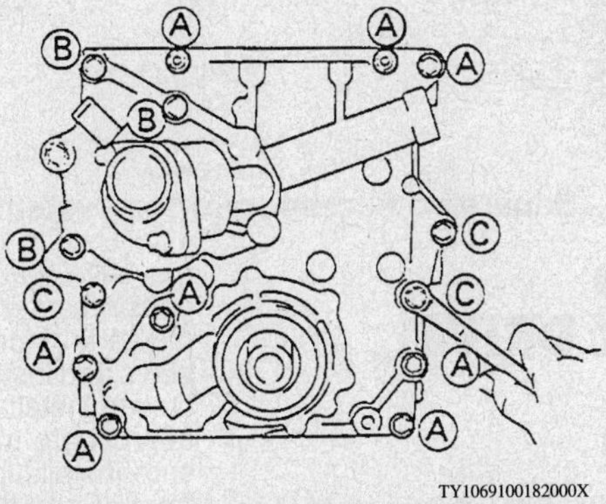
TY1069100182000X

Fig. 19 Timing chain tightening sequence

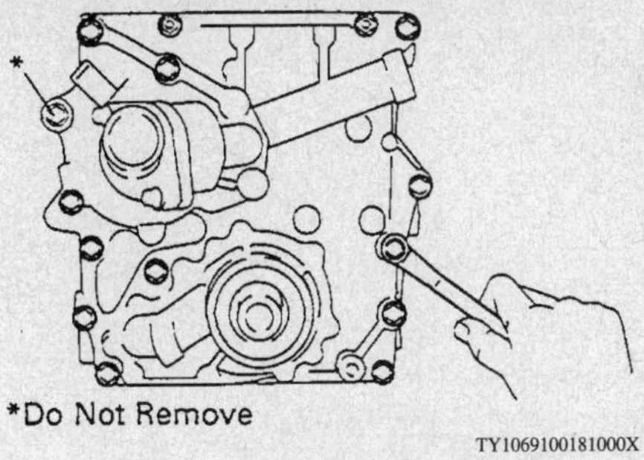
*Do Not Remove
TY1069100181000X

Fig. 18 Timing chain case removal

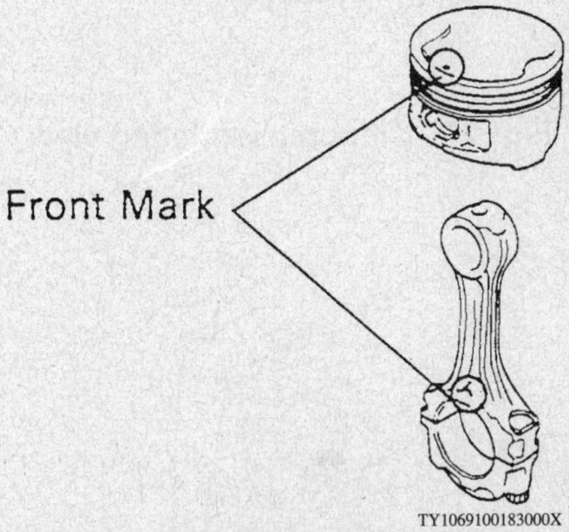
Front Mark
TY1069100183000X

Fig. 20 Piston & connecting rod assembly

aligned with single bright link.

9. Turn camshaft sprocket counterclockwise to remove slack.
10. Install timing chain case, **torque** A, **Fig. 19,** to 14 ft. lbs., B to 21 ft. lbs. and C to 32 ft. lbs.
11. Install new timing case cover O-ring.
12. Install oil filter bracket.
13. Install baffle plate, crankcase assembly, No. 1 oil dipstick guide, ventilation case and engine hanger.
14. Apply Loctite 242, or equivalent to oil pressure switch first two or three threads, then install oil pressure switch.
15. Install left engine mount and stay.
16. Install crankshaft pulley with spline teeth of pulley engaged with large teeth of oil pump.
17. Rotate crankshaft pulley to ensure fit, then install crankshaft pulley bolt.
18. Install cylinder head and engine.

CAMSHAFT

REPLACE

Refer to "Cylinder Head, Replace" for camshaft replacement procedure.

PISTON & ROD ASSEMBLY

Pistons are available in standard and oversize of .020 inch (.50 mm). If the piston bore is not within specifications, replace piston and/or cylinder block. When assembling piston onto connecting rod, ensure mark on top of piston and mark on connecting rod are on same side, **Fig. 20.** When installing piston and connecting rod assembly, ensure mark on top of piston is facing toward front of engine.

MAIN & ROD BEARINGS

Undersize bearings are not available. If crankshaft journals or crankpins are worn or scored, the crankshaft must be replaced.

OIL PUMP

REPLACE

1. Disconnect battery ground cable.
2. Disconnect accessory driveshaft from crankshaft pulley.
3. Using crankshaft pulley holder tool No. 09213-58012 and flange holder tool No. 09330-0021, or equivalents, remove crankshaft pulley.
4. Remove oil pump cover attaching bolts, **Fig. 21,** then the oil pump cover.
5. Remove timing chain case as outlined under "Timing Chain, Replace."
6. Remove oil pump attaching bolts, then the oil pump.

OIL PUMP SERVICE

Oil pump inspection may be performed with oil pump cover removed.

1. Using suitable thickness gauge, measure driven rotor and pump body clearance, **Fig. 22.** Maximum clearance is .0118 inch, if clearance is not as indicated, replace rotor set and/or pump body.
2. Using suitable thickness gauge, measure rotor tip clearance, **Fig. 23.** Maximum clearance is .0138 inch, if

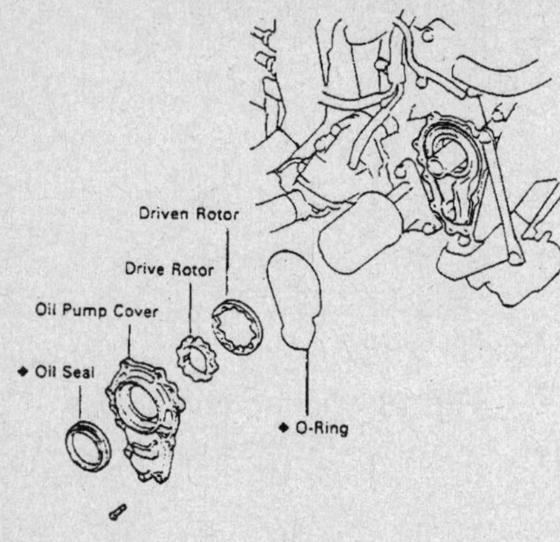
Driven Rotor
Drive Rotor
Oil Pump Cover
◆ Oil Seal
◆ O-Ring
TY1099100019000X

Fig. 21 Oil pump exploded view

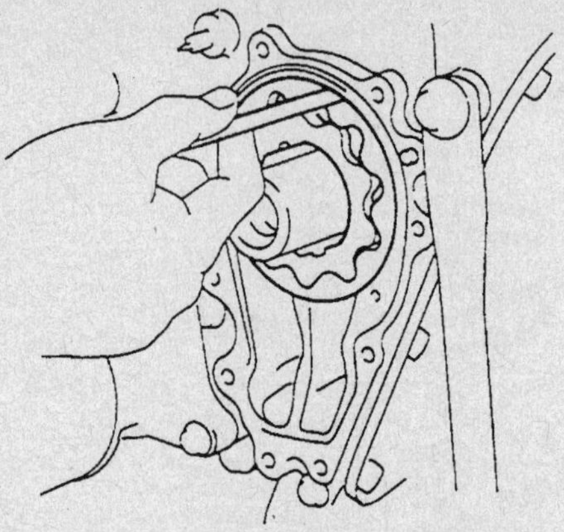
TY1099100020000X

Fig. 22 Oil pump body clearance inspection

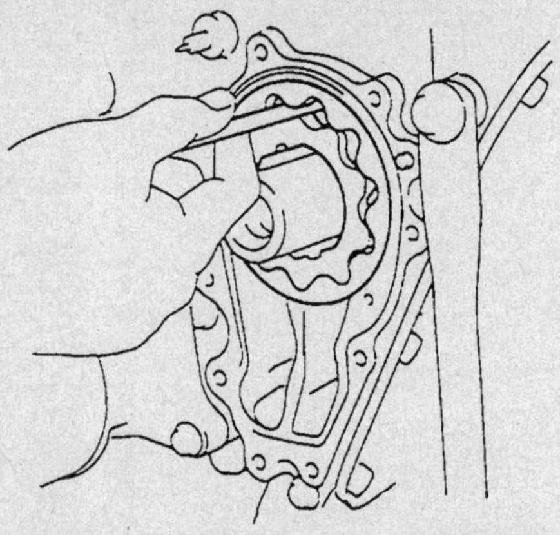
TY1099100021000X

Fig. 23 Oil pump tip clearance inspection

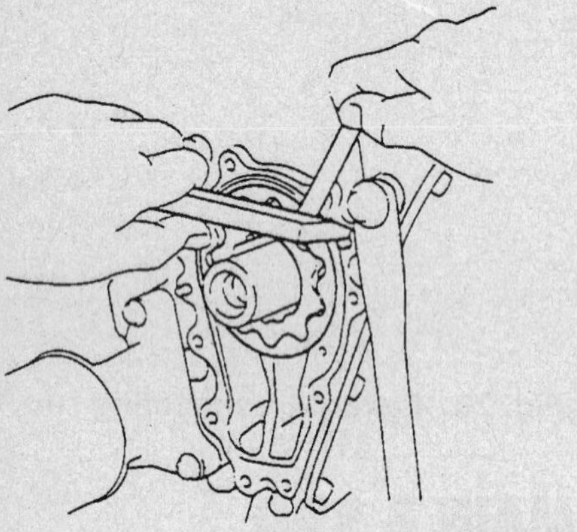
TY1099100022000X

Fig. 24 Oil pump side clearance inspection

TY1069100184000X

Fig. 25 Separated accessory drive system. 2TZ-FE

clearance is not as indicated, replace oil pump rotor set.

3. Using suitable thickness gauge and flat block, measure side clearance, **Fig. 24.** Maximum clearance is .0059 inch, if clearance is not as indicated, replace pump rotor set and/or pump body.

BELT TENSION DATA

Year	Belt	New, lbs.	Used, lbs.
1993	A/C	120–160	100–140
	Alternator	160–180	115–135
	Power Steering	160–180	115–135
1994–96	A/C	139–191	66–110
	Alternator	160–180	115–135
	Power Steering	160–180	115–135
	Super-charger	160–180	115–135

SEPARATED ACCESSORY DRIVE SYSTEM

DESCRIPTION

The cooling fan, alternator, power steering pump and A/C compressor are remotely driven from the engine's crankshaft through a common driveshaft, **Figs. 25 and 26.**

This driveshaft is equipped with a flexible coupling at both ends that compensates for speed variations. The driveshaft and coupling are non-serviceable and should be replaced as a unit.

SERVICE PRECAUTIONS

1. Do not allow rear of driveshaft to hang disconnected. Suspend with suitable sling at horizontal position.
2. Store driveshaft so front coupling is horizontal with shaft, **Fig. 27.**
3. When installing driveshaft, ensure flexible coupling is not malformed, if so, disconnect shaft and install again, **Fig. 28.**
4. When removing driveshaft, do not remove No. 1 and No. 2 equipment drive housing stays unless necessary. If removal is necessary, mark position of stays and install as marked, **Fig. 29.**
5. During installation of driveshaft, using appropriate measuring devices, measure installation angle of driveshaft in front of and behind front flexible coupling, **Fig. 30.** If difference in angle between each section is 2° or more, adjust installation angle by adjusting position of No. 1, No. 2 and/or No. 3 equipment drive housing stays.
6. After service, ensure ground straps between equipment drive housing and body and between alternator and battery ground terminal are connected.

ACCESSORY DRIVESHAFT, REPLACE

Removal

1. Disconnect battery ground cable.
2. Remove fluid coupling with cooling fan as follows:
   a. Remove A/C air intake duct.
   b. Remove fan shroud.

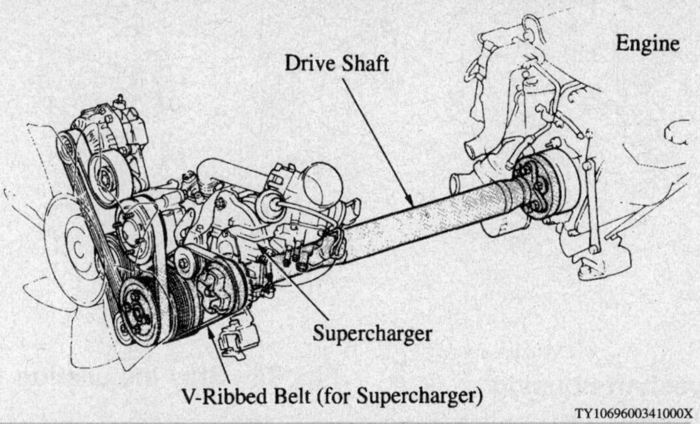
Drive Shaft
Engine
Supercharger
V-Ribbed Belt (for Supercharger)
TY1069600341000X

Fig. 26 Separated accessory drive system. 2TZ-FZE

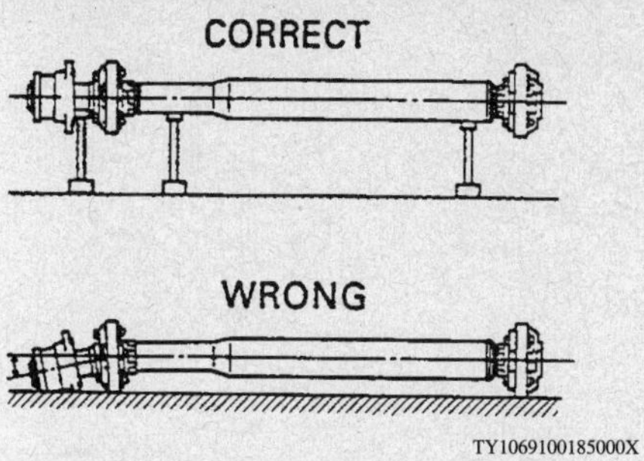
CORRECT
WRONG
TY1069100185000X

Fig. 27 Driveshaft storage

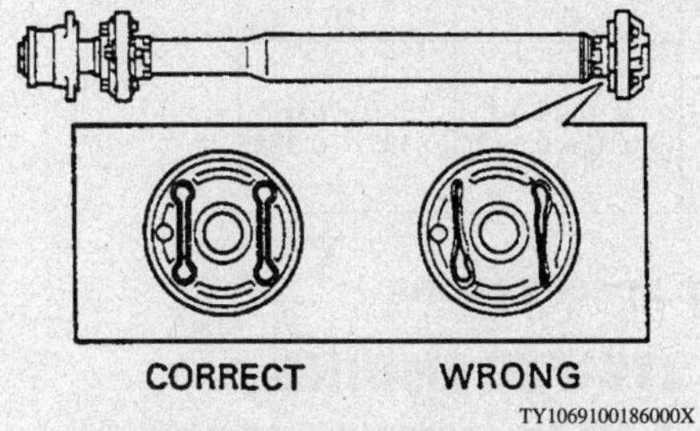
CORRECT
WRONG
TY1069100186000X

Fig. 28 Driveshaft coupling

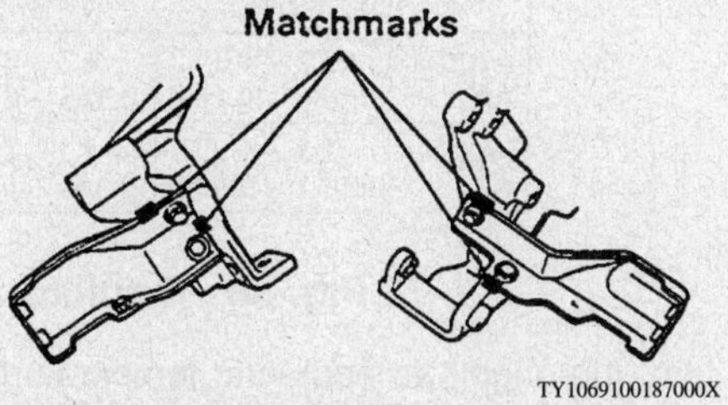
Matchmarks
TY1069100187000X

Fig. 29 Stay matchmarks

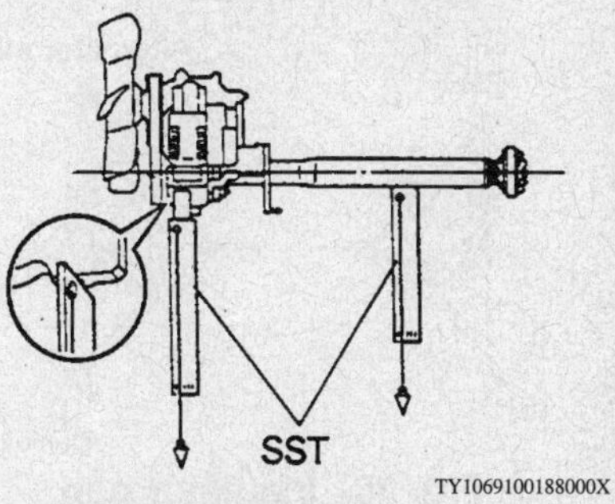
SST
TY1069100188000X

Fig. 30 Driveshaft angle

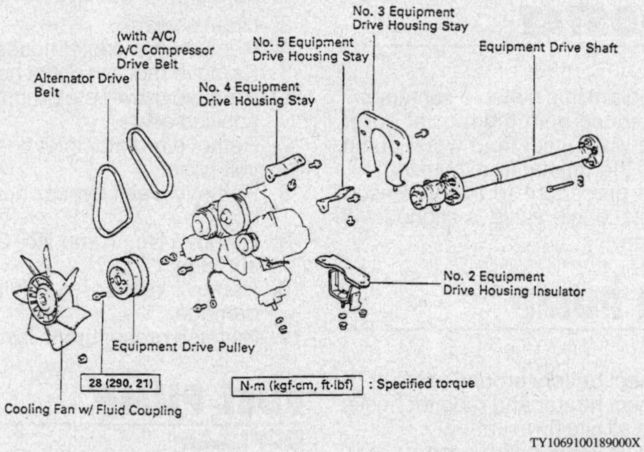
No. 3 Equipment
Drive Housing Stay
(with A/C)
A/C Compressor
Drive Belt
No. 5 Equipment
Drive Housing Stay
Equipment Drive Shaft
Alternator Drive
Belt
No. 4 Equipment
Drive Housing Stay
No. 2 Equipment
Drive Housing Insulator
Equipment Drive Pulley
28 (290, 21)
N·m (kgf·cm, ft·lbf) : Specified torque
Cooling Fan w/ Fluid Coupling
TY1069100189000X

Fig. 31 Exploded view of driveshaft assembly

c. Hold belt down, then loosen nuts of coupling.
d. Remove fluid coupling with cooling fan.

3. Loosen alternator and A/C belt adjusting bolts, then push alternator and A/C compressor as far as possible and remove belts.
4. Remove equipment drive pulley.
5. Remove No. 2 equipment drive housing insulator and No. 3 equipment drive housing stay, **Fig. 31.**
6. Remove No. 4 and No. 5 equipment drive housing stays.
7. Scribe matchmarks on rear flexible coupling flange and crankshaft pulley.
8. Install service bolt and nut to front end of equipment driveshaft, **Fig. 32.**
9. Rotate driveshaft by turning service nut, then remove three A bolts and washers. **Do not remove B bolts.**
10. Remove driveshaft and equipment drive housing retaining bolts, **Fig. 33.**
11. Disconnect equipment drive housing ground strap from body.
12. Remove nuts and washers from No. 1 equipment drive housing insulator and body bracket.
13. Lift up equipment drive housing, then rotate driveshaft approximately 60° clockwise and remove from rear end of driveshaft housing.
14. Lower equipment drive housing, then set in body bracket.

Inspection

1. Check front and rear flexible coupling for cracks and damage.
2. Rotate flange of shaft, ensuring it rotates smoothly without binding or creaking.
3. Using suitable gauge and support, check shaft for runout. Runout should not exceed 0.031 inch.
4. Inspect fluid coupling for leaks.
5. If any of the above criteria is not met, replace the driveshaft.

Installation

1. Lift up equipment drive housing, then insert driveshaft through hole at rear of housing.
2. Align match marks of coupling and pulley, then lower drive housing.
3. Install three front bolts, **torque** to 38 ft. lbs.
4. Install the remaining bolts and **torque** to 25 ft. lbs.
5. Remove the service bolt and nut installed on front end of driveshaft.
6. Secure No. 1 driveshaft housing insulator, then install and **torque** nut to 24 ft. lbs.
7. Install No. 4 and No. 5 driveshaft housing stays.
8. Install the lower bolt, then the upper bolt. **Torque** to 13 ft. lbs.
9. Install No. 2 driveshaft housing insulator.
10. Install No. 3 driveshaft housing stay.
11. Install inboard bolt, then the outboard bolt. **Torque** bolts to 18 ft. lbs.
12. Install No. 1 and No. 2 driveshaft housing stay to No. 3 driveshaft housing stay, then **torque** nuts in several passes to 13 ft. lbs., **Fig. 34.**
13. Install washer and nut of body bracket for No. 2 driveshaft housing insulator. **Torque** to 18 ft. lbs.
14. Check installation angle of driveshaft as follows:
    a. Using appropriate measuring devices, measure installation angle of driveshaft in front of and behind front flexible coupling, **Fig. 30.**
    b. If difference in angle between each section is 2° or more, adjust installation angle by adjusting position of No. 1, No. 2 or No. 3 equipment drive housing stays.

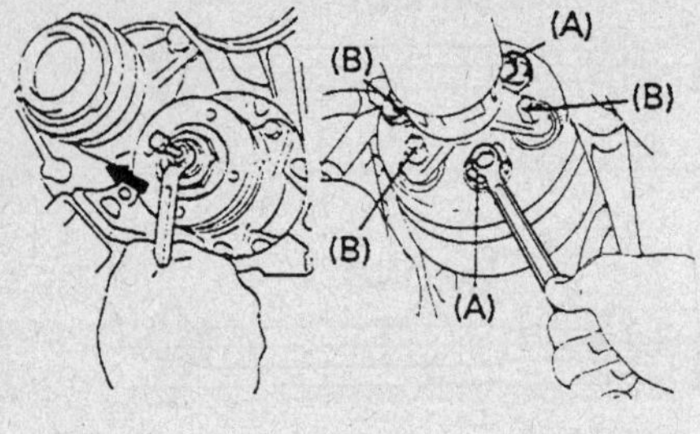
(A)
(B)
(B)
(B)
(A)

TY1069100190000X

Fig. 32 Driveshaft removal

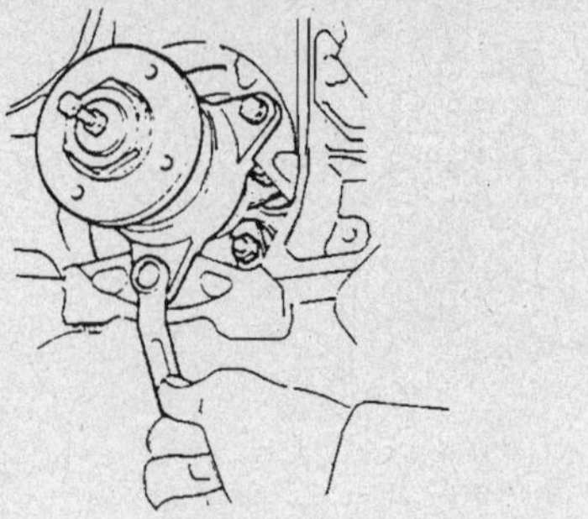

TY1069100191000X

Fig. 33 Driveshaft housing removal

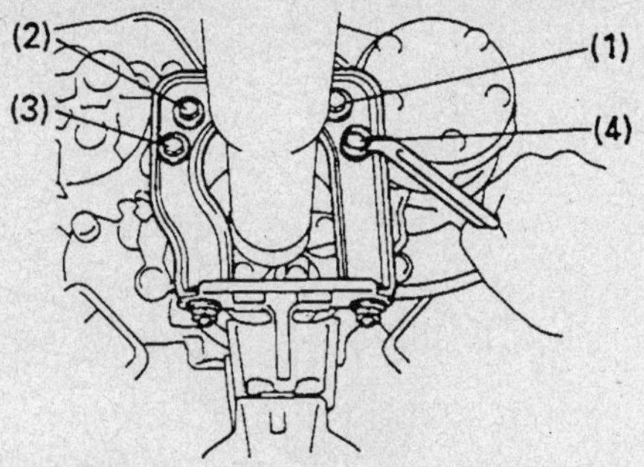
(2)
(1)
(3)
(4)

TY1069100192000X

Fig. 34 Stay Installation

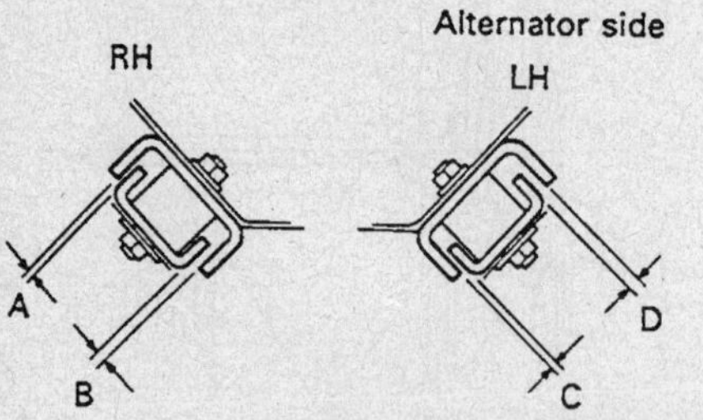
Alternator side
RH
LH
A
D
B
C

TY1069100193000X

Fig. 35 Insulator gap

mm (in.)

	A	B	C	D
with A/C	0.7 – 4.3 (0.028 – 0.169)	4.7 – 8.3 (0.185 – 0.327)	0.4 – 4.0 (0.016 – 0.157)	5.0 – 8.6 (0.197 – 0.339)
without A/C	1.3 – 4.9 (0.051 – 0.193)	4.1 – 7.7 (0.161 – 0.303)		

TY1069100194000X

Fig. 36 Insulator gap specifications

15. Ensure alignment of insulators are correct and gaps are as specified, **Figs. 35 and 36.** Adjust if necessary.
16. Install equipment drive pulley. **Torque** bolts to 21 ft. lbs.
17. Install belts, then the fluid coupling. **Torque** bolts to 10 ft. lbs.
18. Install fan shroud, then A/C air intake duct.
19. Connect battery ground cable.
20. Inspect belt tension.

ACCESSORY DRIVESHAFT HOUSING, REPLACE

1. Disconnect battery ground cable.
2. Remove fluid coupling with cooling fan.
3. Remove alternator, A/C compressor and power steering pump with hose.
4. Remove equipment drive pulley.
5. Remove No. 2 equipment driveshaft housing insulator and No. 3 driveshaft housing.
6. Remove No. 4 and No. 5 driveshaft housing stays.
7. Remove driveshaft as outlined under "Accessory Driveshaft Removal."
8. Mark driveshaft housing for installation reference, then remove No. 1 and No. 2 housing stays, **Fig. 37.**
9. Reverse procedure to install, noting the following:
   a. Align marks made during removal.
   b. Ensure lower surface of equipment drive housing and No. 3 stay are flat and aligned.
   c. **Torque** No. 1 and No. 2 housing stay bolts to 13 ft. lbs.
   d. **Torque** insulators to 18 ft. lbs.

COOLING SYSTEM BLEED

This engine does not require a special bleed procedure. After filling cooling system, run engine to operating temperature with radiator/pressure cap off. Air will then automatically bleed through cap opening.

THERMOSTAT

REPLACE

1. Drain coolant into suitable container.
2. Remove hose from thermostat outlet.
3. Remove water inlet from water pump.
4. Remove thermostat from housing.
5. Reverse procedure to install. Ensure thermostat jiggle valve is aligned with protrusion.

WATER PUMP

REPLACE

1. Disconnect battery ground cable.
2. Disconnect heater and radiator hoses.
3. Remove oil filter bracket.
4. Disconnect water pump hose.
5. Remove water pump attaching bolts, then the water pump, **Fig. 38.**
6. Reverse procedure to install. Refer to **Fig. 39, torque** A bolts to 15 ft. lbs. and B bolts to 21 ft. lbs.

RADIATOR

REPLACE

2TZ-FE ENGINE

1. Remove battery ground cable.
2. Remove air duct and No. 1 engine undercover.
3. Drain coolant.
4. Remove A/C cooler hoses.
5. Remove radiator inlet and outlet hoses.
6. Remove reservoir hose.
7. Remove No. 1 and No. 2 radiator fan shrouds.
8. Remove radiator carefully to prevent damage.
9. Reverse procedure to install.

2TZ-FZE ENGINE

1. Remove battery ground cable.
2. Remove air duct and No. 1 engine undercover.
3. Drain coolant.
4. Remove A/C cooler hoses.
5. Remove radiator outlet hose.
6. Remove power steering reservoir and position aside.
7. Remove radiator inlet hose and reservoir hose.
8. Remove water bypass hose for throttle body.
9. Remove No. 1 and No. 2 radiator fan shrouds.
10. Remove radiator carefully to prevent damage.
11. Reverse procedure to install.

FUEL PUMP

REPLACE

1. Disconnect battery ground cable and relieve fuel system pressure as described under "Precautions."
2. Drain fuel from tank, then remove tank.
3. Remove fuel pump bracket.
4. Disconnect fuel pump electrical connector.
5. Remove fuel pump attaching bolts, then the fuel pump.
6. Separate fuel filter from fuel pump.
7. Reverse procedure to install. Tighten to specification.

FUEL FILTER

REPLACE

1. Disconnect battery ground cable and relieve fuel system pressure as described under "Precautions."
2. Place suitable container under fuel filter/hose connection.
3. Slowly loosen fuel hose to fuel filter. **Place shop towel over connection to avoid fuel spillage on engine.**

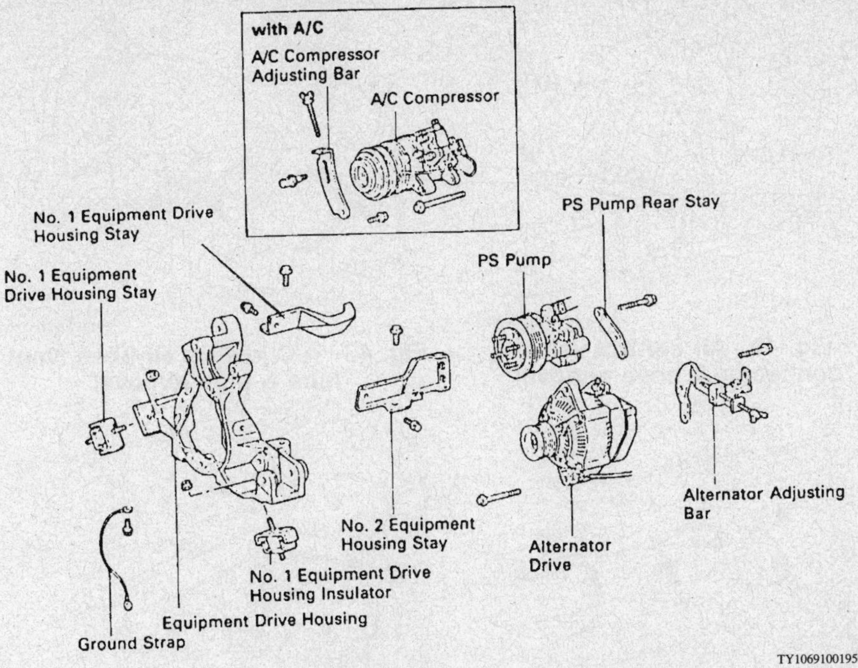
with A/C
A/C Compressor Adjusting Bar
A/C Compressor
No. 1 Equipment Drive Housing Stay
No. 1 Equipment Drive Housing Stay
PS Pump Rear Stay
PS Pump
Alternator Adjusting Bar
No. 2 Equipment Housing Stay
Alternator Drive
No. 1 Equipment Drive Housing Insulator
Equipment Drive Housing
Ground Strap

Fig. 37 Driveshaft housing components

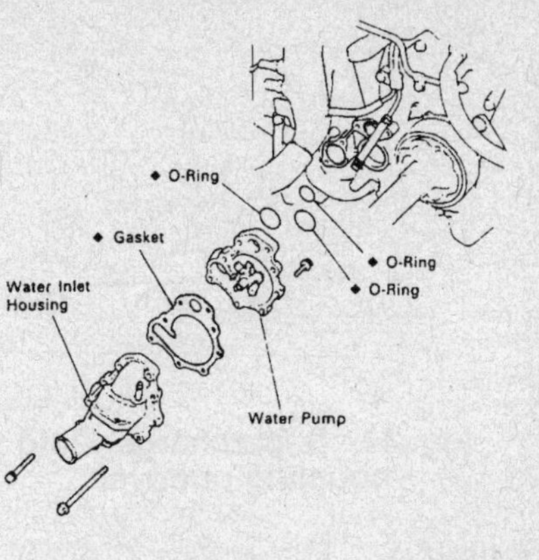
◆ O-Ring
◆ Gasket
◆ O-Ring
◆ O-Ring
Water Inlet Housing
Water Pump

TY1089100017000X

Fig. 38 Exploded view of water pump

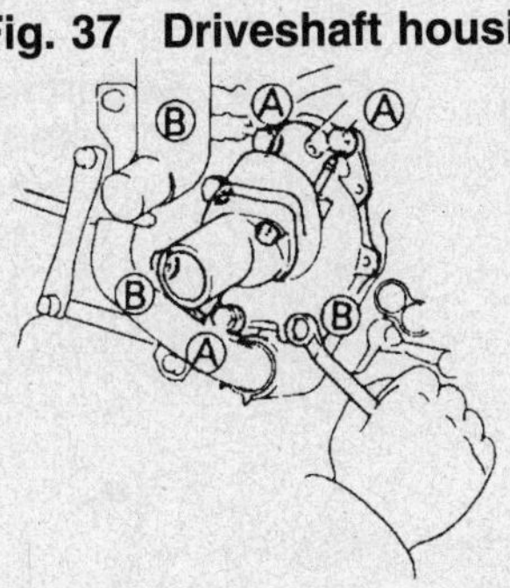
B
A
A
B
A
B

TY1089100018000X

Fig. 39 Water pump installation

TY1069100195000X

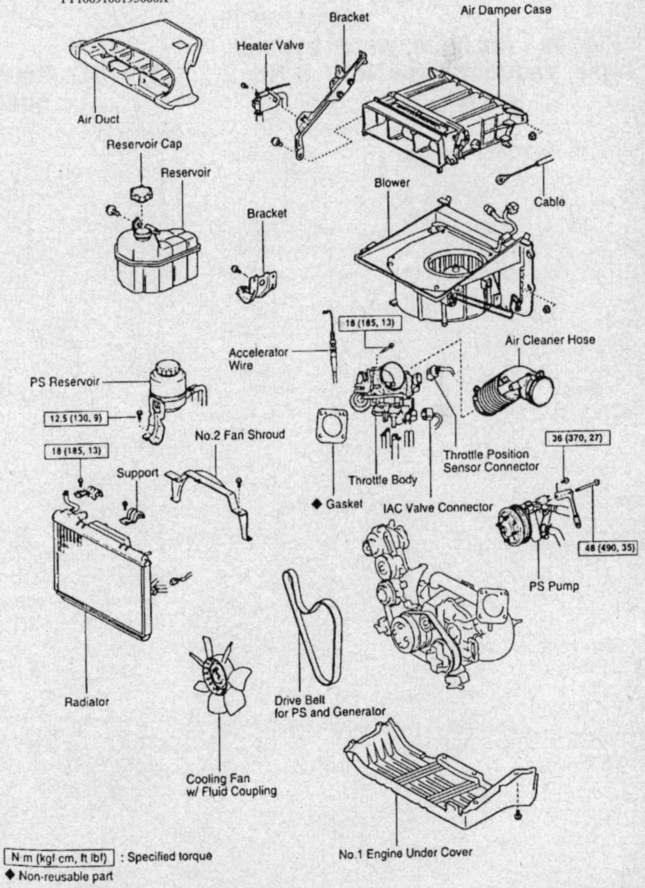
Bracket
Air Damper Case
Heater Valve
Air Duct
Reservoir Cap
Reservoir
Blower
Cable
Bracket
18 (185, 13)
Air Cleaner Hose
Accelerator Wire
PS Reservoir
12.5 (130, 9)
No.2 Fan Shroud
18 (185, 13)
Throttle Position Sensor Connector
36 (370, 27)
Support
Throttle Body
◆ Gasket
IAC Valve Connector
48 (490, 35)
PS Pump
Radiator
Drive Belt for PS and Generator
Cooling Fan w/ Fluid Coupling
N·m (kgf·cm, ft·lbf) : Specified torque
◆ Non-reusable part
No.1 Engine Under Cover

TY1059100003000X

Fig. 40 Supercharger air duct & blower components

4. Remove fuel filter, then plug hose connection.
5. Replace gasket.
6. Reverse procedure to install.

SUPERCHARGER

REPLACE

1. Disconnect battery ground cable and relieve fuel pressure as outlined under "Precautions."
2. Drain engine coolant.
3. Remove air duct, engine coolant reservoir and bracket, **Fig. 40.**
4. Remove air damper case and blower.
5. Disconnect power steering reservoir.
6. Remove radiator and fan shroud.
7. Remove fluid coupling and fan, **Fig. 41.**
8. Disconnect air control valve (ACV) connector and the three ACV hoses **Fig. 42.**
9. Remove No. 1 engine undercover, then disconnect transmission oil cooler hoses.
10. Disconnect radiator outlet, inlet and bypass hoses, then remove the radiator.
11. Disconnect accelerator cable, A/C idle-up air hose, vent tube and vent pipe, then remove air cleaner hose **Fig. 43.**
12. Disconnect throttle position sensor and IAC valve electrical connectors.
13. Disconnect the hoses indicated in **Fig. 44,** then remove throttle body.
14. Disconnect two power steering idle-up hoses, clamp and remove power steering pump with power steering hoses attached, **Fig. 45.**
15. Loosen No. 2 idler pulley nut and adjusting bolt, then remove supercharger drive belt, **Fig. 46.**
16. Remove No. 2 idler pulley, **Fig. 47.**

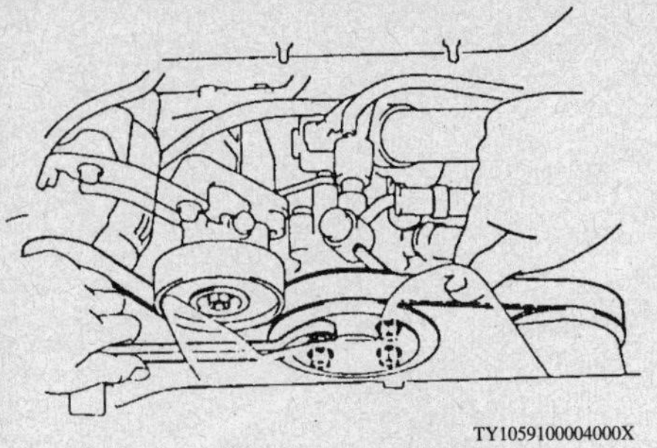
TY1059100004000X

Fig. 41 Supercharger fluid coupling removal

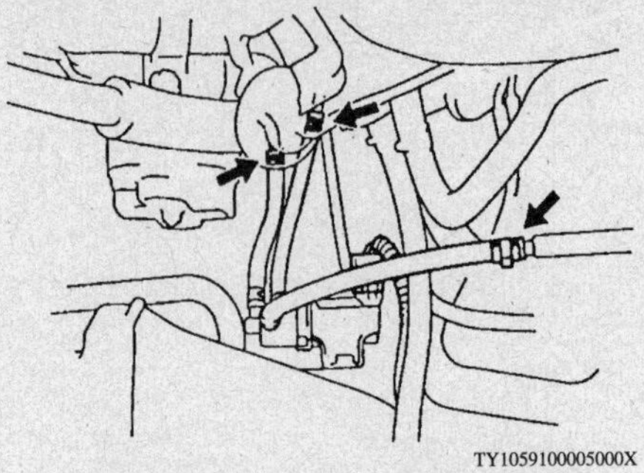
TY1059100005000X

Fig. 42 Air control valve connector & hose removal

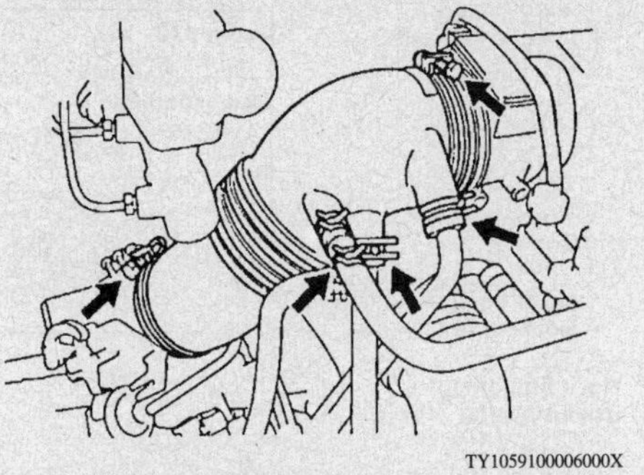
TY1059100006000X

Fig. 43 A/C idle-up air hose, vent tube & pipe removal

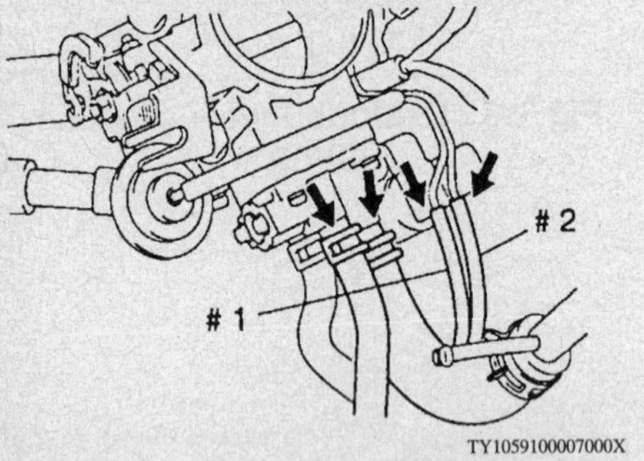
2
1
TY1059100007000X

Fig. 44 Air hose, water bypass hose, vacuum hose No. 1 & No. 2 removal

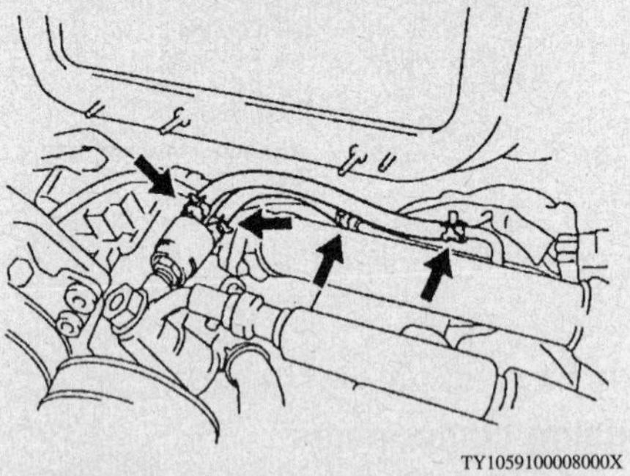
TY1059100008000X

Fig. 45 Power steering idle-up hose removal

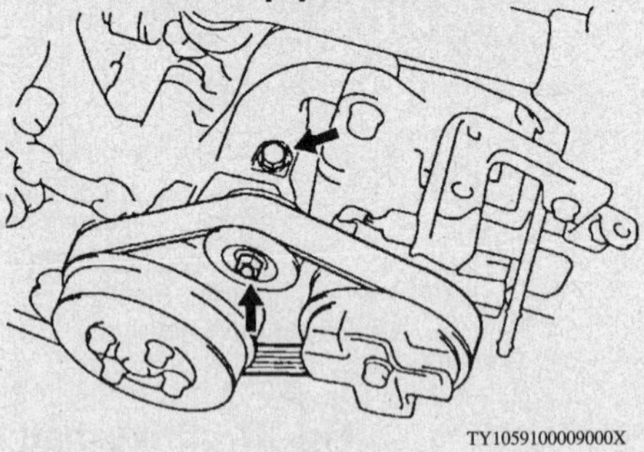
TY1059100009000X

Fig. 46 Supercharger drive belt removal

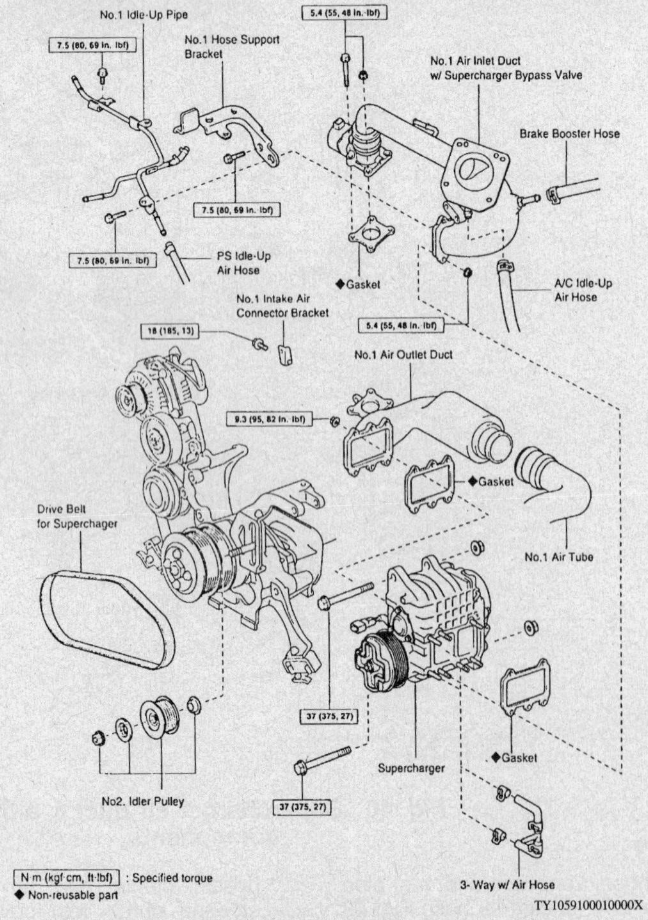
No.1 Idle-Up Pipe
7.5 (80, 69 in. lbf)
No.1 Hose Support Bracket
5.4 (55, 48 in. lbf)
No.1 Air Inlet Duct w/ Supercharger Bypass Valve
Brake Booster Hose
7.5 (80, 69 in. lbf)
7.5 (80, 69 in. lbf)
PS Idle-Up Air Hose
◆Gasket
A/C Idle-Up Air Hose
No.1 Intake Air Connector Bracket
18 (185, 13)
5.4 (55, 48 in. lbf)
No.1 Air Outlet Duct
9.3 (95, 82 in. lbf)
◆Gasket
Drive Belt for Superchager
No.1 Air Tube
37 (375, 27)
◆Gasket
Supercharger
No2. Idler Pulley
37 (375, 27)
N·m (kgf·cm, ft·lbf) : Specified torque
◆ Non-reusable part
3- Way w/ Air Hose
TY1059100010000X

Fig. 47 Supercharger No. 2 idler pulley components

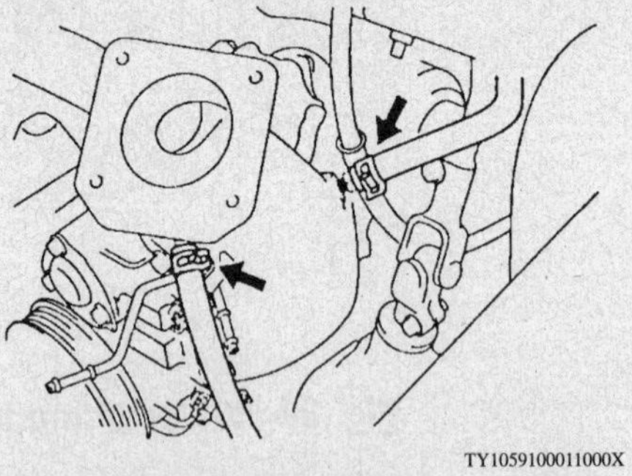
TY1059100011000X

Fig. 48 Brake booster hose, A/C idle-up air hose & magnetic clutch connector

17. Disconnect supercharger bypass valve electrical connector.
18. Disconnect brake booster hose and A/C idle-up air hose, then disconnect supercharger magnetic clutch electrical connector from supercharger and No. 1 hose support bracket, **Fig. 48.**
19. Remove lower hoses and three-way connector, **Fig. 49.**
20. Remove supercharger bypass valve from No. 1 air outlet duct, **Fig. 47.**
21. Remove No. 1 air inlet duct and gaskets with supercharger bypass valve, **Fig. 50.**
22. Remove No. 1 idle-up pipe from equipment drive housing, then disconnect the No. 1 air tube from No. 1 air outlet duct.
23. Remove No. 1 intake air connector bracket, **Fig. 47.**
24. Remove supercharger retaining bolts, **Figs. 51 and 52,** then the supercharger and No. 1 air outlet duct.
25. Reverse procedure to install.

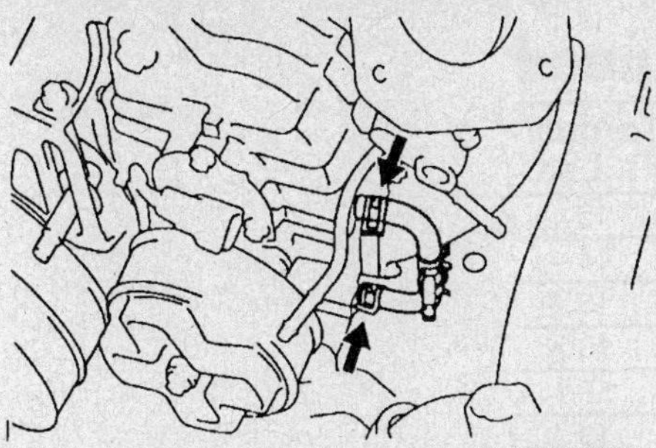
TY1059100012000X

Fig. 49 Air control hoses & three-way connector

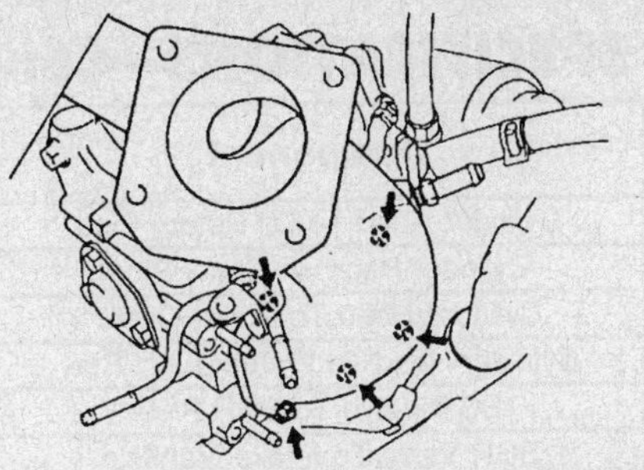
TY1059100013000X

Fig. 50 Supercharger bypass valve

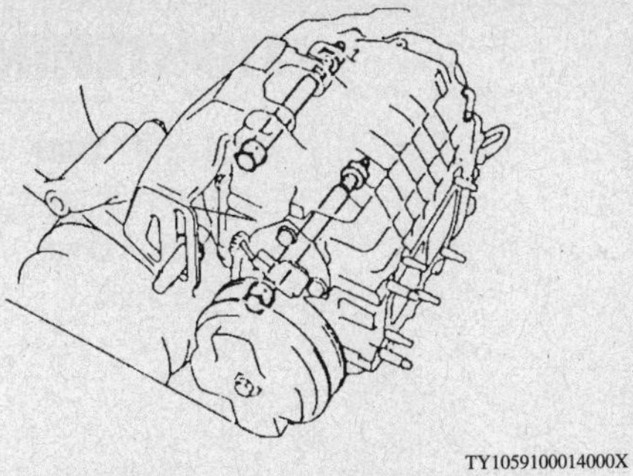
TY1059100014000X

Fig. 51 Supercharger to equipment drive housing removal

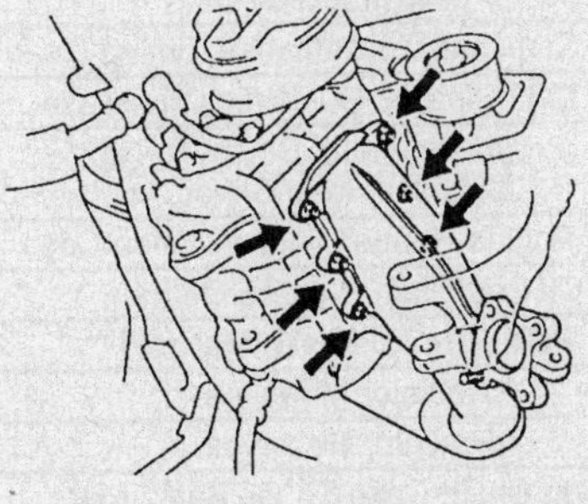
TY1059100015000X

Fig. 52 Supercharger to No. 1 air outlet duct removal

TIGHTENING SPECIFICATIONS

Year	Component	Torque/ Ft. Lbs.
1993–96	Connecting Rod To Connecting Rod Cap	②
	Crankshaft Pulley To Crankshaft	192
	Crankshaft To Driveplate (A/T)	54
	Crankshaft To Flywheel (M/T)	65
	Cylinder Block To Coolant Drain Cock	18
	Cylinder Block To Crankcase	9
	Cylinder Block To Crankshaft Bearing Cap	②
	Cylinder Block To Cylinder Head	②
	Cylinder Block To Damper	13
	Cylinder Block To Engine Mounting Bracket	30
	Cylinder Block To Idle Sprocket	14
	Cylinder Block To No. 2 Engine Hanger	27
	Cylinder Block To Oil Dipstick Guide	13
	Cylinder Block To Oil Nozzle	13
	Cylinder Block To Oil Pan	48①
	Cylinder Block To Oil Strainer	13
	Cylinder Block To Rear Oil Seal Retainer	10
	Cylinder Block To Slipper	20
	Cylinder Head To Camshaft Bearing Cap	12
	Cylinder Head To Chain Tensioner	15
	Cylinder Head To Distributor	14
	Cylinder Head To EGR Pipe	13
	Cylinder Head To Exhaust Manifold	36
	Cylinder Head To Exhaust Manifold Heat Insulator	13
	Cylinder Head To Intake Manifold	15
	Cylinder Head To No. 1 Cylinder Head Cover	6

Continued

TIGHTENING SPECIFICATIONS—Continued

Year	Component	Torque/ Ft. Lbs.
1993–96 Cont.	Cylinder Head To Oil Return Pipe	15
	Cylinder Head To Spark Plug	14
	Cylinder Head To Water Outlet	15
	Cylinder Head To Water Outlet Stay	13
	EGR Valve To EGR Pipe	58
	EGR Valve To Intake Manifold	13
	Engine Mounting To Mounting Insulator	33
	Fuel Pump Bolt	48①
	Fuel Pump Screws	26①
	No. 1 Camshaft To Camshaft Timing Gear	54
	No. 1 Oil Dipstick Guide To Crankcase	22
	No. 2 Cylinder Head Cover To No. 1 Cylinder Head Cover	48①
	No. 2 Engine Hanger To Ventilation Case	6
	Oil Pan Drain Plug To Oil Pan	③
	PCV Pipe To Intake Manifold	43①
	Radiator Mounting	13
	Radiator Reservoir	9
	Timing Chain Case To Oil Baffle Plate	43①
	Timing Chain Case To Oil Filter Bracket	14
	Timing Chain Case To Water Outlet	14
	Ventilation Case To Crankcase	6
	Water Outlet To No. 2 Water By-Pass Pipe	43①
	Water Outlet To Union Bolt	9
	Water Outlet To Water Outlet Stay	15
	Water Pump to Timing Chain Case	④

①— Inch lbs.
②— Refer to "Cylinder Head, Replace."
③— On 1993 models, 18 ft. lbs.; on 1994–96 models, 27 ft. lbs.
④— Refer to "Water Pump, Replace."

Clutch & Manual Transmission

NOTE: On Air Bag Equipped Models, Refer To "Air Bag System Precautions" Located In The Front Of This Manual For System Disarming & Arming Procedures.

INDEX

Page No.
Adjustments 45-18
Clutch Pedal Height............. 45-18
Clutch, Replace 45-19
Hydraulic System Service 45-19
Clutch System Bleed........... 45-19
Slave Cylinder, Replace......... 45-19
Precautions...................... 45-18
Air Bag Systems................ 45-18
Tightening Specifications 45-19
Transmission, Replace 45-19

PRECAUTIONS

AIR BAG SYSTEMS

Refer to "Air Bag System Precautions" in the front of this manual for system disarming and arming procedures.

ADJUSTMENTS

CLUTCH PEDAL HEIGHT

1. Measure clutch pedal height as shown, **Fig. 1.**
2. Clutch pedal height should be 6.46 inches.
3. If clutch pedal height is not as specified, loosen clutch pedal locknut, then rotate stopper bolt until specified height is achieved.

4. Tighten locknut.
5. Measure pushrod play at top of pedal. If pushrod play is not .04–.20 inch, loosen locknut and rotate pushrod until freeplay is as specified. Tighten locknut.
6. Check clutch pedal freeplay by depressing clutch pedal until resistance is felt. Freeplay should be .20–.59 inch.
7. If necessary to adjust freeplay, loosen locknut and rotate pushrod until freeplay is as specified.
8. Tighten locknut.
9. Ensure clutch pedal height and freeplay are as specified.

HYDRAULIC SYSTEM SERVICE

SLAVE CYLINDER, REPLACE

1. Disconnect battery ground cable and drain clutch fluid.
2. Use line removal tool No. 09023-00100, or equivalent, to disconnect clutch line tube.
3. Remove slave cylinder bleeder screw.
4. Remove slave cylinder attaching bolts, then the slave cylinder.
5. Reverse procedure to install and bleed clutch system.

CLUTCH SYSTEM BLEED

If any service is performed on the clutch system or air is suspected in the clutch lines, bleed the system.

1. Fill clutch reservoir with suitable brake fluid. **Do not allow fluid to come in contact with painted surfaces.**
2. Check reservoir frequently, add fluid as required.
3. Connect vinyl tube to bleeder plug, then insert other tube end in half full container of brake fluid.
4. Slowly pump clutch pedal several times.

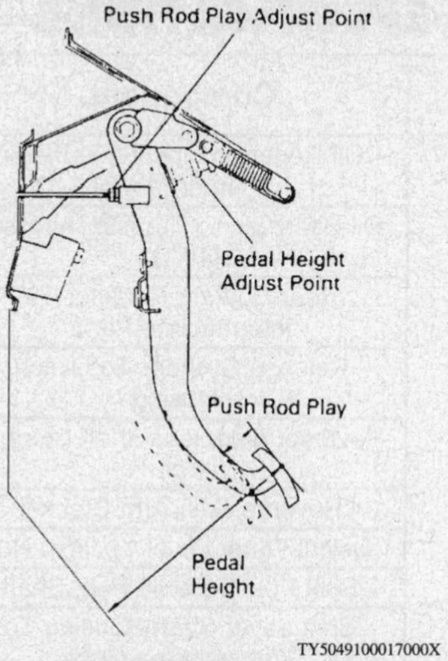
Push Rod Play Adjust Point
Pedal Height Adjust Point
Push Rod Play
Pedal Height
TY5049100017000X

Fig. 1 Clutch pedal height adjustment

5. While depressing pedal, loosen bleeder plug until fluid runs out, then close bleeder plug.
6. Repeat procedure until air bubbles are evident in the fluid. **Do not reuse the fluid that was bled.**

CLUTCH

REPLACE

1. Remove transmission assembly as outlined in "Transmission, Replace."
2. Place installation alignment on clutch cover and flywheel.
3. Loosen each set bolt one turn at a time until spring tension is released.
4. Remove clutch cover attaching bolts, then the cover and disc.
5. Remove release bearing, fork and boot.
6. Using suitable calipers, measure clutch disc rivet head depth. Minimum rivet depth should be .012 inch. If not as indicated, replace clutch disc.
7. Using suitable dial indicator, measure flywheel runout. Maximum runout should be .004 inch. If not as indicated, replace flywheel.
8. Measure clutch disc runout. Maximum runout is .031 inch. If runout is more than specified, replace disc.
9. Using suitable caliper, measure diaphragm spring depth and width. Depth should be .024 inch and width should be .197 inch. If measurement is not as indicated, replace clutch cover.
10. Reverse procedure to install, noting the following:
    a. Using alignment tool No. 09301-20020, or equivalent, install clutch disc.
    b. Match clutch cover and flywheel alignment marks, then tighten cover bolts to specifications one turn at a time in a criss-cross pattern, ensuring clutch disc and pressure plate remain aligned.

TRANSMISSION

REPLACE

1. Raise and support vehicle, then drain transmission fluid.
2. Disconnect propeller shaft.
3. Remove clutch release cylinder hose bracket, then the cylinder.
4. Remove exhaust pipe bracket.
5. Disconnect control cables.
6. Remove control cable bracket.
7. Disconnect speed sensor electrical connector.
8. Remove stiffener plate, then using suitable transmission jack stand, raise transmission.
9. Remove rear engine mount.
10. Using suitable jack, raise rear side of engine.
11. Remove transmission attaching bolts, then the transmission.
12. Reverse procedure to install.

TIGHTENING SPECIFICATIONS

Year	Component	Torque/Ft. Lbs.
1993	Accumulator Bracket To Accumulator Housing	48①
	Accumulator Bracket To Frame	9
	Back-Up Lamp Switch	27
	Bleeder Plug	8
	Clutch Cover To Flywheel	14
	Clutch Housing To Transmission Case	27
	Clutch Line Union	11
	Extension Housing To Transmission Case (2WD)	27
	Flywheel To Crankshaft	65
	Front Bearing Retainer To Transmission Case	12
	Master Cylinder To Mount Bracket	9

Continued

TIGHTENING SPECIFICATIONS—Continued

Year	Component	Torque/Ft. Lbs.
1993	Oil Receiver Pipe To Transfer Adaptor (4WD)	13
	Oil Receiver To Transfer Adaptor (4WD)	9
	Rear Bearing Retainer To Intermediate Plate	13
	Release Cylinder To Clutch Housing	9
	Reverse Idler Gear Shaft Stopper Bolt	13
	Reverse Shift Arm Bracket	13
	Select Outer Lever Lockpin Nut	6
	Shift Fork To Shift Fork Shaft	14
	Shift Lever Shaft Housing To Transmission Case	12
	Shift Outer Lever Lockpin Nut	9
	Speedometer Driver Gear Lock Plate	8
	Straight Screw Plug	14
	Transfer Adapter To Transmission Case (4WD)	27

① — Inch lbs.

Rear Axle & Suspension

INDEX

	Page No.
Axle Shaft Bearing & Oil Seal, Replace	45-20
Installation	45-20
Removal	45-20
Coil Spring, Replace	45-21
Control Arm, Replace	45-21
Lateral Rod, Replace	45-21
Rear Axle Shaft, Replace	45-20
Shock Absorber, Replace	45-21
Tightening Specifications	45-21

REAR AXLE SHAFT

REPLACE

1. Raise and support vehicle, then remove rear wheels.
2. **On models with ABS,** remove speed sensor, **Fig. 1.**
3. **On models with drum brakes,** using brake tube removal tool No. 09751-36011, or equivalent, disconnect brake tube, then remove brake drum, brake shoes and parking brake cable.
4. **On models with disc brakes,** using brake tube removal tool No. 09751-36011, or equivalent, disconnect brake tube, then remove clip, brake hose, cylinder, rotor, parking brake shoes and parking brake cable.
5. **On all models,** remove brake backing plate attaching nuts.
6. Using slide hammer and adapter tool No. 09520-00031, or equivalent, pull out rear axle shaft, then remove backing plate and end gasket.
7. Reverse procedure to install.

AXLE SHAFT BEARING & OIL SEAL

REPLACE

REMOVAL

1. Remove axle shaft as outlined under "Rear Axle Shaft, Replace."
2. **On models with ABS,** using press and bearing holder tool No. 09950-00020, or equivalent, remove oil seal, then using same tool remove speed sensor rotor.
3. **On all models,** grind inner retainer, then using suitable hammer and chisel, cut retainer and remove from shaft.
4. Using bearing housing holder tool No. 09527-30010, or equivalent and suitable press, remove bearing and bearing outer retainer.
5. Using seal removal tool No. 09308-00010, or equivalent, remove oil seal.

INSTALLATION

1. Coat contact surfaces of oil seal with grease, then install oil seal using seal installer tool No. 09517-30010, or equivalent and hammer. Oil seal drive depth for drum brake models is .236 inch and for disc brake models .138 inch.
2. **On models with disc brakes,** assemble bearing outer gasket, retainer and backing plate.
3. **On models with drum brakes,** install bearing outer retainer.
4. **On models with disc brakes,** install backing plate assembly, then using tool No. 09506-30012, or equivalent, and a suitable press, install new bearing.
5. **On all models,** heat inner bearing retainer to about 302°F (150°C) in oil bath, then press inner bearing retainer onto axle shaft with chamfered side facing toward bearing using tool No. 09506-30012, or equivalent.
6. **On models with ABS,** using press and adapter tool No. 09506-30012, or equivalent, and a suitable press, install speed sensor rotor and oil seal.
7. **On all models,** install axle shaft.

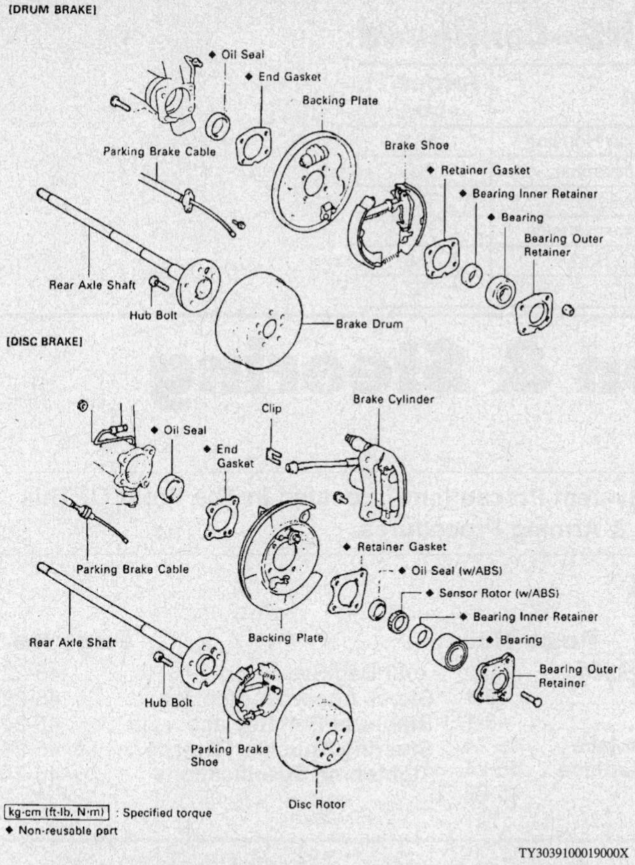
[DRUM BRAKE]
◆ Oil Seal
◆ End Gasket
Backing Plate
Parking Brake Cable
Brake Shoe
◆ Retainer Gasket
◆ Bearing Inner Retainer
◆ Bearing
Bearing Outer Retainer
Rear Axle Shaft
Hub Bolt
Brake Drum
[DISC BRAKE]
Clip
Brake Cylinder
◆ Oil Seal
◆ End Gasket
Parking Brake Cable
◆ Retainer Gasket
◆ Oil Seal (w/ABS)
◆ Sensor Rotor (w/ABS)
◆ Bearing Inner Retainer
◆ Bearing
Rear Axle Shaft
Backing Plate
Bearing Outer Retainer
Hub Bolt
Parking Brake Shoe
Disc Rotor
kg-cm (ft-lb, N·m) : Specified torque
◆ Non-reusable part
TY3039100019000X

Fig. 1 Exploded view of rear axle shaft

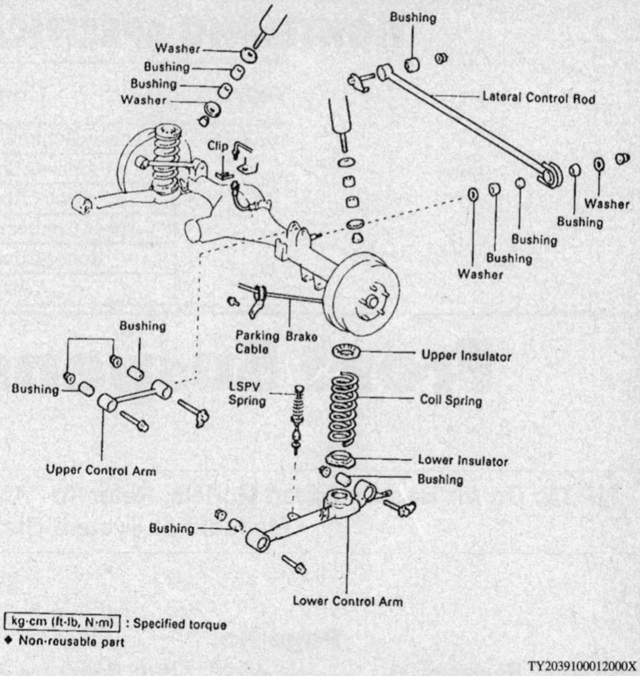
Bushing
Washer
Bushing
Bushing
Washer
Lateral Control Rod
Clip
Washer
Bushing
Bushing
Bushing
Washer
Bushing
Parking Brake Cable
Upper Insulator
Bushing
LSPV Spring
Coil Spring
Upper Control Arm
Lower Insulator
Bushing
Bushing
Lower Control Arm
kg-cm (ft-lb, N·m) : Specified torque
◆ Non-reusable part
TY2039100012000X

Fig. 2 Exploded view of rear suspension

SHOCK ABSORBER

REPLACE

1. Raise and support vehicle and support rear axle assembly using suitable jack.
2. Remove rear wheels.
3. Remove shock absorber lower attaching nut.
4. Remove upper shock attaching bolt, then the shock absorber.
5. Reverse procedure to install, noting the following:
   a. Tighten attaching nuts and bolt to specifications.
   b. Tighten lower shock attaching nut until at least .0059 inch of shock bolt protrudes.

COIL SPRING

REPLACE

Refer to "Control Arm, Replace" for coil spring replacement procedure.

CONTROL ARM

REPLACE

1. Raise and support rear of vehicle and rear axle, using suitable jack stands.
2. Using brake tube removal tool No. 09751-36011, or equivalent, disconnect brake tube from brake hose.
3. **On models with ABS,** remove ABS wire harness bracket.
4. **On all models,** disconnect LSPV spring from lower control arm, **Fig. 2.**
5. Remove shock absorber lower attaching nut.
6. Remove lateral control rod attaching nut and bolt, then the lateral control rod with bushings.
7. Disconnect parking brake cable from lower control arm.
8. Lower rear axle assembly, then remove coil spring with upper and lower insulators.
9. Remove lower control arm attaching nuts and bolts, then the lower control arm.
10. Remove upper control arm attaching nuts and bolts, then the upper control arm.
11. Reverse procedure to install.

LATERAL ROD

REPLACE

Refer to "Control Arm, Replace" for lateral rod replacement procedure.

TIGHTENING SPECIFICATIONS

Year	Component	Torque/Ft. Lbs.
1993–96	Adjusting Nut Lock	9
	Backing Plate Set Nut	53
	Differential Carrier To Axle Housing	20
	Differential Drain Plug	36
	Differential Filler Plug	36
	Lateral Control Rod To Body	156
	Lower Control Arm Body	156

Continued

TIGHTENING SPECIFICATIONS—Continued

Year	Component	Torque/Ft. Lbs.
1993–96	Lower Control Arm To Axle Housing	181
	Propeller Shaft To Differential	54
	Shock Absorber To Body	27
	Upper Control Arm To Axle Housing	156
	Upper Control Arm To Body	156
	Wheel Lug Nut	76

Front Suspension & Steering

NOTE: On Air Bag Equipped Models, Refer To "Air Bag System Precautions" Located In The Front Of This Manual For System Disarming & Arming Procedures.

INDEX

	Page No.
Ball Joint, Replace	45-22
Lower	45-22
Ball Joint Inspection	45-22
Coil Spring, Replace	45-22
Control Arm, Replace	45-24
Lower	45-24
Hub, Bearing & Seal, Replace	45-22
Manual Steering Gears	48-1
Power Steering	48-1
Power Steering Gear, Replace	45-24
Power Steering Pump, Replace	45-24
Precautions	45-22
Air Bag Systems	45-22
Shock Absorber, Replace	45-22
Stabilizer Bar, Replace	45-24
Steering Knuckle, Replace	45-24
Tightening Specifications	45-24

PRECAUTIONS

AIR BAG SYSTEMS

Refer to "Air Bag System Precautions" in the front of this manual for system disarming and arming procedures.

HUB, BEARING & SEAL

REPLACE

1. Raise and support vehicle, then remove front wheels.
2. **On models with ABS,** remove speed sensor, **Fig. 1.**
3. **On 2WD models,** remove brake cylinder from steering knuckle, then using suitable wire, hang cylinder aside. Remove brake rotor.
4. **On models with 4WD,** remove cotter pin and lock cap, then with brakes applied, remove locknut. Remove brake cylinder and rotor.
5. **On all models,** loosen lower shock absorber attaching nuts, but do not remove.
6. Loosen lower ball joint attaching bolts, but do not remove.
7. Remove tie rod end cotter pin and nut, then using ball joint puller tool No. 09628-10011, or equivalent, separate tie rod end from steering knuckle.
8. Remove lower ball joint attaching bolts and separate from steering knuckle.
9. Remove shock absorber lower attaching nuts and bolts.
10. Remove steering knuckle and axle hub. **Do not damage speed sensor rotor, oil seal and driveshaft boot.**
11. **On 2WD models,** remove axle hub grease cap, then using suitable chisel and hammer, release nut caulking and remove locknut.
12. **On 2WD models with ABS,** remove speed sensor rotor. **Do not scratch sensor rotor serrations.**
13. **On 2WD models less ABS,** remove spacer.
14. **On all models,** using axle shaft puller tool No. 09520-00031, or equivalent, remove axle hub.
15. Using bearing remover tools No. 09950-00020 (2WD), 09550-10012 (4WD) or 09550-0020 (4WD), or equivalents, and suitable press, remove axle hub bearing.
16. Remove dust cover.
17. **On 4WD models,** remove dust deflector, then using oil seal puller tool No. 09308-00010, or equivalent, remove inner oil seal.
18. **On all models,** remove steering knuckle snap ring, then using bearing replacer tool Nos. 09223-56010 and 09316-60010, or equivalents, remove bearing.
19. Reverse procedure to install.

BALL JOINT INSPECTION

1. Raise and support vehicle.
2. Ensure front wheels are in straight ahead position, then depress and hold brake pedal.
3. Move control arm up and down. If play is evident, replace ball joint.

BALL JOINT

REPLACE

LOWER

1. Raise and support vehicle, then remove front wheels.
2. Remove ball joint cotter pin and attaching nut.
3. Remove ball join attaching bolts.
4. Using ball joint puller tool No. 09628-62011, or equivalent, remove ball joint.
5. Reverse procedure to install.

COIL SPRING

REPLACE

Refer to "Shock Absorber, Replace" for coil spring replacement procedure.

SHOCK ABSORBER

REPLACE

1. Raise and support vehicle, then remove front wheels.
2. **On models with 4WD,** remove driveshaft cotter pin and lock cap, then with brakes applied, remove locknut and washer, **Fig. 2.**
3. **On all models,** disconnect stabilizer bar link from shock assembly.
4. **On models with ABS,** remove speed sensor.
5. **On all models,** loosen lower shock absorber attaching nuts, but do not remove.
6. Loosen lower ball joint attaching bolts, but do not remove.

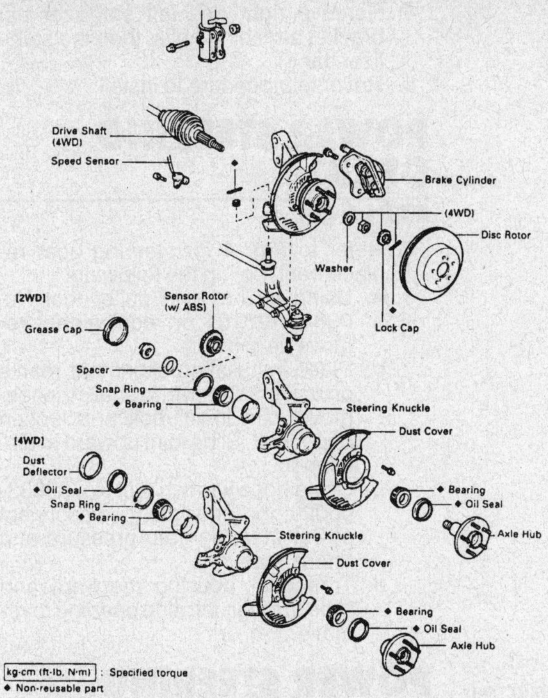
Drive Shaft
(4WD)
Speed Sensor
Brake Cylinder
(4WD)
Disc Rotor
Washer
[2WD]
Sensor Rotor
(w/ ABS)
Lock Cap
Grease Cap
Spacer
Snap Ring
◆ Bearing
Steering Knuckle
Dust Cover
[4WD]
Dust
Deflector
◆ Oil Seal
Snap Ring
◆ Bearing
◆ Bearing
◆ Oil Seal
Axle Hub
Steering Knuckle
Dust Cover
◆ Bearing
◆ Oil Seal
Axle Hub
kg-cm (ft-lb, N·m) : Specified torque
◆ Non-reusable part

TY2049100033000X

Fig. 1 Exploded view of hub, bearing & seal

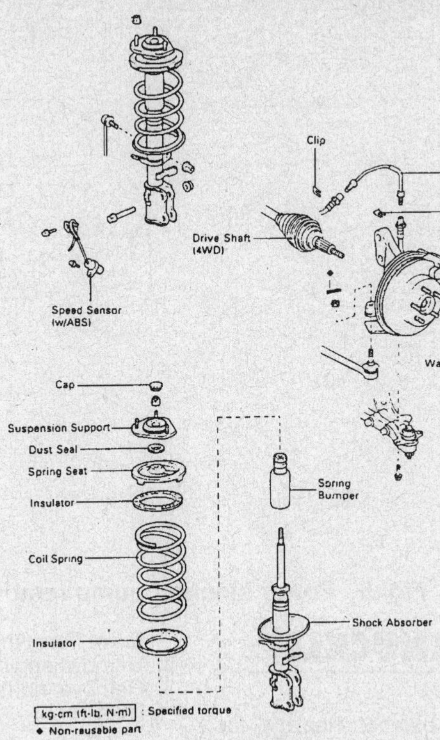
Clip
Brake Tube
Clip
Drive Shaft
(4WD)
(4WD)
Speed Sensor
(w/ABS)
Washer
Lock Cap
Cap
Suspension Support
Dust Seal
Spring Seat
Insulator
Spring
Bumper
Coil Spring
Shock Absorber
Insulator
kg-cm (ft-lb, N·m) : Specified torque
◆ Non-reusable part

TY2029100017000X

Fig. 2 Exploded view of shock absorber

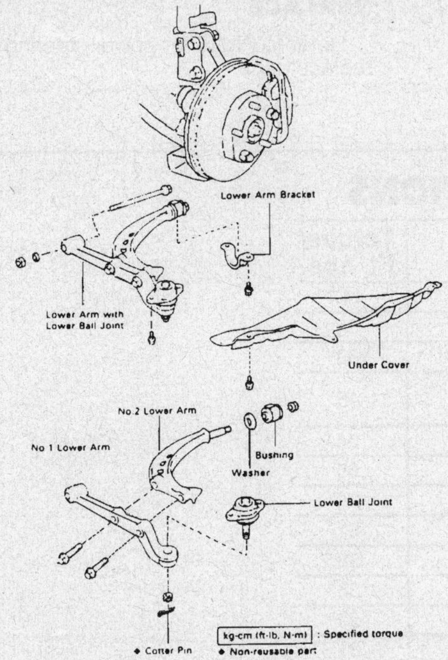
Lower Arm Bracket
Lower Arm with
Lower Ball Joint
Under Cover
No 2 Lower Arm
No 1 Lower Arm
Bushing
Washer
Lower Ball Joint
kg-cm (ft-lb, N·m) : Specified torque
◆ Cotter Pin
◆ Non-reusable part

TY2029100016000X

Fig. 3 Exploded view of lower control arm

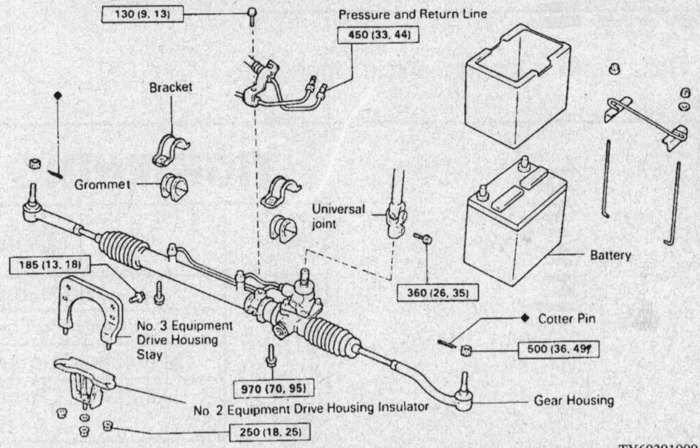
130 (9, 13)
Pressure and Return Line
450 (33, 44)
Bracket
Grommet
Universal
Joint
Battery
185 (13, 18)
360 (26, 35)
Cotter Pin
No. 3 Equipment
Drive Housing
Stay
500 (36, 49)
970 (70, 95)
No. 2 Equipment Drive Housing Insulator
Gear Housing
250 (18, 25)

TY6039100017000X

Fig. 4 Steering gear removal

7. Remove tie rod end cotter pin and nut, then using ball joint puller tool No. 09628-10011, or equivalent, remove tie rod from steering knuckle.
8. Remove lower ball joint attaching nuts.
9. Remove steering knuckle to shock absorber attaching nuts and bolts, then the steering knuckle.
10. Using suitable jack, support shock absorber and coil spring, then remove shock absorber upper attaching nuts.
11. Remove shock absorber and coil spring assembly.
12. Using spring compressor tool No. 09727-30020, or equivalent, compress coil spring.
13. Install bolt and two nuts into shock absorber lower bracket, then install assembly in suitable soft jawed vise.
14. Using upper seat holder tool No. 09729-22031, or equivalent, hold spring seat, then remove nut.
15. Remove suspension support, dust seal, spring seat, upper insulator, coil spring, spring bumper and lower insulator.
16. Reverse procedure to install.

CONTROL ARM

REPLACE

LOWER

1. Raise and support vehicle, then remove front wheels.
2. Remove engine undercover, **Fig. 3.**
3. Remove lower ball joint attaching bolts, then separate from steering knuckle.
4. Remove lower arm bracket attaching bolts.
5. Remove arm shaft attaching nut.
6. Remove lower control arm and lower ball joint assembly.
7. Using ball joint puller tool No. 09628-62011, or equivalent, remove lower ball joint from arm.
8. Reverse procedure to install.

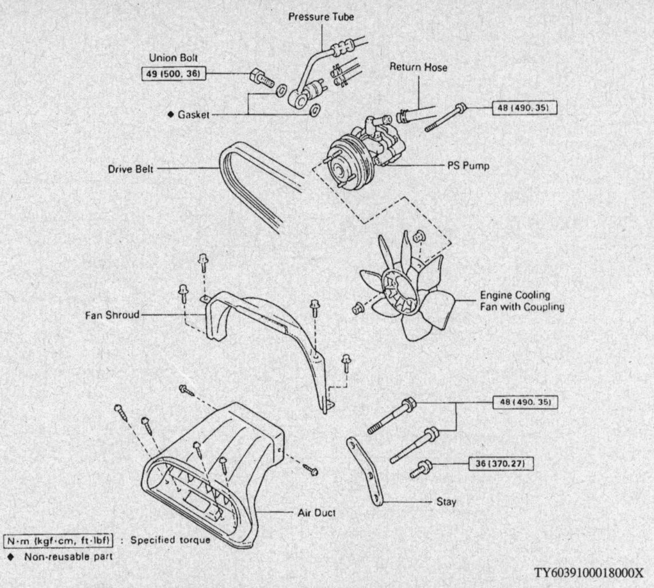
Pressure Tube
Union Bolt
49 (500, 36)
Return Hose
◆ Gasket
48 (490, 35)
Drive Belt
PS Pump
Engine Cooling Fan with Coupling
Fan Shroud
48 (490, 35)
36 (370, 27)
Stay
Air Duct
N·m (kgf·cm, ft·lbf) : Specified torque
◆ Non-reusable part
TY6039100018000X

Fig. 5 Power steering pump removal

STEERING KNUCKLE

REPLACE

Refer to "Shock Absorber, Replace" for steering knuckle replacement procedure.

STABILIZER BAR

REPLACE

1. Raise and support vehicle, then remove front wheels.
2. Remove engine undercovers.
3. Remove right and left stabilizer bar links.
4. Remove right and left stabilizer bar bracket attaching bolts, then the stabilizer bar.
5. Reverse procedure to install.

POWER STEERING GEAR

REPLACE

1. Refer to **Fig. 4** for steering gear replacement, noting the following:
   a. Using tie rod end puller tool No. 09611-12010, or equivalent, remove tie rod end.
   b. Place installation alignment marks on universal joint and shaft, then remove joint lower bolt and loosen upper bolt. Slide joint upward to disconnect.
   c. Using hose wrench tool No. 09633-00020, or equivalent, disconnect power steering gear pressure and return lines.
   d. Turn gear housing rearward and slide through left side opening to remove.

POWER STEERING PUMP

REPLACE

Refer to **Fig. 5** for power steering pump replacement.

TIGHTENING SPECIFICATIONS

Year	Component	Torque/ Ft. Lbs.
1993	Axle Hub Bearing Locknut	147
	Differential Carrier Cover Set Bolt	34
	Differential Carrier To Differential Support	59
	Differential Carrier To No. 2 Differential Support	48
	Differential Support Bolt	54
	Differential Tube To Differential Carrier	65
	Driveshaft Locknut	137
	Driveshaft To Side Gear Shaft	61
	Front Differential Bearing Cap	58
	Front Differential Drain Plug	36
	Front Differential Filler Plug	29
	Front Differential To Propeller Shaft	31
	Lower Arm Bracket To Body	105
	Lower Ball Joint To Lower Arm	76
	No. 1 Differential Support To Differential Tube	51
	No. 1 Lower Arm To Body	121
	No. 1 Lower Arm To No. 2 Lower Arm	136
	No. 2 Lower Arm To Bushing	141
	Ring Gear To Differential Case	71
	Stabilizer Bar Bracket	14
	Stabilizer Bar Link Nut	76
	Steering Knuckle To Lower Ball Joint	94
	Steering Knuckle To Shock Absorber	231
	Suspension Support To Body	47

Continued

TIGHTENING SPECIFICATIONS—Continued

Year	Component	Torque/ Ft. Lbs.
1993 Cont.	Suspension Support To Shock Absorber	34
	Tie Rod End To Steering Knuckle	36
	Wheel Lug Nut	76
1994–96	Axle Hub Bearing Locknut	147
	Differential Carrier Cover Set Bolt	34
	Differential Carrier To Differential Support	116
	Differential Carrier To No. 2 Differential Support	48
	Differential Support Bolt	54
	Differential Tube To Differential Carrier	65
	Driveshaft Locknut	152
	Driveshaft To Side Gear Shaft	51
	Front Differential Bearing Cap	58
	Front Differential Drain Plug	36
	Front Differential Filler Plug	29
	Front Differential To Propeller Shaft	31
	Lower Arm Bracket To Body	105
	Lower Ball Joint To Lower Arm	76
	No. 1 Differential Support To Differential Tube	51
	No. 1 Lower Arm To Body	121
	No. 1 Lower Arm To No. 2 Lower Arm	136
	No. 2 Lower Arm To Bushing	80
	Ring Gear To Differential Case	71
	Stabilizer Bar Bracket	14
	Stabilizer Bar Link Nut	76
	Steering Knuckle To Lower Ball Joint	94
	Steering Knuckle To Shock Absorber	231
	Suspension Support To Body	47
	Suspension Support To Shock Absorber	34
	Tie Rod End To Steering Knuckle	36
	Wheel Lug Nut	76

Wheel Alignment

INDEX

	Page No.
Steering Axis Inclination	45-26
Toe-In	45-26
Preliminary Inspection	45-26
Vehicle Ride Height	45-26
Wheel Alignment Specifications	45-2

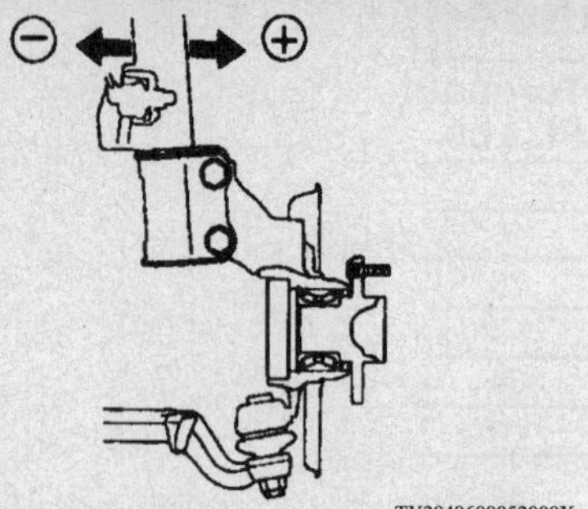
TY2049600052000X

Fig. 1 Camber adjustment

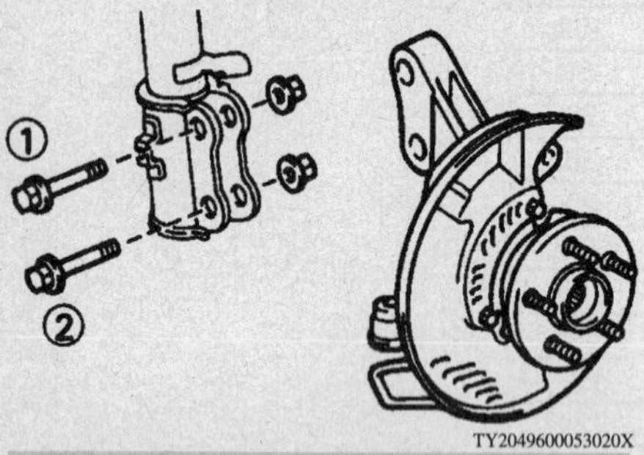
①
②
TY2049600053020X

Fig. 2 Camber adjust bolt selection (Part 2 of 2)

PRELIMINARY INSPECTION

Inspect and repair the following prior to adjusting wheel alignment.

1. Check tires for wear and proper inflation.
2. Check front suspension, steering linkage and ball joints for wear or looseness.
3. Check wheel runout with a dial indicator. Wheel runout should not exceed .039 inch (1.0 mm).
4. Ensure front shock absorbers are functioning properly.

FRONT WHEEL ALIGNMENT

CASTER

Caster is not adjustable. If caster is not within specifications, check for worn or damaged suspension parts and replace as required.

CAMBER

1. Remove front wheels.
2. Remove two nuts from lower side of shock absorber.
3. Coat threads of nuts with engine oil and temporarily install.
4. Adjust camber by pushing or pulling lower side of shock absorber in direction in which camber adjustment is required, **Fig. 1.**

Bolt, Nut / Adjusting Value	Set Bolt		Adjusting Bolt			
	90105-17002		90105-17006		90105-17007	
	11		2 Dots •11•		3 Dots •11•	
	Nut		Nut			
	90179-17001		90179-17002			
	Gold		Silver			
	①	②	①	②	①	②
20'	●			●		
40'	●					●
1°00'				●	●	
1°20'					●	●

TY2049600053010X

Fig. 2 Camber adjust bolt selection (Part 1 of 2)

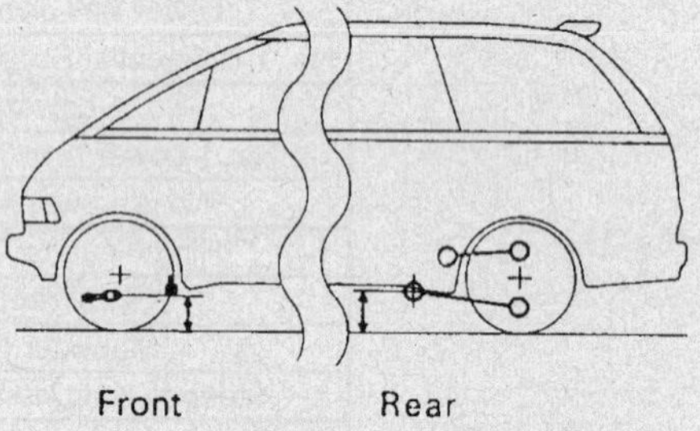
Front
Rear
TY2049100034000X

Fig. 3 Vehicle ride height measurement

5. Tighten nuts, then recheck camber.
6. If camber is not within specifications, estimate how much additional camber adjustment is required and select camber adjusting bolt from chart shown in **Fig. 2.**
7. Install selected bolts and adjust camber by pushing or pulling lower side of shock absorber in direction in which camber adjustment is required.
8. **Torque** set bolt to 232 ft. lbs. and adjusting bolt to 163 ft. lbs.

TOE-IN

1. Rock vehicle up and down to stabilize suspension.
2. Move vehicle forward about 16.4 feet (5 m) with front wheels in straight ahead position on a level surface. **If vehicle is backed up, move forward the same distance.**
3. Mark center of each rear tread and measure distance between marks.
4. Move vehicle forward until marks on rear sides of tires come up to the measuring heights of the gauge on the front side **If tire rolls too far, repeat step 2.**
5. Measure distance between marks on front tires.
6. If toe-in is not to specifications, adjust as follows:
   a. Remove boot clips.
   b. Loosen tie rod end locknut.
   c. Turn left and right tie rod ends an equal amount.
   d. Ensure lengths of left and right tie rod ends are equal.

STEERING AXIS INCLINATION

Steering axis inclination is not adjustable. If steering axis inclination is not within specifications, check for worn or damaged suspension parts and replace as required.

VEHICLE RIDE HEIGHT

Measure vehicle ride height as shown in **Fig. 3.** Ride height for 2WD models with P205/75 R14 tires, should be 9.37 inches front and 11.06 inches rear. On 2WD models with P215/65 R15 tires, ride height should be 9.33 inches front and 10.98 inches rear.

On 4WD models with P205/75 R14 tires, ride height should be 9.76 inches front and 11.46 inches rear. On 4WD models with P215/65 R15 tires, ride height should be 9.72 inches front and 11.38 inches rear.

TOYOTA PASEO & TERCEL

INDEX OF SERVICE OPERATIONS

Page No.

AIR BAG SYSTEM PRECAUTIONS 0-8
AUTOMATIC TRANSMISSIONS/ TRANSAXLES 48-1
BRAKES
- Anti-Lock Brakes 48-1
- Disc Brakes 48-1
- Drum Brakes 48-1
- Hydraulic Brake Systems 48-1
- Power Brake Units 48-1

CLUTCH & MANUAL TRANSAXLE
- Adjustments 46-20
- Clutch, Replace 46-21
- Hydraulic System Service 46-20
- Precautions 46-20
- Tightening Specifications 46-22
- Transaxle, Replace 46-21

ELECTRICAL
- Air Bags 48-1
- Air Conditioning 48-1
- Alternators 48-1
- Blower Motor, Replace 46-8
- Coil Pack, Replace 46-5
- Combination Switch, Replace 46-5
- Cooling Fans 48-1
- Cruise Control 48-1
- Dash Gauges 48-1
- Dash Panels 48-1
- Distributor, Replace 46-4
- Evaporator Core, Replace 46-8
- Fuel Pump Relay Location 46-4
- Fuse Panel & Flasher Location 46-4
- Heater Core, Replace 46-8
- Ignition Lock, Replace 46-5
- Ignition Switch, Replace 46-5
- Instrument Cluster, Replace 46-6
- Neutral Safety Switch, Replace 46-5
- Passive Restraints 48-1
- Precautions 46-4
- Radio, Replace 46-7
- Relay Center Location 46-4
- Speed Controls 48-1
- Starter, Replace 46-4
- Starter Motors 48-1
- Steering Columns 48-1
- Steering Wheel, Replace 46-6
- Stop Light Switch, Replace 46-5
- Wiper Motor, Replace 46-8
- Wiper Switch, Replace 46-8
- Wiper Systems 48-1

ELECTRICAL SYMBOL IDENTIFICATION 0-139
FRONT SUSPENSION & STEERING
- Ball Joint, Replace 46-26
- Ball Joint Inspection 46-26
- Coil Spring, Replace 46-26
- Manual Steering Gear, Replace 46-28
- Manual Steering Gears 48-1
- Power Steering 48-1
- Power Steering Gear, Replace 46-27
- Power Steering Pump, Replace 46-28
- Power Steering System Bleed 46-28
- Precautions 46-25
- Stabilizer Bar, Replace 46-27
- Strut, Replace 46-27
- Suspension Arm, Replace 46-27
- Tightening Specifications 46-29
- Wheel Bearing, Adjust 46-25
- Wheel Hub & Steering Knuckle, Replace 46-25

FRONT WHEEL DRIVE AXLES 48-1
REAR AXLE & SUSPENSION
- Axle Beam, Replace 46-23
- Coil Spring, Replace 46-23
- Hub & Bearing, Replace 46-23
- Lateral Control Bar, Replace 46-24
- Shock Absorber, Replace 46-23
- Tightening Specifications 46-24

SERVICE REMINDER & WARNING LAMP RESET PROCEDURES 0-10
SPECIFICATIONS
- Engine Identification 46-2
- Fluid Capacities & Cooling System Data 46-3
- Front Wheel Alignment Specifications 46-3
- General Engine Specifications 46-2
- Lubricant Data 46-4
- Rear Wheel Alignment Specifications 46-3
- Tune Up Specifications 46-2

VEHICLE IDENTIFICATION 0-1
VEHICLE LIFT POINTS 0-34
VEHICLE MAINTENANCE SCHEDULES 0-69
WHEEL ALIGNMENT
- Front Wheel Alignment 46-30
- Preliminary Inspection 46-30
- Rear Wheel Alignment 46-30
- Vehicle Ride Height 46-30
- Wheel Alignment Specifications 46-3

WIRE COLOR CODE IDENTIFICATION 0-144
3E-E 1.5L & 5E-FE 1.5L ENGINES
- Belt Tension Data 46-17
- Camshaft, Replace 46-16
- Camshaft Lobe Lift Specifications 46-15
- Compression Pressure 46-8
- Cooling System Bleed 46-17
- Cylinder Head, Replace 46-10
- Engine Rebuilding Specifications 48-1
- Engine, Replace 46-8
- Exhaust Manifold, Replace 46-10
- Fuel Filter, Replace 46-17
- Fuel Pump, Replace 46-17
- Hydraulic Lifters, Replace 46-15
- Intake Manifold, Replace 46-10
- Main & Rod Bearings 46-16
- Oil Pan, Replace 46-16
- Oil Pump, Replace 46-16
- Oil Pump Service 46-16
- Piston & Rod Assembly 46-16
- Precautions 46-8
- Radiator, Replace 46-17
- Thermostat, Replace 46-17
- Tightening Specifications 46-17
- Timing Belt, Replace 46-15
- Valve Adjustment 46-15
- Valve Clearance Specifications 46-15
- Valve Guides 46-15
- Water Pump, Replace 46-17

Specifications

ENGINE IDENTIFICATION

Model	Year	Engine Code	Engine, Liter
Tercel	1993–94	3E-E	1.5L
	1995–96	5E-FE	1.5L
Paseo	1993–96	5E-FE	1.5L

GENERAL ENGINE SPECIFICATIONS

Year	Engine	Fuel System	Bore & Stroke, Inches	Compression Ratio	Maximum Brake H.P. @ RPM	Maximum Torque, Ft. Lbs. @ RPM	Normal Oil Pressure, psi
1993	1.5L 3E-E②	Fuel Inj.	2.88 x 3.43	9.3	82 @ 5200	90 @ 4400	①
	1.5L 5E-FE③	Fuel Inj.	2.91 x 3.43	9.4	100 @ 6400	91 @ 3200	①
1994	1.5L 3E-E②	Fuel Inj.	2.88 x 3.43	9.3	82 @ 5200	89 @ 4400	①
	1.5L 5E-FE③	Fuel Inj.	2.91 x 3.43	9.4	100 @ 6400	91 @ 3200	①
1995	1.5L 5E-FE②	Fuel Inj.	2.91 x 3.43	9.4	93 @ 5400	100 @ 4400	①
	1.5L 5E-FE③④	Fuel Inj.	2.91 x 3.43	9.4	100 @ 6400	91 @ 3200	①
	1.5L 5E-FE③⑤	Fuel Inj.	2.91 x 3.43	9.4	93 @ 5400	100 @ 4400	①
1996	1.5L 5E-FE②	Fuel Inj.	2.91 x 3.43	9.4	93 @ 5400	100 @ 4400	①
	1.5L 5E-FE③	Fuel Inj.	2.91 x 3.43	9.4	93 @ 5400	100 @ 4400	①

① — 4.3 psi or more at idle, 36–71 psi at 3000 RPM.
② — Tercel.
③ — Paseo.
④ — Except California.
⑤ — California.

TUNE UP SPECIFICATIONS

The following specifications are published from the latest information available. This data should be used only in the absence of a decal affixed in the engine compartment.

When checking ignition timing, it may be necessary to disconnect certain hoses and/or electrical connectors. Refer to vehicle emission control label for specific instructions.

Before disconnecting spark plug wires from distributor cap, determine location of No. 1 wire in cap, as distributor position may have been altered from that shown.

Year	Engine	Spark Plug Gap, Inch	Ignition Timing			Idle Speed①②		Fuel Pump Pressure, psi.	Valve Clearance, Inch	
			Firing Order	Timing, °BTDC①	Timing Mark, Fig.	Man. Trans.	Auto. Trans.		Int.	Exh.
1993–94	1.5L 3E-E	.043	1-3-4-2	10③	A	750	800N	40.8–41.7	.006–.010	.012–.016
1993–96	1.5L 5E-FE	.043	1-3-4-2	10③	A	750	750N	40.8–41.7	.006–.010	.012–.016

BTDC — Before Top Dead Center.
N — Neutral.
① — With cooling fan off.
② — Controlled by idle air controller.
③ — With check connector terminals TE1 & E1 connected.

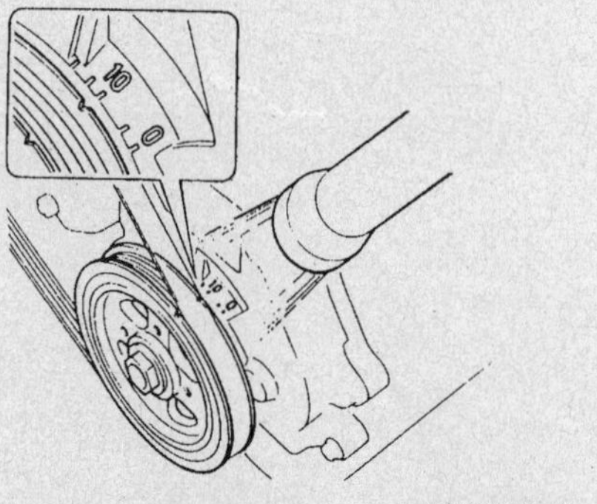

TY1139100121000X

Fig. A

FRONT WHEEL ALIGNMENT SPECIFICATIONS

The specifications listed below are for unloaded vehicles.

Year	Model	Caster Angle, Degrees		Camber Angle, Degrees		Toe-In, Inch①	Toe-Out On Turns, Degrees		Steering Axis Inclination	Ball Joint Wear
		Limits	Desired	Limits	Desired		Outer Wheel	Inner Wheel		
1993	Paseo	+⅔ to +2 ⅙	+1 5/12	-1 ⅙ to +⅓	-5/12	-.04 to +.12	32 1/12	35 ¾	12 ¼	②
	Tercel	+1 to +2 ½	+1 ¾	-1 ⅙ to +⅓	-5/12	-.04 to +.12	32 ¼	36 ⅙	12 ¼	②
1994	Paseo	+⅔ to +2 ⅙	+1 5/12	-1 ⅙ to +⅓	-5/12	-.04 to +.12	32 1/12	35 ¾	12 ¼	②
	Tercel	+½ to +2	+1 ¼	-1 to +½	-¼	-.04 to +.12	32 ¼	36 ⅙	12	②
1995	Paseo	+⅔ to +2 ⅙	+1 5/12	–1 ⅙ to +⅓	–5/12	–.04 to +.12	35 ¾	32 1/12	12 ¼	②
	Tercel	+7/12 to +2 1/12	+1 ⅓	-1 1/12 to +5/12	-⅓	-.04 to +.12	35 11/12	32 ⅙	12 ⅙	②
1996	Paseo	+⅔ to +2 ⅙	+1 ½	–1 ⅙ to +⅓	–5/12	-.04 to +.12	35 ¾	32 1/12	12 ¼	②
	Tercel	+7/12 to +2 1/12	+1 ⅓	-1 1/12 to +5/12	-⅓	-.04 to +.12	35 11/12	32 ⅙	12 ⅙	②

① — Toe-in (+); toe-out (-).
② — Refer to "Ball Joint Inspection" under "Front Suspension & Steering."

REAR WHEEL ALIGNMENT SPECIFICATIONS

The specifications listed below are for unloaded vehicles.

Year	Model	Camber Angle, Degrees		Toe-In, Inch①
		Limits	Desired	
1993	All	-1 ¼ to +¼	-½	0 to +.24
1994–96	Paseo	–1 to 0	–½	0 to +.24
	Tercel	–1 ¼ to +¼	–½	0 to +.24

① — Toe-in (+); toe-out (-).

FLUID CAPACITIES & COOLING SYSTEM DATA

Year	Model	Cooling Capacity, Qts.		Radiator Cap Relief Pressure, Lbs.	Thermo. Opening Temp., °F	Fuel Tank, Gals.	Engine Oil Refill, Qts.①	Transmission/Transaxle Oil			Axle Oil, Pints
		Auto Trans.	Manual Trans					4 Speed, Pints	5 Speed, Pints	Auto. Trans., Qts.	
1993	Paseo	5.7	5.2	13	180	11.9	3.4	5.0	5.0	3.3	—
	Tercel	5.7	5.2	13	180	11.9	3.4	—	5.0	5.8	3
1994	Paseo	5.7	5.2	15	180	11.9	2.9	—	5.0	3.0	-
	Tercel	5.7	5.2	15	180	11.9	2.9	5.0	5.0	5.8	3
1995	Paseo	5.7	5.2	13	180	11.9	2.7	—	5.0	7.6	—
	Tercel	5.7	5.2	13	180	11.9	2.6	5.0	5.0	②	3
1996	Paseo	5.7	5.2	13	180	11.9	2.7	—	4.0	7.6	—
	Tercel	5.7	5.2	13	180	11.9	2.6	5.0	5.0	②	3

① — With filter change.
② — A132L, 5.8 qts.; A242L, 7.6 qts.

LUBRICANT DATA

Year	Model	Lubricant Type				
		Transaxle		Rear Axle	Power Steering	Brake System
		Manual	Automatic			
1993–94	Paseo	SAE 75W-90 or 80W-90	ATF Dexron II	Dexron II	Dexron II	DOT 3
	Tercel	SAE 75W-90 or 80W-90	ATF Dexron II	Dexron II	Dexron II	DOT 3
1995–96	Paseo	75W-90 GL-4/5	Dexron II/IIE/III	—	Dexron II/IIE/III	DOT 3
	Tercel	75W-90 GI-4/5	Dexron II/IIE/III	—	Dexron II/IIE/III	DOT 3

Electrical

NOTE: On Air Bag Equipped Models, Refer To "Air Bag System Precautions" Located In The Front Of This Manual For System Disarming & Arming Procedures.

INDEX

	Page No.
Air Bags	48-1
Air Conditioning	48-1
Alternators	48-1
Blower Motor, Replace	46-8
Coil Pack, Replace	46-5
1995–96	46-5
Combination Switch, Replace	46-5
Replacement	46-5
Service	46-6
Cooling Fans	48-1
Cruise Control	48-1
Dash Gauges	48-1
Dash Panels	48-1
Distributor, Replace	46-4
1993–94	46-4
Evaporator Core, Replace	46-8
Fuel Pump Relay Location	46-4
Fuse Panel & Flasher Location	46-4
Heater Core, Replace	46-8
Ignition Lock, Replace	46-5
Ignition Switch, Replace	46-5
Instrument Cluster, Replace	46-6
Neutral Safety Switch, Replace	46-5
Passive Restraints	48-1
Precautions	46-4
Air Bag Systems	46-4
Radio, Replace	46-7
Relay Center Location	46-4
Speed Controls	48-1
Starter, Replace	46-4
Starter Motors	48-1
Steering Columns	48-1
Steering Wheel, Replace	46-6
Less Air Bag	46-6
With Air Bag	46-6
Stop Light Switch, Replace	46-5
Wiper Motor, Replace	46-8
Wiper Switch, Replace	46-8
Wiper Systems	48-1

PRECAUTIONS

AIR BAG SYSTEMS

Refer to "Air Bag System Precautions" in the front of this manual for system disarming and arming procedures.

FUSE PANEL & FLASHER LOCATION

There are two fuse panels; the first is on the left front kick panel and the second is forward of the left front shock tower. The turn signal/hazard flasher is under the dash, left of the steering column.

FUEL PUMP RELAY LOCATION

The fuel pump relay is located in the engine compartment relay box, **Fig. 1.**

RELAY CENTER LOCATION

There are two relay centers; one is located on the left front kick panel and the other is located forward of the left front shock tower.

STARTER

REPLACE

1. Disconnect battery ground cable.
2. **On Paseo models,** remove air cleaner hose and intake manifold stay.
3. **On all models,** disconnect electrical connectors from starter motor, then remove attaching bolts and starter motor.
4. Reverse procedure to install. **Torque** starter attaching bolts to 29 ft. lbs.

DISTRIBUTOR

REPLACE

1993–94

Removal

1. Disconnect battery ground cable and air intake connector.
2. Disconnect distributor electrical connectors, then high tension cables from distributor cap.
3. Remove distributor attaching bolts, then remove.

Installation

1. Set No. 1 cylinder to TDC, turn crankshaft clockwise and position slits, **Figs. 2 and 3.**
2. Lightly coat distributor O-ring with suitable engine oil, then install O-ring.
3. **On Tercel models,** align housing protrusion coupling side groove, **Fig. 4.**
4. **On Paseo models,** align cutout portion of coupling with groove of housing. **Fig. 5.**
5. **On Tercel models,** install distributor, align flange protrusion with cylinder head cover nut, **Fig. 6.**
6. **On Paseo models,** install distributor, align center of flange with cylinder head cover nut, **Fig. 7.**
7. Install distributor attaching bolts. **Torque** to 13 ft. lbs.
8. Connect high tension cables to distributor cap.
9. Connect battery ground cable.
10. Check and adjust ignition timing as required.

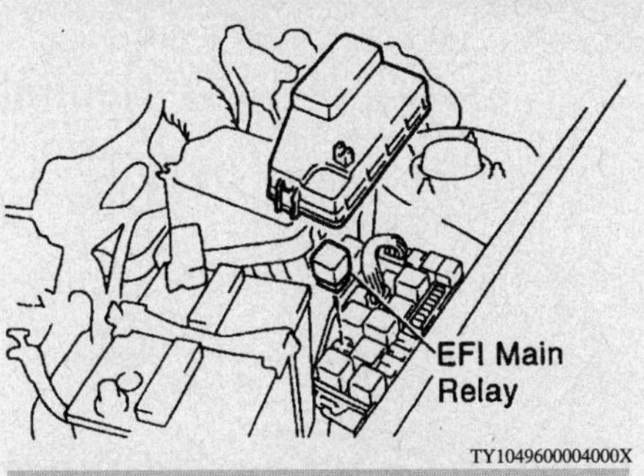
EFI Main
Relay
TY1049600004000X

Fig. 1 Fuel pump relay location

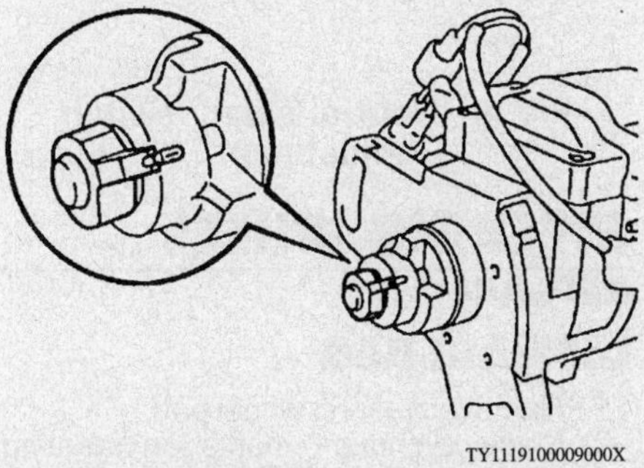
TY1119100009000X

Fig. 4 Distributor housing alignment. Tercel

COIL PACK

REPLACE

1995–96

1. Disconnect battery ground cable.
2. Disconnect high tension cords from ignition coils, **Fig. 8.**
3. Disconnect ignition coil electrical connectors.
4. Remove ignition coil retaining bolts and ignition coils.
5. Reverse procedure to install. **Torque** to 6 ft. lbs.

IGNITION LOCK

REPLACE

1. Disconnect battery ground cable.
2. Turn ignition switch to ACC position.
3. Insert a small diameter rod into hole located on side of lock cylinder, then while holding down pin, remove lock cylinder.
4. Reverse procedure to install. Ensure lock cylinder is in ACC position.

IGNITION SWITCH

REPLACE

1.
2. Remove steering wheel, then upper and lower covers.
3. Disconnect electrical connectors from ignition switch.
4. Turn ignition key to ACC position and remove ignition key cylinder.
5. Remove screw and ignition switch.
6. Reverse procedure to install.

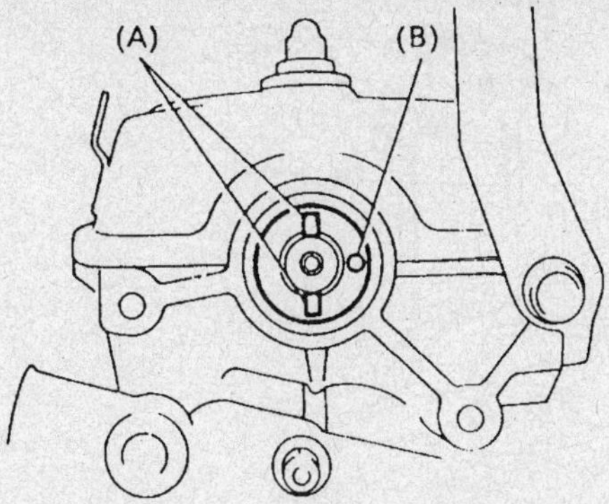
(A)
(B)

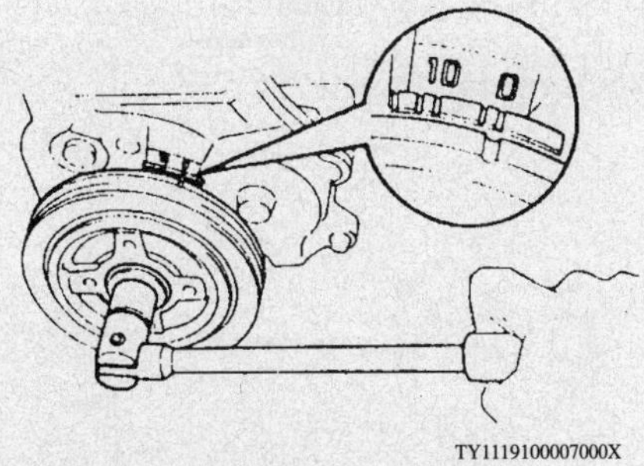
10
0
TY1119100007000X

Fig. 2 Crankshaft alignment. Tercel

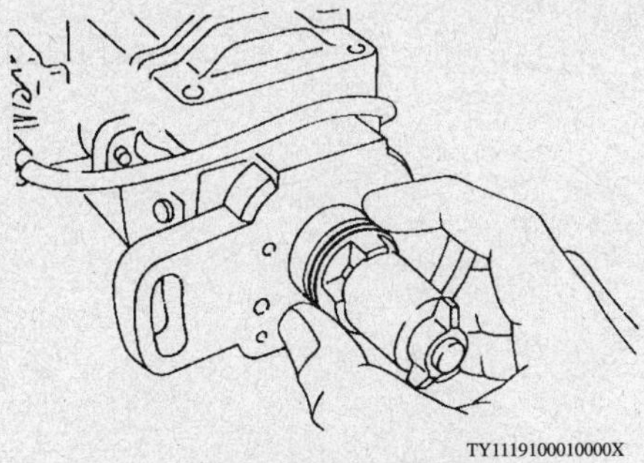
TY1119100010000X

Fig. 5 Distributor housing alignment. Paseo

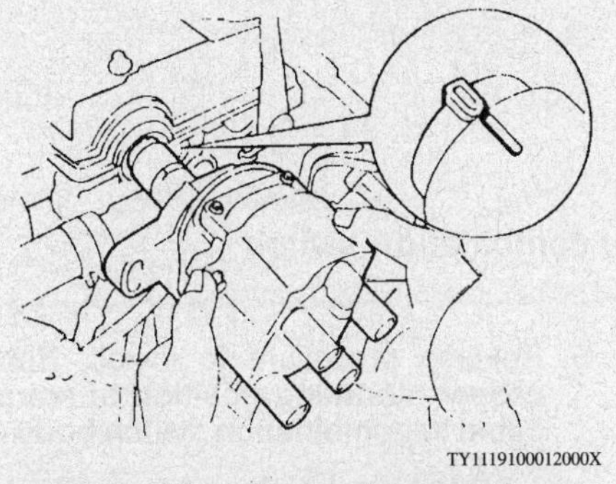
TY1119100012000X

Fig. 7 Distributor installation alignment. Paseo

NEUTRAL SAFETY SWITCH

REPLACE

1. Raise and support vehicle.
2. Loosen neutral safety switch bracket bolt.

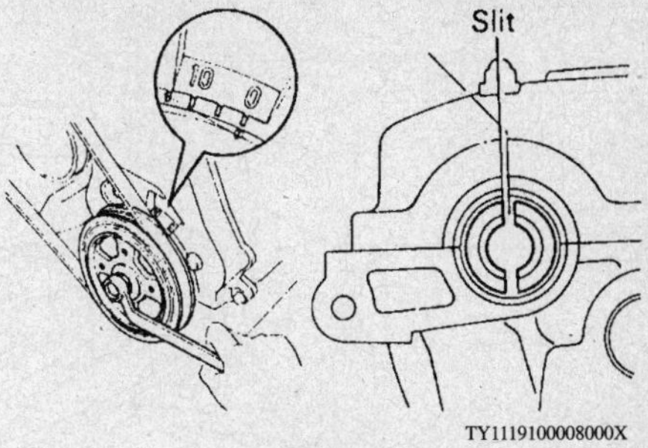
Slit
10
0
TY1119100008000X

Fig. 3 Crankshaft alignment. Paseo

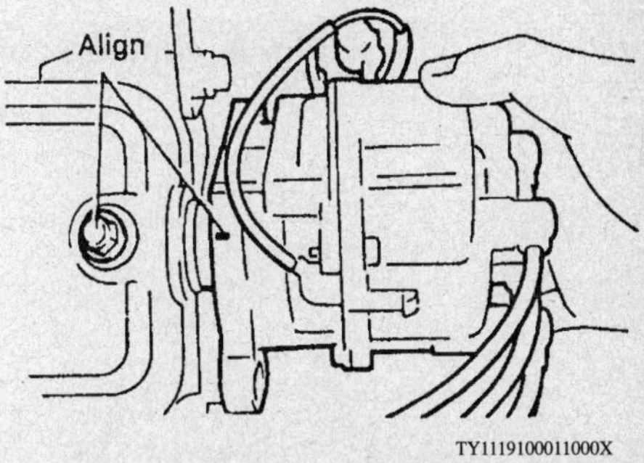
Align
TY1119100011000X

Fig. 6 Distributor installation alignment. Tercel

3. Position transaxle shift lever into Neutral.
4. Align switch shaft groove with neutral base line, **Fig. 9,** then retighten switch bracket bolt. **Torque** bolts to 48 inch lbs.
5. Connect electrical connector to switch.

STOP LIGHT SWITCH

REPLACE

1. Remove brake pedal tension spring.
2. Disconnect switch wire connector.
3. Remove switch mounting nut, then slide switch from mounting bracket.
4. Reverse procedure to install.

COMBINATION SWITCH

REPLACE

REPLACEMENT

1. Disconnect battery ground cable.
2. Remove horn button screws and horn button.
3. Scribe alignment marks on steering wheel and steering shaft.
4. Remove steering wheel nut.
5. Using a steering wheel puller, remove steering wheel.
6. Remove steering column upper and lower covers.
7. Disconnect combination switch harness.
8. **On models with air bag,** disconnect spiral cable connector.
9. **On all models,** remove combination switch.
10. Reverse procedure to install.

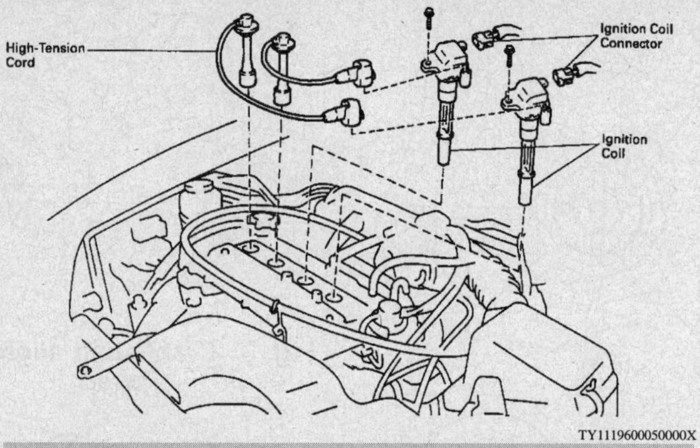
High-Tension Cord
Ignition Coil Connector
Ignition Coil
TY1119600050000X

Fig. 8 Ignition coil pack replacement

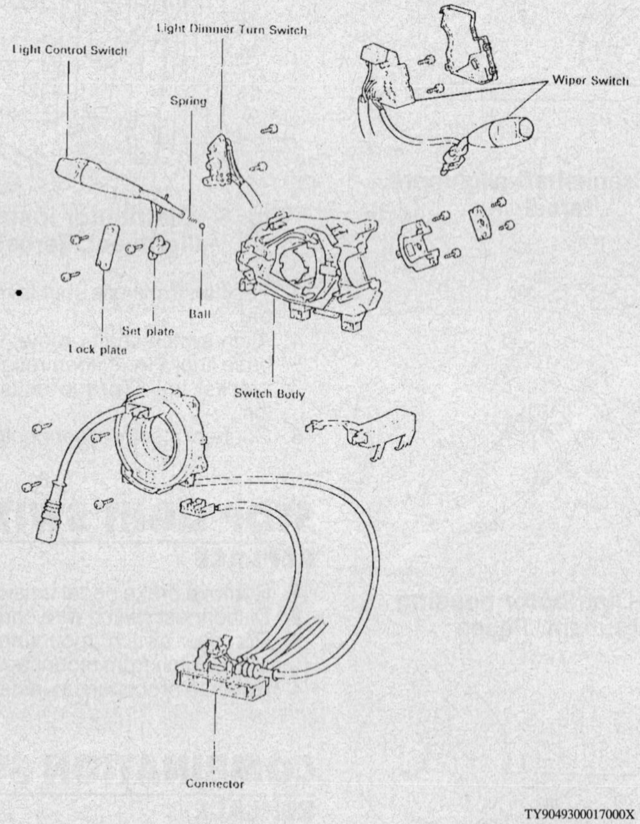
Light Dimmer Turn Switch
Light Control Switch
Spring
Wiper Switch
Ball
Set plate
Lock plate
Switch Body
Connector
TY9049300017000X

Fig. 10 Exploded view of combination switch

SERVICE

Headlamp & Dimmer Switch

1. Remove combination switch as outlined under "Replacement."
2. Remove four spiral cable attaching screws and separate spiral cable from switch body, **Fig 10.**
3. Remove lock plate and ball set plate from switch body, **Fig. 10.**
4. Remove ball from set plate, then slide out light control switch from switch body.
5. Remove light dimmer turn switch attaching screws and light dimmer turn switch unit.
6. Reverse procedure to install. **Note proper mounting position of spiral cable to combination switch body.**

Windshield Wiper/Washer Switch

1. Remove combination switch as outlined under "Replacement."
2. Remove wiper and washer switch attaching screws, then disconnect switch electrical connector and remove switch.
3. Reverse procedure to install.

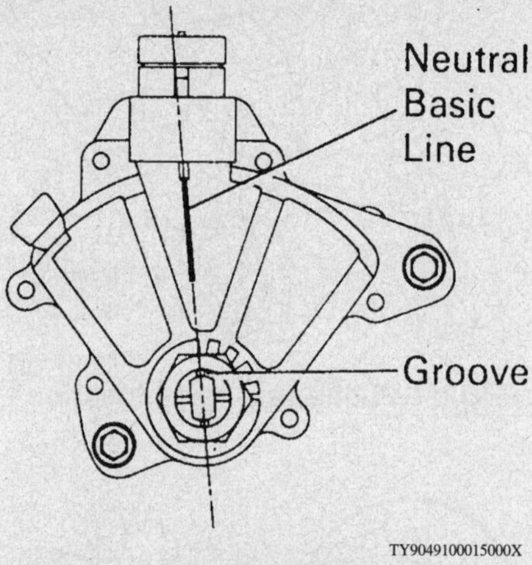
Neutral
Basic
Line
Groove
TY9049100015000X

Fig. 9 Neutral safety switch adjustment

STEERING WHEEL

REPLACE

LESS AIR BAG

1. Remove steering wheel pad.
2. Place alignment marks on steering wheel and mainshaft for assembly reference.
3. Remove nut attaching steering wheel to steering shaft.
4. Using a suitable puller, remove steering wheel.
5. Reverse procedure to install. **Torque** steering wheel attaching nut to 25 ft. lbs.

WITH AIR BAG

1. Place front wheels in straight-ahead position
2. Remove Torx screws holding air bag module to steering wheel, then remove air bag module and disconnect air bag connector.
3. Remove nut attaching steering wheel to steering shaft.
4. Place alignment marks on steering wheel and mainshaft for assembly reference.
5. Using a suitable puller, remove steering wheel.
6. Reverse procedure to install, noting:
   a. Realign marks on steering wheel and mainshaft for proper assembly.
   b. **Torque** steering wheel attaching nut to 25 ft. lbs.
7. Rearm air bag system as outlined under "Precautions. "

INSTRUMENT CLUSTER

REPLACE

1. Remove steering wheel as outlined under "Steering Wheel, Replace."
2. Remove steering column covers, **Figs. 11 and 12.**
3. Remove console box, if necessary.
4. Remove engine hood release lever.
5. Remove instrument finish lower panel retaining screws and lower panel.

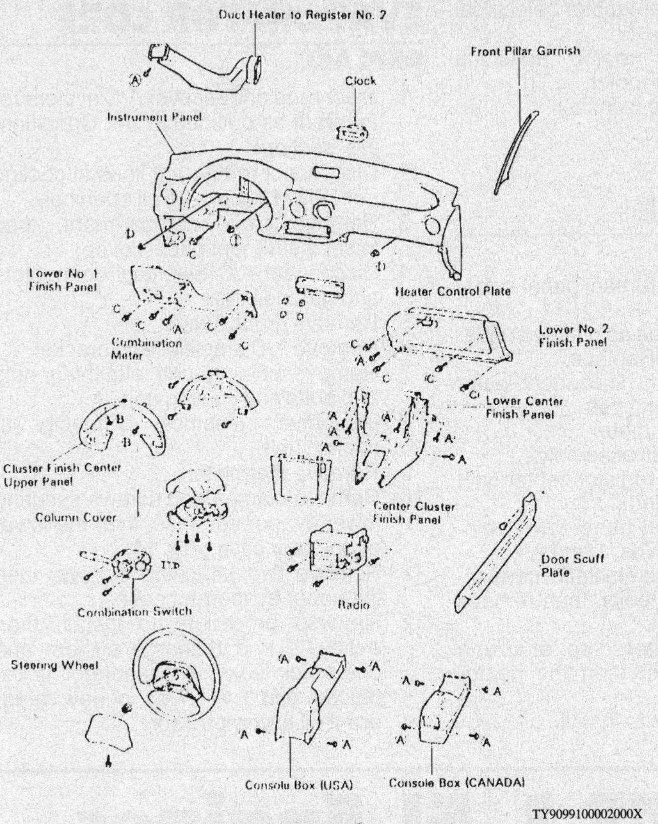
Duct Heater to Register No. 2
Front Pillar Garnish
Clock
Instrument Panel
Lower No. 1 Finish Panel
Heater Control Plate
Combination Meter
Lower No. 2 Finish Panel
Lower Center Finish Panel
Cluster Finish Center Upper Panel
Column Cover
Center Cluster Finish Panel
Door Scuff Plate
Combination Switch
Radio
Steering Wheel
Console Box (USA)
Console Box (CANADA)
TY9099100002000X

Fig. 11 Exploded view of instrument panel. 1993–95

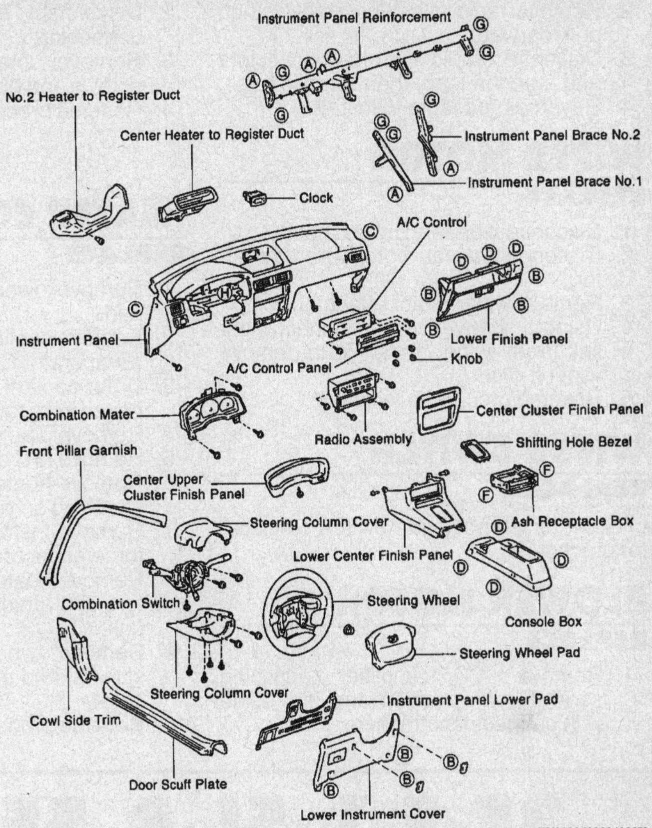
Instrument Panel Reinforcement
No.2 Heater to Register Duct
Center Heater to Register Duct
Instrument Panel Brace No.2
Instrument Panel Brace No.1
Clock
A/C Control
Instrument Panel
Lower Finish Panel
Knob
A/C Control Panel
Combination Mater
Radio Assembly
Center Cluster Finish Panel
Shifting Hole Bezel
Front Pillar Garnish
Center Upper Cluster Finish Panel
Ash Receptacle Box
Steering Column Cover
Lower Center Finish Panel
Combination Switch
Steering Wheel
Console Box
Steering Wheel Pad
Steering Column Cover
Instrument Panel Lower Pad
Cowl Side Trim
Door Scuff Plate
Lower Instrument Cover
TY90996000094000X

Fig. 12 Exploded view of instrument panel. 1996

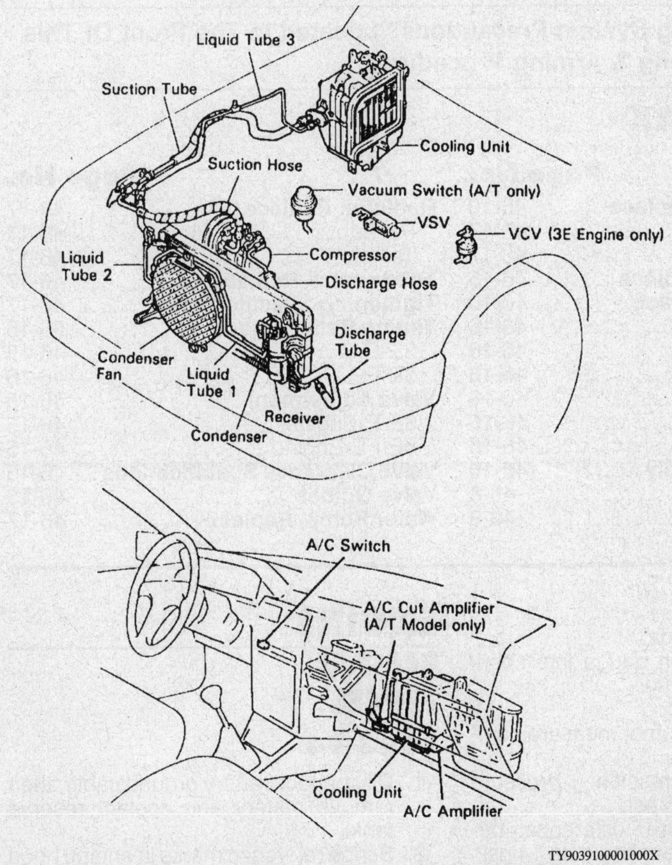
Liquid Tube 3
Suction Tube
Cooling Unit
Suction Hose
Vacuum Switch (A/T only)
VSV
VCV (3E Engine only)
Liquid Tube 2
Compressor
Discharge Hose
Discharge Tube
Condenser Fan
Liquid Tube 1
Receiver
Condenser
A/C Switch
A/C Cut Amplifier (A/T Model only)
Cooling Unit
A/C Amplifier
TY9039100001000X

Fig. 13 A/C system components

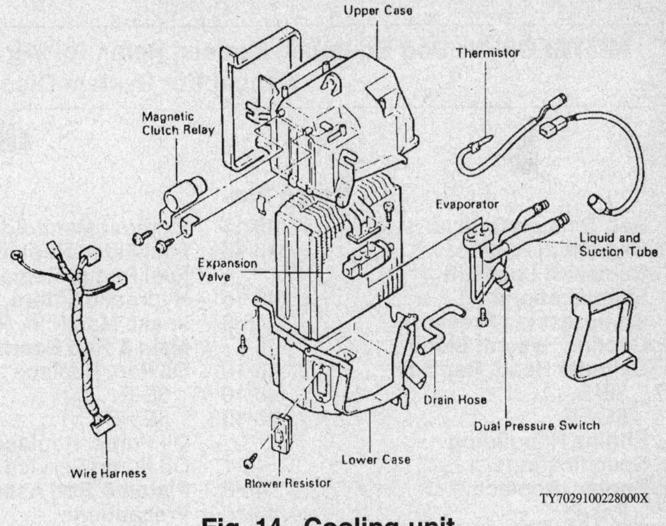
Upper Case
Thermistor
Magnetic Clutch Relay
Evaporator
Expansion Valve
Liquid and Suction Tube
Drain Hose
Dual Pressure Switch
Wire Harness
Lower Case
Blower Resistor
TY7029100228000X

Fig. 14 Cooling unit

6. Remove instrument cluster finish center panel.
7. Remove instrument cluster panel.
8. Remove combination meter retaining screws, disconnect speedometer and electrical connectors, then remove combination meter.
9. Reverse procedure to install.

RADIO

REPLACE

1. Pull center instrument panel finish panel rearward to remove, **Fig. 11.**

2. Remove radio attaching screws, then pull rearward.
3. Disconnect radio electrical connectors and antenna lead, then remove radio.
4. Reverse procedure to install.

WIPER MOTOR

REPLACE

1. Disconnect battery ground cable.
2. Disconnect wiper motor wire connector.
3. Remove wiper motor attaching bolts.
4. Using a screwdriver disconnect wiper link from wiper motor and remove wiper motor.
5. Reverse procedure to install.

WIPER SWITCH

REPLACE

Refer to "Combination Switch, Replace" for procedure.

BLOWER MOTOR

REPLACE

1. Remove A/C amplifier attaching screws, then position amplifier aside with connectors attached.
2. Disconnect blower motor electrical connector.
3. Remove blower motor attaching screws and blower motor.
4. Reverse procedure to install.

HEATER CORE

REPLACE

1. Remove lower instrument panel safety pad.
2. Remove cooling unit as outlined under "Evaporator Core, Replace."
3. Drain coolant, then disconnect water hoses from radiator pipes.
4. Remove pipe grommets.
5. Remove A/C control assembly.
6. Remove heater to register center duct attaching screws and duct.
7. Remove instrument panel lower reinforcements brace Nos. 1 and 2.
8. Remove heater unit electrical connectors and attaching bolts, then remove unit.
9. Remove two heater core attaching screws and plates, then the heater core.
10. Reverse procedure to install.

EVAPORATOR CORE

REPLACE

1. Discharge and recover A/C system refrigerant as outlined in "Air Conditioning" section.
2. Disconnect refrigerant lines at cooling unit, **Fig. 13,** capping all openings.
3. Remove glove compartment, then lower instrument panel cover.
4. Disconnect A/C electrical connectors and ground strap.
5. Remove ground wire.
6. Remove A/C amplifier and bracket.
7. Remove cooling unit attaching nuts and bolts and cooling unit.
8. Disconnect electrical connector at cooling unit.
9. Remove thermistor.
10. Remove clamps and screws securing lower evaporator case, then the lower evaporator case, **Fig. 14.**
11. Remove two attaching screws, then the upper evaporator case.
12. Reverse procedure to install, then evacuate and recharge system and check for leaks. If evaporator is replaced, add 1.4–1.7 oz. of new refrigerant oil to compressor.

3E-E 1.5L & 5E-FE 1.5L Engines

NOTE: On Air Bag Equipped Models, Refer To "Air Bag System Precautions" Located In The Front Of This Manual For System Disarming & Arming Procedures.

INDEX

	Page No.
Belt Tension Data	46-17
Camshaft, Replace	46-16
Camshaft Lobe Lift Specifications	46-15
Compression Pressure	46-8
Cooling System Bleed	46-17
Cylinder Head, Replace	46-10
3E-E	46-10
5E-FE	46-13
Engine Rebuilding Specifications	48-1
Engine, Replace	46-8
Paseo	46-10
Tercel	46-8
Exhaust Manifold, Replace	46-10
Fuel Filter, Replace	46-17
Fuel Pump, Replace	46-17
Hydraulic Lifters, Replace	46-15
Intake Manifold, Replace	46-10
Main & Rod Bearings	46-16
Oil Pan, Replace	46-16
3E-E	46-16
5E-FE	46-16
Oil Pump, Replace	46-16
Oil Pump Service	46-16
Piston & Rod Assembly	46-16
Precautions	46-8
Air Bag Systems	46-8
Radiator, Replace	46-17
Paseo	46-17
Tercel	46-17
Thermostat, Replace	46-17
Tightening Specifications	46-17
Timing Belt, Replace	46-15
3E-E	46-15
5E-FE	46-16
Valve Adjustment	46-15
3E-E Engine	46-15
5E-FE Engine	46-15
Valve Clearance Specifications	46-15
Valve Guides	46-15
Water Pump, Replace	46-17

PRECAUTIONS

AIR BAG SYSTEMS

Refer to "Air Bag System Precautions" in the front of this manual for system disarming and arming procedures.

COMPRESSION PRESSURE

1. Start engine and warm to normal operating temperature.
2. Remove spark plugs.
3. Insert compression gauge into spark plug hole.
4. Fully open throttle.
5. While cranking engine, measure compression pressure.
6. Standard compression pressure should be 142–185 psi.
7. Maximum pressure difference between each cylinder should be 14 psi.

ENGINE

REPLACE

TERCEL

1993–94

1. Disconnect battery ground cable, then remove battery and coolant reserve tank.
2. Scribe reference marks in engine hood

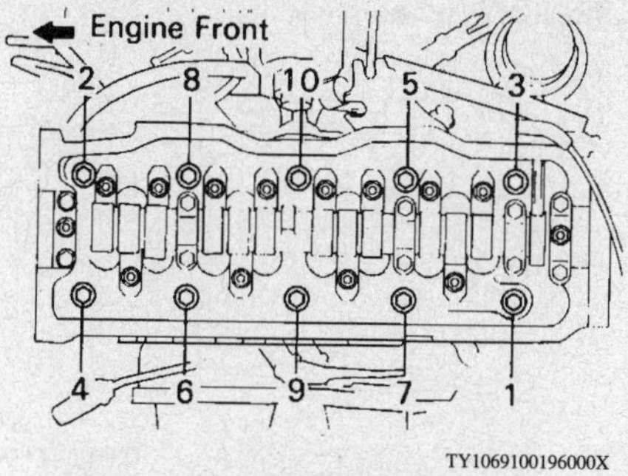
Engine Front
2
8
10
5
3
4
6
9
7
1
TY1069100196000X

Fig. 1 Cylinder head bolt loosening sequence. 3E-E

TY1069100197000X

Fig. 2 Camshaft thrust clearance measurement. 3E-E

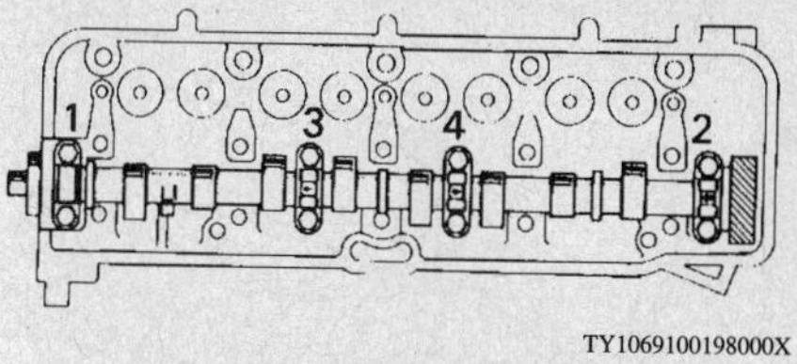
1
3
4
2
TY1069100198000X

Fig. 3 Camshaft bearing cap loosening sequence. 3E-E

hinge area, then remove hood.

3. Remove engine undercovers.
4. Drain engine coolant into suitable container.
5. Remove radiator.
6. **On models with cruise control,** disconnect control cable and connector, then remove actuator attaching bolts and the actuator.
7. **On all models,** disconnect accelerator cable.
8. **On models with automatic transaxle,** disconnect transaxle throttle cable.
9. Remove PCV hoses, then remove air cleaner assembly with air intake.
10. Disconnect fuel hoses from fuel pump and plug open ends.
11. Remove charcoal canister.
12. Disconnect brake booster hose.
13. Disconnect vacuum sensor hose, A/C idle-up hose, idle-up vacuum transmitting hose and power steering idle-up hose.
14. Disconnect heater hoses.
15. Disconnect speedometer cable from transaxle.
16. Disconnect transaxle control cables from transaxle.
17. **On models with automatic transaxle,** remove control cable bracket.
18. **On all models,** remove clutch slave cylinder from transaxle and position aside. **Do not disconnect hydraulic lines.**
19. Remove starter.
20. **On models with manual transaxle,** remove gear selector bell crank.
21. **On all models,** disconnect the following electrical connectors:
    a. Oxygen sensor.
    b. Oil pressure switch.
    c. Water temperature sender gauge.
    d. Water temperature sensor.
    e. **On models with manual transaxle,** back-up light and neutral start switch.
    f. **On all models,** distributor connectors.
    g. Water temperature switch.
    h. **On California models,** throttle opener VSV.
    i. **On models with A/C,** A/C idle-up VSV.
    j. **On all models,** wiper motor.
    k. Vacuum sensor.
    l. Igniter connector.
    m. Four injector connectors.
    n. Throttle position sensor.
    o. Cylinder head ground strap.
    p. Starter and alternator connectors.
22. **On models with power steering,** remove pump from engine with hoses attached and position aside.
23. **On models with A/C,** remove compressor with hoses attached and position aside.
24. **On all models,** disconnect exhaust pipe from exhaust manifold.
25. Disconnect driveshafts from transaxle.
26. Attach suitable engine lifting equipment, then remove rear mount through bolt and insulator.
27. Remove front mount through bolt, then the front mount from the cylinder block.
28. Remove right side mount through bolt and insulator.
29. Disconnect ground strap.
30. Remove left side mount attaching bolts, then the mount.
31. Carefully lift engine and transaxle assembly from vehicle and place on suitable stand.
32. Remove starter from engine.
33. **On models with automatic transaxle,** remove flywheel inspection cover, then rotate crankshaft as necessary to loosen six torque converter attaching bolts.
34. **On all models,** remove transaxle from engine.
35. Reverse procedure to install.

1995-96

1. Disconnect battery ground cable, then remove battery and coolant reserve tank.
2. Scribe reference marks in engine hood hinge area, then remove hood.
3. Remove engine undercovers.
4. Drain engine coolant into suitable container.
5. Remove radiator as outlined under "Radiator, Replace."
6. **On models with cruise control,** disconnect control cable and connector, then remove actuator attaching bolts and the actuator.
7. **On all models,** disconnect accelerator cable.
8. Disconnect fuel hoses from fuel pump and plug open ends.
9. Remove charcoal canister.
10. Disconnect heater hoses.
11. Disconnect MAP sensor hose and brake booster vacuum hose.
12. Disconnect speedometer cable from transaxle.
13. Disconnect vacuum sensor hose and idle-up vacuum transmitting hose.
14. **On models with A/C,** remove A/C idle-up hose.
15. **On models with power steering,** remove power steering idle-up hose.
16. **On all models,** disconnect the following electrical connectors:
    a. Oxygen sensor.
    b. Oil pressure switch.
    c. Engine coolant temperature sender gauge.
    d. Engine coolant temperature sensor.
    e. Camshaft position sensor.
    f. EGR solenoid valve.
    g. Engine coolant temperature switch.
    h. **On models with automatic transaxle,** lock-up solenoid, Park/Neutral position switch, and No. 2 vehicle speed sensor.
    i. **On models with manual transaxles** back-up light switch.
    j. **On all models,** ground strap.
    k. Throttle position sensor.
    l. IAC valve.
    m. Four injector connectors.
    n. Crankshaft position sensor.
    o. Knock sensor.
    p. Starter and alternator connectors.
17. **On models with manual transaxle,** remove clutch slave cylinder from transaxle and position aside. **Do not disconnect hydraulic lines.**
18. **On all models,** disconnect transaxle control cables from transaxle.
19. **On models with power steering,** remove pump from engine with hoses attached and position aside.
20. **On models with A/C,** remove compressor with hoses attached and position aside.
21. **On all models,** disconnect front exhaust pipe from exhaust manifold.
22. Disconnect driveshafts from transaxle.
23. Attach suitable engine lifting equipment, then remove rear mount through bolt and insulator.
24. Disconnect ground strap.
25. Remove right side mount through bolt and insulator.
26. Remove left side mount attaching bolts, then the mount.
27. Carefully lift engine and transaxle assembly from vehicle and place on suitable stand.
28. Remove starter from engine.
29. **On models with power steering,** remove power steering pump adjusting strut.
30. **On models with A/C,** remove compressor mounting bracket.

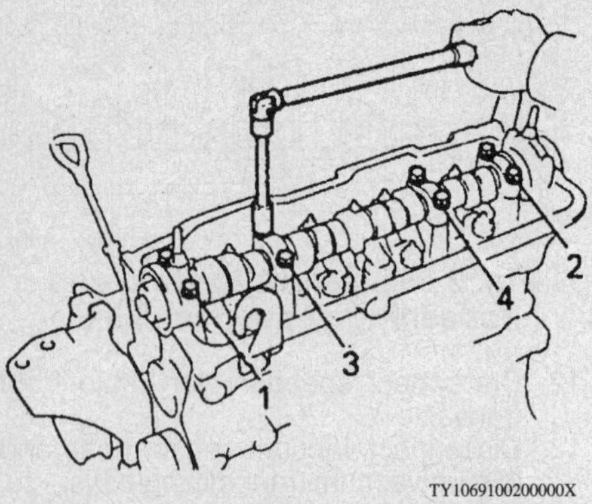
1
2
3
4
TY1069100200000X

Fig. 4 Camshaft bearing cap tightening sequence. 3E-E

31. **On models with automatic transaxle,** remove torque converter clutch mounting bolts.
32. **On all models,** remove transaxle from engine.
33. Reverse procedure to install.

PASEO

1. Disconnect battery ground cable, drain coolant, then remove battery and coolant reservoir tank.
2. Scribe installation reference marks in engine hood hinge area, then remove hood.
3. Remove engine undercovers.
4. Remove air cleaner assembly with air intake connector.
5. Remove radiator assembly.
6. **On models with automatic transaxle,** disconnect throttle cable.
7. **On all models,** disconnect accelerator cable.
8. Remove air cleaner bracket.
9. Disconnect ground strap from lefthand fender apron.
10. Remove charcoal canister, then drain case.
11. Position suitable fuel container, disconnect fuel return hoses, then remove union bolt and gaskets and disconnect fuel inlet hose.
12. Disconnect PCV hose, brake booster vacuum hose, vacuum sensor hose, two idle-up vacuum hoses and two idle-up air hoses, as equipped.
13. Disconnect engine wire harness electrical connectors as follows:
    a. Starter.
    b. Fan water temperature switch.
    c. Water temperature sender gauge.
    d. Water temperature sensor.
    e. **On models with automatic transaxle,** water temperature switch, neutral start switch and ECT solenoid.
    f. **On all models,** oxygen sensor.
    g. Oil pressure switch.
    h. **On with manual transaxle,** back-up light switch.
    i. **On all models,** EGR gas temperature sensor.
    j. Wiper motor.
    k. EGR vacuum switching valve.
    l. Throttle opener VSV.
    m. Alternator.
    n. Fuel injectors.
    o. Distributor.
    p. ECT solenoid.
14. Disconnect ground straps, then remove eight clamps and engine wiring harness.
15. **On models with cruise control,** remove cruise control actuator.
16. **On all models,** disconnect vacuum switching valve vacuum hoses, then remove ground strap and valve assembly.
17. Disconnect heater hoses from heater radiator pipes.
18. Disconnect speedometer cable and control cables from transaxle.
19. **On models with manual transaxle,** remove clutch release cylinder without disconnecting tube.
20. **On models with power steering,** remove power steering belt, remove power steering pump attaching bolts and position aside, then remove power steering pump adjusting strut.
21. **On models with A/C, less power steering,** loosen idler pulley attaching nut, remove compressor belt, then remove idler pulley bracket attaching bolts.
22. **On models with A/C,** disconnect A/C compressor electrical connector, remove compressor attaching bolts and position compressor aside, then remove compressor bracket.
23. **On all models,** remove front exhaust pipe.
24. Remove driveshafts.
25. Install suitable engine lifting equipment, then remove rear engine mount and bracket.
26. Disconnect ground strap, then remove lefthand engine mount.
27. Carefully lift engine from vehicle. Tip transaxle and engine assembly rearward to clear battery carrier support.
28. Position engine and transaxle assembly on suitable stand.
29. Remove engine rear end plate hole cover.
30. Turn crankshaft to gain access to torque converter bolts, then remove six bolts and torque converter assembly.
31. Remove starter assembly.
32. Separate engine and transaxle assembly.
33. Reverse procedure to install. Tighten attaching nuts and bolts to specifications.

INTAKE MANIFOLD

REPLACE

Refer to "Cylinder Head, Replace" for procedure.

EXHAUST MANIFOLD

REPLACE

Refer to "Cylinder Head, Replace" for procedure.

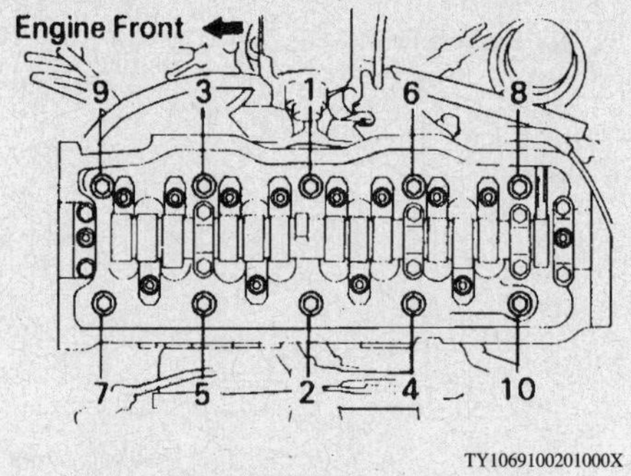
Engine Front
9
3
1
6
8
7
5
2
4
10
TY1069100201000X

Fig. 5 Cylinder head bolt tightening sequence. 3E-E

CYLINDER HEAD

REPLACE

3E-E

Removal

1. Disconnect battery ground cable.
2. Remove right side engine undercover.
3. Drain coolant from engine block and radiator into suitable container. **Engine block drain cock is located near the oil filter.**
4. Remove air cleaner assembly.
5. **On models with power steering,** remove power steering pump and bracket.
6. **On models with A/C, less power steering,** remove idler pulley bracket.
7. **On all models,** disconnect accelerator cable and throttle valve cable.
8. Disconnect radiator, heater and water bypass hoses.
9. Remove air cleaner assembly with air intake connector.
10. Disconnect the following hoses:
    a. Remove pulsation damper, then disconnect fuel inlet and return hoses. **Catch leaking fuel in a suitable container.**
    b. Water bypass hose for auxiliary air valve from water inlet pipe.
    c. Brake booster hose, charcoal canister vacuum hose and vacuum sensor.
    d. A/C idle-up hose.
    e. Power steering air hoses.
    f. Cruise control actuator hose.
11. Disconnect or remove the following:
    a. Disconnect fuel hoses from fuel pump and plug hose ends.
    b. **On California models,** remove air suction hose.
    c. **On models except California,** remove air suction hose and valve.
    d. **On all models,** disconnect brake booster hose from intake manifold.
    e. Disconnect water inlet hose and intake manifold water hose from intake manifold.
    f. Disconnect High Altitude Compensation (HAC) hose (if equipped).
    g. **On models with A/C,** disconnect vacuum switching valve hoses.
    h. **On all models,** disconnect vacuum switch hoses.
    i. Disconnect power steering air hoses.
    j. Disconnect evaporative emission

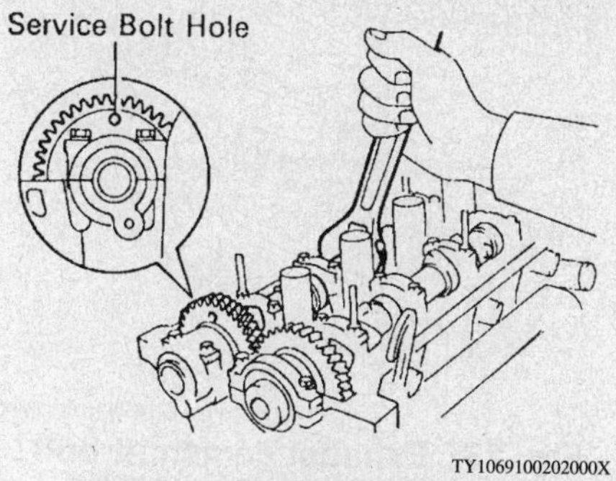
Service Bolt Hole
TY1069100202000X

Fig. 6 Intake camshaft positioning. 5E-FE

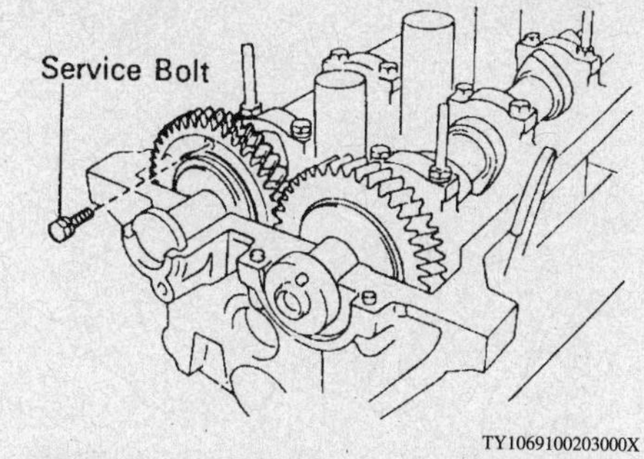
Service Bolt
TY1069100203000X

Fig. 7 Service bolt installation. 5E-FE

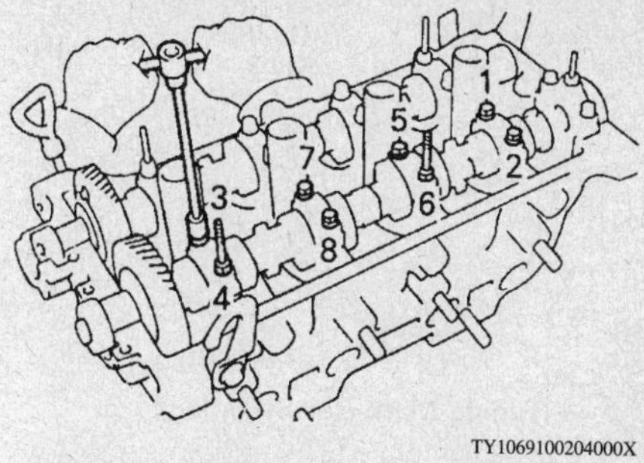
TY1069100204000X

Fig. 8 Exhaust camshaft bolt loosening sequence. 5E-FE

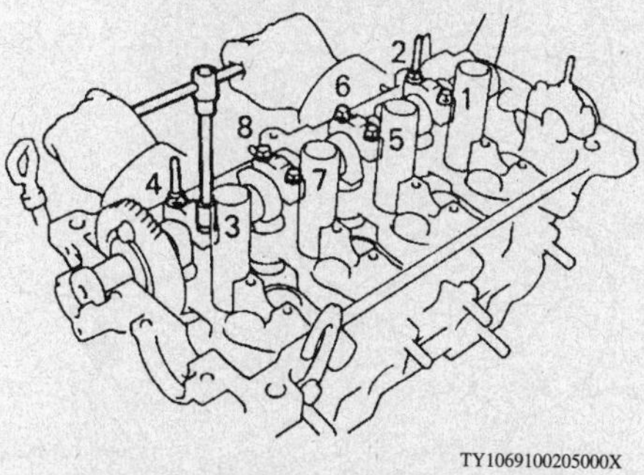
TY1069100205000X

Fig. 9 Intake camshaft bolt loosening sequence. 5E-FE

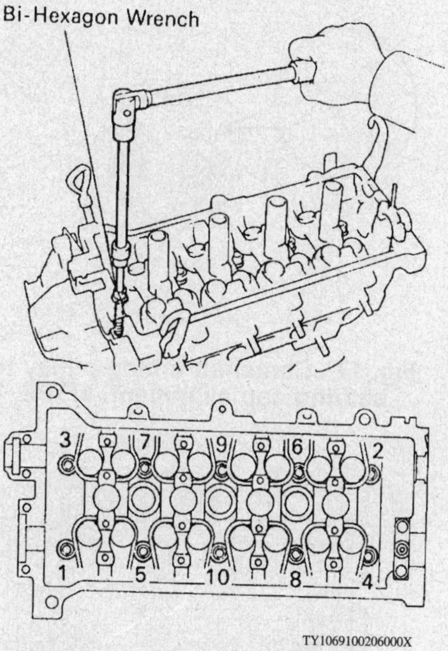
Bi-Hexagon Wrench
TY1069100206000X

Fig. 10 Cylinder head bolt loosening sequence. 5E-FE

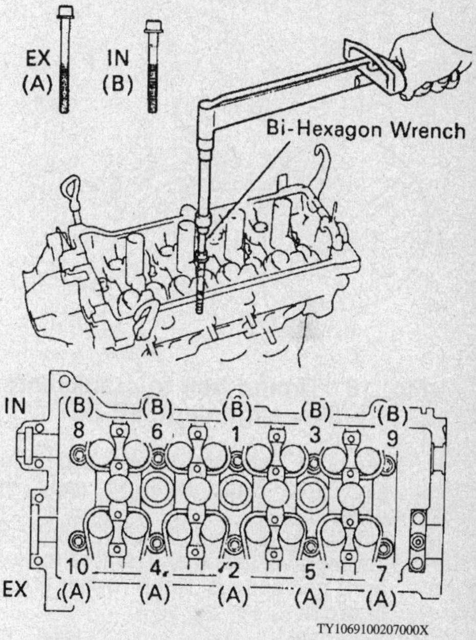
EX
(A)
IN
(B)
Bi-Hexagon Wrench
IN
EX
TY1069100207000X

Fig. 11 Cylinder head bolt tightening sequence. 5E-FE

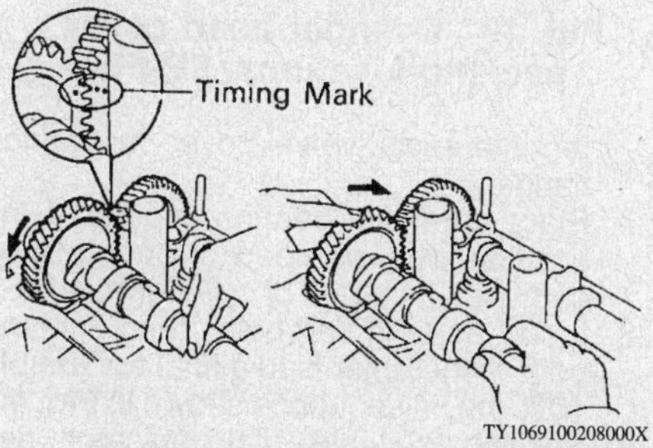
Timing Mark
TY1069100208000X

Fig. 12 Intake & exhaust camshaft timing marks. 5E-FE

control purge (EVAP) hose.
- k. Disconnect outer vent control valve (OVCV) hose.
- l. Remove EVAP and No. 2 cold enrichment breaker vacuum switching valves.
- m. Disconnect water bypass hoses from carburetor.

12. Disconnect the following connectors:
    - a. Three vacuum switching valve (VSV) connectors.
    - b. EGR gas temperature sensor connector.
    - c. A/C idle-up vacuum switching valve connector.
    - d. Acceleration cut vacuum switch connector.
    - e. Vacuum sensor and igniter connectors.
    - f. Four injector connectors.
    - g. Ground strap from cylinder head connector.
    - h. Cold start injector connector.
    - i. Alternator and starter connectors and wires.
    - j. Water temperature sender gauge connector.
    - k. Water temperature sensor and switch connectors.
    - l. Cold start injector time switch connector.
    - m. Distributor connectors.
    - n. Remove six clamps and disconnect engine harness.
13. Remove exhaust pipe to manifold attaching nuts and pipe.
14. Remove intake manifold stay, ground strap and wire harness clamp bolt from intake manifold.
15. Remove timing belt and camshaft timing pulley as outlined in "Timing Belt, Replace."
16. Loosen cylinder head bolts in several passes, using sequence shown in **Fig. 1,** then remove cylinder head bolts. **If loosening sequence is not followed, cylinder head cracking or warpage could result.**
17. Remove cylinder head from engine block and place on suitable wooden blocks. **If cylinder head is difficult to remove, use suitable pry bar between cylinder head and block projection to aid in removal. Take care not to damage cylinder head or engine block deck surfaces.**
18. Disconnect distributor secondary wiring from spark plugs, then remove two distributor hold-down bolts and the distributor, with cap attached.
19. Remove coolant outlet housing, then the engine hangers.
20. **On California models,** remove AS pipe.
21. **On all models,** remove exhaust manifold attaching bolts and manifold.
22. Remove spark plugs, carburetor, accelerator cable bracket, air cleaner bracket and air pipes.
23. Remove fuel pump and intake manifold.
24. Position suitable dial indicator as shown in **Fig. 2,** then measure camshaft thrust clearance by prying camshaft back and forth. Standard clearance is .0031–.0071 inch. If clearance exceeds .0098 inch, cylinder head and/or camshaft should be replaced.
25. Loosen rocker arm adjusting screw locknut and fully loosen adjusting screw.
26. Loosen camshaft bearing cap bolts in several passes, using sequence shown in **Fig. 3,** then remove bearing

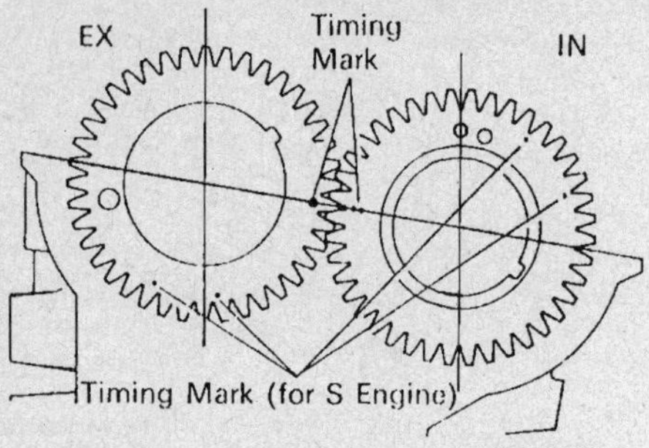
EX
Timing
Mark
IN
Timing Mark (for S Engine)

TY1069100209000X

Fig. 13 Intake & exhaust camshaft alignment. 5E-FE

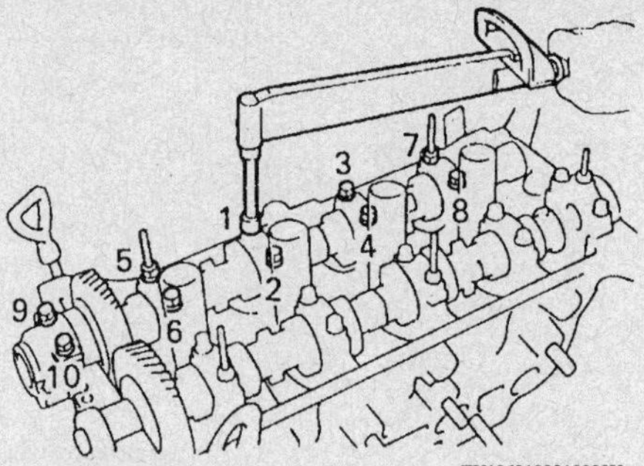
1
2
3
4
5
6
7
8
9
10

TY1069100210000X

Fig. 14 Intake camshaft bolt tightening sequence. 5E-FE

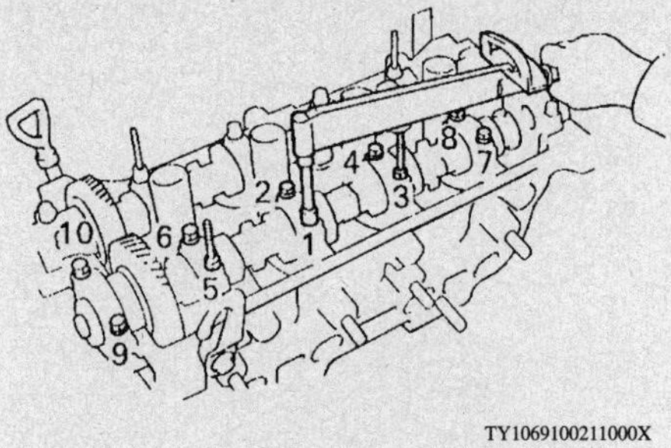
1
2
3
4
5
6
7
8
9
10

TY1069100211000X

Fig. 15 Exhaust camshaft bolt tightening sequence. 5E-FE

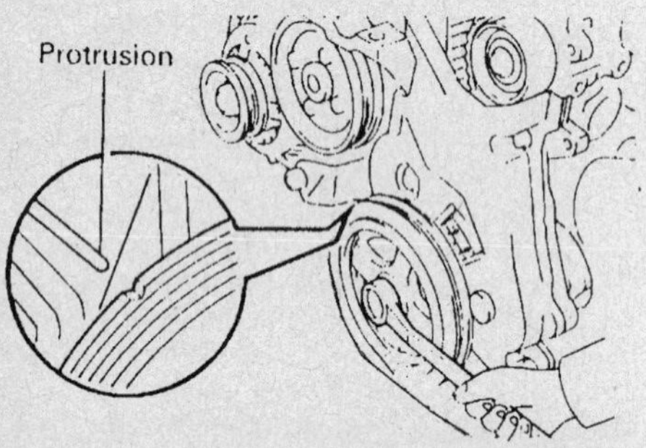
Protrusion

TY1069100212000X

Fig. 16 Timing belt to crankshaft pulley alignment. 5E-FE

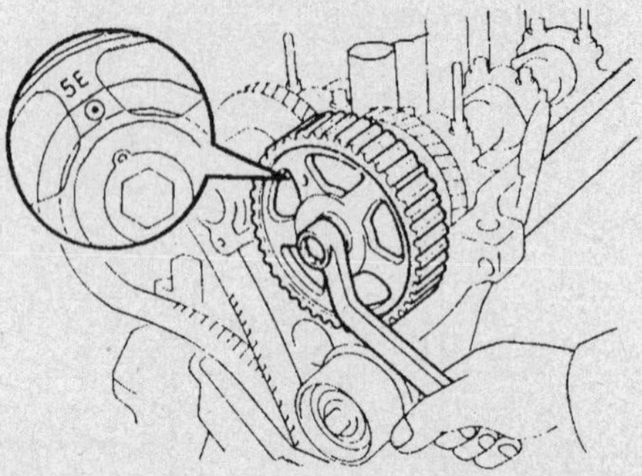
5E

TY1069100213000X

Fig. 17 Camshaft timing pulley to bearing cap alignment. 5E-FE

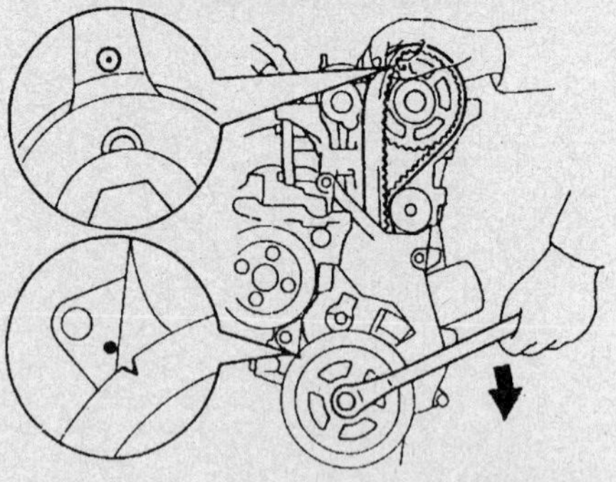

TY1069100214000X

Fig. 18 Timing belt installation. 5E-FE

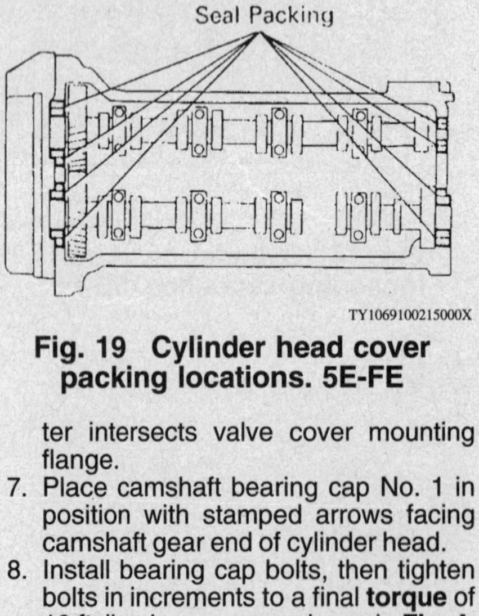
Seal Packing

TY1069100215000X

Fig. 19 Cylinder head cover packing locations. 5E-FE

cap bolts, camshaft, oil seal and bearing caps. **Keep bearing caps in order.**

27. Lifting top of retaining spring, pry out lower part of spring and remove rocker arms and springs. **Keep rocker arms in order.**

Installation

1. Ensure rocker arm adjusting screw is fully backed out, then install new rocker arm spring on rocker arm. Press bottom lip of spring until it fits into the rocker arm pivot groove.
2. Position rocker arm/spring assembly in cylinder head with rocker arm adjusting screw located in rocker arm pivot. Using suitable screwdriver, pry rocker arm spring onto rocker arm pivot. Move rocker arm up and down at pivot end to ensure there is spring tension on rocker arm and that the rocker arm does not rattle.
3. Ensure engine crankshaft is set at TDC compression stoke, then lubricate camshaft journals with engine oil and install camshaft with camshaft gear lockpin at 12 o'clock position. **Set camshaft and crankshaft as noted above to prevent damage to the sub-intake valve and/or piston head.**
4. Place camshaft bearing caps Nos. 2, 3 and 4 in position with stamped arrows facing camshaft gear end of head.
5. Apply oil to camshaft oil seal inner diameter, then apply suitable liquid sealer to seal outer diameter and install seal.
6. Apply small amount of suitable sealer to corners where oil seal outer diameter intersects valve cover mounting flange.
7. Place camshaft bearing cap No. 1 in position with stamped arrows facing camshaft gear end of cylinder head.
8. Install bearing cap bolts, then tighten bolts in increments to a final **torque** of 10 ft. lbs. in sequence shown in **Fig. 4.**
9. Position suitable dial indicator as shown in **Fig. 2,** then measure camshaft thrust clearance by prying camshaft back and forth. Standard clearance is .0031–.0071 inch. If clearance exceeds .0098 inch, cylinder head and/or camshaft should be replaced.
10. Install new grommets on the injectors.
11. Apply a thin coat of gasoline to O-rings and install them onto injectors.
12. Turning injectors left and right, then install them into fuel delivery pipe.
13. Place two spacers and four insulators into position on cylinder head, then position delivery pipe onto cylinder head.
14. Install two fuel delivery pipe attaching bolts and tighten to specifications.
15. Position engine hanger bracket at left front of engine, then apply suitable sealer to bracket attaching bolt threads and install. Tighten attaching bolt to specification.
16. Position engine hanger bracket at right rear of engine, and install attaching bolt. Tighten attaching bolt to specification.
17. Apply suitable sealing compound to coolant outlet housing flange, then install outlet housing.
18. Align distributor coupling groove with lower housing groove. Install distributor into cylinder head while aligning mounting flange groove with valve cover attaching stud. Install hold-down bolt(s) finger tight.
19. Install new cylinder head gasket on cylinder block, then the cylinder head and cylinder head bolts. **Ensure head gasket is installed with proper side up.**
20. **Torque** cylinder head bolts in sequence shown, **Fig. 5,** to 22 ft. lbs., then **torque** again in sequence to 36 ft. lbs. Tighten bolts an additional 90° in sequence to achieve final tightening specification.
21. Install timing belt. Refer to "Timing Belt, Replace" for procedure.
22. Adjust valves. Refer to "Valve Adjustment" for procedure.
23. Install wire harness clamp bolt to intake manifold, then intake manifold to engine block bracket and ground strap.
24. Connect exhaust pipe to exhaust manifold, then the coolant bypass hose to carburetor. Connect belts, hoses,

Engine	Cam Height Limit, Inch.	
	Intake	Exhaust
1.5L 3E-E	1.3453	1.4106
1.5L 5E-FE	1.6283	1.6205

Fig. 20 Camshaft lobe lift specifications

New shim thickness mm (in.)

Shim No.	Thickness	Shim No.	Thickness
02	2.500 (0.0984)	20	2.950 (0.1161)
04	2.550 (0.1004)	22	3.000 (0.1181)
06	2.600 (0.1024)	24	3.050 (0.1201)
08	2.650 (0.1043)	26	3.100 (0.1220)
10	2.700 (0.1063)	28	3.150 (0.1240)
12	2.750 (0.1083)	30	3.200 (0.1260)
14	2.800 (0.1102)	32	3.250 (0.1280)
16	2.850 (0.1122)	34	3.300 (0.1299)
18	2.900 (0.1142)		

TY1069100216000X

Fig. 21 Valve shim thickness chart. 5E-FE

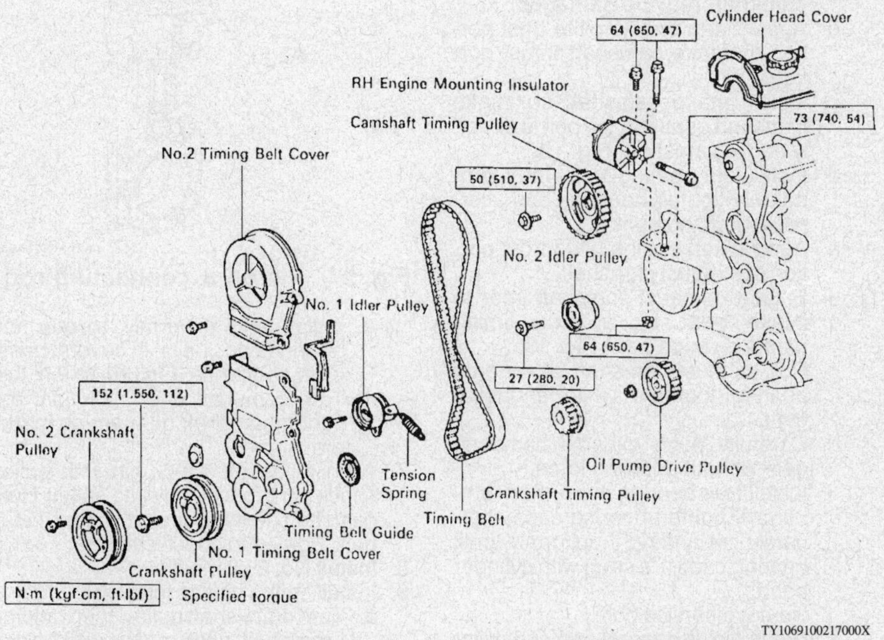
64 (650, 47)
Cylinder Head Cover
RH Engine Mounting Insulator
Camshaft Timing Pulley
73 (740, 54)
No.2 Timing Belt Cover
50 (510, 37)
No. 2 Idler Pulley
No. 1 Idler Pulley
64 (650, 47)
27 (280, 20)
152 (1,550, 112)
No. 2 Crankshaft Pulley
Tension Spring
Oil Pump Drive Pulley
Crankshaft Timing Pulley
Timing Belt
Timing Belt Guide
No. 1 Timing Belt Cover
Crankshaft Pulley
N·m (kgf·cm, ft·lbf) : Specified torque
TY1069100217000X

Fig. 22 Exploded view of timing belt assembly. 3E-E engine

wires and cables that were disconnected during removal procedure.
25. Refill cooling system and crankcase.
26. Connect battery ground cable, then start engine and allow to reach operating temperature while checking for leaks.
27. Readjust valve clearances.
28. Adjust ignition timing and idle speed as necessary.

5E-FE

Removal

1. Remove righthand engine undercover.
2. Drain engine coolant.
3. Disconnect front exhaust pipe, then oxygen sensor electrical connector.
4. **On models with automatic transaxle,** disconnect throttle cable.
5. **On all models,** disconnect accelerator cable.
6. Remove PCV hose.
7. Remove air cleaner assembly with air intake connector.
8. Position suitable fuel container, then disconnect fuel return hose. Remove union bolt, gasket and disconnect fuel inlet hose.
9. **On models with power steering,** remove power steering belt, pump attaching bolts and position pump aside. Remove pump bracket.
10. **On models with A/C, less power steering,** loosen idler pulley nut. Remove drive belt, then the idler pulley bracket.
11. **On all models,** remove distributor or ignition coils with spark plug wires.
12. Remove spark plugs.
13. Disconnect vacuum hoses from throttle opener, EGR valve, EGR vacuum modulator, charcoal canister and idle-up vacuum switching valve.
14. Remove EGR pipe assembly and gasket.
15. **On 1993–95 California and all 1996 models,** disconnect EGR gas temperature sensor electrical connector, then remove sensor and gasket.
16. **On all models,** remove EGR vacuum modulator and bracket, then EGR valve and gasket.
17. Disconnect water temperature sender gauge, water temperature sensor, water temperature switch and fan water temperature switch electrical connectors.
18. Disconnect two radiator hoses, water inlet hose, water outlet hose, water bypass hose and two BVSV vacuum hoses.
19. Remove water inlet and outlet housings.
20. Remove exhaust manifold heat insulator, then manifold and gasket.
21. Disconnect ACV electrical connector and air hose, remove attaching bolts and ground strap, then remove ACV and O-ring.
22. Remove throttle body assembly.
23. Remove delivery pipe and injectors.
24. **On models with power steering,** disconnect two idle-up air hoses from air pipe.
25. **On all models,** remove air pipe attaching bolts and pipe.
26. Remove intake manifold stay, disconnect idle-up vacuum hose, brake booster vacuum hose and vacuum sensor hose, remove intake manifold attaching nuts and bolts, then manifold and gasket.
27. Remove oil filler cap, then the five cylinder head cover attaching cap nuts and seal washers.
28. Remove cover and gasket, then the No. 2 timing belt cover.
29. Loosen alternator pivot and adjusting bolt, then remove belt.
30. Remove No. 3 timing belt cover from No. 1 timing belt cover.
31. If reusing timing belt, place installation alignment marks on timing belt and camshaft timing pulley.
32. Loosen No. 1 idler pulley mount bolt, then shift pulley as far left as possible and temporarily tighten bolt. Remove timing belt.
33. Remove No. 2 idler pulley attaching bolt and pulley. **Support timing belt, ensure crankshaft timing pulley and timing belt do not shift. Do not allow timing belt to come in contact with oil, water or dust.**
34. Hold camshaft hexagonal portion, then remove attaching bolt and timing pulley.
35. Remove camshafts as follows:
    a. **Camshafts must be held level during removal or head or camshaft may be damaged.**
    b. Set intake camshaft, ensuring intake camshaft gear service bolt holes are directly above, **Fig. 6.** Lift exhaust camshaft level and evenly push intake camshaft No. 2 and No. 4 cylinder cam lobes toward valve lifters.
    c. Remove No. 1 and No. 4 bearing caps.
    d. Install service bolt 6 mm thread diameter, 1.0 mm thread pitch and 16–20 mm (.63–.79 inch) long to secure intake camshaft sub-gear to main gear, **Fig. 7.**
    e. Loosen and remove eight No. 3 bearing caps in several passes in

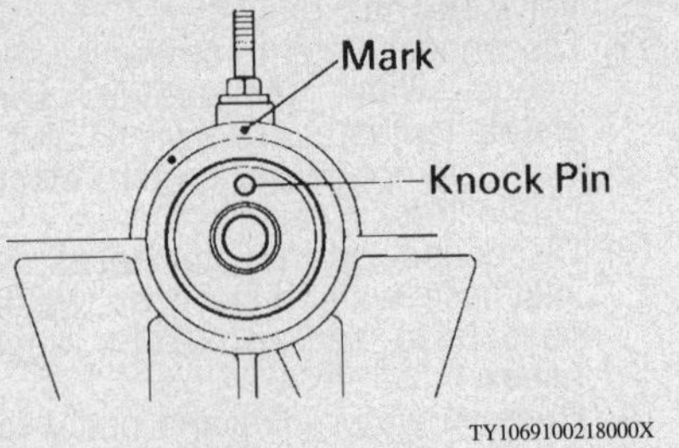
Mark
Knock Pin
TY1069100218000X

Fig. 23 Camshaft & bearing cap alignment. 3E-E engine

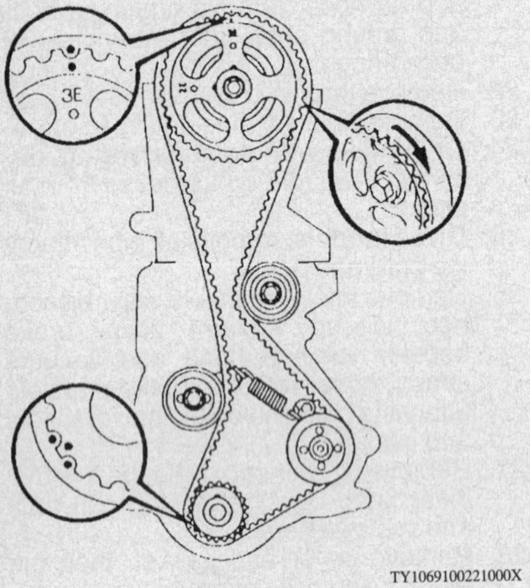
3E
TY1069100221000X

Fig. 26 Timing mark alignment. 3E-E engine

sequence shown, **Fig. 8.**

f. Remove four bearing caps and exhaust camshaft. **Camshaft must be removed straight and level. Do not pry or force camshaft to remove.**

g. Loosen and remove eight No. 3 bearing caps in several passes in sequence shown, **Fig. 9.**

h. Remove four bearing caps and intake camshaft. **Camshaft must be removed straight and level. Do not pry or force camshaft to remove.**

36. Using suitable 8 mm bi-hexagon wrench, loosen ten cylinder head bolts in several passes using sequence shown in **Fig. 10.**
37. Lift cylinder head from dowels to remove.

Installation

1. Thoroughly clean all parts, before installing.
2. Apply clean engine oil to sliding and rotating parts.
3. Replace all gaskets and oil seals.
4. Install cylinder head to block, ensure installation direction is correct.
5. Apply clean engine oil to exhaust and intake bolts, then using suitable 8 mm bi-hexagon wrench, **torque** to 33 ft. lbs. in several passes using sequence shown in **Fig. 11.** Mark front of each bolt with paint, then tighten ten cylinder head bolts an additional 90° in se-

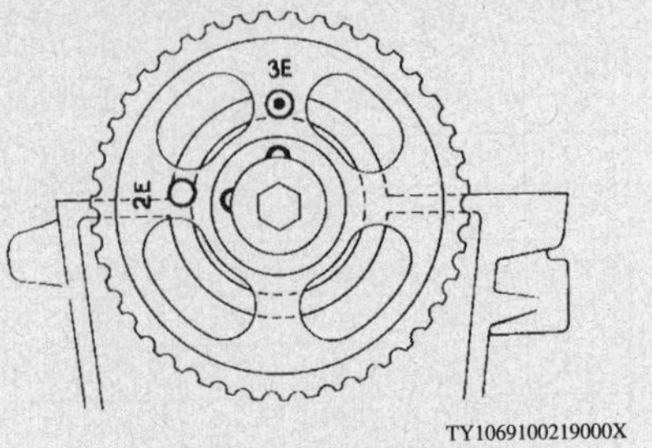
3E
2E
TY1069100219000X

Fig. 24 Camshaft sprocket installation. 3E-E

quence, ensure painted mark is at a 90° angle to front.

6. Install camshafts as follows:
   a. **Camshafts must be held level during installation or head or camshaft may be damaged.**
   b. Apply clean engine oil to trust portion of intake camshaft thrust portion.
   c. Install intake camshaft so intake camshaft gear service bolt is directly above camshaft, **Fig. 12.**
   d. Install four bearing caps, then temporarily tighten bearing caps alternately left and right.
   e. Apply clean engine oil to trust portion of exhaust camshaft.
   f. Engage exhaust camshaft gear to intake gear by aligning timing marks on each gear, **Fig. 13.**
   g. Roll exhaust camshaft down onto bearing journals while engaging gear.
   h. Carefully push exhaust camshaft gear without applying force.
   i. Install four bearing caps, then temporarily tighten bearing caps alternately left and right uniformly, until bearing caps are snug with cylinder head.
   j. Remove service bolt.
   k. Clean No. 2 bearing cap and cylinder head installed surface with suitable cleaner, then apply suitable seal packing to No. 2 bearing cap.
   l. Install No. 2 bearing cap to proper location, ensuring there is no gap between cylinder head and bearing cap contact surface.
   m. Temporarily tighten bearing cap bolts, alternately from right to left uniformly, then install camshaft housing plug.
   n. Install and uniformly **torque** ten bearing cap bolts, in several passes in sequence, **Fig. 14,** to 9 ft. lbs.
   o. Apply suitable MP grease to camshaft oil seal lip, then install as far as deepest part of cylinder head.
   p. Clean No. 1 bearing cap and cylinder head installed surface with suitable cleaner, then apply suitable seal packing to No. 1 bearing cap.
   q. Install No. 1 bearing cap to proper location, ensuring there is no gap between cylinder head and bearing cap contact surface.
   r. Temporarily tighten bearing cap bolts, alternately from right to left uniformly.

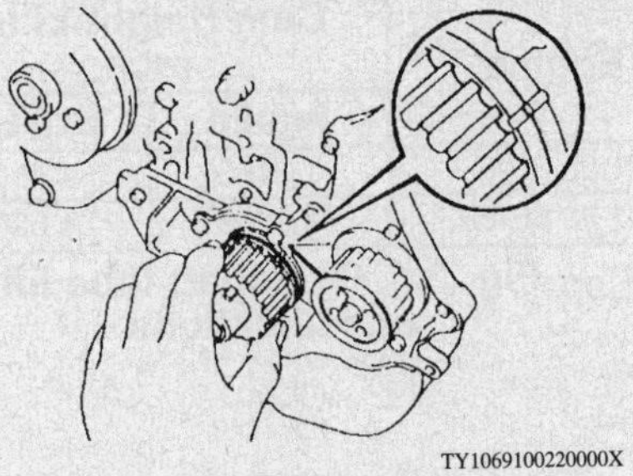
TY1069100220000X

Fig. 25 Crankshaft sprocket & oil pump body TDC mark. 3E-E engine

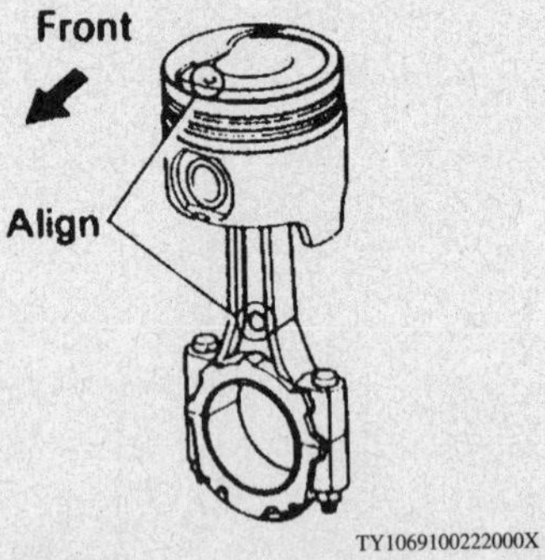
Front
Align
TY1069100222000X

Fig. 27 Piston & connecting rod

   s. Install and uniformly **torque** ten bearing caps bolts, in several passes in sequence, **Fig. 15,** to 9 ft. lbs.
   t. Turn camshaft one revolution, ensuring camshaft gear timing marks are aligned.
7. Align camshaft knock pin with pulley knock pin groove and slide pulley. Hold camshaft hexagonal portion and install bolt. Tighten to specifications.
8. Install No. 2 idler pulley.
9. Install timing belt as follows:
   a. Turn crankshaft pulley, then holding timing belt, align groove with belt installation protrusion of No. 1 timing belt cover, **Fig. 16.**
   b. Turn camshaft and align camshaft timing pulley hole with bearing cap belt installation mark, **Fig. 17.**
   c. Coil timing belt around camshaft timing pulley, turn crankshaft pulley, then install belt to camshaft timing pulley, **Fig. 18.**
   d. Loosen No. 1 idler pulley mount bolt until pulley is moved slightly by spring tension.
   e. Turn crankshaft pulley two revolutions from TDC to TDC. **Always turn crankshaft clockwise.**
   f. Ensure pulleys align with timing marks.
10. Install No. 3 timing belt cover.
11. Install alternator drive belt.
12. Install No. 2 timing belt cover.
13. Apply suitable seal packing to cylinder head cover, **Fig. 19,** then install gasket and cover. Tighten to specifications.
14. Install intake manifold and gasket, connect idle-up vacuum hose, brake booster vacuum hose and vacuum sensor hose, then install manifold stay and tighten attaching nuts and bolts to

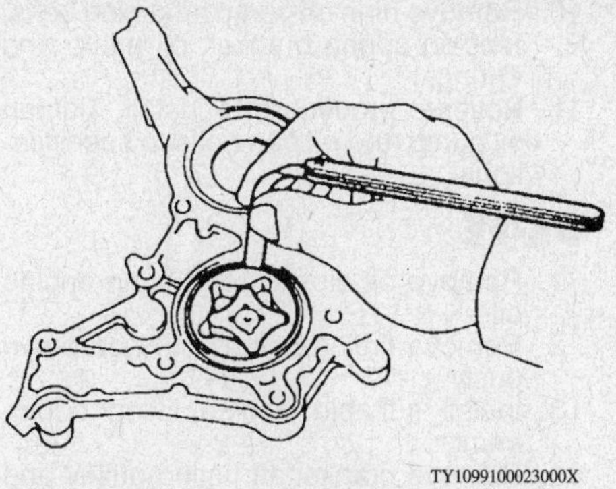
TY1099100023000X

Fig. 28 Oil pump body clearance inspection

specifications.

15. Connect two idle-up air hoses, then install air pipe.
16. Install fuel injectors and delivery pipe.
17. Install throttle body.
18. Install ACV.
19. Install exhaust manifold and gasket and heat insulator.
20. Install water inlet and outlet housings, connect two radiator hoses, water inlet hose, heater outlet hose, water bypass hose, BVSV vacuum hose from throttle body P port and from charcoal canister.
21. Connect water temperature sender, water temperature sensor, water temperature switch and fan water temperature switch electrical connectors.
22. Install EGR valve, vacuum modulator and pipe.
23. **On California models,** install EGR temperature sensor and gasket.
24. **On all models,** connect vacuum hose to throttle opener, EGR valve, EGR vacuum modulator, charcoal canister and idle-up vacuum hoses.
25. Install spark plugs. Tighten to specifications.
26. Install distributor, then spark plug wires.
27. **On models with A/C, less power steering,** install idler pulley bracket.
28. **On models with power steering,** install power steering pump bracket and pump, then install belt.
29. **On all models,** connect fuel hoses.
30. Install air cleaner assembly and air intake connector.
31. Install PCV hose.
32. Install accelerator cable and adjust.
33. **On models with automatic transaxle,** connect throttle cable and adjust.
34. **On all models,** connect front exhaust pipe and tighten to specifications.
35. Install righthand engine undercover.
36. Refill engine coolant, then start engine and inspect for leaks.

CAMSHAFT LOBE LIFT SPECIFICATIONS

Refer to **Fig. 20** for camshaft lobe lift specifications.

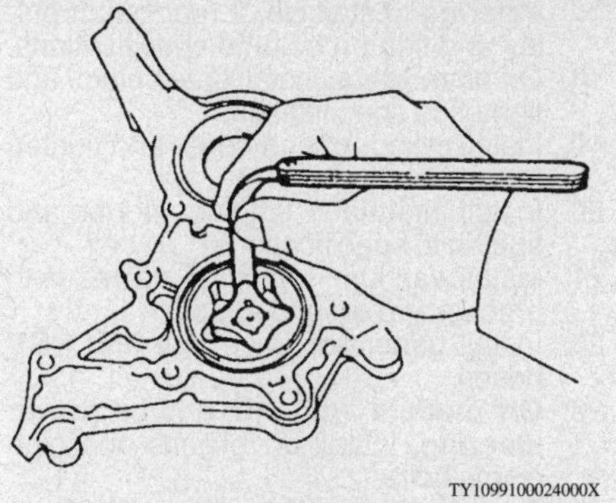
TY1099100024000X

Fig. 29 Oil pump tip clearance inspection

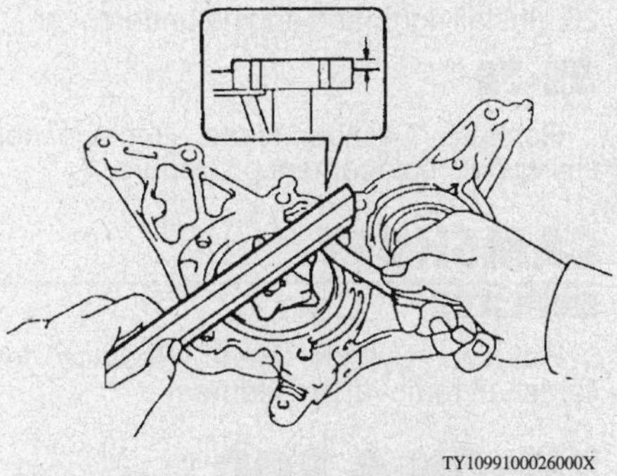
TY1099100026000X

Fig. 31 Oil pump side clearance inspection. 5E-FE engine

VALVE CLEARANCE SPECIFICATIONS

Stem-To-Guide Clearance	
Intake	Exhaust
.006–.010	.012–.016

VALVE ADJUSTMENT

3E-E ENGINE

These engines use an adjusting screw and locknut to adjust the valves.

1. With No. 1 piston at TDC on compression stroke, adjust the following cylinders valves to .008 inch: No. 1 intake and exhaust, No. 2 intake and No. 3 exhaust.
2. Turn crankshaft in normal direction of rotation one full revolution (360°) and adjust the following cylinders valves to .008 inch: No. 2 exhaust, No. 3 intake and No. 4 intake and exhaust.

5E-FE ENGINE

These engines use an adjusting shim to adjust the valves.

1. With No. 1 piston at TDC on compression stroke, measure and record clearance between valve lifter and camshaft: No. 1 intake and exhaust, No. 2 intake and No. 3 exhaust.
2. Turn crankshaft in normal direction of rotation one full revolution (360°) and measure and record clearance between valve lifter and camshaft: No. 2 exhaust, No. 3 intake and No. 4 intake and exhaust.

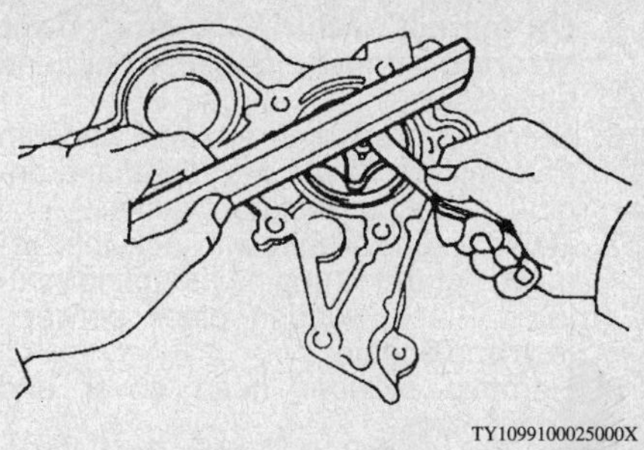
TY1099100025000X

Fig. 30 Oil pump side clearance inspection. 3E-E engine

3. Turn crankshaft to position camshaft cam lobe on adjusting valve upward.
4. Position valve lifter notch, then using suitable small screwdriver, remove adjusting shim.
5. Using suitable micrometer, measure thickness of removed shim.
6. New shim thickness equals measured valve clearance less .006–.010 inch on intake valves or .012–.016 inch on exhaust valves, plus thickness of used shim.
7. Select new shim with thickness as close as possible to values calculated in step 6, **Fig. 21.**
8. Install new shim, then recheck valve clearance.

VALVE GUIDES

1. Using a suitable tool and hammer, strike valve guide bushing to break it off at cylinder head casting.
2. Heat cylinder head to 176–212°F (80–100°C).
3. Using suitable valve guide removal tool, tap out bushing.
4. Install snap ring on new valve guide, then install new valve guide using tool as outlined above and driving in from the reverse side of removal.
5. Ream new valve guide, if necessary. Refer to "Valve Specifications" for stem clearances.

HYDRAULIC LIFTERS

REPLACE

Check lifters for excessive wear and/or damage. Replace worn or damaged valve lifters as required. Lubricate hydraulic valve lifter before installation.

TIMING BELT

REPLACE

3E-E

Removal

Refer to **Fig. 22** for removal and installation of timing belt.

1. Remove righthand engine undercover.
2. Disconnect accelerator cable.
3. **On models with automatic transaxle,** disconnect throttle cable.
4. **On all models,** disconnect PCV hoses.

5. **On models with A/C and/or power steering,** remove pipe clamp bolts and drive belts.
6. Remove ground strap and vacuum transmitting valves with righthand engine mounting insulator bracket.
7. Raise engine slightly with jack, then remove righthand engine mounting insulator. Place wooden block between jack and engine.
8. Remove cylinder head cover and spark plugs.
9. Turn crankshaft to set No. 1 piston to TDC on compression stroke.
10. Install crankshaft pulley holding tool No. 09213-14010, or equivalent, to crankshaft pulley. Loosen pulley bolt with appropriate tool and remove crankshaft pulleys.
11. Remove timing belt covers and timing belt guide.
12. Remove tension spring.
13. Loosen idler pulley bolt. Push bolt far left, then tighten temporarily.
14. Remove timing belt and No. 1 idler pulley.
15. Remove No. 2 idler pulley.
16. Remove crankshaft timing pulley and camshaft pulley.
17. Using adjusting wrench tool No. 09616-12011, or equivalent, remove oil pump pulley.

Installation

1. Align pulley with oil pump driveshaft, then hold pump sprocket with suitable tool and tighten attaching nut to specification.
2. Align camshaft knock pin with No. 1 camshaft bearing cap, **Fig. 23.**
3. Align knock pin hole on 3E mark side with camshaft knock pin hole, then install camshaft pulley to camshaft. Tighten camshaft sprocket bolt to specification, **Fig. 24.**
4. Install crankshaft timing pulley. Align TDC marks on oil pump body with crankshaft timing pulley, **Fig. 25.**
5. Install No. 1 idler pulley. Pry pulley to far left and tighten temporarily.
6. Install No. 2 idler pulley and tighten to specification.
7. Install timing belt. Ensure marks made during removal align and arrows on belt are pointing in direction of engine revolution, **Fig. 26.**
8. Install tension spring.
9. Temporarily install crankshaft pulley bolt, then inspect valve timing and belt tension. Ensure each pulley aligns with marks shown in **Fig. 26.**
10. Tighten No. 1 idler pulley bolt to specification.
11. Remove crankshaft pulley bolt.
12. Install timing belt guide.
13. Install timing belt covers and tighten to specifications.
14. Align crankshaft pulley set key with key groove of crankshaft pulley.
15. Install crankshaft pulley bolt.
16. Hold crankshaft pulley with pulley holding tool No. 09213-14010, or equivalent, while using suitable tool to tighten crankshaft pulley bolt to specification.
17. **On models with A/C and/or power steering,** install No. 2 crankshaft pulley and tighten bolts to specifications.
18. **On all models,** install spark plugs and tighten to specifications.
19. Install cylinder head cover and tighten to specifications.
20. Install righthand engine mount and tighten to specifications.
21. Install vacuum switching valves with bracket and ground strap.
22. Install generator drive belt and PCV hoses.
23. **On models with AC and/or power steering,** install drive belts and pipe clamp bolts.
24. **On models with automatic transaxle,** connect and adjust throttle cable.
25. Connect and adjust accelerator cable.
26. Install righthand engine undercover

5E-FE

Refer to "Cylinder Head, Replace" for timing belt replacement procedure.

CAMSHAFT

REPLACE

Refer to "Cylinder Head, Replace" for camshaft removal procedures.

PISTON & ROD ASSEMBLY

On 3E-E engines, pistons are available in standard and oversize of .020 inch (.50 mm). On all engines, when assembling piston onto connecting rod, ensure mark on top of piston and mark on connecting rod are on same side, **Fig. 27.** When installing piston and connecting rod assembly, ensure mark on top of piston is facing toward front of engine.

MAIN & ROD BEARINGS

Main and connecting rod bearings are available in standard and undersizes of .010 inch (.25 mm).

OIL PAN

REPLACE

3E-E

1. Disconnect battery ground cable, then raise and support vehicle.
2. Remove right side engine undercover.
3. Disconnect front exhaust pipe.
4. Remove timing belt. Refer to "Timing Belt, Replace" for procedure.
5. Remove crankshaft timing pulley and oil pump pulley.
6. Remove oil filler cap and oil dipstick, then drain crankcase into suitable container.
7. Remove oil pan attaching nuts and bolts, then the oil pan.
8. Remove oil strainer attaching bolts, then the strainer and O-ring.
9. Remove pressure regulator valve assembly.
10. Remove nine oil pump attaching bolts, tension spring bracket, oil pump and O-ring.
11. Reverse procedure to install. Tighten oil pump and oil pan bolts to specifications.

5E-FE

1. Remove oil dipstick and drain engine oil.
2. Remove timing belt as outlined previously.
3. Install suitable engine lifting equipment.
4. Remove crankshaft timing pulley and oil pump pulley.
5. **On models with A/C,** disconnect compressor electrical connector, then remove compressor attaching bolts and position compressor aside. Remove compressor mounting bracket.
6. **On all models,** disconnect oxygen sensor electrical connector, then disconnect front exhaust pipe stay and exhaust pipe.
7. Remove two oil pan attaching nuts and eight bolts, then using suitable tool, cut off oil pan sealer and remove pan.
8. Remove oil strainer and O-ring.
9. Remove pressure regulator valve.
10. Remove nine oil pump attaching bolts and tension spring bracket.
11. Using suitable soft faced hammer, remove oil pump and O-ring.
12. Reverse procedure to install.

OIL PUMP

REPLACE

Refer to "Oil Pan, Replace" for procedure.

OIL PUMP SERVICE

1. Using a suitable feeler gauge, measure clearance between driven rotor and pump case, **Fig. 28.**
2. **On 3E-E engines,** standard clearance should be .0039–.0063 inch. If feeler gauge clearance obtained exceeds specified limits, replace oil pump rotor set and/or pump case.
3. **On 5E-FE engines,** standard clearance should be .0039–.0083 inch. If feeler gauge clearance obtained exceeds specified limits, replace oil pump rotor set and/or pump case.
4. **On all models,** using a feeler gauge, measure clearance between both rotor tips, **Fig. 29.** Clearance should be .0024–.0059 inch. If feeler gauge clearance obtained exceeds specified limit, replace oil pump rotor set.
5. **On 3E-E engines,** place suitable straightedge across pump opening and measure side clearance, **Fig. 30.** Side clearance should be .0012–.0035 inch. If clearance is greater than specifications, replace oil pump rotor set and/or pump body.
6. **On 5E-FE engines,** place suitable straightedge across pump opening and measure side clearance, **Fig. 31.** Side clearance should be .1146–.1169

inch. If clearance is greater than specifications, replace oil pump rotor set and/or pump body.

BELT TENSION DATA

Belt	New, lbs.	Used, lbs.
Air Cond.	150–180	90–130
Alternator	140–180	80–120
Power Steer.	①	80–120

① — On 1993, 140–180; 1994–96, 135–185.

COOLING SYSTEM BLEED

These engines do not require a specified bleed procedure. After filling cooling system, run engine to operating temperature with radiator/pressure cap off. Air will then be automatically bled through cap opening.

THERMOSTAT

REPLACE

1. **On Paseo models,** remove air intake connector.
2. **On all models,** remove water inlet attaching nuts, then remove inlet, thermostat and gasket.
3. Reverse procedure to install.

WATER PUMP

REPLACE

1. Remove right side undercover, then drain engine coolant.
2. Remove alternator assembly.
3. Remove intake manifold support bracket.
4. Disconnect water inlet, heater inlet and water hoses.
5. Remove dipstick tube.
6. Remove alternator adjusting bracket.
7. Disconnect coolant hose from intake manifold.
8. Remove water pump attaching nuts and bolts, then the water pump.
9. Reverse procedure to install. Tighten water pump mounting bolts to specifications.

RADIATOR

REPLACE

PASEO

1. Disconnect battery ground cable.
2. Remove engine undercovers.
3. Drain engine coolant.
4. Remove air intake connector.
5. Disconnect cooling fan motor connector.
6. Remove oxygen sensor connector.
7. Disconnect coolant reservoir hose.
8. Disconnect radiator hoses.
9. **On models with automatic transaxle,** disconnect transaxle oil cooler hoses.
10. **On all models,** remove radiator supports and radiator with cooling fans.
11. Reverse procedure to install.

TERCEL

1993–94

1. Disconnect battery ground cable.
2. Remove engine undercovers.
3. Drain engine coolant.
4. Remove air intake connector.
5. Disconnect coolant reservoir hose.
6. Disconnect radiator hoses.
7. **On models with automatic transaxle,** disconnect transaxle oil cooler hoses.
8. **On all models,** disconnect cooling fan motor connector.
9. Remove radiator supports and radiator with cooling fans.
10. Reverse procedure to install.

1995–96

1. Disconnect battery ground cable.
2. Remove engine undercovers.
3. Drain engine coolant.
4. Remove air intake connector.
5. Remove coolant reservoir tank assembly and hose.
6. Disconnect No. 1 cooling fan connector.
7. **On models with A/C,** disconnect No. 2 cooling fan connector.
8. **On all models,** disconnect upper radiator hose at radiator and lower radiator hose at water inlet.
9. **On models with automatic transaxle,** disconnect transaxle oil cooler hoses.
10. **On all models,** remove radiator supports, radiator with cooling fans and lower radiator hose attached.
11. Reverse procedure to install.

FUEL PUMP

REPLACE

1. Remove rear seat cushion.
2. Remove floor service hole attaching screws, then remove cover.
3. Disconnect fuel pump electrical connector.
4. Disconnect fuel lines.
5. Remove fuel pump attaching bolts, then the fuel pump.
6. Reverse procedure to install.

FUEL FILTER

REPLACE

1. Place suitable container under fuel filter/hose connection.
2. Slowly disconnect fuel hose from fuel filter outlet. **Place shop towel over fuel hose to prevent fuel spillage on engine.**
3. Remove fuel filter, then plug fuel hose.
4. Replace gasket and reverse procedure to install.

TIGHTENING SPECIFICATIONS

3E-E

Year	Component	Torque/Ft. Lbs.
1993–94	A/C Compressor	18
	A/C Compressor Bracket	20
	Alternator Adjusting Bar	13
	Alternator Bracket	13
	Connecting Rod Cap Bolts	29
	Camshaft Sprocket	37
	Clutch Release Cylinder	9
	Crankshaft Pulley	112
	Cylinder Head Bolts	①
	Cylinder Head Cover	5
	Distributor	13
	Exhaust Manifold	38
	Exhaust Pipe Bracket To Cylinder Block	14

Continued

TIGHTENING SPECIFICATIONS

3E-E—Continued

1993–94	Exhaust Pipe To Manifold	49
	Fixed Idler Pulley	20
	Flywheel	65
	Fuel Cutoff Valve To Fuel Pump Bracket	13②
	Fuel Delivery Pipe	14
	Fuel Hose Inlet w/Union	22
	Fuel Pump Bracket	30②
	Intake Manifold	14
	Intake Manifold Bracket	13
	Left Front Engine Hanger Bracket	15
	Main Bearing Cap	42
	No. 1 Heat Insulator	6
	No. 1 Idler Pulley	13
	No. 2 Crankshaft Pulley	14
	No. 2 Idler Pulley	20
	Oil Dipstick Guide	13
	Oil Drain Plug	18
	Oil Filter Union	18
	Oil Pan	6
	Oil Pressure Regulator Valve	22
	Oil Pump	5
	Oil Pump Sprocket	27
	Oil Strainer	7
	Power Steering Pump	29–32
	Power Steering Pump Adjusting Strut	15
	Radiator Support	9
	Rear End Plate	7
	Rear Engine Mount Through Bolt	47
	Rear Engine Mount To Body	58
	Rear Oil Seal Retainer	5
	RH Engine Mount Bracket	43
	RH Engine Mount Through Body	54
	RH Engine Mount To Body	47
	RH Rear Engine Hanger Bracket	43
	Spark Plug	13
	Spring Loaded Idler	13
	Timing Belt Cover	5
	Torque Cover Bolts	13
	Transaxle To Engine	47
	Valve Clearance Adjusting Nut To Rocker Arm	14
	Water Inlet To Water Inlet Housing	43②
	Water Pump	13
	Water Outlet Housing	13

① — Refer to "Cylinder Head, Replace."
② — Inch lbs.

TIGHTENING SPECIFICATIONS

5E-FE

Year	Component	Torque/Ft. Lbs.
1993–96	A/C Compressor	18
	A/C Compressor Bracket	20
	Air Pipe To Intake Manifold	48①
	Alternator Bracket	13
	Camshaft Bearing Cap	9
	Camshaft Timing Pulley	37
	Clutch Release Cylinder	9
	Connecting Rod Cap	29
	Crankshaft Pulley	112
	Cylinder Head Bolt	②
	Driveplate To Torque Converter	18
	EGR Pipe Assembly To EGR Valve	29
	EGR Pipe Assembly To Exhaust Manifold	22
	EGR Temperature Sensor	15
	EGR Valve	13
	Exhaust Manifold	35
	Exhaust Pipe Stay	14
	Flywheel To Crankshaft	65
	Front Exhaust Pipe	46
	Fuel Inlet Hose	22
	Fuel Pipe & Hose To Pump Bracket	22
	Fuel Pump Bracket	30①
	Heat Insulator	6
	Idler Pulley Bracket To Cylinder Block	20
	Idler Pulley Bracket To Cylinder Head	27
	Intake Manifold	14
	Intake Manifold To ACV	6
	LH Engine Mount Bracket To Engine Mount	35
	LH Engine Mount Bracket To Ground Strap	35
	LH Engine Mount Bracket To Transaxle	47
	Main Bearing Cap	42
	No. 1 Idler Pulley	13
	No. 2 Crankshaft Pulley	14
	No. 2 Idler Pulley	20
	Oil Drain Plug	18
	Oil Filter Union	18
	Oil Pan	6
	Oil Pressure Regulator Valve	22
	Oil Pump	5
	Oil Pump Pulley	27
	Oil Strainer	7
	Power Steering Pump Adjusting Strut To Cylinder Block	15
	Power Steering Pump Adjusting Strut To Pump Housing	29
	Power Steering Pump Bracket	32
	Radiator Support	9
	Rear Engine Mount Bracket To Engine Mount	47
	Rear Engine Mount Bracket To Transaxle	35

Continued

TIGHTENING SPECIFICATIONS

5E-FE—Continued

1993–96	Rear Oil Seal Retainer	5
	RH Engine Mount Bracket	43
	RH Engine Mount To Bracket	47
	RH Engine Mount To RH Crossmember	54
	Spark Plug	13
	Valve Cover	5
	Water Inlet	43①
	Water Outlet Housing	13
	Water Pump	13

① — Inch lbs.
② — Tighten cylinder head bolts in several passes to 33 ft. lbs., then tighten an additional 90°.

Clutch & Manual Transaxle

NOTE: On Air Bag Equipped Models, Refer To "Air Bag System Precautions" Located In The Front Of This Manual For System Disarming & Arming Procedures.

INDEX

	Page No.		Page No.		Page No.
Adjustments	46-20	Clutch Master Cylinder, Replace	46-20	**Precautions**	46-20
Clutch Pedal	46-20	Clutch Slave Cylinder, Replace	46-20	Air Bag Systems	46-20
Clutch, Replace	46-21	Clutch System Bleed	46-21	**Tightening Specifications**	46-22
Hydraulic System Service	46-20			**Transaxle, Replace**	46-21

PRECAUTIONS

AIR BAG SYSTEMS

Refer to "Air Bag System Precautions" in the front of this manual for system disarming and arming procedures.

ADJUSTMENTS

CLUTCH PEDAL

1. Measure clutch pedal height as shown, **Fig. 1.**
2. Clutch pedal height should be 5.69–6.08 inches on 4-speed transaxles and 5.51–5.91 inches on 5-speed transaxles, measured from the asphalt sheet.
3. If clutch pedal height is not as specified, loosen clutch pedal locknut, then rotate stopper bolt on models less cruise control or clutch switch on models with cruise control, until specified height is achieved.
4. Tighten locknut.
5. Check clutch pedal freeplay by depressing clutch pedal until resistance is felt. Freeplay should be .197–.591 inch. Pushrod play at top of pedal should be .039–.197 inch.
6. If necessary to adjust freeplay, loosen locknut and rotate pushrod until freeplay is as specified.

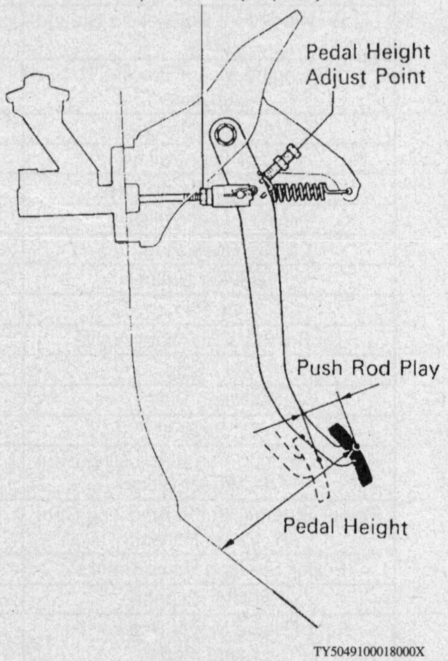

Push Rod Play and Freeplay Adjust Point
Pedal Height Adjust Point
Push Rod Play
Pedal Height
TY5049100018000X

Fig. 1 Clutch pedal adjustment

7. Tighten locknut.
8. Ensure clutch pedal height and freeplay are as specified, then reinstall air duct and finish panel.

HYDRAULIC SYSTEM SERVICE

CLUTCH SLAVE CYLINDER, REPLACE

1. Place suitable container below slave cylinder.
2. Using tube wrench tool No. 09751-36011, or equivalent, disconnect clutch tube from cylinder.
3. Remove slave cylinder attaching bolts, then the slave cylinder.
4. Reverse procedure to install.

CLUTCH MASTER CYLINDER, REPLACE

1. Remove fluid from cylinder with syringe.
2. **On all models,** place suitable container below cylinder, then using tube wrench tool No. 09751-36011, or equivalent, disconnect clutch tube from cylinder.
3. Remove clip, clevis pin and wave washer.
4. Remove master cylinder attaching nuts, then pull rearward to remove.
5. Reverse procedure to install.

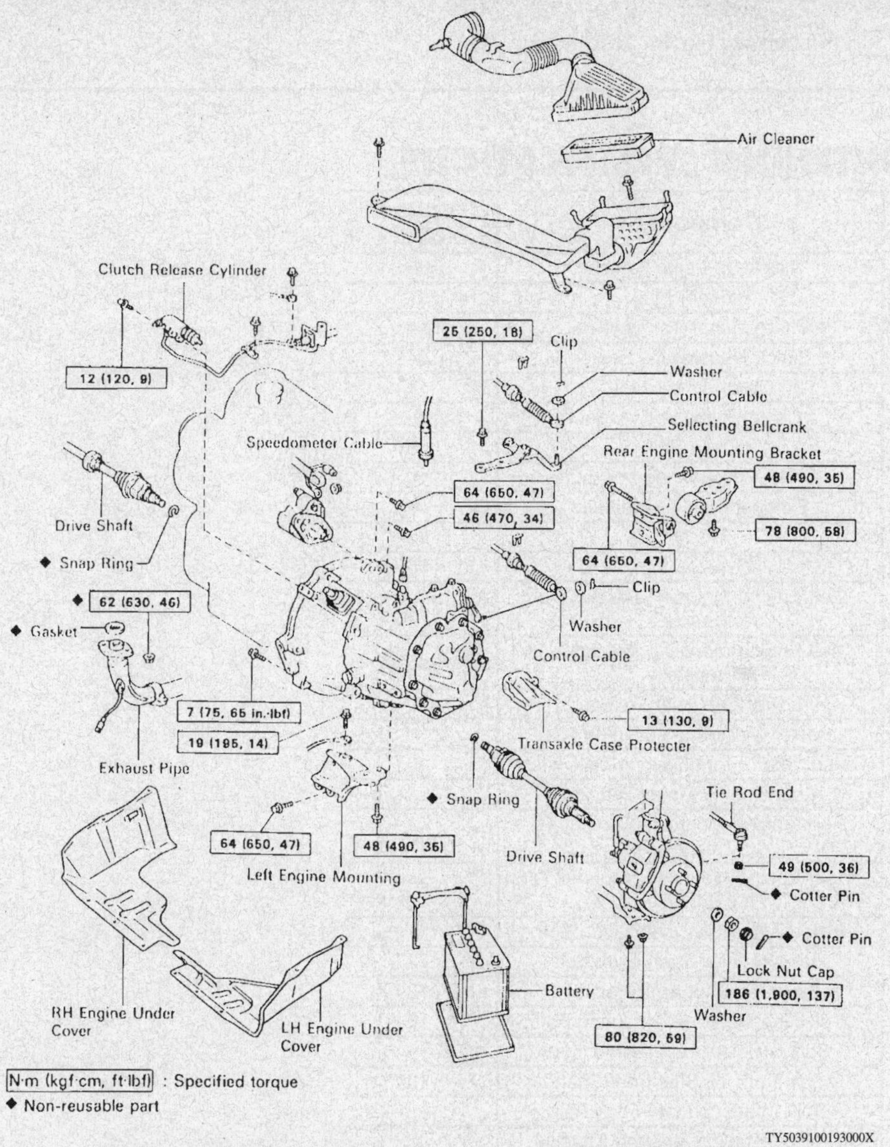
Air Cleaner
Clutch Release Cylinder
12 (120, 9)
25 (250, 18)
Clip
Washer
Control Cable
Selecting Bellcrank
Rear Engine Mounting Bracket
48 (490, 35)
Speedometer Cable
64 (650, 47)
46 (470, 34)
78 (800, 58)
Drive Shaft
◆ Snap Ring
64 (650, 47)
Clip
◆ 62 (630, 46)
◆ Gasket
Washer
Control Cable
7 (75, 65 in.·lbf)
19 (195, 14)
13 (130, 9)
Transaxle Case Protecter
Exhaust Pipe
◆ Snap Ring
Tie Rod End
64 (650, 47)
48 (490, 35)
Drive Shaft
Left Engine Mounting
49 (500, 36)
◆ Cotter Pin
◆ Cotter Pin
Lock Nut Cap
186 (1,900, 137)
Battery
Washer
RH Engine Under Cover
LH Engine Under Cover
80 (820, 59)
N·m (kgf·cm, ft·lbf) : Specified torque
◆ Non-reusable part
TY5039100193000X

Fig. 2 Exploded view of manual transaxle assembly

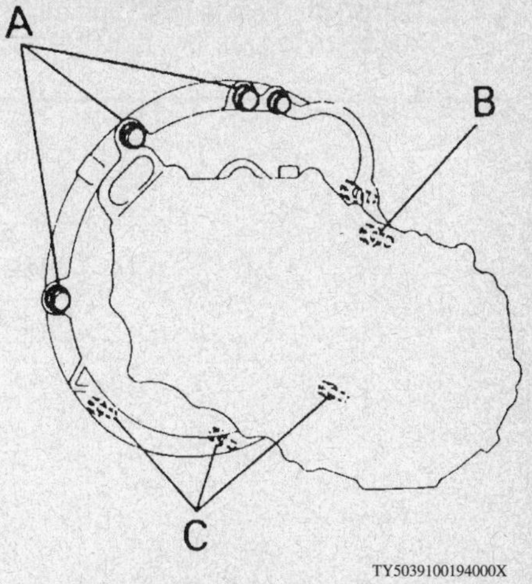
A
B
C
TY5039100194000X

Fig. 3 Transaxle to engine bolt tightening

CLUTCH SYSTEM BLEED

If any service is performed on the clutch system or air is suspected in the clutch lines, bleed the system.

1. Fill clutch reservoir with suitable brake fluid. **Do not allow fluid to come in contact with painted surfaces.**
2. Check reservoir frequently and add fluid as required.
3. Connect vinyl tube to bleeder plug, then insert other tube end in half full container of brake fluid.
4. Slowly pump clutch pedal several times.
5. While depressing pedal, loosen bleeder plug until fluid runs out, then close bleeder plug.
6. Repeat procedure until air bubbles are evident in the fluid. **Do not reuse the fluid that was bled.**

CLUTCH

REPLACE

1. Remove transaxle assembly as previously outlined.
2. Place installation alignment on clutch cover and flywheel.
3. Loosen each set bolt one turn at a time until spring tension is released.
4. Remove clutch cover attaching bolts, then remove cover and disc.
5. Remove release bearing, fork and boot.
6. Using suitable calipers, measure clutch disc rivet head depth. Minimum rivet depth should be .012 inch. If not as indicated, replace clutch disc.
7. Using suitable dial indicator, measure flywheel runout. Maximum runout should be .004 inch. If not as indicated, replace flywheel.
8. Measure clutch disc runout. Maximum runout is .031 inch. If not as indicated, replace disc.
9. Using suitable calipers, measure diaphragm spring depth and width. Maximum depth is .024 inch and maximum width is .0197 inch. If measurements are not as indicated, replace clutch cover.
10. Reverse procedure to install, noting the following:
    a. **On Tercel models,** using clutch guide tool No. 09301–32010, or equivalent, install clutch disc.
    b. **On Paseo models,** using clutch guide tool No. 09301–00210, or equivalent, install clutch disc.
    c. **On all models,** match clutch cover and flywheel alignment marks, then tighten clutch cover bolts to specification in a criss-cross pattern. Ensure clutch disc and pressure plate remain aligned.

TRANSAXLE

REPLACE

Refer to **Fig. 2** when replacing manual transaxle.

1. Disconnect battery ground cable and remove air cleaner assembly with hose.
2. Remove clutch release cylinder and tube clamp, then disconnect back-up lamp switch connector.
3. Remove clips and washers, then the control cable retainers.
4. Remove clutch release cylinder bracket with ground strap.
5. Remove upper transaxle mounting bolts.
6. Raise and support vehicle, then remove undercovers.
7. Drain transaxle fluid.
8. Disconnect speedometer cable, then the driveshafts.
9. Remove front and rear engine mounting brackets, then the starter attaching bolts and starter.
10. Slightly raise engine and transaxle assembly, using suitable jacks, then disconnect left engine mount.
11. Remove transaxle to engine attaching bolts, then lower left side of engine and separate transaxle from engine.
12. Reverse procedure to install, noting the following:
    a. Align input shaft spline with clutch disc, then install transaxle to engine.

b. **Torque** transaxle to engine attaching bolt A to 47 ft. lbs., bolt B, to 34 ft. lbs. and bolt C to 65 inch lbs. as shown in **Fig. 3.**

TIGHTENING SPECIFICATIONS

Year	Component	Torque/Ft. Lbs.
1993–96	Back-Up Lamp Switch	30
	Bleeder Plug	6
	Clutch Cover To Flywheel	14
	Clutch Housing To Engine	34
	Clutch Line Union	11
	Clutch Release Cylinder	9
	Drain Plug	29
	Drive Axle Bearing Locknut	②
	Exhaust Pipe To Manifold	46
	Filler Plug	29
	Flywheel Bolt	65
	Left Engine Mounting Bracket To Frame	47
	Left Engine Mounting Bracket To Transaxle	35
	Lower Ball Joint To Arm	59
	Master Cylinder Installation Nut	①
	Output Shaft Front Bearing Lock Plate	8
	Rear Engine Mount Bracket	58
	Rear Engine Mounting Bracket To Transaxle	35
	Rear Engine Mounting Insulator To Body	58
	Release Cylinder Installation Bolt	9
	Reverse Idler Shaft Lock Bolt	22
	Reverse Shift Arm Bracket	13
	Selecting Bellcrank Mounting Bolt	18
	Shift & Select Lever Assembly	14
	Shift Fork To Shift Fork Shaft	12
	Shift Interlock Plate Lock Bolt	22
	Tie Rod End To Steering Knuckle	36
	Transaxle Case Protector	9
	Transaxle Case To Case Cover	13
	Transaxle Case To Engine	③
	Transaxle Case To Transaxle	22
	Wheel Lug Nut	76

①— Paseo, 69 inch lbs.; Tercel, 9 ft. lbs.

②— 1993 Paseo, 152 ft. lbs.; 1994–96 Paseo, 159 ft. lbs.; Tercel, 166 ft. lbs.

③— Refer to “Transaxle, Replace.”

Rear Axle & Suspension

INDEX

	Page No.
Axle Beam, Replace	46-23
Coil Spring, Replace	46-23
Paseo	46-23
Tercel	46-23
Hub & Bearing, Replace	46-23
Lateral Control Bar, Replace	46-24
Shock Absorber, Replace	46-23
Tightening Specifications	46-24

HUB & BEARING

REPLACE

1. Raise and support rear of vehicle, then remove wheel and tire assembly.
2. Remove grease cap, cotter pin, nut lock and adjusting nut, **Fig. 1.**
3. Remove brake drum/hub assembly with outer bearing and thrust washer from axle shaft.
4. Using a suitable screwdriver, pry oil seal from hub, then remove inner bearing.
5. Inspect inner and outer bearings and races for wear and damage. If necessary, replace race(s) with suitable removal and installation tools.
6. Clean and repack bearings and fill inside of axle hub and grease cap with multi-purpose grease.
7. Install inner bearing in axle hub, then install new oil seal using suitable seal installer. Grease oil seal lips with multi-purpose grease.
8. Install brake drum/hub assembly on axle shaft, then install outer bearing in hub. Apply multi-purpose grease between outer bearing and thrust washer surface, then install thrust washer.
9. Install adjusting nut and tighten to specification, then rotate brake drum/hub assembly to seat bearings. Loosen adjusting nut until hand tight. **Ensure brakes are not dragging.**
10. Attach suitable spring scale to wheel stud and measure oil seal rotation frictional force. Oil seal frictional force should be approximately .9 lb.
11. With spring scale still attached, tighten adjusting nut until bearing preload is 0–2.6 lbs. above the oil seal frictional force determined in step 10.
12. Install locknut, cotter pin and grease cap. **If cotter pin will not line up with axle shaft hole, tighten adjusting nut to align.**
13. Adjust rear brakes as necessary.

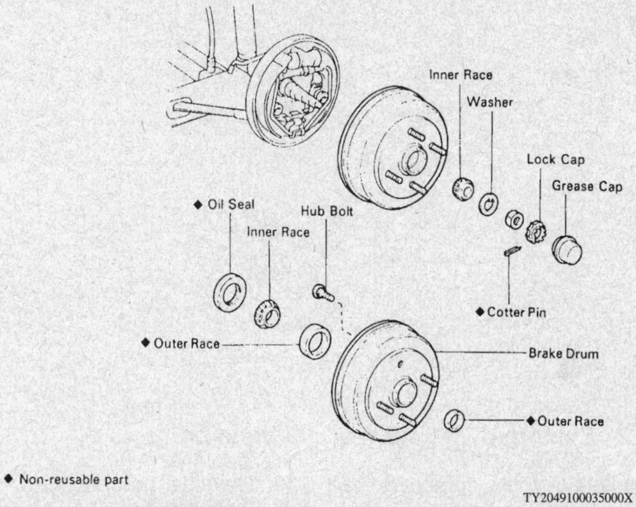

Inner Race
Washer
Lock Cap
Grease Cap
◆ Oil Seal
Hub Bolt
Inner Race
◆ Cotter Pin
◆ Outer Race
Brake Drum
◆ Outer Race
◆ Non-reusable part
TY2049100035000X

Fig. 1 Exploded view of rear wheel bearing

AXLE BEAM

REPLACE

1. Remove rear axle hubs as outlined previously.
2. Remove left and right brake shoes.
3. Disconnect parking brake from backing plate.
4. Using suitable tool, disconnect brake tube from cylinder, then disconnect tube from axle beam.
5. Remove backing plate.
6. Remove lateral control rod attaching nut and bolt, then disconnect rod from body.
7. Remove lateral rod from axle beam.
8. Support axle beam, using suitable equipment.
9. Remove shock absorber lower attaching nuts and bolts.
10. Remove axle beam attaching nuts and bolts, then remove beam.
11. Reverse procedure to install.

SHOCK ABSORBER

REPLACE

Refer to "Coil Spring, Replace" for shock absorber replacement procedures.

COIL SPRING

REPLACE

TERCEL

1. Remove rear seat back and cushion.
2. Working inside vehicle, remove shock absorber cover.
3. Disconnect brake hose from wheel cylinder or caliper, then disconnect brake hose from shock absorber.
4. Working inside vehicle, loosen nut securing suspension support to shock absorber, **Fig. 2. Do not remove nut at this time.**
5. Remove bolts securing shock absorber to axle carrier, then disconnect shock absorber from carrier.
6. Working inside vehicle, remove nuts securing suspension support to vehicle body, then remove shock absorber.
7. Install a bolt and two nuts in shock absorber lower mounting bracket and clamp unit in a suitable vise using lower mounting bracket as clamping surface.
8. Using a suitable spring compressor, compress coil spring.
9. Remove nut securing suspension support to shock absorber, then remove suspension support, coil spring, insulator and spring bumper. Shock absorber is filled with colorless, odorless and non-poisonous high pressure gas. Upon removal, handle shock absorber with care. Do not score or scratch exposed part of piston rod or allow paint or oil to come in contact with it. Do not rotate piston rod and cylinder assembly with shock absorber fully extended. When discarding shock absorber, drill a small hole in bottom of cylinder to relieve pressure.
10. Reverse procedure to install.

PASEO

1. Remove rear seat cushion, seat back and seat lock striker.
2. Remove quarter trim.
3. Disconnect rear seat belt.
4. Disconnect package tray trim.
5. Remove room partition board.
6. Raise and support rear of vehicle.
7. Remove lower shock attaching nut and bolt, then two upper attaching nuts.
8. Remove shock absorber and coil spring assembly.

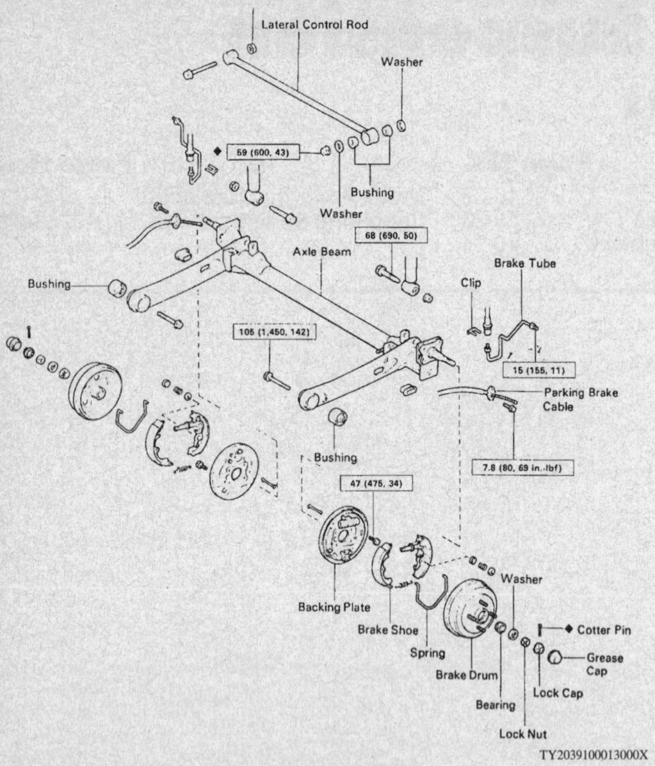
Lateral Control Rod
Washer
59 (600, 43)
Bushing
Washer
68 (690, 50)
Axle Beam
Brake Tube
Clip
Bushing
105 (1,450, 142)
15 (155, 11)
Parking Brake Cable
Bushing
7.8 (80, 69 in.-lbf)
47 (475, 34)
Washer
Backing Plate
Brake Shoe
Cotter Pin
Spring
Grease Cap
Brake Drum
Lock Cap
Bearing
Lock Nut
TY2039100013000X

Fig. 2 Exploded view of rear suspension

9. Using suitable tool, compress coil spring.
10. Remove spring attaching nut, washer, suspension bumper and coil spring.
11. Reverse procedure to install, noting the following:
    a. Align suspension support with shock absorber bracket, **Fig. 3.**

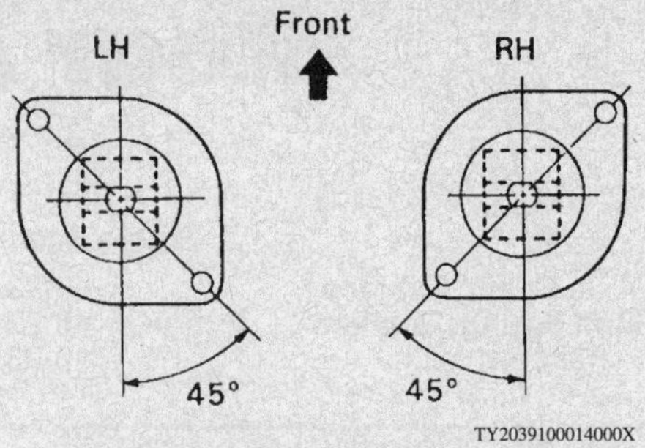
Front
LH
RH
45°
45°
TY2039100014000X

Fig. 3 Suspension support to shock absorber lower bracket alignment. Paseo

    b. Tighten attaching nuts and bolts to specification.
    c. After repairs, bounce rear of vehicle several time to stabilize suspension.

LATERAL CONTROL BAR

REPLACE

1. Raise and support vehicle.
2. Remove lateral control rod attaching nut, retainer and bushing.
3. Disconnect lateral control rod from rear axle beam.
4. Remove bushing and retainer.
5. Remove lateral rod to body attaching nut and bolt, then remove rod.
6. Reverse procedure to install.

TIGHTENING SPECIFICATIONS

Year	Component	Torque/Ft. Lbs.
1993–96	Backing Plate To Axle Beam	34
	Body To Axle Beam	105
	Brake Tube To Flexible Tube	11
	Brake Tube To Wheel Cylinder	11
	Lateral Control Rod To Axle Beam	43
	Lateral Control Rod To Body	83
	Parking Brake Cable To Backing Plate	6
	Piston Rod To Suspension Support	40
	Shock Absorber To Axle Beam	50
	Suspension Support To Body	29
	Wheel Lug Nut	76

Front Suspension & Steering

NOTE: On Air Bag Equipped Models, Refer To "Air Bag System Precautions" Located In The Front Of This Manual For System Disarming & Arming Procedures.

INDEX

	Page No.
Ball Joint, Replace	46-26
Ball Joint Inspection	46-26
Coil Spring, Replace	46-26
Paseo	46-27
Tercel	46-26
Manual Steering Gear, Replace	46-28
Tercel	46-28
Manual Steering Gears	48-1
Power Steering	48-1
Power Steering Gear, Replace	46-27
Paseo	46-27
Tercel	46-27
Power Steering Pump, Replace	46-28
Paseo	46-28
Tercel	46-28
Power Steering System Bleed	46-28
Precautions	46-25
Air Bag Systems	46-25
Stabilizer Bar, Replace	46-27
Strut, Replace	46-27
Suspension Arm, Replace	46-27
Tightening Specifications	46-29
Wheel Bearing, Adjust	46-25
Wheel Hub & Steering Knuckle, Replace	46-25
Paseo	46-26
Tercel	46-25

PRECAUTIONS

AIR BAG SYSTEMS

Refer to "Air Bag System Precautions" in the front of this manual for system disarming and arming procedures.

WHEEL BEARING

ADJUST

These models incorporate lubed for life, sealed front wheel bearings with no provision for adjustment.

WHEEL HUB & STEERING KNUCKLE

REPLACE

TERCEL

1. Raise and support vehicle.
2. Remove front wheels.
3. Remove brake cylinder from steering knuckle, then using suitable wire, hang and position aside.
4. Remove brake rotor.
5. Using suitable dial indicator, measure backlash near center of axle hub in bearing shaft direction. Maximum backlash is .0020 inch (.05 mm). If backlash is greater than indicated, replace bearing.
6. Install brake rotor and cylinder.
7. Remove cotter pin and lock cap, then with brakes applied, remove nut and washer, then remove brake cylinder and rotor, **Fig. 1.**
8. Loosen lower shock attaching bolts, but do not remove.
9. Remove tie rod end cotter pin and nut, then using ball joint puller tool No. 09628-62011, or equivalent, disconnect tie rod end from steering knuckle.
10. Remove lower ball joint to lower arm attaching nuts and bolt, then disconnect joint from arm.
11. Remove lower shock absorber attaching nuts and bolts, then remove steering knuckle with axle hub. **Do not damage driveshaft oil seal.**
12. Place axle hub in suitable vise, then remove ball joint clip and nut. Using ball joint puller tool No. 09628-6201, or equivalent, remove ball joint.
13. Using suitable screwdriver, remove inner oil seal.
14. Remove dust cover attaching bolts.
15. Using tool No. 09950-2001, or equivalent, separate axle hub from steering knuckle and remove dust cover.
16. Using same tool, remove axle hub inner race.
17. Using seal removal tool No. 09308-00010, or equivalent, remove outer oil seal.
18. Remove steering knuckle snap ring, position inner race on outside of bearing, then using suitable brass bar and hammer, remove steering knuckle bearing.

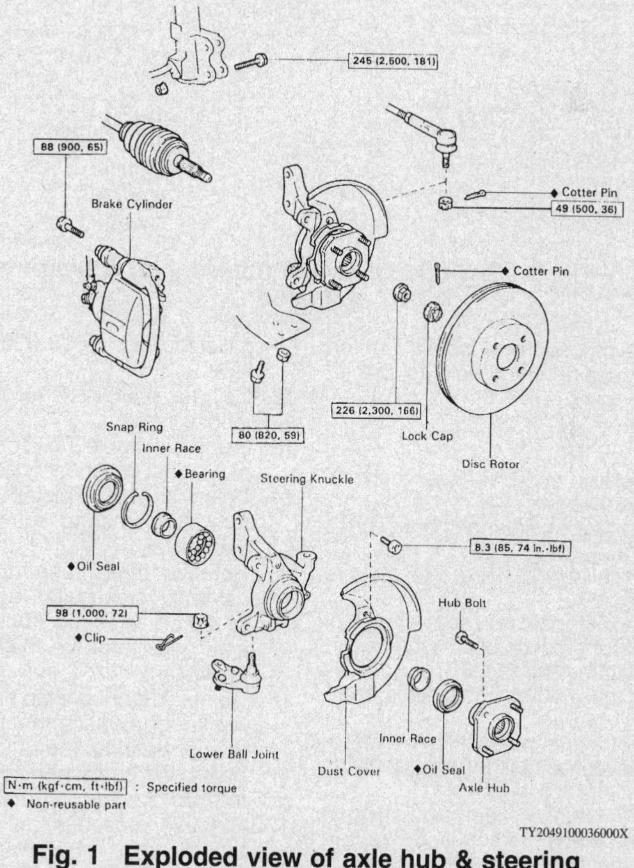

245 (2,500, 181)
88 (900, 65)
Brake Cylinder
◆Cotter Pin
49 (500, 36)
◆Cotter Pin
226 (2,300, 166)
Lock Cap
Disc Rotor
80 (820, 59)
Snap Ring
Inner Race
◆Bearing
Steering Knuckle
◆Oil Seal
8.3 (85, 74 in.·lbf)
Hub Bolt
98 (1,000, 72)
◆Clip
Lower Ball Joint
Inner Race
Dust Cover
◆Oil Seal
Axle Hub
N·m (kgf·cm, ft·lbf) : Specified torque
◆ Non-reusable part
TY2049100036000X

Fig. 1 Exploded view of axle hub & steering knuckle. Tercel

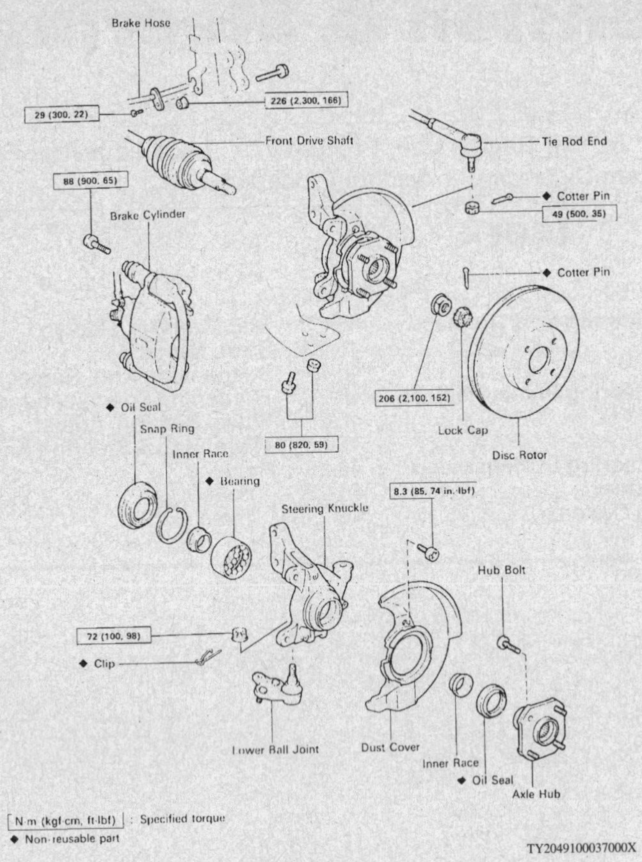
Brake Hose
29 (300, 22)
226 (2,300, 166)
Front Drive Shaft
Tie Rod End
88 (900, 65)
Brake Cylinder
◆ Cotter Pin
49 (500, 35)
◆ Cotter Pin
206 (2,100, 152)
Lock Cap
Disc Rotor
◆ Oil Seal
Snap Ring
Inner Race
◆ Bearing
80 (820, 59)
8.3 (85, 74 in.-lbf)
Steering Knuckle
Hub Bolt
72 (100, 98)
◆ Clip
Lower Ball Joint
Dust Cover
Inner Race
◆ Oil Seal
Axle Hub
N·m (kgf·cm, ft·lbf) : Specified torque
◆ Non-reusable part
TY2049100037000X

Fig. 2 Exploded view of knuckle, hub & bearing. Paseo

19. Reverse procedure to install. Tighten all attaching nuts and bolts to specifications.

PASEO

1. Raise and support vehicle, then remove front wheels.
2. Remove brake caliper and brake hose from strut.
3. Support caliper with wire, then remove rotor, **Fig. 2.**
4. Place a dial indicator near center of axle hub and check backlash in bearing shaft direction, **Fig. 3.** If backlash is greater than .002 inch, replace bearing.
5. Install rotor and brake caliper, then remove driveshaft locknut while applying brakes.
6. Remove brake caliper and support with wire, then the rotor.
7. Loosen nuts on lower side of shock absorber. **Do not remove bolts at this time.**
8. Disconnect tie rod end from steering knuckle using ball joint puller tool No. 09628-62011, or equivalent, then the lower ball joint from lower suspension arm.
9. Using universal puller tool No. 09950-20017, or equivalent, disconnect driveshaft from steering knuckle.
10. Remove bolts on lower side of shock absorber, then the steering knuckle and hub.
11. Remove lower ball joint using ball joint puller tool No. 09628-62011, or equivalent.
12. Using a suitable screwdriver, remove inner oil seal.
13. Using a suitable T30 Torx wrench, remove dust cover set bolts.
14. Using universal puller, remove axle hub from steering knuckle, then the dust cover.
15. Remove inner race from axle hub using universal puller, then the outer oil seal from steering knuckle using oil seal puller tool No. 09308-00010, or equivalent.
16. Remove bearing snap ring from steering knuckle, place inner race on outside of bearing, then using a suitable brass drift and a hammer, drive bearing from steering knuckle.
17. Reverse procedure to install, noting the following:
    a. Press new bearing into steering knuckle using steering knuckle oil seal replacer tool No. 09608-10010, or equivalent.
    b. Install outer oil seal using steering knuckle oil seal replacer.
    c. Press axle hub into steering knuckle using steering knuckle oil seal replacer and universal puller, or equivalents.
    d. Install outer oil seal using steering knuckle oil seal replacer, or equivalent.

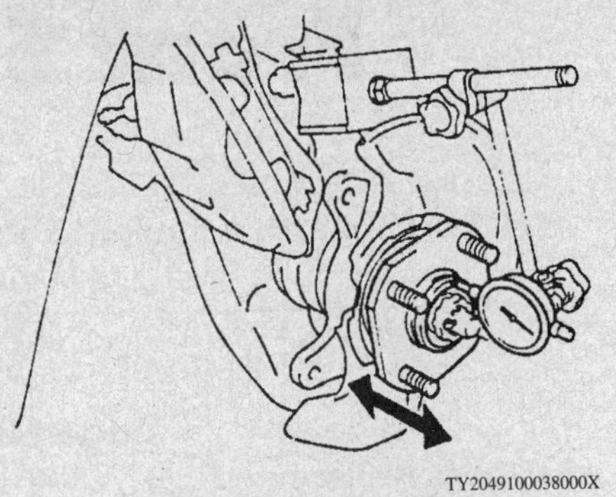
TY2049100038000X

Fig. 3 Bearing backlash measurement. Paseo

BALL JOINT INSPECTION

1. Remove ball joint as outlined under "Ball Joint, Replace."
2. Move ball joint stud back and forth five times, then install nut.
3. Using torque wrench, turn nut continuously one turn every two to four seconds and take torque reading on fifth turn.
4. If torque reading is not 9–26 inch lbs., replace ball joint.

BALL JOINT

REPLACE

1. Raise and support vehicle, then remove front wheels.
2. Remove steering knuckle and hub as outlined under "Wheel Hub & Steering Knuckle, Replace."
3. Remove lower ball joint using ball joint puller tool No. 09628-62011, or equivalent.
4. Inspect ball joint as outlined under "Ball Joint Inspection."
5. Reverse procedure to install.

COIL SPRING

REPLACE

TERCEL

1. Raise and support vehicle.
2. Disconnect brake hose to shock absorber attaching bolt.
3. Scribe alignment marks on strut lower bracket and the camber adjusting cam.
4. Remove two bolts and nuts and disconnect from steering knuckle.
5. Remove three nuts attaching strut to body, then remove strut from body. **Cover driveshaft boot with cloth to avoid damage.**
6. Install bolt and nuts on bracket at lower portion of strut shell and secure assembly in suitable vise.
7. Using spring compressor tool No. 09727-30020, or equivalent, compress coil spring.
8. Using front spring upper seat holder tool No. 09729-22031, or equivalent, hold spring seat, then remove support nut.

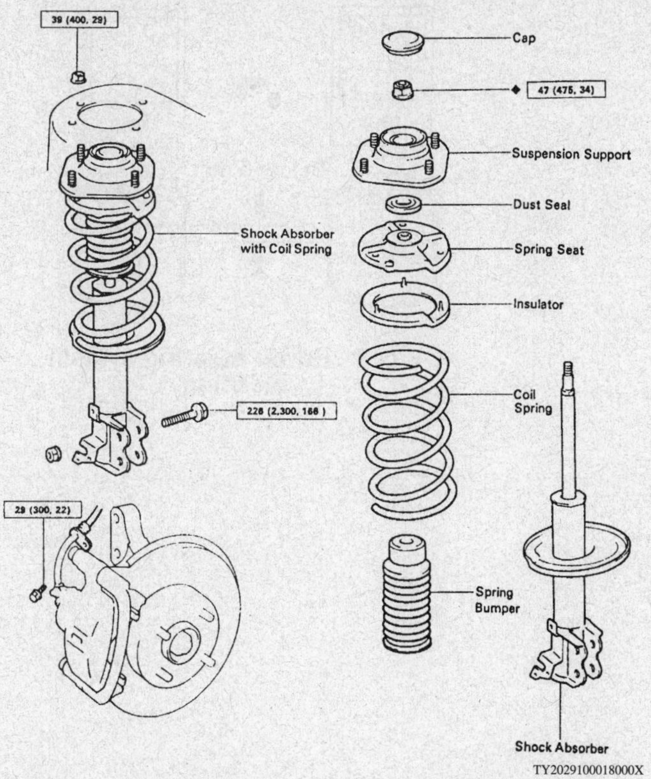
39 (400, 29)
Cap
◆ 47 (475, 34)
Suspension Support
Dust Seal
Shock Absorber with Coil Spring
Spring Seat
Insulator
Coil Spring
228 (2,300, 166)
29 (300, 22)
Spring Bumper
Shock Absorber
TY2029100018000X

Fig. 4 Exploded view of strut assembly. Paseo

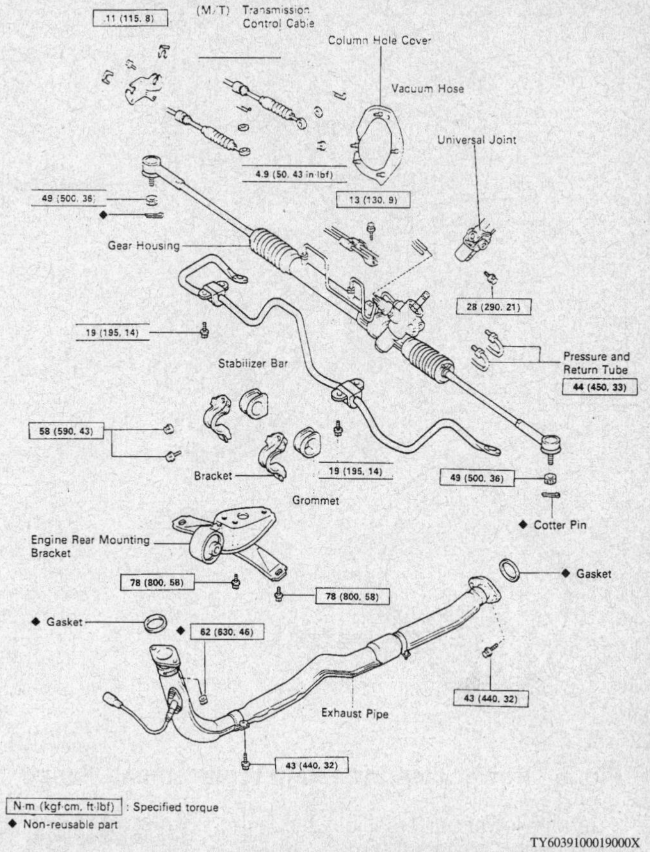
11 (115, 8)
(M/T) Transmission Control Cable
Column Hole Cover
Vacuum Hose
Universal Joint
4.9 (50, 43 in·lbf)
49 (500, 36)
13 (130, 9)
Gear Housing
28 (290, 21)
19 (195, 14)
Stabilizer Bar
Pressure and Return Tube
44 (450, 33)
58 (590, 43)
Bracket
19 (195, 14)
Grommet
49 (500, 36)
◆ Cotter Pin
Engine Rear Mounting Bracket
◆ Gasket
78 (800, 58)
78 (800, 58)
◆ Gasket
◆ 62 (630, 46)
43 (440, 32)
Exhaust Pipe
43 (440, 32)
N·m (kgf·cm, ft·lbf) : Specified torque
◆ Non-reusable part
TY6039100019000X

Fig. 5 Power steering gear replacement. Paseo

9. Remove suspension support, spring seat, spring and dust cover.
10. Reverse procedure to install. Tighten all attaching nuts and bolts to specifications.

PASEO

1. Raise and support vehicle, then remove front wheels.
2. Disconnect brake hose from strut.
3. Remove lower strut attaching nuts and bolts, **Fig. 4,** then disconnect strut from steering knuckle.
4. Remove three nuts holding top of suspension support.
5. Remove strut from body.
6. Using coil spring compressor tool No. 09727-30020, or equivalent, compress coil spring.
7. Install a bolt and two nuts to lower portion of strut shell and secure in vise.
8. Using spring seat holding tool No. 09729-22031, or equivalent, remove nut, suspension upper support, upper insulator, coil spring, spring bumper and lower insulator. **Do not disassemble spring lower seat.**
9. Reverse procedure to install, noting the following:
   a. Fit lower end of coil spring into gap of lower seat.
   b. Tighten all attaching nuts and bolts to specifications.

STRUT

REPLACE

Refer to "Coil Spring, Replace" for procedure.

STABILIZER BAR

REPLACE

1. Disconnect stabilizer bar from front lower suspension arms.
2. Remove stabilizer bar brackets from body structure.
3. Remove stabilizer bar.
4. Reverse procedure to install, tighten bolts to specifications.

SUSPENSION ARM

REPLACE

1. Raise and support vehicle.
2. Remove front wheel.
3. Remove lower ball joint to lower arm attaching bolts, then disconnect ball joint.
4. Remove lower arm attaching bolts, then remove arm.
5. Reverse procedure to install, noting the following:
   a. **On Paseo models,** temporarily install lower arm attaching bolts, then lower vehicle, stabilize suspension and tighten attaching bolts to specifications.

POWER STEERING GEAR

REPLACE

TERCEL

1. Raise and support vehicle, then remove front wheel.
2. Remove tie rod end cotter pin and nut, then using ball joint puller tool No. 09628-62011, or equivalent, disconnect tie rod end from steering knuckle.
3. Remove column hole cover attaching bolts, then remove cover.
4. Place installation alignment mark on universal joint and shaft.
5. Loosen upper and lower universal joint set bolt, then pull joint upward from control valve shaft.
6. Remove exhaust pipe clamp from front bracket, then remove exhaust pipe.
7. Remove rear engine bracket.
8. Remove gear housing attaching nuts and bolts, then slide gear to righthand side, then to lefthand side to remove.
9. Reverse procedure to install.

PASEO

1. Disconnect tie rod ends using ball joint puller tool No. 09628-62011 or equivalent, **Fig. 5.**
2. Place alignment marks on universal joint and control valve shaft.
3. Loosen upper universal joint bolt and

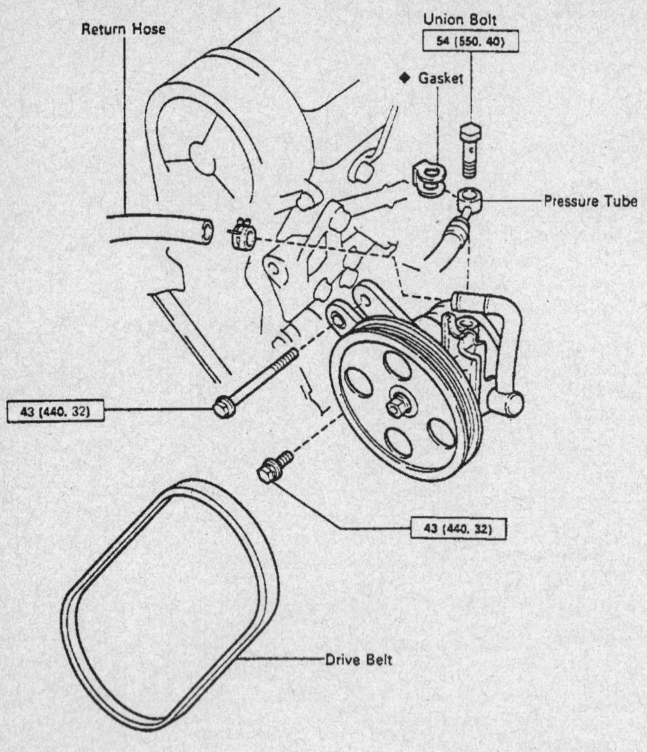
Return Hose
Union Bolt
54 (550, 40)
◆ Gasket
Pressure Tube
43 (440, 32)
43 (440, 32)
Drive Belt
TY6039100020000X

Fig. 6 Power steering pump replacement. Paseo

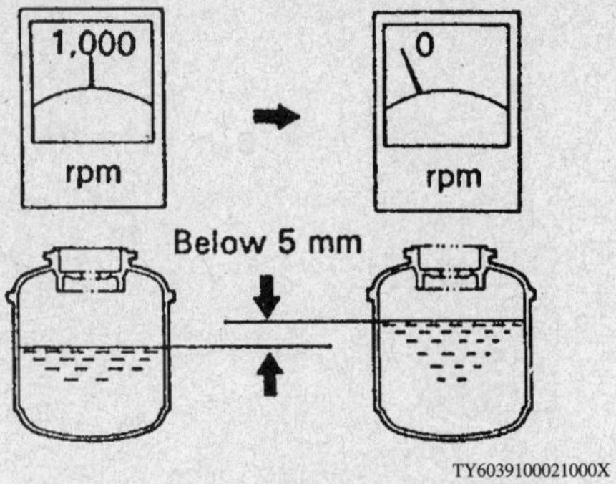
1,000
rpm
0
rpm
Below 5 mm
TY6039100021000X

Fig. 7 Power steering system bleeding

remove lower universal joint bolt, then disconnect universal joint.
4. Disconnect and connect pressure and return tubes using power steering hose nut wrench set tool No. 09631-22020, or equivalent.
5. Slide gear assembly to righthand side, then to lefthand side and remove.
6. Align marks made during removal and connect universal joint.
7. Reverse procedure to install.

POWER STEERING PUMP

REPLACE

TERCEL

1. Using hose wrench tool No. 09631-22020, or equivalent, remove pressure tube.
2. Disconnect return tube.
3. Loosen power steering adjusting bolt.
4. Remove pump attaching bolts, then the pump.
5. Reverse procedure to install.

PASEO

Refer to **Fig. 6** when replacing power steering pump.

MANUAL STEERING GEAR

REPLACE

TERCEL

1. Raise and support front of vehicle, then remove front wheel and tire assemblies.
2. Remove cotter pins and nuts from tie rod ends, then using puller tool No. 09628-62011, or equivalent, separate tie rod ends from steering knuckles.
3. Remove four steering column hole cover attaching bolts and the cover.
4. Place installation alignment marks on universal joint to pinion shaft, then remove steering shaft universal joint attaching bolts and the joint.
5. Remove steering gear attaching nuts and bolts, then slide housing to right-hand side and pull through body panel.
6. Reverse procedure to install. Tighten attaching nuts and bolts specifications.

POWER STEERING SYSTEM BLEED

1. Ensure fluid in reservoir tank is at proper level.
2. With engine speed below 1000 RPM, turn steering wheel from stop to stop three or four times, keeping at full stop position for two to three seconds.
3. Ensure fluid is not foamy or cloudy.
4. Measure fluid lever with engine running, then stop engine and measure fluid level again, **Fig. 7.** Maximum rise of fluid is .20 inch.
5. If a problem is found, proceed as follows:
   a. Disconnect return hose from reservoir tank and drain fluid.
   b. Fill reservoir tank with fresh fluid.
   c. With return hose placed into a suitable container, start engine and run at 1000 RPM. **After one or two seconds, fluid will begin to discharge from the return hose. Stop engine immediately at this time. Ensure some fluid remains in the reservoir tank.**
   d. Repeat steps b and c four or five times until there is no more air in fluid.
   e. Connect return hose and correct fluid level.

TIGHTENING SPECIFICATIONS

Year	Component	Torque/Ft. Lbs.
PASEO		
1993–96	Ball Joint To Lower Suspension Arm	59
	Ball Joint To Steering Knuckle	98
	Brake Caliper Bolts	65
	Brake Hose To Strut Bolt	22
	Driveshaft To Axle Hub Nut	152
	Dust Cover To Steering Knuckle	6
	Front Exhaust Pipe To Converter Nuts	32
	Front Exhaust Pipe To Manifold Nuts	46
	Lower Suspension Arm Bracket Bolts	94
	Lower Suspension Arm Mounting Bolts	105
	Power Steering Pump Mounting Bolts	32
	Power Steering Pump Pressure Tube	40
	Stabilizer Bar Link Nuts	13
	Stabilizer Bar Retainer Bracket Bolts	14
	Steering Rack Line Clamp Nut	9
	Steering Rack Mounting Bolts	43
	Steering Rack Pressure & Return Tubes	33
	Steering Rack Universal Joint Bolt	21
	Strut Nut	34
	Strut To Steering Knuckle	166
	Strut To Strut Tower	29
	Tie Rod End To Steering Knuckle	35
	Wheel Lug Nut	76
TERCEL		
1993–96	Disc Brake Caliper Union Bolt	22
	Front Axle Bearing Locknut	137
	Lower Ball Joint To Lower Suspension Arm	59
	Lower Ball Joint To Steering Knuckle	72
	Lower Suspension Arm To Body (Front)	108
	Lower Suspension Arm To Body (Rear)	94
	Piston Rod To Suspension Support	34
	Steering Knuckle To Shock Absorber	166
	Steering Knuckle To Tie Rod End	36
	Suspension Support To Body	23
	Tie Rod End Locknut	35
	Wheel Lug Nut	76

Wheel Alignment

INDEX

	Page No.
Front Wheel Alignment	46-30
Caster & Camber	46-30
Toe-In	46-30
Preliminary Inspection	46-30
Rear Wheel Alignment	46-30
Camber & Toe-In	46-30
Vehicle Ride Height	46-30
Paseo	46-30
Tercel	46-30
Wheel Alignment Specifications	46-3
Front	46-3
Rear	46-3

PRELIMINARY INSPECTION

Inspect and repair the following prior to adjusting wheel alignment.

1. Check tires for wear and proper inflation.
2. Check wheel runout; .047 inch or less should be indicated.
3. Check front wheel bearings, front suspension, steering linkage and ball joints for wear or looseness.
4. Ensure front shock absorbers are functioning properly.

FRONT WHEEL ALIGNMENT

CASTER & CAMBER

Caster and camber are not adjustable on these models. If caster and camber are not within limits, check for worn or damaged suspension parts and replace as necessary.

TOE-IN

1. Remove clamps from steering gear boots.
2. Loosen tie rod end locknuts.
3. Turn left and right tie rod ends an equal amount to adjust toe-in.
4. Ensure length of both tie rods are equal following adjustment.
5. Following adjustment, install steering boot clamps and **torque** locknut to 35 ft. lbs.

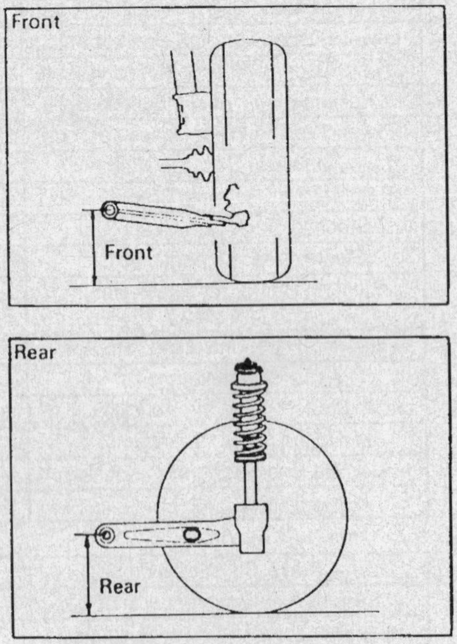
Front
Front
Rear
Rear

TY2049100039000X

Fig. 1 Vehicle ride height measurement. Paseo

Tire size	Height mm (in.) Front	Rear
175/65 R 14	185 (7.28)	244 (9.61)
185/60 R 14	186 (7.32)	245 (9.65)

TY2049100040000X

Fig. 2 Vehicle ride height specifications. Paseo

Tire size	Height mm (in.) Front	Rear
P145/80R13	185 (7.28)	248 (9.76)
155SR13 155SR13AS P155/80R13	192 (7.56)	255 (11.22)

TY2049100041000X

Fig. 3 Vehicle ride height specifications. 1993 Tercel

Tire size	Rear
175/65R14	244 mm (9.61 in.)
185/60R14	245 mm (9.65 in.)

TY2049400042000X

Fig. 4 Vehicle ride height specifications. 1994–96 Tercel

REAR WHEEL ALIGNMENT

CAMBER & TOE-IN

Measure camber angle and toe-in with suitable wheel alignment gauge and adjust to specifications. If reading is not within specification, check for worn or damaged bushings and bent or damaged rear suspension components. Replace parts as necessary.

VEHICLE RIDE HEIGHT

PASEO

Measure vehicle ride height from positions shown in **Fig 1.** Refer to **Fig. 2,** for correct height specifications.

TERCEL

Measure vehicle ride height from positions shown in **Fig 1.** Refer to **Figs. 3 and 4** for correct height specifications.

TOYOTA LAND CRUISER, PICKUPS, RAV4 & 4RUNNER

INDEX OF SERVICE OPERATIONS

	Page No.
AIR BAG SYSTEM PRECAUTIONS	0-8
AUTOMATIC TRANSMISSIONS/ TRANSAXLES	48-1
BRAKES	
Anti-Lock Brakes	48-1
Disc Brakes	48-1
Drum Brakes	48-1
Hydraulic Brake Systems	48-1
Power Brake Units	48-1
CLUTCH & MANUAL TRANSMISSION	
Adjustments	47-64
Clutch, Replace	47-64
Hydraulic System Service	47-64
Precautions	47-64
Tightening Specifications	47-66
Transaxle, Replace	47-66
Transmission, Replace	47-64
ELECTRICAL	
Air Bags	48-1
Air Conditioning	48-1
Alternators	48-1
Blower Motor, Replace	47-15
Coil Pack, Replace	47-12
Combination Switch, Replace	47-14
Combination Switch Service	47-14
Cooling Fans	48-1
Cruise Control	48-1
Dash Gauges	48-1
Dash Panels	48-1
Distributor, Replace	47-11
Evaporator Core, Replace	47-18
Fuel Pump Relay Location	47-10
Fuse Panel & Flasher Location	47-10
Heater Core, Replace	47-17
Ignition Lock, Replace	47-13
Ignition Switch, Replace	47-13
Instrument Cluster, Replace	47-14
Neutral Safety Switch, Adjust	47-13
Passive Restraints	48-1
Precautions	47-9
Radio, Replace	47-14
Relay Center Location	47-10
Speed Controls	48-1
Starter Motors	48-1
Starter, Replace	47-11
Steering Columns	48-1
Steering Wheel, Replace	47-14
Stop Light Switch, Replace	47-14
Wiper Motor, Replace	47-15
Wiper Switch, Replace	47-15
Wiper Systems	48-1
ELECTRICAL SYMBOL IDENTIFICATION	0-139
FRONT SUSPENSION & STEERING	
Ball Joint Inspection	47-73
Coil Spring, Replace	47-73
Lower Control Arm & Torsion Bar, Replace	47-74
Lower Suspension Arm & Shock Absorber, Replace	47-74
Manual Steering Gears	48-1
Power Steering	48-1
Power Steering Gear, Replace	47-75
Power Steering Pump, Replace	47-75
Shock Absorber, Replace	47-73
Stabilizer Bar, Replace	47-73
Strut Bar, Replace	47-74
Tightening Specifications	47-78
Torsion Bar, Replace	47-73
Wheel Bearing, Adjust	47-72
Wheel Hub & Steering Knuckle, Replace	47-73
FRONT WHEEL DRIVE AXLES	48-1
REAR AXLE & SUSPENSION	
Axle Shaft, Bearing & Oil Seal, Replace	47-67
Coil Spring, Replace	47-68
Leaf Spring, Replace	47-69
Rear Axle, Replace	47-67
Shock Absorber, Replace	47-68
Stabilizer Bar, Replace	47-69
Tightening Specifications	47-70
SERVICE REMINDER & WARNING LAMP RESET PROCEDURES	0-10
SPECIFICATIONS	
Fluid Capacities & Cooling System Data	47-7
Front Wheel Alignment Specifications	47-4
General Engine Specifications	47-2
Lubricant Data	47-9
Tune Up Specifications	47-3
VEHICLE IDENTIFICATION	0-1
VEHICLE LIFT POINTS	0-34
VEHICLE MAINTENANCE SCHEDULES	0-69
WHEEL ALIGNMENT	
Front Wheel Alignment	47-80
Rear Wheel Alignment	47-80
Vehicle Ride Height	47-80
Wheel Alignment Specifications	47-4
WIRE COLOR CODE IDENTIFICATION	0-144
1FZ-FE 4.5L ENGINE	
Belt Tension Data	47-61
Camshaft, Replace	47-61
Compression Pressure	47-58
Cooling System Bleed	47-61
Cylinder Head, Replace	47-59
Engine Rebuilding Specifications	48-1
Engine, Replace	47-58
Fuel Filter, Replace	47-62
Fuel Pump, Replace	47-62
Intake Manifold, Replace	47-59
Main & Rod Bearings	47-61
Oil Pan, Replace	47-61
Oil Pump, Replace	47-61
Oil Pump Service	47-61
Piston & Rod Assembly	47-61
Precautions	47-58
Radiator, Replace	47-62
Thermostat, Replace	47-62
Tightening Specifications	47-62
Timing Chain, Replace	47-60
Valve Adjustment	47-60
Valve Clearance Specifications	47-60
Valve Guides	47-60
Water Pump, Replace	47-62
22R-E 2.4L ENGINE	
Belt Tension Data	47-30
Camshaft, Replace	47-29
Compression Pressure	47-27
Cooling System Bleed	47-30
Crankshaft Rear Oil Seal, Replace	47-29
Cylinder Head, Replace	47-28
Engine Rebuilding Specifications	48-1
Engine, Replace	47-27
Front Cover Seal, Replace	47-29
Fuel Filter, Replace	47-30
Fuel Pump, Replace	47-30
Intake Manifold, Replace	47-28
Main & Rod Bearings	47-29
Oil Pan, Replace	47-29
Oil Pump, Replace	47-30
Oil Pump Service	47-30
Piston & Rod Assembly	47-29
Precautions	47-27
Radiator, Replace	47-30
Thermostat, Replace	47-30
Tightening Specifications	47-31
Timing Chain, Replace	47-29
Valve Adjustment	47-29
Valve Clearance Specifications	47-29
Valve Guides	47-29
Water Pump, Replace	47-30
2RZ-FE 2.4L & 3RZ-FE 2.7L ENGINES	
Balance Shaft, Replace	47-36
Belt Tension Data	47-38
Camshaft, Replace	47-36
Compression Pressure	47-33
Cooling System Bleed	47-38
Crankshaft Rear Oil Seal, Replace	47-37
Cylinder Head, Replace	47-34
Engine Rebuilding Specifications	48-1
Engine, Replace	47-33
Front Cover Seal, Replace	47-36
Fuel Filter, Replace	47-40
Fuel Pump, Replace	47-40
Intake Manifold, Replace	47-34
Main & Rod Bearings	47-37
Oil Pan, Replace	47-37
Oil Pump, Replace	47-37
Oil Pump Service	47-37
Piston & Rod Assembly	47-37
Precautions	47-32
Radiator, Replace	47-40
Thermostat, Replace	47-38
Tightening Specifications	47-40
Timing Chain, Replace	47-36
Valve Adjustment	47-35
Valve Clearance Specifications	47-35

Page No.

Valve Guides 47-36
Water Pump, Replace 47-38

3S-FE 2.0L ENGINE

Belt Tension Data 47-25
Camshaft, Replace 47-24
Compression Pressure 47-19
Cooling System Bleed 47-25
Cylinder Head, Replace 47-20
Engine Rebuilding Specifications 48-1
Engine, Replace 47-19
Exhaust Manifold, Replace 47-20
Fuel Filter, Replace 47-25
Fuel Pump, Replace 47-25
Intake Manifold, Replace 47-20
Main & Rod Bearings 47-24
Oil Pan, Replace 47-25
Oil Pump, Replace 47-25
Piston & Rod Assembly 47-24
Precautions 47-19
Radiator, Replace 47-25
Thermostat, Replace 47-25
Tightening Specifications 47-26
Timing Belt, Replace 47-24
Valve Adjustment 47-23
Valve Clearance Specifications 47-23

Water Pump, Replace 47-25

3VZ-E 3.0L ENGINE

Belt Tension Data 47-45
Camshaft, Replace 47-44
Compression Pressure 47-42
Cooling System Bleed 47-45
Crankshaft Rear Oil Seal, Replace 47-44
Cylinder Head, Replace 47-42
Engine Rebuilding Specifications 48-1
Engine, Replace 47-42
Front Cover Seal, Replace 47-43
Fuel Filter, Replace 47-45
Fuel Pump, Replace 47-45
Intake Manifold, Replace 47-42
Main & Rod Bearings 47-44
Oil Pan, Replace 47-44
Oil Pump, Replace 47-44
Oil Pump Service 47-45
Piston & Rod Assembly 47-44
Precautions 47-41
Radiator, Replace 47-45
Thermostat, Replace 47-45
Tightening Specifications 47-46
Timing Belt, Replace 47-44
Valve Adjustment 47-43

Valve Clearance Specifications 47-43
Valve Guides 47-43
Water Pump, Replace 47-45

5VZ-FE 3.4L ENGINE

Belt Tension Data 47-55
Camshaft, Replace 47-54
Compression Pressure 47-47
Cooling System Bleed 47-55
Cylinder Head, Replace 47-49
Engine Rebuilding Specifications 48-1
Engine, Replace 47-47
Fuel Filter, Replace 47-57
Fuel Pump, Replace 47-56
Oil Pan, Replace 47-54
Oil Pump, Replace 47-55
Oil Pump Service 47-55
Precautions 47-47
Radiator, Replace 47-56
Thermostat, Replace 47-55
Tightening Specifications 47-57
Timing Belt, Replace 47-52
Valve Adjustment 47-52
Valve Clearance Specifications 47-52
Water Pump, Replace 47-56

Specifications

GENERAL ENGINE SPECIFICATIONS

Year	Engine	Fuel System	Bore & Stroke	Compression Ratio	Maximum Brake H.P. @ RPM	Maximum Torque Ft. Lbs. @ RPM	Normal Oil Pressure, psi @ 3000 RPM
1993	2.4L 22R-E	Fuel Inj.	3.62 x 3.50	9.3	116 @ 4800	140 @ 2800	36–71
	3.0L 3VZ-E	Fuel Inj.	3.44 x 3.23	9.0	150 @ 4800	180 @ 3400	36–71
	4.5L 1FZ-FE	Fuel Inj.	3.94 x 3.74	9.0	212 @ 4600	275 @ 3200	36–71
1994	2.4L 22R-E	Fuel Inj.	3.62 x 3.50	9.3	116 @ 4800	140 @ 2800	36–71
	2.7L 3RZ-FE	Fuel Inj.	3.74 x 3.74	9.5	150 @ 4800	177 @ 4000	36–71
	3.0L 3VZ-E	Fuel Inj.	3.44 x 3.23	9.0	150 @ 4800	180 @ 3400	36–71
	4.5L 1FZ-FE	Fuel Inj.	3.94 x 3.74	9.0	212 @ 4600	275 @ 3200	36–71
1995	2.4L 2RZ-FE	Fuel Inj.	3.74 x 3.38	9.5	142 @ 5000	160 @ 4000	36–71
	2.4L 22R-E	Fuel Inj.	3.62 x 3.50	9.3	116 @ 4800	140 @ 2800	36–75
	2.7L 3RZ-FE	Fuel Inj.	3.74 x 3.74	9.5	150 @ 4800	177 @ 4000	36–71
	3.0L 3VZ-E	Fuel Inj.	3.44 x 3.23	9.0	150 @ 4800	180 @ 3400	36–71
	3.4L 5VZ-FE	Fuel Inj.	3.68 x 3.23	9.6	190 @ 4800	220 @ 3600	36–75
	4.5L 1FZ-FE	Fuel Inj.	3.94 x 3.74	9.0	212 @ 4600	275 @ 3200	36–71
1996	2.0L 3S-FE	Fuel Inj.	3.40 x 3.40	9.5	120 @ 5400	125 @ 4600	36–71
	2.4L 2RZ-FE	Fuel Inj.	3.74 x 3.38	9.5	142 @ 5000	160 @ 4000	36–71
	2.7L 3RZ-FE	Fuel Inj.	3.74 x 3.74	9.5	150 @ 4800	177 @ 4000	36–71
	3.4L 5VZ-FE	Fuel Inj.	3.68 x 3.23	9.6	190 @ 4800	220 @ 3600	36–75
	4.5L 1FZ-FE	Fuel Inj.	3.94 x 3.74	9.0	212 @ 4600	275 @ 3200	36–71

TUNE UP SPECIFICATIONS

The following specifications are published from the latest information available. This data should be used only in the absence of a decal affixed in the engine compartment.

When checking ignition timing, it may be necessary to disconnect certain hoses and/or electrical connectors. Refer to vehicle emission control label for specific instructions.

Before disconnecting spark plug wires from distributor cap, determine location of No. 1 wire in cap, as distributor position may have been altered from that shown.

Year	Engine	Spark Plug Gap, Inch	Ignition			Curb Idle Speed, RPM③		Fuel Pump Pressure, psi	Valve Clearance, Inch	
			Firing Order	Timing, °BTDC①	Timing Mark Fig.	Man. Trans.	Auto. Trans.		Int.	Exh.
1993	2.4L 22R-R	.031	1-3-4-2	5	A	750	②	36–38	.008	.012
	3.0L	.031	1-2-3-4-5-6	10	C	800	800N	38–44	.007–.011	.009–.013
	4.5L	.031	1-5-3-6-2-4	3	D	—	650N	38–44	.006–.010	.010–.014
1994	2.4L 22R-E	.031	1-3-4-2	5	A	750	②	36–38	.008	.012
	2.7L	.031	1-3-4-2	5	E	700	—	38–44	.006–.010	.010–.014
	3.0L	.031	1-2-3-4-5-6	10	C	800	800N	38–44	.007–.011	.009–.013
	4.5L	.031	1-5-3-6-2-4	3	D	—	650N	38–44	.006–.010	.010–.014
1995	2.4L 2RZ-FE	.031	1-3-4-2	5	A	750	750N	38–44	.006–.010	.010–.014
	2.4L 22R-E	.031	1-3-4-2	5	A	750	②	38–44	.008	.012
	2.7L	.031	1-3-4-2	5	E	700	700N	38–44	.006–.010	.010–.014
	3.0L	.031	1-2-3-4-5-6	10	C	800	800N	38–44	.007–.011	.009–.013
	3.4L	.043	1-2-3-4-5-6	10	D	700	700N	38–44	.006–.009	.011–.014
	4.5L	.031	1-5-3-6-2-4	3	D	650	650N	38–44	.006–.010	.010–.014
1996	2.0L	.043	1-3-4-2	10	B	750	750N	44–50	.007–.011	.011–.015
	2.4L 2RZ-FE	.031	1-3-4-2	5	A	750	750N	38–44	.006–.010	.010–.014
	2.7L	.031	1-3-4-2	5	E	700	700N	38–44	.006–.010	.010–.014
	3.4L	.043	1-2-3-4-5-6	10	D	700	700N	38–44	.006–.009	.011–.014
	4.5L	.031	1-5-3-6-2-4	3	D	650	650N	38–44	.006–.010	.010–.014

N — Neutral.
BTDC — Before Top Dead Center.
① — Terminals T/Te1 & E1 shorted.

② — Less 4WD 750N, w/4WD 850N.

③ — When adjusting idle speed, set parking brake & chock drive wheels.

TY1139100122000X

Fig. A

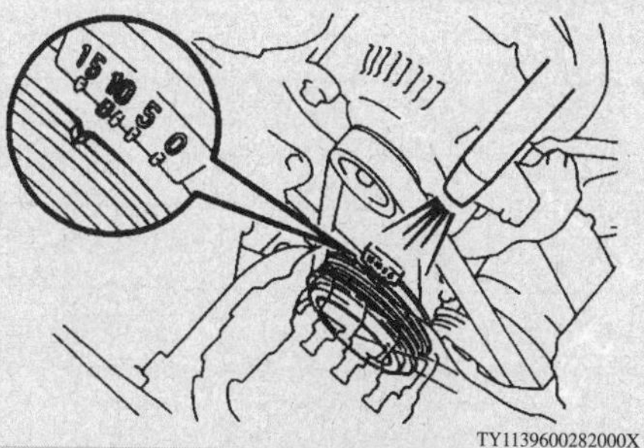
15 10 5 0
TY1139600282000X

Fig. B

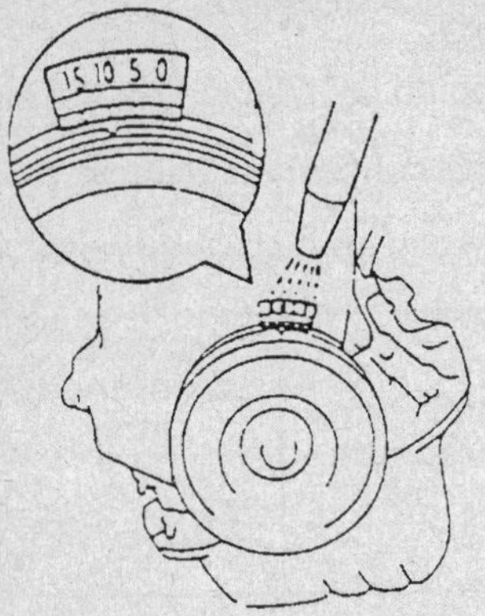
15 10 5 0

TY1139100124000X

Fig. C

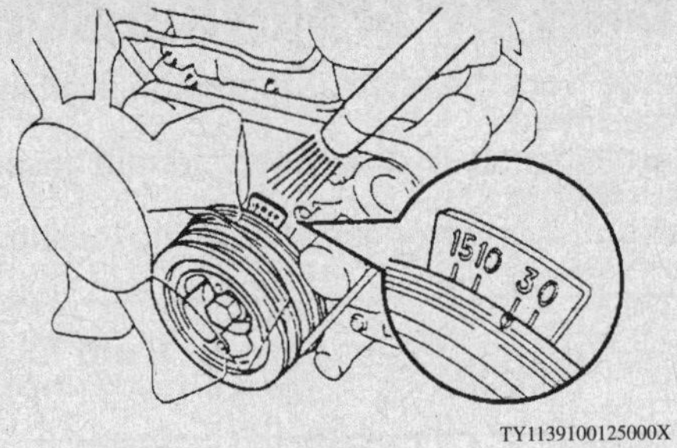
1510 30

TY1139100125000X

Fig. D

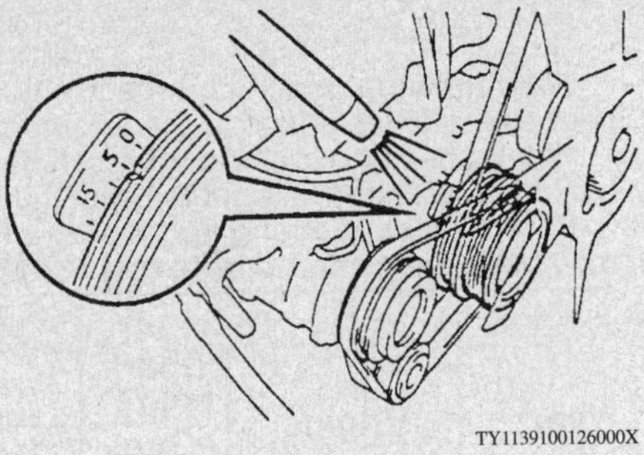
15 5 0

TY1139100126000X

Fig. E

FRONT WHEEL ALIGNMENT SPECIFICATIONS

The specifications listed below are for unloaded vehicles.

LAND CRUISER, RAV4, TACOMA, T100 & 1996 4RUNNER

Year	Model	Caster Angle, Degrees		Camber Angle, Degrees		Toe, Inch①	Toe-Out On Turns, Deg.		Steering Axis Inclination, Deg.	Ball Joint Wear
		Limits	Desired	Limits	Desired		Inner Wheel	Outer Wheel		
1993	Land Cruiser	+2 to +4	+3	+¼ to +1 ¾	+1	−.04 to +.12	35	30	13	②
	T100 2WD④	+1 ¾ to +3 ¼	+2 ½	−¼ to +1 ¼	+½	+.08 to +.16	40 ¾	35 ¼	10	②
	T100 2WD⑤	+2 ¼ to +3 ¾	+3	−¼ to +1 ¼	+½	+.31 to +.39	40 ½	35 ¾	9 ½	②
	T100 4WD	+ ¾ to +2 ¼	+1 ½	0 to +1 ½	+¾	+.04 to +.20	33	30 ½	11 ⅚	②
1994	Land Cruiser	+2 to +4	+3	+¼ to +1 ¾	+1	0 to +.32	35	31	13	②
	T100 2WD④	+1 ⅚ to +3 ⅓	+3	−⅓ to +1 ⅙	+⅖	+.04 to +.20	40 ⅔	35 1/12	12 ⅙	②
	T100 2WD⑤	+1 7/12 to +3 1/12	+2 ⅓	−5/12 to +1 1/12	+¾	+.27 to +.43	40 5/12	35 ½	12 ⅙	②
	T100 4WD	+¾ to +2 ¼	+1 ½	0 to +1 ½	+¾	+.04 to +.20	33	30 ½	11 ⅚	②
1995	Land Cruiser	+2 to +4	+3	+¼ to +1 ¾	+1	0 to +.32	35	31	13	②
	Tacoma 2WD	+1 1/12 to +2 7/12	+1 ⅚	-¾ to +¾	0	-.08 to +.08	36	30 ¾	10	②
	Tacoma 4WD	+2 1/12 to +3 7/12	+2 ⅚	-¾ to +¾	0	-.08 to +.08	37 1/12	32 ⅓	10 ¾	②
	T100 2WD④	⑥	⑦	−⅓ to +1 ⅙	+5/12	+.04 to +.20	40 ⅔	35 ⅙	12 1/12	②
	T100 2WD⑤	+⅚ to +2 ⅓	+1 7/12	-⅓ to +1 ⅙	+5/12	+.20 to +.36	40 5/12	35 7/12	12 ⅙	②
	T100 4WD	⑧	③	-1/12 to +1 5/12	+ ⅔	+.04 to +.20	32 ⅚	30 ½	12	②
1996	Land Cruiser	+2 to +4	+3	+¼ to +1 ¾	+1	0 to +.32	35	31	13	②
	RAV4 2WD	+1 ⅓ to +2 ¼	+1 5/12	-1 1/12 to +5/12	-⅓	-.08 to +.08	33 ¼	28 1/12	11	②
	RAV4 4WD	+5/12 to +2 1/12	+1 ⅓	-1 to +½	-¼	-.08 to +.08	33 ¼	28 1/12	10 ¾	②
	Tacoma 2WD	+1 1/12 to +2 7/12	+1 ⅚	-¾ to +¾	0	-.08 to +.08	36	30 ¾	10	②
	Tacoma 4WD	+2 1/12 to +3 7/12	+2 ⅚	-¾ to +¾	0	-.08 to +.08	37 1/12	32 ⅓	10 ¾	②
	T100 2WD④	⑥	⑦	−⅓ to +1 ⅙	+5/12	+.04 to +.20	40 ⅔	35 ⅙	12 1/12	②
	T100 2WD⑤	+⅚ to +2 ⅓	+1 7/12	-⅓ to +1 ⅙	+5/12	+.20 to +.36	40 5/12	35 7/12	12 ⅙	②

Continued

FRONT WHEEL ALIGNMENT SPECIFICATIONS

The specifications listed below are for unloaded vehicles.

LAND CRUISER, RAV4, TACOMA, T100 & 1996 4RUNNER—Continued

Year	Model	Caster Angle, Degrees		Camber Angle, Degrees		Toe, Inch①	Toe-Out On Turns, Deg.		Steering Axis Inclination, Deg.	Ball Joint Wear
		Limits	Desired	Limits	Desired		Inner Wheel	Outer Wheel		
1996	T100 4WD	⑧	③	-1/12 to +1 5/12	+ 2/3	+.04 to +.20	32 5/6	30 1/2	12	②
	4Runner⑨	+2 3/5 to +4 3/5	+3 1/3	-1 to +8/15	-1/5	-.02 to +.14	35 1/5	31 11/30	10 29/30	②
	4Runner⑩	+1 9/10 to +3 2/5	+2 19/30	-7/12 to +11/12	+1/6	-.01 to +.15	35 3/4	31 11/12	10 7/12	②

① — Toe-in (+); toe-out (-).
② — Refer to "Ball Joint Inspection" in "Front Suspension & Steering."
③ — Standard suspension, +1 1/6; soft ride suspension, +1 7/12.
④ — 1/2 ton models.
⑤ — 1 ton models.
⑥ — Standard suspension, +1 7/12 to +3 1/12 ; soft ride suspension, +1 11/12 to +3 5/12.
⑦ — Standard suspension, +2 1/3; soft ride suspension, +2 2/3.
⑧ — Standard suspension, +5/12 to +1 11/12 ; soft ride suspension, +5/6 to +2 1/3.
⑨ — Tire size, 225/75R15.
⑩ — Tire size, 265/70R16.

1993-95 CAB & CHASSIS, PICKUP & 4RUNNER

Year	Model Code	Caster Angle, Deg.①	Camber Angle, Deg.①	Toe, Inch②	Toe-Out On Turns, Deg.		Steering Axis Inclination, Deg.
					Inner Wheel	Outer Wheel	
TWO WHEEL DRIVE MODELS							
1993	RN80L-TRSDEA, TRSDEK	+43/60	+1/2	+.052	34	30	10
	RN80L-TRMDEA, TRMDEK	+11/15	+1/2	+.052	34	30	10
	RN80L-TRMREA, TRMREK	+2/3	+7/15	+.069	34	30	10 1/60
	RN85L-TRMDEA, TRMDEK	+59/60	+9/20	+.082	34	30	10 1/30
	RN85L-TRSDEA, TRSDEK	+29/30	+9/20	+.082	34	30	10 1/30
	RN90L-CRMDEA, CRMDEK	+1 1/4	+23/60	+.129	34	30	10 1/10
	RN90L-CRSDEA, CRSDEK	+1 1/4	+23/60	+.129	34	30	10 1/10
	VZN85L-THMDEA	+17/30	+29/60	+.221	34	30	10
	VZN85L-THSDEA	+11/20	+1/2	+.191	34	30	10
	VZN85L-TWMREA6	+1 23/30	+29/60	+.226	34	30	10
	VZN85L-TWSREA6	+1 3/4	+29/60	+.226	34	30	10
	VZN90L-CRMDEA, CRMDEK	+1 11/60	+23/60	+.129	34	30	10 1/10
	VZN90L-CRSDEA, CRSDEK	+1 1/5	+23/60	+.129	34	30	10 1/10
	VZN90L-CRMGEA, CRMGEK	+1 13/60	+5/12	+.111	34	30	10 1/15
	VZN90L-CRPGEA	+1 1/5	+5/12	+.111	34	30	10 1/15
	VZN95L-TWMREA6	+1 47/60	+29/60	+.226	34	30	10
	VZN95L-TWSREA6, TWSREK6	+1 23/30	+29/60	+.226	34	30	10
1994–95	RN80L-TRSDEA	+3/4	+1/2	+.052	35	31	10
	RN80L-TRMDEA	+3/4	+1/2	+.052	35	31	10
	RN80L-TRMREA, TRMREK	+3/4	+1/2	+.069	35	31	10
	RN90L-CRMDEA, CRMDEK	+1 1/4	+1/3	+.129	35	31	10 1/12
	RN90L-CRSDEA, CRSDEK	+1 1/4	+1/3	+.129	35	31	10 1/12
	VZN90L-CRMDEA, CRMDEK	+1 1/4	+1/3	+.129	35	31	10 1/12
	VZN90L-CRSDEA, CRSDEK	+1 1/4	+1/3	+.129	35	31	10 1/12
	VZN90L-CRMGEA	+1 1/4	+1/3	+.161	35	31	10 1/6
	VZN90L-CRPGEA	+1 1/4	+1/3	+.161	35	31	10 1/6
FOUR WHEEL DRIVE MODELS							
1993	RN101L-TRLDEA, TRMDEA	+1 19/30	+43/60	+.076	32	31	11 13/15
	RN101L-TRLDEK	+1 37/60	+43/60	+.076	32	31	11 13/15
	RN101L-TRPDEA	+1 41/60	+43/60	+.075	32	31	11 13/15
	RN106L Series	+1 41/60	+7/10	+.087	32	31	11 53/60

Continued

1993-95 CAB & CHASSIS, PICKUP & 4RUNNER—Continued

Year	Model Code	Caster Angle, Deg.①	Camber Angle, Deg.①	Toe, Inch②	Toe-Out On Turns, Deg.		Steering Axis Inclination, Deg.
					Inner Wheel	Outer Wheel	
FOUR WHEEL DRIVE MODELS							
1993	RN110L-CRLDEK	+1 11/15	+2/3	+.106	32	31	11 11/12
	RN110L-CRMDEA, CRLDEA	+1 49/60	+2/3	+.106	32	31	11 11/12
	RN110L-CRPDEA	+1 13/15	+2/3	+.106	32	31	11 11/12
	RN120L Series	+1 9/10	+43/60	+.080	32	31	11 13/15
	RN121L-RKMSEK	+1 43/60	+43/60	+.076	32	31	11 13/15
	RN121L-RKPSEK	+1 23/30	+43/60	+.076	32	31	11 13/15
	RN130L Series	+2 1/60	+43/60	+.081	32	31	11 13/15
	RN131L-RJLSEK	+1 4/5	+43/60	+.078	32	31	11 13/15
	RN131L-RKLSEK, RKPSEK	+1 53/60	+43/60	+.078	32	31	11 13/15
	VZN100L Series	+1 41/60	+43/60	+.075	32	31	11 13/15
	VZN105L Series	+1 3/4	+7/10	+.087	32	31	11 53/60
	VZN110L-CRMDEA	+1 13/15	+2/3	+.106	32	31	11 11/12
	VZN110L-CRMDEK	+1 4/5	+2/3	+.106	32	31	11 11/12
	VZN110L-CRMGEA	+1 11/12	+7/10	+.089	32	31	11 53/60
	VZN110L-CRMGEK	+1 5/6	+7/10	+.089	32	31	11 53/60
	VZN110L-CRMDEK	+1 4/5	+2/3	+.106	32	31	11 11/12
	VZN110L-CRMGEA	+1 11/12	+7/10	+.089	32	31	11 53/60
	VZN110L-CRMGEK	+1 5/6	+7/10	+.089	32	31	11 53/60
	VZN110L-CRPDEA	+1 53/60	+2/3	+.106	32	31	11 11/12
	VZN110L-CRPDEK	+1 49/60	+2/3	+.106	32	31	11 11/12
	VZN110L-CRPGEA	+1 14/15	+7/10	+.089	32	31	11 53/60
	VZV120L Series	+1 14/15	+43/60	+.080	32	31	11 13/15
	VZV130L-GJMGEA	⑬	+43/60	⑭	32	31	11 13/15
	VZV130L-GJPGEA	⑮	+43/60	+.076	32	31	11 13/15
	VZV130L-GKMGEA	⑯	+43/60	+.076	32	31	11 13/15
	VZV130L-GKPGEA	⑰	+43/60	+.076	32	31	11 13/15
	VZV131L-RJMGEK	⑧	+43/60	⑫	32	31	11 13/15
	VZV131L-RJPGEK	⑪	+43/60	⑫	32	31	11 13/15
	VZV131L-RKMGEK	⑩	+43/60	⑫	32	31	11 13/15
	VZV131L-RKPGEK	⑦	+43/60	⑨	32	31	11 13/15
1994–95	RN101L-TRMDEA	+1 7/12	+43/60	+.076	32	31	11 13/15
	RN101L-TRLDEK	+1 7/12	+43/60	+.076	32	31	11 13/15
	RN101L-TRPDEA	+1 19/30	+43/60	+.075	32	31	11 13/15
	RN110L-CRLDEK	+1 4/5	+11/15	+.069	32	31	11 51/60
	RN110L-CRMDEA	+1 49/60	+2/3	+.106	32	31	11 11/12
	RN130L-GKLSEA	+1 23/30	+43/60	+.076	32	31	11 13/15
	RN131L-RKLSEK	+1 23/30	+43/60	+.073	32	31	11 13/15
	RN131L-RKPSEK	+1 47/60	+43/60	+.073	32	31	11 13/15
	VZN110L-CRMDEA, CRMDEK	+1 5/6	+11/15	+.066	32	31	11 51/60
	VZN110L-CRMGEA, CRMGEK	+1 51/60	+11/15	+.065	32	31	11 51/60
	VZN110L-CRPDEA, CRPDEK	+1 13/15	+11/15	+.065	32	31	11 51/60
	VZN110L-CRPGEA	+1 13/15	+11/15	+.065	32	31	11 51/60
	VZN120L-GKPGEA	+1 43/60	+43/60	+.076	32	31	11 13/15
	VZN130L-GKMGEA	⑥	+43/60	+.076	32	31	11 13/15
	VZN130L-GKPGEA	⑤	+43/60	+.076	32	31	11 13/15

Continued

1993–95 CAB & CHASSIS, PICKUP & 4RUNNER—Continued

Year	Model Code	Caster Angle, Deg.(1)	Camber Angle, Deg.(1)	Toe, Inch(2)	Toe-Out On Turns, Deg.		Steering Axis Inclination, Deg.
					Inner Wheel	Outer Wheel	
FOUR WHEEL DRIVE MODELS							
1994–95	VZN131L-RKMGEK	(4)	+43/60	+.074	32	31	11 13/15
	VZN131L-RKPGEK	(3)	+43/60	+.074	32	31	11 13/15

(1) — Plus or minus 3/4°.
(2) — Toe-in (+); toe-out (-).
(3) — With P225/75R 15 tires, +1 59/60; w/30 x 10.50R or 31 x 10.50R 15 tires, +1 57/60.
(4) — With P225/75R 15 tires, +1 3/4; w/30 x 10.50R or 31 x 10.50R 15 tires, +1 11/15.
(5) — With P225/75R 15 tires, +1 4/5; w/30 x 10.50R or 31 x 10.50R 15 tires, +1 47/60.
(6) — With P225/75R 15 tires, +1 47/60; w/30 x 10.50R or 31 x 10.50R 15 tires, +1 23/30.
(7) — With P225/75R 15 tires, +1 47/60; w/30 x 10.50R or 31 x 10.50R 15 tires, +1 49/60.
(8) — With P225/75R 15 tires, +1 37/60; w/30 x 10.50R or 31 x 10.50R 15 tires, +1 41/60.
(9) — With P225/75R 15 tires, +.075; w/30 x 10.50R or 31 x 10.50R 15 tires, +.073.
(10) — With P225/75R 15 tires, +1 37/60; w/30 x 10.50R or 31 x 10.50R 15 tires, +1 2/3.
(11) — With P225/75R 15 tires, +1 39/60; w/30 x 10.50R or 31 x 10.50R 15 tires, +1 7/10.
(12) — With P225/75R 15 tires, +.076; w/30 x 10.50R or 31 x 10.50R 15 tires, +.074.
(13) — With P225/75R 15 tires, +1 49/60; w/30 x 10.50R or 31 x 10.50R 15 tires, +1 51/60.
(14) — With P225/75R 15 tires, +.080; w/30 x 10.50R or 31 x 10.50R 15 tires, +.076.
(15) — With P225/75R 15 tires, +1 5/6; w/30 x 10.50R or 31 x 10.50R 15 tires, +1 13/15.
(16) — With P225/75R 15 tires, +1 41/60; w/30 x 10.50R or 31 x 10.50R 15 tires, +1 43/60.
(17) — With P225/75R 15 tires, +1 2/3; w/30 x 10.50R or 31 x 10.50R 15 tires, +1 43/60.

FLUID CAPACITIES & COOLING SYSTEM DATA

Year	Model	Coolant Capacity, Qts.		Radiator Cap Relief Pressure, Lbs.	Thermo. Opening Temp., °F	Fuel Tank, Gals.	Engine Oil Refill, Qts.(3)	Transmission/ Transaxle Oil		Axle Oil, Pints
		Less A/C	With A/C					5 Speed Man. Trans., Pints	Auto Trans., Qts.	
1993–94	Pickup 2WD(6)	8.9	8.9	12.8	180	17.2	4.5	(8)	(14)	(15)
	Pickup 2WD(7)	(10)	(10)	12.8	180	17.2	4.5	(8)	(14)	(15)
	Pickup 4WD(6)	(12)	(12)	12.8	180	17.2	4.5	(4)(2)	(14)(5)	(16)
	Pickup 4WD(7)	(13)	(13)	12.8	180	17.2	4.8	(4)(2)	(14)(5)	(16)
	4Runner 2WD	8.9	8.9	12.8	180	17.2	4.5	6.4	10.9	(15)
	4Runner 4WD(6)	(12)	(12)	12.8	180	17.2	4.5	6.4	10.9	(16)
	4Runner 4WD(7)	(13)	(13)	12.8	180	17.2	4.8	6.4	10.9	(16)
	Land Cruiser	15	15	12.8	180	25.1	7.8	(46)	(46)	(11)
	T100 2WD(6)	9.2	9.2	13	180	24	5.6	6.4	—	4.34
	T100 2WD(7)	(17)	(17)	13	180	24	5.7	6.4	(19)	4.34
	T100 4WD(7)	(18)	(18)	13	180	24	4.8	6.4(20)	(19)(20)	(1)
1995	4Runner 22-R	(13)	(13)	13	190	17.2	4.5	(8)	(20)(21)	(22)
	4Runner 2WD 3VZ-E	(13)	(13)	13	180	17.2	4.8	(8)	(21)	3.8
	4Runner 4WD 3VZ-E	(13)	(13)	13	180	17.2	4.8	(8)	10.9(20)	(22)
	Land Cruiser	(23)	(23)	13	180	25.1	7.8	—	11.6(24)	(25)
	Tacoma 2WD w/2RZ-FE	(26)	(26)	13	180	15.1	5.8	5.4	(27)	2.84
	Tacoma 4WD w/3RZ-FE	(28)	(28)	13	180	18	5.7	5.2(20)	(20)(27)	(29)
	Tacoma 2WD w/5VZ-FE	(30)	(30)	13	180	15.1	5.7	5.4	(27)	4.38
	Tacoma 4WD w/5VZ-F	(30)	(30)	13	180	18	5.5	4.6(20)	(20)(27)	(29)
	Pickup 2WD w/22R-E	8.9	8.9	13	190	(31)	4.5	5.4	(32)	(15)
	Pickup 4WD w/22R-E	(35)	(35)	13	190	(31)	4.5	(20)(33)	(20)(32)	(16)

Continued

FLUID CAPACITIES & COOLING SYSTEM DATA—Continued

Year	Model	Coolant Capacity, Qts.		Radiator Cap Relief Pressure, Lbs.	Thermo. Opening Temp., °F	Fuel Tank, Gals.	Engine Oil Refill, Qts.(3)	Transmission/ Transaxle Oil		Axle Oil, Pints
		Less A/C	With A/C					5 Speed Man. Trans., Pints	Auto Trans., Qts.	
1995	Pickup 2WD w/3VZ-E	(13)	(13)	13	180	(31)	4.5	5.4	(32)	(15)
	Pickup 4WD w/3VZ-E	(13)	(13)	13	180	(31)	4.8	(20)(33)	(20)(32)	(16)
	T100 w/3RZ-FE	9.2	9.2	13	180	24	5.8	5.4	8	4.34
	T100 2WD w/5VZ-FE	10.6	10.6	13	180	24	5.5	6.4	8	4.34
	T100 4WD w/5VZ-FE	10.8	10.8	13	180	24	5	4.6(20)	8(20)	(34)
1996	4Runner 2WD w/3RZ-FE	(9)	(9)	13	180	18.5	5.6	(37)	(39)	(41)(43)
	4Runner 4WD w/3RZ-FE	(9)	(9)	13	180	18.5	5.7	(38)	(39)(40)	(41)(42)
	4Runner 2WD w/5VZ-FE	(36)	(36)	13	180	18.5	5.5	(37)	(39)	(41)(43)
	4Runner 4WD w/5VZ-FE	(36)	(36)	13	180	18.5	5.5	(38)	(39)(40)	(41)(42)
	Land Cruiser	(23)	(23)	13	180	25.1	7.8	—	11.6(24)	(25)
	RAV4	(44)	(44)	13	180	15.3	4.1	(45)	8.5	2
	Tacoma 2WD w/2RZ-FE	(26)	(26)	13	180	15.1	5.8	5.4	(27)	2.84
	Tacoma 4WD w/3RZ-FE	(28)	(28)	13	180	18	5.7	5.2(20)	(20)(27)	(29)
	Tacoma 2WD w/5VZ-FE	(30)	(30)	13	180	15.1	5.7	5.4	(27)	4.38
	Tacoma 4WD w/5VZ-F	(30)	(30)	13	180	18	5.5	4.6(20)	(20)(27)	(29)
	T100 w/3RZ-FE	9.2	9.2	13	180	24	5.8	5.4	8	4.34
	T100 2WD w/5VZ-FE	10.6	10.6	13	180	24	5.5	6.4	8	4.34
	T100 4WD w/5VZ-FE	10.8	10.8	13	180	24	5	4.6(20)	8(20)	(34)

(1) — Front, std. 3.4 pts., auto. disconnect diff. (ADD), 4 pts.; rear 4.34 pts.
(2) — Countergear type transfer case, 3.4 pts.; planetary type, 2.4 pts.
(3) — With filter change.
(4) — G58, 8.2 pts.; W56, 6.2 pts.; R150F, 6.4 pts.
(5) — A340H Transfer case oil, 1.6 qts.
(6) — With 4-cylinder engine.
(7) — With 6-cylinder engine.
(8) — G55 & W55, 5.0 pts.; R150, 6.4 pts.
(9) — Less rear heater, 10.6 qts.; w/rear heater 11.6 qts.
(10) — With manual trans., 9.9 qts.; w/auto. trans., 9.7 qts.
(11) — Front, 2.6 pts.; rear, 4 pts.
(12) — With manual trans., 9.6 qts.; w/auto. trans., 8.9 qts.
(13) — With manual trans., 10.6 qts.; w/auto. trans., 10.4 qts.
(14) — A43D, 6.9; A340E, 7.6; A340H, 10.9.
(15) — 7.5 inches, 2.8 pts.; 8.0 inches, 3.8 pts.
(16) — Front, 3.4 pts.; rear, 4.6 pts.; ADD, 4.0 pts.
(17) — With manual trans., 10.6 qts.; w/auto. trans., 10.5 qts.
(18) — With manual trans., 10.6 qts.; w/auto. trans., 10.8 qts.
(19) — A340E, 7.6 qts.; A340F, 8 qts.
(20) — Transfer case oil, 2.4 pts.
(21) — A340E, 7.6 qts.; A340F, 8 qts.; A340H, 10.8 qts.
(22) — Front except ADD, 3.4 pts.; ADD, 4 pts.; rear, 4.6 pts.
(23) — Front heater only, 13.2 qts.; front & rear heater, 14.2 qts.
(24) — Transfer case oil, 3.6 pts.
(25) — Front, less differential lock, 6 pts.; w/differential lock, 5.6 pts.; rear, 6.8 pts.
(26) — Man. trans., 8.5 qts.; auto. trans., 8.2 qts.
(27) — A43D, 6.9 qts.; A340E, 7.6 qts.; A340F, 10.5 qts.
(28) — Man. trans., 8.8 qts.; auto. trans., 8.7 qts.
(29) — Front except ADD, 2.32 pts.; ADD, 2.44 pts.; rear, short wheel base, 4.38 pts.; extra long wheel base, 3.32 pts.
(30) — Man. trans., 10.7 qts.; auto. trans., 10.5 qts.
(31) — Short wheel base, 13.7 gals.; long wheel base & short bed models, 17.2 gals.; long bed models, 19.3 gals.
(32) — A43D, 6.9 qts.; A340E, 7.6 qts.; A340F, 8 qts.; A340H, 10.8 qts.
(33) — G58, 8.2 pts.; W56, 6.2 pts.; R150F, 4.6 pts.
(34) — Front, 4 pts.; ADD, 4 pts.; rear, 4.34 pts.
(35) — Man. trans., 8.9 qts.; auto. trans., 9.6 qts.
(36) — Less rear heater, 8.5 qts.; w/rear heater, 9.5 qts.
(37) — W59, 5.4 pts.; R150F, 4.6 pts.
(38) — W59, 5.2 pts.; R150F, 4.6 pts.
(39) — A340E, 7.6 qts.; A340F, 9.3 qts.
(40) — Transfer oil, 2.2 pts.
(41) — Front except ADD, 2.32 pts.; ADD, 2.44 pts.
(42) — Rear less differential lock, 5.2 pts.; w/differential lock, 5.8 pts.
(43) — Rear differential, 5.8 pts.
(44) — Man. trans., 8.5 qts.; auto. trans., 8.1 qts.
(45) — 2WD, 8.2 pts.; 4WD, 10.6 pts.
(46) — Transfer case oil, 2.6 pts.

LUBRICANT DATA

Year	Model	Lubricant Type					
		Transmission		Transfer Case	Rear Axle	Power Steering	Brake System
		Manual	Automatic				
1993–94	All	API GL-4 or GL-5	Dexron II	API GL-4 or GL-5	API GL-5	Dexron II	DOT 3
1995	Land Cruiser	—	Dexron II	75W-90 GL-4/5	API GL-5	Dexron II/IIE/III	DOT 3
	Tacoma	75W-90 GL-3/4/5	Dexron II/IIE/III	75W-90 GL-3/4/5	①	Dexron II/IIE/III	DOT 3
	T100	75W-90 GL-4/5	Dexron II/IIE/III	75W-90 GL-4/5	80W-90/90 GL-5	Dexron II/IIE/III	DOT 3
	Pickup & 4Runner	75W-90 GL-4/5	Dexron II/IIE/III	75W-90 GL-3/4/5	①	Dexron II/IIE/III	DOT 3
1996	Land Cruiser	—	Dexron II	75W-90 GL-4/5	API GL-5	Dexron II/IIE/III	DOT 3
	RAV4	75W-90 GL-4/5	Dexron II	—	API GL-5	Dexron II or III	DOT 3
	Tacoma	75W-90 GL-3/4/5	Dexron II/IIE/III	75W-90 GL-3/4/5	①	Dexron II/IIE/III	DOT 3
	T100	75W-90 GL-4/5	Dexron II/IIE/III	75W-90 GL-4/5	80W-90/90 GL-5	Dexron II/IIE/III	DOT 3
	4Runner	75W-90 GL-4/5	Dexron II/IIE/III	75W-90 GL-4/5	API GL-5	Dexron II or III	DOT 3

① — 2WD & 4WD standard differential, 80W-90/90 GL-5; 4WD ADD front differential, 75W-90 GL-5.

Electrical

NOTE: On Air Bag Equipped Models, Refer To "Air Bag System Precautions" Located In The Front Of This Manual For System Disarming & Arming Procedures.

INDEX

Page No.

Air Bags 48-1
Air Conditioning 48-1
Alternators 48-1
Blower Motor, Replace 47-15
Land Cruiser 47-17
Pickup 47-15
RAV4 & Tacoma 47-16
4Runner 47-16
Coil Pack, Replace 47-12
5VZ-FE Engine 47-12
Combination Switch, Replace ... 47-14
Combination Switch Service 47-14
Cooling Fans 48-1
Cruise Control 48-1
Dash Gauges 48-1
Dash Panels 48-1
Distributor, Replace 47-11
Land Cruiser 47-12
Pickup, Tacoma & 4Runner 47-11
RAV4 47-12
Evaporator Core, Replace 47-18
Land Cruiser 47-18
Pickup & 4Runner 47-18
RAV4 47-18
T100 47-18

Page No.

Tacoma 47-18
Fuel Pump Relay Location 47-10
Land Cruiser 47-10
Pickup 47-10
RAV4 47-10
T100 47-10
Tacoma 47-10
4Runner 47-10
Fuse Panel & Flasher Location .. 47-10
Land Cruiser 47-10
Pickup 47-10
RAV4 47-10
T100 47-10
Tacoma 47-10
4Runner 47-10
Heater Core, Replace 47-17
Land Cruiser 47-17
Pickup & T100 47-17
RAV4 47-17
Tacoma 47-17
4Runner 47-17
Ignition Lock, Replace 47-13
Ignition Switch, Replace 47-13
Instrument Cluster, Replace 47-14
Neutral Safety Switch, Adjust 47-13

Page No.

Passive Restraints 48-1
Precautions 47-9
Air Bag Systems 47-9
Audio Coded Anti-Theft System . 47-9
Radio, Replace 47-14
Land Cruiser 47-15
Pickup, RAV4 & 4Runner 47-14
Relay Center Location 47-10
Land Cruiser 47-10
Pickup 47-11
RAV4 47-11
T100 47-11
Tacoma 47-11
4Runner 47-10
Speed Controls 48-1
Starter Motors 48-1
Starter, Replace 47-11
Steering Columns 48-1
Steering Wheel, Replace 47-14
Stop Light Switch, Replace 47-14
Wiper Motor, Replace 47-15
Front 47-15
Rear 47-15
Wiper Switch, Replace 47-15
Wiper Systems 48-1

PRECAUTIONS

AIR BAG SYSTEMS

Refer to "Air Bag System Precautions" in the front of this manual for system disarming and arming procedures.

AUDIO CODED ANTI-THEFT SYSTEM

Some models are equipped with an audio coded anti-theft system that will disable the radio when the battery cable is disconnected. The system can be identified by the "ANTI-THEFT SYSTEM" on the cassette lid. Obtain three-digit code for input. Reset system after service as follows:

1. Obtain three-digit audio theft code.

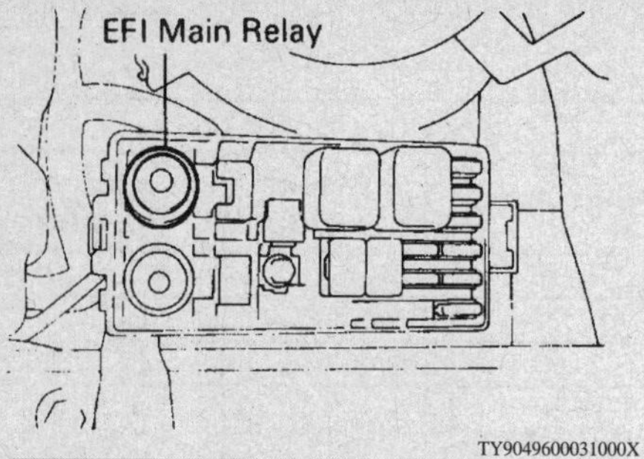
EFI Main Relay
TY9049600031000X

Fig. 1 EFI relay location. Land Cruiser

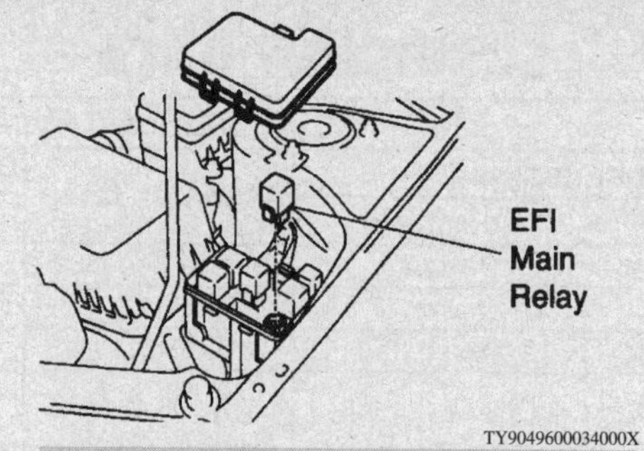
EFI
Main
Relay
TY9049600034000X

Fig. 2 EFI relay location. RAV4

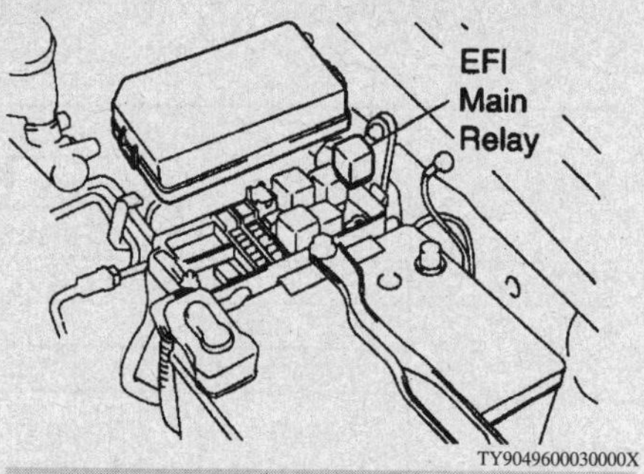
EFI
Main
Relay
TY9049600030000X

Fig. 3 EFI relay location. Tacoma

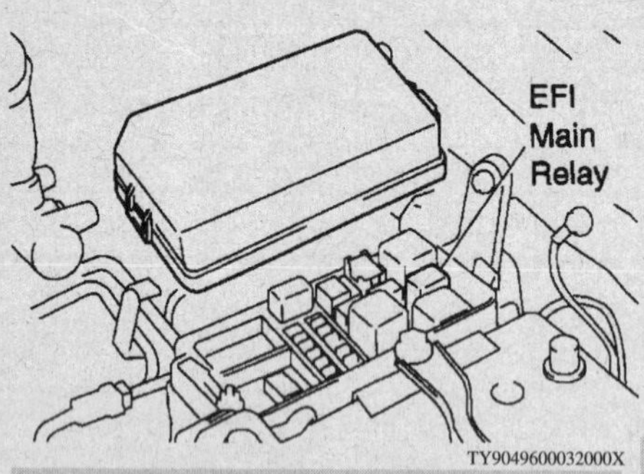
EFI
Main
Relay
TY9049600032000X

Fig. 4 EFI relay location. 4Runner

2. Depress 1 (PROG) button while depressing righthand side of TUNE SEEK button. Three dashes will appear in tape operation display.
3. To enter first digit, depress 1 (PROG) button repeatedly until number of times depressed equals first digit (depress 1 button six times if first digit is five, first press equals 0).
4. To enter second digit, depress 2 (APS) button repeatedly until number of times depressed equals second digit.
5. To enter third digit, depress 3 (RPT) button repeatedly until number of times depressed equals third digit.
6. If three dashes are displayed after inputting digits, repeat procedure.
7. When code appears in display, depress and hold SCAN button until SEC appears.
8. When SEC disappears audio system is operative.
9. If Err is displayed, repeat procedure. **Attempting to input code more than nine times may permanently disable audio system.**

FUSE PANEL & FLASHER LOCATION

LAND CRUISER

The No. 1 fuse panel is located behind the removable instrument panel cover, to the left of the steering column. The No. 2 fuse panel is located in the lefthand side of the engine compartment, behind the battery. The turn signal/hazard flasher is in the No. 1 relay panel, located at the lefthand side kick panel.

4RUNNER

1993-95

The No. 1 fuse panel is located below the lefthand side kick panel. The No. 2 fuse panel is in the righthand side of the engine compartment, behind the battery. Fuse panel No. 3 is behind the righthand side kick panel. The turn signal/hazard flasher is located behind the instrument cluster.

1996

The No. 1 fuse panel is located behind the lower lefthand side of the instrument panel. Fuse/relay panel No. 2 is located in the righthand side of the engine compartment, behind the battery. The turn signal/hazard flasher is at fuse panel No. 1.

PICKUP

The No. 1 fuse panel is located behind the lefthand side kick panel. The No. 2 fuse panel is in the righthand side of the engine compartment, behind the battery. Fuse panel No. 3 is on behind the righthand side kick panel. The turn signal/hazard flasher is located behind the instrument cluster.

RAV4

The No. 1 fuse panel is located behind the lefthand side kick panel. The No. 2 fuse panel is in the righthand side of the engine compartment, near the righthand side shock tower. The turn signal/hazard flasher unit is at the No. 1 fuse panel.

TACOMA

The No. 1 fuse panel is located below the lefthand side kick panel. The No. 2 fuse panel is in engine compartment, on the front lefthand side.

T100

The No. 1 fuse panel is located behind the lefthand side kick panel. The No. 2 fuse panel is in the lefthand side of the engine compartment, behind the battery. The turn signal/hazard flasher is located under the instrument panel, below and to the left of the steering column.

FUEL PUMP RELAY LOCATION

LAND CRUISER

The fuel pump (EFI) relay is located in the engine compartment relay box, **Fig. 1.**

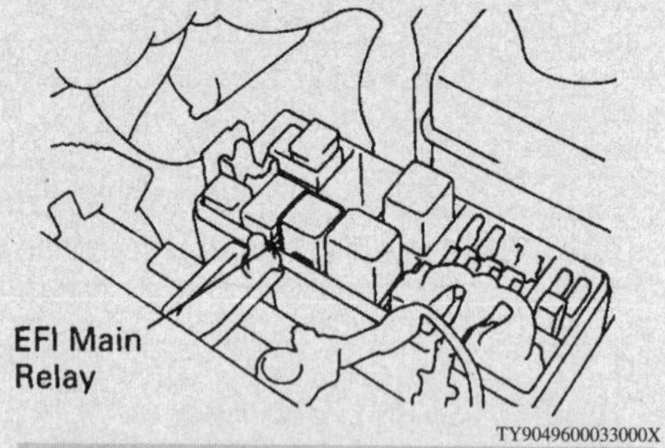
EFI Main
Relay
TY9049600033000X

Fig. 5 EFI relay location. T100

PICKUP

The fuel pump (EFI) relay is located in the righthand side of the engine compartment, in the fuse/relay box.

RAV4

The fuel pump (EFI) relay is located in the engine compartment fuse/relay box, **Fig. 2.**

TACOMA

The fuel pump (EFI) relay is located in the engine compartment fuse/relay box, lefthand side of engine compartment, **Fig. 3.**

4RUNNER

The fuel pump (EFI) relay is located in the engine compartment relay box, **Fig. 4.**

T100

The fuel pump (EFI) relay is located in the engine compartment relay box, **Fig. 5.**

RELAY CENTER LOCATION

LAND CRUISER

The No. 1 relay panel is located behind the removable instrument panel cover, to the left of the steering column. The No. 2 relay panel is located in the lefthand side of the engine compartment, behind the battery. The turn signal/hazard flasher is in the No. 1 relay panel, located at the lefthand side kick panel.

4RUNNER

1993-95

The No. 1 relay panel is located below

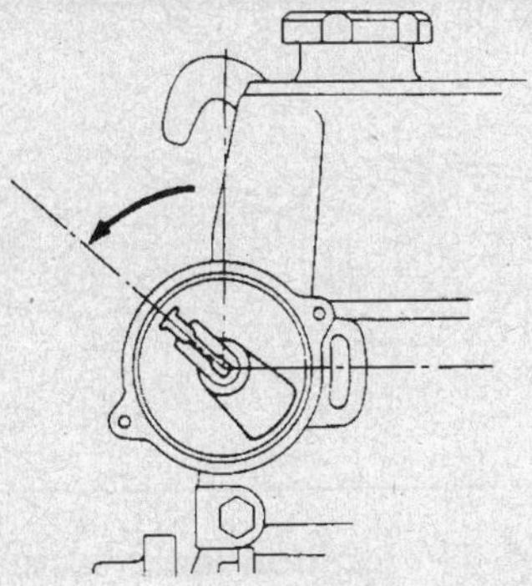
TY1119100013000X

Fig. 6 Installed rotor position. 22R-E

the lefthand side kick panel. The No. 2 relay panel is in the righthand side of the engine compartment, behind the battery. Relay panel No. 3 is behind the righthand side kick panel. The turn signal/hazard flasher is located behind the instrument cluster.

1996

The No. 1 relay panel is located behind the lower lefthand side of the instrument panel. Relay panel No. 2 is located in the righthand side of the engine compartment, behind the battery. The turn signal/hazard flasher is at fuse panel No. 1.

PICKUP

The No. 1 relay panel is located behind the lefthand side kick panel. The No. 2 relay panel is in the righthand side of the engine compartment, behind the battery. Relay panel No. 3 is on behind the righthand side kick panel. The turn signal/hazard flasher is located behind the instrument cluster.

RAV4

The No. 1 relay panel is located behind the lefthand side kick panel. The No. 2 relay panel is in the righthand side of the engine compartment, near the righthand side shock tower. The turn signal flasher unit is at the No. 1 relay panel.

TACOMA

The No. 1 relay panel is located below the lefthand side kick panel. The No. 2 relay panel is in engine compartment, on the front lefthand side.

T100

The No. 1 relay panel is located behind the lefthand side kick panel. The No. 2 relay panel is in the lefthand side of the engine compartment, behind the battery. The turn signal/hazard flasher is located under the instrument panel, below and left of the steering column.

STARTER

REPLACE

1. **On models with audio coded anti-theft system,**obtain three-digit system code.

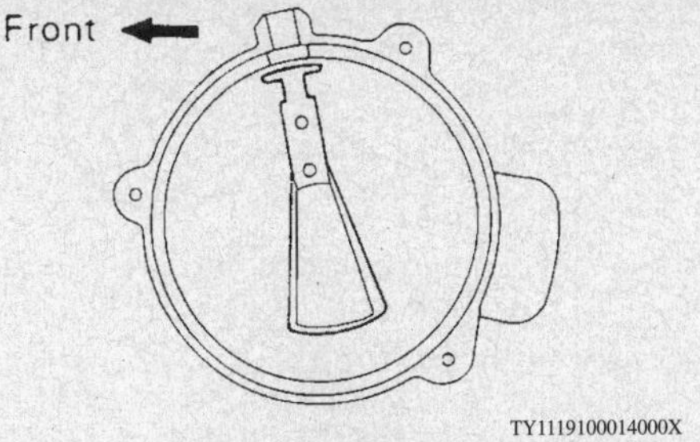
Front
TY1119100014000X

Fig. 7 Rotor position No. 1 TDC. 3VZ-E

2. **On RAV4 models,** remove engine coolant reservoir.
3. **On all models** disconnect battery ground cable.
4. If necessary, remove battery, battery tray and/or igniter bracket.
5. Remove air cleaner assembly, if necessary.
6. Disconnect electrical connectors from starter motor.
7. **On models with automatic transmission,** remove transmission oil filler tube if necessary.
8. **On all models,** remove starter motor attaching bolts, heat shield (if equipped), then the starter motor.
9. Reverse procedure to install. Reset audio coded anti-theft, if equipped, as outlined under "Precautions."

DISTRIBUTOR

REPLACE

PICKUP, TACOMA & 4RUNNER

22R-E ENGINE

Removal

1. Disconnect spark plug wires and wiring connectors from distributor.
2. Remove distributor cap.
3. Remove hold-down bolt, then the distributor from engine.

Installation

1. Turn crankshaft until crankshaft pulley timing mark is aligned with 5° mark. Ensure rocker arms on No. 1 cylinder are loose. If not, rotate crankshaft one full revolution.
2. Fit distributor with a new O-ring, then insert with rotor pointing straight up and mounting hole at center of bolt hole. When fully inserted the rotor will rotate about 10°. Align rotor with pickup coil projection, **Fig. 6. Torque** hold-down bolt to 14 ft. lbs.
3. Install distributor cap and spark plug wires.
4. Connect suitable tachometer and timing light to engine. Start engine and allow to warm up. Do not allow tachometer lead to touch ground.
5. Install jumper wire between terminals TE1 and E1 of check connector.
6. Loosen distributor hold-down bolt and adjust timing to 5° BTDC @ idle.
7. Tighten hold-down bolt. Remove jumper wire. Ensure timing varies between 10–14° BTDC.
8. Remove tachometer and timing light.

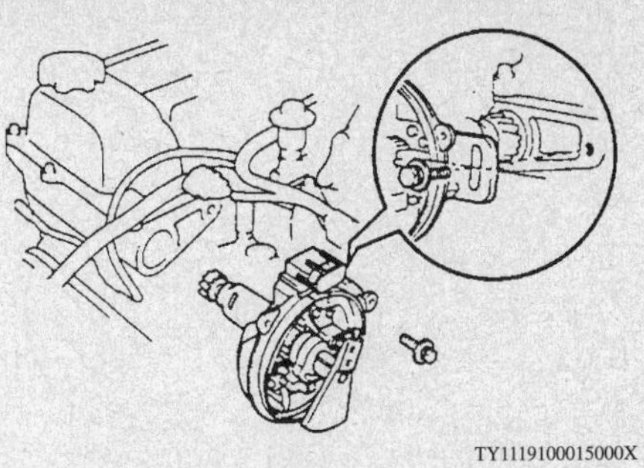
TY1119100015000X

Fig. 8 Distributor flange alignment. Land Cruiser

2RZ-FE & 3RZ-FE ENGINES

Removal

1. **On models with audio coded anti-theft system,**obtain three-digit system code.
2. **On all models** disconnect battery ground cable.
3. Disconnect distributor connector, spark plug wires and distributor cap.
4. Set engine to No. 1 cylinder TDC compression stroke. Distributor rotor should point to about 2 o'clock when alignment is correct.
5. Remove two distributor mounting bolts, then the distributor. Discard O-ring.

Installation

1. Install a new O-ring to distributor body. Lubricate O-ring, then align groove on distributor drive gear to protrusion on distributor body.
2. Install distributor, centering adjustment slots on the two mounting bolts. Lightly tighten bolts.
3. Install distributor cap, spark plug wires and distributor connector. Connect battery ground cable.
4. Connect suitable tachometer to terminal IG– of DLC1 and timing light to engine. Do not allow tachometer lead to touch ground. Start and run engine until normal operating temperature is reached.
5. Connect a jumper between terminals TE1 and E1 of DLC. Set timing to 5° BTDC at idle with air conditioner off. **Torque** bolts to 14 ft. lbs.
6. Disconnect tachometer and timing light.
7. Reset audio coded anti-theft system, if equipped, as outlined under "Precautions."

3VZ-E ENGINE

Removal

1. **On models with audio coded anti-theft system,**obtain three-digit system code.
2. **On all models,** disconnect battery ground cable.
3. Remove spark plug wires from distributor cap and disconnect distributor connector. Remove distributor cap and

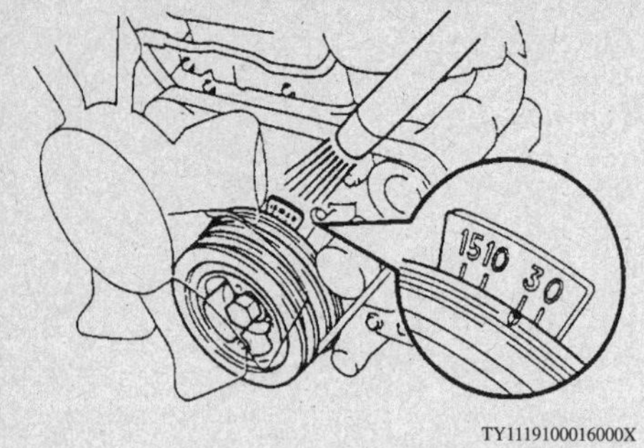
1510 30
TY1119100016000X

Fig. 9 Ignition timing check. Land Cruiser

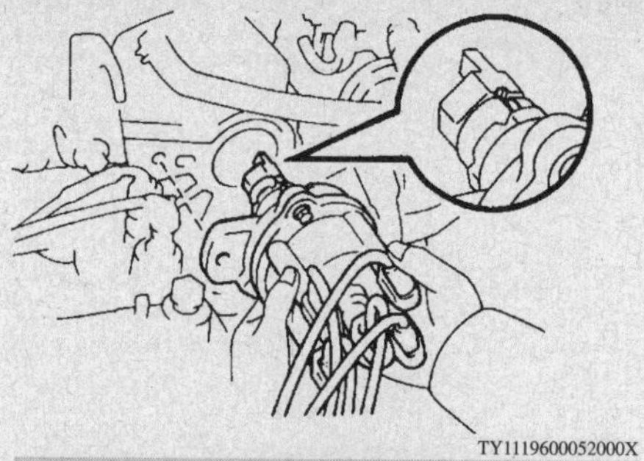
TY1119600052000X

Fig. 10 Distributor rotor alignment. 3S-FE engine

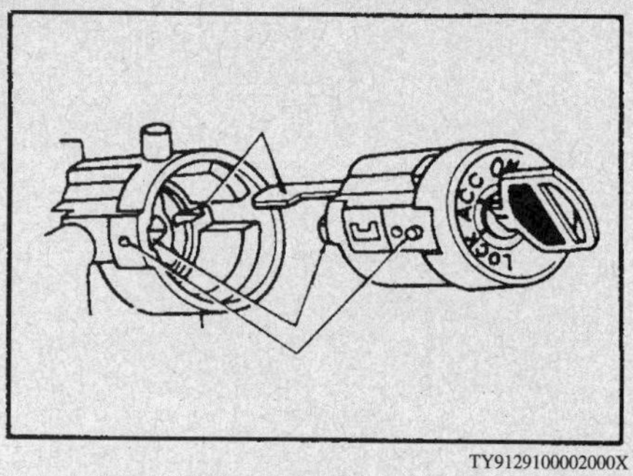
TY9129100002000X

Fig. 11 Ignition lock removal

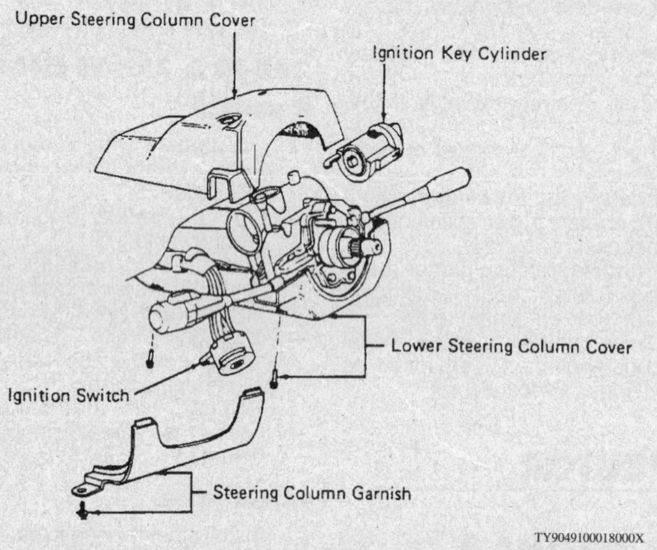
Upper Steering Column Cover
Ignition Key Cylinder
Lower Steering Column Cover
Ignition Switch
Steering Column Garnish
TY9049100018000X

Fig. 12 Steering column & ignition switch assembly

dust proof packing.

4. Turn crankshaft until timing mark is aligned with 0 mark on No. 1 timing belt cover. Ensure rotor position is as in **Fig. 7.** If not, rotate crankshaft one complete revolution.
5. Remove hold-down bolt, then the distributor.

Installation

1. Ensure No. 1 cylinder is at TDC. Align protrusion on driven gear with groove on distributor housing.
2. Use a new O-ring and insert distributor. Align groove on distributor housing with groove on No. 4 camshaft bearing cap. Lightly tighten hold-down bolt.
3. Install dust proof packing and distributor cap.
4. Connect distributor connector and install spark plug wires.
5. Connect battery ground cable.
6. Connect suitable tachometer and timing light to engine.
7. Start and run engine until it reaches normal operating temperature. **Do not allow tachometer lead to touch ground.**
8. Install jumper wire between terminals Te1 and E1 of check connector. Ensure timing is 10° BTDC at idle with transmission in neutral. Adjust if necessary and **torque** hold-down bolt to 13 ft. lbs.
9. Remove jumper wire and ensure timing is 8° BTDC at idle.
10. Disconnect tachometer and timing light from engine.
11. Reset audio coded anti-theft system, if equipped, as outlined under "Precautions."

LAND CRUISER

REMOVAL

1. **On models with audio coded anti-theft system,** obtain three-digit system code.
2. **On all models,** disconnect battery ground cable.
3. Disconnect distributor connectors, then remove distributor cap with spark plug wires attached.
4. Set No. 1 cylinder to TDC on compression stroke.
5. Remove distributor hold-down bolts and pull out distributor.

INSTALLATION

1. Set No. 1 cylinder to TDC on compression stroke by aligning crankshaft pulley grove with zero mark of timing chain cover.
2. Install new O-ring and align distributor housing with protrusion on driven gear
3. Align center of distributor flange with bolt hole on cylinder head, **Fig. 8,** then install distributor.
4. Install distributor cap and connect distributor connector.
5. Connect battery ground cable.
6. Reset audio coded anti-theft system, if equipped, as outlined under "Precautions."
7. Start and warm engine.
8. Connect suitable tachometer and timing light. Do not allow tachometer lead to touch ground. With transmission in neutral and A/C OFF, adjust ignition timing. Ensure timing is 3° BTDC at idle, **Fig. 9.**
9. If no further timing adjusting is necessary, **torque** distributor retaining bolt to 13 ft. lbs.
10. Remove tachometer and timing light.

RAV4

REMOVAL

1. Remove air cleaner cap assembly.
2. Disconnect distributor connector.
3. Disconnect high-tension cord from distributor and spark plugs.
4. Remove distributor mounting bolt and pull out distributor.

INSTALLATION

1. Set No. 1 cylinder to TDC of its compression stroke.
2. Install new distributor O-ring, lightly coated with engine oil.
3. Align cutout of coupling with line of housing, **Fig. 10.**
4. Install distributor, align center of flange with bolt hole on cylinder head.
5. **Torque** distributor mounting bolt to 14 ft. lbs.
6. Connect high-tension cords to spark pugs and distributor.
7. Connect distributor connector and install air cleaner cap assembly.

COIL PACK

REPLACE

5VZ-FE ENGINE

1. **On 4Runner models,** remove air cleaner hose.
2. **On T100 and Tacoma models,** remove air cleaner cap and MAF meter assembly.
3. **On all models,** disconnect three ignition coil connectors from coils.

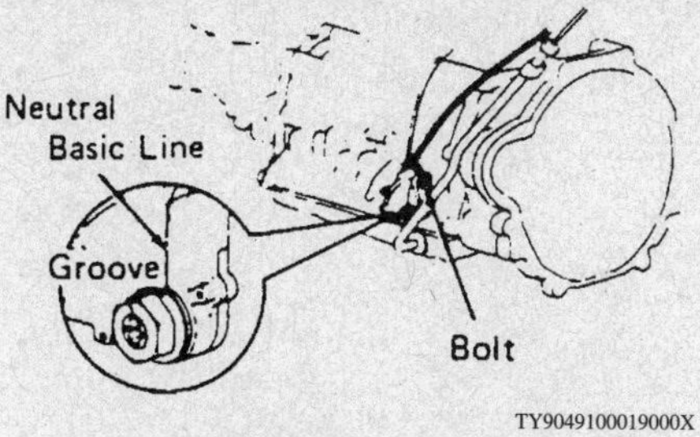
Neutral
Basic Line
Groove
Bolt
TY9049100019000X

Fig. 13 Neutral safety switch adjustment

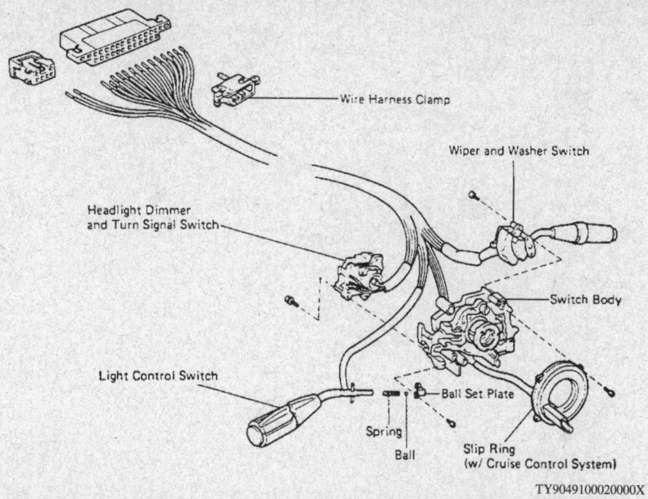
Wire Harness Clamp
Wiper and Washer Switch
Headlight Dimmer and Turn Signal Switch
Switch Body
Light Control Switch
Ball Set Plate
Spring
Ball
Slip Ring (w/ Cruise Control System)
TY9049100020000X

Fig. 14 Combination switch disassembly. Pickup & 1993–95 4Runner

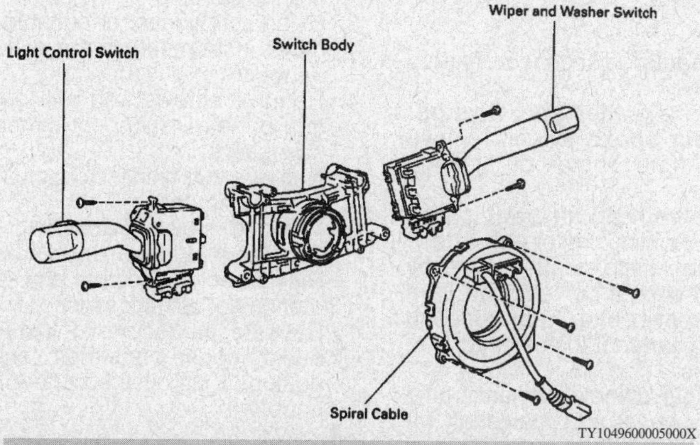
Wiper and Washer Switch
Light Control Switch
Switch Body
Spiral Cable
TY1049600005000X

Fig. 15 Combination switch disassembly. RAV4 & 1996 4Runner

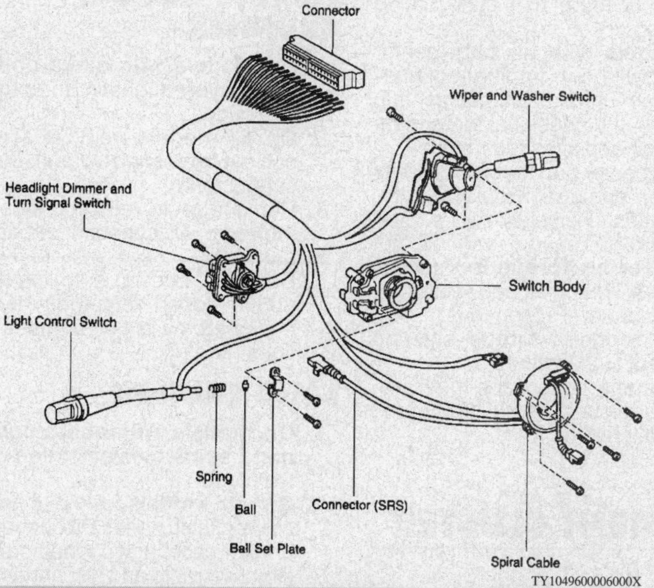
Connector
Wiper and Washer Switch
Headlight Dimmer and Turn Signal Switch
Switch Body
Light Control Switch
Spring
Ball
Connector (SRS)
Ball Set Plate
Spiral Cable
TY1049600006000X

Fig. 16 Combination switch disassembly. Land Cruiser

4. Remove three bolts and three ignition coils from lefthand side cylinder head.
5. Reverse procedure to install. **Torque** to 6 ft. lbs.

IGNITION LOCK

REPLACE

1. **On models with audio coded anti-theft system,**obtain three-digit system code.
2. **On all models,** disconnect battery ground cable.
3. Turn ignition switch to ACC position.
4. Remove steering column covers.
5. Insert a small diameter rod into hole located on side of lock cylinder, then while holding down pin, remove lock cylinder, **Fig. 11.**
6. Reverse procedure to install. Ensure lock cylinder is in ACC position. Reset audio coded anti-theft system, if equipped, as outlined under "Precautions."

IGNITION SWITCH

REPLACE

1. **On models with audio coded anti-theft system,**obtain three-digit system code.
2. **On all models,** disconnect battery ground cable.
3. Remove steering wheel, if necessary, steering column garnish, if equipped, upper and lower covers, **Fig. 12.**
4. Disconnect electrical connectors from ignition switch.
5. Turn ignition key to ACC position and remove ignition key cylinder.
6. Remove screw and ignition switch.
7. Reverse procedure to install. Reset audio coded anti-theft and air bag system, if equipped, as outlined under "Precautions."

NEUTRAL SAFETY SWITCH

ADJUST

1. Raise and support vehicle.

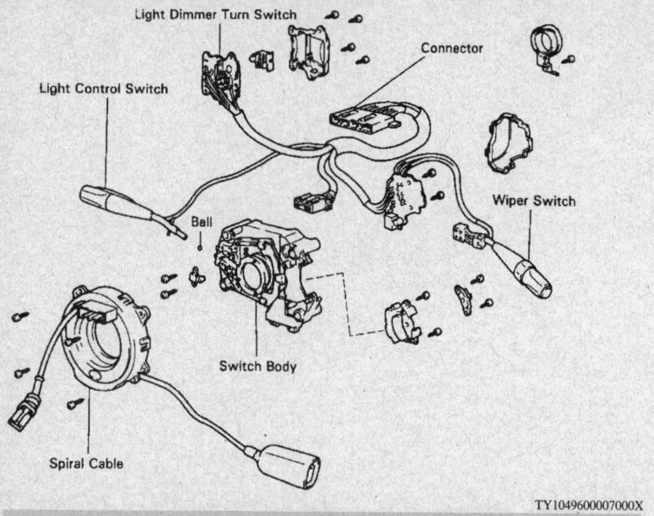

Light Dimmer Turn Switch
Connector
Light Control Switch
Wiper Switch
Ball
Switch Body
Spiral Cable
TY1049600007000X

Fig. 17 Combination switch disassembly. Tacoma & T100 less intermittent/mist wipers

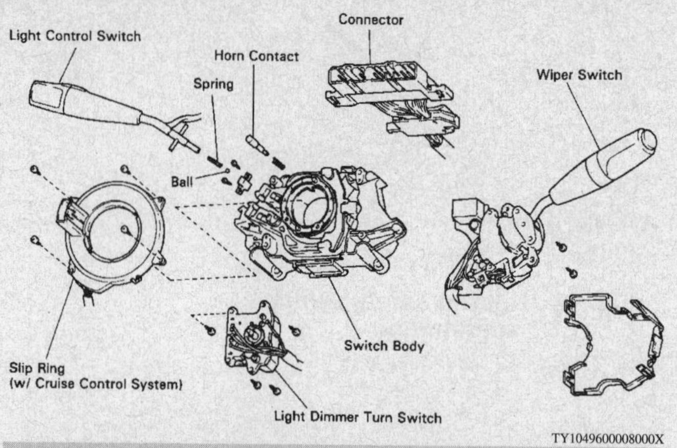

Light Control Switch
Connector
Horn Contact
Spring
Wiper Switch
Ball
Switch Body
Slip Ring
(w/ Cruise Control System)
Light Dimmer Turn Switch
TY1049600008000X

Fig. 18 Combination switch disassembly. T100 w/intermittent & mist wipers

2. Loosen neutral safety switch bracket bolt.
3. Position transmission shift lever into Neutral.
4. Align switch shaft groove with neutral base line, **Fig. 13,** then retighten switch bracket bolt.
5. Connect electrical connector to switch.

STOP LIGHT SWITCH

REPLACE

1. Remove brake pedal tension spring.
2. Disconnect switch wire connector.
3. Remove switch mounting nut, then slide switch from mounting bracket.
4. Reverse procedure to install.

COMBINATION SWITCH

REPLACE

1. **On models with audio coded anti-theft system,**obtain three-digit system code.
2. **On all models,** disconnect battery ground cable.
3. Remove steering wheel as outlined under "Steering Wheel, Replace."
4. Remove steering column upper and lower covers.
5. Disconnect switch connectors, remove screws and combination switch.
6. Reverse procedure to install. Reset audio coded anti-theft system, if equipped, as outlined under "Precautions."

COMBINATION SWITCH SERVICE

Refer to **Figs. 14 through 18** for combination switch disassembly.

STEERING WHEEL

REPLACE

1. **On models with audio coded anti-theft system,** obtain three-digit system code.
2. **On all models,** disconnect battery ground cable.
3. Remove steering wheel pad. **On models with four spoke wheel,** remove trim cover from center of steering wheel.
4. **On models with an air bag,** loosen Torx screws holding center pad. These screws are held into steering wheel by a cage and cannot be removed from wheel. Remove pad from steering wheel using care not to pull on air bag wire harness.
5. **On all models,** place alignment marks on steering wheel and mainshaft for assembly reference.
6. Remove nut attaching steering wheel to steering shaft.
7. Using a puller tool No. 09950-50010, or equivalent, remove steering wheel.
8. Reverse procedure to install, noting the following.
   a. **On models with air bag,** center spiral cable by turning counterclockwise until resistance is felt, then turn and additional three turns clockwise and align red marks.
   b. Inspect center pad for cracks dents or other damage. Replace damaged pads. Reinstall center pad, use care to ensure wire is not pinched or cut. **Torque** Torx screws to 7 ft. lbs. Rearm air bag system as outlined under "Precautions."
   c. **On all models, torque** steering wheel nut to 25 ft. lbs.
   d. Reset audio coded anti-theft system, if equipped, as outlined under "Precautions."

INSTRUMENT CLUSTER

REPLACE

Refer to "Dash Panel Service" for exploded view of instrument panel.

1. **On models with audio coded anti-theft system,**obtain three-digit system code.
2. **On all models,** disconnect battery ground cable.
3. Using screwdriver or suitable tool, remove instrument cluster center finish panel.
4. Remove screws and pull out cluster trim panel. Disconnect connectors, if necessary.
5. Remove cup holder from cluster finish panel, if equipped.
6. Remove cluster attaching screws, then the cluster from instrument panel. Disconnect connectors and speedometer cable, as necessary.
7. Reverse procedure to install. Reset audio coded anti-theft system, if equipped, as outlined under "Precautions."

RADIO

REPLACE

PICKUP, RAV4 & 4RUNNER

1. **On models with audio coded anti-theft system,**obtain three-digit system code.
2. **On all models,** remove screws and pull out center finish panel. Disconnect connectors.
3. Remove radio retaining screws, then the radio. Disconnect connectors and antenna.
4. Reverse procedure to install. Reset audio coded anti-theft system, if equipped, as outlined under "Precautions."

LAND CRUISER

1. **On models with audio coded anti-theft system,**obtain three-digit system code.
2. **On all models,** remove instrument cluster finish panel. Disconnect speedometer cable and connectors.
3. Remove radio and disconnect connectors and antenna.
4. Reverse procedure to install. Reset audio coded anti-theft system, if equipped, as outlined under "Precautions."

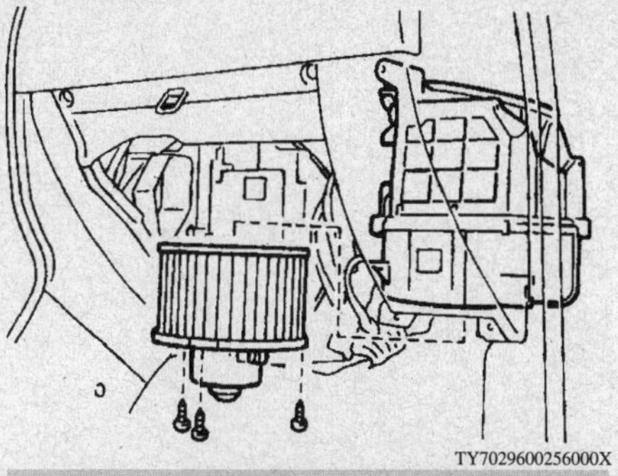

Fig. 19 Front blower motor removal. 4Runner

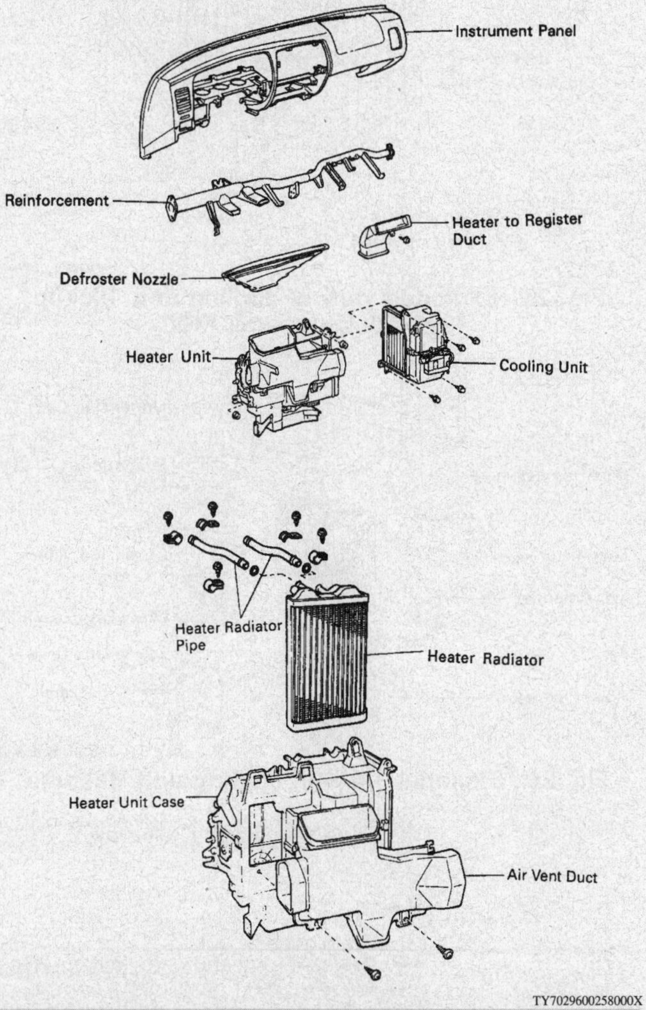
Instrument Panel
Reinforcement
Heater to Register Duct
Defroster Nozzle
Heater Unit
Cooling Unit
Heater Radiator Pipe
Heater Radiator
Heater Unit Case
Air Vent Duct

Fig. 21 Front heater core replacement. 4Runner

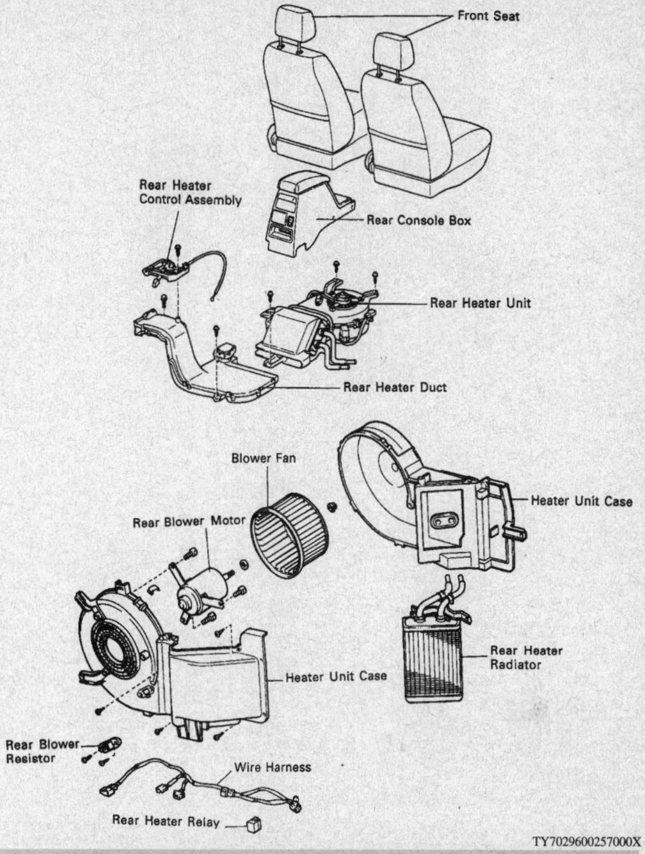
Front Seat
Rear Heater Control Assembly
Rear Console Box
Rear Heater Unit
Rear Heater Duct
Blower Fan
Heater Unit Case
Rear Blower Motor
Rear Heater Radiator
Heater Unit Case
Rear Blower Resistor
Wire Harness
Rear Heater Relay

Fig. 20 Rear heater core & blower motor replacement. 4Runner

WIPER MOTOR

REPLACE

FRONT

1. **On models with audio coded anti-theft system,** obtain three-digit system code.
2. **On all models,** disconnect battery ground cable.
3. Disconnect wiper motor wire connector, then remove wiper motor service cover or cowl vent screen, if equipped.
4. Remove wiper motor attaching bolts.
5. Using a screwdriver disconnect wiper link from wiper motor and remove wiper motor.
6. Reverse procedure to install. Reset audio coded anti-theft system, if equipped, as outlined under "Precautions."

REAR

1. **On models with audio coded anti-theft system,** obtain three-digit system code.
2. **On all models,** disconnect battery ground cable.
3. Remove wiper arm and rear door trim cover.
4. **On RAV4 models,** remove service hole cover.
5. **On all models,** disconnect wiper motor wire connector.
6. Remove wiper motor bracket attaching bolts and wiper motor and bracket.
7. Reverse procedure to install. Reset audio coded anti-theft system, if equipped, as outlined under "Precautions."

WIPER SWITCH

REPLACE

Refer to "Combination Switch Service" and "Combination Switch, Replace" procedures.

BLOWER MOTOR

REPLACE

PICKUP

1. **On models with audio coded anti-theft system,** obtain three-digit system code.
2. **On all models,** disconnect battery ground cable.

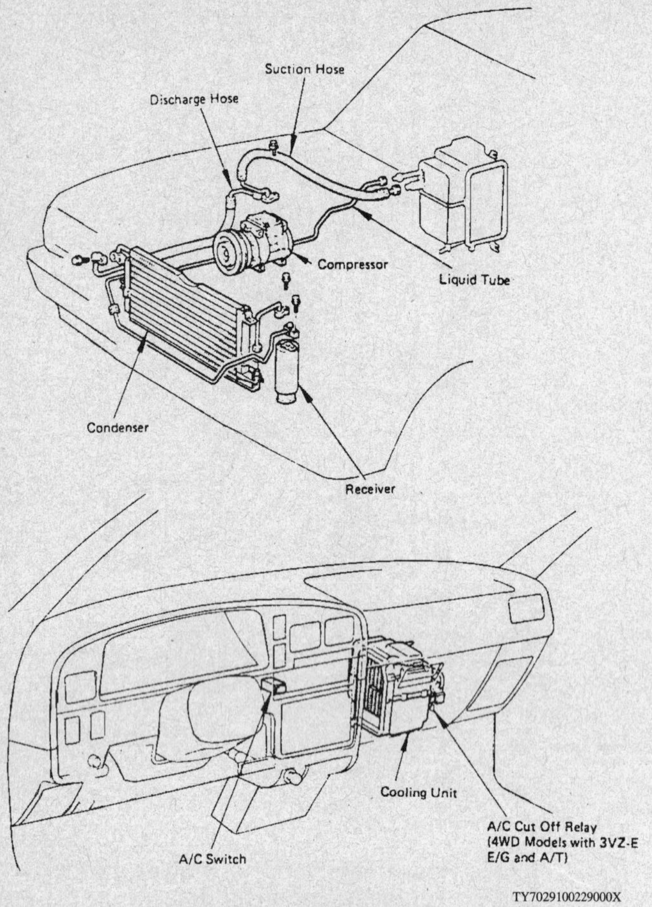

Suction Hose
Discharge Hose
Compressor
Liquid Tube
Condenser
Receiver
Cooling Unit
A/C Cut Off Relay
(4WD Models with 3VZ-E
E/G and A/T)
A/C Switch
TY7029100229000X

Fig. 22 A/C system components. Pickup & 4Runner

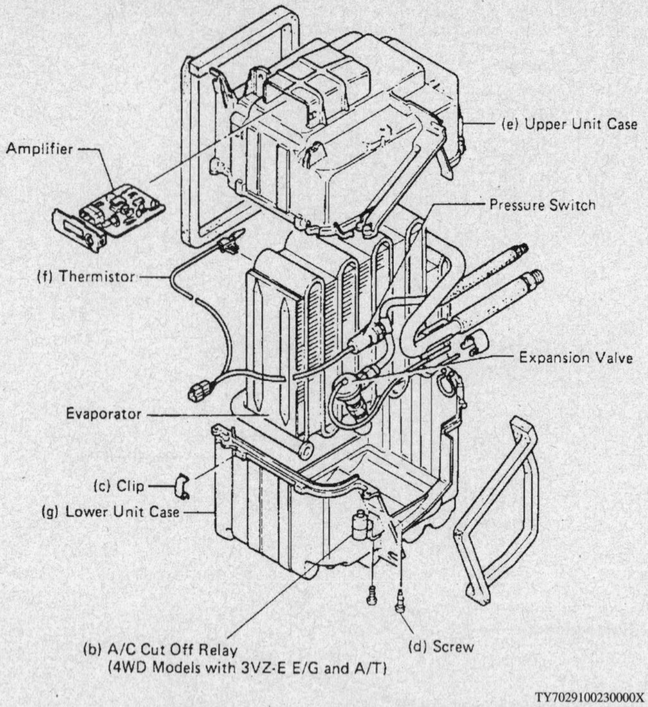

Amplifier
(e) Upper Unit Case
Pressure Switch
(f) Thermistor
Expansion Valve
Evaporator
(c) Clip
(g) Lower Unit Case
(b) A/C Cut Off Relay
(4WD Models with 3VZ-E E/G and A/T)
(d) Screw
TY7029100230000X

Fig. 23 Exploded view of cooling unit. Pickup, 1993–95 4Runner & T100

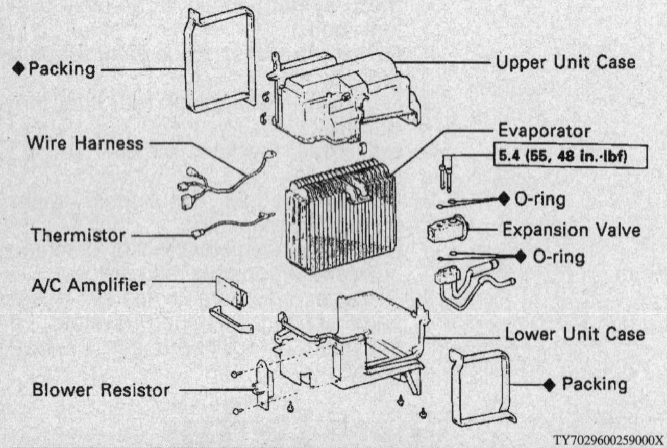

◆Packing
Upper Unit Case
Wire Harness
Evaporator
5.4 (55, 48 in.·lbf)
◆ O-ring
Thermistor
Expansion Valve
◆ O-ring
A/C Amplifier
Lower Unit Case
Blower Resistor
◆ Packing
TY7029600259000X

Fig. 24 Exploded view of cooling unit. 1996 4Runner

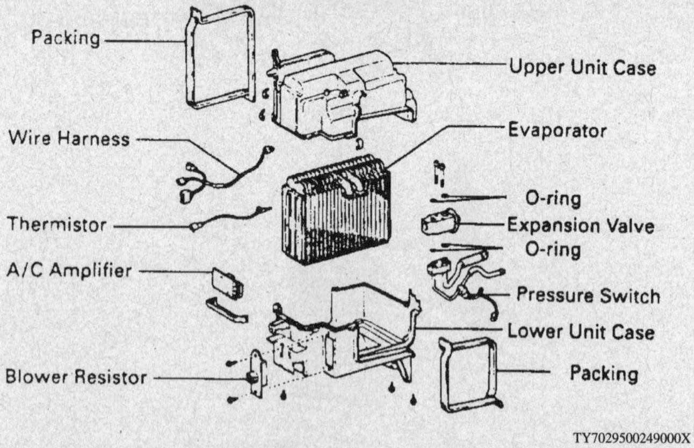

Packing
Upper Unit Case
Wire Harness
Evaporator
O-ring
Thermistor
Expansion Valve
O-ring
A/C Amplifier
Pressure Switch
Lower Unit Case
Blower Resistor
Packing
TY7029500249000X

Fig. 25 Exploded view of cooling unit. Tacoma

3. Disconnect blower motor and blower resistor connectors.
4. Remove blower motor retaining screws, then the blower motor.
5. Reverse procedure to install. Reset audio coded anti-theft system, if equipped, as outlined under "Precautions."

4RUNNER

Front

1. Remove glove compartment.
2. Disconnect blower motor connector.
3. Remove three retaining screws and the blower motor, **Fig. 19.**
4. Reverse procedure to install.

Rear

1. Drain engine coolant.
2. Remove front seats and rear console box, **Fig. 20.**
3. Roll up floor carpet, then disconnect water hoses from rear heater unit.
4. Remove rear heater duct.
5. Remove rear heater control assembly and rear heater unit.
6. Separate heater unit case halves and remove rear blower motor.
7. Reverse procedure to install.

RAV4 & TACOMA

1. Remove glove compartment.
2. Remove pillar brace.

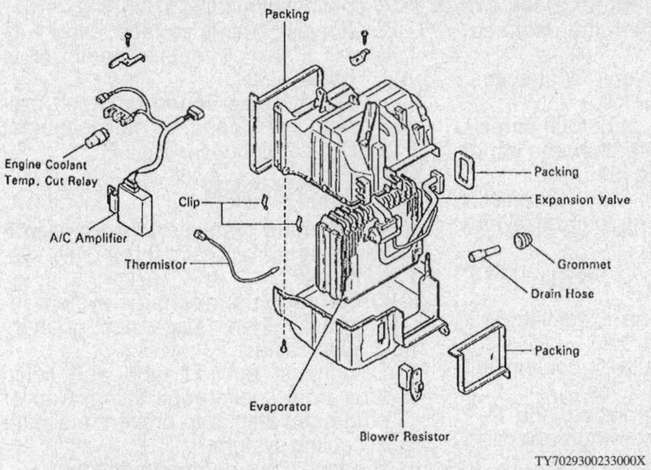
Packing
Engine Coolant Temp. Cut Relay
A/C Amplifier
Clip
Thermistor
Packing
Expansion Valve
Grommet
Drain Hose
Packing
Evaporator
Blower Resistor
TY7029300233000X

Fig. 26 Exploded view of cooling unit. Land Cruiser

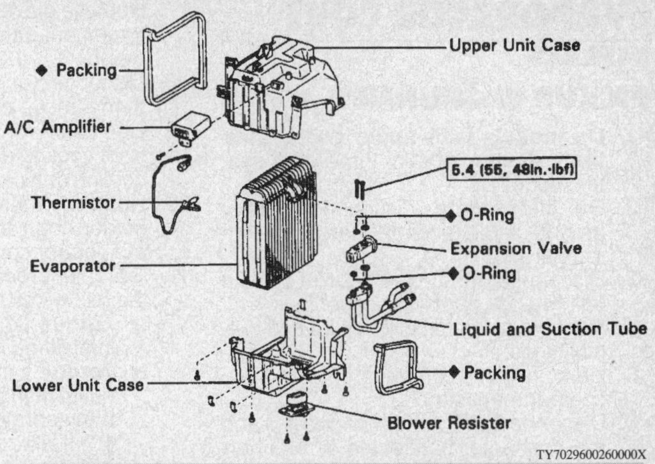
◆ Packing
A/C Amplifier
Thermistor
Evaporator
Lower Unit Case
Upper Unit Case
5.4 (55, 48in.-lbf)
◆ O-Ring
Expansion Valve
◆ O-Ring
Liquid and Suction Tube
◆ Packing
Blower Resister
TY7029600260000X

Fig. 27 Exploded view of cooling unit. RAV4

3. Remove three mounting bolts and the blower unit.
4. Remove three screws from bottom of blower unit, then pull blower motor with fan from blower unit.
5. Reverse procedure to install.

LAND CRUISER

Front

1. **On models with audio coded anti-theft system,**obtain three-digit system code.
2. **On all models,** disconnect battery ground cable.
3. Remove righthand scuff plate.
4. Remove blower motor lower cover.
5. Disconnect blower motor connector, then remove blower motor retaining screws and blower motor.
6. Reverse procedure to install. Reset audio coded anti-theft system, if equipped, as outlined under "Precautions."

Rear

1. **On models with audio coded anti-theft system,**obtain three-digit system code.
2. **On all models,** disconnect battery ground cable.
3. Remove front righthand seat.
4. Disconnect connectors from blower motor and rear heater relay.
5. Remove rear heater relay and blower motor side cover.
6. Remove upper cover with blower motor.
7. Reverse procedure to install. Reset audio coded anti-theft system, if equipped, as outlined under "Precautions."

HEATER CORE

REPLACE

PICKUP & T100

1. Remove cooling unit as outlined under "Evaporator Core, Replace."
2. Drain engine coolant from radiator.
3. Disconnect water hoses from heater core pipes.
4. Remove instrument panel and reinforcement as outlined under "Dash Panel Service."
5. Disconnect control cables from heater unit.
6. Remove heat duct to register No. 4.
7. Remove heater to register center duct.
8. Remove heater unit.
9. Remove heater air duct.
10. Remove heater core retaining screws and plates.
11. Pull heater core from heater unit.
12. Reverse procedure to install.

4RUNNER

Front

1. Remove cooling unit as outlined under "Evaporator Core, Replace."
2. Drain engine coolant from radiator.
3. Disconnect water hoses from heater radiator pipes.
4. Remove instrument panel and reinforcement as outlined under "Dash Panel Service."
5. Remove defroster nozzle and heater to register duct.
6. Remove heater unit.
7. Remove two plates and clamp, then pull heater core from heater unit, **Fig. 21.**
8. Disconnect heater core inlet and outlet pipes.
9. Reverse procedure to install.

Rear

1. Drain engine coolant.
2. Remove front seats and rear console box, **Fig. 20.**
3. Roll up floor carpet, then disconnect water hoses from rear heater unit.
4. Remove rear heater duct.
5. Remove rear heater control assembly and rear heater unit.
6. Separate heater unit case halves and disconnect heater core pipes from rear heater core.
7. Remove rear heater core.
8. Reverse procedure to install.

RAV4

1. Remove cooling unit as outlined under "Evaporator Core, Replace."
2. Drain engine coolant from radiator.
3. Disconnect water hose from heater unit.
4. Remove rear heater duct, then the heater unit.
5. Remove defroster duct from heater unit.
6. Remove two screws and clips from top of heater unit, then pull heater core from heater unit.
7. Reverse procedure to install.

TACOMA

1. Remove cooling unit as outlined under "Evaporator Core, Replace."
2. Drain engine coolant from radiator.
3. Disconnect water hose from heater unit.
4. Remove instrument panel and reinforcement as outlined in "Dash Panel Service."
5. Remove defroster duct heater to register No. 4, then the heater unit.
6. Remove two screws and clips from top of heater unit, then pull heater core from heater unit.
7. Reverse procedure to install.

LAND CRUISER

1. Remove cooling unit as outlined under "Evaporator Core, Replace."
2. Drain engine coolant from radiator.
3. Disconnect water hoses from heater core.
4. Remove pipe grommets.
5. Remove instrument panel and reinforcement as outlined under "Dash Panel Service."
6. Remove duct heater to register No. 3.
7. Remove heater unit.
8. Remove heater core retaining screws and plates.
9. Pull heater core from heater unit.
10. Reverse procedure to install.

EVAPORATOR CORE

REPLACE

PICKUP & 4RUNNER

1. **On models with audio coded anti-theft system,**obtain three-digit system code.
2. **On all models,** disconnect battery ground cable and discharge system refrigerant.
3. Disconnect refrigerant lines at cooling unit **Fig. 22,** capping all openings.
4. Remove grommets from inlet and outlet fittings.
5. Remove glove compartment and glove compartment stay.
6. Disconnect A/C switch connector and the connector connected to A/C harness.
7. Remove four attaching screws and bolt, then the cooling unit.
8. Remove four clamps and four screws securing case halves **Figs. 23 and 24,** then separate case halves and remove evaporator.
9. Pull off clamp and remove thermistor.
10. Remove heat insulator and clamp from outlet tube.
11. Disconnect liquid line tube from inlet fitting of expansion valve.
12. Disconnect expansion valve from inlet fitting of evaporator.
13. Reverse procedure to install, then evacuate the recharge system and check for leaks. If evaporator is replaced, add 1.4–1.7 oz. of new refrigerant oil to compressor. Reset audio coded anti-theft system, if equipped, as outlined under "Precautions."

T100

1. **On models with audio coded anti-theft system,**obtain three-digit system code.
2. **On all models,** disconnect battery ground cable, then discharge system refrigerant.
3. Disconnect suction tube and liquid tube from cooling unit fitting. Cap or plug fitting openings to keep moisture out of system.
4. Remove two grommets and drain pipe grommet.
5. Remove glove compartment door.
6. Remove instrument panel lower center cover.
7. Remove glove compartment door reinforcement screws, then the reinforcement.
8. Disconnect cooling unit connectors, then remove cooling unit.
9. Remove four clips and four screws from cooling unit case, then the upper cooling unit case, **Fig. 23.**
10. Remove thermistor with thermistor holder, then the lower unit case and evaporator core.
11. Reverse procedure to install, noting the following:
    a. **Torque** liquid tube to cooling unit inlet fitting to 10 ft. lbs.
    b. **Torque** suction tube to cooling unit outlet fitting to 24 ft. lbs.
    c. If evaporator is replaced, add 1.4–1.7 fl. oz. of new refrigerant oil to compressor.
    d. Reset audio coded anti-theft system, if equipped, as outlined under "Precautions."

TACOMA

1. **On models with audio coded anti-theft system,**obtain three-digit system code.
2. **On all models,** disconnect battery ground cable, then discharge system refrigerant.
3. Disconnect suction tube and liquid tube from cooling unit fitting. Cap or plug fitting openings to keep moisture out of system.
4. Remove two grommets and drain pipe grommet.
5. Remove glove compartment door.
6. Remove instrument panel lower center cover.
7. Remove glove compartment door reinforcement screws, then the reinforcement.
8. Remove A/C amplifier.
9. Disconnect cooling unit connectors, then the cooling unit.
10. Remove three clips and three screws from cooling unit case, then the upper cooling unit case, **Fig. 25.**
11. Remove thermistor and pressure switch, then the lower unit case and evaporator core.
12. Reverse procedure to install, noting the following:
    a. **Torque** liquid tube to cooling unit inlet fitting to 10 ft. lbs.
    b. **Torque** suction tube to cooling unit outlet fitting to 24 ft. lbs.
    c. If evaporator is replaced, add 1.4–1.7 fl. oz. of new refrigerant oil to compressor.
    d. Reset audio coded anti-theft system, if equipped, as outlined under "Precautions."

LAND CRUISER

1. **On models with audio coded anti-theft system,**obtain three-digit system code.
2. **On all models,** discharge system refrigerant, then disconnect battery ground cable.
3. Disconnect suction tube and liquid tube from cooling unit fitting. Cap or plug open fittings to prevent moisture in cooling system.
4. Remove glove compartment door.
5. Remove engine control module and disconnect electrical connectors.
6. Remove cooling unit and A/C amplifier.
7. Remove blower speed control relay and magnetic clutch relay.
8. Remove upper and lower cooling unit case, then the evaporator core, **Fig. 26.**
9. Reverse procedure to install, noting the following:
    a. **Torque** cooling unit inlet and outlet tube fittings to 48 inch lbs.
    b. If evaporator is replaced, add 1.4–1.7 fl. oz. of new refrigerant oil to compressor.
    c. Reset audio coded anti-theft system, if equipped, as outlined under "Precautions."

RAV4

1. Discharge and recover refrigerant from A/C system.
2. Remove glove compartment.
3. Disconnect suction and liquid tubes from rear of engine compartment, at firewall.
4. Remove three screws, three nuts, and the cooling unit from below lefthand side of instrument panel.
5. Separate upper and lower evaporator case by cutting off packing with a sharp knife, **Fig. 27.**
6. Disconnect thermistor and remove evaporator core.
7. Reverse procedure to install. If evaporator is replaced, add 1.4 fl. oz. of new compressor oil to compressor.

3S-FE 2.0L Engine

INDEX

	Page No.
Belt Tension Data	47-25
Camshaft, Replace	47-24
Compression Pressure	47-19
Cooling System Bleed	47-25
Cylinder Head, Replace	47-20
Installation	47-23
Removal	47-20
Engine Rebuilding Specifications	48-1
Engine, Replace	47-19
Exhaust Manifold, Replace	47-20
Fuel Filter, Replace	47-25
Fuel Pump, Replace	47-25
Intake Manifold, Replace	47-20
Main & Rod Bearings	47-24
Oil Pan, Replace	47-25
Oil Pump, Replace	47-25
Piston & Rod Assembly	47-24
Precautions	47-19
Air Bag Systems	47-19
Audio Coded Anti-Theft System	47-19
Fuel Pressure Relief	47-19
Radiator, Replace	47-25
Thermostat, Replace	47-25
Tightening Specifications	47-26
Timing Belt, Replace	47-24
Valve Adjustment	47-23
Valve Clearance Specifications	47-23
Water Pump, Replace	47-25

PRECAUTIONS

AIR BAG SYSTEMS

Refer to "Air Bag System Precautions" in the front of this manual for system disarming and arming procedures.

AUDIO CODED ANTI-THEFT SYSTEM

Some models are equipped with an audio coded anti-theft system that will disable the radio when the battery cable is disconnected. The system can be identified by the "ANTI-THEFT SYSTEM" on the cassette lid. Obtain three-digit code for input. Reset system after service as follows:

1. Obtain three-digit audio theft code.
2. Depress 1 (PROG) button while depressing righthand side of TUNE SEEK button. Three dashes will appear in tape operation display.
3. To enter first digit, depress 1 (PROG) button repeatedly until number of times depressed equals first digit (depress 1 button six times if first digit is five, first press equals 0).
4. To enter second digit, depress 2 (APS) button repeatedly until number of times depressed equals second digit.
5. To enter third digit, depress 3 (RPT) button repeatedly until number of times depressed equals third digit.
6. If three dashes are displayed after inputting digits, repeat procedure.
7. When code appears in display, depress and hold SCAN button until SEC appears.
8. When SEC disappears audio system is operative.
9. If Err is displayed, repeat procedure. **Attempting to input code more than nine times may permanently disable audio system.**

FUEL PRESSURE RELIEF

1. Remove lefthand side rear seat.
2. Remove floor service hole cover.
3. Disconnect fuel pump electrical connector.
4. Start and run engine until it stalls.
5. Turn ignition switch off.

COMPRESSION PRESSURE

1. Start engine and warm to normal operating temperature.
2. Disconnect distributor connector.
3. Disconnect high tension cords from spark plugs and distributor.
4. Remove spark plugs.
5. Insert compression gauge into spark plug hole.
6. Fully open throttle.
7. While cranking engine, measure compression pressure.
8. Standard compression pressure should be 185 psi. Minimum compression is 135 psi.
9. The difference in compression pressure between each cylinder should not exceed 14 psi.

ENGINE

REPLACE

1. Remove battery, **Fig. 1.**
2. Remove engine compartment hood.
3. Remove engine under covers.
4. Drain engine coolant and engine oil.
5. Drain transaxle oil.
6. Remove air cleaner cap and case.
7. Disconnect accelerator cable from throttle body, cable bracket and clamps.
8. Disconnect engine wire from relay block No. 2.
9. Remove charcoal canister.
10. Remove water inlet.
11. Disconnect heater hoses.
12. Remove alternator.
13. Remove radiator upper and lower hoses.
14. Remove water inlet.
15. Disconnect heater hoses.
16. Disconnect fuel inlet hose.
17. **On models with manual transaxle,** remove starter.
18. **On all models,** disconnect ground cable.
19. **On models with manual transaxle,** proceed as follows:
    a. Disconnect back-up lamp switch connector.
    b. Disconnect clutch release cylinder from transaxle.
20. **On all models,** disconnect transaxle control cables from transaxle.
21. **On models with automatic transaxle,** disconnect transaxle control cable from front suspension crossmember and engine mounting center member.
22. **On all models,** disconnect transaxle oil cooler hoses.
23. Disconnect the following connectors:
    a. Vapor pressure sensor.
    b. Igniter.
    c. Ignition coil.
    d. Noise filter.
    e. High-tension cord from ignition coil.
    f. MAP sensor.
    g. MAP sensor vacuum hose from gas filter on intake manifold.
    h. Brake booster hose from intake manifold.
    i. Differential lock control solenoid, if equipped.
24. Disconnect ground strap from cowl.
25. Remove righthand scuff plate, righthand cowl side trim and righthand floor carpet center cover.
26. Disconnect engine wire from passenger compartment.
27. Disconnect two ECM connectors and connector from junction box No. 4.
28. Remove front exhaust pipe.
29. Disconnect A/C compressor from engine.
30. Remove propeller shaft, if equipped.
31. Remove front driveshaft.
32. Remove stabilizer.
33. Remove front suspension crossmember.
34. Remove engine mounting center member.
35. Remove drive belt and power steering pump from engine.
36. Install suitable engine hanger, then attach engine sling device to engine hanger.
37. Disconnect lefthand engine mounting bracket from mounting insulator.
38. Disconnect ground strap connector.
39. Disconnect righthand engine mounting bracket from mounting insulator.
40. Slowly lower engine and raise vehicle,

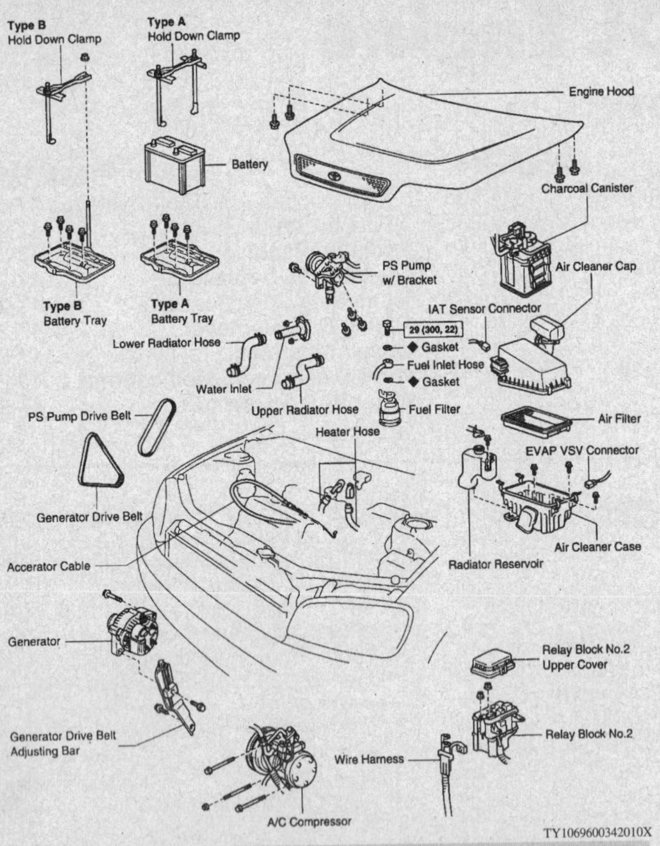
Type B
Hold Down Clamp
Type A
Hold Down Clamp
Engine Hood
Battery
Charcoal Canister
Type B
Battery Tray
Type A
Battery Tray
PS Pump
w/ Bracket
Air Cleaner Cap
IAT Sensor Connector
29 (300, 22)
◆ Gasket
Fuel Inlet Hose
◆ Gasket
Lower Radiator Hose
Water Inlet
Upper Radiator Hose
Fuel Filter
Air Filter
PS Pump Drive Belt
Heater Hose
EVAP VSV Connector
Generator Drive Belt
Air Cleaner Case
Accerator Cable
Radiator Reservoir
Generator
Relay Block No.2
Upper Cover
Relay Block No.2
Generator Drive Belt
Adjusting Bar
Wire Harness
A/C Compressor
TY1069600342010X

Fig. 1 Engine replacement (Part 1 of 2). 3S-FE

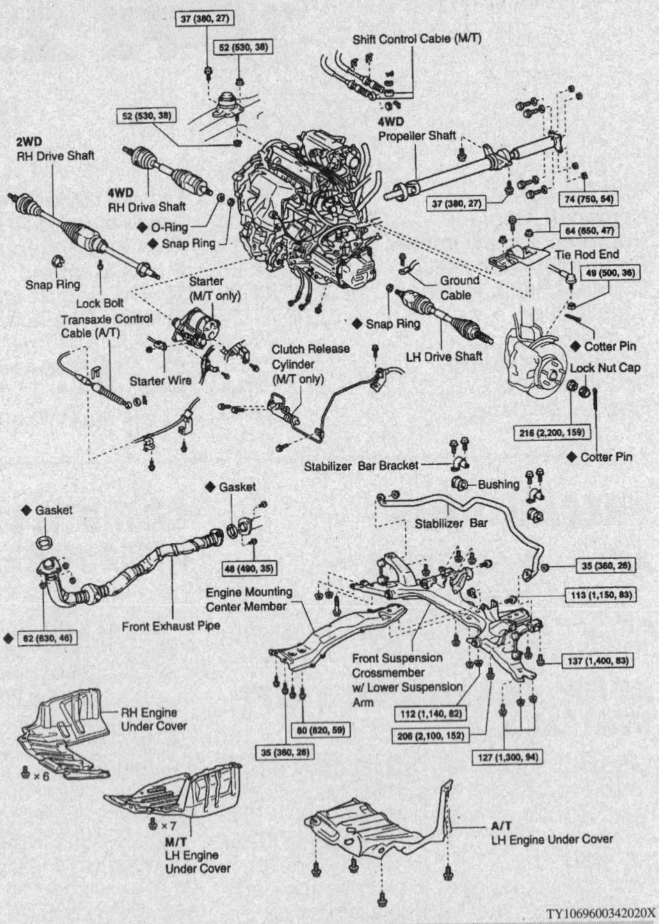
37 (380, 27)
52 (530, 38)
Shift Control Cable (M/T)
52 (530, 38)
4WD
Propeller Shaft
2WD
RH Drive Shaft
4WD
RH Drive Shaft
◆ O-Ring
◆ Snap Ring
37 (380, 27)
74 (750, 54)
64 (650, 47)
Tie Rod End
49 (500, 36)
Snap Ring
Lock Bolt
Starter
(M/T only)
Ground
Cable
Transaxle Control
Cable (A/T)
◆ Snap Ring
LH Drive Shaft
◆ Cotter Pin
Lock Nut Cap
Clutch Release
Cylinder
(M/T only)
Starter Wire
216 (2,200, 159)
◆ Cotter Pin
Stabilizer Bar Bracket
Bushing
◆ Gasket
◆ Gasket
Stabilizer Bar
48 (490, 35)
35 (360, 26)
Engine Mounting
Center Member
113 (1,150, 83)
Front Exhaust Pipe
◆ 62 (630, 46)
Front Suspension
Crossmember
w/ Lower Suspension
Arm
137 (1,400, 83)
RH Engine
Under Cover
112 (1,140, 82)
80 (820, 59)
206 (2,100, 152)
35 (360, 26)
127 (1,300, 94)
× 6
× 7
M/T
LH Engine
Under Cover
A/T
LH Engine Under Cover
TY1069600342020X

Fig. 1 Engine replacement (Part 2 of 2). 3S-FE

ensuring all wiring, hoses and cables are clear.

41. Place engine and transaxle assembly on stand and separate engine from transaxle.
42. Reverse procedure to install. Tighten to specifications.

INTAKE MANIFOLD

REPLACE

Refer to "Cylinder Head, Replace" for procedure.

EXHAUST MANIFOLD

REPLACE

Refer to "Cylinder Head, Replace" for procedure.

CYLINDER HEAD

REPLACE

REMOVAL

1. Remove righthand side engine under cover.
2. Drain engine coolant.
3. **On models with automatic transaxle,** disconnect throttle cable from throttle body.
4. **On all models,** disconnect accelerator cable from throttle body.
5. Remove air cleaner cap and case.
6. Remove alternator.
7. Remove distributor as outlined under "Distributor, Replace" in "Electrical" section.
8. Remove front exhaust pipe.
9. Disconnect oxygen sensor connectors, (bank 1/sensor 1) and (bank 1/sensor 2), **Fig. 2.**
10. Remove exhaust manifold upper heat insulator.
11. Remove two bolts attaching righthand exhaust manifold stay to cylinder block.
12. Remove exhaust manifold and catalytic converter assembly.
13. Remove oxygen sensor (bank 1/sensor 1) from exhaust manifold.
14. Remove oxygen sensor (bank 1/sensor 2) from catalytic converter.
15. Disconnect oil pressure switch connector.
16. Disconnect ECT sensor and ECT sender connectors.
17. Disconnect radiator hose, water bypass hose, heater water hose and IAC valve water bypass hose from water outlet.
18. Remove water outlet and gasket.
19. Remove water bypass pipe.
20. Disconnect IAC valve water bypass hose from water bypass pipe.
21. Disconnect heater water hose from water bypass pipe.
22. Disconnect two oil cooler water bypass hoses from oil cooler.
23. Disconnect water bypass pipe from water pump cover.
24. Remove water bypass pipe.
25. Disconnect IAC valve and throttle position sensor connectors.
26. Disconnect PCV hose and vacuum hoses from throttle body.
27. Remove throttle body from engine.
28. Disconnect vacuum sensor hose from gas filter on intake manifold.
29. Disconnect brake booster vacuum hose from intake manifold.
30. Disconnect ground strap from intake manifold.
31. Disconnect fuel inlet hose from fuel filter.
32. Remove EGR valve and vacuum modulator.
33. Remove intake manifold stay.
34. **On models with automatic transaxle,** disconnect throttle control cable from intake manifold.
35. **On all models,** disconnect power steering idle-up air hoses from air tube.
36. Disconnect knock sensor connector.
37. Remove VSV for EGR.
38. Remove two bolts and accelerator cable bracket.
39. Disconnect PCV hose from intake manifold.
40. Disconnect engine wire protector from two mounting bolts of upper (No. 2)

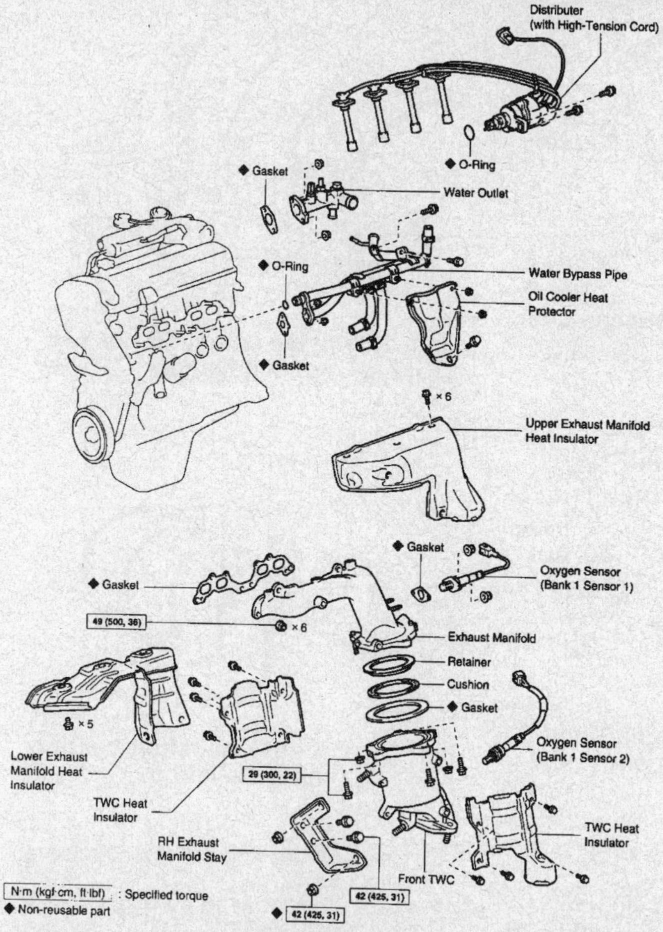

Distributer (with High-Tension Cord)
◆ O-Ring
◆ Gasket
Water Outlet
◆ O-Ring
Water Bypass Pipe
Oil Cooler Heat Protector
◆ Gasket
× 6
Upper Exhaust Manifold Heat Insulator
◆ Gasket
Oxygen Sensor (Bank 1 Sensor 1)
◆ Gasket
49 (500, 36)
× 6
Exhaust Manifold
Retainer
Cushion
◆ Gasket
× 5
Oxygen Sensor (Bank 1 Sensor 2)
Lower Exhaust Manifold Heat Insulator
29 (300, 22)
TWC Heat Insulator
TWC Heat Insulator
RH Exhaust Manifold Stay
Front TWC
N·m (kgf·cm, ft·lbf) : Specified torque
◆ Non-reusable part
42 (425, 31)
42 (425, 31)

TY1069600357000X

Fig. 2 Exhaust manifold removal

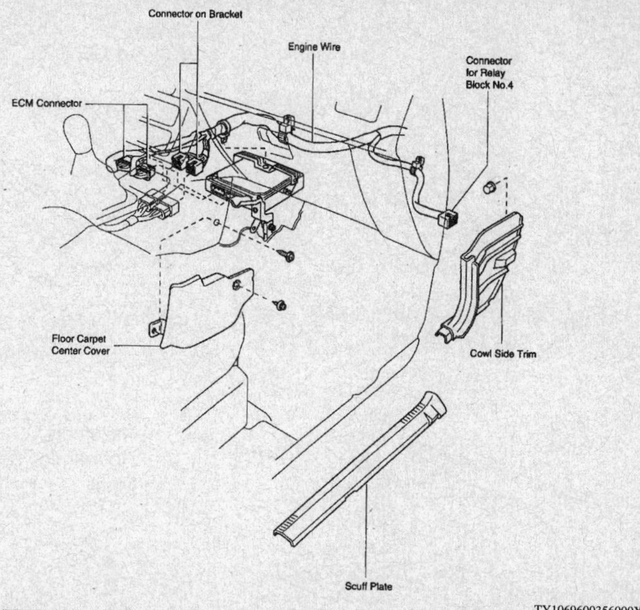

Connector on Bracket
Engine Wire
Connector for Relay Block No.4
ECM Connector
Floor Carpet Center Cover
Cowl Side Trim
Scuff Plate

TY1069600356000X

Fig. 3 Engine wire removal

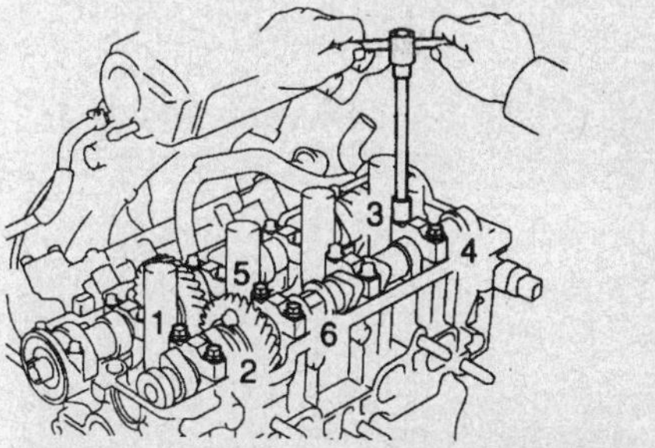

3
4
5
1
6
2

TY1069600345000X

Fig. 6 Exhaust camshaft bearing cap loosening sequence

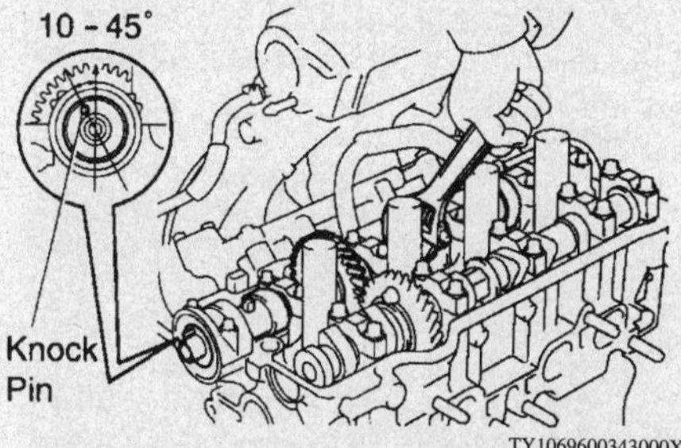

10 - 45°
Knock Pin

TY1069600343000X

Fig. 4 Intake camshaft knock pin

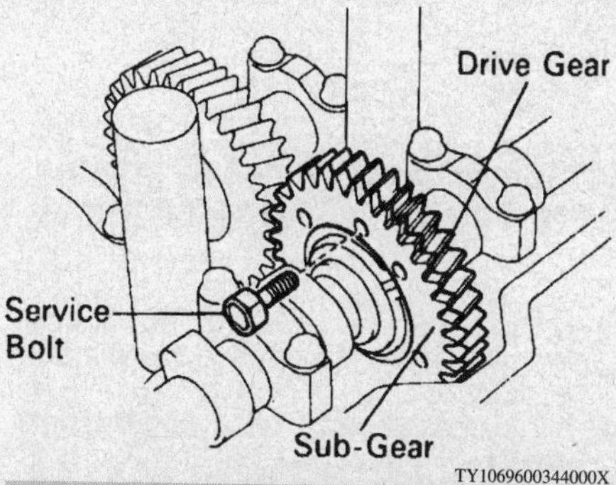

Drive Gear
Service Bolt
Sub-Gear

TY1069600344000X

Fig. 5 Service bolt installation

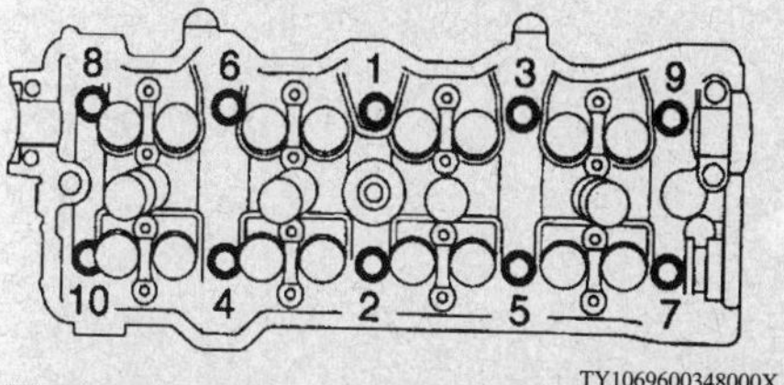

8
6
1
3
9
10
4
2
5
7

TY1069600348000X

Fig. 9 Cylinder head bolt tightening sequence

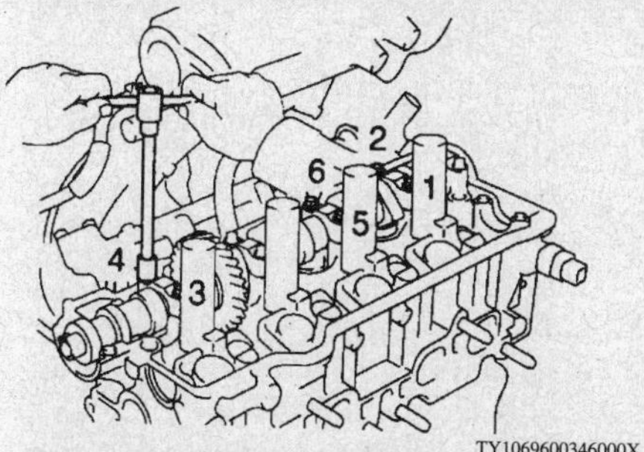

2
6
1
5
4
3

TY1069600346000X

Fig. 7 Intake camshaft bearing cap loosening sequence

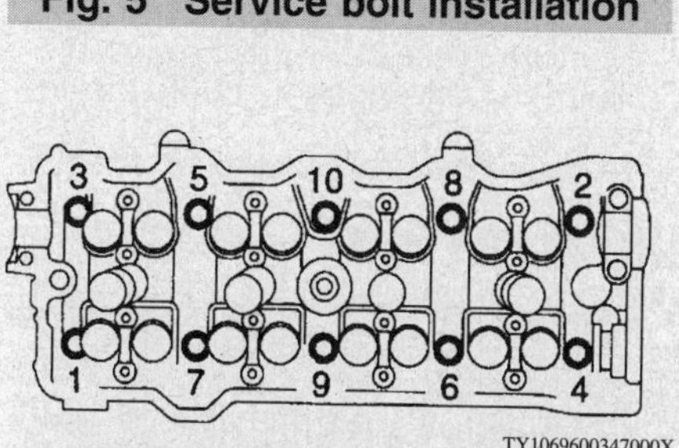

3
5
10
8
2
1
7
9
6
4

TY1069600347000X

Fig. 8 Cylinder head bolt loosening sequence

timing belt cover.

41. Remove four cylinder head cover nuts, head cover and gasket.
42. Disconnect four fuel injector connectors.
43. Disconnect A/C compressor connector, if equipped.
44. Disconnect crankshaft position sensor connector.
45. Remove righthand scuff plate, righthand cowl side trim and righthand floor carpet center cover, **Fig. 3.**
46. Disconnect engine wire from passenger compartment.
47. Disconnect two ECM connectors and connector from junction box No. 4.

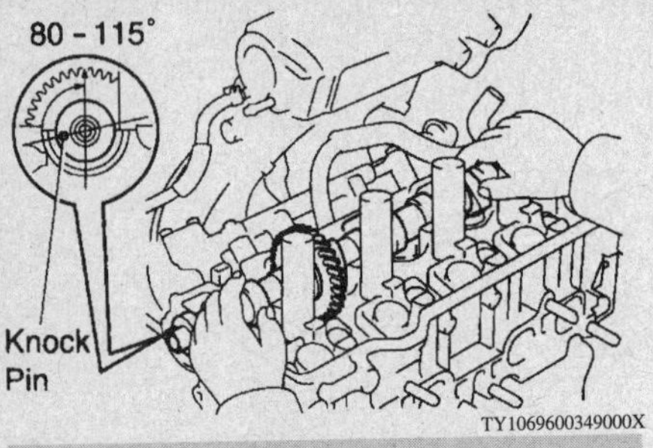
80 - 115°
Knock Pin
TY1069600349000X

Fig. 10 Intake camshaft installation

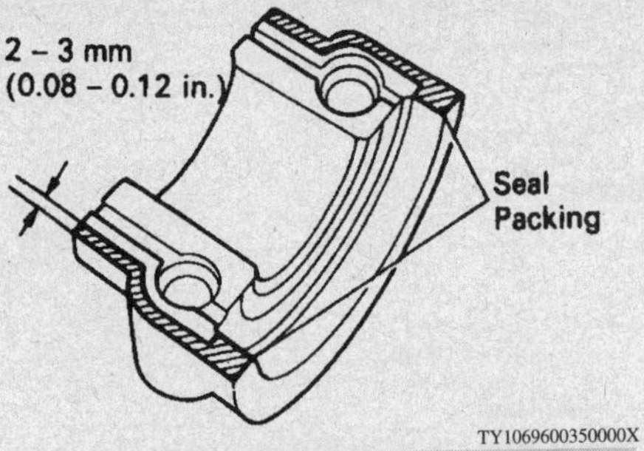
2 – 3 mm
(0.08 – 0.12 in.)
Seal Packing
TY1069600350000X

Fig. 11 No. 1 bearing cap seal packing

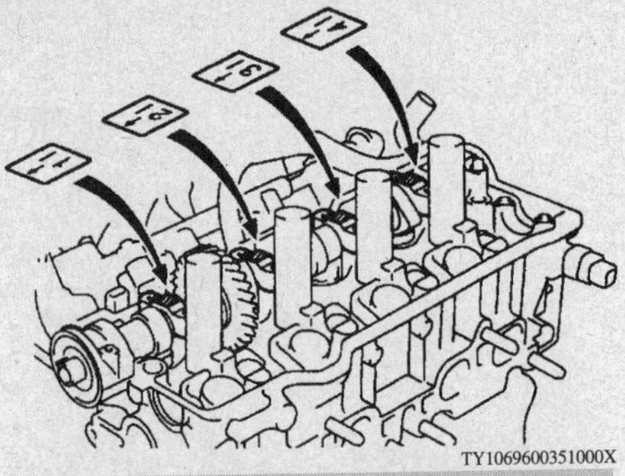
TY1069600351000X

Fig. 12 Intake camshaft bearing cap installation

7
1
8
5
2
3
6
9
4
10
TY1069600352000X

Fig. 13 Intake camshaft bearing cap bolt tightening sequence

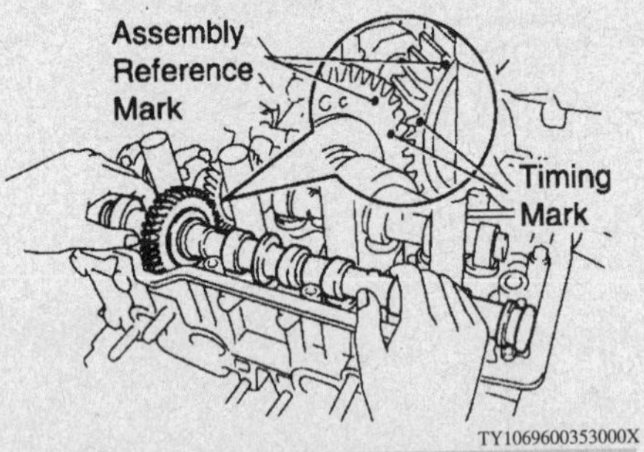
Assembly Reference Mark
Timing Mark
TY1069600353000X

Fig. 14 Camshaft gear timing mark alignment

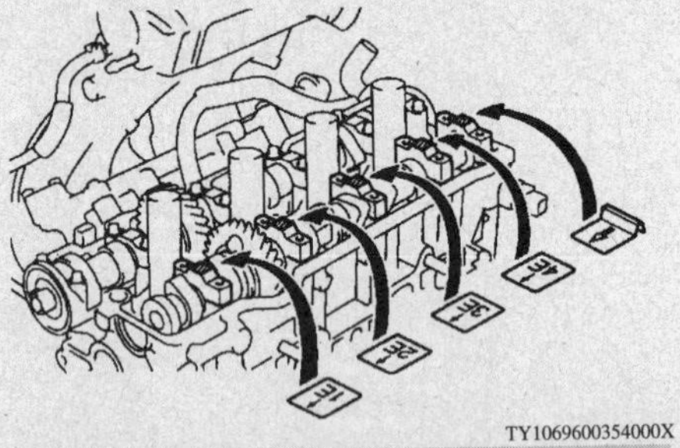
TY1069600354000X

Fig. 15 Exhaust camshaft bearing cap installation

48. Pull engine wire from passenger compartment.
49. Disconnect timing belt from camshaft timing pulley.
50. Remove timing pulley.
51. Remove No. 1 idler pulley and tension spring.
52. Remove camshafts as follows:
    a. Set knock pin of intake camshaft at 10–45° BTDC of camshaft angle, **Fig. 4.** This allows the No. 2 and No. 4 cylinder cam lobes of the exhaust camshaft to push valve lifters evenly.
    b. Secure exhaust camshaft sub gear to drive gear with service bolt, **Fig. 5.**
    c. Remove two bolts and rear bearing cap.
    d. Using sequence shown in **Fig. 6,** uniformly loosen and remove six bolts on No. 1, No. 2 and No. 4 bearing caps.
    e. Remove No. 1, No. 2 and No. 4 bearing caps.
    f. Remove No. 3 bearing cap and exhaust camshaft.
    g. Set knock pin of intake camshaft at 80–115° BTDC of camshaft angle. This allows the No. 1 and No. 3 cylinder cam lobes of the intake camshaft to push valve lifters evenly.
    h. Remove two bolts, front bearing cap and oil seal.
    i. Using sequence shown in **Fig. 7,** uniformly loosen and remove six bolts on No. 1, No. 3 and No. 4 bearing caps.
    j. Remove No. 2 bearing cap and intake camshaft.

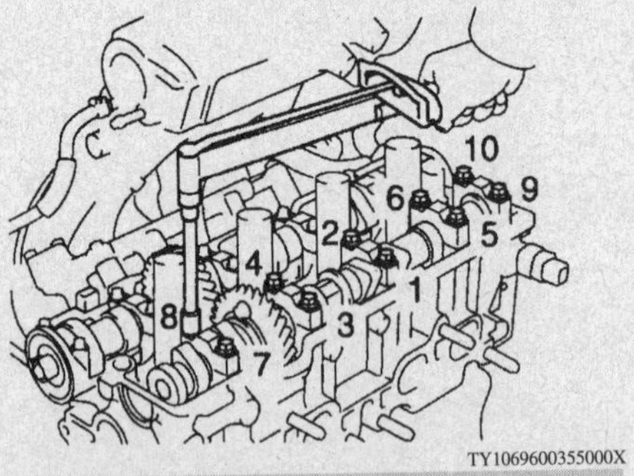
10
6
9
5
2
4
1
8
3
7
TY1069600355000X

Fig. 16 Exhaust camshaft bearing cap bolt tightening sequence

53. Using sequence shown in **Fig. 8,** uniformly loosen and remove 10 cylinder head bolts.
54. Lift cylinder head from cylinder block dowels.
55. Disconnect air hose from intake manifold, then remove air tube.
56. Remove intake manifold and gasket.
57. Remove delivery pipe and fuel injectors.
58. Remove oil pressure switch.

INSTALLATION

1. Install oil pressure switch. Apply suitable adhesive (Three Bond 1344 or equivalent) to switch threads.
2. Install fuel injectors and delivery pipe.
3. Install air hose for air assist system to cylinder head.
4. Install intake manifold with new gasket to cylinder head. Tighten to specifications.
5. Install air tube and connect air hose to intake manifold.
6. Place cylinder head on engine block with new gasket.
7. Install cylinder head bolts, then using sequence shown in **Fig. 9,** tighten bolts in two steps. First step, **torque** bolts 36 ft. lbs.; second step, tighten bolts an additional 90°.
8. Install spark plug tubes and tighten to specifications.
9. Install camshafts as follows:
    a. Apply MP grease to thrust portion of intake camshaft, then place intake camshaft on cylinder head at 80–115° BTDC, **Fig. 10.**
    b. Install new intake camshaft oil seal.
    c. Apply seal packing, part No. 08826-00080, or equivalent, to No. 1 bearing cap, **Fig. 11.**
    d. Install bearing caps in proper locations, **Fig. 12.**
    e. Uniformly tighten bearing cap bolts to specification using sequence shown in **Fig. 13.**
    f. Set knock pin of intake camshaft at 10–45° BTDC of camshaft angle, **Fig. 4.**
    g. Apply MP grease to thrust portion of exhaust camshaft, then engage exhaust camshaft gear to intake camshaft gear by aligning timing marks on each gear, **Fig. 14. Do not use assembly reference marks shown in illustration.**
    h. Install exhaust camshaft bearing caps in proper locations, **Fig. 15.**
    i. Tighten bearing cap bolts to specification using sequence shown in **Fig. 16.**

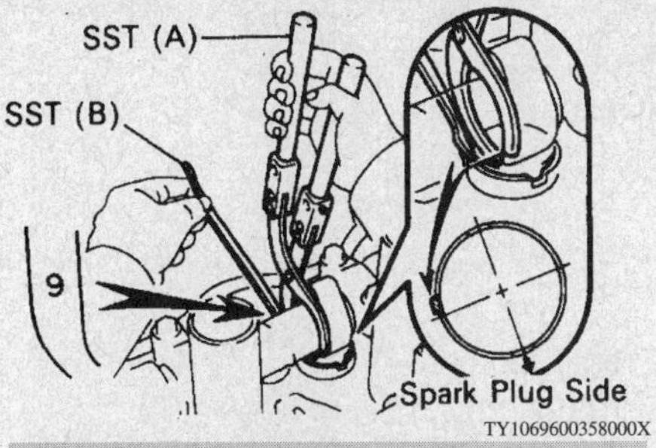
SST (A)
SST (B)
9
Spark Plug Side
TY1069600358000X

Fig. 17 Valve clearance adjustment

New shim thickness mm (in.)

Shim No.	Thickness	Shim No.	Thickness
1	2.500 (0.0984)	10	2.950 (0.1161)
2	2.550 (0.1004)	11	3.000 (0.1181)
3	2.600 (0.1024)	12	3.050 (0.1201)
4	2.650 (0.1043)	13	3.100 (0.1220)
5	2.700 (0.1063)	14	3.150 (0.1240)
6	2.750 (0.1083)	15	3.200 (0.1260)
7	2.800 (0.1102)	16	3.250 (0.1280)
8	2.850 (0.1122)	17	3.300 (0.1299)
9	2.900 (0.1142)		

TY1069600359000X

Fig. 18 Intake adjusting shims

New shim thickness mm (in.)

Shim No.	Thickness	Shim No.	Thickness
1	2.500 (0.0984)	10	2.950 (0.1161)
2	2.550 (0.1004)	11	3.000 (0.1181)
3	2.600 (0.1024)	12	3.050 (0.1201)
4	2.650 (0.1043)	13	3.100 (0.1220)
5	2.700 (0.1063)	14	3.150 (0.1240)
6	2.750 (0.1083)	15	3.200 (0.1260)
7	2.800 (0.1102)	16	3.250 (0.1280)
8	2.850 (0.1122)	17	3.300 (0.1299)
9	2.900 (0.1142)		

TY1069600360000X

Fig. 19 Exhaust adjusting shims

10. Check and adjust valve clearance as outlined under "Valve Adjustment."
11. Apply new packing material to semi-circular plugs and install both plugs to cylinder head.
12. Install No. 3 timing belt cover and tighten to specifications.
13. Temporarily install No. 1 idler pulley and tension spring.
14. Install camshaft timing pulley and timing belt as outlined under "Timing Belt, Replace."
15. Install engine wire protector to two brackets on front of intake manifold.
16. Connect four fuel injector connectors. Nos. 1 and 3 connectors are brown, and Nos. 2 and 4 connectors are gray.
17. Install engine wire protector to lefthand side of intake manifold.
18. Push engine wire through cowl panel, **Fig. 3.**
19. Install engine wire clamp to bracket, then connect wire.
20. Connect ECM connectors, junction box No. 4 connector and two bracket connectors.
21. Install righthand floor carpet cover, righthand cowl side trim and righthand scuff plate.
22. Install cylinder head cover with four grommets and tighten bolts to specifications.
23. Install engine wire protector to two mounting bolts of No. 2 timing belt cover.
24. Connect three clamps to No. 2 timing belt cover and alternator belt adjusting bar.
25. Connect crankshaft position sensor connector.
26. Connect A/C compressor connector.
27. Connect PCV hose to intake manifold.
28. Install accelerator cable bracket.
29. Install VSV for EGR.
30. Connect ground cable to intake manifold.
31. Connect knock sensor connector.
32. Connect power steering idle-up air hose to air tube.
33. **On models with automatic transaxle,** connect throttle control cable to intake manifold.
34. **On all models,** install intake manifold stay and tighten to specifications.
35. Install EGR valve and vacuum modulator.
36. Connect two vacuum hoses to VSV for EGR.
37. Connect fuel inlet hose to fuel filter.
38. Install vacuum sensor hose to gas filter on intake manifold.
39. Install brake booster vacuum hose to intake manifold.
40. Install ground strap to intake manifold.
41. Install throttle body.
42. Install water bypass pipe with new gasket and O-ring.
43. Connect IAC valve water bypass hose to water bypass pipe.
44. Connect heater water hose to water bypass pipe.
45. Connect two oil cooler water bypass hoses to oil cooler.
46. Install oil cooler heat protector.
47. Install water outlet, then connect the following hoses:
    a. Radiator.
    b. Water bypass.
    c. Heater water.
    d. IAC valve water bypass.
48. Connect ECT sensor and sender gauge connectors.
49. Connect oil pressure switch connector.
50. Install catalytic converter to exhaust manifold, then install lower manifold heat insulator.
51. Install two catalytic converter heat insulators.
52. Install oxygen sensor (bank 1/sensor 1) to exhaust manifold.
53. Install oxygen sensor (bank 1/sensor 2) to front of catalytic converter.
54. Install exhaust manifold and front catalytic converter assembly.
55. Connect oxygen sensor electrical connectors, then install front exhaust pipe.
56. Install distributor as outlined under "Distributor, Replace" in "Electrical" section.
57. Install alternator, then the air cleaner case and cap.
58. Connect accelerator cable to throttle body and cable bracket.
59. **On models with automatic transaxle,** connect throttle cable to throttle body and cable bracket.
60. **On all models,** fill engine coolant and oil, then start engine and check for leaks.
61. Install righthand engine under cover.

VALVE CLEARANCE SPECIFICATIONS

Year	Stem-To-Guide Clearance	
	Intake	Exhaust
1996	.007–.011	.011–.015

VALVE ADJUSTMENT

1. Disconnect power steering reservoir.
2. Disconnect accelerator cable from throttle body and clamp on intake manifold.
3. Disconnect accelerator cable from clamp on generator bracket.
4. Disconnect throttle control cable from throttle body.
5. Disconnect PCV hose from air cleaner hose and intake manifold.
6. Disconnect spark plug wires.
7. Remove accelerator cable bracket from intake manifold.
8. Disconnect engine wire protector from two No. 2 timing belt cover mounting bolts.
9. Remove cylinder head cover.
10. Turn crankshaft pulley and align groove with "0"timing mark of timing belt cover. This will set No. 1 cylinder to TDC on compression.
11. Using feeler gauge, measure clearance between valve lifters and camshaft for valve No. 1 intake and exhaust, No. 2 exhaust and No. 3 intake.
12. Turn crankshaft 360° and check clearance of remaining valves.
13. Refer to "Valve Clearance Specifications" for standard cold clearance specifications.
14. If valve clearance falls out of specification, adjust as follows:

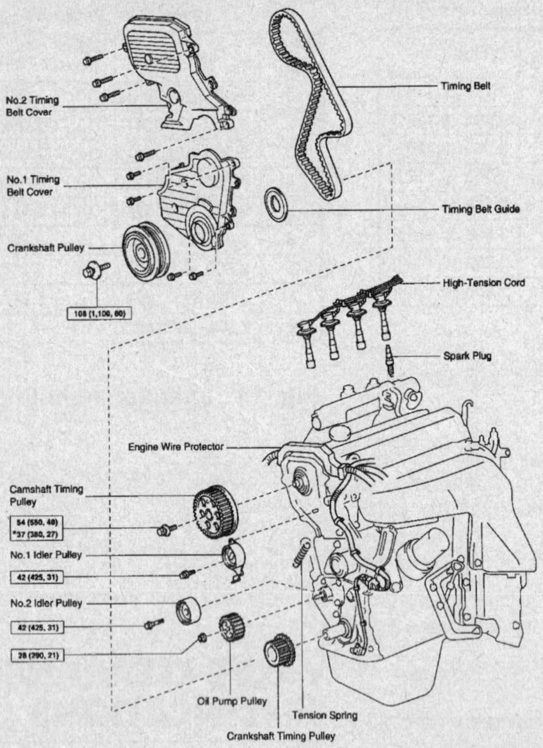
No.2 Timing Belt Cover
Timing Belt
No.1 Timing Belt Cover
Timing Belt Guide
Crankshaft Pulley
High-Tension Cord
108 (1,100, 80)
Spark Plug
Engine Wire Protector
Camshaft Timing Pulley
54 (550, 40)
*37 (380, 27)
No.1 Idler Pulley
42 (425, 31)
No.2 Idler Pulley
42 (425, 31)
28 (290, 21)
Oil Pump Pulley
Tension Spring
Crankshaft Timing Pulley
TY1069600361000X

Fig. 20 Timing belt replacement

a. Turn crankshaft so that cam lobe on adjusting valve points upward.
b. Position notch of valve lifter facing spark plug side.
c. Using tool No. 09248-55040 (A), or equivalent, press down valve lifter and place tool No. 09248-55040 (B), or equivalent, between camshaft and valve lifter, **Fig. 17.**
d. Remove tool (A).
e. Remove adjusting shim with screwdriver and magnetic finger.
f. Using a micrometer, measure thickness of removed shim.
g. Determine difference between desired and actual valve clearance measurement, then add difference to dimension of measured shim. Refer to shim charts, **Figs. 18 and 19,** to select a replacement shim.
h. Place new adjusting shim on valve lifter, then remove tool (B).
i. Recheck valve clearances.

TIMING BELT

REPLACE

1. Disconnect power steering reservoir and remove reservoir bracket.
2. Disconnect wire harness bracket for DLC1.
3. Remove alternator and bracket.
4. **On models with anti-lock brakes,** remove ABS actuator.

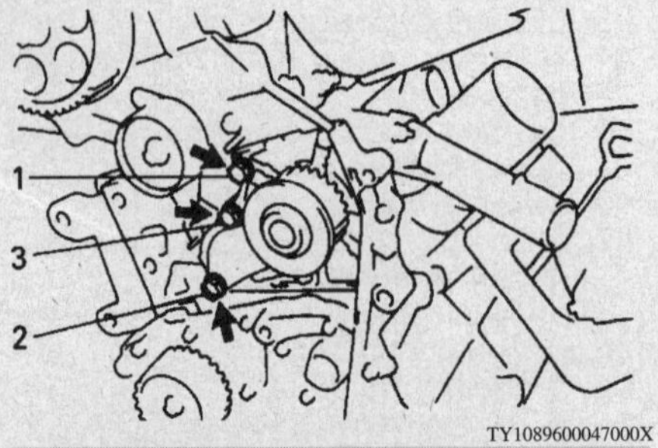
1
3
2
TY1089600047000X

Fig. 22 Water pump bolt removal sequence

5. **On all models,** remove righthand front wheel and righthand engine under cover.
6. Remove power steering pump drive belt.
7. Place jack under oil pan and raise engine enough to remove weight from righthand engine mounting.
8. Remove righthand engine mounting insulator.
9. Remove spark plugs.
10. Using bolt removal tool No. 09213-54015, or equivalent, and bolt (No. 91121-40665), remove crankshaft pulley bolt, **Fig. 20.**
11. Using pulley removal tool No. 09950-50010, or equivalent, remove crankshaft pulley.
12. Remove righthand engine mounting bracket using tool No. 09249-63010, or equivalent.
13. Disconnect engine wire from No. 2 timing belt cover and remove No. 2 timing belt cover.

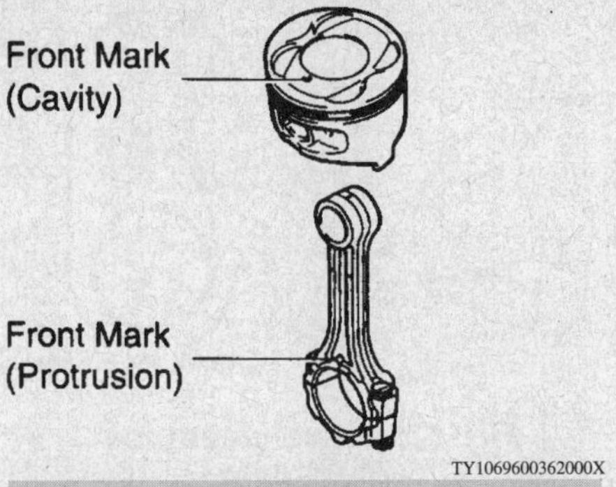
Front Mark (Cavity)
Front Mark (Protrusion)
TY1069600362000X

Fig. 21 Piston & rod assembly

14. Temporarily install crankshaft pulley with pulley set key aligned with key groove of pulley.
15. Turn crankshaft pulley and align its groove with timing mark "0" of No. 1 timing belt cover. This will set No. 1 cylinder to TDC on compression.
16. Loosen mounting bolt of No. 1 idler pulley and shift pulley toward left as far as it will go, then temporarily tighten.
17. Remove timing belt from camshaft timing pulley.
18. Using pulley removal tool Nos. 09249-63010 and 09960-10010, or equivalents, remove camshaft timing pulley.
19. Remove crankshaft pulley.
20. Disconnect engine wire from No. 1 timing belt cover, then remove No. 1 timing belt cover.
21. Remove timing belt guide, then the timing belt.
22. Remove both idler pulleys and tension spring.
23. Remove crankshaft timing pulley and oil pump pulley.
24. Reverse procedure to install. Tighten all fasteners to specifications.

CAMSHAFT

REPLACE

Refer to "Cylinder Head, Replace" for procedure.

PISTON & ROD ASSEMBLY

Piston and rod assemblies are marked as shown in **Fig. 21** to indicate the front. Pistons are available in three standard sizes and one oversize. Oversize pistons are available in 3.4004–3.4016 inches. The top of the piston is marked with either a 1, 2 or 3 to indicate standard sizes as follows:

1. Mark "1" (3.3807–3.3811 inches).
2. Mark "2" (3.3811–3.3815 inches).
3. Mark "3" (3.3815–3.3819 inches).

MAIN & ROD BEARINGS

Main and rod bearings are available in three standard sizes, marked on connecting rod cap with a 1, 2 or 3. Main bearing oil clearance is .0007–.0019 inch for journals

1, 2, 4 and 5, and .0011–.0021 inch for journal 3. Crankshaft thrust clearance is .0008–.0027 inch. Connecting rod bearing oil clearance is .0009–.0022 inch.

OIL PAN

REPLACE

1. Remove hood and righthand engine under cover.
2. Drain engine oil.
3. Remove front exhaust pipe.
4. Remove stiffener plate.
5. Remove engine oil dipstick.
6. Remove oil pan bolts, cut off applied oil pan sealer material and pry pan loose with suitable tool.
7. Reverse procedure to install. Clear old pan gasket material, apply new gasket and tighten oil pan bolts to specifications.

OIL PUMP

REPLACE

1. Remove oil pan as outlined under "Oil Pan, Replace."
2. Remove oil pan baffle plate and oil strainer.
3. Suspend engine with engine hanger and sling device, tool Nos. 12281-74060 and 91611-B1020, or equivalents.
4. Remove timing belt as outlined under "Timing Belt, Replace."
5. Remove oil pump pulley using pulley removal tool No. 09960-10010, or equivalent.
6. Disconnect crankshaft position sensor connector and remove sensor.
7. Remove oil pump mounting bolts, then the oil pump.
8. Reverse procedure to install. Tighten bolts to specifications.

BELT TENSION DATA

Belt	New, Lbs.	Used, Lbs.
Alternator	140-190①	100-120①
	100-150②	75-115②
Power Steer.	95-145	60-100
A/C Comp.	139-192	66-99

①— Models with A/C.
②— Models less A/C.

COOLING SYSTEM BLEED

These engines do not require a specific bleed procedure. After filling cooling system, run engine to operating temperature with radiator/pressure cap off. Air will then be automatically bled through cap opening.

THERMOSTAT

REPLACE

1. Drain engine coolant.
2. Remove oil filter.
3. Remove two nuts and disconnect water inlet from water pump cover.
4. Remove thermostat and gasket.
5. Reverse procedure to install.

WATER PUMP

REPLACE

1. Remove engine under cover and drain engine coolant.
2. Remove timing belt as outlined under "Timing Belt, Replace."
3. Disconnect lower radiator hose from water inlet.
4. Remove timing belt tension spring and No. 2 idler pulley.
5. Remove alternator drive belt adjusting bar.
6. Remove two nuts attaching water pump to water bypass pipe.
7. Remove three bolts from water pump cover in sequence shown, **Fig. 22.**
8. Disconnect water pump cover from water bypass pipe and remove water pump cover assembly.
9. Remove water pump from water pump cover.
10. Reverse procedure to install. Tighten pump cover bolts to specifications in reverse order of removal sequence shown in **Fig. 22.**

RADIATOR

REPLACE

1. Remove engine under covers and drain engine coolant.
2. **On models with A/C,** remove condenser core, then disconnect No. 2 cooling fan connector.
3. **On all models,** disconnect No. 1 cooling fan connector, then the ECT switch connector for the electric cooling fan.
4. Disconnect engine wire clamp from No. 1 cooling fan shroud.
5. Disconnect upper and lower radiator hoses.
6. Disconnect radiator overflow reservoir hose from radiator.
7. Disconnect two automatic transaxle oil cooler hoses from oil cooler pipes, if equipped.
8. Remove upper radiator supports, then the radiator.
9. Remove lower radiator supports.
10. **On models with A/C,** remove three No. 2 cooling fan assembly from radiator.
11. **On all models,** remove No. 1 cooling fan from radiator.
12. Reverse procedure to install.

FUEL PUMP

REPLACE

1. Relieve fuel system pressure as outlined under "Precautions."
2. Remove floor service hole cover.
3. Disconnect fuel pump connector.
4. Start engine and wait for engine to shut off on its own before turning ignition switch off. This will relieve fuel system pressure.
5. Disconnect battery ground cable.
6. Disconnect ground strap from fuel pump clamp.
7. Pull off lower side of fuel pump from pump bracket.
8. Disconnect fuel hose from fuel pump, then remove fuel pump.
9. Reverse procedure to install.

FUEL FILTER

REPLACE

1. Relieve fuel system pressure as outlined under "Precautions."
2. Disconnect battery ground cable.
3. Disconnect ground strap from fuel pump clamp.
4. Pull off lower side of fuel pump from pump bracket.
5. Disconnect fuel hose from fuel pump, then remove fuel pump.
6. Using small screwdriver, remove clip at top of fuel pump and pull out pump filter.
7. Reverse procedure to install.

TIGHTENING SPECIFICATIONS

Component	Torque/Ft. Lbs.
Alternator Bracket	31
Camshaft Bearing Cap	14
Catalytic Converter To Exhaust Manifold	22
Crankshaft Pulley Bolt	80
Cylinder Head Bolts	①
Cylinder Head Cover Bolts	17
Distributor Mounting Bolt	14
Exhaust Manifold Mounting Bolts	36
Intake Manifold Bolts	14
Intake Manifold Stay	14
Main Bearing Cap Bolts	43
No. 1 Idler Pulley Bolt	31
No. 2 Idler Pulley Bolt	31
No. 3 Timing Belt Cover	6
Oil Pump Pulley Bolt	18
Oxygen Sensor (Catalytic Converter)	33
Oxygen Sensor (Exhaust Manifold)	14
Power Steering Pump Adjusting Bolt	29
Power Steering Pump Through Bolt	32
Rear End Plate To Cylinder Block	7
Rear Oil Seal Retainer	9
RH Engine Mounting Bracket To Cylinder Block	38
RH Mounting Insulator To Body	47
RH Mounting Insulator To Mounting Bracket	27
Spark Plug Tube	29
Water Bypass Pipe To Engine	14
Water Bypass Pipe To Pump Cover	7
Water Outlet To Cylinder Head	11

① — Refer to "Cylinder Head, Replace."

22R-E 2.4L Engine

INDEX

	Page No.
Belt Tension Data	47-30
Camshaft, Replace	47-29
Compression Pressure	47-27
Cooling System Bleed	47-30
Crankshaft Rear Oil Seal, Replace	47-29
Cylinder Head, Replace	47-28
Installation	47-29
Removal	47-28
Engine Rebuilding Specifications	48-1
Engine, Replace	47-27
Front Cover Seal, Replace	47-29
Fuel Filter, Replace	47-30
Fuel Pump, Replace	47-30
Intake Manifold, Replace	47-28
Main & Rod Bearings	47-29
Oil Pan, Replace	47-29
Oil Pump, Replace	47-30
Oil Pump Service	47-30
Piston & Rod Assembly	47-29
Precautions	47-27
Audio Coded Anti-Theft System	47-27
Radiator, Replace	47-30
Thermostat, Replace	47-30
Tightening Specifications	47-32
Timing Chain, Replace	47-29
Installation	47-29
Removal	47-29
Valve Adjustment	47-29
Valve Clearance Specifications	47-29
Valve Guides	47-29
Water Pump, Replace	47-30

PRECAUTIONS

AUDIO CODED ANTI-THEFT SYSTEM

Some models are equipped with an audio coded anti-theft system that will disable the radio when the battery cable is disconnected. The system can be identified by the "ANTI-THEFT SYSTEM" on the cassette lid. Obtain three-digit code for input. Reset system after service as follows:

1. Obtain three-digit audio theft code.
2. Depress 1 (PROG) button while depressing righthand side of TUNE SEEK button. Three dashes will appear in tape operation display.
3. To enter first digit, depress 1 (PROG) button repeatedly until number of times depressed equals first digit (depress 1 button six times if first digit is five, first press equals 0).
4. To enter second digit, depress 2 (APS) button repeatedly until number of times depressed equals second digit.
5. To enter third digit, depress 3 (RPT) button repeatedly until number of times depressed equals third digit.
6. If three dashes are displayed after inputting digits, repeat procedure.
7. When code appears in display, depress and hold SCAN button until SEC appears.
8. When SEC disappears audio system is operative.
9. If Err is displayed, repeat procedure. **Attempting to input code more than nine times may permanently disable audio system.**

COMPRESSION PRESSURE

1. Start engine and warm to normal operating temperature.
2. Remove spark plugs.
3. Disconnect distributor connector.
4. Disconnect cold start injector connector.
5. Insert compression gauge into spark plug hole.
6. Fully open throttle.
7. While cranking engine, measure compression pressure.
8. Standard compression pressure should be 171 psi. Minimum compression is 142 psi.
9. The difference in compression pressure between each cylinder should not exceed 14 psi.

ENGINE

REPLACE

1. **On models with audio coded anti-theft system,** obtain three-digit system code.
2. **On all models,** remove battery, hood and engine undercover.
3. Drain engine oil and coolant into suitable container.
4. Remove air cleaner hose, air cleaner and radiator.
5. Remove power steering pump drive belt, generator belt, fluid coupling and fan pulley.
6. Disconnect the following connectors:
   a. Ground strap from lefthand fender apron.
   b. Generator connector and wires.
   c. Coil wire, coil connectors and igniter connectors.
   d. Ground strap from engine rear side.
   e. ECU connectors and check connector.
   f. Starter relay connector and A/C compressor connector.
7. Disconnect following hoses:
   a. Brake booster hose.
   b. Cruise control vacuum.
   c. Charcoal canister hoses.
   d. Air hoses from gas filter and air pipe.
8. Disconnect heater hoses, then the accelerator cable, throttle cable and cruise cables.
9. Identify, then disconnect any cables, hoses or electrical connections that would interfere with engine removal.
10. Remove power steering pump (if equipped) from engine block without disconnecting pressure and return lines and position aside.
11. Disconnect ground strap from power steering bracket.
12. **On models with A/C,** remove A/C compressor without disconnecting high and low side hoses and position aside.
13. **On all models,** disconnect ground straps from engine rear and righthand side.
14. **On manual transmissions,** remove shift linkage from inside of vehicle.
15. **On all models,** remove rear propeller shaft.
16. **On 2WD with automatic transmission,** disconnect shift linkage from neutral start switch.
17. **On 4WD with automatic transmission,** disconnect No. 1 and No. 2 transfer shift linkage from cross shaft. Remove cross shaft from body.
18. **On all models,** disconnect speedometer cable.
19. **On 4WD models,** remove transfer case undercover, stabilizer bar and front propeller shaft.
20. **On all models,** disconnect oxygen sensor and exhaust pipe from exhaust manifold.
21. Remove exhaust pipe clamp from clutch housing and exhaust pipe from catalytic converter.
22. **On models with manual transmission,** remove clutch release cylinder and bracket.
23. **On 4WD models,** remove No. 1 front floor heat insulator and brake tube heat insulator.
24. **On 2WD models,** remove engine rear mounting and bracket.
25. **On 4WD models,** remove No. 2 crossmember from side frame.
26. **On all models,** attach suitable lifting equipment to engine.
27. Remove lefthand and righthand side engine mounts.
28. Slowly and carefully lift engine with transmission from vehicle. Ensure all cables, hoses and electrical connectors are disconnected during removal.
29. Separate transmission from engine.
30. Reverse procedure to install. Reset audio coded anti-theft and air bag system, if equipped, as outlined under

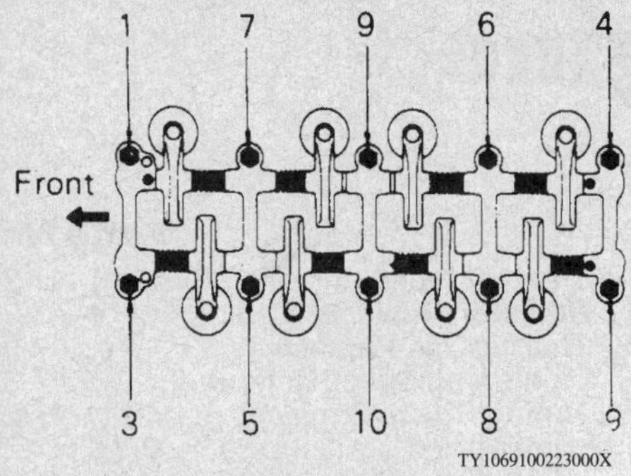
1
7
9
6
4
Front
3
5
10
8
9
TY1069100223000X

Fig. 1 Cylinder head bolt loosening sequence

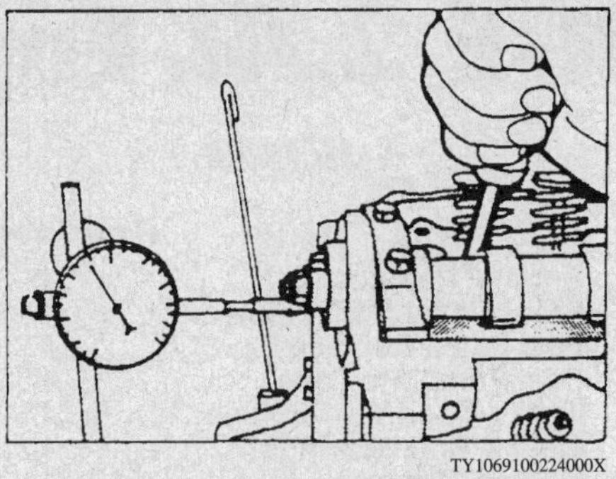
TY1069100224000X

Fig. 2 Camshaft thrust clearance measurement

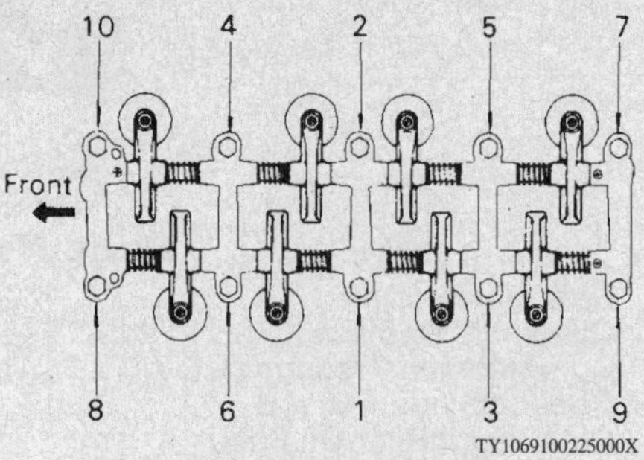
10
4
2
5
7
Front
8
6
1
3
9
TY1069100225000X

Fig. 3 Cylinder head bolt tightening sequence

"Precautions."

INTAKE MANIFOLD

REPLACE

Refer to "Cylinder Head, Replace" for procedure.

CYLINDER HEAD

REPLACE

REMOVAL

1. **On models with audio coded anti-theft system,**obtain three-digit system code.
2. **On all models,** disconnect battery ground cable, then drain coolant from radiator and engine block.
3. Disconnect air cleaner hose from air cleaner.
4. Disconnect exhaust pipe from exhaust manifold.
5. Remove oil dipstick, distributor, spark plugs and radiator inlet hose, then disconnect heater water inlet hose from heater water inlet pipe.
6. Disconnect cruise control actuator (if equipped), accelerator cable and engine ground strap from cylinder head. Disconnect throttle cable, if equipped, from cylinder head.
7. Disconnect the following hoses.
   a. No. 1 and No. 2 PCV hoses.
   b. Brake booster hose.
   c. Air control valve hoses.
   d. Evaporative emission hose.
   e. EGR vacuum modulator hose and EGR valve hose.
   f. Fuel pressure up hose and pressure regulator hose.
   g. Vacuum hoses from throttle body.
   h. Water bypass hoses from throttle body and intake manifold.
8. Remove EGR vacuum modulator.
9. Remove cold start and throttle position wires.
10. **On California models,** remove EGR gas temperature sensor wire.
11. **On all models,** remove bolts, air intake chamber and throttle body.
12. Remove pulsation damper and disconnect fuel hose from fuel line.
13. Disconnect the following wires:
    a. Knock sensor wire.
    b. Oil pressure sender gauge wire.
    c. Starter wire (terminal 50)
    d. Transmission, injector and A/C compressor wires (if equipped).
    e. Engine coolant temperature gauge wire.
    f. **On models with automatic transaxle,** overdrive temperature switch wire.
    g. **On all models,** igniter wire and vacuum switching valve wire
    h. Start injector time switch wire.
    i. Engine coolant temperature sensor wire.
14. Disconnect air bypass hose from air valve and remove air valve from intake manifold.
15. Remove auxiliary air valve.
16. **On models with power steering,** remove drive belt, bolts and pulley. Remove power steering pump mounting bolts and position pump aside. Do not disconnect power steering pump hoses.
17. **On all models,** remove ground strap and cylinder head cover.
18. Rotate crankshaft until No. 1 cylinder is set at TDC compression stroke. Place reference marks on timing chain and camshaft sprocket.
19. Remove semi-circular plug, camshaft sprocket bolt, distributor drive gear and camshaft thrust plate.
20. Remove camshaft sprocket and timing chain from camshaft, leaving lower part of chain engaged on lower sprocket. Remove timing chain cover bolt from front inside of cylinder head. **Timing chain cover bolt must be removed prior to removing head bolts.**
21. Gradually loosen and remove cylinder head bolts in two or three steps as shown in **Fig. 1.**
22. Remove rocker arm assembly from cylinder head, then the cylinder head. **If rocker arm assembly is difficult to remove, a pry bar can be inserted at front or rear of rocker arm assembly to aid in separation.**
23. Remove intake manifold.
24. Remove EGR valve and exhaust manifold, if not previously removed.
25. Remove engine hangers, ground straps and cylinder head rear cover.
26. Using suitable dial indicator positioned at front of cylinder head, measure camshaft thrust clearance, **Fig. 2.** Standard camshaft thrust clearance is .0031–.0071 inch, with a maximum clearance of .0098 inch. If measurement exceeds maximum clearance, replace cylinder head.
27. Remove camshaft bearing cap bolts, then the bearing caps and camshaft.

INSTALLATION

1. Install camshaft in cylinder head, then install bearing caps in numbered order from front of cylinder head with arrows facing forward. Install bearing cap bolts and **torque** to 14 ft. lbs.
2. Rotate camshaft to position alignment pin away from cylinder head.
3. Install cylinder head rear cover, engine hangers and ground straps.
4. Install intake manifold, EGR valve and exhaust manifold.
5. Apply a suitable sealer to where timing cover and front of engine block intersect, then install a new cylinder head gasket.
6. If camshaft sprocket was removed from timing chain, position sprocket in chain while aligning reference marks made during Removal. Install cylinder head onto engine block.
7. Install rocker arm assembly, then using sequence shown in **Fig. 3, torque** cylinder head bolts in three steps to 58 ft. lbs.
8. Install timing chain cover bolt. Tighten bolt to specification.
9. Ensure camshaft alignment pin faces upward. If not, rotate camshaft as necessary to position alignment pin upwards.
10. While holding tension on camshaft sprocket and timing chain, rotate crankshaft to ensure cylinders Nos. 1 and 4 are set at TDC.
11. Position camshaft sprocket and chain onto camshaft. **If timing chain appears too short, rotate crankshaft back and forth while pulling up on chain and sprocket.**
12. Install distributor drive gear and bolt. Tighten bolt to specification.
13. Adjust valve clearances, refer to "Valve Adjustment" for procedure.
14. Install half circular plug, gasket and cylinder head cover.
15. Install power steering pump bolts, pulley and drive belt. Tighten bolts to specification.
16. Reverse steps 1 through 14 of removal procedures to complete installation.

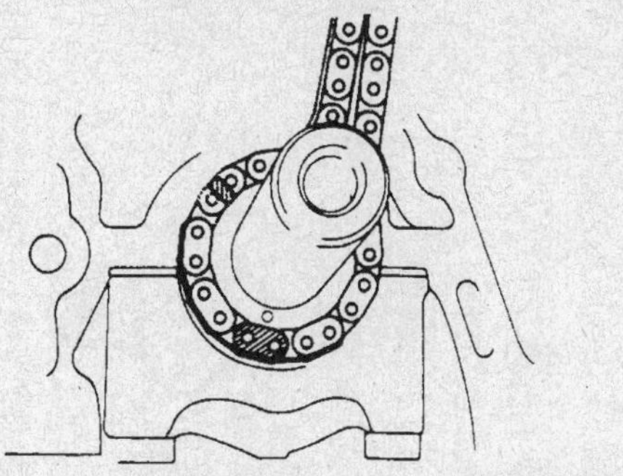
TY1069100226000X

Fig. 4 Timing chain to crankshaft sprocket alignment

Reset audio coded anti-theft system, if equipped, as outlined under "Precautions."

VALVE CLEARANCE SPECIFICATIONS

Year	Stem-To-Guide Clearance	
	Intake	Exhaust
1993–95	.008	.012

VALVE ADJUSTMENT

Valves are adjusted by use of an adjustment screw and locknut. With engine at operating temperature,

1. Crank engine until No. 1 cylinder is at TDC compression stroke and adjust cylinder No. 1 and cylinder No. 2 intake valves, then exhaust Nos. 1 and 3.
2. Rotate engine one complete revolution clockwise and adjust cylinder No. 3 and cylinder No. 4 intake valves, then exhaust Nos. 2 and 4.

VALVE GUIDES

1. Using a suitable tool and hammer, strike valve guide bushing to break it off at cylinder head casting.
2. Heat cylinder head to 176–212°F (80–100°C).
3. Using suitable valve guide removal tool, tap out bushing.
4. Install snap ring on new valve guide, then install new valve guide using tool as above and driving in from reverse side of removal.
5. Ream new valve guide, if necessary. Refer to "Valve Clearance Specifications" for stem clearances.

FRONT COVER SEAL

REPLACE

1. Remove accessory drive belts, then the crankshaft pulley.
2. Cut seal lip and pry out seal using a screwdriver.
3. Apply suitable grease to seal lip, then using seal installer tool No. 09223-50010, or equivalent, install new seal.
4. Install crankshaft pulley and drive belts.

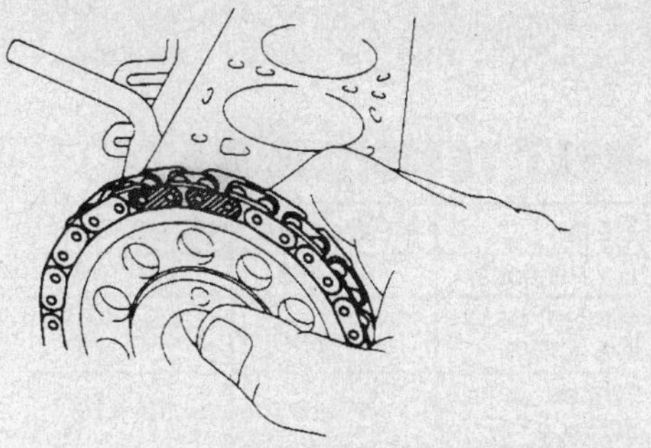
TY1069100227000X

Fig. 5 Timing chain to camshaft sprocket alignment

TIMING CHAIN

REPLACE

REMOVAL

1. Remove cylinder head as outlined under "Cylinder Head, Replace."
2. Remove radiator, oil pan and all drive belts.
3. **On 4WD models,** remove front differential.
4. **On all models,** remove air pump (if equipped), A/C compressor and bracket, generator adjuster bracket, cooling fan, water pump pulley and crankshaft pulley.
5. Remove water bypass tube, then the heater water outlet tube.
6. Remove fan belt adjusting bar.
7. Remove timing chain cover bolts, then, using plastic mallet, loosen timing chain cover and remove.
8. Remove chain from damper, then the camshaft sprocket and chain.
9. Remove oil pump drive spline, then the camshaft sprocket. **If spline and sprocket cannot be removed by hand, use a suitable puller.**

INSTALLATION

1. Rotate crankshaft until keyway is at TDC. Install sprocket onto crankshaft, then the chain onto the sprocket with light colored link aligned with sprocket timing mark, **Fig. 4.**
2. Install chain onto camshaft sprocket with sprocket timing mark between two light colored links, **Fig. 5.**
3. Slide oil pump drive spline over crankshaft and key. **If installation is difficult, drive spline on with hammer and suitable socket.**
4. Install timing cover gasket, then the timing cover. Tighten bolts specifications.
5. Install fan belt adjusting bar and tighten to specification.
6. Install crankshaft pulley and tighten bolt to specification. **Do not rotate crankshaft while tightening bolt.**
7. Install water bypass tube, then the heater water outlet tube.
8. Install air pump (if equipped), A/C compressor and bracket, generator adjuster bracket, cooling fan, water pump pulley and crankshaft pulley.
9. Install cylinder head as outlined under "Cylinder Head, Replace."

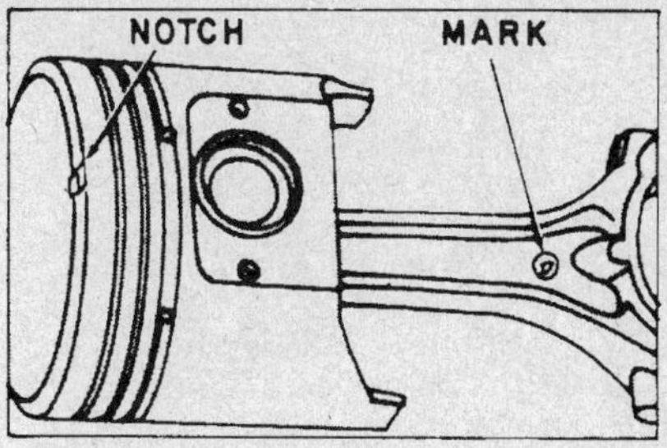
NOTCH
MARK
TY1069100228000X

Fig. 6 Piston & connecting rod assembly

10. Install radiator, oil pan and all drive belts.

CAMSHAFT

REPLACE

Refer to "Cylinder Head, Replace" for camshaft removal procedures.

PISTON & ROD ASSEMBLY

Pistons are available in standard and oversize of .020 inch (.50 mm) and .040 inch (1.00 mm). When assembling piston onto connecting rod, ensure mark on top of piston and mark on connecting rod are on same side, **Fig. 6.** When installing piston and connecting rod assembly, ensure mark on top of piston is facing toward front of engine. **When tightening connecting rods, ensure bolt does not rotate inside rod as this will result in lower torque than specified.**

MAIN & ROD BEARINGS

Main and connecting rod bearings are available in standard and undersizes of .010 inch (.25 mm).

CRANKSHAFT REAR OIL SEAL

REPLACE

1. Remove engine as outlined under "Engine, Replace."
2. Cut seal lip and pry out seal using a screwdriver.
3. Apply suitable grease to seal lip, then using seal installer tool No. 09223-41020, or equivalent, install new seal.
4. Install engine into vehicle.

OIL PAN

REPLACE

1. Remove oil pan and oil strainer.
2. Remove crankshaft bolt and pulley.
3. Remove drive belts and crankshaft pulley.
4. **On models with A/C,** remove A/C compressor and bracket.
5. **On all models,** remove oil pump assembly.

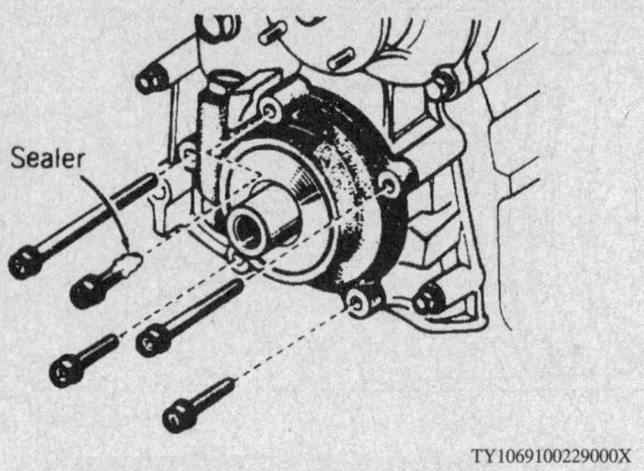
Sealer
TY1069100229000X

Fig. 7 Sealed bolt location

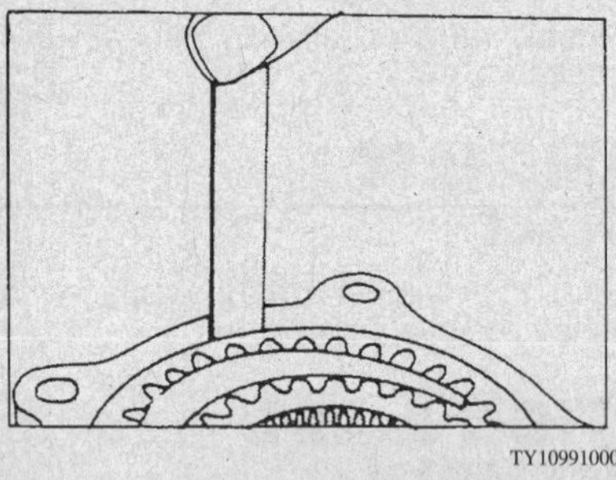
TY1099100028000X

Fig. 9 Driven rotor & pump body clearance inspection

6. Reverse procedure to install. Apply sealer to bolt shown in **Fig. 7.**

OIL PUMP

REPLACE

Refer to "Oil Pan, Replace" for procedure.

OIL PUMP SERVICE

1. To disassemble pump, remove oil pump drive spline and O-ring, then the relief valve plug, spring, relief valve piston and gears, **Fig. 8.**
2. Inspect drive spline, drive and driven gears, pump body and timing chain cover for excessive wear or damage.
3. Measure driven gear to body clearance, **Fig. 9.** Maximum clearance is .008 inch (.2 mm).
4. Measure clearances between drive gear and crescent and driven gear and crescent, **Fig. 10.** Maximum clearance is .012 inch.
5. Using a feeler gauge, measure side clearance using a straightedge placed across housing and gears, **Fig. 11.** Clearance should be .006 inch (.15 mm).
6. Check relief valve piston, oil passages and sliding surfaces for burrs or scoring.
7. Inspect crankshaft front oil seal and replace if worn, damaged or cracked.

BELT TENSION DATA

Belt	New, Lbs.	Used, Lbs.
Conventional	100–150	60–100
Ribbed, Less A/C & P/S	90–140	65–105
Ribbed, w/A/C & P/S	140–180	80–120

COOLING SYSTEM BLEED

These engines do not require a specified bleed procedure. After filling cooling system, run engine to operating temperature with radiator/pressure cap off. Air will then be automatically bled through cap opening.

THERMOSTAT

REPLACE

1. Drain cooling system, then disconnect vacuum and PCV hoses.
2. Disconnect radiator inlet hose, then remove thermostat housing.
3. Remove thermostat and gasket.
4. Reverse procedure to install.

WATER PUMP

REPLACE

1. Drain cooling system and remove fan belt.
2. Remove fan clutch attaching nuts, then the fan pulley and fan clutch as an assembly, **Fig. 12.**
3. If necessary, remove fan from fan clutch.
4. Remove bolts and water pump.
5. Reverse procedure to install.

RADIATOR

REPLACE

1. Disconnect battery ground cable.
2. Drain engine coolant.
3. Remove engine under covers.
4. Remove air intake connector.
5. Disconnect coolant reservoir hose.
6. Disconnect radiator hoses.
7. **On models with A/C,** remove No. 2 fan shroud.
8. **On all models,** remove No. 1 fan shroud.
9. **On models with automatic transmission,** disconnect transmission oil cooler hoses.

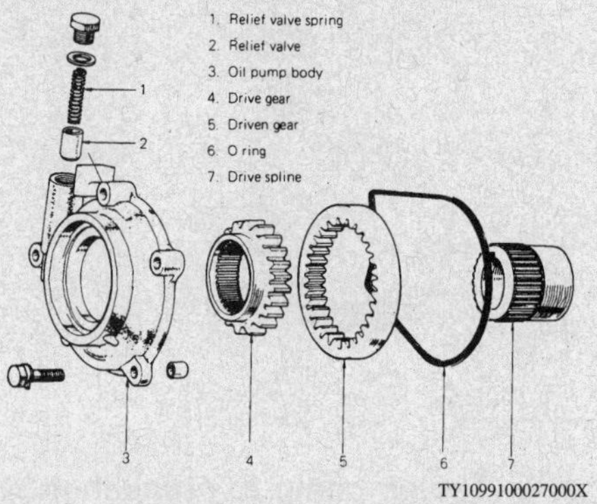
1. Relief valve spring
2. Relief valve
3. Oil pump body
4. Drive gear
5. Driven gear
6. O ring
7. Drive spline
1
2
3
4
5
6
7
TY1099100027000X

Fig. 8 Exploded view of oil pump

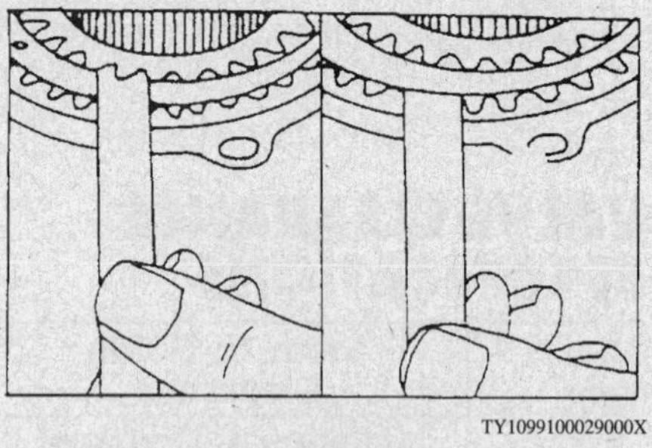
TY1099100029000X

Fig. 10 Oil pump drive gear clearance inspection

10. **On all models,** remove radiator supports and radiator.
11. Reverse procedure to install.

FUEL PUMP

REPLACE

1. Drain fuel from tank.
2. Remove fuel tank, then the fuel pump bracket from tank.
3. Remove fuel pump from fuel pump bracket. Disconnect wires.
4. Remove fuel pump from fuel hose, then the filter from pump.
5. Reverse procedure to install.

FUEL FILTER

REPLACE

1. **On models with audio coded anti-theft system**refer to "Precautions." **On all models,** disconnect battery ground cable.
2. Place suitable container under fuel filter to allow fuel drainage.
3. Slowly disconnect fuel hose from fuel filter, **Fig. 13. Place shop towel over connection to avoid fuel spilling on engine.**
4. Remove fuel filter and cap or plug fuel hose.
5. Reverse procedure to install.

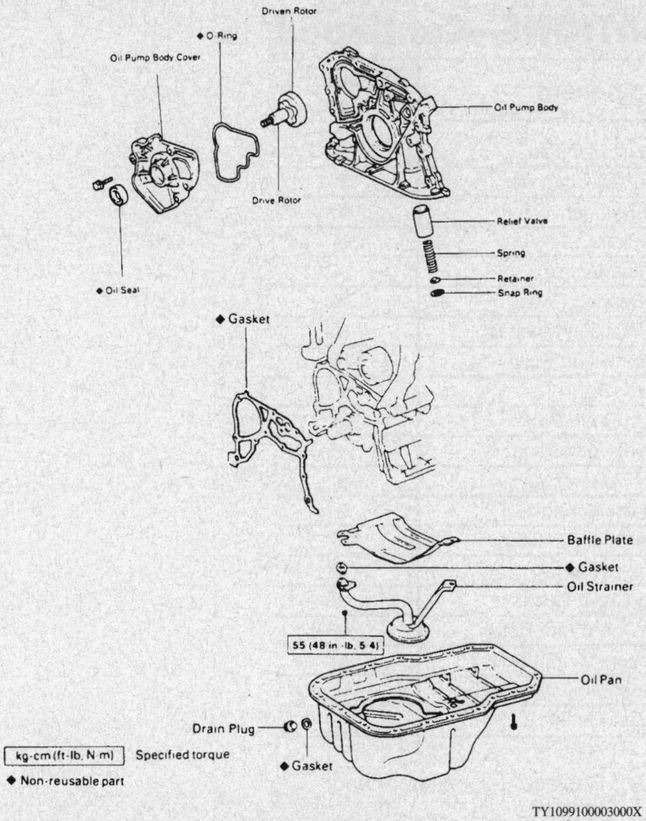
Driven Rotor
◆ O-Ring
Oil Pump Body Cover
Oil Pump Body
Drive Rotor
Relief Valve
Spring
Retainer
Snap Ring
◆ Oil Seal
◆ Gasket
Baffle Plate
◆ Gasket
Oil Strainer
55 (48 in.-lb, 5.4)
Oil Pan
Drain Plug
kg-cm (ft-lb, N·m) Specified torque
◆ Gasket
◆ Non-reusable part
TY1099100003000X

Fig. 11 Side clearance between rotor & cover inspection

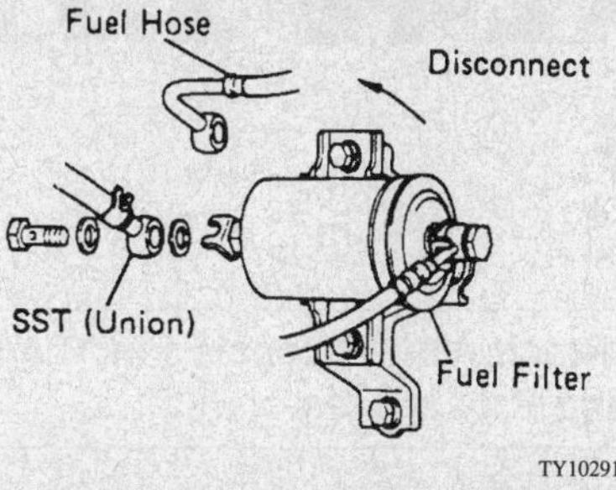
Fuel Hose
Disconnect
SST (Union)
Fuel Filter
TY1029100014000X

Fig. 13 Fuel filter replacement

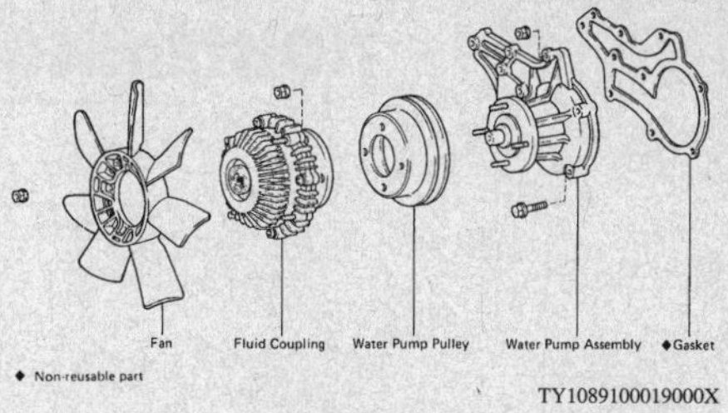
Fan
Fluid Coupling
Water Pump Pulley
Water Pump Assembly
◆ Gasket
◆ Non-reusable part
TY1089100019000X

Fig. 12 Exploded view of water pump

TIGHTENING SPECIFICATIONS

Year	Component	Torque/Ft. Lbs.
1993–95	Camshaft Bearing Cap	14
	Chain Damper	16
	Chain Tensioner	14
	Connecting Rod Cap	51
	Crankshaft Pulley	116
	Cylinder Head	②
	Cylinder Head Cover	52①
	Cylinder Head Rear Cover	9
	Distributor Drive Gear	58
	Driveplate	61
	EGR Valve	9
	Engine Mounting Bolts	29
	Engine Mounting Bracket	33

Continued

TIGHTENING SPECIFICATIONS—Continued

Year	Component	Torque/Ft. Lbs.
1993–95	Exhaust Manifold	33
	Fan Belt Adjusting Bar	9
	Flywheel	80
	Fuel Filter Bracket	14
	Intake Manifold	14
	Main Bearing Caps	76
	No. 1 Air Injection Manifold	9
	No. 2 Crankshaft Pulley	14
	Oil Pan	9
	Oil Pan Drain Plug	18
	Oil Relief Valve Plug	27
	Oil Strainer	9
	Radiator Support	9
	Rear Oil Seal Retainer	13
	Spark Plug	13
	Timing Chain Cover	9
	Timing Cover, 8 mm Bolts	9
	Timing Cover, 10 mm Bolts	29
	Valve Clearance Adjusting Screw	18
	Water Outlet	14

① — Inch lbs.
② — Refer to "Cylinder Head, Replace" for cylinder head cover tightening specifications.

2RZ-FE 2.4L & 3RZ-FE 2.7L Engines

NOTE: On Air Bag Equipped Models, Refer To "Air Bag System Precautions" Located In The Front Of This Manual For System Disarming & Arming Procedures.

INDEX

	Page No.
Balance Shaft, Replace	47-36
Belt Tension Data	47-38
Camshaft, Replace	47-36
Compression Pressure	47-33
Cooling System Bleed	47-38
Crankshaft Rear Oil Seal, Replace	47-37
Cylinder Head, Replace	47-36
Engine Rebuilding Specifications	48-1
Engine, Replace	47-33
Front Cover Seal, Replace	47-36
Fuel Filter, Replace	47-40
Fuel Pump, Replace	47-40
Intake Manifold, Replace	47-34
Main & Rod Bearings	47-37
Oil Pan, Replace	47-37
Oil Pump, Replace	47-37
Oil Pump Service	47-37
Piston & Rod Assembly	47-37
Precautions	47-32
Air Bag Systems	47-32
Audio Coded Anti-Theft System	47-32
Radiator, Replace	47-40
Thermostat, Replace	47-38
Tightening Specifications	47-41
Timing Chain, Replace	47-36
Valve Adjustment	47-36
Valve Clearance Specifications	47-36
Valve Guides	47-36
Water Pump, Replace	47-38

PRECAUTIONS

AIR BAG SYSTEMS

Refer to "Air Bag System Precautions" in the front of this manual for system disarming and arming procedures.

AUDIO CODED ANTI-THEFT SYSTEM

Some models are equipped with an audio coded anti-theft system that will disable the radio when the battery cable is disconnected. The system can be identified by the "ANTI-THEFT SYSTEM" on the cassette lid. Obtain three-digit code for input. Reset system after service as follows:

1. Obtain three-digit audio theft code.

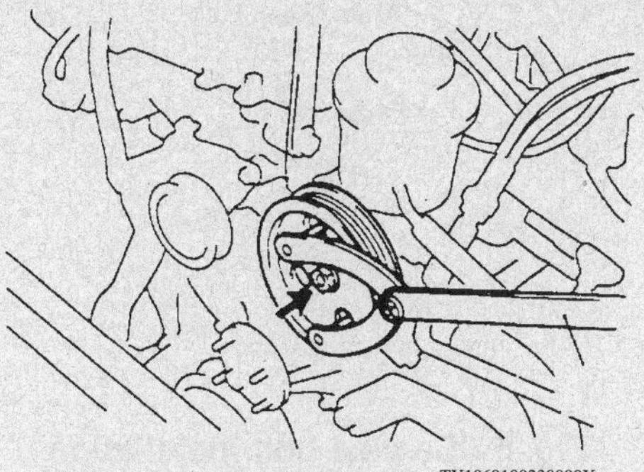

TY1069100230000X

Fig. 1 Power steering pump pulley removal

2. Depress 1 (PROG) button while depressing righthand side of TUNE SEEK button. Three dashes will appear in tape operation display.
3. To enter first digit, depress 1 (PROG) button repeatedly until number of times depressed equals first digit (depress 1 button six times if first digit is five, first press equals 0).
4. To enter second digit, depress 2 (APS) button repeatedly until number of times depressed equals second digit.
5. To enter third digit, depress 3 (RPT) button repeatedly until number of times depressed equals third digit.
6. If three dashes are displayed after inputting digits, repeat procedure.
7. When code appears in display, depress and hold SCAN button until SEC appears.
8. When SEC disappears audio system is operative.
9. If Err is displayed, repeat procedure. **Attempting to input code more than nine times may permanently disable audio system.**

COMPRESSION PRESSURE

1. Start engine and warm to normal operating temperature.
2. Disconnect intake air connector.
3. Disconnect high tension cords from spark plugs and distributor.
4. Remove spark plugs.
5. Insert compression gauge into spark plug hole.
6. Fully open throttle.
7. While cranking engine, measure compression pressure.
8. Standard compression pressure should be 178 psi. Minimum compression is 127 psi.
9. The difference in compression pressure between each cylinder should not exceed 14 psi.

ENGINE

REPLACE

1. **On models with audio coded anti-theft system,** obtain three-digit system code.
2. **On all models,** remove battery, then the engine under covers.

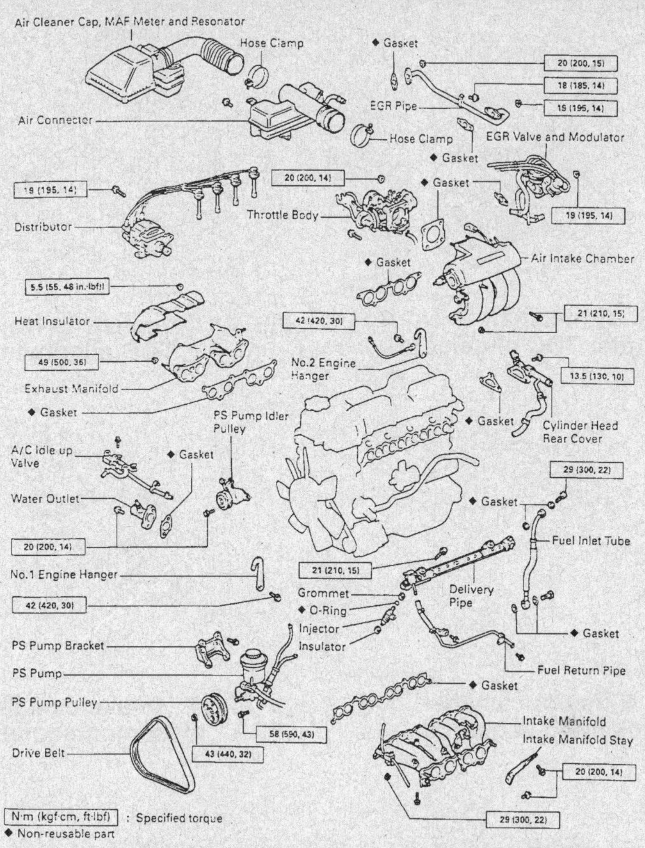

Air Cleaner Cap, MAF Meter and Resonator
Hose Clamp
◆ Gasket
Air Connector
EGR Pipe
Hose Clamp
EGR Valve and Modulator
◆ Gasket
◆ Gasket
Distributor
Throttle Body
Air Intake Chamber
◆ Gasket
Heat Insulator
Exhaust Manifold
◆ Gasket
No.2 Engine Hanger
PS Pump Idler Pulley
◆ Gasket
Cylinder Head Rear Cover
A/C Idle-up Valve
◆ Gasket
Water Outlet
◆ Gasket
Fuel Inlet Tube
No.1 Engine Hanger
Grommet
◆ O-Ring
Injector
Insulator
Delivery Pipe
◆ Gasket
PS Pump Bracket
PS Pump
Fuel Return Pipe
PS Pump Pulley
◆ Gasket
Intake Manifold
Intake Manifold Stay
Drive Belt
N·m (kgf·cm, ft·lbf) : Specified torque
◆ Non-reusable part

TY1069100231000X

Fig. 2 Exploded view of engine components

3. Drain engine coolant and oil, drain transmission oil.
4. Make alignment marks on hood hinges, then remove hood.
5. Remove grill and radiator as follows:
   a. Remove two screws holding lefthand and righthand clearance lights, then the lights.
   b. Remove four screws and 11 clips holding grill, then the grill.
   c. Remove radiator hoses, then the radiator reservoir tank.
   d. Remove drive belts, then the cooling fan and fan shroud as a unit.
   e. Remove four radiator mounting bolts, then the radiator.
6. Remove MAF sensor, IAT sensor, air hose and upper air cleaner as a unit, then the lower air cleaner housing.
7. Disconnect throttle cable from throttle body, then remove intake air connector tube.
8. **On models with A/C,** remove compressor without disconnecting hoses or discharging system. Move and secure compressor aside. Remove compressor mount bracket from engine.
9. **On all models** disconnect heater hoses, brake booster hose and emission system hoses. Disconnect fuel system pressure and return hoses,
10. **On models with power steering,** remove power steering pump pulley using flexible Y wrench, tool No. 09960-10010, or equivalent, to hold pulley, **Fig. 1.** Then, without disconnecting hoses, remove power steering pump and position aside.
11. **On all models** disconnect wires from alternator.
12. Remove righthand side door scuff plate and kick panel trim. Remove ECM, then disconnect engine compartment wiring, prepare wiring to be pulled through cowl into engine compartment.
13. In engine compartment disconnect engine harness from igniter. Remove ground strap bolt, disconnect harness support clamps, then pull engine harness through firewall.
14. Remove gear shift knob and boot, then the lever by removing six bolts holding shifter housing to transmission.
15. Remove front anti-sway bar, then the complete driveshaft. Place matchmarks on driveshaft and differential flanges. Install suitable sealing tool into transmission tailshaft housing to prevent leakage.
16. Disconnect speedometer cable and both oxygen sensor connectors, then remove front exhaust pipe.
17. Remove clutch slave cylinder, then disconnect starter wiring.
18. Support transmission using suitable equipment, then remove transmission mount bracket from frame and transmission.
19. Attach suitable equipment to engine, remove righthand and lefthand motor mount bolts, then lift engine and transmission from vehicle.
20. Separate engine from transmission.
21. Reverse procedure to install. Reset audio coded anti-theft system, if

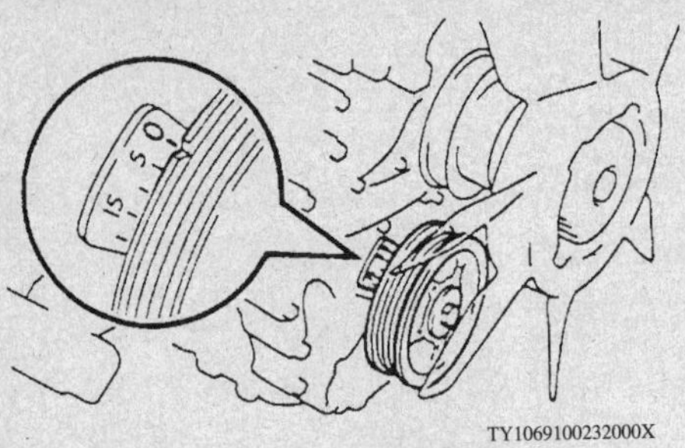
TY1069100232000X

Fig. 3 Crankshaft to No. 1 cylinder TDC alignment

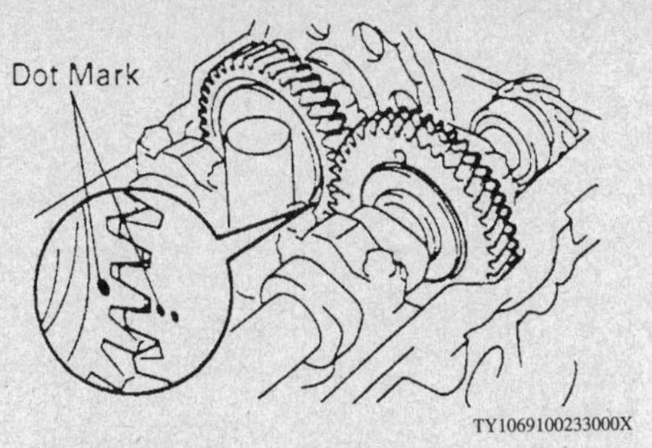
Dot Mark
TY1069100233000X

Fig. 4 Camshaft to No. 1 cylinder TDC alignment

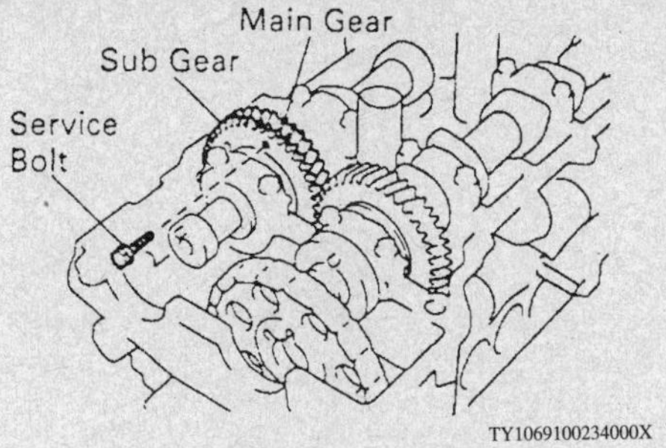
Main Gear
Sub Gear
Service Bolt
TY1069100234000X

Fig. 5 Service bolt installation

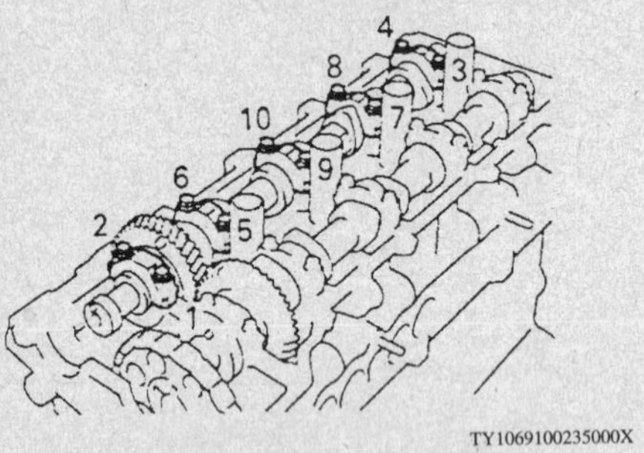
4
8
3
10
7
6
9
2
5
1
TY1069100235000X

Fig. 6 Exhaust camshaft bolt loosening sequence

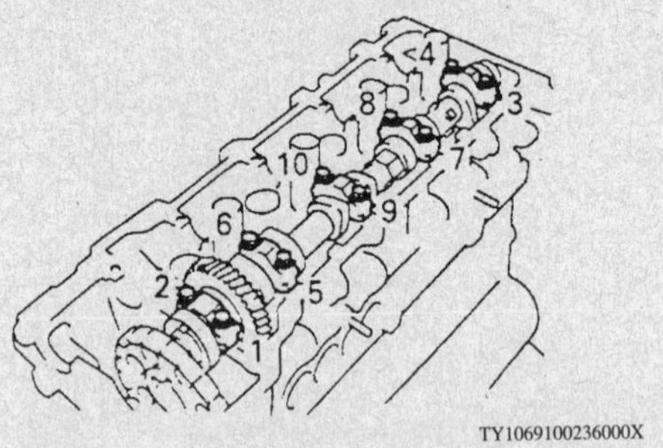
4
8
3
7
10
9
6
2
5
1
TY1069100236000X

Fig. 7 Intake camshaft bolt loosening sequence

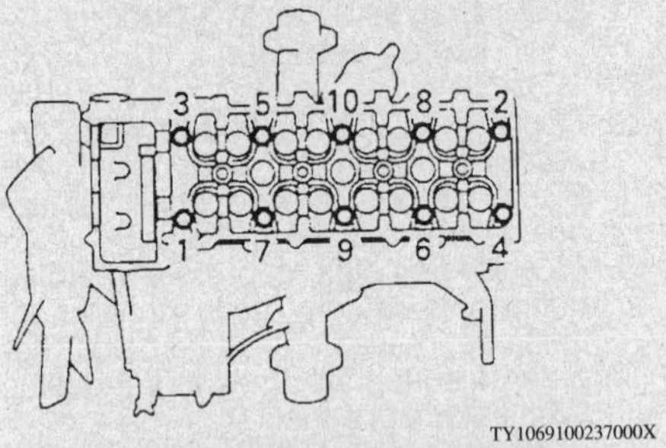
3 5 10 8 2
1 7 9 6 4
TY1069100237000X

Fig. 8 Cylinder head bolt loosening sequence

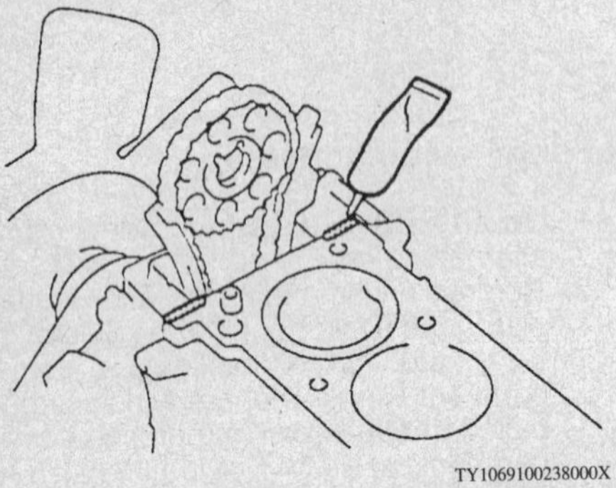
TY1069100238000X

Fig. 9 Cylinder head sealer application

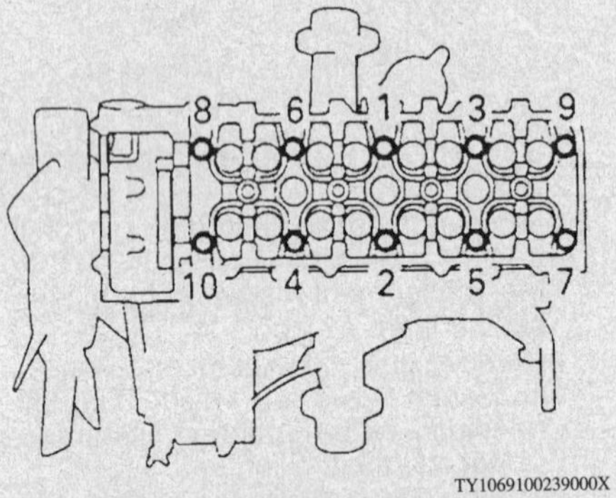
8 6 1 3 9
10 4 2 5 7
TY1069100239000X

Fig. 10 Cylinder head bolt tightening sequence

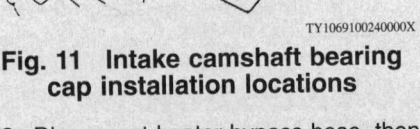

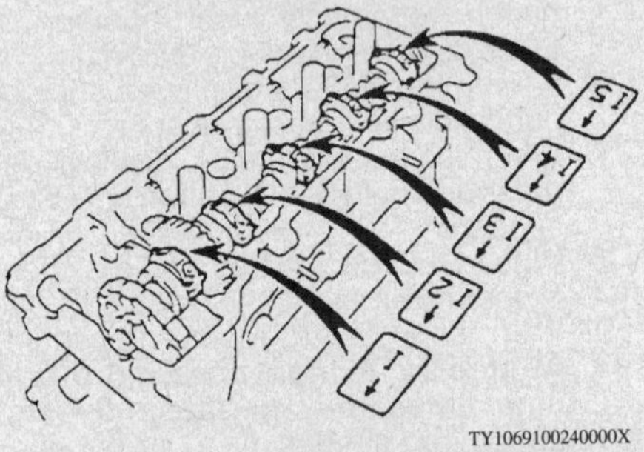
TY1069100240000X

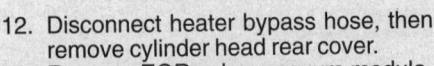

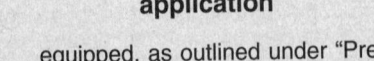

Fig. 11 Intake camshaft bearing cap installation locations

equipped, as outlined under "Precautions."

INTAKE MANIFOLD

REPLACE

Refer to "Cylinder Head, Replace" for procedure.

CYLINDER HEAD

REPLACE

1. **On models with audio coded anti-theft system,** obtain three-digit system code.
2. **On all models,** disconnect battery ground cable.
3. Drain coolant from engine.
4. Remove MAF sensor, IAT sensor, air hose and upper air cleaner as a unit, then the lower air cleaner housing, **Fig. 2.**
5. Disconnect throttle cable from throttle body, then remove intake air connector tube.
6. **On models with A/C,** remove A/C idle-up valve.
7. **On models with power steering,** proceed as follows:
   a. Remove power steering belt and idler pulley.
   b. Remove power steering pump pulley using flexible Y wrench, tool No. 09960-10010, or equivalent, to hold pulley, **Fig. 1.**
   c. Then, without disconnecting hoses, remove power steering pump and position aside.
   d. Remove power steering pump mounting bracket.
8. **On all models,** disconnect spark plug wires, then disconnect and remove complete distributor.
9. Disconnect and remove water outlet and ECT sender form engine as a unit.
10. Disconnect and remove all connectors and hoses from throttle body, then remove throttle body.
11. Disconnect all electrical connectors and wiring attached to cylinder head and components.
12. Disconnect heater bypass hose, then remove cylinder head rear cover.
13. Remove EGR valve, vacuum modulator and connecting pipe, disconnecting necessary water and vacuum lines.
14. Remove intake chamber stay, then the fuel return pipe. When disconnecting fuel lines use a suitable container to collect any spilled fuel, loosen fuel connections slowly to allow pressure to bleed off.
15. Remove bolts to remove intake air chamber from intake manifold, then the fuel inlet tube.
16. Remove fuel delivery pipe and injectors as a unit, then the intake manifold.
17. Disconnect both oxygen sensor connectors, then remove front exhaust pipe.
18. Remove exhaust manifold, then the No. 1 and No. 2 engine hanger hooks.
19. Remove cylinder head cover, then the spark plugs.
20. Turning engine clockwise, set No. 1 cylinder to TDC compression stroke **Figs. 3 and 4.** Remove timing chain tensioner.
21. Remove two rubber semi-circular

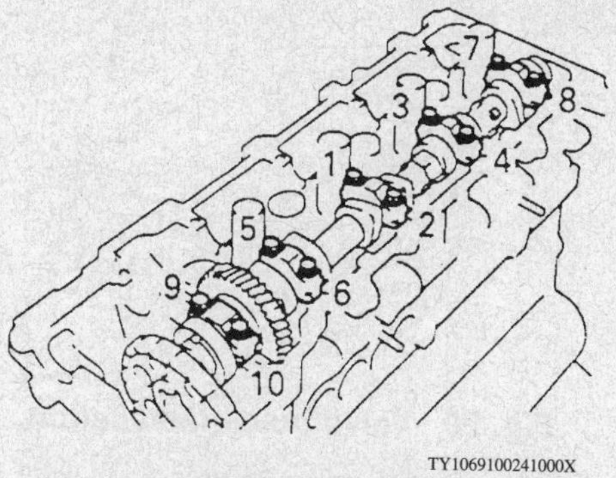
7
3
8
1
4
5
2
9
6
10
TY1069100241000X

Fig. 12 Intake camshaft bearing cap bolt tightening sequence

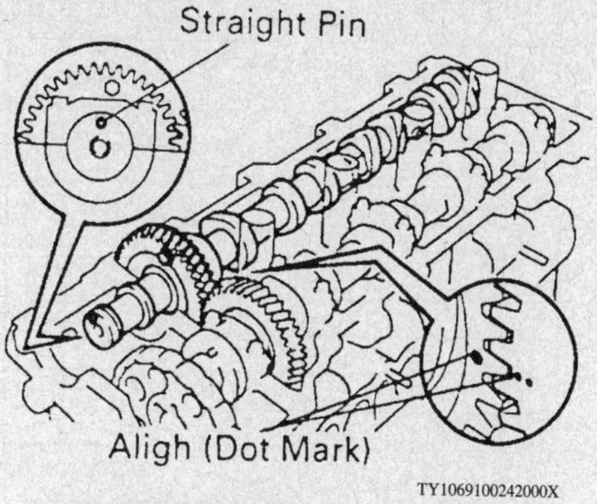
Straight Pin
Aligh (Dot Mark)
TY1069100242000X

Fig. 13 Exhaust to intake camshaft timing marks

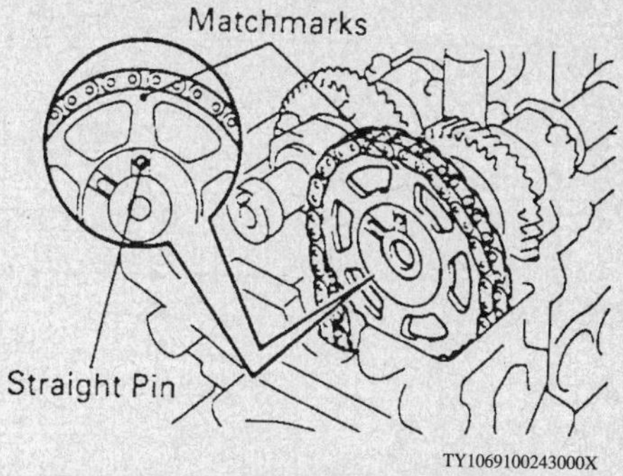
Matchmarks
Straight Pin
TY1069100243000X

Fig. 14 Camshaft alignment marks

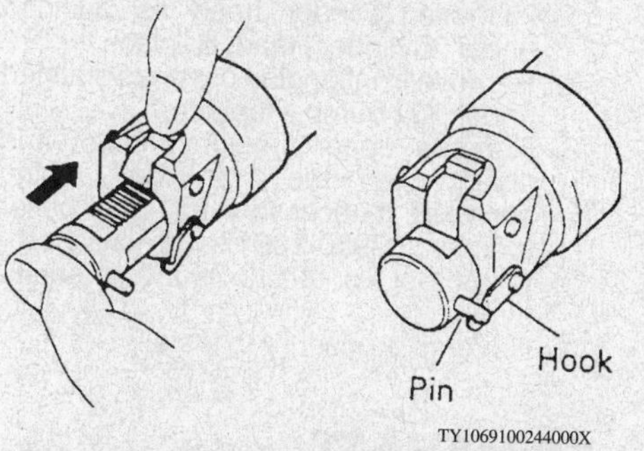
Hook
Pin
TY1069100244000X

Fig. 15 Timing chain tensioner

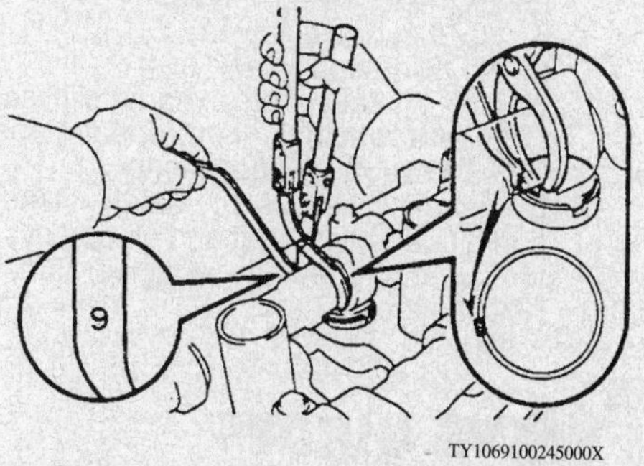
9
TY1069100245000X

Fig. 16 Compressing valve lifter

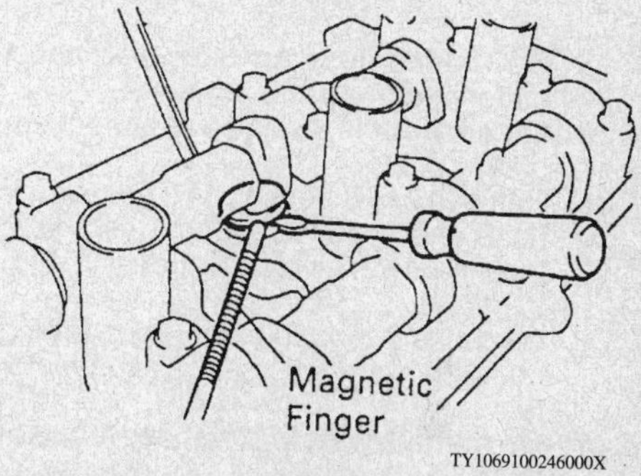
Magnetic
Finger
TY1069100246000X

Fig. 17 Valve adjustment shim removal

plugs from head, then place a suitable wrench on the hex part of exhaust camshaft, remove distributor gear and bolt.

22. Place a suitable wrench on hex part of intake camshaft, then remove cam drive sprocket and bolt. Allow chain and sprocket to rest on chain guide rails.
23. Turn exhaust camshaft with a suitable wrench until service bolt hole is accessible, **Fig. 5.**Install a 6 X 1.0 X 16-20 mm bolt into service hole to secure spring loaded sub gear to main exhaust camshaft gear.
    a. Loosen camshaft bearing caps in several stages in sequence shown in **Fig. 6,** then remove bearing caps.
    b. Camshaft must be lifted from head straight and level. **Do not pry or use force. Due to tight tolerances, if cam is not lifted out of cylinder head straight and level, cam or head breakage could occur.** If binding occurs reinstall No. 3 bearing cap, lightly tighten bolts, then while lifting cam gear, loosen bearing cap bolts evenly to allow camshaft to come out of head straight and level.
    c. Repeat steps a and b above to remove intake camshaft, using sequence shown in **Fig. 7** to loosen bearing caps.
24. Remove two cylinder head bolts located inside front of cam chain passage, then loosen cylinder head bolts in several stages in sequence shown in **Fig. 8.**
25. Lift cylinder head up off of dowel pins to remove from engine.
26. Remove and store, keeping together in order, lifters, adjustment shims, valves, valve springs and retainers.
27. Reverse procedure to install, noting the following:
    a. Tighten all fasteners to specifications. Before installing head gasket, apply a suitable sealer to areas shown in **Fig. 9,** then place head gasket and cylinder head onto block.
    b. Install cylinder head bolts with lightly oiled threads. Using sequence shown in **Fig. 10, torque** bolts in three steps: first, to 29 ft. lbs.; then an additional 90°; and finally, an additional 90°.
    c. Install two cylinder head bolts located at front of cam chain well. **Torque** bolts to 15 ft. lbs.
    d. Install intake camshaft first. Lightly grease thrust bearing surfaces with a MP grease. Ensure bearing caps are installed as shown in **Fig. 11** with dowel pin, on drive sprocket flange pointing up. Tighten bearing cap bolts in several stages, **Fig. 12,** then **torque** bearing cap bolts to 12 ft. lbs. in sequence shown.
    e. Install exhaust camshaft using above procedure. Ensure timing marks on camshaft gears are aligned, **Fig. 13.** After bearing cap bolts have been tightened, remove exhaust camshaft gear service bolt.
    f. Set engine to TDC No. 1 cylinder, **Fig. 3.**
    g. Align matchmarks on timing chain to sprocket, then install sprocket to camshaft, **Fig. 14.**
    h. Holding intake camshaft with suitable wrench **torque** sprocket bolt to 54 ft. lbs. Install distributor drive gear, then holding exhaust camshaft with a suitable wrench **torque** drive gear bolt to 34 ft. lbs.
    i. Compress and hook chain tensioner pin, **Fig. 15,** then install tensioner. Release tensioner by turning crankshaft counterclockwise or by pressing in on tensioner rail with a screwdriver so that tensioner hook is released.
    j. Use new O-rings when installing fuel injectors and distributor. Refer to "Distributor, Replace" in "Electrical" section for distributor procedures. Refer to " Valve Adjustment" for procedures.
    k. Reset audio coded anti-theft system, if equipped, as outlined under "Precautions."

VALVE CLEARANCE SPECIFICATIONS

Year	Stem-To-Guide Clearance	
	Intake	Exhaust
1994–96	.006–.010	.010–.014

VALVE ADJUSTMENT

1. **On models with audio coded anti-theft system,**obtain three-digit system code.
2. **On models with air bag,** disable system as outlined under "Precautions."

New shim thickness mm (in.)

Shim No.	Thickness	Shim No.	Thickness
1	2.500 (0.0984)	10	2.950 (0.1161)
2	2.550 (0.1004)	11	3.000 (0.1181)
3	2.600 (0.1024)	12	3.050 (0.1201)
4	2.650 (0.1043)	13	3.100 (0.1220)
5	2.700 (0.1063)	14	3.150 (0.1240)
6	2.750 (0.1083)	15	3.200 (0.1260)
7	2.800 (0.1102)	16	3.250 (0.1280)
8	2.850 (0.1122)	17	3.300 (0.1299)
9	2.900 (0.1142)		

TY1069100247000X

Fig. 18 Intake camshaft shim table

New shim thickness mm (in.)

Shim No.	Thickness	Shim No.	Thickness
1	2.500 (0.0984)	10	2.950 (0.1161)
2	2.550 (0.1004)	11	3.000 (0.1181)
3	2.600 (0.1024)	12	3.050 (0.1201)
4	2.650 (0.1043)	13	3.100 (0.1220)
5	2.700 (0.1063)	14	3.150 (0.1240)
6	2.750 (0.1083)	15	3.200 (0.1260)
7	2.800 (0.1102)	16	3.250 (0.1280)
8	2.850 (0.1122)	17	3.300 (0.1299)
9	2.900 (0.1142)		

TY1069100248000X

Fig. 19 Exhaust camshaft shim table

3. **On models less air bag,** disconnect battery ground cable.
4. **On all models,** drain coolant from engine.
5. Remove MAF sensor, IAT sensor, air hose and upper air cleaner as a unit, then the lower air cleaner housing, **Fig. 2.**
6. Disconnect throttle cable from throttle body, then remove intake air connector tube.
7. **On models with A/C,** remove A/C idle-up valve.
8. **On all models,** disconnect spark plug wires.
9. Disconnect and remove all connectors and hoses from throttle body, then remove throttle body.
10. Disconnect electrical connectors and wiring attached to cylinder head cover, then remove cylinder head cover.
11. With engine cold, set engine to No. 1 cylinder TDC compression stroke by aligning matchmarks shown in **Figs. 3 and 13.**
12. With engine in this position check clearance of the following valves:
    a. No. 1 intake and exhaust valves.
    b. No. 2 intake valves.
    c. No. 3 exhaust valves.
    d. Record these readings.
13. If any measurement was found outside specifications, remove valve adjustment shim using valve lifter cam wrench set tool No. SST 09248-55040, or equivalent, to depress lifter and a magnet to remove shim, **Figs. 16 and 17.**
14. Using a micrometer measure thickness of removed shim, record this dimension.
15. Determine difference between desired and actual valve clearance measurement, add difference to dimension of measured shim. Refer to shim charts, **Figs. 18 and 19** to select a replacement.
16. Install new shim in lifter, then remove lifter tools. Repeat steps 13 through 16 for any other valves found out of adjustment.
17. Rotate crankshaft pulley two full turns, recheck valves as outlined in steps 11 through 14.
18. Turn crankshaft pulley 360° (one complete revolution) and align timing marks as outlined previously and check the following valves:
    a. No. 2 exhaust valves.
    b. No. 3 intake valves.
    c. No. 4 intake and exhaust valves, record readings, then repeat steps 13 through 16 if necessary.
19. Reverse procedure to install. Reset audio coded anti-theft and air bag system, if equipped, as outlined under "Precautions."

VALVE GUIDES

Valve stem to guide oil clearance should not exceed 0.0031 inch for intake valves and 0.0039 inch for exhaust. If valve replacement will not bring clearance within standards, guide replacement will be necessary.

1. Using a suitable method, gradually heat cylinder head to 176–212°F.
2. Using valve guide driver tool No. 09201-10000, or equivalent, tap out guide from cylinder side.
3. Using a suitable measuring tool measure bore in cylinder head and select correct guide. Bore measurements between .4331 to .4341 inch. Use a standard guide. Measurements above .4341 require valve guide hole to be rebored to .4350 to .4361 inch and use of an oversize guide.
4. Heat cylinder head as outlined in step 1. Install new valve guide using tool as above and driving in from camshaft side leaving a protrusion of .0323 to .339 inch, **Fig. 20.**
5. Using a sharp .234 inch reamer, ream new valve guide if necessary. Refer to "Valve Specifications" for stem clearances.

FRONT COVER SEAL

REPLACE

1. Remove crankshaft pulley as outlined under "Oil Pump Replace."
2. Using a suitable tool pry out seal, using care not to damage crankshaft or seal housing.
3. Lubricate lips of new seal, then using seal driver tool No. 09223-50010, or equivalent, drive new seal into place.
4. Reverse procedure to install.

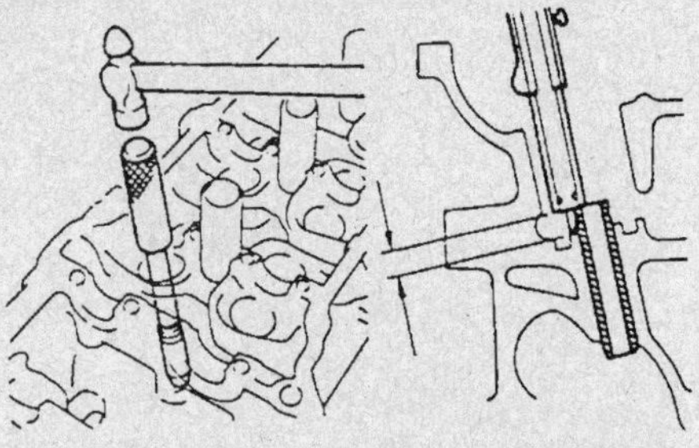

TY1069100249000X

Fig. 20 Valve guide installation

TIMING CHAIN

REPLACE

1. Remove cylinder head as outlined under "Cylinder Head, Replace."
2. Remove front engine cover as outlined under "Oil Pump, Replace."
3. Remove upper timing sprocket and chain, then the crankshaft timing sprocket. If necessary, use gear puller tool No. 09950-20017 with shaft protector tool No. 09213-36020, or equivalents.
4. Reverse procedure to install.

CAMSHAFT

REPLACE

Refer to "Cylinder Head, Replace" for camshaft replacement procedures.

BALANCE SHAFT

REPLACE

1. Remove camshaft/No. 1 timing chain as outlined under "Timing Chain, Replace."
2. Remove camshaft/No. 1 timing chain tension slipper and vibration damper, **Fig. 21.**
3. Install a pin into balance shaft/No. 2 timing chain tensioner, **Fig. 22.** Remove No. 2 and No. 3 balance shaft timing chain dampers, **Fig. 21.** Remove tensioner unit.
4. Remove balance shaft drive gear with shaft, lift off chain, slide sprocket off crankshaft.
5. Remove No. 4 balance shaft timing chain dampner.
6. Remove thrust plate retainer bolts, then slide the No. 1 and No. 2 balance shaft from the block.
7. Reverse procedure to install, noting the following:
    a. Fit balance shaft timing chain to crankshaft and balance shaft with sprocket, align match links and marks on sprockets, **Fig. 23.**
    b. Install balance shaft drive gear into chain aligning match link on chain to mark on sprocket part of drive gear, then align match marks of drive gear and balance shaft, **Fig. 23.**
    c. **Torque** drive gear shaft bolt to 18 ft. lbs.
    d. Tighten fasteners to specifications.

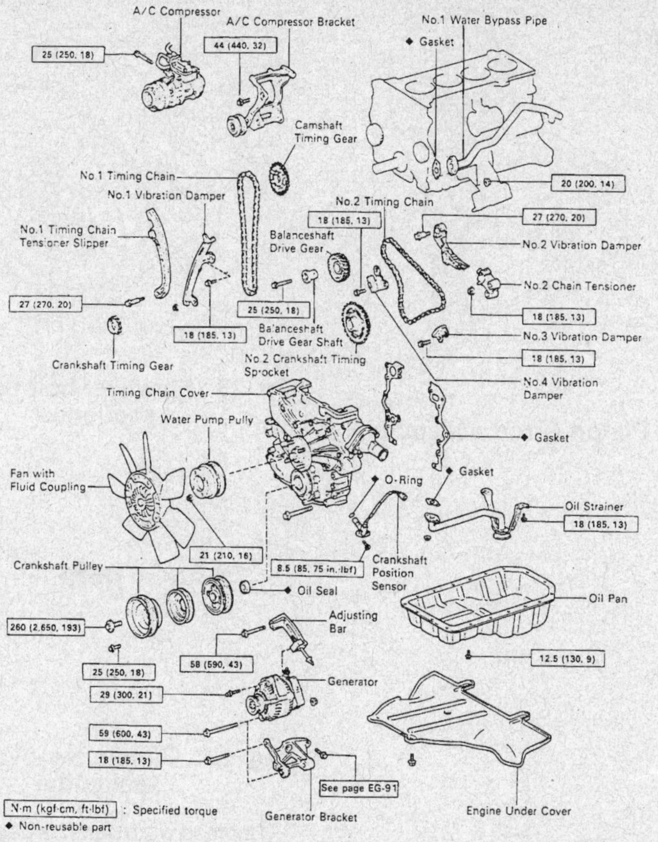
A/C Compressor
A/C Compressor Bracket
No.1 Water Bypass Pipe
◆ Gasket
25 (250, 18)
44 (440, 32)
Camshaft Timing Gear
No.1 Timing Chain
No.1 Vibration Damper
20 (200, 14)
No.2 Timing Chain
18 (185, 13)
27 (270, 20)
No.1 Timing Chain Tensioner Slipper
Balanceshaft Drive Gear
No.2 Vibration Damper
No.2 Chain Tensioner
27 (270, 20)
25 (250, 18)
18 (185, 13)
Balanceshaft Drive Gear Shaft
18 (185, 13)
No.3 Vibration Damper
Crankshaft Timing Gear
No.2 Crankshaft Timing Sprocket
18 (185, 13)
Timing Chain Cover
No.4 Vibration Damper
Water Pump Pully
◆ Gasket
Fan with Fluid Coupling
◆ O-Ring
Gasket
Oil Strainer
18 (185, 13)
21 (210, 16)
Crankshaft Pulley
8.5 (85, 75 in.·lbf)
Crankshaft Position Sensor
◆ Oil Seal
Oil Pan
260 (2,650, 193)
Adjusting Bar
12.5 (130, 9)
25 (250, 18)
58 (590, 43)
Generator
29 (300, 21)
59 (600, 43)
18 (185, 13)
See page EG-91
N·m (kgf·cm, ft·lbf) : Specified torque
◆ Non-reusable part
Generator Bracket
Engine Under Cover
TY1069100250000X

Fig. 21 Auxiliary engine components

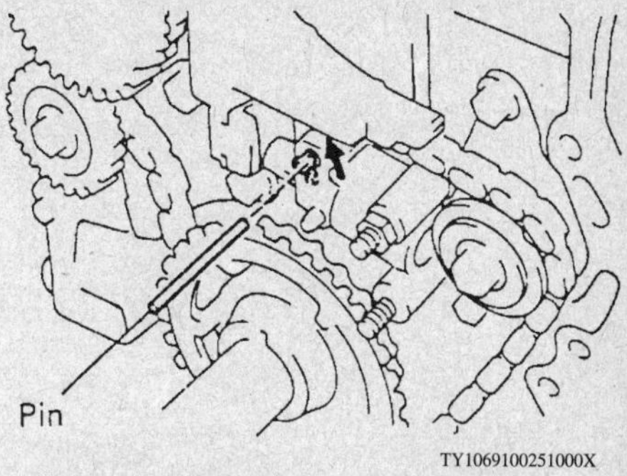
Pin
TY1069100251000X

Fig. 22 Balance shaft timing chain tensioner removal

PISTON & ROD ASSEMBLY

Pistons are available in standard and one oversize of .020 inch (.50 mm). Place match marks on connecting rod, cap and piston before disassembly. Pistons and rods are marked with a dimple to indicate front, **Fig. 24.**

MAIN & ROD BEARINGS

Main and rod bearings are available in standard and one undersize of .010 inch (.25 mm). Main bearing oil clearance is .0009 to .0019 inch for journals 1, 2, 4 and 5 and .0012 to .0022 inch for journal 3. Crankshaft thrust clearance is .0008 to 0.0087 inch. Connecting rod bearing oil clearance is .0012 to .0022 inch.

CRANKSHAFT REAR OIL SEAL

REPLACE

1. Remove engine as outlined under "Engine, Replace."
2. Remove clutch as outlined under "Clutch, Replace."
3. Remove flywheel, then using a suitable tool pry out seal, using care not to damage crankshaft or seal housing.
4. Lubricate lips of new seal, then using seal installer tool No. 09223-15030, or equivalent, drive new seal into place.
5. Reverse procedure to install. **Torque** flywheel bolts to 19 ft. lbs. in several stages in pattern shown in **Fig. 25,** then tighten an additional 90° using this pattern. Tighten fasteners to specifications.

OIL PAN

REPLACE

Refer to "Oil Pump Replace" for procedures.

OIL PUMP

REPLACE

1. Remove cylinder head as outlined in "Cylinder Head, Replace."
2. Remove engine undercover, then the belts.
3. Remove radiator shroud bolts.
4. Remove water pump pulley bolts, then the fan, fan coupling, water pump pulley, and fan shroud.
5. **On models with A/C,** without discharging refrigerant, remove compressor and secure aside, then the compressor mounting bracket.
6. **On all models,** remove alternator, adjusting bracket and mounting bracket.
7. Remove crankshaft position sensor, **Fig. 26.**
8. Remove two engine to transmission stiffener plates, then the oil pan bolts and nuts.
9. Using sealer cutter tool No. 09032-00100, or equivalent, **Fig. 27,** cut sealer to release oil pan. Use caution not to damage flanges.
10. Remove oil strainer and pick-up tube.
11. **On models with A/C,** remove bolts securing V-belt pulley to crankshaft pulley and remove pulley.
12. **On all models,** remove crankshaft pulley nut using holding tool Nos. 09213-54015 and 09330-00021, or equivalents, then the pulley, using gear puller and shaft protector tool Nos. 09213-60017 and 09950-20017, or equivalents, if necessary.
13. Remove two water bypass pipe bolts and two timing chain cover bolts, **Fig. 28,** then the nine bolts and two nuts holding timing chain cover to block.
14. Using a soft face hammer, tap loose timing chain cover, then slide assembly off crankshaft.
15. Reverse procedure to install, noting the following:
    a. **Torque** timing chain cover fasteners as follows, **Fig. 29,** bolt A to 14 ft. lbs., bolt B to 18 ft. lbs., bolt C to 32 ft. lbs. and nut D to 14 ft. lbs.
    b. Tighten fasteners to specifications.
    c. Apply sealer No. 08826-00080, or equivalent, to oil pan flange as shown in **Fig. 30.**

OIL PUMP SERVICE

1. With timing chain cover removed, remove nine screws holding pump cover to timing chain cover, then the cover, O-ring, drive and driven rotors.
2. Remove oil pressure relief valve snap ring, then the relief valve with spring.
3. Inspect oil relief valve piston and bore for sticking wear. Inspect case and pump cover for wear, cracks or breakage.
4. Measure driven rotor to body clearance, **Fig. 31.** Standard is .0039 to .0069 inch, worn is .0118 inch.
5. Measure rotor side clearance, **Fig. 32.** Standard is 0.0012 to 0.0035 inch, limit is 0.0059 inch.
6. Inspect rotor tip clearance, **Fig. 33.** Standard is .0043 to .0094 inch, limit is .0098 inch.

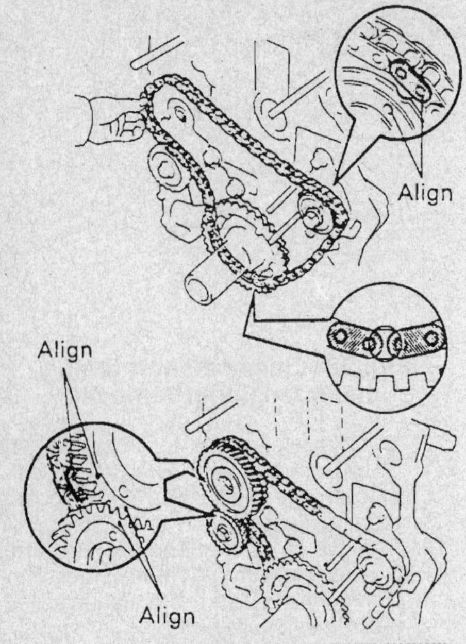
Align
Align
Align
TY1069100252000X

Fig. 23 Balance shaft timing mark alignment

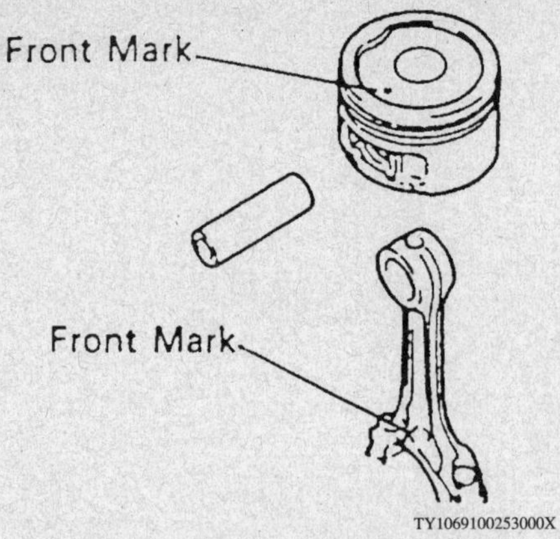
Front Mark
Front Mark
TY1069100253000X

Fig. 24 Piston & rod assembly

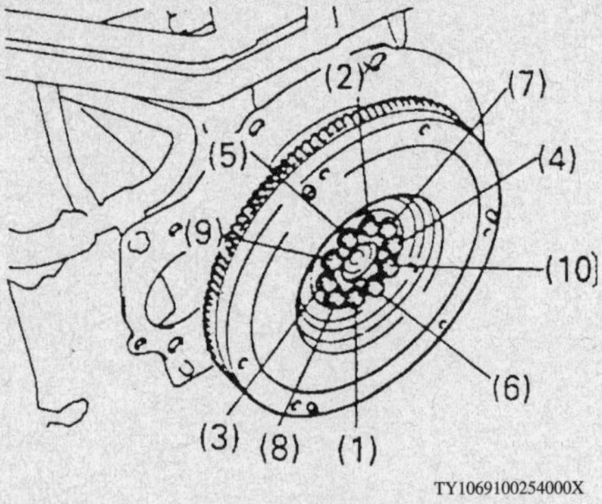
(2)
(7)
(5)
(4)
(9)
(10)
(6)
(3)
(8)
(1)
TY1069100254000X

Fig. 25 Flywheel bolt tightening sequence

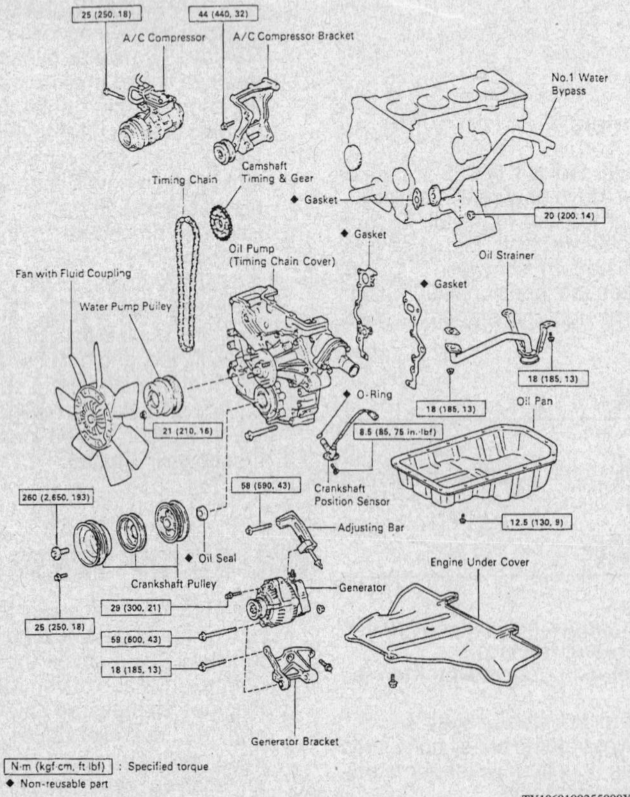
25 (250, 18)
44 (440, 32)
A/C Compressor
A/C Compressor Bracket
No.1 Water Bypass
Camshaft Timing & Gear
Timing Chain
◆ Gasket
20 (200, 14)
◆ Gasket
Oil Pump (Timing Chain Cover)
Oil Strainer
Fan with Fluid Coupling
◆ Gasket
Water Pump Pulley
18 (185, 13)
◆ O-Ring
Oil Pan
18 (185, 13)
21 (210, 16)
8.5 (85, 75 in.-lbf)
260 (2,650, 193)
58 (590, 43)
Crankshaft Position Sensor
12.5 (130, 9)
Adjusting Bar
◆ Oil Seal
Engine Under Cover
Crankshaft Pulley
Generator
29 (300, 21)
25 (250, 18)
59 (600, 43)
18 (185, 13)
Generator Bracket
N·m (kgf·cm, ft·lbf) : Specified torque
◆ Non-reusable part
TY1069100255000X

Fig. 26 Crankshaft position sensor removal

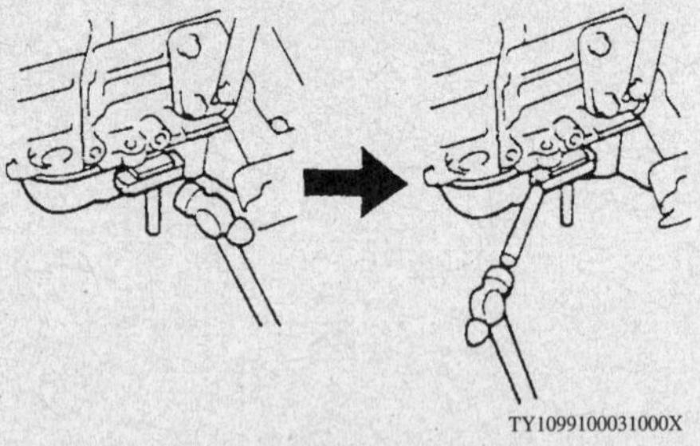
TY1099100031000X

Fig. 27 Oil pan removal using seal cutter

7. Replace worn parts as necessary. Reassemble in reverse order, using a new O-ring.

BELT TENSION DATA

Belt	New, Lbs.	Used, Lbs.
Alternator	145–175	765–125
Power Steer.	135–185	80–120
A/C Comp.	100–150	60–100

COOLING SYSTEM BLEED

These engines do not require a specific bleed procedure. After filling cooling system, run engine to operating temperature with radiator/pressure cap off. Air will then be automatically bled through cap opening.

THERMOSTAT

REPLACE

1. Drain engine coolant, then remove upper radiator hose from engine.
2. Remove engine water inlet, thermostat and O-ring gasket.
3. Reverse procedure to install. Use new O-ring. Ensure bleed hole or valve is facing upward.

WATER PUMP

REPLACE

1. Drain cooling system, remove upper radiator hose.
2. **On models with A/C,** remove A/C belt.

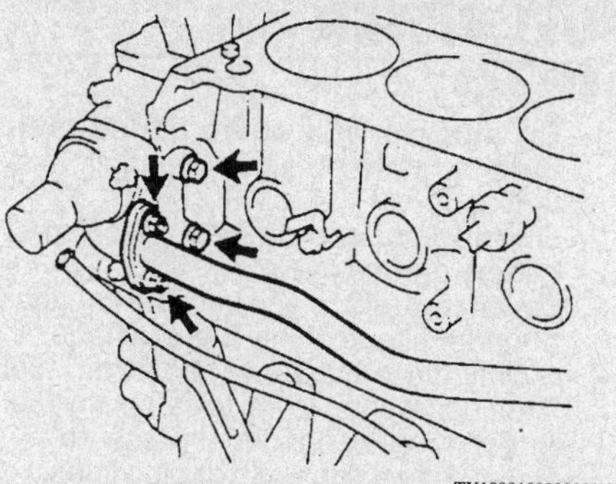
TY1099100032000X

Fig. 28 Water bypass & rear bolts timing chain cover

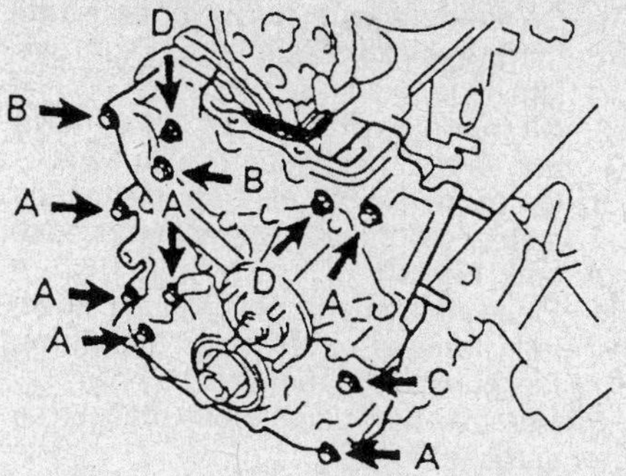
D
B
A
A
A
B
A
D
A
C
A
TY1099100033000X

Fig. 29 Bolt tightening, timing chain cover

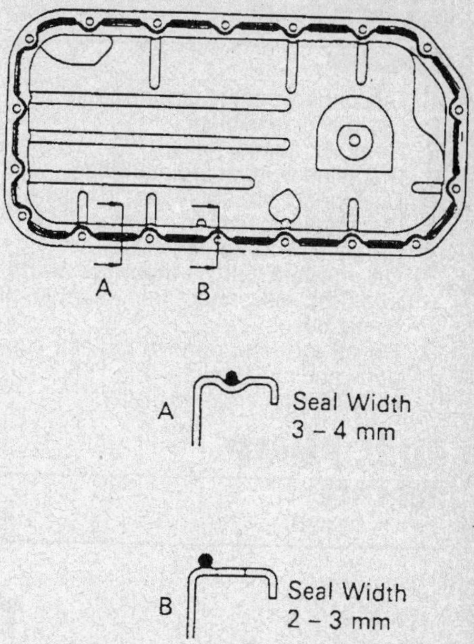
A
B
A
Seal Width
3 – 4 mm
B
Seal Width
2 – 3 mm
TY1099100034000X

Fig. 30 Oil pan sealer application

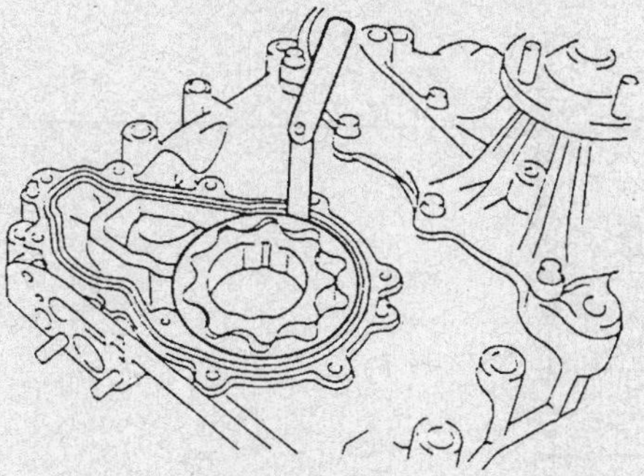
TY1099100035000X

Fig. 31 Oil pump rotor to body measurement

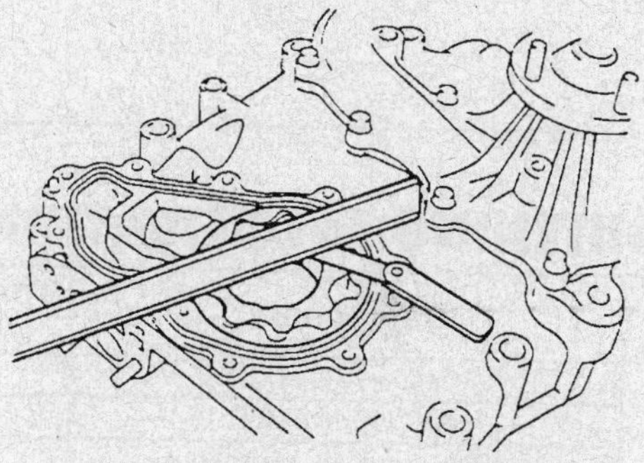
TY1099100036000X

Fig. 32 Oil pump rotor side clearance measurement

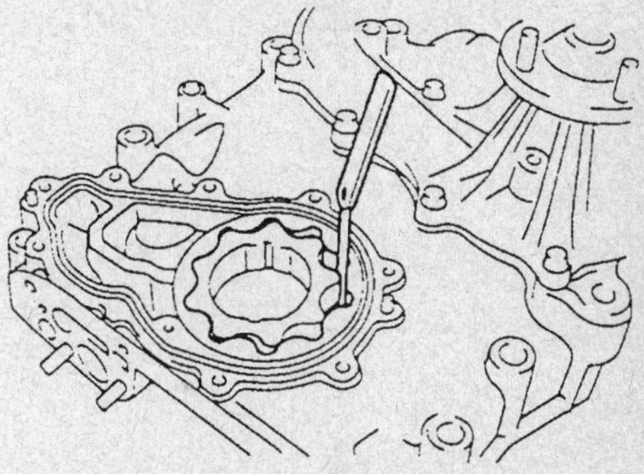
TY1099100037000X

Fig. 33 Oil pump tip clearance measurement

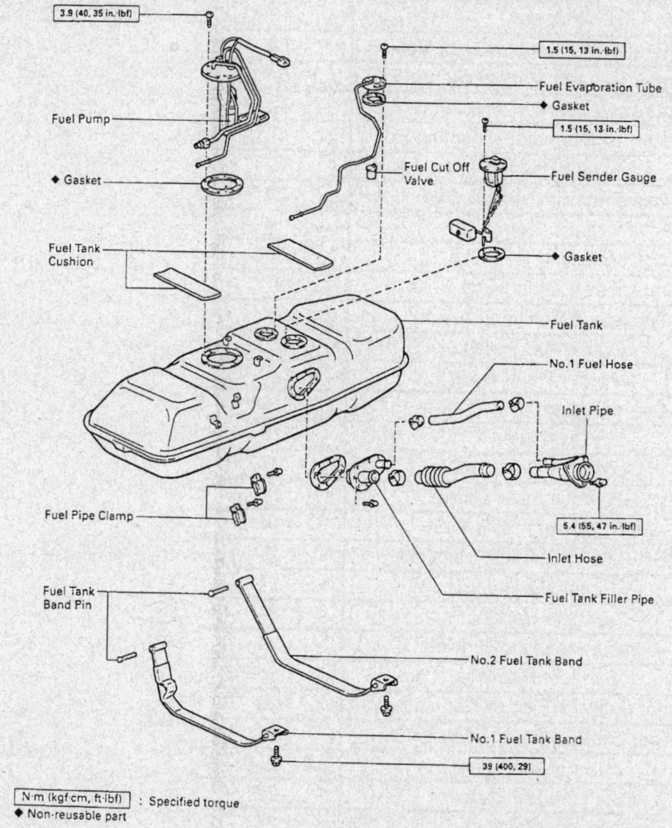
3.9 (40, 35 in.·lbf)
Fuel Pump
◆ Gasket
Fuel Tank Cushion
1.5 (15, 13 in.·lbf)
Fuel Evaporation Tube
◆ Gasket
1.5 (15, 13 in.·lbf)
Fuel Cut Off Valve
Fuel Sender Gauge
◆ Gasket
Fuel Tank
No.1 Fuel Hose
Inlet Pipe
Fuel Pipe Clamp
5.4 (55, 47 in.·lbf)
Inlet Hose
Fuel Tank Filler Pipe
Fuel Tank Band Pin
No.2 Fuel Tank Band
No.1 Fuel Tank Band
39 (400, 29)
N·m (kgf·cm, ft·lbf) : Specified torque
◆ Non-reusable part
TY1029100015000X

Fig. 34 Fuel tank removal

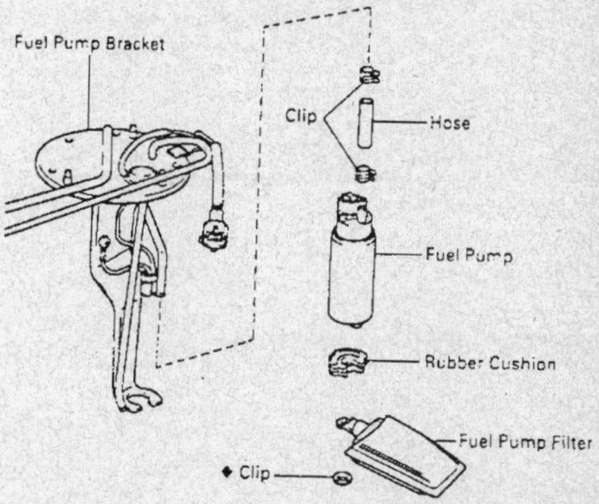
Fuel Pump Bracket
Clip
Hose
Fuel Pump
Rubber Cushion
Fuel Pump Filter
◆ Clip
TY1029100016000X

Fig. 35 Fuel pump service

3. **On all models,** loosen drive belt tension, then remove radiator fan shroud bolts.
4. Remove water pump pulley bolts, then the fan, fan coupling, pulley and fan shroud.
5. Remove water pump ten attaching bolts, then the pump and gasket.
6. Reverse procedure to install. Use new water pump gasket.

RADIATOR

REPLACE

1. Disconnect battery ground cable.
2. Drain engine coolant.
3. Remove radiator grille.
4. Disconnect upper radiator hose.
5. Disconnect coolant reservoir hose.
6. Disconnect lower radiator hose.
7. Remove No. 2 fan shroud.
8. **On models with automatic transmission,** disconnect transmission oil cooler hoses.
9. **On all models,** remove radiator supports and radiator.
10. Reverse procedure to install.

FUEL PUMP

REPLACE

1. **On models with audio coded anti-theft system,**obtain three-digit system code.
2. **On models with air bag,** disable system as outlined under "Precautions."
3. **On models less air bag,** disconnect battery ground cable, then remove fuel tank, **Fig. 34.**
4. Place matchmarks on fuel pump cover, then remove seven bolts and lift out fuel pump and bracket assembly.
5. Remove fuel pump from bracket assembly, **Fig. 35.**
6. Reverse procedure to install. Reset audio coded anti-theft and air bag system, if equipped, as outlined under "Precautions."

FUEL FILTER

REPLACE

1. **On models with audio coded anti-theft system,**obtain three-digit system code.
2. **On models less air bag,** disconnect battery ground cable.
3. **On all models,** place suitable container under filter to allow fuel drainage.
4. Slowly disconnect fuel hose from fuel filter, use a shop towel to catch any fuel that may spray out under pressure.
5. Remove fuel filter, cap or plug lines.
6. Reverse procedure to install. Reset audio coded anti-theft system, if equipped, as outlined under "Precautions."

TIGHTENING SPECIFICATIONS

Year	Component	Torque/Ft. Lbs.
1994–96	Accessory Pulley Bolt	18
	A/C Compressor	18
	A/C Compressor Bracket	32
	Air Intake Chamber	15
	Balance Shaft/No. 2 Chain Tensioner	13
	Generator to Alternator Adjusting Bracket	43
	Generator to Alternator Lock Bolt	54
	Generator to Alternator Bracket Bolt A	54
	Generator to Alternator Bracket Bolt B	13
	Generator to Alternator Mounting Bolt	54
	Camshaft Bearing Cap	12
	Camshaft Timing Sprocket	54
	Clutch Cover	14
	Connecting Rod Cap	33②
	Crankshaft Bearing Cap Bolts	29②
	Crankshaft Position Sensor	6
	Crankshaft Pulley	193
	Cylinder Head Bolts	③
	Cylinder Head, Rear Cover	10
	Distributor	13
	Distributor Drive Gear	37
	EGR Valve to Air Intake	14
	EGR Valve to EGR Pipe	14
	EGR Pipe to Exhaust Manifold	15
	EGR Pipe to Cylinder Head	14
	Engine Hanger	30
	Engine Mounting Bracket	34
	Exhaust Manifold	36
	Front Exhaust Pipe to Convertor	29
	Front Exhaust Pipe to Manifold	46
	Flywheel	19②
	Fuel Line Banjo Bolts	22
	Intake Manifold	22

Continued

TIGHTENING SPECIFICATIONS—Continued

Year	Component	Torque/Ft. Lbs.
1994–96	Knock Sensor	27
	Oil Drain Bolt	18
	Oil Pan Bolt & Nut	9
	Oil Strainer	13
	P/S Pulley Nut	32
	P/S Pump Bracket to Head	14
	P/S Pump to Bracket	43
	P/S Idler Pulley	14
	Throttle Body	14
	Timing/No. 1 Chain Tensioner	13
	Timing Chain Cover	①
	Radiator Support	9
	Rear Oil Seal Retainer	10
	Spark Plug	13
	Water Bypass Pipe	14
	Water Inlet	15
	Water Pump, Short Bolt	18
	Water Pump, Long Bolt	7
	Water Pump Pulley	16

①— Refer to "Timing Chain, Replace."
②— Turn an additional 90°.
③— Refer to "Cylinder Head, Replace."

3VZ-E 3.0L Engine

NOTE: On Air Bag Equipped Models, Refer To "Air Bag System Precautions" Located In The Front Of This Manual For System Disarming & Arming Procedures.

INDEX

	Page No.
Belt Tension Data	47-45
Camshaft, Replace	47-44
Compression Pressure	47-42
Cooling System Bleed	47-45
Crankshaft Rear Oil Seal, Replace	47-44
Cylinder Head, Replace	47-43
Engine Rebuilding Specefications	48-1
Engine, Replace	47-42
Front Cover Seal, Replace	47-43
Fuel Filter, Replace	47-45
Fuel Pump, Replace	47-45
Intake Manifold, Replace	47-42
Main & Rod Bearings	47-44
Oil Pan, Replace	47-44
Oil Pump, Replace	47-44
Oil Pump Service	47-45
Piston & Rod Assembly	47-44
Precautions	47-41
Air Bag Systems	47-41
Audio Coded Anti-Theft System	47-41
Radiator, Replace	47-45
Thermostat, Replace	47-45
Tightening Specifications	47-46
Timing Belt, Replace	47-44
Installation	47-44
Removal	47-44
Valve Adjustment	47-43
Valve Clearance Specifications	47-43
Valve Guides	47-43
Water Pump, Replace	47-45

PRECAUTIONS

AIR BAG SYSTEMS

Refer to "Air Bag System Precautions" in the front of this manual for system disarming and arming procedures.

AUDIO CODED ANTI-THEFT SYSTEM

Some models are equipped with an audio coded anti-theft system that will disable the radio when the battery cable is disconnected. The system can be identified by the "ANTI-THEFT SYSTEM" on the cassette lid. Obtain three-digit code for input. Reset system after service as follows:

1. Obtain three-digit audio theft code.
2. Depress 1 (PROG) button while depressing righthand side of TUNE SEEK button. Three dashes will appear in tape operation display.
3. To enter first digit, depress 1 (PROG) button repeatedly until number of times depressed equals first digit (depress 1 button six times if first digit is five, first press equals 0).
4. To enter second digit, depress 2 (APS) button repeatedly until number of times depressed equals second digit.
5. To enter third digit, depress 3 (RPT) button repeatedly until number of times depressed equals third digit.
6. If three dashes are displayed after inputting digits, repeat procedure.
7. When code appears in display, depress and hold SCAN button until SEC appears.
8. When SEC disappears audio system is operative.
9. If Err is displayed, repeat procedure. **Attempting to input code more than**

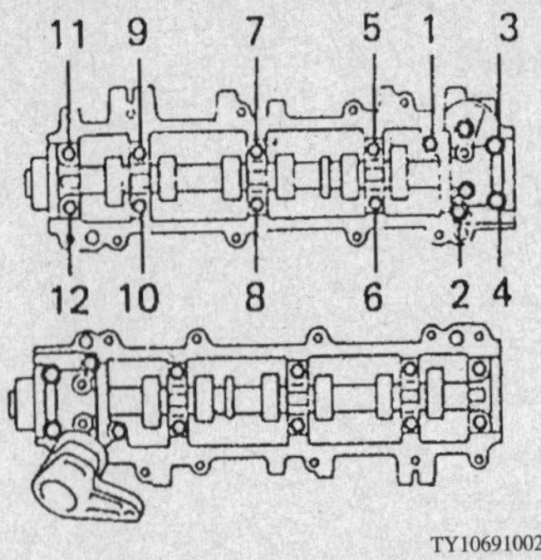
11 9 7 5 1 3
12 10 8 6 2 4
TY1069100256000X

Fig. 1 Camshaft bearing cap bolt loosening sequence

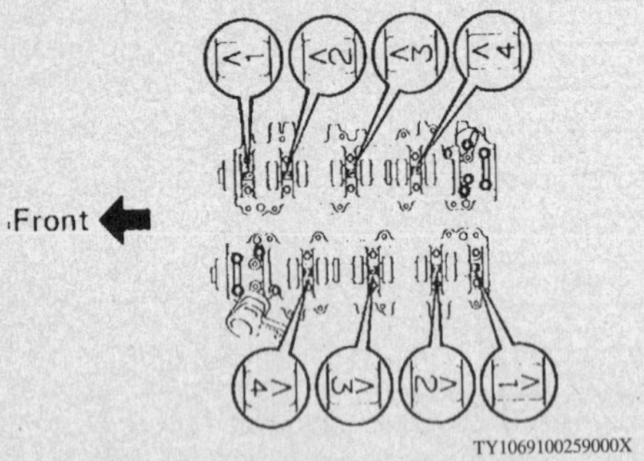
Front
TY1069100259000X

Fig. 4 Bearing cap locations

nine times may permanently disable audio system.

COMPRESSION PRESSURE

1. Start engine and warm to normal operating temperature.
2. Disconnect cold start injector connector.
3. Disconnect igniter connector.
4. Disconnect high tension cords from spark plugs.
5. Insert compression gauge into spark plug hole.
6. Fully open throttle.
7. While cranking engine, measure compression pressure.
8. Standard compression pressure should be 171 psi. Minimum compression is 142 psi.
9. The difference in compression pressure between each cylinder should not exceed 14 psi.

ENGINE

REPLACE

1. **On models with audio coded anti-theft system,** obtain three-digit system code.
2. **On all models,** disconnect battery ground cable.
3. Scribe hood hinge locations, then remove hood.
4. Remove engine undercover.
5. Drain coolant from radiator and engine.
6. Drain oil from engine.
7. Remove air cleaner case and hose.
8. Remove radiator.
9. Remove power steering drive belt.

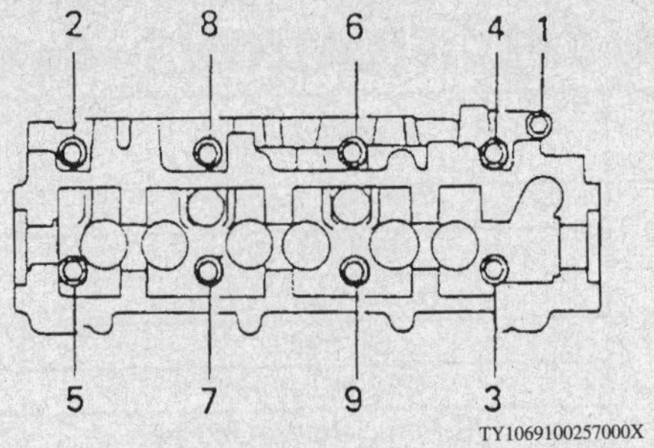
2 8 6 4 1
5 7 9 3
TY1069100257000X

Fig. 2 Cylinder head bolt loosening sequence

10. Remove air conditioner compressor drive belt, if equipped.
11. Remove generator drive belt, fluid coupling and fan pulley.
12. Label locations, then disconnect all electrical connectors, wires and vacuum lines from engine/transaxle assembly.
13. Disconnect accelerator cable, throttle cable and cruise control cable, if equipped.
14. Remove power steering pump and lines.
15. Remove air conditioner compressor, if equipped.
16. Disconnect clutch release cylinder line, if equipped.
17. Disconnect heater hoses.
18. Disconnect and cap fuel lines.
19. **On manual transmission,** remove shift control levers.
20. **On all models,** remove rear driveshaft.
21. Disconnect speedometer cable.
22. **On 4WD models,** remove transfer undercover, stabilizer bar and front driveshaft.
23. **On all models,** remove front crossmember.
24. Remove front exhaust pipe.
25. Remove No. 1 front floor heat insulator.
26. **On 4WD models,** remove brake tube heat insulator.
27. **On 2WD models,** remove engine rear mounting and bracket.
28. **On 4WD models,** remove No. 2 frame crossmember from side frame.
29. **On all models,** attach suitable engine lifting equipment onto engine assembly.
30. Remove engine/transmission assembly from vehicle.
31. Reverse procedure to install. Reset audio coded anti-theft system, if equipped, as outlined under "Precautions."

INTAKE MANIFOLD

REPLACE

Refer to "Cylinder Head, Replace" for procedure.

CYLINDER HEAD

REPLACE

1. **On models with audio coded anti-theft system,** obtain three-digit system code.

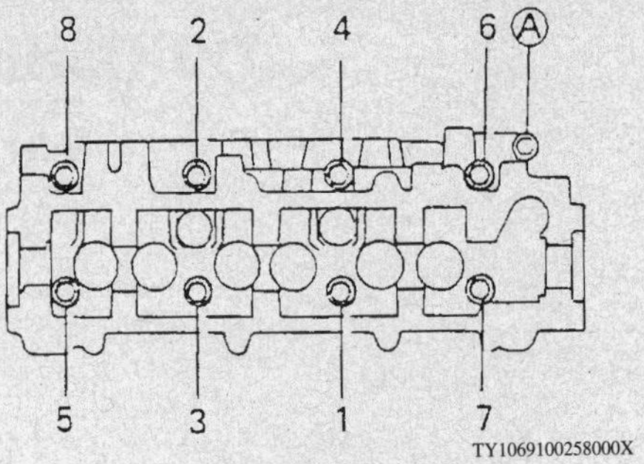
8 2 4 6 A
5 3 1 7
TY1069100258000X

Fig. 3 Cylinder head bolt tightening sequence

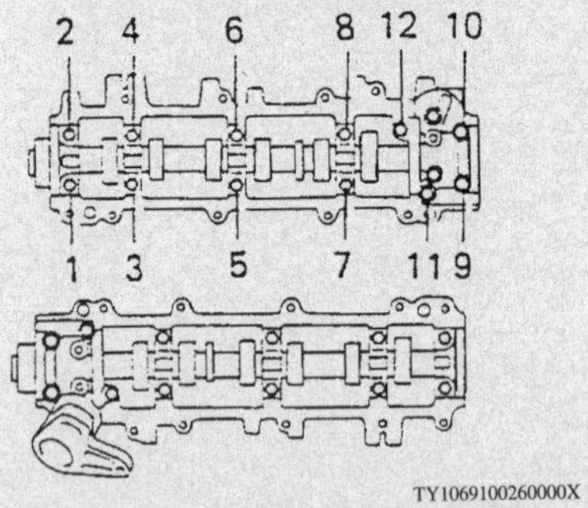
2 4 6 8 12 10
1 3 5 7 11 9
TY1069100260000X

Fig. 5 Bearing cap bolt tightening sequence

2. **On all models,** disconnect battery ground cable.
3. Remove air cleaner assembly and hose.
4. Drain coolant and oil from engine.
5. Remove radiator from vehicle.
6. Remove power steering pump and position aside. Do not disconnect lines.
7. Remove air conditioner compressor drive belt, if equipped.
8. Remove generator drive belt, fluid coupling and fan pulley.
9. Label, then disconnect all electrical connectors, wires, vacuum lines and hoses from cylinder head.
10. Disconnect accelerator, throttle and cruise control cables, if equipped.
11. Disconnect clutch release cylinder line, if equipped.
12. Disconnect heater hoses.
13. Disconnect and cap fuel lines.
14. Disconnect front exhaust pipe from exhaust manifold.
15. Remove timing belt as follows:
    a. Place No. 1 cylinder to TDC of compression stroke by turning crankshaft pulley and align its groove with "0" mark on No. 1 timing belt cover.
    b. Ensure alignment marks on camshaft timing pulley (sprocket) and No. 3 timing belt cover are properly aligned. If not, turn crankshaft pulley one complete revolution (360°). If original timing belt is going to be used, draw a direction arrow on timing belt (in direction of engine rotation) and place alignment marks on sprockets and timing belt for correct assembly alignment.

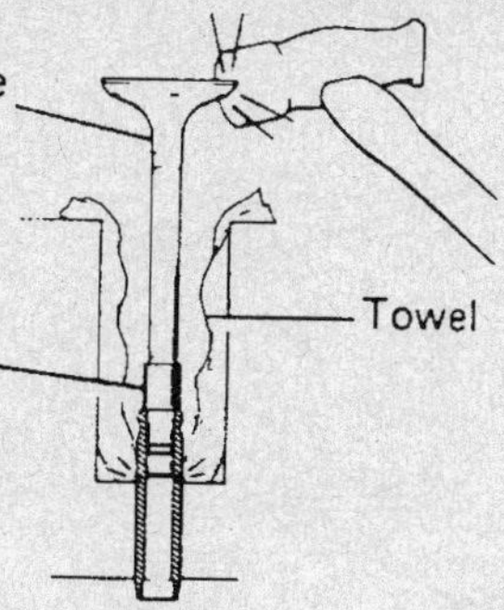
Old Valve
Towel
Tape
TY1069100261000X

Fig. 6 Breaking valve guide

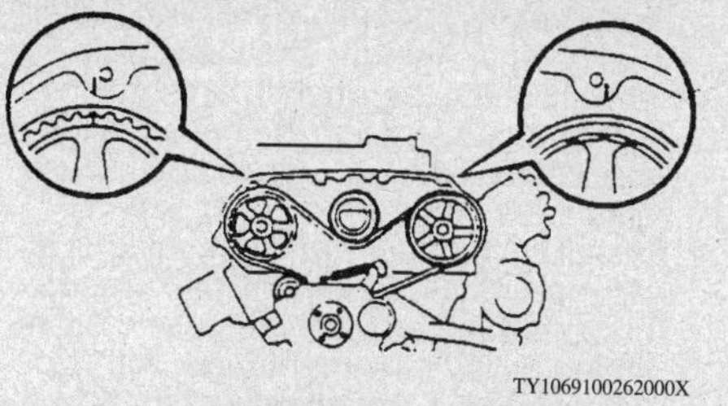
TY1069100262000X

Fig. 7 Timing mark alignment

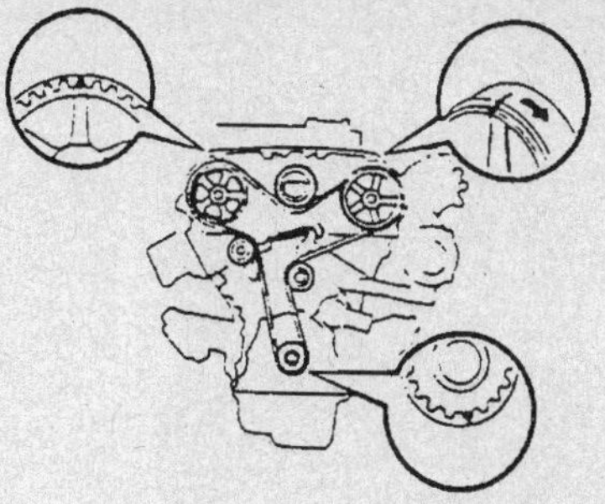
TY1069100263000X

Fig. 8 Placing marks on sprockets & timing belt

16. Remove distributor and spark plug wires.
17. Remove air intake chamber.
18. Remove No. 2 and No. 3 fuel lines.
19. Remove No. 4 timing belt cover.
20. Remove No. 2 idler pulley and No. 3 timing belt cover.
21. Remove righthand delivery pipe and injectors.
22. Remove lefthand delivery pipe and injectors.
23. Remove water bypass outlet and intake manifold.
24. Disconnect knock sensor electrical connector and remove crossover pipe.
25. To remove righthand side cylinder head, proceed as follows:
    a. Remove reed valve with No. 1 air injector manifold.
    b. Remove water bypass pipe mounting bolt, then the generator.
    c. Remove cylinder head cover.
    d. Remove two attaching bolts and camshaft housing rear cover.
    e. Loosen each bearing cap bolts in several passes, in sequence shown in **Fig. 1.** Remove camshaft bearing caps, camshaft housing plug, oil seal and camshaft from cylinder head.
    f. Remove righthand cylinder head. Remove nine attaching bolts in several passes, in sequence shown in **Fig. 2.**
26. To remove lefthand cylinder head, proceed as follows:
    a. Remove oil dipstick guide.
    b. Remove cylinder head cover.
    c. Remove two attaching bolts and camshaft housing rear cover.
    d. Loosen bearing cap bolts in several passes, in sequence shown in **Fig. 1.** Remove camshaft bearing caps, camshaft housing plug, oil seal and camshaft from cylinder head.
    e. Remove lefthand cylinder head. Remove nine attaching bolts in several passes, in sequence shown in **Fig. 2.**
27. Reverse procedure to install, noting the following:
    a. Install righthand cylinder head. Place a new gasket onto cylinder block. Apply a light coat of engine oil on bolt threads and under bolt heads. Using a 12 sided socket, alternately **torque** head bolts in several passes in sequence shown in **Fig. 3,** to 33 ft. lbs. If any bolts do not meet tightening specification, replace bolt. Mark front side of top bolt with paint, then **torque** bolts an additional 90°. Ensure paint mark is facing side of engine. **Torque** bolts an additional 90° and ensure paint mark is now facing rear of engine. **Torque** bolt (A) to 27 ft. lbs.
    b. Install camshaft. Coat all bearing journals with clean engine oil. Place camshaft onto cylinder head. Apply engine oil to lip of new seal. Install oil seal and camshaft housing plug onto camshaft. Apply seal packing No. 08826-00080, or equivalent, to No. 1 and No. 3 bearings caps. Install caps immediately after applying seal packing. Place bearing caps on each journal with arrows point toward front (for righthand side camshaft assembly) or rear (for lefthand side camshaft), **Fig. 4.**
    c. Using sequence shown in **Fig. 5,** temporarily tighten each bearing cap bolt in several passes uniformly.
    d. Using seal installation tool No. 09214-60010, or equivalent, drive in camshaft oil seals and camshaft housing plug. Install camshaft housing rear cover and attaching bolts.
    e. **Torque** bearing cap bolts in several passes uniformly in sequence shown in **Fig. 5,** to 12 ft. lbs.
    f. Reset audio coded anti-theft and air bag system, if equipped, as outlined under "Precautions."

VALVE CLEARANCE SPECIFICATIONS

Year	Stem-To-Guide Clearance	
	Intake	Exhaust
1993–95	.007–.011	.009–.013

VALVE ADJUSTMENT

1. With engine cold, place No. 1 cylinder at TDC of compression stroke by turning crankshaft pulley and aligning its groove with "0" mark on No. 1 timing belt cover.
2. With engine in this position, ensure valves on No. 1 cylinder are loose and valves on No. 4 cylinder are tight.
3. Using a suitable feeler gauge measure valve clearance on No. 6 intake and No. 2 exhaust valves.
4. Turn crankshaft pulley ⅓ of a revolution (120°) and measure clearance of No. 1 intake and No. 3 exhaust valves.
5. Turn crankshaft pulley ⅓ of a revolution (120°) and measure clearance of No. 2 intake and No. 4 exhaust valves.
6. Turn crankshaft pulley ⅓ of a revolution (120°) and measure clearance of No. 3 intake and No. 5 exhaust valves.
7. Turn crankshaft pulley ⅓ of a revolution (120°) and measure clearance of No. 4 intake and No. 6 exhaust valves.
8. Turn crankshaft pulley ⅓ of a revolution (120°) and measure clearance of No. 5 intake and No. 1 exhaust valves.

VALVE GUIDES

Valve stem to guide oil clearance should not exceed .0031 inch for intake valves and .0039 inch for exhaust. If valve replacement will not bring clearance within standards, guide replacement will be necessary.

1. Using a suitable tool, **Fig. 6,** and hammer, strike valve guide to break it off at cylinder head casting.
2. Using a suitable method, gradually heat cylinder head to 176–212°F.
3. Using valve guide driver tool No. 09201-60011, or equivalent, tap out guide from camshaft side.
4. Using a suitable measuring tool, measure bore in cylinder head and select correct guide. Bore measurements between .5118 to .5129 inch and use a standard guide. Measurements above .5129 inch require valve guide hole to be rebored to .5138 to .5148 inch. Use of an oversize guide. Install snap ring on new valve guide. Heat cylinder head as outlined in step 2. Install new valve guide.
5. Using a sharp .310 inch reamer, ream new valve guide if necessary. Refer to "Valve Clearance Specifications" for stem clearances.

FRONT COVER SEAL

REPLACE

1. Remove timing belt and crankshaft pulley as outlined under "Timing Belt, Replace."
2. Using a screwdriver, pry seal from timing cover.
3. Apply MP grease to seal lip and using seal installer tool No. 09309-37010, or equivalent, install seal.

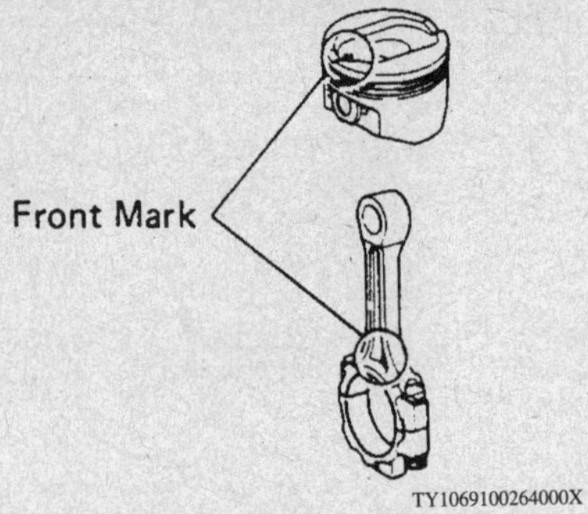
Front Mark
TY1069100264000X

Fig. 9 Piston & connecting rod assembly

4. Install timing belt and crankshaft pulley.

TIMING BELT

REPLACE

REMOVAL

1. **On models with audio coded anti-theft system,** obtain three-digit system code.
2. **On models less air bag,** disconnect battery ground cable.
3. **On all models** drain oil and coolant from engine. Drain coolant from radiator.
4. Remove radiator.
5. Remove power steering pump drive belt and pump.
6. Remove spark plugs.
7. Disconnect No. 2 and No. 3 air hoses from air pipe.
8. Remove water outlet.
9. Remove air conditioning compressor drive belt, if equipped.
10. Remove generator drive belt, fluid coupling, belt guide and fan pulley.
11. Remove No. 2 timing belt cover.
12. Place No. 1 cylinder at TDC of compression stroke by turning crankshaft pulley and aligning pulley groove with "0" mark on No. 1 timing belt cover. Ensure alignment marks on camshaft timing sprockets and No. 3 timing belt cover are correctly aligned, **Fig. 7.**
13. If not, turn crankshaft pulley one complete revolution.
14. Remove crankshaft pulley.
15. Remove fan pulley bracket.
16. Remove No. 1 timing belt cover.
17. Remove timing belt. If original timing belt is going to be used, draw a direction arrow on timing belt (in direction of engine rotation) and place alignment marks on pulley and timing belt, **Fig. 8.**
18. Remove timing belt guide.
19. Remove tension spring. Loosen idler pulley attaching bolt and shift it toward the left as far as it will go. Temporarily tighten set bolt and then relieve timing belt tension. Remove belt from each timing pulley/sprocket.
20. If necessary, remove camshaft timing sprocket, No. 1 idler pulley and crankshaft timing sprocket.

INSTALLATION

1. If removed, install crankshaft timing sprocket, temporarily install No. 1 idler pulley and tighten attaching bolt to specification, then install camshaft timing sprockets. Align camshaft alignment holes with No. 3 timing belt cover alignment marks.
2. Install timing pulley and attaching bolt. Do not install alignment pin. Ensure bolt head is not touching pulley. Align timing pulley alignment mark with No. 3 timing belt cover alignment mark.
3. Install timing belt as follows:
   a. If original timing belt is going to be used, align points marked during removal and install timing belt with arrow mark pointing in direction of engine rotation.
   b. Install timing belt onto camshaft timing sprockets, idler pulleys, water pump pulley and crankshaft timing sprocket.
   c. Pry No. 1 idler pulley toward the right as far as it will go and temporarily tighten it.
   d. Install tension spring and loosen idler pulley attaching bolt to where idler pulley lightly moves with tension spring force.
4. Check valve timing and timing belt tension, as follows:
   a. Temporarily install crankshaft pulley attaching bolt and turn crankshaft two complete revolutions from TDC to TDC. **Always turn crankshaft clockwise.**
   b. Check that each pulley aligns with timing marks.
   c. Tighten No. 1 idler pulley attaching bolt to specification.
   d. Remove camshaft timing sprocket attaching bolts, then align camshaft alignment pin holes.
   e. Tighten camshaft timing sprocket attaching bolt to specification.
   f. Install timing belt guide. Remove crankshaft pulley attaching bolt, then place belt guide onto crankshaft timing sprocket with cup side facing outward.
5. Reverse procedure to complete installation. Reset audio coded anti-theft system, if equipped, as outlined under "Precautions."

CAMSHAFT

REPLACE

Refer to "Cylinder Head, Replace" for camshaft removal procedures.

PISTON & ROD ASSEMBLY

Pistons are available in standard and oversizes of .020 inch (.50 mm). When assembling piston onto connecting rod, ensure mark on top of piston and mark on connecting rod are on same side, **Fig. 9.** When installing piston and connecting rod assembly, ensure mark on top of piston is facing toward front of engine. **When tightening connecting rods, ensure bolt does not rotate inside rod as this will result in lower torque than specified.**

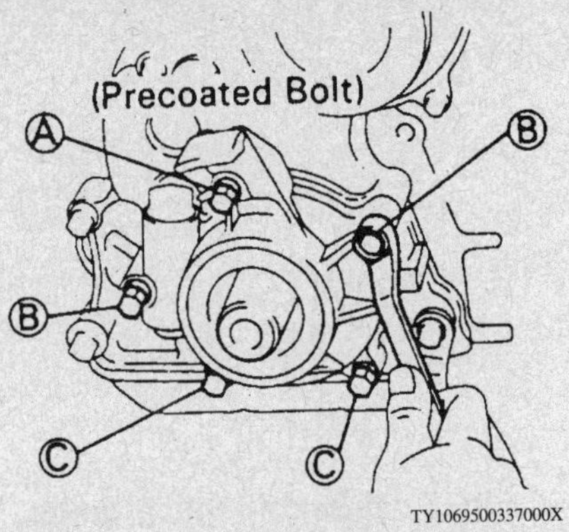
(Precoated Bolt)
A
B
B
C
C
TY1069500337000X

Fig. 10 Oil pump tightening

MAIN & ROD BEARINGS

Main and connecting rod bearings are available in standard and undersizes of .010 inch (.25 mm) and .020 inch (.50 mm).

CRANKSHAFT REAR OIL SEAL

REPLACE

1. Remove engine as previously described.
2. Cut seal lip using a knife, then pry out seal using a screwdriver.
3. Apply MP grease to seal lip. Using seal installer tool No. 09223-56010, or equivalent, and install seal.
4. Install engine as previously described.

OIL PAN

REPLACE

1. **On models with audio coded anti-theft system,** obtain three-digit system code.
2. **On all models,** disconnect battery ground cable, then remove engine undercover.
3. **On 4WD models,** remove front differential.
4. **On all models,** drain oil from engine. Remove timing belt. Refer to "Timing Belt, Replace" for removal procedure.
5. Remove crankshaft timing sprocket.
6. Remove oil pan attaching bolts, then the oil pan.
7. Remove oil strainer, oil baffle plate, then the oil pump.
8. Reverse procedure to install. Reset audio coded anti-theft system, if equipped, as outlined under "Precautions."

OIL PUMP

REPLACE

1. Remove oil pan as outlined under "Oil Pan, Replace. "
2. Remove oil strainer.
3. Remove drive belts.
4. Remove crankshaft pulley.
5. **On models with A/C,** remove compressor and bracket.

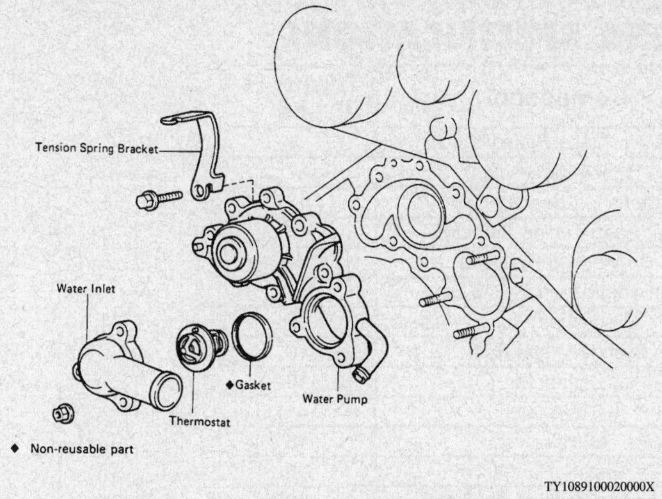
Tension Spring Bracket
Water Inlet
◆Gasket
Water Pump
Thermostat
◆ Non-reusable part
TY1089100020000X

Fig. 11 Water pump assembly

6. **On all models,** remove oil pump assembly and O-ring.
7. Reverse procedure to install, noting the following:
   a. Install new O-ring.
   b. **Torque** bolt "A" to 18 ft. lbs., bolts "B" to 14 ft. lbs. and bolts "C" to 9 ft. lbs., **Fig. 10.**

OIL PUMP SERVICE

1. Remove driven and drive rotor, then the relief valve.
2. Inspect relief valve. Replace if worn or damaged.
3. Using a suitable feeler gauge, measure clearance between driven rotor and pump body. Clearance obtained should be .0039–.0069 inch and should not exceed .0118 inch. If not, replace oil pump rotor set and/or pump body.
4. Using a feeler gauge, measure clearance between both rotor tips. Clearance obtained should be .0043–.0094 inch and should not exceed .0138 inch. If not, replace oil pump rotor set.
5. Using a suitable feeler gauge and a flat block, measure side clearance by placing flat block (square edge) across pump body and measuring (using feeler gauge) between flat edge and top of rotor assembly. Clearance obtained should be .0012–.0035 inch and should not exceed .0059 inch. If not, replace oil pump rotor set and/or pump body assembly.

BELT TENSION DATA

Belt	New, Lbs.	Used, Lbs.
Generator	140–180	80–120
Power Steer.	100–150	60–100
A/C Comp.	100–150	60–100

COOLING SYSTEM BLEED

These engines do not require a specific bleed procedure. After filling cooling system, run engine to operating temperature with radiator/pressure cap off. Air will then be automatically bled through cap opening.

THERMOSTAT

REPLACE

1. Drain cooling system.
2. Disconnect radiator outlet hose, then remove water inlet.
3. Remove thermostat and gasket.
4. Reverse procedure to install. Use a new thermostat gasket and tighten inlet nuts to specifications.

WATER PUMP

REPLACE

1. **On models with audio coded anti-theft system,** obtain three-digit system code.
2. **On all models,** disconnect battery ground cable.
3. Remove timing belt as outlined under "Timing Belt Replace."
4. Remove No. 1 idler pulley.
5. Remove thermostat.
6. Remove water pump, **Fig. 11.**
7. Reverse procedure to install. Reset audio coded anti-theft system, if equipped, as outlined under "Precautions."

RADIATOR

REPLACE

1. Disconnect battery ground cable.
2. Drain engine coolant.
3. Remove engine under cover.
4. Disconnect coolant reservoir hose.
5. Disconnect radiator hoses.
6. Remove No. 2 fan shroud.
7. Remove No. 1 fan shroud.
8. **On models with automatic transmission,** disconnect transmission oil cooler hoses.
9. **On all models,** remove radiator supports and radiator.
10. Reverse procedure to install.

FUEL PUMP

REPLACE

1. Drain and remove fuel tank.
2. Remove fuel pump bracket bolts and fuel pump bracket.
3. Remove fuel pump from bracket. Remove filter from pump.
4. Reverse procedure to install.

FUEL FILTER

REPLACE

1. **On models with audio coded anti-theft system,**obtain three-digit system code.
2. **On models with air bag,** disable system as outlined under "Precautions."
3. **On models less air bag,** disconnect battery ground cable.
4. **On all models,** place suitable container under fuel filter to allow fuel drainage.
5. Slowly disconnect fuel hose from fuel filter. **Place shop towel over connection to avoid fuel spilling on engine.**
6. Remove fuel filter and cap or plug fuel hose.
7. Reverse procedure to install. Reset audio coded anti-theft and air bag system, if equipped, as outlined under "Precautions."

TIGHTENING SPECIFICATIONS

Year	Component	Torque/Ft. Lbs.
1993–95	Air Intake Chamber	9
	Generator Bracket	27
	Camshaft Bearing Cap	12
	Camshaft Timing Sprocket	80
	Connecting Rod Cap	18②
	Crankshaft Bearing Cap Bolts	45②
	Crankshaft Pulley	181
	Cylinder Head Bolts	①
	Distributor	13
	Driveplate	61
	EGR Valve	13
	Engine Hanger	30
	Engine Mounting Bracket	30
	Exhaust Manifold	29
	Fan Pulley Bracket	30
	Flywheel	65
	Intake Manifold	13
	No. 1 Idler Pulley	27
	No. 2 Idler Pulley	6
	No. 3 Timing Belt Cover	6
	Oil Drain Bolt	18
	Oil Pressure Switch	11
	Oil Pump	14
	Oil Strainer	5
	Radiator Support	9
	Rear Oil Seal Retainer	6
	Spark Plug	13
	Water Inlet	14
	Water Pump, Short Bolt	14
	Water Pump, Long Bolt	13

① — Refer to "Cylinder Head, Replace."
② — Turn an additional 90°.

5VZ-FE 3.4L Engine

NOTE: On Air Bag Equipped Models, Refer To "Air Bag System Precautions" Located In The Front Of This Manual For System Disarming & Arming Procedures.

INDEX

	Page No.
Belt Tension Data	47-55
Camshaft, Replace	47-54
Compression Pressure	47-47
Cooling System Bleed	47-55
Cylinder Head, Replace	47-49
Inspection	47-50
Installation	47-52
Removal	47-49
Engine Rebuilding Specifications	48-1
Engine, Replace	47-47
2WD	47-47
4WD	47-48
Fuel Filter, Replace	47-57
Fuel Pump, Replace	47-56
Oil Pan, Replace	47-54
Oil Pump, Replace	47-55
Oil Pump Service	47-55
Precautions	47-47
Air Bag Systems	47-47
Audio Coded Anti-Theft System	47-47
Radiator, Replace	47-56
Thermostat, Replace	47-56
Tightening Specifications	47-58
Timing Belt, Replace	47-52
Installation	47-53
Removal	47-52
Valve Adjustment	47-52
Valve Clearance Specifications	47-52
Water Pump, Replace	47-56

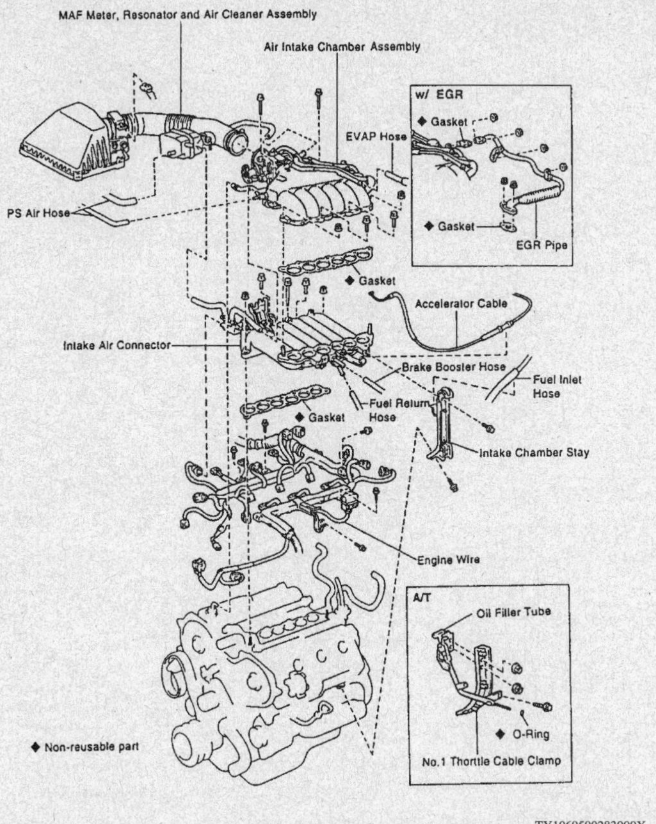
MAF Meter, Resonator and Air Cleaner Assembly
Air Intake Chamber Assembly
w/ EGR
◆ Gasket
EVAP Hose
PS Air Hose
◆ Gasket
EGR Pipe
◆ Gasket
Accelerator Cable
Intake Air Connector
Brake Booster Hose
Fuel Inlet Hose
Fuel Return Hose
◆ Gasket
Intake Chamber Stay
Engine Wire
A/T
Oil Filler Tube
◆ O-Ring
No.1 Throttle Cable Clamp
◆ Non-reusable part

TY1069500283000X

Fig. 1 Exploded view of cylinder head mounted components.

PRECAUTIONS

AIR BAG SYSTEMS

Refer to "Air Bag System Precautions" in the front of this manual for system disarming and arming procedures.

AUDIO CODED ANTI-THEFT SYSTEM

Some models are equipped with an audio coded anti-theft system that will disable the radio when the battery cable is disconnected. The system can be identified by the "ANTI-THEFT SYSTEM" on the cassette lid. Obtain three-digit code for input. Reset system after service as follows:

1. Obtain three-digit audio theft code.
2. Depress 1 (PROG) button while depressing righthand side of TUNE SEEK button. Three dashes will appear in tape operation display.
3. To enter first digit, depress 1 (PROG) button repeatedly until number of times depressed equals first digit (depress 1 button six times if first digit is five, first press equals 0).
4. To enter second digit, depress 2 (APS) button repeatedly until number of times depressed equals second digit.
5. To enter third digit, depress 3 (RPT) button repeatedly until number of times depressed equals third digit.
6. If three dashes are displayed after inputting digits, repeat procedure.
7. When code appears in display, depress and hold SCAN button until SEC appears.
8. When SEC disappears audio system is operative.
9. If Err is displayed, repeat procedure. **Attempting to input code more than nine times may permanently disable audio system.**

COMPRESSION PRESSURE

1. Start engine and warm to normal operating temperature.
2. Remove ignition coils as outlined under "Coil Pack, Replace."
3. Remove spark plugs.
4. Insert compression gauge into spark plug hole.
5. Fully open throttle.
6. While cranking engine, measure compression pressure.
7. Standard compression pressure should be 178 psi. Minimum compression is 127 psi.
8. The difference in compression pressure between each cylinder should not exceed 14 psi.

ENGINE

REPLACE

2WD

1. **On models with audio coded anti-theft system,**obtain three-digit system code.
2. **On all models,** disconnect battery cables.
3. Scribe hood hinge locations, then remove hood.
4. Remove engine under cover.
5. Drain coolant from radiator and engine.
6. Drain engine oil.
7. Drain transmission fluid.
8. Remove radiator as outlined in "Radiator, Replace. "
9. Remove belt drive for power steering pump:
   a. Stretch belt and loosen fan pulley mounting nuts.
   b. Loosen lock bolt, pivot bolt and adjusting bolt, then remove drive belt.
10. **On models with A/C,** loosen compressor idle pulley nut and adjusting bolt, then remove drive belt.
11. **On all models,** loosen alternator lock bolt, pivot bolt and adjusting bolt, then remove drive belt.
12. Remove No. 2 fan shroud.
13. Remove fan with fluid coupling and fan pulleys.
14. Disconnect power steering pump from engine and position aside.
15. **On models with A/C,** disconnect compressor from mounting bracket and position aside. Remove compressor mounting bracket.
16. Remove air cleaner cap, MAF meter and resonator.
17. **On models with cruise control,** disconnect actuator cable.
18. **On all models,** disconnect accelerator cable.
19. **On models with automatic transmission,** disconnect throttle cable.
20. **On all models,** disconnect heater hose.
21. Disconnect brake booster vacuum hose and EVAP hose.
22. Disconnect fuel return and inlet hoses.
23. Disconnect starter harness and connector.
24. Disconnect alternator harness and connector.
25. **On Tacoma and 4Runner models,** remove glove compartment door and lower No. 2 finish panel to disconnect ECM connectors.
26. **On T100 models,** remove front door scuff plate and cowl to disconnect ECM connectors.
27. **On all models,** disconnect igniter connector and ground strap.
28. **On models with manual transmission,** remove shift lever assembly.
29. **On all models,** disconnect propeller shaft.
30. Disconnect speedometer cable.
31. Remove front exhaust pipe.
32. **On models with manual transmission,** remove clutch release cylinder.
33. **On Tacoma and 4Runner models with automatic transmission,** remove control cable.
34. **On T100 models with automatic transmission,**remove cross shaft.
35. **On all models,** place suitable jack under transmission, then remove rear mounting bracket.
36. Attach engine hangers No. 12282–62030, or equivalent, to engine block.

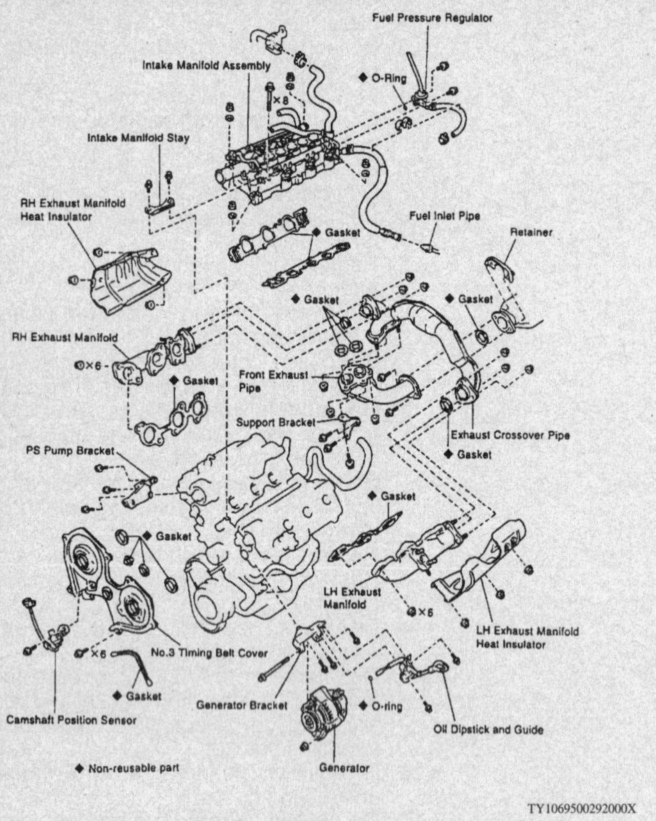

Fuel Pressure Regulator
Intake Manifold Assembly
◆ O-Ring
Intake Manifold Stay
RH Exhaust Manifold Heat Insulator
Fuel Inlet Pipe
Retainer
◆ Gasket
RH Exhaust Manifold
Front Exhaust Pipe
Support Bracket
Exhaust Crossover Pipe
PS Pump Bracket
LH Exhaust Manifold
LH Exhaust Manifold Heat Insulator
No.3 Timing Belt Cover
Camshaft Position Sensor
Generator Bracket
◆ O-ring
Oil Dipstick and Guide
◆ Non-reusable part
Generator
TY1069500292000X

Fig. 2 Exploded view of intake & exhaust components

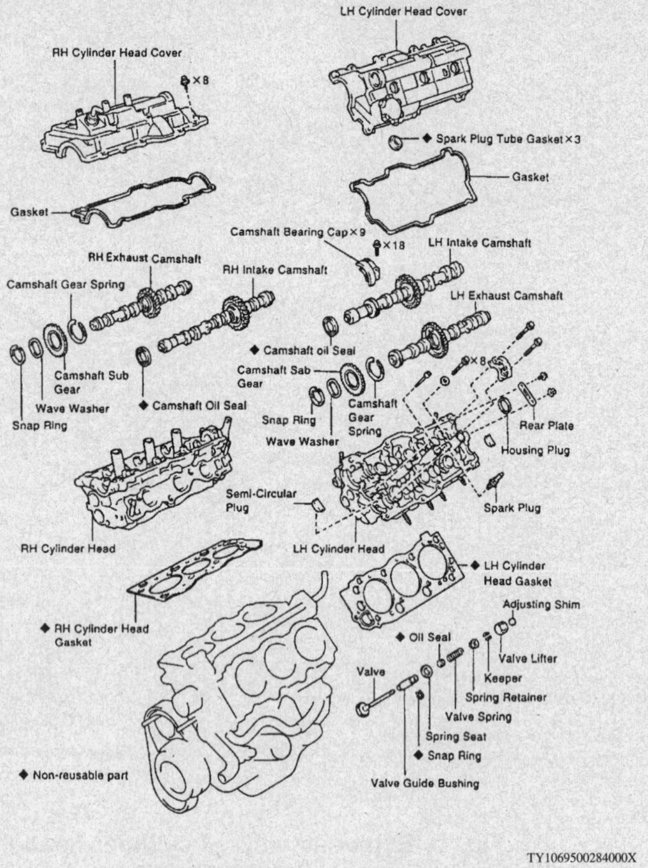

LH Cylinder Head Cover
RH Cylinder Head Cover
◆ Spark Plug Tube Gasket×3
Gasket
Camshaft Bearing Cap×9
RH Exhaust Camshaft
LH Intake Camshaft
Camshaft Gear Spring
RH Intake Camshaft
LH Exhaust Camshaft
◆ Camshaft oil Seal
Camshaft Sub Gear
Camshaft Sab Gear
Wave Washer
◆ Camshaft Oil Seal
Snap Ring
Camshaft Gear Spring
Rear Plate
Housing Plug
Semi-Circular Plug
Spark Plug
RH Cylinder Head
LH Cylinder Head
◆ LH Cylinder Head Gasket
Adjusting Shim
◆ RH Cylinder Head Gasket
◆ Oil Seal
Valve Lifter
Valve
Keeper
Spring Retainer
Valve Spring
Spring Seat
◆ Snap Ring
◆ Non-reusable part
Valve Guide Bushing
TY1069500284000X

Fig. 3 Exploded view of cylinder heads

Install chain hoist to engine hangers.

37. Remove front engine mounting insulators, then lift engine with transmission out of vehicle.
38. Reverse procedure to install.

4WD

1. **On models with audio coded anti-theft system,**obtain three-digit system code.
2. **On all models,** disconnect battery cables.
3. Scribe hood hinge locations, then remove hood.
4. Remove engine under cover.
5. Drain coolant from radiator and engine.
6. Drain engine oil.
7. Remove radiator as outlined in "Radiator, Replace."
8. Remove belt drive for power steering pump:
   a. Stretch belt and loosen fan pulley mounting nuts.
   b. Loosen lock bolt, pivot bolt and adjusting bolt, then remove drive belt.
9. **On models with A/C,** loosen compressor idle pulley nut and adjusting bolt, then remove drive belt.
10. **On all models,** loosen alternator lock bolt, pivot bolt and adjusting bolt, then remove drive belt.
11. Remove fan with fluid coupling and fan pulleys.
12. Disconnect power steering pump from engine and position aside.
13. **On models with A/C,** disconnect compressor from mounting bracket and position aside.

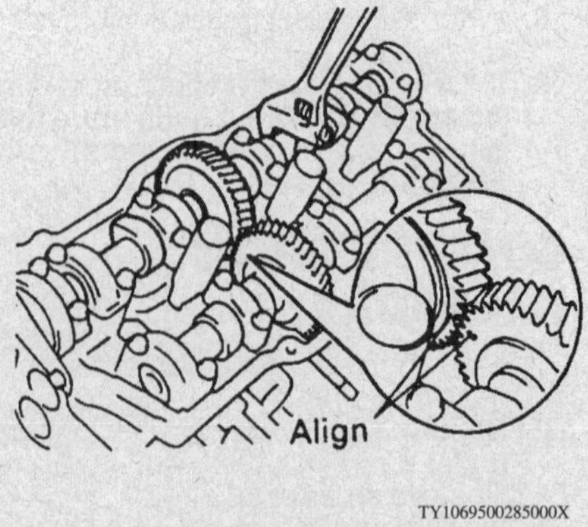

Align
TY1069500285000X

Fig. 4 Camshaft gear alignment

14. Remove air cleaner cap, MAF meter and resonator.
15. Remove air cleaner case and filter.
16. **On models with cruise control,** disconnect actuator cable.
17. **On all models,** disconnect accelerator cable.
18. **On models with automatic transmission,** disconnect throttle cable.
19. **On all models,** disconnect heater hose.
20. Disconnect brake booster vacuum hose, automatic disconnect differential vacuum hose and EVAP hose.
21. Disconnect fuel return and inlet hoses.
22. Disconnect starter harness and connector.
23. Disconnect alternator harness and connector.
24. **On Tacoma and 4Runner models,** remove glove compartment door and lower No. 2 finish panel to disconnect ECM connectors.
25. **On T100 models,** remove front door scuff plate and cowl to disconnect ECM connectors.
26. **On all models,** disconnect igniter connector and ground strap.
27. **On models with manual transmission,** remove shift lever assembly.
28. **On all models,** disconnect propeller shafts.
29. Disconnect speedometer cable.
30. Remove front exhaust pipe.
31. **On models with manual transmission,** remove clutch release cylinder.
32. **On Tacoma and 4Runner models with automatic transmission,** remove control cable.
33. **On T100 models w/automatic transmission,** remove cross shaft.
34. **On all models,** place suitable jack under transmission, then remove rear mounting bracket.
35. Attach engine hangers No. 12282–62030, or equivalent, to engine block. Install chain hoist to engine hangers.
36. Remove front engine mounting insulators, then lift engine with transmission out of vehicle.
37. Reverse procedure to install.

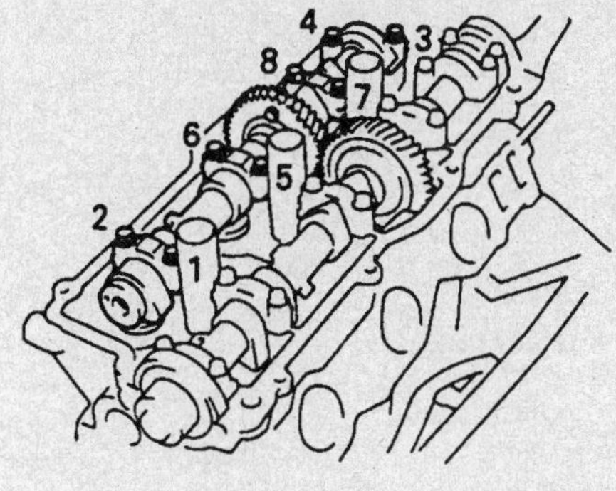
4
8
3
7
6
5
2
1

TY1069500286000X

Fig. 5 RH exhaust camshaft removal

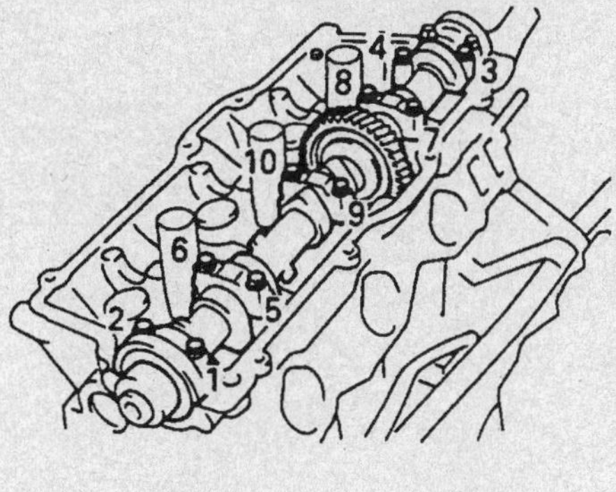
4
8
3
10
9
6
2
5
1

TY1069500287000X

Fig. 6 RH intake camshaft removal

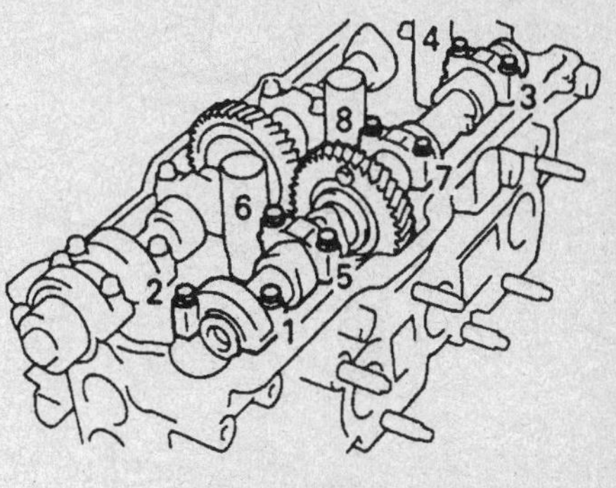
4
3
8
6
7
2
5
1

TY1069500288000X

Fig. 7 LH exhaust camshaft removal

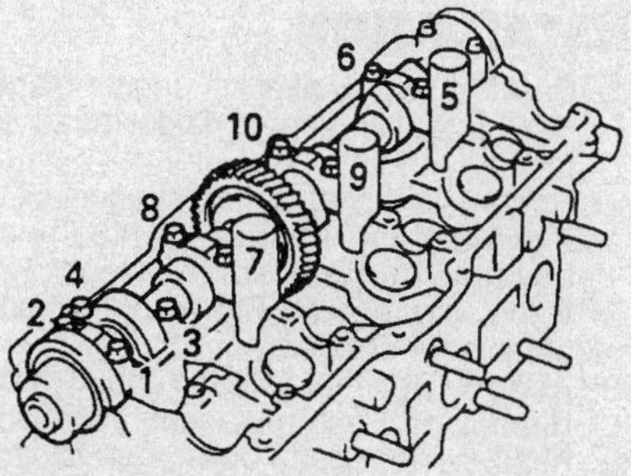
6
5
10
9
8
7
4
2
3
1

TY1069500289000X

Fig. 8 LH intake camshaft removal

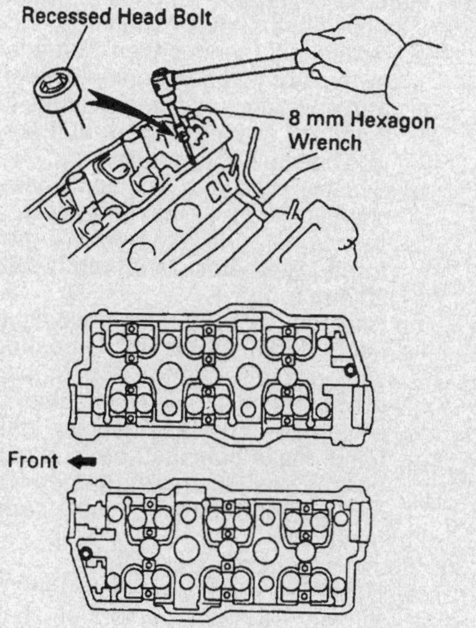
Recessed Head Bolt
8 mm Hexagon
Wrench
Front

TY1069500290000X

Fig. 9 Recessed head bolt removal

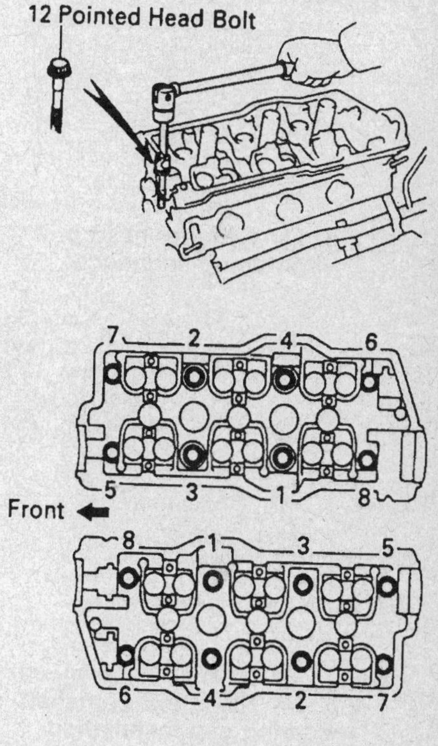
12 Pointed Head Bolt
7
2
4
6
Front
5
3
1
8
8
1
3
5
6
4
2
7

TY1069500291000X

Fig. 10 Cylinder head bolt loosening sequence

CYLINDER HEAD

REPLACE

REMOVAL

1. **On models with audio coded anti-theft system,** obtain three-digit system code.
2. **On all models,** disconnect battery ground cable.
3. Scribe hood hinge locations, then remove hood.
4. Remove engine under cover.
5. Drain coolant from radiator and engine.
6. Remove front exhaust pipe.
7. Remove air cleaner cap, MAF meter and resonator, **Fig. 1.**
8. **On models with cruise control,** disconnect actuator cable.
9. **On all models,** disconnect accelerator cable.
10. **On models with automatic transmission,** disconnect throttle cable.
11. **On all models,** disconnect heater hose.
12. Disconnect upper radiator hose.
13. Remove belt drive for power steering pump:
    a. Stretch belt and loosen fan pulley mounting nuts.
    b. Loosen lock bolt, pivot bolt and adjusting bolt, then remove drive belt.
14. **On all models,** remove spark plug wires with ignition coils, then the spark plugs.
15. Remove timing belt as outlined under "Timing Belt, Replace", then the camshaft timing pulleys.
16. Remove alternator.
17. **On models with EGR,** remove EGR pipe.
18. **On all models,** remove intake chamber stay.
19. Disconnect the following connectors:
    a. VSV connector for fuel pressure control.
    b. Throttle position sensor.
    c. IAC valve
    d. **On models with EGR,** EGR gas temperature sensor and VSV connectors.
20. **On all models,** disconnect the following hoses:
    a. Two PCV hoses.
    b. Two water bypass hoses.
    c. Air assist hose from throttle body.
    d. Two vacuum sensing hoses from VSV.
    e. EVAP hose.
    f. Air hose from power steering pump.
    g. **On models with A/C,** air hose from A/C idle-up valve.
21. Remove air intake chamber assembly.
22. Remove intake air connector as follows:
    a. Disconnect engine wire harness.
    b. Disconnect fuel return hoses.
    c. Disconnect brake booster vacuum hose from intake air connector.
    d. Disconnect ground strap.
    e. Disconnect data link connector (DLC1) from bracket.
    f. **On models with A/C,** disconnect A/C idle-up valve connector.
    g. **On all models,** disconnect intake air connector and gasket.
23. Disconnect following engine harness connectors:
    a. Oil pressure sensor.

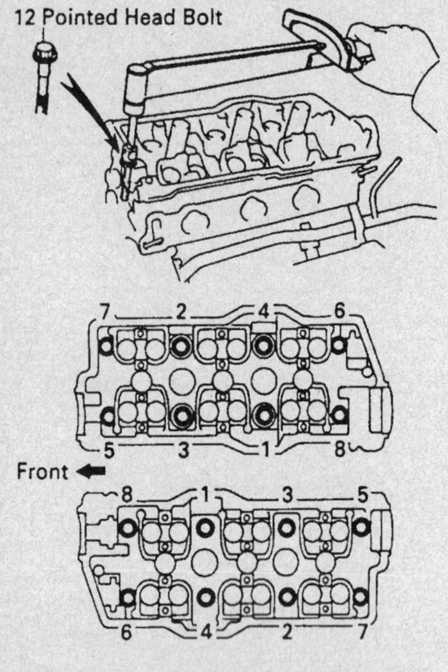
12 Pointed Head Bolt
7 2 4 6
5 3 1 8
Front
8 1 3 5
6 4 2 7
TY1069500293000X

Fig. 11 Cylinder head bolt tightening sequence

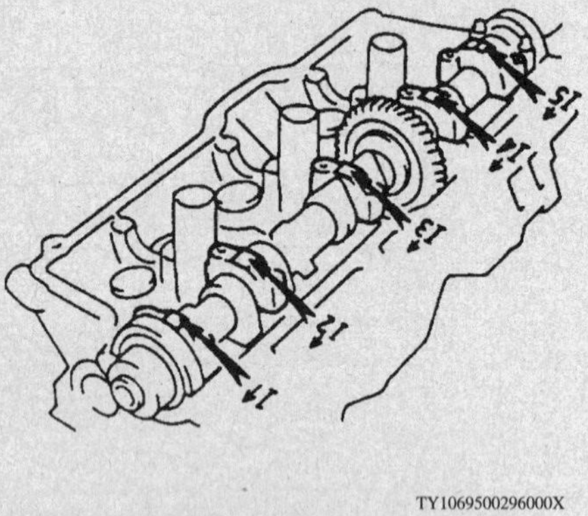
TY1069500296000X

Fig. 14 RH intake camshaft bearing cap installation

b. Crankshaft position sensor.
c. Fuel injectors.
d. ECT sender gauge.
e. ECT sensor.
f. Knock sensor.
g. Camshaft position sensor.

24. Disconnect engine harness from cylinder head.
25. Remove camshaft position sensor.
26. Remove No. 3 timing belt cover **Fig. 2.**
27. Remove fuel pressure regulator.
28. Remove intake manifold assembly:
    a. Disconnect fuel inlet hose.
    b. Remove intake manifold stay.
    c. Remove intake manifold with delivery pipes and injectors. Remove gaskets.
29. Remove power steering pump bracket.
30. Remove oil dipstick and tube.
31. Remove alternator bracket.
32. Remove exhaust crossover pipe.
33. Remove exhaust manifolds.

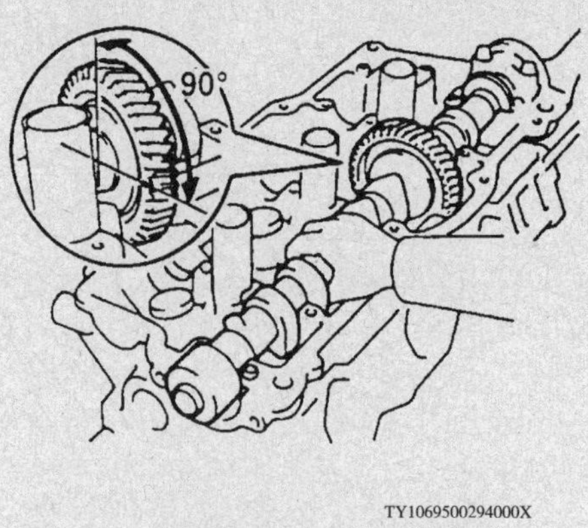
90°
TY1069500294000X

Fig. 12 RH intake camshaft installation

34. Remove cylinder head covers, **Fig. 3.**
35. Remove righthand camshafts:
    a. Rotate righthand driven sub-gear by turning hexagon portion of shaft with a wrench until timing marks (2 dots) are aligned, **Fig. 4,** and service bolt hole is accessible.
    b. Secure righthand exhaust camshaft sub-gear to main gear with a service bolt. **Service bolt is 6 mm thread diameter, 1 mm pitch, 16–20 mm long.**
    c. Uniformly loosen and remove righthand exhaust camshaft bearing cap bolts in sequence, **Fig. 5,** then the righthand exhaust camshaft.
    d. Uniformly loosen and remove righthand intake camshaft bearing cap bolts in sequence, **Fig. 6,** then the oil seal and righthand intake camshaft.
36. Remove lefthand camshafts:
    a. Rotate lefthand driven sub-gear by turning hexagon portion of shaft with a wrench until timing marks (1 dot) are aligned and service bolt hole is accessible.
    b. Secure lefthand exhaust camshaft sub-gear to main gear with a service bolt.
    c. Uniformly loosen and remove lefthand exhaust camshaft bearing cap bolts in sequence, **Fig. 7,**then the lefthand exhaust camshaft.
    d. Uniformly loosen and remove the lefthand intake camshaft bearing cap bolts in sequence, **Fig. 8,** then the oil seal and lefthand intake camshaft.
    e. Using a suitable 8 mm Allen wrench, remove recessed head cylinder head bolts, **Fig. 9.**
    f. Uniformly loosen and remove eight cylinder head bolts in sequence, **Fig. 10. These bolts have 12–pointed heads.**
37. Pry cylinder head from engine block dowels using suitable pry bar, ensuring to not damage contact surfaces.

INSPECTION

1. Inspect cylinder head for cracks wear or damage.
2. Using a straightedge and feeler gauge, measure for warpage across contact

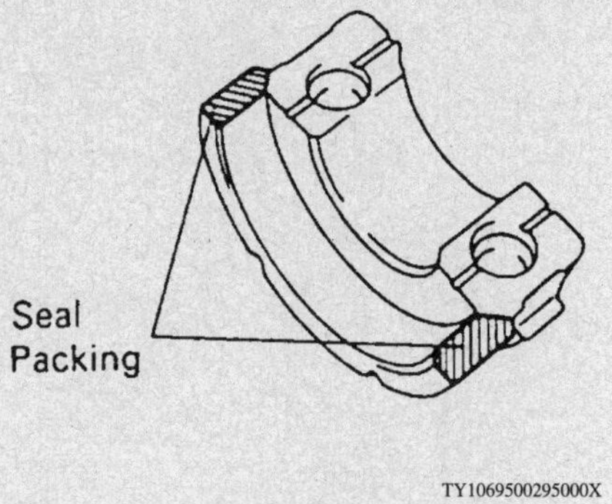
Seal
Packing
TY1069500295000X

Fig. 13 No. 1 bearing cap seal packing

surface of cylinder head at all angles. If warpage is greater than .0039 inch, replace cylinder head.

INSTALLATION

1. Position new gasket on engine block, then carefully place cylinder head on gasket.
2. Apply a light coat of clean engine oil to threads of the eight 12–pointed head bolts and **torque** in several steps to 25 ft. lbs. in sequence, **Fig. 11.** Final tighten an additional 90°.
3. Apply a light coat of clean engine oil to threads of 8 mm hexagonal recessed head cylinder head bolts, then **torque** to 13 ft. lbs.
4. Install ground strap.
5. Install righthand intake camshaft:
    a. Apply a light coat of clean engine oil to thrust portion and journal of camshaft.
    b. Place camshaft at 90° angle of timing mark (2 dots) on cylinder head, **Fig. 12.**
    c. Apply suitable grease to lip of new oil seal and install seal to camshaft.
    d. Apply seal packing No. 08826–00080, or equivalent, to No. 1 bearing cap, **Fig. 13.**
    e. Install bearing caps in their proper locations, **Fig. 14.**
    f. Apply a light coat of clean engine oil to threads and under head of bearing cap bolts. Install and **torque** bearing cap bolts in several passes to 12 ft. lbs. in sequence, **Fig. 15.**
6. Install righthand exhaust camshaft:
    a. Apply a light coat of clean engine oil to thrust portion and journal of camshaft.
    b. Install camshaft and align timing marks (one dot) on gear with timing marks on intake camshaft gear, **Fig. 16.**
    c. Install four bearing caps in their proper locations, **Fig. 17.**
    d. Apply a light coat of clean engine oil to threads and under head of bearing cap bolts. Install and **torque** bearing cap bolts in several passes to 12 ft. lbs. in sequence, **Fig. 18.**
    e. Remove service bolt and adjust alignment of timing marks, if necessary, with wrench.
7. Install lefthand intake camshaft:
    a. Apply a light coat of clean engine oil

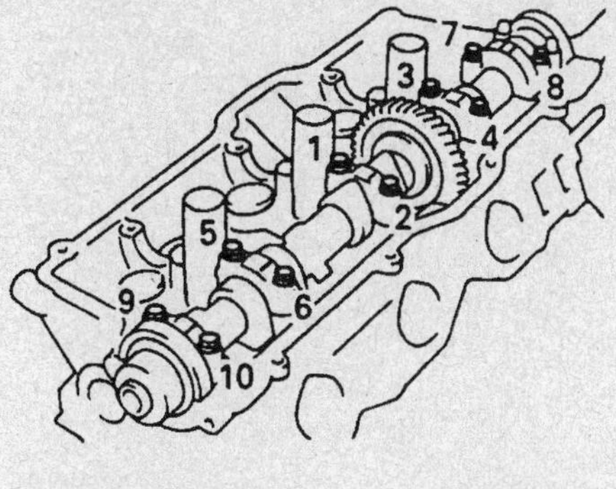

7
3
8
1
4
2
5
9
6
10

TY1069500297000X

Fig. 15 RH intake camshaft bearing cap tightening sequence

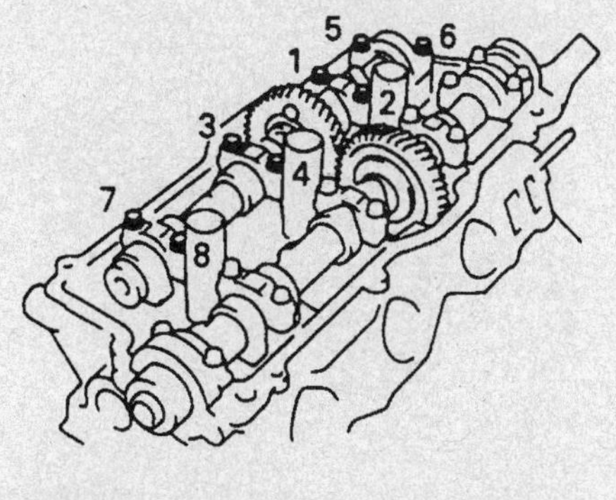

5
6
1
2
3
4
7
8

TY1069500300000X

Fig. 18 RH exhaust camshaft bearing cap tightening sequence

to thrust portion and journal of camshaft.

b. Place camshaft at 90° angle of timing mark (1 dot) on cylinder head, **Fig. 19.**
c. Apply suitable grease to lip of new oil seal and install seal to camshaft.
d. Apply seal packing No. 08826–00080, or equivalent, to No. 1 bearing cap, **Fig. 13.**
e. Install five bearing caps in their proper locations, **Fig. 20.**
f. Apply a light coat of clean engine oil to threads and under head of bearing cap bolts. Install and **torque** bearing cap bolts in several passes to 12 ft. lbs. in sequence, **Fig. 21.**

8. Install lefthand exhaust camshaft:
   a. Apply a light coat of clean engine oil to thrust portion and journal of camshaft.
   b. Install camshaft and align timing marks (one dot) on gear with timing marks on intake camshaft gear, **Fig. 22.**
   c. Install four bearing caps in their proper locations, **Fig. 23.**
   d. Apply a light coat of clean engine oil to threads and under head of bearing cap bolts. Install and **torque** bearing cap bolts in several passes to 12 ft. lbs. in sequence, **Fig. 24.**
   e. Remove service bolt and adjust alignment of timing marks, if necessary, with wrench.
   f. Check and adjust valves as outlined under "Valve Clearance Specifications" and "Valve Adjustment."

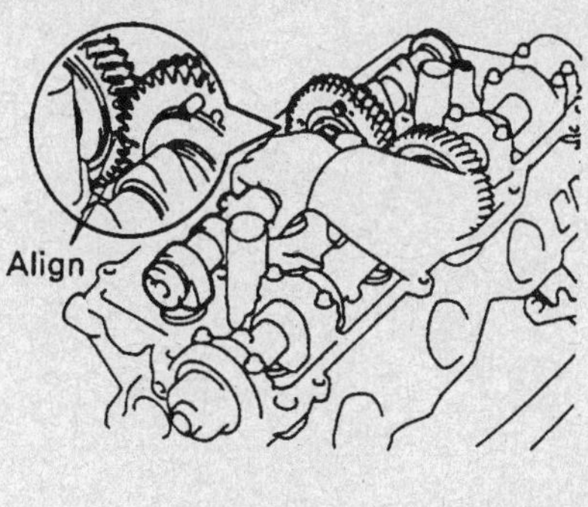

Align

TY1069500298000X

Fig. 16 RH exhaust camshaft timing mark alignment

9. Apply seal packing No. 08826–00080, or equivalent, to semi-circular plug grooves in cylinder heads, then install the semi-circular plugs.
10. Apply seal packing No. 08826–00080, or equivalent, to cylinder heads, then install cylinder head covers. Tighten to specification.
11. Install righthand exhaust manifold, using a new gasket. Tighten to specification.
12. Install righthand exhaust manifold heat insulator and tighten to specification.
13. Install lefthand exhaust manifold, using a new gasket. Tighten to specification.
14. Install lefthand exhaust manifold heat insulator and tighten to specification.
15. Install exhaust crossover pipe and tighten to specification.
16. Install alternator bracket and tighten to specification.
17. Install oil dipstick, guide and power steering pump bracket.
18. Install intake manifold assembly and stay. Tighten to specification.
19. Install fuel pressure regulator. Apply a light coat of gasoline to new O-ring before installation. Tighten to specification.
20. Inspect No. 3 timing belt cover gaskets for cracks, wear or damage. Replace if necessary. Install cover and tighten to specification.
21. Install camshaft position sensor and tighten to specification.
22. Install engine harness connectors:
    a. Oil pressure sensor.
    b. Crankshaft position sensor.
    c. Fuel injectors.
    d. ECT sender gauge.
    e. ECT sensor.
    f. Knock sensor
    g. Camshaft position sensor.
23. Install harness in wire hold down clamps.
24. Install intake air connector, **Fig. 25:**
    a. Install new gasket to unit and install. Tighten to specification.
    b. Connect DLC1 to bracket.
    c. Connect ground strap to intake air connector.
    d. Connect brake booster hose to intake air connector.
    e. Connect two fuel return hoses.
    f. **On models with A/C,** connect A/C idle-up valve connector.

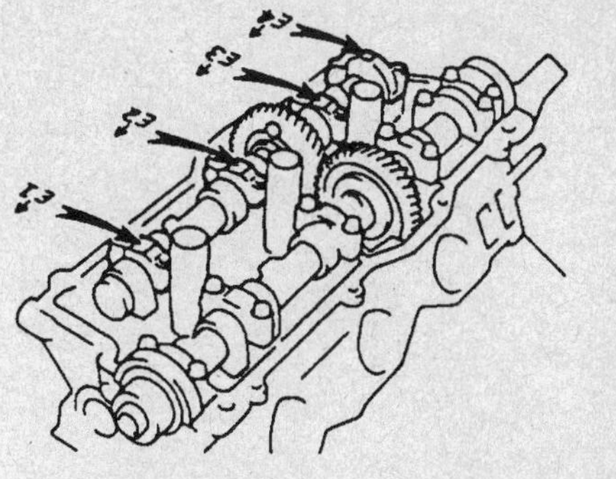

TY1069500299000X

Fig. 17 RH exhaust camshaft bearing cap installation

25. Install new gasket to air intake chamber assembly and tighten to specification. Connect the following:
    a. Two PCV hoses
    b. Two water bypass hoses.
    c. Air assist hose to throttle body.
    d. Two vacuum sensing hoses to VSV.
    e. EVAP hose.
    f. Air hose to power steering pump.
    g. Air hose to A/C idle-up valve, if equipped.
    h. VSV connector for fuel pressure control.
    i. Throttle position sensor connector.
    j. IAC valve connector.
    k. **On models with EGR,** gas temperature sensor connector and VSV connector.
26. Install air intake chamber stay and tighten to specification.
27. **On models with EGR, install EGR pipe. Torque** nuts (A), **Fig. 26,** to 14 ft. lbs., and nuts (B) to 6 ft. lbs.
28. **On all models,** temporarily install alternator.
29. Install timing belt idler No. 2 and tighten to specification.
30. Install lefthand camshaft timing pulley:
    a. Position pulley, with flange facing outward.
    b. Align knock pin hole of camshaft with knock pin groove of timing pulley, **Fig. 27,** then install knock pin. Using pin wrench tool set No. 09960–10010, or equivalent, tighten pulley bolt to specification.
31. Set No. 1 cylinder to TDC on compression stroke:
    a. Turn crankshaft pulley and align groove with "O"timing mark of No. 1 timing belt cover, **Fig. 28.**
    b. Turn camshaft and align knock pin hole of righthand camshaft with timing mark of No. 3 timing belt cover, **Fig. 29.**
    c. Turn camshaft and align timing mark of lefthand camshaft timing pulley with timing mark of No. 3 timing belt cover, **Fig. 29.**
32. Install timing belt as outlined under "Timing Belt, Replace."
33. Install spark plugs.
34. Install spark plug wires with ignition coils.
35. **On models with A/C,** install compressor bracket and connect compressor.

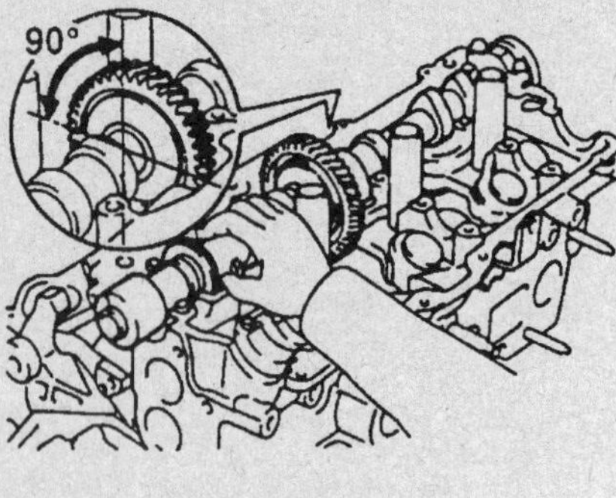
90°

TY1069500301000X

Fig. 19 LH intake camshaft installation

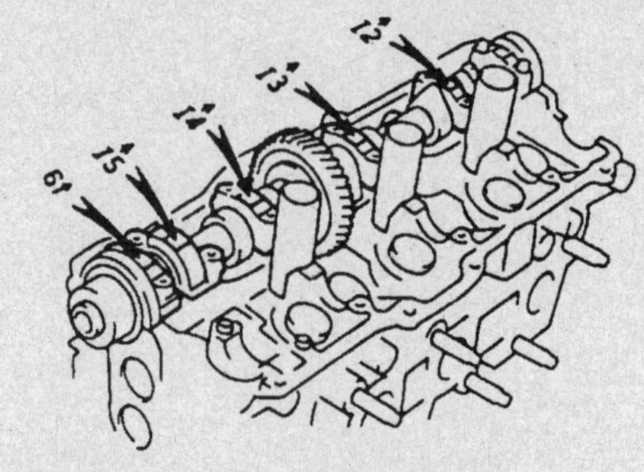
12
13
14
15
19

TY1069500302000X

Fig. 20 LH intake camshaft bearing cap installation

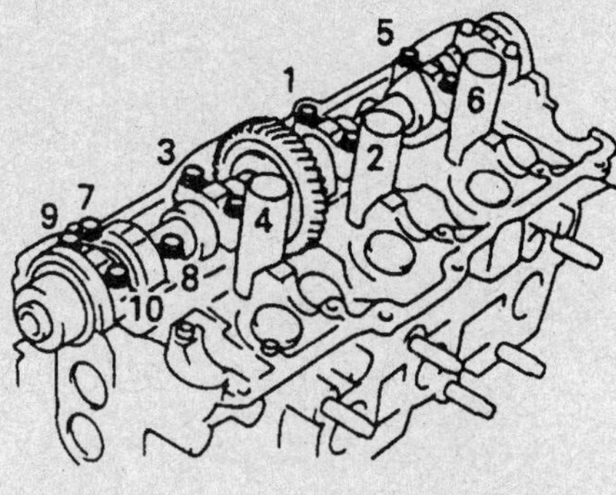
5
1
6
3
2
9
7
4
8
10

TY1069500303000X

Fig. 21 LH intake camshaft bearing cap tightening sequence

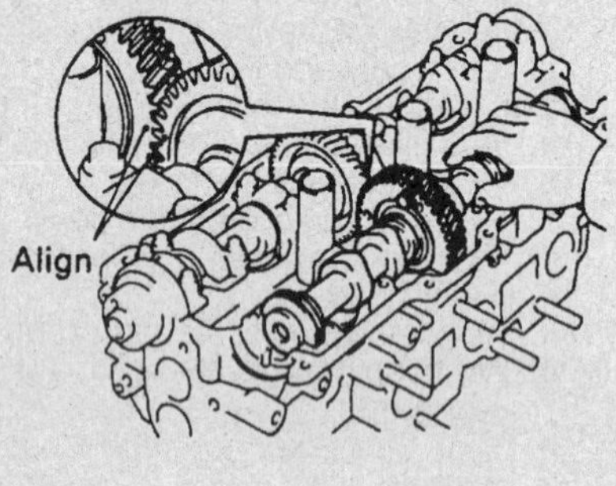
Align

TY1069500304000X

Fig. 22 LH exhaust camshaft installation

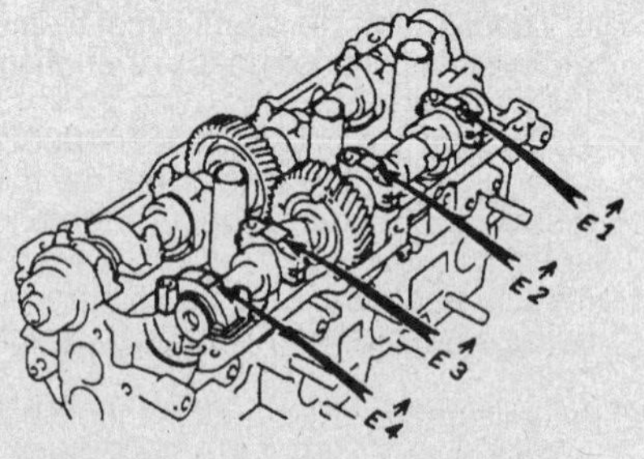
E1
E2
E3
E4

TY1069500305000X

Fig. 23 LH exhaust camshaft bearing cap installation

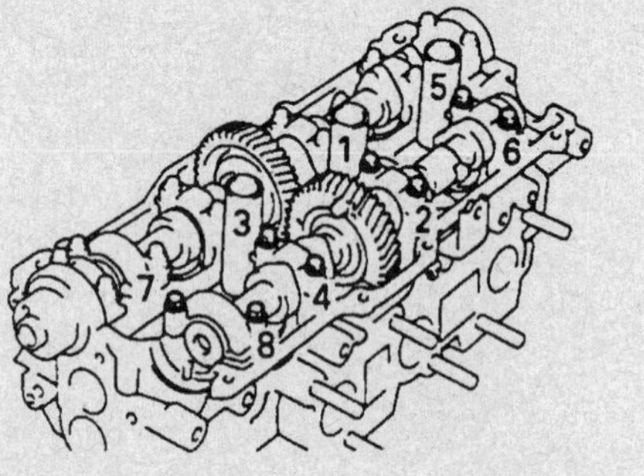
5
1
6
3
2
7
4
8

TY1069500306000X

Fig. 24 LH exhaust camshaft bearing cap tightening sequence

36. Install power steering pump.
37. Install fan with fluid coupling and fan pulleys. Tighten to specification.
38. Install No. 2 fan shroud.
39. Install and adjust alternator drive belt.
40. **On models with A/C,** install and adjust compressor drive belt.
41. **On all models,** install and adjust power steering pump drive belt.
42. Connect upper radiator hose and heater hose.
43. **On models with cruise control,** connect actuator cable.
44. **On models with automatic transmission,** connect throttle cable.
45. **On all models,** connect accelerator cable.
46. Install MAF meter, resonator and air cleaner cap.
47. Install front exhaust pipe.
48. Fill radiator with engine coolant. Start engine and check for coolant leaks. Refill coolant as necessary.
49. Install engine under cover.

VALVE CLEARANCE SPECIFICATIONS

Year	Stem-To-Guide Clearance	
	Intake	Exhaust
1995–96	.006–.009	.011–.014

VALVE ADJUSTMENT

1. Disconnect battery ground cable.

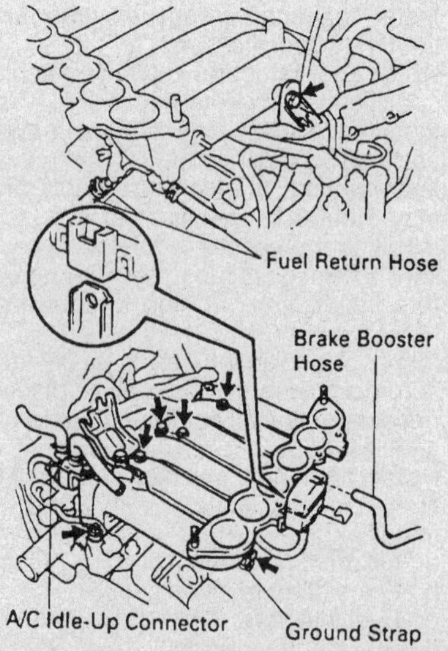
Fuel Return Hose
Brake Booster Hose
A/C Idle-Up Connector
Ground Strap

TY1069500307000X

Fig. 25 Intake air connector

2. Drain engine coolant.
3. Remove intake air connector.
4. Remove cylinder head covers as outlined under "Cylinder Head, Replace."
5. Turn crankshaft pulley and align groove with "O"timing mark of No. 1 timing belt cover, **Fig. 28.**
6. Ensure timing marks (1 dot) of camshaft drive and driven gears are in line, **Fig. 30.**
7. Measure valve clearance:
   a. Using suitable feeler gauge, measure clearance between valve lifter and camshaft. Measure only those valves indicated in **Fig. 31.** Refer to "Valve Clearance Specifications."
   b. Turn crankshaft 240° and measure only those valves indicated in **Fig. 32.**
   c. Turn crankshaft an additional 240° and measure only those valves indicated in **Fig. 33.**
8. Adjust valve clearance:
   a. Remove adjusting shim.
   b. Turn camshaft until cam lobe faces up, **Fig. 34.**
   c. Turn valve lifter with screwdriver until notches are perpendicular to camshaft.
   d. Using valve clearance adjusting tool set No. 09248–55040, or equivalent, remove and replace adjusting shim until proper clearance is obtained. Shims are available in increments of .0020 inch, from .0984 inch to .1299 inch.
9. Install cylinder head cover.
10. Fill cooling system.
11. Install air intake connector.
12. Connect battery ground cable.

TIMING BELT

REPLACE

REMOVAL

1. **On models with audio coded anti-theft system,**obtain three-digit system code.

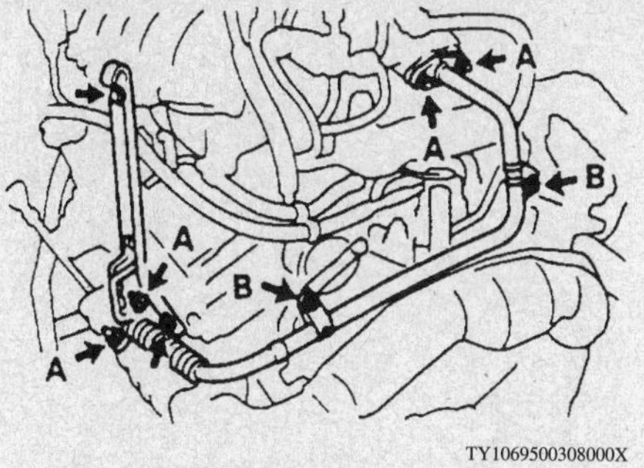
A
B
A
A
B
A
B
A
TY1069500308000X

Fig. 26 EGR pipe installation

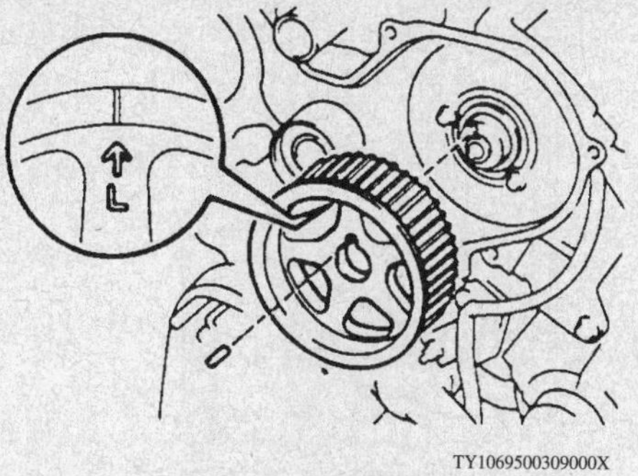
L
TY1069500309000X

Fig. 27 LH camshaft knock pin alignment

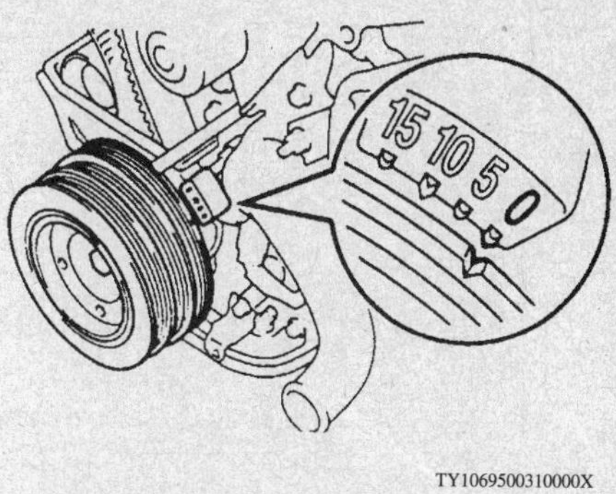
15 10 5 0
TY1069500310000X

Fig. 28 Timing mark of No. 1 timing belt cover

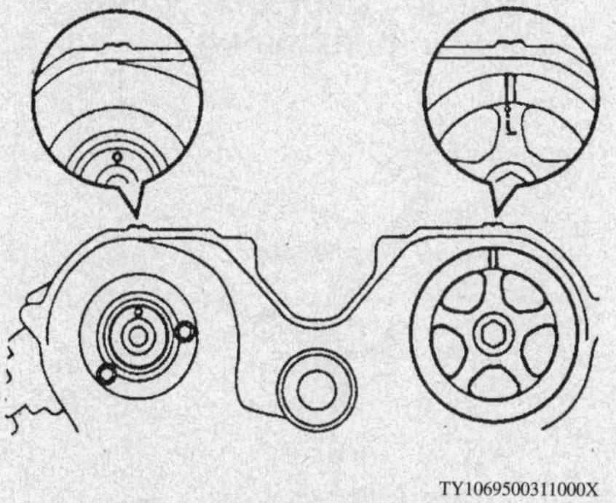
TY1069500311000X

Fig. 29 Camshaft timing positions

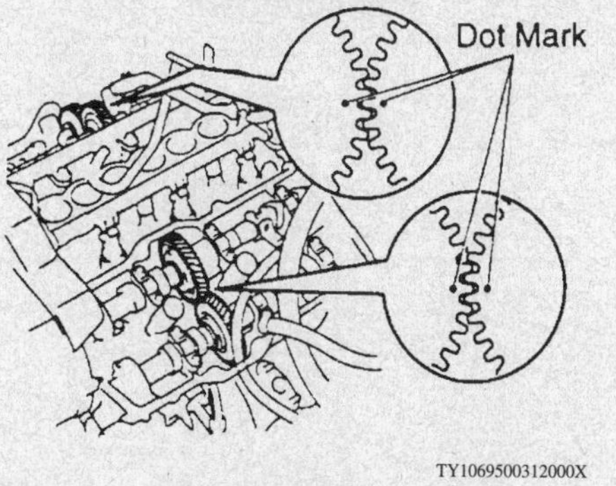
Dot Mark
TY1069500312000X

Fig. 30 Camshaft gear alignment.

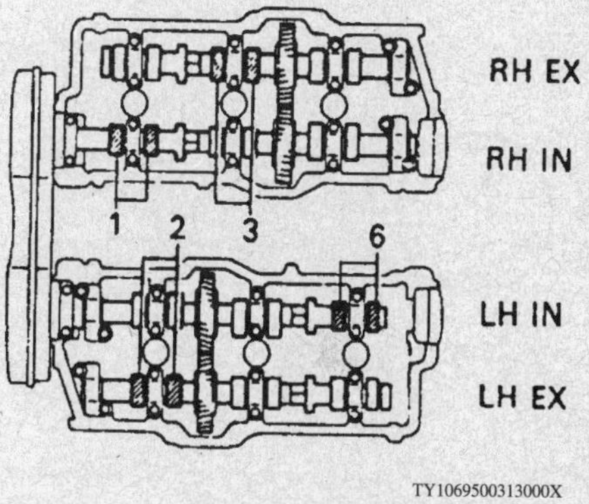
RH EX
RH IN
1 2 3 6
LH IN
LH EX
TY1069500313000X

Fig. 31 1st valve clearance measurement

2. **On all models,** disconnect battery ground cable.
3. Remove engine under cover.
4. Drain engine coolant.
5. Disconnect upper radiator hose.
6. Remove belt drive for power steering pump:
   a. Stretch belt and loosen fan pulley mounting nuts.
   b. Loosen lock bolt, pivot bolt and adjusting bolt, then remove drive belt.
7. **On models with A/C,** loosen idle pulley nut and adjusting bolt, then remove drive belt.
8. **On all models,** loosen alternator lock bolt, pivot bolt and adjusting bolt, then remove drive belt.
9. Remove No. 2 fan shroud.
10. Remove fan with fluid coupling and fan pulleys.
11. Disconnect power steering pump from engine and position aside.
12. **On models with A/C,** disconnect compressor from mounting bracket and position aside. Remove compressor mounting bracket.
13. **On all models,** remove No. 2 timing belt cover.
14. Remove fan bracket.
15. Turn crankshaft pulley and align groove with "O"timing mark of No. 1 timing belt cover and ensure timing marks of camshaft timing pulleys and No. 3 timing belt cover are aligned, **Fig. 35.**
16. Remove timing belt tensioner.
17. Remove righthand camshaft timing pulley with using removal wrench tool No. 09962–01000, or equivalent.
18. Remove lefthand camshaft timing pulley using removal wrench tool No. 09962–01000, or equivalent.
19. Remove crankshaft pulley using flange tool No. 09213–54015, or equivalent.
20. Remove starter wire bracket and No. 1 timing belt cover, **Fig. 36.**
21. Remove timing belt guide.
22. Remove timing belt.
23. Remove timing belt idlers No. 1 and No. 2.

INSTALLATION

1. Install timing belt idlers No. 1 and No. 2. Tighten to specification.
2. Temporarily install timing belt:
   a. Ensure engine is cold.
   b. Align timing marks on crankshaft timing pulley and oil pump body, **Fig. 37.**
   c. Remove any oil or water on pulleys.
   d. Align installation mark on timing belt with drilled mark on crankshaft timing pulley, **Fig. 38.**
   e. Install timing belt on crankshaft timing pulley, No. 1 idler and water pump pulleys.
3. Install timing belt guide.
4. Install No. 1 timing belt cover and starter wire bracket. Tighten to specification.
5. Install crankshaft pulley using flange tool No. 09213–54015, or equivalent. Tighten to specification.
6. Install lefthand camshaft timing pulley ensuring to align with knock pin groove, **Fig. 39.**Tighten to specification.
7. Turn crankshaft pulley and align groove with "O"timing mark of No. 1 timing belt cover and ensure timing marks of camshaft timing pulleys and No. 3 timing belt cover are aligned, **Fig. 35.**
8. Turn camshaft and align knock pin hole of righthand camshaft with timing mark of No. 3 timing belt cover, **Fig. 29.**
9. Turn camshaft and align timing mark of lefthand camshaft timing pulley with timing mark of No. 3 timing belt cover, **Fig. 29.**
10. Install timing belt to lefthand camshaft timing pulley:
   a. Ensure installation mark on timing belt matches end of No. 1 timing belt cover, **Fig. 40.**If installation mark does not align, shift meshing of timing belt and crankshaft timing pulley until they align.
   b. Remove any oil or water on lefthand camshaft timing pulley.
   c. Using wrench tool No. 09960–10010, or equivalent, slightly turn lefthand camshaft timing pulley clockwise. Align timing mark on timing belt with timing mark on lefthand camshaft timing pulley, **Fig. 41,** and hang timing belt on lefthand camshaft timing pulley.
   d. Using wrench tool No. 09960–10010, or equivalent, align timing mark of lefthand camshaft pulley

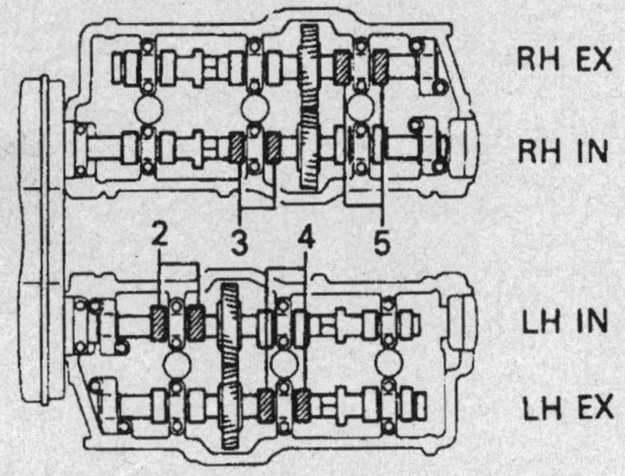
RH EX
RH IN
2
3
4
5
LH IN
LH EX

TY1069500314000X

Fig. 32 2nd valve clearance measurement

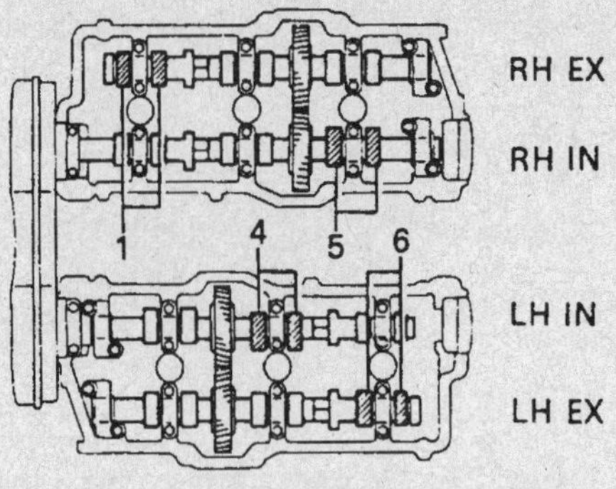
RH EX
RH IN
1
4
5
6
LH IN
LH EX

TY1069500315000X

Fig. 33 3rd valve clearance measurement

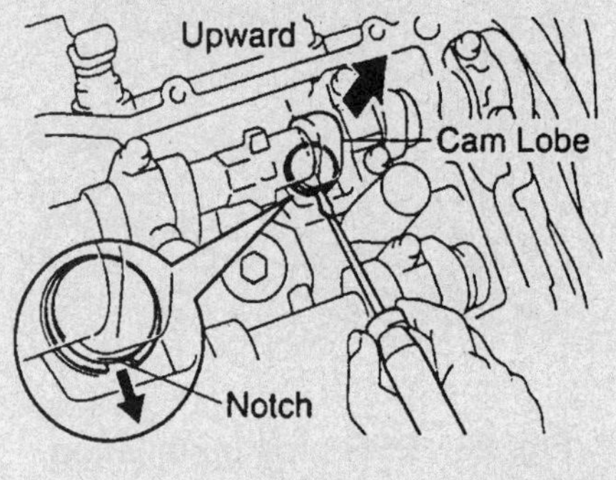
Upward
Cam Lobe
Notch

TY1069500316000X

Fig. 34 Cam lobe & lifter positioning

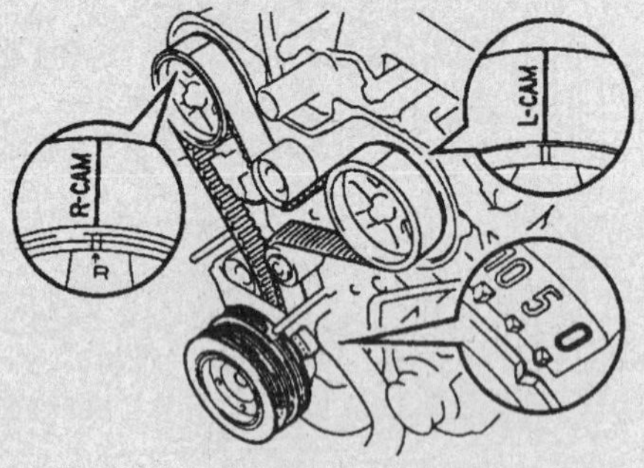
L-CAM
R-CAM
R
0 5 0

TY1069500317000X

Fig. 35 Timing pulley alignment

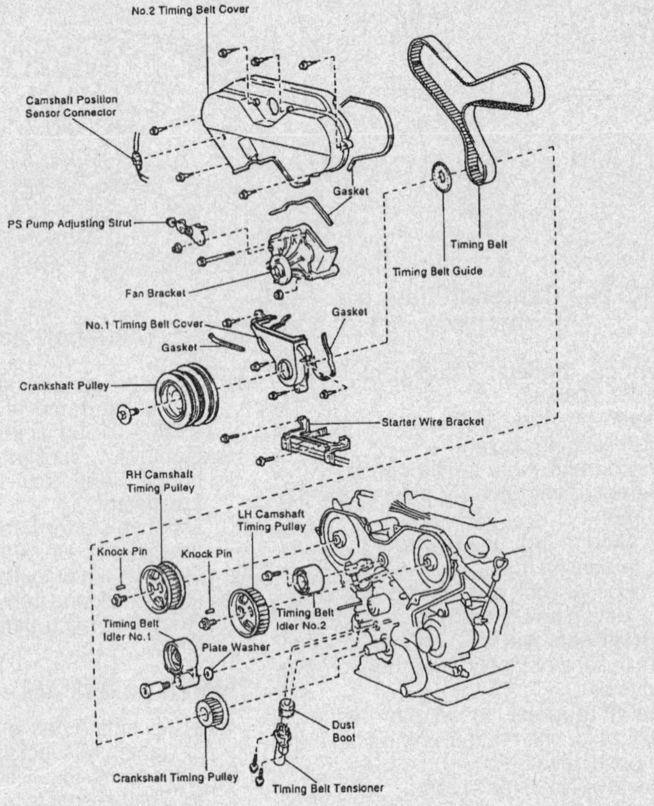
No.2 Timing Belt Cover
Camshaft Position Sensor Connector
Gasket
PS Pump Adjusting Strut
Timing Belt
Timing Belt Guide
Fan Bracket
Gasket
No.1 Timing Belt Cover
Gasket
Crankshaft Pulley
Starter Wire Bracket
RH Camshaft Timing Pulley
LH Camshaft Timing Pulley
Knock Pin
Knock Pin
Timing Belt Idler No.1
Timing Belt Idler No.2
Plate Washer
Dust Boot
Crankshaft Timing Pulley
Timing Belt Tensioner

TY1069500318000X

Fig. 36 Exploded view of timing belt assembly

and No. 3 timing belt cover, **Fig. 42.**

11. Install righthand camshaft timing pulley and timing belt:
    a. Remove any oil or water on righthand camshaft timing pulley and No. 2 idler pulley.
    b. Align installation mark on timing belt with timing mark on righthand camshaft timing pulley, **Fig. 43.**
    c. Hang timing belt on righthand camshaft timing pulley.
    d. Align timing marks of righthand camshaft timing pulley and No. 3 timing belt cover.
    e. Slide righthand camshaft timing pulley onto camshaft.
    f. Using wrench tool No. 09960–10010, or equivalent, align knock pin hole of camshaft with knock pin groove marked "R"on pulley and install knock pin.
    g. Install pulley bolt and tighten to specification.
12. Install timing belt tensioner:
    a. Using shop press, compress push rod into tensioner body, then insert 1.5 mm hex wrench through collar to retain push rod. Release press.
    b. Install dust boot to tensioner.
    c. Install tensioner and tighten to specification, then remove hex wrench.
13. Check valve timing:
    a. Turn crankshaft two complete revolutions clockwise from TDC to TDC.
    b. Ensure each pulley realigns with timing marks, **Fig. 44. If marks do not realign, remove and reinstall timing belt.**
14. Install fan bracket and power steering pump adjusting bracket.
15. Install No. 2 timing belt cover.
16. **On models with A/C,** install compressor bracket and mount compressor.
17. **On all models,** install power steering pump.
18. Install fan and pulley assembly. Tighten to specification.
19. Install No. 2 fan shroud.
20. Install and adjust drive belt for alternator.
21. **On models with A/C,** install and adjust drive belt for A/C compressor.
22. **On all models,** install and adjust drive belt for power steering pump.
23. Connect upper radiator hose.
24. Fill engine with coolant.
25. Install engine under cover.

CAMSHAFT

REPLACE

Refer to "Cylinder Head , Replace" for camshaft replacement procedure.

OIL PAN

REPLACE

1. Drain engine oil.
2. Remove pan bolts and nuts.
3. Using seal cutter tool No. 09032–00100, or equivalent, remove oil pan from engine block. Ensure to not damage oil pan flange.
4. Remove all remaining seal material from mating surfaces of pan and engine block.

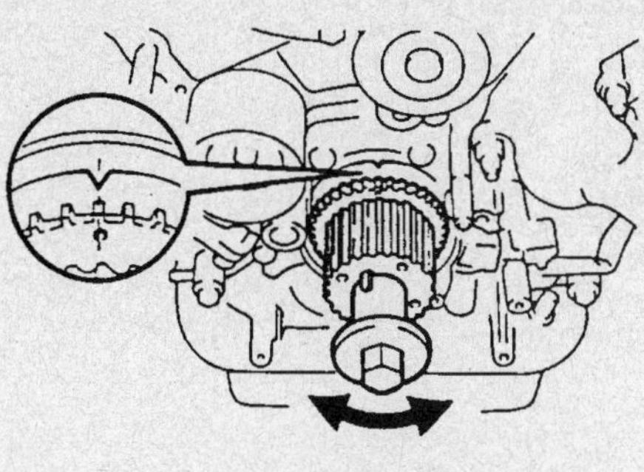

TY1069500319000X

Fig. 37 Crankshaft timing pulley alignment

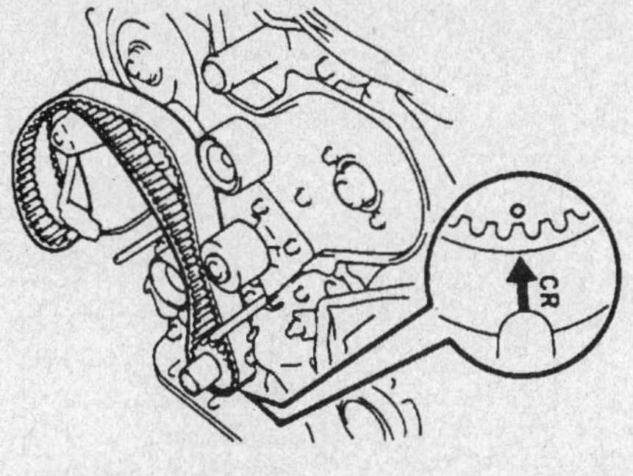
CR

TY1069500320000X

Fig. 38 Timing belt & crankshaft timing pulley alignment

TY1069500321000X

Fig. 39 LH camshaft timing pulley & knock pin groove alignment

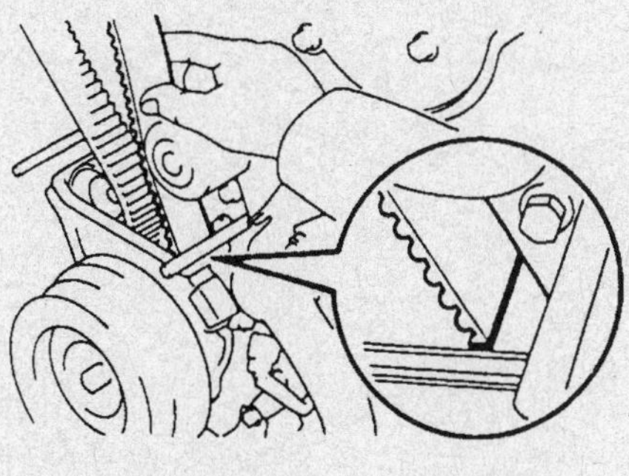

TY1069500322000X

Fig. 40 Timing belt & No. 1 timing belt cover alignment

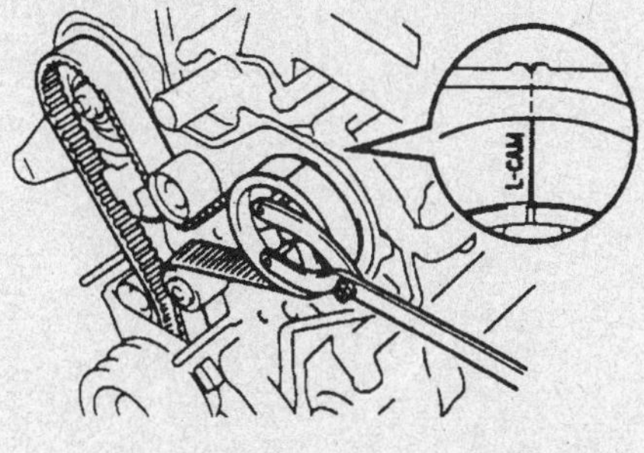
L-CAM

TY1069500323000X

Fig. 41 Timing belt & lefthand camshaft timing pulley alignment

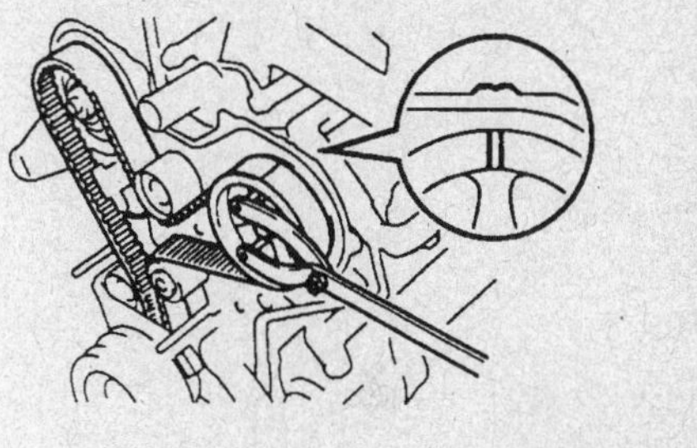

TY1069500324000X

Fig. 42 LH camshaft timing pulley & No. 3 timing belt cover alignment

5. Install new seal No. 08826–00080, or equivalent, to oil pan.
6. Install pan to engine and tighten to specification.

OIL PUMP

REPLACE

1. Remove crankshaft timing pulley as outlined under "Timing Belt, Replace."
2. **On 4WD models,** remove front differential.
3. **On models with automatic transmission,** remove transmission fluid cooler lines and clamp.
4. **On all models,** remove stiffener plate, **Fig. 45.**
5. Remove flywheel housing under cover and dust cover.
6. Disconnect starter harness connector.
7. Remove crankshaft position sensor.
8. Remove oil pan as outlined under "Oil Pan, Replace."
9. Remove oil strainer and oil pan baffle plate.
10. Remove oil pump and discard O-ring.
11. Reverse procedure to install, noting the following:
    a. Install new O-ring.
    b. **Torque** oil pump bolts "A" to 15 ft. lbs. and bolts "B" to 31 ft. lbs., **Fig. 46.**

OIL PUMP SERVICE

1. Remove oil pump as outlined under "Oil Pump, Replace."
2. Remove relief valve, **Fig. 47.**
3. Measure body clearance between driven rotor and pump body. Clearance should be .0039—.0069 inch. Replace rotor set or body if not as specified.

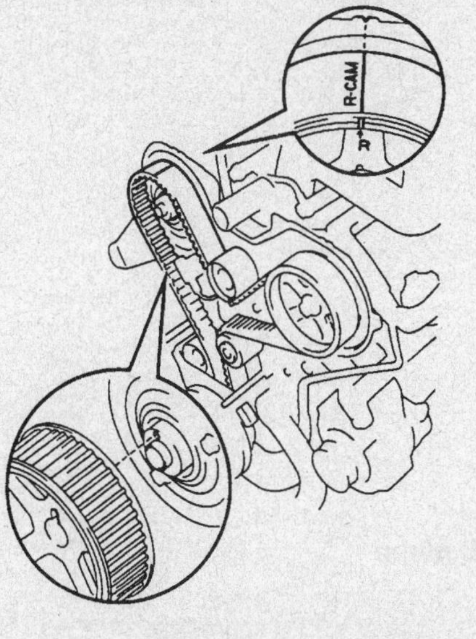
R-CAM
R

TY1069500325000X

Fig. 43 LH camshaft timing pulley & No. 2 idler pulley alignment

4. Measure tip clearance between drive and driven rotors. Clearance should be .0043—.0094 inch. Replace rotor set if not as specified.
5. Using a straight edge, measure side clearance between rotor set and body. Clearance should be .0012—.0035 inch. Replace rotor set and/or body if not as specified.
6. Inspect relief valve for damage or wear. Coat relief valve with engine oil and ensure it falls smoothly into valve hole by its own weight. Replace valve and/or body if not as specified.
7. Replace crankshaft front oil seal.
    a. Using a screwdriver, pry out old seal.
    b. Using seal setting tool No. 09309–37010, or equivalent, and a hammer, install new seal. Seat seal flush with pump body.
    c. Apply multi-purpose grease to seal lip.
8. Install oil pump as outlined under "Oil Pump, Replace."

BELT TENSION DATA

Belt	New, Lbs.	Used, Lbs.
Alternator	140–180	80–120
Power Steer.	135-180	85-120
A/C Comp.	135-185	80-120

COOLING SYSTEM BLEED

These engines do not require a specific bleed procedure. After filling cooling system, run engine to operating temperature with radiator/pressure cap off. Air will then be automatically bled through cap opening.

THERMOSTAT

REPLACE

1. Drain cooling system.

15 10 5 0

TY1069500334000X

Fig. 44 Valve timing marks

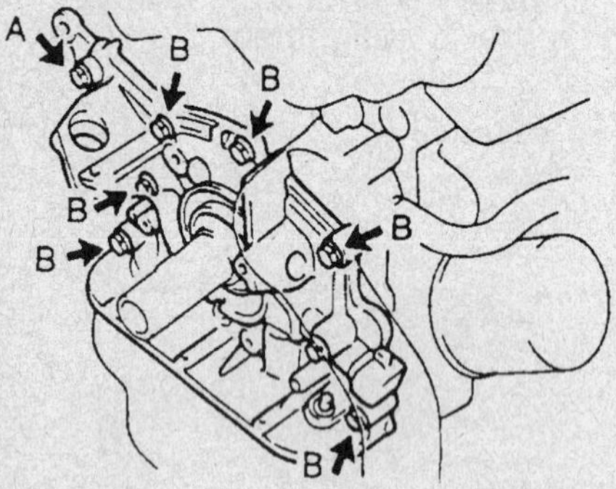
A
B
B
B
B
C
B
B

TY1069500336000X

Fig. 46 Oil pump tightening

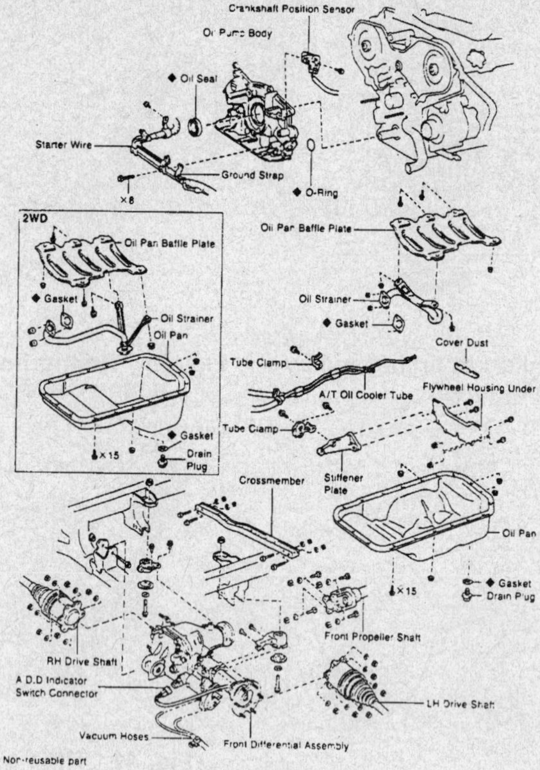
Crankshaft Position Sensor
Oil Pump Body
◆ Oil Seal
Starter Wire
Ground Strap
×8
◆ O-Ring
2WD
Oil Pan Baffle Plate
◆ Gasket
Oil Strainer
Oil Pan
◆ Gasket
×15
Drain Plug
Oil Pan Baffle Plate
Oil Strainer
◆ Gasket
Cover Dust
Tube Clamp
A/T Oil Cooler Tube
Flywheel Housing Under
Tube Clamp
Crossmember
Stiffener Plate
Oil Pan
◆ Gasket
Drain Plug
×15
Front Propeller Shaft
RH Drive Shaft
A.D.D Indicator Switch Connector
LH Drive Shaft
Vacuum Hoses
Front Differential Assembly
◆ Non-reusable part

TY1069500335000X

Fig. 45 Lubrication system

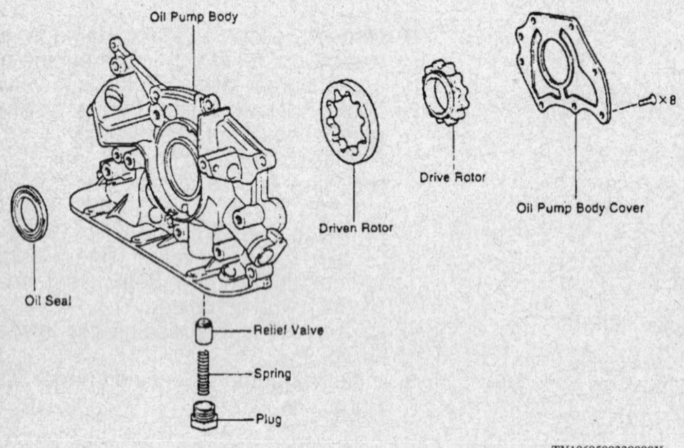
Oil Pump Body
Drive Rotor
×8
Oil Pump Body Cover
Driven Rotor
Oil Seal
Relief Valve
Spring
Plug

TY1069500338000X

Fig. 47 Exploded view of oil pump

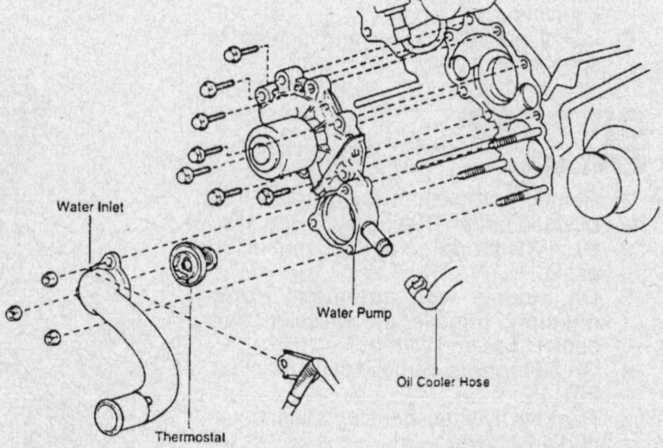
Water Inlet
Water Pump
Oil Cooler Hose
Thermostat

TY1069500339000X

Fig. 48 Water pump removal

2. Disconnect lower radiator hose.
3. Remove thermostat and gasket.
4. Reverse procedure to install. Use a new thermostat gasket and tighten inlet nuts to specifications.

WATER PUMP

REPLACE

1. **On models with audio coded anti-theft system,**obtain three-digit system code.
2. **On all models,** disconnect battery ground cable.
3. Remove timing belt as outlined under "Timing Belt, Replace."
4. Remove thermostat, **Fig. 48.**
5. **On models with oil cooler,** remove oil cooler hose.
6. **On all models,** remove water pump,
7. Reverse procedure to install. Reset audio coded anti-theft system, if equipped, as outlined under "Precautions."

RADIATOR

REPLACE

1. Disconnect battery ground cable.
2. Drain engine coolant.
3. **On Tacoma models,** remove front bumper filler.
4. **On all models,** remove radiator grille.
5. Disconnect upper radiator hose.
6. Disconnect coolant reservoir hose.
7. Disconnect lower radiator hose.
8. Remove fan shroud No. 2.
9. **On models with automatic transmission,** disconnect transmission oil cooler hoses.
10. **On all models,** remove radiator supports and radiator.
11. Reverse procedure to install.

FUEL PUMP

REPLACE

1. **On models with audio coded anti-theft system,**obtain three-digit system code.
2. **On all models,** disconnect battery ground cable.
3. Remove fuel tank.

4. Remove fuel pump harness connector.
5. Remove fuel pump bracket mounting bolts and pull out pump bracket assembly.
6. Remove and discard gasket.
7. Reverse procedure to install, noting:
   a. Install new gasket.
   b. Reset audio coded anti-theft system, if equipped, as outlined under "Precautions."

FUEL FILTER

REPLACE

1. Remove fuel pump as outlined under "Fuel Pump, Replace."
2. Using a small screwdriver, remove fuel filter clip.
3. Install new filter using new clip.
4. Reverse procedure to install.

TIGHTENING SPECIFICATIONS

Year	Component	Torque/ Ft. Lbs.
1995–96	Air Intake Chamber Assembly	13
	Air Intake Chamber Stay	30
	Alternator Bracket	14
	Alternator Pulley	81
	Camshaft Bearing Cap	②
	Camshaft Position Sensor	6
	Camshaft Pulley	81
	Clutch Release Cylinder	9
	Connecting Rod Cap	18⑤
	Crankshaft Main Bearing	45⑤
	Crankshaft Pulley	184
	Cylinder Head Bolts (12 Point)	②
	Cylinder Head Bolts (8 mm Recessed Head)	13
	Cylinder Head Cover	53①
	Cylinder Head Rear Plate	6
	Drive Plate	61
	EGR Pipe (Nut A)	14
	EGR Pipe (Nut B)	6
	Fan Assembly	48①
	Engine Front Mounting Bracket	28
	Engine Rear Mounting Bracket	43
	Exhaust Crossover Pipe	33
	Exhaust Manifold	30
	Exhaust Manifold Insulator	6
	Fan Mounting	48①
	Fuel Tank Mounting	③
	Fuel Pressure Regulator	71
	Fuel Pump	④
	Intake Air Connector	13
	Intake Manifold & Stay	13
	Knock Sensor	29
	No.1 Idler Pulley	26
	No. 2 Idler Pulley	30
	Oil Dipstick Guide	6
	Oil Pan	6
	Oil Pump	②
	Power Steering Pump Bracket	14
	Radiator Support	9
	Thermostat	14
	Timing Belt Covers	7
	Timing Belt Idler No. 1	26

Continued

TIGHTENING SPECIFICATIONS—Continued

Year	Component	Torque/ Ft. Lbs.
1995–96	Timing Belt Idler No. 2	30
	Timing Belt Tensioner	20

① — Inch lbs.
② — Refer to "Cylinder Head, Replace."
③ — Tacoma, 45 ft. lbs.; T100, 29 ft. lbs.
④ — Tacoma, 30 inch lbs.; T100, 35 inch lbs.
⑤ — Tighten each bolt an additional 90°.

1FZ-FE 4.5L Engine

NOTE: On Air Bag Equipped Models, Refer To "Air Bag System Precautions" Located In The Front Of This Manual For System Disarming & Arming Procedures.

INDEX

	Page No.
Belt Tension Data	47-61
Camshaft, Replace	47-61
Compression Pressure	47-58
Cooling System Bleed	47-61
Cylinder Head, Replace	47-59
Installation	47-60
Removal	47-59
Engine Rebuilding Specifications	48-1
Engine, Replace	47-58
Fuel Filter, Replace	47-62
Fuel Pump, Replace	47-62
Intake Manifold, Replace	47-59
Main & Rod Bearings	47-61
Oil Pan, Replace	47-61
Oil Pump, Replace	47-61
Oil Pump Service	47-61
Inspection	47-61
Overhaul	47-61
Piston & Rod Assembly	47-61
Precautions	47-58
Air Bag Systems	47-58
Audio Coded Anti-Theft System	47-58
Radiator, Replace	47-62
Thermostat, Replace	47-62
Tightening Specifications	47-63
Timing Chain, Replace	47-60
Installation	47-61
Removal	47-60
Valve Adjustment	47-60
Valve Clearance Specifications	47-60
Valve Guides	47-60
Water Pump, Replace	47-62

PRECAUTIONS

AIR BAG SYSTEMS

Refer to "Air Bag System Precautions" in the front of this manual for system disarming and arming procedures.

AUDIO CODED ANTI-THEFT SYSTEM

Some models are equipped with an audio coded anti-theft system that will disable the radio when the battery cable is disconnected. The system can be identified by the "ANTI-THEFT SYSTEM" on the cassette lid. Obtain three-digit code for input. Reset system after service as follows:

1. Obtain three-digit audio theft code.
2. Depress 1 (PROG) button while depressing righthand side of TUNE SEEK button. Three dashes will appear in tape operation display.
3. To enter first digit, depress 1 (PROG) button repeatedly until number of times depressed equals first digit (depress 1 button six times if first digit is five, first press equals 0).
4. To enter second digit, depress 2 (APS) button repeatedly until number of times depressed equals second digit.
5. To enter third digit, depress 3 (RPT) button repeatedly until number of times depressed equals third digit.
6. If three dashes are displayed after inputting digits, repeat procedure.
7. When code appears in display, depress and hold SCAN button until SEC appears.
8. When SEC disappears audio system is operative.
9. If Err is displayed, repeat procedure. **Attempting to input code more than nine times may permanently disable audio system.**

COMPRESSION PRESSURE

1. Start engine and warm to normal operating temperature.
2. Disconnect distributor connector.
3. Disconnect igniter connector.
4. Disconnect high tension cords from spark plugs.
5. Remove spark plugs, then insert compression gauge into spark plug hole.
6. Fully open throttle.
7. While cranking engine, measure compression pressure.
8. Standard compression pressure should be 171 psi. Minimum compression is 128 psi.
9. The difference in compression pressure between each cylinder should not exceed 14 psi.

ENGINE

REPLACE

1. **On models with audio coded anti-theft system,** obtain three-digit system code.
2. **On all models,** remove battery and battery tray.
3. Drain engine coolant and engine oil.
4. Scribe hood hinge locations, then remove hood.
5. Remove radiator grille.
6. Remove fan with fluid coupling, water pump pulley and fan shroud.
7. Remove drive belts.
8. Disconnect radiator hoses and remove radiator.
9. Disconnect volume airflow meter connector and wire clamp.
10. Loosen No. 2 air hose clamp and disconnect hose.
11. Remove air cleaner cap, resonator and volume airflow meter.
12. Remove air filter and air cleaner case.
13. Disconnect cruise control actuator and accelerator cables from throttle body.
14. Disconnect heater hoses.
15. Disconnect brake booster vacuum hose, EVAP hose and fuel hoses.
16. Disconnect engine wires and connectors.
17. Disconnect A/C compressor and

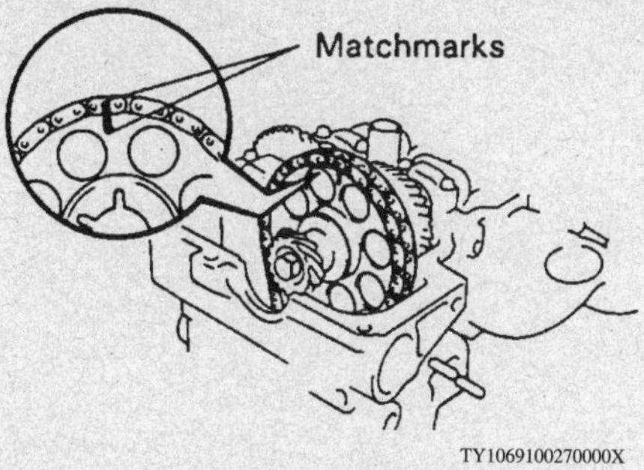
Matchmarks
TY1069100270000X

Fig. 1 Camshaft timing gear & chain matchmarks

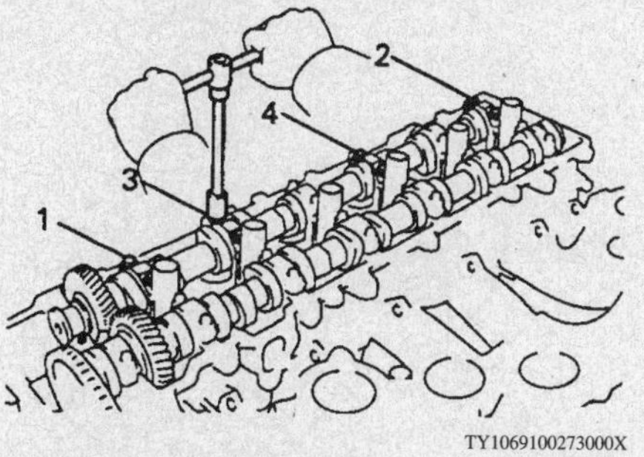
2
4
3
1
TY1069100273000X

Fig. 4 Remove bearing cap bolts

bracket, if equipped. Place compressor aside and suspend it.
18. Disconnect No. 2 radiator hose from water inlet, then remove radiator pipe.
19. Disconnect power steering pressure hose and return hose.
20. Remove heater valve, then disconnect ground strap and engine wire from cowl panel.
21. Remove glove compartment door.
22. Remove ECM retaining screws and disconnect ECM. Disconnect ECM connectors.
23. Disconnect cowl wire connectors, then pull engine wire from cabin.
24. Remove stabilizer bar.
25. Remove front and rear propeller shafts. Put alignment marks on flanges.
26. Remove transmission control rod from shift lever.
27. Remove shift lever knob, console and boot, then the console box.
28. Disconnect shift lever connectors, then remove transmission shift lever assembly.
29. Pull out shift rod pin and disconnect shift rod.
30. Remove hose clamp and transfer shift lever.
31. Remove front exhaust pipe assembly.
32. Disconnect ground strap from heat insulator.
33. Remove transfer undercover.
34. Place jack under transmission, then remove frame crossmember.
35. Slowly lift engine with transmission from vehicle. Ensure all cables, hoses and electrical connectors are disconnected during removal.
36. Separate transmission from engine.
37. Reverse procedure to install. Reset audio coded anti-theft system, if

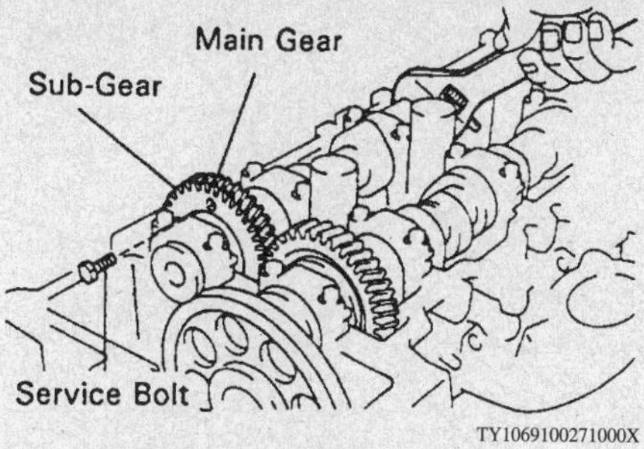
Main Gear
Sub-Gear
Service Bolt
TY1069100271000X

Fig. 2 Service bolt hole

equipped, as outlined under "Precautions."

INTAKE MANIFOLD

REPLACE

Refer to "Cylinder Head, Replace" for procedure.

CYLINDER HEAD

REPLACE

REMOVAL

1. **On models with audio coded anti-theft system,** obtain three-digit system code.
2. **On all models,** disconnect battery ground cable, then drain coolant from radiator and engine block.
3. Remove PCV hoses.
4. Remove air cleaner cap, volume air flow meter and resonator.
5. Disconnect cruise control actuator, throttle and accelerator cables from throttle body.
6. Disconnect engine ground straps.
7. Disconnect connector on intake manifold from lefthand fender apron.
8. Disconnect heater hoses.
9. Disconnect heater valve and engine wire from cowl panel.
10. Remove No. 2 and No. 3 cylinder head covers.
11. Disconnect distributor wires and connector, then remove distributor.
12. Disconnect power steering reservoir tank.
13. Disconnect radiator inlet hose.
14. Disconnect No. 3 water bypass hose.
15. Remove generator and generator bracket.
16. Remove water outlet.
17. Disconnect throttle body connectors and remove throttle body.
18. Remove No. 2 water bypass pipe with hoses.
19. Disconnect connector for emission control valve set assembly.
20. Disconnect hoses and connectors from EGR valve, then remove EGR valve and vacuum modulator.
21. Remove heater inlet pipe and air intake chamber retaining bolt.
22. Remove oil dipsticks, engine guides and transmission guides.
23. Remove hoses from air intake chamber, then the air intake chamber.
24. Remove fuel return pipe, No. 1 water bypass hose and No. 1 fuel pipe.

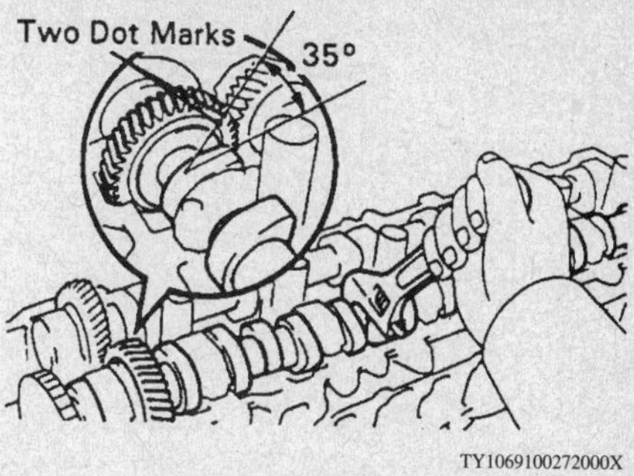
Two Dot Marks
35°
TY1069100272000X

Fig. 3 Camshaft gear timing mark

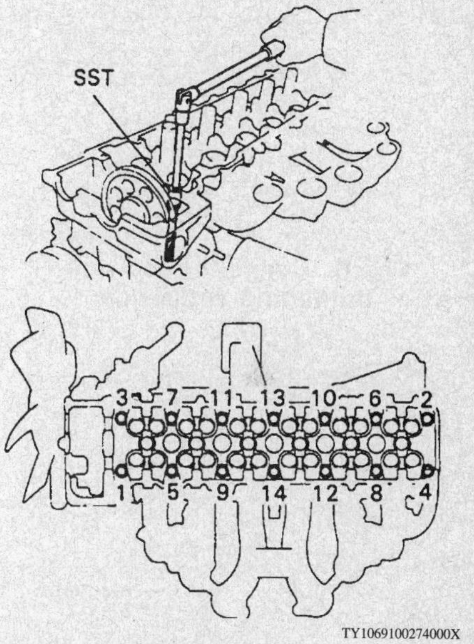
SST
3 7 11 13 10 6 2
1 5 9 14 12 8 4
TY1069100274000X

Fig. 5 Cylinder head bolt removal sequence

25. Disconnect fuel inlet hose.
26. Remove delivery pipe and injectors.
27. Disconnect engine connectors and engine wire.
28. Remove front exhaust pipe assembly.
29. Remove heater pipe, air pipe and pair reed valve.
30. Remove No. 1 and No. 2 exhaust manifolds.
31. Remove engine hangers.
32. Remove water outlet bypass and pipe.
33. Remove cylinder head cover and spark plugs.
34. Turn crankshaft pulley to set No. 1 cylinder to TDC on compression stroke.
35. Place matchmarks on camshaft timing gear and timing chain, then remove chain tensioner and camshaft timing gear, **Fig. 1.**
36. Remove camshafts as follows:
    a. Turn hexagon portion of intake camshaft with wrench to bring service bolt hole of driven sub-gear upward, **Fig. 2.**
    b. Attach exhaust camshaft sub-gear to driven gear with service bolt.
    c. Set timing mark of camshaft driven gear at a 35° angle by turning hexagon wrench head portion of intake camshaft, **Fig. 3.**
    d. Gently push camshaft toward rear of engine. Loosen and remove

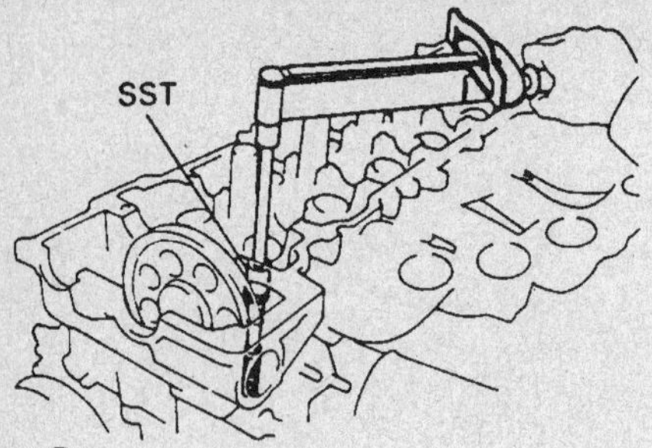
SST

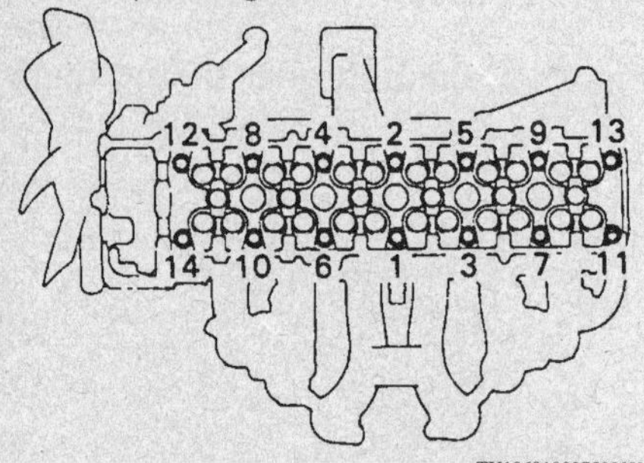
12 8 4 2 5 9 13
14 10 6 1 3 7 11

TY1069100275000X

Fig. 6 Cylinder head bolt tightening sequence

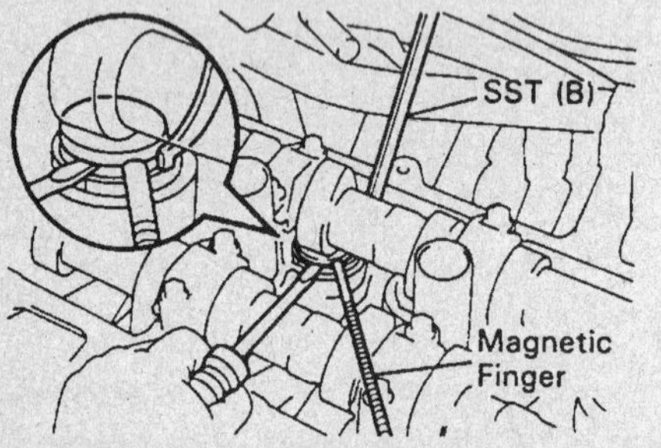
SST (B)
Magnetic Finger

TY1069100278000X

Fig. 9 Valve adjusting shim

bearing cap bolts as shown in **Fig. 4.**

e. Remove two remaining bearing cap bolts and remove exhaust camshaft.

f. Set timing mark on intake camshaft drive gear at a 25° angle, then lightly push camshaft toward front of engine.

g. Remove bearing caps and exhaust camshaft.

37. Remove cylinder head bolts in sequence shown in **Fig. 5,** then the cylinder head.
38. Remove heater inlet pipe and hose.
39. Remove intake manifold with fuel filter.

INSTALLATION

1. Install fuel filter and intake manifold. Tighten to specifications.
2. Install heater inlet pipe and hose.
3. Install cylinder head, then using sequence shown in **Fig. 6,** tighten bolts in three steps: first, **torque** cylinder head bolts to 29 ft. lbs.; then tighten an additional 90°; and finally tighten an additional 90°.
4. Install intake and exhaust camshafts and bearing caps. Tighten bearing caps to specifications, then remove service bolt.

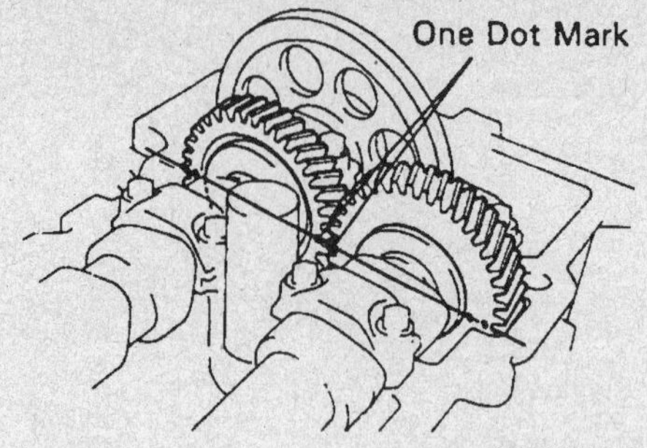
One Dot Mark

TY1069100276000X

Fig. 7 Camshaft gear alignment

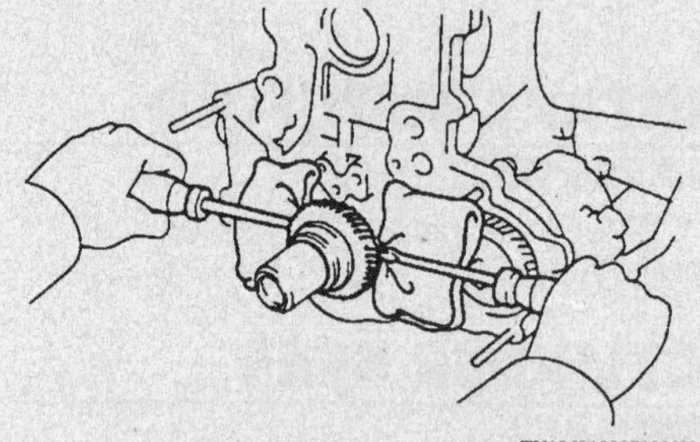

TY1069100279000X

Fig. 10 Driveshaft gear removal

5. Set No. 1 cylinder to TDC on compression stroke.
6. Turn camshafts until timing marks align as in **Fig. 7.**
7. Install camshaft gear over straight pin of intake camshaft.
8. Align straight pin of distributor gear with straight pin groove of intake camshaft, **Fig. 8,** then install and tighten bolt to specification.
9. Install and set chain tensioner, then check valve timing.
10. Reverse steps 1 through 32 of removal procedure to complete installation. Reset audio coded anti-theft system, if equipped, as outlined under "Precautions."

VALVE CLEARANCE SPECIFICATIONS

With the engine cold, intake valve clearance should be .006–.010 inch and exhaust clearance should be .010–.014 inch.

VALVE ADJUSTMENT

Valve clearance is adjusted by removing or installing adjusting shims. Shims are removed and inserted with a screwdriver and magnetic finger, **Fig. 9.**

1. Turn crankshaft until No. 1 cylinder is at TDC on compression stroke. Adjust valves of cylinders except No. 6.
2. Before adjusting rear valves of No. 6 cylinder, remove distributor, and camshafts.

VALVE GUIDES

1. Heat cylinder head to 176–212°F.
2. Using suitable tool and hammer, tap out valve guide bushing.
3. Using suitable tool and hammer, tap in new guide bushing until .323–.339 inch is protruding from cylinder head.

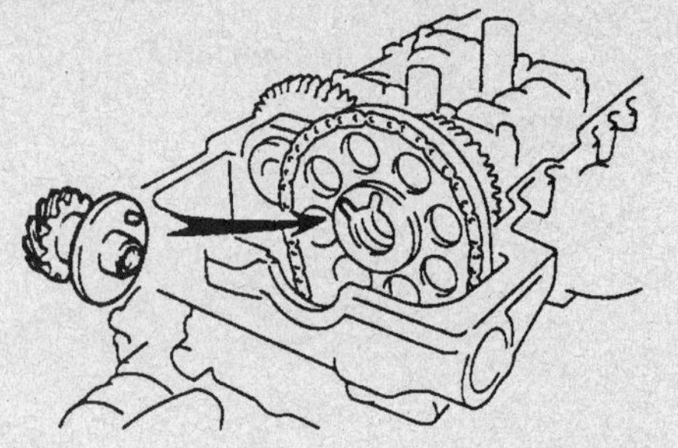

TY1069100277000X

Fig. 8 Distributor gear alignment

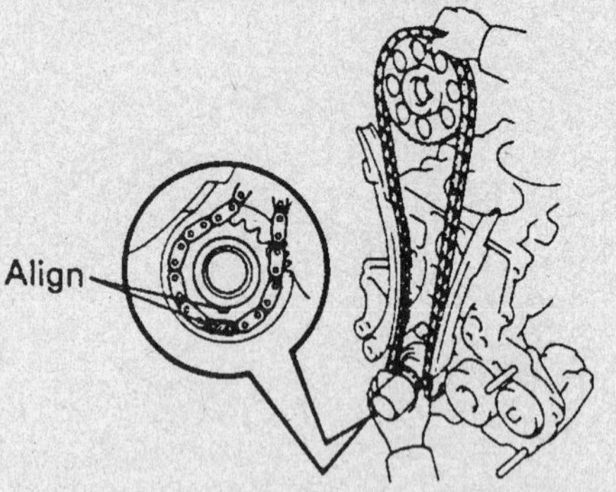
Align

TY1069100280000X

Fig. 11 Crankshaft timing gear alignment

TIMING CHAIN

REPLACE

REMOVAL

1. Drain engine oil and coolant.
2. Remove engine undercover and radiator.
3. Leaving pressure hoses connected, remove A/C compressor and bracket. Position aside.
4. Disconnect radiator hose from water inlet, then remove radiator pipe.
5. Remove water pump retaining bolts and water pump.
6. Remove cylinder head as outlined under "Cylinder Head, Replace."
7. Disconnect oil cooler pipe bracket from No. 1 oil pan.
8. Remove oil level sensor.
9. Remove No. 1 oil pan attaching bolts, then the oil pan.
10. Remove crankshaft pulley and drive belt idler pulley.
11. Remove timing chain cover attaching bolts and drive belt adjusting bar.
12. Remove timing chain cover with oil pump.
13. Remove timing chain and camshaft timing gear.
14. Remove crankshaft timing gear.
15. Remove chain tensioner slipper and vibration damper.
16. Remove oil jet and oil pump driveshaft gear. **Position shop towels as shown in Fig. 10 to prevent damage.**

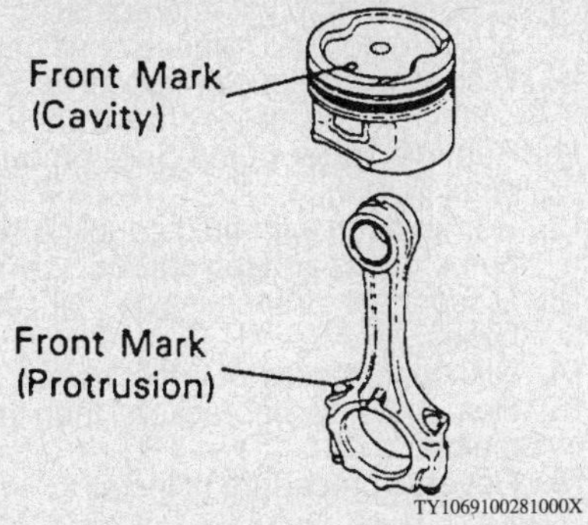
Front Mark
(Cavity)
Front Mark
(Protrusion)
TY1069100281000X

Fig. 12 Piston & connecting rod

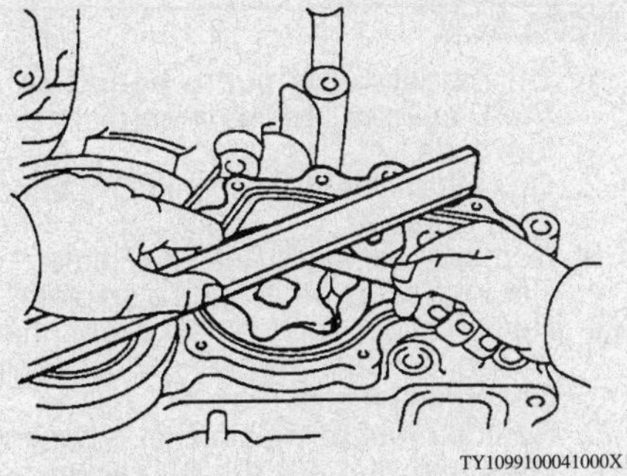
TY1099100041000X

Fig. 13 Oil pump inspection

INSTALLATION

1. Rotate crankshaft until set key faces downward.
2. Install pump driveshaft gear.
3. Install oil pump driveshaft gear and oil jet.
4. Install chain tensioner slipper and vibration damper.
5. Install crankshaft timing gear.
6. Install timing chain on camshaft timing gear. Align bright colored link on timing chain with timing mark on camshaft timing gear.
7. Install timing chain on crankshaft timing gear. Align bright colored link on timing chain with timing mark on crankshaft timing gear, **Fig. 11.**
8. Apply seal packing to timing chain cover, then install timing chain cover with oil pump.
9. Install drive belt idler pulley and tighten bolt to specification.
10. Install crankshaft pulley and tighten bolt to specification.
11. Install No. 1 and No. 2 oil pans and tighten bolts to specifications.
12. Install oil level sensor.
13. Connect oil cooler pipe bracket to No. 1 oil pan.
14. Install cylinder head as outlined under "Cylinder Head, Replace."
15. Install water pump and radiator pipe.
16. Install A/C compressor and bracket.
17. Install radiator. Fill engine with oil and check for leaks.
18. Install engine undercover.

CAMSHAFT

REPLACE

Refer to "Cylinder Head, Replace" for camshaft removal procedures.

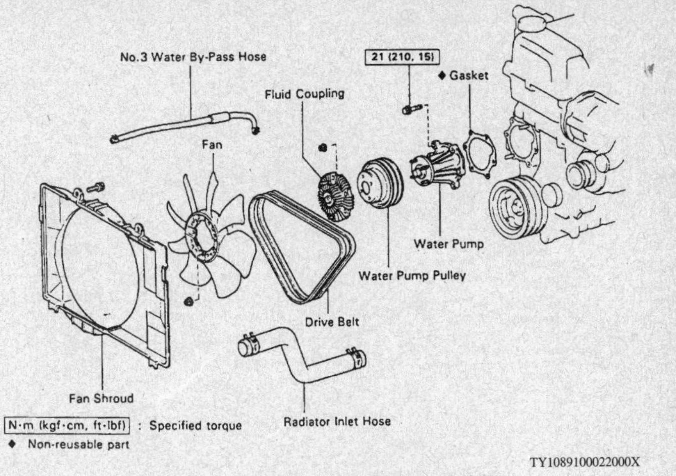
No.3 Water By-Pass Hose
21 (210, 15)
◆ Gasket
Fluid Coupling
Fan
Water Pump
Water Pump Pulley
Drive Belt
Fan Shroud
Radiator Inlet Hose
N·m (kgf·cm, ft·lbf) : Specified torque
◆ Non-reusable part
TY1089100022000X

Fig. 14 Water pump removal

PISTON & ROD ASSEMBLY

Pistons are available in standard and oversize of .020 (.50 mm) and .040 inch (1.00 mm). When assembling piston onto connecting rod, align front marks of piston and connecting rod, **Fig. 12.** When installing piston and connecting rod assembly, ensure mark on top of piston is facing toward front of engine.

MAIN & ROD BEARINGS

Main and connecting rod bearings are available in standard and undersize of .010 inch (.25 mm) and .020 inch (.50 mm).

OIL PAN

REPLACE

1. Drain engine oil and engine coolant.
2. Remove engine undercover.
3. Remove radiator.
4. Disconnect A/C compressor and bracket. Place compressor aside and suspend it.
5. Disconnect No. 2 radiator hose from water inlet, then remove radiator pipe.
6. Remove water pump.
7. Remove cylinder head as outlined under "Cylinder Head, Replace."
8. Disconnect oil cooler pipe bracket from No. 1 oil pan.
9. Remove oil level sensor.
10. Remove No. 1 oil pan to transmission housing attaching bolts.
11. Remove No. 2 oil pan mounting bolts and oil pan.
12. Remove No. 2 oil pan mounting bolts and oil pan.
13. Remove oil pan baffle plate and oil strainer.
14. Remove crankshaft pulley and drive belt idler pulley.
15. Remove oil pump with timing chain cover.
16. Reverse procedure to install. Tighten oil pump and oil pan mounting bolts to specifications.

OIL PUMP

REPLACE

Refer to "Oil Pan, Replace" for procedure.

OIL PUMP SERVICE

OVERHAUL

1. Remove pump cover, drive rotor, driven rotor and gasket.
2. Remove relief valve plug, gasket and spring.
3. Reverse procedure to assemble.

INSPECTION

1. Check relief valve for scoring or wear. Replace if damaged.
2. Using thickness gauge, measure clearance between driven rotor and body. If clearance is greater than .0118 inch, replace oil pump assembly.
3. Using thickness gauge and straightedge, measure clearance between rotors and straightedge, **Fig. 13.** If clearance is greater than .0059 inch, replace oil pump assembly.
4. Using thickness gauge, measure clearance between drive and driven rotor tips. If clearance is greater than .0098 inch, replace rotor set.

BELT TENSION DATA

Belt	New, Lbs.	Used, Lbs.
Generator	100–150	60–100
Power Steer.	100–150	60–100
A/C Comp.	100–150	60–100

COOLING SYSTEM BLEED

These engines do not require a specific bleed procedure. After filling cooling system, run engine to operating temperature with radiator/pressure cap off. Air will then be automatically bled through cap opening.

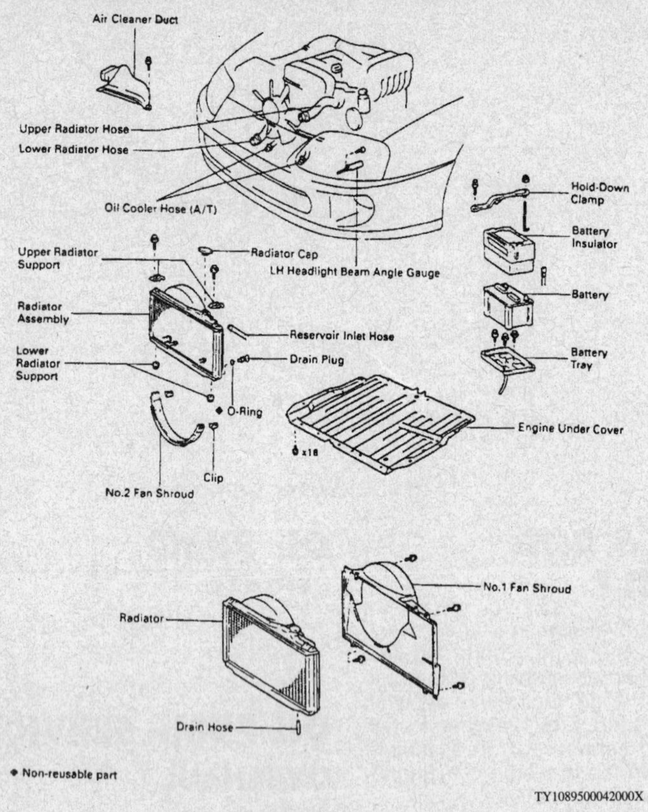
Air Cleaner Duct
Upper Radiator Hose
Lower Radiator Hose
Oil Cooler Hose (A/T)
Upper Radiator Support
Radiator Cap
LH Headlight Beam Angle Gauge
Radiator Assembly
Reservoir Inlet Hose
Lower Radiator Support
Drain Plug
O-Ring
Engine Under Cover
Clip
No.2 Fan Shroud
Hold-Down Clamp
Battery Insulator
Battery
Battery Tray
No.1 Fan Shroud
Radiator
Drain Hose
◆ Non-reusable part
TY1089500042000X

Fig. 15 Radiator removal

THERMOSTAT

REPLACE

1. Drain engine coolant.
2. Disconnect water inlet and remove thermostat from water pump.
3. Remove gasket and inspect thermostat.
4. Reverse procedure to install.

WATER PUMP

REPLACE

1. Drain engine coolant, then disconnect radiator inlet and water bypass hoses.
2. Remove drive belts and fan with fluid coupling, **Fig. 14.**
3. Remove water pump pulley and fan shroud.
4. Remove water pump mounting bolts and water pump.
5. Reverse procedure to install. Tighten water pump mounting bolts to specifications.

RADIATOR

REPLACE

1. Disconnect battery ground cable.
2. Drain engine coolant.
3. Remove battery and tray, **Fig. 15.**
4. Remove radiator grille
5. Disconnect No. 3 water bypass hose.
6. Disconnect radiator inlet hose.
7. Disconnect coolant reservoir hose.
8. Loosen water pump pulley mounting bolts.
9. Loosen lock, pivot and adjusting bolts of alternator and remove drive belts.
10. Disconnect oil cooler hose from clamp on fan shroud, then remove shroud.
11. Remove water pump pulley mounting nuts.
12. Remove fan with fluid coupling, water pump pulley and fan shroud.
13. Disconnect transmission oil cooler hoses.
14. Disconnect radiator outlet hose.
15. Remove radiator brackets, then the radiator.
16. Reverse procedure to install.

FUEL PUMP

REPLACE

1. **On models with audio coded anti-theft system,**obtain three-digit system code.
2. **On all models,** disconnect battery ground cable.
3. Remove rear seats and scuff plate.
4. Remove side garnish and step plate.
5. Remove floor service hole cover, then disconnect fuel pipe and hose from fuel pump bracket.
6. Remove fuel pump bracket mounting bolts and pull out pump bracket assembly.
7. Reverse procedure to install. Reset audio coded anti-theft system, if equipped, as outlined under "Precautions."

FUEL FILTER

REPLACE

1. **On models with audio coded anti-theft system,**obtain three-digit system code.
2. **On all models,** disconnect battery ground cable.
3. Place suitable container under fuel filter to allow fuel drainage.
4. Slowly disconnect fuel pipe and fuel hose from fuel filter. **Place shop towel over connection to avoid fuel spilling on engine.**
5. Remove fuel filter and cap or plug fuel hose.
6. Reverse procedure to install. Reset audio coded anti-theft system, if equipped, as outlined under "Precautions."

TIGHTENING SPECIFICATIONS

Year	Component	Torque/Ft. Lbs.
1993–96	A/C Compressor	18
	Air Intake Chamber	14
	Air Pipe Bolt	14
	Air Pipe Nut	15
	Bearing cap bolts	12
	Chain Tensioner Slipper	51
	Crankshaft Pulley	304
	Cylinder Head Bolts	②

Continued

TIGHTENING SPECIFICATIONS—Continued

Year	Component	Torque/Ft. Lbs.
1993–96	Delivery Pipe To Intake Manifold	15
	Distributor	15
	Drive Belt Idler Pulley	32
	EGR Pipe	15
	EGR Union Nut	47
	EGR Valve	14
	Engine Hanger	30
	Engine To Transmission	43
	Exhaust Manifold	29
	Exhaust Pipe Assembly	46
	Exhaust Pipe Clamp Bolt	14
	Exhaust Pipe Support Bracket	29
	Front Propeller Shaft	54
	Fuel Inlet Hose	22
	Fuel Pipe Bolt	14
	Fuel Pipe To Fuel Pump Bracket	22
	Fuel Pipe Union Bolt	22
	Fuel Return Pipe	14
	Generator Bracket	32
	Heat Insulator Bolts	14
	Heater Inlet Pipe	15
	Heater Pipe Bolt	14
	Heater Pipe Nut	15
	No. 1 Oil Pan, 14 mm Bolts	32
	No. 1 Oil Pan, 12 mm Bolts	14
	No. 2 Oil Pan Bolts	6
	No. 2 Oil Pan Nuts	7
	No. 1 Oil Pan To Transmission Housing	53
	Oil Jet Bolt	14
	Oil Pan Drain Bolt	18
	Oil Pan Baffle Plate	69
	Oil Pump	15
	Pair Reed Valve	14
	Power Steering Hose	33
	Radiator Bolts	13
	Radiator Nuts	9
	Radiator Pipe	15
	Rear Propeller Shaft	65
	Starter	29
	Throttle Body	15
	Timing Chain Cover	32
	Timing Chain Tensioner	15
	Torque Converter Clutch	41
	Transfer Shift Lever	13
	Transmission Control Rod	9
	Transmission Shift Lever	14
	Vibration Damper	14
	Water Bypass Pipe	15
	Water Pump Bolts	15

① — Refer to "Cylinder Head, Replace."

Clutch & Manual Transmission

NOTE: On Air Bag Equipped Models, Refer To "Air Bag System Precautions" Located In The Front Of This Manual For System Disarming & Arming Procedures.

INDEX

	Page No.
Adjustments	47-64
Clutch Pedal	47-64
Clutch, Replace	47-64
Hydraulic System Service	47-64
Clutch Master Cylinder, Replace	47-64
Clutch Slave Cylinder, Replace	47-64
Clutch System Bleed	47-64
Precautions	47-64
Air Bag Systems	47-64
Audio Coded Anti-Theft System	47-64
Tightening Specifications	47-67
Transaxle, Replace	47-66
RAV4	47-66
Transmission, Replace	47-64
Pickup & 4Runner	47-64
T100	47-66

PRECAUTIONS

AIR BAG SYSTEMS

Refer to "Air Bag System Precautions" in the front of this manual for system disarming and arming procedures.

AUDIO CODED ANTI-THEFT SYSTEM

Some models are equipped with an audio coded anti-theft system that will disable the radio when the battery cable is disconnected. The system can be identified by the "ANTI-THEFT SYSTEM" on the cassette lid. Obtain three-digit code for input. Reset system after service as follows:

1. Obtain three-digit audio theft code.
2. Depress 1 (PROG) button while depressing righthand side of TUNE SEEK button. Three dashes will appear in tape operation display.
3. To enter first digit, depress 1 (PROG) button repeatedly until number of times depressed equals first digit (depress 1 button six times if first digit is five, first press equals 0).
4. To enter second digit, depress 2 (APS) button repeatedly until number of times depressed equals second digit.
5. To enter third digit, depress 3 (RPT) button repeatedly until number of times depressed equals third digit.
6. If three dashes are displayed after inputting digits, repeat procedure.
7. When code appears in display, depress and hold SCAN button until SEC appears.
8. When SEC disappears audio system is operative.
9. If Err is displayed, repeat procedure. **Attempting to input code more than nine times may permanently disable audio system.**

ADJUSTMENTS

CLUTCH PEDAL

1. Check clutch pedal height, **Fig. 1.** Clutch pedal height should be 6.2 inches. If height is not as specified, loosen locknut, then rotate adjusting bolt until specified height is obtained. Tighten locknut.
2. Check clutch pedal freeplay, **Fig. 1.** Depress clutch pedal until resistance is felt, then measure freeplay distance. Freeplay should be .20–.59 inch.
3. Check clutch cylinder pushrod play at top of pedal. Play should be .039–.197 inch.
4. If clutch pedal freeplay is not as specified, loosen locknut, then rotate pushrod adjusting screw until specified freeplay is obtained.
5. Tighten locknut, then recheck pedal height.

HYDRAULIC SYSTEM SERVICE

CLUTCH MASTER CYLINDER, REPLACE

Pickups & 4Runner

1. Remove pushrod pin.
2. Disconnect clutch line using line wrench tool No. 09751-36011, or equivalent.
3. Remove mounting nuts and master cylinder.
4. Reverse procedure to install. Bleed clutch system.

RAV4

1. **On models with cruise control,** remove cruise control actuator cover and actuator.
2. **On all models,** draw out fluid with syringe.
3. Disconnect reservoir hose from master cylinder.
4. Remove clip and pin.
5. Remove two mounting nuts and pull out master cylinder.
6. Reverse procedure to install.

CLUTCH SLAVE CYLINDER, REPLACE

1. Disconnect clutch line using line wrench tool No. 09751-36011, or equivalent.
2. Remove two bolts and release cylinder.
3. Reverse procedure to install. Bleed clutch system.

CLUTCH SYSTEM BLEED

1. Fill clutch reservoir with fluid. Check reservoir frequently, add if necessary.
2. Connect vinyl tube to bleeder plug, insert opposite end in container half full of fluid.
3. Pump clutch pedal several times. Hold pedal down and open bleeder plug. Close bleeder plug and repeat this step until no more air bubbles are in fluid.

CLUTCH

REPLACE

1. Remove transmission or transaxle from vehicle. Refer to "Transmission, Replace" for procedure.
2. Loosen pressure plate attaching bolts one turn at a time, then remove bolts, pressure plate and clutch disc.
3. Install new clutch disc and pressure plate assembly, checking to ensure disc and plate are properly aligned. Tighten attaching bolts one turn at a time while ensuring clutch disc and pressure plate remain aligned. Refer to "Tightening Specifications" for torque values.
4. Install transmission or transaxle and adjust clutch as outlined under "Clutch Pedal" under "Adjustments."

TRANSMISSION

REPLACE

PICKUP & 4RUNNER

R150F TRANSMISSION

1. **On models with audio coded anti-theft system,** obtain three-digit system code.
2. **On all models,** disconnect battery ground cable, then remove starter upper mount bolt.

3. Remove shift lever from inside vehicle, then, if equipped, the shift lever retainer.
4. Raise and support vehicle, then drain transmission fluid.
5. Disconnect propeller shaft, then the speedometer cable, back-up lamp switch and light switch connector.
6. Remove exhaust pipe clamp and exhaust pipe.
7. Remove clutch release cylinder, tube bracket and lower starter attaching bolt. Position starter aside.
8. Remove four rear engine mount attaching bolts, then slightly raise transmission, using a suitable jack.
9. Remove four attaching bolts from support member, then the rear mount bracket.
10. Remove engine rear mount from transmission.
11. Place a piece of wood, approximately .8 inch (20 mm) thick, between engine oil pan and front crossmember, then lower transmission.
12. Remove exhaust pipe bracket and stiffener plate bolts.
13. Remove remaining transmission attaching bolts.
14. Rotate transmission clockwise approximately 45°, then slide transmission rearward. Lower transmission forward and away from vehicle.
15. Reverse procedure to install. Reset audio coded anti-theft system, if equipped, as outlined under "Precautions."

G57 & G58 TRANSMISSIONS

1. **On models with audio coded anti-theft system,**obtain three-digit system code.
2. **On all models,** disconnect battery ground cable.
3. Remove shift lever from inside vehicle.
4. Raise and support vehicle, then drain transmission fluid.
5. Disconnect propeller shaft, then the speedometer cable, back-up lamp switch and light switch connector.
6. Remove exhaust pipe clamp from bracket, then the exhaust pipe from manifold. Remove exhaust pipe clamp from No. 2 crossmember frame.
7. Remove clutch release cylinder and tube bracket. **Do not remove clutch line.**
8. Remove four rear engine mount attaching bolts, then slightly raise transmission, using a suitable jack.
9. Remove four attaching bolts from support member, then the rear mount bracket.
10. Remove engine rear mount from transmission.
11. Place a piece of wood, approximately .8 inch (20 mm) thick, between engine oil pan and front crossmember, then lower transmission.
12. Remove starter, then the exhaust pipe bracket and stiffener plate bolts.
13. Remove remaining transmission attaching bolts.
14. Pull transmission assembly toward rear of vehicle, then lower transmission forward and away from vehicle, using care not to damage extension housing dust deflector.
15. Reverse procedure to install. Reset audio coded anti-theft system, if equipped, as outlined under "Precautions."

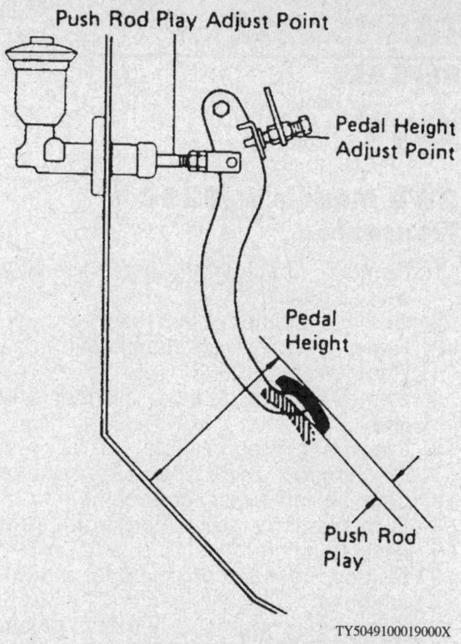

Push Rod Play Adjust Point
Pedal Height
Adjust Point
Pedal
Height
Push Rod
Play
TY5049100019000X

Fig. 1 Clutch pedal adjustments

W55 & W56 TRANSMISSIONS

2WD Models

1. Remove shift lever boot retainer and boot.
2. Remove shift lever using gear shift lever remover tool No. 09305-20012, or equivalent.
3. Disconnect battery ground cable.
4. Drain cooling system, then disconnect upper radiator hose.
5. Remove clutch release cylinder hose bracket.
6. Remove accelerator torque rod.
7. Remove starter, then the clutch slave cylinder.
8. Disconnect speedometer cable and back-up switch electrical connector.
9. Disconnect exhaust pipe from exhaust manifold, then remove exhaust pipe bracket and heat insulator, if equipped.
10. Release parking brake, then disconnect parking brake cable from intermediate lever.
11. Mark driveshaft and pinion flanges for reassembly, then remove driveshaft.
12. Support transmission using suitable jack, then remove rear crossmember.
13. Lower jack and remove clutch housing to engine block attaching bolts. **To prevent oil pan from striking suspension member or EGR valve from striking instrument panel, position wooden block and suitable jack under oil pan for support.**
14. Pull transmission rearward and lower from vehicle.
15. Reverse procedure to install.

4WD Models

1. Disconnect battery ground cable.
2. Using gear shift lever remover tool No. 09305-20012, or equivalent, remove gear shift lever.
3. Using suitable long nosed pliers, remove transfer case lever retaining clip, then the shift lever.
4. Raise and support vehicle.
5. If transmission or transfer case is to be disassembled, drain lubricant into suitable container.
6. Scribe alignment marks, then remove front and rear driveshafts.
7. Remove clutch release cylinder, then the starter and position both aside.
8. Disconnect back-up light switch wiring and four wheel drive indicator switch wiring.
9. Disconnect speedometer cable.
10. Disconnect exhaust pipe clamp from transmission housing.
11. Remove bolts securing rear engine mount to crossmember.
12. Support transmission using suitable jack, then remove crossmember from frame rails.
13. Lower transmission slightly.
14. Position a suitable support and wooden block under engine, then remove bolts securing transmission to engine block.
15. Remove jack supporting transmission, then pull transmission and transfer case down and rearward to remove.
16. If necessary, remove transfer case from transmission by removing mounting bolts, then pulling transfer case away from transmission.
17. Reverse procedure to install.

Models w/V6 Engine

1. **On models with audio coded anti-theft system,**obtain three-digit system code.
2. **On all models,** disconnect battery ground cable.
3. Scribe hood hinge locations, then remove hood.
4. Remove engine undercover.
5. Drain coolant from radiator and engine.
6. Drain oil from engine.
7. Remove air cleaner case and hose.
8. Remove radiator.
9. Remove power steering drive belt.
10. Remove air conditioner compressor drive belt, if equipped.
11. Remove generator drive belt, fluid coupling and fan pulley.
12. Label locations, then disconnect all electrical connectors, wires and vacuum lines from engine/transaxle assembly.
13. Disconnect accelerator cable, throttle cable and cruise control cable, if equipped.
14. Remove power steering pump and lines.
15. Remove air conditioner compressor, if equipped.
16. Disconnect clutch release cylinder line, if equipped.
17. Disconnect heater hoses.
18. Disconnect and cap fuel lines.
19. Remove shift control levers, if equipped.
20. Remove rear driveshaft.
21. Disconnect speedometer cable.

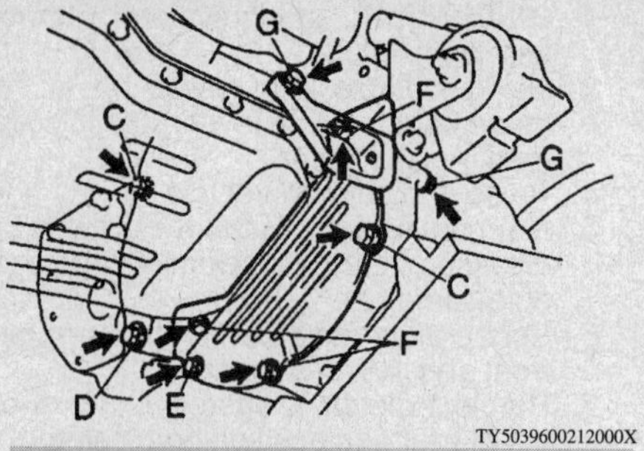
G
C
F
G
C
F
D
E
TY5039600212000X

Fig. 2 Rear end plate bolts. 2WD models w/E250 transaxle

22. Remove transfer undercover.
23. Remove stabilizer bar.
24. Remove front driveshaft shaft.
25. Remove front crossmember.
26. Remove front exhaust pipe.
27. Remove No. 1 front floor heat insulator and brake tube heat insulator.
28. Remove No. 2 frame crossmember from side frame.
29. Attach suitable engine lifting equipment onto engine assembly.
30. Remove engine/transmission assembly from vehicle.
31. Reverse procedure to install. Reset audio coded anti-theft system, if equipped, as outlined under "Precautions."

T100

1. **On models with audio coded anti-theft system,**obtain three-digit system code.
2. **On all models,** remove transmission with engine as outlined under "Engine, Replace" in "3VZ-FE Engine" section.
3. Remove stiffener plate.
4. Separate transmission from engine.
5. Reverse procedure to install. Reset audio coded anti-theft system, if equipped, as outlined under "Precautions."

TRANSAXLE

REPLACE

RAV4

2WD Models w/E250 Transaxle

1. Remove air cleaner case assembly with air hose.
2. Remove engine coolant reservoir tank.
3. Remove engine wire clamp set nut.
4. Remove starter.
5. Remove clutch release cylinder and line.
6. Disconnect ground cable.
7. Disconnect vehicle speed sensor and back-up light switch connector.
8. Disconnect control cable from transaxle housing.
9. Remove four transaxle upper mounting bolts.
10. Remove set bolt and two nuts of engine lefthand mounting insulator.
11. Install engine support fixture.
12. Tie power steering gear assembly to engine support fixture.
13. Remove front wheel, then raise and support vehicle.
14. Remove lefthand and righthand engine under covers.
15. Drain transaxle oil.
16. Remove lefthand and righthand driveshafts.
17. Remove front exhaust pipe.
18. Remove front suspension crossmember with stabilizer bar.
19. Remove engine mounting center member.
20. Slightly raise transaxle.
21. Disconnect lefthand side engine mounting bracket from lefthand side engine mounting insulator.
22. Remove stiffener plate, No. 2 rear end plate and transaxle lower side mounting bolt.
23. Lower engine lefthand side and remove transaxle from engine.
24. Reverse procedure to install. Refer to **Fig. 2** and tighten No. 2 rear end plate bolts as follows:

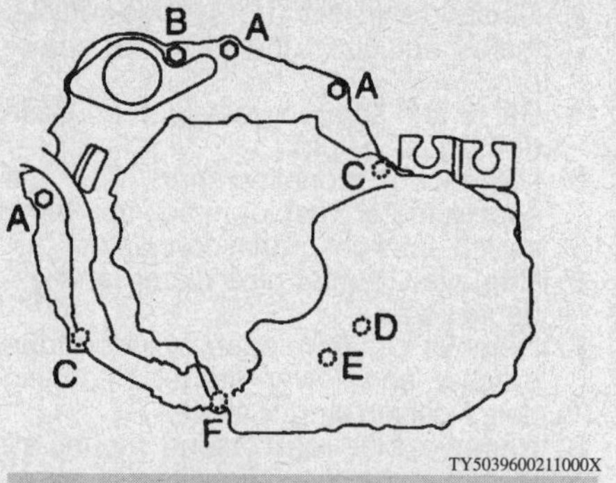
B
A
A
C
A
D
E
C
F
TY5039600211000X

Fig. 3 Transaxle mounting bolts. 4WD models w/E250F transaxle

a. **Torque** bolt C to 22 ft. lbs.
b. **Torque** bolt D to 34 ft. lbs.
c. **Torque** bolt E to 18 ft. lbs.
d. **Torque** bolt F to 7 ft. lbs.
e. **Torque** bolt G to 27 ft. lbs.

4WD Models w/E250F Transaxle

1. Remove engine with transaxle as outlined under "Engine, Replace" in "3S-FE Engine" section.
2. Remove transaxle case protector.
3. Remove starter.
4. Disconnect differential lock indicator switch, back-up light switch and vehicle speed sensor connector.
5. Remove transfer vacuum actuator bracket.
6. Disconnect vacuum actuator solenoid connectors and remove transfer vacuum actuator assembly.
7. Remove righthand transfer stiffener plate.
8. Remove center transfer stiffener plate.
9. Remove transaxle from engine.
10. Reverse procedure to install. Refer to **Fig. 3,** and tighten transaxle mounting bolts to following specifications:
 a. **Torque** bolt A to 47 ft. lbs.
 b. **Torque** bolt B to 26 ft. lbs.
 c. **Torque** bolt C to 22 ft. lbs.
 d. **Torque** bolt D to 34 ft. lbs.
 e. **Torque** bolt E to 18 ft. lbs.
 f. **Torque** bolt F to 7 ft. lbs.

TIGHTENING SPECIFICATIONS

Year	Component	Torque/Ft. Lbs.
EXCEPT RAV4		
1993–96	Bleeder Plug	8
	Clutch Line	11
	Crossmember	70
	Engine Rear Mounting	19
	Engine Rear Mounting To Transmission	19
	Flywheel To Crankshaft	①
	Master Cylinder	9
	No. 2 Crossmember To Frame, 4WD	70
	Pressure Plate	14
	Release Cylinder	9

Continued

TIGHTENING SPECIFICATIONS—Continued

Year	Component	Torque/Ft. Lbs.
EXCEPT RAV4		
1993–96	Starter	29
	Stiffener Plate To Transmission	27
	Transfer Vacuum Actuator Bracket	27
	Transmission To Engine	53
RAV4 4WD		
1996	Clutch Line Union	11
	Clutch Master Cylinder Nut	9
	Flywheel Set Bolt	65
	Starter Bolts	29
	Stiffener Plates To Transaxle	27
	Transaxle Case Protector	18
	Transaxle To Engine	②
	Transfer Vacuum Actuator	27
RAV4 2WD		
1996	Clutch Line Union	11
	Clutch Master Cylinder Nut	9
	Engine LH Mounting Bracket To Mounting Insulator	47
	Flywheel Set Bolt	65
	Starter Bolts	29
	Stiffener Plates To Transaxle	②
	Transaxle Case Protector	18
	Transaxle To Engine Upper Mounting Bolts	47

①— Except 3RZ-FE engine, to 65 ft. lbs.; 3RZ-FE engine, to 19 ft. lbs., then turn an additional 90°.
②— Refer to "Transaxle, Replace."

Rear Axle & Suspension

INDEX

	Page No.
Axle Shaft, Bearing & Oil Seal, Replace	47-67
Land Cruiser	47-68
Pickup & 4Runner	47-67
Coil Spring, Replace	47-68
Leaf Spring, Replace	47-69
Rear Axle, Replace	47-67
Models w/Coil Springs	47-67
Models w/Leaf Springs	47-67
Shock Absorber, Replace	47-68
Stabilizer Bar, Replace	47-69
Tightening Specifications	47-70

REAR AXLE

REPLACE

MODELS w/COIL SPRINGS

RAV4 & 4Runner

1. Raise and support vehicle.
2. Remove wheel and brake drum.
3. Remove ABS speed sensor.
4. Remove rear brake assembly, then disconnect parking brake cable and brake tube.
5. Remove lock nut and rear axle shaft assembly.
6. Reverse procedure to install.

Land Cruiser

1. Raise and support vehicle.
2. Remove wheel and brake drum.
3. Remove drain plug and drain differential oil.
4. Remove load sensing proportioning valve shackle bracket from differential cover.
5. Remove parking brake cable clamp and differential cover.
6. Remove pinion shaft and spacer.
7. Remove axle shaft lock and axle shaft, then the oil deflector.
8. Reverse procedure to install.

MODELS w/LEAF SPRINGS

Pickup, Tacoma & T100

1. Raise and support vehicle.
2. Remove wheel and brake drum.
3. Disconnect brake tube and parking brake cable.
4. Remove backing plate mounting nuts.
5. Remove axle shaft from rear axle housing.
6. Remove snap ring, then the rear axle shaft from backing plate.
7. Reverse procedure to install.

AXLE SHAFT, BEARING & OIL SEAL

REPLACE

PICKUP & 4RUNNER

1. Raise and support vehicle.
2. Remove rear wheel and brake drum.
3. **On 4Runner,** remove rear brake assembly.
4. **On all models,** disconnect parking brake cable and using line wrench tool

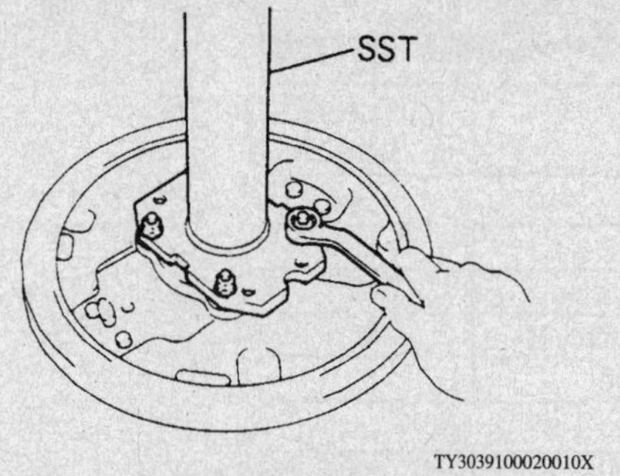
SST
TY3039100020010X

Fig. 1 Backing plate removal (Part 1 of 2). Pickup & 4Runner

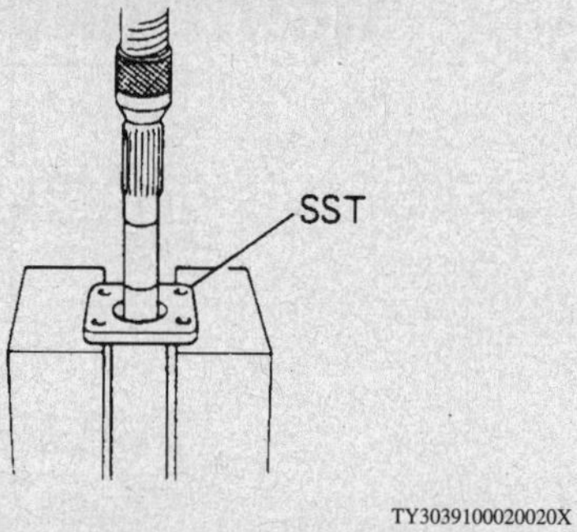
SST
TY3039100020020X

Fig. 1 Backing plate removal (Part 2 of 2). Pickup & 4Runner

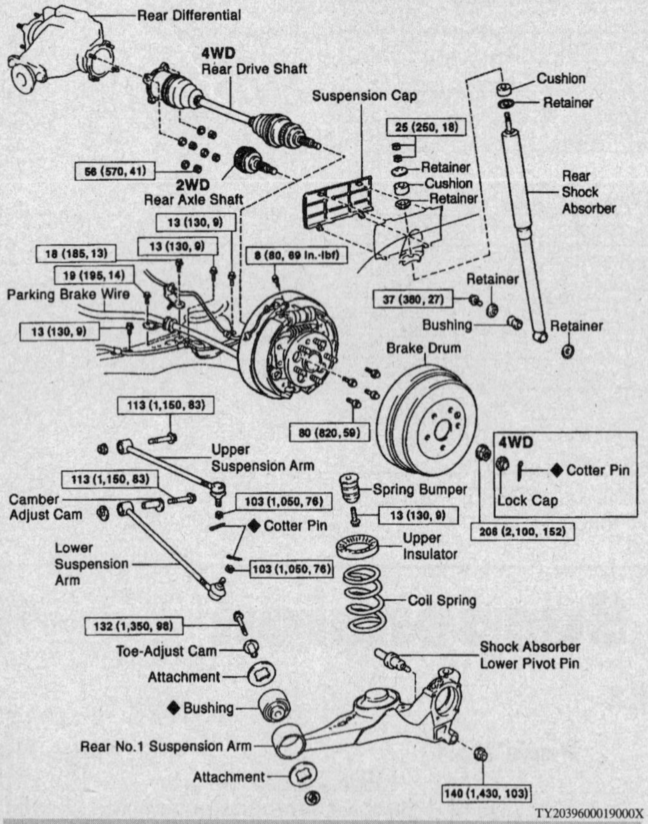
Rear Differential
4WD
Rear Drive Shaft
Suspension Cap
Cushion
Retainer
25 (250, 18)
56 (570, 41)
2WD
Rear Axle Shaft
Retainer
Cushion
Retainer
Rear
Shock
Absorber
13 (130, 9)
18 (185, 13)
13 (130, 9)
8 (80, 69 in.-lbf)
19 (195, 14)
Parking Brake Wire
Retainer
37 (380, 27)
13 (130, 9)
Bushing
Retainer
Brake Drum
113 (1,150, 83)
80 (820, 59)
Upper
Suspension Arm
4WD
Cotter Pin
113 (1,150, 83)
Spring Bumper
Lock Cap
Camber
Adjust Cam
103 (1,050, 76)
Cotter Pin
13 (130, 9)
Lower
Suspension
Arm
Upper
Insulator
208 (2,100, 152)
103 (1,050, 76)
Coil Spring
132 (1,350, 98)
Toe-Adjust Cam
Shock Absorber
Lower Pivot Pin
Attachment
Bushing
Rear No.1 Suspension Arm
Attachment
140 (1,430, 103)
TY2039600019000X

Fig. 2 Exploded view of coil spring rear suspension. RAV4

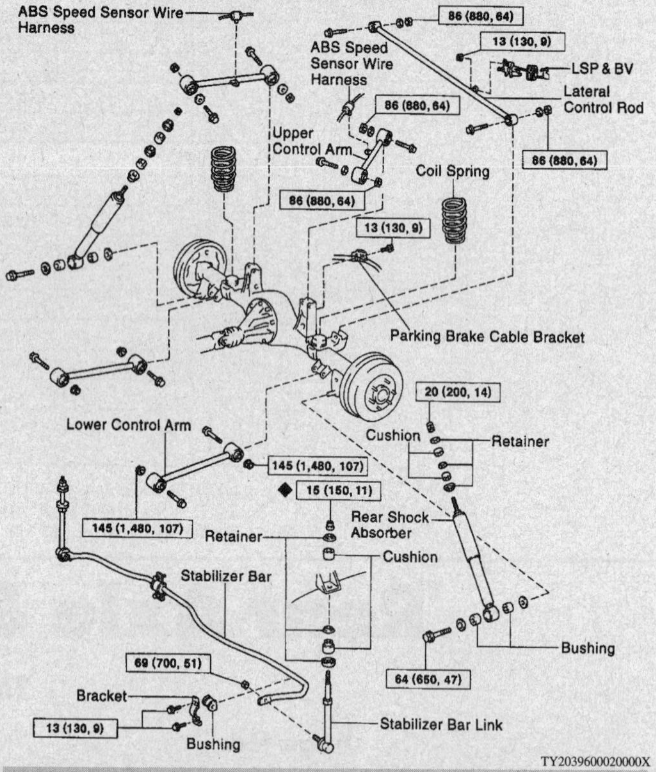
ABS Speed Sensor Wire
Harness
86 (880, 64)
13 (130, 9)
ABS Speed
Sensor Wire
Harness
LSP & BV
Lateral
Control Rod
86 (880, 64)
Upper
Control Arm
86 (880, 64)
Coil Spring
86 (880, 64)
13 (130, 9)
Parking Brake Cable Bracket
20 (200, 14)
Lower Control Arm
Cushion
Retainer
145 (1,480, 107)
15 (150, 11)
145 (1,480, 107)
Retainer
Rear Shock
Absorber
Cushion
Stabilizer Bar
Bushing
64 (650, 47)
69 (700, 51)
Bracket
13 (130, 9)
Stabilizer Bar Link
Bushing
TY2039600020000X

Fig. 3 Exploded view of coil spring rear suspension. Pickup & 4Runner

No. 09751-36011, or equivalent, remove brake line.

5. Remove four backing plate mounting bolts and pull out axle.
6. Remove snap ring from axle shaft.
7. Install adapter tool No. 09521-25011, or equivalent, and press axle from backing plate, **Fig. 1**.
8. Pry out outer seal using screwdriver.
9. Using bearing remover tool Nos. 09223-56010 and 09608-35014, or equivalents, press bearing from backing plate.
10. Grind down bearing inner retainer, then cut off using a hammer and chisel.
11. Reverse procedure to install.

LAND CRUISER

1. Raise and support vehicle.
2. Remove rear wheel and brake drum, then drain differential oil.
3. Remove LSPV shackle bracket, then the parking brake cable clamp.
4. Remove differential cover.
5. Remove pinion shaft and spacer. Push axle toward differential and remove lock from axle located in differential. Remove axle.
6. Using seal puller tool No. 09308-00010, or equivalent, remove axle seal.
7. Using bearing puller tool No. 09514-35011, or equivalent, remove bearing.
8. Reverse procedure to install.

SHOCK ABSORBER

REPLACE

1. Raise rear of vehicle and support rear axle housing on stands.
2. Disconnect shock absorber from lower mounting.
3. Disconnect shock absorber from upper mounting and remove from vehicle.

COIL SPRING

REPLACE

1. Raise rear of vehicle and support rear axle housing on stands.
2. Disconnect shock absorber from lower mounting, **Figs. 2 through 4,** then the lateral control rod from axle housing.
3. If equipped with rear stabilizer, remove bolts securing stabilizer bar to rear housing.
4. Lower jack until spring tension is relieved, then remove coil spring with insulator.

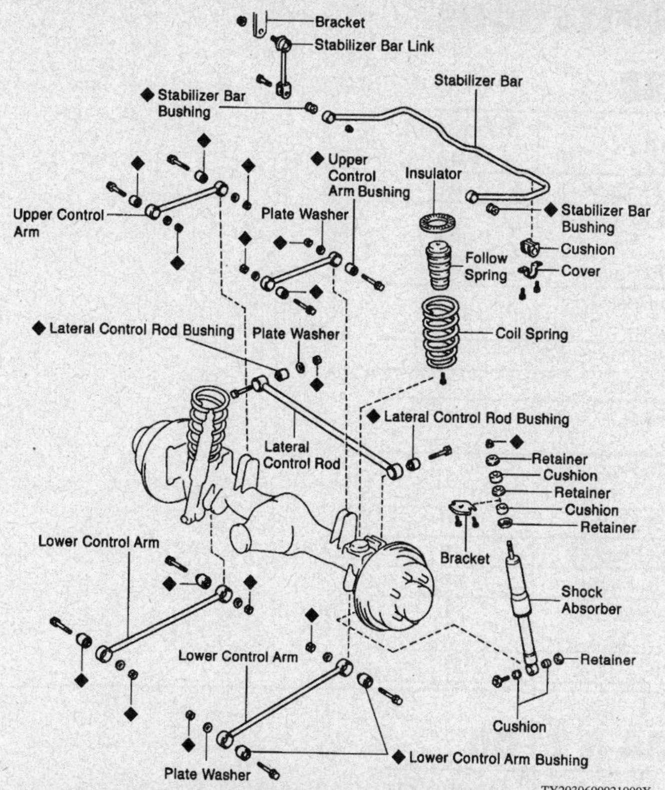
Bracket
Stabilizer Bar Link
Stabilizer Bar
◆ Stabilizer Bar Bushing
◆ Upper Control Arm Bushing
Insulator
Upper Control Arm
Plate Washer
◆ Stabilizer Bar Bushing
Cushion
Cover
Follow Spring
◆ Lateral Control Rod Bushing
Plate Washer
Coil Spring
◆ Lateral Control Rod Bushing
Lateral Control Rod
Retainer
Cushion
Retainer
Cushion
Retainer
Bracket
Lower Control Arm
Shock Absorber
Lower Control Arm
Retainer
Cushion
◆ Lower Control Arm Bushing
Plate Washer

TY2039600021000X

Fig. 4 Exploded view of coil spring rear suspension. Land Cruiser

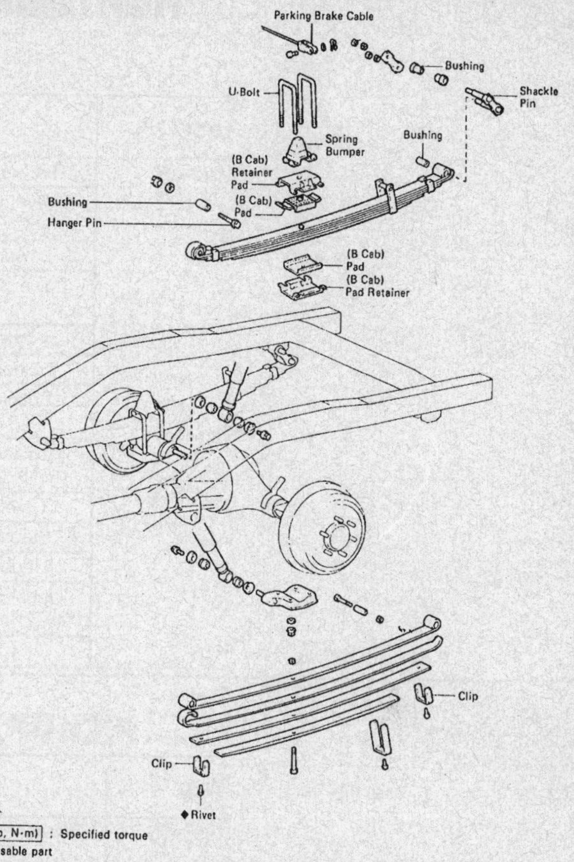
Parking Brake Cable
Bushing
U-Bolt
Shackle Pin
Spring Bumper
Bushing
(B Cab) Retainer Pad
(B Cab) Pad
Bushing
Hanger Pin
(B Cab) Pad
(B Cab) Pad Retainer
Clip
Clip
◆ Rivet
kg-cm (ft-lb, N·m) : Specified torque
◆ Non-reusable part

TY2039100016000X

Fig. 5 Exploded view of leaf spring rear suspension

5. Reverse procedure to install.

LEAF SPRING

REPLACE

1. Raise rear of vehicle and place stands under frame and rear axle housing.
2. Disconnect shock absorber from upper and lower mountings and remove shock absorber from vehicle, **Fig. 5.**
3. Disconnect parking brake equalizer from parking brake intermediate lever.
4. Remove U-bolts and spring seats
5. **On 4WD models,** remove spring bumper.
6. **On all models,** position a suitable jack under rear axle housing and raise housing to relieve weight from rear springs.
7. Remove spring shackle nuts and inner plate, then, using a suitable pry bar, remove spring shackle.
8. Remove two bolts retaining spring bracket and hanger pin nut, then drive out spring hanger pin.
9. Remove spring assembly from vehicle.
10. Reverse procedure to install.

STABILIZER BAR

REPLACE

1. Raise and support rear of vehicle, then remove rear wheels.
2. Disconnect bolts securing stabilizer bar to axle housing, **Figs. 2 through 4.**
3. Disconnect bolts securing stabilizer bar to frame, then remove stabilizer bar.
4. Reverse procedure to install.

TIGHTENING SPECIFICATIONS

4RUNNER

Year	Component	Torque/Ft. Lbs.
1993–96	Lateral Control Rod To Frame	101
	Lateral Control Rod To Rear Axle Housing	83
	Lower Control Arm To Frame	148
	Lower Control Arm To Rear Axle Housing	148
	Rear Axle Housing To Backing Plate	51
	Shock Absorber To Frame	18
	Shock Absorber To Rear Axle Housing	47
	Stabilizer Bar Bracket To Rear Axle Housing	9
	Stabilizer Bar Link Stabilizer	70
	Stabilizer Bar Link To Bracket	13
	Upper Control Arm To Frame	148
	Upper Control Arm To Rear Axle Housing	148
	Wheel Lug Nut	76

PICKUP, TACOMA & T100

Year	Component	Torque/Ft. Lbs.
1993–96	Differential Carrier To Axle Housing (Double Tire)	23
	Differential Carrier To Axle Housing (Single Tire)	18
	Front Spring Bracket To Hanger Pin (Press Installed Bushing)	116
	Front Spring Bracket To Hanger Pin (Rubber Bushing)	67
	Rear Shock Absorber To Frame (2WD)	19
	Rear Shock Absorber To Frame (4WD)	53
	Rear Shock Absorber To Spring Seat (2WD)	19
	Rear Shock Absorber To Spring Seat (4WD)	53
	Rear Spring Shackle To Leaf Spring	67
	Spring Center Bolt	33
	Stabilizer Bar Bracket To Axle Housing	9
	Stabilizer Bar To Stabilizer Bar Link	26
	U Bolt (½ Ton 2WD)	108
	U Bolt (1 Ton 2WD Cab & Chassis)	90
	U Bolt (4WD)	①
	Wheel Lug Nut	76

LAND CRUISER

Year	Component	Torque/Ft. Lbs.
1993–96	Differential Cover	9
	Lateral Control Rod To Frame	130
	Lateral Control Rod To Rear Axle Housing	181
	Lower Control Arm To Frame	130
	Lower Control Arm To Rear Axle Housing	130
	LSPV Shackle Bracket	9
	Parking Brake Cable Clamp	9
	Pinion Shaft Pin	20
	Rear Axle Housing To Backing Plate	51
	Shock Absorber To Frame	37
	Shock Absorber To Rear Axle Housing	47
	Stabilizer Bar Bracket To Rear Axle Housing	13
	Stabilizer Bar To Link	19
	Stabilizer Link To Frame	11
	Upper Control Arm To Frame	130
	Upper Control Arm To Rear Axle Housing	130
	Wheel Lug Nut	108

RAV4

Year	Component	Torque/Ft. Lbs.
1996	ABS Speed Sensor	6
	Axle Hub Bolt	59
	Axle Shaft Lock Nut	152
	Brake Line	11
	Differential Rear Mount Cushion	48
	Differential Carrier To Side Bearing Cap	58
	Differential Carrier To Differential Case Cover	34
	Lower Suspension Arm	83
	Shock Absorber Bolts	18
	Shock Absorber Lower Pivot Pin	103
	Rear No. 1 Suspension Arm To Body	98
	Rear No. 1 Suspension Arm To Brake Line Bracket	13
	Upper Suspension Arm	76
	Wheel Lug Nut	76

①—Regular Cab, 108 ft. lbs.; extra cab, 90 ft. lbs.

Front Suspension & Steering

INDEX

	Page No.
Ball Joint Inspection	47-73
Coil Spring, Replace	47-73
Lower Control Arm & Torsion Bar, Replace	47-74
Pickup, Tacoma & T100 w/2WD & 4Runner	47-74
Lower Suspension Arm & Shock Absorber, Replace	47-74
Pickup, Tacoma & T100 w/2WD	47-74
Pickup, Tacoma & T100 w/4WD & 4Runner	47-74
Manual Steering Gears	48-1
Power Steering	48-1
Power Steering Gear, Replace	47-75
Land Cruiser	47-75
Pickup, Tacoma, T100 & 4Runner	47-75
RAV4	47-75
Power Steering Pump, Replace	47-75
Shock Absorber, Replace	47-73
Stabilizer Bar, Replace	47-73
Land Cruiser	47-73
Pickup, Tacoma & T100 w/2WD	47-73
Pickup, Tacoma, T100 w/4WD & 4Runner	47-73
RAV4	47-73
Strut Bar, Replace	47-74
Pickup, Tacoma & T100 w/2WD	47-74
Tightening Specifications	47-80
Torsion Bar, Replace	47-73
Pickup, Tacoma, T100 & 4Runner w/4WD	47-73
Wheel Bearing, Adjust	47-72
2WD	47-72
4WD	47-72
Wheel Hub & Steering Knuckle, Replace	47-72
RAV4	47-73

WHEEL BEARING

ADJUST

2WD

1. Raise and support front of vehicle, then remove wheel and tire assembly and brake caliper. Wire brake caliper aside without stretching brake hose.
2. Remove hub grease cap, cotter pin and locknut, then loosen hub nut.
3. Tighten hub nut to 22 ft. lbs., then rotate hub and disc assembly several times to ensure bearings are seated.
4. Loosen hub nut until it can be turned with fingers, then retighten nut finger tight.
5. Using a suitable spring scale, measure frictional force of axle seal and make note of it, **Fig. 1.** Frictional force should be 12.35–30.69 ounces (350–870 g).
6. Tighten hub nut slightly, then measure wheel bearing preload with spring scale. Preload should be 21–64 ounces, in addition to axle seal frictional force measured in step 5.
7. If preload is not as specified, tighten or loosen hub nut as necessary until proper preload is obtained.
8. Install locknut, cotter pin, grease cap, caliper and wheel and tire assembly. **If cotter pin holes do not line up, tighten nut by the least amount possible until holes are aligned.**

4WD

1. Raise and support vehicle, then remove tire and wheel assembly and brake caliper.
2. Remove manual locking hub as follows:
   a. Place control handle in "Free" position.
   b. Remove cover attaching bolts, then the cover.
   c. Remove axle bolt with washer, then the hub body attaching nuts and washers.
   d. Remove cone washer by tapping on heads of bolts using a hammer and suitable drift.
   e. Remove manual locking hub body.

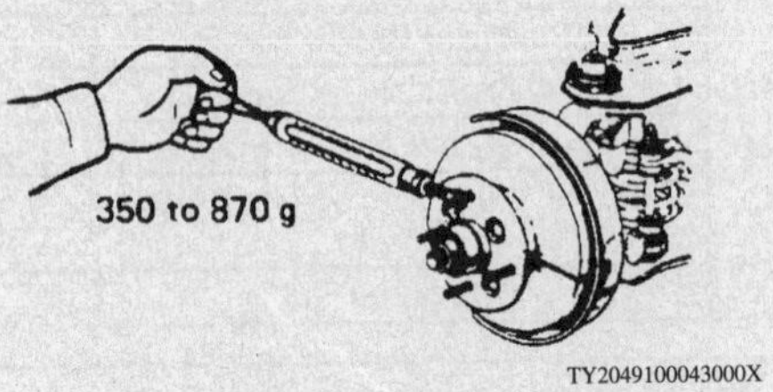

350 to 870 g
TY2049100043000X

Fig. 1 Wheel bearing preload inspection

3. **On models with automatic locking hubs,** remove hub as follows:
   a. Remove hub cover.
   b. Remove axle bolt, then the washer.
   c. Remove hub body attaching nuts.
   d. Remove cone washer by tapping on heads of bolts, using a hammer and suitable drift.
   e. Remove automatic locking hub body.
4. **On models less automatic locking hubs,** remove hub as follows:
   a. Remove grease cap from hub flange.
   b. Remove hub bolt and washer, then the hub flange attaching nuts.
   c. Tap hub flange attaching studs with brass drift and hammer to remove cone washers.
   d. Install two bolts into hub flange opposite from each other, then tighten evenly to remove hub flange.
5. **On models with automatic locking hubs,** proceed as follows:
   a. Release lock washer, then remove locknut and lock washer.
   b. Loosen hub nut.
   c. Tighten hub nut to 43 ft. lbs., then rotate hub and disc assembly several times to ensure bearings are seated.
   d. Loosen hub nut until it can be turned with fingers, then **torque** to 18 ft. lbs.
   e. Using a suitable spring scale, measure wheel bearing starting preload with spring scale, **Fig. 1.** Preload should be 9–17 ft. lbs. If preload is not as specified, tighten or loosen adjusting nut as necessary.
6. **On models less automatic locking hubs,** proceed as follows:
   a. Install lock washer and locknut.
   b. Tighten locknut to specification.
   c. Using a suitable spring scale, measure wheel bearing starting preload with spring scale, **Fig. 1.** Preload should be 9–17 ft. lbs. If preload is not as specified, tighten or loosen adjusting nut as necessary.
   d. If preload is within specifications, bend over lock washer.
7. **On all models,** install freewheeling hub as follows:
   a. Place new gasket on front axle hub.
   b. Install hub body with six cone washers and nuts, then **torque** attaching nuts to 23 ft. lbs.
   c. Install hub bolt with washer, then tighten to specification.
   d. Apply a suitable grease to inner hub splines, then place control handle in "Free" position.
   e. Install new gasket on cover, then install cover on body with follower pawl tabs aligned with non-toothed portions of body.
   f. Install cover attaching bolts and tighten to specification.
8. **On models with automatic locking hubs,** install hub as follows:
   a. Position new gasket on axle hub, then apply suitable multipurpose grease to automatic locking hub splines.
   b. Align spring ends of brake assembly in hub with hub flange alignment pins.
   c. Ensure locking hub outer cam stopper is securely in inner cam groove, then position inner cam protrusion so it is centered between outer cam protrusions and aligned with hub alignment pin holes.
   d. Install locking hub to axle hub ensuring inner cam protrusion is set between ends of hub brake spring.
   e. Install six cone washers and nuts and tighten nuts to specification. **If hub does not fit perfectly on axle hub, remove and reinstall.**

f. Install cover, then insert attaching bolts and tighten to specification.

9. **On models less automatic locking hubs,** install hubs as follows:
   a. Position new gasket on axle hub, then install hub flange on axle.
   b. Install cone washers and attaching nuts. **Torque** attaching nuts to 23 ft. lbs.
   c. Install grease cap on hub flange.
10. **On all models,** install brake caliper, wheel and tire assembly.

WHEEL HUB & STEERING KNUCKLE

REPLACE

RAV4

1. Remove front wheel and drive shaft locknut, **Fig. 2.**
2. Remove ABS speed sensor and wire harness from steering knuckle.
3. Loosen lower shock absorber nuts.
4. Remove tie rod end cotter pin.
5. Using tie rod end remover tool No. 09610-20012, or equivalent, disconnect lower ball joint from lower arm.
6. Remove steering knuckle with hub.
7. Reverse procedure to install. Tighten to specifications.

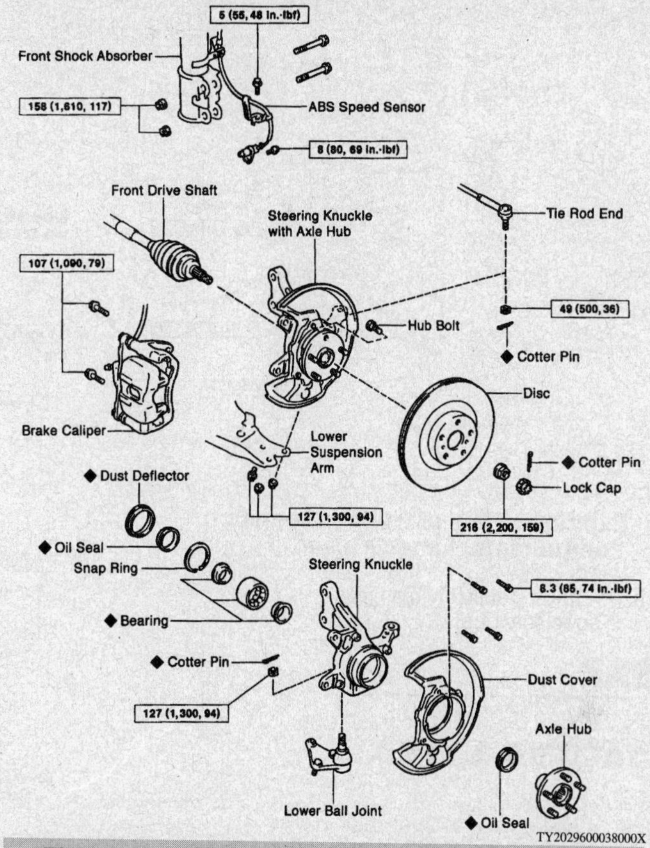
5 (55, 48 in.-lbf)
Front Shock Absorber
158 (1,610, 117)
ABS Speed Sensor
8 (80, 69 in.-lbf)
Front Drive Shaft
Steering Knuckle with Axle Hub
Tie Rod End
107 (1,090, 79)
49 (500, 36)
Hub Bolt
◆ Cotter Pin
Disc
Brake Caliper
Lower Suspension Arm
◆ Cotter Pin
◆ Dust Deflector
Lock Cap
127 (1,300, 94)
216 (2,200, 159)
◆ Oil Seal
Snap Ring
Steering Knuckle
8.3 (85, 74 in.-lbf)
◆ Bearing
◆ Cotter Pin
Dust Cover
127 (1,300, 94)
Axle Hub
Lower Ball Joint
◆ Oil Seal
TY2029600038000X

Fig. 2 Exploded view of front axle hub. RAV4

BALL JOINT INSPECTION

1. Raise and support vehicle.
2. Ensure front wheels are in straight ahead position and depress and hold brake pedal to eliminate wheel bearing play.
3. Move lower control arm up and down and check that lower ball joint play does not exceed 0 inch.

COIL SPRING

REPLACE

Refer to "Shock Absorber, Replace" for procedure.

SHOCK ABSORBER

REPLACE

1. Raise and support front of vehicle and remove front wheel.
2. Disconnect brake hose and ABS speed sensor from shock absorber.
3. Disconnect shock absorber from upper and lower mountings, **Figs. 3 through 5.**
4. Remove shock absorber with coil spring from vehicle.
5. Reverse procedure to install.

TORSION BAR

REPLACE

PICKUP, TACOMA, T100 & 4RUNNER w/4WD

1. Remove boots, then mark relative position between torsion bar, anchor arm and torque arm, **Fig. 6.**
2. Measure protruding bolt end dimension "A," **Fig. 7.**
3. Loosen adjusting nut, then remove anchor arm and torsion bar. **At rear end of torsion bar there are right and left indication marks that are not to be interchanged.**
4. Apply a suitable lubricant to torsion bar spline.
5. Align matchmarks made during removal.
6. Install and tighten adjusting nut to length noted during removal, dimension "A," **Fig. 7.**

STABILIZER BAR

REPLACE

RAV4

1. Raise and support vehicle, then remove front wheels.
2. Remove both stabilizer bar links.
3. Remove stabilizer bar brackets and bushings.
4. Remove stabilizer bar from righthand side.
5. Reverse procedure to install

PICKUP, TACOMA, T100 w/4WD & 4RUNNER

1. Remove stabilizer bar to lower suspension arms retaining nuts, cushions and retainers.
2. Disconnect stabilizer bar.
3. Remove stabilizer bar brackets and cushions, then the stabilizer bar.
4. Place stabilizer bar in position, then install new cushion and brackets to frame and insert attaching bolts.
5. Connect stabilizer bar on both sides to lower arms with attaching bolts, retainers and nuts, then **torque** nuts to 19 ft. lbs.
6. **Torque** bracket set bolts to 22 ft. lbs.

PICKUP, TACOMA & T100 w/2WD

1. Remove one torsion bar as outlined under "Lower Control Arm & Torsion Bar, Replace."
2. Remove stabilizer bar from lower control arms.
3. Remove stabilizer brackets and bushings from frame, then the stabilizer bar.
4. Reverse procedure to install.

LAND CRUISER

1. Raise and support vehicle.
2. Remove stabilizer bar brackets from axle housing, **Fig. 3.**
3. Remove nuts, cushions and bolts retaining both sides of stabilizer bar to frame, then the stabilizer.
4. Reverse procedure to install. Tighten

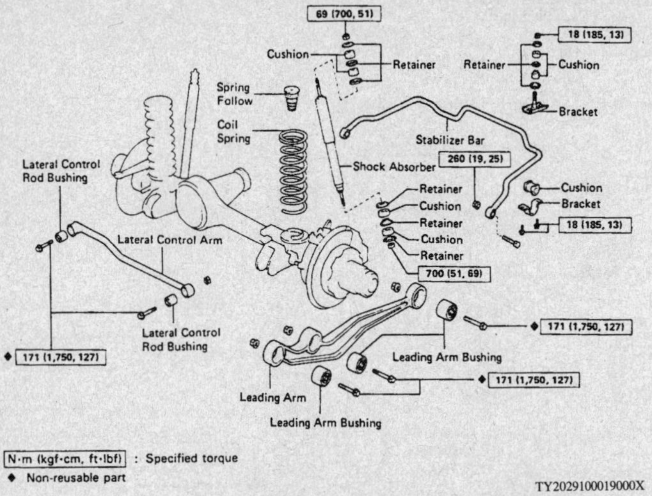
69 (700, 51)
Cushion
Retainer
Retainer
Cushion
18 (185, 13)
Spring Follow
Bracket
Coil Spring
Stabilizer Bar
Lateral Control Rod Bushing
Shock Absorber
260 (19, 25)
Retainer
Cushion
Retainer
Cushion
Retainer
Cushion
Bracket
18 (185, 13)
Lateral Control Arm
700 (51, 69)
Lateral Control Rod Bushing
◆ 171 (1,750, 127)
◆ 171 (1,750, 127)
Leading Arm Bushing
◆ 171 (1,750, 127)
Leading Arm
Leading Arm Bushing
N·m (kgf·cm, ft·lbf) : Specified torque
◆ Non-reusable part
TY2029100019000X

Fig. 3 Exploded view of front suspension components. Land Cruiser

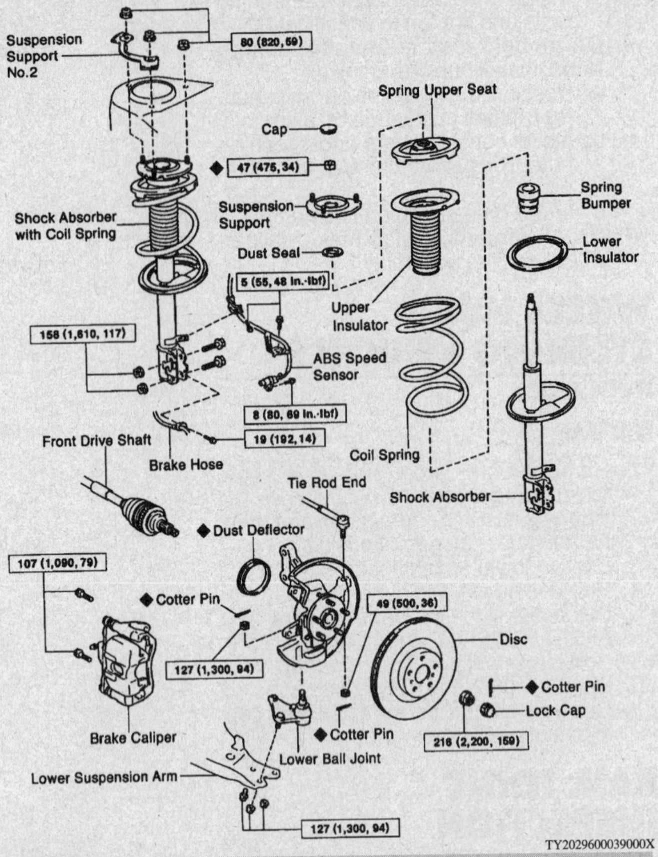
Suspension Support No.2
80 (820, 59)
Spring Upper Seat
Cap
◆ 47 (475, 34)
Spring Bumper
Shock Absorber with Coil Spring
Suspension Support
Lower Insulator
Dust Seal
5 (55, 48 in.-lbf)
Upper Insulator
158 (1,610, 117)
ABS Speed Sensor
8 (80, 69 in.-lbf)
Front Drive Shaft
19 (192, 14)
Brake Hose
Coil Spring
Tie Rod End
Shock Absorber
◆ Dust Deflector
107 (1,090, 79)
◆ Cotter Pin
49 (500, 36)
Disc
127 (1,300, 94)
◆ Cotter Pin
Lock Cap
Brake Caliper
◆ Cotter Pin
216 (2,200, 159)
Lower Ball Joint
Lower Suspension Arm
127 (1,300, 94)
TY2029600039000X

Fig. 4 Exploded view of front suspension components. RAV4

bracket bolts and stabilizer bar to frame nuts to specifications.

STRUT BAR

REPLACE

PICKUP, TACOMA & T100 w/2WD

Mark position of staked nut to strut rod prior to removing strut rod bracket retaining bolt and washers, then disconnect strut bar from frame bracket and lower arm and remove from vehicle. When installing strut rod, check to ensure staked nut is in proper position to strut rod.

LOWER CONTROL ARM & TORSION BAR

REPLACE

PICKUP, TACOMA & T100 w/2WD & 4RUNNER

1. Raise and support vehicle.
2. Remove torsion bar boots, then place alignment mark across torsion bar, anchor arm and torque arm, **Fig. 8.**
3. Remove locknut from torsion bar adjusting bolt and measure height of exposed bolt end. Record this value for reference when adjusting vehicle height.
4. Loosen adjusting nut, then remove anchor arm and torsion bar from vehicle.
5. Disconnect stabilizer bar end from lower suspension arm.
6. Disconnect strut bar end from lower suspension arm.
7. Remove shock absorber, refer "Shock Absorber, Replace."
8. Remove bolts securing lower ball joint to lower suspension arm, then separate ball joint from suspension arm.
9. Remove lower arm shaft nut, torque arm and lower arm shaft from lower arm, then the lower suspension arm.
10. To install lower suspension arm, reverse steps 1 through 9. To install torsion bar, follow remaining steps below.
11. If original torsion bar is to be installed, apply suitable grease to splines, then align marks made during removal and install torsion bar. Check to ensure adjusting bolt protrusion is equal to value obtained prior to removal of torsion bar.
12. If new torsion bar is to be installed, position block of wood 7.09–7.87 inches (180–200 mm) under front tire on side of vehicle from which torsion bar was removed.
13. Lower vehicle unit clearance between spring bumper on lower arm and frame is .051 inch (13 mm), **Fig. 9.** Install anchor arm onto torsion bar until adjusting bolt protrusion dimension A is .31–1.10 inch (8–28 mm), **Fig. 10,** on ½ ton models or .43–1.22 inch (11–31 mm) on ¾ ton and Cab and Chassis models. Remove wooden block, then tighten adjusting nut until bolt protrusion dimension B, **Fig. 11,** is 2.72–3.50 inches (69–89 mm).
14. Install torsion bar boots and locknut, then **torque** locknut to 51–65 ft. lbs. **Torque** lower suspension arm shaft nuts to 145–216 ft. lbs. with vehicle suspension loaded.

LOWER SUSPENSION ARM & SHOCK ABSORBER

REPLACE

PICKUP, TACOMA & T100 w/4WD & 4RUNNER

1. Remove shock absorber.
2. Disconnect stabilizer bar from lower suspension arm.
3. Remove four attaching bolts, then disconnect lower suspension arm from lower ball joint.
4. Mark relative position between front and rear adjusting cams, then remove attaching nut, adjusting cams and lower suspension arm.
5. Reverse procedure to install. Tighten lower suspension arm to ball joint nut, shock absorber to lower suspension arm bracket and adjusting cam nuts to specifications.

PICKUP, TACOMA & T100 w/2WD

1. Raise and support vehicle.

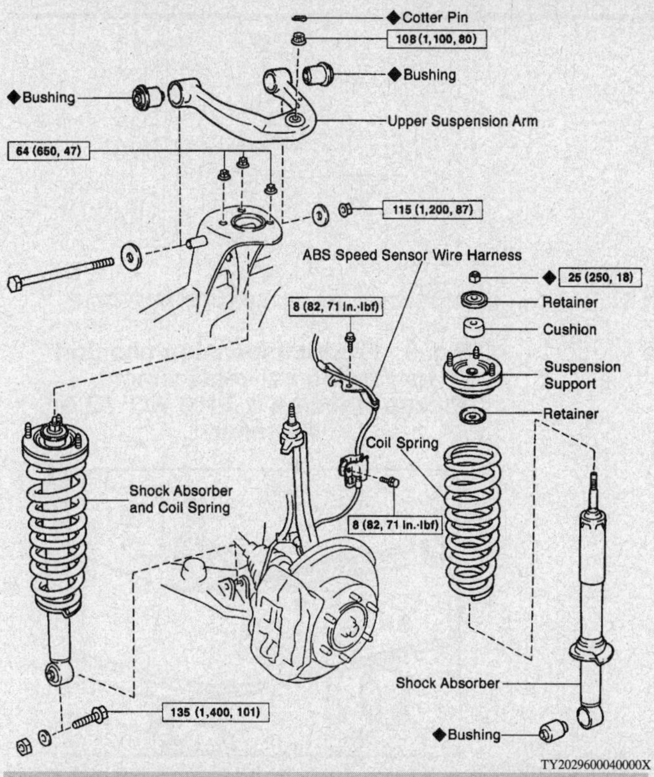
◆Cotter Pin
108 (1,100, 80)
◆Bushing
◆Bushing
Upper Suspension Arm
64 (650, 47)
115 (1,200, 87)
ABS Speed Sensor Wire Harness
◆ 25 (250, 18)
Retainer
Cushion
8 (82, 71 in.-lbf)
Suspension Support
Retainer
Coil Spring
Shock Absorber and Coil Spring
8 (82, 71 in.-lbf)
Shock Absorber
135 (1,400, 101)
◆Bushing
TY2029600040000X

Fig. 5 Exploded view of front suspension components. Pickup, Tacoma, T100 & 4Runner

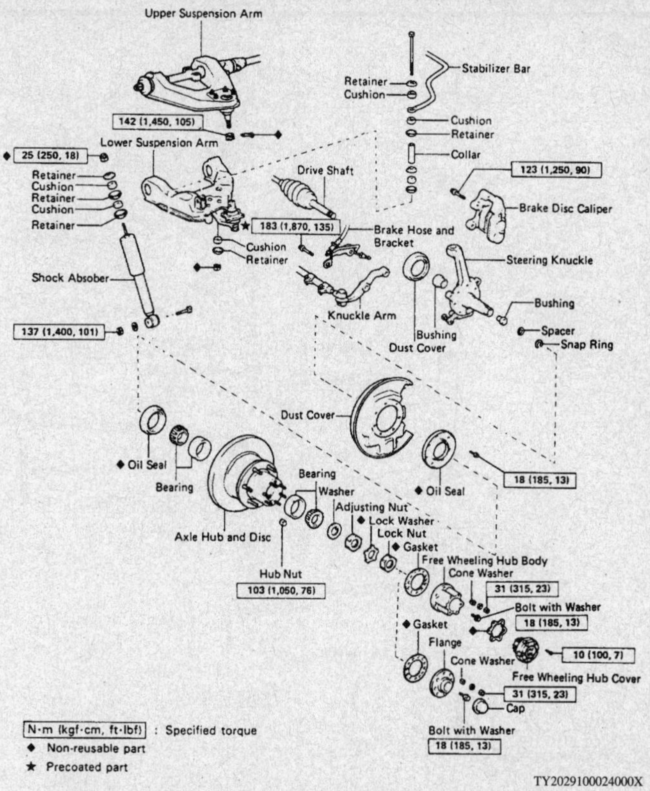
Upper Suspension Arm
Stabilizer Bar
Retainer
Cushion
142 (1,450, 105)
Cushion
Retainer
Lower Suspension Arm
Collar
◆ 25 (250, 18)
Retainer
Cushion
Retainer
Cushion
Retainer
Drive Shaft
123 (1,250, 90)
Brake Disc Caliper
183 (1,870, 135)
Brake Hose and Bracket
Cushion
Retainer
Shock Absober
Steering Knuckle
Knuckle Arm
Bushing
137 (1,400, 101)
Bushing
Dust Cover
Spacer
Snap Ring
Dust Cover
◆ Oil Seal
Bearing
18 (185, 13)
Bearing
Washer
◆ Oil Seal
Adjusting Nut
◆ Lock Washer
Axle Hub and Disc
Lock Nut
◆ Gasket
Hub Nut
103 (1,050, 76)
Free Wheeling Hub Body
Cone Washer
31 (315, 23)
Bolt with Washer
◆ Gasket
18 (185, 13)
Flange
Cone Washer
10 (100, 7)
Free Wheeling Hub Cover
31 (315, 23)
Cap
N·m (kgf·cm, ft·lbf) : Specified torque
◆ Non-reusable part
★ Precoated part
Bolt with Washer
18 (185, 13)
TY2029100024000X

Fig. 6 Exploded view of front suspension components. Pickup, Tacoma, T100 & 4Runner w/4WD

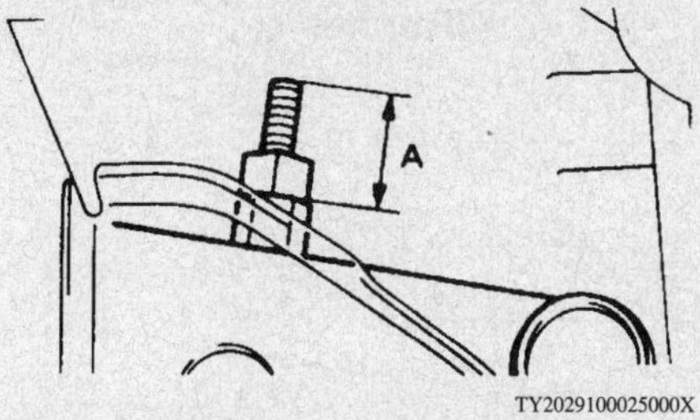
A
TY2029100025000X

Fig. 7 Measuring protruding bolt dimension "A." Pickup, Tacoma, T100 & 4Runner w/4WD

2. Remove engine undercover and torsion bar spring.
3. Remove shock absorber, then disconnect strut bar from lower arm.
4. Disconnect lower ball joint, then remove lower suspension arm.
5. Reverse procedure to install.

POWER STEERING GEAR

REPLACE

RAV4

1. Remove steering wheel as outlined under "Steering Wheel, Replace" in "Electrical" section.
2. Remove righthand and lefthand engine under covers.
3. Disconnect righthand and lefthand tie rod ends.
4. Remove front exhaust pipe.
5. Remove stabilizer bar with link.
6. Disconnect No. 2 intermediate shaft.
7. Disconnect pressure feed and return tubes, then remove tube clamps.
8. Disconnect righthand and lefthand lower suspension arms.
9. Remove two power steering gear assembly set bolts and nuts.
10. Remove front suspension crossmember assembly.
11. Reverse procedure to install. Tighten to specifications.

PICKUP, TACOMA, T100 & 4RUNNER

2WD

1. Mark relative position between coupling and worm shaft, then remove coupling attaching bolt.
2. Loosen pitman arm mount nut, then disconnect relay rod from pitman arm, using tie rod end puller tool No. 09611-22012, or equivalent.
3. Remove gear housing attaching bolts, then the gear housing.
4. Reverse procedure to install.

4WD

1. Remove joint protector set bolt, then mark relative position between universal joint and worm shaft.
2. Remove two universal joint attaching bolts, then disconnect universal joint from worm shaft.
3. Remove pitman arm set nut, then disconnect pitman arm from steering gear housing, using ball joint puller tool No. 09628-62011, or equivalent.
4. Remove gear housing attaching bolts, then the gear housing.

LAND CRUISER

1. Raise and support vehicle, then remove front tire and wheel assembly.
2. Make alignment marks between universal joint and worm shaft. **Fig. 12.**
3. Remove universal joint retaining bolts, then slide the intermediate shaft to main shaft side, then disconnect from worm shaft.
4. **On models with power steering,** remove pressure line clamp bolts, then using wrench tool No. 09631-22020, or equivalent, disconnect power steering lines.
5. **On all models,** remove cotter pin and set nut retaining pitman arm onto relay rod, then using ball joint puller tool No. 09628-62011, or equivalent, disconnect pitman arm from relay rod.
6. Remove steering gear retaining bolts, then the steering gear.
7. Reverse procedure to install. Tighten set nut to specification.

POWER STEERING PUMP

REPLACE

Refer to **Figs. 13 through 16** for power steering pump replacement.

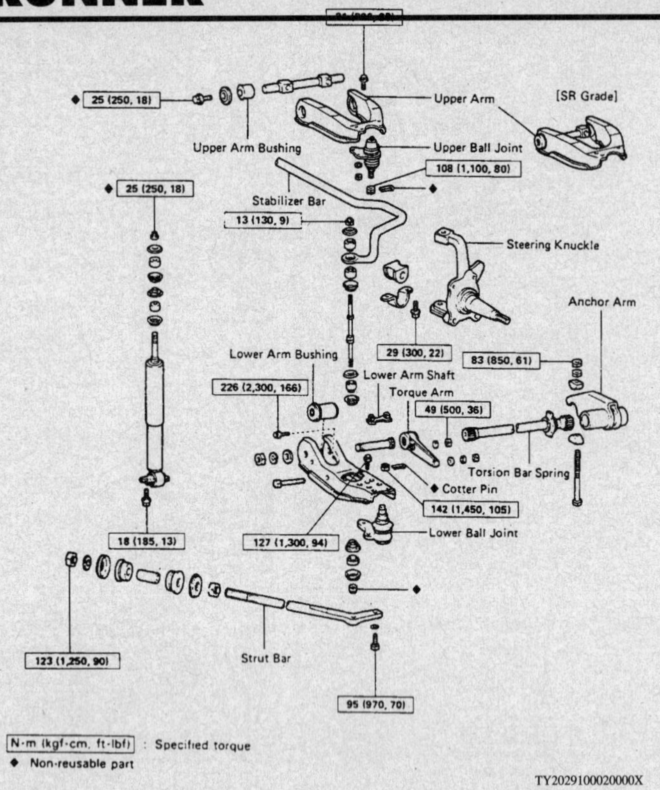
25 (250, 18)
Upper Arm
[SR Grade]
Upper Arm Bushing
Upper Ball Joint
108 (1,100, 80)
25 (250, 18)
Stabilizer Bar
13 (130, 9)
Steering Knuckle
Anchor Arm
Lower Arm Bushing
29 (300, 22)
83 (850, 61)
Lower Arm Shaft
226 (2,300, 166)
Torque Arm
49 (500, 36)
Torsion Bar Spring
Cotter Pin
142 (1,450, 105)
18 (185, 13)
127 (1,300, 94)
Lower Ball Joint
123 (1,250, 90)
Strut Bar
95 (970, 70)
N·m (kgf·cm, ft·lbf) : Specified torque
◆ Non-reusable part
TY2029100020000X

Fig. 8 Exploded view of front suspension. Pickup, Tacoma & T100 w/2WD & 4Runner

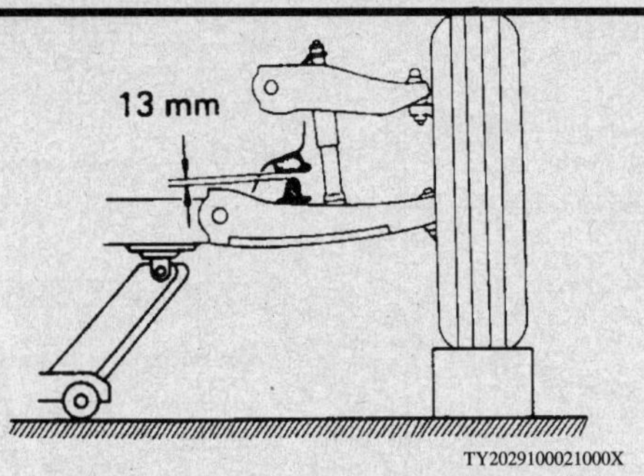
13 mm
TY2029100021000X

Fig. 9 Front suspension position for torsion bar replacement. Pickup, Tacoma & T100 w/2WD & 4Runner

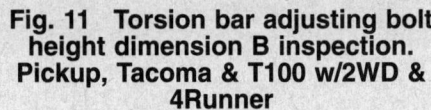

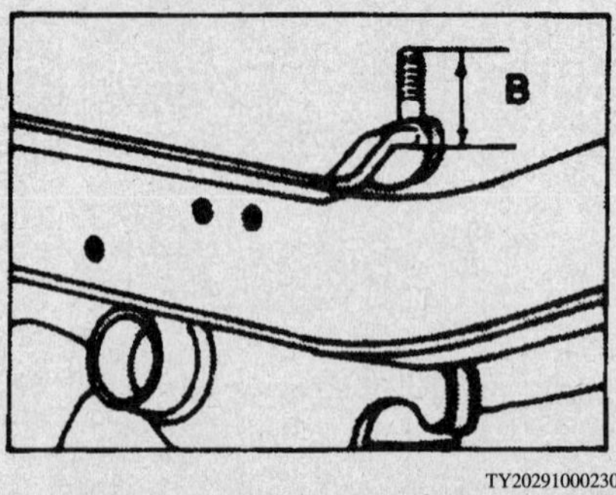
B
TY2029100023000X

Fig. 11 Torsion bar adjusting bolt height dimension B inspection. Pickup, Tacoma & T100 w/2WD & 4Runner

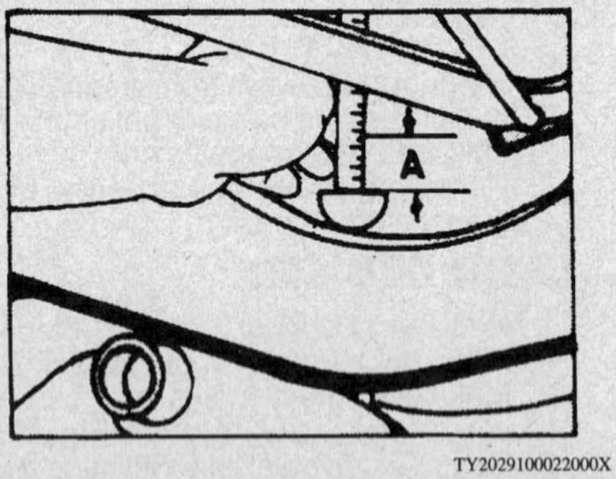
A
TY2029100022000X

Fig. 10 Torsion bar adjusting bolt height dimension A inspection. Pickup, Tacoma & T100 w/2WD & 4Runner

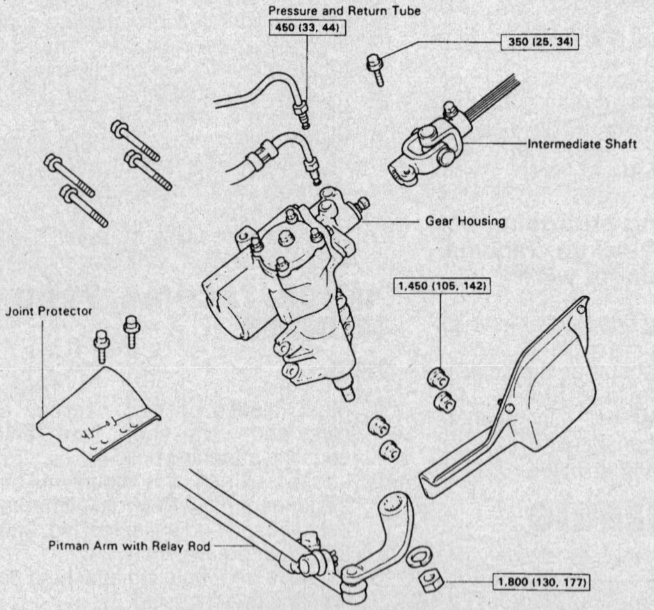
Pressure and Return Tube
450 (33, 44)
350 (25, 34)
Intermediate Shaft
Gear Housing
1,450 (105, 142)
Joint Protector
Pitman Arm with Relay Rod
1,800 (130, 177)
TY6039100022000X

Fig. 12 Exploded view of steering gear components. Land Cruiser

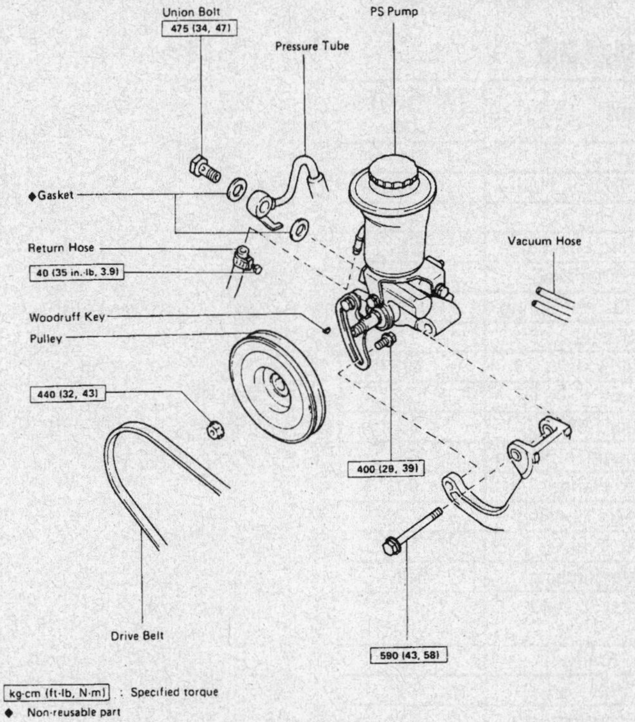
Union Bolt
475 (34, 47)
PS Pump
Pressure Tube
◆Gasket
Return Hose
40 (35 in.-lb, 3.9)
Vacuum Hose
Woodruff Key
Pulley
440 (32, 43)
400 (29, 39)
Drive Belt
590 (43, 58)
kg-cm (ft-lb, N·m) : Specified torque
◆ Non-reusable part

TY6039100023000X

Fig. 13 Power steering pump removal. Pickup, Tacoma, T100 & 4Runner, VZN Series

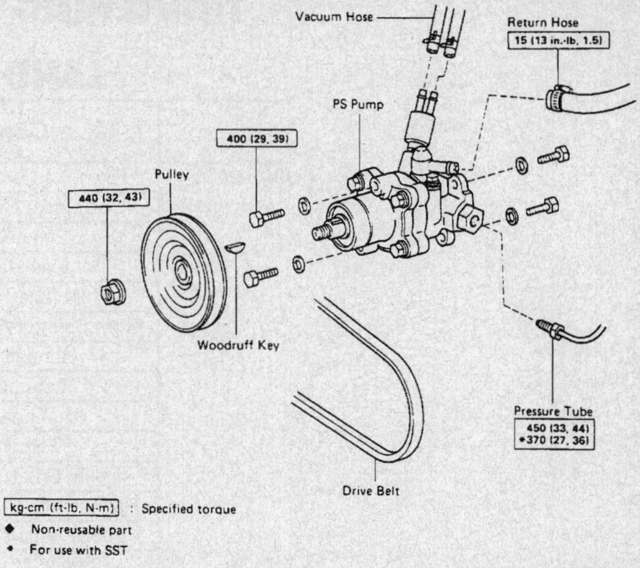
Vacuum Hose
Return Hose
15 (13 in.-lb, 1.5)
PS Pump
400 (29, 39)
Pulley
440 (32, 43)
Woodruff Key
Pressure Tube
450 (33, 44)
*370 (27, 36)
Drive Belt
kg-cm (ft-lb, N·m) : Specified torque
◆ Non-reusable part
* For use with SST

TY6039100024000X

Fig. 14 Power steering pump removal. Pickup, Tacoma, T100 & 4Runner, RN Series

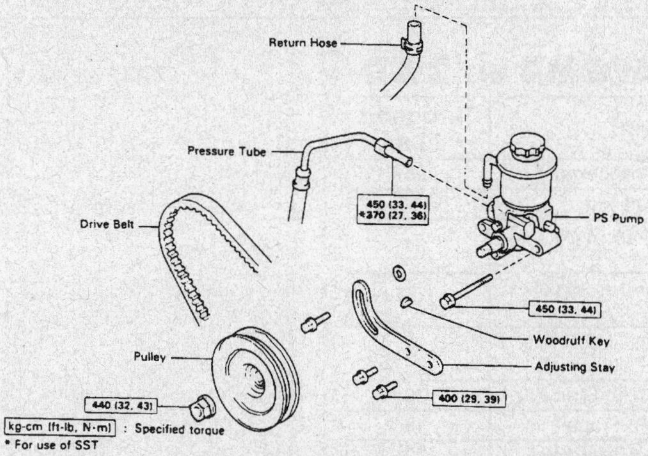
Return Hose
Pressure Tube
450 (33, 44)
*370 (27, 36)
PS Pump
Drive Belt
450 (33, 44)
Woodruff Key
Adjusting Stay
Pulley
440 (32, 43)
400 (29, 39)
kg-cm (ft-lb, N·m) : Specified torque
* For use of SST

TY6039100025000X

Fig. 15 Power steering pump removal. Land Cruiser

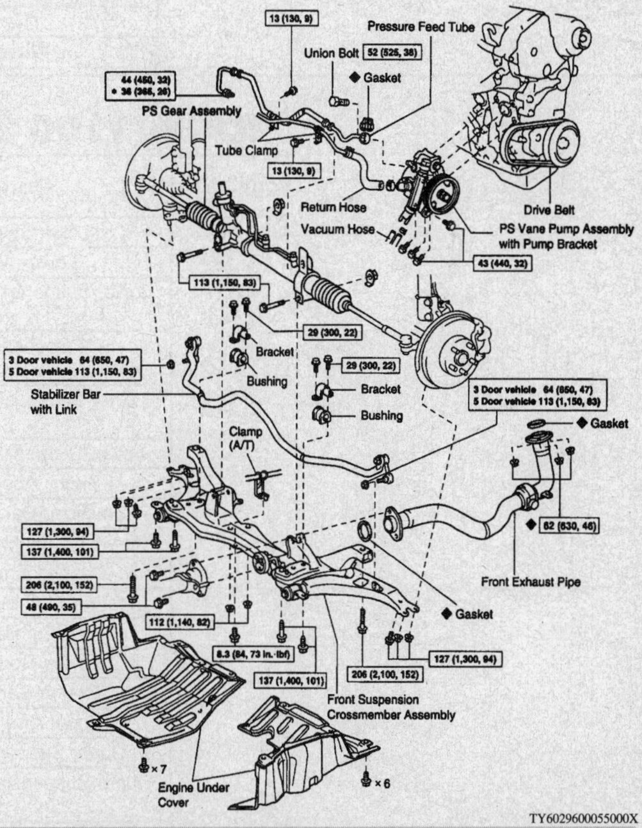
13 (130, 9)
Pressure Feed Tube
Union Bolt 52 (525, 38)
44 (450, 32)
* 36 (366, 26)
◆ Gasket
PS Gear Assembly
Tube Clamp
13 (130, 9)
Return Hose
Drive Belt
Vacuum Hose
PS Vane Pump Assembly with Pump Bracket
43 (440, 32)
113 (1,150, 83)
29 (300, 22)
Bracket
Bushing
3 Door vehicle 64 (650, 47)
5 Door vehicle 113 (1,150, 83)
29 (300, 22)
Stabilizer Bar with Link
Bracket
Bushing
3 Door vehicle 64 (650, 47)
5 Door vehicle 113 (1,150, 83)
◆ Gasket
Clamp (A/T)
◆ 62 (630, 46)
127 (1,300, 94)
137 (1,400, 101)
206 (2,100, 152)
Front Exhaust Pipe
48 (490, 35)
◆ Gasket
112 (1,140, 82)
8.3 (84, 73 in.·lbf)
127 (1,300, 94)
137 (1,400, 101)
206 (2,100, 152)
Front Suspension Crossmember Assembly
×7
×6
Engine Under Cover

TY6029600055000X

Fig. 16 Power steering pump removal. RAV4

TIGHTENING SPECIFICATIONS

LAND CRUISER

Year	Component	Torque/Ft. Lbs.
1993–96	Brake Line	11
	Disc Brake Cylinder To Axle Hub	90
	Flange To Axle Hub	26
	Front Axle Hub Bearing Locknut	65
	Front Axle Hub To Rotor Disc	54
	Front Spring Shackle To Leaf Spring	67
	Hanger Pin To Frame	17
	Lateral Control Rod	127
	Leading Arm	127
	LH Spring Center Bolt	36
	Propeller Shaft To Companion Flange	54
	Rear Spring Bracket To Hanger Pin	90
	Shock Absorber To Axle Housing	47
	Shock Absorber To Frame	19
	Spring U-Bolt To Axle Housing	105
	Stabilizer Bar Bracket To Axle Housing	9
	Stabilizer Bar To Frame	13
	Steering Knuckle To Bearing Cap	71
	Steering Knuckle To Knuckle Arm	71
	Steering Knuckle To Knuckle Spindle	34
	Tie Rod End	67
	Wheel Lug Nuts	108

PICKUP, T100 & TACOMA w/2WD

Year	Component	Torque/Ft. Lbs.
1993–96	Knuckle Stopper Bolt locknut	25
	Lower Arm Shaft Nut	166
	Lower Suspension Arm To Lower Ball Joint	94
	Lower Suspension Arm To Shock Absorber	13
	Lower Suspension Arm To Stabilizer Bar	9
	Lower Suspension Arm To Strut Bar	70
	Shock Absorber To Frame	18
	Stabilizer Bar Bracket To Frame	22
	Steering Knuckle To Lower Ball Joint	105
	Steering Knuckle To Tie Rod	67
	Steering Knuckle To Upper Ball Joint	80
	Strut Bar To Frame	90
	Tie Rod Clamp Bolt	19
	Torsion Bar Spring Locknut	61
	Upper Arm Shaft To Frame	71
	Upper Suspension Arm Set Bolt	93
	Upper Suspension Arm To Upper Ball Joint	23
	Wheel Lug Nut	76

PICKUP, TACOMA, T100 & 4RUNNER w/4WD

Year	Component	Torque/ Ft. Lbs.
1993–96	Axle Hub Bearing locknut	35
	Brake Caliper To Steering Knuckle	90
	Differential Carrier To Carrier Cover	34
	Differential Carrier To Side Bearing Cap	58
	Differential Tube To Bracket	94
	Free Wheeling Hub Body To Axle Hub	23
	Free Wheeling Hub Body To Cover	7
	Free Wheeling Hub Body To Front Driveshaft	13
	Front Differential Front Mounting Bolt	108
	Front Differential Rear LH Mounting Bolt	123
	Front Differential Rear RH Mounting Bolt	123
	Front Differential To Bracket	94
	Front Driveshaft To Side Gear Shaft	61
	Knuckle Stopper Bolt Locknut	35
	Lower Suspension Arm To Frame	145
	Lower Suspension Arm To Lower Ball Joint	105
	Lower Suspension Arm To Shock Absorber	101
	Lower Suspension Arm To Stabilizer Bar	19
	Ring Gear To Differential Case	71
	Shock Absorber To Frame	18
	Stabilizer Bar Bracket To Frame	22
	Steering Knuckle Arm To Steering Knuckle	135
	Upper Ball Joint To Steering Knuckle	105
	Upper Suspension Arm Shaft Locknut	166
	Upper Suspension Arm Shaft To Frame	131
	Upper Suspension Arm To Torque Arm	64
	Upper Suspension Arm To Upper Ball Joint	18
	Wheel Lug Nut	76

RAV4

Year	Component	Torque/Ft. Lbs.
1996	ABS Speed Sensor To Steering Knuckle	6
	Brake Hose Set Bolt	14
	Center Bearing Bracket Set Bolt	47
	Center Bearing Lock Bolt	24
	Driveshaft Locknut	159
	Lower Ball Joint To Lower Suspension Arm	94
	Lower Ball Joint To Steering Knuckle	94
	Lower Suspension Arm Bracket To Body	101
	Stabilizer Bar Link To Lower Suspension Arm	①
	Stabilizer Bar To Stabilizer Bar Link	①
	Steering Knuckle To Tie Rod End	36
	Suspension Crossmember To Body	152
	Tie Rod End Locknut	41
	Transmission Case Protector Set Bolt	13
	Wheel Lug Nuts	76

① — 3-door model, 47 ft. lbs.; 5-door model, 83 ft. lbs.

Wheel Alignment

INDEX

	Page No.
Front Wheel Alignment	47-80
Caster & Camber	47-80
Toe-In, Adjustment	47-80
Rear Wheel Alignment	47-80
Except RAV4	47-80
RAV4	47-80
Vehicle Ride Height	47-80
Land Cruiser	47-81
Pickup, Tacoma, T100 & 1993–95 4Runner	47-81
RAV4	47-80
1996 4Runner	47-81
Wheel Alignment Specifications	47-4

FRONT WHEEL ALIGNMENT

Prior to checking and resetting front wheel alignment, check tire pressure to ensure it is correct, check wheel bearings for looseness and correct as necessary, and check wheel runout with a dial indicator. Wheel runout should not exceed .047 inch (1.2 mm) on Pickup and 1993–95 4Runner, .118 inch (3.0 mm) on Land Cruiser, T100, Tacoma and 1996 4Runner, or .039 inch (1.0 mm) on RAV4.

CASTER & CAMBER

Land Cruiser

Caster and camber are not adjustable on these models. If caster and camber are not within limits, check for worn or damaged suspension parts and replace as necessary.

Pickup, Tacoma & T100 w/2WD

Caster and camber are adjusted by increasing or decreasing the number of shims between upper arm shaft and frame mounting surface. The thickness difference between front and rear shim packs should not exceed .16 inch (4 mm).

Pickup, Tacoma & T100 w/4WD & 1993–95 4Runner

Caster and camber are adjusted by rotating front and/or rear adjusting cams as shown, **Figs. 1 and 2.**

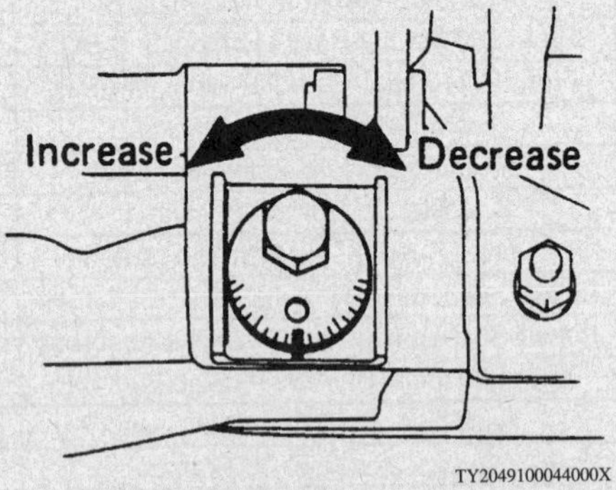

Increase
Decrease
TY2049100044000X

Fig. 1 Front camber angle adjustment. Pickup, Tacoma & T100 w/4WD & 1993–95 4Runner

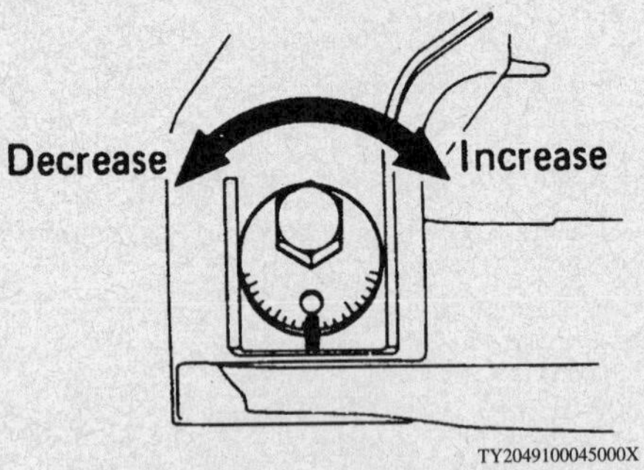

Decrease
Increase
TY2049100045000X

Fig. 2 Rear camber angle adjustment. Pickup, Tacoma & T100 w/4WD & 1993–95 4Runner

1996 4Runner

Caster and camber are adjusted by rotating front and/or rear adjusting cams as shown, **Fig. 3.**

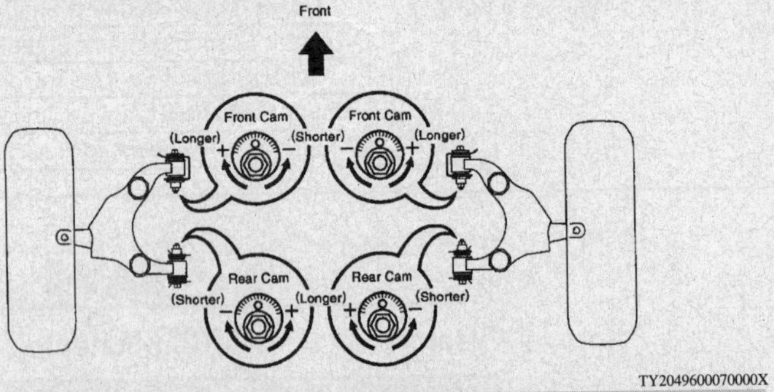

Front
Front Cam
Front Cam
(Longer)
(Shorter)
(Shorter)
(Longer)
Rear Cam
Rear Cam
(Shorter)
(Longer)
(Longer)
(Shorter)
TY2049600070000X

Fig. 3 Caster & camber adjustment cams. 1996 4Runner

RAV4

Caster is not adjustable. If caster is out of specification, check for worn or damaged suspension parts.

Adjust front camber as follows:

1. Remove front wheels.
2. Remove two lower shock absorber attaching nuts, then coat threads of nuts with engine oil and temporarily reinstall nuts.
3. Adjust camber by pulling or pushing lower side of shock absorber in direction in which camber adjustment is required.
4. **Torque** two lower shock absorber nuts to 117 ft. lbs. and install front wheels.
5. Check camber. If camber is not within specifications, estimate how much additional camber is required and select adjusting bolt from **Fig. 4.**
6. Repeat procedure, substituting proper adjusting bolt(s) for lower shock absorber bolts.

TOE-IN, ADJUSTMENT

Measure length of tie rod on each side and adjust to be equal. Adjust toe-in by turning adjusting tubes equal amounts. Clamp adjusting tubes after aligning clamps with tube slots. Lock tie rod ends so that inner and outer ends are at right angles to each other.

REAR WHEEL ALIGNMENT

EXCEPT RAV4

Vehicles with solid rear axles are non-adjustable.

RAV4

Camber and toe-in are adjusted by loosening the adjustment cam lock bolt and turning cam, **Fig. 5.**

VEHICLE RIDE HEIGHT

RAV4

Measure front vehicle ride height from

Bolt / Adjusting Value	Set Bolt		Adjusting Bolt					
	Original		OD=13.9 mm		OD=13.3 mm		OD=12.4 mm	
			1 Dot		2 Dots		3 Dots	
	11		•11		•11		•11	
	①	②	①	②	①	②	①	②
15'	●			●				
30'	●					●		
45'	●							●
1°00'			●					●
1°15'					●			●
1°30'							●	●

TY2049600071010X

Fig. 4 Front camber adjusting bolt selection (Part 1 of 2). RAV4

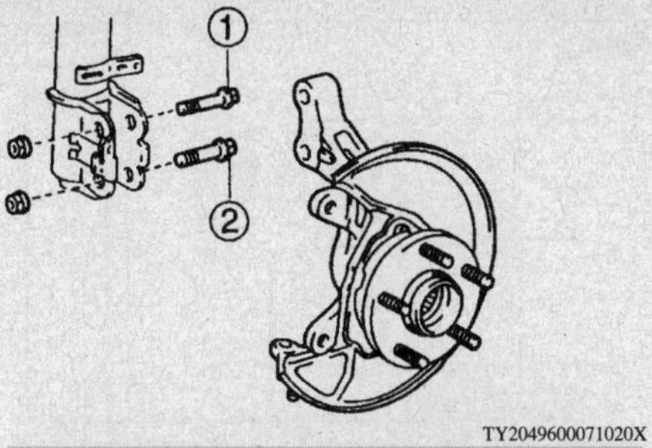
①
②

TY2049600071020X

Fig. 4 Front camber adjusting bolt selection (Part 2 of 2). RAV4

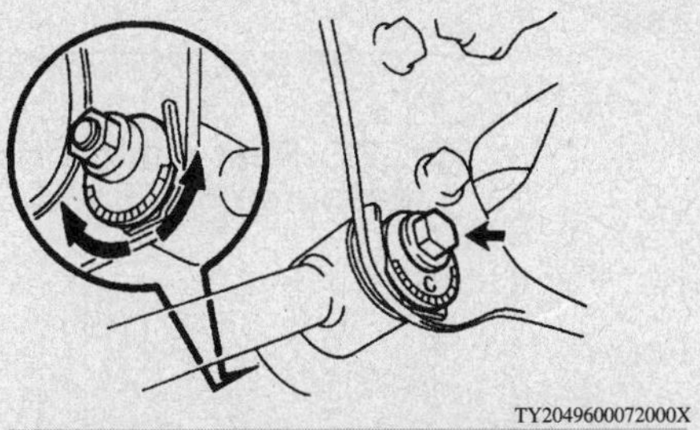

TY2049600072000X

Fig. 5 Rear camber & toe-in adjustment cam. RAV4

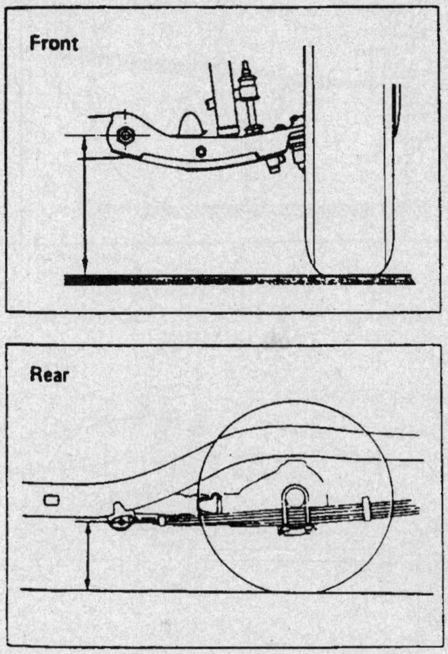
Front
Rear

TY2049100046000X

Fig. 6 Vehicle ride height measurement. Pickup, Tacoma & T100 w/2WD

ground to the center of the lower suspension arm front mounting bolt. Front vehicle ride height should be 8.94 inches on 2WD models and 9.33 inches on 4WD models.

Measure rear vehicle ride height from ground to the center of the body side No. 1 suspension arm mounting bolt. Rear vehicle ride height should be 13.90 inches on 2WD models and 14.17 inches on 4WD models.

PICKUP, TACOMA, T100 & 1993-95 4RUNNER

Trim height on these models will vary depending on option package. For measurement, refer to **Figs. 6 through 8.**

1996 4RUNNER

Refer to **Figs. 9 and 10** for ride height check locations. For models with tire size 225/75R15, the front should measure (A-B)=2.740 inches and the rear should measure (C-D)=1.953 inches. For models with tire size 265/70R16, the front should measure (A-B)=1.870 inches and the rear should measure (C-D)=1.157 inches.

LAND CRUISER

Refer to **Figs. 11 and 12** for vehicle ride height check locations. For models with tire size P235/75 R15, the front and rear should measure 13.193 inches. For models with tire size 31x10.50 R15LT (C), the front and rear should measure 14.193 inches.

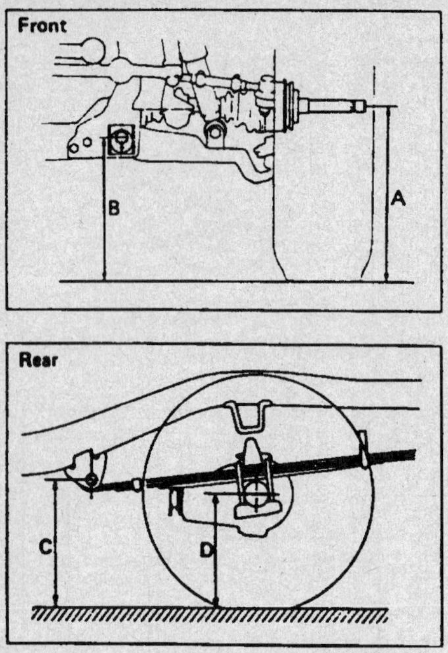
Front
A
B
Rear
C
D
TY2049100047000X

Fig. 7 Vehicle ride height measurement. Pickup, Tacoma & T100 w/4WD

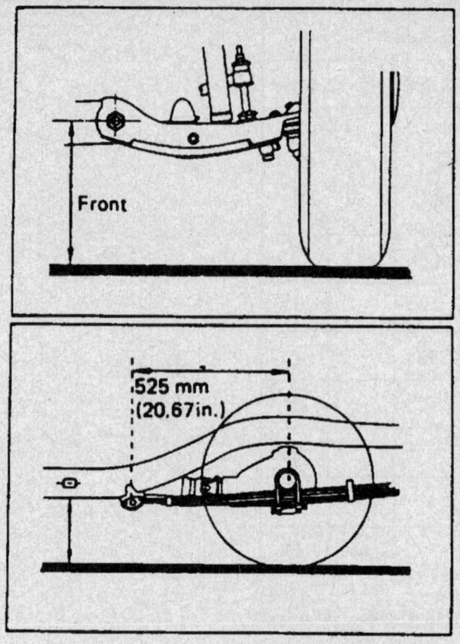
525 mm
(20.67in.)
Front
TY2049100048000X

Fig. 8 Vehicle ride height measurement. 1993–95 4Runner

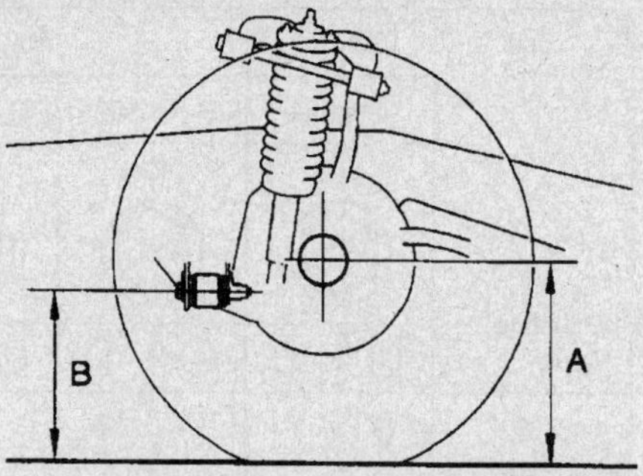
A
B
TY2049600073000X

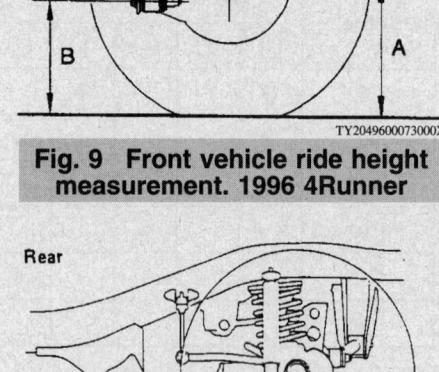

Fig. 9 Front vehicle ride height measurement. 1996 4Runner

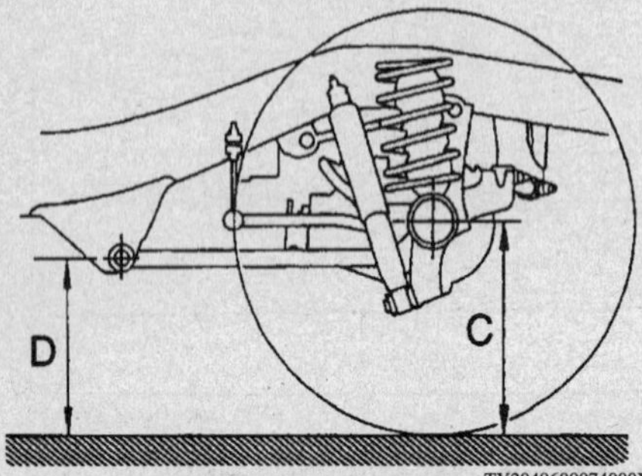
C
D
TY2049600074000X

Fig. 10 Rear vehicle ride height measurement. 1996 4Runner

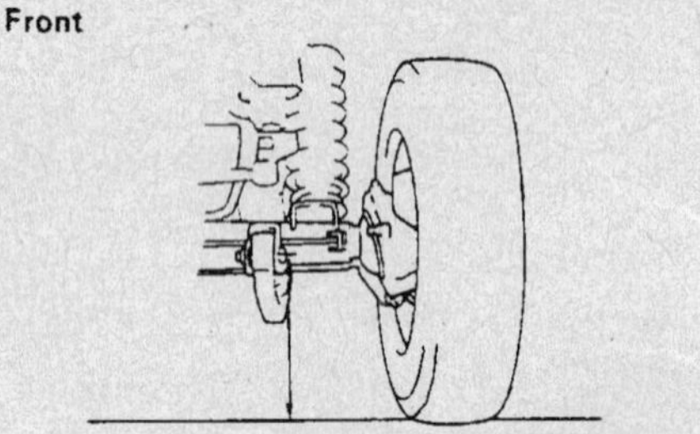
Front
TY2049100049000X

Fig. 11 Front vehicle ride height measurement. Land Cruiser

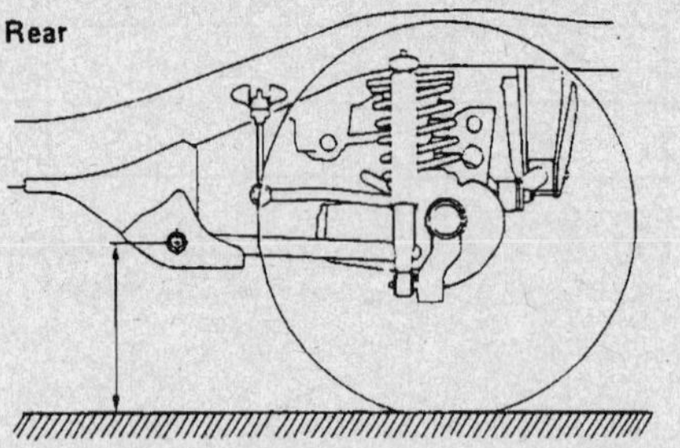
Rear
TY2049100050000X

Fig. 12 Rear vehicle ride height measurement. Land Cruiser

TOYOTA UNIT REPAIR

TABLE OF CONTENTS

	Page No.
AIR BAG SYSTEM	48-50
AIR CONDITIONING	48-1
ALL-WHEEL DRIVE AXLES	48-319
ALTERNATORS	48-33
ANTI-LOCK BRAKES	48-154
AUTOMATIC TRANSMISSIONS/TRANSAXLES	48-257
COOLING FANS	48-9
DASH GAUGES	48-17
DASH PANEL SERVICE	48-69
DISC BRAKES	48-130
DRIVE AXLES	48-325
DRUM BRAKES	48-142
ENGINE REBUILDING SPECIFICATIONS	48-334
FRONT WHEEL DRIVE AXLES	48-309
HYDRAULIC BRAKE SYSTEM	48-150
MANUAL STEERING GEAR	48-88
POWER BRAKE UNITS	48-152
POWER STEERING	48-92
SPEED CONTROL SYSTEMS	48-37
STARTER MOTORS	48-28
STEERING COLUMNS	48-81
WIPER SYSTEMS	48-44

Air Conditioning

INDEX

	Page No.
A/C Specifications	48-7
Belt Tension	48-9
Charging System	48-7
Charging Station Method	48-7
Disposable Can Method	48-7
Description	48-2
Automatic System	48-2
Discharging System	48-6
Discharging System	48-6
Evacuating System	48-6
Refrigerant Recovery	48-6
Exercise System	48-4
Leak Test	48-5
Electronic Leak Detectors	48-5
Flame-Type (Halide) Leak Detectors	48-6
Fluid Leak Detectors	48-6
R-12 Systems	48-5
R-134a Systems	48-5
Oil Charge	48-7
Oil Level Check	48-7
Performance Test	48-4
1993	48-4
1994–96	48-4
Precautions	48-1
Cleanliness	48-1
General Service	48-2
R-12 Systems	48-1
R-134a Systems	48-1
System Flush	48-7
Troubleshooting	48-2
Automatic System	48-2
Manual System	48-3

PRECAUTIONS

R-134A SYSTEMS

R-134a is a non-toxic, non-flammable, clear, odorless, liquified gas.

R-134a refrigerant is not compatible with R-12 refrigerant. Even small amounts of R-12 in a R134a system can cause lubricant contamination, improper A/C performance or compressor failure. Never add R-12 to a R-134a system.

New service ports have been added to the compressor to prevent charging the system with R-12 refrigerant. **R-134a systems require a special compressor lubricant. Use ND8 PAG compressor oil part No. 82300102, or equivalent, when servicing system.**

Avoid breathing A/C refrigerant and lubricant vapor and mist. Exposure may irritate eyes, nose and throat. Use only approved service equipment to discharge R-134a systems.

R-12 SYSTEMS

The refrigerant used in car air conditioners is also known as R-12. It is colorless and odorless both as a gas and a liquid. Since it boils (vaporizes) at –21.7°F, it will usually be in a vapor state when being handled in a repair shop. But if a portion of the liquid coolant should come in contact with the hands or face, note that its temperature momentarily will be at least 22° below zero.

Protective goggles should be worn when opening any refrigerant lines. If liquid coolant does touch the eyes, bathe the eyes quickly in cold water. Then apply a bland disinfectant oil to the eyes. See an eye doctor.

When checking a system for leaks with a torch type leak detector, do not breathe the vapors coming from the flame. Do not discharge refrigerant in the area of a live flame. A poisonous phosgene gas is produced when R-12 is burned. While the small amount of this gas produced by a leak detector is not harmful unless inhaled directly at the flame, the quantity of refrigerant released into the air when a system is purged can be extremely dangerous if allowed to come in contact with an open flame.

Never allow the temperature of refrigerant drums to exceed 125°F. The result increase in temperature will cause a corresponding increase in pressure which may cause the safety plug to release or the drum to burst.

If it is necessary to heat a drum of refrigerant when charging a system, the drum should be placed in water that is no hotter than 125°F. Never use a blowtorch, or other open flame. If possible, a pressure release mechanism should be attached before the drum is heated.

CLEANLINESS

Air conditioning systems are extremely sensitive to moisture and dirt. The importance of clean working conditions is extremely important, as the smallest particle of foreign matter in an air conditioning system will contaminate the refrigerant, causing rust, ice or damage to the compressor. For this reason, all replacement parts are sold in vacuum sealed containers and should not be opened until they are to be installed in the system. If, for any reason, a part has been removed from its container for any length of time, the part must be completely flushed using only refrigerant to remove any dust or moisture that may have accumulated during storage. In cases of collision repairs where the system has been open for any length of time, the entire system must be purged completely and a new receiver-dehydrator must be installed because the element of the existing unit will have become saturated and unable to remove any moisture from the system once the system is recharged.

When making gauge connections, purge the gauge lines first by cracking the charging valve and allowing a small amount of refrigerant to flow through the lines, then connect the lines immediately.

Cleanliness is especially important when servicing compressors because of the very close tolerances used in these units. Consequently, repairs to the compressor itself should not be attempted unless all proper tools are at hand and a virtually spotless work area is provided.

GENERAL SERVICE

Use care when disconnecting or connecting refrigerant lines; always use a back-up wrench and be careful not to over-tighten any connection. Over-tightening will result inline and flare seat distortion and a system leak.

When making pressure checks on systems having service valves, be sure valve is in the intermediate position. If turned in too far, the hose connection will be closed, a position used for isolating the compressor. When closing the gauge port, do not over-tighten the valve or damage to the seat will result.

After disconnecting gauge lines, check the valve areas to be sure service valves are correctly seated and Schrader valves, if used, are not leaking.

DESCRIPTION

AUTOMATIC SYSTEM

The automatic A/C system automatically controls operation of the A/C compressor, air inlet door, water valve and blower fan in order to maintain passenger compartment temperature within the range selected by the operator.

The system control circuit consists of a feedback potentiometer, temperature control rheostat and ambient and in-car temperature sensors which are connected in series to provide a variable resistance to system input voltage. The output voltage of this control circuit is applied to an amplifier which transforms the control signal into an operating voltage that is proportional to the control circuit voltage signal. The amplifier output voltage is converted to a modulated vacuum signal in the vacuum valve, the vacuum signal is applied to the power servo, and the power servo controls system operation.

TROUBLESHOOTING

AUTOMATIC SYSTEM

BLOWER MOTOR DOES NOT OPERATE

1. Blown circuit breaker or fuse.
2. Defective blower motor.
3. Defective blower relay.
4. Defective blower or A/C cutoff relay.
5. Defective blower switch.
6. Defective A/C auto relay.
7. Defective water temperature switch.
8. Defective blower resistor.
9. Defective wiring connection.
10. Defective power transistor.
11. Defective ambient temperature sensor.
12. Defective A/C control assembly.
13. Defective air flow mode control servo.

NO BLOWER MOTOR CONTROL

1. Defective blower motor resistor.
2. Defective blower switch.
3. Defective in-car and/or ambient sensors.
4. Defective rheostat.
5. Defective servo motor.
6. Defective vacuum valves.
7. Defective blower control relay.
8. Defective amplifier.
9. Defective heater mode switch.
10. Defective coolant temperature switch.
11. Defective wiring or ground connections.
12. Defective vacuum circuit.

INTERIOR TEMPERATURE DOES NOT LOWER

1. Blown fuse or circuit breaker.
2. Defective magnetic clutch.
3. Defective compressor.
4. Defective pressure switch.
5. Defective expansion valve.
6. Defective EPR valve.
7. Insufficient refrigerant in system.
8. Defective A/C switch.
9. Defective temperature sensors.
10. Defective rheostat.
11. Defective servo motor.
12. Defective vacuum valves.
13. Defective A/C amplifier.
14. Defective magnetic clutch relay.
15. Defective wiring or ground connections.
16. Defective vacuum circuit.
17. Defective water valve.

INTERIOR TEMPERATURE DOES NOT RISE

1. Defective water valve.
2. Defective temperature sensors.
3. Defective rheostat.
4. Defective power servo motor.
5. Defective vacuum valves.
6. Defective A/C amplifier.
7. Defective wiring or ground connections.
8. Defective vacuum circuit.

UNSTABLE SYSTEM OPERATION

1. Defective vacuum circuit.
2. Improperly connected rheostat.
3. Defective power servo motor.
4. Defective vacuum valves.
5. Defective A/C amplifier.
6. Defective wiring or ground connection.

IMPROPER SHIFTING OF DAMPER DOORS

1. Control damper or rod improperly adjusted.
2. Defective vacuum circuit.
3. Defective dampers.
4. Defective vacuum valves.

NO COOL AIR COMES OUT

1. Incorrect volume of refrigerant.
2. Fault in cooling fan system.
3. Faulty revolution detecting sensor.
4. Faulty pressure switch.
5. Faulty magnetic clutch.
6. Faulty igniter circuit.
7. Faulty A/C amplifier.
8. Fault in A/C control assembly.
9. Faulty room temperature sensor.
10. Faulty air mix control servo motor.
11. Faulty ambient temperature sensor.

NO WARM AIR COMES OUT

1. Faulty air mix control servo motor.
2. Faulty ambient temperature sensor.
3. Faulty room temperature sensor.
4. Faulty evaporator temperature sensor.
5. Fault in A/C control assembly.
6. Fault in A/C amplifier.

OUTPUT AIR DIFFERS FROM SET TEMPERATURE OR RESPONSE IS SLOW

1. Improper refrigerant volume.
2. Improper drive belt tension.
3. Faulty ambient temperature sensor.
4. Faulty room temperature sensor.
5. Faulty evaporator temperature sensor.
6. Faulty air mix control servo motor.
7. Fault in A/C control assembly.
8. Faulty A/C amplifier.
9. Faulty compressor, condenser, evaporator or receiver.
10. Fault in heater core.
11. Faulty expansion valve.

NO AIR TEMPERATURE CONTROL (ONLY PROVIDES MAX COOL & MAX WARM)

1. Faulty air mix control servo motor.
2. Fault in A/C control assembly.
3. Faulty A/C amplifier.

NO AIR INLET CONTROL

1. Faulty air inlet control servo motor.
2. Fault in A/C control assembly.
3. Faulty A/C amplifier.

NO AIR OUTLET CONTROL

1. Faulty air outlet control servo motor.
2. Fault in A/C control assembly.
3. Faulty A/C amplifier.

ENGINE IDLE-UP DOES NOT OCCUR, OR IS CONTINUOUS

1. Fault in A/C control assembly.
2. Faulty igniter circuit.
3. Faulty magnetic clutch.

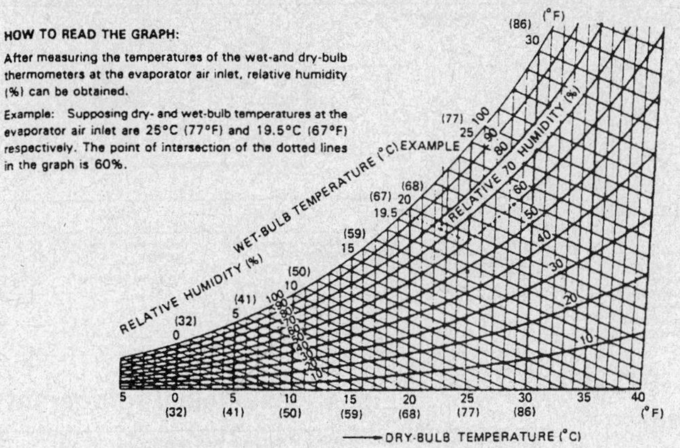
HOW TO READ THE GRAPH:
After measuring the temperatures of the wet-and dry-bulb thermometers at the evaporator air inlet, relative humidity (%) can be obtained.
Example: Supposing dry- and wet-bulb temperatures at the evaporator air inlet are 25°C (77°F) and 19.5°C (67°F) respectively. The point of intersection of the dotted lines in the graph is 60%.
WET-BULB TEMPERATURE (°C)
RELATIVE HUMIDITY (%)
EXAMPLE
RELATIVE HUMIDITY (%)
DRY-BULB TEMPERATURE (°C)
(°F)

TY7029100235000X

Fig. 1 Relative humidity graph

4. Faulty A/C amplifier.

BLINKING OF A/C INDICATOR

1. Faulty revolution detecting sensor.
2. Fault in A/C control assembly

MANUAL SYSTEM

EXCEPT MR2

System Cools Intermittently

1. Slipping magnetic clutch.
2. Defective expansion valve.
3. Faulty wiring connections.
4. Excess moisture in system.
5. Faulty revolution detecting sensor.
6. Faulty A/C amplifier.

Insufficient Cooling At High Speeds

1. Faulty thermistor.

System Cools At High Speeds Only

1. Condenser fins partially clogged.
2. Slipping compressor drive belt.
3. Defective compressor.
4. Insufficient or excess refrigerant in system.
5. Air in system.

Insufficient Cooling (All Speeds)

1. Clogged condenser fins.
2. Slipping compressor drive belt.
3. Slipping magnetic clutch.
4. Defective compressor.
5. Defective expansion valve.
6. Improperly adjusted temperature control lever.
7. Defective thermistor.
8. Defective temperature control resistor (if equipped).
9. Air or excessive compressor oil in system.
10. Clogged receiver.
11. Faulty vent mode switch.
12. Water valve cable set faulty.

Insufficient Velocity Of Cool Air

1. Blocked air inlet.
2. Clogged evaporator fins.
3. Frosted evaporator.
4. Air leakage from cooling unit or air duct.
5. Defective blower motor.
6. Faulty wiring connections.

System Produces Little Or No Heat

1. Defective water valve.
2. Improperly adjusted temperature control lever.
3. Disconnected control wire.
4. Insufficient coolant.
5. Clogged heater core.
6. Clogged or collapsed heater hoses.
7. Defective vacuum switching valve.

Improper Shifting Of Damper Doors

1. Improperly adjusted control lever.
2. Disconnected control wire.

Noisy System Operation

1. Piping noise:
   a. Loose or broken piping clamp.
   b. Defective compressor.
   c. Defective expansion valve.
2. Blower noise:
   a. Blower touching case.
   b. Defective blower motor bearing.
3. Compressor noise:
   a. Compressor mount or mounting bolts loose or broken.
   b. Defective compressor.
   c. Improper amount of compressor oil.
   d. Insufficient amount of refrigerant.
4. Magnetic clutch noise:
   a. Seized or worn bearings.
   b. Insufficient clearance between pressure plate and rotor.
5. Compressor drive belt noise:
   a. Loose drive belt.
6. Idle pulley noise:
   a. Seized or worn bearing.

Engine Overheats

1. Loose or broken fan belt.
2. Clogged radiator or condenser fins.
3. Defective radiator cap.
4. Defective water pump.
5. Incorrect ignition timing.
6. Low coolant level.
7. Faulty thermostat.

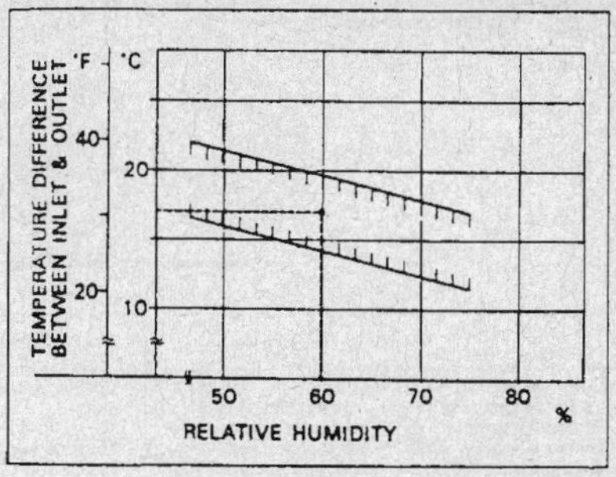
TEMPERATURE DIFFERENCE BETWEEN INLET & OUTLET
°F
°C
40
20
20
10
50
60
70
80
%
RELATIVE HUMIDITY

TY7029100236000X

Fig. 2 Typical system performance graph

8. Cracked block.
9. Cracked cylinder head.

No Blower Operation With Fan On

1. Blown heater fuse.
2. Faulty heater relay.
3. Faulty heater blower switch.
4. Faulty heater blower resistor.
5. Faulty heater blower motor.
6. Faulty wiring or ground.

Incorrect Water Temperature Output

1. Broken or binding control cables.
2. Leaking or clogged heater hoses.
3. Faulty water valve.
4. Broken air dampers.
5. Clogged air ducts.
6. Leaking or clogged heater core.
7. Faulty heater control unit.

A/C Switch Indicator Flashing

1. Slipping compressor drive belt.
2. Faulty revolution sensor.
3. Faulty A/C amplifier.

MR2

Blower Motor Does Not Operate

1. Blown fuse.
2. Defective blower motor.
3. Defective blower relay.
4. Defective blower switch.
5. Defective blower resistor.
6. Defective wiring connection.

No Blower Motor Control

1. Defective blower motor resistor.
2. Defective blower switch.
3. Defective servo motor.
4. Defective blower control relay.
5. Defective amplifier.
6. Defective a/c amplifier.
7. Defective wiring or ground connections.

Interior Temperature Does Not Lower

1. Blown fuse or circuit breaker.
2. Defective magnetic clutch.
3. Defective compressor.
4. Defective pressure switch.
5. Insufficient refrigerant in system.
6. Defective A/C switch.
7. Defective servo motor.

Condition: Periodically cools and then fails to cool

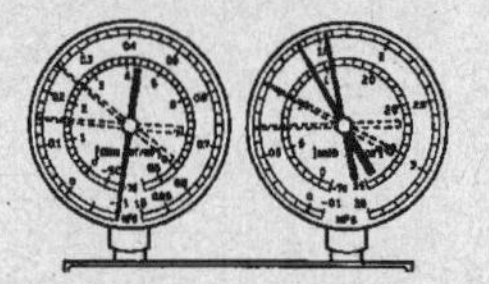

Symptom seen in refrigeration system	Probable cause	Diagnosis	Remedy
• During operation, pressure on low pressure side sometimes becomes a vacuum and sometimes normal	• Moisture entered in refrigeration system freezes at expansion valve orifice and temporarily stops cycle, but normal state is restored after a time when the ice melts	• Drier in oversaturated state ↓ • Moisture in refrigeration system freezes at expansion valve orifice and blocks circulation of refrigerant	(1) Replace receiver/drier (2) Remove moisture in cycle through repeatedly evacuating air (3) Charge proper amount of new refrigerant

TY7029100237000X

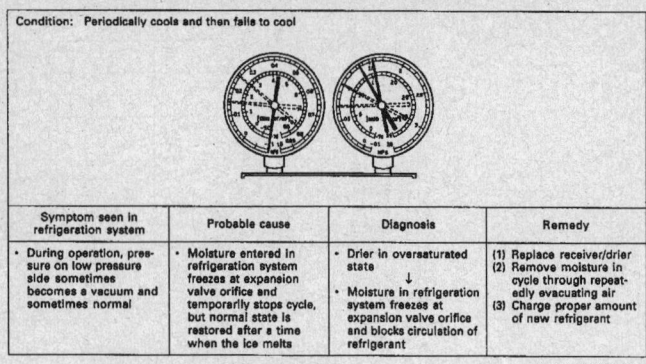

Fig. 3 Moisture present in refrigeration system

Condition: Insufficient cooling

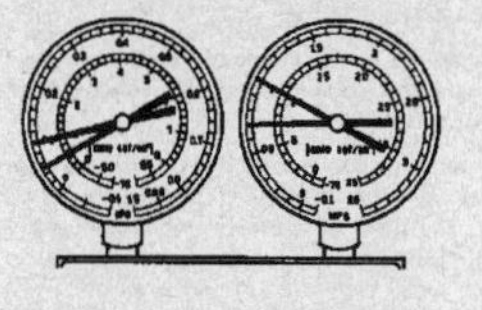

Symptom seen in refrigeration system	Probable cause	Diagnosis	Remedy
• Pressure low on both low and high pressure sides • Bubbles seen in sight glass continuously • Insufficient cooling performance	• Gas leakage at some place in refrigeration system	• Insufficient refrigerant in system ↓ • Refrigerant leaking	(1) Check for gas leakage with leak detector and repair if necessary (2) Charge proper amount of refrigerant (3) If indicated pressure value is near 0 when connected to gauge, create the vacuum after inspecting and repairing the location of the leak

TY7029100238000X

Fig. 4 Insufficient refrigerant

Condition: Insufficient cooling

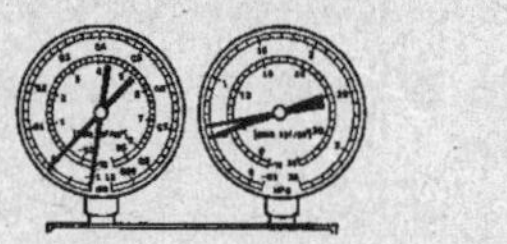

Symptom seen in refrigeration system	Probable cause	Diagnosis	Remedy
• Pressure low on both low and high pressure sides • Frost on tubes from receiver to unit	• Refrigerant flow obstructed by dirt in receiver	• Receiver clogged	• Replace receiver

TY7029100239000X

Fig. 5 Poor recirculation of refrigerant

Condition: Does not cool (Cools from time to time in some cases)

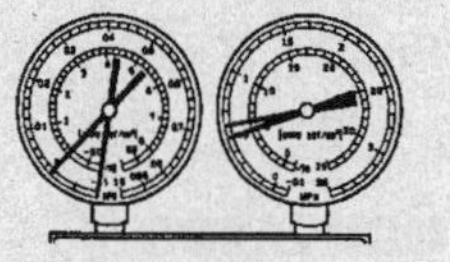

Symptom seen in refrigeration system	Probable cause	Diagnosis	Remedy
• Vacuum indicated on low pressure side, very low pressure indicated on high pressure side • Frost or dew seen on piping before and after receiver/drier or expansion valve	• Refrigerant flow obstructed by moisture or dirt in refrigeration system • Refrigerant flow obstructed by gas leakage from expansion valve heat sensing tube	• Refrigerant does not circulate	(1) Check heat sensing tube, expansion valve and EPR (2) Clean out dirt in expansion valve by blowing with air If not able to remove dirt, replace expansion valve (3) Replace receiver (4) Evacuate air and charge new refrigerant to proper amount. For gas leakage from heat sensing tube, replace expansion valve.

TY7029100240000X

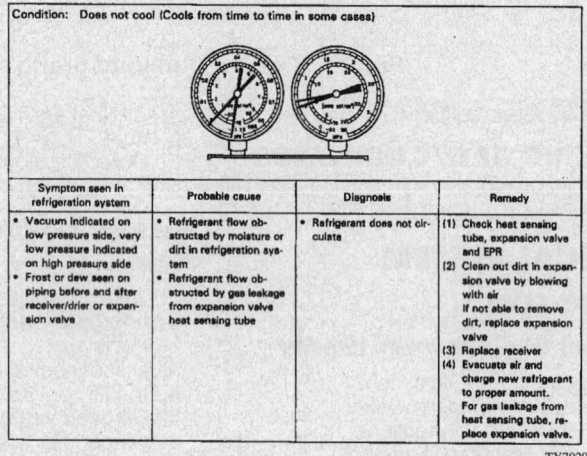

Fig. 6 Refrigerant does not circulate

8. Defective system amplifier.
9. Defective A/C amplifier.
10. Defective magnetic clutch relay.
11. Defective wiring or ground connections.
12. Defective water valve.

Interior Temperature Does Not Rise

1. Defective water valve.
2. Defective power servo motor.
3. Defective system amplifier.
4. Defective A/C amplifier.
5. Defective wiring or ground connections.

Unstable System Operation

1. Defective power servo motor.
2. Defective system amplifier.
3. Defective A/C amplifier.
4. Defective wiring or ground connection.

EXERCISE SYSTEM

An important fact most car owners ignore is that A/C systems must be used periodically. Car manufacturers recommend that when the air conditioner is not used regularly, particularly during cold months, it should be turned on for a few minutes once every two or three weeks while the engine is running. This keeps the system in good operating condition.

Checking out the system for the effects of disuse before the onset of summer is one of the most important aspects of A/C system servicing.

First clean out the condenser core. All obstructions, such as leaves, bugs and dirt, must be removed as they will reduce heat transfer and impair the efficiency of the system. Make sure the space between the condenser and the radiator also is free of foreign matter.

Make certain the evaporator water drain is open. Certain systems have two evaporators, one in the engine compartment and one in the trunk. The evaporator cools and dehumidifies the air before it enters the car; there the refrigerant is changed from a liquid to a vapor. As the core cools the air, moisture condenses on it but is prevented from collecting in the evaporator by the water drain.

PERFORMANCE TEST

1993

1. Connect manifold gauge set to high and low sides of system at compressor service valves.
2. Start engine and allow to run at approximately 2000 RPM , then activate air conditioner.
3. Set blower switch at "HI," temperature lever at "COOL" and the selector levers at "VENT" and "RECIR."
4. Open all windows and doors, then position dry bulb thermometer in cool air outlet and psychrometer (combination dry/wet bulb thermometer) near to evaporator inlet.
5. Check that high pressure gauge reading is within specified range as outlined under "System Diagnosis." **If high pressure gauge reading is above specified range, pour water on condenser until specified range is reached. If gauge reading is below specified range, cover condenser front surface area.**
6. Making sure that dry bulb portion of psychrometer is 77°–95°F, operate system until all gauges and thermometers have stabilized.
7. Compare temperatures of dry and wet bulb portions of psychrometer, then determine relative humidity using graph, **Fig. 1.** Record reading.
8. Measure the difference in dry bulb temperatures at cool air outlet and evaporator inlet. Record reading.
9. Using information gathered in steps 8 and 9, determine if system is operating properly by using graph, **Fig. 2.** Intersection of the two points should be within the diagonal lines as shown.

1994–96

1. Connect manifold gauge set as follows:
   a. Connect charging hoses to manifold gauge set.
   b. Connect quick connectors to charging hoses.
   c. Close both hand valves of manifold gauge set.
   d. Remove caps from service valves on refrigerant line.
   e. Connect quick connectors to service valves.
2. Read manifold gauge pressure when the following conditions are established:
   a. Temperature at air inlet with the switch set at RECIRC is 86–95°F.

Condition: Insufficient Cooling

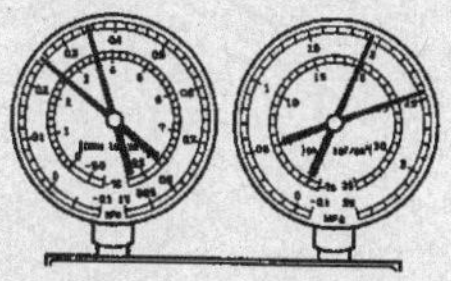

Symptom seen in refrigeration system	Probable cause	Diagnosis	Remedy
• Pressure too high on both low and high pressure sides • No air bubbles seen through the sight glass even when the engine rpm is lowered.	• Unable to develop sufficient performance due to excessive refrigerant in system • Insufficient cooling of condenser	• Excessive refrigerant in cycle → refrigerant overcharged • Condenser cooling insufficient → condenser fins clogged or fan motor faulty	(1) Clean condenser (2) Check fan motor operation (3) If (1) and (2) are in normal state, check amount of refrigerant Charge proper amount of refrigerant

TY7029100241000X

Fig. 7 Refrigerant overcharge or insufficient cooling of condenser

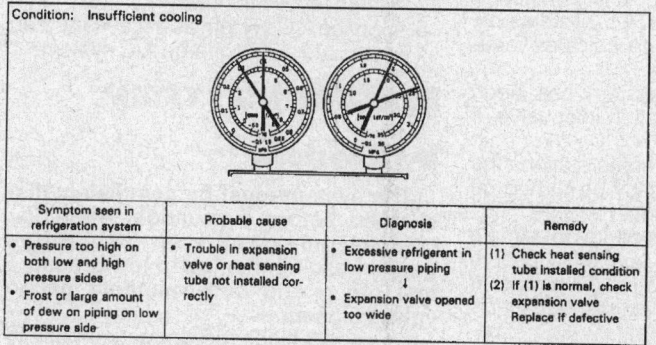

Condition: Insufficient cooling

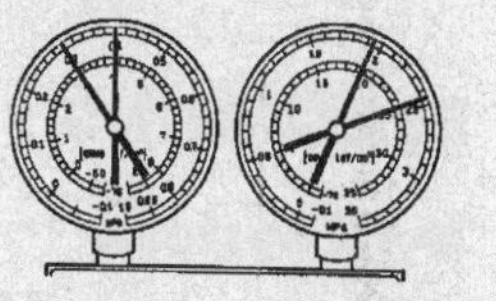

Symptom seen in refrigeration system	Probable cause	Diagnosis	Remedy
• Pressure too high on both low and high pressure sides • Frost or large amount of dew on piping on low pressure side	• Trouble in expansion valve or heat sensing tube not installed correctly	• Excessive refrigerant in low pressure piping ↓ • Expansion valve opened too wide	(1) Check heat sensing tube installed condition (2) If (1) is normal, check expansion valve Replace if defective

TY7029100243000X

Fig. 9 Expansion valve improperly mounted/heat sensing tube defective

Condition: Insufficient cooling

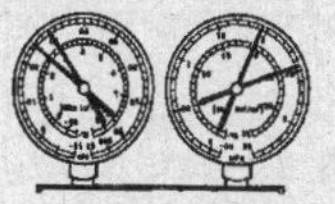

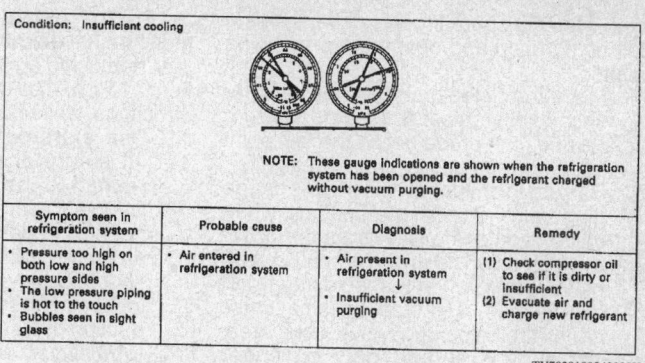

NOTE: These gauge indications are shown when the refrigeration system has been opened and the refrigerant charged without vacuum purging.

Symptom seen in refrigeration system	Probable cause	Diagnosis	Remedy
• Pressure too high on both low and high pressure sides • The low pressure piping is hot to the touch • Bubbles seen in sight glass	• Air entered in refrigeration system	• Air present in refrigeration system ↓ • Insufficient vacuum purging	(1) Check compressor oil to see if it is dirty or insufficient (2) Evacuate air and charge new refrigerant

TY7029100242000X

Fig. 8 Air present in refrigeration system

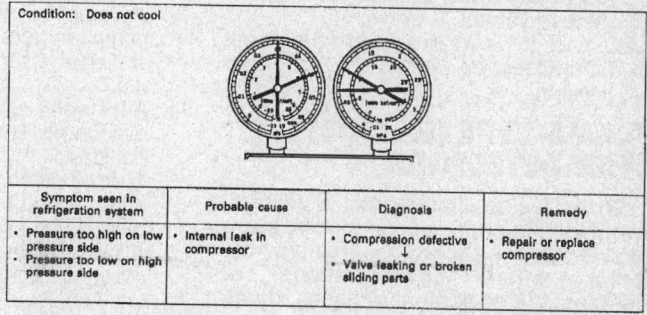

Condition: Does not cool

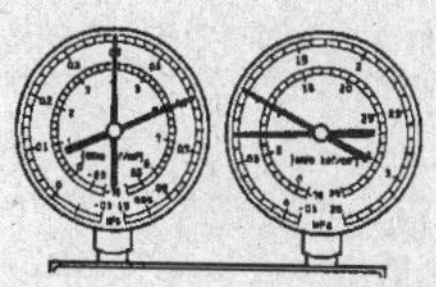

Symptom seen in refrigeration system	Probable cause	Diagnosis	Remedy
• Pressure too high on low pressure side • Pressure too low on high pressure side	• Internal leak in compressor	• Compression defective ↓ • Valve leaking or broken sliding parts	• Repair or replace compressor

TY7029100244000X

Fig. 10 Defective compression compressor

b. Engine running at 1,500 RPM .
c. Blower speed control switch set at high.
d. Temperature control set at MAX COOL.

3. For a normally functioning refrigeration system, the gauge reading should be 21–35 psi for the low pressure side, and 198–228 psi for the high pressure side.
4. Refer to **Figs. 3 through 10** for problems that may cause abnormal gauge readings.

LEAK TEST

R-12 SYSTEMS

Testing the refrigerant system for leaks is one of the most important phases of troubleshooting. One or more of the methods outlined will prove useful in detecting leaks or checking connections if service work is performed. Before beginning any leak test, attach a manifold gauge set and note pressure. If little or no pressure is indicated, a partial charge must be installed. Check all connections, compressor head gasket, oil filler plug and compressor shaft seal for leaks. Prior to performing any leak test, prepare the vehicle as follows:

1. Attach suitable gauge manifold to system and observe pressure readings.
2. If little or no pressure is indicated, system must be partially charged.
3. If gauges indicate pressure, set engine to run at fast idle and operate system at maximum cooling for 10–15 minutes, then stop engine and perform leak tests.

R-134A SYSTEMS

When servicing R-134a air conditioning systems always use the R-134a manifold gauges, gas leak detector assembly, tool No. 07116-38360, or equivalent, and vacuum pump adapter. Use R-134a manifold gauges to prevent R12 and R12 compressor oil contaminating the R-134a system. The R12 leak detector is not sufficiently sensitive, always use the R-134a gas leak detector assembly tool. By adapting a vacuum pump adapter, the vacuum pump can be used for both R-134a and R-12 air conditioning systems. The vacuum pump adapter has an internal magnetic valve. When evacuation is completed and the vacuum pump switch is turned off, the magnetic valve opens allowing atmospheric air into the manifold gauges to prevent the back flow of oil from the vacuum pump into the gauge hose. Be sure to turn off manifold gauge immediately after evacuating system. If not, the line will temporarily open to atmosphere.

System Empty

Do not pressure test the R-134a system with compressed air. Some mixtures of R-134a refrigerant have been shown be to combustible at higher pressures. Use gas leak detector assembly, tool No. 07116-38360, or equivalent, designed for R-134a systems.

1. Evacuate A/C system.
2. Prepare 10 oz. R-134a refrigerant charge to be injected into system. Refer to "Charging System" for procedure.
3. With engine Off, use the gas leak detector assembly, tool No. 07116-38360, or equivalent, designed for R-134a system and inspect for leaks. Fittings, lines or components that appear to be oily may indicate a refrigerant leak. To inspect the evaporator core for leaks, it is possible to insert the leak detector probe into the recirculating air door opening. With the blower at low speed and the selector in FLOOR and RECIRC mode check for leaks at left and right heater outlets. If no leak is present, fill system as outlined under "Performance Test."

Low Level

1. Start engine with A/C On for five minutes to allow system to reach operating temperature and pressure.
2. With engine Off, use the gas leak detector assembly, tool No. 07116-38360, or equivalent, designed for R-134a system and inspect for leaks. Fittings, lines or components that appear to be oily may indicate a refrigerant leak. To inspect the evaporator core for leaks, it is possible to insert the leak detector probe into the recirculating air door opening. With the blower at low speed and the selector in FLOOR and RECIRC mode check for leaks at left and right heater outlets. If no leak is present, fill system as outlined under "Performance Test."

ELECTRONIC LEAK DETECTORS

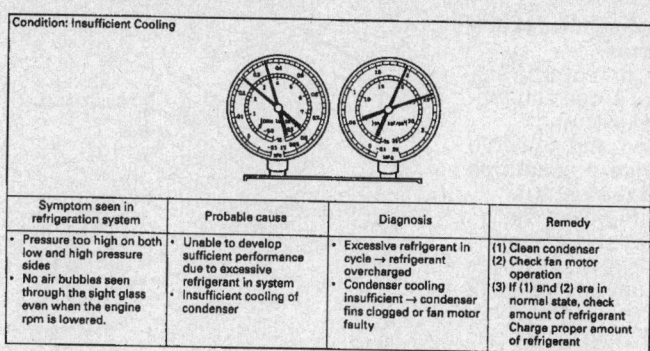

There is a number of electronic leak detectors, **Fig. 11,** available to perform leak tests. Refer to operating instructions for the unit being used and observe the following points:

1. Move the detector probe one inch per second in areas of suspected leaks.
2. Position the probe below the test point as refrigerant gas is heavier than air.
3. Be sure to check service access gauge port valve fittings (particularly when valve caps are missing) as dirt accumulations can destroy the sealing area of valve core when manifold gauge set is attached. Replace missing valve caps after cleaning valve core area. **Valve caps should only be finger tightened. Using pliers to tighten valve caps may distort sealing surface of valve.**
4. Check for leaks in manifold gauge set and hoses, as well as the rest of the system.

FLAME-TYPE (HALIDE) LEAK DETECTORS

When using flame-type detectors, avoid inhaling fumes produced by burning refrigerant. Do not use this type detector where concentrations of combustible or explosive gases, dusts or vapors may exist.

1. Adjust detector flame as low as possible to obtain maximum sensitivity. Be sure copper element is cherry red and not burned away. The flame will be almost colorless.
2. Slowly move detector along areas of suspected leaks. A slight leak will cause the flame to change to a bright yellow-green color. A significant leak will be indicated by a brilliant blue flame. Position detector under areas being tested as refrigerant gas is heavier than air. **The presence of dust in the pickup hose may cause a change in the color of the flame. If not recognized, a false diagnosis could be made. Store leak detector in a clean place and ensure hose is free of dust before leak testing.**
3. Check for leaks in the manifold gauge set and hoses, as well as the rest of the system.
4. Use a small fan to ventilate areas where the leak detector indicates refrigerant constantly. These areas are contaminated with refrigerant and must be ventilated before leak can be pinpointed.

FLUID LEAK DETECTORS

Apply leak detector solution around joints to be tested. A cluster of bubbles will form immediately if there is a leak. A white foam that forms after a short while will indicate an extremely small leak. In some confined areas such as sections of the evaporator and condenser, electronic leak detectors will be more useful.

DISCHARGING SYSTEM

REFRIGERANT RECOVERY

The use of refrigerant recovery and recycling stations allows the recovery and reuse of refrigerant after contaminants and moisture have been removed.

When using a recovery or recycling station , follow manufacturer's operating instructions, while noting the following:

1. **Use extreme caution and observe all safety and service precautions related to the use of refrigerant.**
2. Connect refrigerant recycling station hose(s) to vehicle A/C service port(s) and recovery station inlet fitting. Hoses should have shutoff devices within 12 inches of hose ends to minimize introduction of air into recycling station and to minimize amount of refrigerant release when hose(s) are disconnected.
3. Turn on recycling station to start recovery process. Allow recycling station to pump refrigerant from A/C system until station pressure gauge indicates vacuum.
4. After vehicle A/C system has been evacuated, close station inlet valve, if equipped.
5. Turn off station. On some stations the pump will automatically be turned off by a low pressure switch.
6. Allow vehicle A/C system to remain closed for about two minutes. Observe vacuum level indicated on gauge. If pressure does not rise, disconnect recycling station hose(s).
7. If system pressure rises, repeat steps 3 through 6 until vacuum level remains stable for two minutes.
8. Service A/C system as necessary, then evacuate and recharge A/C system.

DISCHARGING SYSTEM

The use of refrigerant recovery and recycling stations allows the recovery and reuse of refrigerant after contaminants and moisture have been removed.

When using a recovery or recycling station, follow the manufacturer's operating instructions, noting the following:

1. **Use extreme caution and observe all safety and service precautions related to use of refrigerants.**
2. Connect refrigerant recycling station hose(s) to vehicle A/C service port(s) and recovery station inlet fitting. Hoses used should have shutoff devices or check valve within 12 inches of hose ends to minimize introduction of air into recycling station and to minimize amount of refrigerant release when hose(s) is disconnected.
3. Turn on recycling station to start recovery process. Allow recycling station to pump refrigerant from A/C system until station pressure gauge indicates vacuum.
4. After vehicle A/C system has been evacuated, close station inlet valve, if equipped.
5. Turn station Off. On some stations the pump will automatically be turned off by a low pressure switch.
6. Allow vehicle A/C system to remain closed for approximately two minutes. Observe vacuum level indicated on gauge. If pressure does not rise, disconnect recycling station hose(s).
7. If system pressure rises, repeat steps 3 through 6 until vacuum level remains stable for two minutes.

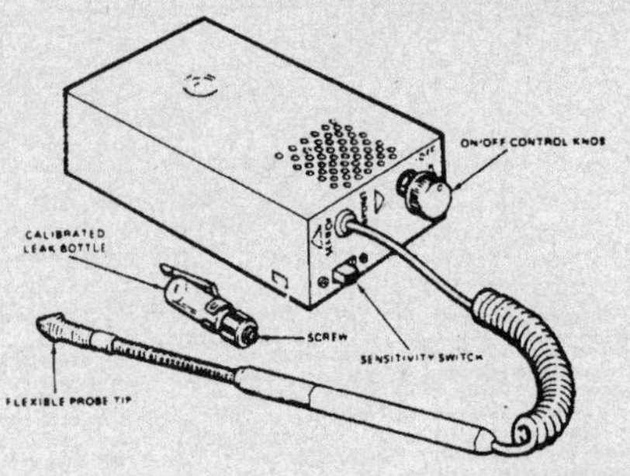
ON/OFF CONTROL KNOB
CALIBRATED LEAK BOTTLE
SCREW
SENSITIVITY SWITCH
FLEXIBLE PROBE TIP

TY7029100234000X

Fig. 11 Typical electronic leak detector

8. Service A/C system as necessary. then evacuate and recharge A/C system.

EVACUATING SYSTEM

R-12 Systems

The system must be completely discharged before evacuation. After discharging the system, keep low pressure gauge hose connected to low pressure test fitting and both manifold gauge valves closed.

1. Connect high pressure gauge hose to vacuum pump.
2. Connect center manifold gauge hose to refrigerant source with tapping valve closed.
3. Open high and low side gauge valves with vacuum pump operating.
4. Continue to operate pump for approximately 15–20 minutes after low side gauge reaches 29 or more inches of vacuum. **If the system has been left open for any period of time, it should be partially charged, then evacuated again.**
5. Close both gauge valves and turn vacuum pump off. Ensure vacuum does not drop more than 2 inches in 5 minutes. If vacuum does drop more than 2 inches, check all system connections for leaks and correct as necessary.
6. Open valve on refrigerant container and allow 14 ounces of refrigerant to enter system. Close refrigerant container and low pressure valve and recheck system for leaks. Repair as necessary.
7. Discharge refrigerant, then evacuate system. **Do not discharge refrigerant through vacuum pump.**
8. Operate vacuum pump for approximately 20 minutes at a minimum of 28 inches vacuum, then close both gauge valves and shutoff vacuum pump.

R-134a Systems

Keep all R-134a components capped to prevent moisture from entering the system. If the refrigerant system has been opened to the atmosphere, it must be evacuated.

The system must be completely discharged before it can be evacuated. Damage to the vacuum pump may result if pressurized refrigerant is allowed to enter.

1. Connect suitable charging station, refrigerant recovery machine and a manifold gauge set with vacuum pump.
2. Open suction and discharge valves and start vacuum pump. The vacuum pump should run a minimum of 45 minutes before charging to eliminate all moisture in system. When suction gauge reads 26 inch Hg or greater for 45 minutes, close all valves and turn off vacuum pump. If system fails to reach specified vacuum, refrigerant system likely has a leak that must be corrected. If refrigerant system maintains specified vacuum for at least 30 minutes, start vacuum pump and open discharge and suction valves, and allow system to evacuate for an additional 10 minutes.
3. Close all valves, turn off and disconnect pump and charge with refrigerant.

SYSTEM FLUSH

Several factors, particularly compressor failure can cause contamination of the A/C system. If the A/C system is suspected of being contaminated, or if any system components have been stored in open air for extended periods, the entire system should be flushed. If contamination or moisture is minimal, the system can be flushed with nitrogen. If contamination is more extensive, the system should be flushed with refrigerant. The receiver drier or accumulator should be replaced and a full charge of oil should be added any time the system is flushed.

CHARGING SYSTEM

DISPOSABLE CAN METHOD

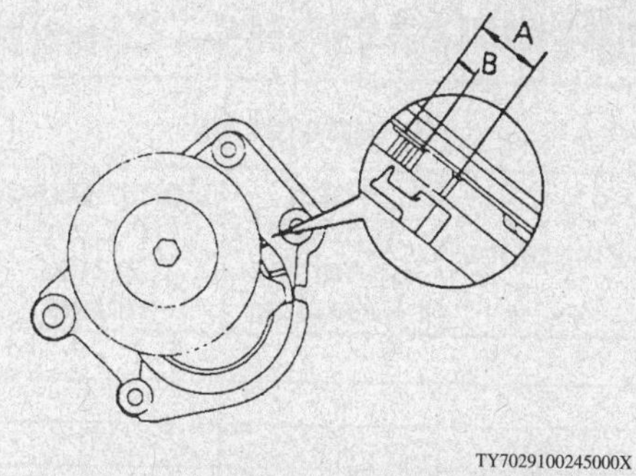
A
B
TY7029100245000X

Fig. 12 A/C belt auto tensioner scale. 2JZ-GE & 2JZ-GTE

1. Connect a suitable refrigerant dispensing valve to refrigerant can, then connect manifold gauge set to system.
2. Connect center line of gauge set to fitting on container valve.
3. Purge air from center line by loosening connection at center fitting on gauge set, then slightly opening valve at container for a second or two. Retighten connection at gauge and close valve on container.
4. Open manifold gauge set low side valve and allow refrigerant to enter system. **The refrigerant can must be kept upright if vehicle low pressure service gauge port is not on suction accumulator-drier, or suction accumulator fitting.**
5. When can is empty, close valve and remove can. Connect new can, open valve and continue charging until correct weight of refrigerant has entered system.
6. If system stops drawing refrigerant in before system is completely charged, start engine, turn A/C on and operate blower at high speed until remaining refrigerant is drawn into system.
7. When charging is complete, close valve at container and run engine for approximately 30 seconds to clear lines and gauges, then close low side valve on gauge set and disconnect refrigerant can from center hose.

CHARGING STATION METHOD

To charge system using a charging station, use manufacturers instructions provided with the unit. Observe the following precautions:

1. Do not connect high pressure line to A/C system.
2. Always keep high pressure valve on charging station closed.
3. Perform all evacuation and charging through low side pressure service fitting.

OIL CHARGE

Drain and measure amount of oil present in old compressor, then add same amount plus 0.7 ounce to new compressor. When replacing other components, add the following amounts of oil to system: condenser, 1.4–1.7 ounces; evaporator, 1.4–1.7 ounces; receiver/drier, 2.9 ounces on all models except Previa and .7 ounce on Previa.

OIL LEVEL CHECK

No provision is made for checking oil level on these vehicles. Oil is added according to component(s) being replaced. Refer to "Oil Charge."

A/C SPECIFICATIONS

Model	System	Refrigerant Capacity, Lbs.	Refrigerant Oil			Compressor Clutch Air Gap, Inch	Charging Valve Locations	
			Viscosity	Total System Capacity, Ounces	Compressor Oil Level Check, Inches		High Press.	Low Press.
1993								
Camry	R-12	2.09	①	4.3	②	.014–.026	③	④
Celica	R-12	1.59	①	4.1	②	.014–.026	⑥	④
Corolla	R-12	1.65	⑩	4.1	②	.014–.026	③	④
Land Cruiser	R-12	1.98	①	4.1	②	.014–.026	⑥	④
MR2	R-12	1.87	⑩	4.2	②	.024–.040	③	④
Paseo	R-12	1.65	⑦	4.1	②	.014–.026	⑤	⑤
Pickup	R-12	1.80	①	4.1	②	⑨	⑤	⑤
Previa	R-12	⑪	①	—	②	.014–.026	③	④
Supra	R-134a	1.56	⑫	4.1	②	.014–.026	③	④
Tercel	R-12	1.65	⑦	4.1	②	.014–.026	③	④
T100	R-134a	1.43	⑫	4.8	②	.014–.026	③	④
4Runner	R-12	1.9	①	4.1	②	⑨	⑤	⑤
1994								
Camry	R-134a	1.88	⑫	4.9	②	.014–.026	③	④

Continued

A/C SPECIFICATIONS—Continued

Model	System	Refrigerant Capacity, Lbs.	Refrigerant Oil			Compressor Clutch Air Gap, Inch	Charging Valve Locations	
			Viscosity	Total System Capacity, Ounces	Compressor Oil Level Check, Inches		High Press.	Low Press.
1994								
Celica	R-134a	1.43	⑫	4.1	②	.014–.026	③	④
Corolla	R-134a	1.65	⑫	4.1	②	.014–.026	③	④
Land Cruiser	R-134a	1.88	⑫	4.1	②	.014–.026	③	④
MR2	R-134a	1.61	⑫	4.1	②	.014–.026	③	④
Paseo	R-134a	1.56	⑫	4.1	②	.014–.026	③	④
Pickup	R-134a	1.65	⑫	4.1	②	.014–.026	⑤	⑤
Previa	R-134a	⑬	⑫	—	②	.014–.026	③	④
Supra	R-134a	1.56	⑫	4.1	②	.014–.026	③	④
Tercel	R-134a	1.54	⑫	4.1	②	.014–.026	③	④
T100	R-134a	1.43	⑫	4.8	②	.014–.026	③	④
4Runner	R-134a	1.56	⑫	—	②	.014–.026	③	④
1995								
Avalon	R-134a	1.88	⑫	—	②	.014–.026	③	④
Camry	R-134a	1.88	⑫	4.9	②	.014–.026	③	④
Celica	R-134a	1.43	⑫	4.1	②	.014–.026	③	④
Corolla	R-134a	1.54	⑫	4.1	②	.014–.026	③	④
Land Cruiser	R-134a	1.88	⑫	4.1	②	.014–.026	③	④
MR2	R-134a	1.61	⑫	4.1	②	.014–.026	③	④
Paseo	R-134a	1.56	⑧	4.1	②	.014–.026	③	④
Pickup	R-134a	1.27	⑫	4.1	②	.014–.026	⑤	⑤
Previa	R-134a	⑬	⑫	—	②	.014–.026	③	④
Supra	R-134a	1.56	⑫	4.1	②	.014–.026	③	④
Tacoma	R-134a	1.32	⑫	4.1	②	.014–.026	③	④
Tercel	R-134a	1.43	⑧	4.1	②	.014–.026	③	④
T100	R-134a	1.43	⑫	4.8	②	.014–.026	③	④
4Runner	R-134a	1.56	⑫	4.1	②	.014–.026	③	④
1996								
Avalon	R-134a	1.88	⑫	—	②	.014–.026	③	④
Camry	R-134a	1.88	⑫	4.9	②	.014–.026	③	④
Celica	R-134a	1.43	⑫	4.1	②	.014–.026	③	④
Corolla	R-134a	1.54	⑫	4.1	②	.014–.026	③	④
Land Cruiser	R-134a	1.88	⑫	4.1	②	.014–.026	③	④
Paseo	R-134a	1.56	⑧	4.1	②	.014–.026	③	④
Previa	R-134a	⑬	⑫	—	②	.014–.026	③	④
RAV4	R-134a	1.56	⑫	4.1	②	.014–.026	③	④
Supra	R-134a	1.56	⑫	4.1	②	.014–.026	③	④
Tacoma	R-134a	1.32	⑫	4.1	②	.014–.026	③	④
Tercel	R-134a	1.43	⑧	4.1	②	.014–.026	③	④
T100	R-134a	1.43	⑫	4.8	②	.014–.026	③	④
4Runner	R-134a	1.56	⑫	4.1	②	.014–.026	③	④

① — Denso oil 6 or Suniso 5GS, or equivalent.
② — Oil level cannot be checked.
③ — On high pressure line.
④ — On low pressure line.
⑤ — On compressor.
⑥ — On receiver/dryer.
⑦ — Denso oil 7, or equivalent.
⑧ — ND oil 9, or equivalent.
⑨ — Less air pump, 0.024–0.039 inch; w/air pump, 0.014–0.026 inch.
⑩ — Denso oil 6, or equivalent.
⑪ — Less rear A/C, 2.09 lbs.; w/rear A/C, 2.65 lbs.
⑫ — ND oil 8, or equivalent.
⑬ — Less rear A/C, 198 lbs.; w/rear A/C, 2.54 lbs.

BELT TENSION

Engine	Belt Tension, Lbs.	
	New	Used
1FZ-FE & 3VZ-E	100–150	60–100
1MZ-FE	140–190	66–100
2JZ-GE & 2JZ-GTE	①	①
2RZ-FE & 2TZ-FE	120–160	100–140
3E-E	150–180	90–130
3RZ-FE & 3S-GTE	135–185	80–120
3S-FE	139–192	66–99
3VZ-E	100–150	60–100
4A-FE	140–180	80–120
5S-FE	170–180	120–140
5VZ-FE	135–185	80–120
7A-FE	140–180	80–120

① — Belt tension should be within the "A" range on the auto tensioner scale, Fig. 12.

Cooling Fans

INDEX

Page No.
Electric Cooling Fans 48-9
Variable Speed Cooling Fans 48-16

Electric Cooling Fans

INDEX

Page No.
Component Replacement........ 48-14
Cooling Fan/Motor 48-14
Avalon........................ 48-14
Camry 48-15
Celica 48-15
Corolla........................ 48-15
MR2........................... 48-15
Paseo 48-15
RAV4.......................... 48-15
Supra w/2JZ-GTE Engine..... 48-15
Tercel......................... 48-15
Precautions...................... 48-9
Air Bag Systems................ 48-9
Audio Coded Anti-Theft System. 48-9
Troubleshooting 48-9
Avalon......................... 48-9
Camry w/1MZ-FE Engine 48-10
Camry w/5S-FE Engine......... 48-10
Celica 48-11
Corolla......................... 48-11
MR2............................ 48-12
Paseo 48-12
RAV4........................... 48-13
Supra w/2JZ-GTE Engine....... 48-13
Tercel.......................... 48-14

PRECAUTIONS

AIR BAG SYSTEMS

Refer to "Air Bag System Precautions" in the front of this manual for system disarming and arming procedures.

AUDIO CODED ANTI-THEFT SYSTEM

Some models are equipped with an audio coded anti-theft system that will disable the radio when the battery cable is disconnected. The system can be identified by the "ANTI-THEFT SYSTEM" on the cassette tape lid. Obtain 3 digit customer code for input. Reset system after service as follows:

1. Obtain 3 digit audio anti-theft code.
2. Depress 1 (PROG) while depressing righthand side of TUNE SEEK button, - - - will appear in tape operation display.
3. To enter the first digit, depress 1 (PROG) button repeatedly until the number of times depressed equals the first digit beginning with zero (depress the 1 button six times if the first digit if five).
4. To enter second digit, depress 2 (APS) button repeatedly until the number of times depressed equals the second digit beginning with zero.
5. To enter third digit, depress 3 (RPT) button repeatedly until the number of times depressed equals the second digit beginning with zero.
6. If - - - is displayed during code input, repeat procedure.
7. When code appears in display, depress and hold SCAN button until SEC appears.
8. When SEC disappears audio system should be operative.
9. If Err is displayed, repeat procedure. **Attempting to input code more than nine times may permanently disable audio system.**

TROUBLESHOOTING

AVALON

On-Vehicle Inspection

1. Check cooling fan operation with temperature below 190°F as follows:
   a. Turn ignition switch to On.
   b. Check that cooling fan stops. If not, check cooling fan relay and ECT

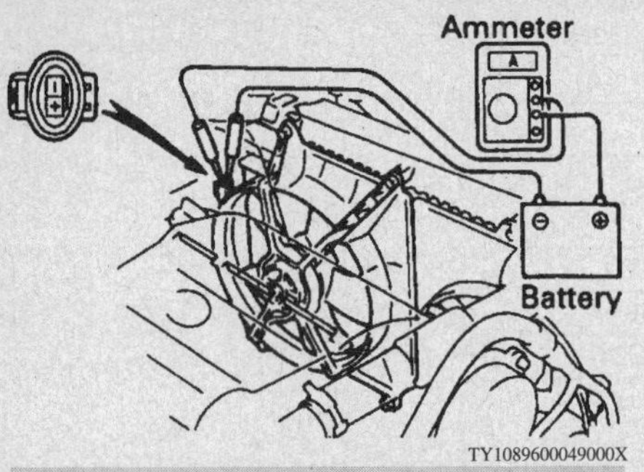
Ammeter
Battery
TY1089600049000X

Fig. 1 No. 1 fan motor inspection. Avalon & Camry w/1MZ-FE Engine

switch and check for separated connector or severed wire between cooling fan relay and ECT switch.
c. Disconnect No. 1 ECT switch connector.
d. Check that cooling fan operates. If not, check the fuses, engine main relay, cooling fan relay, cooling fan and check for a short between cooling fan relay and ECT switch.
e. Reconnect No.1 ECT switch connector.
2. Check cooling fan operation with high temperature above 208°F as follows:
a. Start engine and raise coolant temperature to above 208°F.
b. Check that cooling fan operates. If not, replace No. 1 ECT switch.

No. 1 Cooling Fan Motor Inspection

1. Disconnect cooling fan connector.
2. Connect battery and ammeter to connector, **Fig. 1.**
3. Ensure cooling fan rotates smoothly and reading on ammeter is 6.1–7.3 amps.

No. 2 Cooling Fan Motor Inspection

1. Disconnect cooling fan connector.
2. Connect battery and ammeter to connector, **Fig. 2.**
3. Ensure cooling fan rotates smoothly and reading on ammeter is 9.2–11.0 amps.

Cooling Fan Relay Inspection

1. Inspect No. 1 cooling fan relay as follows:
   a. Ensure continuity exists between terminals 85 and 86, **Fig. 3.**
   b. Ensure continuity exists between terminals 30 and 87.
   c. Apply battery voltage across terminals 85 and 86, then ensure no continuity exists between terminals 30 and 87.
2. Inspect No. 2 cooling fan relay as follows:
   a. Ensure continuity exists between terminals 85 and 86, **Fig. 4.**
   b. Ensure continuity exists between terminals 30 and 87.
   c. Ensure continuity does not exist between terminals 30 and 87.
   d. Apply battery voltage across terminals 85 and 86.
   e. Ensure continuity does not exist between terminals 30 and 87.
   f. Ensure continuity exists between terminals 30 and 87.
3. Inspect No. 3 cooling fan relay as follows:
   a. Ensure continuity exists between terminals 85 and 86, **Fig. 5.**
   b. Ensure continuity does not exist between terminals 30 and 87.
   c. Apply battery voltage across terminals 85 and 86.
   d. Ensure continuity exists between terminals 30 and 87.

CAMRY W/1MZ-FE ENGINE

On-Vehicle Inspection

1. Check cooling fan operation with temperature below 190°F as follows:
   a. Turn ignition switch to On.
   b. Check that cooling fan stops. If not, check cooling fan relay and ECT switch and check for separated connector or severed wire between cooling fan relay and ECT switch.
   c. Disconnect No. 1 ECT switch connector.
   d. Check that cooling fan operates. If not, check the fuses, engine main relay, cooling fan relay, cooling fan and check for a short between cooling fan relay and ECT switch.
   e. Reconnect No.1 ECT switch connector.
2. Check cooling fan operation with high temperature above 208°F as follows:
   a. Start engine and raise coolant temperature to above 208°F.
   b. Check that cooling fan operates. If not, replace No. 1 ECT switch.

No. 1 Cooling Fan Motor Inspection

1. Disconnect cooling fan connector.
2. Connect battery and ammeter to connector, **Fig. 1.**
3. Ensure cooling fan rotates smoothly and reading on ammeter is 6.1–7.3 amps.

No. 2 Cooling Fan Motor Inspection

1. Disconnect cooling fan connector.
2. Connect battery and ammeter to connector, **Fig. 2.**
3. Ensure cooling fan rotates smoothly and reading on ammeter is 9.2–11.0 amps.

Cooling Fan Relay Inspection

1. Inspect No. 1 cooling fan relay as follows:
   a. Ensure continuity exists between terminals 1 and 2, **Fig. 6.**
   b. Ensure continuity exists between terminals 3 and 4.
   c. Apply battery voltage across terminals 1 and 2.
   d. Ensure continuity does not exist between terminals 3 and 4.
   e. If continuity is not as specified, replace relay.

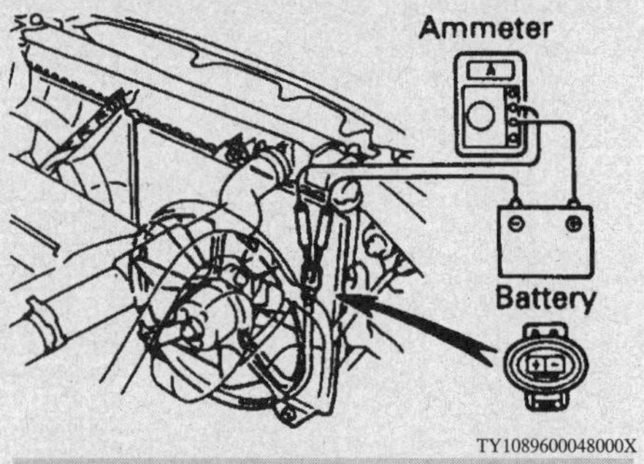
Ammeter
Battery
TY1089600048000X

Fig. 2 No. 2 fan inspection. Avalon & Camry w/1MZ-FE engine

2. Inspect No. 2 cooling fan relay as follows:
   a. Ensure continuity exists between terminals 1 and 2, **Fig. 7.**
   b. Ensure continuity exists between terminals 3 and 4.
   c. Ensure continuity does not exist between terminals 3 and 5
   d. Apply battery voltage across terminals 1 and 2.
   e. Ensure continuity does not exist between terminals 3 and 4.
   f. Ensure continuity exists between terminals 3 and 5.
   g. If continuity is not as specified, replace relay.
3. Inspect No. 3 cooling fan relay as follows:
   a. Ensure continuity exists between terminals 1 and 2, **Fig. 8.**
   b. Ensure continuity does not exist between terminals 3 and 5.
   c. Apply battery voltage across terminals 1 and 2.
   d. Ensure continuity exists between terminals 3 and 5.
   e. If continuity is not as specified, replace relay.

CAMRY W/5S-FE ENGINE

On-Vehicle Inspection

1. If coolant temperature is low (below 181°F), proceed as follows:
   a. Turn ignition switch on and check that cooling fan does not operate.
   b. If fan is operating, check for faulty fan relay and/or temperature switch. Check too for separated electrical connectors or severed wire between fan relay and temperature switch.
   c. Disconnect temperature switch wire, then check that fan rotates.
   d. If fan does not rotate, check fan relay, fan motor, engine main relay and fuse. Check also for short circuit between fan relay and temperature switch.
   e. Connect temperature switch connector.
2. If coolant temperature is high (above 199°F), proceed as follows:
   a. Raise engine temperature to at least 200°F, then check that fan rotates.
   b. If fan does not rotate, replace temperature switch.

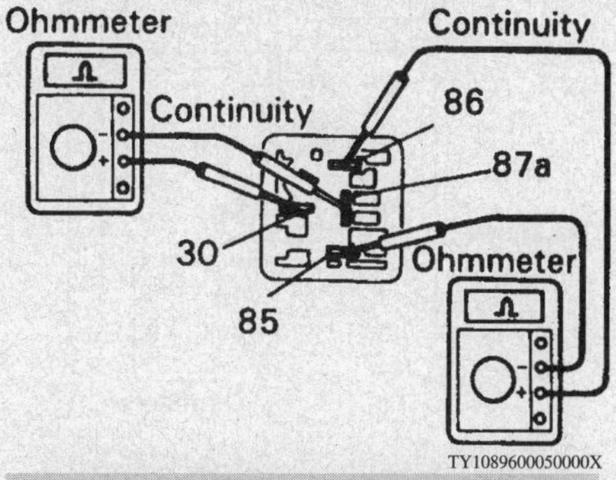
Ohmmeter
Continuity
Continuity
86
87a
30
Ohmmeter
85
TY1089600050000X

Fig. 3 No. 1 cooling fan relay inspection. Avalon

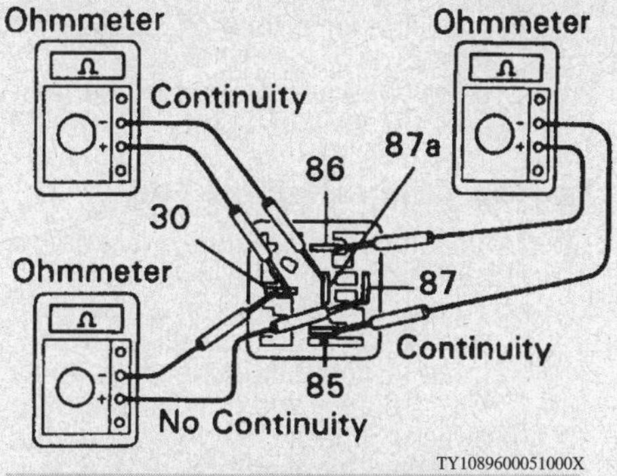
Ohmmeter
Continuity
30
Ohmmeter
86
87a
Ohmmeter
87
Continuity
85
No Continuity
TY1089600051000X

Fig. 4 No. 2 cooling fan relay inspection. Avalon

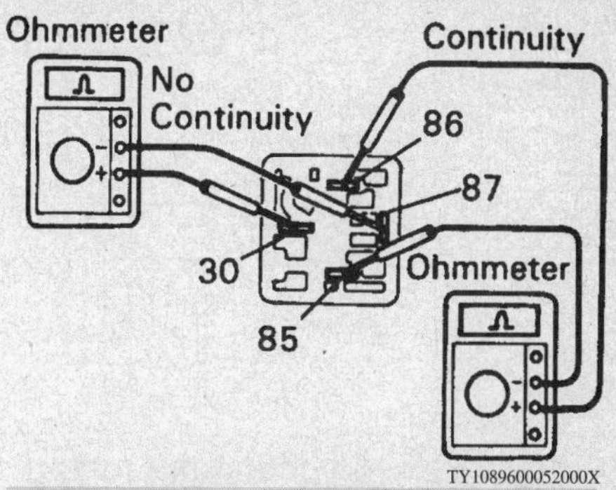
Ohmmeter
No Continuity
Continuity
86
87
30
Ohmmeter
85
TY1089600052000X

Fig. 5 No. 3 cooling fan relay inspection. Avalon

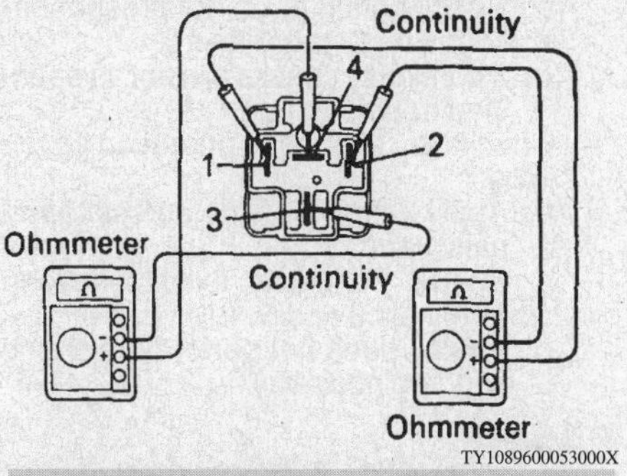
Continuity
4
1
2
3
Ohmmeter
Continuity
Ohmmeter
TY1089600053000X

Fig. 6 No. 1 cooling fan relay inspection. Camry w/1MZ-FE engine & Celica

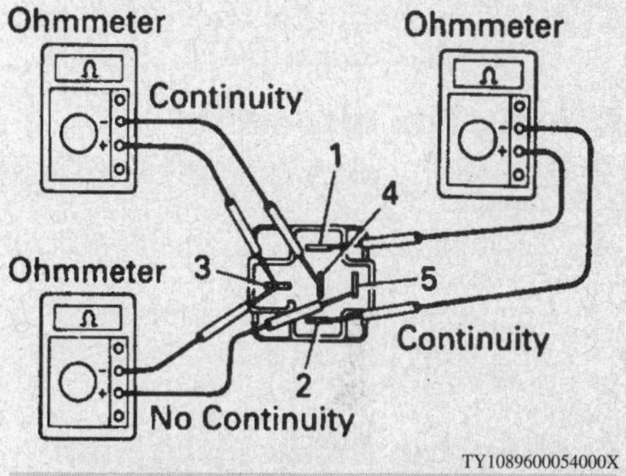
Ohmmeter
Ohmmeter
Continuity
1
4
Ohmmeter
3
5
Continuity
2
No Continuity
TY1089600054000X

Fig. 7 No. 2 cooling fan relay inspection. Camry w/1MZ-FE engine & Celica

Cooling Fan Inspection

1. Disconnect cooling fan electrical connector.
2. Connect battery and ammeter to cooling fan connector.
3. Ensure cooling fan operates smoothly and reading on measurement is 5.8–7.4 amps.

Cooling Fan Relay Inspection

1. Ensure continuity exists between terminals 1 and 2, **Fig. 9.**
2. Ensure continuity exists between terminals 3 and 4.
3. Apply battery voltage across terminals 1 and 2.
4. Ensure continuity does not exist between terminals 3 and 4.
5. If continuity is not as specified, replace relay.

CELICA

On-Vehicle Inspection

1. If coolant temperature is low (below 181°F), proceed as follows:
   a. Turn on ignition switch and check that cooling fan is not operating.
   b. If fan is operating, check for faulty fan relay and/or temperature switch. Check too for separated electrical connectors or severed wire between relay and temperature switch.
   c. Disconnect temperature switch wire, then check that fan rotates.
   d. If fan does not rotate, check fan relay, fan motor, engine main relay and fuse. Check also for short circuit between fan relay and temperature switch.
   e. Connect temperature switch wire.
2. Raise engine temperature at least 200°F, then check that fan rotates. If fan does not rotate, replace temperature switch.

No. 1 Cooling Fan Inspection

1. Disconnect cooling fan electrical connector.
2. Connect battery and ammeter to cooling fan connector.
3. Ensure cooling fan operates smoothly and reading on measurement is 5.8–7.4 amps.

No. 2 Cooling Fan Inspection

1. Disconnect cooling fan electrical connector.
2. Connect battery and ammeter to cooling fan connector.
3. Ensure cooling fan operates smoothly and reading on measurement is 5.7–7.7 amps.

Cooling Fan Relay Inspection

1. Inspect No. 1 cooling fan relay as follows:
   a. Ensure continuity exists between terminals 1 and 2, **Fig. 6.**
   b. Ensure continuity exists between terminals 3 and 4.
   c. Apply battery voltage across terminals 1 and 2.
   d. Ensure continuity does not exist between terminals 3 and 4.
   e. If continuity is not as specified, replace relay.
2. Inspect No. 2 cooling fan relay as follows:
   a. Ensure continuity exists between terminals 1 and 2, **Fig. 7.**
   b. Ensure continuity exists between terminals 3 and 4.
   c. Ensure continuity does not exist between terminals 3 and 5
   d. Apply battery voltage across terminals 1 and 2.
   e. Ensure continuity does not exist between terminals 3 and 4.
   f. Ensure continuity exists between terminals 3 and 5.
   g. If continuity is not as specified, replace relay.
3. Inspect No. 3 cooling fan relay as follows:
   a. Ensure continuity exists between terminals 1 and 2, **Fig. 8.**
   b. Ensure continuity does not exist between terminals 3 and 5.
   c. Apply battery voltage across terminals 1 and 2.
   d. Ensure continuity exists between terminals 3 and 5.
   e. If continuity is not as specified, replace relay.

COROLLA

On-Vehicle Inspection

1. If coolant temperature is low (below 181°F), proceed as follows:
   a. Turn ignition switch on and check that cooling fan does not operate. If fan runs, check for faulty fan relay and/or temperature switch (ECT). Check too for separated electrical connectors or severed wire between relay and temperature switch (ECT).
   b. Disconnect temperature switch wire, then check that fan rotates. If fan does not run, check fan relay, fan motor, ignition relay and temperature switch (ECT).
   c. Connect temperature switch wire.
2. If coolant temperature is high (above 199°F), proceed as follows:
   a. Raise engine temperature to at least 200°F, then confirm that fan rotates.

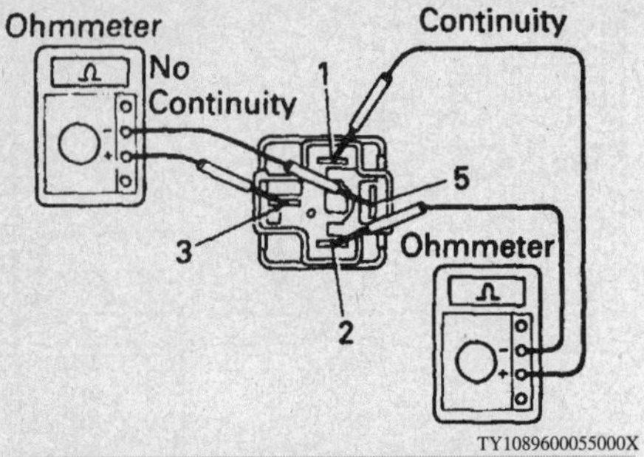
Ohmmeter
No Continuity
Continuity
1
5
3
Ohmmeter
2
TY1089600055000X

Fig. 8 No. 3 cooling fan relay inspection. Camry w/1MZ-FE engine & Celica

b. If fan does not rotate, replace temperature switch (ECT).

Cooling Fan Inspection

1. Disconnect cooling fan electrical connector.
2. Connect battery and ammeter to cooling fan connector.
3. Ensure cooling fan operates smoothly and reading on measurement is 5.7–7.7 amps.

Cooling Fan Relay Inspection

1. Check fan motor relay, located in engine compartment relay box, as follows:
   a. Using an ohmmeter, check relay continuity. If in either case continuity is absent, replace relay. Check for continuity first between terminals 1 and 2, then between terminals 3 and 4, **Fig. 10.**
   b. Apply battery voltage across terminals 1 and 2, then confirm that continuity is not present between terminals 3 and 4. If continuity is found, replace relay.

MR2

Radiator Fan

1. If coolant temperature is low (below 181°F on models less A/C; below 185°F on A/C-equipped models), proceed as follows:
   a. Turn ignition switch on and check that cooling fan is not operating.
   b. If fan is operating, check for faulty fan relay and/or temperature switch. Check too for separated electrical connectors or severed wire between relay and temperature switch.
   c. Disconnect temperature switch wire, then check that fan rotates.
   d. If fan does not rotate, check fan relay, fan motor, ignition relay and fuse. Check for short circuit between fan relay and temperature switch.
   e. Connect temperature switch wire.
2. If coolant temperature is high (above 194°F on A/C-equipped models; above 199°F on models less A/C) proceed as follows:
   a. Raise engine temperature above specified limit, then check that fan rotates.
   b. If fan does not rotate, replace temperature switch.

Engine Compartment Fan

1. If coolant temperature is below 113.9°F, proceed as follows:
   a. Turn ignition switch on and ensure cooling fan is not operating.
   b. If fan is operating, check for faulty fan relay and/or temperature switch. Check too for separated electrical connectors or severed wire between relay and temperature switch.
   c. Disconnect temperature switch wire, then check that fan rotates.
   d. If fan does not rotate, check fan relays, fan motor, ignition main relay, fuses and cooling fan ECU. Check also for short circuit between fan relay and temperature switch.
   e. Connect temperature switch wire.
2. If coolant temperature is above 144.5°F, proceed as follows:
   a. Raise engine temperature above 144.5°F, then check that fan rotates.
   b. If fan does not rotate, replace coolant temperature sensor.

Cooling Fan Relay Inspection

1. Check No. 1 fan relay, located in No. 5 junction block of front luggage compartment, as follows. If continuity checks are not as specified, replace relay.
   a. Check that continuity is present between terminals 1 and 2, **Fig. 11.**
   b. Ensure continuity exists between terminals 3 and 4.
2. Check No. 1 fan relay operation as follows:
   a. Apply battery voltage across terminals 1 and 2.
   b. No continuity should exist between terminals 3 and 4.
   c. If continuity is not as specified, replace relay.
3. **On models with A/C,** check No. 2 fan relay as follows:
   a. Using an ohmmeter, check continuity is present between terminals 1 and 2, **Fig. 12.**
   b. Ensure continuity exists between terminals 3 and 4.
   c. Ensure continuity does not exist between terminals 3 and 5.
   d. If continuity checks are not as specified, replace relay.
4. **On models less A/C,** check No. 2 fan relay operation as follows:
   a. Apply battery voltage across terminals 1 and 2.
   b. Check continuity is absent between terminals 3 and 4.
   c. Check continuity is present between terminals 3 and 5.
   d. If continuity is not as specified, replace relay.
5. **On all models,** check no. 3 fan relay as follows:
   a. Ensure continuity is present between terminals 1 and 2, **Fig. 13.**

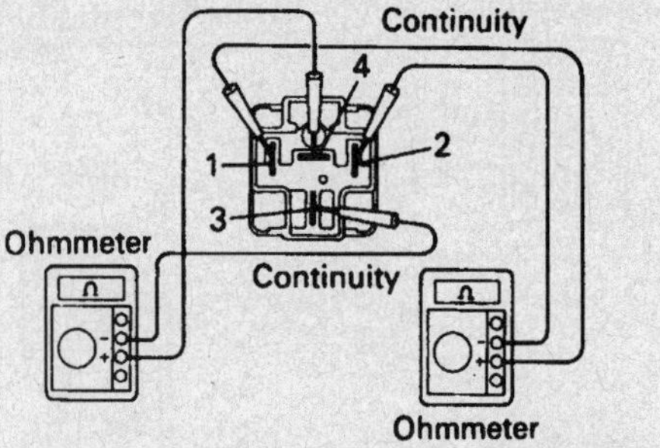
Continuity
4
1
2
3
Ohmmeter
Continuity
Ohmmeter
TY1089600056000X

Fig. 9 Cooling fan relay inspection. Camry w/5S-FE engine

   b. Check continuity is not present between terminals 3 and 5.
   c. If continuity checks are not as specified, replace relay.
6. Check No. 3 fan relay operation as follows:
   a. Apply battery voltage across terminals 1 and 2.
   b. Ensure continuity exists between terminals 3 and 5.
   c. If relay does not perform as specified, replace relay.

PASEO

On-Vehicle Inspection

1. If coolant temperature is low (below 181°F), proceed as follows:
   a. Turn ignition switch On and check cooling fan does not operate.
   b. If fan runs, check for fan motor relay and/or water temperature switch failure. Check for separated connectors or broken wire between fan motor relay and temperature switch.
   c. Disconnect water temperature switch connector, then check that fan runs.
   d. If fan does not operate, check cooling fan, fan motor relays, engine main relay and fuse. Check for short circuit between fan motor relay and water temperature switch.
2. If coolant temperature is high (above 199°F), check that cooling fan rotates. If fan does not operate, replace water temperature switch.

No. 1 Fan Inspection

1. Disconnect cooling fan electrical connector.
2. Connect battery and ammeter to cooling fan connector.
3. Ensure cooling fan operates smoothly and reading on measurement is 5.7–7.7 amps on models with manual transaxle and 8.8–10.8 amps on models with automatic transaxle.

No. 2 Fan Inspection

1. Disconnect cooling fan electrical connector.
2. Connect battery and ammeter to cooling fan connector.
3. Ensure cooling fan operates smoothly and reading on measurement is 6.0–

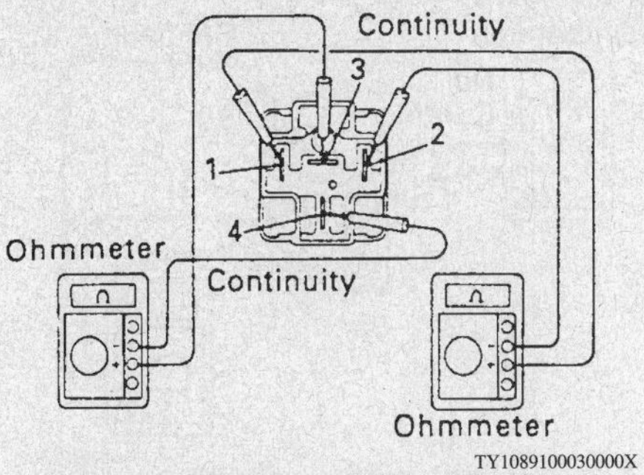
Continuity
3
2
1
4
Ohmmeter
Continuity
Ohmmeter
TY1089100030000X

Fig. 10 Cooling fan motor relay inspection. Corolla

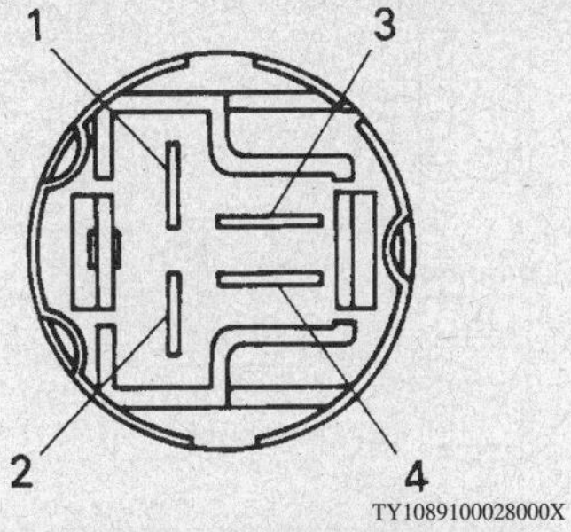
1
3
2
4
TY1089100028000X

Fig. 11 No. 1 Cooling fan motor relay inspection. MR2

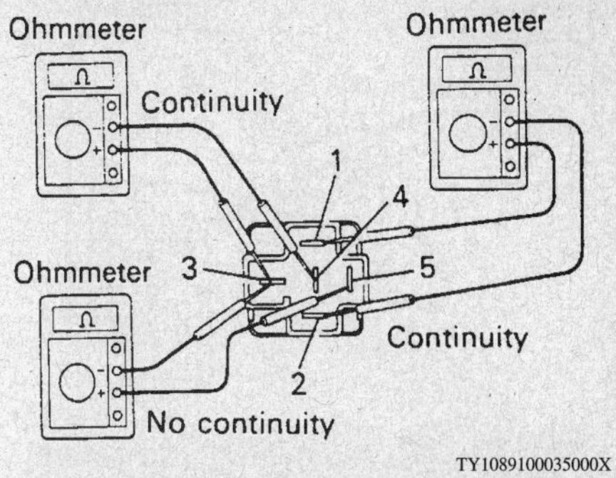
Ohmmeter
Ohmmeter
Continuity
1
4
Ohmmeter
3
5
Continuity
2
No continuity
TY1089100035000X

Fig. 12 No. 2 cooling fan relay connector. MR2

7.4 amps.

Cooling Fan Relay Inspection

1. Inspect No. 1 cooling fan relay as follows:
   a. Ensure continuity exists between terminals 85 and 86, **Fig. 14.**
   b. Ensure continuity exists between terminals 30 and 87.
   c. Apply battery voltage across terminals 85 and 86.
   d. Ensure continuity does not exist between terminals 30 and 87.
   e. If continuity is not as specified, replace relay.
2. Inspect No. 2 cooling fan relay as follows:
   a. Ensure continuity exists between terminals 85 and 86, **Fig. 15.**
   b. Ensure continuity exists between terminals 30 and 87.
   c. Ensure continuity does not exist between terminals 30 and 87.
   d. Apply battery voltage across terminals 85 and 86.
   e. Ensure continuity does not exist between terminals 30 and 87.
   f. Ensure continuity exists between terminals 30 and 87.
   g. If continuity is not as specified, replace relay.
3. Inspect No. 3 cooling fan relay as follows:
   a. Ensure continuity exists between terminals 85 and 86, **Fig. 16.**
   b. Ensure continuity does not exist between terminals 30 and 87.
   c. Apply battery voltage across terminals 85 and 86.
   d. Ensure continuity exists between terminals 30 and 87.
   e. If continuity is not as specified, replace relay.

RAV4

On-Vehicle Inspection

1. If coolant temperature is low (below 181°F), proceed as follows:
   a. Turn ignition switch On and check that cooling fan does not operate.
   b. If fan runs, check for fan motor relay and/or engine coolant temperature (ECT) switch failure. Check for separated connectors or broken wire between fan motor relay and temperature switch.
   c. Disconnect ECT switch connector, then ensure fan runs.

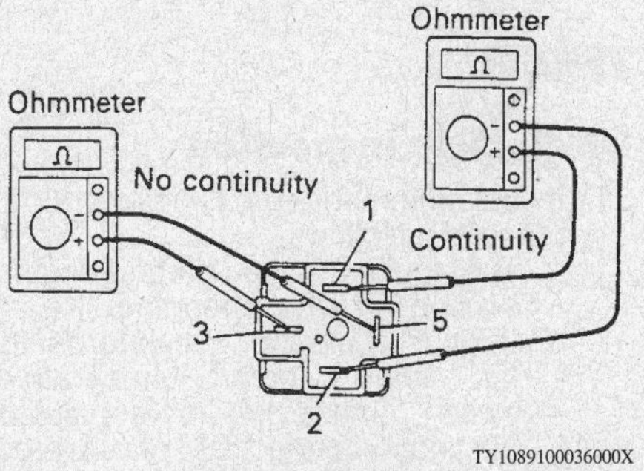
Ohmmeter
Ohmmeter
No continuity
1
Continuity
3
5
2
TY1089100036000X

Fig. 13 No. 3 cooling fan relay connector. MR2

   d. If fan does not operate, check cooling fan, fan motor relays, engine main relay and fuse. Check for short circuit between fan motor relay and ECT switch.
2. If coolant temperature is high (above 199°F), check that cooling fan rotates. If fan does not operate, replace ECT switch.

No. 1 Fan Inspection

1. Disconnect cooling fan electrical connector.
2. Connect battery and ammeter to cooling fan connector.
3. Ensure cooling fan operates smoothly and reading on measurement is 10.9–13.9 amps.

No. 2 Fan Inspection

1. Disconnect cooling fan electrical connector.
2. Connect battery and ammeter to cooling fan connector.
3. Ensure cooling fan operates smoothly and reading on measurement is 9.1–11.1 amps.

Cooling Fan Relay Inspection

1. Inspect No. 1 cooling fan relay as follows:
   a. Ensure continuity exists between terminals 1 and 2, **Fig. 17.**
   b. Ensure continuity exists between terminals 3 and 4.
   c. Apply battery voltage across terminals 1 and 2.
   d. Ensure continuity does not exist between terminals 3 and 4.
2. Inspect No. 2 cooling fan relay as follows:
   a. Ensure continuity exists between terminals 1 and 2, **Fig. 18.**
   b. Ensure continuity exists between terminals 3 and 4.
   c. Ensure continuity does not exist between terminals 3 and 5.
   d. Apply battery voltage across terminals 1 and 2.
   e. Ensure continuity does not exist between terminals 3 and 4.
   f. Ensure continuity exists between terminals 3 and 5.
3. Inspect No. 3 cooling fan relay as follows:
   a. Ensure continuity exists between terminals 1 and 2, **Fig. 19.**
   b. Ensure continuity does not exists between terminals 3 and 5.
   c. Apply battery voltage across terminals 1 and 2.
   d. Ensure continuity does not exist between terminals 3 and 5.
4. If continuity is not as specified, replace relay.

SUPRA W/2JZ-GTE ENGINE

On-Vehicle Inspection

1. If coolant temperature is below 190°F, proceed as follows:
   a. Turn ignition switch on and ensure cooling fan is not operating.
   b. If fan is operating, check for faulty fan relay and/or temperature (ECT) switch. Check too for separated electrical connectors or severed wire between radiator fan relay and temperature switch.
   c. Disconnect temperature switch wire, then check that fan rotates.
   d. If fan does not rotate, check No. 1 radiator relay, No. 2 radiator fan relay, cooling fan and fuses. Check also for short circuit between No. 1 fan relay and temperature switch.
   e. Connect temperature switch connector.
2. If coolant temperature is above 207°F, proceed as follows:
   a. Raise engine temperature above 207°F, then check that fan rotates.
   b. If fan does not rotate, replace temperature (ECT) switch.
   c. Allow coolant temperature to drop below 190°F. Fan should stop rotating.
   d. If fan does not stop rotating, replace temperature (ECT) switch.

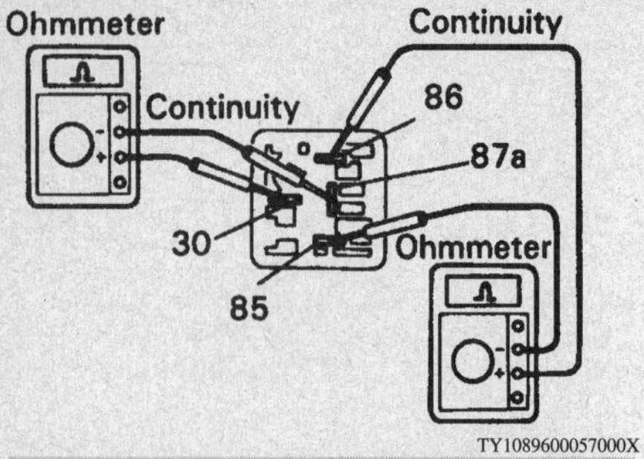
Ohmmeter
Continuity
Continuity
86
87a
30
Ohmmeter
85
TY1089600057000X

Fig. 14 No. 1 cooling fan relay inspection. Paseo & Tercel

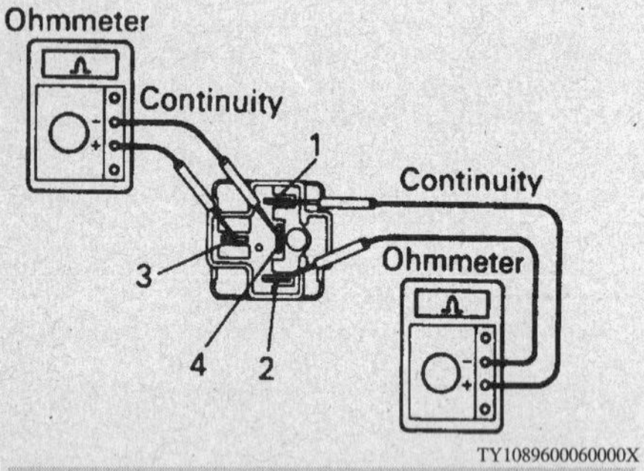
Ohmmeter
Continuity
1
Continuity
Ohmmeter
3
4
2
TY1089600060000X

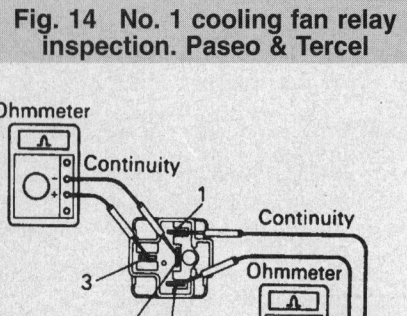

Fig. 17 No. 1 cooling fan relay inspection. RAV4

Cooling Fan Inspection

1. Disconnect cooling fan electrical connector.
2. Connect battery and ammeter to cooling fan connector.
3. Ensure cooling fan operates smoothly and reading on measurement is 2.5–4.5 amps.

Cooling Fan Relay Inspection

1. Disconnect No. 1 cooling fan relay electrical connector and remove relay from mounting clip, then inspect as follows:
   a. Ensure continuity exists between terminals 3 and 4, **Fig. 20.**
   b. Ensure continuity does not exists between terminals 1 and 2.
   c. Apply battery voltage across terminals 3 and 4.
   d. Ensure continuity exists between terminals 1 and 2.
2. Disconnect No. 2 cooling fan relay electrical connector and remove relay from mounting clip, then inspect as follows:
   a. Ensure continuity exists between terminals 1 and 6, **Fig. 21.**
   b. Ensure continuity exists between terminals 3 and 5.
   c. Ensure continuity does not exist between terminals 2 and 5.
   d. Apply battery voltage across terminals 1 and 6.
   e. Ensure continuity does not exist between terminals 3 and 5.
   f. Ensure continuity exists between terminals 2 and 5.
3. If continuity is not as specified, replace relay.

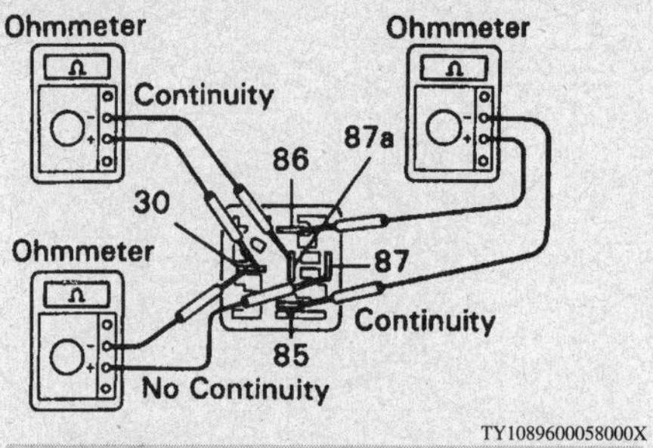
Ohmmeter
Ohmmeter
Continuity
86
87a
30
Ohmmeter
87
Continuity
85
No Continuity
TY1089600058000X

Fig. 15 No. 2 cooling fan relay inspection. Paseo & Tercel

TERCEL

On-Vehicle Inspection

1. If coolant temperature is below 181°F, proceed as follows:
   a. Turn ignition switch on and ensure cooling fan is not operating.
   b. If fan is operating, check for faulty fan relay and/or temperature switch. Check too for separated electrical connectors or severed wire between relay and temperature switch.
   c. Disconnect temperature switch wire, then check that fan rotates.
   d. If fan does not rotate, check fan relay, fan motor, engine main relay and fuse. Check also for short circuit between fan relay and temperature switch.
   e. Connect temperature switch wire.
2. If coolant temperature is above 201°F, proceed as follows:
   a. Raise engine temperature above 201°F, then check that fan rotates.
   b. If fan does not rotate, replace temperature switch.
   c. Allow coolant temperature to drop below 181°F. Fan should stop rotating.
   d. If fan does not stop rotating, replace temperature switch.

Cooling Fan Inspection

1. Disconnect cooling fan electrical connector.
2. Connect battery and ammeter to cooling fan connector.
3. Ensure cooling fan operates smoothly and reading on measurement is 5.7–7.7 amps on models with manual transaxle and 8.6–11.6 amps on models with automatic transaxle.

Cooling Fan Relay Inspection

1. Inspect No. 1 cooling fan relay as follows:
   a. Ensure continuity exists between terminals 85 and 86, **Fig. 14.**
   b. Ensure continuity exists between terminals 30 and 87.
   c. Apply battery voltage across terminals 85 and 86.
   d. Ensure continuity does not exist between terminals 30 and 87.
   e. If continuity is not as specified, replace relay.

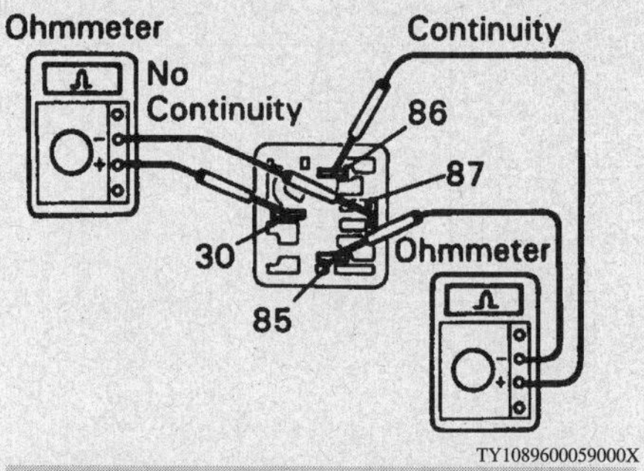
Ohmmeter
Continuity
No
Continuity
86
87
30
Ohmmeter
85
TY1089600059000X

Fig. 16 No. 3 cooling fan relay inspection. Paseo & Tercel

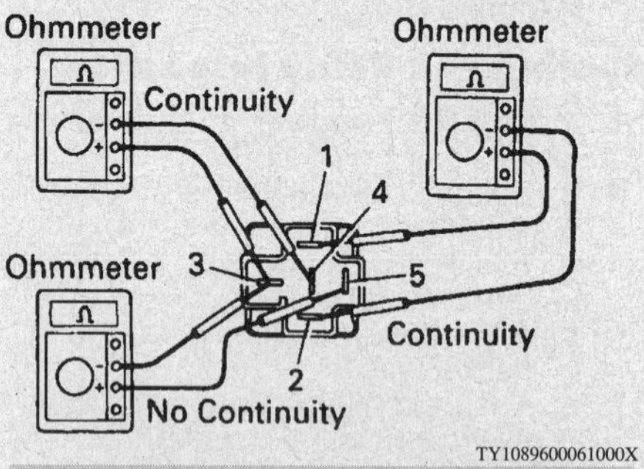
Ohmmeter
Ohmmeter
Continuity
1
4
Ohmmeter
3
5
Continuity
2
No Continuity
TY1089600061000X

Fig. 18 No. 2 cooling fan relay inspection. RAV4

2. Inspect No. 2 cooling fan relay as follows:
   a. Ensure continuity exists between terminals 85 and 86, **Fig. 15.**
   b. Ensure continuity exists between terminals 30 and 87.
   c. Ensure continuity does not exist between terminals 30 and 87.
   d. Apply battery voltage across terminals 85 and 86.
   e. Ensure continuity does not exist between terminals 30 and 87.
   f. Ensure continuity exists between terminals 30 and 87.
   g. If continuity is not as specified, replace relay.
3. Inspect No. 3 cooling fan relay as follows:
   a. Ensure continuity exists between terminals 85 and 86, **Fig. 16.**
   b. Ensure continuity does not exist between terminals 30 and 87.
   c. Apply battery voltage across terminals 85 and 86.
   d. Ensure continuity exists between terminals 30 and 87.
   e. If continuity is not as specified, replace relay.

COMPONENT REPLACEMENT

Cooling Fan/Motor

AVALON

No. 1 Cooling Fan

1. Remove battery and tray.

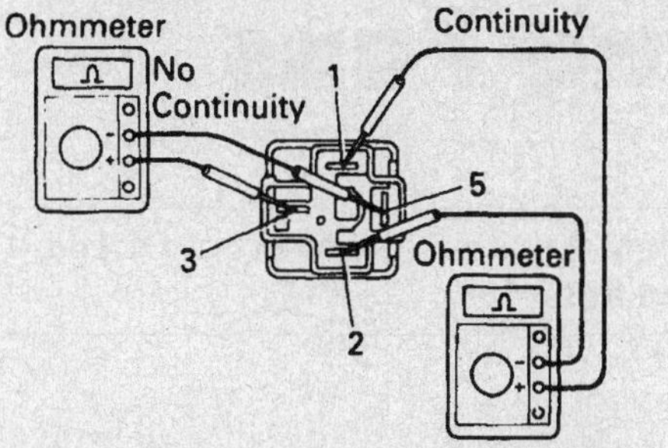
Ohmmeter
Continuity
No Continuity
1
5
3
Ohmmeter
2
TY1089600062000X

Fig. 19 No. 3 cooling fan relay inspection. RAV4

2. Disconnect cruise control actuator from body.
3. Remove No. 1 cooling fan from left hand side of engine compartment.
4. Disconnect cruise control actuator wire from clamp on fan shroud.
5. Disconnect cooling fan connector.
6. Remove four retaining bolts from cooling fan assembly.
7. Remove fan blade attaching nut and fan.
8. Remove three fan motor to assembly attaching screws and remove motor.
9. Reverse procedure to install, **torquing** fan assembly bolts to 44 inch. lbs. and fan blade attaching nut to 55 inch. lbs.

No. 2 Cooling Fan

1. Drain engine coolant.
2. Disconnect upper radiator hose from radiator.
3. Remove three attaching bolts and No. 2 cooling fan assembly.
4. Disconnect cooling fan connector.
5. Remove clip from fan blade.
6. Remove three motor to fan assembly attaching screws and motor.
7. Reverse procedure to install, **torquing** fan assembly bolts to 44 inch. lbs.

CAMRY

1. Drain engine coolant.
2. **On models with cruise control,** remove cruise control actuator cover.
3. **On all models,** disconnect cooling fan motor electrical connectors from both fan assemblies.
4. Remove cooling fan assembly attaching screws, then the fan assembly.
5. Reverse procedure to install.

CELICA

1. Drain engine coolant, then disconnect coolant reservoir hose from radiator.
2. Disconnect upper radiator hose from radiator.
3. Disconnect engine relay box from battery, then the electrical connector from the cooling fan.
4. Remove three fan motor attaching bolts, then the cooling fan.
5. Reverse procedure to install.

COROLLA

1. Disconnect battery ground cable.

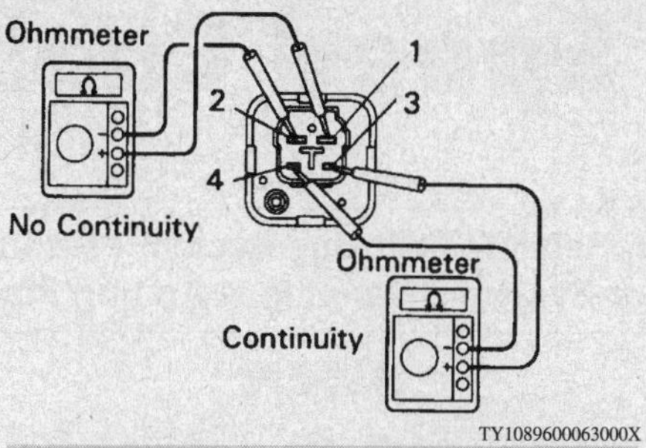
Ohmmeter
1
2
3
4
No Continuity
Ohmmeter
Continuity
TY1089600063000X

Fig. 20 No. 1 cooling fan relay inspection. Supra w/2JZ-GTE engine

2. Disconnect electrical connector from fan motor.
3. Remove reservoir tank.
4. Drain coolant, then remove upper radiator hose.
5. Remove front grille.
6. Remove cooling fan assembly.
7. Remove attaching nut, then separate fan blade and spacer from motor.
8. Remove bushings and attaching screws, then separate fan motor from shroud.
9. Reverse procedure to assemble and install.

MR2

Radiator Fan Replacement

1. **On models with 3S-GTE engine,** remove righthand engine hood side panel, then disconnect air intake electrical connectors Nos. 1 and 2.
2. **On models less 3S-GTE engine,** remove engine undercovers, then upper radiator support seal.
3. **On all models,** disconnect cooling fan electrical connectors.
4. Remove three cooling fan attaching bolts, then fan assembly.
5. Reverse to install.

Engine Compartment Fan Replacement

1. Remove righthand engine hood side panel.
2. Remove No. 1 and No. 2 air intake connectors.
3. Disconnect fan connector.
4. Remove three bolts, then fan motor assembly.
5. Reverse procedure to install.

PASEO

1. Disconnect battery ground cable.
2. Remove righthand and lefthand engine undercovers.
3. Drain engine coolant, then remove three bolts and air intake connector.
4. Remove three bolts and exhaust manifold heat shield.
5. Disconnect radiator inlet hose from radiator.
6. Disconnect oxygen sensor and cooling fan connectors, then remove four bolts and cooling fan.

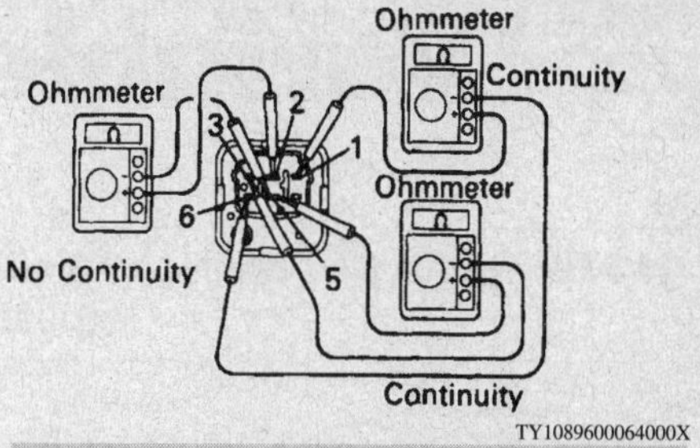
Ohmmeter
Ohmmeter
Continuity
3
2
1
Ohmmeter
6
No Continuity
5
Continuity
TY1089600064000X

Fig. 21 No. 2 cooling fan relay inspection. Supra w/2JZ-GTE engine

7. Reverse procedure to install.

SUPRA W/2JZ-GTE ENGINE

1. Remove engine under cover.
2. Disconnect cooling fan connector.
3. Remove three bolts and cooling fan shroud with fan attached.
4. Remove three attaching screws and separate fan motor from fan shroud.
5. Reverse procedure to install.

RAV4

1. Remove engine under covers.
2. **On models with A/C,** remove condenser core from radiator.
3. **On all models,** remove upper radiator supports.
4. Disconnect cooling fan connectors.
5. Push radiator forward and remove fan shroud mounting bolts.
6. **On models with A/C,** remove No. 2 cooling fan by pushing forward and pulling upward.
7. **On all models,** remove No. 1 cooling fan.
8. Reverse procedure to install. **Torque** upper radiator supports to 9 ft. lbs.

TERCEL

1. Remove engine under covers.
2. Drain engine coolant.
3. Remove air intake connector.
4. Remove reservoir tank assembly.
5. Remove No. 1 cooling fan from left hand side of engine compartment as follows:
   a. Disconnect upper radiator hose from radiator.
   b. Disconnect cooling fan connector.
   c. Remove two bolts and cooling fan.
6. Remove No. 2 cooling fan from right hand side of engine compartment as follows:
   a. Disconnect cooling fan connector.
   b. Remove three bolts and cooling fan.
7. Remove fan attaching nut from No. 1 fan and three attaching screws from No. 2 fan and remove fan blades.
8. Remove three fan motor to fan shroud attaching bolts and motor.
9. Reverse procedure to install.

Variable Speed Cooling Fans

NOTE: On Air Bag Equipped Models, Refer To "Air Bag System Precautions" Located In The Front Of This Manual For System Disarming & Arming Procedures.

INDEX

	Page No.
Component Replacement	48-17
Hydraulic Fan Motor	48-17
Oil Cooler	48-17
Component Service	48-17
Hydraulic/Power Steering Pump Overhaul	48-17
Cooling Fan System Bleed	48-16
Description	48-16
Precautions	48-16
Air Bag Systems	48-16
Audio Coded Anti-Theft System	48-16
System Diagnosis & Testing	48-17
Solenoid Valve	48-17
System ECU	48-17
Water Temperature Sensor	48-17
System Pressure Check	48-16

PRECAUTIONS

AIR BAG SYSTEMS

Refer to "Air Bag System Precautions" in the front of this manual for system disarming and arming procedures.

AUDIO CODED ANTI-THEFT SYSTEM

Some models are equipped with an audio coded anti-theft system that will disable the radio when the battery cable is disconnected. The system can be identified by the "ANTI-THEFT SYSTEM" on the cassette tape lid. Obtain 3 digit customer code for input. Reset system after service as follows:

1. Obtain 3 digit audio anti-theft code.
2. Depress 1 (PROG) while depressing righthand side of TUNE SEEK button, - - - will appear in tape operation display.
3. To enter the first digit, depress 1 (PROG) button repeatedly until the number of times depressed equals the first digit beginning with zero (depress the 1 button six times if the first digit if five).
4. To enter second digit, depress 2 (APS) button repeatedly until the number of times depressed equals the second digit beginning with zero.
5. To enter third digit, depress 3 (RPT) button repeatedly until the number of times depressed equals the third digit beginning with zero.
6. If - - - is displayed during code input, repeat procedure.
7. When code appears in display, depress and hold SCAN button until SEC appears.
8. When SEC disappears audio system should be operative.
9. If Err is displayed, repeat procedure. **Attempting to input code more than nine times may permanently disable audio system.**

DESCRIPTION

The electronically controlled hydraulic cooling fan system consists of a belt-driven hydraulic pump, a pump solenoid valve, a hydraulic fan motor and an electronic system controller (ECU), **Fig. 1.** The cooling fan processor (controller) determines hydraulic pressure by monitoring engine and air conditioner operation. A processor-controlled solenoid valve regulates oil flow from the integrated power steering/hydraulic pump to the fan motor. After leaving the fan motor, heated oil is then cooled by an oil cooler before returning to the power steering pump reservoir.

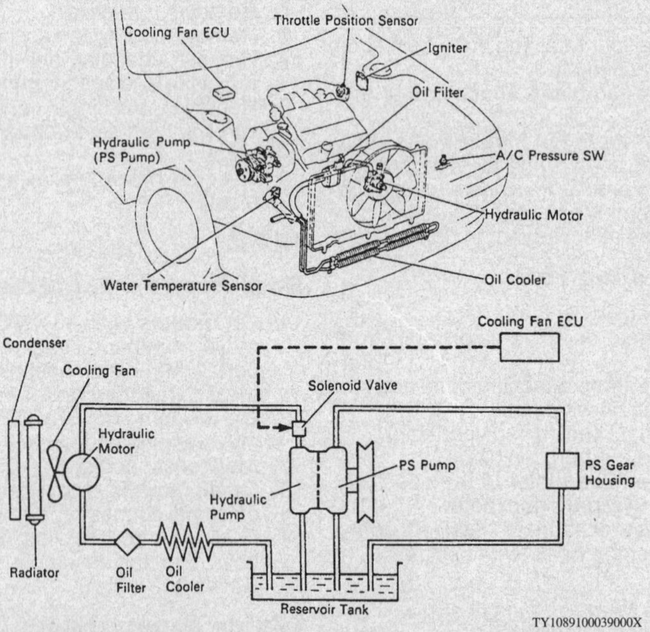

Throttle Position Sensor
Cooling Fan ECU
Igniter
Oil Filter
Hydraulic Pump
(PS Pump)
A/C Pressure SW
Hydraulic Motor
Water Temperature Sensor
Oil Cooler
Cooling Fan ECU
Condenser
Cooling Fan
Solenoid Valve
Hydraulic Motor
PS Pump
PS Gear Housing
Hydraulic Pump
Radiator
Oil Filter
Oil Cooler
Reservoir Tank
TY1089100039000X

Fig. 1 Cooling fan system components

COOLING FAN SYSTEM BLEED

1. Check reservoir fluid level. Add as necessary.
2. Locate underhood check connector behind righthand strut tower, then ground terminals OP1 and E1.
3. Without depressing accelerator pedal, start engine and let it run for several seconds. Check that there is no foaming of fluid in reservoir.

SYSTEM PRESSURE CHECK

1. Remove the union bolt and gasket, then disconnect the pressure hose from fan motor.
2. Connect a pressure gauge to pressure hose and fan motor.
3. With A/C Off, bleed system as directed in "Cooling Fan System Bleed."
4. Run engine at 2000 RPM until fluid temperature measures 158°F–195°F, then check fluid level.
5. Measure oil pressure at idle. With check connector terminals grounded oil pressure should fall within a 142–284 psi range.
6. Remove jumper from check connector and check that oil pressure decreases.

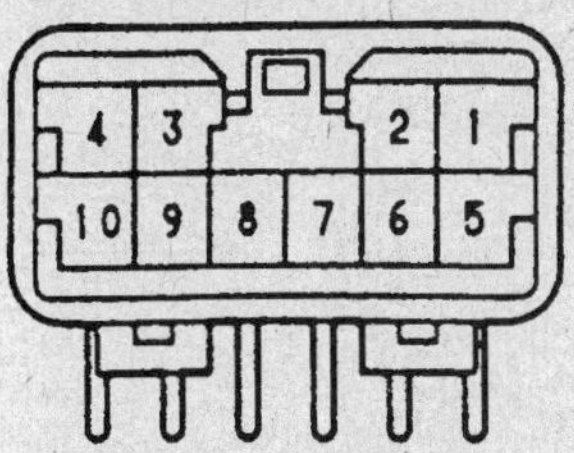
4
3
2
1
10
9
8
7
6
5

TY1089100040000X

Fig. 2 Cooling fan ECU connector

Check for	Tester connection	Condition	Specified value
Voltage	1 – Ground	Ignition switch ON	Battery voltage
Resistance	2 – 3	Solenoid valve at cold (25°C (77°F))	7.6 – 8.0 Ω
Continuity	4 – Ground	–	Continuity
Continuity	5 – Ground	Throttle valve open	No continuity
		Throttle valve closed	Continuity
Continuity	8 – Ground	A/C pressure SW connector disconnected	No continuity
		A/C pressure SW connector connected	Continuity
Resistance	9 – 10	Coolant temperature at 80°C (176°F)	1.48 – 1.58 kΩ

TY1089100041000X

Fig. 3 Cooling fan ECU values

SYSTEM DIAGNOSIS & TESTING

SOLENOID VALVE

Using an ohmmeter, measure solenoid valve resistance. Resistance should be 7.6–8.0 ohms at 77°F. If resistance is not as specified, replace solenoid valve.

SYSTEM ECU

Refer to **Figs. 2 and 3** when inspecting cooling fan ECU.

WATER TEMPERATURE SENSOR

Using an ohmmeter, measure sensor resistance. Resistance should be 1480–1580 ohms at 176°F. If resistance is not as specified, replace sensor.

COMPONENT REPLACEMENT

HYDRAULIC FAN MOTOR

1. Drain engine coolant.
2. Remove cruise control actuator cover.
3. Remove union bolt and gasket, then disconnect pressure hose at fan motor.
4. Disconnect radiator inlet hose, then coolant reservoir hose.
5. Disconnect hydraulic motor return hose.
6. Remove six bolts and hydraulic cooling fan assembly, then separate fan, shroud and motor.
7. Reverse procedure to install.

OIL COOLER

1. Remove fourteen clips and upper radiator seal.
2. Remove two screws and radiator grille.
3. Remove righthand parking lamp and headlamp assemblies, then disconnect inlet and outlet hoses from oil cooler.
4. Remove engine undercover and oil cooler.

COMPONENT SERVICE

HYDRAULIC/POWER STEERING PUMP OVERHAUL

Refer to "Power Steering Service" section, for pump overhaul procedure.

Dash Gauges

NOTE: Refer To The "Dash Panel Service" Section For Dash Panel Removal Procedures.

NOTE: Refer To The "Electronic Instrumentation" Section In MOTOR'S "Imported Engine Performance & Driveability Manual" For Information Related To Electronic Instrumentation.

NOTE: On Air Bag Equipped Models, Refer To "Air Bag System Precautions" Located In The Front Of This Manual For System Disarming & Arming Procedures.

INDEX

	Page No.
Gauges	48-18
Engine Coolant Temperature	48-25
Fuel	48-18
Low Oil Pressure	48-27
Precautions	48-18
Air Bag Systems	48-18
Audio Coded Anti-Theft System	48-18

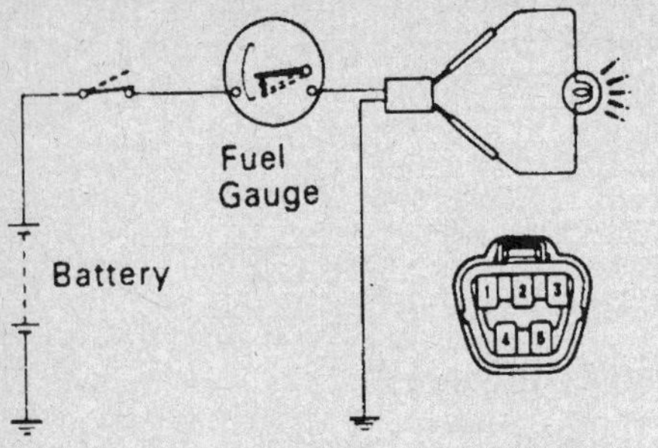
Fuel
Gauge
Battery
1 2 3
4 5

TY9099500087000X

Fig. 1 Fuel receiver gauge inspection. Avalon

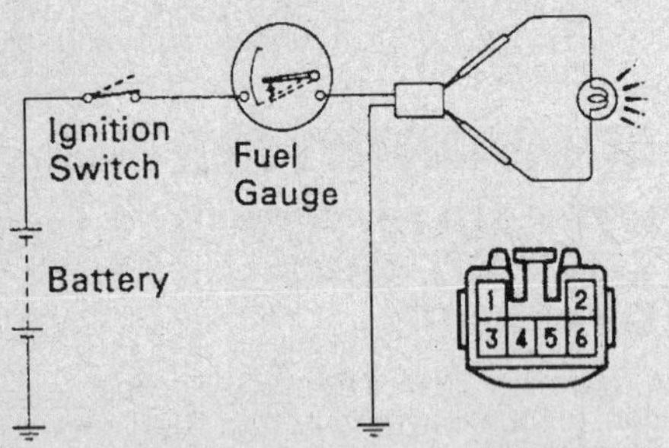
Ignition
Switch
Fuel
Gauge
Battery
1 2
3 4 5 6

TY9099100003000X

Fig. 4 Fuel receiver gauge inspection. 1993 Celica

PRECAUTIONS

AIR BAG SYSTEMS

Refer to "Air Bag System Precautions" in the front of this manual for system disarming and arming procedures.

AUDIO CODED ANTI-THEFT SYSTEM

Some models are equipped with an audio coded anti-theft system that will disable the radio when the battery cable is disconnected. The system can be identified by the "ANTI-THEFT SYSTEM" on the cassette tape lid. Obtain 3 digit customer code for input. Reset system after service as follows:

1. Obtain 3 digit audio anti-theft code.
2. Depress 1 (PROG) while depressing righthand side of TUNE SEEK button, - - - will appear in tape operation display.
3. To enter the first digit, depress 1 (PROG) button repeatedly until the number of times depressed equals the first digit beginning with zero (depress the 1 button six times if the first digit if five).
4. To enter second digit, depress 2 (APS) button repeatedly until the number of times depressed equals the second digit beginning with zero.
5. To enter third digit, depress 3 (RPT) button repeatedly until the number of times depressed equals the third digit beginning with zero.
6. If - - - is displayed during code input, repeat procedure.
7. When code appears in display, depress and hold SCAN button until SEC appears.
8. When SEC disappears audio system

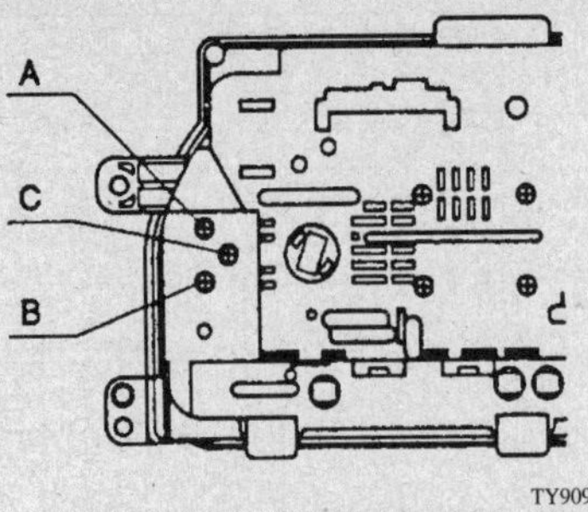
A
C
B

TY9099500088000X

Fig. 2 Fuel gauge terminal locations. Avalon

should be operative.

9. If Err is displayed, repeat procedure. **Attempting to input code more than nine times may permanently disable audio system.**

GAUGES

FUEL

AVALON

1. Disconnect connector from sender gauge.
2. Turn ignition switch to On position, then check receiver gauge needle indicates Empty.
3. Connect terminals 2 and 3 on wire harness side connector through a 3.4W test bulb, **Fig. 1.**
4. Turn ignition switch On, then ensure bulb lights and receiver gauge needle moves toward full side.
5. Measure resistance between terminals A, B and C, **Fig. 2.** Resistance should be as follows:
   a. A–B: about 151.0 ohms.
   b. A–C: about 306.0 ohms.
   c. B–C: about 154.0 ohms.
   d. If resistance is not as specified, replace receiver gauge.
6. Measure resistance between terminal 2 and 3 for each float position, **Fig. 3.**
7. Ensure voltage rises between terminals 2 and 3 as the float is moved from top to bottom position.
8. Measure resistance between terminals 2 and 3 for each float position. Resistance should be as follows:
   a. Full position: about 3.0 ohms.
   b. Half position: about 30.8 ohms.
   c. Empty position: about 110.0 ohms.
   d. If resistance is not as specified, replace sender gauge.

CELICA

1993

1. Disconnect connector from sender gauge.
2. Turn ignition switch to On position, then check receiver gauge needle indicates Empty.
3. Connect terminals 3 and 4 on wire harness side connector through a 3.4W test bulb, **Fig. 4.**
4. Turn ignition switch On, then ensure bulb lights and receiver gauge needle moves toward full side.
5. Measure resistance between terminals A, B and C, **Fig. 5.**

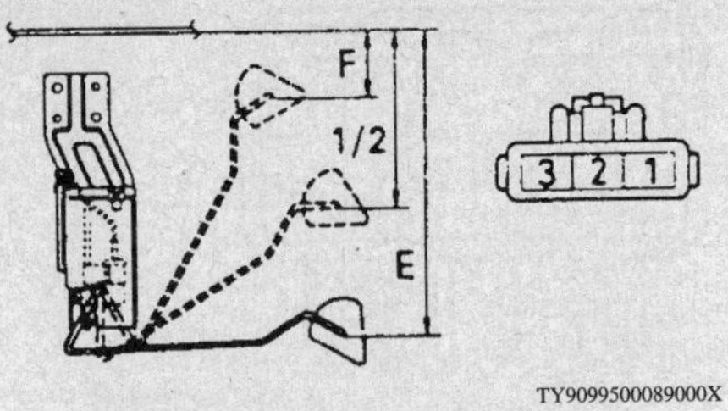
F
1/2
E
3 2 1

TY9099500089000X

Fig. 3 Fuel sender gauge inspection. Avalon

6. **On models with 4A-FE and 5S-FE engines,** resistance should be as follows:
   a. A–B: about 86.0 ohms.
   b. A–C: about 275.0 ohms.
   c. B–C: about 189.0 ohms.
7. **On models with 3S-GTE engines,** resistance should be as follows:
   a. A–B: about 101.0 ohms.
   b. A–C: about 252.0 ohms.
   c. B–C: about 151.0 ohms.
8. **On all models,** if resistance is not as specified, replace receiver gauge.
9. Connect a series of three 1.5 volt dry cell batteries, then connect the positive lead from the dry cell batteries to terminal 3 through a 3.4W test bulb and the negative lead to terminal 4, **Figs. 6 and 7.**
10. Ensure voltage rises between terminals 3 and 4 as the float is moved from top to bottom position.
11. Measure resistance between terminals 3 and 4 for each float position. Resistance should be as follows:
    a. Full position: about 3.0 ohms.
    b. Empty position: about 110.0 ohms.
    c. If resistance is not as specified, replace sender gauge.

1994–96

1. Disconnect connector from sender gauge.
2. Turn ignition switch to On position, then check receiver gauge needle indicates Empty.
3. Connect terminals 2 and 3 on wire harness side connector through a 3.4W test bulb, **Fig. 8.**
4. Turn ignition switch On, then ensure bulb lights and receiver gauge needle moves toward full side.
5. Measure resistance between terminals A, B and C, **Fig. 9.**
6. **On 7A-FE and 5S-FE engines,** resistance should be as follows:
   a. A–B: about 154.3 ohms.
   b. A–C: about 126.2 ohms.
   c. B–C: about 280.5 ohms.
7. **On all models,** if resistance is not as specified, replace fuel receiver gauge.
8. Connect a series of three 1.5 volt dry cell batteries, then connect the positive lead from the dry cell batteries to terminal 2 through a 3.4W test bulb and the negative lead to terminal 1, **Fig. 10.**
9. Ensure voltage rises between terminals 1 and 2 as the float is moved from top to bottom position.
10. Measure resistance between terminals 2 and 3 for each float position. Resistance should be as follows:

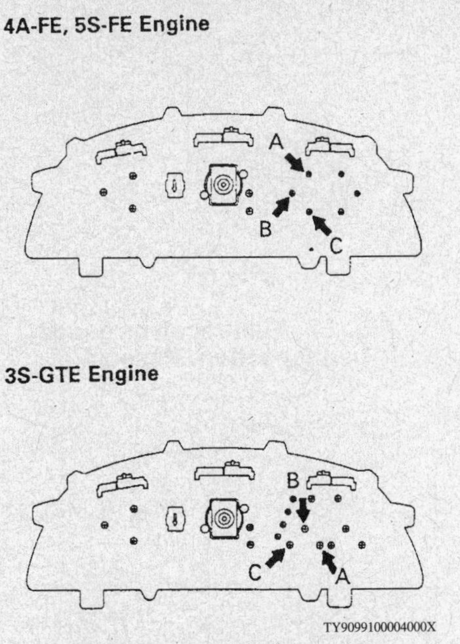
4A-FE, 5S-FE Engine
A
B
C
3S-GTE Engine
B
C
A
TY9099100004000X

Fig. 5 Fuel gauge terminal locations. 1993 Celica

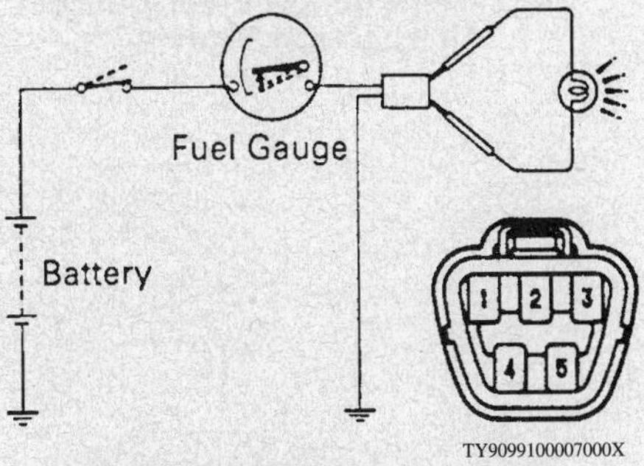
Fuel Gauge
Battery
1 2 3
4 5
TY9099100007000X

Fig. 8 Fuel receiver gauge inspection. 1994–96 Celica

a. Full position: about 3.0 ohms.
b. ½ position: about 31.6 ohms.
c. Empty position: about 110.0 ohms.
d. If resistance is not as specified, replace sender gauge.

MR2

1. Disconnect connector from sender gauge.
2. Turn ignition switch to On position, then check receiver gauge needle indicates Empty.
3. Connect terminals 1 and 3 on wire harness side connector through a 3.4W test bulb, **Fig. 11.**
4. Turn ignition switch On, then ensure bulb lights and receiver gauge needle moves toward full side.
5. Measure resistance between terminals A, B and C, **Fig. 12.** Resistance should be as follows:
   a. A–B: about 101.9 ohms.
   b. A–C: about 203.2 ohms.
   c. B–C: about 101.3 ohms.
   d. If resistance is not as specified, replace receiver gauge.
6. Connect a series of three 1.5 volt dry cell batteries, then connect the positive lead from the dry cell batteries to terminal 1 through a 3.4W test bulb and the negative lead to terminal 3, **Fig. 13.**

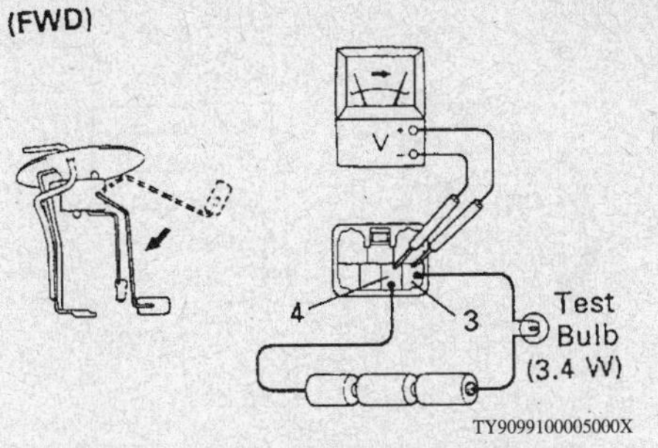
(FWD)
V
4
3
Test
Bulb
(3.4 W)
TY9099100005000X

Fig. 6 Fuel sender gauge inspection. 1993 Celica w/FWD models

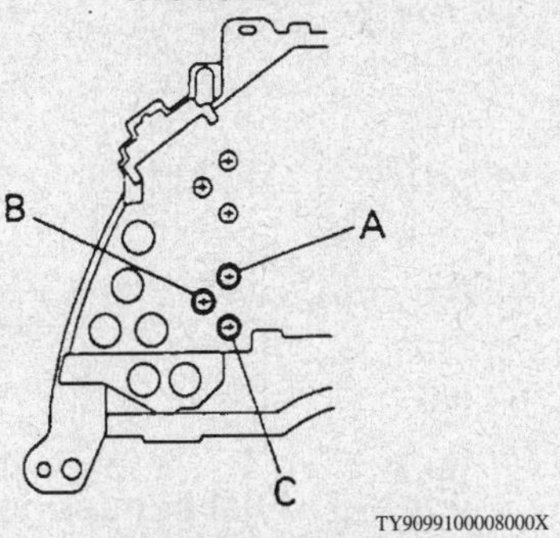
B
A
C
TY9099100008000X

Fig. 9 Fuel gauge terminal locations. 1994–96 Celica

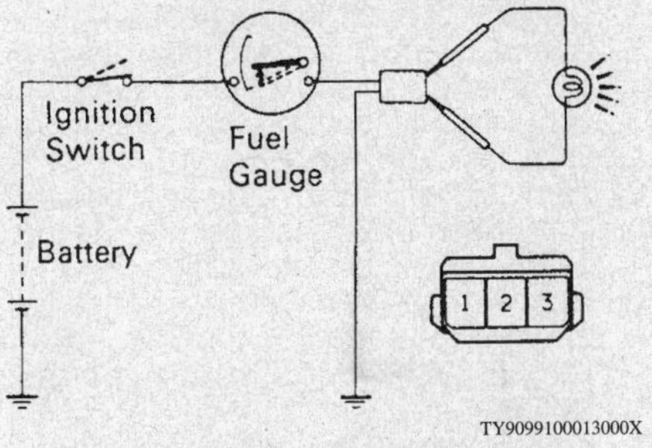
Ignition
Switch
Fuel
Gauge
Battery
1 2 3
TY9099100013000X

Fig. 11 Fuel receiver gauge inspection. MR2

7. Ensure voltage rises between terminals 1 and 3 as the float is moved from top to bottom position.
8. Measure resistance between terminals 1 and 3 for each float position. Resistance should be as follows:
   a. Full position: about 2.0–4.0 ohms.
   b. Empty position: about 103.0–117.0 ohms.
   c. If resistance is not as specified, replace sender gauge.

PASEO

1. Disconnect connector from sender gauge.
2. Turn ignition switch to On position, then check receiver gauge needle indicates Empty.
3. Connect terminals 1 and 4 on wire harness side connector through a 3.4W test bulb, **Fig. 14.**
4. Turn ignition switch On, then ensure bulb lights and receiver gauge needle moves toward full side.
5. Measure resistance between terminals A, B and C, **Fig. 15.** Resistance should be as follows:

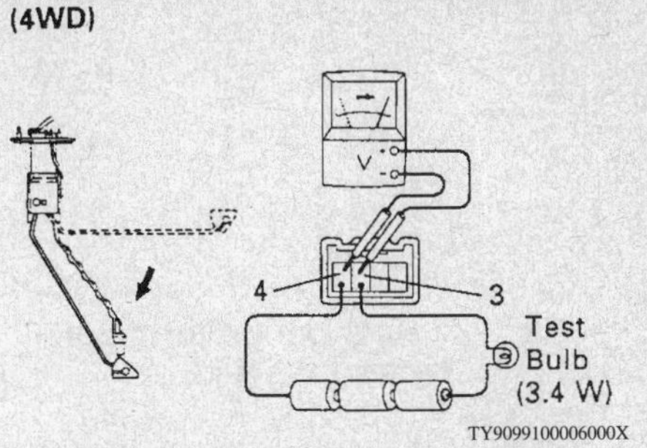
(4WD)
V
4
3
Test
Bulb
(3.4 W)
TY9099100006000X

Fig. 7 Fuel sender gauge inspection. 1993 Celica w/4WD models

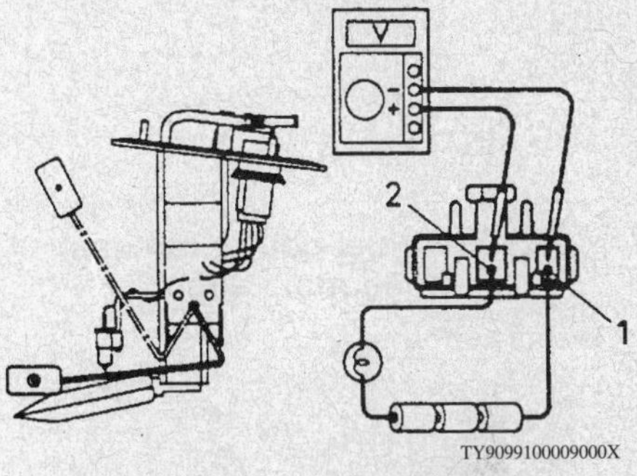
V
2
1
TY9099100009000X

Fig. 10 Fuel sender gauge inspection. 1994–96 Celica

a. A–B: about 101.9 ohms.
b. A–C: about 203.4 ohms.
c. B–C: about 101.5 ohms.
d. If resistance is not as specified, replace receiver gauge.

6. Connect a series of three 1.5 volt dry cell batteries, then connect the positive lead from the dry cell batteries to terminal 1 through a 3.4W test bulb and the negative lead to terminal 4, **Fig. 16.**
7. Connect positive lead from voltmeter to terminal and negative lead to terminal. Ensure voltage rises between terminals 1 and 4 as the float is moved from top to bottom position.
8. Measure resistance between terminals 1 and 4 for each float position. Resistance should be as follows:
   a. Full position: about 2.0–4.0 ohms.
   b. Half position: about 25.0–34.0 ohms.
   c. Empty position: about 103.0–117.0 ohms.
   d. If resistance is not as specified, replace sender gauge.

PREVIA

1. Disconnect connector from sender gauge.
2. Turn ignition switch to On position, then check receiver gauge needle indicates Empty.
3. Connect terminals 2 and 3 on wire harness side connector through a 3.4W test bulb, **Fig. 17.**
4. Turn ignition switch On, then ensure bulb lights and receiver gauge needle moves toward full side.
5. Measure resistance between terminals A, B and C, **Fig. 18.** Resistance should be as follows:
   a. A–B: about 101.3 ohms.

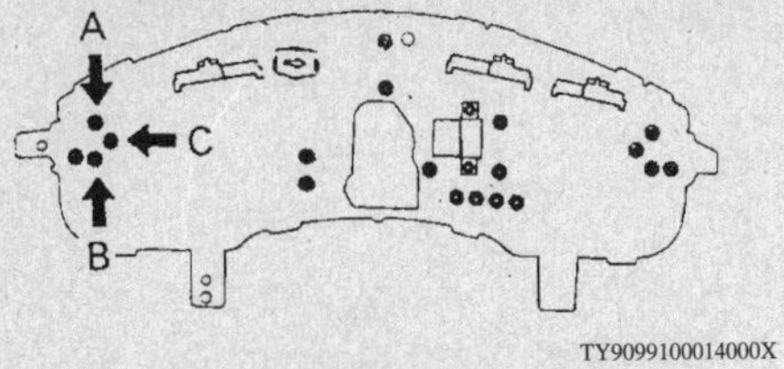
A
C
B
TY9099100014000X

Fig. 12 Fuel gauge terminal locations. MR2

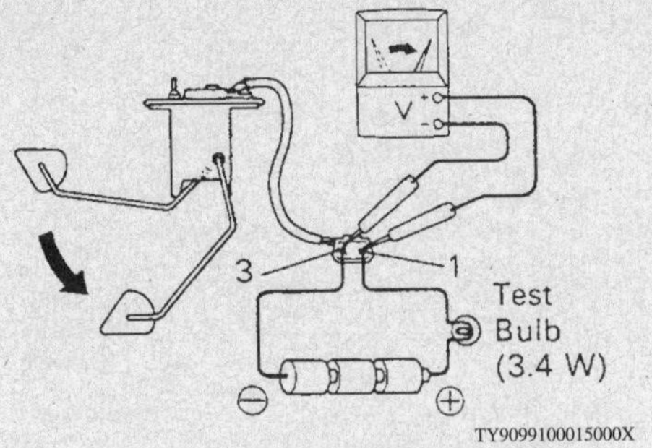
V
3
1
Test
Bulb
(3.4 W)
TY9099100015000X

Fig. 13 Fuel sender gauge inspection. MR2

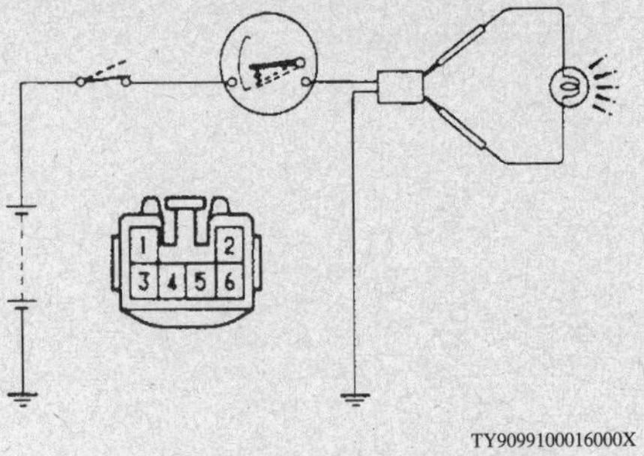
1
2
3
4
5
6
TY9099100016000X

Fig. 14 Fuel receiver gauge inspection. Paseo

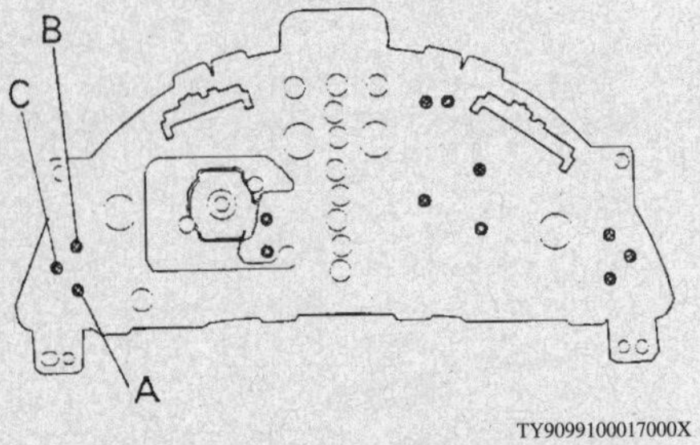
B
C
A
TY9099100017000X

Fig. 15 Fuel gauge terminal locations. Paseo

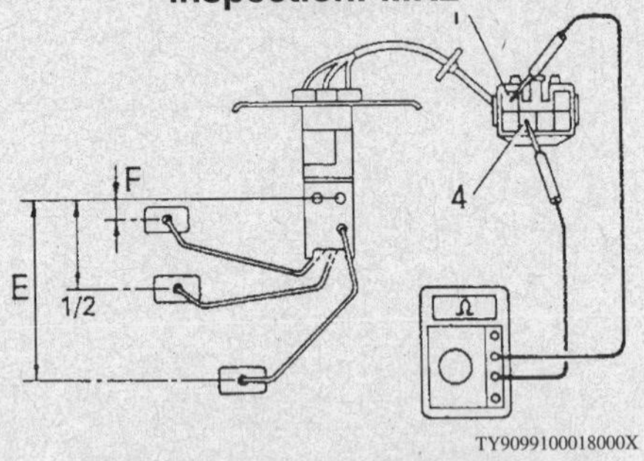
1
F
4
E
1/2
Ω
TY9099100018000X

Fig. 16 Fuel sender gauge inspection. Paseo

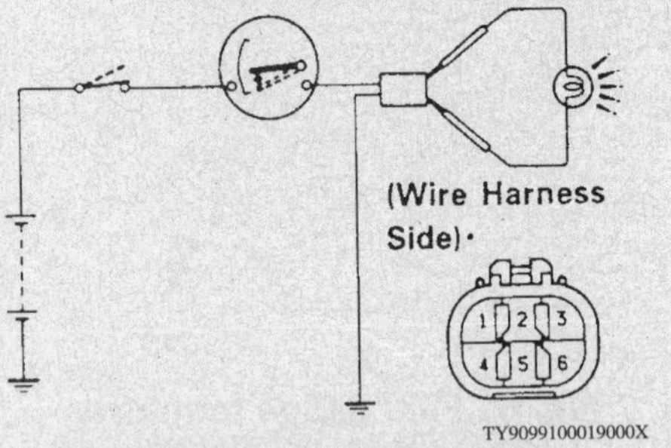
(Wire Harness
Side)
1
2
3
4
5
6
TY9099100019000X

Fig. 17 Fuel receiver gauge inspection. Previa

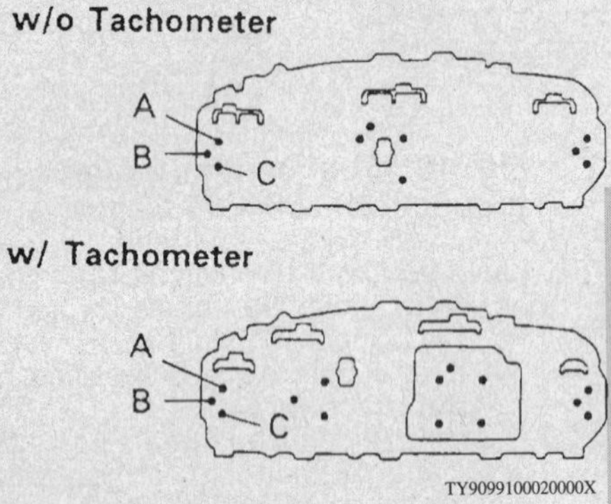
w/o Tachometer
A
B
C
w/ Tachometer
A
B
C
TY9099100020000X

Fig. 18 Fuel gauge terminal locations. Previa

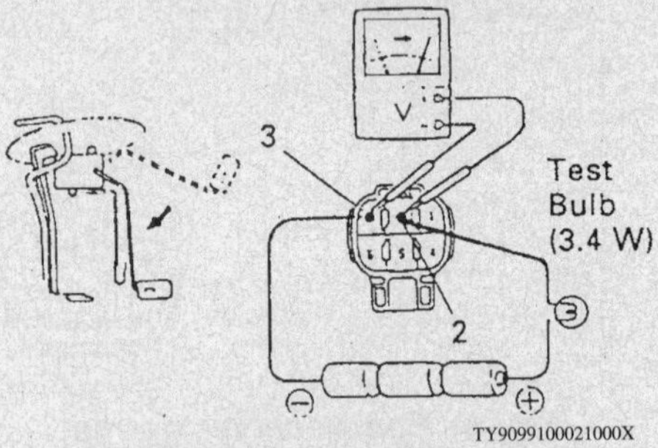
V
3
Test
Bulb
(3.4 W)
2
TY9099100021000X

Fig. 19 Fuel sender gauge inspection. Previa

b. A–C: about 101.9 ohms.
c. B–C: about 203.2 ohms.
d. If resistance is not as specified, replace receiver gauge.

6. Connect a series of three 1.5 volt dry cell batteries, then connect the positive lead from the dry cell batteries to terminal 3 through a 3.4W test bulb and the negative lead to terminal 2, **Fig. 19.**
7. Ensure voltage rises between terminals 2 and 3 as the float is moved from top to bottom position.
8. Measure resistance between terminals 2 and 3 for each float position. Resistance should be as follows:
   a. Full position: about 3.0 ohms.
   b. Empty position: about 110.0 ohms.
   c. If resistance is not as specified, replace sender gauge.

RAV4

1. Disconnect connector from main fuel sender gauge assembly.
2. Turn ignition switch On and ensure receiver gauge needle indicates Empty, **Fig. 20.**
3. Connect main sender gauge, then disconnect sub sender gauge assembly connector.
4. Turn ignition switch On and ensure receiver gauge needle indicates Empty, **Fig. 21.**
5. Disconnect main sender gauge.
6. Connect terminals 3 of main sender gauge and A of sub sender gauge, on harness side connectors, through a 3.4W test bulb, **Fig. 22.**
7. Turn ignition switch On and ensure bulb illuminates and receiver gauge needle moves toward full side.
8. Inspect receiver gauge resistance by measuring between terminal locations, **Fig. 23.** Resistance should be as follows:
   a. A-B: about 106 ohms.
   b. A-C: about 256.3 ohms.
   c. B-C: about 150.3 ohms.
9. Inspect main sender gauge resistance by measuring resistance between terminals 2 and 3 with float in high position and low position. Resistance should be about 2 ohms with float in high position and about 74 ohms with float in low position.
10. Inspect sub sender gauge resistance by measuring resistance between terminals with float in high position and low position. Resistance should be about 2 ohms with float in high position and about 32.9 ohms with float in low position.
11. If resistance is not as specified, replace sender gauge.

SUPRA

1. Disconnect connector from sender gauge.
2. Turn ignition switch to On position, then check receiver gauge needle indicates Empty.
3. Connect terminals 2 and 3 on wire harness side connector through a 3.4W test bulb, **Fig. 24.**
4. Turn ignition switch On, then ensure bulb lights and receiver gauge needle moves toward full side.
5. **On 1993 models,** measure resistance between terminals A, B and C, **Fig. 25.** Resistance should be as follows:
   a. A–B: about 261.5 ohms.
   b. A–C: about 107.2 ohms.
   c. B–C: about 154.3 ohms.
6. **On 1994–96 models,** measure resistance between terminals A, B and C, **Fig. 25.** Resistance should be as follows:
   a. A–B: about 269.7 ohms.
   b. A–C: about 123.5 ohms.
   c. B–C: about 146.2 ohms.
7. If resistance is not as specified, replace receiver gauge.
8. **On 1993 models,** connect a series of three 1.5 volt dry cell batteries, then connect the positive lead from the dry cell batteries to terminal 3 through a 3.4W test bulb and the negative lead to terminal 1, **Fig. 26.**
9. **On 1994–96 models,** connect a series of three 1.5 volt dry cell batteries, then connect the positive lead from the dry cell batteries to terminal 2 through a 3.4W test bulb and the negative lead to terminal 3, **Fig. 26.**
10. **On 1993 models,** ensure voltage rises

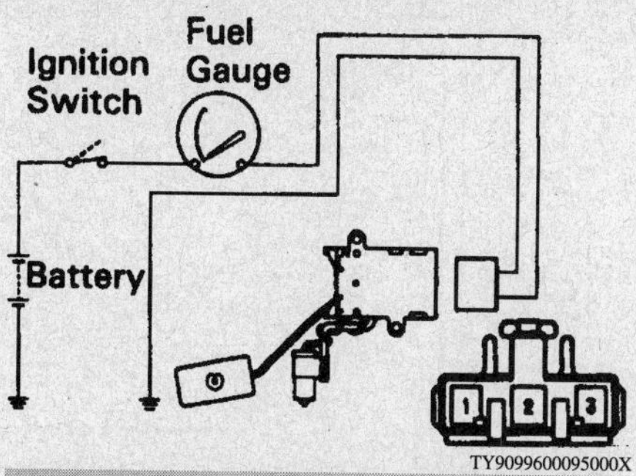
Ignition Switch
Fuel Gauge
Battery
1
2
3
TY9099600095000X

Fig. 20 Main fuel sender gauge inspection. RAV4

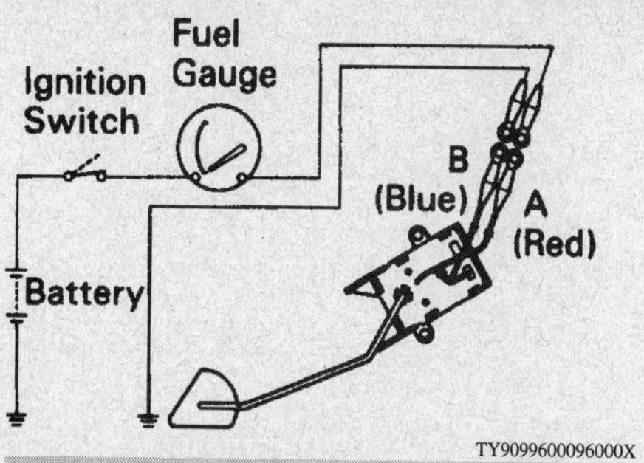
Ignition Switch
Fuel Gauge
B (Blue)
A (Red)
Battery
TY9099600096000X

Fig. 21 Sub fuel sender gauge inspection. RAV4

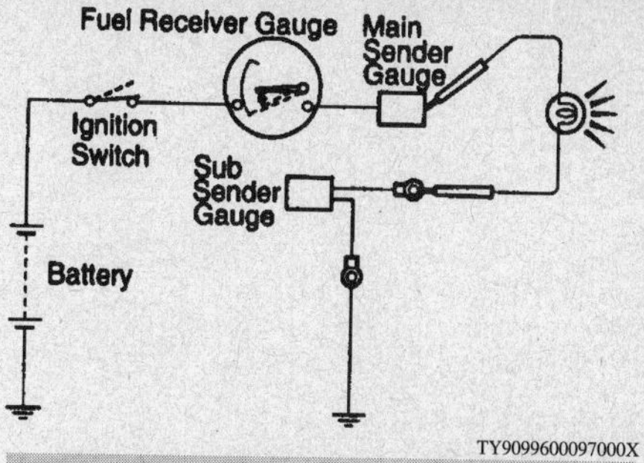
Fuel Receiver Gauge
Main Sender Gauge
Ignition Switch
Sub Sender Gauge
Battery
TY9099600097000X

Fig. 22 Fuel gauge test bulb check. RAV4

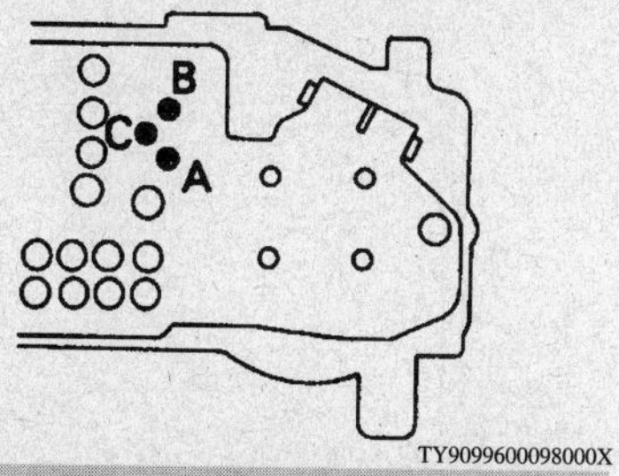
B
C
A
TY9099600098000X

Fig. 23 Fuel gauge terminal locations. RAV4

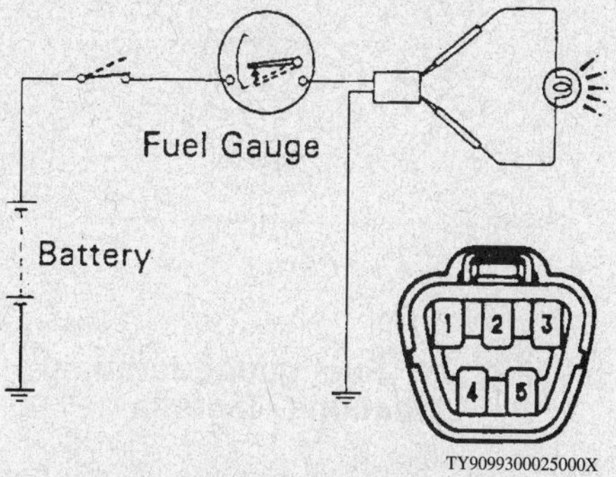
Fuel Gauge
Battery
1
2
3
4
5
TY9099300025000X

Fig. 24 Fuel receiver gauge inspection. Supra

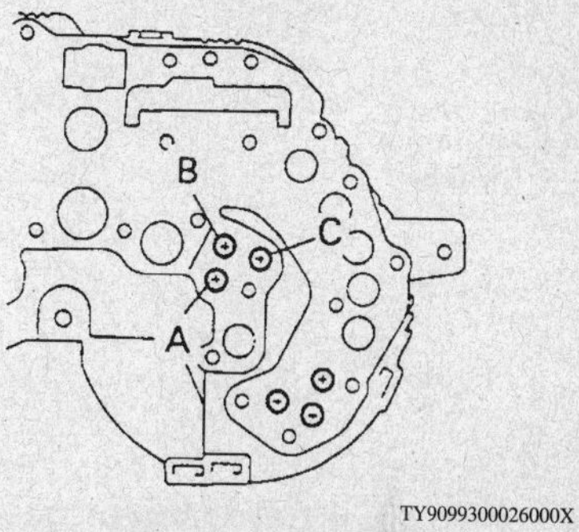
B
C
A
TY9099300026000X

Fig. 25 Fuel gauge terminal locations. Supra

between terminals 1 and 3 as the float is moved from top to bottom position.

11. **On 1994–96 models,** ensure voltage rises between terminals 2 and 3 as the float is moved from top to bottom position.
12. **On 1993 models,** measure resistance between terminals 2 and 3 for each float position, **Fig. 26.** Resistance should be as follows:
    a. Full position: about 3.0 ohms.
    b. ½ position: about 31.5 ohms.
    c. Empty position: about 110.0 ohms.
13. **On 1994–96 models,** measure resistance between terminals 2 and 3 for each float position, **Fig. 26.** Resistance should be as follows:
    a. Full position: about 4.0 ohms.
    b. ½ position: about 55.0 ohms.
    c. Empty position: about 107.0 ohms.
14. **On all models,** if resistance is not as specified, replace sender gauge.

TACOMA

1. Disconnect connector from sender gauge.
2. Turn ignition switch to On position, then check receiver gauge needle indicates Empty.
3. Connect terminals 1 and 3 on wire harness side connector through a 3.4W test bulb, **Fig. 27.**
4. Turn ignition switch On, then ensure bulb lights and receiver gauge needle moves toward full side.
5. Measure resistance between terminals A, B and C, **Fig. 28.** Resistance should be as follows with tachometer:
    a. A–B: about 137.0 ohms.
    b. A–C: about 123.0 ohms.
    c. B–C: about 260.0 ohms.
6. Resistance should be as follows without tachometer:

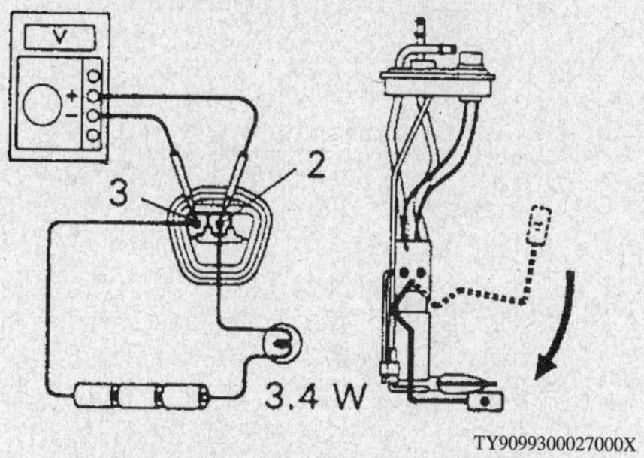
V
3
2
3.4 W
TY9099300027000X

Fig. 26 Fuel sender gauge inspection. Supra

    a. A–B: about 150.0 ohms.
    b. A–C: about 80.0 ohms.
    c. B–C: about 55.0 ohms.
    d. If resistance is not as specified, replace receiver gauge.
7. Connect a series of three 1.5 volt dry cell batteries, then connect the positive lead from the dry cell batteries to terminal 2 through a 3.4W test bulb and the negative lead to terminal 1, **Fig. 29.**
8. Connect positive lead from voltmeter to terminal 2 and negative lead to terminal 1. Ensure voltage rises between terminals 1 and 2 as the float is moved from top to bottom position.
9. Measure resistance between terminals 1 and 2 for each float position. Resistance should be as follows:
    a. Full position: about 3.0 ohms.
    b. Half position: about 32.5 ohms.
    c. Empty position: about 110.0 ohms.
    d. If resistance is not as specified, replace sender gauge.

T100

1. Disconnect connector from sender gauge.
2. Turn ignition switch to On position, then check receiver gauge needle indicates Empty.
3. Connect terminals 1 and 3 on wire harness side connector through a 3.4W test bulb, **Fig. 30.**
4. Turn ignition switch On, then ensure bulb lights and receiver gauge needle moves toward full side.
5. Measure resistance between terminals A, B and C, **Fig. 31.** Resistance should be as follows with tachometer:
    a. A–B: about 137.0 ohms.
    b. A–C: about 123.0 ohms.
    c. B–C: about 260.0 ohms.
6. Resistance should be as follows without tachometer:
    a. A–B: about 150.0 ohms.
    b. A–C: about 80.0 ohms.
    c. B–C: about 55.0 ohms.
    d. If resistance is not as specified, replace receiver gauge.
7. Connect a series of three 1.5 volt dry cell batteries, then connect the positive lead from the dry cell batteries to terminal 2 through a 3.4W test bulb and the negative lead to terminal 1, **Fig. 32.**
8. Connect positive lead from voltmeter to terminal 2 and negative lead to terminal 1. Ensure voltage rises between terminals 1 and 2 as the float is moved from top to bottom position.
9. Measure resistance between terminals 1 and 2 for each float position. Resistance should be as follows:
    a. Full position: about 3.0 ohms.

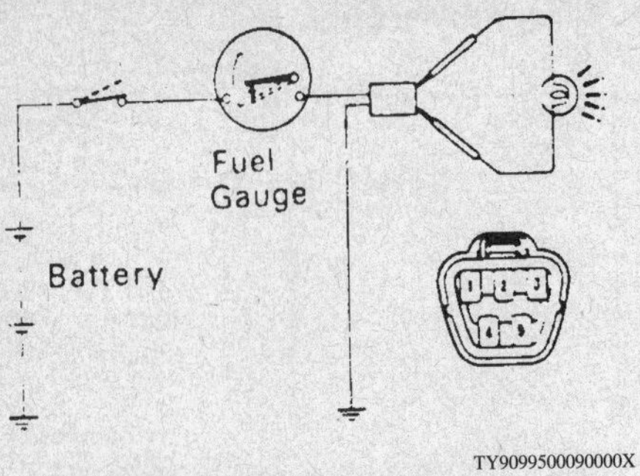
Fuel
Gauge
Battery
TY9099500090000X

Fig. 27 Fuel receiver gauge inspection. Tacoma

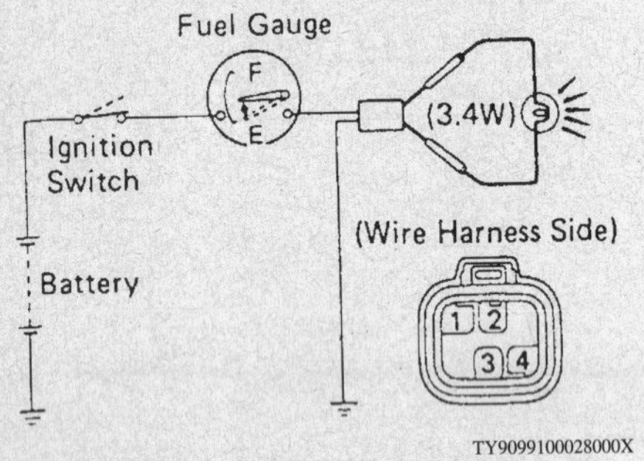
Fuel Gauge
F
E
(3.4W)
Ignition
Switch
Battery
(Wire Harness Side)
1 2
3 4
TY9099100028000X

Fig. 30 Fuel receiver gauge inspection. T100 & 4Runner

b. Half position: about 32.5 ohms.
c. Empty position: about 110.0 ohms.
d. If resistance is not as specified, replace sender gauge.

4RUNNER

1. Disconnect connector from sender gauge.
2. Turn ignition switch to On position, then check receiver gauge needle indicates Empty.
3. Connect terminals 2 and 4 on wire harness side connector through a 3.4W test bulb, **Fig. 30.**
4. Turn ignition switch On, then ensure bulb lights and receiver gauge needle moves toward full side.
5. Measure resistance between terminals A, B and C, **Fig. 33.** Resistance should be as follows:
   a. A–B: about 123.0 ohms.
   b. A–C: about 260.0 ohms.
   c. B–C: about 137.0 ohms.
   d. If resistance is not as specified, replace receiver gauge.
6. Connect a series of three 1.5 volt dry cell batteries, then connect the positive lead from the dry cell batteries to terminal 4 through a 3.4W test bulb and the negative lead to terminal 2, **Fig. 34.**
7. Connect positive lead from voltmeter to terminal 4 and negative lead to terminal 2. Ensure voltage rises between terminals 2 and 4 as the float is moved from top to bottom position.
8. Measure resistance between terminals 2 and 4 for each float position. Resistance should be as follows:
   a. Full position: about 3.0 ohms.
   b. Half position: about 32.5 ohms.
   c. Empty position: about 110.0 ohms.
   d. If resistance is not as specified, replace sender gauge.

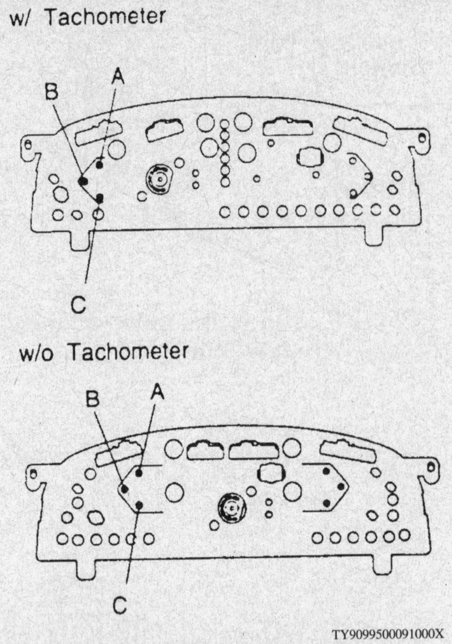
w/ Tachometer
B
A
C
w/o Tachometer
B
A
C
TY9099500091000X

Fig. 28 Fuel gauge terminal locations. Tacoma

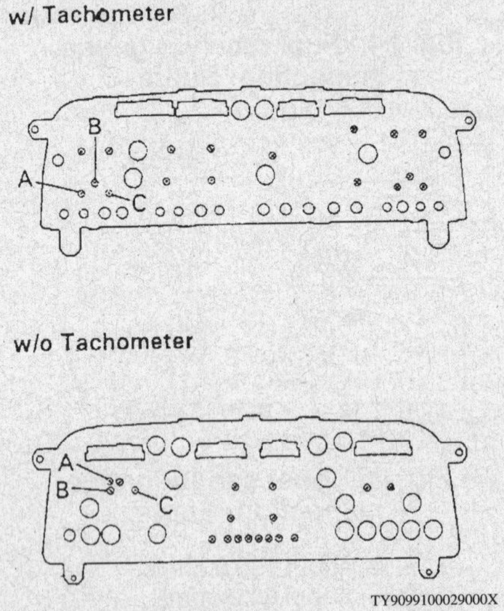
w/ Tachometer
B
A
C
w/o Tachometer
A
B
C
TY9099100029000X

Fig. 31 Fuel gauge terminal locations. T100

CAMRY

1993

1. Disconnect connector from sender gauge.
2. Turn ignition switch to On position, then check receiver gauge needle indicates Empty.
3. Connect 1 and 2 on wire harness side connector through a 3.4W test bulb, **Fig. 35.**
4. Turn ignition switch On, then ensure bulb lights and receiver gauge needle moves toward full side.
5. Measure resistance between terminals A, B and C, **Fig. 36.**
6. Resistance should be as follows:
   a. A–B: about 126.0 ohms.
   b. A–C: about 281.0 ohms.
   c. B–C: about 154.0 ohms.

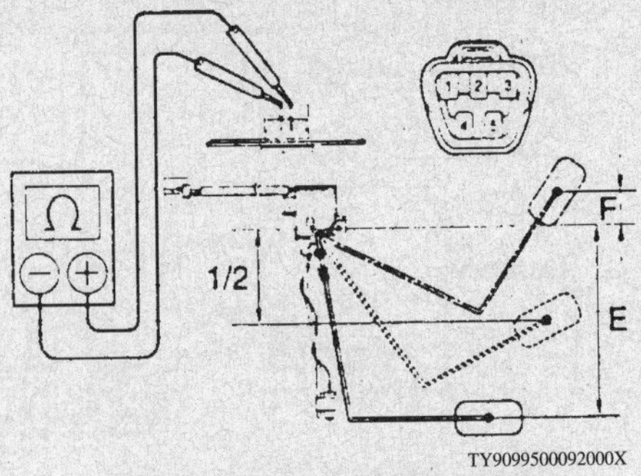
Ω
1/2
F
E
TY9099500092000X

Fig. 29 Fuel sender gauge inspection. Tacoma

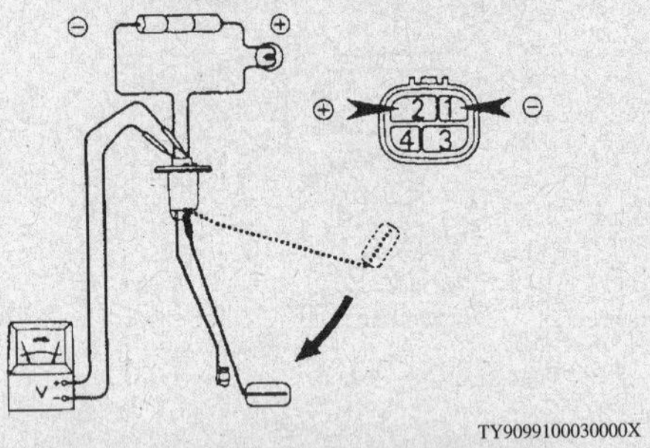
2 1
4 3
V
TY9099100030000X

Fig. 32 Fuel sender gauge inspection. T100

d. If resistance is not as specified, replace receiver gauge.

7. Connect a series of three 1.5 volt dry cell batteries.
8. Connect positive lead from dry cell batteries to terminal 2 through a 3.4W test bulb and negative lead to terminal 1, **Fig. 37.**
9. Ensure voltage rises between terminals 1 and 2 as float is moved from top to bottom position.
10. Measure resistance between terminals 1 and 2 for each float position. Resistance should be as follows:
    a. Full position: about 3.0 ohms.
    b. Empty position: about 110.0 ohms.
    c. If resistance is not as specified, replace sender gauge.

1994-96

1. Disconnect connector from sender gauge.
2. Turn ignition switch to On position, then check receiver gauge needle indicates Empty.
3. Connect terminals 2 and 3 on wire harness side connector through a 3.4W test bulb, **Fig. 35.**
4. Turn ignition switch On, then ensure bulb lights and receiver gauge needle moves toward full side.
5. Measure resistance between terminals A, B and C, **Fig. 36.** Resistance should be as follows:
   a. A–B: about 126.0 ohms.
   b. A–C: about 281.0 ohms.
   c. B–C: about 154.0 ohms.
   d. If resistance is not as specified, replace receiver gauge.
6. Connect a series of three 1.5 volt dry cell batteries.
7. Connect the positive lead from the dry cell batteries to terminal 2 through a

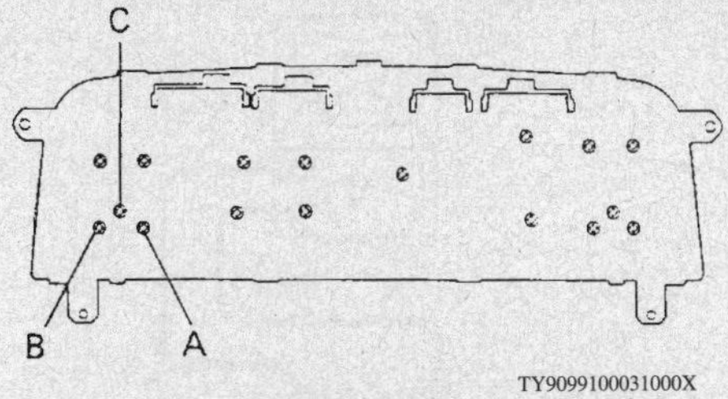
C
B
A
TY9099100031000X

Fig. 33 Fuel gauge terminal locations. 4Runner

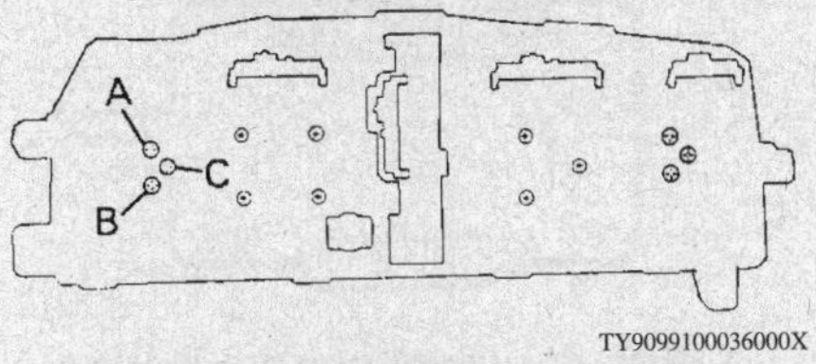
A
C
B
TY9099100036000X

Fig. 36 Fuel gauge terminal locations. Camry

3.4W test bulb and the negative lead to terminal 3, **Fig. 38.**

8. Ensure voltage rises between terminals 2 and 3 as the float is moved from top to bottom position.
9. Measure resistance between terminals 2 and 3 for each float position. Resistance should be as follows:
   a. Full position: about 3.0 ohms.
   b. Empty position: about 110.0 ohms.
   c. If resistance is not as specified, replace sender gauge.

COROLLA

1. Disconnect connector from sender gauge.
2. Turn ignition switch to On position, then check receiver gauge needle indicates Empty.
3. Connect terminals 1 and 3 on wire harness side connector through a 3.4W test bulb, **Fig. 39.**
4. Turn ignition switch On, then ensure bulb lights and receiver gauge needle moves toward full side.
5. If gauge does not operate as specified, check receiver gauge resistance.
6. Measure resistance between terminals A, B and C, **Fig. 40.**
7. **On models with tachometer,** resistance should be as follows:
   a. A–B: about 154.3 ohms.
   b. A–C: about 107.2 ohms.
   c. B–C: about 261.5 ohms.
   d. If resistance is not as specified, replace receiver gauge.
8. **On models less tachometer,** resistance should be as follows:
   a. A–B: about 280.5 ohms.
   b. A–C: about 126.2 ohms.
   c. B–C: about 154.3 ohms.
   d. If resistance is not as specified, replace receiver gauge.
9. **On 1993 models,** check fuel sender gauge as follows:
   a. Connect a series of three 1.5 volt dry cell batteries.
   b. Connect positive lead from dry cell batteries to terminal 2 through a 3.4W test bulb, **Fig. 41.**
   c. Connect negative lead from dry cell

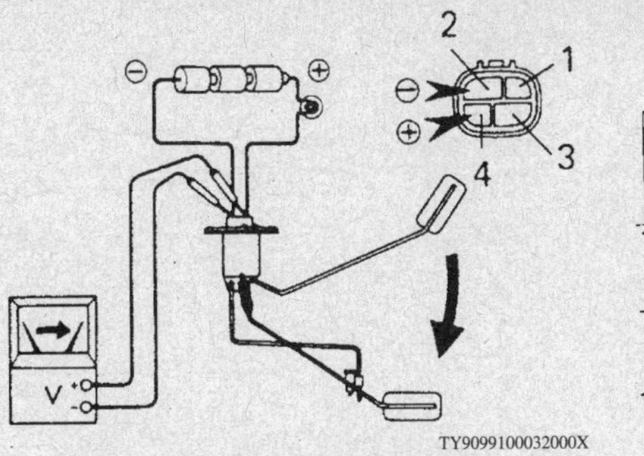
2
1
3
4
V
TY9099100032000X

Fig. 34 Fuel sender gauge inspection. 4Runner

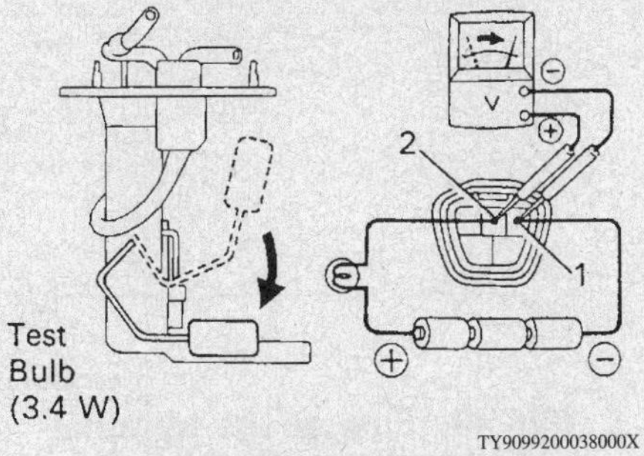
2
V
1
Test
Bulb
(3.4 W)
TY9099200038000X

Fig. 37 Fuel sender gauge inspection. 1993 Camry

batteries to terminal 1.

   d. Connect positive lead of a voltmeter to terminal 1 and negative lead to terminal 2.
   e. Ensure voltage rises between terminals as float is moved from top to bottom.
   f. If voltage does not rise as specified, replace fuel sender gauge.
10. **On 1994–96 models,** check fuel sender gauge as follows:
   a. Connect a series of three 1.5 volt dry cell batteries.
   b. Connect positive lead from dry cell batteries to terminal 2 through a 3.4W test bulb, **Fig. 42.**
   c. Connect negative lead from dry cell batteries to terminal 3.
   d. Connect positive lead from voltmeter to terminal 1 and negative lead to terminal 3.
   e. Ensure voltage rises between terminals as float is moved from top to bottom position.
   f. If voltage does not rise as specified, replace fuel sender gauge.
11. **On 1993 models,** measure resistance between terminals 1 and 3 for each float position. Resistance should be as follows:
   a. Full position: about 3.0 ohms.
   b. Half position: about 30.8 ohms.
   c. Empty position: about 110.0 ohms.
   d. If resistance is not as specified, replace sender gauge.
12. **On 1994–96 models,** measure resistance between terminals 2 and 3 for each float position. Resistance should be as follows:
   a. Full position: about 4.0 ohms.
   b. Half position: about 55.0 ohms.
   c. Empty position: about 111.0 ohms.
   d. If resistance is not as specified, re-

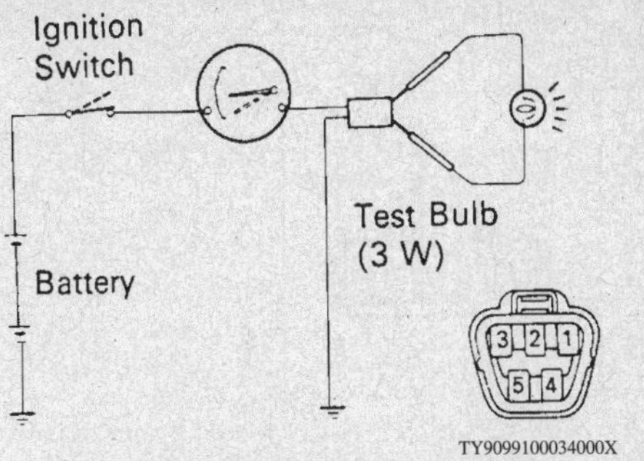
Ignition
Switch
Battery
Test Bulb
(3 W)
3 2 1
5 4
TY9099100034000X

Fig. 35 Fuel receiver gauge inspection. Camry

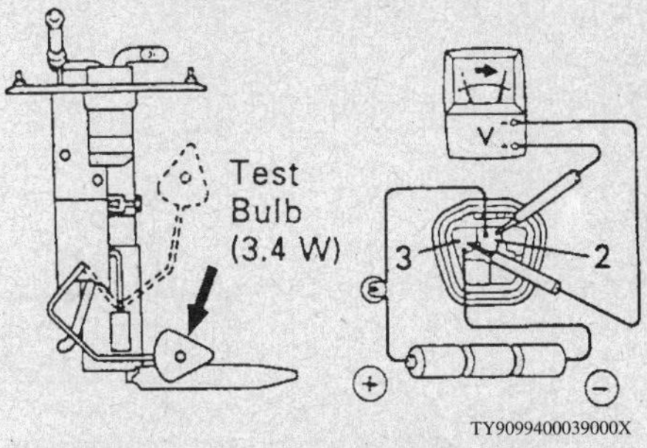
Test
Bulb
(3.4 W)
V
3
2
TY9099400039000X

Fig. 38 Fuel sender gauge inspection. 1994–96 Camry

place sender gauge.

TERCEL

1. Disconnect connector from sender gauge.
2. Turn ignition switch to On position, ensure gauge needle indicates Empty.
3. Connect terminals 3 and 4 on wire harness side of the connector through a 3.4W test bulb, **Fig. 43.**
4. Turn ignition switch On, ensure bulb lights and gauge needle moves towards Full.
5. If gauge does not operate as specified, check receiver gauge resistance.
6. Measure resistance between terminals A, B and C, **Figs. 44 and 45.**
7. **On models with tachometer,** resistance should be as follows:
   a. A–B: about 101.9 ohms.
   b. A–C: about 203.4 ohms.
   c. B–C: about 101.5 ohms.
   d. If resistance is not as specified, replace receiver gauge.
8. **On models less tachometer,** resistance should be as follows:
   a. A–B: about 55.0 ohms.
   b. A–C: about 70.0 ohms.
   c. B–C: about 125.0 ohms.
   d. If resistance is not as specified, replace receiver gauge.
9. **On all models,** connect an ohmmeter between red and black cable terminals of fuel gauge sender connector, **Fig. 46.**
10. Measure resistance for each float position, resistance should be as follows:
   a. Full position: about 2.0–4.0 ohms.
   b. Empty position: about 102.3–117.7 ohms.
   c. If resistance is not as specified, replace sender gauge.

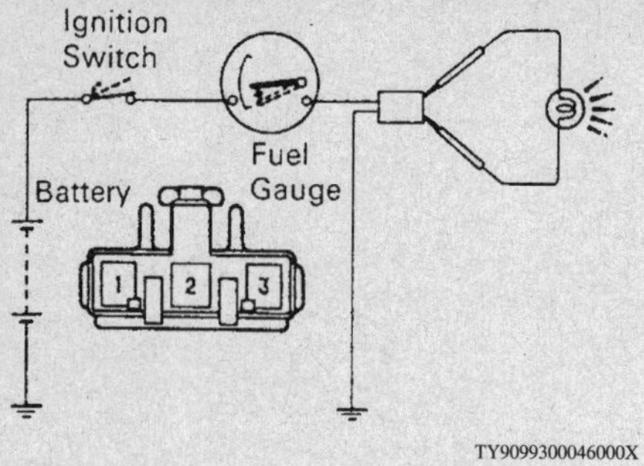
Ignition
Switch
Fuel
Gauge
Battery
1
2
3
TY9099300046000X

Fig. 39 Fuel receiver gauge inspection. Corolla

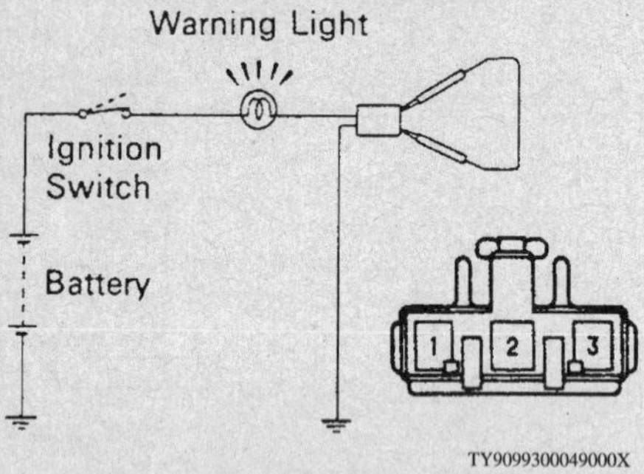
Warning Light
Ignition
Switch
Battery
1
2
3
TY9099300049000X

Fig. 42 Fuel sender gauge inspection (terminals 1 and 3). 1994–96 Corolla

LAND CRUISER

1. Disconnect connector from sender gauge.
2. Turn ignition switch to On position, then check receiver gauge needle indicates Empty.
3. Connect terminals 4 and 5 on wire harness side connector through a 3.4W test bulb, **Fig. 47.**
4. Turn ignition switch On, ensure bulb lights and receiver gauge needle moves towards Full.
5. If gauge does not operate as specified, check receiver gauge resistance.
6. Measure resistance between terminals A, B and C, **Fig. 48.** Resistance should be as follows:
   a. A–B: about 85.5–105.5 ohms.
   b. A–C: about 126.0–150.0 ohms.
   c. B–C: about 90.0–110.0 ohms.
   d. If resistance is not as specified, replace receiver gauge.
7. Connect a series of three 1.5 volt dry cell batteries, then connect the positive lead from the dry cell batteries to terminal 4 through a 3.4W test bulb and the negative lead to terminal 5, **Fig. 49.**
8. Connect the positive lead from the voltmeter to terminal 5 and the negative lead to terminal 4.
9. Ensure voltage rises between terminals as float is moved from top to bottom position.
10. Measure resistance between terminals 4 and 5 for each float position. Resistance should be as follows:
    a. Full position: about 3.0 ohms.
    b. Empty position: about 110.0 ohms.
    c. If resistance is not as specified, replace sender gauge.

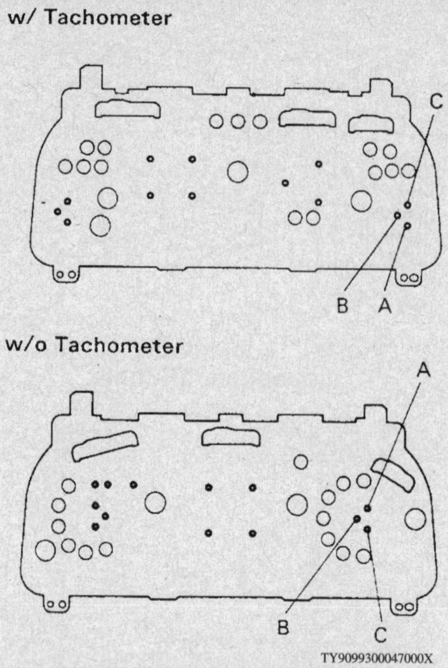
w/ Tachometer
C
B
A
w/o Tachometer
A
B
C
TY9099300047000X

Fig. 40 Fuel gauge terminal locations. Corolla

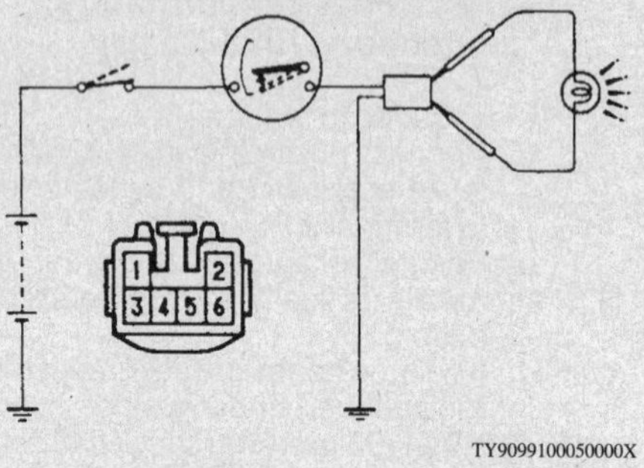
1
2
3
4
5
6
TY9099100050000X

Fig. 43 Fuel receiver gauge inspection. Tercel

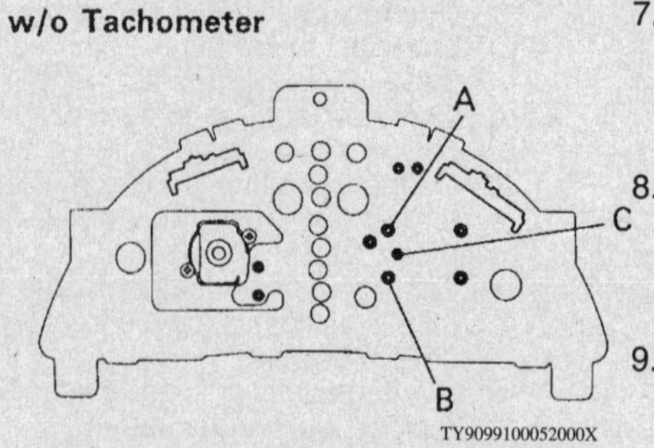
w/o Tachometer
A
C
B
TY9099100052000X

Fig. 45 Fuel gauge terminal locations. Tercel less tachometer

PICKUP

1. Disconnect connector from sender gauge.
2. Turn ignition switch to On position, then check receiver gauge needle indicates Empty.
3. Connect terminals 1 and 2 on wire harness side connector through a 3.4W test bulb, **Fig. 50.**
4. Turn ignition switch On, ensure bulb lights and receiver gauge needle

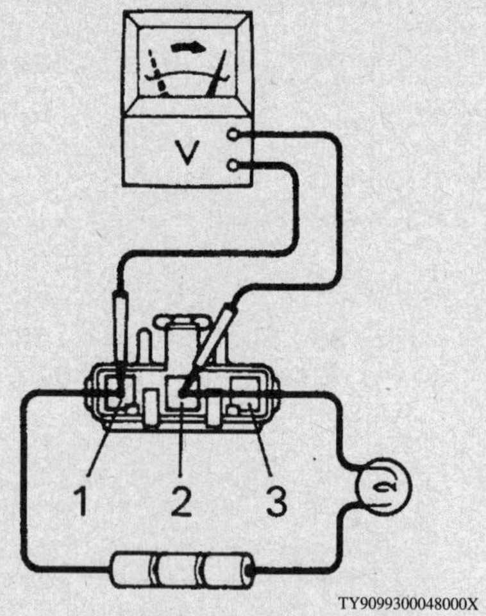
V
1
2
3
TY9099300048000X

Fig. 41 Fuel sender gauge inspection (terminals 2 and 4). 1993 Corolla

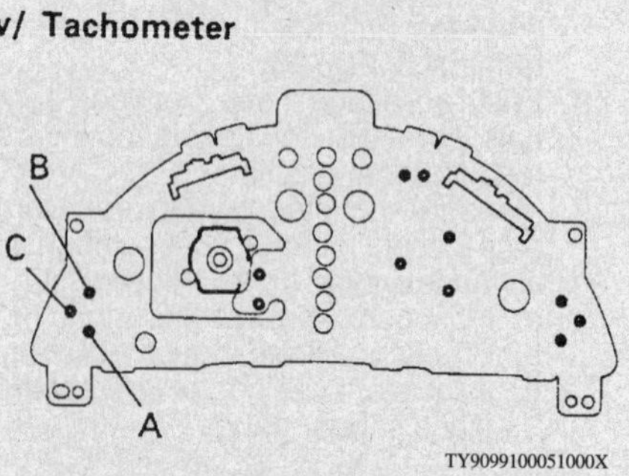
w/ Tachometer
B
C
A
TY9099100051000X

Fig. 44 Fuel gauge terminal locations. Tercel w/tachometer

moves towards Full position.

5. If gauge doe not operate as specified, check receiver gauge resistance.
6. Measure resistance between terminals A, B and C, **Figs. 51 and 52.**
7. **On models with tachometer,** resistance should be as follows:
   a. A–B: about 123.0 ohms.
   b. A–C: about 260.0 ohms.
   c. B–C: about 137.0 ohms.
8. **On models less tachometer,** resistance should be as follows:
   a. A–B: about 55.0 ohms.
   b. If resistance is not as specified, replace receiver gauge.
9. Connect a series of three 1.5 volt dry cell batteries, then connect the positive lead from the dry cell batteries to terminal 2, then the negative lead to terminal 1, **Fig. 53.**
10. Connect the positive lead from the voltmeter to terminal 2, then the negative lead to terminal 1.
11. Ensure voltage rises between terminals as the float is moved from top to bottom position.
12. Measure resistance between terminals 2 and 3 for each float position. Resistance should be as follows:
    a. Full position: about 3.0 ohms.
    b. Empty position: about 110.0 ohms.
    c. If resistance is not as specified, replace sender gauge.

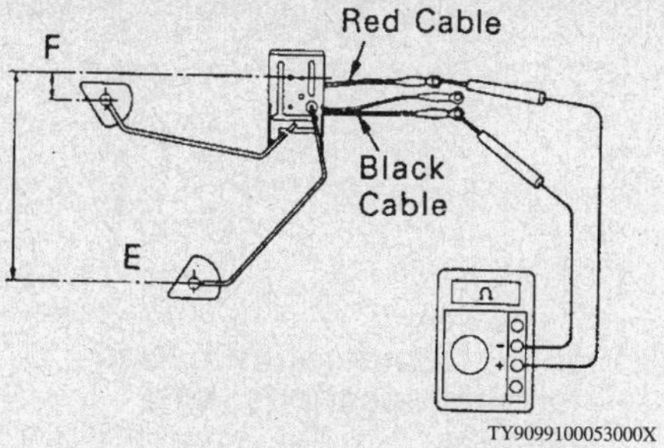
Red Cable
F
Black
Cable
E
Ω
TY9099100053000X

Fig. 46 Fuel sender gauge inspection. Tercel

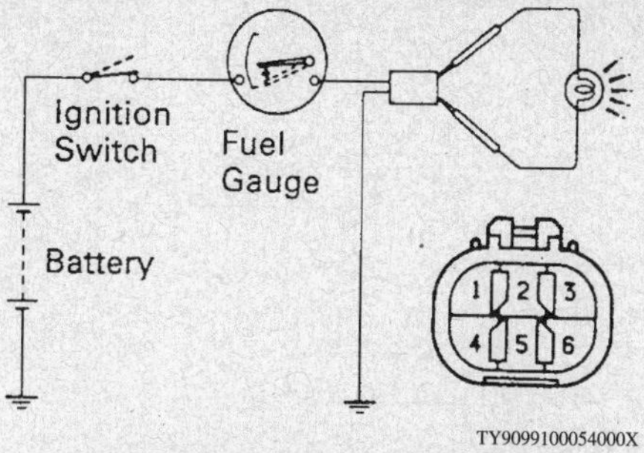
Ignition
Switch
Fuel
Gauge
Battery
1
2
3
4
5
6
TY9099100054000X

Fig. 47 Fuel receiver gauge inspection. Land Cruiser

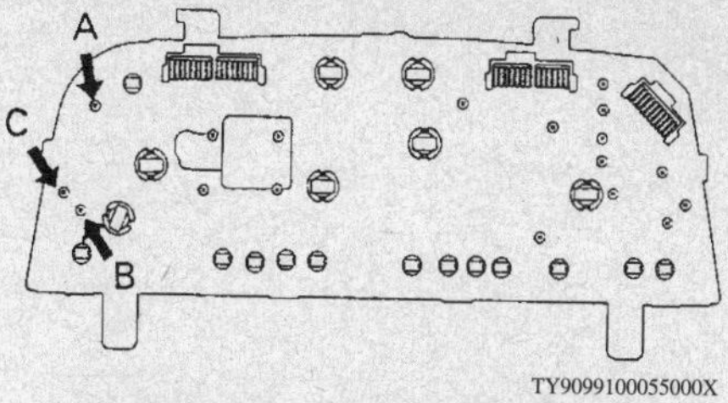
A
C
B
TY9099100055000X

Fig. 48 Fuel gauge terminal locations. Land Cruiser

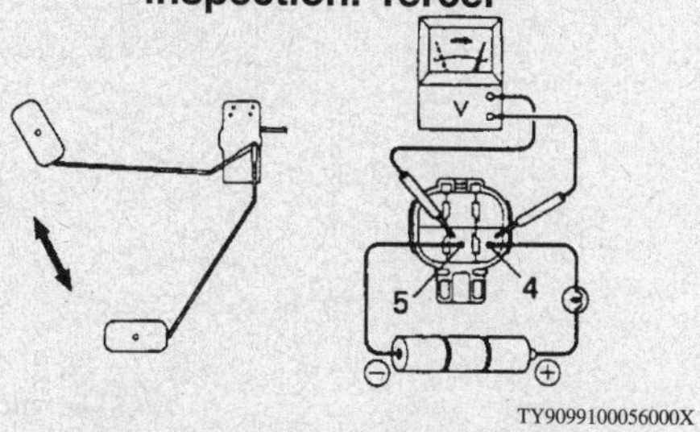
V
5
4
TY9099100056000X

Fig. 49 Fuel sender gauge inspection. Land Cruiser

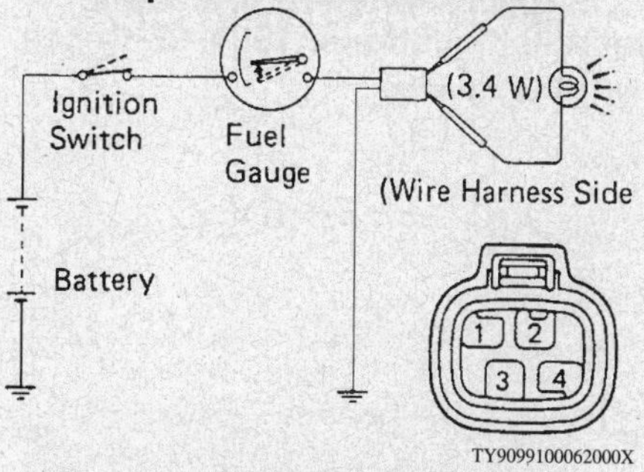
Ignition
Switch
Fuel
Gauge
(3.4 W)
(Wire Harness Side
Battery
1
2
3
4
TY9099100062000X

Fig. 50 Fuel receiver gauge inspection. Pickup

w/o Tachometer

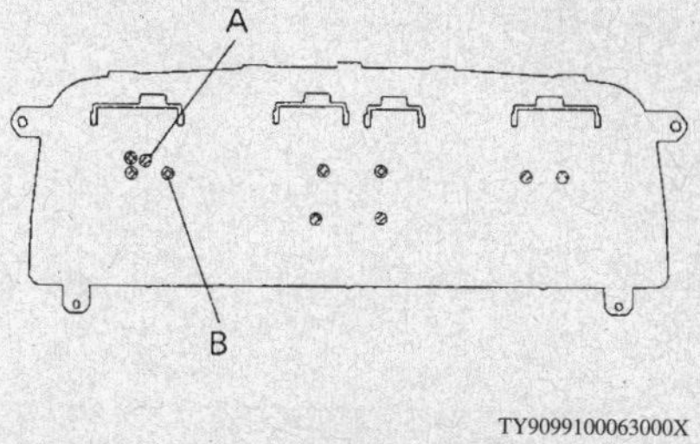
A
B
TY9099100063000X

Fig. 51 Fuel gauge terminal locations. Pickup less tachometer

w/ Tachometer

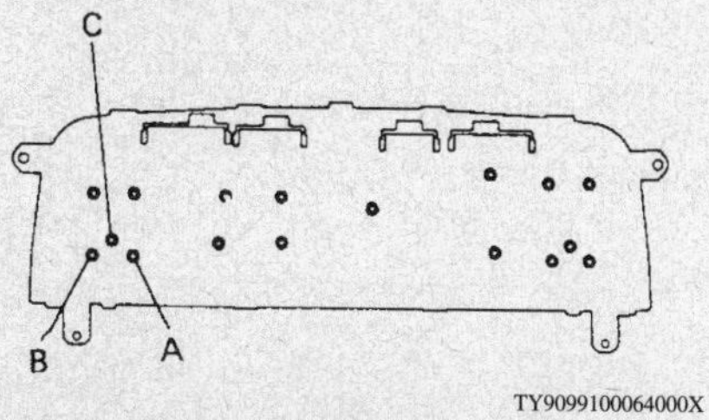
C
B
A
TY9099100064000X

Fig. 52 Fuel gauge terminal locations. Pickup w/tachometer

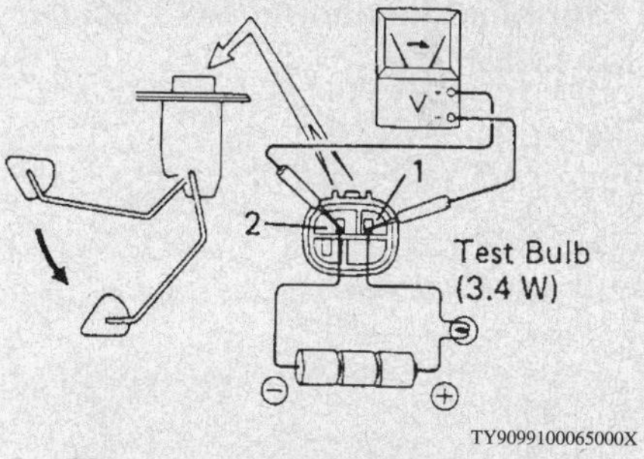
V
1
2
Test Bulb
(3.4 W)
TY9099100065000X

Fig. 53 Fuel sender gauge inspection. Pickup

ENGINE COOLANT TEMPERATURE

Refer to **Figs. 54 through 70** for terminal locations on engine coolant temperature gauges.

1. Disconnect connector from sender gauge.
2. Turn ignition switch On, then check receiver gauge needle indicates COOL.
3. Ground terminal on wire harness side connector through a 3.4W test bulb.
4. Turn ignition switch On, then check bulb lights up and receiver gauge needle moves toward hot side.
5. If operation is as specified, replace sender gauge, then recheck system.
6. If operation is not as specified, measure receiver gauge resistance between terminals A, B and C.
7. **On Avalon and Camry models,** resistance should be as follows:
   a. A–B: about 54.0 ohms.
   b. A–C: about 176.0 ohms.
   c. B–C: about 230.0 ohms.
8. **On 1993 Celica models,** resistance should be as follows:
   a. A–B: about 182.0 ohms.
   b. A–C: about 131.0 ohms.
   c. B–C: about 51.0 ohms.
9. **On 1994–96 Celica models,** resistance should be as follows:
   a. A–B: about 230.0 ohms.
   b. A–C: about 54.0 ohms.
   c. B–C: about 176.0 ohms.
10. **On Corolla models less tachometer,** resistance should be as follows:
    a. A–B: about 176.0 ohms.
    b. A–C: about 54.0 ohms.
    c. B–C: about 230.0 ohms.
11. **On Corolla models with tachometer,** resistance should be as follows:
    a. A–B: about 230.0 ohms.
    b. A–C: about 54.0 ohms.
    c. B–C: about 176.0 ohms.
12. **On Land Cruiser models,** resistance should be as follows:
    a. A–B: about 71.0–79.0 ohms.
    b. A–C: about 117.0–141.0 ohms.
    c. B–C: about 185.0–215.0 ohms.
13. **On MR2 models,** resistance should be as follows:
    a. A–B: about 54.0 ohms.
    b. A–C: about 176.0 ohms.
    c. B–C: about 230.0 ohms.
14. **On Paseo models,** resistance should be as follows:
    a. A–B: about 54.0 ohms.
    b. A–C: about 146.0 ohms.
    c. B–C: about 200.0 ohms.
15. **On Previa models,** resistance should be as follows:
    a. A–B: about 200.0 ohms.
    b. A–C: about 54.0 ohms.
    c. B–C: about 146.0 ohms.
16. **On Pickup models with tachometer,** resistance should be as follows;
    a. A–B: about 57.0 ohms.
    b. A–C: about 135.0 ohms.
    c. B–C: about 217.0 ohms.
17. **On RAV4 models,** resistance should be as follows:
    a. A-B: about 54 ohms.
    b. A-C: about 175.7 ohms.
    c. B-C: about 229.7 ohms.
18. **On Pickup models less tachometer,** resistance should be as follows;
    a. A–B: about 25.0 ohms.
19. **On Supra models,** measure resistance between terminals A, B and C. Resistance should be as follows:
    a. A–B: about 229.7 ohms.
    b. A–C: about 54.0 ohms.
    c. B–C: about 175.7 ohms.
20. **On 1993 Previa models,** measure resistance between terminal and gauge body. Resistance should be about 226 ohms at 122°F and about 26 ohms at 239°F.
21. **On 1994–96 Previa models,** measure resistance between terminals A, B and C. Resistance should be as follows:
    a. A–B: about 200.3 ohms.
    b. A–C: about 54.0 ohms.
    c. B–C: about 146.3 ohms.
22. **On 1993–94 Tercel models with tachometer,** resistance should be as follows:
    a. A-B: about 51.0 ohms.
    b. A–C: about 149.0 ohms.
    c. B–C: about 200.0 ohms.
23. **On 1993–94 Tercel models less tachometer,** resistance should be as follows:
    a. A–B: about 55.0 ohms.
    b. A–C: about 70.0 ohms.
    c. B–C: about 125.0 ohms.
24. **On 1995–96 Tercel models with tachometer,** resistance should be as follows:

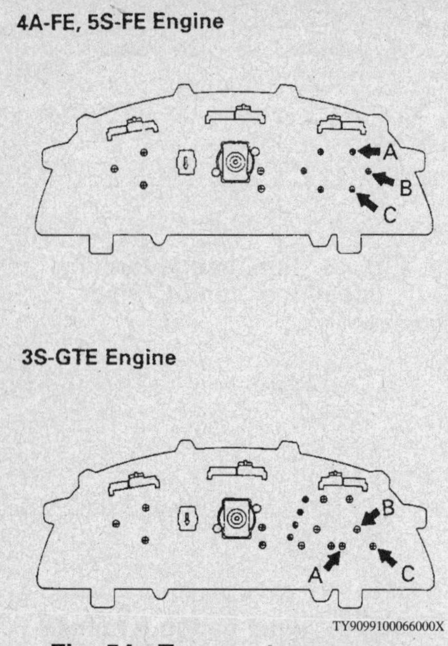
4A-FE, 5S-FE Engine
A
B
C
3S-GTE Engine
B
A
C
TY9099100066000X

Fig. 54 Temperature gauge terminal locations. 1993 Celica

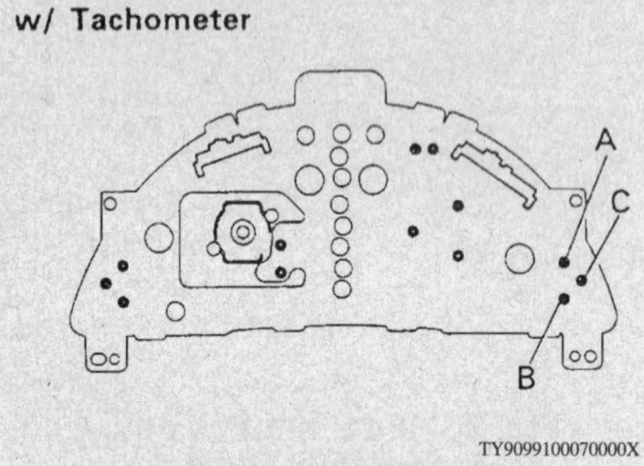
w/ Tachometer
A
C
B
TY9099100070000X

Fig. 57 Temperature gauge terminal locations. Paseo

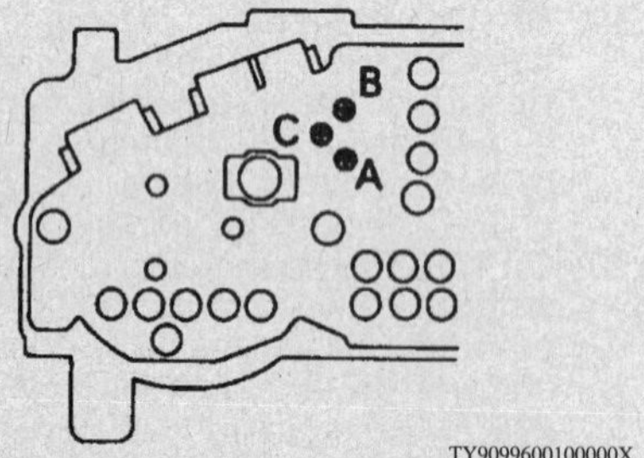
B
C
A
TY9099600100000X

Fig. 60 Temperature gauge terminal locations. RAV4

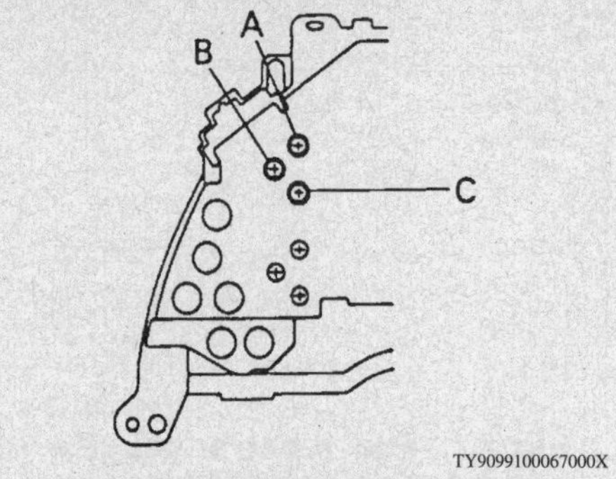
A
B
C
TY9099100067000X

Fig. 55 Temperature gauge terminal locations. 1994–96 Celica

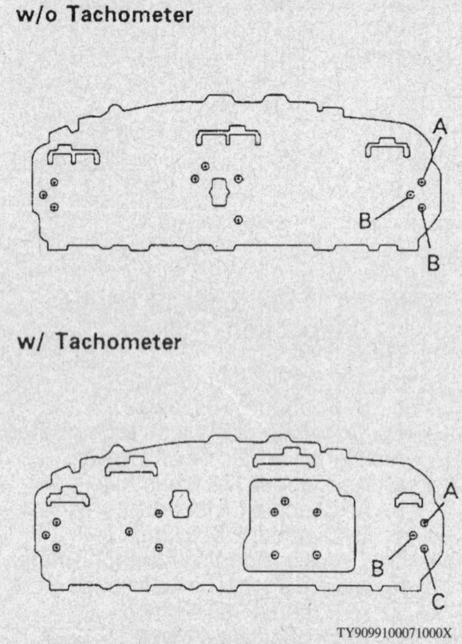
w/o Tachometer
A
B
B
w/ Tachometer
A
B
C
TY9099100071000X

Fig. 58 Temperature gauge terminal locations. Previa

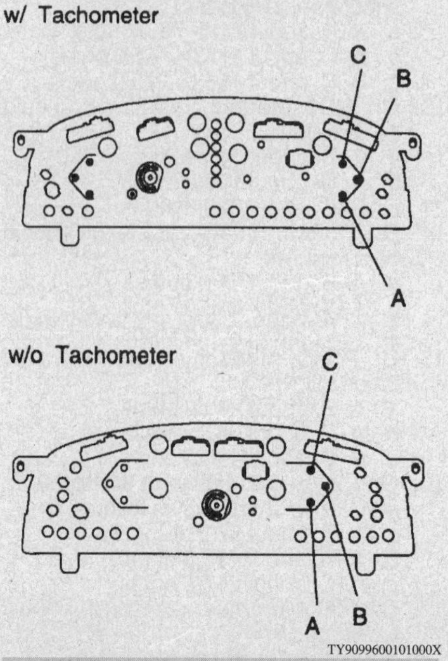
w/ Tachometer
C
B
A
w/o Tachometer
C
A
B
TY9099600101000X

Fig. 61 Temperature gauge terminal locations. Tacoma

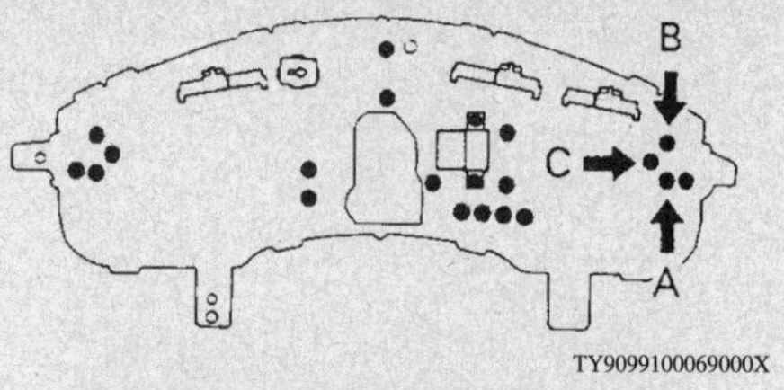
B
C
A
TY9099100069000X

Fig. 56 Temperature gauge terminal locations. MR2

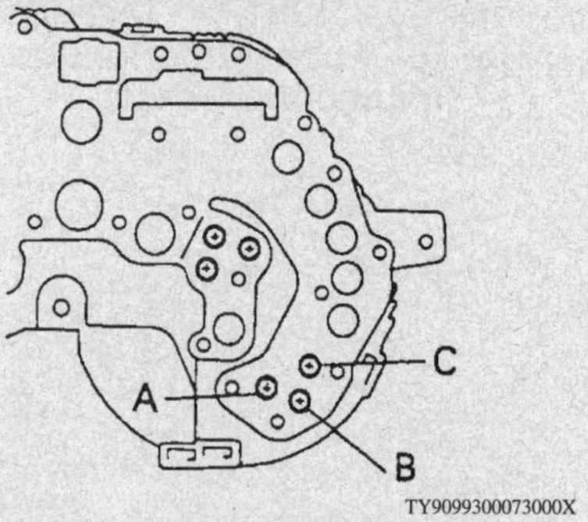
C
A
B
TY9099300073000X

Fig. 59 Temperature gauge terminal locations. Supra

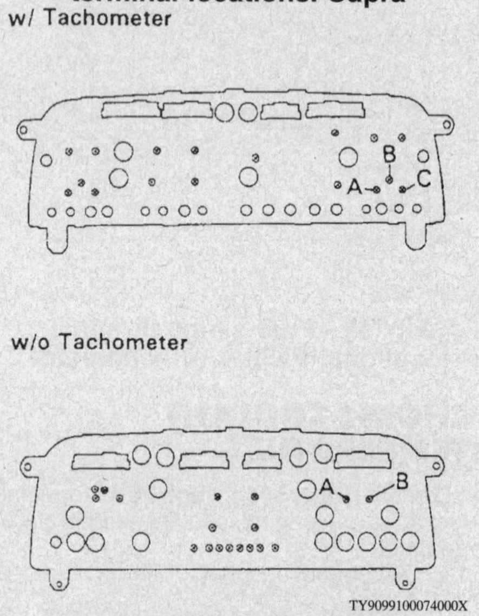
w/ Tachometer
B
A
C
w/o Tachometer
A
B
TY9099100074000X

Fig. 62 Temperature gauge terminal locations. T100

a. D-E: about 51.0 ohms.
b. D–F: about 149.0 ohms.
c. E–F: about 200.0 ohms.

25. **On 1995–96 Tercel models less tachometer,** resistance should be as follows:
    a. A–B: about 54.0 ohms.
    b. A–C: about 176.0 ohms.
    c. B–C: about 230.0 ohms.
26. **On Tacoma models with tachometer,** resistance should be as follows:
    a. D-E: about 85.0–95.0 ohms.
    b. D–F: about 158.0–192.0 ohms.
    c. E–F: about 215.0–255.0 ohms.
27. **On Tacoma models less tachometer,** resistance should be as follows:
    a. A–B: about 85.0–95.0 ohms.
    b. A–C: about 158.0–192.0 ohms.
    c. B–C: about 215.0–255.0 ohms.
28. **On T100 models with tachometer,** resistance should be as follows:
    a. A–B: about 150.0 ohms.
    b. A–C: about 54.0 ohms.
    c. B–C: about 138.0 ohms.
29. **On T100 models less tachometer,** resistance should be as follows:
    a. A–B: about 25.0 ohms.
30. **On 4Runner models,** resistance should be as follows:
    a. A–B: about 57.0 ohms.
    b. A–C: about 135.0 ohms.
    c. B–C: about 217.0 ohms.
31. **On all models,** if resistance is not as specified, replace receiver gauge.
32. Measure sender resistance between terminal and ground. Resistance

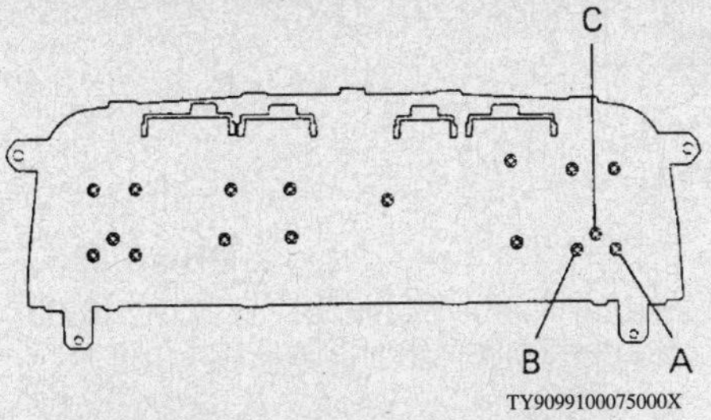
C
B
A
TY9099100075000X

Fig. 63 Temperature gauge terminal locations. 4Runner

w/ Tachometer

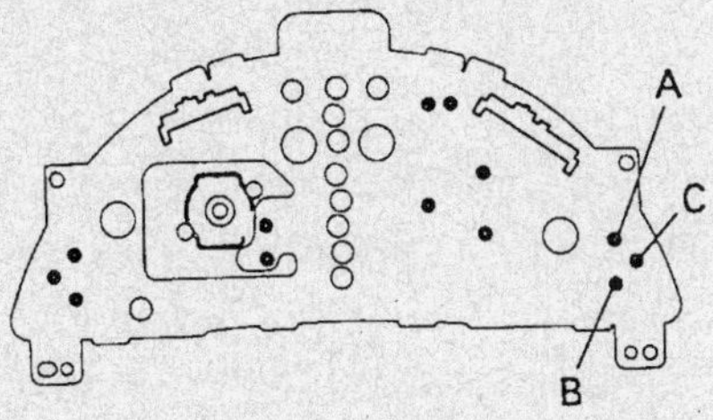
A
C
B
TY9099100080000X

Fig. 66 Temperature gauge terminal locations. Tercel w/ tachometer

w/o Tachometer

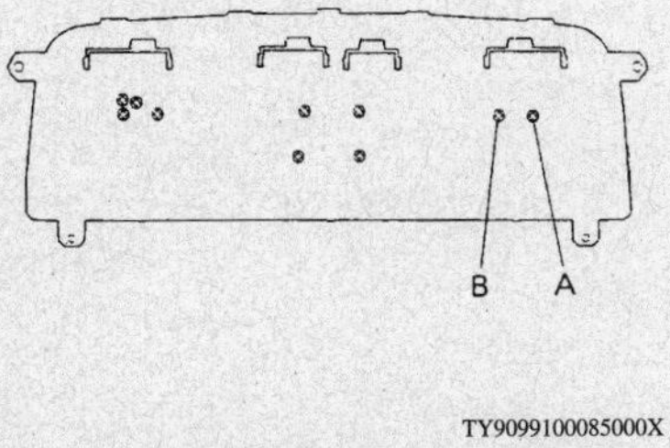
B
A
TY9099100085000X

Fig. 69 Temperature gauge terminal locations. Pickup less tachometer

should be 160–314 ohms at 122°F and 17–30 ohms at 248°F.

33. If resistance is not as specified, replace sender gauge.

LOW OIL PRESSURE

1. Disconnect connector from warning switch and ground terminal on wire harness side connector.
2. Turn ignition switch to On position, then check warning light illuminates. If not, test bulb.
3. Ensure there is continuity between terminal and ground with engine stopped.

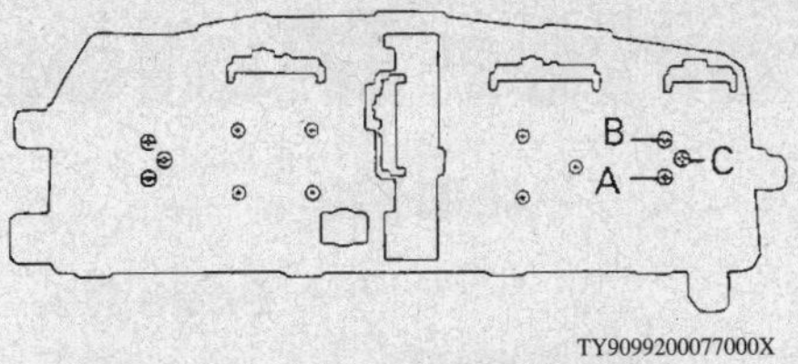
B
A
C
TY9099200077000X

Fig. 64 Temperature gauge terminal locations. Camry

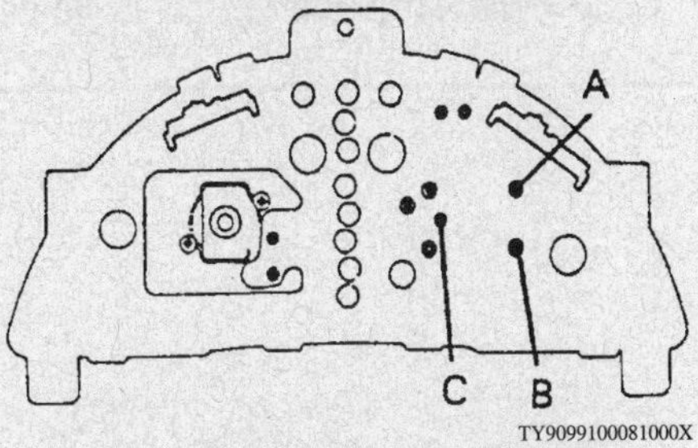
A
C
B
TY9099100081000X

Fig. 67 Temperature gauge terminal locations. Tercel less tachometer

4. Ensure there is no continuity between terminal and ground with engine running.
5. Oil pressure should be as follows:
   a. **On Avalon, Previa, Supra and 1994–96 Camry,** over 4.3 psi.
   b. **On Paseo models,** over 2.8 psi.
   c. **On Celica models,** over 2.9 psi.
   d. **On RAV4 models,** over 3.6 psi.
   e. **On MR2, Tacoma, Tercel, T100, 1993 Camry and Corolla models,** over 7.1 psi.
6. **On 4Runner, Pickup and Land Cruiser models,** disconnect connector from sender gauge.
7. **On all models,** turn ignition switch to On position, then check receiver gauge needle indicates Low.
8. Ground terminal on wire harness side connector through a 3.4W test bulb.
9. Turn ignition switch to On position, then check bulb illuminates and receiver gauge needle moves to high side.
10. **On 4Runner and Pickup models,** measure resistance between terminals A and B. Resistance should be about 25.0 ohms. If not as specified, replace receiver gauge.
11. **On 1993 Land Cruiser models,** measure resistance between terminals. Resistance should be 22.0–28.0 ohms. If not as specified, replace receiver gauge.
12. **On 1994–96 Land Cruiser models,** measure resistance between terminals. Resistance should be 40.0–48.0 ohms. If not as specified, replace receiver gauge.
13. If resistance is not as specified, replace sender gauge.

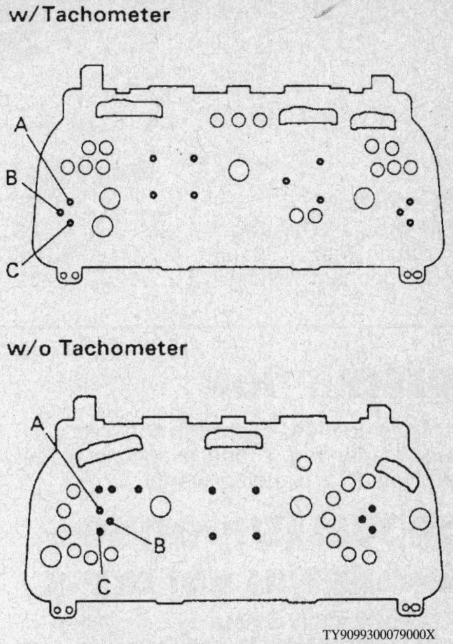
w/Tachometer
A
B
C
w/o Tachometer
A
B
C
TY9099300079000X

Fig. 65 Temperature gauge terminal locations. Corolla

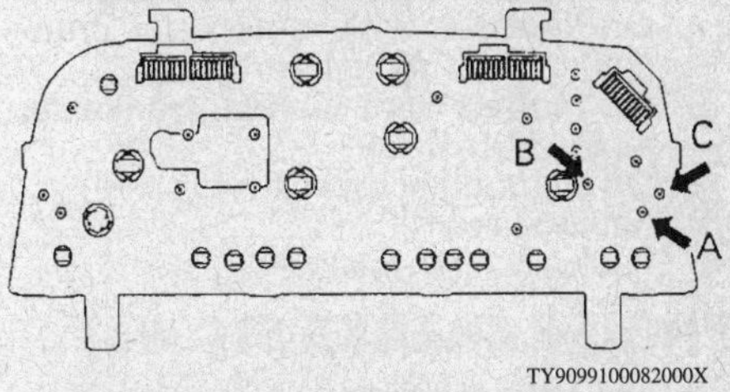
B
C
A
TY9099100082000X

Fig. 68 Temperature gauge terminal locations. Land Cruiser

w/ Tachometer

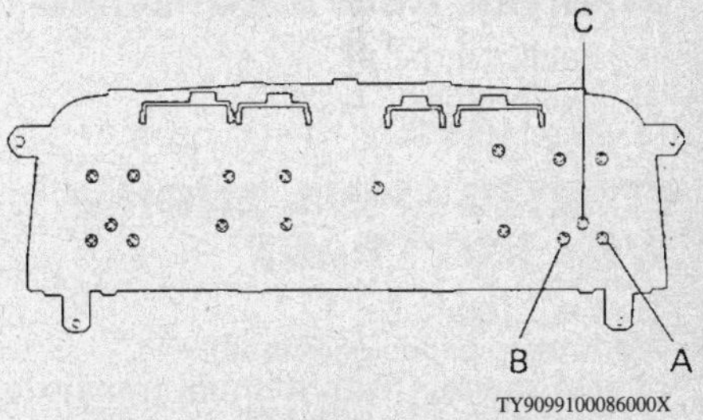
C
B
A
TY9099100086000X

Fig. 70 Temperature gauge terminal locations. Pickup w/ tachometer

Starter Motors

INDEX

	Page No.
Description	48-28
Diagnosis & Testing	48-28
Bench Test	48-28
Component Testing	48-29
Starter Specifications	48-31
Troubleshooting	48-28
Engine Cranks Slowly	48-28
Engine Will Not Crank	48-28
Starter Keeps Running	48-28
Starter Spins, Engine Will Not Crank	48-28

DESCRIPTION

Refer to **Figs. 1 through 6** for reduction type starter, **Fig. 7** for conventional starter and **Fig. 8** for planetary starter.

TROUBLESHOOTING

ENGINE WILL NOT CRANK

1. Low battery charge.
2. Battery cables loose or corroded.
3. **On models with manual transaxle,** faulty clutch start switch.
4. **On models with automatic transaxle,** faulty neutral start switch.
5. **On models with manual transaxle,** faulty starter relay.
6. **On all models,** blown fusible link.
7. Faulty starter.
8. Faulty ignition switch.

ENGINE CRANKS SLOWLY

1. Low battery charge.
2. Battery cables loose, corroded or worn.
3. Faulty starter.

STARTER KEEPS RUNNING

1. Faulty starter.
2. Faulty ignition switch.
3. Electrical wiring short or open.

STARTER SPINS, ENGINE WILL NOT CRANK

1. Faulty starter.
2. Broken pinion gear teeth.
3. **On models with manual transaxle,** broken flywheel teeth.
4. **On models with automatic transaxle,** broken driveplate teeth.

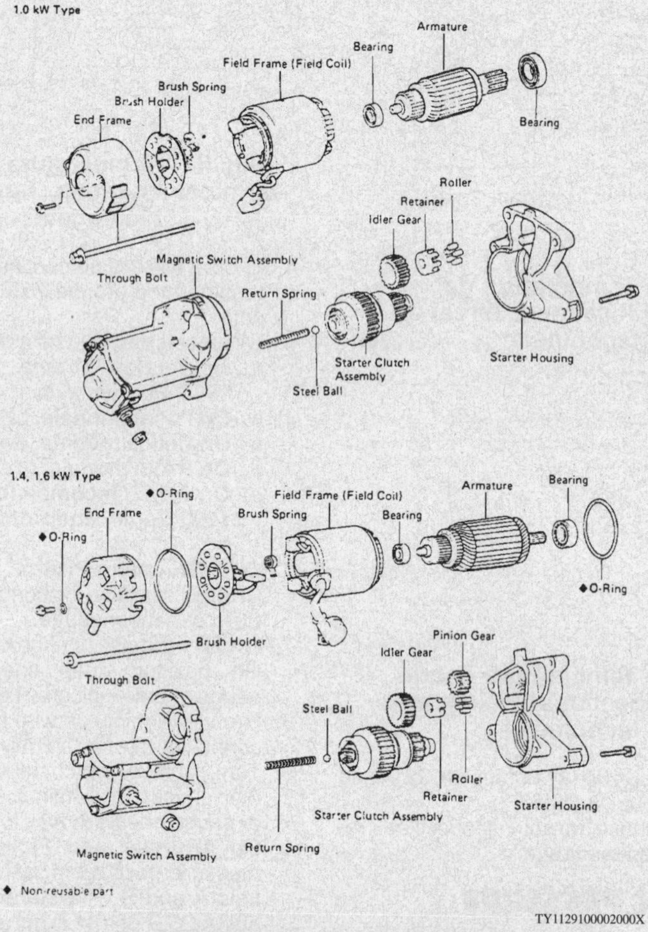

1.0 kW Type
Armature
Bearing
Field Frame (Field Coil)
Brush Spring
Brush Holder
End Frame
Bearing
Roller
Retainer
Idler Gear
Magnetic Switch Assembly
Through Bolt
Return Spring
Starter Clutch Assembly
Steel Ball
Starter Housing
1.4, 1.6 kW Type
O-Ring
Field Frame (Field Coil)
Armature
Bearing
End Frame
Brush Spring
Bearing
O-Ring
O-Ring
Brush Holder
Pinion Gear
Idler Gear
Through Bolt
Steel Ball
Roller
Retainer
Starter Housing
Starter Clutch Assembly
Magnetic Switch Assembly
Return Spring
Non-reusable part
TY1129100002000X

Fig. 1 Exploded view of reduction type starter. Pickup, Previa, Tacoma, T100 & 4Runner

DIAGNOSIS & TESTING

BENCH TEST

These tests must be performed within 3 to 5 seconds to avoid burning out the coil.

Pull-In Test

1. Disconnect field coil wire from terminal C.
2. Connect negative battery voltage to both magnetic switch body and terminal C.
3. Connect positive battery voltage to starter terminal 50, **Fig. 9.**
4. Ensure pinion gear moves outward.
5. If pinion gear movement is not as indicated, replace magnetic switch.

Hold-In Test

1. Install test equipment as outlined under "Pull-In Test."
2. With pinion gear out, disconnect negative lead from terminal C.
3. Ensure pinion gear remains out.
4. If pinion gear returns inward, replace magnetic switch.

Plunger Return

1. Install test equipment as outlined under "Pull-In Test."
2. Disconnect negative lead from magnetic switch body.
3. Ensure pinion gear moves inward.
4. If pinion gear movement is not as indicated, replace magnetic switch.

No-Load Performance

1. Connect suitable ammeter negative lead to terminals both 30 and 50.
2. Connect ammeter positive terminal to positive battery terminal.
3. Ensure starter rotates smoothly and steadily with pinion gear moving out.
4. Refer to "Starter Specifications" for

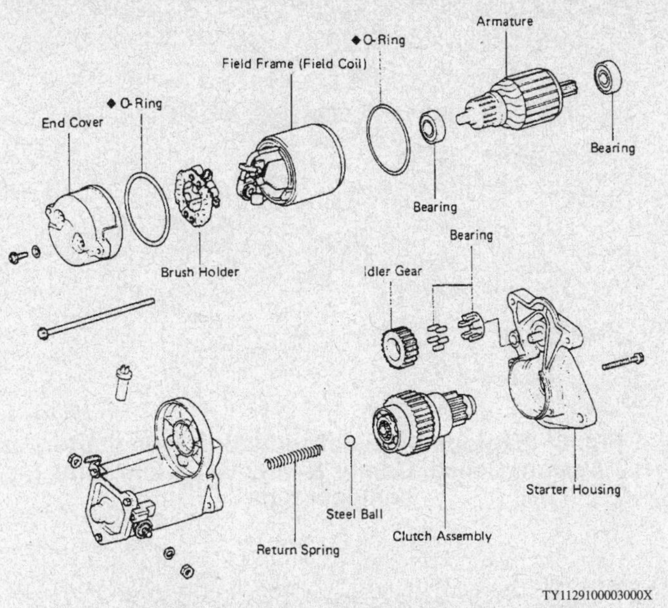
Armature
O-Ring
Field Frame (Field Coil)
O-Ring
End Cover
Bearing
Bearing
Bearing
Brush Holder
Idler Gear
Starter Housing
Steel Ball
Clutch Assembly
Return Spring
TY1129100003000X

Fig. 2 Exploded view of reduction type starter. Celica, Corolla, Land Cruiser, Paseo, Pickup, 4Runner, Previa, Supra, T100 & Tercel

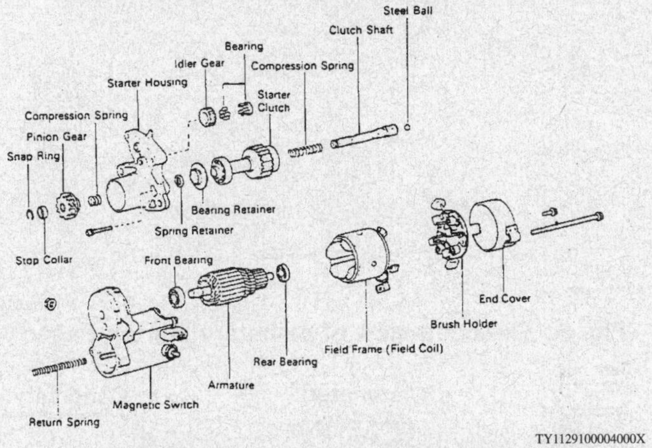
Steel Ball
Clutch Shaft
Bearing
Idler Gear
Compression Spring
Starter Housing
Starter Clutch
Compression Spring
Pinion Gear
Snap Ring
Bearing Retainer
Spring Retainer
Stop Collar
Front Bearing
End Cover
Brush Holder
Field Frame (Field Coil)
Rear Bearing
Armature
Magnetic Switch
Return Spring
TY1129100004000X

Fig. 4 Exploded view of reduction type starter. Celica w/1.0 kilowatts

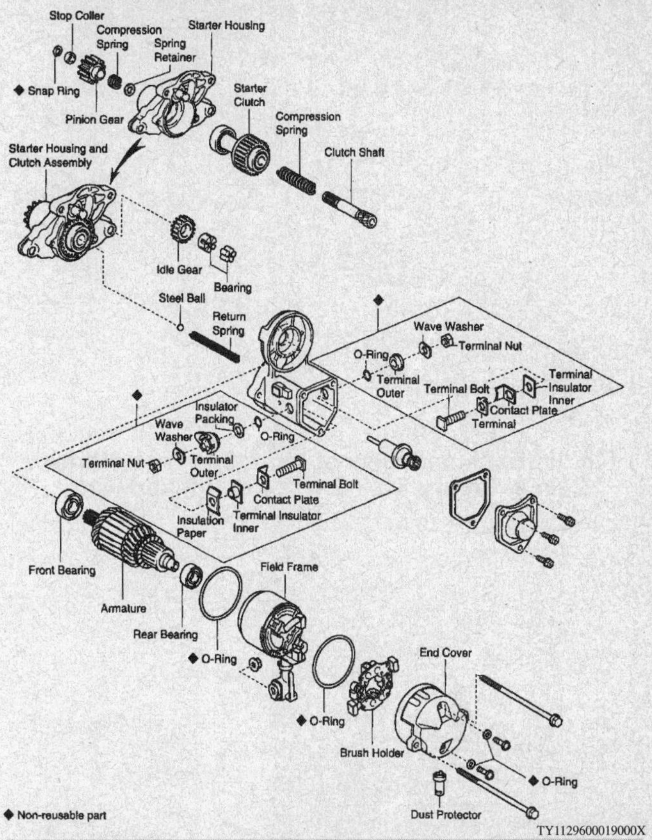
Stop Collar
Compression Spring
Spring Retainer
Starter Housing
Snap Ring
Pinion Gear
Starter Clutch
Compression Spring
Starter Housing and Clutch Assembly
Clutch Shaft
Idle Gear
Bearing
Steel Ball
Return Spring
Wave Washer
Terminal Nut
O-Ring
Terminal Outer
Terminal Bolt
Terminal Insulator Inner
Contact Plate
Terminal
Insulator Packing
Wave Washer
O-Ring
Terminal Nut
Terminal Outer
Terminal Bolt
Contact Plate
Insulation Paper
Terminal Insulator Inner
Front Bearing
Field Frame
Armature
Rear Bearing
O-Ring
End Cover
O-Ring
Brush Holder
O-Ring
Dust Protector
Non-reusable part
TY1129600019000X

Fig. 3 Exploded view of reduction type starter. RAV4

standard amperage.

COMPONENT TESTING

Starter Relay

1. **On 1993 Camry models,** starter relay is located behind the center of the instrument panel.
2. **On Avalon and 1994–96 Camry models,** starter relay is located in the front lefthand side of the engine compartment (lefthand side of battery), at junction block No. 2.
3. **On 1993 Celica models,** starter relay is located behind the righthand kick panel.
4. **On 1994–96 Celica models,** starter relay is located in the front lefthand side of the engine compartment, at relay block No. 2.
5. **On Corolla models,** starter relay is located behind the lefthand side kick panel.
6. **On Land Cruiser and RAV4 models,** starter relay is located in the engine compartment relay box.
7. **On MR2 models,** starter relay is located at the rear center of engine compartment.
8. **On Pickup and 4Runner models,** the starter relay is located in the righthand front of the engine compartment, in the No. 2 relay box.
9. **On Paseo and Tercel models,** starter relay is located behind the lower lefthand side of the center dash cluster, behind radio.
10. **On Previa models,** starter relay is located below the lefthand side of instrument panel.
11. **On Supra and Tacoma models,** starter relay is located in the lefthand side of the engine compartment, at relay block No. 2.
12. **On MR2 and Previa models,** using a suitable ohmmeter, check relay continuity as follows:
    a. Ensure continuity between terminal Nos. 1 and 3, **Fig. 10.**
    b. No continuity should exist between terminal Nos. 2 and 4.
    c. If continuity is not as indicated, replace relay.
13. Using suitable ohmmeter, inspect relay operation as follows:
    a. Apply battery voltage across terminal Nos. 1 and 3.
    b. Using suitable ohmmeter, ensure continuity exists between terminal Nos. 2 and 4.
    c. If continuity is not as indicated, replace relay.
14. **On Paseo and Tercel models,** using a suitable ohmmeter, check relay continuity as follows:
    a. Ensure continuity exists between terminals 85 and 86, **Fig. 11.**
    b. Ensure continuity exists between terminals 30 and 87.
    c. Apply battery voltage across terminals 85 and 86.
    d. Ensure continuity does not exist between terminals 30 and 87.
    e. If continuity is not as specified, replace relay.
15. **On models except MR2, Paseo, Previa and Tercel models,** using a suitable ohmmeter, check relay continuity as follows:
    a. Ensure continuity exists between terminals 1 and 2, **Fig. 12.**
    b. Ensure continuity does not exist between terminals 3 and 5.
    c. Apply battery voltage across terminals 1 and 2.
    d. Ensure continuity exists between terminals 3 and 5.

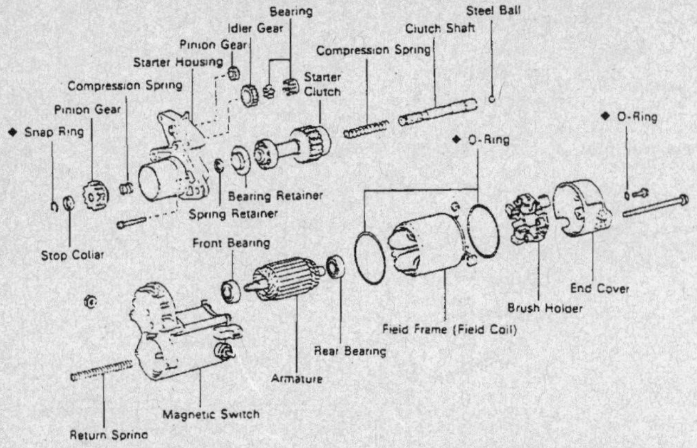
Bearing
Steel Ball
Idler Gear
Clutch Shaft
Pinion Gear
Compression Spring
Starter Housing
Starter Clutch
Compression Spring
Pinion Gear
◆ O-Ring
◆ Snap Ring
◆ O-Ring
Bearing Retainer
Spring Retainer
Stop Collar
Front Bearing
End Cover
Brush Holder
Field Frame (Field Coil)
Rear Bearing
Armature
Magnetic Switch
Return Spring

TY1129100005000X

Fig. 5 Exploded view of reduction type starter. Celica, Camry & MR2 w/1.4 or 1.6 kilowatts

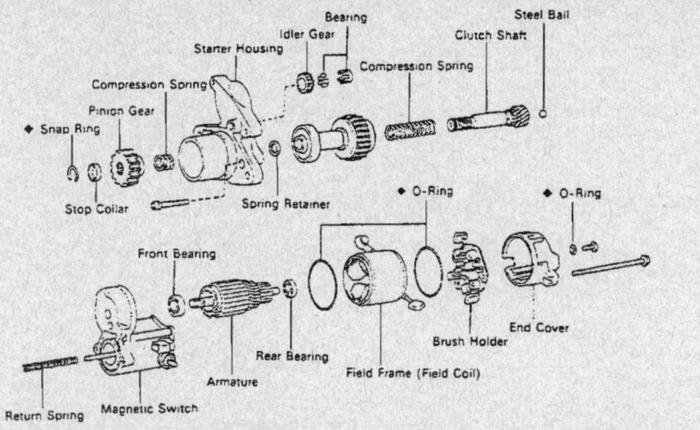
Bearing
Steel Ball
Idler Gear
Clutch Shaft
Starter Housing
Compression Spring
Compression Spring
Pinion Gear
◆ Snap Ring
Stop Collar
Spring Retainer
◆ O-Ring
◆ O-Ring
Front Bearing
End Cover
Brush Holder
Rear Bearing
Field Frame (Field Coil)
Armature
Return Spring
Magnetic Switch

TY1129100006000X

Fig. 6 Exploded view of reduction type starter. Avalon, Celica, Camry & MR2 w/1.4 kilowatts compact type

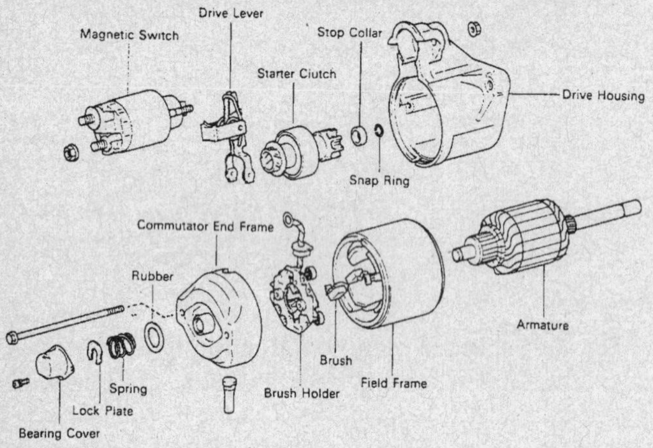
Drive Lever
Magnetic Switch
Stop Collar
Starter Clutch
Drive Housing
Snap Ring
Commutator End Frame
Rubber
Armature
Brush
Field Frame
Spring
Brush Holder
Lock Plate
Bearing Cover

TY1129100007000X

Fig. 7 Exploded view of conventional starter. Tercel

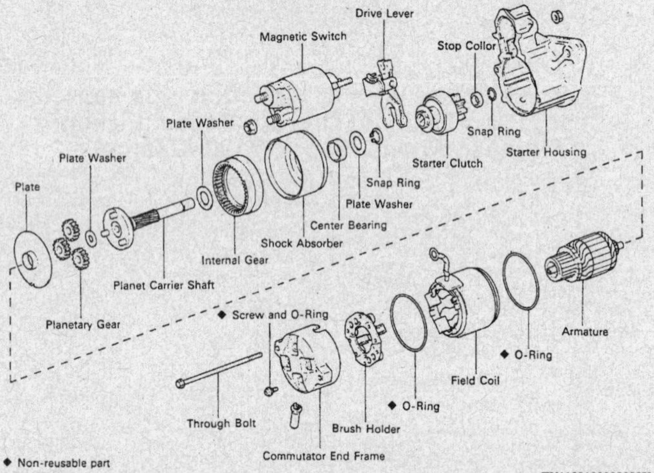
Drive Lever
Magnetic Switch
Stop Collar
Plate Washer
Snap Ring
Starter Housing
Plate Washer
Starter Clutch
Plate
Snap Ring
Plate Washer
Center Bearing
Shock Absorber
Internal Gear
Planet Carrier Shaft
◆ Screw and O-Ring
Planetary Gear
Armature
◆ O-Ring
Field Coil
◆ O-Ring
Through Bolt
Brush Holder
Commutator End Frame
◆ Non-reusable part

TY1129100008000X

Fig. 8 Exploded view of planetary starter. Paseo

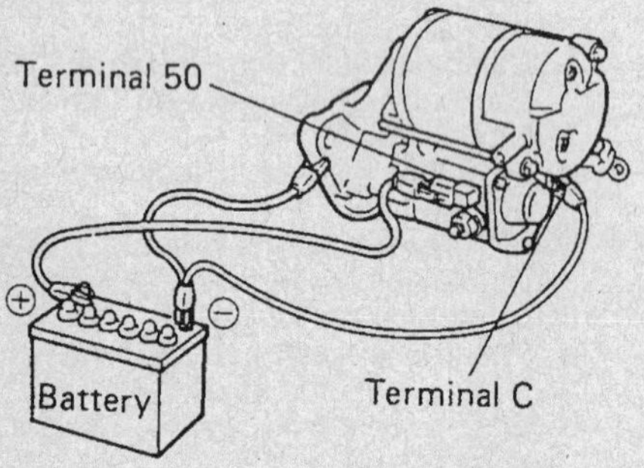
Terminal 50
Battery
Terminal C

TY1129100009000X

Fig. 9 Bench test connectors

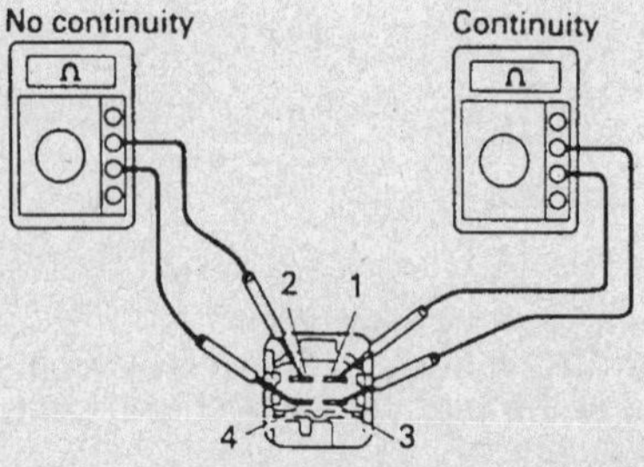
No continuity
Continuity
2
1
4
3

TY1129100010000X

Fig. 10 Starter relay inspection. MR2 & Previa

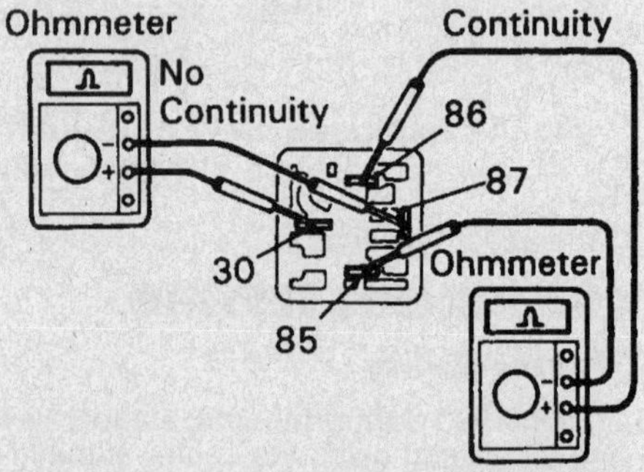
Ohmmeter
Continuity
No
Continuity
86
87
30
Ohmmeter
85

TY1129600018000X

Fig. 11 Starter relay inspection. Paseo & Tercel

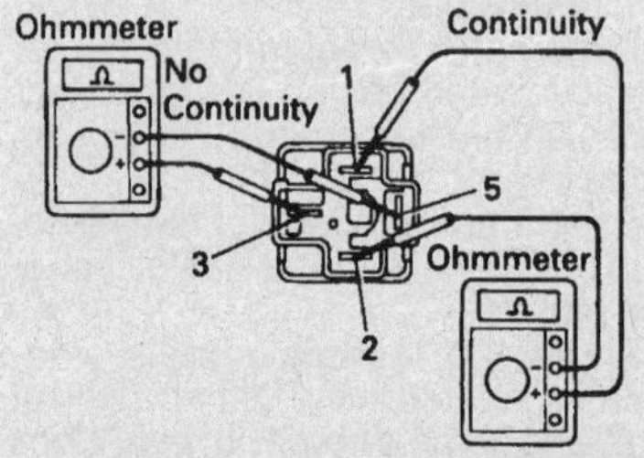
Ohmmeter
Continuity
No
Continuity
1
5
3
Ohmmeter
2

TY1129600021000X

Fig. 12 Starter relay inspection. Except MR2, Paseo, Previa & Tercel

STARTER SPECIFICATIONS

Year	Engine	Brush Spring Tension, Ounces	No Load Test		
			Amperes	Volts	RPM
1993	1FZ-FE⑥	62–84	90	11.5	3000
	1FZ-FE⑨	43–84	100	11.5	2500
	2JZ-GE, 2JZ-GTE⑥	62–84	90	11.5	3000
	2TZ-FE⑥	62–85	90	11.5	3000
	2TZ-FE⑧	62–85	90	11.5	3500
	3E-E③	56	50	11	5000
	3E-E④	62–85	90	11.5	3000
	3S-GTE⑦	62–85	90	11.5	3500
	3S-GTE②	62–85	90	11.5	3000
	3VZ-E④	62–85	90	11.5	3000
	3VZ-E⑥	62–85	90	11.5	3500
1993	3VZ-FE②	62–85	90	11.5	3000
	4A-FE④	62–85	90	11.5	3000
	4A-FE⑥	62–85	90	11.5	3500
	5E-FE⑤	56	90	11.5	3000
	5E-FE④	62–85	90	11.5	3000
	5S-FE⑦	62–85	90	11.5	3500
	5S-FE②	62–85	90	11.5	3000
	7A-FE⑥	62–84	90	11.5	3000
	22R-E④	62–85	90	11.5	3000
	22R-E⑥	62–85	90	11.5	3500
1994	1FZ-FE⑥	62–84	90	11.5	3000
	1FZ-FE⑨	43–84	100	11.5	2500
	1MZ-FE⑥	62–84	90	11.5	3000
	2JZ-GE, 2JZ-GTE⑥	62–84	90	11.5	3000
	2TZ-FE⑥	62–85	90	11.5	3000
	2TZ-FE⑧	62–85	90	11.5	3500
	3E-E③	56	50	11	5000
	3E-E④	62–85	90	11.5	3000
	3RZ-FE⑩	35–62	90	11.5	3000
	3RZ-FE⑪	43–84	100	11.5	2500
	3S-GTE⑦	62–85	90	11.5	3500
	3S-GTE②	62–85	90	11.5	3000
	3VZ-E④	62–85	90	11.5	3000
	3VZ-E⑥	62–85	90	11.5	3500
	3VZ-FE②	62–85	90	11.5	3000
	4A-FE④	62–85	90	11.5	3000
	4A-FE⑥	62–85	90	11.5	3500
	5E-FE⑤	56	90	11.5	3000
	5E-FE④	62–85	90	11.5	3000
	5S-FE⑦	62–85	90	11.5	3500
	5S-FE②	62–85	90	11.5	3000
	7A-FE⑥	62–84	90	11.5	3000
	22R-E④	62–85	90	11.5	3000
	22R-E⑥	62–85	90	11.5	3500
1995	1FZ-FE⑥	62–84	90	11.5	3000
	1FZ-FE⑨	43–84	100	11.5	2500
	1MZ-FE⑥	62–84	90	11.5	3000
	2JZ-GE, 2JZ-GTE⑥	62–84	90	11.5	3000
	2TZ-FE⑥	62–85	90	11.5	3000
	2TZ-FE⑧	62–85	90	11.5	3500

Continued

STARTER SPECIFICATIONS—Continued

Year	Engine	Brush Spring Tension, Ounces	No Load Test		
			Amperes	Volts	RPM
1995	2RZ-FE④	42–72	90	11.5	3000
	2RZ-FE⑥	34–60	90	11.5	3000
	2RZ-FE⑨	43–85	100	11.5	2500
	3RZ-FE⑩	34–60	90	11.5	3000
	3RZ-FE⑪	43–85	100	11.5	2500
	3S-GTE⑦	62–85	90	11.5	3500
	3S-GTE②	62–85	90	11.5	3000
	3VZ-E④	62–85	90	11.5	3000
	3VZ-E⑥	62–85	90	11.5	3500
	3VZ-FE②	62–85	90	11.5	3000
	4A-FE④	62–85	90	11.5	3000
	4A-FE⑥	62–85	90	11.5	3500
	5E-FE⑤	56	90	11.5	3000
	5E-FE④	62–85	90	11.5	3000
	5S-FE⑦	62–85	90	11.5	3500
	5S-FE②	62–85	90	11.5	3000
	5VZ-FE⑥	33–60	90	11.5	3000
	5VZ-FE①	43–85	100	11.5	2500
	7A-FE⑥	62–84	90	11.5	3000
	22R-E④	62–85	90	11.5	3000
	22R-E⑥	62–85	90	11.5	3500
1996	1FZ-FE⑥	62–84	90	11.5	3000
	1FZ-FE⑨	43–84	100	11.5	2500
	1MZ-FE⑥	62–84	90	11.5	3000
	2JZ-GE, 2JZ-GTE⑥	62–84	90	11.5	3000
	2TZ-FZE⑥	62–85	90	11.5	3000
	2TZ-FZE⑧	62–85	90	11.5	3500
	2RZ-FE④	42–72	90	11.5	3000
	2RZ-FE⑥	34–60	90	11.5	3000
	2RZ-FE⑨	43–85	100	11.5	2500
	3RZ-FE⑩	34–60	90	11.5	3000
	3RZ-FE①	43–85	100	11.5	2500
	3S-FE⑪	49–70	90	11.5	3000
	4A-FE④	62–85	90	11.5	3000
	4A-FE⑥	62–85	90	11.5	3500
	5E-FE⑤	56	90	11.5	3000
	5E-FE④	62–85	90	11.5	3000
	5S-FE⑦	62–85	90	11.5	3500
	5S-FE②	62–85	90	11.5	3000
	5VZ-FE⑥	33–60	90	11.5	3000
	5VZ-FE①	43–85	100	11.5	2500
	7A-FE⑥	64–85	90	11.5	3000

① — Reduction type starter, 1.8 kilowatt rating.
② — Compact reduction type starter, 1.4 kilowatt rating.
③ — Conventional starter, .8 kilowatt rating.
④ — Reduction type starter, 1.0 kilowatt rating.
⑤ — Planetary starter, .8 kilowatt rating.
⑥ — Reduction type starter, 1.4 kilowatt rating.
⑦ — Reduction type starter, 1.4 or 1.6 kilowatt rating.
⑧ — Reduction type starter, 1.6 kilowatt rating.
⑨ — Reduction type starter, 2.0 kilowatt rating.
⑩ — Reduction type starter, 1.2 kilowatt rating.
⑪ — Reduction type starter, 1.2 or 1.4 kilowatt rating.

Alternators

INDEX

	Page No.
Alternator Specifications	48-34
Description	48-33
Diagnosis & Testing	48-33
Regulator Test	48-33
System Test	48-33
Troubleshooting	48-33
Warning Light Does Not Go Out w/Engine Running	48-33
Warning Light Does Not Light w/Ignition On & Engine Off	48-33

DESCRIPTION

Refer to **Figs. 1 through 6,** for alternator exploded views.

TROUBLESHOOTING

WARNING LIGHT DOES NOT LIGHT W/IGNITION ON & ENGINE OFF

1. Blown fuse.
2. Lamp burned out.
3. Loose electrical connection.
4. Faulty main ignition relay.
5. Faulty IC regulator.

WARNING LIGHT DOES NOT GO OUT W/ENGINE RUNNING

1. Worn or loose drive belt.
2. Loose, corroded or worn battery cables.
3. Blow fuse.
4. Faulty alternator.
5. Faulty IC regulator.
6. Faulty wiring.

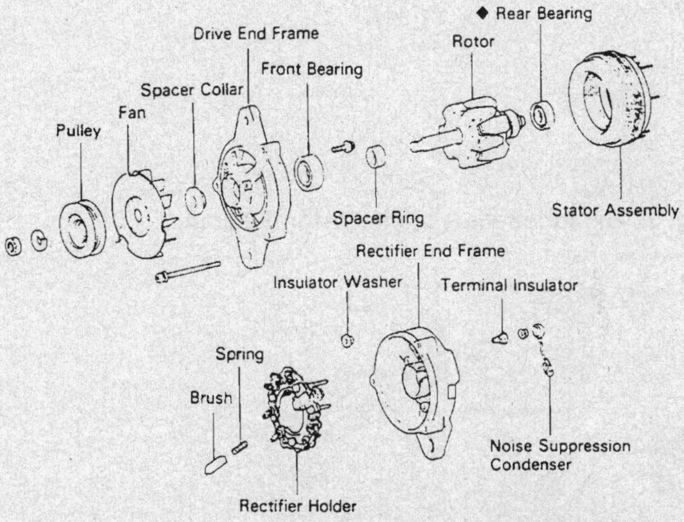

◆ Rear Bearing
Drive End Frame
Rotor
Front Bearing
Spacer Collar
Fan
Pulley
Spacer Ring
Stator Assembly
Rectifier End Frame
Insulator Washer
Terminal Insulator
Spring
Brush
Noise Suppression Condenser
Rectifier Holder
TY1129100011000X

Fig. 1 Exploded view of alternator. Less IC regulator

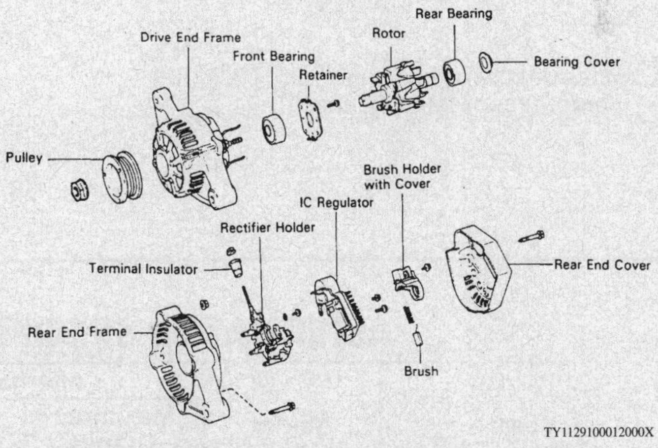

Rear Bearing
Drive End Frame
Rotor
Front Bearing
Retainer
Bearing Cover
Pulley
Brush Holder with Cover
IC Regulator
Rectifier Holder
Terminal Insulator
Rear End Cover
Rear End Frame
Brush
TY1129100012000X

Fig. 2 Exploded view of alternator. 50 amp

DIAGNOSIS & TESTING

SYSTEM TEST

1. Connect ammeter and voltmeter as follows:
   a. Disconnect wire from terminal B of alternator, then connect ammeter negative probe to the wire.
   b. Connect ammeter positive probe to B terminal of alternator.
   c. Connect voltmeter positive probe to B terminal and the negative probe to ground.
2. Start engine and allow to run at 2000 RPM , then check reading of ammeter and voltmeter. Ammeter should read less than 10 amps. At 77°F, voltmeter should read to specifications under "Alternator Specifications. "
3. If voltage reading is greater than specified voltage, replace IC regulator. If voltage reading is less than specified, check IC regulator and alternator as follows:
   a. With engine running and F terminal grounded, check voltage reading at B terminal.
   b. If voltage is greater than specified, replace IC regulator. If voltage reading is less than specified, check alternator.
4. With engine running at 2000 RPM , turn on high beam headlights and place heater in HI position.
5. Check ammeter reading. If reading is less than 30 amps, repair alternator.

REGULATOR TEST

1. Connect voltmeter and fast charger to battery.
2. Turn ignition switch On and slowly increase charge rate. Indicator lamp in vehicle will begin to dim when voltage setting is reached.
3. Observe voltmeter, light should dim at 13.5–16.9 volts.
4. If no voltage is present, replace voltage regulator.

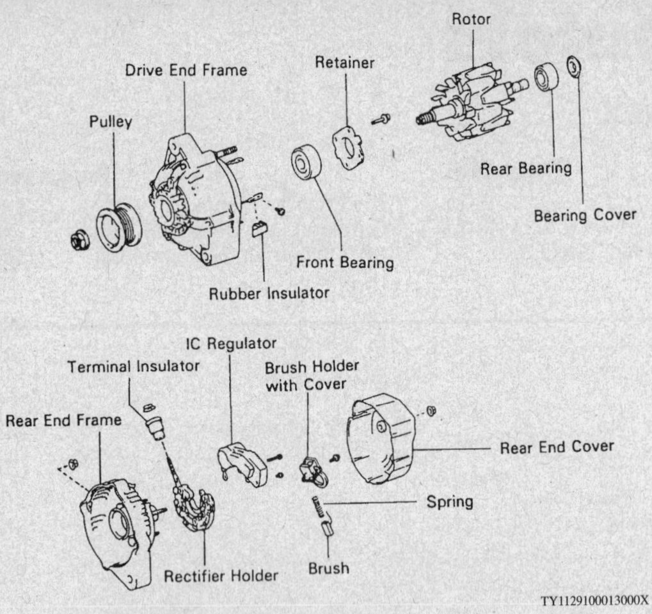
Rotor
Drive End Frame
Retainer
Pulley
Rear Bearing
Bearing Cover
Front Bearing
Rubber Insulator
IC Regulator
Terminal Insulator
Brush Holder with Cover
Rear End Frame
Rear End Cover
Spring
Rectifier Holder
Brush
TY1129100013000X

Fig. 3 Exploded view of alternator. 55 amp

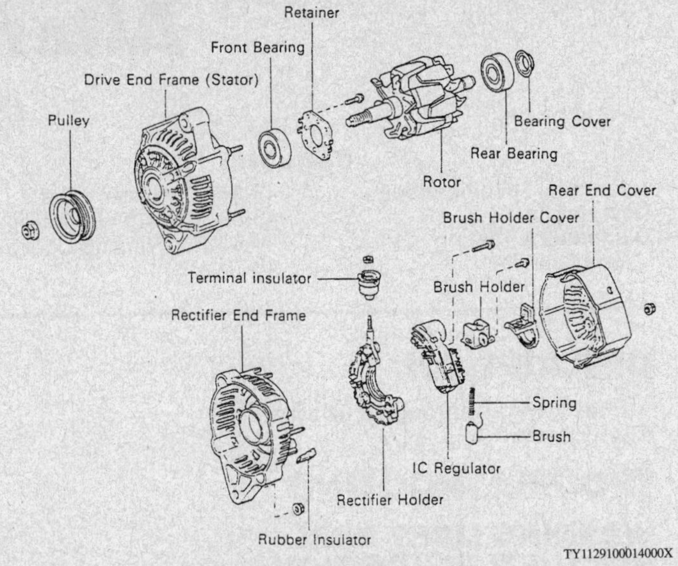
Retainer
Front Bearing
Drive End Frame (Stator)
Pulley
Bearing Cover
Rear Bearing
Rotor
Rear End Cover
Brush Holder Cover
Terminal insulator
Brush Holder
Rectifier End Frame
Spring
Brush
IC Regulator
Rectifier Holder
Rubber Insulator
TY1129100014000X

Fig. 4 Exploded view of alternator. 60 & 70 amp

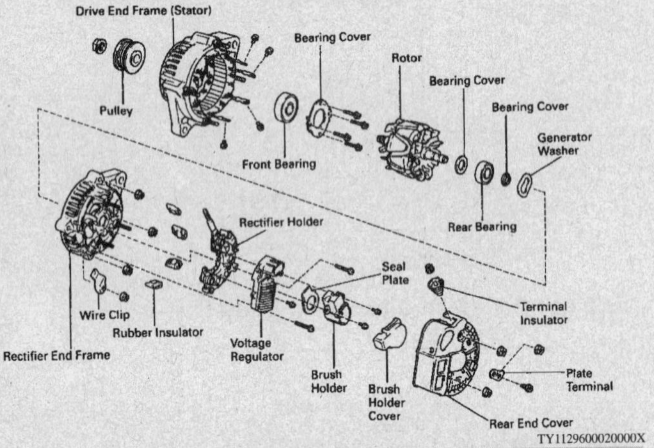
Drive End Frame (Stator)
Bearing Cover
Rotor
Bearing Cover
Pulley
Bearing Cover
Generator Washer
Front Bearing
Rectifier Holder
Rear Bearing
Seal Plate
Terminal Insulator
Wire Clip
Rubber Insulator
Rectifier End Frame
Voltage Regulator
Brush Holder
Brush Holder Cover
Plate Terminal
Rear End Cover
TY1129600020000X

Fig. 5 Exploded view of alternator. 80, 90 & 100 amp except Land Cruiser

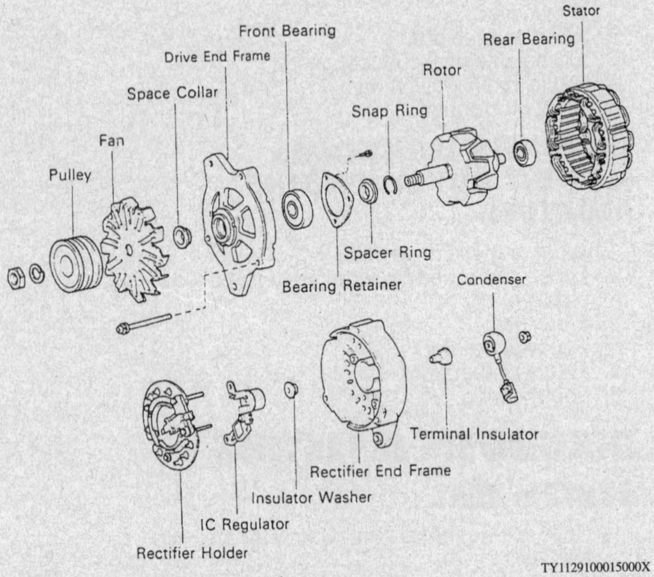
Stator
Front Bearing
Rear Bearing
Drive End Frame
Rotor
Space Collar
Snap Ring
Fan
Pulley
Spacer Ring
Bearing Retainer
Condenser
Terminal Insulator
Rectifier End Frame
Insulator Washer
IC Regulator
Rectifier Holder
TY1129100015000X

Fig. 6 Exploded view of alternator. Land Cruiser w/80 amp

ALTERNATOR SPECIFICATIONS

Year	Model	Alternator		Voltage Regulator Voltage
		Maximum Output Amps	Rotor Coil Resistance Ohms	
1993	1FZ-FE	80	2.9	②
	2JZ-GE	80	2.9	④
	2JZ-GTE	80	2.9	④
	2TZ-FE	70	2.9	③
	3E-E	60	2.9	③
	3E-E	70	2.9	③
	3S-GTE	70	2.9	③
	3S-GTE	80	2.9	③
	3VZ-E	60	2.9	③

Continued

ALTERNATOR SPECIFICATIONS—Continued

Year	Model	Alternator		Voltage Regulator Voltage
		Maximum Output Amps	Rotor Coil Resistance Ohms	
1993	3VZ-FE	80	2.9	①
	4A-FE⑦	70	2.9	③
	4A-FE⑤	80	2.9	③
	5E-FE	70	2.9	③
	5S-FE⑤	70	2.9	③
	5S-FE⑥	70	2.9	③
	5S-FE⑧	70	2.9	②
	5S-FE⑤	80	2.9	③
	5S-FE⑥	80	2.9	③
	5S-FE⑥	90	2.9	③
	7A-FE⑥	70	2.9	②
	22R-E	70	2.9	③
1994	1FZ-FE	80	2.9	②
	1MZ-FE	80	2.9	②
	2JZ-GE	80	2.9	④
	2JZ-GTE	80	2.9	④
	2TZ-FE	70	2.9	③
	2TZ-FZE	70	2.9	③
	3E-E	60	2.9	③
	3E-E	70	2.9	③
	3RZ-FE	60	2.9	②
	3S-GTE	70	2.9	③
	3S-GTE	80	2.9	③
	3VZ-E	60	2.9	③
	3VZ-FE	80	2.9	①
	4A-FE⑦	70	2.9	③
	4A-FE⑤	80	2.9	③
	5E-FE	70	2.9	③
	5S-FE⑤	70	2.9	③
	5S-FE⑥	70	2.9	③
	5S-FE⑧	70	2.9	②
	5S-FE⑤	80	2.9	③
	5S-FE⑥	80	2.9	③
	5S-FE⑥	90	2.9	③
	7A-FE⑥	70	2.9	②
	22R-E	70	2.9	③
1995	1FZ-FE	80	2.9	②
	1MZ-FE	80	2.9	②
	2JZ-GE	80	2.9	④
	2JZ-GTE	80	2.9	④
	2RZ-FE	60	2.9	②
	2TZ-FE	70	2.9	③
	2TZ-FZE	70	2.9	③
	3E-E	60	2.9	③
	3E-E	70	2.9	③
	3RZ-FE	60	2.9	②
	3S-GTE	70	2.9	③
	3S-GTE	80	2.9	③
	3VZ-E	60	2.9	③
	3VZ-FE	80	2.9	①
	4A-FE⑦	70	2.9	③
	4A-FE⑤	80	2.9	③
	5E-FE	70	2.9	③
	5S-FE⑤	70	2.9	③

Continued

ALTERNATOR SPECIFICATIONS—Continued

Year	Model	Alternator		Voltage Regulator Voltage
		Maximum Output Amps	Rotor Coil Resistance Ohms	
1995	5S-FE⑥	70	2.9	③
	5S-FE⑧	70	2.9	②
	5S-FE⑤	80	2.9	③
	5S-FE⑥	80	2.9	③
	5S-FE⑥	90	2.9	③
	5VZ-FE	60	2.9	③
	7A-FE⑥	70	2.9	②
	22R-E	70	2.9	③
1996	1FZ-FE	80	2.9	②
	1MZ-FE	80	2.9	②
	2JZ-GE	80	2.9	④
	2JZ-GTE	80	2.9	④
	2RZ-FE	60	2.9	②
	2TZ-FZE	70	2.9	③
	3RZ-FE	60	2.9	②
	3S-GTE	70	2.9	③
	3S-GTE	80	2.9	③
	3S-FE	80	2.9	②
	4A-FE⑦	70	2.9	③
	4A-FE⑤	80	2.9	③
	5E-FE	70	2.9	③
	5S-FE⑤	70	2.9	③
	5S-FE⑥	70	2.9	③
	5S-FE⑧	70	2.9	②
	5S-FE⑤	80	2.9	③
	5S-FE⑥	80	2.9	③
	5S-FE⑥	90	2.9	③
	5VZ-FE	60	2.9	③
	7A-FE⑥	70	2.9	②

① — 14–14.3 volts at 77°F, 13.5–14.3 volts at 239°F.

② — 14–15 volts at 77°F, 13.5–14.3 volts at 239°F.

③ — 13.9–15.1 volts at 77°F, 13.5–14.3 volts at 239°F.

④ — 13.6–14.8 volts at 77°F, 13.2–14.0 volts at 239°F.

⑤ — Celica.

⑥ — MR2.

⑦ — Corolla.

⑧ — Camry.

Speed Control Systems

INDEX

	Page No.
System Diagnosis & Testing	48-37
Circuit Testing	48-37
Diagnostic Trouble Codes	48-37
Toyota Diagnostic Tester	48-37

No.	Operation Method	CRUISE MAIN Indicator Light Blinking Pattern	Diagnosis
1	Turn SET/COAST switch ON.	Light ON OFF 0.25 0.25	SET/COAST switch circuit is normal.
2	Turn RES/ACC switch ON.	Light ON OFF	RES/ACC switch circuit is normal.
3	Turn CANCEL switch ON.	Light ON OFF switch OFF switch ON	CANCEL switch circuit is normal.
4	Turn stop light switch ON. (Depress brake pedal)		Stop light switch circuit is normal.
5	Turn parking brake switch ON.		Parking brake switch circuit is normal.
6	Turn park/neutral position switch ON. (Shift to N or P position.)		Park/Neutral Position switch circuit is normal.
7	Turn clutch start switch ON. (Depress clutch pedal.)		Clutch switch circuit is normal.
8	Drive at 40 km/h (25 mph) or higher.	Light ON OFF	Speed sensor is normal.
9	Drive at 40 km/h (25 mph) or below.	Light ON OFF	

TY1109400002000X

Fig. 1 Type A diagnostic codes. Camry & Paseo

No.	Operation Method	CRUISE MAIN Indicator Light Blinking Pattern	Diagnosis
1	Turn SET/COAST switch ON.	Light ON BE4006 OFF 0.25 0.25	SET/COAST switch circuit is normal.
2	Turn RES/ACC switch ON.	Light ON BE4006 OFF	RES/ACC switch circuit is normal.
3	Turn CANCEL switch ON.	Light ON OFF Switch OFF Switch ON BE4006	CANCEL switch circuit is normal.
	Turn stop light switch ON. (Depress brake pedal)		Stop light switch circuit is normal.
	Turn parking brake switch ON. (Release parking brake)		Parking brake switch circuit is normal.
	Turn neutral start switch ON. (Shift to N or P range)		Park/Neutral Position Switch is normal.
4	Drive at 40 km/h (25 mph) or higher.	Light ON BE4006 OFF	Vehicle speed sensor is normal.
	Drive at 40 km/h (25 mph) or below.	Light ON BE4006 OFF	

TY1109300005000X

Fig. 2 Type A diagnostic codes. Avalon & Corolla

SYSTEM DIAGNOSIS & TESTING

DIAGNOSTIC TROUBLE CODES

INPUT SIGNAL CHECK (TYPE A CODES)

1. On models except T100, proceed as follows:
   a. Place ignition switch to On position.
   b. Push set/coast switch to on and hold it there.
   c. Place main switch in on position, then push set/coast switch to off.
   d. Read diagnostic code by watching main switch indicator flash.
   e. Refer to **Figs. 1 through 8,** for description of codes.
2. On T100 models, proceed as follows:
   a. Using tool No. 09843-18020, or equivalent, connect Data Link Connector (DLC) check terminals Tc and E1, **Fig. 9.**
   b. Read trouble code on cruise main indicator lamp, **Fig. 6.**
   c. After reading codes, disconnect terminals Tc and E1, then turn off display.

DTC (TYPE B CODES)

Except Avalon, Camry, Celica, RAV4 & Supra

1. Drive vehicle at a speed of less then 10 mph, then press set/coast switch three time in two seconds. **Inspect system for codes with ignition and main switches in on position. Loss of system power will cause codes to be cleared from computers memory.**
2. **On MR2, Paseo, Pickup, Tacoma, T100 and 4Runner,** with vehicle stopped, with suitable jumper wire, connect check terminals 3 and 11 of data link connector (DLC).
3. **On Land Cruiser and Previa models,** with vehicle stopped, with suitable jumper wire, connect check terminals 3 and 15.
4. **On all models,** read the codes by watching the main switch indicator flash.
5. Refer to **Figs. 10 through 18,** for description of codes.

Avalon, Camry & Supra

1. Turn ignition switch On.
2. Using tool No. 09843-18020, or equivalent, connect Data Link Connector (Toyota Diagnostic Communication Link (TDCL)) check terminals Tc and E1, **Fig. 19.**
3. Read trouble code on cruise main indicator lamp, **Fig. 20.**
4. Refer to **Figs. 10, 12 and 21,** for diagnostic trouble code interpretation.
5. After reading codes, disconnect terminals Tc and E1, then turn off display.

Celica & RAV4

1. Using tool No. 09843-18020, or equivalent, connect Data Link Connector (DLC) check terminals Tc and E1, **Figs. 9 and 22.**
2. Read trouble code on cruise main indicator lamp, **Figs. 10 and 23.**
3. After reading codes, disconnect terminals Tc and E1, then turn off display.

CLEARING CODES

1. After repairs are complete, with ignition switch Off, remove DOME or ECU-B fuse for 10 or more seconds.
2. Install fuse, ensure normal code is output.

TOYOTA DIAGNOSTIC TESTER

Diagnostic trouble codes can be retrieved using the Toyota Hand-Held Diagnostic Tester. The tester can be hooked up directly to the data link connector (DLC), **Fig. 24.** ECU data may then be monitored by following prompts on the tester screen.

CIRCUIT TESTING

Refer to **Figs. 25 through 34,** for testing of cruise control system circuits.

No.	Operation Method	CRUISE MAIN Indicator Light Blinking Pattern	Diagnosis
1	Turn SET/COAST switch ON.	Light ON / OFF 0.25 0.25	SET COAST switch circuit is normal.
2	Turn RES/ACC switch ON.	Light ON / OFF	RES ACC switch circuit is normal.
3	Turn CANCEL switch ON.	Light ON Switch OFF / OFF Switch ON	CANCEL switch circuit is normal.
4	Turn stop light switch ON. (Depress brake pedal)		Stop light switch circuit is normal.
5	Turn parking brake switch ON.		Parking brake switch circuit is normal.
6	Turn park/neutral position switch ON. (Shift to N or P range.)		Park/Neutral position switch circuit is normal.
7	Drive at 40 km/h (25 mph) or higher.	Light ON / OFF	No.1 Vehicle speed sensor is normal.
8	Drive at 40 km/h (25 mph) or below.	Light ON / OFF	

TY1109300008000X

Fig. 3 Type A diagnostic codes. Land Cruiser

No.	Conditions	Indication code	Diagnosis
1	Turn the control switch to SET/COAST position.	ON / OFF 1S 0.25S 0.25S	SET/COAST circuit is normal.
2	Turn the control switch to RES/ACC position.	ON / OFF	RES/ACC circuit is normal.
3	Each cancel switch is turned ON. • Control switch (to CANCEL) • Stop light switch • Parking brake switch • Clutch Switch (M/T) • Neutral Start Switch (A/T)	ON / OFF	Each cancel switch is normal.
4	Drive at approx. 40 km/h (25 mph) or below.	ON / OFF	Speed sensor circuit is normal.
	Drive at approx. 40 km/h (25 mph) or over	ON / OFF	Speed sensor circuit is normal.

TY1109100009000X

Fig. 5 Type A diagnostic codes. MR2

No.	Conditions	Indication code	Diagnosis
1	Turn the control switch to SET/COAST position	ON 1S 0.25S 0.25S / OFF	SET/COAST circuit is normal.
2	Turn the control switch to RES/ACC position.	ON / OFF	RES/ACC circuit is normal.
3	Each cancel switch is turned ON. • Control switch (to CANCEL) • Stop light switch • Parking brake switch • Neutral start switch (to N or P range)	ON / OFF	Each cancel switch is normal.
4	Drive approx. 40 km/h (25 mph) or below.	ON / OFF	Speed sensor circuit is normal.
5	Drive approx. 40 km/h (25 mph) or over. (w/o ECT)	ON / OFF	Speed sensor (in meter) circuit is normal.

TY1109100011000X

Fig. 7 Type A diagnostic codes. Previa

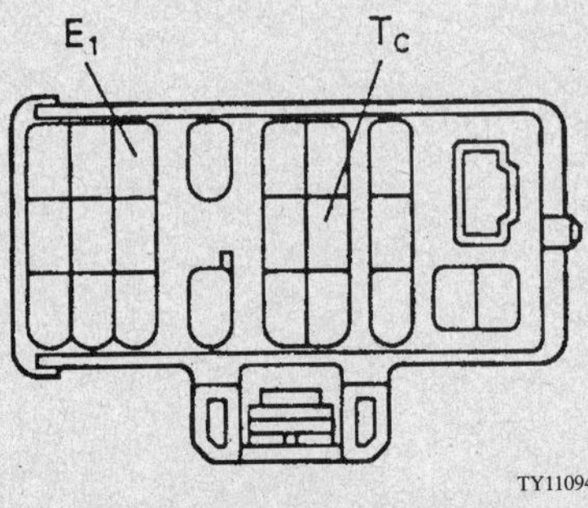
E_1
T_C

TY1109400018000X

Fig. 9 Data link connector. T100

No.	Operation Method	CRUISE MAIN Indicator Light Blinking Pattern	Diagnosis
1	Turn SET/COAST switch ON.	Light ON / OFF 0.25 1 sec. 0.25	SET/COAST switch circuit is normal.
2	Turn RES/ACC switch ON.	Light ON / OFF	RES/ACC switch circuit is normal.
3	Turn CANCEL switch ON.	Light ON Switch OFF / OFF Switch ON	CANCEL switch circuit is normal.
	Turn stop light switch ON. (Depress brake pedal)		Stop light switch circuit is normal.
	Turn park/neutral position switch OFF. (Shift to except D position)	Light ON Switch ON / OFF Switch OFF	Park/neutral position switch circuit is normal.
	Turn clutch switch OFF. (Depress clutch pedal)		Clutch switch circuit is normal.
4	Drive at about 40 km/h (25 mph) or higher.	Light ON / OFF	Vehicle speed sensor is normal.
	Drive at about 40 km/h (25 mph) or below.	Light ON / OFF	

TY1109600071000X

Fig. 4 Type A diagnostic codes. Celica & RAV4

No.	Conditions	Indication code	Diagnosis
1	Push the speed control switch SET/COAST on.	ON / OFF 1S 0.25S 0.25S	SET/COAST circuit is normal.
2	Push the speed control switch RESUME/ACCEL on.	ON / OFF	RESUME/ACCEL circuit is normal.
3	Vacuum switch is turned ON.	ON / OFF	Vacuum switch circuit is normal.
4	Each cancel switch turned ON. • Speed control switch (to CANCEL) • Stop light switch • Neutral start switch (to N or P range) • Clutch switch • Parking brake switch	ON / OFF	Each cancel switch is normal.
5	Drive approx. 40 km/h (25 mph) or over.	ON / OFF	Speed sensor circuit is normal.
6	Drive approx. 40 km/h (25 mph) or below.	ON / OFF	Speed sensor circuit is normal.

TY1109100010000X

Fig. 6 Type A diagnostic codes. Pickup, T100 & 4Runner

No.	Operation Method	CRUISE MAIN Indicator Light Blinking Pattern	Diagnosis
1	Turn SET/COAST switch ON.	Light ON / OFF 0.25 1 sec. 0.25	SET/COAST switch circuit is normal.
2	Turn RES/ACC switch ON.	Light ON / OFF	RES/ACC switch circuit is normal.
3	Turn CANCEL switch ON.	Light ON Switch OFF / OFF Switch ON	CANCEL switch circuit is normal.
	Turn stop light switch ON. (Depress brake pedal)		Stop light switch circuit is normal.
	Turn parking brake switch ON. (Pull up the parking brake lever).		Parking brake switch circuit is normal.
	Turn neutral start swtich OFF. (Shift to EXCEPT D RANGE)	ON Switch ON / OFF Switch OFF	Neutral start switch circuit is normal.
	Turn clutch switch OFF. (Depress clutch pedal)		Clutch switch circuit is normal.
4	Drive at 40 km/h (25 mph) or higher.	Light ON / OFF	Speed sensor is normal.
	Drive at 40 km/h (25 mph) or below.	Light ON / OFF	

TY1109300013000X

Fig. 8 Type A diagnostic codes. Supra & Tacoma

DTC	CRUISE MAIN Indicator Light Blinking Pattern	Diagnosis
-	ON / OFF	Normal
11	ON / OFF	• Overcurrent (short) in motor circuit.
12	ON / OFF	• Overcurrent (short) in magnetic clutch circuit. • Open in magnet clutch circuit for 0.8 sec.
13	ON / OFF	• Position sensor detects abnormal voltage.
14	ON / OFF	• Open in actuator motor circuit. • Position sensor signal value does not change when the motor operates.
21	ON / OFF	• Speed signal is not input to the ECU while cruise control is set.
*23	ON / OFF	• Actual vehicle speed has dropped by 16 km/h (10 mph) or more below the set speed. • Vehicle speed sensor pulse is abnormal.
32	ON / OFF	• Short in control switch circuit.
34	ON / OFF	• Voltage abnormality in control switch.
41	ON / OFF	• Duty ratio of 100% out put to motor acceleration side.
42	ON / OFF	• Source voltage drop.

HINT: When two or more codes are indicated, the lowest numbered code will be displayed first.
(*) When the vehicle speed is reduced on uphill roads, the speed can be set again and driving continued. (This is not a malfunction.)

TY1109400019000X

Fig. 10 Type B diagnostic codes. Avalon, Celica, Tacoma & 1994–95 MR2

	Indication Code	Diagnosis
	ON / OFF (0.25S, 0.25S)	Normal.
11	ON / OFF (0.5S, 1.5S, 4S)	Actuator circuit is abnormal.
21	ON / OFF (0.5S, 1.5S)	Speed sensor signal circuit is abnormal.
23	ON / OFF	* Vehicle speed decreases to 16 km/h (10 mph) or more below set speed.
31	ON / OFF	Resume/accel switch circuit is abnormal

*: If the set speed can be maintained when the speed control switch is again set at SET/COAST, there is no malfunction.

TY1109100021000X

Fig. 12 Type B diagnostic codes. Supra

	Indication code	Diagnosis
	0.25S 0.25S	Normal
11	4S 1.5S 0.5S	Excessive current flowed to motor or safety magnetic clutch drive circuit.
12	1.5S 0.5S	Open circuit in safety magnetic clutch circuit.
13		• Position sensor circuit abnormal. • Open circuit in motor.
21		Vehicle speed signal not sent for 140 msec. or longer
22		(A/T) Speed sensor (in ECT) circuit is abnormal.
23		* Vehicle speed has decreased by 16 km/h (10 mph) or more from the set speed during cruising.
31		RESUME/ACCEL switch is ON always when MAIN switch is pushed ON.
32		Short circuit in control switch circuit.
33		SET/COAST switch signal and RES/ACC switch signal turned on simultaneously.
34		Control switch does not turn off before switching.
41		ECU malfunction.

* If the set speed can be maintained when the speed control switch is again set at SET/COAST, there is no malfunction.

TY1109100028000X

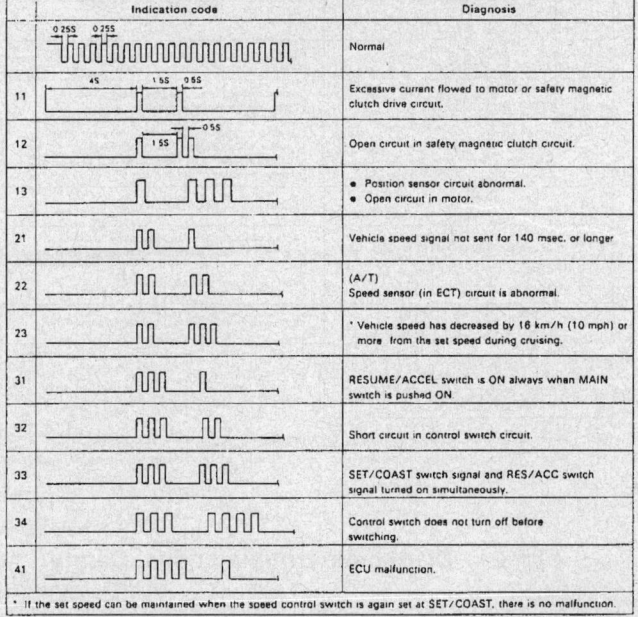

Fig. 14 Type B diagnostic codes. 1993 MR2

	Indication code	Diagnosis
	ON / OFF (0.25S, 0.25S)	Normal.
11	ON / OFF (0.5S, 1.5S, 4S)	Actuator circuit is abnormal.
21	ON / OFF (0.5S, 1.5S)	Speed sensor signal circuit is abnormal.
23	ON / OFF	*Vehicle speed decreases to 16 km/h (10 mph) or more below set speed.
31	ON / OFF	Resume/accel switch circuit is abnormal.
33	ON / OFF	Resume/accel switch and set/coast switch circuit is abnormal.

*If the set speed can be maintained when the speed control switch is again set at SET COAST, there is no malfunction.

TY1109100020000X

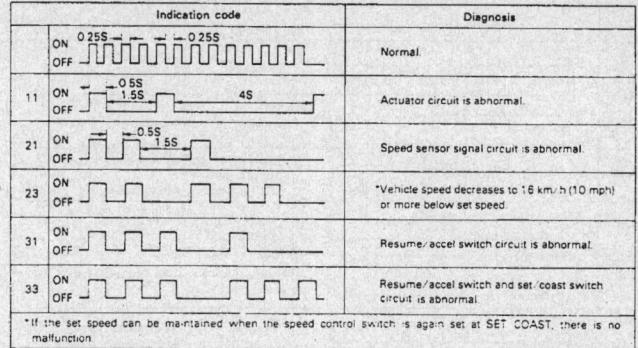

Fig. 11 Type B diagnostic codes. Corolla

Code No.	CRUISE MAIN Indicator Light Blinking Pattern	Diagnosis
–	ON / OFF	Normal
11	ON / OFF	• Duty ratio of 100 % output to motor acceleration side. • Overcurrent (short) in motor circuit.
12	ON / OFF	• Overcurrent (short) in magnet clutch circuit. • Open in magnet clutch circuit for 0.8 sec.
13	ON / OFF	• Open in actuator motor circuit. • Position sensor detects abnormal voltage. • Position sensor signal value does not change when the motor operates.
21	ON / OFF	• Speed signal is not input to the ECU while cruise control is set.
*23	ON / OFF	• Actual vehicle speed has dropped by 16 km/h (10 mph) or more below the set speed.
32	ON / OFF	• Short in control switch circuit.
34	ON / OFF	• Voltage abnormality in control switch.
41	ON / OFF	• When 41 code is indicated, replace the cruise control ECU.

TY1109100027000X

Fig. 13 Type B diagnostic codes. Land Cruiser

	Indication code	Diagnosis
	0.25S 0.25S	Normal
11	4S 1.5S 0.5S	Excessive current flowed to motor or motor output is 100 % duty.
12	1.5S 0.5S	• Open circuit in safety magnetic clutch circuit. • Overcurrent output by magnetic clutch.
13		• Position sensor circuit abnormal. • Open circuit in motor.
21		Vehicle speed signal not sent for 140 msec. or longer
23		* Vehicle speed has decreased by 16 km/h (10 mph) or more from the set speed during cruising.
32		Short circuit in control switch circuit.
34		Control switch does not turn off before switching.
When 41 code is indicated, replace the cruise control ECU.		
41		ECU malfunction.

* If the set speed can be maintained when the speed control switch is again set at SET/COAST, there is no malfunction.

HINT:
- Indication codes appear in order from No. 11.
- If there is no indication code, perform troubleshooting and inspection.

TY1109100029000X

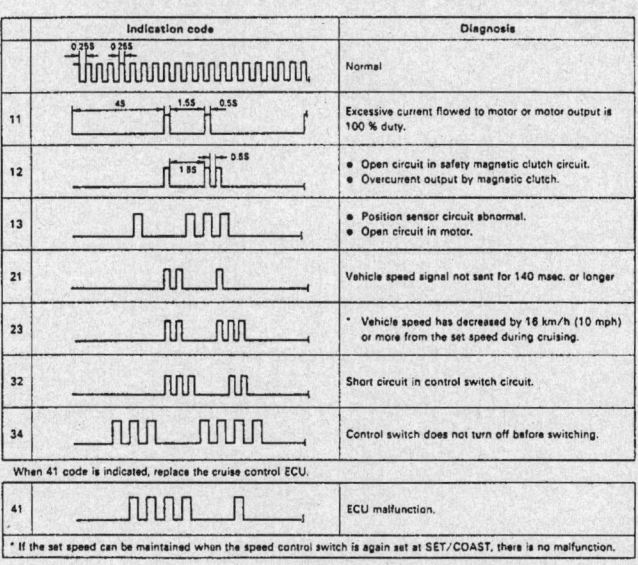

Fig. 15 Type B diagnostic codes. Paseo

	Indication code	Diagnosis
	0.25S 0.25S	Normal
11	4S 1.5S 0.5S	Excessive current flowed to motor drive circuit.
12	1.5S 0.5S	• Excessive current flowed to magnetic clutch drive circuit. • Open circuit magnetic clutch circuit.
13		• Position sensor circuit abnormal. • Open circuit in motor.
21		Vehicle speed signal not sent for 140 msec. or longer
23		Vehicle speed has decreased by 16 km/h (10 mph) or more from the set speed during cruising.
32		Short circuit in control switch circuit.
34		Control switch does not turn off before switching
41		ECU malfunction.

• If the set speed can be maintained when the speed control switch is again set at SET/COAST, there is no malfunction.

HINT:
- Indication codes appear in order from No.11.
- If there is no indication code, perform troubleshooting and inspection.

TY1109200031000X

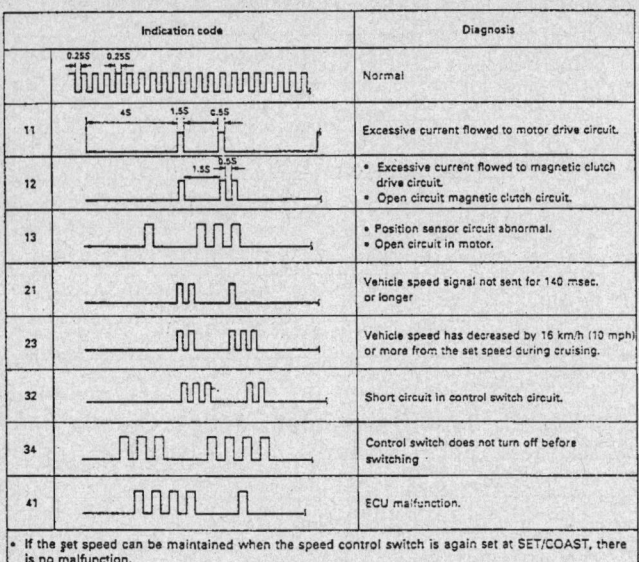

Fig. 16 Type B diagnostic codes. Previa

	Indication code	Diagnosis
	0.25S 0.25S	Normal.
11	4S 1.5S 0.5S	Control valve circuit of actuator is abnormal.
12	1.5S 0.5S	Release valve circuit of actuator is abnormal.
* 21		Speed sensor circuit is abnormal.
23		*Vehicle speed has decreased by 16 km/h (10 mph) or more from the set speed.
32		SET/COAST switch signal and RESUME/ACCEL switch signal stay on simultaneously.
34		Control switch does not turn off before switching.

* If the set speed can be maintained when the speed control switch is again set at SET/COAST, there is no malfunction.

TY1109300033000X

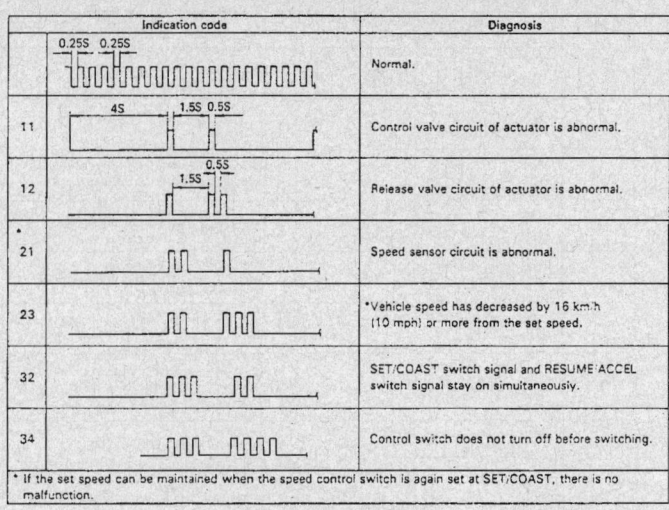

Fig. 17 Type B diagnostic codes. Pickup & 4Runner

Code No.	CRUISE MAIN Indicator Light Blinking Pattern	Diagnosis
–	ON OFF (BE3931)	Normal
11	ON OFF (BE3931)	• Duty ratio of 100% output to motor acceleration side. • Overcurrent (short) in motor circuit.
12	ON OFF (BE3931)	• Overcurrent (short) in magnet clutch circuit. • Open in magnet clutch circuit.
13	ON OFF (BE3931)	• Open in actuator motor circuit. • Position sensor detects abnormal voltage. • Position sensor signal value does not change when the motor operates.
21	ON OFF (BE3932)	• Speed signal is not input to the Cruise Control ECU.
*23	ON OFF (BE3932)	• Actual vehicle speed has dropped by 16 km/h (10 mph)or more below the set speed during crusing.
32	ON OFF (BE3933)	• Short in control switch circuit.
34	ON OFF (BE3933)	• Voltage abnormality in control switch circuit.
41	ON OFF (BE4345)	• When 41 code is indicated, replace the cruise control ECU.

TY1109100034000X

Fig. 18 Type B diagnostic codes. T100

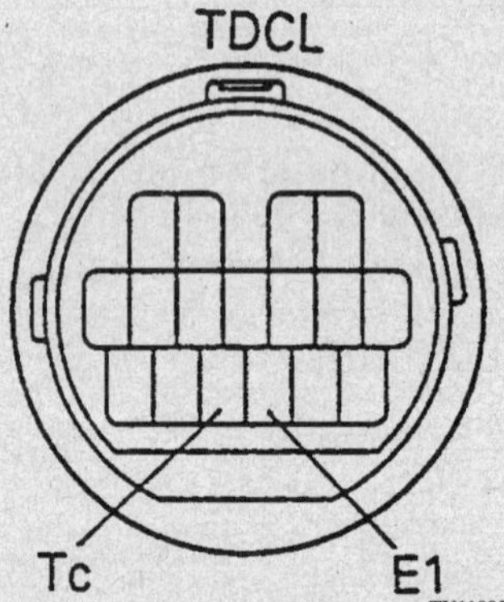
TDCL
Tc
E1

TY1109200035000X

Fig. 19 Data link connector. Avalon, Camry & Supra

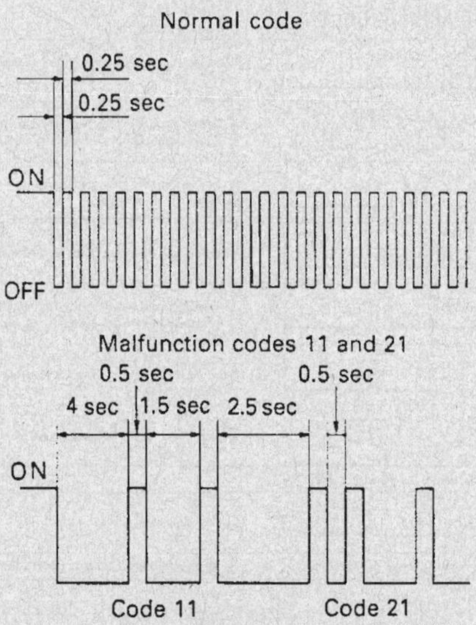
Normal code
0.25 sec
0.25 sec
ON
OFF
Malfunction codes 11 and 21
0.5 sec
0.5 sec
4 sec
1.5 sec
2.5 sec
ON
Code 11
Code 21

TY1109200036000X

Fig. 20 Diagnostic trouble code output. Camry

Code No.	CRUISE MAIN Indicator Light Blinking Pattern	Diagnosis
–	ON OFF	Normal
11	ON OFF	• Continuous output to motor acceleration side. • Overcurrent (short) in motor circuit.
12	ON OFF	• Overcurrent (short) in magnet clutch circuit. • Open in magnet clutch circuit.
13	ON OFF	• Open in actuator motor circuit. • Position sensor detects abnormal voltage. • Position sensor signal value does not change when the motor operates.
21	ON OFF	• Speed signal is not input to the ECU.
*23	ON OFF	• Actual vehicle speed has dropped by 16 km/h (10 mph) or more below the set speed during crusing.
32	ON OFF	• Short in control switch circuit.
34	ON OFF	• Voltage abnormality in control switch circuit.

When 41 code is indicated, replace the cruise control ECU.

41	ON OFF	

HINT: When two or more codes are indicated, the lowest numbered code will be displayed first.
(*) When the vehicle speed is reduced on uphill roads, the speed can be set again and driving continued. (This is not a malfunction.)

TY1109200037000X

Fig. 21 Diagnostic trouble codes. Camry

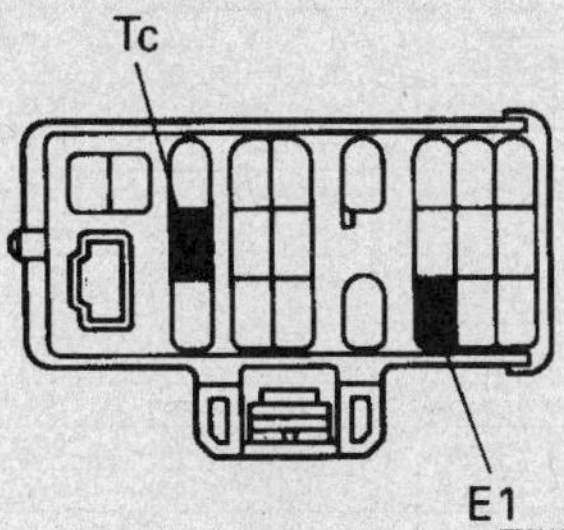
Tc
E1

TY1109600073000X

Fig. 22 Data link connector. RAV4

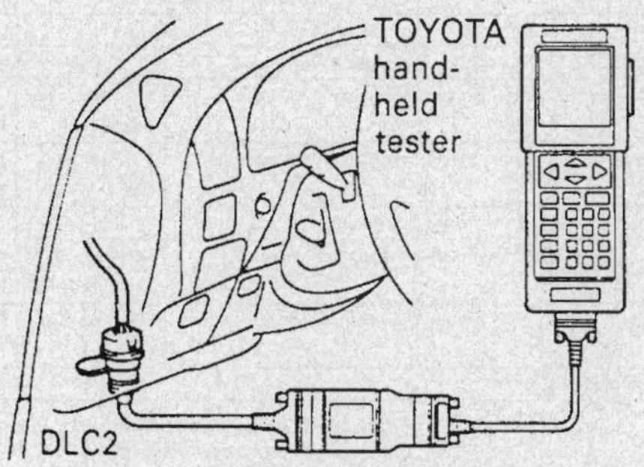
TOYOTA hand-held tester
DLC2

TY1109100038000X

Fig. 24 Hand-Held Tester

Connection or measure item	Check for	Tester connection	Condition	Specified value
Stop Fuse	Voltage	16 – Body ground	——	Battery voltage
Stop Light Switch	Voltage	15 – Body ground	Brake pedal depressed	Battery voltage
			Brake pedal released	No voltage
Stop Light Switch and Release Valve	Resistance	2 – 14	Brake pedal released	Approx. 68 Ω
Control Valve	Resistance	4 – 14	——	Approx. 30 Ω
Control Switch	Voltage	10 – Body ground	Turn ignition switch and main switch on	Battery voltage
			Turn ignition switch and main switch off	No voltage
Control Switch (indicator circuit)	Voltage	3 – Body ground	Turn ignition switch and main switch on	Battery voltage
			Turn ignition switch and main switch off	No voltage
Control Switch (set/coast)	Continuity	5 – Body ground	Turn set/coast switch on	Continuity
			Turn set/coast switch off	No continuity
Control Switch (resume/accel)	Continuity	17 – Body ground	Turn resume/accel switch on	Continuity
			Turn resume/accel switch off	No continuity
Speed Sensor	Continuity	7 – Body ground	Vehicle moving slowly	1 pulse each 40 cm (15.75 in.)
Clutch Switch (M/T) or Neutral Start Switch (A/T)	Continuity	11 – Body ground	Clutch pedal depressed or shifted into "N" range	Continuity
			Clutch pedal released or shifted into only range except "N" and "P" range	No continuity
Parking Brake Switch	Voltage	12 – Body ground	Remove CHARGE fuse and ignition switch turned on with parking brake lever pulled up	No voltage
			Remove CHARGE fuse and ignition switch turned on with parking brake lever released	Battery voltage
Vacuum Switch	Continuity	9 – Body ground	Apply vacuum approx. 170 mmHg (6.69 in.Hg, 22.7 kPa)	No continuity
			No vacuum	Continuity
Vacuum Pump	Continuity	1 – Body ground	——	Continuity
Body Ground	Continuity	13 – Body ground	——	Continuity

TY1109100059000X

Fig. 25 System circuit test. Avalon, Camry & Corolla

DTC No.	Detection Item	Trouble Area
–	• Normal	–
11	• Actuator Motor Circuit	• Cruise control actuator motor • Harness or connector between actuator motor and ECU • ECU
12	• Actuator Magnetic Clutch Circuit	• Cruise control actuator magnetic clutch • Harness or connector between ECU and magnetic clutch, magnetic clutch and body ground • ECU • STOP Fuse
13	• Actuator Position Sensor Circuit	• Cruise control actuator position sensor • Harness or connector between actuator position sensor and ECU • ECU
14	• Actuator Motor Circuit • Actuator Position Sensor Circuit	• Cruise control actuator motor • Cruise control actuator position sensor • Harness or connector between actuator position sensor and body ground • Harness or connector between actuator motor and ECU • ECU
*21	• Vehicle Speed Sensor Circuit	• Vehicle speed sensor • Combination meter • Harness or connector between vehicle speed sensor and combination meter, combination meter and ECU • ECU
32	• Control Switch Circuit (Cruise Control Switch)	• Cruise control switch • Harness and connector between control switch and ECU • ECU
41	• Cruise Control ECU	• ECU
42	• Source Voltage Drop	• Battery

TY1109600072000X

Fig. 23 Type B diagnostic trouble codes. RAV4

Check for	Measured item	Tester connection	Condition		Specified value
Continuity	Neutral start switch (A/T)	A-4 – ground	Shift lever position	N or P	Continuity
				L, 2, D or R	No continuity
	Clutch switch (M/T)	A-4 – ground	Clutch pedal position	released	No continuity
				depressed	Continuity
	Parking brake switch	A-5 – ground	Parking brake lever position	released	No continuity
				pulled	Continuity
	Control switch	A-8 – ground	Main switch position	OFF	No continuity
				ON	Continuity
	Ground connection	A-9 – ground	Constant		Continuity
	Water temp. switch and O/D main switch	B-2 – ground	Engine coolant temp. is Cold		Continuity
			Engine coolant temp. is Hot		
			O/D main switch position	OFF	No continuity
				ON	Continuity
	Actuator (motor)	B-4 – B-10	Actuator arm position	max. OPEN	(B-4 → B-10) Continuity
				max. CLOSE	(B-10 → B-4) Continuity
				any position except above position	(B-4 ↔ B-10) Continuity
	TDCL circuit	B-7 – ground	Constant		Continuity
			Terminals Tc and E1 connected		Continuity
	Throttle position sensor (IDL)	B-9 – ground	Acceleration pedal position	released	Continuity
				depressed	No continuity
Resistance	Actuator (position sensor)	A-10 – A-12	Constant		Approx. 2 kΩ
		A-10 – A-11	Actuator arm turned		Resistance change even
	ECT No. 2 solenoid valve	B-1 – ground	Constant		Approx. 13 Ω
	Actuator (Safety magnetic clutch)	B-3 – ground	Brake pedal position	released	Approx. 38.5 Ω
				depressed	No continuity
	Control switch	B-8 – ground	Control switch position	OFF	No continuity
				RES/ACC	Approx. 68 Ω
				SET/COAST	Approx. 198 Ω
				CANCEL	Approx. 418 Ω
Voltage	Power source	A-1 – ground	Ignition switch position	LOCK or ACC	No voltage
				ON	Battery voltage
	STOP fuse	A-2 – ground	Constant		Battery voltage
	Stop light	A-3 – ground	Brake pedal position	released	No voltage
				depressed	Battery voltage
	Speed sensor	A-7 – ground	With ignition switch ON, speedometer shaft or speed sensor shaft turned.		Voltage changes repeatedly

TY1109100060000X

Fig. 26 System circuit test. Celica w/motor actuator

Check for	Measured item	Tester connection	Condition		Specified value
Continuity	TDCL circuit	1 - ground	Constant		No continuity
			Terminal Tc and E1 connected		Continuity
	Control switch (main switch)	6 - ground	Main switch position	OFF	No continuity
				ON	Continuity
	Water temp. switch and O/D main switch	7 - ground	Engine coolant is Cold		Continuity
			Engine coolant is Hot		
			O/D main switch position	OFF	No continuity
				ON	Continuity
	Neutral start switch (A/T)	13 - ground	Shift lever position	N or P	Continuity
				L, 2, D or R	No continuity
	Clutch switch (M/T)	13 - ground	Clutch pedal position	released	No continuity
				depressed	Continuity
	Parking brake switch	14 - ground	Parking brake lever position	released	No continuity
				pulled	Continuity
	Ground connection	15 - ground	Constant		Continuity
Resistance	Actuator (release valve)	3 - 16	Brake pedal position	released	Approx. 68 Ω
				depressed	No continuity
	Actuator (control valve)	5 - 16	Constant		Approx. 30 Ω
	ECT No. 2 solenoid valve	9 - ground	Constant		Approx. 13 Ω
	Control switch	19 - ground	Control switch position	OFF	No continuity
				RES/ACC	Approx. 68 Ω
				SET/COAST	Approx. 198 Ω
				CANCEL	Approx. 418 Ω
Voltage	CC indicator	4 - ground	Ignition switch position	LOCK or ACC	No voltage
				ON	Battery voltage
	Speed sensor	8 - ground	With ignition switch on, speedometer shaft or speed sensor shaft turned.		Voltage changes repeatedly
	Power source	12 - ground	Ignition switch position	LOCK or ACC	No voltage
				ON	Battery voltage
	Stop light	17 - ground	Brake pedal position	released	No voltage
				depressed	Battery voltage
	STOP fuse	18 - ground	Constant		Battery voltage

TY1109100061000X

Fig. 27 System circuit test. Celica w/vacuum actuator

Check for	Measured item	Tester connection	Condition		Specified value
Continuity	Neutral start switch	2 – ground	Shift lever position	N or P	Continuity
				L, 2, D or R	No continuity
	Parking brake switch	3 – ground	Parking brake lever position	released	No continuity
				pulled	Continuity
	Control switch	4 – ground	Main switch position	OFF	No continuity
				ON	Continuity
	Ground connection	13 – ground	Constant		Continuity
	Control switch	18 – ground	Control switch position	RES/ACC	Continuity
		19 – ground	Control switch position	SET/COAST	Continuity
		17 – ground	Control switch position	CANCEL	Continuity
	Actuator (motor)	*11 – 12	Actuator arm position	max. OPEN	(12 → 11) Continuity
				max. CLOSE	(11 → 12) Continuity
				any position except above position	(12 → 11) Continuity
	TDCL circuit	8 – ground	Constant		No continuity
			Terminals Tc and E1 connected		Continuity
	Throttle position sensor (IDL)	23 – ground	Acceleration pedal position	released	Continuity
				depressed	No continuity
	Speed sensor	20 – ground	With ignition switch ON, speedometer shaft or speed sensor shaft turned.		Continuity ↕ No continuity
Resistance	Actuator (position sensor)	24 – 26	Constant		Approx. 2 kΩ
		24 – 25	Actuator arm turned		Resistance change even
	Actuator (Safety magnetic clutch)	10 – ground	Brake pedal position	released	Approx. 38.5 Ω
				depressed	No continuity
Voltage	Power source	14 – ground	Ignition switch position	LOCK or ACC	No voltage
				ON	Battery voltage
	STOP fuse	1 – ground	Constant		Battery voltage
	Stop light	16 – ground	Brake pedal position	released	No voltage
				depressed	Battery voltage
	O/D solenoid	9 – ground	Ignition switch position	LOCK or ACC	No voltage
				ON	Battery voltage

*: This circuit include the diode.

If circuit is as specified, try another ECU.
If circuit is not as specified, refer to wiring diagram and inspect the circuits connected to other parts.

TY1109100064000X

Fig. 28 System circuit test. Land Cruiser & Tacoma

Terminals	Symbols	Condition	Standard Value
2 – 13	D ↔ GND	(M/T) Depress clutch pedal. (A/T) Shift to except D position.	Below 1 V
		(M/T) Release clutch pedal. (A/T) shift to D position	10 – 16 V
7 – 13	Pi ↔ GND	IG ON. Main Switch ON. Main indicator light ON.	Below 1.2 V
		IG ON. Main switch OFF. Main indicator light OFF.	10 – 16 V
8 – 13	Tc ↔ GND	Ignition switch ON.	10 – 16 V
9 – 13	O/D ↔ GND	Except during cruise control driving.	10 – 16 V
		O/D Switch ON. During cruise control driving. (Driving on flat road).	10 – 16 V
		O/D Switch OFF. During cruise control driving. (3rd driving).	Below 1 V
10 – 13	L ↔ GND	During cruise control driving.	9 – 15 V
		Except during cruise control driving.	Below 1 V
11 – 13	MC ↔ GND	During cruise control driving. COAST switch hold ON.	9 – 16 V
		During cruise control driving. ACCEL switch hold ON.	Below 1 V
12 – 13	MO ↔ GND	During cruise control driving. ACCEL switch hold ON.	9 – 15 V
		During cruise control driving. COAST switch hold ON.	Below 1 V
13 – Body Ground	GND ↔ Body Ground	Always.	Below 1 V
14 – 13	B ↔ GND	Ignition switch ON.	10 – 16 V
15 – 13	BATT ↔ GND	Always.	10 – 16 V
16 – 13	STP– ↔ GND	Depress brake pedal.	10 – 16 V
		Release brake pedal.	Below 1 V

TY1109600074010X

Fig. 29 System circuit test (Part 1 of 2). RAV4

Terminals	Symbols	Condition	Standard Value
18 – 13	CCS ↔ GND	IG ON. Main switch ON. Switch neutral position.	10 – 16 V
		IG ON. Main switch ON. CANCEL switch hold ON.	5.1 – 8.3 V
		IG ON. Main switch ON. SET/COAST switch hold ON.	2.4 – 4.0 V
		IG ON. Main switch ON. RESUME/ACCEL switch hold ON.	0.8 – 1.4 V
19 – 13	CMS ↔ GND	IG ON. Main switch hold ON. (Indicator light ON)	Below 1 V
		IG ON. Main switch OFF. (Indicator Light OFF)	10 – 16 V
20 – 13	SPD ↔ GND	Engine start. Car stationary.	4.7 – 5.2 V
		During driving. (Pulse generated)	3 – 7 V
21 – 13	IDL ↔ GND	IG ON. Throttle valve fully opened.	Below 1 V
		IG ON. Throttle valve fully closed.	10 – 16 V
22 – 13	ECT ↔ GND	During cruise control driving. O/D switch ON.	Below 1 V
		During cruise control driving. O/D switch OFF (3rd driving).	10 – 16 V
23 – 13	VR1 ↔ GND	Ignition switch ON.	4.7 – 5.2 V
24 – 25	VR2 ↔ VR3	During cruise control driving.	1.0 – 4.7 V
		IG ON. Control plate fully opened.	4.2 – 4.7 V
		IG ON. Control plate fully closed.	1.0 – 1.2 V
25 – 13	VR3 ↔ GND	Always.	Below 1 V
26 – 13	L– ↔ GND	Always.	Below 1 V

TY1109600074020X

Fig. 29 System circuit test (Part 2 of 2). RAV4

Check for	Measured item	Tester connection	Condition		Specified Value
Continuity	Clutch Switch (M/T)	2 – ground	Clutch pedal Position	released	No continuity
				depressed	Continuity
	Neutral start switch (A/T)	2 – ground	Shift lever position	N or P	Continuity
				L,2,D or R	No continuity
	Parking brake switch	3 – ground	Parking brake lever position	released	No continuity
				pulled	Continuity
	Control switch	4 – ground	Main switch position	pushed	Continuity
				released	No continuity
	Actuator (motor)	11 – 12	Actuator arm position	max. OPEN	(12→11) Continuity
					(11→12) No continuity
				max. CLOSE	(11→12) Continuity
					(12→11) No continuity
				any position except above position	(11→12) Continuity
	Ground connection	13 – ground	Constant		Continuity
Resistance	Actuator (Safety magnetic clutch)	10 – ground	Brake pedal position	released	Approx. 38.5 Ω
				depressed	No continuity
	Control switch	18 – ground	Control switch position	OFF	No continuity
				RES/ACC	Approx. 68 Ω
				SET/COAST	Approx. 198 Ω
				CANCEL	Approx. 418 Ω
	ECT No. 2 solenoid valve (A/T)	22 – ground	Constant		Approx. 13 Ω
	Actuator (position sensor)	24 – 26	Constant		Approx. 2 kΩ
		25 – 26	Actuator arm turned		Resistance change even
Voltage	STOP fuse	1 – ground	Constant		Battery voltage
	Power source	14 – ground	Ignition switch position	LOCK or ACC	No voltage
				ON	Battery voltage
	Stop light	16 – ground	Brake pedal position	released	No voltage
				depressed	Battery voltage
	Speed sensor	20 – ground	With ignition switch ON, speedometer shaft or speed sensor shaft turned.		Voltage changes repeatedly

TY1109100065000X

Fig. 30 System circuit test. MR2

Check for	Tester connection	Condition	Specified Value
Continuity	1 – Ground	Luggage door unlocked with key	Continuity
		Other positions	No continuity
	3 – Ground	Front LH door lock lever unlocked	Continuity
		Front LH door lock lever locked	No continuity
	4 – Ground	RH front door opened	Continuity
		RH front door closed	No continuity
	5 – Ground	LH front door opened	Continuity
		LH front door closed	No continuity
Voltage	6 – Ground	Turn ignition switch to ACC or ON	Battery Voltage
Continuity	7 – Ground	Constant	Continuity
Voltage	8 – Ground	Constant	Battery Voltage
	9 – Ground	Constant	Battery Voltage
Continuity	10 – Ground	LH or RH front door unlocked with key	Continuity
		Other positions	No continuity
	11 – Ground	LH or RH front door locked with key	Continuity
		Other positions	No continuity
	12 – Ground	Front RH door lock lever unlocked	Continuity
		Front RH door lock lever locked	No continuity
	13 – Ground	Luggage door opened	Continuity
		Luggage door closed	No continuity
	*14 – Ground	Front door or rear door or engine hood opened	Continuity
		Front door and rear door and engine hood closed	No continuity
	15 – Ground	Ignition key set to ignition switch	Continuity
		Ignition key removed from ignition switch	No continuity
	*16 – Ground	Constant	Continuity
Voltage	17 – Ground	Constant	Battery Voltage
	18 – Ground	Turn ignition switch to ST with clutch pedal depressed	Battery Voltage
	19 – Ground	Constant	Battery Voltage
	20 – Ground	Constant	Battery Voltage

This circuit includes the LED or diode. If the circuit shows no continuity, change the positive and negative probes and recheck the circuit.

TY1109100066000X

Fig. 31 System circuit test. Paseo

Connection or Measure item	Check for	Tester Connection	Condition		Specified valve
TOYOTA Diagnostic Communication Link	Continuity	1 – Ground	Short terminals between "Tc" and "E_1"		Continuity
			Released		No continuity
Vacuum pump		2 – Ground	Constant		Continuity *1
Speed sensor (in combination meter)		8 – Ground	Vehicle moving slowly		1 pulse each 40 cm approx. (15.75 in.)
Vacuum switch		11 – Ground	Vacuum	No vacuum	Continuity
				More than 70 ± 30 mmHg (6.69 ± 1.18 in.Hg / 22.66 ± 4.0 kPa)	No continuity
Neutral start switch (A/T)		13 – Ground	Shift position	"N" or "P" range	Continuity
				"L", "2", "D" or "R" range	No continuity
Clutch switch (M/T)		13 – Ground	Clutch pedal position	Depressed	Continuity
				Released	No continuity
Parking brake switch		14 – Ground	Parking brake lever position	Pulled	Continuity
				Released	No continuity
Body ground		15 – Ground	Constant		Continuity
Stop light switch		17 – 18	Brake pedal position	Depressed	Continuity *1
				Released	No continuity
CANCEL switch	Resistance	19 – Ground	Speed control switch position	CANCEL switch is pushed	Approx. 418 Ω
				Released	No continuity
RESUME/ACCEL switch		19 – Ground		RESUME/ACCEL switch is pushed	Approx. 68 Ω
				Released	No continuity
SET/COAST switch		19 – Ground		SET/COAST switch is pushed	Approx. 198 Ω
				Released	No continuity
Stop light switch and actuator (release valve)		3 – 16	Brake pedal position	Depressed	No continuity
				Released	Approx. 71 Ω
Actuator (control valve)		5 – 16	Constant		Approx. 38 Ω
No.2 solenoid valve		9 – Ground	Constant		less than 15 Ω
GAUGE fuse and indicator light	Voltage	4 – Ground	Ignition switch position	ON	Battery voltage
				LOCK, ACC	No voltage
ENGINE fuse		6 – Ground	Ignition switch position	ON	Battery voltage
				LOCK, ACC	No voltage
O/D circuit		7 – Ground	Ignition switch position	ON	Approx. 5 V or more
				LOCK or ACC	No voltage
ENGINE fuse, main switch and main relay		10 – Ground	Ignition switch ON and main switch position	ON	less than 0.3 V
				OFF	No voltage
		12 – Ground	Ignition switch ON and main switch position	ON	Battery voltage
				OFF	No voltage
Engine signal		20 – Ground	Ignition switch position	ON or ST	Battery voltage
				LOCK or ACC	No voltage

*1 There is resistance in the circuit.

If circuit is as specified, replace the ECU.

TY1109100067000X

Fig. 32 System circuit test. Pickup & 4Runner

Check for	Measured Item	Tester connection	Condition		Specified value
Continuity	Clutch switch	2 – ground	Clutch pedal position	Released	No continuity
				Depressed	Continuity
	Parking brake switch	3 – ground	Parking brake lever position	Released	No continuity
				Pulled	Continuity
	MAIN switch*[1]	4 – ground	Main switch position	Pushed	Continuity
				Released	No continuity
	Actuator (motor)	11 – 12	Actuator arm position	Max. OPEN	(12 → 11) Continuity
					(11 → 12) No continuity
				Max. CLOSE	(11 → 12) Continuity
					(12 → 11) No continuity
				Any position except above position	(11 ↔ 12) Continuity
	Ground connection	13 – ground	Constant		Continuity
Resistance	Control switch	18 – ground	Control switch position	OFF	No continuity
				RES/ACC	Approx. 68 Ω
				SET/COAST	Approx. 198 Ω
				CANCEL	Approx. 418 Ω
	Actuator (Safety magnetic clutch)	10 – Ground	Brake pedal position	Released	Approx. 38.5 Ω
				Depressed	No continuity
	Actuator (position sensor)	24 – 26	Constant		Approx. 2 kΩ
		25 – 26	Actuator arm turned		Resistance change even
Voltage	STOP fuse	1 – ground	Constant		Battery voltage
	Power source	14 – ground	Ignition switch position	LOCK or ACC	No voltage
				ON	Battery voltage
	Stop light	16 – ground	Brake pedal position	Released	No voltage
				Depressed	Battery voltage
	Speed sensor	20 – ground	With ignition switch ON, speedometer shaft or speed sensor shaft turned.		Voltage changes repeatedly

TY1109200069000X

Fig. 33 System circuit test. Previa

Connection or Measure Item	Check For	Tester Connection	Condition	Specified Value
Stop Fuse	Voltage	18 – Body ground	———	Battery voltage
Stop Light Switch	Voltage	17 – Body ground	Brake pedal depressed	Battery voltage
			Brake pedal released	No voltage
Stop Light Switch and Release Valve	Resistance	3 – 16	Brake pedal released	Approx. 68 Ω
Control Valve	Resistance	5 – 16	———	Approx. 30 Ω
Cruise Control Indicator	Voltage	4 – Body ground	Turn ignition switch on	Battery voltage
			Turn ignition switch off	No voltage
Control Switch (set/coast)	Resistance	6 – Body ground	Push set/coast switch on	Approx. 198 Ω
Control Switch (resume/accel)	Resistance	6 – Body ground	Push resume/accel switch on	Approx. 68 Ω
Control Switch (cancel)	Resistance	6 – Body ground	Push cancel switch on	Approx. 418 Ω
Speed Sensor	Continuity	10 – Body ground	Vehicle moving slowly	1 pulse each 40 cm (15.75 in.)
Clutch Switch (M/T) or Neutral Start Switch (A/T)	Continuity	13 – Body ground	Clutch pedal depressed or shifted into "N" range	Continuity
			Clutch pedal released or shifted into only range except "N" and "P" range	No continuity
Parking Brake Switch	Voltage	14 – Body ground	Disconnect alternator connector and ignition switch turned on with parking brake lever pulled up.	No voltage
			Disconnect alternator connector and ignition switch turned on with parking brake lever released.	Battery voltage
Vacuum Switch (7M-GTE only)	Continuity	11 – Body ground	Apply vacuum about 170 mmHg (6.69 in.Hg, 22.7 kPa)	No continuity
			No vacuum	Continuity
Vacuum Pump (7M-GTE only)	Continuity	2 – Body ground	———	Continuity
Body Ground	Continuity	15 – Body ground	———	Continuity

TY1109100070000X

Fig. 34 System circuit test. Supra

Wiper Systems

INDEX

	Page No.
Component Diagnosis & Testing	48-44
Front Wiper & Washer Switch	48-44
Front Wiper Motor	48-47
Intermittent & Washer Switch	48-44
Rear Motor & Relay	48-48
Rear Wiper & Washer Switch	48-48
Washer Motor	48-47
Wiper Relay	48-46
Troubleshooting	48-44
Front Wiper	48-44
Rear Wiper	48-44

TROUBLESHOOTING

FRONT WIPER

Wiper Does Not Operate Or Return To Off Position

1. Wiper fuse blown.
2. Wiper motor faulty.
3. Wiper switch faulty.
4. Wiring or ground faulty.

Wiper Does Not Operate In Mist Position

1. Wiper motor faulty.
2. Wiper switch faulty.
3. Wiring or ground faulty.
4. Wiper relay faulty.

REAR WIPER

On 4Runner models, ensure there is no malfunction in the back door power window control system.

Wiper Does Not Operate Or Return To Off Position

1. Circuit breaker off.
2. Wiper fuse blown.
3. Wiper motor faulty.
4. Rear door power window and wiper relay faulty.
5. Wiring or ground faulty.

Wiper Does Not Operate In Intermittent Position

1. Wiper motor faulty.
2. Wiper switch faulty.
3. Wiring or ground faulty.
4. Wiper relay faulty.

COMPONENT DIAGNOSIS & TESTING

FRONT WIPER & WASHER SWITCH

1. Using suitable ohmmeter, inspect continuity between terminals, **Fig. 1 through 17.**
2. If continuity is not as indicated, replace switch.

INTERMITTENT & WASHER SWITCH

Avalon, Camry, Celica, Previa, Land Cruiser, MR2 & Tacoma

1. Inspect intermittent switch operation as follows:
   a. Place wiper switch in INT position.
   b. **On models with variable type,** place INT switch to Fast position.
   c. **On all models,** connect battery positive lead to terminal (B)18 and negative lead to terminal (B)16.
   d. Connect voltmeter positive lead to terminal (B)7 and negative lead to terminal (B)16, needle sweep indicates battery voltage.
   e. Using suitable wire, connect terminals (B)4 and (B)18, then connect terminal (B)16.
   f. Battery voltage should rise from zero volts to battery voltage, as shown in **Fig. 18.**
   g. If operation is not as indicated, replace wiper and washer switch.

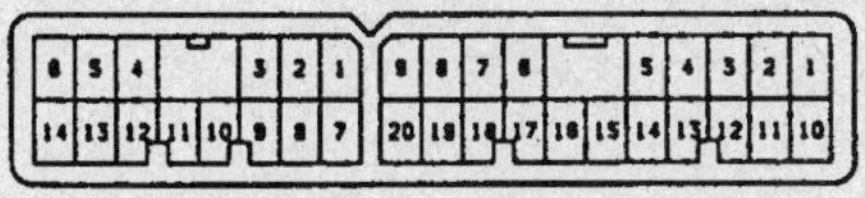

Connector "A" Connector "B"

Terminal (Color) / Switch position		B-4 (L-R)	B-7 (L-B)	B-13 (L-O)	B-18 (L-W)	B-8 (L)	B-16 (B)
Wiper	MIST		O	—	O		
	OFF	O	O				
	INT	O	O				
	LO		O	—	O		
	HI			O	O		
Washer	OFF						
	ON					O	O

TY9029100002000X

Fig. 1 Front wiper & washer switch inspection. Corolla & Tacoma

Connector "A" Connector "B"

Switch position	Tester connection	Specified condition
Wiper OFF	B4 – B7	Continuity
Wiper OFF and MIST	B4 – B7 B16 – B18	Continuity
Wiper INT	B4 – B7 B14 – B16	Continuity
Wiper INT and MIST	B4 – B7 B14 – B16 – B18	Continuity
Wiper LO	B7 – B18	Continuity
Wiper LO and MIST	B7 – B18	Continuity
Wiper HI	B6 – B16 B13 – B18	Continuity
Wiper HI and MIST	B6 – B16 B13 – B18	Continuity
Washer ON	B8 – B16	Continuity

TY9029600040000X

Fig. 2 Front wiper & washer switch inspection. Camry

Connector "A" Connector "B"

Terminal (Color) / Switch position			B-4 (L-R)	B-7 (L-B)	B-8 (L)	B-13 (R-O)	B-16 (B)	B-18 (L-W)
Wiper	OFF	OFF	O	O				
		MIST		O	—	—	—	O
	INT	OFF	O	O				
		MIST		O	—	—	—	O
	LO	OFF		O	—	—	—	O
		MIST		O	—	—	—	O
	HI	OFF				O	—	O
		MIST		O	—	O	—	O
Washer	OFF							
	ON				O	—	O	

TY9029300003000X

Fig. 3 Front wiper & washer switch inspection. MR2

Connector "A" Connector "B"

Terminal (Color) / Switch position			B-4 (L-R)	B-7 (L-B)	B-8 (L)	B-13 (R-O)	B-16 (B)	B-18 (L-W)
Wiper	OFF	OFF	O	O				
		MIST		O	—	—	—	O
	INT	OFF	O	O				
		MIST		O	—	—	—	O
	LO	OFF		O	—	—	—	O
		MIST		O	—	—	—	O
	HI	OFF				O	—	O
		MIST		O	—	O	—	O
Washer	OFF							
	ON				O	—	O	

TY9029100005000X

Fig. 4 Front wiper & washer switch inspection. 1993–95 Celica

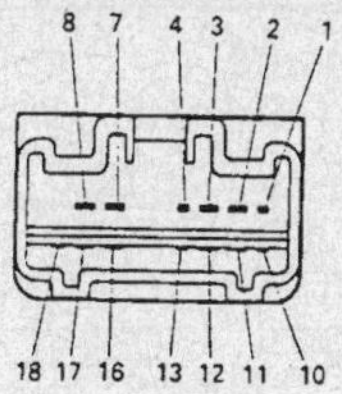
8 7 4 3 2 1
18 17 16 13 12 11 10

Switch position	Tester connection to terminal number	Specified condition
Wiper OFF	7 – 16	Continuity
Wiper INT	7 – 16	Continuity
Wiper LO	7 – 17	Continuity
Wiper HI	8 – 17	Continuity
Washer ON	2 – 11	Continuity

TY9029500038000X

Fig. 5 Front wiper & washer switch inspection. Avalon, RAV4, 1996 Celica, Paseo & Tercel

Connector "A" Connector "B"

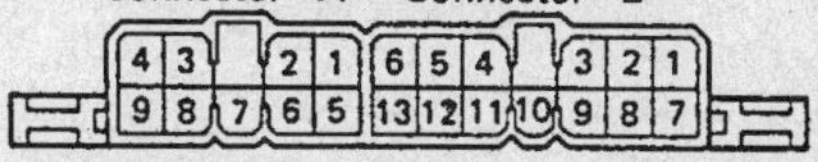

Terminal (Color) / Switch position		A-1 (B)	A-2 (L)	A-4 (L-W)	A-7 (L-R)	A-8 (L-B)	A-9 (L-O)
Wiper	MIST			O	—	O	
	OFF				O	O	
	LO			O	—	O	
	HI			O	—	—	O
Washer	OFF						
	ON	O	O				

TY9029100006000X

Fig. 6 Front wiper & washer switch inspection. Pickup & T100 w/mist wiper

2. Inspect washer switch operation as follows:
   a. Connect positive battery lead to terminal (B)18 and negative to terminal (B)16.
   b. Connect voltmeter positive lead to terminal (B)7 and negative to terminal (B)16.
   c. Depress washer switch, ensuring voltage is as indicated in **Fig. 19.**
   d. If operation is not as indicated, replace wiper and washer switch.

RAV4

Use the following procedure to inspect intermittent switch operation.

1. Place wiper switch in INT position.
2. Place INT switch to Fast position.
3. Connect battery positive lead to terminal 17 and negative lead to terminal 16.
4. Connect voltmeter positive lead to terminal 7 and negative lead to terminal 16, needle sweep indicates battery voltage.
5. Using suitable wire, connect terminals 2 and 17, then connect terminal 16.
6. Battery voltage should rise from zero volts to battery voltage, as shown in **Fig. 20.**
7. If operation is not as specified, replace wiper/washer switch.

1996 4Runner

1. Inspect intermittent switch operation as follows:
   a. Place wiper switch in INT position.
   b. Place INT switch to Fast position.
   c. Connect battery positive lead to terminal 16 and negative lead to terminal 2.
   d. Connect voltmeter positive lead to terminal 7 and negative lead to terminal 2, needle sweep indicates battery voltage.
   e. Battery voltage should rise from zero volts to battery voltage, as shown in **Fig. 20.**
   f. If operation is not as specified, replace wiper/washer switch.

Corolla

1. Inspect intermittent switch operation as follows:
   a. Place wiper switch in INT position.
   b. Connect battery positive lead to terminal (B)18 and negative lead to terminal (B)16.
   c. Connect voltmeter positive lead to terminal (B)13 and negative lead to terminal (B)16, needle sweep indicates battery voltage.
   d. Using suitable wire, connect terminals (B)4 and (B)16, then connect terminal (B)18.
   e. Battery voltage should rise from zero volts to battery voltage as indicated, **Fig. 21.**
   f. If operation is not as indicated, replace wiper and washer switch.

1993–95 Paseo & Tercel

1. Inspect intermittent switch operation as follows:
   a. Place wiper switch in INT position.
   b. Turn intermittent time control switch to fast position.
   c. Connect battery positive lead to terminal 5 and negative lead to terminal 3.
   d. Connect voltmeter positive lead to terminal 1 and negative lead to terminal 3, needle sweep indicates battery voltage.
   e. Using suitable wire, connect terminals 6 and 5, then connect terminal 3.
   f. Battery voltage should rise from zero volts to battery voltage as shown in **Figs. 21 and 22.**
   g. If operation is not as indicated, replace switch.

1996 Paseo

1. Inspect intermittent switch operation as follows:
   a. Place wiper switch in INT position.
   b. Connect battery positive lead to terminal 17 and negative lead to terminal 2.
   c. Connect voltmeter positive lead to terminal 16 and negative lead to terminal 7, needle sweep indicates battery voltage.
   d. Using suitable wire, connect terminals 16 and 17, then connect terminals 16 and 2.
   e. Battery voltage should rise from zero volts to battery voltage as shown in **Fig. 23.**
   f. If operation is not as indicated, replace switch.

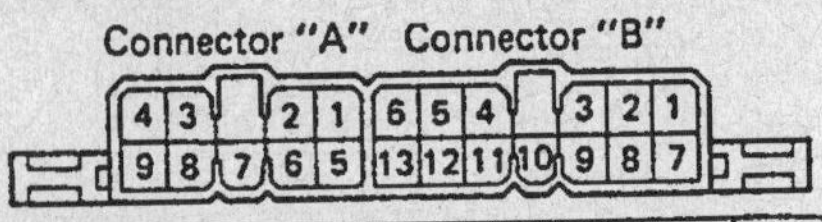
Connector "A"
Connector "B"

Terminal (Color) / Switch position		A-1 (B)	A-2 (L)	A-4 (L-W)	A-7 (L-R)	A-8 (L-B)	A-9 (L-O)
Wiper	MIST				○	○	
	INT			○		○	
	LO			○		○	
	HI			○			○
Washer	OFF						
	ON	○	○				

TY9029100007000X

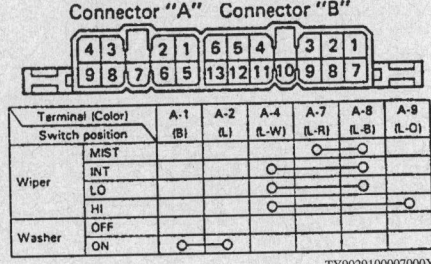

Fig. 7 Front wiper & washer switch inspection. Pickup & T100 w/intermittent wiper

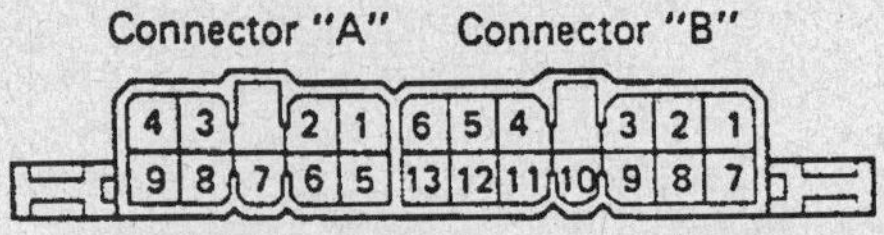
Connector "A"
Connector "B"

Terminal (Color) / Switch position		A-1 (B)	A-2 (L)	A-4 (L-W)	A-7 (L-R)	A-8 (L-B)	A-9 (L-O)
Wiper	OFF				○	○	
	INT				○	○	
	LO			○		○	
	HI			○			○
Washer	OFF						
	ON	○	○				

TY9029100008000X

Fig. 8 Front wiper & washer switch inspection. 1993–95 4Runner

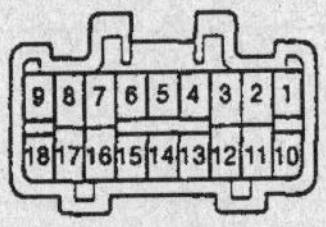

Switch position	Tester connection	Specified condition
OFF	7 – 16	Continuity
MIST	7 – 17	Continuity
LO	7 – 17	Continuity
HI	8 – 17	Continuity
Washer ON	2 – 11	Continuity

TY9029600043000X

Fig. 9 Front wiper & washer switch inspection. 1996 4Runner w/mist wiper

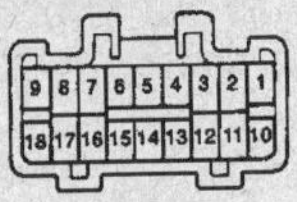

Switch position	Tester connection	Specified condition
OFF	7 – 16	Continuity
INT	7 – 16	Continuity
LO	7 – 17	Continuity
HI	8 – 17	Continuity
Washer ON	2 – 11	Continuity

TY9029600044000X

Fig. 10 Front wiper & washer switch inspection. 1996 4Runner w/intermittent wiper

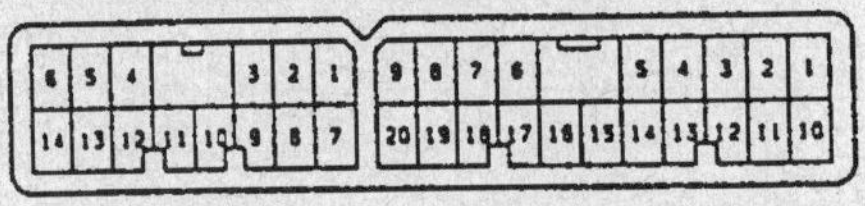

Connector "A" Connector "B"

(Front Wiper and Washer Switch/ Continuity)

Terminal (Color) / Switch position		B4 (L-R)	B7 (L-B)	B8 (L)	B12 (Y-B)	B13 (L-O)	B16 (B)	B18 (L-W)
Wiper	OFF	○	○					
	INT	○	○		○		○	
	LO		○					○
	HI					○		○
Washer	OFF							
	ON			○			○	

(Rear Wiper and Washer Switch/ Continuity)

Terminal (Color) / Switch position		B1 (G)	B2 (V)	B10 (O)	B16 (B)
Washer	ON		○		○
Wiper	OFF				
	INT			○	○
	ON	○			○
Washer	ON	○	○		○

TY9029100009000X

Fig. 11 Front wiper & washer switch inspection. 1993 Previa

Connector "A" Connector "B"

Switch position	Tester connection	Specified condition
Wiper OFF	B4 – B7	Continuity
Wiper INT	B4 – B7 B12 – B16	Continuity
Wiper LO	B7 – B18	Continuity
Wiper HI	B13 – B18	Continuity
Washer ON	B8 – B16	Continuity

TY9029600041000X

Fig. 12 Front wiper & washer switch inspection. 1994–96 Previa

1996 Tercel

1. Inspect intermittent switch operation as follows:
   a. Place wiper switch in INT position.
   b. Connect battery positive lead to terminal 17 and negative lead to terminal 2.
   c. Connect voltmeter positive lead to terminal 7 and negative lead to terminal 2, needle sweep indicates battery voltage.
   d. Using suitable wire, connect terminals 16 and 17, then connect terminals 17 and 2.
   e. Battery voltage should rise from zero volts to battery voltage as shown in **Fig. 21.**
   f. If operation is not as indicated, replace switch.

Supra

1. Inspect intermittent switch operation as follows:
   a. Connect battery positive lead to terminal 5 and negative lead to terminal 7, **Fig. 24.**
   b. Using suitable wire, connect terminals 7 and 8, check continuity between terminals 1 and 5, as shown in **Fig. 25.**
2. Inspect washer circuit relay as follows:
   a. Connect battery positive lead to terminal 5 and negative lead to terminal 7.
   b. Check continuity between terminals 1 and 5 as shown in **Fig. 26.**
   c. If operation is not as indicated, replace relay.

Pickup, T100 & 4Runner

1. Inspect intermittent switch operation as follows:
   a. Place wiper switch in INT position.
   b. **On models with variable type,** place INT switch to Fast position.
   c. **On all models,** connect battery positive lead to terminal (A)4 and negative lead to terminal (A)1.
   d. Connect voltmeter positive lead to terminal (A)8 and negative lead to terminal (A)1, needle sweep indicates battery voltage.
   e. Using suitable wire, connect terminals (A)7 and (A)4, then connect terminal (A)1.
   f. Battery voltage should rise from zero volts to battery voltage, as shown in **Fig. 27.**
   g. If operation is not as indicated, replace wiper and washer switch.

WIPER RELAY

Corolla

1. Ensure there is no continuity between terminals 3 and 4, **Fig. 28.**
2. Ensure continuity exists between terminals 4 and 5.
3. If continuity is not as indicated, replace relay.
4. Inspect front wiper relay operation as follows:
   a. Connect battery positive lead to terminal 3 and negative to terminal 6.
   b. Connect positive lead from voltmeter to terminal 5 and negative lead to terminal 6. Ensure the meter indicates 0 Volts.
   c. Connect positive lead from voltmeter to terminal 4 and negative lead to terminal 6. Ensure meter indicates positive voltage.

Land Cruiser

1. Inspect rear wiper relay operation as follows:
   a. Ensure no continuity exists between terminals 1 and 3.
   b. Continuity should exist between terminals 2 and 3.
   c. If continuity is not as indicated, replace relay.
   d. Connect positive battery lead to terminal 1 and negative to terminal 6.
   e. Connect voltmeter positive lead to terminal 2 and negative to terminal 6, ensure meter indicates zero volts.
   f. Connect voltmeter positive lead to terminal 3 and negative to terminal 6, ensure meter indicates battery voltage volts.
   g. Connect positive battery lead to terminal 2 and negative to terminal 4.
   h. Connect voltmeter positive lead to terminal 3 and negative to terminal 4.
   i. Disconnect positive lead from terminal 2, then connect to terminal 1, ensure meter needle rises from zero volts to battery voltage within 6–10 seconds.

Switch position	Tester connection to terminal number	Specified value
Wiper OFF	B4 – B7	Continuity
Wiper OFF and MIST	B7 – B18	Continuity
Wiper INT	B4 – B7	Continuity
Wiper INT and MIST	B7 – B18	Continuity
Wiper LO	B7 – B18	Continuity
Wiper LO and MIST	B7 – B18	Continuity
Wiper HI	B13 – B18	Continuity
Wiper HI and MIST	B7 – B13 B13 – B18	Continuity
Washer ON	B8 – B18	Continuity

TY9029300011000X

Fig. 13 Front wiper & washer switch inspection. Supra

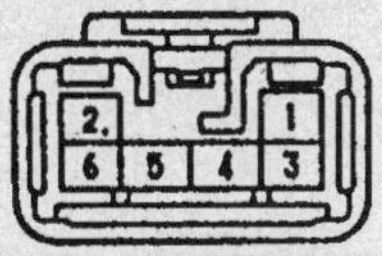
2
1
6 5 4 3

Switch position		1	2	5	6	3	4
Wiper	MIST	O	—	O			
	OFF	O	—	—	O		
	LO	O	—	O			
	HI		O	O			
Washer	OFF						
	ON					O	O

TY9029300013000X

Fig. 16 Front wiper & washer switch inspection. 1993–95 Tercel w/mist wiper

j. If operation is not as indicated, replace relay.

Previa

1. Inspect front wiper relay for continuity between terminals 1 and 4, no continuity should be indicated.
2. Ensure continuity between terminals 1 and 3, **Fig. 29.**
3. If continuity is not as indicated, replace relay.
4. Inspect front wiper relay operation as follows:
   a. Connect battery positive lead to terminal 4 and negative lead to terminal 5.
   b. Connect voltmeter positive lead to terminal 3 and negative to terminal 5.
   c. Connect battery negative lead to terminal 6, ensure voltage changes from battery voltage to no voltage.
   d. Disconnect negative lead from terminal 6, ensuring voltage changes from no voltage to battery voltage in about 2.5 seconds.
   e. If operation is not as indicated, replace relay.

FRONT WIPER MOTOR

Except Previa

1. Inspect low speed motor operation as follows:
   a. Disconnect wiper motor electrical connector.
   b. Connect positive battery lead to terminal 2 and negative to motor body, **Fig. 30.**

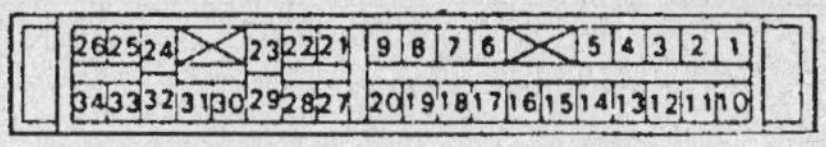

Switch	Switch position	18	13	7	4	16	8
Wiper	MIST	O	—	O			
	OFF			O	O		
	INT			O	O		
	LO	O	—	O			
	HI	O	O				
Washer	OFF						
	ON					O	O

TY9029300012000X

Fig. 14 Front wiper & washer switch inspection. 1993 Land Cruiser

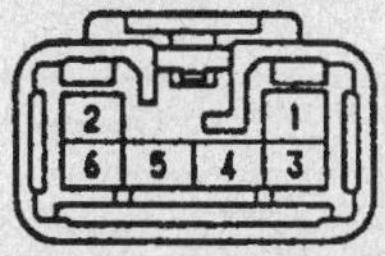
2
1
6 5 4 3

Switch position		1	2	5	6	3	4
Wiper	OFF	O	—	—	O		
	INT	O	—	—	O		
	LO	O	—	O			
	HI		O	O			
Washer	OFF						
	ON					O	O

TY9029100014000X

Fig. 17 Front wiper & washer switch inspection. 1993–95 Paseo & Tercel w/intermittent wiper

   c. Ensure motor operates at low speed.
2. Inspect high speed motor operation as follows:
   a. Connect positive battery lead to terminal 1 and negative to motor body.
   b. Ensure motor operates at high speed.
3. Inspect motor operation, stopping at stop position, as follows:
   a. Operate motor at low speed.
   b. Disconnect terminal 2 to stop motor operation.
   c. Connect terminals 2 and 3.
   d. Connect battery positive lead to terminal 4.
   e. Ensure motor stops running in Off position after motor operates again.
4. If motor operation is not as indicated, replace motor.

Previa

1. Inspect low speed motor operation as follows:
   a. Disconnect wiper motor electrical connector.
   b. Connect positive battery lead to terminal 3 and negative to terminal 1, **Fig. 31.**
   c. Ensure motor operates at low speed.
2. Inspect high speed motor operation as follows:
   a. Connect positive battery lead to terminal 2 and negative to terminal 1.

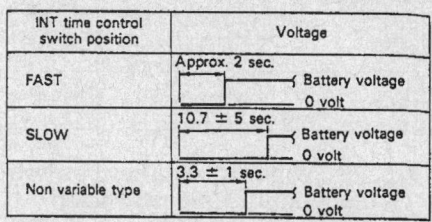

Connector "A"
Connector "B"

Switch position	Tester connection	Specified condition
Wiper OFF	B4 – B7	Continuity
Wiper INT	B4 – B7	Continuity
Wiper LO	B7 – B18	Continuity
Wiper HI	B13 – B18	Continuity
Washer OFF	–	No continuity
Washer ON	B8 – B16	Continuity

TY9029600042000X

Fig. 15 Front wiper & washer switch inspection. 1994–96 Land Cruiser

INT time control switch position	Voltage
FAST	Approx. 2 sec. Battery voltage / 0 volt
SLOW	10.7 ± 5 sec. Battery voltage / 0 volt
Non variable type	3.3 ± 1 sec. Battery voltage / 0 volt

TY9029100015000X

Fig. 18 Wiper intermittent switch inspection. Avalon, Camry, Celica, Previa, Land Cruiser, MR2 & Tacoma

   b. Ensure motor operates at high speed.
3. Inspect motor stop operation, as follows:
   a. Operate motor at low speed.
   b. Disconnect positive lead from terminal 3 to stop motor operation.
   c. Connect terminals 3 and 4.
   d. Connect battery positive lead to terminal 5 and negative lead to terminal 1.
   e. Ensure motor stops running in Off position after motor operates again.
4. If motor operation is not as indicated, replace motor.

WASHER MOTOR

Celica Less Rear Wiper, Camry, Corolla, Land Cruiser, Paseo, Pickup, Supra, 4Runner, MR2, T100 & Tercel

Perform test within 20 seconds to prevent coil damage.

1. Connect battery positive lead to terminal 2 and negative to terminal 1.
2. Ensure motor operates.
3. If motor operation is not as indicated, replace motor.

Celica w/Rear Wiper

Perform test within 20 seconds to prevent coil damage.

1. Connect battery positive lead to terminal 2 and negative to terminal 1.
2. Ensure motor operates.
3. Disconnect negative lead from terminal 1 and connect to terminal 3.
4. Ensure motor operates.
5. If motor operation is not as indicated, replace motor.

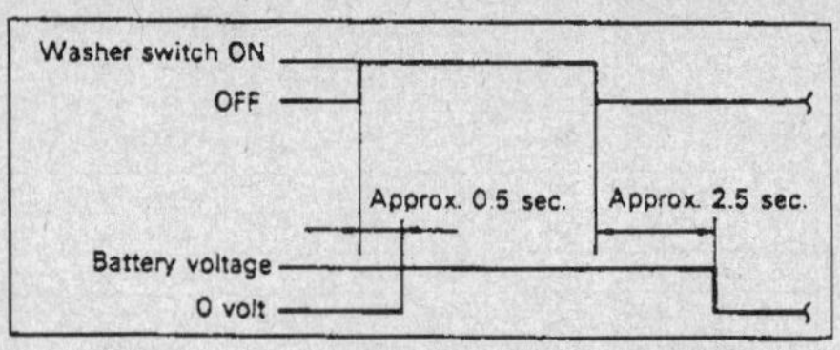
Washer switch ON
OFF
Approx. 0.5 sec.
Approx. 2.5 sec.
Battery voltage
0 volt

TY9029100016000X

Fig. 19 Washer intermittent switch inspection. Avalon, Camry, Celica, Previa, Land Cruiser, MR2 & Tacoma

INT time control switch position	Voltage
FAST	1.6 ± 1 sec. Battery voltage 0 volts
SLOW	10.7 ± 5 sec. Battery voltage 0 volts

TY9029100017000X

Fig. 22 Wiper intermittent switch inspection. 1993–95 Paseo

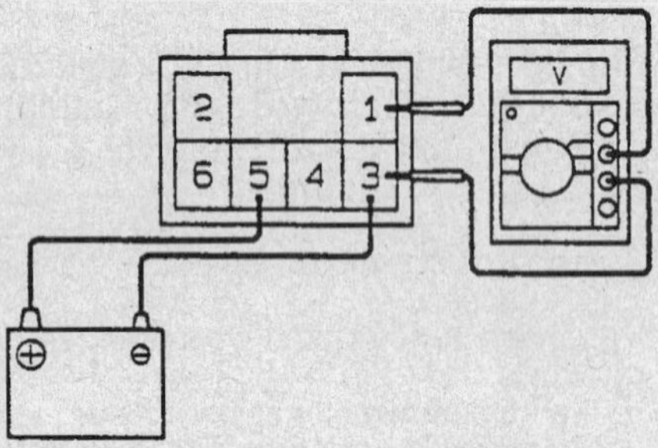
2
1
6
5
4
3
V

TY9029100020000X

Fig. 25 Wiper relay intermittent operation inspection. Supra

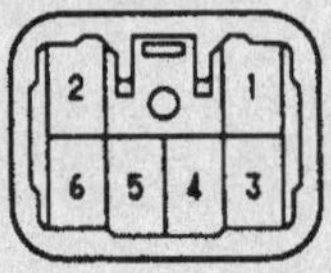
2
1
6
5
4
3

TY9029100024000X

Fig. 28 Wiper relay. Corolla

REAR WIPER & WASHER SWITCH

1. Inspect for continuity as shown in **Figs. 32 through 35.**
2. If continuity is not as indicated, replace switch.

REAR MOTOR & RELAY

Celica & Supra

1. Inspect relay and motor operation as follows:
   a. Connect battery positive lead to terminal 1 and negative to terminal 3 and motor body, **Fig. 36.**
   b. Ensure motor operation.
2. Inspect motor operation, stopping at stop position, as follows:
   a. Connect battery positive lead to terminal 1 and negative to both terminal 3 and motor body to start motor operation.
   b. **On models except Celica,** disconnect terminal 1 to stop motor operation.
   c. **On all models,** connect battery positive lead to terminal 1 and negative lead to motor body.
   d. Ensure motor stops running at stop position after motor operates again.
   e. If operation is not as indicated, replace motor.
3. Inspect intermittent relay operation as follows:
   a. Connect battery positive lead to terminal 1 and negative to terminal 2 and motor body.
   b. Ensure motor operates intermittently for 9–15 seconds.
   c. If operation is not as indicated, replace relay.

INT time control switch position	Voltage
FAST	Approx. 1–3 sec. Battery positive voltage 0 volt
SLOW	Approx. 10–15 sec. Battery positive voltage 0 volt

TY9029600045000X

Fig. 20 Wiper intermittent switch inspection. RAV4 & 1996 4Runner

Switch position	Specified value
INT	4.1 ± 1 sec. Battery voltage 0 volts

TY9029600046000X

Fig. 23 Wiper intermittent switch inspection. 1996 Paseo

Time (seconds)	Between terminals 1 and 5	Time (seconds)	Between terminals 1 and 5
Connect terminals 6 and 7 0.5 ± 0.1	No Continuity → Continuity	Disconnect terminals 6 and 7 2.5 ± 0.5	Continuity → No Continuity

TY9029100021000X

Fig. 26 Wiper relay washer circuit inspection. Supra

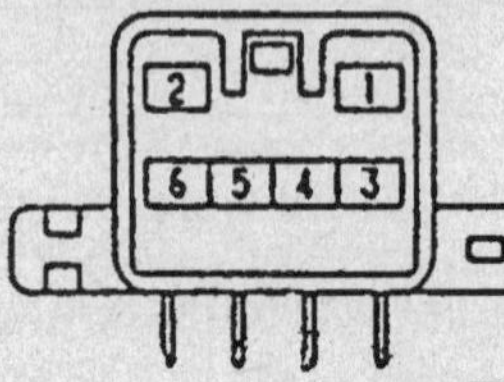
2
1
6
5
4
3

TY9029100028000X

Fig. 29 Wiper relay. Previa

Corolla

1. Inspect motor operation as follows:
   a. Connect battery positive lead to terminal 2 and negative to motor body.
   b. Ensure motor operation.
2. Inspect motor operation, stopping at stop position, as follows:
   a. Operate motor, then disconnect terminal 2 to stop motor operation.
   b. Connect terminals 2 and 3.
   c. Connect battery positive lead to terminal 1 and negative lead to motor body.
   d. Ensure motor stops running at stop position after motor operates again.
   e. If operation is not as indicated, replace motor.

Switch position	Voltage
INT	3.3 ± 1 sec. Battery voltage No voltage

TY9029100018000X

Fig. 21 Wiper intermittent switch inspection. Corolla & Tercel

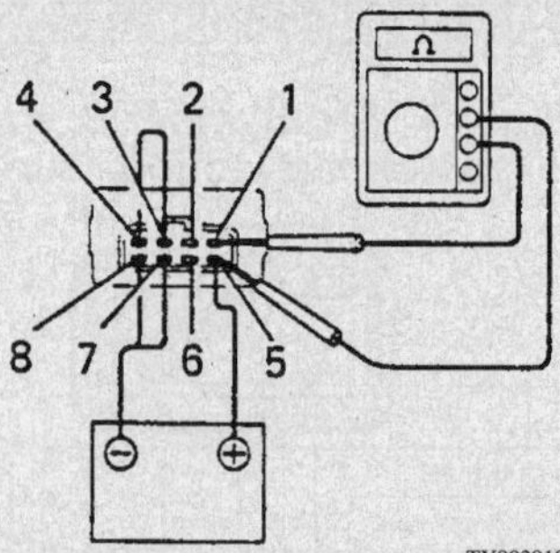
4
3
2
1
Ω
8
7
6
5

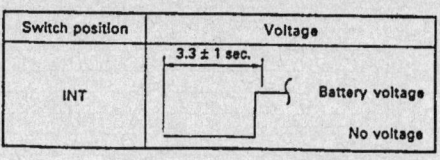

TY9029100019000X

Fig. 24 Wiper relay. Supra

Non Variable Type

Switch position	Specifed value
INT	3.3 ± 1 sec. Battery voltage 0 volts

Variable Type

Switch position		Specifed value
INT	FAST	1.6 ± 1 sec. Battery voltage 0 volts
	LOW	10.7 ± 5 sec. Battery voltage 0 volts

TY9029100022000X

Fig. 27 Wiper & washer intermittent switch inspection. Pickup, T100 & 4Runner

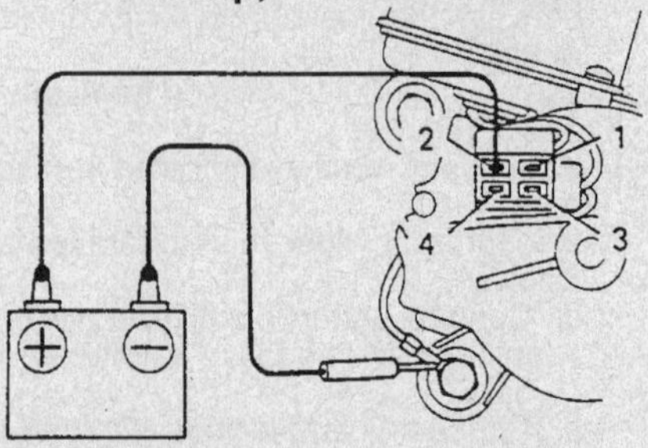
2
1
4
3

TY9029100029000X

Fig. 30 Front wiper motor connector. Except Previa

Previa & Land Cruiser

1. Inspect low speed motor operation as follows:
   a. Connect battery positive lead to terminal 3 and negative to terminal 2.
   b. Ensure motor operation.
2. Inspect motor operation, stopping at stop position, as follows:
   a. Operate motor, then disconnect terminal 3 to stop motor operation.
   b. Connect terminals 3 and 4.
   c. Connect battery positive lead to terminal 1 and negative lead to terminal 2.
   d. Ensure motor stops running at stop position after motor operates again.
   e. If operation is not as indicated, replace motor.

3
2
1
5
4

TY9029100030000X

Fig. 31 Front Wiper motor connector. Previa

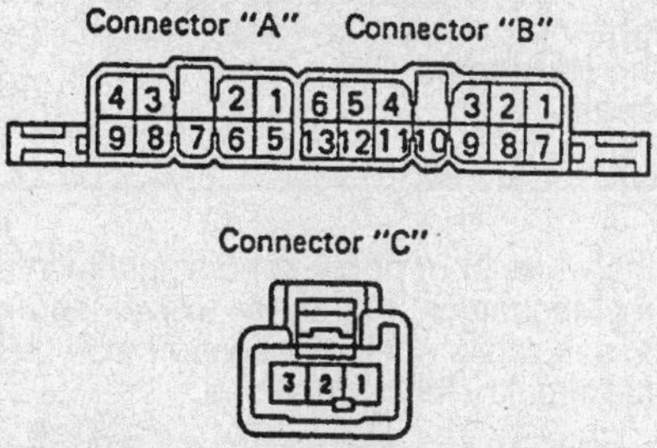
Connector "A"
Connector "B"
Connector "C"

Terminal (Color) / Switch position	A-1	C-1	C-2	C-3
Washer	o			o
OFF				
INT	o		o	
ON	o	o		
Washer	o	o		o

TY9029100034000X

Fig. 34 Rear wiper & washer switch. 1993–95 4Runner

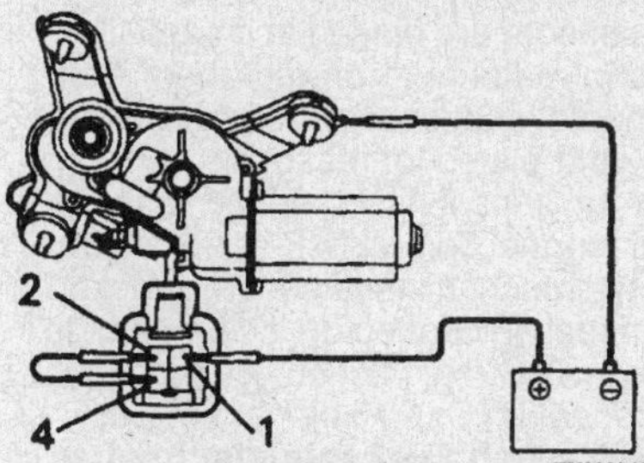
2
4
1

TY9029600048000X

Fig. 37 Rear wiper motor connector. RAV4

RAV4

1. Connect battery positive lead to terminal 4 and negative battery lead to motor, **Fig. 37.**
2. Ensure motor operates.
3. Inspect motor operation, stopping at stop position, as follows:
   a. Operate motor, then disconnect terminal 4 to stop motor operation.
   b. Connect terminals 2 and 4.
   c. Connect battery positive lead to terminal 1 and negative lead to motor body.

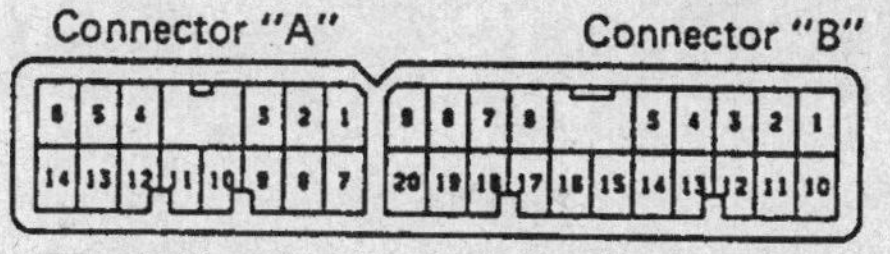
Connector "A"
Connector "B"

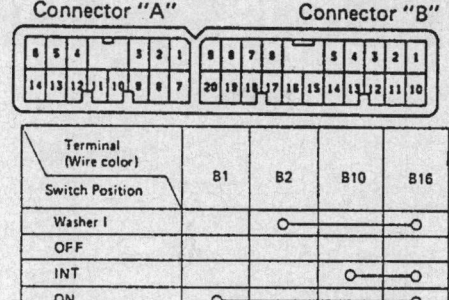

Terminal (Wire color) / Switch Position	B1	B2	B10	B16
Washer I		o		o
OFF				
INT			o	o
ON	o			o
Washer II	o	o		o

TY9029100031000X

Fig. 32 Rear wiper & washer switch. Previa, Celica, Land Cruiser, RAV4 & Supra

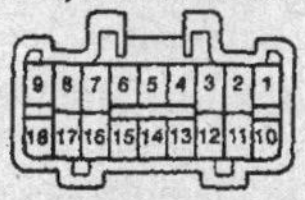

Switch position	Tester connection	Specified condition
Washer 1	2 – 12	Continuity
Wiper OFF	–	No continuity
Wiper INT	2 – 13	Continuity
Wiper ON	2 – 10	Continuity
Washer 2	2 – 10 – 12	Continuity

TY9029600047000X

Fig. 35 Rear wiper & washer switch. 1996 4Runner

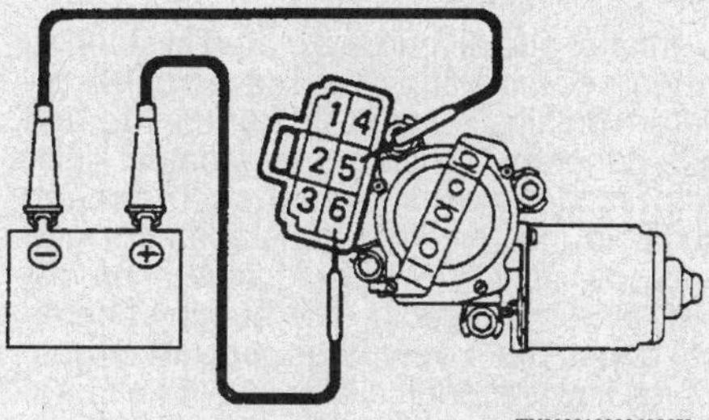
1
4
2
5
3
6

TY9029100036000X

Fig. 38 Rear wiper motor connector. 4Runner

   d. Ensure motor stops running at stop position after motor operates again.
   e. If operation is not as indicated, replace motor.
4. Connect battery positive lead to terminal 2 and negative lead to terminal 1.
5. Ensure motor operates.

4Runner

1. Inspect low speed motor operation as follows:
   a. Connect battery positive lead to terminal 1 and negative to terminal 3, **Fig. 38.**
   b. Ensure motor turns clockwise.
   c. Reverse polarity, ensure motor turn counterclockwise.

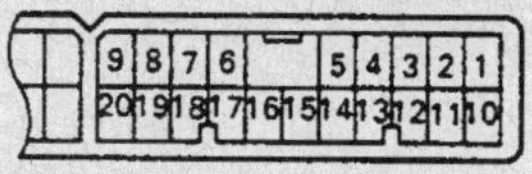

Terminal / Switch position		1	2	10	16
Washer 1			o		o
Wiper	OFF				
	INT			o	o
	ON	o			o
Washer 2		o	o		o

TY9029100033000X

Fig. 33 Rear wiper & washer switch Corolla

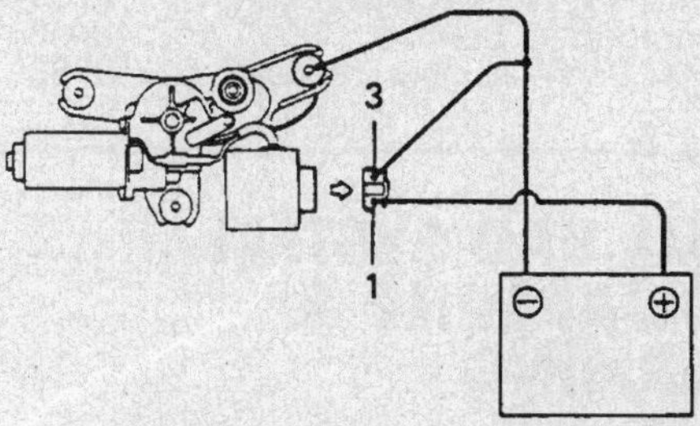
3
1

TY9029100035000X

Fig. 36 Rear wiper motor connector. Celica & Supra

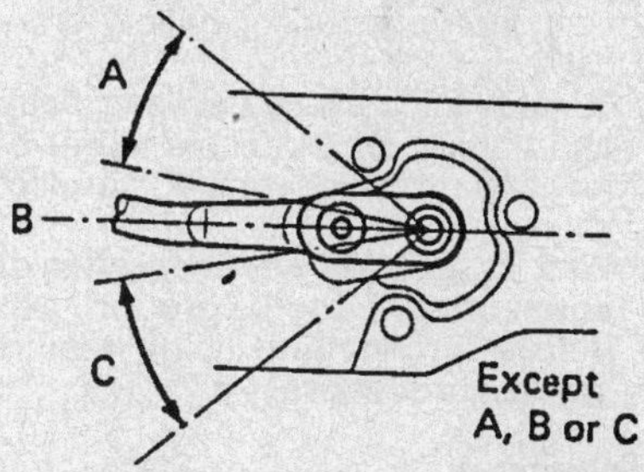
A
B
C
Except
A, B or C

Terminal / Motor link position	4	5	6
A		o	o
B	o	o	o
C		o	o
Except A, B or C			

TY9029100037000X

Fig. 39 Rear wiper motor inspection. 4Runner

   d. If operation is not as indicated, replace motor.
2. Inspect motor continuity as follows:
   a. Connect battery positive lead to terminal 3 and negative to terminal 1, inspect continuity between terminals, **Fig. 39.**
   b. If continuity is not as indicated, replace motor.

Air Bag System

INDEX

	Page No.
Air Bag System Disarming & Arming	48-50
Arming	48-50
Disarming	48-50
Collision Inspection	48-52
Air Bag Is Deployed	48-52
Air Bag Not Deployed	48-52
Component Service	48-52
Air Bag Assembly Disposal	48-56
Air Bag Module, Replace	48-52
Air Bag Sensor Assembly, Replace	48-54
Front Air Bag Sensor, Replace	48-54
Spiral Cable, Replace	48-53
Description & Operation	48-50
System Components	48-50
Diagnosis & Testing	48-52
Precautions	48-51
Audio Coded Anti-Theft System	48-51
Center Air Bag Sensor Assembly	48-51
Front Air Bag Sensor	48-51
Spiral Cable	48-51
Steering Wheel Pad	48-51
Tightening Specifications	48-67
Wire Harness & Connector Repair	48-51

AIR BAG SYSTEM DISARMING & ARMING

Disarming

1. Place ignition switch in the Lock position, then disconnect battery ground cable.
2. To prevent contact between battery and battery ground cable, cover battery ground cable terminal with electrical tape.
3. **Wait at least 90 seconds after disconnecting battery ground cable before proceeding with required service procedures.**

Arming

1. Ensure ignition switch is in the Lock position.
2. Reconnect battery ground cable.
3. **Wait at least 10 seconds before turning the ignition switch from the Lock position.**
4. Place ignition switch in the Acc or On position. Ensure the air bag light illuminates. After approximately 6 seconds, the light should go off. If not, there is a code stored in the system memory.

DESCRIPTION & OPERATION

The Supplemental Restraint System (SRS) works together with seat belts to protect driver and, if equipped, front seat passenger by deploying air bag(s) during certain frontal collisions. The SRS consists of a series of sensors, air bag module(s), spiral cable, steering wheel pad, diagnosis system, ignition control, drive circuit, SRS warning lamp, connectors and wires, **Figs. 1 through 20.**

Sensors are set in line. They work in separate, redundant circuits. Power supply and ground circuits also have built-in redundancy.

Air bag deployment occurs instantaneously when a safing sensor and a front air bag sensor and/or air bag sensor simultaneously detect deceleration greater than a specified valve. When a deceleration force acts on sensors, electric current is sent through air bag squib to igniter. This generates gas, rapidly increasing pressure inside bag. The inflated bag breaks open steering wheel pad or instrument panel. Inflation ends as gas discharges through rear and/or side bag holes and the air bag deflates.

SYSTEM COMPONENTS

AIR BAG MODULE

Driver Side

Inflator and air bag are stored in steering wheel pad that cannot be disassembled. Inflator contains a squib, igniter charge and gas generant. When sensors detect sufficient impact, electric current is sent through squib in inflator. This heats filament and sets off igniter, which ignites chemical packed around squib. The burning chemical generates a very large amount of gas, which flows through a filter into the air bag, inflating it within .1 second.

Passenger Side

Inflator and air bag are stored in passenger side instrument panel on Avalon, Camry, Celica, Corolla, MR2, Previa and Supra, 1995–96 Land Cruiser and Tercel, and 1996 Paseo, 4Runner and RAV4 models. Passenger's air bag module cannot be disassembled. Inflator contains a squib, igniter charge and gas generant. When sensors detect sufficient impact, electric current is sent through squib in inflator. This heats filament and sets off igniter, which ignites chemical packed around driver's squib. The burning chemical generates a very large amount of gas, which flows through a filter into the air bag, inflating it within .1 second.

SPIRAL CABLE

The spiral cable is an electrical joint between vehicle body side and steering wheel. It is located in steering column combination switch.

SENSOR

Sensor detect impacts sever enough to set off inflator, varying with collision type and vehicle speed. G sensors measure speed and degree of deceleration to determine whether or not to send signal to inflator. Mechanical sensors utilize sprung masses, while analogue sensors use electrical circuitry for calculations.

Front Air Bag Sensor

The front air bag sensor unit is a mechanical G sensor that cannot be disassembled. The G sensor is an eccentric mass rotating on a fixed axis and held in place by a spring. If deceleration exceeds a predetermine value, the rotor moves and at a certain point turns a switch On. If the safety switch is also On, the air bag inflator is ignited.

Front sensors are placed in a case filled with potting material to protect them from the elements and assure reliability. The switch is gold-plated for reliability.

The front sensor is equipped with an electrical connection check mechanism. Ensure this mechanism is securely locked when connecting connector. If connector is not locked, SRS malfunction or diagnostic trouble codes (DTCs) will be generated.

On Celica and MR2 models, front air bag sensors are located on upper radiator mount.

On Camry, Supra, T100, 1994 Tercel, 1994–95 Corolla, Paseo and Previa models, front air bag sensors are located on inside of each front fender.

Air Bag Sensor Assembly

The air bag sensor assembly consists of an air bag sensor, safing sensor, ignition control, drive circuit and diagnostic circuit. The assembly receives signals from air bag sensors, judges whether air bag must be activated or not and diagnoses system malfunctions.

The air bag sensor use semiconductors to detect deceleration rate. A semiconductor acceleration sensor has a silicon base with a lever on one side. Resistance bridges detect lever change amounts and an amplifier circuit boosts output for readability. Even if there is a circuitry breakdown, the safety sensor will not complete the circuit and send the ignitor signal to the squib unless there is an actual collision.

On Avalon, Camry, Celica, Corolla, Land Cruiser, MR2, Paseo, Previa,

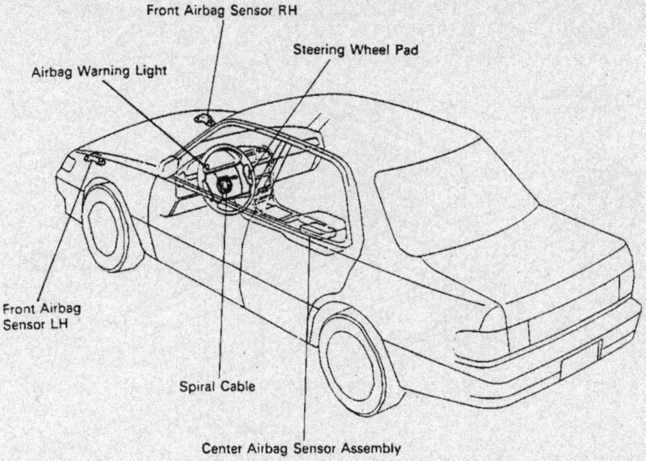
Front Airbag Sensor RH
Steering Wheel Pad
Airbag Warning Light
Front Airbag Sensor LH
Spiral Cable
Center Airbag Sensor Assembly

TY8019300118000X

Fig. 1 SRS component locations. 1993 Camry, Corolla, Paseo & Tercel

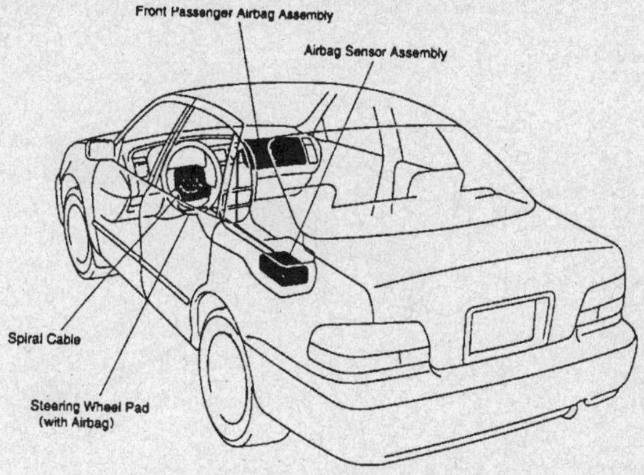
Front Passenger Airbag Assembly
Airbag Sensor Assembly
Spiral Cable
Steering Wheel Pad
(with Airbag)

TY8019500140000X

Fig. 2 SRS component locations. Avalon

RAV4, Supra, Tercel and 1994 T100 models, the air bag sensor assembly is located inside center console on floor.

On Tacoma, 4Runner and 1995–96 T100 models, the air bag sensor assembly is located on floor behind center of instrument panel.

SRS WARNING LAMP

SRS warning lamp is located in instrument cluster and lights to alert driver if a malfunction is detected by air bag sensor assembly self-diagnosis feature. In normal operating conditions, when ignition is turned to Acc or On positions, the lamp goes on for about six seconds, then goes off.

DIAGNOSIS CIRCUIT

When ignition is turned on, diagnosis circuit lights SRS warning lamp for about six seconds while running primary check of every part of system. If everything checks out, the circuit turns the lamp off. The diagnosis circuit continues to check system functions during operation. If anything is amiss, the circuit turns the SRS warning lamp on and memorizes the problem as a diagnostic trouble code (DTC).

AIR BAG CONNECTORS

SRS wire harness is integrated with cowl wire harness and luggage compartment wire harness assembly. SRS harnesses are encased in a yellow corrugated tube. All SRS wiring connectors are yellow colored. Connectors having special functions and specifically designed for air bags are used in these locations to ensure high reliability. These connectors use durable gold plated terminals.

PRECAUTIONS

AUDIO CODED ANTI-THEFT SYSTEM

Some models are equipped with an audio coded anti-theft system that will disable the radio when the battery cable is disconnected. The system can be identified by the "ANTI-THEFT SYSTEM" on the cassette tape lid. Obtain 3 digit customer code for input. Reset system after service as follows:

1. Obtain 3 digit audio anti-theft code.
2. Depress 1 (PROG) while depressing righthand side of TUNE SEEK button, - - - will appear in tape operation display.
3. To enter the first digit, depress 1 (PROG) button repeatedly until the number of times depressed equals the first digit beginning with zero (depress the 1 button six times if the first digit if five).
4. To enter second digit, depress 2 (APS) button repeatedly until the number of times depressed equals the second digit beginning with zero.
5. To enter third digit, depress 3 (RPT) button repeatedly until the number of times depressed equals the second digit beginning with zero.
6. If - - - is displayed during code input, repeat procedure.
7. When code appears in display, depress and hold SCAN button until SEC appears.
8. When SEC disappears audio system should be operative.
9. If Err is displayed, repeat procedure. **Attempting to input code more than nine times may permanently disable audio system.**

FRONT AIR BAG SENSOR

Never reuse front air bag sensors that have been involved in a collision when the air bag has been deployed. Do not disassemble front air bag sensors. Install the front air bag sensor with the arrow on the sensor facing toward the front of the vehicle. The front air bag sensor set bolts and nuts have been anti-rust treated, when then sensor is removed, always replace set bolt and nut.

SPIRAL CABLE

The spiral cable must be installed in the neutral position for air bag deployment may occur.

STEERING WHEEL PAD

When remove steering wheel pad or handling new pad, place on level surface with pad top facing upward. The twin-lock connector lock lever should be in the lock position. Do not damage connector. Do not disassemble steering wheel pad assembly. Do not store steering wheel pads on top of another. Store pad where ambient temperature remains below 200°F without humidity and away from electrical noise. Do not apply grease to pad and pad should not be cleaned with detergents. When using electric welding, disconnect air bag connector below steering column near combination switch before performing service.

CENTER AIR BAG SENSOR ASSEMBLY

The center air bag sensor assembly contains mercury, after replacement or service, do not destroy old part, dispose of as toxic waste. Do not disassemble center air bag sensor assembly. When disconnecting sensor assembly electrical connectors, ensure assembly is properly mounted to floor or accidental air bag deployment may occur.

WIRE HARNESS & CONNECTOR REPAIR

Wires for air bag wiring harness are encased in a yellow conduit, with yellow electrical connectors.

When required, replace either wiring harness or connector. If harness has been damaged, replace entire harness assembly. If only connector has been damaged, replace only connector.

Whenever repairing wiring, always use special repair wire kit (part No. 82988-50010), which is manufactured specifically for this operation.

1. Disarm air bag as outlined under "Air Bag System Disarming and Arming."
2. Remove connector from sensor, then open rear of connector to expose wiring. Cut wires behind connector housing, leaving long strands for easier repair.
3. Strip away .31–.43 inch from each wire

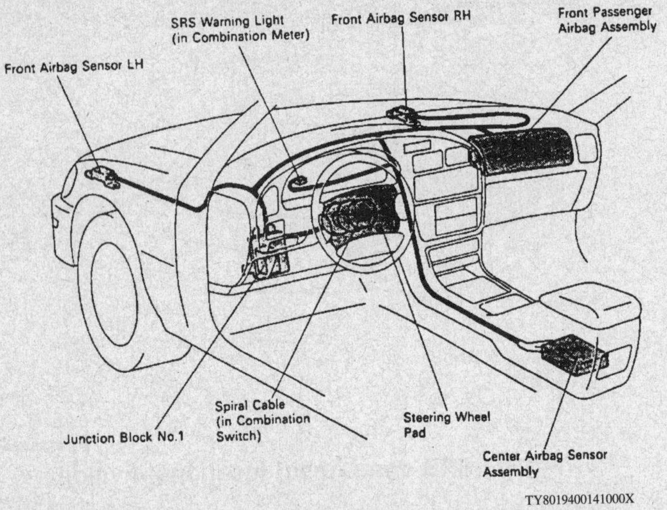
SRS Warning Light
(in Combination Meter)
Front Airbag Sensor RH
Front Passenger
Airbag Assembly
Front Airbag Sensor LH
Junction Block No.1
Spiral Cable
(in Combination
Switch)
Steering Wheel
Pad
Center Airbag Sensor
Assembly
TY8019400141000X

Fig. 3 SRS component locations. 1994–96 Camry

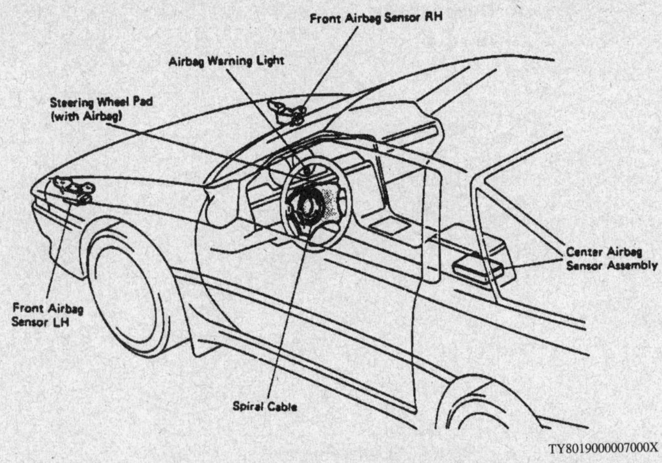
Front Airbag Sensor RH
Airbag Warning Light
Steering Wheel Pad
(with Airbag)
Center Airbag
Sensor Assembly
Front Airbag
Sensor LH
Spiral Cable
TY8019000007000X

Fig. 4 SRS component locations. 1993 Celica

end. Overlap two stripped pieces of wire and place in pressure sleeve, **Fig. 21.**

4. Crimp pressure sleeve closed at center.
5. Once crimped, pull at both ends of wire to ensure wires are secure in pressure sleeve.
6. Crimp both of pressure sleeve outside edges.
7. Wrap repair with silicone tape.
8. Wrap ends of corrugated tube with silicone tape, then wrap tube with vinyl tape. Final repair should be as shown in **Fig. 22.**

DIAGNOSIS & TESTING

Refer to Motor's "Air Bag Manual" for complete diagnosis and testing information.

COLLISION INSPECTION

AIR BAG NOT DEPLOYED

1. Perform diagnostic system check.
2. With driver and passenger side air bag units removed, perform visual check for the following items:
   a. Check for cuts and cracks in, or discoloration of steering wheel pad top surface and its grooved portion.
   b. Check for cuts or cracks in wire harnesses, and for chipping in connectors.
   c. Check for deformation of horn button contact plate of steering wheel. Replace steering wheel assembly if deformation has occurred.
   d. Check passenger side instrument panel and air bag mounting for damage.
   e. There should be no interference between steering wheel pad and steering wheel, and clearance should be uniform all the way around when new steering wheel pad is installed.

AIR BAG IS DEPLOYED

1. Perform diagnostic system check.
2. With driver and passenger side air bag units removed, perform visual check for the following items:
   a. Check for deformation of horn button contact plate of steering wheel. Replace steering wheel assembly if deformation has occurred
   b. There should be no interference between steering wheel pad and steering wheel, and clearance should be uniform all the way around when new steering wheel pad is installed.
   c. Check passenger side instrument panel and air bag mounting for damage.
3. Replace the air bag unit, both front sensors and center air bag sensor after a collision.

COMPONENT SERVICE

AIR BAG MODULE, REPLACE

DRIVER SIDE

Removal

1. Disarm SRS as outlined under "Air Bag System Disarming and Arming."
2. Position front wheels in straight-ahead position.
3. Remove steering wheel lower covers.
4. Using a suitable Torx socket wrench, loosen Torx screws until screw circumference grooves catch screw case, **Figs. 23 through 35.**
5. Pull steering pad rearward, then disconnect air bag electrical connector.
6. Remove air bag module and store with pad facing upward.

Installation

1. Connect air bag electrical connector.
2. Ensure Torx screw circumference grooves are caught in screw case, then install air bag module.
3. Ensure wiring does not interfere with other parts and is not pinched, then tighten mounting screws to specifications.
4. Install steering wheel lower covers.
5. Ensure steering wheel is centered.
6. Arm SRS as outlined under "Air Bag System Disarming and Arming."

PASSENGER SIDE

Avalon

1. Disarm SRS as outlined under "Air Bag System Disarming and Arming."
2. Remove glove compartment door finish plate.
3. Disconnect passenger air bag electrical connector.
4. Remove instrument panel, **Fig. 36.**
5. Remove passenger air bag mounting nuts.
6. Carefully remove passenger air bag module.
7. Remove screws and air bag door.
8. Reverse procedure to install, and tighten to specifications.

Camry

1. Disarm SRS as outlined under "Air Bag System Disarming and Arming."
2. Remove glove compartment door finish plate.
3. Remove driver side air bag module as outlined under "Air Bag Module, Replace."
4. Remove steering wheel as outlined under "Spiral Cable, Replace."
5. Remove under cover No. 2, instrument lower panel, glove compartment panel and door, combination switch, center cluster finish panel, radio, cluster finish panel and heater control panel, **Fig. 37.**
6. Remove passenger side air bag module righthand side mounting bolt, then remove remaining air bag module mounting bolts.
7. Remove air bag module and store with air bag door facing up.
8. Reverse procedure to install and tighten bolts to specifications.

Celica

1. Disarm SRS as outlined under "Air Bag System Disarming and Arming."

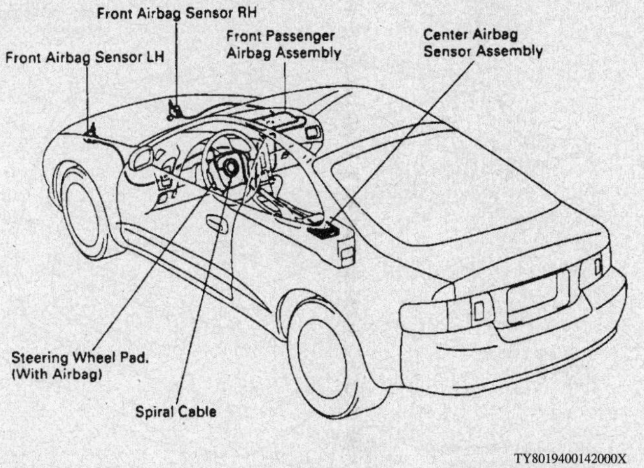
Front Airbag Sensor RH
Front Passenger Airbag Assembly
Center Airbag Sensor Assembly
Front Airbag Sensor LH
Steering Wheel Pad. (With Airbag)
Spiral Cable
TY8019400142000X

Fig. 5 SRS component locations. 1994–96 Celica

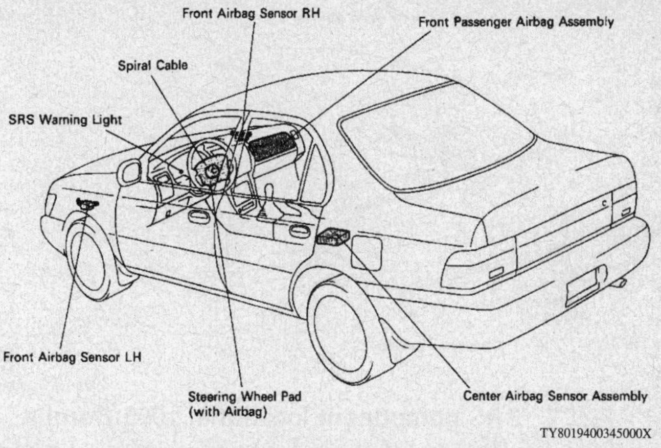
Front Airbag Sensor RH
Front Passenger Airbag Assembly
Spiral Cable
SRS Warning Light
Front Airbag Sensor LH
Steering Wheel Pad (with Airbag)
Center Airbag Sensor Assembly
TY8019400345000X

Fig. 6 SRS component locations. 1994–95 Corolla

2. Remove glove compartment door finish plate.
3. Disconnect passenger air bag electrical connector.
4. Remove instrument panel, **Figs. 36 through 46.**
5. Remove passenger air bag mounting bolts and nuts.
6. Carefully remove passenger air bag module.
7. Remove screws and air bag door.
8. Reverse procedure to install, and tighten to specifications.

Corolla

1. Disarm SRS as outlined under "Air Bag System Disarming and Arming."
2. Remove glove compartment door finish plate.
3. Disconnect passenger air bag electrical connector.
4. Remove glove compartment door, **Fig. 39.**
5. Remove front passenger air bag module mounting bolts and clips, then module.
6. Reverse procedure to install and tighten bolts to specifications.

Land Cruiser

1. Disarm SRS as outlined under "Air Bag System Disarming and Arming."
2. Remove glove compartment door.
3. Remove air bag electrical connector from bracket and disconnect
4. Remove instrument panel, **Fig. 40.**
5. Remove front passenger air bag mounting nuts and bolts, then assembly.
6. Remove clips and air bag door.
7. Reverse procedure to install, and tighten bolts and nuts to specifications.

MR2

1. Disarm SRS as outlined under "Air Bag System Disarming and Arming."
2. Remove glove compartment door finish plate.
3. Disconnect passenger air bag electrical connector.
4. Remove righthand door scuff plate, glove compartment door and lower insert, **Fig. 41.**
5. Remove passenger air bag mounting bolts and nuts.
6. Carefully remove passenger air bag module.
7. Reverse procedure to install, and tighten nuts and bolts to specifications.

Paseo

1. Disarm SRS as outlined under "Air Bag System Disarming and Arming."
2. Remove lower finish panel
3. Disconnect air bag electrical connector.
4. Remove instrument panel reinforcement bolts and instrument panel, **Fig. 42.**
5. Remove front passenger air bag mounting nuts and bolts, then assembly.
6. Remove air bag door.
7. Reverse procedure to install, and tighten to specifications.

Previa

1. Disarm SRS as outlined under "Air Bag System Disarming and Arming."
2. Remove glove compartment door finish plate.
3. Disconnect air bag connector.
4. Remove glove compartment door and lock striker, **Fig. 43**
5. Remove passenger air bag module mounting bolts and nuts.
6. Remove air bag module and store with air bag door facing up.
7. Reverse procedure to install, and tighten to specifications.

RAV4 & 4Runner

1. Disarm SRS as outlined under "Air Bag System Disarming and Arming."
2. Remove glove compartment door.
3. Remove air bag electrical connector from bracket and disconnect
4. Remove instrument panel, **Fig. 44.**
5. Remove front passenger air bag mounting bolts, then assembly.
6. Remove bolts and pry off clips, then remove air bag door.
7. Reverse procedure to install and tighten bolts to specifications.

Supra

1. Disarm SRS as outlined under "Air Bag System Disarming and Arming."
2. Remove glove compartment door finish plate.
3. Disconnect passenger air bag electrical connector.
4. Remove glove compartment panel and heater to register duct No. 4, **Fig. 45.**
5. Remove passenger air bag mounting bolts.
6. Carefully remove passenger air bag module.
7. Reverse procedure to install and tighten bolts to specifications.

Tercel

1. Disarm SRS as outlined under "Air Bag System Disarming and Arming."
2. Remove lower finish panel
3. Disconnect air bag electrical connector.
4. Remove instrument panel, **Fig. 46.**
5. Remove front passenger air bag mounting nuts and bolts, then assembly.
6. Remove air bag door.
7. Reverse procedure to install, and tighten to specifications.

SPIRAL CABLE, REPLACE

REMOVAL

1. Ensure front wheels are straight-ahead.
2. Disarm SRS as outlined under "Air Bag System Disarming and Arming."
3. Removal air bag module as outlined under "Air Bag Module, Replace."
4. Disconnect connector and remove steering wheel set nut.
5. Place alignment marks on steering wheel and steering shaft for use during installation.
6. Remove steering wheel with suitable puller tool.
7. Remove steering column covers.
8. **On MR2 models,** remove instrument panel No. 1 lower finish panel and insert.
9. **On all models,** remove combination switch.

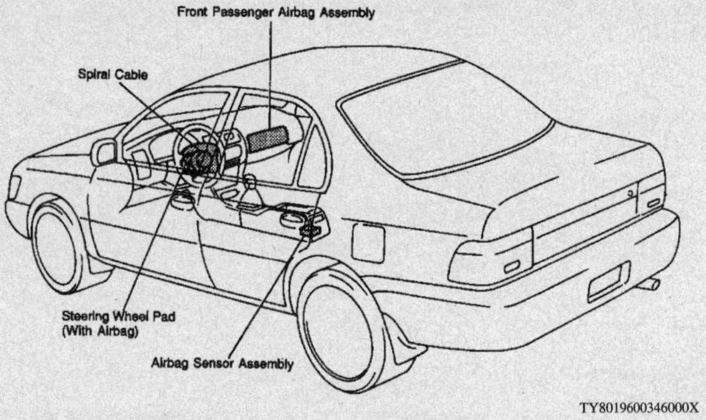
Front Passenger Airbag Assembly
Spiral Cable
Steering Wheel Pad
(With Airbag)
Airbag Sensor Assembly
TY8019600346000X

Fig. 7 SRS component locations. 1996 Corolla

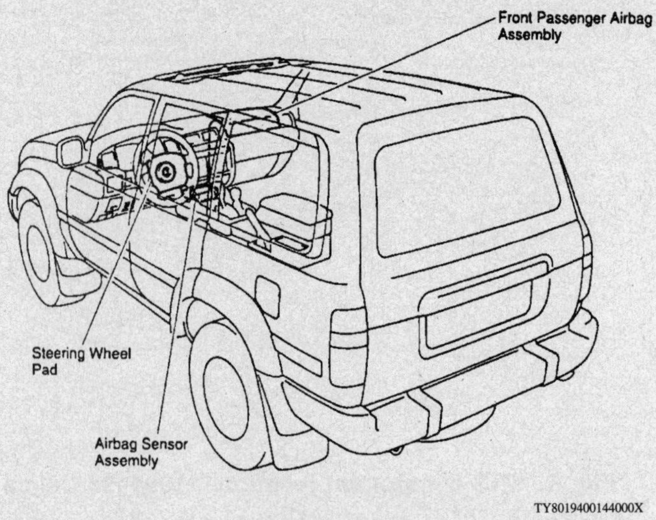
Front Passenger Airbag
Assembly
Steering Wheel
Pad
Airbag Sensor
Assembly
TY8019400144000X

Fig. 8 SRS component locations. Land Cruiser & 4Runner

10. Remove mounting screws and spiral cable from combination switch.

INSTALLATION

1. Ensure front wheel are in straight-ahead position.
2. Install spiral cable
3. Turn spiral cable counterclockwise by hand until cable becomes difficult to turn.
4. **On Avalon, Camry, Corolla, Land Cruiser, Previa, Supra, Tacoma and T100, 1993–94 Tercel, 1993–95 Celica and Paseo, and 1996 4Runner models,** turn spiral cable clockwise approximately three turns to align red mark, **Fig. 47.** Spiral cable will rotate about three turns either left or right of center.
5. **On MR2, RAV4, 1995–96 Tercel, and 1996 Paseo models,** turn spiral cable clockwise approximately two and one-half turns to align red mark, **Fig. 47.** Spiral cable will rotate about 2½ turns either left or right of center.
6. **On all models,** install combination switch.
7. **On MR2 models,** install instrument panel No. 1 lower finish panel and insert.
8. **On all models,** install steering column covers.
9. Align steering wheel and steering shaft marks, then install steering wheel mounting nut and tighten to specifications.
10. Install air bag module as outlined under "Air Bag Module, Replace."
11. Arm SRS system as outlined under "Air Bag System Disarming and Arming."

FRONT AIR BAG SENSOR, REPLACE

CAMRY, COROLLA, PASEO & SUPRA

1. Disarm SRS as outlined under "Air Bag System Disarming and Arming."
2. Remove inner fender liners, **Figs. 48 through 55.**
3. **On Supra models,** remove headlamps.
4. **On all models,** disconnect sensor electrical connectors.
5. Remove sensor mounting bolt and sensor.
6. Reverse procedure to install, noting following:
   a. Ensure sensor arrow points toward vehicle front.
   b. Tighten new mounting bolts to specifications. **Do not reuse old mounting bolts.**
   c. Shake sensor and ensure there is no looseness.
   d. Lock electrical connection check mechanism securely or diagnosis circuit may generate diagnostic trouble code (DTC).

CELICA

1. Disarm SRS as outlined under "Air Bag System Disarming and Arming."
2. **On 1996 models,** remove under engine cover No. and front fender liners.
3. **On all models,** remove front bumper cover, **Fig. 52.**
4. **On 1993–95 models,** remove upper radiator support.
5. **On all models,** remove condenser bolt and nut.
6. Disconnect front air bag sensor electrical connectors.
7. Till radiator and condenser back.
8. Remove sensor mounting screws with suitable Torx wrench tool, then sensor.
9. Reverse procedure to install, ensuring sensor arrow points toward vehicle front and tighten screws to specifications.

MR2

1. Disarm SRS as outlined under "Air Bag System Disarming and Arming."
2. Remove hood lock protector rear plate and headlamp door covers, **Fig. 53.**
3. Disconnect sensor electrical connectors.
4. Remove sensor mounting nut and bolt, then sensor.
5. Reverse procedure to install, ensuring sensor arrow points toward vehicle front and tighten nuts and bolts to specifications.

PREVIA

1. Disarm SRS as outlined under "Air Bag System Disarming and Arming."
2. Disconnect sensor electrical connectors, **Fig. 54.**
3. Remove sensor mounting screws with suitable Torx wrench, then sensor.
4. Reverse procedure to install, ensure sensor arrow points toward vehicle front and tighten mounting screws to specifications.

T100

1. Disarm SRS as outlined under "Air Bag System Disarming and Arming."
2. Remove battery and air cleaner assembly, **Fig. 55.**
3. Disconnect sensor electrical connectors.
4. Loosen sensor mounting screws with suitable Torx wrench and remove sensor.
5. Reverse procedure to install, noting following:
   a. Ensure sensor arrow points toward vehicle front.
   b. Tighten mounting screws to specifications.
   c. Shake sensor and ensure there is no looseness.
   d. Lock electrical connection check mechanism securely or diagnosis circuit may generate diagnostic trouble code (DTC).

AIR BAG SENSOR ASSEMBLY, REPLACE

AVALON

1. Disarm SRS as outlined under "Air Bag System Disarming and Arming."
2. **On models with floor shift,** remove front seat, upper console box, center cluster finish panel, lower finish panel assembly, lower No. 2 finish panel, glove compartment door, glove compartment and front console box, **Fig. 56.**

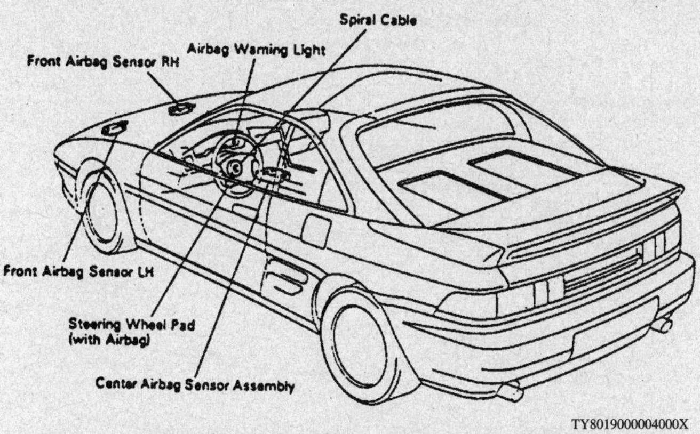
Spiral Cable
Airbag Warning Light
Front Airbag Sensor RH
Front Airbag Sensor LH
Steering Wheel Pad (with Airbag)
Center Airbag Sensor Assembly
TY8019000004000X

Fig. 9 SRS component locations. 1993 MR2

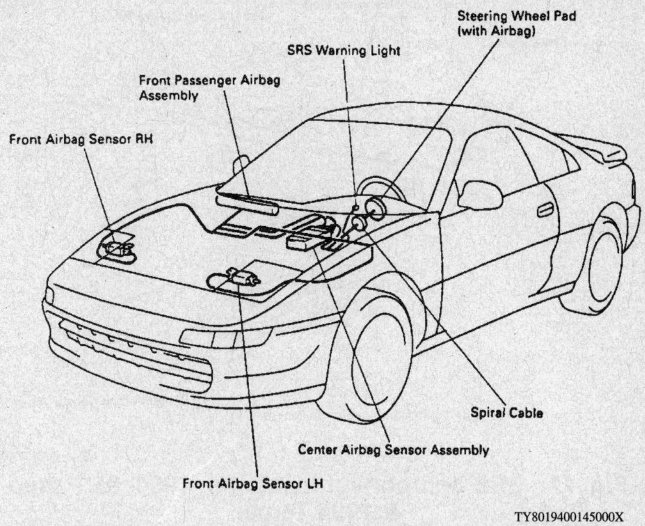
Steering Wheel Pad (with Airbag)
SRS Warning Light
Front Passenger Airbag Assembly
Front Airbag Sensor RH
Spiral Cable
Center Airbag Sensor Assembly
Front Airbag Sensor LH
TY8019400145000X

Fig. 10 SRS component locations. 1994–96 MR2

3. **On models with column shift,** remove front seat, center seat belt, center cluster finish panel, lower No. 2 finish panel, glove compartment door, glove compartment, finish panel, center pillar garnish, cowl side trim, front door inside scuff plate and protector, then peel back floor carpet, **Fig. 57.**
4. Remove connector for sensor assembly, then remove mounting screws with suitable Torx wrench and remove air bag sensor assembly.
5. Reverse procedure to install and tighten bolts to specifications.

CAMRY

1. Disarm SRS as outlined under "Air Bag System Disarming and Arming."
2. Remove front door inside scuff plate and opening cover, cowl side trim, coin box and bezel, lower center cover, No. 2 cover and finish panel, console upper panel, rear console box and front console box, **Fig. 58.**
3. Loosen air bag sensor assembly mounting screws with suitable Torx wrench.
4. Remove connector for sensor assembly and remove air bag sensor assembly.
5. Reverse procedure to install and tighten bolts to specifications.

CELICA

1. Disarm SRS as outlined under "Air Bag System Disarming and Arming."
2. Remove center console panel and box, **Fig. 59**
3. Remove electrical connector from air bag sensor assembly.
4. Remove mounting screws with suitable Torx wrench and sensor assembly.
5. Reverse procedure to install and tighten mounting screws to specifications.

COROLLA

1. Disarm SRS as outlined under "Air Bag System Disarming and Arming."
2. Remove console box, **Fig. 60.**
3. Loosen air bag sensor assembly mounting screws with suitable Torx wrench.
4. Remove electrical connector for air bag sensor assembly, then remove assembly.
5. Reverse procedure to install and tighten mounting screws to specifications.

LAND CRUISER

1. Disarm SRS as outlined under "Air Bag System Disarming and Arming."
2. Remove transfer shift knob and front console box, **Fig. 61.**
3. Remove air bag sensor assembly electrical connector.
4. Remove assembly mounting screws with suitable Torx wrench, then remove assembly.
5. Reverse procedure to install and tighten mounting screws to specifications.

MR2

1. Disarm SRS as outlined under "Air Bag System Disarming and Arming."
2. Remove shift lever knob and boot, shift hole cover, ash tray, instrument cluster center finish panel, radio and heater control, **Fig. 62.**
3. Remove air bag sensor electrical connector.
4. Remove sensor mounting screws with suitable Torx wrench, then assembly.
5. Reverse procedure to install and tighten mounting screws to specifications.

PASEO

1. Disarm SRS as outlined under "Air Bag System Disarming and Arming."
2. **On 1993–95 models,** remove console box, lower No. 1 and No. 2 finish panels, radio and lower center finish panel, **Fig. 63.**
3. **On 1996 models,** remove console box and lower center finish panel, **Fig. 64.**
4. **On all models,** remove air bag sensor assembly electrical connector.
5. Loosen assembly screws with suitable Torx wrench and remove assembly.
6. Reverse procedure to install and tighten mounting screws to specifications.

PREVIA

1. Disarm SRS as outlined under "Air Bag System Disarming and Arming."
2. Remove cool or console box, **Fig. 65.**
3. Loosen air bag sensor assembly mounting screws with suitable Torx wrench.
4. Remove air bag sensor assembly electrical connector and assembly.
5. Reverse procedure to install and tighten mounting screws to specifications.

RAV4

1. Disarm SRS as outlined under "Air Bag System Disarming and Arming."
2. Remove shift lever knob, shifting hole cover, console box hole cover and console box, **Fig. 66.**
3. Remove air bag sensor assembly electrical connector.
4. Remove sensor assembly mounting screws with suitable Torx wrench, then assembly.
5. Reverse procedure to install and tighten screws to specifications.

SUPRA

1. Disarm SRS as outlined under "Air Bag System Disarming and Arming."
2. Remove console panel upper and console box, **Fig. 67.**
3. Remove air bag sensor assembly electrical connector.
4. Remove air bag sensor assembly mounting screws with suitable Torx wrench and assembly.
5. Reverse procedure to install and tighten mounting screws to specifications.

TACOMA

1. Disarm SRS as outlined under "Air Bag System Disarming and Arming."
2. Remove lower center cover and anti-lock brake system (ABS) electrical control unit (ECU), **Fig. 68.**
3. Remove air bag sensor assembly electrical connector.
4. Remove air bag sensor assembly mounting screws with suitable Torx wrench and assembly.
5. Reverse procedure to install and tighten mounting screws to specifications.

TERCEL

1. Disarm SRS as outlined under "Air Bag

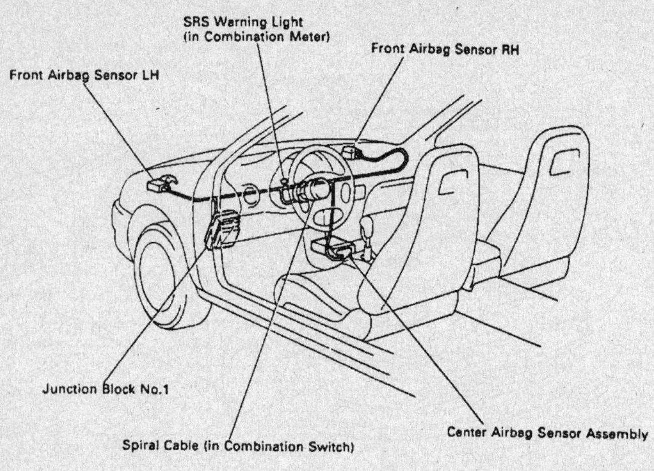

SRS Warning Light
(in Combination Meter)
Front Airbag Sensor RH
Front Airbag Sensor LH
Junction Block No.1
Spiral Cable (in Combination Switch)
Center Airbag Sensor Assembly

TY8019400146000X

Fig. 11 SRS component locations. 1994–95 Paseo & 1994 Tercel

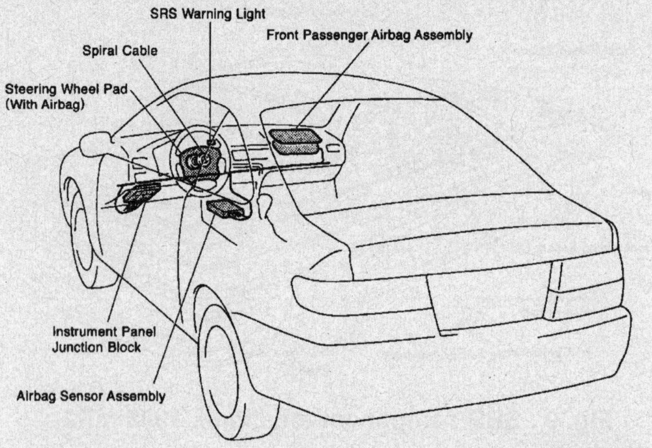

SRS Warning Light
Front Passenger Airbag Assembly
Spiral Cable
Steering Wheel Pad
(With Airbag)
Instrument Panel
Junction Block
Airbag Sensor Assembly

TY8019600347000X

Fig. 12 SRS component locations. 1996 Paseo

System Disarming and Arming."

2. Remove console box, center cluster and lower center finish panels, and rear air duct No. 3, **Figs. 69 and 70.**
3. Remove electrical connector.
4. Remove air bag sensor assembly screws with suitable Torx wrench and assembly.
5. Reverse procedure to install and tighten mounting screws to specifications, then arm SRS as outlined under "Air Bag System Disarming and Arming."

T100

1. Disarm SRS as outlined under "Air Bag System Disarming and Arming."
2. **On 1994 models,** remove tool box lid and air bag sensor assembly cover, **Fig. 71.**
3. **On 1995–96 models,** remove lower center cover and cruise control electrical control unit (ECU), **Fig. 72.**
4. **On all models,** remove air bag sensor assembly mounting screws with suitable Torx wrench, then remove assembly.
5. Reverse procedure to install and tighten mounting screws to specifications.

4RUNNER

1. Disarm SRS as outlined under "Air Bag System Disarming and Arming."
2. Remove upper console panel, rear console box, console panel garnish, ash tray, heater control panel and center cluster finish panel, **Fig. 73.**
3. Disconnect air bag sensor assembly connector.
4. Remove air bag sensor assembly mounting screws with suitable Torx wrench, then remove assembly.
5. Reverse procedure to install and tighten mounting screws to specifications.

AIR BAG ASSEMBLY DISPOSAL

When handling a deployed air bag assembly, a face shield and rubber gloves should be worn. Vehicle interior and HVAC ducts should be vacuumed. If sinus or throat irritation is encountered during air bag removal, exit vehicle and breath fresh air. If skin irritation is encountered, flush affected area with cool water. If sinus, throat, skin or any other type of irritation continues, consult a physician. Wash hands and rinse thoroughly with water after handling a deployed air bag assembly.

All deployed air bag units must be removed as outlined under "Air Bag Module, Replace." After unit has been removed, it should be placed in a heavy duty plastic bag, sealed securely, then discarded with automotive scrap.

An undeployed air bag unit must be deployed prior to disposal.

If vehicle is not being scrapped, air bag assembly should be deployed outside of vehicle. If vehicle is to be scrapped, air bag may be deployed while still installed.

DRIVER SIDE AIR BAG

Outside Vehicle Deployment

1. Disarm SRS as outlined under "Air Bag System Disarming and Arming."
2. Remove driver's air bag as outlined under "Air Bag Module, Replace."
3. Using bolts and washers, mount driver's air bag to a discarded tire and rim.
4. Using three pieces of thick wire, wrap wire at least two times around each air bag bolt. Wrap harness through wheel lug holes and securely tie off, **Fig. 74.**
5. Connect deployment tool No. 09082-00700, or equivalent, to air bag connector from underneath wheel. Move deployment tool at least 33 feet away from wheel.
6. Ensure wheel pad is facing upward. Cover wheel and pad with a large cardboard box. Weigh box down in four places.
7. Ensure no people, animals or objects are within 33 feet of air bag.
8. Connect deployment tool's battery terminals to a fully charged 12 volt battery.
9. Press deployment button and deploy air bag.
10. If air bag assembly does not deploy, consult Toyota for disposal procedures.

Inside Vehicle Deployment

If a vehicle with an undeployed air bag is to be scrapped, air bag must be deployed before scrapping.

1. Disarm SRS as outlined under "Air Bag System Disarming and Arming."
2. Remove No. 1 undercover and disconnect air bag connector from spiral cable.
3. Connect deployment tool No. 09082-00700, or equivalent, to spiral cable connector.
4. Close all vehicle doors and windows.
5. Move deployment tool at least 33 feet from vehicle.
6. Ensure no people, animals or objects are within 33 feet of air bag.
7. Connect deployment tool's battery terminals to a fully charged 12 volt battery.
8. Press deployment button and deploy air bag.
9. If air bag assembly does not deploy, consult Toyota for disposal procedures.

PASSENGER AIR BAG

Outside Vehicle Deployment

1. Disarm SRS as outlined under "Air Bag System Disarming and Arming."
2. Remove passenger air bag as outlined under "Air Bag Module, Replace."
3. Using thick wire, secure passenger air bag to a discarded tire and wheel, **Fig. 75.**
4. Position tire with air bag on top of two tires, then place two more tires on top of tires containing air bag.
5. Use thick wire to secure tires together.
6. Connect deployment tool No. 09082-00700, or equivalent, to air bag connector from underneath wheel. Move deployment tool at least 33 feet away from wheel.
7. Ensure no people, animals or objects are within 33 feet of air bag.
8. Connect battery terminals of deployment tool to battery source.
9. Press deployment button and deploy air bag.

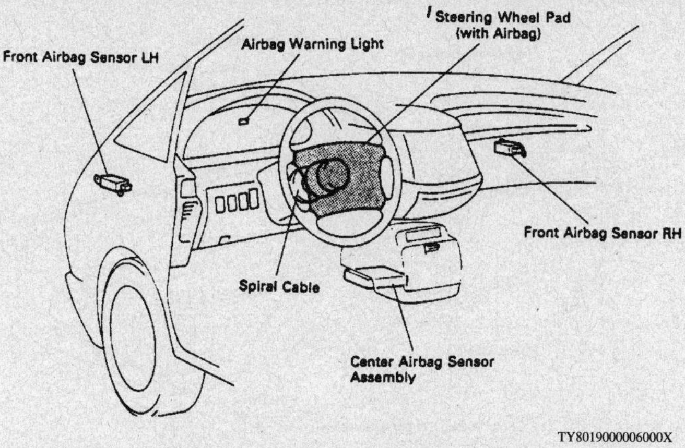
Front Airbag Sensor LH
Airbag Warning Light
Steering Wheel Pad (with Airbag)
Front Airbag Sensor RH
Spiral Cable
Center Airbag Sensor Assembly
TY8019000006000X

Fig. 13 SRS component locations. 1993 Previa

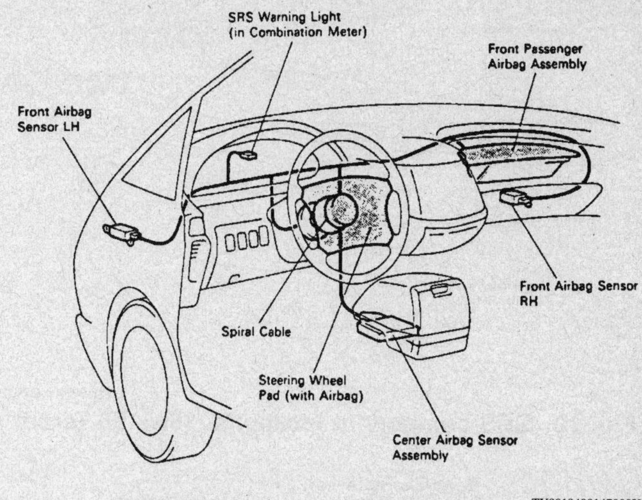
SRS Warning Light (in Combination Meter)
Front Passenger Airbag Assembly
Front Airbag Sensor LH
Front Airbag Sensor RH
Spiral Cable
Steering Wheel Pad (with Airbag)
Center Airbag Sensor Assembly
TY8019400147000X

Fig. 14 SRS component locations. 1994–95 Previa

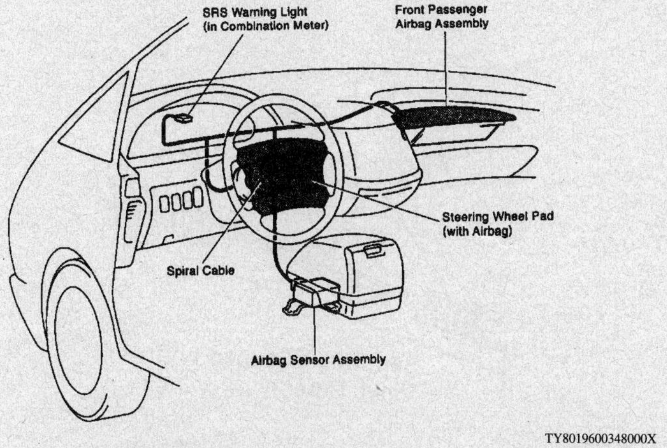
SRS Warning Light (in Combination Meter)
Front Passenger Airbag Assembly
Steering Wheel Pad (with Airbag)
Spiral Cable
Airbag Sensor Assembly
TY8019600348000X

Fig. 15 SRS component locations. 1996 Previa

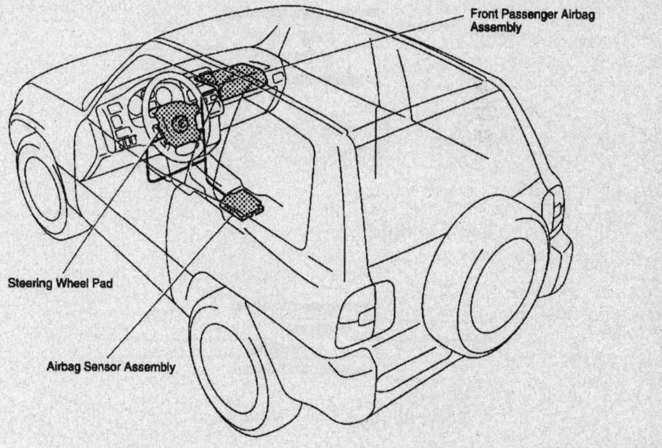
Front Passenger Airbag Assembly
Steering Wheel Pad
Airbag Sensor Assembly
TY8019600349000X

Fig. 16 SRS component locations. RAV4

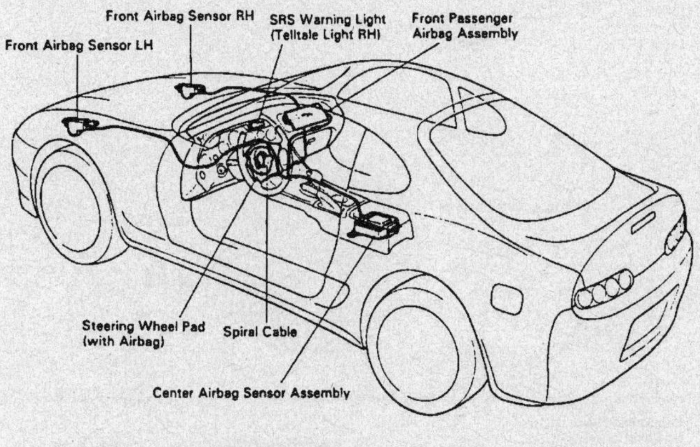
Front Airbag Sensor RH
SRS Warning Light (Telltale Light RH)
Front Passenger Airbag Assembly
Front Airbag Sensor LH
Steering Wheel Pad (with Airbag)
Spiral Cable
Center Airbag Sensor Assembly
TY8019400148000X

Fig. 17 SRS component locations. Supra

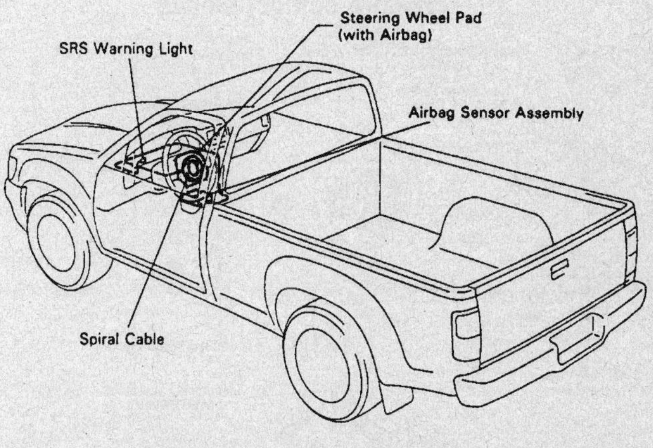
Steering Wheel Pad (with Airbag)
SRS Warning Light
Airbag Sensor Assembly
Spiral Cable
TY8019500149000X

Fig. 18 SRS component locations. Tacoma

10. If air bag assembly does not deploy, consult Toyota for disposal procedures.

Inside Vehicle Deployment

If a vehicle with an undeployed air bag is to be scrapped , air bag must be deployed before scrapping.

1. Disarm SRS as outlined under "Air Bag System Disarming and Arming."
2. Remove glove compartment door trim plate, then disconnect passenger air bag connector.
3. Connect air bag deployment tool No. 09082-00700, or equivalent, to air bag connector, **Fig. 76.**
4. Close all vehicle doors and windows.
5. Move deployment tool at least 33 feet from vehicle.
6. Ensure no people, animals or objects are within 33 feet of air bag.
7. Connect deployment tool's battery terminals to a fully charged 12 volt battery.
8. Press deployment button and deploy air bag.
9. If air bag assembly does not deploy, consult Toyota for disposal procedures.

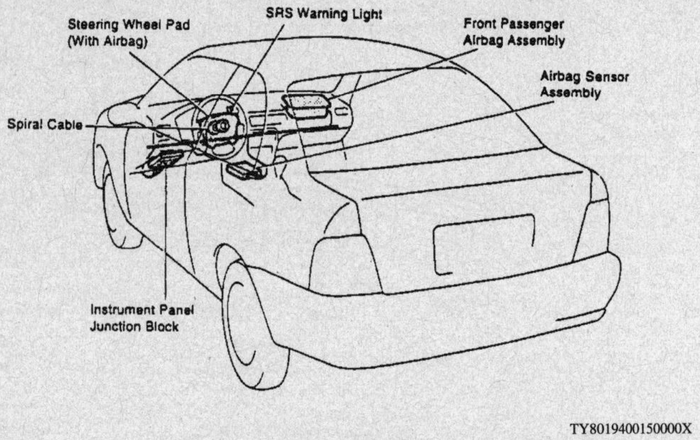
Steering Wheel Pad
(With Airbag)
SRS Warning Light
Front Passenger
Airbag Assembly
Airbag Sensor
Assembly
Spiral Cable
Instrument Panel
Junction Block

TY8019400150000X

Fig. 19 SRS component locations. 1995–96 Tercel

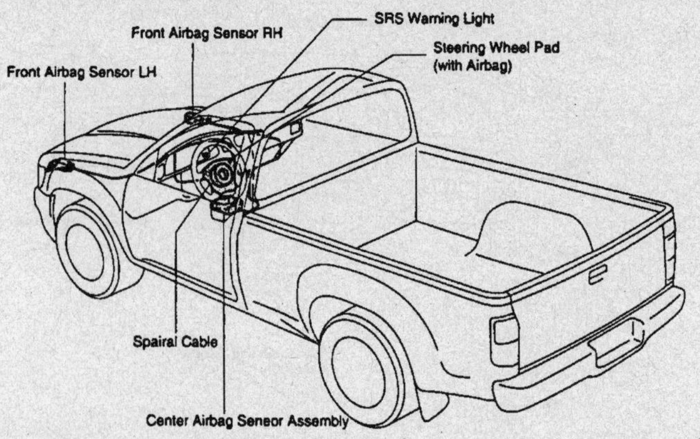
SRS Warning Light
Front Airbag Sensor RH
Steering Wheel Pad
(with Airbag)
Front Airbag Sensor LH
Spairal Cable
Center Airbag Sensor Assembly

TY8019400151000X

Fig. 20 SRS component locations. T100

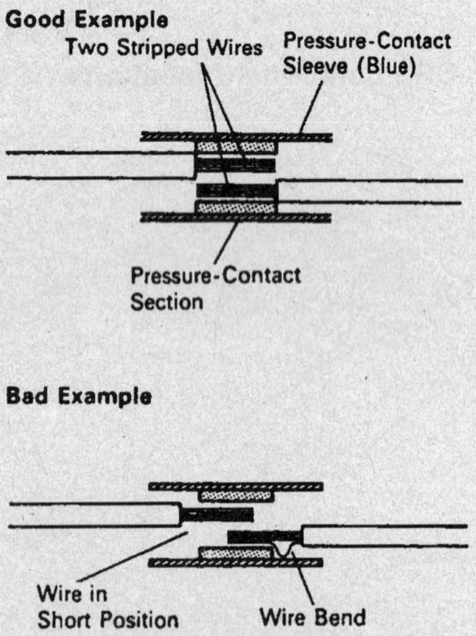
Good Example
Two Stripped Wires
Pressure-Contact
Sleeve (Blue)
Pressure-Contact
Section
Bad Example
Wire in
Short Position
Wire Bend

TY8019400167000X

Fig. 21 Positioning SRS wire in pressure contact sleeve

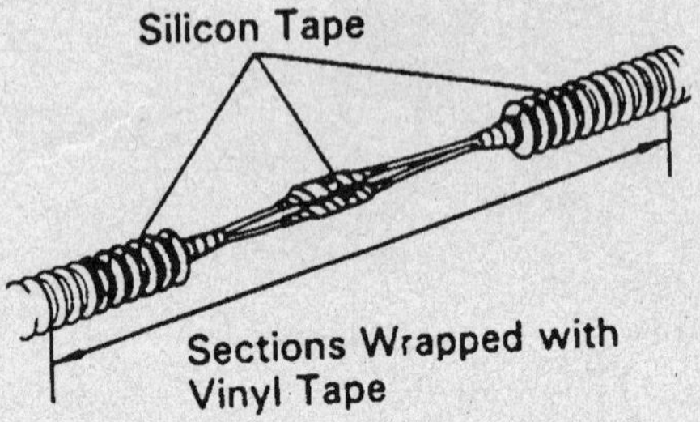
Silicon Tape
Sections Wrapped with
Vinyl Tape

TY8019400168000X

Fig. 22 Completed wire repair

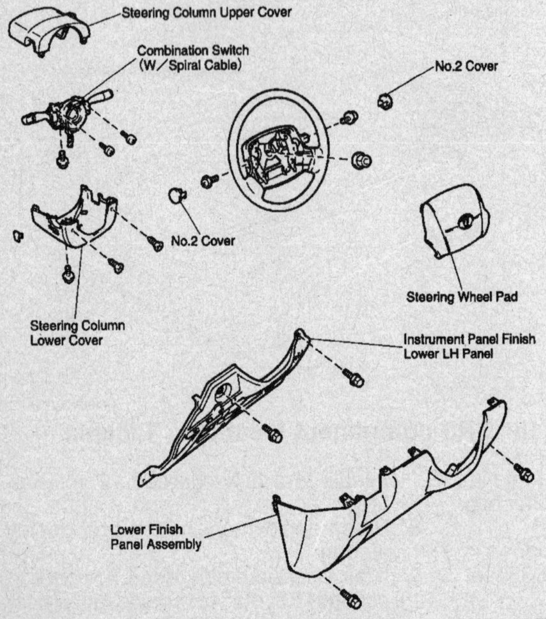
Steering Column Upper Cover
Combination Switch
(W/Spiral Cable)
No.2 Cover
No.2 Cover
Steering Wheel Pad
Steering Column
Lower Cover
Instrument Panel Finish
Lower LH Panel
Lower Finish
Panel Assembly

TY8019500350000X

Fig. 23 Driver side air bag module replacement. Avalon

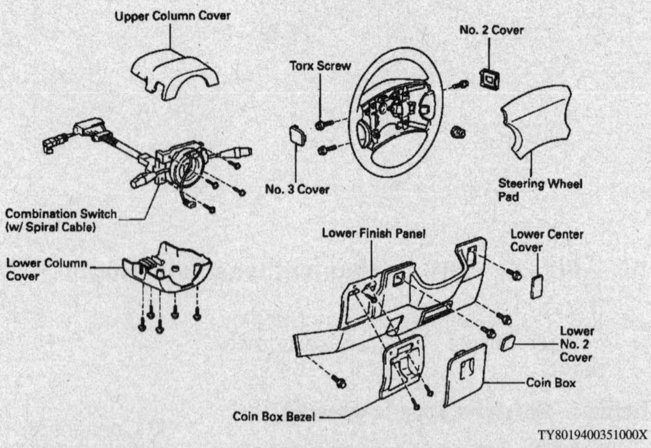
Upper Column Cover
No. 2 Cover
Torx Screw
No. 3 Cover
Steering Wheel
Pad
Combination Switch
(w/ Spiral Cable)
Lower Finish Panel
Lower Center
Cover
Lower Column
Cover
Lower
No. 2
Cover
Coin Box
Coin Box Bezel

TY8019400351000X

Fig. 24 Driver side air bag module replacement. Camry

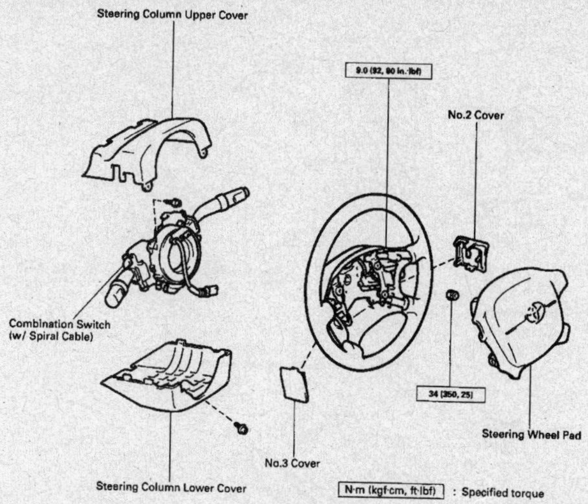
Steering Column Upper Cover
9.0 (92, 80 in.·lbf)
No.2 Cover
Combination Switch
(w/ Spiral Cable)
34 (350, 25)
Steering Wheel Pad
No.3 Cover
Steering Column Lower Cover
N·m (kgf·cm, ft·lbf) : Specified torque

TY8019400352000X

Fig. 25 Driver side air bag module replacement. Celica & RAV4

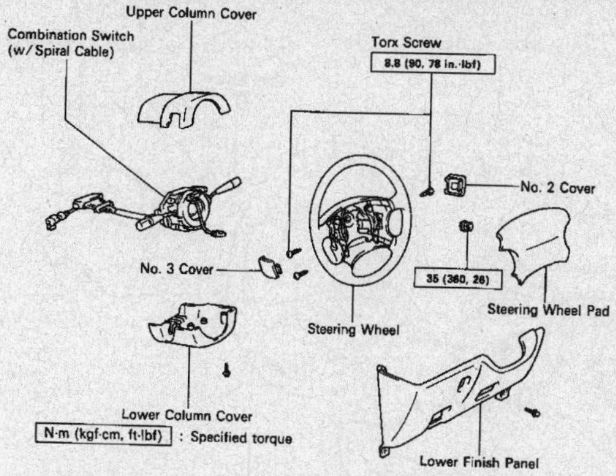
Upper Column Cover
Combination Switch
(w/ Spiral Cable)
Torx Screw
8.8 (90, 78 in.·lbf)
No. 2 Cover
No. 3 Cover
35 (360, 26)
Steering Wheel Pad
Steering Wheel
Lower Column Cover
N·m (kgf·cm, ft·lbf) : Specified torque
Lower Finish Panel

TY8019400353000X

Fig. 26 Driver side air bag module replacement. Corolla

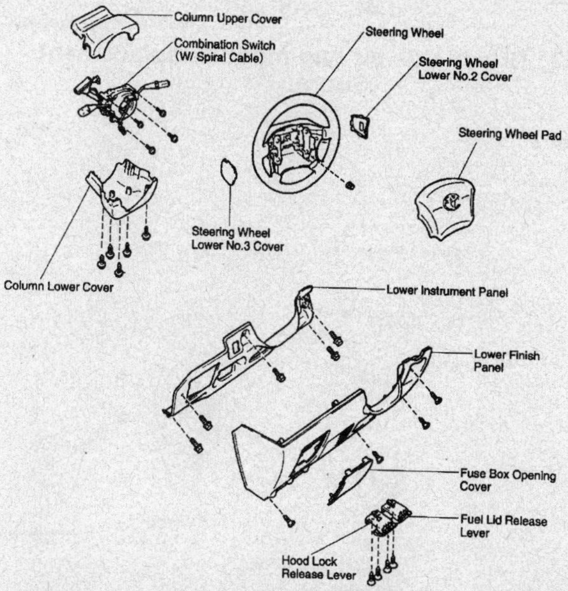
Column Upper Cover
Combination Switch
(W/ Spiral Cable)
Steering Wheel
Steering Wheel
Lower No.2 Cover
Steering Wheel Pad
Steering Wheel
Lower No.3 Cover
Column Lower Cover
Lower Instrument Panel
Lower Finish
Panel
Fuse Box Opening
Cover
Fuel Lid Release
Lever
Hood Lock
Release Lever

TY8019500354000X

Fig. 27 Driver side air bag module replacement. Land Cruiser

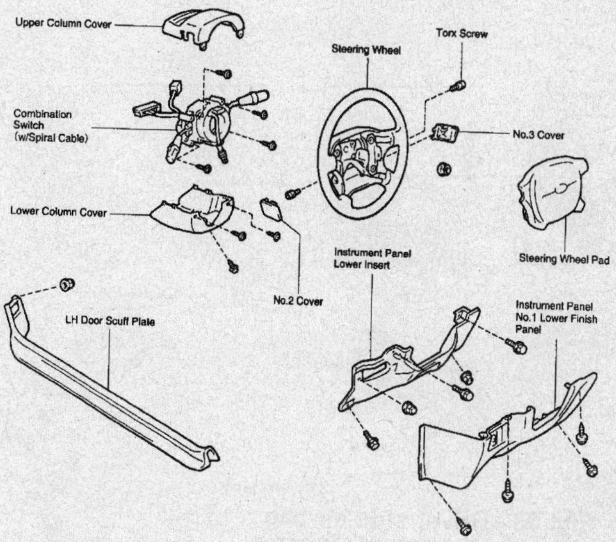
Upper Column Cover
Torx Screw
Steering Wheel
Combination
Switch
(w/Spiral Cable)
No.3 Cover
Lower Column Cover
Instrument Panel
Lower Insert
Steering Wheel Pad
No.2 Cover
LH Door Scuff Plate
Instrument Panel
No.1 Lower Finish
Panel

TY8019400355000X

Fig. 28 Driver side air bag module replacement. MR2

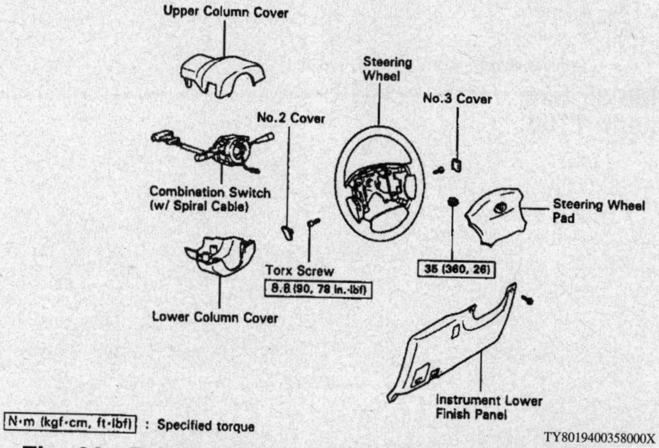
Upper Column Cover
Steering
Wheel
No.3 Cover
No.2 Cover
Combination Switch
(w/ Spiral Cable)
Steering Wheel
Pad
Torx Screw
8.8 (90, 78 in.·lbf)
35 (360, 26)
Lower Column Cover
Instrument Lower
Finish Panel
N·m (kgf·cm, ft·lbf) : Specified torque

TY8019400358000X

Fig. 29 Driver side air bag module replacement. 1993–94 Tercel & 1993–95 Paseo

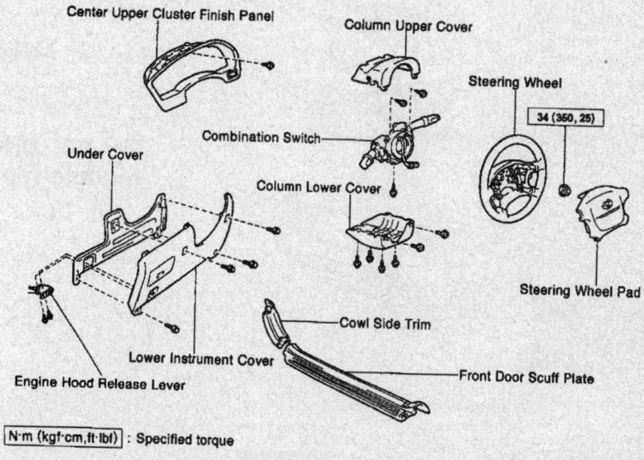
Center Upper Cluster Finish Panel
Column Upper Cover
Steering Wheel
34 (350, 25)
Combination Switch
Under Cover
Column Lower Cover
Steering Wheel Pad
Cowl Side Trim
Lower Instrument Cover
Front Door Scuff Plate
Engine Hood Release Lever
N·m (kgf·cm,ft·lbf) : Specified torque

TY8019600359000X

Fig. 30 Driver side air bag module replacement. 1995–96 Tercel & 1996 Paseo

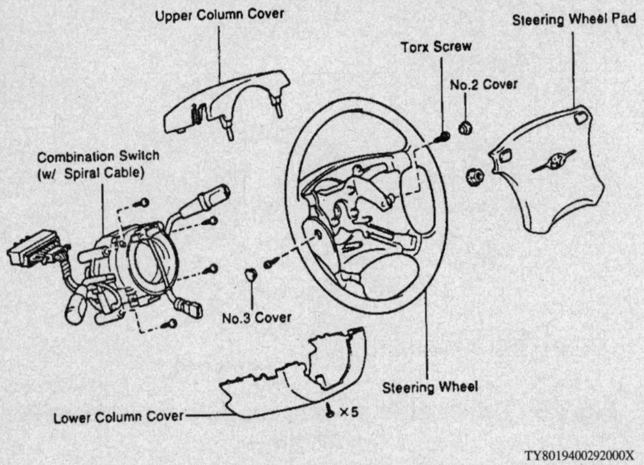
Upper Column Cover
Steering Wheel Pad
Torx Screw
No.2 Cover
Combination Switch
(w/ Spiral Cable)
No.3 Cover
Steering Wheel
Lower Column Cover
×5

TY8019400292000X

Fig. 31 Driver side air bag module removal. Previa

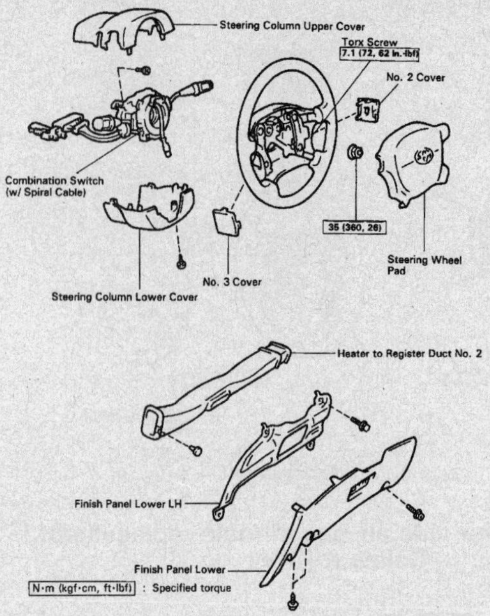
Steering Column Upper Cover
Torx Screw
7.1 (72, 62 in.-lbf)
No. 2 Cover
Combination Switch
(w/ Spiral Cable)
35 (360, 26)
Steering Wheel
Pad
No. 3 Cover
Steering Column Lower Cover
Heater to Register Duct No. 2
Finish Panel Lower LH
Finish Panel Lower
N·m (kgf·cm, ft·lbf) : Specified torque

TY8019400362000X

Fig. 32 Driver side air bag module replacement. Supra

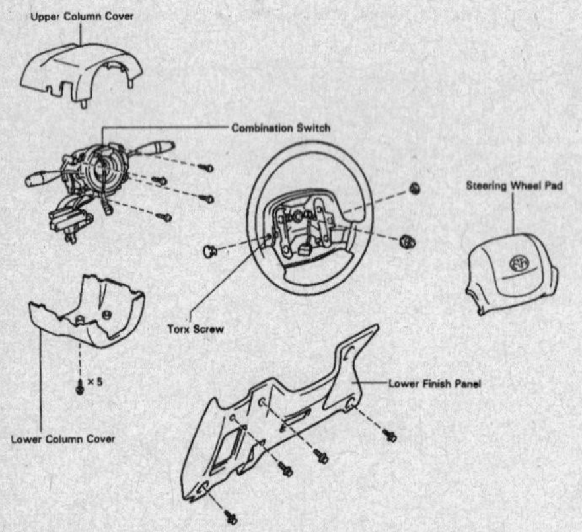
Upper Column Cover
Combination Switch
Steering Wheel Pad
Torx Screw
×5
Lower Finish Panel
Lower Column Cover

TY8019600306000X

Fig. 33 Driver side air bag module replacement. Tacoma

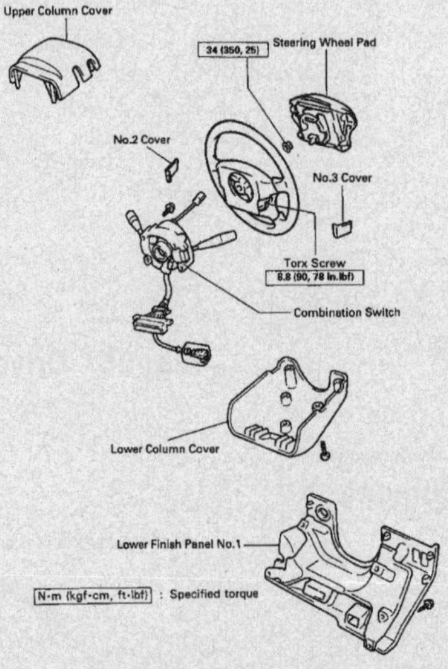
Upper Column Cover
34 (350, 25)
Steering Wheel Pad
No.2 Cover
No.3 Cover
Torx Screw
8.8 (90, 78 in.-lbf)
Combination Switch
Lower Column Cover
Lower Finish Panel No.1
N·m (kgf·cm, ft·lbf) : Specified torque

TY8019400365000X

Fig. 34 Driver side air bag module replacement. T100

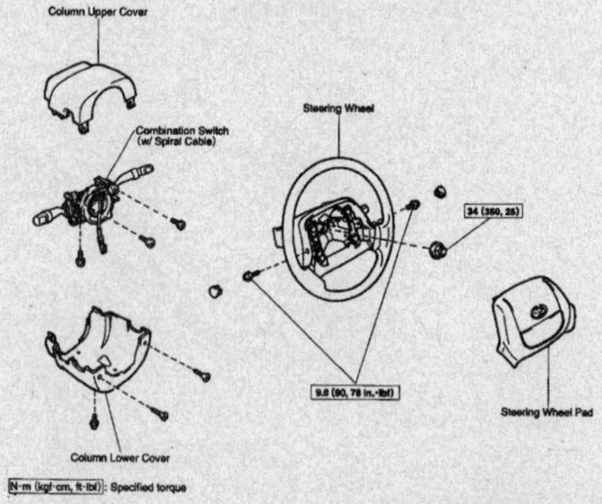
Column Upper Cover
Combination Switch
(w/ Spiral Cable)
Steering Wheel
34 (350, 25)
8.8 (90, 78 in.-lbf)
Steering Wheel Pad
Column Lower Cover
N·m (kgf·cm, ft·lbf): Specified torque

TY8019600367000X

Fig. 35 Driver side air bag module replacement. 4Runner

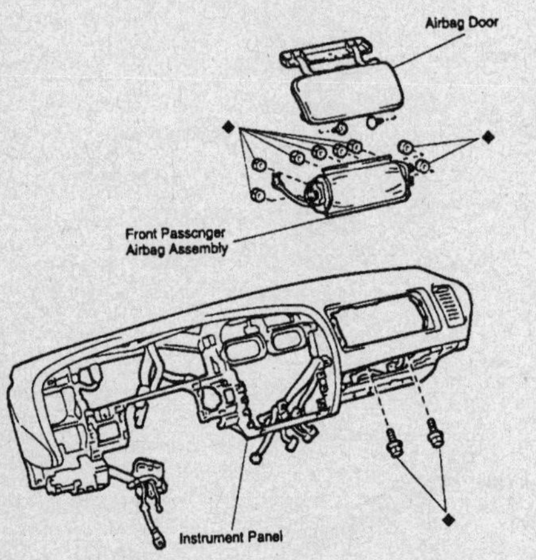
Airbag Door
Front Passenger
Airbag Assembly
Instrument Panel

TY8019529400OX

Fig. 36 Passenger air bag module replacement. Avalon

mm (in.)

Code	Shape	Size	Code	Shape	Size
Ⓐ		ϕ = 8 (0.32) L=18 (0.71)	Ⓑ		ϕ = 6 (0.24) L=16 (0.63)

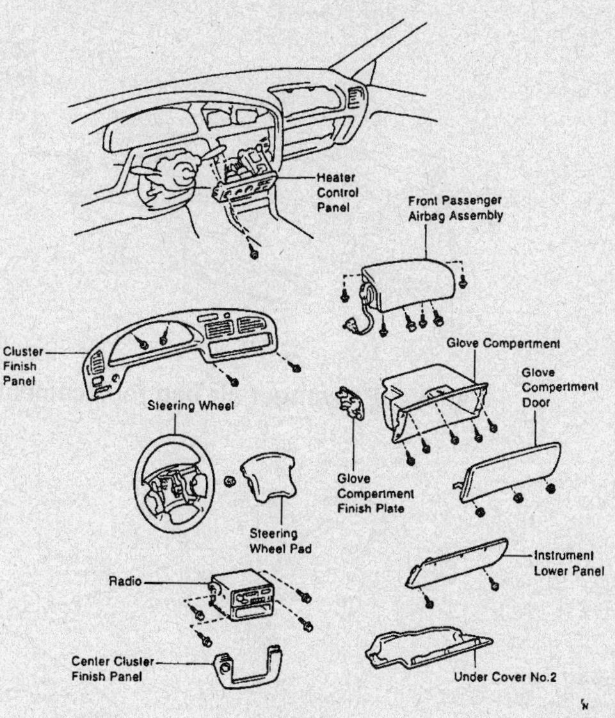
Heater
Control
Panel
Front Passenger
Airbag Assembly
Cluster
Finish
Panel
Glove Compartment
Glove
Compartment
Door
Steering Wheel
Glove
Compartment
Finish Plate
Steering
Wheel Pad
Radio
Instrument
Lower Panel
Center Cluster
Finish Panel
Under Cover No.2

TY8019400295000X

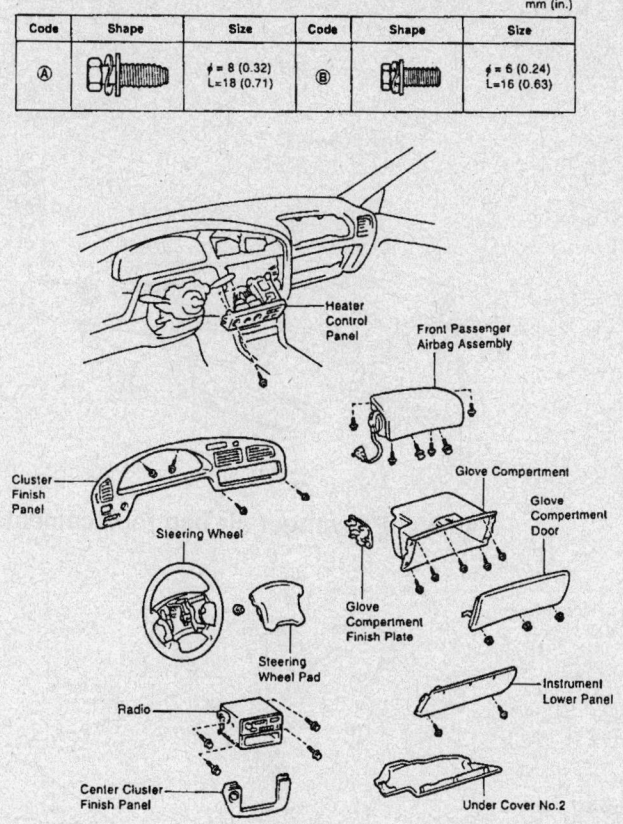

Fig. 37 Passenger air bag module replacement. Camry

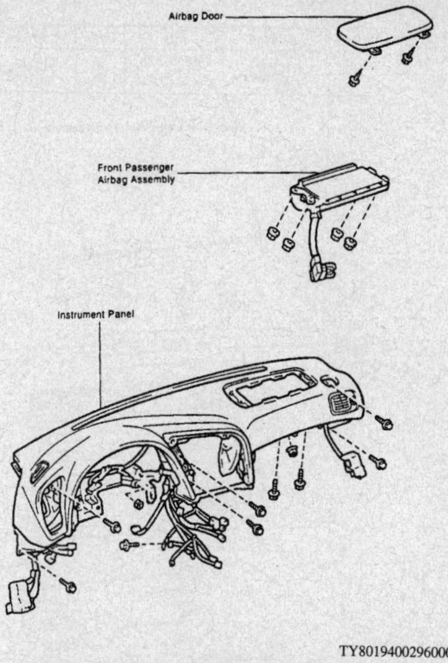
Airbag Door
Front Passenger
Airbag Assembly
Instrument Panel

TY8019400296000X

Fig. 38 Passenger air bag module replacement. Celica

Code	Shape	Size	Code	Shape	Size
Ⓐ		ϕ = 8 (0.31) L= 18 (0.71)	Ⓑ		ϕ = 6 (0.24)

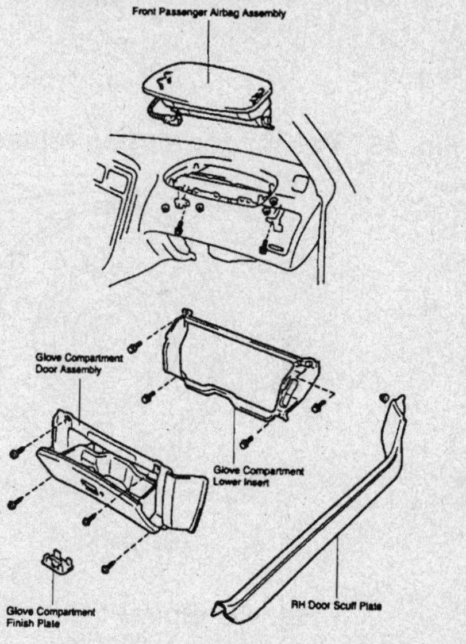
Front Passenger Airbag Assembly
Glove Compartment
Door Assembly
Glove Compartment
Lower Insert
Glove Compartment
Finish Plate
RH Door Scuff Plate

TY8019400299000X

Fig. 41 Passenger air bag replacement. MR2

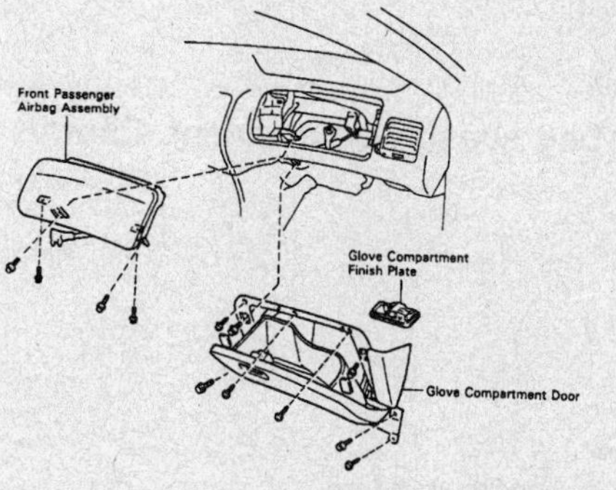
Front Passenger
Airbag Assembly
Glove Compartment
Finish Plate
Glove Compartment Door

TY8019500297000X

Fig. 39 Passenger side air bag replacement. Corolla

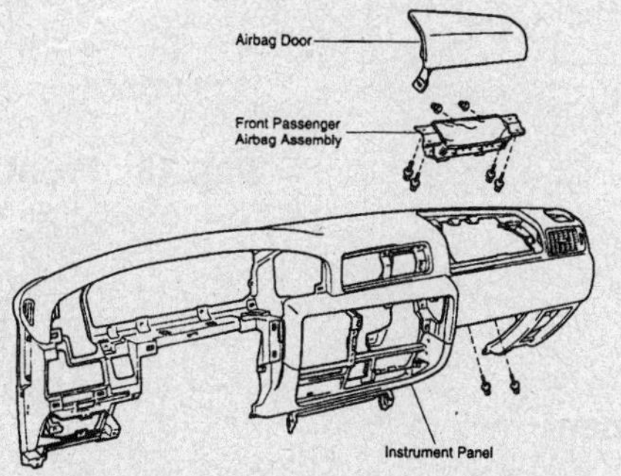
Airbag Door
Front Passenger
Airbag Assembly
Instrument Panel

TY8019400298000X

Fig. 40 Passenger air bag replacement. Land Cruiser

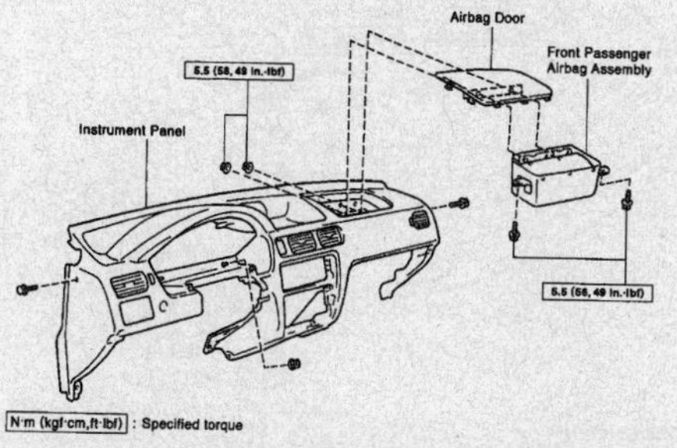
Airbag Door
Front Passenger
Airbag Assembly
5.5 (56, 49 in.-lbf)
Instrument Panel
5.5 (56, 49 in.-lbf)
N·m (kgf·cm,ft·lbf) : Specified torque

TY8019600360000

Fig. 42 Passenger's air bag module replacement. Paseo

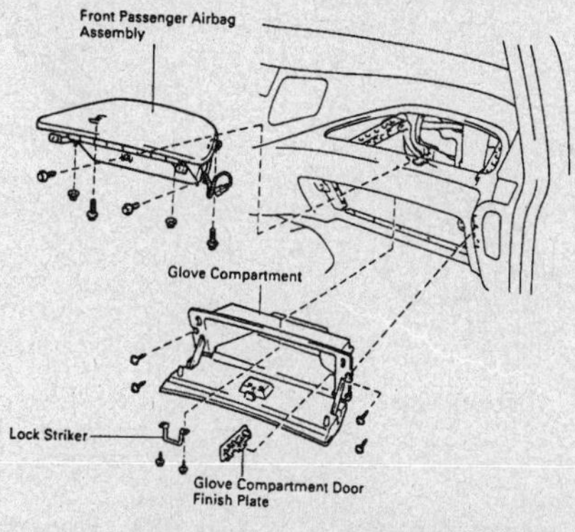
Front Passenger Airbag
Assembly
Glove Compartment
Lock Striker
Glove Compartment Door
Finish Plate

TY8019400300000X

Fig. 43 Passenger air bag replacement. Previa

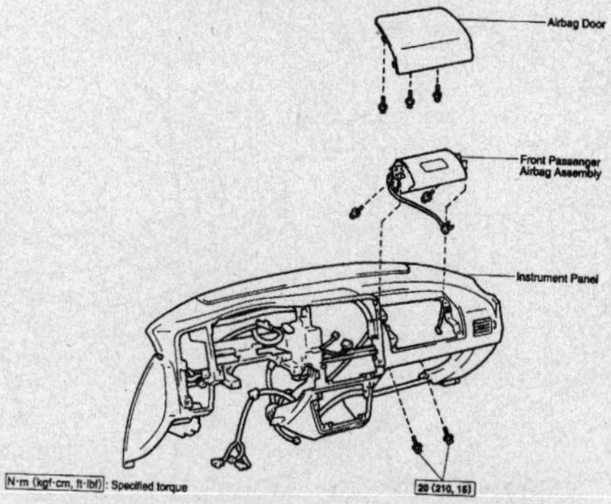
Airbag Door
Front Passenger
Airbag Assembly
Instrument Panel
N·m (kgf·cm, ft·lbf) : Specified torque
20 (210, 15)

TY8019600356000X

Fig. 44 Passenger air bag module replacement. RAV4 & 4Runner

mm (in.)

Code	Shape	Size	Code	Shape	Size
Ⓐ		ϕ=8 (0.32) L=18 (0.71)	Ⓑ		ϕ=6 (0.24) L=22 (0.87)

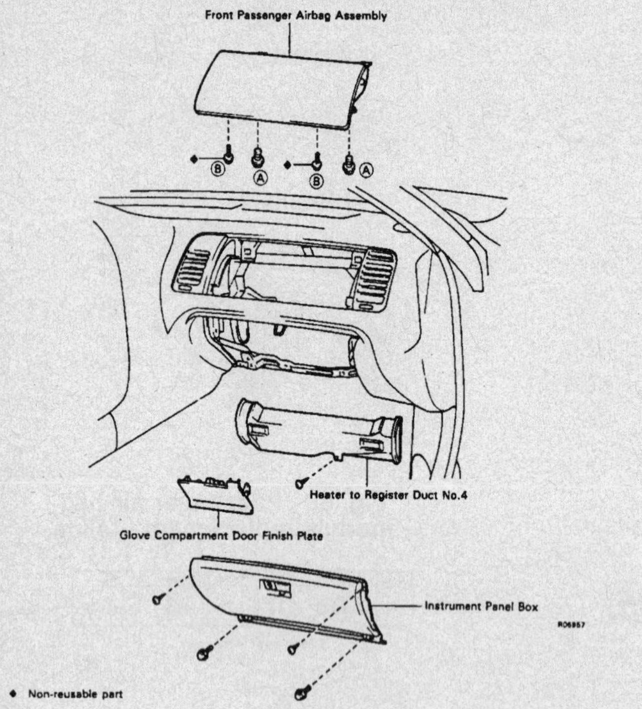
Front Passenger Airbag Assembly
Heater to Register Duct No.4
Glove Compartment Door Finish Plate
Instrument Panel Box
R06957
◆ Non-reusable part

TY8019400301000X

Fig. 45 Passenger air bag replacement. Supra

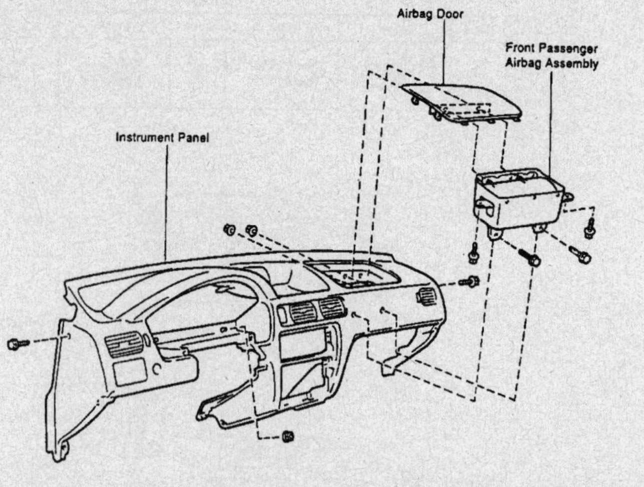
Airbag Door
Front Passenger Airbag Assembly
Instrument Panel

TY8019400302000X

Fig. 46 Passenger air bag replacement. Tercel

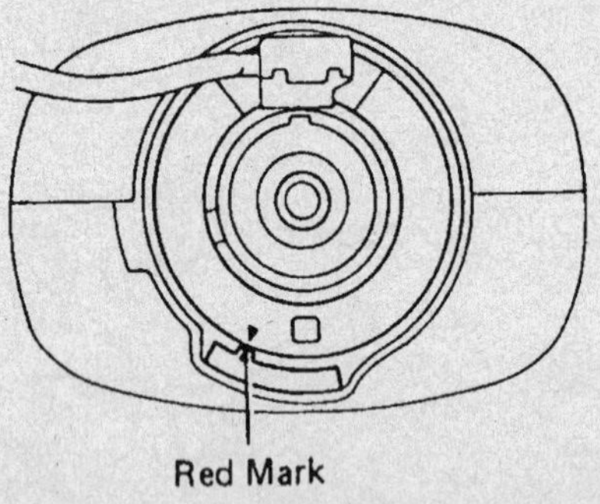
Red Mark

TY8019400293000X

Fig. 47 Spiral cable alignment marks

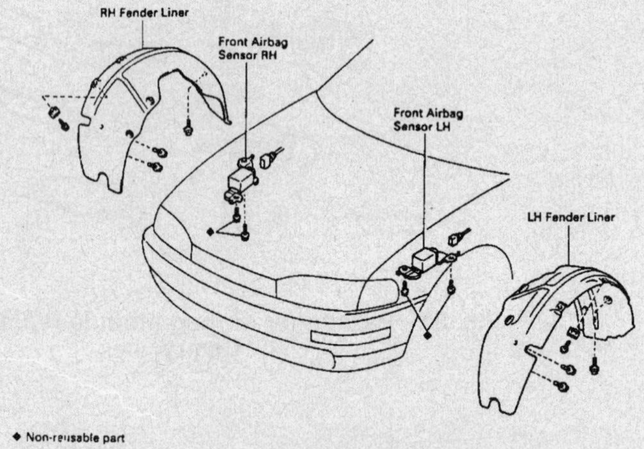
RH Fender Liner
Front Airbag Sensor RH
Front Airbag Sensor LH
LH Fender Liner
◆ Non-reusable part

TY8019400303000X

Fig. 48 Front air bag sensor replacement. Camry

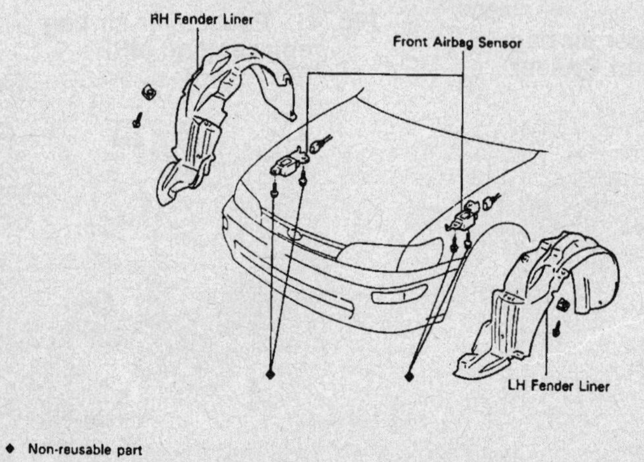
RH Fender Liner
Front Airbag Sensor
LH Fender Liner
◆ Non-reusable part

TY8019400304000X

Fig. 49 Front air bag sensor replacement. Corolla

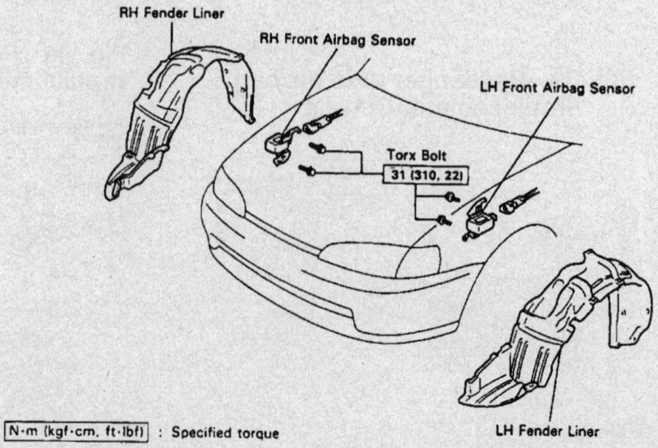
RH Fender Liner
RH Front Airbag Sensor
LH Front Airbag Sensor
Torx Bolt
31 (310, 22)
LH Fender Liner
N·m (kgf·cm, ft·lbf) : Specified torque

TY8019400305000X

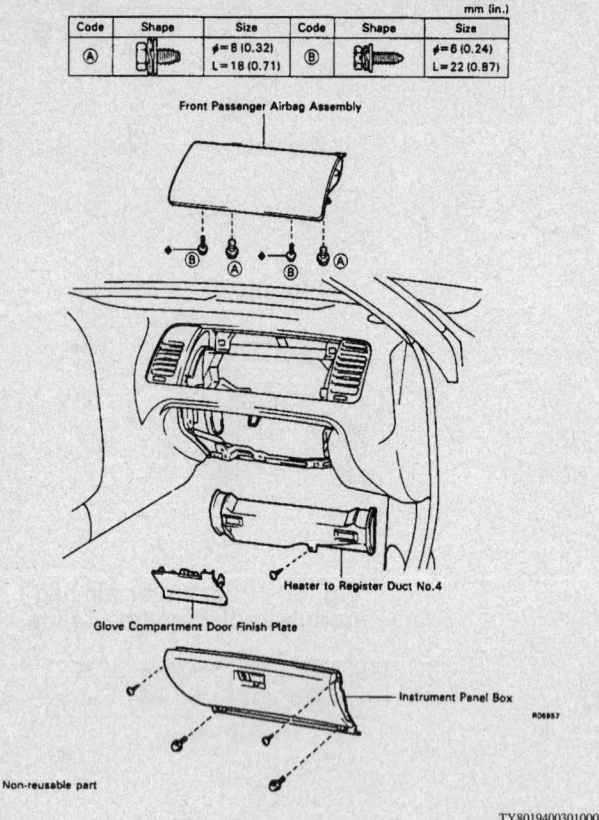

Fig. 50 Front air bag sensor replacement. Paseo & Tercel

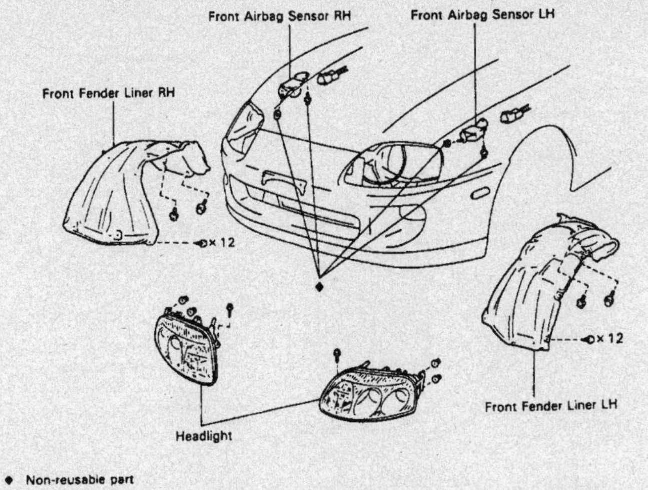
Front Airbag Sensor RH
Front Airbag Sensor LH
Front Fender Liner RH
×12
×12
Front Fender Liner LH
Headlight
◆ Non-reusable part

TY8019400306000X

Fig. 51 Front air bag sensor replacement. Supra

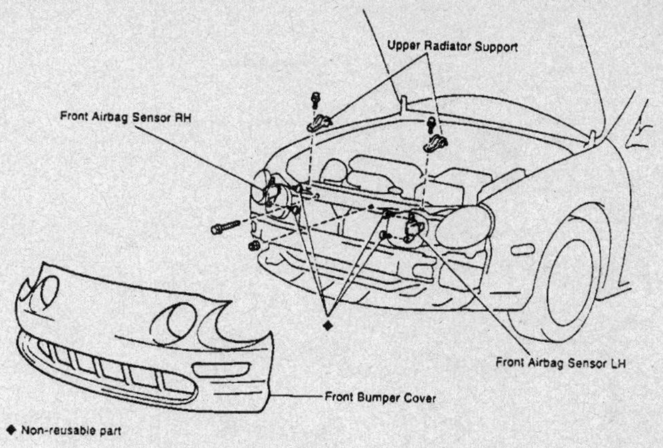
Upper Radiator Support
Front Airbag Sensor RH
Front Airbag Sensor LH
Front Bumper Cover
◆ Non-reusable part

TY8019400308000X

Fig. 52 Front air bag sensor replacement. Celica

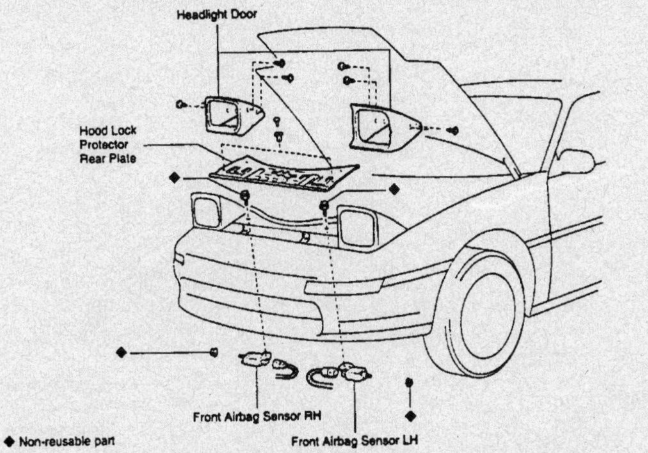
Headlight Door
Hood Lock Protector Rear Plate
Front Airbag Sensor RH
Front Airbag Sensor LH
◆ Non-reusable part

TY8019400309000X

Fig. 53 Front air bag sensor replacement. MR2

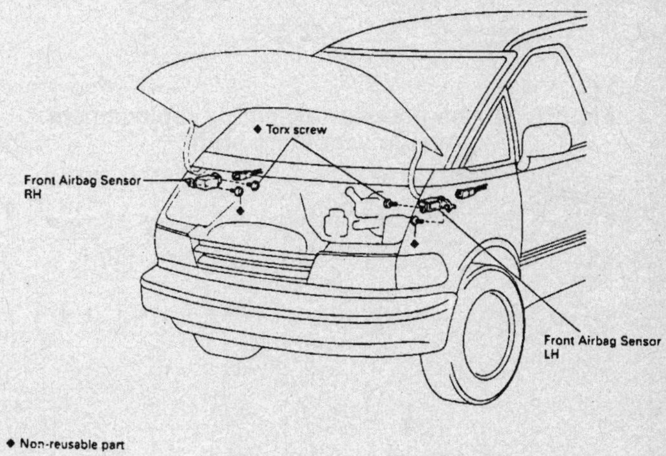
◆ Torx screw
Front Airbag Sensor RH
Front Airbag Sensor LH
◆ Non-reusable part

TY8019400310000X

Fig. 54 Front air bag sensor replacement. Previa

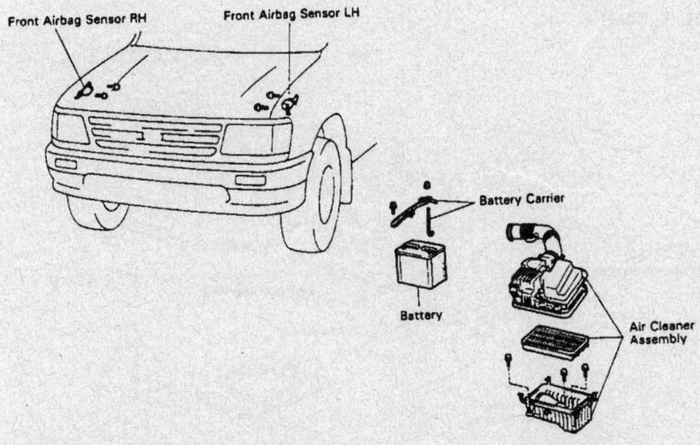
Front Airbag Sensor RH
Front Airbag Sensor LH
Battery Carrier
Battery
Air Cleaner Assembly

TY8019400307000X

Fig. 55 Front air bag sensor replacement. T100

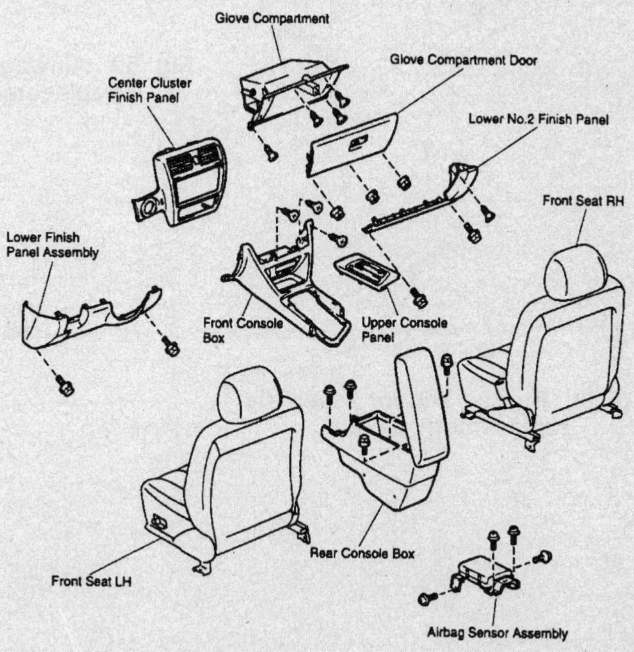
Glove Compartment
Glove Compartment Door
Center Cluster Finish Panel
Lower No.2 Finish Panel
Front Seat RH
Lower Finish Panel Assembly
Front Console Box
Upper Console Panel
Rear Console Box
Front Seat LH
Airbag Sensor Assembly

TY8019500311000X

Fig. 56 Air bag sensor assembly replacement. Avalon w/floor shift

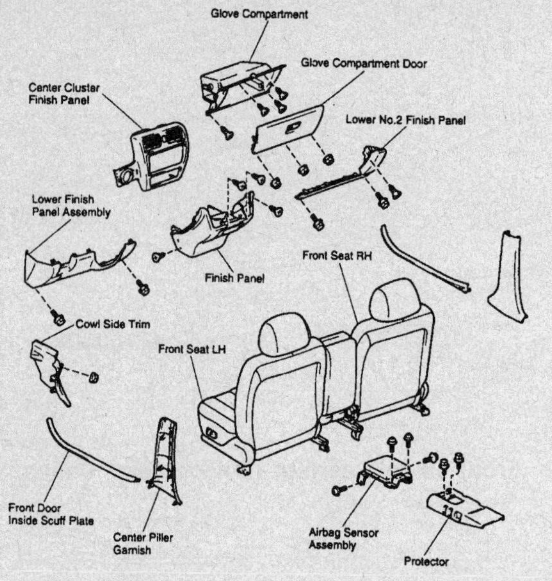
Glove Compartment
Glove Compartment Door
Center Cluster Finish Panel
Lower No.2 Finish Panel
Lower Finish Panel Assembly
Front Seat RH
Finish Panel
Cowl Side Trim
Front Seat LH
Front Door Inside Scuff Plate
Center Piller Garnish
Airbag Sensor Assembly
Protector

TY8019500312000X

Fig. 57 Air bag sensor assembly replacement. Avalon w/column shift

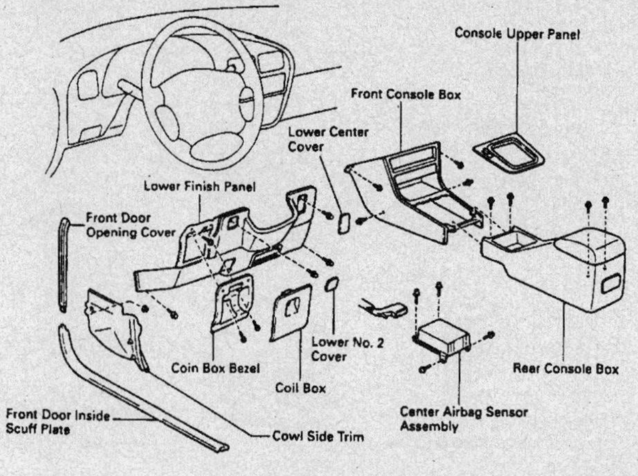
Console Upper Panel
Front Console Box
Lower Center Cover
Lower Finish Panel
Front Door Opening Cover
Lower No. 2 Cover
Coin Box Bezel
Coil Box
Rear Console Box
Front Door Inside Scuff Plate
Cowl Side Trim
Center Airbag Sensor Assembly

TY8019400313000X

Fig. 58 Air bag sensor assembly replacement. Camry

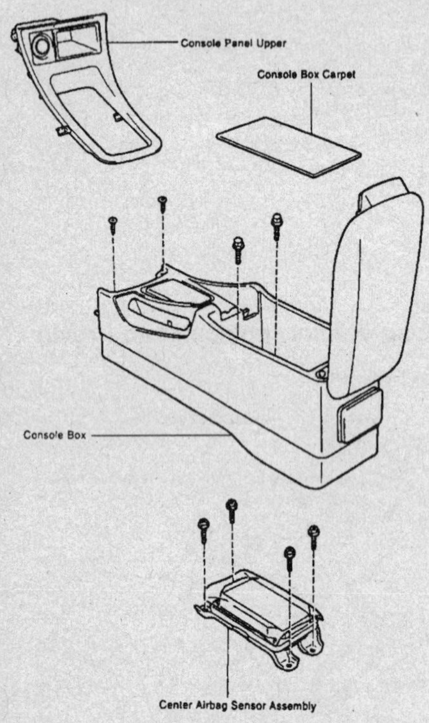
Console Panel Upper
Console Box Carpet
Console Box
Center Airbag Sensor Assembly

TY8019400314000X

Fig. 59 Air bag sensor assembly replacement. Celica

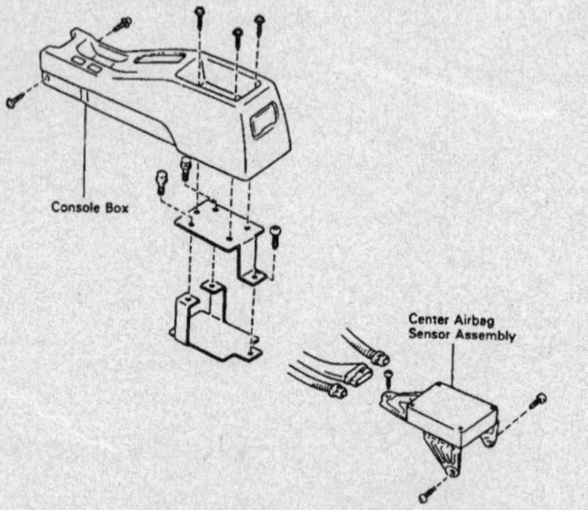
Console Box
Center Airbag Sensor Assembly

TY8019400315000X

Fig. 60 Air bag sensor assembly replacement. Corolla

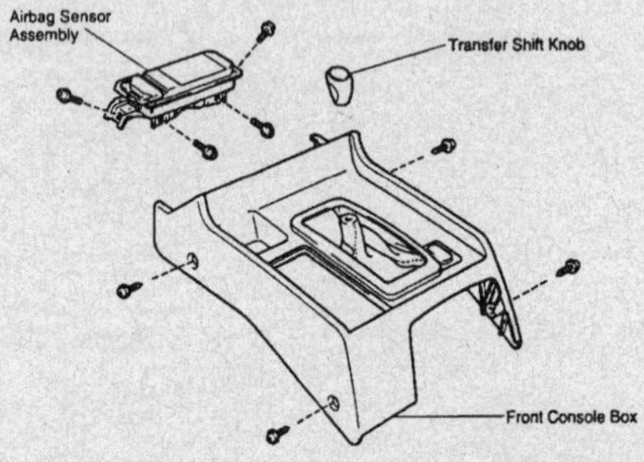
Airbag Sensor Assembly
Transfer Shift Knob
Front Console Box

TY8019400316000X

Fig. 61 Air bag sensor assembly replacement. Land Cruiser

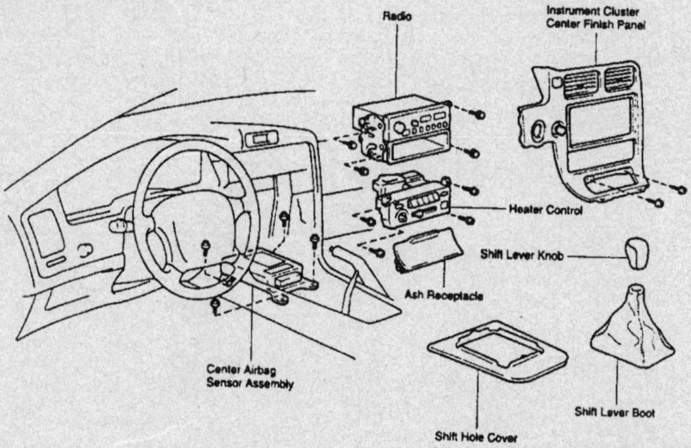
Radio
Instrument Cluster Center Finish Panel
Heater Control
Shift Lever Knob
Ash Receptacle
Center Airbag Sensor Assembly
Shift Lever Boot
Shift Hole Cover

TY8019400317000X

Fig. 62 Air bag sensor assembly replacement. MR2

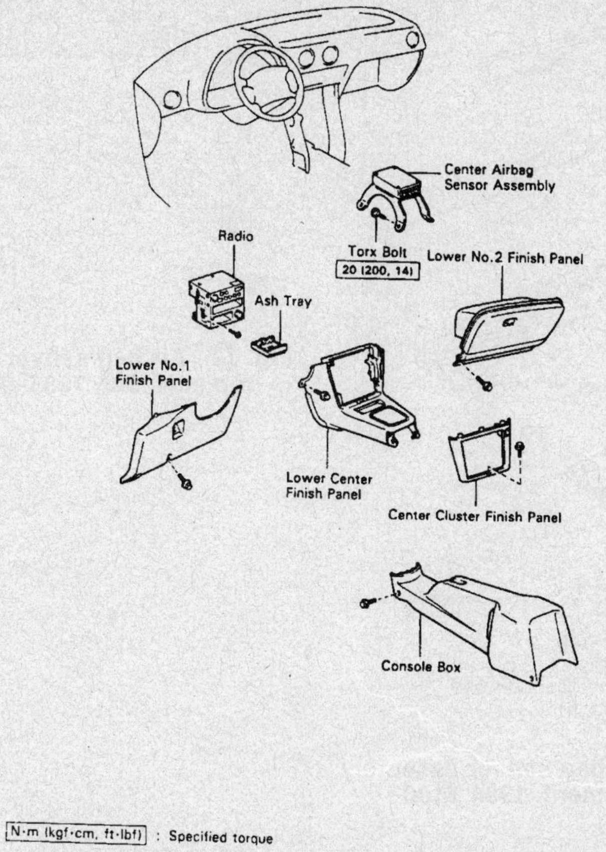
Center Airbag
Sensor Assembly
Radio
Torx Bolt
20 (200, 14)
Lower No.2 Finish Panel
Ash Tray
Lower No.1
Finish Panel
Lower Center
Finish Panel
Center Cluster Finish Panel
Console Box
N·m (kgf·cm, ft·lbf) : Specified torque

TY8019400318000X

Fig. 63 Air bag sensor assembly replacement. 1993–95 Paseo

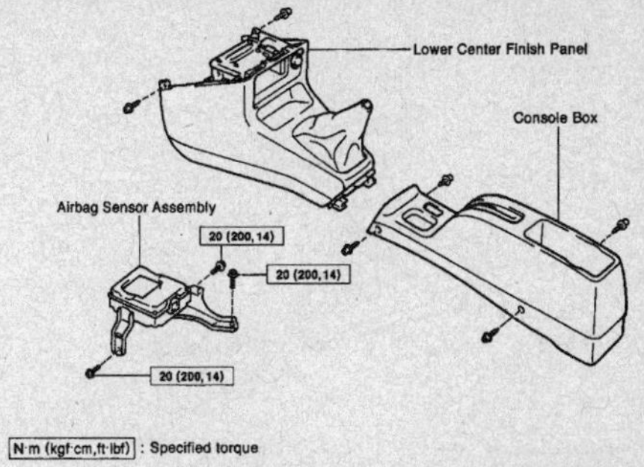
Lower Center Finish Panel
Console Box
Airbag Sensor Assembly
20 (200,14)
20 (200,14)
20 (200,14)
N·m (kgf·cm,ft·lbf) : Specified torque

TY8019600361000X

Fig. 64 Air bag sensor assembly replacement. 1996 Paseo

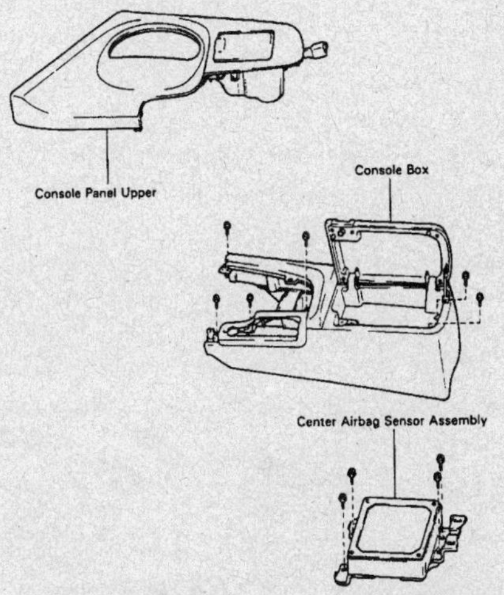
Console Panel Upper
Console Box
Center Airbag Sensor Assembly

TY8019400320000X

Fig. 67 Air bag sensor assembly replacement. Supra

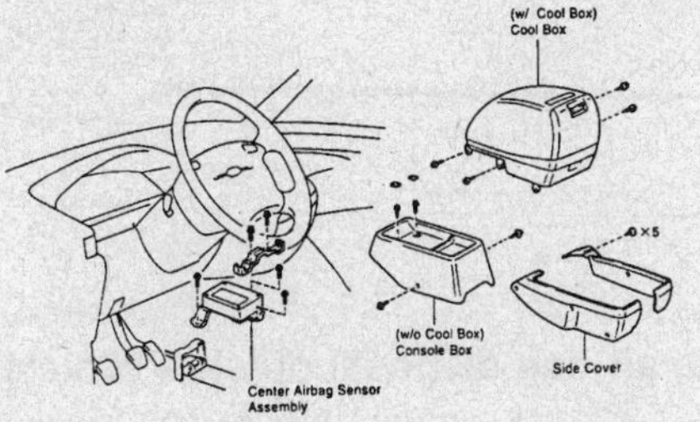
(w/ Cool Box)
Cool Box
×5
(w/o Cool Box)
Console Box
Side Cover
Center Airbag Sensor
Assembly

TY8019400319000X

Fig. 65 Air bag sensor assembly replacement. Previa

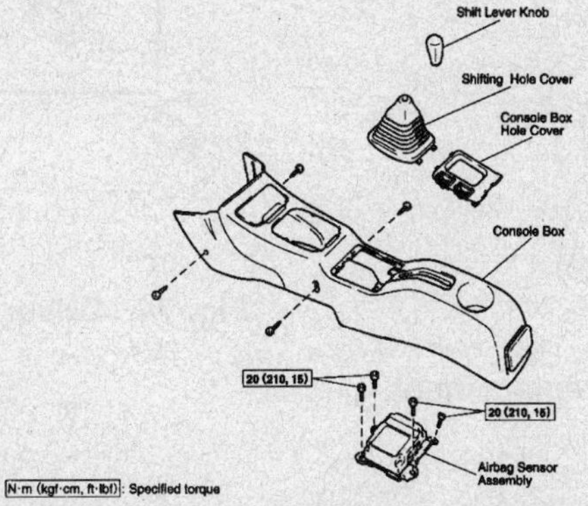
Shift Lever Knob
Shifting Hole Cover
Console Box
Hole Cover
Console Box
20 (210, 15)
20 (210, 15)
Airbag Sensor
Assembly
N·m (kgf·cm, ft·lbf): Specified torque

TY8019600357000X

Fig. 66 Air bag sensor assembly replacement. RAV4

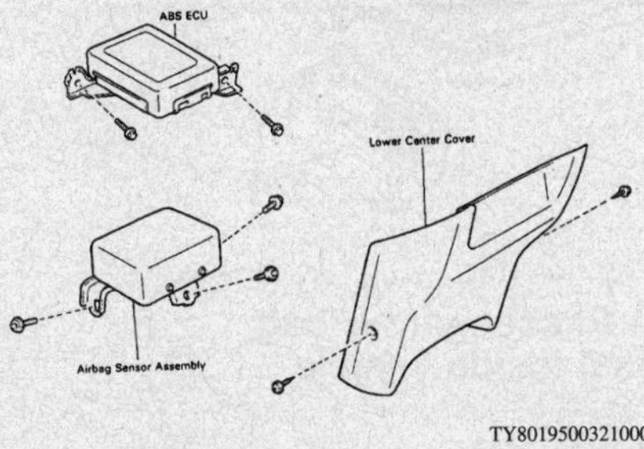
ABS ECU
Lower Center Cover
Airbag Sensor Assembly

TY8019500321000X

Fig. 68 Air bag sensor assembly replacement. Tacoma

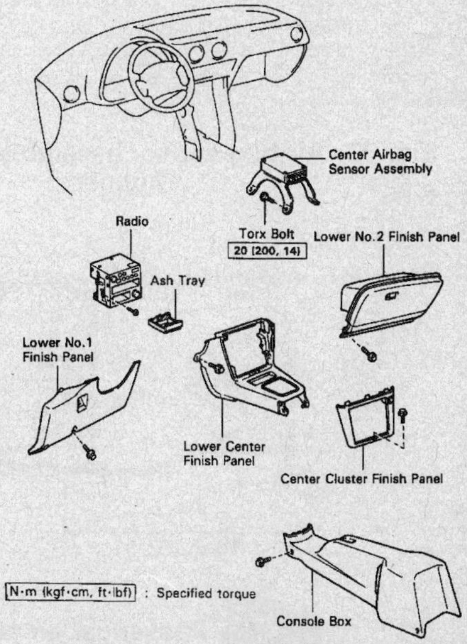
Center Airbag
Sensor Assembly
Radio
Torx Bolt
20 (200, 14)
Lower No.2 Finish Panel
Ash Tray
Lower No.1
Finish Panel
Lower Center
Finish Panel
Center Cluster Finish Panel
N·m (kgf·cm, ft·lbf) : Specified torque
Console Box

TY8019400364000X

Fig. 69 Air bag sensor assembly replacement. 1993–94 Tercel

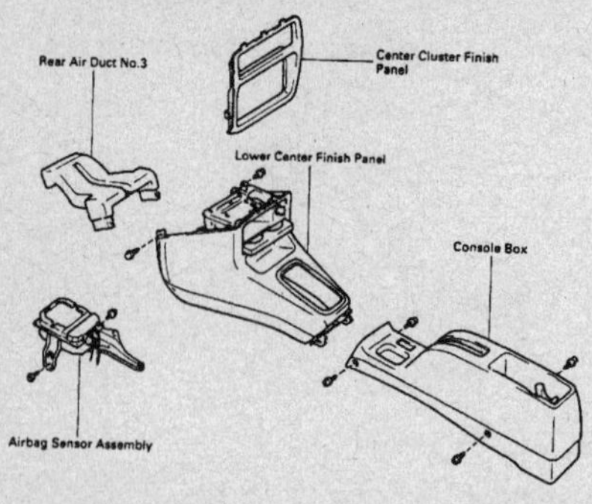
Rear Air Duct No.3
Center Cluster Finish Panel
Lower Center Finish Panel
Console Box
Airbag Sensor Assembly

TY8019400322000X

Fig. 70 Air bag sensor assembly replacement. 1995–96 Tercel

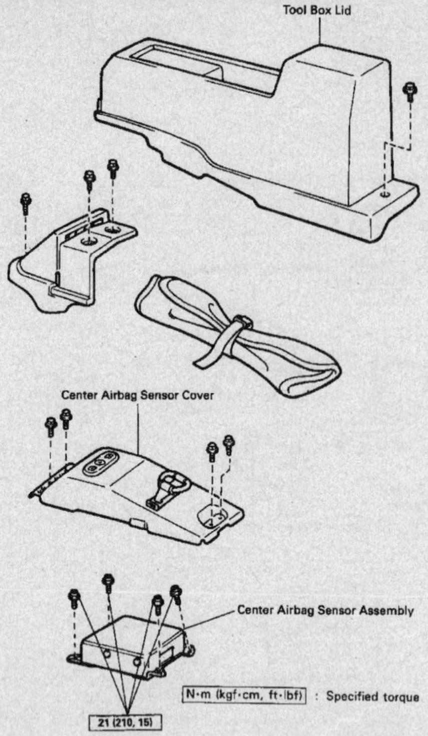
Tool Box Lid
Center Airbag Sensor Cover
Center Airbag Sensor Assembly
N·m (kgf·cm, ft·lbf) : Specified torque
21 (210, 15)

TY8019400366000X

Fig. 71 Air bag sensor assembly replacement. 1994 T100

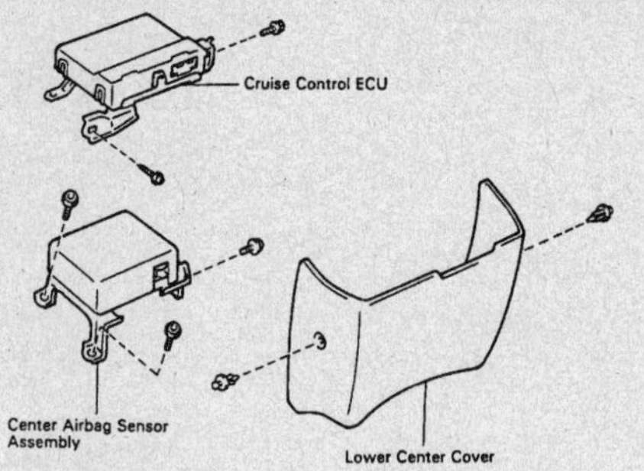
Cruise Control ECU
Center Airbag Sensor Assembly
Lower Center Cover

TY8019400323000X

Fig. 72 Air bag sensor assembly replacement. 1995–96 T100

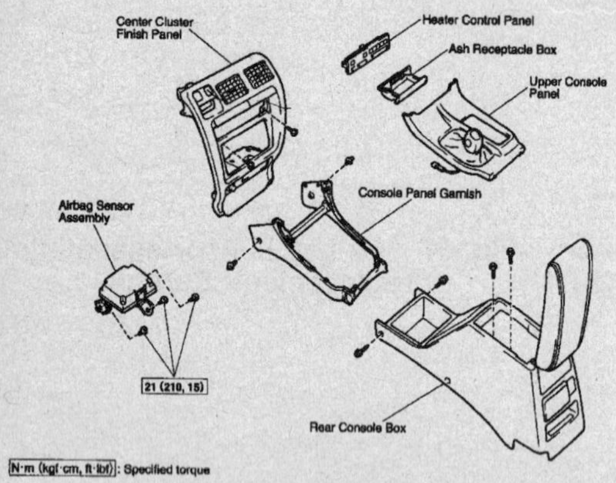
Center Cluster Finish Panel
Heater Control Panel
Ash Receptacle Box
Upper Console Panel
Console Panel Garnish
Airbag Sensor Assembly
21 (210, 15)
Rear Console Box
N·m (kgf·cm, ft·lbf): Specified torque

TY8019600368000X

Fig. 73 Air bag sensor assembly replacement. 4Runner

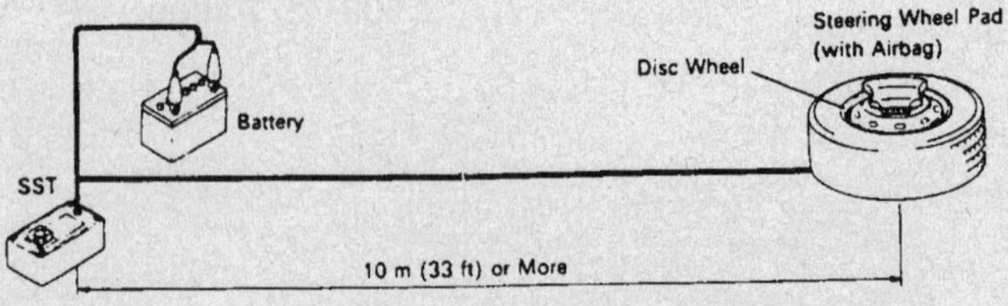
Steering Wheel Pad (with Airbag)
Disc Wheel
Battery
SST
10 m (33 ft) or More

TY8019400324000X

Fig. 74 Driver side air bag disposal outside vehicle

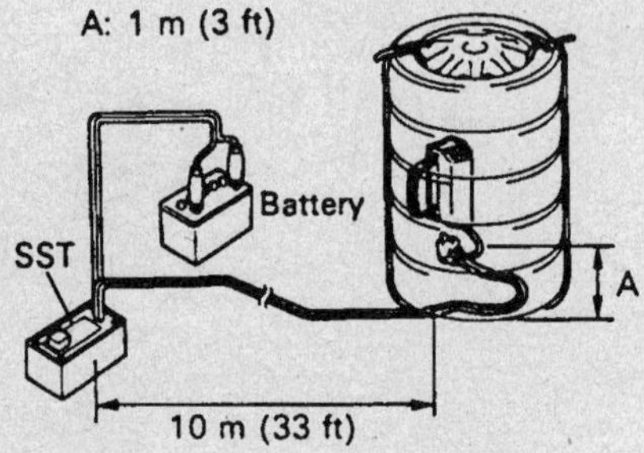
A: 1 m (3 ft)
Battery
SST
A
10 m (33 ft)

TY8019400325000X

Fig. 75 Passenger air bag disposal outside vehicle

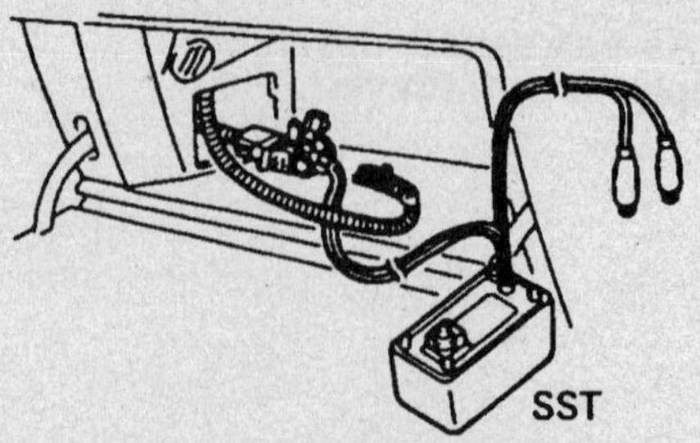
SST

TY8019400326000X

Fig. 76 Passenger air bag disposal inside vehicle

TIGHTENING SPECIFICATIONS

Year	Component	Torque/Ft. Lbs
AVALON & CAMRY		
1993	Center Air Bag Sensor	9
	Front Air Bag Sensor	19
	Steering Wheel Retaining Nut	26
	Steering Wheel Side Torx Screws	78①
1994–96	Center Air Bag Sensor	15
	Front Air Bag Sensor	19
	Front Passenger Air Bag To Instrument Panel Reinforcement Screws	15
	Front Passenger Air Bag To Instrument Panel Screws	52①
	Steering Wheel Retaining Nut	26
	Steering Wheel Side Torx Screws	78①
CELICA		
1993	Center Air Bag Sensor	9
	Front Air Bag Sensor	19
	Steering Wheel Retaining Nut	26
	Steering Wheel Side Torx Screws	65①
1994–96	Center Air Bag Sensor	15
	Front Air Bag Sensor	22
	Front Passenger Air Bag Assembly	15
	Steering Wheel Retaining Nut	25
	Steering Wheel Side Torx Screws	80①
COROLLA		
1993	Center Air Bag Sensor	9
	Front Air Bag Sensor	19
	Steering Wheel Retaining Nut	26
	Steering Wheel Side Torx Screws	78①
1994–96	Air Bag Sensor Assembly Mounting Screws	③
	Front Passenger Air Bag To Instrument Panel Reinforcement Screws	15
	Front Passenger Air Bag To Instrument Panel Screws	49①
	Steering Wheel Retaining Nut	26
	Steering Wheel Side Torx Screws	78①
MR2		
1993	Center Air Bag Sensor	9
	Front Air Bag Sensor	19
	Steering Wheel Retaining Nut	26
	Steering Wheel Side Torx Screws	65①
1994–95	Center Air Bag Sensor	9
	Front Air Bag Sensor	19
	Front Passenger Air Bag To Instrument Panel Reinforcement Screws	14
	Front Passenger Air Bag To Instrument Panel Screws	52①
	Steering Wheel Retaining Nut	26
	Steering Wheel Side Torx Screws	65①
PASEO & TERCEL		
1993–96	Center Air Bag Sensor	14
	Front Air Bag Sensor	22
	Steering Wheel Retaining Nut	26
	Steering Wheel Side Torx Screws	78①

Continued

TIGHTENING SPECIFICATIONS—Continued

Year	Component	Torque/Ft. Lbs
PREVIA		
1993	Center Air Bag Sensor	14
	Front Air Bag Sensor	22
	Steering Wheel Retaining Nut	25
	Steering Wheel Side Torx Screws	65①
1994–96	Center Air Bag Sensor	14
	Front Air Bag Sensor	22
	Front Passenger Air Bag Assembly Bolts	14
	Front Passenger Air Bag Assembly Nuts	52①
	Steering Wheel Retaining Nut	26
	Steering Wheel Side Torx Screws	78①
RAV4		
1996	Air Bag Module Screws (Driver)	6.5
	Air Bag Module Bolts (Passenger)	②
	Air Bag Sensor Assembly Mounting Screws	15
	Instrument Panel Reinforcement Bolts	15
	Steering Wheel Nut	26
SUPRA		
1993–96	Center Air Bag Sensor	15
	Front Air Bag Sensor	22
	Steering Wheel Retaining Nut	26
	Steering Wheel Side Torx Screws	62①
	Front Passenger Air Bag To Instrument Panel Reinforcement Screws	15
	Front Passenger Air Bag To Instrument Panel Screws	78①
TACOMA, T100 & LAND CRUISER		
1994–96	Center Air Bag Sensor	15
	Front Air Bag Sensor	22
	Steering Wheel Retaining Nut	25
	Passenger air bag assembly	80①
	Steering Wheel Side Torx Screws	78①
4RUNNER		
1996	Air Bag Module Screws (Driver)	6.5
	Air Bag Module Bolts (Passenger)	②
	Air Bag Sensor Assembly Mounting Screws	15
	Instrument Panel Reinforcement Bolts	15
	Steering Wheel Nut	26

① — Inch lbs.

② — 6 mm, 6.5 ft. lbs.; 8 mm, 15 ft. lbs.

③ — 1994–95, 11 ft. lbs.; 1996, 15 ft. lbs.

Dash Panel Service

NOTE: On Air Bag Equipped Models, Refer To "Air Bag System Precautions" Located In The Front Of This Manual For System Disarming & Arming Procedures.

NOTE: Refer To The "Dash Gauges" Section For Related Information.

INDEX

	Page No.
Dash Panel, Replace	48-69
Avalon	48-69
Camry	48-73
Celica	48-74
Corolla	48-70
Land Cruiser	48-75
MR2	48-73
Paseo	48-70
Pickup & 1993–95 4Runner	48-70
Previa	48-75
RAV4	48-71
Supra	48-69
Tacoma	48-71
Tercel	48-72
T100	48-72
1996 4Runner	48-71
Precautions	48-69
Air Bag Systems	48-69
Audio Coded Anti-Theft System	48-69

PRECAUTIONS

AIR BAG SYSTEMS

Refer to "Air Bag System Precautions" in the front of this manual for system disarming and arming procedures.

AUDIO CODED ANTI-THEFT SYSTEM

Some models are equipped with an audio coded anti-theft system that will disable the radio when the battery cable is disconnected. The system can be identified by the "ANTI-THEFT SYSTEM" on the cassette tape lid. Obtain 3 digit customer code for input. Reset system after service as follows:

1. Obtain 3 digit audio anti-theft code.
2. Depress 1 (PROG) while depressing righthand side of TUNE SEEK button, - - - will appear in tape operation display.
3. To enter the first digit, depress 1 (PROG) button repeatedly until the number of times depressed equals the first digit beginning with zero (depress the 1 button six times if the first digit if five).
4. To enter second digit, depress 2 (APS) button repeatedly until the number of times depressed equals the second digit beginning with zero.
5. To enter third digit, depress 3 (RPT) button repeatedly until the number of times depressed equals the third digit beginning with zero.
6. If - - - is displayed during code input, repeat procedure.
7. When code appears in display, depress and hold SCAN button until SEC appears.
8. When SEC disappears audio system should be operative.
9. If Err is displayed, repeat procedure. **Attempting to input code more thannine times may permanently disable audio system.**

DASH PANEL

REPLACE

AVALON

1. Remove front pillar garnish and door inside scuff plate, **Fig. 1.**
2. Remove hood lock release lever and cowl side trim.
3. Remove steering wheel, steering column cover and combination switch.
4. Remove lower finish panel assembly and instrument panel finish lower lefthand panel.
5. Remove fuse box bolt and parking brake release lever.
6. Remove No. 2 duct heater to register and No. 2 under cover and lower finish panel.
7. Remove glove compartment door and glove compartment.
8. Remove glove compartment door finish plate inside instrument panel box.
9. Pull up and disconnect air bag connector.
10. Remove four screws and compartment by pulling and disconnect the connectors.
11. Remove center cluster finish panel, radio and heater control assembly.
12. **On models with floor shift,** remove the following parts:
    a. Upper console panel.
    b. Rear console box.
    c. Front console box.
13. **On models with column shift,** remove finish panel.
14. **On all models,** remove steering column.
15. Remove cluster finish panel, assembly and combination meter.
16. Remove and disconnect attaching bolts and connectors, then remove instrument panel from vehicle.
17. Remove instrument panel reinforcement.
18. Reverse procedure to install.

SUPRA

1. Remove front pillar garnishes with assist grip.
2. Remove foot rest and front door scuff inside plates.
3. Remove air bag, steering wheel and steering column cover.
4. Remove console upper panel, **Fig. 2.**
5. Remove parking brake hole cover.
6. Remove console box.
7. Remove lower finish panel, below steering column.
8. Remove center, lefthand and righthand dash gauge finish panels.
9. Remove combination meter.
10. Remove heater to register duct No. 2.
11. Remove combination switch.
12. Remove audio receiver assembly and computer cover.
13. Remove glove compartment door finish plate.
14. Pull up and disconnect passenger air bag connector.
15. Remove glove compartment and finish panel mounting brackets.
16. Remove heater to register duct No. 4.
17. Remove front passenger air bag assembly.
18. Remove parking brake lever, steering column and side defroster nozzle No. 2.
19. Disconnect instrument panel electrical connectors, then remove instrument panel and instrument panel reinforcement.
20. Remove instrument panel brace No. 1 and side bracket No. 3.
21. Reverse procedure to install, noting the following:
    a. **Torque** steering column bolts to 19 ft. lbs.
    b. **Torque** passenger air bag assembly to instrument panel reinforcement screws to 15 ft. lbs.
    c. **Torque** passenger air bag assembly to instrument panel screws to 78 inch lbs.

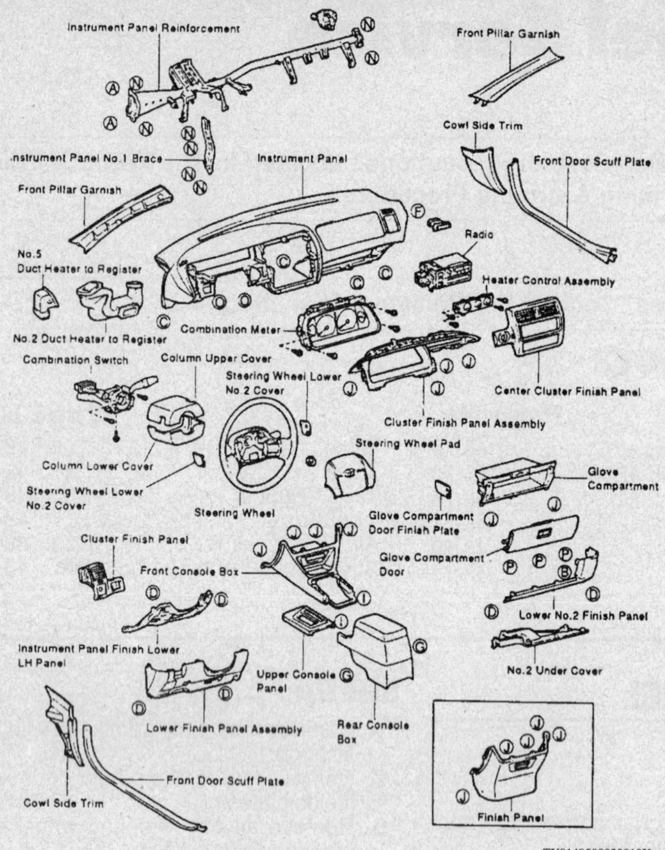
Instrument Panel Reinforcement
Front Pillar Garnish
Cowl Side Trim
Instrument Panel No.1 Brace
Instrument Panel
Front Door Scuff Plate
Front Pillar Garnish
No.5 Duct Heater to Register
Radio
Heater Control Assembly
No.2 Duct Heater to Register
Combination Meter
Combination Switch
Column Upper Cover
Steering Wheel Lower No.2 Cover
Center Cluster Finish Panel
Cluster Finish Panel Assembly
Steering Wheel Pad
Column Lower Cover
Steering Wheel Lower No.2 Cover
Glove Compartment
Steering Wheel
Glove Compartment Door Finish Plate
Cluster Finish Panel
Front Console Box
Glove Compartment Door
Lower No.2 Finish Panel
Instrument Panel Finish Lower LH Panel
Upper Console Panel
No.2 Under Cover
Lower Finish Panel Assembly
Rear Console Box
Front Door Scuff Plate
Cowl Side Trim
Finish Panel
TY9149500023010X

Fig. 1 Exploded view of instrument panel & components (Part 1 of 2). Avalon

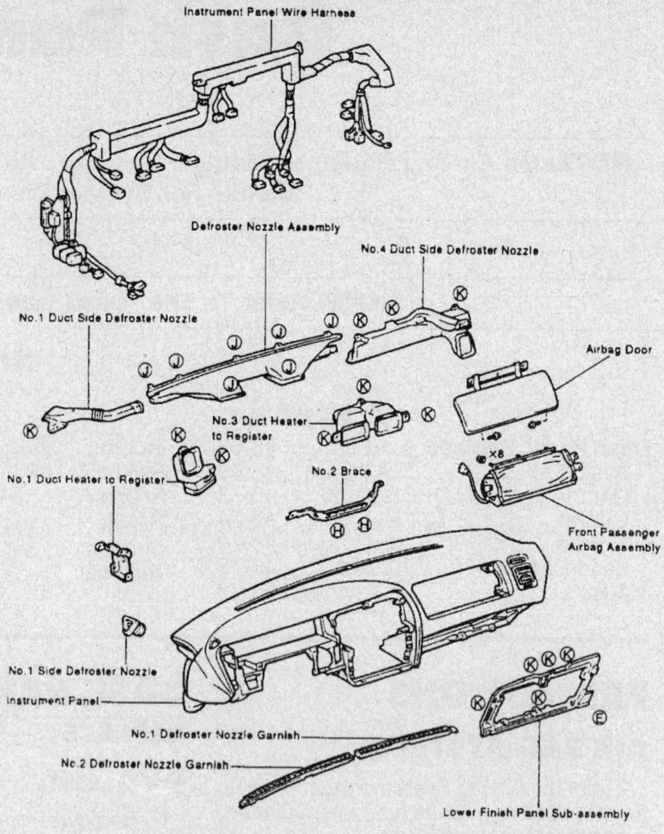
Instrument Panel Wire Harness
Defroster Nozzle Assembly
No.4 Duct Side Defroster Nozzle
No.1 Duct Side Defroster Nozzle
Airbag Door
No.3 Duct Heater to Register
No.1 Duct Heater to Register
No.2 Brace
Front Passenger Airbag Assembly
No.1 Side Defroster Nozzle
Instrument Panel
No.1 Defroster Nozzle Garnish
No.2 Defroster Nozzle Garnish
Lower Finish Panel Sub-assembly
TY9149500023020X

Fig. 1 Exploded view of instrument panel & components (Part 2 of 2). Avalon

d. **Torque** steering wheel set nut to 26 ft. lbs.
e. **Torque** steering wheel pad to 62 inch lbs.

COROLLA

1. Remove front pillar garnish and door scuff plate.
2. Remove steering wheel and steering column covers, **Fig. 3.**
3. Remove shifting hole bezel, hood release lever and rear console box.
4. Remove lower finish panel, combination switch and glove compartment door.
5. Remove center cluster finish lower panel.
6. Remove heater control knobs, then remove center cluster finish panel.
7. Remove radio and heater control.
8. Remove two attaching screws and dash cluster finish panel.
9. Remove finish lower center panel, then remove defroster nozzle No. 2 and heat ducts.
10. **On models with passenger side air bag,** disconnect air bag electrical connector, remove attaching bolts and clips, then pull out passenger air bag assembly.
11. **On all models,** disconnect instrument panel electrical connectors, them remove instrument panel and panel reinforcement.
12. Reverse procedure to install.

PASEO

1. Disconnect battery ground cable.
2. Disarm anti-theft system as outlined under "Precautions."
3. Remove front garnish clip, **Figs. 3, 4 and 5.**
4. Remove door scuff plate.
5. Remove steering wheel.
6. Remove steering column cover.
7. Remove console box.
8. Remove hood lever release.
9. Using suitable screwdriver with taped tip, remove lower No. 1 finish panel opening covers, then remove lower No. 1 finish panel.
10. Remove combination switch.
11. Remove cluster finish center upper panel.
12. Remove instrument cluster attaching bolt and screws, pull cluster rearward, disconnect electrical connectors, then remove cluster.
13. Using suitable screwdriver with taped tip, remove lower No. 2 finish panel opening covers, then remove lower No. 2 finish panel.
14. Remove center cluster finish panel.
15. Remove radio.
16. Remove lower center finish panel.
17. Remove clock.
18. Remove heater control knobs.
19. **On models with A/C,** pry out A/C switch.
20. **On all models,** pry out heater control plate, then remove heater control.
21. Remove duct heater to register No. 2 duct.
22. Remove junction block No. 1.
23. Remove instrument panel attaching bolt and three nuts, then remove instrument panel.
24. Reverse procedure to install.

PICKUP & 1993-95 4RUNNER

1. Disconnect battery ground cable.
2. Remove steering wheel and column covers.
3. Remove engine hood release.
4. Remove cowl side trim, instrument lower center cover and key cylinder cover.
5. Remove lower finish No. 1 panel, then duct heater to register No. 2, **Fig. 6.**
6. Remove knee panel and heater control plate.
7. **On all models except 4 speed,** remove cluster finish panel retaining screws, then disconnect electrical connectors, then finish panel and cup holder.
8. **On 4 speed models,** remove cluster finish panel with meter hood, retaining screws, disconnect electrical connectors, then cluster finish panel and cup holder.
9. **On all models,** remove instrument panel No. 1 register.
10. Remove combination meter retaining screws, disconnect electrical connectors, then remove combination meter.
11. Remove lower finish No. 2 panel with

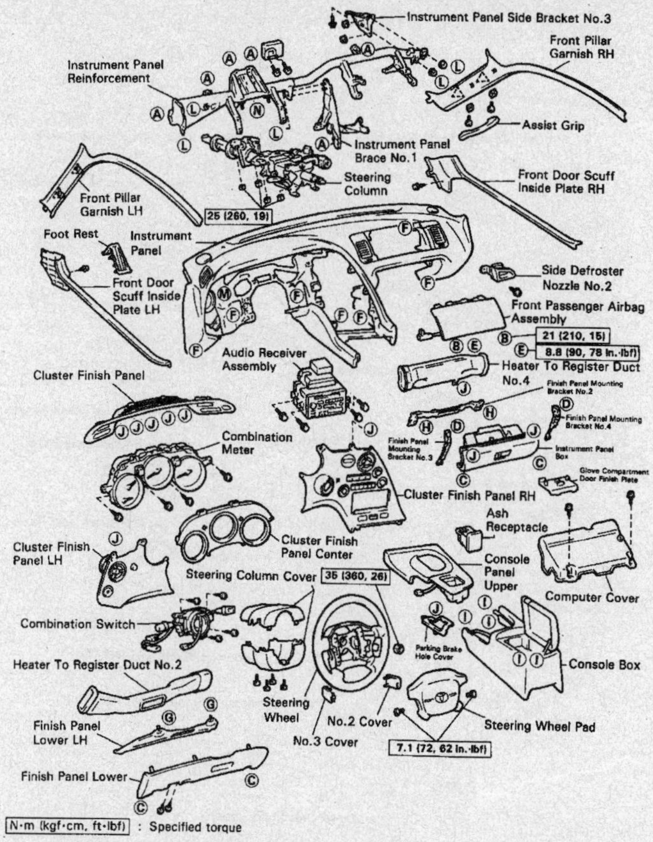

Instrument Panel Side Bracket No.3
Front Pillar Garnish RH
Instrument Panel Reinforcement
Assist Grip
Instrument Panel Brace No.1
Steering Column
Front Door Scuff Inside Plate RH
Front Pillar Garnish LH
25 (260, 19)
Foot Rest
Instrument Panel
Front Door Scuff Inside Plate LH
Side Defroster Nozzle No.2
Front Passenger Airbag Assembly
21 (210, 15)
8.8 (90, 78 in.-lbf)
Heater To Register Duct No.4
Audio Receiver Assembly
Cluster Finish Panel
Combination Meter
Cluster Finish Panel RH
Ash Receptacle
Cluster Finish Panel LH
Cluster Finish Panel Center
Steering Column Cover
35 (360, 26)
Console Panel Upper
Computer Cover
Combination Switch
Heater To Register Duct No.2
Console Box
Steering Wheel
No.2 Cover
No.3 Cover
Steering Wheel Pad
7.1 (72, 62 in.-lbf)
Finish Panel Lower LH
Finish Panel Lower
N·m (kgf·cm, ft·lbf) : Specified torque

TY9149300002000X

Fig. 2 Exploded view of instrument panel & components. Supra

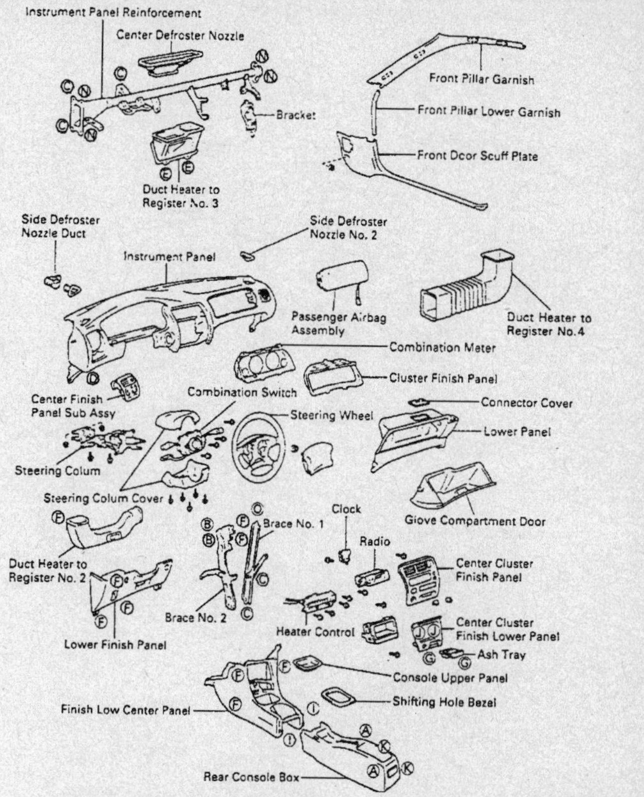

Instrument Panel Reinforcement
Center Defroster Nozzle
Front Pillar Garnish
Bracket
Front Pillar Lower Garnish
Front Door Scuff Plate
Duct Heater to Register No. 3
Side Defroster Nozzle Duct
Side Defroster Nozzle No. 2
Instrument Panel
Passenger Airbag Assembly
Duct Heater to Register No.4
Combination Meter
Cluster Finish Panel
Center Finish Panel Sub Assy
Combination Switch
Connector Cover
Steering Wheel
Lower Panel
Steering Colum
Steering Colum Cover
Clock
Glove Compartment Door
Brace No. 1
Radio
Duct Heater to Register No. 2
Center Cluster Finish Panel
Brace No. 2
Heater Control
Center Cluster Finish Lower Panel
Lower Finish Panel
Ash Tray
Console Upper Panel
Shifting Hole Bezel
Finish Low Center Panel
Rear Console Box

TY9149300004000X

Fig. 3 Exploded view of instrument panel & components. Corolla

glove compartment door.

12. Remove lower center finish panel, heater control and radio.
13. Remove instrument panel retaining bolts, then instrument panel.
14. Reverse procedure to install.

1996 4RUNNER

1. Disconnect battery ground cable.
2. Remove steering wheel as outlined under "Steering Wheel, Replace" in "Electrical" section of "Land Cruiser, 4Runner & Pickup" chassis chapter, **Fig. 7.**
3. Remove cowl side trim and front door scuff plate.
4. Remove hood and fuel tank release lever.
5. Remove lower finish panel.
6. Remove starter switch bezel.
7. Remove No. 1 and No. 2 heater register ducts.
8. Remove four screws and instrument cluster finish panel.
9. Disconnect combination meter connectors and remove combination meter.
10. Remove A/C switch, heater control knob and heater control panel.
11. Remove center cluster finish panel and disconnect A/C control cable.
12. Remove glove compartment door.
13. Remove lower No. 2 finish panel.
14. Remove glove compartment door reinforcement.
15. Remove No. 4 heater to register duct.
16. Remove radio and side bracket.
17. Disconnect air bag connector, then remove instrument panel.
18. Remove defroster nozzle.
19. Remove instrument panel reinforcement No. 1 and No. 2 brace.
20. Remove steering column assembly.
21. Remove center heater to register duct.
22. Remove instrument panel reinforcement.
23. Reverse procedure to install.

RAV4

1. Disconnect battery ground cable.
2. Remove door scuff plate and cowl side trim board, **Fig. 8.**
3. Remove steering wheel as outlined under "Steering Wheel, Replace" in "Electrical" section of "RAV4" chassis chapter.
4. Remove steering column cover.
5. Remove cluster finish panel and combination meter.
6. Remove hood lock release lever.
7. Remove lower finish panel.
8. Remove instrument panel lower finish panel and lower insert.
9. Remove No. 2 heater to register duct.
10. Remove steering column assembly as outlined under "Steering Columns."
11. Remove center cluster finish panel.
12. Remove heater control knobs and the heater control name plate.
13. Pry off cluster instrument panel, then remove three screws from heater control assembly.
14. Disconnect connectors, then remove cluster panel.
15. Remove heater control and accessory assembly.
16. Remove radio and console box.
17. Remove lower center cluster finish panel.
18. Remove stereo opening cover.
19. Remove two mounting screws and glove compartment door.
20. Remove kick panel covers.
21. Remove instrument panel retaining screws and nuts.
22. Disconnect instrument panel electrical connectors and remove instrument panel.
23. Remove instrument panel reinforcement.
24. Reverse procedure to install.

TACOMA

1. Disconnect battery ground cable.
2. Remove air bag, steering wheel, column cover and combination switch, **Fig. 9.**
3. Remove hood lock release lever and fuse box opening cover.
4. Remove four bolts, one screw and lower left hand finish panel.
5. Remove starter switch bezel.
6. Remove No. 2 heater to register duct.
7. Remove steering column. Refer to "Steering Column" section.
8. Remove clock.
9. Remove the center cluster finish panel as follows:

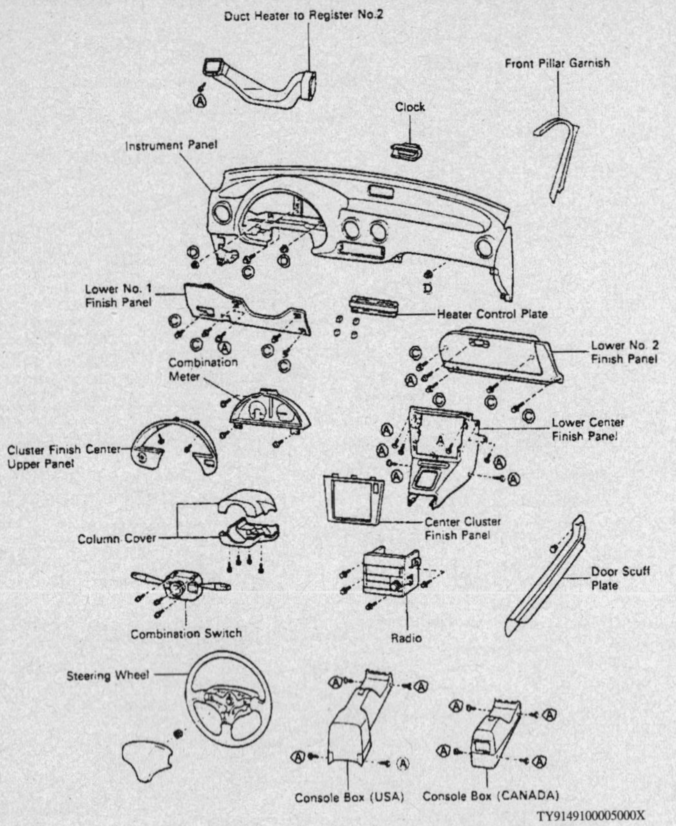
Duct Heater to Register No.2
Front Pillar Garnish
Clock
Instrument Panel
Lower No. 1 Finish Panel
Heater Control Plate
Lower No. 2 Finish Panel
Combination Meter
Lower Center Finish Panel
Cluster Finish Center Upper Panel
Center Cluster Finish Panel
Column Cover
Door Scuff Plate
Combination Switch
Radio
Steering Wheel
Console Box (USA)
Console Box (CANADA)
TY9149100005000X

Fig. 4 Exploded view of instrument panel & components. 1993–95 Paseo

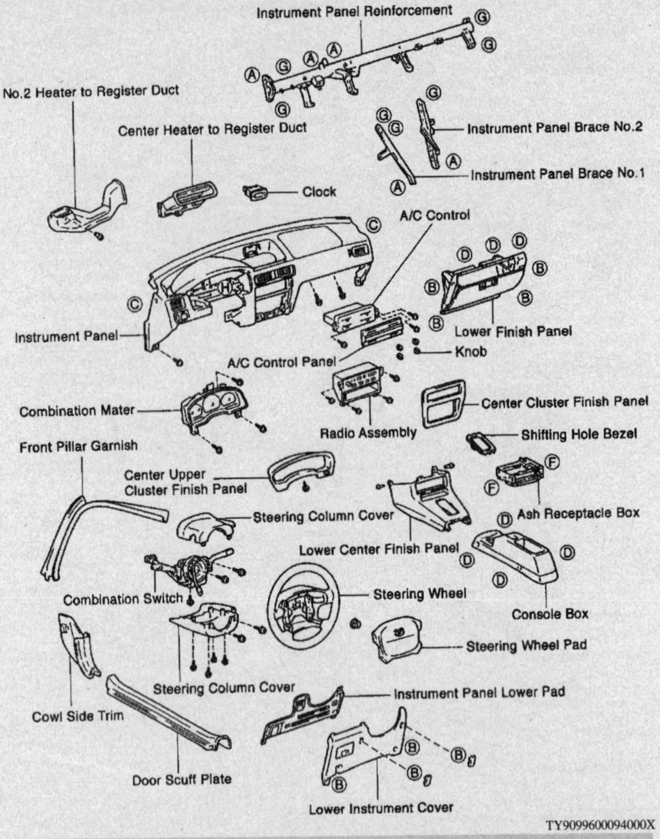
Instrument Panel Reinforcement
No.2 Heater to Register Duct
Center Heater to Register Duct
Instrument Panel Brace No.2
Instrument Panel Brace No.1
Clock
A/C Control
Lower Finish Panel
Instrument Panel
Knob
A/C Control Panel
Combination Mater
Center Cluster Finish Panel
Radio Assembly
Shifting Hole Bezel
Front Pillar Garnish
Center Upper Cluster Finish Panel
Steering Column Cover
Ash Receptacle Box
Lower Center Finish Panel
Combination Switch
Steering Wheel
Console Box
Steering Wheel Pad
Steering Column Cover
Instrument Panel Lower Pad
Cowl Side Trim
Door Scuff Plate
Lower Instrument Cover
TY9099600094000X

Fig. 5 Exploded view of instrument panel & components. 1996 Paseo

a. Remove cup holder and heater control knobs.
b. Using a screwdriver, or equivalent, remove heater control panel.
c. Disconnect hazard connector.
d. Remove two screws and center cluster finish panel.
e. Remove heater control and radio.

10. Remove three screws and three clips, then cluster finish panel.
11. Remove and disconnect four screws, four connectors, speedometer cable and combination meter.
12. Remove No. 1 register and No. 1 heater to register duct.
13. Remove two screws and glove compartment door.
14. Remove two screws, bolt and glove compartment door reinforcement.
15. Remove two clips and lower center instrument cover.
16. Remove three screws and lower No. 2 finish panel.
17. Remove ash receptacle box and retainer.
18. Remove and disconnect stereo opening cover, screw, cigar lighter connector and center lower cluster finish panel.
19. Remove instrument panel side bracket, two nuts and instrument panel.
20. Remove instrument panel No. 1 and No. two brace.
21. Remove center heater to register duct and defroster nozzle.
22. Remove four nuts, three bolts and instrument panel reinforcement.

T100

1. Disconnect battery ground cable.
2. Disarm anti-theft system as outlined under "Precautions."
3. Remove pillar garnish, scuff plate and cowl side trim.
4. Remove steering wheel and steering column covers.
5. Remove hood release lever, lower finish panels, lower center cover and glove compartment door, **Fig. 10.**
6. Remove combination switch and heater control knobs.
7. Remove center cluster finish panel, then remove radio and heater control.
8. Remove center cluster lower finish panel.
9. Remove dash cluster finish panel. Remove heating ducts and registers as necessary.
10. Reverse procedure to install.

TERCEL

1993-94

Refer to **Fig. 11,** for assistance in the following procedure.

1. Disconnect battery ground cable.
2. Disarm anti-theft system as outlined under "Precautions."
3. Remove front pillar garnishes by pulling. Then remove door scuff plates.
4. Remove steering wheel as outlined in the "Electrical" section.
5. Remove steering column covers, console box and hood release lever.
6. Remove No. 1 lower finish panel.
7. Remove combination switch as outlined in the "Electrical" section.
8. Remove instrument cluster as outlined in the "Electrical" section.
9. Remove No. 2 lower finish panel. Then remove radio.
10. Remove lower center finish panel. Remove clock and disconnect connector.
11. Remove heater control plate by prying off A/C switch, pulling off knobs and then removing screws and heater plate.
12. Remove heater to register duct No. 2 and No. 1 junction block.
13. Remove a bolt, three nuts and then the instrument panel.
14. Reverse procedure to install.

1995-96

Refer to **Fig. 12,** for assistance in the following procedure.

1. Disconnect battery ground cable.
2. Disarm anti-theft system as outlined under "Precautions."
3. Remove front pillar garnishes by pulling.
4. Remove cowl side trim and door scuff plates.
5. Remove drivers side air bag and steering wheel as outlined in the "Electrical" section.
6. Remove steering column covers, console box and hood release lever.
7. Remove No. 1 lower finish panel.
8. Remove combination switch as outlined in the "Electrical" section.

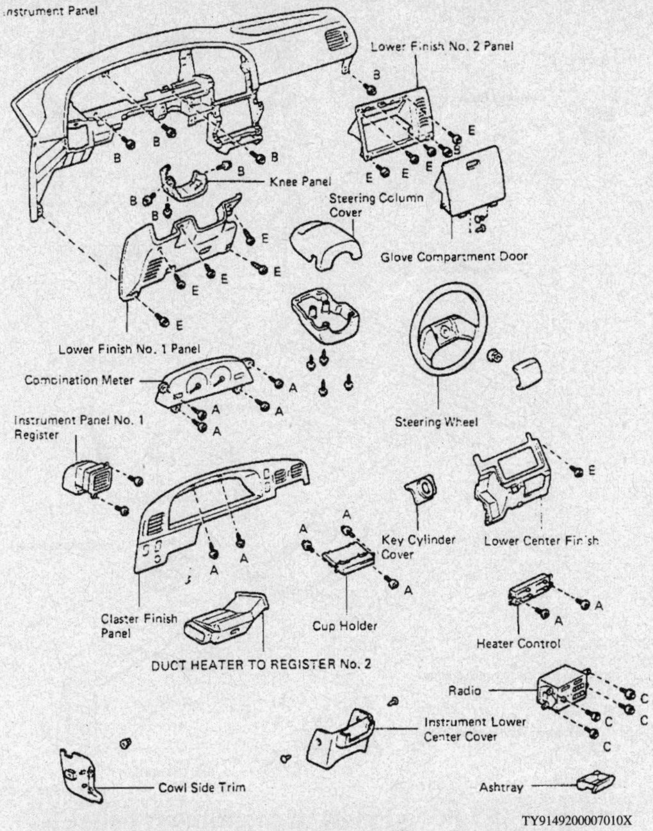

Instrument Panel
Lower Finish No. 2 Panel
Knee Panel
Steering Column Cover
Glove Compartment Door
Lower Finish No. 1 Panel
Combination Meter
Instrument Panel No. 1 Register
Steering Wheel
Key Cylinder Cover
Lower Center Finish
Cluster Finish Panel
Cup Holder
Heater Control
DUCT HEATER TO REGISTER No. 2
Radio
Instrument Lower Center Cover
Cowl Side Trim
Ashtray
TY9149200007010X

Fig. 6 Exploded view of instrument panel & components (Part 1 of 2). Pickup & 1993–95 4Runner less 4 speed manual transmission

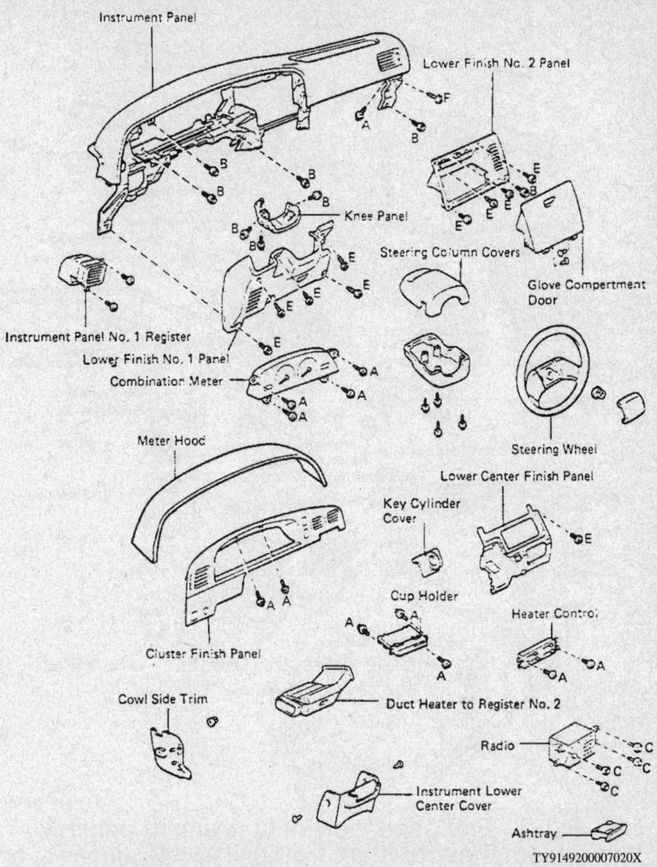

Instrument Panel
Lower Finish No. 2 Panel
Knee Panel
Steering Column Covers
Glove Compertment Door
Instrument Panel No. 1 Register
Lower Finish No. 1 Panel
Combination Meter
Meter Hood
Steering Wheel
Lower Center Finish Panel
Key Cylinder Cover
Cup Holder
Heater Control
Cluster Finish Panel
Cowl Side Trim
Duct Heater to Register No. 2
Radio
Instrument Lower Center Cover
Ashtray
TY9149200007020X

Fig. 6 Exploded view of instrument panel & components (Part 2 of 2). Pickup w/4 speed manual transmission

9. Remove instrument cluster as outlined in the "Electrical" section.
10. Remove No. 2 lower finish panel. Then remove radio.
11. Remove passenger side air bag module.
12. Remove lower center finish panel. Remove clock and disconnect connector.
13. Remove heater control plate by prying off A/C switch, pulling off knobs and then removing screws and heater plate.
14. Remove heater to register duct No. 2 and No. 1 junction block.
15. Remove four bolts, two nuts and then the instrument panel.
16. Reverse procedure to install.

CAMRY

1. Pry out front pillar garnish retaining clips, then remove garnish by pulling upwards by hand.
2. Remove front door inside scuff plate, **Fig. 13.**
3. Remove front door opening cover.
4. Remove engine hood release lever attaching screws, then the lever.
5. Remove cowl side trim.
6. Remove steering wheel.
7. Remove steering column upper and lower covers.
8. Remove console upper panel.
9. Remove rear console box.
10. Remove coil box and bezel.
11. Remove instrument panel lower pad.
12. Remove combination switch.
13. Remove No. 2 undercover.
14. Remove instrument lower panel.
15. Remove front console box.
16. Remove glove compartment door.
17. **On models with passenger side air bag,** remove glove compartment door finish plate, then pull up and disconnect air bag connector.
18. Remove glove compartment attaching screws, then pull out glove compartment.
19. **On all models,** remove center cluster finish panel.
20. Remove four cluster finish panel attaching screws, pry panel rearward, disconnect electrical connectors, then remove panel.
21. Remove register No. 1 and 2 attaching screws, then remove registers.
22. Remove radio attaching screws, disconnect electrical connector, then remove radio.
23. Remove instrument cluster attaching screws, disconnect electrical connector, then remove cluster.
24. Remove heater control knobs, remove heater control attaching screws, disconnect air mix damper control cable, then remove heater control.
25. Remove duct heater to register No. 2.
26. **On models with passenger side air bag,** remove front passenger air bag assembly.
27. **On all models,** remove side defroster nozzle No. 2.
28. Disconnect instrument panel right and left electrical connectors, remove connector holder attaching bolt, then remove connector holder.
29. Remove instrument panel six attaching bolts and three nuts, then remove instrument panel.
30. Reverse procedure to install, noting the following:
    a. **Torque** passenger air bag assembly to instrument panel reinforcement screws to 15 ft. lbs.
    b. **Torque** passenger air bag assembly to instrument panel screws to 69 inch lbs.

MR2

Refer to **Figs. 14 and 15,** for assistance.

1. Remove front pillar garnish and door scuff plate. Then remove steering wheel, combination switch and turn signal bracket as outlined in the "Electrical" section.
2. Remove rear console box, console upper panel and console box.
3. Remove No. 1 lower finish panel and lower insert.
4. Remove No. 2 heater to register duct, No. 2 undercover and No. 2 lower finish panel.
5. Remove center cluster finish panel, cluster finish panel and instrument cluster.
6. Remove radio, heater control, ashtray receptacle retainer and clock. Disconnect necessary connectors.

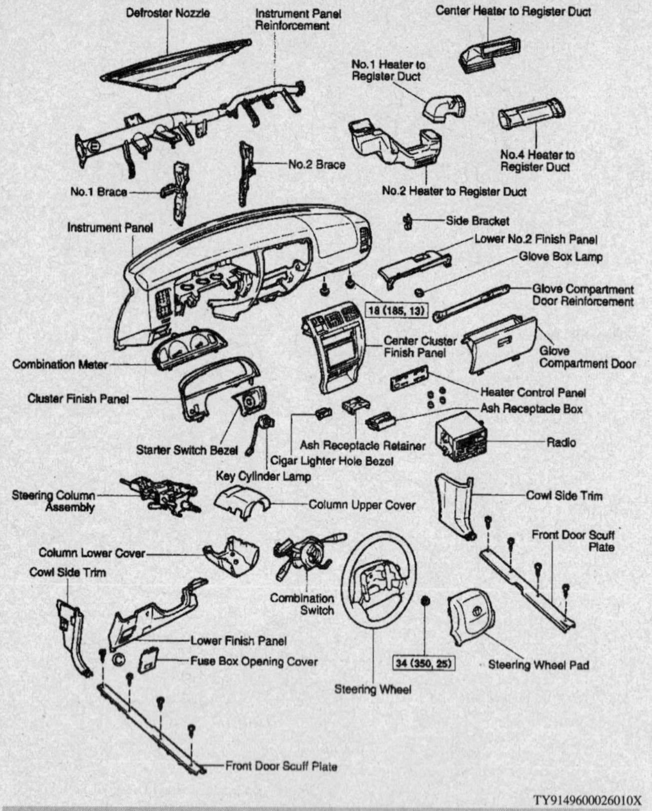
Defroster Nozzle
Instrument Panel Reinforcement
Center Heater to Register Duct
No.1 Heater to Register Duct
No.4 Heater to Register Duct
No.2 Brace
No.1 Brace
No.2 Heater to Register Duct
Instrument Panel
Side Bracket
Lower No.2 Finish Panel
Glove Box Lamp
18 (185, 13)
Glove Compartment Door Reinforcement
Center Cluster Finish Panel
Glove Compartment Door
Combination Meter
Heater Control Panel
Cluster Finish Panel
Ash Receptacle Box
Ash Receptacle Retainer
Radio
Starter Switch Bezel
Cigar Lighter Hole Bezel
Key Cylinder Lamp
Steering Column Assembly
Column Upper Cover
Cowl Side Trim
Front Door Scuff Plate
Column Lower Cover
Cowl Side Trim
Combination Switch
Lower Finish Panel
Fuse Box Opening Cover
34 (350, 25)
Steering Wheel Pad
Steering Wheel
Front Door Scuff Plate
TY9149600026010X

Fig. 7 Exploded view of instrument panel & components (Part 1 of 2). 1996 4Runner

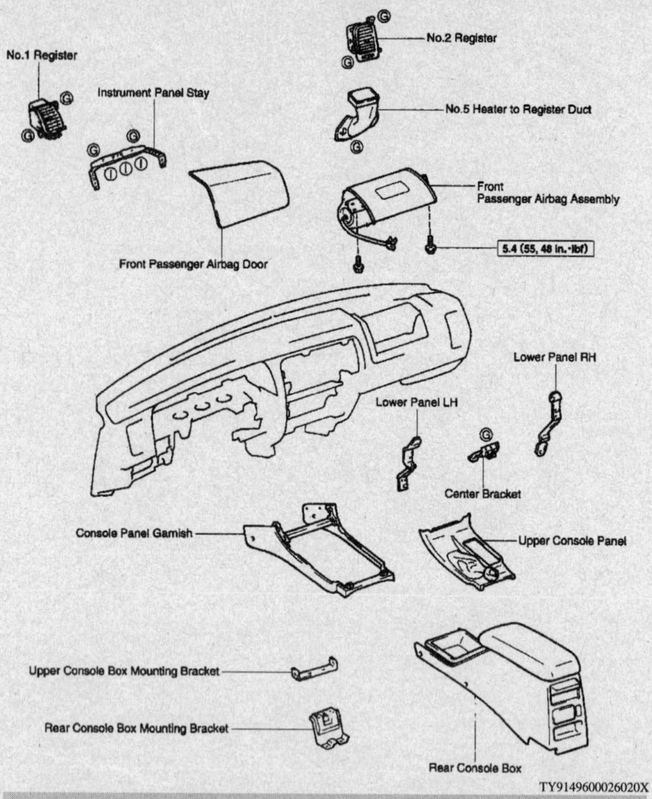
No.2 Register
No.1 Register
Instrument Panel Stay
No.5 Heater to Register Duct
Front Passenger Airbag Assembly
5.4 (55, 48 in.-lbf)
Front Passenger Airbag Door
Lower Panel RH
Lower Panel LH
Center Bracket
Console Panel Garnish
Upper Console Panel
Upper Console Box Mounting Bracket
Rear Console Box Mounting Bracket
Rear Console Box
TY9149600026020X

Fig. 7 Exploded view of instrument panel & components (Part 2 of 2). 1996 4Runner

7. **On models with passenger side air bag,** remove glove compartment door finish plate, then pull up and disconnect air bag connector.
8. Remove glove compartment door assembly.
9. Remove front air bag assembly.
10. Remove No. 2 side defroster nozzle and bracket.
11. **On all models,** remove steering column.
12. Remove five bolts, five screws, a nut and then the dash panel.
13. Reverse procedure to install.

CELICA

1993

Refer to **Fig. 16,** when performing the following procedure.

1. Pull wheel pad out from steering wheel and disconnect air bag connector. **When removing wheel pad, take care not to pull air bag wire harness. When storing wheel pad, keep upper surface of the pad facing upward. Never disassemble wheel pad.**
2. Remove steering wheel, then upper and lower steering column covers.
3. Remove console upper panel, then using a screwdriver remove four console cap screws.
4. Remove four screws and two bolts that attach console box to floor.
5. Disconnect all electrical connectors, then remove console box.
6. Remove glove box door scuff plate, then the four attaching screws from the lower finish trim panel.
7. Disconnect electrical connectors and remove finish panel.
8. Remove engine hood release lever from lower part of instrument panel.
9. Using a screwdriver, pry out cluster finish panel cover.
10. Remove scuff plate, then the six lower No. 1 finish panel attaching screws.
11. Remove two center cluster finish panel attaching screws, then using the screwdriver remove center cluster finish panel and disconnect electrical connector.
12. Remove four radio attaching screws, then disconnect antenna lead, speaker and electrical connectors and remove radio.
13. Using a screwdriver, remove screw caps from lower center finish panel.
14. Remove four lower center finish panel attaching screws and the panel.
15. Remove five instrument cluster finish panel attaching screws, then the panel.
16. Remove four combination meter attaching screws.
17. Disconnect electrical connectors from rear of combination meter and remove meter.
18. Remove speedometer cable by pushing on pawls on right and left sides of the meter bracket.
19. Remove five lower lefthand finish panel retaining bolts, then the panel.
20. Using a screwdriver, remove center register.
21. Remove clip and No. 2 heater to register duct.
22. Using a screwdriver, remove No. 2 side defroster nozzle.
23. Remove five bolts and three nuts that attach instrument panel to cowl, then remove instrument panel.
24. Reverse procedure to install.

1994–96

Refer to **Fig. 17,** when performing the following procedure.

1. Remove front pillar lower garnish and front pillar garnish.
2. Remove front door inside scuff plate.
3. Remove cowl side trim board.
4. Remove steering column cover.
5. Remove upper console panel and console box.
6. Remove lower finish panel No. 1.
7. Remove finish panel.
8. Remove heater to register duct No. 2.
9. Remove combination switch.
10. Remove lower cluster finish panel.
11. Remove heater register No. 1 and combination meter.
12. Remove center cluster finish panel.
13. Remove audio receiver assembly.
14. Disconnect cable to air mix damper control.
15. Disconnect cable to water valve in engine compartment.
16. Remove A/C control assembly.
17. Remove glove compartment door finish plate, then pull up and disconnect

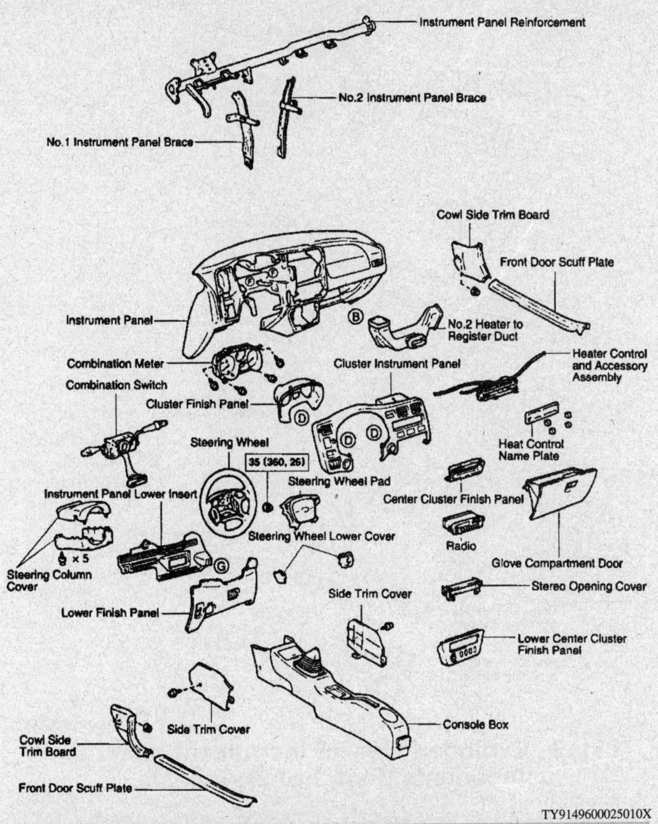
Instrument Panel Reinforcement
No.2 Instrument Panel Brace
No.1 Instrument Panel Brace
Cowl Side Trim Board
Front Door Scuff Plate
Instrument Panel
No.2 Heater to Register Duct
Combination Meter
Cluster Instrument Panel
Heater Control and Accessory Assembly
Combination Switch
Cluster Finish Panel
Steering Wheel
35 (360, 26)
Heat Control Name Plate
Steering Wheel Pad
Instrument Panel Lower Insert
Center Cluster Finish Panel
Steering Wheel Lower Cover
Radio
× 5
Steering Column Cover
Glove Compartment Door
Stereo Opening Cover
Side Trim Cover
Lower Finish Panel
Lower Center Cluster Finish Panel
Side Trim Cover
Console Box
Cowl Side Trim Board
Front Door Scuff Plate
TY9149600025010X

Fig. 8 Exploded view of instrument panel & components (Part 1 of 2). RAV4

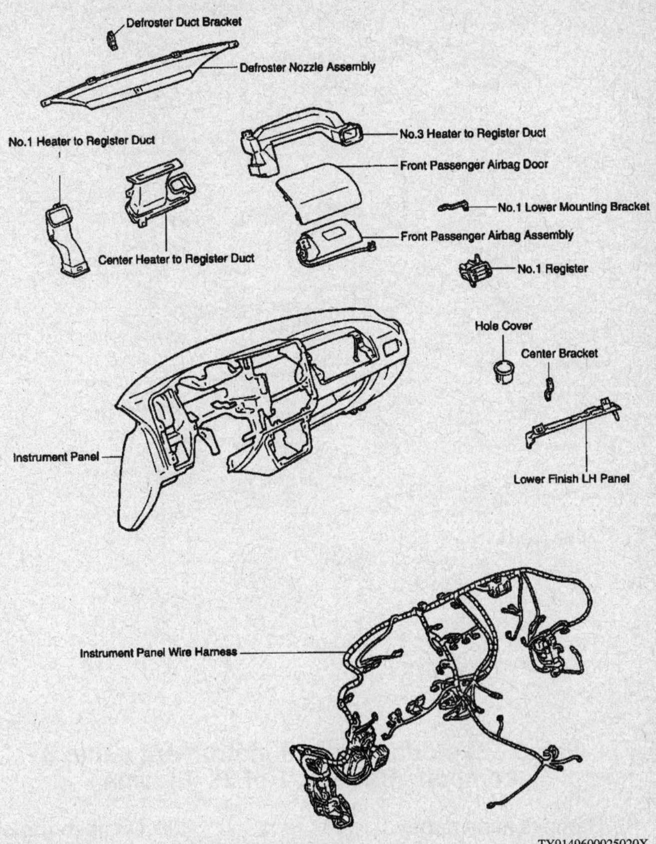
Defroster Duct Bracket
Defroster Nozzle Assembly
No.1 Heater to Register Duct
No.3 Heater to Register Duct
Front Passenger Airbag Door
No.1 Lower Mounting Bracket
Front Passenger Airbag Assembly
Center Heater to Register Duct
No.1 Register
Hole Cover
Center Bracket
Instrument Panel
Lower Finish LH Panel
Instrument Panel Wire Harness
TY9149600025020X

Fig. 8 Exploded view of instrument panel & components (Part 2 of 2). RAV4

passenger side air bag connector.
18. Remove glove compartment.
19. Remove lower center finish panel.
20. Remove side defroster No. 2.
21. Remove steering column.
22. Disconnect instrument panel electrical connectors, then remove instrument panel.
23. Remove center console bracket No. 1.
24. Remove instrument panel brace No. 2.
25. Remove brake spring and center console bracket support.
26. Remove cowl top inner brace.
27. Reverse procedure to install, noting the following:
    a. **Torque** steering column attaching bolts to 19 ft. lbs.
    b. **Torque** passenger air bag assembly bolts to 15 ft. lbs.
    c. **Torque** steering wheel set nut to 25 ft. lbs.
    d. **Torque** steering wheel pad to 80 inch lbs.

LAND CRUISER

1993–94

Refer to **Fig. 18,** for assistance.

1. Disconnect battery ground cable
2. Remove steering wheel, combination switch and turn signal bracket as outlined in the "Electrical" section.
3. Apply protection tape to roof pillars.
4. Remove hood and fuel filler release levers. Then remove lower finish panel.
5. Remove No. 2 heater to register duct.
6. Remove choke knob, ashtray, ashtray receptacle and instrument cluster center finish panel.
7. Remove instrument cluster finish panel.
8. Remove instrument cluster. Then remove heater control unit and radio. Disconnect necessary connectors.
9. Remove front console box, then instrument panel speaker. Disconnect connectors.
10. Remove glove compartment door. Then remove engine ECU.
11. Remove ten bolts, six screws and instrument panel.
12. Reverse procedure to install.

1995–96

Refer to **Fig. 19,** for assistance.

1. Disconnect battery ground cable
2. Remove driver side air bag assembly, steering wheel, combination switch and turn signal bracket as outlined in the "Electrical " section.
3. Apply protection tape to roof pillars.
4. Remove hood and fuel filler release levers. Then remove lower finish and instrument panels.
5. Remove No. 2 heater to register duct.
6. Loosen DLC 3 and fuse block.
7. Remove ashtray, ashtray receptacle and No. 2 instrument cluster center finish panel and clock.
8. Remove instrument cluster finish panel and combination meter.
9. Remove instrument cluster. Then remove heater control unit and radio. Disconnect necessary connectors.
10. Remove front console box, then instrument panel speaker. Disconnect connectors.
11. Remove glove compartment door. Then remove engine ECU.
12. Disconnect passenger air bag electrical connector and remove air bag module.
13. Remove nine bolts, five screws and instrument panel.
14. Reverse procedure to install, noting the following:
    a. **Torque** steering column attaching bolts to 19 ft. lbs.
    b. **Torque** passenger air bag assembly bolts to 15 ft. lbs.
    c. **Torque** steering wheel set nut to 25 ft. lbs.
    d. **Torque** steering wheel pad to 80 inch lbs.

PREVIA

1993

1. Remove assist grips, front pillar garnish and side defroster nozzle, **Fig. 20.**
2. Remove steering wheel and steering column cover.
3. Remove front door scuff plate, side panel, hood release lever and cluster finish lower panel.

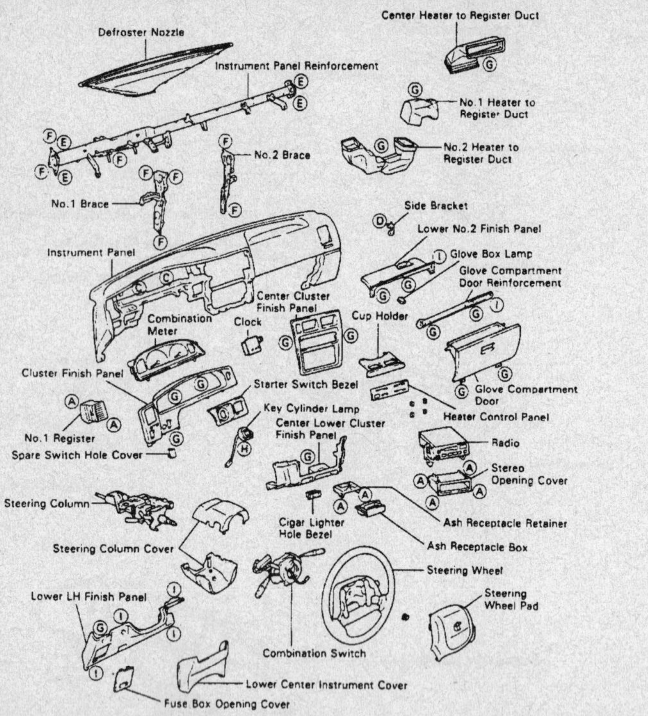
Center Heater to Register Duct
Defroster Nozzle
Instrument Panel Reinforcement
No.1 Heater to Register Duct
No.2 Brace
No.2 Heater to Register Duct
No.1 Brace
Side Bracket
Lower No.2 Finish Panel
Instrument Panel
Glove Box Lamp
Glove Compartment Door Reinforcement
Center Cluster Finish Panel
Combination Meter
Clock
Cup Holder
Cluster Finish Panel
Starter Switch Bezel
Glove Compartment Door
No.1 Register
Key Cylinder Lamp
Center Lower Cluster Finish Panel
Heater Control Panel
Spare Switch Hole Cover
Radio
Stereo Opening Cover
Steering Column
Cigar Lighter Hole Bezel
Ash Receptacle Retainer
Steering Column Cover
Ash Receptacle Box
Steering Wheel
Lower LH Finish Panel
Steering Wheel Pad
Combination Switch
Lower Center Instrument Cover
Fuse Box Opening Cover
TY9149500024010X

Fig. 9 Exploded view of instrument panel & components (Part 1 of 2). Tacoma

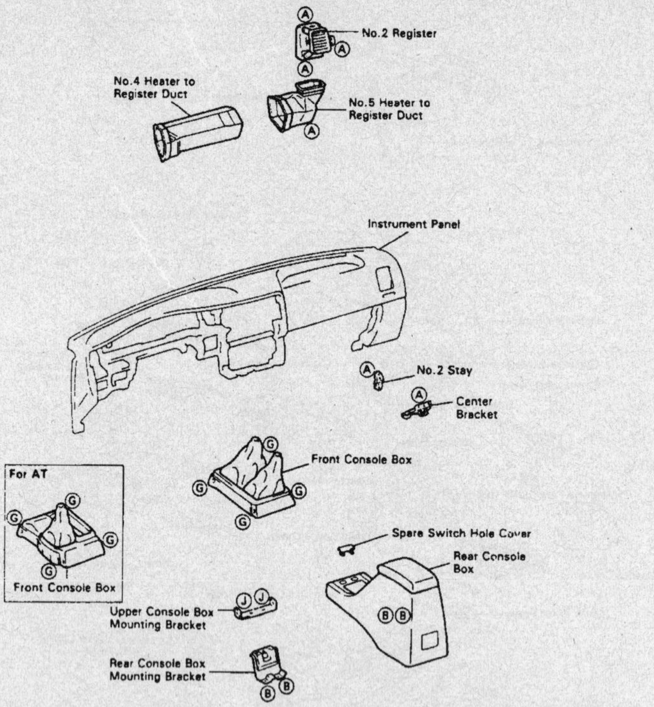
No.2 Register
No.4 Heater to Register Duct
No.5 Heater to Register Duct
Instrument Panel
No.2 Stay
Center Bracket
Front Console Box
For AT
Front Console Box
Spare Switch Hole Cover
Rear Console Box
Upper Console Box Mounting Bracket
Rear Console Box Mounting Bracket
TY9149500024020X

Fig. 9 Exploded view of instrument panel & components (Part 2 of 2). Tacoma

4. Remove knee panel.
5. Remove combination switch with spiral cable and turn signal bracket.
6. Remove cluster finish center upper panel. Then remove console box, ash receptacle retainer and cup holder.
7. Remove cluster finish center panel with radio. Remove cluster finish end panel.
8. Remove cluster finish panel and combination meter.
9. Remove glove compartment door and heater control. Disconnect connectors.
10. Remove No. 1 junction and relay block.
11. **On models with automatic transmission,** remove two bolts and the detent plate. Then remove the through bolt, nut and the shift lever. Disconnect connectors.
12. **On all models,** remove ten bolts, three screws, three nuts and the instrument panel.
13. Reverse procedure to install.

1994–96

1. Remove assist grips, front pillar garnish and side defroster nozzle, **Fig. 21.**
2. Remove steering wheel and steering column cover.
3. Remove front door scuff plate, side panel, hood release lever and cluster finish lower panel.
4. Remove knee panel.
5. Remove combination switch with spiral cable and turn signal bracket.
6. Remove cluster finish center upper panel. Then remove console box, ash receptacle retainer and cup holder.
7. Remove cluster finish center panel with radio. Remove cluster finish end panel.
8. Remove cluster finish panel and combination meter.
9. Remove glove compartment door finish plate, then pull up and disconnect air bag connector.
10. Remove glove compartment lock striker.
11. Remove glove compartment door.
12. Remove passenger air bag assembly, then the heater control.
13. Remove No. 1 junction and relay block.
14. Remove two bolts and the detent plate. Then remove the through bolt, nut and the shift lever. Disconnect connectors.
15. Remove ten bolts, three screws, three nuts and the instrument panel.
16. Reverse procedure to install.

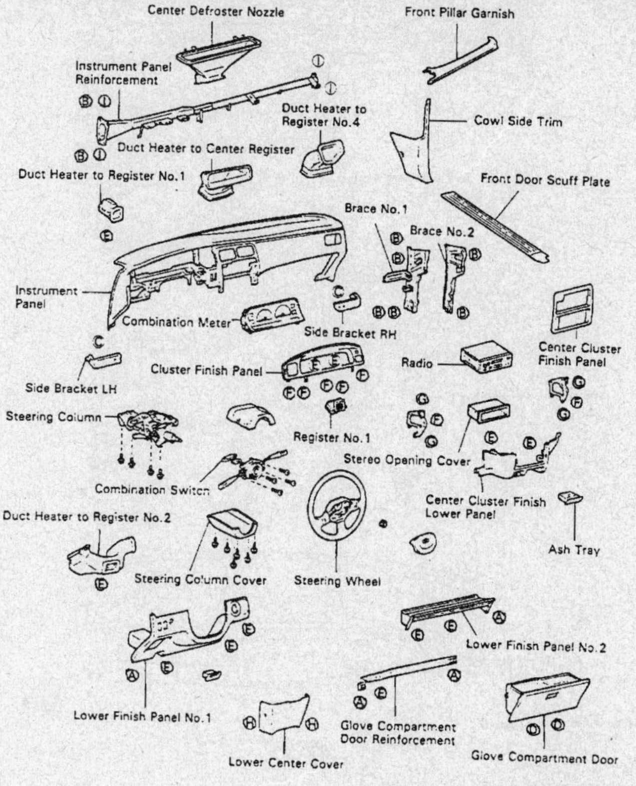
Center Defroster Nozzle
Front Pillar Garnish
Instrument Panel Reinforcement
Duct Heater to Register No.4
Cowl Side Trim
Duct Heater to Center Register
Duct Heater to Register No.1
Front Door Scuff Plate
Brace No.1
Brace No.2
Instrument Panel
Combination Meter
Side Bracket RH
Side Bracket LH
Cluster Finish Panel
Radio
Center Cluster Finish Panel
Steering Column
Register No.1
Stereo Opening Cover
Combination Switch
Center Cluster Finish Lower Panel
Duct Heater to Register No.2
Ash Tray
Steering Column Cover
Steering Wheel
Lower Finish Panel No.2
Lower Finish Panel No.1
Glove Compartment Door Reinforcement
Lower Center Cover
Glove Compartment Door
TY9149100008000X

Fig. 10 Exploded view of instrument panel & components. T100

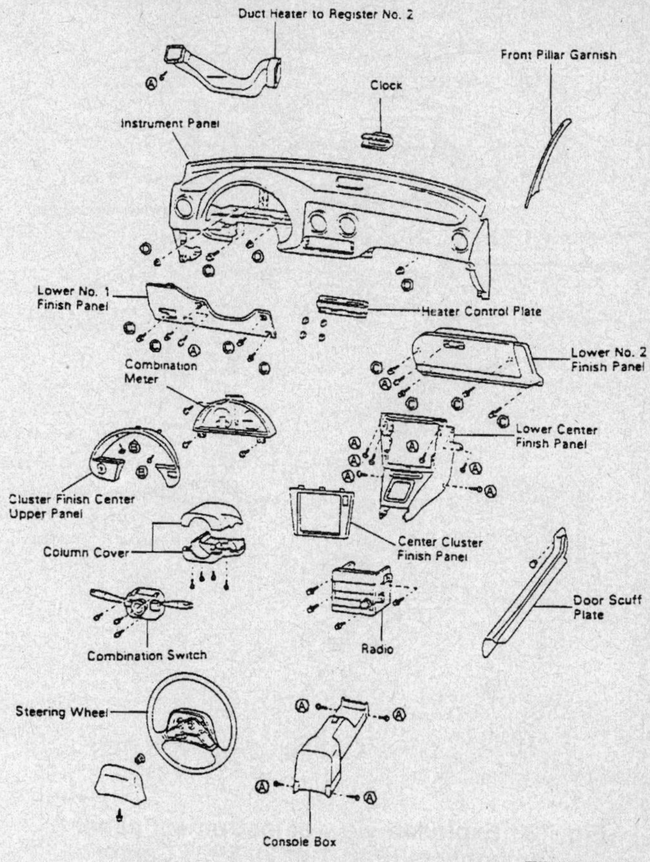
Duct Heater to Register No. 2
Front Pillar Garnish
Clock
Instrument Panel
Lower No. 1 Finish Panel
Heater Control Plate
Combination Meter
Lower No. 2 Finish Panel
Lower Center Finish Panel
Cluster Finish Center Upper Panel
Column Cover
Center Cluster Finish Panel
Door Scuff Plate
Radio
Combination Switch
Steering Wheel
Console Box
TY9149100009000X

Fig. 11 Exploded view of instrument panel. 1993–94 Tercel

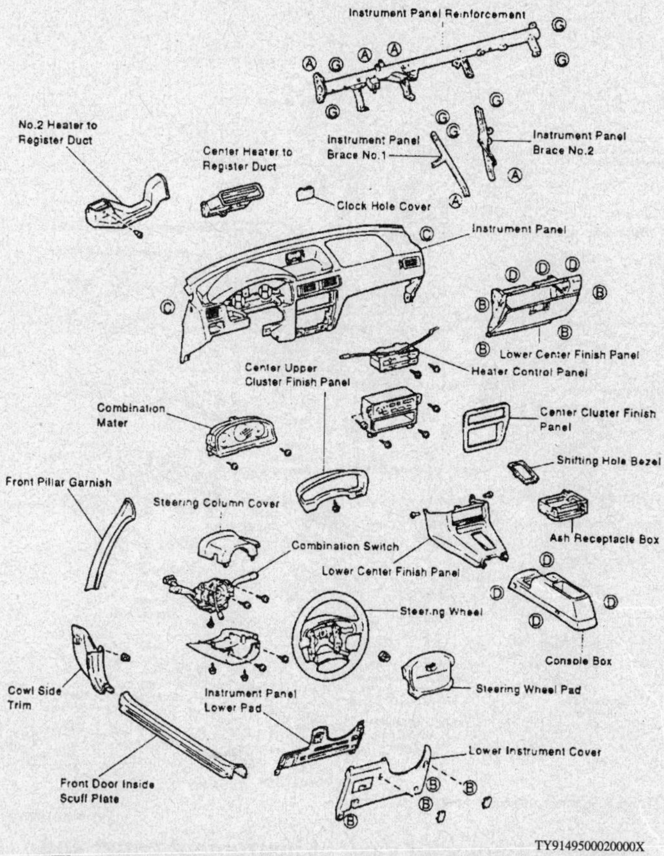
Instrument Panel Reinforcement
No.2 Heater to Register Duct
Center Heater to Register Duct
Instrument Panel Brace No.1
Instrument Panel Brace No.2
Clock Hole Cover
Instrument Panel
Lower Center Finish Panel
Center Upper Cluster Finish Panel
Heater Control Panel
Combination Meter
Center Cluster Finish Panel
Shifting Hole Bezel
Front Pillar Garnish
Steering Column Cover
Ash Receptacle Box
Combination Switch
Lower Center Finish Panel
Steering Wheel
Console Box
Steering Wheel Pad
Cowl Side Trim
Instrument Panel Lower Pad
Lower Instrument Cover
Front Door Inside Scuff Plate
TY9149500020000X

Fig. 12 Exploded view of instrument panel. 1995–96 Tercel

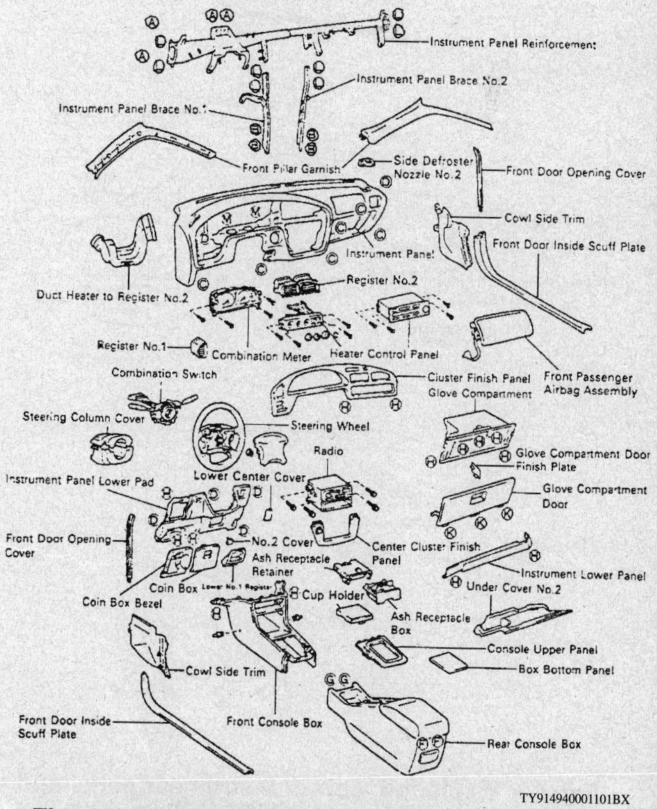
Instrument Panel Reinforcement
Instrument Panel Brace No.2
Instrument Panel Brace No.1
Front Pillar Garnish
Side Defroster Nozzle No.2
Front Door Opening Cover
Cowl Side Trim
Front Door Inside Scuff Plate
Instrument Panel
Register No.2
Duct Heater to Register No.2
Register No.1
Combination Meter
Heater Control Panel
Combination Switch
Cluster Finish Panel
Glove Compartment
Front Passenger Airbag Assembly
Steering Column Cover
Steering Wheel
Radio
Glove Compartment Door Finish Plate
Instrument Panel Lower Pad
Lower Center Cover
Glove Compartment Door
Front Door Opening Cover
No.2 Cover
Ash Receptacle Retainer
Center Cluster Finish Panel
Instrument Lower Panel
Under Cover No.2
Coin Box
Coin Box Bezel
Cup Holder
Ash Receptacle Box
Console Upper Panel
Box Bottom Panel
Cowl Side Trim
Front Door Inside Scuff Plate
Front Console Box
Rear Console Box
TY914940001101BX

Fig. 13 Exploded view of instrument panel & components (Part 1 of 2). 1994–96 Camry

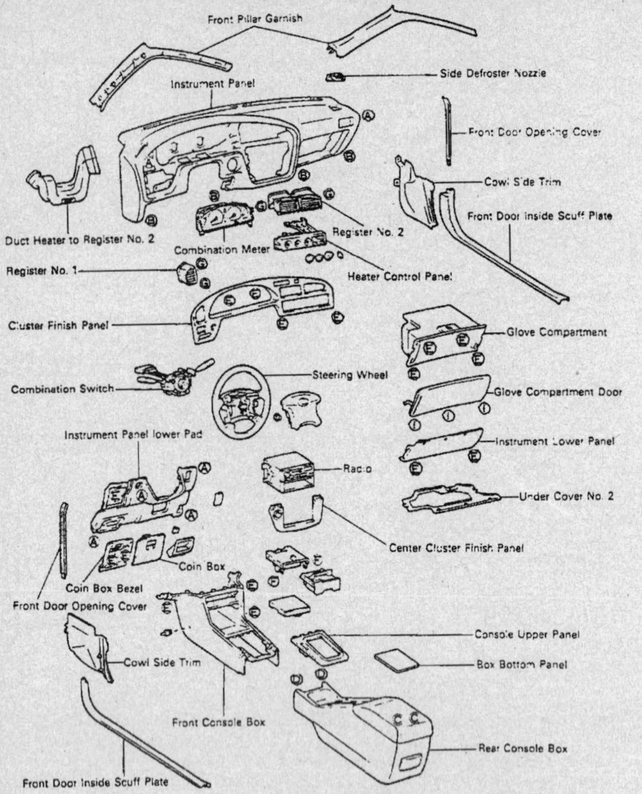
Front Pillar Garnish
Side Defroster Nozzle
Instrument Panel
Front Door Opening Cover
Cowl Side Trim
Front Door Inside Scuff Plate
Duct Heater to Register No. 2
Register No. 2
Combination Meter
Register No. 1
Heater Control Panel
Cluster Finish Panel
Glove Compartment
Combination Switch
Steering Wheel
Glove Compartment Door
Instrument Panel lower Pad
Instrument Lower Panel
Radio
Under Cover No. 2
Center Cluster Finish Panel
Coin Box
Coin Box Bezel
Front Door Opening Cover
Console Upper Panel
Cowl Side Trim
Box Bottom Panel
Front Console Box
Rear Console Box
Front Door Inside Scuff Plate

TY914920001101AX

Fig. 13 Exploded view of instrument panel & components (Part 1 of 2). 1993 Camry

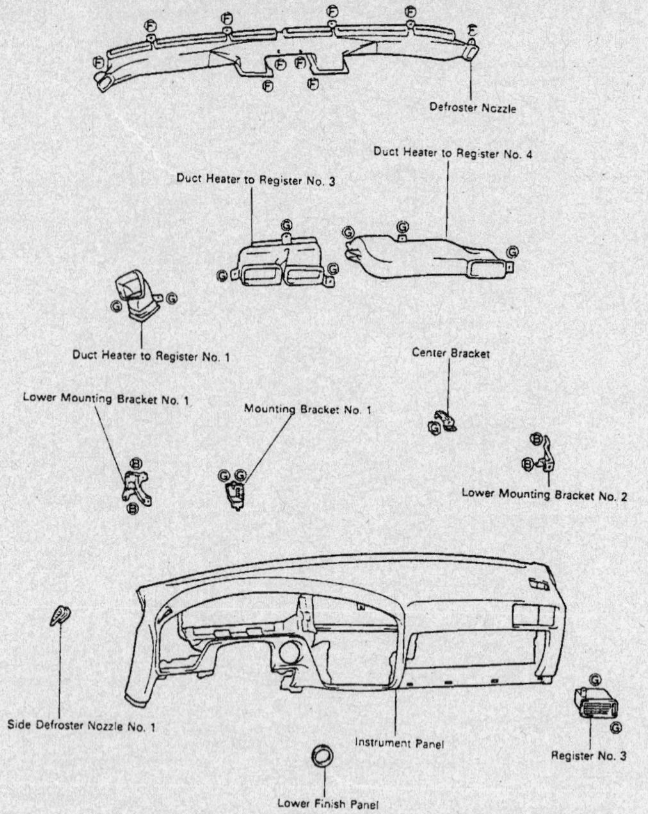
Defroster Nozzle
Duct Heater to Register No. 4
Duct Heater to Register No. 3
Duct Heater to Register No. 1
Center Bracket
Lower Mounting Bracket No. 1
Mounting Bracket No. 1
Lower Mounting Bracket No. 2
Side Defroster Nozzle No. 1
Instrument Panel
Register No. 3
Lower Finish Panel

TY9149200011020X

Fig. 13 Exploded view of instrument panel & components (Part 2 of 2). Camry

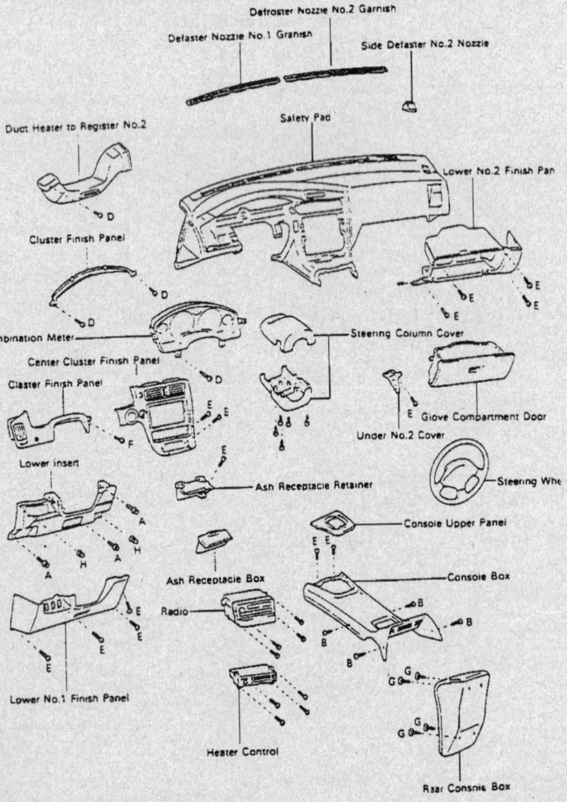
Defroster Nozzle No.2 Garnish
Defaster Nozzle No.1 Granish
Side Defaster No.2 Nozzle
Duct Heater to Register No.2
Safety Pad
Lower No.2 Finish Pan
Cluster Finish Panel
Combination Meter
Steering Column Cover
Center Cluster Finish Panel
Claster Finish Panel
Glove Compartment Door
Under No.2 Cover
Lower insert
Ash Receptacle Retainer
Steering Whe
Console Upper Panel
Ash Receptacle Box
Console Box
Radio
Lower No.1 Finish Panel
Heater Control
Rear Console Box

TY9149100014000X

Fig. 14 Exploded view of instrument panel and components. 1993 MR2

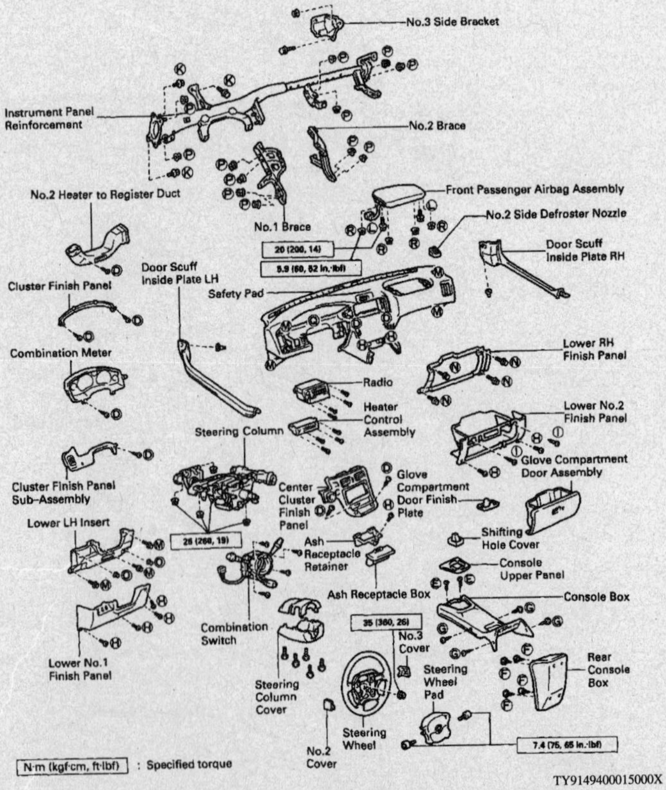
No.3 Side Bracket
Instrument Panel Reinforcement
No.2 Brace
No.2 Heater to Register Duct
Front Passenger Airbag Assembly
No.1 Brace
No.2 Side Defroster Nozzle
20 (200, 14)
5.9 (60, 52 in.·lbf)
Door Scuff Inside Plate RH
Door Scuff Inside Plate LH
Cluster Finish Panel
Safety Pad
Combination Meter
Lower RH Finish Panel
Radio
Heater Control Assembly
Lower No.2 Finish Panel
Steering Column
Glove Compartment Door Assembly
Cluster Finish Panel Sub-Assembly
Center Cluster Finish Panel
Glove Compartment Door Finish Plate
Lower LH Insert
26 (260, 19)
Ash Receptacle Retainer
Shifting Hole Cover
Console Upper Panel
Ash Receptacle Box
Console Box
Combination Switch
35 (360, 26)
No.3 Cover
Lower No.1 Finish Panel
Steering Wheel Pad
Rear Console Box
Steering Column Cover
Steering Wheel
No.2 Cover
7.4 (75, 65 in.·lbf)
N·m (kgf·cm, ft·lbf) : Specified torque

TY9149400015000X

Fig. 15 Exploded view of instrument panel and components. 1994–95 MR2

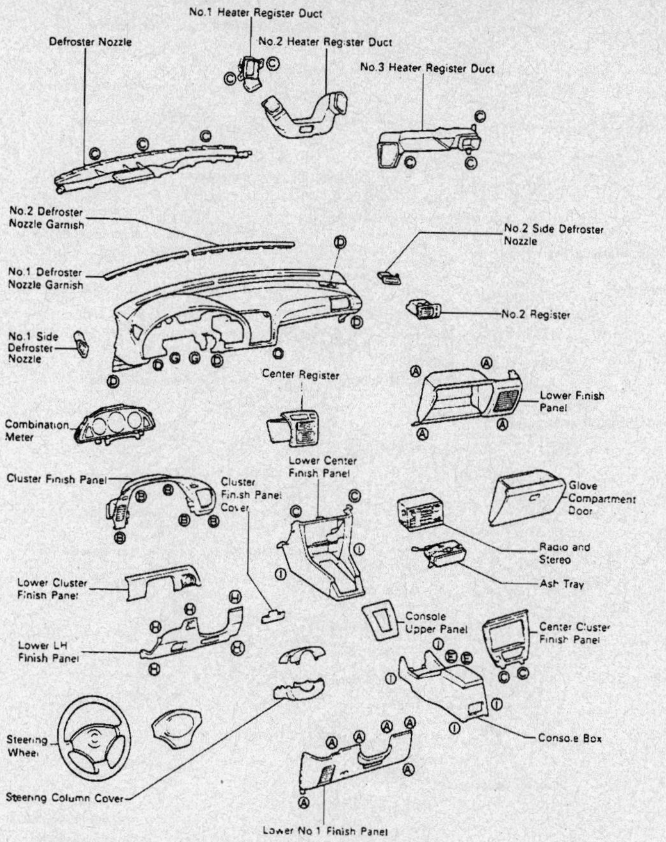
No.1 Heater Register Duct
Defroster Nozzle
No.2 Heater Register Duct
No.3 Heater Register Duct
No.2 Defroster Nozzle Garnish
No.2 Side Defroster Nozzle
No.1 Defroster Nozzle Garnish
No.2 Register
No.1 Side Defroster Nozzle
Center Register
Lower Finish Panel
Combination Meter
Lower Center Finish Panel
Cluster Finish Panel
Cluster Finish Panel Cover
Glove Compartment Door
Radio and Stereo
Ash Tray
Lower Cluster Finish Panel
Console Upper Panel
Center Cluster Finish Panel
Lower LH Finish Panel
Console Box
Steering Wheel
Steering Column Cover
Lower No.1 Finish Panel

TY9149100016000X

Fig. 16 Exploded view of instrument panel and components. 1993 Celica

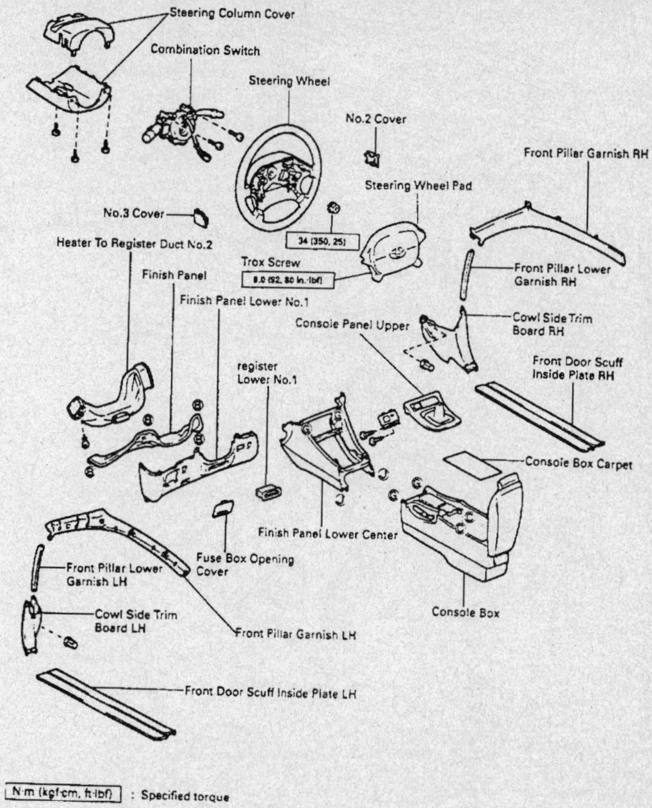
Steering Column Cover
Combination Switch
Steering Wheel
No.2 Cover
Front Pillar Garnish RH
Steering Wheel Pad
No.3 Cover
34 (350, 25)
Heater To Register Duct No.2
Trox Screw
8.0 (82, 80 in.·lbf)
Front Pillar Lower Garnish RH
Finish Panel
Finish Panel Lower No.1
Console Panel Upper
Cowl Side Trim Board RH
register Lower No.1
Front Door Scuff Inside Plate RH
Console Box Carpet
Finish Panel Lower Center
Fuse Box Opening Cover
Front Pillar Lower Garnish LH
Console Box
Cowl Side Trim Board LH
Front Pillar Garnish LH
Front Door Scuff Inside Plate LH
N·m (kgf·cm, ft·lbf) : Specified torque

TY9149400017010X

Fig. 17 Exploded view of instrument panel and components (Part 1 of 3). 1994–96 Celica

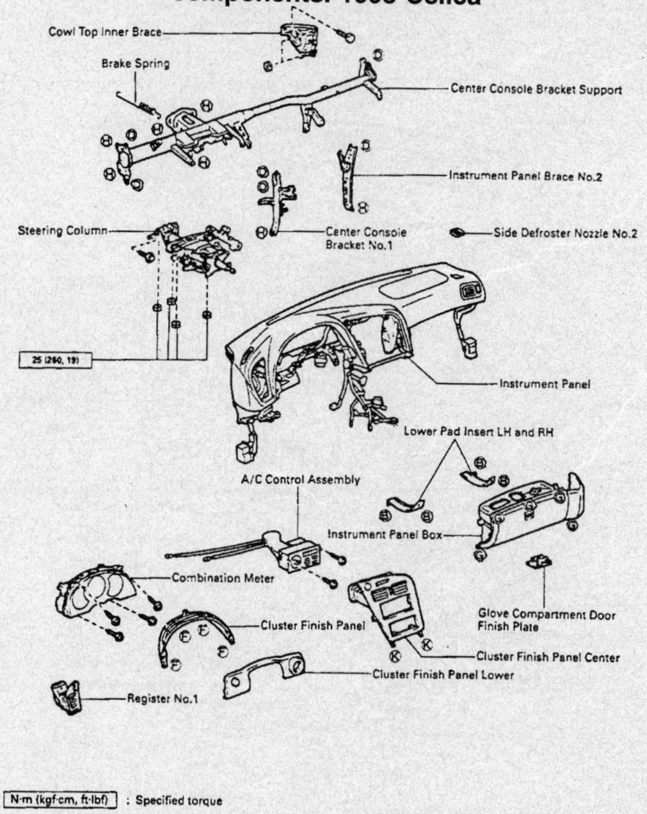
Cowl Top Inner Brace
Brake Spring
Center Console Bracket Support
Instrument Panel Brace No.2
Steering Column
Center Console Bracket No.1
Side Defroster Nozzle No.2
25 (260, 19)
Instrument Panel
Lower Pad Insert LH and RH
A/C Control Assembly
Instrument Panel Box
Combination Meter
Cluster Finish Panel
Glove Compartment Door Finish Plate
Cluster Finish Panel Center
Cluster Finish Panel Lower
Register No.1
N·m (kgf·cm, ft·lbf) : Specified torque

TY9149400017020X

Fig. 17 Exploded view of instrument panel and components (Part 2 of 3). 1994–96 Celica

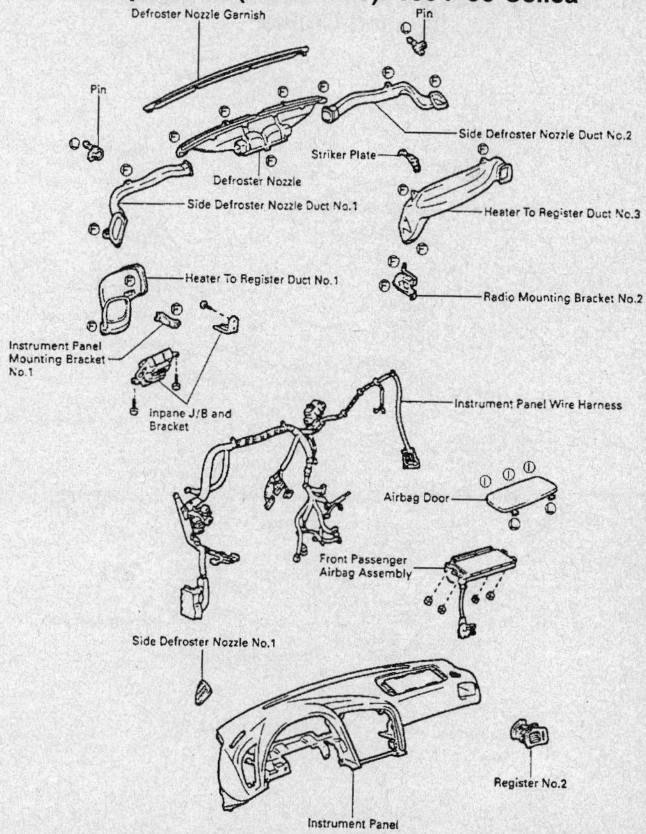
Defroster Nozzle Garnish
Pin
Pin
Side Defroster Nozzle Duct No.2
Striker Plate
Defroster Nozzle
Side Defroster Nozzle Duct No.1
Heater To Register Duct No.3
Heater To Register Duct No.1
Radio Mounting Bracket No.2
Instrument Panel Mounting Bracket No.1
Inpane J/B and Bracket
Instrument Panel Wire Harness
Airbag Door
Front Passenger Airbag Assembly
Side Defroster Nozzle No.1
Register No.2
Instrument Panel

TY9149100017030X

Fig. 17 Exploded view of instrument panel and components (Part 3 of 3). 1994–95 Celica

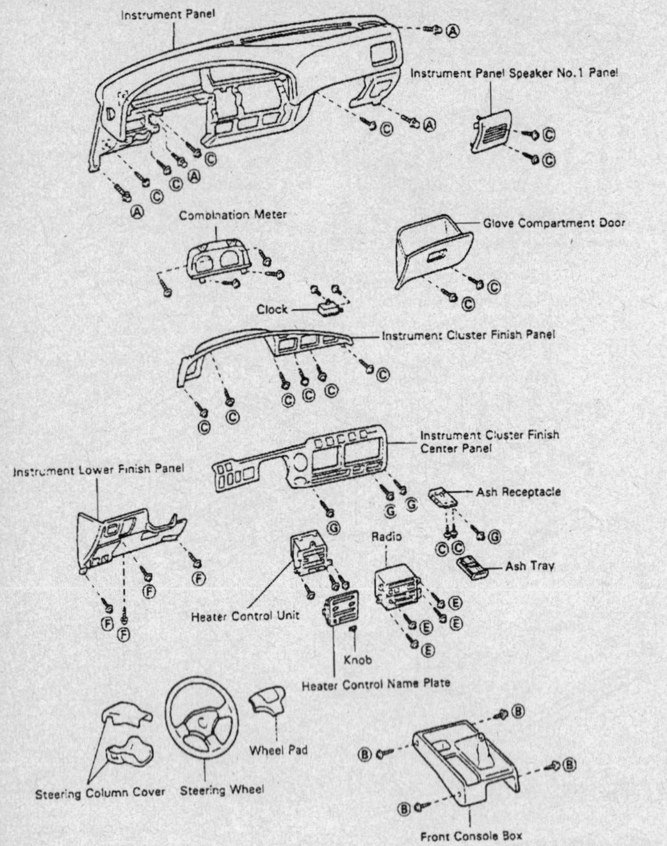
Instrument Panel
Instrument Panel Speaker No.1 Panel
Combination Meter
Glove Compartment Door
Clock
Instrument Cluster Finish Panel
Instrument Cluster Finish Center Panel
Instrument Lower Finish Panel
Ash Receptacle
Radio
Ash Tray
Heater Control Unit
Knob
Heater Control Name Plate
Wheel Pad
Steering Column Cover
Steering Wheel
Front Console Box

TY9149100018000X

Fig. 18 Exploded view of instrument panel. 1993–94 Land Cruiser

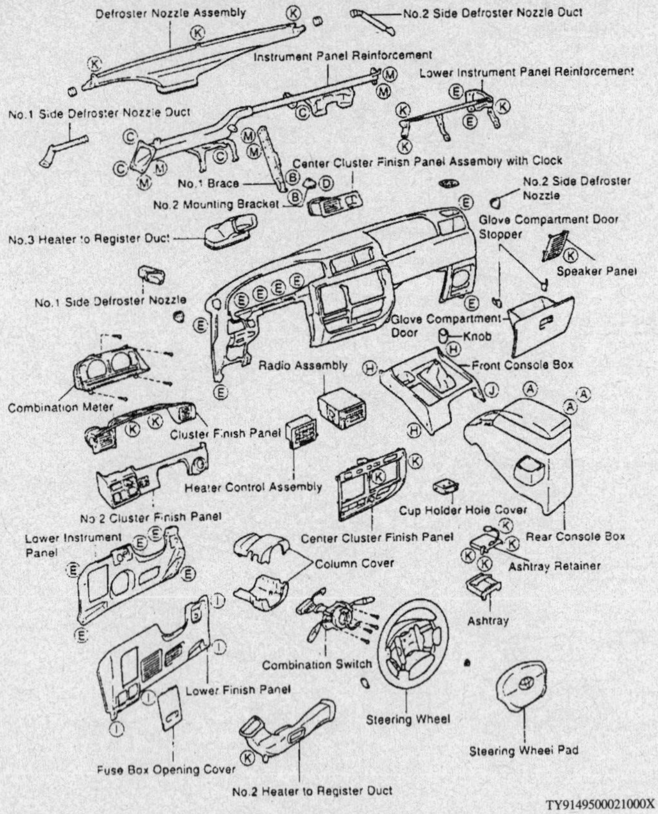
Defroster Nozzle Assembly
No.2 Side Defroster Nozzle Duct
Instrument Panel Reinforcement
Lower Instrument Panel Reinforcement
No.1 Side Defroster Nozzle Duct
Center Cluster Finish Panel Assembly with Clock
No.1 Brace
No.2 Mounting Bracket
No.2 Side Defroster Nozzle
No.3 Heater to Register Duct
Glove Compartment Door Stopper
Speaker Panel
No.1 Side Defroster Nozzle
Glove Compartment Door
Knob
Radio Assembly
Front Console Box
Combination Meter
Cluster Finish Panel
Heater Control Assembly
Cup Holder Hole Cover
No 2 Cluster Finish Panel
Lower Instrument Panel
Center Cluster Finish Panel
Rear Console Box
Column Cover
Ashtray Retainer
Ashtray
Combination Switch
Lower Finish Panel
Steering Wheel
Steering Wheel Pad
Fuse Box Opening Cover
No.2 Heater to Register Duct

TY9149500021000X

Fig. 19 Exploded view of instrument panel. 1995–96 Land Cruiser

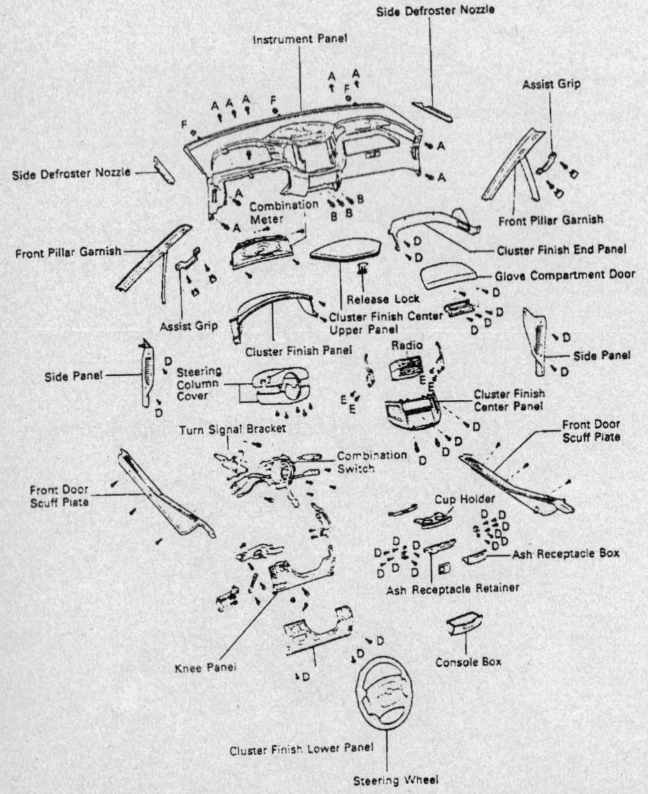
Side Defroster Nozzle
Instrument Panel
Assist Grip
Side Defroster Nozzle
Combination Meter
Front Pillar Garnish
Front Pillar Garnish
Cluster Finish End Panel
Glove Compartment Door
Release Lock
Assist Grip
Cluster Finish Center Upper Panel
Cluster Finish Panel
Radio
Side Panel
Side Panel
Steering Column Cover
Cluster Finish Center Panel
Turn Signal Bracket
Front Door Scuff Plate
Combination Switch
Front Door Scuff Plate
Cup Holder
Ash Receptacle Box
Ash Receptacle Retainer
Knee Panel
Console Box
Cluster Finish Lower Panel
Steering Wheel

TY9149200019000X

Fig. 20 Exploded view of instrument panel & components. 1993 Previa

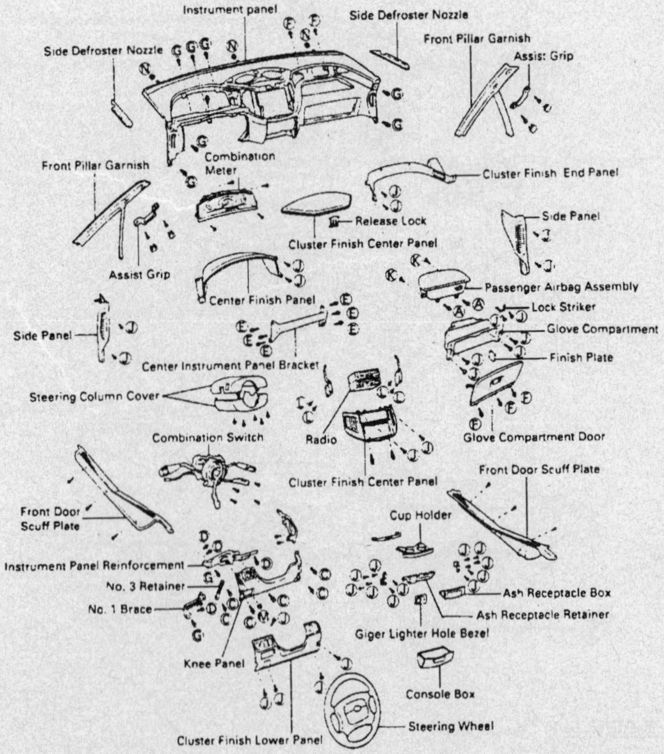
Instrument panel
Side Defroster Nozzle
Side Defroster Nozzle
Front Pillar Garnish
Assist Grip
Front Pillar Garnish
Combination Meter
Cluster Finish End Panel
Release Lock
Side Panel
Cluster Finish Center Panel
Assist Grip
Passenger Airbag Assembly
Center Finish Panel
Lock Striker
Side Panel
Glove Compartment
Finish Plate
Center Instrument Panel Bracket
Steering Column Cover
Glove Compartment Door
Combination Switch
Radio
Cluster Finish Center Panel
Front Door Scuff Plate
Front Door Scuff Plate
Cup Holder
Instrument Panel Reinforcement
No. 3 Retainer
Ash Receptacle Box
No. 1 Brace
Ash Receptacle Retainer
Giger Lighter Hole Bezel
Knee Panel
Console Box
Steering Wheel
Cluster Finish Lower Panel

TY9149500022010X

Fig. 21 Exploded view of instrument panel & components (Part 1 of 2). 1994–96 Previa

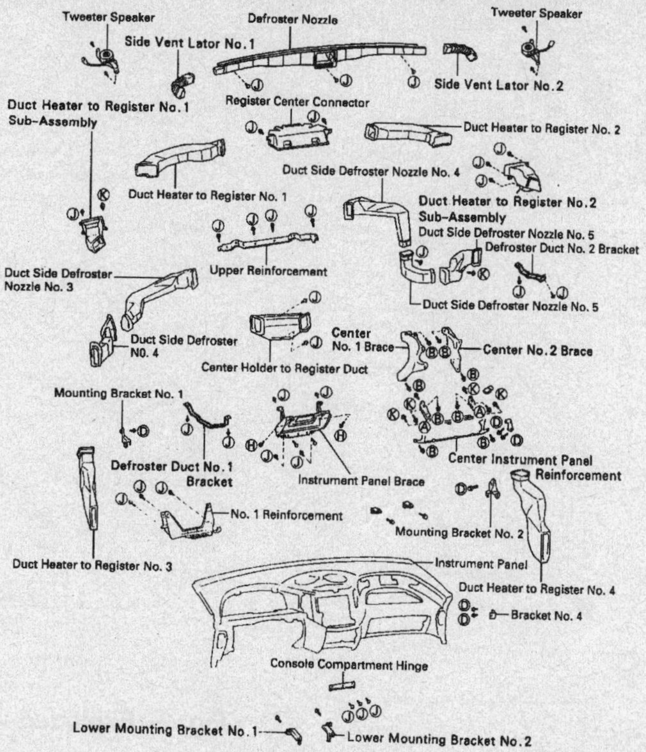
Tweeter Speaker
Defroster Nozzle
Tweeter Speaker
Side Vent Lator No.1
Side Vent Lator No.2
Duct Heater to Register No.1 Sub-Assembly
Register Center Connector
Duct Heater to Register No. 2
Duct Side Defroster Nozzle No. 4
Duct Heater to Register No. 1
Duct Heater to Register No.2 Sub-Assembly
Duct Side Defroster Nozzle No. 5
Defroster Duct No. 2 Bracket
Duct Side Defroster Nozzle No. 3
Upper Reinforcement
Duct Side Defroster Nozzle No. 5
Duct Side Defroster NO. 4
Center No. 1 Brace
Center No.2 Brace
Center Holder to Register Duct
Mounting Bracket No. 1
Defroster Duct No.1 Bracket
Instrument Panel Brace
Center Instrument Panel Reinforcement
No. 1 Reinforcement
Mounting Bracket No. 2
Duct Heater to Register No. 3
Instrument Panel
Duct Heater to Register No. 4
Bracket No. 4
Console Compartment Hinge
Lower Mounting Bracket No. 1
Lower Mounting Bracket No. 2

TY9149500022020X

Fig. 21 Exploded view of instrument panel & components (Part 2 of 2). 1994–96 Previa

Steering Columns

NOTE: On Air Bag Equipped Models, Refer To "Air Bag System Precautions" Located In The Front Of This Manual For System Disarming & Arming Procedures.

INDEX

	Page No.
Precautions	48-81
Air Bag Systems	48-81
Audio Coded Anti-Theft System	48-81
Steering Column Service	48-81

PRECAUTIONS

AIR BAG SYSTEMS

Refer to "Air Bag System Precautions" in the front of this manual for system disarming and arming procedures.

AUDIO CODED ANTI-THEFT SYSTEM

Some models are equipped with an audio coded anti-theft system that will disable the radio when the battery cable is disconnected. The system can be identified by the "ANTI-THEFT SYSTEM" on the cassette tape lid. Obtain 3 digit customer code for input. Reset system after service as follows:

1. Obtain 3 digit audio anti-theft code.
2. Depress 1 (PROG) while depressing righthand side of TUNE SEEK button, - - - will appear in tape operation display.
3. To enter the first digit, depress 1 (PROG) button repeatedly until the number of times depressed equals the first digit beginning with zero (depress the 1 button six times if the first digit if five).
4. To enter second digit, depress 2 (APS) button repeatedly until the number of times depressed equals the second digit beginning with zero.
5. To enter third digit, depress 3 (RPT) button repeatedly until the number of times depressed equals the third digit beginning with zero.
6. If - - - is displayed during code input, repeat procedure.
7. When code appears in display, depress and hold SCAN button until SEC appears.
8. When SEC disappears audio system should be operative.
9. If Err is displayed, repeat procedure. **Attempting to input code more than nine times may permanently disable audio system.**

STEERING COLUMN SERVICE

On models with air bags and/or anti-theft system, disarm systems as outlined under "Precautions." For steering column service, refer to **Figs. 1 through 26.**

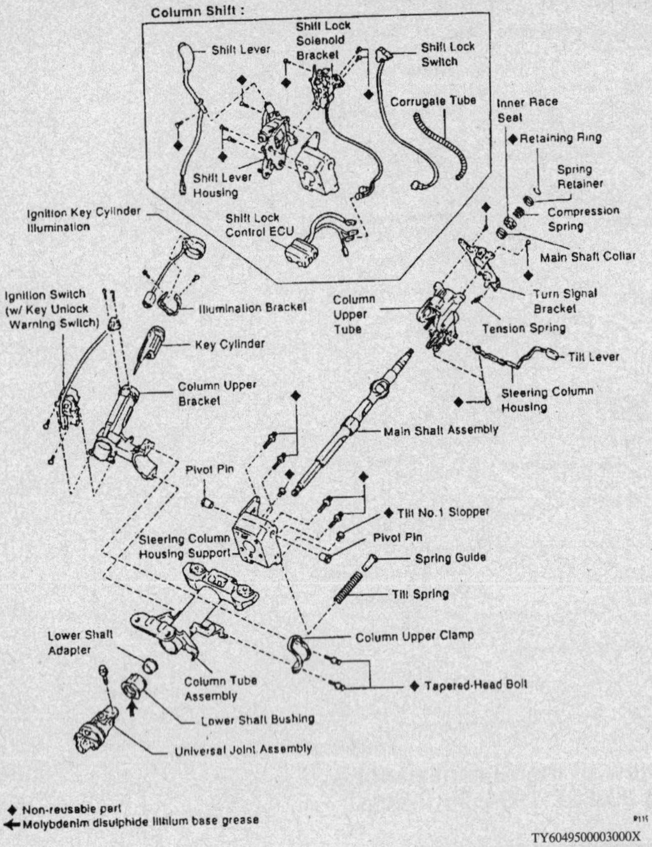

Column Shift :
Shift Lever
Shift Lock Solenoid Bracket
Shift Lock Switch
Corrugate Tube
Shift Lever Housing
Shift Lock Control ECU
Inner Race Seat
◆ Retaining Ring
Spring Retainer
Compression Spring
Main Shaft Collar
Ignition Key Cylinder Illumination
Ignition Switch (w/ Key Unlock Warning Switch)
Illumination Bracket
Key Cylinder
Column Upper Bracket
Column Upper Tube
Turn Signal Bracket
Tension Spring
Tilt Lever
Steering Column Housing
Main Shaft Assembly
Pivot Pin
◆ Tilt No.1 Stopper
Pivot Pin
Steering Column Housing Support
Spring Guide
Tilt Spring
Column Upper Clamp
Lower Shaft Adapter
Column Tube Assembly
◆ Tapered-Head Bolt
Lower Shaft Bushing
Universal Joint Assembly
◆ Non-reusable part
← Molybdenim disulphide lithium base grease
TY6049500003000X

Fig. 1 Exploded view of steering column. Avalon

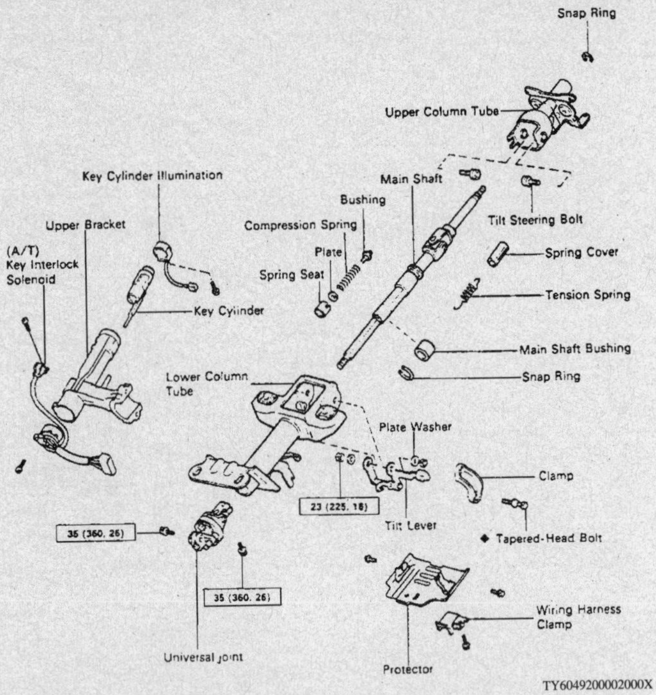

Snap Ring
Upper Column Tube
Key Cylinder Illumination
Main Shaft
Bushing
Tilt Steering Bolt
Upper Bracket
Compression Spring
Plate
Spring Cover
(A/T) Key Interlock Solenoid
Spring Seat
Key Cylinder
Tension Spring
Main Shaft Bushing
Snap Ring
Lower Column Tube
Plate Washer
Clamp
23 (225, 18)
35 (360, 26)
Tilt Lever
◆ Tapered-Head Bolt
35 (360, 26)
Wiring Harness Clamp
Universal joint
Protector
TY6049200002000X

Fig. 2 Exploded view of steering column. Camry

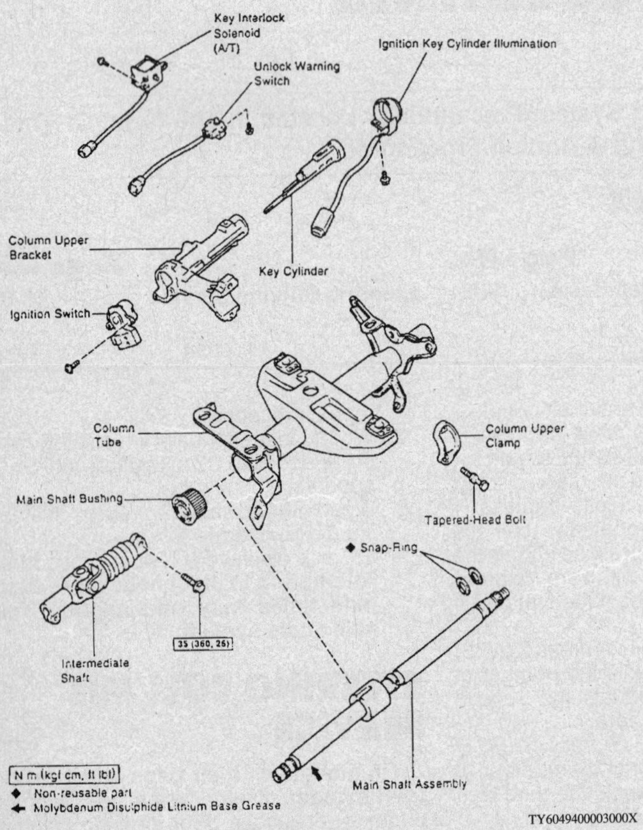

Key Interlock Solenoid (A/T)
Unlock Warning Switch
Ignition Key Cylinder Illumination
Column Upper Bracket
Key Cylinder
Ignition Switch
Column Tube
Column Upper Clamp
Main Shaft Bushing
Tapered-Head Bolt
◆ Snap-Ring
Intermediate Shaft
35 (360, 26)
Main Shaft Assembly
N·m (kgf·cm, ft·lbf)
◆ Non-reusable part
← Molybdenum Disulphide Lithium Base Grease
TY6049400003000X

Fig. 3 Exploded view of steering column. 1994–96 Celica less tilt column

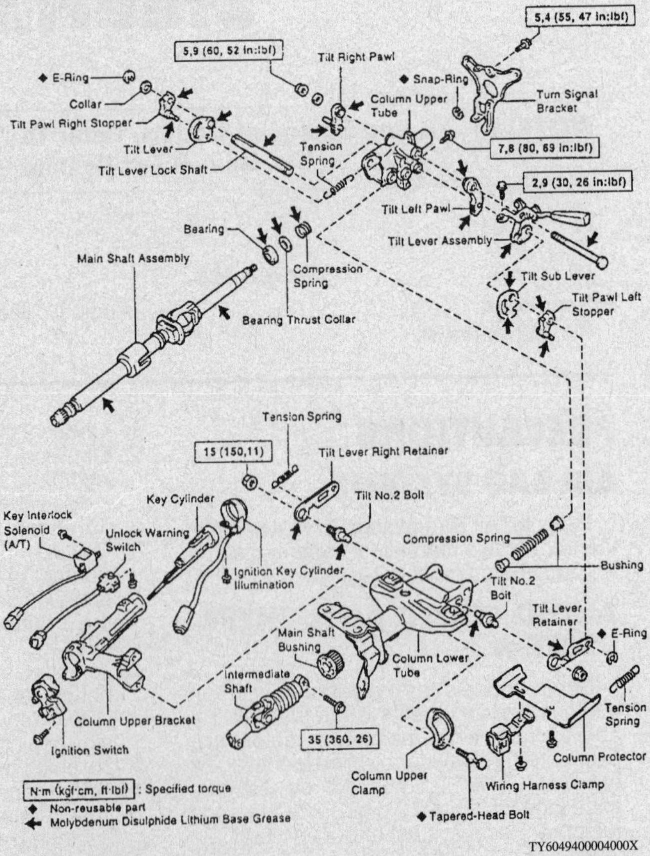

5,4 (55, 47 in·lbf)
5,9 (60, 52 in·lbf)
Tilt Right Pawl
◆ E-Ring
Collar
◆ Snap-Ring
Column Upper Tube
Turn Signal Bracket
Tilt Pawl Right Stopper
Tilt Lever
Tension Spring
7,8 (80, 69 in·lbf)
Tilt Lever Lock Shaft
2,9 (30, 26 in·lbf)
Tilt Left Pawl
Bearing
Tilt Lever Assembly
Main Shaft Assembly
Compression Spring
Tilt Sub Lever
Tilt Pawl Left Stopper
Bearing Thrust Collar
Tension Spring
15 (150,11)
Tilt Lever Right Retainer
Key Cylinder
Tilt No.2 Bolt
Key Interlock Solenoid (A/T)
Unlock Warning Switch
Compression Spring
Ignition Key Cylinder Illumination
Bushing
Tilt No.2 Bolt
Main Shaft Bushing
Tilt Lever Retainer
◆ E-Ring
Column Lower Tube
Intermediate Shaft
Tension Spring
Column Upper Bracket
35 (360, 26)
Ignition Switch
Column Protector
Column Upper Clamp
Wiring Harness Clamp
N·m (kgf·cm, ft·lbf) : Specified torque
◆ Non-reusable part
← Molybdenum Disulphide Lithium Base Grease
◆ Tapered-Head Bolt
TY6049400004000X

Fig. 4 Exploded view of steering column. 1994–96 Celica w/tilt column

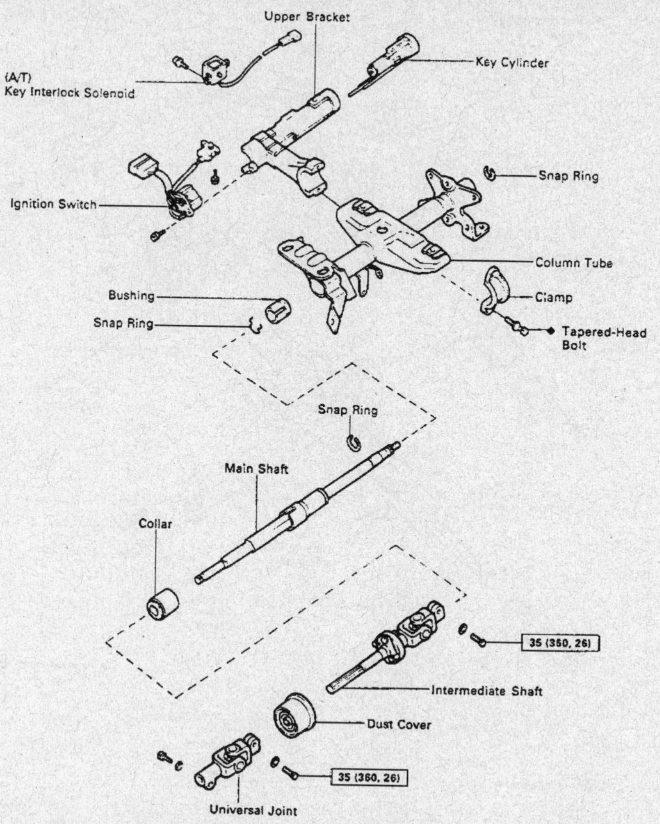
Upper Bracket
Key Cylinder
(A/T)
Key Interlock Solenoid
Snap Ring
Ignition Switch
Column Tube
Bushing
Clamp
Snap Ring
Tapered-Head Bolt
Snap Ring
Main Shaft
Collar
35 (350, 26)
Intermediate Shaft
Dust Cover
35 (350, 26)
Universal Joint

TY6049200005000X

Fig. 5 Exploded view of steering column. 1993 Celica less tilt column

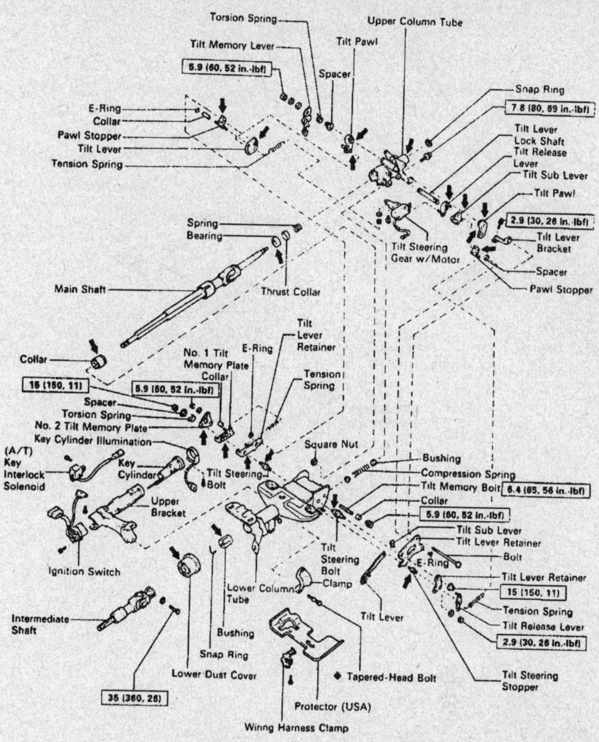
Torsion Spring
Upper Column Tube
Tilt Memory Lever
Tilt Pawl
5.9 (60, 52 in.-lbf)
Spacer
Snap Ring
7.8 (80, 69 in.-lbf)
E-Ring
Collar
Pawl Stopper
Tilt Lever
Tension Spring
Tilt Lever Lock Shaft
Tilt Release Lever
Tilt Sub Lever
Tilt Pawl
2.9 (30, 26 in.-lbf)
Tilt Lever Bracket
Spring
Bearing
Tilt Steering Gear w/Motor
Spacer
Pawl Stopper
Main Shaft
Thrust Collar
Collar
No. 1 Tilt Memory Plate
Collar
E-Ring
Tilt Lever Retainer
Tension Spring
15 (150, 11)
5.9 (60, 52 in.-lbf)
Spacer
Torsion Spring
No. 2 Tilt Memory Plate
Key Cylinder Illumination
Square Nut
(A/T)
Key Interlock Solenoid
Key Cylinder
Tilt Steering Bolt
Bushing
Compression Spring
Tilt Memory Bolt
6.4 (65, 56 in.-lbf)
Collar
5.9 (60, 52 in.-lbf)
Upper Bracket
Tilt Sub Lever
Tilt Lever Retainer
Bolt
Ignition Switch
Tilt Steering Bolt
E-Ring
Lower Column Tube
Clamp
Tilt Lever Retainer
15 (150, 11)
Tension Spring
Tilt Release Lever
2.9 (30, 26 in.-lbf)
Intermediate Shaft
Tilt Lever
Bushing
Snap Ring
Lower Dust Cover
Tapered-Head Bolt
Tilt Steering Stopper
35 (360, 26)
Protector (USA)
Wiring Harness Clamp

TY6049100006000X

Fig. 6 Exploded view of steering column. 1993 Celica w/tilt column

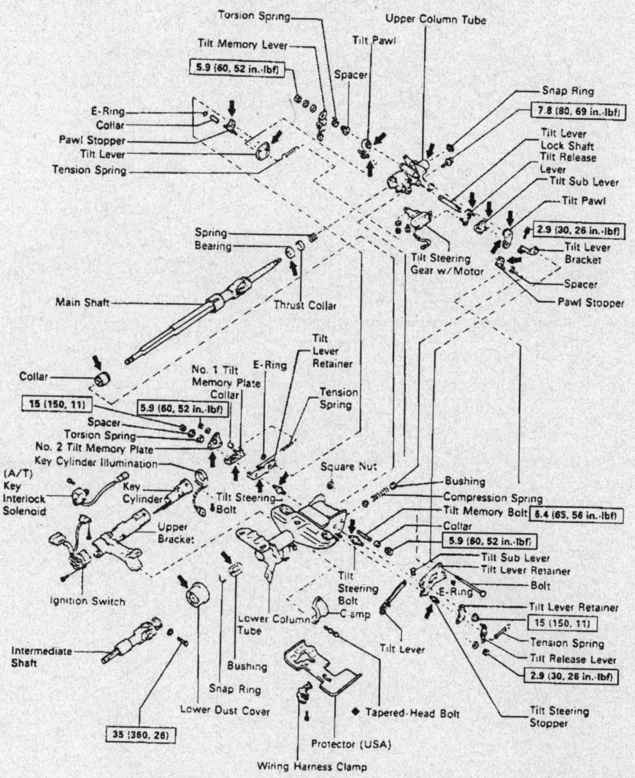
Torsion Spring
Upper Column Tube
Tilt Memory Lever
Tilt Pawl
5.9 (60, 52 in.-lbf)
Spacer
Snap Ring
7.8 (80, 69 in.-lbf)
E-Ring
Collar
Pawl Stopper
Tilt Lever
Tension Spring
Tilt Lever Lock Shaft
Tilt Release Lever
Tilt Sub Lever
Tilt Pawl
2.9 (30, 26 in.-lbf)
Tilt Lever Bracket
Spring
Bearing
Tilt Steering Gear w/Motor
Spacer
Pawl Stopper
Main Shaft
Thrust Collar
Collar
No. 1 Tilt Memory Plate
Collar
E-Ring
Tilt Lever Retainer
Tension Spring
15 (150, 11)
5.9 (60, 52 in.-lbf)
Spacer
Torsion Spring
No. 2 Tilt Memory Plate
Key Cylinder Illumination
Square Nut
(A/T)
Key Interlock Solenoid
Key Cylinder
Tilt Steering Bolt
Bushing
Compression Spring
Tilt Memory Bolt
6.4 (65, 56 in.-lbf)
Collar
5.9 (60, 52 in.-lbf)
Upper Bracket
Tilt Sub Lever
Tilt Lever Retainer
Bolt
Ignition Switch
Tilt Steering Bolt
E-Ring
Lower Column Tube
Clamp
Tilt Lever Retainer
15 (150, 11)
Tension Spring
Tilt Release Lever
2.9 (30, 26 in.-lbf)
Intermediate Shaft
Tilt Lever
Bushing
Snap Ring
Lower Dust Cover
Tapered-Head Bolt
Tilt Steering Stopper
35 (360, 26)
Protector (USA)
Wiring Harness Clamp

TY6049100007000X

Fig. 7 Exploded view of steering column. 1993 Celica w/telescopic column

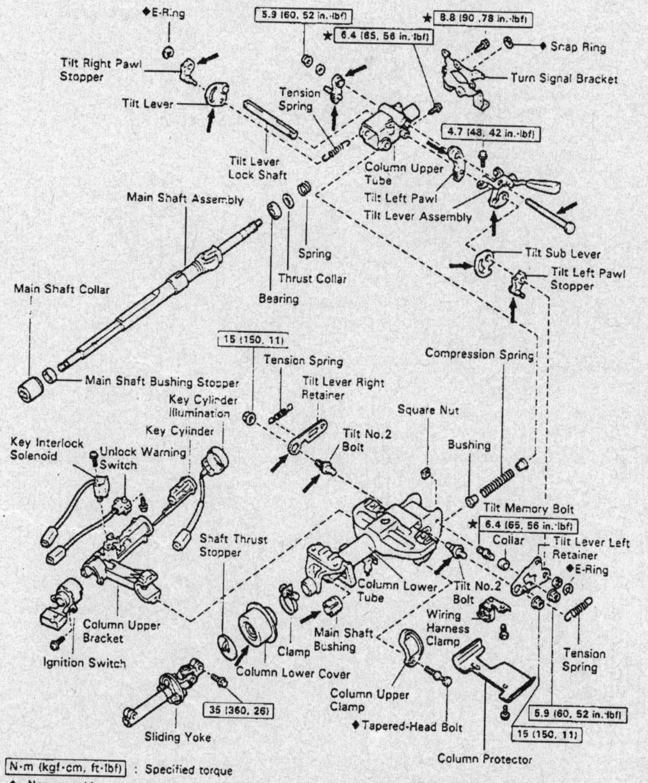
E-Ring
5.9 (60, 52 in.-lbf)
8.8 (90, 78 in.-lbf)
6.4 (65, 56 in.-lbf)
Snap Ring
Tilt Right Pawl Stopper
Turn Signal Bracket
Tension Spring
Tilt Lever
4.7 (48, 42 in.-lbf)
Tilt Lever Lock Shaft
Column Upper Tube
Main Shaft Assembly
Tilt Left Pawl
Tilt Lever Assembly
Spring
Tilt Sub Lever
Thrust Collar
Tilt Left Pawl Stopper
Main Shaft Collar
Bearing
15 (150, 11)
Compression Spring
Tension Spring
Main Shaft Bushing Stopper
Tilt Lever Right Retainer
Key Cylinder Illumination
Square Nut
Key Cylinder
Tilt No.2 Bolt
Key Interlock Solenoid
Unlock Warning Switch
Bushing
Tilt Memory Bolt
6.4 (65, 56 in.-lbf)
Collar
Tilt Lever Left Retainer
E-Ring
Shaft Thrust Stopper
Column Lower Tube
Tilt No.2 Bolt
Column Upper Bracket
Wiring Harness Clamp
Main Shaft Bushing
Clamp
Ignition Switch
Tension Spring
Column Lower Cover
Column Upper Clamp
35 (360, 26)
5.9 (60, 52 in.-lbf)
Tapered-Head Bolt
15 (150, 11)
Sliding Yoke
Column Protector

N·m (kgf·cm, ft·lbf) : Specified torque

◆ Non-reusable part

★ Precoated part

:Apply Molybdenum Disulphide Lithium Base Grease

TY6049300009000X

Fig. 8 Exploded view of steering column. Supra

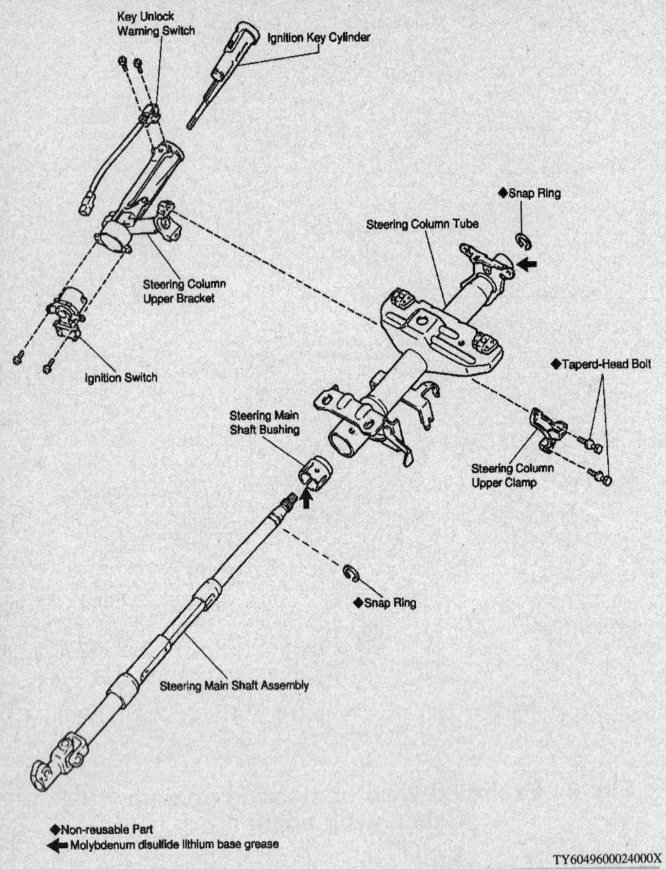
Key Unlock Warning Switch
Ignition Key Cylinder
Snap Ring
Steering Column Tube
Steering Column Upper Bracket
Ignition Switch
Taperd-Head Bolt
Steering Main Shaft Bushing
Steering Column Upper Clamp
Snap Ring
Steering Main Shaft Assembly
◆Non-reusable Part
Molybdenum disulfide lithium base grease
TY6049600024000X

Fig. 9 Exploded view of steering column. RAV4

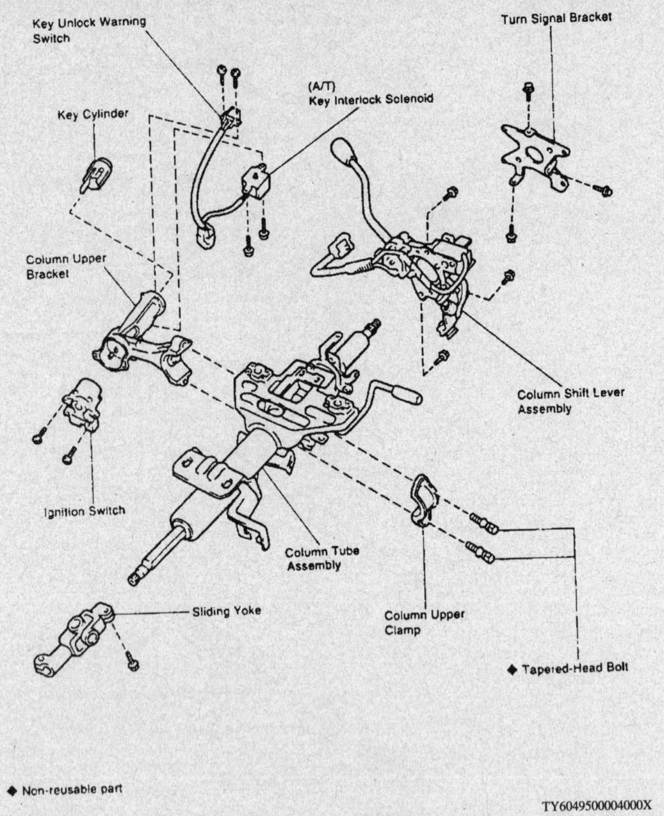
Key Unlock Warning Switch
Turn Signal Bracket
(A/T) Key Interlock Solenoid
Key Cylinder
Column Upper Bracket
Column Shift Lever Assembly
Ignition Switch
Column Tube Assembly
Sliding Yoke
Column Upper Clamp
◆ Tapered-Head Bolt
◆ Non-reusable part
TY6049500004000X

Fig. 10 Exploded view of steering column. Tacoma w/tilt column

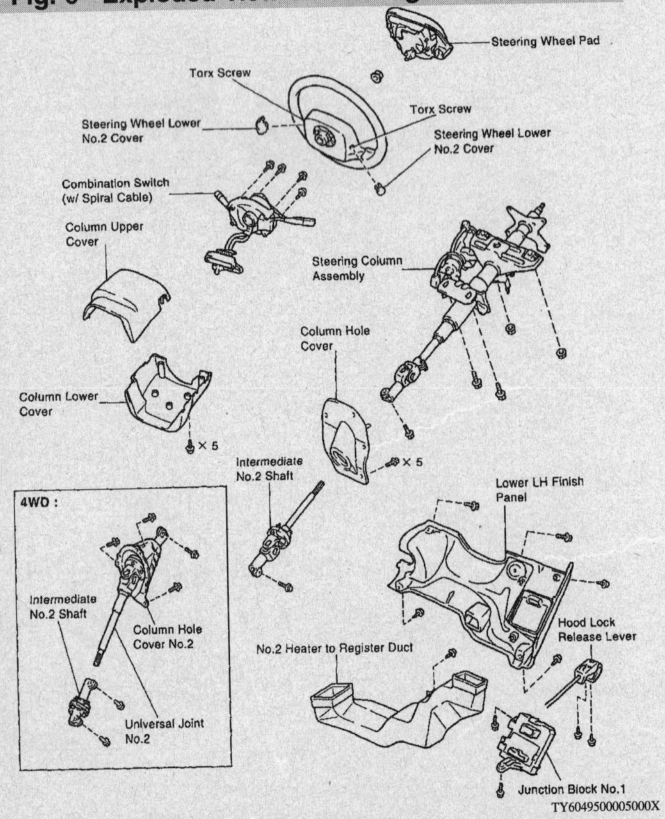
Steering Wheel Pad
Torx Screw
Steering Wheel Lower No.2 Cover
Torx Screw
Steering Wheel Lower No.2 Cover
Combination Switch (w/ Spiral Cable)
Column Upper Cover
Steering Column Assembly
Column Hole Cover
Column Lower Cover
×5
×5
Intermediate No.2 Shaft
Lower LH Finish Panel
4WD :
Intermediate No.2 Shaft
Column Hole Cover No.2
Universal Joint No.2
No.2 Heater to Register Duct
Hood Lock Release Lever
Junction Block No.1
TY6049500005000X

Fig. 11 Exploded view of steering column. Tacoma less tilt column

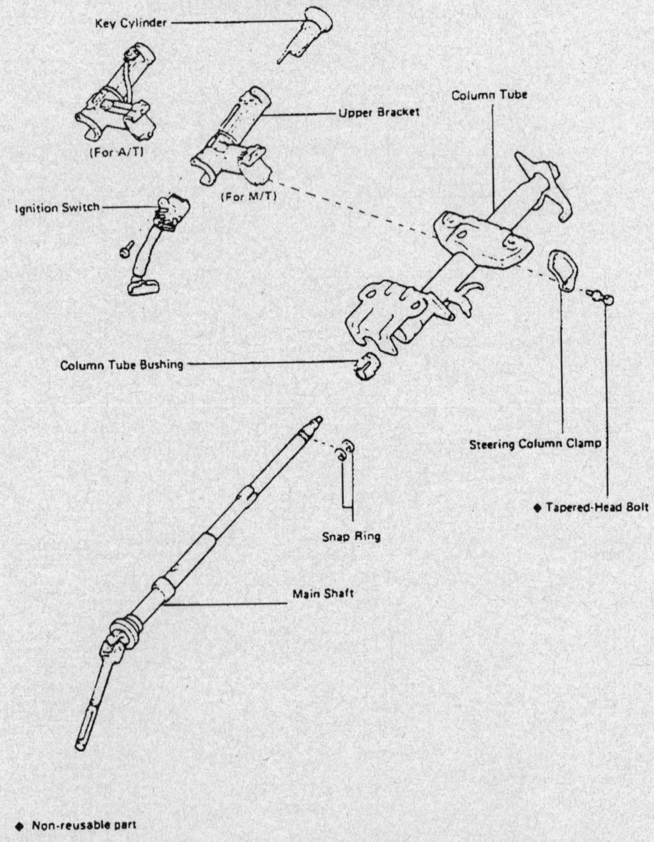
Key Cylinder
Upper Bracket
Column Tube
(For A/T)
(For M/T)
Ignition Switch
Column Tube Bushing
Steering Column Clamp
◆ Tapered-Head Bolt
Snap Ring
Main Shaft
◆ Non-reusable part
TY6049100010000X

Fig. 12 Exploded view of steering column. 1993 Corolla less tilt column

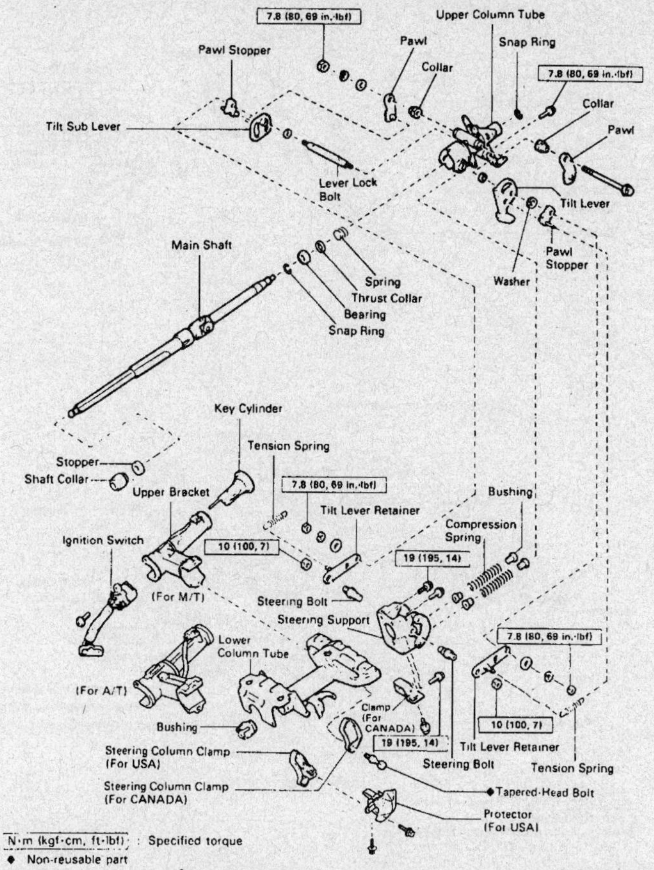
7.8 (80, 69 in.-lbf)
Upper Column Tube
Pawl Stopper
Pawl
Snap Ring
Collar
7.8 (80, 69 in.-lbf)
Collar
Tilt Sub Lever
Pawl
Lever Lock Bolt
Tilt Lever
Main Shaft
Pawl Stopper
Spring
Washer
Thrust Collar
Bearing
Snap Ring
Key Cylinder
Tension Spring
Stopper
Shaft Collar
Upper Bracket
7.8 (80, 69 in.-lbf)
Bushing
Tilt Lever Retainer
Ignition Switch
Compression Spring
10 (100, 7)
19 (195, 14)
(For M/T)
Steering Bolt
Steering Support
Lower Column Tube
7.8 (80, 69 in.-lbf)
(For A/T)
Clamp (For CANADA)
10 (100, 7)
Bushing
19 (195, 14)
Tilt Lever Retainer
Steering Column Clamp (For USA)
Steering Bolt
Tension Spring
Steering Column Clamp (For CANADA)
◆Tapered-Head Bolt
Protector (For USA)
N·m (kgf·cm, ft·lbf) : Specified torque
◆ Non-reusable part

TY6049100011000X

Fig. 13 Exploded view of steering column. 1993 Corolla w/tilt column

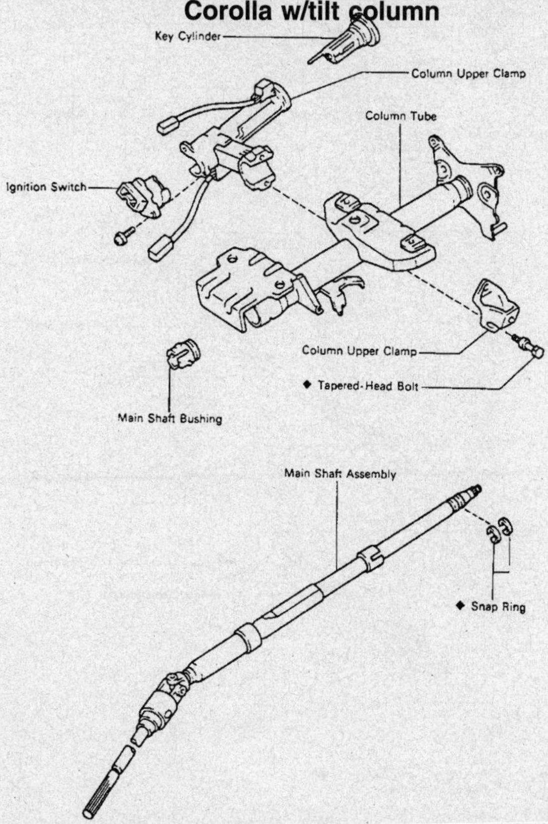
Key Cylinder
Column Upper Clamp
Column Tube
Ignition Switch
Column Upper Clamp
◆ Tapered-Head Bolt
Main Shaft Bushing
Main Shaft Assembly
◆ Snap Ring

TY6049400013000X

Fig. 15 Exploded view of steering column (Toyota). 1994–96 Corolla less tilt column

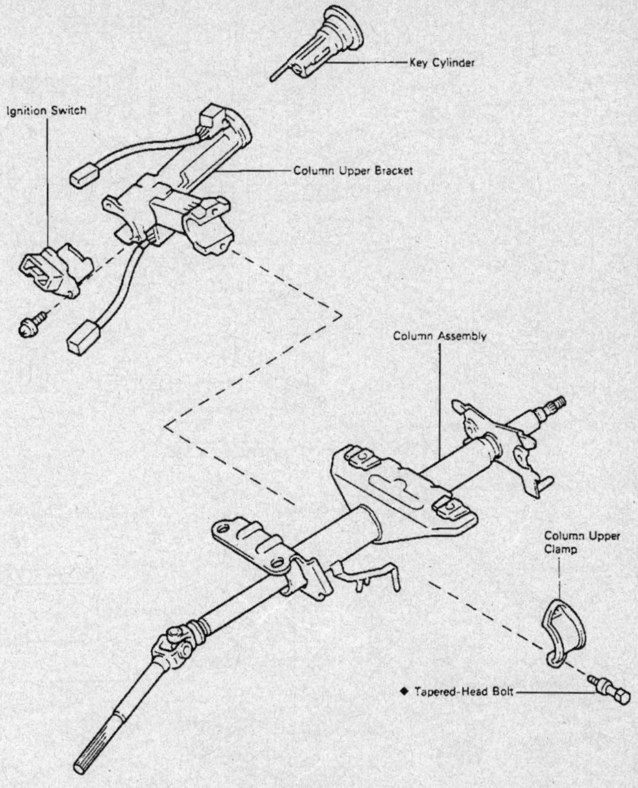
Key Cylinder
Ignition Switch
Column Upper Bracket
Column Assembly
Column Upper Clamp
◆ Tapered-Head Bolt

TY6049400012000X

Fig. 14 Exploded view of steering column (Nastech). 1994–96 Corolla less tilt column

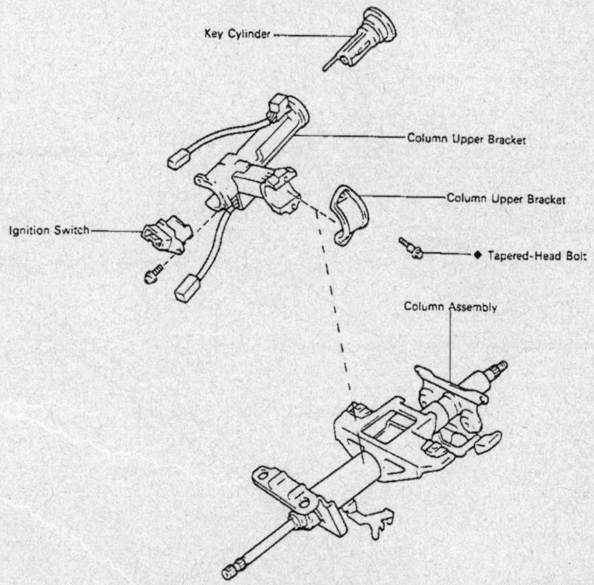
Key Cylinder
Column Upper Bracket
Column Upper Bracket
Ignition Switch
◆ Tapered-Head Bolt
Column Assembly

TY6049400014000X

Fig. 16 Exploded view of steering column. 1994–96 Corolla w/tilt column

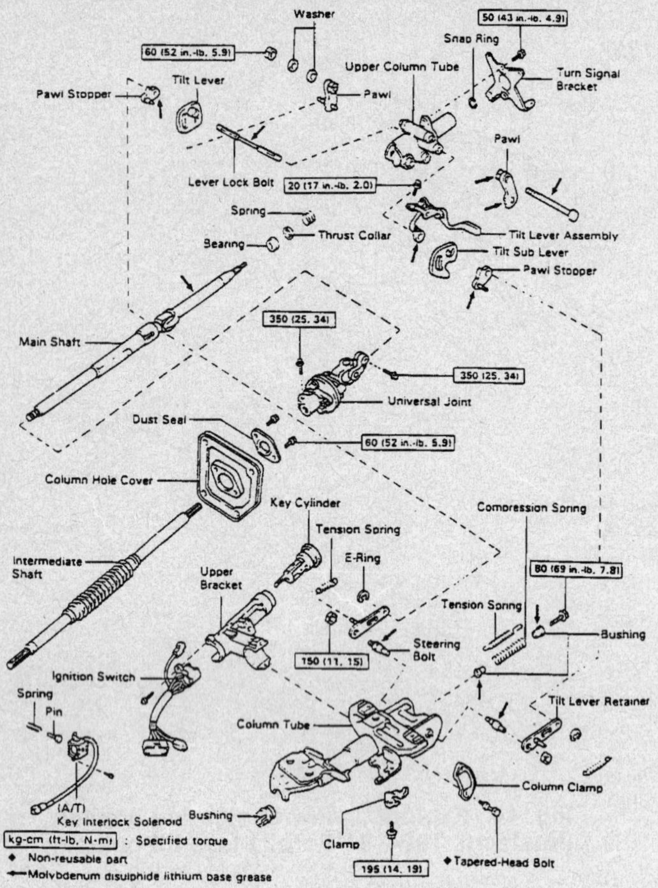

Washer
50 (43 in.-lb. 4.9)
Snap Ring
60 (52 in.-lb. 5.9)
Upper Column Tube
Turn Signal Bracket
Tilt Lever
Pawl Stopper
Pawl
Pawl
Lever Lock Bolt
20 (17 in.-lb. 2.0)
Spring
Thrust Collar
Bearing
Tilt Lever Assembly
Tilt Sub Lever
Pawl Stopper
Main Shaft
350 (25, 34)
350 (25, 34)
Universal Joint
Dust Seal
60 (52 in.-lb. 5.9)
Column Hole Cover
Key Cylinder
Compression Spring
Tension Spring
Intermediate Shaft
E-Ring
Upper Bracket
80 (69 in.-lb. 7.8)
Tension Spring
Bushing
Steering Bolt
150 (11, 15)
Ignition Switch
Spring
Pin
Column Tube
Tilt Lever Retainer
Column Clamp
(A/T)
Key Interlock Solenoid
Bushing
kg-cm (ft-lb, N-m) : Specified torque
◆ Non-reusable part
Molybdenum disulphide lithium base grease
Clamp
195 (14, 19)
◆ Tapered-Head Bolt

TY6049100016000X

Fig. 17 Exploded view of steering column. Land Cruiser

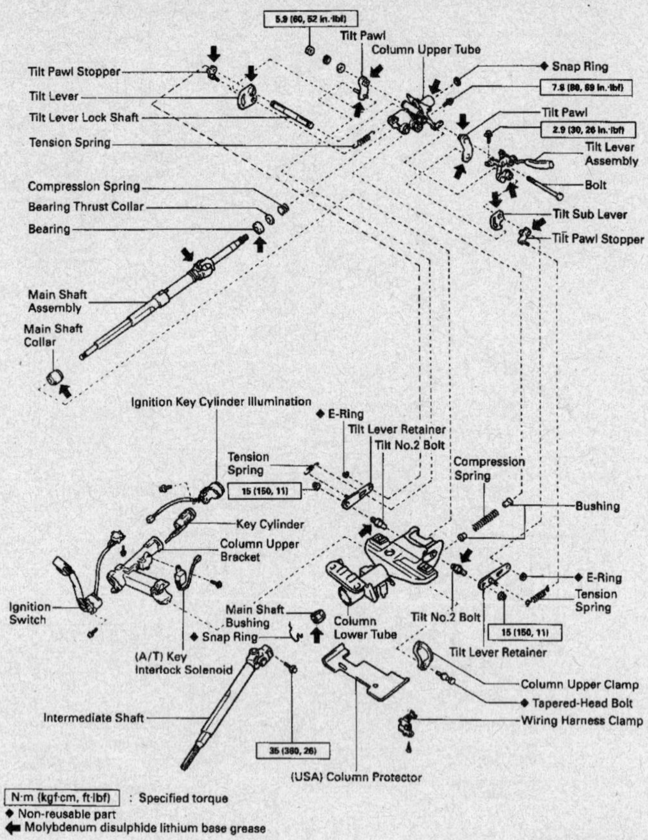

5.9 (60, 52 in.·lbf)
Tilt Pawl
Column Upper Tube
Tilt Pawl Stopper
◆ Snap Ring
7.8 (80, 69 in.·lbf)
Tilt Lever
Tilt Pawl
Tilt Lever Lock Shaft
2.9 (30, 26 in.·lbf)
Tension Spring
Tilt Lever Assembly
Bolt
Compression Spring
Bearing Thrust Collar
Tilt Sub Lever
Bearing
Tilt Pawl Stopper
Main Shaft Assembly
Main Shaft Collar
Ignition Key Cylinder Illumination
◆ E-Ring
Tilt Lever Retainer
Tilt No.2 Bolt
Tension Spring
Compression Spring
15 (150, 11)
Bushing
Key Cylinder
Column Upper Bracket
◆ E-Ring
Tension Spring
Ignition Switch
Main Shaft Bushing
Column Lower Tube
Tilt No.2 Bolt
◆ Snap Ring
15 (150, 11)
(A/T) Key Interlock Solenoid
Tilt Lever Retainer
Column Upper Clamp
◆ Tapered-Head Bolt
Intermediate Shaft
Wiring Harness Clamp
35 (360, 26)
(USA) Column Protector
N·m (kgf·cm, ft·lbf) : Specified torque
◆ Non-reusable part
Molybdenum disulphide lithium base grease

TY6049100017000X

Fig. 18 Exploded view of steering column. MR2

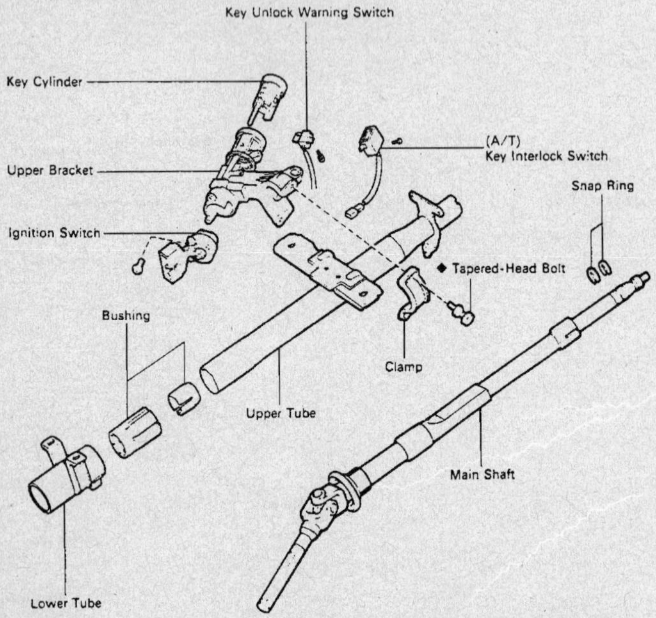

Key Unlock Warning Switch
Key Cylinder
(A/T)
Key Interlock Switch
Upper Bracket
Snap Ring
Ignition Switch
◆ Tapered-Head Bolt
Bushing
Clamp
Upper Tube
Main Shaft
Lower Tube

TY6049100018000X

Fig. 19 Exploded view of steering column. Paseo

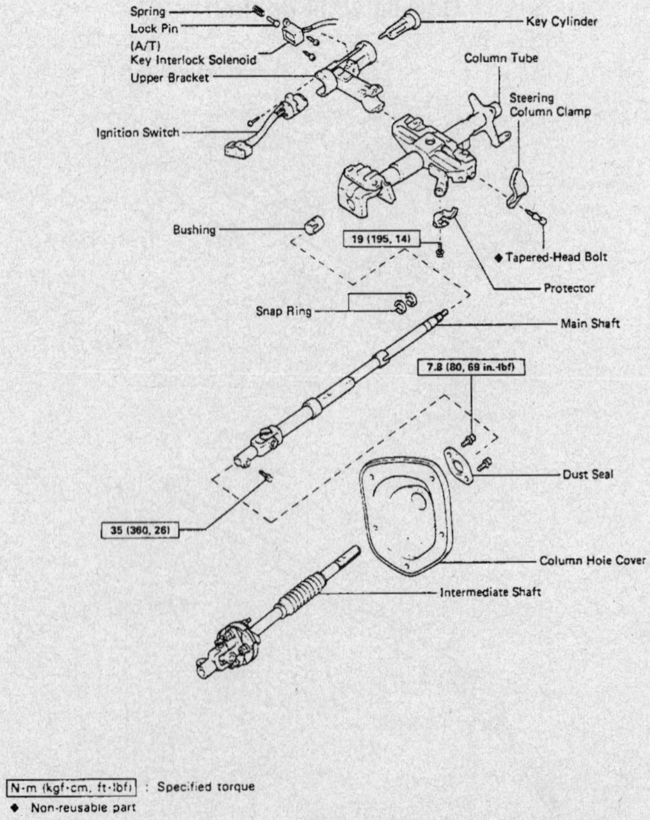

Spring
Lock Pin
Key Cylinder
(A/T)
Key Interlock Solenoid
Column Tube
Upper Bracket
Steering Column Clamp
Ignition Switch
Bushing
19 (195, 14)
◆ Tapered-Head Bolt
Protector
Snap Ring
Main Shaft
7.8 (80, 69 in.·lbf)
Dust Seal
35 (360, 26)
Column Hole Cover
Intermediate Shaft
N·m (kgf·cm, ft·lbf) : Specified torque
◆ Non-reusable part

TY6049100019000X

Fig. 20 Exploded view of steering column. Pickup, T100 & 1993–95 4Runner less tilt column

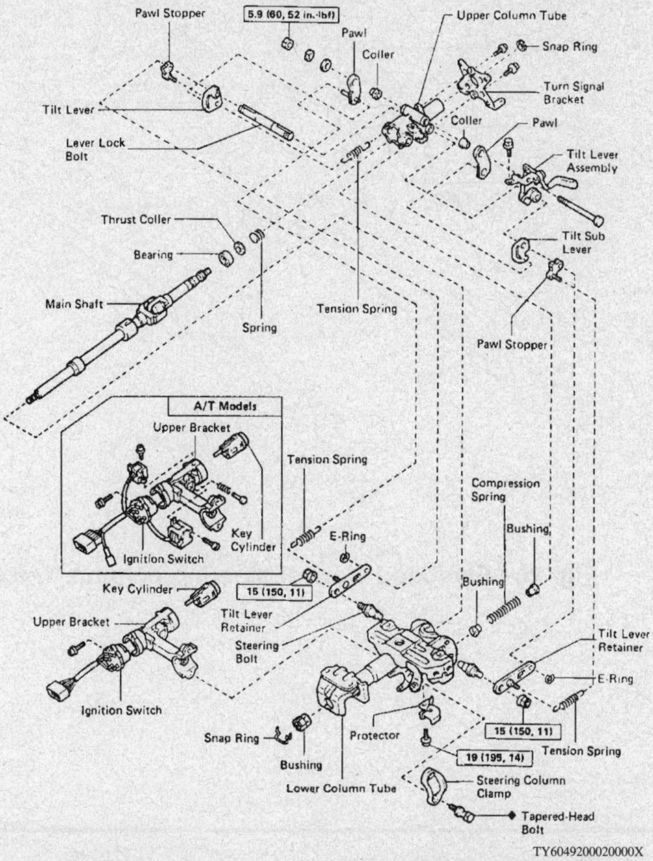
Pawl Stopper
5.9 (60, 52 in.-lbf)
Upper Column Tube
Pawl
Coller
Snap Ring
Turn Signal Bracket
Tilt Lever
Coller
Pawl
Lever Lock Bolt
Tilt Lever Assembly
Thrust Coller
Bearing
Tilt Sub Lever
Main Shaft
Tension Spring
Spring
Pawl Stopper
A/T Models
Upper Bracket
Tension Spring
Key Cylinder
Ignition Switch
Compression Spring
E-Ring
Bushing
Key Cylinder
15 (150, 11)
Bushing
Upper Bracket
Tilt Lever Retainer
Steering Bolt
Tilt Lever Retainer
E-Ring
Ignition Switch
Snap Ring
Protector
15 (150, 11)
19 (195, 14)
Tension Spring
Bushing
Lower Column Tube
Steering Column Clamp
Tapered-Head Bolt
TY6049200020000X

Fig. 21 Exploded view of steering column. Pickup, T100 & 1993–95 4Runner w/tilt column

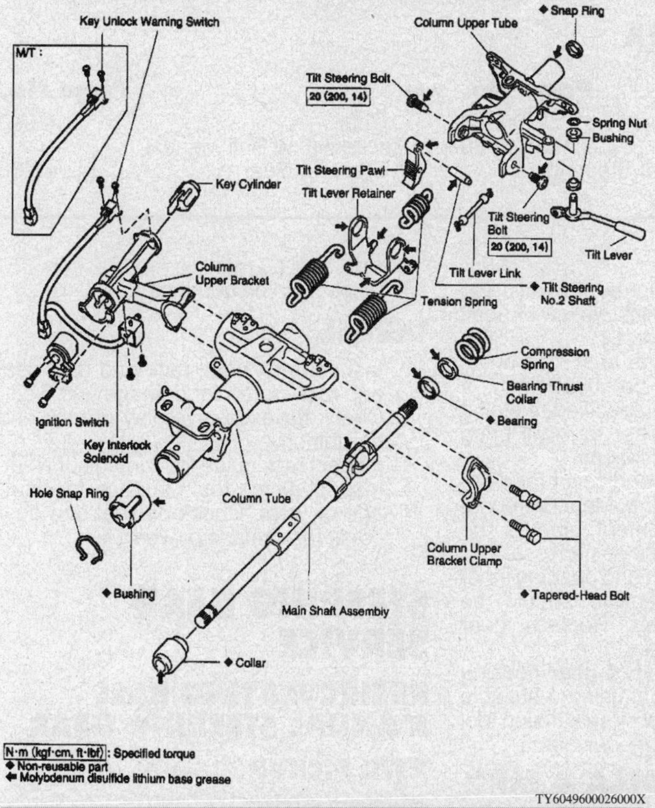
Key Unlock Warning Switch
M/T :
Column Upper Tube
Snap Ring
Tilt Steering Bolt
20 (200, 14)
Spring Nut
Bushing
Tilt Steering Pawl
Key Cylinder
Tilt Lever Retainer
Tilt Steering Bolt
20 (200, 14)
Tilt Lever
Column Upper Bracket
Tilt Lever Link
Tilt Steering No.2 Shaft
Tension Spring
Compression Spring
Bearing Thrust Collar
Bearing
Ignition Switch
Key Interlock Solenoid
Hole Snap Ring
Column Tube
Column Upper Bracket Clamp
Bushing
Tapered-Head Bolt
Main Shaft Assembly
Collar
N·m (kgf·cm, ft·lbf) : Specified torque
Non-reusable part
Molybdenum disulfide lithium base grease
TY6049600026000X

Fig. 23 Exploded view of steering column. 1996 4Runner w/tilt column

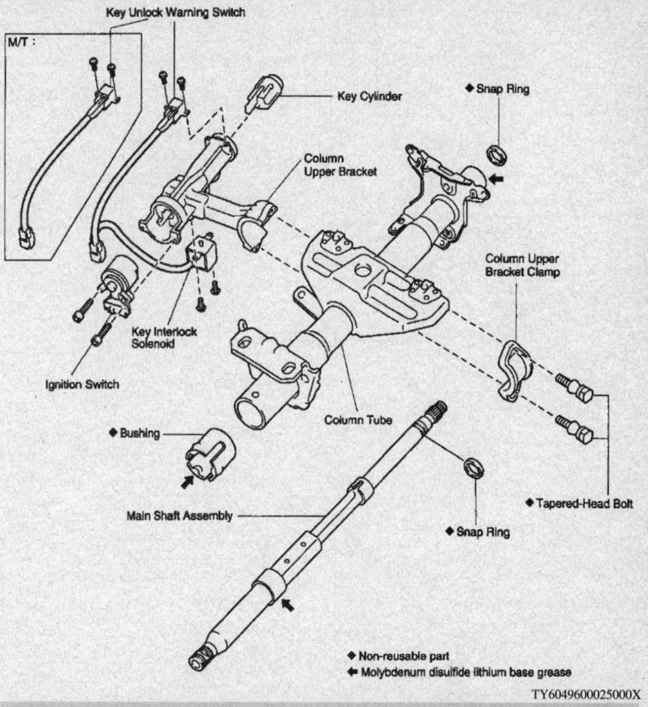
Key Unlock Warning Switch
M/T :
Key Cylinder
Snap Ring
Column Upper Bracket
Column Upper Bracket Clamp
Key Interlock Solenoid
Ignition Switch
Column Tube
Bushing
Tapered-Head Bolt
Main Shaft Assembly
Snap Ring
Non-reusable part
Molybdenum disulfide lithium base grease
TY6049600025000X

Fig. 22 Exploded view of steering column. 1996 4Runner less tilt column

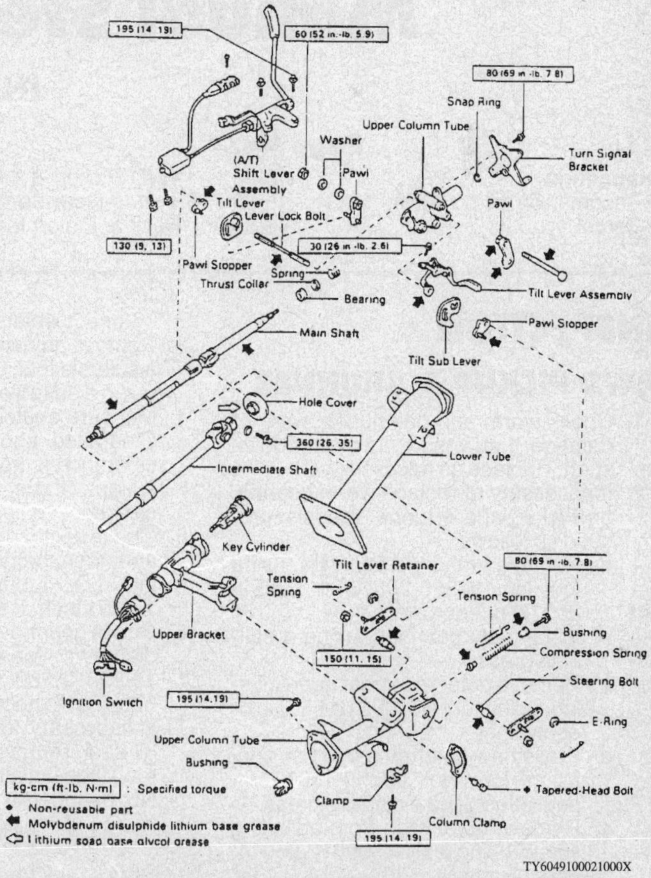
195 (14, 19)
60 (52 in.-lb, 5.9)
80 (69 in.-lb, 7.8)
Snap Ring
Upper Column Tube
Turn Signal Bracket
Washer
(A/T) Shift Lever Assembly
Pawl
Tilt Lever
Lever Lock Bolt
Pawl
130 (9, 13)
30 (26 in.-lb, 2.6)
Pawl Stopper
Spring
Thrust Collar
Bearing
Tilt Lever Assembly
Main Shaft
Pawl Stopper
Tilt Sub Lever
Hole Cover
360 (26, 35)
Intermediate Shaft
Lower Tube
Key Cylinder
Tilt Lever Retainer
80 (69 in.-lb, 7.8)
Tension Spring
Tension Spring
Upper Bracket
Bushing
150 (11, 15)
Compression Spring
Steering Bolt
Ignition Switch
195 (14, 19)
E-Ring
Upper Column Tube
Bushing
kg-cm (ft-lb, N·m) : Specified torque
Non-reusable part
Molybdenum disulphide lithium base grease
Lithium soap base glycol grease
Clamp
Tapered-Head Bolt
Column Clamp
195 (14, 19)
TY6049100021000X

Fig. 24 Exploded view of steering column. 1993 Previa w/tilt column

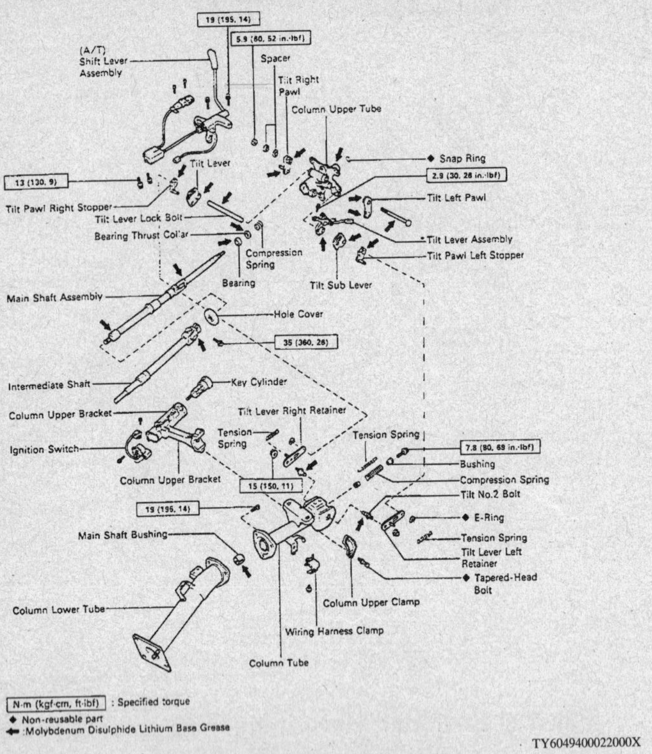
19 (195, 14)
5.9 (60, 52 in.-lbf)
(A/T) Shift Lever Assembly
Spacer
Tilt Right Pawl
Column Upper Tube
Snap Ring
2.9 (30, 26 in.-lbf)
13 (130, 9)
Tilt Lever
Tilt Left Pawl
Tilt Pawl Right Stopper
Tilt Lever Lock Bolt
Bearing Thrust Collar
Compression Spring
Tilt Lever Assembly
Tilt Pawl Left Stopper
Bearing
Tilt Sub Lever
Main Shaft Assembly
Hole Cover
35 (360, 26)
Intermediate Shaft
Key Cylinder
Column Upper Bracket
Tilt Lever Right Retainer
Tension Spring
Ignition Switch
Tension Spring
7.8 (80, 69 in.-lbf)
Bushing
Compression Spring
Column Upper Bracket
15 (150, 11)
Tilt No.2 Bolt
19 (195, 14)
E-Ring
Main Shaft Bushing
Tension Spring
Tilt Lever Left Retainer
Tapered-Head Bolt
Column Upper Clamp
Column Lower Tube
Wiring Harness Clamp
Column Tube
N·m (kgf-cm, ft-lbf) : Specified torque
◆ Non-reusable part
Molybdenum Disulphide Lithium Base Grease
TY6049400022000X

Fig. 25 Exploded view of steering column. 1994–96 Previa

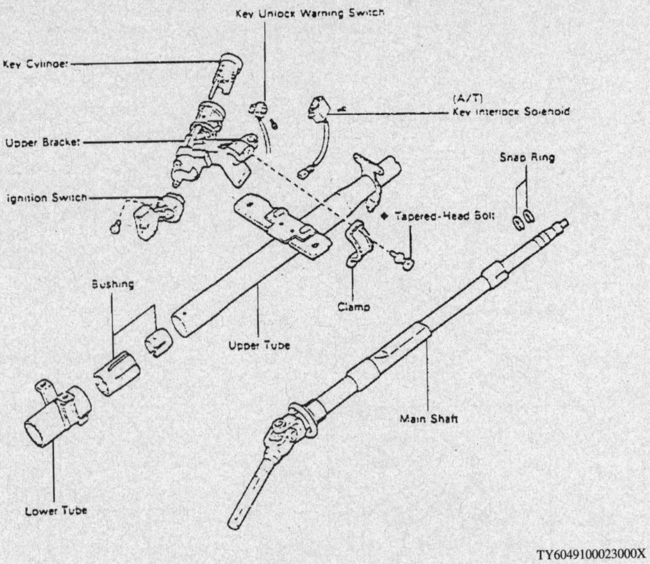
Key Unlock Warning Switch
Key Cylinder
(A/T) Key Interlock Solenoid
Upper Bracket
Snap Ring
Ignition Switch
Tapered-Head Bolt
Bushing
Clamp
Upper Tube
Main Shaft
Lower Tube
TY6049100023000X

Fig. 26 Exploded view of steering column. Tercel

Manual Steering Gears

INDEX

	Page No.
Inspection	48-88
Tacoma, Corolla & MR2	48-88
Tercel	48-88
4WD Pickup & 4Runner	48-88
Steering Gear Service	48-88
Rack & Pinion Manual Steering Gear	48-90
Recirculating Ball Manual Steering Gear	48-88

INSPECTION

4WD PICKUP & 4RUNNER

1. Check worm and ball nut for wear or damage, then ensure nut rotates down shaft. Replace as necessary.
2. If necessary to replace worm bearing, on Pickup and 4Runner models, proceed as follows:
   a. Remove both side bearings, using tool No. 09950-20016 or 09950-20017, or equivalent.
   b. Install new bearings, using a suitable press.
   c. Remove outer race from gear housing, using tool No. 09612-65014, or equivalent.
   d. Press new outer race into housing, using tool No. 09550-10012, or equivalent, and a suitable press.
   e. Remove outer race from adjusting screw, using tool No. 09612-65014, or equivalent.
   f. Press in new adjusting screw outer race, using tool No. 09550-10012, or equivalent.
3. Remove adjusting screw oil seal, using a suitable tool, then install new oil seal, using a suitable socket.
4. Measure sector shaft trust clearance. Clearance should be .0020 inch. If clearance is not as specified, install a suitable thrust washer that will bring clearance to specifications.
5. Check sector shaft end cover for damage, then the bushing. Measure bushing I.D. Measurement should be 1.4201 inch. Replace as necessary.
6. Check gear housing and bushing inner diameter. Measurement should be 1.2598–1.2608 inch. Replace gear housing as necessary.
7. If necessary to replace gear housing oil seal, remove seal using a suitable tool, then install new oil seal, using tool No. 09550-10012, or equivalent.

TACOMA, COROLLA & MR2

1. Check rack teeth and back for wear or damage.
2. Ensure rack runout does not exceed .012 inch (.3 mm).
3. Inspect pinion bearings.

TERCEL

1. Inspect rack boot, rack end dust seal and rack clamp for damage and wear.
2. Check for excessive play in rack end ball joint.
3. Inspect rack guide for damage or wear.
4. Inspect pinion tooth surface for damage or wear. Check oil seal and dust cover for damage or wear.

STEERING GEAR SERVICE

RECIRCULATING BALL MANUAL STEERING GEAR

2WD PICKUP

Disassemble

1. Remove pitman arm using a suitable puller, **Figs. 1 and 2.**

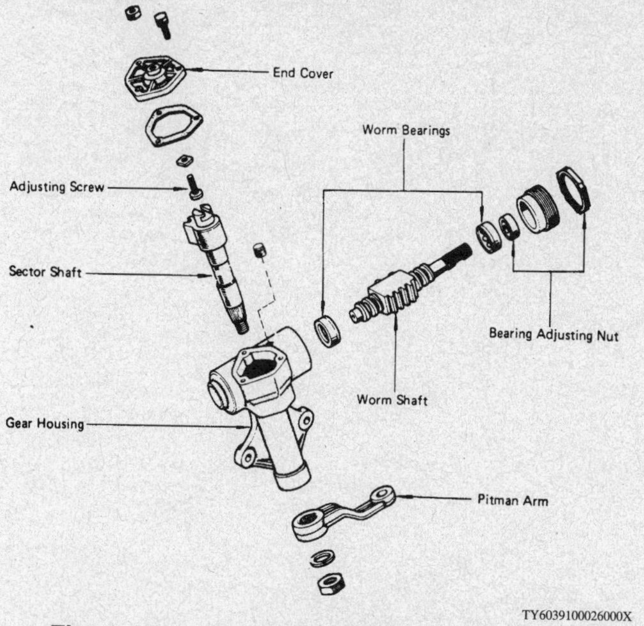
End Cover
Worm Bearings
Adjusting Screw
Sector Shaft
Bearing Adjusting Nut
Worm Shaft
Gear Housing
Pitman Arm
TY6039100026000X

Fig. 1 Manual steering gear. Pickup 2WD

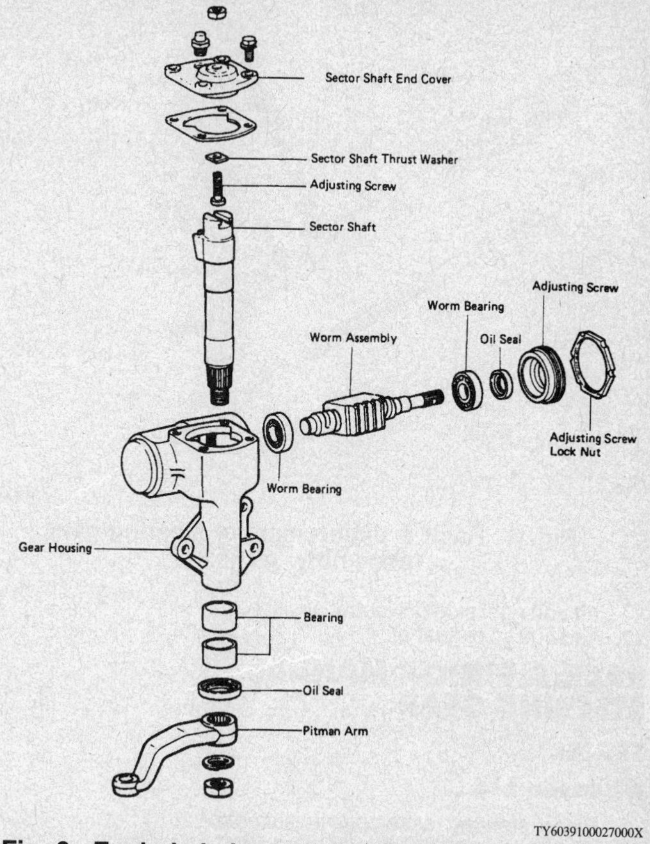
Sector Shaft End Cover
Sector Shaft Thrust Washer
Adjusting Screw
Sector Shaft
Adjusting Screw
Worm Bearing
Worm Assembly
Oil Seal
Adjusting Screw Lock Nut
Worm Bearing
Gear Housing
Bearing
Oil Seal
Pitman Arm
TY6039100027000X

Fig. 2 Exploded view of manual steering gear. 4WD Pickup & 4Runner

2. Remove sector shaft adjusting screw locknut.
3. Remove end cover attaching bolts, then remove end cover and sector shaft. Drain oil from gear housing.
4. Loosen worm bearing adjusting screw locknut using suitable tool.
5. Using suitable tool, remove worm bearing adjusting screw from gear housing.
6. Remove worm assembly with bearing from gear housing. **Do not disassemble ball nut from worm assembly. If found to be defective, replace the entire assembly.**

Assemble & Adjustment

Apply grease to oil seal lips and a light coat of grease or gear oil to bearing and sliding surfaces before assembling.

1. Install worm and assemble adjusting screw and locknut, **Fig. 1.**
2. Using suitable tool, tighten adjusting screw within turning range of steering worm and allow bearings to seat.
3. Loosen adjusting screw and adjust bearing preload by gradually tightening adjusting screw until preload value is 2.6–4.3 inch lbs.
4. Tighten locknuts.
5. Recheck worm bearing preload to ensure adjustment has not changed.
6. Position ball nut at center, then insert sector shaft so that sector shaft gear will center mesh with worm.
7. Install adjusting screw, gasket and end cover.
8. Adjust overall preload by turning in sector shaft adjusting screw. Preload should be 6.9–9.1 inch lbs. Perform measurement with gear at center position.
9. Check sector shaft to ensure there is no backlash within 100° of either side of center.
10. Measure backlash by installing pitman arm and check arm deflection at arm end with a dial indicator. After making measurement tighten adjusting screw locknut.
11. Align marks on pitman arm and sector shaft, then tighten attaching nut.

4WD PICKUP & 4RUNNER

Disassemble

1. Remove breather plug, then drain gear oil, **Fig. 2.**
2. Remove adjusting screw locknut, then the four end cover attaching nuts.
3. Rotate adjusting screw clockwise, and remove end cover.
4. Remove sector shaft, using a suitable tool.
5. Remove worm bearing adjusting screw locknut, using tool No. 09617-60010, or equivalent.
6. Remove worm bearing adjusting screw, using suitable tool, then remove worm shaft from gear housing. **Do not disassemble ball nut from worm assembly. If found to be defective, replace entire assembly.**

Assemble & Adjustment

Apply a suitable lubricant to oil seal lips, bushings and bearings prior to assembly.

1. Insert worm shaft into gear housing, **Fig. 2.**
2. Apply a suitable sealant to adjusting screw, then install and tighten screw.
3. Measure bearing preload, in both directions, using a suitable torque wrench. **Rotate adjusting screw until preload is 3.0–4.3 inch lbs.**
4. Retain adjusting screw with tool No. 09616-22010, or equivalent, then torque locknut with tool No. 09617-60010, or equivalent, to specifications. Check for proper bearing preload.
5. Install adjusting screw and thrust washer onto sector shaft, then insert sector into gear housing.
6. Place ball nut at center of worm shaft and mesh center teeth.
7. Apply a suitable sealant to new end cover gasket and end cover, then install end cover with new gasket. Loosen adjusting screw as far as possible, then **torque** four cover bolts to 72 ft. lbs.
8. Count total shaft rotation, then turn shaft back half number counted. With worm shaft in this position (Neutral), mark relative position between worm shaft and housing.
9. Rotate adjusting screw, using a suitable torque wrench, until preload is 6.9–9.5 inch lbs.
10. Hold adjusting screw using a suitable screwdriver, then torque locknut to specifications.
11. Align marks on sector shaft with marks on pitman arm, then ensure sector shaft has no backlash within 100° of

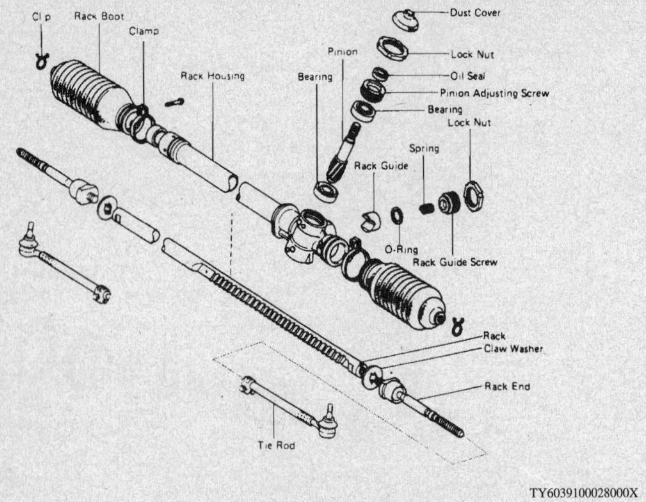

Clip
Rack Boot
Clamp
Rack Housing
Pinion
Bearing
Dust Cover
Lock Nut
Oil Seal
Pinion Adjusting Screw
Bearing
Lock Nut
Spring
Rack Guide
O-Ring
Rack Guide Screw
Rack
Claw Washer
Rack End
Tie Rod
TY6039100028000X

Fig. 3 Rack & pinion manual steering gear assembly. Tercel

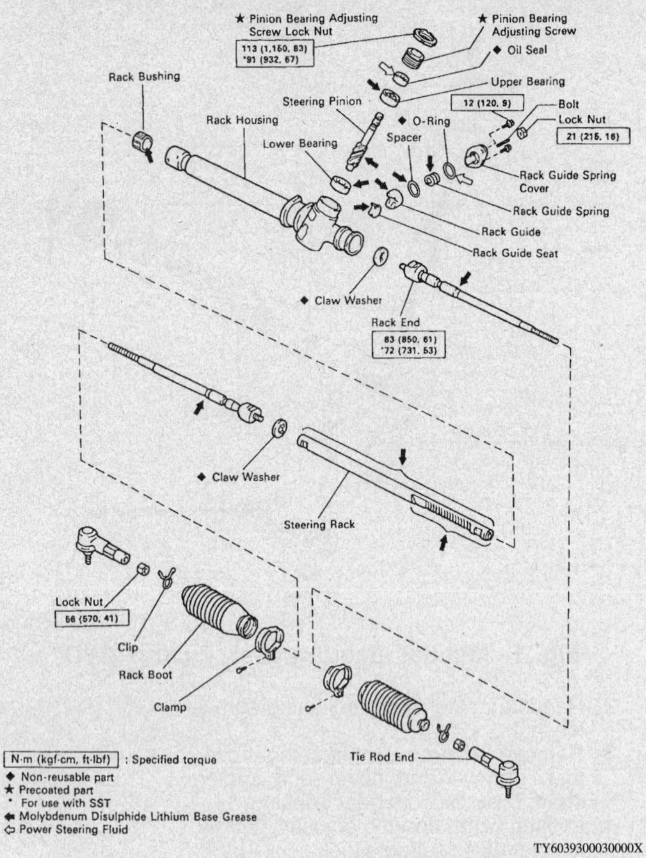

★ Pinion Bearing Adjusting Screw Lock Nut
113 (1,150, 83)
*91 (932, 67)
★ Pinion Bearing Adjusting Screw
◆ Oil Seal
Rack Bushing
Upper Bearing
Steering Pinion
12 (120, 9)
Bolt
Rack Housing
◆ O-Ring
Lock Nut
21 (215, 16)
Spacer
Lower Bearing
Rack Guide Spring Cover
Rack Guide Spring
Rack Guide
Rack Guide Seat
◆ Claw Washer
Rack End
83 (850, 61)
*72 (731, 53)
◆ Claw Washer
Steering Rack
Lock Nut
56 (570, 41)
Clip
Rack Boot
Clamp
Tie Rod End
N·m (kgf·cm, ft·lbf) : Specified torque
◆ Non-reusable part
★ Precoated part
* For use with SST
Molybdenum Disulphide Lithium Base Grease
Power Steering Fluid
TY6039300030000X

Fig. 4 Rack & pinion manual steering gear assembly. Corolla

left and right side of Neutral position.

12. Add 400 cc of gear oil.

RACK & PINION MANUAL STEERING GEAR

TERCEL

Disassemble

1. Place steering assembly in suitable vise, then mark position of tie rod and rack end for reference during assembly. Remove tie rod ends, **Fig. 3.**
2. Remove clip and clamp, then remove rack boot.
3. Remove rack end dust seal, then remove claw washer. Remove rack end using suitable tool and a wrench. Use caution not to scratch outside of rack with wrench.
4. Remove rack guide spring cap locknut, rack guide spring cap and spring.
5. Remove rack guide, dust cover, locknut and pinion bearing adjusting screw.
6. Pull rack from rack housing side and align rack notched portion with pinion. Remove pinion, upper bearing and washer.
7. Remove rack from pinion side, using caution not to rotate rack as it is being removed.

Assemble

1. To replace pinion upper bearing, remove and install using suitable puller and press. Check to ensure spacer is installed before installing bearing.
2. To replace lower bearing, heat rack housing to above 176°F, then tap bearing from shaft. Heat housing again when installing bearing.
3. Measure rack runout using dial indicator. Runout should be no more than .012 inch (.3 mm).
4. Apply suitable grease to pinion lower bearing, and rack bushing. Install rack into rack housing. Position rack notched area so that pinion can be installed.
5. Apply grease to pinion bearing and tooth surfaces, then install pinion and spacer.
6. Install pinion bearing adjusting screw and adjust preload to 3.2 inch lbs. on all vehicles. Loosen adjusting screw until preload is 2–2.9 inch lbs. on all vehicles.
7. Install adjusting screw locknut and tighten to specifications. Check for pinion preload of 2.0–2.9 inch lbs. on 1993 models.
8. Apply grease to rack guide, then install spring and rack guide spring cap. torque spring cap to 43 inch lbs. Check for preload of 5.2–10.4 inch lbs. on 1993 models. Adjust by rotating spring cap.
9. Install locknut and tighten to specifications. Recheck preload as outlined in step 13.
10. Install dust cover and claw washer, aligning claw on washer with rack groove, then torque rack end to specifications. on all models except Tercel, or 43 ft. lbs. on Tercel. Stake claw washer in position.
11. Install rack end seal and dust boot. Check to ensure tube hole is not blocked.
12. Install rack boot clamp with tapered edge toward tube side. Install rack boot clip.
13. Install tie rod end aligning marks made during disassembly.

COROLLA & MR2

1. Clamp steering gear housing in soft jawed vise, **Figs. 4 through 5.**
2. Remove tie rod ends after making alignment marks.
3. Remove clips, clamps and rack boots.
4. Unstake claw washers and remove rack ends using suitable tools. Mark left and right ends and remove claw washers.
5. Using suitable tool, remove locknut and rack guide spring cap.
6. Remove rack guide spring, rack guide with spacer, then dust cover.
7. Using suitable tool, remove locknut and pinion bearing adjusting screw.
8. Pull rack fully from housing side and align pinion with notched portion of rack. Remove pinion and upper bearing as an assembly.
9. Remove rack from pinion side without turning it.
10. Reverse procedure to assemble, noting the following:
    a. If necessary, replace pinion upper bearing using suitable tools.
    b. If necessary, replace lower pinion bearing by heating rack housing to over 176 °F and using a plastic hammer to tap housing and free bearing. Then reheat rack housing to over 176 °F and using a suitable tool, install new lower bearing, noting correct bearing direction.
    c. If necessary, replace rack bushing

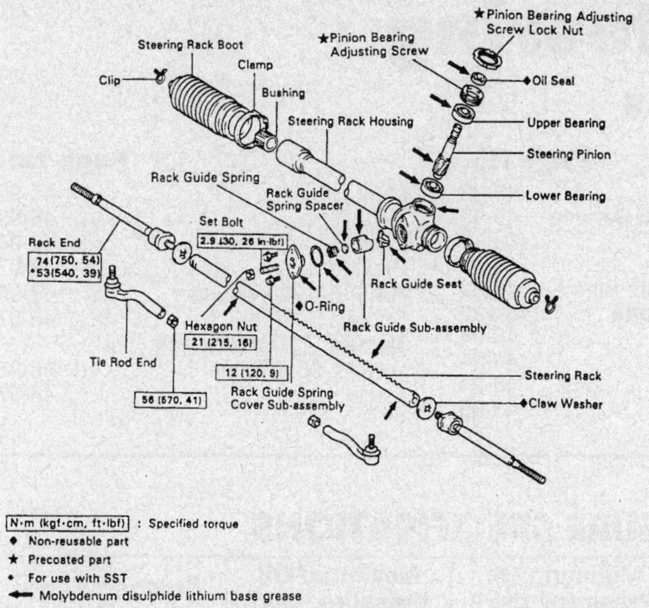

★Pinion Bearing Adjusting Screw Lock Nut
★Pinion Bearing Adjusting Screw
Steering Rack Boot
Clamp
Clip
Bushing
◆Oil Seal
Steering Rack Housing
Upper Bearing
Steering Pinion
Rack Guide Spring
Rack Guide Spring Spacer
Lower Bearing
Set Bolt
2.9 (30, 26 in·lbf)
Rack End
74 (750, 54)
*53 (540, 39)
◆O-Ring
Rack Guide Seat
Hexagon Nut
21 (215, 16)
Rack Guide Sub-assembly
Tie Rod End
12 (120, 9)
Steering Rack
56 (570, 41)
Rack Guide Spring Cover Sub-assembly
◆Claw Washer
N·m (kgf·cm, ft·lbf) : Specified torque
◆ Non-reusable part
★ Precoated part
* For use with SST
Molybdenum disulphide lithium base grease
TY6039100031000X

Fig. 5 Rack & pinion manual steering gear assembly. MR2

using suitable tools. **Ensure tube hole is not blocked with grease. Press new bushing in until edge**

TACOMA

1. Using vise mounted steering gear assembly holder tool No. 09612–00012, or equivalent, and two bolts, secure gear assembly in a vise, or clamp steering gear housing in soft jawed vise, being careful not to damage the gear housing.
2. Remove tie rod ends and lock nuts, after making alignment marks, **Fig. 6.**
3. Remove clips, clamps and rack boots.
4. Unstake claw washers and remove rack ends using suitable tools. Mark left and right ends and remove claw washers.

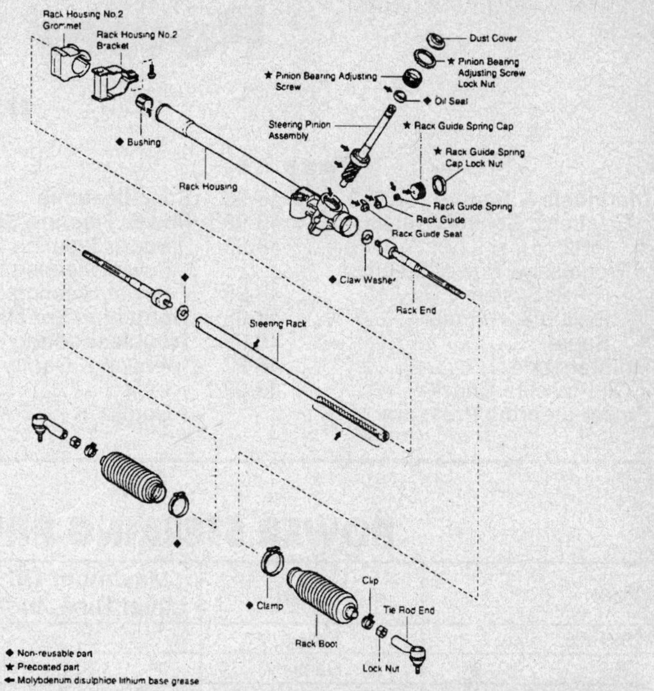

Rack Housing No.2 Grommet
Rack Housing No.2 Bracket
Dust Cover
★ Pinion Bearing Adjusting Screw Lock Nut
★ Pinion Bearing Adjusting Screw
◆ Oil Seal
Steering Pinion Assembly
★ Rack Guide Spring Cap
★ Rack Guide Spring Cap Lock Nut
◆ Bushing
Rack Housing
Rack Guide Spring
Rack Guide
Rack Guide Seat
◆ Claw Washer
Rack End
Steering Rack
Clip
◆ Clamp
Tie Rod End
Rack Boot
Lock Nut
◆ Non-reusable part
★ Precoated part
Molybdenum disulphide lithium base grease
TY6039500032000X

Fig. 6 Rack & pinion manual steering gear assembly. Tacoma

5. Remove rack housing No. 2 bracket and grommet after placing alignment marks on rack and housing.
6. Using suitable tool, remove locknut and rack guide spring cap.
7. Remove rack guide spring, rack guide with spacer, rack guide seat, then dust cover.
8. Using suitable tool, remove locknut and pinion bearing adjusting screw.
9. Pull rack fully from housing side and align pinion with notched portion of rack. Remove pinion and upper bearing as an assembly.
10. Remove rack from pinion side without turning it.
11. Reverse procedure to assemble, noting the following:
    a. If necessary, replace pinion upper bearing using suitable tools.
    b. If necessary, replace lower pinion bearing by heating rack housing to over 176 °F and using a plastic hammer to tap housing and free bearing. Then reheat rack housing to over 176 °F and using a suitable tool, install new lower bearing, noting correct bearing direction.
    c. If necessary, replace rack bushing using suitable tools. **Ensure tube hole is not blocked with grease. Press new bushing in until edge.**

Power Steering

INDEX

	Page No.
Diagnosis & Testing	48-98
Electronic Control System	48-98
MR2	48-98
Progressive Power Steering (PPS) System	48-98
Pickup & 4Runner	48-98
Supra	48-99
Maintenance	48-92
Oil Pressure Check	48-92
Power Steering Pressure Specifications	48-92
Power Steering System Service	48-99
Power Steering Gear	48-112
Power Steering Pump	48-99
Power Steering System Bleed	48-99
Tightening Specifications	48-122
Troubleshooting	48-94
Avalon & Camry	48-94
Celica	48-94
Corolla	48-95
Land Cruiser	48-95
MR2	48-95
Paseo	48-96
Previa	48-97
RAV4 & 1996 4Runner	48-96
Supra	48-97
Tacoma, T100, Pickup & 1993–95 4Runner	48-96
Tercel	48-97

POWER STEERING PRESSURE SPECIFICATIONS

Year	Model	Maximum Oil Level Rise, Inch	Minimum Oil Pressure, psi①	Maximum Oil Pressure, psi①	Steering Effort
1995–96	Avalon	.20	1138	—	52②
1993	Camry	.20	③	—	8.8④
1994–96	Camry	.20	⑦	—	52②
1993	Celica	.20	⑤	—	8.8④
1994–96	Celica	.20	⑧	—	61②
1993	Corolla	.20	853	—	11④
1994–96	Corolla	.20	924	—	11④
1993–95	Land Cruiser	.20	1138	—	8.8④
1996	Land Cruiser	.20	1351	—	73②
1993–95	MR2	.20	711	782	9.9④
1993–95	Paseo/Tercel	.20	853	—	69②
1996	Paseo/Tercel	.20	925	—	69②
1993	Pickup & 4Runner	.20	1067	—	⑥
1994–95	Pickup & 4Runner	.20	⑨	—	8.8④
1996	4Runner	.20	1209	—	43②
1993–96	Previa	.20	1067	—	8.8④
1996	RAV4	.20	1067	—	52②
1993–96	Supra	.20	1140	—	9.0④
1995–96	Tacoma	.20	1209	—	43②
1993–95	T100	.20	1138	—	73②
1996	T100	.20	⑩	—	73②

① — SV models, 924 psi, VZV models, 1067 psi.
② — Inch lbs.
③ — 3VZ-FE, 1351 psi, 5S-FE, 1209 psi.
④ — Ft. lbs.
⑤ — 4A-FE, 996 psi, 5S-FE, 1068 psi, 3S-GTE, 1138 psi.
⑥ — Less Progressive Power Steering (PPS), 8.8 ft. lbs., w/PPS 6.6 ft. lbs.
⑦ — 1MZ-FE, 1138 psi, 5S-FE, 1209 psi.
⑧ — 7A-FE, 996 psi, 5S-FE, 1280 psi.
⑨ — 3VZ-E, 1138 psi, except 3VZ-E, 1067 psi.
⑩ — 2WD models, 1138 psi, 4WD models, 1209 psi.

MAINTENANCE

OIL PRESSURE CHECK

Avalon & Camry

1. **On models with 3VZ-FE engine,** using suitable tool, disconnect power steering pressure joint line.
2. **On models less 3VZ-FE engine,** disconnect pressure tube from power steering pump.
3. **On all models,** connect gauge side of pressure gauge to power steering pump side and valve side to gear housing side.
4. Bleed power steering system as outlined under "Power Steering System Bleed."
5. Start engine, turn steering wheel from lock to lock three or four times, ensuring proper fluid level.
6. Allow fluid temperature to reach at least 176°F.
7. Start engine and allow to idle.
8. Close pressure valve and observe valve reading. **Do not keep valve closed for more then 10 seconds. Do not allow fluid temperature to become too high.**
9. If observed pressure is below specifications, replace power steering pump.

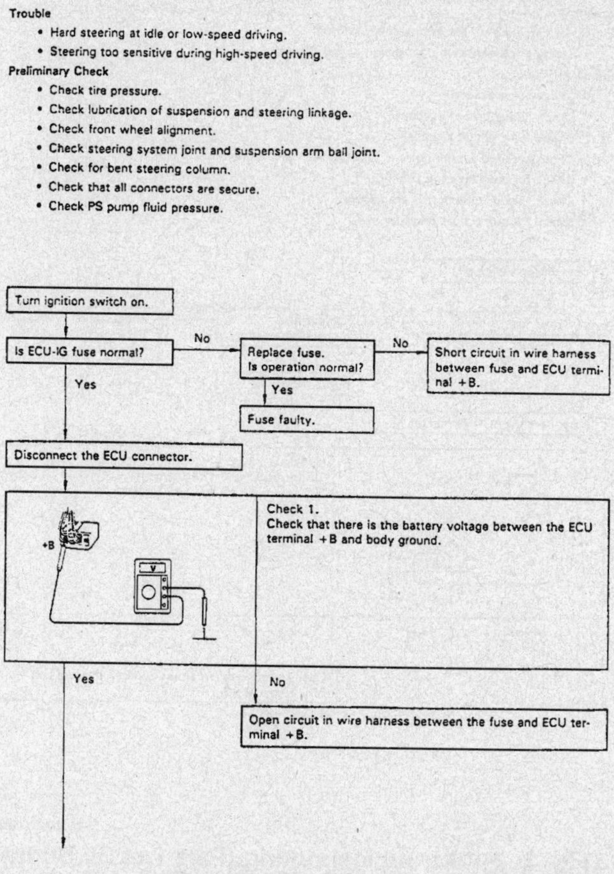
Trouble
• Hard steering at idle or low-speed driving.
• Steering too sensitive during high-speed driving.
Preliminary Check
• Check tire pressure.
• Check lubrication of suspension and steering linkage.
• Check front wheel alignment.
• Check steering system joint and suspension arm ball joint.
• Check for bent steering column.
• Check that all connectors are secure.
• Check PS pump fluid pressure.
Turn ignition switch on.
Is ECU-IG fuse normal?
No
Replace fuse. Is operation normal?
No
Short circuit in wire harness between fuse and ECU terminal +B.
Yes
Yes
Fuse faulty.
Disconnect the ECU connector.
Check 1.
Check that there is the battery voltage between the ECU terminal +B and body ground.
+B
Yes
No
Open circuit in wire harness between the fuse and ECU terminal +B.
TY6029100001010X

Fig. 1 PPS troubleshooting (Part 1 of 3). Pickup & 4Runner

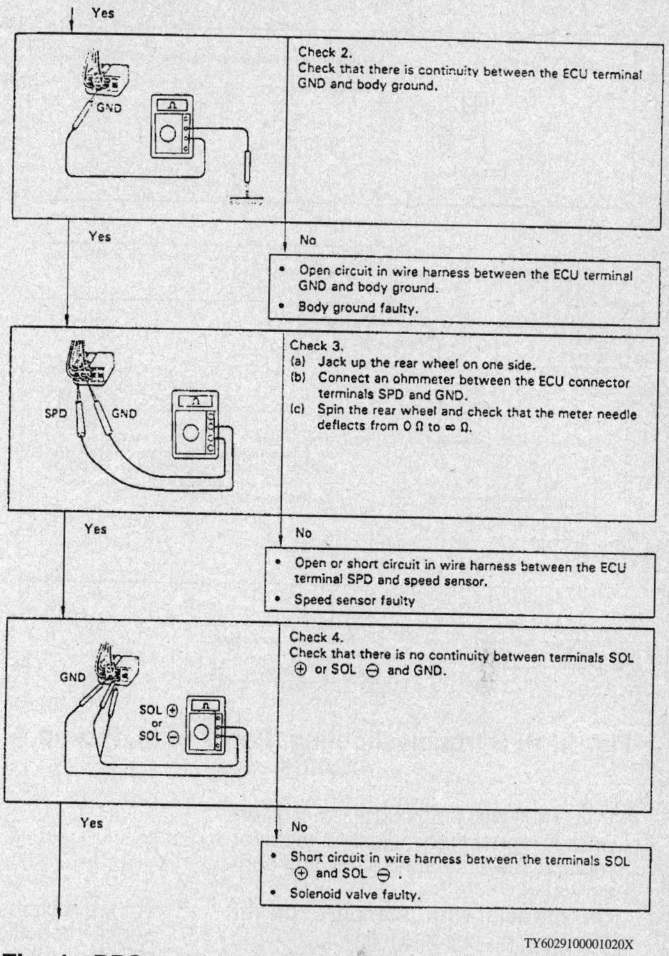
Yes
Check 2.
Check that there is continuity between the ECU terminal GND and body ground.
GND
Yes
No
• Open circuit in wire harness between the ECU terminal GND and body ground.
• Body ground faulty.
Check 3.
(a) Jack up the rear wheel on one side.
(b) Connect an ohmmeter between the ECU connector terminals SPD and GND.
(c) Spin the rear wheel and check that the meter needle deflects from 0 Ω to ∞ Ω.
SPD
GND
Yes
No
• Open or short circuit in wire harness between the ECU terminal SPD and speed sensor.
• Speed sensor faulty
Check 4.
Check that there is no continuity between terminals SOL ⊕ or SOL ⊖ and GND.
GND
SOL ⊕
or
SOL ⊖
Yes
No
• Short circuit in wire harness between the terminals SOL ⊕ and SOL ⊖.
• Solenoid valve faulty.
TY6029100001020X

Fig. 1 PPS troubleshooting (Part 2 of 3). Pickup & 4Runner

10. Open valve fully.
11. Check and record pressure reading at 1000 RPM and 3000 RPM , less then 71 psi difference should be indicated from 1000 RPM to 3000 RPM . If difference is higher than indicated, repair or replace power steering pump flow control valve.
12. Ensure valve is fully open with engine at idle, check pressure with steering wheel at full lock. **Do not maintain full lock position for more than 10 seconds. Do not allow fluid temperature to become too high.**
13. If pressure is below specifications, internal gear housing leak is indicated and must be repaired or replaced.
14. Center steering wheel and allow engine to idle.
15. Using suitable spring scale, measure steering effort in both directions. If steering effort is above specifications, repair power steering unit.

Celica, Corolla, MR2, Paseo, RAV4, Supra & Tercel

1. Disconnect pressure feed tube from power steering pump.
2. Connect gauge side of pressure gauge to power steering pump side and valve side to gear housing side.
3. Bleed power steering system as outlined under “Power Steering System Bleed.”
4. Start engine, turn steering wheel from lock to lock three or four times, ensuring proper fluid level.
5. Allow fluid temperature to reach at least 176°F.
6. Start engine and allow to idle.
7. Close pressure valve and observe valve reading. **Do not keep valve closed for more then 10 seconds. Do not allow fluid temperature to become too high.**
8. If observed pressure is below specifications, replace power steering pump.
9. Open valve fully.
10. Check and record pressure reading at 1000 RPM and 3000 RPM, less then 71 psi difference should be indicated from 1000 RPM to 3000 RPM. If difference is higher than indicated, repair or replace power steering pump flow control valve.
11. Ensure valve is fully open with engine at idle, check pressure with steering wheel at full lock. **Do not maintain full lock position for more than 10 seconds. Do not allow fluid temperature to become too high.**
12. If pressure is below specifications, internal gear housing leak is indicated and must be repaired or replaced.
13. Center steering wheel and allow engine to idle.
14. Using suitable spring scale, measure steering effort in both directions. If steering effort is above specifications, repair power steering unit.

Land Cruiser, Pickup, T100, Tacoma & 4Runner

1. Using suitable tool, disconnect pressure line from power steering pump.
2. Connect gauge side of pressure gauge to power steering pump side and valve side to pressure line side.
3. Bleed power steering system as outlined under “Power Steering System Bleed.”
4. Start engine, turn steering wheel from lock to lock three or four times, ensuring proper fluid level.
5. Allow fluid temperature to reach at least 176°F.
6. Start engine and allow to idle.
7. Close pressure valve and observe valve reading. **Do not keep valve closed for more then 10 seconds. Do not allow fluid temperature to become too high.**
8. If observed pressure is below specifications, replace power steering pump.
9. Open valve fully.
10. Check and record pressure reading at 1000 RPM and 3000 RPM, less then 71 psi difference should be indicated

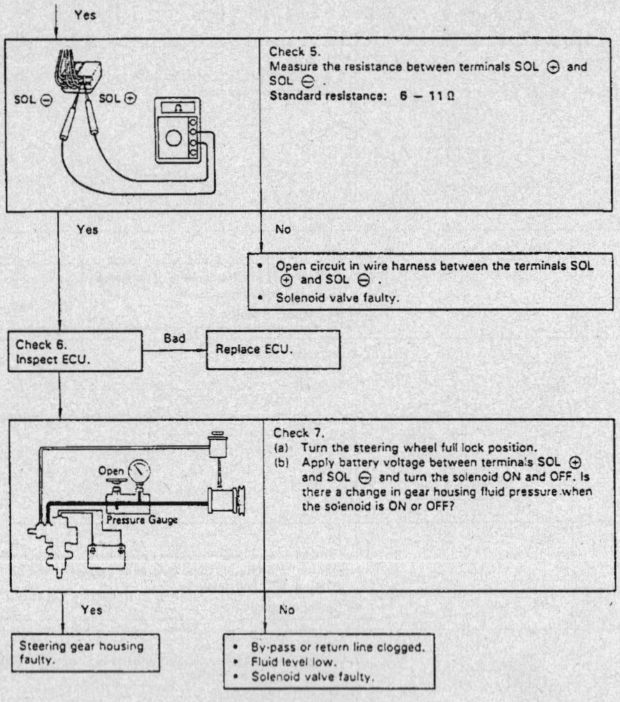
Yes
Check 5.
Measure the resistance between terminals SOL ⊕ and SOL ⊖.
Standard resistance: 6 – 11 Ω
SOL ⊖
SOL ⊕
Yes
No
• Open circuit in wire harness between the terminals SOL ⊕ and SOL ⊖.
• Solenoid valve faulty.
Check 6.
Inspect ECU.
Bad
Replace ECU.
Check 7.
(a) Turn the steering wheel full lock position.
(b) Apply battery voltage between terminals SOL ⊕ and SOL ⊖ and turn the solenoid ON and OFF. Is there a change in gear housing fluid pressure when the solenoid is ON or OFF?
Open
Pressure Gauge
Yes
No
Steering gear housing faulty.
• By-pass or return line clogged.
• Fluid level low.
• Solenoid valve faulty.
TY6029100001030X

Fig. 1 PPS troubleshooting (Part 3 of 3). Pickup & 4Runner

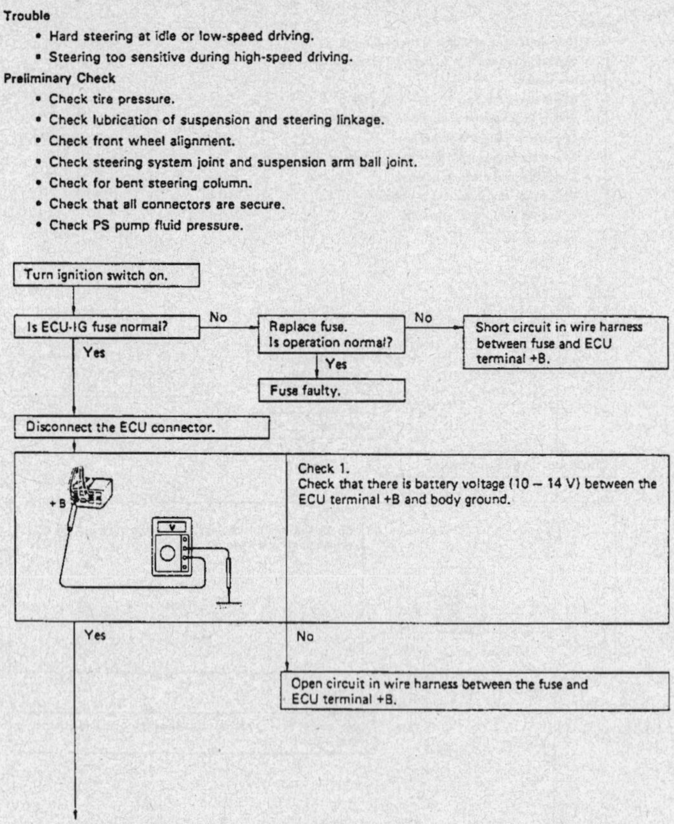
Trouble
• Hard steering at idle or low-speed driving.
• Steering too sensitive during high-speed driving.
Preliminary Check
• Check tire pressure.
• Check lubrication of suspension and steering linkage.
• Check front wheel alignment.
• Check steering system joint and suspension arm ball joint.
• Check for bent steering column.
• Check that all connectors are secure.
• Check PS pump fluid pressure.
Turn ignition switch on.
Is ECU-IG fuse normal?
No
Replace fuse.
Is operation normal?
No
Short circuit in wire harness between fuse and ECU terminal +B.
Yes
Yes
Fuse faulty.
Disconnect the ECU connector.
Check 1.
Check that there is battery voltage (10 – 14 V) between the ECU terminal +B and body ground.
+B
Yes
No
Open circuit in wire harness between the fuse and ECU terminal +B.
TY6029100002010X

Fig. 2 PPS troubleshooting (Part 1 of 3). Supra

from 1000 RPM to 3000 RPM. If difference is higher than indicated, repair or replace power steering pump flow control valve.

11. **On models with standard power steering,** proceed as follows:
    a. Ensure valve is fully open with engine at idle, check pressure with steering wheel at full lock. **Do not maintain full lock position for more than 10 seconds. Do not allow fluid temperature to become too high.**
    b. If pressure is below specifications, internal gear housing leak is indicated and must be repaired or replaced.
12. **On models with Progressive Power Steering (PPS),** proceed as follows:
    a. Turn steering wheel to full lock, disconnect solenoid electrical connector, ensure pressure gauge valve is fully opened and engine is running at 1000 RPM.
    b. If pressure is below specifications, internal gear housing leak or faulty solenoid is indicated.
    c. Apply battery voltage to solenoid. **Do not apply voltage for more than 30 seconds to avoid burning out solenoid.** Inspect oil pressure, maximum pressure should be 569 psi., if pressure is high, inspect solenoid.
    d. Connect solenoid electrical connector, then inspect oil pressure. If pressure is below specifications, PPS system is faulty.
13. **On all models,** center steering wheel and allow engine to idle. Using suitable spring scale, measure steering effort in both directions. If steering effort is above specifications, repair power steering unit.
14. **On models with PPS,** apply battery voltage to solenoid. **Do not apply voltage for more than 30 seconds to avoid burning out solenoid.** Recheck steering effort. Maximum steering effort should be 26 ft. lbs.
15. **On models with PPS,** if steering effort is not heavier then specification, inspect solenoid.

TROUBLESHOOTING

AVALON & CAMRY

Hard Steering

1. Improperly inflated tires.
2. Incorrect front wheel alignment.
3. Worn steering system joints.
4. Worn lower arm ball joints.
5. Steering column binding.
6. Steering gear housing.
7. Improperly adjusted power steering belt.
8. Low reservoir fluid level.

Poor Return

1. Improperly inflated tires.
2. Incorrect wheel alignment.
3. Steering column binding.
4. Steering gear out of adjustment or faulty.

Excessive Play

1. Worn steering system joints.
2. Worn suspension ball joints.
3. Worn sliding yoke.
4. Worn front wheel bearing.
5. Steering gear housing.

Abnormal Noise

1. Low reservoir fluid level.
2. Worn steering system joints.
3. Steering gear housing.

CELICA

Hard Steering

1. Improperly inflated tires.
2. Insufficient front end lubrication.
3. Excessive caster.
4. Worn steering system joints.
5. Worn lower arm ball joints.
6. Steering column binding.
7. Steering gear out of adjustment or faulty.
8. Improperly adjusted power steering belt.
9. Low reservoir fluid level.
10. Faulty power steering unit.

Poor Return

1. Improperly inflated tires.
2. Insufficient front end lubrication.
3. Incorrect wheel alignment.
4. Steering column binding.
5. Steering gear out of adjustment or faulty.

Excessive Play

1. Worn front wheel bearing.

Yes
Check 2.
Check that there is continuity between the ECU terminal GND and body ground.
GND
Yes
No
• Open circuit in wire harness between the ECU terminal GND and body ground.
• Body ground faulty.
Check 3.
(a) Jack up the rear wheel on one side.
(b) Connect an ohmmeter between the ECU connector terminals SPD and GND.
(c) Spin the rear wheel and check that the meter needle deflects from 0 Ω to ∞ Ω.
SPD
GND
Yes
No
• Open or short circuit in wire harness between the ECU terminal SPD and speed sensor.
• Speed sensor faulty
Check 4.
Check that there is no continuity between terminals SOL ⊕ or SOL ⊖ and GND.
GND
SOL⊕
or
SOL⊖
Yes
No
• Short circuit in wire harness between the terminals SOL ⊕ and SOL ⊖.
• Solenoid valve faulty.

TY6029100002020X

Fig. 2 PPS troubleshooting (Part 2 of 3). Supra

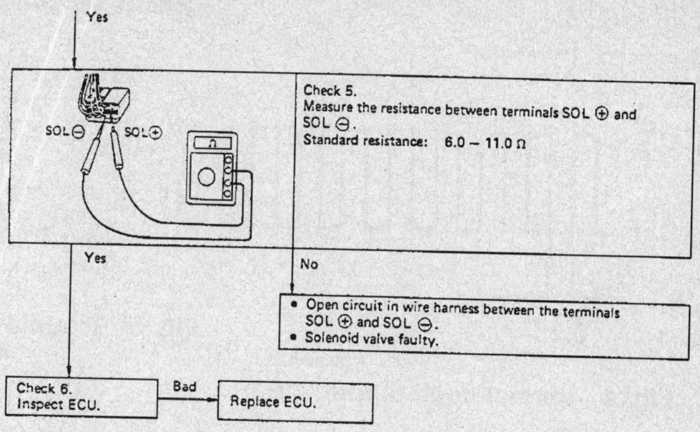
Yes
Check 5.
Measure the resistance between terminals SOL ⊕ and SOL ⊖.
Standard resistance: 6.0 – 11.0 Ω
SOL⊖
SOL⊕
Yes
No
• Open circuit in wire harness between the terminals SOL ⊕ and SOL ⊖.
• Solenoid valve faulty.
Check 6.
Inspect ECU.
Bad
Replace ECU.

TY6029100002030X

Fig. 2 PPS troubleshooting (Part 3 of 3). Supra

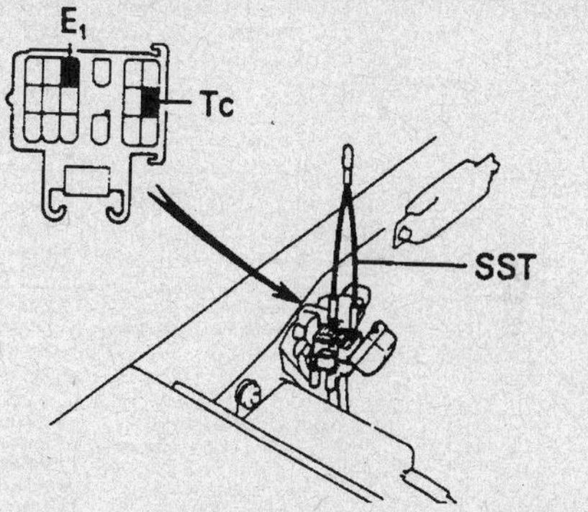
E1
Tc
SST

TY6029100006000X

Fig. 3 Check connector terminal. MR2

2. Worn main shaft yoke or intermediate shaft yoke.
3. Worn lower ball joints.
4. Worn steering system joints.
5. Steering gear out of adjustment or faulty.

Abnormal Noise

1. Loose steering linkage.
2. Worn steering system joints.
3. Steering gear out of adjustment or faulty.

COROLLA

Hard Steering

1. Improperly inflated tires.
2. Insufficient front end lubrication.
3. Excessive caster.
4. Worn steering system joints.
5. Worn lower arm ball joints.
6. Steering column binding.
7. Steering gear out of adjustment or faulty.
8. Improperly adjusted power steering belt.
9. Low reservoir fluid level.
10. Faulty power steering unit.

Poor Return

1. Improperly inflated tires.
2. Insufficient front end lubrication.
3. Incorrect wheel alignment.
4. Steering column binding.
5. Steering gear out of adjustment or faulty.

Excessive Play

1. Worn front wheel bearing.
2. Worn main shaft yoke or intermediate shaft yoke.
3. Worn lower ball joints.
4. Worn steering system joints.
5. Steering gear out of adjustment or faulty.

Abnormal Noise

1. Loose steering linkage.
2. Worn steering system joints.
3. Steering gear out of adjustment or faulty.

LAND CRUISER

Hard Steering

1. Improperly inflated tires.
2. Insufficient front end lubrication.
3. Excessive caster.
4. Worn steering system joints.
5. Worn lower arm ball joints.
6. Steering column binding.
7. Steering gear out of adjustment or faulty.
8. Improperly adjusted power steering belt.
9. Low reservoir fluid level.
10. Faulty power steering unit.

Poor Return

1. Improperly inflated tires.
2. Insufficient front end lubrication.
3. Incorrect wheel alignment.
4. Steering column binding.
5. Steering gear out of adjustment or faulty.

Excessive Play

1. Worn front wheel bearing.
2. Worn main shaft yoke or intermediate shaft yoke.
3. Worn lower ball joints.
4. Worn steering system joints.
5. Steering gear out of adjustment or faulty.

Abnormal Noise

1. Loose steering linkage.
2. Worn steering system joints.
3. Steering gear out of adjustment or faulty.

MR2

Hard Steering

1. Improperly inflated tires.
2. Insufficient front end lubrication.
3. Excessive caster.
4. Worn steering system joints.
5. Worn lower arm ball joints.
6. Steering column binding.
7. Steering gear out of adjustment or faulty.

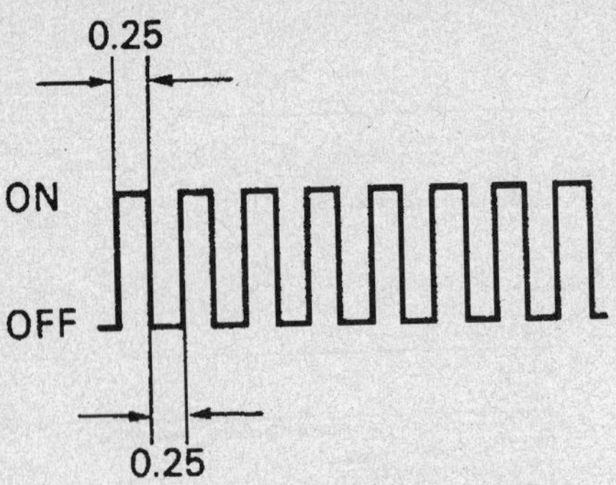
0.25
ON
OFF
0.25

TY6029100007000X

Fig. 4 Normal code output. MR2

Code 11 and 31

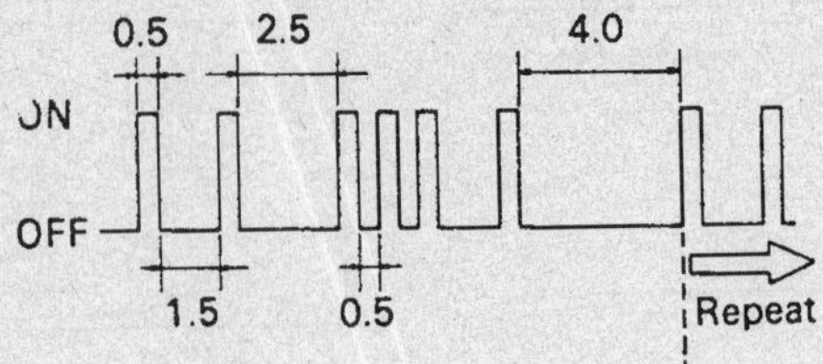
0.5
2.5
4.0
ON
OFF
1.5
0.5
Repeat

TY6029100008000X

Fig. 5 Trouble code output. 1993 MR2

Code 11 and 21

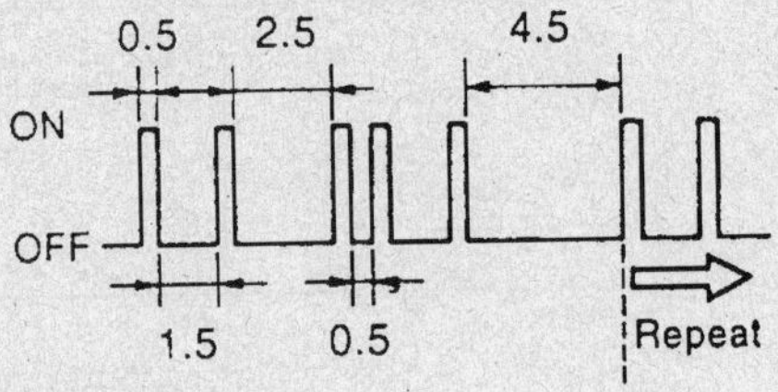
0.5
2.5
4.5
ON
OFF
1.5
0.5
Repeat

TY6029400003000X

Fig. 6 Trouble code output. 1994–95 MR2

Code No.	Blink Pattern	Diagnosis	Trouble Area	Warning Light	PS Operation
11	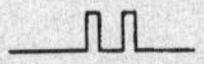	No electric current being supplied to power steering motor	• Wire harness and connector between battery and power steering motor • Wire harness and connector between ECU and power steering motor • Power steering relay • Power steering motor • ECU	ON	Stopped (*1)
12	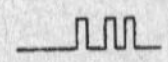	Short-circuit in power steering relay coil circuit	• Wire harness and connector between ECU and power steering relay • Power steering relay • ECU	ON	Stopped (*1)
21	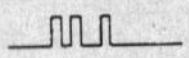	Power steering motor temperature is abnormally high	• Wire harness and connector between ECU and power steering motor • Power steering motor • ECU	OFF	Disconti-nued (*2)
22	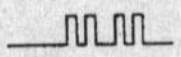	Abnormally high current being supplied to power steering motor	• Wire harness and connector between ECU and power steering driver • Power steering driver • ECU	ON	Stopped (*1)
31	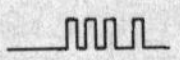	Wearing out of power steering motor brush	• Wire harness and connector between ECU and power steering motor • Power steering motor • ECU	ON	Continues

*1: Until fault is fixed and ignition is turned OFF, then ON.
*2: Returns when temp. of PS pump drops.

TY6029100009000X

Fig. 7 Trouble codes. 1993 MR2

8. Improperly adjusted power steering belt.
9. Low reservoir fluid level.
10. Faulty power steering unit.

Poor Return

1. Improperly inflated tires.
2. Insufficient front end lubrication.
3. Incorrect wheel alignment.
4. Steering column binding.
5. Steering gear out of adjustment or faulty.

Excessive Play

1. Worn front wheel bearing.
2. Worn main shaft yoke or intermediate shaft yoke.
3. Worn lower ball joints.
4. Worn steering system joints.
5. Steering gear out of adjustment or faulty.

Abnormal Noise

1. Loose steering linkage.
2. Worn steering system joints.
3. Steering gear out of adjustment or faulty.

PASEO

Hard Steering

1. Improperly inflated tires.
2. Incorrect front wheel alignment.
3. Worn steering system joints.
4. Worn lower arm ball joints.
5. Steering column binding.
6. Steering gear housing.
7. Improperly adjusted power steering belt.
8. Low reservoir fluid level.

Poor Return

1. Improperly inflated tires.
2. Incorrect wheel alignment.
3. Steering column binding.
4. Steering gear out of adjustment or faulty.

Excessive Play

1. Worn steering system joints.
2. Worn suspension ball joints.
3. Worn sliding yoke.
4. Worn front wheel bearing.
5. Steering gear housing.

Abnormal Noise

1. Low reservoir fluid level.
2. Worn steering system joints.
3. Steering gear housing.

TACOMA, T100, PICKUP & 1993-95 4RUNNER

Hard Steering

1. Improperly inflated tires.
2. Incorrect front wheel alignment.
3. Worn steering system joints.
4. Worn lower arm ball joints.
5. Steering column binding.
6. Steering gear out of adjustment of faulty.
7. Improperly adjusted power steering belt.
8. Low reservoir fluid level.
9. Insufficient front end lubrication.
10. Faulty power steering unit.
11. Faulty solenoid valve.
12. Faulty electronic control.

Poor Return

1. Improperly inflated tires.
2. Incorrect wheel alignment.
3. Steering column binding.
4. Steering gear out of adjustment or faulty.
5. Insufficient front end lubrication.

Excessive Play

1. Worn steering system joints.
2. Worn lower arm ball joints.
3. Worn main shaft yoke or intermediate shaft yoke.
4. Worn front wheel bearing.
5. Steering gear out of adjustment or faulty.

Abnormal Noise

1. Loose steering linkage.
2. Worn steering system joints.
3. Steering gear out of adjustment or faulty.

Progressive Power Steering (PPS) System

Refer to **Fig. 1**, for troubleshooting PPS system.

RAV4 & 1996 4RUNNER

Hard Steering

1. Improperly inflated tires.
2. Low power steering fluid level.
3. Loose drive belt.

DTC No.	Blink Pattern	Diagnosis	Trouble Area ( ): Terminal Name	Warning Light	PS Operation
11		No electric current being supplied to power steering motor	• Wire harness and connector between battery and power steering motor (MB) • Wire harness and connector between ECU (MTH) and power steering motor (MTH) • Power steering relay • Wire harness and connector between ECU (MRLY) and power steering relay (MRLY) and GND • Power steering motor (+) • ECU	ON	Stopped (*1)
12		Short-circuit in power steering relay coil circuit	• Power steering relay coil • Wire harness and connector between ECU (MRLY) and power steering relay (MRLY) • ECU	ON	Stopped (*1)
13		• Open or short circuit between ECU and power steering motor • Wearing out of power steering motor brush	• Wire harness and connector between ECU (MTL) and power steering motor (MTL) • Wire harness and connector between power steering driver (M−) and power steering motor (M−) • Wire harness and connector between power steering driver (PGND) and GND • Power steering motor (−) • Power steering motor brush • ECU • Power steering driver	ON	Stopped (*1)
21		Power steering temperature is abnormally high	• Power steering motor • Power steering oil pressure • Wire harness and connector between ECU (IFB) and power steering driver (IFB) • ECU • Power steering driver	OFF	Discontinued (*2)
22		Abnormally high current being supplied to power steering motor	• Wire harness and connector between ECU (IOUR) and power steering driver (IOUR) • Power steering motor • ECU • Power steering driver	ON	Stopped (*1)

*1: Until fault is fixed and ignition is turned OFF, then ON.
*2: Returns when temp. of PS pump drops.

TY6029400010000X

Fig. 8 Trouble codes. 1994–95 MR2

4. Incorrect front wheel alignment.
5. Worn steering system joints.
6. Worn suspension arm ball joints.
7. Binding steering column.
8. Faulty power steering vane pump.
9. Faulty power steering gear.

Poor Return

1. Improperly inflated tires.
2. Incorrect front wheel alignment.
3. Binding steering column.
4. Faulty power steering gear.

Excessive Play

1. Worn steering system joints.
2. Worn suspension arm ball joints.
3. Worn intermediate shaft or sliding yoke.
4. Faulty power steering gear.
5. Worn front wheel bearing.

Abnormal Noise

1. Low power steering fluid level.
2. Worn steering system joints.
3. Faulty power steering vane pump.
4. Faulty power steering gear.

PREVIA

Hard Steering

1. Improperly inflated tires.
2. Incorrect front wheel alignment.
3. Worn steering system joints.
4. Worn lower arm ball joints.
5. Steering column binding.
6. Steering gear housing.
7. Improperly adjusted power steering belt.
8. Low reservoir fluid level.

Poor Return

1. Improperly inflated tires.
2. Incorrect wheel alignment.
3. Steering column binding.
4. Steering gear out of adjustment or faulty.

Excessive Play

1. Worn steering system joints.
2. Worn suspension ball joints.
3. Worn sliding yoke.
4. Worn front wheel bearing.
5. Steering gear housing.

Abnormal Noise

1. Low reservoir fluid level.
2. Worn steering system joints.
3. Steering gear housing.

SUPRA

Hard Steering

1. Improperly inflated tires.
2. Insufficient front end lubrication.
3. Excessive caster.
4. Worn steering system joints.
5. Worn lower arm ball joints.
6. Steering column binding.
7. Steering gear out of adjustment or faulty.
8. Improperly adjusted power steering belt.
9. Low reservoir fluid level.
10. Faulty power steering unit.

Poor Return

1. Improperly inflated tires.
2. Insufficient front end lubrication.
3. Incorrect wheel alignment.
4. Steering column binding.
5. Steering gear out of adjustment or faulty.

Excessive Play

1. Worn front wheel bearing.
2. Worn main shaft yoke or intermediate shaft yoke.
3. Worn lower ball joints.
4. Worn steering system joints.
5. Steering gear out of adjustment or faulty.

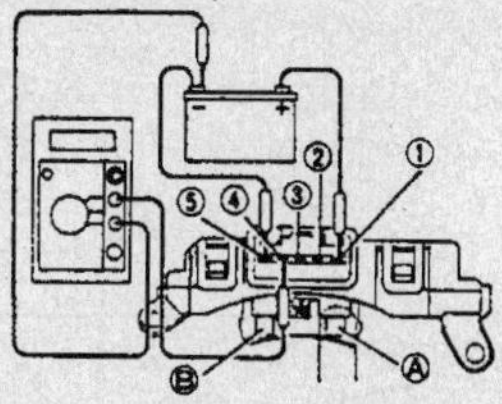

Light Exposure Condition	Terminal ② – Ground	Terminal ④ – Ground
Ⓐ and Ⓑ exposed	Approx. 100 Ω	Approx. 100 Ω
Ⓐ and Ⓑ cut out	∞	∞
Only Ⓐ is cut out	∞	Approx. 100 Ω
Only Ⓑ is cut out	Approx. 100 Ω	∞

TY6029100011000X

Fig. 9 Steering sensor inspection. MR2

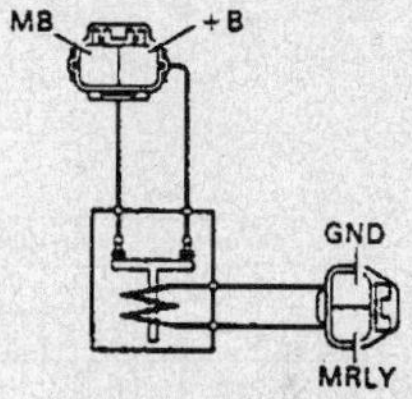
MB
+B
GND
MRLY

MRLY	GND	+B	MB
O——	——O		

TY6029100012000X

Fig. 10 Power steering relay inspection. MR2

Abnormal Noise

1. Loose steering linkage.
2. Worn steering system joints.
3. Steering gear out of adjustment or faulty.

PPS System

Refer to **Fig. 2,** for troubleshooting procedures.

TERCEL

Hard Steering

1. Improperly inflated tires.
2. Incorrect front wheel alignment.
3. Worn steering system joints.
4. Worn lower arm ball joints.
5. Steering column binding.
6. Steering gear housing.
7. Improperly adjusted power steering belt.
8. Low reservoir fluid level.

Poor Return

1. Improperly inflated tires.
2. Incorrect wheel alignment.
3. Steering column binding.
4. Steering gear out of adjustment or faulty.

Excessive Play

1. Worn steering system joints.
2. Worn suspension ball joints.
3. Worn sliding yoke.
4. Worn front wheel bearing.

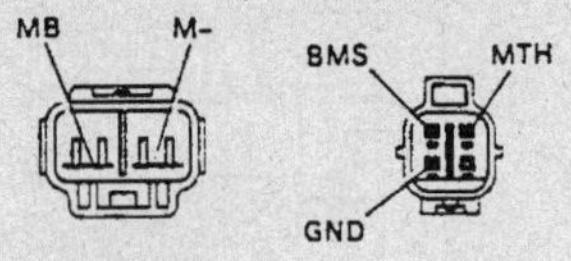
MB
M-
BMS
MTH
GND

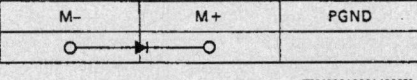

Condition \ Terminal	MB	M–	MTH	BMS	GND
Motor brushes installed	○—	—○—	—○	○—	—○
Motor brushes removed	○—	—○—	—○		

TY6029100013000X

Fig. 11 Power steering motor inspection. MR2

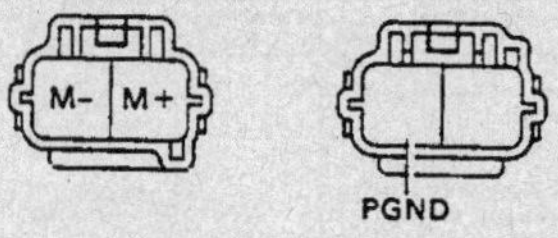
M-
M+
PGND

M–	M+	PGND
○——▶——○		

TY6029100014000X

Fig. 12 Power steering connector inspection. MR2

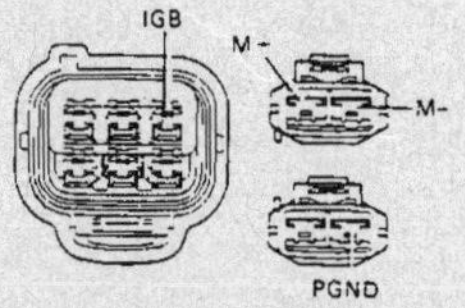
IGB
M-
M-
PGND

Check for	Tester Connection	Condition		Specified Value
Continuity	PGND – Ground	Constant		Continuity
	M– – M–	Constant		Continuity
Voltage	IGB – Ground	Ignition switch	OFF	0 V
			ON	Battery voltage

TY6029100015000X

Fig. 13 Power steering wire harness connector inspection. MR2

5. Steering gear housing.

Abnormal Noise

1. Low reservoir fluid level.
2. Worn steering system joints.
3. Steering gear housing.

DIAGNOSIS & TESTING

Electronic Control System

MR2

Do not open ECU or other computer covers or cases except as required, If IC terminals are touched, the IC may be destroyed by static electricity.

Power Steering Warning Lamp Inspection

1. Turn ignition switch On, ensure lamp comes On.
2. Warning lamp should go Off after about two seconds.
3. If lamp stays On, a malfunction is indicated.

Steering Sensor Inspection

Do not perform the following test when a diagnostic code has been stored.

1. Turn ignition switch On.
2. Using suitable jumper wire, connect check terminals Tc and E [1], **Fig. 3.**
3. Inspect power steering warning lamp condition changes as follows:
   a. When vehicle speed is below 12 mph and steering angle is less then 36°, lamp should blink.
   b. When vehicle speed is below 12 mph and steering angle is more then 36°, lamp should be Off.
   c. When vehicle speed is above 12 mph and steering angle is less then 36°, lamp should be On.
   d. When vehicle speed is above 12 mph and steering angle is more then 36°, lamp should be Off.

Reading Trouble Codes

1. Turn ignition switch On.
2. Using suitable jumper wire, connect check terminals Tc and E [1], **Fig. 3.**
3. Lamp will blink two times per second for a normal code, **Fig. 4.**
4. If a trouble code is indicted, the lamp will blink, the first number will equal the first digit of a two digit trouble code, after a 1.5 second pause the second digit will be flashed, **Figs. 5 and 6.**
5. If two or more codes are present, the will be a 2.5 second pause between codes.
6. Codes will appear from smallest to largest.
7. After all codes have been output, there will be a four second pause and they will be repeated.
8. Refer to **Figs. 7 and 8,** for codes and possible fault areas.

Steering Sensor

1. Connect positive battery voltage to steering sensor terminal 1 and negative to terminal 5, **Fig. 9.**
2. Install suitable ohmmeter as shown.
3. Install thick card at parts A and B and measure resistance between ground and terminals 2 and 4 when light is cut out.

Power Steering Relay

1. Inspect relay continuity as shown in **Fig. 10.**
2. Connect positive battery voltage to terminal MRLY and negative to terminal GND.
3. Ensure continuity between terminals +B and MB.

Power Steering Motor

1. Inspect continuity between motor connector terminals as shown in **Fig. 11.**
2. Connect positive battery voltage to terminal MB and negative to terminal M–, ensure motor turns. **Do not run motor more than is necessary.**

Power Steering Driver

1. Inspect continuity between driver side connector terminals, **Fig. 12.**
2. Disconnect harness side electrical connector and inspect as shown in **Fig. 13.**

Power Steering ECU

1. Ensure continuity between terminals GND and SGND, **Fig. 14.**
2. Disconnect wire harness side electrical connector, then inspect as shown in **Fig. 15.**
3. With wire harness side electrical connector connected, inspect as shown in **Fig. 16.**
4. Measure output voltage (M+) of power steering driver on power steering motor as shown, **Fig. 17. Do not allow tester to contact anything other than terminals, a short between terminals and housing may cause blown fuse or incorrect test readings.**

Progressive Power Steering (PPS) System

PICKUP & 4RUNNER

Solenoid Valve

1. Disconnect solenoid electrical connector.
2. Measure resistance between terminals SOL+ and SOL–, **Fig. 18.**
3. Reconnect electrical connector.

Solenoid Operation

1. Remove solenoid valve from gear housing.
2. Connect positive battery voltage to solenoid terminal SOL+.
3. Connect negative battery voltage to solenoid terminal SOL–.
4. Needle valve should withdraw .79 inch during step 2 and 3, if not as indicated, replace solenoid valve.
5. Install solenoid valve and bleed power steering line.

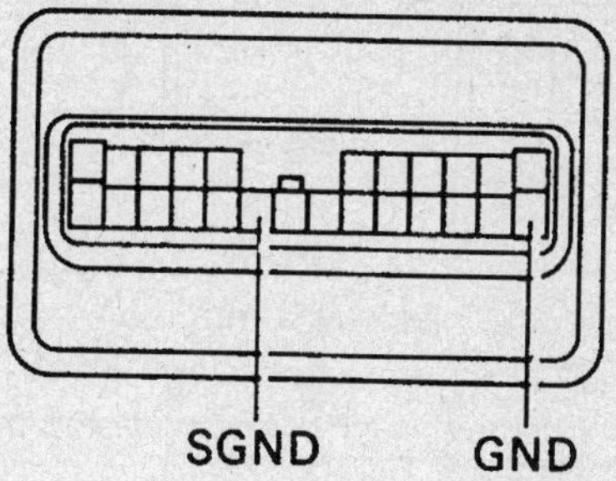
SGND
GND

TY6029100016000X

Fig. 14 ECU connector continuity inspection. MR2

Check for	Tester Connection	Condition		Specified Value
Continuity	GND – Ground	Constant		Continuity
	MRLY – Ground	Constant		Continuity
	BMS – Ground	Power steering motor brushes installed		Continuity
		Power steering motor brushes removed		No continuity
	CHK – Ground	Normal		No continuity
		Connect terminals Tc and E_1 of check connector		Continuity
	SPD – Ground	Ignition switch ON and spin slowly rear wheel		Continuity ↕ No continuity
Voltage	IGB – Ground	Ignition switch	OFF	0 V
			ON	Battery voltage
	WL – Ground	Ignition switch	OFF	0 V
			ON	Battery voltage

TY6029100017000X

Fig. 15 ECU connector inspection w/connector disconnected. MR2

Tester Connection	Condition	Voltage
EFI – Ground	Ignition switch ON and engine stopped	1.5 V or less
	Engine running	4.5 V or more
MRLY – Ground	Engine running	5 V or more
BMS – Ground	Ignition switch ON and power steering motor brushes installed	1.5 V or less
	Ignition switch ON and power steering motor brushes removed	4.5 V or more
SPD – Ground	Ignition switch ON and spin slowly rear wheel	1.5 V or less ↕ 4.5 V or more
SS1 – Ground	Ignition switch ON and turn slowly steering wheel	1.5 V or less ↕ 5 V or more
SS2 – Ground		
CHK – Ground	Connect terminals Tc and E_1 of check connector	1.5 V or less
	Normal	4.5 V or more
ICTR – SGND	Steering wheel operated with engine running and vehicle speed at 0 km/h (0 mph)	2.3 – 4.8 V
	Steering wheel operated with vehicle speed at 65 km/h (40 mph)	1.8 – 2.4 V

TY6029100018000X

Fig. 16 ECU connector inspection w/connector connected. MR2

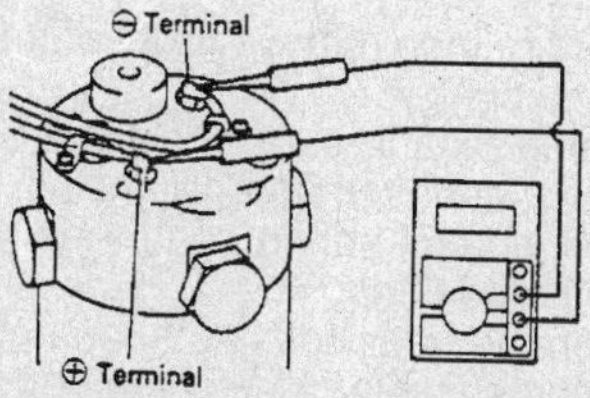
⊖ Terminal
⊕ Terminal

Condition	Voltage
Steering wheel operated with engine running and vehicle speed at 0 km/h (0 mph)	9 – 11 V
Steering wheel operated with vehicle speed at 65 km/h (40 mph)	3 – 5 V

TY6029100019000X

Fig. 17 Power steering motor output voltage inspection. MR2

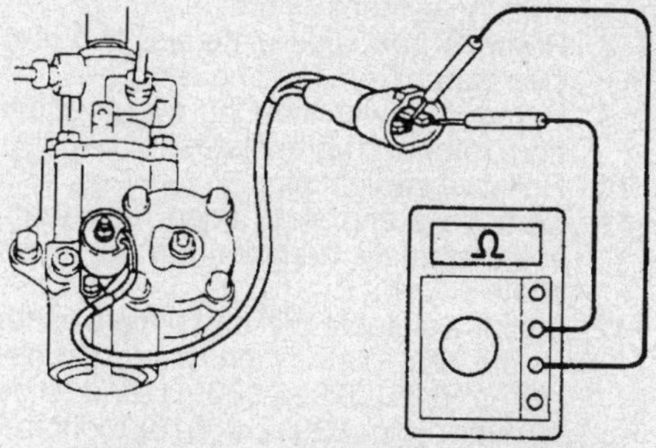
Ω

TY6029100020000X

Fig. 18 Solenoid valve inspection. Pickup & 4Runner

Power Steering ECU

1. Using suitable stands, raise and support vehicle.
2. Remove center console. **Do not disconnect ECU electrical connector.**
3. Start engine.
4. Using suitable voltmeter, measure voltage between terminals GND and SOL– with engine at idle, **Fig. 19,** 0–.05 volts should be indicated.
5. Place transmission in gear and while running at 31 mph, measure voltage between terminals GND and SOL–.
6. Total voltage should be voltage measured in step 4 plus an additional .12–.24 volts.
7. If no voltage is indicated, replace ECU.
8. Install center console and lower vehicle.

SUPRA

Solenoid Valve

1. Disconnect solenoid electrical connector.
2. Measure resistance between terminals SOL+ and SOL–, **Fig. 20,** resistance should be 6.0–11.0 ohms.
3. Reconnect electrical connector.

Solenoid Operation

1. Connect positive battery voltage to solenoid terminal SOL+.
2. Connect negative battery voltage to solenoid terminal SOL–.
3. Solenoid valve should click, if not as indicated, replace pressure control valve with solenoid. **Do not apply voltage for more than 30 seconds to avoid burning out solenoid.**
4. Connect electrical connector.

POWER STEERING SYSTEM SERVICE

POWER STEERING SYSTEM BLEED

1. Ensure fluid in reservoir tank is at proper level.
2. With engine speed below 1000 RPM, turn steering wheel from stop to stop three or four times, keeping at full stop position for two to three seconds.
3. Ensure fluid is not foamy or cloudy.
4. Measure fluid lever with engine running then stop engine and measure fluid level again, **Fig. 21.** Maximum rise of fluid is .20 inch.
5. If a problem is found, proceed as follows:
   a. Disconnect return hose from reservoir tank and drain fluid.
   b. Fill reservoir tank with fresh fluid.
   c. With return hose placed into a suitable container, start engine and run at 1000 RPM. **After 1 or 2 seconds, fluid will begin to discharge from the return hose. Stop engine immediately at this time. Ensure some fluid remains in the reservoir tank.**
   d. Repeat steps b and c four or five times until there is no more air in fluid.
   e. Connect return hose and correct fluid level.

POWER STEERING PUMP

1993 CAMRY w/5S-FE ENGINE

Disassemble

1. Position power steering pump in suitable soft-jawed vise.
2. Using suitable tool, remove pump pulley.
3. Remove end plate, **Fig. 22.**
4. Remove air control valve and union seat.
5. Remove suction port union and O-ring.
6. Remove pressure port union and

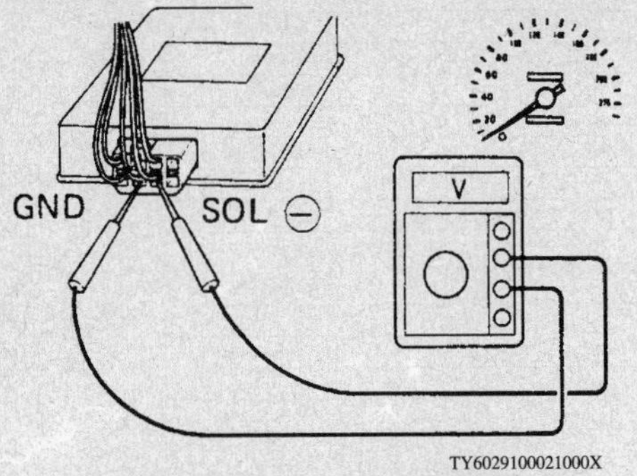
GND
SOL ⊖
V
TY6029100021000X

Fig. 19 ECU connector inspection. Pickup & 4Runner

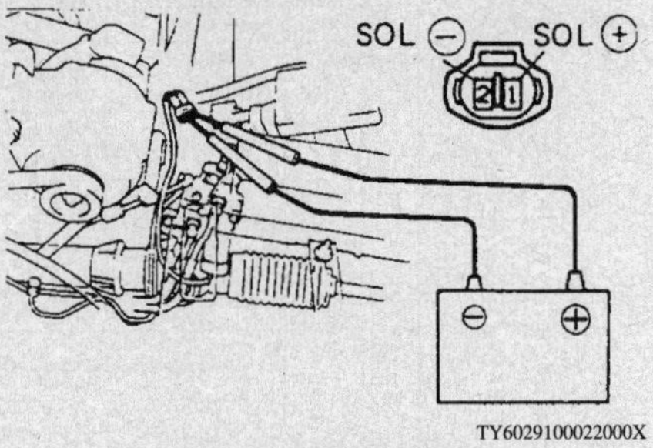
SOL ⊖
SOL ⊕
TY6029100022000X

Fig. 20 Solenoid valve inspection. Supra

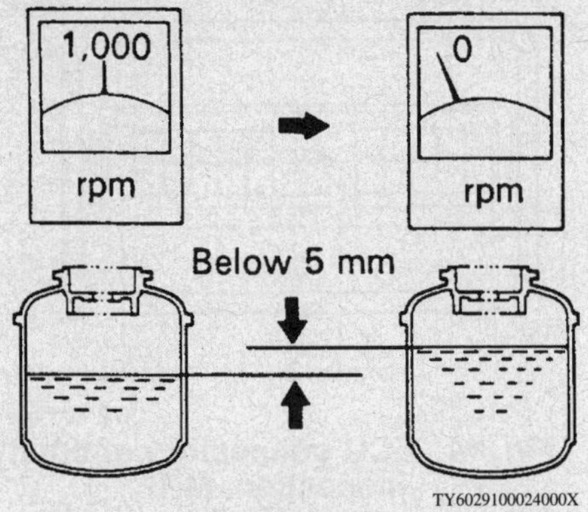
1,000
rpm
0
rpm
Below 5 mm
TY6029100024000X

Fig. 21 Power steering system bleed

O-ring, then remove flow control valve and spring.
7. Using suitable snap ring pliers, remove snap ring, temporarily install bolt to flow control spring seat, then remove seat and O-ring.
8. Remove rear housing snap ring, then using suitable plastic hammer, tap out rear housing, wave washer and O-ring.
9. Using suitable plastic hammer, tap out end shaft, then remove rear side plate and O-ring.
10. Remove pump shaft, cam ring and vane plates.
11. Using suitable screwdriver, remove pump shaft snap ring, remove rotor and front plate from pump shaft.
12. Remove front plate O-rings, then using suitable pin punch and hammer, drive out straight pin.

Inspection & Repair

1. Using suitable micrometer and calipers, measure oil clearance between shaft and bushing, .0028 inch or less should be indicated, if not replace entire power steering pump.
2. Using suitable micrometer, measure height, thickness and length of vane plates. Minimum height should be .315 inch, thickness, .0697 inch and length .5894 inch.
3. Using suitable feeler gauge, measure clearance between rotor groove and vane plate, maximum indicated should be .0012 inch.
4. If measurements are not as indicated in steps 2 and 3, replace vane plate and/or rotor with one having the same mark stamped on cam ring.
5. Coat flow control valve with power steering fluid, ensuring it falls smoothly into valve hole.
6. Close one flow control valve hole, then apply compressed air (57–71 psi) to opposite side, ensuring air does not come out end holes.
7. If inspections are not as indicated in steps 6 and 7, replace flow control valve with one having same letter as on front housing.
8. Using suitable scale, measure flow control spring free length, 1.42–1.49 inch should be indicated, if not replace spring.
9. If required, replace oil seal as follows:
   a. Using suitable screwdriver, pry out oil seal.
   b. Using suitable socket and hammer, drive in new oil seal.

Assemble

1. Coat all sliding surfaces with power steering fluid.
2. Using suitable plastic hammer, drive short straight pin to front plate.
3. Install O-rings to front plate, then install front plate, rotor and snap ring to pump shaft.
4. Coat oil seal lip with MP grease, install long straight pin to front housing, align front plate hole and straight pin, then using suitable plastic hammer, tap in pump shaft. **Do not damage oil seal and O-rings.**
5. Align cam ring holes with straight pins, then install cam ring with inscribed marks facing outward.
6. Install vane plates with round end facing outward.
7. Install side plate O-ring, then align side plate holes with pins and install side plate.
8. Install rear housing wave washer, O-ring, then using suitable plastic hammer, tap in rear housing, install snap ring.
9. Ensure pump shaft rotates smoothly without abnormal noise.
10. Temporarily install pulley nut and check rotating torque, 2.4 inch lbs. or less should be indicated.
11. Install O-ring to flow control spring seat, install spring seat with bolt hole facing outward to housing, then install snap ring.
12. Install spring, flow control valve, O-ring and pressure port union, tighten to specifications.
13. Install suction port O-ring and suction port union to housing, tightening to specifications.
14. Install air control valve.
15. Install woodruff key to power steering pulley shaft, then install pulley and nut, tighten to specifications.
16. Install end plate.

CAMRY w/3VZ-FE ENGINE

Disassemble

1. Mount pump in suitable soft jawed vise, with a suitable puller, remove pump pulley set nut and then pulley.
2. Using tool No. 09617-24030, or equivalent, remove control valve from pump rear housing, **Fig. 23.**
3. Remove three bolts, two suction port unions and union O-rings.
4. Remove pressure port union and union O-ring, then power steering flow control valve and spring. Label valve so that it is not later mistaken for cooling fan system flow control valve.
5. Remove pressure port union and union O-ring, then cooling fan system flow control valve and spring.
6. Using suitable 8 mm wrench remove pump rear housing and discard gasket.
7. Remove cooling fan system cam ring, rotor and vane plates. Do not confuse these parts with those of the power steering system.
8. Remove front side plate and two rear side plates from front housing.
9. Remove power steering system cam ring, rotor and vane plates.
10. Remove straight pins.
11. Remove pump shaft snap ring, then, using a plastic hammer, tap out pump shaft.
12. Install a suitable bolt and plate washer to the rear plate, then, using special clamp (No. 09911-00011) and slide hammer (No. 09912-00010) tools, remove rear side plate from rear housing.

Inspection

1. Using a micrometer and calipers, measure pump shaft and bushing oil clearance. Standard clearance is .0012–.0020 inch. If clearance exceeds maximum of .0028 inch., pump assembly is beyond repair and must be replaced.
2. Using a micrometer, measure power steering system vane plates (minimum height: .339 inch; minimum thickness: .055 inch; minimum length: .5902 inch), then cooling fan system vane plates (minimum height: .319 inch; minimum thickness: .071 inch; minimum length: .5898 inch).
3. Using suitable feeler gauge, measure rotor groove and vane plate clearance. When clearance exceeds .0014 inch maximum, replace vane plate and/or rotor.
4. Inspect power steering and cooling fan system control valves by performing

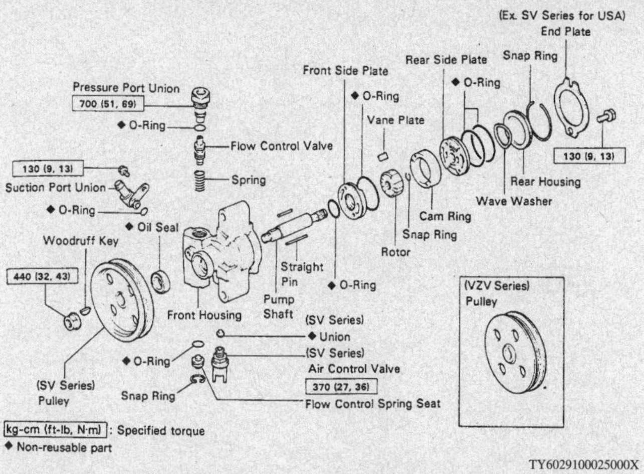
(Ex. SV Series for USA)
End Plate
Rear Side Plate
Snap Ring
Front Side Plate
◆ O-Ring
◆ O-Ring
Pressure Port Union
700 (51, 69)
◆ O-Ring
Vane Plate
Flow Control Valve
130 (9, 13)
130 (9, 13)
Spring
Suction Port Union
Rear Housing
◆ O-Ring
Wave Washer
Cam Ring
◆ Oil Seal
Snap Ring
Woodruff Key
Rotor
440 (32, 43)
Straight Pin
◆ O-Ring
Pump Shaft
Front Housing
(VZV Series) Pulley
(SV Series)
◆ Union
◆ O-Ring
(SV Series)
Air Control Valve
370 (27, 36)
(SV Series) Pulley
Snap Ring
Flow Control Spring Seat
kg-cm (ft-lb, N·m) : Specified torque
◆ Non-reusable part
TY6029100025000X

Fig. 22 Exploded view of power steering pump. 1993 Camry except 3VZ-FE engine & Celica except 4A-FE engine

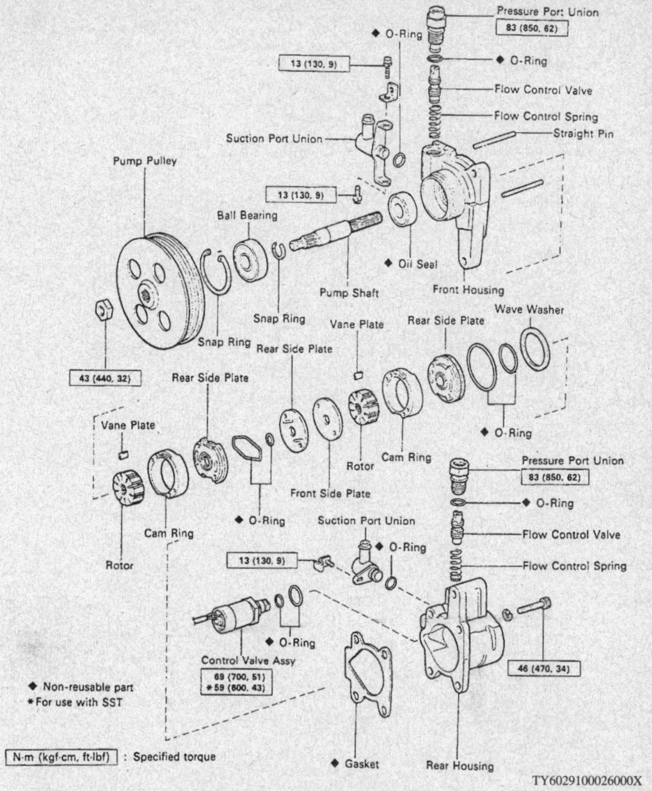
Pressure Port Union
◆ O-Ring
83 (850, 62)
13 (130, 9)
◆ O-Ring
Flow Control Valve
Flow Control Spring
Straight Pin
Suction Port Union
Pump Pulley
13 (130, 9)
Ball Bearing
◆ Oil Seal
Pump Shaft
Front Housing
Snap Ring
Vane Plate
Rear Side Plate
Wave Washer
Snap Ring
Rear Side Plate
43 (440, 32)
Rear Side Plate
Vane Plate
◆ O-Ring
Pressure Port Union
83 (850, 62)
Rotor
Cam Ring
Front Side Plate
◆ O-Ring
◆ O-Ring
Cam Ring
Suction Port Union
◆ O-Ring
Flow Control Valve
13 (130, 9)
Rotor
Flow Control Spring
◆ O-Ring
Control Valve Assy
69 (700, 51)
✱59 (600, 43)
46 (470, 34)
◆ Non-reusable part
✱For use with SST
N·m (kgf·cm, ft·lbf) : Specified torque
◆ Gasket
Rear Housing
TY6029100026000X

Fig. 23 Exploded view of power steering pump. Camry w/3VZ-FE engine

the following tests:

a. Coat flow control valve in power steering fluid, then drop valve into valve bore, valve should fall smoothly to bottom.
b. Check flow control valves for leakage by closing one hole and applying compressed air (57–71 psi) to the other. Ensure vacuum does not escape from the end holes.

5. Using a scale, check flow control valve spring length. Specified length is 1.46–1.54 inch.
6. Using a hammer and seal remover tool No. 09631–10030, or equivalent, drive out pump shaft oil seal.
7. Drive in a new oil seal with suitable hammer and 24 mm socket.
8. Using suitable press, remove ball bearing from pump shaft, then discard shaft snap ring and install a new one.
9. Using suitable press and 17 mm deep socket, install a new ball bearing.

Assemble

1. Coat all sliding surfaces with suitable power steering fluid.
2. Using tool No. 09238-47012, or equivalent, install pump shaft and bearing, then using suitable snap ring pliers, install snap ring.
3. Using suitable plastic hammer, drive straight pins to front plate.
4. Align cam ring holes with long straight pins, then install cam ring with inscribed marks facing outward.
5. Install rotor to shaft with inscribed mark facing outward.
6. Coat vane plates with power steering fluid.
7. Install vane plates with round end facing outward.
8. Install rear side plate O-ring, then align rear side plate holes with pins and install side plate.
9. Install rear housing wave washer, install rear housing and gasket.
10. Ensure pump shaft rotates smoothly without abnormal noise.
11. Temporarily install pulley nut and check rotating torque, 2.4 inch lbs. or less should be indicated.
12. Install spring, flow control valve, O-ring and pressure port union, tighten to specifications.
13. Install suction port union O-rings and union, then tighten union to specifications.
14. Install rear housing O-ring, air control valve O-ring and valve, using suitable tool tighten air control valve to specifications.
15. Install woodruff key to power steering pulley shaft, then install pulley and nut to shaft, using suitable tool, hold pulley and tighten attaching nut to specifications.

AVALON & 1994–96 CAMRY

Disassemble

1. Position power steering pump in suitable soft-jawed vise.
2. Using suitable tool, remove pump pulley.
3. Remove end plate, **Fig. 24**.
4. Remove air control valve and union seat.
5. Remove suction port union and O-ring.
6. Remove pressure port union and O-ring, then remove flow control valve and spring.
7. Using suitable snap ring pliers, remove snap ring, temporarily install bolt to flow control spring seat, then remove seat and O-ring.
8. Remove rear housing snap ring, then using suitable plastic hammer, tap out rear housing, wave washer and O-ring.
9. Using suitable plastic hammer, tap out end shaft, then remove rear side plate and O-ring.
10. Remove pump shaft, cam ring and vane plates.
11. Using suitable screwdriver, remove pump shaft snap ring, remove rotor and front plate from pump shaft.
12. Remove front plate O-rings, then using suitable pin punch and hammer, drive out straight pin.

Inspection & Repair

1. Using suitable micrometer and calipers, measure oil clearance between shaft and bushing, .0028 inch or less should be indicated, if not replace entire power steering pump.
2. Using suitable micrometer, measure height, thickness and length of vane plates. Minimum height should be .315 inch, thickness, .0697 inch and length .5894 inch.
3. Using suitable feeler gauge, measure clearance between rotor groove and vane plate, maximum indicated should be .0012 inch.
4. If measurements are not as indicated in steps 2 and 3, replace vane plate and/or rotor with one having the same mark stamped on cam ring.
5. Coat flow control valve with power steering fluid, ensuring it falls smoothly into valve hole.
6. Close one flow control valve hole, then apply compressed air (57–71 psi) to opposite side, ensuring air does not come out end holes.
7. If inspections are not as indicated in steps 6 and 7, replace flow control

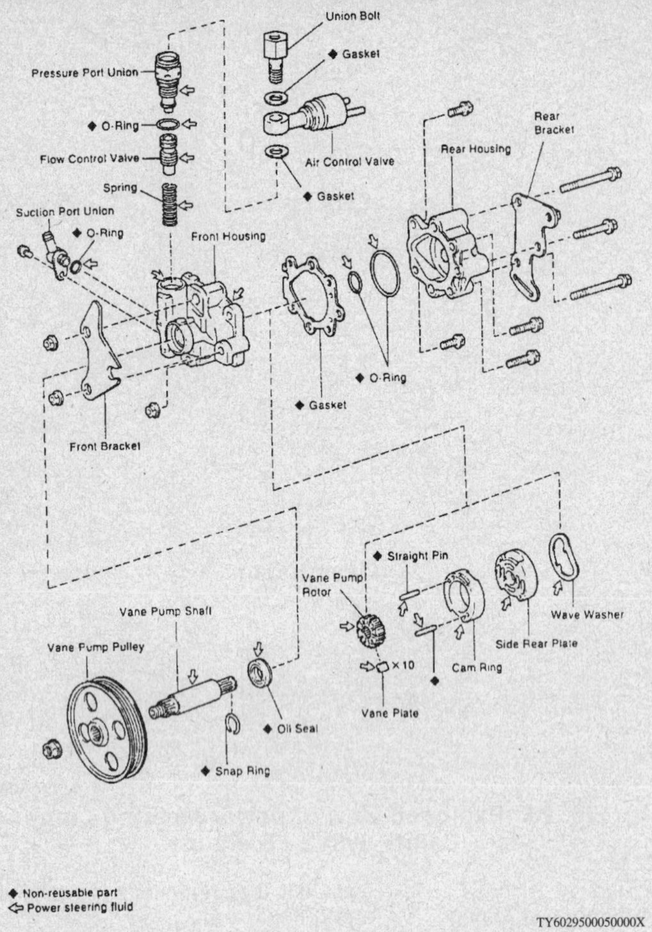

Union Bolt
Gasket
Pressure Port Union
O-Ring
Flow Control Valve
Air Control Valve
Spring
Gasket
Suction Port Union
O-Ring
Front Housing
Rear Bracket
Rear Housing
O-Ring
Gasket
Front Bracket
Straight Pin
Vane Pump Rotor
Vane Pump Shaft
Vane Pump Pulley
Wave Washer
Side Rear Plate
Cam Ring
×10
Vane Plate
Oil Seal
Snap Ring
◆ Non-reusable part
Power steering fluid
TY6029500050000X

Fig. 24 Exploded view of power steering pump. Avalon & 1994–96 Camry w/5S-FE (1MZ-FE Similar)

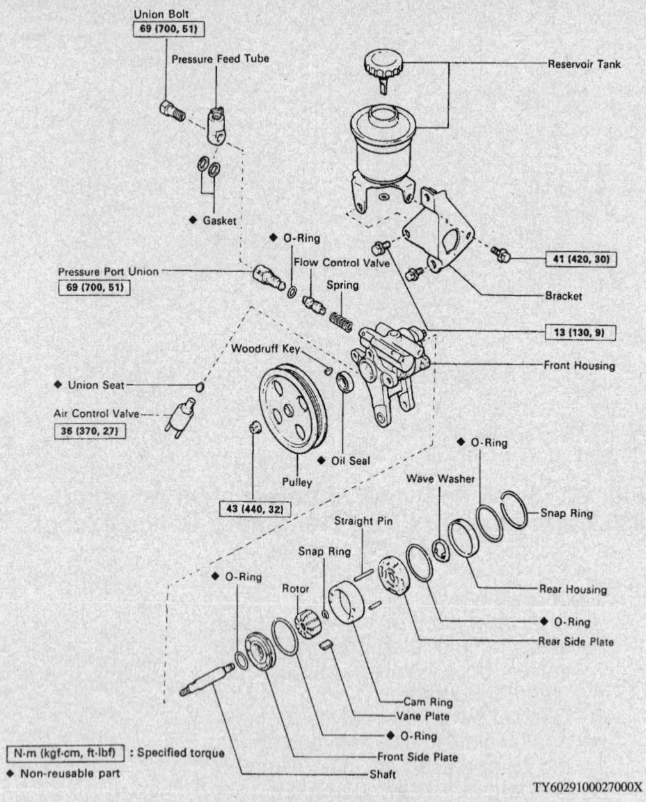

Union Bolt
69 (700, 51)
Pressure Feed Tube
Reservoir Tank
Gasket
O-Ring
Flow Control Valve
41 (420, 30)
Pressure Port Union
69 (700, 51)
Spring
Bracket
13 (130, 9)
Woodruff Key
Front Housing
Union Seat
Air Control Valve
36 (370, 27)
Oil Seal
O-Ring
Pulley
Wave Washer
43 (440, 32)
Snap Ring
Straight Pin
Snap Ring
O-Ring
Rotor
Rear Housing
O-Ring
Rear Side Plate
Cam Ring
Vane Plate
O-Ring
Front Side Plate
Shaft
N·m (kgf-cm, ft-lbf) : Specified torque
◆ Non-reusable part
TY6029100027000X

Fig. 25 Exploded view of power steering pump. Celica w/4A-FE engine

valve with one having same letter as on front housing.

8. Using suitable scale, measure flow control spring free length, 1.42–1.49 inch should be indicated, if not replace spring.
9. If required, replace oil seal as follows:
   a. Using suitable screwdriver, pry out oil seal.
   b. Using suitable socket and hammer, drive in new oil seal.

Assemble

1. Coat all sliding surfaces with power steering fluid.
2. Using suitable plastic hammer, drive short straight pin to front plate.
3. Install O-rings to front plate, then install front plate, rotor and snap ring to pump shaft.
4. Coat oil seal lip with MP grease, install long straight pin to front housing, align front plate hole and straight pin, then using suitable plastic hammer, tap in pump shaft. **Do not damage oil seal and O-rings.**
5. Align cam ring holes with straight pins, then install cam ring with inscribed marks facing outward.
6. Install vane plates with round end facing outward.
7. Install side plate O-ring, then align side plate holes with pins and install side plate.
8. Install rear housing wave washer, O-ring, then using suitable plastic hammer, tap in rear housing, install snap ring.
9. Ensure pump shaft rotates smoothly without abnormal noise.
10. Temporarily install pulley nut and check rotating torque, 2.4 inch lbs. or less should be indicated.
11. Install O-ring to flow control spring seat, install spring seat with bolt hole facing outward to housing, then install snap ring.
12. Install spring, flow control valve, O-ring and pressure port union, tighten to specifications.
13. Install suction port O-ring and suction port union to housing, tightening to specifications.
14. Install air control valve.
15. Install woodruff key to power steering pulley shaft, then install pulley and nut, tighten to specifications.
16. Install end plate.

CELICA LESS 4A-FE ENGINE

Refer to "5S-FE Engine," for power steering pump service.

CELICA w/4A-FE ENGINE

Disassemble

1. Position power steering pump in suitable soft-jawed vise.
2. Using suitable tool, remove pump pulley and woodruff key.
3. Remove reservoir tank, bracket and O-ring.
4. Remove air control valve, **Fig. 25.**
5. Remove pressure feed tube, pressure port union and O-ring, then remove flow control valve and spring.
6. Remove rear housing snap ring, then using suitable plastic hammer, tap out rear housing, wave washer and O-ring.
7. Using suitable plastic hammer, tap out shaft end, then remove rear side plate and O-ring.
8. Remove pump shaft, cam ring and vane plates.
9. Using suitable screwdriver, remove pump shaft snap ring, remove rotor and front plate from pump shaft.
10. Remove front plate O-rings, then using suitable pin punch and hammer, drive out straight pin.

Inspection

1. Using suitable micrometer and calipers, measure oil clearance between shaft and bushing, .0028 inch or less should be indicated, if not replace entire power steering pump.
2. Using suitable micrometer, measure height, thickness and length of vane plates. Minimum height should be .315

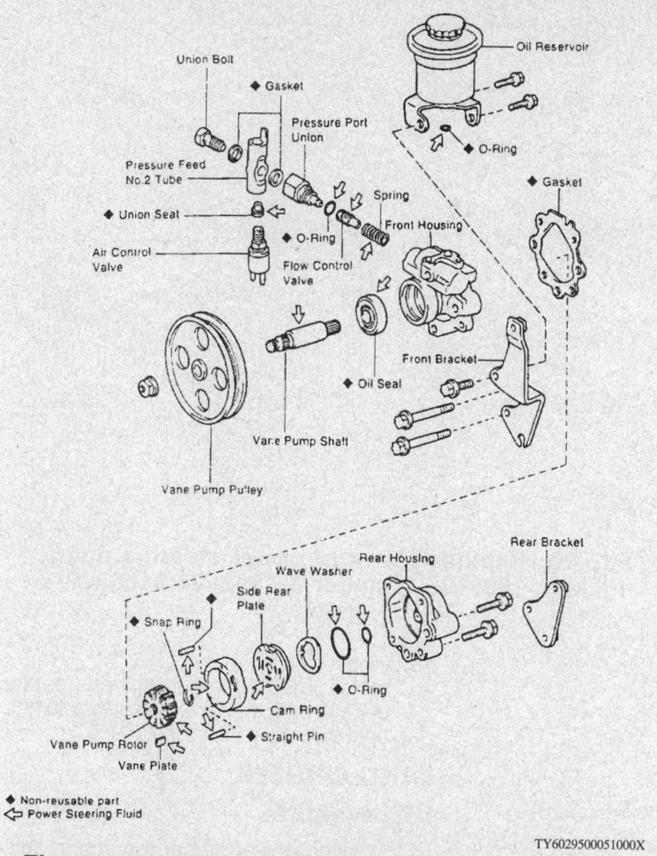
Union Bolt
◆ Gasket
Pressure Port Union
Oil Reservoir
◆ O-Ring
Pressure Feed No.2 Tube
◆ Union Seat
Air Control Valve
◆ O-Ring
Flow Control Valve
Spring
Front Housing
◆ Gasket
Front Bracket
◆ Oil Seal
Vane Pump Shaft
Vane Pump Pulley
Rear Bracket
Rear Housing
Wave Washer
Side Rear Plate
◆ Snap Ring
◆ O-Ring
Cam Ring
◆ Straight Pin
Vane Pump Rotor
Vane Plate
◆ Non-reusable part
⇦ Power Steering Fluid
TY6029500051000X

Fig. 26 Exploded view of power steering pump. Corolla

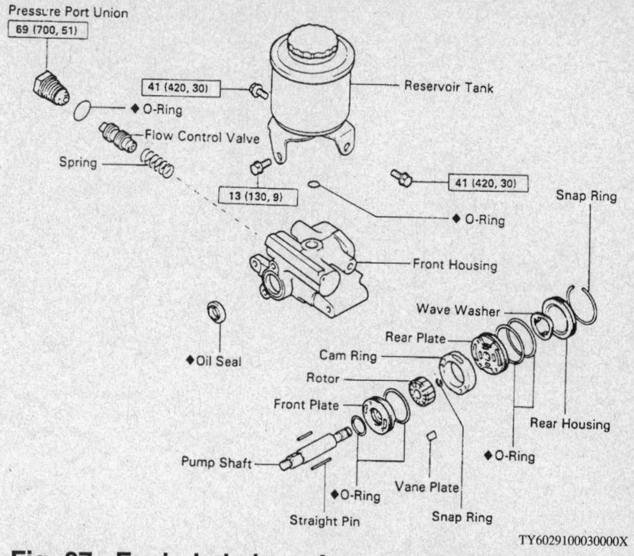
Pressure Port Union
69 (700, 51)
41 (420, 30)
◆ O-Ring
Reservoir Tank
Flow Control Valve
Spring
13 (130, 9)
41 (420, 30)
Snap Ring
◆ O-Ring
Front Housing
Wave Washer
Rear Plate
◆ Oil Seal
Cam Ring
Rotor
Front Plate
Rear Housing
◆ O-Ring
Pump Shaft
Vane Plate
◆ O-Ring
Straight Pin
Snap Ring
TY6029100030000X

Fig. 27 Exploded view of power steering pump. 1993 Land Cruiser

inch, thickness, .0697 inch and length .5894 inch.

3. Using suitable feeler gauge, measure clearance between rotor groove and vane plate, maximum indicated should be .0012 inch.
4. If measurements are not as indicated in steps 2 and 3, replace vane plate and/or rotor with one having the same mark stamped on cam ring.
5. Coat flow control valve with power steering fluid, ensuring it falls smoothly into valve hole.
6. Close one flow control valve hole, then apply compressed air (57–71 psi) to opposite side, ensuring air does not come out end holes.
7. If inspections are not as indicated in steps 6 and 7, replace flow control valve with one having same letter as on front housing.
8. Using suitable scale, measure flow control spring free length, 1.42–1.49 inch should be indicated, if not replace spring.
9. If required, replace oil seal as follows:
   a. Using suitable screwdriver, pry out oil seal.
   b. Using suitable socket and hammer, drive in new oil seal.

Assemble

1. Coat all sliding surfaces with power steering fluid.
2. Using suitable plastic hammer, drive short straight pin to front plate.
3. Install O-rings to front plate, then install front plate, rotor with inscribed mark facing toward rear and snap ring to pump shaft.
4. Coat oil seal lip with MP grease, install long straight pin to front housing, align front plate hole and straight pin, then using suitable plastic hammer, tap in pump shaft. **Do not damage oil seal and O-rings.**
5. Align cam ring holes with long straight pins, then install cam ring with inscribed marks facing outward.
6. Install vane plates with round end facing outward.
7. Install side plate O-ring, then align side plate holes with pins and install side plate.
8. Install rear housing wave washer so washer protrusions fit into slots on rear side of plate, O-ring, then using suitable press, install rear housing, press wave washer hard enough to compress it, then install snap ring.
9. Ensure pump shaft rotates smoothly without abnormal noise.
10. Temporarily install pulley nut and check rotating torque, 2.4 inch lbs. or less should be indicated.
11. Install spring, flow control valve, O-ring and pressure port union, tighten to specifications.
12. Install pressure feed tube, new gaskets and union bolt, tighten to specifications.
13. Install air control valve.
14. Install O-ring to reservoir tank, then install tank and bracket, tighten to specifications.
15. Install woodruff key to power steering pulley shaft, then install pulley and nut to shaft, using suitable tool, hold pulley and tighten attaching nut to specifications.

COROLLA

Disassemble

1. Position power steering pump in suitable soft-jawed vise.
2. Using suitable tool, remove pump pulley.
3. Remove air control valve, **Fig. 26.**
4. Remove reservoir tank, bracket and O-ring.
5. Remove pressure port union and O-ring, then remove flow control valve and spring.
6. Remove rear housing snap ring, then using suitable plastic hammer, tap out rear housing, wave washer and O-ring.
7. Using suitable plastic hammer, tap out shaft end, rear side plate and O-ring.
8. Remove pump shaft, cam ring and vane plates.
9. Using suitable screwdriver, remove pump shaft snap ring, remove rotor and front plate from pump shaft.
10. Remove front plate O-rings, then using suitable pin punch and hammer, drive out straight pin.

Inspection

1. Using suitable micrometer and calipers, measure oil clearance between shaft and bushing, .0028 inch or less should be indicated, if not replace entire power steering pump.
2. Using suitable micrometer, measure height, thickness and length of vane

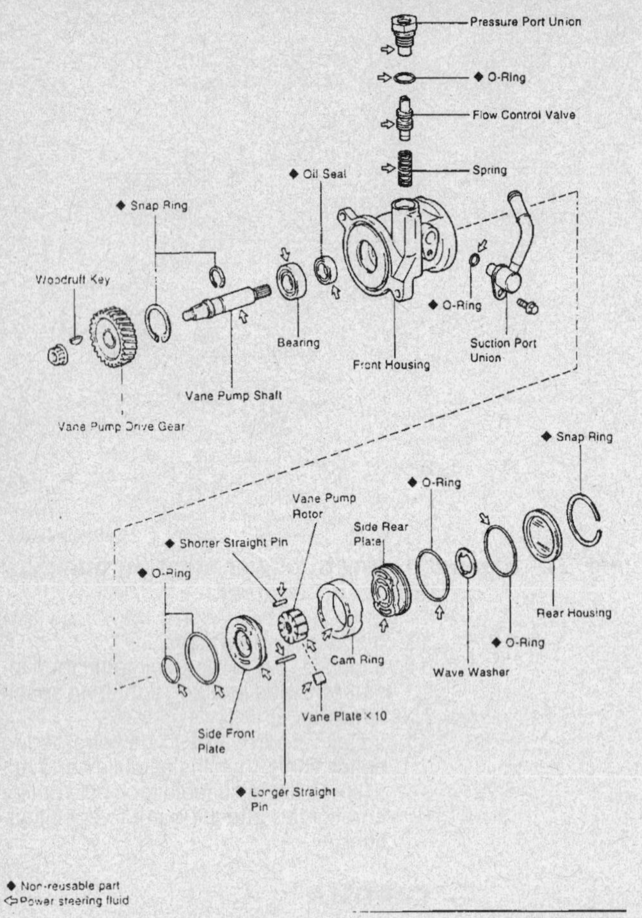
Pressure Port Union
◆ O-Ring
Flow Control Valve
Spring
◆ Oil Seal
◆ Snap Ring
Woodruff Key
◆ O-Ring
Bearing
Suction Port Union
Front Housing
Vane Pump Shaft
Vane Pump Drive Gear
◆ Snap Ring
◆ O-Ring
Vane Pump Rotor
Side Rear Plate
◆ Shorter Straight Pin
◆ O-Ring
Rear Housing
◆ O-Ring
Cam Ring
Wave Washer
Vane Plate × 10
Side Front Plate
◆ Longer Straight Pin
◆ Non-reusable part
⇦ Power steering fluid
TY6029500052000X

Fig. 28 Exploded view of power steering pump. 1994–96 Land Cruiser

plates. Minimum height should be .339 inch, thickness, .055 inch and length .5902 inch.
3. Using suitable feeler gauge, measure clearance between rotor groove and vane plate, maximum indicated should be .014 inch.
4. If measurements are not as indicated in steps 2 and 3, replace vane plate and/ or rotor with one having the same mark stamped on cam ring.
5. Coat flow control valve with power steering fluid, ensuring it falls smoothly into valve hole.
6. Close one flow control valve hole, then apply compressed air (57–71 psi) to opposite side, ensuring air does not come out end holes.
7. If inspections are not as indicated in steps 6 and 7, replace flow control valve with one having same letter as on front housing.
8. Using suitable scale, measure flow control spring free length. Length should be 1.28–1.34 inches.
9. If required, replace oil seal as follows:
   a. Using suitable screwdriver, pry out oil seal.
   b. Using suitable socket and hammer, drive in new oil seal.

Assemble

1. Coat all sliding surfaces with power steering fluid.
2. Using suitable plastic hammer, drive short straight pin to front plate.
3. Install O-rings to front plate, then install front plate, rotor and snap ring to pump shaft.
4. Coat oil seal lip with MP grease, install long straight pin to front housing, align front plate hole and straight pin, then using suitable plastic hammer, tap in pump shaft. **Do not damage oil seal and O-rings.**
5. Align cam ring holes with straight pins, then install cam ring with inscribed marks facing outward.
6. Install vane plates with round end facing outward.
7. Install side plate O-ring, then align side plate holes with pins and install side plate.
8. Install rear housing wave washer, O-ring, then using suitable plastic hammer, tap in rear housing, install snap ring.
9. Ensure pump shaft rotates smoothly without abnormal noise.
10. Temporarily install pulley nut and check rotating torque, 2.2 or less should be indicated.
11. Install spring, flow control valve, O-ring and pressure port union, tighten to specifications.
12. Install reservoir tank O-ring, tank and bracket, tighten to specifications.

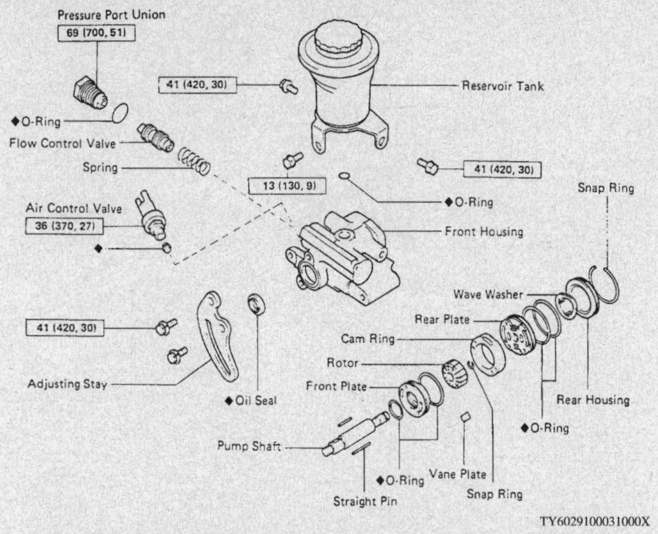
Pressure Port Union
69 (700, 51)
41 (420, 30)
Reservoir Tank
◆O-Ring
Flow Control Valve
Spring
41 (420, 30)
Snap Ring
13 (130, 9)
◆O-Ring
Air Control Valve
36 (370, 27)
Front Housing
Wave Washer
Rear Plate
41 (420, 30)
Cam Ring
Rotor
Front Plate
Rear Housing
Adjusting Stay
◆Oil Seal
◆O-Ring
Pump Shaft
◆O-Ring
Vane Plate
Snap Ring
Straight Pin
TY6029100031000X

Fig. 29 Exploded view of power steering pump. Pickup, 1993–95 4Runner & 1993–94 T100 w/VZ series

13. Install air control valve.
14. Install woodruff key to power steering pulley shaft, then install pulley and nut, tighten to specifications.

LAND CRUISER

Disassemble

1. Position power steering pump in suitable soft-jawed vise.
2. Remove reservoir tank and O-ring.
3. Remove pressure port union and O-ring, then remove flow control valve and spring **Figs. 27 and 28.**
4. Remove rear housing snap ring, then using suitable plastic hammer, tap out rear housing, wave washer and O-ring.
5. Using suitable plastic hammer, tap shaft end, rear side plate and O-ring.
6. Using suitable snap ring pliers, remove snap ring, temporarily install bolt to flow control spring seat, then remove seat and O-ring.
7. Remove pump shaft, cam ring and vane plates.
8. Using suitable screwdriver, remove pump shaft snap ring, remove rotor and front plate from pump shaft.
9. Remove front plate O-rings, then remove straight pin.

Inspection

1. Using suitable micrometer and calipers, measure oil clearance between shaft and bushing, .0028 inch or less should be indicated, if not replace entire power steering pump.
2. Using suitable micrometer, measure height, thickness and length of vane plates. Minimum height should be .319 inch, thickness, .0707 inch and length .5901 inch.
3. Using suitable feeler gauge, measure clearance between rotor groove and vane plate, maximum indicated should be .0011 inch.
4. If measurements are not as indicated in steps 2 and 3, replace vane plate and/ or rotor with one having the same

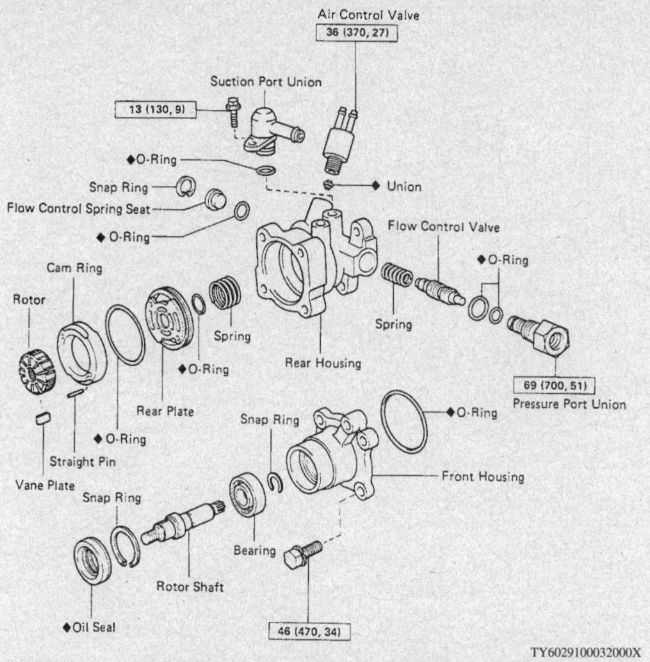
Air Control Valve
36 (370, 27)
Suction Port Union
13 (130, 9)
◆O-Ring
Snap Ring
Union
Flow Control Spring Seat
◆O-Ring
Flow Control Valve
◆O-Ring
Cam Ring
Rotor
Spring
Spring
◆O-Ring
Rear Housing
69 (700, 51)
Pressure Port Union
Rear Plate
◆O-Ring
Snap Ring
◆O-Ring
Straight Pin
Vane Plate
Front Housing
Snap Ring
Bearing
Rotor Shaft
◆Oil Seal
46 (470, 34)
TY6029100032000X

Fig. 30 Exploded view of power steering pump. Pickup, 1993–95 4Runner & 1993–94 T100 (RZ Series)

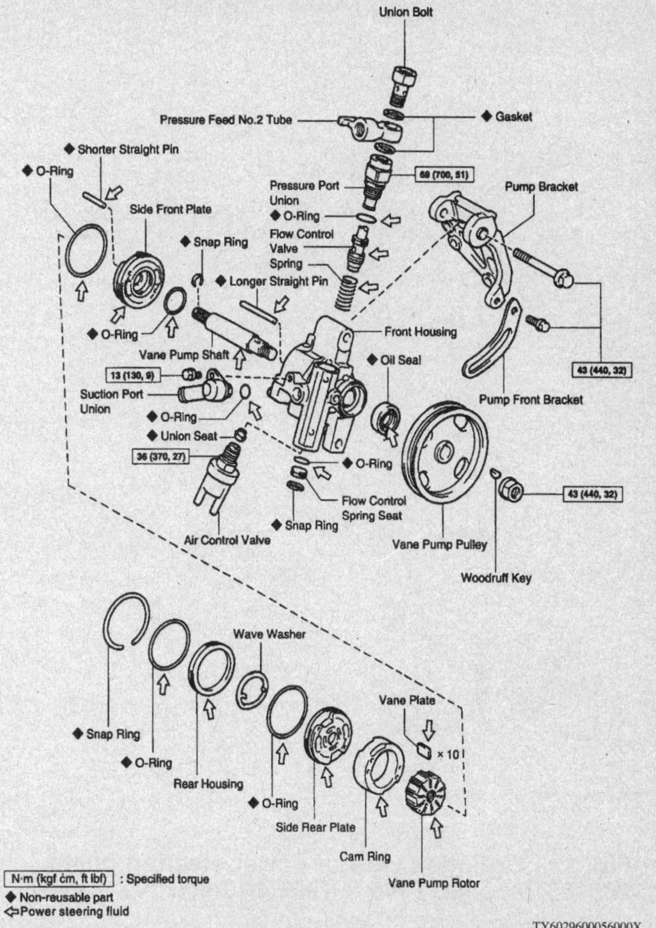
Union Bolt
Pressure Feed No.2 Tube
◆ Gasket
◆ Shorter Straight Pin
◆ O-Ring
69 (700, 51)
Pressure Port Union
Pump Bracket
Side Front Plate
◆ O-Ring
◆ Snap Ring
Flow Control Valve
Spring
◆ Longer Straight Pin
◆ O-Ring
Front Housing
Vane Pump Shaft
◆ Oil Seal
13 (130, 9)
43 (440, 32)
Suction Port Union
Pump Front Bracket
◆ O-Ring
◆ Union Seat
36 (370, 27)
◆ O-Ring
43 (440, 32)
Flow Control Spring Seat
◆ Snap Ring
Air Control Valve
Vane Pump Pulley
Woodruff Key
Wave Washer
Vane Plate
× 10
◆ Snap Ring
◆ O-Ring
Rear Housing
◆ O-Ring
Side Rear Plate
Cam Ring
Vane Pump Rotor
N·m (kgf·cm, ft·lbf) : Specified torque
◆ Non-reusable part
⇦Power steering fluid
TY6029600056000X

Fig. 31 Exploded view of power steering pump. RAV4

mark stamped on cam ring.

5. Coat flow control valve with power steering fluid, ensuring it falls smoothly into valve hole.
6. Close one flow control valve hole, then apply compressed air (57–71 psi) to opposite side, ensuring air does not come out end holes.
7. If inspections are not as indicated in steps 6 and 7, replace flow control valve with one having same letter as on front housing.
8. Using suitable scale, measure flow control spring free length, 1.38–1.46 inch should be indicated, if not replace spring.
9. If required, replace oil seal as follows:
   a. Using suitable screwdriver, pry out oil seal.
   b. Using suitable socket and hammer, drive in new oil seal.

Assemble

1. Coat all sliding surfaces with power steering fluid.
2. Using suitable plastic hammer, drive short straight pin to front plate.
3. Install O-rings to front plate, install front plate to pump shaft, then rotor to pump shaft with inscribed mark facing outward, then install snap ring.
4. Coat oil seal lip with MP grease, install long straight pin to front housing, align front plate hole and straight pin, then using suitable plastic hammer, tap in pump shaft. **Do not damage oil seal and O-rings.**
5. Align cam ring holes with straight pins, then install cam ring with inscribed marks facing outward.
6. Install vane plates with round end facing outward.
7. Install side plate O-ring, then align rear plate holes with pins and install rear plate.
8. Install rear housing wave washer, O-ring, then using suitable plastic hammer, tap in rear housing, install snap ring.
9. Ensure pump shaft rotates smoothly without abnormal noise.
10. Temporarily install pulley nut and check rotating torque, 2.4 inch lbs. or less should be indicated.
11. Install O-ring to flow control spring seat, install spring seat with bolt hole facing outward to housing, then install snap ring.
12. Install spring, flow control valve, O-ring and pressure port union, tighten to specifications.
13. Install reservoir tank and O-ring.
14. Install suction port O-ring and suction port union to housing, tightening to specifications.

PASEO

Refer to "Tercel Power Steering Pump," for power steering pump service. On Paseo models, vane plate height should be .319 inch, thickness should be .0708 inch and length should be .5901 inch.

PICKUP, 1993–95 4RUNNER & 1993–94 T100 (VZ SERIES)

Disassemble

1. Position power steering pump in suitable soft-jawed vise.
2. Remove air control valve, then remove reservoir tank and O-ring.
3. Remove pressure port union and O-ring, then remove flow control valve and spring **Fig. 29.**
4. Remove rear housing snap ring, then using suitable plastic hammer, tap out rear housing, wave washer and O-ring.
5. Using suitable plastic hammer, tap shaft end, rear side plate and O-ring.
6. Remove pump shaft, cam ring and vane plates.
7. Using suitable screwdriver, remove pump shaft snap ring, remove rotor and front plate from pump shaft.
8. Remove front plate O-rings, then remove straight pin.
9. Remove adjusting stay.

Inspection

1. Using suitable micrometer and calipers, measure oil clearance between shaft and bushing, .0028 inch or less

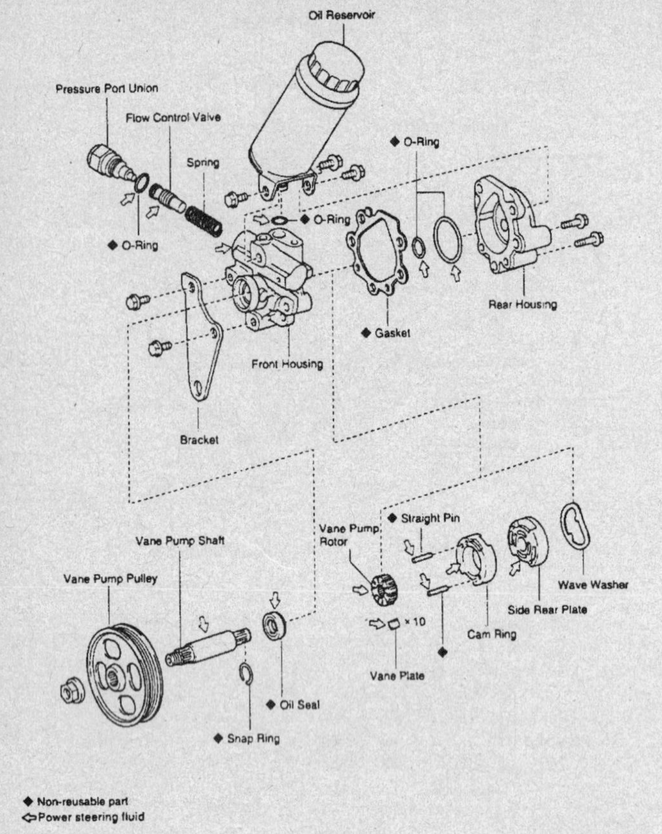
Oil Reservoir
Pressure Port Union
Flow Control Valve
Spring
◆ O-Ring
◆ O-Ring
◆ O-Ring
Rear Housing
◆ Gasket
Front Housing
Bracket
Vane Pump Shaft
Vane Pump Pulley
Vane Pump Rotor
◆ Straight Pin
Wave Washer
Side Rear Plate
Cam Ring
× 10
Vane Plate
◆ Oil Seal
◆ Snap Ring
◆ Non-reusable part
⇦ Power steering fluid
TY6029500054000X

Fig. 32 Exploded view of power steering pump. 1995–96 Tacoma, T100 & 1996 4Runner (VZ series)

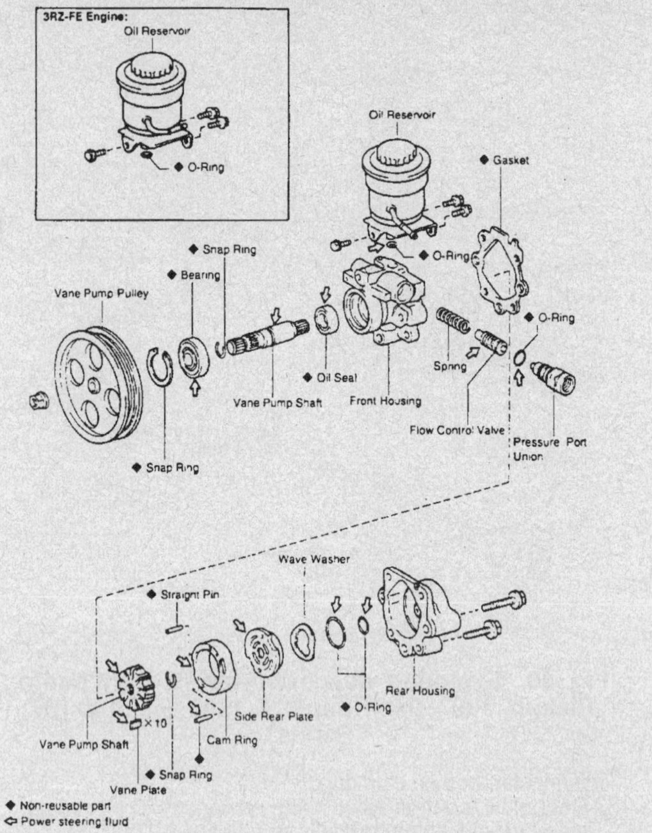
3RZ-FE Engine:
Oil Reservoir
◆ O-Ring
Oil Reservoir
◆ Gasket
◆ Snap Ring
◆ Bearing
◆ O-Ring
Vane Pump Pulley
◆ O-Ring
Spring
◆ Oil Seal
Vane Pump Shaft
Front Housing
Flow Control Valve
Pressure Port Union
◆ Snap Ring
Wave Washer
◆ Straight Pin
Rear Housing
◆ O-Ring
Side Rear Plate
× 10
Cam Ring
Vane Pump Shaft
◆ Snap Ring
Vane Plate
◆ Non-reusable part
⇦ Power steering fluid
TY6029500053000X

Fig. 33 Exploded view of power steering pump. 1995–96 Tacoma, T100 w/RZ series & 1996 4Runner w/3RZ-FE Engine

should be indicated, if not replace entire power steering pump.

2. Using suitable micrometer, measure height, thickness and length of vane plates. Minimum height should be .319 inch, thickness, .0707 inch and length .5901 inch.
3. Using suitable feeler gauge, measure clearance between rotor groove and vane plate, maximum indicated should be .0012 inch.
4. If measurements are not as indicated in steps 2 and 3, replace vane plate and/ or rotor with one having the same mark stamped on cam ring.
5. Coat flow control valve with power steering fluid, ensuring it falls smoothly into valve hole.
6. Close one flow control valve hole, then apply compressed air (57–71 psi) to opposite side, ensuring air does not come out end holes.
7. If inspections are not as indicated in steps 6 and 7, replace flow control valve with one having same letter as on front housing.
8. Using suitable scale, measure flow control spring free length, 1.38–1.46 inch should be indicated, if not replace spring.
9. If required, replace oil seal as follows:
   a. Using suitable screwdriver, pry out oil seal.
   b. Using suitable socket and hammer, drive in new oil seal.

Assemble

1. Coat all sliding surfaces with power steering fluid, then install adjusting stay.
2. Using suitable plastic hammer, drive short straight pin to front plate.
3. Install O-rings to front plate, install front plate to pump shaft, then rotor to pump shaft with inscribed mark facing outward, then install snap ring.
4. Coat oil seal lip with MP grease, install long straight pin to front housing, align front plate hole and straight pin, then using suitable plastic hammer, tap in pump shaft. **Do not damage oil seal and O-rings.**
5. Align cam ring holes with straight pins, then install cam ring with inscribed marks facing outward.
6. Install vane plates with round end facing outward.
7. Install side plate O-ring, then align rear plate holes with pins and install rear plate.
8. Install rear housing wave washer, O-ring, then using suitable plastic hammer, tap in rear housing, install snap ring.
9. Ensure pump shaft rotates smoothly without abnormal noise.
10. Temporarily install pulley nut and check rotating torque, 2.4 inch lbs. or less should be indicated.
11. Install O-ring to flow control spring seat, install spring seat with bolt hole facing outward to housing, then install snap ring.
12. Install spring, flow control valve, O-ring and pressure port union, tighten to specifications.
13. Install reservoir tank and O-ring.
14. Install air control valve and tighten to specifications.

PICKUP, 1993–95 4RUNNER & 1993–94 T100 (RZ SERIES)

Disassemble

1. Position power steering pump in suitable soft-jawed vise.
2. Remove air control valve and union seat.
3. Remove suction port union and O-ring, **Fig. 30.**
4. Remove front housing attaching bolts, place installation alignment mark on front and rear housing, then using suitable plastic hammer, tap off front housing. **Do not allow vane plates, rotor or cam ring to fall out.**
5. Remove cam ring, rotor and vane plates.
6. Position front housing in suitable soft jawed vise.
7. Using suitable hammer and chisel, pry off oil seal, then remove snap ring.
8. Using suitable plastic hammer, remove rotor shaft from front housing.
9. Using suitable plastic hammer, tap bottom end of rear housing and remove rear plate and spring. **Do not grip rear**

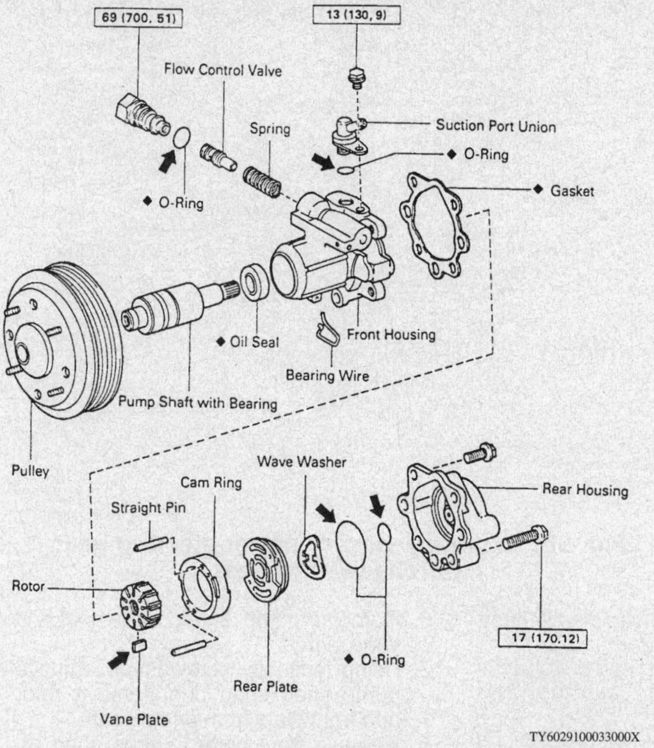
69 (700, 51)
13 (130, 9)
Flow Control Valve
Spring
Suction Port Union
O-Ring
O-Ring
Gasket
Oil Seal
Front Housing
Bearing Wire
Pump Shaft with Bearing
Pulley
Wave Washer
Cam Ring
Straight Pin
Rear Housing
Rotor
17 (170, 12)
O-Ring
Rear Plate
Vane Plate
TY6029100033000X

Fig. 34 Exploded view of power steering pump. Previa

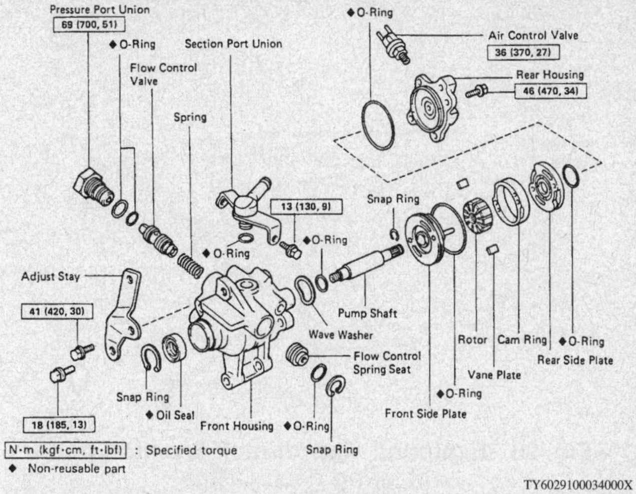
Pressure Port Union
69 (700, 51)
O-Ring
Section Port Union
Flow Control Valve
Spring
O-Ring
Air Control Valve
36 (370, 27)
Rear Housing
46 (470, 34)
13 (130, 9)
Snap Ring
O-Ring
O-Ring
Adjust Stay
41 (420, 30)
Pump Shaft
Wave Washer
Flow Control Spring Seat
Rotor
Cam Ring
O-Ring
Rear Side Plate
Vane Plate
O-Ring
Snap Ring
Oil Seal
Front Housing
O-Ring
Front Side Plate
18 (185, 13)
N·m (kgf·cm, ft·lbf) : Specified torque
Non-reusable part
Snap Ring
TY6029100034000X

Fig. 35 Exploded view of power steering pump. Supra

plate with pliers as damage may occur.

10. Temporarily install bolt to spring seat, using suitable snap ring pliers, remove snap ring, pull out bolt, using suitable tool, remove spring seat, then remove O-ring.

Inspection & Repair

1. Using suitable micrometer and calipers, measure oil clearance between shaft and bushing, .0028 inch or less should be indicated, if not replace entire power steering pump.
2. If required, replace rotor shaft bearing as follows:
   a. Using suitable snap ring pliers, remove snap ring.
   b. Using suitable press, press out bearing.
   c. Using suitable press, press in bearing.
   d. Using suitable snap ring pliers, install snap ring.
3. Using suitable feeler gauge, measure cam ring clearance, maximum should be .0024 inch, if difference is not as indicated, replace cam ring with one with same letter as on rotor.
4. Using suitable micrometer, measure height, thickness and length of vane plates. Minimum height should be .319 inch, thickness, .0707 inch and length .5901 inch.
5. Using suitable feeler gauge, measure clearance between rotor groove and vane plate, maximum indicated should be .0012 inch.
6. If measurements are not as indicated in steps 5 and 6, replace vane plate and/ or rotor with one having the same mark stamped on cam ring.
7. Coat flow control valve with power steering fluid, ensuring it falls smoothly into valve hole.
8. Close one flow control valve hole, then apply compressed air (57–71 psi) to opposite side, ensuring air does not come out end holes.
9. If inspections are not as indicated in steps 8 and 9, replace flow control valve with one having same letter as on front housing.
10. Using suitable scale, measure flow control spring free length, 1.38–1.46 inch should be indicated, if not replace spring.

Assemble

1. Coat all sliding surfaces with power steering fluid.
2. Install O-ring to flow control spring seat, install spring seat to housing, then install snap ring.
3. Install spring, flow control valve, O-ring and pressure port union, tighten to specifications.
4. Using suitable plastic hammer, tap in rotor shaft to front housing, then install snap ring.
5. Coat oil seal lip with MP grease, using suitable tool and hammer, install oil seal.
6. Install O-ring and pin to front housing.
7. Align and install cam ring fluid passages and front housing and install cam ring.
8. Install rotor with inscribed letters facing upward.
9. Install vane plates with round end facing outward.
10. Install rear plate O-ring, then align rear plate fluid passages with cam ring and install rear plate and spring.
11. Align front and rear housing matchmarks, install reservoir tank and O-ring, install and temporarily tighten front housing bolts.
12. Position rear housing in suitable soft jawed vise, then tighten housing attaching bolts uniformly in several passes to specifications.
13. Install suction port union and O-ring and tighten to specifications.
14. Install new union seat, then air control valve.
15. Temporarily install pulley nut and check rotating torque, 2.4 inch lbs. or less should be indicated.

RAV4

Disassemble

1. Position power steering pump in suitable soft-jawed vise.
2. Remove pump front bracket and pump bracket, **Fig. 31.**
3. Using tool No. 09960-10010, or equivalent, remove pump pulley set bolt and pulley.
4. Remove O-ring from pulley.
5. Remove woodruff key from pump shaft.
6. Remove air control valve.
7. Remove pressure feed No. 2 tube.
8. Remove union set bolt, union and union O-ring.
9. Remove pressure port union.
10. Remove flow control valve and spring.
11. Using snap ring pliers, remove flow control snap ring.
12. Partially install a 6 mm normal diameter bolt (Part No. 91651-60650, or equivalent) into flow control spring seat, then remove bolt and spring seat from front pump housing.
13. Remove O-ring from flow control spring seat.
14. Using a plastic hammer, tap out rear housing, wave washer and side rear plate.
15. Remove cam ring and 10 vane plates.
16. Remove vane pump shaft with vane pump rotor and side front plate.

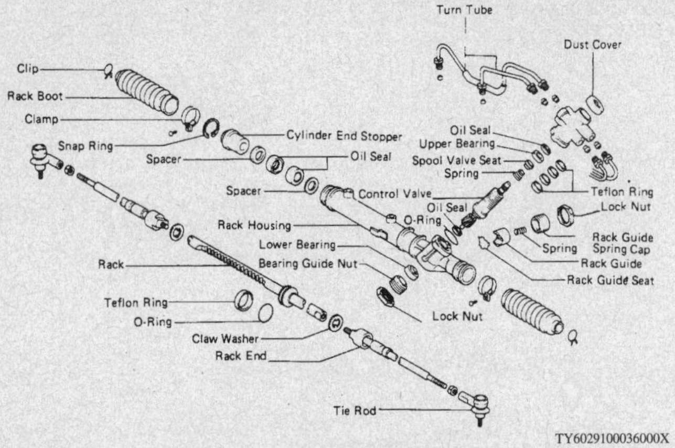
Turn Tube
Dust Cover
Clip
Rack Boot
Clamp
Snap Ring
Spacer
Cylinder End Stopper
Oil Seal
Oil Seal
Upper Bearing
Spool Valve Seat
Spring
Spacer
Control Valve
Teflon Ring
Lock Nut
Oil Seal
O-Ring
Rack Housing
Lower Bearing
Bearing Guide Nut
Rack Guide Spring Cap
Spring
Rack Guide
Rack Guide Seat
Rack
Teflon Ring
O-Ring
Lock Nut
Claw Washer
Rack End
Tie Rod
TY6029100036000X

Fig. 36 Exploded view of rack & pinion power steering gear. Celica

17. Using pliers, remove shorter straight pin from side front plate and longer straight pin from front housing.

Inspection

1. Using a micrometer and caliper gauge, measure oil clearance between vane pump shaft and bushing.
2. Standard oil clearance should be .0012–.0020 inch. Maximum oil clearance is .0028 inch.
3. Using a micrometer, measure the height, thickness and length of 10 pump plates. Height should be .319 inch. Thickness should be .0707 inch and plate length should be .59008 inch.
4. Using a feeler gauge, measure clearance between rotor groove and plate. Maximum clearance should be .0012 inch.
5. If plate and/or rotor must be replaced, use replacement part with the same mark inscribed on cam ring (1, 2, 3, 4 or none).
6. Inpect flow control valve by coating with power steering fluid and ensuring it falls smoothly into valve hole by its own weight.
7. Check flow control valve for leakage by closing one hole and applying compressed air into opposite side.
8. If necessary, replace valve with one having the same letter inscribed (A, B, C, D, E or F).
9. Using calipers, measure free length of spring.
10. Spring length should be at least 1.42 inches.

Assemble

1. Coat parts with power steering fluid.
2. Using plastic hammer, tap new long straight pin into front pump housing.
3. Using plastic hammer, tap new short straight pin into side front plate.
4. Place new O-rings on side front plate and install plate to pump shaft.
5. Install rotor to pump shaft with inscribed mark facing outward.
6. Using snap ring pliers, install new snap ring to vane pump shaft.
7. Align hole of plate and longer straight pin, then tap in shaft with plastic hammer.
8. Align holes of cam ring and two straight pins, then install ring with inscribed mark facing outward.
9. Install 10 vane plates with round end facing outward.
10. Align holes of side rear plate and two straight pins, then install side rear plate.
11. Install wave washer so that its protrusions fit into slots in side rear plate.
12. Using plastic hammer, tap rear housing to front housing and install new snap ring.
13. Install flow control spring seat into rear housing, then remove bolt.
14. Install spring and flow control valve.
15. Install pressure port union and **torque** to 51 ft. lbs.
16. Install suction port union and **torque** to 9 ft. lbs.
17. Install pressure feed No. 2 tube.
18. Install air control valve. **Torque** to 27 ft. lbs.
19. Install woodruff key to vane pump shaft.
20. Using tool No. 09960-10010, or equivalent, install pump pulley and **torque** set nut to 32 ft. lbs.
21. Install pump bracket and pump front bracket.

1995–96 TACOMA, T100 & 1996 4RUNNER (VZ SERIES)

Disassemble

1. Position power steering pump in suitable soft-jawed vise.
2. Remove air control valve, then remove reservoir tank and O-ring.
3. Remove suction port union and O-ring, then remove flow control valve and spring **Fig. 32.**
4. Remove rear housing snap ring, then using suitable plastic hammer, tap out rear housing, wave washer and O-ring.
5. Using suitable plastic hammer, tap shaft end, rear side plate and O-ring.

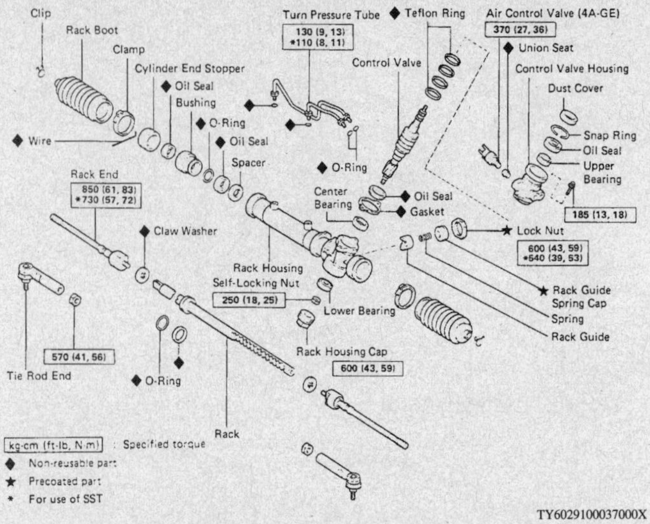
Clip
Rack Boot
Clamp
Cylinder End Stopper
◆ Oil Seal
Bushing
◆ O-Ring
◆ Oil Seal
Spacer
◆ Wire
Rack End
850 (61, 83)
*730 (57, 72)
◆ Claw Washer
Turn Pressure Tube
130 (9, 13)
*110 (8, 11)
◆ Teflon Ring
Control Valve
Air Control Valve (4A-GE)
370 (27, 36)
◆ Union Seat
Control Valve Housing
Dust Cover
Snap Ring
Oil Seal
Upper Bearing
185 (13, 18)
◆ O-Ring
Center Bearing
◆ Oil Seal
◆ Gasket
★ Lock Nut
600 (43, 59)
*540 (39, 53)
Rack Housing
Self-Locking Nut
250 (18, 25)
Lower Bearing
★ Rack Guide Spring Cap
Spring
Rack Guide
Rack Housing Cap
600 (43, 59)
570 (41, 56)
Tie Rod End
◆ O-Ring
Rack
kg-cm (ft-lb, N·m) : Specified torque
◆ Non-reusable part
★ Precoated part
* For use of SST
TY6029100037000X

Fig. 37 Exploded view of power steering gear. Corolla w/Koyo gear

6. Remove pump shaft, cam ring and vane plates.
7. Using suitable screwdriver, remove pump shaft snap ring, remove rotor and front plate from pump shaft.
8. Remove front plate O-rings, then remove straight pin.
9. Remove adjusting stay.

Inspection

1. Using suitable micrometer and calipers, measure oil clearance between shaft and bushing, .0028 inch or less should be indicated, if not replace entire power steering pump.
2. Using suitable micrometer, measure height, thickness and length of vane plates. Minimum height should be .319 inch, thickness, .0707 inch and length .5901 inch.
3. Using suitable feeler gauge, measure clearance between rotor groove and vane plate, maximum indicated should be .0012 inch.
4. If measurements are not as indicated in steps 2 and 3, replace vane plate and/ or rotor with one having the same mark stamped on cam ring.
5. Coat flow control valve with power steering fluid, ensuring it falls smoothly into valve hole.
6. Close one flow control valve hole, then apply compressed air (57–71 psi) to opposite side, ensuring air does not come out end holes.
7. If inspections are not as indicated in steps 6 and 7, replace flow control valve with one having same letter as on front housing.
8. Using suitable scale, measure flow control spring free length, 1.38–1.46 inch should be indicated, if not replace spring.
9. If required, replace oil seal as follows:
   a. Using suitable screwdriver, pry out oil seal.
   b. Using suitable socket and hammer, drive in new oil seal.

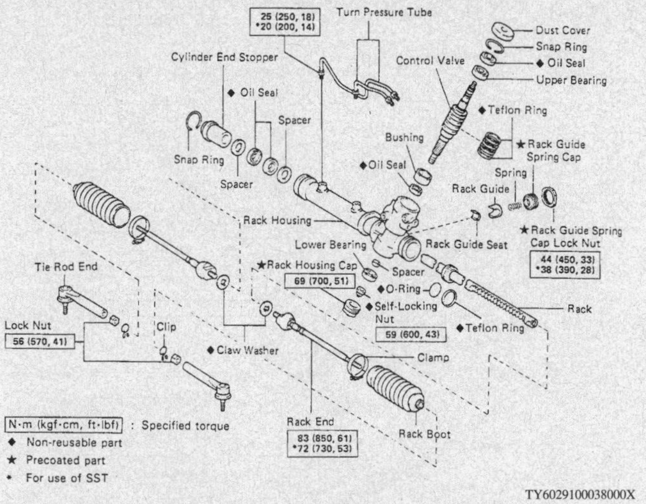

25 (250, 18)
*20 (200, 14)
Turn Pressure Tube
Dust Cover
Snap Ring
◆ Oil Seal
Upper Bearing
Cylinder End Stopper
Control Valve
◆ Oil Seal
Spacer
◆ Teflon Ring
Snap Ring
Bushing
★ Rack Guide Spring Cap
◆ Oil Seal
Spring
Spacer
Rack Guide
Rack Housing
★ Rack Guide Spring Cap Lock Nut
Lower Bearing
Rack Guide Seat
44 (450, 33)
*38 (390, 28)
Tie Rod End
★ Rack Housing Cap
Spacer
69 (700, 51)
◆ O-Ring
◆ Self-Locking Nut
Rack
Lock Nut
56 (570, 41)
Clip
59 (600, 43)
◆ Teflon Ring
◆ Claw Washer
Clamp
N·m (kgf·cm, ft·lbf) : Specified torque
◆ Non-reusable part
★ Precoated part
* For use of SST
Rack End
83 (850, 61)
*72 (730, 53)
Rack Boot
TY6029100038000X

Fig. 38 Exploded view of power steering gear. Corolla w/Toyota gear

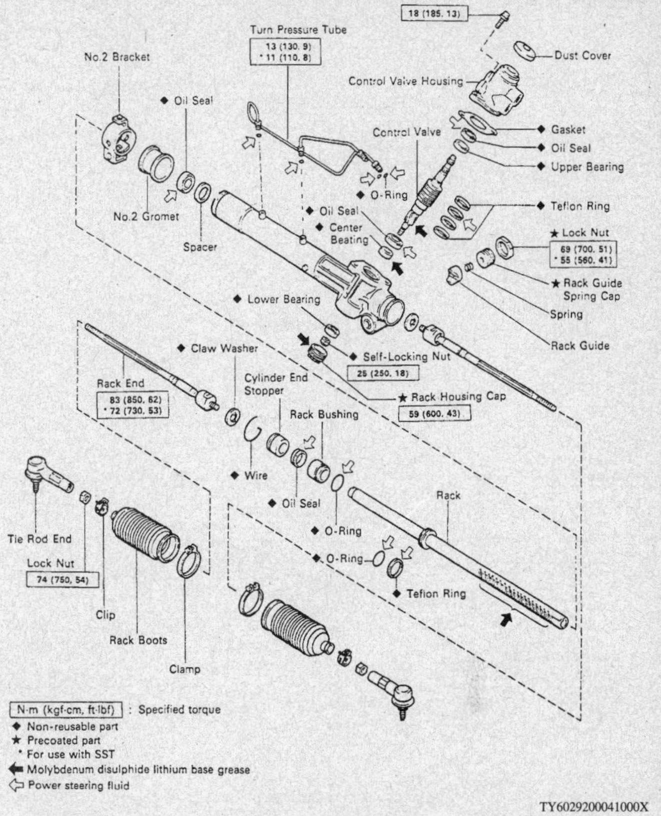

18 (185, 13)
Turn Pressure Tube
13 (130, 9)
* 11 (110, 8)
No.2 Bracket
Dust Cover
Control Valve Housing
◆ Oil Seal
Control Valve
◆ Gasket
◆ Oil Seal
◆ Upper Bearing
No.2 Gromet
◆ O-Ring
◆ Oil Seal
◆ Teflon Ring
◆ Center Bearing
★ Lock Nut
69 (700, 51)
* 55 (560, 41)
Spacer
★ Rack Guide Spring Cap
Spring
◆ Lower Bearing
Rack Guide
◆ Claw Washer
◆ Self-Locking Nut
25 (250, 18)
Rack End
83 (850, 62)
* 72 (730, 53)
Cylinder End Stopper
★ Rack Housing Cap
Rack Bushing
59 (600, 43)
◆ Wire
◆ Oil Seal
Rack
◆ O-Ring
◆ O-Ring
Tie Rod End
Lock Nut
74 (750, 54)
◆ Teflon Ring
Clip
Rack Boots
Clamp
N·m (kgf·cm, ft·lbf) : Specified torque
◆ Non-reusable part
★ Precoated part
* For use with SST
Molybdenum disulphide lithium base grease
Power steering fluid
TY6029200041000X

Fig. 39 Exploded view of power steering gear. Avalon & Camry

Assemble

1. Coat all sliding surfaces with power steering fluid, then install adjusting stay.
2. Using suitable plastic hammer, drive short straight pin to front plate.
3. Install O-rings to front plate, install front plate to pump shaft, then rotor to pump shaft with inscribed mark facing outward, then install snap ring.
4. Coat oil seal lip with MP grease, install long straight pin to front housing, align front plate hole and straight pin, then using suitable plastic hammer, tap in pump shaft. **Do not damage oil seal and O-rings.**
5. Align cam ring holes with straight pins, then install cam ring with inscribed marks facing outward.
6. Install vane plates with round end facing outward.
7. Install side plate O-ring, then align rear plate holes with pins and install rear plate.
8. Install rear housing wave washer, O-ring, then using suitable plastic hammer, tap in rear housing, install snap ring.
9. Ensure pump shaft rotates smoothly without abnormal noise.
10. Temporarily install pulley nut and check rotating torque, 2.4 inch lbs. or less should be indicated.
11. Install O-ring to flow control spring seat, install spring seat with bolt hole facing outward to housing, then install snap ring.
12. Install spring, flow control valve, O-ring and pressure port union, tighten to specifications.
13. Install reservoir tank and O-ring.
14. Install air control valve and tighten to specifications.

1995–96 TACOMA, T100 (RZ SERIES) & 1996 4RUNNER W/3RZ-FE ENGINE

Disassemble

1. Position power steering pump in suitable soft-jawed vise.
2. Remove air control valve and union seat.
3. Remove suction port union and O-ring, **Fig. 33.**
4. Remove front housing attaching bolts, place installation alignment mark on front and rear housing, then using suitable plastic hammer, tap off front housing. **Do not allow vane plates, rotor or cam ring to fall out.**
5. Remove cam ring, rotor and vane plates.
6. Position front housing in suitable soft jawed vise.
7. Using suitable hammer and chisel, pry off oil seal, then remove snap ring.
8. Using suitable plastic hammer, remove rotor shaft from front housing.
9. Using suitable plastic hammer, tap bottom end of rear housing and remove rear plate and spring. **Do not grip rear plate with pliers as damage may occur.**
10. Temporarily install bolt to spring seat, using suitable snap ring pliers, remove snap ring, pull out bolt, using suitable tool, remove spring seat, then remove O-ring.

Inspection & Repair

1. Using suitable micrometer and calipers, measure oil clearance between shaft and bushing, .0028 inch or less should be indicated, if not replace entire power steering pump.
2. If required, replace rotor shaft bearing as follows:
   a. Using suitable snap ring pliers, remove snap ring.
   b. Using suitable press, press out bearing.
   c. Using suitable press, press in bearing.
   d. Using suitable snap ring pliers, install snap ring.
3. Using suitable feeler gauge, measure cam ring clearance, maximum should be .0024 inch, if difference is not as indicated, replace cam ring with one with same letter as on rotor.
4. Using suitable micrometer, measure height, thickness and length of vane plates. Minimum height should be .319 inch, thickness, .0707 inch and length .5901 inch.
5. Using suitable feeler gauge, measure clearance between rotor groove and vane plate, maximum indicated should be .0012 inch.
6. If measurements are not as indicated in steps 5 and 6, replace vane plate and/ or rotor with one having the same mark stamped on cam ring.
7. Coat flow control valve with power steering fluid, ensuring it falls smoothly into valve hole.
8. Close one flow control valve hole, then apply compressed air (57–71 psi) to opposite side, ensuring air does not come out end holes.
9. If inspections are not as indicated in steps 8 and 9, replace flow control

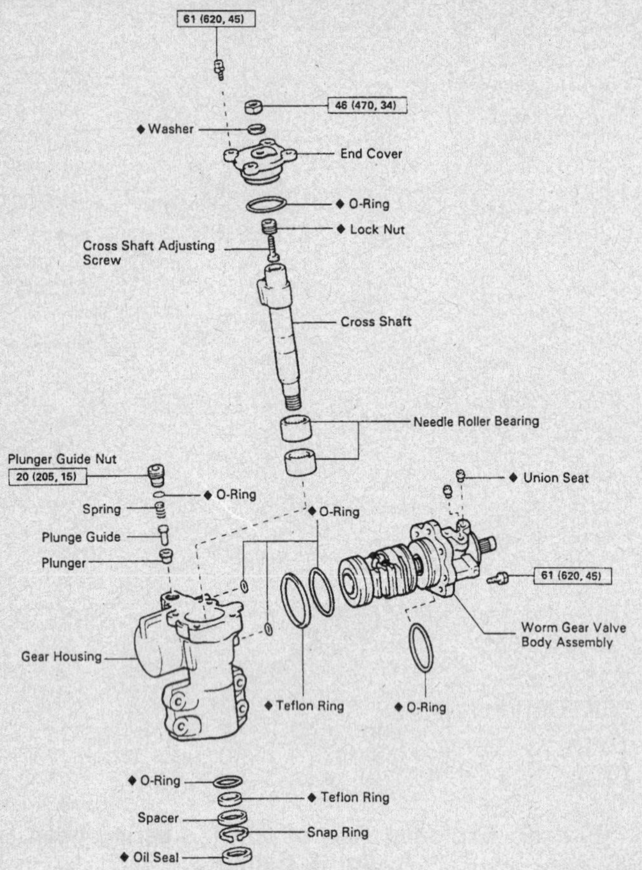
61 (620, 45)
46 (470, 34)
◆ Washer
End Cover
◆ O-Ring
◆ Lock Nut
Cross Shaft Adjusting Screw
Cross Shaft
Needle Roller Bearing
Plunger Guide Nut
20 (205, 15)
◆ O-Ring
Spring
◆ O-Ring
Plunge Guide
Plunger
◆ Union Seat
61 (620, 45)
Worm Gear Valve Body Assembly
Gear Housing
◆ Teflon Ring
◆ O-Ring
◆ O-Ring
◆ Teflon Ring
Spacer
Snap Ring
◆ Oil Seal

TY6029100042000X

Fig. 40 Exploded view of power steering gear. Land Cruiser

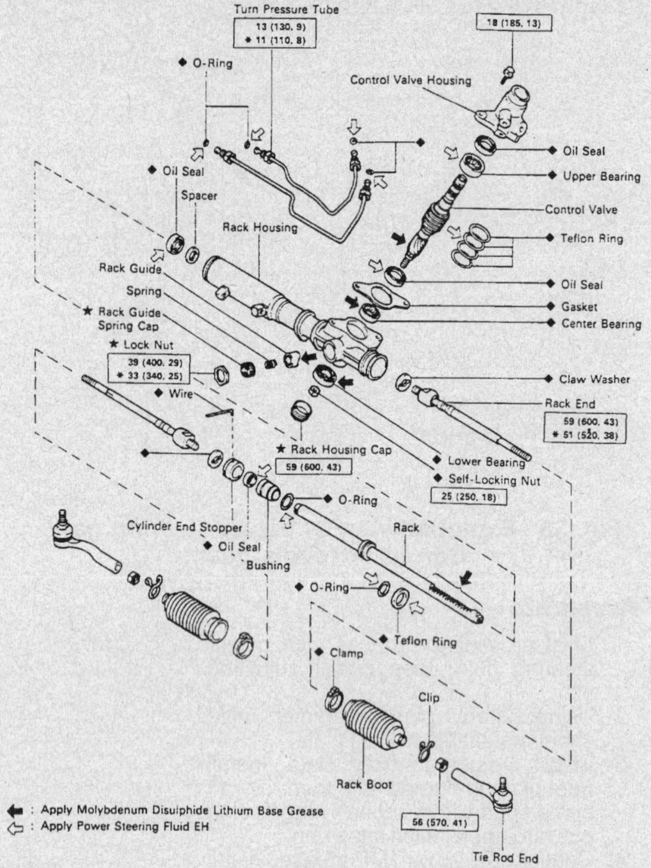
Turn Pressure Tube
13 (130, 9)
★ 11 (110, 8)
18 (185, 13)
◆ O-Ring
Control Valve Housing
◆ Oil Seal
◆ Oil Seal
◆ Upper Bearing
Spacer
Control Valve
Rack Housing
◆ Teflon Ring
Rack Guide
◆ Oil Seal
Spring
◆ Gasket
★ Rack Guide Spring Cap
◆ Center Bearing
★ Lock Nut
39 (400, 29)
★ 33 (340, 25)
◆ Wire
◆ Claw Washer
Rack End
59 (600, 43)
★ 51 (520, 38)
★ Rack Housing Cap
59 (600, 43)
◆ Lower Bearing
◆ Self-Locking Nut
25 (250, 18)
◆ O-Ring
Cylinder End Stopper
Rack
◆ Oil Seal
Bushing
◆ O-Ring
◆ Teflon Ring
◆ Clamp
Clip
Rack Boot
: Apply Molybdenum Disulphide Lithium Base Grease
: Apply Power Steering Fluid EH
56 (570, 41)
Tie Rod End

TY6029100043000X

Fig. 41 Exploded view of power steering gear. MR2

valve with one having same letter as on front housing.

10. Using suitable scale, measure flow control spring free length, 1.38–1.46 inch should be indicated, if not replace spring.

Assemble

1. Coat all sliding surfaces with power steering fluid.
2. Install O-ring to flow control spring seat, install spring seat to housing, then install snap ring.
3. Install spring, flow control valve, O-ring and pressure port union, tighten to specifications.
4. Using suitable plastic hammer, tap in rotor shaft to front housing, then install snap ring.
5. Coat oil seal lip with MP grease, using suitable tool and hammer, install oil seal.
6. Install O-ring and pin to front housing.
7. Align and install cam ring fluid passages and front housing and install cam ring.
8. Install rotor with inscribed letters facing upward.
9. Install vane plates with round end facing outward.
10. Install rear plate O-ring, then align rear plate fluid passages with cam ring and install rear plate and spring.
11. Align front and rear housing matchmarks, install reservoir tank and O-ring, install and temporarily tighten front housing bolts.
12. Position rear housing in suitable soft jawed vise, then tighten housing attaching bolts uniformly in several passes to specifications.
13. Install suction port union and O-ring and tighten to specifications.
14. Install new union seat, then air control valve.
15. Temporarily install pulley nut and check rotating torque, 2.4 inch lbs. or less should be indicated.

PREVIA

Disassemble

1. Position power steering pump in suitable soft-jawed vise.
2. Using suitable tool, remove pump pulley.
3. Remove suction port union and O-ring, **Fig. 34.**
4. Remove pressure port union and O-ring, then remove flow control valve and spring.
5. Place installation alignment marks on front and rear housing, then remove rear housing attaching bolts, O-rings and gasket.
6. Remove wave washer and rear plate.
7. Remove cam ring, rotor and vane plates.
8. Using suitable pliers, remove straight pins from front housing.
9. Using suitable pliers, remove bearing wire.
10. Using tool No. 09515-21010, or equivalent, and an extension bar, press out pump shaft with bearing. Do not allow assembly to drop.

Inspection & Repair

1. Using suitable micrometer, measure height, thickness and length of vane plates. Minimum height should be .315 inch, thickness, .0697 inch and length .5894 inch.
2. Using suitable feeler gauge, measure clearance between rotor groove and vane plate, maximum indicated should be .0012 inch.
3. If measurements are not as indicated in steps 1 and 2, replace vane plate and/ or rotor with one having the same mark stamped on cam ring.
4. Coat flow control valve with power steering fluid, ensuring it falls smoothly into valve hole.
5. Close one flow control valve hole, then apply compressed air (57–71 psi) to opposite side, ensuring air does not come out end holes.
6. If inspections are not as indicated in steps 4 and 5, replace flow control valve with one having same letter as on front housing.
7. Using suitable scale, measure flow control spring free length, 1.42 inch should be indicated, if not replace spring.

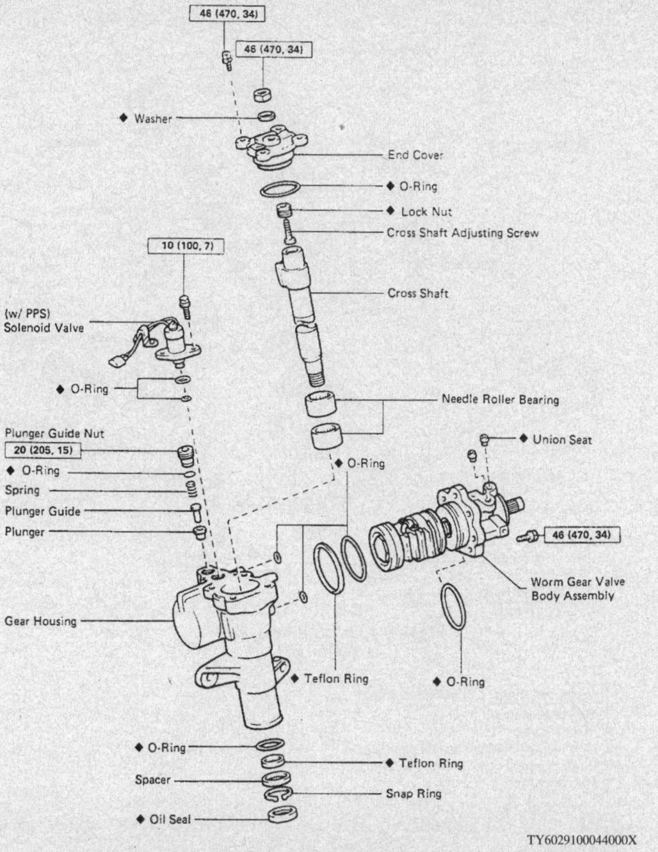
46 (470, 34)
46 (470, 34)
◆ Washer
End Cover
◆ O-Ring
◆ Lock Nut
Cross Shaft Adjusting Screw
10 (100, 7)
Cross Shaft
(w/ PPS)
Solenoid Valve
◆ O-Ring
Needle Roller Bearing
Plunger Guide Nut
20 (205, 15)
◆ O-Ring
Spring
Plunger Guide
Plunger
◆ Union Seat
◆ O-Ring
46 (470, 34)
Worm Gear Valve
Body Assembly
Gear Housing
◆ Teflon Ring
◆ O-Ring
◆ O-Ring
◆ Teflon Ring
Spacer
Snap Ring
◆ Oil Seal
TY6029100044000X

Fig. 42 Exploded view of power steering gear. 2WD Pickup & 4Runner

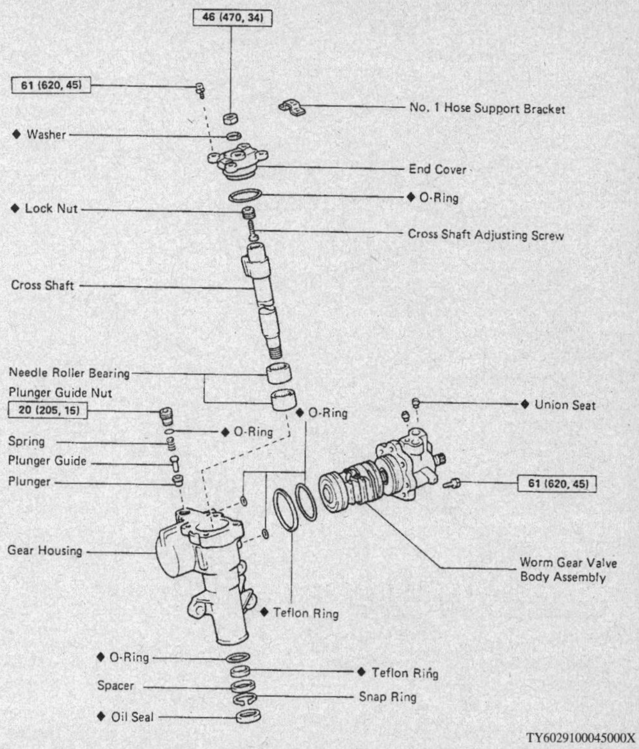
46 (470, 34)
61 (620, 45)
No. 1 Hose Support Bracket
◆ Washer
End Cover
◆ O-Ring
◆ Lock Nut
Cross Shaft Adjusting Screw
Cross Shaft
Needle Roller Bearing
Plunger Guide Nut
20 (205, 15)
◆ O-Ring
◆ Union Seat
◆ O-Ring
Spring
Plunger Guide
Plunger
61 (620, 45)
Gear Housing
Worm Gear Valve
Body Assembly
◆ Teflon Ring
◆ O-Ring
◆ Teflon Ring
Spacer
Snap Ring
◆ Oil Seal
TY6029100045000X

Fig. 43 Exploded view of power steering gear. 4WD Pickup, 4Runner, Tacoma & T100

8. If required, replace oil seal as follows:
   a. Using suitable tool, pry out oil seal.
   b. Using suitable socket and hammer, drive in new oil seal.

Assemble

1. Coat all sliding surfaces with power steering fluid.
2. Install pump shaft with bearing into front housing.
3. Using suitable plastic hammer, drive short straight pin to front plate.
4. Align cam ring holes with straight pins and install cam ring with inscribed mark facing upward.
5. Install rotor with inscribed marks facing outward.
6. Coat vane plates with power steering fluid, then install vane plates with round end facing outward.
7. Install rear plate O-ring, then align rear plate holes with pins and install rear plate.
8. Install suction port union.
9. Install spring, flow control valve, O-ring and pressure port union, tighten to specifications.
10. Install suction port O-ring and suction port union to housing, tightening to specifications.
11. Using tool No. 09613–00012, or equivalent, press pulley to pump shaft until .071–.087 inch of shaft is above pulley.
12. Ensure pump shaft rotates smoothly without abnormal noise.
13. Install pulley nut and check rotating torque, 2.4 inch lbs. or less should be indicated.

SUPRA

Disassemble

1. Position power steering pump in suitable soft-jawed vise.
2. Remove adjust stay.
3. Remove air control valve and union seat, **Fig. 35.**
4. Remove suction port union and O-ring.
5. Remove pressure port union and O-ring, then remove flow control valve and spring.
6. Using suitable snap ring pliers, remove snap ring, temporarily install bolt to flow control spring seat, then remove seat and O-ring.
7. Place installation alignment marks on front and rear housing, then remove rear housing.
8. Using suitable plastic hammer, tap out end shaft, then remove rear side plate and O-ring.
9. Using suitable plastic hammer, tap out rotor shaft assembly, then remove wave washer.
10. Remove cam ring and vane plates.
11. Using suitable pliers, remove pump shaft snap ring, remove rotor and front plate from pump shaft.

Inspection & Repair

1. Using suitable micrometer and calipers, measure oil clearance between shaft and bushing, .0028 inch or less should be indicated, if not replace entire power steering pump.
2. Using suitable micrometer, measure height, thickness and length of vane plates. Minimum height should be .319 inch, thickness, .0707 inch and length .5901 inch.
3. Using suitable feeler gauge, measure clearance between rotor groove and vane plate, maximum indicated should be .0012 inch.
4. If measurements are not as indicated in steps 2 and 3, replace vane plate and/or rotor with one having the same mark stamped on cam ring.
5. Coat flow control valve with power steering fluid, ensuring it falls smoothly into valve hole.
6. Close one flow control valve hole, then apply compressed air (57–71 psi) to opposite side, ensuring air does not come out end holes.
7. If inspections are not as indicated in steps 6 and 7, replace flow control valve with one having same letter as on front housing.
8. Using suitable scale, measure flow control spring free length, 1.46–1.54 inch should be indicated, if not replace spring.
9. If required, replace oil seal as follows:
   a. Using suitable screwdriver, pry out oil seal.
   b. Using suitable socket and hammer, drive in new oil seal.

Assemble

1. Coat all sliding surfaces with power steering fluid.
2. Using suitable plastic hammer, drive

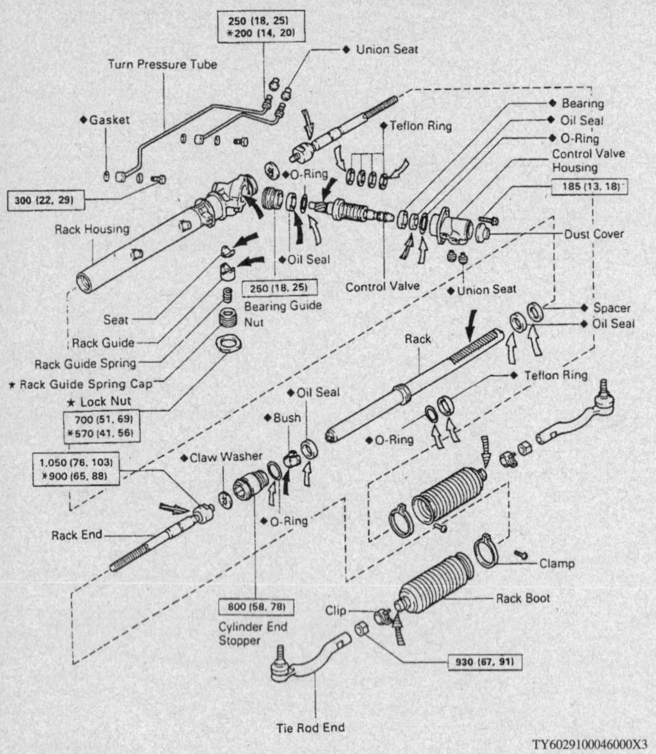
250 (18, 25)
*200 (14, 20)
Turn Pressure Tube
◆ Union Seat
◆Gasket
◆ Bearing
◆ Oil Seal
◆Teflon Ring
◆ O-Ring
Control Valve
Housing
185 (13, 18)
◆O-Ring
300 (22, 29)
Rack Housing
Dust Cover
◆Oil Seal
250 (18, 25)
Bearing Guide
Nut
Control Valve
◆Union Seat
Seat
◆ Spacer
◆ Oil Seal
Rack Guide
Rack
Rack Guide Spring
★ Rack Guide Spring Cap
◆ Teflon Ring
★ Lock Nut
◆Oil Seal
700 (51, 69)
*570 (41, 56)
◆Bush
◆O-Ring
1,050 (76, 103)
*900 (65, 88)
◆Claw Washer
Rack End
◆O-Ring
Clamp
Rack Boot
800 (58, 78)
Cylinder End
Stopper
Clip
930 (67, 91)
Tie Rod End
TY6029100046000X3

Fig. 44 Exploded view of power steering gear. Previa

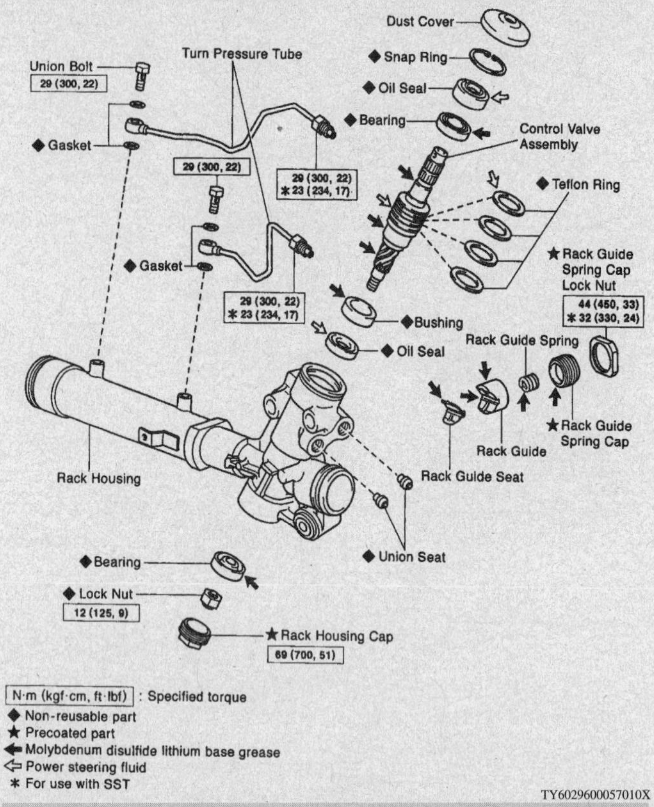
Dust Cover
Union Bolt
29 (300, 22)
Turn Pressure Tube
◆Snap Ring
◆Oil Seal
◆Bearing
◆ Gasket
Control Valve
Assembly
29 (300, 22)
29 (300, 22)
★23 (234, 17)
◆Teflon Ring
◆ Gasket
★Rack Guide
Spring Cap
Lock Nut
44 (450, 33)
★32 (330, 24)
29 (300, 22)
★23 (234, 17)
◆Bushing
Rack Guide Spring
◆Oil Seal
★Rack Guide
Spring Cap
Rack Guide
Rack Housing
Rack Guide Seat
◆Union Seat
◆Bearing
◆Lock Nut
12 (125, 9)
★Rack Housing Cap
69 (700, 51)
N·m (kgf·cm, ft·lbf) : Specified torque
◆ Non-reusable part
★ Precoated part
Molybdenum disulfide lithium base grease
Power steering fluid
* For use with SST
TY6029600057010X

Fig. 45 Exploded view of power steering gear (Part 1 of 2). RAV4

short straight pin to front plate.

3. Install O-rings to front plate, then install front plate, rotor and snap ring to pump shaft.
4. Coat oil seal lip with MP grease, install long straight pin to front housing, align front plate hole and straight pin, then using suitable plastic hammer, tap in pump shaft. **Do not damage oil seal and O-rings.**
5. Align cam ring holes with straight pins, then install cam ring with inscribed marks facing outward.
6. Install vane plates with round end facing outward.
7. Install side plate O-ring, then align side plate holes with pins and install side plate.
8. Install rear housing wave washer, O-ring, then using suitable plastic hammer, tap in rear housing, install snap ring.
9. Ensure pump shaft rotates smoothly without noise.
10. Temporarily install pulley nut and check rotating torque, 2.4 inch lbs. or less should be indicated.
11. Install O-ring to flow control spring seat, install spring seat with bolt hole facing outward to housing, then install snap ring.
12. Install spring, flow control valve, O-ring and pressure port union, tighten to specifications.
13. Install suction port O-ring and suction port union to housing, tightening to specifications.
14. Install air control valve.
15. Install adjusting stay.

POWER STEERING GEAR

CELICA

Disassemble

1. Connect a suitable holding fixture to gear housing, then place fixture in a suitable vise, **Fig. 36.**
2. Remove air control valve, then the right and left pressure tubes.
3. Loosen locknut, then mark relative position between tie rod end and rack end. Remove tie rod end and locknut.
4. Remove rack boots clips and clamps, then the rack boots.
5. Unstake claw washer, then remove rack ends. Mark left and right ends respectively, then remove claw washers.
6. Remove rack guide spring cap locknut, then the rack guide spring cap.
7. Remove rack guide spring, then the rack guide and seat.
8. Remove bearing guide locknut, then the bearing guide nut.
9. Remove dust cover.
10. Mark relative position between valve housing and rack housing, then remove two retaining bolts. Pull out valve with valve housing, then remove O-ring from rack housing.
11. Remove spool valve spring seat and spring, then the control valve with bearing.
12. Remove snap ring from end stopper, then press out cylinder end stopper until end stopper slightly touches press block.
13. Pull out rack together with cylinder end stopper, spacer and oil seal.

Inspection & Repair

1. Inspect rack for excessive runout, tooth wear, or damage and replace as necessary. Maximum runout should be .012 inch.
2. If necessary to replace cylinder housing oil seal, drive out spacer and oil seal, then install new spacer and oil seal.
3. If necessary, to replace rack housing oil seal, pry out oil seal, using a suitable tool, then install new seal.
4. If necessary to replace control valve housing oil seal, proceed as follows:
   a. Press out oil seal with bearing.
   b. Press in new oil seal.
5. If necessary to replace Teflon ring and O-ring, proceed as follows:
   a. Remove Teflon ring and O-ring.
   b. Install new Teflon ring onto suitable tool to expand it.
   c. Insert tool with ring onto rack, then install ring onto piston.
   d. Apply a suitable lubricant to Teflon ring, then ensure proper installation position.
6. If necessary to replace control valve Teflon ring, proceed as follows:
   a. Remove ring, using a suitable tool.
   b. Place new ring onto suitable tool to expand it.
   c. Install rings onto control arm, then ensure proper installation position.
   d. Apply a suitable lubricant to Teflon

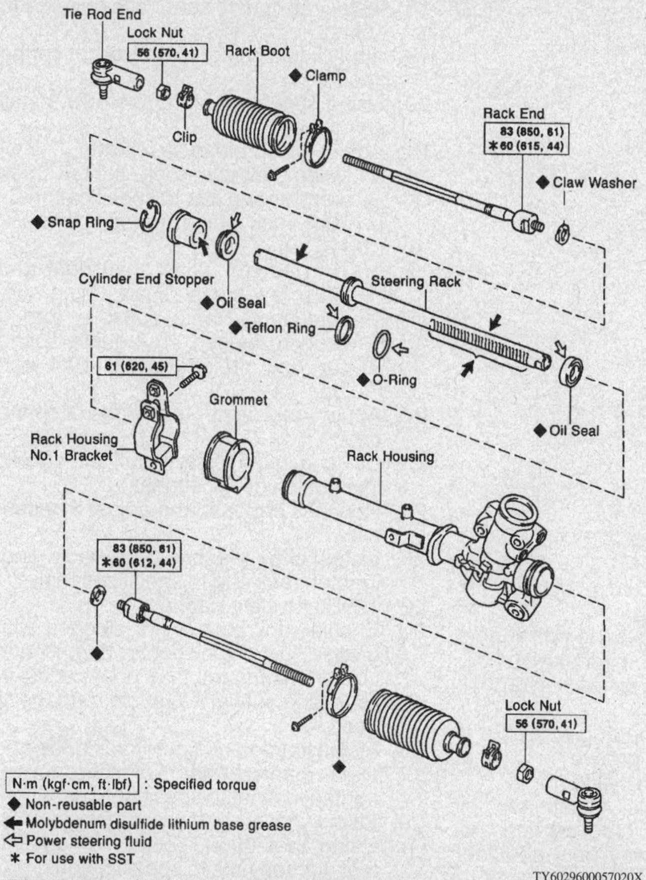
Tie Rod End
Lock Nut
56 (570, 41)
Rack Boot
◆ Clamp
Clip
Rack End
83 (850, 61)
✱60 (615, 44)
◆ Claw Washer
◆ Snap Ring
Cylinder End Stopper
◆ Oil Seal
Steering Rack
◆ Teflon Ring
◆ O-Ring
◆ Oil Seal
61 (620, 45)
Grommet
Rack Housing No.1 Bracket
Rack Housing
83 (850, 61)
✱60 (612, 44)
Lock Nut
56 (570, 41)
N·m (kgf·cm, ft·lbf) : Specified torque
◆ Non-reusable part
Molybdenum disulfide lithium base grease
Power steering fluid
✱ For use with SST
TY6029600057020X

Fig. 45 Exploded view of power steering gear (Part 2 of 2). RAV4

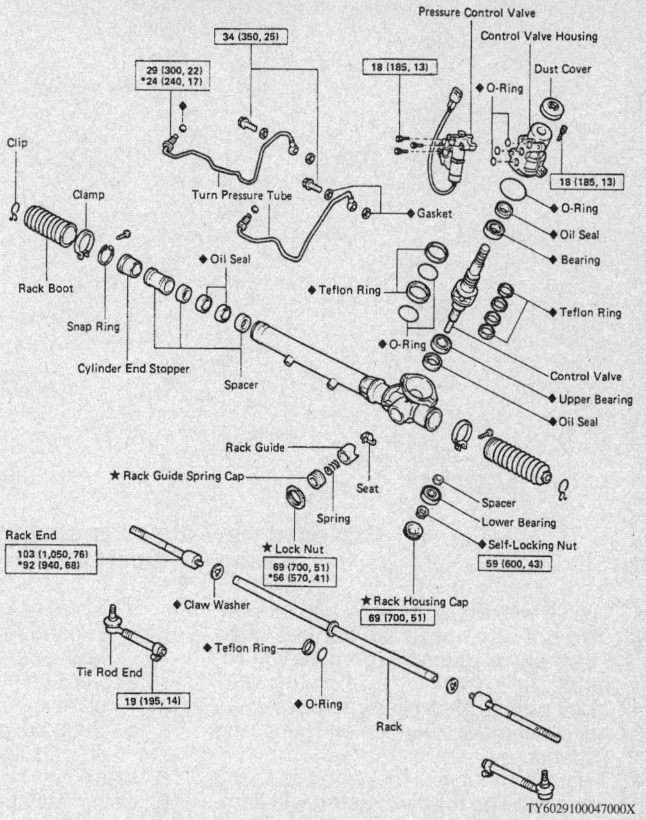
Pressure Control Valve
Control Valve Housing
34 (350, 25)
29 (300, 22)
*24 (240, 17)
18 (185, 13)
◆O-Ring
Dust Cover
Clip
Clamp
Turn Pressure Tube
18 (185, 13)
◆Gasket
◆O-Ring
◆Oil Seal
◆Bearing
◆Oil Seal
Rack Boot
◆Teflon Ring
◆Teflon Ring
Snap Ring
◆O-Ring
Cylinder End Stopper
Spacer
Control Valve
◆Upper Bearing
◆Oil Seal
Rack Guide
★Rack Guide Spring Cap
Seat
Spacer
Spring
Lower Bearing
Rack End
103 (1,050, 76)
*92 (940, 68)
★Lock Nut
69 (700, 51)
*56 (570, 41)
◆Self-Locking Nut
59 (600, 43)
★Rack Housing Cap
69 (700, 51)
◆Claw Washer
◆Teflon Ring
Tie Rod End
19 (195, 14)
◆O-Ring
Rack
TY6029100047000X

Fig. 46 Exploded view of power steering gear. Supra

ring, then slide tapered end of tool over ring and seat ring.

7. If necessary to replace union seat, remove it with suitable screw extractor, then tap new union seat into place, using a hammer and suitable drift.

Assemble

During assembly, coat all moving parts, bearings, and bushings with molybdenum disulfide lithium based grease, and all O-rings and Teflon rings with power steering fluid.

1. Install tool No. 09631-20100, or equivalent, onto rack, then apply a suitable lubricant. Insert rack into cylinder, then remove tool.
2. Wrap vinyl tape around steering rack end, then apply a suitable lubricant. Install oil seal, pushing seal into cylinder.
3. Install spacer and cylinder end stopper, then seat components, using tool No. 09612-22011, or equivalent. Install snap ring.
4. Ensure cylinder is air tight. Connect tool No. 09631-12070, or equivalent, to union of cylinder housing, then apply 15.75 inches Hg vacuum for approximately 30 seconds. There should be no drop in vacuum.
5. Apply a suitable lubricant to Teflon ring, then insert control valve into housing.
6. Apply a suitable lubricant, then install O-ring, spring and spring seat.
7. Align match marks on valve housing and rack housing, then insert two attaching bolts and tighten specifications.
8. Install control valve lower bearing, then apply a suitable sealant to 2 or 3 threads of bearing guide nut. Install nut, then tighten to specifications. Using a suitable torque meter, loosen guide nut until preload of 3.9–5.6 inch lbs. is obtained.
9. Apply Loctite 242, or equivalent to 2 or 3 threads of bearing guide locknut, then install locknut and tighten to specifications. Install rack guide seat, rack guide, then the rack guide spring.
10. Apply a suitable sealant to 2 or 3 threads of spring cap, then tighten cap to specifications.
11. Adjust total preload as follows:
    a. Back off spring cap 15°, then rotate control valve shaft right and left two to three times.
    b. Loosen spring cap until rack guide compression spring is not functional.
    c. Tighten rack guide spring cap until preload of 7.8–10.4 inch lbs. is obtained.
12. Apply a suitable sealant to 2 or 3 threads of locknut, then install rack guide spring cap locknut and tighten to specifications. Recheck total preload.
13. Install new claw washer and rack end, then tighten rack end specifications. Stake claw washer, using a hammer and suitable drift.
14. Install rack boots, clamps and clips, ensuring holes in tube are not clogged, and that clip ends face outward.
15. Screw locknuts and tie rod ends onto rack ends until match marks are aligned.
16. Install new union seats. Install right and left turn tubes, then tighten fittings to specifications.

Corolla w/Koyo Type

Disassemble

1. Remove right and left turn pressure lines, **Fig. 37.**
2. Mount steering gear housing in soft jawed vise.
3. Remove tie rod ends.
4. Remove clips, clamps and rack boots.
5. Remove rack ends and claw washers.
6. Using suitable tool, remove rack guide spring cap locknut.
7. Using suitable tool, remove rack guide spring cap.
8. Remove rack guide spring, rack guide, and seat.
9. Remove dust cover.
10. Remove rack housing cap.
11. Using suitable tool, remove self-locking nut. Remove lower bearing and spacer.
12. Using suitable snap ring pliers, remove snap ring.
13. Using suitable tool, remove control

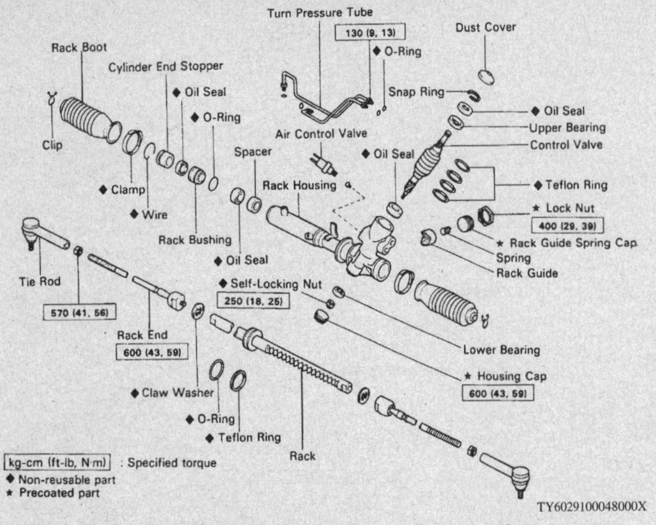
Turn Pressure Tube
130 (9, 13)
◆ O-Ring
Dust Cover
Rack Boot
Cylinder End Stopper
◆ Oil Seal
◆ O-Ring
Snap Ring
◆ Oil Seal
Upper Bearing
Control Valve
Air Control Valve
Clip
Spacer
◆ Oil Seal
Rack Housing
◆ Teflon Ring
◆ Clamp
★ Lock Nut
400 (29, 39)
◆ Wire
Rack Bushing
★ Rack Guide Spring Cap
Spring
Rack Guide
◆ Oil Seal
Tie Rod
◆ Self-Locking Nut
250 (18, 25)
570 (41, 56)
Rack End
600 (43, 59)
Lower Bearing
★ Housing Cap
600 (43, 59)
◆ Claw Washer
◆ O-Ring
◆ Teflon Ring
Rack
kg-cm (ft-lb, N·m) : Specified torque
◆ Non-reusable part
★ Precoated part
TY6029100048000X

Fig. 47 Exploded view of power steering gear. Paseo & Tercel

valve with upper bearing and oil seal. **Do not attempt to tap control valve out, since damage to valve will result.**

14. Using snap ring pliers, remove snap ring. Remove cylinder end stop and spacer.
15. Temporarily install rack end and tie rod on rack. **The following step will damage the cylinder oil seal. Seal will require replacement.**
16. Pull rack out with oil seal.
17. Remove cylinder oil seal with spacer using suitable tools.

Inspection & Assemble

During assembly, coat all moving parts, bearings, and bushings with molybdenum disulfide lithium base grease, and all O-rings and Teflon rings with power steering fluid.

1. Check back surface of rack or teeth for wear or damage.
2. Ensure rack runout does not exceed .012 inch (.3 mm).
3. If necessary, replace bushing and oil seal as follows:
   a. Using service tool 09612-65014, or equivalent, remove bushing.
   b. Using suitable brass bar, remove oil seal.
   c. Coat oil seal lip with power steering fluid.
   d. Using 24 mm socket and extension, tap oil seal into housing.
   e. Using suitable tool 09515-21010, 24 mm socket, and extension, carefully press bushing in to depth of 2.736 inch (69.5 mm). **If bushing is pressed in too far, deformation of the housing will result. If bushing is not pressed in far enough, interference with the control valve will result. Therefore, a press should be used to ensure proper installation. Temporarily install control valve to check that it turns properly.**
4. If necessary, replace Teflon ring and O-ring as follows:
   a. Remove Teflon ring and O-ring.
   b. Install new O-ring.
   c. Expand new Teflon ring with fingers taking care not to over stretch ring.
   d. Position ring into piston ring groove of rack.
   e. Snug down Teflon ring with fingers so it fits tightly in groove.
5. Install new spacer in cylinder.
6. Using suitable tools, install new oil seal. Position seal onto service tool with closed side away from shoulder on tool.
7. Mount service tool on rack. If tool can not be inserted smoothly, remove any burrs on rack with fine emery cloth.
8. Coat service tool with power steering fluid and insert rack into cylinder.
9. Remove service tool.
10. Install oil seal, spacer and cylinder end stop as follows:
    a. Mount service tool on opposite end of rack.
    b. Coat service tool with power steering fluid.
    c. Install oil seal on rack.
    d. Remove service tool.
    e. Using suitable tool, tap in oil seal, spacer and end stop into cylinder.
    f. Using snap ring pliers, install snap ring.
11. Check seal tightness as follows:
    a. Install suitable tool to fluid fittings on cylinder housing.
    b. Apply 15.75 inches Hg. (400 mm Hg) of vacuum for about 30 seconds.
    c. Ensure there is no drop in vacuum for approximately 30 seconds.
12. Place control valve in housing.
13. Using suitable tool, install upper bearing with press.
14. Install oil seal and snap ring, using suitable tool.
15. Install dust cover.
16. Install spacer, lower bearing, and self-locking nut on control valve shaft. Tighten nut to specifications.
17. Apply liquid seal to threads of new housing cap. Install and tighten cap to specifications. Using hammer and chisel, stake housing cap.
18. Install rack guide seat, rack guide, and spring.
19. Apply liquid sealer to threads of spring cap.
20. Using suitable tool, temporarily install spring cap.
21. Adjust total preload as follows:
    a. Using suitable tool, tighten rack guide spring cap to specifications.
    b. Turn rack guide spring cap back 12°.
    c. Turn control valve shaft right and left a few times. Then, using suitable tools, and suitable torque wrench, loosen rack guide spring cap until preload is 7.8–10.4 inch lbs.
22. Apply liquid sealer to threads of spring cap.
23. Using suitable tools, install and tighten locknut to specifications.
24. Recheck preload, and adjust if necessary.
25. Install claw washer, and rack end. Tighten rack end to specifications.
26. 129Stake claw washer.
27. Ensure rack hole is not clogged with grease. Install rack boots, clamps, and clips. Make sure that open ends of clips face outward to avoid damage to boots.
28. Install tie rod ends onto rack ends and align marks. After adjusting toe-in, tighten locknut to specifications.
29. Install right and left turn pressure lines. Using tool 09633-00020, or equivalent, tighten nuts to specifications.

Corolla w/Toyota Type

Disassemble

1. Using tool 09631-22020, or equivalent, remove pressure lines, **Fig. 38.**
2. Mount steering gear housing in soft jawed vise.
3. Remove tie rod ends.
4. Using screwdriver, loosen staked part of clamp and remove clamps. Remove clips and rack boots.
5. Remove rack ends and claw washers.
6. Remove dust cover.
7. Remove rack guide spring cap using tool 09612-24012, or equivalent.
8. Remove rack guide spring and rack guide.
9. Remove rack housing cap.
10. Using tool 09616-00010, or equivalent, remove self-locking nut.
11. Place alignment marks on control valve housing and rack housing. Remove 2 bolts and pull out valve and housing as an assembly.
12. Using hammer and chisel, loosen staked part of claw washer.
13. Using tool 09631-16010, or equivalent, remove stopper nut and claw washer.
14. Place alignment marks on housing and tube.
15. Using hammer and chisel, loosen staked portion of locknut. Using tool 09617-16010, or equivalent, turn set nut to separate housing and cylinder.
16. Using plastic hammer, knock out rack, end stop and wave washer.
17. Pull control valve out of housing.

Inspection & Assemble

During assembly, coat all moving parts, bearings, and bushings with molybdenum disulfide lithium base grease, and all O-rings and Teflon rings with power steering fluid.

1. Check back surface of rack and teeth for wear or damage.
2. Ensure rack runout does not exceed .012 inch (.3 mm).
3. Using suitable micrometer and cylinder gauge, measure shaft O.D. and bushing I.D., shaft O.D. should be 1.0925 inch and bushing I.D. should be 1.1102 inch.
4. If necessary, replace control valve, bearing, and oil seal as follows:
   a. Remove snap ring and oil seal.
   b. Using suitable tools and a press, remove bearing.
   c. Using suitable tool, press in new bearing.
   d. Using socket and press, install new oil seal.
   e. Using snap ring pliers, install snap ring.
5. If necessary, replace pinion bearing as follows:
   a. Using suitable tool, remove bearing.
   b. Using same tool and hammer, install new bearing.
   c. Tighten rack housing cap to snug down bearing.
   d. Remove rack housing cap.
6. If necessary, replace housing oil seal as follows:
   a. Using suitable tool, remove oil seal.
   b. Using suitable tool, install new oil seal.
7. If necessary, replace cylinder end stop oil seal as follows:
   a. Using suitable tool, remove oil seal.
   b. Using suitable tool and hammer, install new oil seal.
8. If necessary, replace Teflon ring and O-ring as follows:
   a. Remove Teflon ring and O-ring.
   b. Install new O-ring.
   c. Using fingers only, stretch new Teflon ring just enough to install into groove of rack.
   d. Using fingers, smooth Teflon ring down so it fits tightly in groove.
9. Mount tool 09631-16020 on end of rack.
10. Coat tool with power steering fluid.
11. Insert rack into cylinder.
12. Remove tool.
13. Install new O-ring on end stop.
14. Push end stop into cylinder.
15. Assemble rack housing and cylinder as follows:
    a. Mount housing in vise.
    b. Install pin and new O-ring on housing.
    c. Align marks on housing and cylinder.
    d. Assemble housing, cylinder, and new set nut.
    e. Using suitable tool, tighten set nut to specifications.
    f. Using hammer and chisel, stake nut.
16. Install cylinder end stop nut with new claw washer.
17. Using suitable tool, tighten stop nut to specifications.
18. Stake claw washer.
19. Push control valve into housing.
20. Place new O-ring on control valve assembly, align marks on valve housing and rack housing, and install valve. Tighten bolts to specifications.
21. Install new self-locking nut and tighten to specifications using suitable tool.
22. Apply liquid sealer to threads of new rack housing cap and install and tighten cap to specifications. Stake housing cap.
23. Install rack guide and spring.
24. Apply liquid sealer to spring cap threads and temporarily install spring cap.
25. Using suitable tool, tighten rack guide spring cap to specifications.
26. Using same tool, turn rack guide spring cap back 12°. Turn control valve shaft right and left, once or twice.
27. Using suitable tools and torque wrench, loosen rack guide spring cap until preload is 6.9–11.3 inch lbs.
28. Apply liquid sealer to spring cap threads.
29. Using suitable tool, install and tighten locknut to specifications.
30. Recheck total preload, adjust if necessary.
31. Install rack ends.
32. Install dust cover.
33. Ensure rack hole is not clogged with grease and install rack boots, clamps, and clips.
34. Install tie rods and tighten locknuts to specifications.
35. Place new O-rings on pressure lines and install right and left turn pressure lines. Using suitable tool, tighten fittings to specifications.

AVALON & CAMRY

Disassemble

1. Position rack in suitable soft jawed vise.
2. Using suitable tool, remove turn tubes and O-rings, **Fig. 39.**
3. Loosen tie rod end locknut, then place installation alignment marks on tie rod end and rack end, remove tie rod end.
4. Remove back boots. **Do not damage rack boots or rack housing.**
5. Unstake claw washers, then using suitable tool, remove rack ends, mark right and left rack ends and remove claw washers.
6. Using suitable tool, remove rack guide spring cap locknut.
7. Using suitable tool, remove rack guide spring cap.
8. Remove rack guide spring, rack guide and seat.
9. Remove rack housing cap.
10. Using suitable tool to hold control valve, remove self locking nut.
11. Remove control valve housing dust cover, place installation alignment marks on valve and rack housing, remove valve housing, valve and rack housing gasket.
12. Tap out control valve and oil seal.
13. Place installation alignment marks on No. 2 bracket and rack housing, then using suitable screwdriver, pry No. 2 bracket clasp apart, remove bushing and bracket.
14. Using suitable tool, turn cylinder end stopper clockwise until wire end comes out, then turn cylinder end stopper counterclockwise and remove wire.
15. Using suitable brass bar, tap out rack with rack bushing and remove O-ring.
16. Using suitable tool and brass bar, drive out oil seal and spacer.

Inspection & Repair

1. Using suitable dial indicator, inspect rack for runout and tooth wear or damage. Maximum runout is .012 inch, if measurement is not as indicated or damaged, replace rack.
2. If required, replace control valve housing oil seal and upper bearing.
3. If required, replace control valve lower bearing and center bearing.
4. If required, replace rack bushing oil seal, using suitable tool, remove oil seal, coat new oil seal with power steering fluid, then install.
5. If required, replace Teflon ring and O-ring as follows:
   a. Remove Teflon ring and O-ring. **Do not damage steering rack.**
   b. Coat new O-ring with power steering fluid, then install.
   c. Coat new Teflon ring with power steering fluid.
   d. Install Teflon ring to tool No. 09630-24013, or equivalent, then expand ring.
   e. Install expanded ring to steering rack and snug down by hand to fit tightly in groove.
6. If required, replace control valve Teflon ring as follows:
   a. Using suitable screwdriver, remove Teflon ring. **Do not damage control valve.**
   b. Install new rings to tool No. 09631-20070, or equivalent, then expand rings.
   c. Install expanded rings to control valve and snug down by hand.
   d. Coat ring with power steering fluid, then carefully slide tapered end of tool No. 09631-20081, or equivalent, over rings to seat rings.

Assemble

1. Coat cylinder side oil seal lip with power steering fluid, then press in cylinder side oil seal and spacer.
2. Install tool No. 09631-33010, or equivalent, to rack, scrape burrs from rack teeth end and burnish as required, coat tool with power steering fluid, the install rack to cylinder, remove tool.
3. Install rack bushing and cylinder end stopper pushing in until wire installation hole appears.
4. Install wire end to hole, then using suitable tool, turn cylinder end stopper clockwise until wire end disappears.
5. Install suitable vacuum tool to cylinder

housing unions, apply 15.75 inch Hg. vacuum for about 30 seconds, ensure no change in vacuum, if change is indicated, inspect rack housing oil seal installation.
6. Install No. 2 bracket and bushing, aligning matchmarks.
7. Place suitable vinyl tape on control valve, coat Teflon rings with power steering fluid, then install control valve into housing and press in new oil seal.
8. Position new gasket on rack housing, align valve and rack housing matchmarks, install attaching bolts and tighten to specifications, then install dust cover.
9. Using suitable tool, hold control valve, install new self locking nut and tighten to specifications.
10. Apply Loctite 242, or equivalent to two or three rack housing cap threads, then install cap, using suitable center punch, stake housing in two places.
11. Install rack guide seat, rack guide and spring.
12. Apply Loctite 242, or equivalent to two or three spring cap threads, then install cap, tighten to specifications.
13. Return rack guide spring cap 12°, turn control valve shaft right and left one or two times, loosen spring cap until rack guide compression spring is not functioning, then using suitable tool, tighten rack guide spring cap until turning preload of 6.9–12.2 ft. lbs. is indicated.
14. Apply Loctite 242, or equivalent to two or three rack guide spring cap locknut threads, then install locknut, tighten to specifications, then recheck preload as outlined in step 13.
15. Install claw washer and rack ends, then using suitable brass bar and hammer, stake claw washer.
16. Ensure tube hole is not clogged, then install rack boots.
17. Install tie rod ends, align matchmarks.
18. Install right and left turn pressure tubes.

LAND CRUISER

Disassemble

1. Place gear in suitable soft jawed vise.
2. Remove end cover adjusting screw locknut and seal washer, remove end cover attaching bolts, **Fig. 40,** screw in adjusting screw until cover is removed.
3. Using suitable plastic hammer, tap out cross shaft end and remove shaft.
4. Using tool No. 09043-38100, or equivalent, remove plunger guide nut, then remove spring, plunger, plunger guide and O-ring.
5. Remove four valve body cap bolts, then using tool No. 09616-00010, or equivalent, turn shaft clockwise to disconnect worm gear valve body from gear housing.
6. Hold power piston so it cannot move, turn wormshaft clockwise, then remove valve body and power piston assembly and O-ring. **Ensure power piston nut does not come off with worm shaft.**

Inspection & Repair

1. Place valve body in suitable soft jawed vise, using suitable dial indicator, inspect ball clearance, moving worm gear up and down, maximum ball clearance should be .00059 inch, if clearance is not as indicated, replace power control valve assembly.
2. Place cross shaft in suitable soft jawed vise, then using suitable dial indicator, measure thrust clearance, .0012–.0020 inch should be indicated, is not as indicated, adjust thrust clearance.
3. Adjust thrust clearance as follows:
   a. Using suitable hammer and chisel, remove locknut stake.
   b. Using tool No. 09630–00012, or equivalent, loosen locknut.
   c. Turn adjusting screw for correct thrust clearance, then tighten locknut.
   d. Stake locknut.
4. If required, replace needle roller bearings as follows:
   a. Using suitable screw driver, remove oil seal.
   b. Using suitable snap ring pliers, remove snap ring.
   c. Remove metal spacer, O-ring and Teflon ring.
   d. Using tool No. 09630-00012, or equivalent, press out bearings.
   e. Install new lower bearing, ensuring it is positioned .909 inch away from lower end of housing.
   f. Press in new upper bearing, ensuring top end is installed so it aligns with end of housing hole.
   g. Install O-ring and metal spacer.
   h. Using suitable snap ring pliers, install snap ring.
   i. Form Teflon ring into heart shape and install with fingers.
   j. Using tool No. 09630–00012, or equivalent, form Teflon ring, Teflon ring must be formed before sector shaft installation or damage may occur.
   k. Drive in new oil seal, then apply MP grease to oil seal lip.
5. If required, replace control valve Teflon rings as follows:
   a. Using suitable screwdriver, remove Teflon ring and O-ring. **Do not damage control valve.**
   b. Install new O-ring.
   c. Expand Teflon ring by hand, do not over expand Teflon ring.
   d. Install Teflon ring.
   e. Coat Teflon ring with power steering fluid and snug down with piston ring compressor for 5–7 minutes.
6. If required, replace union set as follows:
   a. Using suitable screw extractor, remove union seat.
   b. Using suitable plastic hammer and extension bar, tap in new union seat.

Assemble

1. Install O-rings to gear housing and valve body, mount gear housing to tool No. 09630–00012, or equivalent, then install tool to suitable soft jawed vise. Install worm gear valve body. **Do not damage Teflon ring.**
2. Hold power piston nut to prevent turning, then using tool No. 09616-00010, or equivalent, check worm gear preload, starting preload should be 2.6–4.8 inch lbs. If preload is not as indicated, replace worm gear assembly.
3. Install plunger, plunger guide and spring.
4. Install plunger guide nut O-ring, then using tool No. 09043-38100, or equivalent, install plunger guide nut and tighten specifications.
5. Install end cover O-ring, fully loosen adjusting screw, using suitable screwdriver, assemble cross shaft to end cover.
6. Set worm gear at center of gear housing.
7. Install and push cross shaft into gear housing so center teeth mesh together, install four cap bolts tightening to specifications in diagonal pattern.
8. Using tool No. 09616-00010, or equivalent, turn worm shaft to full lock in both directions to determine exact center, place matchmarks on worm shaft and housing to show neutral position.
9. Install tool No. 09616-0010, or equivalent with suitable torque meter to worm shaft, turn adjusting screw while measuring preload, total starting preload should be 6.5–9.6 inch lbs.
10. Install washer, then install and tighten locknut while holding adjusting screw.
11. Recheck total preload.

MR2

Disassemble

1. Position rack in suitable soft jawed vise.
2. Using suitable tool, remove turn tubes and O-rings, **Fig. 41.**
3. Loosen tie rod end locknut, then place installation alignment marks on tie rod end and rack end, remove tie rod end.
4. Remove back boots. **Do not damage rack boots or rack housing.**
5. Unstake claw washers, then using suitable tool, remove rack ends, mark right and left rack ends and remove claw washers.
6. Using suitable tool, remove rack guide spring cap locknut.
7. Using suitable tool, remove rack guide spring cap.
8. Remove rack guide spring, rack guide and seat.
9. Remove rack housing cap.
10. Using suitable tool to hold control valve, remove self locking nut.
11. Remove control valve housing dust cover, place installation alignment marks on valve and rack housing, remove valve housing, valve and rack housing gasket.
12. Tap out control valve and oil seal.
13. Using suitable tool, turn cylinder end stopper clockwise until wire end comes out, then turn cylinder end stopper counterclockwise and remove wire.
14. Pull out steering rack, remove cylinder

end stopper, rack bushing and O-ring.
15. Using suitable tool and brass bar, drive out oil seal and spacer.

Inspection & Repair

When coating gear housing components with power steering fluid, use Toyota power steering fluid EH, or equivalent.

1. Using suitable dial indicator, inspect rack for runout and tooth wear or damage. Maximum runout is .012 inch, if measurement is not as indicated or damaged, replace rack.
2. If required, replace control valve housing oil seal and upper bearing.
3. If required, replace control valve lower bearing and center bearing.
4. If required, replace rack bushing oil seal, using suitable tool, remove oil seal, coat new oil seal with power steering fluid, then install.
5. If required, replace Teflon ring and O-ring as follows:
   a. Remove Teflon ring and O-ring. **Do not damage steering rack.**
   b. Coat new O-ring with power steering fluid, then install.
   c. Coat new Teflon ring with power steering fluid.
   d. Expand Teflon ring by hand. **Do not over expand Teflon ring.**
   e. Install expanded ring to steering rack and snug down by hand to fit tightly in groove.
6. If required, replace control valve Teflon ring as follows:
   a. Using suitable screwdriver, remove Teflon ring. **Do not damage control valve.**
   b. Install new rings to tool No. 09631-20070, or equivalent, then expand rings.
   c. Install expanded rings to control valve and snug down by hand.
   d. Coat ring with power steering fluid, then carefully slide tapered end of tool No. 09631-20081, or equivalent, over rings to seat rings.

Assemble

When coating gear housing components with power steering fluid, use Toyota power steering fluid EH, or equivalent.

1. Coat cylinder side oil seal lip with power steering fluid, then press in rack housing oil seal and spacer.
2. Install tool No. 09631-10040, or equivalent to rack, scrape burrs from rack teeth end and burnish as required, coat tool with power steering fluid, the install rack to cylinder, remove tool.
3. Install rack bushing and cylinder end stopper pushing in until wire installation hole appears.
4. Install wire end to hole, then using suitable tool, turn cylinder end stopper clockwise until wire end disappears.
5. Install suitable vacuum tool to cylinder housing unions, apply 15.75 inch Hg. vacuum for about 30 seconds, ensure no change in vacuum, if change is indicated, inspect rack housing oil seal installation.
6. Place suitable vinyl tape on control valve, coat Teflon rings with power steering fluid, then install control valve into housing and press in new oil seal.
7. Position new gasket on rack housing, align valve and rack housing matchmarks, install attaching bolts and tighten to specifications, then install dust cover.
8. Using suitable tool, hold control valve, install new self locking nut and tighten to specifications.
9. Apply Loctite 242, or equivalent to two or three rack housing cap threads, then install cap, using suitable center punch, stake housing in two places.
10. Install rack guide seat, rack guide and spring.
11. Apply Loctite 242, or equivalent to two or three spring cap threads, then install cap, tighten to specifications.
12. Return rack guide spring cap 12°, turn control valve shaft right and left one or two times, loosen spring cap until rack guide compression spring is not functioning, then using suitable tool, tighten rack guide spring cap until turning preload of 7.8–11.3 ft. lbs. is indicated.
13. Apply Loctite 242, or equivalent to two or three rack guide spring cap locknut threads, then install locknut, tighten to specifications, then recheck preload as outlined in step 12.
14. Install claw washer and rack ends, then using suitable brass bar and hammer, stake claw washer.
15. Ensure tube hole is not clogged, then install rack boots.
16. Install tie rod ends, align matchmarks.
17. Install right and left turn pressure tubes.

PASEO

Refer to "Tercel," "Power Steering Gear" for power steering gear service. Total preload for Paseo models, is 7.8–12.0 inch lbs.

2WD PICKUP & 4RUNNER

Disassemble

1. Place gear in suitable soft jawed vise.
2. **On models with PPS,** remove solenoid valve.
3. **On all models,** remove end cover adjusting screw locknut and seal washer, remove end cover attaching bolts, **Fig. 42,** screw in adjusting screw until cover is removed.
4. Using suitable plastic hammer, tap out cross shaft end and remove shaft.
5. Using tool No. 09043-38100, or equivalent, remove plunger guide nut, then remove spring, plunger, plunger guide and O-ring.
6. Remove four valve body cap bolts, then using tool No. 09616-00010, or equivalent, turn shaft clockwise to disconnect worm gear valve body from gear housing.
7. Hold power piston so it cannot move, turn wormshaft clockwise, then remove valve body and power piston assembly and O-ring. **Ensure power piston nut does not come off with worm shaft.**

Inspection & Repair

1. Place valve body in suitable soft jawed vise, using suitable dial indicator, inspect ball clearance, moving worm gear up and down, maximum ball clearance should be .00059 inch, if clearance is not as indicated, replace power control valve assembly.
2. Place cross shaft in suitable soft jawed vise, then using suitable dial indicator, measure thrust clearance, .0012–.0020 inch should be indicated, is not as indicated, adjust thrust clearance.
3. Adjust thrust clearance as follows:
   a. Using suitable hammer and chisel, remove locknut stake.
   b. Using tool No. 09630–00012, or equivalent, loosen locknut.
   c. Turn adjusting screw for correct thrust clearance, then tighten locknut.
   d. Stake locknut.
4. If required, replace needle roller bearings as follows:
   a. Using suitable screw driver, remove oil seal.
   b. Using suitable snap ring pliers, remove snap ring.
   c. Remove metal spacer, O-ring and Teflon ring.
   d. Using tool No. 09630-00012, or equivalent, press out bearings.
   e. Install new lower bearing, ensuring it is positioned .909 inch away from lower end of housing.
   f. Press in new upper bearing, ensuring top end is installed so it aligns with end of housing hole.
   g. Install O-ring and metal spacer.
   h. Using suitable snap ring pliers, install snap ring.
   i. Form Teflon ring into heart shape and install with fingers.
   j. Using tool No. 09630–00012, or equivalent, form Teflon ring, Teflon ring must be formed before sector shaft installation or damage may occur.
   k. Drive in new oil seal, then apply MP grease to oil seal lip.
5. If required, replace control valve Teflon rings as follows:
   a. Using suitable screwdriver, remove Teflon ring and O-ring. **Do not damage control valve.**
   b. Install new O-ring.
   c. Expand Teflon ring by hand, do not over expand Teflon ring.
   d. Install Teflon ring.
   e. Coat Teflon ring with power steering fluid and snug down with piston ring compressor for 5–7 minutes.
6. If required, replace union set as follows:
   a. Using suitable screw extractor, remove union seat.
   b. Using suitable plastic hammer and extension bar, tap in new union seat.

Assemble

1. Install O-rings to gear housing and valve body, mount gear housing to tool No. 09630–00012, or equivalent, then install tool to suitable soft jawed vise. Install worm gear valve body. **Do not damage Teflon ring.**

2. Hold power piston nut to prevent turning, then using tool No. 09616-00010, or equivalent, check worm gear preload, starting preload should be 2.6–4.8 inch lbs. If preload is not as indicated, replace worm gear assembly.
3. Install plunger, plunger guide and spring.
4. Install plunger guide nut O-ring, then using tool No. 09043-38100, or equivalent, install plunger guide nut and tighten specifications.
5. Install end cover O-ring, fully loosen adjusting screw, using suitable screwdriver, assemble cross shaft to end cover.
6. Set worm gear at center of gear housing.
7. Install and push cross shaft into gear housing so center teeth mesh together, install four cap bolts tightening to specifications in diagonal pattern.
8. Using tool No. 09616-00010, or equivalent, turn worm shaft to full lock in both directions to determine exact center, place matchmarks on worm shaft and housing to show neutral position.
9. Install tool No. 09616-0010, or equivalent with suitable torque meter to worm shaft, turn adjusting screw while measuring preload, total starting preload should be 4.3–8.3 inch lbs.
10. **On models with PPS,** install solenoid valve.
11. **On all models,** install washer, then install and tighten locknut while holding adjusting screw.
12. Recheck total preload.

2WD TACOMA & T100

Disassemble

1. Remove turn pressure tube bracket, then using power steering hose nut wrench tool No. 09633-00020, or equivalent, remove turn pressure tubes and O-rings.
2. Secure gear housing in a vise.
3. Loosen locknut and place matchmarks on tie rod and rack ends, then remove tie rod ends and locknuts.
4. Remove rack boot clips and clamps, then rack boots. Mark left and right boots accordingly.
5. Unstake claw washers, **avoid any impact to rack,** using variable open wrench No. 09922-10010, remove rack ends.
6. Mark left and right rack ends accordingly, then remove claw washers.
7. Remove rack guide spring cap locknut, then rack guide spring cap.
8. Remove rack guide spring cap and rack guide, then O-ring from rack guide.
9. Remove rack housing cap.
10. Using steering worm bearing adjusting socket tool No. 09616-00010, or equivalent to hold control valve, remove self-locking nut.
11. Remove control valve housing as follows:
    a. Place matchmarks on valve housing and rack housing, then remove dust cover and two bolts.
    b. Pull out valve with valve housing.
    c. Remove gasket from rack housing.
    d. Remove control valve housing and oil seal.
12. Using cylinder end stopper nut wrench tool No. 09631-16010, or equivalent, turn cylinder end stopper clockwise until wire end comes out, then turn cylinder end stopper counterclockwise and remove wire.
13. Using a brass bar, tap out rack with rack bushing and remove O-ring from bushing.
14. Using steering gearbox replacer set tool No. 09620-30010, or equivalent, and a brass bar, drive out oil seal.

Inspection & Repair

1. Check rack runout; maximum runout is .012 inch. Check back surface for wear or damage; if faulty, replace rack.
2. If necessary, replace control valve housing oil seal and upper bearing as follows:
    a. Using steering gearbox replacer set tool No. 09620-30010, or equivalent, tap out oil seal and upper bearing.
    b. Coat new seal lip with MP grease.
    c. Using steering gearbox replacer set tool No. 09620-3001, or equivalent, press in oil seal. the install new upper bearing in valve housing.
    d. Using steering gearbox replacer set tool No. 09620-30010, or equivalent, press in new upper bearing.
3. If necessary, replace control valve lower bearing as follows:
    a. Using a brass bar, drive out lower bearing.
    b. Using steering gear housing overhaul set tool No. 09612-24014, or equivalent, remove center bearing.
    c. Using steering gearbox replacer set tool No. 09620-30010, or equivalent, press in new center bearing.
    d. Using steering gear rack oil tool set tool No. 09630-24013, or equivalent, press in new lower bearing.
4. If necessary, replace rack bushing oil seal as follows:
    a. Using water pump overhaul set tool No. 09236-00101, or equivalent, remove oil seal.
    b. Coat new seal with power steering fluid.
    c. Using oil seal replacer tool No. 09631-32010, or equivalent, press in new oil seal.
5. If necessary, replace teflon ring and O-ring as follows:
    a. Remove teflon ring and O-ring. **Ensure not to damage steering rack.**
    b. Coat with power steering fluid, then install new O-ring.
    c. Expand new teflon ring. **Ensure not to over-expand ring.**
    d. Install teflon ring to steering rack, then coat teflon ring with power steering fluid and snug it down with fingers.
6. If necessary, replace control valve teflon ring as follows:
    a. Using a screwdriver, remove teflon rings. **Ensure not to damage control valve.**
    b. Install new teflon rings to seal ring guide No. 09631-20070 and expand them.
    c. Install expanded teflon rings to control valve and snug them down with fingers, then carefully slide tapered end of tool over teflon rings to seat them.

Assemble

1. Coat new cylinder housing seal with power steering fluid, install seal onto front hub and drive pinion bearing replacer set tool No. 09608-12010, or equivalent, and press seal in.
2. Install rack as follows:
    a. Install rack to steering rack cover "I" tool No. 09631-33010, or equivalent, then coat tool with power steering fluid.
    b. Insert rack into cylinder.
    c. Remove tool.
3. To prevent damage to oil seal lip, wrap vinyl tape around steering rack end and apply power steering fluid.
4. Coat new O-ring with power steering fluid and install it to rack bushing. Push rack bushing and cylinder end stopper until wire installation hole appears.
5. Insert a new wire into hole, then using cylinder end stopper wrench tool No. 09631-16010, or equivalent, turn cylinder end clockwise until wire end disappears.
6. Install suitable hand vacuum pump to unions of cylinder housing, then apply 15.75 inch vacuum for about 30 seconds. Ensure of no change in vacuum; if vacuum changes, check installation of rack housing oil seal.
7. Wind vinyl tape on control valve and coat teflon rings with power steering fluid. Push control valve into housing, **ensure not to damage teflon rings and oil seal. Using tilt bearing handle replacer tool No. 09612-22011, or equivalent, press in new oil seal.**
8. Install new control valve housing gasket on rack housing, then control valve housing and two bolts and dust cover. Tighten housing bolts to specifications.
9. Using steering worm bearing adjusting socket tool No. 09616-00010, or equivalent to hold control valve, install new self-locking nut. Tighten to specifications.
10. Apply sealant (Loctite 242, or equivalent) to two or three threads of housing cap, then install cap. Using a center punch, stake housing at two places.
11. Install O-ring to rack guide, then install rack guide and spring.
12. Adjust total preload as follows:
    a. Apply sealant (Loctite 242, or equivalent) to two or three threads of spring cap, then install spring cap.
    b. Set rack at rack stroke center.
    c. Using steering gear housing overhaul set tool No. 09612-24014, or equivalent, install and **torque** spring cap to specifications.
    d. Using steering gear housing overhaul set tool No. 09612-24014, or

equivalent, return rack guide spring cap 10° to 12°.
   e. Using steering worm bearing adjusting socket tool No. 09616-00010, or equivalent and torque meter, check total preload; preload (turning) should be 11.3 inch lbs. or less. If preload is 11.3 inch lbs. or more, return rack guide spring cap another 5°.
13. Install rack guide spring cap locknut as follows:
   a. Apply sealant (Loctite 242, or equivalent) to two or three threads of locknut, then using steering gear housing overhaul tool set tool No. 09612-24014, or equivalent, install and **torque** locknut to specifications; use torque wrench with a fulcrum length of 13.39 inch.
   b. Recheck total preload.
14. Install rack ends as follows:
   a. Install a new claw washer.
   b. Using variable open wrench tool No. 09922-10010, or equivalent, install rack ends; use torque wrench with a fulcrum length of 13.39 inch.
   c. Using a brass bar and a hammer, stake claw washers.
15. Install rack boots as follows:
   a. Ensure tube hole is not clogged with grease. If tube hole is clogged, pressure inside boot will change after it is assembled and steering wheel is turned.
   b. Install boots. **Ensure not to damage to twist boots.**
   c. Install clips and clamps.
16. Screw locknuts and tie rod ends onto rack ends until matchmarks are aligned. After adjusting toe-in, **torque** locknut to specifications.
17. Install right and left turn pressure tubes as follows:
   a. Install new O-rings to tube.
   b. Using power steering hose nut wrench tool No. 09633-0020, or equivalent, install and **torque** tubes to specifications; use torque wrench with a fulcrum length of 11.81 inch.
   c. Install turn pressure tube bracket.

4WD PICKUP, TACOMA, T100 & 4RUNNER2

Disassemble

1. Place gear in suitable soft jawed vise.
2. Remove end cover adjusting screw locknut and seal washer, remove end cover attaching bolts and No. 1 hose support bracket, **Fig. 43**, screw in adjusting screw until cover is removed.
3. Using suitable plastic hammer, tap out cross shaft end and remove shaft.
4. Using tool No. 09043-38100, or equivalent, remove plunger guide nut, then remove spring, plunger, plunger guide and O-ring.
5. Remove four valve body cap bolts, then using tool No. 09616-00010, or equivalent, turn shaft clockwise to disconnect worm gear valve body from gear housing.
6. Hold power piston so it cannot move, turn wormshaft clockwise, then remove valve body and power piston assembly and O-ring. **Ensure power piston nut does not come off with worm shaft.**

Inspection & Repair

1. Place valve body in suitable soft jawed vise, using suitable dial indicator, inspect ball clearance, moving worm gear up and down, maximum ball clearance should be .00059 inch, if clearance is not as indicated, replace power control valve assembly.
2. Place cross shaft in suitable soft jawed vise, then using suitable dial indicator, measure thrust clearance, .0012–.0020 inch should be indicated, is not as indicated, adjust thrust clearance.
3. Adjust thrust clearance as follows:
   a. Using suitable hammer and chisel, remove locknut stake.
   b. Using tool No. 09630–00012, or equivalent, loosen locknut.
   c. Turn adjusting screw for correct thrust clearance, then tighten locknut.
   d. Stake locknut.
4. If required, replace needle roller bearings as follows:
   a. Using suitable screw driver, remove oil seal.
   b. Using suitable snap ring pliers, remove snap ring.
   c. Remove metal spacer, O-ring and Teflon ring.
   d. Using tool No. 09630-00012, or equivalent, press out bearings.
   e. Install new lower bearing, ensuring it is positioned .909 inch away from lower end of housing.
   f. Press in new upper bearing, ensuring top end is installed so it aligns with housing end surface.
   g. Install O-ring and metal spacer.
   h. Using suitable snap ring pliers, install snap ring.
   i. Form Teflon ring into heart shape and install with fingers.
   j. Using tool No. 09630–00012, or equivalent, form Teflon ring, Teflon ring must be formed before sector shaft installation or damage may occur.
   k. Drive in new oil seal.
5. If required, replace control valve Teflon rings as follows:
   a. Using suitable screwdriver, remove Teflon ring and O-ring. **Do not damage control valve.**
   b. Install new O-ring.
   c. Expand Teflon ring by hand, do not over expand Teflon ring.
   d. Install Teflon ring.
   e. Coat Teflon ring with power steering fluid and snug down with piston ring compressor for 5–7 minutes.
6. If required, replace union set as follows:
   a. Using suitable screw extractor, remove union seat.
   b. Using suitable plastic hammer and extension bar, tap in new union seat.

Assemble

1. Install O-rings to gear housing and valve body, mount gear housing to tool No. 09630–00012, or equivalent, then install tool to suitable soft jawed vise. Install worm gear valve body. **Do not damage Teflon ring.**
2. Hold power piston nut to prevent turning, then using tool No. 09616-00010, or equivalent, check worm gear preload, starting preload should be 2.6–4.8 inch lbs. If preload is not as indicated, replace worm gear assembly.
3. Install plunger, plunger guide and spring.
4. Install plunger guide nut O-ring, then using tool No. 09043-38100, or equivalent, install plunger guide nut and tighten specifications.
5. Install end cover O-ring, fully loosen adjusting screw, using suitable screwdriver, assemble cross shaft to end cover.
6. Set worm gear at center of gear housing.
7. Install and push cross shaft into gear housing so center teeth mesh together, install four cap bolts tightening to specifications in diagonal pattern.
8. Using tool No. 09616-00010, or equivalent, turn worm shaft to full lock in both directions to determine exact center, place matchmarks on worm shaft and housing to show neutral position.
9. Install tool No. 09616-0010, or equivalent with suitable torque meter to worm shaft, turn adjusting screw while measuring preload, total starting preload should be 4.3–8.3 inch lbs.
10. Install washer, then install and tighten locknut while holding adjusting screw.
11. Recheck total preload.

PREVIA

Disassemble

1. Connect a suitable holding fixture to gear housing, then place fixture in a suitable vise, **Fig. 44.**
2. Remove right and left turn pressure tubes, using tool No. 09633-00020.
3. Loosen locknut, then mark relative position between tie rod end and rack end. Remove tie rod end and locknut.
4. Remove rack boots clips and clamps, then the rack boots.
5. Unstake claw washers, then remove rack ends. Mark left and right ends respectively, then remove claw washer.
6. Remove rack guide spring cap locknut, then the rack guide spring cap.
7. Remove rack guide, spring, then the rack guide seat.
8. Mark relative position between valve housing and rack housing, then remove two attaching bolts. Remove control valve with housing, then the O-rings.
9. Remove cylinder end stopper nut, using tool No. 09631-20120.
10. Using tool No. 09612-24013 and a suitable press, remove rack and oil seal. Pull out steering rack with oil seal and rack end guide from cylinder.

Inspection & Repair

1. Inspect rack for runout, tooth wear and damage and replace as necessary. Maximum runout should be .012 inch.
2. Check needle roller bearing for wear or damage and replace cylinder housing assembly as necessary.
3. If necessary to replace control valve bearing oil seal, press out oil seal and bearing, using tool Nos. 09630-24013 and 09631-12020. Press in new oil seal, using tool Nos. 09631-12020 and 09630-24013 and a suitable press.
4. If necessary, replace rack teflon ring and O-ring coating with fluid and snug down.
5. If necessary to replace control valve Teflon ring, proceed as follows:
   a. Remove ring, using a suitable tool.
   b. Place new ring onto tool No. 09631-20070 to expand it.
   c. Install rings onto control valve, then ensure proper installation position.
   d. Apply a suitable lubricant to Teflon ring, then slide tapered end of tool over ring and seat ring.
6. If necessary to replace union seat, remove it, using a suitable screw extractor, then tap new union seat into place, using a hammer and suitable drift.

Assemble

During assembly, coat all moving parts, bearings, and bushings with molybdenum disulfide lithium based grease, and all O-rings and Teflon rings with power steering fluid.

1. Install spacer to rack housing, then using tool No. 09631-12020 tap in new seal horizontally.
2. Coat tool No. 09631-20111 with power steering fluid, then insert rack and tool into cylinder and remove tool.
3. Coat tool No. 09631-20111 with power steering fluid, then insert rack into opposite end and install oil seal by pushing over tool horizontally.
4. Secure rack onto vise, then install O-ring to end stopper and tap into rack housing using a block of wood and hammer.
5. Using tool No. 09631-20120 install stopper. Tighten to specifications, then stake rack housing.
6. Install new O-ring into control valve, then apply a suitable lubricant to Teflon ring and O-ring. Carefully push control valve into housing, then install bearing guide nut and tighten to specification.
7. Fill bottom of housing cavity with suitable grease, then align matchmarks and install control valve assembly onto rack housing.
8. Install rack guide, then rack guide spring and rack guide spring cap. tighten to specifications.
9. Adjust total preload as follows:
   a. Back off spring cap 30°, then rotate control valve shaft right and left two to three times.
   b. Loosen spring cap until rack guide compression spring is not functional.
   c. Tighten rack guide spring cap until preload of 6.1–11.3 inch lbs. is obtained.
10. Apply a suitable sealant to spring cap screws, then install and tighten locknut to specifications. Recheck total preload. Stake locknut and cap.
11. Install claw washers, rack and rack ends. Tighten rack ends to specifications. Stake claw washer.
12. Install rack boots, clamp and clips. Ensure rack hole is not clogged with grease, and that open end of clips face outward.
13. Install tie rods, aligning match marks, then adjust toe-in.
14. Install right and left turn pressure tubes, then tighten to specifications.

RAV4

Disassemble

1. Secure power steering gear in suitable soft-jawed vise.
2. Remove two turn pressure tubes using tool No. 09633-00020, or equivalent, **Fig. 45.**
3. Place matchmarks on tie rod end and rack end, then remove righthand and lefthand tie rod ends and lock nuts.
4. Remove righthand and lefthand clips, rack boots and clamps.
5. Using tool No. 09922-10010, or equivalent, remove rack ends and claw washers. Use a spanner to hold steering rack steady.
6. Place matchmarks on rack housing No. 1 bracket and rack housing.
7. Remove grommet from rack housing No. 1 bracket.
8. Remove rack guide spring cap lock nut using tool No. 09922-10010, or equivalent.
9. Remove rack guide spring cap, spring, guide and guide seat.
10. Remove rack housing cap.
11. Using tool No. 09616-00010, or equivalent to stop control valve shaft rotation, remove nut.
12. Remove dust cover.
13. Using snap ring pliers, remove snap ring from rack housing.
14. Using tool No. 09613-12010, or equivalent, remove control valve with oil seal and bearing.
15. Remove oil seal and bearing from control valve.
16. Remove bearing and spacer from rack housing.
17. Using tool No. 09612-10093, or equivalent, press out steering rack and end stopper.
18. Press oil seat from steering rack using tool Nos. 09950-60010 and 09950-70010, or equivalents.

Inspection

1. Using a dial indicator, check rack for runout. Maximum runout is .0118 inch.
2. Check rack teeth for wear and damage.
3. Check back surface for wear and damage.
4. Using a cylinder gauge and micrometer, measure inside diameter of bushing and outside diameter of valve assembly.
5. Maximum inside diameter of bushing should be 1.11 inches. Minimum outside diameter of valve assembly should be 1.0925 inches.

Assemble

1. Using tool Nos. 09950-60010 and 09950-70010, or equivalents, install new oil seal.
2. Install tool No. 09631-16020, or equivalent to steering rack, then install rack into rack housing and remove tool.
3. Install oil seal into rack housing.
4. Install cylinder end stopper and new snap ring to rack housing.
5. Install control valve assembly.
6. Using tool No. 09612-22011, or equivalent, press in new bearing.
7. Install dust cover, spacer and new bearing into rack housing.
8. Using tool No. 09616-00010, or equivalent to stop control valve shaft rotation, install lock nut and tighten to specifications.
9. Install rack housing cap with suitable sealant.
10. Install rack guide seat, rack guide, spring and spring cap.
11. Adjust preload as follows:
    a. Using hexagon wrench, **torque** rack guide spring cap to 18 ft. lbs., then turn cap back 12°.
    b. Temporarily install righthand and lefthand rack ends to prevent steering rack teeth from damaging oil seal lip.
    c. Using tool No. 09616-00010, or equivalent, turn control valve shaft left and right a few times.
    d. Loosen rack guide spring cap until rack guide spring is not functioning.
    e. Using tool No. 09616-00010, or equivalent and a hexagon wrench, tighten cap until preload is 6.9–11.3 inch lbs.
12. Install rack guide spring cap lock nut and tighten to specification.
13. Remove righthand and lefthand rack ends.
14. Install new washer and lefthand and righthand rack ends.
15. Install grommet to rack housing No. 1 bracket. Align matchmarks on bracket and housing.
16. Install righthand and lefthand rack boots, clamps and clips.
17. Install righthand and lefthand tie rod ends and lock nuts. Align matchmarks on tie rod end and rack.
18. Install turn pressure tubes and tighten to specifications.

SUPRA

Disassemble

1. Position rack in suitable soft jawed vise.
2. Using suitable tool, remove turn tubes and O-rings, **Fig. 46.**
3. Loosen tie rod end locknut, then place installation alignment marks on tie rod end and rack end, remove tie rod end.
4. Remove back boots. **Do not damage rack boots or rack housing.**
5. Unstake claw washers, then using suitable tool, remove rack ends, mark

right and left rack ends and remove claw washers.
6. Using suitable tool, remove rack guide spring cap locknut.
7. Using suitable tool, remove rack guide spring cap.
8. Remove rack guide spring, rack guide and seat.
9. Remove rack housing gap.
10. Using suitable tool to hold control valve, remove self locking nut.
11. Remove control valve housing dust cover, place installation alignment marks on valve and rack housing, remove valve housing, valve and rack housing gasket.
12. Tap out control valve and oil seal.
13. Remove lower bearing and spacer.
14. Using suitable tool, remove snap ring, then using suitable tool, press rack until end stopper slightly touches press block, pull out rack with cylinder end stopper, two spacers and oil seal.
15. Using suitable tool, tap cylinder housing oil seal and spacer.

Inspection & Repair

1. Using suitable dial indicator, inspect rack for runout and tooth wear or damage. Maximum runout is .012 inch, if measurement is not as indicated or damaged, replace rack.
2. If required, replace rack housing oil seal and bearing.
3. If required, replace control valve housing oil seal and bearing.
4. If required, replace rack bushing oil seal, using suitable tool, remove oil seal, coat new oil seal with power steering fluid, then install.
5. If required, replace Teflon ring and O-ring as follows:
   a. Remove Teflon ring and O-ring. **Do not damage steering rack.**
   b. Coat new O-ring with power steering fluid, then install.
   c. Coat new Teflon ring with power steering fluid.
   d. Install Teflon ring then expand ring by hand.
   e. Install expanded ring to steering rack and snug down by hand to fit tightly in groove.
6. If required, replace control valve Teflon ring as follows:
   a. Using suitable screwdriver, remove Teflon ring. **Do not damage control valve.**
   b. Install new rings to tool No. 09631-20070, or equivalent, then expand rings.
   c. Install expanded rings to control valve and snug down by hand.
   d. Coat ring with power steering fluid, then carefully slide tapered end of tool No. 09631-20081, or equivalent, over rings to seat rings.
7. If required, replace hydraulic reaction chamber Teflon rings and O-rings as follows:
   a. Remove Teflon ring and O-rings. **Do not damage control valve.**
   b. Install new O-rings.
   c. Expand Teflon rings by hand. **Do not over expand Teflon rings.**
   d. Install expanded Teflon rings to control valve.
   e. Coat Teflon rings with power steering fluid and snug down by hand.
   f. Slide tapered end of tool No. 09631-32020, or equivalent, over Teflon rings to seat rings.
8. If required, replace pressure control valve.

Assemble

1. Coat cylinder housing oil seal lip with power steering fluid, then using suitable tool, tap in cylinder housing oil seal and spacer.
2. Install tool No. 09631-20102 equivalent to rack, scrape burrs from rack teeth end and burnish as required, coat tool with power steering fluid, the install rack to cylinder, remove tool.
3. Install cylinder end stopper, oil seal and spacers as follows:
   a. Apply suitable vinyl tape to steering rack end to prevent oil seal lip damage.
   b. Push oil seal into cylinder without tilting seal.
   c. Install two spacers.
   d. Using tool No. 09620-30010, or equivalent, drive in cylinder end stopper.
   e. Using suitable snap ring pliers, install snap ring.
4. Install tool No. 09631-12070 or 09631-12071 equivalent to cylinder housing, apply 15.75 inch Hg vacuum for about 30 seconds, ensure no change in vacuum, if vacuum changes, inspect oil seal installation.
5. Coat Teflon rings with power steering fluid, then install control valve into housing.
6. Coat O-ring with power steering fluid and install, align valve and rack housing matchmarks, install attaching bolts and tighten to specifications.
7. Install lower bearing and spacer.
8. Using suitable tool, install new self locking nut and tighten to specifications.
9. Apply Loctite 242, or equivalent to two or three rack housing cap threads, then install cap, using suitable center punch, stake housing in two places.
10. Install rack guide seat, rack guide and spring.
11. Apply Loctite 242, or equivalent to two or three spring cap threads, then install spring cap, tighten to specifications.
12. Return rack guide spring cap 15°, turn control valve shaft right and left one or two times, loosen spring cap until rack guide compression spring is not functioning, then using suitable tool, tighten rack guide spring cap until turning preload of 7.8–10.4 ft. lbs. is indicated.
13. Apply Loctite 242, or equivalent to two or three rack guide spring cap locknut threads, then install locknut, tighten to specifications, then recheck preload as outlined in step 13.
14. Install dust cover, install claw washer and rack ends, then using suitable brass bar and hammer, stake claw washer.
15. Ensure tube hole is not clogged, then install rack boots.
16. Install tie rod ends, align matchmarks.
17. Install right and left turn pressure tubes.

TERCEL

Disassemble

1. Place steering gear in suitable vice, then remove pressure lines using suitable tool, **Fig. 47.**
2. Remove the air control valve.
3. Mark position of tie-rod and rack end for reference during assembly, then remove tie-rods.
4. Remove rack boots, then unstake claw washer.
5. Using suitable tool, remove rack ends, then the claw washer.
6. Using suitable tool, remove rack guide spring cap locknut.
7. Remove rack guide spring cap, using suitable tool.
8. Remove rack guide spring, rack guide and rack housing cap.
9. Using suitable tool, remove self locking nut.
10. Remove control valve dust cover, then the snap ring. Using suitable tool, remove the control valve with oil seal and bearing, then the oil seal from the control valve.
11. Using suitable tool, remove upper bearing from the control valve.
12. Using suitable tool, turn the cylinder end stopper clockwise until the wire end comes out of the opening, then turn the cylinder and stopper counterclockwise and remove wire, then pull out cylinder end stopper.
13. Remove rack bushing and rack, then the cylinder side oil seal and spacer.

Inspection & Repair

1. Check rack for damage, wear or excessive runout. If runout exceeds .012 inch, replace rack assembly.
2. If necessary replace cylinder control valve lower bearing and oil seal as follows:
   a. Drive out bearing, then using suitable tool, remove oil seal. Using suitable tool, install new oil seal.
   b. Install new bearing with rack housing cap, tighten cap to specifications, then remove rack housing cap.
3. If necessary, replace rack bushing oil seal by prying out the oil seal, then using a 24 mm socket wrench, drive in a new oil seal.
4. If necessary, replace rack Teflon ring and O-ring, coating Teflon ring with power steering fluid.
5. If necessary, replace control valve Teflon ring as follows:
   a. Pry off Teflon ring with suitable tool.
   b. Install Teflon ring onto suitable tool, then install Teflon rings to control valve and snug down with fingers.
   c. Coat ring with power steering fluid, then slide tapered end of tool over the Teflon ring to seat ring.
6. If necessary, remove control valve housing union seat with suitable screw

extractor. Drive new seat fully into position using an extension bar and hammer.

Assemble

During assembly, coat all moving parts, bearings and bushings with molybdenum disulfide lithium base grease, and all O-rings and Teflon rings with power steering fluid.

1. Install rack housing cylinder side oil seal and spacer by coating new oil seal with power steering fluid, then install oil seal and spacer to suitable tool, and drive into cylinder.
2. Install suitable tool onto rack assembly, coat tool with power steering fluid, then remove tool.
3. Install new O-ring onto the rack bushing, then install rack bushing in the rack cylinder.
4. Push cylinder end stopper into rack cylinder until wire installation hole appears. Insert a new wire end into hole, then using suitable tool, turn cylinder end stopper clockwise until wire end disappears.
5. Ensure cylinder is air tight. Connect suitable tool, to union of cylinder housing, then apply 15.75 inches Hg vacuum for at least 30 seconds. There should be no drop in vacuum.
6. Install control valve assembly as follows:
   a. Push control valve into housing.
   b. Using suitable tool, press in the upper bearing.
   c. Using suitable tool press in oil seal until snug with bearing.
   d. Install snap ring, then dust cover.
7. Using suitable tool, install self-locknut into lower control valve housing. Tighten nut to specifications.
8. Apply Loctite 242, or equivalent to rack housing cap, then install cap, tighten to specifications. Using a center punch, stake the housing cap at opposite ends of cap.
9. Install rack guide and rack guide spring.
10. Apply Loctite 242, or equivalent, to spring cap locknut, then install locknut and tighten specifications. Recheck preload as specified in previous step.
11. Install new rack end claw washers, then rack ends. Tighten rack ends to specifications.
12. Stake claw washers into position, then ensuring that tube hole is not clogged with grease, install rack boots, clamps and clips. Ensure clip ends face outward.
13. Install tie-rod ends, ensuring marks made during disassembly are aligned. After adjusting toe-in, tighten locknuts to specifications.
14. Install new pressure line O-rings, then the pressure lines. Tighten to specifications.
15. Install air control valve. Tighten to specifications.

TIGHTENING SPECIFICATIONS

Year	Component	Torque/Ft. Lbs.
4WD PICKUP & 4RUNNER		
1993–96	Adjusting Stay To Pump Housing (VZN Series)	30
	Air Control Valve To Rear Housing	27
	Ball Guide Clamp Setscrew	26②
	Bleeder Plug	34
	Cross Shaft Adjusting Screw Locknut	34
	Cross Shaft End Cover To Gear Housing	34
	Cross Shaft End Cover To Gear Housing	72②
	Front Housing To rear Housing	34
	Gear Housing To Frame	105
	Idler Arm Bracket To Frame	105
	Idler Arm To Idler Arm Bracket	135
	Intermediate Shaft To Worm Shaft	26
	Knuckle Arm To Steering Knuckle	56
	Pitman Arm To Relay Rod	67
	Pitman Arm To Sector Shaft	130
	Plunger Guide Nut	69①
	Pressure Line To Gear Housing	33
	Pressure Port Union To Rear Housing	51
	Pressure Tube	33
	Pressure Tube To Pressure Port Union	27
	PS Pump Pulley To Rotor Shaft	32
	PS Pump To Adjusting Stay (VZN Series)	30
	PS Pump To Bracket (RN Series)	29
	Relay Rod To Idler Arm	43
	Relay Rod To Steering Damper	43
	Reservoir Tank To Pump Housing (VZN, 12 mm)	9

Continued

TIGHTENING SPECIFICATIONS—Continued

Year	Component	Torque/Ft. Lbs.
4WD PICKUP & 4RUNNER		
1993–96	Reservoir Tank To Pump Housing (VZN, 14 mm)	30
	Return Hose Clamp (RN Series)	13①
	Return Hose Clamp (VZN Series)	35①
	Return Line To Gear Housing	36
	Return Tube (Except Union Bolt)	36
	Return Tube (Union Bolt)	34
	Solenoid Valve Seat Bolt (PPS)	7
	Suction Port Union To Rear Housing	9
	Tie Rod End Clamp Bolt	19
	Tie Rod To Knuckle Arm	67
	Tie Rod To Relay Rod	67
	Union Bolt To Pressure Tube	34
	Worm Bearing Adjusting Screw Locknut	31
	Worm Gear Valve Body To Gear Housing	34
	Worm Gear Valve Body To Gear Housing	45②
TACOMA, T100 & 2WD PICKUP		
1993–96	Air Control Valve To Rear Housing	27
	Bleeder Plug	34
	Control Valve Housing	13
	Cross Shaft Adjusting Screw Locknut	34
	Cross Shaft End Cover To Gear Housing	34
	Front Housing To Rear Housing	34
	Gear Housing To Body	87
	Idler Arm Bracket To Frame	87
	Idler Arm To Idler Arm Bracket	58
	Knuckle Arm To Steering Knuckle	80
	Pitman Arm To Relay Rod	67
	Pitman Arm To Sector Shaft	130
	Plunger Guide Nut	69①
	Pressure Port Union To Rear Housing	51
	Pressure Tube To Pressure Port Union	27
	PS Pump Pulley To Rotor Shaft	32
	PS Pump To Bracket	29
	Rack Ends	44
	Rack Guide Spring Cap locknut	35
	Rack Housing Cap	51
	Relay Rod To Idler Arm	43
	Return Hose Clamp (RN Series)	13①
	Return Hose Clamp (VZN Series)	35①
	Self-Locking Nut	18
	Spring Cap	18
	Steering Damper To Frame	9
	Steering Damper To Relay Rod	43
	Suction Port Union To Rear Housing	9
	Tie Rod End Clamp Bolt	19
	Tie Rod Ends	41
	Tie Rod To Knuckle Arm	67
	Tie Rod To Relay Rod	67

Continued

TIGHTENING SPECIFICATIONS—Continued

Year	Component	Torque/Ft. Lbs.
TACOMA, T100 & 2WD PICKUP		
1993–96	Turn Pressure Tubes	8
	Worm Gear Valve Body To Gear Housing	34
AVALON & CAMRY		
1993–96	Control Valve Assy (3VZ-FE)	43
	Control Valve Housing To Rack Housing	13
	Control Valve Self-Locking Nut	18
	Control Valve Shaft To Universal Joint	26
	Front Housing To Rear Housing (3VZ-FE)	34
	Gear Housing To Sub Frame	134
	Locknut	41
	Pressure & Return Tube To Gear Housing	18
	Pressure Port Union To Pump Housing (3VZ-FE)	62
	Pressure Port Union To Pump Housing (5S-FE)	51
	Pressure Tube To Pressure Port Union (3VZ-FE)	33
	PS Pump Adjusting Bolt (5S-FE)	29
	PS Pump Bolt (3VZ-FE)	32
	PS Pump Through Bolt (5S-FE)	32
	PS Pump To Pressure Tube (5S-FE)	38
	Pump Pulley To Pump Shaft (3VZ-FE)	32
	Pump Pulley To Pump Shaft (5S-FE)	32
	Rack Housing Cap	43
	Rack To Rack End	53
	Suction Port Union To Pump Housing (3VZ-FE)	9
	Suction Port Union To Pump Housing (5S-FE)	9
	Tie Rod End Locknut	54
	Tie Rod End To Steering Knuckle	36
	Turn Pressure Tube Union Nut	8
CELICA		
1993–96	Air Control Valve To Pump Housing	27
	Bearing Guide Locknut	41
	Center Member To Body	38
	Control Valve Housing To Rack Housing	23
	Control Valve Shaft To Universal Joint	26
	Drive Pulley Nut	32
	Engine Mounting To Center Member (4A-FE)	47
	Engine Mounting To Center Member (5S-FE, 3S-GTE)	54
	Engine Mounting To Insulator	64
	Engine To Engine Mounting	57
	Exhaust Front Pipe To Center Pipe	32
	Exhaust Front Pipe To Manifold	46
	Gear Housing To Body	43

Continued

TIGHTENING SPECIFICATIONS—Continued

Year	Component	Torque/Ft. Lbs.
CELICA		
1993–96	Gear Housing To Pressure Line	33
	Gear Housing To Return Line	33
	Lower Crossmember (Center)	29
	Lower Crossmember (RH & LH Sides)	112
	Pressure Port Union To Front Housing	51
	Pressure Tube Joint Bolt	38
	Pressure Tube Union Nut (5S-FE & 3S-GTE)	27
	Propeller Shaft To Intermediate Shaft	54
	PS Pump To Bracket (4A-FE)	29
	PS Pump To Bracket (Lower, 5S-FE, 3S-GTE)	29
	PS Pump To Bracket (Upper, 5S-FE, 3S-GTE)	32
	Rack Guide Spring Cap Locknut	41
	Rack To Rack End	53
	Reservoir Tank & Housing, 12mm (4A-FE)	9
	Reservoir Tank & Housing, 14mm (4A-FE)	9
	Stabilizer Bar Bracket	13
	Stabilizer Bar To Link	26
	Suction Port Union To Pump Housing (5S-FE)	9
	Tie Rod End Locknut	41
	Tie Rod End To Knuckle Arm	36
	Tube Clamp Set Bolt	9
	Turn Pressure Tube To Gear Housing	14
	Union Bolt (4A-FE)	51
COROLLA		
1993–96	Control Valve Self-Locking Nut	18
	Control Valve Shaft To Universal Joint	26
	Drive Pulley To Rotor Shaft	32
	Gear Housing Bracket To Body	43
	Power Steering Pump Installation Bolt	32
	Pressure & Return Tube To Gear Housing	9
	Pressure Port Union To Pump Housing	51
	Pressure Tube To Pressure Port Union	40
	Rack Guided Spring Cap Locknut	43
	Rack Housing Cap	43
	Rack To Rack End	61
	Reservoir Installation Bolt	30
	Steering Main Shaft To Universal Joint	26
	Tie Rod End Locknut	41
	Tie Rod End To Steering Knuckle	36
	Turn Pressure Tube Union Nut	9

Continued

TIGHTENING SPECIFICATIONS—Continued

Year	Component	Torque/Ft. Lbs.
LAND CRUISER		
1993–96	Adjusting Stay To Bracket	29
	Cross Shaft Adjusting Screw Set Nut	34
	Cross Shaft End Cover Lock Bolt	45
	Damper Hinge To Body	29
	Gear Housing To Body	105
	Gear Housing To Pitman Arm	130
	Pitman Arm To Relay Rod	67
	Plunger Guide Nut	15
	Pressure & Return Tube	33
	Pressure Port Union	51
	Pressure Tube To PS Pump	27
	PS Pump To Adjusting Stay	29
	PS Pump To Bracket	33
	Pulley Set Nut	32
	Relay Rod To Knuckle Arm	67
	Relay Rod To Steering Damper	54
	Reservoir Set Bolt (12 mm Bolt)	9
	Reservoir Set Bolt (14 mm Bolt)	30
	Steering Damper To Damper Hinge	54
	Tie Or Relay Rod Clamp	27
	Tie Rod To Knuckle Arm	67
	Universal Joint	25
	Worm Gear Valve Body Set Bolt	45
MR2		
1993–95	Control Valve Housing To Rack Housing	13
	Control Valve Shaft Self-Locking Nut	18
	Gear Housing Bracket To Body	32
	Pressure Tube Union Bolt	36
	Pressure Tube Union Nut	27
	PS Pump To Crossmember	19
	Rack Guide Spring Cap Locknut	25
	Rack Housing Cap	43
	Rack To Rack End	38
	Rear Pump Stay To Body	13
	Rear Pump Stay To PS Pump	13
	Return Tube	18
	Tie Rod End Locknut	41
	Tie Rod End To Steering Knuckle	36
	Turn Pressure Tube To Housing	8
	Universal Joint Bolt	26
PASEO		
1993–96	Air Control Valve To Gear Housing	22
	Column Hole Cover To Body	43①
	Control Valve Self-Locking Nut	43
	Control Valve Shaft To Universal Joint	21
	Cylinder End Stopper	43
	Drive Pulley To Rotor Shaft	32
	Engine Rear Mounting Bracket To Body	58
	Engine Rear Mounting Bracket To Transaxle	35
	Exhaust Pipe To Converter	32
	Exhaust Pipe To Exhaust Manifold	46

Continued

TIGHTENING SPECIFICATIONS—Continued

Year	Component	Torque/Ft. Lbs.
PASEO		
1993–96	Gear Housing Bracket To Body	43
	Pressure & Return Tube Clamp To Gear Housing	9
	Pressure & Return Tube To Gear Housing	33
	Pressure Port Union To Pump Housing	51
	Pressure Tube To Pressure Port Union	40
	PS Pump Installation Bolt	32
	Rack Guide Spring Cap Locknut	27
	Rack Housing Cap	43
	Rack To Rack End	38
	Steering Main Shaft To Universal Joint	21
	Suction Port Union To Pump Housing	9
	Tie Rod End Locknut	35
	TIe Rod End To Steering Knuckle	36
	Transaxle Case To Control Cable Bracket (M/T)	8
	Turn Pressure Tube Union Nut	14
PREVIA		
1993–96	Bearing Guide Nut	18
	Control Valve Housing To Rack Housing	13
	Cylinder End Stopper	58
	Front Differential To Body	54
	Front Differential To Driveshaft	50
	Front Differential To Propeller Shaft	31
	Gear Housing Set Bolt	58
	No. 2 Equipment Drive Housing Insulator	18
	No. 2 Equipment Drive Housing Mount	13
	Pressure & Return Lines	33
	PS Pump Bracket To Stay	27
	PS Pump Front To Rear Housing	12
	PS Pump Pressure Port Union	51
	PS Pump Set Bolt	35
	PS Pump Suction Port Union	9
	PS Pump Union	36
	Rack Guide Spring Cap Locknut	41
	Return & Pressure Line To Gear Housing	33
	Steering Rack To Rack End	65
	Tie Rod End To Knuckle	36
	Tie Rod End Locknut	67
	Torque Shaft To Pinion Shaft	26
	Turn Pressure Tubes (Control Valve Side)	14
	Turn Pressure Tubes (Rack Housing Guide)	22
	Universal Joint	26

Continued

TIGHTENING SPECIFICATIONS—Continued

Year	Component	Torque/Ft. Lbs.
RAV4		
1996	Air Control Valve	27
	Drive Belt Adjusting Bolt	32
	Pressure Feed Tube Union Bolt	32
	Pump Bracket Set Bolt	32
	Pump Suction Port Union Set Bolt	9
	Rack Guide Spring Cap	18
	Rack Guide Spring Cap Lock Nut	33
	Rack Housing No. 1 Bracket Set Bolt	45
	Tie Rod End Lock Nut	41
SUPRA		
1993–96	Air Control Valve To Pump Housing	27
	Bearing Guide Locknut (Less PPS)	41
	Control Valve Housing To Rack Housing (Less PPS)	23
	Control Valve Housing To Rack Housing (w/PPS)	13
	Control Valve Self-Locking Nut (w/PPS)	43
	Control Valve Shaft To Universal Joint	24
	Drive Belt Adjust Stay Bolt (12 mm Bolt)	13
	Drive Belt Adjust Stay Bolt (14 mm Bolt)	30
	Front Housing To Rear Housing	34
	Gear Housing To Body	56
	Gear Housing To Pressure Line (Less PPS)	36
	Gear Housing To Pressure Line (w/PPS)	38
	Gear Housing To Return Line (Less PPS)	33
	Gear Housing To Return Line (w/PPS)	38
	Pressure Control Valve To Control Valve Housing (w/PPS)	13
	Pressure Port Union To Pump Housing	51
	PS Pump Pulley To Rotor Shaft	32
	PS Pump To Adjust Bracket	27
	PS Pump To Bracket	43
	PS Pump To Pressure Tube	36
	Rack Guide Spring Cap Locknut	41
	Rack Housing Cap (w/PPS)	51
	Rack To Rack End	68
	Suction Port Union To Pump Housing	9
	Tie Rod End Clamp Bolt	14
	Tie Rod End To Steering Knuckle	36
	Turn Pressure Tube To Rack Housing	17
	Turn Pressure Tube To Valve Housing (Less PPS)	14
	Turn Pressure Tube To Valve Housing (w/PPS)	25

Continued

TIGHTENING SPECIFICATIONS—Continued

Year	Component	Torque/Ft. Lbs.
TERCEL		
1993–96	Air Control Valve To Gear Housing	22
	Column Hole Cover To Body	43①
	Column Valve Shaft To Universal Joint	21
	Control Valve Self-Locking Nut	43
	Cylinder End Stopper	43
	Engine Rear Mount Bracket To Body	58
	Engine Rear Mount Bracket To Transaxle	35
	Exhaust Pipe To Converter	32
	Exhaust Pipe To Exhaust Manifold	46
	Gear Housing Bracket To Body	43
	Pressure & Return Tube Clamp To Gear Housing	9
	Pressure & Return Tube To Gear Housing	33
	PS Pump Drive Pulley To Rotor Shaft	32
	PS Pump Mounting Bolt	32
	PS Pump Pressure Port Union To Housing	51
	PS Pump Pressure Tube To Pressure Port Union	40
	PS Pump Suction Port Union To Housing	9
	Rack Guide Spring Cap Locknut	27
	Rack Housing Cap	43
	Rack To Rack End	38
	Steering Main Shaft To Universal Joint	21
	Tie Rod End Locknut	35
	Tie Rod End To Steering Knuckle	36
	Transaxle Case To Control Cable Bracket (M/T)	8
	Turn Pressure Tube Union Nut	14

① — Inch lbs.

② — T100.

Disc Brakes

INDEX

Page No.
Front Disc Brakes 48-130
Rear Disc & Parking Brakes 48-137

Front Disc Brakes

INDEX

Page No.
Brake Pad Service 48-130
Avalon, Camry, Corolla & Celica 48-131
Land Cruiser, 4WD Tacoma, 4WD Pickup, 1993–95 4Runner & T100 48-130
Paseo 48-130
Pickup & 1993–95 4Runner w/FS17 & F18 Type Disc, 2WD 48-130
Pickup & 1993–95 4Runner w/PD60 & PD66 Type Disc & T100, 2WD 48-130
Previa & Supra 48-131
RAV4 48-131
Tacoma, 2WD 48-130
Tercel 48-131
1996 4Runner 48-131
Caliper Service 48-131
Avalon, Camry, Corolla & Celica 48-133
Land Cruiser, 4WD Pickup, 1993–95 4Runner & T100 48-132
Paseo 48-131
Pickup & 1993–95 4Runner w/FS17 & F18 Type Disc, 2WD 48-132
Pickup & 1993–95 4Runner w/PD60 & PD66 Type Disc & T100, 2WD 48-132
Previa & Supra 48-133
RAV4 48-133
Tacoma 2WD 48-132
Tercel 48-131
1996 4Runner 48-133
Disc Brake Specifications 48-134
Tightening Specifications 48-135

BRAKE PAD SERVICE

TERCEL

1. Raise and support front of vehicle, then remove wheel and tire assembly.
2. Remove two caliper mounting bolts, then remove caliper. **Do not allow caliper to hang by brake hose.**
3. Remove inner pad, then remove outer pad and anti-squeal shim(s), **Fig. 1.**
4. Remove anti-rattle spring and pad guide plate.
5. Remove pad support plate and anti-squeal shim(s).
6. Reverse procedure to install.

PASEO

1. Raise and support vehicle, then remove wheel and tire assembly.
2. Reinstall two wheel lug nuts to retain disc.
3. Remove two attaching bolts and the caliper from torque plate, **Fig. 2,** then suspend from chassis.
4. Remove brake pads, anti-squeal shims, pad wear indicator plates and support plates.
5. Reverse procedure to install, **torque** caliper attaching bolts to 18 ft. lbs.

TACOMA, 2WD

1. Check that pad thickness is no less than .039 inch. Replace pads if thinner.
2. Raise and support vehicle and remove front wheel.
3. Remove caliper pin on subpin side, **Fig. 3.**
4. Pivot caliper up and support, leaving brake hose connected.
5. Remove brake pads, anti-squeal shim(s), pad wear indicator plate and 4 support plates.
6. Reverse procedure to install.

PICKUP & 1993-95 4RUNNER w/FS17 & F18 TYPE DISC, 2WD

1. Check that pad thickness is no less than .039 inch. Replace pads if thinner.
2. Raise and support vehicle and remove front wheel.
3. Remove caliper pin on subpin side, **Fig. 4.**
4. Pivot caliper up and support, leaving brake hose connected.
5. Remove brake pads, anti-squeal shim(s) and 4 support plates.
6. Reverse procedure to install.

PICKUP & 1993-95 4RUNNER w/PD60 & PD66 TYPE DISC & T100, 2WD

1. Raise and support vehicle and remove tire and wheel assembly.
2. Remove caliper attaching bolts, **Figs. 5 and 6,** and the caliper, supporting caliper out of way so that brake hose is not stretched.
3. Remove two anti-rattle springs, brake pads, anti-squeal shims and the four support plates.
4. Reverse procedure to install, **torquing** caliper mounting bolts to 29 ft. lbs.

LAND CRUISER, 4WD PICKUP, 4WD TACOMA, 1993-95 4RUNNER & T100

1. Raise and support front of vehicle, then remove tire and wheel assembly.
2. Remove clip and hole pins, **Fig. 7.**
3. Remove anti-rattle spring and shim(s) if equipped, then remove brake pads.
4. Lubricate caliper housing with suitable brake grease at pad contact points.
5. Reverse procedure to install.

Disc, Replace

1. Remove caliper as outlined under "Caliper, Replace."
2. Remove cap and snap ring, **Fig. 8,** then remove cone washers with tapered punch.
3. Insert suitable length bolts into flange bolt holes, then tighten bolts evenly and remove flanges.
4. Remove free wheel hub cover and snap ring, then remove nut, spring washer and cone washer with suitable tapered punch.
5. Remove free wheel hub body and gasket.
6. Remove locknut, lock washer and adjusting nut.
7. Remove axle hub and brake disc as an assembly.
8. Remove oil seal and inner bearing from hub.
9. Reverse procedure to install. **Torque** adjusting nut to 43 ft. lbs., then back off nut. **Torque** nut to 18 ft. lbs. Using

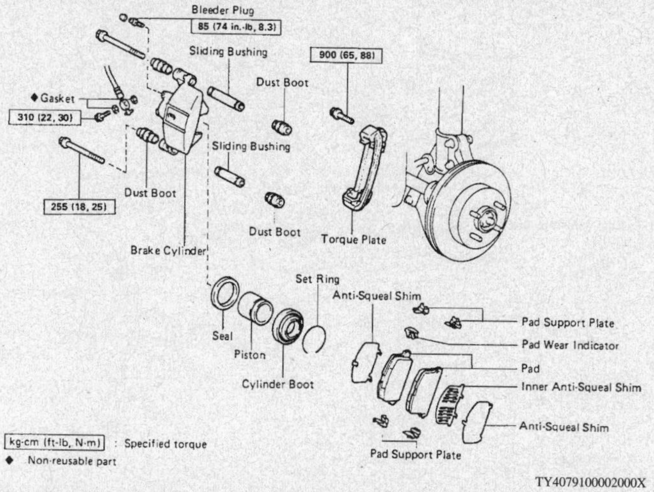
Bleeder Plug
85 (74 in.-lb, 8.3)
Sliding Bushing
900 (65, 88)
Dust Boot
◆Gasket
310 (22, 30)
Sliding Bushing
Dust Boot
255 (18, 25)
Dust Boot
Torque Plate
Brake Cylinder
Set Ring
Anti-Squeal Shim
Seal
Piston
Cylinder Boot
Pad Support Plate
Pad Wear Indicator
Pad
Inner Anti-Squeal Shim
Anti-Squeal Shim
Pad Support Plate
kg-cm (ft-lb, N·m) : Specified torque
◆ Non-reusable part
TY4079100002000X

Fig. 1 Exploded view of disc brake assembly. Tercel

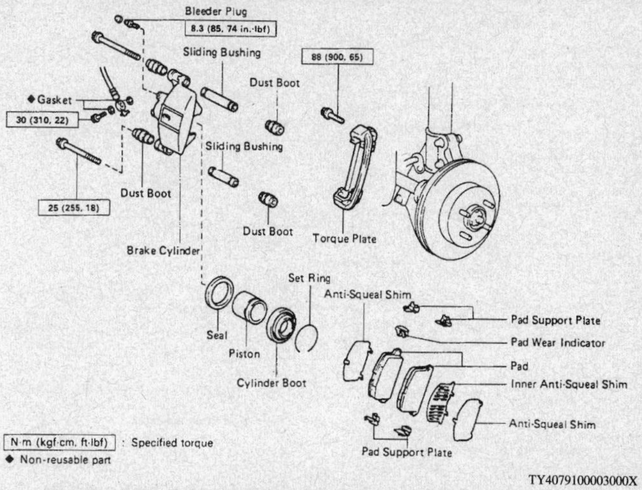
Bleeder Plug
8.3 (85, 74 in.-lbf)
Sliding Bushing
88 (900, 65)
Dust Boot
◆Gasket
30 (310, 22)
Sliding Bushing
Dust Boot
25 (255, 18)
Dust Boot
Torque Plate
Brake Cylinder
Set Ring
Anti-Squeal Shim
Seal
Piston
Cylinder Boot
Pad Support Plate
Pad Wear Indicator
Pad
Inner Anti-Squeal Shim
Anti-Squeal Shim
Pad Support Plate
N·m (kgf·cm, ft·lbf) : Specified torque
◆ Non-reusable part
TY4079100003000X

Fig. 2 Exploded view of disc brake assembly. Paseo

spring scale attached to hub bolt, check that preload is 1.4–12.6. Install lockwasher and locknut, if equipped. **Torque** locknut to 35 ft. lbs., and recheck preload. Secure lockwasher by bending one tab inward and one tab outward.

1996 4RUNNER

1. Raise and support vehicle, then remove front wheel.
2. Inspect brake pad lining thickness. Minimum thickness should be .039 inch.
3. Remove pad retaining clip and two pins, **Fig. 9.**
4. Remove anti-rattle spring, brake pads and four anti-squeal shims.
5. Reverse procedure to install.

RAV4

1. Raise and support vehicle, then remove front wheel.
2. Inspect brake pad lining thickness. Minimum thickness should be .039 inch.
3. Lift caliper and remove flexible hose bracket, **Fig. 10.**
4. Hold sliding pin on bottom and loosen installation bolt.
5. Remove installation bolt.
6. Lift and suspend caliper with brake hose attached.
7. Remove brake pads, anti-squeal shims and pad support plates.
8. Reverse procedure to install. If caliper pistons are difficult to push in, loosen bleeder plug and let some brake fluid escape.

PREVIA & SUPRA

1. Raise and support front of vehicle, then remove tire and wheel assembly. Temporarily install lug nuts to hold rotor in place.
2. Remove brake hose bracket attaching bolts from steering knuckle, if necessary.
3. While holding the sliding bushing, remove cylinder installation bolt, **Figs. 11 and 12.**
4. Rotate caliper upwards and remove. Suspend caliper with wire using caution not to stretch brake hose.
5. Remove pads and anti-squeal shim(s).
6. Remove anti-rattle springs, support and pad guide plates.
7. Install new anti-rattle springs, support and pad guide plates.
8. Siphon a small amount of fluid from master cylinder reservoir.
9. Slowly force piston into caliper bore.
10. Install new pads and anti-squeal shim(s). **If pads are equipped with wear indicators, install outside pad so indicator is at top side of caliper.**
11. Rotate caliper into place, then install cylinder installation bolt and **torque** to 27 ft. lbs.
12. Install brake hose bracket attaching bolts. **Torque** attaching bolts to 14 ft. lbs.
13. Fill master cylinder, then pump brake pedal until a firm pedal is obtained.

AVALON, CAMRY, COROLLA & CELICA

1. Remove front wheel and reinstall lug nuts to locate disc temporarily.
2. Check that brake pad thickness is at least .039 inch (1 mm). Replace pads if too thin.
3. Remove caliper from torque plate and suspend so brake hose is not under tension. Do not disconnect brake hose.
4. Refer to **Fig. 13** and remove the following components:
   a. Brake pads.
   b. Anti-squeal shims.
   c. Pad wear indicator plates.
   d. Support plates.
   e. Anti-squeal springs.
5. Install new pad support plates.
6. Install new pad wear indicator plates on each pad with arrow pointing in direction of disc rotation.
7. Install new anti-squeal shims on each pad.
8. Install each brake pad on to each support plate.
9. Install anti-squeal springs.
10. Siphon out a small amount of brake fluid from reservoir and press caliper piston in with hammer handle. Change one brake pad at a time to prevent chance of opposite piston from flying out.
11. Install caliper taking care not to wedge dust boot.
12. Install wheel and check that brake fluid level is at MAX line.

CALIPER SERVICE

TERCEL

Caliper, Replace

1. Raise and support front of vehicle, then remove wheel and tire assembly.
2. Disconnect brake hydraulic line from frame bracket and from caliper using line wrench tool No. 09751-36011, or equivalent.
3. Remove caliper mounting bolts, then the caliper.
4. Reverse procedure to install and bleed brake system.

Overhaul

1. Remove caliper as outlined under "Caliper, Replace. "
2. Remove anti-squeal shim(s) and cylinder boot set ring, **Fig. 1.**
3. Remove cylinder boot, then remove piston using compressed air.
4. Remove piston seal, caliper sliding bolt, dust boot, collar and union.
5. Install union onto caliper and tighten to specification.
6. Apply rubber grease to piston seal, then install piston seal onto piston.
7. Apply rubber grease to piston, then install piston into caliper.
8. Install cylinder boot and set ring, then lubricate collar and dust boot and assemble onto caliper.
9. Install caliper sliding bolt and anti-squeal shim(s).

PASEO

Caliper, Replace

Remove caliper as in "Brake Pad Service" and remove brake line union.

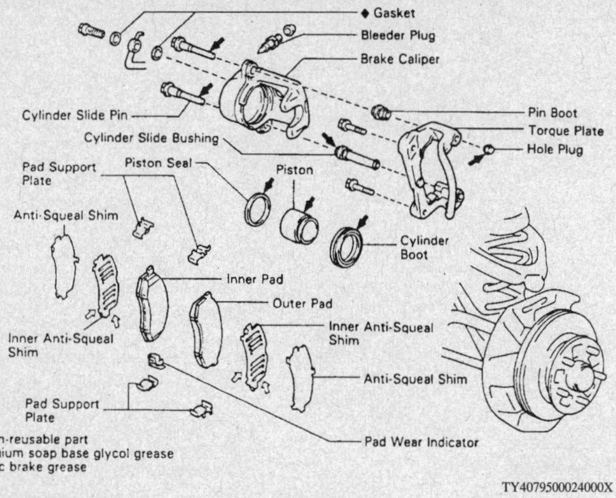
Gasket
Bleeder Plug
Brake Caliper
Cylinder Slide Pin
Cylinder Slide Bushing
Pin Boot
Torque Plate
Hole Plug
Pad Support Plate
Piston Seal
Piston
Anti-Squeal Shim
Cylinder Boot
Inner Pad
Outer Pad
Inner Anti-Squeal Shim
Inner Anti-Squeal Shim
Anti-Squeal Shim
Pad Support Plate
Pad Wear Indicator
◆ Non-reusable part
Lithium soap base glycol grease
Disc brake grease
TY4079500024000X

Fig. 3 Exploded view of disc brake assembly. Tacoma

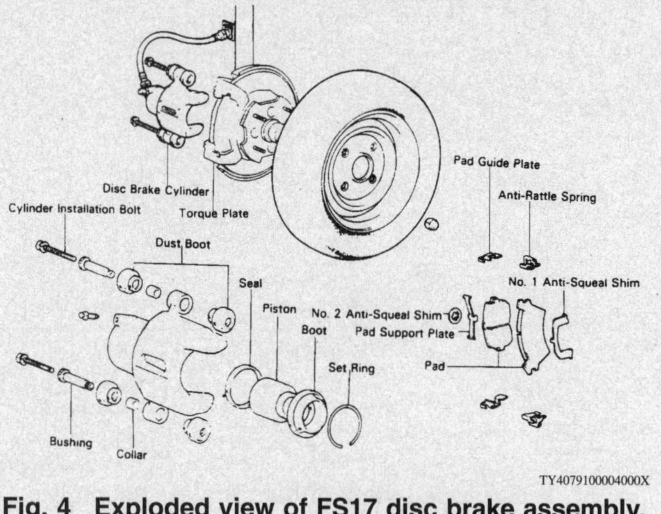
Disc Brake Cylinder
Cylinder Installation Bolt
Torque Plate
Dust Boot
Pad Guide Plate
Anti-Rattle Spring
No. 1 Anti-Squeal Shim
Seal
Piston
Boot
No. 2 Anti-Squeal Shim
Pad Support Plate
Set Ring
Pad
Bushing
Collar
TY4079100004000X

Fig. 4 Exploded view of FS17 disc brake assembly. 2WD Pickup & 1993–95 4Runner

Overhaul

1. Remove caliper as in "Brake Pad Service."
2. Remove two caliper siding bushings and four dust boots.
3. Using screwdriver, remove cylinder boot set ring and cylinder boot.
4. Place a piece of cloth between piston and cylinder and using compressed air, remove piston from cylinder.
5. Using screwdriver, remove piston seal.
6. Apply lithium soap base glycol grease to all movable parts.
7. Install piston seal and piston in cylinder.
8. Install cylinder boot and set ring in cylinder.
9. Install collar and dust boot, ensuring that boot is secured firmly to bushing groove.

TACOMA 2WD

Caliper, Replace

1. Raise and support vehicle and remove front wheel.
2. Disconnect brake hose and use suitable container to catch brake fluid.
3. Remove bracket from caliper.
4. Remove 2 slide pins and caliper.
5. Remove brake pads, anti-squeal shim(s), pad wear indicator plate and 4 support plates.
6. If necessary, remove slide bushing and pin boots.

Overhaul

1. Remove caliper as outlined under "Caliper, Replace."
2. Using screwdriver, remove cylinder boot set ring and boot.
3. Place suitable rag or block between caliper and piston. Using compressed air, remove piston.
4. Using screwdriver, remove piston seal.
5. Apply lithium soap base glycol grease to caliper boot, piston, piston seal, and both slide pins.
6. Install piston seal and piston in caliper.
7. Install caliper boot and set ring in cylinder.
8. Install pin boots to torque plate of main pin side.
9. Using a suitable driver, install slide bushing into torque plate of sub-pin side.

PICKUP & 1993–95 4RUNNER w/FS17 & F18 TYPE DISC, 2WD

Caliper, Replace

1. Raise and support vehicle and remove front wheel.
2. Disconnect brake hose and use suitable container to catch brake fluid.
3. Remove bracket from caliper.
4. Remove 2 slide pins and caliper.
5. Remove brake pads, anti-squeal shim(s), and 4 support plates.
6. If necessary, remove slide bushing and pin boots.

Overhaul

1. Remove caliper as outlined under "Caliper, Replace."
2. Using screwdriver, remove cylinder boot set ring and boot.
3. Place suitable rag or block between caliper and piston. Using compressed air, remove piston.
4. Using screwdriver, remove piston seal.
5. Apply lithium soap base glycol grease to caliper boot, piston, piston seal, and both slide pins.
6. Install piston seal and piston in caliper.
7. Install caliper boot and set ring in cylinder.
8. Install pin boots to torque plate of main pin side.
9. Using a suitable driver, install slide bushing into torque plate of sub-pin side.

PICKUP & 1993–95 4RUNNER w/PD60 & PD66 TYPE DISC & T100, 2WD

Caliper, Replace

1. Raise and support vehicle and remove tire and wheel assembly.
2. Disconnect brake line at caliper.
3. Remove bracket from caliper.
4. Remove two caliper attaching bolts and the caliper.
5. Remove anti-rattle springs, brake pads, anti-squeal shims and support plates.
6. Reverse procedure to install. **Torque** bracket attaching bolts to 13 ft. lbs. and the brake line to 11 ft. lbs.

Overhaul

1. Remove caliper as previously described.
2. Remove two cylinder slide bushings, four dust boots and two collars.
3. Using screwdriver, remove cylinder boot set ring and boot.
4. Place a piece of cloth between piston and cylinder and, using compressed air, remove piston from cylinder.
5. Using screwdriver, remove piston seal from brake cylinder.
6. Apply lithium soap base glycol grease to all movable components.
7. Install piston seal and piston in cylinder.
8. Install cylinder boot and set ring in cylinder.
9. Install collar and dust boot in caliper, ensuring that boots are secured firmly to each brake cylinder groove.
10. Install bushing into boots, ensuring boots are secured firmly to each bushing groove.

LAND CRUISER, 4WD PICKUP, 1993–95 4RUNNER & T100

Caliper, Replace

1. Remove pads as outlined under "Brake Pad Service."
2. Disconnect brake hydraulic line from caliper.
3. Remove caliper retaining bolts, then the caliper.
4. Reverse procedure to install, then bleed brake system.

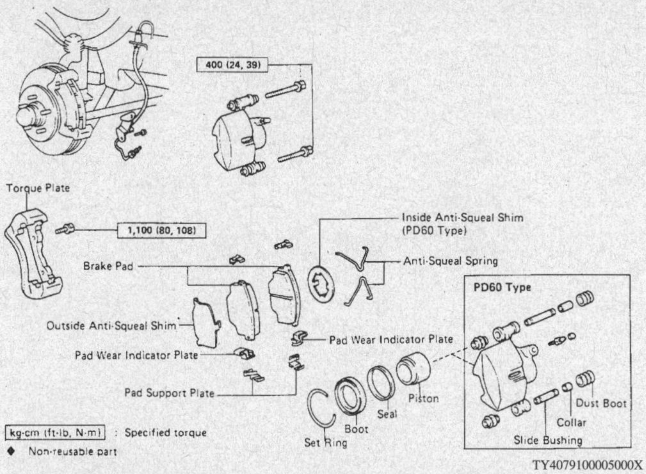
400 (24, 39)
Torque Plate
1,100 (80, 108)
Inside Anti-Squeal Shim (PD60 Type)
Brake Pad
Anti-Squeal Spring
PD60 Type
Outside Anti-Squeal Shim
Pad Wear Indicator Plate
Pad Wear Indicator Plate
Pad Support Plate
Piston
Seal
Dust Boot
Boot
Collar
Set Ring
Slide Bushing
kg-cm (ft-lb, N·m) : Specified torque
◆ Non-reusable part

TY4079100005000X

Fig. 5 Exploded view of PD60 disc brake assembly. 2WD Pickup & 1993–95 4Runner

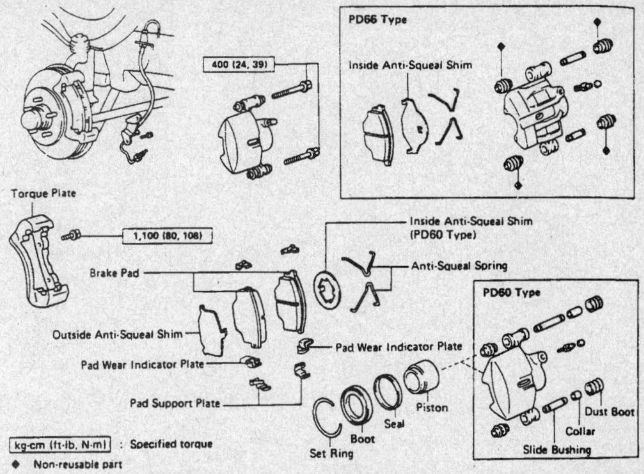
PD66 Type
400 (24, 39)
Inside Anti-Squeal Shim
Torque Plate
1,100 (80, 108)
Inside Anti-Squeal Shim (PD60 Type)
Brake Pad
Anti-Squeal Spring
PD60 Type
Outside Anti-Squeal Shim
Pad Wear Indicator Plate
Pad Wear Indicator Plate
Pad Support Plate
Piston
Seal
Dust Boot
Boot
Collar
Set Ring
Slide Bushing
kg-cm (ft-lb, N·m) : Specified torque
◆ Non-reusable part

TY4079100006000X

Fig. 6 Exploded view of PD60 & PD66 disc brake assembly. 2WD Pickup, 1993–95 4Runner & T100

Overhaul

1. Remove caliper as outlined under "Caliper, Replace."
2. Fabricate block of wood to dimensions shown in **Fig. 14.**
3. Remove snap ring and boot, **Fig. 7.**
4. Position block of wood between pistons, then remove pistons using compressed air.
5. Remove piston seals.
6. Lubricate piston and seal with suitable grease, then reverse procedure to assemble.

PREVIA & SUPRA

Caliper, Replace

1. Disconnect brake hydraulic hose at frame bracket, then at caliper.
2. Remove caliper attaching bolts, then lift caliper up and pull away from torque plate main pin, removing brake pads and components in the process, **Figs. 11 and 12.**
3. Reverse procedure to install.

Overhaul

1. Remove caliper as outlined under "Caliper, Replace."
2. Remove pads, anti-squeal shims, anti-rattle springs, support and pad guide plates.
3. Remove sliding bushing and boot, **Figs. 11 and 12.**
4. Remove main pin boot.
5. Remove caliper boot, set ring and piston seal from caliper.
6. Remove piston using compressed air. **When using compressed air to remove piston, keep fingers clear of piston to avoid injury.**
7. Lubricate main pin boot, sliding pin and boot, piston seal and boot and dust boot with suitable brake lubricant.
8. Install piston seal and piston in caliper.
9. Install cylinder boot and seat in caliper.
10. Using a 21 mm socket, press in main pin boot, then install dust and sliding bushing.
11. Install caliper.

AVALON, CAMRY, COROLLA & CELICA

Caliper, Replace

1. Raise and support vehicle and remove front wheel.
2. Remove union bolt and disconnect brake hose. Use suitable container to catch brake fluid.
3. Remove caliper, **Fig. 13.**
4. Remove anti-squeal shims and brake pad wear indicator plates.
5. Remove support plates.
6. Reverse procedure to install.

Overhaul

1. Remove caliper as outlined under "Caliper, Replace."
2. Remove the following parts:
   a. Caliper slide bushings.
   b. Dust boots.
   c. Collars.
3. Using screwdriver, remove caliper boot set ring and boot.
4. Place suitable rag between caliper and piston and using compressed air, remove pistons.
5. Using screwdriver, remove piston seal.
6. Apply suitable lubricant to following parts: boot, piston seal, piston, slide bushing, collar, and dust boot.
7. Install piston seal(s) and piston(s) in caliper.
8. Install caliper boot and set ring in caliper.
9. Install collar and dust boots in caliper.
10. Check that boots are firmly seated in caliper grooves.
11. Install bushing into boots.
12. Check that boots are firmly secured to each bushing groove.

RAV4

Caliper, Replace

1. Disconnect flexible brake hose from caliper and drain brake fluid into suitable container.
2. Hold sliding pin and loosen installation bolts, **Fig. 10.**
3. Remove installation bolts and caliper from torque plate.
4. Remove brake pads and support plates as outlined under "Brake Pad Service."
5. Reverse procedure to install.

Overhaul

1. Remove caliper as outlined under "Caliper, Replace."
2. Remove cylinder boot set ring.
3. Place a piece of cloth between piston and caliper, then use compressed air to remove piston from cylinder.
4. Remove piston seal.
5. Remove sliding pins and dust boots.
6. Reverse procedure to assemble. Apply lithium soap base glycol grease to all movable parts.

1996 4RUNNER

Caliper, Replace

1. Raise and support vehicle, then remove front wheel.
2. Disconnect brake line from caliper, **Fig. 9.**
3. Remove caliper mounting bolts and caliper.
4. Remove clip, pins, anti-rattle spring, pads and anti-squeal shims as outlined under "Brake Pad Service."
5. Reverse procedure to install.

Overhaul

1. Remove caliper and brake pads as outlined under "Caliper, Replace."
2. Using a screwdriver, remove cylinder boot set rings and boots.
3. Fabricate wooden block, **Fig. 14,** to hold pistons, then place block between pistons and insert a brake pad on side of block opposite pistons.
4. Use compressed air to remove pistons from cylinder.
5. Remove piston seals from cylinder.
6. Reverse procedure to assemble. Apply lithium soap base glycol grease

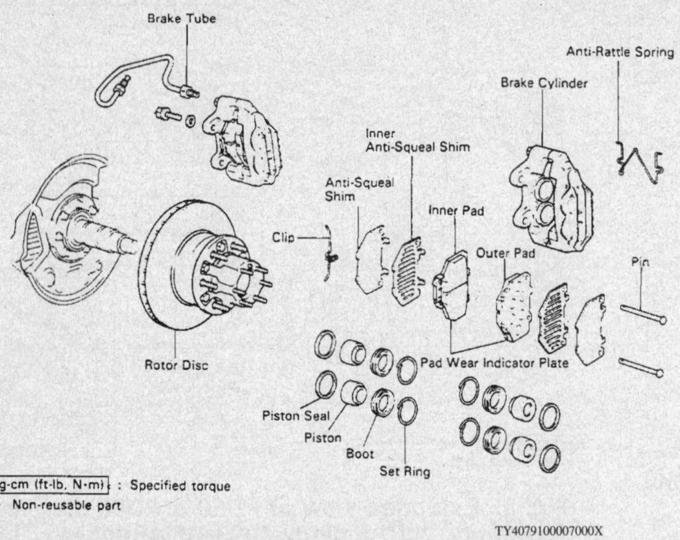
Brake Tube
Anti-Rattle Spring
Brake Cylinder
Inner
Anti-Squeal Shim
Anti-Squeal
Shim
Inner Pad
Clip
Outer Pad
Pin
Rotor Disc
Pad Wear Indicator Plate
Piston Seal
Piston
Boot
Set Ring
kg-cm (ft-lb, N·m) : Specified torque
◆ Non-reusable part
TY4079100007000X

Fig. 7 Exploded view of disc brake assembly. Land Cruiser, Tacoma, 4WD Pickup, 1993–95 4Runner & T100

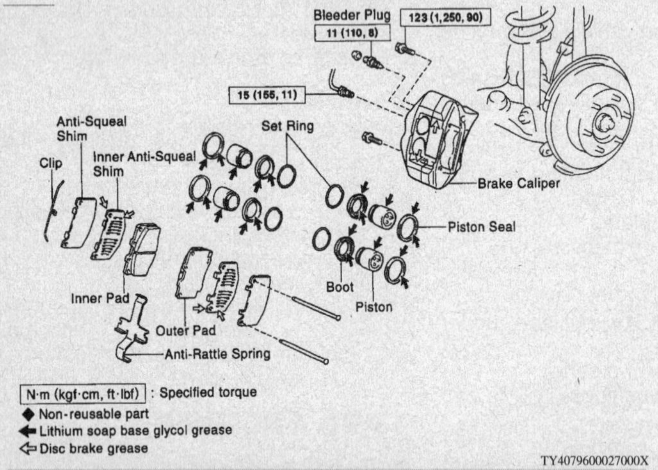
Bleeder Plug
11 (110, 8)
123 (1,250, 90)
15 (155, 11)
Anti-Squeal
Shim
Set Ring
Clip
Inner Anti-Squeal
Shim
Brake Caliper
Piston Seal
Inner Pad
Boot
Piston
Outer Pad
Anti-Rattle Spring
N·m (kgf·cm, ft·lbf) : Specified torque
◆ Non-reusable part
Lithium soap base glycol grease
Disc brake grease
TY4079600027000X

Fig. 9 Exploded view of disc brake assembly. 1996 4Runner

to all movable parts.

DISC BRAKE SPECIFICATIONS

Refer to the disc brake specifications under "Rear Disc & Parking Brakes" for rotor thickness and lateral runout specifications.

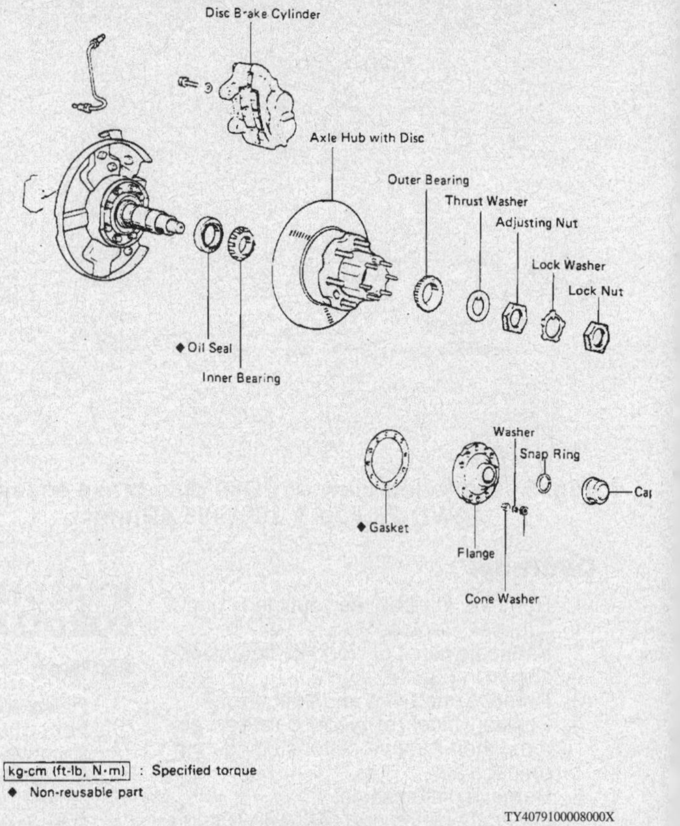
Disc Brake Cylinder
Axle Hub with Disc
Outer Bearing
Thrust Washer
Adjusting Nut
Lock Washer
Lock Nut
◆ Oil Seal
Inner Bearing
Washer
Snap Ring
◆ Gasket
Flange
Cone Washer
kg-cm (ft-lb, N·m) : Specified torque
◆ Non-reusable part
TY4079100008000X

Fig. 8 Exploded view of front axle hub. Land Cruiser, 4WD Pickup, 1993–95 4Runner & T100

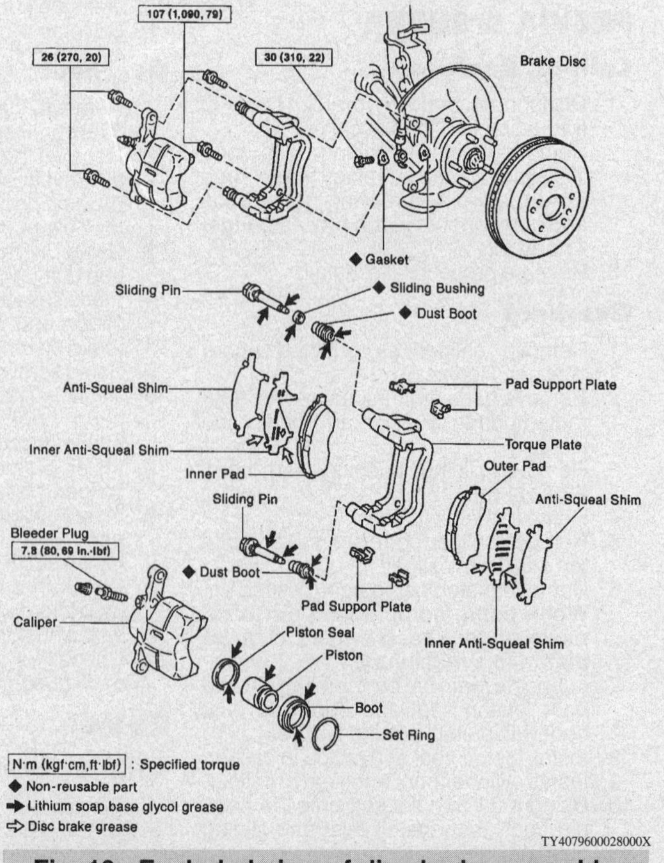
107 (1,090, 79)
26 (270, 20)
30 (310, 22)
Brake Disc
◆ Gasket
Sliding Pin
◆ Sliding Bushing
◆ Dust Boot
Anti-Squeal Shim
Pad Support Plate
Inner Anti-Squeal Shim
Torque Plate
Inner Pad
Outer Pad
Sliding Pin
Anti-Squeal Shim
Bleeder Plug
7.8 (80, 69 in.-lbf)
◆ Dust Boot
Pad Support Plate
Caliper
Piston Seal
Piston
Inner Anti-Squeal Shim
Boot
Set Ring
N·m (kgf·cm, ft·lbf) : Specified torque
◆ Non-reusable part
Lithium soap base glycol grease
Disc brake grease
TY4079600028000X

Fig. 10 Exploded view of disc brake assembly. RAV4

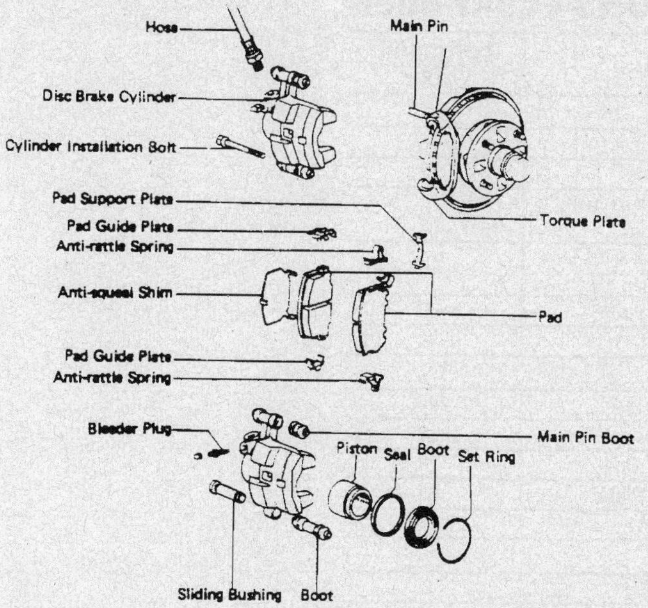
Hose
Main Pin
Disc Brake Cylinder
Cylinder Installation Bolt
Pad Support Plate
Torque Plate
Pad Guide Plate
Anti-rattle Spring
Anti-squeal Shim
Pad
Pad Guide Plate
Anti-rattle Spring
Bleeder Plug
Main Pin Boot
Piston
Seal
Boot
Set Ring
Sliding Bushing
Boot

TY4079100009000X

Fig. 11 Exploded view of AD disc brake assembly. Supra

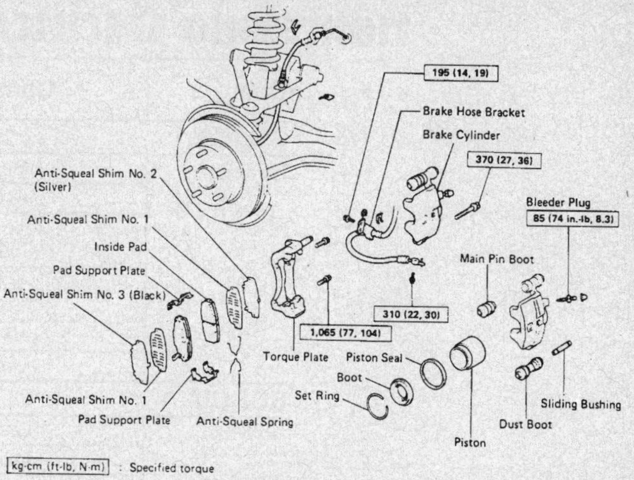
195 (14, 19)
Brake Hose Bracket
Brake Cylinder
370 (27, 36)
Anti-Squeal Shim No. 2 (Silver)
Bleeder Plug
85 (74 in.-lb, 8.3)
Anti-Squeal Shim No. 1
Inside Pad
Main Pin Boot
Pad Support Plate
Anti-Squeal Shim No. 3 (Black)
310 (22, 30)
1,065 (77, 104)
Torque Plate
Piston Seal
Boot
Set Ring
Sliding Bushing
Anti-Squeal Shim No. 1
Dust Boot
Pad Support Plate
Anti-Squeal Spring
Piston
kg-cm (ft-lb, N·m) : Specified torque

TY4079100010000X

Fig. 12 Exploded view of front disc brake assembly. Supra

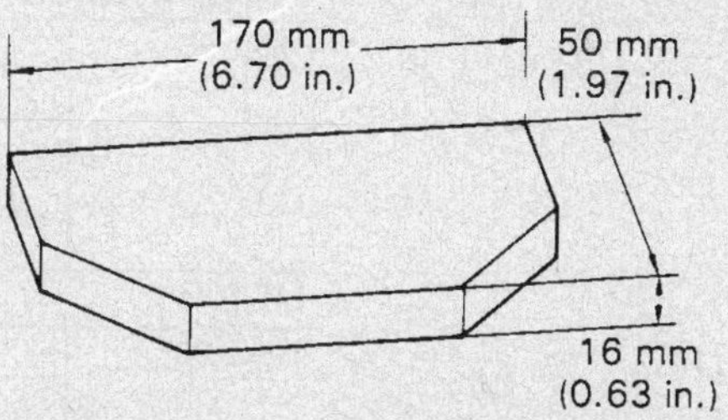
170 mm
(6.70 in.)
50 mm
(1.97 in.)
16 mm
(0.63 in.)

TY4079100014000X

Fig. 14 Dimensions for fabricating block of wood for piston removal. Land Cruiser, 4WD Pickup, 1993-95 4Runner & T100

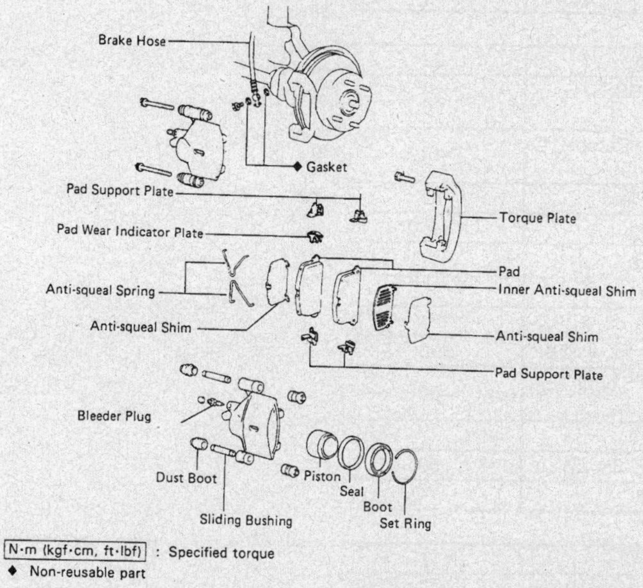
Brake Hose
Gasket
Pad Support Plate
Torque Plate
Pad Wear Indicator Plate
Pad
Anti-squeal Spring
Inner Anti-squeal Shim
Anti-squeal Shim
Anti-squeal Shim
Pad Support Plate
Bleeder Plug
Dust Boot
Piston
Seal
Boot
Sliding Bushing
Set Ring
N·m (kgf·cm, ft·lbf) : Specified torque
◆ Non-reusable part

TY4079100011000X

Fig. 13 Exploded view of disc brake assembly. Avalon, Camry, Corolla & Celica

TIGHTENING SPECIFICATIONS

Year	Component	Torque/Ft. Lbs.
CAMRY		
1993–96	Bleeder Plug	74①
	Flexible Hose	22
	Union Nut	11
	Front Caliper Bolt	25
	Front Torque Plate	79

Continued

TIGHTENING SPECIFICATIONS—Continued

Year	Component	Torque/Ft. Lbs.
CELICA		
1993–96	Bleeder Plug	74①
	Flexible Hose	22
	Front Caliper Bolt (13 Inch Wheel)	18
	Front Caliper Bolt (14 & 15 Inch Wheel)	29
	Front Torque Plate	79
	Union Nut	11
COROLLA		
1993–96	Bleeder Plug	74①
	Flexible Hose	22
	Front Caliper Bolt	18
	Front Torque Plate	65
	Union Nut	11
LAND CRUISER		
1993–96	Bleeder Plug	8
	Caliper Bolts	90
	Disc To Hub	34
	Torque Plate	90
	Union Nut	11
MR2		
1993–95	Flexible Hose	22
	Front Caliper Bolt (3S-GTE Engine)	25
	Front Caliper Bolt (Except 3S-GTE Engine)	18
	Front Torque Plate	65
	Bleeder Plug	74①
PICKUP & 1993–95 4RUNNER		
1993–96	Bleeder Plug	8
	Caliper Bolts (PD60 & 66, 2WD)	24
	Caliper Bolts (S12 & 12, 4WD)	90
	Caliper Sliding Pin (FS17 & 18, 2WD)	65
	Disc To Hub	47
	Torque Plate (PD60 & 66, 2WD)	80
	Union Nut	11
1996 4RUNNER		
1996	Bleeder Plug	8
	Front Brake Hose	11
	Front Caliper Bolts	90
PREVIA		
1993–96	Bleeder Plug	74①
	Front Brake Hose	22
	Front Caliper Bolt	27
	Front Torque Plate	65
RAV4		
1996	Bleeder Plug	74①
	Brake Line Union Nut	11
	Front Brake Hose	22
	Front Caliper Bolt	20

Continued

TIGHTENING SPECIFICATIONS—Continued

Year	Component	Torque/Ft. Lbs.
SUPRA		
1993–96	Front Caliper Bolt	27
	Front Dust Cover	14
	Front Flexible Hose	22
	Front Torque Plate	77
TACOMA		
1995–96	Bleeder Plug	8
	Caliper Bolts (2WD)	24
	Caliper Bolts (4WD)	90
	Caliper Sliding Pin	65
	Disc To Hub	47
	Torque Plate	80
	Union Nut	11

① — Inch Lbs.

Rear Disc & Parking Brakes

INDEX

	Page No.
Brake Pad Service	48-137
Camry, Previa & 1993–94 Supra	48-137
Land Cruiser	48-137
MR2	48-137
1995–96 Avalon & Supra	48-137
Caliper Service	48-137
Avalon & 1995–96 Supra	48-137
Camry, Previa & 1993–94 Supra	48-138
Land Cruiser	48-139
MR2	48-138
Disc Brake Specifications	48-141
Parking Brake Service	48-139
Avalon, Previa, Supra, Celica & Camry	48-139
Land Cruiser	48-140
Tightening Specifications	48-141

BRAKE PAD SERVICE

1995–96 AVALON & SUPRA

1. Raise and support rear of vehicle, then remove tire and wheel assembly.
2. Remove caliper attaching bolts, then the caliper, **Figs. 1 and 2.** Do not allow caliper to hang unsupported or damage to the brake hose may occur.
3. Remove pads and anti-squeal shim(s).
4. Remove anti-rattle springs, pad guide plates and support plate.
5. Reverse procedure to install. Tighten caliper attaching bolts to specifications.

CAMRY, PREVIA & 1993–94 SUPRA

1. Raise and support rear of vehicle, then remove tire and wheel assembly.
2. Remove caliper attaching bolts, then the caliper, **Fig. 3.** Do not allow caliper to hang unsupported or damage to the brake hose may occur.
3. Remove pads and anti-squeal shim(s).
4. Remove anti-rattle springs, pad guide plates and support plate.
5. Reverse procedure to install. Tighten caliper attaching bolts to specifications.

MR2

1. Raise and support vehicle and remove tire and wheel assembly.
2. Temporarily install lug nuts to restrain brake disc.
3. Remove caliper attaching bolts from torque plate, **Fig. 4.**
4. Lift caliper up out of way and suspend it. Do not remove cylinder from main pin or disconnect brake hose.
5. Remove brake pads, anti-squeal shims, anti-rattle springs, pad support plate and pad guide plate.
6. Reverse procedure to install. Tighten caliper attaching bolts to specifications.

LAND CRUISER

1. Raise and support rear of vehicle, then remove tire and wheel assembly.
2. Check pad thickness through caliper inspection hole and replace pads if measured thickness is less than .039 inch.
3. Remove caliper sliding main pin and sliding sub pin, **Fig. 5.**
4. Remove brake caliper and suspend it so hose is not stretched. **Do not disconnect brake hose.**
5. Remove brake pads, anti-squeal shim, support plates and pad wear indicators, **Fig. 5.**
6. Reverse procedure to install. Tighten caliper sliding main pin and sliding sub pin to specifications.

CALIPER SERVICE

AVALON & 1995–96 SUPRA

Caliper, Replace

1. Raise and support rear of vehicle, then remove tire and wheel assembly.
2. Disconnect brake hose from brake tube and caliper using a suitable tool.
3. Remove caliper attaching bolts, then the caliper, **Figs. 1 and 2.**
4. Remove anti-squeal shim(s), brake pad, anti-rattle spring, pad guide plate and pad support plate.
5. Reverse procedure to install, then bleed brake system.

Overhaul

1. Remove sliding bushing and boot, **Figs. 1 and 2.**
2. Remove main pin boot using a suitable chisel.
3. Remove piston using compressed air. **When using air pressure to remove caliper piston, place a shop towel over piston to prevent it from flying out.**
4. Remove caliper boot, set ring and piston seal from caliper.

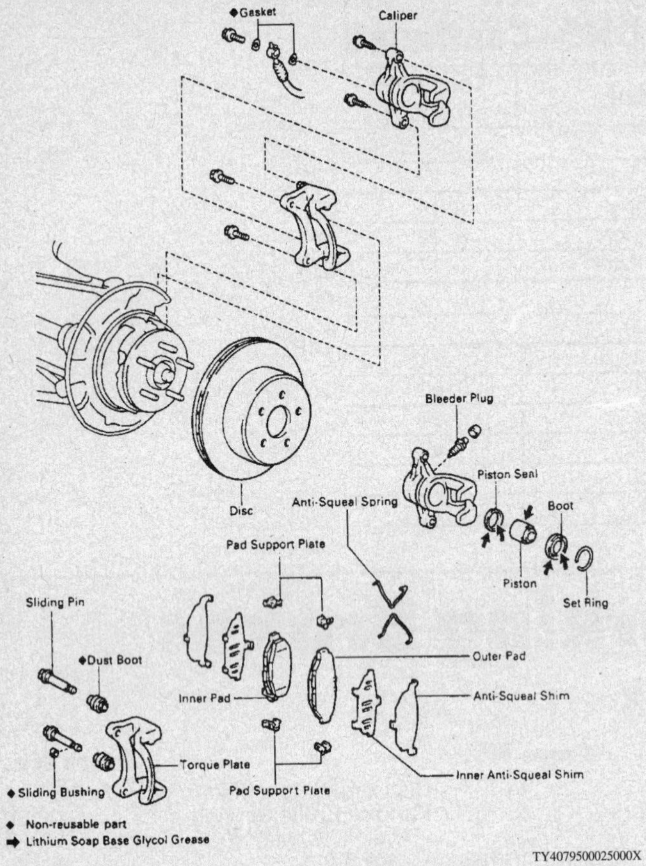
◆Gasket
Caliper
Bleeder Plug
Piston Seal
Boot
Disc
Anti-Squeal Spring
Pad Support Plate
Piston
Set Ring
Sliding Pin
◆Dust Boot
Outer Pad
Inner Pad
Anti-Squeal Shim
Torque Plate
◆Sliding Bushing
Pad Support Plate
Inner Anti-Squeal Shim
◆ Non-reusable part
Lithium Soap Base Glycol Grease
TY4079500025000X

Fig. 1 Exploded view of rear disc brake caliper assembly. 1995–96 Avalon & Supra w/2JZ-GE

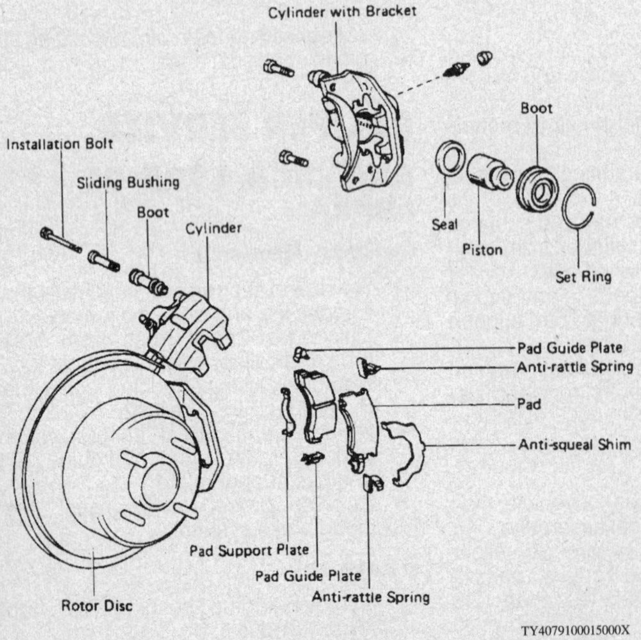
Cylinder with Bracket
Boot
Installation Bolt
Sliding Bushing
Boot
Cylinder
Seal
Piston
Set Ring
Pad Guide Plate
Anti-rattle Spring
Pad
Anti-squeal Shim
Pad Support Plate
Pad Guide Plate
Rotor Disc
Anti-rattle Spring
TY4079100015000X

Fig. 3 Exploded view of rear disc brake caliper assembly. Camry, Previa & 1993–94 Supra

5. Reverse procedure to install, noting the following:
   a. Apply suitable grease to the main pin boot, sliding pin and boot, piston seal and piston and dust boot.
   b. Install main pin boot using a press and suitable socket.
   c. Ensure dust boot does not fold under during installation.

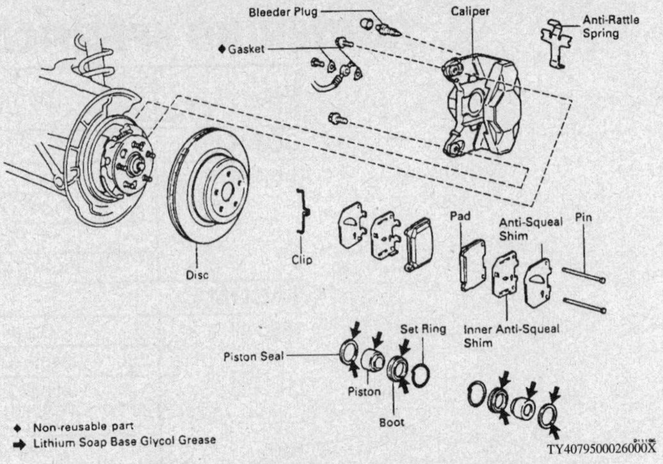
Bleeder Plug
Caliper
Anti-Rattle Spring
◆Gasket
Clip
Disc
Pad
Anti-Squeal Shim
Pin
Set Ring
Inner Anti-Squeal Shim
Piston Seal
Piston
Boot
◆ Non-reusable part
Lithium Soap Base Glycol Grease
TY4079500026000X

Fig. 2 Exploded view of rear disc brake caliper assembly. 1995–96 Supra w/2JZ-GTE

CAMRY, PREVIA & 1993-94 SUPRA

Caliper, Replace

1. Raise and support rear of vehicle, then remove tire and wheel assembly.
2. Disconnect brake hose from brake tube and caliper using a suitable tool.
3. Remove caliper attaching bolts, then the caliper, **Fig. 3.**
4. Remove anti-squeal shim(s), brake pad, anti-rattle spring, pad guide plate and pad support plate.
5. Reverse procedure to install, then bleed brake system.

Overhaul

1. Remove sliding bushing and boot, **Fig. 3.**
2. Remove main pin boot using a suitable chisel.
3. Remove piston using compressed air. **When using air pressure to remove caliper piston, place a shop towel over piston to prevent it from flying out.**
4. Remove caliper boot, set ring and piston seal from caliper.
5. Reverse procedure to install, noting the following:
   a. Apply suitable grease to the main pin boot, sliding pin and boot, piston seal and piston and dust boot.
   b. Install main pin boot using a press and suitable socket.
   c. Ensure dust boot does not fold under during installation.

MR2

Caliper, Replace

1. Raise and support vehicle and remove wheel and tire assembly.
2. Remove union bolt and two gaskets and disconnect brake hose from caliper.
3. Disconnect parking brake cable as follows:
   a. Remove clip.
   b. Pull out hole pin while pushing parking brake cable.

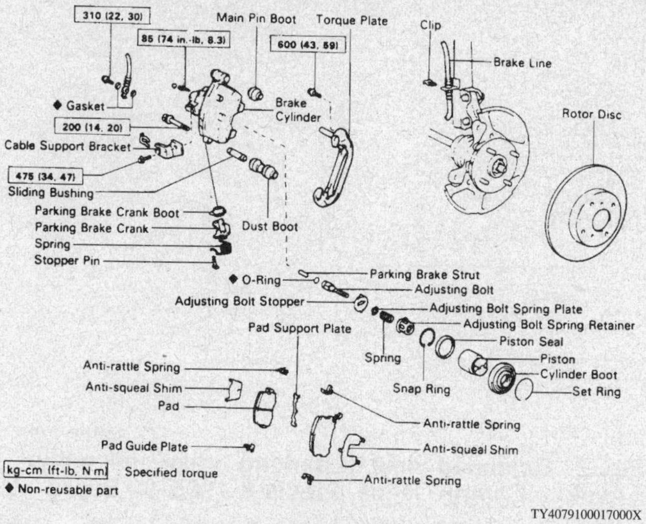
310 (22, 30)
Main Pin Boot
Torque Plate
Clip
85 (74 in.-lb, 8.3)
600 (43, 59)
Brake Line
◆ Gasket
Brake Cylinder
Rotor Disc
200 (14, 20)
Cable Support Bracket
475 (34, 47)
Sliding Bushing
Parking Brake Crank Boot
Parking Brake Crank
Dust Boot
Spring
Stopper Pin
◆ O-Ring
Parking Brake Strut
Adjusting Bolt
Adjusting Bolt Stopper
Adjusting Bolt Spring Plate
Pad Support Plate
Adjusting Bolt Spring Retainer
Piston Seal
Spring
Piston
Anti-rattle Spring
Cylinder Boot
Anti-squeal Shim
Snap Ring
Set Ring
Pad
Anti-rattle Spring
Pad Guide Plate
Anti-squeal Shim
kg-cm (ft-lb, N·m) Specified torque
◆ Non-reusable part
Anti-rattle Spring
TY4079100017000X

Fig. 4 Exploded view of rear disc brake assembly. MR2

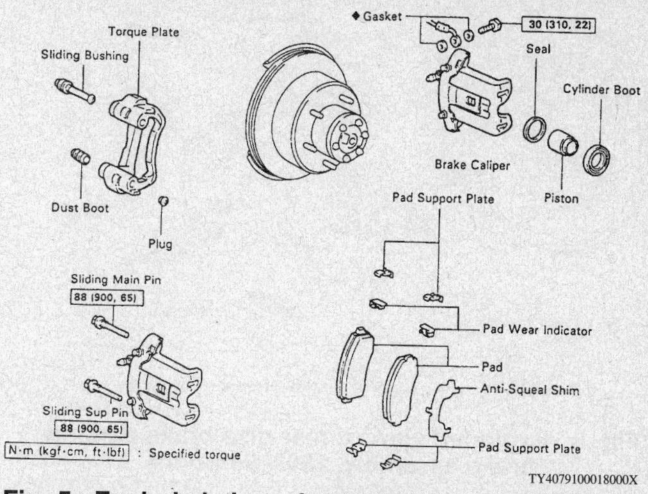
◆ Gasket
30 (310, 22)
Torque Plate
Sliding Bushing
Seal
Cylinder Boot
Brake Caliper
Dust Boot
Pad Support Plate
Piston
Plug
Sliding Main Pin
88 (900, 65)
Pad Wear Indicator
Pad
Anti-Squeal Shim
Sliding Sup Pin
88 (900, 65)
N·m (kgf·cm, ft·lbf) : Specified torque
Pad Support Plate
TY4079100018000X

Fig. 5 Exploded view of rear disc brake assembly. Land Cruiser

   c. Remove retainer.
   d. Remove parking brake cable from cable support bracket.
4. Remove caliper attaching bolt and the caliper.
5. Remove brake pads, anti-squeal shims, anti-rattle springs, pad support plate and pad guide plate.
6. Reverse procedure to install, **torquing** brake hose union bolt to 22 ft. lbs.

Overhaul

1. Remove caliper as previously described.
2. Remove sliding bushing and boot, then the main pin boot.
3. Using screwdriver, remove cylinder boot set ring and cylinder boot.
4. Using tool 09719–14020, or equivalent, turn piston counterclockwise to remove.
5. Using screwdriver, remove piston seal.
6. Place tool 09756–00010, or equivalent, onto adjusting bolt and lightly tighten bolt using 14 mm socket. **Always use tool, or equivalent or spring may fly out and cause personal injury or damage interior surface of caliper. Do not tighten tool too tightly as this may damage spring retainer.**
7. Using suitable tool, remove snap ring from cylinder.
8. Pull spring retainer, spring, spring plate and stopper out of cylinder together with adjusting bolt, being careful not to damage O-ring.
9. Disassemble adjusting bolt as follows:
   a. Remove adjusting bolt guide nut tool No. 09756-00010, or equivalent.
   b. Remove spring retainer, spring, spring plate and stopper from adjusting bolt.
   c. Remove O-ring from adjusting bolt.
10. Remove parking brake strut, then on Corolla models, the parking brake cable support bracket.
11. Remove torsion spring from parking brake crank.
12. Remove parking brake crank from caliper.
13. If parking brake crank boot is to be replaced, use screwdriver to lightly tap on metal portion of boot to remove it. **If crank boot is not to be replaced, do not remove it.**
14. Remove cable support bracket.
15. Using pin punch, tap out the stopper pin.
16. Apply lithium soap base glycol grease to all moving parts.
17. Tap stopper pin into caliper until pin extends .98 inch.
18. Press surface of cable support bracket flush against cylinder wall and **torque** bolt to 34 ft. lbs.
19. If removed, install parking brake crank boot in caliper.
20. Install parking brake crank in caliper, securely matching crank boot with groove of crank seal.
21. Install torsion spring, ensuring that parking brake crank subassembly is in touch with stopper pin.
22. Install parking brake strut after adjusting rollers of needle roller bearing so they do not catch on caliper hole.
23. Install new O-ring on adjusting bolt.
24. Assemble adjusting bolt as follows:
   a. Assemble stopper, plate, spring and spring retainer to adjusting bolt and, using adjusting bolt guide nut tool No. 09756-00010, or equivalent, fully tighten components down manually. **Position scribed surface of stopper upward and align notches of spring case with notches of stopper.**
   b. Install adjusting bolt subassembly into cylinder.
25. Using suitable tool, install snap ring, facing snap ring opening toward bleeder side, then remove tool from adjusting bolt and firmly pull up adjusting bolt manually to ensure it does not move.
26. Manually move parking brake crank to ensure adjusting bolt moves smoothly.
27. Install piston seal in cylinder.
28. Assemble piston in cylinder as follows:
   a. Using rear disc brake tool No. 09719-14020, or equivalent, slowly screw in piston clockwise until it will not descend any further.
   b. Align center of piston stopper groove with positioning protrusion of cylinder.
29. Install cylinder boot and set ring in cylinder.
30. Install main pin boot.
31. Install dust boot, ensuring that seal does not fold under, then install bushing into boot with flange facing inside.
32. Install master cylinder.
33. Fill reservoir with brake fluid and bleed system.

LAND CRUISER

Caliper, Replace

1. Remove union bolt and gaskets from brake caliper, then disconnect flexible hose. **Use suitable container to catch brake fluid.**
2. Remove caliper sliding pins, then the caliper.
3. Reverse procedure to install, Tighten caliper mounting bolt to specification.

Overhaul

1. Using suitable screwdriver, remove cylinder boot from caliper.
2. Place cloth between piston and caliper, then use compressed air to remove piston from caliper.
3. Using suitable screwdriver, remove piston seal from caliper.
4. Remove pin boot and sliding bushing using screwdriver and suitable hammer.

PARKING BRAKE SERVICE

AVALON, PREVIA, SUPRA, CELICA & CAMRY

Shoes, Replace

1. Raise and support rear of vehicle, then remove tire and wheel assembly.

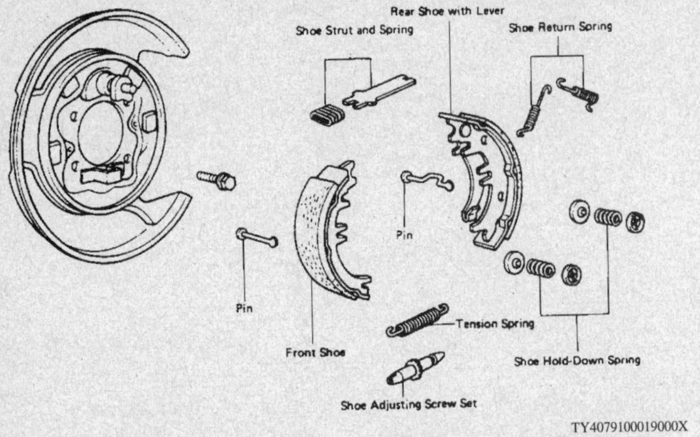
Rear Shoe with Lever
Shoe Strut and Spring
Shoe Return Spring
Pin
Pin
Front Shoe
Tension Spring
Shoe Hold-Down Spring
Shoe Adjusting Screw Set
TY4079100019000X

Fig. 6 Exploded view of rear disc brake parking brake assembly. 1993–94 Supra

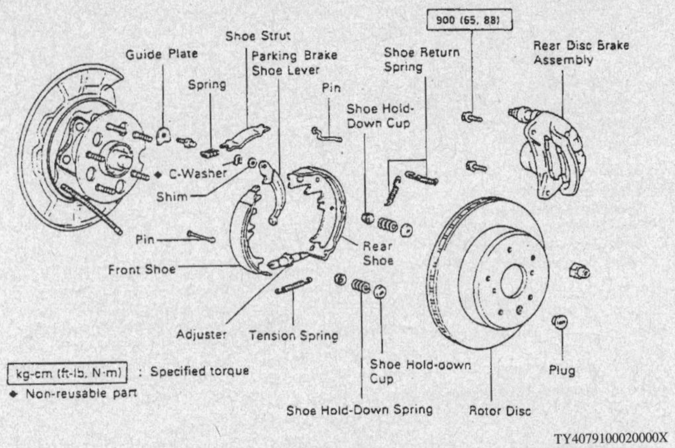
900 (65, 88)
Shoe Strut
Guide Plate
Parking Brake Shoe Lever
Shoe Return Spring
Rear Disc Brake Assembly
Spring
Pin
Shoe Hold-Down Cup
◆ C-Washer
Shim
Pin
Rear Shoe
Front Shoe
Adjuster
Tension Spring
kg-cm (ft-lb, N·m) : Specified torque
◆ Non-reusable part
Shoe Hold-Down Cup
Plug
Shoe Hold-Down Spring
Rotor Disc
TY4079100020000X

Fig. 7 Exploded view of parking brake assembly. Avalon, Camry, Celica, Previa & 1995–96 Supra

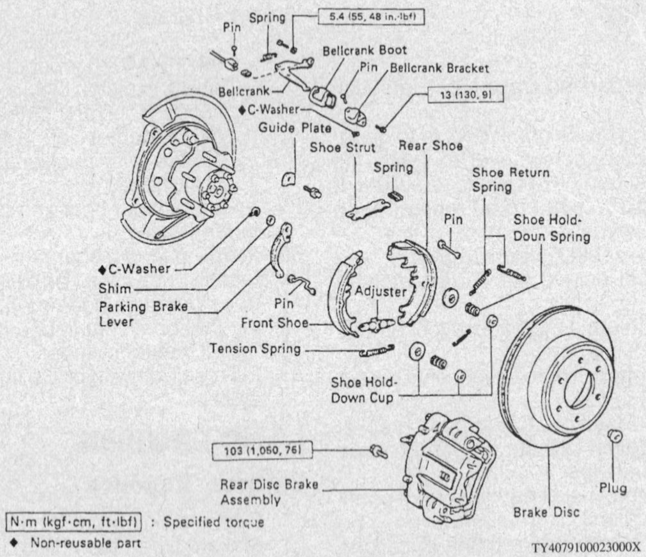
Pin
Spring
5.4 (55, 48 in.-lbf)
Bellcrank Boot
Pin
Bellcrank Bracket
Bellcrank
◆C-Washer
13 (130, 9)
Guide Plate
Shoe Strut
Rear Shoe
Spring
Shoe Return Spring
Pin
Shoe Hold-Doun Spring
◆C-Washer
Shim
Parking Brake Lever
Pin
Adjuster
Front Shoe
Tension Spring
Shoe Hold-Down Cup
103 (1,050, 76)
Rear Disc Brake Assembly
Plug
Brake Disc
N·m (kgf·cm, ft·lbf) : Specified torque
◆ Non-reusable part
TY4079100023000X

Fig. 8 Exploded view of rear disc brake parking brake assembly. Land Cruiser

2. Remove rear caliper, refer to "Caliper, Replace."
3. Remove rotor disc.
4. Remove shoe return springs, **Figs. 6 and 7.**
5. Using strut remover 09717–20010, or equivalent, remove shoe strut and spring.
6. Slide front shoe from under shoe hold-down spring, then remove shoe adjusting screw, tension spring and remove shoe.
7. Slide rear from shoe hold-down spring, then disconnect parking brake cable from shoe lever.
8. Apply non-melting grease on brake backing plate shoe flats, then on shoe sliding surface.
9. Lubricate adjusting screw with non-melting lubricant.
10. Connect parking brake lever to cable.
11. Slide rear shoe into position under shoe hold-down spring, then install tension spring.
12. Install adjusting screw on rear shoe and partially install on front shoe.
13. Slide front shoe into position under shoe hold-down spring. Ensure adjusting screw and tension spring are positioned properly.
14. Install front shoe return spring, then rear return spring.
15. Lightly sand brake drum inner surface, then align the service hole on disc with groove on axle shaft and install disc.
16. Install caliper, then adjust parking brake.

LAND CRUISER

1. Raise and support rear of vehicle, then remove tire and wheel assembly.
2. Remove rear disc brake assembly.
3. Place matchmarks on disc and rear hub, then remove disc, **Fig 8.**
4. Remove tension spring using suitable pliers.
5. Remove shoe return springs.
6. Remove shoe strut with spring.
7. Remove rear shoe, adjuster and tension spring, **Fig 8.**
8. Remove front shoe hold-down spring cups, springs and pin.
9. Slide out front shoe.
10. Disconnect parking brake cable from parking brake shoe lever.
11. Measure clearance between parking brake shoe and lever. If clearance is greater than .0138 inch, replace shim to obtain correct clearance.
12. Apply high temperature grease to the backing plate, adjusting screw and sliding surfaces of the shoe.
13. Install parking brake cable to front shoe using suitable pliers.
14. Install front shoe pin to backing plate, then slide in front shoe.
15. Install front shoe hold-down spring and cups.
16. Install tension spring, rear shoe and adjuster.
17. Install front shoe hold-down spring and cups.
18. Install strut with spring.
19. Install shoe return springs.
20. Install disc brake assembly.

DISC BRAKE SPECIFICATIONS

Year	Model	Nominal Thickness, Inch	Minimum Thickness, Inch	Lateral Runout (T.I.R.), Inch
1995–96	Avalon	1.102	1.024	.0020
1993–96	Camry①	.394③	.354	.006
1993–96	Celica⑥	1.102	1.024	.002
1993–96	Celica⑦	.984	.906	.002
1993–96	Corolla	.866	.787	.002
1993–96	Land Cruiser	.709	.630	.006
1993	MR2⑤	.984	.945	.003
1994–95	MR2⑤	.866	.828	.004
1993–95	MR2⑥①	.630	.591	.004
1993–96	Paseo	.709	.669	.002
1993–96	Previa⑧	.866	.787	.003
1993–96	Previa⑨	.984	.906	.003
1993–96	Previa①	.709②	.630	.004
1996	RAV4	.709	.630	.002
1993–96	Supra①	.630②	.591	.002
1995–96	Tacoma	.866	.787	.0028
1993–96	Tercel	.709	.669	.004
1993–96	T100	.984	.906	④
1993–95	4Runner	.787	.709	.003
1996	4Runner	.866	.787	.002

① — Rear disc brakes.
② — Parking brake drum I.D., 7.49–7.52 inch.
③ — Parking brake drum I.D., 6.69–6.73 inch.
④ — 1 ton models, .0035 inch; ½ ton models, .0028 inch.
⑤ — 3S-GTE engine.
⑥ — 5S-FE engine.
⑦ — 7A-FE engine.
⑧ — Single piston type.
⑨ — Two piston type.

TIGHTENING SPECIFICATIONS

Year	Component	Torque/ Ft.Lbs.
AVALON		
1995–96	Bleeder Plug	74①
	Flexible Hose	21
	Rear Caliper Bolt	25
	Rear Speed Sensor Bolt	69①
	Rear Torque Plate	34
	Union Nut	11
CAMRY		
1993–96	Bleeder Plug	74①
	Flexible Hose	22
	Rear Caliper Bolt	14
	Rear Torque Plate	34
	Union Nut	11
LAND CRUISER		
1993–96	Bleeder Plug	8
	Caliper Bolts	90
	Disc To Hub	34
	Torque Plate	90
	Union Nut	11
MR2		
1993–95	Flexible Hose	22
	Bleeder Plug	74①
	Rear Caliper Bolt	14
	Rear Torque Plate	43

Continued

TIGHTENING SPECIFICATIONS—Continued

Year	Component	Torque/ Ft.Lbs.
PICKUP & 4RUNNER		
1993–96	Bleeder Plug	8
	Caliper Bolts (PD60 & 66, 2WD)	24
	Caliper Bolts (S12 & 12, 4WD)	90
	Caliper Sliding Pin (FS17 & 18, 2WD)	65
	Disc To Hub	47
	Torque Plate (PD60 & 66, 2WD)	80
	Union Nut	11
PREVIA		
1993–96	Bleeder Plug	74①
	Rear Brake Hose	22
	Rear Caliper Bolt	18
	Rear Dust Cover	18
	Rear Torque Plate	18
SUPRA		
1993–96	Bleeder Plug	8
	Flexible Hose Union Bolt	22
	Rear Caliper Bolt	25
	Rear Torque Plate	77

① — Inch Lbs.

Drum Brakes

INDEX

Page No.

Adjustments 48-147
Parking Brake 48-147
Shoe Adjustment 48-148
Application Chart 48-142
Brake Service 48-143
Type 1 (2WD Duo Servo Type) .48-143
Type 2 (2WD Leading-Trailing Type) 48-143
Type 3.........................48-143
Type 4.........................48-144
Type 5.........................48-145
Type 6.........................48-145
Type 7.........................48-146
Type 8.........................48-147
Drum Brake Specifications 48-148
Tightening Specifications 48-149

APPLICATION CHART

Model	Type
Camry	7
Celica	6
Corolla	6
Land Cruiser	4
Paseo	3
Previa	5
RAV4	8
Tercel	3
2WD Tacoma	2
4WD Tacoma	4
2WD T100	2
4WD T100	4
2WD Pickup①	1
2WD Pickup②	2
4Runner	4
4WD Pickup	4

① — Duo Servo brakes.
② — Leading Trailing brakes.

BRAKE SERVICE

TYPE 1 (2WD DUO SERVO TYPE)

Removal

1. Raise and support rear of vehicle, then remove wheel and tire assembly.
2. Remove brake drum. If brake drum cannot be remove easily, insert a suitable screwdriver through hole in backing plate, then push adjuster lever away from adjuster and back of adjustment tension.
3. Remove two shoe return springs, using suitable tool, **Fig. 1.**
4. Push lever upward, then remove cable, shoe guide, plate and cable guide.
5. Remove spring from lever, then the lever and spring.
6. Remove two tension springs, using a suitable tool, then the shoe hold-down springs and pins.
7. Remove shoes, adjuster and strut, then disconnect parking brake cable from parking brake lever.

Inspection

1. Measure brake drum inside diameter. Inside diameter should be 10.08 inches, **Fig. 2.**
2. Measure brake shoe lining thickness, **Fig. 3.** Minimum thickness should be .04 inch.
3. Inspect brake lining and drum for proper contact and replace drum or shoes as necessary.
4. Inspect wheel cylinder for corrosion or damage.
5. Inspect backing plate for wear or damage.
6. Apply a suitable lubricant to backing plate contact areas.

Installation

1. Assemble parking brake cable to parking brake lever, **Fig. 1.**
2. Position rear brake in place with end of shoe inserted in piston rod, then install shoe hold-down spring and pin, using a suitable brake tool.
3. Install strut with spring rearward, then position front brake in place with end of shoe inserted in piston rod and strut in place. Install shoe hold-down spring and pin, using suitable tool.
4. Install tension springs.
5. Apply a suitable lubricant to adjuster, then install adjuster by opening shoes with screwdriver and inserting adjuster between pads.
6. Install shoe guide plate, cable guide and adjusting cable, then the front return spring and rear return spring, using a suitable tool.
7. Install tension spring to rear shoe, then hook adjusting lever with cable and insert lever. Retain adjusting lever with tension spring.
8. Pull adjusting lever cable rearward, then release and ensure adjusting bolt rotates. If bolt does not rotate, check for improper installation of rear brakes.
9. Adjust strut to shortest possible length, then install drum.
10. Rotate brake drum in reverse direction and depress brake pedal. Repeat process several times.
11. Remove drum, then check for proper clearance, **Fig. 4.** Clearance should be .024 inch. If clearance is not as specified, check parking brake system.
12. Install brake drum, then bleed and refill brake system.
13. Install wheel and tire assembly, then lower vehicle.

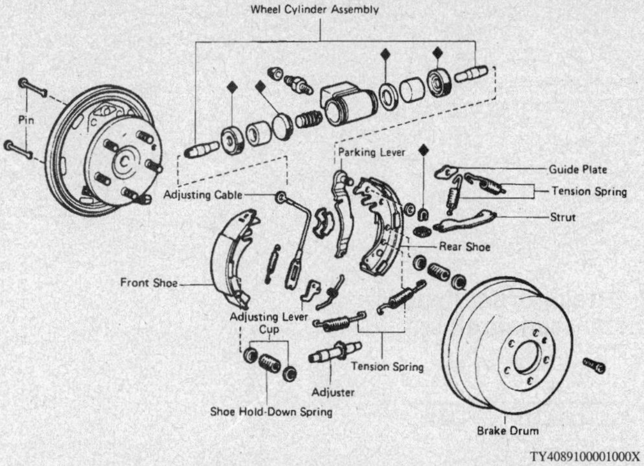
Wheel Cylinder Assembly
Pin
Parking Lever
Guide Plate
Tension Spring
Strut
Adjusting Cable
Rear Shoe
Front Shoe
Adjusting Lever
Cup
Tension Spring
Adjuster
Shoe Hold-Down Spring
Brake Drum
TY4089100001000X

Fig. 1 Exploded view of type 1 (2WD duo servo) brake assembly

TYPE 2 (2WD LEADING/ TRAILING TYPE)

Removal

1. Raise and support rear of vehicle, then remove wheel and tire assembly.
2. Remove brake drum. If brake drum cannot be remove easily, insert a suitable screwdriver through hole in backing plate, then push adjuster lever away from adjuster and back of adjustment tension.
3. Remove return spring adjuster, using a suitable tool, then the front shoe hold-down spring and pin, **Fig. 5.**
4. Remove front brake shoe, then the anchor spring.
5. Remove hold-down spring and pin, then the rear shoe, using a suitable tool.
6. Remove strut and spring from parking brake lever, then the adjusting lever spring.
7. Remove parking brake cable from parking brake lever.

Inspection

1. Measure brake drum inside diameter. Inside diameter should be 10.00 inches, **Fig. 2.**
2. Measure brake shoe lining thickness, **Fig. 3.** Minimum thickness should be .04 inch.
3. Inspect brake lining and drum for proper contact and replace drum or shoes as necessary.
4. Inspect wheel cylinder for corrosion or damage.
5. Inspect backing plate for wear or damage.
6. Apply a suitable lubricant to backing plate contact areas.

Installation

1. Apply a suitable lubricant to adjuster bolt threads and end.
2. Connect parking brake cable, then assemble strut and return spring to lever. Install adjusting lever spring using a suitable tool.
3. Position rear shoe in place with one end of shoe inserted in wheel cylinder and the other end in anchor plate. Using a suitable tool, install pin and shoe hold-down spring.
4. Insert anchor spring between front and rear shoes, then position front shoe in place with end of shoe in wheel cylinder and strut in place. Using a suitable tool, install pin and shoe hold-down spring.
5. Install return spring.
6. Pull adjusting lever cable upward, then release and ensure adjusting bolt rotates. If bolt does not rotate, check for improper installation of rear brakes.
7. Adjust strut to shortest possible length, then install drum.
8. Pull parking brake lever fully upward. Repeat process several times.
9. Remove drum, then check for proper clearance, **Fig. 4.** Clearance should be .024 inch. If clearance is not as specified, check parking brake system.
10. Install brake drum, then bleed and refill brake system.
11. Install wheel and tire assembly, then lower vehicle.

TYPE 3

Removal

1. Raise and support rear of vehicle, then remove wheel and tire assembly.
2. Remove brake drum. If brake drum cannot be remove easily, insert a suitable screwdriver through hole in backing plate, then push adjuster lever away from adjuster and back of adjustment tension.
3. Remove shoe return spring, using suitable tool, then remove return spring clamp, **Fig. 6.**

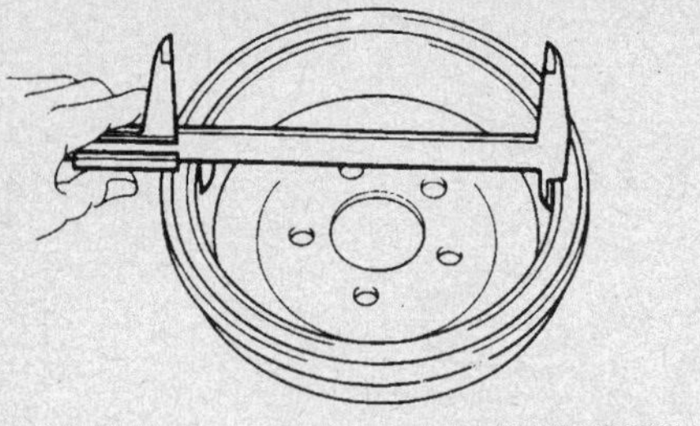

TY4089100002000X

Fig. 2 Brake drum inside diameter measurement

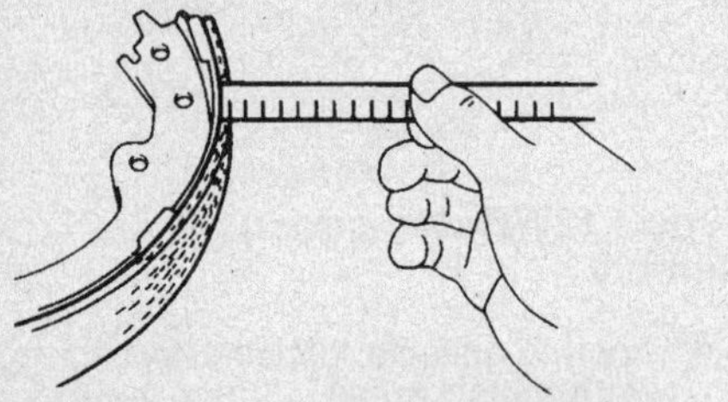

TY4089100003000X

Fig. 3 Brake shoe lining thickness measurement

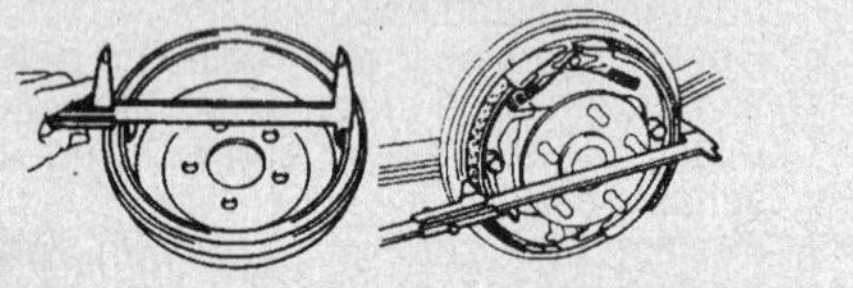

TY4089100004000X

Fig. 4 Clearance between shoes & drum measurement

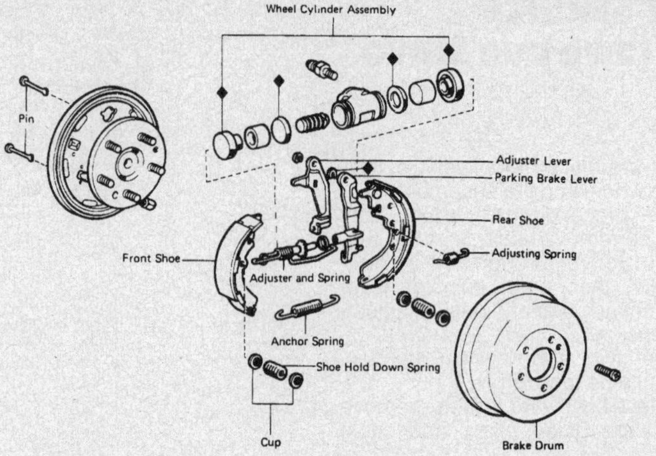
Wheel Cylinder Assembly
Pin
Adjuster Lever
Parking Brake Lever
Rear Shoe
Adjusting Spring
Front Shoe
Adjuster and Spring
Anchor Spring
Shoe Hold Down Spring
Cup
Brake Drum

TY4089100005000X

Fig. 5 Exploded view of type 2 (2WD leading/ trailing) brake assembly

4. Remove front shoe hold-down spring, retainers and pin.
5. Disconnect anchor spring, then remove front brake shoe and anchor spring.
6. Remove rear shoe hold-down spring, retainers and pin using suitable tool.
7. Disconnect parking brake cable from lever, then remove rear shoe with strut.
8. Remove adjusting lever spring and strut from rear shoe.
9. Remove C-washer, then the shims, parking brake lever and automatic adjusting lever from rear shoe.
10. Position a suitable container to catch fluid, then disconnect brake line.
11. Remove two attaching bolts, then the wheel cylinder.
12. Remove two boots, two pistons, two piston cups and spring from wheel cylinder.

Inspection

1. Measure brake drum inside diameter. Inside diameter should be 7.09 inches, **Fig. 2.**
2. Measure brake shoe lining thickness, **Fig. 3.** Minimum thickness should be .04 inch.
3. Inspect brake lining and drum for proper contact and replace drum or shoes as necessary.
4. Inspect wheel cylinder for corrosion or damage.
5. Inspect backing plate for wear or damage.
6. Inspect bellcrank components for bending, wear or damage.
7. Apply a suitable lubricant to backing plate contact areas.

Installation

1. Apply a suitable lubricant to pistons and cups, then install spring and two piston cups into wheel cylinder. Apply a suitable lubricant to inside of boots, then insert them into cylinder, **Fig. 6.**
2. Install wheel cylinder onto backing plate, then insert attaching bolts and **torque** to 7 ft. lbs.
3. Connect brake tube to wheel cylinder, then **torque** nut to 11 ft. lbs.
4. Apply a suitable lubricant to adjuster bolt contact points, then install levers, shim and new C-washer.
5. Measure clearance between shoe and lever. Clearance should be .014 inch. If clearance is not as specified, select a suitable shim to bring clearance to specified value.
6. Place strut and return spring on rear shoe, then install adjusting lever spring.
7. Connect parking brake cable to lever, then position one end of rear shoe in wheel cylinder and the other end in anchor plate.
8. Install rear shoe pin and hold-down spring.
9. Insert anchor spring between front and rear shoes, then position end of front shoe in wheel cylinder with strut in place.
10. Install front shoe hold-down spring, retainers and pin.
11. Install shoe return spring clamp, then the shoe return spring.
12. Ensure adjusting bolt rotates while pulling parking brake upward. If bolt does not turn, check installation of rear brakes.
13. Adjust strut to shortest possible length, then install drum.
14. Pull parking brake lever fully upward then repeat step several times.
15. Remove drum, then check for proper clearance, **Fig. 4.** Clearance should be .024 inch. If clearance is not as specified, check parking brake system.
16. Install brake drum, then bleed and refill brake system.
17. Install wheel and tire assembly, then lower vehicle.

TYPE 4

Removal

1. Raise and support rear of vehicle, then remove wheel and tire assembly.
2. Remove brake drum. If brake drum cannot be removed easily, insert a suitable screwdriver through hole in backing plate, then push adjuster lever away from adjuster and back of adjustment tension.
3. Remove tension spring, using a suitable tool, then remove rear shoe hold-down spring and pin. Remove rear brake shoe and anchor spring, **Fig. 7.**
4. **On Land Cruiser models,** remove front hold-down spring using a suitable tool, then disconnect the parking brake cable from the parking brake bellcrank, **Fig. 7.**
5. **On Pickup, 4Runner, 4WD T100 and 4WD Tacoma models,** remove front shoe hold-down spring and pin, using a suitable tool, then disconnect No. 1 parking brake cable from No. 3 parking brake bellcrank.
6. **On 2WD T100 models,** proceed as follows:
   a. Remove E-ring, then automatic adjusting lever and C-washer, then parking brake lever. Disconnect brake line from wheel cylinder using a suitable container to catch fluid.
   b. Remove wheel cylinder. Remove following parts from wheel cylinder: two boots, two pistons, two pistons cups and spring.
7. **On models except 2WD T100,** remove front brake with strut, then disconnect parking brake cable from front shoe. Remove parking brake cable No. 2.
8. Remove adjusting lever spring, then the adjuster from front shoe.

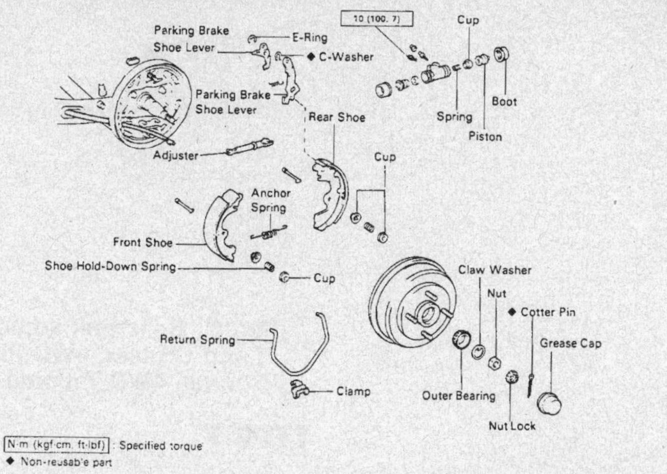
Parking Brake Shoe Lever
E-Ring
◆ C-Washer
10 (100, 7)
Cup
Parking Brake Shoe Lever
Rear Shoe
Boot
Spring
Piston
Adjuster
Cup
Anchor Spring
Front Shoe
Shoe Hold-Down Spring
Cup
Claw Washer
Nut
◆ Cotter Pin
Grease Cap
Return Spring
Clamp
Outer Bearing
Nut Lock
N·m (kgf·cm, ft·lbf) : Specified torque
◆ Non-reusable part

TY4089100006000X

Fig. 6 Exploded view of type 3 brake assembly. Tercel & Paseo

Inspection

1. Measure brake drum inside diameter. Inside diameter should be 11.61 inches, **Fig. 2.**
2. Measure brake shoe lining thickness, **Fig. 3.** Minimum thickness should be .04 inch on models except on T100 models and .039 inch on T100 models.
3. Inspect brake lining and drum for proper contact and replace drum or shoes as necessary.
4. Inspect wheel cylinder for corrosion or damage.
5. Inspect backing plate for wear or damage.
6. Inspect bellcrank components for bending, wear or damage.
7. Apply a suitable lubricant to backing plate contact areas.

Installation

1. **On 2WD T100 models,** proceed as follows:
   a. Apply lithium soap base glycol grease to piston cups, pistons and boots.
   b. Assemble and install wheel cylinder.
   c. Connect brake line to cylinder.
2. Apply high temperature grease to following parts:
   a. Backing plate and brake shoe contact points.
   b. Anchor plate and brake shoe contact points.
   c. Adjusting bolt.
   d. Adjuster and brake shoe contact points.
3. Apply a suitable lubricant to adjuster bolt threads and end.
4. Assemble adjuster to lever, then install adjuster lever spring.
5. **On Land Cruiser models,** install parking brake lever cable to parking brake shoe, then attach cable to bellcrank.
6. **On Pickup, 4Runner, 4WD T100 and 4WD Tacoma models,** install No. 1 parking brake cable to parking brake lever shoe, then attach the other side of cable to No. 3 bellcrank.
7. **On all models,** position front shoe in place with end of shoe inserted into piston, then install shoe hold-down spring and pin using a suitable tool.
8. Assemble anchor spring to front and rear shoe, then install rear shoe with end inserted in piston.
9. Install rear shoe hold-down spring and pin, then the tension spring.
10. If necessary, adjust bellcrank as follows:
    a. Lightly pull bellcrank in direction "A," **Fig. 8,** until there is no slack in part "B."
    b. Rotate adjusting bolt until dimension "C" is .016–.031 inch.
    c. Lock adjusting bolt with locknut, when connect parking brake cable to bellcrank.
    d. Install tension spring.
11. Ensure proper parking brake travel.
12. Pull adjusting lever cable upward, then release and ensure adjusting bolt rotates. If bolt does not rotate, check for improper installation of rear brakes.
13. Adjust strut to shortest possible length, then install drum.
14. Pull parking brake lever fully upward. Repeat process several times.
15. Remove drum, then check for proper clearance, **Fig. 4.** Clearance should be .024 inch. If clearance is not as specified, check parking brake system.
16. Install brake drum, then bleed and refill brake system.
17. Install wheel and tire assembly, then lower vehicle.

TYPE 5

Removal

1. Raise and support rear of vehicle, then remove wheel and tire assembly.
2. Remove brake drum. If brake drum cannot be remove easily, insert a suitable screwdriver through hole in backing plate, then push adjuster lever away from adjuster and back of adjustment tension.
3. Remove tension spring, using a suitable tool, then remove rear shoe hold-down spring and pin. Remove rear brake shoe and anchor spring, **Fig. 9.**
4. Remove rear shoe hold-down spring and pin, using suitable tool, then disconnect parking brake cable from lever.
5. Remove adjusting lever spring and strut from rear shoe.
6. Position a suitable container to catch fluid, then remove two boots, two pistons, two piston cups and spring from wheel cylinder.

Inspection

1. Measure brake drum inside diameter. Inside diameter should be 9.00 inches, **Fig. 2.**
2. Measure brake shoe lining thickness, **Fig. 3.** Minimum thickness should be .04 inch.
3. Inspect brake lining and drum for proper contact and replace drum or shoes as necessary.
4. Inspect wheel cylinder for corrosion or damage.
5. Inspect backing plate for wear or damage.
6. Apply a suitable lubricant to backing plate contact areas.

Installation

1. Apply a suitable lubricant to piston cups, then insert spring and two piston cups into wheel cylinder. Apply a suitable lubricant to inside of boots, then insert them into cylinder, **Fig. 9.**
2. Apply a suitable lubricant to adjuster bolt threads and end, then install strut and adjusting lever spring.
3. Connect parking brake cable to lever, then position one end of rear shoe in wheel cylinder and the other end in anchor plate.
4. Install rear shoe pin and hold-down spring.
5. Insert anchor spring between front and rear shoes, then position end of front shoe in wheel cylinder with strut in place.
6. Install front shoe hold-down spring and pin.
7. Install tension spring.
8. Ensure adjusting bolt rotates while pulling parking brake upward. If bolt does not turn, check installation of rear brakes.
9. Adjust strut to shortest possible length, then install drum.
10. Pull parking brake lever fully upward then repeat step several times.
11. Remove drum, then check for proper clearance, **Fig. 4.** Clearance should be .024 inch. If clearance is not as specified, check parking brake system.
12. Install brake drum, then bleed and refill brake system.
13. Install wheel and tire assembly, then lower vehicle.

TYPE 6

Removal

1. Raise and support rear of vehicle, then remove wheel and tire assembly.
2. Remove brake drum. If brake drum

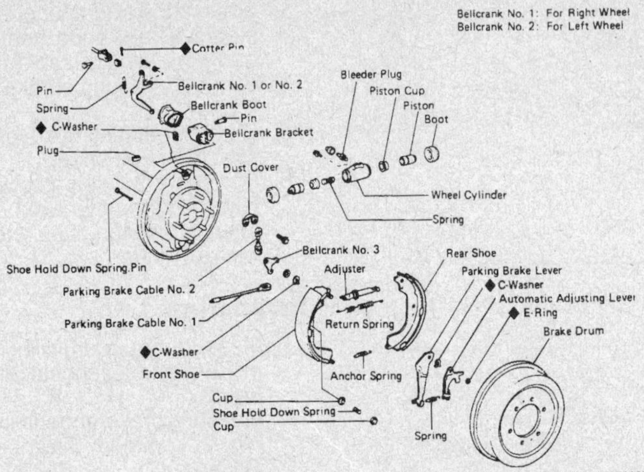
Bellcrank No. 1: For Right Wheel
Bellcrank No. 2: For Left Wheel
Cotter Pin
Pin
Spring
Bellcrank No. 1 or No. 2
Bellcrank Boot
Pin
C-Washer
Bellcrank Bracket
Plug
Bleeder Plug
Piston Cup
Piston
Boot
Dust Cover
Wheel Cylinder
Spring
Bellcrank No. 3
Shoe Hold Down Spring Pin
Adjuster
Rear Shoe
Parking Brake Lever
C-Washer
Automatic Adjusting Lever
E-Ring
Brake Drum
Parking Brake Cable No. 2
Parking Brake Cable No. 1
Return Spring
C-Washer
Front Shoe
Anchor Spring
Cup
Shoe Hold Down Spring
Cup
Spring

TY4089100007000X

Fig. 7 Exploded view of type 4 drum brake assembly. Land Cruiser, Pickup, 4Runner, 4WD Tacoma & 4WD T100

cannot be remove easily, insert a suitable screwdriver through hole in backing plate, then push automatic adjuster lever away from adjuster and back of adjustment tension.
3. Disconnect return spring, using a suitable tool, then remove front shoe hold-down spring, retainers and pin.
4. Disconnect anchor spring, then remove front brake shoe and anchor spring, **Fig. 10.**
5. Remove rear shoe hold-down spring, retainers and pin, using suitable a tool, then disconnect parking brake cable from anchor plate.
6. Disconnect parking brake cable from lever, then remove rear shoe with strut.
7. Remove adjusting lever spring, strut and return spring from rear shoe.
8. Remove C-washer, then the shims, parking brake lever and automatic adjusting lever from rear shoe.
9. Position a suitable container to catch fluid, then disconnect brake line.
10. Remove two attaching bolts, then the wheel cylinder.
11. Remove two boots, two pistons, two piston cups and spring from wheel cylinder.

Inspection

1. Measure brake drum inside diameter. Inside diameter should be 7.87 inches, **Fig. 2.**
2. Measure brake shoe lining thickness, **Fig. 3.** Minimum thickness should be .04 inch.
3. Inspect brake lining and drum for proper contact and replace drum or shoes as necessary.
4. Inspect wheel cylinder for corrosion or damage.
5. Inspect backing plate for wear or damage.
6. Inspect bellcrank components for bending, wear or damage.
7. Apply a suitable lubricant to backing plate contact areas.

Installation

1. Apply a suitable lubricant to pistons and cups, then install spring and two piston cups into wheel cylinder. Apply a suitable lubricant to inside of boots, then insert them into cylinder, **Fig. 10.**
2. Install wheel cylinder onto backing plate, then insert attaching bolts and **torque** to 7 ft. lbs.
3. Connect brake tube to wheel cylinder, then **torque** nut to 11 ft. lbs.
4. Apply a suitable lubricant to adjuster bolt contact points, then install levers, shim and new C-washer.
5. Measure clearance between shoe and lever. Clearance should be .014 inch. If clearance is not as specified, select a suitable shim to bring clearance to specified value.
6. Place strut and return spring on rear shoe, then install adjusting lever spring.
7. Connect parking brake cable to lever, then insert cable through notch in anchor plate.
8. Position one end of rear shoe in wheel cylinder and the other end in anchor plate.
9. Install rear shoe pin and hold-down spring and retainers.
10. Insert anchor spring between front and rear shoes, then position end of front shoe in wheel cylinder with strut in place.
11. Install front shoe hold-down spring, retainers and pin.
12. Install return spring.
13. Ensure adjusting bolt rotates while pulling parking brake upward. If bolt does not turn, check installation of rear brakes.
14. Adjust strut to its shortest possible length, then install drum.
15. Pull parking brake lever fully upward, then repeat step several times.
16. Remove drum, then check for proper clearance, **Fig. 4.** Clearance should be .024 inch. If clearance is not as specified, check parking brake system.
17. Install brake drum, then bleed and refill brake system.
18. Install wheel and tire assembly, then lower vehicle.

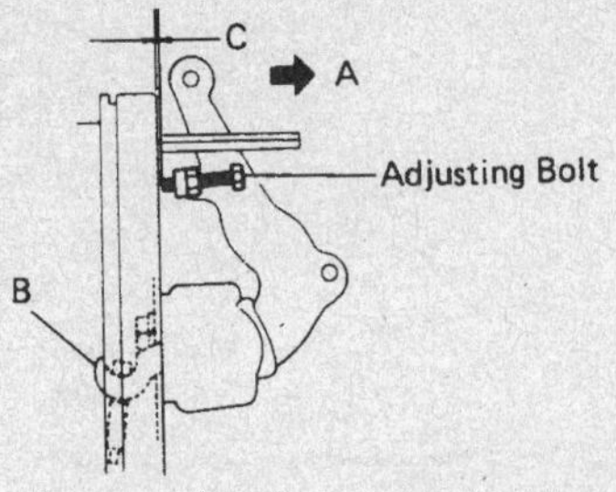
C
A
Adjusting Bolt
B

TY4089100008000X

Fig. 8 Bellcrank adjustment. Land Cruiser, 4WD Pickup, 4Runner, 4WD Tacoma & T100

TYPE 7

Removal

1. Raise and support rear of vehicle, then remove wheel and tire assembly.
2. Remove brake drum. If brake drum cannot be remove easily, insert a suitable screwdriver through hole in backing plate, then push adjuster lever away from adjuster and back of adjustment tension.
3. Disconnect return spring, using a suitable tool, then remove front shoe hold-down spring, retainers and pin.
4. Disconnect anchor spring, then remove front brake shoe and anchor spring, **Fig. 11.**
5. Remove rear shoe hold-down spring, retainers and pin, using suitable tool, then disconnect parking brake cable from anchor plate.
6. Disconnect parking brake cable from lever, then remove rear shoe with strut.
7. Remove adjusting lever spring, strut and return spring from rear shoe.
8. Remove C-washer, then the shims, parking brake lever and automatic adjusting lever from rear shoe.
9. Position a suitable container to catch fluid, then disconnect brake line.
10. Remove two attaching bolts, then the wheel cylinder.
11. Remove two boots, two pistons, two piston cups and spring from wheel cylinder.

Inspection

1. Measure brake drum inside diameter. Inside diameter should be 7.87 inches, **Fig. 2.**
2. Measure brake shoe lining thickness, **Fig. 3.** Minimum thickness should be .04 inch.
3. Inspect brake lining and drum for proper contact and replace drum or shoes as necessary.
4. Inspect wheel cylinder for corrosion or damage.
5. Inspect backing plate for wear or damage.
6. Inspect bellcrank components for bending, wear or damage.
7. Apply a suitable lubricant to backing plate contact areas.

Installation

1. Apply a suitable lubricant to pistons

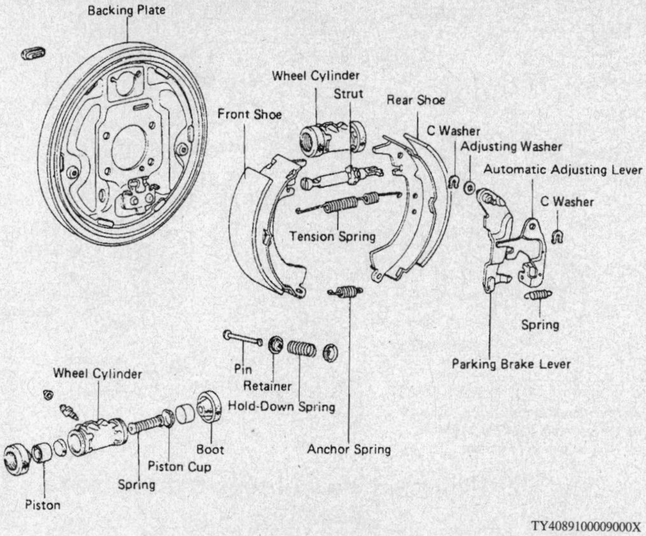
Backing Plate
Wheel Cylinder
Strut
Rear Shoe
Front Shoe
C Washer
Adjusting Washer
Automatic Adjusting Lever
C Washer
Tension Spring
Spring
Parking Brake Lever
Pin
Retainer
Hold-Down Spring
Wheel Cylinder
Boot
Anchor Spring
Piston Cup
Spring
Piston
TY4089100009000X

Fig. 9 Exploded view of type 5 drum brake assembly

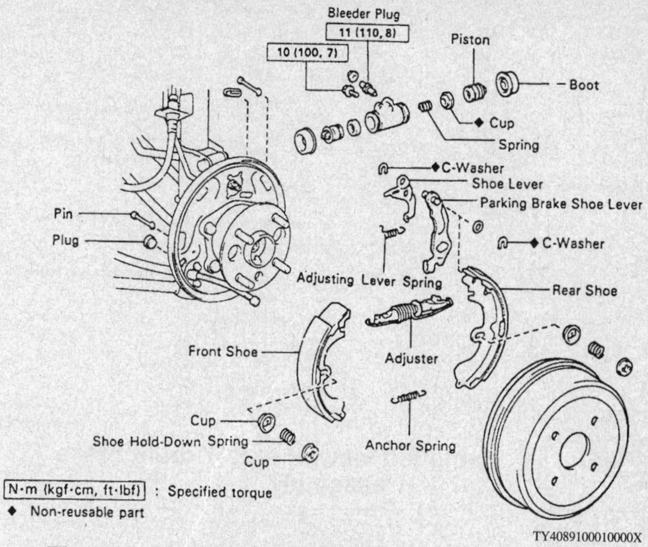
Bleeder Plug
11 (110, 8)
10 (100, 7)
Piston
Boot
Cup
Spring
C-Washer
Shoe Lever
Parking Brake Shoe Lever
Pin
Plug
C-Washer
Adjusting Lever Spring
Rear Shoe
Front Shoe
Adjuster
Cup
Shoe Hold-Down Spring
Cup
Anchor Spring
N·m (kgf·cm, ft·lbf) : Specified torque
◆ Non-reusable part
TY4089100010000X

Fig. 10 Exploded view of type 6 drum brake assembly

and cups, then install spring and two piston cups into wheel cylinder. Apply a suitable lubricant to inside of boots, then insert them into cylinder, **Fig. 11.**

2. Install wheel cylinder onto backing plate, then insert attaching bolts and **torque** to 7 ft. lbs.
3. Connect brake tube to wheel cylinder, then **torque** nut to 11 ft. lbs.
4. Apply a suitable lubricant to adjuster bolt contact points, then install levers, shim and new C-washer.
5. Measure clearance between shoe and lever. Clearance should be .014 inch. If clearance is not as specified, select a suitable shim to bring clearance to specified value.
6. Place strut and return spring on rear shoe, then install adjusting lever spring.
7. Connect parking brake cable to lever, then insert cable through notch in anchor plate.
8. Position one end of rear shoe in wheel cylinder and the other end in anchor plate.
9. Install rear shoe pin and hold-down spring and retainers.
10. Insert anchor spring between front and rear shoes, then position end of front shoe in wheel cylinder with strut in place.
11. Install front shoe hold-down spring, retainers and pin.
12. Install return spring.
13. Ensure adjusting bolt rotates while pulling parking brake upward. If bolt does not turn, check installation of rear brakes.
14. Adjust strut to its shortest possible length, then install drum.
15. Pull parking brake lever fully upward then repeat step several times.
16. Remove drum, then check for proper clearance, **Fig. 4.** Clearance should be .024 inch. If clearance is not as specified, check parking brake system.
17. Install brake drum, then bleed and refill brake system.
18. Install wheel and tire assembly, then lower vehicle.

TYPE 8

Removal

1. Raise and support vehicle, then remove rear wheel.
2. Remove brake drum. If drum cannot easily be removed, insert bent wire through hole in drum and hold automatic adjusting lever away from adjuster.
3. Remove front shoe return spring using tool No. 09703-30010, or equivalent, **Fig. 12.**
4. Using tool No. 09718-00010, or equivalent, remove front shoe hold-down spring, cups and pin.
5. Disconnect anchor spring from front shoe and remove front shoe.
6. Using tool No. 09718-00010, or equivalent, remove rear shoe hold-down spring, cups and pin.
7. Using a screwdriver, disconnect parking cable from anchor plate.
8. Using pliers, disconnect parking brake cable from lever and remove rear shoe together with adjuster.
9. Remove adjusting lever spring and adjuster from rear shoe.
10. Disconnect brake line from wheel cylinder using tool No. 09023-00100, or equivalent.
11. Remove wheel cylinder.

Inspection

1. Inspect parts for wear, rust or damage.
2. Using a ruler, measure brake shoe lining. Standard thickness is .197 inch. Minimum thickness is .039 inch.
3. Using vernier calipers, measure inside drum diameter. Standard diameter should be 9 inches. Maximum inner diameter is 9.08 inches.
4. If brake drum is scored or worn, it may be lathed to maximum inside diameter.
5. Inspect brake lining and drum for proper contact and replace drum or shoes as necessary.

Installation

1. Reverse removal procedure to install, noting the following:
   a. Move parking brake lever of rear shoe back and forth. Ensure adjuster turns.
   b. If adjuster does not turn, check for incorrect installation of rear brakes.
   c. Adjust length of adjuster to shortest length possible.
   d. Check clearance between brake shoes and drum. Clearance should be .024 inch.

ADJUSTMENTS

PARKING BRAKE

Camry, Celica, Corolla, Paseo, Previa, Tercel

1. Apply parking brake and count number of notches on parking brake sector. Specified number of notches should be as follows: 4–7 for Celica, 5–8 for Corolla, 5–8 for Camry, 4–5 for Previa, 5–8 for Tercel sedans and 6–8 for Tercel wagons.
2. **On Camry, Celica, Corolla and Tercel,** adjust parking brake as follows:
   a. Remove console box, and if necessary, the shift knob.
   b. Loosen locknut and turn adjustment screw until lever travel is correct.
   c. Tighten locknut and reinstall console.
3. **On Previa models,** proceed as follows:
   a. Raise and support vehicle.
   b. Tighten or loosen adjusting nut at parking brake equalizer as necessary to bring parking brake adjustment within specifications.
   c. Lower vehicle.

Pickup, T100, Tacoma & 4Runner, 2WD

1. Release parking brake and check to

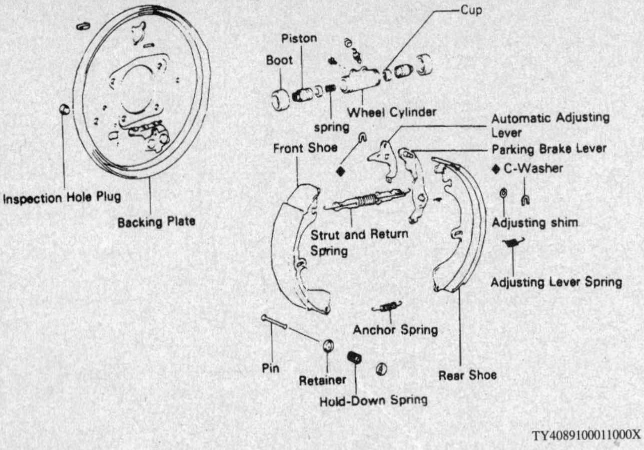

Cup
Piston
Boot
spring
Wheel Cylinder
Automatic Adjusting Lever
Parking Brake Lever
◆ C-Washer
Front Shoe
Inspection Hole Plug
Backing Plate
Strut and Return Spring
Adjusting shim
Adjusting Lever Spring
Anchor Spring
Pin
Retainer
Rear Shoe
Hold-Down Spring
TY4089100011000X

Fig. 11 Exploded view of type 7 drum brake assembly

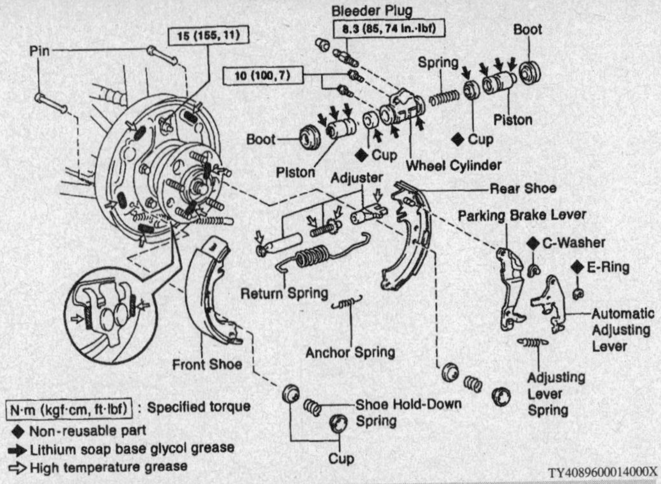

Bleeder Plug
8.3 (85, 74 in.·lbf)
Boot
15 (155, 11)
Pin
10 (100, 7)
Spring
Piston
◆ Cup
Boot
Piston
◆ Cup
Wheel Cylinder
Adjuster
Rear Shoe
Parking Brake Lever
◆ C-Washer
◆ E-Ring
Automatic Adjusting Lever
Return Spring
Anchor Spring
Front Shoe
Adjusting Lever Spring
Shoe Hold-Down Spring
Cup
N·m (kgf·cm, ft·lbf) : Specified torque
◆ Non-reusable part
Lithium soap base glycol grease
High temperature grease
TY4089600014000X

Fig. 12 Exploded view of type 8 drum brake assembly

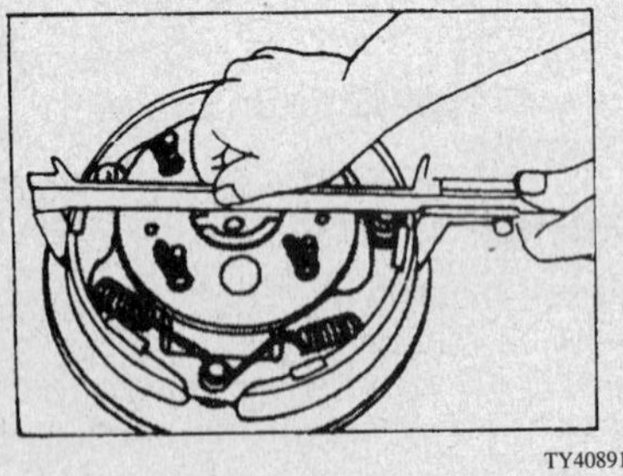

TY4089100013000X

Fig. 13 Brake shoe to brake drum clearance measurement. Land Cruiser, Pickup, Tacoma, T100 & 4Runner

ensure warning light switch is off. If adjustment is required, loosen parking brake warning light switch bracket and position switch.

2. Adjust nut at parking brake cable equalizer so that there is no looseness at No. 2 and No. 3 parking brake cables. Check to ensure both rear wheels rotate freely.
3. After adjusting, apply parking brake lever and count number of notches on brake lever. Specified number of notches should be 10–16.

Land Cruiser, Pickup, T100, Tacoma & 4Runner, 4WD

1. Tighten bellcrank stopper screw until there is no play in rear brake link. Back off screw one turn, then tighten screw locknut.
2. Tighten one intermediate lever adjusting nut while loosening the other until lever travel of 9–17 clicks is obtained. Tighten both adjusting nuts.
3. Check to ensure bellcrank stopper screw contacts backing plate.

SHOE ADJUSTMENT

Land Cruiser, Pickup, Tacoma, T100 & 4Runner

Measure brake drum inside diameter and maximum diameter of brake shoes using brake shoe clearance gauge, **Fig. 13.** Turn adjuster so that brake shoe diameter will be .012–.024 inch (.3–.6 mm) smaller than brake drum inner diameter.

Raise and support rear of vehicle, ensure rear wheels move freely. Remove brake shoe adjusting hole plug from backing plate, then using a suitable brake tool, expand adjuster until wheel is locked. Working through backing plate, insert a narrow tool to move self-adjuster lever away from adjuster, then loosen adjuster wheel approximately 10–12 notches. Install brake shoe adjusting hole plug.

DRUM BRAKE SPECIFICATIONS

Year	Model	Brake Drum Inside Dia. Inch	Maximum Refinish Dia. Inch
1993–96	Camry①	9.000	9.079
1993–96	Celica	7.874②③	7.913④
1993–96	Corolla	7.874	7.913
1993–94	Land Cruiser	11.614	11.693
1993–96	Paseo & Tercel	7.087	7.126
1996	RAV4	9.000	9.079
1993–96	Tacoma, Pickup & 4Runner⑤	10.000	10.079
1993–96	Tacoma, Pickup & 4Runner⑥	11.614	11.693
1993–96	Previa	10.000	10.079
1993–96	T100	11.61	11.69

① — Except All Trac 4WD system.
② — With rear disc brakes, parking brake drum I.D, 6.69 inch.
③ — With rear disc brake, rear disc brake rotor, .394 inch.
④ — With rear disc brake, rear disc brake rotor, .354 inch.
⑤ — Except 4WD.
⑥ — 4WD

TIGHTENING SPECIFICATIONS

Year	Component	Torque/Ft.Lbs.
CAMRY		
1993–96	Bleeder Plug	74①
	Wheel Cylinder	7
CELICA		
1993–96	Bleeder Plug	74①
	Union Nut	11
	Wheel Cylinder	7
COROLLA		
1993–96	Bleeder Plug	74①
	Union Nut	11
	Wheel Cylinder	7
LAND CRUISER		
1993–94	Backing Plate	90
	Bleeder Plug	8
	Parking Brake To Backing Plate	9
	Union Nut	11
	Wheel Cylinder	7
PICKUP & 4RUNNER		
1993–96	Bleeder Plug	8
	Backing Plate	51
	Union Nut	11
	Wheel Cylinder (Duo Servo Brakes)	10
	Wheel Cylinder (Leading-Trailing Brakes)	7
PREVIA		
1993–96	Bleeder Plug	74①
	Parking Brake Bracket	69①
	Wheel Cylinder	7
RAV4		
1996	Backing Plate	7
	Bleeder Plug	74①
TERCEL & PASEO		
1993–96	Backing Plate	51
	Wheel Cylinder	7
T100 & TACOMA		
1993–96	Backing Plate	51
	Wheel Cylinder	7
	Parking Brake Bellcrank Bracket To Backing Plate	9

① — Inch lbs.

Hydraulic Brake Systems

NOTE: On Vehicles Equipped With Anti-Lock Brakes Refer To "Anti-Lock Brakes" Section Of This Manual.

INDEX

	Page No.
Brake System Bleed	48-151
Brake Lines	48-151
Master Cylinder	48-151
Component Replacement	48-150
Master Cylinder	48-150
Proportioning Valve	48-150
Wheel Cylinders	48-150
Component Service	48-150
Master Cylinder	48-150
Wheel Cylinders	48-151
Description	48-150
Tightening Specifications	48-151
Troubleshooting	48-150

DESCRIPTION

When the brake pedal is depressed, a vacuum builds up in the booster which amplifies the pedal force, pressing on the piston in the master cylinder. The piston raises the hydraulic pressure in the cylinder. This hydraulic pressure is then applied to each respective brake caliper, and acts to press the brake pads and shoes against the rotating discs and drums. The resulting friction converts the rotational energy to thermal energy, stopping the vehicle.

TROUBLESHOOTING

Refer to **Fig. 1** for general troubleshooting of the brake system.

Trouble \ Part Name	Brake system (Fluid leaks)	Brake system (Air in)	Brake pad (Worn)	Piston seal (Worn or damaged)	Brake pedal (Freeplay minimal)	Master cylinder (Faulty)	Parking brake (Shoe clearance out of adjustment)	Parking brake (Pedal travel out of adjustment)	Parking-brake wire (Sticking)	Booster push rod (Out of adjustment)	Tension or return spring (Faulty)	Pad (Cracked or distorted)	Piston (Stuck)	Pad (Oily)	Piston (Frozen)	Booster system (Vacuum leaks)	Pad support plate (Loose)	Installation bolt (Loose)	Sliding pin (Worn)	Disc (Scored)	Pad (Dirty)	Pad (Glazed)	Anti-squeal shim (Damaged)	Hold-down spring (Damaged)
Low pedal or spongy pedal	1	2		3		4				5														
Brake drag					1	11	4	2	3	9	8	5	6		7	10								
Brake pull												5	1	2	3					4				
Hard pedal but brake inefficient	1	2	3							8		4		5		9				7		6		
Noise from brakes											8	1					4	2	5	3	6	7	9	10

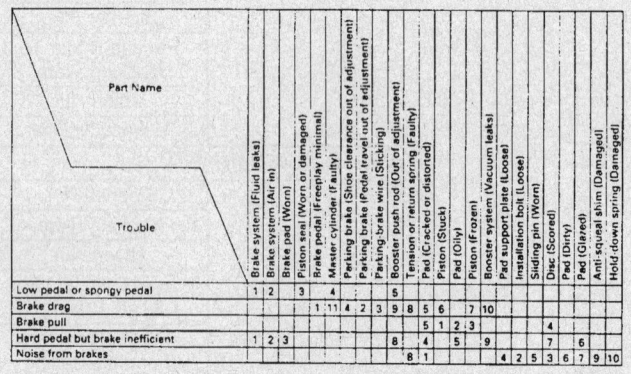

The numbers indicate the priority of the likely cause of the problem.
Check each part in order. If necessary, replace these parts.

TY4099500006000X

Fig. 1 Troubleshooting chart

COMPONENT REPLACEMENT

MASTER CYLINDER

1. **On MR2,** remove luggage compartment trim cover by removing two clips after disengaging inner part of clip.
2. **On all models,** remove brake fluid with syringe.
3. **On RAV4,** remove air cleaner cover with air cleaner hose.
4. **On all models,** label and disconnect brake lines using line wrench 09751-36011, 09023–00100, or equivalent. Then cap brake lines from master cylinder.
5. Disconnect wire connector from brake pressure switch and then disconnect level warning switch connector, if equipped.
6. Remove master cylinder to brake unit attaching nuts, then remove master cylinder, wire clamp, gasket and 3-way union, as needed.
7. Reverse procedure to install. Bleed brake system.

WHEEL CYLINDERS

1. Remove brake shoes as outlined under "Drum Brakes."
2. Disconnect brake line using line wrench 09751–36011, or equivalent. Then remove two wheel cylinder attaching bolts and wheel cylinder.
3. Reverse procedure to install. **Torque** wheel cylinder bolts to 7 ft. lbs. Bleed brakes.

PROPORTIONING VALVE

EXCEPT LAND CRUISER, PICKUP & 4RUNNER

Models w/Load Sensing Proportioning Valve (LSPV)

1. Disconnect brake lines using line wrench 09751–36011, or equivalent.
2. Remove proportioning valve adjusting nut, then the spring from rear suspension arm.
3. Remove bolts and proportioning valve from mounting assembly.
4. Reverse procedure to install. Bleed brakes.

Models w/Proportioning & By-Pass Valve (P-BV)

The proportioning valve is located nest to the master cylinder. Remove brake lines with line wrench 09751–36011, or equivalent. Then remove attaching bolts and valve. Reverse necessary steps to install, then bleed system.

LAND CRUISER, PICKUP & 4RUNNER

1. Disconnect shackle No. 2 from bracket.
2. Disconnect brake lines using line wrench 09751–36011, or equivalent.
3. Remove mounting bolts and valve.
4. Reverse procedure to install. Bleed system.

COMPONENT SERVICE

MASTER CYLINDER

Disassembly

For the following procedures, refer to **Fig. 2** for assistance.

1. Remove master cylinder boot.
2. Remove setscrew and then reservoir tank. Remove cap and strainer from reservoir.
3. Remove two grommets. Then place cylinder in vise.
4. Push piston in and remove stopper bolt, **Fig. 3.**
5. Push pistons in and remove snap ring. Then carefully remove No. 1 piston by hand.
6. Place cylinder on edges of two wooden blocks and tap on cylinder until No. 2 piston comes out.

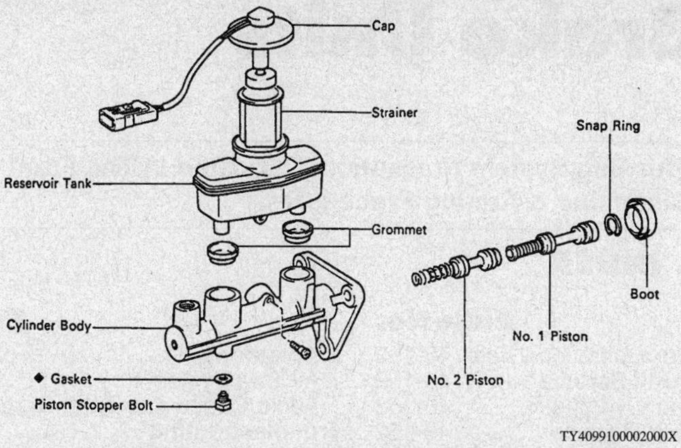
Cap
Strainer
Reservoir Tank
Grommet
Snap Ring
Boot
Cylinder Body
No. 1 Piston
◆ Gasket
Piston Stopper Bolt
No. 2 Piston
TY4099100002000X

Fig. 2 Exploded view of master cylinder. Typical

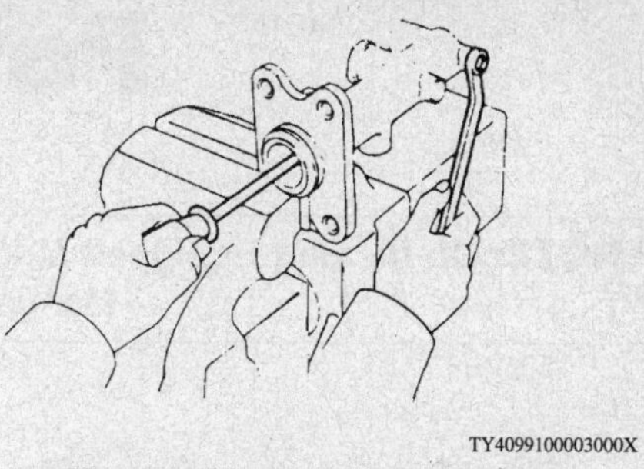
TY4099100003000X

Fig. 3 Piston stopper bolt removal

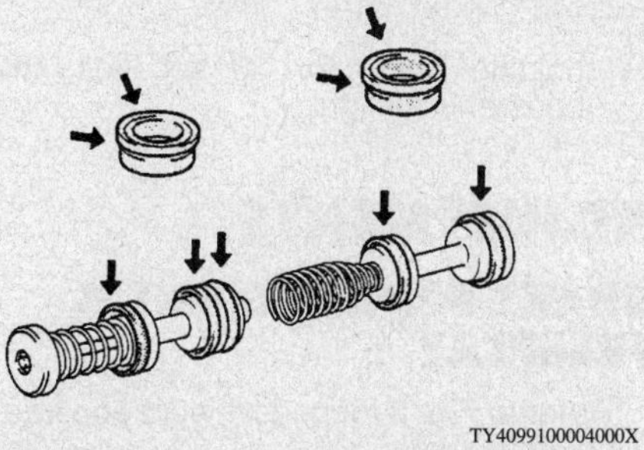
TY4099100004000X

Fig. 4 Master cylinder lubrication locations. Typical

Inspection

Clean parts with compressed air. Inspect cylinder bore for rust and scoring. Also, inspect for wear or damage to bore. If necessary, replace. Refer to **Fig. 4** for master cylinder lubricant locations.

Assembly

1. Install two grommets.
2. Install reservoir, while pushing down on reservoir, install setscrew. **Torque** setscrew to 15.2 inch lbs.
3. Install master cylinder boot, then the master cylinder as previously described.

WHEEL CYLINDERS

Refer to Fig. 5 for disassembled view of a typical wheel cylinder.

1. Remove boots, pistons, piston cups and spring from wheel cylinder.
2. Clean all parts using suitable brake cleaner. Inspect cylinder bore for rust, scoring or wear. If necessary, replace cylinder.
3. Apply suitable grease to all rubber parts and mating surfaces.
4. Install piston cups to pistons. Then install spring and pistons into wheel cylinder. **Ensure flanges of cups are pointed upward.** Install boots.

BRAKE SYSTEM BLEED

MASTER CYLINDER

1. Fill reservoir with fluid.
2. Disconnect tubes from master cylinder. Then slowly depress brake pedal and hold.

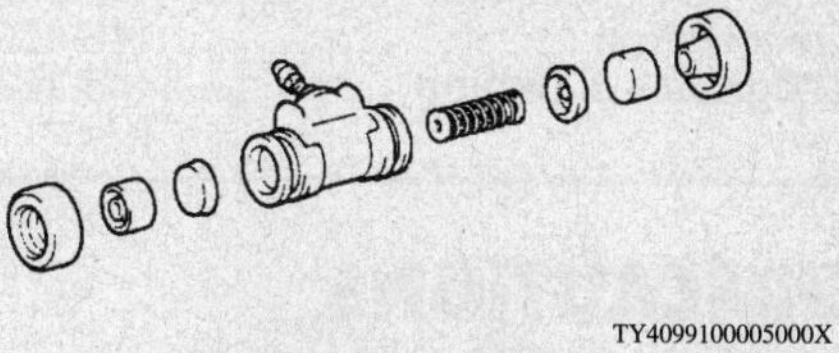
TY4099100005000X

Fig. 5 Exploded view of wheel cylinder. Typical

3. Block off outlet holes with fingers, and release pedal. Repeat three or four times.

BRAKE LINES

Bleed wheel with longest brake line first, then work your way back to the master cylinder according to brake line length.

1. Connect tube to brake cylinder.
2. Depress pedal several times and hold. Loosen bleeder plug.
3. When fluid stops coming out, tighten bleeder plug and release pedal. Repeat several times.
4. Repeat entire procedure for each wheel. Fill reservoir.

TIGHTENING SPECIFICATIONS

Year	Component	Torque/ Ft. Lbs.
1993–96	Brake Line To Master Cylinder Union Nuts	11
	Master Cylinder Bolts	9
	Piston Stopper Bolt	6–7
	Reservoir Set Screw	13–15.5①
	Wheel Cylinder Bolts	7

① — Inch Lbs.

Power Brake Units

NOTE: On Air Bag Equipped Models, Refer To "Air Bag System Precautions" Located In The Front Of This Manual For System Disarming & Arming Procedures.

INDEX

	Page No.
Adjustments	48-152
Brake Pedal Height & Freeplay	48-152
Description	48-152
Diagnosis & Testing	48-152
Brake Booster Operational Test	48-152
Power Brake Unit Service	48-152
Brake Booster Overhaul	48-153
Brake Booster, Replace	48-152
Precautions	48-152
Air Bag Systems	48-152
Audio Coded Anti-Theft System	48-152
Troubleshooting	48-152

PRECAUTIONS

AIR BAG SYSTEMS

Refer to "Air Bag System Precautions" in the front of this manual for system disarming and arming procedures.

AUDIO CODED ANTI-THEFT SYSTEM

Some models are equipped with an audio coded anti-theft system that will disable the radio when the battery cable is disconnected. The system can be identified by the "ANTI-THEFT SYSTEM" on the cassette tape lid. Obtain 3 digit customer code for input. Reset system after service as follows:

1. Obtain 3 digit audio anti-theft code.
2. Depress 1 (PROG) while depressing righthand side of TUNE SEEK button, - - - will appear in tape operation display.
3. To enter the first digit, depress 1 (PROG) button repeatedly until the number of times depressed equals the first digit beginning with zero (depress the 1 button six times if the first digit if five).
4. To enter second digit, depress 2 (APS) button repeatedly until the number of times depressed equals the second digit beginning with zero.
5. To enter third digit, depress 3 (RPT) button repeatedly until the number of times depressed equals the third digit beginning with zero.
6. If - - - is displayed during code input, repeat procedure.
7. When code appears in display, depress and hold SCAN button until SEC appears.
8. When SEC disappears audio system should be operative.
9. If Err is displayed, repeat procedure. **Attempting to input code more than nine times may permanently disable audio system.**

DESCRIPTION

When the brake pedal is depressed, a vacuum builds up in the booster which amplifies the pedal force, pressing on the piston in the master cylinder. The piston raises the hydraulic pressure in the cylinder. This hydraulic pressure is then applied to each respective brake cylinder, and acts to press the brake pads against the rotating rotor discs. the resulting friction converts the rotational energy to thermal energy, stopping the vehicle.

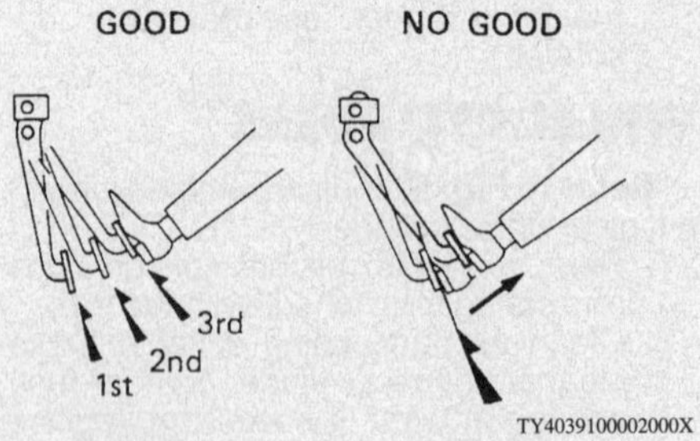

GOOD
NO GOOD
3rd
2nd
1st
TY4039100002000X

Fig. 1 Air tightness check

TROUBLESHOOTING

Refer to "Hydraulic Brake Systems" for general brake system troubleshooting charts.

DIAGNOSIS & TESTING

BRAKE BOOSTER OPERATIONAL TEST

Operating Check

1. Depress brake pedal several times with engine stopped, and ensure pedal reserve distance has no change, **Fig. 1.**
2. Depress brake pedal and start engine. If pedal drops slightly, operation is normal.

Air Tightness Check

1. Start engine and stop after one or two minutes.
2. Depress brake pedal several times slowly. If pedal drops the most on the first time, but gradually rises after the second or third time, booster is air tight, **Fig. 2.**
3. Depress brake pedal with engine running, then while depressing brake pedal stop engine. If there is no change in pedal reserve travel after holding pedal for 30 seconds, the booster is air tight.

ADJUSTMENTS

BRAKE PEDAL HEIGHT & FREEPLAY

Refer to **Fig. 3** for pedal height and freeplay references.

1. Loosen stop light switch, then the clevis locknut.
2. Adjust pedal height by turning pushrod.
3. Tighten locknut and adjust stop light switch .02–.09 inch from pedal stopper.
4. Depress pedal several times to relieve vacuum.
5. Push pedal until beginning of resistance is felt. Adjust freeplay by turning pushrod, if necessary.

POWER BRAKE UNIT SERVICE

BRAKE BOOSTER, REPLACE

Removal

1. Remove master cylinder as outlined under "Master Cylinder, Replace" in the "Hydraulic Brake Systems " section.
2. **On Camry and Celica models,** push away charcoal vapor canister for better access.
3. **On Supra,** remove cruise actuator.
4. **On Supra and Celica models,** remove lower finish panel or lower pad as outlined in "Dash Panel Service. "
5. **On all models,** remove pedal return spring, clip, clevis pin and clevis locknut, **Fig. 4.**
6. **On Celica,** remove ignition coil and igniter.
7. **On Celica,** use wrench and service tool No. 09751-36011, or equivalent to disconnect brake line from lefthand front brake hose, then remove brake line grommet from wheelhouse.
8. **On all models,** remove brake booster nuts. Pull out booster and gasket.

Year	Model	Pedal Height, Inch	Pedal Freeplay, Inch
1995–96	Avalon	5.81–6.20	.04–.24
1993–96	Camry	5.81–6.20	.04–.24
1993	Celica w/Man. Trans.	6.64–7.03	.04–.24
1993	Celica w/Auto. Trans.	6.61–7.01	.04–.24
1994–96	Celica	5.98–6.37	.02–.09
1993	Corolla	5.47–5.87	.12–.24
1994–96	Corolla	5.65–6.05	.04–.24
1993–96	Land Cruiser	6.59–6.99	.12–.24
1993–95	MR2	6.96–7.36	.12–.20
1993–95	Pickup w/2WD	5.83–6.02	.12–.24
1993–95	Pickup w/4WD	5.71–5.91	.12–.24
1993–96	Paseo	5.45–5.85	.04–.24
1993–96	Previa	5.71–6.10	.04–.24
1993–95	4Runner w/2WD	5.91–6.10	.12–.24
1993–95	4Runner w/4WD	5.71–5.91	.12–.24
1996	4Runner	6.22–6.62	.12–.24
1993–96	T100 Std.	6.06	.12–.24
1993–96	T100 SR5	5.91	.12–.24
1993–96	Supra	5.92–6.31	.04–.24
1996	RAV4	6.19–6.58	.04–.24
1995–96	Tacoma	6.34–6.74	.12–.24
1993	Tercel w/4-Man. Trans.	5.63–6.03	.12–.24
1993	Tercel w/Auto. Trans.	5.45–5.85	.12–.24
1994–96	Tercel w/Auto. Trans.	5.63–6.03	.04–.24
1994–96	Tercel w/Auto. Trans.	5.45–5.85	.04–.24

Fig. 2 Brake pedal height & freeplay chart

Installation

1. Adjust length of booster pushrod as follows:
   a. Install gasket on master cylinder.
   b. Install brake booster pushrod gauge tool No. 09737-00010, or equivalent on gasket.
   c. Lower pin until its tip slightly touches the piston.
   d. Turn gauge tool upside down and set it on booster.
   e. Measure clearance between booster pushrod and pin head of gauge tool.
   f. Adjust booster pushrod length until the pushrod slightly touches the pin head.
2. Install booster and gasket.
3. Install clevis to operating rod.
4. Install clevis pin into clevis and brake pedal then install clip to clevis pin.
5. **On Celica,** connect vacuum hose to brake booster.
6. Install lower finish panel and undercover.

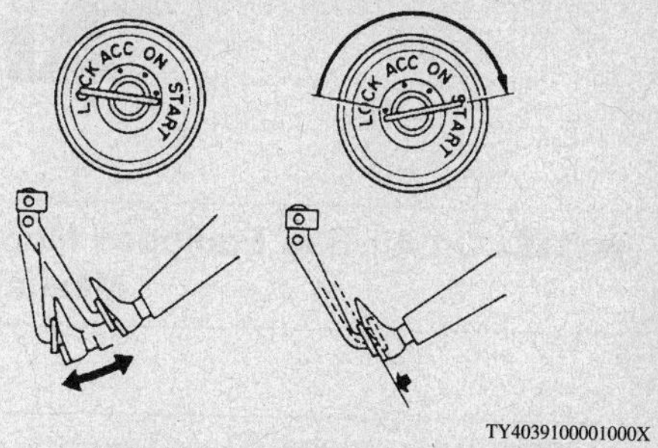
LOCK ACC ON START
LOCK ACC ON START
TY4039100001000X

Fig. 3 Operational test

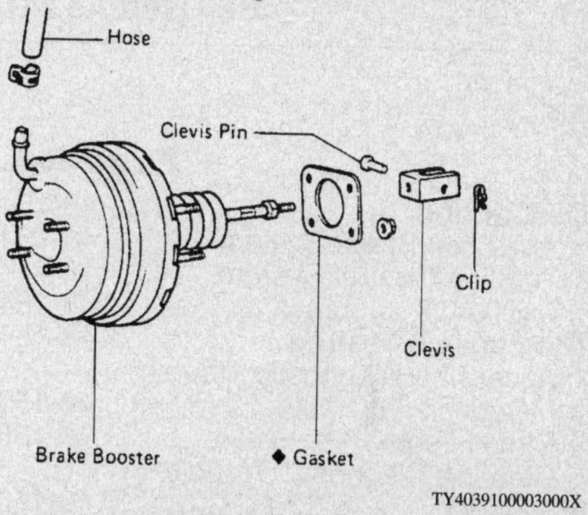
Hose
Clevis Pin
Clip
Clevis
Brake Booster
◆ Gasket
TY4039100003000X

Fig. 4 Brake booster pushrod connections. Typical

7. **On Supra,** install cruise actuator.
8. **On all models,** install master cylinder, fill and bleed brake system as outlined under "Hydraulic Brake System."
9. Check and adjust pedal height and freeplay.
10. Ensure brake system is operating correctly.

BRAKE BOOSTER OVERHAUL

The brake booster on these models cannot be overhauled and must be replaced as a complete unit.

Anti-Lock Brakes

NOTE: On Air Bag Equipped Models, Refer To "Air Bag System Precautions" Located In The Front Of This Manual For System Disarming & Arming Procedures.

NOTE: Wire Color Code Identification And Symbol Identification Located In The Front Of This Manual May Be Used As An Aid When Using Wiring Circuits Found In This Section.

INDEX

	Page No.
Description	48-154
Anti-Lock Brake System	48-154
Traction Control System (TRAC)	48-154
Diagnosis & Testing	48-154
Accessing Diagnostic Trouble Codes	48-155
Circuit Tests	48-155
Clearing Diagnostic Trouble Codes	48-155
Diagnostic System Inspection	48-154
Diagnostic Tests	48-155
Self Diagnostic System	48-154
Wiring Diagrams	48-154
Diagnostic Chart Index	48-197
Precautions	48-154
Air Bag Systems	48-154
System Service	48-155
Anti-Lock Brake System Circuit Check	48-158
Brake Actuator	48-156
Brake System Bleed	48-158
Brake Lines	48-158
Master Cylinder	48-158
Component Replacement	48-159
ABS Computer	48-160
Brake Actuator	48-159
Control Relays	48-157
Front Speed Sensor	48-157
Rear Speed Sensor	48-158
Speed Sensor Diagnostic System	48-155
Troubleshooting	48-154

PRECAUTIONS

AIR BAG SYSTEMS

Refer to "Air Bag System Precautions" in the front of this manual for system disarming and arming procedures.

DESCRIPTION

ANTI-LOCK BRAKE SYSTEM

By use of a micro-computer, this anti-lock brake system controls brake fluid pressure to prevent wheel lock. With this system, directional stability is improved and steerability maintained even at panic braking on wet, sandy, snowy or icy road conditions.

TRACTION CONTROL SYSTEM (TRAC)

The traction control system controls the engine torque and rear wheel braking. It helps avoid wheel slippage and maintain optimal driving force according to road surface conditions.

TROUBLESHOOTING

Refer to **Figs. 1 through 12,** for troubleshooting of the anti-lock brake system.

Problem		No.
"ABS" warning light	Always comes on after ignition switch is turned on.	1
	Does not come on for 3 seconds after ignition switch on.	2
	Comes on and off.	3
	Comes on while running.	1
Brake condition	Brakes pull.	4
	Braking inefficient.	4
	ABS operates at ordinary braking.	4
	ABS operates just before stopping at ordinary braking.	4
	Brake pedal pulsates abnormally while ABS is operating.	4
	Skidding noise occurs while ABS operating. (ABS operates inefficiently)	5

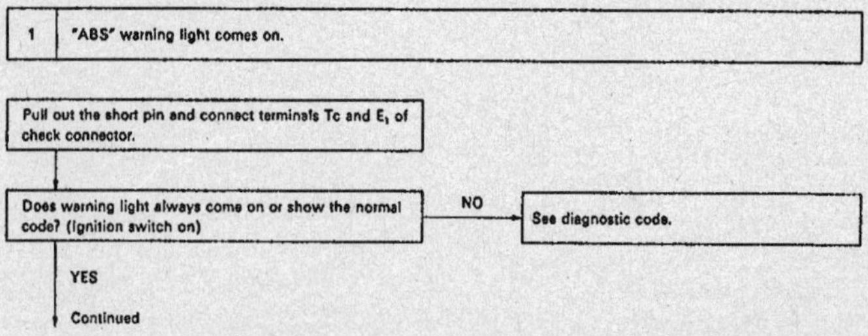

1
"ABS" warning light comes on.
Pull out the short pin and connect terminals Tc and E1 of check connector.
Does warning light always come on or show the normal code? (Ignition switch on)
NO
See diagnostic code.
YES
Continued
TY4029100015010X

Fig. 1 Troubleshooting (Part 1 of 5). 1993 Camry

DIAGNOSIS & TESTING

WIRING DIAGRAMS

Refer to wiring circuits in **Figs. 13 through 36,** when diagnosing anti-lock brake system.

SELF DIAGNOSTIC SYSTEM

The anti-lock brake system is equipped with a self diagnosis system capable of reading and storing specific diagnostic trouble codes, which may indicate component failure or system malfunction.

DIAGNOSTIC SYSTEM INSPECTION

1. Ensure battery voltage is about 12 volts.
2. Turn ignition switch on.
3. Ensure "ANTI-LOCK" warning light

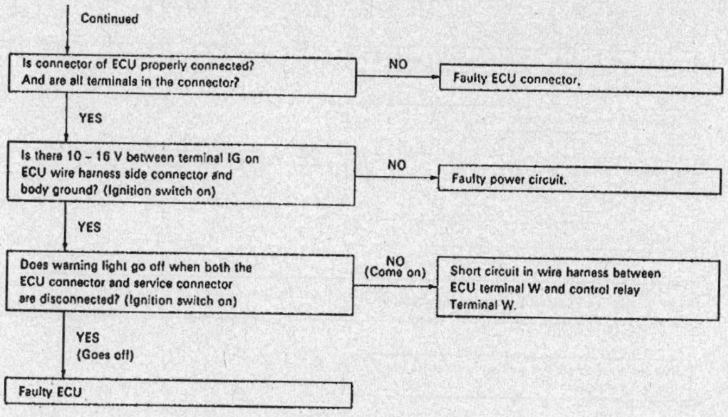
Continued
Is connector of ECU properly connected? And are all terminals in the connector?
NO
Faulty ECU connector.
YES
Is there 10 - 16 V between terminal IG on ECU wire harness side connector and body ground? (Ignition switch on)
NO
Faulty power circuit.
YES
Does warning light go off when both the ECU connector and service connector are disconnected? (Ignition switch on)
NO (Come on)
Short circuit in wire harness between ECU terminal W and control relay Terminal W.
YES (Goes off)
Faulty ECU

TY4029100015020X

Fig. 1 Troubleshooting (Part 2 of 5). 1993 Camry

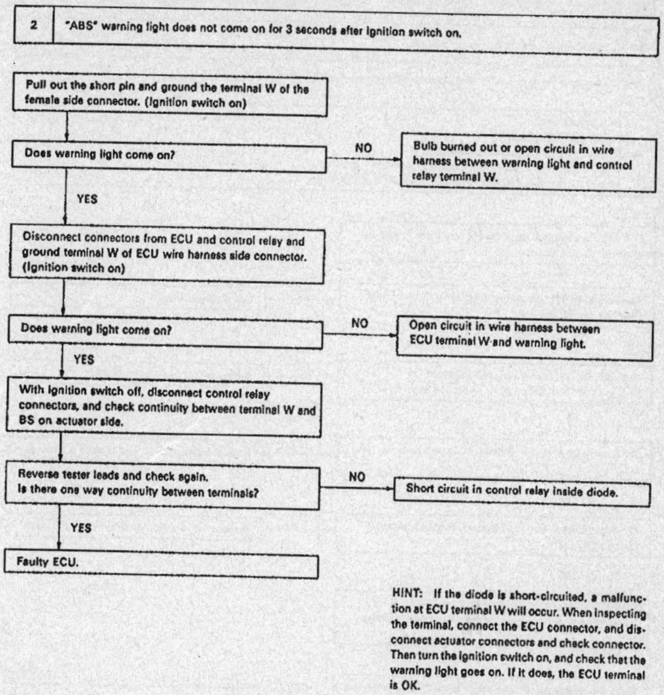
2
"ABS" warning light does not come on for 3 seconds after ignition switch on.
Pull out the short pin and ground the terminal W of the female side connector. (Ignition switch on)
Does warning light come on?
NO
Bulb burned out or open circuit in wire harness between warning light and control relay terminal W.
YES
Disconnect connectors from ECU and control relay and ground terminal W of ECU wire harness side connector. (Ignition switch on)
Does warning light come on?
NO
Open circuit in wire harness between ECU terminal W and warning light.
YES
With ignition switch off, disconnect control relay connectors, and check continuity between terminal W and BS on actuator side.
Reverse tester leads and check again. Is there one way continuity between terminals?
NO
Short circuit in control relay inside diode.
YES
Faulty ECU.
HINT: If the diode is short-circuited, a malfunction at ECU terminal W will occur. When inspecting the terminal, connect the ECU connector, and disconnect actuator connectors and check connector. Then turn the ignition switch on, and check that the warning light goes on. If it does, the ECU terminal is OK.

TY4029100015030X

Fig. 1 Troubleshooting (Part 3 of 5). 1993 Camry

turns On for three seconds. If not, inspect and repair or replace fuse, bulb or wire harness.

ACCESSING DIAGNOSTIC TROUBLE CODES

LESS SUPER MONITOR

1. **On Land Cruiser models,** ensure center differential is free.
2. **On all models,** turn ignition switch to On position.
3. Disconnect short pin from data link connector 1 (DLC1).
4. Connect terminals Tc and E1 of DLC1 using tool No. 09843-18020, or equivalent, **Fig. 37.**
5. Read and record number of times the "ANTI-LOCK" warning light flashes. Refer to **Figs. 38 through 52,** to diagnosis light pattern and possible trouble area.
6. If the system is operation properly, (no malfunction) the warning light will blink once every .5 seconds.
7. Connect actuator check connector and ensure proper operation.

WITH SUPER MONITOR

1. Turn ignition switch to Off position.
2. Disconnect actuator connector.
3. Turn ignition switch to On position then set monitor display to calendar mode.
4. Push and hold the in SELECT and INPUT (M) buttons, **Fig. 53,** at the same time for more than three seconds.
5. Ensure display changes to "DIAG."
6. Push and hold the SET button for more than three seconds and ensure display changes to "ENG-."
7. Push the SET button twice and ensure the display changes to ABS.
8. Read diagnosis code. If code reads "OK" ABS computer is operating normally. If code reads "00" a faulty ABS computer or a short or open circuit in the wire harness between the ABS computer and the super monitor computer.

WITH TOYOTA HAND-HELD TESTER

1. Hook up tester and breakout box to vehicle harness.
2. Read ECU input/output values by following prompts on tester screen.

CLEARING DIAGNOSTIC TROUBLE CODES

LESS SUPER MONITOR

1. Turn ignition switch to On position.
2. Disconnect actuator check connector.
3. Using suitable jumper wire, connect check terminals Tc and E1.
4. **On models except 1996 Celica, Corolla and RAV4 with 2WD,** clear diagnostic trouble codes stored in memory by depressing the brake pedal eight or more times within three seconds.
5. **On 1996 Celica, Corolla and RAV4 with 2WD,** clear diagnostic trouble codes stored in memory by depressing the brake pedal eight or more times within five seconds.
6. **On all models,** ensure the warning light shows normal code.
7. Connect actuator connector.
8. Ensure warning light goes Off.

WITH SUPER MONITOR

1. While monitor showing diagnostic Trouble codes, push and hold the SET button then push the INPUT (H) button, **Fig. 54.** Ensure display changes to "CLEAR ?."
2. Hold the buttons in step 1 until display changes to "OK."
3. Turn ignition switch to Off position then connect actuator check connector. Then follow inspection and testing procedures.

CIRCUIT TESTS

AVALON, CAMRY, TACOMA, TERCEL, SUPRA, 1993–95 COROLLA & 1994–95 CELICA

Stop Light Switch

Refer to **Figs. 55 through 64,** for stop light switch inspection and testing procedure.

ABS Warning Light

Refer to **Figs. 65 through 73,** for ABS warning light inspection and testing procedure.

Tc Terminal

Refer to **Figs. 74 through 82,** for Tc terminal inspection and testing procedure.

Ts Terminal

Refer to **Figs. 83 through 91,** for Ts inspection and terminal testing procedure.

DIAGNOSTIC TESTS

Refer to **Figs. 92 through 164,** for diagnostic testing procedures.

SYSTEM SERVICE

SPEED SENSOR DIAGNOSTIC SYSTEM

Except Land Cruiser, Pickup, Tacoma, T100 & 4Runner

1. Turn ignition switch to OFF.

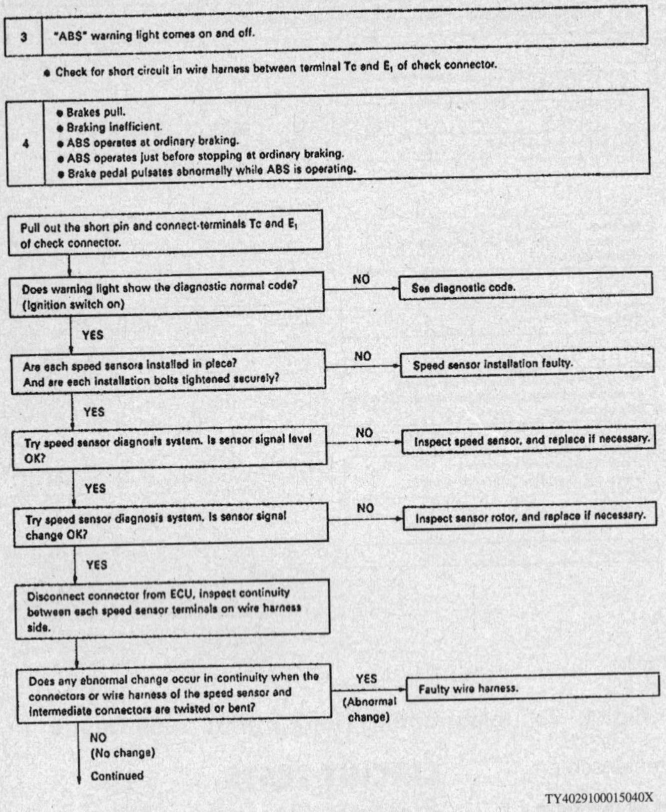
3
"ABS" warning light comes on and off.
• Check for short circuit in wire harness between terminal Tc and E1 of check connector.
4
• Brakes pull.
• Braking inefficient.
• ABS operates at ordinary braking.
• ABS operates just before stopping at ordinary braking.
• Brake pedal pulsates abnormally while ABS is operating.
Pull out the short pin and connect terminals Tc and E1 of check connector.
Does warning light show the diagnostic normal code? (Ignition switch on)
NO
See diagnostic code.
YES
Are each speed sensors installed in place? And are each installation bolts tightened securely?
NO
Speed sensor installation faulty.
YES
Try speed sensor diagnosis system. Is sensor signal level OK?
NO
Inspect speed sensor, and replace if necessary.
YES
Try speed sensor diagnosis system. Is sensor signal change OK?
NO
Inspect sensor rotor, and replace if necessary.
YES
Disconnect connector from ECU, inspect continuity between each speed sensor terminals on wire harness side.
Does any abnormal change occur in continuity when the connectors or wire harness of the speed sensor and intermediate connectors are twisted or bent?
YES
(Abnormal change)
Faulty wire harness.
NO
(No change)
Continued
TY4029100015040X

Fig. 1 Troubleshooting (Part 4 of 5). 1993 Camry

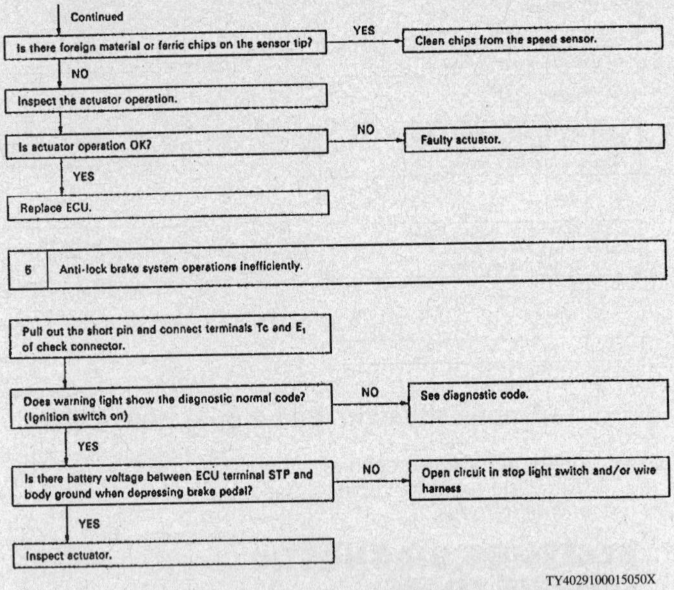
Continued
Is there foreign material or ferric chips on the sensor tip?
YES
Clean chips from the speed sensor.
NO
Inspect the actuator operation.
Is actuator operation OK?
NO
Faulty actuator.
YES
Replace ECU.
5
Anti-lock brake system operations inefficiently.
Pull out the short pin and connect terminals Tc and E1 of check connector.
Does warning light show the diagnostic normal code? (Ignition switch on)
NO
See diagnostic code.
YES
Is there battery voltage between ECU terminal STP and body ground when depressing brake pedal?
NO
Open circuit in stop light switch and/or wire harness
YES
Inspect actuator.
TY4029100015050X

Fig. 1 Troubleshooting (Part 5 of 5). 1993 Camry

2. Connect terminals E1 and Ts of data link connector (DLC1).
3. Start engine and ensure ABS warning light blinks.
4. Drive vehicle straight ahead at least 28 mph for several seconds, then stop vehicle.
5. Connect terminals E1 and Tc of DLC1.
6. Read number of blinks of ABS warning light to obtain diagnostic trouble codes.
7. After performing check, remove DLC1 terminal connections, then turn ignition off.

Land Cruiser, Pickup, Tacoma, T100 & 4Runner

1. Turn ignition switch on and ensure ABS warning lamp turns on for 3 seconds then turns off.
2. Turn ignition switch off.
3. Connect terminals E1 and Ts of data link connector (DLC1).
4. Check that ABS warning light blinks about 4 times every second.
5. Inspect speed sensor signal change by driving vehicle at least 28 mph for several seconds.
6. Check ABS warning light signal. If warning light signal is abnormal, stop vehicle. Warning light will begin to blink.
7. Read number of blinks of ABS warning light to obtain diagnostic trouble codes, **Figs. 165 and 166.**
8. If the system is operating normally, the light will blink once every 0.5 seconds.
9. After any malfunctioning component has been repaired, clear diagnostic trouble codes from ECU, then remove DLC1 terminal connections.

BRAKE ACTUATOR

1. Ensure battery voltage is approximately 12 volts.
2. **On 4WD Celica models,** remove vinyl tube covering wire harness of actuator checker tool No. 0990–00150, then tape separated harness.
3. **On all models,** disconnect actuator connectors.
4. **On T100 models,** disconnect solenoid relay connector.
5. **On all models,** connect actuator checker, tool Nos. 09990–00150, 09990–00200, 09990–00205 or 09990–00210 to actuator and inspect as follows:
   a. **On Celica 2WD models,** connect actuator checker to actuator control relay and body side wire harness using sub-wire harness No. 09990–00165.
   b. **On 4WD Celica, Supra, Pickup, 4Runner and MR2 and Previa models,** connect actuator checker to actuator and body side wire harness using sub-wire harness.
   c. **On Camry models,** connect actuator checker to actuator control relay and body side wire harness through sub wire harness C and E.
   d. **On T100 models,** connect actuator checker to actuator control relay, solenoid relay and body side wire harness using sub-wire harness.
   e. **On all models,** connect red cable of checker to battery positive terminal and black to negative terminal. Connect black cable of sub-wire harness to battery negative terminal or body ground.
   f. **On Celica, Camry and Corolla,** place checker "Sheet A" tool No. 09990–00163 on actuator checker.
   g. **On Supra ,** substitute "motor" for "sub-motor," and "solenoid" for "main" switch on actuator when referring to following steps.
   h. **On all models,** start engine and run at idle.
   i. **On models with four wheel ABS,** turn selector switch of actuator checker to "Front RH" position.
   j. **On models with four wheel ABS,** press and hold in "motor" switch for a few seconds, then press brake pedal and hold it for 15 seconds. Press motor switch for a few seconds and ensure brake pedal does not pulsate.
   k. **On models equipped with rear wheel ABS,** turn selector switch to "Rear" position.
   l. **On all models,** depress brake pedal and hold, then press power switch, ensure brake pedal does not go down. **Do not press power switch for more than 10 seconds.** Release power switch, ensure brake pedal goes down, then press motor or sub motor switch, ensuring pedal returns.
   m. Release pedal.
   n. Inspect other wheels by repeating steps F through I.
   o. After testing has been completed remove "Sheet A " from actuator checker and sub-wire harness from actuator. Connect actuator and/or

Problem		No.
"ABS" warning light	Always comes on after ignition switch is turned on.	1
	Does not come on for 3 seconds after ignition switch on.	2
	Comes on and off.	3
	Comes on while running.	1
Brake working	Brakes pull.	4
	Braking inefficient.	4
	ABS operates at ordinary braking.	4
	ABS operates just before stopping at ordinary braking.	4
	Brake pedal pulsates abnormally while ABS is operating.	4
	Skidding noise occurs while ABS working. (ABS works inefficiently)	5

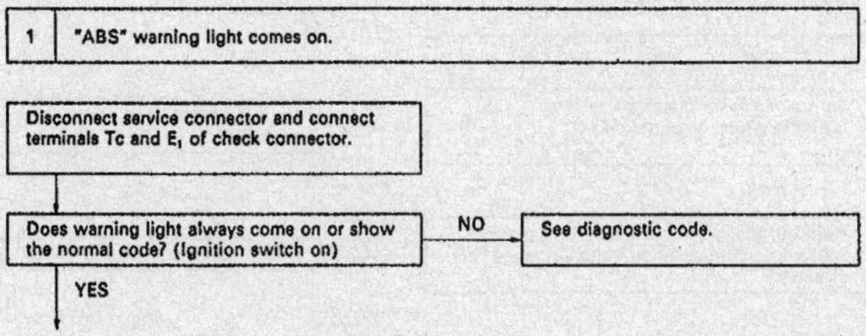
1 "ABS" warning light comes on.
Disconnect service connector and connect terminals Tc and E1 of check connector.
Does warning light always come on or show the normal code? (Ignition switch on)
NO
See diagnostic code.
YES

TY4029100016010X

Fig. 2 Troubleshooting (Part 1 of 6). 1993–95 Celica

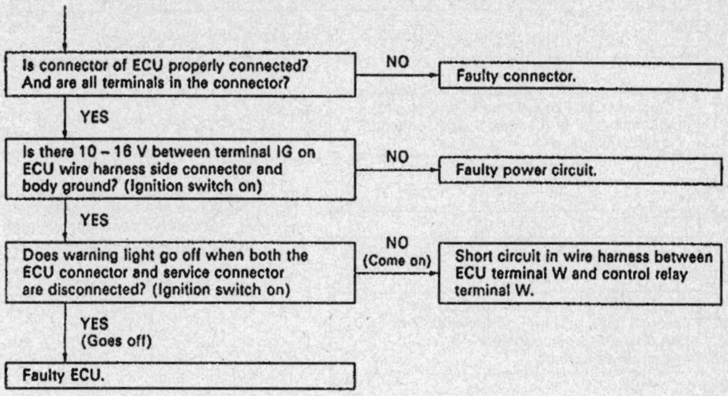
Is connector of ECU properly connected? And are all terminals in the connector?
NO
Faulty connector.
YES
Is there 10 – 16 V between terminal IG on ECU wire harness side connector and body ground? (Ignition switch on)
NO
Faulty power circuit.
YES
Does warning light go off when both the ECU connector and service connector are disconnected? (Ignition switch on)
NO (Come on)
Short circuit in wire harness between ECU terminal W and control relay terminal W.
YES (Goes off)
Faulty ECU.

TY4029100016020X

Fig. 2 Troubleshooting (Part 2 of 6). 1993–95 Celica

control relay connectors.
p. Clear diagnostic Trouble codes.

CONTROL RELAYS

Except Celica, Pickup, Tacoma, T100, 4Runner, Avalon, Camry & Land Cruiser

1. Remove control relays, **Figs. 167 and 168.**
2. Inspect pump motor relay continuity as follows:
   a. Ensure there is continuity between terminals 1 and 2.
   b. Ensure there is no continuity between terminals 3 and 4.
   c. **On MR2, Previa and Supra models,** ensure there is no continuity between terminals 1 and 4.
3. **On all models,** inspect pump motor relay operation as follows:
   a. Apply battery voltage to terminals 1 and 2.
   b. Ensure there is continuity between terminals 3 and 4.
   c. Ensure there is no continuity between terminals 1 and 4.
4. Inspect solenoid relay continuity as follows:
   a. Ensure there is continuity between terminals 1 and 3.
   b. Ensure there is continuity between terminals 2 and 4.
   c. Ensure there is no continuity between terminals 4 and 5.
5. Inspect solenoid relay operation as follows:
   a. Apply battery voltage to terminals 1 and 3.
   b. Ensure there is continuity between terminals 4 and 5.
   c. Ensure there is no continuity between terminals 2 and 4.
   d. If operation is not as specified, replace relay.

Avalon, Camry & Land Cruiser

1. Inspect continuity of motor relay circuit as follows:
   a. Ensure there is continuity between terminals 9 and 10.
   b. Ensure there is no continuity between terminals 7 and 8.
   c. If continuity is not as specified, replace relay.
2. Inspect operation of motor relay circuit as follows:
   a. Connect positive lead from battery to terminal 10 and negative lead to terminal 9.
   b. Ensure there is continuity between terminals 7 and 8.
   c. If operation is not as specified, replace relay.
3. Inspect continuity of solenoid relay circuit as follows:
   a. Ensure there is continuity between terminals 1 and 9.
   b. Ensure there is no continuity between terminals 2 and 5.
   c. **On Land Cruiser models,** connect positive lead from ohmmeter to terminal 5 and connect negative lead to terminal 4. Ensure there is continuity between terminals.
   d. **On all models,** connect two leads in reverse, and ensure there is no continuity between terminals.
   e. If continuity is not as specified, replace relay.
4. Inspect operation of solenoid relay circuit as follows:
   a. Connect positive lead from battery to terminal 1 and negative lead to terminal 9.
   b. Ensure there is continuity between terminals 2 and 5.
   c. **On Camry and Land Cruiser models,** ensure there is no continuity between terminals 2 and 6.
   d. **On all models,** if operation is not as specified, replace relay.

Celica

Refer to **Fig. 169,** for control relay testing procedure.

Pickup, Tacoma, 4Runner & T100

Refer to **Fig. 170,** for control relay testing procedure.

FRONT SPEED SENSOR

Except Avalon, RAV4, Supra, 1994–96 Camry & Celica

1. Remove screws and/or bolt retaining sensor wiring harness, if necessary. Disconnect speed sensor connector at speed sensor.
2. Measure resistance between terminals. **On 1993 Celica models,** resistance should be 800–1300 ohms. **On Land Cruiser,** resistance should be 870–1270 ohms. **On Previa, 1993 Camry and Corolla models,** resistance should be 920–1200 ohms. **On MR2 models,** resistance should be 900–1500 ohms. If resistance is not as specified, replace sensor.
3. Ensure there is no continuity between each terminal and sensor body. If there is continuity, replace sensor.
4. Connect speed sensor connector and install sensor connector retaining screws and/or bolts.
5. Ensure sensor installation bolt is secure and torqued to specification. **On Celica 4WD and 2WD and Camry models, torque** to 9 ft. lbs. **On 1993 Land Cruiser models, torque** to 13 ft. lbs. **On Supra, torque** to 14 ft. lbs. **On MR2, Pickup, 4Runner, 1993 Celica, 1993 Corolla and Previa models, torque** to 69 inch lbs.
6. **On all models,** visually inspect sensor rotor serrations by removing torque plate retaining bolts and torque plate with brake cylinder, then the disc.
7. Inspect sensor rotor serrations for scratches, cracks, warping or missing teeth.

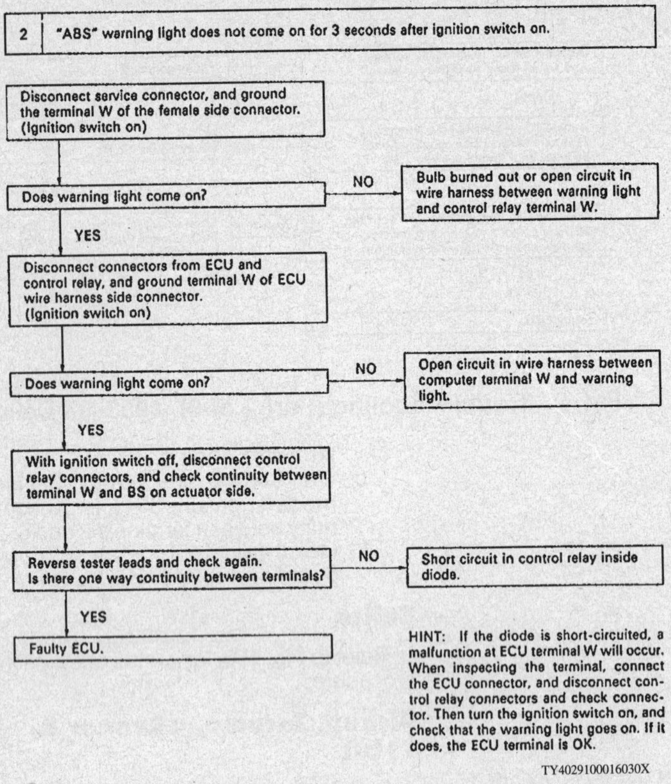
2
"ABS" warning light does not come on for 3 seconds after ignition switch on.
Disconnect service connector, and ground the terminal W of the female side connector. (Ignition switch on)
Does warning light come on?
NO
Bulb burned out or open circuit in wire harness between warning light and control relay terminal W.
YES
Disconnect connectors from ECU and control relay, and ground terminal W of ECU wire harness side connector. (Ignition switch on)
Does warning light come on?
NO
Open circuit in wire harness between computer terminal W and warning light.
YES
With ignition switch off, disconnect control relay connectors, and check continuity between terminal W and BS on actuator side.
Reverse tester leads and check again. Is there one way continuity between terminals?
NO
Short circuit in control relay inside diode.
YES
Faulty ECU.
HINT: If the diode is short-circuited, a malfunction at ECU terminal W will occur. When inspecting the terminal, connect the ECU connector, and disconnect control relay connectors and check connector. Then turn the ignition switch on, and check that the warning light goes on. If it does, the ECU terminal is OK.
TY4029100016030X

Fig. 2 Troubleshooting (Part 3 of 6). 1993–95 Celica

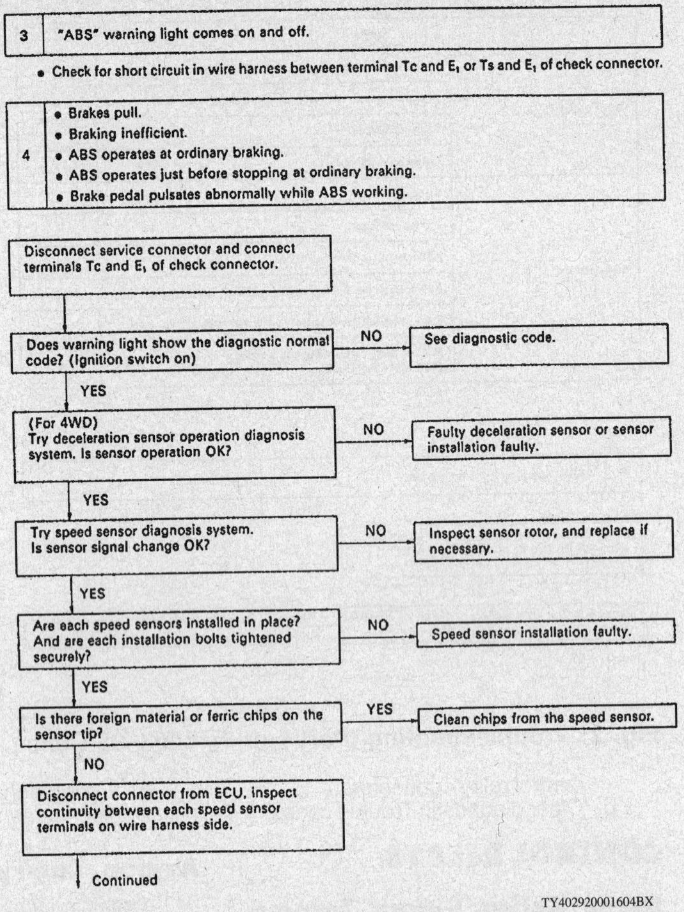
3
"ABS" warning light comes on and off.
• Check for short circuit in wire harness between terminal Tc and E1 or Ts and E1 of check connector.
4
• Brakes pull.
• Braking inefficient.
• ABS operates at ordinary braking.
• ABS operates just before stopping at ordinary braking.
• Brake pedal pulsates abnormally while ABS working.
Disconnect service connector and connect terminals Tc and E1 of check connector.
Does warning light show the diagnostic normal code? (Ignition switch on)
NO
See diagnostic code.
YES
(For 4WD) Try deceleration sensor operation diagnosis system. Is sensor operation OK?
NO
Faulty deceleration sensor or sensor installation faulty.
YES
Try speed sensor diagnosis system. Is sensor signal change OK?
NO
Inspect sensor rotor, and replace if necessary.
YES
Are each speed sensors installed in place? And are each installation bolts tightened securely?
NO
Speed sensor installation faulty.
YES
Is there foreign material or ferric chips on the sensor tip?
YES
Clean chips from the speed sensor.
NO
Disconnect connector from ECU, inspect continuity between each speed sensor terminals on wire harness side.
Continued
TY402920001604BX

Fig. 2 Troubleshooting (Part 4 of 6). 1993–95 Celica

8. Install rotor disc and brake assembly. **On Corolla models, torque** bolts to 65 ft. lbs. **On Celica and Previa with 2WD, and Camry 2WD models, torque** bolts to 69 ft. lbs. **On Celica and Previa with 4WD models, torque** bolts 73 ft. lbs. **On Supra models, torque** bolts to 77 ft. lbs. **On Land Cruiser, torque** bolts to 90 ft. lbs.

Avalon, Supra, 1994–96 Camry & Celica

1. Connect oscilloscope to speed sensor connector.
2. Run vehicle at 12.4 mph and inspect speed sensor output wave, **Fig. 171.**
3. Ensure "C" is at least 0.5 volts, **Fig. 171.** If it is not, replace speed sensor.
4. Ensure "B" is 30% more of "A". If it is not, replace driveshaft.

REAR SPEED SENSOR

Except Avalon, Supra, 1994–96 Camry & Celica

1. Disconnect speed sensor connector removing necessary brake assemblies as required.
2. Measure resistance between terminals. On 1993 Celica 4WD models, resistance should be 800–1500 ohms. On Previa, 1993 Camry and 1993 Corolla models, resistance should be 1050–1450 ohms. On MR2 models, resistance should be 900–1500 ohms. On Land Cruiser models, resistance should be 700–1000 ohms. On T100 models, resistance should be 770–890 ohms. On Pickup and 4Runner models, resistance should be 580–700 ohms. If resistance is not as specified, replace sensor.
3. **On Supra models,** proceed as follows:
   a. Disconnect speed sensor connector, then ensure there is no continuity between each terminal and sensor body.
   b. Remove speed sensor from transmission, then the terminals from connector.
   c. Using a resistor, 2,000–10,000 ohms, complete circuit as shown in **Fig. 172.** Ensure voltmeter shows 2 volts or less as a cloth covered screwdriver is brought near sensor.
4. **On all models,** Inspect sensor rotor serrations visually as follows:
   a. Drain transmission fluid, then remove propeller shaft and extension housing.
   b. **On A340, R154 transmission models,** inspect sensor rotor serration, mounted on main shaft. **On W58 models,** inspect reverse gear serrations.
   c. **On all models,** install extension housing, propeller shaft, then fill transmission with proper fluid, then check level.

Supra, 1994–96 Camry & Celica

1. Connect oscilloscope to speed sensor connector.
2. Run vehicle at 12.4 mph and inspect speed sensor output wave, **Fig. 171.**
3. Ensure "C" is at least 0.5 volts, **Fig. 171.** If it is not, replace speed sensor.
4. Ensure "B" is 30% more of "A". If it is not, replace rear axle hub.

ANTI-LOCK BRAKE SYSTEM CIRCUIT CHECK

1. Remove glove box or ECU cover, as required, and pull out ABS computer.
2. Using a multimeter with high impedance (10,000 ohms minimum), measure voltage and resistance at each terminal shown in **Figs. 173 through 197,** and body ground.
3. Ensure results are as shown.

Brake System Bleed

MASTER CYLINDER

1. Fill reservoir with fluid.
2. Disconnect tubes from master cylinder. Then slowly depress brake pedal and hold.
3. Block off outlet holes with fingers, and release pedal. Repeat three or four times.

BRAKE LINES

Bleed wheel with longest brake line first, then work your way back to the master cylinder according to brake line length.

1. Connect tube to brake cylinder.

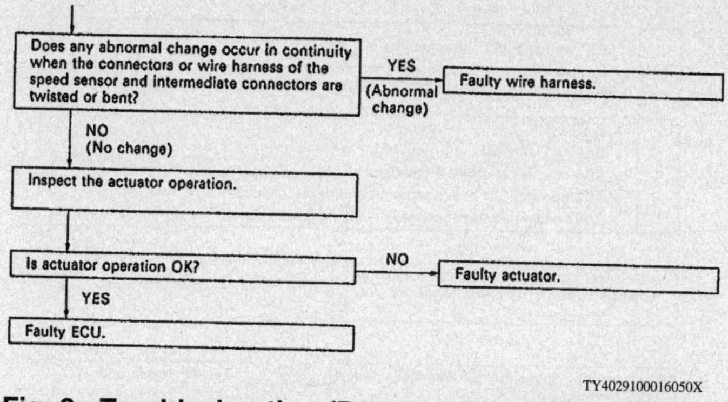
Does any abnormal change occur in continuity when the connectors or wire harness of the speed sensor and intermediate connectors are twisted or bent?
YES (Abnormal change)
Faulty wire harness.
NO (No change)
Inspect the actuator operation.
Is actuator operation OK?
NO
Faulty actuator.
YES
Faulty ECU.
TY4029100016050X

Fig. 2 Troubleshooting (Part 5 of 6). 1993–95 Celica

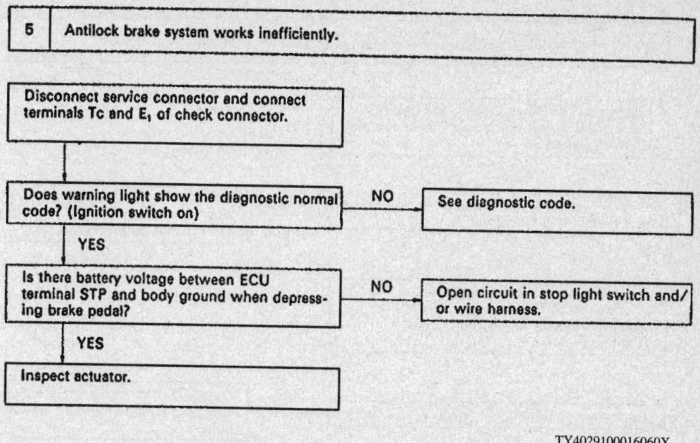
5 Antilock brake system works inefficiently.
Disconnect service connector and connect terminals Tc and E1 of check connector.
Does warning light show the diagnostic normal code? (Ignition switch on)
NO
See diagnostic code.
YES
Is there battery voltage between ECU terminal STP and body ground when depressing brake pedal?
NO
Open circuit in stop light switch and/or wire harness.
YES
Inspect actuator.
TY4029100016060X

Fig. 2 Troubleshooting (Part 6 of 6). 1993–95 Celica

Problem		No.
"ABS" warning light	Always comes on after ignition switch is turned on.	1
	Does not come on for 3 seconds after ignition switch on.	2
	Comes on and off.	3
	Comes on while running.	1
Brake working	Brakes pull.	4
	Braking inefficient.	4
	ABS operates at ordinary braking.	4
	ABS operates just before stopping at ordinary braking.	4
	Brake pedal pulsates abnormally while ABS is operating.	4
	Skidding noise occurs while ABS working. (ABS works inefficiently)	5

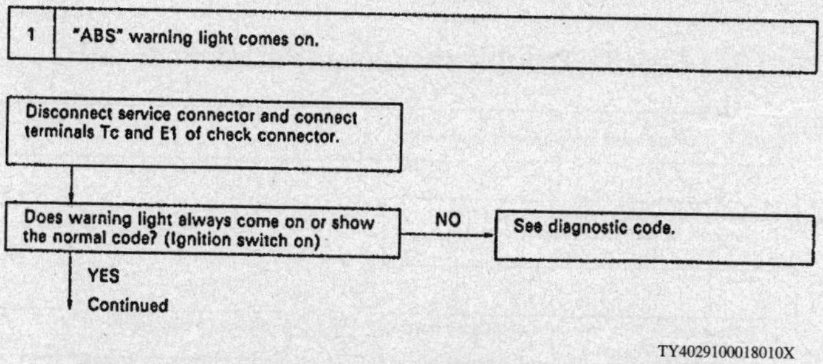
1 "ABS" warning light comes on.
Disconnect service connector and connect terminals Tc and E1 of check connector.
Does warning light always come on or show the normal code? (Ignition switch on)
NO
See diagnostic code.
YES
Continued
TY4029100018010X

Fig. 3 Troubleshooting (Part 1 of 6). MR2

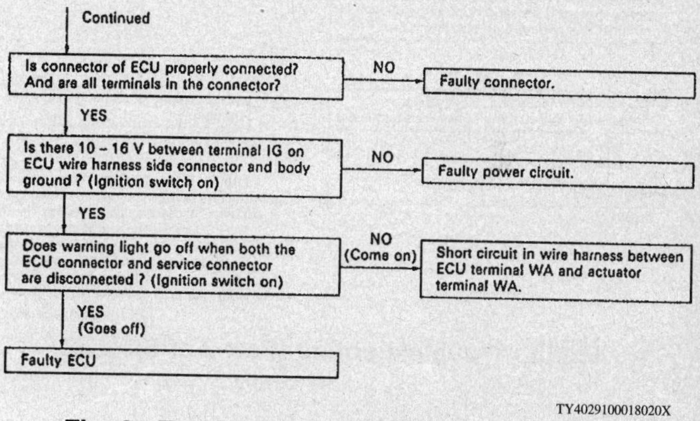
Continued
Is connector of ECU properly connected? And are all terminals in the connector?
NO
Faulty connector.
YES
Is there 10 – 16 V between terminal IG on ECU wire harness side connector and body ground ? (Ignition switch on)
NO
Faulty power circuit.
YES
Does warning light go off when both the ECU connector and service connector are disconnected ? (Ignition switch on)
NO (Come on)
Short circuit in wire harness between ECU terminal WA and actuator terminal WA.
YES (Goes off)
Faulty ECU
TY4029100018020X

Fig. 3 Troubleshooting (Part 2 of 6). MR2

2. Depress pedal several times and hold. Loosen bleeder plug.
3. When fluid stops coming out, tighten bleeder plug and release pedal. Repeat several times.
4. Repeat entire procedure for each wheel. Fill reservoir.

Component Replacement

BRAKE ACTUATOR

Except Celica 4WD, RAV4 & 1993–94 Land Cruiser

1. Remove brake fluid from actuator using a suitable tool.
2. **On Pickup, 4Runner and T100 models,** remove battery.
3. **On all models,** disconnect connectors from actuator.
4. Remove brake tubes from actuator using suitable wrench.
5. **On Pickup, 4Runner and T100 models,** turn steering wheel clockwise until it locks, then disconnect power steering lines from actuator.
6. **On all models,** remove actuator bracket attaching bolt, then remove actuator and bracket assembly.
7. Remove actuator mounting nuts and actuator.
8. Reverse procedure to install, noting the following:
   a. **On all models, except Pickup, 4Runner and T100, torque** actuator mounting nuts to 48 inch lbs.
   b. **On Pickup, 4Runner and T100 models, torque** actuator mounting nuts to 9 ft. lbs.
   c. **Torque** actuator bracket bolt to 21 ft. lbs.
   d. **Torque** five brake lines to 11 ft. lbs.
   e. Fill brake fluid reservoir and bleed brakes.
   f. Check for fluid leakage and proper brake operation.

Celica 4WD

1. Remove brake fluid from reservoir, using syringe, or equivalent.
2. Remove rear seat cushion, seat brackets and luggage compartment cover.
3. Disconnect actuator electrical connector.
4. Raise vehicle, then disconnect four brake lines from actuator brake line connectors.
5. Remove actuator cover and rubber gasket, then disconnect two brake lines from actuator.
6. Remove actuator and mounting bracket.
7. Reverse procedure to install. Fill reservoir with brake fluid and bleed system.

RAV4

1. Disconnect brake lines from ABS actuator using tool No. 09023-00100, or equivalent.
2. Disconnect power steering fluid reservoir.
3. Remove ABS actuator assembly.
4. Remove ABS actuator from bracket.
5. Remove three holders and cushions.
6. Reverse procedure to install, noting the following:
   a. **Torque** brake lines to 11 ft. lbs.
   b. **Torque** ABS actuator to bracket nuts to 48 inch lbs.
   c. **Torque** actuator assembly retaining bolts to 14 ft. lbs.

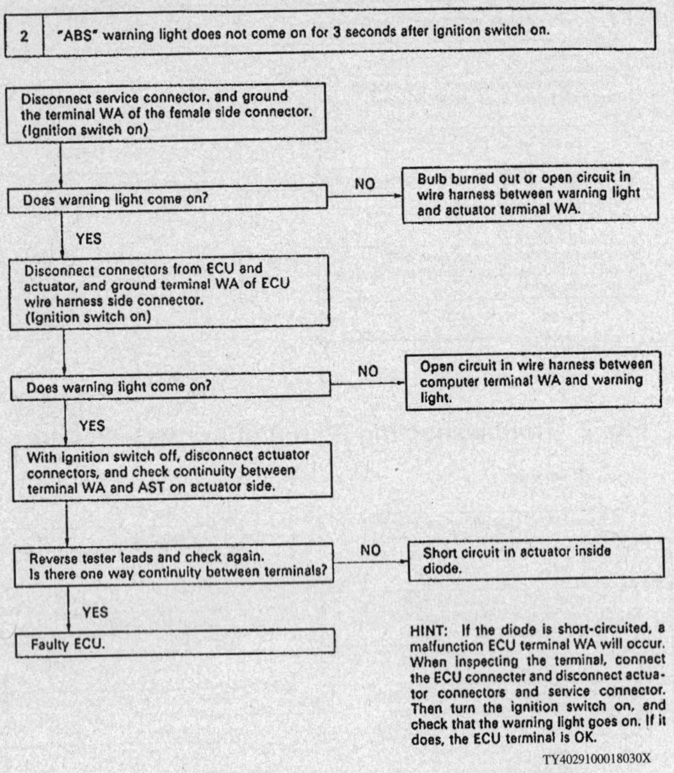
2 "ABS" warning light does not come on for 3 seconds after ignition switch on.
Disconnect service connector, and ground the terminal WA of the female side connector. (Ignition switch on)
Does warning light come on?
NO
Bulb burned out or open circuit in wire harness between warning light and actuator terminal WA.
YES
Disconnect connectors from ECU and actuator, and ground terminal WA of ECU wire harness side connector. (Ignition switch on)
Does warning light come on?
NO
Open circuit in wire harness between computer terminal WA and warning light.
YES
With ignition switch off, disconnect actuator connectors, and check continuity between terminal WA and AST on actuator side.
Reverse tester leads and check again. Is there one way continuity between terminals?
NO
Short circuit in actuator inside diode.
YES
Faulty ECU.
HINT: If the diode is short-circuited, a malfunction ECU terminal WA will occur. When inspecting the terminal, connect the ECU connecter and disconnect actuator connectors and service connector. Then turn the ignition switch on, and check that the warning light goes on. If it does, the ECU terminal is OK.
TY4029100018030X

Fig. 3 Troubleshooting (Part 3 of 6). MR2

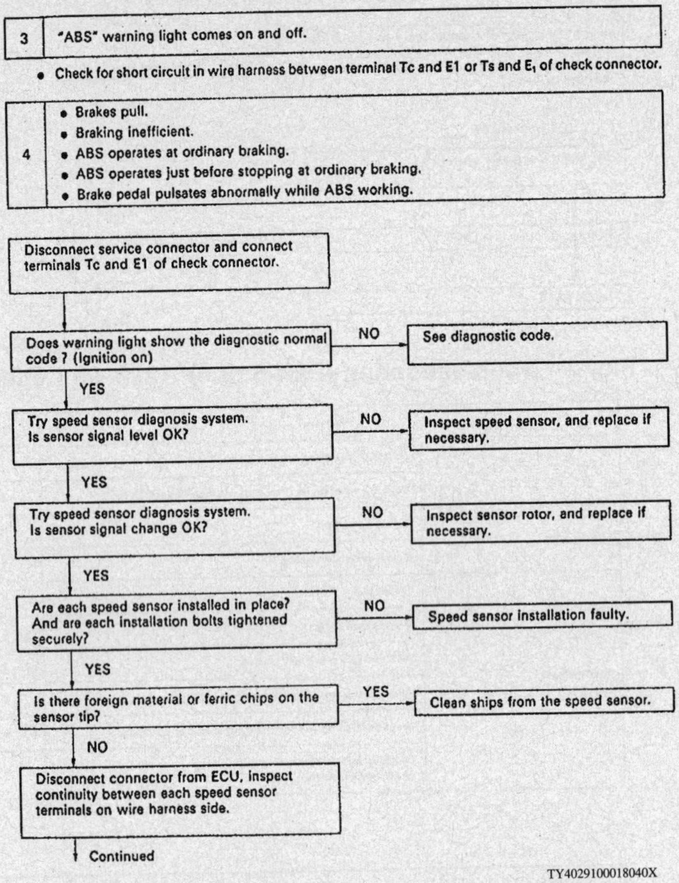
3 "ABS" warning light comes on and off.
• Check for short circuit in wire harness between terminal Tc and E1 or Ts and E1 of check connector.
4
• Brakes pull.
• Braking inefficient.
• ABS operates at ordinary braking.
• ABS operates just before stopping at ordinary braking.
• Brake pedal pulsates abnormally while ABS working.
Disconnect service connector and connect terminals Tc and E1 of check connector.
Does warning light show the diagnostic normal code ? (Ignition on)
NO
See diagnostic code.
YES
Try speed sensor diagnosis system. Is sensor signal level OK?
NO
Inspect speed sensor, and replace if necessary.
YES
Try speed sensor diagnosis system. Is sensor signal change OK?
NO
Inspect sensor rotor, and replace if necessary.
YES
Are each speed sensor installed in place? And are each installation bolts tightened securely?
NO
Speed sensor installation faulty.
YES
Is there foreign material or ferric chips on the sensor tip?
YES
Clean ships from the speed sensor.
NO
Disconnect connector from ECU, inspect continuity between each speed sensor terminals on wire harness side.
Continued
TY4029100018040X

Fig. 3 Troubleshooting (Part 4 of 6). MR2

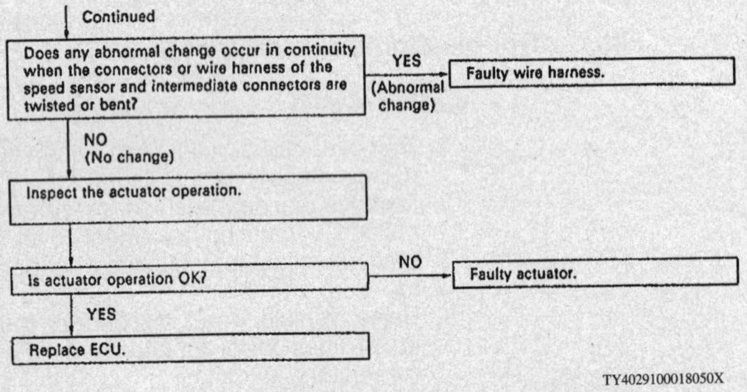
Continued
Does any abnormal change occur in continuity when the connectors or wire harness of the speed sensor and intermediate connectors are twisted or bent?
YES (Abnormal change)
Faulty wire harness.
NO (No change)
Inspect the actuator operation.
Is actuator operation OK?
NO
Faulty actuator.
YES
Replace ECU.
TY4029100018050X

Fig. 3 Troubleshooting (Part 5 of 6). MR2

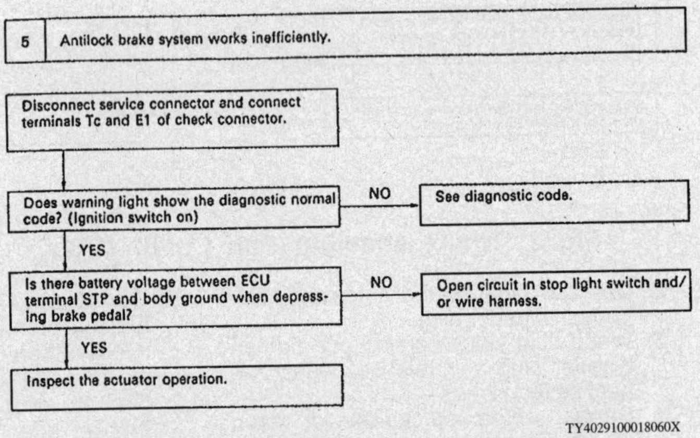
5 Antilock brake system works inefficiently.
Disconnect service connector and connect terminals Tc and E1 of check connector.
Does warning light show the diagnostic normal code? (Ignition switch on)
NO
See diagnostic code.
YES
Is there battery voltage between ECU terminal STP and body ground when depressing brake pedal?
NO
Open circuit in stop light switch and/or wire harness.
YES
Inspect the actuator operation.
TY4029100018060X

Fig. 3 Troubleshooting (Part 6 of 6). MR2

1993–94 Land Cruiser

Refer to **Fig. 198** for replacement procedure.

ABS COMPUTER

Except Celica 4WD

1. **On models equipped with CD player,** remove audio power amplifier attaching screws, then remove.
2. **On Pickup, 4Runner and T100 models,** remove glove box assembly.
3. **On all models,** remove computer cover, as required, then the computer retaining screws.
4. Pull out wire harness from clamp on bracket, then pull out connector from clamp on bracket.
5. Disconnect electrical connectors, then remove computer.
6. Reverse procedure to install.

Celica 4WD

1. Remove rear seat cushion. then the mounting bracket retaining bolts and ground terminal.
2. Disconnect electrical connectors, then remove computer retaining bolts.
3. Remove computer from bracket.
4. Reverse procedure to install.

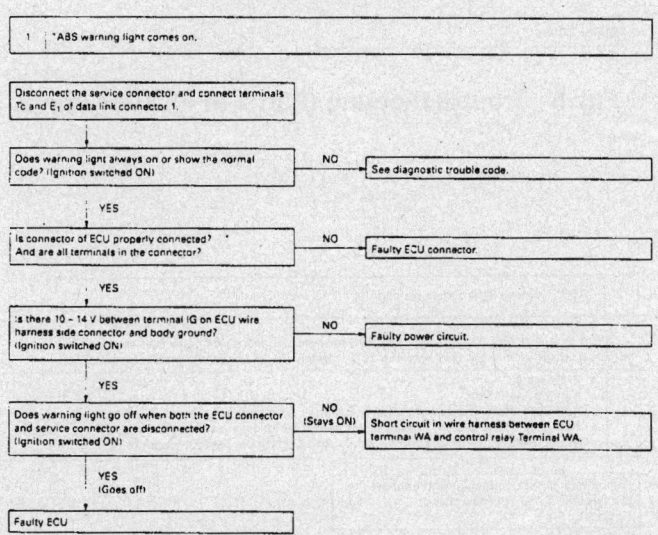

	Problem	No.
"ABS" warning light	Always comes on after ignition switched ON.	1
	Does not come on for 3 seconds after ignition switched ON.	2
	Goes on and off.	3
	Comes on while running.	1
Brake condition	Brakes pull. *	4
	Braking inefficient. *	4
	ABS operates during normal braking.	4
	ABS operates just before stopping during normal braking.	4
	Brake pedal pulsates abnormally while ABS is operating.	4
	Skidding noise occurs while ABS operating. (ABS operates inefficiently)	5

* Also check the parts of the brake system (brake cylinders, pads, hydraulic lines, etc.) not specifically part of the ABS.

1 "ABS warning light comes on.

Disconnect the service connector and connect terminals Tc and E_1 of data link connector 1.

Does warning light always on or show the normal code? (Ignition switched ON) — NO → See diagnostic trouble code.

YES

Is connector of ECU properly connected? And are all terminals in the connector? — NO → Faulty ECU connector.

YES

Is there 10 – 14 V between terminal IG on ECU wire harness side connector and body ground? (Ignition switched ON) — NO → Faulty power circuit.

YES

Does warning light go off when both the ECU connector and service connector are disconnected? (Ignition switched ON) — NO (Stays ON) → Short circuit in wire harness between ECU terminal WA and control relay Terminal WA.

YES (Goes off)

Faulty ECU

TY4029500147010X

Fig. 4 Troubleshooting (Part 1 of 4). 1993–95 Paseo & Tercel

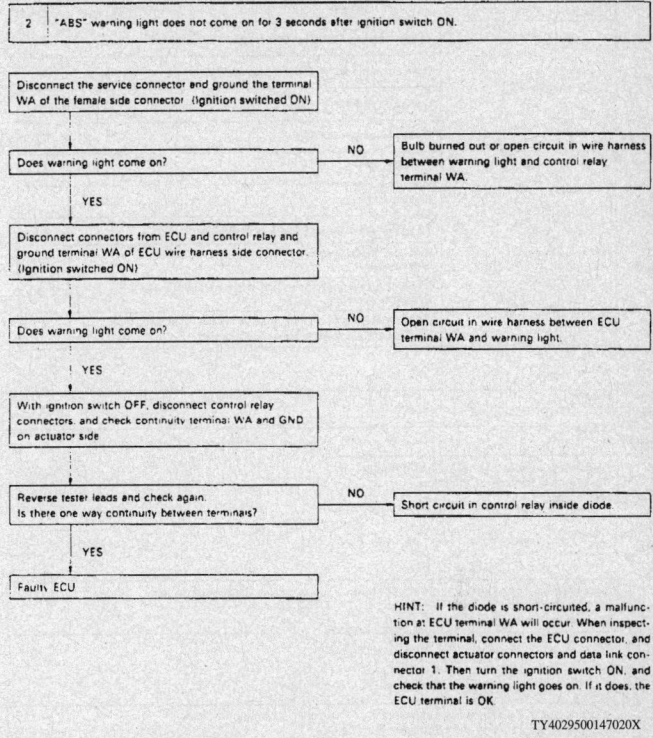

2 "ABS" warning light does not come on for 3 seconds after ignition switch ON.

Disconnect the service connector and ground the terminal WA of the female side connector. (Ignition switched ON)

Does warning light come on? — NO → Bulb burned out or open circuit in wire harness between warning light and control relay terminal WA.

YES

Disconnect connectors from ECU and control relay and ground terminal WA of ECU wire harness side connector. (Ignition switched ON)

Does warning light come on? — NO → Open circuit in wire harness between ECU terminal WA and warning light.

YES

With ignition switch OFF, disconnect control relay connectors, and check continuity terminal WA and GND on actuator side.

Reverse tester leads and check again. Is there one way continuity between terminals? — NO → Short circuit in control relay inside diode.

YES

Faulty ECU

HINT: If the diode is short-circuited, a malfunction at ECU terminal WA will occur. When inspecting the terminal, connect the ECU connector, and disconnect actuator connectors and data link connector 1. Then turn the ignition switch ON, and check that the warning light goes on. If it does, the ECU terminal is OK.

TY4029500147020X

Fig. 4 Troubleshooting (Part 2 of 4). 1993–95 Paseo & Tercel

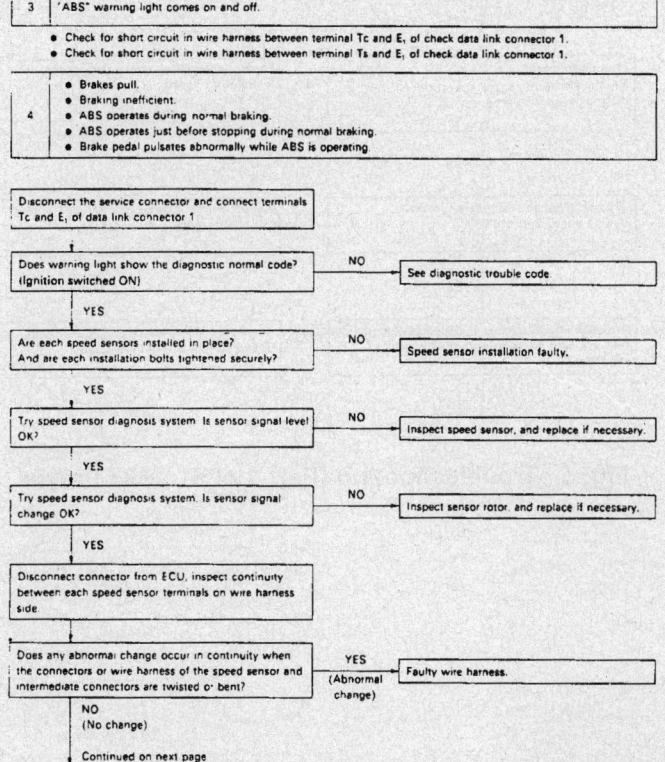

3 "ABS" warning light comes on and off.

- Check for short circuit in wire harness between terminal Tc and E_1 of check data link connector 1.
- Check for short circuit in wire harness between terminal Ts and E_1 of check data link connector 1.

4
- Brakes pull.
- Braking inefficient.
- ABS operates during normal braking.
- ABS operates just before stopping during normal braking.
- Brake pedal pulsates abnormally while ABS is operating.

Disconnect the service connector and connect terminals Tc and E_1 of data link connector 1.

Does warning light show the diagnostic normal code? (Ignition switched ON) — NO → See diagnostic trouble code.

YES

Are each speed sensors installed in place? And are each installation bolts tightened securely? — NO → Speed sensor installation faulty.

YES

Try speed sensor diagnosis system. Is sensor signal level OK? — NO → Inspect speed sensor, and replace if necessary.

YES

Try speed sensor diagnosis system. Is sensor signal change OK? — NO → Inspect sensor rotor, and replace if necessary.

YES

Disconnect connector from ECU, inspect continuity between each speed sensor terminals on wire harness side.

Does any abnormal change occur in continuity when the connectors or wire harness of the speed sensor and intermediate connectors are twisted or bent? — YES (Abnormal change) → Faulty wire harness.

NO (No change)

Continued on next page

TY4029500147030X

Fig. 4 Troubleshooting (Part 3 of 4). 1993–95 Paseo & Tercel

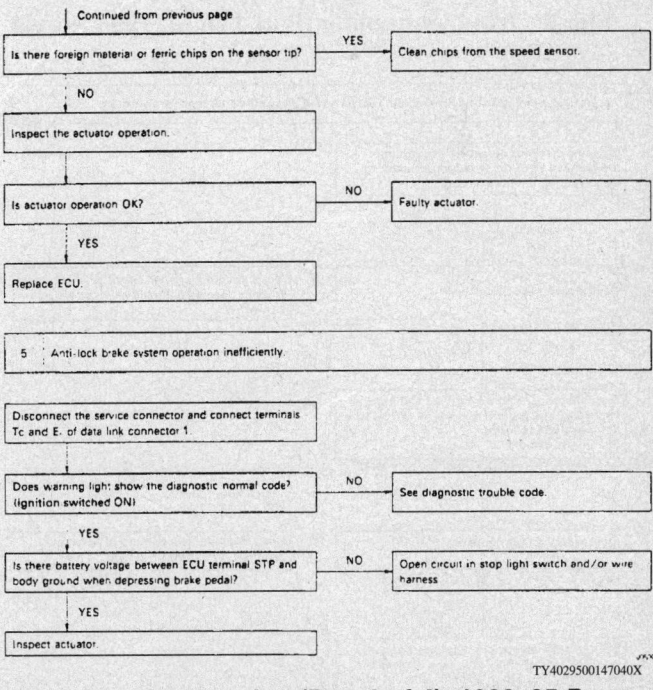

Continued from previous page

Is there foreign material or ferric chips on the sensor tip? — YES → Clean chips from the speed sensor.

NO

Inspect the actuator operation.

Is actuator operation OK? — NO → Faulty actuator.

YES

Replace ECU.

5 Anti-lock brake system operation inefficiently.

Disconnect the service connector and connect terminals Tc and E_1 of data link connector 1.

Does warning light show the diagnostic normal code? (Ignition switched ON) — NO → See diagnostic trouble code.

YES

Is there battery voltage between ECU terminal STP and body ground when depressing brake pedal? — NO → Open circuit in stop light switch and/or wire harness

YES

Inspect actuator.

TY4029500147040X

Fig. 4 Troubleshooting (Part 4 of 4). 1993–95 Paseo & Tercel

Problem		No.
"ABS" warning light	Always comes on after ignition switch is turned to ON.	1
	Does not come on for about 3 seconds after ignition switch on.	2
	Comes on and off.	3
	Comes on while running.	1
Brake working	Brakes pull.	4
	Braking inefficient.	4
	Anti-Lock Brake System operates at ordinary braking.	4
	Anti-Lock Brake System operates just before stopping at ordinary braking.	4
	Brake pedal pulsates abnormally while Anti-Lock Brake System is operating.	4
	Skidding noise occurs while Anti-Lock Brake System working. (Anti-Lock Brake System works inefficiently)	5

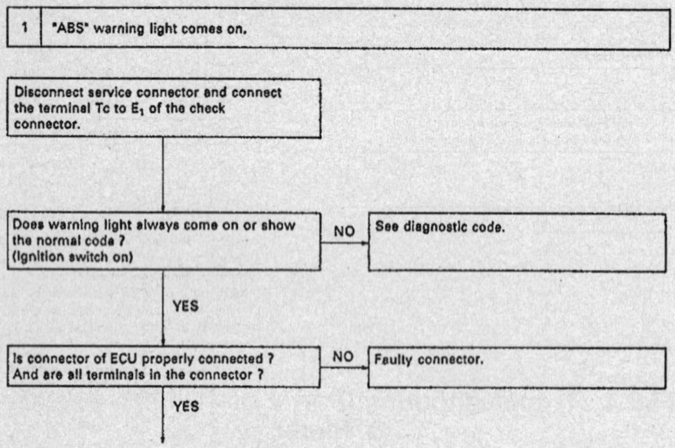
1 "ABS" warning light comes on.
Disconnect service connector and connect the terminal Tc to E1 of the check connector.
Does warning light always come on or show the normal code ? (Ignition switch on)
NO
See diagnostic code.
YES
Is connector of ECU properly connected ? And are all terminals in the connector ?
NO
Faulty connector.
YES

TY4029100019010X

Fig. 5 Troubleshooting (Part 1 of 6). 1993 Previa

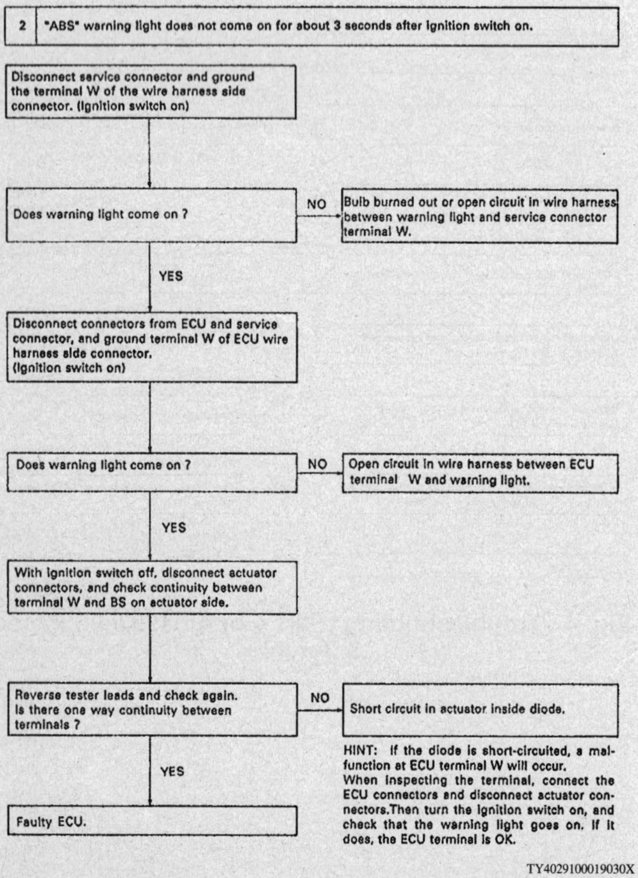
2 "ABS" warning light does not come on for about 3 seconds after ignition switch on.
Disconnect service connector and ground the terminal W of the wire harness side connector. (Ignition switch on)
Does warning light come on ?
NO
Bulb burned out or open circuit in wire harness between warning light and service connector terminal W.
YES
Disconnect connectors from ECU and service connector, and ground terminal W of ECU wire harness side connector. (Ignition switch on)
Does warning light come on ?
NO
Open circuit in wire harness between ECU terminal W and warning light.
YES
With ignition switch off, disconnect actuator connectors, and check continuity between terminal W and BS on actuator side.
Reverse tester leads and check again. Is there one way continuity between terminals ?
NO
Short circuit in actuator inside diode.
YES
Faulty ECU.
HINT: If the diode is short-circuited, a malfunction at ECU terminal W will occur.
When inspecting the terminal, connect the ECU connectors and disconnect actuator connectors.Then turn the ignition switch on, and check that the warning light goes on. If it does, the ECU terminal is OK.

TY4029100019030X

Fig. 5 Troubleshooting (Part 3 of 6). 1993 Previa

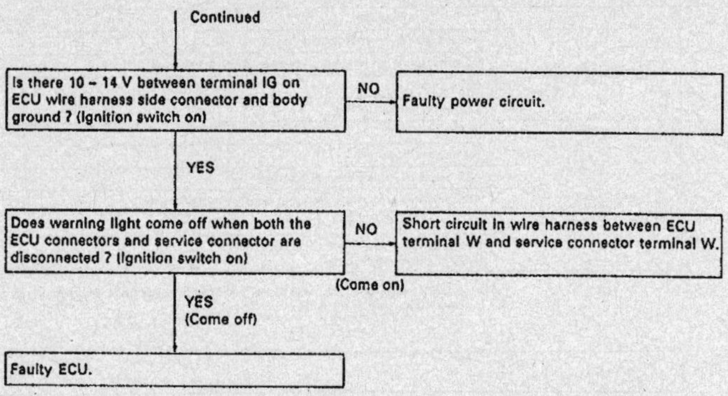
Continued
Is there 10 – 14 V between terminal IG on ECU wire harness side connector and body ground ? (Ignition switch on)
NO
Faulty power circuit.
YES
Does warning light come off when both the ECU connectors and service connector are disconnected ? (Ignition switch on)
NO
Short circuit in wire harness between ECU terminal W and service connector terminal W.
(Come on)
YES
(Come off)
Faulty ECU.

TY4029100019020X

Fig. 5 Troubleshooting (Part 2 of 6). 1993 Previa

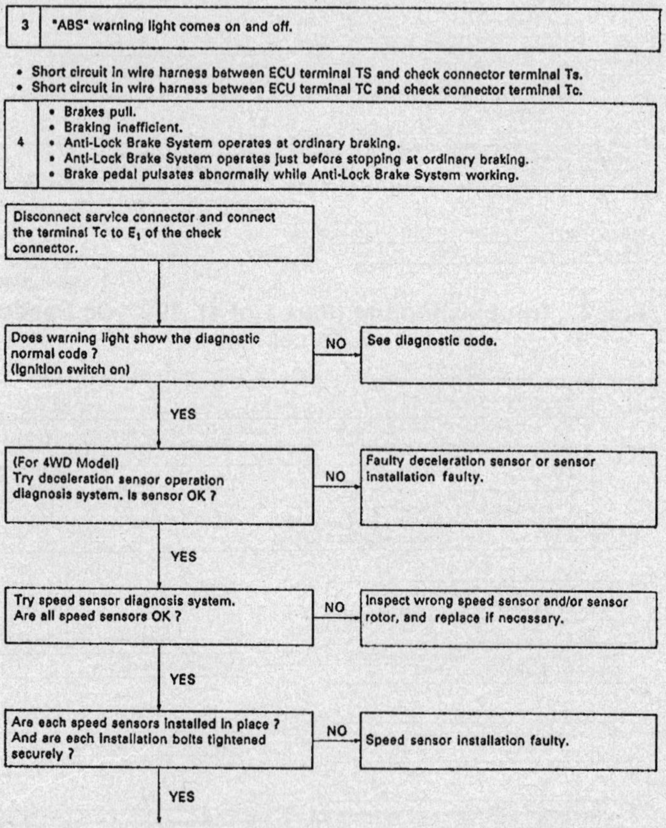
3 "ABS" warning light comes on and off.
• Short circuit in wire harness between ECU terminal TS and check connector terminal Ts.
• Short circuit in wire harness between ECU terminal TC and check connector terminal Tc.
4
• Brakes pull.
• Braking inefficient.
• Anti-Lock Brake System operates at ordinary braking.
• Anti-Lock Brake System operates just before stopping at ordinary braking.
• Brake pedal pulsates abnormally while Anti-Lock Brake System working.
Disconnect service connector and connect the terminal Tc to E1 of the check connector.
Does warning light show the diagnostic normal code ? (Ignition switch on)
NO
See diagnostic code.
YES
(For 4WD Model) Try deceleration sensor operation diagnosis system. Is sensor OK ?
NO
Faulty deceleration sensor or sensor installation faulty.
YES
Try speed sensor diagnosis system. Are all speed sensors OK ?
NO
Inspect wrong speed sensor and/or sensor rotor, and replace if necessary.
YES
Are each speed sensors installed in place ? And are each installation bolts tightened securely ?
NO
Speed sensor installation faulty.
YES

TY4029100019040X

Fig. 5 Troubleshooting (Part 4 of 6). 1993 Previa

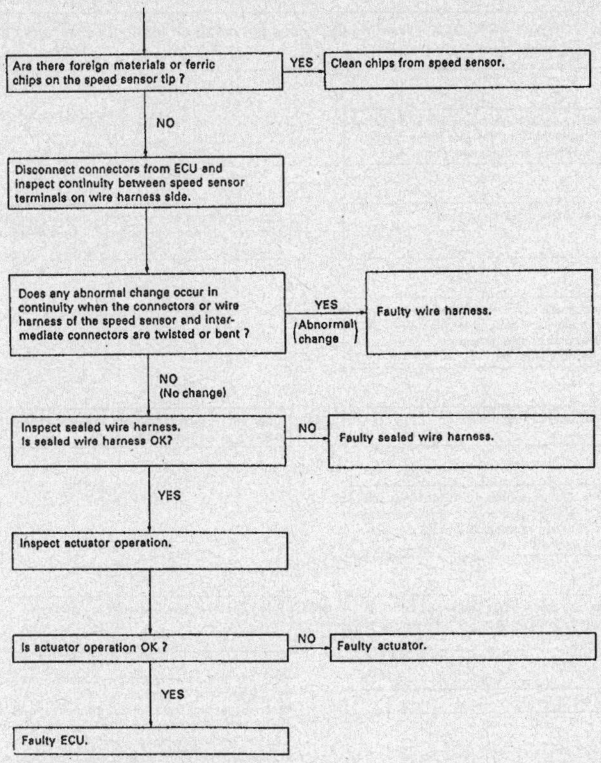
Are there foreign materials or ferric chips on the speed sensor tip ?
YES
Clean chips from speed sensor.
NO
Disconnect connectors from ECU and inspect continuity between speed sensor terminals on wire harness side.
Does any abnormal change occur in continuity when the connectors or wire harness of the speed sensor and intermediate connectors are twisted or bent ?
YES (Abnormal change)
Faulty wire harness.
NO (No change)
Inspect sealed wire harness. Is sealed wire harness OK?
NO
Faulty sealed wire harness.
YES
Inspect actuator operation.
Is actuator operation OK ?
NO
Faulty actuator.
YES
Faulty ECU.

TY4029100019050X

Fig. 5 Troubleshooting (Part 5 of 6). 1993 Previa

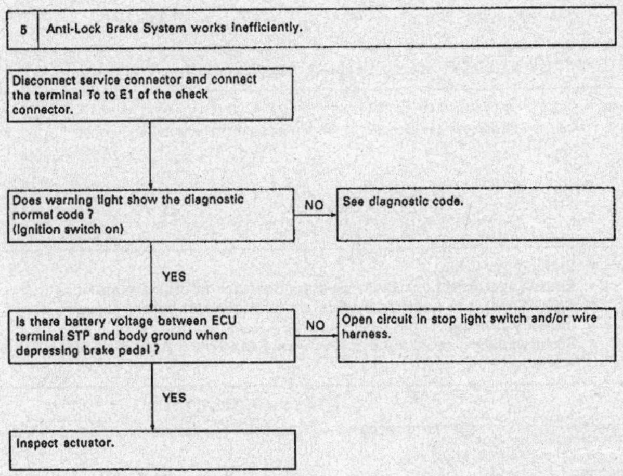
5 Anti-Lock Brake System works inefficiently.
Disconnect service connector and connect the terminal Tc to E1 of the check connector.
Does warning light show the diagnostic normal code ? (Ignition switch on)
NO
See diagnostic code.
YES
Is there battery voltage between ECU terminal STP and body ground when depressing brake pedal ?
NO
Open circuit in stop light switch and/or wire harness.
YES
Inspect actuator.

TY4029100019060X

Fig. 5 Troubleshooting (Part 6 of 6). 1993 Previa

Problem		No.
"ABS" warning light	Always comes on after ignition switch is turned on.	1
	Does not come on for 3 seconds after ignition switched on.	2
	Goes on and off.	3
	Comes on while running.	1
Brake condition	Brakes pull. ※	4
	Braking inefficient. ※	4
	ABS operates during normal braking.	4
	ABS operates just before stopping during normal braking.	4
	Brake pedal pulsates abnormally while ABS is operating.	4
	Skidding noise occurs while ABS operating. (ABS operates inefficiently)	5

※ Also check the parts of the brake system (brake cylinders, pads, hydraulic lines, etc.) not specifically part of the ABS.

TY4029400020010X

Fig. 6 Troubleshooting (Part 1 of 5). 1994–96 Previa

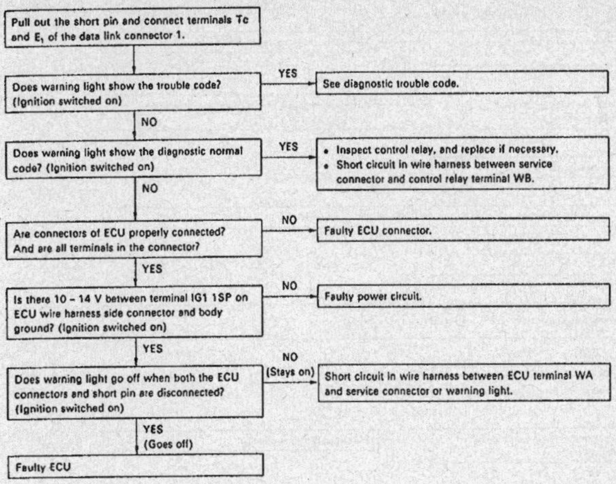
Pull out the short pin and connect terminals Tc and E1 of the data link connector 1.
Does warning light show the trouble code? (Ignition switched on)
YES
See diagnostic trouble code.
NO
Does warning light show the diagnostic normal code? (Ignition switched on)
YES
• Inspect control relay, and replace if necessary.
• Short circuit in wire harness between service connector and control relay terminal WB.
NO
Are connectors of ECU properly connected? And are all terminals in the connector?
NO
Faulty ECU connector.
YES
Is there 10 – 14 V between terminal IG1 1SP on ECU wire harness side connector and body ground? (Ignition switched on)
NO
Faulty power circuit.
YES
Does warning light go off when both the ECU connectors and short pin are disconnected? (Ignition switched on)
NO (Stays on)
Short circuit in wire harness between ECU terminal WA and service connector or warning light.
YES (Goes off)
Faulty ECU

TY4029400020020X

Fig. 6 Troubleshooting (Part 2 of 5). 1994–96 Previa

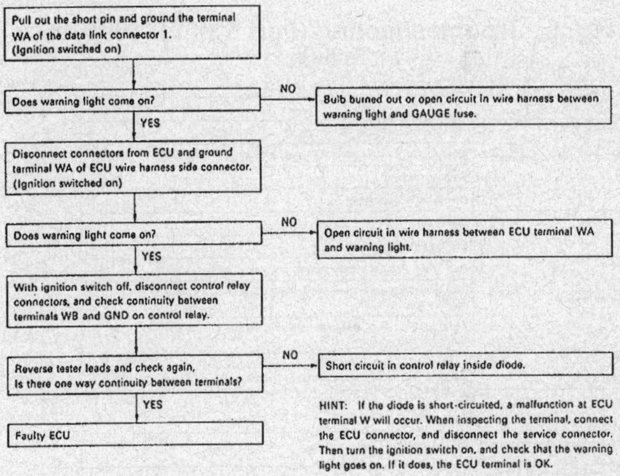
Pull out the short pin and ground the terminal WA of the data link connector 1. (Ignition switched on)
Does warning light come on?
NO
Bulb burned out or open circuit in wire harness between warning light and GAUGE fuse.
YES
Disconnect connectors from ECU and ground terminal WA of ECU wire harness side connector. (Ignition switched on)
Does warning light come on?
NO
Open circuit in wire harness between ECU terminal WA and warning light.
YES
With ignition switch off, disconnect control relay connectors, and check continuity between terminals WB and GND on control relay.
Reverse tester leads and check again. Is there one way continuity between terminals?
NO
Short circuit in control relay inside diode.
YES
Faulty ECU
HINT: If the diode is short-circuited, a malfunction at ECU terminal W will occur. When inspecting the terminal, connect the ECU connector, and disconnect the service connector. Then turn the ignition switch on, and check that the warning light goes on. If it does, the ECU terminal is OK.

TY4029400020030X

Fig. 6 Troubleshooting (Part 3 of 5). 1994–96 Previa

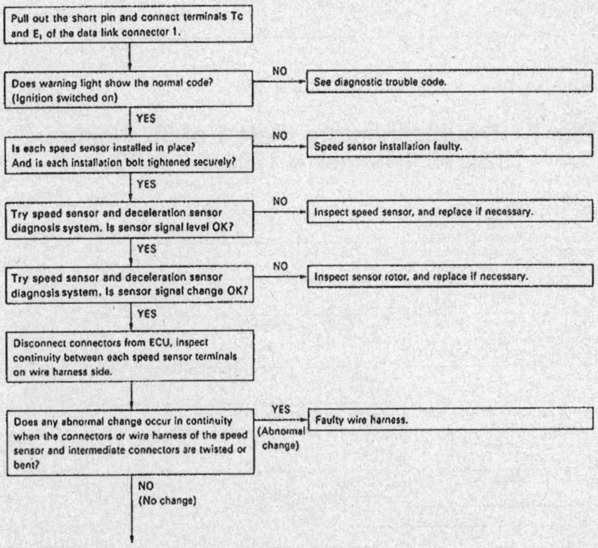
Pull out the short pin and connect terminals Tc and E1 of the data link connector 1.
Does warning light show the normal code? (Ignition switched on)
NO
See diagnostic trouble code.
YES
Is each speed sensor installed in place? And is each installation bolt tightened securely?
NO
Speed sensor installation faulty.
YES
Try speed sensor and deceleration sensor diagnosis system. Is sensor signal level OK?
NO
Inspect speed sensor, and replace if necessary.
YES
Try speed sensor and deceleration sensor diagnosis system. Is sensor signal change OK?
NO
Inspect sensor rotor, and replace if necessary.
YES
Disconnect connectors from ECU, inspect continuity between each speed sensor terminals on wire harness side.
Does any abnormal change occur in continuity when the connectors or wire harness of the speed sensor and intermediate connectors are twisted or bent?
YES (Abnormal change)
Faulty wire harness.
NO (No change)

TY4029400020040X

Fig. 6 Troubleshooting (Part 4 of 5). 1994–96 Previa

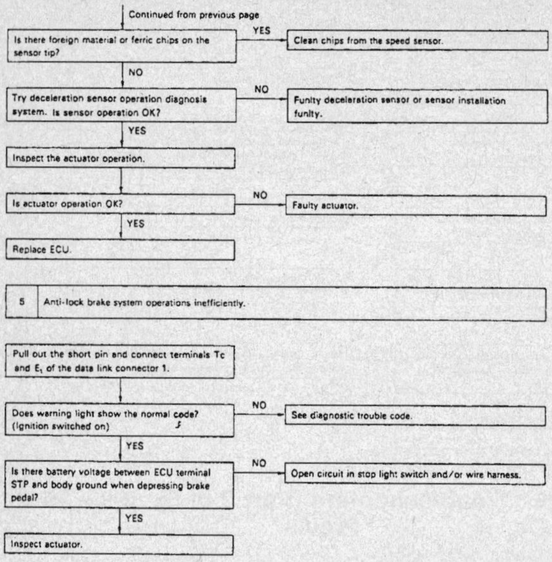

Continued from previous page
Is there foreign material or ferric chips on the sensor tip?
YES
Clean chips from the speed sensor.
NO
Try deceleration sensor operation diagnosis system. Is sensor operation OK?
NO
Funlty deceleration sensor or sensor installation funlty.
YES
Inspect the actuator operation.
Is actuator operation OK?
NO
Faulty actuator.
YES
Replace ECU.
5 Anti-lock brake system operations inefficiently.
Pull out the short pin and connect terminals Tc and E1 of the data link connector 1.
Does warning light show the normal code? (Ignition switched on)
NO
See diagnostic trouble code.
YES
Is there battery voltage between ECU terminal STP and body ground when depressing brake pedal?
NO
Open circuit in stop light switch and/or wire harness.
YES
Inspect actuator.

TY4029400020050X

Fig. 6 Troubleshooting (Part 5 of 5). 1994–96 Previa

Problem		No.
"REAR ANTILOCK" warning light	Always comes on after ignition switch is turned to ON.	1
	Does not come on for about 2 seconds after ignition switch on.	2
	Comes on and off.	3
	Comes on while running.	1
Brake working	Brakes pull.	4
	Braking inefficient.	4
	Rear-Wheel Anti-Lock Brake System operates at ordinary braking.	4
	Rear-Wheel Anti-Lock Brake System operates just before stopping at ordinary braking.	4
	Brake pedal pulsates abnormally while Rear-Wheel Anti-Lock Brake System is operating.	4
	Skidding noise occurs while Rear-Wheel Anti-Lock Brake System working. (Rear-Wheel Anti-Lock Brake System works inefficiently)	5

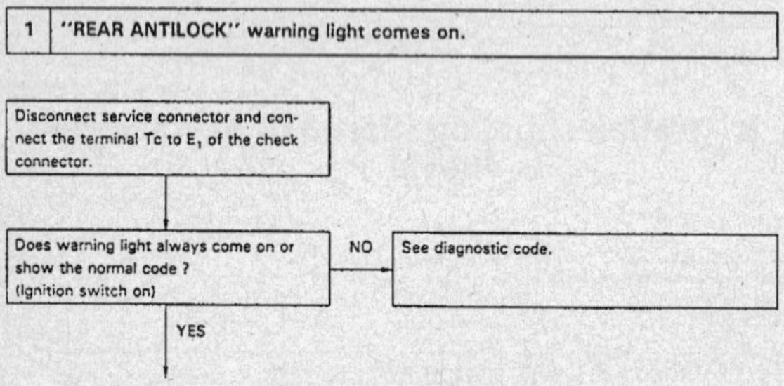

1 "REAR ANTILOCK" warning light comes on.
Disconnect service connector and connect the terminal Tc to E1 of the check connector.
Does warning light always come on or show the normal code ? (Ignition switch on)
NO
See diagnostic code.
YES

TY4029100021010X

Fig. 7 Troubleshooting (Part 1 of 6). Pickup, 1993–95 4Runner & 1993–94 T100

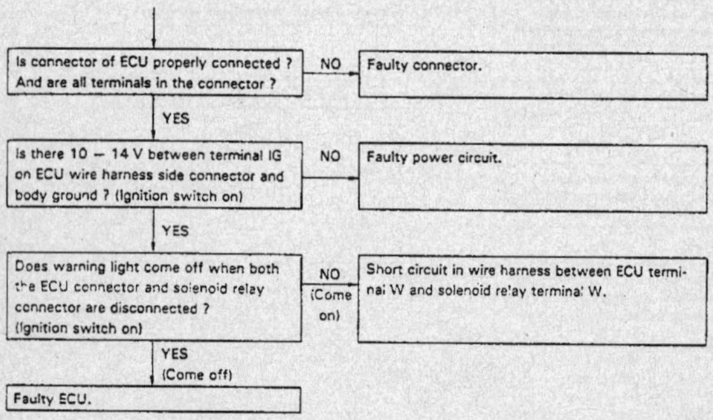

Is connector of ECU properly connected ? And are all terminals in the connector ?
NO
Faulty connector.
YES
Is there 10 — 14 V between terminal IG on ECU wire harness side connector and body ground ? (Ignition switch on)
NO
Faulty power circuit.
YES
Does warning light come off when both the ECU connector and solenoid relay connector are disconnected ? (Ignition switch on)
NO (Come on)
Short circuit in wire harness between ECU terminal W and solenoid relay terminal W.
YES (Come off)
Faulty ECU.

TY4029100021020X

Fig. 7 Troubleshooting (Part 2 of 6). Pickup, 1993–95 4Runner & 1993–94 T100

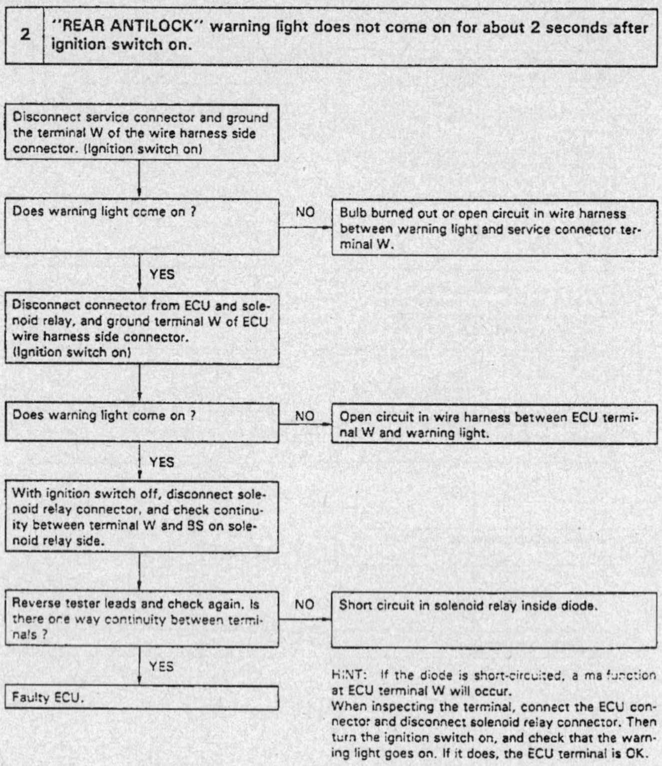

2 "REAR ANTILOCK" warning light does not come on for about 2 seconds after ignition switch on.
Disconnect service connector and ground the terminal W of the wire harness side connector. (Ignition switch on)
Does warning light come on ?
NO
Bulb burned out or open circuit in wire harness between warning light and service connector terminal W.
YES
Disconnect connector from ECU and solenoid relay, and ground terminal W of ECU wire harness side connector. (Ignition switch on)
Does warning light come on ?
NO
Open circuit in wire harness between ECU terminal W and warning light.
YES
With ignition switch off, disconnect solenoid relay connector, and check continuity between terminal W and BS on solenoid relay side.
Reverse tester leads and check again. Is there one way continuity between terminals ?
NO
Short circuit in solenoid relay inside diode.
YES
Faulty ECU.
HINT: If the diode is short-circuited, a malfunction at ECU terminal W will occur.
When inspecting the terminal, connect the ECU connector and disconnect solenoid relay connector. Then turn the ignition switch on, and check that the warning light goes on. If it does, the ECU terminal is OK.

TY4029100021030X

Fig. 7 Troubleshooting (Part 3 of 6). Pickup, 1993–95 4Runner & 1993–94 T100

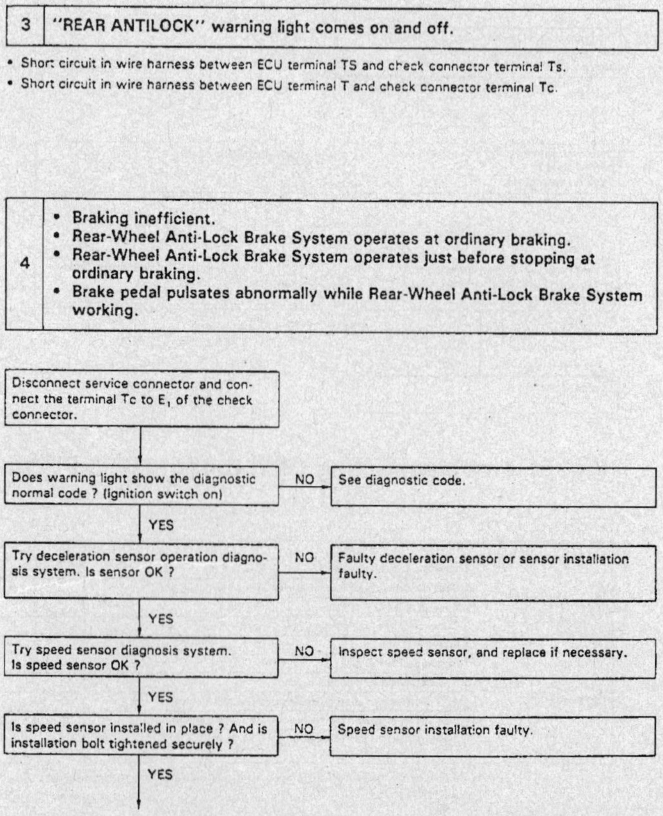

3 "REAR ANTILOCK" warning light comes on and off.
• Short circuit in wire harness between ECU terminal TS and check connector terminal Ts.
• Short circuit in wire harness between ECU terminal T and check connector terminal Tc.
4
• Braking inefficient.
• Rear-Wheel Anti-Lock Brake System operates at ordinary braking.
• Rear-Wheel Anti-Lock Brake System operates just before stopping at ordinary braking.
• Brake pedal pulsates abnormally while Rear-Wheel Anti-Lock Brake System working.
Disconnect service connector and connect the terminal Tc to E1 of the check connector.
Does warning light show the diagnostic normal code ? (Ignition switch on)
NO
See diagnostic code.
YES
Try deceleration sensor operation diagnosis system. Is sensor OK ?
NO
Faulty deceleration sensor or sensor installation faulty.
YES
Try speed sensor diagnosis system. Is speed sensor OK ?
NO
Inspect speed sensor, and replace if necessary.
YES
Is speed sensor installed in place ? And is installation bolt tightened securely ?
NO
Speed sensor installation faulty.
YES

TY4029100021040X

Fig. 7 Troubleshooting (Part 4 of 6). Pickup, 1993–95 4Runner & 1993–94 T100

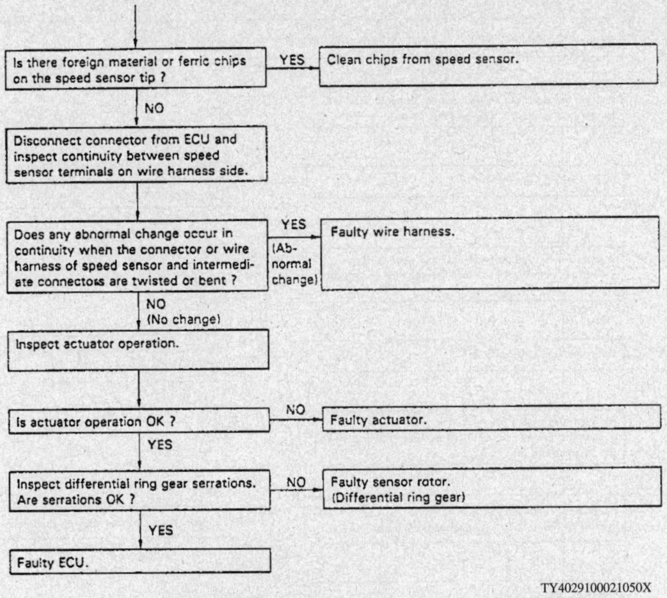
Is there foreign material or ferric chips on the speed sensor tip ?
YES
Clean chips from speed sensor.
NO
Disconnect connector from ECU and inspect continuity between speed sensor terminals on wire harness side.
Does any abnormal change occur in continuity when the connector or wire harness of speed sensor and intermediate connectors are twisted or bent ?
YES (Abnormal change)
Faulty wire harness.
NO (No change)
Inspect actuator operation.
Is actuator operation OK ?
NO
Faulty actuator.
YES
Inspect differential ring gear serrations. Are serrations OK ?
NO
Faulty sensor rotor. (Differential ring gear)
YES
Faulty ECU.
TY4029100021050X

Fig. 7 Troubleshooting (Part 5 of 6). Pickup, 1993–95 4Runner & 1993–94 T100

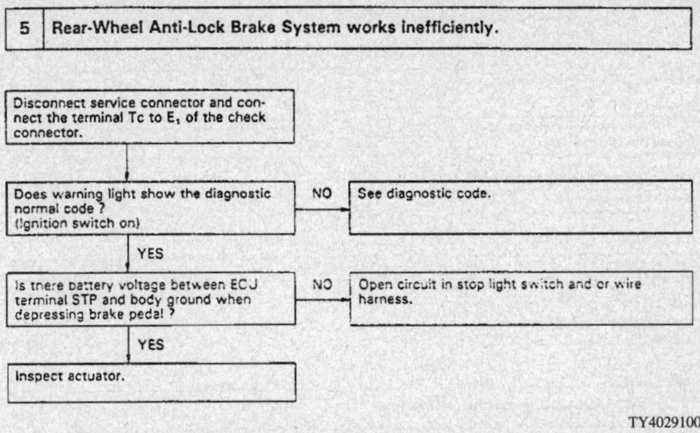
5 Rear-Wheel Anti-Lock Brake System works inefficiently.
Disconnect service connector and connect the terminal Tc to E1 of the check connector.
Does warning light show the diagnostic normal code ? (Ignition switch on)
NO
See diagnostic code.
YES
Is there battery voltage between ECU terminal STP and body ground when depressing brake pedal ?
NO
Open circuit in stop light switch and or wire harness.
YES
Inspect actuator.
TY4029100021060X

Fig. 7 Troubleshooting (Part 6 of 6). Pickup, 1993–95 4Runner & 1993–94 T100

Problem		No.
"ABS" warning light	Always comes on after ignition switched ON.	1
	Does not come on for 3 seconds after ignition switched ON.	2
	Goes on and off.	3
	Comes on while running.	1
Brake condition	Brakes pull. ✱	4
	Braking inefficient. ✱	4
	ABS operates during normal braking.	4
	ABS operates just before stopping during normal braking.	4
	Brake pedal pulsates abnormally while ABS is operating.	4
	Skidding noise occurs while ABS operating. (ABS operates inefficiently)	5

✱ Also check the parts of the brake system (brake cylinders, pads, hydraulic lines, etc.) not specifically part of the ABS.

TY4029500146010X

Fig. 8 Troubleshooting (Part 1 of 5). 1995–96 T100

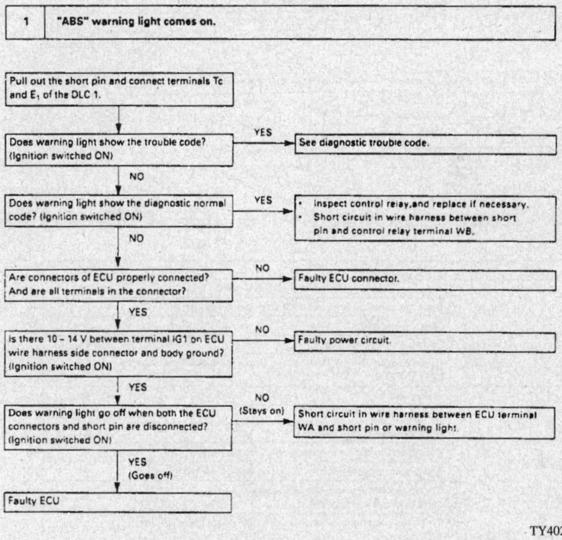
1 "ABS" warning light comes on.
Pull out the short pin and connect terminals Tc and E1 of the DLC 1.
Does warning light show the trouble code? (Ignition switched ON)
YES
See diagnostic trouble code.
NO
Does warning light show the diagnostic normal code? (Ignition switched ON)
YES
• Inspect control relay,and replace if necessary.
• Short circuit in wire harness between short pin and control relay terminal WB.
NO
Are connectors of ECU properly connected? And are all terminals in the connector?
NO
Faulty ECU connector.
YES
Is there 10 – 14 V between terminal IG1 on ECU wire harness side connector and body ground? (Ignition switched ON)
NO
Faulty power circuit.
YES
Does warning light go off when both the ECU connectors and short pin are disconnected? (Ignition switched ON)
NO (Stays on)
Short circuit in wire harness between ECU terminal WA and short pin or warning light.
YES (Goes off)
Faulty ECU
TY4029500146020X

Fig. 8 Troubleshooting (Part 2 of 5). 1995–96 T100

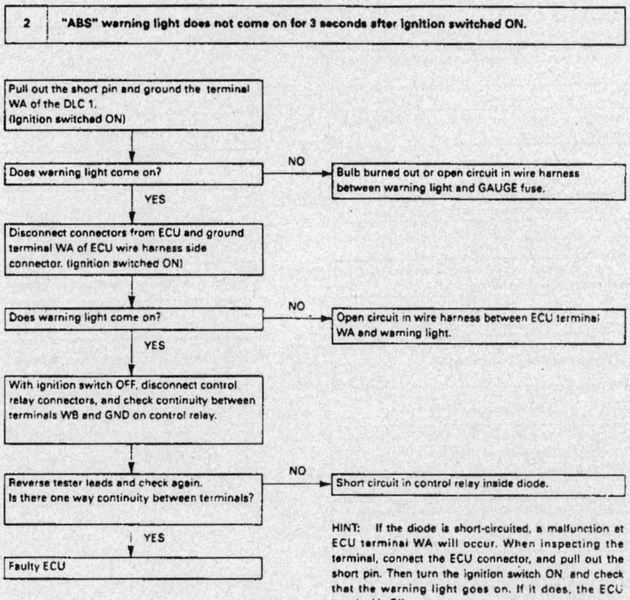
2 "ABS" warning light does not come on for 3 seconds after ignition switched ON.
Pull out the short pin and ground the terminal WA of the DLC 1. (Ignition switched ON)
Does warning light come on?
NO
Bulb burned out or open circuit in wire harness between warning light and GAUGE fuse.
YES
Disconnect connectors from ECU and ground terminal WA of ECU wire harness side connector. (Ignition switched ON)
Does warning light come on?
NO
Open circuit in wire harness between ECU terminal WA and warning light.
YES
With ignition switch OFF, disconnect control relay connectors, and check continuity between terminals WB and GND on control relay.
Reverse tester leads and check again. Is there one way continuity between terminals?
NO
Short circuit in control relay inside diode.
YES
Faulty ECU

HINT: If the diode is short-circuited, a malfunction at ECU terminal WA will occur. When inspecting the terminal, connect the ECU connector, and pull out the short pin. Then turn the ignition switch ON and check that the warning light goes on. If it does, the ECU terminal is OK.

TY4029500146030X

Fig. 8 Troubleshooting (Part 3 of 5). 1995–96 T100

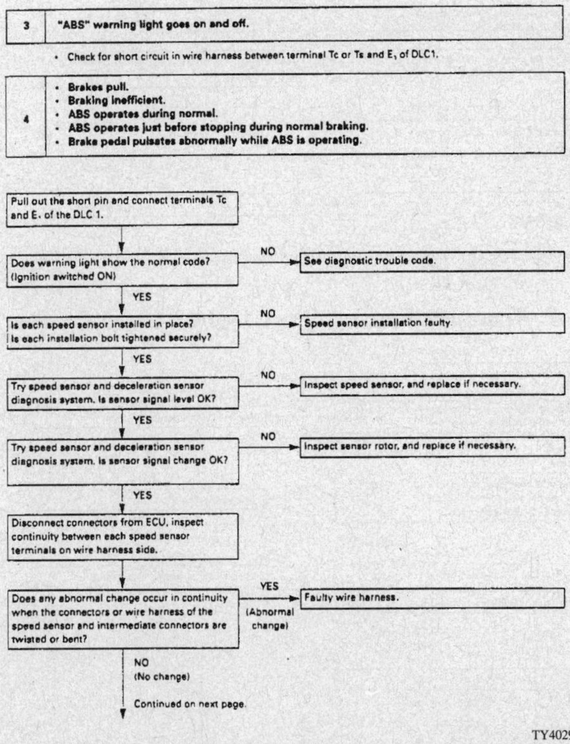
3 "ABS" warning light goes on and off.
• Check for short circuit in wire harness between terminal Tc or Ts and E1 of DLC1.
4
• Brakes pull.
• Braking inefficient.
• ABS operates during normal.
• ABS operates just before stopping during normal braking.
• Brake pedal pulsates abnormally while ABS is operating.
Pull out the short pin and connect terminals Tc and E1 of the DLC 1.
Does warning light show the normal code? (Ignition switched ON)
NO
See diagnostic trouble code.
YES
Is each speed sensor installed in place? Is each installation bolt tightened securely?
NO
Speed sensor installation faulty.
YES
Try speed sensor and deceleration sensor diagnosis system. Is sensor signal level OK?
NO
Inspect speed sensor, and replace if necessary.
YES
Try speed sensor and deceleration sensor diagnosis system. Is sensor signal change OK?
NO
Inspect sensor rotor, and replace if necessary.
YES
Disconnect connectors from ECU, inspect continuity between each speed sensor terminals on wire harness side.
Does any abnormal change occur in continuity when the connectors or wire harness of the speed sensor and intermediate connectors are twisted or bent?
YES (Abnormal change)
Faulty wire harness.
NO (No change)
Continued on next page.
TY4029500146040X

Fig. 8 Troubleshooting (Part 4 of 5). 1995–96 T100

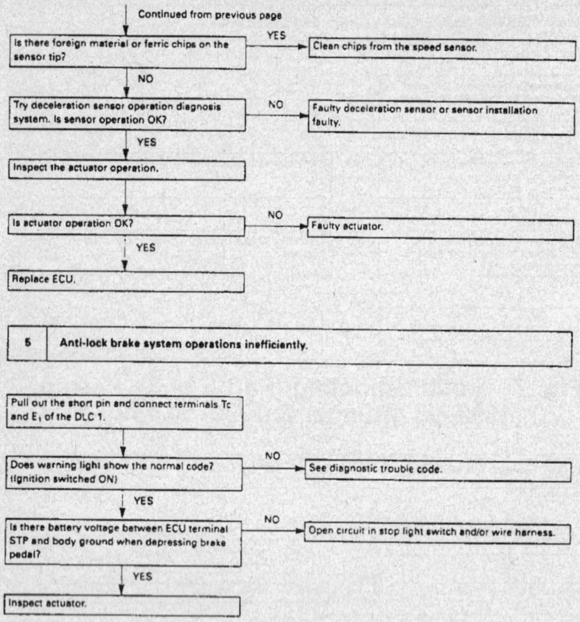
Continued from previous page
Is there foreign material or ferric chips on the sensor tip?
YES
Clean chips from the speed sensor.
NO
Try deceleration sensor operation diagnosis system. Is sensor operation OK?
NO
Faulty deceleration sensor or sensor installation faulty.
YES
Inspect the actuator operation.
Is actuator operation OK?
NO
Faulty actuator.
YES
Replace ECU.
5 Anti-lock brake system operations inefficiently.
Pull out the short pin and connect terminals Tc and E_1 of the DLC 1.
Does warning light show the normal code? (Ignition switched ON)
NO
See diagnostic trouble code.
YES
Is there battery voltage between ECU terminal STP and body ground when depressing brake pedal?
NO
Open circuit in stop light switch and/or wire harness.
YES
Inspect actuator.

TY4029500146050X

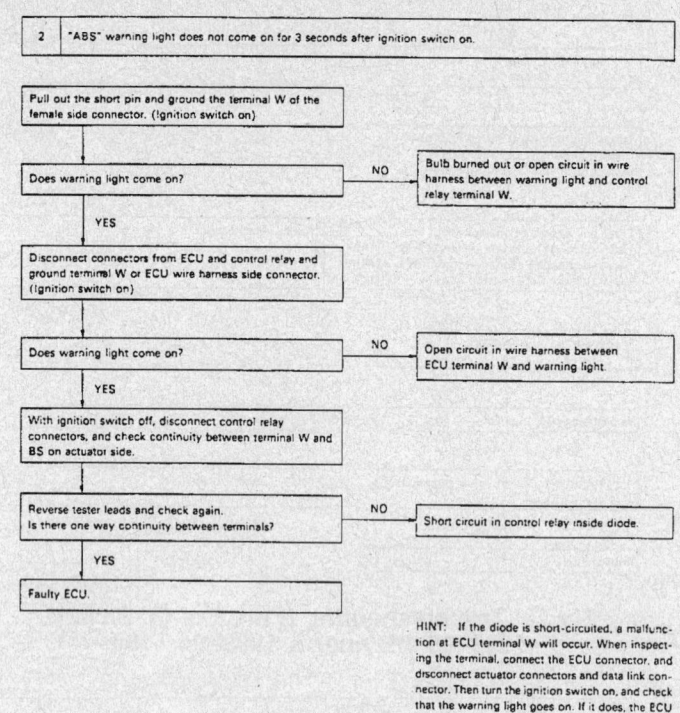

Fig. 8 Troubleshooting (Part 5 of 5). 1995–96 T100

Problem		No.
"ABS" warning light	Always comes on after ignition switch is turned on.	1
	Does not come on for 3 seconds after ignition switch on.	2
	Goes on and off.	3
	Comes on while running.	1
	Does not light up when the transfer is in L (center differential lock) position.	6
Brake condition	Brakes pull.*	4
	Braking inefficient.*	4
	ABS operates at ordinary braking.	4
	ABS operates just before stopping at ordinary braking	4
	Brake pedal pulsates abnormally while ABS is operating.	4
	Skidding noise occurs while ABS operating. (ABS operates inefficiently)	5
	When the transfer is in L (center differential lock) position, the ABS operates.	6

* Also check the parts of the brake system (brake cylinders, pads, hydraulic lines, etc.) not specifically part of the ABS.

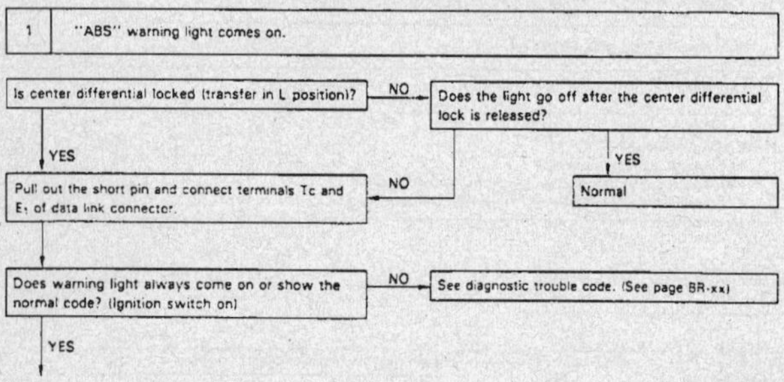
1 "ABS" warning light comes on.
Is center differential locked (transfer in L position)?
NO
Does the light go off after the center differential lock is released?
YES
Normal
YES
Pull out the short pin and connect terminals Tc and E_1 of data link connector.
NO
Does warning light always come on or show the normal code? (Ignition switch on)
NO
See diagnostic trouble code. (See page BR-xx)
YES

TY4029300022010X

Fig. 9 Troubleshooting (Part 1 of 6). Land Cruiser

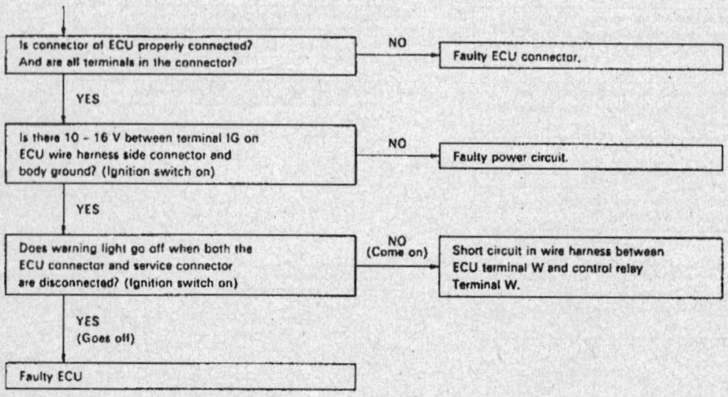
Is connector of ECU properly connected? And are all terminals in the connector?
NO
Faulty ECU connector.
YES
Is there 10 - 16 V between terminal IG on ECU wire harness side connector and body ground? (Ignition switch on)
NO
Faulty power circuit.
YES
Does warning light go off when both the ECU connector and service connector are disconnected? (Ignition switch on)
NO (Come on)
Short circuit in wire harness between ECU terminal W and control relay Terminal W.
YES (Goes off)
Faulty ECU

TY4029300022020X

Fig. 9 Troubleshooting (Part 2 of 6). Land Cruiser

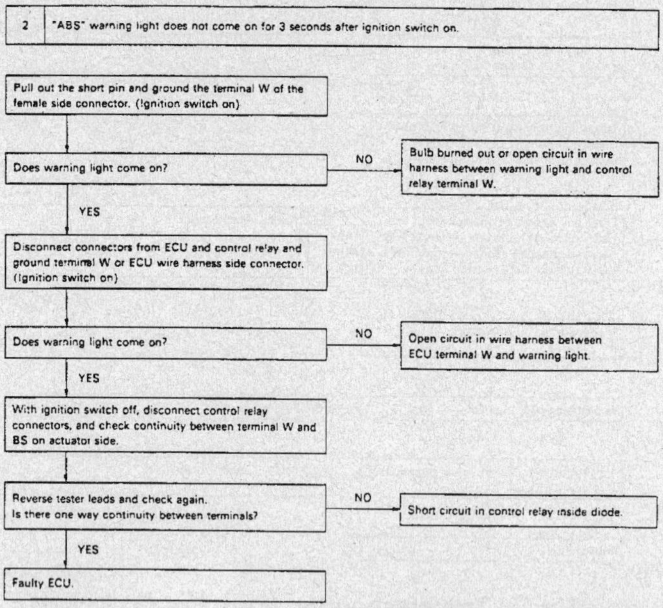
2 "ABS" warning light does not come on for 3 seconds after ignition switch on.
Pull out the short pin and ground the terminal W of the female side connector. (Ignition switch on)
Does warning light come on?
NO
Bulb burned out or open circuit in wire harness between warning light and control relay terminal W.
YES
Disconnect connectors from ECU and control relay and ground terminal W or ECU wire harness side connector. (Ignition switch on)
Does warning light come on?
NO
Open circuit in wire harness between ECU terminal W and warning light.
YES
With ignition switch off, disconnect control relay connectors, and check continuity between terminal W and BS on actuator side.
Reverse tester leads and check again. Is there one way continuity between terminals?
NO
Short circuit in control relay inside diode.
YES
Faulty ECU.

HINT: If the diode is short-circuited, a malfunction at ECU terminal W will occur. When inspecting the terminal, connect the ECU connector, and disconnect actuator connectors and data link connector. Then turn the ignition switch on, and check that the warning light goes on. If it does, the ECU terminal is OK.

TY4029300022030X

Fig. 9 Troubleshooting (Part 3 of 6). Land Cruiser

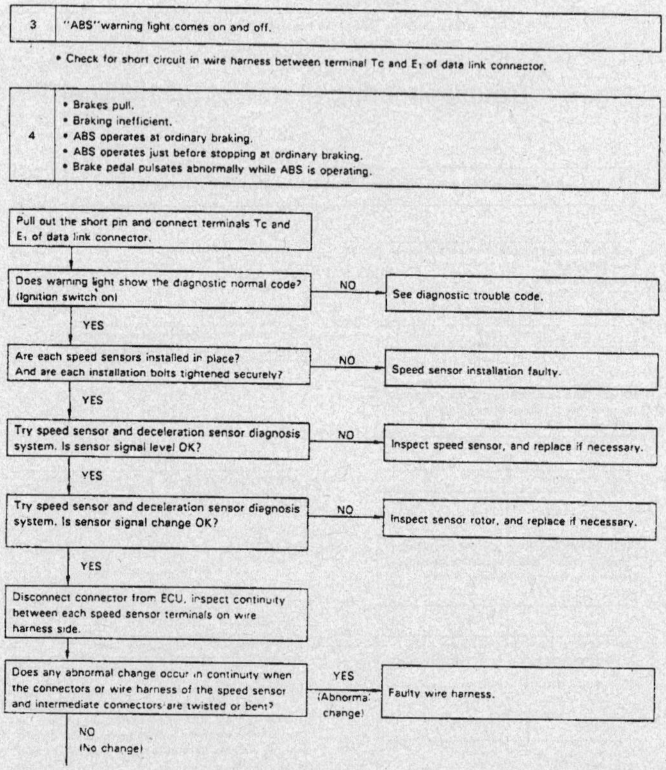
3 "ABS" warning light comes on and off.
• Check for short circuit in wire harness between terminal Tc and E_1 of data link connector.
4
• Brakes pull.
• Braking inefficient.
• ABS operates at ordinary braking.
• ABS operates just before stopping at ordinary braking.
• Brake pedal pulsates abnormally while ABS is operating.
Pull out the short pin and connect terminals Tc and E_1 of data link connector.
Does warning light show the diagnostic normal code? (Ignition switch on)
NO
See diagnostic trouble code.
YES
Are each speed sensors installed in place? And are each installation bolts tightened securely?
NO
Speed sensor installation faulty.
YES
Try speed sensor and deceleration sensor diagnosis system. Is sensor signal level OK?
NO
Inspect speed sensor, and replace if necessary.
YES
Try speed sensor and deceleration sensor diagnosis system. Is sensor signal change OK?
NO
Inspect sensor rotor, and replace if necessary.
YES
Disconnect connector from ECU, inspect continuity between each speed sensor terminals on wire harness side.
Does any abnormal change occur in continuity when the connectors or wire harness of the speed sensor and intermediate connectors are twisted or bent?
YES (Abnormal change)
Faulty wire harness.
NO (No change)

TY4029300022040X

Fig. 9 Troubleshooting (Part 4 of 6). Land Cruiser

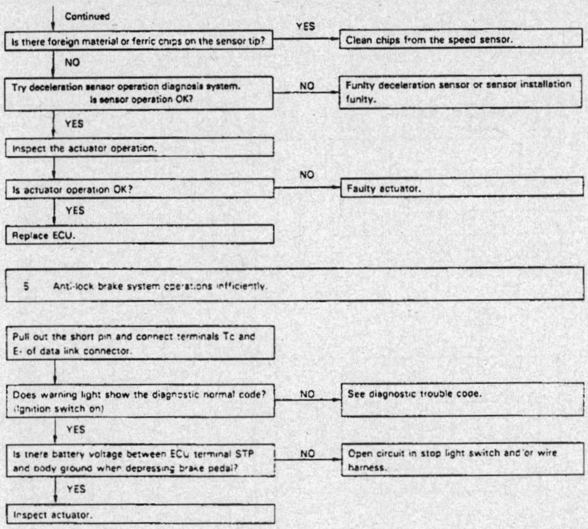
Continued
Is there foreign material or ferric chips on the sensor tip?
YES
Clean chips from the speed sensor.
NO
Try deceleration sensor operation diagnosis system.
Is sensor operation OK?
NO
Funlty deceleration sensor or sensor installation funlty.
YES
Inspect the actuator operation.
Is actuator operation OK?
NO
Faulty actuator.
YES
Replace ECU.
5 Anti-lock brake system operations inefficiently.
Pull out the short pin and connect terminals Tc and E- of data link connector.
Does warning light show the diagnostic normal code? (Ignition switch on)
NO
See diagnostic trouble code.
YES
Is there battery voltage between ECU terminal STP and body ground when depressing brake pedal?
NO
Open circuit in stop light switch and/or wire harness.
YES
Inspect actuator.

TY4029300022050X

Fig. 9 Troubleshooting (Part 5 of 6). Land Cruiser

Symptoms	Inspection Circuit
ABS does not operate.	Only when 1. ~ 4. are all normal and the problem is still occuring, replace the ABS (& TRAC) ECU. 1. Check the DTC, reconfirming that the normal code is output. 2. IG power source circuit. 3. Speed sensor circuit. 4. Check the ABS actuator with a checker. If abnormal, check the hydraulic circuit for leakage.
ABS does not operate efficiently.	Only when 1. ~ 4. are all normal and the problem is still occuring, replace the ABS (& TRAC) ECU. 1. Check the DTC, reconfirming that the normal code is output. 2. Speed sensor circuit. 3. Stop light switch circuit. 4. Check the ABS actuator with a checker. If abnormal, check the hydraulic circuit for leakage.
ABS warning light abnormal.	1. ABS warning light circuit. 2. ABS (& TRAC) ECU.
DTC check cannot be done.	Only when 1. and 2. are all normal and the problem is still occuring, replace the ABS (& TRAC) ECU. 1. ABS warning light circuit. 2. Tc terminal circuit.
Speed sensor signal check cannot be done.	1. Ts terminal circuit. 2. ABS (& TRAC) ECU.

TY4029600188000X

Fig. 10 Troubleshooting. Supra

Symptoms	Inspection Circuit
ABS does not operate.	Only when 1. ~ 4. are all normal and the problem is still occurring, replace the ABS ECU. 1. Check the DTC reconfirming that the normal code is output. 2. +BS power source circuit. 3. Speed sensor circuit. 4. Check the hydraulic circuit for leakage.
ABS does not operate efficiently.	Only when 1. ~ 4, are all normal and the problem is still occurring, replace the ABS ECU. 1. Check the DTC reconfirming that the normal code is output. 2. Speed sensor circuit. 3. Stop light switch circuit. 4. Check the hydraulic circuit for leakage.
ABS warning light abnormal.	1. ABS warning light circuit. 2. ABS ECU.
DTC check cannot be done.	Only when 1. and 2. are all normal and the problem is still occurring, replace the ABS ECU. 1. ABS warning light circuit. 2. Tc terminal circuit.
Speed sensor signal check cannot be done.	1. Ts terminal circuit. 2. ABS ECU.

TY4029600190000X

Fig. 12 Troubleshooting. Avalon & 1996 Camry w/Bosch ABS

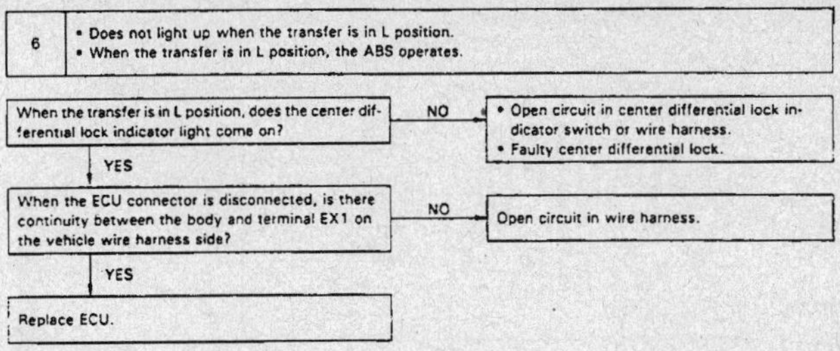
6
• Does not light up when the transfer is in L position.
• When the transfer is in L position, the ABS operates.
When the transfer is in L position, does the center differential lock indicator light come on?
NO
• Open circuit in center differential lock indicator switch or wire harness.
• Faulty center differential lock.
YES
When the ECU connector is disconnected, is there continuity between the body and terminal EX1 on the vehicle wire harness side?
NO
Open circuit in wire harness.
YES
Replace ECU.

TY4029300022060X

Fig. 9 Troubleshooting (Part 6 of 6). Land Cruiser

Symptoms	Inspection Circuit
ABS does not operate.	Only when 1. ~ 4. are all normal and the problem is still occuring, replace the ABS ECU. 1. Check the DTC reconfirming that the normal code is output. 2. IG power source circuit. 3. Speed sensor circuit. 4. Check the ABS actuator with a checker. If abnormal, check the hydraulic circuit for leakage.
ABS does not operate efficiently	Only when 1. ~ 4. are all normal and the problem is still occuring, replace the ABS ECU. 1. Check the DTC reconfirming that the normal code is output. 2. Speed sensor circuit. 3. Stop light switch circuit. 4. Check the ABS actuator with a checker. If abnormal, check the hydraulic circuit for leakage.
ABS warning light abnormal.	1. ABS warning light circuit. 2. ABS ECU.
DTC check cannot be done	Only when 1. and 2. are all normal and the problem is still occuring, replace the ABS ECU. 1. ABS warning light circuit. 2. Tc terminal circuit.
Speed sensor signal check cannot be done	1. Ts terminal circuit. 2. ABS ECU.

TY4029600189000X

Fig. 11 Troubleshooting. Corolla, RAV4, 1996 Celica, Camry w/Nippondenso ABS, Paseo, Tacoma, Tercel & 4Runner

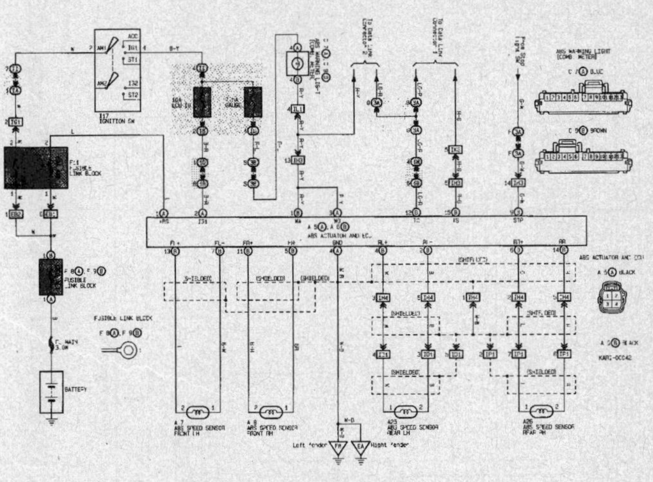

TY4029500148000X

Fig. 13 Wiring diagram. Avalon

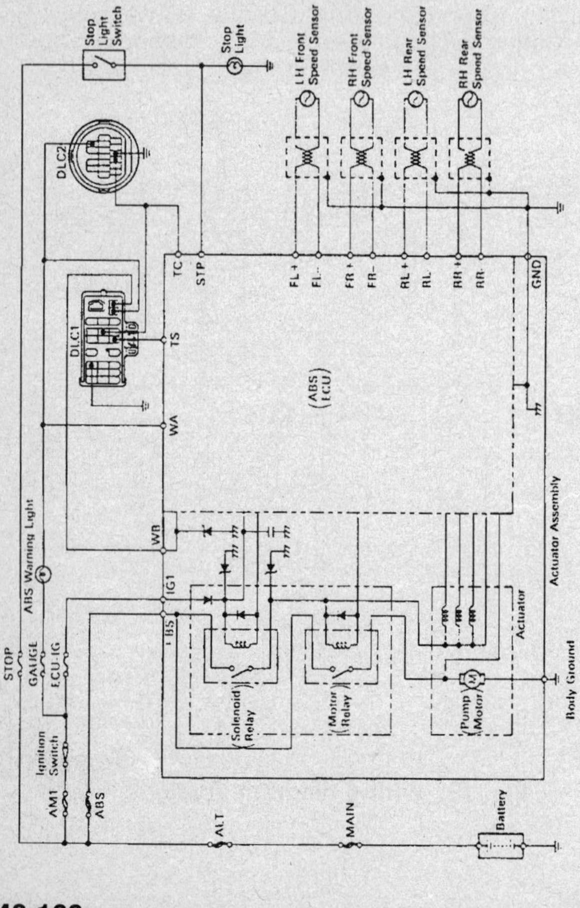
Stop Light Switch
Stop Light
DLC2
LH Front Speed Sensor
RH Front Speed Sensor
LH Rear Speed Sensor
RH Rear Speed Sensor
DLC1
TC
STP
TS
WA
WB
IG1
BS
FL+
FL-
FR+
FR-
RL+
RL
RR+
RR-
GND
(ABS ECU)
ABS Warning Light
STOP
GAUGE
ECU-IG
Ignition Switch
AM1
ABS
ALT
MAIN
Battery
Solenoid Relay
Motor Relay
Pump Motor
Actuator
Actuator Assembly
Body Ground
TY4029200029000X

Fig. 14 Wiring diagram. Camry w/Bosch ABS

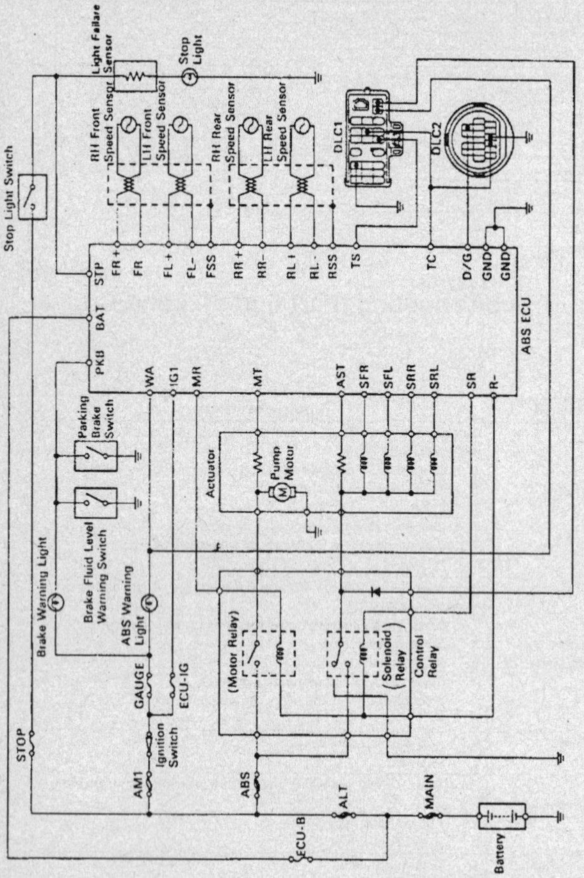
Stop Light Switch
Light Failure Sensor
Stop Light
RH Front Speed Sensor
LH Front Speed Sensor
RH Rear Speed Sensor
LH Rear Speed Sensor
DLC1
DLC2
STP
FR+
FR-
FL+
FL-
FSS
RR+
RR-
RL+
RL-
RSS
TS
TC
D/G
GND
ABS ECU
BAT
PKB
WA
IG1
MR
MT
AST
SFR
SFL
SRR
SRL
SR
R-
Parking Brake Switch
Brake Fluid Level Warning Switch
Brake Warning Light
ABS Warning Light
Actuator
Pump Motor
(Motor Relay)
(Solenoid Relay)
Control Relay
STOP
GAUGE
ECU-IG
Ignition Switch
AM1
ABS
ALT
MAIN
ECU-B
Battery
TY4029200030000X

Fig. 15 Wiring diagram. Camry w/Nippondenso ABS

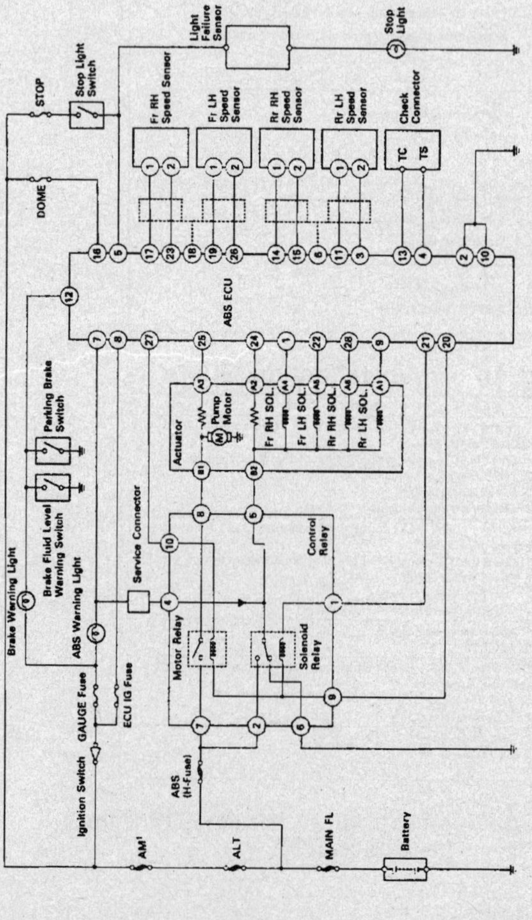
STOP
Stop Light Switch
Light Failure Sensor
Stop Light
Fr RH Speed Sensor
Fr LH Speed Sensor
Rr RH Speed Sensor
Rr LH Speed Sensor
Check Connector
TC
TS
DOME
ABS ECU
Brake Warning Light
Brake Fluid Level Warning Switch
Parking Brake Switch
ABS Warning Light
Service Connector
Actuator
Pump Motor
Fr RH SOL
Fr LH SOL
Rr RH SOL
Rr LH SOL
Control Relay
Motor Relay
Solenoid Relay
GAUGE Fuse
ECU IG Fuse
Ignition Switch
ABS (H-Fuse)
AM1
ALT
MAIN FL
Battery
SOL: Solenoid
TY4029200026000X

Fig. 16 Wiring diagram. 1993 Celica FWD

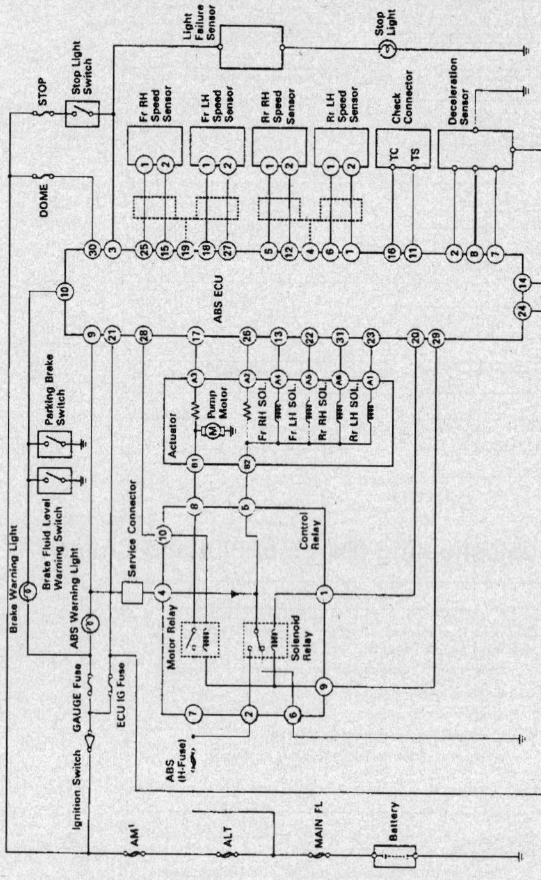
STOP
Stop Light Switch
Light Failure Sensor
Stop Light
Fr RH Speed Sensor
Fr LH Speed Sensor
Rr RH Speed Sensor
Rr LH Speed Sensor
Check Connector
TC
TS
Deceleration Sensor
DOME
ABS ECU
Brake Warning Light
Brake Fluid Level Warning Switch
Parking Brake Switch
ABS Warning Light
Service Connector
Actuator
Pump Motor
Fr RH SOL
Fr LH SOL
Rr RH SOL
Rr LH SOL
Control Relay
Motor Relay
Solenoid Relay
GAUGE Fuse
ECU IG Fuse
Ignition Switch
ABS (H-Fuse)
AM1
ALT
MAIN FL
Battery
SOL: Solenoid
TY4029200027000X

Fig. 17 Wiring diagram. 1993 Celica AWD

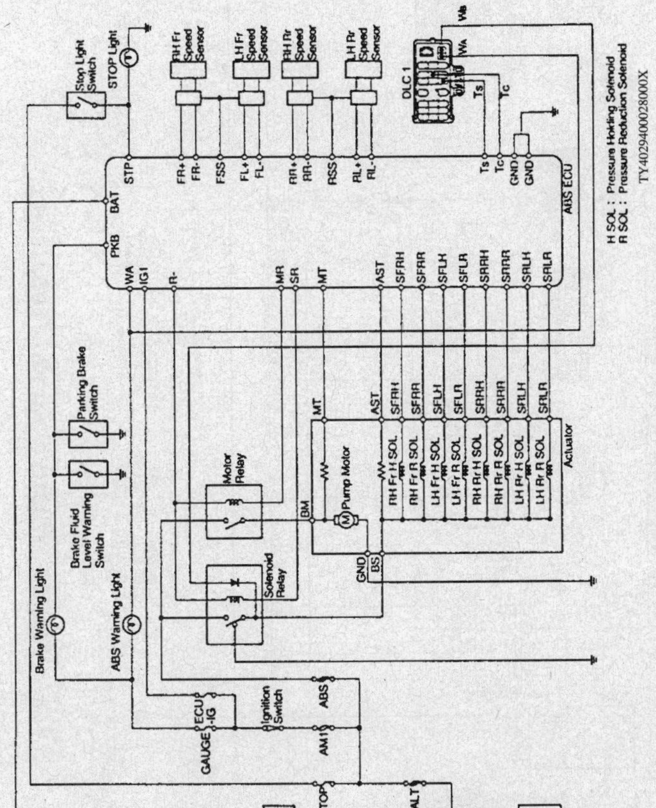
Brake Warning Light
ABS Warning Light
Brake Fluid Level Warning Switch
Parking Brake Switch
Motor Relay
Solenoid Relay
Pump Motor
Actuator
ABS ECU
DLC 1
Stop Light Switch
STOP Light
ECU-B
Short Pin
MAIN
FL MAIN
Battery
GAUGE
ECU-IG
Ignition Switch
AM1
ABS
ALT
STOP
H SOL : Pressure Holding Solenoid
R SOL : Pressure Reduction Solenoid
TY4029400028000X

Fig. 18 Wiring diagram. 1994–96 Celica

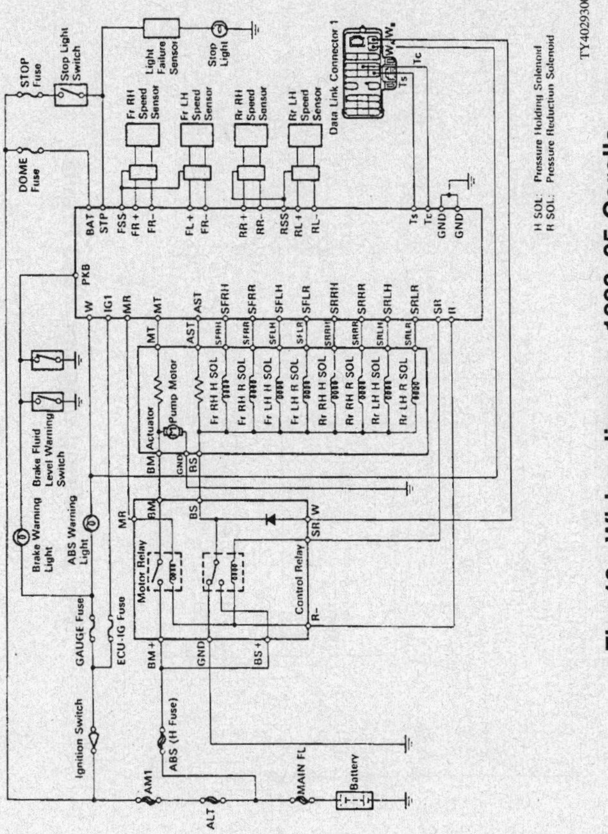
DOME Fuse
STOP Fuse
Stop Light Switch
Light Failure Sensor
Stop Light
Brake Warning Light
Brake Fluid Level Warning Switch
ABS Warning Light
Motor Relay
Control Relay
Actuator
Pump Motor
Data Link Connector 1
Ignition Switch
GAUGE Fuse
ECU-IG Fuse
ABS (H Fuse)
AM1
ALT
MAIN FL
Battery
H SOL : Pressure Holding Solenoid
R SOL : Pressure Reduction Solenoid
TY4029300036000X

Fig. 19 Wiring diagram. 1993–95 Corolla

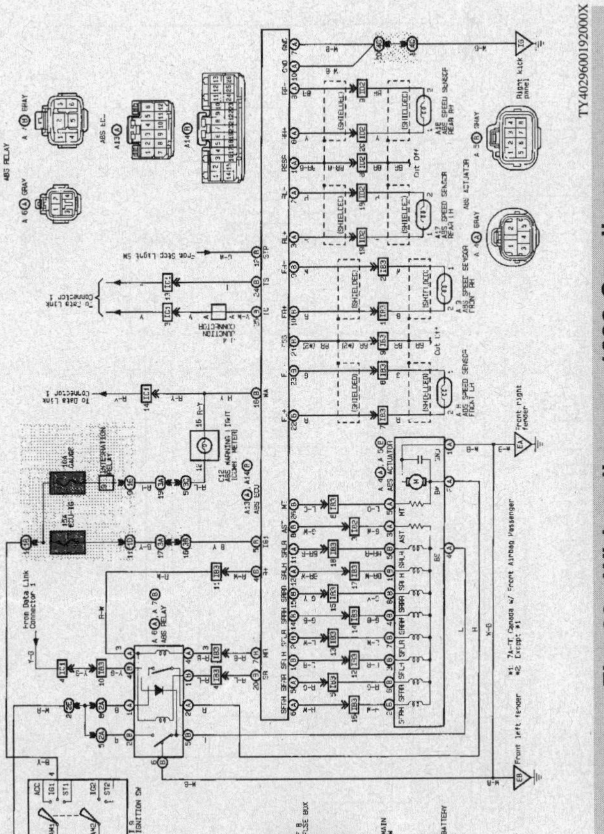
IGNITION SW
FUSE BOX
BATTERY
ABS RELAY
ABS ACTUATOR
ABS ECU
To Data Link Connector 1
From Stop Light SW
TY4029600192000X

Fig. 20 Wiring diagram. 1996 Corolla

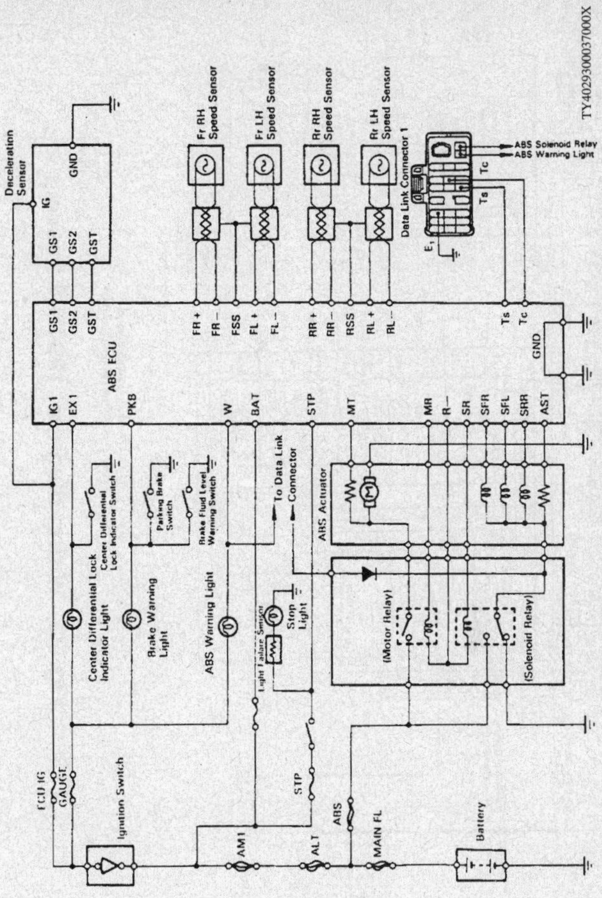
Deceleration Sensor
ABS ECU
Fr RH Speed Sensor
Fr LH Speed Sensor
Rr RH Speed Sensor
Rr LH Speed Sensor
Data Link Connector 1
ABS Solenoid Relay
ABS Warning Light
Center Differential Lock Indicator Light
Brake Warning Light
ABS Warning Light
Stop Light
Light Failure Sensor
To Data Link Connector
ABS Actuator
(Motor Relay)
(Solenoid Relay)
Ignition Switch
Battery
TY4029300037000X

Fig. 21 Wiring diagram. Land Cruiser

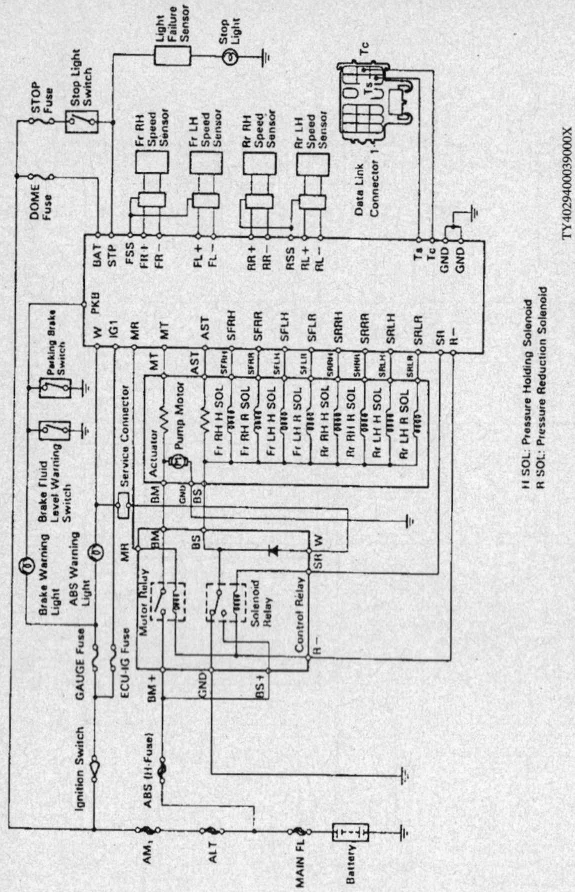
STOP Fuse
Stop Light Switch
Light Failure Sensor
Stop Light
DOME Fuse
Fr RH Speed Sensor
Fr LH Speed Sensor
Rr RH Speed Sensor
Rr LH Speed Sensor
Data Link Connector 1
Parking Brake Switch
Brake Fluid Level Warning Switch
Service Connector
Brake Warning Light
ABS Warning Light
Actuator
Pump Motor
Motor Relay
Solenoid Relay
Control Relay
GAUGE Fuse
ECU-IG Fuse
Ignition Switch
ABS (H-Fuse)
AM1
ALT
MAIN FL
Battery
H SOL: Pressure Holding Solenoid
R SOL: Pressure Reduction Solenoid
TY4029400039000X

Fig. 23 Wiring diagram. 1994–95 Paseo

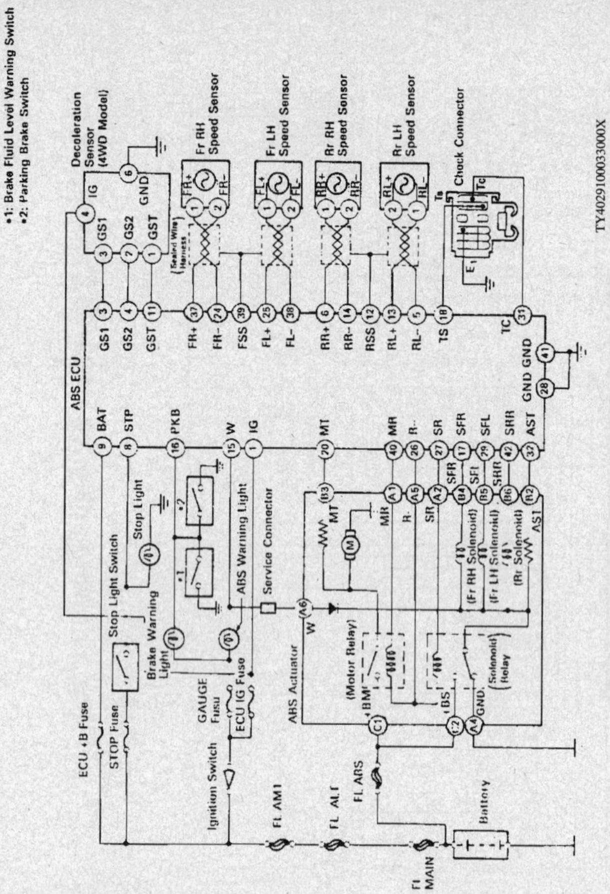
*1: Brake Fluid Level Warning Switch
*2: Parking Brake Switch
Deceleration Sensor (4WD Model)
Fr RH Speed Sensor
Fr LH Speed Sensor
Rr RH Speed Sensor
Rr LH Speed Sensor
Check Connector
ABS ECU
Stop Light
Stop Light Switch
ABS Warning Light
Service Connector
Brake Warning Light
ECU +B Fuse
STOP Fuse
GAUGE Fuse
ECU IG Fuse
Ignition Switch
ABS Actuator
(Motor Relay)
(Solenoid) (Relay)
FL AM1
FL ALT
FL ABS
FL MAIN
Battery
TY4029100033000X

Fig. 25 Wiring diagram. 1993 Previa

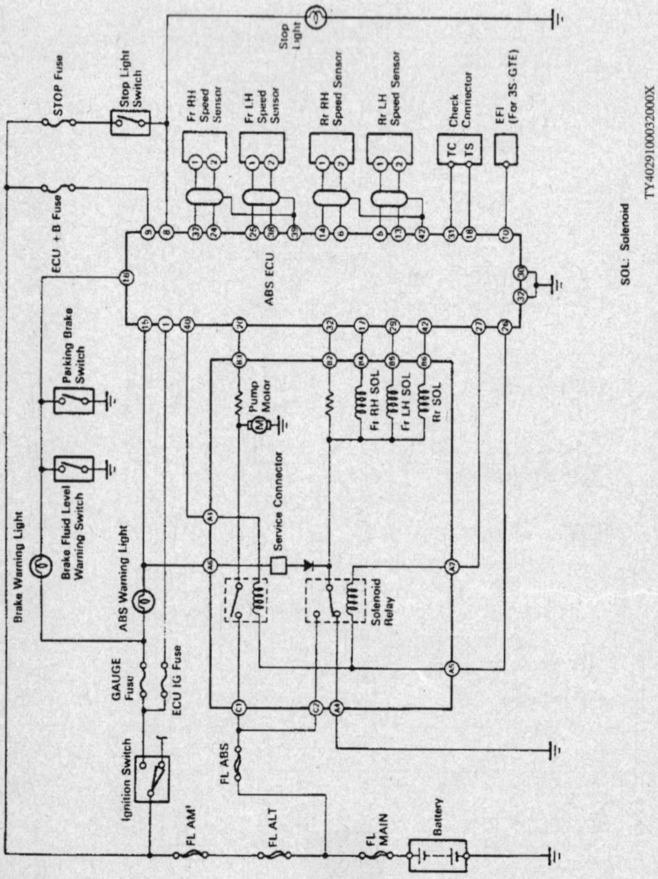
STOP Fuse
Stop Light Switch
Stop Light
ECU +B Fuse
Fr RH Speed Sensor
Fr LH Speed Sensor
Rr RH Speed Sensor
Rr LH Speed Sensor
Check Connector
EFI (For 3S-GTE)
ABS ECU
Parking Brake Switch
Brake Warning Light
Brake Fluid Level Warning Switch
ABS Warning Light
Pump Motor
Fr RH SOL
Fr LH SOL
Rr SOL
Service Connector
Solenoid Relay
GAUGE Fuse
ECU IG Fuse
Ignition Switch
FL ABS
FL AM1
FL ALT
FL MAIN
Battery
SOL: Solenoid
TY4029100032000X

Fig. 22 Wiring diagram. MR2

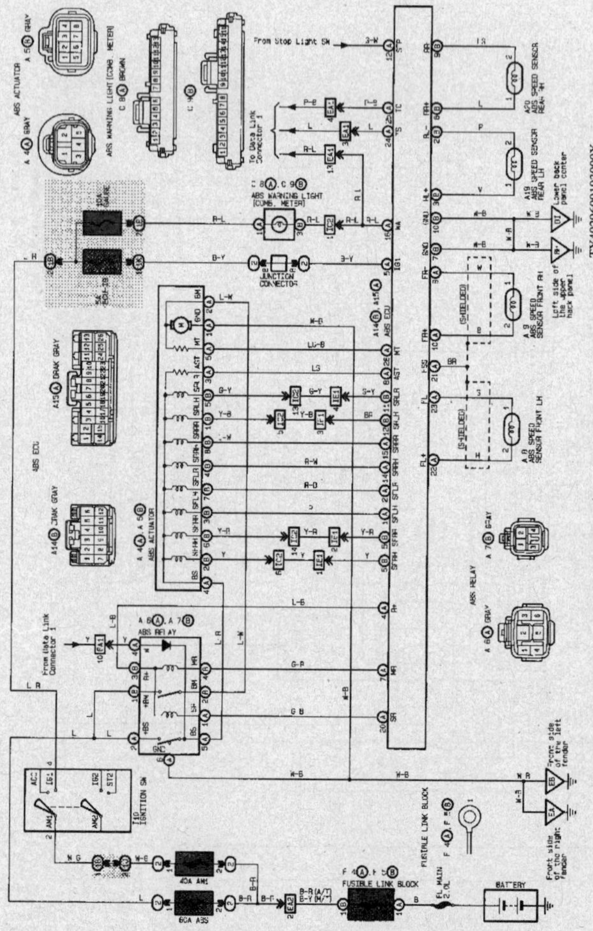
ABS ACTUATOR
ABS WARNING LIGHT
JUNCTION CONNECTOR
ABS ECU
ABS RELAY
IG IGNITION SW
FUSIBLE LINK BLOCK
BATTERY
40A AM1
60A ABS
TY4029600193000X

Fig. 24 Wiring diagram. 1996 Paseo

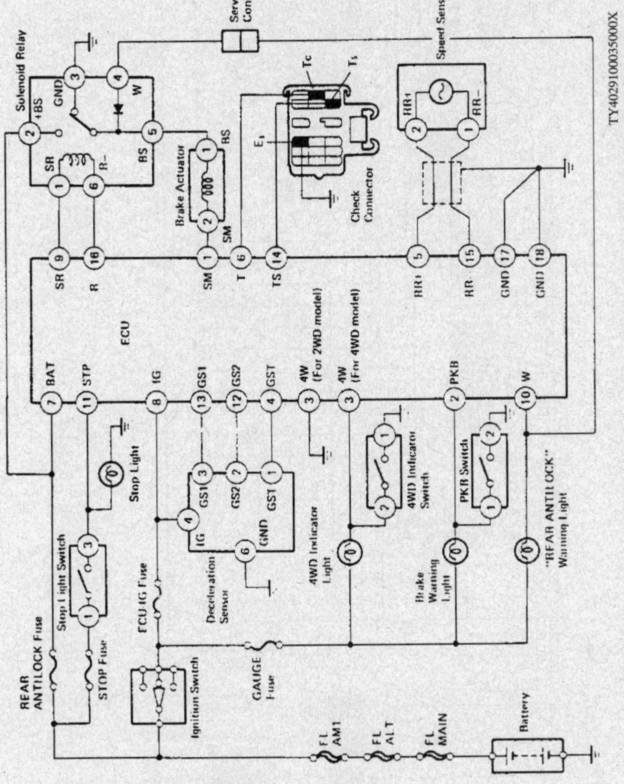
Solenoid Relay
Service Connector
Speed Sensor
Brake Actuator
Check Connector
ECU
REAR ANTILOCK Fuse
STOP Fuse
Ignition Switch
GAUGE Fuse
Stop Light Switch
ECU IG Fuse
Stop Light
Deceleration Sensor
4WD Indicator Light
4WD Indicator Switch
PKB Switch
Brake Warning Light
"REAR ANTI LOCK" Warning Light
Battery
FL AM1
FL ALT
FL MAIN
TY40291000350000X

Fig. 27 Wiring diagram. Pickup & 1993–95 4Runner

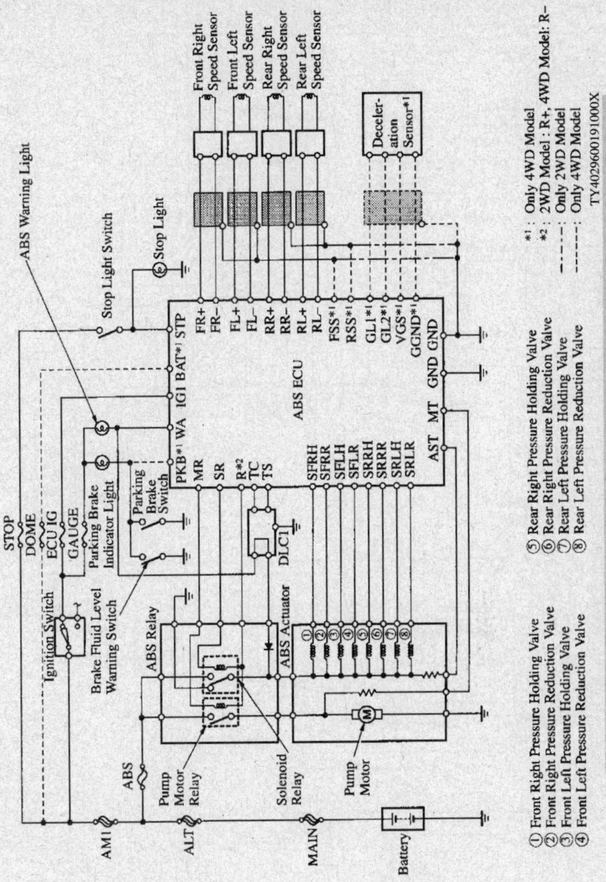
Front Right Speed Sensor
Front Left Speed Sensor
Rear Right Speed Sensor
Rear Left Speed Sensor
Deceleration Sensor*1
Stop Light
Stop Light Switch
ABS Warning Light
ABS ECU
STOP
DOME
ECU IG
GAUGE
Ignition Switch
Parking Brake Indicator Light
Parking Brake Switch
Brake Fluid Level Warning Switch
ABS Relay
ABS Actuator
DLC1
Pump Motor Relay
Solenoid Relay
Pump Motor
AM1
ALT
ABS
MAIN
Battery
① Front Right Pressure Holding Valve
② Front Right Pressure Reduction Valve
③ Front Left Pressure Holding Valve
④ Front Left Pressure Reduction Valve
⑤ Rear Right Pressure Holding Valve
⑥ Rear Right Pressure Reduction Valve
⑦ Rear Left Pressure Holding Valve
⑧ Rear Left Pressure Reduction Valve
*1 : Only 4WD Model
*2 : 2WD Model : R+, 4WD Model: R–
----- : Only 2WD Model
-·-·- : Only 4WD Model
TY40296001910000X

Fig. 29 Wiring diagram. RAV4

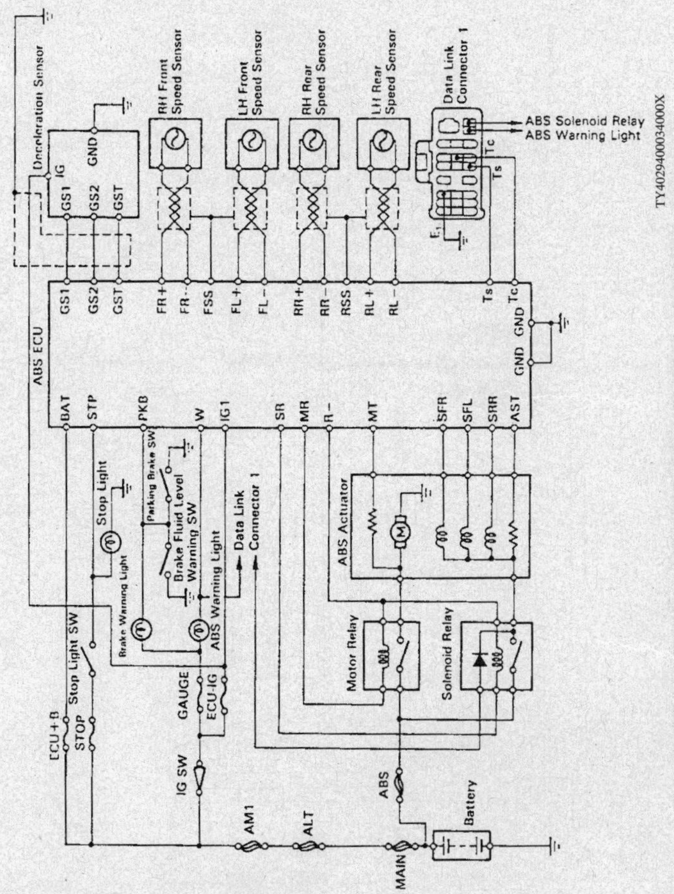
Deceleration Sensor
RH Front Speed Sensor
LH Front Speed Sensor
RH Rear Speed Sensor
LH Rear Speed Sensor
Data Link Connector 1
ABS Solenoid Relay
ABS Warning Light
ABS ECU
Stop Light
Parking Brake SW
Brake Fluid Level Warning SW
Brake Warning Light
ABS Warning Light
Data Link Connector 1
ABS Actuator
Motor Relay
Solenoid Relay
Stop Light SW
ECU+B
STOP
GAUGE
ECU-IG
IG SW
AM1
ALT
ABS
MAIN
Battery
TY40294000340000X

Fig. 26 Wiring diagram. 1994–96 Previa

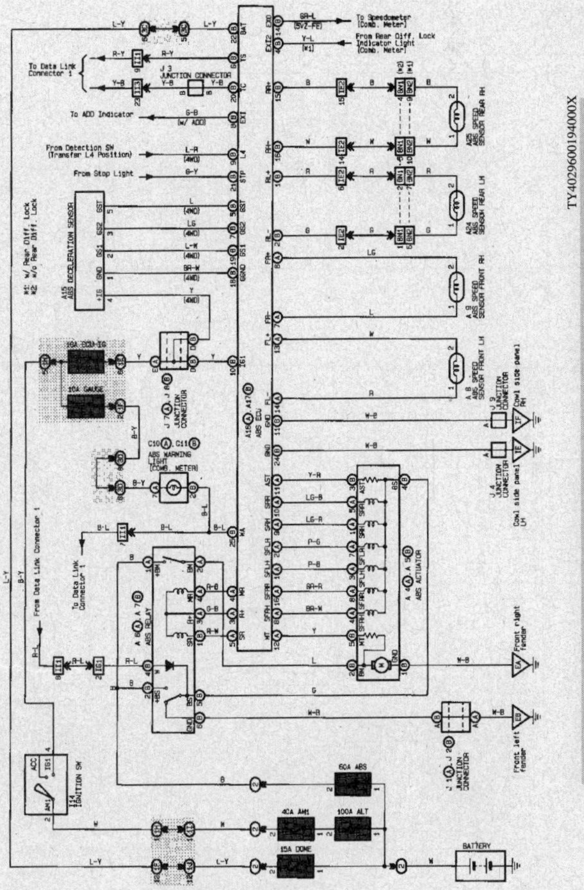
To Speedometer (Comb. Meter)
From Rear Diff. Lock Indicator Light (Comb. Meter)
To Data Link Connector 1
To ADD Indicator
From Detection SW (Transfer L4 Position)
From Stop Light
ABS Deceleration Sensor
ABS Speed Sensor Rear RH
ABS Speed Sensor Rear LH
ABS Speed Sensor Front RH
ABS Speed Sensor Front LH
ABS ECU
ABS Warning Light (Comb. Meter)
ABS Relay
ABS Actuator
Junction Connector
Ignition SW
Front Right Fender
Front Left Fender
Battery
10A ECU-IG
10A GAUGE
60A ABS
40A AM1
100A ALT
15A DOME
TY40296001940000X

Fig. 28 Wiring diagram. 1996 4Runner

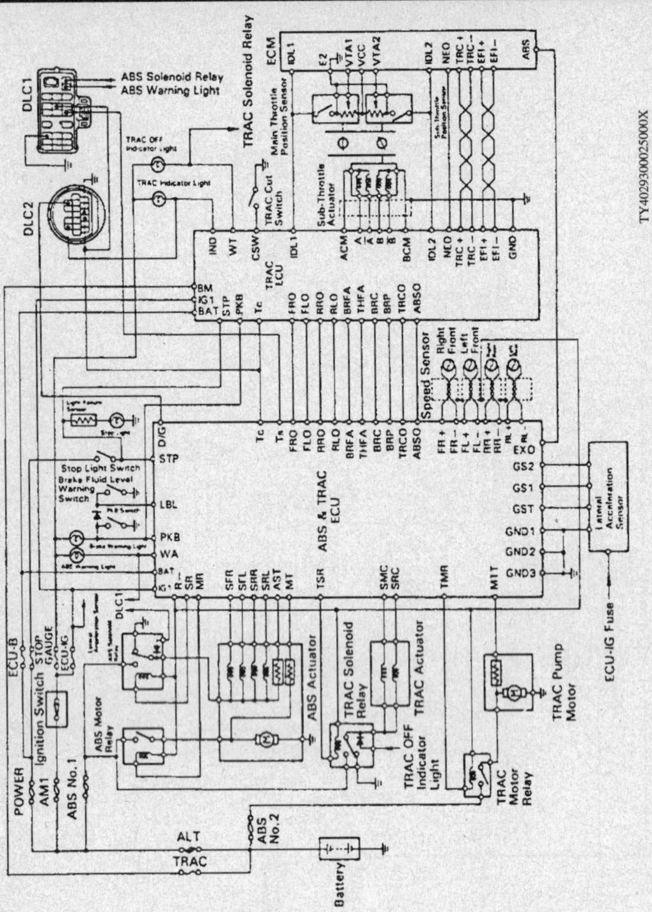
TY4029300025000X
ECM
TRAC Solenoid Relay
ABS Solenoid Relay
ABS Warning Light
DLC1
DLC2
TRAC OFF Indicator Light
TRAC Indicator Light
TRAC Cut Switch
Main Throttle Position Sensor
Sub-Throttle Actuator
Sub-Throttle Position Sensor
TRAC ECU
Stop Light Switch
Brake Fluid Level Warning Switch
ABS & TRAC ECU
Speed Sensor
Right Front
Left Front
Lateral Acceleration Sensor
ECU-IG Fuse
POWER
AM1
Ignition Switch
ECU-B
STOP
GAUGE
ECU-IG
ABS No.1
ABS Motor Relay
ABS Actuator
TRAC Solenoid Relay
TRAC Actuator
TRAC OFF Indicator Light
TRAC Motor Relay
TRAC Pump Motor
ALT
ABS No.2
TRAC
Battery
Fig. 31 Wiring diagram. Supra w/Traction Control

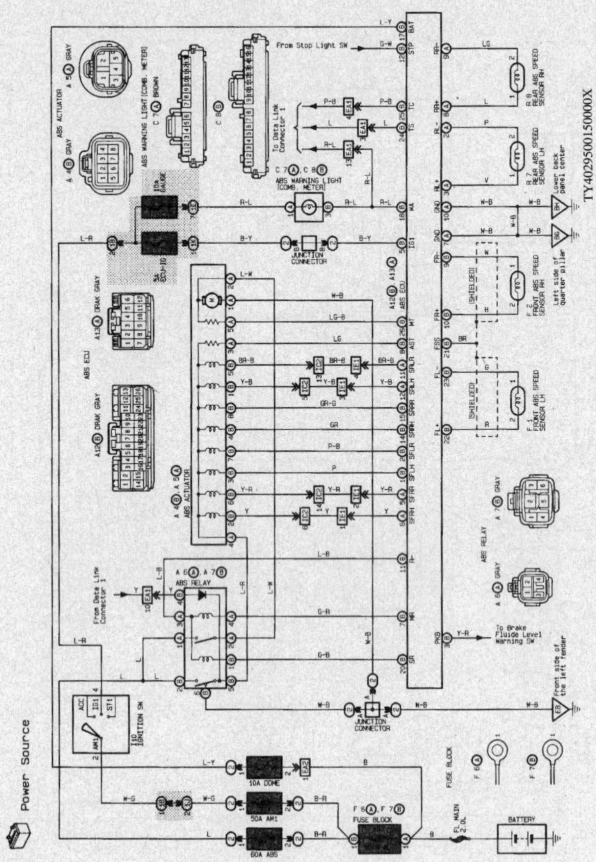
TY4029500150000X
Power Source
ABS ACTUATOR
ABS WARNING LIGHT (COMB. METER)
JUNCTION CONNECTOR
ABS ECU
ABS RELAY
IGNITION SW
FUSE BLOCK
BATTERY
10A DOME
50A AM1
60A ABS
From Stop Light SW
To Data Link Connector 1
REAR ABS SPEED SENSOR RH
REAR ABS SPEED SENSOR LH
FRONT ABS SPEED SENSOR RH
FRONT ABS SPEED SENSOR LH
To Brake Fluide Level Warning SW
Front side of left fender
Fig. 33 Wiring diagram. 1993–95 Tercel

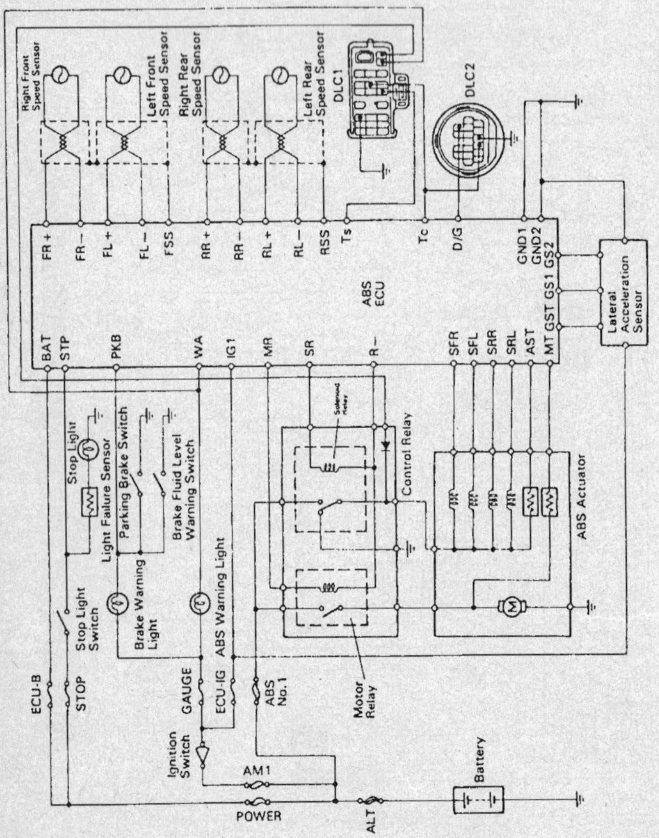
TY4029300024000X
Right Front Speed Sensor
Left Front Speed Sensor
Right Rear Speed Sensor
Left Rear Speed Sensor
DLC1
DLC2
ABS ECU
Lateral Acceleration Sensor
Stop Light
Light Failure Sensor
Parking Brake Switch
Brake Fluid Level Warning Switch
Stop Light Switch
Brake Warning Light
ABS Warning Light
Control Relay
ABS Actuator
Motor Relay
ECU-B
STOP
GAUGE
ECU-IG
ABS No.1
Ignition Switch
AM1
POWER
ALT
Battery
Fig. 30 Wiring diagram. Supra less Traction Control

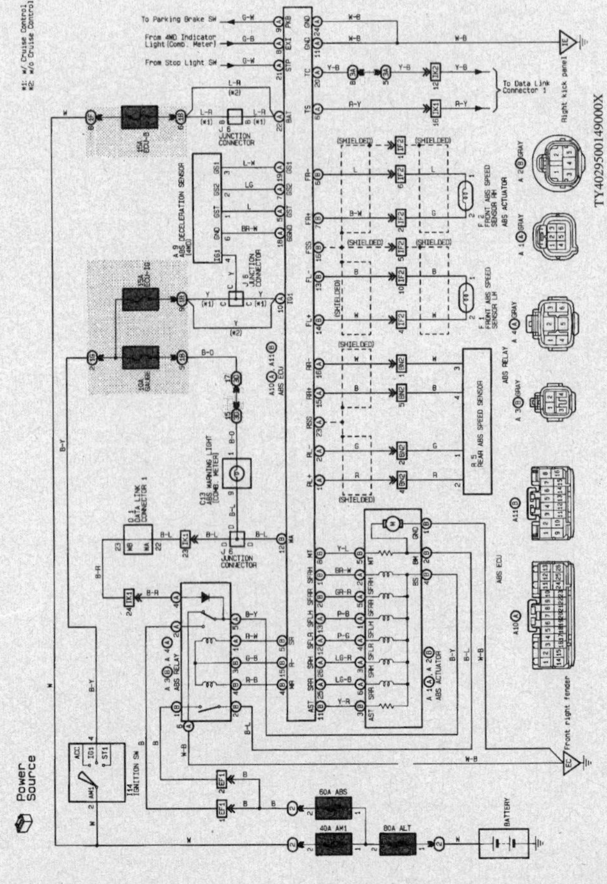
TY4029500149000X
Power Source
To Parking Brake SW
From 4WD Indicator Light (Comb. Meter)
From Stop Light SW
To Data Link Connector 1
ABS DECELERATION SENSOR
JUNCTION CONNECTOR
ABS WARNING LIGHT (COMB. METER)
ABS RELAY
ABS ACTUATOR
ABS ECU
REAR ABS SPEED SENSOR
FRONT ABS SPEED SENSOR RH
FRONT ABS SPEED SENSOR LH
IGNITION SW
60A ABS
40A AM1
80A ALT
BATTERY
Right kick panel
Front right fender
Fig. 32 Wiring diagram. Tacoma

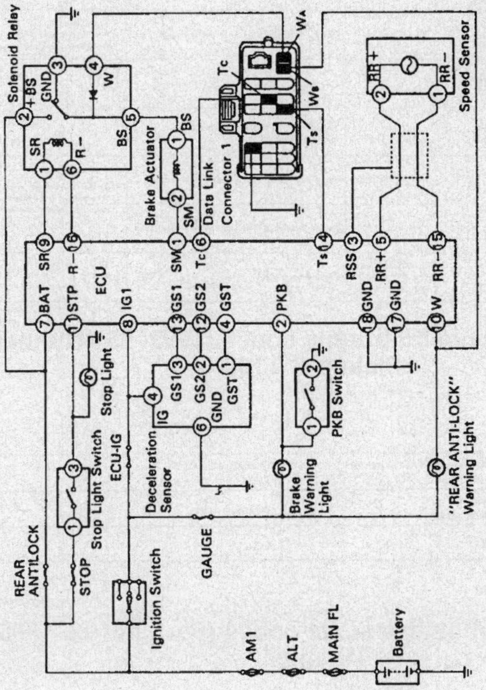

Solenoid Relay
BS
GND
SR
R-
BS
Brake Actuator
SM
BS
Data Link Connector 1
Tc
Ts
Ws
WA
RR+
RR-
Speed Sensor
BAT
SR
STP
R-
ECU
IG1
GS1
SM
GS2
Tc
GST
PKB
Ts
RSS
GND
RR+
GND
W
RR-
Stop Light
Deceleration Sensor
IG
GS1
GS2
GND
GST
PKB Switch
REAR ANTILOCK
Stop Light Switch
ECU-IG
STOP
Ignition Switch
GAUGE
Brake Warning Light
"REAR ANTI-LOCK" Warning Light
AM1
ALT
MAIN FL
Battery

TY40293000380000X

Fig. 35 Wiring diagram. 1993–94 T100

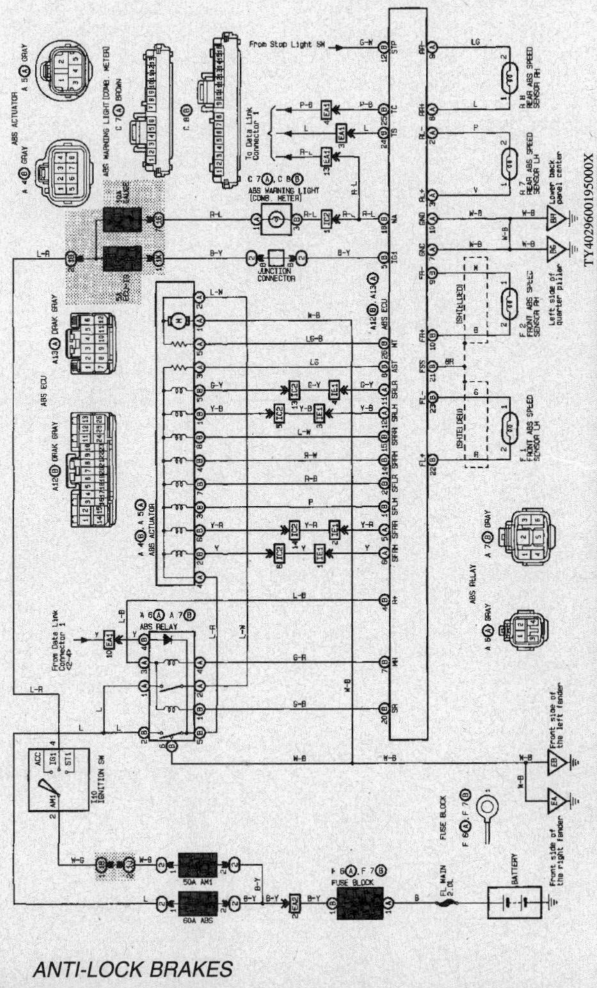
TY40296001950000X

Fig. 34 Wiring diagram. 1996 Tercel

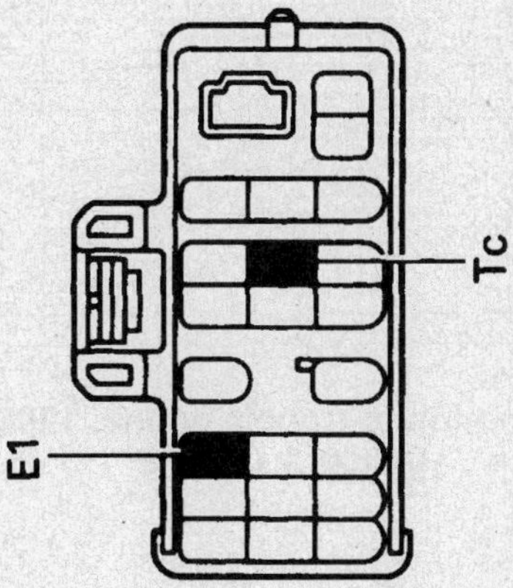

E1
Tc

TY40296001960000X

Fig. 37 Data link connector (DLC1)

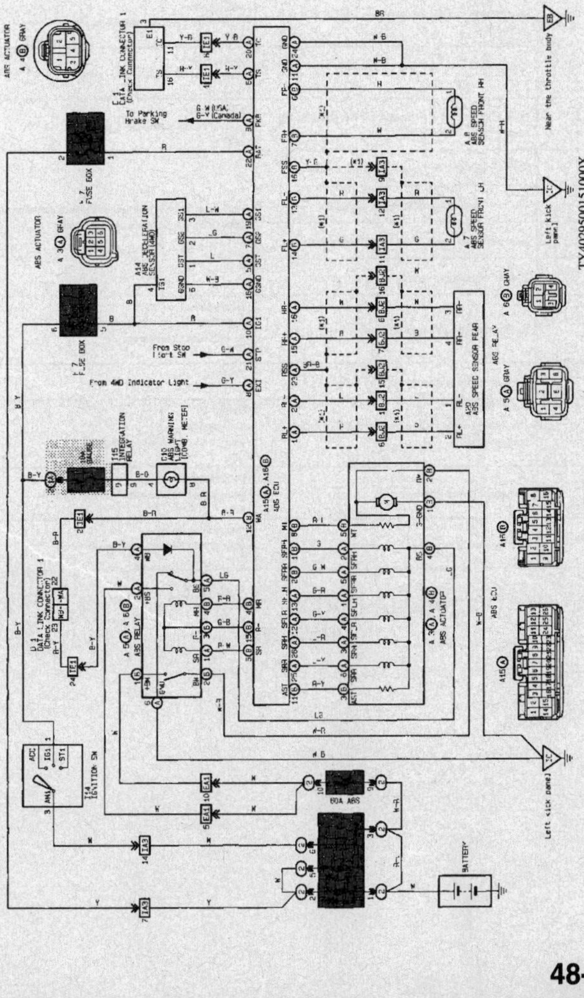
TY40295001510000X

Fig. 36 Wiring diagram. 1995–96 T100

Code No.	Light Pattern	Diagnosis	Trouble Part
11	ON OFF	Open circuit in control relay circuit	• Actuator inside wire harness • Control relay • Wire harness and connector of control relay circuit
12		Short circuit in control relay circuit	
13		Open circuit in control relay circuit	• Actuator inside wire harness • Control relay • Wire harness and connector of control relay circuit
14		Short circuit in control relay circuit	
21		Open or short circuit in 3 position solenoid of front right wheel	• Actuator solenoid • Wire harness and connector of actuator solenoid circuit
22		Open or short circuit in 3 position solenoid of front left wheel	
23		Open or short circuit in 3 position solenoid of rear right wheel	
24		Open or short circuit in 3 position solenoid of rear left wheel	
31		Front right wheel speed sensor signal malfunction	• Speed sensor • Sensor rotor • Wire harness and connector of speed sensor
32		Front left wheel speed sensor signal malfunction	
33		Rear right wheel speed sensor signal malfunction	
34		Rear left wheel speed sensor signal malfunction	
35		Open circuit in front left or rear right wheel speed sensor	
36		Open circuit in front right or rear left wheel speed sensor	
*37		Wrong both rear axle hubs	• Rear sensor rotors
41		Abnormal battery positive voltage (9.5 V less than or 16.2 V more than)	• Battery • Voltage regulator
*43		Malfunction in deceleration sensor	• Deceleration sensor • Deceleration sensor installation • Wire harness and connector of deceleration sensor
*44		Open or short circuit in deceleration sensor	
51		Pump motor of actuator locked or open circuit in pump motor circuit in actuator	• Pump motor, relay and battery • Wire harness, connector and ground bolt or actuator pump motor circuit
Always on		Malfunction in ECU	• ECU

*: For 2WD *: For 4WD

TY4029100040000X

Fig. 38 Diagnostic trouble codes. 1993 Camry, Celica & Corolla

Code No.	Light Pattern	Diagnosis	Trouble Part
11	ON OFF	Open circuit in solenoid relay circuit or solenoid circuit	• Solenoid • Solenoid relay • Wire harness and connector of solenoid and/or solenoid relay circuit
12		Short circuit in solenoid relay circuit	
25		Short circuit in solenoid circuit	
33		Open or short circuit in speed sensor circuit	• Speed sensor • Wire harness and connector of speed sensor circuit
41		Low battery positive voltage (9.5 V or lower)	• Battery
42		Abnormally high battery positive voltage (17 V or higher)	
43		Mechanical malfunction in deceleration sensor	• Deceleration sensor • Wire harness and connector of deceleration sensor circuit
44		Electrical malfunction in deceleration sensor circuit	
Always ON		Malfunction in ECU	• ECU

TY4029300042000X

Fig. 39 Diagnostic trouble codes. 1993–95 4Runner, Pickup & T100

DTC No.	Detection Item	Trouble Area
11	Open circuit in ABS control (solenoid) relay circuit	• ABS control (solenoid) relay • Open or short in ABS control (solenoid) relay circuit • ECU
12	Short circuit in ABS control (solenoid) relay circuit	• ABS control (solenoid) relay • B+ short in ABS control (solenoid) relay circuit • ECU
13	Open circuit in ABS control (motor) relay circuit	• ABS control (motor) relay • Open or short in ABS control (motor) relay circuit • ECU
14	Short circuit in ABS control (motor) relay circuit	• ABS control (motor) relay • B+ short in ABS control (motor) relay circuit • ECU
21	Open or short circuit in 2-position solenoid circuit for right front wheel	• ABS actuator • Open or short in SFRR or SFRH circuit • ECU
22	Open or short circuit in 2-position solenoid circuit for left front wheel	• ABS actuator • Open or short in SFLR or SFLH circuit • ECU
23	Open or short circuit in 2-position solenoid circuit for rear wheel	• ABS actuator • Open or short in SRR or SRH circuit • ECU
31	Right front wheel speed sensor signal malfunction	• Right front, left front, right rear and left rear speed sensor • Open or short in each speed sensor circuit • ECU
32	Left front wheel speed sensor signal malfunction	
33	Right rear wheel speed sensor signal malfunction	
34	Left rear wheel speed sensor signal malfunction	
37	Neither front speed sensor rotor missing	• Front axle hub • Right front, left front speed sensor • Wire harness for sensor system • ECU
37	Some tire is different size from the other tires	• Tire size • ECU
41	Low battery positive voltage or abnormally high battery positive voltage	• Battery • IC regulator • Open or short in power source circuit • ECU
43*1	Malfunction in deceleration sensor	• Deceleration sensor • Wire harness for deceleration sensor circuit • ECU
44*1	Open or short in deceleration sensor circuit	• Deceleration sensor • Open or short in deceleration sensor circuit • ECU

TY4029600199010X

Fig. 40 Diagnostic trouble codes (Part 1 of 2). 1996 4Runner

48*2	Open or short circuit in rear differential lock circuit Rear differential is locking	• Rear differential lock • ECU
51	Pump motor is locked Open in pump motor ground	• ABS pump motor
Always ON	Malfunction in ECU	• ECU

*1: 4WD models
*2: w/ Rear differential lock

TY4029600199020X

Fig. 41 Diagnostic trouble codes (Part 2 of 2). 1996 4Runner

Code No.	Light Pattern	Diagnosis	Trouble Part
11	ON OFF	Open circuit in solenoid relay circuit	• Actuator inside wire harness • Control relay • Wire harness and connector of solenoid relay circuit
12		Short circuit in solenoid relay circuit	
13		Open circuit in pump motor relay circuit	• Actuator inside wire harness • Control relay • Wire harness and connector of pump motor relay circuit
14		Short circuit in pump motor relay circuit	
21		Open or short circuit in 3 position solenoid of front right wheel	• Actuator solenoid • Wire harness and connector of actuator solenoid circuit
22		Open or short circuit in 3 position solenoid of front left wheel	
23		Open or short circuit in 3 position solenoid of rear right wheel	
24		Open or short circuit in 3 position solenoid of rear left wheel	
31		Front right wheel speed sensor signal malfunction	• Speed sensor • Sensor rotor • Wire harness and connector of speed sensor
32		Front left wheel speed sensor signal malfunction	
33		Rear right wheel speed sensor signal malfunction	
34		Rear left wheel speed sensor signal malfunction	
35		Open circuit in front left or rear right wheel speed sensor	
36		Open circuit in front right or rear left wheel speed sensor	
37		Wrong both rear axle hubs	• Rear sensor rotors
41		Abnormal battery voltage (less than 9 5 V/more than 16 2 V)	• Battery • Voltage regulator
51		Pump motor of actuator locked or open circuit in pump motor circuit in actuator	• Pump motor, relay and battery • Wire harness, connector and ground bolt or actuator pump motor circuit
Always on		Malfunction in ECU	• ECU

TY4029200044000X

Fig. 42 Diagnostic trouble codes. 1993 MR2

Code	ABS Warning Light Blinking Pattern	Indicator			Diagnosis
		ABS Warning Light	TRAC Indicator Light	TRAC OFF Light	
11		ON	OFF	ON	Open or short in ABS solenoid relay circuit
12		ON	OFF	ON	B+ short in ABS solenoid relay circuit
13		ON	OFF	ON	Open or short in ABS motor relay circuit
14		ON	OFF	ON	B+ short in ABS motor relay circuit
⑮		ON	ON	ON	Open or short in TRAC solenoid relay circuit
⑯		ON	ON	OFF	B+ short in TRAC solenoid relay circuit
⑰		OFF*	ON	ON	Open or short in TRAC motor relay circuit
⑱		OFF*	ON	ON	B+ short in TRAC motor relay circuit
21		ON	OFF	ON	Open or short in ABS actuator solenoid circuit (SFR circuit)
22		ON	OFF	ON	Open or short in ABS actuator solenoid circuit (SFL circuit)
23		ON	OFF	ON	Open or short in ABS actuator solenoid circuit (SRR circuit)
24		ON	OFF	ON	Open or short in ABS actuator solenoid circuit (SRL circuit)
㉕		ON	ON	ON	Open or short in TRAC actuator solenoid circuit (SMC circuit)
㉗		ON	ON	ON	Open or short in TRAC actuator solenoid circuit (SRC circuit)
31		ON	OFF	ON	Right front wheel speed sensor signal malfunction
32		ON	OFF	ON	Left front wheel speed sensor signal malfunction
33		ON	OFF	ON	Right rear wheel speed sensor signal malfunction
34		ON	OFF	ON	Left rear wheel speed sensor signal malfunction

TY4029300046010X

Fig. 43 Diagnostic trouble codes (Part 1 of 2). Supra

Code	ABS Warning Light Blinking Pattern	Indicator			Diagnosis
		ABS Warning Light	TRAC Indicator Light	TRAC OFF Light	
35		ON	OFF	ON	Open circuit in left front or right rear speed sensor circuit
36		ON	OFF	ON	Open circuit in right front or left rear speed sensor circuit
41		ON	OFF	ON	Low battery positive voltage or abnormally high battery positive voltage
44		ON	OFF	OFF	Open or short in lateral acceleration sensor circuit
51		ON	OFF	ON	ABS pump motor is locked Open in ABS pump motor ground
㊺		OFF*	ON	ON	Brake fluid reservoir level low
㊽		OFF*	ON	ON	Open circuit in TRAC pump motor circuit
61 (circled)		OFF*	ON	ON	TRAC ECU communication abnormal
62 (circled)		OFF*	ON	ON	Wheel speed sensor signal malfunction
Always ON		ON	ON	ON	Malfunction in ABS (& TRAC) ECU

○: Only vehicles with TRAC

*: When a malfunction causing code No. 17, 18, 55, 58, 61 or 62 is detected, the ABS warning light does not light up, but the TRAC indicator light does. However, when checking the DTC, check the blinking pattern of the ABS warning light.

TY4029300046020X

Fig. 43 Diagnostic trouble codes (Part 2 of 2). Supra

Code No.	Light Pattern	Diagnosis	Trouble Part
11	ON OFF	Open circuit in solenoid relay circuit	• Actuator inside wire harness • Solenoid relay • Wire harness and connector of solenoid relay circuit (Include AST circuit)
12		Short circuit in solenoid relay circuit	
13		Open circuit in pump motor relay circuit	• Actuator inside wire harness • Pump motor relay • Wire harness and connector of pump motor relay circuit (include MT circuit)
14		Short circuit in pump motor relay circuit	
21		Open or short circuit in 3 position solenoid of front right wheel	• Actuator solenoid • Wire harness and connector of actuator solenoid circuit
22		Open or short circuit in 3 position solenoid of front left wheel	
23		Open or short circuit in 3 position solenoid of rear wheel	
31		Right front wheel speed sensor signal malfunction	• Speed sensor • Sensor rotor • Wire harness and connector of speed sensor
32		Left front wheel speed sensor signal malfunction	
33		Right rear wheel speed sensor signal malfunction	
34		Left rear wheel speed sensor signal malfunction	
35		Open circuit in left front or right rear wheel speed sensor	
36		Open circuit in right front or left rear wheel speed sensor	
41		Abnormally high or low battery voltage	• Battery • Voltage regulator
*43		Malfunction in deceleration sensor	• Deceleration sensor • Deceleration sensor installation • Wire harness and connector of deceleration sensor
*44		Open or short circuit in deceleration sensor	
51		Pump motor of actuator locked or open circuit in pump motor circuit in actuator	• Pump motor, relay and battery • Wire harness, connector and ground bolt or actuator pump motor circuit (Include MT circuit)
Always on		Malfunction in ECU	• ECU

*: For 4WD Model

TY4029200049000X

Fig. 44 Diagnostic trouble codes. Previa

Code No.	Light Pattern	Diagnosis	Trouble Part
11	ON OFF	Open circuit in solenoid relay circuit	• Actuator inside wire harness • Solenoid relay • Wire harness and connector of solenoid relay circuit (Include AST circuit)
12		Short circuit in solenoid relay circuit	
13		Open circuit in pump motor relay circuit	• Actuator inside wire harness • Pump motor relay • Wire harness and connector of pump motor relay circuit (include MT circuit)
14		Short circuit in pump motor relay circuit	
21		Open or short circuit in 3 position solenoid of front right wheel	• Actuator solenoid • Wire harness and connector of actuator solenoid circuit
22		Open or short circuit in 3 position solenoid of front left wheel	
23		Open or short circuit in 3 position solenoid of rear wheel	
31		Front right wheel speed sensor signal malfunction	• Speed sensor • Sensor rotor • Wire harness and connector of speed sensor
32		Front left wheel speed sensor signal malfunction	
33		Rear right wheel speed sensor signal malfunction	
34		Rear left wheel speed sensor signal malfunction	
35		Open circuit in front left or rear right wheel speed sensor	
36		Open circuit in front right or rear left wheel speed sensor	
41		Abnormally high or low battery voltage	• Battery • Voltage regulator
43		Malfunction in deceleration sensor	• Deceleration sensor • Deceleration sensor installation • Wire harness and connector of deceleration sensor
44		Open or short circuit in deceleration sensor	
48		Open or short circuit in center differential lock indicator	• Center differental lock • Center differential lock indicator light • Center differential lock indicator switch • Wire harness and connector of center differential lock
51		Pump motor of actuator locked or open circuit in pump motor circuit in actuator	• Pump motor, relay and battery • Wire harness, connector and ground bolt or actuator pump motor circuit (Include MT circuit)
Always on		Malfunction in ECU	• ECU

TY4029300050000X

Fig. 45 Diagnostic trouble codes. Land Cruiser

Code No.	Light Pattern	Diagnosis	Trouble Part
11	ON OFF	Open circuit in solenoid relay circuit	• Actuator inside wire harness • Control relay • Wire harness and connector of solenoid relay circuit
12		Short circuit in solenoid relay circuit	
13		Open circuit in pump motor relay circuit	• Actuator inside wire harness • Control relay • Wire harness and connector of pump motor relay circuit
14		Short circuit in pump motor relay circuit	
21		Open or short circuit in solenoid of front right wheel	• Actuator solenoid • Wire harness and connector of actuator solenoid circuit
22		Open or short circuit in solenoid of front left wheel	
23		Open or short circuit in solenoid of rear right wheel	
24		Open or short circuit in solenoid of rear left wheel	
31		Front right wheel speed sensor signal malfunction	• Speed sensor • Sensor rotor • Wire harness and connector of speed sensor
32		Front left wheel speed sensor signal malfunction	
33		Rear right wheel speed sensor signal malfunction	
34		Rear left wheel speed sensor signal malfunction	
35		Open circuit in front left or rear right wheel speed sensor	
36		Open circuit in front right or rear left wheel speed sensor	
37		Wrong both rear axle hubs	• Rear sensor rotors
41		Abnormal battery voltage (less than 9.5 V/more than 16.2 V)	• Battery • Voltage regulator
51		Actuator pump motor locked or open circuit in pump motor	• Pump motor, relay and battery • Wire harness, connector and ground bolt or actuator pump motor circuit
Always on		Malfunction in ECU	• ECU

TY4029300051000X

Fig. 46 Diagnostic trouble codes. 1993–95 Paseo & Tercel

Code	ABS Warning Light Blinking Pattern	Diagnosis
11	ON OFF	Open circuit in ABS solenoid relay circuit
12	ON OFF	Short circuit in ABS solenoid relay circuit
13	ON OFF	Open circuit in ABS motor relay circuit
14	ON OFF	Short circuit in ABS motor relay circuit
21	ON OFF	Open or short circuit in solenoid circuit for right front wheel
22	ON OFF	Open or short circuit in solenoid circuit for left front wheel
23	ON OFF	Open or short circuit in solenoid circuit for right rear wheel
24	ON OFF	Open or short circuit in solenoid circuit for left rear wheel
31	ON OFF	Right front wheel speed sensor signal malfunction
32	ON OFF	Left front wheel speed sensor signal malfunction
33	ON OFF	Right rear wheel speed sensor signal malfunction
34	ON OFF	Left rear wheel speed sensor signal malfunction
35	ON OFF	Open circuit in left front or right rear speed sensor circuit
36	ON OFF	Open circuit in right front or left rear speed sensor circuit
37	ON OFF	Faulty rear speed sensor rotor
41	ON OFF	Low battery positive voltage or abnormally high battery positive voltage
51	ON OFF	Pump motor is locked Open in pump motor ground
Always ON	ON OFF	Malfunction in ECU

TY4029400052000X

Fig. 48 Diagnostic trouble codes. 1994–95 MR2, 1994–96 Celica, Corolla & Camry w/Nippondenso ABS

DTC No.	Detection Item	Trouble Area
11	Open circuit in ABS control (solenoid) relay circuit	• ABS control (solenoid) relay • Open or short in ABS control (solenoid) relay circuit • ECU
12	Short circuit in ABS control (solenoid) relay circuit	• ABS control (solenoid) relay • B+ short in ABS control (solenoid) relay circuit • ECU
13	Open circuit in ABS control (motor) relay circuit	• ABS control (motor) relay • Open or short in ABS control (motor) relay circuit • ECU
14	Short circuit in ABS control (motor) relay circuit	• ABS control (motor) relay • B+ short in ABS control (motor) relay circuit • ECU
21	Open or short circuit in solenoid circuit for right front wheel	• ABS actuator • Open or short in SFR circuit • ECU
22	Open or short circuit in solenoid circuit for left front wheel	• ABS actuator • Open or short in SFL circuit • ECU
23	Open or short circuit in solenoid circuit for right rear wheel	• ABS actuator • Open or short in SRR circuit • ECU
24	Open or short circuit in solenoid circuit for left rear wheel	• ABS actuator • Open or short in SRL circuit • ECU
31	Right front wheel speed sensor signal malfunction	• Right front, left front, right rear and left rear speed sensor • Open or short in each speed sensor circuit • ECU
32	Left front wheel speed sensor signal malfunction	
33	Right rear wheel speed sensor signal malfunction	
34	Left rear wheel speed sensor signal malfunction	
41	Low battery positive voltage or abnormally high battery positive voltage	• Battery • IC regulator • Open or short in power source circuit • ECU
51	Pump motor is locked Open in pump motor ground	• ABS pump motor
Always ON	Malfunction in ECU	• ECU

TY4029600200000X

Fig. 47 Diagnostic trouble codes. 1996 Paseo & Tercel

DTC No.	Detection Item	Trouble Area
11	Open or short circuit in ABS solenoid relay circuit	• Open or short in ABS solenoid relay circuit • ECU
13	Open or short circuit in ABS motor relay circuit	• Pump motor • Open in ABS motor relay circuit • ECU
21	Open or short circuit in 3-position solenoid circuit for right front wheel	• ABS actuator (solenoid valve) • Open or short in right front solenoid circuit • ECU
22	Open or short circuit in 3-position solenoid circuit for left front wheel	• ABS actuator (solenoid valve) • Open or short in left front solenoid circuit • ECU
23	Open or short circuit in 3-position solenoid circuit for rear wheels	• ABS actuator (solenoid valve) • Open or short in rear solenoid circuit • ECU
31	Right front wheel speed sensor signal malfunction	• Right front, left front, right rear and left rear speed sensor • Open in each speed sensor circuit • Sensor installation • Sensor rotor • ECU
32	Left front wheel speed sensor signal malfunction	
33	Right rear wheel speed sensor signal malfunction	
34	Left rear wheel speed sensor signal malfunction	
35	Open circuit in right front speed sensor circuit	• Right front, left front, right rear and left rear speed sensor • Open in each speed sensor circuit • ECU
36	Open circuit in left front speed sensor circuit	
37	Faulty one of 4 speed sensor rotors	• Sensor rotor • Speed sensor • Wire harness for sensor circuit • Tires • ECU
38	Open circuit in right rear speed sensor circuit	• Right front, left front, right rear and left rear speed sensor • Open in each speed sensor circuit • ECU
39	Open circuit in left rear speed sensor circuit	
41	Low battery positive voltage	• Battery • IC regulator • Open or short in power source circuit • ECU
51	Pump motor is locked Open in pump motor circuit in actuator	• ABS pump motor
62	Malfunction in ECU	• ECU

TY4029600197000X

Fig. 49 Diagnostic trouble codes. Camry w/Bosch ABS

Code	ABS Warning Light Blinking Pattern	Diagnosis
11	ON OFF	Open or short circuit in ABS solenoid relay circuit
13	ON OFF	Open or short circuit in ABS motor relay circuit
21	ON OFF	Open or short circuit in 3-position solenoid circuit for right front wheel
22	ON OFF	Open or short circuit in 3-position solenoid circuit for left front wheel
23	ON OFF	Open or short circuit in 3-position solenoid circuit for rear wheels
31	ON OFF	Right front wheel speed sensor signal malfunction
32	ON OFF	Left front wheel speed sensor signal malfunction
33	ON OFF	Right rear wheel speed sensor signal malfunction
34	ON OFF	Left rear wheel speed sensor signal malfunction
35	ON OFF	Open circuit in right front speed sensor circuit
36	ON OFF	Open circuit in left front speed sensor circuit
37	ON OFF	Faulty front or rear speed sensor rotor
38	ON OFF	Open circuit in right rear speed sensor circuit
39	ON OFF	Open circuit in left rear speed sensor circuit
41	ON OFF	Low battery positive voltage
51	ON OFF	Pump motor is locked Open in pump motor circuit in actuator
62	ON OFF	Malfunction in ECU

TY4029500152000X

Fig. 50 Diagnostic trouble codes. Avalon

DTC No.	Detection Item	Trouble Area
11	Open circuit in ABS control (solenoid) relay circuit	• ABS control (solenoid) relay • Open or short in ABS control (solenoid) relay circuit
12	Short circuit in ABS control (solenoid) relay circuit	• ABS control (solenoid) relay • B+ short in ABS control (solenoid) relay circuit
13	Open circuit in ABS control (motor) relay circuit	• ABS control (motor) relay • Open or short in ABS control (motor) relay circuit
14	Short circuit in ABS control (motor) relay circuit	• ABS control (motor) relay • B+ short in ABS control (motor) relay circuit
21	Open or short circuit in 2-position solenoid circuit for right front wheel	• ABS actuator • Open or short in SFRR or SFRH circuit
22	Open or short circuit in 2-position solenoid circuit for left front wheel	• ABS actuator • Open or short in SFLR or SFLH circuit
23	Open or short circuit in 2-position solenoid circuit for right rear wheel	• ABS actuator • Open or short in SRRR or SRRH circuit
24	Open or short circuit in 2-position solenoid circuit for left rear wheel	• ABS actuator • Open or short in SRLR or SRLH circuit
31	Right front wheel speed sensor signal malfunction	• Right front, left front, right rear and left rear speed sensor • Open or short in each speed sensor circuit • Speed sensor
32	Left front wheel speed sensor signal malfunction	
33	Right rear wheel speed sensor signal malfunction	
34	Left rear wheel speed sensor signal malfunction	
35	Open circuit in left speed sensor circuit	• Open in speed sensor circuit
*1 37	Some tire is different size from the other tires	• Tire size
41	Low battery positive voltage. Abnormally high battery positive voltage (4WD)	• Battery • IC regulator • Open or short in power source circuit
*2 43	Malfunction in deceleration sensor (constant output)	• Deceleration sensor • Wire harness for deceleration sensor system
*2 44	Open or short in deceleration sensor circuit	• Deceleration sensor • Open or short in deceleration sensor circuit
*2 45	Malfunction in deceleration sensor	• Deceleration sensor • Wire harness for deceleration sensor system
51	Pump motor is locked Open in pump motor ground	• ABS pump motor
Always ON	Malfunction in ECU Abnormal high battery positive voltage (2WD)	• ECU

*1: 2WD models
*2: 4WD models

TY4029600198000X

Fig. 51 Diagnostic trouble codes. RAV4

Code	ABS Warning Light Blinking Pattern	Diagnosis
11		Open circuit in ABS control (solenoid) relay circuit
12		Short circuit in ABS control (solenoid) relay circuit
13		Open circuit in ABS control (motor) relay circuit
14		Short circuit in ABS control (motor) relay circuit
21		Open or short circuit in 2-position solenoid circuit for right front wheel
22		Open or short circuit in 2-position solenoid circuit for left front wheel
23		Open or short circuit in 2-position solenoid circuit for rear wheel
31		Right front wheel speed sensor signal malfunction
32		Left front wheel speed sensor signal malfunction
33		Right rear wheel speed sensor signal malfunction
34		Left rear wheel speed sensor signal malfunction
35		Open circuit in left front or right rear speed sensor circuit
36		Open circuit in right front or left rear speed sensor circuit
37		• Neither front speed sensor rotor missing *1 • Some tire is different size from the other tires
41		Low battery positive voltage or abnormally high battery positive voltage
*2 43		Malfunction in deceleration sensor
*2 44		Open or short in deceleration sensor circuit
51		Pump motor is locked Open in pump motor ground
Always ON		Malfunction in ECU

*1: 2WD models
*2: 4WD models

TY4029500153000X

Fig. 52 Diagnostic trouble codes. Tacoma & 1996 T100

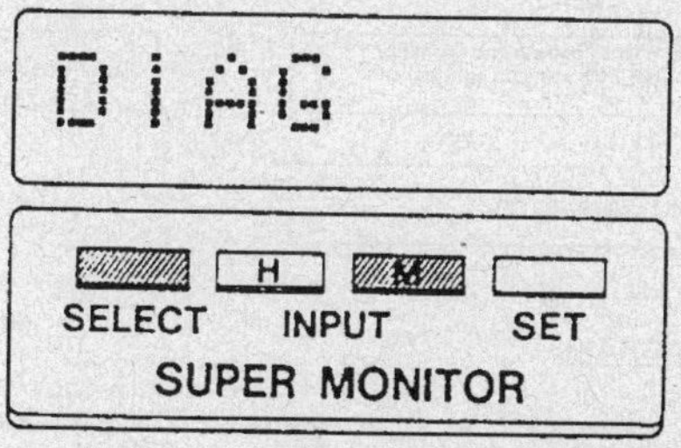
DIAG
H
M
SELECT
INPUT
SET
SUPER MONITOR

TY4029100053000X

Fig. 53 Accessing diagnostic trouble codes. Models w/super monitor

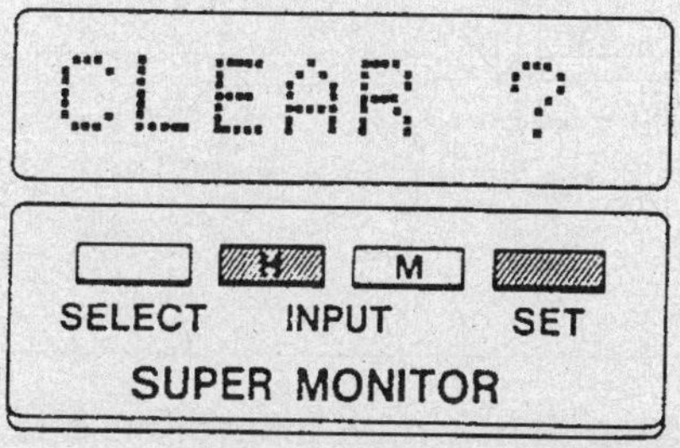
CLEAR ?
H
M
SELECT
INPUT
SET
SUPER MONITOR

TY4029100054000X

Fig. 54 Clearing diagnostic trouble codes. Models w/super monitor

CIRCUIT DESCRIPTION

This stop light switch senses whether the brake pedal is depressed or released, and sends the signal to the ECU.

WIRING DIAGRAM

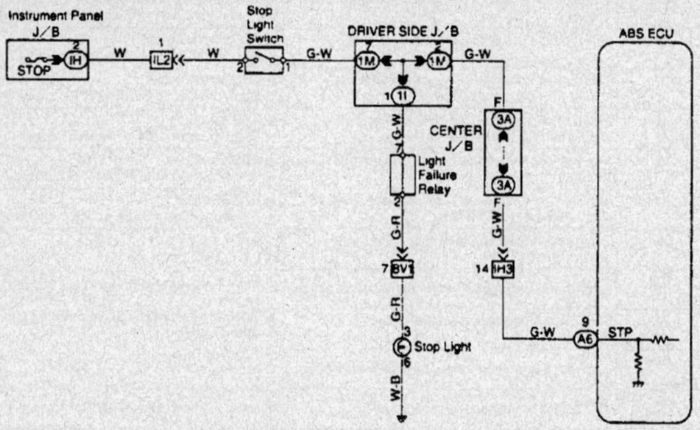
Instrument Panel J/B
STOP
IH
W
IL2
Stop Light Switch
DRIVER SIDE J/B
1M
1M
1V
G-W
ABS ECU
CENTER J/B
3A
3A
Light Failure Relay
G-W
G-R
8V1
IH3
G-W
A6
STP
Stop Light
W-B

TY4029500160010X

Fig. 55 Stop light switch circuit inspection & testing (Part 1 of 2). Avalon

1	Check operation of stop light.

C Check that stop light lights up when brake pedal is depressed and turns off when brake pedal is released.

OK

NG 〉 Repair stop light circuit

2	Check voltage between terminal STP of ABS ECU connector and body ground.

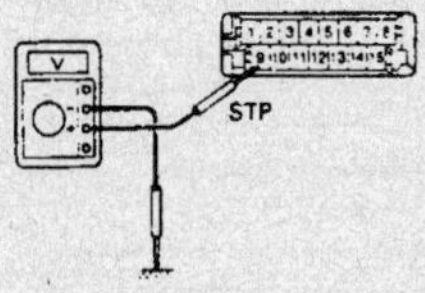
V
STP

P Disconnect ABS ECU connector.

C Measure voltage between terminal STP and body ground.

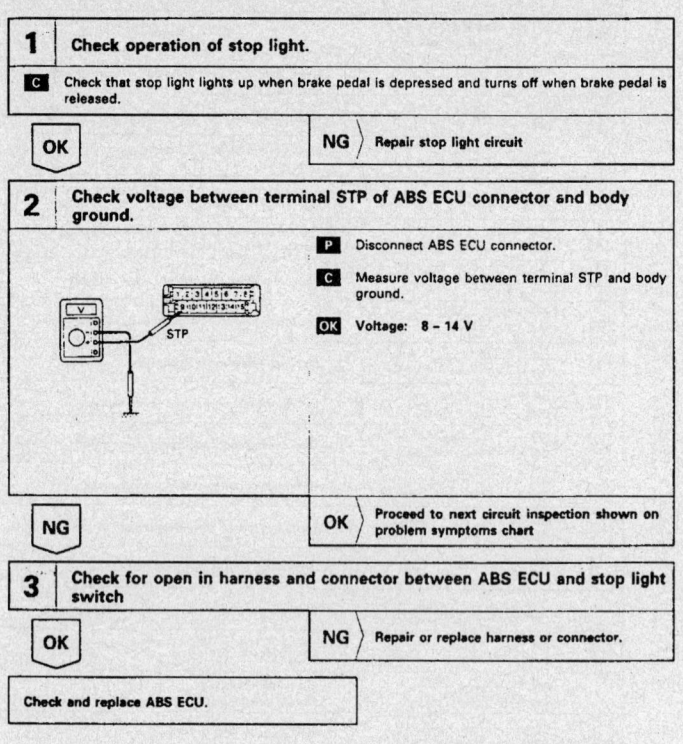

OK Voltage: 8 – 14 V

NG

OK 〉 Proceed to next circuit inspection shown on problem symptoms chart

3	Check for open in harness and connector between ABS ECU and stop light switch

OK

NG 〉 Repair or replace harness or connector.

Check and replace ABS ECU.

TY4029500160020X

Fig. 55 Stop light switch circuit inspection & testing (Part 2 of 2). Avalon

CIRCUIT DESCRIPTION

This stop light switch senses whether the brake pedal is depressed or released, and sends the signal to the ECU.

DIAGNOSTIC CHART

1. Check operation or stop light. — NG → Repair stop light circuit
   - ↓ OK
2. Check voltage of terminal STP. — OK → Proceed to next circuit inspection shown on problem symptoms chart
   - ↓ NG
3. Check for open in harness and connector between ABS ECU and stop light switch — NG → Repair or replace harness or connector.
   - ↓ OK

Check and replace ABS ECU.

WIRING DIAGRAM

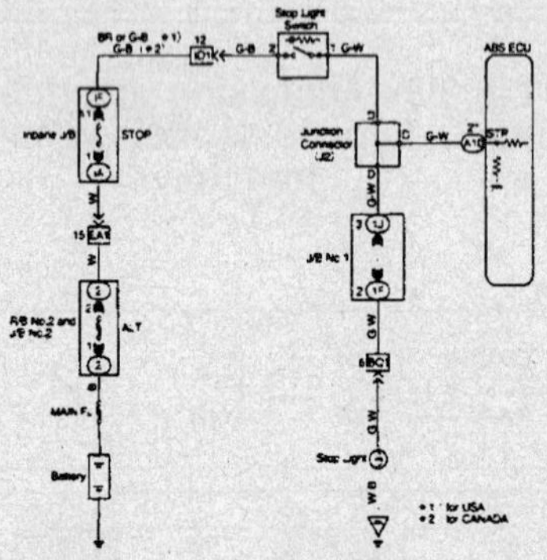
Stop Light Switch
ABS ECU
STOP
Junction Connector
G-W
STP
J/B No.1
ALT
Battery
Stop Light
*1 : for USA
*2 : for CANADA

TY4029400058010X

Fig. 56 Stop light circuit inspection & testing (Part 1 of 2). Celica

1	Check operation of stop light.

C Check that stop light lights up when brake pedal is depressed and turns off when brake pedal is released.

OK

NG 〉 Repair stop light circuit

2	Check voltage between terminal STP of ABS ECU and body ground.

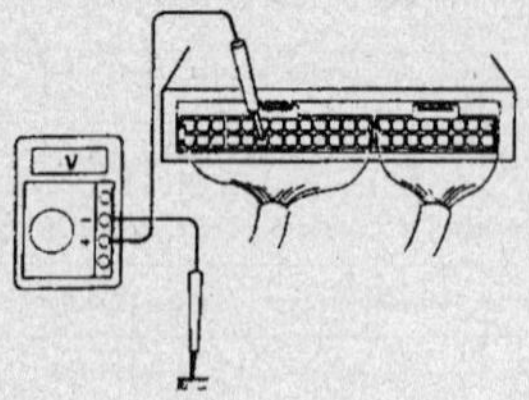
V

P Remove ABS ECU with connectors still connected.

C Measure voltage between terminal STP of ABS ECU and body ground when brake pedal is depressed.

OK Voltage: 8 ~ 14 V

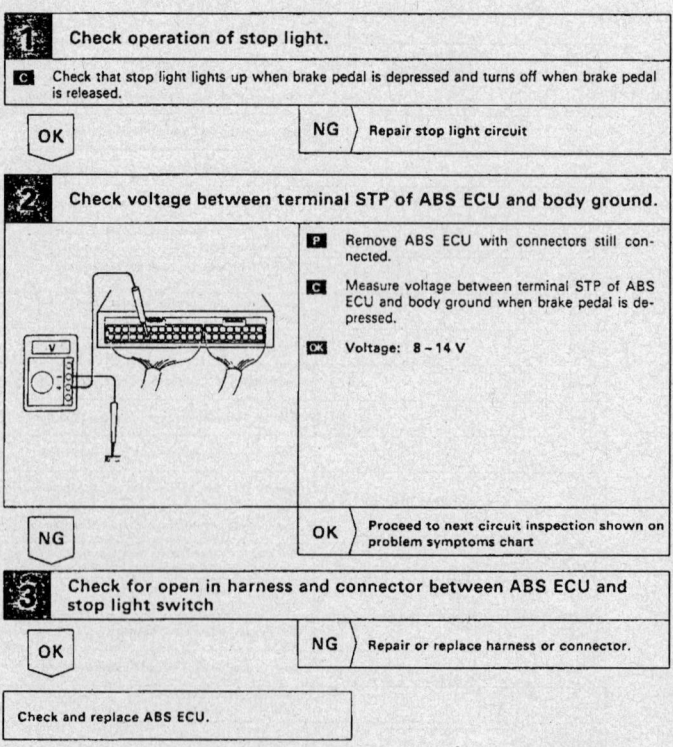

NG

OK 〉 Proceed to next circuit inspection shown on problem symptoms chart

3	Check for open in harness and connector between ABS ECU and stop light switch

OK

NG 〉 Repair or replace harness or connector.

Check and replace ABS ECU.

TY4029400058020X

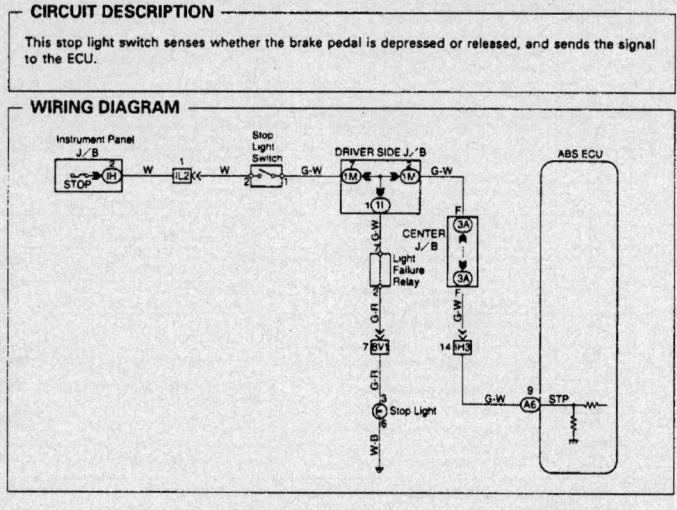

Fig. 56 Stop light circuit inspection & testing (Part 2 of 2). Celica

CIRCUIT DESCRIPTION

This stop light switch senses whether the brake pedal is depressed or released, and send the signal to the ECU.

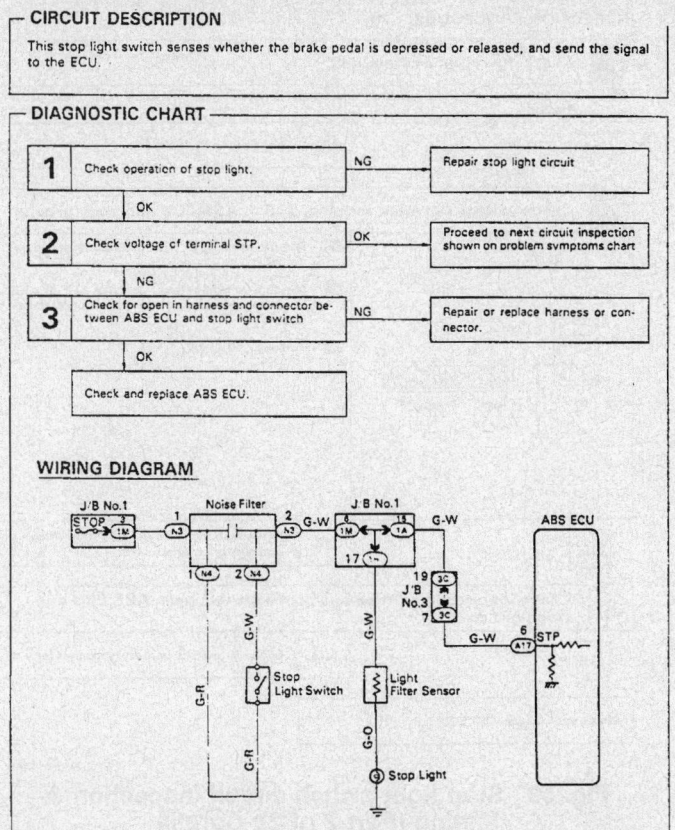

DIAGNOSTIC CHART

1. Check operation of stop light. — NG → Repair stop light circuit
   - OK ↓
2. Check voltage of terminal STP. — OK → Proceed to next circuit inspection shown on problem symptoms chart
   - NG ↓
3. Check for open in harness and connector between ABS ECU and stop light switch — NG → Repair or replace harness or connector.
   - OK ↓

Check and replace ABS ECU.

WIRING DIAGRAM

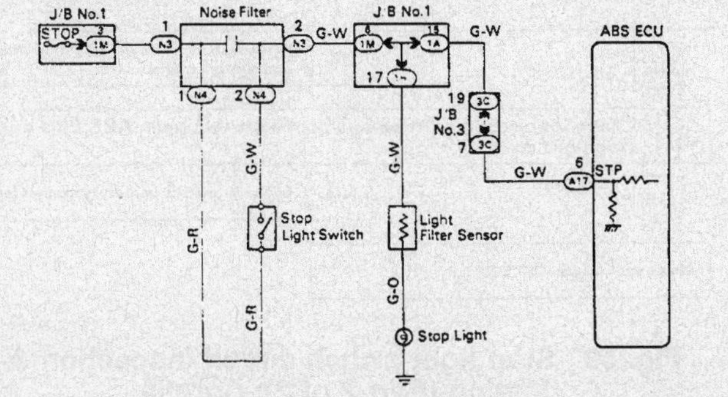

J/B No.1
STOP
Noise Filter
J/B No.1
G-W
ABS ECU
J/B No.3
STP
G-W
G-R
Stop Light Switch
Light Filter Sensor
G-O
Stop Light

TY4029200056010X

Fig. 57 Stop light circuit inspection & testing (Part 1 of 2). Camry Less TRAC

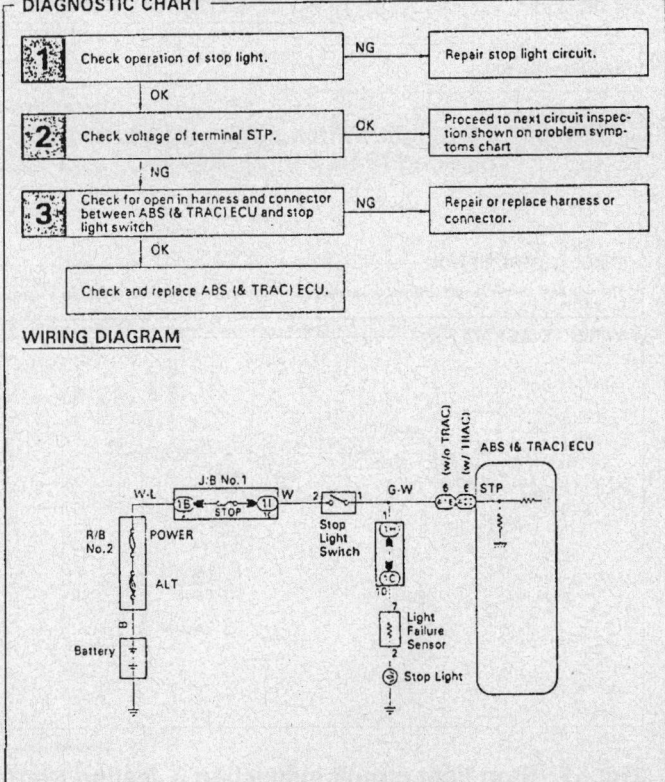

DIAGNOSTIC CHART

1. Check operation of stop light. — NG → Repair stop light circuit.
   - OK ↓
2. Check voltage of terminal STP. — OK → Proceed to next circuit inspection shown on problem symptoms chart
   - NG ↓
3. Check for open in harness and connector between ABS (& TRAC) ECU and stop light switch — NG → Repair or replace harness or connector.
   - OK ↓

Check and replace ABS (& TRAC) ECU.

WIRING DIAGRAM

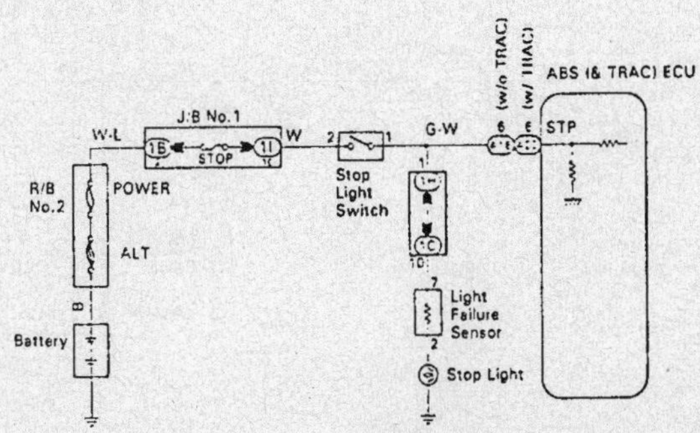

(w/o TRAC)
(w/ TRAC)
ABS (& TRAC) ECU
J/B No.1
W-L
W
STOP
G-W
STP
R/B No.2
POWER
ALT
Battery
Stop Light Switch
Light Failure Sensor
Stop Light

TY4029200057010X

Fig. 58 Stop light circuit inspection & testing (Part 1 of 2). Camry w/TRAC

INSPECTION PROCEDURE

1 Check operation of stop light.

C Check that stop light lights up when brake pedal is depressed and turns off when brake pedal is released.

- OK ↓
- NG → Repair stop light circuit

2 Check voltage between terminal STP of ABS ECU and body ground.

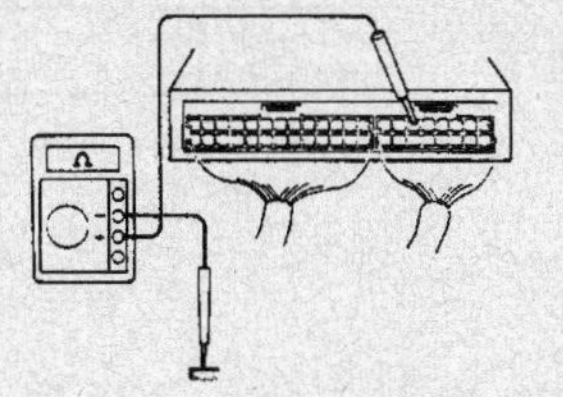

P Remove ABS ECU with connectors still connected.

C Measure voltage between terminal.

OK Voltage: 10 – 14 V

- NG ↓
- OK → Proceed to next circuit inspection shown on problem symptoms chart

3 Check for open in harness and connector between ABS ECU and stop light switch

- OK ↓
- NG → Repair or replace harness or connector.

Check and replace ABS ECU.

TY4029200056020X

Fig. 57 Stop light circuit inspection & testing (Part 2 of 2). Camry Less TRAC

1 Check operation of stop light.

C Check that stop light lights up when brake pedal is depressed and turns off when brake pedal is released.

- OK ↓
- NG → Repair stop light circuit.

2 Check voltage between terminal STP of ABS (& TRAC) ECU and body ground.

w/o TRAC

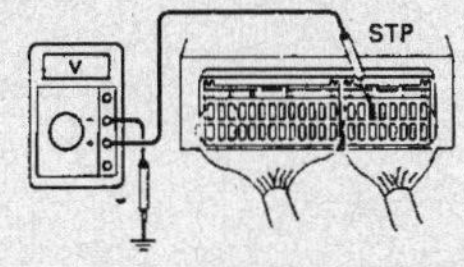

STP

w/ TRAC

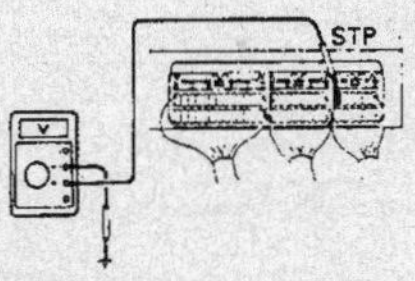

STP

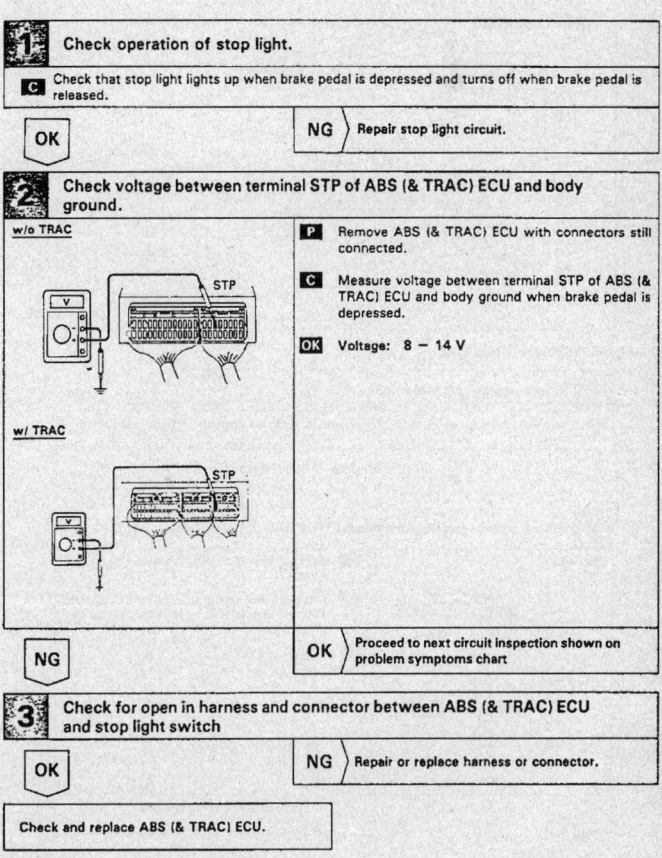

P Remove ABS (& TRAC) ECU with connectors still connected.

C Measure voltage between terminal STP of ABS (& TRAC) ECU and body ground when brake pedal is depressed.

OK Voltage: 8 – 14 V

- NG ↓
- OK → Proceed to next circuit inspection shown on problem symptoms chart

3 Check for open in harness and connector between ABS (& TRAC) ECU and stop light switch

- OK ↓
- NG → Repair or replace harness or connector.

Check and replace ABS (& TRAC) ECU.

TY4029200057020X

Fig. 58 Stop light circuit inspection & testing (Part 2 of 2). Camry w/TRAC

CIRCUIT DESCRIPTION

This stop light switch senses whether the brake pedal is depressed or released, and send the signal to the ECU.

DIAGNOSTIC CHART

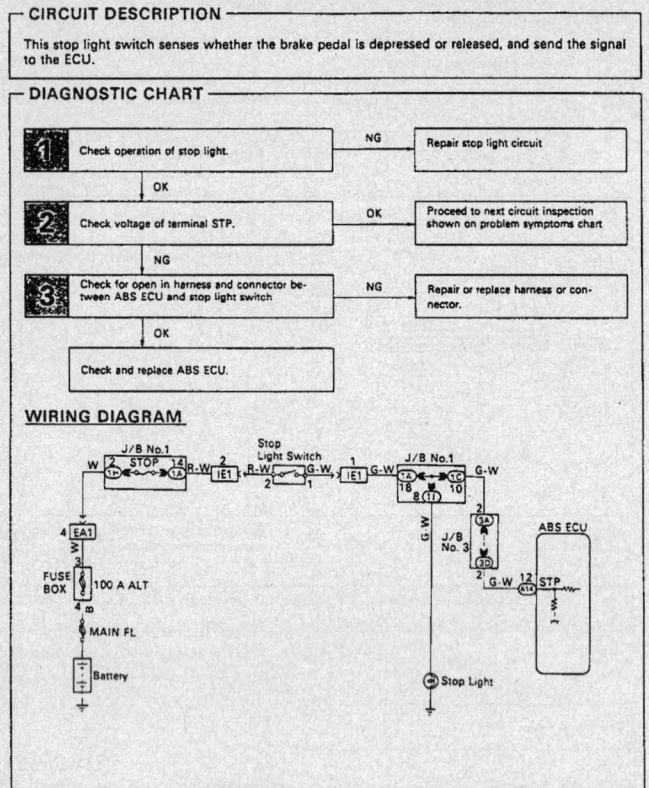

1. Check operation of stop light. — NG → Repair stop light circuit
   - OK ↓
2. Check voltage of terminal STP. — OK → Proceed to next circuit inspection shown on problem symptoms chart
   - NG ↓
3. Check for open in harness and connector between ABS ECU and stop light switch — NG → Repair or replace harness or connector.
   - OK ↓

Check and replace ABS ECU.

WIRING DIAGRAM

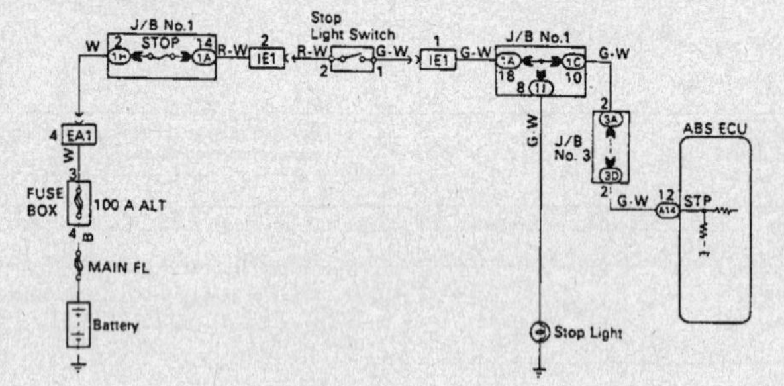

J/B No.1
STOP
Stop Light Switch
J/B No.1
EA1
FUSE BOX
100 A ALT
MAIN FL
Battery
J/B No. 3
ABS ECU
STP
Stop Light

TY4029300055010X

Fig. 59 Stop light switch circuit inspection & testing (Part 1 of 2). Corolla

INSPECTION PROCEDURE

1 Check operation of stop light.

C Check that stop light lights up when brake pedal is depressed and turns off when brake pedal is released.

OK | NG → Repair stop light circuit

2 Check voltage between terminal STP of ABS ECU and body ground.

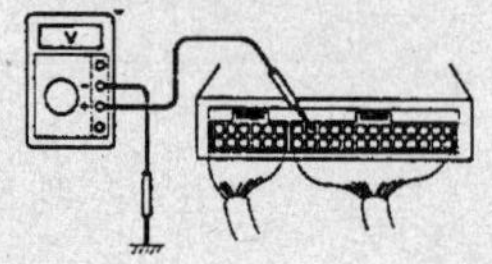

P Remove ABS ECU with connectors still connected.

C Measure voltage between terminal STP of ABS ECU and body ground when brake pedal is depressed.

OK Voltage: 10 – 14 V

NG | OK → Proceed to next circuit inspection shown on problem symptoms chart

3 Check for open in harness and connector between ABS ECU and stop light switch

OK | NG → Repair or replace harness or connector.

Check and replace ABS ECU.

TY4029300055020X

Fig. 59 Stop light switch circuit inspection & testing (Part 2 of 2). Corolla

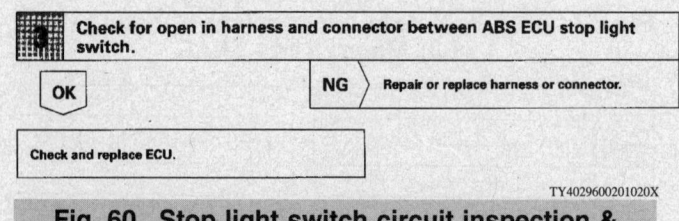

WIRING DIAGRAM

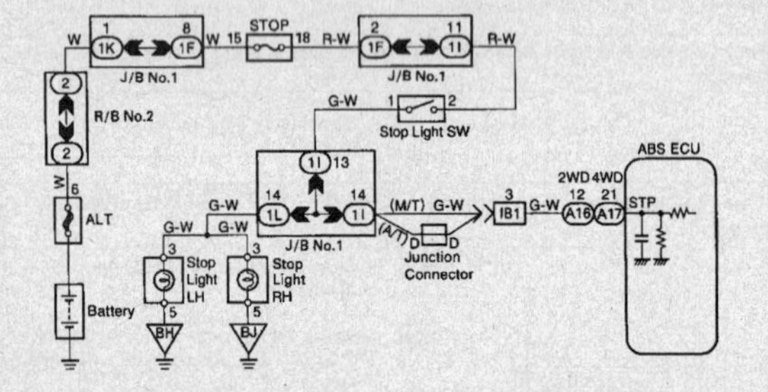

J/B No.1
STOP
J/B No.1
R/B No.2
Stop Light SW
ABS ECU
2WD 4WD
STP
ALT
J/B No.1
Junction Connector
Stop Light LH
Stop Light RH
Battery

INSPECTION PROCEDURE

1 Check operation of stop light.

C Check that stop light lights up when brake pedal is depressed and turns off when brake pedal is released.

OK | NG → Repair stop light circuit.

2 Check voltage between terminal STP of ABS ECU and body ground.

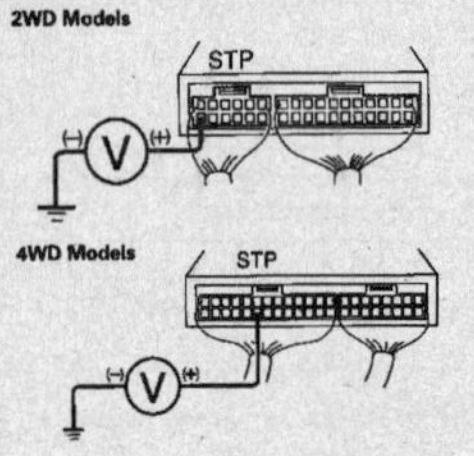

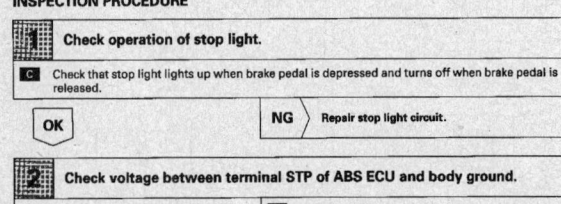

2WD Models
STP
4WD Models
STP

P Remove ABS ECU with connectors still connected.

C Measure voltage between terminal STP of ABS ECU and body ground when brake pedal is depressed.

OK Voltage: 8 – 14 V

OK | NG → Proceed to next circuit inspection.

TY4029600201010X

Fig. 60 Stop light switch circuit inspection & testing (Part 1 of 2). RAV4

3 Check for open in harness and connector between ABS ECU stop light switch.

OK | NG → Repair or replace harness or connector.

Check and replace ECU.

TY4029600201020X

Fig. 60 Stop light switch circuit inspection & testing (Part 2 of 2). RAV4

CIRCUIT DESCRIPTION

The stop light switch senses whether the brake pedal is depressed or released, and sends a signal to the ECU.

WIRING DIAGRAM

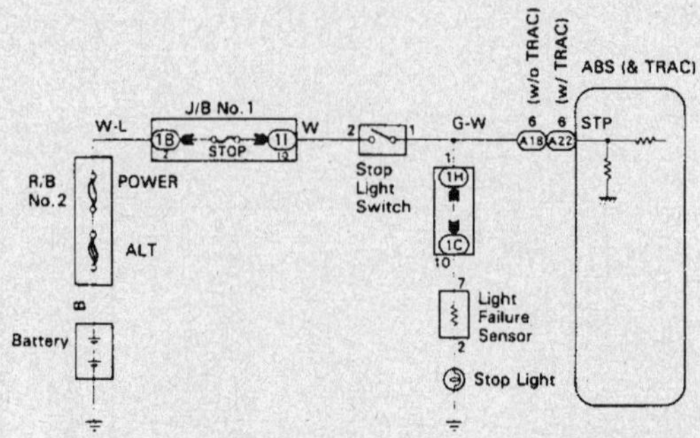

(w/o TRAC)
(w/ TRAC)
ABS (& TRAC) ECU
J/B No. 1
STOP
STP
R/B No. 2
POWER
ALT
Stop Light Switch
Battery
Light Failure Sensor
Stop Light

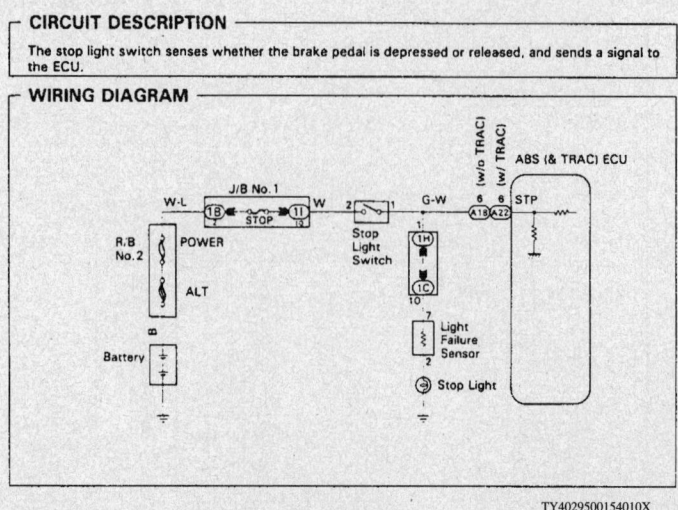

TY4029500154010X

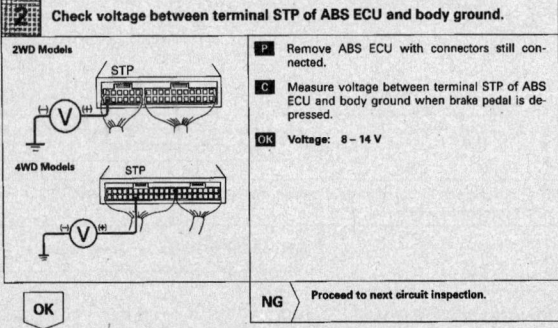

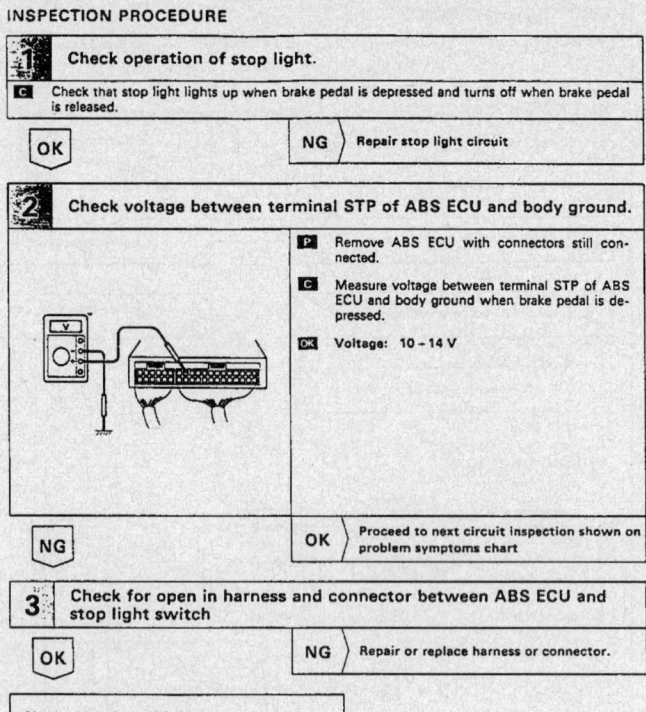

Fig. 61 Stop light circuit inspection & testing (Part 1 of 2). Supra

1 Check operation of stop light.

C Check that stop light lights up when brake pedal is depressed and turns off when brake pedal is released.

OK

NG — Repair stop light circuit.

2 Check voltage between terminal STP of ABS (& TRAC) ECU and body ground.

w/o TRAC

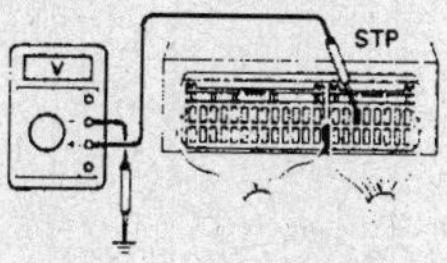
STP
V

w/ TRAC

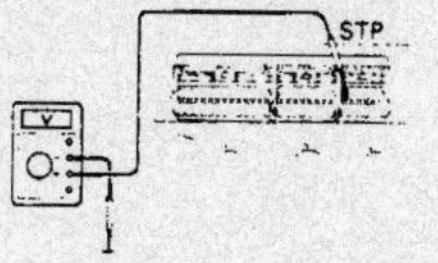
STP
V

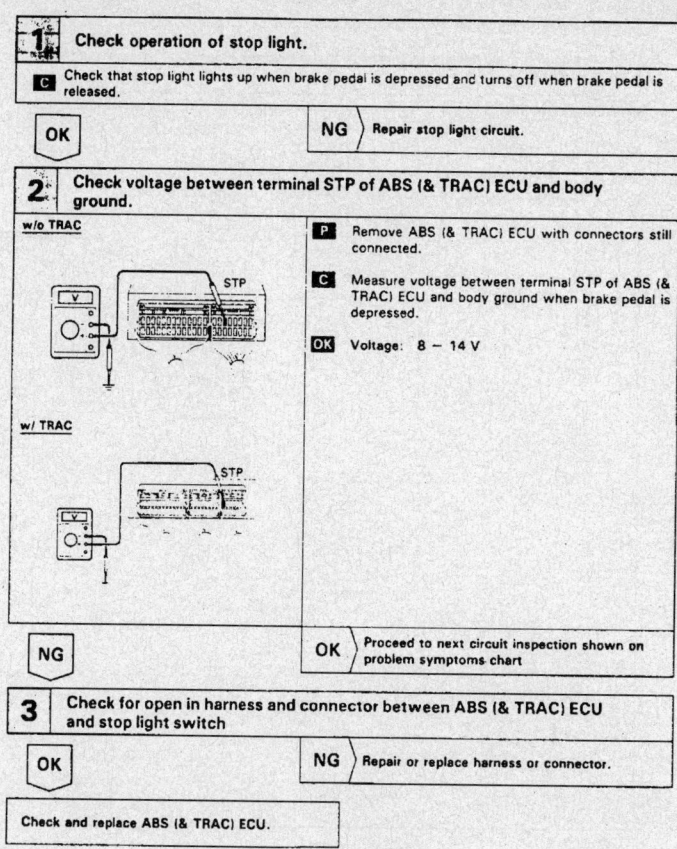

P Remove ABS (& TRAC) ECU with connectors still connected.

C Measure voltage between terminal STP of ABS (& TRAC) ECU and body ground when brake pedal is depressed.

OK Voltage: 8 – 14 V

NG

OK — Proceed to next circuit inspection shown on problem symptoms chart

3 Check for open in harness and connector between ABS (& TRAC) ECU and stop light switch

OK

NG — Repair or replace harness or connector.

Check and replace ABS (& TRAC) ECU.

TY4029500154020X

Fig. 61 Stop light circuit inspection & testing (Part 2 of 2). Supra

2 Check voltage between terminal STP of ABS ECU and body ground.

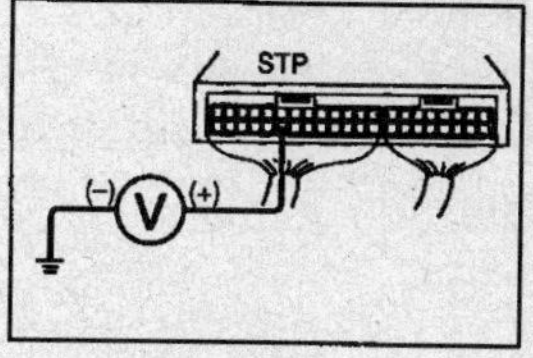
STP
(–)
V
(+)

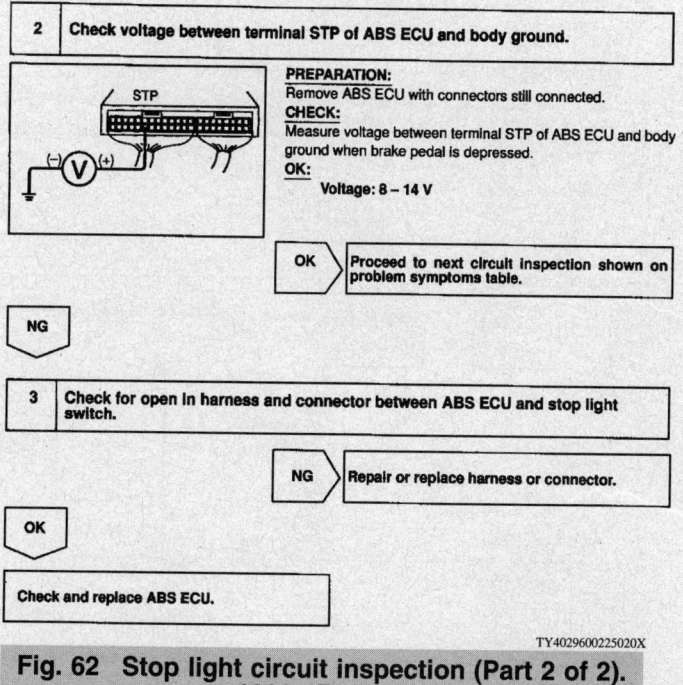

PREPARATION:
Remove ABS ECU with connectors still connected.

CHECK:
Measure voltage between terminal STP of ABS ECU and body ground when brake pedal is depressed.

OK:
Voltage: 8 – 14 V

OK — Proceed to next circuit inspection shown on problem symptoms table.

NG

3 Check for open in harness and connector between ABS ECU and stop light switch.

NG — Repair or replace harness or connector.

OK

Check and replace ABS ECU.

TY4029600225020X

Fig. 62 Stop light circuit inspection (Part 2 of 2). 1996 4Runner

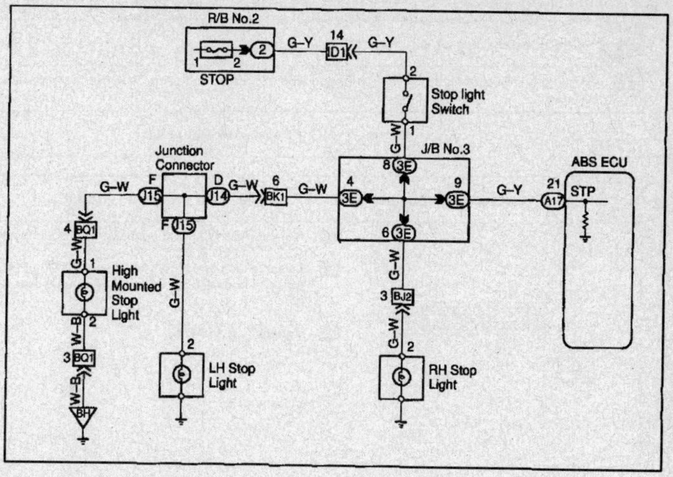
R/B No.2
STOP
G–Y
G–Y
Stop light Switch
Junction Connector
J/B No.3
ABS ECU
STP
G–W
High Mounted Stop Light
LH Stop Light
RH Stop Light
W–B

INSPECTION PROCEDURE

1 Check operation of stop light.

CHECK:
Check that stop light lights up when brake pedal is depressed and turns off when brake pedal is released.

NG — Repair stop light circuit.

OK

TY4029600225010X

Fig. 62 Stop light circuit inspection (Part 1 of 2). 1996 4Runner

CIRCUIT DESCRIPTION

This stop light switch senses whether the brake pedal is depressed or released, and sends the signal to the ECU.

WIRING DIAGRAM

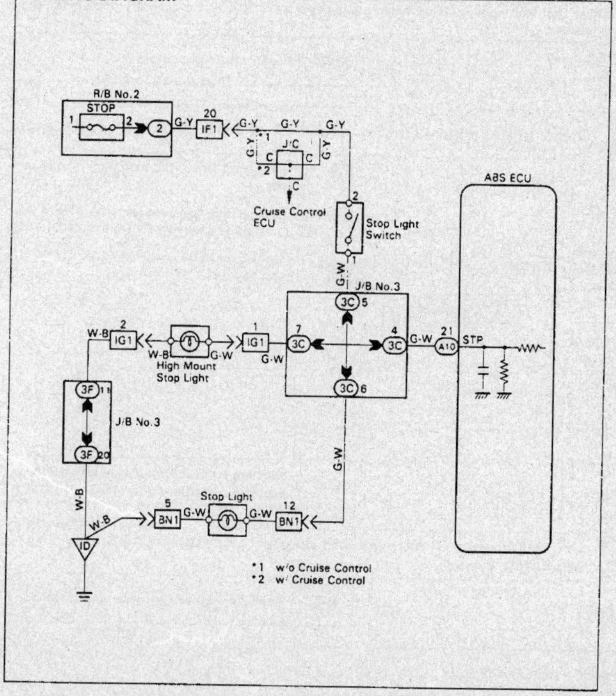
R/B No.2
STOP
Cruise Control ECU
Stop Light Switch
ABS ECU
J/B No.3
High Mount Stop Light
STP
Stop Light
*1 w/o Cruise Control
*2 w/ Cruise Control

TY4029500174010X

Fig. 63 Stop light circuit inspection & testing (Part 1 of 2). Tacoma

1 Check operation of stop light.

C Check that stop light lights up when brake pedal is depressed and turns off when brake pedal is released.

OK | NG Repair stop light circuit

2 Check voltage between terminal STP of ABS ECU and body ground.

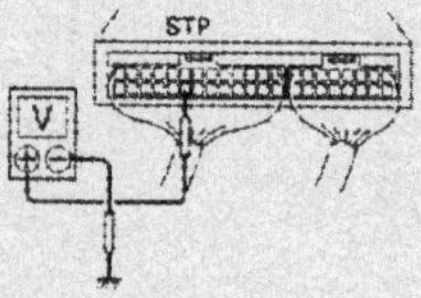
STP
V

P Remove ABS ECU with connectors still connected.

C Measure voltage between terminal STP of ABS ECU and body ground when brake pedal is depressed.

OK Voltage: 8 – 14 V

NG | OK Proceed to next circuit inspection shown on problem symptoms chart

3 Check for open in harness and connector between ABS ECU and stop light switch

OK | NG Repair or replace harness or connector.

Check and replace ABS ECU.

TY4029500174020X

Fig. 63 Stop light circuit inspection & testing (Part 2 of 2). Tacoma

CIRCUIT DESCRIPTION

This stop light switch senses whether the brake pedal is depressed or released, and sends the signal to the ECU.

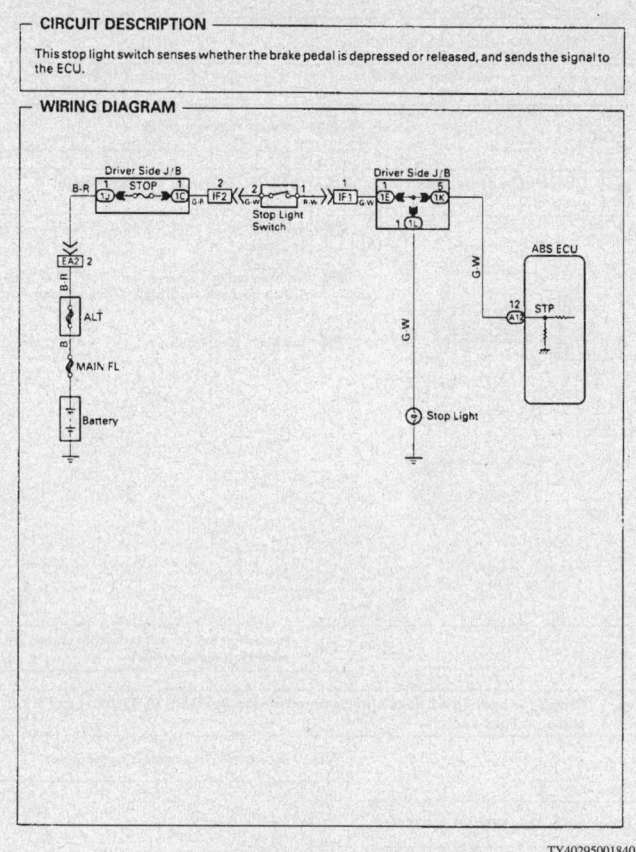

WIRING DIAGRAM

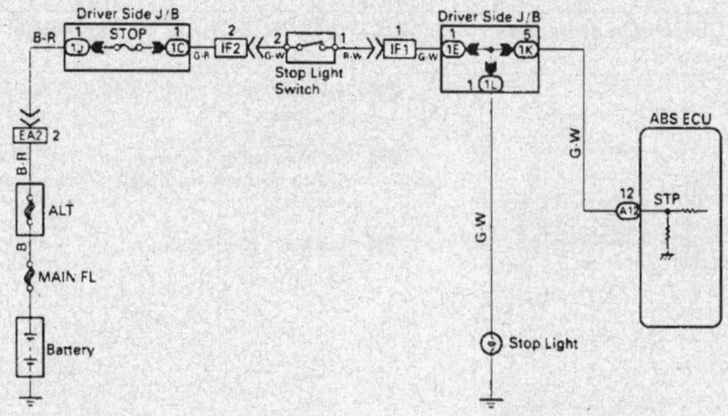
Driver Side J/B
STOP
B-R
IF2
Stop Light Switch
IF1
Driver Side J/B
G-W
ABS ECU
STP
A12
EA2
ALT
MAIN FL
Battery
Stop Light

TY4029500184010X

Fig. 64 Stop light circuit inspection & testing (Part 1 of 2). 1995–96 Tercel

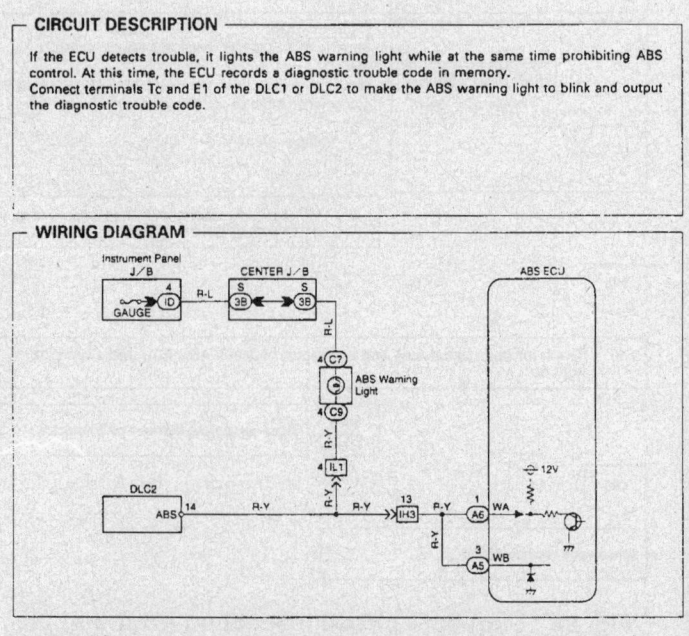

1 Check operation of stop light.

C Check that stop light lights up when brake pedal is depressed and turns off when brake pedal is released.

OK | NG Repair stop light circuit

2 Check voltage between terminal STP of ABS ECU and body ground.

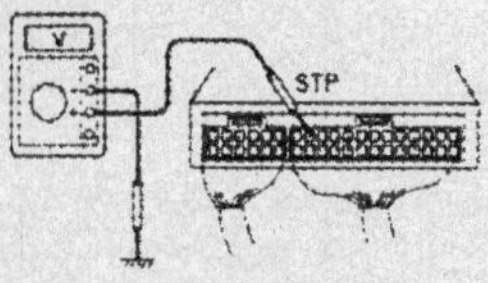
V
STP

P Remove ABS ECU with connectors still connected.

C Measure voltage between terminal STP of ABS ECU and body ground when brake pedal is depressed.

OK Voltage: 8 - 14 V

NG | OK Proceed to next circuit inspection shown on problem symptoms chart (See page BR-43).

3 Check for open in harness and connector between ABS ECU and stop light switch

OK | NG Repair or replace harness or connector.

Check and replace ABS ECU.

TY4029500184020X

Fig. 64 Stop light circuit inspection & testing (Part 2 of 2). 1995–96 Tercel

CIRCUIT DESCRIPTION

If the ECU detects trouble, it lights the ABS warning light while at the same time prohibiting ABS control. At this time, the ECU records a diagnostic trouble code in memory.
Connect terminals Tc and E1 of the DLC1 or DLC2 to make the ABS warning light to blink and output the diagnostic trouble code.

WIRING DIAGRAM

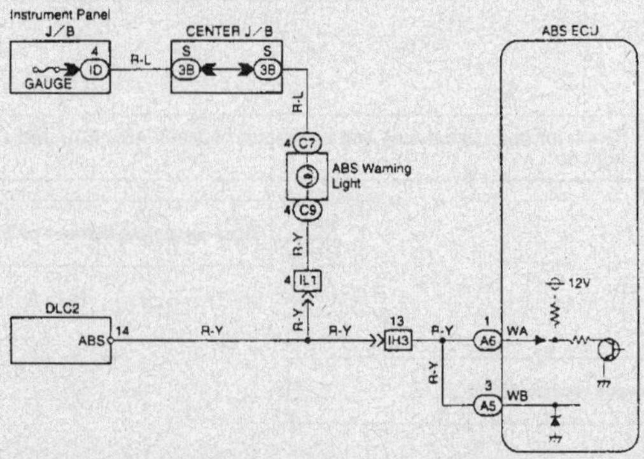
Instrument Panel J/B
GAUGE
CENTER J/B
R-L
ABS Warning Light
ABS ECU
12V
WA
WB
DLC2
ABS
R-Y
IH3
A6
A5

TY4029500161010X

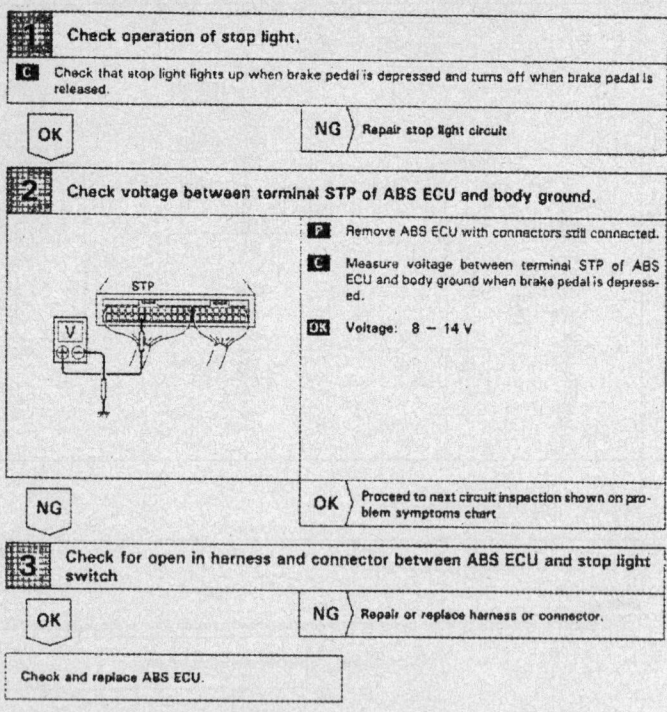

Fig. 65 ABS warning light circuit inspection & testing (Part 1 of 2). Avalon

Troubleshoot in accordance with the chart below for each trouble symptom.

ABS warning light does not light up	Go to step 1
ABS warning light remains on	Go to step 2

1 Check ABS warning light.

See Combination Meter Troubleshooting

OK — NG: **Replace bulb or combination meter assembly.**

Check for open in harness and connector between GAUGE fuse and ECU

2 Is diagnostic trouble code output?

Check diagnostic trouble code

NO — YES: **Repair circuit indicated by the code output.**

Check for short in harness and connector between warning light and ECU terminal WB, DLC 2 and ECU terminal WA

TY4029500161020X

Fig. 65 ABS warning light circuit inspection & testing (Part 2 of 2). Avalon

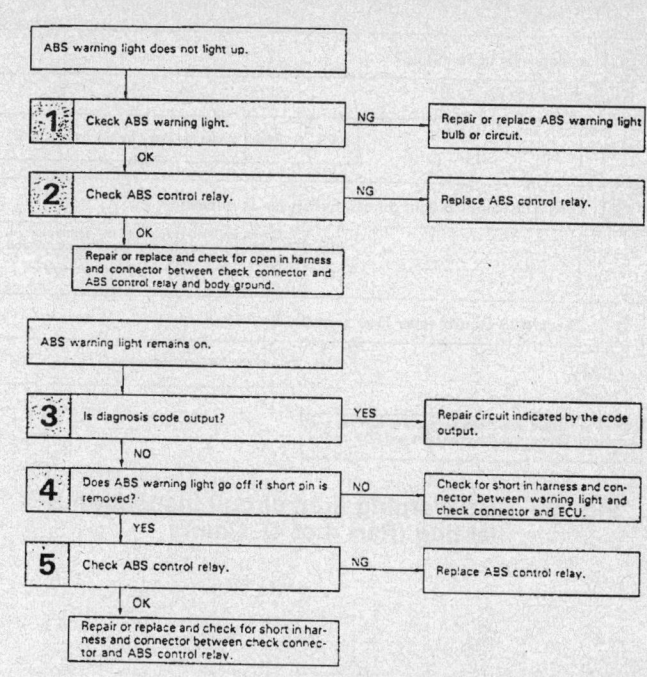

ABS warning light does not light up.

1. Ckeck ABS warning light. — NG: Repair or replace ABS warning light bulb or circuit.
   OK
2. Check ABS control relay. — NG: Replace ABS control relay.
   OK

Repair or replace and check for open in harness and connector between check connector and ABS control relay and body ground.

ABS warning light remains on.

3. Is diagnosis code output? — YES: Repair circuit indicated by the code output.
   NO
4. Does ABS warning light go off if short pin is removed? — NO: Check for short in harness and connector between warning light and check connector and ECU.
   YES
5. Check ABS control relay. — NG: Replace ABS control relay.
   OK

Repair or replace and check for short in harness and connector between check connector and ABS control relay.

TY4029200059020X

Fig. 66 ABS warning light circuit inspection & testing (Part 2 of 4). Camry

CIRCUIT DESCRIPTION

If the ECU detects trouble, it lights the ABS warning light while at the same time prohibiting ABS control. At this time, the ECU records a diagnostic code in memory.
After removing the short pin of the check connector, connect a check connector or connect between Tc and E1 of the TDCL to cause the ABS warning light to blink and output the diagnosis code is output.

DIAGNOSTIC CHART

Perform troubleshooting in accordance with the chart below for each trouble symptom.

ABS warning light does not light up	Go to step 1
ABS warning light remains on	Go to step 3

WIRING DIAGRAM

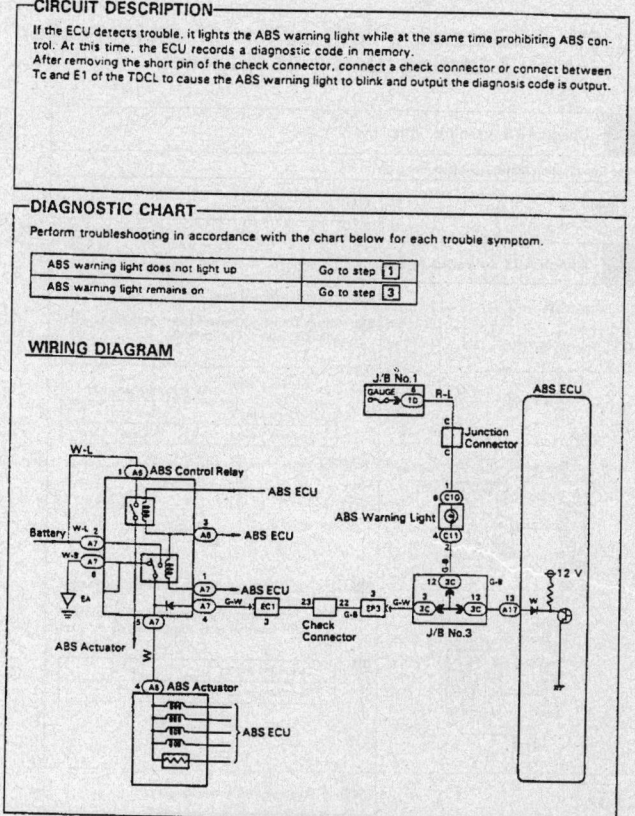

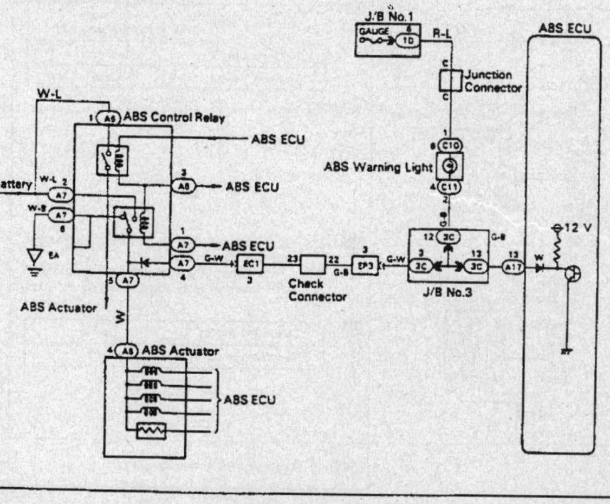

J/B No.1
GAUGE
R-L
ABS ECU
Junction Connector
W-L
ABS Control Relay
ABS ECU
ABS Warning Light
Battery
ABS ECU
ABS ECU
12 V
Check Connector
J/B No.3
ABS Actuator
ABS Actuator
ABS ECU

TY4029200059010X

Fig. 66 ABS warning light circuit inspection & testing (Part 1 of 4). Camry

INSPECTION PROCEDURE

1 Check ABS warning light.

OK — NG: Replace bulb or combination meter assembly.

2 Check ABS (control) relay.

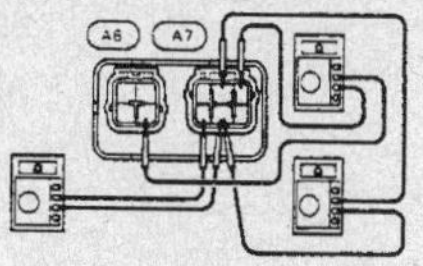

P
1. Remove the washer tank and control relay.
2. Disconnect the connectors from control relay.

C Check continuity between each terminal of ABS control relay shown below.

OK

Terminals (A7) 1 and (A6) 3	Continuity (Reference value 80 Ω)
Terminals (A7) 5 and (A7) 6	Continuity
Terminals (A7) 2 and (A7) 5	Open

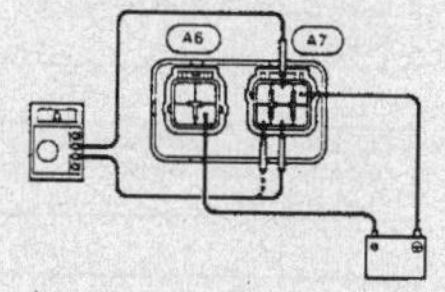

C
1. Apply battery voltage between terminals (A7) 1 and (A6) 3.
2. Check continuity between each terminal of ABS control relay shown below.

OK

Terminals (A7) 5 and (A7) 6	Open
Terminals (A7) 2 and (A7) 5	Continuity

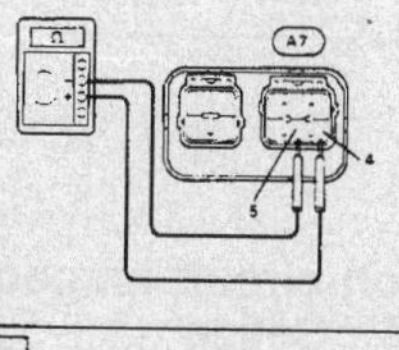

C Connect the ⊕ test lead to terminal 4 of (A7) and the ⊖ lead to terminal 5 of (A7). Check continuity between the terminals.

OK Continuity
If there is no continuity, connect the ⊖ test lead to terminal 4 of (A7) and the ⊕ lead to terminal 5 of (A7). Recheck continuity between terminals.

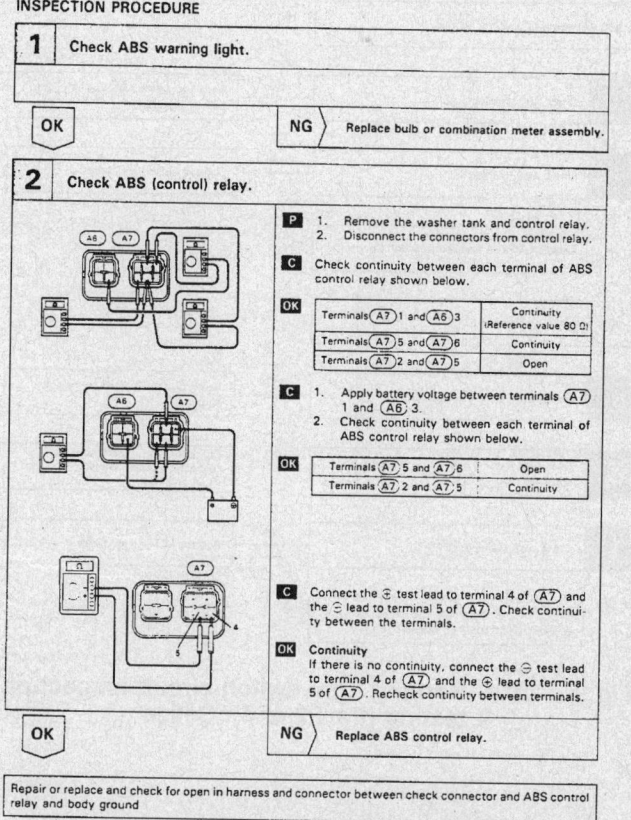

OK — NG: Replace ABS control relay.

Repair or replace and check for open in harness and connector between check connector and ABS control relay and body ground

TY4029200059030X

Fig. 66 ABS warning light circuit inspection & testing (Part 3 of 4). Camry

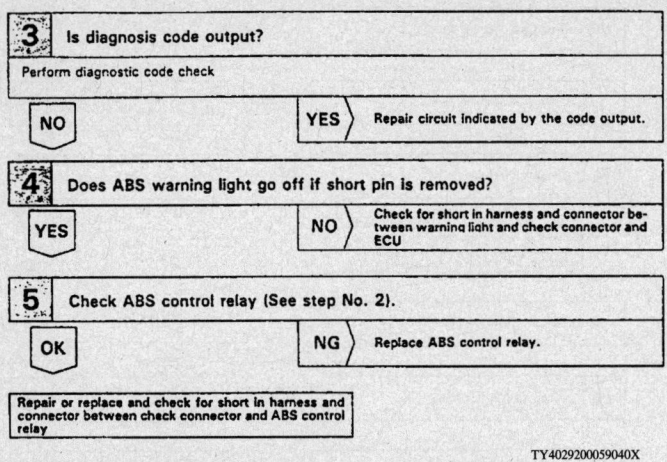

3	Is diagnosis code output?
	Perform diagnostic code check

NO

YES — Repair circuit indicated by the code output.

4	Does ABS warning light go off if short pin is removed?

YES

NO — Check for short in harness and connector between warning light and check connector and ECU

5	Check ABS control relay (See step No. 2).

OK

NG — Replace ABS control relay.

Repair or replace and check for short in harness and connector between check connector and ABS control relay

TY4029200059040X

Fig. 66 ABS warning light circuit inspection & testing (Part 4 of 4). Camry

ABS warning light does not light up.

1. Check ABS warning light. — NG → Repair or replace ABS warning light bulb or circuit.
   - OK
2. Check ABS solenoid relay. — NG → Replace ABS solenoid relay.
   - OK

Check for open in harness and connector between GAUGE fuse and Junction Connector (J7).

ABS warning light remains on.

3. Is diagnostic trouble code output? — YES → Repair circuit indicated by the code output.
   - NO
4. Does ABS warning light go off if short pin is removed? — NO → Check for short in harness and connector between warning light and DLC1 and ECU.
   - YES
5. Check ABS solenoid relay. — NG → Replace ABS solenoid relay.
   - OK

Check for short in harness and connector between DLC1 and ABS solenoid relay.

TY4029400062020X

Fig. 67 ABS warning light switch circuit inspection & testing (Part 2 of 4). Celica

CIRCUIT DESCRIPTION

If the ECU detects trouble, it lights the ABS warning light while at the same time prohibiting ABS control. At this time, the ECU records a diagnostic trouble code in memory.
After removing the short pin of the DLC1 connect terminals Tc and E1 of DLC1 to make the ABS warning light blink and output the diagnostic trouble code.

DIAGNOSTIC CHART

Perform troubleshooting in accordance with the chart below for each trouble symptom.

ABS warning light does not light up	Go to step [illegible]
ABS warning light remains on	Go to step [illegible]

WIRING DIAGRAM

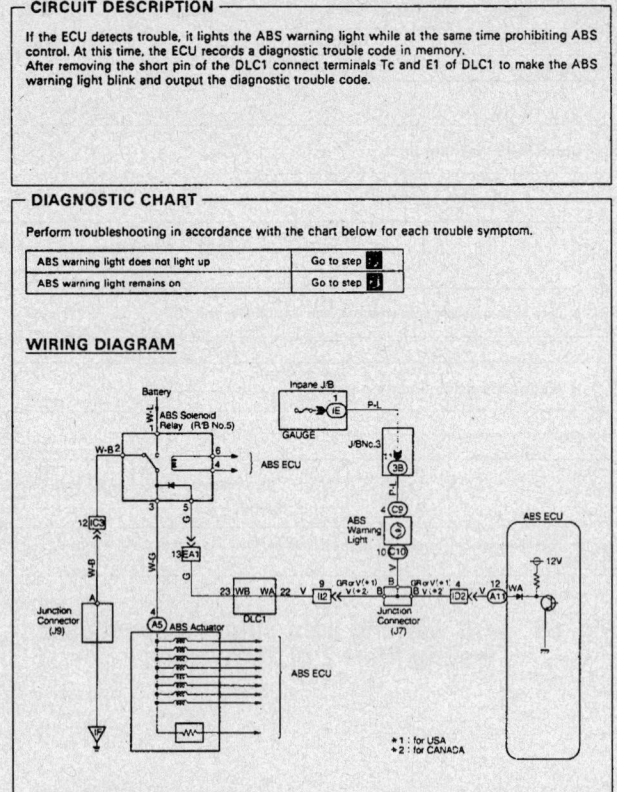

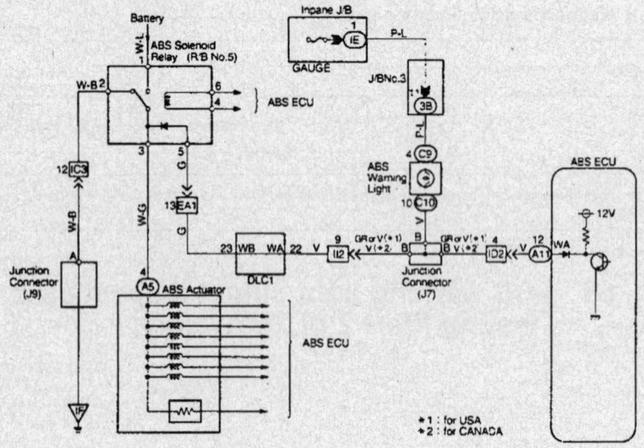

Battery
W-L
ABS Solenoid Relay (R/B No.5)
W-B
ABS ECU
Inpane J/B
GAUGE
P-L
J/BNo.3
3B
C9
ABS Warning Light
C10
IC3
W-B
W-G
G
EA1
Junction Connector (J9)
A5 ABS Actuator
DLC1
WB
WA
II2
GR or V(*1)
V(*2)
Junction Connector (J7)
ID2
A11
ABS ECU
12V
*1 : for USA
*2 : for CANADA

TY4029400062010X

Fig. 67 ABS warning light switch circuit inspection & testing (Part 1 of 4). Celica

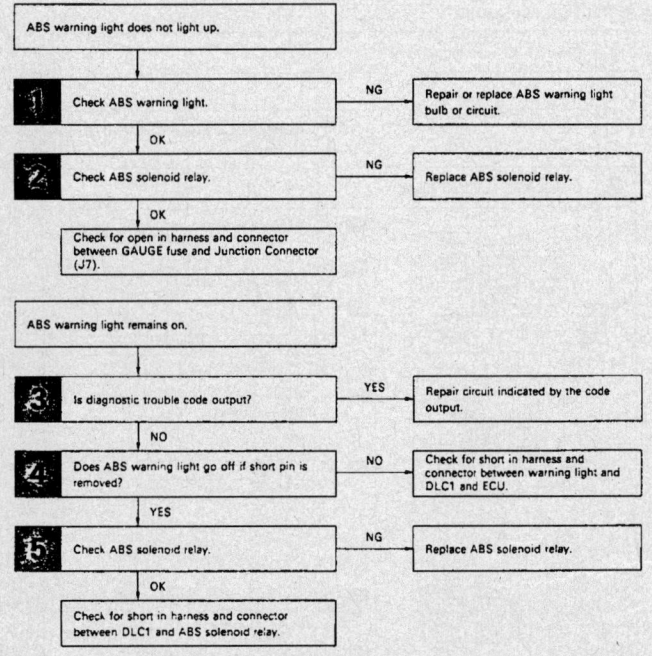

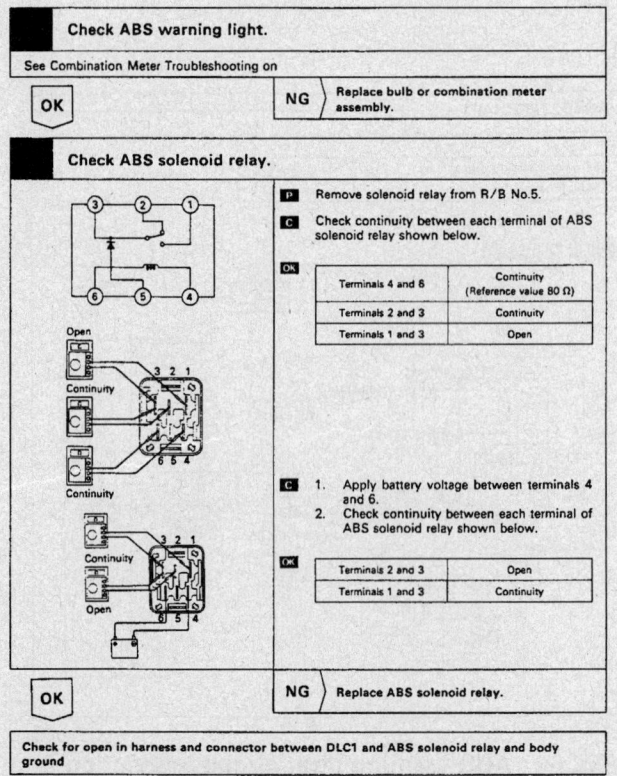

1	Check ABS warning light.
	See Combination Meter Troubleshooting on

OK

NG — Replace bulb or combination meter assembly.

2	Check ABS solenoid relay.

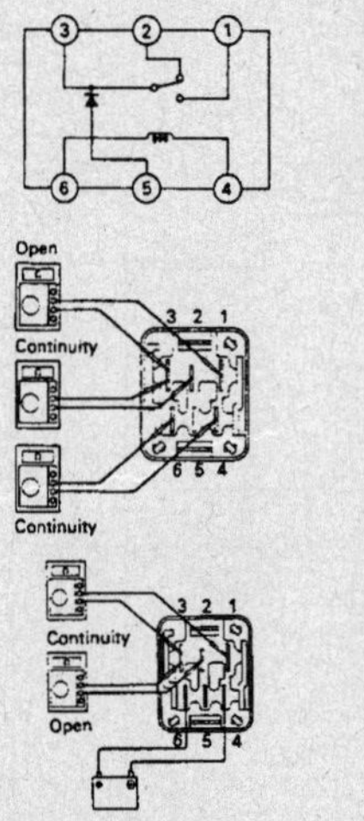

Open
Continuity
Continuity
Continuity
Open

P Remove solenoid relay from R/B No.5.

C Check continuity between each terminal of ABS solenoid relay shown below.

OK

Terminals 4 and 6	Continuity (Reference value 80 Ω)
Terminals 2 and 3	Continuity
Terminals 1 and 3	Open

C
1. Apply battery voltage between terminals 4 and 6.
2. Check continuity between each terminal of ABS solenoid relay shown below.

OK

Terminals 2 and 3	Open
Terminals 1 and 3	Continuity

OK

NG — Replace ABS solenoid relay.

Check for open in harness and connector between DLC1 and ABS solenoid relay and body ground

TY4029400062030X

Fig. 67 ABS warning light switch circuit inspection & testing (Part 3 of 4). Celica

Is diagnostic trouble code output?	
Perform diagnostic trouble code check	
NO	YES — Repair circuit indicated by the code output.

Does ABS warning light go off if short pin is removed?	
YES	NO — Check for short in harness and connector between warning light and DLC1 and ECU.

Check ABS solenoid relay (See step No. [illegible]).	
OK	NG — Replace ABS solenoid relay.

Check for short in harness and connector between DLC1 and ABS solenoid relay

TY4029400062040X

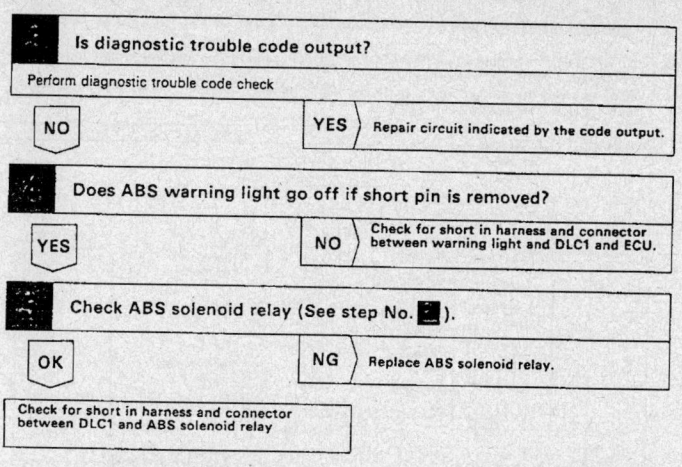

Fig. 67 ABS warning light switch circuit inspection & testing (Part 4 of 4). Celica

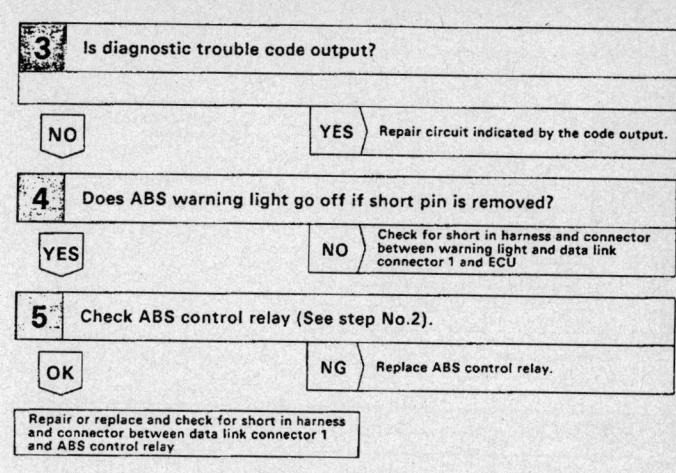

CIRCUIT DESCRIPTION

If the ECU detects trouble, it lights the ABS warning light while at the same time prohibiting ABS control. At this time, the ECU records a diagnostic trouble code in memory.
After removing the short pin of the data link connector 1, connect between terminals Tc and E1 of the data link connector 1 to cause the ABS warning light to blink and output the diagnostic trouble code.

DIAGNOSTIC CHART

ABS warning light does not light up	Go to step 1
ABS warning light remains on	Go to step 3

WIRING DIAGRAM

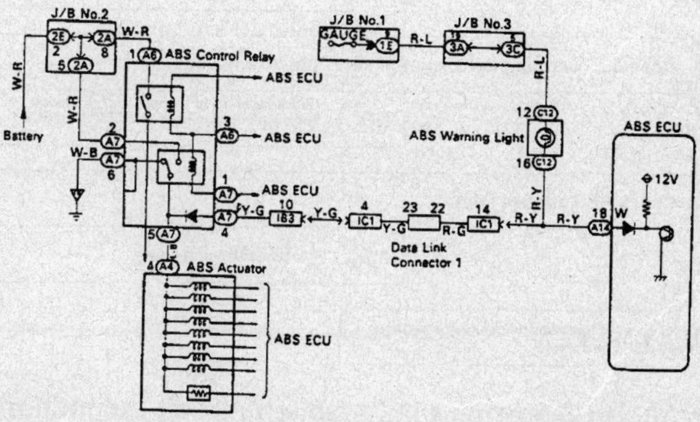

J/B No.2
W-R
A6 ABS Control Relay
ABS ECU
Battery
W-B
J/B No.1
GAUGE
R-L
J/B No.3
ABS Warning Light
ABS ECU
12V
Y-G
R-G
R-Y
Data Link Connector 1
ABS Actuator

TY4029300060010X

Fig. 68 ABS warning light switch circuit inspection & testing (Part 1 of 4). Corolla

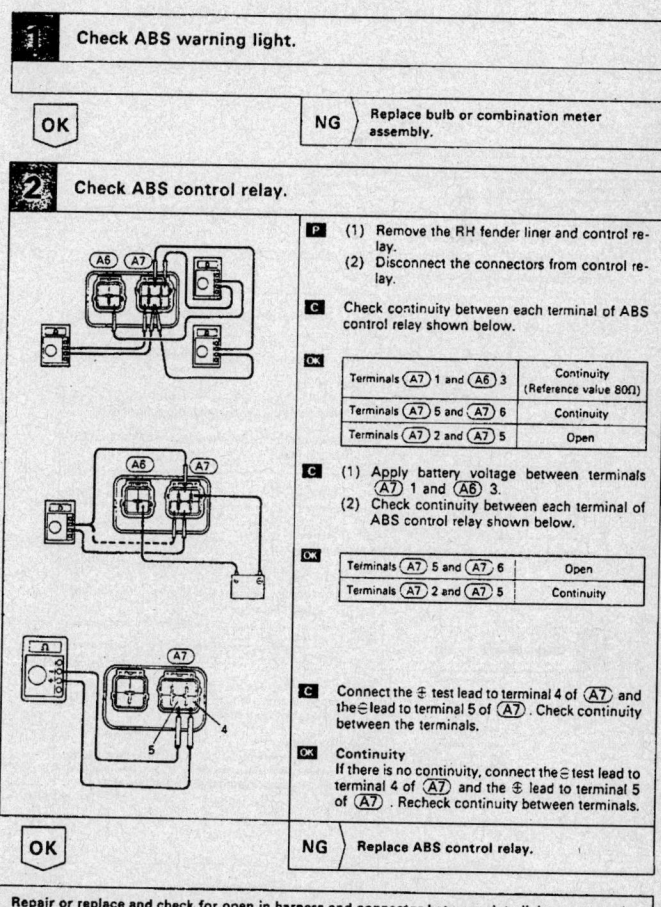

3 Is diagnostic trouble code output?	
NO	YES — Repair circuit indicated by the code output.

4 Does ABS warning light go off if short pin is removed?	
YES	NO — Check for short in harness and connector between warning light and data link connector 1 and ECU

5 Check ABS control relay (See step No.2).	
OK	NG — Replace ABS control relay.

Repair or replace and check for short in harness and connector between data link connector 1 and ABS control relay

TY4029300060020X

Fig. 68 ABS warning light switch circuit inspection & testing (Part 2 of 4). Corolla

1 Check ABS warning light.	
OK	NG — Replace bulb or combination meter assembly.

2 Check ABS control relay.

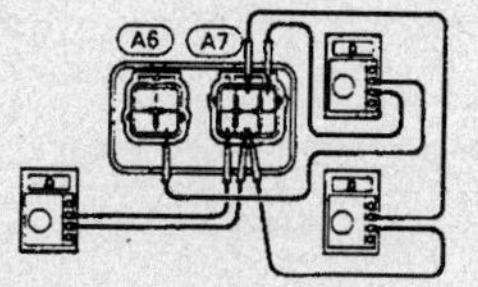

P (1) Remove the RH fender liner and control relay.
(2) Disconnect the connectors from control relay.

C Check continuity between each terminal of ABS control relay shown below.

OK

Terminals (A7) 1 and (A6) 3	Continuity (Reference value 80Ω)
Terminals (A7) 5 and (A7) 6	Continuity
Terminals (A7) 2 and (A7) 5	Open

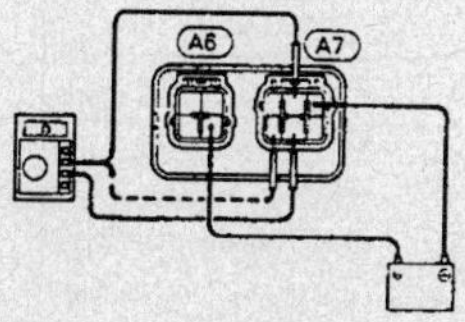

C (1) Apply battery voltage between terminals (A7) 1 and (A6) 3.
(2) Check continuity between each terminal of ABS control relay shown below.

OK

Terminals (A7) 5 and (A7) 6	Open
Terminals (A7) 2 and (A7) 5	Continuity

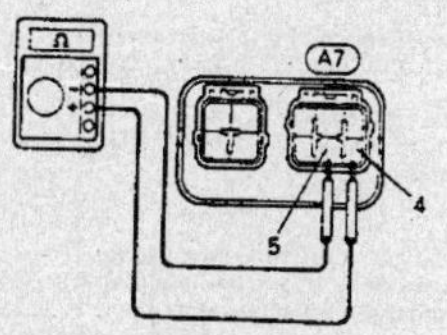

C Connect the ⊕ test lead to terminal 4 of (A7) and the ⊖ lead to terminal 5 of (A7). Check continuity between the terminals.

OK Continuity
If there is no continuity, connect the ⊖ test lead to terminal 4 of (A7) and the ⊕ lead to terminal 5 of (A7). Recheck continuity between terminals.

OK	NG — Replace ABS control relay.

Repair or replace and check for open in harness and connector between data link connector 1 and ABS control relay and body ground

TY4029300060030X

Fig. 68 ABS warning light switch circuit inspection & testing (Part 3 of 4). Corolla

ABS warning light does not light up.

1 Check ABS warning light. — NG → Repair or replace ABS warning light bulb or circuit.

OK

2 Check ABS control relay. — NG → Replace ABS control relay.

OK

Repair or replace and check for open in harness and connector between data link connector 1 and ABS control relay and body ground.

ABS warning light remains on.

3 Is diagnostic trouble code output? — YES → Repair circuit indicated by the code output.

NO

4 Does ABS warning light go off if short pin is removed? — NO → Check for short in harness and connector between warning light and data link connector 1 and ECU.

YES

5 Check ABS control relay. — NG → Replace ABS control relay.

OK

Repair or replace and check for short in harness and connector between data link connector 1 and ABS control relay.

TY4029300060040X

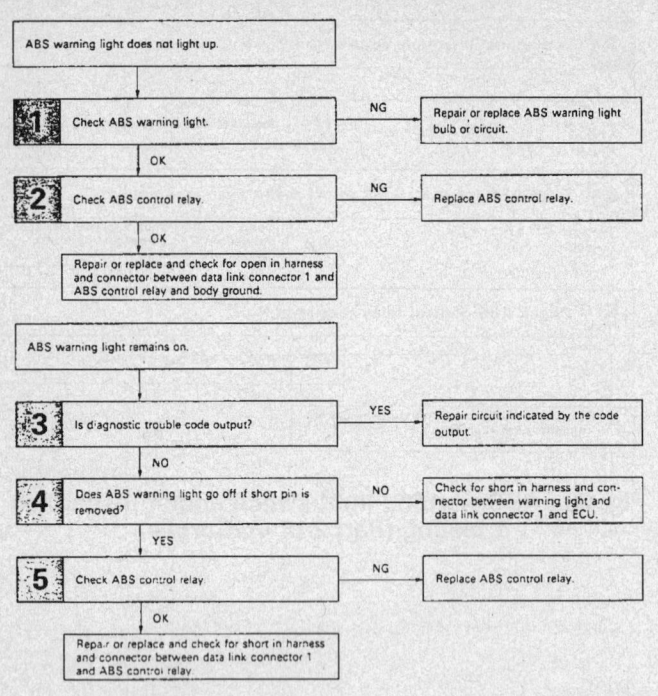

Fig. 68 ABS warning light switch circuit inspection & testing (Part 4 of 4). Corolla

CIRCUIT DESCRIPTION

If the ECU detects trouble, it lights the ABS warning light while at the same time prohibiting ABS control. At this time, the ECU records a DTC in memory.
After removing the short pin of the DLC1, connect terminals Tc and E1 of the DLC1 to make the ABS warning light blink and output the DTC.

WIRING DIAGRAM

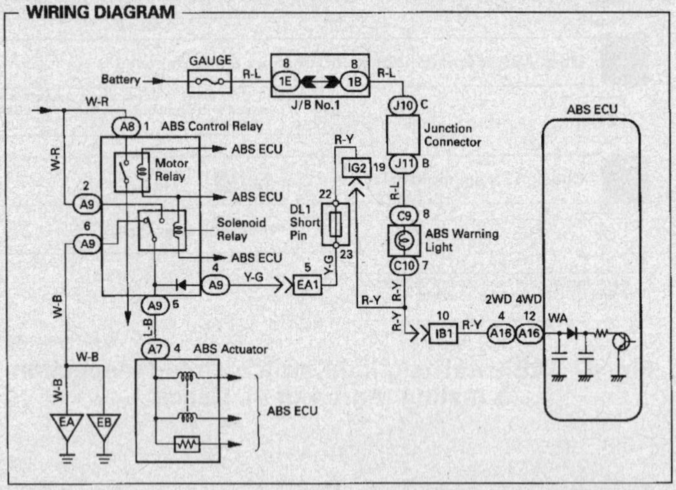

GAUGE
Battery
R-L
1E
1B
J/B No.1
W-R
A8
ABS Control Relay
ABS ECU
Motor Relay
Solenoid Relay
R-Y
IG2
J10
J11
Junction Connector
DL1 Short Pin
C9
ABS Warning Light
C10
A9
EA1
Y-G
L-B
W-B
A7
ABS Actuator
IB1
A16
2WD 4WD
WA
EA
EB
ABS ECU

TY4029600202010X

Fig. 69 ABS warning light switch circuit inspection & testing (Part 1 of 3). RAV4

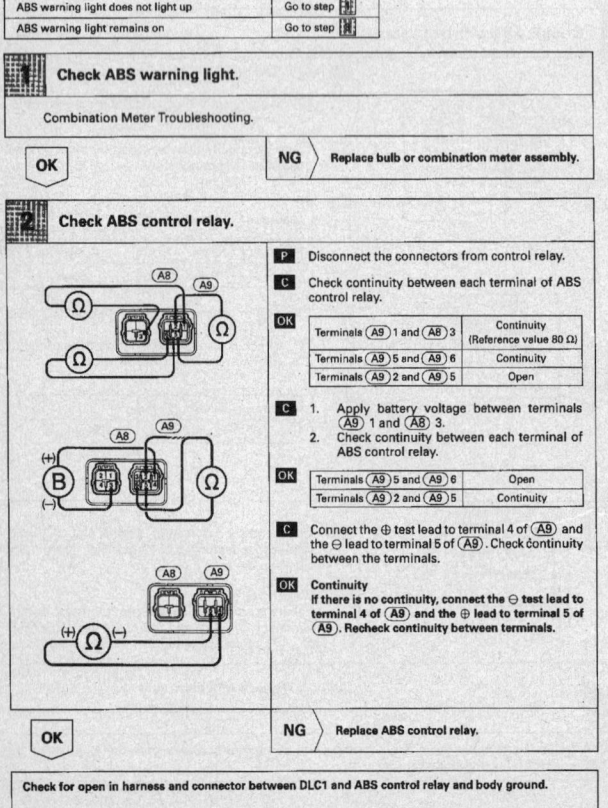

ABS warning light does not light up	Go to step 1
ABS warning light remains on	Go to step 3

1 **Check ABS warning light.**

Combination Meter Troubleshooting.

OK — NG → **Replace bulb or combination meter assembly.**

2 **Check ABS control relay.**

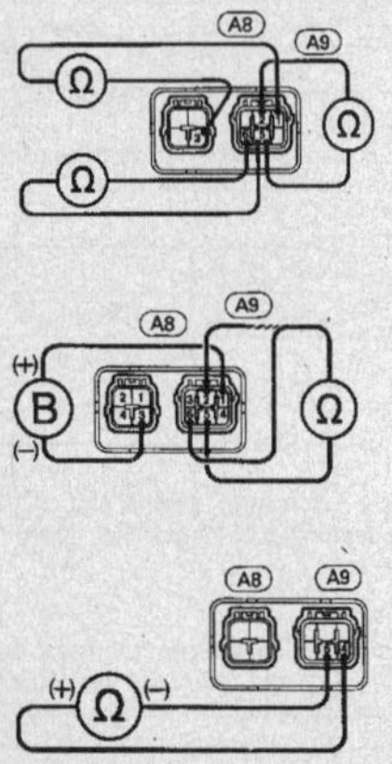

A8
A9
Ω
(+)
B
(−)

P Disconnect the connectors from control relay.

C Check continuity between each terminal of ABS control relay.

OK

Terminals A9 1 and A8 3	Continuity (Reference value 80 Ω)
Terminals A9 5 and A9 6	Continuity
Terminals A9 2 and A9 5	Open

C
1. Apply battery voltage between terminals A9 1 and A8 3.
2. Check continuity between each terminal of ABS control relay.

OK

Terminals A9 5 and A9 6	Open
Terminals A9 2 and A9 5	Continuity

C Connect the ⊕ test lead to terminal 4 of A9 and the ⊖ lead to terminal 5 of A9. Check continuity between the terminals.

OK **Continuity**
If there is no continuity, connect the ⊖ test lead to terminal 4 of A9 and the ⊕ lead to terminal 5 of A9. Recheck continuity between terminals.

OK — NG → **Replace ABS control relay.**

Check for open in harness and connector between DLC1 and ABS control relay and body ground.

TY4029600202020X

Fig. 69 ABS warning light switch circuit inspection & testing (Part 2 of 3). RAV4

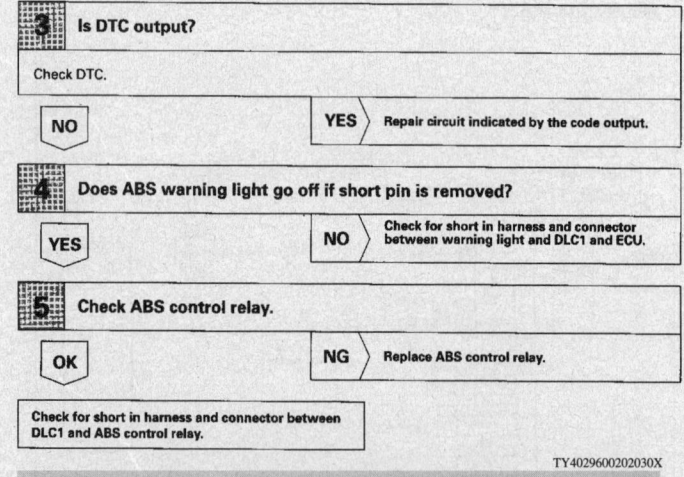

3 **Is DTC output?**

Check DTC.

NO — YES → **Repair circuit indicated by the code output.**

4 **Does ABS warning light go off if short pin is removed?**

YES — NO → **Check for short in harness and connector between warning light and DLC1 and ECU.**

5 **Check ABS control relay.**

OK — NG → **Replace ABS control relay.**

Check for short in harness and connector between DLC1 and ABS control relay.

TY4029600202030X

Fig. 69 ABS warning light switch circuit inspection & testing (Part 3 of 3). RAV4

CIRCUIT DESCRIPTION

If the ECU detects trouble, it lights the ABS warning light while at the same time prohibiting ABS control. At this time, the ECU records a diagnostic trouble code in memory.
After removing the short pin of the DLC1, connect terminals Tc and E1 of the DLC1 or DLC2 to make the ABS warning light to blink and output the diagnostic trouble code.

DIAGNOSTIC CHART

Perform troubleshooting in accordance with the chart below for each trouble symptom.

ABS warning light does not light up	Go to step 1
ABS warning light remains on	Go to step 3

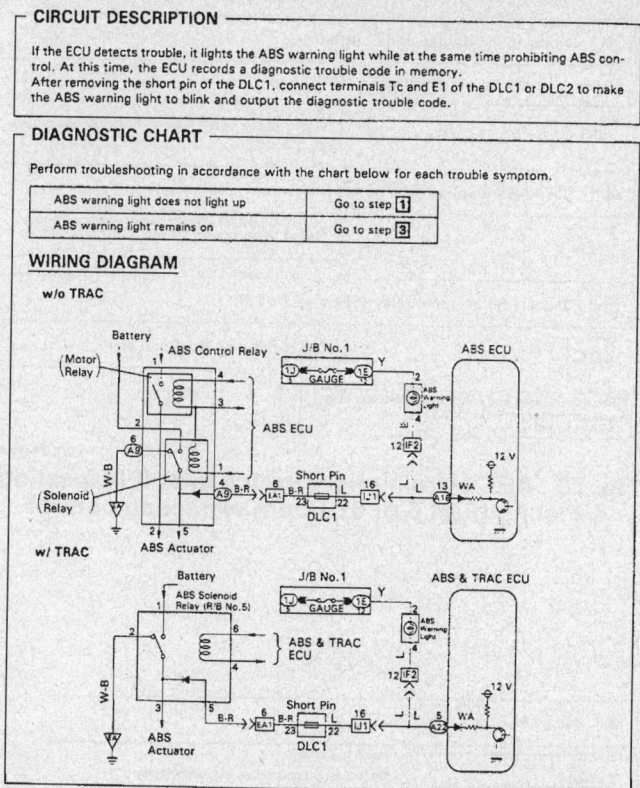

WIRING DIAGRAM

w/o TRAC

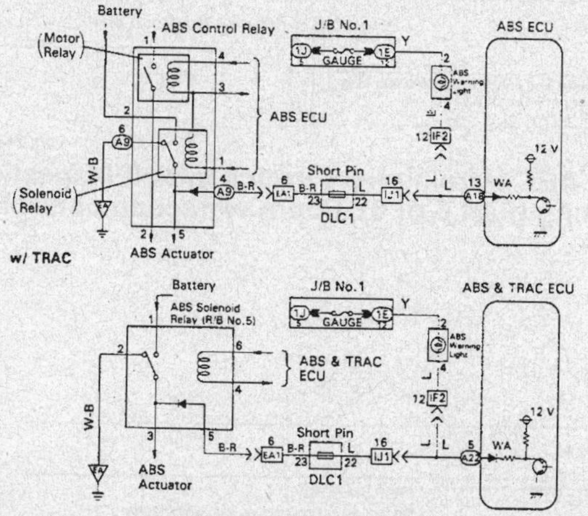

Battery
ABS Control Relay
Motor Relay
J/B No.1
GAUGE
ABS ECU
ABS Warning Light
ABS ECU
W-B
Solenoid Relay
Short Pin
DLC1
ABS Actuator
w/ TRAC
Battery
ABS Solenoid Relay (R/B No.5)
J/B No.1
GAUGE
ABS & TRAC ECU
ABS & TRAC ECU
Short Pin
DLC1
ABS Actuator
12 V

TY4029300061010X

Fig. 70 ABS warning light switch circuit inspection & testing (Part 1 of 6). Supra

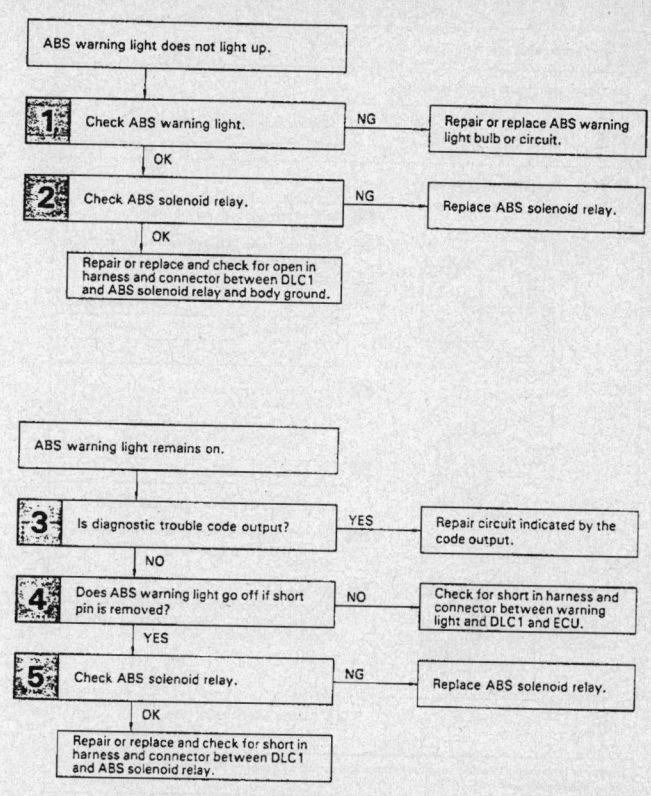

ABS warning light does not light up.

1 Check ABS warning light. — NG → Repair or replace ABS warning light bulb or circuit.
OK ↓

2 Check ABS solenoid relay. — NG → Replace ABS solenoid relay.
OK ↓

Repair or replace and check for open in harness and connector between DLC1 and ABS solenoid relay and body ground.

TY4029300061020X

Fig. 70 ABS warning light switch circuit inspection & testing (Part 2 of 6). Supra

ABS warning light remains on.

3 Is diagnostic trouble code output? — YES → Repair circuit indicated by the code output.
NO ↓

4 Does ABS warning light go off if short pin is removed? — NO → Check for short in harness and connector between warning light and DLC1 and ECU.
YES ↓

5 Check ABS solenoid relay. — NG → Replace ABS solenoid relay.
OK ↓

Repair or replace and check for short in harness and connector between DLC1 and ABS solenoid relay.

INSPECTION PROCEDURE (w/o TRAC)

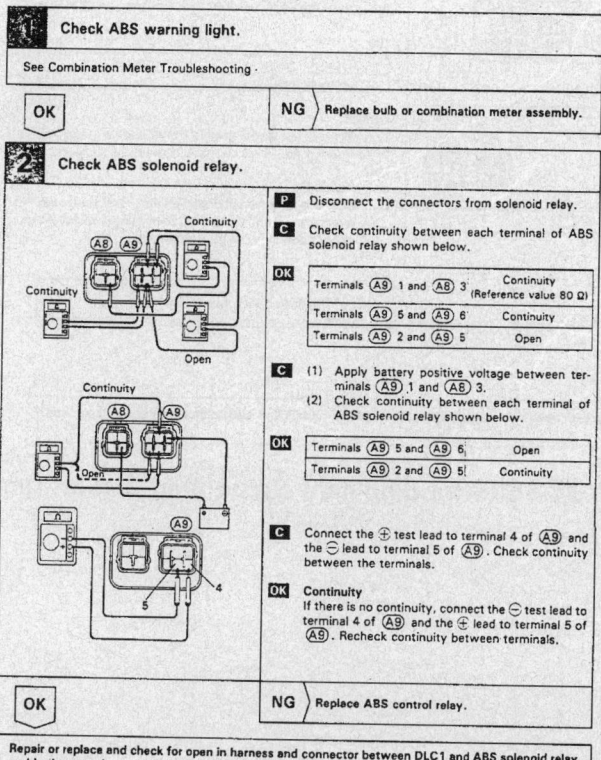

1 Check ABS warning light.

See Combination Meter Troubleshooting.

OK | NG → Replace bulb or combination meter assembly.

2 Check ABS solenoid relay.

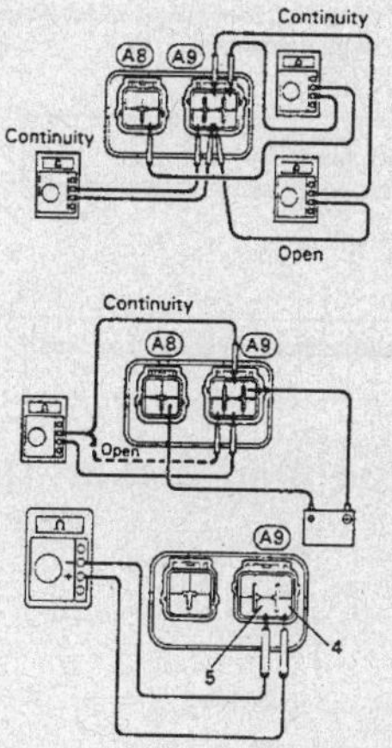

Continuity
A8
A9
Continuity
Open
Continuity
A8
A9
Open
A9
5
4

P Disconnect the connectors from solenoid relay.

C Check continuity between each terminal of ABS solenoid relay shown below.

OK

Terminals A9 1 and A8 3	Continuity (Reference value 80 Ω)
Terminals A9 5 and A9 6	Continuity
Terminals A9 2 and A9 5	Open

C (1) Apply battery positive voltage between terminals A9 1 and A8 3.
(2) Check continuity between each terminal of ABS solenoid relay shown below.

OK

Terminals A9 5 and A9 6	Open
Terminals A9 2 and A9 5	Continuity

C Connect the ⊕ test lead to terminal 4 of A9 and the ⊖ lead to terminal 5 of A9. Check continuity between the terminals.

OK Continuity
If there is no continuity, connect the ⊖ test lead to terminal 4 of A9 and the ⊕ lead to terminal 5 of A9. Recheck continuity between terminals.

OK | NG → Replace ABS control relay.

Repair or replace and check for open in harness and connector between DLC1 and ABS solenoid relay and body ground

TY4029300061030X

Fig. 70 ABS warning light switch circuit inspection & testing (Part 3 of 6). Supra less traction control

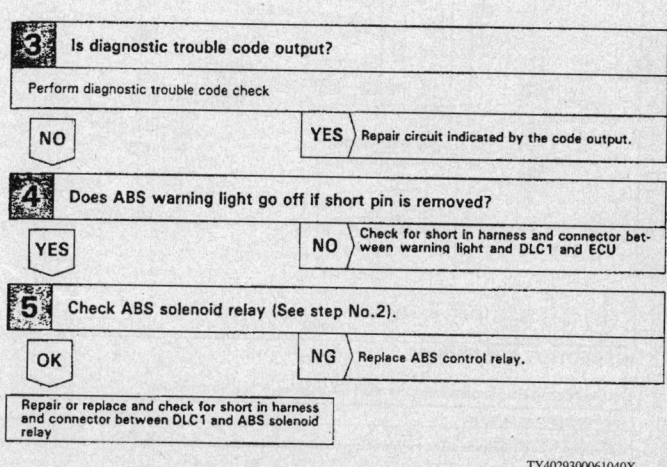

3 Is diagnostic trouble code output?

Perform diagnostic trouble code check

NO | YES → Repair circuit indicated by the code output.

4 Does ABS warning light go off if short pin is removed?

YES | NO → Check for short in harness and connector between warning light and DLC1 and ECU

5 Check ABS solenoid relay (See step No.2).

OK | NG → Replace ABS control relay.

Repair or replace and check for short in harness and connector between DLC1 and ABS solenoid relay

TY4029300061040X

Fig. 70 ABS warning light switch circuit inspection & testing (Part 4 of 6). Supra less traction control

1 Check ABS warning light.

See Combination Meter Troubleshooting

NG → Replace bulb or combination meter assembly.

OK ↓

2 Check ABS solenoid relay.

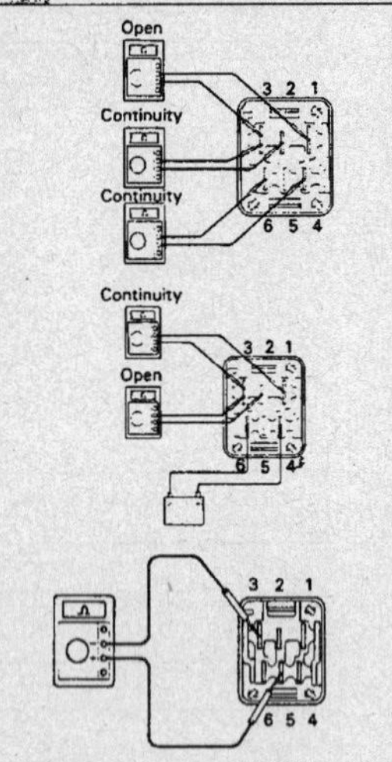

Open
Continuity
Continuity
3 2 1
6 5 4
Continuity
Open
3 2 1
6 5 4
3 2 1
6 5 4

P Remove solenoid relay from R/B No.5.

C Check continuity between each terminal of ABS solenoid relay shown below.

OK

Terminals 4 and 6	Continuity (Reference value 80 Ω)
Terminals 2 and 3	Continuity
Terminals 1 and 3	Open

C
1. Apply battery positive voltage between terminals 4 and 6.
2. Check continuity between each terminal of ABS solenoid relay shown below.

OK

Terminals 2 and 3	Open
Terminals 1 and 3	Continuity

C Connect the ⊕ test lead to terminal 5 and the ⊖ lead to terminal 3. Check continuity between the terminals.

OK **Continuity**
If there is no continuity, connect the ⊖ test lead to terminal 5 and the ⊕ lead to terminal 3. Recheck continuity between terminals.

NG → Replace ABS solenoid relay.

OK ↓

Repair or replace and check for open in harness and connector between DLC1 and ABS solenoid relay and body ground

TY4029300061050X

Fig. 70 ABS warning light switch circuit inspection & testing (Part 5 of 6). Supra w/traction control

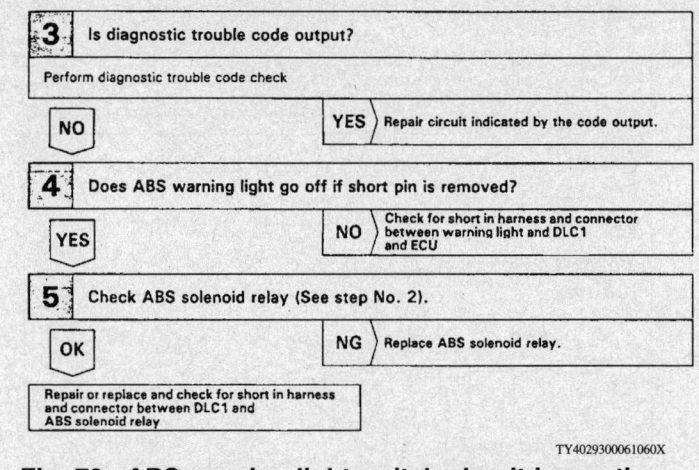

3 Is diagnostic trouble code output?

Perform diagnostic trouble code check

YES → Repair circuit indicated by the code output.

NO ↓

4 Does ABS warning light go off if short pin is removed?

NO → Check for short in harness and connector between warning light and DLC1 and ECU

YES ↓

5 Check ABS solenoid relay (See step No. 2).

NG → Replace ABS solenoid relay.

OK ↓

Repair or replace and check for short in harness and connector between DLC1 and ABS solenoid relay

TY4029300061060X

Fig. 70 ABS warning light switch circuit inspection & testing (Part 6 of 6). Supra w/traction control

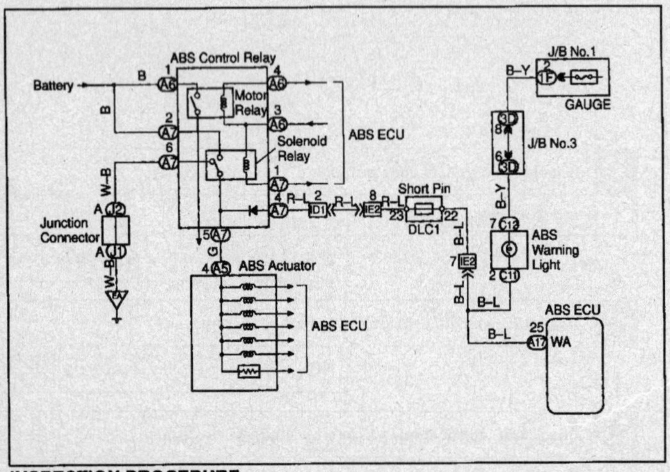

ABS Control Relay
Battery
Motor Relay
Solenoid Relay
ABS ECU
J/B No.1
GAUGE
J/B No.3
Short Pin
DLC1
Junction Connector
ABS Actuator
ABS ECU
ABS Warning Light
ABS ECU
WA

INSPECTION PROCEDURE

Troubleshooting in accordance with the chart below for each trouble symptom.

ABS warning light does not light up	Go to step 1
ABS warning light remains on	Go to step 3

1 Check ABS warning light.

See Combination Meter Troubleshooting.

NG → Repair bulb or combination meter assembly.

OK ↓

TY4029600226010X

Fig. 71 ABS warning light circuit (Part 1 of 3). 1996 4Runner

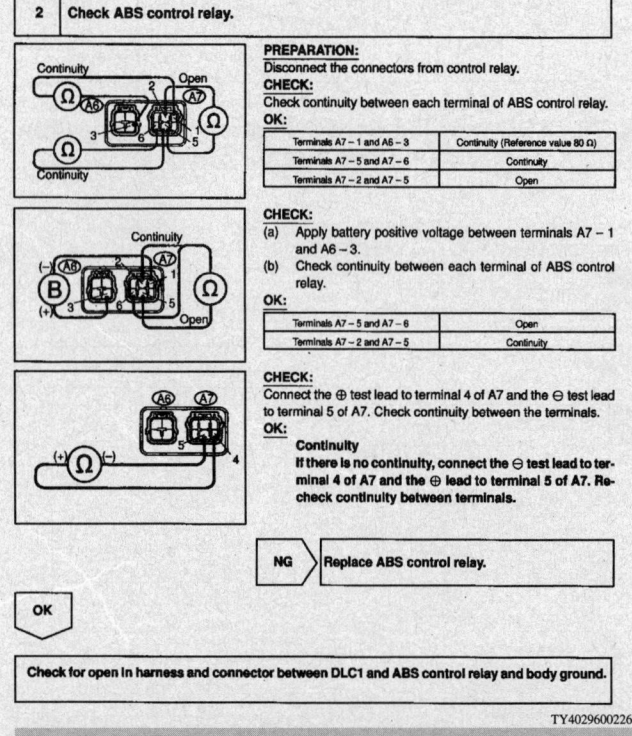

2 Check ABS control relay.

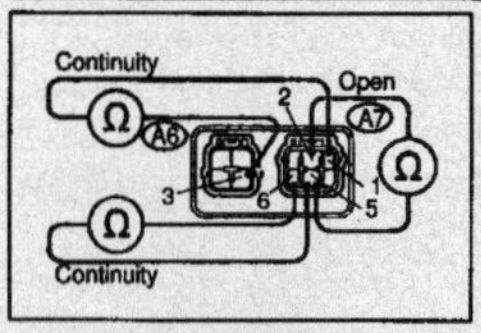

Continuity
Open
Continuity

PREPARATION:
Disconnect the connectors from control relay.

CHECK:
Check continuity between each terminal of ABS control relay.

OK:

Terminals A7 – 1 and A6 – 3	Continuity (Reference value 80 Ω)
Terminals A7 – 5 and A7 – 6	Continuity
Terminals A7 – 2 and A7 – 5	Open

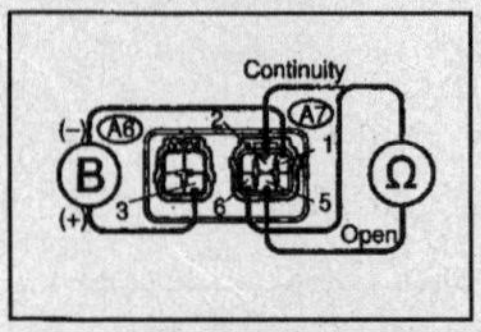

Continuity
Open

CHECK:
(a) Apply battery positive voltage between terminals A7 – 1 and A6 – 3.
(b) Check continuity between each terminal of ABS control relay.

OK:

Terminals A7 – 5 and A7 – 6	Open
Terminals A7 – 2 and A7 – 5	Continuity

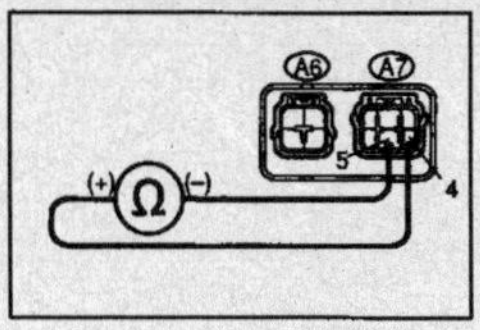

CHECK:
Connect the ⊕ test lead to terminal 4 of A7 and the ⊖ test lead to terminal 5 of A7. Check continuity between the terminals.

OK:
Continuity
If there is no continuity, connect the ⊖ test lead to terminal 4 of A7 and the ⊕ lead to terminal 5 of A7. Recheck continuity between terminals.

NG → Replace ABS control relay.

OK ↓

Check for open in harness and connector between DLC1 and ABS control relay and body ground.

TY4029600226020X

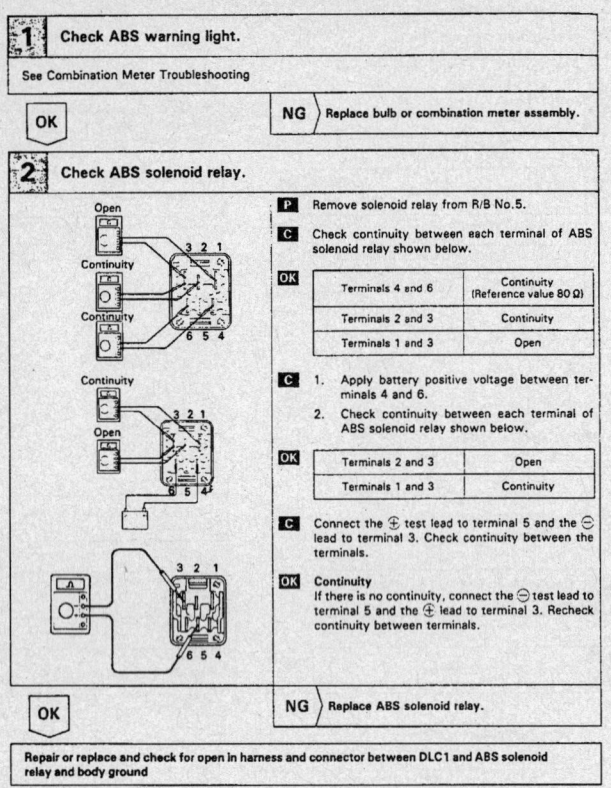

Fig. 71 ABS warning light circuit (Part 2 of 3). 1996 4Runner

3	**Is DTC output?**

Check DTC.

YES ⟩ **Repair circuit indicated by the code output.**

NO

4	**Does ABS warning light go off if short pin is removed?**

NO ⟩ **Check for short in harness and connector between warning light and DLC1 and ECU.**

YES

5	**Check ABS control relay (See step 2).**

NG ⟩ **Replace ABS control relay.**

OK

Check for short in harness and connector between DLC1 and ABS control relay.

TY4029600226030X

Fig. 71 ABS warning light circuit (Part 3 of 3). 1996 4Runner

CIRCUIT DESCRIPTION

If the ECU detects trouble, it lights the ABS warning light while at the same time prohibiting ABS control. At this time, the ECU records a DTC in memory.
After removing the short pin of the DLC1, connect terminals Tc and E1 of the DLC1 to make the ABS warning light blink and output the DTC.

WIRING DIAGRAM

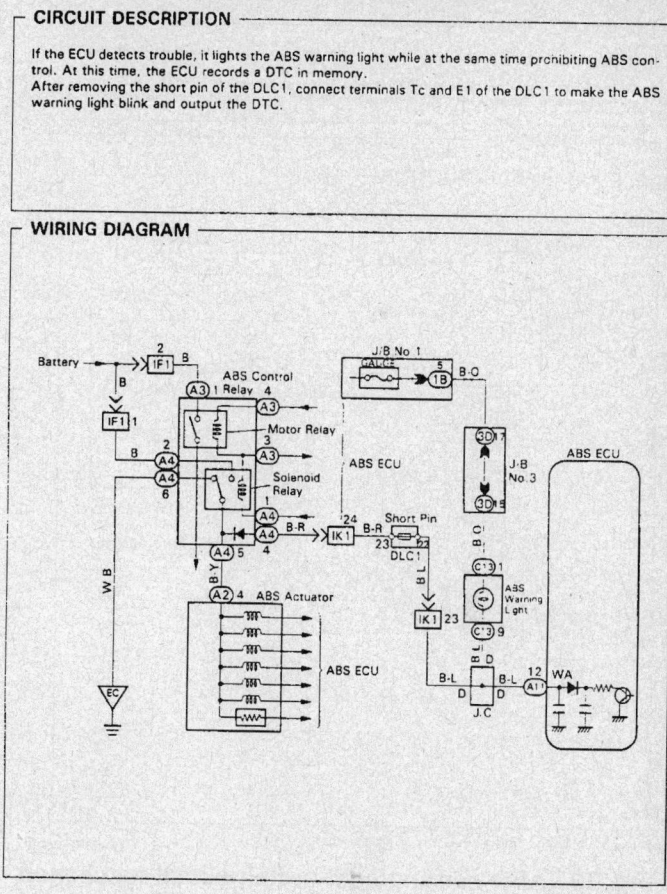

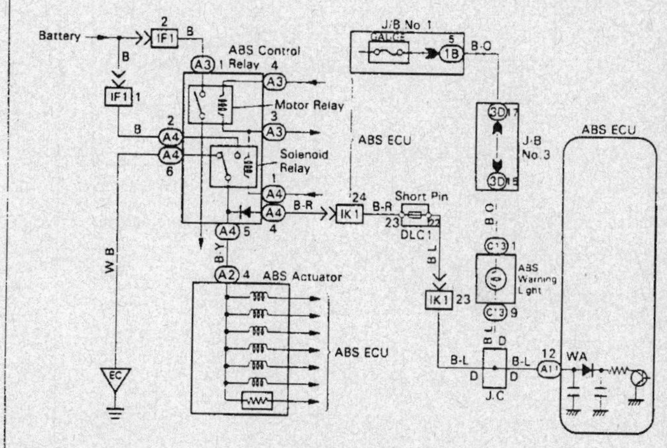

Battery
IF1
ABS Control Relay
Motor Relay
Solenoid Relay
ABS ECU
J/B No. 1
GAUGE
J/B No.3
Short Pin
DLC1
ABS Warning Light
ABS Actuator
J.C
WA

TY4029500175010X

Fig. 72 ABS warning light switch circuit inspection & testing (Part 1 of 3). Tacoma

Troubleshoot in accordance with the chart below for each trouble symptom.

ABS warning light does not light up	Go to step 1
ABS warning light remains on	Go to step 2

1	**Check ABS warning light.**

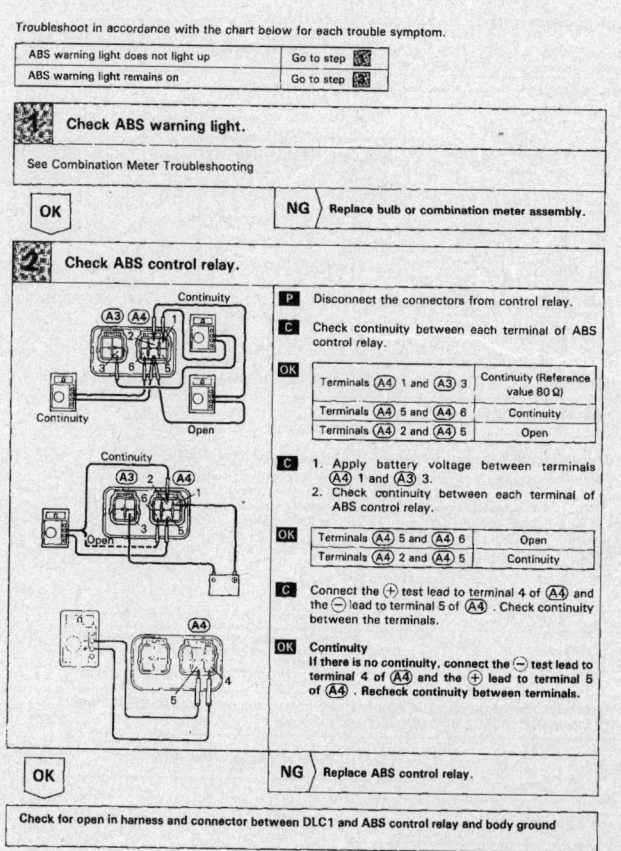

See Combination Meter Troubleshooting

OK | **NG** ⟩ **Replace bulb or combination meter assembly.**

2	**Check ABS control relay.**

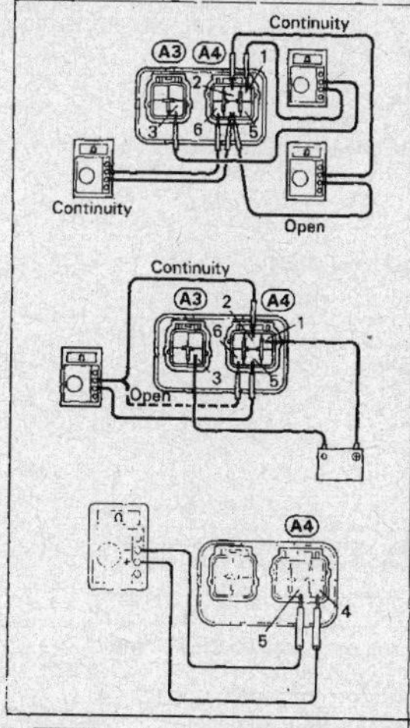

Continuity
Open

P Disconnect the connectors from control relay.

C Check continuity between each terminal of ABS control relay.

OK

Terminals (A4) 1 and (A3) 3	Continuity (Reference value 80 Ω)
Terminals (A4) 5 and (A4) 6	Continuity
Terminals (A4) 2 and (A4) 5	Open

C
1. Apply battery voltage between terminals (A4) 1 and (A3) 3.
2. Check continuity between each terminal of ABS control relay.

OK

Terminals (A4) 5 and (A4) 6	Open
Terminals (A4) 2 and (A4) 5	Continuity

C Connect the (+) test lead to terminal 4 of (A4) and the (−) lead to terminal 5 of (A4). Check continuity between the terminals.

OK **Continuity**
If there is no continuity, connect the (−) test lead to terminal 4 of (A4) and the (+) lead to terminal 5 of (A4). Recheck continuity between terminals.

OK | **NG** ⟩ **Replace ABS control relay.**

Check for open in harness and connector between DLC1 and ABS control relay and body ground

TY4029500175020X

Fig. 72 ABS warning light switch circuit inspection & testing (Part 2 of 3). Tacoma

3	**Is DTC output?**

Check DTC

NO | **YES** ⟩ **Repair circuit indicated by the code output.**

4	**Does ABS warning light go off if short pin is removed?**

YES | **NO** ⟩ **Check for short in harness and connector between warning light and DLC1 and ECU**

5	**Check ABS control relay (See step No.2).**

OK | **NG** ⟩ **Replace ABS control relay.**

Check for short in harness and connector between DLC1 and ABS control relay

TY4029500175030X

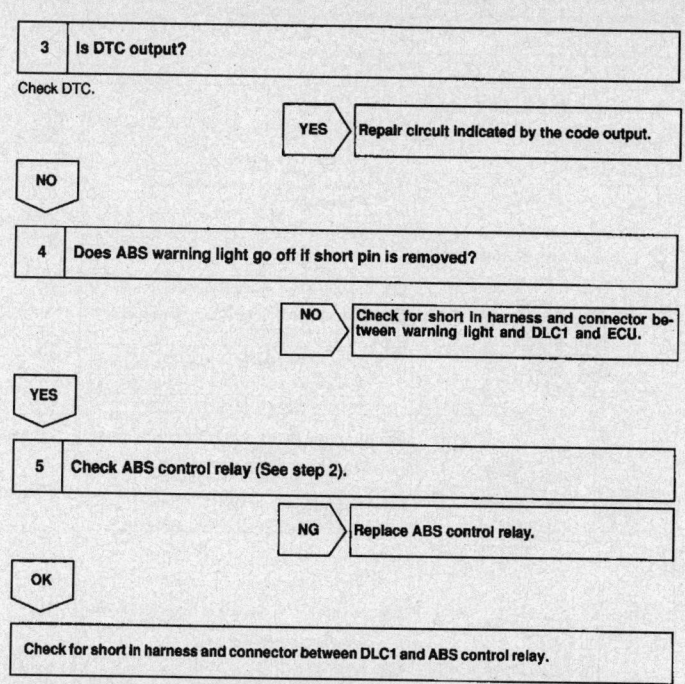

Fig. 72 ABS warning light switch circuit inspection & testing (Part 3 of 3). Tacoma

CIRCUIT DESCRIPTION

If the ECU detects trouble, it lights the ABS warning light while at the same time prohibiting ABS control. At this time, the ECU records a diagnostic trouble code in memory.
After removing the short pin of the data link connector 1, connect between terminals Tc and E1 of the data link connector 1 to make the ABS warning light blink and output the diagnostic trouble code.

WIRING DIAGRAM

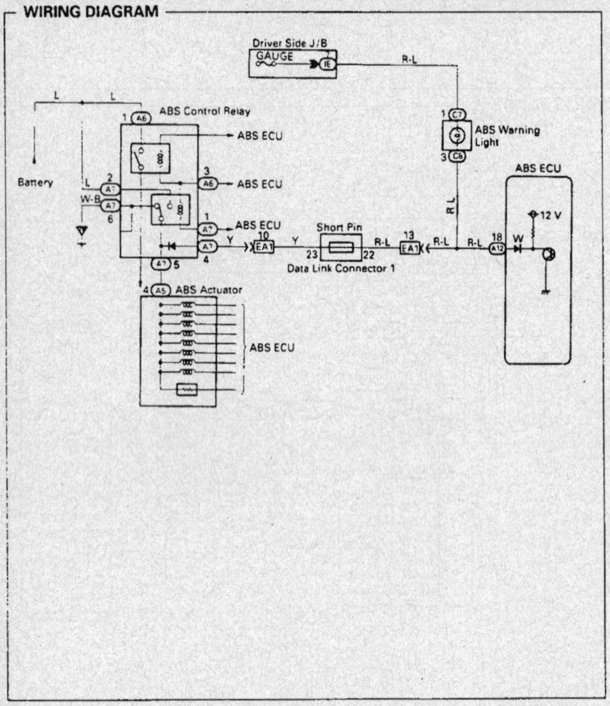

Driver Side J/B
GAUGE
R-L
ABS Control Relay
ABS ECU
ABS Warning Light
Battery
ABS ECU
Short Pin
Data Link Connector 1
ABS Actuator
12 V

TY4029500185010X

Fig. 73 ABS warning light switch circuit inspection & testing (Part 1 of 3). 1995–96 Tercel

Troubleshoot in accordance with the chart below for each trouble symptom.

ABS warning light does not light up	Go to step 1
ABS warning light remains on	Go to step 3

1 Check ABS warning light.

See Combination Meter

OK

NG — Replace bulb or combination meter assembly.

2 Check ABS control relay.

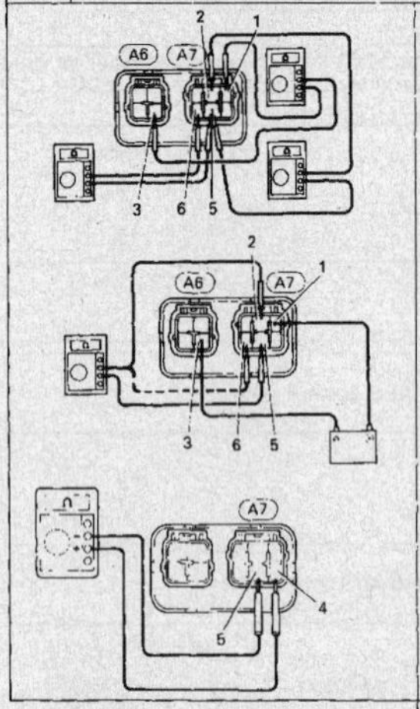

P Disconnect the connectors from control relay.

C Check continuity between each terminal of ABS control relay shown below.

OK

Terminals (A7) 1 and (A6) 3	Continuity (Reference value 80 Ω)
Terminals (A7) 5 and (A7) 6	Continuity
Terminals (A7) 2 and (A7) 5	Open

C (1) Apply battery voltage between terminals (A7) 1 and (A6) 3.
(2) Check continuity between each terminal of ABS control relay shown below.

OK

Terminals (A7) 5 and (A7) 6	Open
Terminals (A7) 2 and (A7) 5	Continuity

C Connect the ⊕ test lead to terminal 4 of (A7) and the ⊖ lead to terminal 5 of (A7). Check continuity between the terminals.

OK **Continuity**
If there is no continuity, connect the ⊖ test lead to terminal 4 of (A7) and the ⊕ lead to terminal 5 of (A7). Recheck continuity between terminals.

OK

NG — Replace ABS control relay.

Repair or replace and check for open in harness and connector between data link connector 1 and ABS control relay and body ground

TY4029500185020X

Fig. 73 ABS warning light switch circuit inspection & testing (Part 2 of 3). 1995–96 Tercel

3 Is diagnostic trouble code output?

Check diagnostic trouble code

NO

YES — Repair circuit indicated by the code output.

4 Does ABS warning light go off if short pin is removed?

YES

NO — Check for short in harness and connector between warning light and data link connector 1 and ECU

5 Check ABS control relay (See step 2).

OK

NG — Replace ABS control relay.

Repair or replace and check for short in harness and connector between data link connector 1 and ABS control relay

TY4029500185030X

Fig. 73 ABS warning light switch circuit inspection & testing (Part 3 of 3). 1995–96 Tercel

CIRCUIT DESCRIPTION

Connecting terminals Tc and E1 of the DLC1 or the DLC2 causes the ECU to display the diagnostic trouble code by flasing the ABS warning light.

WIRING DIAGRAM

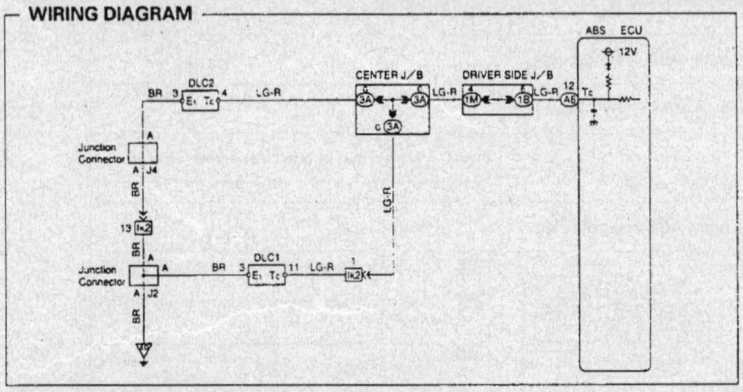

ABS ECU
12V
CENTER J/B
DRIVER SIDE J/B
DLC2
Junction Connector
DLC1
Junction Connector

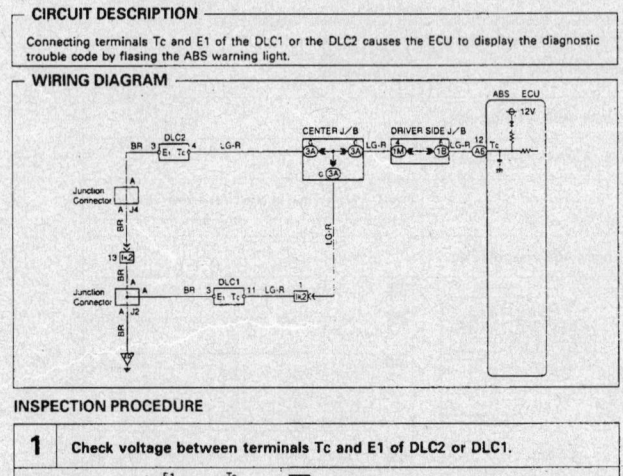

INSPECTION PROCEDURE

1 Check voltage between terminals Tc and E1 of DLC2 or DLC1.

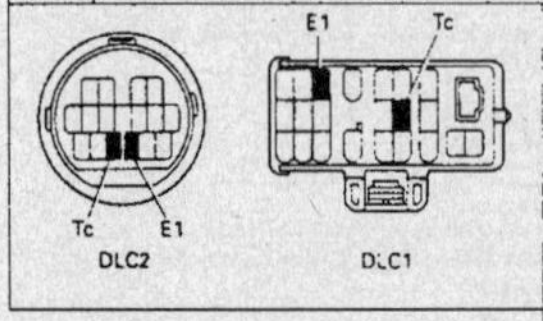

E1
Tc
Tc
E1
DLC2
DLC1

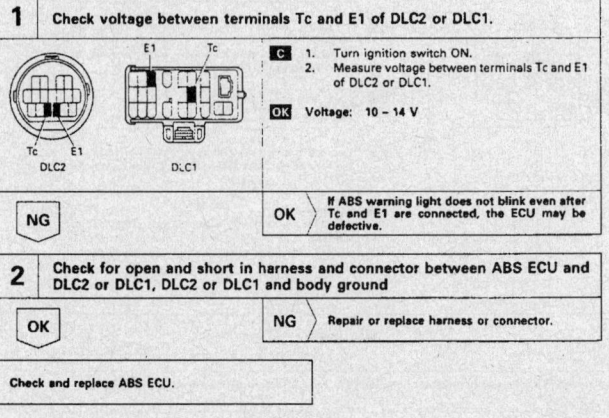

C 1. Turn ignition switch ON.
2. Measure voltage between terminals Tc and E1 of DLC2 or DLC1.

OK **Voltage: 10 – 14 V**

NG

OK — If ABS warning light does not blink even after Tc and E1 are connected, the ECU may be defective.

2 Check for open and short in harness and connector between ABS ECU and DLC2 or DLC1, DLC2 or DLC1 and body ground

OK

NG — Repair or replace harness or connector.

Check and replace ABS ECU.

TY4029500162000X

Fig. 74 Tc terminal circuit inspection & testing. Avalon

CIRCUIT DESCRIPTION

Connecting between terminals Tc and E1 of the check connector or the TDCL causes the ECU to display the diagnostic code by flashing the ABS warning light.

DIAGNOSTIC CHART

1 Check voltage between terminals Tc and E1 of TDCL or check connector.
- OK → If ABS warning light does not blink even after Tc and E1 are connected, the ECU may be defective.*
- NG ↓

2 Check for open and short in harness and connector between ABS ECU and TDCL or check connector, TDCL or check connector and body ground
- NG → Repair or replace harness or connector.
- OK ↓

Check and replace ABS ECU.

*: Provided that the harness between terminal Tc of TDCL or check connector and terminal Tc of ECU is not open.

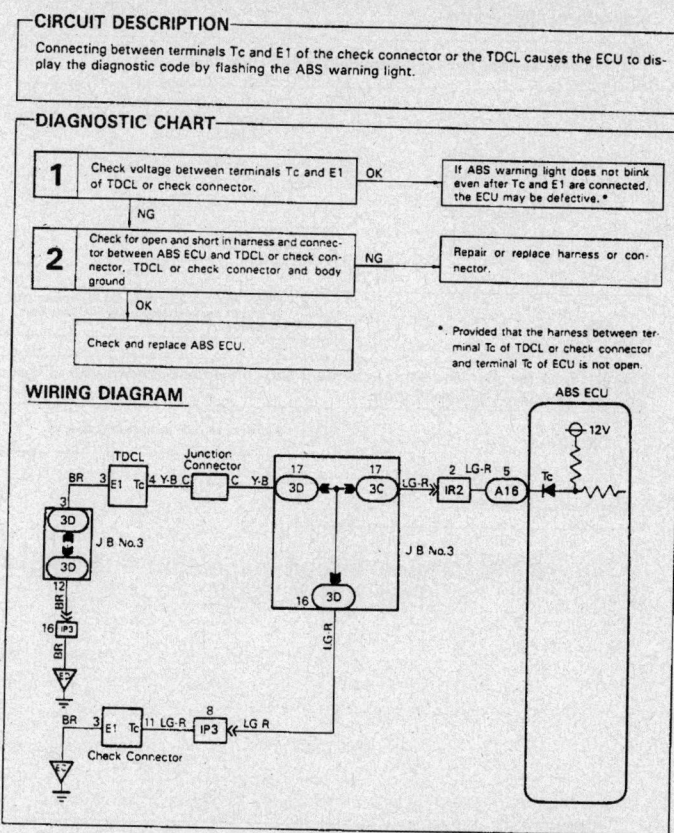

WIRING DIAGRAM

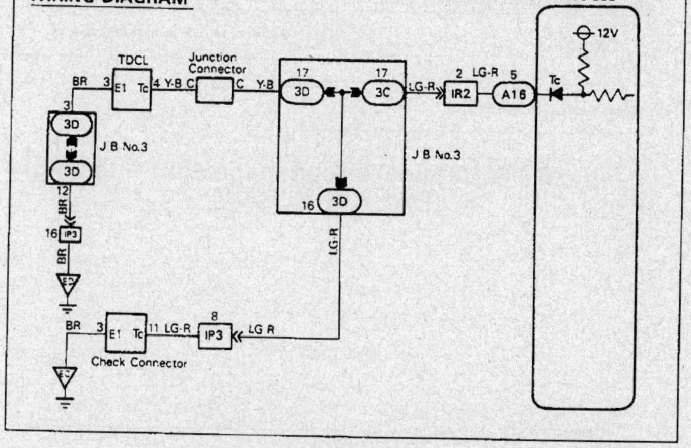

ABS ECU
12V
TDCL
Junction Connector
BR
E1
Tc
Y-B
3D
3C
LG-R
IR2
A16
J B No.3
IP3
Check Connector

TY4029200063010X

Fig. 75 Tc terminal circuit inspection & testing (Part 1 of 2). Camry

INSPECTION PROCEDURE

1 Check voltage between terminals Tc and E1 of TDCL or Check Connector.

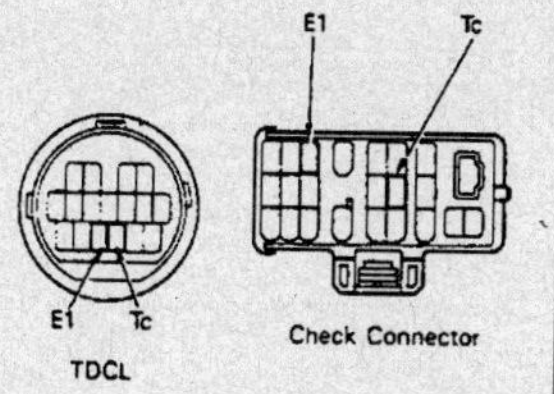

E1
Tc
E1
Tc
TDCL
Check Connector

C (1) Turn ignition switch ON.
(2) Measure voltage between terminals Tc and E1 of TDCL or check connector.

OK Voltage: 10 – 14 V

- NG ↓
- OK → If ABS warning light does not blink even after Tc and E1 are connected, the ECU may be defective.

2 Check for open and short in harness and connector between ABS ECU and TDCL or check connector, TDCL or check connector and body ground

- OK ↓
- NG → Repair or replace harness or connector.

Check and replace ABS ECU.

TY4029200063020X

Fig. 75 Tc terminal circuit inspection & testing (Part 2 of 2). Camry

CIRCUIT DESCRIPTION

DTC No.	Diagnostic Trouble Code Detecting Condition	Trouble Area
51	Pump motor is not operating normally during initial check.	• ABS pump motor.

Fail safe function: If trouble occurs in the ABS pump motor, the ECU cuts off the current to the control (solenoid) relay and prohibits ABS control.

DIAGNOSTIC CHART

See inspection of ABS actuator

WIRING DIAGRAM

(Reference)

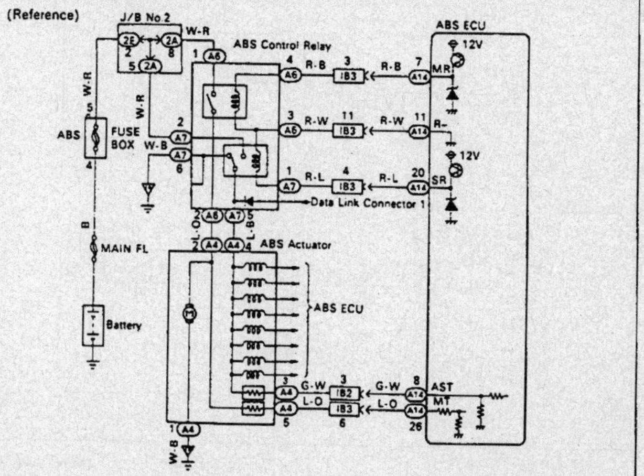

J/B No.2
ABS Control Relay
ABS ECU
12V
ABS
FUSE BOX
MAIN FL
Battery
Data Link Connector 1
ABS Actuator
ABS ECU
AST
MT

TY4029300064010X

Fig. 76 Tc terminal circuit inspection & testing (Part 1 of 2). Corolla

INSPECTION PROCEDURE

1 Check voltage between terminals Tc and E1 of Data Link Connector 1.

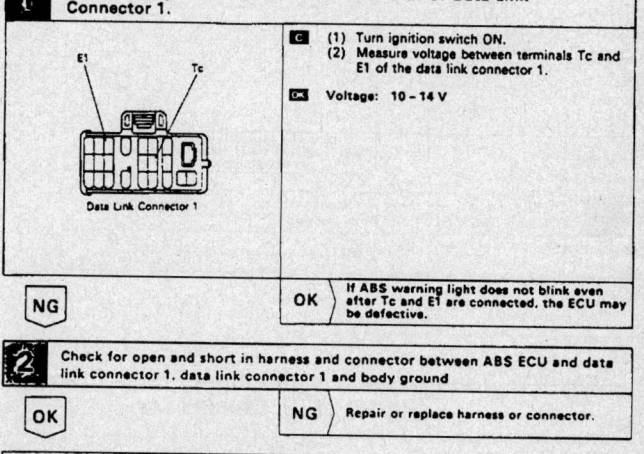

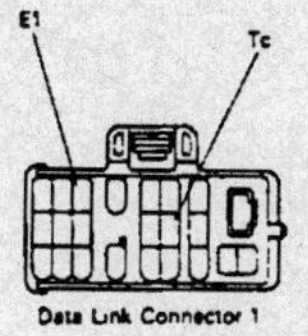

E1
Tc
Data Link Connector 1

C (1) Turn ignition switch ON.
(2) Measure voltage between terminals Tc and E1 of the data link connector 1.

OK Voltage: 10 – 14 V

- NG ↓
- OK → If ABS warning light does not blink even after Tc and E1 are connected, the ECU may be defective.

2 Check for open and short in harness and connector between ABS ECU and data link connector 1, data link connector 1 and body ground

- OK ↓
- NG → Repair or replace harness or connector.

Check and replace ABS ECU.

TY4029300064020X

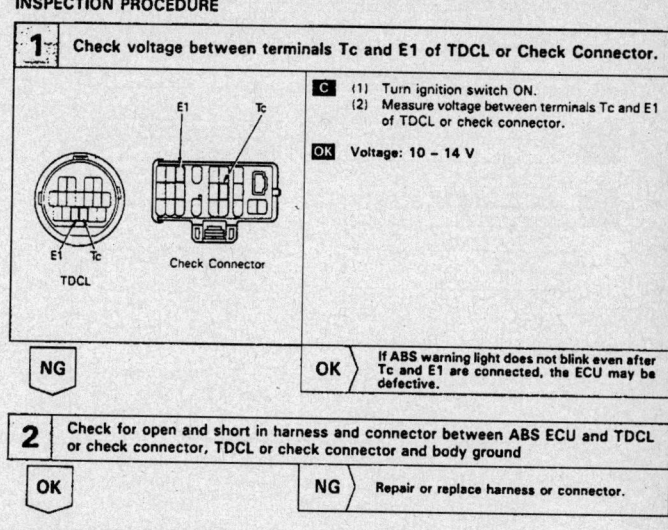

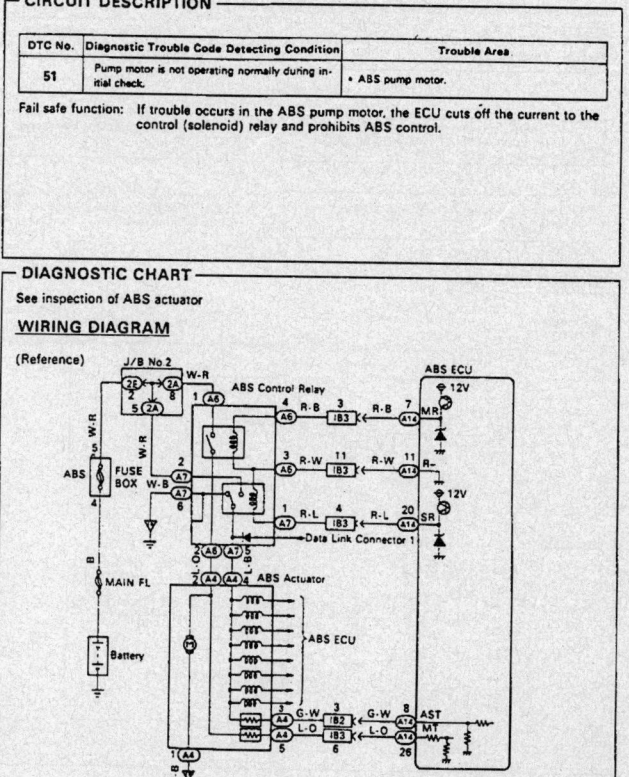

Fig. 76 Tc terminal circuit inspection & testing (Part 2 of 2). Corolla

CIRCUIT DESCRIPTION

Connecting terminals Tc and E1 of the DLC1 causes the ECU to display the diagnostic trouble code by flashing the ABS warning light.

DIAGNOSTIC CHART

1. Check voltage between terminals Tc and E1 of DLC1. — OK → If ABS warning light does not blink even after Tc and E1 are connected, the ECU may be defective.*
   - NG ↓
2. Check for open and short in harness and connector between ABS ECU and DLC1, DLC1 and body ground. — NG → Repair or replace harness or connector.
   - OK ↓
3. Check and replace ABS ECU.

*: Provided that the harness between terminal Tc of DLC1 and terminal Tc of ECU is not open.

WIRING DIAGRAM

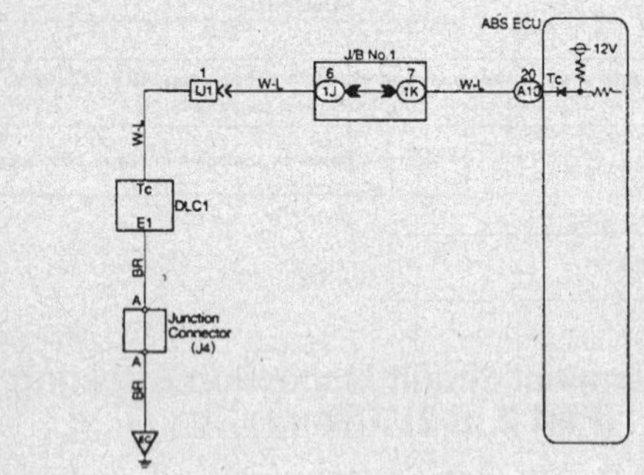

ABS ECU
J/B No.1
12V
Tc
W-L
DLC1
Junction Connector (J4)
BR

TY4029400066010X

Fig. 77 Tc terminal circuit inspection & testing (Part 1 of 2). Celica

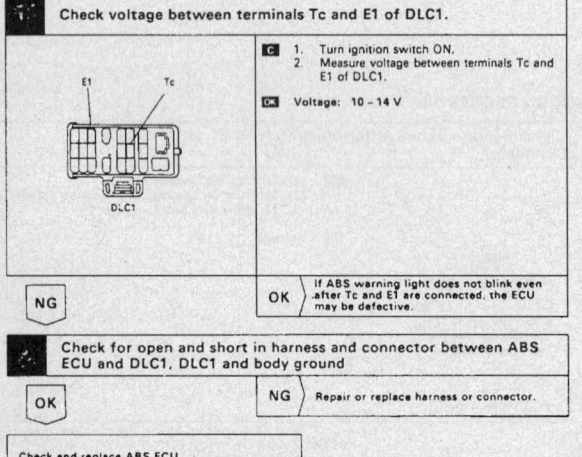

1 Check voltage between terminals Tc and E1 of DLC1.

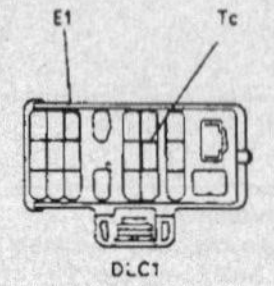

E1
Tc
DLC1

C
1. Turn ignition switch ON.
2. Measure voltage between terminals Tc and E1 of DLC1.

OK Voltage: 10 – 14 V

OK → If ABS warning light does not blink even after Tc and E1 are connected, the ECU may be defective.

NG ↓

2 Check for open and short in harness and connector between ABS ECU and DLC1, DLC1 and body ground

NG → Repair or replace harness or connector.

OK ↓

Check and replace ABS ECU.

TY4029400066020X

Fig. 77 Tc terminal circuit inspection & testing (Part 2 of 2). Celica

CIRCUIT DESCRIPTION

Connecting terminals Tc and E1 of the DLC1 causes the ECU to display the DTC by flasing the ABS warning light.

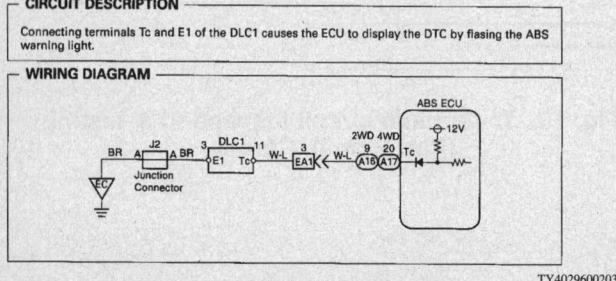

WIRING DIAGRAM

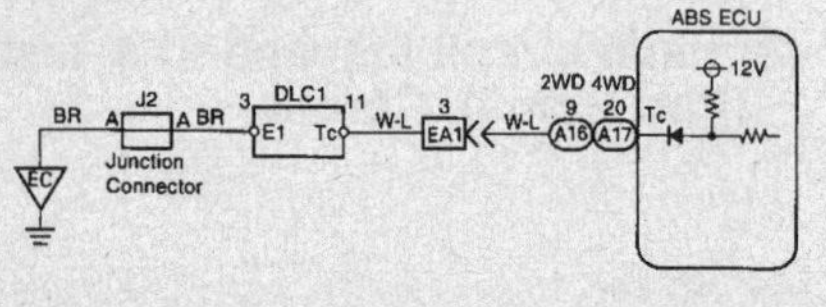

ABS ECU
2WD 4WD
12V
BR
J2
DLC1
E1
Tc
W-L
EA1
A16
A17
Junction Connector
EC

TY4029600203010X

Fig. 78 Tc terminal circuit inspection & testing (Part 1 of 2). RAV4

INSPECTION PROCEDURE

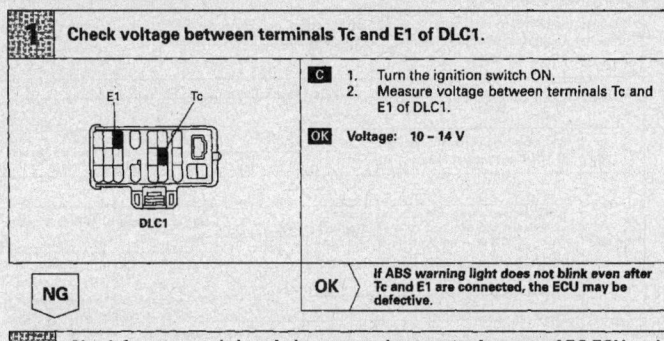

1 Check voltage between terminals Tc and E1 of DLC1.

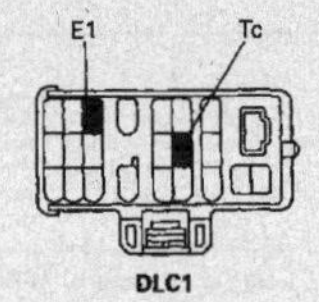

E1
Tc
DLC1

C
1. Turn the ignition switch ON.
2. Measure voltage between terminals Tc and E1 of DLC1.

OK **Voltage: 10 – 14 V**

OK → **If ABS warning light does not blink even after Tc and E1 are connected, the ECU may be defective.**

NG ↓

2 Check for open and short in harness and connector between ABS ECU and DLC1, DLC1 and body ground.

NG → **Repair or replace harness or connector.**

OK ↓

Check and replace ABS ECU.

TY4029600203020X

Fig. 78 Tc terminal circuit inspection & testing (Part 2 of 2). RAV4

CIRCUIT DESCRIPTION

Connecting terminals Tc and E1 of the DLC1 or the DLC2 causes the ECU to display the diagnostic trouble code by flashing the ABS warning light.

DIAGNOSTIC CHART

HINT: First confirm that the ABS warning light is operating normally.

1. Check voltage between terminals Tc and E1 of DLC2 or DLC1. — OK → If ABS warning light does not blink even after Tc and E1 are connected, the ECU may be defective.*
   - NG ↓
2. Check for open and short in harness and connector of systems connected to Tc terminal — NG → Repair or replace harness or connector.
   - OK ↓
3. Check and replace ABS (& TRAC) ECU.

*: Provided that the harness between terminal Tc of DLC2 or DLC1 and terminal Tc of ECU is not open.

WIRING DIAGRAM

w/o TRAC

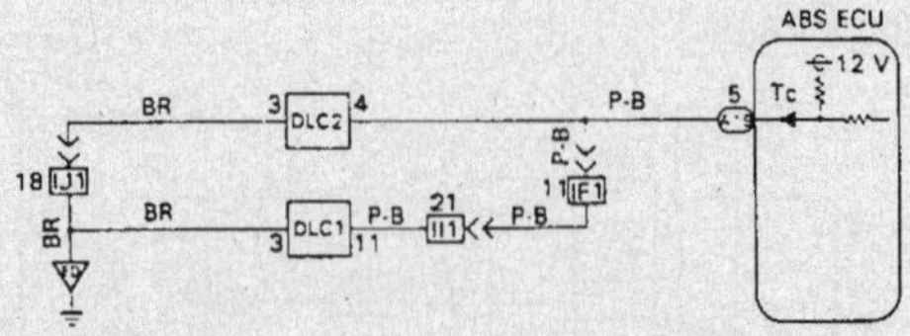

ABS ECU
12 V
Tc
BR
DLC2
P-B
DLC1
IJ1
II1
IF1

w/ TRAC

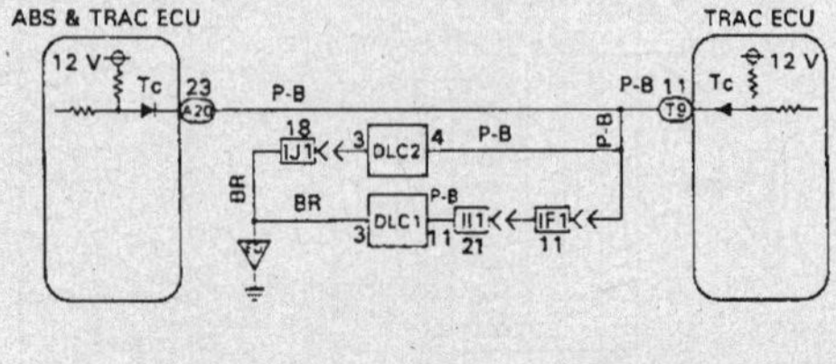

ABS & TRAC ECU
TRAC ECU
12 V
Tc
P-B
BR
DLC2
DLC1
IJ1
II1
IF1

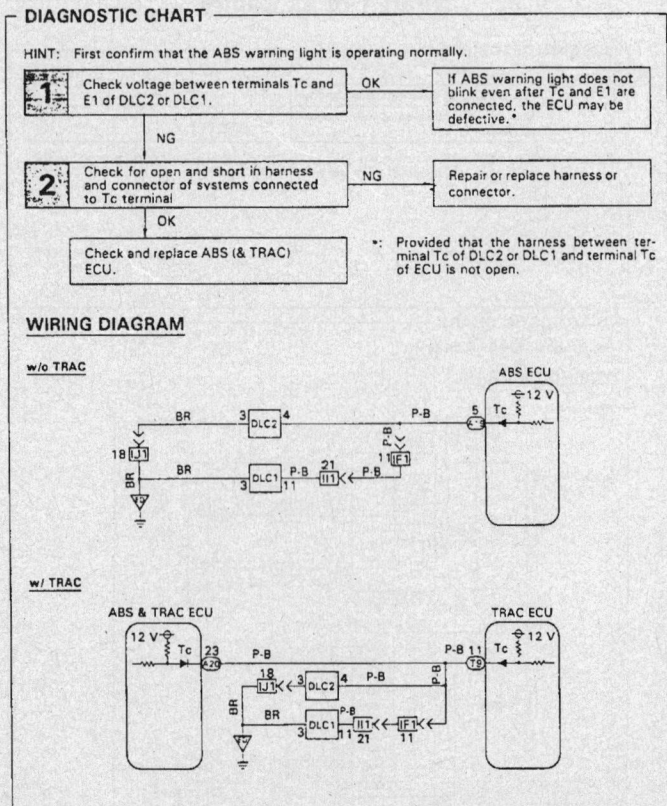

TY4029300065010X

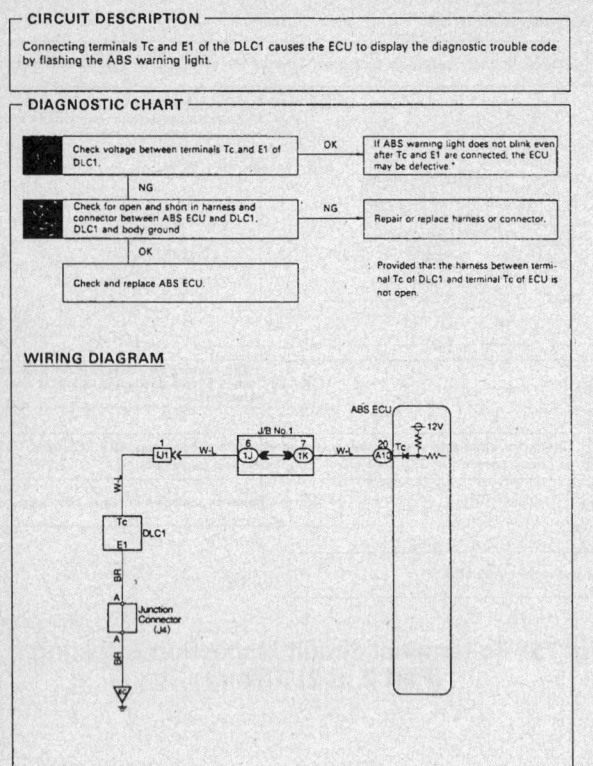

Fig. 79 Tc terminal circuit inspection & testing (Part 1 of 2). Supra

1 Check voltage between terminals Tc and E1 of DLC2 or DLC1.

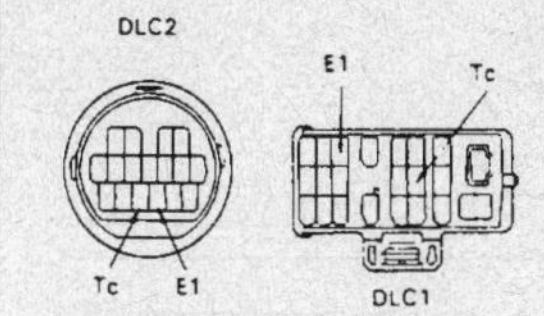
DLC2
E1
Tc
Tc
E1
DLC1

P Turn ignition switch ON.

C Measure voltage between terminals Tc and E1 of DLC2 or DLC1.

OK Voltage: 10 – 14 V

NG

OK 〉 If ABS warning light does not blink even after Tc and E1 are connected, the ECU may be defective.

2 Check for open and short in harness and connector of systems connected to Tc terminal

OK

NG 〉 Repair or replace harness or connector.

Check and replace ABS (& TRAC) ECU.

TY4029300065020X

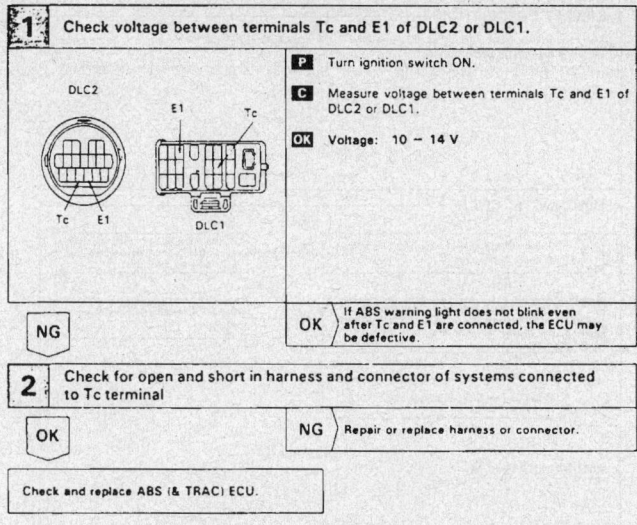

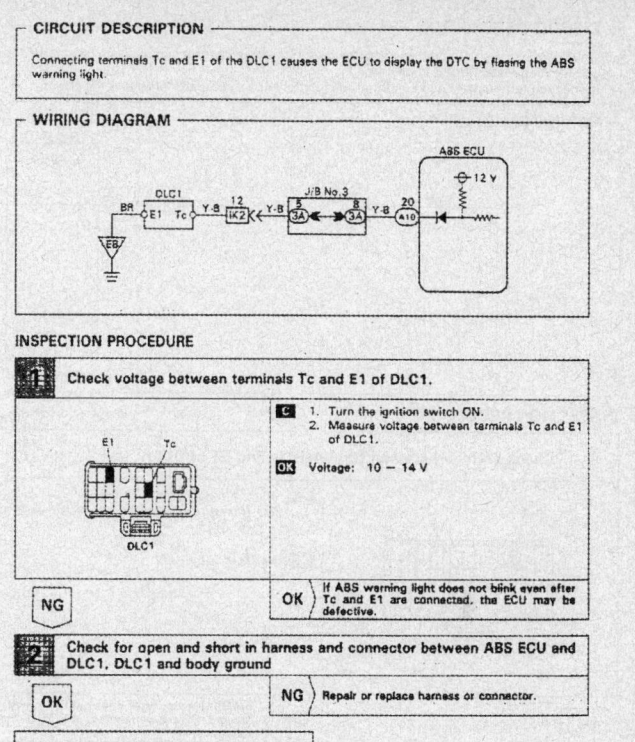

Fig. 79 Tc terminal circuit inspection & testing (Part 2 of 2). Supra

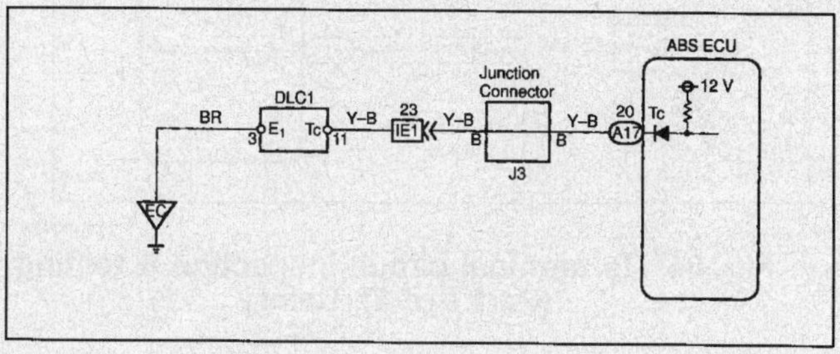
ABS ECU
Junction Connector
12 V
DLC1
BR
E1
Tc
Y–B
23
IE1
Y–B
B
Y–B
B
20
Tc
A17
J3
EC

INSPECTION PROCEDURE

1 Check voltage between terminals Tc and E_1 of DLC1.

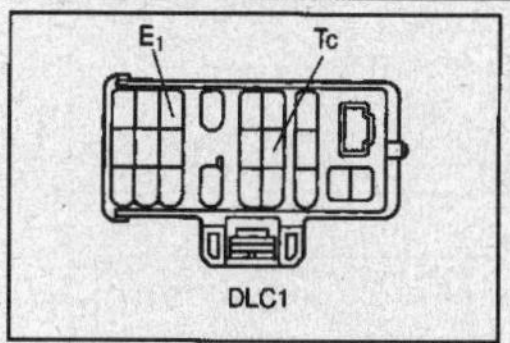
E1
Tc
DLC1

CHECK:

(a) Turn the ignition switch ON.

(b) Measure voltage between terminals Tc and E_1 of DLC1.

OK:

Voltage: 10 – 14 V

OK 〉 If ABS warning light does not blink even after Tc and E_1 are connected, the ECU may be defective.

NG

TY4029600227010X

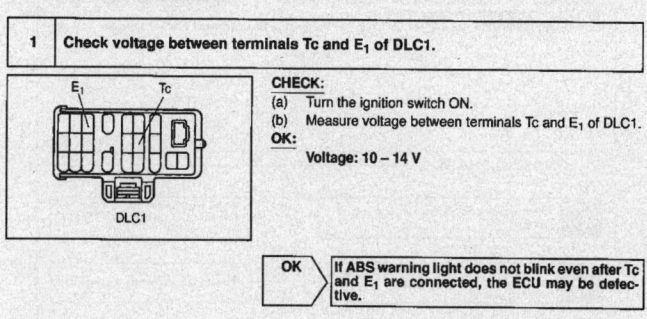

Fig. 80 Tc terminal circuit (Part 1 of 2). 1996 4Runner

2 Check for open and short in harness and connector between ABS ECU and DLC1, DLC1 and body ground.

NG 〉 Repair or replace harness or connector.

OK

Check and replace ABS ECU.

TY4029600227020X

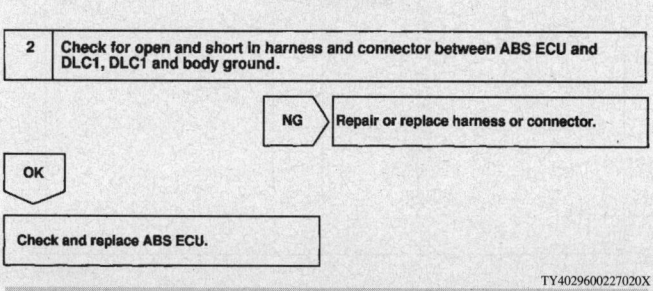

Fig. 80 Tc terminal circuit (Part 2 of 2). 1996 4Runner

CIRCUIT DESCRIPTION

Connecting terminals Tc and E1 of the DLC1 causes the ECU to display the DTC by flasing the ABS warning light.

WIRING DIAGRAM

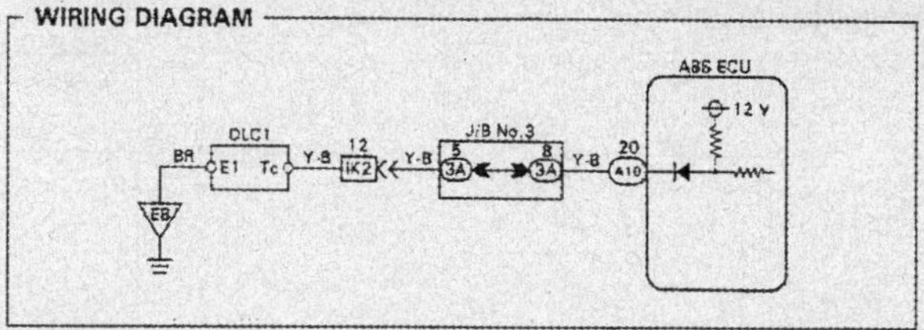
ABS ECU
12 V
DLC1
J/B No.3
BR
E1
Tc
Y-B
12
IK2
Y-B
5
3A
8
3A
Y-B
20
A10
EB

INSPECTION PROCEDURE

1 Check voltage between terminals Tc and E1 of DLC1.

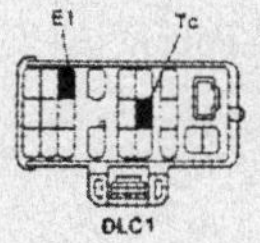
E1
Tc
DLC1

C 1. Turn the ignition switch ON.
2. Measure voltage between terminals Tc and E1 of DLC1.

OK Voltage: 10 – 14 V

NG

OK 〉 If ABS warning light does not blink even after Tc and E1 are connected, the ECU may be defective.

2 Check for open and short in harness and connector between ABS ECU and DLC1, DLC1 and body ground

OK

NG 〉 Repair or replace harness or connector.

Check and replace ABS ECU.

TY4029500176000X

Fig. 81 Tc terminal circuit inspection & testing. Tacoma

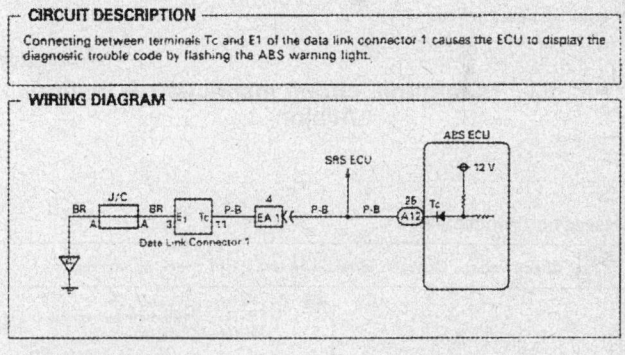

CIRCUIT DESCRIPTION

Connecting between terminals Tc and E1 of the data link connector 1 causes the ECU to display the diagnostic trouble code by flashing the ABS warning light.

WIRING DIAGRAM

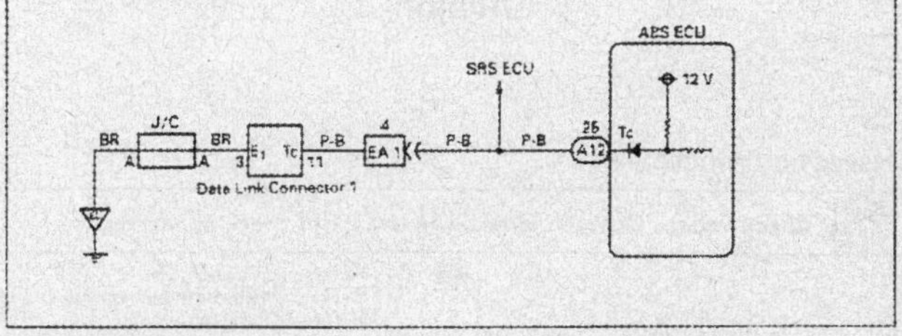
ABS ECU
SRS ECU
12 V
J/C
BR
BR
P-B
4
EA1
P-B
P-B
25
Tc
A12
Data Link Connector 1

INSPECTION PROCEDURE

1 Check voltage between terminals Tc and E1 of Data Link Connector 1.

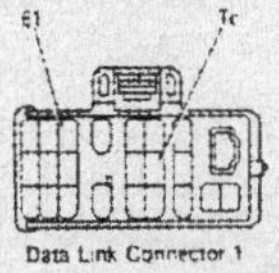
E1
Tc
Data Link Connector 1

C (1) Turn ignition switch ON.
(2) Measure voltage between terminals Tc and E1 of the data link connector 1.

OK Voltage: 10 - 14 V

NG

OK 〉 If ABS warning light does not blink even after Tc and E1 are connected, the ECU may be defective.

2 Check for open and short in harness and connector between ABS ECU and data link connector 1, data link connector 1 and body ground

OK

NG 〉 Repair or replace harness or connector.

Check and replace ABS ECU.

TY4029500186000X

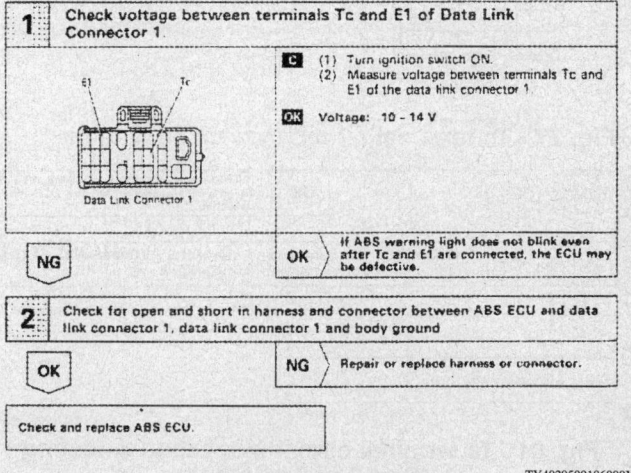

Fig. 82 Tc terminal circuit inspection & testing. 1995–96 Tercel

CIRCUIT DESCRIPTION

The sensor check circuit detects abnormalities in the speed sensor signal which cannot be detected with the diagnostic trouble code check.
Connecting terminals Ts and E1 of the DLC1 in the engine compartment starts the check.

WIRING DIAGRAM

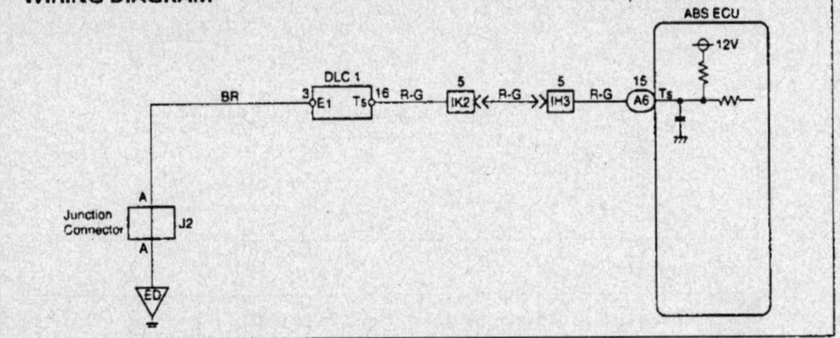
ABS ECU
12V
DLC 1
BR
3
E1
Ts
16
R-G
5
IK2
R-G
5
IH3
R-G
15
A6
Ts
A
Junction Connector
J2
A
ED

INSPECTION PROCEDURE

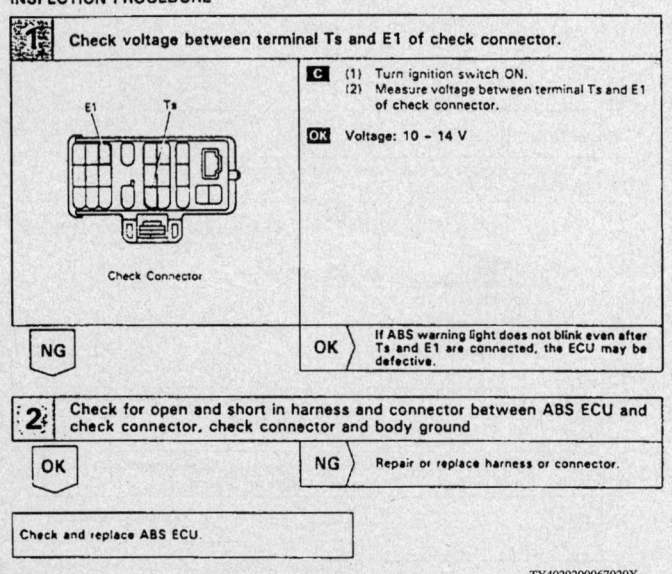

1 Check voltage between terminals Ts and E1 of DLC1.

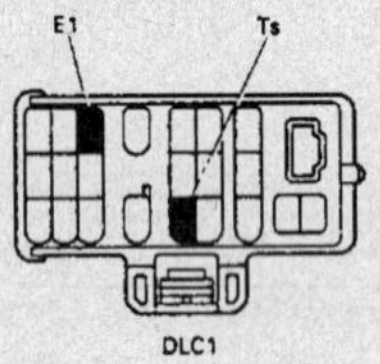
E1
Ts
DLC1

C
1. Turn ignition switch ON.
2. Measure voltage between terminals Ts and E1 of DLC1.

OK Voltage: 10 – 14 V

NG

OK → If ABS warning light does not blink even after Ts and E1 are connected, the ECU may be defective.

2 Check for open and short in harness and connector between ABS ECU and DLC1, DLC1 and body ground

OK

NG → Repair or replace harness or connector.

Check and replace ABS ECU.

TY4029500163000X

Fig. 83 Ts terminal circuit inspection & testing. Avalon

CIRCUIT DESCRIPTION

The sensor check circuit detects abnormalities in the speed sensor signal which can not be detected with the diagnostic code check.
Connecting terminals Tc and E1 of the check connector in the engine compartment starts the check.

DIAGNOSTIC CHART

1 Check voltage between terminals Ts and E1 of check connector. — OK → If ABS warning light does not blink even after Ts and E1 connected, the ECU may be defective.

NG

2 Check for open and short in harness and connector between ABS ECU and check connector, check connector and body ground — NG → Repair or replace harness or connector.

OK

Check and replace ABS ECU.

WIRING DIAGRAM

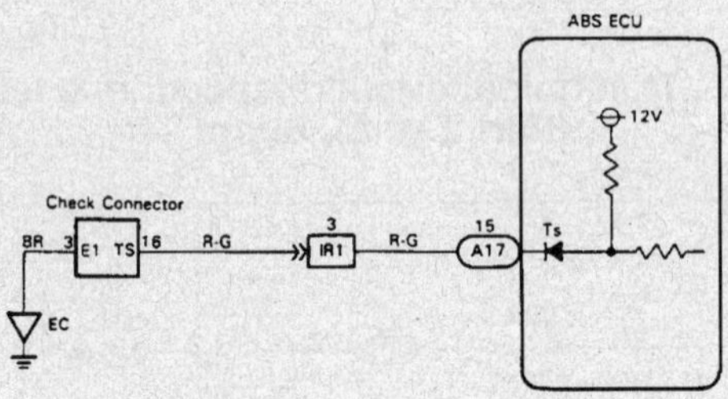
ABS ECU
12V
Check Connector
BR
3
E1
TS
16
R-G
3
IR1
R-G
15
A17
Ts
EC

TY4029200067010X

Fig. 84 Ts terminal circuit inspection & testing (Part 1 of 2). Camry

INSPECTION PROCEDURE

1 Check voltage between terminal Ts and E1 of check connector.

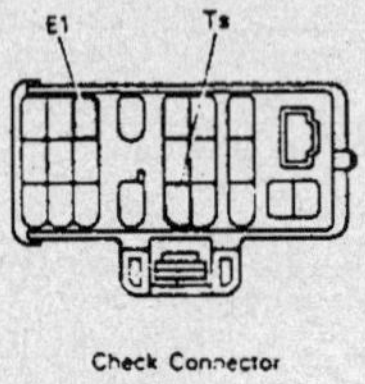
E1
Ts
Check Connector

C
(1) Turn ignition switch ON.
(2) Measure voltage between terminal Ts and E1 of check connector.

OK Voltage: 10 – 14 V

NG

OK → If ABS warning light does not blink even after Ts and E1 are connected, the ECU may be defective.

2 Check for open and short in harness and connector between ABS ECU and check connector, check connector and body ground

OK

NG → Repair or replace harness or connector.

Check and replace ABS ECU.

TY4029200067020X

Fig. 84 Ts terminal circuit inspection & testing (Part 2 of 2). Camry

CIRCUIT DESCRIPTION

The sensor check circuit detects abnormalities in the speed sensor signal which cannot be detected with the diagnostic trouble code check.
Connecting terminals Ts and E1 of the DLC1 in the engine compartment starts the check.

DIAGNOSTIC CHART

1 Check voltage between terminals Ts and E1 of DLC1. — OK → If ABS warning light does not blink even after Ts and E1 are connected, the ECU may be defective.

NG

2 Check for open and short in harness and connector between ABS ECU and DLC1, DLC1 and body ground — NG → Repair or replace harness or connector.

OK

Check and replace ABS ECU.

WIRING DIAGRAM

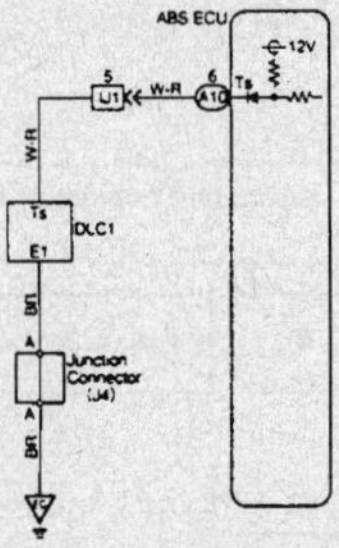
ABS ECU
12V
5
U1
W-R
6
A10
Ts
W-R
Ts
DLC1
E1
BR
Junction Connector
(J4)
BR

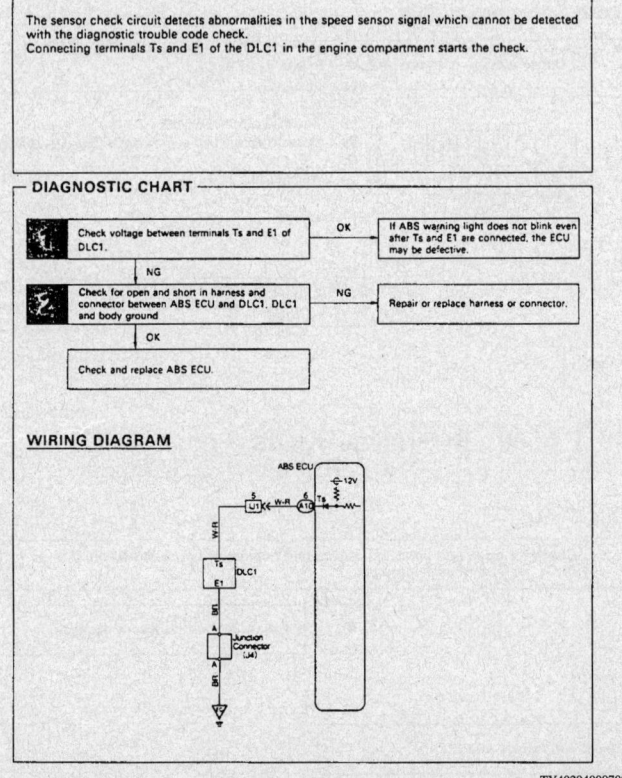

TY4029400070010X

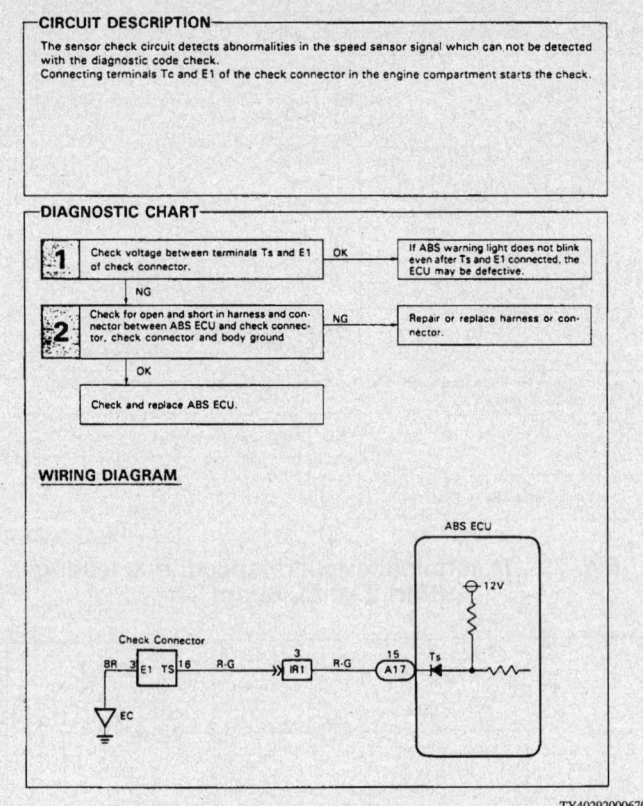

Fig. 85 Ts terminal circuit inspection & testing (Part 1 of 2). Celica

CIRCUIT DESCRIPTION

This relay supplies power to each ABS solenoid. After the ignition switch is turned on, if the initial check is OK, the relay goes on.

Code No.	Diagnostic Code Detecting Condition	Trouble area
11	Conditions (1) and (2) continue for 0.2 sec. or more: (1) ABS control (solenoid) relay: ON (2) ABS control (solenoid) relay monitor terminal (AST) voltage: 0 V	• ABS control (solenoid) relay. • Open or short in ABS control (solenoid) relay circuit. • ECU.
12	Conditions (1) and (2) continue for 0.2 sec. or more: (1) ABS control (solenoid) relay: OFF (2) ABS control (solenoid) relay monitor terminal (AST) voltage: Battery voltage.	• ABS control (solenoid) relay. • +B short in ABS control (solenoid) relay circuit. • ECU.

Fail safe function: If trouble occurs in the control (solenoid) relay circuit, the ECU cuts off current to the ABS control (solenoid) relay and prohibits ABS control.

DIAGNOSTIC CHART

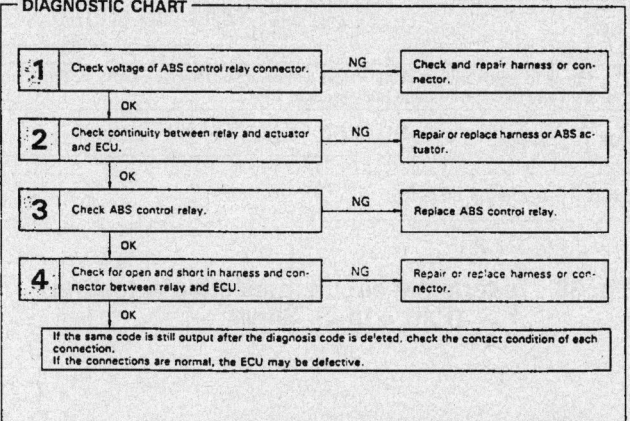

1. Check voltage of ABS control relay connector. — NG → Check and repair harness or connector.
   OK
2. Check continuity between relay and actuator and ECU. — NG → Repair or replace harness or ABS actuator.
   OK
3. Check ABS control relay. — NG → Replace ABS control relay.
   OK
4. Check for open and short in harness and connector between relay and ECU. — NG → Repair or replace harness or connector.
   OK

If the same code is still output after the diagnosis code is deleted, check the contact condition of each connection.
If the connections are normal, the ECU may be defective.

TY4029400070020X

Fig. 85 Ts terminal circuit inspection & testing (Part 2 of 2). Celica

CIRCUIT DESCRIPTION

The sensor check circuit detects abnormalities in the speed sensor signal which can not be detected with the diagnostic trouble code check.
Connecting terminals Ts and E1 of the data link connector 1 in the engine compartment starts the check.

DIAGNOSTIC CHART

1. Check voltage between terminals Ts and E1 of the data link connector 1. — OK → If ABS warning light does not blink even after Ts and E1 are connected, the ECU may be defective.
   NG
2. Check for open and short in harness and connector between ABS ECU and data link connector 1, data link connector 1 and body ground — NG → Repair or replace harness or connector.
   OK

Check and replace ABS ECU.

WIRING DIAGRAM

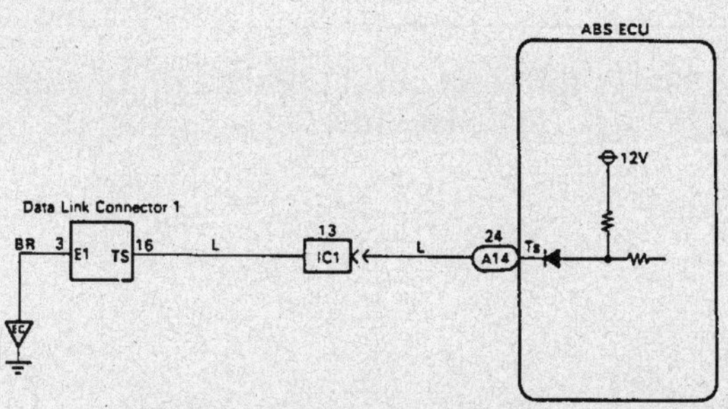

ABS ECU
12V
Data Link Connector 1
BR
3
E1
TS
16
L
13
IC1
L
24
A14
Ts

TY4029300068010X

Fig. 86 Ts terminal circuit inspection & testing (Part 1 of 2). Corolla

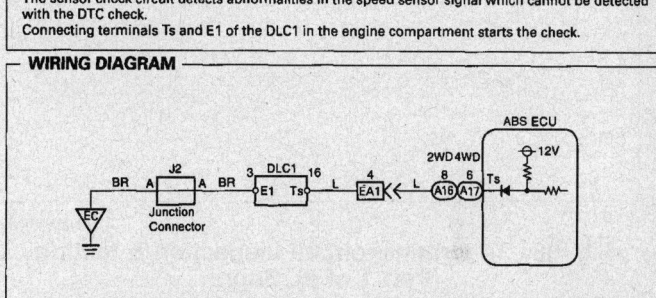

INSPECTION PROCEDURE

1 Check voltage between terminals Ts and E1 of data link connector 1.

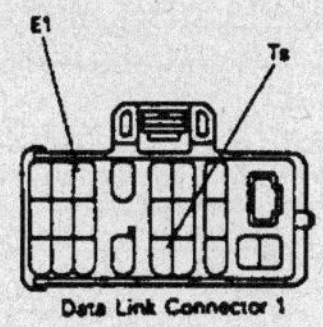

E1
Ts
Data Link Connector 1

C (1) Turn ignition switch ON.
(2) Measure voltage between terminals Ts and E1 of the data link connector 1.

OK Voltage: 10 – 14 V

NG

OK → If ABS warning light does not blink even after Ts and E1 are connected, the ECU may be defective.

2 Check for open and short in harness and connector between ABS ECU and data link connector 1, data link connector 1 and body ground

OK

NG → Repair or replace harness or connector.

Check and replace ABS ECU.

TY4029300068020X

Fig. 86 Ts terminal circuit inspection & testing (Part 2 of 2). Corolla

CIRCUIT DESCRIPTION

The sensor check circuit detects abnormalities in the speed sensor signal which cannot be detected with the DTC check.
Connecting terminals Ts and E1 of the DLC1 in the engine compartment starts the check.

WIRING DIAGRAM

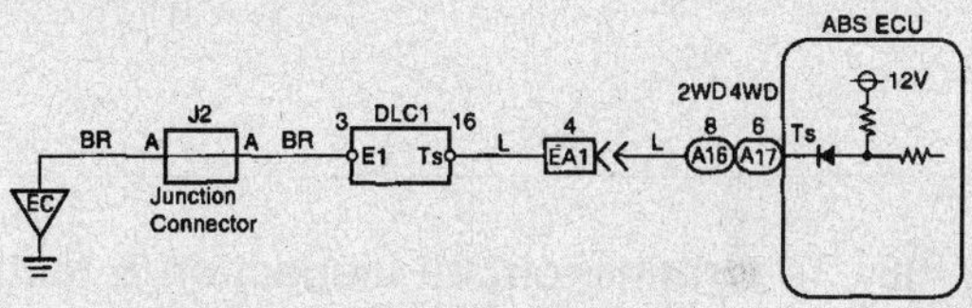

ABS ECU
12V
2WD 4WD
8 6
Ts
BR
A
J2
A
BR
3
DLC1
16
E1
Ts
L
4
EA1
L
A16
A17
EC
Junction Connector

TY4029600204010X

Fig. 87 Ts terminal circuit inspection & testing (Part 1 of 2). RAV4

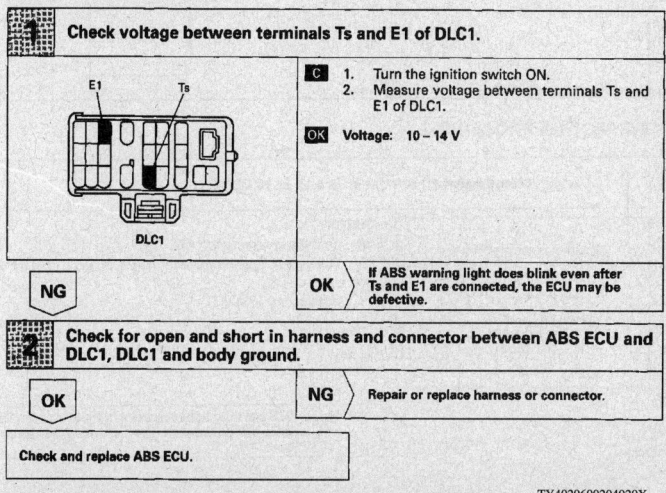

INSPECTION PROCEDURE

1 Check voltage between terminals Ts and E1 of DLC1.

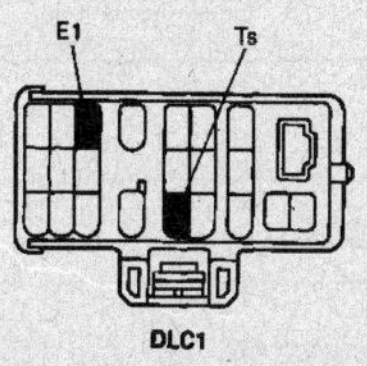

E1
Ts
DLC1

C 1. Turn the ignition switch ON.
2. Measure voltage between terminals Ts and E1 of DLC1.

OK Voltage: 10 – 14 V

NG

OK → If ABS warning light does blink even after Ts and E1 are connected, the ECU may be defective.

2 Check for open and short in harness and connector between ABS ECU and DLC1, DLC1 and body ground.

OK

NG → Repair or replace harness or connector.

Check and replace ABS ECU.

TY4029600204020X

Fig. 87 Ts terminal circuit inspection & testing (Part 2 of 2). RAV4

CIRCUIT DESCRIPTION

The sensor check circuit detects abnormalities in the speed sensor signal which can not be detected with the diagnostic trouble code check.
Connecting terminals Ts and E1 of the DLC1 in the engine compartment starts the check.

DIAGNOSTIC CHART

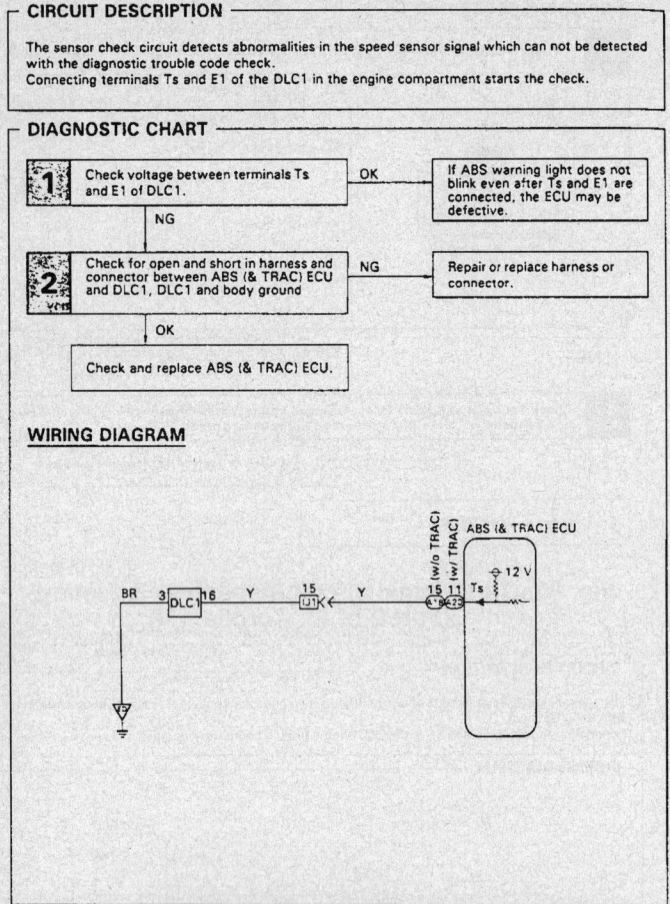

1. Check voltage between terminals Ts and E1 of DLC1.
   - OK → If ABS warning light does not blink even after Ts and E1 are connected, the ECU may be defective.
   - NG → go to 2
2. Check for open and short in harness and connector between ABS (& TRAC) ECU and DLC1, DLC1 and body ground
   - NG → Repair or replace harness or connector.
   - OK → Check and replace ABS (& TRAC) ECU.

WIRING DIAGRAM

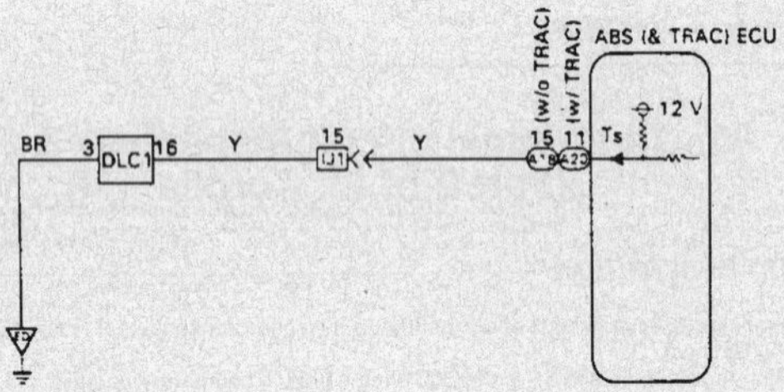

ABS (& TRAC) ECU
(w/o TRAC)
(w/ TRAC)
12 V
BR
3
DLC1
16
Y
15
IJ1
Y
15
11
Ts

TY4029300069010X

Fig. 88 Ts terminal circuit inspection & testing (Part 1 of 2). Supra

1	Check voltage between terminals Ts and E1 of DLC1.

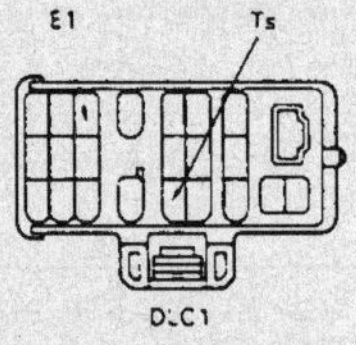

E1
Ts
DLC1

P Turn ignition switch ON.

C Measure voltage between terminals Ts and E1 of DLC1.

OK Voltage: 10 – 14 V

OK → If ABS warning light does not blink even after Ts and E1 are connected, the ECU may be defective.

NG ↓

2	Check for open and short in harness and connector between ABS (& TRAC) ECU and DLC1, DLC1 and body ground

NG → Repair or replace harness or connector.

OK ↓

Check and replace ABS (& TRAC) ECU.

TY4029300069020X

Fig. 88 Ts terminal circuit inspection & testing (Part 2 of 2). Supra

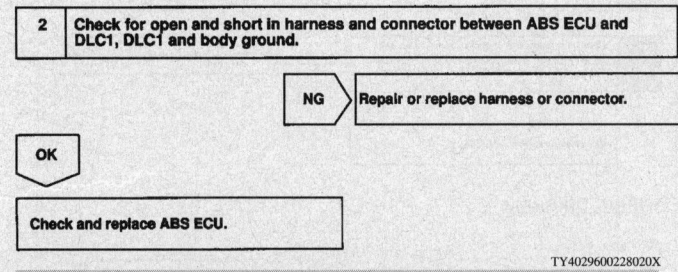

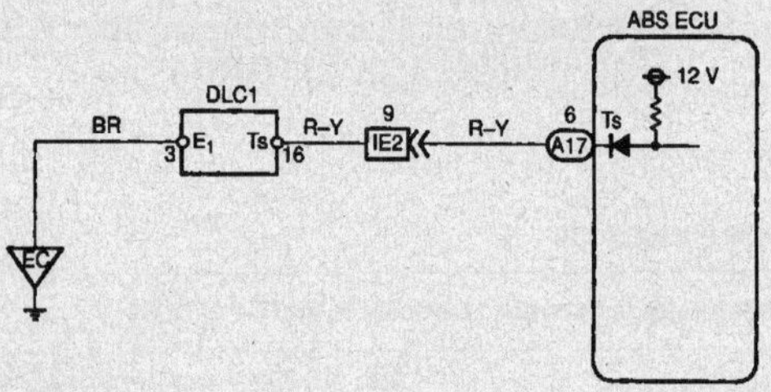

ABS ECU
12 V
DLC1
BR
3
E_1
Ts
16
R–Y
9
IE2
R–Y
6
A17
Ts
EC

INSPECTION PROCEDURE

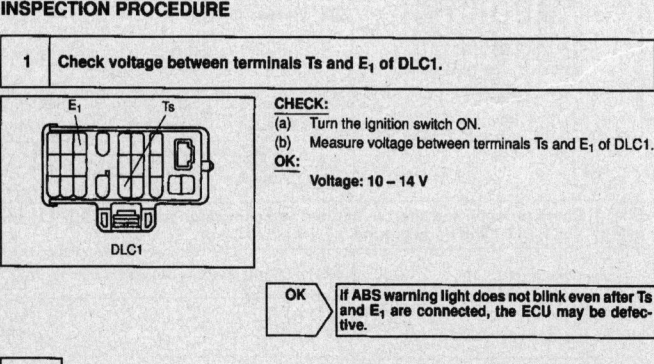

1	Check voltage between terminals Ts and E_1 of DLC1.

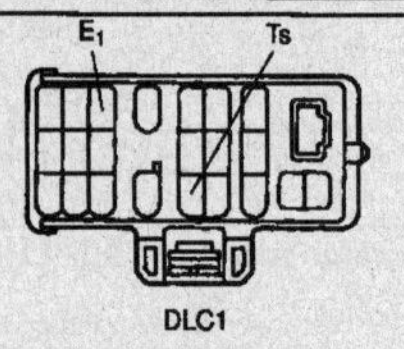

E_1
Ts
DLC1

CHECK:
(a) Turn the ignition switch ON.
(b) Measure voltage between terminals Ts and E_1 of DLC1.

OK:
Voltage: 10 – 14 V

OK → If ABS warning light does not blink even after Ts and E_1 are connected, the ECU may be defective.

NG ↓

TY4029600228010X

Fig. 89 Ts terminal circuit (Part 1 of 2). 1996 4Runner

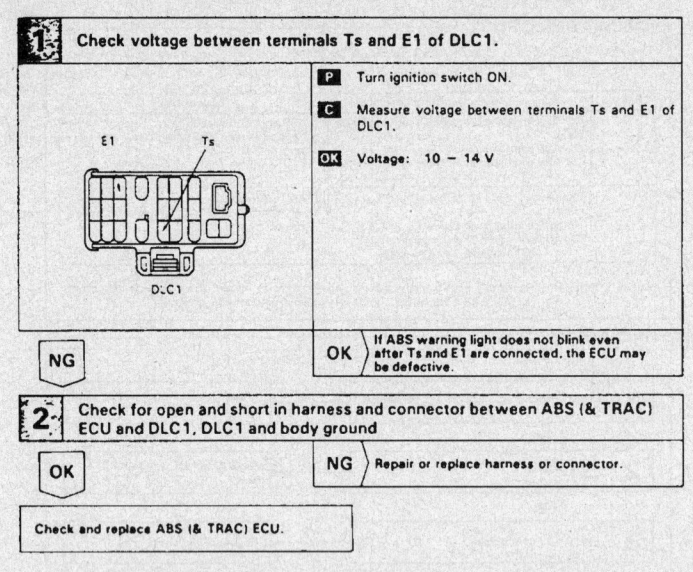

2	Check for open and short in harness and connector between ABS ECU and DLC1, DLC1 and body ground.

NG → Repair or replace harness or connector.

OK ↓

Check and replace ABS ECU.

TY4029600228020X

Fig. 89 Ts terminal circuit (Part 2 of 2). 1996 4Runner

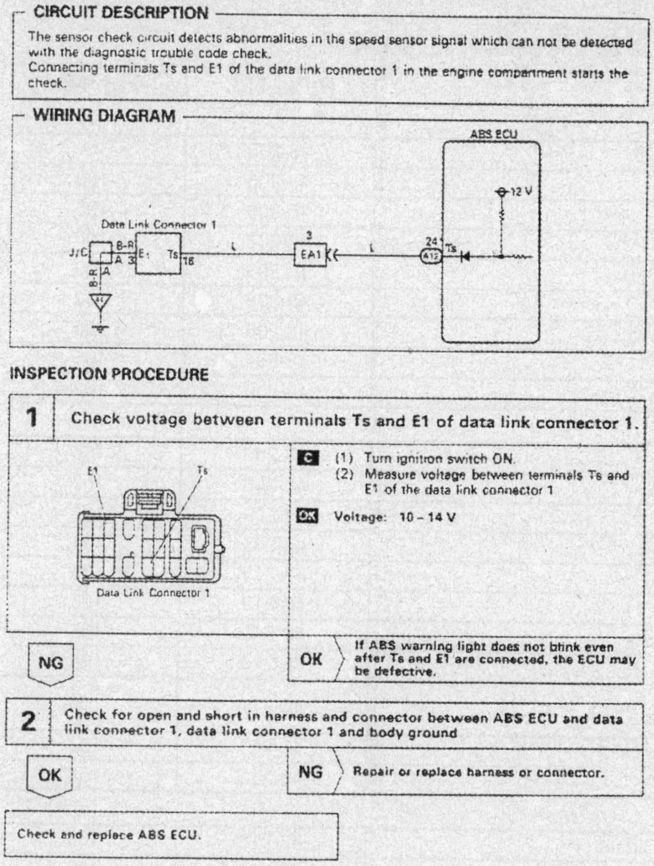
CIRCUIT DESCRIPTION
The sensor check circuit detects abnormalities in the speed sensor signal which can not be detected with the diagnostic trouble code check.
Connecting terminals Ts and E1 of the data link connector 1 in the engine compartment starts the check.
WIRING DIAGRAM
ABS ECU
12 V
Data Link Connector 1
J/C
B-R
A
E1
Ts
16
3
EA1
L
24
A12
Ts
INSPECTION PROCEDURE
1
Check voltage between terminals Ts and E1 of data link connector 1.
E1
Ts
Data Link Connector 1
C (1) Turn ignition switch ON.
(2) Measure voltage between terminals Ts and E1 of the data link connector 1
OK Voltage: 10 – 14 V
NG
OK
If ABS warning light does not blink even after Ts and E1 are connected, the ECU may be defective.
2
Check for open and short in harness and connector between ABS ECU and data link connector 1, data link connector 1 and body ground
OK
NG
Repair or replace harness or connector.
Check and replace ABS ECU.
TY4029500187000X

Fig. 91 Ts terminal circuit inspection & testing. 1995–96 Tercel

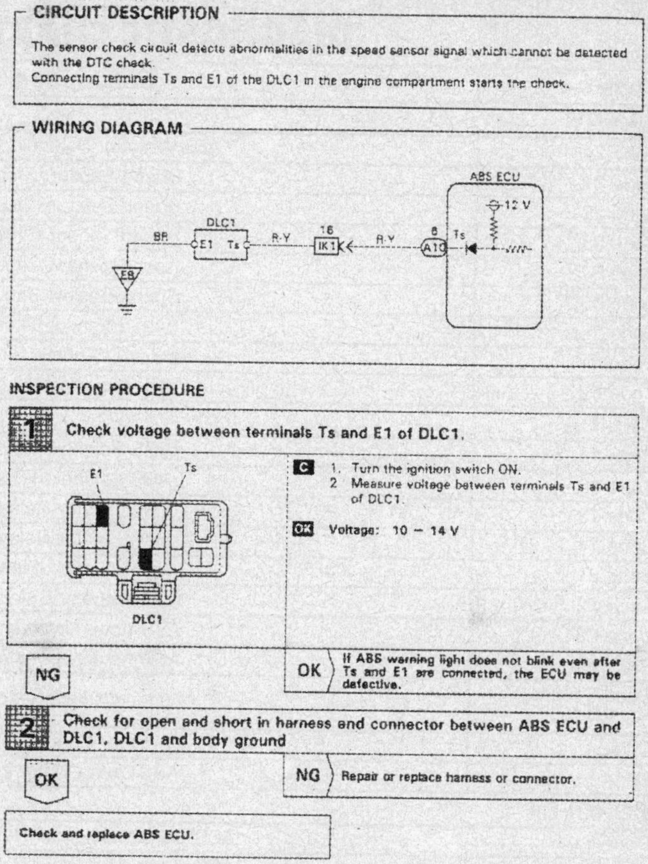
CIRCUIT DESCRIPTION
The sensor check circuit detects abnormalities in the speed sensor signal which cannot be detected with the DTC check.
Connecting terminals Ts and E1 of the DLC1 in the engine compartment starts the check.
WIRING DIAGRAM
ABS ECU
12 V
DLC1
BR
E1
Ts
R-Y
16
IK1
R-Y
6
A10
Ts
EB
INSPECTION PROCEDURE
1
Check voltage between terminals Ts and E1 of DLC1.
E1
Ts
DLC1
C 1. Turn the ignition switch ON.
2. Measure voltage between terminals Ts and E1 of DLC1.
OK Voltage: 10 – 14 V
NG
OK
If ABS warning light does not blink even after Ts and E1 are connected, the ECU may be defective.
2
Check for open and short in harness and connector between ABS ECU and DLC1, DLC1 and body ground
OK
NG
Repair or replace harness or connector.
Check and replace ABS ECU.
TY4029500177000X

Fig. 90 Ts terminal circuit inspection & testing. Tacoma

DIAGNOSTIC CHART INDEX

Code	Description	Page No.	Fig. No.
AVALON			
Code 11	ABS Solenoid & Motor Relay Circuit	48-201	92
Code 13	ABS Solenoid & Motor Relay Circuit	48-201	92
Code 21	ABS Actuator Solenoid Circuit	48-201	93
Code 22	ABS Actuator Solenoid Circuit	48-201	93
Code 23	ABS Actuator Solenoid Circuit	48-201	93
Code 31	Speed Sensor Circuit	48-202	94
Code 32	Speed Sensor Circuit	48-202	94
Code 33	Speed Sensor Circuit	48-202	94
Code 34	Speed Sensor Circuit	48-202	94
Code 35	Speed Sensor Circuit	48-202	94
Code 36	Speed Sensor Circuit	48-202	94
Code 38	Speed Sensor Circuit	48-202	94
Code 39	Speed Sensor Circuit	48-202	94
Code 41	+BS Power Source Circuit	48-203	95
Code 51	ABS Pump Motor Lock	48-203	96
CAMRY			
Code 11	ABS Control Solenoid Relay Circuit	48-203	97
Code 12	ABS Control Solenoid Relay Circuit	48-203	97
Code 13	ABS Control Motor Relay Circuit	48-204	98
Code 14	ABS Control Motor Relay Circuit	48-204	98
Code 21	ABS Actuator Solenoid Circuit	48-205	99
Code 22	ABS Actuator Solenoid Circuit	48-205	99
Code 23	ABS Actuator Solenoid Circuit	48-205	99

Continued

DIAGNOSTIC CHART INDEX—Continued

Code	Description	Page No.	Fig. No.
CAMRY			
Code 24	ABS Actuator Solenoid Circuit	48-205	99
Code 31	Speed Sensor Circuit	48-206	100
Code 32	Speed Sensor Circuit	48-206	100
Code 33	Speed Sensor Circuit	48-206	100
Code 34	Speed Sensor Circuit	48-206	100
Code 35	Speed Sensor Circuit	48-206	100
Code 36	Speed Sensor Circuit	48-206	100
Code 41	IG Power Source Circuit	48-207	101
Code 52	ABS Pump Motor Lock	48-208	102
CELICA			
Code 11	ABS Solenoid Relay	48-208	103
Code 12	ABS Solenoid Relay	48-208	103
Code 13	ABS Motor Relay	48-209	104
Code 14	ABS Motor Relay	48-209	104
Code 21	ABS Actuator Solenoid	48-210	105
Code 22	ABS Actuator Solenoid	48-210	105
Code 23	ABS Actuator Solenoid	48-210	105
Code 24	ABS Actuator Solenoid	48-210	105
Code 31 through 36	Speed Sensor Circuit	48-211	106
Code 41	IG Power Source Circuit	48-212	107
Code 51	ABS Pump Motor Lock	48-213	108
COROLLA			
Code 11	ABS Control Solenoid Relay Circuit	48-213	109
Code 12	ABS Control Solenoid Relay Circuit	48-213	109
Code 13	ABS Control Motor Relay Circuit	48-214	110
Code 14	ABS Control Motor Relay Circuit	48-214	110
Code 21	ABS Actuator Solenoid Circuit	48-215	111
Code 22	ABS Actuator Solenoid Circuit	48-215	111
Code 23	ABS Actuator Solenoid Circuit	48-215	111
Code 24	ABS Actuator Solenoid Circuit	48-215	111
Code 31	Speed Sensor Circuit	48-216	112
Code 32	Speed Sensor Circuit	48-216	112
Code 33	Speed Sensor Circuit	48-216	112
Code 34	Speed Sensor Circuit	48-216	112
Code 35	Speed Sensor Circuit	48-216	112
Code 36	Speed Sensor Circuit	48-216	112
Code 41	IG Power Source	48-217	113
Code 51	ABS Pump Motor Lock	48-218	114
RAV4			
Code 11	ABS Control Solenoid Relay Circuit	48-218	115
Code 12	ABS Control Solenoid Relay Circuit	48-218	115
Code 13	ABS Control Motor Relay Circuit	48-219	116
Code 14	ABS Control Motor Relay Circuit	48-219	116
Code 21	ABS Actuator Solenoid Circuit	48-219	117
Code 22	ABS Actuator Solenoid Circuit	48-219	117
Code 23	ABS Actuator Solenoid Circuit	48-219	117
Code 24	ABS Actuator Solenoid Circuit	48-219	117
Code 31	Speed Sensor Circuit	48-220	118
Code 32	Speed Sensor Circuit	48-220	118
Code 33	Speed Sensor Circuit	48-220	118
Code 34	Speed Sensor Circuit	48-220	118
Code 35	Speed Sensor Circuit	48-220	118
Code 37	Tires Of Different Size	48-220	119
Code 41	IG Power Source Circuit	48-220	120
Code 43	Malfunction In Deceleration Sensor	48-221	121

Continued

DIAGNOSTIC CHART INDEX—Continued

Code	Description	Page No.	Fig. No.
RAV4			
Code 45	Malfunction In Deceleration Sensor	48-221	121
Code 44	Deceleration Sensor Circuit	48-221	122
Code 51	ABS Pump Motor Lock	48-222	123
SUPRA			
Code 11	ABS Solenoid Relay	48-222	124
Code 12	ABS Solenoid Relay	48-222	124
Code 13①	ABS Motor Relay	48-223	125
Code 14①	ABS Motor Relay	48-223	125
Code 15	TRAC Solenoid Relay	48-225	126
Code 16	TRAC Solenoid Relay	48-225	126
Code 17	TRAC Motor Relay	48-226	127
Code 18	TRAC Motor Relay	48-226	127
Code 21	ABS Actuator Solenoid	48-227	128
Code 22	ABS Actuator Solenoid	48-227	128
Code 23	ABS Actuator Solenoid	48-227	128
Code 24	ABS Actuator Solenoid	48-227	128
Code 25	TRAC Actuator Solenoid	48-228	129
Code 27	TRAC Actuator Solenoid	48-228	129
Code 31 through 36	Speed Sensor	48-228	130
Code 41	IG Power Source Circuit	48-229	131
Code 44	Lateral Acceleration Sensor Circuit	48-230	132
Code 51	ABS Pump Motor Lock	48-231	133
Code 55	Brake Fluid Level Warning Switch	48-231	134
Code 58	TRAC Pump Motor	48-232	135
Code 61	TRAC ECU Communication Circuit Malfunction	48-232	136
Code 62	TRAC Vehicle Speed Malfunction	48-233	137
1996 4RUNNER			
Code 11	ABS Control Solenoid Relay Circuit	48-233	138
Code 12	ABS Control Solenoid Relay Circuit	48-233	138
Code 13	ABS Control Motor Relay Circuit	48-234	139
Code 14	ABS Control Motor Relay Circuit	48-234	139
Code 21	ABS Actuator Solenoid Circuit	48-235	140
Code 22	ABS Actuator Solenoid Circuit	48-235	140
Code 23	ABS Actuator Solenoid Circuit	48-235	140
Code 31	Speed Sensor Circuit	48-235	141
Code 32	Speed Sensor Circuit	48-235	141
Code 33	Speed Sensor Circuit	48-235	141
Code 34	Speed Sensor Circuit	48-235	141
Code 37	Neither Front Speed Sensor Rotor Missing	48-236	142
Code 37	Tires Of Different Size	48-236	143
Code 41	IG Power Source Circuit	48-236	144
Code 43	Malfunction In Deceleration Sensor	48-237	145
Code 44	Deceleration Sensor Circuit	48-237	146
Code 48	Rear Differential Lock Circuit	48-237	147
Code 51	ABS Pump Motor Lock	48-238	148
TACOMA			
Code 11	ABS Control Solenoid Relay Circuit	48-238	149
Code 12	ABS Control Solenoid Relay Circuit	48-238	149
Code 13	ABS Control Motor Relay Circuit	48-239	150
Code 14	ABS Control Motor Relay Circuit	48-239	150
Code 21	ABS Actuator Solenoid Circuit	48-240	151
Code 22	ABS Actuator Solenoid Circuit	48-240	151
Code 23	ABS Actuator Solenoid Circuit	48-240	151
Code 31	Speed Sensor Circuit	48-240	152
Code 32	Speed Sensor Circuit	48-240	152

Continued

DIAGNOSTIC CHART INDEX—Continued

Code	Description	Page No.	Fig. No.
TACOMA			
Code 33	Speed Sensor Circuit	48-240	152
Code 34	Speed Sensor Circuit	48-240	152
Code 35	Speed Sensor Circuit	48-240	152
Code 36	Speed Sensor Circuit	48-240	152
Code 37	Neither Front Speed Sensor Rotor Missing	48-241	153
Code 37	Tires Of Different Size On 2WD Vehicles	48-241	154
Code 41	IG Power Source Circuit	48-241	155
Code 43	Malfunction In Deceleration Sensor	48-242	156
Code 44	Deceleration Sensor Circuit	48-242	157
Code 51	ABS Pump Motor Lock	48-243	158
1995–96 TERCEL			
Code 11	ABS Control Solenoid Relay Circuit	48-243	159
Code 12	ABS Control Solenoid Relay Circuit	48-243	159
Code 13	ABS Control Motor Relay Circuit	48-244	160
Code 14	ABS Control Motor Relay Circuit	48-244	160
Code 21	ABS Actuator Solenoid Circuit	48-245	161
Code 22	ABS Actuator Solenoid Circuit	48-245	161
Code 23	ABS Actuator Solenoid Circuit	48-245	161
Code 24	ABS Actuator Solenoid Circuit	48-245	161
Code 31	Speed Sensor Circuit	48-245	162
Code 32	Speed Sensor Circuit	48-245	162
Code 33	Speed Sensor Circuit	48-245	162
Code 34	Speed Sensor Circuit	48-245	162
Code 35	Speed Sensor Circuit	48-245	162
Code 36	Speed Sensor Circuit	48-245	162
Code 41	IG Power Source Circuit	48-246	163
Code 51	ABS Pump Motor Lock	48-247	164

① — Supra less traction control.

CIRCUIT DESCRIPTION

The solenoid relay supplies power to each ABS solenoid. After the ignition switch is turned ON, if the initial check is OK, the relay goes on. The motor relay supplies power to the ABS pump motor. While the ABS is activated, the ECU switches the motor relay ON and operates the ABS pump motor.

DTC No.	Diagnostic Trouble Code Detecting Condition	Trouble area
11	(1) 5V is applied to the solenoid voltage monitor terminal (AST) for 30 sec. or more, with the IG switch ON and the warning light on. (2) 5V is applied to the solenoid voltage monitor terminal (AST) for 0.02 sec. or more, after the warning light goes off.	• Open or short in ABS solenoid relay circuit • ECU
13	(1) The motor voltage monitor terminal (MT) is ON for 5 sec. or more, with the motor relay operation signal OFF. (2) The motor voltage monitor terminal (MT) is OFF for 0.04 sec. with the motor relay operation signal ON.	• Pump motor • Open in ABS motor relay circuit • ECU

Fail safe function: If trouble occurs in the control (solenoid) relay circuit, the ECU cuts off current to the ABS solenoid relay and prohibits ABS control.

WIRING DIAGRAM

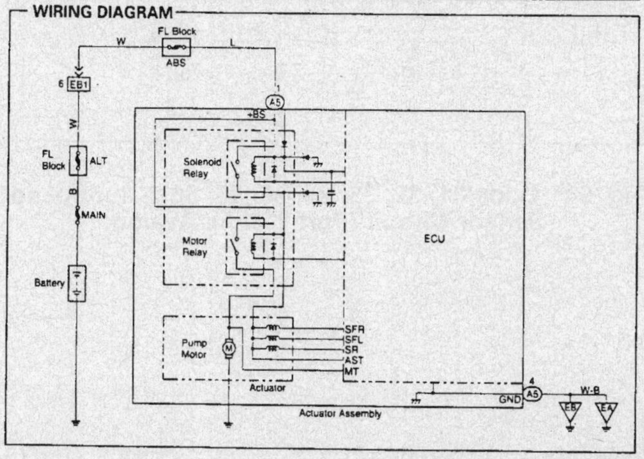
FL Block
W
L
ABS
6
EB1
A5
+BS
W
FL Block
ALT
B
MAIN
Battery
Solenoid Relay
Motor Relay
ECU
Pump Motor
SFR
SFL
SR
AST
MT
Actuator
4
GND
W-B
EB
EA
Actuator Assembly

TY4029500155010X

Fig. 92 Code 11 & 13: ABS Solenoid & Motor Relay Circuit (Part 1 of 2). Avalon

1	Check voltage between terminals (A5) 1 and (A5) 4 of ABS ECU connector.

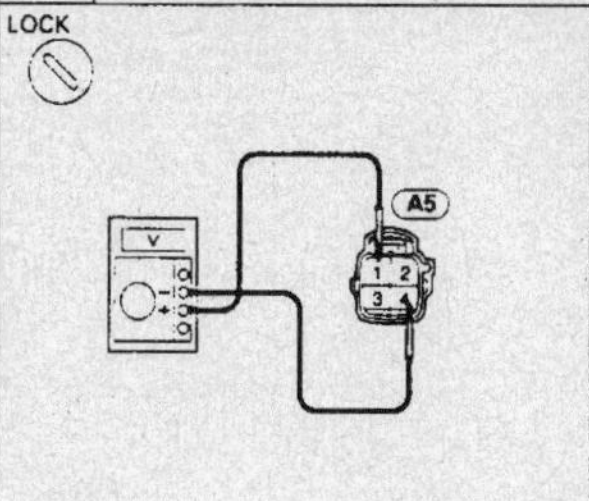
LOCK
V
A5
1
2
3
4

P Disconnect the ABS ECU connector.

C Measure voltage between terminals (A5) 1 and (A5) 4 of ABS ECU harness side connector.

OK Voltage: 10 – 14 V

OK

NG 〉 Check and repair harness or connector.

If the same code is still output after the diagnostic trouble code is deleted, check the contact condition of each connection.
If the connections are normal, the ECU may be defective.

TY4029500155020X

Fig. 92 Code 11 & 13: ABS Solenoid & Motor Relay Circuit (Part 2 of 2). Avalon

CIRCUIT DESCRIPTION

This solenoid goes on when signals are received from the ECU and controls the pressure acting on the wheel cylinders, thus controlling the braking force.

DTC No.	Diagnostic Trouble Code Detecting Condition	Trouble area
21	(1) 0V is applied to terminal SFR for 0.035 sec. while battery voltage is applied to the solenoid voltage monitor terminal (AST) and the ECM power transistor is OFF. (2) Battery voltage is applied to terminal SFR for 0.035 sec. while battery voltage is applied to the solenoid voltage monitor terminal (AST) and the ECM power transistor is ON.	• ABS actuator (soldnoid valve) • Open or short in right front solenoid circuit • ECU
22	(1) 0V is applied to terminal SFL for 0.035 sec. while battery voltage is applied to the solenoid voltage monitor terminal (AST) and the ECM power transistor is OFF. (2) Battery voltage is applied to terminal SFL for 0.035 sec. while battery voltage is applied to the solenoid voltage monitor terminal (AST) and the ECM power transistor is ON.	• ABS actuator (soldnoid valve) • Open or short in left front solenoid circuit • ECU
23	(1) 0V is applied to terminal SRA for 0.035 sec. while battery voltage is applied to the solenoid voltage monitor terminal (AST) and the ECM power transistor is OFF. (2) Battery voltage is applied to terminal SRA for 0.035 sec. while battery voltage is applied to the solenoid voltage monitor terminal (AST) and the ECM power transistor is ON.	• ABS actuator (solenoid valve) • Open or short in rear solenoid circuit • ECU

Fail safe function: If trouble occurs in the actuator solenoid circuit, the ECU cuts off current to the solenoid relay and prohibits ABS control.

TY4029500156010X

Fig. 93 Code 21, 22 & 23: ABS Actuator Solenoid Circuit (Part 1 of 2). Avalon

WIRING DIAGRAM

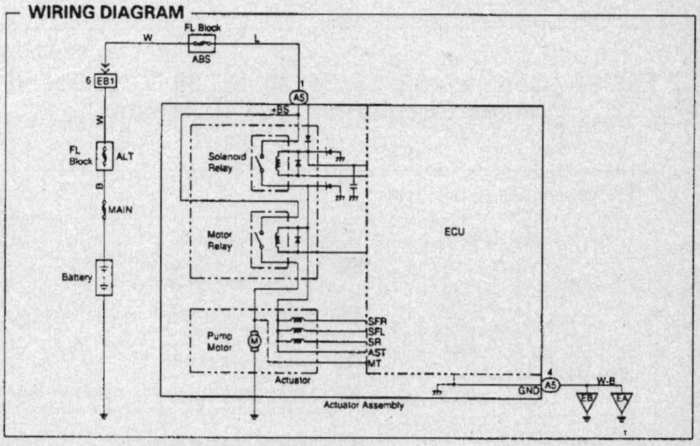
FL Block
W
L
ABS
6
EB1
A5
+BS
W
FL Block
ALT
B
MAIN
Battery
Solenoid Relay
Motor Relay
ECU
Pump Motor
SFR
SFL
SR
AST
MT
Actuator
4
GND
W-B
EB
EA
Actuator Assembly

INSPECTION PROCEDURE

1	Check ABS actuator solenoid.

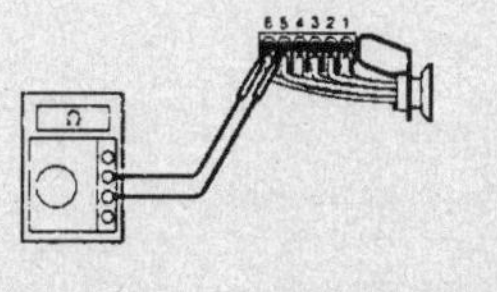
6 5 4 3 2 1

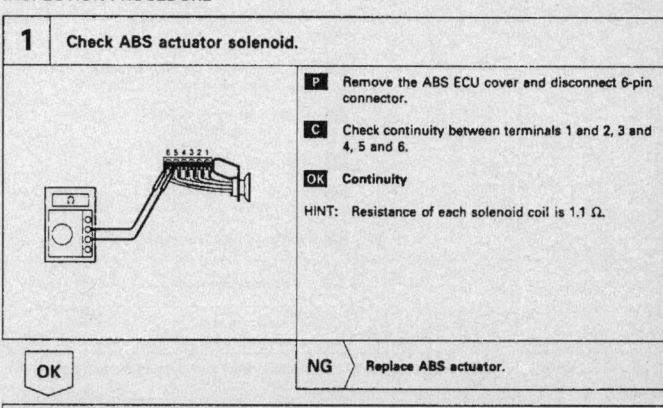

P Remove the ABS ECU cover and disconnect 6-pin connector.

C Check continuity between terminals 1 and 2, 3 and 4, 5 and 6.

OK Continuity

HINT: Resistance of each solenoid coil is 1.1 Ω.

OK

NG 〉 Replace ABS actuator.

If the same code is still output after the diagnostic trouble code is deleted, check the contact condition of each connection.
If the connections are normal, the ECU may be defective.

TY4029500156020X

Fig. 93 Code 21, 22 & 23: ABS Actuator Solenoid Circuit (Part 2 of 2). Avalon

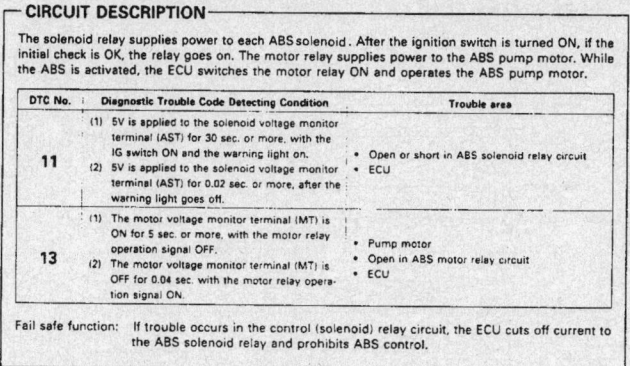

CIRCUIT DESCRIPTION

The speed sensor detects the wheel speed and sends the appropriate signals to the ECU. These signals are used to control the ABS system. The front and rear rotors each have 48 serrations.
When the rotors rotate, the magnetic field emitted by the permanent magnet in the speed sensor generates an AC voltage. Since the frequency of this AC voltage changes in direct proportion to the speed of the rotor, the frequency is used by the ECU to detect the speed of each wheel.

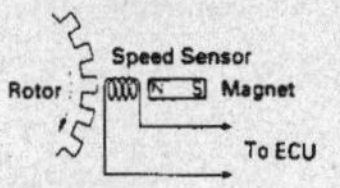
Speed Sensor
Rotor
N S Magnet
To ECU

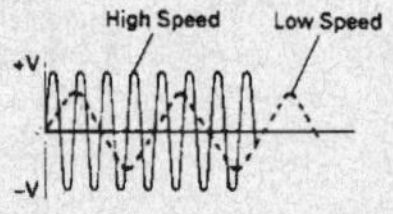
High Speed
Low Speed
+V
-V

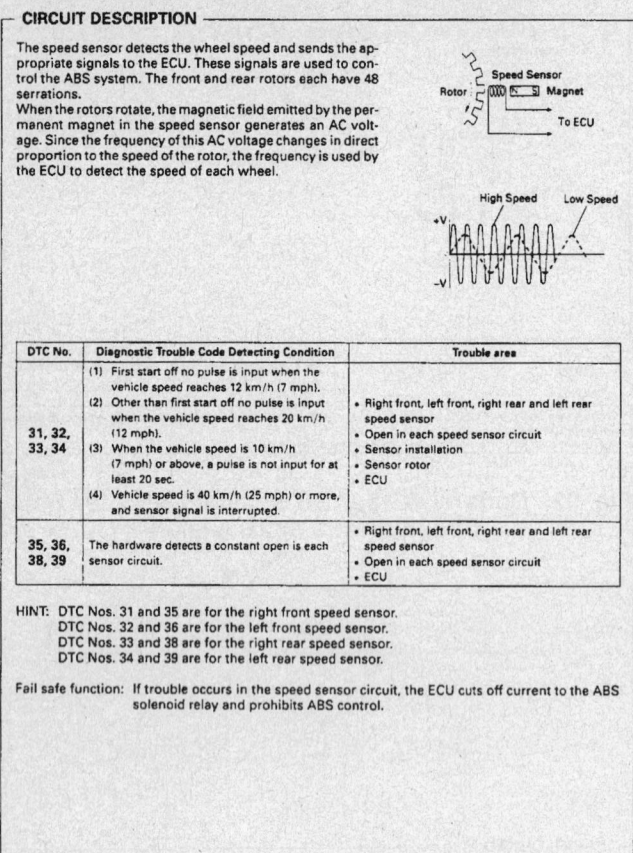

DTC No.	Diagnostic Trouble Code Detecting Condition	Trouble area
31, 32, 33, 34	(1) First start off no pulse is input when the vehicle speed reaches 12 km/h (7 mph). (2) Other than first start off no pulse is input when the vehicle speed reaches 20 km/h (12 mph). (3) When the vehicle speed is 10 km/h (7 mph) or above, a pulse is not input for at least 20 sec. (4) Vehicle speed is 40 km/h (25 mph) or more, and sensor signal is interrupted.	• Right front, left front, right rear and left rear speed sensor • Open in each speed sensor circuit • Sensor installation • Sensor rotor • ECU
35, 36, 38, 39	The hardware detects a constant open is each sensor circuit.	• Right front, left front, right rear and left rear speed sensor • Open in each speed sensor circuit • ECU

HINT: DTC Nos. 31 and 35 are for the right front speed sensor.
DTC Nos. 32 and 36 are for the left front speed sensor.
DTC Nos. 33 and 38 are for the right rear speed sensor.
DTC Nos. 34 and 39 are for the left rear speed sensor.

Fail safe function: If trouble occurs in the speed sensor circuit, the ECU cuts off current to the ABS solenoid relay and prohibits ABS control.

TY4029500157010X

Fig. 94 Code 31, 32, 33, 34, 35, 36, 38 & 39: Speed Sensor Circuit (Part 1 of 4). Avalon

WIRING DIAGRAM

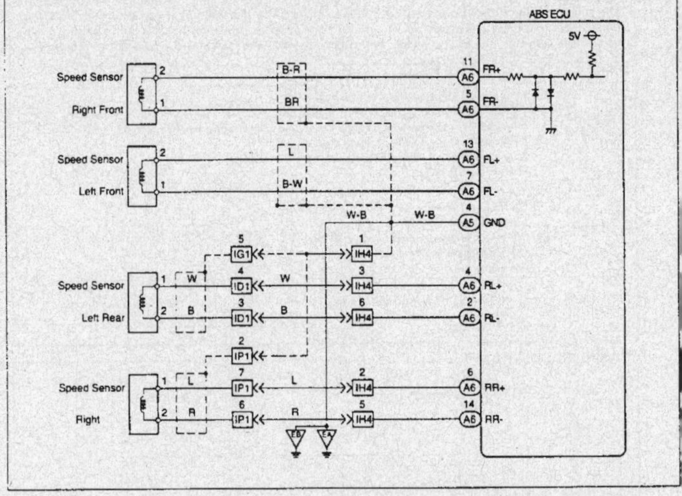
ABS ECU
5V
Speed Sensor
Right Front
B-R
BR
FR+
FR-
Speed Sensor
Left Front
L
B-W
FL+
FL-
W-B
W-B
GND
IG1
IH4
Speed Sensor
Left Rear
W
B
ID1
RL+
RL-
IP1
Speed Sensor
Right
L
R
RR+
RR-
EB
EA

TY4029500157020X

Fig. 94 Code 31, 32, 33, 34, 35, 36, 38 & 39: Speed Sensor Circuit (Part 2 of 4). Avalon

1 Check speed sensor.

Front

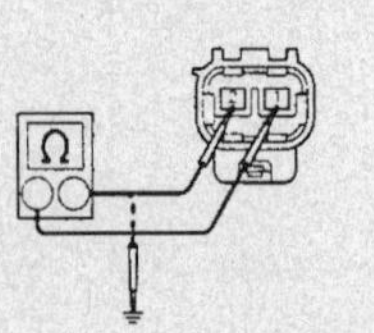

Front

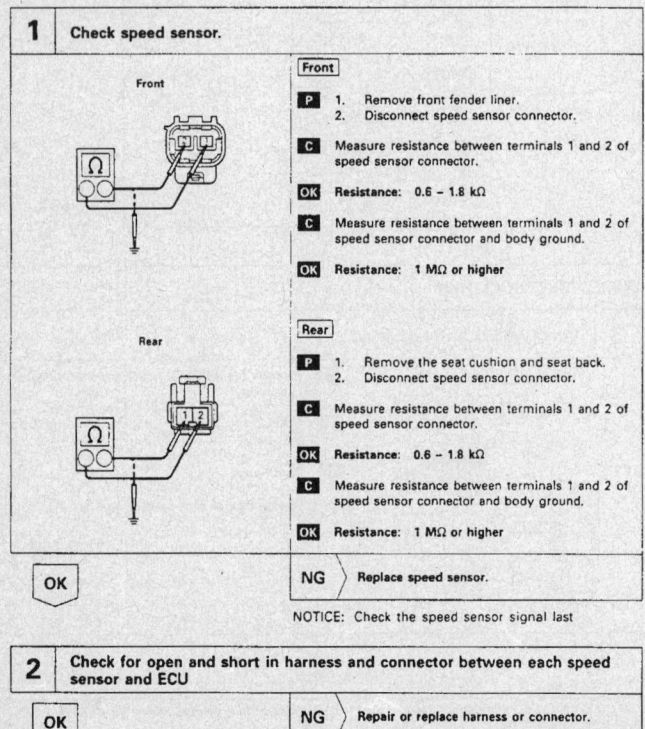

P 1. Remove front fender liner.
2. Disconnect speed sensor connector.

C Measure resistance between terminals 1 and 2 of speed sensor connector.

OK **Resistance: 0.6 – 1.8 kΩ**

C Measure resistance between terminals 1 and 2 of speed sensor connector and body ground.

OK **Resistance: 1 MΩ or higher**

Rear

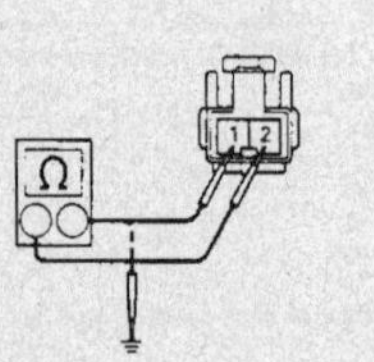
1 2

Rear

P 1. Remove the seat cushion and seat back.
2. Disconnect speed sensor connector.

C Measure resistance between terminals 1 and 2 of speed sensor connector.

OK **Resistance: 0.6 – 1.8 kΩ**

C Measure resistance between terminals 1 and 2 of speed sensor connector and body ground.

OK **Resistance: 1 MΩ or higher**

OK | NG **Replace speed sensor.**

NOTICE: Check the speed sensor signal last

2 Check for open and short in harness and connector between each speed sensor and ECU

OK | NG **Repair or replace harness or connector.**

TY4029500157030X

Fig. 94 Code 31, 32, 33, 34, 35, 36, 38 & 39: Speed Sensor Circuit (Part 3 of 4). Avalon

3 Check sensor rotor and sensor installation.

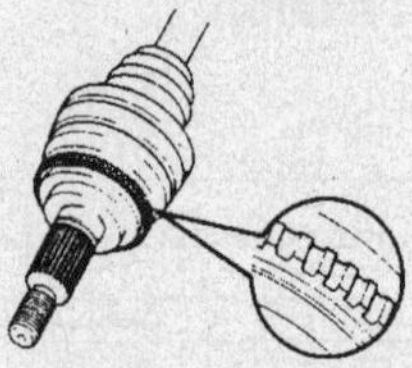

Front

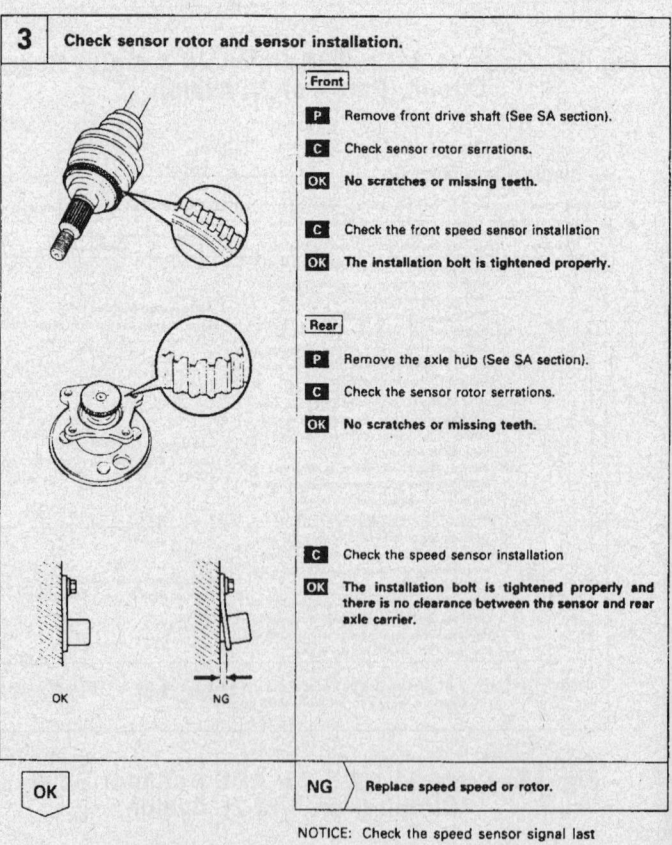

P Remove front drive shaft (See SA section).

C Check sensor rotor serrations.

OK **No scratches or missing teeth.**

C Check the front speed sensor installation

OK **The installation bolt is tightened properly.**

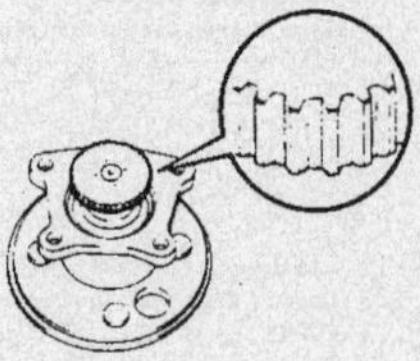

Rear

P Remove the axle hub (See SA section).

C Check the sensor rotor serrations.

OK **No scratches or missing teeth.**

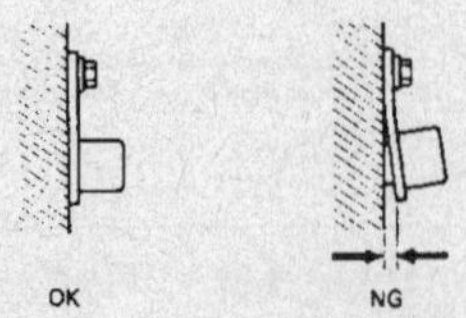
OK
NG

C Check the speed sensor installation

OK **The installation bolt is tightened properly and there is no clearance between the sensor and rear axle carrier.**

OK | NG **Replace speed speed or rotor.**

NOTICE: Check the speed sensor signal last

Check and replace ABS ECU.

TY4029500157040X

Fig. 94 Code 31, 32, 33, 34, 35, 36, 38 & 39: Speed Sensor Circuit (Part 4 of 4). Avalon

CIRCUIT DESCRIPTION

This is the power source for the ECU, hence the CPU, and the actuators.

DTC No.	Diagnostic Trouble Code Detecting Condition	Trouble area
41	(1) Voltage from 5V to 9.4V, is applied for at least 60 sec. to terminal +BS before the ABS primary check and ABS operation. (2) Voltage from 5V to 9.4V, is applied to terminal +BS for 0.2 sec. or more, after the ABS primary check and before ABS operation. (3) During ABS operation, voltage from 5V to 8.8V, is applied to terminal +BS for 0.2 sec. or more.	• Battery • IC regulator • Open or short in power source circuit • ECU

Fail safe function: If trouble occurs in the power source circuit, the ECU cuts off current to the ABS solenoid relay and prohibits ABS control. If the voltage applied to terminal +BS becomes 9.9V or more, the warning light goes off and ABS control becomes possible.

WIRING DIAGRAM

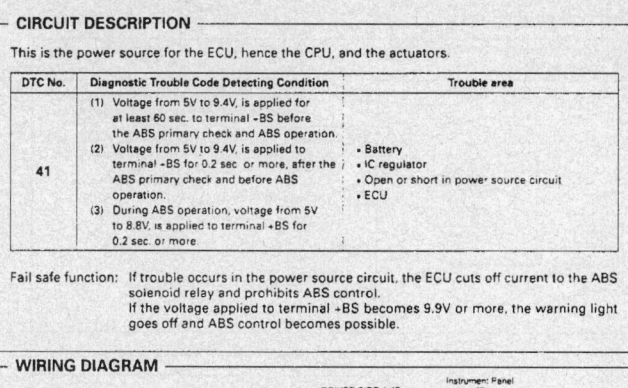

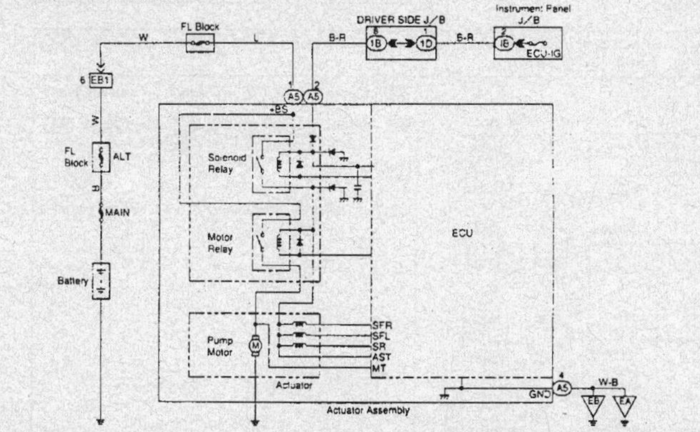

FL Block
W
L
B-R
DRIVER SIDE J/B
Instrument Panel J/B
ECU-IG
EB1
+BS
A5
FL Block
ALT
MAIN
Battery
Solenoid Relay
Motor Relay
ECU
Pump Motor
SFR
SFL
SR
AST
MT
Actuator
Actuator Assembly
GND
W-B
EB
EA

TY4029500158010X

Fig. 95 Code 41: +BS Power Source Circuit (Part 1 of 3). Avalon

1 Check battery positive voltage.

OK Voltage: 10 – 14 V

OK | NG → Check and repair the charging system.

2 Check voltage between terminals +BS and GND of ABS ECU connector.

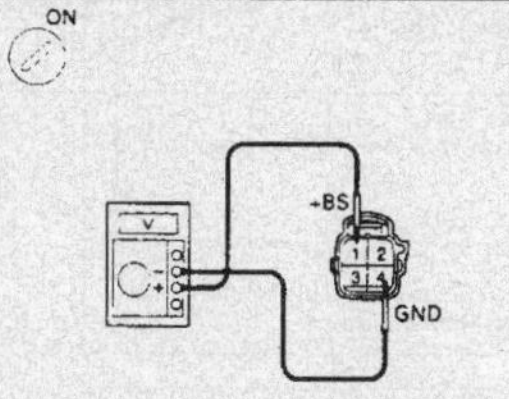

ON
V
+BS
1
2
3
4
GND

P Disconnect ABS ECU connector.

C 1. Turn ignition switch ON.
2. Measure voltage between terminals +BS and GND of ABS ECU connector.

OK Voltage: 10 – 14 V

OK | NG → Check and replace ABS ECU.

3 Check continuity between terminal GND of ABS ECU connector and body ground.

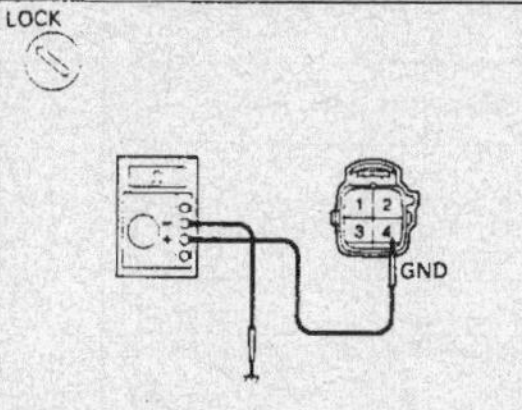

LOCK
1
2
3
4
GND

C Measure resistance between terminal GND of ABS ECU connector and body ground.

OK Resistance: 1 Ω or less

OK | NG → Repair or replace harness or connector.

TY4029500158020X

Fig. 95 Code 41: +BS Power Source Circuit (Part 2 of 3). Avalon

4 Check ECU-IG fuse.

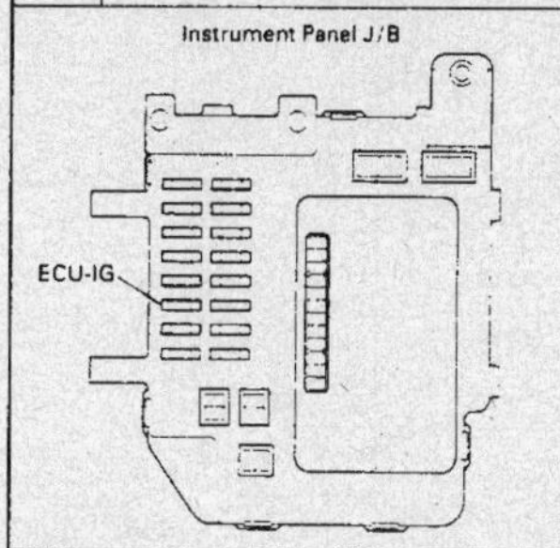

Instrument Panel J/B
ECU-IG

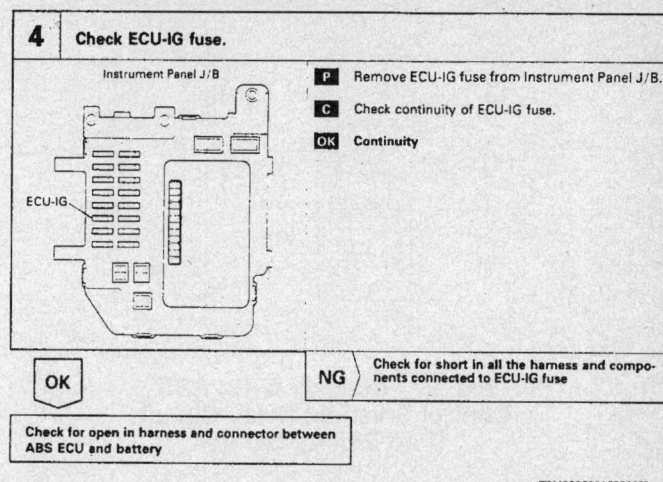

P Remove ECU-IG fuse from Instrument Panel J/B.

C Check continuity of ECU-IG fuse.

OK Continuity

OK | NG → Check for short in all the harness and components connected to ECU-IG fuse

Check for open in harness and connector between ABS ECU and battery

TY4029500158030X

Fig. 95 Code 41: +BS Power Source Circuit (Part 3 of 3). Avalon

CIRCUIT DESCRIPTION

DTC No.	Diagnostic Trouble Code Detecting Condition	Trouble area
51	Pump motor is not operating normally during initial check.	• ABS pump motor

Fail safe function: If trouble occurs in the ABS pump motor, the ECU cuts off current to the solenoid relay and prohibits ABS control.

INSPECTION PROCEDURE

Check that the pump motor ground wire is installed correctly.
If it is OK, replace the ABS actuator assembly.

TY4029500159000X

Fig. 96 Code 51: ABS Pump Motor Lock. Avalon

1 Check voltage between terminal Ts and E1 of DLC1.

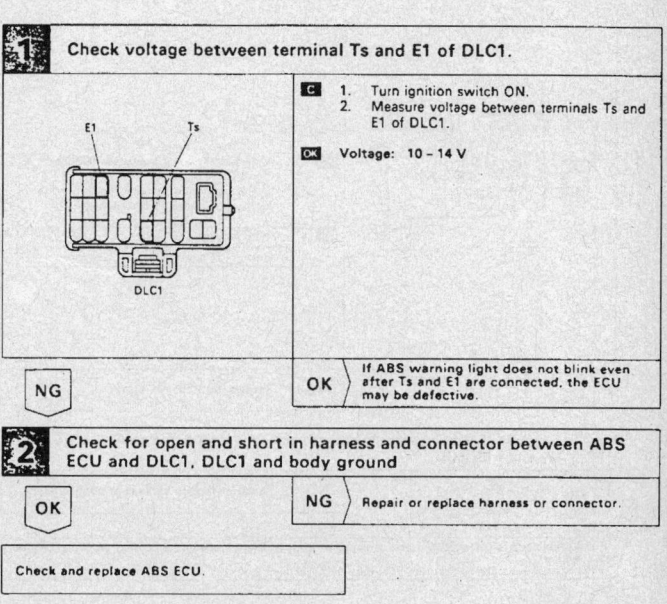

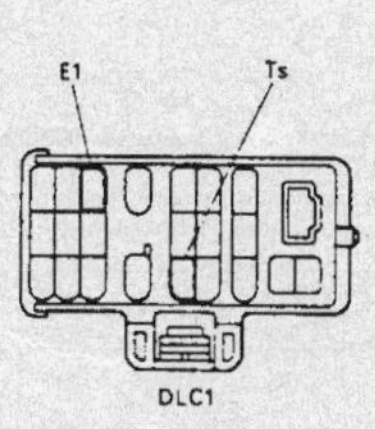

E1
Ts
DLC1

C 1. Turn ignition switch ON.
2. Measure voltage between terminals Ts and E1 of DLC1.

OK Voltage: 10 – 14 V

NG | OK → If ABS warning light does not blink even after Ts and E1 are connected, the ECU may be defective.

2 Check for open and short in harness and connector between ABS ECU and DLC1, DLC1 and body ground

OK | NG → Repair or replace harness or connector.

Check and replace ABS ECU.

TY4029200071010X

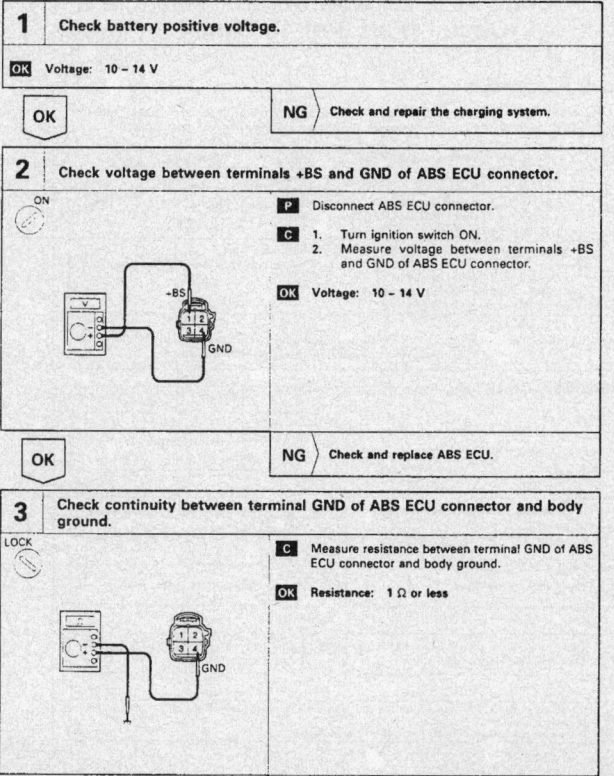

Fig. 97 Code 11 & 12: ABS Control Solenoid Relay Circuit (Part 1 of 4). Camry

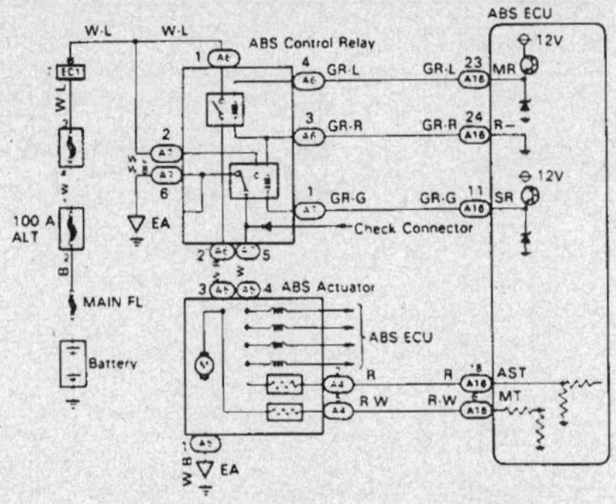
ABS ECU
W-L
ABS Control Relay
GR-L
MR
12V
GR-R
R-
GR-G
SR
Check Connector
100 A ALT
MAIN FL
Battery
EA
ABS Actuator
ABS ECU
R
R-W
AST
MT

TY4029200071020X

Fig. 97 Code 11 & 12: ABS Control Solenoid Relay Circuit (Part 2 of 4). Camry

INSPECTION PROCEDURE

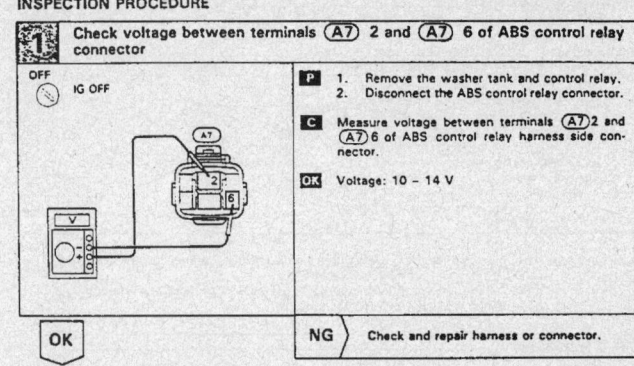

1 Check voltage between terminals (A7) 2 and (A7) 6 of ABS control relay connector

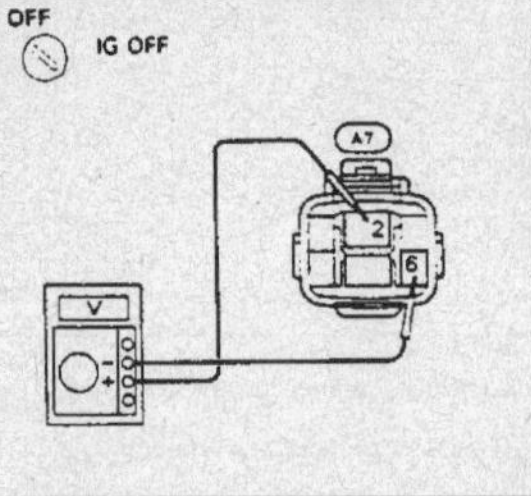
OFF
IG OFF
A7
2
6
V

P 1. Remove the washer tank and control relay.
2. Disconnect the ABS control relay connector.

C Measure voltage between terminals (A7) 2 and (A7) 6 of ABS control relay harness side connector.

OK Voltage: 10 – 14 V

OK

NG Check and repair harness or connector.

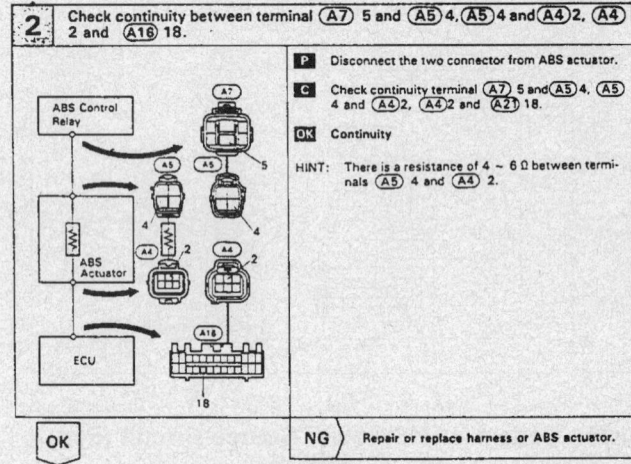

2 Check continuity between terminal (A7) 5 and (A5) 4, (A5) 4 and (A4) 2, (A4) 2 and (A16) 18.

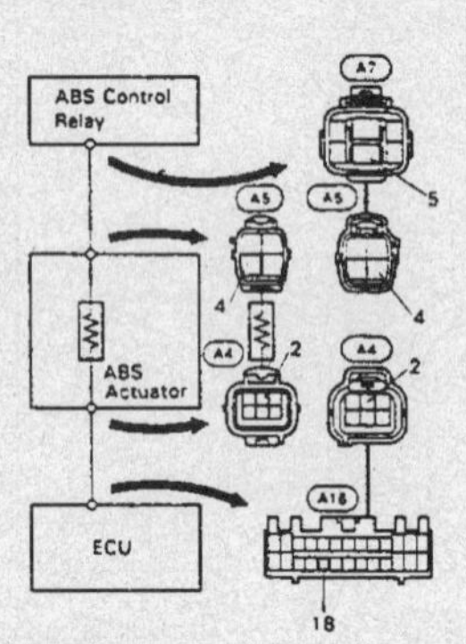
ABS Control Relay
A7
5
A5
4
ABS Actuator
A4
2
ECU
A16
18

P Disconnect the two connector from ABS actuator.

C Check continuity terminal (A7) 5 and (A5) 4, (A5) 4 and (A4) 2, (A4) 2 and (A21) 18.

OK Continuity

HINT: There is a resistance of 4 ~ 6 Ω between terminals (A5) 4 and (A4) 2.

OK

NG Repair or replace harness or ABS actuator.

TY4029200071030X

Fig. 97 Code 11 & 12: ABS Control Solenoid Relay Circuit (Part 3 of 4). Camry

3 Check ABS control relay.

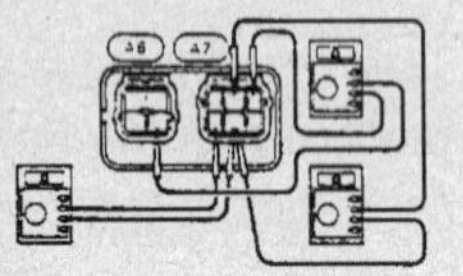
A6
A7

C Check continuity between each terminal of ABS control relay shown below.

OK

Terminals (A7) 1 and (A6) 3	Continuity (Reference value 80 Ω)
Terminals (A7) 5 and (A7) 6	Continuity
Terminals (A7) 2 and (A7) 5	Open

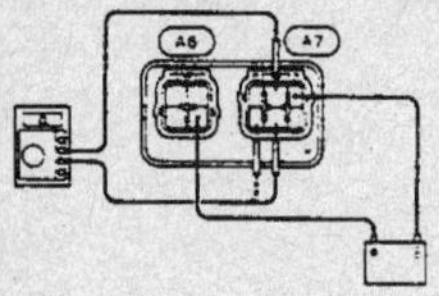
A6
A7

C 1. Apply battery voltage between terminals (A7) 1 and (A6) 3.
2. Check continuity between each terminal of ABS control relay shown below.

OK

Terminals (A7) 5 and (A7) 6	Open
Terminals (A7) 2 and (A7) 5	Continuity

OK

NG Replace ABS control relay.

4 Check for open and short in harness and connector between ABS control relay and ABS ECU

OK

NG Repair or replace harness or connector.

If the same code is still output after the diagnosis code is deleted, check the contact condition of each connection.
If the connections are normal, the ECU may be defective.

TY4029200071040X

Fig. 97 Code 11 & 12: ABS Control Solenoid Relay Circuit (Part 4 of 4). Camry

CIRCUIT DESCRIPTION

The ABS control (motor) relay supplies power to the ABS pump motor. If the accumulator pressure drops, the ECU switches the control (motor) relay ON and operates the ABS pump motor.

Code No.	Diagnostic Code Detecting Condition	Trouble area
13	Conditions (1) and (2) continued for 0.2 sec. or more: (1) ABS control (motor) relay: ON (2) ABS control (motor) relay monitor terminal (MT) voltage: 0 V	• ABS control (motor) relay. • Open or short in ABS control (motor) relay circuit. • ECU.
14	Conditions (1) and (2) continued for 4 sec. or more: (1) ABS control (motor) relay: OFF (2) ABS control (motor) relay monitor terminal (MT) voltage: Battery voltage.	• ABS motor relay. • +B short in ABS control (motor) relay circuit. • ECU.

Fail safe function: If trouble occurs in the control (motor) relay circuit, the ECU cuts off the current to the ABS control (motor) relay and prohibits ABS control.

DIAGNOSTIC CHART

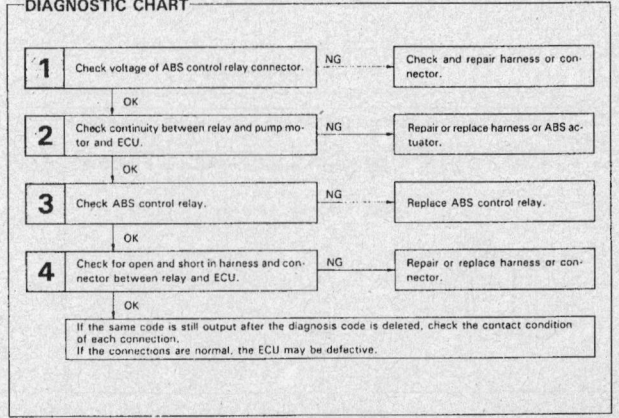

Step	Check	Result	Action
1	Check voltage of ABS control relay connector.	NG	Check and repair harness or connector.
	OK		
2	Check continuity between relay and pump motor and ECU.	NG	Repair or replace harness or ABS actuator.
	OK		
3	Check ABS control relay.	NG	Replace ABS control relay.
	OK		
4	Check for open and short in harness and connector between relay and ECU.	NG	Repair or replace harness or connector.
	OK		

If the same code is still output after the diagnosis code is deleted, check the contact condition of each connection.
If the connections are normal, the ECU may be defective.

TY4029200072010X

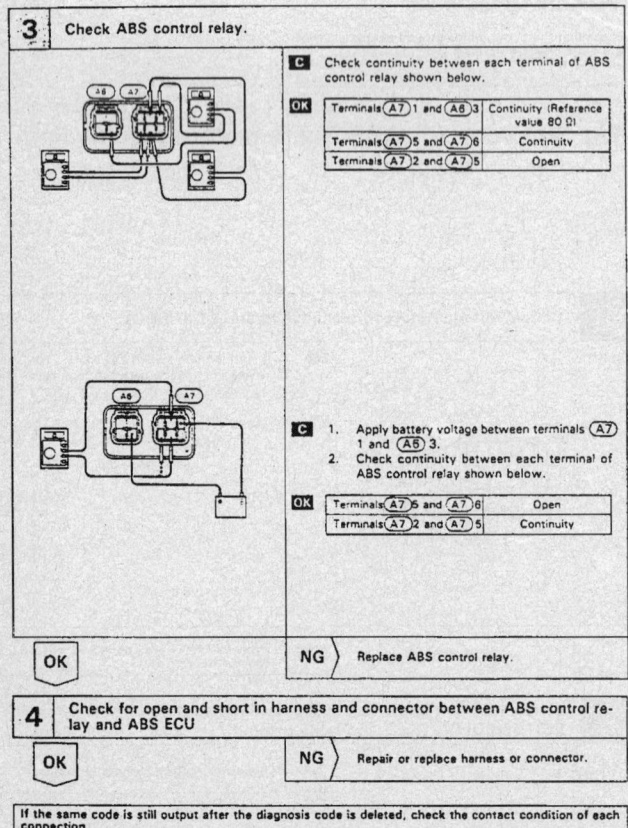

Fig. 98 Code 13 & 14: ABS Control Motor Relay Circuit (Part 1 of 4). Camry

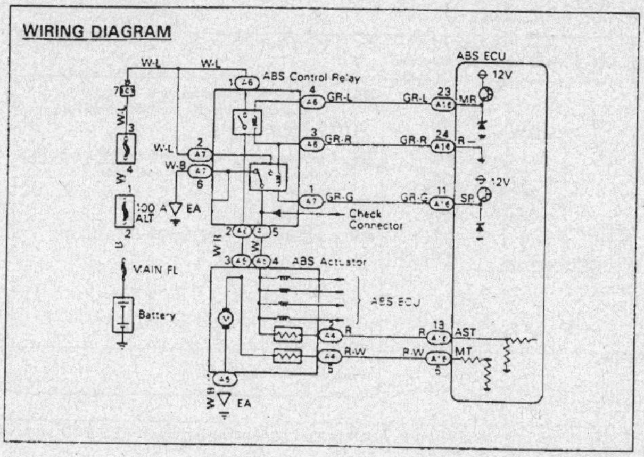
WIRING DIAGRAM
ABS ECU
ABS Control Relay
12V
GR-L
GR-R
GR-G
MR
R
SR
Check Connector
ABS Actuator
ABS ECU
AST
MT
R-W
W-L
W-B
100 A ALT
EA
MAIN FL
Battery

TY4029200072020X

Fig. 98 Code 13 & 14: ABS Control Motor Relay Circuit (Part 2 of 4). Camry

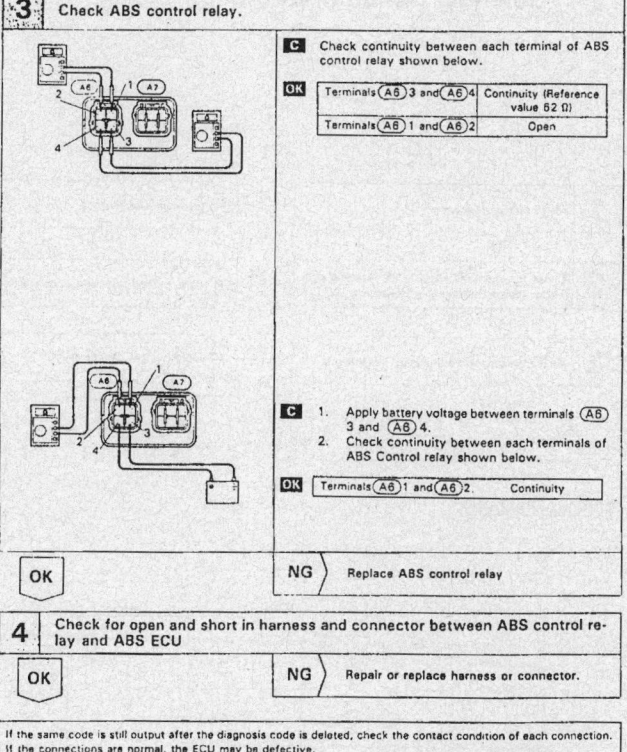

3	Check ABS control relay.

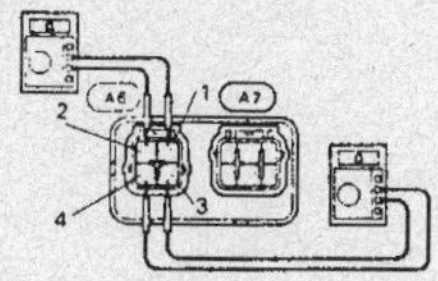

C Check continuity between each terminal of ABS control relay shown below.

OK

Terminals (A6) 3 and (A6) 4	Continuity (Reference value 62 Ω)
Terminals (A6) 1 and (A6) 2	Open

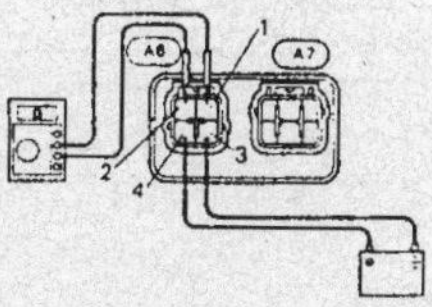

C
1. Apply battery voltage between terminals (A6) 3 and (A6) 4.
2. Check continuity between each terminals of ABS Control relay shown below.

OK

Terminals (A6) 1 and (A6) 2.	Continuity

OK | NG › Replace ABS control relay

4	Check for open and short in harness and connector between ABS control relay and ABS ECU

OK | NG › Repair or replace harness or connector.

If the same code is still output after the diagnosis code is deleted, check the contact condition of each connection. If the connections are normal, the ECU may be defective.

TY4029200072040X

Fig. 98 Code 13 & 14: ABS Control Motor Relay Circuit (Part 4 of 4). Camry

INSPECTION PROCEDURE

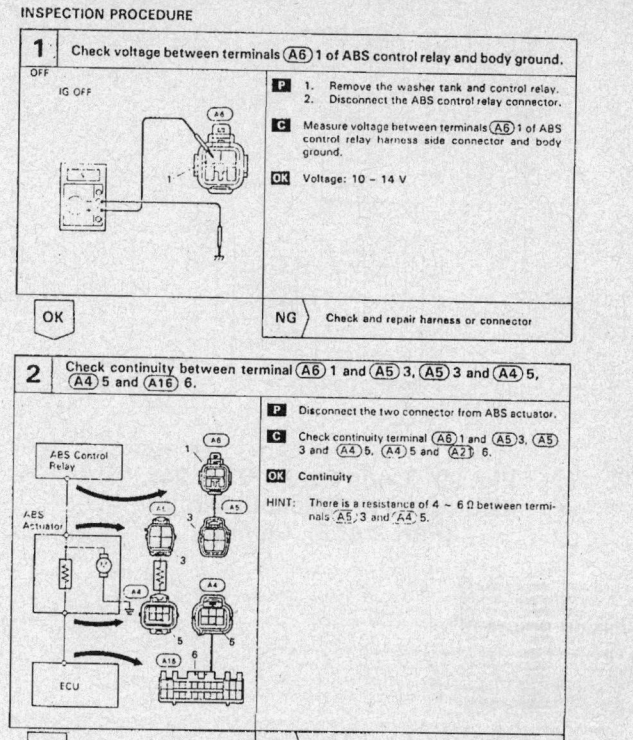

1	Check voltage between terminals (A6) 1 of ABS control relay and body ground.

OFF

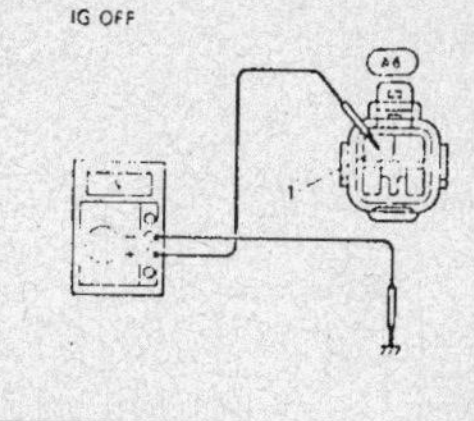
IG OFF

P
1. Remove the washer tank and control relay.
2. Disconnect the ABS control relay connector.

C Measure voltage between terminals (A6) 1 of ABS control relay harness side connector and body ground.

OK Voltage: 10 – 14 V

OK | NG › Check and repair harness or connector

2	Check continuity between terminal (A6) 1 and (A5) 3, (A5) 3 and (A4) 5, (A4) 5 and (A16) 6.

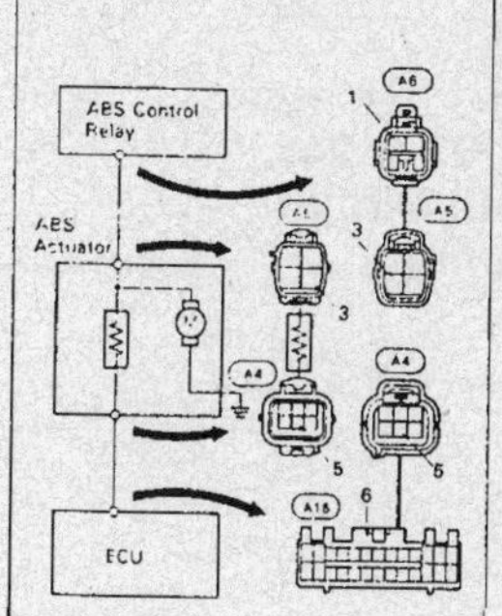
ABS Control Relay
ABS Actuator
ECU

P Disconnect the two connector from ABS actuator.

C Check continuity terminal (A6) 1 and (A5) 3, (A5) 3 and (A4) 5, (A4) 5 and (A21) 6.

OK Continuity

HINT: There is a resistance of 4 ~ 6 Ω between terminals (A5) 3 and (A4) 5.

OK | NG › Repair or replace harness or ABS actuator.

TY4029200072030X

Fig. 98 Code 13 & 14: ABS Control Motor Relay Circuit (Part 3 of 4). Camry

CIRCUIT DESCRIPTION

This solenoid goes on when signals are received from the ECU and controls the pressure acting on the wheel cylinders, thus controlling the turning of the wheels.

Code No.	Diagnostic Code Detecting Condition	Trouble area
21	Conditions (1) through (3) continue for 0.05 sec. or more: (1) ABS control (solenoid) relay: ON (2) Voltage of ABS ECU terminal AST: Battery voltage (3) When power transistor of ECU is ON, voltage of terminal SFR is 0 V or battery voltage.	• ABS actuator. • Open or short in SFR circuit. • ECU.
22	Conditions (1) through (3) continue for 0.05 sec. or more: (1) ABS control (solenoid) relay: ON (2) Voltage of ABS ECU terminal AST: Battery voltage (3) When power transistor of ECU is ON, voltage of terminal SFL is 0 V or battery voltage.	• ABS actuator. • Open or short in SFL circuit. • ECU.
23	Conditions (1) through (3) continue for 0.05 sec. or more: (1) ABS control (solenoid) relay: ON (2) Voltage of ABS ECU terminal AST: Battery voltage (3) When power transistor of ECU is ON, voltage of terminal SRR is 0 V or battery voltage.	• ABS actuator. • Open or short in SRR circuit. • ECU.
24	Conditions (1) through (3) continue for 0.05 sec. or more: (1) ABS control (solenoid) relay: ON (2) Voltage of ABS ECU terminal AST: Battery voltage (3) When power transistor of ECU is ON, voltage of terminal SRL is 0 V or battery voltage.	• ABS actuator. • Open or short in SRL circuit. • ECU.

Fail safe function: If trouble occurs in the actuator solenoid circuit, the ECU cuts off current to the control (solenoid) relay and prohibits ABS control.

DIAGNOSTIC CHART

Step	Check	Result	Action
1	Check ABS actuator solenoid.	NG	Replace ABS actuator.
	↓ OK		
2	Check for open and short in harness and connector between ECU and actuator.	NG	Repair or replace harness or connector.
	↓ OK		

If the same code is still output after the diagnosis code is deleted, check the contact condition of each connection. If the connections are normal, the ECU may be defective.

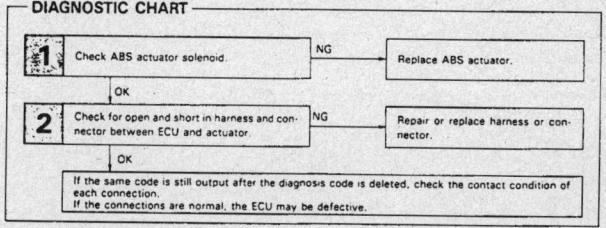

TY4029200073010X

Fig. 99 Code 21, 22, 23 & 24: ABS Actuator Solenoid Circuit (Part 1 of 3). Camry

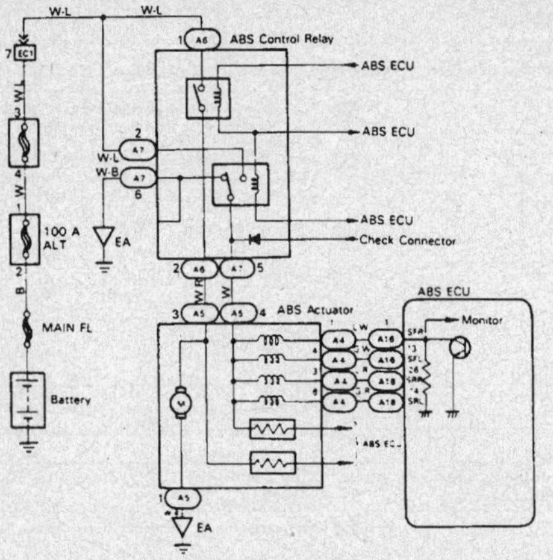
W-L
ABS Control Relay
ABS ECU
ABS ECU
ABS ECU
Check Connector
100 A ALT
EA
MAIN FL
Battery
ABS Actuator
ABS ECU
Monitor
EA

TY4029200073020X

Fig. 99 Code 21, 22, 23 & 24: ABS Actuator Solenoid Circuit (Part 2 of 3). Camry

INSPECTION PROCEDURE

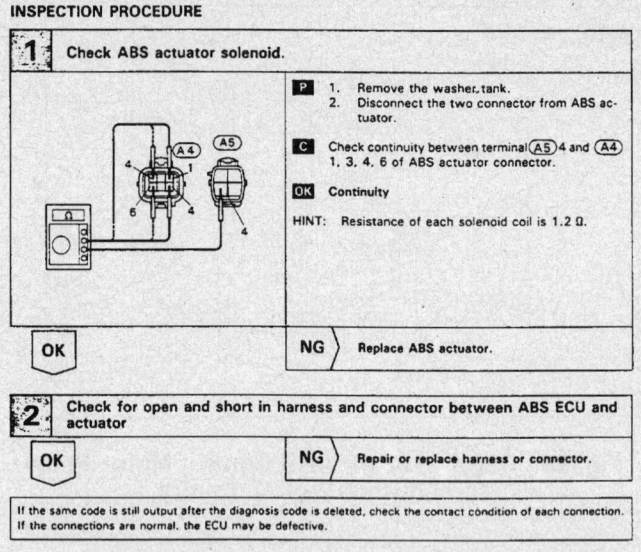

1 Check ABS actuator solenoid.

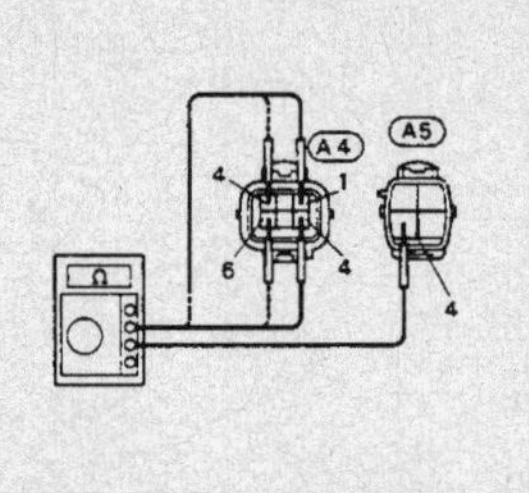
A4
A5

P 1. Remove the washer tank.
2. Disconnect the two connector from ABS actuator.

C Check continuity between terminal (A5) 4 and (A4) 1, 3, 4, 6 of ABS actuator connector.

OK Continuity

HINT: Resistance of each solenoid coil is 1.2 Ω.

OK — NG: Replace ABS actuator.

2 Check for open and short in harness and connector between ABS ECU and actuator

OK — NG: Repair or replace harness or connector.

If the same code is still output after the diagnosis code is deleted, check the contact condition of each connection. If the connections are normal, the ECU may be defective.

TY4029200073030X

Fig. 99 Code 21, 22, 23 & 24: ABS Actuator Solenoid Circuit (Part 3 of 3). Camry

CIRCUIT DESCRIPTION

The speed sensor detects the wheel speed and sends the appropriate signals to the ECU. These signals are used for control of both the ABS and system. The front rotor and rear rotor have 48 serrations. When the rotors rotate, the magnetic field emitted by the permanent magnet in the speed sensor generates an AC voltage. Since the frequency of this AC voltage changes in proportion to the speed of the rotors (wheels), the frequency is used by the ECU to detect the speed of each wheel.

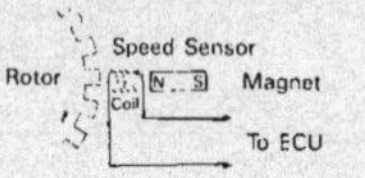
Speed Sensor
Rotor
Coil
Magnet
To ECU

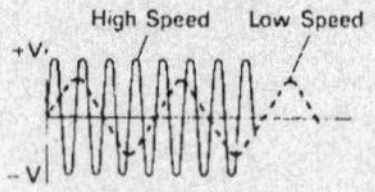
High Speed
Low Speed
+V
-V

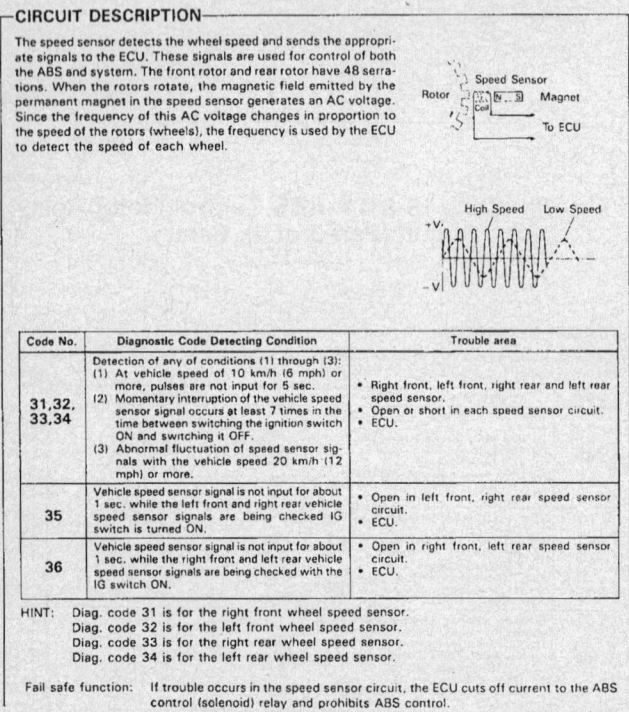

Code No.	Diagnostic Code Detecting Condition	Trouble area
31,32, 33,34	Detection of any of conditions (1) through (3): (1) At vehicle speed of 10 km/h (6 mph) or more, pulses are not input for 5 sec. (2) Momentary interruption of the vehicle speed sensor signal occurs at least 7 times in the time between switching the ignition switch ON and switching it OFF. (3) Abnormal fluctuation of speed sensor signals with the vehicle speed 20 km/h (12 mph) or more.	• Right front, left front, right rear and left rear speed sensor. • Open or short in each speed sensor circuit. • ECU.
35	Vehicle speed sensor signal is not input for about 1 sec. while the left front and right rear vehicle speed sensor signals are being checked IG switch is turned ON.	• Open in left front, right rear speed sensor circuit. • ECU.
36	Vehicle speed sensor signal is not input for about 1 sec. while the right front and left rear vehicle speed sensor signals are being checked with the IG switch ON.	• Open in right front, left rear speed sensor circuit. • ECU.

HINT: Diag. code 31 is for the right front wheel speed sensor.
Diag. code 32 is for the left front wheel speed sensor.
Diag. code 33 is for the right rear wheel speed sensor.
Diag. code 34 is for the left rear wheel speed sensor.

Fail safe function: If trouble occurs in the speed sensor circuit, the ECU cuts off current to the ABS control (solenoid) relay and prohibits ABS control.

TY4029200074010X

Fig. 100 Code 31, 32, 33, 34, 35 & 36: Speed Sensor Circuit (Part 1 of 4). Camry

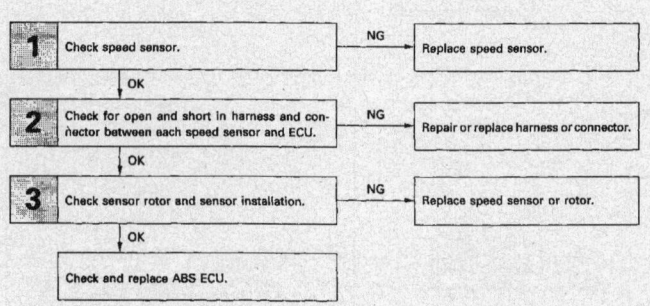

1 Check speed sensor. — NG → Replace speed sensor.

↓ OK

2 Check for open and short in harness and connector between each speed sensor and ECU. — NG → Repair or replace harness or connector.

↓ OK

3 Check sensor rotor and sensor installation. — NG → Replace speed sensor or rotor.

↓ OK

Check and replace ABS ECU.

WIRING DIAGRAM

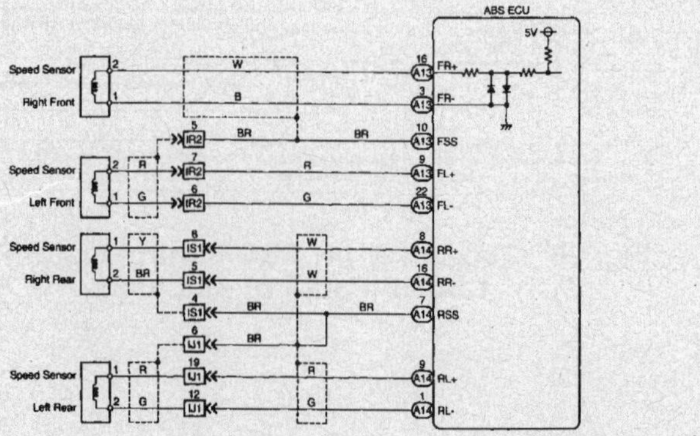
ABS ECU
5V
Speed Sensor
Right Front
Speed Sensor
Left Front
Speed Sensor
Right Rear
Speed Sensor
Left Rear
FR+
FR-
FSS
FL+
FL-
RR+
RR-
RSS
RL+
RL-

TY4029200074020X

Fig. 100 Code 31, 32, 33, 34, 35 & 36: Speed Sensor Circuit (Part 2 of 4). Camry

INSPECTION PROCEDURE

1 Speed sensor check.

P See speed sensor check

NG

OK — When diag. Code 31-36 are displayed, check and replace ABS ECU.

2 Check speed sensor.

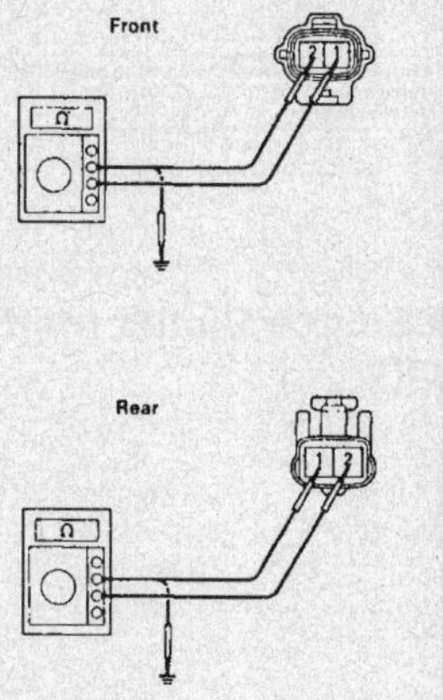

Front
Rear

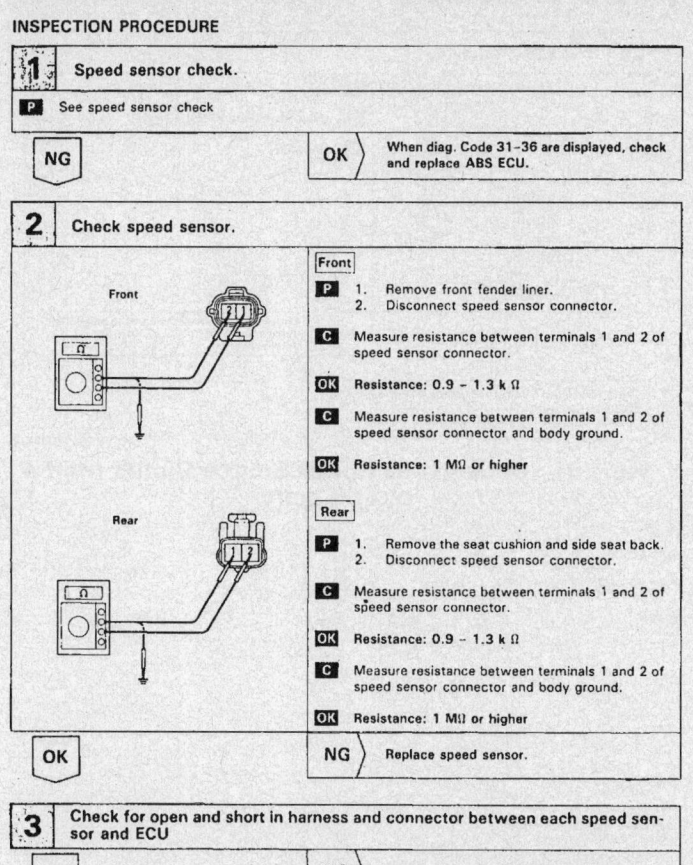

Front

P 1. Remove front fender liner.
2. Disconnect speed sensor connector.

C Measure resistance between terminals 1 and 2 of speed sensor connector.

OK Resistance: 0.9 – 1.3 k Ω

C Measure resistance between terminals 1 and 2 of speed sensor connector and body ground.

OK Resistance: 1 MΩ or higher

Rear

P 1. Remove the seat cushion and side seat back.
2. Disconnect speed sensor connector.

C Measure resistance between terminals 1 and 2 of speed sensor connector.

OK Resistance: 0.9 – 1.3 k Ω

C Measure resistance between terminals 1 and 2 of speed sensor connector and body ground.

OK Resistance: 1 MΩ or higher

OK

NG — Replace speed sensor.

3 Check for open and short in harness and connector between each speed sensor and ECU

OK

NG — Repair or replace harness or connector.

TY4029200074030X

Fig. 100 Code 31, 32, 33, 34, 35 & 36: Speed Sensor Circuit (Part 3 of 4). Camry

4 Check sensor rotor and sensor installation.

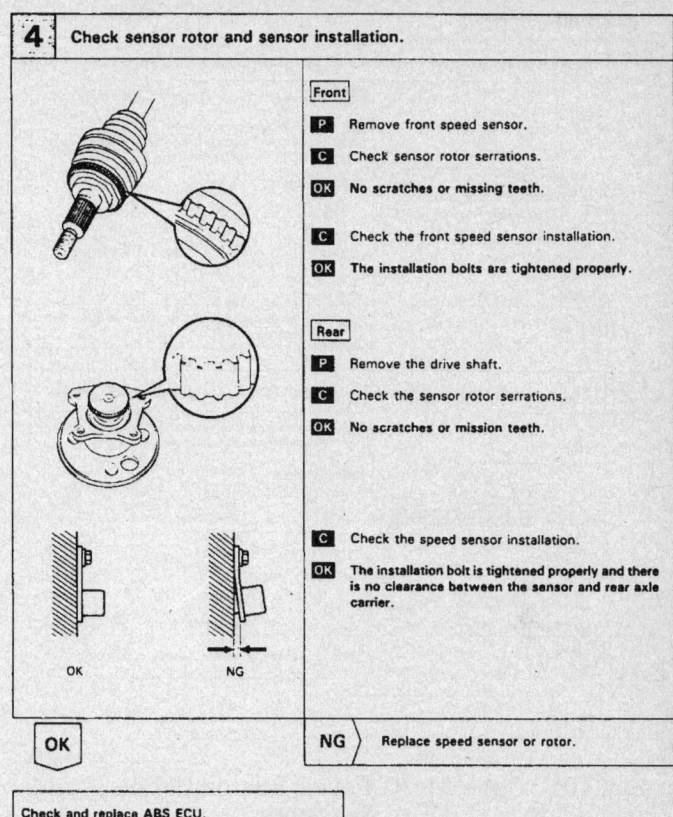

OK
NG

Front

P Remove front speed sensor.

C Check sensor rotor serrations.

OK No scratches or missing teeth.

C Check the front speed sensor installation.

OK The installation bolts are tightened properly.

Rear

P Remove the drive shaft.

C Check the sensor rotor serrations.

OK No scratches or mission teeth.

C Check the speed sensor installation.

OK The installation bolt is tightened properly and there is no clearance between the sensor and rear axle carrier.

OK

NG — Replace speed sensor or rotor.

Check and replace ABS ECU.

TY4029200074040X

Fig. 100 Code 31, 32, 33, 34, 35 & 36: Speed Sensor Circuit (Part 4 of 4). Camry

CIRCUIT DESCRIPTION

This is the power source for the ECU and becomes power source for the CPU and actuators.

Code No.	Diagnostic Code Detecting Condition	Trouble area
41	Vehicle speed is 3 km/h (1.9 mph) or more and voltage of ECU terminal IG remains at more than 17 V or below 9.5 V for more than 10 sec.	• Battery. • IC regulator. • Open or short in power source circuit. • ECU.

Fail safe function: If trouble occurs in the power source circuit, the ECU cuts off current to the ABS control (solenoid) relay and prohibits ABS control.

DIAGNOSTIC CHART

First check battery voltage. If the voltage is not between 10 V and 14 V, check and repair the charging system.

1 Check voltage between terminals IG and GND of ABS ECU connector. — OK → When diag. code 41 is displayed, check and replace ABS ECU.

NG ↓

2 Check continuity between terminal GND of ABS ECU connector and body ground. — NG → Repair or replace harness or connector.

OK ↓

3 Check ECU-IG fuse. — NG → Check for short in all the harness and components connected to ECU-IG fuse (See wiring diagram).

OK ↓

Check for open in harness and connector between ABS ECU and battery.

TY4029200075010X

Fig. 101 Code 41: IG Power Source Circuit (Part 1 of 4). Camry

WIRING DIAGRAM

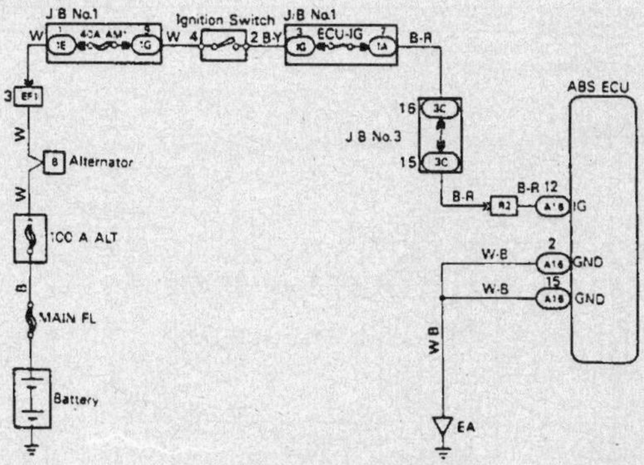

J B No.1
Ignition Switch
J B No.1
ECU-IG
B-R
ABS ECU
J B No.3
Alternator
100 A ALT
MAIN FL
Battery
IG
GND
GND
W-B
EA

TY4029200075020X

Fig. 101 Code 41: IG Power Source Circuit (Part 2 4 of 4). Camry

INSPECTION PROCEDURE

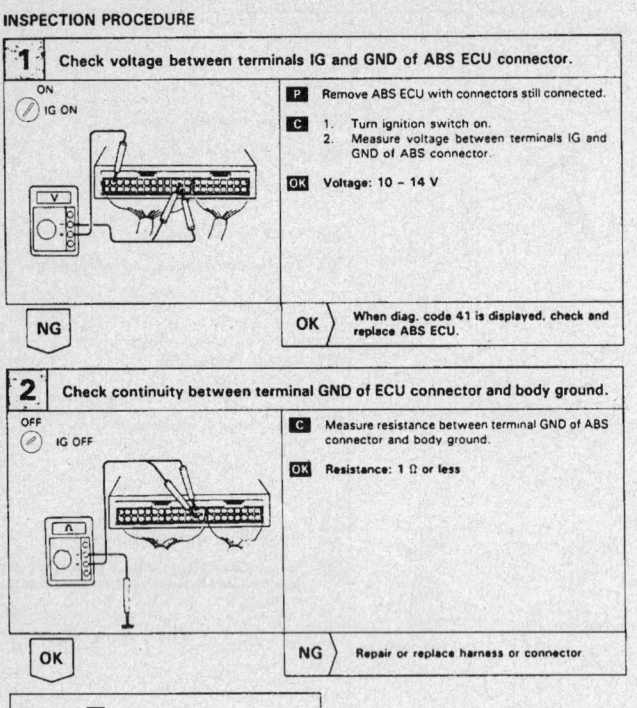

1 Check voltage between terminals IG and GND of ABS ECU connector.

ON
IG ON

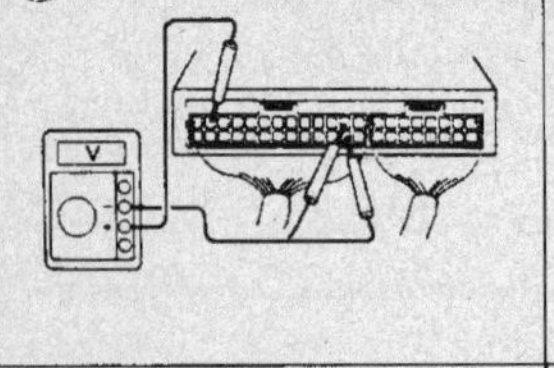
V

P Remove ABS ECU with connectors still connected.

C 1. Turn ignition switch on.
2. Measure voltage between terminals IG and GND of ABS connector.

OK Voltage: 10 – 14 V

NG

OK — When diag. code 41 is displayed, check and replace ABS ECU.

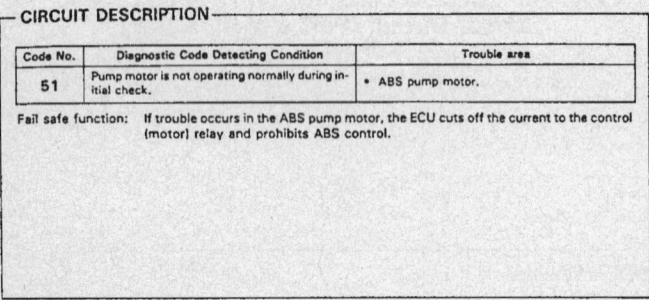

2 Check continuity between terminal GND of ECU connector and body ground.

OFF
IG OFF

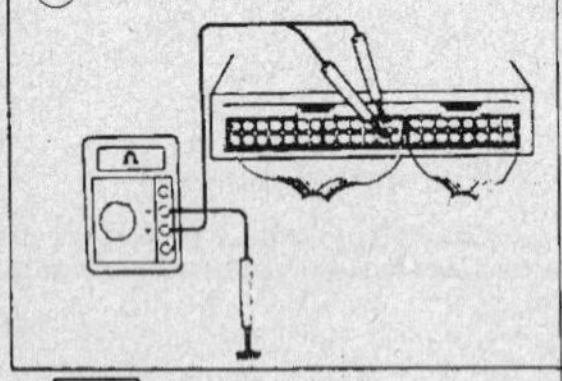
Ω

C Measure resistance between terminal GND of ABS connector and body ground.

OK Resistance: 1 Ω or less

OK

NG — Repair or replace harness or connector.

Go to step 3

TY4029200075030X

Fig. 101 Code 41: IG Power Source Circuit (Part 3 of 4). Camry

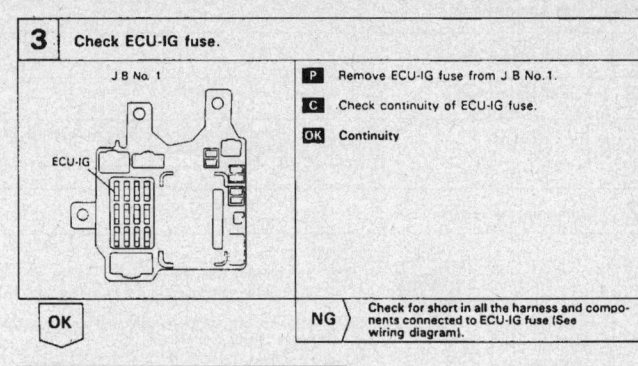

3 Check ECU-IG fuse.

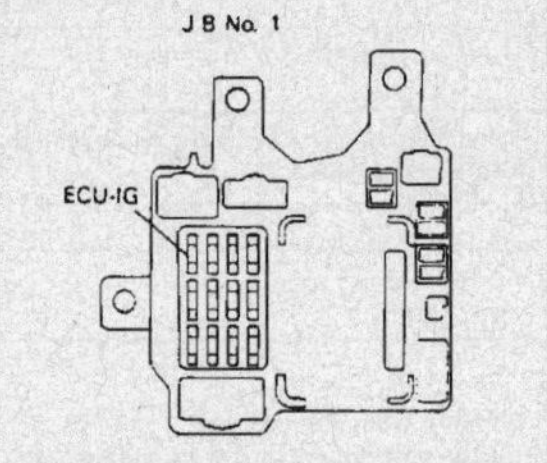
J B No. 1
ECU-IG

P Remove ECU-IG fuse from J B No.1.

C Check continuity of ECU-IG fuse.

OK Continuity

OK

NG — Check for short in all the harness and components connected to ECU-IG fuse (See wiring diagram).

Check for open in harness and connector between ABS ECU and battery.

TY4029200075040X

Fig. 101 Code 41: IG Power Source Circuit (Part 4 of 4). Camry

CIRCUIT DESCRIPTION

Code No.	Diagnostic Code Detecting Condition	Trouble area
51	Pump motor is not operating normally during initial check.	• ABS pump motor.

Fail safe function: If trouble occurs in the ABS pump motor, the ECU cuts off the current to the control (motor) relay and prohibits ABS control.

DIAGNOSTIC CHART

See inspection of ABS pump motor

WIRING DIAGRAM

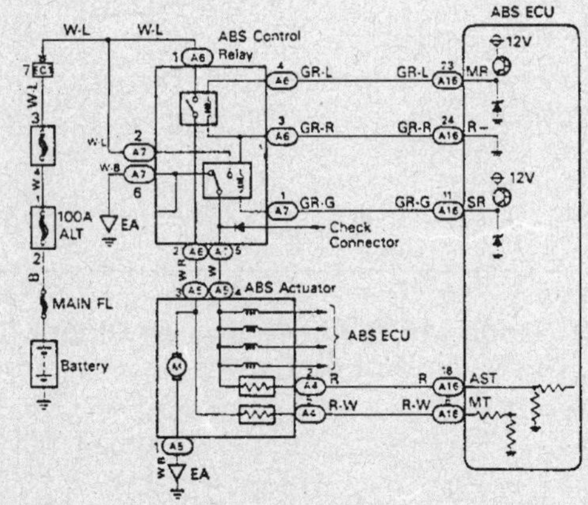
ABS ECU
W-L
W-L
ABS Control Relay
12V
GR-L
GR-L
MR
GR-R
GR-R
R-
W-L
W-B
12V
EA
GR-G
GR-G
SR
100A ALT
Check Connector
ABS Actuator
MAIN FL
ABS ECU
Battery
R
R
AST
R-W
R-W
MT
EA

TY4029200076000X

Fig. 102 Code 52: ABS Pump Motor Lock. Camry

CIRCUIT DESCRIPTION

This relay supplies power to each ABS solenoid. After the ignition switch is turned ON, if the initial check is OK, the relay goes on.

DTC No.	Diagnostic Trouble Code Detecting Condition	Trouble area
11	Conditions (1) and (2) continue for 0.2 sec. or more: (1) ABS solenoid relay terminal (SR) voltage: Battery positive voltage (2) Solenoid relay monitor terminal (AST) voltage: 0 V	• ABS solenoid relay • Open or short in ABS solenoid relay circuit • ECU
12	Conditions (1) and (2) continue for 0.2 sec. or more: (1) ABS solenoid relay terminal (SR) voltage: 0 V (2) Solenoid relay monitor terminal (AST) voltage: Battery positive voltage	• ABS solenoid relay • B+ short in ABS solenoid relay circuit. • ECU

Fail safe function: If trouble occurs in the solenoid relay circuit, the ECU cuts off current to the solenoid relay and prohibits ABS control.

DIAGNOSTIC CHART

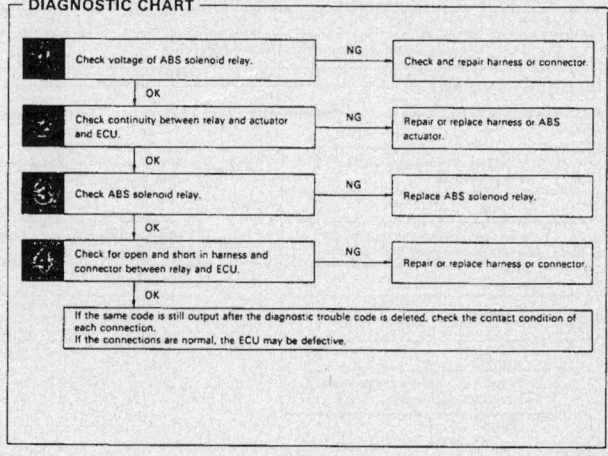

1. Check voltage of ABS solenoid relay. — NG → Check and repair harness or connector.
   OK ↓
2. Check continuity between relay and actuator and ECU. — NG → Repair or replace harness or ABS actuator.
   OK ↓
3. Check ABS solenoid relay. — NG → Replace ABS solenoid relay.
   OK ↓
4. Check for open and short in harness and connector between relay and ECU. — NG → Repair or replace harness or connector.
   OK ↓

If the same code is still output after the diagnostic trouble code is deleted, check the contact condition of each connection.
If the connections are normal, the ECU may be defective.

TY4029400097010X

Fig. 103 Code 11 & 12: ABS Solenoid Relay (Part 1 of 4). Celica

WIRING DIAGRAM

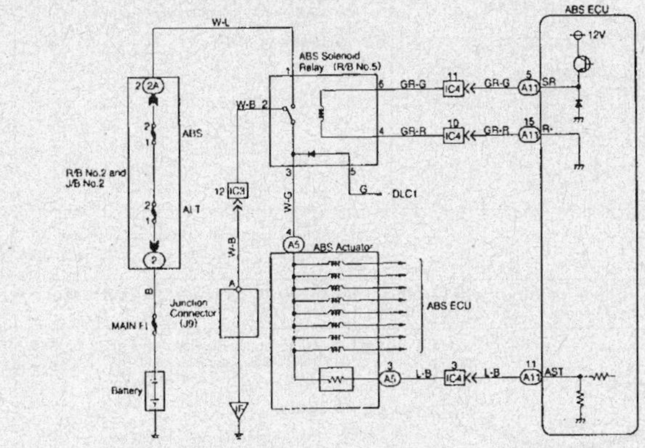
ABS ECU
12V
ABS Solenoid Relay (R/B No.5)
R/B No.2 and J/B No.2
ABS
ALT
MAIN FL
Battery
Junction Connector (J9)
ABS Actuator
DLC1

TY4029400097020X

Fig. 103 Code 11 & 12: ABS Solenoid Relay (Part 2 of 4). Celica

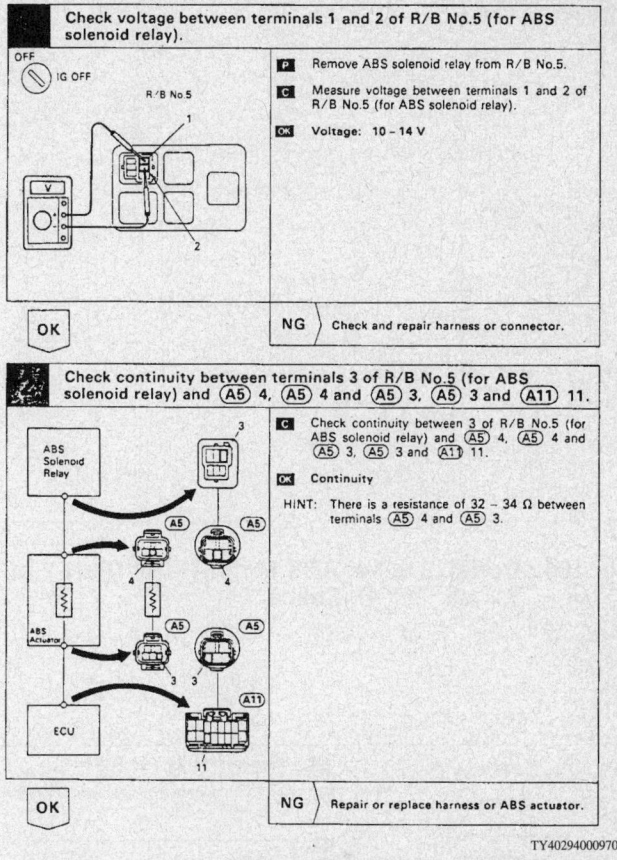

Check voltage between terminals 1 and 2 of R/B No.5 (for ABS solenoid relay).

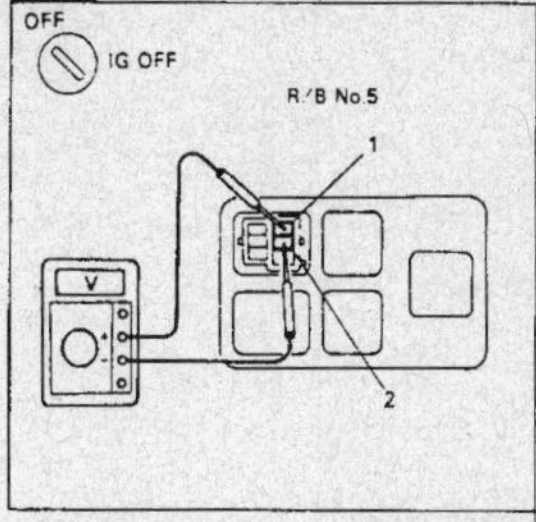
OFF
IG OFF
R/B No.5
1
2

P Remove ABS solenoid relay from R/B No.5.

C Measure voltage between terminals 1 and 2 of R/B No.5 (for ABS solenoid relay).

OK **Voltage: 10 – 14 V**

OK | NG — Check and repair harness or connector.

Check continuity between terminals 3 of R/B No.5 (for ABS solenoid relay) and (A5) 4, (A5) 4 and (A5) 3, (A5) 3 and (A11) 11.

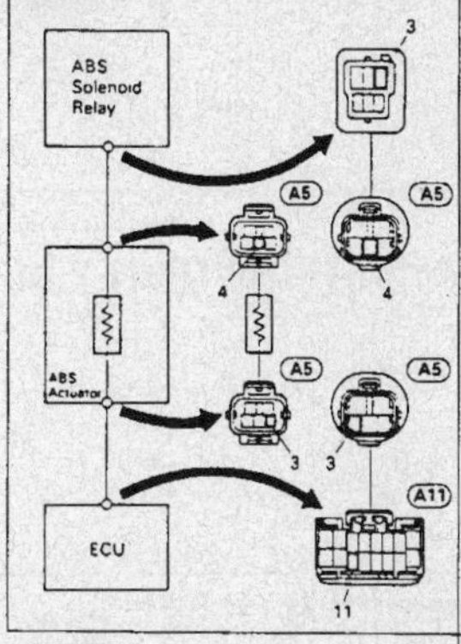
ABS Solenoid Relay
ABS Actuator
ECU
A5
A11
3
4
11

C Check continuity between 3 of R/B No.5 (for ABS solenoid relay) and (A5) 4, (A5) 4 and (A5) 3, (A5) 3 and (A11) 11.

OK Continuity

HINT: There is a resistance of 32 – 34 Ω between terminals (A5) 4 and (A5) 3.

OK | NG — Repair or replace harness or ABS actuator.

TY4029400097030X

Fig. 103 Code 11 & 12: ABS Solenoid Relay (Part 3 of 4). Celica

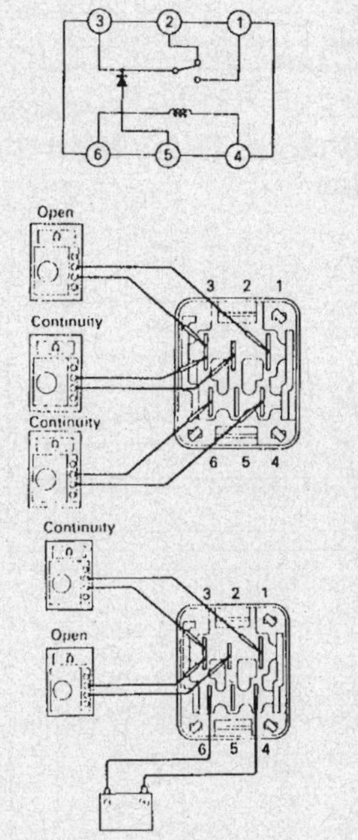
Open
Continuity
Continuity
Continuity
Open
3 2 1
6 5 4

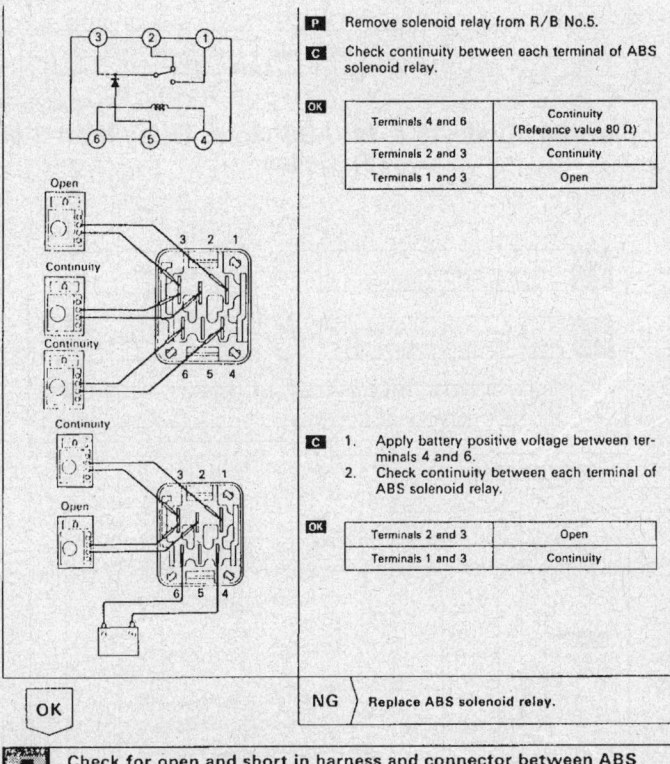

P Remove solenoid relay from R/B No.5.

C Check continuity between each terminal of ABS solenoid relay.

OK

Terminals 4 and 6	Continuity (Reference value 80 Ω)
Terminals 2 and 3	Continuity
Terminals 1 and 3	Open

C
1. Apply battery positive voltage between terminals 4 and 6.
2. Check continuity between each terminal of ABS solenoid relay.

OK

Terminals 2 and 3	Open
Terminals 1 and 3	Continuity

OK | NG — Replace ABS solenoid relay.

4 Check for open and short in harness and connector between ABS solenoid relay and ABS ECU

OK | NG — Repair or replace harness or connector.

If the same code is still output after the diagnostic trouble code is deleted, check the contact condition of each connection.
If the connections are normal, the ECU may be defective.

TY4029400097040X

Fig. 103 Code 11 & 12: ABS Solenoid Relay (Part 4 of 4). Celica

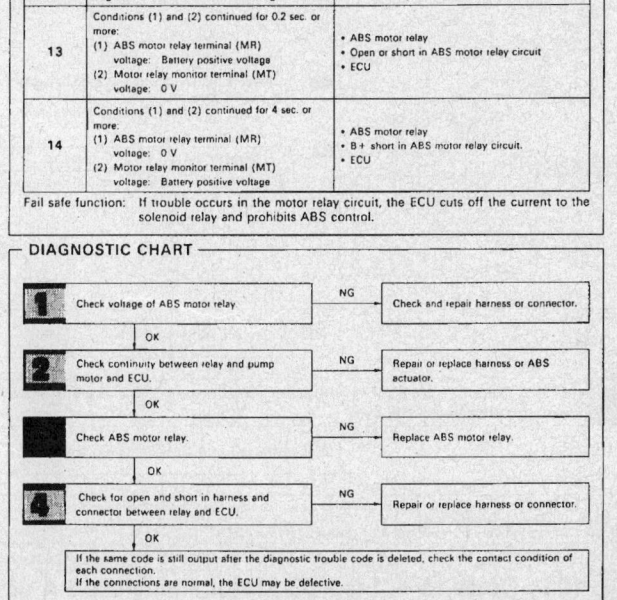

The ABS motor relay supplies power to the ABS pump motor. While the ABS activated, the ECU switches the motor relay ON and operates the ABS pump motor.

DTC No.	Diagnostic Trouble Code Detecting Condition	Trouble area
13	Conditions (1) and (2) continued for 0.2 sec. or more: (1) ABS motor relay terminal (MR) voltage: Battery positive voltage (2) Motor relay monitor terminal (MT) voltage: 0 V	• ABS motor relay • Open or short in ABS motor relay circuit • ECU
14	Conditions (1) and (2) continued for 4 sec. or more: (1) ABS motor relay terminal (MR) voltage: 0 V (2) Motor relay monitor terminal (MT) voltage: Battery positive voltage	• ABS motor relay • B+ short in ABS motor relay circuit. • ECU

Fail safe function: If trouble occurs in the motor relay circuit, the ECU cuts off the current to the solenoid relay and prohibits ABS control.

DIAGNOSTIC CHART

1. Check voltage of ABS motor relay. — NG → Check and repair harness or connector. — OK ↓
2. Check continuity between relay and pump motor and ECU. — NG → Repair or replace harness or ABS actuator. — OK ↓
3. Check ABS motor relay. — NG → Replace ABS motor relay. — OK ↓
4. Check for open and short in harness and connector between relay and ECU. — NG → Repair or replace harness or connector. — OK ↓

If the same code is still output after the diagnostic trouble code is deleted, check the contact condition of each connection.
If the connections are normal, the ECU may be defective.

TY4029400098010X

Fig. 104 Code 13 & 14: ABS Motor Relay (Part 1 of 4). Celica

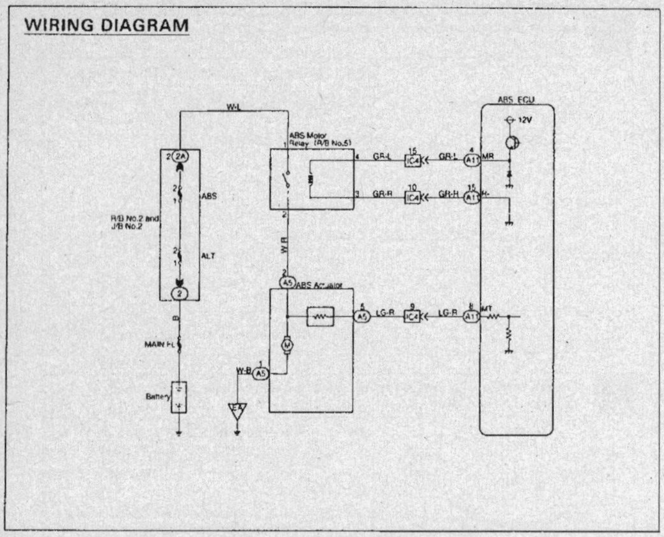
WIRING DIAGRAM
W-L
ABS ECU
12V
ABS Motor Relay (R/B No.5)
GR-L
GR-R
W-R
ABS
ALT
R/B No.2 and J/B No.2
ABS Actuator
LG-R
MAIN FL
W-B
Battery

TY4029400098020X

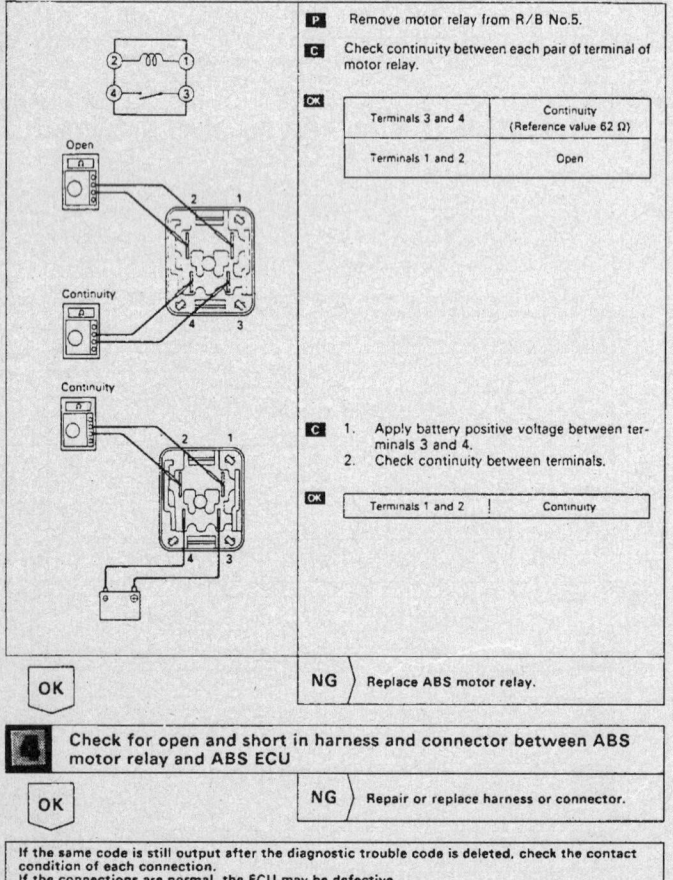

Fig. 104 Code 13 & 14: ABS Motor Relay (Part 2 of 4). Celica

1 Check voltage between terminal 1 of R/B No.5 (for ABS motor relay) and body ground.

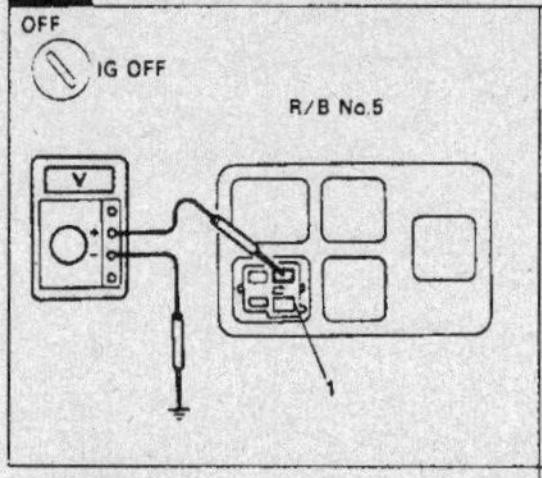
OFF
IG OFF
R/B No.5
V
1

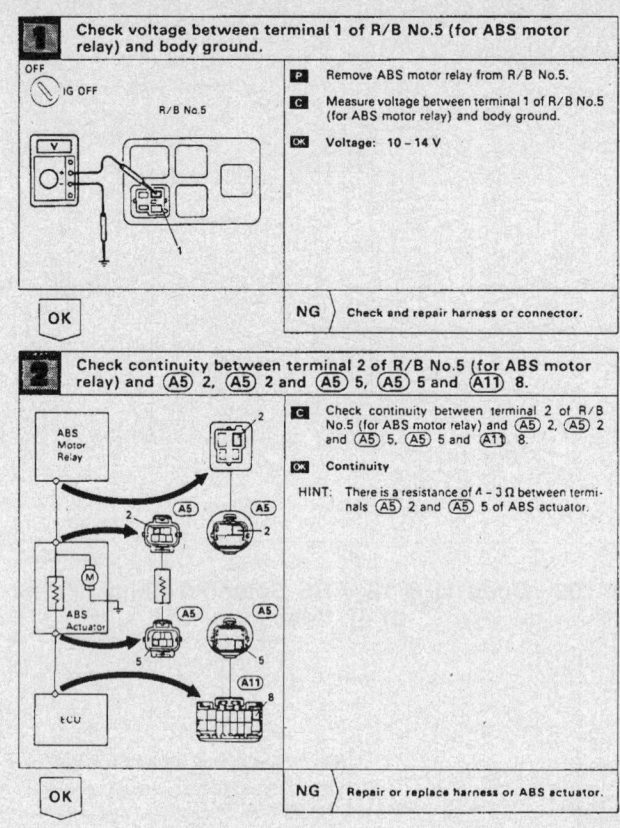

P Remove ABS motor relay from R/B No.5.

C Measure voltage between terminal 1 of R/B No.5 (for ABS motor relay) and body ground.

OK Voltage: 10 – 14 V

OK

NG Check and repair harness or connector.

2 Check continuity between terminal 2 of R/B No.5 (for ABS motor relay) and (A5) 2, (A5) 2 and (A5) 5, (A5) 5 and (A11) 8.

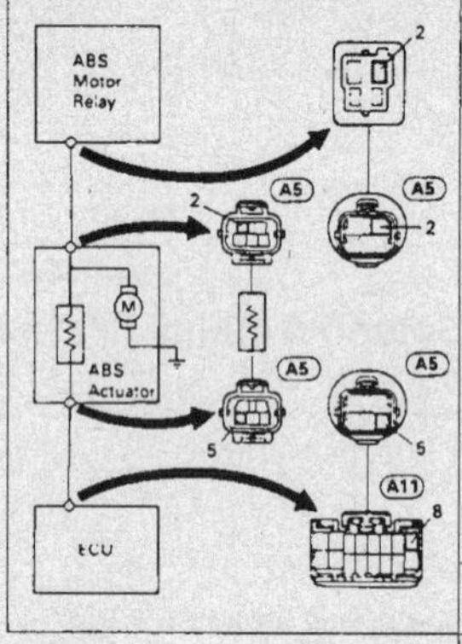
ABS Motor Relay
2
A5
ABS Actuator
5
A11
8
ECU

C Check continuity between terminal 2 of R/B No.5 (for ABS motor relay) and (A5) 2, (A5) 2 and (A5) 5, (A5) 5 and (A11) 8.

OK Continuity

HINT: There is a resistance of 4 – 3 Ω between terminals (A5) 2 and (A5) 5 of ABS actuator.

OK

NG Repair or replace harness or ABS actuator.

TY4029400098030X

Fig. 104 Code 13 & 14: ABS Motor Relay (Part 3 of 4). Celica

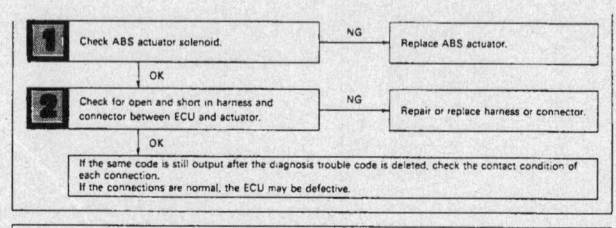

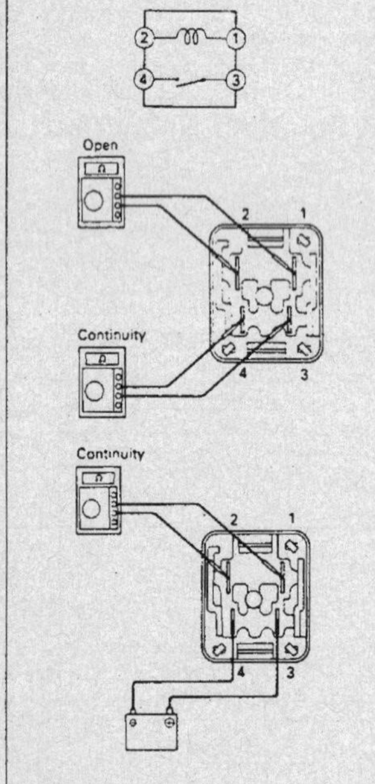
2
1
4
3
Open
Continuity
Continuity

P Remove motor relay from R/B No.5.

C Check continuity between each pair of terminal of motor relay.

OK

Terminals 3 and 4	Continuity (Reference value 62 Ω)
Terminals 1 and 2	Open

C 1. Apply battery positive voltage between terminals 3 and 4.
2. Check continuity between terminals.

OK

Terminals 1 and 2	Continuity

OK

NG Replace ABS motor relay.

4 Check for open and short in harness and connector between ABS motor relay and ABS ECU

OK

NG Repair or replace harness or connector.

If the same code is still output after the diagnostic trouble code is deleted, check the contact condition of each connection.
If the connections are normal, the ECU may be defective.

TY4029400098040X

Fig. 104 Code 13 & 14: ABS Motor Relay (Part 4 of 4). Celica

1 Check ABS actuator solenoid.	NG	Replace ABS actuator.
OK		
2 Check for open and short in harness and connector between ECU and actuator.	NG	Repair or replace harness or connector.
OK		

If the same code is still output after the diagnosis trouble code is deleted, check the contact condition of each connection.
If the connections are normal, the ECU may be defective.

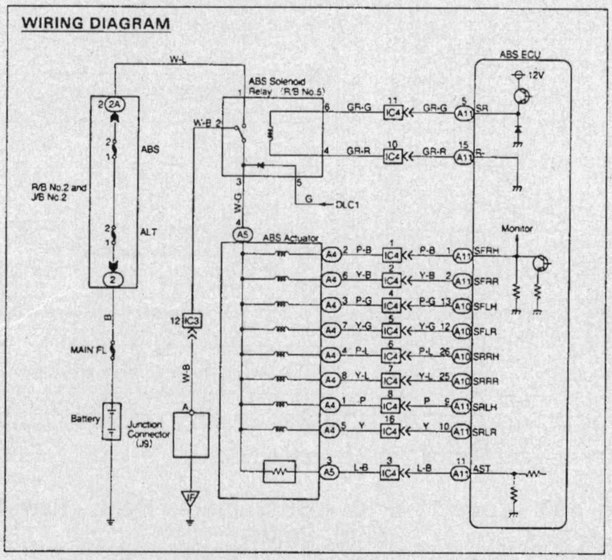
WIRING DIAGRAM
W-L
ABS ECU
12V
ABS Solenoid Relay (R/B No.5)
GR-G
GR-R
W-B
ABS
ALT
R/B No.2 and J/B No.2
DLC1
W-G
ABS Actuator
Monitor
P-B
Y-B
P-G
Y-G
P-L
Y-L
P
Y
L-B
SFRH
SFRR
SFLH
SFLR
SRRH
SRRR
SRLH
SRLR
AST
MAIN FL
W-B
Battery
Junction Connector (J9)

TY4029400099010X

Fig. 105 Code 21, 22, 23, 24: ABS Actuator Solenoid (Part 1 of 3). Celica

CIRCUIT DESCRIPTION

This solenoid goes on when signals are received from the ECU and controls the fluid pressure acting on the brake cylinders, thus controlling the braking force.

DTC No.	Diagnostic Trouble Code Detecting Condition	Trouble area
21	Conditions (1) through (3) continue for 0.05 sec. or more: (1) ABS solenoid relay terminal (SR) voltage: Battery positive voltage (2) Voltage of ABS ECU terminal AST: Battery positive voltage (3) When power transistor of ECU is ON, voltage of terminal SFRH or SFRR is 0 V or battery positive voltage.	• ABS actuator. • Open or short in SFRH or SFRR circuit. • ECU.
22	Conditions (1) through (3) continue for 0.05 sec. or more: (1) ABS solenoid relay terminal (SR) voltage: Battery positive voltage (2) Voltage of ABS ECU terminal AST: Battery positive voltage (3) When power transistor of ECU is ON, voltage of terminal SFLH or SFLR is 0 V or battery positive voltage.	• ABS actuator. • Open or short in SFLH or SFLR circuit. • ECU.
23	Conditions (1) through (3) continue for 0.05 sec. or more: (1) ABS solenoid relay terminal (SR) voltage: Battery positive voltage (2) Voltage of ABS ECU terminal AST: Battery positive voltage (3) When power transistor of ECU is ON, voltage of terminal SRRH or SRRR is 0 V or battery positive voltage.	• ABS actuator. • Open or short in SRRH or SRRR circuit. • ECU.
24	Conditions (1) through (3) continue for 0.05 sec. S solenoid relay terminal (SR) voltage: Battery positive voltage (2) Voltage of ABS ECU terminal AST: Battery positive voltage (3) When power transistor of ECU is ON, voltage of terminal SRLH or SRLR is 0 V or battery positive voltage.	• ABS actuator. • Open or short in SRLH or SRLR circuit. • ECU.

Fail safe function: If trouble occurs in the actuator solenoid circuit, the ECU cuts off current to the solenoid relay and prohibits ABS control.

TY4029400099020X

Fig. 105 Code 21, 22, 23, 24: ABS Actuator Solenoid (Part 2 of 3). Celica

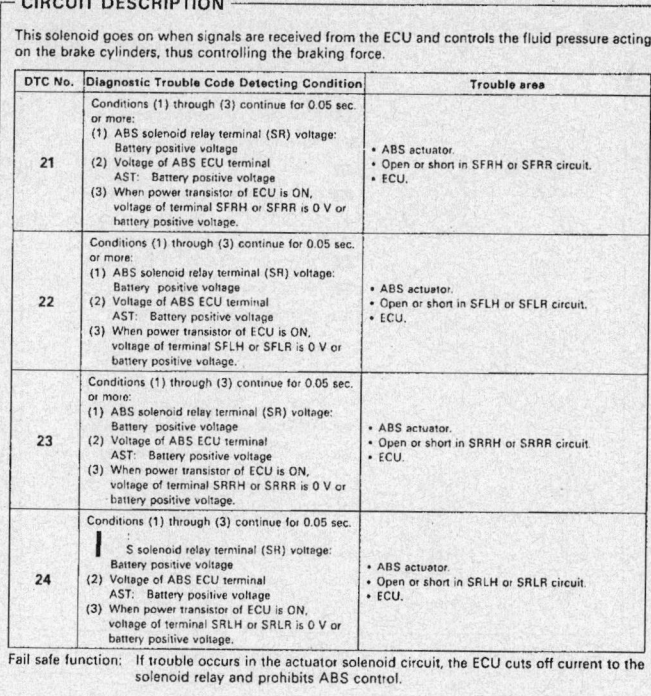

1 Check ABS actuator solenoid.

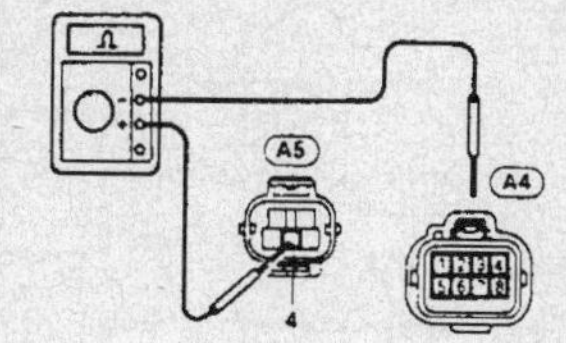

A5
A4
4

C Check continuity between terminal (A5) 4 and (A4) 1, 2, 3, 4, 5, 6, 7, 8 of ABS actuator connector.

OK Continuity

HINT: Resistance of each of the solenoids SFRH, SFLH, SRRH and SRLH is 5.0 Ω. Resistance of each of the solenoids SFRR, SFLR, SRRR and SRLR is 2.2 Ω.

OK

NG — Replace ABS actuator.

2 Check for open and short in harness and connector between ABS ECU and actuator

OK

NG — Repair or replace harness or connector.

If the same code is still output after the diagnostic trouble code is deleted, check the contact condition of each connection.
If the connections are normal, the ECU may be defective.

TY4029400099030X

Fig. 105 Code 21, 22, 23, 24: ABS Actuator Solenoid (Part 3 of 3). Celica

CIRCUIT DESCRIPTION

The speed sensor detects the wheel speed and sends the appropriate signals to the ECU. These signals are used to control the ABS system. The front and rear rotors each have 48 serrations. When the rotors rotate, the magnetic field emitted by the permanent magnet in the speed sensor generates an AC voltage. Since the frequency of this AC voltage changes in direct proportion to the speed of the rotor, the frequency is used by the ECU to detect the speed of each wheel.

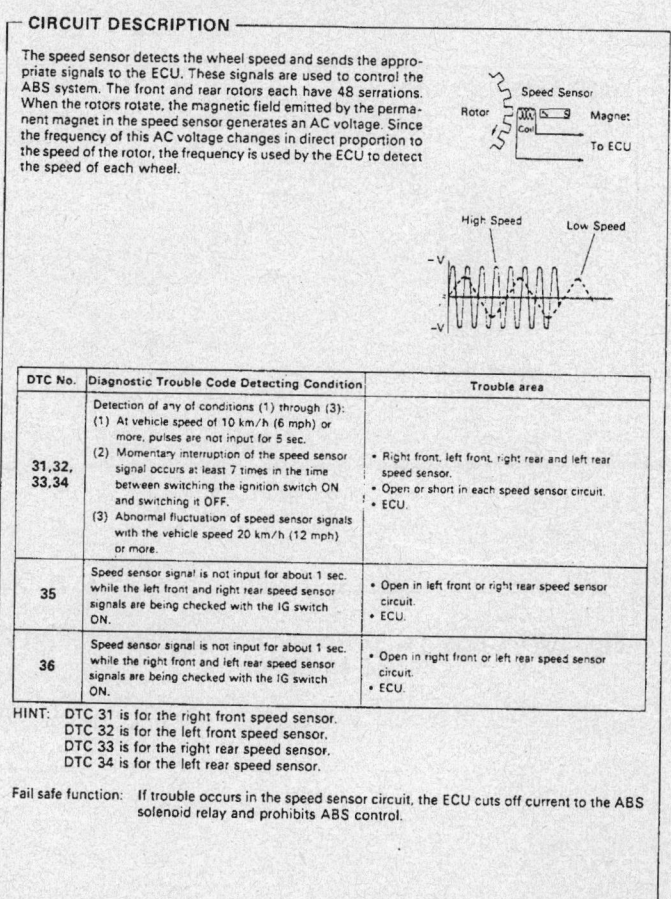

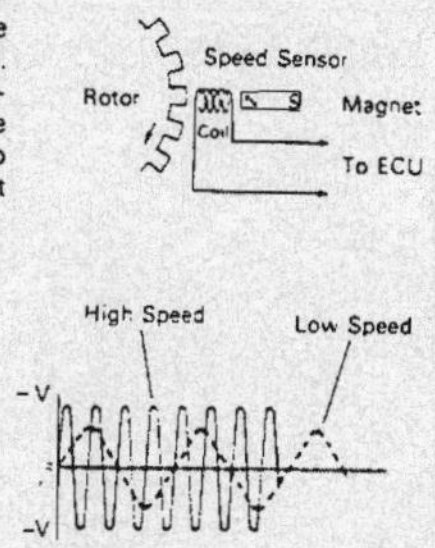

Speed Sensor
Rotor
Coil
Magnet
To ECU
High Speed
Low Speed
–V
–V

DTC No.	Diagnostic Trouble Code Detecting Condition	Trouble area
31,32, 33,34	Detection of any of conditions (1) through (3): (1) At vehicle speed of 10 km/h (6 mph) or more, pulses are not input for 5 sec. (2) Momentary interruption of the speed sensor signal occurs at least 7 times in the time between switching the ignition switch ON and switching it OFF. (3) Abnormal fluctuation of speed sensor signals with the vehicle speed 20 km/h (12 mph) or more.	• Right front, left front, right rear and left rear speed sensor. • Open or short in each speed sensor circuit. • ECU.
35	Speed sensor signal is not input for about 1 sec. while the left front and right rear speed sensor signals are being checked with the IG switch ON.	• Open in left front or right rear speed sensor circuit. • ECU.
36	Speed sensor signal is not input for about 1 sec. while the right front and left rear speed sensor signals are being checked with the IG switch ON.	• Open in right front or left rear speed sensor circuit. • ECU.

HINT: DTC 31 is for the right front speed sensor.
DTC 32 is for the left front speed sensor.
DTC 33 is for the right rear speed sensor.
DTC 34 is for the left rear speed sensor.

Fail safe function: If trouble occurs in the speed sensor circuit, the ECU cuts off current to the ABS solenoid relay and prohibits ABS control.

TY4029400100010X

Fig. 106 Code 31 through 36: Speed Sensor Circuit (Part 1 of 4). Celica

DIAGNOSTIC CHART

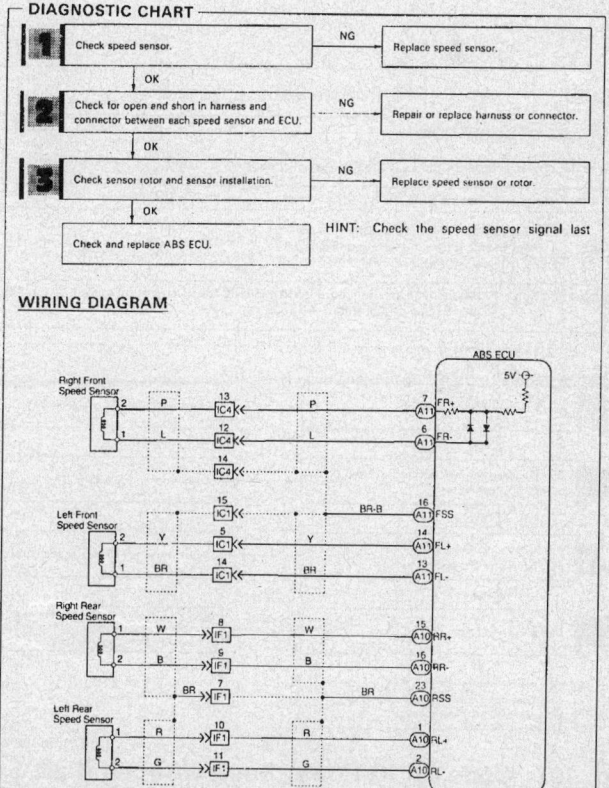

1 Check speed sensor. — NG → Replace speed sensor.

↓ OK

2 Check for open and short in harness and connector between each speed sensor and ECU. — NG → Repair or replace harness or connector.

↓ OK

3 Check sensor rotor and sensor installation. — NG → Replace speed sensor or rotor.

↓ OK

Check and replace ABS ECU.

HINT: Check the speed sensor signal last

WIRING DIAGRAM

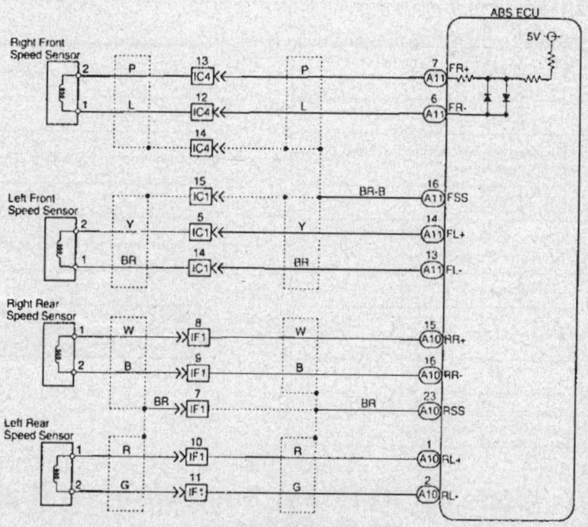

ABS ECU
Right Front Speed Sensor
Left Front Speed Sensor
Right Rear Speed Sensor
Left Rear Speed Sensor
5V
FR+
FR-
FSS
FL+
FL-
RR+
RR-
RSS
RL+
RL-

TY4029400100020X

Fig. 106 Code 31 through 36: Speed Sensor Circuit (Part 2 of 4). Celica

INSPECTION PROCEDURE

1 Check speed sensor.

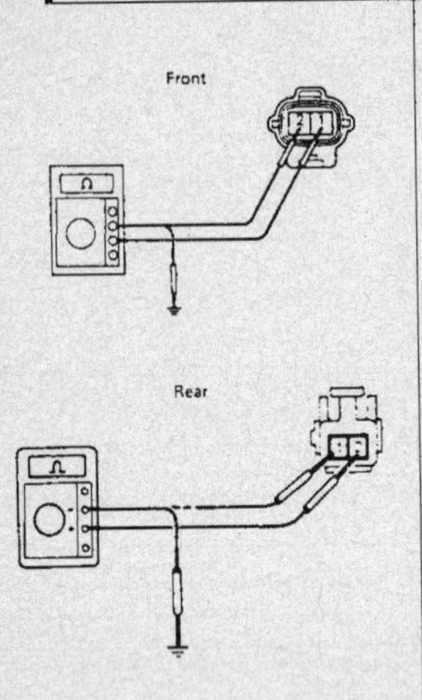
Front
Rear

Front

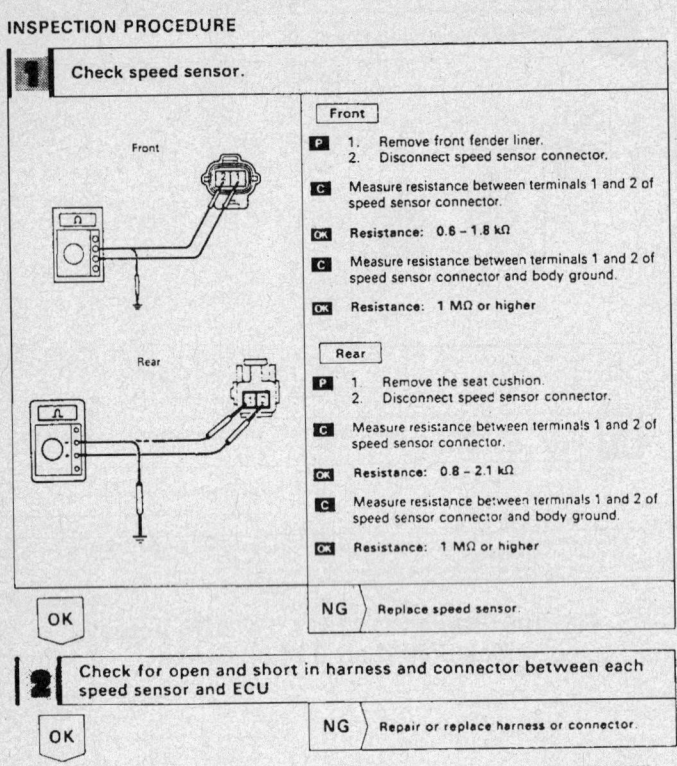

P 1. Remove front fender liner.
2. Disconnect speed sensor connector.

C Measure resistance between terminals 1 and 2 of speed sensor connector.

OK **Resistance: 0.6 – 1.8 kΩ**

C Measure resistance between terminals 1 and 2 of speed sensor connector and body ground.

OK **Resistance: 1 MΩ or higher**

Rear

P 1. Remove the seat cushion.
2. Disconnect speed sensor connector.

C Measure resistance between terminals 1 and 2 of speed sensor connector.

OK **Resistance: 0.8 – 2.1 kΩ**

C Measure resistance between terminals 1 and 2 of speed sensor connector and body ground.

OK **Resistance: 1 MΩ or higher**

OK ↓ | NG → **Replace speed sensor.**

2 Check for open and short in harness and connector between each speed sensor and ECU

OK ↓ | NG → **Repair or replace harness or connector.**

TY4029400100030X

Fig. 106 Code 31 through 36: Speed Sensor Circuit (Part 3 of 4). Celica

3 Check sensor rotor and sensor installation.

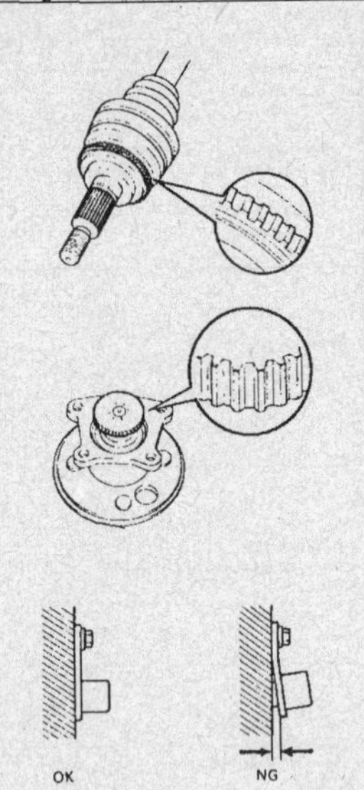
OK
NG

Front

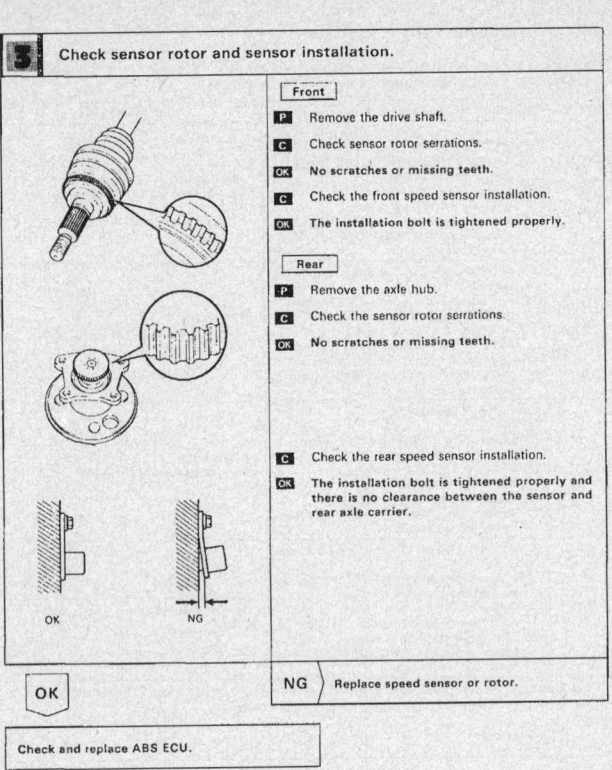

P Remove the drive shaft.

C Check sensor rotor serrations.

OK **No scratches or missing teeth.**

C Check the front speed sensor installation.

OK **The installation bolt is tightened properly.**

Rear

P Remove the axle hub.

C Check the sensor rotor serrations.

OK **No scratches or missing teeth.**

C Check the rear speed sensor installation.

OK **The installation bolt is tightened properly and there is no clearance between the sensor and rear axle carrier.**

OK ↓ | NG → **Replace speed sensor or rotor.**

Check and replace ABS ECU.

TY4029400100040X

Fig. 106 Code 31 through 36: Speed Sensor Circuit (Part 4 of 4). Celica

DTC	41	IG Power Source Circuit

CIRCUIT DESCRIPTION

This is the power source for the ECU, hence the CPU, and the actuators.

DTC No.	Diagnostic Trouble Code Detecting Condition	Trouble area
41	Vehicle speed is 3 km/h (1.9 mph) or more and voltage of ECU terminal IG1 remains at more than 17 V or below 9.5 V for more than 10 sec.	• Battery. • IC regulator. • Open or short in power source circuit. • ECU.

Fail safe function: If trouble occurs in the power source circuit, the ECU cuts off current to the ABS solenoid relay and prohibits ABS control.

DIAGNOSTIC CHART

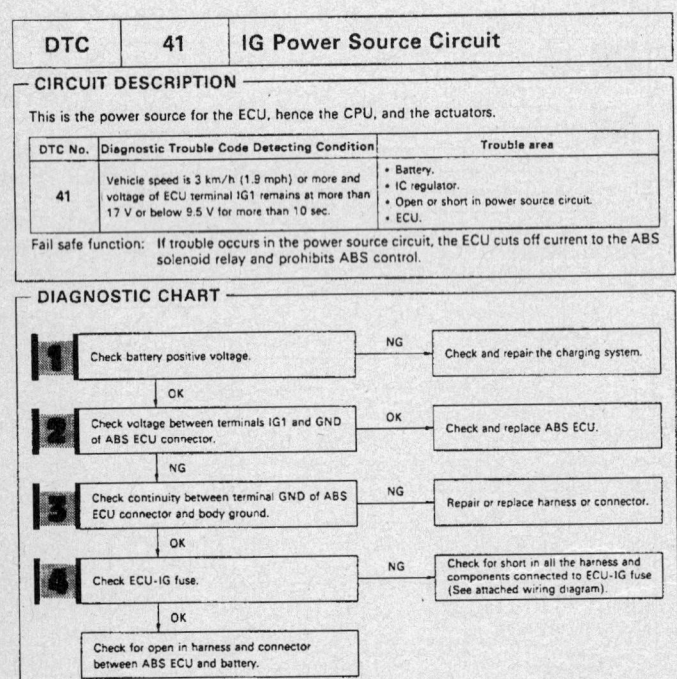

1 Check battery positive voltage. — NG → Check and repair the charging system.

OK ↓

2 Check voltage between terminals IG1 and GND of ABS ECU connector. — OK → Check and replace ABS ECU.

NG ↓

3 Check continuity between terminal GND of ABS ECU connector and body ground. — NG → Repair or replace harness or connector.

OK ↓

4 Check ECU-IG fuse. — NG → Check for short in all the harness and components connected to ECU-IG fuse (See attached wiring diagram).

OK ↓

Check for open in harness and connector between ABS ECU and battery.

TY4029400101010X

Fig. 107 Code 41: IG Power Source Circuit (Part 1 of 4). Celica

WIRING DIAGRAM

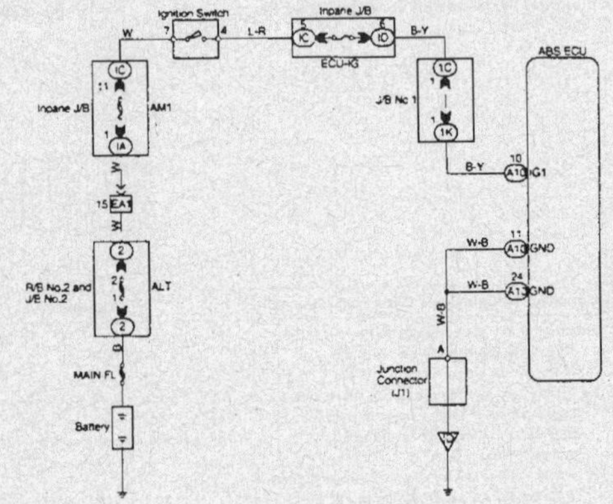
Ignition Switch
Inpane J/B
ECU-IG
J/B No.1
ABS ECU
AM1
B-Y
L-R
W
IG1
W-B
GND
R/B No.2 and J/B No.2
ALT
MAIN FL
Battery
Junction Connector (J1)

TY4029400101020X

Fig. 107 Code 41: IG Power Source Circuit (Part 2 of 4). Celica

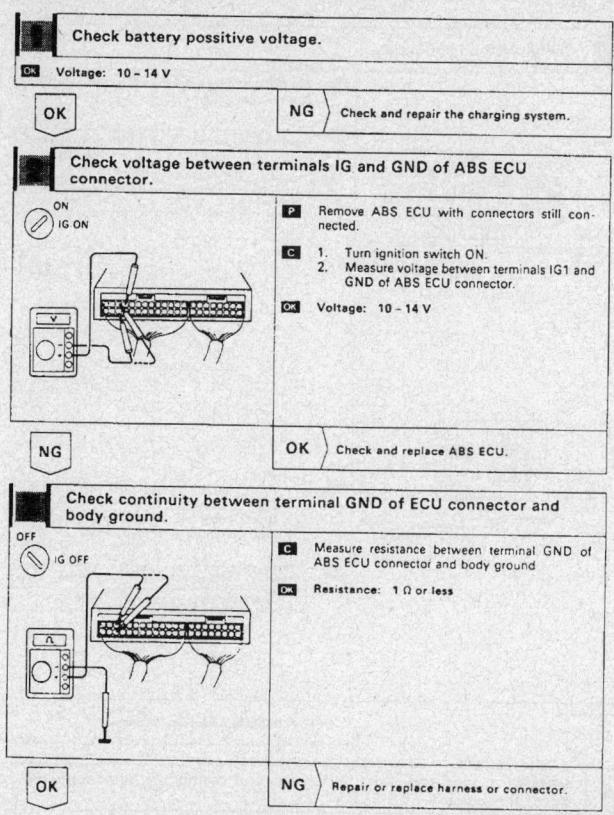

1 Check battery possitive voltage.

OK Voltage: 10 – 14 V

OK

NG Check and repair the charging system.

2 Check voltage between terminals IG and GND of ABS ECU connector.

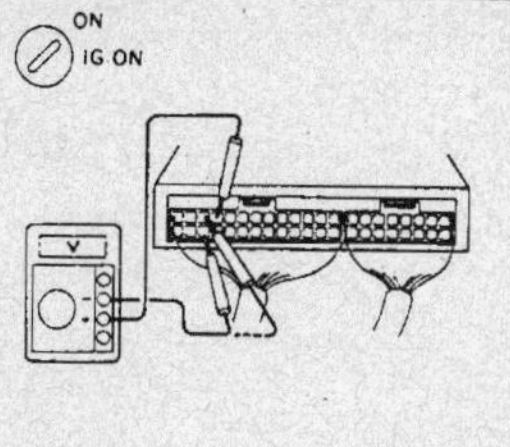
ON
IG ON

P Remove ABS ECU with connectors still connected.

C 1. Turn ignition switch ON.
2. Measure voltage between terminals IG1 and GND of ABS ECU connector.

OK Voltage: 10 – 14 V

NG

OK Check and replace ABS ECU.

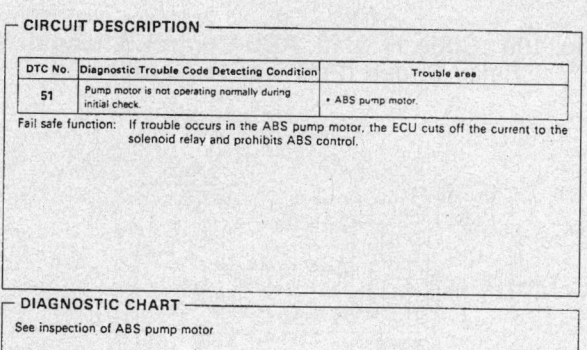

3 Check continuity between terminal GND of ECU connector and body ground.

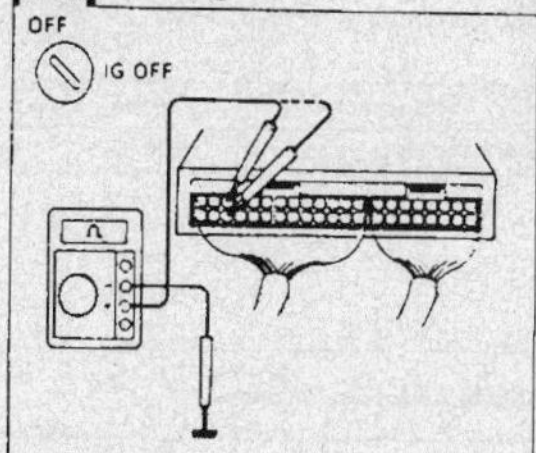
OFF
IG OFF

C Measure resistance between terminal GND of ABS ECU connector and body ground

OK Resistance: 1 Ω or less

OK

NG Repair or replace harness or connector.

TY4029400101030X

Fig. 107 Code 41: IG Power Source Circuit (Part 3 of 4). Celica

CIRCUIT DESCRIPTION

DTC No.	Diagnostic Trouble Code Detecting Condition	Trouble area
51	Pump motor is not operating normally during initial check.	• ABS pump motor.

Fail safe function: If trouble occurs in the ABS pump motor, the ECU cuts off the current to the solenoid relay and prohibits ABS control.

DIAGNOSTIC CHART

See inspection of ABS pump motor

WIRING DIAGRAM

(Reference)

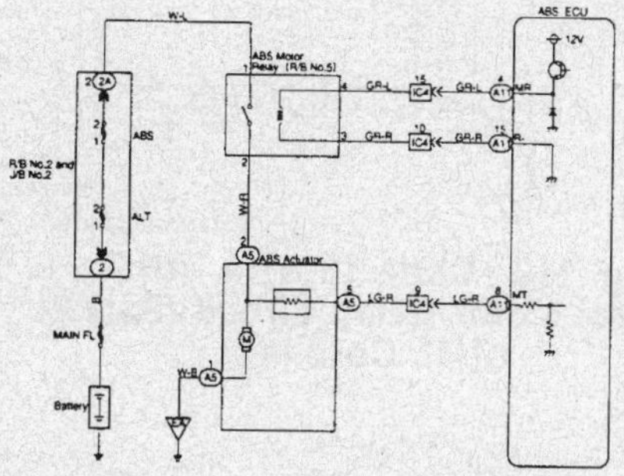
W-L
ABS Motor Relay (R/B No.5)
ABS ECU
12V
GR-L
IC4
A11
MR
GR-R
R-
R/B No.2 and J/B No.2
ABS
ALT
W-R
A5
ABS Actuator
LG-R
MT
MAIN FL
W-B
Battery

TY4029400102000X

Fig. 108 Code 51: ABS Pump Motor Lock. Celica

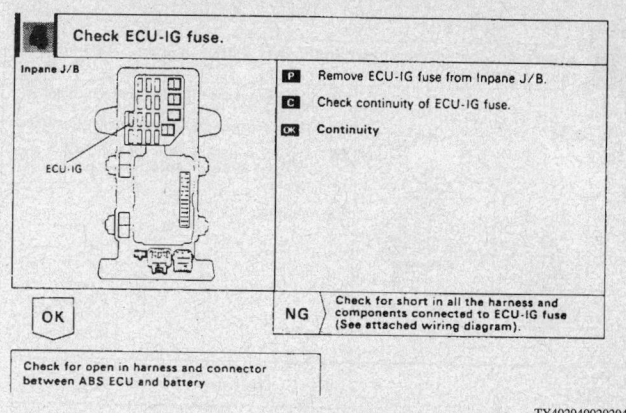

4 Check ECU-IG fuse.

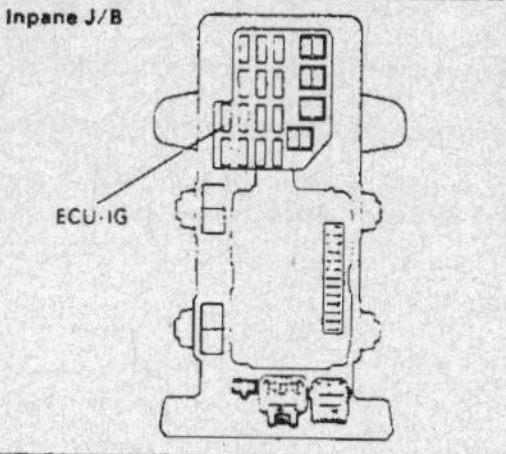
Inpane J/B
ECU-IG

P Remove ECU-IG fuse from Inpane J/B.

C Check continuity of ECU-IG fuse.

OK Continuity

OK

NG Check for short in all the harness and components connected to ECU-IG fuse (See attached wiring diagram).

Check for open in harness and connector between ABS ECU and battery

TY4029400202040X

Fig. 107 Code 41: IG Power Source Circuit (Part 4 of 4). Celica

CIRCUIT DESCRIPTION

This relay supplies power to each ABS solenoid. After the ignition switch is turned on, if the initial check is OK, the relay goes on.

DTC No.	Diagnostic Trouble Code Detecting Condition	Trouble Area
11	Conditions (1) and (2) continue for 0.2 sec. or more: (1) ABS control (solenoid) relay: ON (2) ABS control (solenoid) relay monitor terminal (AST) voltage: 0 V	• ABS control (solenoid) relay. • Open or short in ABS control (solenoid) relay circuit. • ECU.
12	Conditions (1) and (2) continue for 0.2 sec. or more: (1) ABS control (solenoid) relay: OFF (2) ABS control (solenoid) relay monitor terminal (AST) voltage: Battery voltage	• ABS control (solenoid) relay. • B+ short in ABS control (solenoid) relay circuit. • ECU.

Fail safe function: If trouble occurs in the control (solenoid) relay circuit, the ECU cuts off current to the ABS control (solenoid) relay and prohibits ABS control.

DIAGNOSTIC CHART

1 Check voltage of ABS control relay connector. — NG → Check and repair harness or connector.

OK

2 Check continuity between relay and actuator and ECU. — NG → Repair or replace harness or ABS actuator.

OK

3 Check ABS control relay. — NG → Replace ABS control relay.

OK

4 Check for open and short in harness and connector between relay and ECU. — NG → Repair or replace harness or connector.

OK

If the same code is still output after the diagnostic trouble code is deleted, check the contact condition of each connection.
If the connections are normal, the ECU may be defective.

TY4029300077010X

Fig. 109 Code 11 & 12: ABS Control Solenoid Relay Circuit (Part 1 of 4). Corolla

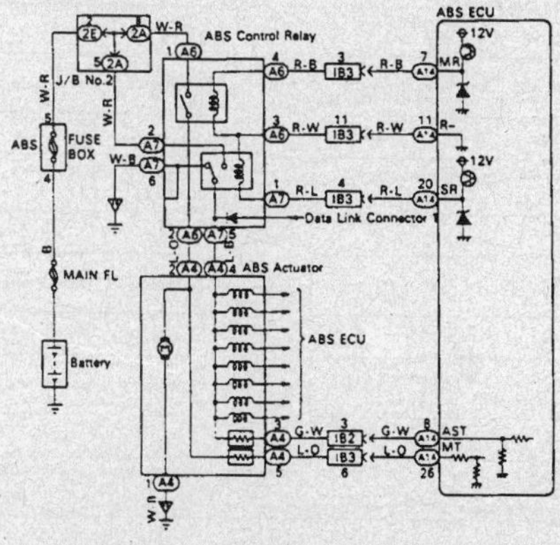
W-R
ABS Control Relay
ABS ECU
12V
J/B No.2
R-B
IB3
MR
R-W
R-
ABS
FUSE BOX
W-B
R-L
SR
Data Link Connector 1
MAIN FL
ABS Actuator
ABS ECU
Battery
G-W
IB2
AST
L-O
MT

TY4029300077020X

Fig. 109 Code 11 & 12: ABS Control Solenoid Relay Circuit (Part 2 of 4). Corolla

INSPECTION PROCEDURE

1 Check voltage between terminals (A7) 2 and (A7) 6 of ABS control relay connector

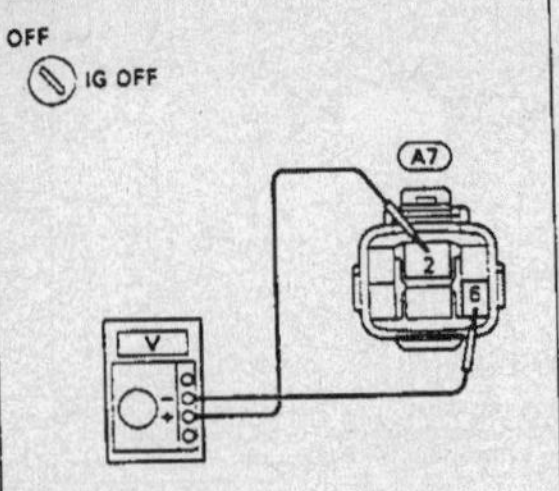
OFF
IG OFF
A7
2
6
V

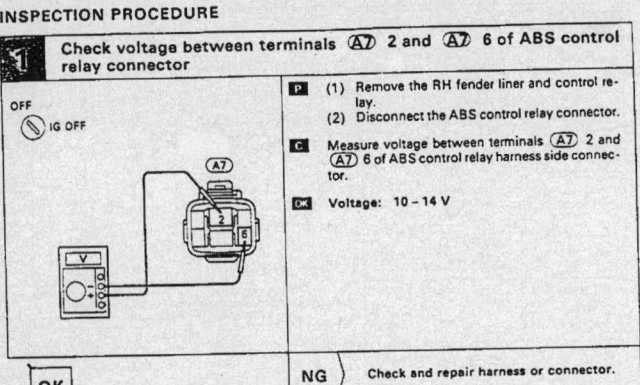

P (1) Remove the RH fender liner and control relay.
(2) Disconnect the ABS control relay connector.

C Measure voltage between terminals (A7) 2 and (A7) 6 of ABS control relay harness side connector.

OK Voltage: 10 – 14 V

OK

NG ⟩ Check and repair harness or connector.

2 Check continuity between terminal (A7) 5 and (A4) 4, (A4) 4 and (A4) 3, (A4) 3 and (A14) 8.

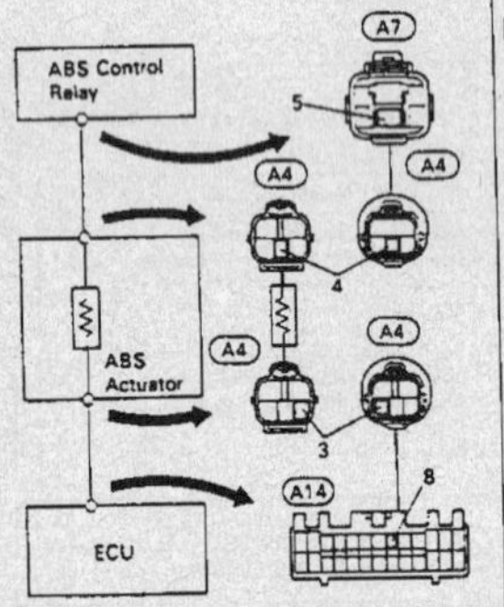
ABS Control Relay
A7
5
A4
A4
4
ABS Actuator
A4
A4
3
A14
8
ECU

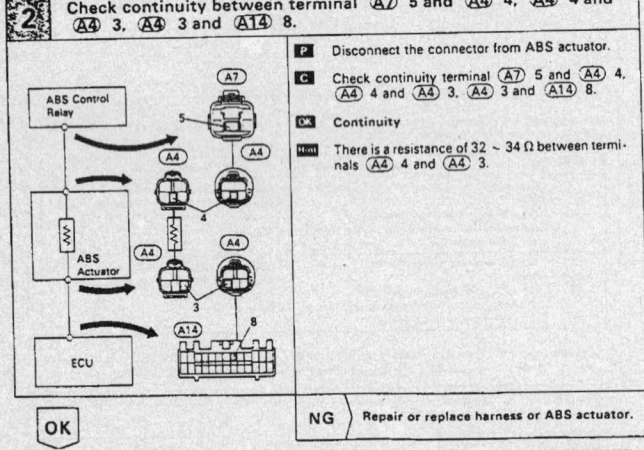

P Disconnect the connector from ABS actuator.

C Check continuity terminal (A7) 5 and (A4) 4, (A4) 4 and (A4) 3, (A4) 3 and (A14) 8.

OK Continuity

Hint There is a resistance of 32 ~ 34 Ω between terminals (A4) 4 and (A4) 3.

OK

NG ⟩ Repair or replace harness or ABS actuator.

TY4029300077030X

Fig. 109 Code 11 & 12: ABS Control Solenoid Relay Circuit (Part 3 of 4). Corolla

3 Check ABS control relay.

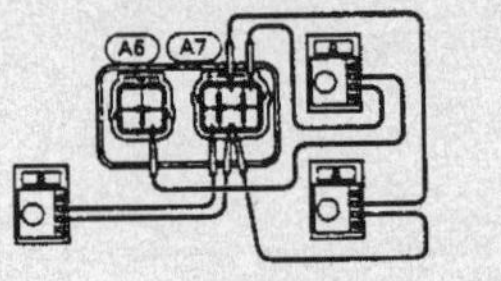
A6
A7

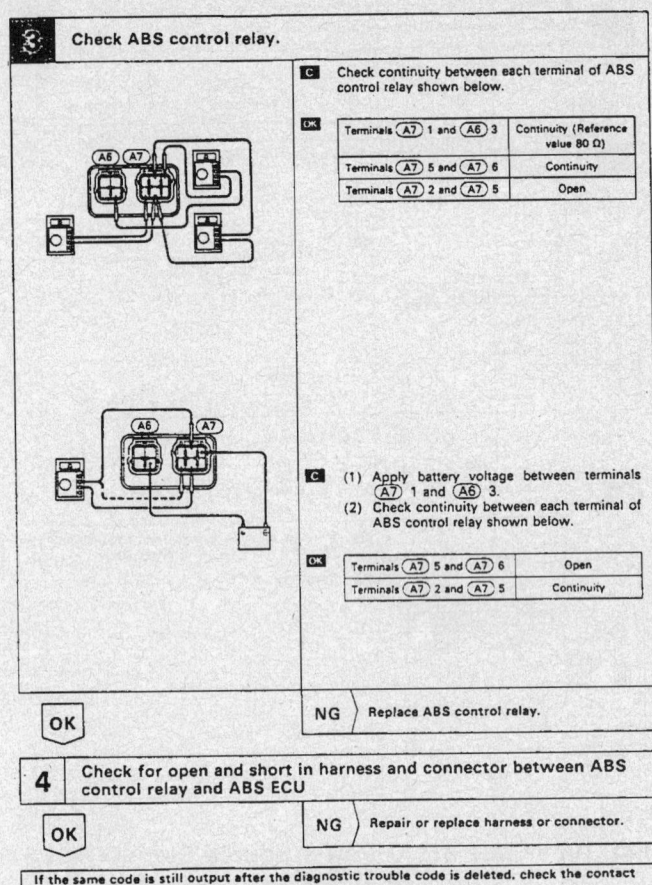

C Check continuity between each terminal of ABS control relay shown below.

OK

Terminals (A7) 1 and (A6) 3	Continuity (Reference value 80 Ω)
Terminals (A7) 5 and (A7) 6	Continuity
Terminals (A7) 2 and (A7) 5	Open

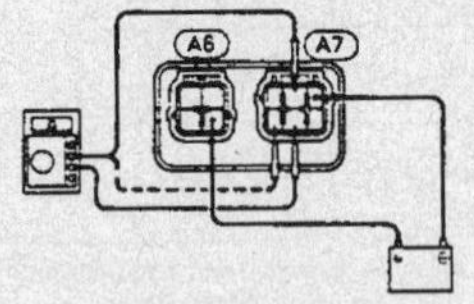
A6
A7

C (1) Apply battery voltage between terminals (A7) 1 and (A6) 3.
(2) Check continuity between each terminal of ABS control relay shown below.

OK

Terminals (A7) 5 and (A7) 6	Open
Terminals (A7) 2 and (A7) 5	Continuity

OK

NG ⟩ Replace ABS control relay.

4 Check for open and short in harness and connector between ABS control relay and ABS ECU

OK

NG ⟩ Repair or replace harness or connector.

If the same code is still output after the diagnostic trouble code is deleted, check the contact condition of each connection.
If the connections are normal, the ECU may be defective.

TY4029300077040X

Fig. 109 Code 11 & 12: ABS Control Solenoid Relay Circuit (Part 4 of 4). Corolla

CIRCUIT DESCRIPTION

The ABS control (motor) relay supplies power to the ABS pump motor. If the accumulator pressure drops, the ECU switches the control (motor) relay ON and operates the ABS pump motor.

DTC No.	Diagnostic Trouble Code Detecting Condition	Trouble Area
13	Conditions (1) and (2) continue for 0.2 sec. or more: (1) ABS control (motor) relay: ON (2) ABS control (motor) relay monitor terminal (MT) voltage: 0 V	• ABS control (motor) relay. • Open or short in ABS control (motor) relay circuit. • ECU.
14	Conditions (1) and (2) continue for 4 sec. or more: (1) ABS control (motor) relay: OFF (2) ABS control (motor) relay monitor terminal (MT) voltage: Battery voltage	• ABS control (motor) relay. • B+ short in ABS control (motor) relay circuit. • ECU.

Fail safe function: If trouble occurs in the control (motor) relay circuit, the ECU cuts off the current to the ABS control (solenoid) relay and prohibits ABS control.

DIAGNOSTIC CHART

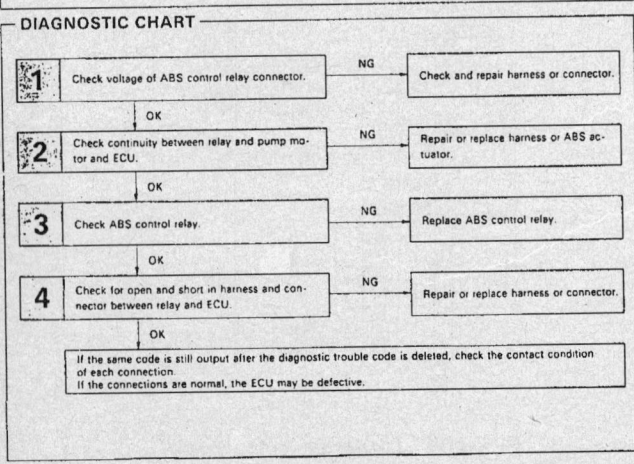

1 Check voltage of ABS control relay connector. — NG → Check and repair harness or connector.

OK

2 Check continuity between relay and pump motor and ECU. — NG → Repair or replace harness or ABS actuator.

OK

3 Check ABS control relay. — NG → Replace ABS control relay.

OK

4 Check for open and short in harness and connector between relay and ECU. — NG → Repair or replace harness or connector.

OK

If the same code is still output after the diagnostic trouble code is deleted, check the contact condition of each connection.
If the connections are normal, the ECU may be defective.

TY4029300078010X

Fig. 110 Code 13 & 14: ABS Control Motor Relay Circuit (Part 1 of 4). Corolla

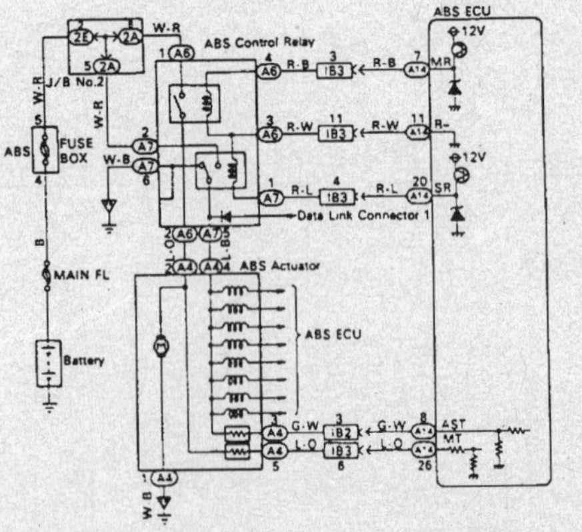
ABS ECU
W-R
ABS Control Relay
J/B No.2
FUSE BOX
ABS
W-B
R-B
R-W
R-L
Data Link Connector 1
MAIN FL
ABS Actuator
ABS ECU
Battery
G-W
L-O

TY4029300078020X

Fig. 110 Code 13 & 14: ABS Control Motor Relay Circuit (Part 2 of 4). Corolla

INSPECTION PROCEDURE

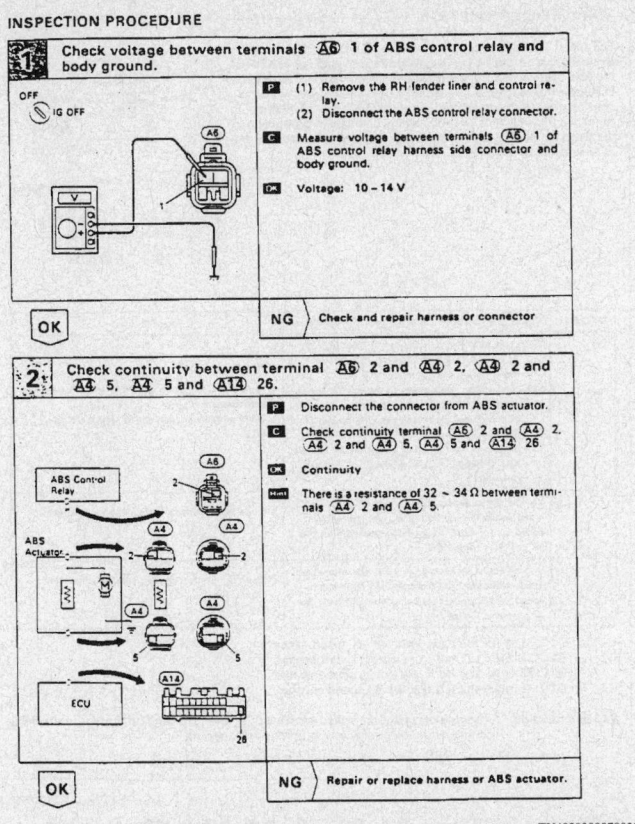

1 Check voltage between terminals (A6) 1 of ABS control relay and body ground.

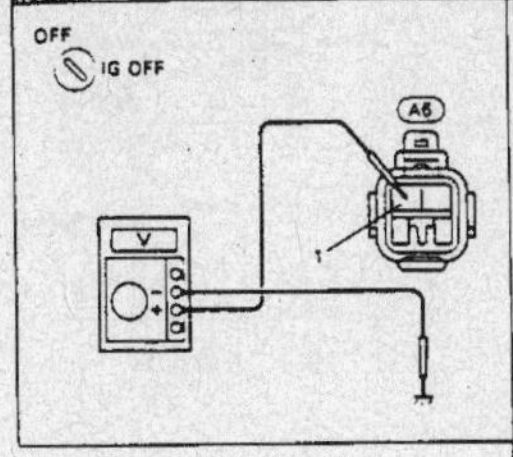
OFF
IG OFF
A6
V
1

P (1) Remove the RH fender liner and control relay.
(2) Disconnect the ABS control relay connector.

C Measure voltage between terminals (A6) 1 of ABS control relay harness side connector and body ground.

OK Voltage: 10 – 14 V

OK

NG 〉 Check and repair harness or connector

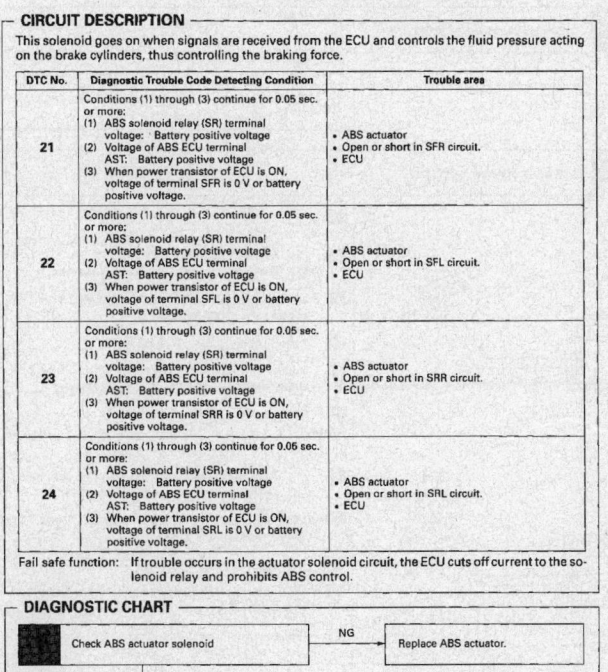

2 Check continuity between terminal (A6) 2 and (A4) 2, (A4) 2 and (A4) 5, (A4) 5 and (A14) 26.

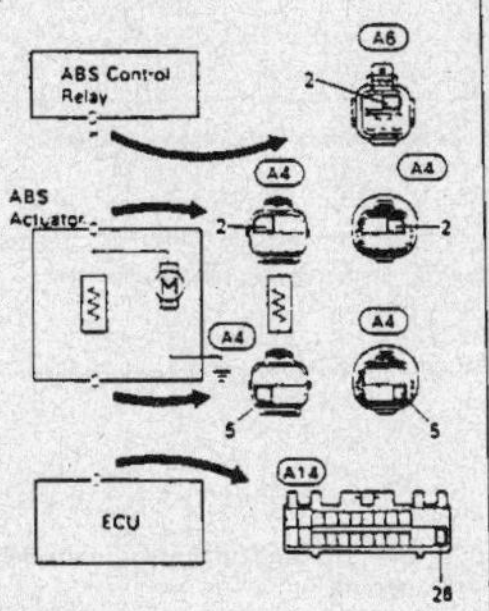
ABS Control Relay
A6
2
ABS Actuator
A4
2
A4
A4
5
A14
ECU
26

P Disconnect the connector from ABS actuator.

C Check continuity terminal (A6) 2 and (A4) 2, (A4) 2 and (A4) 5, (A4) 5 and (A14) 26.

OK Continuity

Hint There is a resistance of 32 ~ 34 Ω between terminals (A4) 2 and (A4) 5.

OK

NG 〉 Repair or replace harness or ABS actuator.

TY4029300078030X

Fig. 110 Code 13 & 14: ABS Control Motor Relay Circuit (Part 3 of 4). Corolla

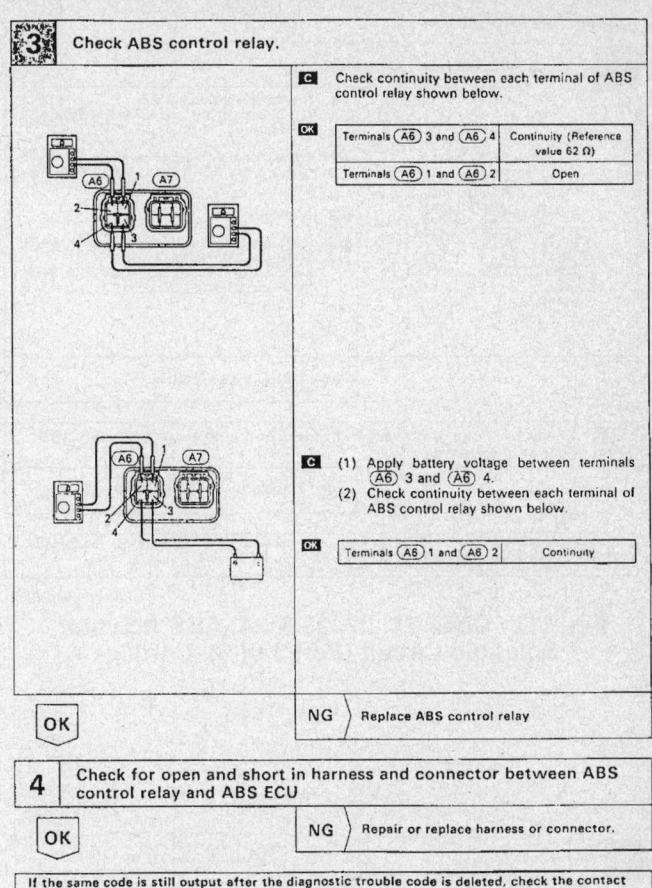

3 Check ABS control relay.

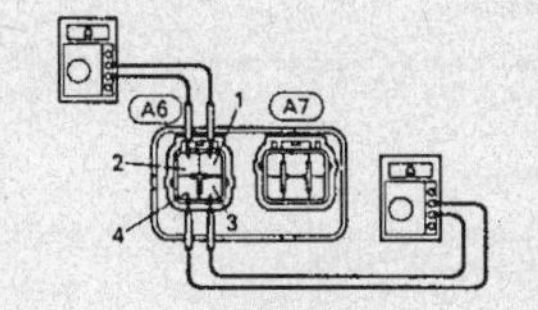
A6
A7
1
2
3
4

C Check continuity between each terminal of ABS control relay shown below.

OK

Terminals (A6) 3 and (A6) 4	Continuity (Reference value 62 Ω)
Terminals (A6) 1 and (A6) 2	Open

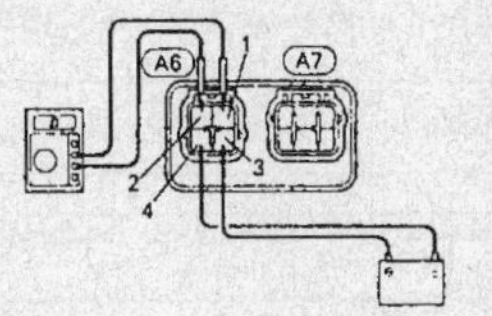
A6
A7
1
2
3
4

C (1) Apply battery voltage between terminals (A6) 3 and (A6) 4.
(2) Check continuity between each terminal of ABS control relay shown below.

OK

Terminals (A6) 1 and (A6) 2	Continuity

OK

NG 〉 Replace ABS control relay

4 Check for open and short in harness and connector between ABS control relay and ABS ECU

OK

NG 〉 Repair or replace harness or connector.

If the same code is still output after the diagnostic trouble code is deleted, check the contact condition of each connection.
If the connections are normal, the ECU may be defective.

TY4029300078040X

Fig. 110 Code 13 & 14: ABS Control Motor Relay Circuit (Part 4 of 4). Corolla

CIRCUIT DESCRIPTION

This solenoid goes on when signals are received from the ECU and controls the fluid pressure acting on the brake cylinders, thus controlling the braking force.

DTC No.	Diagnostic Trouble Code Detecting Condition	Trouble area
21	Conditions (1) through (3) continue for 0.05 sec. or more: (1) ABS solenoid relay (SR) terminal voltage: Battery positive voltage (2) Voltage of ABS ECU terminal AST: Battery positive voltage (3) When power transistor of ECU is ON, voltage of terminal SFR is 0 V or battery positive voltage.	• ABS actuator • Open or short in SFR circuit. • ECU
22	Conditions (1) through (3) continue for 0.05 sec. or more: (1) ABS solenoid relay (SR) terminal voltage: Battery positive voltage (2) Voltage of ABS ECU terminal AST: Battery positive voltage (3) When power transistor of ECU is ON, voltage of terminal SFL is 0 V or battery positive voltage.	• ABS actuator • Open or short in SFL circuit. • ECU
23	Conditions (1) through (3) continue for 0.05 sec. or more: (1) ABS solenoid relay (SR) terminal voltage: Battery positive voltage (2) Voltage of ABS ECU terminal AST: Battery positive voltage (3) When power transistor of ECU is ON, voltage of terminal SRR is 0 V or battery positive voltage.	• ABS actuator • Open or short in SRR circuit. • ECU
24	Conditions (1) through (3) continue for 0.06 sec. or more: (1) ABS solenoid relay (SR) terminal voltage: Battery positive voltage (2) Voltage of ABS ECU terminal AST: Battery positive voltage (3) When power transistor of ECU is ON, voltage of terminal SRL is 0 V or battery positive voltage.	• ABS actuator • Open or short in SRL circuit. • ECU

Fail safe function: If trouble occurs in the actuator solenoid circuit, the ECU cuts off current to the solenoid relay and prohibits ABS control.

DIAGNOSTIC CHART

Check ABS actuator solenoid —NG→ Replace ABS actuator.

↓ OK

Check for open and short in harness and connector between ECU and actuator. —NG→ Repair or replace harness or connector.

↓ OK

If the same code is still output after the diagnostic trouble code is deleted, check the contact condition of each connection.
If the connections are normal, the ECU may be defective.

TY4029300079010X

Fig. 111 Code 21, 22, 23 & 24: ABS Actuator Solenoid Circuit (Part 1 of 3). Corolla

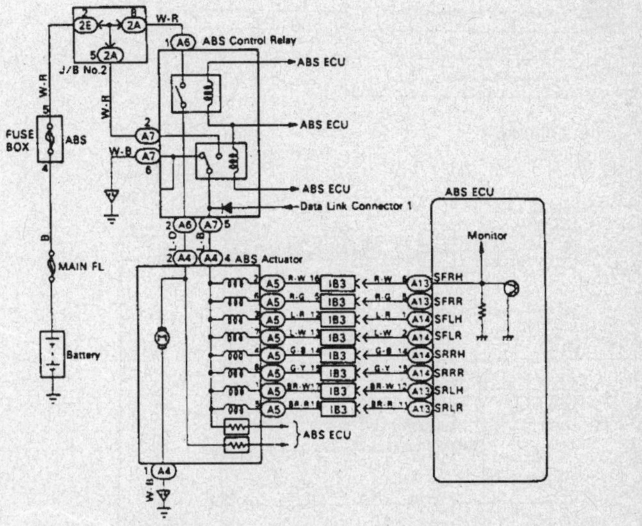
W-R
ABS Control Relay
ABS ECU
J/B No.2
FUSE BOX
ABS
W-B
ABS ECU
ABS ECU
Data Link Connector 1
ABS ECU
Monitor
MAIN FL
ABS Actuator
SFRH
SFRR
SFLH
SFLR
SRRH
SRRR
SRLH
SRLR
Battery
ABS ECU

TY4029300079020X

Fig. 111 Code 21, 22, 23 & 24: ABS Actuator Solenoid Circuit (Part 2 of 3). Corolla

INSPECTION PROCEDURE

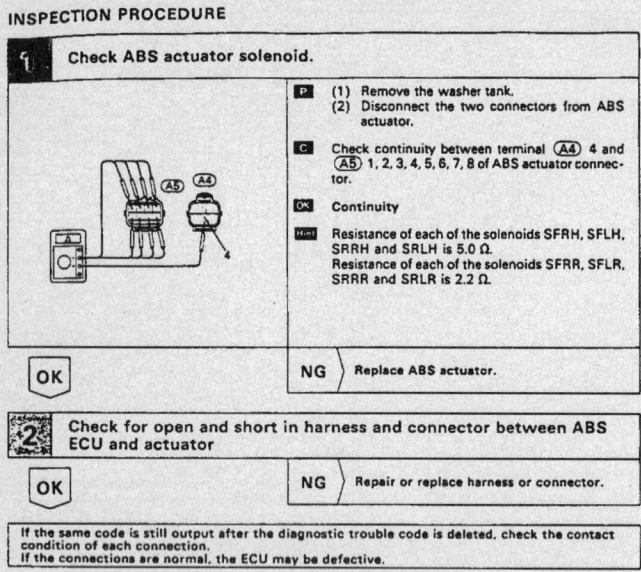

1 Check ABS actuator solenoid.

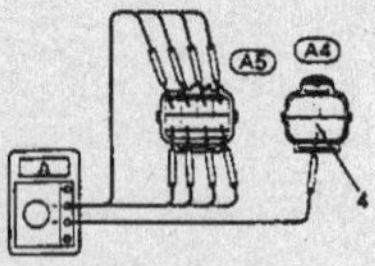
A5
A4
4

P (1) Remove the washer tank.
(2) Disconnect the two connectors from ABS actuator.

C Check continuity between terminal (A4) 4 and (A5) 1, 2, 3, 4, 5, 6, 7, 8 of ABS actuator connector.

OK **Continuity**

Hint Resistance of each of the solenoids SFRH, SFLH, SRRH and SRLH is 5.0 Ω.
Resistance of each of the solenoids SFRR, SFLR, SRRR and SRLR is 2.2 Ω.

OK

NG **Replace ABS actuator.**

2 Check for open and short in harness and connector between ABS ECU and actuator

OK

NG **Repair or replace harness or connector.**

If the same code is still output after the diagnostic trouble code is deleted, check the contact condition of each connection.
If the connections are normal, the ECU may be defective.

TY4029300079030X

Fig. 111 Code 21, 22, 23 & 24: ABS Actuator Solenoid Circuit (Part 3 of 3). Corolla

CIRCUIT DESCRIPTION

The speed sensor detects the wheel speed and sends the appropriate signals to the ECU. These signals are used for control of the ABS system. The front rotor and rear rotor have 48 serrations. When the rotors rotate, the magnetic field emitted by the permanent magnet in the speed sensor generates an AC voltage. Since the frequency of this AC voltage changes in proportion to the speed of the rotors (wheels), the frequency is used by the ECU to detect the speed of each wheel.

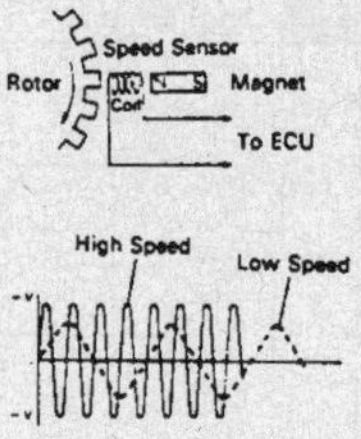
Speed Sensor
Rotor
Coil
Magnet
To ECU
High Speed
Low Speed

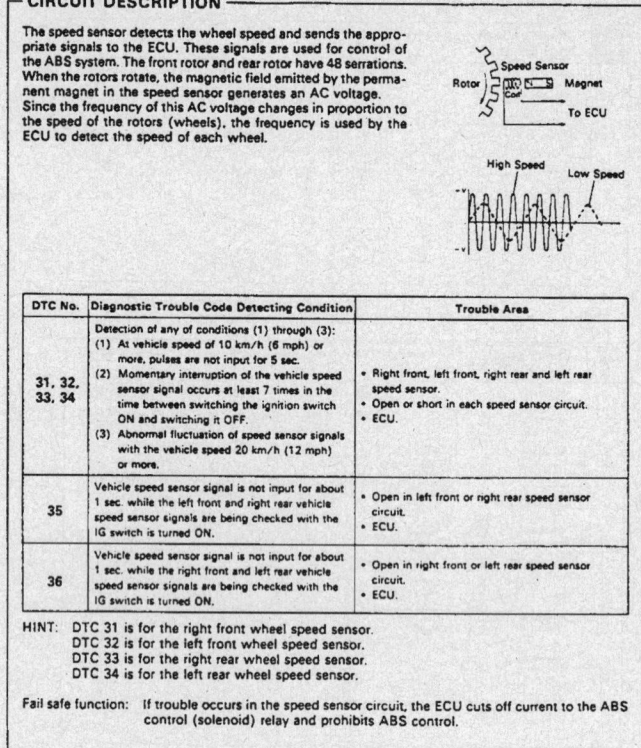

DTC No.	Diagnostic Trouble Code Detecting Condition	Trouble Area
31, 32, 33, 34	Detection of any of conditions (1) through (3): (1) At vehicle speed of 10 km/h (6 mph) or more, pulses are not input for 5 sec. (2) Momentary interruption of the vehicle speed sensor signal occurs at least 7 times in the time between switching the ignition switch ON and switching it OFF. (3) Abnormal fluctuation of speed sensor signals with the vehicle speed 20 km/h (12 mph) or more.	• Right front, left front, right rear and left rear speed sensor. • Open or short in each speed sensor circuit. • ECU.
35	Vehicle speed sensor signal is not input for about 1 sec. while the left front and right rear vehicle speed sensor signals are being checked with the IG switch is turned ON.	• Open in left front or right rear speed sensor circuit. • ECU.
36	Vehicle speed sensor signal is not input for about 1 sec. while the right front and left rear vehicle speed sensor signals are being checked with the IG switch is turned ON.	• Open in right front or left rear speed sensor circuit. • ECU.

HINT: DTC 31 is for the right front wheel speed sensor.
DTC 32 is for the left front wheel speed sensor.
DTC 33 is for the right rear wheel speed sensor.
DTC 34 is for the left rear wheel speed sensor.

Fail safe function: If trouble occurs in the speed sensor circuit, the ECU cuts off current to the ABS control (solenoid) relay and prohibits ABS control.

TY4029300080010X

Fig. 112 Code 31, 32, 33, 34, 35 & 36: Speed Sensor Circuit (Part 1 of 4). Corolla

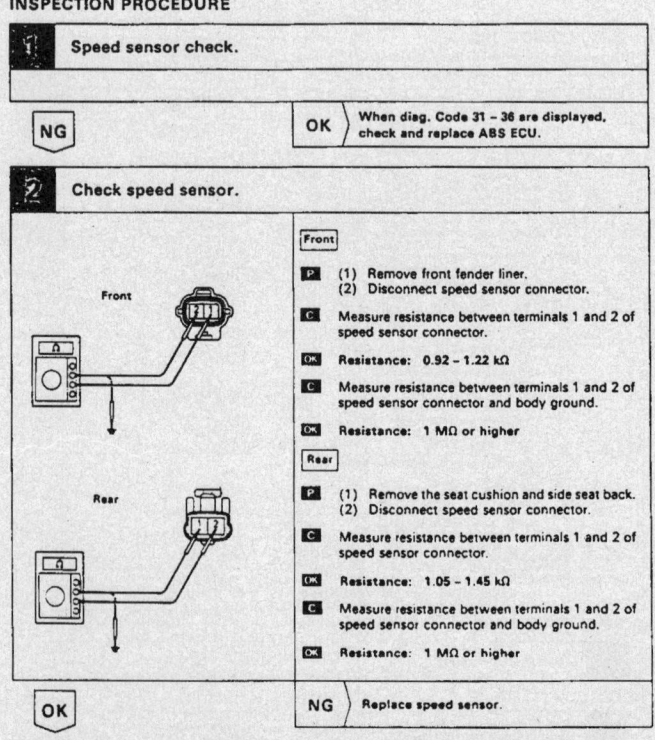

1 Speed sensor check — OK → When diag. code 31 – 36 are displayed, check and replace ABS ECU.
↓ NG
2 Check speed sensor. — NG → Replace speed sensor.
↓ OK
3 Check for open and short in harness and connector between each speed sensor and ECU. — NG → Repair or replace harness or connector.
↓ OK
4 Check sensor rotor and sensor installation — NG → Replace speed sensor or rotor.
↓ OK
Check and replace ABS ECU.

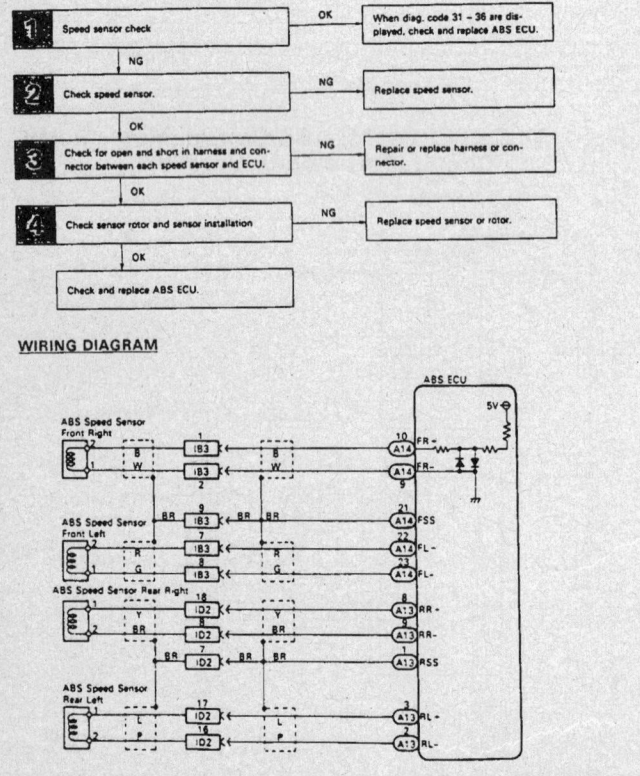

WIRING DIAGRAM

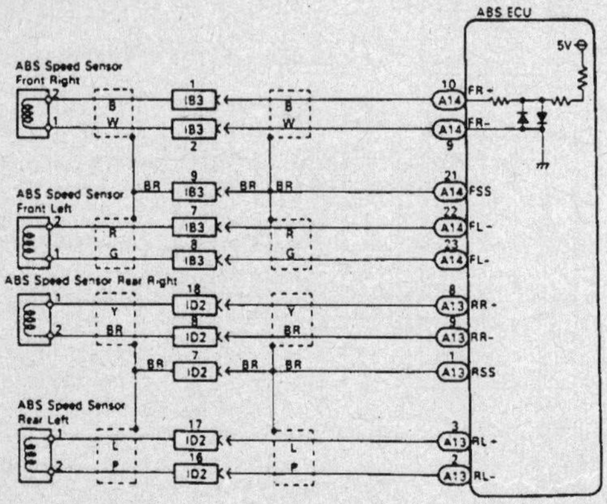
ABS ECU
5V
ABS Speed Sensor Front Right
ABS Speed Sensor Front Left
ABS Speed Sensor Rear Right
ABS Speed Sensor Rear Left
B
W
R
G
Y
BR
L
P
IB3
ID2
A14
A13
FR+
FR-
FSS
FL+
FL-
RR+
RR-
RSS
RL+
RL-

TY4029300080020X

Fig. 112 Code 31, 32, 33, 34, 35 & 36: Speed Sensor Circuit (Part 2 of 4). Corolla

INSPECTION PROCEDURE

1 Speed sensor check.

NG

OK **When diag. Code 31 – 36 are displayed, check and replace ABS ECU.**

2 Check speed sensor.

Front

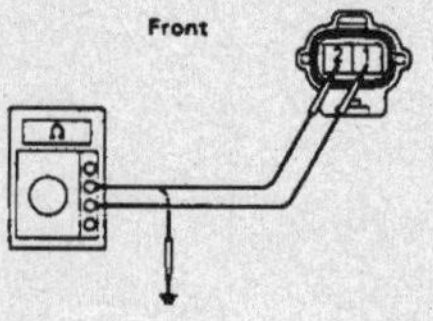
Front

P (1) Remove front fender liner.
(2) Disconnect speed sensor connector.

C Measure resistance between terminals 1 and 2 of speed sensor connector.

OK **Resistance: 0.92 – 1.22 kΩ**

C Measure resistance between terminals 1 and 2 of speed sensor connector and body ground.

OK **Resistance: 1 MΩ or higher**

Rear

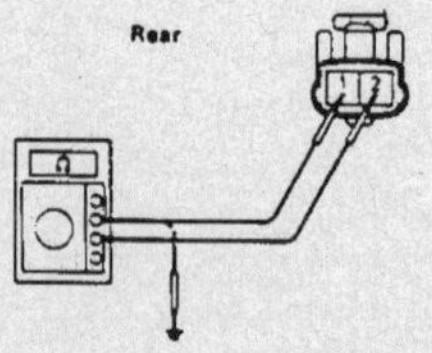
Rear

P (1) Remove the seat cushion and side seat back.
(2) Disconnect speed sensor connector.

C Measure resistance between terminals 1 and 2 of speed sensor connector.

OK **Resistance: 1.05 – 1.45 kΩ**

C Measure resistance between terminals 1 and 2 of speed sensor connector and body ground.

OK **Resistance: 1 MΩ or higher**

OK

NG **Replace speed sensor.**

3 Check for open and short in harness and connector between each speed sensor and ECU

OK

NG **Repair or replace harness or connector.**

TY4029300080030X

Fig. 112 Code 31, 32, 33, 34, 35 & 36: Speed Sensor Circuit (Part 3 of 4). Corolla

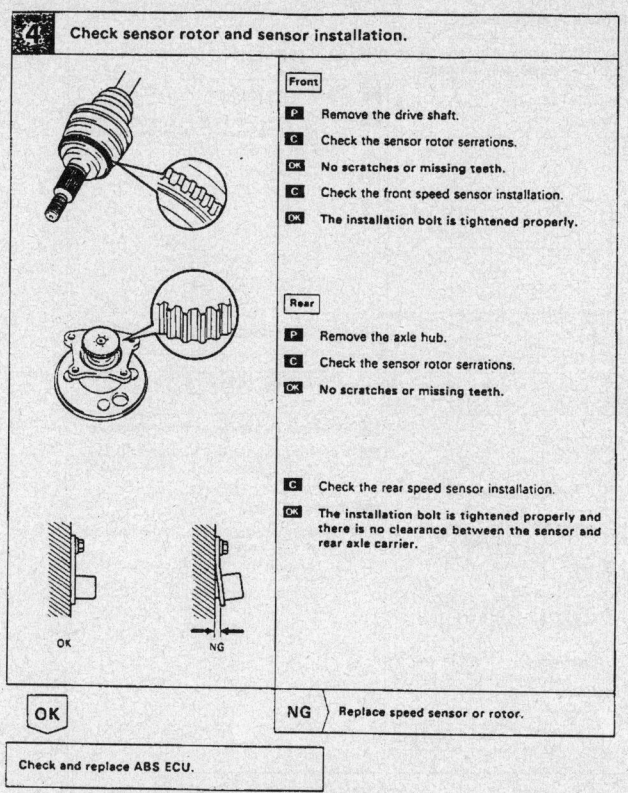

4 Check sensor rotor and sensor installation.

OK
NG

Front

- P Remove the drive shaft.
- C Check the sensor rotor serrations.
- OK No scratches or missing teeth.
- C Check the front speed sensor installation.
- OK The installation bolt is tightened properly.

Rear

- P Remove the axle hub.
- C Check the sensor rotor serrations.
- OK No scratches or missing teeth.
- C Check the rear speed sensor installation.
- OK The installation bolt is tightened properly and there is no clearance between the sensor and rear axle carrier.

NG — Replace speed sensor or rotor.

OK — Check and replace ABS ECU.

TY4029300080040X

Fig. 112 Code 31, 32, 33, 34, 35 & 36: Speed Sensor Circuit (Part 4 of 4). Corolla

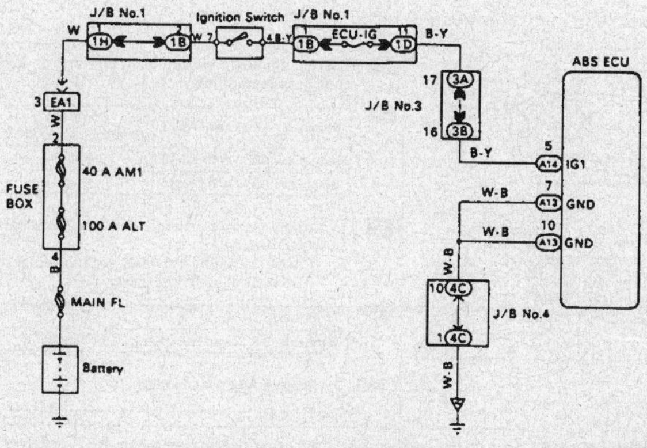
J/B No.1
Ignition Switch
J/B No.1
W
1H
1B
W
7
4
B-Y
1B
ECU-IG
1D
B-Y
ABS ECU
17
3A
J/B No.3
16
3B
3
EA1
W
2
FUSE BOX
40 A AM1
100 A ALT
4
B
MAIN FL
Battery
B-Y
5
A14
IG1
W-B
7
A13
GND
W-B
10
A13
GND
W-B
10
4C
J/B No.4
1
4C
W-B

TY4029300081020X

Fig. 113 Code 41: IG Power Source (Part 2 of 4). Corolla

CIRCUIT DESCRIPTION

This is the power source for the ECU and becomes power source for the CPU and actuators.

DTC No.	Diagnostic Trouble Code Detecting Condition	Trouble Area
41	Vehicle speed is 3 km/h (1.9 mph) or more and voltage of ECU terminal IG1 remains at more than 17 V or below 9.5 V for more than 10 sec.	• Battery. • IC regulator. • Open or short in power source circuit. • ECU.

Fail safe function: If trouble occurs in the power source circuit, the ECU cuts off current to the ABS control (solenoid) relay and prohibits ABS control.

DIAGNOSTIC CHART

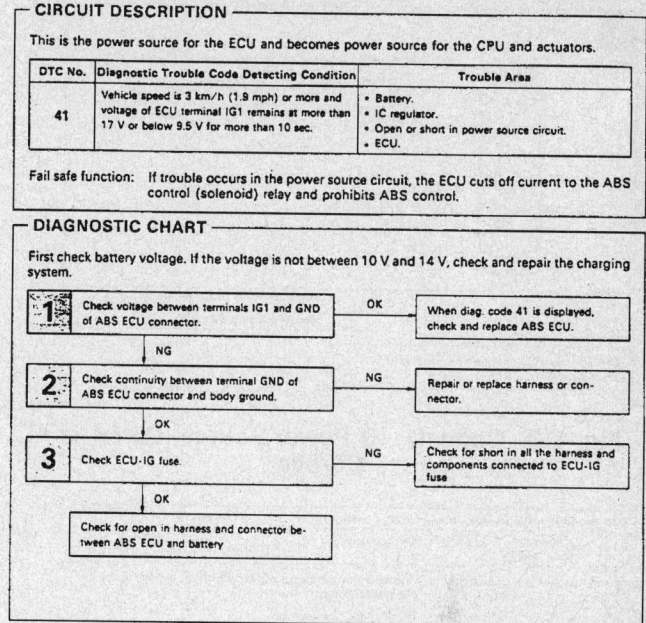

First check battery voltage. If the voltage is not between 10 V and 14 V, check and repair the charging system.

- **1** Check voltage between terminals IG1 and GND of ABS ECU connector.
  - OK → When diag. code 41 is displayed, check and replace ABS ECU.
  - NG ↓
- **2** Check continuity between terminal GND of ABS ECU connector and body ground.
  - NG → Repair or replace harness or connector.
  - OK ↓
- **3** Check ECU-IG fuse.
  - NG → Check for short in all the harness and components connected to ECU-IG fuse
  - OK ↓
- Check for open in harness and connector between ABS ECU and battery

TY4029300081010X

Fig. 113 Code 41: IG Power Source (Part 1 of 4). Corolla

INSPECTION PROCEDURE

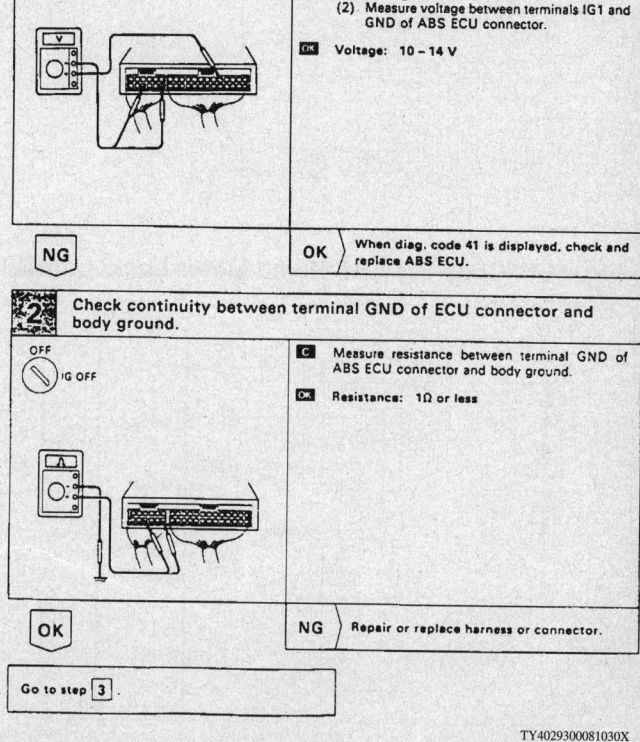

1 Check voltage between terminals IG1 and GND of ABS ECU connector.

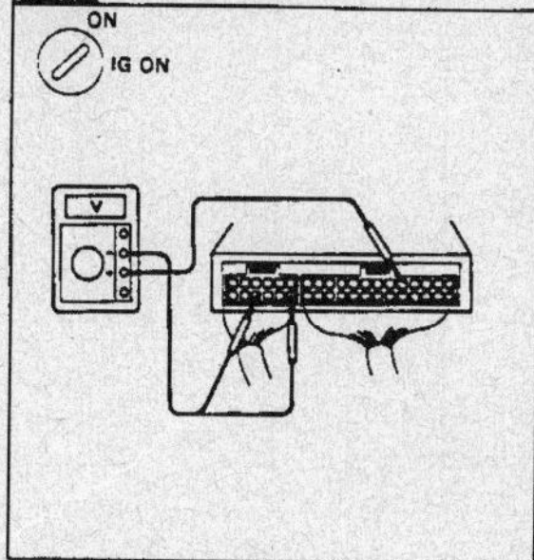
ON
IG ON
V

- P Remove ABS ECU with connectors still connected.
- C (1) Turn ignition switch on.
  (2) Measure voltage between terminals IG1 and GND of ABS ECU connector.
- OK Voltage: 10 – 14 V

NG

OK — When diag. code 41 is displayed, check and replace ABS ECU.

2 Check continuity between terminal GND of ECU connector and body ground.

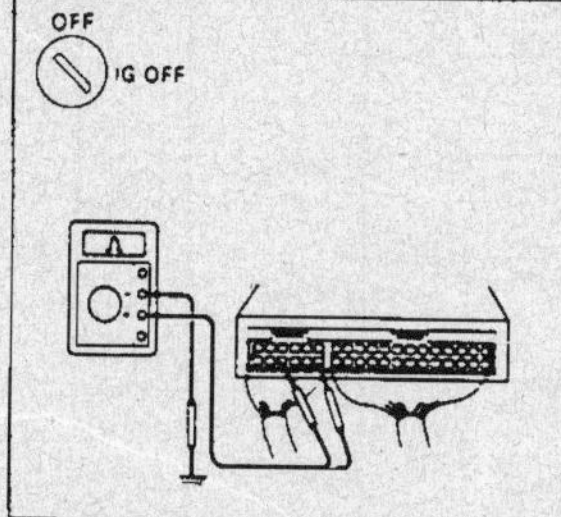
OFF
IG OFF

- C Measure resistance between terminal GND of ABS ECU connector and body ground.
- OK Resistance: 1Ω or less

NG — Repair or replace harness or connector.

OK — Go to step 3.

TY4029300081030X

Fig. 113 Code 41: IG Power Source (Part 3 of 4). Corolla

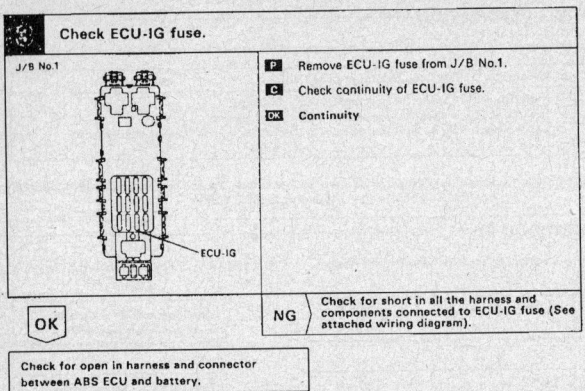

3 Check ECU-IG fuse.

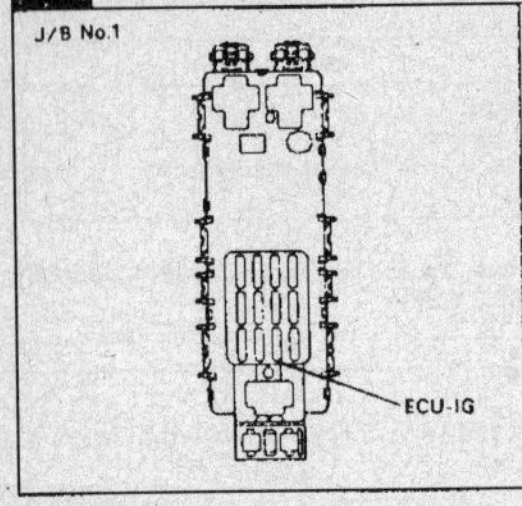
J/B No.1
ECU-IG

P Remove ECU-IG fuse from J/B No.1.

C Check continuity of ECU-IG fuse.

OK Continuity

OK

NG — Check for short in all the harness and components connected to ECU-IG fuse (See attached wiring diagram).

Check for open in harness and connector between ABS ECU and battery.

TY4029300081040X

Fig. 113 Code 41: IG Power Source (Part 4 of 4). Corolla

DTC No.	Diagnostic Trouble Code Detecting Condition	Trouble Area
51	Pump motor is not operating normally during initial check.	• ABS pump motor.

Fail safe function: If trouble occurs in the ABS pump motor, the ECU cuts off the current to the solenoid relay and prohibits ABS control.

DIAGNOSTIC CHART

See inspection of ABS actuator

WIRING DIAGRAM

(Reference)

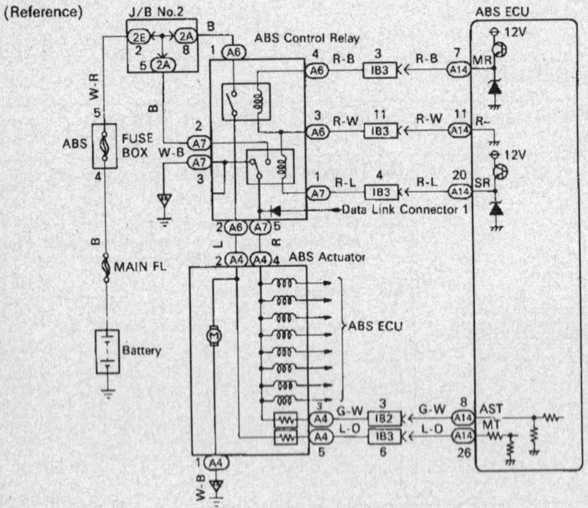
J/B No.2
ABS Control Relay
ABS ECU
ABS
FUSE BOX
MAIN FL
Battery
ABS Actuator
ABS ECU
Data Link Connector 1

TY4029300082000X

Fig. 114 Code 51: ABS Pump Motor Lock. Corolla

WIRING DIAGRAM

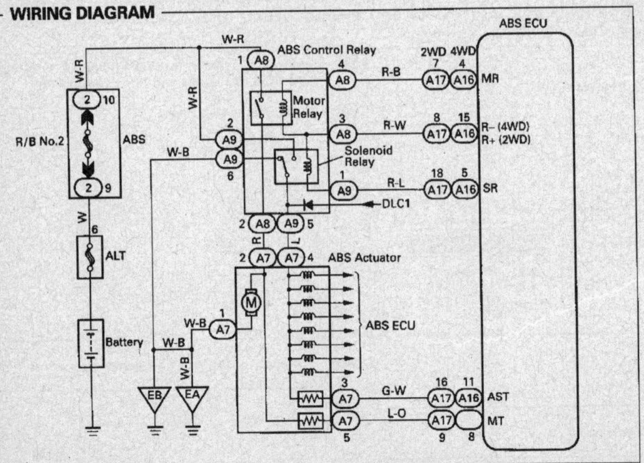
ABS ECU
ABS Control Relay
Motor Relay
Solenoid Relay
R/B No.2
ABS
ALT
Battery
ABS Actuator
ABS ECU
DLC1

TY4029600205010X

Fig. 115 Code 11 & 12: ABS Control Solenoid Relay Circuit (Part 1 of 3). RAV4

INSPECTION PROCEDURE

1 **Check voltage between terminals (A9) 2 and (A9) 6 of ABS control (solenoid) relay connector.**

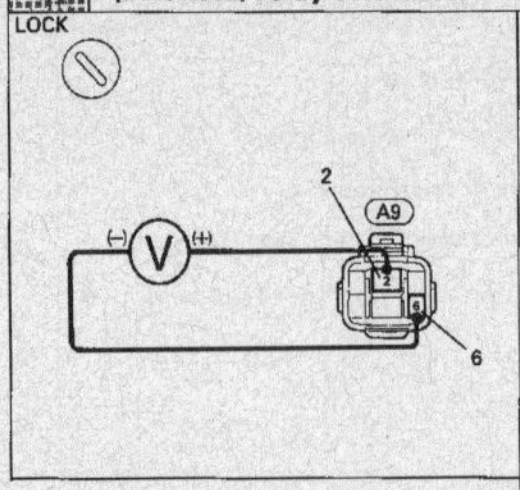
LOCK
A9

P Disconnect the ABS control relay connector.

C Measure the voltage between terminals (A9) 2 and (A9) 6 of ABS control relay harness side connector.

OK Voltage: 10 – 14 V

OK

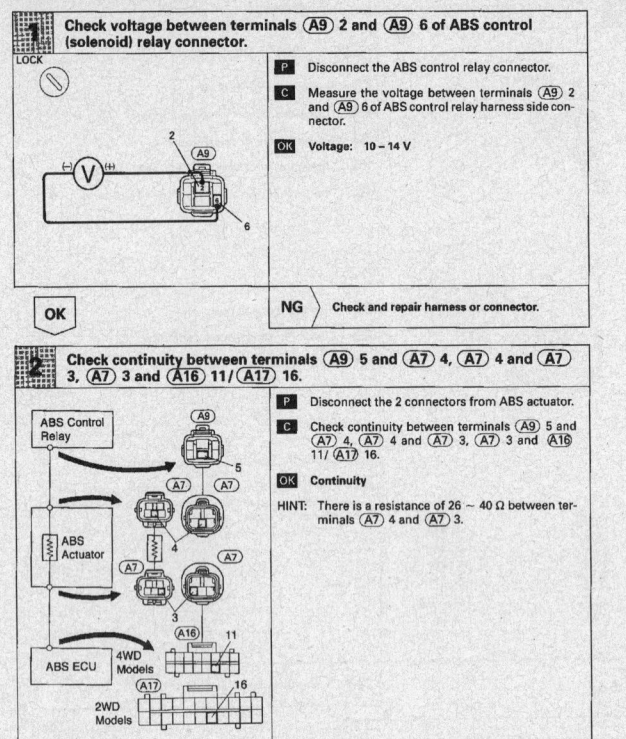

NG — Check and repair harness or connector.

2 **Check continuity between terminals (A9) 5 and (A7) 4, (A7) 4 and (A7) 3, (A7) 3 and (A16) 11/(A17) 16.**

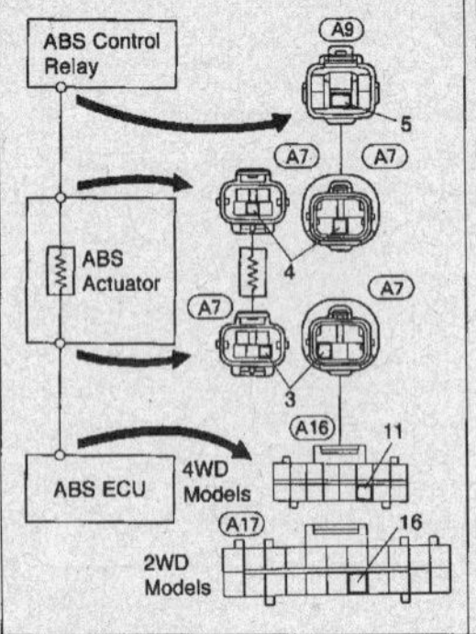
ABS Control Relay
ABS Actuator
ABS ECU
4WD Models
2WD Models

P Disconnect the 2 connectors from ABS actuator.

C Check continuity between terminals (A9) 5 and (A7) 4, (A7) 4 and (A7) 3, (A7) 3 and (A16) 11/(A17) 16.

OK Continuity

HINT: There is a resistance of 26 ~ 40 Ω between terminals (A7) 4 and (A7) 3.

OK

NG — Repair or replace harness or ABS actuator.

TY4029600205020X

Fig. 115 Code 11 & 12: ABS Control Solenoid Relay Circuit (Part 2 of 3). RAV4

3 **Check ABS control (solenoid) relay.**

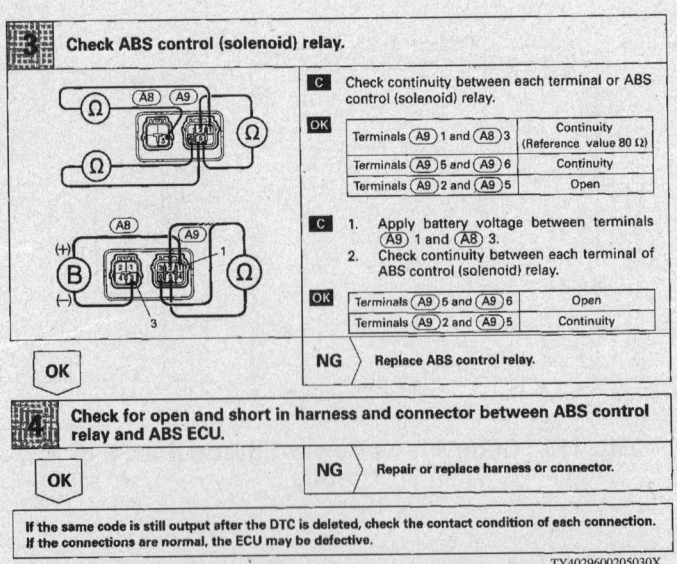

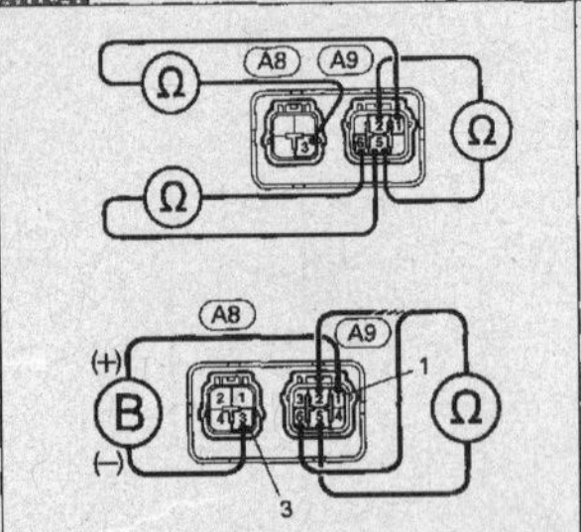

C Check continuity between each terminal or ABS control (solenoid) relay.

OK

Terminals (A9) 1 and (A8) 3	Continuity (Reference value 80 Ω)
Terminals (A9) 5 and (A9) 6	Continuity
Terminals (A9) 2 and (A9) 5	Open

C
1. Apply battery voltage between terminals (A9) 1 and (A8) 3.
2. Check continuity between each terminal of ABS control (solenoid) relay.

OK

Terminals (A9) 5 and (A9) 6	Open
Terminals (A9) 2 and (A9) 5	Continuity

OK

NG — Replace ABS control relay.

4 **Check for open and short in harness and connector between ABS control relay and ABS ECU.**

OK

NG — Repair or replace harness or connector.

If the same code is still output after the DTC is deleted, check the contact condition of each connection. If the connections are normal, the ECU may be defective.

TY4029600205030X

Fig. 115 Code 11 & 12: ABS Control Solenoid Relay Circuit (Part 3 of 3). RAV4

WIRING DIAGRAM

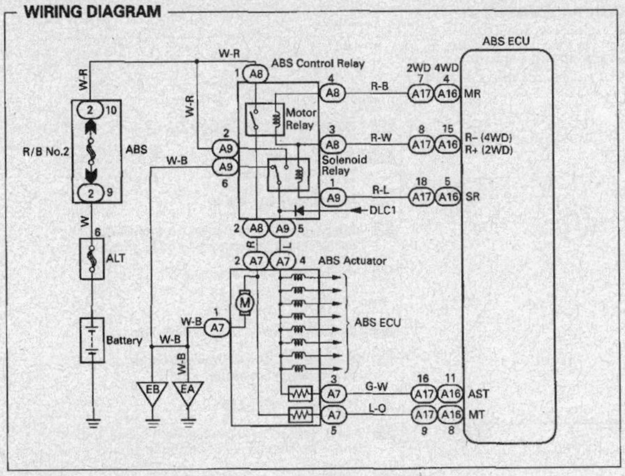
ABS ECU
W-R
ABS Control Relay
2WD 4WD
A8
R-B
A17 A16 MR
Motor Relay
R/B No.2
ABS
W-B
A9
R-W
R- (4WD)
R+ (2WD)
Solenoid Relay
R-L
SR
DLC1
ALT
ABS Actuator
ABS ECU
Battery
W-B
G-W
L-O
AST
MT
EB
EA

INSPECTION PROCEDURE

1 Check voltage between terminal (A8) 1 of ABS control (motor) relay and body ground.

LOCK

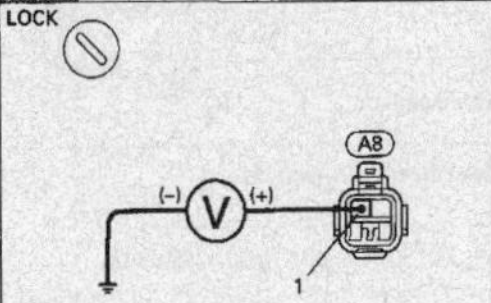
A8
(-)
V
(+)
1

P Disconnect the ABS control relay connector.

C Measure voltage between terminal (A8) 1 of ABS control relay harness side connector and body ground.

OK **Voltage: 10 – 14 V**

OK

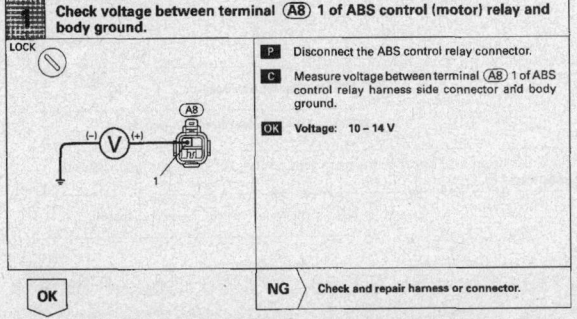

NG **Check and repair harness or connector.**

TY4029600206010X

Fig. 116 Code 13 & 14: ABS Control Motor Relay Circuit (Part 1 of 3). RAV4

2 Check continuity between terminals (A8) 2 and (A7) 2, (A7) 2 and (A7) 5, (A7) 5 and (A16) 8/(A17) 9.

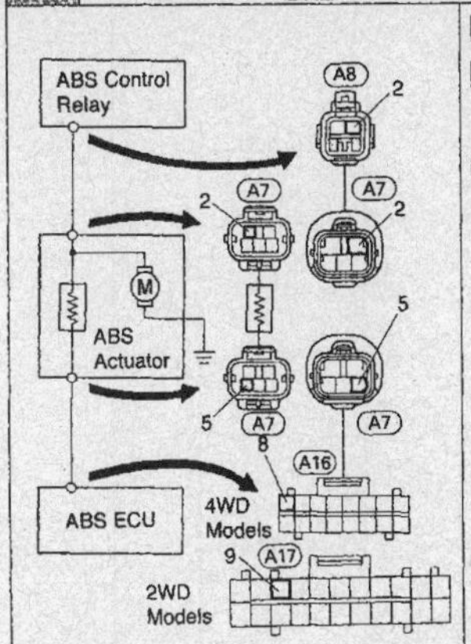
ABS Control Relay
A8
2
A7
ABS Actuator
5
A16
8
ABS ECU
4WD Models
9
A17
2WD Models

P Disconnect the 2 connectors from ABS actuator.

C Check continuity between terminals (A8) 2 and (A7) 2, (A7) 2 and (A7) 5, (A7) 5 and (A16) 8/(A17) 9.

OK **Continuity**

HINT: There is a resistance of 26 ~ 40 Ω between terminals (A7) 2 and (A7) 5.

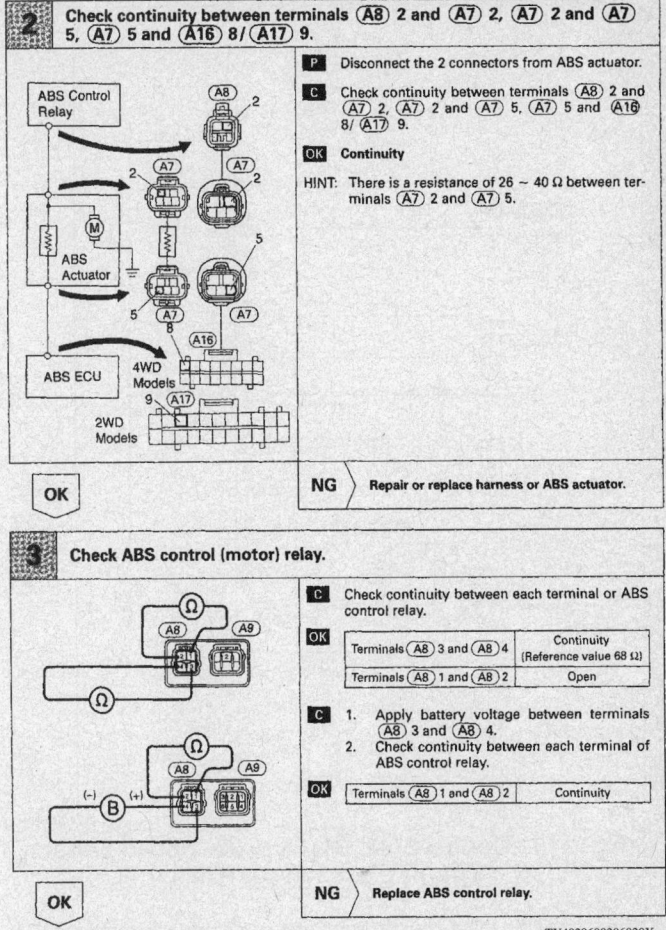

OK

NG **Repair or replace harness or ABS actuator.**

3 Check ABS control (motor) relay.

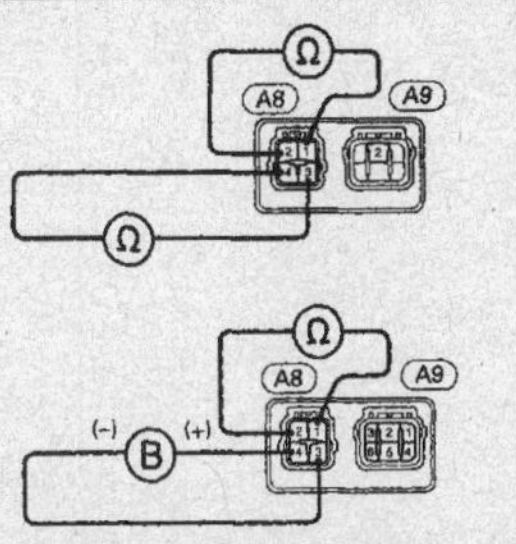
Ω
A8
A9
(-)
B
(+)

C Check continuity between each terminal or ABS control relay.

OK

Terminals (A8) 3 and (A8) 4	Continuity (Reference value 68 Ω)
Terminals (A8) 1 and (A8) 2	Open

C 1. Apply battery voltage between terminals (A8) 3 and (A8) 4.
2. Check continuity between each terminal of ABS control relay.

OK

Terminals (A8) 1 and (A8) 2	Continuity

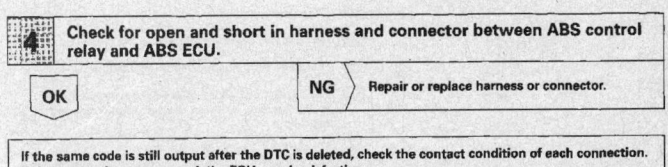

OK

NG **Replace ABS control relay.**

TY4029600206020X

Fig. 116 Code 13 & 14: ABS Control Motor Relay Circuit (Part 2 of 3). RAV4

4 Check for open and short in harness and connector between ABS control relay and ABS ECU.

OK

NG **Repair or replace harness or connector.**

If the same code is still output after the DTC is deleted, check the contact condition of each connection. If the connections are normal, the ECU may be defective.

TY4029600206030X

Fig. 116 Code 13 & 14: ABS Control Motor Relay Circuit (Part 3 of 3). RAV4

WIRING DIAGRAM

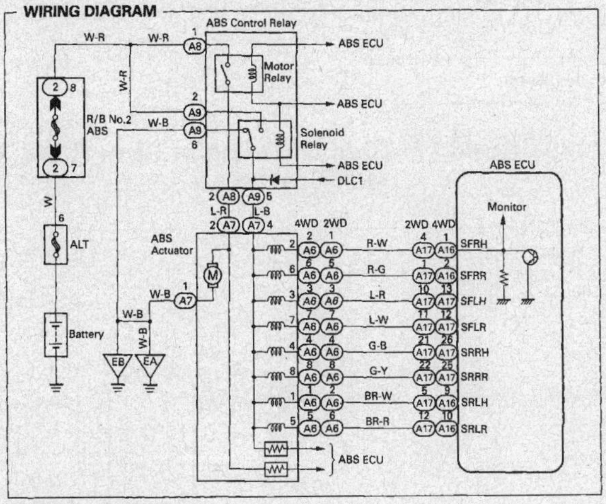
ABS Control Relay
W-R
A8
ABS ECU
Motor Relay
R/B No.2
ABS
W-B
A9
Solenoid Relay
DLC1
ABS ECU
Monitor
ALT
ABS Actuator
4WD 2WD
2WD 4WD
R-W
SFRH
R-G
SFRR
L-R
SFLH
L-W
SFLR
G-B
SRRH
G-Y
SRRR
BR-W
SRLH
BR-R
SRLR
Battery
EB
EA
ABS ECU

INSPECTION PROCEDURE

1 Check ABS actuator solenoid.

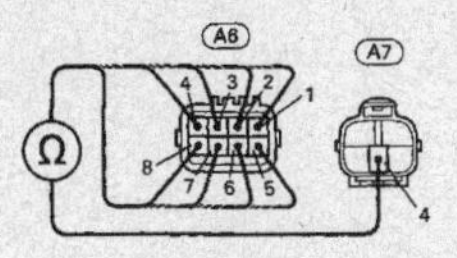
A6
A7
Ω
1
4

P Disconnect the 2 connectors from ABS actuator.

C Check continuity between terminals (A7) 4 and (A6) 1, 2, 3, 4, 5, 6, 7, 8 of ABS actuator connector.

OK **Continuity**

HINT: Resistance of each solenoid coil
SFRH, SFLH, SRRH, SRLH:
(4WD Models) 5.0 Ω
(2WD models) 8.8 Ω
SFRR, SFLR, SRRR, SRLR:
(4WD Models) 2.2 Ω
(2WD models) 4.3 Ω

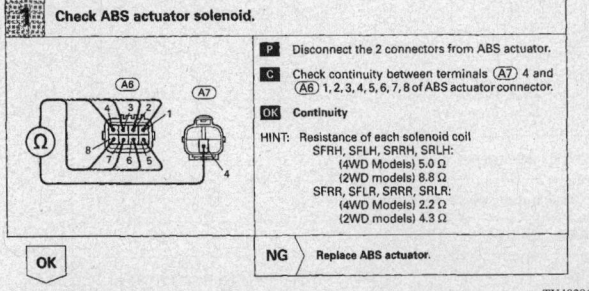

OK

NG **Replace ABS actuator.**

TY4029600207010X

Fig. 117 Code 21, 22, 23 & 24: ABS Actuator Solenoid Circuit (Part 1 of 2). RAV4

2 Check for open and short in harness and connector between ABS ECU and actuator.

OK

NG **Repair or replace harness or connector.**

If the same code is still output after the DTC is deleted, check the contact condition of each connection. If the connections are normal, the ECU may be defective.

TY4029600207020X

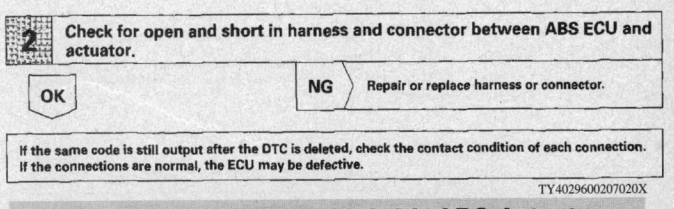

Fig. 117 Code 21, 22, 23 & 24: ABS Actuator Solenoid Circuit (Part 2 of 2). RAV4

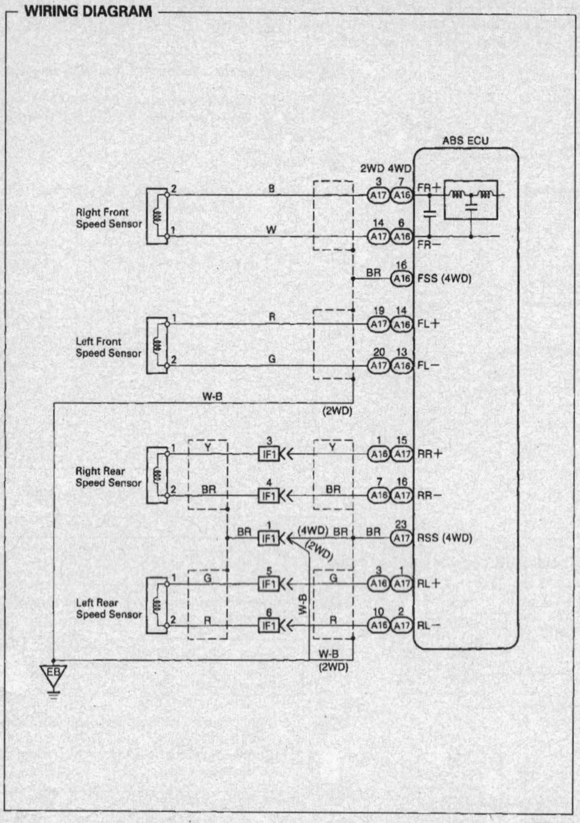
WIRING DIAGRAM
ABS ECU
2WD 4WD
Right Front Speed Sensor
Left Front Speed Sensor
Right Rear Speed Sensor
Left Rear Speed Sensor
FR+
FR−
FSS (4WD)
FL+
FL−
RR+
RR−
RSS (4WD)
RL+
RL−
W-B
(2WD)
EB

TY4029600208010X

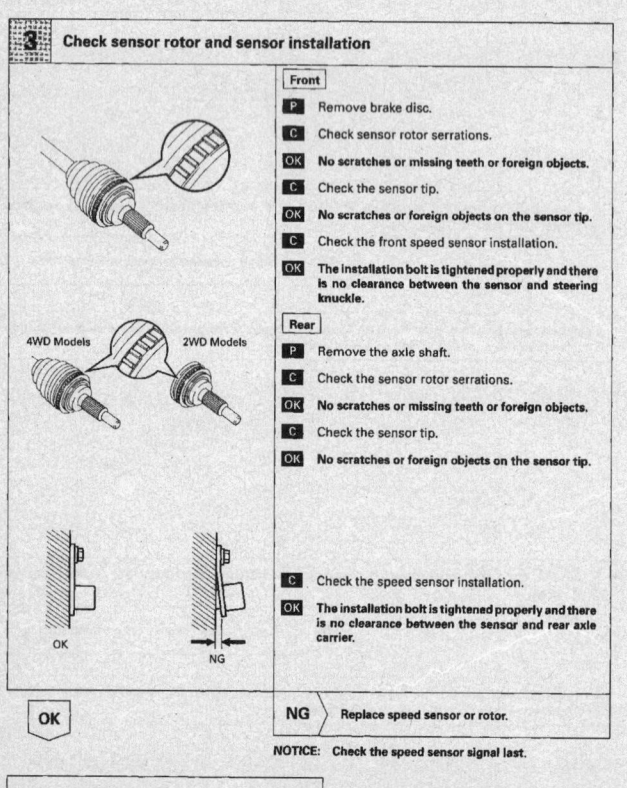

Fig. 118 Code 31, 32, 33, 34 & 35: Speed Sensor Circuit (Part 1 of 3). RAV4

INSPECTION PROCEDURE

1 **Check speed sensor.**

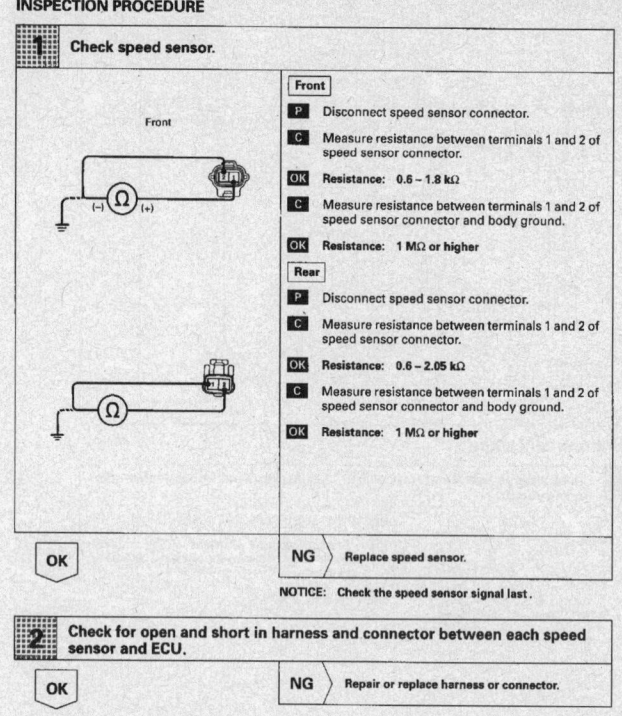

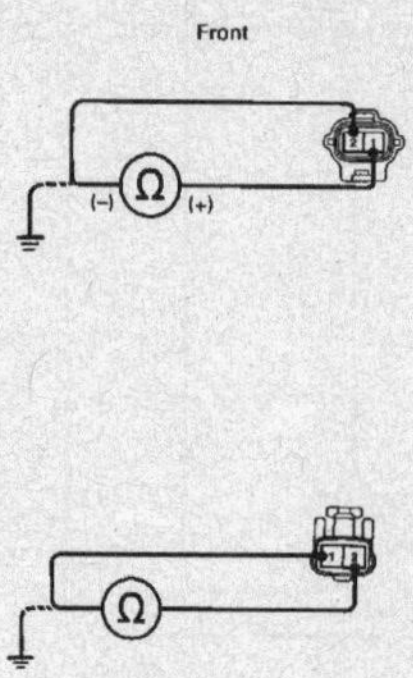
Front

Front

P Disconnect speed sensor connector.

C Measure resistance between terminals 1 and 2 of speed sensor connector.

OK **Resistance: 0.6 – 1.8 kΩ**

C Measure resistance between terminals 1 and 2 of speed sensor connector and body ground.

OK **Resistance: 1 MΩ or higher**

Rear

P Disconnect speed sensor connector.

C Measure resistance between terminals 1 and 2 of speed sensor connector.

OK **Resistance: 0.6 – 2.05 kΩ**

C Measure resistance between terminals 1 and 2 of speed sensor connector and body ground.

OK **Resistance: 1 MΩ or higher**

OK

NG **Replace speed sensor.**

NOTICE: Check the speed sensor signal last.

2 **Check for open and short in harness and connector between each speed sensor and ECU.**

OK

NG **Repair or replace harness or connector.**

TY4029600208020X

Fig. 118 Code 31, 32, 33, 34 & 35: Speed Sensor Circuit (Part 2 of 3). RAV4

3 **Check sensor rotor and sensor installation**

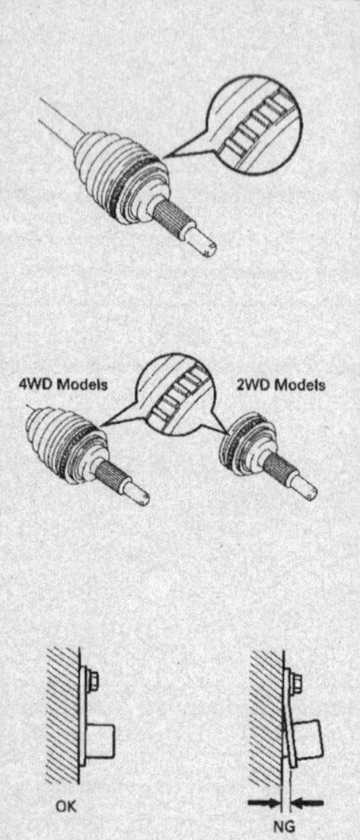
4WD Models
2WD Models
OK
NG

Front

P Remove brake disc.

C Check sensor rotor serrations.

OK **No scratches or missing teeth or foreign objects.**

C Check the sensor tip.

OK **No scratches or foreign objects on the sensor tip.**

C Check the front speed sensor installation.

OK **The installation bolt is tightened properly and there is no clearance between the sensor and steering knuckle.**

Rear

P Remove the axle shaft.

C Check the sensor rotor serrations.

OK **No scratches or missing teeth or foreign objects.**

C Check the sensor tip.

OK **No scratches or foreign objects on the sensor tip.**

C Check the speed sensor installation.

OK **The installation bolt is tightened properly and there is no clearance between the sensor and rear axle carrier.**

OK

NG **Replace speed sensor or rotor.**

NOTICE: Check the speed sensor signal last.

Check and replace ABS ECU.

TY4029600208030X

Fig. 118 Code 31, 32, 33, 34 & 35: Speed Sensor Circuit (Part 3 of 3). RAV4

INSPECTION PROCEDURE

1 **Check tire size.**

OK

NG **Replace tires so that all 4 tires are of the same size.**

Check and replace ABS ECU.

TY4029600209000X

Fig. 119 Code 37: Tires Of Different Size. RAV4 w/2WD

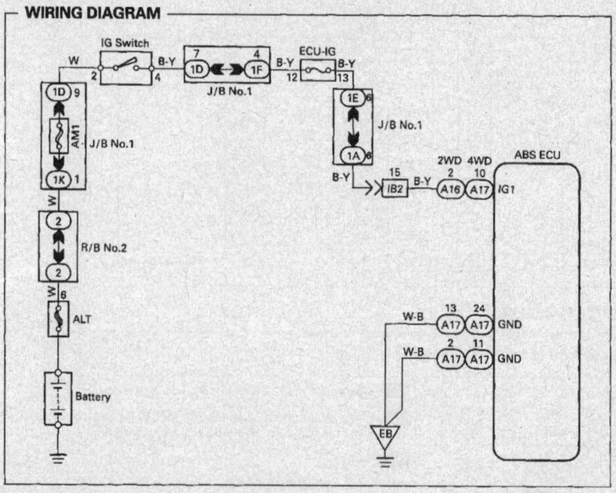
WIRING DIAGRAM
IG Switch
ECU-IG
J/B No.1
AM1
R/B No.2
ALT
Battery
2WD 4WD
ABS ECU
IG1
GND
GND
W-B
EB

INSPECTION PROCEDURE

1 **Check battery positive voltage.**

OK **Voltage: 10 – 14 V**

OK

NG **Check and repair the charging system.**

TY4029600210010X

Fig. 120 Code 41: IG Power Source Circuit (Part 1 of 3). RAV4

2 **Check voltage between terminals IG1 and GND of ABS ECU connector.**

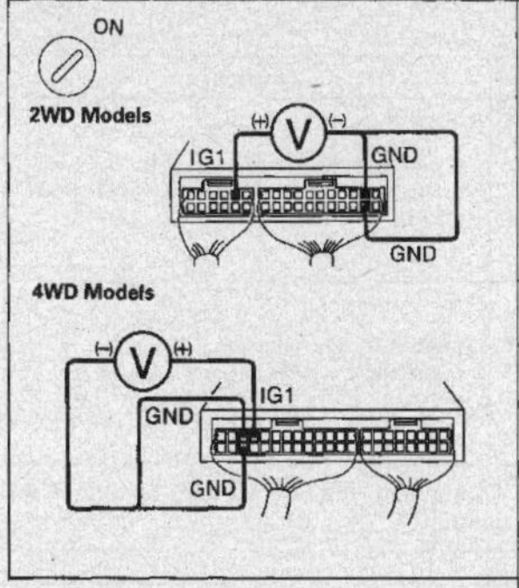
ON
2WD Models
(+)
(-)
V
IG1
GND
GND
4WD Models
(-)
(+)
V
IG1
GND
GND

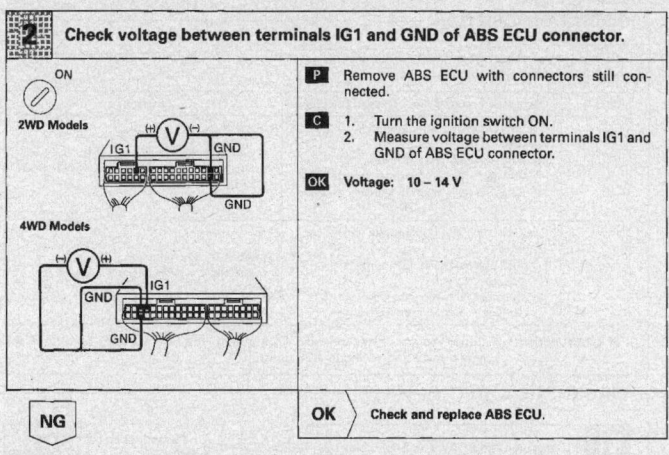

P Remove ABS ECU with connectors still connected.

C
1. Turn the ignition switch ON.
2. Measure voltage between terminals IG1 and GND of ABS ECU connector.

OK **Voltage: 10 – 14 V**

NG

OK 〉 **Check and replace ABS ECU.**

3 **Check continuity between terminals GND of ABS ECU connector and body ground.**

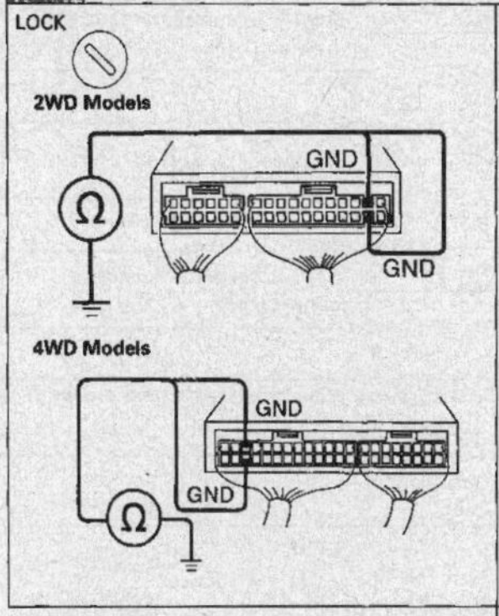
LOCK
2WD Models
GND
Ω
GND
4WD Models
GND
GND
Ω

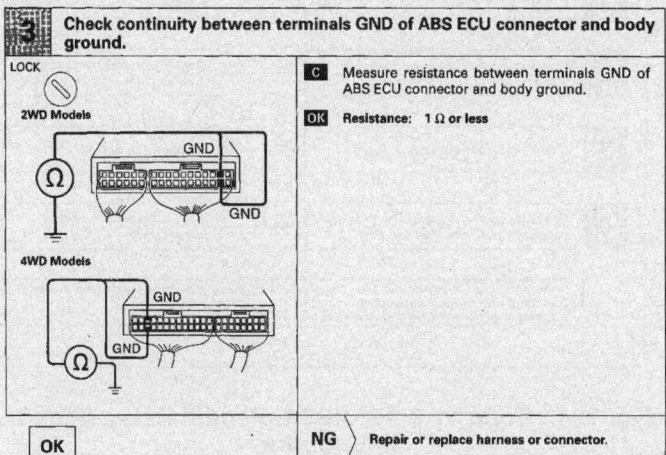

C Measure resistance between terminals GND of ABS ECU connector and body ground.

OK **Resistance: 1 Ω or less**

OK

NG 〉 **Repair or replace harness or connector.**

TY4029600210020X

Fig. 120 Code 41: IG Power Source Circuit (Part 2 of 3). RAV4

4 **Check ECU-IG fuse.**

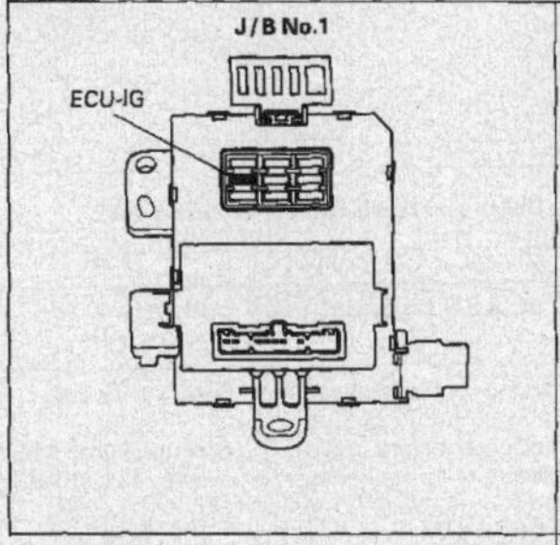
J/B No.1
ECU-IG

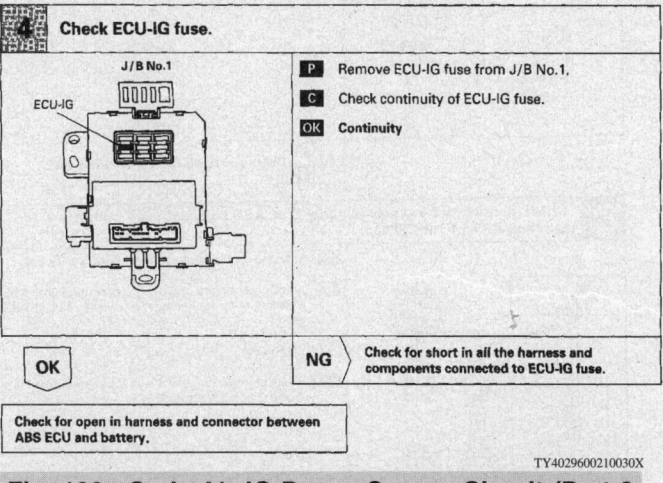

P Remove ECU-IG fuse from J/B No.1.

C Check continuity of ECU-IG fuse.

OK **Continuity**

OK

NG 〉 **Check for short in all the harness and components connected to ECU-IG fuse.**

Check for open in harness and connector between ABS ECU and battery.

TY4029600210030X

Fig. 120 Code 41: IG Power Source Circuit (Part 3 of 3). RAV4

INSPECTION PROCEDURE

1 **Check deceleration sensor.**

OK

NG 〉 **Replace deceleration sensor.**

2 **Check for open or short in harness and connector between sensor and ECU.**

OK

NG 〉 **Repair or replace harness and connector.**

Check and replace ABS ECU.

TY4029600211000X

Fig. 121 Code 43 & 45: Malfunction In Deceleration Sensor. RAV4 w/4WD

WIRING DIAGRAM

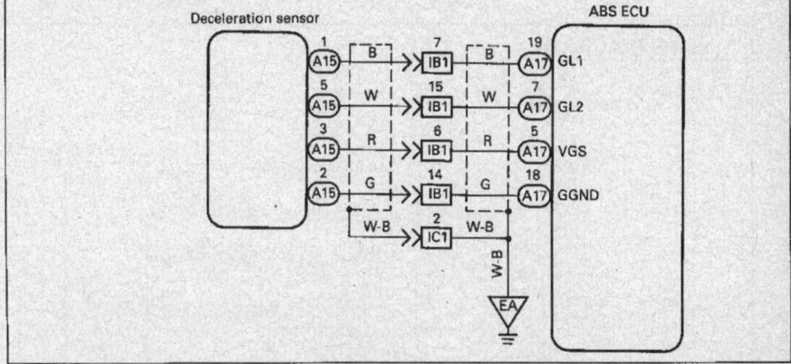
Deceleration sensor
ABS ECU
1
A15
B
7
IB1
B
19
A17
GL1
5
A15
W
15
IB1
W
7
A17
GL2
3
A15
R
6
IB1
R
5
A17
VGS
2
A15
G
14
IB1
G
18
A17
GGND
W-B
2
IC1
W-B
W-B
EA

TY4029600212010X

Fig. 122 Code 44: Deceleration Sensor Circuit (Part 1 of 2). RAV4

INSPECTION PROCEDURE

1 **Check for open and short in harness and connector between sensor and ECU.**

OK

NG 〉 **Repair or replace harness or connector.**

2 **Check voltage between terminals GL1, GL2, VGS of ECU and body ground.**

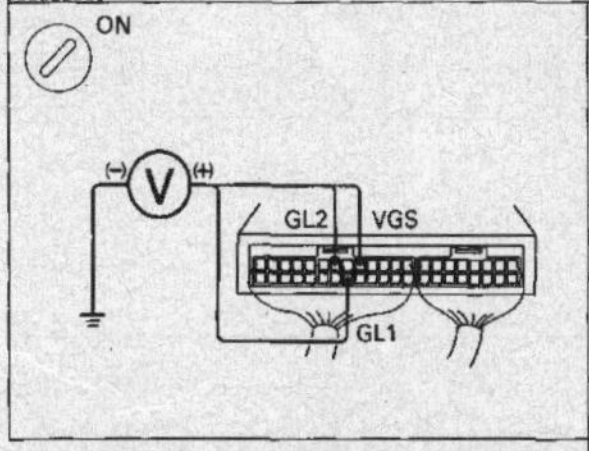
ON
(-)
V
(+)
GL2
VGS
GL1

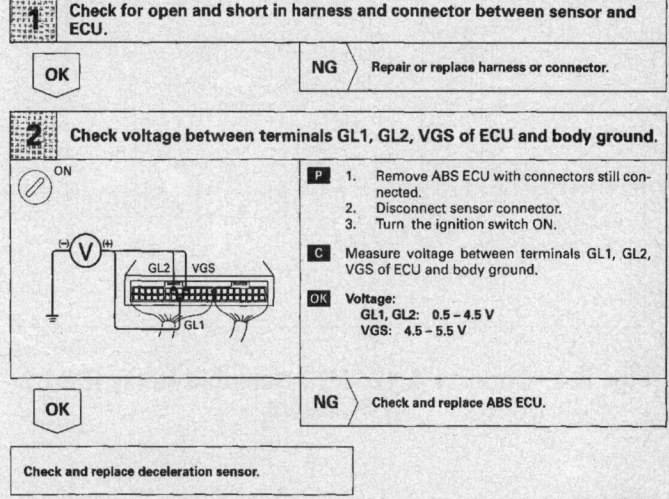

P
1. Remove ABS ECU with connectors still connected.
2. Disconnect sensor connector.
3. Turn the ignition switch ON.

C Measure voltage between terminals GL1, GL2, VGS of ECU and body ground.

OK **Voltage:**
GL1, GL2: 0.5 – 4.5 V
VGS: 4.5 – 5.5 V

OK

NG 〉 **Check and replace ABS ECU.**

Check and replace deceleration sensor.

TY4029600212020X

Fig. 122 Code 44: Deceleration Sensor Circuit (Part 2 of 2). RAV4

CIRCUIT DESCRIPTION

DTC No.	DTC Detecting Condition	Trouble area
51	Pump motor is not operating normally during initial check.	• ABS pump motor

Fail safe function: If trouble occurs in the ABS pump motor, the ECU cuts off current to the control (solenoid) relay and prohibits ABS control.

TY4029600213000X

Fig. 123 Code 51: ABS Pump Motor Lock. RAV4

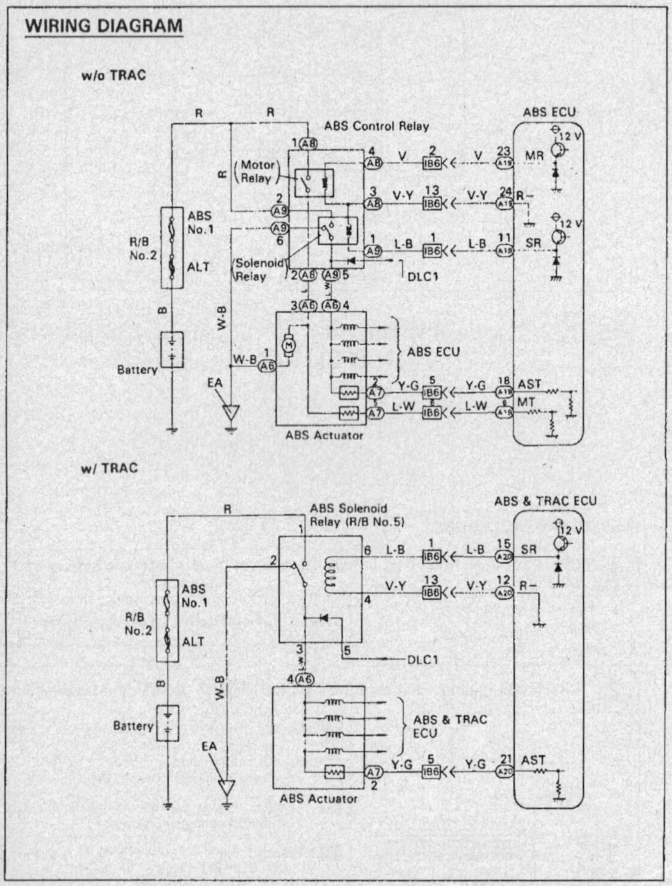

WIRING DIAGRAM
w/o TRAC
ABS Control Relay
Motor Relay
Solenoid Relay
ABS ECU
ABS No.1
R/B No.2
ALT
Battery
EA
DLC1
ABS Actuator
MR
SR
AST
MT
12 V
w/ TRAC
ABS Solenoid Relay (R/B No.5)
ABS & TRAC ECU

TY4029300083020X

Fig. 124 Code 11 & 12: ABS Solenoid Relay (Part 2 of 6). Supra

CIRCUIT DESCRIPTION

This relay supplies power to each ABS solenoid. After the ignition switch is turned on, if the initial check is OK, the relay goes on.

DTC No.	Diagnostic Trouble Code Detecting Condition	Trouble area
11	Conditions (1) and (2) continue for 0.2 sec. or more: (1) ABS solenoid relay (SR) terminal voltage: Battery positive voltage (2) Solenoid relay monitor terminal (AST) voltage: 0 V	• ABS solenoid relay • Open or short in ABS solenoid relay circuit • ECU
12	Conditions (1) and (2) continue for 0.2 sec. or more: (1) ABS solenoid relay (SR) terminal voltage: 0 V (2) Solenoid relay monitor terminal (AST) voltage: Battery positive voltage	• ABS solenoid relay • B+ short in ABS solenoid relay circuit • ECU

Fail safe function: If trouble occurs in the solenoid relay circuit, the ECU cuts off current to the solenoid relay and prohibits ABS control.

DIAGNOSTIC CHART

1. Check voltage of ABS solenoid relay. — NG → Check and repair harness or connector.
   OK ↓
2. Check continuity between relay and actuator and ECU. — NG → Repair or replace harness or ABS actuator.
   OK ↓
3. Check ABS solenoid relay. — NG → Replace ABS solenoid relay.
   OK ↓
4. Check for open and short in harness and connector between relay and ECU. — NG → Repair or replace harness or connector.
   OK ↓

If the same code is still output after the diagnostic trouble code is deleted, check the contact condition of each connection.
If the connections are normal, the ECU may be defective.

TY4029300083010X

Fig. 124 Code 11 & 12: ABS Solenoid Relay (Part 1 of 6). Supra

INSPECTION PROCEDURE (w/o TRAC)

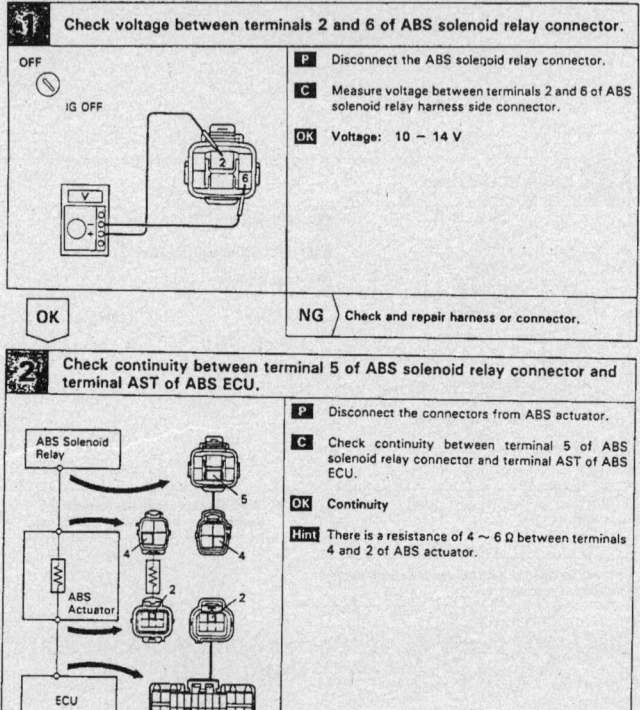

1 Check voltage between terminals 2 and 6 of ABS solenoid relay connector.

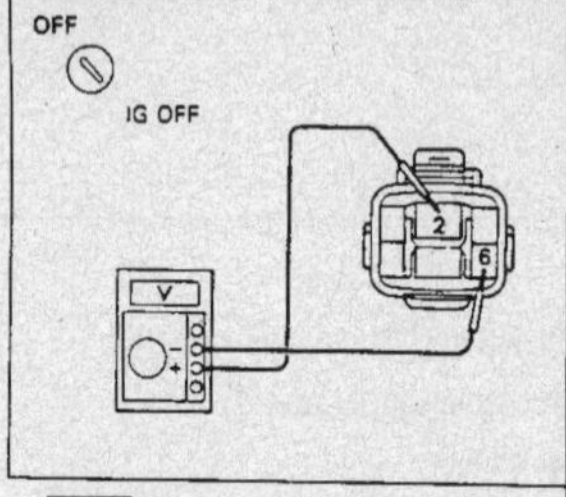

OFF
IG OFF
2
6
V

P Disconnect the ABS solenoid relay connector.

C Measure voltage between terminals 2 and 6 of ABS solenoid relay harness side connector.

OK Voltage: 10 – 14 V

OK

NG — Check and repair harness or connector.

2 Check continuity between terminal 5 of ABS solenoid relay connector and terminal AST of ABS ECU.

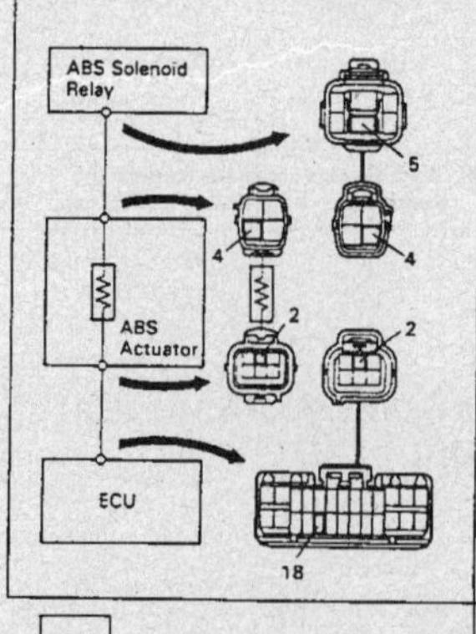

ABS Solenoid Relay
5
4
4
2
2
ABS Actuator
ECU
18

P Disconnect the connectors from ABS actuator.

C Check continuity between terminal 5 of ABS solenoid relay connector and terminal AST of ABS ECU.

OK Continuity

Hint There is a resistance of 4 ~ 6 Ω between terminals 4 and 2 of ABS actuator.

OK

NG — Repair or replace harness or ABS actuator.

TY4029300083030X

Fig. 124 Code 11 & 12: ABS Solenoid Relay (Part 3 of 6). Supra Less Traction Control

3 Check ABS solenoid relay.

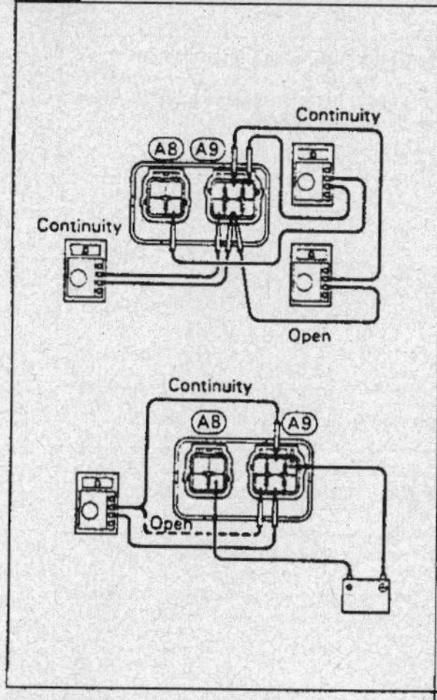
Continuity
A8
A9
Continuity
Open
Continuity
A8
A9
Open

C Check continuity between each terminal of ABS solenoid relay shown below.

OK

Terminals (A9) 1 and (A8) 3	Continuity (Reference value 80 Ω)
Terminals (A9) 5 and (A9) 6	Continuity
Terminals (A9) 2 and (A9) 5	Open

C (1) Apply battery positive voltage between terminals (A9) 1 and (A8) 3.
(2) Check continuity between each terminal of ABS solenoid relay shown below.

OK

Terminals (A9) 5 and (A9) 6	Open
Terminals (A9) 2 and (A9) 5	Continuity

OK

NG — Replace ABS control relay.

4 Check for open and short in harness and connector between ABS solenoid relay and ABS ECU

OK

NG — Repair or replace harness or connector.

If the same code is still output after the diagnostic trouble code is deleted, check the contact condition of each connection.
If the connections are normal, the ECU may be defective.

TY4029300083040X

Fig. 124 Code 11 & 12: ABS Solenoid Relay (Part 4 of 6). Supra Less Traction Control

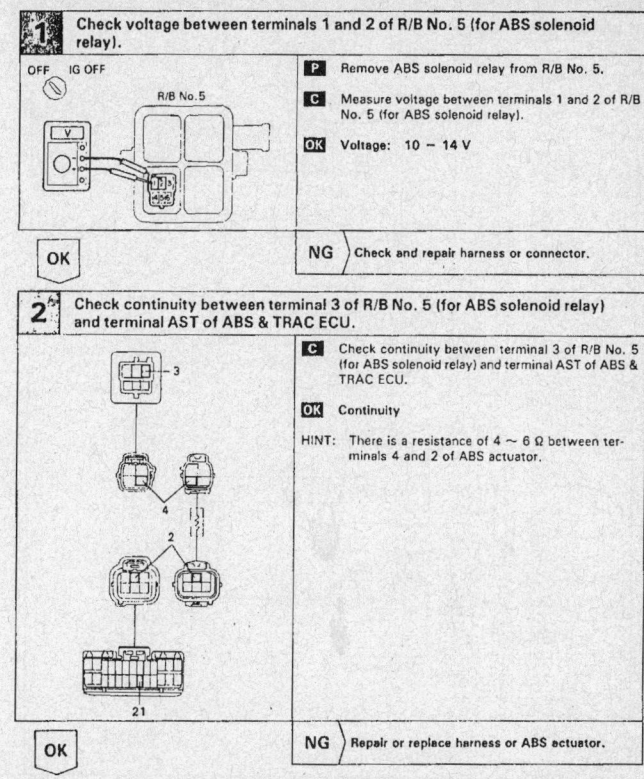

1 Check voltage between terminals 1 and 2 of R/B No. 5 (for ABS solenoid relay).

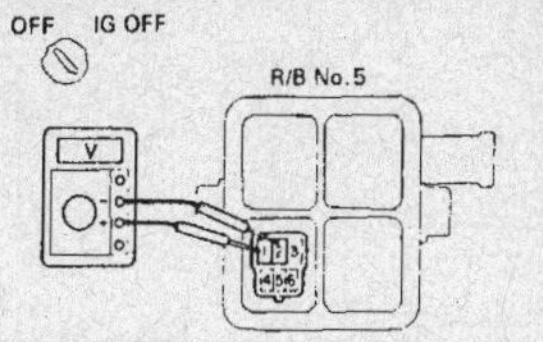
OFF
IG OFF
R/B No.5
V

P Remove ABS solenoid relay from R/B No. 5.

C Measure voltage between terminals 1 and 2 of R/B No. 5 (for ABS solenoid relay).

OK Voltage: 10 – 14 V

OK

NG — Check and repair harness or connector.

2 Check continuity between terminal 3 of R/B No. 5 (for ABS solenoid relay) and terminal AST of ABS & TRAC ECU.

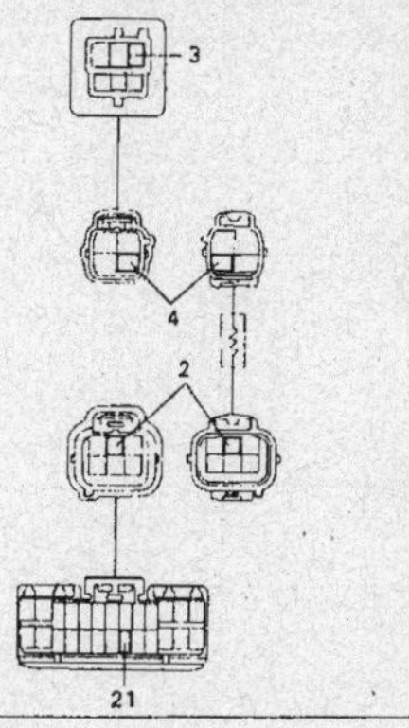
3
4
2
21

C Check continuity between terminal 3 of R/B No. 5 (for ABS solenoid relay) and terminal AST of ABS & TRAC ECU.

OK Continuity

HINT: There is a resistance of 4 ~ 6 Ω between terminals 4 and 2 of ABS actuator.

OK

NG — Repair or replace harness or ABS actuator.

TY4029300083050X

Fig. 124 Code 11 & 12: ABS Solenoid Relay (Part 5 of 6). Supra w/Traction Control

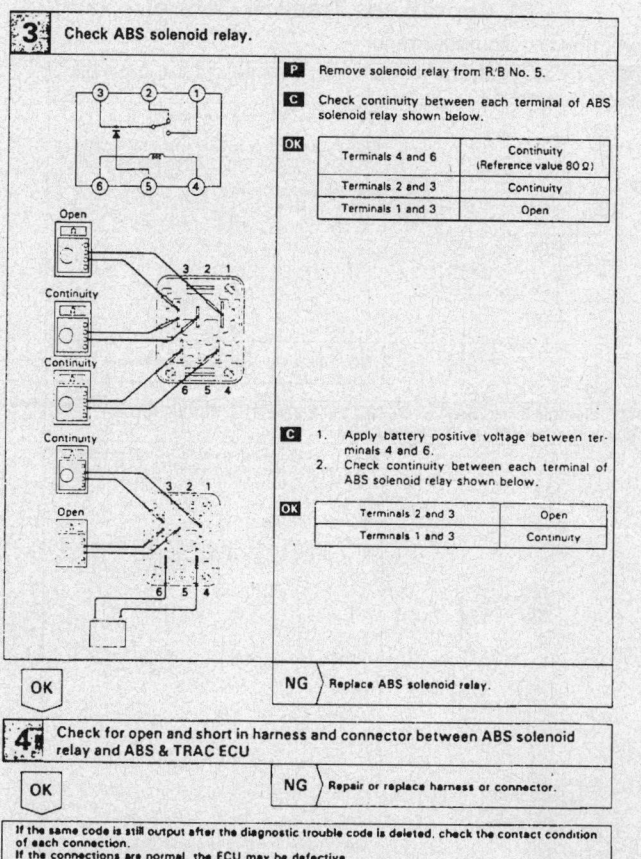

3 Check ABS solenoid relay.

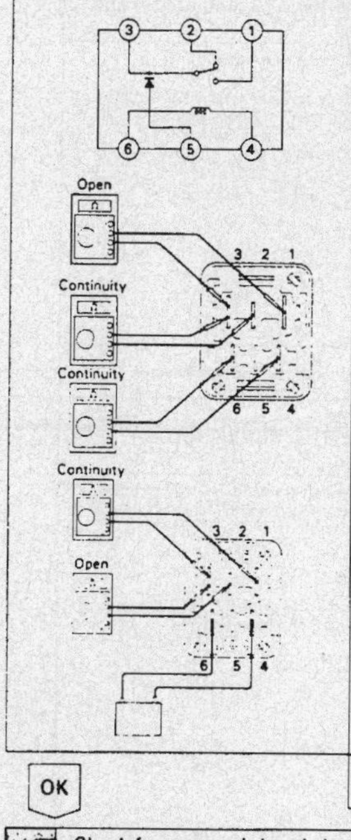
3
2
1
6
5
4
Open
3 2 1
Continuity
Continuity
6 5 4
Continuity
3 2 1
Open
6 5 4

P Remove solenoid relay from R/B No. 5.

C Check continuity between each terminal of ABS solenoid relay shown below.

OK

Terminals 4 and 6	Continuity (Reference value 80 Ω)
Terminals 2 and 3	Continuity
Terminals 1 and 3	Open

C 1. Apply battery positive voltage between terminals 4 and 6.
2. Check continuity between each terminal of ABS solenoid relay shown below.

OK

Terminals 2 and 3	Open
Terminals 1 and 3	Continuity

OK

NG — Replace ABS solenoid relay.

4 Check for open and short in harness and connector between ABS solenoid relay and ABS & TRAC ECU

OK

NG — Repair or replace harness or connector.

If the same code is still output after the diagnostic trouble code is deleted, check the contact condition of each connection.
If the connections are normal, the ECU may be defective.

TY4029300083060X

Fig. 124 Code 11 & 12: ABS Solenoid Relay (Part 6 of 6). Supra w/Traction Control

CIRCUIT DESCRIPTION

The ABS motor relay supplies power to the ABS pump motor. While the ABS is activated, the ECU switches the motor relay ON and operates the ABS pump motor.

DTC No.	Diagnostic Trouble Code Detecting Condition	Trouble area
13	Conditions (1) and (2) continue for 0.2 sec. or more: (1) ABS motor relay (MR) terminal voltage: Battery positive voltage (2) Motor relay monitor terminal (MT) voltage: 0 V	• ABS motor relay • Open or short in ABS motor relay circuit • ECU
14	Conditions (1) and (2) continue for 4 sec. or more: (1) ABS motor relay (MR) terminal voltage: 0 V (2) Motor relay monitor terminal (MT) voltage: Battery positive voltage	• ABS motor relay • B+ short in ABS motor relay circuit • ECU

Fail safe function: If trouble occurs in the motor relay circuit, the ECU cuts off the current to the solenoid relay and prohibits ABS control.

DIAGNOSTIC CHART

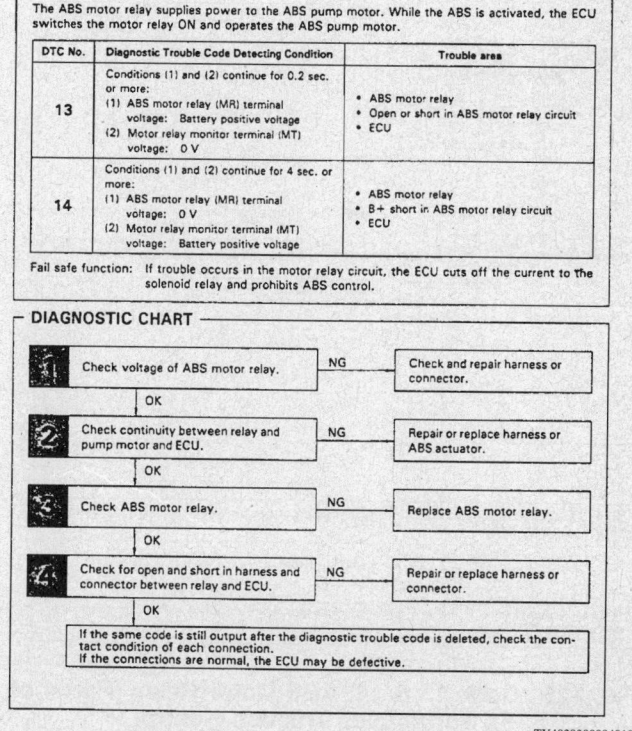

Step	Check	NG
1	Check voltage of ABS motor relay.	Check and repair harness or connector.
2	Check continuity between relay and pump motor and ECU.	Repair or replace harness or ABS actuator.
3	Check ABS motor relay.	Replace ABS motor relay.
4	Check for open and short in harness and connector between relay and ECU.	Repair or replace harness or connector.

OK

If the same code is still output after the diagnostic trouble code is deleted, check the contact condition of each connection.
If the connections are normal, the ECU may be defective.

TY4029300084010X

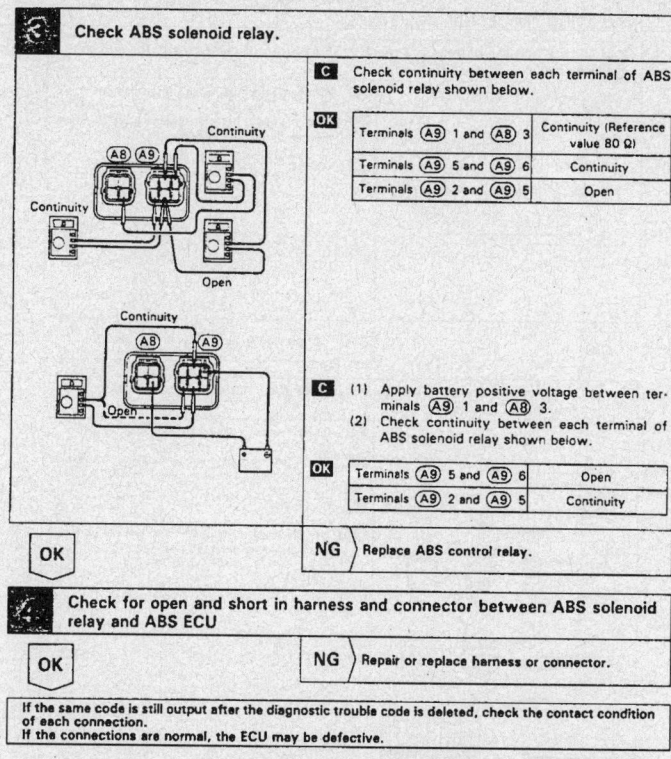

Fig. 125 Code 13 & 14: ABS Motor Relay (Part 1 of 6). Supra Less Traction Control

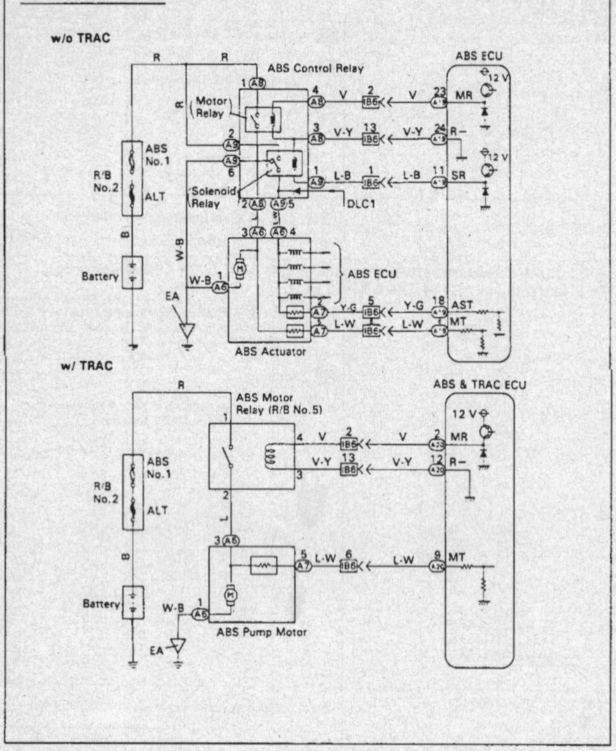
WIRING DIAGRAM
w/o TRAC
ABS Control Relay
ABS ECU
Motor Relay
Solenoid Relay
ABS No. 1
R/B No. 2
ALT
Battery
DLC1
ABS ECU
ABS Actuator
EA
MR
SR
AST
MT
12 V
w/ TRAC
ABS Motor Relay (R/B No. 5)
ABS & TRAC ECU
ABS No. 1
R/B No. 2
ALT
Battery
EA
ABS Pump Motor
MR
MT
12 V

TY4029300084020X

Fig. 125 Code 13 & 14: ABS Motor Relay (Part 2 of 6). Supra Less Traction Control

INSPECTION PROCEDURE (w/o TRAC)

1 Check voltage between terminal 1 of ABS motor relay connector and body ground.

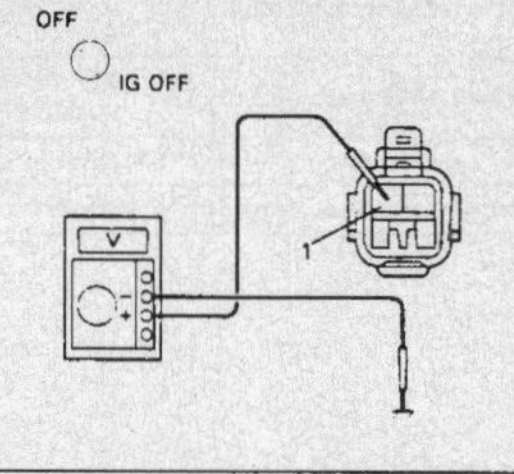
OFF
IG OFF
V
1

P Disconnect the ABS motor relay connector.

C Measure voltage between terminal 1 of ABS motor relay connector and body ground.

OK Voltage: 10 – 14 V

OK

NG 〉 Check and repair harness or connector.

2 Check continuity between terminal 2 of ABS motor relay connector and terminal MT of ABS ECU.

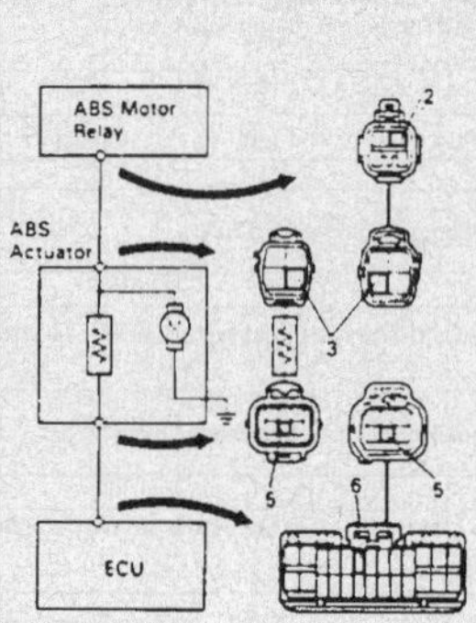
ABS Motor Relay
ABS Actuator
ECU
2
3
5
6
5

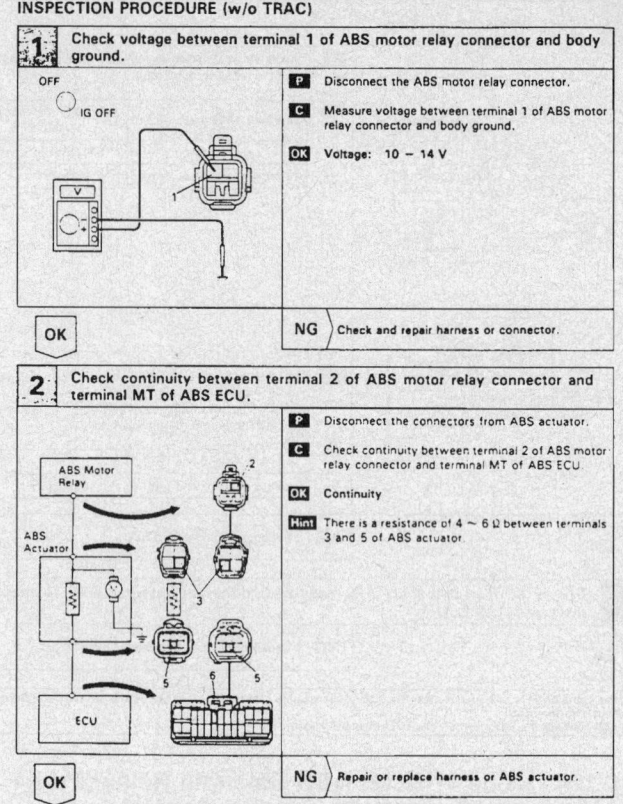

P Disconnect the connectors from ABS actuator.

C Check continuity between terminal 2 of ABS motor relay connector and terminal MT of ABS ECU.

OK Continuity

Hint There is a resistance of 4 ~ 6 Ω between terminals 3 and 5 of ABS actuator.

OK

NG 〉 Repair or replace harness or ABS actuator.

TY4029300084030X

Fig. 125 Code 13 & 14: ABS Motor Relay (Part 3 of 6). Supra Less Traction Control

3 Check ABS motor relay.

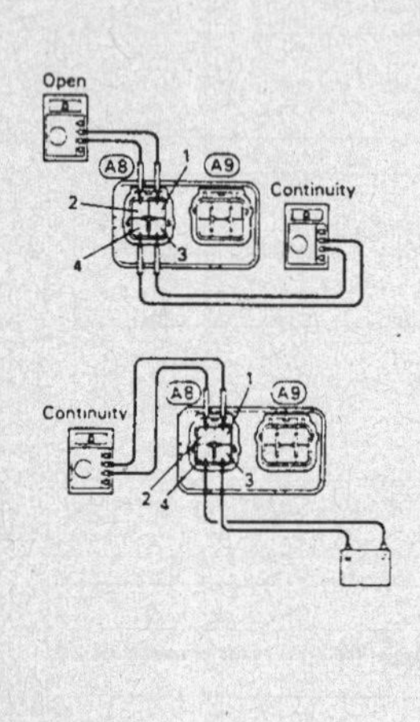
Open
A8
A9
1
2
3
4
Continuity
Continuity
A8
A9
1
2
3
4

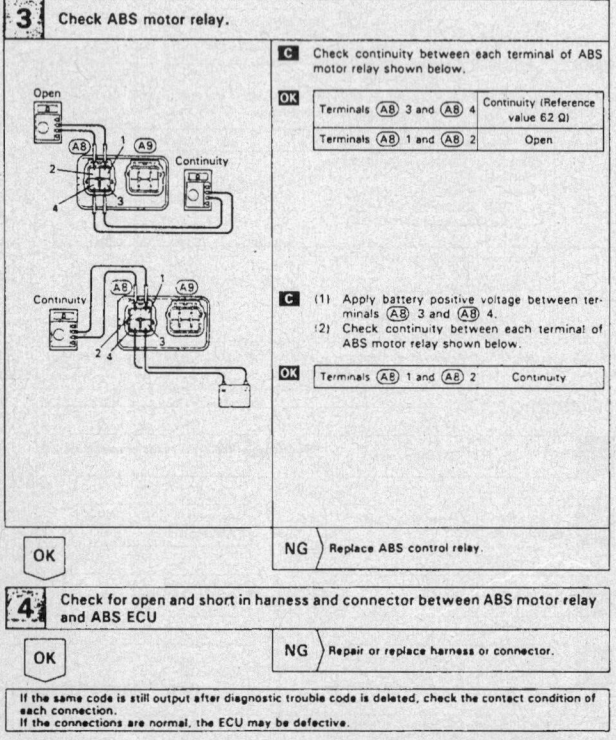

C Check continuity between each terminal of ABS motor relay shown below.

OK

Terminals	Continuity
Terminals (A8) 3 and (A8) 4	Continuity (Reference value 62 Ω)
Terminals (A8) 1 and (A8) 2	Open

C (1) Apply battery positive voltage between terminals (A8) 3 and (A8) 4.
(2) Check continuity between each terminal of ABS motor relay shown below.

OK

Terminals	Continuity
Terminals (A8) 1 and (A8) 2	Continuity

OK

NG 〉 Replace ABS control relay.

4 Check for open and short in harness and connector between ABS motor relay and ABS ECU

OK

NG 〉 Repair or replace harness or connector.

If the same code is still output after diagnostic trouble code is deleted, check the contact condition of each connection.
If the connections are normal, the ECU may be defective.

TY4029300084040X

Fig. 125 Code 13 & 14: ABS Motor Relay (Part 4 of 6). Supra Less Traction Control

INSPECTION PROCEDURE (w/ TRAC)

1 Check voltage between terminal 1 of R/B No. 5 (for ABS motor relay) and body ground.

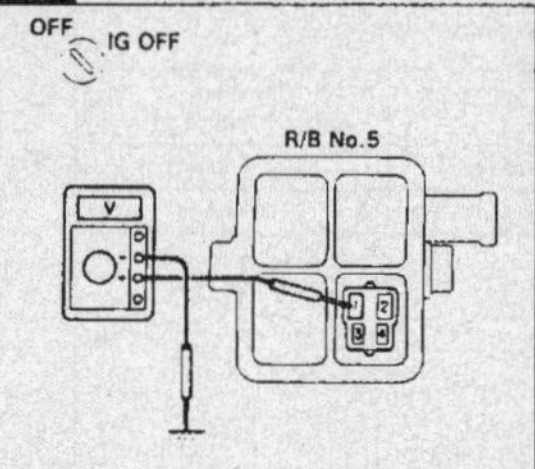
OFF
IG OFF
R/B No.5
V

P Remove ABS motor relay from R/B No. 5.

C Measure voltage between terminal 1 of R/B No. 5 (for ABS motor relay) and body ground.

OK Voltage: 10 – 14 V

OK

NG 〉 Check and repair harness or connector.

2 Check continuity between terminal 2 of R/B No. 5 (for ABS motor relay) and terminal MT of ABS & TRAC ECU.

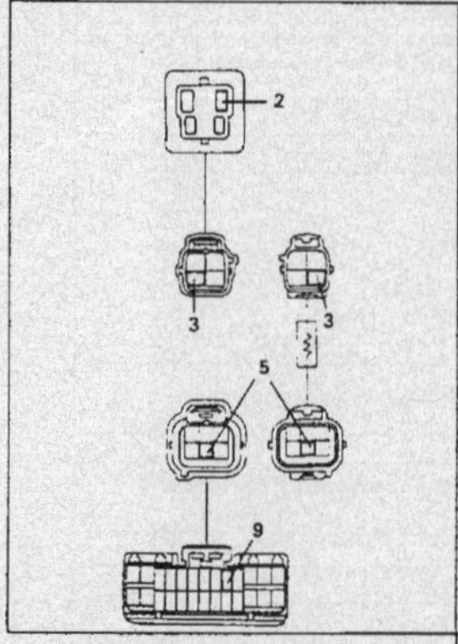
2
3
3
5
9

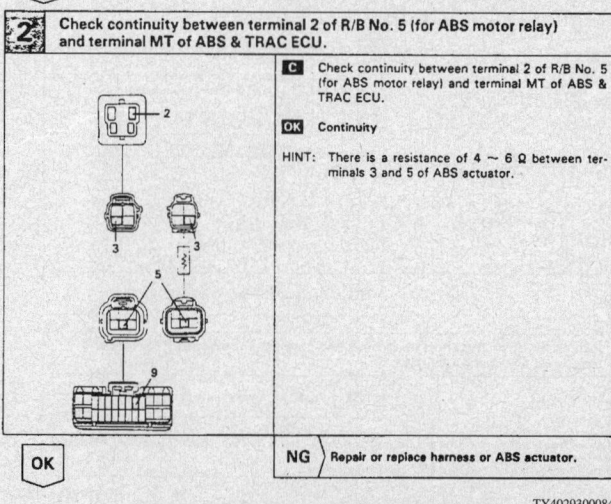

C Check continuity between terminal 2 of R/B No. 5 (for ABS motor relay) and terminal MT of ABS & TRAC ECU.

OK Continuity

HINT: There is a resistance of 4 ~ 6 Ω between terminals 3 and 5 of ABS actuator.

OK

NG 〉 Repair or replace harness or ABS actuator.

TY4029300084050X

Fig. 125 Code 13 & 14: ABS Motor Relay (Part 5 of 6). Supra w/Traction Control

3 **Check ABS motor relay.**

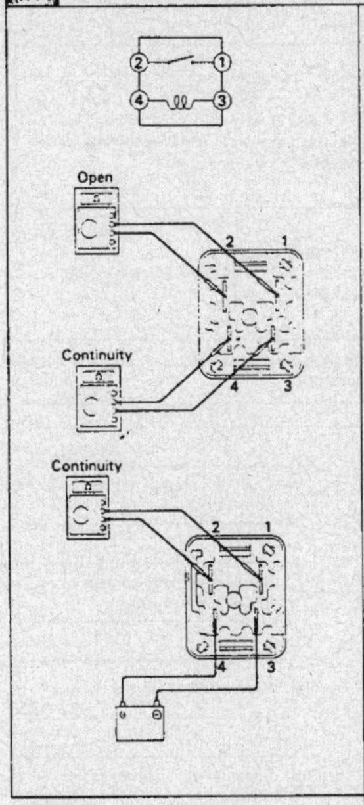
Open
2
1
Continuity
4
3
Continuity
2
1
4
3

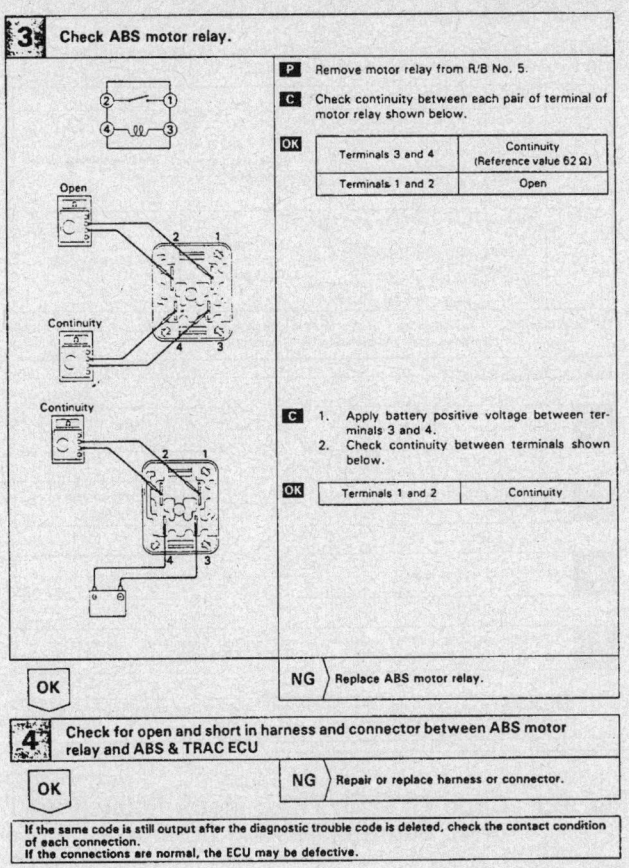

P Remove motor relay from R/B No. 5.

C Check continuity between each pair of terminal of motor relay shown below.

OK

Terminals 3 and 4	Continuity (Reference value 62 Ω)
Terminals 1 and 2	Open

C 1. Apply battery positive voltage between terminals 3 and 4.
2. Check continuity between terminals shown below.

OK

Terminals 1 and 2	Continuity

OK

NG 〉 **Replace ABS motor relay.**

4 **Check for open and short in harness and connector between ABS motor relay and ABS & TRAC ECU**

OK

NG 〉 **Repair or replace harness or connector.**

If the same code is still output after the diagnostic trouble code is deleted, check the contact condition of each connection.
If the connections are normal, the ECU may be defective.

TY4029300084060X

Fig. 125 Code 13 & 14: ABS Motor Relay (Part 6 of 6). Supra w/Traction Control

WIRING DIAGRAM

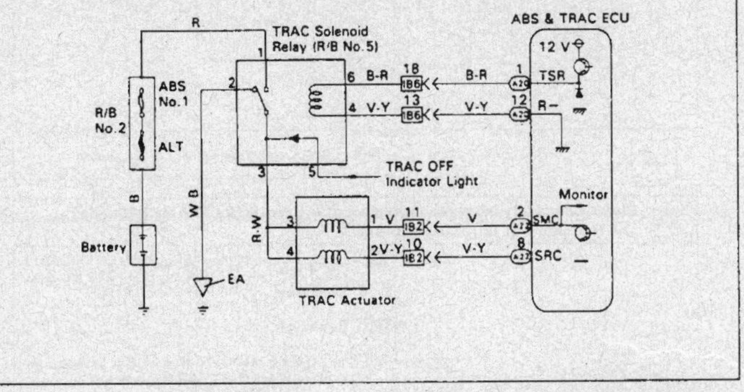
R
TRAC Solenoid Relay (R/B No. 5)
ABS & TRAC ECU
12 V
ABS No. 1
R/B No. 2
ALT
6 B-R 18 IB6
B-R
1 TSR
4 V-Y 13 IB6
V-Y
12 R−
TRAC OFF Indicator Light
Monitor
B
W-B
R-W
1 V 11 IB2
V
2 SMC
2 V-Y 10 IB2
V-Y
8 SRC
Battery
EA
TRAC Actuator

TY4029300085020X

Fig. 126 Code 15 & 16: TRAC Solenoid Relay (Part 2 of 4). Supra w/Traction Control

CIRCUIT DESCRIPTION

This relay circuit supplies power to each traction actuator solenoid.
When the ignition switch is turned on, the relay goes on.

DTC No.	Diagnostic Trouble Code Detecting Condition	Trouble area
15	Conditions (1) through (3) continue for 0.2 sec. or more: (1) TRAC solenoid relay (TSR) terminal voltage: Battery positive voltage (2) All TRAC actuator solenoids: OFF (3) All TRAC actuator solenoid monitor voltages (in ECU): 0 V	• TRAC solenoid relay • Open or short in TRAC solenoid relay circuit • ECU
16	Conditions (1) through (3) continue for 0.2 sec. or more: (1) TRAC solenoid relay (TSR) terminal voltage: 0 V (2) All TRAC actuator solenoids: OFF (3) TRAC actuator solenoid monitor voltage (in ECU): Battery positive voltage	• TRAC solenoid relay • B+ short in TRAC solenoid relay circuit • ECU

Fail safe function: If trouble occurs in this relay circuit, the ECU cuts off current to the ABS and TRAC solenoid relays and prohibits ABS and TRAC control.

DIAGNOSTIC CHART

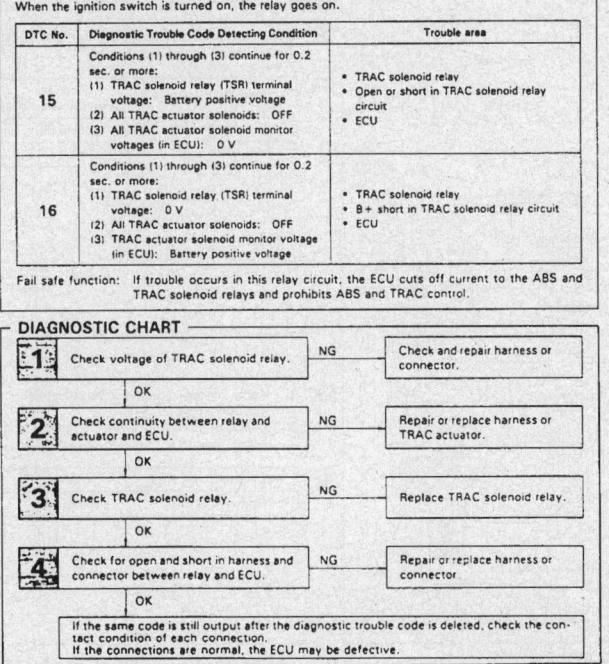

1 Check voltage of TRAC solenoid relay. — NG → Check and repair harness or connector.
↓ OK
2 Check continuity between relay and actuator and ECU. — NG → Repair or replace harness or TRAC actuator.
↓ OK
3 Check TRAC solenoid relay. — NG → Replace TRAC solenoid relay.
↓ OK
4 Check for open and short in harness and connector between relay and ECU. — NG → Repair or replace harness or connector.
↓ OK

If the same code is still output after the diagnostic trouble code is deleted, check the contact condition of each connection.
If the connections are normal, the ECU may be defective.

TY4029300085010X

Fig. 126 Code 15 & 16: TRAC Solenoid Relay (Part 1 of 4). Supra w/Traction Control

1 **Check voltage between terminals 1 and 2 of R/B No. 5 (for TRAC solenoid relay).**

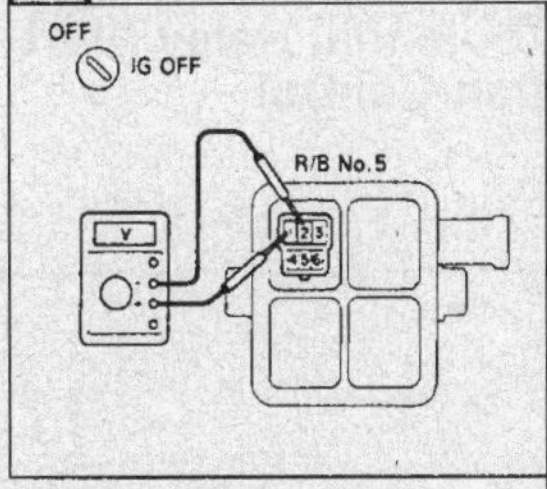
OFF
IG OFF
R/B No.5
V

P Remove TRAC solenoid relay from R/B No. 5.

C Measure voltage between terminals 1 and 2 of R/B No. 5 (for TRAC solenoid relay).

OK **Voltage: 10 – 14 V**

OK

NG 〉 **Repair or replace harness or connector.**

2 **Check continuity between terminal 3 of R/B No. 5 (for TRAC solenoid relay) and terminals SMC and SRC of ABS & TRAC ECU.**

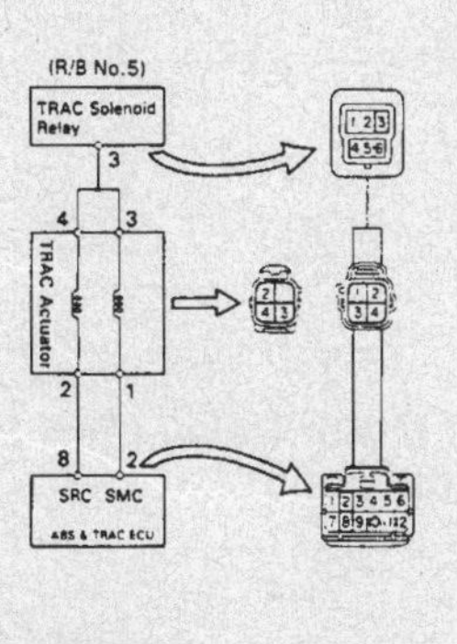
(R/B No.5)
TRAC Solenoid Relay
3
4
3
TRAC Actuator
2
1
8
2
SRC SMC
ABS & TRAC ECU

C Check continuity between terminal 3 of R/B No. 5 (for TRAC solenoid relay) and terminals SMC and SRC of ABS & TRAC ECU.

OK **Continuity**

HINT: Resistance of the TRAC actuator solenoid is 2 Ω.

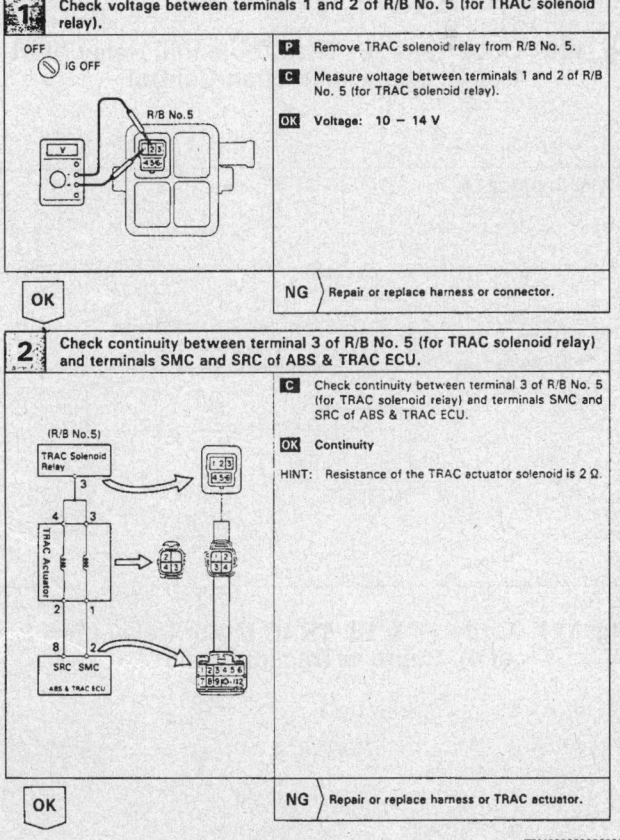

OK

NG 〉 **Repair or replace harness or TRAC actuator.**

TY4029300085030X

Fig. 126 Code 15 & 16: TRAC Solenoid Relay (Part 3 of 4). Supra w/Traction Control

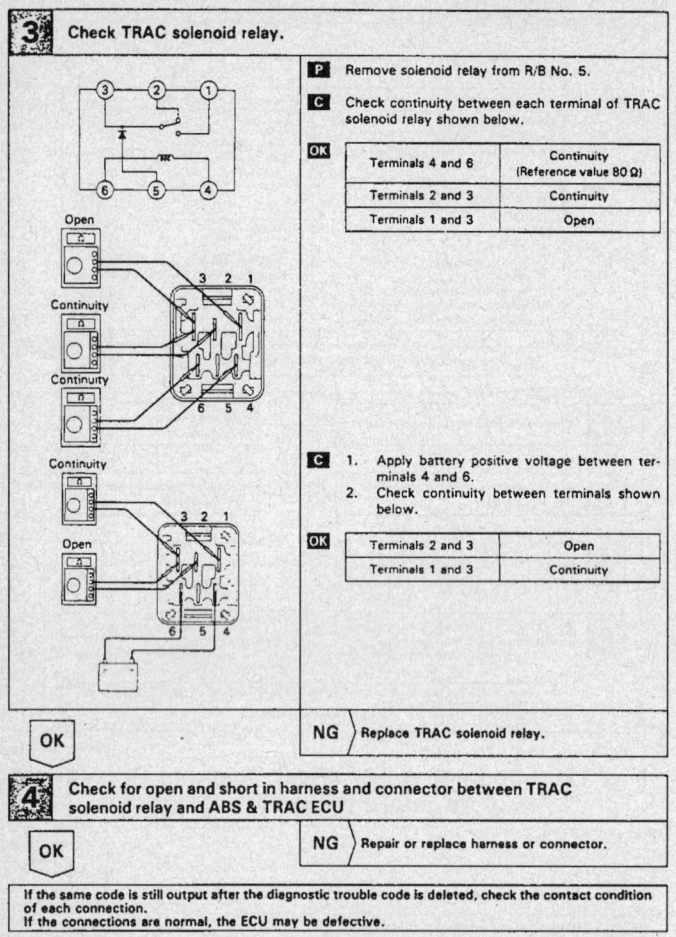

3 Check TRAC solenoid relay.

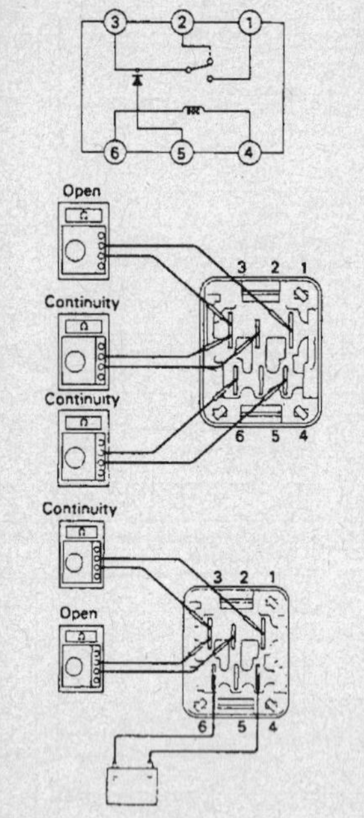
3
2
1
6
5
4
Open
Continuity
Continuity
3 2 1
6 5 4
Continuity
Open
3 2 1
6 5 4

P Remove solenoid relay from R/B No. 5.

C Check continuity between each terminal of TRAC solenoid relay shown below.

OK

Terminals 4 and 6	Continuity (Reference value 80 Ω)
Terminals 2 and 3	Continuity
Terminals 1 and 3	Open

C
1. Apply battery positive voltage between terminals 4 and 6.
2. Check continuity between terminals shown below.

OK

Terminals 2 and 3	Open
Terminals 1 and 3	Continuity

OK

NG 〉 Replace TRAC solenoid relay.

4 Check for open and short in harness and connector between TRAC solenoid relay and ABS & TRAC ECU

OK

NG 〉 Repair or replace harness or connector.

If the same code is still output after the diagnostic trouble code is deleted, check the contact condition of each connection.
If the connections are normal, the ECU may be defective.

TY4029300085040X

Fig. 126 Code 15 & 16: TRAC Solenoid Relay (Part 4 of 4). Supra w/Traction Control

WIRING DIAGRAM

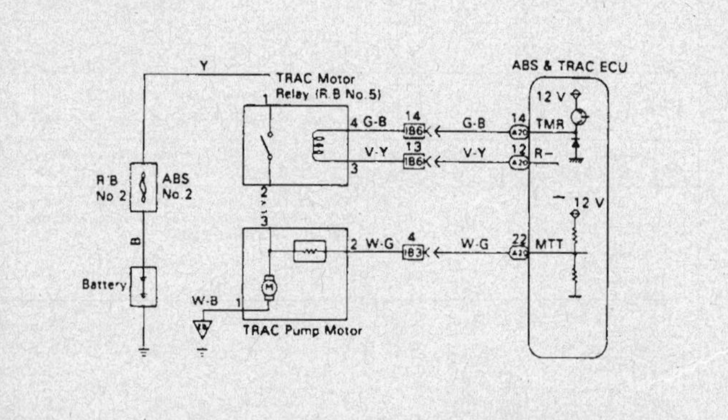
Y
TRAC Motor Relay (R/B No.5)
ABS & TRAC ECU
12 V
4 G-B
14
IB6
G-B
14
A20
TMR
V-Y
13
IB6
V-Y
12
A20
R−
R/B No. 2
ABS No. 2
B
12 V
2 W-G
4
IB3
W-G
22
A20
MTT
Battery
W-B
TRAC Pump Motor

TY4029300086020X

Fig. 127 Code 17 & 18: TRAC Motor Relay (Part 2 of 4). Supra w/Traction Control

CIRCUIT DESCRIPTION

This relay circuit supplies power to the TRAC pump motor. While the TRAC is activated, the ECU switches the motor relay ON and operates the TRAC pump motor.

DTC No.	Diagnostic Trouble Code Detecting Condition	Trouble area
17	Conditions (1) and (2) continue for 0.2 sec. or more: (1) TRAC motor relay (TMR) terminal voltage: Battery positive voltage (2) Voltage of ABS & TRAC ECU terminal MTT: 0 V	• TRAC motor relay • Open or short in TRAC motor relay circuit • ECU
18	Conditions (1) and (2) continue for 2 sec. or more: (1) TRAC motor relay (TMR) terminal voltage: 0 V (2) Voltage of ABS & TRAC ECU terminal MTT: Battery positive voltage	• TRAC motor relay • B+ short in TRAC motor relay circuit • ECU

Fail safe function: If trouble occurs in this relay circuit, the ECU cuts off current to the TRAC solenoid relay and prohibits TRAC control.

DIAGNOSTIC CHART

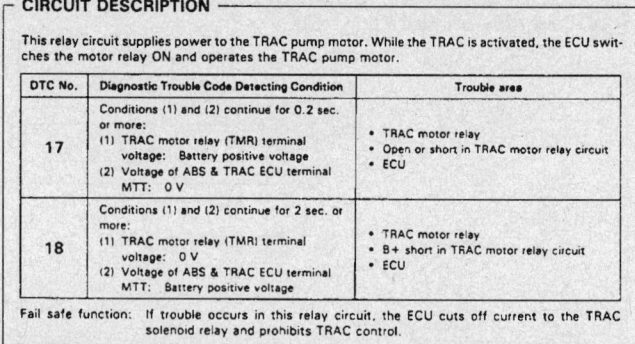

1 Check voltage of TRAC motor relay. — NG → Check and repair harness or connector.

OK

2 Check continuity between relay and pump motor. — NG → Repair or replace harness or TRAC pump motor.

OK

3 Check TRAC motor relay. — NG → Replace TRAC motor relay.

OK

4 Check for open and short in harness and connector between relay and ECU. — NG → Repair or replace harness or connector.

OK

If the same code is still output after the diagnostic trouble code is deleted, check the contact condition of each connection.
If the connections are normal, the ECU may be defective.

TY4029300086010X

Fig. 127 Code 17 & 18: TRAC Motor Relay (Part 1 of 4). Supra w/Traction Control

INSPECTION PROCEDURE

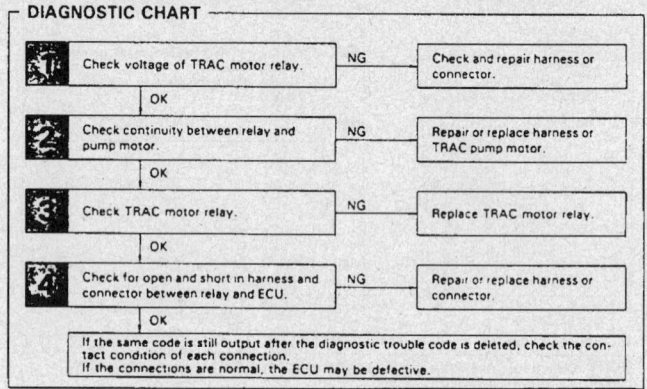

1 Check voltage between terminal 1 of R/B No. 5 (for TRAC motor relay) and body ground.

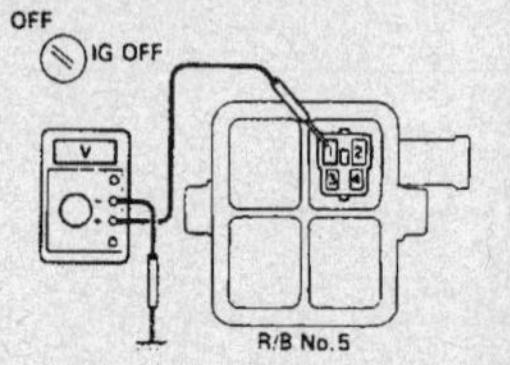
OFF
IG OFF
V
R/B No.5

P Remove TRAC motor relay from R/B No. 5.

C Measure voltage between terminal 1 of R/B No. 5 (for TRAC motor relay) and body ground.

OK **Voltage: 10 – 14 V**

OK

NG 〉 Check and repair harness or connector.

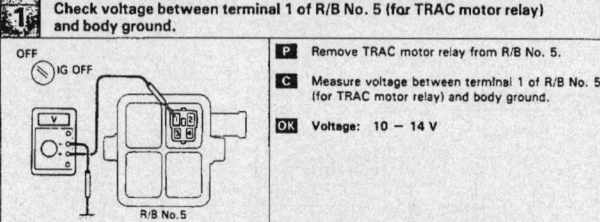

2 Check continuity between terminal 2 of R/B No. 5 (for TRAC motor relay) and terminal 2 of TRAC pump motor.

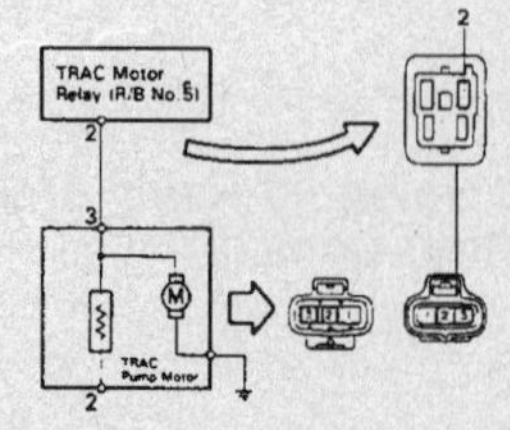
TRAC Motor Relay (R/B No. 5)
2
3
2
TRAC Pump Motor
2

C Check continuity between terminal 2 of R/B No. 5 (for TRAC motor relay) and terminal 2 of TRAC pump motor.

OK Continuity

HINT: There is a resistance of 4 – 6 Ω between terminals 2 and 3 of TRAC pump motor.

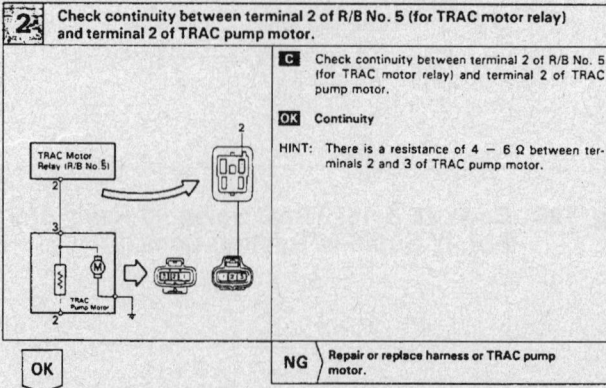

OK

NG 〉 Repair or replace harness or TRAC pump motor.

TY4029300086030X

Fig. 127 Code 17 & 18: TRAC Motor Relay (Part 3 of 4). Supra w/Traction Control

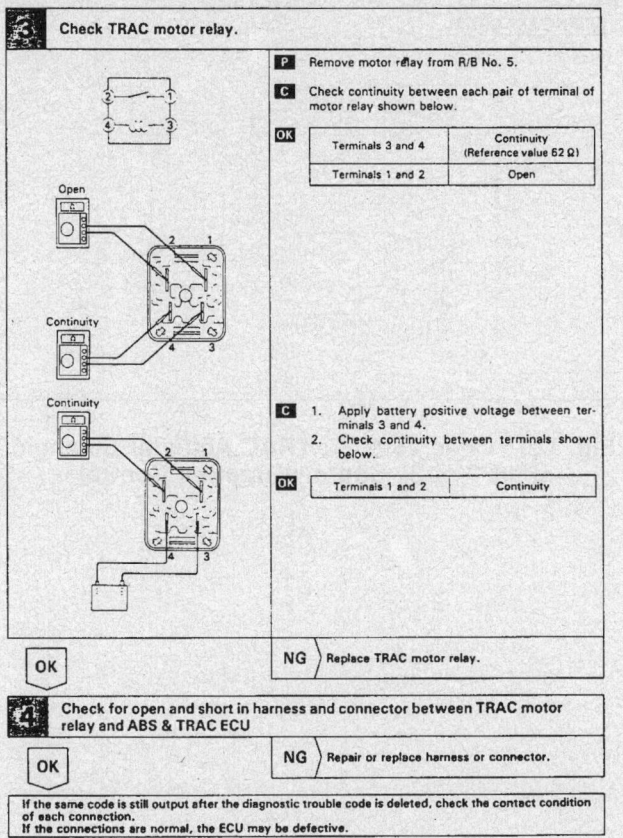

3 Check TRAC motor relay.

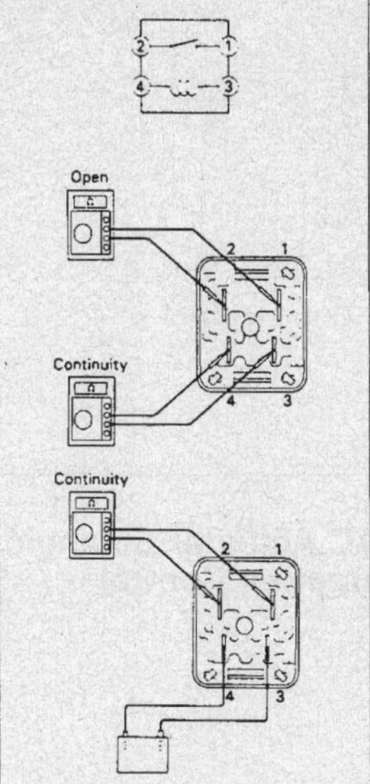
Open
Continuity
Continuity

P Remove motor relay from R/B No. 5.

C Check continuity between each pair of terminal of motor relay shown below.

OK

Terminals 3 and 4	Continuity (Reference value 62 Ω)
Terminals 1 and 2	Open

C 1. Apply battery positive voltage between terminals 3 and 4.
2. Check continuity between terminals shown below.

OK

Terminals 1 and 2	Continuity

OK

NG 〉 Replace TRAC motor relay.

4 Check for open and short in harness and connector between TRAC motor relay and ABS & TRAC ECU

OK

NG 〉 Repair or replace harness or connector.

If the same code is still output after the diagnostic trouble code is deleted, check the contact condition of each connection.
If the connections are normal, the ECU may be defective.

TY4029300086040X

Fig. 127 Code 17 & 18: TRAC Motor Relay (Part 4 of 4). Supra w/Traction Control

WIRING DIAGRAM

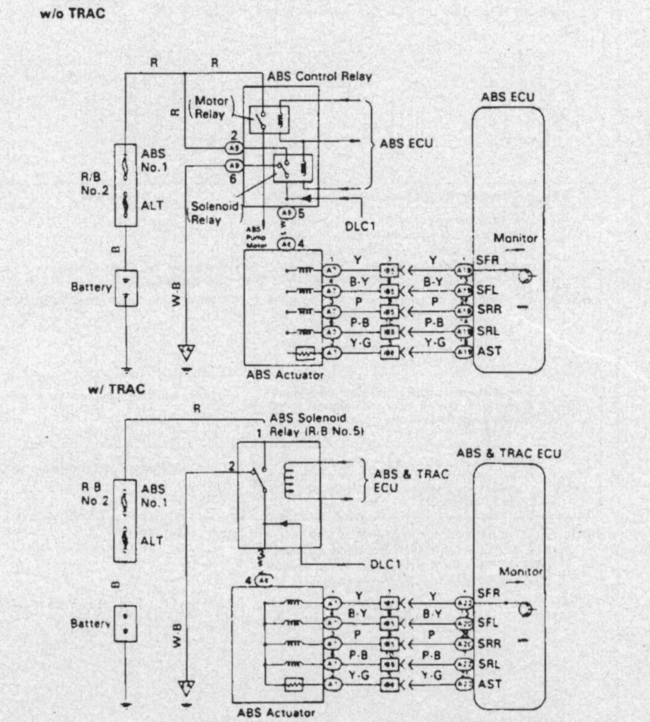
w/o TRAC
ABS Control Relay
Motor Relay
ABS ECU
R/B No.2
ABS No.1
ALT
Solenoid Relay
DLC1
Monitor
Battery
SFR
SFL
SRR
SRL
AST
ABS Actuator
w/ TRAC
ABS Solenoid Relay (R/B No.5)
ABS & TRAC ECU
ABS & TRAC ECU
R B No 2
ABS No.1
ALT
DLC1
Monitor
Battery
SFR
SFL
SRR
SRL
AST
ABS Actuator

TY4029300087020X

Fig. 128 Code 21, 22, 23 & 24: ABS Actuator Solenoid (Part 2 of 3). Supra

CIRCUIT DESCRIPTION

This solenoid goes on when signals are received from the ECU and controls the fluid pressure acting on the brake cylinders, thus controlling the braking force.

DTC No.	Diagnostic Trouble Code Detecting Condition	Trouble area
21	Conditions (1) through (3) continue for 0.05 sec. or more: (1) ABS solenoid relay (SR) terminal voltage: Battery positive voltage (2) Voltage of ABS (& TRAC) ECU terminal AST: Battery positive voltage (3) When power transistor of ECU is ON, voltage of terminal SFR is 0 V or battery positive voltage.	• ABS actuator • Open or short in SFR circuit. • ECU
22	Conditions (1) through (3) continue for 0.05 sec. or more: (1) ABS solenoid relay (SR) terminal voltage: Battery positive voltage (2) Voltage of ABS (& TRAC) ECU terminal AST: Battery positive voltage (3) When power transistor of ECU is ON, voltage of terminal SFL is 0 V or battery positive voltage.	• ABS actuator • Open or short in SFL circuit. • ECU
23	Conditions (1) through (3) continue for 0.05 sec. or more: (1) ABS solenoid relay (SR) terminal voltage: Battery positive voltage (2) Voltage of ABS (& TRAC) ECU terminal AST: Battery positive voltage (3) When power transistor of ECU is ON, voltage of terminal SRR is 0 V or battery positive voltage.	• ABS actuator • Open or short in SRR circuit. • ECU
24	Conditions (1) through (3) continue for 0.05 sec. or more: (1) ABS solenoid relay (SR) terminal voltage: Battery positive voltage (2) Voltage of ABS (& TRAC) ECU terminal AST: Battery positive voltage (3) When power transistor of ECU is ON, voltage of terminal SRL is 0 V or battery positive voltage.	• ABS actuator • Open or short in SRL circuit. • ECU

Fail safe function: If trouble occurs in the actuator solenoid circuit, the ECU cuts off current to the solenoid relay and prohibits ABS control.

DIAGNOSTIC CHART

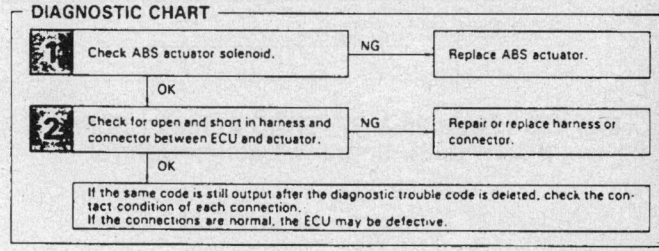

Step	Check	NG
1	Check ABS actuator solenoid. (OK ↓)	Replace ABS actuator.
2	Check for open and short in harness and connector between ECU and actuator. (OK ↓)	Repair or replace harness or connector.

If the same code is still output after the diagnostic trouble code is deleted, check the contact condition of each connection.
If the connections are normal, the ECU may be defective.

TY4029300087010X

Fig. 128 Code 21, 22, 23 & 24: ABS Actuator Solenoid (Part 1 of 3). Supra

1 Check ABS actuator solenoid.

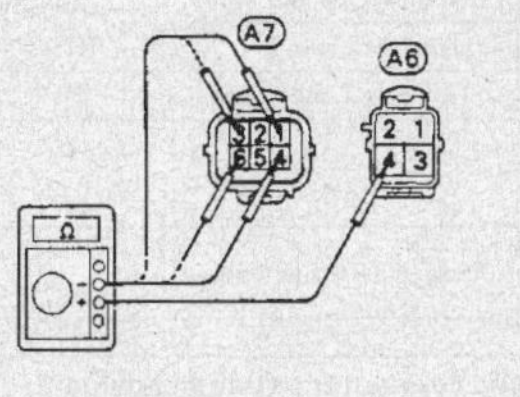
A7
A6
Ω

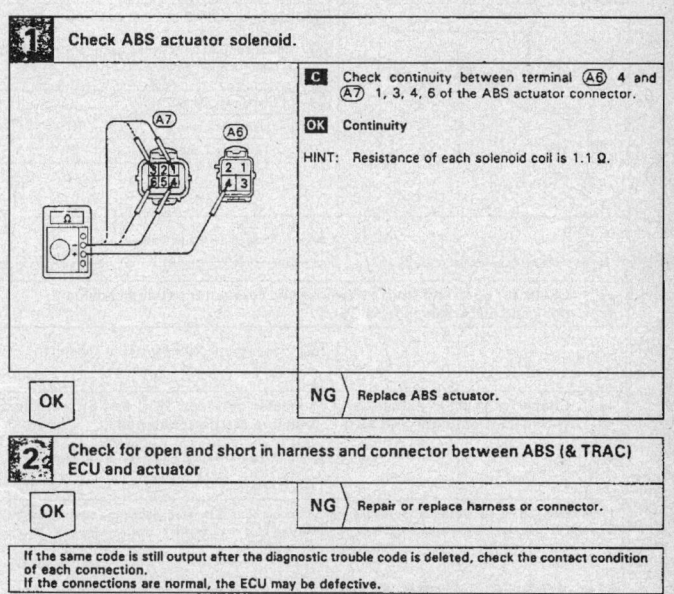

C Check continuity between terminal (A6) 4 and (A7) 1, 3, 4, 6 of the ABS actuator connector.

OK Continuity

HINT: Resistance of each solenoid coil is 1.1 Ω.

OK

NG 〉 Replace ABS actuator.

2 Check for open and short in harness and connector between ABS (& TRAC) ECU and actuator

OK

NG 〉 Repair or replace harness or connector.

If the same code is still output after the diagnostic trouble code is deleted, check the contact condition of each connection.
If the connections are normal, the ECU may be defective.

TY4029300087030X

Fig. 128 Code 21, 22, 23 & 24: ABS Actuator Solenoid (Part 3 of 3). Supra

CIRCUIT DESCRIPTION

The TRAC actuator solenoid operates in accordance with signals from the ECU and raises the fluid pressure in and releases it from the brake cylinders.

DTC No.	Diagnostic Trouble Code Detecting Condition	Trouble area
25	Conditions (1) and (2) continue for 0.05 sec. or more: (1) TRAC solenoid relay (TSR) terminal voltage: Battery positive voltage (2) Voltage of ABS & TRAC ECU terminal SMC: 0 V	• TRAC actuator • Open or short in SMC circuit • ECU
27	Conditions (1) and (2) continue for 0.05 sec. or more: (1) TRAC solenoid relay (TSR) terminal voltage: Battery positive voltage (2) Voltage of ABS & TRAC ECU terminal SRC: 0V	• TRAC actuator • Open or short in SRC circuit • ECU

Fail safe function: If trouble occurs in this solenoid circuit, the ECU cuts off current to the ABS and TRAC solenoid relays and prohibits ABS and TRAC control.

DIAGNOSTIC CHART

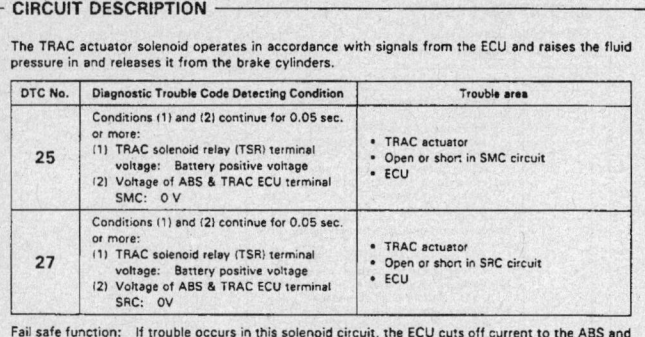

1 Check TRAC actuator solenoid. — NG → Replace TRAC actuator.

OK

2 Check for open and short in harness and connector between solenoid relay and ECU. — NG → Repair or replace harness or connector.

OK

3 Check for short in harness and connector between SMC and SRC terminals with TRAC actuator and ECU connectors are disconnected. — NG → Repair or replace harness or connector.

OK

If the same code is still output after the diagnostic trouble code is deleted, check the contact condition of each connection.
If the connections are normal, the ECU may be defective.

TY4029300088010X

Fig. 129 Code 25 & 27: TRAC Actuator Solenoid (Part 1 of 3). Supra w/Traction Control

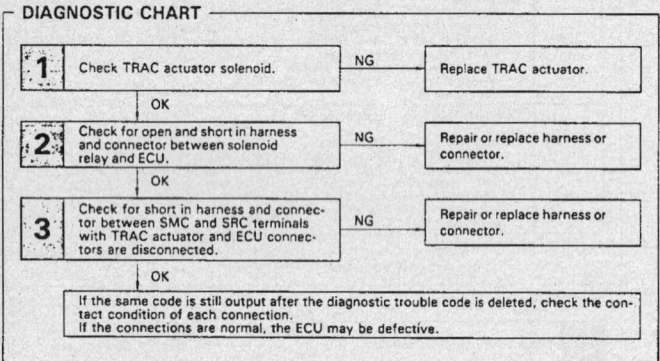

WIRING DIAGRAM

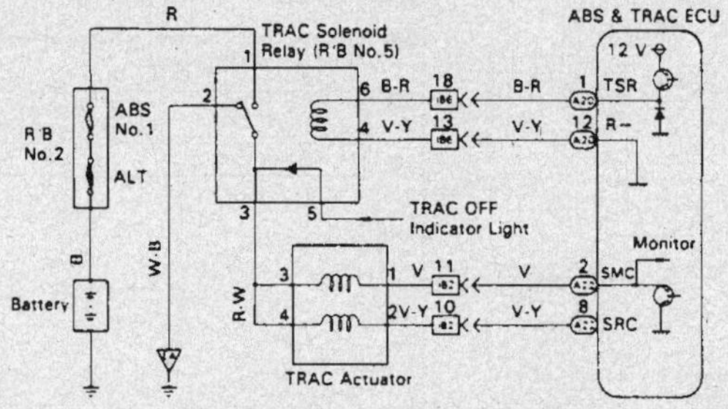
R
TRAC Solenoid
Relay (R/B No.5)
ABS & TRAC ECU
12 V
R/B
No.2
ABS
No.1
ALT
B-R
V-Y
TSR
R-
TRAC OFF
Indicator Light
Monitor
SMC
SRC
Battery
W-B
R-W
V
V-Y
TRAC Actuator

TY4029300088020X

Fig. 129 Code 25 & 27: TRAC Actuator Solenoid (Part 2 of 3). Supra w/Traction Control

1 Check TRAC actuator solenoid.

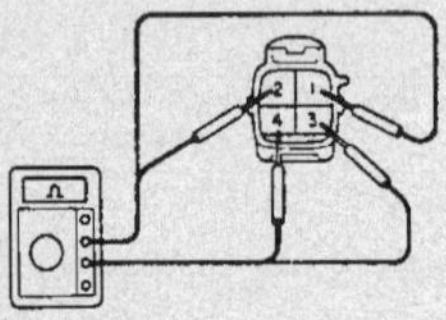

P Disconnect TRAC actuator connector.

C Check continuity between each terminal of TRAC actuator shown below.

OK

Terminals 1 and 3	Continuity (Reference value 2 Ω)
Terminals 2 and 4	
Terminals 1 and 2	Open

OK — NG Replace TRAC actuator.

2 Check for open and short in harness and connector between solenoid relay and ECU (See page IN-35).

OK — NG Repair or replace harness or connector.

3 Check for short in harness and connector between SMC and SRC terminals with TRAC actuator and ECU connectors are disconnected.

OK — NG Repair or replace harness or connector.

If the same code is still output after the diagnostic trouble code is deleted, check the contact condition of each connection. If the connections are normal, the ECU may be defective.

TY4029300088030X

Fig. 129 Code 25 & 27: TRAC Actuator Solenoid (Part 3 of 3). Supra w/Traction Control

CIRCUIT DESCRIPTION

The speed sensor detects the wheel speed and sends the appropriate signals to the ECU. These signals are used to control both the ABS and TRAC control systems. The front and rear rotors each have 48 serrations. When the rotors rotate, the magnetic field emitted by the permanent magnet in the speed sensor generates an AC voltage. Since the frequency of this AC voltage changes in direct proportion to the speed of the rotor, the frequency is used by the ECU to detect the speed of each wheel.

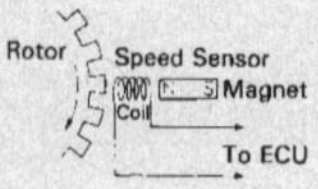
Rotor
Speed Sensor
Coil
Magnet
To ECU

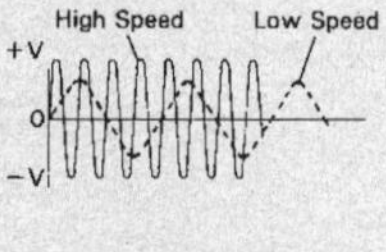
High Speed
Low Speed
+V
0
-V

DTC No.	Diagnostic Trouble Code Detecting Condition	Trouble area
31, 32 33, 34	Detection of any of conditions (1) through (3): (1) At vehicle speed of 10 km/h (6 mph) or more, pulses are not input for 5 sec. (2) Momentary interruption of the vehicle speed sensor signal occurs at least 7 times in the time between switching the ignition switch ON and switching it OFF. (3) Abnormal fluctuation of speed sensor signals with the vehicle speed 20 km/h (12 mph) or more.	• Right front, left front, right rear and left rear speed sensor. • Open or short in each speed sensor circuit. • ECU
35	Speed sensor signal is not input for about 1 sec. while the left front and right rear speed sensor signals are being checked with the IG switch ON.	• Open in left front, right rear speed sensor circuit. • ECU
36	Speed sensor signal is not input for about 1 sec. while the right front and left rear speed sensor signals are being checked with the IG switch ON.	• Open in right front, left rear speed sensor circuit. • ECU

HINT: DTC No.31 is for the right front speed sensor.
DTC No.32 is for the left front speed sensor.
DTC No.33 is for the right rear speed sensor.
DTC No.34 is for the left rear speed sensor.

Fail safe function: If trouble occurs in the speed sensor circuit, the ECU cuts off current to the ABS solenoid relay and prohibits ABS control.

TY4029300089010X

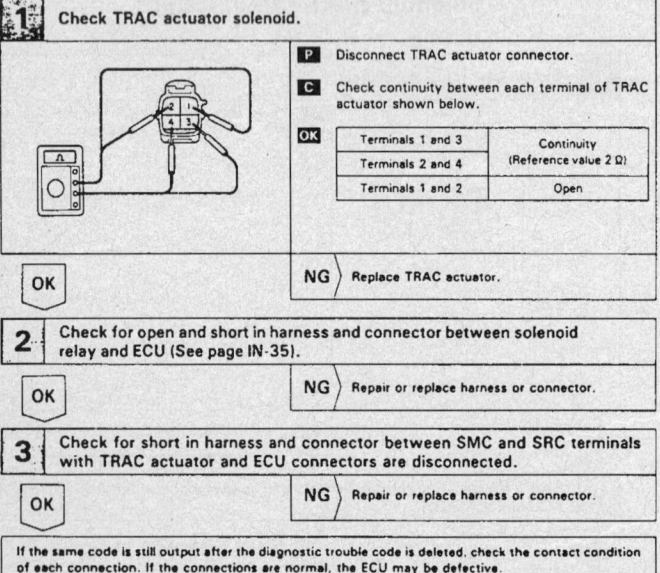

Fig. 130 Code 31 through 36: Speed Sensor (Part 1 of 4). Supra

DIAGNOSTIC CHART

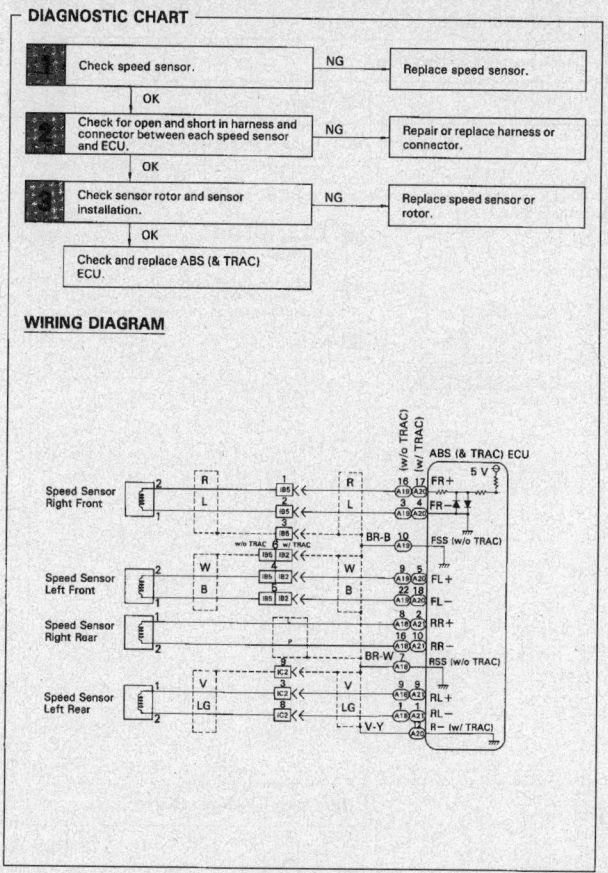

Step	Check	Result	Action
1	Check speed sensor.	NG	Replace speed sensor.
	↓ OK		
2	Check for open and short in harness and connector between each speed sensor and ECU.	NG	Repair or replace harness or connector.
	↓ OK		
3	Check sensor rotor and sensor installation.	NG	Replace speed sensor or rotor.
	↓ OK		
	Check and replace ABS (& TRAC) ECU.		

WIRING DIAGRAM

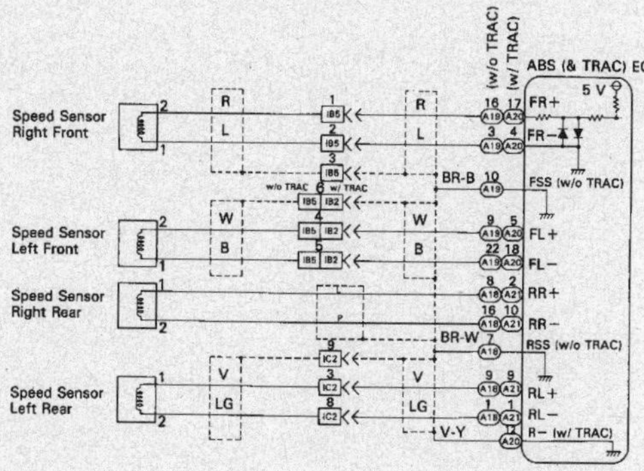

ABS (& TRAC) ECU
Speed Sensor Right Front
Speed Sensor Left Front
Speed Sensor Right Rear
Speed Sensor Left Rear
(w/o TRAC)
(w/ TRAC)
FR+
FR−
FSS (w/o TRAC)
FL+
FL−
RR+
RR−
RSS (w/o TRAC)
RL+
RL−
R− (w/ TRAC)
BR-B
BR-W
V-Y
5 V

TY4029300089020X

Fig. 130 Code 31 through 36: Speed Sensor (Part 2 of 4). Supra

1 Check speed sensor.

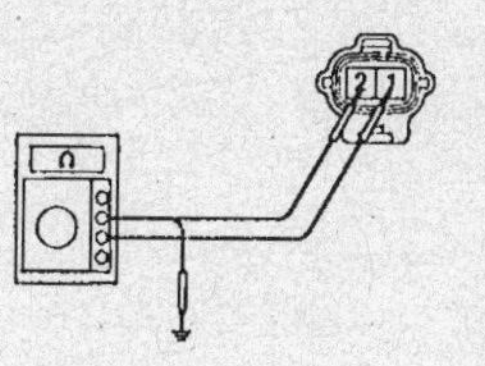

Front

Front

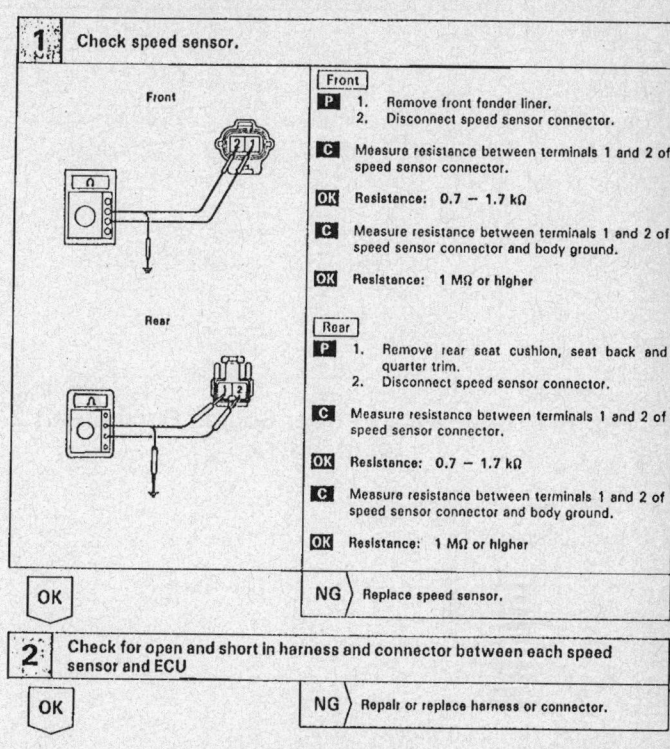

P 1. Remove front fender liner.
2. Disconnect speed sensor connector.

C Measure resistance between terminals 1 and 2 of speed sensor connector.

OK Resistance: 0.7 – 1.7 kΩ

C Measure resistance between terminals 1 and 2 of speed sensor connector and body ground.

OK Resistance: 1 MΩ or higher

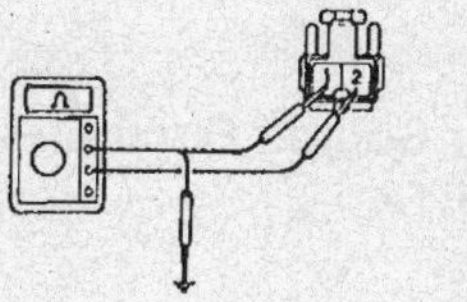

Rear

Rear

P 1. Remove rear seat cushion, seat back and quarter trim.
2. Disconnect speed sensor connector.

C Measure resistance between terminals 1 and 2 of speed sensor connector.

OK Resistance: 0.7 – 1.7 kΩ

C Measure resistance between terminals 1 and 2 of speed sensor connector and body ground.

OK Resistance: 1 MΩ or higher

OK | NG 〉 Replace speed sensor.

2 Check for open and short in harness and connector between each speed sensor and ECU

OK | NG 〉 Repair or replace harness or connector.

TY4029300089030X

Fig. 130 Code 31 through 36: Speed Sensor (Part 3 of 4). Supra

3 Check sensor rotor and sensor installation.

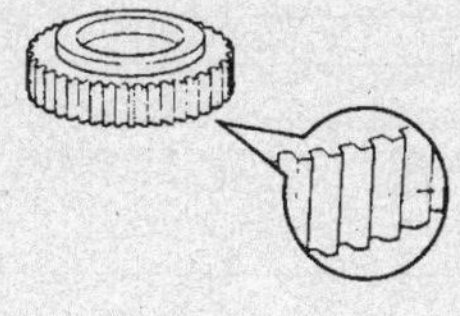

Front

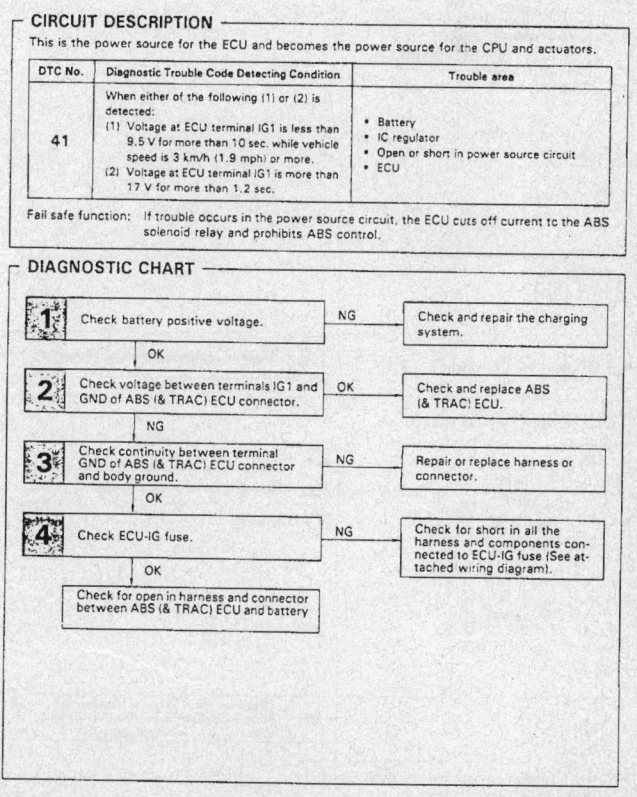

P Remove front speed sensor rotor

C Check sensor rotor serrations.

OK No scratches or missing teeth.

C Check the front speed sensor installation.

OK The installation bolt is tightened properly.

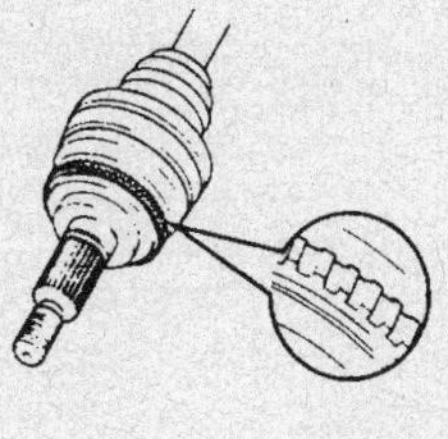

Rear

P Remove the drive shaft

C Check the sensor rotor serrations.

OK No scratches or missing teeth.

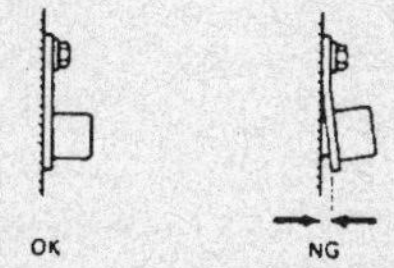

OK
NG

C Check the rear speed sensor installation.

OK The installation bolt is tightened properly and there is no clearance between the sensor and rear axle carrier.

OK | NG 〉 Replace speed sensor or rotor.

Check and replace ABS (& TRAC) ECU.

TY4029300089040X

Fig. 130 Code 31 through 36: Speed Sensor (Part 4 of 4). Supra

CIRCUIT DESCRIPTION

This is the power source for the ECU and becomes the power source for the CPU and actuators.

DTC No.	Diagnostic Trouble Code Detecting Condition	Trouble area
41	When either of the following (1) or (2) is detected: (1) Voltage at ECU terminal IG1 is less than 9.5 V for more than 10 sec. while vehicle speed is 3 km/h (1.9 mph) or more. (2) Voltage at ECU terminal IG1 is more than 17 V for more than 1.2 sec.	• Battery • IC regulator • Open or short in power source circuit • ECU

Fail safe function: If trouble occurs in the power source circuit, the ECU cuts off current to the ABS solenoid relay and prohibits ABS control.

DIAGNOSTIC CHART

Step	Check	Result	Action
1	Check battery positive voltage.	NG	Check and repair the charging system.
	↓ OK		
2	Check voltage between terminals IG1 and GND of ABS (& TRAC) ECU connector.	OK	Check and replace ABS (& TRAC) ECU.
	↓ NG		
3	Check continuity between terminal GND of ABS (& TRAC) ECU connector and body ground.	NG	Repair or replace harness or connector.
	↓ OK		
4	Check ECU-IG fuse.	NG	Check for short in all the harness and components connected to ECU-IG fuse (See attached wiring diagram).
	↓ OK		
	Check for open in harness and connector between ABS (& TRAC) ECU and battery		

TY4029300090010X

Fig. 131 Code 41: IG Power Source Circuit (Part 1 of 4). Supra

WIRING DIAGRAM

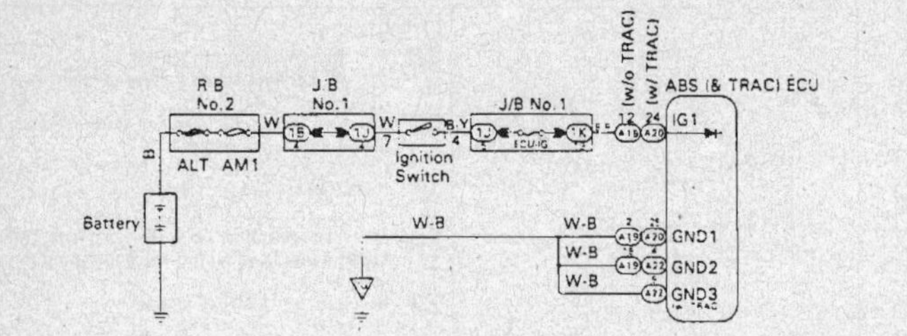
R/B No.2
J/B No.1
ALT
AM1
B
W
Ignition Switch
J/B No.1
ECU-IG
B-Y
(w/o TRAC)
(w/ TRAC)
ABS (& TRAC) ECU
IG1
Battery
W-B
GND1
GND2
GND3

TY4029300090020X

Fig. 131 Code 41: IG Power Source Circuit (Part 2 of 4). Supra

INSPECTION PROCEDURE

1 Check battery positive voltage.

OK Voltage: 10 – 14 V

OK

NG Check and repair the charging system.

2 Check voltage between terminals IG1 and GND of ABS (& TRAC) ECU connector.

w/o TRAC

ON IG ON

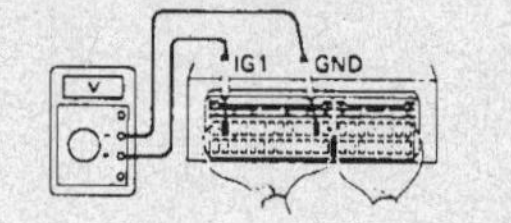
IG1
GND

w/ TRAC

ON IG ON

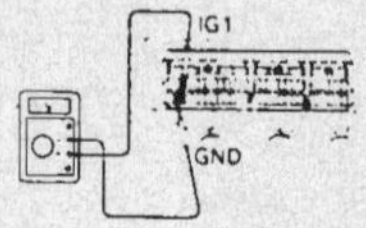
IG1
GND

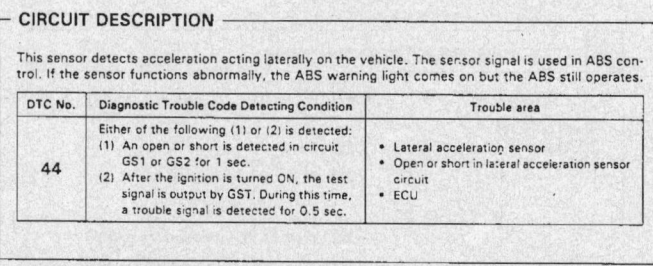

P Remove ABS (& TRAC) ECU with connectors still connected.

C 1. Turn ignition switch on.
2. Measure voltage between terminals IG1 and GND of ABS (& TRAC) ECU connector.

OK Voltage: 10 – 14 V

NG

OK Check and replace ABS (& TRAC) ECU.

TY4029300090030X

Fig. 131 Code 41: IG Power Source Circuit (Part 3 of 4). Supra

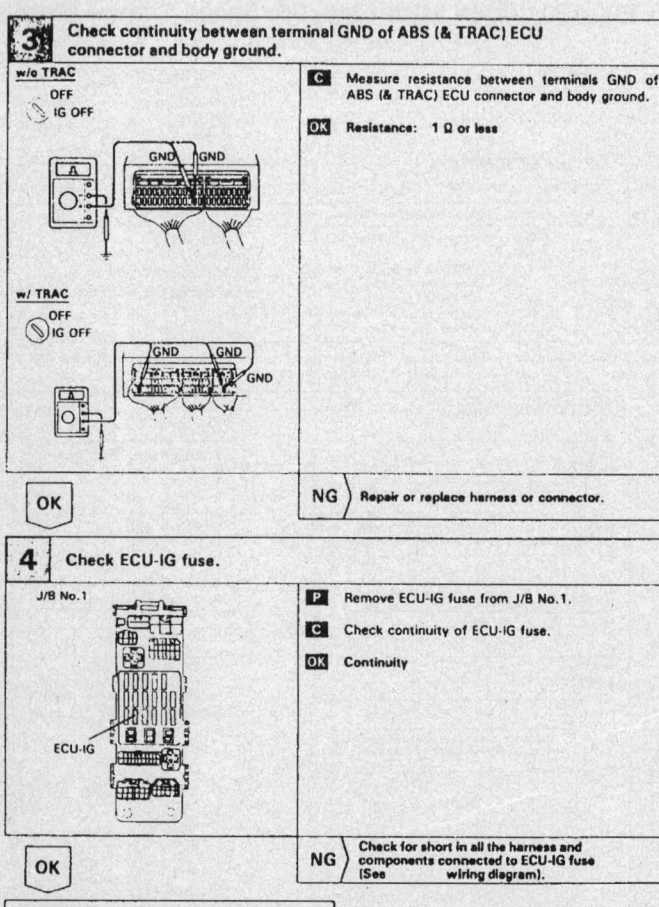

3 Check continuity between terminal GND of ABS (& TRAC) ECU connector and body ground.

w/o TRAC

OFF IG OFF

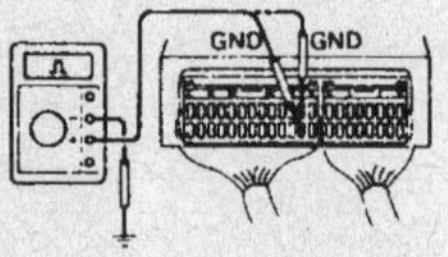
GND
GND

w/ TRAC

OFF IG OFF

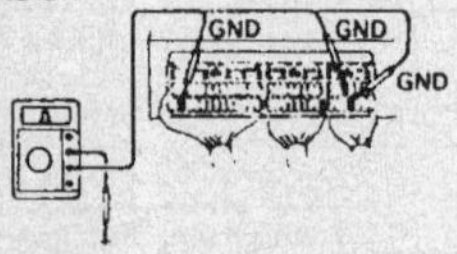
GND
GND
GND

C Measure resistance between terminals GND of ABS (& TRAC) ECU connector and body ground.

OK Resistance: 1 Ω or less

OK

NG Repair or replace harness or connector.

4 Check ECU-IG fuse.

J/B No.1

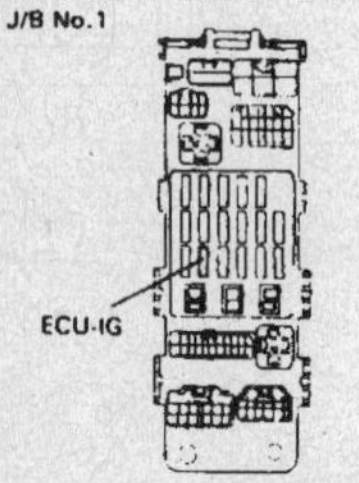
ECU-IG

P Remove ECU-IG fuse from J/B No.1.

C Check continuity of ECU-IG fuse.

OK Continuity

OK

NG Check for short in all the harness and components connected to ECU-IG fuse (See wiring diagram).

Check for open in harness and connector between ABS (& TRAC) ECU and battery

TY4029300090040X

Fig. 131 Code 41: IG Power Source Circuit (Part 4 of 4). Supra

CIRCUIT DESCRIPTION

This sensor detects acceleration acting laterally on the vehicle. The sensor signal is used in ABS control. If the sensor functions abnormally, the ABS warning light comes on but the ABS still operates.

DTC No.	Diagnostic Trouble Code Detecting Condition	Trouble area
44	Either of the following (1) or (2) is detected: (1) An open or short is detected in circuit GS1 or GS2 for 1 sec. (2) After the ignition is turned ON, the test signal is output by GST. During this time, a trouble signal is detected for 0.5 sec.	• Lateral acceleration sensor • Open or short in lateral acceleration sensor circuit • ECU

DIAGNOSTIC CHART

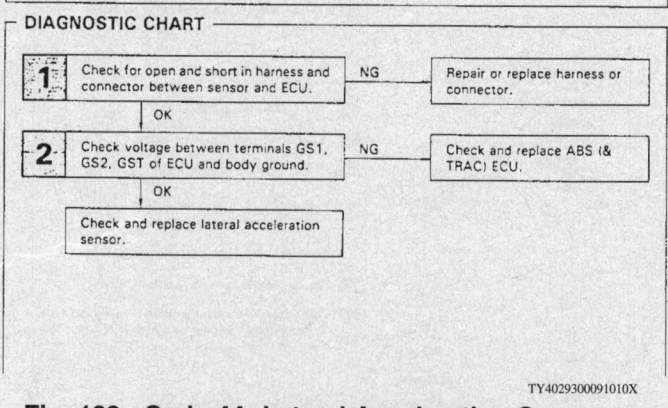

1. Check for open and short in harness and connector between sensor and ECU. — NG → Repair or replace harness or connector.
   - OK ↓
2. Check voltage between terminals GS1, GS2, GST of ECU and body ground. — NG → Check and replace ABS (& TRAC) ECU.
   - OK ↓

Check and replace lateral acceleration sensor.

TY4029300091010X

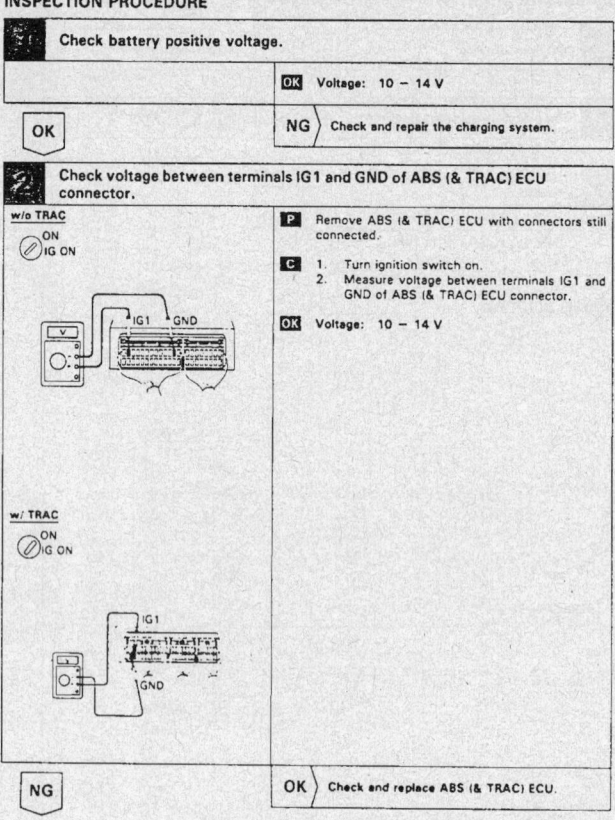

Fig. 132 Code 44: Lateral Acceleration Sensor Circuit (Part 1 of 3). Supra

WIRING DIAGRAM

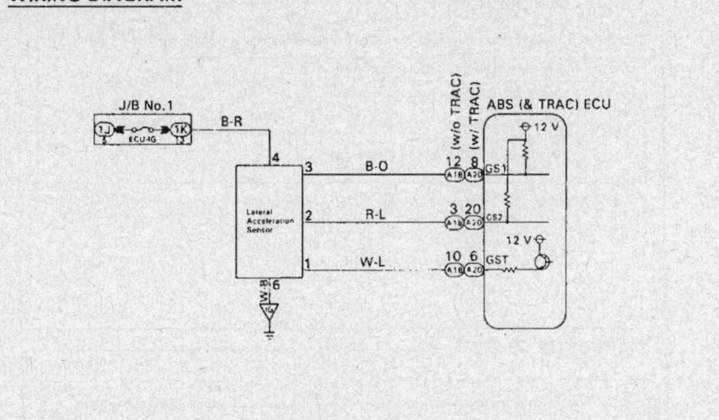
J/B No.1
B-R
ABS (& TRAC) ECU
(w/o TRAC)
(w/ TRAC)
12 V
B-O
R-L
W-L
GS1
GS2
GST
Lateral Acceleration Sensor

TY4029300091020X

Fig. 132 Code 44: Lateral Acceleration Sensor Circuit (Part 2 of 3). Supra

1	Check for open and short in harness and connector between sensor and ECU
OK	NG: Repair or replace harness or connector.

2	Check voltage between terminals GS1, GS2, GST of ECU and body ground.

w/o TRAC

ON
IG ON

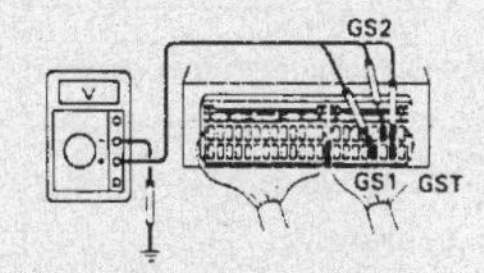
GS2
GS1
GST

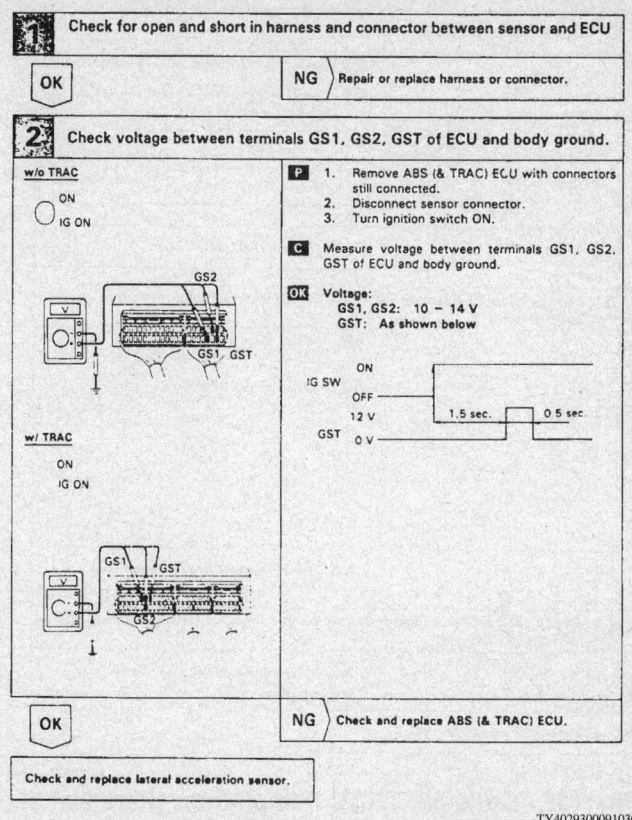

P
1. Remove ABS (& TRAC) ECU with connectors still connected.
2. Disconnect sensor connector.
3. Turn ignition switch ON.

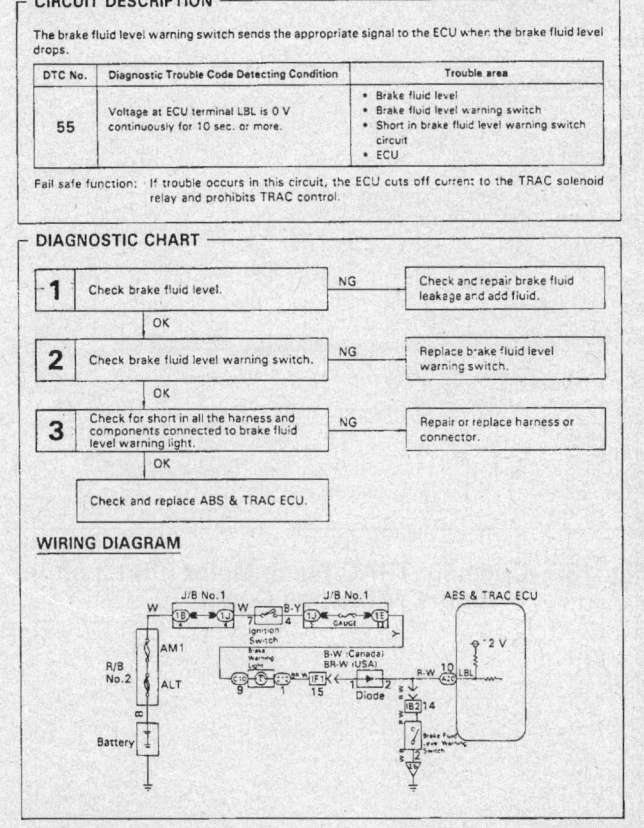

C Measure voltage between terminals GS1, GS2, GST of ECU and body ground.

OK **Voltage:**
GS1, GS2: 10 – 14 V
GST: As shown below

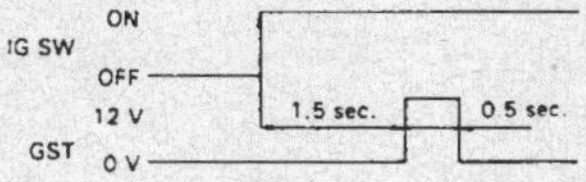
ON
IG SW
OFF
12 V
GST
0 V
1.5 sec.
0.5 sec.

w/ TRAC

ON
IG ON

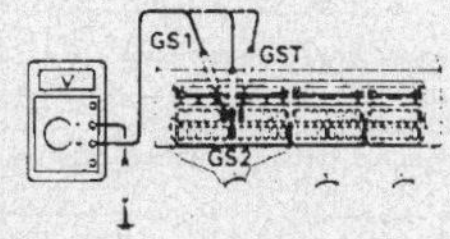
GS1
GST
GS2

OK	NG: Check and replace ABS (& TRAC) ECU.

Check and replace lateral acceleration sensor.

TY4029300091030X

Fig. 132 Code 44: Lateral Acceleration Sensor Circuit (Part 3 of 3). Supra

CIRCUIT DESCRIPTION

DTC No.	Diagnostic Trouble Code Detecting Condition	Trouble area
51	Pump motor is not operating normally during initial check.	• ABS pump motor

Fail safe function: If trouble occurs in the ABS pump motor, the ECU cuts off the current to the solenoid relay and prohibits ABS control.

TY4029300092000X

Fig. 133 Code 51: ABS Pump Motor Lock. Supra

CIRCUIT DESCRIPTION

The brake fluid level warning switch sends the appropriate signal to the ECU when the brake fluid level drops.

DTC No.	Diagnostic Trouble Code Detecting Condition	Trouble area
55	Voltage at ECU terminal LBL is 0 V continuously for 10 sec. or more.	• Brake fluid level • Brake fluid level warning switch • Short in brake fluid level warning switch circuit • ECU

Fail safe function: If trouble occurs in this circuit, the ECU cuts off current to the TRAC solenoid relay and prohibits TRAC control.

DIAGNOSTIC CHART

Step	Check	NG
1	Check brake fluid level.	Check and repair brake fluid leakage and add fluid.
2	Check brake fluid level warning switch.	Replace brake fluid level warning switch.
3	Check for short in all the harness and components connected to brake fluid level warning light.	Repair or replace harness or connector.

OK → Check and replace ABS & TRAC ECU.

WIRING DIAGRAM

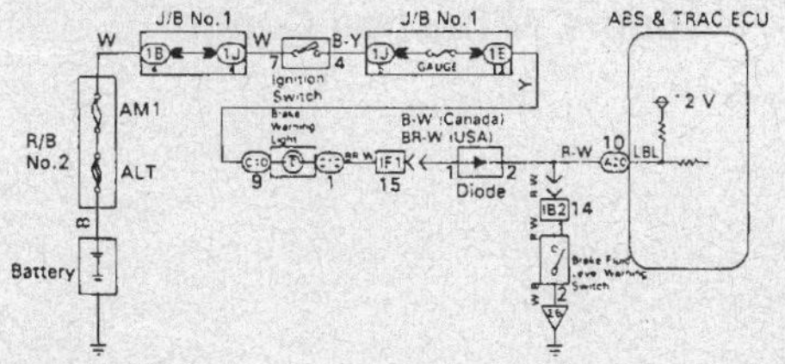
J/B No.1
J/B No.1
ABS & TRAC ECU
W
B-Y
Ignition Switch
GAUGE
AM1
R/B No.2
ALT
Brake Warning Light
B-W (Canada)
BR-W (USA)
R-W
LBL
12 V
Diode
Battery
Brake Fluid Level Warning Switch

TY4029300093010X

Fig. 134 Code 55: Brake Fluid Level Warning Switch (Part 1 of 2). Supra

INSPECTION PROCEDURE

1	Check brake fluid level.
C	Check the amount of fluid in the brake reservoir.
OK	NG: Check and repair brake fluid leakage and add fluid.

2	Check brake fluid level warning switch.
OK	NG: Replace brake fluid level warning switch.

3	Check for short in all the harness and components connected to brake fluid level warning light
OK	NG: Repair or replace harness or connector.

Check and replace ABS & TRAC ECU.

TY4029300093020X

Fig. 134 Code 55: Brake Fluid Level Warning Switch (Part 2 of 2). Supra

1	Check TRAC pump motor.

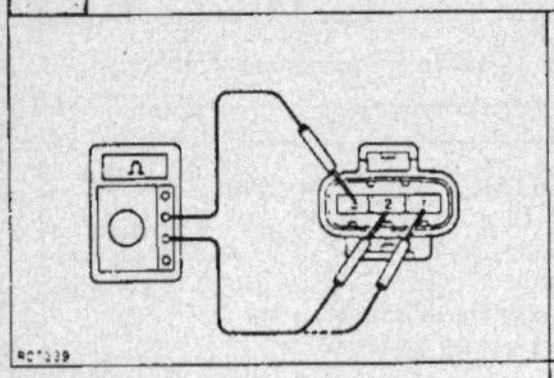

P Disconnect TRAC pump motor connector.

C Check continuity between each terminal of TRAC pump motor shown below.

OK

Terminals 1 and 3	Continuity (Reference value 100 Ω or less)
Terminals 2 and 3	Continuity (Reference value 4 ~ 6 Ω)

OK

NG 〉 Replace TRAC pump motor.

2	Check continuity between terminal GND of TRAC pump motor connector and body ground.

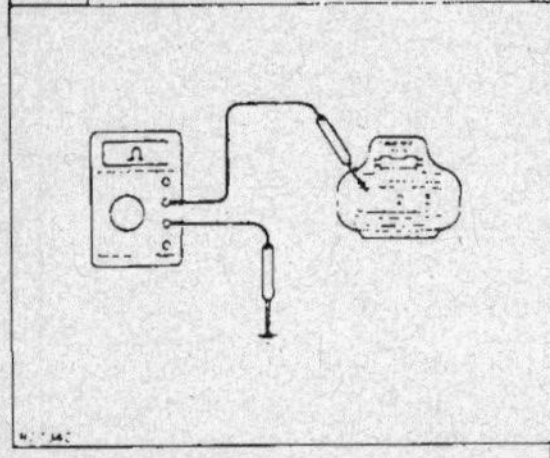

C Measure resistance between terminal GND of TRAC pump motor connector and body ground.

OK Resistance: 1 Ω or less

OK

NG 〉 Repair or replace harness or connector.

3	Check for open and short in harness and connector between TRAC pump motor and ECU

OK

NG 〉 Repair or replace harness or connector.

Check and replace ABS & TRAC ECU.

TY4029300094010X

Fig. 135 Code 58: TRAC Pump Motor (Part 1 of 3). Supra w/Traction Control

WIRING DIAGRAM

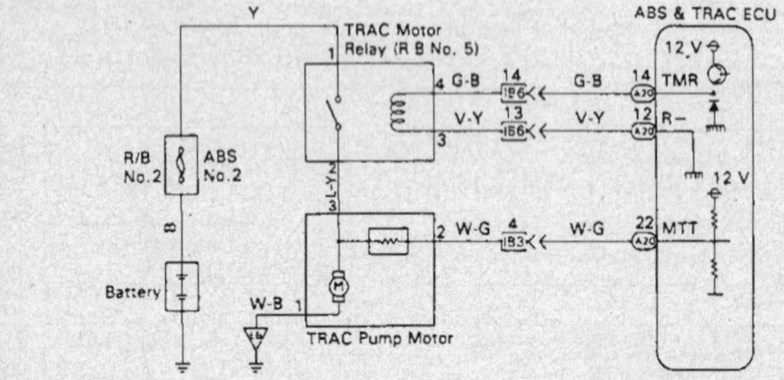
Y
TRAC Motor Relay (R B No. 5)
ABS & TRAC ECU
12 V
G-B
14
IB6
G-B
14
A20
TMR
V-Y
13
IB6
V-Y
12
A20
R-
R/B No. 2
ABS No. 2
12 V
L-Y
2 W-G
4
IB3
W-G
22
A20
MTT
Battery
W-B
TRAC Pump Motor

TY4029300094030X

Fig. 135 Code 58: TRAC Pump Motor (Part 3 of 3). Supra w/Traction Control

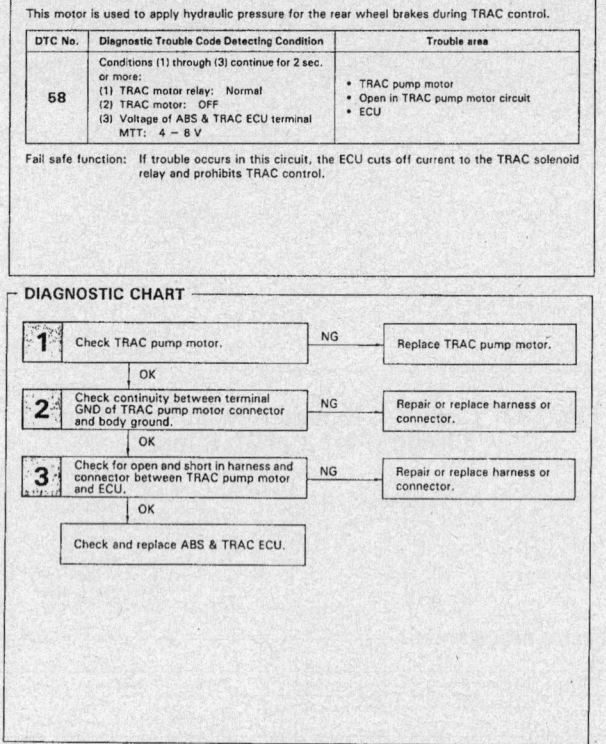

CIRCUIT DESCRIPTION

This motor is used to apply hydraulic pressure for the rear wheel brakes during TRAC control.

DTC No.	Diagnostic Trouble Code Detecting Condition	Trouble area
58	Conditions (1) through (3) continue for 2 sec. or more: (1) TRAC motor relay: Normal (2) TRAC motor: OFF (3) Voltage of ABS & TRAC ECU terminal MTT: 4 – 8 V	• TRAC pump motor • Open in TRAC pump motor circuit • ECU

Fail safe function: If trouble occurs in this circuit, the ECU cuts off current to the TRAC solenoid relay and prohibits TRAC control.

DIAGNOSTIC CHART

Step	Check	Result	Action
1	Check TRAC pump motor.	NG	Replace TRAC pump motor.
	OK		
2	Check continuity between terminal GND of TRAC pump motor connector and body ground.	NG	Repair or replace harness or connector.
	OK		
3	Check for open and short in harness and connector between TRAC pump motor and ECU.	NG	Repair or replace harness or connector.
	OK		
	Check and replace ABS & TRAC ECU.		

TY4029300094020X

Fig. 135 Code 58: TRAC Pump Motor (Part 2 of 3). Supra w/Traction Control

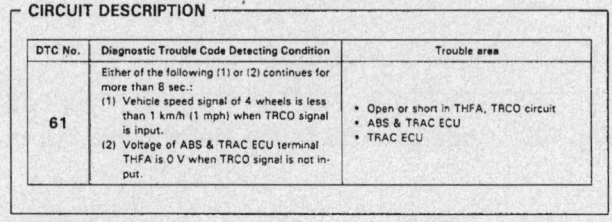

CIRCUIT DESCRIPTION

DTC No.	Diagnostic Trouble Code Detecting Condition	Trouble area
61	Either of the following (1) or (2) continues for more than 8 sec.: (1) Vehicle speed signal of 4 wheels is less than 1 km/h (1 mph) when TRCO signal is input. (2) Voltage of ABS & TRAC ECU terminal THFA is 0 V when TRCO signal is not input.	• Open or short in THFA, TRCO circuit • ABS & TRAC ECU • TRAC ECU

DIAGNOSTIC CHART

Step	Check	Result	Action
1	Check voltage of terminals THFA, TRCO of ABS & TRAC ECU.	OK	Check and replace ABS & TRAC ECU.
	NG		
2	Check voltage of terminals THFA, TRCO of ABS & TRAC ECU with ABS & TRAC ECU connector is disconnected.	OK	Check and replace ABS & TRAC ECU.
	NG		
3	Check for open and short in harness and connector between ABS & TRAC ECU and TRAC ECU.	NG	Repair or replace harness or connector.
	OK		
	Check and replace TRAC ECU.		

WIRING DIAGRAM

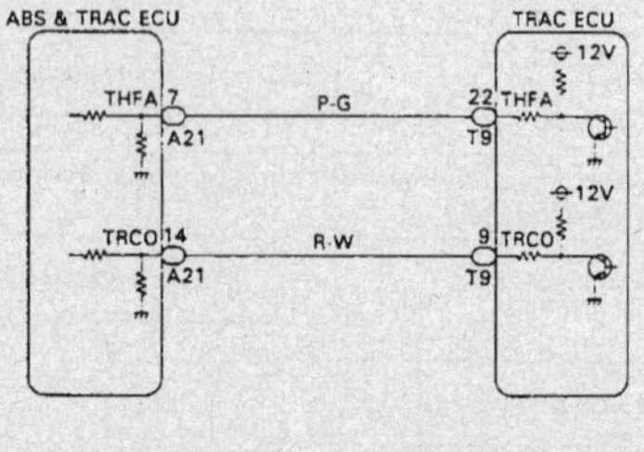
ABS & TRAC ECU
TRAC ECU
THFA 7
A21
P-G
22 THFA
T9
12V
TRCO 14
A21
R-W
9 TRCO
T9
12V

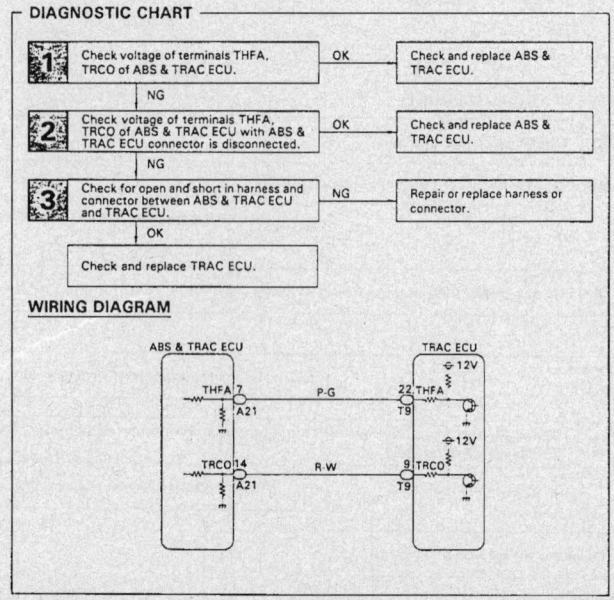

TY4029300095010X

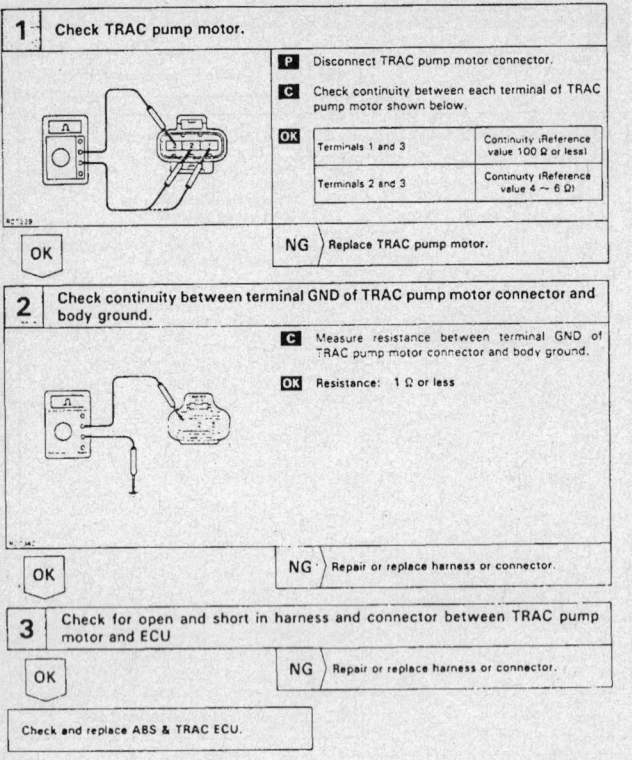

Fig. 136 Code 61: TRAC ECU Communication Circuit Malfunction (Part 1 of 2). Supra w/Traction Control

1 Check voltage between terminals THFA, TRCO of ABS & TRAC ECU and body ground.

ON
IG ON

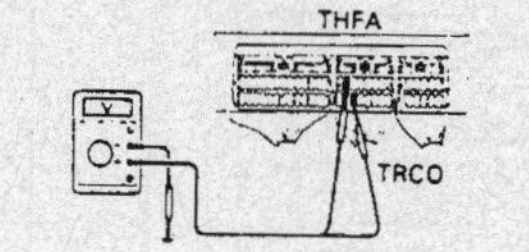
THFA
V
TRCO

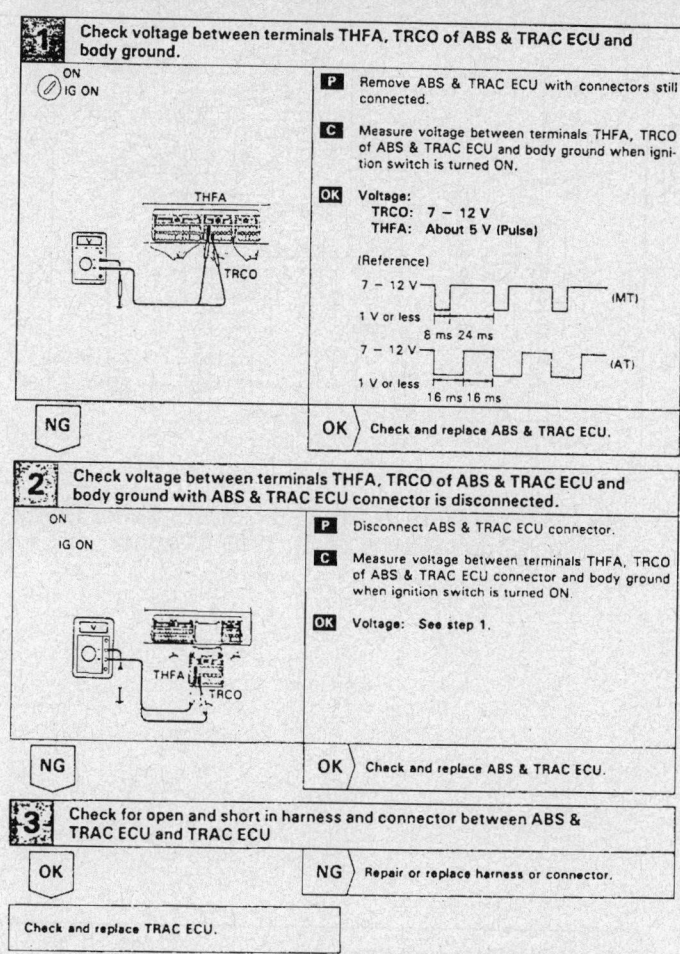

P Remove ABS & TRAC ECU with connectors still connected.

C Measure voltage between terminals THFA, TRCO of ABS & TRAC ECU and body ground when ignition switch is turned ON.

OK Voltage:
TRCO: 7 – 12 V
THFA: About 5 V (Pulse)

(Reference)

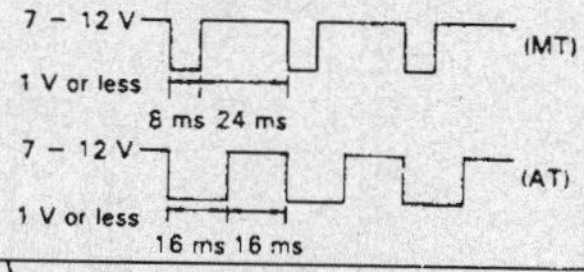
7 – 12 V
1 V or less
8 ms 24 ms
(MT)
7 – 12 V
1 V or less
16 ms 16 ms
(AT)

NG

OK → Check and replace ABS & TRAC ECU.

2 Check voltage between terminals THFA, TRCO of ABS & TRAC ECU and body ground with ABS & TRAC ECU connector is disconnected.

ON
IG ON

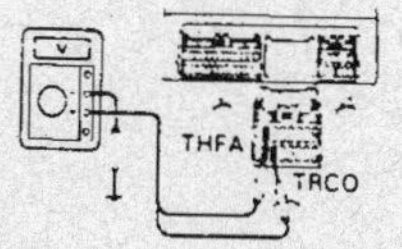
V
THFA
TRCO

P Disconnect ABS & TRAC ECU connector.

C Measure voltage between terminals THFA, TRCO of ABS & TRAC ECU connector and body ground when ignition switch is turned ON.

OK Voltage: See step 1.

NG

OK → Check and replace ABS & TRAC ECU.

3 Check for open and short in harness and connector between ABS & TRAC ECU and TRAC ECU

OK

NG → Repair or replace harness or connector.

Check and replace TRAC ECU.

TY4029300095020X

Fig. 136 Code 61: TRAC ECU Communication Circuit Malfunction (Part 2 of 2). Supra w/Traction Control

CIRCUIT DESCRIPTION

DTC No.	Diagnostic Trouble Code Detecting Condition	Trouble area
62	At vehicle speed of 10 km/h (6 mph) or more, pulses are not input for 5 sec.	• ECU

HINT: When DTC Nos.31 – 36 are recorded in memory, DTC No.62 is not recorded.

DIAGNOSTIC CHART

1 Are there any other codes (besides DTC No.62) being output? — YES → Go to relevant DTC chart.

NO → Replace ABS & TRAC ECU.

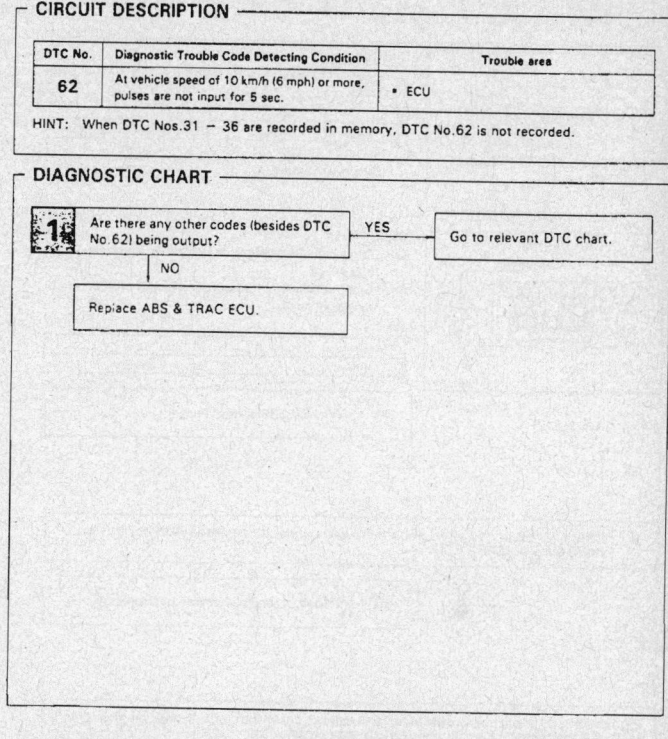

TY4029300096000X

Fig. 137 Code 62: TRAC Vehicle Speed Malfunction. Supra w/Traction Control

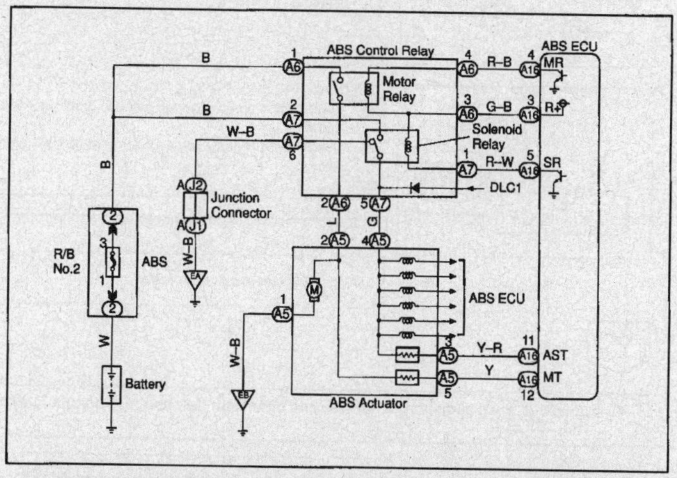
B
1
A6
ABS Control Relay
4
A6
R–B
4
A16
MR
ABS ECU
Motor Relay
B
2
A7
3
A6
G–B
3
A16
R+
W–B
A7
6
Solenoid Relay
1
A7
R–W
5
A16
SR
DLC1
B
J2
Junction Connector
J1
2 A6
5 A7
L
G
W–B
2 A5
4 A5
EA
R/B No.2
3
1
ABS
2
2
M
1
A5
ABS ECU
W
W–B
Y–R
11
A5
A16
AST
Y
A5
A16
MT
3
5
12
Battery
ABS Actuator
EB

TY4029600214010X

Fig. 138 Code 11 & 12: ABS Control Solenoid Relay Circuit (Part 1 of 3). 1996 4Runner

1 Check voltage between terminals A7 – 2 and A7 – 6 of ABS control (solenoid) relay connector.

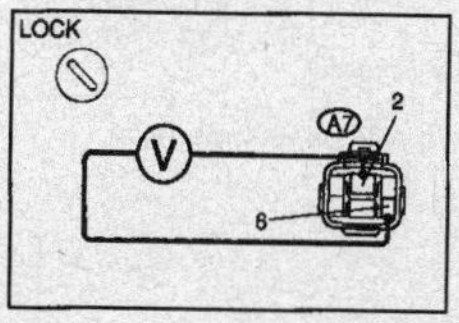
LOCK
V
A7
2
6

PREPARATION:
Disconnect the ABS control relay connector.

CHECK:
Measure the voltage between terminals A7 – 2 and A7 – 6 of ABS control relay harness side connector.

OK:
Voltage: 10 – 14 V

NG → Check and repair harness or connector.

OK

2 Check continuity between terminals A7 – 5 and A5 – 4, A5 – 4 and A5 – 3, A5 – 3 and A16 – 11.

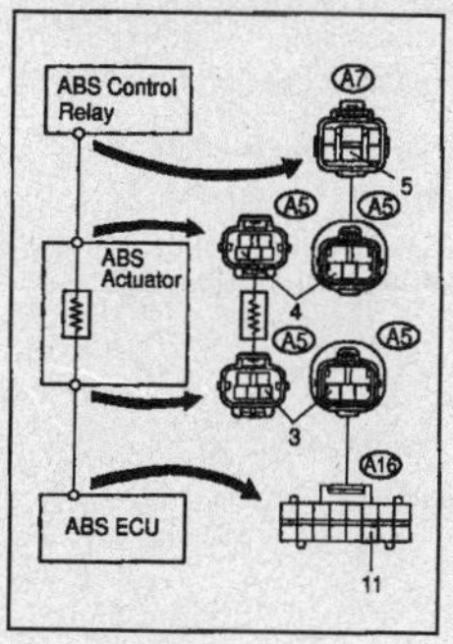
ABS Control Relay
A7
5
A5
A5
ABS Actuator
4
A5
A5
3
A16
ABS ECU
11

PREPARATION:
Disconnect the 2 connectors from ABS actuator.

CHECK:
Check continuity between terminals A7 – 5 and A5 – 4, A5 – 4 and A5 – 3, A5 – 2 and A16 – 11.

OK:
Continuity

HINT: There is a resistance of 26 ~ 40 Ω between terminals A5 – 4 and A5 – 3.

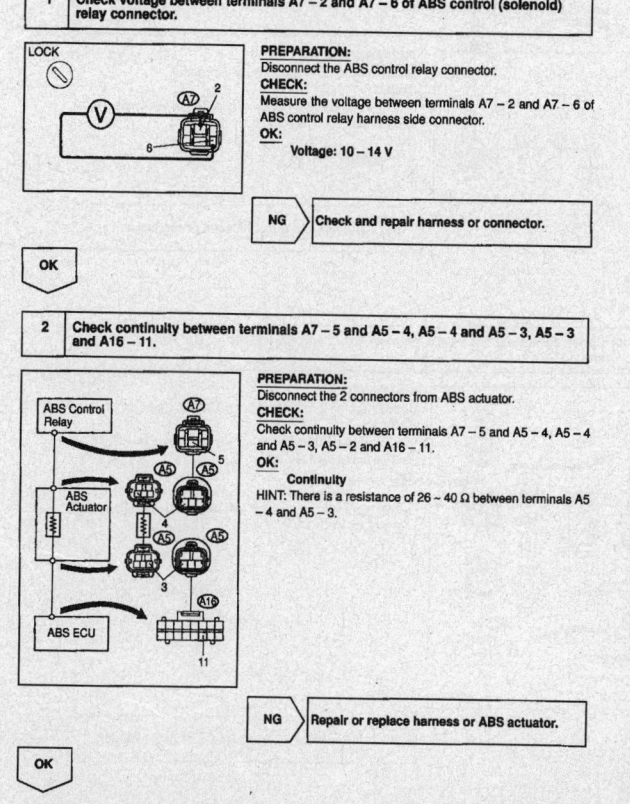

NG → Repair or replace harness or ABS actuator.

OK

TY4029600214020X

Fig. 138 Code 11 & 12: ABS Control Solenoid Relay Circuit (Part 2 of 3). 1996 4Runner

3 Check ABS control (solenoid) relay.

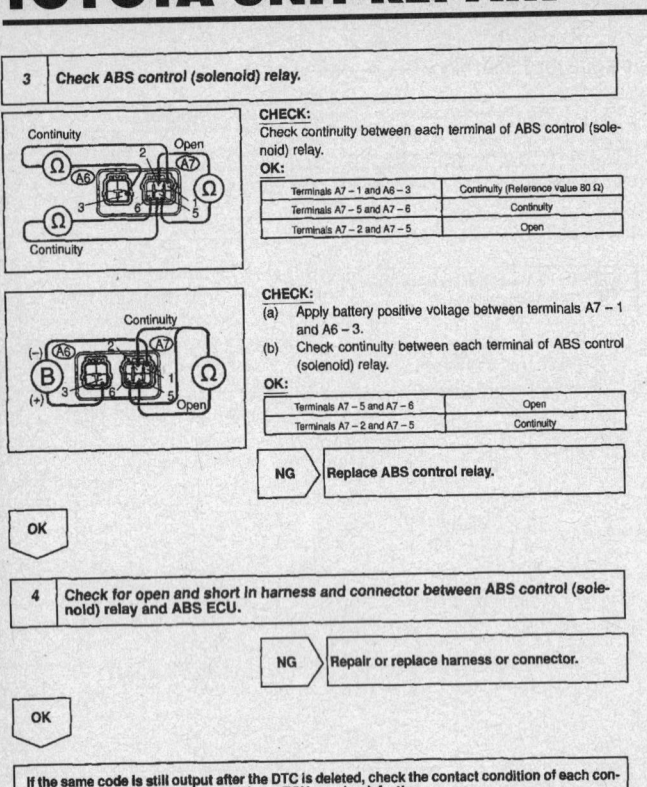

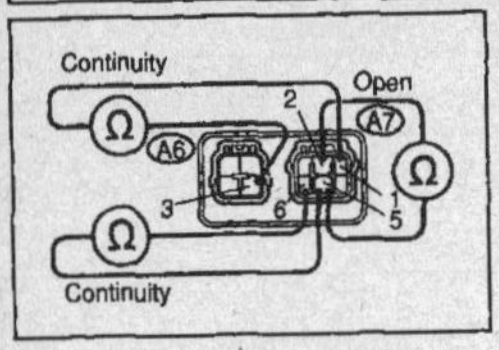
Continuity
Open
2
A7
A6
3
6
1
5
Continuity

CHECK:
Check continuity between each terminal of ABS control (solenoid) relay.
OK:

Terminals A7 – 1 and A6 – 3	Continuity (Reference value 80 Ω)
Terminals A7 – 5 and A7 – 6	Continuity
Terminals A7 – 2 and A7 – 5	Open

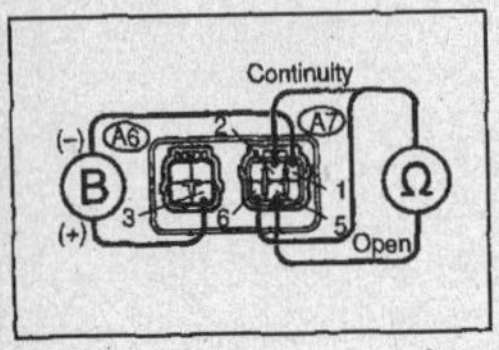
Continuity
(–)
A6
A7
B
(+)
2
3
6
1
5
Open

CHECK:
(a) Apply battery positive voltage between terminals A7 – 1 and A6 – 3.
(b) Check continuity between each terminal of ABS control (solenoid) relay.
OK:

Terminals A7 – 5 and A7 – 6	Open
Terminals A7 – 2 and A7 – 5	Continuity

NG → Replace ABS control relay.

OK

4 Check for open and short in harness and connector between ABS control (solenoid) relay and ABS ECU.

NG → Repair or replace harness or connector.

OK

If the same code is still output after the DTC is deleted, check the contact condition of each connection. If the connector are normal, the ECU may be defective.

TY4029600214030

Fig. 138 Code 11 & 12: ABS Control Solenoid Relay Circuit (Part 3 of 3). 1996 4Runner

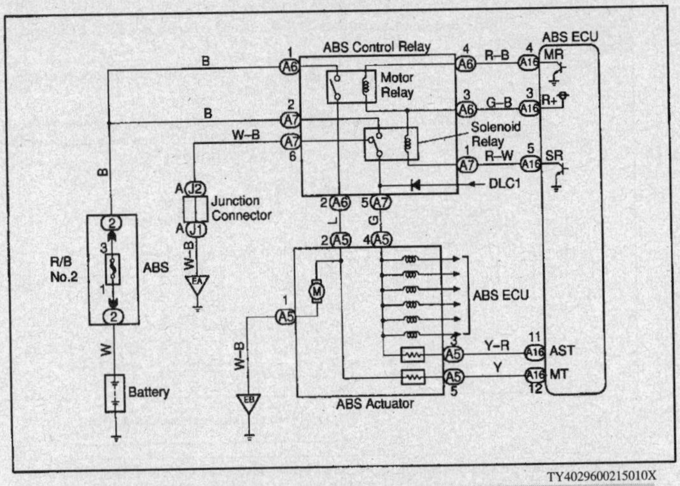
ABS Control Relay
ABS ECU
Motor Relay
Solenoid Relay
MR
R+
SR
R–B
G–B
R–W
B
W–B
DLC1
Junction Connector
R/B No.2
ABS
Battery
ABS Actuator
Y–R
Y
AST
MT

TY4029600215010X

Fig. 139 Code 13 & 14: ABS Control Motor Relay Circuit (Part 1 of 3). 1996 4Runner

1 Check voltage between terminal A6 – 1 of ABS control (motor) relay and body ground.

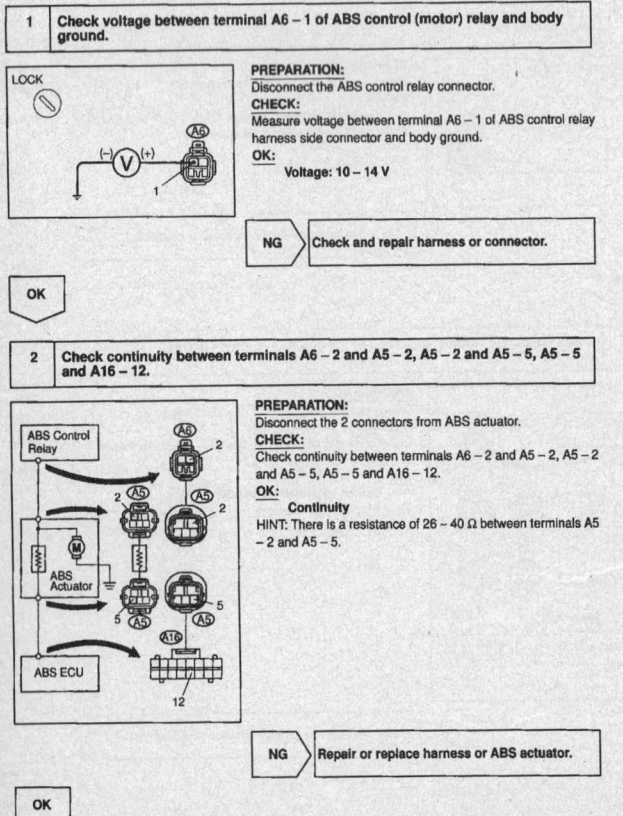

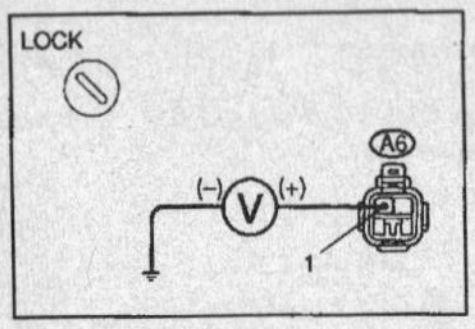
LOCK
A6
(–)
V
(+)
1

PREPARATION:
Disconnect the ABS control relay connector.
CHECK:
Measure voltage between terminal A6 – 1 of ABS control relay harness side connector and body ground.
OK:
Voltage: 10 – 14 V

NG → Check and repair harness or connector.

OK

2 Check continuity between terminals A6 – 2 and A5 – 2, A5 – 2 and A5 – 5, A5 – 5 and A16 – 12.

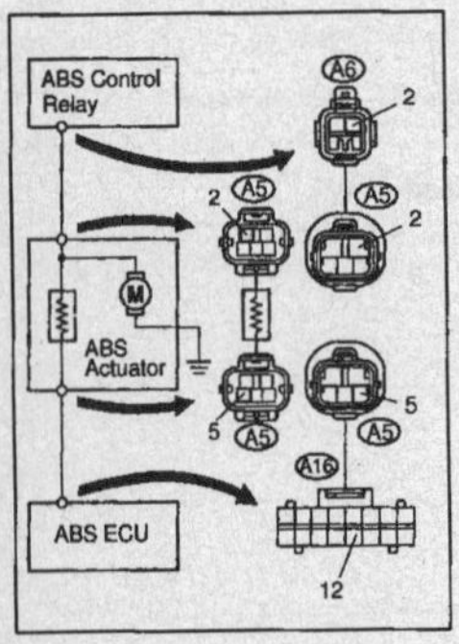
ABS Control Relay
A6
A5
ABS Actuator
A16
ABS ECU
12

PREPARATION:
Disconnect the 2 connectors from ABS actuator.
CHECK:
Check continuity between terminals A6 – 2 and A5 – 2, A5 – 2 and A5 – 5, A5 – 5 and A16 – 12.
OK:
Continuity
HINT: There is a resistance of 26 – 40 Ω between terminals A5 – 2 and A5 – 5.

NG → Repair or replace harness or ABS actuator.

OK

TY4029600215020X

Fig. 139 Code 13 & 14: ABS Control Motor Relay Circuit (Part 2 of 3). 1996 4Runner

3 Check ABS control (motor) relay.

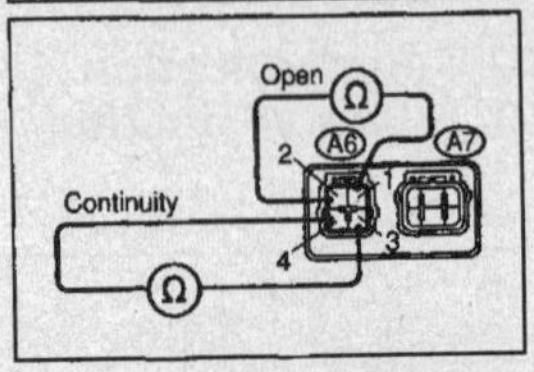
Open
Continuity
A6
A7
2
3
4

CHECK:
Check continuity between each terminal of ABS control (motor) relay.
OK:

Terminals A6 – 3 and A6 – 4	Continuity (Reference value 62 Ω)
Terminals A6 – 1 and A6 – 2	Open

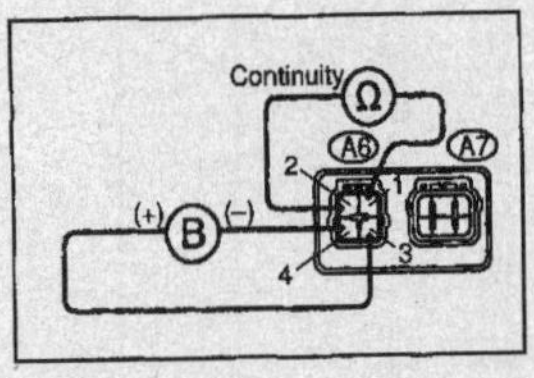
Continuity
A6
A7
(+)
B
(–)
2
1
3
4

CHECK:
(a) Apply battery positive voltage between terminals A6 – 3 and A6 – 4.
(b) Check continuity between each terminal of ABS control relay.
OK:

Terminals A6 – 1 and A6 – 2	Continuity

NG → Replace ABS control relay.

OK

4 Check for open and short in harness and connector between ABS control relay and ABS ECU.

NG → Repair or replace harness or connector.

OK

If the same code is still output after the DTC is deleted, check the contact condition of each connection. If the connections are normal, the ECU may be defective.

TY4029600215030X

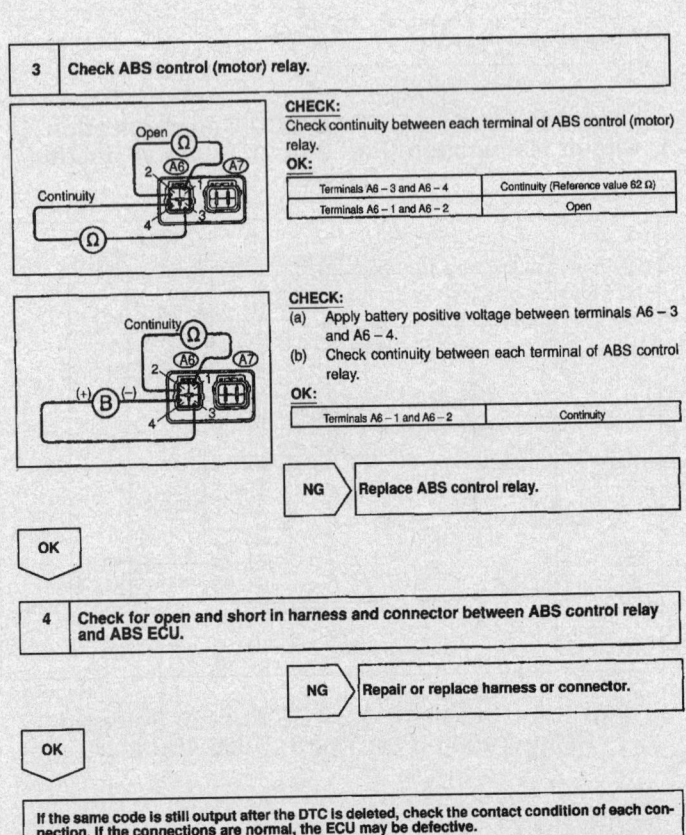

Fig. 139 Code 13 & 14: ABS Control Motor Relay Circuit (Part 3 of 3). 1996 4Runner

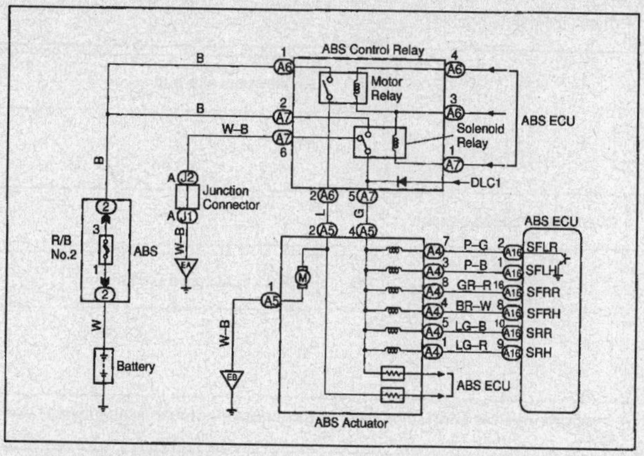
ABS Control Relay
Motor Relay
Solenoid Relay
ABS ECU
DLC1
Junction Connector
R/B No.2
ABS
Battery
ABS Actuator
SFLR
SFLH
SFRR
SFRH
SRR
SRH
P-G
P-B
GR-R
BR-W
LG-B
LG-R
W-B
B
W
L
G

INSPECTION PROCEDURE

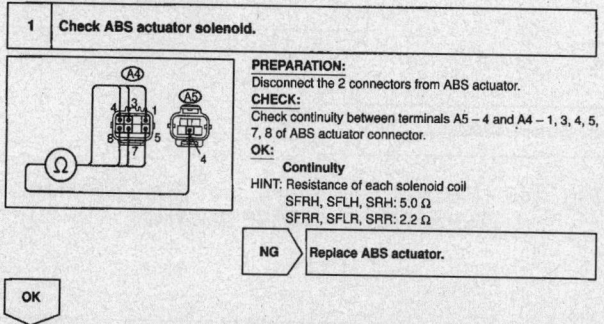

1	Check ABS actuator solenoid.

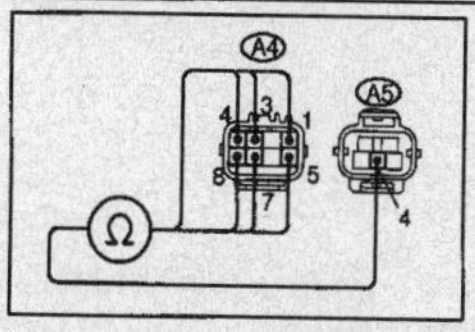
A4
A5

PREPARATION:
Disconnect the 2 connectors from ABS actuator.
CHECK:
Check continuity between terminals A5 – 4 and A4 – 1, 3, 4, 5, 7, 8 of ABS actuator connector.
OK:
Continuity
HINT: Resistance of each solenoid coil
SFRH, SFLH, SRH: 5.0 Ω
SFRR, SFLR, SRR: 2.2 Ω

NG → Replace ABS actuator.

OK

TY4029600216010X

Fig. 140 Code 21, 22 & 23: ABS Actuator Solenoid Circuit (Part 1 of 2). 1996 4Runner

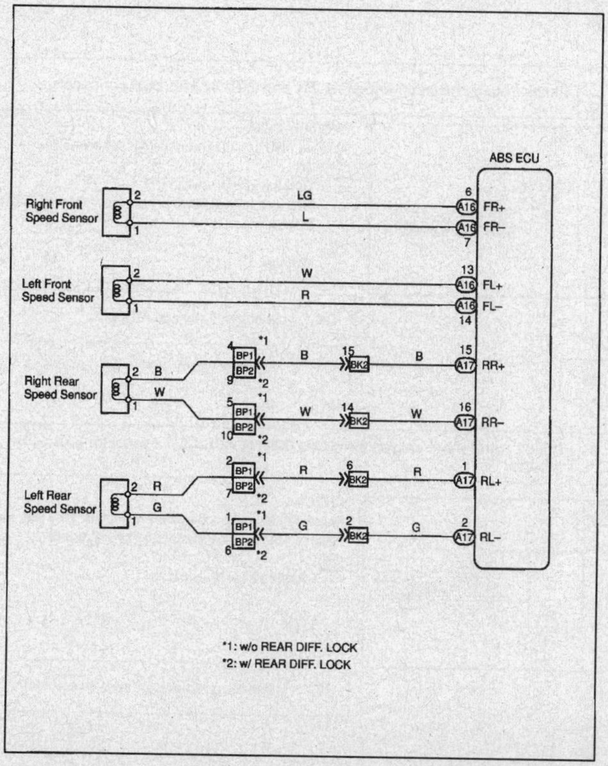
ABS ECU
Right Front Speed Sensor
Left Front Speed Sensor
Right Rear Speed Sensor
Left Rear Speed Sensor
FR+
FR–
FL+
FL–
RR+
RR–
RL+
RL–
BP1
BP2
BK2
*1: w/o REAR DIFF. LOCK
*2: w/ REAR DIFF. LOCK

TY4029600217010X

Fig. 141 Code 31, 32, 33, 34: Speed Sensor Circuit (Part 1 of 3). 1996 4Runner

2	Check for open and short in harness and connector between ABS ECU and actuator.

NG → Repair or replace harness or connector.

OK

If the same code is still output after the DTC is deleted, check the contact condition of each connection. If the connector are normal, the ECU may be defective.

TY4029600216020X

Fig. 140 Code 21, 22 & 23: ABS Actuator Solenoid Circuit (Part 2 of 2). 1996 4Runner

1	Check speed sensor.

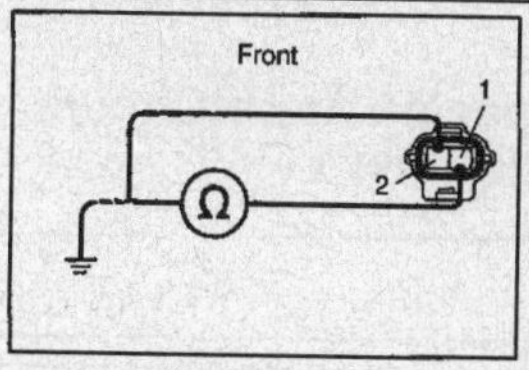
Front

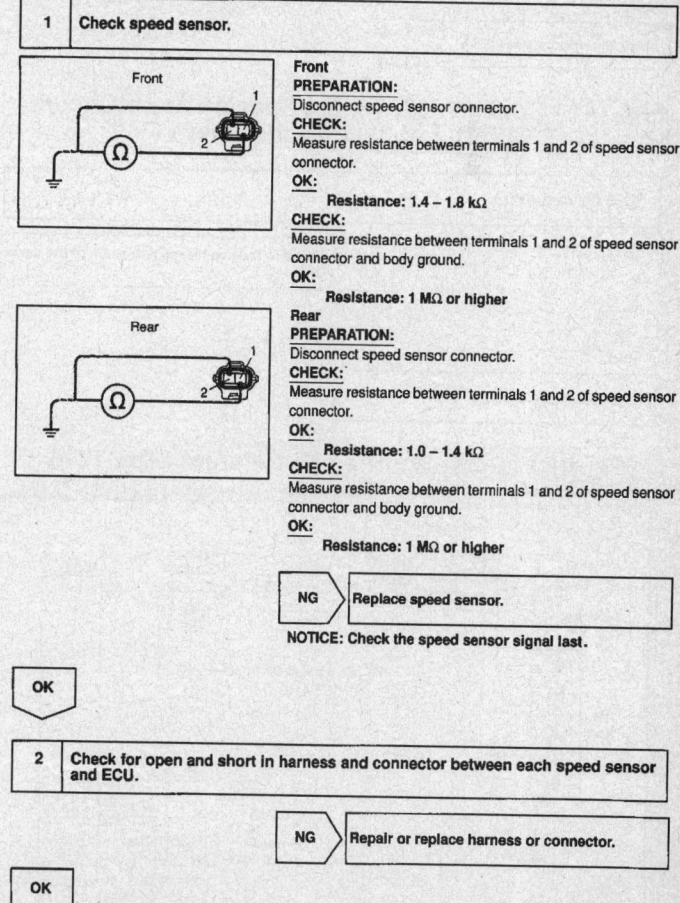

Front
PREPARATION:
Disconnect speed sensor connector.
CHECK:
Measure resistance between terminals 1 and 2 of speed sensor connector.
OK:
Resistance: 1.4 – 1.8 kΩ
CHECK:
Measure resistance between terminals 1 and 2 of speed sensor connector and body ground.
OK:
Resistance: 1 MΩ or higher

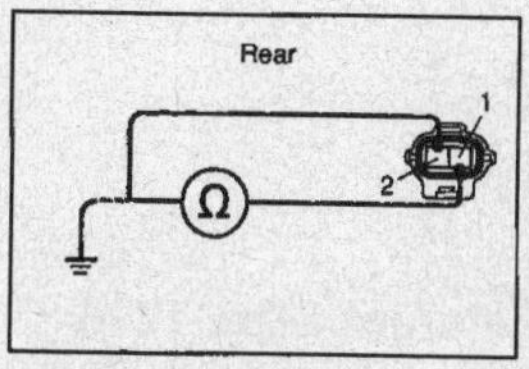
Rear

Rear
PREPARATION:
Disconnect speed sensor connector.
CHECK:
Measure resistance between terminals 1 and 2 of speed sensor connector.
OK:
Resistance: 1.0 – 1.4 kΩ
CHECK:
Measure resistance between terminals 1 and 2 of speed sensor connector and body ground.
OK:
Resistance: 1 MΩ or higher

NG → Replace speed sensor.

NOTICE: Check the speed sensor signal last.

OK

2	Check for open and short in harness and connector between each speed sensor and ECU.

NG → Repair or replace harness or connector.

OK

TY4029600217020X

Fig. 141 Code 31, 32, 33, 34: Speed Sensor Circuit (Part 2 of 3). 1996 4Runner

3 Check sensor rotor and sensor installation.

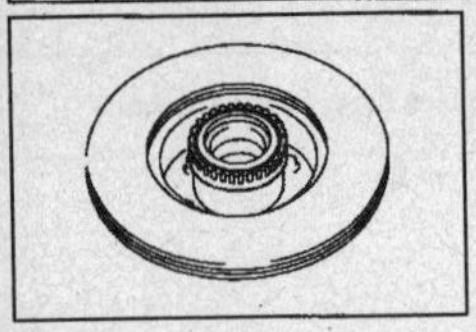

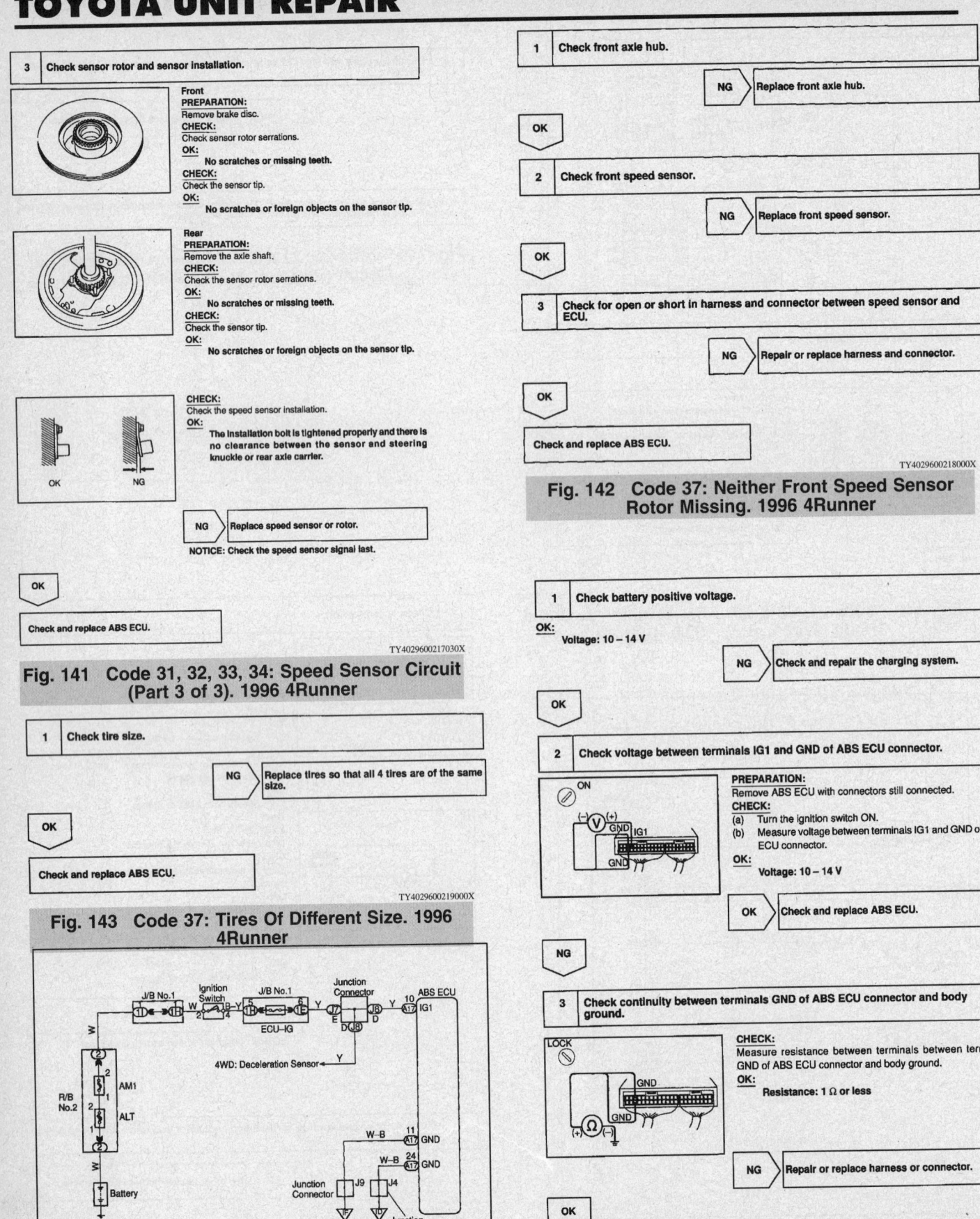

Front
PREPARATION:
Remove brake disc.
CHECK:
Check sensor rotor serrations.
OK:
No scratches or missing teeth.
CHECK:
Check the sensor tip.
OK:
No scratches or foreign objects on the sensor tip.

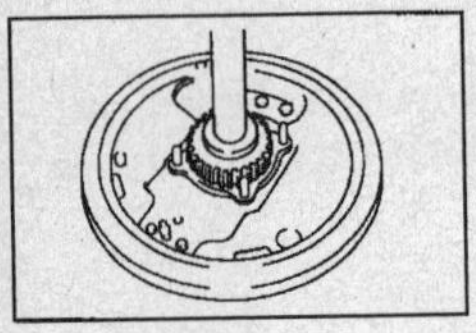

Rear
PREPARATION:
Remove the axle shaft.
CHECK:
Check the sensor rotor serrations.
OK:
No scratches or missing teeth.
CHECK:
Check the sensor tip.
OK:
No scratches or foreign objects on the sensor tip.

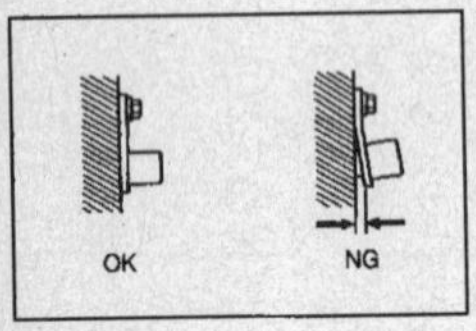
OK
NG

CHECK:
Check the speed sensor installation.
OK:
The installation bolt is tightened properly and there is no clearance between the sensor and steering knuckle or rear axle carrier.

NG → Replace speed sensor or rotor.

NOTICE: Check the speed sensor signal last.

OK ↓

Check and replace ABS ECU.

TY4029600217030X

Fig. 141 Code 31, 32, 33, 34: Speed Sensor Circuit (Part 3 of 3). 1996 4Runner

1 Check tire size.

NG → Replace tires so that all 4 tires are of the same size.

OK ↓

Check and replace ABS ECU.

TY4029600219000X

Fig. 143 Code 37: Tires Of Different Size. 1996 4Runner

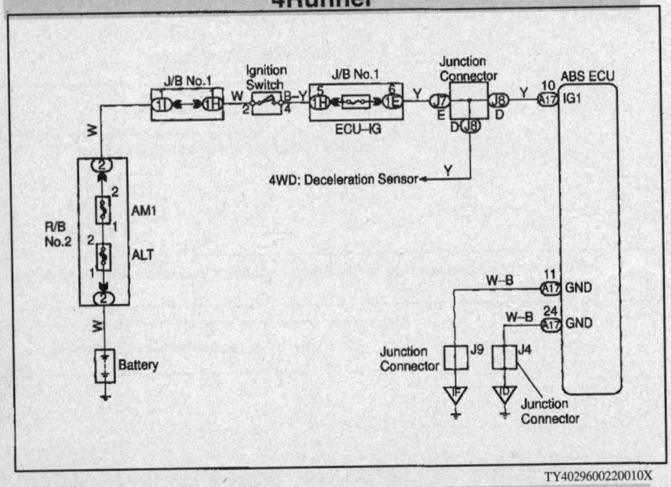
J/B No.1
Ignition Switch
J/B No.1
Junction Connector
ABS ECU
1I
1H
W
B–Y
2
4
5
1H
6
1E
Y
J7
E
D
J8
D
J8
Y
10
A17
IG1
ECU–IG
W
4WD: Deceleration Sensor
Y
2
2
AM1
1
R/B No.2
2
ALT
1
2
W
Battery
W–B
11
A17
GND
W–B
24
A17
GND
Junction Connector
J9
J4
IF
ID
Junction Connector

TY4029600220010X

Fig. 144 Code 41: IG Power Source Circuit (Part 1 of 3). 1996 4Runner

1 Check front axle hub.

NG → Replace front axle hub.

OK ↓

2 Check front speed sensor.

NG → Replace front speed sensor.

OK ↓

3 Check for open or short in harness and connector between speed sensor and ECU.

NG → Repair or replace harness and connector.

OK ↓

Check and replace ABS ECU.

TY4029600218000X

Fig. 142 Code 37: Neither Front Speed Sensor Rotor Missing. 1996 4Runner

1 Check battery positive voltage.

OK:
Voltage: 10 – 14 V

NG → Check and repair the charging system.

OK ↓

2 Check voltage between terminals IG1 and GND of ABS ECU connector.

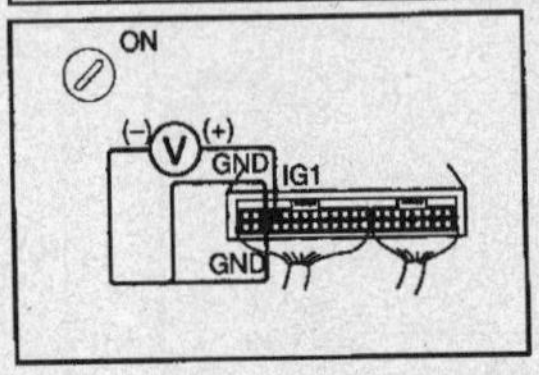
ON
(–)
V
(+)
GND
IG1
GND

PREPARATION:
Remove ABS ECU with connectors still connected.
CHECK:
(a) Turn the ignition switch ON.
(b) Measure voltage between terminals IG1 and GND of ABS ECU connector.
OK:
Voltage: 10 – 14 V

OK → Check and replace ABS ECU.

NG ↓

3 Check continuity between terminals GND of ABS ECU connector and body ground.

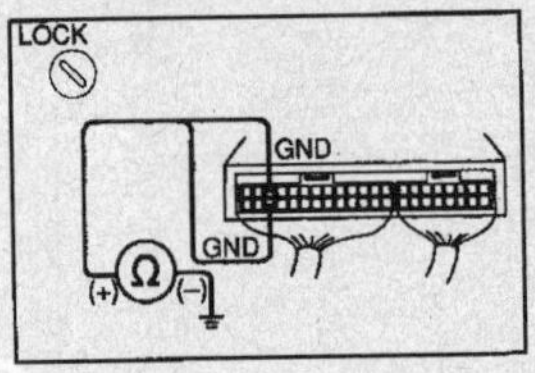
LOCK
GND
GND
(+)
Ω
(–)

CHECK:
Measure resistance between terminals between terminals GND of ABS ECU connector and body ground.
OK:
Resistance: 1 Ω or less

NG → Repair or replace harness or connector.

OK ↓

TY4029600220020X

Fig. 144 Code 41: IG Power Source Circuit (Part 2 of 3). 1996 4Runner

4	Check ECU–IG fuse.

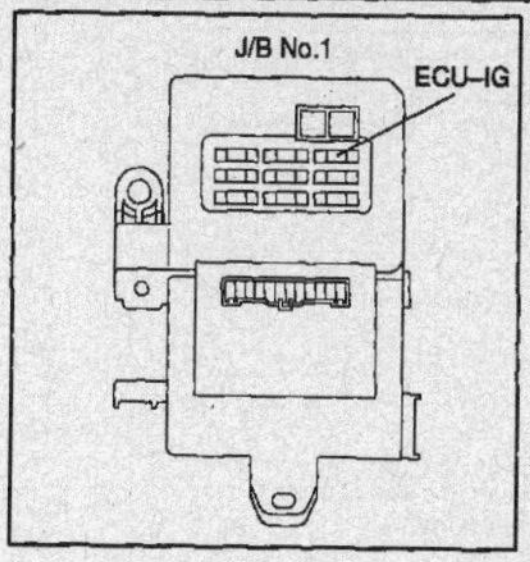
J/B No.1
ECU–IG

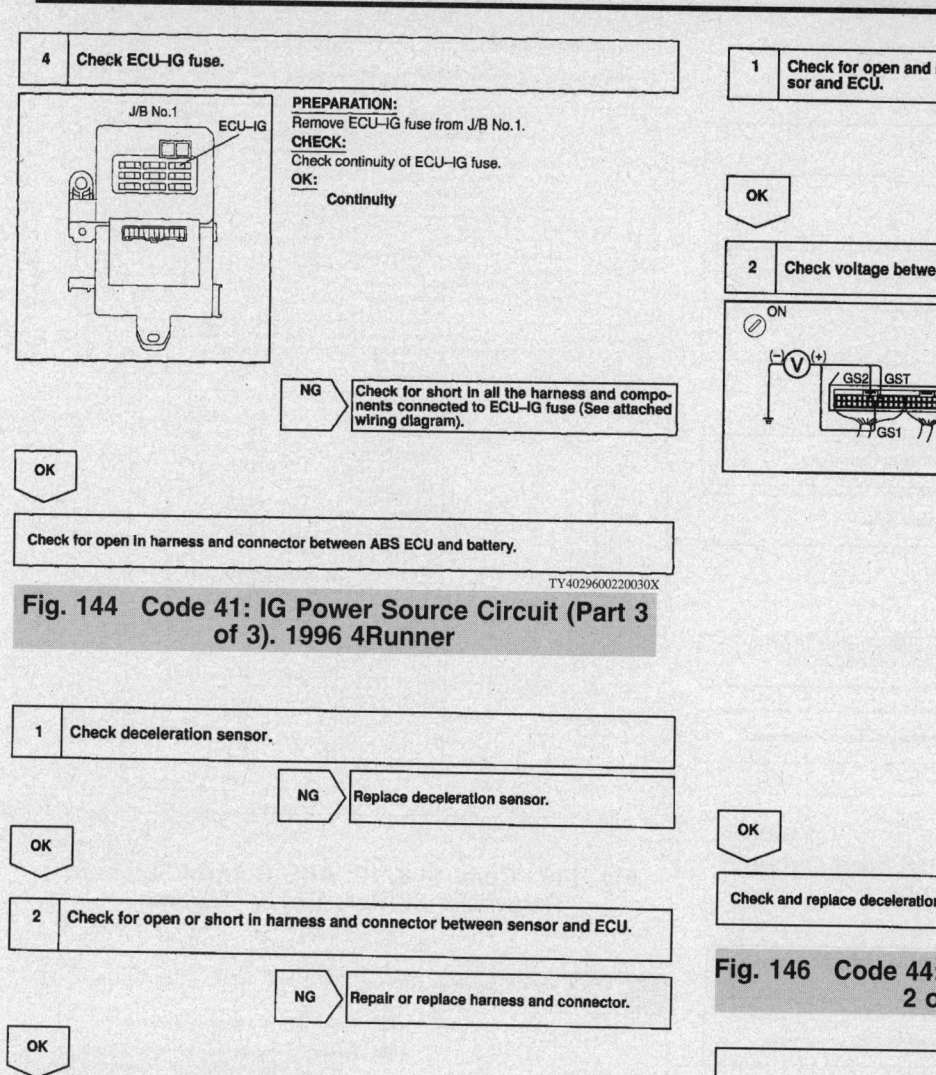

PREPARATION:
Remove ECU–IG fuse from J/B No.1.
CHECK:
Check continuity of ECU–IG fuse.
OK:
Continuity

NG → Check for short in all the harness and components connected to ECU–IG fuse (See attached wiring diagram).

OK ↓

Check for open in harness and connector between ABS ECU and battery.

TY4029600220030X

Fig. 144 Code 41: IG Power Source Circuit (Part 3 of 3). 1996 4Runner

1	Check deceleration sensor.

NG → Replace deceleration sensor.

OK ↓

2	Check for open or short in harness and connector between sensor and ECU.

NG → Repair or replace harness and connector.

OK ↓

Check and replace ABS ECU.

TY4029600221000X

Fig. 145 Code 43: Malfunction In Deceleration Sensor. 1996 4Runner

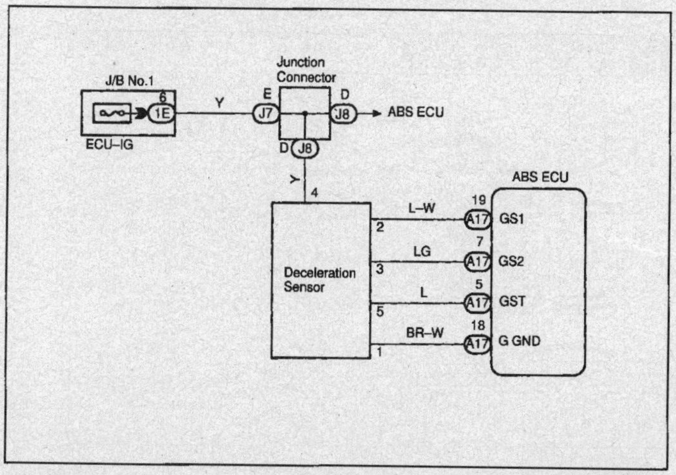
J/B No.1
ECU–IG
6
1E
Y
Junction Connector
E
J7
D
J8
ABS ECU
D
J8
Y
4
ABS ECU
Deceleration Sensor
L–W
19
A17
GS1
2
LG
7
A17
GS2
3
L
5
A17
GST
5
BR–W
18
A17
G GND
1

TY4029600222010X

Fig. 146 Code 44: Deceleration Sensor Circuit (Part 1 of 2). 1996 4Runner

1	Check for open and short in harness and connector between Deceleration sensor and ECU.

NG → Repair or replace harness or connector.

OK ↓

2	Check voltage between terminals GS1, GS2, GST of ABS ECU and body ground.

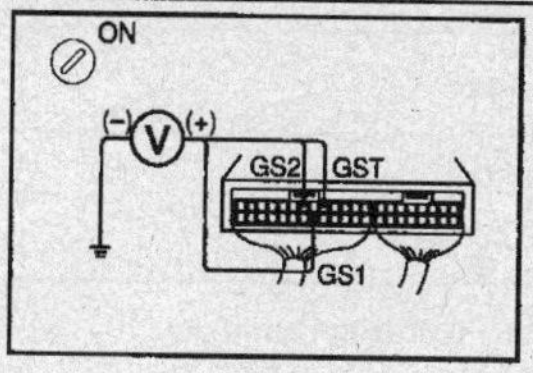
ON
(–)
V
(+)
GS2
GST
GS1

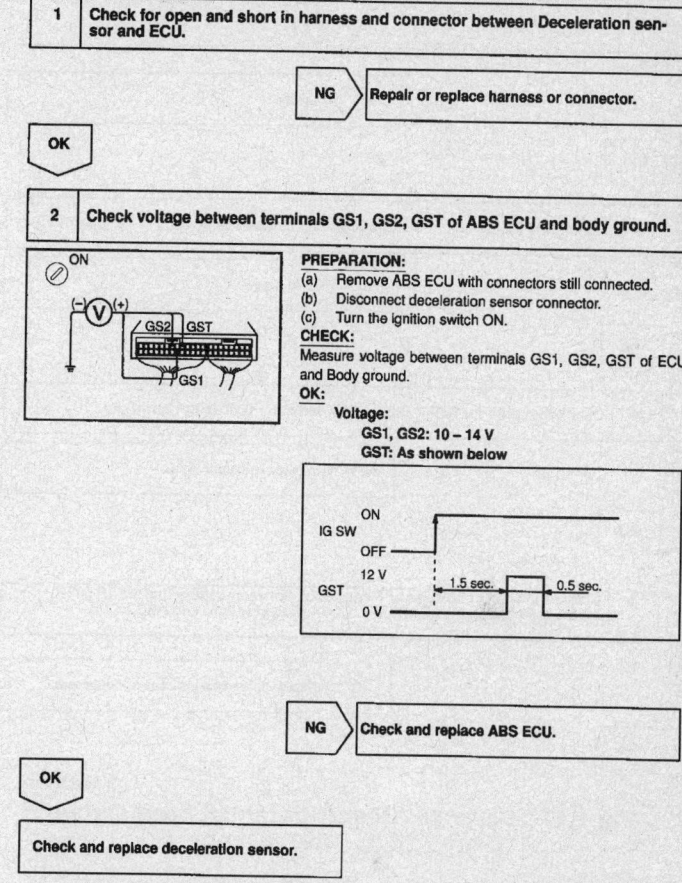

PREPARATION:
(a) Remove ABS ECU with connectors still connected.
(b) Disconnect deceleration sensor connector.
(c) Turn the ignition switch ON.
CHECK:
Measure voltage between terminals GS1, GS2, GST of ECU and Body ground.
OK:
Voltage:
GS1, GS2: 10 – 14 V
GST: As shown below

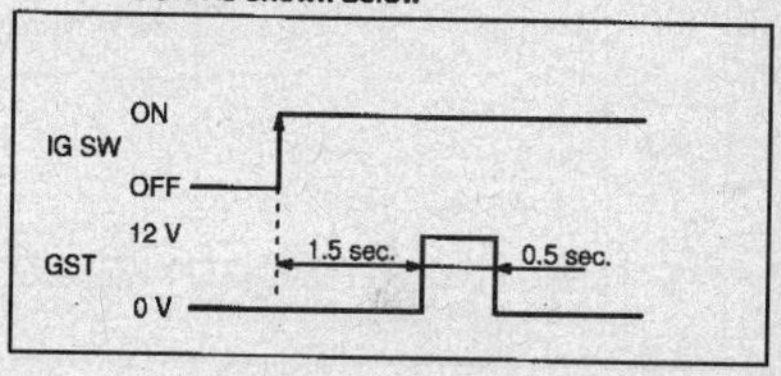
ON
IG SW
OFF
12 V
GST
0 V
1.5 sec.
0.5 sec.

NG → Check and replace ABS ECU.

OK ↓

Check and replace deceleration sensor.

TY4029600222020X

Fig. 146 Code 44: Deceleration Sensor Circuit (Part 2 of 2). 1996 4Runner

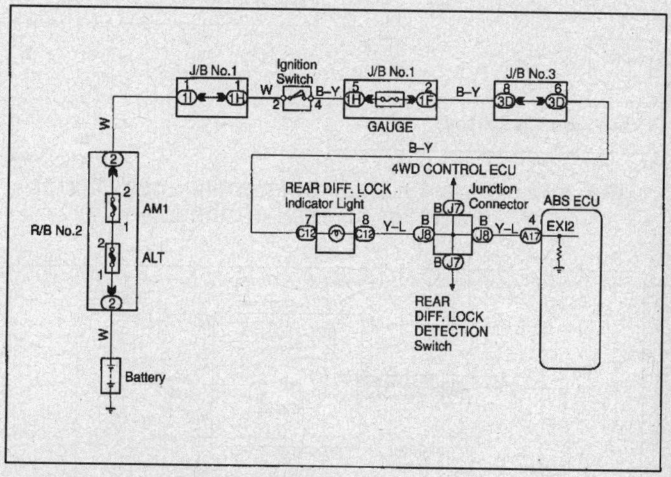
J/B No.1
Ignition Switch
J/B No.1
J/B No.3
W
B–Y
B–Y
GAUGE
B–Y
4WD CONTROL ECU
REAR DIFF. LOCK Indicator Light
Junction Connector
ABS ECU
EXI2
Y–L
Y–L
R/B No.2
AM1
ALT
W
W
Battery
REAR DIFF. LOCK DETECTION Switch

INSPECTION PROCEDURE

HINT: Rear differential lock switch is OFF.

1	Check the rear differential lock is free.

NG → Repair the rear differential lock system.

OK ↓

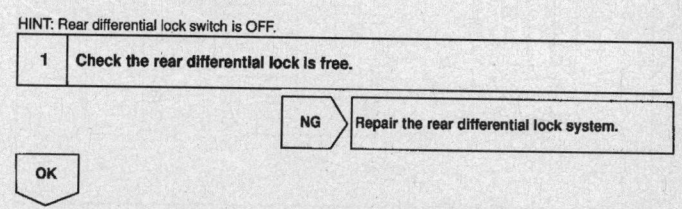

TY4029600223010X

Fig. 147 Code 48: Rear Differential Lock Circuit (Part 1 of 3). 1996 4Runner

2 | **Is DTC output?**

Check DTC.

NO → **Normal.**

YES

3 | **Check that REAR DIFF. LOCK indicator light does not go off.**

NO → **Go to step 6.**

YES

4 | **Check that bulb for REAR DIFF. LOCK indicator light is not burnt out.**

YES → **Replace indicator light.**

NO

5 | **Check for open in harness and connector between battery and REAR DIFF. LOCK indicator light, REAR DIFF. LOCK indicator light and ABS ECU.**

NG → **Repair or replace harness or connector.**

OK

TY4029600223020X

Fig. 147 Code 48: Rear Differential Lock Circuit (Part 2 of 3). 1996 4Runner

6 | **Check for short in harness and connector between REAR DIFF. LOCK indicator light and ABS ECU.**

NG → **Repair or replace harness or connector.**

OK

Check and replace ABS ECU.

TY4029600223030X

Fig. 147 Code 48: Rear Differential Lock Circuit (Part 3 of 3). 1996 4Runner

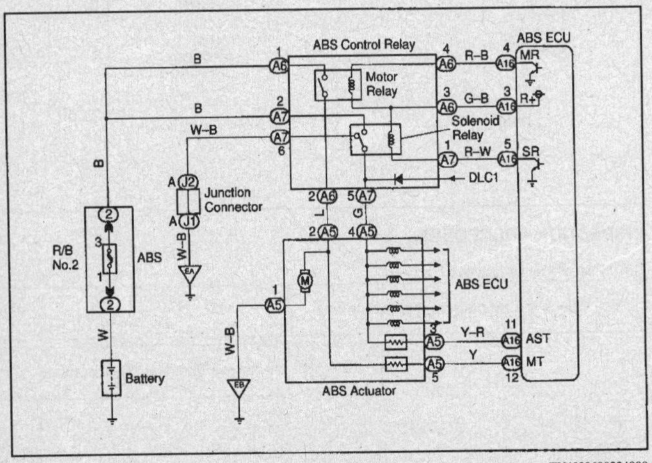

ABS Control Relay
Motor Relay
Solenoid Relay
ABS ECU
DLC1
Junction Connector
R/B No.2
ABS
Battery
ABS Actuator
AST
MT
MR
SR

TY4029600224000

Fig. 148 Code 51: ABS Pump Motor Lock. 1996 4Runner

CIRCUIT DESCRIPTION

This relay supplies power to each ABS solenoid. After the ignition switch is turned ON, if the initial check is OK, the relay goes on.

DTC No.	DTC Detecting Condition	Trouble area
11	Conditions (1) and (2) continue for 0.2 sec. or more: (1) ABS control (solenoid) relay terminal (SR) voltage: Battery positive voltage (2) ABS control (solenoid) relay monitor terminal (AST) voltage: 0 V	• ABS control (solenoid) relay • Open or short in ABS control (solenoid) relay circuit • ECU
12	Conditions (1) and (2) continue for 0.2 sec. or more: (1) ABS control (solenoid) relay terminal (SR) voltage: 0 V (2) ABS control (solenoid) relay monitor terminal (AST) voltage: Battery positive voltage	• ABS control (solenoid) relay • B+ short in ABS control (solenoid) relay circuit • ECU

Fail safe function: If trouble occurs in the control (solenoid) relay circuit, the ECU cuts off current to the ABS control (solenoid) relay and prohibits ABS control.

WIRING DIAGRAM

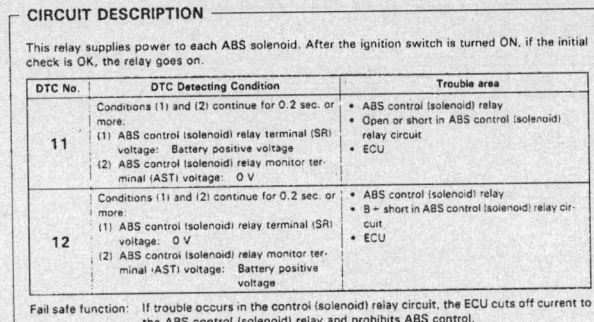

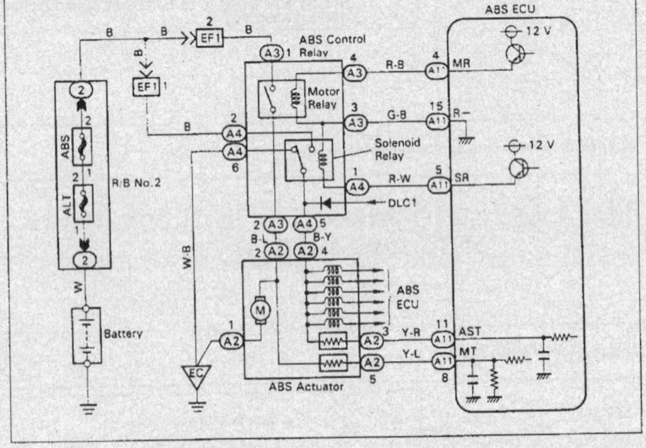

ABS ECU
ABS Control Relay
Motor Relay
Solenoid Relay
DLC1
R/B No.2
ABS
ALT
Battery
ABS Actuator
12 V
MR
SR
AST
MT

TY4029500164010X

Fig. 149 Code 11 & 12: ABS Control Solenoid Relay Circuit (Part 1 of 3). Tacoma

1 | Check voltage between terminals (A4) 2 and (A4) 6 of ABS control (solenoid) relay connector.

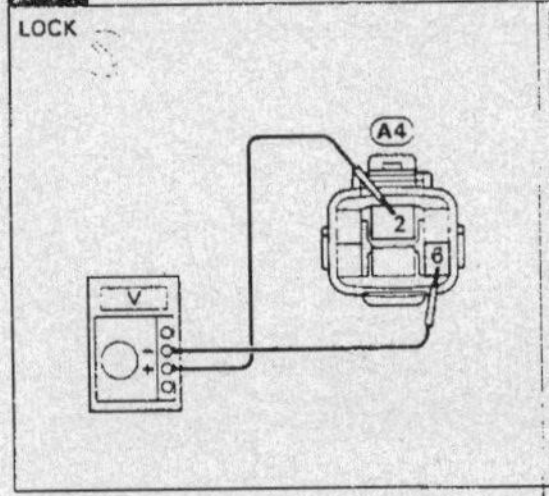

LOCK
A4
V

P Disconnect the ABS control relay connector.

C Measure the voltage between terminals (A4) 2 and (A4) 6 of ABS control relay harness side connector.

OK Voltage: 10 – 14 V

NG → Check and repair harness or connector.

OK

2 | Check continuity between terminals (A4) 5 and (A2) 4, (A2) 4 and (A2) 3, (A2) 3 and (A11) 11.

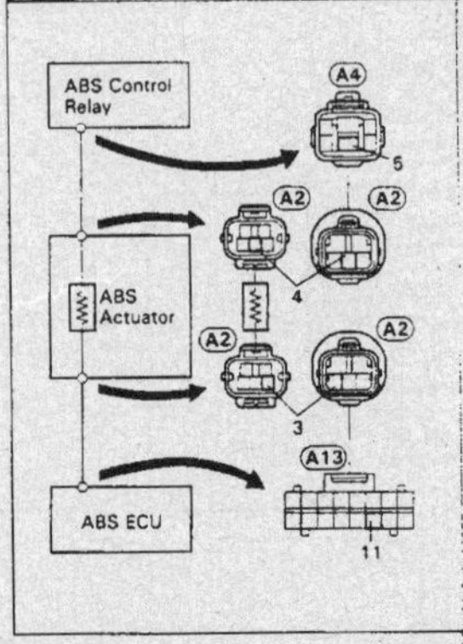

ABS Control Relay
ABS Actuator
ABS ECU
A4
A2
A13

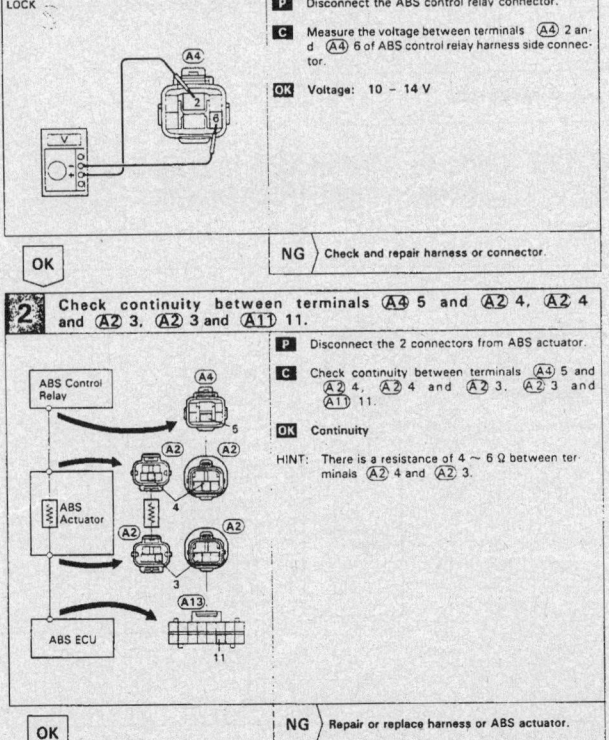

P Disconnect the 2 connectors from ABS actuator.

C Check continuity between terminals (A4) 5 and (A2) 4, (A2) 4 and (A2) 3, (A2) 3 and (A11) 11.

OK Continuity

HINT: There is a resistance of 4 ~ 6 Ω between terminals (A2) 4 and (A2) 3.

NG → Repair or replace harness or ABS actuator.

OK

TY4029500164020X

Fig. 149 Code 11 & 12: ABS Control Solenoid Relay Circuit (Part 2 of 3). Tacoma

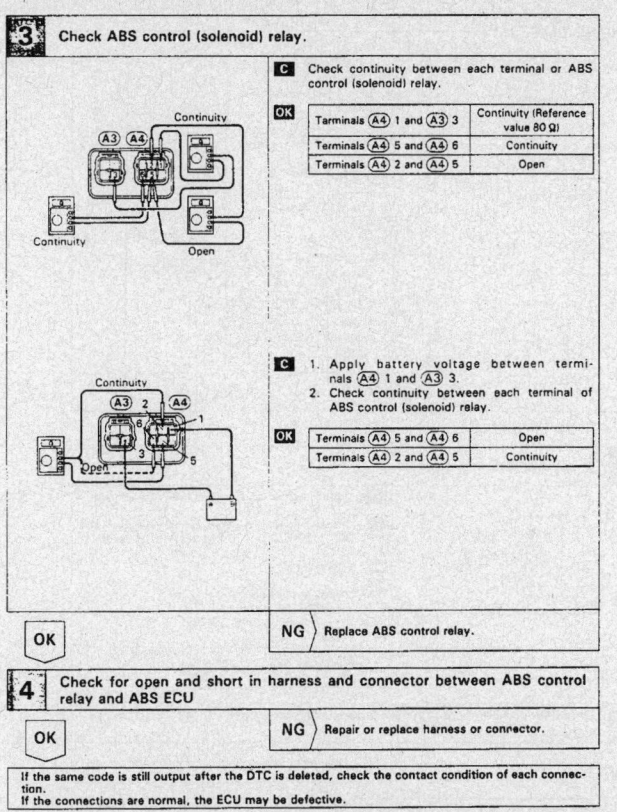

3 Check ABS control (solenoid) relay.

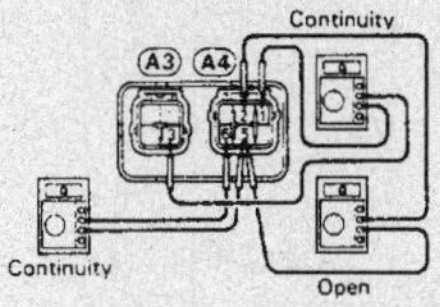
Continuity
A3
A4
Continuity
Open

C Check continuity between each terminal or ABS control (solenoid) relay.

OK

Terminals A4 1 and A3 3	Continuity (Reference value 80 Ω)
Terminals A4 5 and A4 6	Continuity
Terminals A4 2 and A4 5	Open

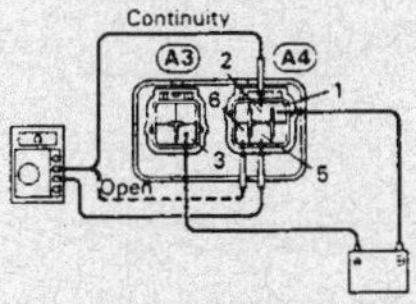
Continuity
A3
A4
Open

C
1. Apply battery voltage between terminals A4 1 and A3 3.
2. Check continuity between each terminal of ABS control (solenoid) relay.

OK

Terminals A4 5 and A4 6	Open
Terminals A4 2 and A4 5	Continuity

OK

NG 〉 Replace ABS control relay.

4 Check for open and short in harness and connector between ABS control relay and ABS ECU

OK

NG 〉 Repair or replace harness or connector.

If the same code is still output after the DTC is deleted, check the contact condition of each connection.
If the connections are normal, the ECU may be defective.

TY4029500164030X

Fig. 149 Code 11 & 12: ABS Control Solenoid Relay Circuit (Part 3 of 3). Tacoma

CIRCUIT DESCRIPTION

The ABS control (motor) relay supplies power to the ABS pump motor. While the ABS is activated, the ECU switches the control (motor) relay ON and operates the ABS pump motor.

DTC No.	DTC Detecting Condition	Trouble area
13	Conditions (1) and (2) continued for 0.2 sec. or more: (1) ABS control (motor) relay terminal (MR) voltage: Battery positive voltage (2) ABS control (motor) relay monitor terminal (MT) voltage: 0 V	• ABS control (motor) relay • Open or short in ABS control (motor) relay circuit • ECU
14	Conditions (1) and (2) continued for 4 sec. or more: (1) ABS control (motor) relay terminal (MR) voltage: 0 V (2) ABS control (motor) relay monitor terminal (MT) voltage: Battery positive voltage	• ABS control (motor) relay • B+ short in ABS control (motor) relay circuit • ECU

Fail safe function: If trouble occurs in the control (motor) relay circuit, the ECU cuts off current to the ABS control (solenoid) relay and prohibits ABS control.

WIRING DIAGRAM

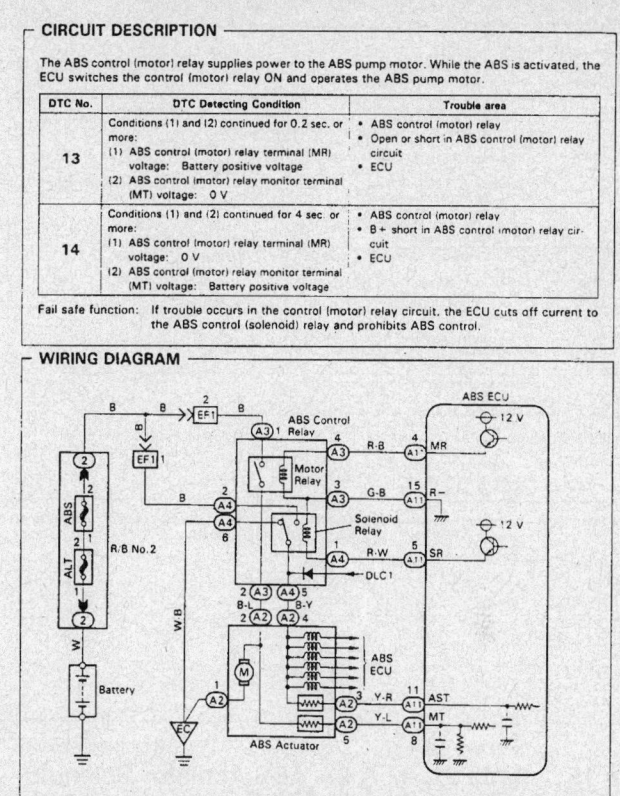

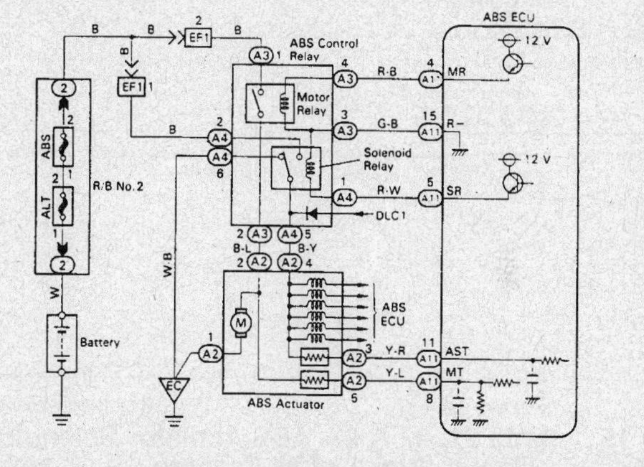
ABS ECU
12 V
ABS Control Relay
Motor Relay
Solenoid Relay
EF1
R/B No. 2
ABS
ALT
Battery
R-B
G-B
R-W
Y-R
Y-L
MR
R–
SR
AST
MT
DLC1
ABS ECU
ABS Actuator
W-B
B-L
B-Y
EC

TY4029500165010X

Fig. 150 Code 13 & 14: ABS Control Motor Relay Circuit (Part 1 of 3). Tacoma

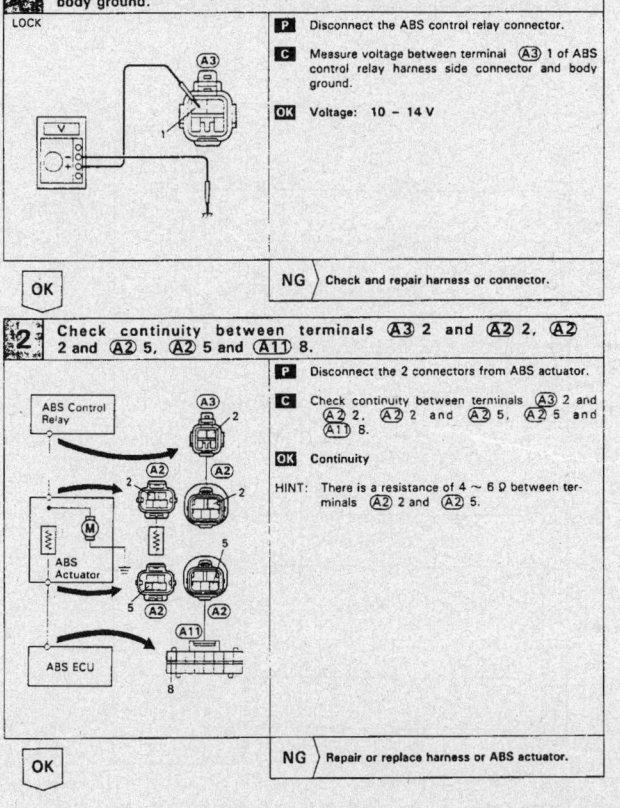

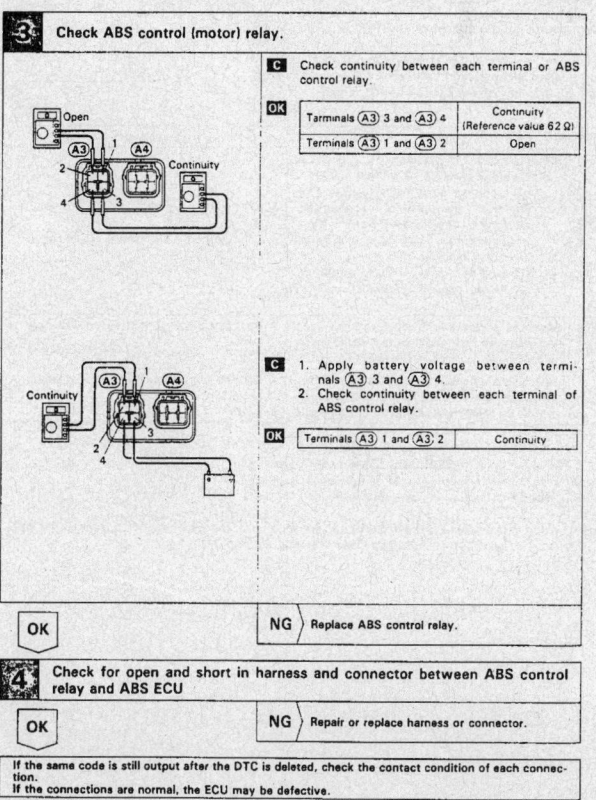

1 Check voltage between terminal A3 1 of ABS control (motor) relay and body ground.

LOCK

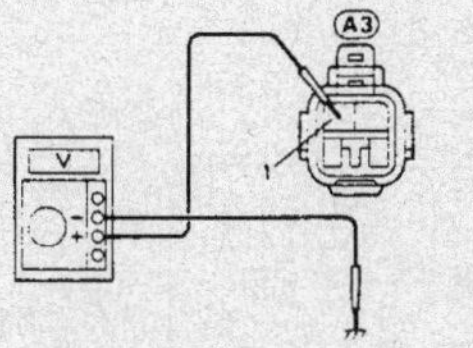
A3
V

P Disconnect the ABS control relay connector.

C Measure voltage between terminal A3 1 of ABS control relay harness side connector and body ground.

OK Voltage: 10 – 14 V

OK

NG 〉 Check and repair harness or connector.

2 Check continuity between terminals A3 2 and A2 2, A2 2 and A2 5, A2 5 and A11 8.

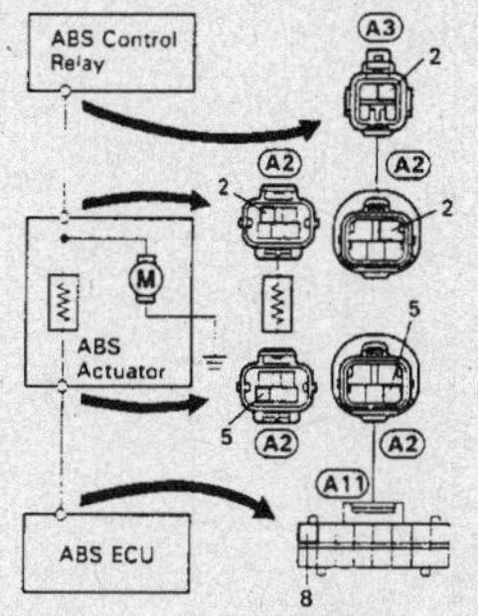
ABS Control Relay
A3
A2
ABS Actuator
A11
ABS ECU

P Disconnect the 2 connectors from ABS actuator.

C Check continuity between terminals A3 2 and A2 2, A2 2 and A2 5, A2 5 and A11 8.

OK Continuity

HINT: There is a resistance of 4 ~ 6 Ω between terminals A2 2 and A2 5.

OK

NG 〉 Repair or replace harness or ABS actuator.

TY4029500165020X

Fig. 150 Code 13 & 14: ABS Control Motor Relay Circuit (Part 2 of 3). Tacoma

3 Check ABS control (motor) relay.

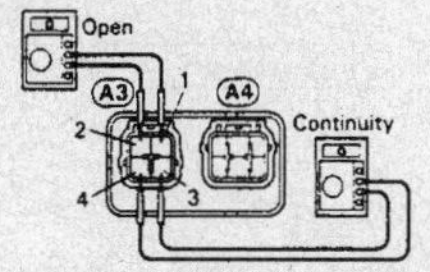
Open
A3
A4
Continuity

C Check continuity between each terminal or ABS control relay.

OK

Terminals A3 3 and A3 4	Continuity (Reference value 62 Ω)
Terminals A3 1 and A3 2	Open

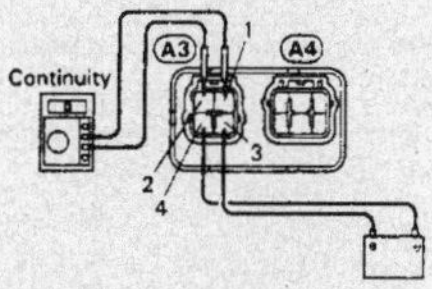
Continuity
A3
A4

C
1. Apply battery voltage between terminals A3 3 and A3 4.
2. Check continuity between each terminal of ABS control relay.

OK

Terminals A3 1 and A3 2	Continuity

OK

NG 〉 Replace ABS control relay.

4 Check for open and short in harness and connector between ABS control relay and ABS ECU

OK

NG 〉 Repair or replace harness or connector.

If the same code is still output after the DTC is deleted, check the contact condition of each connection.
If the connections are normal, the ECU may be defective.

TY4029500165030X

Fig. 150 Code 13 & 14: ABS Control Motor Relay Circuit (Part 3 of 3). Tacoma

CIRCUIT DESCRIPTION

This solenoid goes on when signals are received from the ECU and controls the pressure acting on the wheel cylinders, thus controlling the braking force.

DTC No.	DTC Detecting Condition	Trouble area
21	Conditions (1) through (3) continue for 0.05 sec.or more: (1) ABS control (solenoid) relay terminal (SR) voltage: Battery positive voltage (2) Voltage of ABS ECU terminal AST: Battery positive voltage (3) When power transistor of ECU is ON, voltage of terminal SFRR or SFRH is 0 V or battery positive voltage.	• ABS actuator • Open or short in SFRR or SFRH circuit • ECU
22	Conditions (1) through (3) continue for 0.05 sec. or more: (1) ABS control (solenoid) relay terminal (SR) voltage: Battery positive voltage (2) Voltage of ABS ECU terminal AST: Battery positive voltage (3) When power transistor of ECU is ON, voltage of terminal SFLR or SFLH is 0 V or battery positive voltage.	• ABS actuator • Open or short in SFLR or SFLH circuit • ECU
23	Conditions (1) through (3) continue for 0.05 sec. or more: (1) ABS control (solenoid) relay terminal (SR) voltage: Battery positive voltage (2) Voltage of ABS ECU terminal AST: Battery positive voltage (3) When power transistor of ECU is ON, voltage of terminal SRR or SRH is 0 V or battery positive voltage.	• ABS actuator • Open or short in SRR or SRH circuit • ECU

Fail safe function: If trouble occurs in the actuator solenoid circuit, the ECU cuts off current to the control (solenoid) relay and prohibits ABS control.

TY4029500166010X

Fig. 151 Code 21, 22 & 23: ABS Actuator Solenoid Circuit (Part 1 of 2). Tacoma

WIRING DIAGRAM

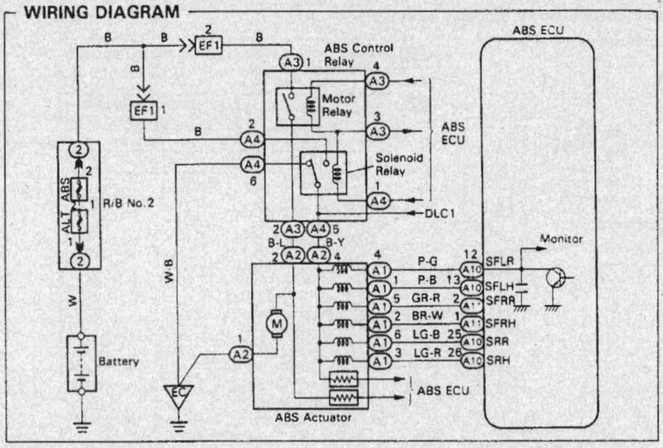
ABS ECU
ABS Control Relay
Motor Relay
Solenoid Relay
ABS ECU
DLC1
EF1
R/B No. 2
ALT ABS
Battery
Monitor
SFLR
SFLH
SFRR
SFRH
SRR
SRH
ABS ECU
ABS Actuator

INSPECTION PROCEDURE

1 Check ABS actuator solenoid.

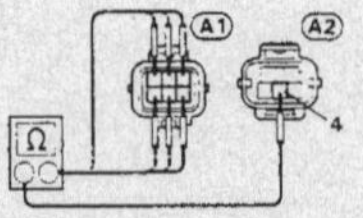
A1
A2
4

P Disconnect the 2 connectors from ABS actuator.

C Check continuity between terminals (A2) 4 and (A1) 1, 2, 3, 4, 5, 6 of ABS actuator connector.

OK Continuity

HINT: Resistance of each solenoid coil
SFRH, SFLH, SRH: 5.0 Ω
SFRR, SFLR, SRR: 2.2 Ω

OK

NG — Replace ABS actuator.

2 Check for open and short in harness and connector between ABS ECU and actuator

OK

NG — Repair or replace harness or connector.

If the same code is still output after the DTC is deleted, check the contact condition of each connection.
If the connections are normal, the ECU may be defective.

TY4029500166020X

Fig. 151 Code 21, 22 & 23: ABS Actuator Solenoid Circuit (Part 2 of 2). Tacoma

CIRCUIT DESCRIPTION

The speed sensor detects the wheel speed and sends the appropriate signals to the ECU. These signals are used to control the ABS system. The front and rear rotors each have 48 serrations.

When the rotors rotate, the magnetic field emitted by the permanent magnet in the speed sensor generates an AC voltage. Since the frequency of this AC voltage changes in direct proportion to the speed of the rotor, the frequency is used by the ECU to detect the speed of each wheel.

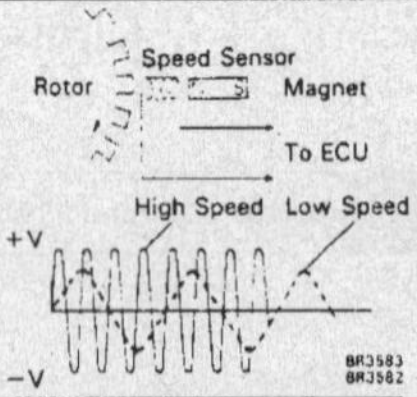
Speed Sensor
Rotor
Magnet
To ECU
High Speed
Low Speed
+V
-V

DTC No.	DTC Detecting Condition	Trouble area
31, 32, 33, 34	Detection of any of conditions (1) through (3): (1) At vehicle speed of 10 km/h (6 mph) or more, pulses are not input for 5 sec. (2) Momentary interruption of the speed sensor signal occurs at least 7 times in the time between switching the ignition switch ON and switching it OFF. (3) Abnormal fluctuation of speed sensor signals with the vehicle speed 20 km/h (12 mph) or more.	• Right front, left front, right rear and left rear speed sensor • Open or short in each speed sensor circuit • ECU
35	Speed sensor signal is not input for about 1 sec. while the left front and right rear speed sensor signals are being checked with the IG switch ON.	• Open in left front or right rear speed sensor circuit • ECU
36	Speed sensor signal is not input for about 1 sec. while the right front and left rear speed sensor signals are being checked with the IG switch ON.	• Open in right front or left rear speed sensor circuit • ECU

HINT: DTC No.31 is for the right front speed sensor.
DTC No.32 is for the left front speed sensor.
DTC No.33 is for the right rear speed sensor.
DTC No.34 is for the left rear speed sensor.

Fail safe function: If trouble occurs in the speed sensor circuit, the ECU cuts off current to the ABS control (solenoid) relay and prohibits ABS control.

TY4029500167010X

Fig. 152 Code 31, 32, 33, 34, 35 & 36: Speed Sensor Circuit (Part 1 of 4). Tacoma

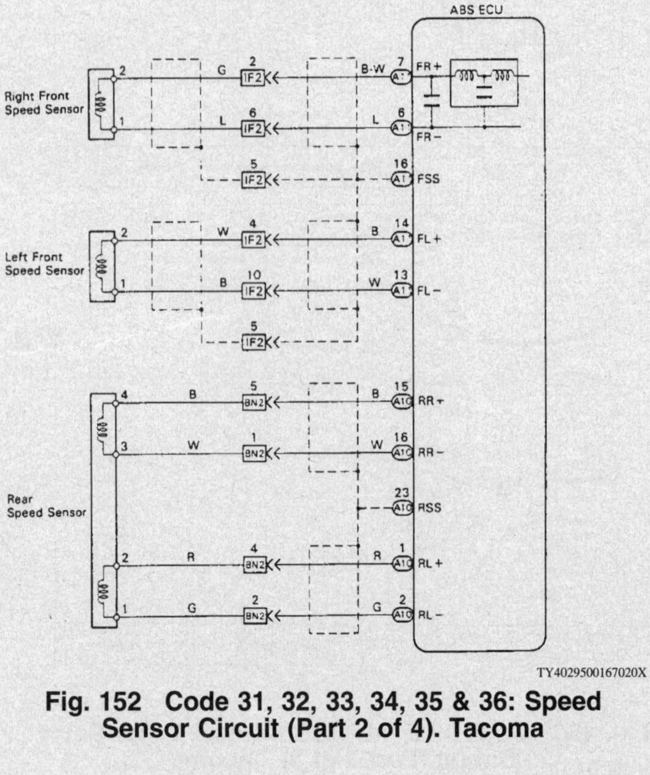
ABS ECU
Right Front Speed Sensor
Left Front Speed Sensor
Rear Speed Sensor
FR+
FR−
FSS
FL+
FL−
RR+
RR−
RSS
RL+
RL−

TY4029500167020X

Fig. 152 Code 31, 32, 33, 34, 35 & 36: Speed Sensor Circuit (Part 2 of 4). Tacoma

INSPECTION PROCEDURE

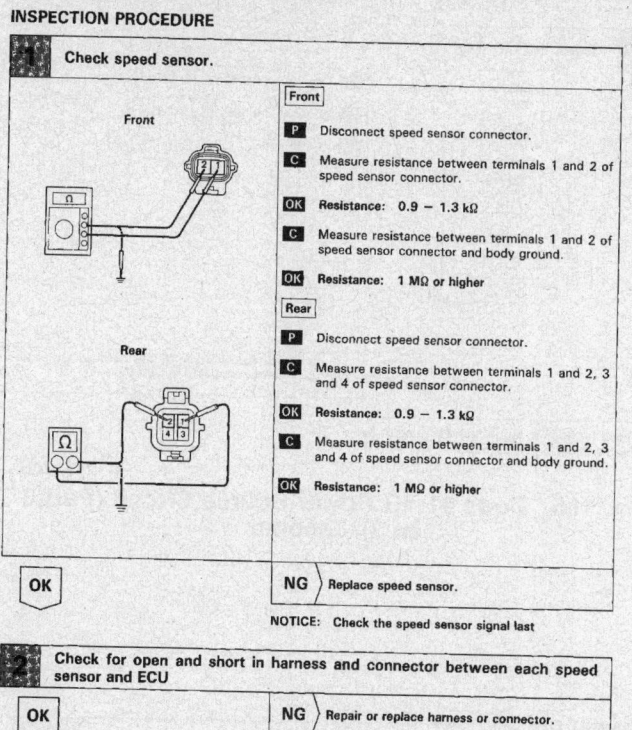

1 Check speed sensor.

Front

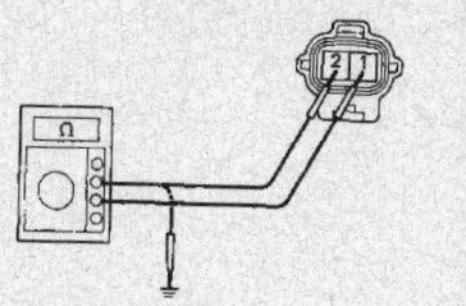

Front

- **P** Disconnect speed sensor connector.
- **C** Measure resistance between terminals 1 and 2 of speed sensor connector.
- **OK** **Resistance: 0.9 – 1.3 kΩ**
- **C** Measure resistance between terminals 1 and 2 of speed sensor connector and body ground.
- **OK** **Resistance: 1 MΩ or higher**

Rear

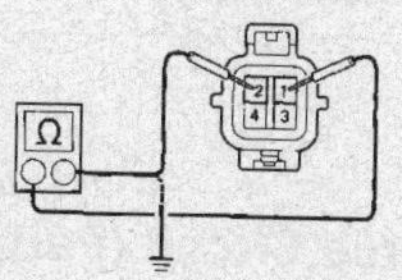

Rear

- **P** Disconnect speed sensor connector.
- **C** Measure resistance between terminals 1 and 2, 3 and 4 of speed sensor connector.
- **OK** **Resistance: 0.9 – 1.3 kΩ**
- **C** Measure resistance between terminals 1 and 2, 3 and 4 of speed sensor connector and body ground.
- **OK** **Resistance: 1 MΩ or higher**

OK | NG: **Replace speed sensor.**

NOTICE: **Check the speed sensor signal last**

2 Check for open and short in harness and connector between each speed sensor and ECU

OK | NG: **Repair or replace harness or connector.**

TY4029500167030X

Fig. 152 Code 31, 32, 33, 34, 35 & 36: Speed Sensor Circuit (Part 3 of 4). Tacoma

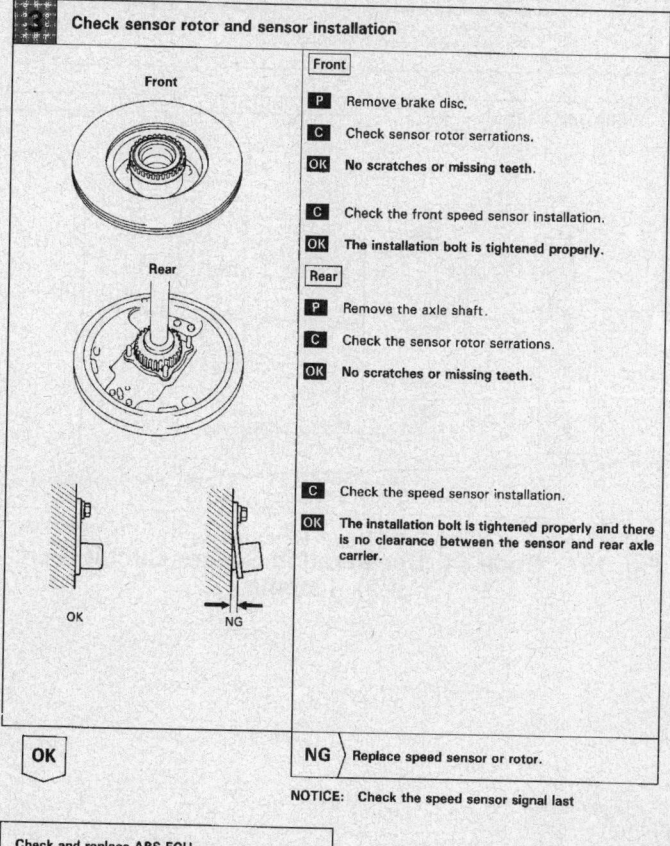

3 Check sensor rotor and sensor installation

Front

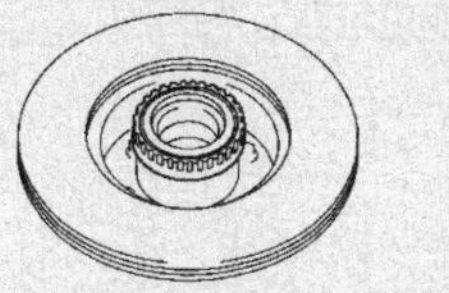

Front

- **P** Remove brake disc.
- **C** Check sensor rotor serrations.
- **OK** **No scratches or missing teeth.**
- **C** Check the front speed sensor installation.
- **OK** **The installation bolt is tightened properly.**

Rear

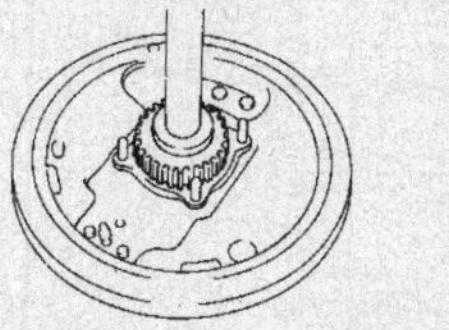

Rear

- **P** Remove the axle shaft.
- **C** Check the sensor rotor serrations.
- **OK** **No scratches or missing teeth.**

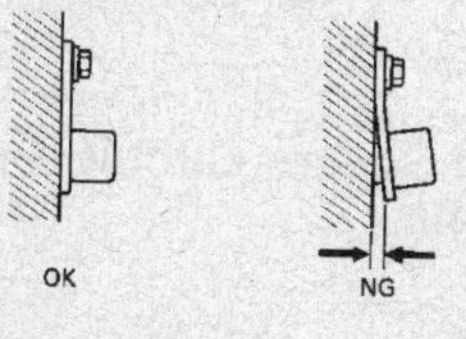
OK
NG

- **C** Check the speed sensor installation.
- **OK** **The installation bolt is tightened properly and there is no clearance between the sensor and rear axle carrier.**

OK | NG: **Replace speed sensor or rotor.**

NOTICE: **Check the speed sensor signal last**

Check and replace ABS ECU.

TY4029500167040X

Fig. 152 Code 31, 32, 33, 34, 35 & 36: Speed Sensor Circuit (Part 4 of 4). Tacoma

CIRCUIT DESCRIPTION

DTC No.	DTC Detecting Condition	Trouble area
37	With the rear wheels stationary and front wheels rotating at 20+ km/h (12+ mph) for 10+ secs, turn ignition switch ON then OFF 8 times, in succession.	• Front axle hub • Right front, left front speed sensor • Wire harness for sensor system • ECU

INSPECTION PROCEDURE

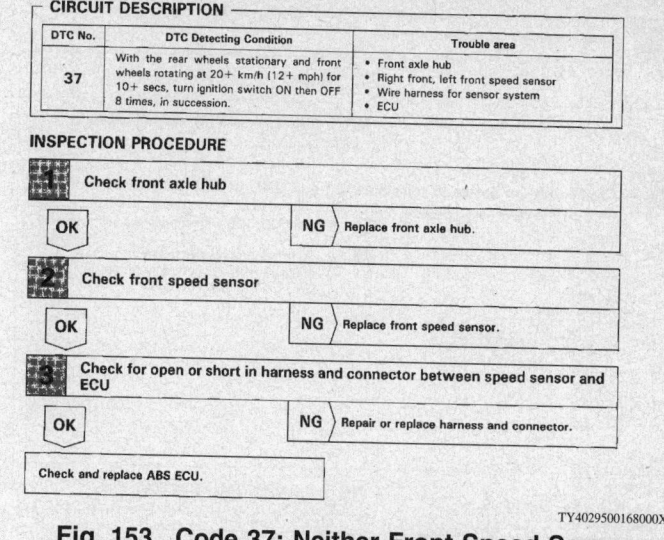

1 Check front axle hub

OK | NG: **Replace front axle hub.**

2 Check front speed sensor

OK | NG: **Replace front speed sensor.**

3 Check for open or short in harness and connector between speed sensor and ECU

OK | NG: **Repair or replace harness and connector.**

Check and replace ABS ECU.

TY4029500168000X

Fig. 153 Code 37: Neither Front Speed Sensor Rotor Missing. Tacoma

CIRCUIT DESCRIPTION

DTC No.	DTC Detecting Condition	Trouble area
37	Driving at more than 30 km/h (19 mph) for more than 60 seconds with 1 or 2 tires of different size.	• Tire size • ECU

INSPECTION PROCEDURE

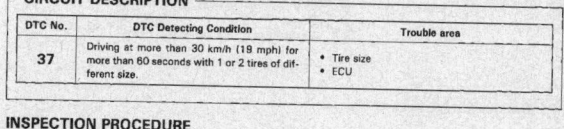

1 Check tire size.

OK | NG: **Replace tires so that all 4 tires are of the same size.**

Check and replace ABS ECU.

TY4029500169000X

Fig. 154 Code 37: Tires Of Different Size On 2WD Vehicles. Tacoma

CIRCUIT DESCRIPTION

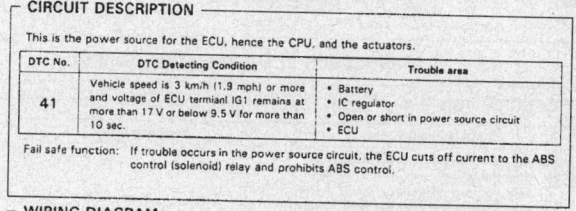

This is the power source for the ECU, hence the CPU, and the actuators.

DTC No.	DTC Detecting Condition	Trouble area
41	Vehicle speed is 3 km/h (1.9 mph) or more and voltage of ECU termianl IG1 remains at more than 17 V or below 9.5 V for more than 10 sec.	• Battery • IC regulator • Open or short in power source circuit • ECU

Fail safe function: If trouble occurs in the power source circuit, the ECU cuts off current to the ABS control (solenoid) relay and prohibits ABS control.

WIRING DIAGRAM

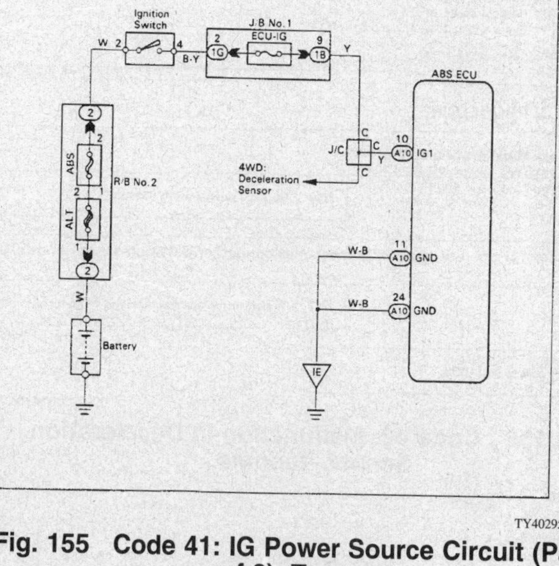
Ignition Switch
J/B No.1
ECU-IG
W
B-Y
1G
1B
Y
ABS ECU
ABS
ALT
R/B No.2
J/C
IG1
4WD: Deceleration Sensor
W-B
GND
Battery
IE

TY4029500170010X

Fig. 155 Code 41: IG Power Source Circuit (Part 1 of 3). Tacoma

1 Check battery positive voltage.

OK Voltage: 10 – 14 V

OK

NG Check and repair the charging system.

2 Check voltage between terminals IG1 and GND of ABS ECU connector.

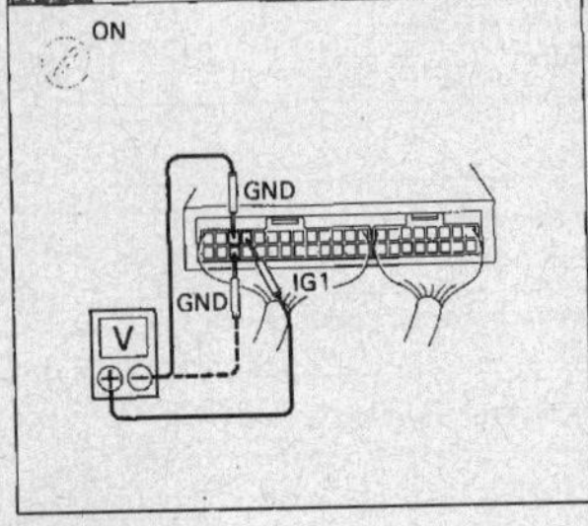

ON
GND
IG1
GND
V

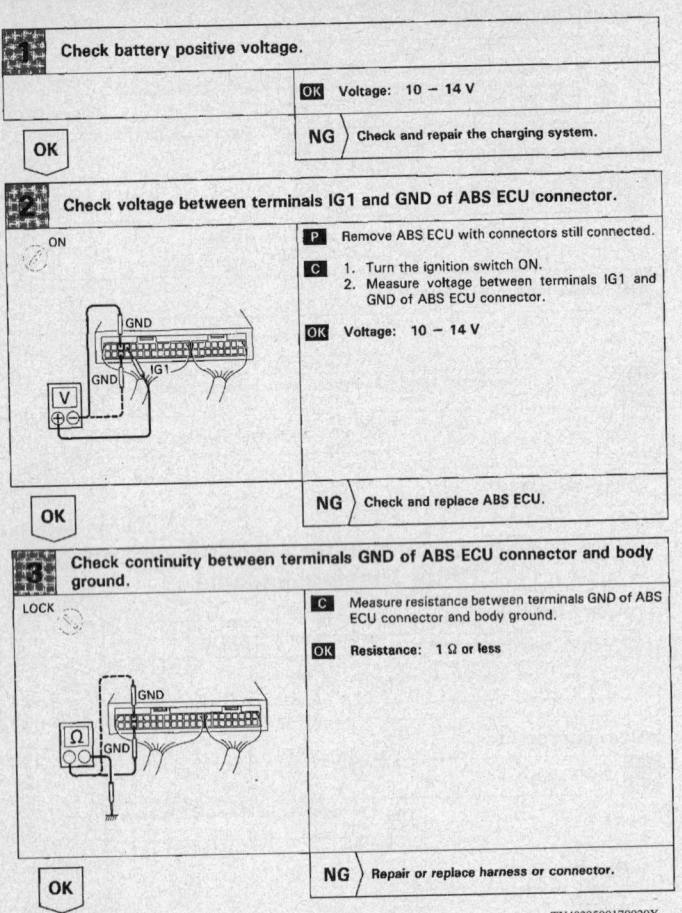

P Remove ABS ECU with connectors still connected.

C 1. Turn the ignition switch ON.
2. Measure voltage between terminals IG1 and GND of ABS ECU connector.

OK Voltage: 10 – 14 V

OK

NG Check and replace ABS ECU.

3 Check continuity between terminals GND of ABS ECU connector and body ground.

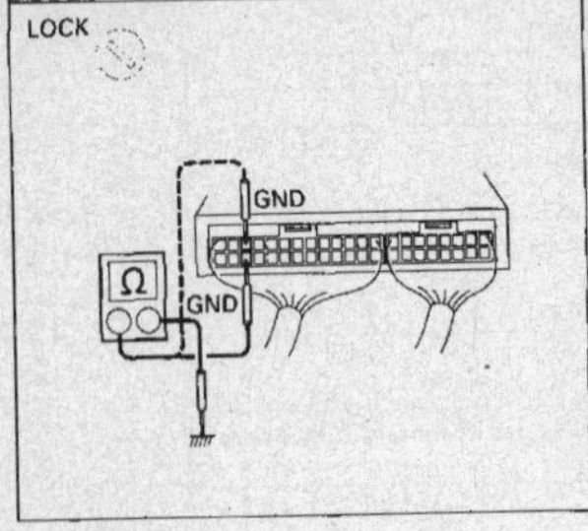

LOCK
GND
Ω
GND

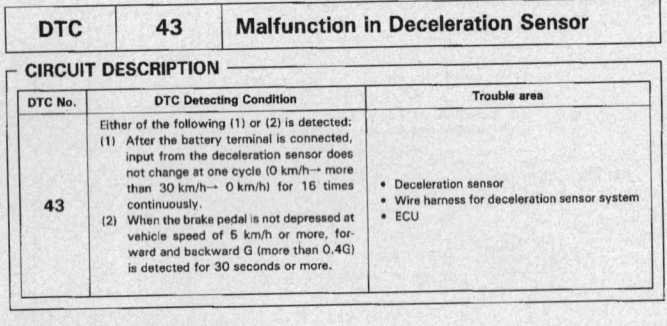

C Measure resistance between terminals GND of ABS ECU connector and body ground.

OK Resistance: 1 Ω or less

OK

NG Repair or replace harness or connector.

TY4029500170020X

Fig. 155 Code 41: IG Power Source Circuit (Part 2 of 3). Tacoma

4 Check ECU-IG fuse.

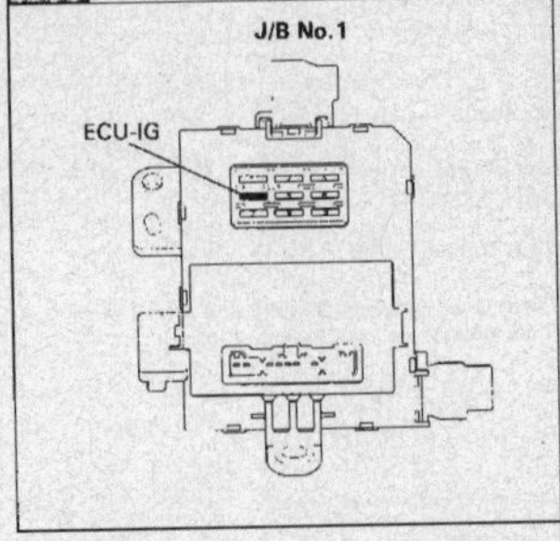

J/B No.1
ECU-IG

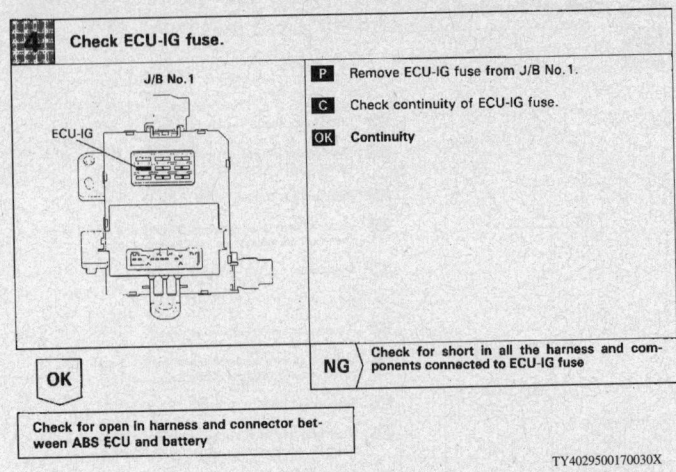

P Remove ECU-IG fuse from J/B No.1.

C Check continuity of ECU-IG fuse.

OK Continuity

OK

NG Check for short in all the harness and components connected to ECU-IG fuse

Check for open in harness and connector between ABS ECU and battery

TY4029500170030X

Fig. 155 Code 41: IG Power Source Circuit (Part 3 of 3). Tacoma

DTC	43	Malfunction in Deceleration Sensor

CIRCUIT DESCRIPTION

DTC No.	DTC Detecting Condition	Trouble area
43	Either of the following (1) or (2) is detected: (1) After the battery terminal is connected, input from the deceleration sensor does not change at one cycle (0 km/h→ more than 30 km/h→ 0 km/h) for 16 times continuously. (2) When the brake pedal is not depressed at vehicle speed of 5 km/h or more, forward and backward G (more than 0.4G) is detected for 30 seconds or more.	• Deceleration sensor • Wire harness for deceleration sensor system • ECU

INSPECTION PROCEDURE

1 Check deceleration sensor

OK

NG Replace deceleration sensor.

2 Check for open or short in harness and connector between sensor and ECU

OK

NG Repair or replace harness and connector.

Check and replace ABS ECU.

TY4029500171000X

Fig. 156 Code 43: Malfunction In Deceleration Sensor. Tacoma

CIRCUIT DESCRIPTION

This sensor detects deceleration on the vehicle. The sensor signal is used in ABS control. If the sensor functions abnormally, the ABS warning light comes on but the ABS still operates.

DTC No.	DTC Detecting Condition	Trouble area
44	Either of the following (1) or (2) is detected: (1) An open or short is detected in circuit GS1 or GS2 for 1 sec. (2) After the ignition is turned ON, the test signal is output by GST. During this time, a trouble signal is detected for 0.5 sec.	• Deceleration sensor • Open or short in deceleration sensor circuit • ECU

WIRING DIAGRAM

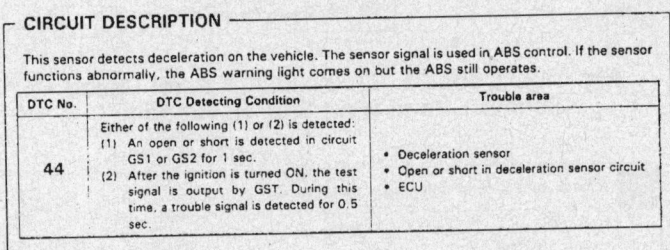

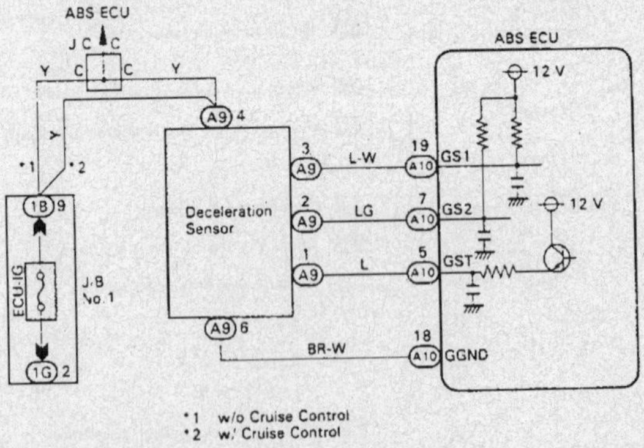

ABS ECU
J C C
Y C C Y
A9 4
Y
*1 *2
1B 9
ECU-IG
J/B No.1
1G 2
Deceleration Sensor
3 A9
2 A9
1 A9
A9 6
L-W
LG
L
BR-W
19 A10 GS1
7 A10 GS2
5 A10 GST
18 A10 GGND
ABS ECU
12 V
12 V
*1 w/o Cruise Control
*2 w/ Cruise Control

TY4029500172010X

Fig. 157 Code 44: Deceleration Sensor Circuit (Part 1 of 2). Tacoma

1 Check for open and short in harness and connector between sensor and ECU

OK	NG 〉 Repair or replace harness or connector.

2 Check voltage between terminals GS1, GS2, GST of ECU and body ground.

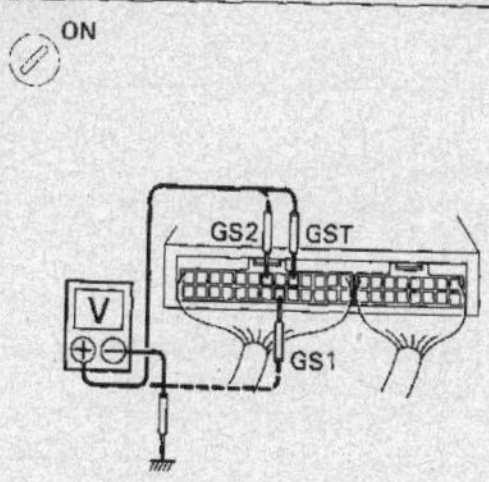

ON
GS2
GST
V
GS1

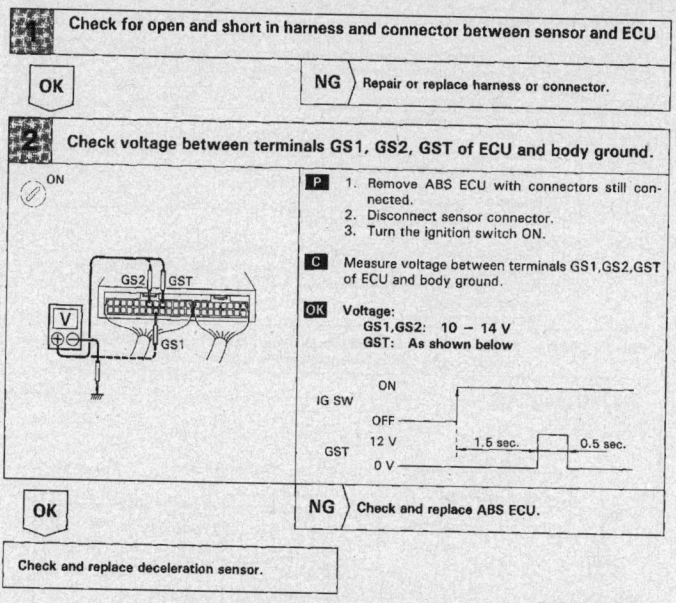

P 1. Remove ABS ECU with connectors still connected.
2. Disconnect sensor connector.
3. Turn the ignition switch ON.

C Measure voltage between terminals GS1,GS2,GST of ECU and body ground.

OK Voltage:
GS1,GS2: 10 – 14 V
GST: As shown below

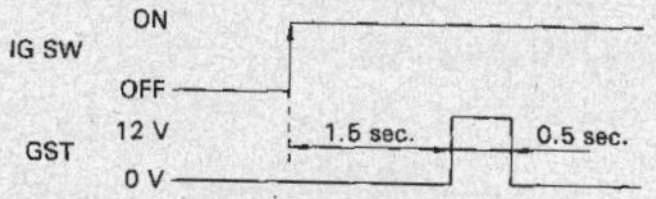

ON
IG SW
OFF
12 V
GST
0 V
1.5 sec.
0.5 sec.

OK	NG 〉 Check and replace ABS ECU.

Check and replace deceleration sensor.

TY4029500172020X

Fig. 157 Code 44: Deceleration Sensor Circuit (Part 2 of 2). Tacoma

CIRCUIT DESCRIPTION

This relay supplies power to each ABS solenoid. After the ignition switch is turned ON, if the initial check is OK, the relay goes on.

DTC No.	DTC Detecting Condition	Trouble Area
11	Conditions (1) and (2) continue for 0.2 sec. or more: (1) ABS control (solenoid) relay terminal (SR) voltage: Battery positive voltage (2) ABS control (solenoid) relay monitor terminal (AST) voltage: 0 V	• ABS control (solenoid) relay • Open or short in ABS control (solenoid) relay circuit • ECU
12	Conditions (1) and (2) continue for 0.2sec. or more: (1) ABS control (solenoid) relay terminal (SR) voltage: 0 V (2) ABS control (solenoid) relay monitor terminal (AST) voltage: Battery positive voltage	• ABS control (solenoid) relay • B+ short in ABS control (solenoid) relay circuit • ECU

Fail safe function: If trouble occurs in the ABS control (solenoid) relay circuit, the ECU cuts off current to the ABS control (solenoid) relay and prohibits ABS control.

WIRING DIAGRAM

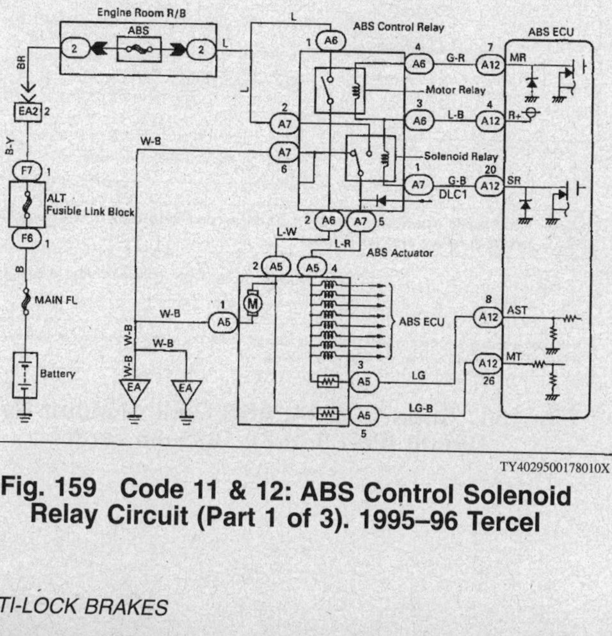

Engine Room R/B
ABS
ABS Control Relay
ABS ECU
Motor Relay
Solenoid Relay
DLC1
ABS Actuator
ALT
Fusible Link Block
MAIN FL
Battery
MR
SR
AST
MT
LG
LG-B

TY4029500178010X

Fig. 159 Code 11 & 12: ABS Control Solenoid Relay Circuit (Part 1 of 3). 1995–96 Tercel

CIRCUIT DESCRIPTION

DTC No.	DTC Detecting Condition	Trouble area
51	Pump motor is not operating normally during initial check.	• ABS pump motor

Fail safe function: If trouble occurs in the ABS pump motor, the ECU cuts off current to the control (solenoid) relay and prohibits ABS control.

WIRING DIAGRAM

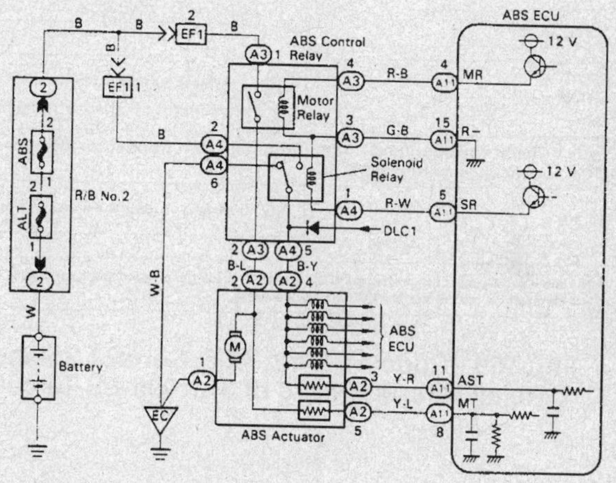

ABS ECU
ABS Control Relay
Motor Relay
Solenoid Relay
R/B No. 2
DLC1
ABS ECU
Battery
ABS Actuator
MR
SR
AST
MT
12 V

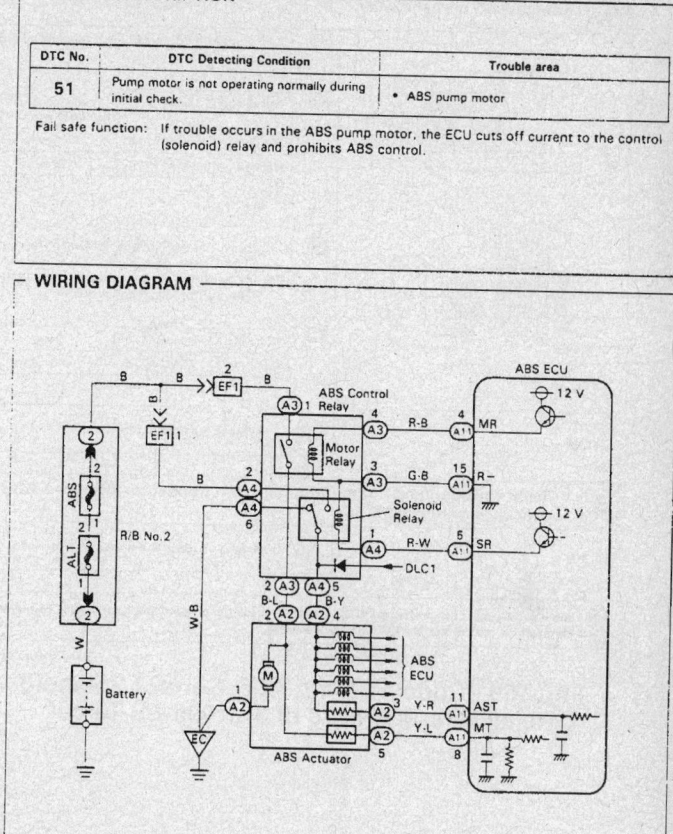

TY4029500173000X

Fig. 158 Code 51: ABS Pump Motor Lock. Tacoma

1 Check voltage between terminals (A7)2 and (A7)6 of ABS control relay connector.

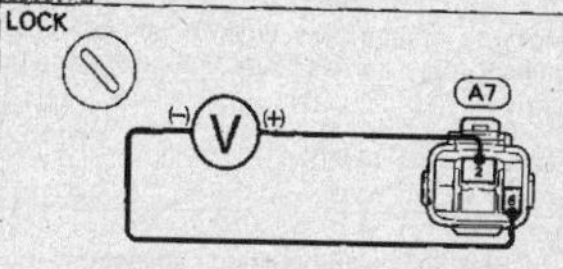

LOCK
V
A7

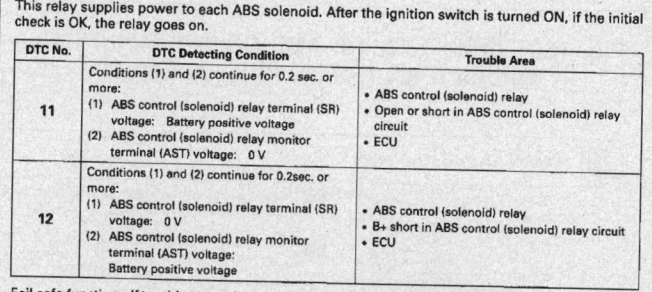

P Disconnect the ABS control relay connector.

C Measure voltage between terminals (A7)2 and (A7)6 of ABS control relay harness side connector.

OK Voltage: 10 – 14 V

OK	NG 〉 Check and repair harness or connector.

2 Check continuity between terminal (A7)5 and (A5)4, (A5)4 and (A5)3, (A5)3 and (A12)8.

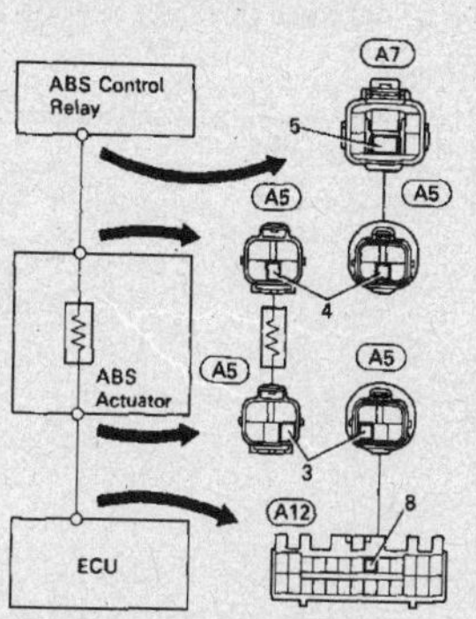

ABS Control Relay
A7
A5
ABS Actuator
A12
ECU

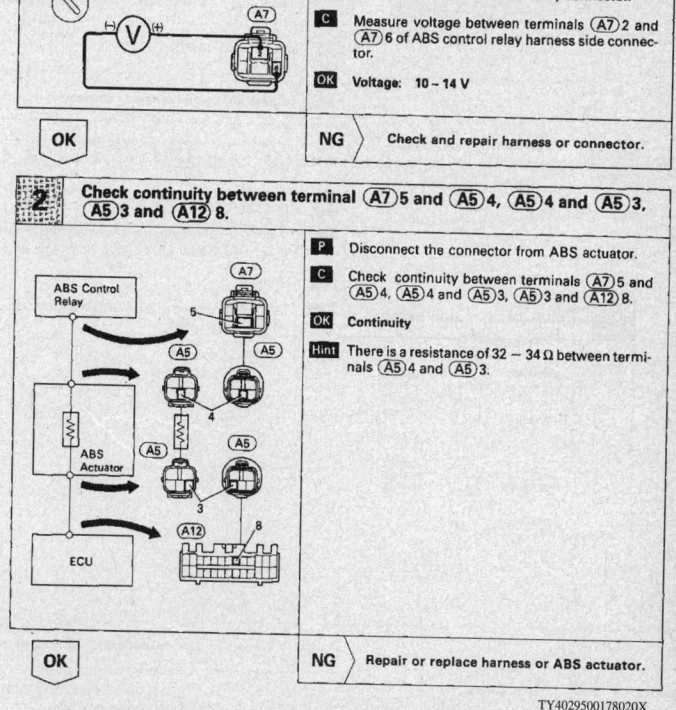

P Disconnect the connector from ABS actuator.

C Check continuity between terminals (A7)5 and (A5)4, (A5)4 and (A5)3, (A5)3 and (A12)8.

OK Continuity

Hint There is a resistance of 32 ~ 34 Ω between terminals (A5)4 and (A5)3.

OK	NG 〉 Repair or replace harness or ABS actuator.

TY4029500178020X

Fig. 159 Code 11 & 12: ABS Control Solenoid Relay Circuit (Part 2 of 3). 1995–96 Tercel

3 Check ABS control relay.

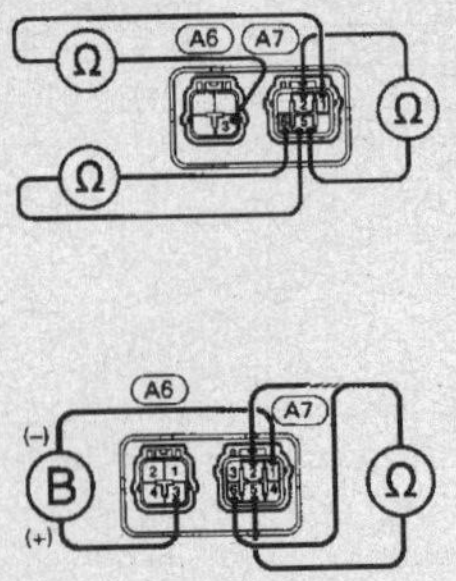
A6
A7
(–)
B
(+)

C Check continuity between each terminal of ABS control relay shown below.

OK

Terminals (A7) 1 and (A6) 3	Continuity (Reference value 80 Ω)
Terminals (A7) 5 and (A7) 6	Continuity
Terminals (A7) 2 and (A7) 5	Open

C (1) Apply battery voltage between terminals (A7) 1 and (A6) 3.
(2) Check continuity between each terminal of ABS control relay shown below.

OK

Terminals (A7) 5 and (A7) 6	Open
Terminals (A7) 2 and (A7) 5	Continuity

OK

NG Replace ABS control relay.

4 Check for open and short in harness and connector between ABS control relay and ABS ECU

OK

NG Repair or replace harness or connector.

If the same code is still output after the DTC is deleted, check the contact condition of each connection. If the connections are normal, the ECU may be defective.

TY4029500178030X

Fig. 159 Code 11 & 12: ABS Control Solenoid Relay Circuit (Part 3 of 3). 1995–96 Tercel

1 Check voltage between terminals (A6) 1 of ABS control relay and body ground.

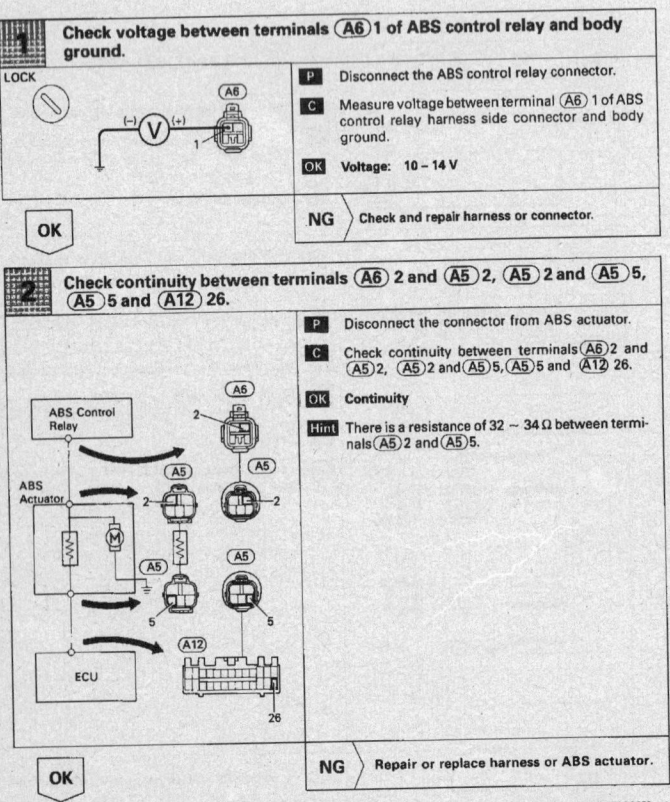

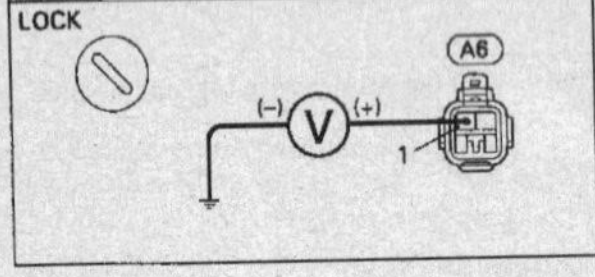
LOCK
A6
(–)
(+)
V
1

P Disconnect the ABS control relay connector.

C Measure voltage between terminal (A6) 1 of ABS control relay harness side connector and body ground.

OK **Voltage: 10 – 14 V**

OK

NG Check and repair harness or connector.

2 Check continuity between terminals (A6) 2 and (A5) 2, (A5) 2 and (A5) 5, (A5) 5 and (A12) 26.

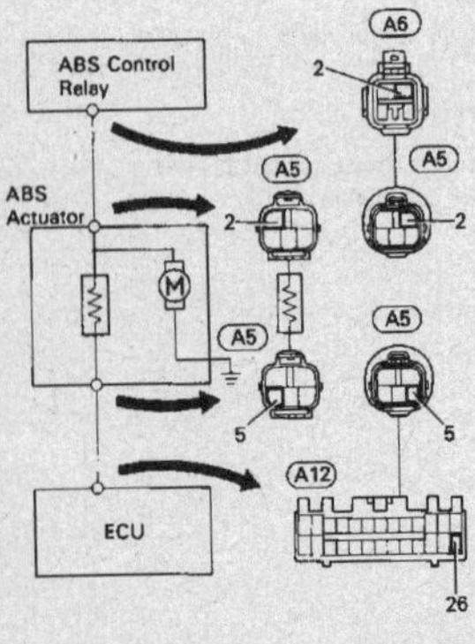
ABS Control Relay
ABS Actuator
ECU
A6
A5
A12
M
26

P Disconnect the connector from ABS actuator.

C Check continuity between terminals (A6) 2 and (A5) 2, (A5) 2 and (A5) 5, (A5) 5 and (A12) 26.

OK **Continuity**

Hint There is a resistance of 32 ~ 34 Ω between terminals (A5) 2 and (A5) 5.

OK

NG Repair or replace harness or ABS actuator.

TY4029500179020X

Fig. 160 Code 13 & 14: ABS Control Motor Relay Circuit (Part 2 of 3). 1995–96 Tercel

CIRCUIT DESCRIPTION

The ABS control (motor) relay supplies power to the ABS pump motor. While the ABS is activated, the ECU switches the ABS control (motor) relay on and operates the ABS pump motor.

DTC No.	DTC Detecting Condition	Trouble Area
13	Conditions (1) and (2) continue for 0.2 sec. or more: (1) ABS control (motor) relay terminal (MR) voltage: Battery positive voltage (2) ABS control (motor) relay monitor terminal (MT) voltage: 0 V	• ABS control (motor) relay • Open or short in ABS control (motor) relay circuit • ECU
14	Conditions (1) and (2) continued for 4 sec. or more: (1) ABS control (motor) relay terminal (MR) voltage: 0 V (2) ABS control (motor) relay monitor terminal (MT) voltage: Battery positive voltage	• ABS control (motor) relay • B+ short in ABS control (motor) relay circuit • ECU

Fail safe function: If trouble occurs in the ABS control (motor) relay circuit, the ECU cuts off the current to the ABS control (solenoid) relay and prohibits ABS control.

WIRING DIAGRAM

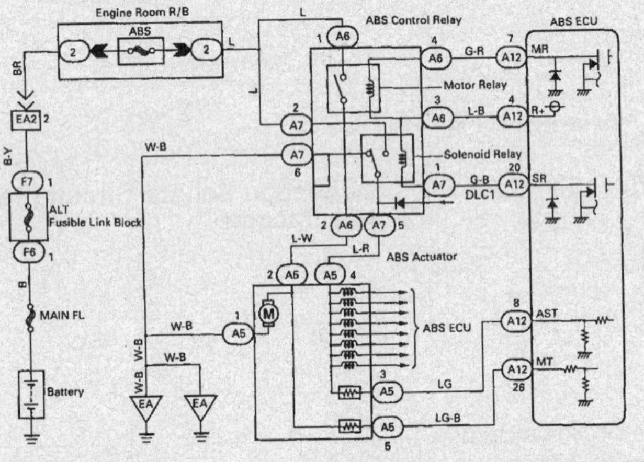
Engine Room R/B
ABS
ABS Control Relay
ABS ECU
Motor Relay
Solenoid Relay
DLC1
ALT
Fusible Link Block
MAIN FL
Battery
ABS Actuator
ABS ECU
MR
R+
SR
AST
MT
G-R
L-B
G-B
W-B
B-Y
BR
L-W
L-R
LG
LG-B

TY4029500179010X

Fig. 160 Code 13 & 14: ABS Control Motor Relay Circuit (Part 1 of 3). 1995–96 Tercel

3 Check ABS control relay.

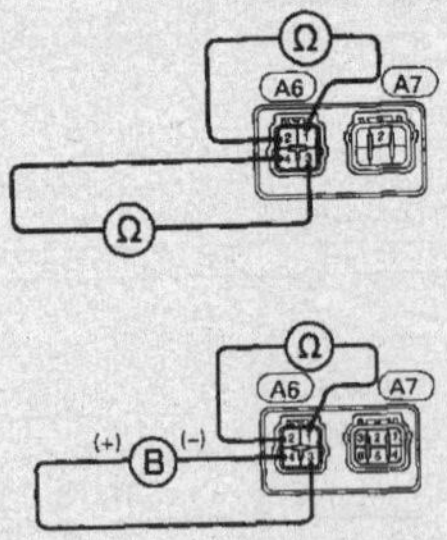
A6
A7
(+)
B
(–)

C Check continuity between each terminal of ABS control relay shown below.

OK

Terminals (A6) 3 and (A6) 4	Continuity (Reference value 62 Ω)
Terminals (A6) 1 and (A6) 2	Open

C (1) Apply battery voltage between terminals (A6) 3 and (A6) 4.
(2) Check continuity between each terminal of ABS control relay shown below.

OK

Terminals (A6) 1 and (A6) 2	Continuity

OK

NG Replace ABS control relay.

4 Check for open and short in harness and connector between ABS control relay and ABS ECU

OK

NG Repair or replace harness or connector.

If the same code is still output after the DTC is deleted, check the contact condition of each connection. If the connections are normal, the ECU may be defective.

TY4029500179030X

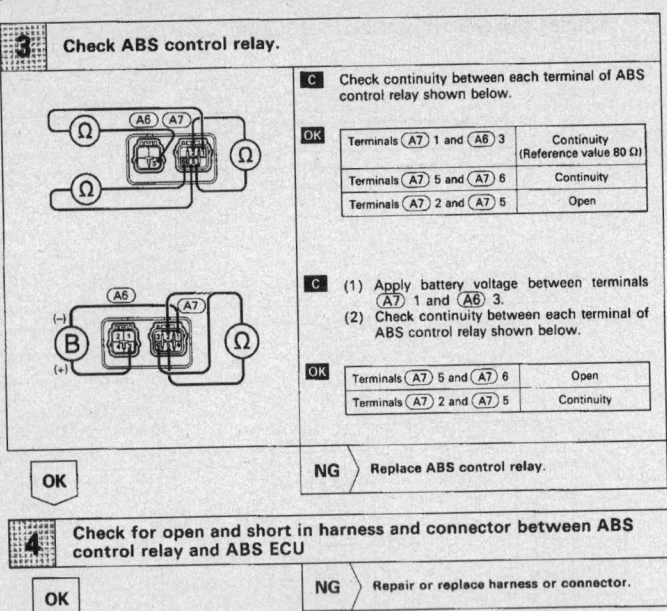

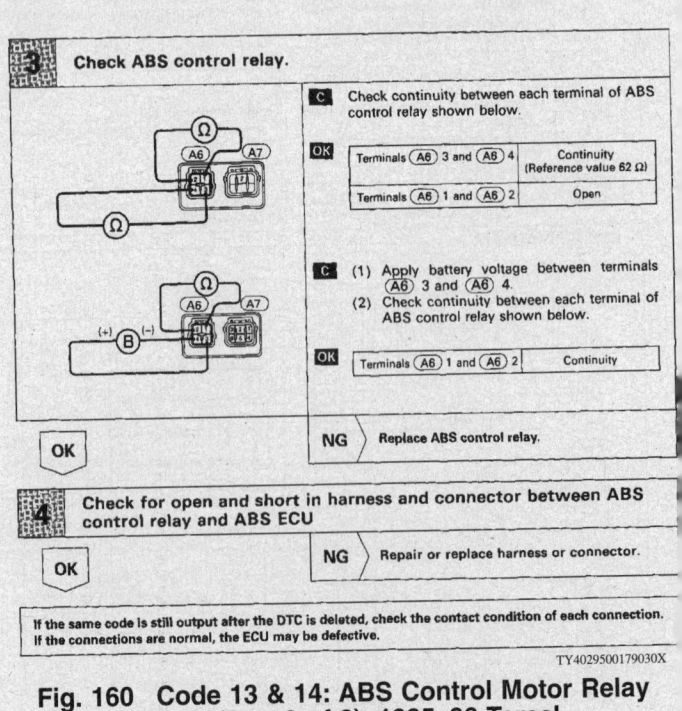

Fig. 160 Code 13 & 14: ABS Control Motor Relay Circuit (Part 3 of 3). 1995–96 Tercel

CIRCUIT DESCRIPTION

This solenoid goes on when signals are received from the ECU and controls the pressure acting on the brake cylinders, thus controlling the braking force.

DTC No.	DTC Detecting Condition	Trouble Area
21	Conditions (1) through (3) continue for 0.05 sec. or more: (1) ABS control (solenoid) relay terminal (SR) voltage: Battery positive voltage (2) Voltage or ABS ECU terminal AST: Battery positive voltage (3) When power transistor of ECU is ON, voltage of terminal SFR is 0 V or battery positive voltage.	• ABS actuator • Open or short in SFR circuit • ECU
22	Conditions (1) through (3) continue for 0.05 sec. or more: (1) ABS control (solenoid) relay terminal (SR) voltage: Battery positive voltage (2) Voltage of ABS ECU terminal AST: Battery positive voltage (3) When power transistor of ECU is ON, voltage of terminal SFL is 0 V or battery positive voltage.	• ABS actuator • Open or short in SFL circuit • ECU
23	Conditions (1) through (3) continue for 0.05 sec. or more: (1) ABS control (solenoid) relay terminal (SR) voltage: Battery positive voltage (2) Voltage of ABS ECU terminal AST: Battery positive voltage (3) When power transistor of ECU is ON, voltage of terminal SRR is 0 V or battery positive voltage.	• ABS actuator • Open or short in SRR circuit • ECU
24	Conditions (1) through (3) continue for 0.05 sec. or more: (1) ABS control (solenoid) relay terminal (SR) voltage: Battery positive voltage (2) Voltage of ABS ECU terminal AST: Battery positive voltage (3) When power transistor of ECU is ON, voltage of terminal SRL is 0 V or battery positive voltage.	• ABS actuator • Open or short in SRL circuit • ECU

Fail safe function: If trouble occurs in the actuator solenoid circuit, the ECU cuts off current to the ABS control (solenoid) relay and prohibits ABS control.

TY4029500180010X

Fig. 161 Code 21, 22, 23 & 24: ABS Actuator Solenoid Circuit (Part 1 of 3). 1995–96 Tercel

WIRING DIAGRAM

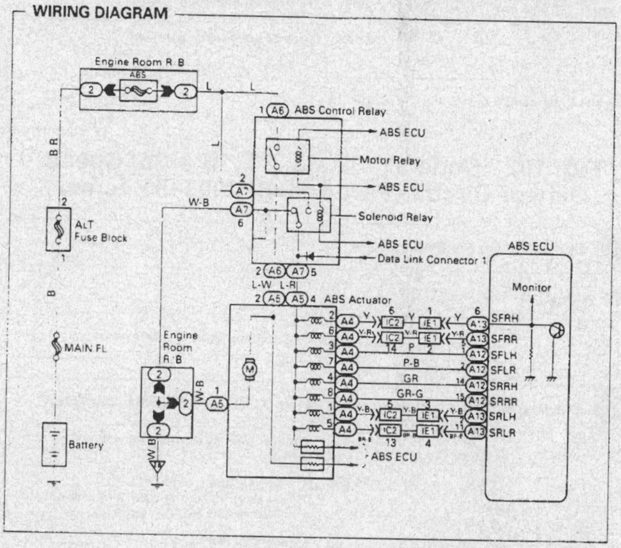
Engine Room R/B
ABS
ABS Control Relay
ABS ECU
Motor Relay
ABS ECU
Solenoid Relay
ABS ECU
Data Link Connector 1
ABS ECU
ALT
Fuse Block
MAIN FL
Battery
Engine Room R/B
ABS Actuator
Monitor
SFRH
SFRR
SFLH
SFLR
SRRH
SRRR
SRLH
SRLR
ABS ECU

TY4029500180020X

Fig. 161 Code 21, 22, 23 & 24: ABS Actuator Solenoid Circuit (Part 2 of 3). 1995–96 Tercel

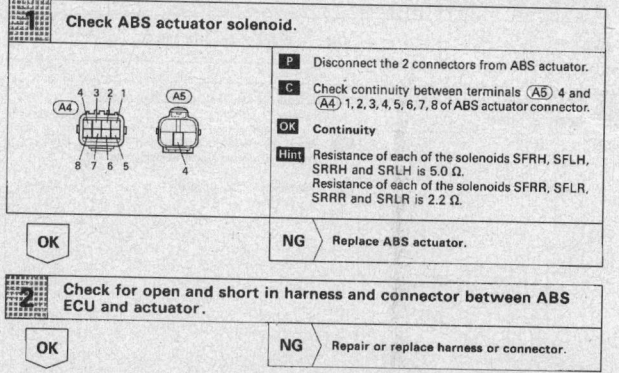

1 Check ABS actuator solenoid.

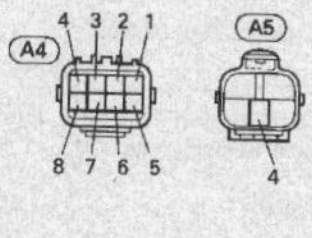
A4
4 3 2 1
8 7 6 5
A5
4

P Disconnect the 2 connectors from ABS actuator.

C Check continuity between terminals (A5) 4 and (A4) 1, 2, 3, 4, 5, 6, 7, 8 of ABS actuator connector.

OK Continuity

Hint Resistance of each of the solenoids SFRH, SFLH, SRRH and SRLH is 5.0 Ω. Resistance of each of the solenoids SFRR, SFLR, SRRR and SRLR is 2.2 Ω.

OK | NG > Replace ABS actuator.

2 Check for open and short in harness and connector between ABS ECU and actuator.

OK | NG > Repair or replace harness or connector.

If the same code is still output after the DTC is deleted, check the contact condition of each connection. If the connections are normal, the ECU may be defective.

TY4029500180030X

Fig. 161 Code 21, 22, 23 & 24: ABS Actuator Solenoid Circuit (Part 3 of 3). 1995–96 Tercel

CIRCUIT DESCRIPTION

The speed sensor detects the wheel speed and sends the appropriate signals to the ECU. These signals are used to control the ABS system. The front and rear rotors each have 48 serrations. When the rotors rotate, the magnetic field emitted by the permanent magnet in the speed sensor generates an AC voltage. Since the frequency of this AC voltage changes in direct proportion to the speed of the rotors, the frequency is used by the ECU to detect the speed of each wheel.

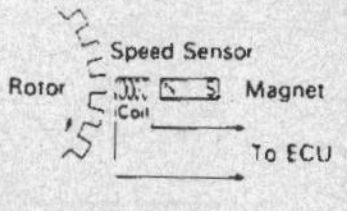
Speed Sensor
Rotor
Coil
Magnet
To ECU

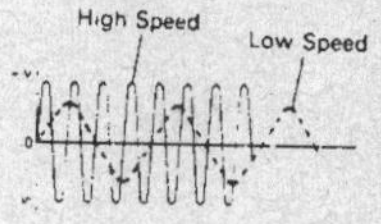
High Speed
Low Speed

DTC No.	Diagnostic Trouble Code Detecting Condition	Trouble Area
31, 32, 33, 34	Detection of any of conditions (1) through (3): (1) At vehicle speed of 10 km/h (6 mph) or more, pulses are not input for 5 sec. (2) Momentary interruption of the speed sensor signal occurs at least 7 times in the time between switching the ignition switch ON and switching it OFF. (3) Abnormal fluctuation of speed sensor signals with the vehicle speed 20 km/h (12 mph) or more.	• Right front, left front, right rear and left rear speed sensor • Open or short in each speed sensor circuit • ECU
35	Speed sensor signal is not input for about 1 sec. while the left front and right rear speed sensor signals are being checked with the IG switch ON.	• Open in left front or right rear speed sensor circuit • ECU
36	Vehicle speed sensor signal is not input for about 1 sec. while the right front and left rear speed sensor signals are being checked with the IG switch ON.	• Open in right front of left rear speed sensor circuit • ECU

HINT: DTC 31 is for the right front speed sensor.
DTC 32 is for the left front speed sensor.
DTC 33 is for the right rear speed sensor.
DTC 34 is for the left rear speed sensor.

Fail safe function: If trouble occurs in the speed sensor circuit, the ECU cuts off current to the ABS control (solenoid) relay and prohibits ABS control.

TY4029500181010X

Fig. 162 Code 31, 32, 33, 34, 35 & 36: Speed Sensor Circuit (Part 1 of 4). 1995–96 Tercel

WIRING DIAGRAM

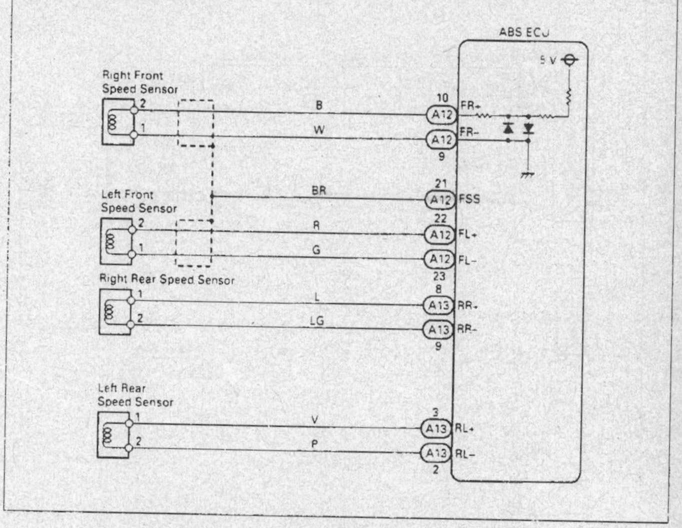
ABS ECU
5 V
Right Front Speed Sensor
B
W
FR+
FR-
Left Front Speed Sensor
BR
FSS
R
G
FL+
FL-
Right Rear Speed Sensor
L
LG
RR+
RR-
Left Rear Speed Sensor
V
P
RL+
RL-

TY4029500181020X

Fig. 162 Code 31, 32, 33, 34, 35 & 36: Speed Sensor Circuit (Part 2 of 4). 1995–96 Tercel

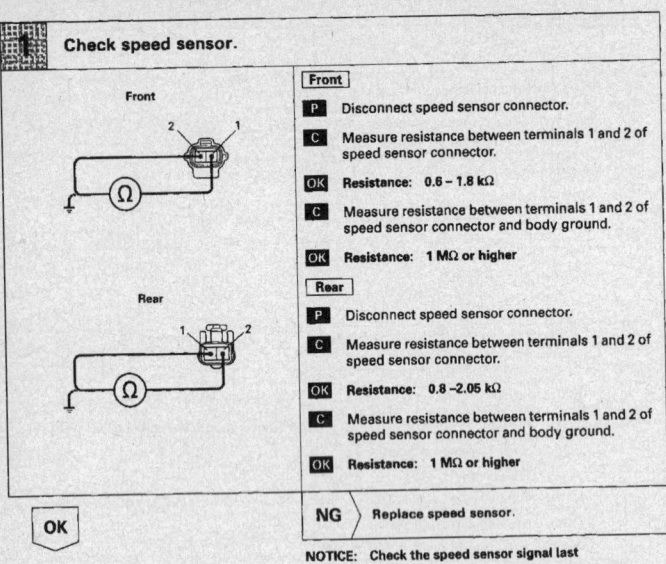

1 **Check speed sensor.**

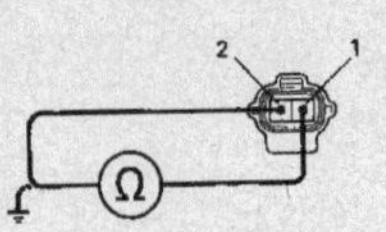
Front
2
1
Ω

Front

P Disconnect speed sensor connector.

C Measure resistance between terminals 1 and 2 of speed sensor connector.

OK **Resistance: 0.6 – 1.8 kΩ**

C Measure resistance between terminals 1 and 2 of speed sensor connector and body ground.

OK **Resistance: 1 MΩ or higher**

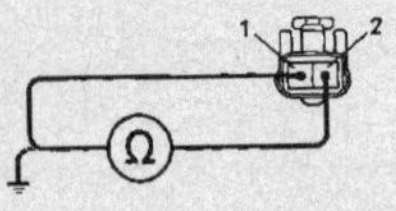
Rear
1
2
Ω

Rear

P Disconnect speed sensor connector.

C Measure resistance between terminals 1 and 2 of speed sensor connector.

OK **Resistance: 0.8 –2.05 kΩ**

C Measure resistance between terminals 1 and 2 of speed sensor connector and body ground.

OK **Resistance: 1 MΩ or higher**

OK

NG **Replace speed sensor.**

NOTICE: **Check the speed sensor signal last**

TY4029500181030X

Fig. 162 Code 31, 32, 33, 34, 35 & 36: Speed Sensor Circuit (Part 3 of 4). 1995–96 Tercel

2 **Check for open and short in harness and connector between each speed sensor and ECU.**

OK

NG **Repair or replace harness or connector.**

3 **Check sensor rotor and sensor installation.**

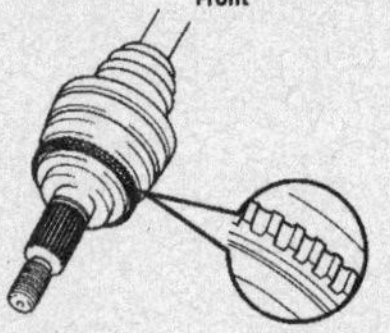
Front

Front

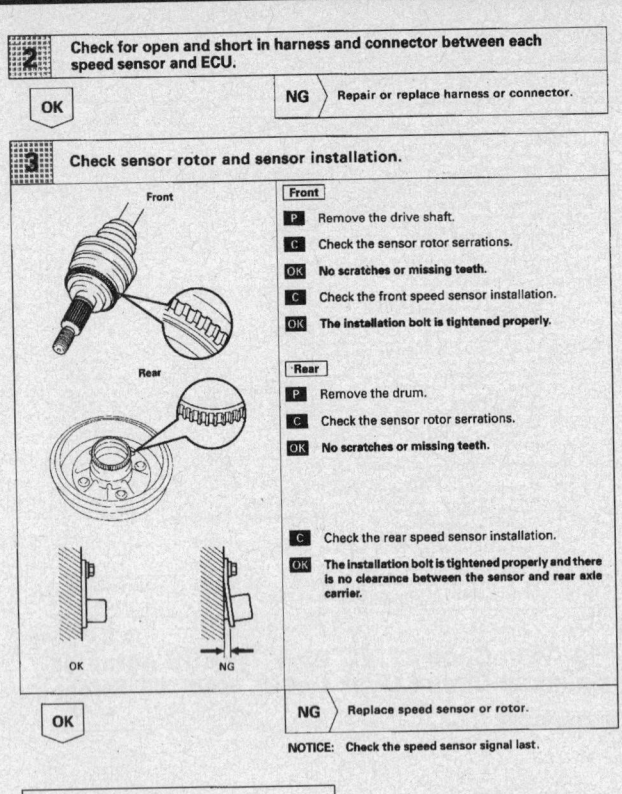

P Remove the drive shaft.

C Check the sensor rotor serrations.

OK **No scratches or missing teeth.**

C Check the front speed sensor installation.

OK **The installation bolt is tightened properly.**

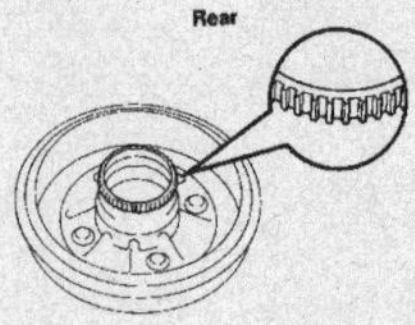
Rear

Rear

P Remove the drum.

C Check the sensor rotor serrations.

OK **No scratches or missing teeth.**

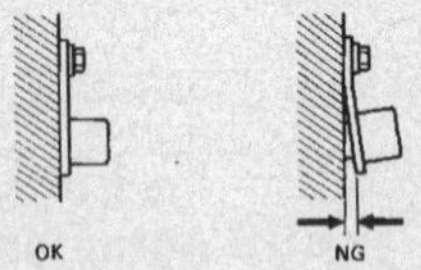
OK
NG

C Check the rear speed sensor installation.

OK **The installation bolt is tightened properly and there is no clearance between the sensor and rear axle carrier.**

OK

NG **Replace speed sensor or rotor.**

NOTICE: **Check the speed sensor signal last.**

Check and replace ABS ECU.

TY4029500181040X

Fig. 162 Code 31, 32, 33, 34, 35 & 36: Speed Sensor Circuit (Part 4 of 4). 1995–96 Tercel

CIRCUIT DESCRIPTION

This is the power source for the ECU and , hence the CPU and the actuators.

DTC No.	Diagnostic Trouble Code Detecting Condition	Trouble Area
41	Vehicle speed is 3 km/h (1.9 mph) or more and voltage of ECU terminal IG1 remains at more than 17 V or below 9.5 V for more than 10 sec.	• Battery • IC regulator • Open or short in power source circuit • ECU

Fail safe function: If trouble occurs in the power source circuit, the ECU cuts off current to the ABS control (solenoid) relay and prohibits ABS control.

WIRING DIAGRAM

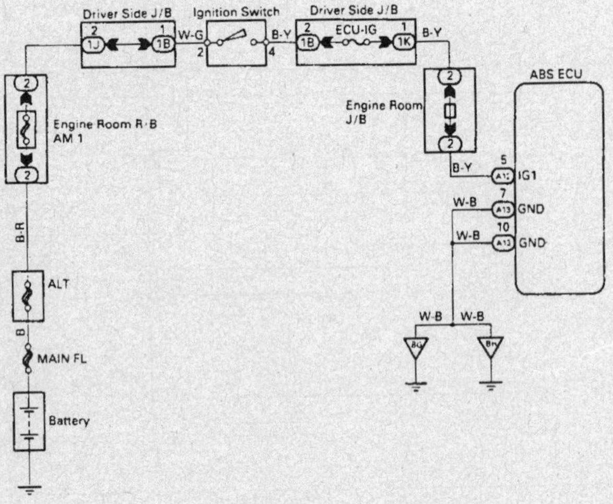
Driver Side J/B
Ignition Switch
Driver Side J/B
ECU-IG
W-G
B-Y
B-Y
1J
1B
1B
1K
2
4
ABS ECU
Engine Room R/B
AM 1
Engine Room J/B
B-Y
IG1
W-B
GND
W-B
GND
A13
B-R
ALT
B
MAIN FL
W-B
W-B
Battery

TY4029500182010X

Fig. 163 Code 41: IG Power Source Circuit (Part 1 of 3). 1995–96 Tercel

1 **Check battery positive voltage**

OK **Voltage: 10 – 14 V**

OK

NG **Check and repair the charging system.**

2 **Check voltage between terminals IG1 and GND of ABS ECU connector.**

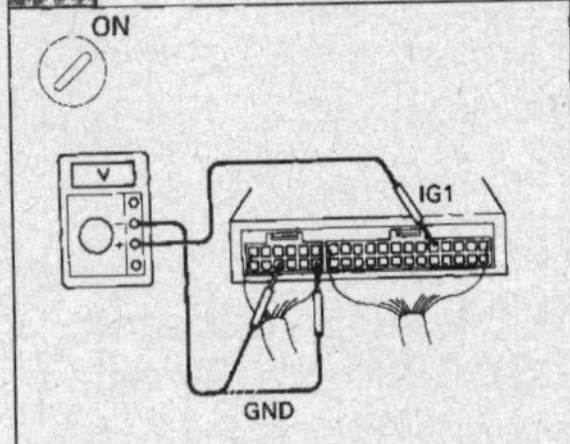
ON
V
IG1
GND

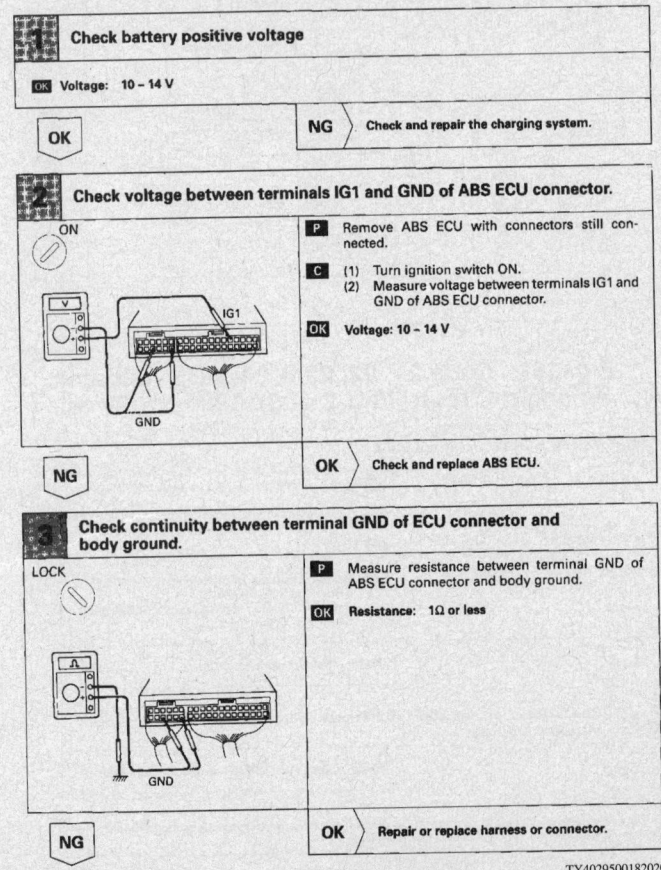

P Remove ABS ECU with connectors still connected.

C (1) Turn ignition switch ON.
(2) Measure voltage between terminals IG1 and GND of ABS ECU connector.

OK **Voltage: 10 – 14 V**

NG

OK **Check and replace ABS ECU.**

3 **Check continuity between terminal GND of ECU connector and body ground.**

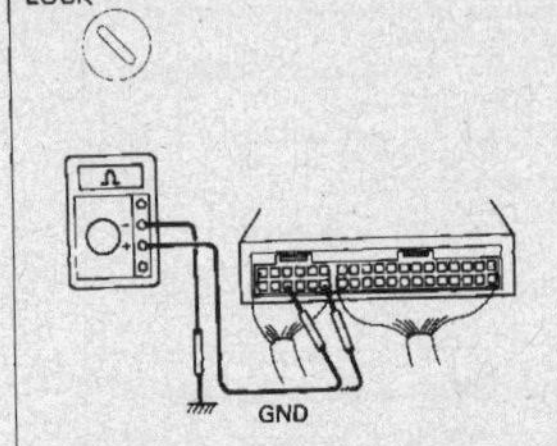
LOCK
Ω
GND

P Measure resistance between terminal GND of ABS ECU connector and body ground.

OK **Resistance: 1Ω or less**

NG

OK **Repair or replace harness or connector.**

TY4029500182020X

Fig. 163 Code 41: IG Power Source Circuit (Part 2 of 3). 1995–96 Tercel

4 Check ECU-IG fuse.

Driver Side J/B

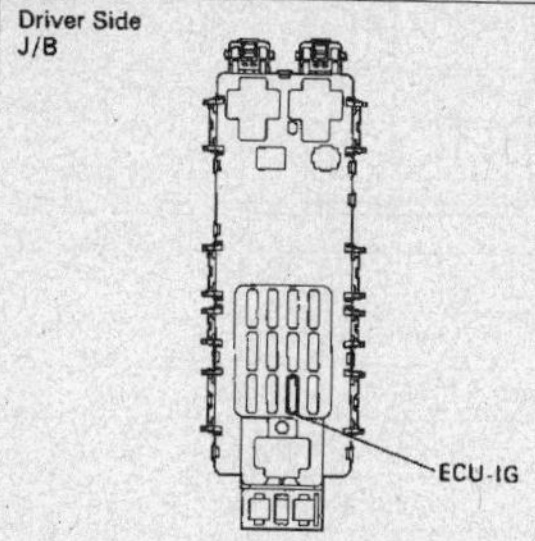
ECU-IG

P Remove ECU-IG fuse from driver side J/B.

C Check continuity of ECU-IG fuse.

OK Continuity

OK → Check for open in harness and connector between ABS ECU and battery

NG → Check for short in all the harness and components connected to ECU-IG fuse

TY4029500182030X

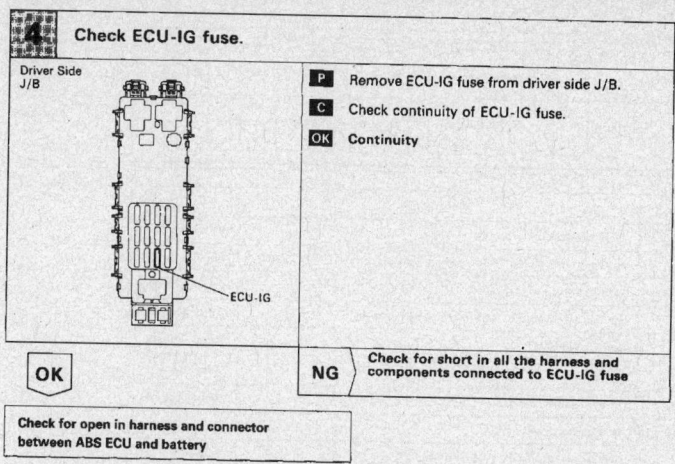

Fig. 163 Code 41: IG Power Source Circuit (Part 3 of 3). 1995–96 Tercel

DTC	51	ABS Pump Motor Lock

CIRCUIT DESCRIPTION

DTC No.	Diagnostic Trouble Code Detecting Condition	Trouble Area
51	Pump motor is not operating normally during initial check.	• ABS pump motor

Fail safe function: If trouble occurs in the ABS pump motor, the ECU cuts off the current to the ABS control (solenoid) relay and prohibits ABS control.

WIRING DIAGRAM

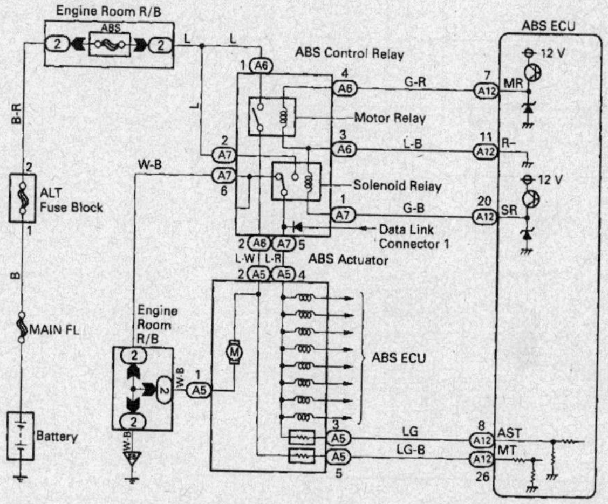
Engine Room R/B
ABS
L
ABS Control Relay
ABS ECU
12 V
G-R
MR
Motor Relay
L-B
R-
B-R
W-B
Solenoid Relay
ALT
Fuse Block
G-B
SR
Data Link Connector 1
L-W
L-R
ABS Actuator
B
Engine Room R/B
MAIN FL
ABS ECU
W-B
Battery
LG
LG-B
AST
MT

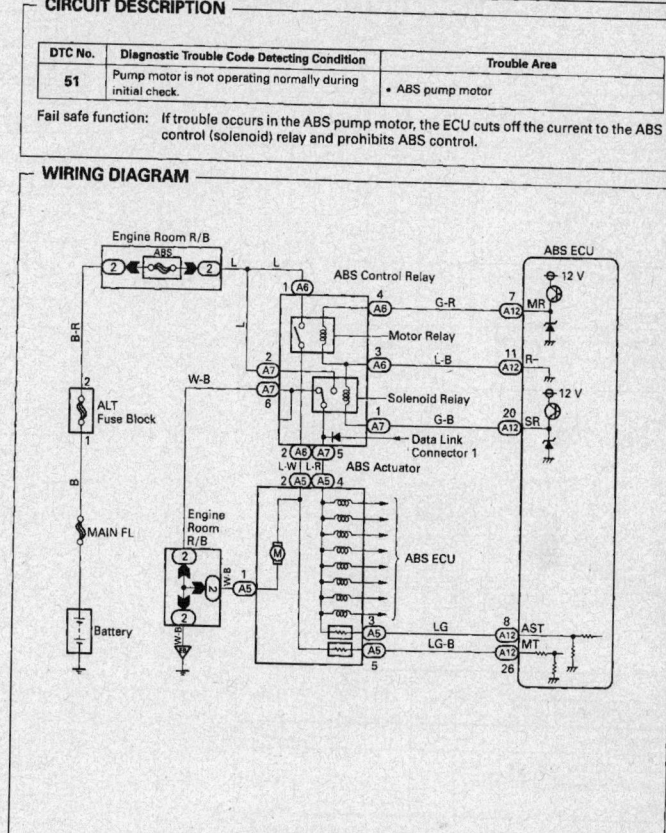

TY4029500183000X

Fig. 164 Code 51: ABS Pump Motor Lock. 1995–96 Tercel

Code No.	Light Pattern	Diagnosis	Mulfunctioning Part
	ON OFF	Speed sensor and sensor rotor are normal	
73		Low output voltage of speed sensor signal	Speed sensor Sensor rotor (Differential ring gear)
77		Abnormal change of output voltage of speed sensor signal	Sensor rotor (Differential ring gear)
79		Sticking of deceleration sensor pendulum	Deceleration sensor

TY4029200205000X

Fig. 165 Speed sensor diagnostic trouble codes. 1993 Pickup, 4Runner & T100

Code No.	Light Pattern	Diagnosis	Malfunctioning Part
	ON OFF	All speed sensors and sensor rotors are normal	
71		Low voltage of front right speed sensor signal	• Front right speed sensor • Sensor installation
72		Low voltage of front left speed sensor signal	• Front left speed sensor • Sensor installation
73		Low voltage of rear right speed sensor signal	• Rear right speed sensor • Sensor installation
74		Low voltage of rear left speed sensor signal	• Rear left speed sensor • Sensor installation
75		Abnormal change of front right speed sensor signal	• Front right sensor rotor
76		Abnormal change of front left speed sensor signal	• Front left sensor rotor
77		Abnormal change of rear right speed sensor signal	• Rear right sensor rotor
78		Abnormal change of rear left speed sensor signal	• Rear left sensor rotor
79		Deceleration sensor is faulty	• Deceleration sensor • Sensor installation

TY4029300106000X

Fig. 166 Speed sensor diagnostic trouble codes. Land Cruiser, 1994–96 Pickup, Tacoma, T100 & 4Runner

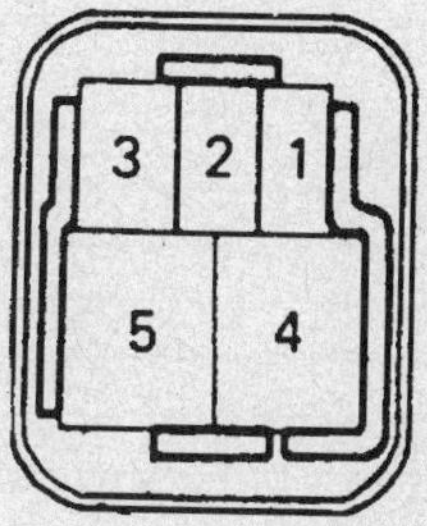
3
2
1
5
4

TY4029100111000X

Fig. 167 Solenoid relay. Except Celica, Pickup, Tacoma, T100, 4Runner, Avalon, Camry & Land Cruiser

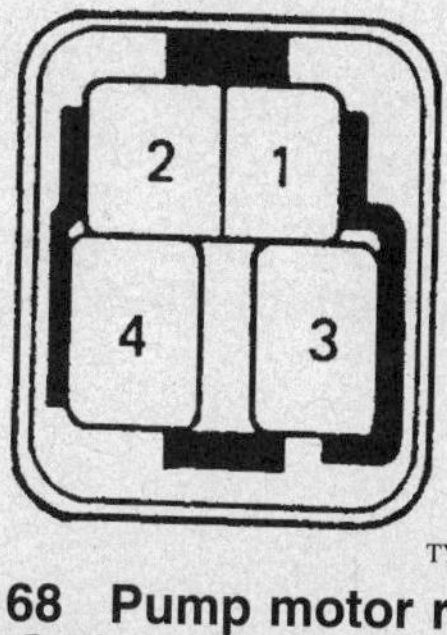
2
1
4
3

TY4029100112000X

Fig. 168 Pump motor relay. Except Celica, Pickup, Tacoma, T100, 4Runner, Avalon, Camry & Land Cruiser

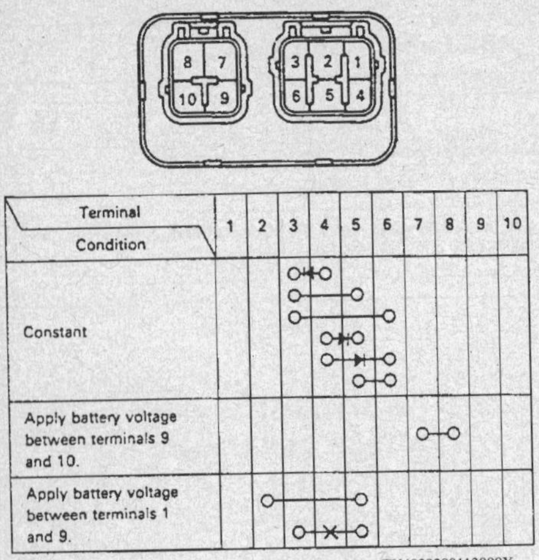
8
7
10
9
3
2
1
6
5
4
Terminal
Condition
1 2 3 4 5 6 7 8 9 10
Constant
Apply battery voltage between terminals 9 and 10.
Apply battery voltage between terminals 1 and 9.

TY4029200113000X

Fig. 169 Control relay. Celica

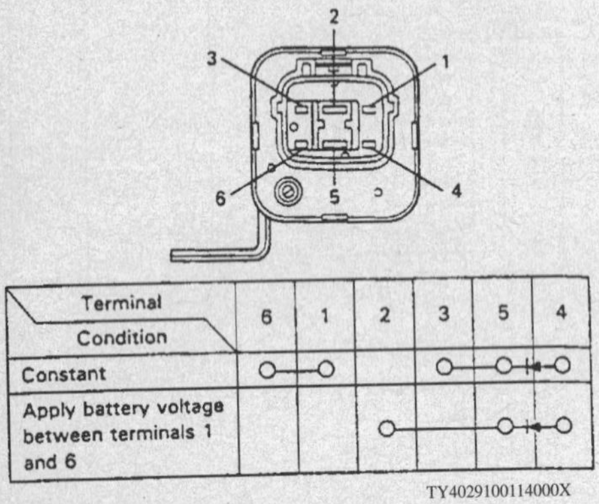
2
3
1
6
5
4
Terminal
Condition
6 1 2 3 5 4
Constant
Apply battery voltage between terminals 1 and 6

TY4029100114000X

Fig. 170 Control relay. Pickup, Tacoma, 4Runner & T100

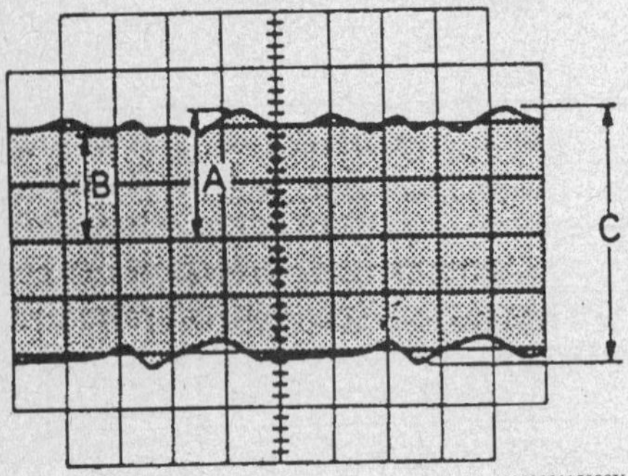
B
A
C

TY4029300115000X

Fig. 171 Front & rear speed sensor inspection. Avalon, RAV4, Supra, 1994–96 Camry & Celica

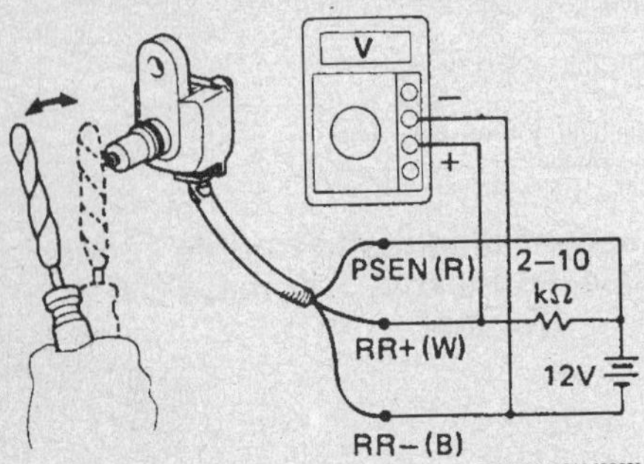
V
−
+
PSEN (R)
2–10 kΩ
RR+ (W)
12V
RR− (B)

TY4029100116000X

Fig. 172 Rear speed sensor circuit test

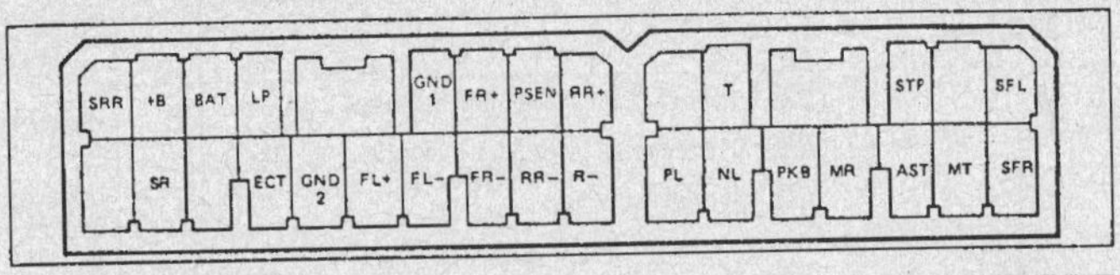
SRR
+B
BAT
LP
GND 1
FR+
PSEN
RR+
T
STP
SFL
SR
ECT
GND 2
FL+
FL−
FR−
RR−
R−
PL
NL
PKB
MR
AST
MT
SFR

Tester Connection	Condition	Voltage
SFL – Body ground	Ignition switch on	Battery voltage
	Ignition switch on and "ABS" warning light goes on	About 0 V
SFR – Body ground	Ignition switch on	Battery voltage
	Ignition switch on and "ABS" warning light goes on	About 0 V
AST – Body ground	Ignition switch on	Battery voltage
	Ignition switch on and "ABS" warning light goes on	About 0 V
PESN – Body ground	Ignition switch on	Battery voltage
LP – Body ground	Ignition switch on	Battery voltage
	Ignition switch on and "ABS" warning light goes on	About 0 V
SRR – Body ground	Ignition switch on	Battery voltage
	Ignition switch on and "ABS" warning light goes on	About 0 V

TY4029200117000X

Fig. 173 Anti-lock brake system circuit test (w/ computer connector connected). 1993 Supra

Tester Connection	Check Item	Condition	Voltage or Resistance Value
SFL – AST	Resistance	Ignition switch off	About 1 Ω
STP – Body ground	Voltage	Ignition switch off and brake pedal depressed	Battery voltage
	Continuity	Ignition switch off and brake pedal returned	Continuity
T – Body ground	Continuity	Ignition switch off	Continuity
SFR – AST	Resistance	Ignition switch off	About 1 Ω
MT – Body ground	Continuity	Ignition switch off	Continuity
AST – Body ground	Continuity	Ignition switch off	Continuity
MR – R ⊖	Resistance	Ignition switch off	50 – 80 Ω
PKB – Body ground	Voltage	Ignition switch on and PKB lever pulled	About 0 V
		Engine running and PKB lever returned	Battery voltage
NL – Body ground	Voltage	Ignition switch on and shift into "N" range	Battery voltage
PL – Body ground	Voltage	Ignition switch on and shift into "P" range	Battery voltage
FR ⊕ – FR ⊖	Resistance	Ignition switch off	0.8 – 1.3 kΩ
GND1 – Body ground	Continuity	Ignition switch off	Continuity
BAT – Body ground	Voltage	–	Battery voltage
+B – Body ground	Voltage	Ignition switch on	Battery voltage
SRR – AST	Resistance	Ignition switch off	About 1 Ω
R ⊖ – Body ground	Continuity	Ignition switch off	No continuity
RR ⊖ – Body ground	Continuity	Ignition switch off	No continuity
FR ⊖ – Body ground	Continuity	Ignition switch off	No continuity
FL ⊖ – Body ground	Continuity	Ignition switch off	No continuity
FL ⊕ – FL ⊖	Resistance	Ignition switch off	0.8 – 1.3 kΩ
GND2 – Body ground	Continuity	Ignition switch off	Continuity
ECT – Body ground	Voltage	Ignition switch on and shift into "N" or "P" range	About 5 V
SR – R ⊖	Resistance	Ignition switch off	65 – 100 Ω

TY4029200127000X

Fig. 174 Anti-lock brake system circuit test (w/ computer connector disconnected). 1993 Supra

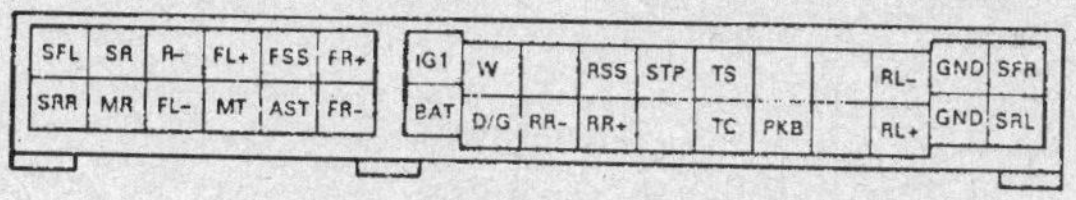
SFL SR R- FL+ FSS FR+
SRR MR FL- MT AST FR-
IG1 W RSS STP TS RL- GND SFR
BAT D/G RR- RR+ TC PKB RL+ GND SRL

Tester Connection	Check Item	Condition	Specified Value	Trouble Part
SFR	Voltage	IG switch on and "ABS" warning light goes on	About 0V	Actuator
		IG switch on and "ABS" warning light goes off	Battery voltage	
RL-	Continuity	IG switch off	Continuity	ABS ECU
TS	Voltage	IG switch on and check connector Ts-E, not connected	Battery voltage	
		IG switch on and check connector Ts-E, connected	About 0V	
STP	Voltage	IG switch off and brake pedal depressed	Battery voltage	Stop light switch
	Continuity	IG switch off and brake pedal returned	Continuity	Stop light
RSS	Continuity	IG switch off	Continuity	ABS ECU
W	Voltage	IG switch on and "ABS" warning light goes on	About 0V	ABS ECU
		IG switch on and "ABS" warning light goes off	Battery voltage	"ABS" warning light
IG1	Voltage	IG switch on	Battery voltage	ECU-IG Fuse
SRL	Voltage	IG switch on and "ABS" warning light goes on	About 0V	Actuator
		IG switch on and "ABS" warning light goes off	Battery voltage	
GND	Continuity	IG switch off	Continuity	Wiring harness
PKB	Voltage	IG switch on and PKB lever pulled	About 0V	Parking brake switch
		IG switch on and PKB lever returned	Battery voltage	Level warning switch
TC	Voltage	IG switch on and check connector Tc-E, not connected	Battery voltage	ABS ECU
		IG switch on and check connector Tc-E, connected	About 0V	
RR-	Continuity	IG switch off	Continuity	
D/G	Voltage	IG switch on and check connector Ts-E, not connected	About 0V	
BAT	Voltage	IG switch off	Battery voltage	DOME Fuse
FSS	Continuity	IG switch off	Continuity	ABS ECU
R-	Continuity	IG switch off	Continuity	

TY4029200118010X

Fig. 175 Anti-lock brake system circuit test (w/ computer connector connected, Part 1 of 2). 1993 Celica w/2WD

Tester Connection	Check Item	Condition	Specified Value	Trouble Part
SR	Voltage	IG switch on and "ABS" warning light goes on	About 0V	ABS ECU
		IG switch on and "ABS" warning light goes off	Battery voltage	
SFL	Voltage	IG switch on and "ABS" warning light goes on	About 0V	Actuator
		IG switch on and "ABS" warning light goes off	Battery voltage	
FR-	Continuity	IG switch off	Continuity	ABS ECU
AST	Voltage	IG switch on and "ABS" warning light goes on	About 0V	Actuator
		IG switch on and "ABS" warning light goes off	Battery voltage	
FL-	Continuity	IG switch off	Continuity	ABS ECU
SRR	Voltage	IG switch on and "ABS" warning light goes on	About 0V	Actuator
		IG switch on and "ABS" warning light goes off	Battery voltage	

TY4029200118020X

Fig. 175 Anti-lock brake system circuit test (w/ computer connector connected, Part 2 of 2). 1993 Celica w/2WD

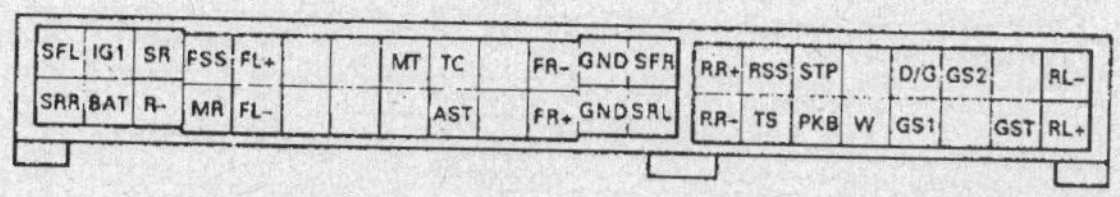
SFL IG1 SR FSS FL+ MT TC FR- GND SFR
SRR BAT R- MR FL- AST FR+ GND SRL
RR+ RSS STP D/G GS2 RL-
RR- TS PKB W GS1 GST RL+

Tester Connection	Check Item	Condition	Specified Value	Trouble Part
RL-	Continuity	IG switch off	Continuity	ABS ECU
GS2	Voltage	IG switch on	4 ~ 6 V	Deceleration Sensor
D/G	Voltage	IG switch on and check connector Ts-E, not connected	About 0V	ABS ECU
STP	Voltage	IG switch off and brake pedal depressed	Battery voltage	Stop light switch
	Continuity	IG switch off and brake pedal returned	Continuity	Stop light
RSS	Continuity	IG switch off	Continuity	ABS ECU
GS1	Voltage	IG switch on	4 ~ 6 V	Deceleration Sensor
W	Voltage	IG switch on and "ABS" warning light goes on	About 0V	ABS ECU
		IG switch on and "ABS" warning light goes off	Battery voltage	"ABS" warning light
PKB	Voltage	IG switch on and PKB lever pulled	About 0V	Parking brake switch
		IG switch on and PKB lever returned	Battery voltage	Level warning switch
TS	Voltage	IG switch on and check connector Ts-E, not connected	Battery voltage	ABS ECU
		IG switch on and check connector Ts-E, connected	About 0V	
RR-	Continuity	IG switch off	Continuity	
SFR	Voltage	IG switch on and "ABS" warning light goes on	About 0V	Actuator
		IG switch on and "ABS" warning light goes off	Battery voltage	
GND	Continuity	IG switch off	Continuity	Wiring harness
FR-	Continuity	IG switch off	Continuity	ABS ECU
TC	Voltage	IG switch on and check connector Tc-E, not connected	Battery voltage	
		IG switch on and check connector Tc-E, connected	About 0V	
FSS	Continuity	IG switch off	Continuity	
SR	Voltage	IG switch on and "ABS" warning light goes on	About 0V	
		IG switch on and "ABS" warning light goes off	Battery voltage	
IG1	Voltage	IG switch on	Battery voltage	ECU-IG Fuse

TY4029200119010X

Fig. 176 Anti-lock brake system circuit test (w/ computer connector connected, Part 1 of 2). 1993 Celica w/4WD

Tester Connection	Check Item	Condition	Specified Value	Trouble Part
SFL	Voltage	IG switch on and "ABS" warning light goes on	About 0V	Actuator
		IG switch on and "ABS" warning light goes off	Battery voltage	
SRL	Voltage	IG switch on and "ABS" warning light goes on	About 0V	
		IG switch on and "ABS" warning light goes off	Battery voltage	
AST	Voltage	IG switch on and "ABS" warning light goes on	About 0V	
		IG switch on and "ABS" warning light goes off	Battery voltage	
FL-	Continuity	IG switch off	Continuity	ABS ECU
R-	Continuity	IG switch off	Continuity	
BAT	Voltage	IG switch off	Battery voltage	DOME Fuse
SRR	Voltage	IG switch on and "ABS" warning light goes on	About 0V	Actuator
		IG switch on and "ABS" warning light goes off	Battery voltage	

TY4029200119020X

Fig. 176 Anti-lock brake system circuit test (w/ computer connector connected, Part 2 of 2). 1993 Celica w/4WD

Tester Connection	Check Item	Specified Value	Trouble Part	Tester Connection	Check Item	Specified Value	Trouble Part
SFR ↔ AST	Resistance	About 6 Ω	Actuator	SR ↔ R-	Resistance	60 ~ 100 Ω	Control relay
SRL ↔ AST	Resistance	About 6 Ω	Actuator	SFL ↔ AST	Resistance	About 6 Ω	Actuator
RL+ ↔ RL-	Resistance	1.1 ~ 1.7 kΩ	Rear LH speed sensor	AST ↔ Body ground	Resistance	About 5 Ω	Actuator
RR+ ↔ RR-	Resistance	1.1 ~ 1.7 kΩ	Rear RH speed sensor	MT ↔ Body ground	Continuity	Continuity	Actuator
FR+ ↔ FR-	Resistance	0.8 ~ 1.3 kΩ	Front RH speed sensor	MR ↔ R-	Resistance	50 ~ 80 Ω	Control relay
FL+ ↔ FL-	Resistance	0.8 ~ 1.3 kΩ	Front LH speed sensor	SRR ↔ AST	Resistance	About 6 Ω	Actuator

TY4029100128000X

Fig. 177 Anti-lock brake system circuit test (w/ computer connector disconnected). 1993 Celica w/2WD

Tester Connection	Check Item	Specified Value	Trouble Part	Tester Connection	Check Item	Specified Value	Trouble Part
RR+ ↔ RR-	Resistance	1.1 ~ 1.7 kΩ	Rear RH speed sensor	SFL ↔ AST	Resistance	About 6 Ω	Actuator
RL+ ↔ RL-	Resistance	1.1 ~ 1.7 kΩ	Rear LH speed sensor	SRL ↔ AST	Resistance	About 6 Ω	Actuator
SFR ↔ AST	Resistance	About 6 Ω	Actuator	FR+ ↔ FR-	Resistance	0.8 ~ 1.3 kΩ	Front RH speed sensor
MT ↔ Body ground	Continuity	Continuity	Actuator	AST ↔ Body ground	Resistance	About 5 Ω	Actuator
FL+ ↔ FL-	Resistance	0.8 ~ 1.3 kΩ	Front LH speed sensor	MR ↔ R-	Resistance	50 ~ 80 Ω	Control relay
SR ↔ R-	Resistance	60 ~ 100 Ω	Control relay	SRR ↔ AST	Resistance	About 6 Ω	Actuator

TY4029100129000X

Fig. 178 Anti-lock brake system circuit test (w/ computer connector disconnected). 1993 Celica w/4WD

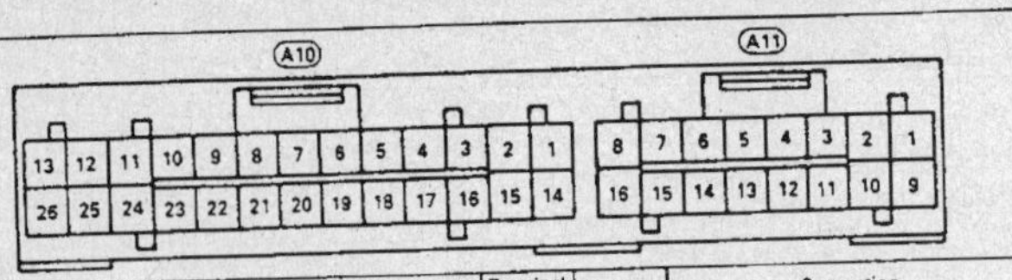
A10
A11
13
12
11
10
9
8
7
6
5
4
3
2
1
26
25
24
23
22
21
20
19
18
17
16
15
14
8
7
6
5
4
3
2
1
16
15
14
13
12
11
10
9

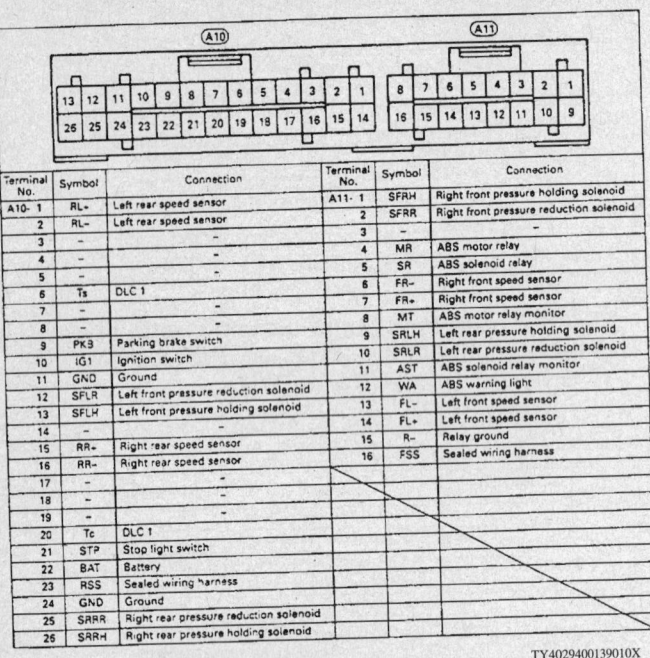

Terminal No.	Symbol	Connection	Terminal No.	Symbol	Connection
A10- 1	RL+	Left rear speed sensor	A11- 1	SFRH	Right front pressure holding solenoid
2	RL-	Left rear speed sensor	2	SFRR	Right front pressure reduction solenoid
3	-	-	3	-	-
4	-	-	4	MR	ABS motor relay
5	-	-	5	SR	ABS solenoid relay
6	Ts	DLC 1	6	FR-	Right front speed sensor
7	-	-	7	FR+	Right front speed sensor
8	-	-	8	MT	ABS motor relay monitor
9	PKB	Parking brake switch	9	SRLH	Left rear pressure holding solenoid
10	IG1	Ignition switch	10	SRLR	Left rear pressure reduction solenoid
11	GND	Ground	11	AST	ABS solenoid relay monitor
12	SFLR	Left front pressure reduction solenoid	12	WA	ABS warning light
13	SFLH	Left front pressure holding solenoid	13	FL-	Left front speed sensor
14	-	-	14	FL+	Left front speed sensor
15	RR+	Right rear speed sensor	15	R-	Relay ground
16	RR-	Right rear speed sensor	16	FSS	Sealed wiring harness
17	-	-			
18	-	-			
19	-	-			
20	Tc	DLC 1			
21	STP	Stop light switch			
22	BAT	Battery			
23	RSS	Sealed wiring harness			
24	GND	Ground			
25	SRRR	Right rear pressure reduction solenoid			
26	SRRH	Right rear pressure holding solenoid			

TY4029400139010X

Fig. 179 Anti-lock brake system circuit test (Part 1 of 2). 1994–96 Celica

Symbols (Terminals No.)	STD Voltage (V)	Condition
BAT (A10-22) - GND (A10-11/24)	10 - 14	Always
IG1 (A10-10) - GND (A10-11/24)	10 - 14	IG switch ON
SR (A11-5) - R- (A11-5)	9 - 14	IG switch ON
MR (A11-4) - R- (A11-15)	Below 1.0	IG switch ON
SFRR (A11-2) - GND (A10-11/24)	10 - 14	IG switch ON, ABS warning light OFF
SFRH (A11-1) - GND (A10-11/24)	10 - 14	IG switch ON, ABS warning light OFF
SFLR (A10-12) - GND (A10-11/24)	10 - 14	IG switch ON, ABS warning light OFF
SFLH (A10-13) - GND (A10-11/24)	10 - 14	IG switch ON, ABS warning light OFF
SRRR (A10-25) - GND (A10-11/24)	10 - 14	IG switch ON, ABS warning light OFF
SRRH (A10-26) - GND (A10-11/24)	10 - 14	IG switch ON, ABS warning light OFF
SRLR (A11-10) - GND (A10-11/24)	10 - 14	IG switch ON, ABS warning light OFF
SRLH (A11-9) - GND (A10-11/24)	10 - 14	IG switch ON, ABS warning light OFF
AST (A11-11) - GND (A10-11/24)	10 - 14	IG switch ON, ABS warning light OFF
WA (A11-12) - GND (A10-11/24)	Below 2.0	IG switch ON, ABS warning light ON
	10 - 14	IG switch ON, ABS warning light OFF
PKB (A10-9) - GND (A10-11/24)	Below 1.5	IG switch ON, PKB switch ON
	10 - 14	IG switch ON, PKB switch OFF
STP (A10-21) - GND (A10-11/24)	Below 1.5	Stop light switch OFF
	8 - 14	Stop light switch ON
Tc (A10-20) - GND (A10-11/24)	10 - 14	IG switch ON
Ts (A10-6) - GND (A10-11/24)	10 - 14	IG switch ON
FR+ (A11-7) - FR- (A11-6)	AC generation	IG switch ON Slowly turn right front wheel
FL+ (A11-14) - FL- (A11-13)	AC generation	IG switch ON Slowly turn left front wheel
RR+ (A10-15) - RR- (A10-16)	AC generation	IG switch ON Slowly turn right rear wheel
RL+ (A10-1) - RL- (A10-2)	AC generation	IG switch ON Slowly turn left rear wheel

TY4029400139020X

Fig. 179 Anti-lock brake system circuit test (Part 2 of 2). 1994–96 Celica

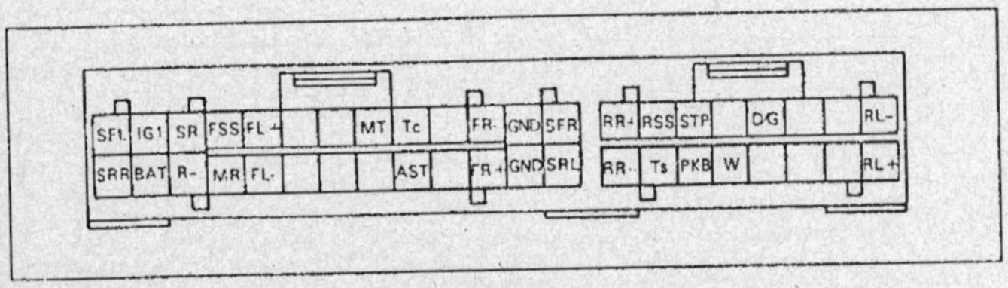
SFL
IG1
SR
FSS
FL+
MT
Tc
FR-
GND
SFR
RR+
RSS
STP
DG
RL-
SRR
BAT
R-
MR
FL-
AST
FR+
GND
SRL
RR-
Ts
PKB
W
RL+

Tester Connection	Check Item	Condition	Specified Value	Trouble Part
RL -	Continuity	IG switch off	Continuity	ABS ECU
D/G	Voltage	IG switch on and check connector T_s-E_1 not connected	About 0V	
STP	Voltage	IG switch off and brake pedal depressed	Battery voltage	Stop Light switch Stop light
	Continuity	IG switch off and brake pedal returned	Continuity	
RSS	Continuity	IG switch off	Continuity	ABS ECU
W	Voltage	IG switch on and "ABS" warning light goes on	About 0V	ABS ECU "ABS"warning light
		IG switch on and "ABS" warning light goes off	Battery voltage	
PKB	Voltage	IG switch on and PKB	About 0V	Parking brake switch Level warning switch
		IG switch on and PKB	Battery voltage	
TS	Voltage	IG switch on and check connector T_s-E_1 not connected	Battery voltage	ABS ECU
		IG switch on and check connector T_s-E_1 connected	About 0V	
RR -	Continuity	IG switch off	Continuity	
SFR	Voltage	IG switch on and "ABS" warning light goes on	About 0V	Actuator
		IG switch on and "ABS" warning light goes off	Battery voltage	
GND	Continuity	IG switch off	Continuity	Wiring harness
FR -	Continuity	IG switch off	Continuity	ABS ECU
TC	Voltage	IG switch on and check connector T_s-E_1 not connected	Battery voltage	
		IG switch on and check connector T_s-E_1 connected	About 0V	
FSS	Continuity	IG switch off	Continuity	
SR	Voltage	IG switch on and "ABS" warning light goes on	About 0V	
		IG switch on and "ABS" warning light goes off	Battery voltage	
IG1	Voltage	IG switch on	Battery voltage	ECU-IG Fuse
SFL	Voltage	IG switch on and "ABS" warning light goes on	About 0V	Actuator
		IG switch on and "ABS" warning light goes off	Battery voltage	

TY4029200120010X

Fig. 180 Anti-lock brake system circuit test (w/computer connector connected, Part 1 of 2). 1993 Camry

Tester Connection	Check Item	Condition	Specified Value	Trouble Part
SRL	Voltage	IG switch on and "ABS" warning light goes on	About 0V	Actuator
		IG switch on and "ABS" warning light goes off	Battery voltage	
AST	Voltage	IG switch on and "ABS" warning light goes on	About 0V	
		IG switch on and "ABS' warning light goes off	Battery voltage	
FL -	Continuity	IG switch off	Continuity	ABS ECU
R -	Continuity	IG switch off	Continuity	
BAT	Voltage	IG switch off	Battery voltage	DOME Fuse
SRR	Voltage	IG switch on and "ABS" warning light goes on	About 0V	Actuator
		IG switch on and "ABS" warning light goes off	Battery voltage	

TY4029200120020X

Fig. 180 Anti-lock brake system circuit test (w/computer connector connected, Part 2 of 2). 1993 Camry

Tester Connection	Check Item	Specified Value	Trouble Part	Tester Connection	Check Item	Specified Value	Trouble Part
RR+ ↔ RR -	Resistance	1.1 ~ 1.5 kΩ	Rear RH speed sensor	SFL ↔ AST	Resistance	About 6 Ω	Actuator
RL+ ↔ RL -	Resistance	1.1 ~ 1.5 kΩ	Rear LH speed sensor	SRL ↔ AST	Resistance	About 6 Ω	Actuator
SFR ↔ AST	Resistance	About 6 Ω	Actuator	AST ↔ Body ground	Resistance	About 5 Ω	Actuator
MT ↔ Body ground	Continuity	Continuity	Actuator	FR+ ↔ FR -	Resistance	0.8 ~ 1.3 Ω	Front RH speed sensor
FL+ ↔ FL -	Resistance	0.8 ~ 1.3 kΩ	Front LH speed sensor	MR ↔ R -	Resistance	50 ~ 80 Ω	Control relay
SR ↔ R -	Resistance	60 ~ 100 Ω	Control relay	SRR ↔ AST	Resistance	About 6 Ω	Actuator

TY4029200130000X

Fig. 181 Anti-lock brake system circuit test (w/computer connector disconnected). 1993 Camry

Tester Connection	Check Item	Condition	Specified Value	Trouble Part
TC	Voltage	IG switch on and check connector T_c-E_1 not connected	Battery voltage	ABS ECU
		IG switch on and check connector T_c-E_1 connected	About 0V	
AST	Voltage	IG switch on and "ABS" warning light goes on	About 0V	Actuator
		IG switch on and "ABS" warning light goes off	Battery voltage	
FL-	Continuity	IG switch off	Continuity	ABS ECU
FSS	Continuity	IG switch off	Continuity	
SRR	Voltage	IG switch on and "ABS" warning light goes on	About 0V	Actuator
		IG switch on and "ABS" warning light goes off	Battery voltage	

TY4029100122020X

Fig. 182 Anti-lock brake system circuit test (w/computer connector connected, Part 2 of 2). MR2

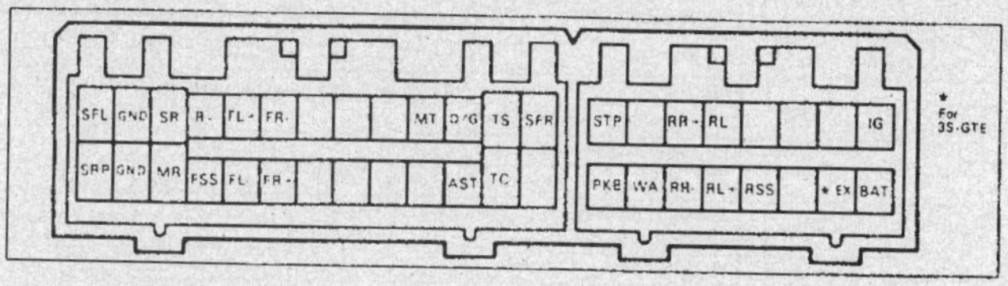
SFL
GND
SR
R-
FL+
FR-
MT
D/G
TS
SFR
STP
RR-
RL
IG
* For 3S-GTE
SRR
GND
MR
RSS
FL
FR+
AST
TC
PKB
WA
RR-
RL+
RSS
* EX
BAT

Tester Connection	Check Item	Condition	Specified Value	Trouble Part
IG	Voltage	IG switch on	Battery voltage	ECU-IG Fuse
RL-	Continuity	IG switch off	Continuity	ABS ECU
STP	Voltage	IG switch off and brake pedal depressed	Battery voltage	Stop light switch Stop light
	Continuity	IG switch off and brake pedal returned	Continuity	
BAT	Voltage	IG switch off	Battery voltage	ECU +B Fuse
EX	Voltage	IG switch on	Battery voltage	ABS ECU, EFI ECU
RSS	Continuity	IG switch off	Continuity	ABS ECU
RR-	Continuity	IG switch off	Continuity	ABS ECU
WA	Voltage	IG switch on and "ABS" warning light goes on	About 0V	ABS ECU "ABS" warning light
		IG switch on and "ABS" warning light goes off	Battery voltage	
PKB	Voltage	IG switch on and PKB lever pulled	About 0V	Parking brake switch Level warning switch
		Engine running on and PKB lever returned	Battery voltage	
SFR	Voltage	IG switch on and "ABS" warning light goes on	About 0V	Actuator
		IG switch on and "ABS" warning light goes off	Battery voltage	
TS	Voltage	IG switch on and check connector Ts-E, not connected	Battery voltage	ABS ECU
		IG switch on and check connector Ts-E, connector	About 0V	
FR-	Continuity	IG switch off	Continuity	
R-	Continuity	IG switch off	Continuity	
SR	Voltage	IG switch on and "ABS" warning light goes on	About 0V	ABS ECU
		IG switch on and "ABS" warning light goes off	Battery voltage	
GND	Continuity	IG switch off	Continuity	Wiring harness
SFL	Voltage	IG switch on and "ABS" warning light goes on	About 0V	Actuator
		IG switch on and "ABS" warning light goes off	Battery voltage	

TY402910012010X

Fig. 182 Anti-lock brake system circuit test (w/computer connector connected, Part 1 of 2). MR2

Tester Connection	Check Item	Specified Value	Trouble Part	Tester Connection	Check Item	Specified Value	Trouble Part
RR+ ↔ RR-	Resistance	0.9 ~ 1.5 kΩ	Rear RH speed sensor	SFL ↔ AST	Resistance	About 6 Ω	Actuator
RL+ ↔ RL-	Resistance	0.9 ~ 1.5 kΩ	Rear LH speed sensor	AST ↔ Body ground	Resistance	About 5 Ω	Actuator
SFR ↔ AST	Resistance	About 6 Ω	Actuator	FR+ ↔ FR-	Resistance	0.8 ~ 1.5 Ω	Front RH speed sensor
MT ↔ Body ground	Resistance	About 5 Ω	Actuator	MR ↔ R-	Resistance	50 ~ 80 Ω	Control relay
FL+ ↔ FL-	Resistance	0.8 ~ 1.5 kΩ	Front LH speed sensor	SRR ↔ AST	Resistance	About 6 Ω	Actuator
SR ↔ R-	Resistance	60 ~ 100 Ω	Control relay				

TY4029100132000X

Fig. 183 Anti-lock brake system circuit test (w/computer connector disconnected). MR2

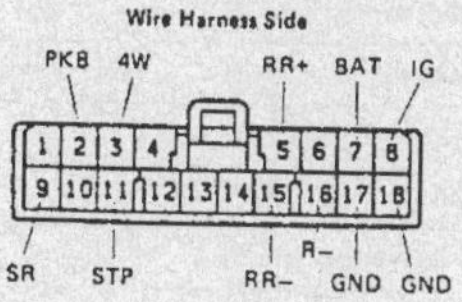
Wire Harness Side
PKB
4W
RR+
BAT
IG
1
2
3
4
5
6
7
8
9
10
11
12
13
14
15
16
17
18
SR
STP
R-
RR-
GND
GND

Tester Connection	Check Item	Condition	Voltage or Resistance Value	Trouble Part
PKB – Body ground	Voltage	Ignition SW on and PKB lever pulled	About 0 V	PKB switch, level warning switch
		Ignition SW on and PKB lever returned	Battery voltage	
*1 4W – Body ground	Voltage	Ignition SW on and 4WD indicator SW on	About 0 V	4WD indicator switch
		Ignition SW on and 4WD indicator SW off	Battery voltage	
*2 4W – Body ground	Continuity	–	Continuity	Wire harness
RR+ – RR–	Resistance	–	580 – 700 Ω	Speed sensor
BAT – Body ground	Voltage	–	Battery voltage	Wire harness
IG – Body ground	Voltage	Ignition SW on	Battery voltage	ECU-IG fuse, wire harness
		Ignition SW off	About 0 V	
SR – R–	Resistance	–	80 Ω	Solenoid relay
STP – Body ground	Voltage	Ignition SW off and brake pedal depressed	Battery voltage	Stop light switch, stop light
	Continuity	Ignition SW off and brake pedal returned	Continuity	
GND – Body ground	Continuity	–	Continuity	Wire harness

*1: For 4WD model only
*2: For 2WD model only

TY4029100124000X

Fig. 184 Anti-lock brake system circuit test (w/computer connector connected). Pickup, Tacoma & 1993–95 4Runner

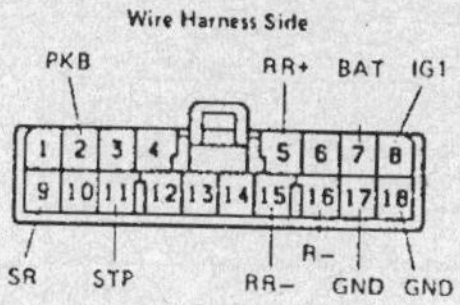
Wire Harness Side
PKB
RR+
BAT
IG1
1
2
3
4
5
6
7
8
9
10
11
12
13
14
15
16
17
18
SR
STP
R-
RR-
GND
GND

Tester Connection	Check Item	Condition	Voltage or Resistance Value	Trouble Part
PKB – Body ground	Voltage	Ignition SW on and PKB lever pulled	About 0 V	PKB switch, level warning switch
		Ignition SW on and PKB lever returned	Battery voltage	
RR+ – RR–	Resistance	–	580 – 700 Ω	Speed sensor
BAT – Body ground	Voltage	–	Battery voltage	Wire harness
IG1 – Body ground	Voltage	Ignition SW on	Battery voltage	ECU-IG fuse, wire harness
		Ignition SW off	About 0 V	
SR – R–	Resistance	–	80 Ω	Solenoid relay
STP – Body ground	Voltage	Ignition SW off and brake pedal depressed	Battery voltage	Stop light switch, stop light
	Continuity	Ignition SW off and brake pedal returned	Continuity	
GND – Body ground	Continuity	–	Continuity	Wire harness

TY4029200134000X

Fig. 185 Anti-lock brake system circuit test (w/computer connector disconnected). Pickup, Tacoma & 1993–95 4Runner

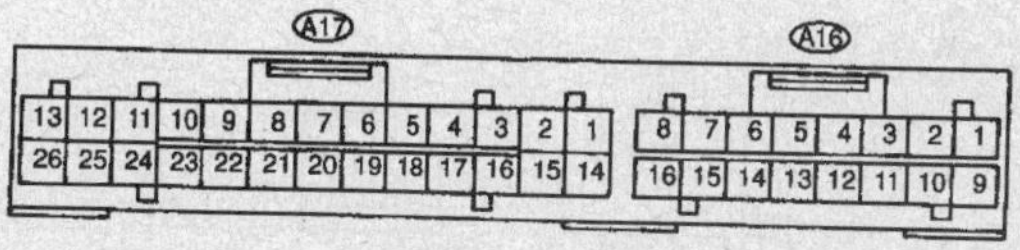
A17
A16
13
12
11
10
9
8
7
6
5
4
3
2
1
26
25
24
23
22
21
20
19
18
17
16
15
14
8
7
6
5
4
3
2
1
16
15
14
13
12
11
10
9

Symbols (Terminals No.)	STD Voltage (V)	Condition
BAT (A17 – 22) – GND (A17 – 11, 24)	10 – 14	Always
IG1 (A17 – 10) – GND (A17 – 11, 24)	10 – 14	IG switch ON
SR (A16 – 5) – R+ (A16 – 3)	9 – 14	IG switch ON, ABS warning light OFF
MR (A16 – 4) – R+ (A16 – 3)	Below 1.0	IG switch ON
SFRH (A16 – 8) – GND (A17 – 11, 24)	10 – 14	IG switch ON, ABS warning light OFF
SFRR (A16 – 16) – GND (A17 – 11, 24)	10 – 14	IG switch ON, ABS warning light OFF
SFLH (A16 – 1) – GND (A17 – 11, 24)	10 – 14	IG switch ON, ABS warning light OFF
SFLR (A17 – 2) – GND (A17 – 11, 24)	10 – 14	IG switch ON, ABS warning light OFF
SRR (A17 – 10) – GND (A17 – 11, 24)	10 – 14	IG switch ON, ABS warning light OFF
SRH (A17 – 9) – GND (A17 – 11, 24)	10 – 14	IG switch ON, ABS warning light OFF
AST (A16 – 11) – GND (A17 – 11, 24)	10 – 14	IG switch ON, ABS warning light OFF
WA (A17 – 25) – GND (A17 – 11, 24)	Below 2.0	IG switch ON, ABS warning light ON
	10 – 14	IG switch ON, ABS warning light OFF
STP (A17 – 21) – GND (A17 – 11, 24)	Below 1.5	Stop light switch OFF
	8 – 14	Stop light switch ON
Tc (A17 – 20) – GND (A17 – 11, 24)	10 – 14	IG switch ON
Ts (A17 – 6) – GND (A17 – 11, 24)	10 – 14	IG switch ON
FR+ (A16 – 6) – FR– (A16 – 7)	AC generation	IG switch ON Slowly turn right front wheel
FL+ (A16 – 13) – FL– (A16 – 14)	AC generation	IG switch on Slowly turn left front wheel
RR+ (A17 – 15) – RR– (A17 – 16)	AC generation	IG switch ON Slowly turn right rear wheel
RL+ (A17 – 1) – RL– (A17 – 2)	AC generation	IG switch ON Slowly turn left rear wheel
GS1 (A17 – 19) – GND (A17 – 11, 24)	4 – 6 or 7 – 11	IG switch ON
GS2 (A17 – 7) – GND (A17 – 11, 24)	4 – 6	IG switch ON
EXI (A17 – 8) – GND (A17 – 11, 24)	Below 2.0	IG switch ON, center differential is locked
	10 – 14	IG switch ON, center differential is free
EXI2 (A17 – 4) – GND (A17 – 11, 24)	Below 2.0	IG switch ON, rear differential is locked (4WD)
	12 – 14	IG switch ON, rear differential is free (4WD)
	Below 2.0	Always (2WD)
EXI3 (A17 – 9) – GND (A17 – 11, 24)	Below 2.0	IG switch ON, transfer is in L4 position
	10 – 14	IG switch ON, transfer is in a position other than L4

TY4029600229000X

Fig. 186 Anti-lock brake system circuit test. 1996 4Runner

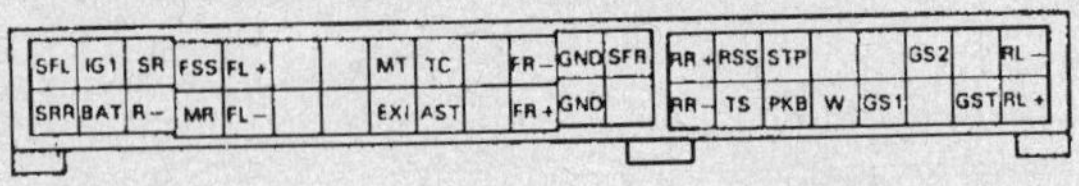
SFL IG1 SR FSS FL+ MT TC FR− GND SFR RR+ RSS STP GS2 RL−
SRR BAT R− MR FL− EXI AST FR+ GND RR− TS PKB W GS1 GST RL+

Tester Connection	Check Item	Condition	Specified Value	Trouble Part
RL	Continuity	IG switch off	Continuity	ABS ECU
GS2	Voltage	IG switch on	4 ~ 6 V	Deceleration Sensor
STP	Voltage	IG switch off and brake pedal depressed	10 ~ 14 V	Stop light switch Stop light
	Continuity	IG switch off and brake pedal returned	Continuity	
RSS	Continuity	IG switch off	Continuity	ABS ECU
GS1	Voltage	IG switch on	4 ~ 6 V or 7 ~ 12 V	Deceleration Sensor
W	Voltage	IG switch on and "ABS" warning light goes on	About 0 V	ABS ECU "ABS" warning light
		IG switch on and "ABS" warning light goes off	10 ~ 14 V	
PKB	Voltage	IG switch on and PKB lever pulled	About 0 V	Parking brake switch Level warning switch
		IG switch on and PKB lever returned	10 ~ 14 V	
TS	Voltage	IG switch on and data link connector Tc − E_1 connected	About 0 V	ABS ECU
RR	Continuity	IG switch off	Continuity	
SFR	Voltage	IG switch on and "ABS" warning light goes on	About 0 V	Actuator
		IG switch on and "ABS" warning light goes off	10 ~ 14 V	
GND	Continuity	IG switch off	Continuity	Wiring harness
FR	Continuity	IG switch off	Continuity	ABS ECU
TC	Voltage	IG switch on and data link connector Tc − E_1 not connected	10 ~ 14 V	
		IG switch on and data link connector Tc − E_1 connected	About 0 V	
FSS	Continuity	IG switch off	Continuity	
SR	Voltage	IG switch on and "ABS" warning light goes on	About 0 V	
		IG switch on and "ABS" warning light goes off	10 ~ 14 V	
IG1	Voltage	IG switch on	10 ~ 14 V	ECU-IG Fuse

TY4029300125010X

Fig. 187 Anti-lock brake system circuit test (w/computer connector connected, Part 1 of 2). Land Cruiser

Tester Connection	Check Item	Condition	Specified Value	Trouble Part
SFL	Voltage	IG switch on and "ABS" warning light goes on	About 0 V	Actuator
		IG switch on and "ABS" warning light goes off	10 ~ 14 V	
AST	Voltage	IG switch on and "ABS" warning light goes on	About 0 V	
		IG switch on and "ABS" warning light goes off	Battery voltage	
EXI	Voltage	IG switch on and center differential lock indicator light goes off	10 ~ 14 V	GAUGE Fuse
FL −	Continuity	IG switch off	Continuity	ABS ECU
R −	Continuity	IG switch off	Continuity	
BAT	Voltage	IG switch off	10 ~ 14 V	DOME Fuse
SRR	Voltage	IG switch on and "ABS" warning light goes on	About 0 V	Actuator
		IG switch on and "ABS" warning light goes off	10 ~ 14 V	

TY4029300125020X

Fig. 187 Anti-lock brake system circuit test (w/computer connector connected, Part 2 of 2). Land Cruiser

Tester Connection	Check Item	Specified Value	Trouble Part	Tester Connection	Check Item	Specified Value	Trouble Part
RR + ↔ RR −	Resistance	*0.7 ~ 1.1 kΩ	Rear RH speed sensor	SFL ↔ AST	Resistance	*About 6 Ω	Actuator
RL + ↔ RL −	Resistance	*0.7 ~ 1.1 kΩ	Rear LH speed sensor	FR + ↔ FR −	Resistance	*0.87 ~ 1.27 kΩ	Front RH speed sensor
SFR ↔ AST	Resistance	*About 6 Ω	Actuator	AST ↔ Body ground	Resistance	*About 5 Ω	Actuator
MT ↔ Body ground	Continuity	Continuity	Actuator	MR ↔ R −	Resistance	*55.8 ~ 68.2 Ω	Control relay
FL + ↔ FL −	Resistance	*0.87 ~ 1.27 kΩ	Front LH speed sensor	SRR ↔ AST	Resistance	*About 6 Ω	Actuator
SR ↔ R −	Resistance	*80 ~ 100 Ω	Control relay				

*: 20°C (68°F)

TY4029300135000X

Fig. 188 Anti-lock brake system circuit test (w/computer connector disconnected). Land Cruiser

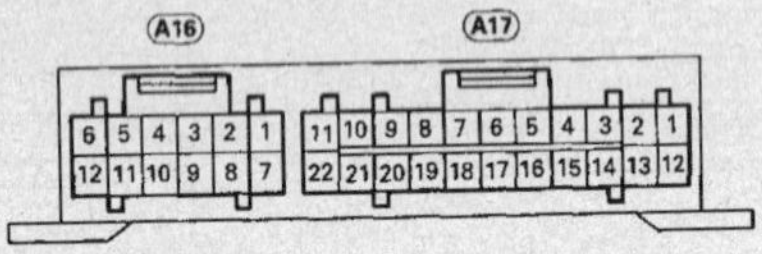
A16
A17
6 5 4 3 2 1
12 11 10 9 8 7
11 10 9 8 7 6 5 4 3 2 1
22 21 20 19 18 17 16 15 14 13 12

Symbols (Terminals No.)			STD Voltage (V)	Condition
IG1 (A16-2)	−	GND (A17-2/13)	10 − 14	IG switch ON
SR (A17-18)	−	R+ (A17-8)	Below 1.5	IG switch ON, ABS warning light OFF
MR (A17-7)	−	R+ (A17-8)	10 − 14	IG switch ON
SFRH (A17-4)	−	GND (A17-2/13)	10 − 14	IG switch ON, ABS warning light OFF
SFRR (A17-1)	−	GND (A17-2/13)	10 − 14	IG switch ON, ABS warning light OFF
SFLH (A17-10)	−	GND (A17-2/13)	10 − 14	IG switch ON, ABS warning light OFF
SFLR (A17-11)	−	GND (A17-2/13)	10 − 14	IG switch ON, ABS warning light OFF
SRRR (A17-22)	−	GND (A17-2/13)	10 − 14	IG switch ON, ABS warning light OFF
SRRH (A17-21)	−	GND (A17-2/13)	10 − 14	IG switch ON, ABS warning light OFF
SRLR (A17-12)	−	GND (A17-2/13)	10 − 14	IG switch ON, ABS warning light OFF
SRLH (A17-5)	−	GND (A17-2/13)	10 − 14	IG switch ON, ABS warning light OFF
AST (A17-16)	−	GND (A17-2/13)	10 − 14	IG switch ON, ABS warning light OFF
WA (A16-4)	−	GND (A17-2/13)	Below 2.0	IG switch ON, ABS, warning light ON
			10 − 14	IG switch ON, ABS warning light OFF
STP (A16-12)	−	GND (A17-2/13)	Below 1.5	Stop light switch OFF
			8 − 14	Stop light switch ON
Tc (A16-9)	−	GND (A17-2/13)	10 − 14	IG switch ON
Ts (A16-8)	−	GND (A17-2/13)	10 − 14	IG switch ON
FR+ (A17-3)	−	FR− (A17-14)	AC generation	IG switch ON Slowly turn right front wheel
FL+ (A17-19)	−	FL− (A17-20)	AC generation	IG switch ON Slowly turn left front wheel
RR+ (A16-1)	−	RR− (A16-7)	AC generation	IG switch ON Slowly turn right rear wheel
RL+ (A16-3)	−	RL− (A16-10)	AC generation	IG switch ON Slowly turn left rear wheel

TY4029600230000X

Fig. 189 Anti-lock brake system circuit test. RAV4 w/2WD

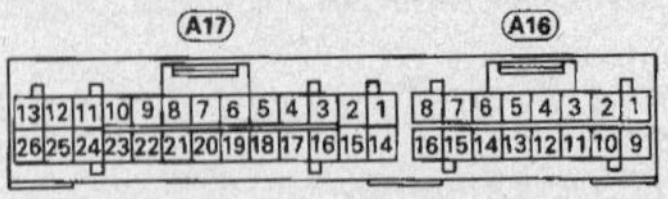
A17
A16
13 12 11 10 9 8 7 6 5 4 3 2 1
26 25 24 23 22 21 20 19 18 17 16 15 14
8 7 6 5 4 3 2 1
16 15 14 13 12 11 10 9

Symbols (Terminals No.)			STD Voltage (V)	Condition
BAT (A17-22)	−	GND (A17-11/24)	10 − 14	Always
IG1 (A17-10)	−	GND (A17-11/24)	10 − 14	IG switch ON
SR (A16-5)	−	R− (A16-15)	10 − 14	IG switch ON, ABS warning light OFF
MR (A16-4)	−	R− (A16-15)	Below 1.0	IG switch ON
SFRH (A16-1)	−	GND (A17-11/24)	10 − 14	IG switch ON, ABS warning light OFF
SFRR (A16-2)	−	GND (A17-11/24)	10 − 14	IG switch ON, ABS warning light OFF
SFLH (A17-13)	−	GND (A17-11/24)	10 − 14	IG switch ON, ABS warning light OFF
SFLR (A17-12)	−	GND (A17-11/24)	10 − 14	IG switch ON, ABS warning light OFF
SRRH (A17-26)	−	GND (A17-11/24)	10 − 14	IG switch ON, ABS warning light OFF
SRRR (A17-25)	−	GND (A17-11/24)	10 − 14	IG switch ON, ABS warning light OFF
SRLH (A16-9)	−	GND (A17-11/24)	10 − 14	IG switch ON, ABS warning light OFF
SRLR (A16-10)	−	GND (A17-11/24)	10 − 14	IG switch ON, ABS warning light OFF
AST (A16-11)	−	GND (A17-11/24)	10 − 14	IG switch ON, ABS warning light OFF
WA (A16-12)	−	GND (A17-11/24)	Below 2.0	IG switch ON, ABS warning light ON
			10 − 14	IG switch ON, ABS warning light OFF
PKB (A17-9)	−	GND (A17-11/24)	Below 1.5	IG switch ON, PKB switch ON
			10 − 14	IG switch ON, PKB switch OFF
STP (A17-21)	−	GND (A17-11/24)	Below 1.5	Stop light switch OFF
			8 − 14	Stop light switch ON
Tc (A17-20)	−	GND (A17-11/24)	10 − 14	IG switch ON
Ts (A17-6)	−	GND (A17-11/24)	10 − 14	IG switch ON
FR+ (A16-7)	−	FR− (A16-6)	AC generation	IG switch ON Slowly turn right front wheel
FL+ (A16-14)	−	FL− (A16-13)	AC generation	IG switch ON Slowly turn left front wheel
RR+ (A17-15)	−	RR− (A17-16)	AC generation	IG switch ON Slowly turn right rear wheel
RL+ (A17-1)	−	RL− (A17-2)	AC generation	IG switch ON Slowly turn left rear wheel
GL1 (A17-19)	−	GND (A17-11/24)	0.5 − 4.5 V	IG switch ON
GL2 (A17-7)	−	GND (A17-11/24)	0.5 − 4.5 V	IG switch ON
VGS (A17-5)	−	GND (A17-11/24)	4.5 − 5.5 V	IG switch ON

TY4029600231000X

Fig. 190 Anti-lock brake system circuit test. RAV4 w/4WD

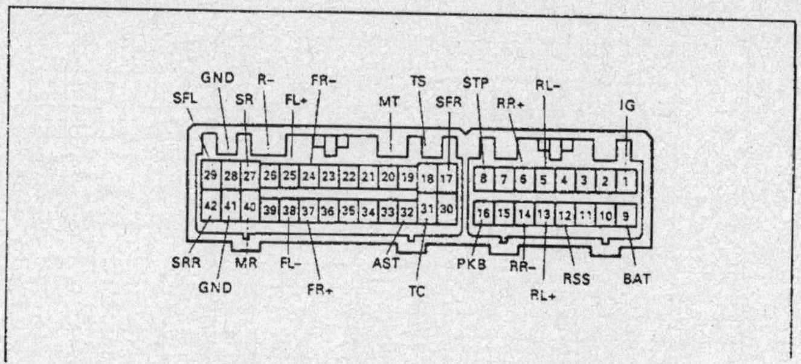
GND
R–
FR–
TS
STP
RL–
SFL
SR
FL+
MT
SFR
RR+
IG
SRR
MR
FL–
AST
PKB
RR–
RSS
BAT
GND
FR+
TC
RL+

Tester connection	Check item	Condition	Voltage or resistance value	Trouble part
IG – Body ground	Voltage	Ignition SW on	Battery voltage	ECU-IG fuse, wire harness
		Ignition SW off	About 0 V	
RL– – Body ground	Continuity	—	No continuity	Rear LH speed sensor or wire harness
RL– – RL+	Resistance	—	1.05–1.45 kΩ	
RL+ – Body ground	Continuity	—	No continuity	
RR+ – Body ground	Continuity	—	No continuity	Rear RH speed sensor or wire harness
RR+ – RR–	Resistance	—	1.05–1.45 kΩ	
RR– – Body ground	Continuity	—	No continuity	
STP – Body ground	Voltage	Ignition SW off and brake pedal depressed	Battery voltage	Stop light switch or stop light
	Continuity	Ignition SW off and brake pedal returned	Continuity	
BAT – Body ground	Voltage	—	Battery voltage	Wire harness
RSS – *	Continuity	—	Continuity	Sealed wire

*: Terminals 1 and 6 of the intermediate connector on the fuel tank.

TY4029100133010X

Fig. 191 Anti-lock brake system circuit test (w/computer connector disconnected, Part 1 of 2). 1993–95 Previa

Tester connection	Check item	Condition	Voltage or resistance value	Trouble part
PKB – Body ground	Voltage	Ignition SW on and PKB lever pulled	About 0 V	PKB switch, level warning switch
		Ignition SW on and PKB lever returned	Battery voltage	
SFR – AST	Resistance	Ignition SW off	About 6 Ω	Actuator
TS – Body ground	Continuity	—	No continuity	Check connector or wire harness
		Check connector terminals Ts and E_1 are connected	Continuity	
MT – Body ground	Continuity	—	Continuity	Actuator
FR– – Body ground	Continuity	—	No continuity	Front RH speed sensor or wire harness
FR– – FR+	Resistance	—	0.92–1.22 kΩ	
FR+ – Body ground	Continuity	—	No continuity	
FL+ – Body ground	Continuity	—	No continuity	Front LH speed sensor or wire harness
FL+ – FL–	Resistance	—	0.92–1.22 kΩ	
FL– – Body ground	Continuity	—	No continuity	
R– – Body ground	Continuity	—	No continuity	Wire harness
R– – MR	Continuity	—	Continuity	Motor relay
R– – SR	Continuity	—	Continuity	Solenoid relay
GND – Body ground	Continuity	—	Continuity	Wire harness
SFL – AST	Resistance	Ignition SW off	About 6 Ω	Actuator
TC – Body ground	Continuity	—	No continuity	Check connector or wire harness
		Terminal Tc of check connector shorted	Continuity	
AST – Body ground	Resistance	—	About 5 Ω	Actuator
SRR – AST	Resistance	Ignition SW off	About 6 Ω	

TY4029100133020X

Fig. 191 Anti-lock brake system circuit test (w/computer connector disconnected, Part 2 of 2). 1993–95 Previa

Tester Connection	Check Item	Condition	Specified Value	Trouble Part
GND	Continuity	IG switch OFF	Continuity	Wiring harness
AST	Voltage	IG switch ON and "ABS" warning light goes OFF	10 ~ 14 V	ABS ECU
		IG switch ON and "ABS" warning light goes ON	About 0 V	
FL–	Continuity	IG switch OFF	Continuity	
R–	Continuity	IG switch OFF	Continuity	
BAT	Voltage	IG switch ON	10 ~ 14 V	ECU-B Fuse
SRR	Voltage	IG switch ON and "ABS" warning light goes OFF	10 ~ 14 V	Actuator

TY4029600232020X

Fig. 192 Anti-lock brake system circuit test (w/computer connector connected, Part 2 of 2). 1996 Previa

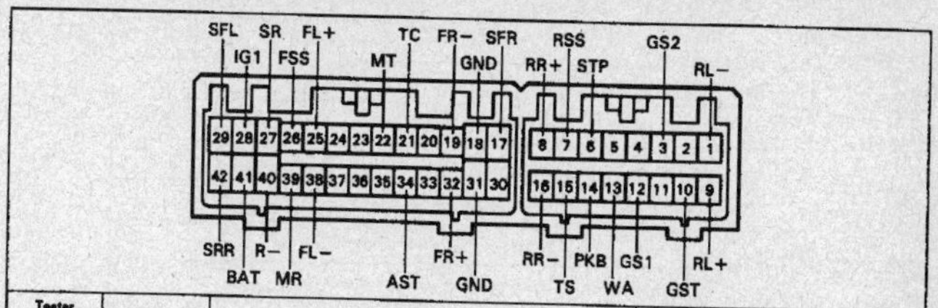
SFL
SR
FL+
TC
FR–
SFR
RSS
GS2
IG1
FSS
MT
GND
RR+
STP
RL–
SRR
R–
FL–
FR+
RR–
PKB
GS1
RL+
BAT
MR
AST
GND
TS
WA
GST

Tester Connection	Check Item	Condition	Specified Value	Trouble Part
RL–	Continuity	IG switch OFF	Continuity	ABS ECU
GS2	Voltage	IG switch ON	4 ~ 6 V	Deceleration sensor
STP	Voltage	IG switch OFF and brake pedal depressed	8 ~ 14 V	Stop light switch Stop light
	Voltage	IG switch OFF and brake pedal returned	Below 1.5 V	
RSS	Continuity	IG switch OFF	Continuity	ABS ECU
SFR	Voltage	IG switch ON and "ABS" warning light goes OFF	10 ~ 14 V	Actuator
GND	Continuity	IG switch OFF	Continuity	Wiring harness
FR–	Continuity	IG switch OFF	Continuity	ABS ECU
TC	Voltage	IG switch ON and data link connector 1 Tc – E_1 not connected	10 ~ 14 V	
		IG switch ON and data link connector 1 Tc – E_1 connected	About 0 V	
FSS	Continuity	IG switch OFF	Continuity	
SR	Voltage	IG switch ON and "ABS" warning light goes ON	About 0 V	
		IG switch ON and "ABS" warning light goes OFF	9 ~ 14 V	
IG1	Voltage	IG switch ON	10 ~ 14 V	ECU-IG Fuse
SFL	Voltage	IG switch ON and "ABS" warning light goes OFF	10 ~ 14 V	Actuator
GS1	Voltage	IG switch ON	4 ~ 6 V or 7 ~ 11V	Deceleration sensor
WA	Voltage	IG switch ON and "ABS" warning light goes ON	Below 2.0 V	ABS ECU "ABS" warning light
		IG switch ON and "ABS" warning light goes OFF	10 ~ 14 V	
PKB	Voltage	IG switch ON and PKB lever pulled	Below 1.5 V	Parking brake switch Level warning switch
		IG switch ON and PKB lever returned	10 ~ 14 V	
TS	Voltage	IG switch ON and data link connector 1 Ts – E_1 not connected	10 ~ 14 V	ABS ECU
		IG switch ON and data link connector 1 Ts – E_1 connected	Below 1.0 V	
RR–	Continuity	IG switch OFF	Continuity	

TY4029600232010X

Fig. 192 Anti-lock brake system circuit test (w/computer connector connected, Part 1 of 2). 1996 Previa

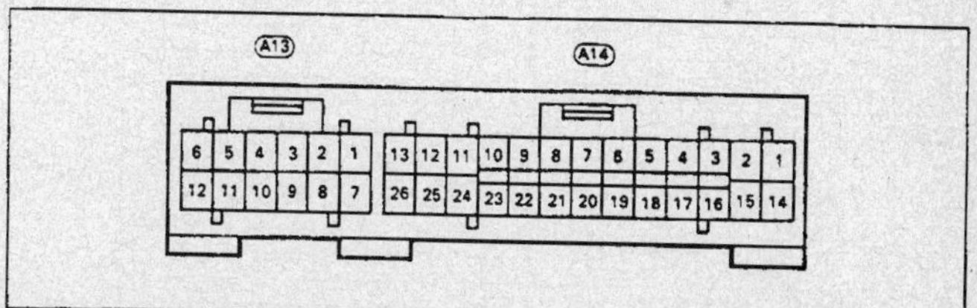
A13
A14

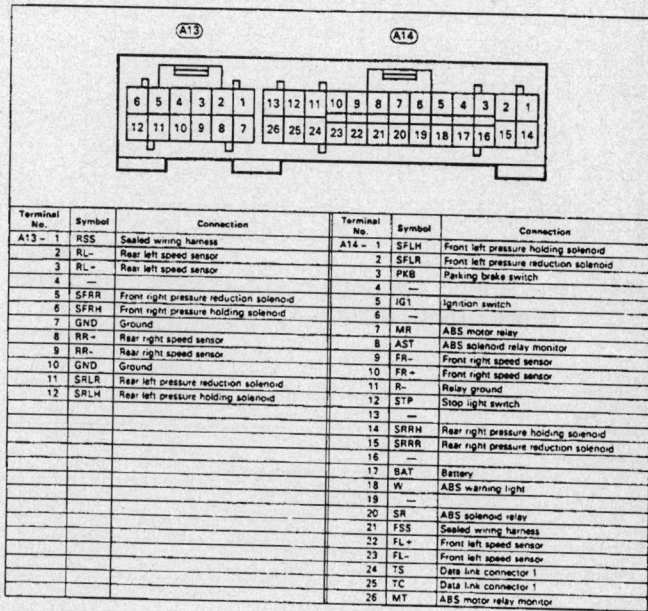

Terminal No.	Symbol	Connection	Terminal No.	Symbol	Connection
A13 – 1	RSS	Sealed wiring harness	A14 – 1	SFLH	Front left pressure holding solenoid
2	RL–	Rear left speed sensor	2	SFLR	Front left pressure reduction solenoid
3	RL+	Rear left speed sensor	3	PKB	Parking brake switch
4	—		4	—	
5	SFRR	Front right pressure reduction solenoid	5	IG1	Ignition switch
6	SFRH	Front right pressure holding solenoid	6	—	
7	GND	Ground	7	MR	ABS motor relay
8	RR+	Rear right speed sensor	8	AST	ABS solenoid relay monitor
9	RR–	Rear right speed sensor	9	FR–	Front right speed sensor
10	GND	Ground	10	FR+	Front right speed sensor
11	SRLR	Rear left pressure reduction solenoid	11	R–	Relay ground
12	SRLH	Rear left pressure holding solenoid	12	STP	Stop light switch
			13	—	
			14	SRRH	Rear right pressure holding solenoid
			15	SRRR	Rear right pressure reduction solenoid
			16	—	
			17	BAT	Battery
			18	W	ABS warning light
			19	—	
			20	SR	ABS solenoid relay
			21	FSS	Sealed wiring harness
			22	FL+	Front left speed sensor
			23	FL–	Front left speed sensor
			24	TS	Data link connector 1
			25	TC	Data link connector 1
			26	MT	ABS motor relay monitor

TY4029300137010X

Fig. 193 Anti-lock brake system circuit test (Part 1 of 2). Corolla

Symbols (Terminals No.)	STD Voltage (V)	Condition
BAT (A14 - 7) - GND (A13 - 7)	10 - 14	Always
IG1 (A14 - 5) - GND (A13 - 7)	10 - 14	IG switch ON
SR (A14 - 20) - R- (A14 - 11)	10 - 14	IG switch ON
MR (A14 - 7) - R- (A14 - 11)	Below 1.0	IG switch ON
SFRR (A13 - 5) - GND (A13 - 7)	10 - 14	IG switch ON, ABS warning light OFF
SFRH (A13 - 6) - GND (A13 - 7)	10 - 14	IG switch ON, ABS warning light OFF
SFLR (A14 - 2) - GND (A13 - 7)	10 - 14	IG switch ON, ABS warning light OFF
SFLH (A14 - 1) - GND (A13 - 7)	10 - 14	IG switch ON, ABS warning light OFF
SRRR (A14 - 5) - GND (A13 - 7)	10 - 14	IG switch ON, ABS warning light OFF
SRRH (A14 - 4) - GND (A13 - 7)	10 - 14	IG switch ON, ABS warning light OFF
SRLR (A13 - 11) - GND (A13 - 7)	10 - 14	IG switch ON, ABS warning light OFF
SRLH (A13 - 12) - GND (A13 - 7)	10 - 14	IG switch ON, ABS warning light OFF
AST (A14 - 8) - GND (A13 - 7)	10 - 14	IG switch ON, ABS warning light OFF
W (A14 - 18) - GND (A13 - 7)	Below 1.0	IG switch ON, ABS warning light ON
	10 - 14	IG switch ON, ABS warning light OFF
PKB (A14 - 3) - GND (A13 - 7)	Below 1.0	IG switch ON, PKB switch ON
	10 - 14	IG switch ON, PKB switch OFF
STP (A14 - 12) - GND (A13 - 7)	Below 1.0	Stop light switch OFF
	10 - 14	Stop light switch ON
Tc (A14 - 25) - GND (A13 - 7)	10 - 14	IG switch ON
Ts (A14 - 24) - GND (A13 - 7)	10 - 14	IG switch ON
FR+ (A14 - 10) - FR- (A14 - 9)	AC generation	IG switch ON Slowly turn front right wheel
FL+ (A14 - 22) - FL- (A14 - 23)	AC generation	IG switch ON Slowly turn front left wheel
RR+ (A13 - 8) - RR- (A13 - 9)	AC generation	IG switch ON Slowly turn rear right wheel
RL+ (A13 - 3) - RL- (A13 - 2)	AC generation	IG switch ON Slowly turn rear left wheel

TY4029300137020X

Fig. 193 Anti-lock brake system circuit test (Part 2 of 2). Corolla

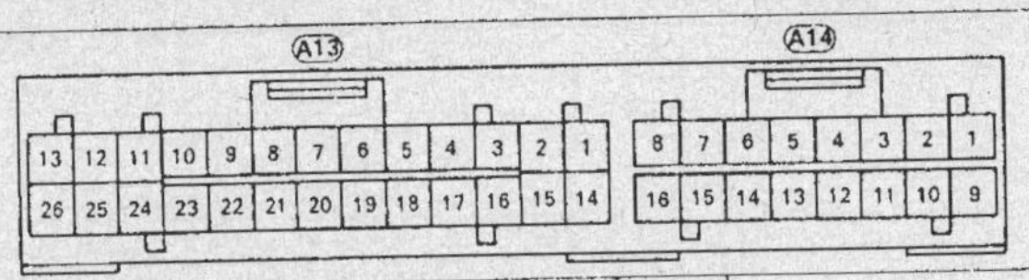
A13
A14

Terminal No.	Symbol	Connection	Terminal No.	Symbol	Connection
A13- 1	SFR	Right front solenoid	A14- 1	RL-	Left rear speed sensor
2	GND	Ground	2	-	-
3	FR-	Right front speed sensor	3	-	-
4	-	-	4	D/G	DLC2
5	TC	DLC1, DLC2	5	-	-
6	MT	ABS control (motor) relay monitor	6	STP	Stop light switch
7	-	-	7	RSS	Sealed wiring harness
8	-	-	8	RR+	Right rear speed sensor
9	FL+	Left front speed sensor	9	RL+	Left rear speed sensor
10	FSS	Sealed wiring harness	10	-	-
11	SR	ABS control (solenoid) relay	11	-	-
12	IG1	Ignition switch	12	-	-
13	SFL	Left front solenoid	13	WA	ABS warning light
14	SRL	Left rear solenoid	14	PKB	Parking brake switch
15	GND	Ground	15	TS	DLC1
16	FR+	Right front speed sensor	16	RR-	Right rear speed sensor
17	-	-			
18	AST	ABS control (solenoid) relay monitor			
19	-	-			
20	-	-			
21	-	-			
22	FL-	Left front speed sensor			
23	MR	ABS control (motor) relay			
24	R-	Relay ground			
25	BAT	Battery			
26	SRR	Right rear solenoid			

TY4029400138030X

Fig. 194 Nippondenso Anti-lock brake system circuit test (Part 3 of 4). Avalon & 1994–96 Camry

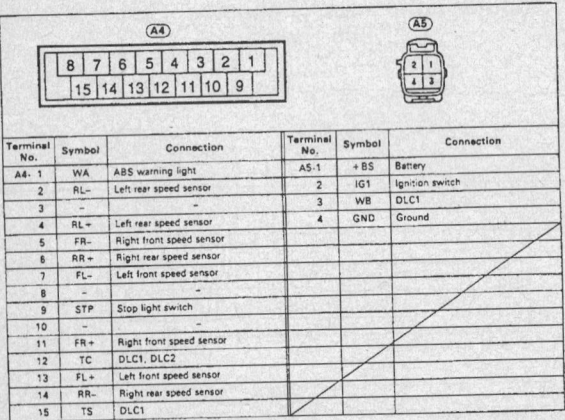

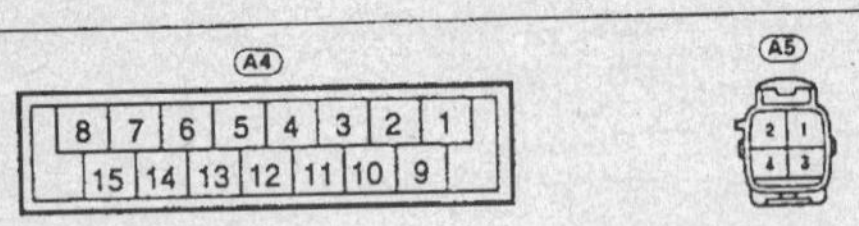
A4
A5

Terminal No.	Symbol	Connection	Terminal No.	Symbol	Connection
A4- 1	WA	ABS warning light	A5-1	+BS	Battery
2	RL-	Left rear speed sensor	2	IG1	Ignition switch
3	-	-	3	WB	DLC1
4	RL+	Left rear speed sensor	4	GND	Ground
5	FR-	Right front speed sensor			
6	RR+	Right rear speed sensor			
7	FL-	Left front speed sensor			
8	-	-			
9	STP	Stop light switch			
10	-	-			
11	FR+	Right front speed sensor			
12	TC	DLC1, DLC2			
13	FL+	Left front speed sensor			
14	RR-	Right rear speed sensor			
15	TS	DLC1			

TY4029400138010X

Fig. 194 Bosch Anti-lock brake system circuit test (Part 1 of 4). Avalon & 1994–96 Camry

Symbols (Terminals No.)	STD Voltage (V)	Condition
+BS (A5-1) - GND (A5-4)	10 - 14	Always
IG1 (A5-2) - GND (A5-4)	10 - 14	IG switch ON
WA (A4-1) - GND (A5-4)	Below 2.6	IG switch ON, ABS warning light ON
	10 - 14	IG switch ON, ABS warning light OFF
WB (A5-3) - GND (A5-4)	Below 2.6	IG switch ON, ABS warning light ON
	10 - 14	IG switch ON, ABS warning light OFF
STP (A4-9) - GND (A5-4)	Below 1.5	Stop light switch OFF
	5 - 14	Stop light switch ON
Tc (A4-12) - GND (A5-4)	5.7 - 8.1	IG switch ON
Ts (A4-15) - GND (A5-4)	5.7 - 8.1	IG switch ON
FR+ (A4-11) - FR- (A4-5)	AC generation	IG switch ON, slowly turn right front wheel
FL+ (A4-13) - FL- (A4-7)	AC generation	IG switch ON, slowly turn left front wheel
RR+ (A4-6) - RR- (A4-14)	AC generation	IG switch ON, slowly turn right rear wheel
RL+ (A4-4) - RL- (A4-2)	AC generation	IG switch ON, slowly turn left rear wheel

TY4029400138020X

Fig. 194 Bosch Anti-lock brake system circuit test (Part 2 of 4). Avalon & 1994–96 Camry

Symbols (Terminals No.)	STD Voltage (V)	Condition
BAT (A13-25) - GND (A13- 2/15)	10 - 14	Always
IG1 (A13-12) - GND (A13- 2/15)	10 - 14	IG switch ON
SR (A13-11) - R- (A13-24)	8.4 - 14	IG switch ON, ABS warning light OFF
MR (A13-23) - R- (A13-24)	Below 1.0	IG switch ON
SFR (A13-1) - GND (A13- 2/15)	10 - 14	IG switch ON, ABS warning light OFF
SFL (A13-13) - GND (A13- 2/15)	10 - 14	IG switch ON, ABS warning light OFF
SRR (A13-26) - GND (A13- 2/15)	10 - 14	IG switch ON, ABS warning light OFF
AST (A13-18) - GND (A13- 2/15)	10 - 14	IG switch ON, ABS warning light OFF
WA (A14-13) - GND (A13- 2/15)	Below 2.0	IG switch ON, ABS warning light ON
	10 - 14	IG switch ON, ABS warning light OFF
PKB (A14-14) - GND (A13- 2/15)	Below 1.5	IG switch ON, PKB switch ON, Fluid in M/C reservoir above MIN level
	10 - 14	IG switch ON, PKB switch OFF, Fluid in M/C reservoir above MIN level
STP (A14-6) - GND (A13- 2/15)	Below 1.5	Stop light switch OFF
	8 - 14	Stop light switch ON
D/G (A14-4) - GND (A13- 2/15)	10 - 14	IG switch ON, ABS warning light OFF
TC (A13-5) - GND (A13- 2/15)	10 - 14	IG switch ON
TS (A14-15) - GND (A13- 2/15)	10 - 14	IG switch ON
FR+ (A13-16) - FR- (A13-3)	AC generation	IG switch ON Slowly turn right front wheel
FL+ (A13-9) - FL- (A13-22)	AC generation	IG switch ON Slowly turn left front wheel
RR+ (A14-8) - RR- (A14-16)	AC generation	IG switch ON Slowly turn right rear wheel
RL+ (A14-9) - RL- (A14-1)	AC generation	IG switch ON Slowly turn left rear wheel

TY4029400138040X

Fig. 194 Nippondenso Anti-lock brake system circuit test (Part 4 of 4). Avalon & 1994–96 Camry

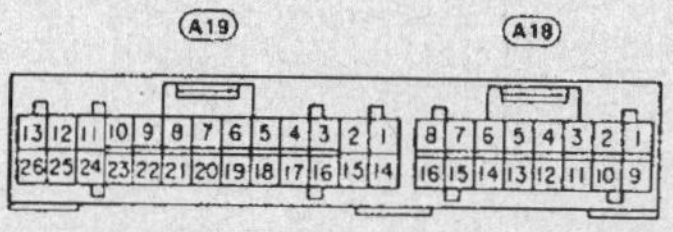
A19
A18
13 12 11 10 9 8 7 6 5 4 3 2 1
26 25 24 23 22 21 20 19 18 17 16 15 14
8 7 6 5 4 3 2 1
16 15 14 13 12 11 10 9

Terminal No.	Symbol	Connection	Terminal No.	Symbol	Connection
A19- 1	SFR	Right front solenoid	A18- 1	RL–	Left rear speed sensor
2	GND1	Ground	2	–	–
3	FR–	Right front speed sensor	3	GS2	Lateral acceleration sensor
4	–	–	4	D/G	DLC2
5	Tc	DLC1, DLC2	5	–	–
6	MT	ABS motor relay monitor	6	STP	Stop light switch
7	–	–	7	RSS	Sealed wiring harness
8	–	–	8	RR+	Right rear speed sensor
9	FL+	Left front speed sensor	9	RL+	Left rear speed sensor
10	FSS	Sealed wiring harness	10	GST	Lateral acceleration sensor
11	SR	ABS solenoid relay	11	–	–
12	IG1	Ignition switch	12	GS1	Lateral acceleration sensor
13	SFL	Left front solenoid	13	WA	ABS warning light
14	SRL	Left rear solenoid	14	PKB	Parking brake switch
15	GND2	Ground	15	Ts	DLC1
16	FR+	Right front speed sensor	16	RR–	Right rear speed sensor
17	–	–			
18	AST	ABS solenoid relay monitor			
19	–	–			
20	–	–			
21	–	–			
22	FL–	Left front speed sensor			
23	MR	ABS motor relay			
24	R–	Relay ground			
25	BAT	Battery			
26	SRR	Right rear solenoid			

TY4029400140010X

Fig. 195 Anti-lock brake system circuit test (Part 1 of 5). 1994–96 Supra less traction control

Symbols (Terminals No.)	STD Voltage (V)	Condition
BAT (A19-25) – GND (A19-15)	10 – 14	Always
IG 1 (A19-12) – GND (A19-2)	10 – 14	IG switch ON
SR (A19-11) – R– (A19-24)	9 – 14	IG switch ON, ABS warning light OFF
MR (A19-23) – R– (A19-24)	Below 1.0	IG switch ON
SFR (A19-1) – GND (A19-2)	10 – 14	IG switch ON, ABS warning light OFF
SFL (A19-13) – GND (A19-2)	10 – 14	IG switch ON, ABS warning light OFF
SRR (A19-26) – GND (A19-15)	10 – 14	IG switch ON, ABS warning light OFF
SRL (A19-14) – GND (A19-15)	10 – 14	IG switch ON, ABS warning light OFF
AST (A19-18) – GND (A19-15)	10 – 14	IG switch ON, ABS warning light OFF
WA (A18-13) – GND (A19-15)	Below 2.0	IG switch ON, ABS warning light ON
	10 – 14	IG switch ON, ABS warning light OFF
PKB (A18-14) – GND (A19-15)	Below 1.5	IG switch ON, PKB switch ON
	10 – 14	IG switch ON, PKB switch OFF
STP (A18-6) – GND (A19-2)	Below 1.5	Stop light switch OFF
	10 – 14	Stop light switch ON
D/G (A18-4) – GND (A19-2)	10 – 14	IG switch ON, ABS warning light OFF
Tc (A19-5) – GND (A19-2)	10 – 14	IG switch ON
Ts (A18-15) – GND (A19-15)	10 – 14	IG switch ON
FR+ (A19-16) – FR– (A19-3)	AC generation	IG switch ON Slowly turn right front wheel
FL+ (A19-9) – FL– (A19-22)	AC generation	IG switch ON Slowly turn left front wheel
RR+ (A18-8) – RR– (A18-16)	AC generation	IG switch ON Slowly turn right rear wheel
RL+ (A18-9) – RL– (A18-1)	AC generation	IG switch ON Slowly turn left rear wheel
GS 1 (A18-12) – GND (A19-15)	4 – 6 or 7 – 11	IG switch ON, Vehicle parked on a level surface
GS 2 (A18-3) – GND (A19-2)	4 – 6	IG switch ON, Vehicle parked on a level surface

TY4029400140020X

Fig. 195 Anti-lock brake system circuit test (Part 2 of 5). 1994–96 Supra less traction control

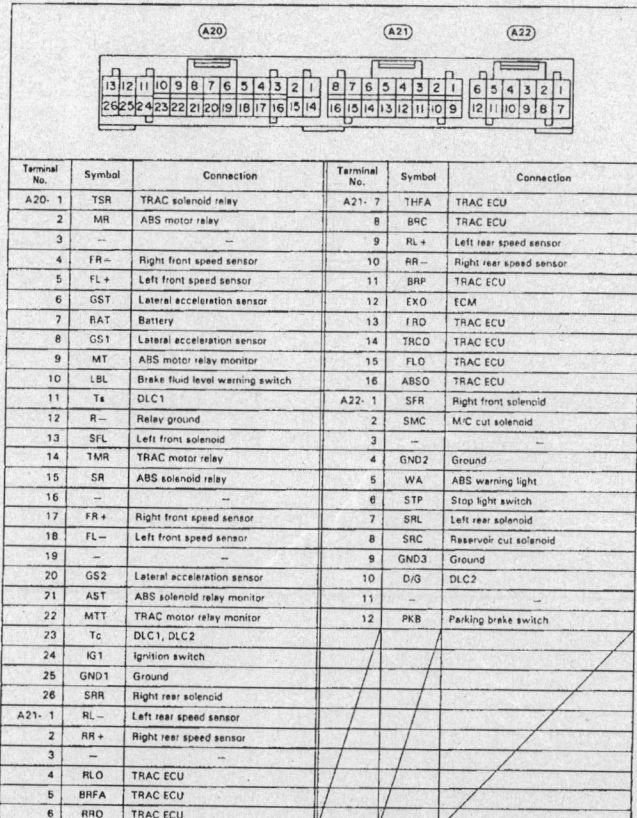

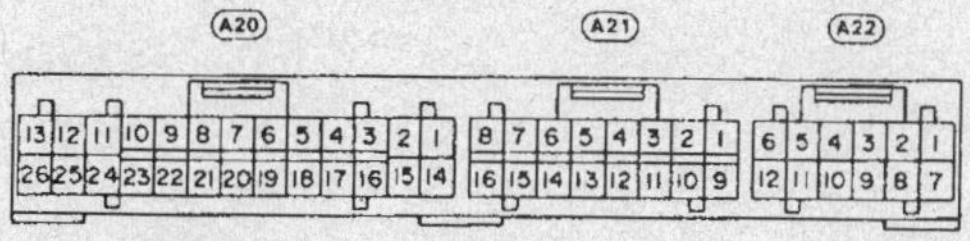
A20
A21
A22
13 12 11 10 9 8 7 6 5 4 3 2 1
26 25 24 23 22 21 20 19 18 17 16 15 14
8 7 6 5 4 3 2 1
16 15 14 13 12 11 10 9
6 5 4 3 2 1
12 11 10 9 8 7

Terminal No.	Symbol	Connection	Terminal No.	Symbol	Connection
A20- 1	TSR	TRAC solenoid relay	A21- 7	THFA	TRAC ECU
2	MR	ABS motor relay	8	BRC	TRAC ECU
3	–	–	9	RL+	Left rear speed sensor
4	FR–	Right front speed sensor	10	RR–	Right rear speed sensor
5	FL+	Left front speed sensor	11	BRP	TRAC ECU
6	GST	Lateral acceleration sensor	12	EXO	ECM
7	BAT	Battery	13	FRO	TRAC ECU
8	GS1	Lateral acceleration sensor	14	TRCO	TRAC ECU
9	MT	ABS motor relay monitor	15	FLO	TRAC ECU
10	LBL	Brake fluid level warning switch	16	ABSO	TRAC ECU
11	Ts	DLC1	A22- 1	SFR	Right front solenoid
12	R–	Relay ground	2	SMC	M/C cut solenoid
13	SFL	Left front solenoid	3	–	–
14	TMR	TRAC motor relay	4	GND2	Ground
15	SR	ABS solenoid relay	5	WA	ABS warning light
16	–	–	6	STP	Stop light switch
17	FR+	Right front speed sensor	7	SRL	Left rear solenoid
18	FL–	Left front speed sensor	8	SRC	Reservoir cut solenoid
19	–	–	9	GND3	Ground
20	GS2	Lateral acceleration sensor	10	D/G	DLC2
21	AST	ABS solenoid relay monitor	11	–	–
22	MTT	TRAC motor relay monitor	12	PKB	Parking brake switch
23	Tc	DLC1, DLC2			
24	IG1	Ignition switch			
25	GND1	Ground			
26	SRR	Right rear solenoid			
A21- 1	RL–	Left rear speed sensor			
2	RR+	Right rear speed sensor			
3	–	–			
4	RLO	TRAC ECU			
5	BRFA	TRAC ECU			
6	RRO	TRAC ECU			

TY4029400140030X

Fig. 195 Anti-lock brake system circuit test (Part 3 of 5). 1994–96 Supra w/traction control

Symbols (Terminals No.)	STD Voltage (V)	Condition
BAT (A20-7) – GND (A20-25)	10 – 14	Always
IG 1 (A20-24) – GND (A20-25)	10 – 14	IG switch ON
SR (A20-15) – R– (A20-12)	8.3 – 14	IG switch ON, ABS warning light OFF
MR (A20-2) – R– (A20-12)	Below 1.0	IG switch ON
TSR (A20-1) – R– (A20-12)	8.3 – 14	IG switch ON, TRAC and TRAC OFF indicator light OFF
TMR (A20-14) – R– (A20-12)	Below 1.0	IG switch ON
SFR (A22-1) – GND (A22-9)	10 – 14	IG switch ON, ABS warning light OFF
SFL (A20-13) – GND (A20-25)	10 – 14	IG switch ON, ABS warning light OFF
SRR (A20-26) – GND (A20-25)	10 – 14	IG switch ON, ABS warning light OFF
SRL (A22-7) – GND (A22-9)	10 – 14	IG switch ON, ABS warning light OFF
AST (A20-21) – GND (A20-25)	10 – 14	IG switch ON, ABS warning light OFF
SMC (A22-2) – GND (A22-9)	10 – 14	IG switch ON, TRAC and TRAC OFF indicator light OFF
SRC (A22-8) – GND (A22-9)	10 – 14	IG switch ON, TRAC and TRAC OFF indicator light OFF
WA (A22-5) – GND (A22-4)	Below 2.0	IG switch ON, ABS warning light ON
	10 – 14	IG switch ON, ABS warning light OFF
PKB (A22-12) – GND (A22-4)	Below 1.5	IG switch ON, PKB switch ON Fluid in M/C reservoir above MIN level.
	10 – 14	IG switch ON, PKB switch OFF Fluid in M/C reservoir above MIN level.
LBL (A20-10) – GND (A20-25)	10 – 14	IG switch ON Fluid in M/C reservoir above MIN level.
STP (A22-6) – GND (A22-4)	Below 1.5	Stop light switch OFF
	8 – 14	Stop light switch ON
D/G (A22-10) – GND (A22-9)	10 – 14	IG switch ON, ABS warning light OFF
Tc (A20-23) – GND (A20-25)	10 – 14	IG switch ON
Ts (A20-11) – GND (A20-25)	10 – 14	IG switch ON
FR+ (A20-17) – FR– (A20-4)	10 – 14	IG switch ON Slowly turn right front wheel.

TY4029400140040X

Fig. 195 Anti-lock brake system circuit test (Part 4 of 5). 1994–96 Supra w/traction control

Symbols (Terminal No.)	STD Voltage (V)	Conditions
FL+ (A20-5) – FL– (A20-18)	AC generation	IG switch ON Slowly turn left front wheel.
RR+ (A21-2) – RR– (A21-10)	AC generation	IG switch ON Slowly turn right rear wheel.
RL+ (A21-9) – RL– (A21-1)	AC generation	IG switch ON Slowly turn left rear wheel.
FRO (A21-13) – GND (A22-4)	Pulse generation	IG switch ON Slowly turn right front wheel.
FLO (A21-15) – GND (A22-4)	Pulse generation	IG switch ON Slowly turn left front wheel.
RRO (A21-6) – GND (A22-4)	Pulse generation	IG switch ON Slowly turn right rear wheel.
RLO (A21-4) – GND (A22-4)	Pulse generation	IG switch ON Slowly turn left rear wheel.
GS 1 (A20-8) – GND (A20-25)	4 – 6 or 7 – 11	IG switch ON, Vehicle parked on a level surface
GS 2 (A20-20) – GND (A20-25)	4 – 6	IG switch ON, Vehicle parked on a level surface
EXO (A21-12) – GND (A22-4)	10 – 14	IG switch ON

TY4029400140050X

Fig. 195 Anti-lock brake system circuit test (Part 5 of 5). 1994–96 Supra w/traction control

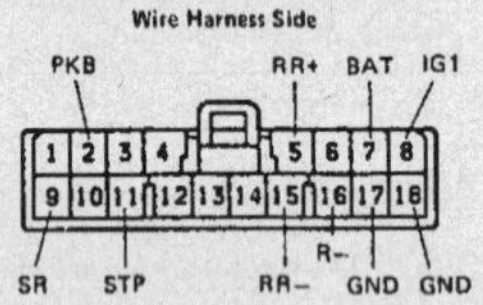
Wire Harness Side
PKB
RR+
BAT
IG1
1 2 3 4 5 6 7 8
9 10 11 12 13 14 15 16 17 18
R–
SR
STP
RR–
GND
GND

Tester Connection	Check Item	Condition	Voltage or Resistance Value	Trouble Part
PKB – Body ground	Voltage	Ignition SW on and PKB lever pulled	About 0 V	PKB switch, level warning switch
		Ignition SW on and PKB lever returned	Battery voltage	
RR+ – RR–	Resistance	–	770 – 890 Ω	Speed sensor
BAT – Body ground	Voltage	–	Battery voltage	Wire harness
IG1 – Body ground	Voltage	Ignition SW on	Battery voltage	ECU-IG fuse, wire harness
		Ignition SW off	About 0 V	
SR – R–	Resistance	–	80 Ω	Solenoid relay
STP – Body ground	Voltage	Ignition SW off and brake pedal depressed	Battery voltage	Stop light switch, stop light
	Continuity	Ignition SW off and brake pedal returned	Continuity	
GND – Body ground	Continuity	–	Continuity	Wire harness

TY4029300136000X

Fig. 197 Anti-lock brake system circuit test (w/ computer connector disconnected). T100

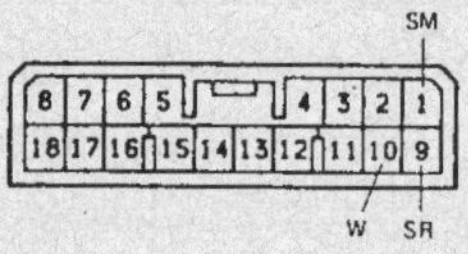
SM
8 7 6 5 4 3 2 1
18 17 16 15 14 13 12 11 10 9
W
SR

Tester Connection	Condition	Voltage	Trouble Part
SM – Body ground	Ignition switch ON	Battery voltage	Solenoid relay, Actuator
	Ignition switch ON and "REAR ANTILOCK" warning light goes on	About 0 V	
SR – Body ground	Ignition switch ON	Battery voltage	
	Ignition switch ON and "REAR ANTILOCK" warning light goes on	About 0 V	
W – Body ground	Ignition switch ON	Battery voltage	Warning light bulb
	Ignition switch ON and "REAR ANTILOCK" warning light goes on	About 0 V	

TY4029300126000X

Fig. 196 Anti-lock brake system circuit test (w/ computer connector connected). T100

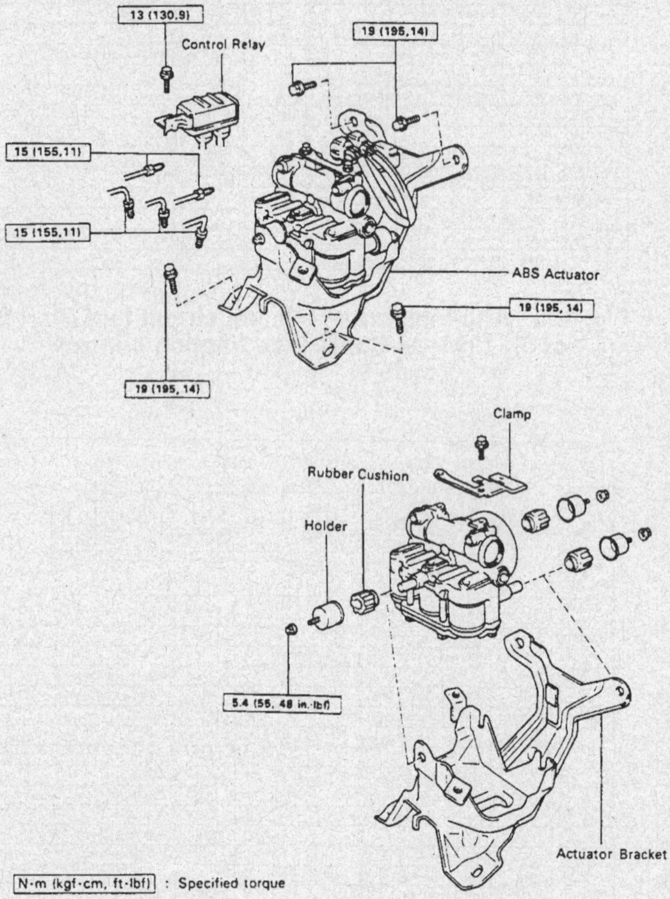
13 (130,9)
Control Relay
19 (195,14)
15 (155,11)
15 (155,11)
ABS Actuator
19 (195, 14)
19 (195, 14)
Clamp
Rubber Cushion
Holder
5.4 (55, 48 in.·lbf)
Actuator Bracket
N·m (kgf·cm, ft·lbf) : Specified torque

TY4029300141000X

Fig. 198 ABS actuator removal. 1993–94 Land Cruiser

Automatic Transmissions/ Transaxles

NOTE: On Air Bag Equipped Models, Refer To "Air Bag System Precautions" Located In The Front Of This Manual For System Disarming & Arming Procedures.

INDEX

	Page No.
Application Chart	48-257
A131L, A241E, A243L, A244E, A245E & A246E Automatic Transaxles	48-265
A132L & A242L Automatic Transaxle	48-275
A140E Automatic Transaxles	48-279
A340E, A340F & A340H Automatic Transmissions	48-285
A343F Automatic Transmission	48-299
A43D, A46DE & A46DF Automatic Transmissions	48-258
A440F & A442F Automatic Transmissions	48-296
A540E, A540H & A541E Automatic Transaxles	48-304

Application Chart

Models	Transaxle/Transmission
1993	
Camry	A140E, A540E
Celica	A241E, A243L
Corolla	A131L, A245E
Land Cruiser	A440F
MR2	A241E
Paseo	A244E
Pickup	A43D, A340E, A340F, A340H
Previa	A46DE, A46DF
Supra	A340E
Tercel	A132L
T100	A340E, A340F
4Runner	A340E, A340F, A340H
1994	
Camry	A140E, A540E
Celica	A140E, A246E
Corolla	A131L, A245E
Land Cruiser	A442F
MR2	A241E
Paseo	A244E
Pickup	A43D, A340E, A340F, A340H
Previa	A46DE, A46DF
Supra	A340E
Tercel	A132L
T100	A340E, A340F
4Runner	A340E, A340F, A340H
1995	
Avalon	A541E
Camry	A140E, A541E
Celica	A140E, A246E
Corolla	A131L, A245E
Land Cruiser	A343F
MR2	A241E
Paseo	A244E
Pickup/Tacoma	A43D, A340E, A340F, A340H
Previa	A46DE, A46DF, A340E, A340F

Continued

Models	Transaxle/Transmission
1995	
Supra	A340E
Tercel	A132L, A242L
T100	A340E, A340F, A340H
4Runner	A340E, A340F, A340H
1996	
Avalon	A541E
Camry	A140E, A541E
Celica	A140E, A246E
Corolla	A131L, A245E
Land Cruiser	A343F
Paseo	A244E
Previa	A340E, A340F
RAV4	A241E, A540H
Supra	A340E
Tacoma	A43D, A340E, A340F, A340H
Tercel	A132L, A242L
T100	A340E, A340F
4Runner	A340E, A340F

A43D, A46DE & A46DF Automatic Transmissions

INDEX

Page No.

Adjustments 48-260
Manual Shift Linkage 48-260
Neutral Start Switch 48-261
Park Lock Cable 48-261
Throttle Cable 48-260
In-Vehicle Repairs 48-261
Governor Or Rotor Sensor, Replace 48-262
Throttle Cable, Replace 48-261
Valve Body, Replace 48-261
Maintenance 48-260
Fluid Change 48-260
Fluid Check 48-260
Precautions 48-258
Air Bag Systems 48-258
Audio Coded Anti-Theft System 48-258
Tightening Specifications 48-263
Transmission, Replace 48-262
Pickup & 4Runner 48-262
Previa 48-263
Tacoma 48-262
Troubleshooting 48-258
Delayed Shifting-Up Or Down 48-259
Drag, Binding Or Tie-Up On 1-2, 2-3 Or 3-O/D Upshift 48-260
Fluid Smells, Discolored Or Burned 48-259
Harsh Downshift 48-259
Harsh Engagement Into Any Range 48-259
Incorrect Coast Downshift 48-260
Incorrect Shift Lever Position 48-260
No Coast Downshift 48-260
No Engine Braking In 2nd Range 48-260
No Kickdown 48-260
No Lock-Up In 2nd, 3rd Or O/D 48-260
Shift Lock System 48-258
Slips On Upshift-Slips Or Shudders On Acceleration 48-259
Vehicle Does Not Hold In Park 48-260
Vehicle Does Not Move In Any Range 48-259

PRECAUTIONS

AIR BAG SYSTEMS

Refer to "Air Bag System Precautions" in the front of this manual for system disarming and arming procedures.

AUDIO CODED ANTI-THEFT SYSTEM

Some models are equipped with an audio coded anti-theft system that will disable the radio when the battery cable is disconnected. The system can be identified by the "ANTI-THEFT SYSTEM" on the cassette lid. Obtain 3 digit code for input. Reset system after service as follows:

1. Obtain 3 digit audio theft code.
2. Depress 1 (PROG) while depressing righthand side of TUNE SEEK button, - - - will appear in tape operation display.
3. To enter the first digit, depress 1 (PROG) button repeatedly until the number of times depressed equals the first digit (depress the 1 button six times if the first digit if five, first press equals 0).
4. To enter second digit, depress 2 (APS) button repeatedly until the number of times depressed equals the second digit.
5. To enter third digit, depress 3 (RPT) button repeatedly until the number of times depressed equals the third digit.
6. If - - - is displayed after inputting digits, repeat procedure.
7. When code appears in display, depress and hold SCAN button until SEC appears.
8. When SEC disappears audio system is operative.
9. If Err is displayed, repeat procedure. **Attempting to input code more than 9 times may permanently disable audio system.**

TROUBLESHOOTING

SHIFT LOCK SYSTEM

PICKUP W/A43D

The shift lock system, **Fig. 1,** is mechanical and requires replacement of the shift lock mechanism, if faulty.

PREVIA W/A46DE & A46DF

The shift lock system, **Fig. 2,** is mechanical and requires adjustment of the shift lock pin, if faulty.

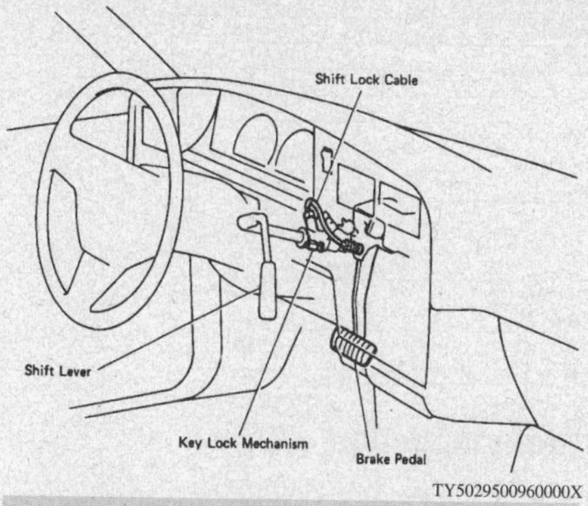
Shift Lock Cable
Shift Lever
Key Lock Mechanism
Brake Pedal
TY5029500960000X

Fig. 1 Shift lock system components. Pickup w/A43D

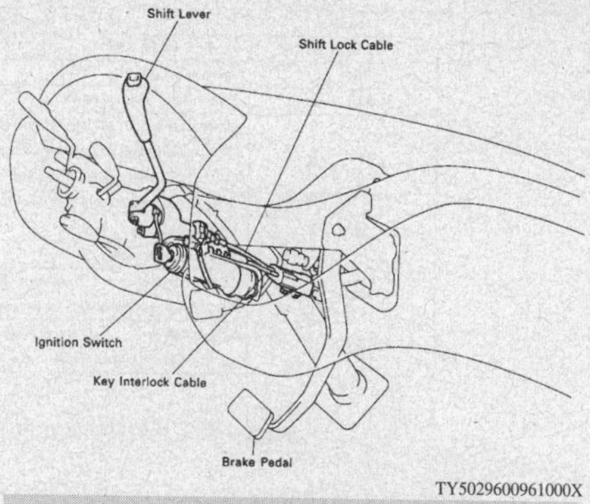
Shift Lever
Shift Lock Cable
Ignition Switch
Key Interlock Cable
Brake Pedal
TY5029600961000X

Fig. 2 Shift Lock System Components. Previa w/A46DE & A46DF

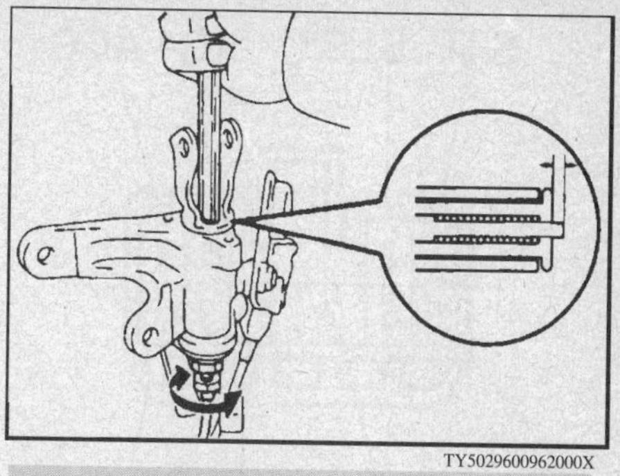
TY5029600962000X

Fig. 3 Shift lock pin adjustment

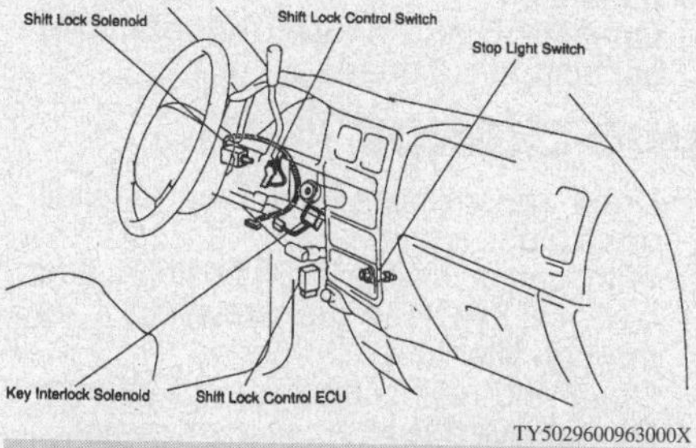
Shift Lock Solenoid
Shift Lock Control Switch
Stop Light Switch
Key Interlock Solenoid
Shift Lock Control ECU
TY5029600963000X

Fig. 4 Shift lock system components. Tacoma w/A43D

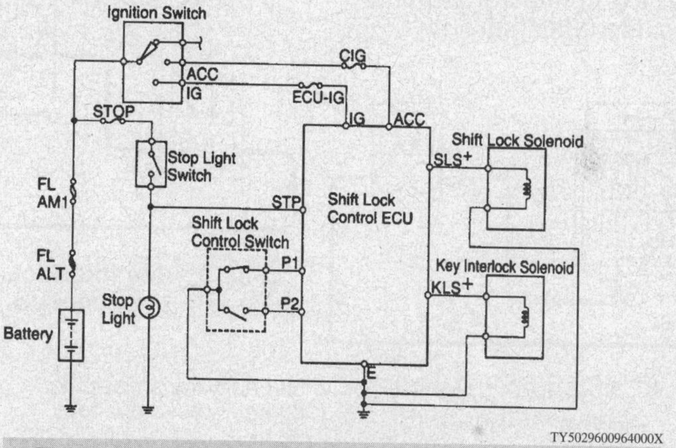
Ignition Switch
CIG
ACC
IG
ECU-IG
STOP
IG
ACC
Shift Lock Solenoid
SLS+
Stop Light Switch
FL AM1
STP
Shift Lock Control ECU
Shift Lock Control Switch
P1
P2
FL ALT
Key Interlock Solenoid
KLS+
Stop Light
Battery
E
TY5029600964000X

Fig. 5 Shift lock system wiring circuit. Tacoma w/A43D

Shift Lock Pin Adjustment

1. Adjust pin length by tightening and loosening nut. Pin should be above or below shift lever assembly surface, **Fig. 3,** within the following limits:
   a. Above surface: 0.0118 inch max.
   b. Below surface: 0.0276 inch max.
2. **Torque** nut to 18 ft. lbs.
3. Check shift lock system operation.

TACOMA W/A43D

The shift lock system, **Figs. 4 and 5,** is electronically controlled and requires testing of shift lock electronic control components, if faulty.

Shift Lock Control ECU Inspection

Using a suitable voltmeter, measure voltage at each terminal of the ECU connector, **Fig. 6.** Refer to **Fig. 7** for measuring conditions and voltage specifications.

Shift Lock Solenoid Inspection

1. Disconnect solenoid connector.
2. Using suitable ohmmeter, measure resistance between terminals 5 and 6, **Fig. 8.** Resistance should be 29-35 ohms.
3. Apply battery positive voltage between terminals. Ensure operating noise can be heard from solenoid.

Key Interlock Solenoid Inspection

1. Disconnect solenoid connector.
2. Using suitable ohmmeter, measure resistance between terminals 3 and 4, **Fig. 9.**
3. Apply battery positive voltage between terminals. Ensure operating noise can be heard from solenoid.

Shift Lock Control Switch Inspection

Using a suitable ohmmeter, check for continuity between terminals indicated in **Figs. 10 and 11.**

FLUID SMELLS, DISCOLORED OR BURNED

1. Contaminated fluid.
2. Faulty torque convertor.
3. Faulty transmission.

VEHICLE DOES NOT MOVE IN ANY RANGE

1. Disconnected or improperly adjusted manual shift linkage.
2. Faulty valve body or primary regulator.
3. Faulty parking lock pawl.
4. Faulty torque converter or broken driveplate.
5. Clogged oil pump inlet screen.
6. Faulty electronic controls.
7. Faulty transmission.

HARSH ENGAGEMENT INTO ANY RANGE

1. Improperly adjusted throttle cable.
2. Faulty valve body or primary regulator.
3. Faulty accumulator pistons.
4. Faulty transmission.

HARSH DOWNSHIFT

1. Improperly adjusted throttle cable.
2. Faulty throttle cable and/or cam.
3. Faulty accumulator pistons.
4. Faulty valve body.
5. Faulty transmission.

DELAYED SHIFTING-UP OR DOWN

1. Improperly adjusted throttle cable.
2. Faulty throttle cable and/or cam.
3. Faulty governor.
4. Faulty valve body.
5. Faulty electronic controls.
6. Faulty solenoid valve.

SLIPS ON UPSHIFT-SLIPS OR SHUDDERS ON ACCELERATION

1. Improperly adjusted shift linkage.
2. Improperly adjusted throttle cable.
3. Faulty valve body.

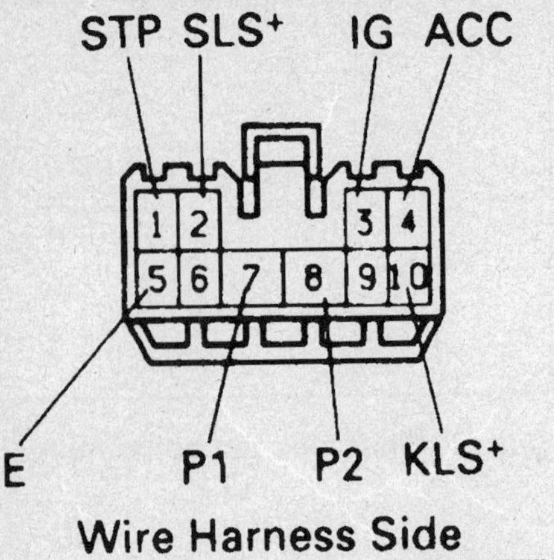
STP SLS+ IG ACC
1 2 3 4
5 6 7 8 9 10
E P1 P2 KLS+
Wire Harness Side

TY5029600965000X

Fig. 6 ECU connector terminal identification

Terminal	Measuring Condition	Voltage (V)
ACC – E	Ignition switch ACC	10 – 14
IG – E	Ignition switch ON	10 – 14
STP – E	Depressing brake pedal	10 – 14
KLS+ – E	① Ignition switch ACC and P position	0
	② Ignition switch ACC and except P position	10 – 14
	③ (After approx 1 second)	6 – 9
SLS+ – E	① Ignition switch ON and P position	0
	② Depress brake pedal	8.5 – 13.5
	③ Except P position	0
P1 – E	① Ignition switch ON, P position and depress brake pedal	0
	② Shift except P position under conditions above	9 – 13.5
P2 – E	① Ignition switch ACC and P position	9 – 13.5
	② Shift except P position under conditions above	0

TY5029600966000X

Fig. 7 Shift lock control inspection

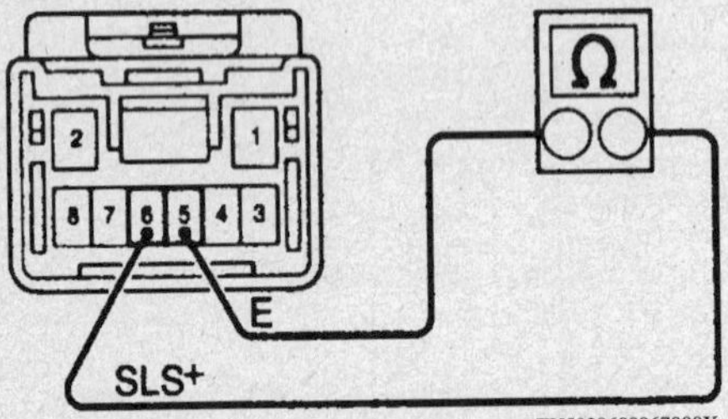
2
1
8 7 6 5 4 3
E
SLS+
Ω

TY5029600967000X

Fig. 8 Shift lock solenoid inspection

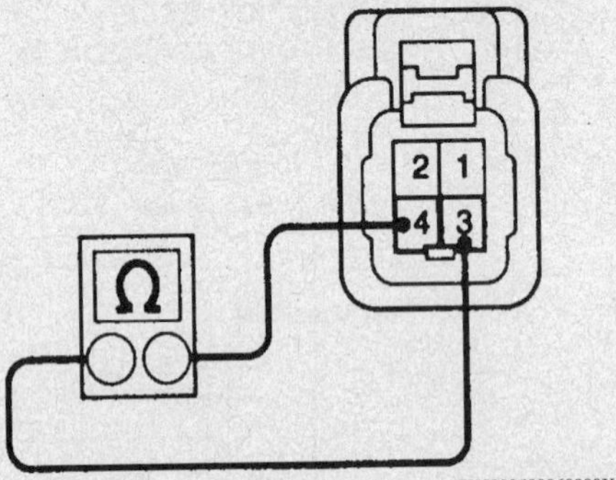
2 1
4 3
Ω

TY5029600968000X

Fig. 9 Key interlock solenoid inspection

4. Faulty solenoid valve.
5. Faulty transmission.

VEHICLE DOES NOT HOLD IN PARK

1. Improperly adjusted manual linkage.
2. Faulty parking lock pawl, cam or spring.

NO ENGINE BRAKING IN 2ND RANGE

1. Faulty valve body.
2. Faulty electronic control.
3. Faulty solenoid valve.
4. Faulty transmission.

NO KICKDOWN

1. Improperly adjusted throttle cable.
2. Faulty governor body.
3. Faulty valve body.
4. Faulty transmission.

NO COAST DOWNSHIFT

1. Faulty governor.
2. Faulty valve body.
3. Faulty solenoid valve.
4. Faulty electronic control.

INCORRECT COAST DOWNSHIFT

1. Improperly adjusted throttle cable.
2. Faulty valve body.
3. Faulty solenoid valve.
4. Faulty electric control.

5. Faulty transmission.
6. Faulty governor body.

NO LOCK-UP IN 2ND, 3RD OR O/D

1. Faulty electric control.
2. Faulty valve body.
3. Faulty solenoid valve.
4. Faulty transmission.

DRAG, BINDING OR TIE-UP ON 1-2, 2-3 OR 3-O/D UPSHIFT

1. Improperly adjusted manual linkage.
2. Faulty valve body.
3. Faulty transmission.

INCORRECT SHIFT LEVER POSITION

1. Improperly adjusted manual linkage.
2. Faulty manual valve and lever.
3. Faulty transmission.

MAINTENANCE

FLUID CHECK

1. Operate vehicle, allow transmission fluid to reach normal operating temperature, 158–176°F.
2. Position vehicle on level surface, then apply parking brake.
3. With engine idling, depress brake pedal, then move shift lever through all positions from P to L, then return to P position.
4. Remove transmission dipstick and clean, then return dipstick, remove and check fluid level in HOT range.
5. **On A43D models,** total capacity is 6.9 quarts.
6. **On A46DE and A46DF models,** total capacity is 6.0 quarts.

FLUID CHANGE

1. Drain transmission fluid, then reinstall drain plug.
2. With ignition switch in Off position, add ATF DEXRON II transmission fluid through filler tube.
3. Drain and refill capacity is 2.5 quarts. **Do not overfill.**
4. Start engine, then move shift lever through all positions.
5. With engine idling, check fluid level, add fluid to COOL level.
6. Operate vehicle, allow transmission fluid to reach normal operating temperature, 158–176°F, then recheck.

ADJUSTMENTS

MANUAL SHIFT LINKAGE

1. Remove cross shaft rod attaching nut.
2. Push cross shaft rod fully downward.
3. Return rod three notches to N position.
4. Set shift lever to N position.
5. While lightly holding shift lever toward R position, adjust cross shaft rod nut.
6. Tighten cross shaft rod nut.
7. Start engine, check transmission operation in all selector positions.

THROTTLE CABLE

1. Remove air cleaner, fully depress accelerator pedal and inspect throttle plate.
2. If throttle plate does not open fully with accelerator pedal depressed, adjust accelerator linkage.
3. With accelerator pedal held fully depressed, loosen adjusting nuts on throttle cable, **Fig. 12.**
4. Adjust cable to obtain 0–0.04 inch (0–1 mm) clearance between cable housing and cable stop or painted mark, **Fig. 12. Service replacement cables do not have a cable stop, and a mark must be painted on the inner cable for adjustment reference. If cable installed in vehicle does not have the stop or reference mark, refer to "Throttle Cable, Replace."**
5. Tighten adjuster nuts and release accelerator pedal.

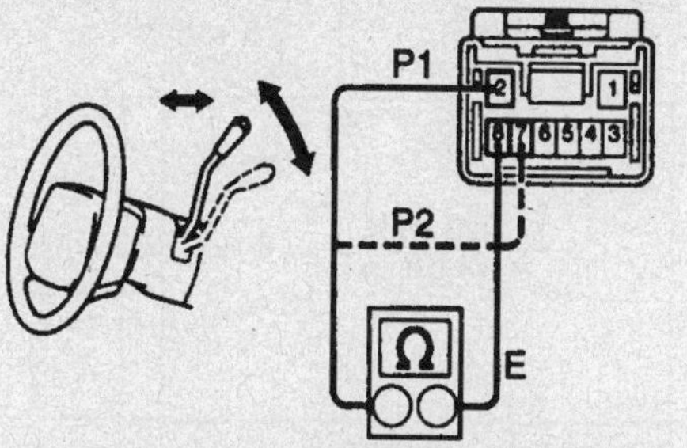
P1
P2
E
Ω

TY5029600969000X

Fig. 10 Shift lock switch connector terminal identification

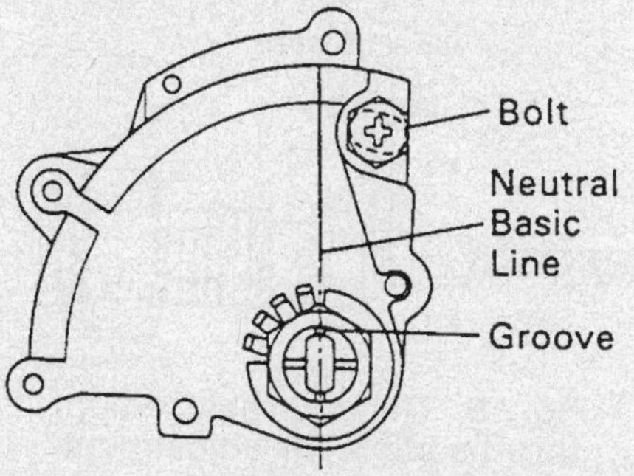
Bolt
Neutral
Basic
Line
Groove

TY5029100749000X

Fig. 13 Neutral safety switch adjustment

6. Fully depress accelerator pedal and recheck adjustment, then install air cleaner.

NEUTRAL START SWITCH

1. Ensure engine can be started on in N or P range.
2. Loosen neutral switch attaching bolt, then set shift lever in N position.
3. Align groove and neutral basic line, **Fig. 13.**
4. Hold position, then **torque** attaching bolt to 48 inch lbs.

PARK LOCK CABLE

1. Move shift lever to P position.
2. Turn ignition switch to lock position.
3. Loosen lower nuts, then ensure slide pin strikes rubber cushion.
4. **Torque** attaching nuts to 48 inch lbs.

IN-VEHICLE REPAIRS

VALVE BODY, REPLACE

A43D

Removal

1. Raise and support vehicle, clean exterior of transmission and drain fluid.
2. Remove bolt from filler tube support, if equipped.
3. Remove oil pan retaining bolts, pan and gasket, and filler tube. **Use care when removing filler tube, so as not to distort tube or damage seal.**
4. Remove oil feed tubes, if equipped, by prying at both ends with suitable levers.

Shift position	Tester condition to terminal number	Specified value
P position	E – P1	Continuity
P position (Pull the shift lever toward you)	E – P1 E – P2	Continuity
R, N, D, 2, L position	E – P2	Continuity

TY5029600970000X

Fig. 11 Shift lock control switch inspection

5. Remove oil strainer retaining bolts, strainer and gasket.
6. Support valve body and remove 17 retaining bolts, noting position of each bolt for assembly reference, then lower valve body.
7. Disconnect throttle cable from cam, **Fig. 14,** and remove valve body.

Installation

1. Push throttle cable fitting into cam, position valve body with manual valve aligned with manual lever and loosely install several retaining bolts to hold valve body. **Valve body retaining bolts are of different lengths, and must be properly positioned to avoid transmission damage. Proper position is shown in Fig. 15. Bolt lengths are given in millimeters.**
2. Remove accumulator piston retaining plate, install remaining valve body bolts and tighten all bolts hand tight.
3. Evenly tighten valve body bolts to specifications.
4. Ensure oil strainer is clean, install strainer using a new gasket and tighten to specifications.
5. Press oil feed tubes into position by hand, if equipped.
6. Install oil pan using a new gasket, evenly tighten to specifications, then install filler tube retaining bolts, if equipped.
7. Install drain plug and tighten to specifications.
8. Refill transmission to specified level and check transmission operation.

A46DE & A46DF

Removal

1. Fabricate a plate from aluminum or plastic to retain accumulator pistons as shown in **Fig. 16.**
2. Raise and support vehicle, clean exterior of transmission and drain fluid.
3. Remove bolt from oil filler tube support.
4. Remove oil pan retaining bolts, oil pan and gasket, and filler tube. **Use care when removing filler tube, so as not to distort tube or damage seal.**
5. Remove oil feed tubes in sequence shown in **Fig. 17,** using suitable levers to pry both ends of each tube.
6. Disconnect electrical connectors from solenoids, then remove oil strainer and gasket.
7. Support valve body and remove valve body retaining bolts, noting position of bolts for reassembly, **Fig. 18.**
8. Lower valve body slightly, remove

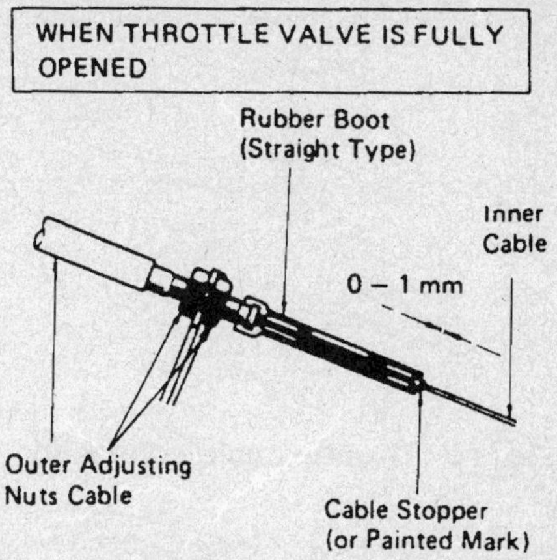
WHEN THROTTLE VALVE IS FULLY OPENED
Rubber Boot
(Straight Type)
Inner
Cable
0 – 1 mm
Outer Adjusting
Nuts Cable
Cable Stopper
(or Painted Mark)

TY5029100748000X

Fig. 12 Throttle cable adjustment

C-accumulator piston spring, then install accumulator piston retaining plate using pan bolts to hold plate.
9. Disconnect throttle cable from cam, **Fig. 14,** then remove valve body.

Installation

1. Connect throttle cable to cam, **Fig. 14,** then remove accumulator retaining plate.
2. Position valve body so that manual valve is aligned with manual lever and install C-accumulator piston spring.
3. Install valve body retaining bolts in proper positions, **Fig. 18,** and tighten bolts hand tight. **Valve body retaining bolts are of different lengths and must be properly positioned to avoid transmission damage. Proper position is shown in Fig. 18, with lengths given in millimeters and inches A is 25 mm (0.98 inch), B is 30 mm (1.18 inch), C is 47 mm (1.85 inch) and D is 60 mm (2.36 inch).**
4. Evenly tighten valve body bolts to specifications.
5. Install oil strainer using a new gasket and tighten to specifications.
6. Connect electrical connectors to solenoids.
7. Press oil feed tubes into position by hand reversing removal sequence, **Fig. 17. Ensure tubes and sediment magnets are positioned so that oil pan can be installed.**
8. Install oil pan using new gasket, evenly tighten to specifications, and install filler tube retaining bolt.
9. Install drain plug and tighten to specifications.
10. Refill transmission to specified level and check transmission operation.

THROTTLE CABLE, REPLACE

1. Remove air cleaner, as required.
2. Disconnect cable housing from bracket and retaining clips, and cable from throttle lever.
3. Raise and support vehicle and remove valve body as outlined.
4. Press cable out of transmission housing using a 10mm socket.

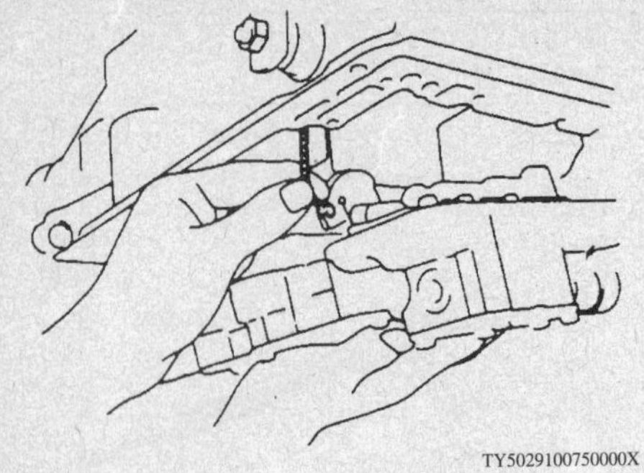
TY5029100750000X

Fig. 14 Throttle cable connection

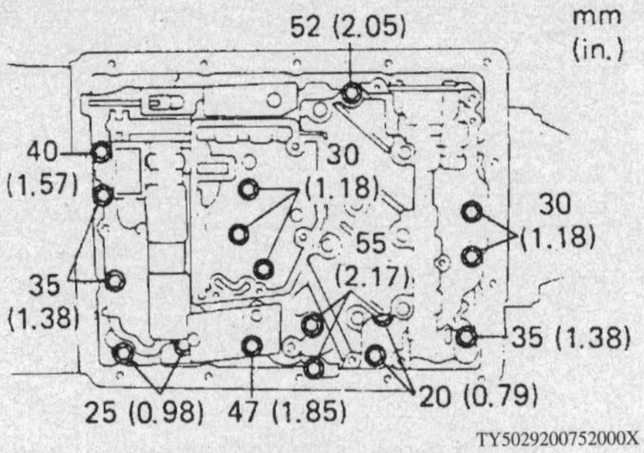
mm
(in.)
52 (2.05)
40
(1.57)
30
(1.18)
30
(1.18)
55
(2.17)
35
(1.38)
35 (1.38)
25 (0.98)
47 (1.85)
20 (0.79)
TY5029200752000X

Fig. 15 Valve body bolt identification. A43D

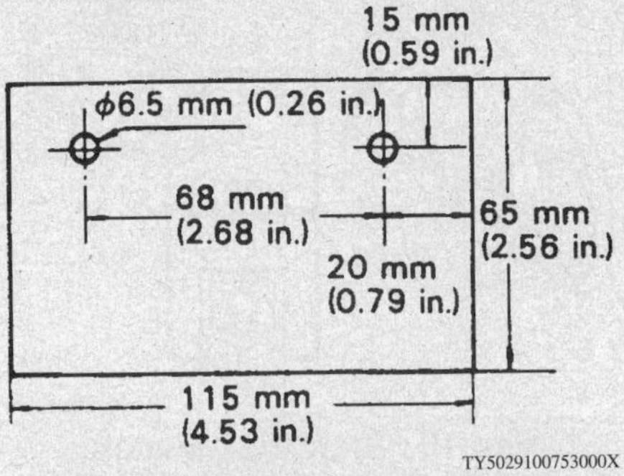
15 mm
(0.59 in.)
ϕ6.5 mm (0.26 in.)
68 mm
(2.68 in.)
65 mm
(2.56 in.)
20 mm
(0.79 in.)
115 mm
(4.53 in.)
TY5029100753000X

Fig. 16 Accumulator piston retaining plate. A46DE & A46DF

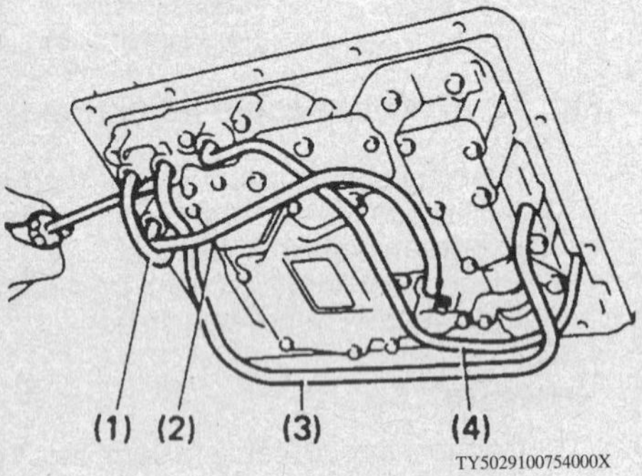
(1)
(2)
(3)
(4)
TY5029100754000X

Fig. 17 Oil feed tube removal sequence. A46DE & A46DF

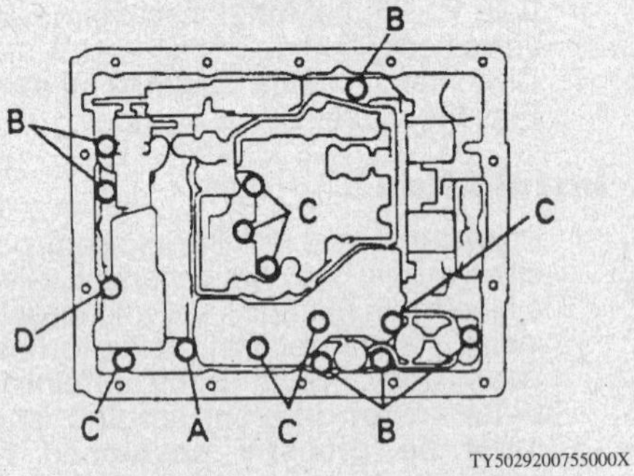
B
B
C
C
D
C
A
C
B
TY5029200755000X

Fig. 18 Valve body bolt identification. A46DE & A46DF

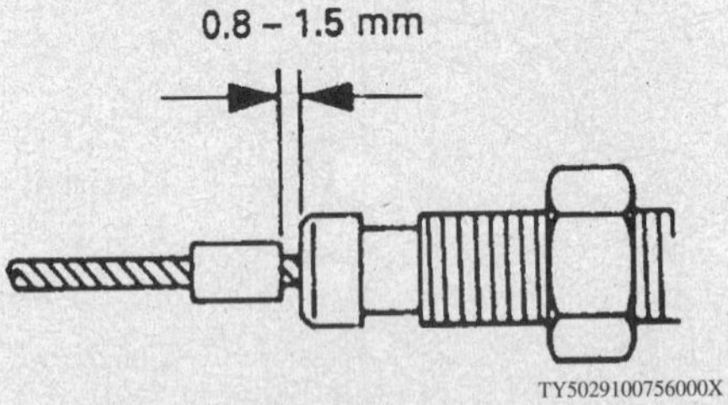
0.8 – 1.5 mm
TY5029100756000X

Fig. 19 Marking replacement throttle cable for adjustment

5. Install replacement cable in transmission housing ensure cable housing is fully seated.
6. Reinstall valve body as outlined, then lower vehicle.
7. Mark replacement cable for adjustment as follows:
   a. Pull inner cable from housing until slight resistance can be felt, and hold in this position. **Replacement cable does not have a cable stop, stake stopper.**
   b. Pull inner cable lightly until slight resistance is felt and hold it.
   c. Stake stopper .031–.059 inch, **Fig. 19.**
8. Reconnect cable to throttle lever and brackets, then adjust cable as outlined.
9. Ensure transmission is filled to specified level and road test vehicle.

GOVERNOR OR ROTOR SENSOR, REPLACE

Except Pickup

1. Raise and support vehicle and remove driveshaft.
2. Using a suitable jack, raise transmission just enough to take weight off rear mount.
3. Disconnect speedometer cable and remove cable drive gear assembly.
4. Disconnect ground strap and rubber exhaust hanger from crossmember and remove crossmember.
5. Remove extension housing retaining bolts, extension housing and seal.
6. Remove outer snap ring and speedometer drive gear from output shaft.
7. Remove lock ball and inner snap ring, if equipped.
8. Remove governor lock bolt, pry up retaining clip with a suitable lever and slide governor off output shaft.
9. Reverse procedure to install, noting the following:
   a. Ensure retaining clip is seated in shaft, **torque** governor lock bolt to 27–43 inch lbs., then stake lock plate.
   b. Renew extension housing and speedometer gear seals as needed.
   c. **Torque** extension housing bolts to 25 ft. lbs.
   d. Fill transmission fluid to specified level then road test vehicle.

Pickup

1. Raise and support vehicle and remove driveshaft.
2. Disconnect speedometer cable and remove cable drive gear assembly.
3. Remove bolts securing rear mount to bracket, then raise transmission using a suitable jack.
4. Remove rear mount from extension housing.
5. Remove extension housing retaining bolts, housing and gasket, noting position of bolts for assembly reference.
6. Remove and replace governor from output shaft as outlined for passenger cars.
7. Reverse procedure to complete installation.

TRANSMISSION

REPLACE

TACOMA

1. Remove transmission with engine as described in "Toyota Land Cruiser, 4Runner & Pickups" chapter.
2. Remove RH and LH stiffener plates and rear end plate, **Fig. 20.**
3. Remove starter.
4. Remove transmission mounting bolts and pull transmission toward rear.
5. Reverse procedure to install.

PICKUP & 4RUNNER

1. **On models with coded audio antitheft system,** disarm system as described under "Precautions."
2. **On all models** disconnect battery ground cable.
3. Remove air cleaner, then disconnect throttle cable from bracket and throttle lever.
4. Remove upper starter mounting bolt or nut.
5. Raise and support vehicle and drain transmission.
6. Disconnect electrical connectors to back-up lamp and neutral start switches and overdrive solenoid. Connectors are located near starter.
7. Remove lower starter mounting bolt and secure starter alongside engine.
8. Remove propeller shaft assembly.
9. Disconnect cooler lines, manual linkage and speedometer cable from transmission.
10. Remove exhaust pipe brace and transmission filler tube.
11. Support weight of transmission with a suitable jack and remove rear mount and bracket.
12. **On 4Runner models,** remove stabilizer bar attaching nut, then the stabilizer bar.
13. **On all models,** remove cover from under engine.
14. Position wooden block between engine oil pan and crossmember, then lower jack supporting transmission

until engine rests on block.

15. **On 4Runner models,** remove rear support member attaching bolts, then the rear support member.
16. **On all models,** pry out access hole cover from rear engine plate and remove 6 bolts securing torque converter to driveplate.
17. Fabricate guide pin by cutting head from spare torque converter bolt and install pin in 1 converter bolt hole.
18. Remove both side stiffener braces and all transmission mounting bolts. **Ensure transmission is properly supported on jack.**
19. Pry against converter guide pin to separate transmission from engine and remove transmission.
20. Reverse procedure to install, noting that **on models with coded audio anti-theft systems,** rearm as outlined under "Precautions."

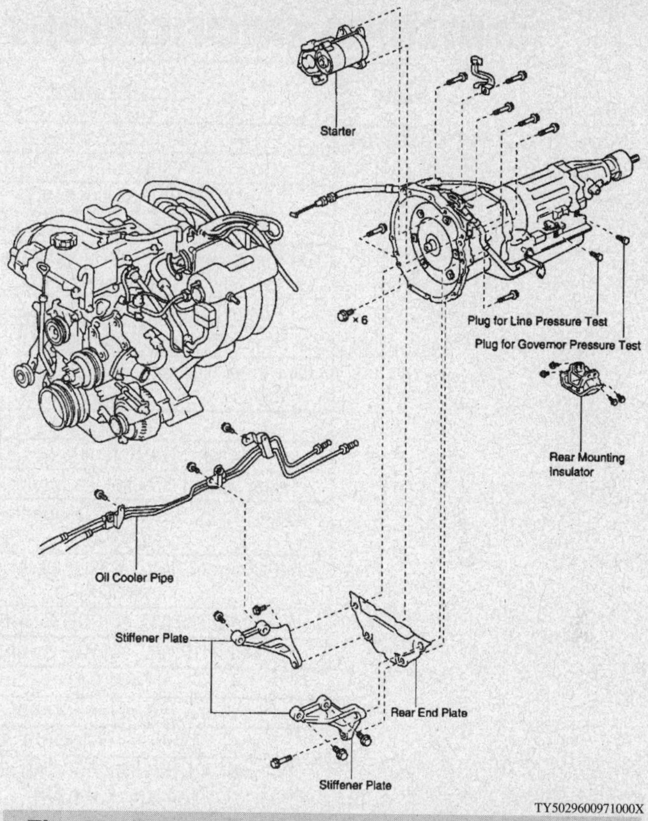
Starter
×6
Plug for Line Pressure Test
Plug for Governor Pressure Test
Rear Mounting Insulator
Oil Cooler Pipe
Stiffener Plate
Rear End Plate
Stiffener Plate
TY5029600971000X

Fig. 20 Transaxle replacement. Tacoma w/A43D

PREVIA

1. **On models with coded audio anti-theft system,** obtain three digit code.
2. **On all models** disconnect battery ground cable.
3. Remove transmission oil level gauge.
4. Remove throttle cable attaching clamp, then disconnect cable.
5. Raise and support vehicle.
6. Remove filler tube.
7. **On 4WD models,** remove front propeller shaft.
8. **On all models,** remove shift control cable, then bracket.
9. **On 2WD models,** remove starter connector attaching nut, disconnect electrical connectors, remove starter attaching nuts and bolts, then remove.
10. **On 4WD models,** disconnect starter electrical connector, remove starter attaching nuts and bolts, remove starter and front propeller shaft center bracket assembly.
11. **On all models,** remove stiffener plates.
12. Remove torque convertor cover, then turn crankshaft to remove torque convertor attaching bolts.
13. Remove oil cooler tubes, then remove exhaust pipe bracket.
14. **On 2WD models,** remove propeller shaft.
15. **On 4WD models,** remove rear propeller shaft.
16. **On all models,** using suitable transmission jack stands, raise transmission, then remove rear mount.
17. Remove transmission attaching bolts, then remove.
18. Reverse procedure to install, noting that **on models with coded audio anti-theft systems,** rearm as outlined under "Precautions."

TIGHTENING SPECIFICATIONS

Year	Component	Torque/ Ft. Lbs.
1993–96	Auxiliary Crossmember (A43D)	70
	Center Support (A43D)	19
	Center Support To Transmission (A46DE & A46DF)	19
	Driveplate (A43D)	61
	Driveplate (A46DE & A46DF)	54
	Exhaust Pipe To Manifold (A43D)	46
	Extension Housing To Case (A46DE & A46DF)	25
	Extension Housing	25
	Governor Body (A43D)	9
	Governor Body (A46DE & A46DF)	35①
	Governor Lock Bolt	27–43①
	Neutral Start Switch (Bolt)	48①
	Neutral Start Switch (Nut)	35①

Continued

TIGHTENING SPECIFICATIONS—Continued

Year	Component	Torque/ Ft. Lbs.
1993–96	Oil Cooler Lines	25
	Oil Drain Plug	15
	Oil Pan Bolts (A43D)	39①
	Oil Pan Bolts (A46DE & A46DF)	48①
	Oil Pump Body To Oil Pump Cover (A46DE & A46DF)	65①
	Oil Pump To Front Case (A46DE & A46DF)	8
	Oil Pump To Stator Shaft (A46DE & A46DF)	65①
	Oil Pump To Transmission Case (A46DE & A46DF)	16
	Oil Strainer	48①
	Overdrive Solenoid (A43D)	61①
	Rear Mount Bracket To Mount (A43D)	22
	Rear Mount Bracket To Support Member (A43D)	43
	Shift Control Shaft To Shift Lever (A46DE & A46DF)	14
	Starter (2WD, A46DE & A46DF)	30
	Starter (4WD, A46DE & A46DF)	40
	Test Plug	65①
	Torque Converter (A43D)	20
	Torque Converter (A46DE & A46DF)	30
	Transfer Adapter To Transmission Case (A46DE & A46DF)	25
	Transfer (A46DE & A46DF)	33
	Transmission Housing To Case (12 mm, A46DE & A46DF)	42
	Transmission Housing To Case (10 mm, A46DE & A46DF)	25
	Transmission Housing To Converter (12mm, A43D)	42
	Transmission Housing To Converter (10mm, A43D)	25
	Transmission Mounting (A43D)	47
	Upper Valve Body To Lower (A43D)	48①
	Valve Body Bolts	7

① — Inch lbs.

A131L, A241E, A243L, A244E, A245E & A246E Automatic Transaxles

INDEX

Page No.

Adjustments 48-268
Manual Shift Linkage 48-268
Neutral Safety Switch 48-268
Park Lock Cable 48-268
Throttle Cable 48-268
In-Vehicle Repairs 48-268
Differential Case, Replace 48-269
Governor Valve, Replace 48-269
Second Brake Servo Assembly, Replace 48-269
Throttle Cable, Replace 48-268
Valve Body, Replace 48-268
Maintenance 48-267
Fluid Change 48-267
Fluid Check 48-267
Precautions 48-265
Air Bag Systems 48-265

Page No.

Audio Coded Anti-Theft System . 48-265
Tightening Specifications 48-274
Transaxle, Replace 48-270
Celica 48-270
Corolla, 2WD Models 48-270
Corolla, 4WD Models 48-271
MR2 48-272
Paseo 48-273
RAV4 48-273
Troubleshooting 48-265
Delayed Upshifts & Downshifts .. 48-266
Drag Or Binding On Upshifts 48-266
Fluid Discolored Or Smells Burned 48-266
Harsh Downshift 48-266
Harsh Engagement Into Any

Page No.

Drive Range 48-266
Incorrect Downshift 48-267
Incorrect Shift Lever Position 48-266
No Center Differential Control ... 48-267
No Downshift When Coasting ... 48-266
No Engine Braking In 2 48-267
No Hold In P 48-267
No Kickdown 48-267
No Lock-Up In 2, 3 OR O/D 48-267
Shift Lock System 48-265
Slips On Upshifts Or Shudders On Takeoffs 48-266
Vehicle Does Not Move In Any Drive Gear 48-266
Vehicle Does Not Move In Any Range 48-266

PRECAUTIONS

AIR BAG SYSTEMS

Refer to "Air Bag System Precautions" in the front of this manual for system disarming and arming procedures.

AUDIO CODED ANTI-THEFT SYSTEM

Some models are equipped with an audio coded anti-theft system that will disable the radio when the battery cable is disconnected. The system can be identified by the "ANTI-THEFT SYSTEM" on the cassette lid. Obtain 3 digit code for input. Reset system after service as follows:

1. Obtain 3 digit audio theft code.
2. Depress 1 (PROG) while depressing righthand side of TUNE SEEK button, - - - will appear in tape operation display.
3. To enter the first digit, depress 1 (PROG) button repeatedly until the number of times depressed equals the first digit (depress the 1 button six times if the first digit if five, first press equals 0).
4. To enter second digit, depress 2 (APS) button repeatedly until the number of times depressed equals the second digit.
5. To enter third digit, depress 3 (RPT) button repeatedly until the number of times depressed equals the third digit.
6. If - - - is displayed after inputting digits, repeat procedure.
7. When code appears in display, depress and hold SCAN button until SEC appears.
8. When SEC disappears audio system is operative.
9. If Err is displayed, repeat procedure. **Attempting to input code more than 9 times may permanently disable audio system.**

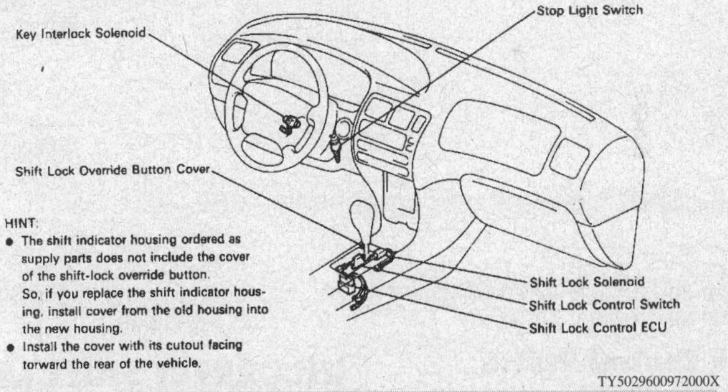

Key Interlock Solenoid
Stop Light Switch
Shift Lock Override Button Cover
HINT:
• The shift indicator housing ordered as supply parts does not include the cover of the shift-lock override button.
So, if you replace the shift indicator housing, install cover from the old housing into the new housing.
• Install the cover with its cutout facing torward the rear of the vehicle.
Shift Lock Solenoid
Shift Lock Control Switch
Shift Lock Control ECU
TY5029600972000X

Fig. 1 Shift lock system components. Corolla & RAV4

TROUBLESHOOTING

SHIFT LOCK SYSTEM

Refer to **Figs. 1 through 4** for shift lock system component locations and **Figs. 5 through 8** wiring circuits.

Shift Lock Control ECU Inspection

Using a suitable voltmeter, measure voltage at each ECU connector terminal, **Figs. 9 through 12.** Refer to **Figs. 13 through 17** for measuring conditions and voltage specifications.

Shift Lock Solenoid Inspection

1. Disconnect solenoid connector.
2. Using suitable ohmmeter, measure resistance between both terminals.
3. Resistance should be as follows:
   a. Corolla and MR2: 21–27 ohms.
   b. RAV4: 26–33 ohms.
   c. Celica: 30–37 ohms.
4. Apply battery positive voltage between terminals and ensure solenoid operating noise can be heard.

Key Interlock Solenoid Inspection

1. Disconnect solenoid connector.
2. Using suitable ohmmeter, measure resistance between both terminals.
3. Resistance should be 12.5–16.5 ohms for all models.
4. Apply battery positive voltage between

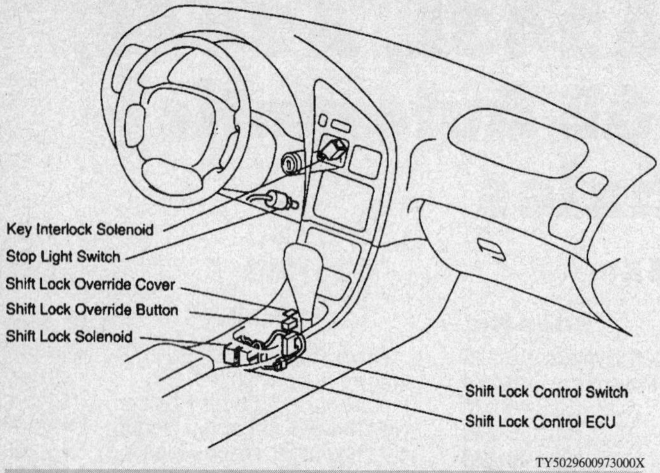
Key Interlock Solenoid
Stop Light Switch
Shift Lock Override Cover
Shift Lock Override Button
Shift Lock Solenoid
Shift Lock Control Switch
Shift Lock Control ECU
TY5029600973000X

Fig. 2 Shift lock system components. Celica

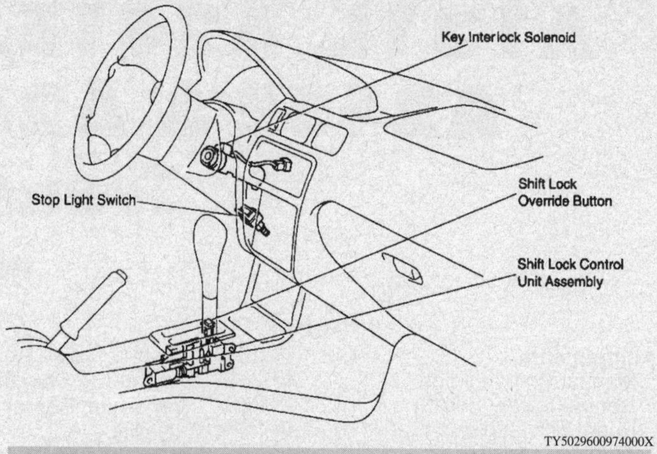
Key Interlock Solenoid
Stop Light Switch
Shift Lock
Override Button
Shift Lock Control
Unit Assembly
TY5029600974000X

Fig. 3 Shift lock system components. Paseo

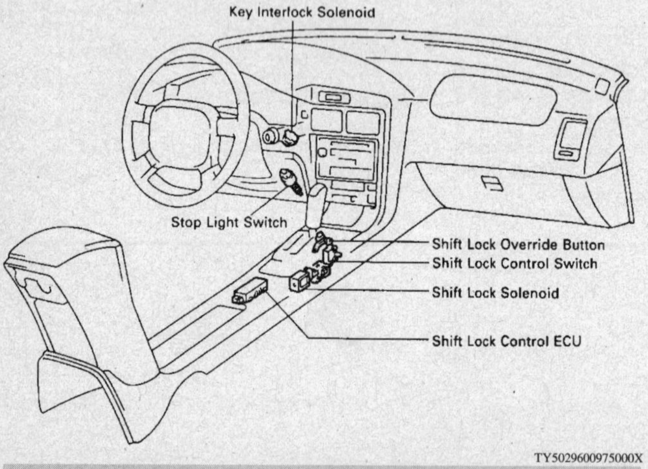
Key Interlock Solenoid
Stop Light Switch
Shift Lock Override Button
Shift Lock Control Switch
Shift Lock Solenoid
Shift Lock Control ECU
TY5029600975000X

Fig. 4 Shift lock system components. MR2

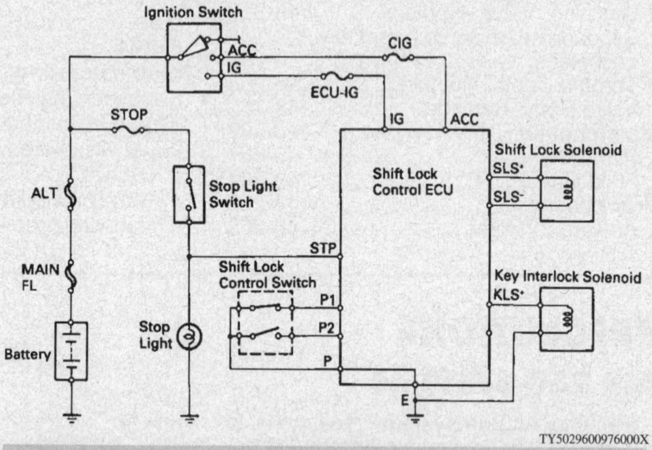
Ignition Switch
ACC
IG
CIG
ECU-IG
STOP
IG
ACC
Shift Lock Solenoid
SLS+
SLS-
ALT
Stop Light
Switch
Shift Lock
Control ECU
STP
MAIN
FL
Shift Lock
Control Switch
P1
P2
P
Key Interlock Solenoid
KLS+
Stop
Light
Battery
E
TY5029600976000X

Fig. 5 Shift lock system wiring circuit. Corolla & RAV4

terminals and ensure solenoid operating noise can be heard.

Shift Lock Control Switch Inspection

Using a suitable ohmmeter, check for continuity at terminals as shown in **Figs. 18 through 20.**

FLUID DISCOLORED OR SMELLS BURNED

1. Contaminated fluid.
2. Faulty torque converter.
3. Faulty transaxle.

VEHICLE DOES NOT MOVE IN ANY DRIVE GEAR

1. Incorrectly adjusted transaxle control cable.
2. Faulty valve body or primary regulator.
3. Faulty transaxle.

VEHICLE DOES NOT MOVE IN ANY RANGE

1. Faulty park lock pawl.
2. Faulty valve body or Primary regulator.
3. Faulty torque converter.
4. Broken converter driveplate.
5. Blocked oil pump intake strainer.
6. Faulty transaxle.

INCORRECT SHIFT LEVER POSITION

1. Incorrectly adjusted transaxle control cable.
2. Faulty manual valve and lever.
3. Faulty transaxle.

HARSH ENGAGEMENT INTO ANY DRIVE RANGE

1. Incorrectly adjusted throttle cable.
2. Incorrectly adjusted transaxle control cable.
3. Faulty valve body or primary regulator.
4. Faulty accumulator pistons.
5. Faulty transaxle.

DELAYED UPSHIFTS & DOWNSHIFTS

1. Incorrectly adjusted throttle cable.
2. Faulty governors.
3. Faulty valve body.
4. Faulty solenoid valve.

SLIPS ON UPSHIFTS OR SHUDDERS ON TAKEOFFS

1. Incorrectly adjusted transaxle control cable.
2. Incorrectly adjusted throttle cable.
3. Faulty valve body.
4. Faulty transaxle.
5. Faulty solenoid valve.

DRAG OR BINDING ON UPSHIFTS

1. Incorrectly adjusted transaxle control cable.
2. Faulty valve body.
3. Faulty transaxle.

HARSH DOWNSHIFT

1. Incorrectly adjusted throttle cable.
2. Faulty accumulator pistons.
3. Faulty valve body.
4. Faulty transaxle.
5. Faulty throttle cable and cam.

NO DOWNSHIFT WHEN COASTING

1. Faulty governor.
2. Faulty valve body.

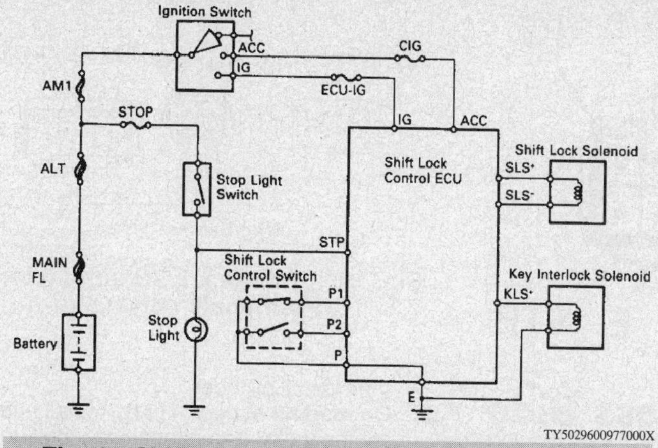
Ignition Switch
ACC
IG
CIG
AM1
ECU-IG
STOP
IG
ACC
Shift Lock Solenoid
ALT
Shift Lock
Control ECU
SLS+
SLS-
Stop Light
Switch
MAIN
FL
STP
Shift Lock
Control Switch
Key Interlock Solenoid
P1
KLS+
Stop
Light
P2
Battery
P
E
TY5029600977000X

Fig. 6 Shift lock system wiring circuit. Celica

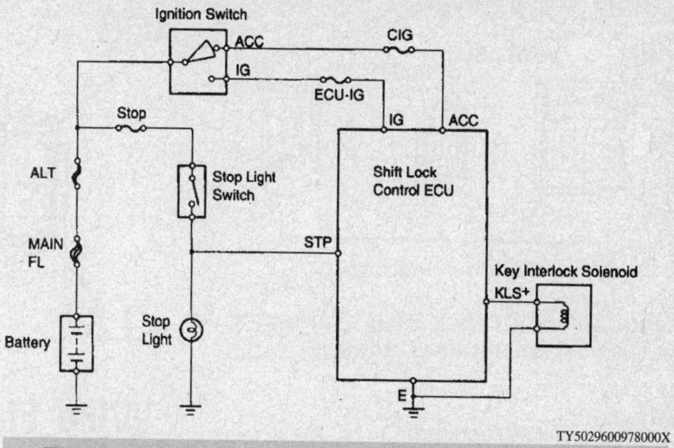
Ignition Switch
ACC
CIG
IG
ECU-IG
Stop
IG
ACC
ALT
Stop Light
Switch
Shift Lock
Control ECU
MAIN
FL
STP
Key Interlock Solenoid
KLS+
Stop
Light
Battery
E
TY5029600978000X

Fig. 7 Shift lock system wiring circuit. Paseo

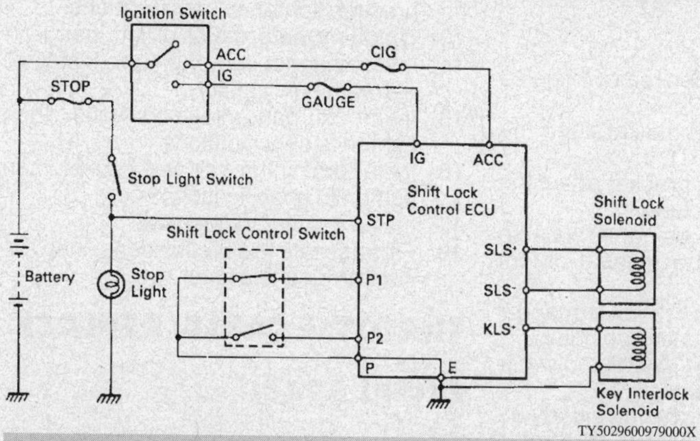
Ignition Switch
ACC
CIG
IG
STOP
GAUGE
IG
ACC
Stop Light Switch
Shift Lock
Control ECU
Shift Lock
Solenoid
STP
Shift Lock Control Switch
SLS+
Battery
Stop
Light
P1
SLS-
KLS+
P2
P
E
Key Interlock
Solenoid
TY5029600979000X

Fig. 8 Shift lock system wiring circuit. MR2

3. Faulty solenoid valve.
4. Faulty electronic controls.

INCORRECT DOWNSHIFT

1. Incorrectly adjusted throttle cable.
2. Faulty governor.
3. Faulty valve body.
4. Faulty transaxle.
5. Faulty solenoid valve.
6. Faulty electronic control.

NO LOCK-UP IN 2, 3 OR O/D

1. Faulty valve body.
2. Faulty transaxle.
3. Faulty solenoid valve.
4. Faulty electronic control.
5. Faulty torque converter.

NO KICKDOWN

1. Incorrectly adjusted throttle cable.
2. Faulty governor.
3. Faulty valve body.
4. Faulty solenoid valve.
5. Faulty electronic control.

NO ENGINE BRAKING IN 2

1. Faulty valve body.
2. Faulty transaxle.
3. Faulty solenoid valve.
4. Faulty electronic control.

NO HOLD IN P

1. Incorrectly adjusted transaxle control cable.
2. Faulty parking lock pawl and rod.

NO CENTER DIFFERENTIAL CONTROL

1. Faulty electronic controls.
2. Faulty valve body.
3. Faulty transfer.
4. Faulty C/D clutch.

MAINTENANCE

On all units, use DEXRON II transaxle fluid.

FLUID CHECK

1. Start engine, allow transaxle fluid to reach 158–176°F.
2. Position vehicle on level surface, then set parking brake.
3. With engine idling, brake pedal depressed, move shift lever through all positions.
4. Remove transaxle dipstick, wipe clean, then replace.

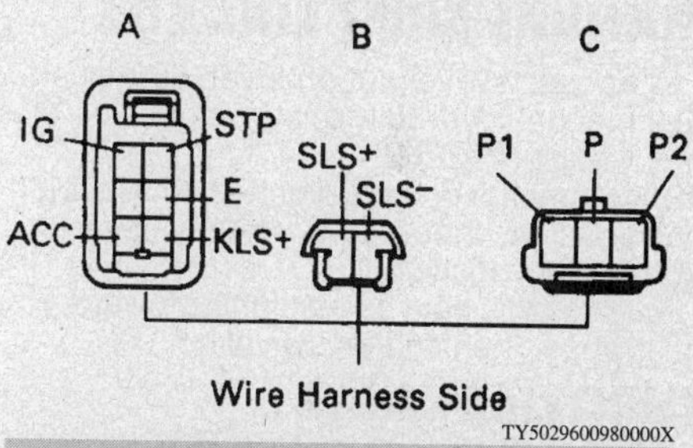
A
B
C
IG
STP
SLS+
P1
P
P2
E
SLS-
ACC
KLS+
Wire Harness Side
TY5029600980000X

Fig. 9 Shift lock ECU connector terminals. Corolla & RAV4

5. Remove dipstick again, check fluid at HOT level.
6. **On A131L units,** dry fill capacity is 5.8 US quarts.
7. **On A241E units,** dry fill capacity is 8.5 US quarts.
8. **On A244E units,** dry fill capacity is 7.6 US quarts.
9. **On A243L units,** dry fill capacity is 8.1 US quarts.
10. **On A245E & A246E units,** dry fill capacity is 8.0 US quarts.

FLUID CHANGE

1. **On all units except A131L,** drain transaxle fluid.
2. **On A131L units,** using wrench tool No. 09043–38100, or equivalent, remove drain plug, then drain fluid.
3. **On all models,** install drain plug and new gasket.
4. Add fluid through filler tube. **Do not overfill.**
5. **On A131L units,** drain and refill capacity is 2.6 US quarts.
6. **On A241E and A243L units,** drain and refill capacity is 3.5 US quarts.
7. **On A244E units,** drain and refill capacity is 3.3 US quarts.
8. **On A245E & A246E units,** drain and refill capacity is 3.5 US quarts.
9. **On all models,** start engine, ensure smooth shift operation in all positions.
10. With engine at idle, check fluid COOL

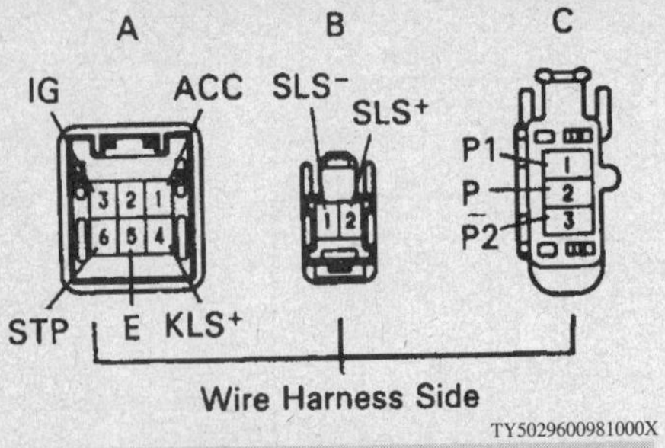
A
B
C
IG
ACC
SLS−
SLS+
P1
P
P2
STP
E
KLS+
Wire Harness Side
TY5029600981000X

Fig. 10 Shift lock ECU connector terminals. Celica

level, fill as required.

11. Allow vehicle to reach normal operating temperatures, then recheck level.

ADJUSTMENTS

MANUAL SHIFT LINKAGE

1. Loosen swivel nut on lever, then push manual lever fully toward right side of vehicle, **Fig. 21.**
2. Return lever two notches to Neutral position, then place selector lever in Neutral position.
3. Manually hold lever tightly toward R range, then tighten swivel nut.

THROTTLE CABLE

1. Hold accelerator pedal in fully depressed position, then loosen cable adjusting nuts, **Fig. 22.**
2. Adjust cable to obtain .040 inch between end of boot and stopper on cable, then tighten adjusting nut.
3. Fully depress accelerator pedal and recheck adjustment, then road test vehicle.

NEUTRAL SAFETY SWITCH

1. Loosen neutral safety switch attaching bolts.
2. Place selector lever in Neutral position.
3. Disconnect electrical connector.
4. Align groove in with neutral basic line, **Fig. 23.**
5. Tighten switch retaining bolts to specifications to secure adjustment.
6. Reconnect electrical connector to switch, then ensure engine starts with selector lever in "N" and "P" only.

PARK LOCK CABLE

1. Remove slide key, then lightly pull park lock cable, to remove looseness.
2. Do not strongly pull on cable.
3. Install lock cable slide key.
4. Push set cable lever inward, **Fig. 24,** set cable lever should go down.
5. Move shift lever to P range.
6. While pushing shift lock override button, push shift lever knob, then release it. Ensure set cable lever is released.

IN-VEHICLE REPAIRS

VALVE BODY, REPLACE

Removal

1. Clean area around pan, then drain

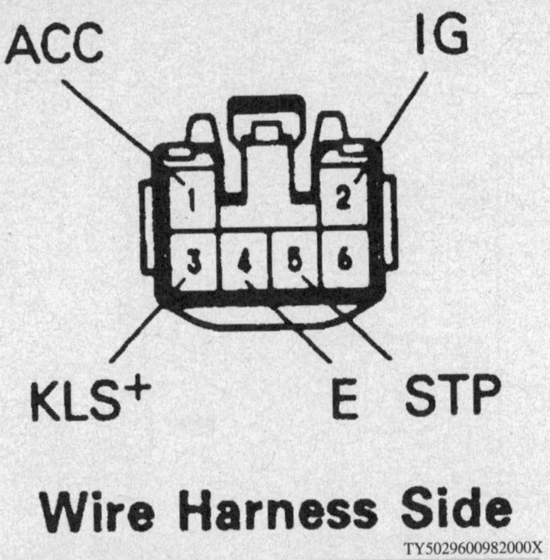
ACC
IG
1
2
3
4
5
6
KLS+
E
STP
Wire Harness Side
TY5029600982000X

Fig. 11 Shift lock ECU connector terminals. Paseo

transmission fluid, then remove engine undercover.

2. Remove oil pan and gasket, then the oil strainer.
3. Remove apply tube bracket attaching bolts, then the apply tube.
4. Remove oil tubes using a suitable screwdriver, then the manual detent spring.
5. **On A131L models,** remove manual valve, then the manual valve body.
6. **On models except A131L,** disconnect solenoid connector.
7. **On all models,** remove valve body attaching bolts, then disconnect throttle cable.
8. **On models except A131L,** disconnect manual valve connecting rod.
9. **On all models,** remove valve body, then the governor apply gasket.
10. **On A131L models,** remove governor oil strainer.

Installation

1. **On A131L models,** install governor oil strainer.
2. **On all models,** install governor apply gasket.
3. **On models except A131L,** connect manual valve connecting rod.
4. **On all models,** hold valve body in place, then manually retain cam in downward position and slip cable end into slot.
5. Position valve body in installation position, then insert and finger tighten attaching bolts. Tighten to specifications. Attaching bolt lengths (mm) are indicated in, **Figs. 25 through 28.**
6. **On models except A131L,** connect solenoid connector.
7. **On A131L models,** align manual valve with pin on manual valve lever, then install manual valve body.
8. Insert and finger tighten attaching bolts, then tighten to specifications.
9. **On all models,** install detent spring, then insert and finger tighten attaching bolt. Tighten attaching bolts to specifications.
10. Ensure manual lever is in contact with center of roller at tip of detent spring,

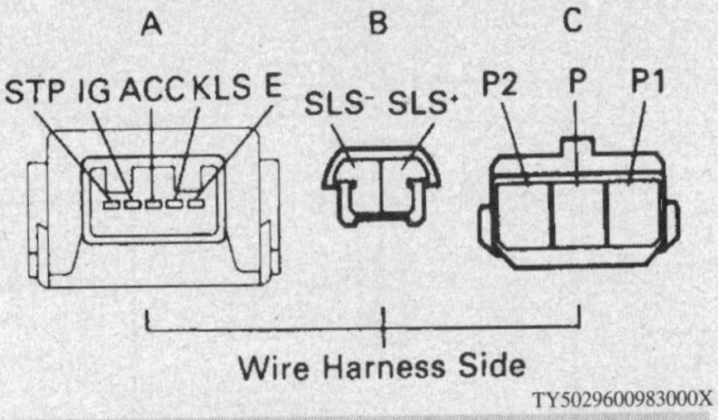
A
B
C
STP IG ACC KLS E
SLS− SLS+
P2
P
P1
Wire Harness Side
TY5029600983000X

Fig. 12 Shift lock ECU connector terminals. MR2

then install oil tubes.

11. **On models except A131L,** install and tighten tube clamp attaching bolt to specifications.
12. **On A131L models,** install apply tube bracket, tighten to specifications.
13. **On all models,** install oil strainer.
14. Insert magnet into pan, then install oil pan with new gasket.
15. Insert oil pan attaching bolts, then tighten to specifications.
16. Install drain plug with new gasket, then tighten to specifications.
17. Install engine undercover.
18. Fill transaxle to specifications, then ensure proper fluid level.

THROTTLE CABLE, REPLACE

EXCEPT A243L

Removal

1. Disconnect throttle cable from engine, then the transaxle control cable from manual shift lever.
2. Remove manual shift lever, then the neutral safety switch.
3. Remove retaining plate bolt and retaining plate, then the valve body as previously described.
4. Pull cable from transaxle case.

Installation

1. Insert cable into transaxle case, then install retaining plate and bolt.
2. Install valve body as previously described, then position cable stop for adjustment reference as follows:
   a. Bend cable to a radius of approximately 7.87 inches as shown, **Fig. 29. Cable stop is not staked in place on replacement cable.**
   b. Lightly pull inner cable from housing until a slight resistance is felt, then hold in position.
   c. Stake stopper onto inner cable so that .031–.059 inch clearance exists between stop and cable housing.
   d. Connect and adjust throttle cable as described previously.
3. Install neutral safety switch, then the manual shift lever. Adjust switch as previously described.
4. Connect transaxle control cable.
5. Ensure transaxle fluid level is to specifications, then road test vehicle.

Connector	Terminal	Measuring condition	Voltage (V)
A	ACC – E	Ignition switch ACC	10 – 14
	IG – E	Ignition switch ON	10 – 14
	STP – E	Depress brake pedal	10 – 14
	KLS+ – E	1 Ignition switch ACC and P position	0
		2 Ignition switch ACC and except P position	10 – 14
		3 (After approx 1 second)	6 – 9
B	SLS+ – SLS−	1 Ignition switch ON and P position	0
		2 Depress brake pedal	8.5 – 13.5
		3 (After approx 20 seconds)	5.5 – 9.5
		4 Except P position	0
C	P1 – P	1 Ignition switch ON, P position and depress brake pedal	9 – 13.5
		2 Shift except P position under conditions above	0
	P2 – P	1 Ignition switch ACC and P position	0
		2 Shift except P position under condition above	9 – 13.5

TY5029600984000X

Fig. 13 Shift lock control ECU inspection. Corolla

Connector	Terminal	Measuring condition	Voltage (V)
A	ACC – E	Ignition switch ACC	10 – 14
	IG – E	Ignition switch ON	10 – 14
	STP – E	Depress brake pedal	10 – 14
	KLS+ – E	1 Ignition switch ACC and P position	0
		2 Ignition switch ACC and except P position	7.5 – 11
		3 (After approx 1 second)	5.5 – 10
B	SLS+ – SLS−	1 Ignition switch ON and P position	0
		2 Depress brake pedal	8.5 – 14
		4 Except P position	0
C	P1 – P	1 Ignition switch ON, P position and depress brake pedal	0
		2 Shift except P position under condition above	10 – 14
	P2 – P	1 Ignition switch ACC and P position	10 – 14
		2 Shift except P position under condition above	0

TY5029600985000X

Fig. 14 Shift lock control ECU inspection. RAV4

Connector	Terminal	Measuring condition	Voltage (V)
A	ACC – E	IG SW ACC	10 – 14
	IG – E	IG SW ON	10 – 14
	STP – E	Depress brake pedal	10 – 14
	KLS+ – E	① IG SW ACC and shift lever at P position	0
		② IG SW ACC and shift lever at R, N, D, 2, L position	10 – 14
		③ (After approx. 1 second)	6 – 9
B	SLS+ – SLS−	① IG SW ON and shift lever at P position	0
		② Depress brake pedal	8.5 – 13.5
		③ Shift lever at R, N, D, 2, L position	0
C	P1 – P	① IG SW ON, shift lever at P position and depress brake pedal	0
		② Shift lever at R, N, D, 2, L position	9 – 13.5
	P2 – P	① IG SW ACC and shift lever at position	9 – 13.5
		② Shift lever at R, N, D, 2, L position	0

TY5029600986000X

Fig. 15 Shift lock control ECU inspection. Celica

Terminal	Measuring Condition	Voltage (V)
ACC – E	Ignition switch ACC	10 – 14
IG – E	Ignition switch ON	10 – 14
STP – E	Depress brake pedal	10 – 14
KLS+ – E	1 Ignition switch ACC and P position	0
	2 Ignition switch ACC and except P position	7 – 12
	3 (After–approx. 1 second)	6 – 9

TY5029600987000X

Fig. 16 Shift lock control ECU inspection. Paseo

A243L

Removal

1. Disconnect throttle cable from engine.
2. Drain transaxle fluid.
3. Remove engine undercover.
4. Remove neutral start switch.
5. Remove oil pan and gasket.
6. Disconnect throttle cable from cam.
7. Remove throttle cable attaching plate, then remove.

Installation

1. Install throttle cable, then plate.
2. Connect throttle cable to cam.
3. Install oil pan and drain plug.
4. Install and adjust neutral start switch.
5. Install engine undercover.
6. Position cable stop for reference as follows:
   a. Bend cable to a radius of approximately 7.87 inches as shown, **Fig. 29. Cable stop is not staked in place on replacement cable.**
   b. Lightly pull inner cable from housing until a slight resistance is felt, then hold in position.
   c. Stake stopper onto inner cable so that .031–.059 inch clearance exists between stop and cable housing.
   d. Connect and adjust throttle cable as described previously.
7. Ensure correct transaxle fluid level, then road test vehicle.

GOVERNOR VALVE, REPLACE

EXCEPT A245E & A246E

Removal

1. **On A131L models,** remove transaxle dust cover, then the LH driveshaft.
2. **On A241E models,** disconnect speedometer cable.
3. **On all models,** remove governor cover, then the O-ring.
4. Remove governor body with thrust washer.
5. **On A131L models,** remove washer, then the governor body adapter.
6. **On A241E models,** remove gasket.

Installation

1. **On A241E models,** install new gasket on governor body adapter.
2. **On all models,** install governor body adapter.
3. **On A131L models,** install washer on governor body.
4. **On A241E models,** install governor body with thrust washer.
5. **On all models,** install governor cover with O-ring.
6. **On A241E models,** connect speedometer cable.
7. **On A131L models,** install LH driveshaft, then the transaxle dust cover.
8. **On all models,** ensure transaxle fluid level is to specifications, then road test vehicle.

DIFFERENTIAL CASE, REPLACE

Removal

1. Remove neutral start switch, then the speedometer driven gear.
2. Remove governor body, then the oil pan.
3. Remove valve body, then the 11 transaxle rear cover attaching bolts. Tap cover from case using a suitable mallet.
4. Remove intermediate shaft, then the parking lock pawl bracket and rod.
5. Remove parking lock pawl, then the manual shaft and lever.
6. Remove manual shaft and lever, then the governor pressure adapter.
7. Remove carrier cover.

Installation

1. Install governor pressure adapter, then the manual shaft and lever.
2. Install parking lock pawl.
3. Install parking lock rod, then the bracket.
4. Install intermediate shaft.
5. Install transaxle rear cover with new gasket, then insert retaining bolts and tighten to specifications.
6. Install valve body, then the governor body.
7. Install oil pan.
8. Install speedometer driven gear, then the neutral start switch.

SECOND BRAKE SERVO ASSEMBLY, REPLACE

Removal

1. Raise and support vehicle, then remove shift cable bracket at transaxle.
2. Remove snap ring.
3. Remove cover.
4. Remove piston, then the outer spring.

Connector	Terminal	Measured Item	Measuring Condition	Specified Value
A	ACC – E	Voltage	Ignition switch ACC position	10 – 14 V
	IG – E	Voltage	Ignition switch ON position	10 – 14 V
	KLS – E	Voltage	① Ignition switch ACC position and "P" position	0 V
			② Ignition switch ACC position and other than "P" position	7.5 – 11.5 V
			③ ② and approx-after one second	6 – 9 V
	E – Ground	Continuity	All conditions	Continuity
	STP – E	Voltage	Release brake pedal	0 V
			Depress brake pedal	10 – 14 V
B	SLS⁺ – E	Continuity	All conditions	Continuity
	SLS⁻ – E	Voltage	① Ignition switch ON position and "P" position	0 V
			② ① and depress brake pedal	8.5 – 13.5 V
			③ ② and release brake pedal or ② and shift to position other than "P" position	0 V
C	P2 – E	Voltage	① Ignition switch ACC position and "P" position	0 – 13.5 V
			② ① and push the shift lever knob, or ignition switch ACC position and shift to position other than "P" position	0 V
	P – E	Continuity	All conditions	Continuity
	P1 – E	Voltage	Ignition switch ON position, "P" position and brake pedal depressed	0 V
			Ignition switch ON position brake pedal depressed and shift to position other than "P" position	9 – 13.5 V

TY5029600988000X

Fig. 17 Shift lock control ECU inspection. MR2

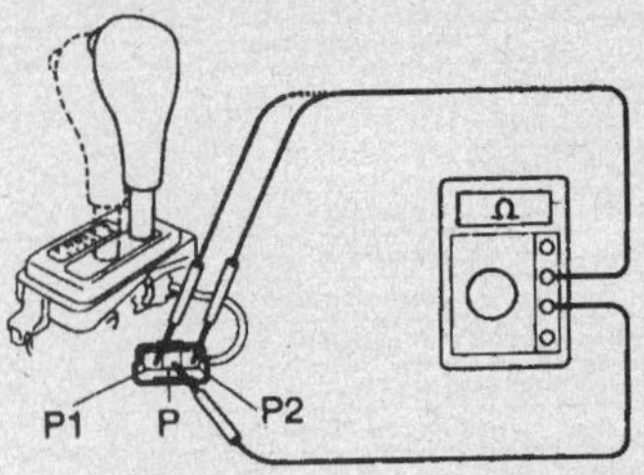

P1
P
P2

TY5029600989000X

Fig. 18 Shift lock control switch connector. Celica, Corolla & RAV4

Shift position	Tester condition to terminal number	Specified value
P position (Release button is not pushed)	P – P 1	Continuity
P position (Release button is pushed)	P – P 1 P – P 2	Continuity
R, N, D, 2, L position	P – P 2	Continuity

TY5029600991000X

Fig. 20 Shift lock control switch inspection

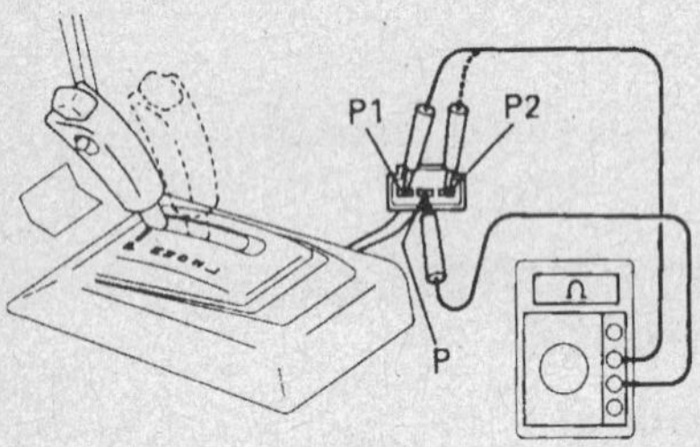

P1
P2
P

TY5029600990000X

Fig. 19 Shift lock control switch connector. MR2

Installation

1. Insert piston, less outer spring, then install snap ring.
2. Install tool No. J-35679, or equivalent, then observe groove on plunger of tool.
3. Press button on tool, to allow tool to push brake apply rod into case. If groove is visible, piston stroke is correct (.059–.118 inch). If stroke is greater than specified, replace piston rod with 2.870 or 2.811 inch rod as needed.
4. Remove snap ring, then install piston and outer spring.
5. Install tool No. J-34955, or equivalent, to compress spring, then insert snap ring.
6. Install cover, then the shift cable bracket.
7. Lower vehicle.

TRANSAXLE

REPLACE

CELICA

1993

1. **On models with coded audio anti-theft system,** obtain three digit code.
2. **On all models,** raise and support vehicle, then drain transaxle fluid.
3. Remove transaxle as shown in, **Fig. 30.**
4. Reverse to procedure install noting that **on models with coded audio anti-theft systems,** rearm as outlined under "Precautions."

1994–96

1. **On models with coded audio anti-theft system,** obtain three digit code.
2. **On all models,** raise and support vehicle, then drain transaxle fluid.
3. Lower vehicle, then remove battery and air cleaner.
4. Disconnect throttle cable and level gauge **Fig. 31.**
5. Remove following:
   a. Bolt from upper left engine mount.
   b. Throttle cable mounting and wiring harness clamps.
   c. Upper starter bolt and two upper transaxle to engine bolts.
   d. Filler tube bolt, then remove filler tube.
6. Disconnect transmission oil cooler lines.
7. Disconnect steering intermediate shaft, then disconnect both power steering lines.
8. Install suitable engine support fixture **Fig. 32,** then raise and support vehicle.
9. Remove engine undercovers, then drain transaxle.
10. Remove right and left drive axles.
11. Using suitable equipment support transaxle, then relieve tension from rear mount and remove bolt.
12. Disconnect all components and brackets attached to subframe except steering gear. Remove protective grommets where necessary to reach attaching bolts.
13. Remove subframe mounting bolts **Figs. 31 and 33,** then lower subframe assembly with steering gear.
14. Disconnect and remove starter, then disconnect speed sensor connection at transaxle.
15. Disconnect shift cable, shift solenoid and neutral safety switch connectors, then remove torque convertor bolt access cover.
16. Turning engine in direction of rotation, align and remove six torque convertor bolts.
17. Remove two bolts from lower left engine mounting.
18. Remove five remaining engine to transaxle bolts, then lower transaxle from vehicle.
19. Reverse procedures to install, noting the following:
   a. Tighten all fasteners to specifications.
   b. **Torque** subframe attaching bolt **Fig. 33** A to 94 ft. lbs., B bolt to 130 ft. lbs. and bolt C to 127 ft. lbs.
   c. **On models with coded audio anti-theft systems,** rearm as outlined under "Precautions."

COROLLA, 2WD MODELS

A131L Transaxle

1. **On models with coded audio anti-theft system,** obtain three digit code
2. **On all models** disconnect battery ground cable.
3. Remove level gauge, throttle cable, engine upper side mounting bolts and ground cable.
4. Disconnect harness wire and throttle cable clamps.
5. Remove speed sensor connectors, then raise vehicle.
6. Remove engine undercover, then disconnect driveshaft and suspend by cord.
7. Jack up transaxle.
8. Remove exhaust pipe, then install engine support fixture.
9. Remove suspension cover.
10. Remove starter, then disconnect neutral start switch.
11. Remove nut from control shaft lever, disconnect clip and remove shift control cable.

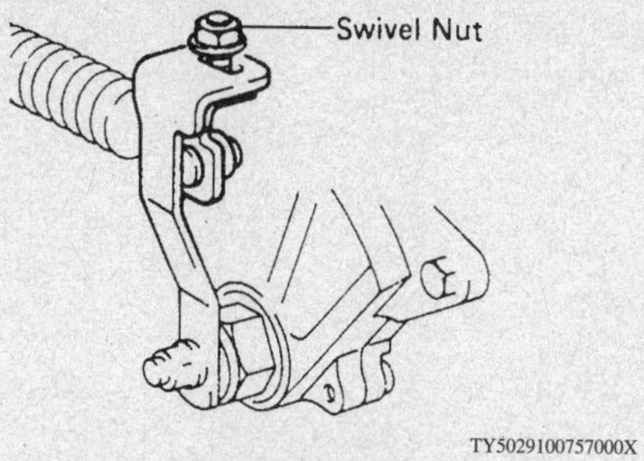
Swivel Nut
TY5029100757000X

Fig. 21 Manual shift linkage adjustment

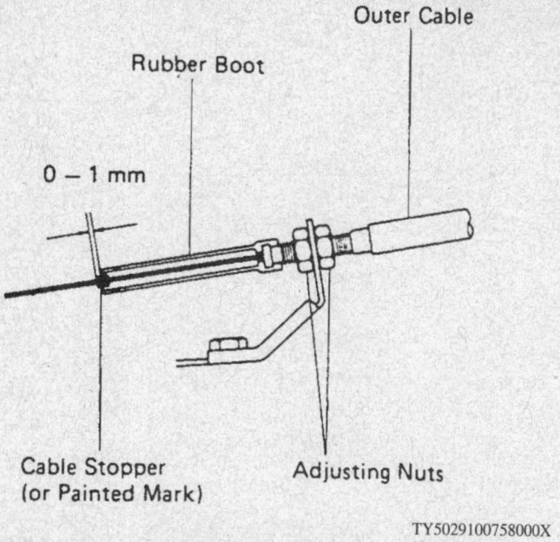
Outer Cable
Rubber Boot
0 – 1 mm
Cable Stopper
(or Painted Mark)
Adjusting Nuts
TY5029100758000X

Fig. 22 Throttle cable adjustment

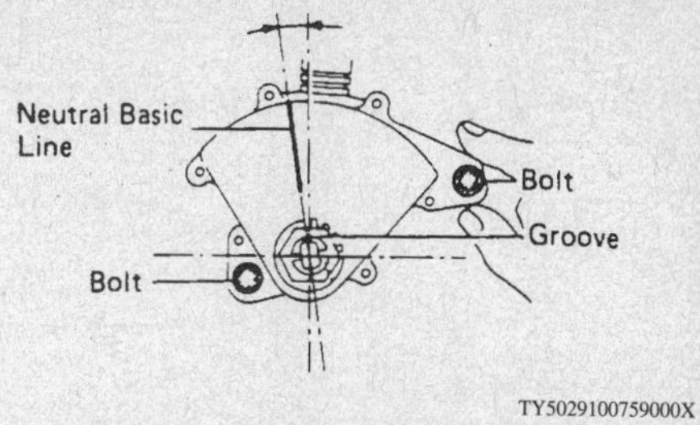
Neutral Basic Line
Bolt
Groove
Bolt
TY5029100759000X

Fig. 23 Neutral start switch adjustment

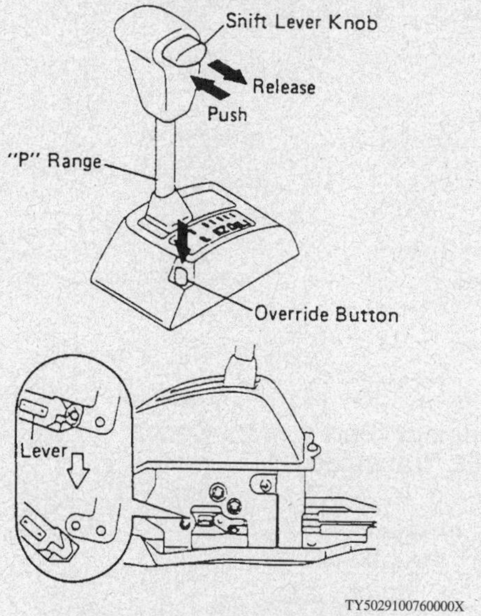
Shift Lever Knob
Release
Push
"P" Range
Override Button
Lever
TY5029100760000X

Fig. 24 Park lock cable adjustment

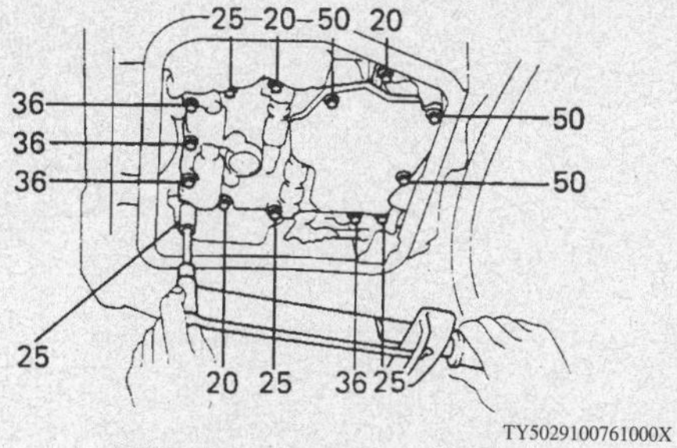
25–20–50 20
36
36
36
50
50
25
20 25
36 25
TY5029100761000X

Fig. 25 Valve body bolt identification. A131L

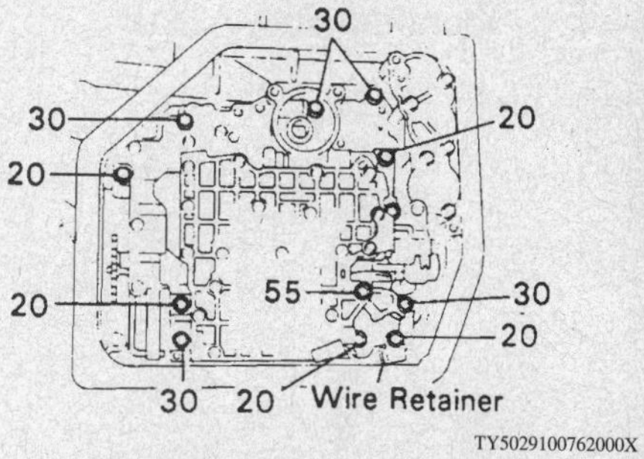
30
30
20
20
20
55
30
20
30 20
Wire Retainer
TY5029100762000X

Fig. 26 Valve body bolt identification. A243L

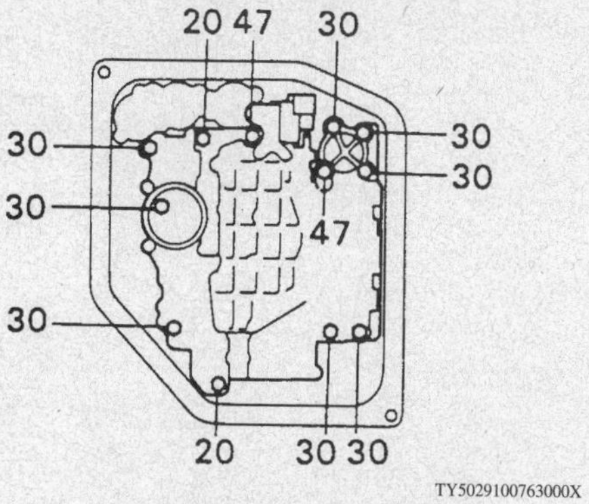
20 47 30
30
30
30
30
47
30
20 30 30
TY5029100763000X

Fig. 27 Valve body bolt identification. A244E

12. Remove two oil cooler tubes and filler tube.
13. Remove converter cover, turn crankshaft to gain access to remove six bolts, then remove seven bolts and transaxle.
14. Reverse procedure to install, noting that **on models with coded audio anti-theft systems,** rearm as outlined under "Precautions."

A245E Transaxle

The A245E transaxle is serviced as an assembly only.

1. **Disarm anti-theft system as outlined under "Precautions."**
2. **On all models** disconnect battery ground cable.
3. Remove lever gauge and coolant reservoir tank.
4. Disconnect throttle cable, then remove air cleaner assembly.
5. Remove engine upper left side mounting bolts, and left engine mounting stay.
6. Disconnect wire harness and throttle cable clamps.
7. Remove starter upper side mounting bolt and two transaxle mounting bolts on transaxle side.
8. Raise and support vehicle, then remove engine undercover and driveshaft. Suspend driveshaft by cord.
9. Using suitable tool, raise transaxle.
10. Remove exhaust pipe, then install engine support fixture.
11. Remove suspension member and starter.
12. Disconnect following connectors: vehicle speed sensor, solenoid and Park/Neutral switch.
13. Remove nut from control shaft lever, disconnect clip and remove shift control cable.
14. Remove two oil cooler tubes and filler tube.
15. Remove converter cover, turn crankshaft to gain access to remove six bolts, then remove seven bolts and transaxle.
16. Reverse procedure to install, noting that **on models with coded audio anti-theft systems,** rearm as outlined under "Precautions."

COROLLA, 4WD MODELS

1. **On models with coded audio anti-theft system,** obtain three digit code.
2. **On all models,** remove battery and hood.
3. Remove right and left side engine undercovers.
4. Drain engine oil and coolant from radiator and engine.
5. Drain fluid from transaxle.
6. Disconnect air intake hose and air intake temperature sensor, then remove air cleaner hose and air cleaner.
7. Remove coolant reservoir tank, then remove radiator with cooling fan.
8. Disconnect accelerator and throttle cables from the bracket, then remove cruise control actuator.
9. Disconnect the following connectors:
   a. No. 2 junction block connectors.
   b. Ground strap connector and bolt.
   c. Check connector.
   d. Vacuum sensor connector.
   e. Vacuum sensor connector.
   f. Oxygen sensor connector.
   g. A/C Wiring connector.
10. Disconnect brake booster, power steering and A/C vacuum hoses.
11. Disconnect vacuum sensor, charcoal canister and vacuum switch vacuum hoses.
12. Remove glove box and ECU, then disconnect three connectors and pull out ECU wiring harness from cowl panel.
13. Disconnect heater hoses.
14. **On models with power steering,** loosen adjusting and pivot bolts and remove drive belt. Remove adjusting and pivot bolts, then vane pump.
15. **On models with A/C,** loosen adjusting bolt and remove drive belt. Remove four compressor mounting bolts, then compressor.

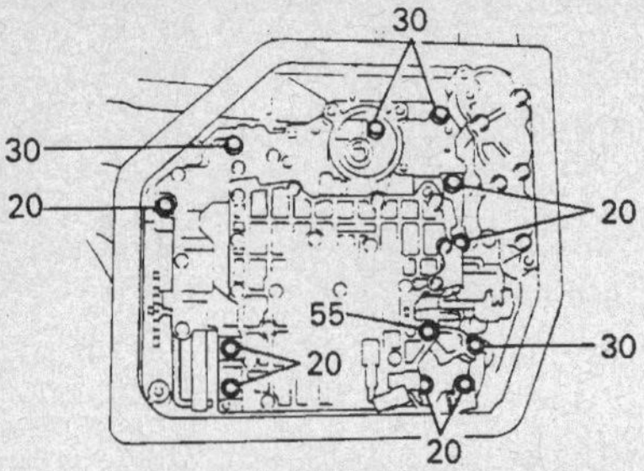
30
30
20
20
55
20
30
20
TY5029200764000X

Fig. 28 Valve body bolt identification. A241E

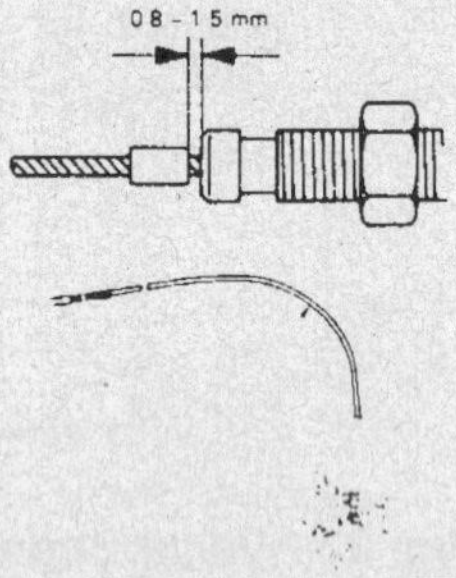
0.8 - 1.5 mm
TY5029100765000X

Fig. 29 Throttle cable stopper installation

16. **On all models,** disconnect speedometer cable from transaxle.
17. Disconnect control cable from shift lever.
18. Disconnect oil cooler hoses.
19. Remove front exhaust pipe, then disconnect driveshafts from transaxle.
20. Disconnect propeller shaft.
21. Attach a suitable engine hoist chain to lifting brackets on engine.
22. Remove hole covers, then disconnect front and rear mountings from center member.
23. Remove center member and front subframe, then remove front and rear mounting bolts and remove mounting.
24. Remove three bolts and mounting stay.
25. Remove bolt, two nuts, through bolt and mounting.
26. Remove air cleaner bracket, then disconnect LH mounting bracket from transaxle bracket.
27. Remove through bolt and mounting.
28. Lift engine with transaxle from vehicle, clear RH mounting while lowering transaxle.
29. Ensure engine is clear of all wiring, hoses and cables.
30. Place engine with transaxle onto stand.
31. Disconnect back-up lamp switch and neutral start switch, then remove rear end plate.
32. Remove six torque convertor mounting bolts, then remove the starter.
33. Remove transaxle from engine.
34. Reverse procedure to install, noting that **on models with coded audio anti-theft systems,** rearm as outlined under "Precautions."

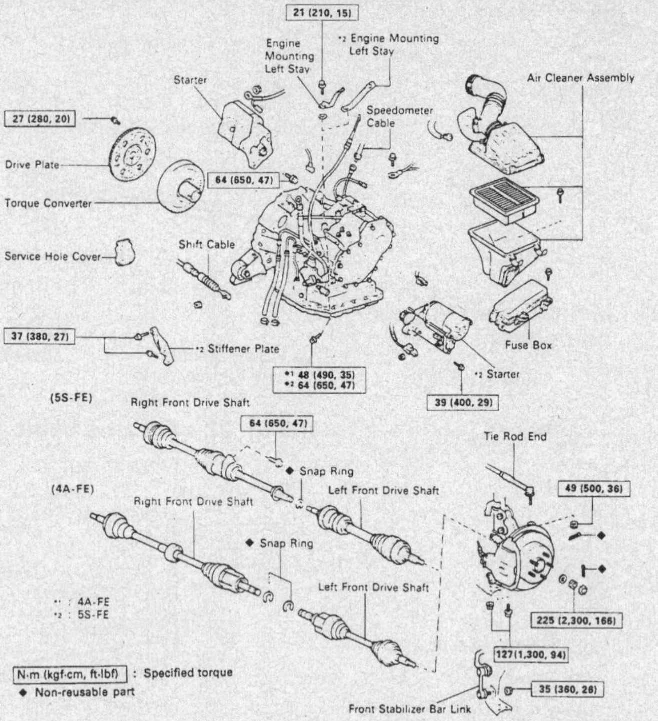
21 (210, 15)
Engine Mounting Left Stay
*2 Engine Mounting Left Stay
Starter
Air Cleaner Assembly
27 (280, 20)
Speedometer Cable
Drive Plate
64 (650, 47)
Torque Converter
Shift Cable
Service Hole Cover
37 (380, 27)
*2 Stiffener Plate
Fuse Box
*1 48 (490, 35)
*2 64 (650, 47)
*2 Starter
39 (400, 29)
(5S-FE)
Right Front Drive Shaft
64 (650, 47)
Tie Rod End
Snap Ring
(4A-FE)
Left Front Drive Shaft
49 (500, 36)
Right Front Drive Shaft
Snap Ring
Left Front Drive Shaft
*1 : 4A-FE
*2 : 5S-FE
225 (2,300, 166)
127 (1,300, 94)
N·m (kgf·cm, ft·lbf) : Specified torque
◆ Non-reusable part
35 (360, 26)
Front Stabilizer Bar Link
TY5029100766010X

Fig. 30 Transaxle replacement (Part 1 of 2). Celica Except A246E Transaxle

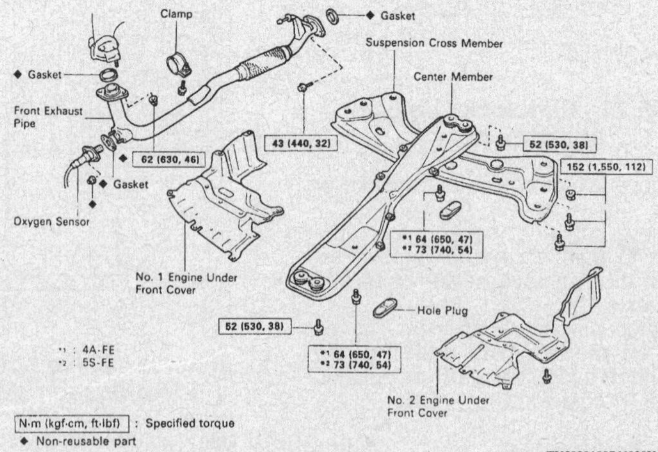
Clamp
Gasket
Suspension Cross Member
Gasket
Center Member
Front Exhaust Pipe
43 (440, 32)
52 (530, 38)
62 (630, 46)
152 (1,550, 112)
Gasket
Oxygen Sensor
*1 64 (650, 47)
*2 73 (740, 54)
No. 1 Engine Under Front Cover
Hole Plug
52 (530, 38)
*1 : 4A-FE
*2 : 5S-FE
*1 64 (650, 47)
*2 73 (740, 54)
No. 2 Engine Under Front Cover
N·m (kgf·cm, ft·lbf) : Specified torque
◆ Non-reusable part
TY5029100766020X

Fig. 30 Transaxle replacement (Part 2 of 2). Celica Except A246E Transaxle

MR2

1. **On models with coded audio anti-theft system,** obtain three digit code, obtain three digit code.
2. **On all models** disconnect battery ground cable.
3. Remove air cleaner assembly with air hose.
4. Remove level gauge and disconnect breather hose.
5. Remove throttle cable and starter.
6. Disconnect No. 1 vehicle speed pulse generator connector.
7. Remove harness wire clamp, then disconnect No. 2 vehicle speed pulse generator connector.
8. Remove engine lateral control assembly, upper transaxle mounting bolts on transaxle side and rear wheels.
9. Raise and support vehicle.
10. Remove engine undercover, then drain transaxle fluid into suitable container.
11. Remove driveshaft.
12. Remove nut from control shaft lever, disconnect clip and remove shift control cable.
13. Remove two oil cooler tubes and filler tube.
14. Disconnect Park/Neutral switch connector.
15. Remove exhaust pipe, then install engine support fixture.

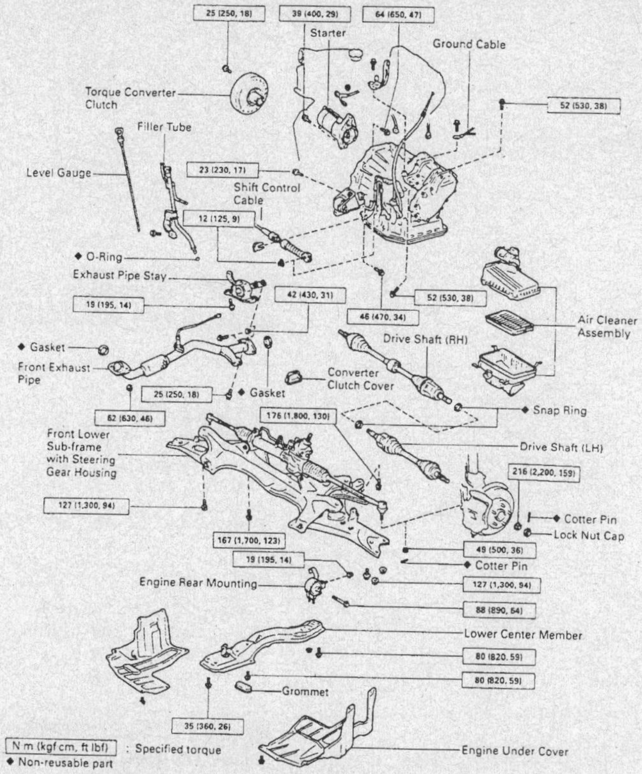
25 (250, 18)
39 (400, 29)
64 (650, 47)
Starter
Ground Cable
Torque Converter Clutch
52 (530, 38)
Filler Tube
Level Gauge
23 (230, 17)
Shift Control Cable
12 (125, 9)
◆ O-Ring
Exhaust Pipe Stay
42 (430, 31)
52 (530, 38)
19 (195, 14)
46 (470, 34)
Air Cleaner Assembly
Drive Shaft (RH)
◆ Gasket
Front Exhaust Pipe
Converter Clutch Cover
25 (250, 18)
◆ Gasket
◆ Snap Ring
62 (630, 46)
176 (1,800, 130)
Front Lower Sub-frame with Steering Gear Housing
Drive Shaft (LH)
216 (2,200, 159)
127 (1,300, 94)
◆ Cotter Pin
Lock Nut Cap
167 (1,700, 123)
49 (500, 36)
19 (195, 14)
◆ Cotter Pin
Engine Rear Mounting
127 (1,300, 94)
88 (890, 64)
Lower Center Member
80 (820, 59)
80 (820, 59)
Grommet
35 (360, 26)
N·m (kgf·cm, ft·lbf) : Specified torque
◆ Non-reusable part
Engine Under Cover

TY5029100767000X

Fig. 31 Component removal. Celica w/A246E transaxle

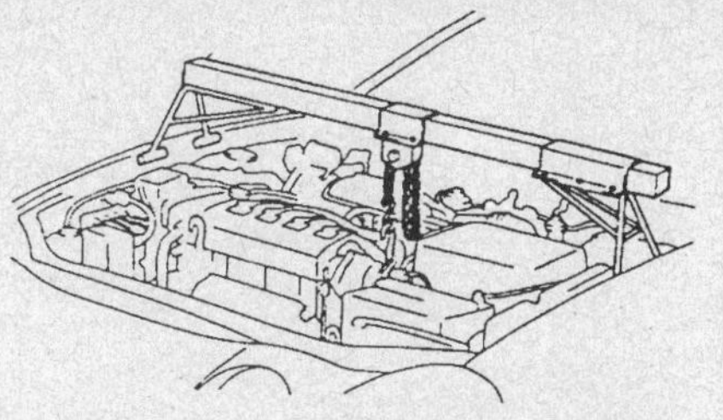

TY5029100768000X

Fig. 32 Engine support fixture

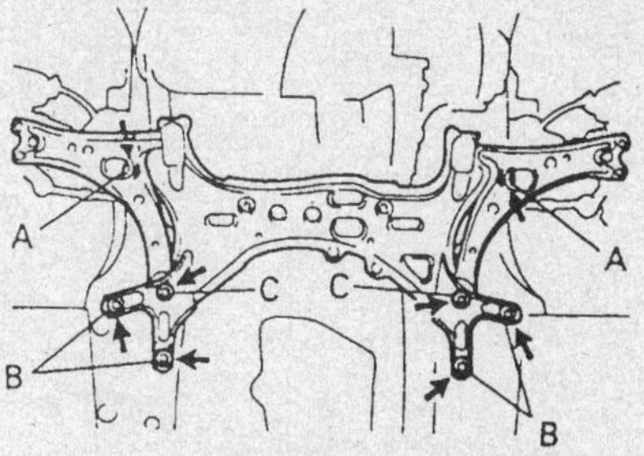
A
A
C
C
B
B

TY5029400769000X

Fig. 33 Tighten subframe bolts. Celica w/A246E transaxle

16. Remove front and rear engine mountings.
17. Remove nut, bolt and suspension arm from rear axle hub.
18. Remove bolt and disconnect speed sensor bracket from rear suspension crossmember.
19. Remove four bolts, then rear suspension crossmember.
20. Remove left engine mount set bolts, stiffener plate, rear end plate and torque converter mounting bolts.
21. Remove transaxle mounting bolts from engine, then lower left side of engine and remove transaxle.
22. Reverse procedure to install, noting that **on models with coded audio anti-theft systems,** rearm as outlined under "Precautions."

PASEO

1. Disconnect battery ground cable, then remove oil level gauge and air duct.
2. Remove air cleaner element. Remove bolts retaining air cleaner lower case assembly, then the case assembly.
3. Remove throttle cable, wire harness and upper side mounting bolts.
4. Attach hoist to engine hangers, then raise vehicle and remove front wheels.
5. Remove engine cover, then drain differential and transaxle fluid.
6. Remove cotter pin and lock cap, then apply brakes and remove driveshaft locknut.
7. Using ball joint puller, tool No. 09628-62011, or equivalent, disconnect tie rod end from steering knuckle, then the lower ball joint from lower arm.
8. Using universal puller, tool No. 09950-20017, or equivalent, disconnect driveshaft steering knuckle. **Be careful not to damage driveshaft boot and inner oil seal.**
9. Remove driveshaft and snap ring, then disconnect solenoid connector and control cable.
10. Disconnect connector from park/neutral position switch (neutral start switch), then remove oil cooler tube and ground wire.
11. Remove bolts from engine mounting left side bracket, then remove starter and speedometer cable.
12. Disconnect No. 2 speed sensor, raise transaxle, then remove bolt from rear mount No. 1 bracket.
13. Remove hole plug and bolts, then the torque converter and transaxle housing mounting bolts. Remove torque converter.
14. Reverse procedure to install, noting the following:
    a. Drain, wash and refill torque converter with ATF.
    b. **Torque** transaxle mounting bolts to 47 ft. lbs., converter mounting bolts to 13 ft. lbs. starter nuts and bolt to 29 ft. lbs., engine mounting and ground wire bolt to 32 ft. lbs.
    c. When installing driveshaft, **be careful not to damage boots or oil seal.**
    d. **Torque** lower arm nuts and bolt to 59 ft. lbs., steering knuckle nut to 36 ft. lbs., driveshaft locknut to 152 ft. lbs.
    e. Inspect front wheel alignment, then install differential and transaxle drain plugs.
    f. Fill transaxle with 7.6 qts. ATF, then check fluid level.

RAV4

1. Disconnect throttle cable.
2. Remove engine coolant reservoir tank, **Fig. 34.**
3. Disconnect electrical connector and ABS relay from air cleaner assembly.
4. Remove air cleaner assembly.
5. Remove transaxle ground cable.
6. Remove set nut of engine wire clamp.
7. Disconnect starter electrical connector.
8. Disconnect engine wire, then remove starter.
9. Remove three upper side transaxle mounting bolts.
10. Install engine support fixture over engine compartment.
11. Remove two engine LH mounting bolts and nuts.
12. Remove LH and RH engine under covers.
13. Drain transmission fluid.
14. Remove LH and RH driveshafts.
15. Remove front exhaust pipe and gaskets.
16. Remove nut from shift control shaft lever.
17. Remove retaining clip and disconnect control cable.
18. Remove two shift cable mounting bolts.
19. Disconnect shift solenoid valve SL connector.
20. Disconnect park/neutral position switch connector.
21. Disconnect vehicle speed sensor connector.
22. Disconnect oil cooler hoses.
23. Remove front suspension crossmember assembly with stabilizer bar.
24. Remove stiffener plate.
25. Remove rear end plate.

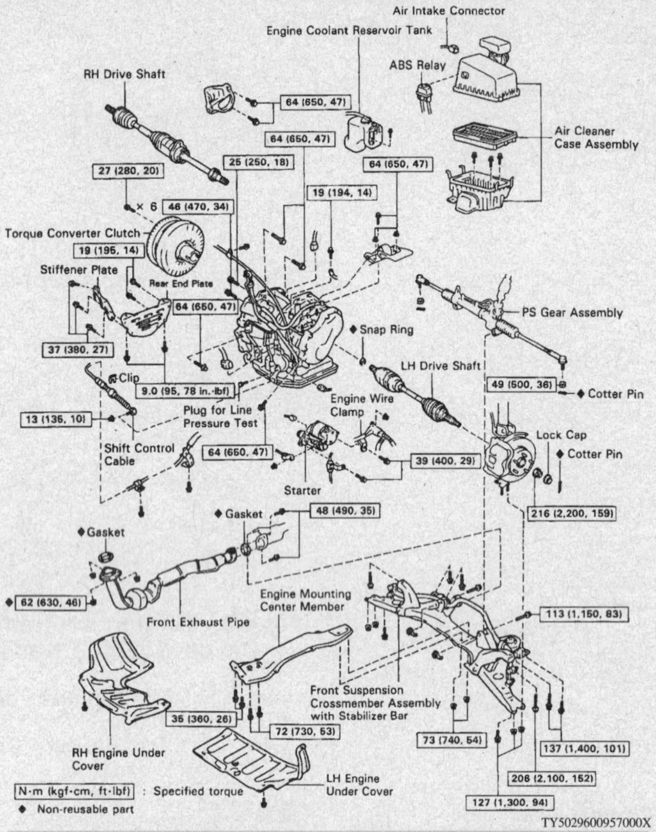

Air Intake Connector
Engine Coolant Reservoir Tank
ABS Relay
RH Drive Shaft
64 (650, 47)
64 (650, 47)
Air Cleaner Case Assembly
25 (250, 18)
64 (650, 47)
27 (280, 20)
19 (194, 14)
× 6
46 (470, 34)
Torque Converter Clutch
19 (195, 14)
Stiffener Plate
Rear End Plate
64 (650, 47)
PS Gear Assembly
Snap Ring
37 (380, 27)
LH Drive Shaft
Clip
9.0 (95, 78 in.·lbf)
49 (500, 36)
Cotter Pin
Plug for Line Pressure Test
Engine Wire Clamp
13 (136, 10)
Lock Cap
Shift Control Cable
64 (650, 47)
39 (400, 29)
Cotter Pin
Starter
Gasket
48 (490, 35)
216 (2,200, 159)
Gasket
62 (630, 46)
Engine Mounting Center Member
113 (1,150, 83)
Front Exhaust Pipe
Front Suspension Crossmember Assembly with Stabilizer Bar
36 (360, 26)
72 (730, 53)
73 (740, 54)
137 (1,400, 101)
RH Engine Under Cover
LH Engine Under Cover
206 (2,100, 152)
N·m (kgf·cm, ft·lbf) : Specified torque
127 (1,300, 94)
Non-reusable part
TY5029600957000X

Fig. 34 Transaxle replacement. RAV4 w/A241E Transaxle

26. Turn crankshaft to gain access to torque converter clutch mounting bolts. Remove six TCC mounting bolts.
27. Raise and support transaxle using suitable jack.
28. Remove transaxle mounting bolts and separate transaxle from engine.
29. Inspect torque converter and drive plate as follows:
    a. Install one-way test tool No. 09350-32014, or equivalent, in inner race of one-way clutch.
    b. With clutch converter on its side, turn test tool. Clutch should lock counterclockwise and rotate freely clockwise.
    c. Using a suitable dial indicator, measure driveplate runout. If greater than .0079 inch or if ring gear is damaged, replace driveplate.
    d. Using a suitable dial indicator, measure torque converter clutch sleeve runout. If greater than .0118 inch, reorient installation of converter clutch. If not corrected, replace torque converter clutch.

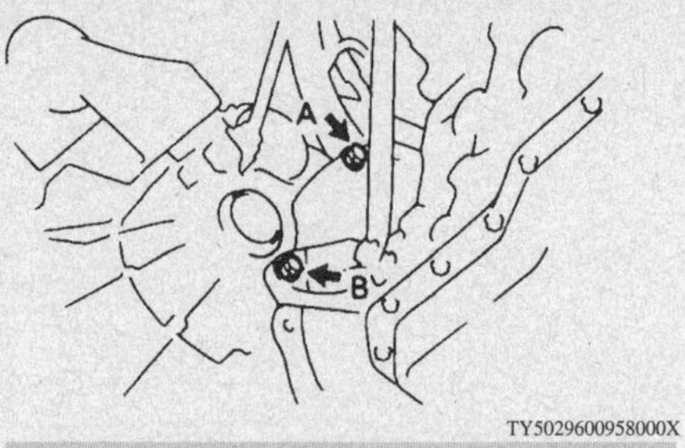

A
B
TY5029600958000X

Fig. 35 Transaxle rear mounting bolts. RAV4 w/A241E Transaxle

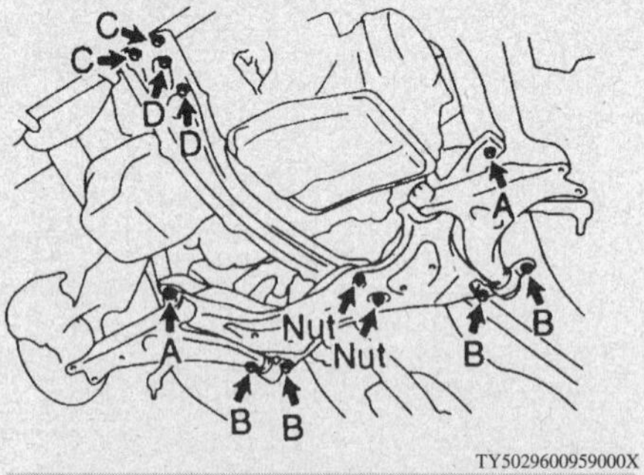

C
C
D
D
A
A
Nut
Nut
B
B
B
B
TY5029600959000X

Fig. 36 Crossmember & stabilizer bar bolts/nut. 4RAV w/A241E Transaxle

30. Reverse procedure to install, noting the following:
    a. **Torque** rear side transaxle mounting bolt "A" to 18 ft. lbs. and "B" to 34 ft. lbs., **Fig. 35.**
    b. **Torque** front suspension crossmember/stabilizer bar "A" bolts to 152 ft. lbs., "B" bolts to 101 ft. lbs., "C" bolts to 26 ft. lbs. and "D" bolts to 53 ft. lbs. **Torque** crossmember nuts to 54 ft. lbs., **Fig. 36.**
    c. Tighten all remaining bolts and nuts to specifications.
    d. After installation, adjust shift lever and throttle cable as described under "Adjustments."

TIGHTENING SPECIFICATIONS

Year	Component	Torque/ Ft. Lbs.
1993–96	Apply Tube Bracket	7
	Control Cable Bolt	9
	Cooler Lines	20
	Exhaust Pipe Nut	46
	Kickdown Pressure Solenoid	56①
	Kickdown Pressure Switch	56①
	LH Engine Mount Bracket	32
	Neutral Safety Switch	58①
	Neutral Start Switch Bolt	48①
	Neutral Start Switch Nut	61①

Continued

TIGHTENING SPECIFICATIONS—Continued

Year	Component	Torque/ Ft. Lbs.
1993–96	Oil Drain Plug (A131L)	36
	Oil Drain Plug (Except A131L)	13
	Oil Pan Bolts	43①
	Oil Pump Body To Stator Shaft	7
	Oil Pump To Transaxle Case	18
	Oil Strainer	7
	Oil Tube	7
	Parking Lock Pawl Bracket	65①
	Rear Engine Mount Bracket To Body	54
	Rear Engine Mount Bracket To Engine	43
	Rear Transaxle Cover	18
	Solenoid Wire Assembly Clamp	7
	Speed Sensor	48①
	Speed Sensor Cover Bracket	9
	Starter	29
	Test Plug	65①
	Torque Converter To Driveplate (Except A131E)	18
	Torque Converter To Driveplate (A131E)	20
	Transaxle Bolts (10 mm)	25
	Transaxle Bolts (12 mm)	47
	Transaxle Housing To Case	22
	Transaxle Rear Cover To Rear Case	18
	Valve Body Bolt	7
	Valve Body Detent Spring	7
	Valve Body To Case	7

① — Inch lbs.

A132L & A242L Automatic Transaxle

INDEX

Page No.

Adjustments 48-277
Manual Shift Linkage 48-277
Neutral Safety Switch 48-277
Throttle Cable 48-277
In-Vehicle Repairs 48-277
Differential Case, Replace 48-278
Governor Valve, Replace 48-277
Throttle Cable, Replace......... 48-277
Valve Body, Replace 48-277
Maintenance 48-276
Fluid Change 48-276
Fluid Check..................... 48-276
Precautions 48-275

Page No.

Air Bag Systems 48-275
Audio Coded Anti-Theft System . 48-275
Tightening Specifications 48-278
Transaxle, Replace 48-278
Troubleshooting 48-276
Delayed Upshifts & Downshifts. . 48-276
Drag Or Binding On Upshift..... 48-276
Fluid Discolored Or Smells Burned 48-276
Harsh Downshift 48-276
Harsh Engagement Into Any Drive Range 48-276
Incorrect Downshift 48-276

Page No.

Incorrect Shift Lever Position.... 48-276
No Downshift When Coasting ... 48-276
No Engine Braking In 2 48-276
No Hold In P.................... 48-276
No Kickdown 48-276
Shift Lock System 48-276
Slips On Upshifts Or Shudders On Takeoff.................... 48-276
Vehicle Does Not Move In Any Drive Gear.................... 48-276
Vehicle Does Not Move In Any Range 48-276

PRECAUTIONS

AIR BAG SYSTEMS

Refer to "Air Bag System Precautions" in the front of this manual for system disarming and arming procedures.

AUDIO CODED ANTI-THEFT SYSTEM

Some models are equipped with an audio coded anti-theft system that will disable the radio when the battery cable is disconnected. The system can be identified by the "ANTI-THEFT SYSTEM" on the cassette lid. Obtain 3 digit code for input. Reset system after service as follows:

1. Obtain 3 digit audio theft code.
2. Depress 1 (PROG) while depressing righthand side of TUNE SEEK button, - - - will appear in tape operation display.

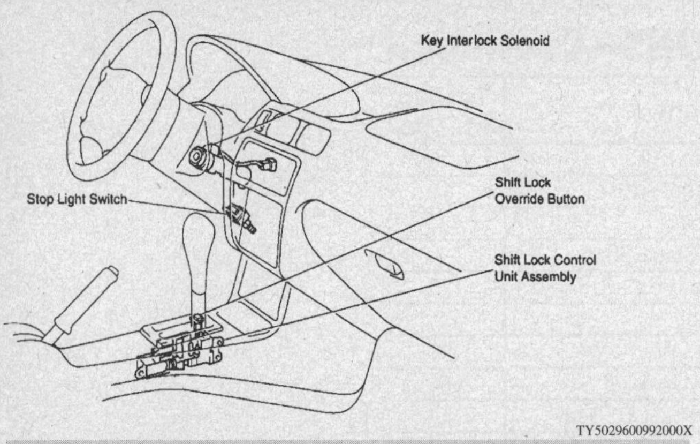
Key Interlock Solenoid
Stop Light Switch
Shift Lock Override Button
Shift Lock Control Unit Assembly
TY5029600992000X

Fig. 1 Shift lock system components. Tercel

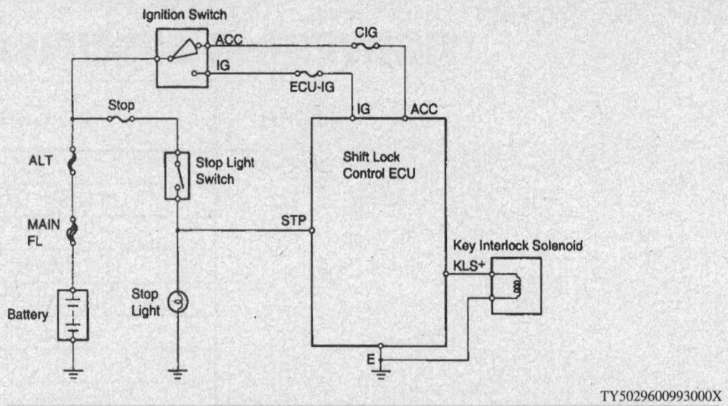
Ignition Switch
ACC
IG
CIG
ECU-IG
Stop
IG
ACC
ALT
Stop Light Switch
Shift Lock Control ECU
MAIN FL
STP
Key Interlock Solenoid
KLS+
Battery
Stop Light
E
TY5029600993000X

Fig. 2 Shift lock wiring circuit. Tercel

3. To enter the first digit, depress 1 (PROG) button repeatedly until the number of times depressed equals the first digit (depress the 1 button six times if the first digit if five, first press equals 0).
4. To enter second digit, depress 2 (APS) button repeatedly until the number of times depressed equals the second digit.
5. To enter third digit, depress 3 (RPT) button repeatedly until the number of times depressed equals the third digit.
6. If - - - is displayed after inputting digits, repeat procedure.
7. When code appears in display, depress and hold SCAN button until SEC appears.
8. When SEC disappears audio system is operative.
9. If Err is displayed, repeat procedure. **Attempting to input code more than 9 times may permanently disable audio system.**

TROUBLESHOOTING

SHIFT LOCK SYSTEM

Refer to **Figs. 1 and 2** for shift lock system component locations and wiring circuit.

Shift Lock Control ECM Inspection

Using a suitable voltmeter, measure voltage at each terminal of the shift lock ECM connector, **Fig. 3.** Refer to **Fig. 4** for measuring conditions and voltage specifications.

Key Interlock Solenoid Inspection

1. Disconnect solenoid connector.
2. Using suitable ohmmeter, measure resistance between connector terminals.
3. Resistance should be 12.5–16.5 ohms.
4. Apply battery positive voltage between terminals and ensure solenoid operating noise can be heard.

FLUID DISCOLORED OR SMELLS BURNED

1. Contaminated fluid.
2. Faulty torque converter.
3. Faulty transaxle.

VEHICLE DOES NOT MOVE IN ANY DRIVE GEAR

1. Improperly adjusted transaxle control cable.
2. Faulty valve body or primary regulator.
3. Faulty transaxle.

VEHICLE DOES NOT MOVE IN ANY RANGE

1. Faulty park lock pawl.
2. Faulty valve body or primary regulator.
3. Faulty torque converter.
4. Broken converter driveplate.
5. Blocked oil pump intake strainer.
6. Faulty transaxle.

INCORRECT SHIFT LEVER POSITION

1. Improperly adjusted transaxle control cable.
2. Faulty manual valve and lever.
3. Faulty transaxle.

HARSH ENGAGEMENT INTO ANY DRIVE RANGE

1. Improperly adjusted transaxle control cable.
2. Faulty valve body or primary regulator.
3. Faulty accumulator pistons.
4. Faulty transaxle.

DELAYED UPSHIFTS & DOWNSHIFTS

1. Improperly adjusted throttle cable.
2. Faulty governors.
3. Faulty valve body.

SLIPS ON UPSHIFTS OR SHUDDERS ON TAKEOFF

1. Improperly adjusted transaxle control cable.
2. Improperly adjusted throttle cable.
3. Faulty valve body.
4. Faulty transaxle.

DRAG OR BINDING ON UPSHIFT

1. Improperly adjusted transaxle control cable.
2. Faulty valve body.
3. Faulty transaxle.

HARSH DOWNSHIFT

1. Improperly adjusted throttle cable.
2. Faulty accumulator pistons.
3. Faulty valve body.
4. Faulty transaxle.

NO DOWNSHIFT WHEN COASTING

1. Faulty governor.
2. Faulty valve body.

INCORRECT DOWNSHIFT

1. Improperly adjusted throttle cable.
2. Faulty governor.
3. Faulty valve body.
4. Faulty transaxle.

NO KICKDOWN

1. Improperly adjusted throttle cable.
2. Faulty governor.
3. Faulty valve body.

NO ENGINE BRAKING IN 2

1. Faulty valve body.
2. Faulty transaxle.

NO HOLD IN P

1. Improperly adjusted transaxle Control Cable.
2. Faulty parking lock pawl and rod.

MAINTENANCE

FLUID CHECK

1. Allow vehicle to reach operating temperature, 158–176°F.
2. Position vehicle on level surface, then apply parking brake.
3. With engine idling, move shift selector through all positions.
4. Remove transmission dipstick, wipe clean, then replace.
5. Remove dipstick again, check HOT fluid level.
6. Total dry fill system capacity is 5.7 quarts.

FLUID CHANGE

1. Using wrench, tool No. 09043–38100, or equivalent, remove drain plug and drain fluid.

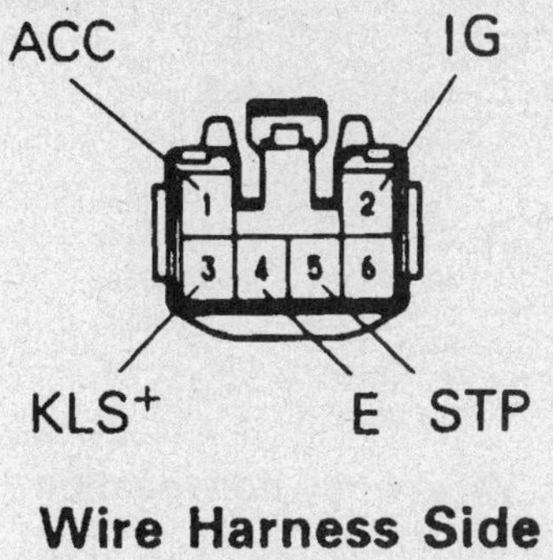
ACC
IG
1
2
3
4
5
6
KLS+
E
STP
Wire Harness Side

TY5029600994000X

Fig. 3 Shift lock ECM connector terminals. Tercel

Terminal	Measuring Condition	Voltage (V)
ACC – E	Ignition switch ACC	10 – 14
IG – E	Ignition switch ON	10 – 14
STP – E	Depressing brake pedal	10 – 14
KLS+ – E	1 Ignition switch ACC and P position	0
	2 Ignition switch ACC and except P position	10 – 14
	3 (After approx 1 second)	6 – 9

TY5029600995000X

Fig. 4 Shift lock control ECM inspection. Tercel

2. Install drain plug, add fluid through filler tube, using ATF DEXRON II. **Do not overfill.**
3. Total drain and refill capacity is 2.6 quarts.
4. Start engine, move shift selector through all positions.
5. Allow engine to idle, check fluid at COOL level.

ADJUSTMENTS

MANUAL SHIFT LINKAGE

1. Loosen swivel nut on lever, then push manual lever fully toward right side of vehicle, **Fig. 5.**
2. Return lever two notches to Neutral position, then place selector lever in Neutral position.
3. Manually hold lever tightly toward R range, then tighten swivel nut.

THROTTLE CABLE

1. Hold accelerator pedal in fully depressed position, then loosen cable adjusting nuts, **Fig. 6.**
2. Adjust cable to obtain 0–.04 inch between end of boot and stopper on cable, then tighten adjusting nut.
3. Fully depress accelerator pedal and recheck adjustment, then road test vehicle.

NEUTRAL SAFETY SWITCH

1. Loosen neutral safety switch attaching bolts.
2. Place selector lever in Neutral position.
3. Disconnect electrical connector.
4. Align groove in with neutral basic line, **Fig. 7.**
5. **Torque** switch retaining bolts to 48 inch lbs. to secure adjustment.
6. Reconnect electrical connector to switch, then ensure engine starts with selector lever in "N" and "P" only.

IN-VEHICLE REPAIRS

VALVE BODY, REPLACE

Removal

1. Clean area around pan, then drain transmission fluid.
2. Remove oil pan and gasket, then the oil strainer.
3. Remove apply tube bracket attaching bolts, then the apply tube.
4. Remove oil tubes using a suitable screwdriver, then the manual detent spring.
5. Remove manual valve, then the manual valve body.
6. Remove valve body attaching bolts, then disconnect throttle cable.
7. Remove valve body, then the governor apply gasket.
8. Remove governor oil strainer.

Installation

1. Install governor oil strainer.
2. Install governor apply gasket.
3. Hold valve body in place, then manually retain cam in downward position and slip cable end into slot.
4. Position valve body in installation position, then insert and finger tighten attaching bolts. Tighten to specifications. Attaching millimeter bolt lengths are indicated in **Fig. 8.**
5. Align manual valve with pin on manual valve lever, then install manual valve body.
6. Insert and finger tighten manual valve body attaching bolts, then tighten to specifications. Attaching bolt lengths (mm) are indicated in **Fig. 9.**
7. Install detent spring, then insert and finger tighten attaching bolt. Tighten to specifications.
8. Ensure manual lever is in contact with center of roller at tip of detent spring, then install oil tubes.
9. Install apply tube bracket, then the oil strainer.
10. Insert magnet into pan, then install oil pan with new gasket.
11. Insert oil pan attaching bolts, then tighten to specifications.
12. Install drain plug with new gasket, then tighten to specifications.
13. Fill transaxle to specifications, then ensure proper fluid level.

THROTTLE CABLE, REPLACE

Removal

1. Disconnect throttle cable from throttle linkage.
2. Disconnect transaxle control cable from manual shift lever, then remove lever.
3. Remove neutral safety switch, then the valve body as previously described.
4. Remove cable retaining bolt, then the retaining plate.
5. Pull cable from transaxle case.

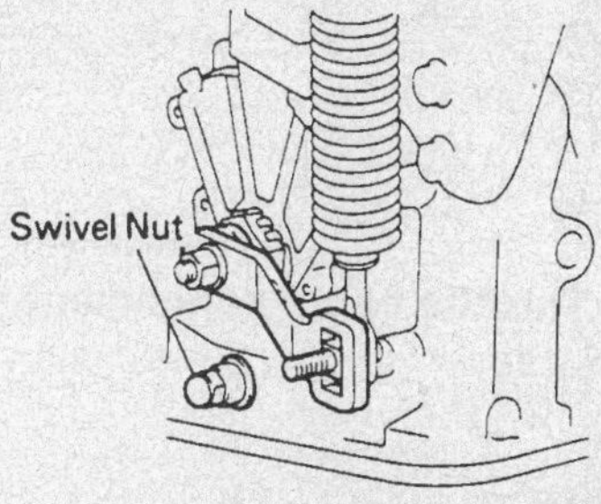
Swivel Nut

TY5029100770000X

Fig. 5 Manual shift linkage adjustment

Installation

1. Insert cable into transaxle case, then install retaining plate and bolt.
2. Install valve body as previously described, then position cable stop for adjustment reference as follows:
   a. Bend cable to a radius of approximately 7.87 inches as shown, **Fig. 10.** Cable stop is not staked in place on replacement cable.
   b. Lightly pull inner cable from housing until a slight resistance is felt, then hold in position.
   c. Stake stopper onto inner cable so that .031–.059 inch clearance exists between stop and cable housing.
   d. Connect and adjust throttle cable as previously described.
3. Install neutral safety switch, then the manual shift lever. Adjust switch as previously described.
4. Connect transaxle control cable.
5. Ensure transaxle fluid level is to specifications, then road test vehicle.

GOVERNOR VALVE, REPLACE

Removal

1. Remove transaxle dust cover, then the LH driveshaft and governor bracket.
2. Remove governor cover, then the O-ring.
3. Remove governor body with thrust washer.
4. Remove washer, then the governor body adapter.

Installation

1. Install governor body adapter.
2. Install washer on governor body.
3. Install governor cover with O-ring.
4. Install LH driveshaft, then the transaxle dust cover.
5. Ensure transaxle fluid level is to specifications, then road test vehicle.

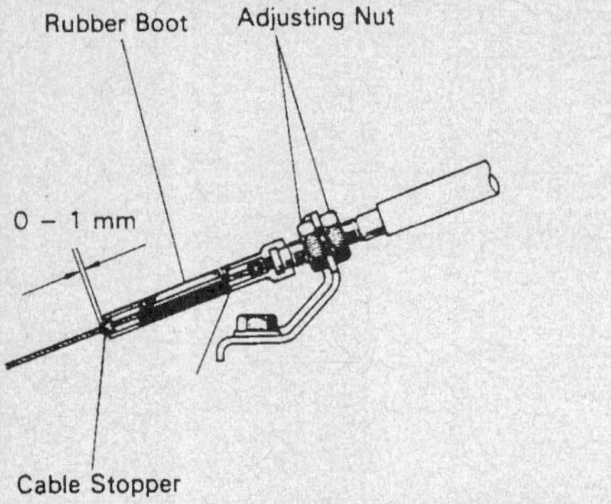
Rubber Boot
Adjusting Nut
0 – 1 mm
Cable Stopper

TY5029100771000X

Fig. 6 Throttle cable adjustment

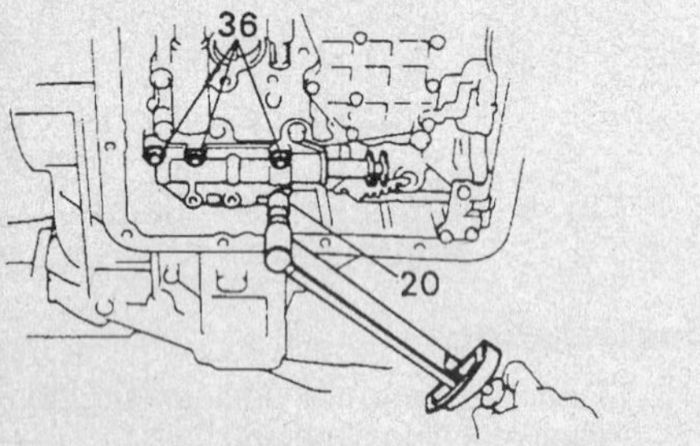
36
20

TY5029100775000X

Fig. 9 Manual valve body bolt location

DIFFERENTIAL CASE, REPLACE

Removal

1. Remove neutral start switch, then the speedometer driven gear.
2. Remove governor body, then the oil pan.
3. Remove valve body, then the 11 transaxle rear cover attaching bolts. Tap cover from case using a suitable mallet.
4. Remove intermediate shaft, then the parking lock pawl bracket and rod.
5. Remove parking lock pawl, then the manual shaft and lever.
6. Remove manual shaft and lever, then the governor pressure adapter.
7. Remove carrier cover.

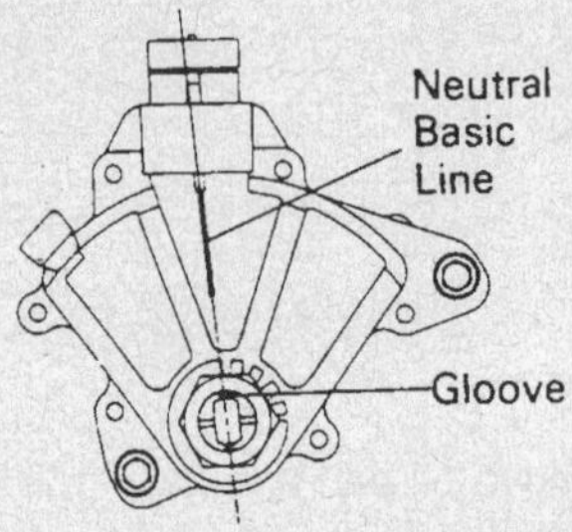
Neutral
Basic
Line
Gloove

TY5029100772000X

Fig. 7 Neutral safety switch adjustment

Installation

1. Install governor pressure adapter, then the manual shaft and lever.
2. Install parking lock pawl.
3. Install parking lock rod, then the bracket.
4. Install intermediate shaft.
5. Install transaxle rear cover with new gasket, then insert retaining bolts and tighten to specifications.
6. Install valve body, then the governor body.
7. Install oil pan.
8. Install speedometer driven gear, then the neutral start switch.

TRANSAXLE

REPLACE

1. **On models with coded audio anti-theft system,** obtain three digit code.
2. **On all models,** disconnect battery ground cable, then remove air duct.
3. Disconnect speedometer cable, then remove throttle cable from throttle link.
4. Remove upper side mounting bolts.
5. Disconnect starter cable and electrical connector, then the starter attaching bolts and starter.
6. Raise and support vehicle.
7. Drain transmission fluid, then the differential fluid.
8. Remove engine undercover.
9. Remove clip from control cable, then disconnect control cable from lever.

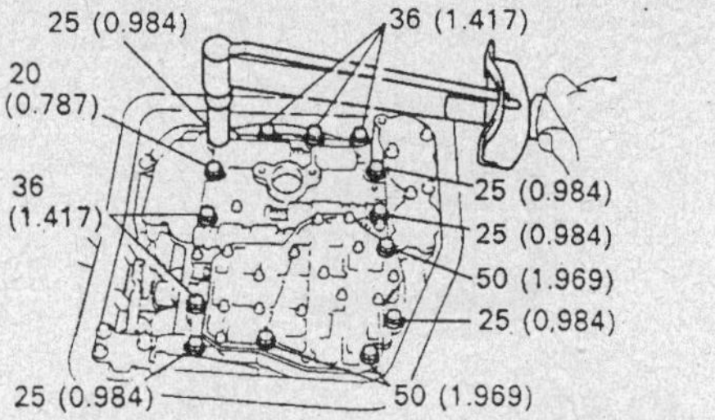
25 (0.984)
36 (1.417)
20
(0.787)
36
(1.417)
25 (0.984)
25 (0.984)
50 (1.969)
25 (0.984)
25 (0.984)
50 (1.969)

TY5029200774000X

Fig. 8 Valve body bolt location

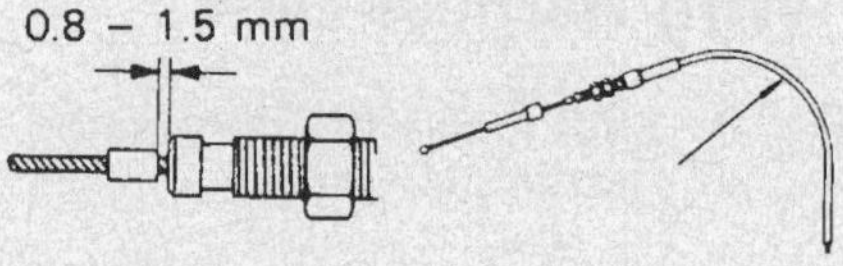
0.8 – 1.5 mm

TY5029100776000X

Fig. 10 Throttle cable installation position

10. Disconnect driveshafts, then suspend using suitable wire or cord.
11. Disconnect oil cooler hose from pipe.
12. Remove exhaust pipe to engine attaching bolts, disconnect oxygen sensor electrical connector, then remove rear exhaust pipe attaching bolts, then remove.
13. Disconnect neutral start switch electrical connector.
14. Remove six torque converter attaching bolts. **Rotate crankshaft to gain access to each bolt.**
15. Disconnect bond cable from LH engine mounting bracket, then remove LH mounting attaching bolts and LH mount.
16. Support engine and transaxle with two suitable jacks, then remove four support bolts and disconnect rear mount bracket from body. Remove three bolts and engine rear mounting bracket.
17. Remove transaxle mount bolts, then separate torque converter from transaxle.
18. Reverse procedure to install, noting that **on models with coded audio anti-theft systems,** rearm as outlined under "Precautions."

TIGHTENING SPECIFICATIONS

Year	Component	Torque/ Ft. Lbs.
1993–96	Cooler Lines	20
	Exhaust Pipe Nut	46
	LH Engine Mount Bracket	32
	Neutral Start Switch (Bolt)	48①
	Neutral Start Switch (Nut)	61①
	Oil Drain Plug	36
	Oil Pan	43①
	Oil Strainer	7
	Parking Lock Pawl Bracket	65①
	Rear Cover	18

Continued

TIGHTENING SPECIFICATIONS—Continued

Year	Component	Torque/ Ft. Lbs.
1993–96	Rear Engine Mount Bracket To Body	54
	Rear Engine Mount Bracket To Engine	43
	Test Plug	65①
	Torque Converter To Driveplate	13
	Transaxle Bolts (10 mm)	25
	Transaxle Bolts (12 mm)	47
	Valve Body To Case	7

① — Inch lbs.

A140E Automatic Transaxles

INDEX

Page No.
Adjustments 48-280
Neutral Start Switch............ 48-280
Throttle Cable 48-280
Transaxle Control Cable 48-280
In-Vehicle Repairs 48-280
Governor Pressure Adapter, Replace 48-282
Manual Valve Lever & Shaft, Replace 48-281
Speed Sensor, Replace.......... 48-280
Throttle Cable, Replace......... 48-280
Transaxle Oil Seal, Replace 48-282
Valve Body, Replace............ 48-281
Maintenance 48-280
Fluid Change 48-280
Fluid Check..................... 48-280

Page No.
Precautions...................... 48-279
Air Bag Systems................ 48-279
Audio Coded Anti-Theft System . 48-279
Tightening Specifications 48-284
Transaxle, Replace 48-282
Camry 48-282
Celica 48-283
Troubleshooting 48-279
Delayed Upshifts, Or Downshifts 4-3 Then Back To 4, Or 3-2 Then Back To 3.............. 48-280
Drags Or Binds On Upshift...... 48-280
Erratic Upshifts 48-280
Fluid Discolored Or Smells Burned 48-279
Harsh Downshifts 48-280

Page No.
Harsh Shifting 48-279
Incorrect Shift Lever Position.... 48-279
No Downshift When Coasting... 48-280
No Engine Braking In "2" Or "L" Range 48-280
No Kickdown 48-280
No Lock-Up In 2nd, 3rd, Or O/D.......................... 48-280
Premature Or Retarded Downshift When Coasting..... 48-280
Shift Lock System 48-279
Slips On Upshifts, Or Slips Or Shudders On Take-Off 48-280
Vehicle Does Not Move In Any Range 48-279
Vehicle Moves In "P"........... 48-280

PRECAUTIONS

AIR BAG SYSTEMS

Refer to "Air Bag System Precautions" in the front of this manual for system disarming and arming procedures.

AUDIO CODED ANTI-THEFT SYSTEM

Some models are equipped with an audio coded anti-theft system that will disable the radio when the battery cable is disconnected. The system can be identified by the "ANTI-THEFT SYSTEM" on the cassette lid. Obtain 3 digit code for input. Reset system after service as follows:

1. Obtain 3 digit audio theft code.
2. Depress 1 (PROG) while depressing righthand side of TUNE SEEK button, - - - will appear in tape operation display.
3. To enter the first digit, depress 1 (PROG) button repeatedly until the number of times depressed equals the first digit (depress the 1 button six times if the first digit if five, first press equals 0).
4. To enter second digit, depress 2 (APS) button repeatedly until the number of times depressed equals the second digit.
5. To enter third digit, depress 3 (RPT) button repeatedly until the number of times depressed equals the third digit.
6. If - - - is displayed after inputting digits, repeat procedure.
7. When code appears in display, depress and hold SCAN button until SEC appears.
8. When SEC disappears audio system is operative.
9. If Err is displayed, repeat procedure. **Attempting to input code more than 9 times may permanently disable audio system.**

TROUBLESHOOTING

SHIFT LOCK SYSTEM

Refer to **Figs. 1 through 3** for shift lock system component locations and wiring circuit.

Shift Lock Control ECU Inspection

Using a suitable voltmeter, measure voltage at each terminal of the shift lock control ECU, **Figs. 4 and 5.** Refer to **Figs. 6 and 7** for measuring conditions and voltage specifications.

FLUID DISCOLORED OR SMELLS BURNED

1. Contaminated or incorrect fluid.
2. Faulty torque converter.
3. Faulty transaxle.

VEHICLE DOES NOT MOVE IN ANY RANGE

1. Malfunctioning electrical controls.
2. Improperly adjusted control cable.
3. Faulty park lock control.
4. Faulty valve body or primary regulator.
5. Faulty torque converter.
6. Broken converter driveplate.
7. Clogged oil strainer.
8. Faulty transaxle.

INCORRECT SHIFT LEVER POSITION

1. Improperly adjusted control cable.
2. Faulty manual valve and lever.
3. Faulty transaxle.

HARSH SHIFTING

1. Improperly adjusted throttle cable.
2. Faulty valve body or primary regulator.
3. Faulty accumulator pistons.
4. Faulty transaxle.

NO DOWNSHIFT WHEN COASTING

1. Faulty valve body.
2. Faulty solenoid valve.
3. Malfunctioning electrical controls.

PREMATURE OR RETARDED DOWNSHIFT WHEN COASTING

1. Faulty throttle cable.
2. Faulty valve body.
3. Faulty transaxle.
4. Faulty solenoid valve.
5. Malfunctioning electrical controls.

NO KICKDOWN

1. Faulty solenoid valve.
2. Malfunctioning electrical controls.
3. Faulty valve body.

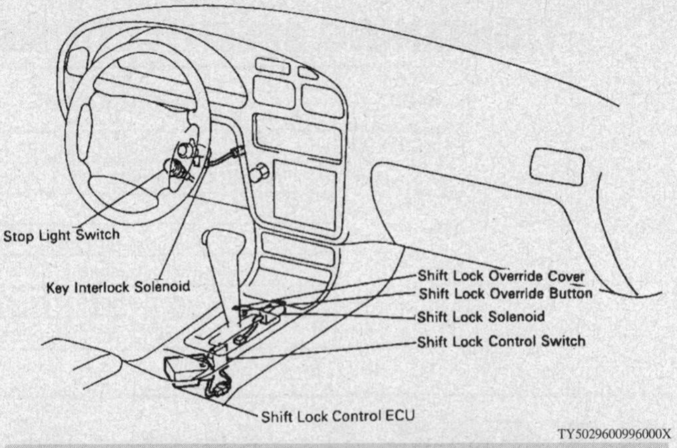
Stop Light Switch
Key Interlock Solenoid
Shift Lock Override Cover
Shift Lock Override Button
Shift Lock Solenoid
Shift Lock Control Switch
Shift Lock Control ECU
TY5029600996000X

Fig. 1 Shift lock system components. Camry

NO ENGINE BRAKING IN "2" OR "L" RANGE

1. Faulty solenoid valve.
2. Malfunctioning electrical controls.
3. Faulty valve body.
4. Faulty transaxle.

VEHICLE MOVES IN "P"

1. Improperly adjusted control cable.
2. Faulty parking lock pawl cam and spring.

DELAYED UPSHIFTS, OR DOWNSHIFTS 4-3 THEN BACK TO 4, OR 3-2 THEN BACK TO 3

1. Malfunctioning electrical controls.
2. Faulty valve body.
3. Faulty clutches and/or bands.
4. Faulty solenoid valve.

SLIPS ON UPSHIFTS, OR SLIPS OR SHUDDERS ON TAKE-OFF

1. Improperly adjusted control cable.
2. Improperly adjusted throttle cable.
3. Faulty valve body.
4. Faulty solenoid valve.
5. Faulty clutches and/or bands.
6. Faulty transaxle.

ERRATIC UPSHIFTS

1. Improperly adjusted control cable.
2. Faulty valve body.
3. Faulty clutches and/or bands.

NO LOCK-UP IN 2ND, 3RD, OR O/D

1. Malfunctioning electrical controls.
2. Faulty valve body.
3. Faulty solenoid valve.
4. Faulty clutches and/or bands.
5. Faulty transaxle.

HARSH DOWNSHIFTS

1. Improperly adjusted throttle cable.
2. Faulty throttle cable and cam.
3. Faulty accumulator pistons.
4. Faulty valve body.
5. Faulty clutches and/or bands.
6. Faulty transaxle.

DRAGS OR BINDS ON UPSHIFT

1. Improperly adjusted shift cable.
2. Faulty valve body.
3. Faulty transaxle.

MAINTENANCE

FLUID CHECK

1. Operate vehicle, allow transaxle fluid temperature to reach 158–176°F.
2. Position vehicle on level surface, apply parking brake.
3. With engine at idle, move shift lever through all positions.
4. Remove transaxle dipstick, wipe clean, then replace.
5. Remove dipstick again, then check fluid level in HOT range.
6. Dry fill capacity is 5.9 US quarts.

FLUID CHANGE

1. Drain transaxle fluid, then install drain plug and new gasket.
2. With engine Off, add fluid through dipstick tube. **Do not overfill.**
3. Drain and refill capacity is 2.6 US quarts.
4. Start engine, then move shift selector through all positions, ensuring smooth operation.
5. Allow to idle, then check at COOL level.
6. Allow to reach normal operating temperature, then recheck.

ADJUSTMENTS

THROTTLE CABLE

1. Remove air intake hose, fully depress accelerator pedal and ensure throttle valve is fully open. If not, adjust accelerator linkage.
2. Hold accelerator pedal fully depressed, and adjust cable to obtain 0–0.04 inch clearance between end of housing and inner cable stop, **Fig. 8.**
3. Tighten adjusting nuts to secure adjustment and release accelerator pedal.
4. Fully depress accelerator pedal and recheck adjustment.
5. Install air hose and road test vehicle.

TRANSAXLE CONTROL CABLE

1. Loosen swivel nut on selector lever control lever at transaxle.
2. Push manual lever fully toward right side of vehicle, then return lever two notches to neutral position.
3. Place selector lever at "N."
4. Hold lever slightly toward "R" range side and tighten swivel nut.

NEUTRAL START SWITCH

1. Loosen neutral start switch attaching bolts.
2. Place transaxle selector lever to "N" position.
3. Align groove in neutral basic line, **Fig. 9.**
4. Maintain groove in position, then **torque** attaching bolts to 48 inch lbs.
5. Adjust idle speed to specifications.

IN-VEHICLE REPAIRS

SPEED SENSOR, REPLACE

1. Remove transmission case protector.
2. Disconnect speed sensor connector, then remove bracket.
3. Remove speed sensor and O-ring.
4. Reverse procedure to install, tighten to specifications.

THROTTLE CABLE, REPLACE

1. Disconnect throttle cable housing from bracket.
2. Disconnect throttle cable from throttle linkage.
3. Remove neutral start switch as follows:
   a. Disconnect clip, then the control cable from manual shift lever.
   b. Remove manual shift lever.
   c. Remove neutral start switch.
4. Remove valve body as described under "Valve Body, Replace."
5. Remove bolt and retaining plate, then pull throttle cable out of transaxle.
6. Install new cable in transaxle case,

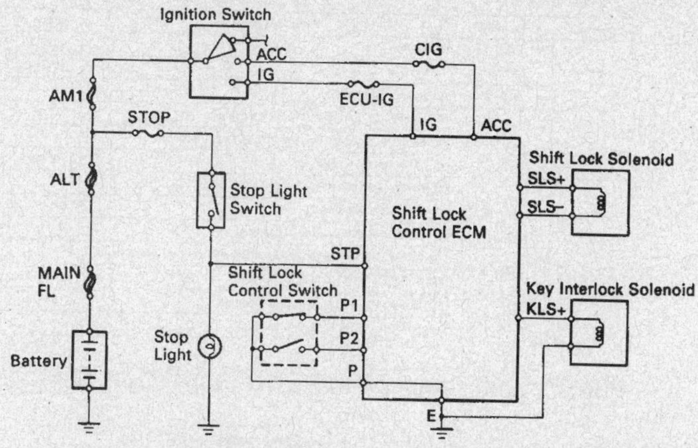
Ignition Switch
ACC
IG
CIG
AM1
ECU-IG
STOP
IG
ACC
Shift Lock Solenoid
SLS+
SLS-
ALT
Stop Light
Switch
Shift Lock
Control ECM
STP
MAIN
FL
Shift Lock
Control Switch
Key Interlock Solenoid
KLS+
P1
P2
P
Battery
Stop
Light
E

TY5029600997000X

Fig. 2 Shift lock system components. Celica

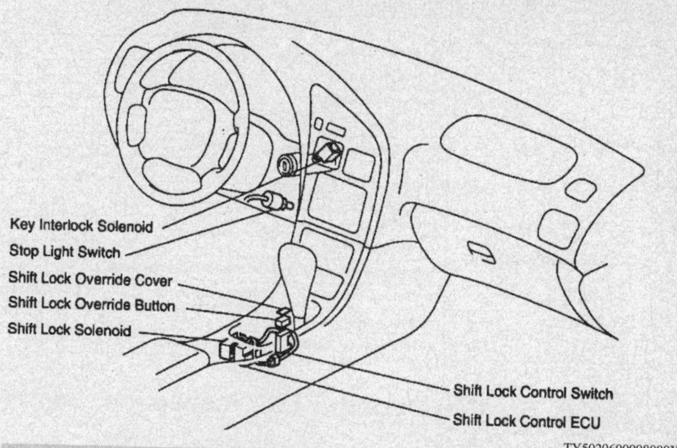
Key Interlock Solenoid
Stop Light Switch
Shift Lock Override Cover
Shift Lock Override Button
Shift Lock Solenoid
Shift Lock Control Switch
Shift Lock Control ECU

TY5029600998000X

Fig. 3 Shift lock system wiring circuit

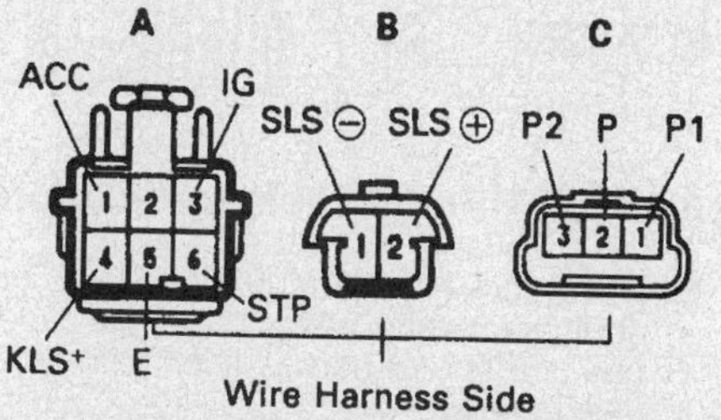
A
B
C
ACC
IG
SLS ⊖
SLS ⊕
P2
P
P1
1 2 3
4 5 6
1 2
3 2 1
STP
KLS+
E
Wire Harness Side

TY5029600999000X

Fig. 4 Shift lock ECU connector terminals. Camry

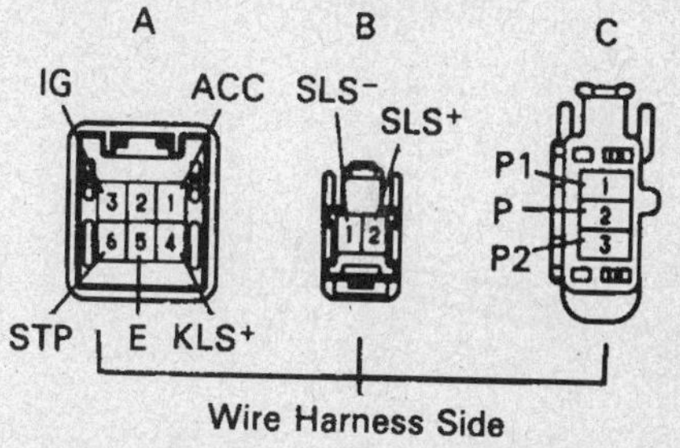
A
B
C
IG
ACC
SLS−
SLS+
P1
P
P2
3 2 1
6 5 4
1 2
1
2
3
STP
E
KLS+
Wire Harness Side

TY5029601001000X

Fig. 5 Shift lock ECU connector terminals. Celica

being sure to push cable all the way in, then install retaining plate and bolt.

7. Install valve body as described under "Valve Body, Replace."
8. Install new stopper on inner cable of new throttle cable as follows:
   a. Bend cable approximately 7.87 inches in radius.
   b. Pull inner cable lightly until a slight resistance is felt, and hold cable in position.
   c. Stake stopper on cable .031–.059 inch from end of outer cable, **Fig. 10.**
9. Connect throttle cable to throttle linkage.
10. Connect throttle cable housing to bracket.
11. Adjust throttle cable as previously described.
12. Install neutral start switch as follows:
    a. Install neutral start switch.
    b. Install manual shift lever.
    c. Adjust neutral start switch as previously described.
    d. Connect transaxle control cable.
    e. Adjust transaxle control cable as previously described.
13. Test drive vehicle.

VALVE BODY, REPLACE

Removal

1. Raise and support vehicle.
2. Clean outside of transaxle and drain transmission fluid.
3. Remove oil pan and gasket, then discard gasket.
4. Remove oil strainer.
5. Remove two bolts and apply tube bracket.
6. Disconnect solenoid electrical connectors.
7. Remove oil tubes.
8. Remove manual detent spring.
9. Remove manual valve with valve body.
10. Remove valve body attaching bolts, disconnect throttle cable from cam, and remove valve body.
11. Remove governor apply gasket.

Installation

1. Install new governor apply gasket.
2. Hold cam down and slip throttle cable end into slot, then install valve body, being careful not to trap kickdown switch wire.
3. Install valve body attaching bolts in their proper locations, **Fig. 11,** finger tighten bolts and tighten to specifications. **Numbers in Fig. 11, indicate bolt lengths in mm.**
4. Connect solenoid electrical connectors.
5. Install manual valve and body as follows:
   a. Align manual valve with pin on manual shift lever.
   b. Install and finger tighten manual valve body with attaching bolts, **Fig. 12. Numbers in figure, indicate bolt lengths in mm.**
   c. Tighten bolts to specifications.
6. Install detent spring, then tighten to specifications.
7. Ensure manual valve lever is in contact with center of roller at tip of detent spring.
8. Using suitable plastic hammer, tap oil tubes in proper locations, being careful not to bend or damage oil tubes.
9. Install apply tube bracket, then the oil strainer.
10. Install magnets in pan, ensuring magnets do not interfere with oil tubes.
11. Install oil pan with new gasket and **torque** bolts to 43 inch lbs.
12. Install drain plug with new gasket and **torque** plug to 36 ft. lbs.
13. Add transmission fluid, referring to specifications.

MANUAL VALVE LEVER & SHAFT, REPLACE

Removal

1. Remove valve body as described in "Valve Body, Replace."
2. Remove parking lock pawl bracket, then remove parking lock rod and retaining spring.
3. Remove manual valve shaft as follows:
   a. Using a hammer and chisel, pry and turn the collar.
   b. With the hammer and a punch, drive out the pin, **Fig. 13.**
   c. Slide out the shaft and remove detent plate.
4. If necessary, replace oil seal of manual shaft.

Installation

1. Install manual valve shaft into case as follows:
   a. Assemble a new collar to the manual lever.
   b. Install manual valve shaft to the transmission case through the manual valve lever.
   c. Drive in roll pin with slot at a right angle to the shaft.
   d. Match collar hole to lever calking hollow and calk collar to the lever.
2. Install retaining spring, then ensure lever moves smoothly.
3. Install parking lock rod and parking lock pawl bracket.
4. Install valve body as described in "Valve Body, Replace."

Connector	Terminal	Measuring condition	Voltage (V)
A	ACC – E	Ignition switch ACC	10 – 14
	IG – E	Ignition switch ON	10 – 14
	STP – E	Depress brake pedal	10 – 14
	KLS+ – E	① Ignition switch ACC and P position	0
		② Ignition switch ACC and except P position	7.5 – 11
		③ (After-approx. 1 second)	6 – 9
B	SLS+ – SLS−	① Ignition switch ON and P position	0
		② Depress brake pedal	8.5 – 13.5
		③ Except P position	0
C	P1 – P	① Ignition switch ON, P position and depress brake pedal	0
		② Shift except P position under conditions above	9 – 13.5
	P2 – P	① Ignition switch ACC and P position	9 – 13.5
		② Shift except P position under condition above	0

TY5029601000000X

Fig. 6 Shift lock control ECU inspection. Camry

Connector	Terminal	Measuring condition	Voltage (V)
A	ACC – E	IG SW ACC	10 – 14
	IG – E	IG SW ON	10 – 14
	STP – E	Depress brake pedal	10 – 14
	KLS+ – E	① IG SW ACC and shift lever at P position	0
		② IG SW ACC and shift lever at R, N, D, 2, L position	10 – 14
		③ (After approx. 1 second)	6 – 9
B	SLS+ – SLS−	① IG SW ON and shift lever at P position	0
		② Depress brake pedal	8.5 – 13.5
		③ Shift lever at R, N, D, 2, L position	0
C	P1 – P	① IG SW ON, shift lever at P position and depress brake pedal	0
		② Shift lever at R, N, D, 2, L position	9 – 13.5
	P2 – P	① IG SW ACC and shift lever at position	9 – 13.5
		② Shift lever at R, N, D, 2, L position	0

TY5029601002000X

Fig. 7 Shift lock control ECU inspection. Celica

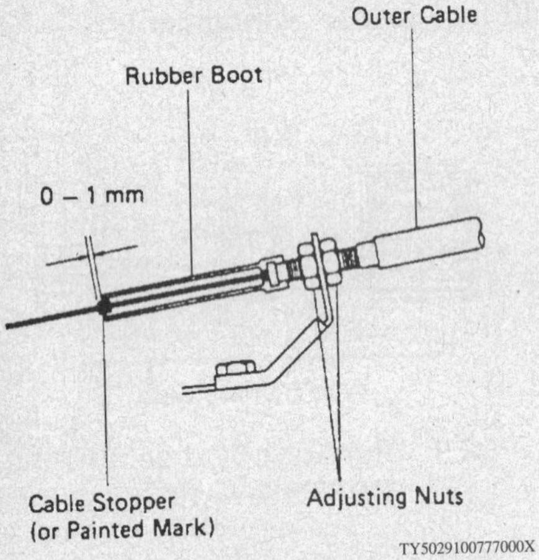
Outer Cable
Rubber Boot
0 – 1 mm
Cable Stopper
(or Painted Mark)
Adjusting Nuts

TY5029100777000X

Fig. 8 Throttle cable adjustment

GOVERNOR PRESSURE ADAPTER, REPLACE

1. Remove valve lever and shaft as described in "Manual Valve Lever & Shaft, Replace."
2. Remove torsion spring, then governor pressure adapter.
3. Reverse procedure to install noting the following:
   a. Align hole of adapter with hole of case and install torsion spring.
   b. Check that adapter does not slide or the spring does not fall out when pulled by hand.
   c. Install valve lever and shaft as described in "Manual Valve Lever & Shaft, Replace."

TRANSAXLE OIL SEAL, REPLACE

Lefthand Side

1. Remove dust cover and fender apron seal.
2. Drain out approximately one quart of transaxle fluid.
3. Remove lefthand driveshaft as described under "Speed Sensor, Replace."
4. Remove speed sensor as described under "Speed Sensor, Replace."
5. Using tool No. SST 09350-32010, or equivalent, drive out side gear shaft.
6. Remove side bearing retainer.
7. Press oil seal out of retainer, and using

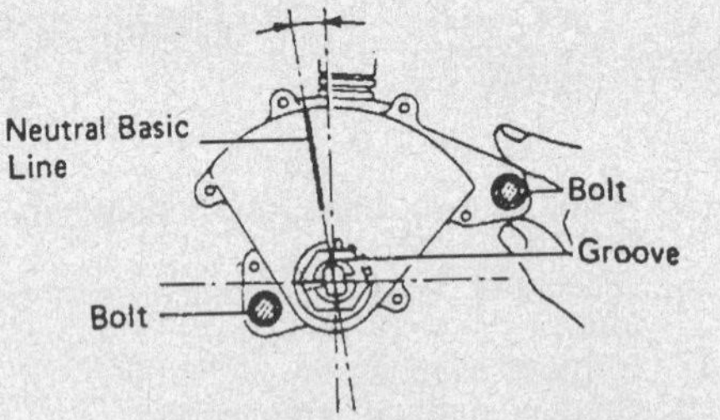
Neutral Basic
Line
Bolt
Groove
Bolt

TY5029100778000X

Fig. 9 Neutral safety switch adjustment

tool No. SST 09359-32010, or equivalent, press in new seal to depth of .106 inch.
8. Coat lip of oil seal with suitable grease.
9. Clean bolt and case threads of side bearing retainer attaching bolts, coat threads of bolts with suitable sealer, and tighten to specifications.
10. Using tool No. SST 09520-32010, or equivalent, drive in side gear shaft until it contacts pinion shaft.
11. Install speed sensor as described under "Speed Sensor, Replace."
12. Install driveshaft as described under "Speed Sensor, Replace."
13. Fill transaxle with approximately one quart of transaxle fluid.

Righthand Side

1. Remove fender apron seal.
2. Drain approximately one quart of transaxle fluid from transaxle.
3. Remove driveshaft and intermediate shaft as follows:
   a. Remove cotter pin, dust cover, and bearing locknut.
   b. Loosen six nuts attaching driveshaft to intermediate shaft flange.
   c. Remove brake caliper from steering knuckle and secure out of way.
   d. Remove disc rotor.
   e. Using tool No. SST 09950-20014, or equivalent, pull axle hub from driveshaft.
   f. Remove bearing bracket bolts and bracket from cylinder block.
   g. Remove intermediate shaft from universal joint.
4. Using tools No. SST 09520-32010 and No. SST 09520-32030, or equivalents, drive out universal joint.
5. Using tool No. SST 09308-00010, or equivalent, drive oil seal from case.

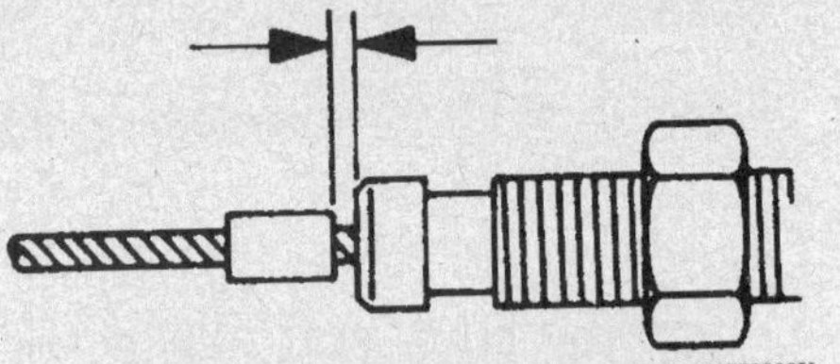

TY5029100779000X

Fig. 10 Throttle cable installation

6. Using tool No. SST 09350-32010, or equivalent, drive new oil seal into case until surface of seal is flush with surface of case.
7. Coat lip of seal with suitable grease.
8. Using tools No. SST 09520-32010 and No. SST 09520-32030, or equivalents, drive in universal joint until joint contacts pinion shaft.
9. Install intermediate shaft and driveshaft as follows:
   a. Install intermediate shaft to universal joint.
   b. Install bearing bracket onto cylinder block.
   c. Install outboard joint side of driveshaft to axle hub.
   d. Finger tighten six nuts connecting driveshaft to intermediate shaft flange.
   e. Install disc rotor.
   f. Install brake caliper to steering knuckle.
   g. Installing bearing locknut, dust cover, and cotter pin.
   h. Tighten six driveshaft to intermediate shaft flange attaching nuts to specifications.
   i. Fill transaxle with approximately one quart of transaxle fluid.
10. Install fender apron seal.

TRANSAXLE

REPLACE

CAMRY

1. Disconnect battery ground cable, remove air cleaner assembly, then the throttle cable.
2. **On models equipped with cruise control,** remove cruise control actuator cover, then disconnect connector from cruise control actuator.
3. **On all models,** remove ground cable from transmission, then disconnect Nos. 1 and 2 speed sensor electrical connectors.

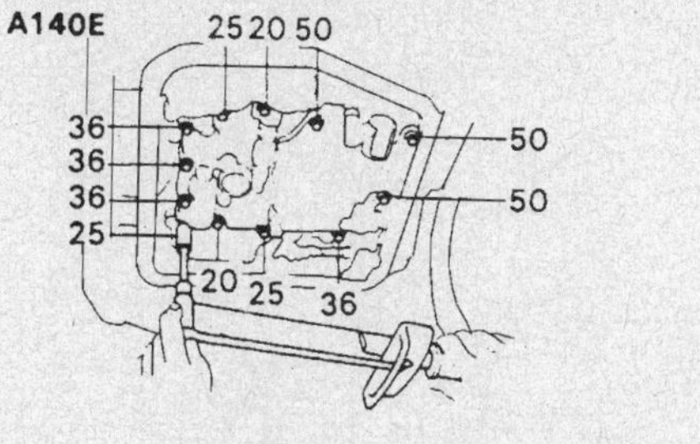
A140E
25 20 50
36
36
36
25
50
50
20
25
36

TY5029100780000X

Fig. 11 Valve body bolt locations.

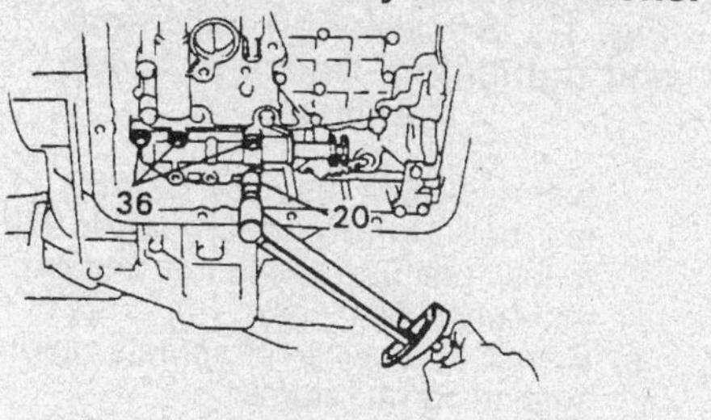
36
20

TY5029100782000X

Fig. 12 Manual valve body bolt locations

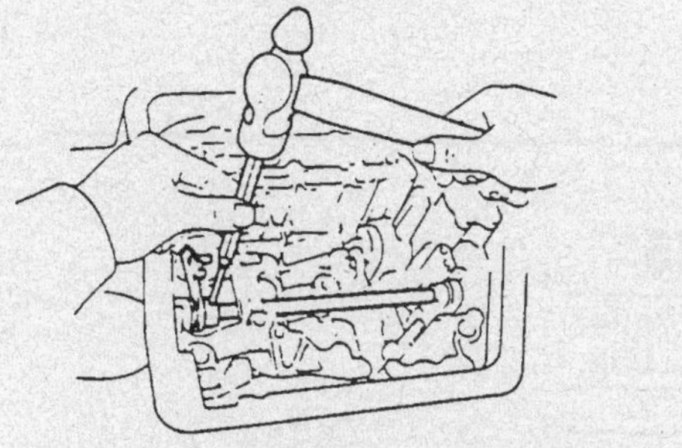

TY5029100783000X

Fig. 13 Manual valve shaft removal

4. Disconnect starter electrical connector, then remove starter.
5. Disconnect park/neutral position (neutral start) switch connector, then the solenoid connector and oil cooler hose.
6. Remove retaining clip and nut, then the disconnect shift control cable.
7. Remove front side engine mounting bolts, then the bolts and clamp from front frame assembly.
8. Remove upper transaxle to engine bolts, then install suitable engine support fixture.
9. Tie steering gear housing to engine support fixture with a suitable cord, then raise and support vehicle.
10. Remove front wheel, then the exhaust pipe.
11. Remove differential drain plug and gasket, then drain fluid.
12. Remove right and left engine side cover No. 2, then the engine under front cover Nos. 1 and 2.
13. Remove driveshaft.
14. Remove front and rear side engine mounting nuts, then the transaxle mounting bolts.
15. Remove bolts, then disconnect stabilizer bar bush bracket from front frame assembly.

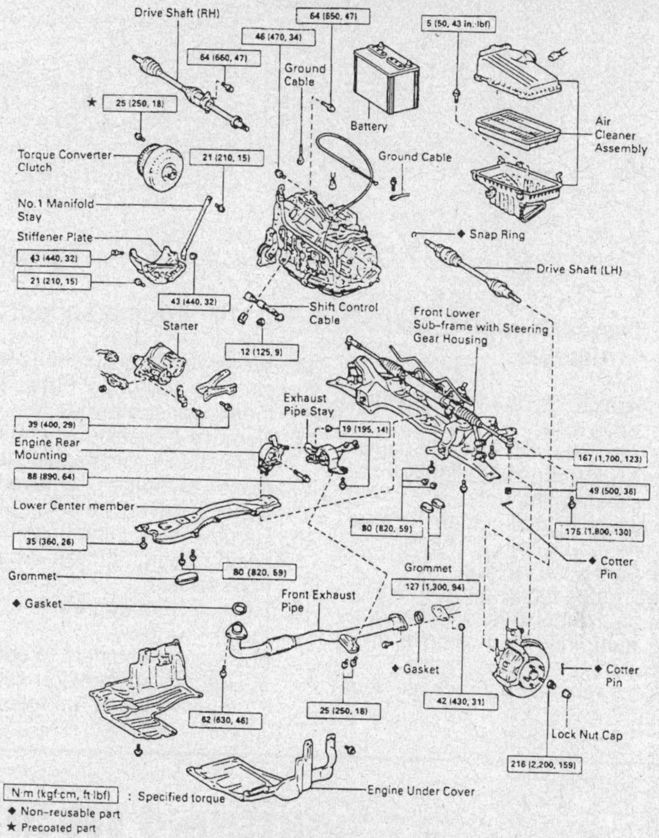
Drive Shaft (RH)
64 (650, 47)
46 (470, 34)
5 (50, 43 in.·lbf)
64 (660, 47)
Ground Cable
★ 25 (250, 18)
Battery
Air Cleaner Assembly
Torque Converter Clutch
21 (210, 15)
Ground Cable
No.1 Manifold Stay
Stiffener Plate
43 (440, 32)
21 (210, 15)
◆ Snap Ring
Drive Shaft (LH)
43 (440, 32)
Shift Control Cable
Starter
Front Lower Sub-frame with Steering Gear Housing
12 (125, 9)
Exhaust Pipe Stay
39 (400, 29)
19 (195, 14)
Engine Rear Mounting
167 (1,700, 123)
88 (890, 64)
49 (500, 36)
Lower Center member
80 (820, 59)
175 (1,800, 130)
35 (360, 26)
◆ Cotter Pin
Grommet
80 (820, 59)
Grommet
127 (1,300, 94)
◆ Gasket
Front Exhaust Pipe
◆ Gasket
◆ Cotter Pin
42 (430, 31)
25 (250, 18)
62 (630, 46)
Lock Nut Cap
216 (2,200, 159)
Engine Under Cover
N·m (kgf·cm, ft·lbf) : Specified torque
◆ Non-reusable part
★ Precoated part

TY5029100784000X

Fig. 14 Component removal. Celica w/A140E transaxle

16. Remove bolts and nuts from steering gear housing, then the housing.
17. Using a suitable jack, raise front frame assembly, then remove screws from right and left fender liners.
18. Remove bolts and nuts, then the front frame assembly.
19. Using a suitable jack, raise transaxle, then remove bolts and stiffener plate.
20. Remove bolts, then the rear end plate.
21. Turning crankshaft to gain access to each bolt, remove bolts starting with the dark green bolt first.
22. Remove transaxle to engine bolts, then separate transaxle and engine.
23. Lower transaxle and remove torque converter clutch from transaxle.
24. Reverse procedure to install, noting the following:
    a. After torque converter clutch has been drained and washed, refill with ATF.
    b. Ensure distance from the installed surface to the front surface of the transaxle housing is 0.51 inch.
    c. **Torque** the 12 mm transaxle to engine bolts to 47 ft. lbs., then the 10 mm bolts to 34 ft. lbs.
    d. **Torque** converter clutch mounting bolts to 20 ft. lbs., then the stiffener plate bolts to 27 ft. lbs.
    e. **Torque** the 19 mm front assembly bolts to 134 ft. lbs., then the 12 mm bolts to 24 ft. lbs.
    f. **Torque** steering gear housing and transaxle mounting bolts to 38 ft. lbs., rear side engine mounting nuts to 48 ft. lbs. and front side engine mounting nut to 59 ft. lbs.
    g. **Torque** exhaust pipe bolts to 76 ft. lbs., upper transaxle to engine bolts to 47 ft. lbs., then front side engine mounting bolts to 59 ft. lbs.
    h. **Torque** starter bolts to 29 ft. lbs. and throttle cable to engine nuts to 11 ft. lbs.
    i. Checking fluid level, inspect front wheel alignment, then perform road test.

CELICA

1. **On models with coded audio anti-theft system,** obtain three digit code.
2. **On all models,** remove battery.
3. Disconnect throttle cable. **On models with cruise control,** remove cruise control actuator.
4. **On all models,** remove air cleaner assembly **Fig. 14,** then disconnect ground cable from transaxle.
5. Remove left engine mount upper bolts, then disconnect and remove starter.
6. Disconnect speed sensor, neutral switch and 2 shift solenoid connectors from transmission.
7. Remove three transaxle mounting bolts **Fig 15.**
8. Disconnect hoses from power steering oil cooler, then install suitable engine support fixture **Fig. 16.**
9. Raise and support vehicle, then remove engine undercovers.

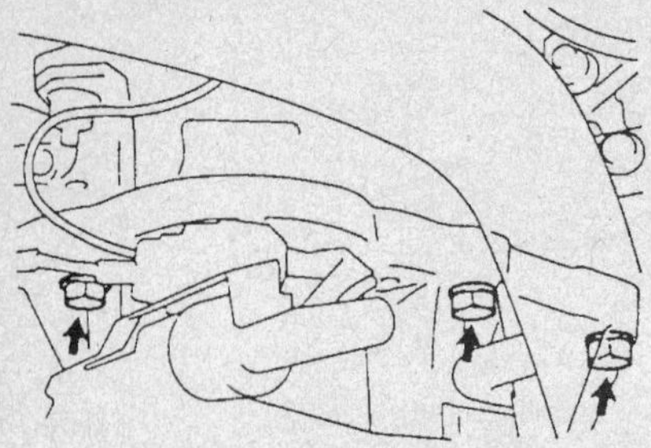
TY5029100785000X

Fig. 15 Transaxle mount bolt removal

10. Drain transaxle oil, then remove left and right drive axle.
11. Support transaxle with suitable equipment, then raise transaxle slightly to release tension from mounts.
12. Disconnect shift cable, then remove rear engine mount bolt.
13. Remove front exhaust pipe.
14. Disconnect steering shaft from steering gearbox, then disconnect power steering fluid lines and remove their support clamps.
15. Disconnect remaining brackets from subframe.

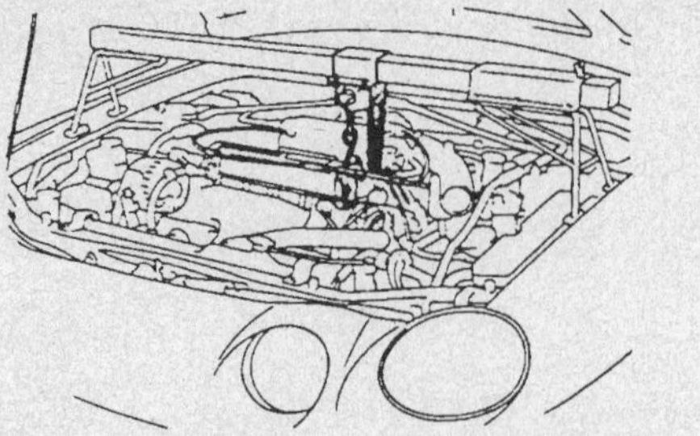
TY5029100786000X

Fig. 16 Engine support fixture

16. Remove remaining bolts holding suspension subframe **Figs. 15 and 17,** then lower subframe.
17. Remove transaxle to engine stiffener plate, then turning engine in normal direction of rotation, remove torque converter to driveplate bolts.
18. Remove remaining bolts holding transaxle to engine, then lower transaxle from vehicle.
19. Reverse procedures to install, noting the following:
    a. Tighten fasteners to specifications.
    b. Tighten suspension subframe fasteners **Fig. 17** as follows; **Torque** bolt A to 26 ft. lbs., bolt B to 59 ft. lbs., bolt C to 130 ft. lbs., bolt D to 94 ft. lbs., bolt E to 123 ft. lbs. and the two nuts to 59 ft. lbs.
    c. Reinstall sealing grommets into suspension subframe.
    d. **On models with coded audio anti-theft systems,** rearm as outlined under "Precautions."

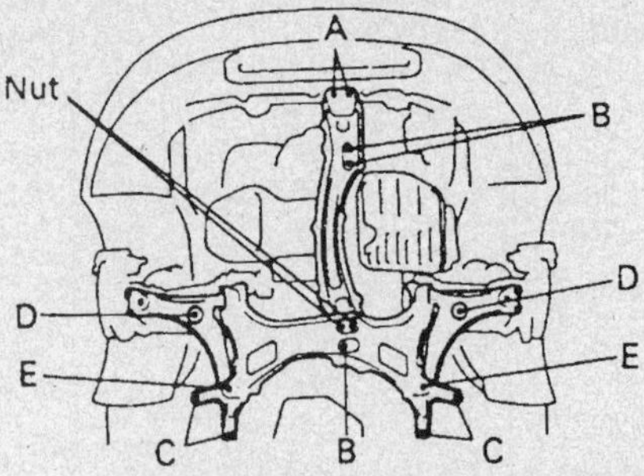
A
Nut
B
D
D
E
E
C
B
C
TY5029100787000X

Fig. 17 Suspension subframe bolt tightening. Celica w/A140E transaxle

TIGHTENING SPECIFICATIONS

Year	Component	Torque/ Ft. Lbs.
1993–96	Accumulator Cover	7
	Apply Tube Bracket	7
	Driveplate	61
	Driveshaft To Intermediate Flange	25
	Front Engine Mount	59
	Front Exhaust Pipe	46
	Front Transaxle Assembly (12 mm Bolt)	24
	Front Transaxle Assembly (19 mm Bolt)	134
	Front Transaxle Assembly (Nut)	27
	Neutral Start Switch Bolt	48①
	Neutral Start Switch Nut	61①
	Oil Cooler Lines	25
	Oil Drain Plug	36
	Oil Pan	43①
	Oil Pump Body	7
	Oil Pump	16
	Oil Strainer	7
	Overdrive Case	48①
	Rear Engine Mount	48
	Rear Exhaust Pipe	76
	Speed Sensor Bracket	9
	Stabilizer Bar Bushing Bracket	14
	Starter	29
	Steering Gear Housing To Frame	134
	Stiffener Plate	27
	Test Plug	65①
	Throttle Cable	11

Continued

TIGHTENING SPECIFICATIONS—Continued

Year	Component	Torque/ Ft. Lbs.
1993–96	Torque Converter	20
	Transaxle Case To Engine (10 mm)	34
	Transaxle Case To Engine (12 mm)	47
	Transaxle Mount	38
	Transaxle Rear Cover To Case	27
	Upper Valve Body To Lower	48①
	Valve Body	7
	Valve Detent Spring	7

① — Inch lbs.

A340E, A340F & A340H Automatic Transmissions

INDEX

Page No.

Adjustments 48-288
Neutral Safety Switch 48-288
Shift Linkage 48-288
Throttle Cable 48-288
Transfer Linkage 48-288
Transfer Position Switch 48-288
In-Vehicle Repairs 48-288
Extension Housing, Replace 48-290
Parking Lock Pawl, Replace 48-290
Rear Oil Seal, Replace 48-290
Sensor Rotor, Replace 48-290
Throttle Cable, Replace 48-289
Transfer Valve Body, Replace ... 48-289
Valve Body, Replace 48-288
Maintenance 48-287
Fluid Change 48-287

Page No.

Fluid Check 48-287
Precautions 48-285
Air Bag Systems 48-285
Audio Coded Anti-Theft System . 48-285
Tightening Specifications 48-295
Transmission, Replace 48-290
Pickup, Tacoma & 4Runner 48-290
Supra 48-291
T100 48-291
Troubleshooting 48-285
Delayed Upshifts & Downshifts. . 48-286
Drag Or Binding On Upshifts 48-286
Fluid Discolored Or Smells Burned 48-286
Harsh Downshift 48-287
Harsh Engagement Into Any

Page No.

Drive Range 48-286
Incorrect Downshift 48-287
Incorrect Shift Lever Position 48-286
No Downshift When Coasting ... 48-287
No Engine Braking In 2 Or L 48-287
No Hold In P 48-287
No Kickdown 48-287
No Lock Up In 2nd, 3rd Or O/D . 48-287
Shift Lock System 48-285
Slips On Upshifts Or Shudders On Takeoff 48-286
Vehicle Does Not Move In Any Drive Gear 48-286
Vehicle Does Not Move In Any Range 48-287

PRECAUTIONS

AIR BAG SYSTEMS

Refer to "Air Bag System Precautions" in the front of this manual for system disarming and arming procedures.

AUDIO CODED ANTI-THEFT SYSTEM

Some models are equipped with an audio coded anti-theft system that will disable the radio when the battery cable is disconnected. The system can be identified by the "ANTI-THEFT SYSTEM" on the cassette lid. Obtain 3 digit code for input. Reset system after service as follows:

1. Obtain 3 digit audio theft code.
2. Depress 1 (PROG) while depressing righthand side of TUNE SEEK button, - - - will appear in tape operation display.
3. To enter the first digit, depress 1 (PROG) button repeatedly until the number of times depressed equals the first digit (depress the 1 button six times if the first digit if five, first press equals 0).
4. To enter second digit, depress 2 (APS) button repeatedly until the number of times depressed equals the second digit.
5. To enter third digit, depress 3 (RPT) button repeatedly until the number of times depressed equals the third digit.
6. If - - - is displayed after inputting digits, repeat procedure.
7. When code appears in display, depress and hold SCAN button until SEC appears.
8. When SEC disappears audio system is operative.
9. If Err is displayed, repeat procedure. **Attempting to input code more than 9 times may permanently disable audio system.**

TROUBLESHOOTING

SHIFT LOCK SYSTEM

MECHANICAL

Refer to **Figs. 1 and 2** for mechanical shift lock control system components.

If a fault exists in the shift lock system, the shift lock mechanism must be replaced.

ELECTRICAL

Refer to **Figs. 3 through 12** for shift lock system component locations and wiring circuits.

Shift Lock Control ECU Inspection

Using a suitable voltmeter, measure voltage at each shift lock control ECU connector terminal, **Figs. 13 through 18.** Refer to **Figs. 19 through 23** for measuring conditions and voltage specifications.

Shift Lock Solenoid Inspection

1. Disconnect solenoid connector.
2. Using suitable ohmmeter, measure resistance between terminals, **Figs. 24 through 28.**
3. Resistance should be as follows:
   a. Supra and Tacoma: 20–28 ohms.
   b. 4Runner: 21–27 ohms.
   c. Pickup: 29–36 ohms.
4. Apply battery positive voltage to shift

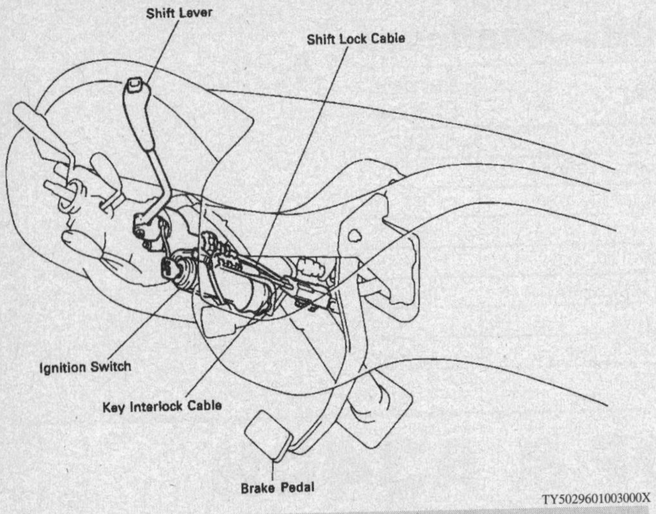
Shift Lever
Shift Lock Cable
Ignition Switch
Key Interlock Cable
Brake Pedal
TY5029601003000X

Fig. 1 Shift lock system components. Previa

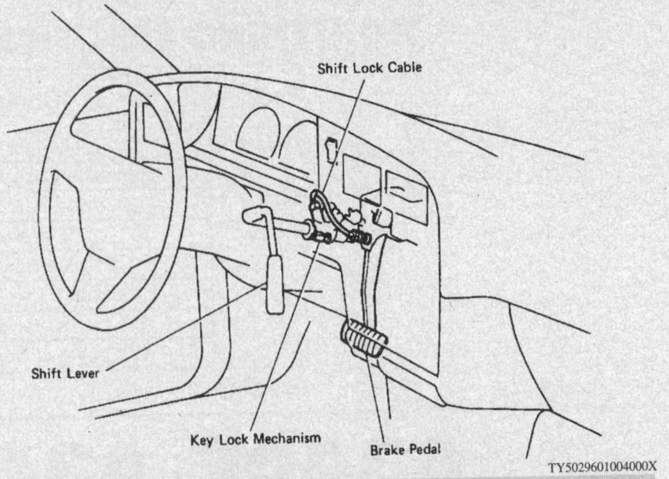
Shift Lock Cable
Shift Lever
Key Lock Mechanism
Brake Pedal
TY5029601004000X

Fig. 2 Shift lock system components. Pickup w/mechanical shift lock

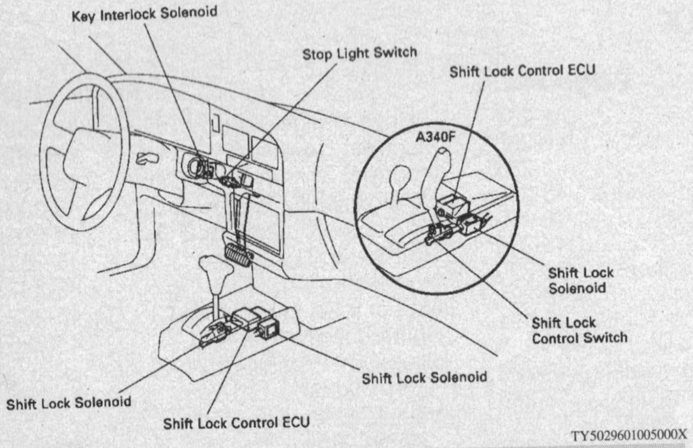
Key Interlock Solenoid
Stop Light Switch
Shift Lock Control ECU
A340F
Shift Lock Solenoid
Shift Lock Control Switch
Shift Lock Solenoid
Shift Lock Solenoid
Shift Lock Control ECU
TY5029601005000X

Fig. 3 Shift lock system components. Pickup w/electronic shift lock

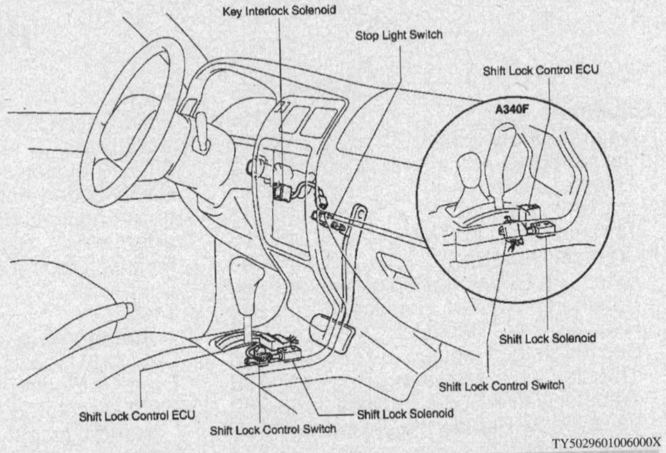
Key Interlock Solenoid
Stop Light Switch
Shift Lock Control ECU
A340F
Shift Lock Solenoid
Shift Lock Control Switch
Shift Lock Control ECU
Shift Lock Solenoid
Shift Lock Control Switch
TY5029601006000X

Fig. 4 Shift lock system components. 4Runner

lock solenoid terminals and ensure operating noise can be heard.

Key Interlock Solenoid Inspection

1. Disconnect solenoid connector.
2. Using suitable ohmmeter, measure resistance between solenoid connector terminals, **Figs. 29 through 32.**
3. Resistance should be 12–17 ohms.
4. Apply battery positive voltage to key interlock solenoid terminals and ensure operating noise can be heard.

Shift Lock Control Switch

Disconnect switch connector and check for continuity at connector terminals indicated in **Figs. 33 through 40.**

FLUID DISCOLORED OR SMELLS BURNED

1. Contaminated fluid.
2. Faulty torque converter.
3. Faulty transmission.

VEHICLE DOES NOT MOVE IN ANY DRIVE GEAR

1. Improperly adjusted transmission control cable.
2. Faulty valve body or primary regulator.
3. Faulty parking lock pawl.
4. Faulty torque converter.
5. Broken converter driveplate.
6. Blocked oil pump intake screen.
7. Faulty transmission.

INCORRECT SHIFT LEVER POSITION

1. Improperly adjusted transmission control cable.
2. Faulty manual valve and lever.
3. Faulty transmission.

HARSH ENGAGEMENT INTO ANY DRIVE RANGE

1. Improperly adjusted transmission control cable.
2. Faulty valve body or primary regulator.
3. Faulty accumulator pistons.
4. Faulty transmission.

DELAYED UPSHIFTS & DOWNSHIFTS

1. Faulty electronic control.
2. Faulty valve body.
3. Faulty solenoid valve.

SLIPS ON UPSHIFTS OR SHUDDERS ON TAKEOFF

1. Improperly adjusted transmission control cable.
2. Improperly adjusted throttle cable.
3. Faulty valve body.
4. Faulty solenoid valve.
5. Faulty transmission.

DRAG OR BINDING ON UPSHIFTS

1. Improperly adjusted transmission control cable.
2. Faulty valve body.
3. Faulty transmission.

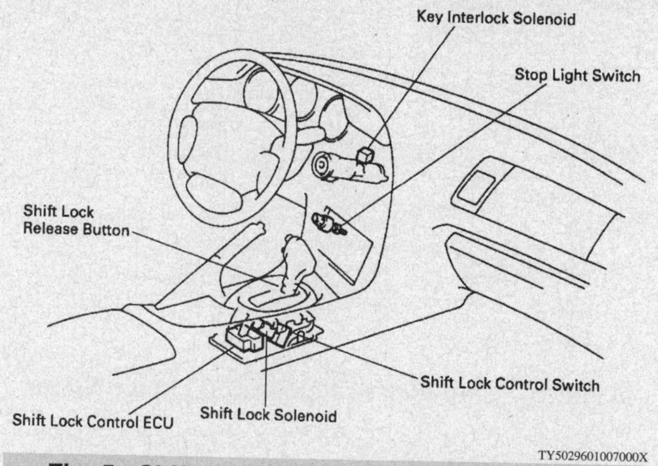
Key Interlock Solenoid
Stop Light Switch
Shift Lock
Release Button
Shift Lock Control Switch
Shift Lock Control ECU
Shift Lock Solenoid
TY5029601007000X

Fig. 5 Shift lock system components. Supra

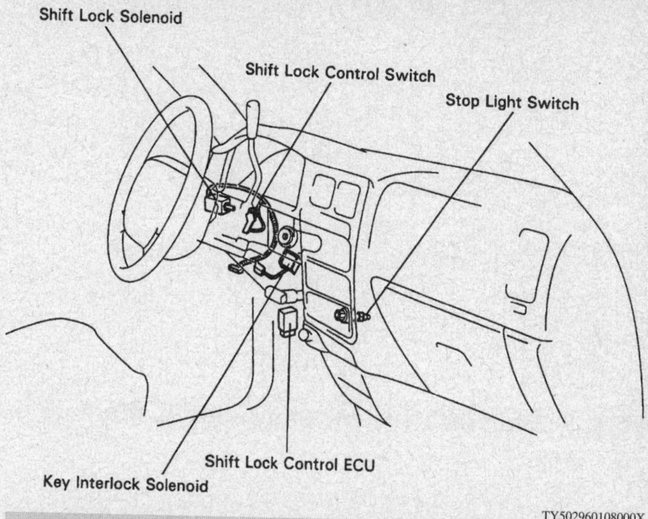
Shift Lock Solenoid
Shift Lock Control Switch
Stop Light Switch
Shift Lock Control ECU
Key Interlock Solenoid
TY502960108000X

Fig. 6 Shift lock system components. Tacoma w/column shift

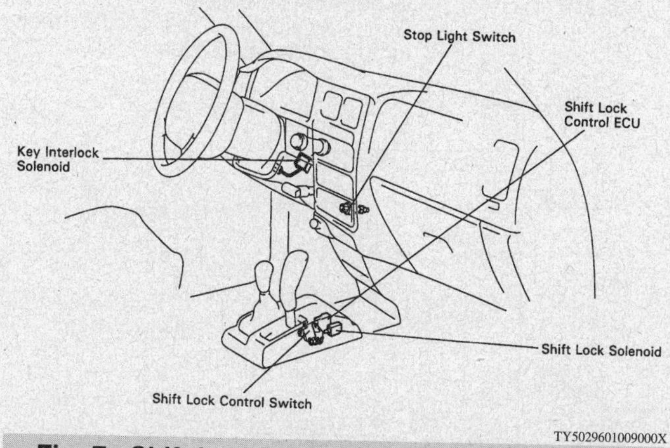
Stop Light Switch
Shift Lock
Control ECU
Key Interlock
Solenoid
Shift Lock Solenoid
Shift Lock Control Switch
TY5029601009000X

Fig. 7 Shift lock system components. Tacoma w/floor shift

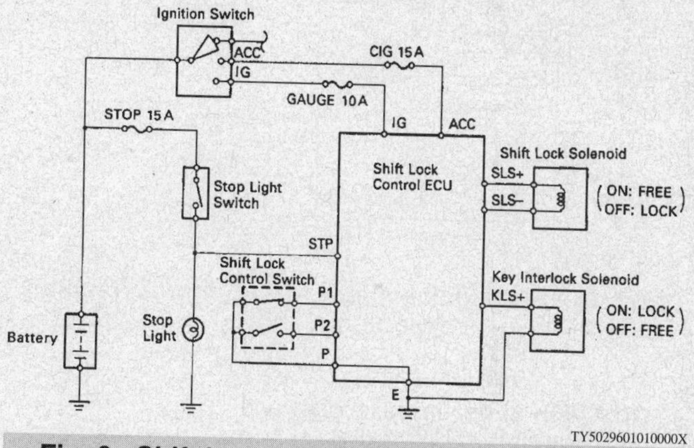
Ignition Switch
ACC
IG
CIG 15A
GAUGE 10A
STOP 15A
IG
ACC
Shift Lock
Control ECU
Shift Lock Solenoid
SLS+
SLS–
ON: FREE
OFF: LOCK
Stop Light
Switch
STP
Shift Lock
Control Switch
P1
P2
P
Key Interlock Solenoid
KLS+
ON: LOCK
OFF: FREE
Battery
Stop
Light
E
TY5029601010000X

Fig. 8 Shift lock system wiring circuit. Pickup

NO LOCK UP IN 2ND, 3RD OR O/D

1. Faulty electronic control
2. Faulty valve body.
3. Faulty solenoid valve.
4. Faulty transmission.

HARSH DOWNSHIFT

1. Improperly adjusted throttle cable.
2. Faulty throttle cable and cam.
3. Faulty accumulator pistons.
4. Faulty valve body.
5. Faulty transmission.

NO DOWNSHIFT WHEN COASTING

1. Faulty valve body.
2. Faulty solenoid valve.
3. Faulty electronic control.

INCORRECT DOWNSHIFT

1. Improperly adjusted throttle cable.
2. Faulty valve body.
3. Faulty transmission.
4. Faulty solenoid valve.
5. Faulty electronic control.

NO KICKDOWN

1. Faulty solenoid valve.
2. Faulty electronic control.
3. Faulty valve body.

NO ENGINE BRAKING IN 2 OR L

1. Faulty solenoid valve.
2. Faulty electronic control.
3. Faulty valve body.
4. Faulty transmission.

NO HOLD IN P

1. Improperly adjusted transmission control cable.
2. Faulty parking lock pawl cam and spring.

VEHICLE DOES NOT MOVE IN ANY RANGE

1. Improperly adjusted transfer linkage.
2. Faulty electronic control.
3. Faulty transfer valve body.
4. Faulty torque converter.
5. Faulty transmission.
6. Faulty transfer.

MAINTENANCE

FLUID CHECK

1. Operate vehicle, allow transaxle fluid temperature to reach 158–176°F.
2. Position vehicle on level surface, apply parking brake.
3. Allow engine to idle, depress brake pedal, then move shift lever through all positions.
4. Remove transaxle dipstick, wipe clean, then replace.
5. Remove again, then check fluid level in HOT range.
6. **On A340E units,** dry capacity is 7.6 US quarts.
7. **On A340F units,** dry capacity is 8.0 US quarts.
8. **On A340H units,** dry capacity for transaxle and transfer is 10.9 US quarts.

FLUID CHANGE

1. Drain transaxle fluid, then reinstall drain plugs.
2. With engine Off, add fluid through filler tube. **Do not overfill.**
3. **On A340E and A340F units,** drain and refill capacity is 1.7 US quarts.

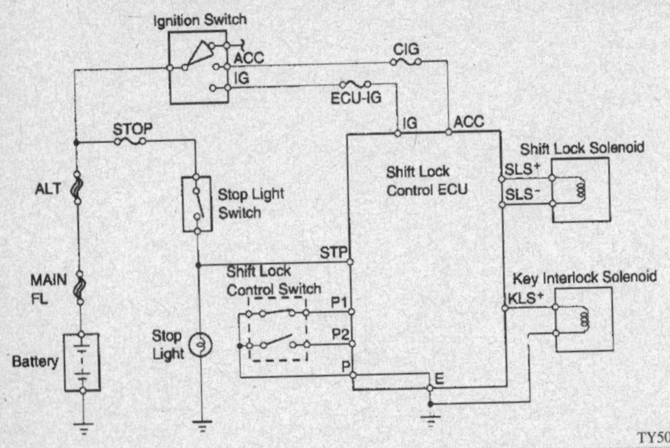
Ignition Switch
ACC
IG
CIG
ECU-IG
STOP
IG
ACC
Shift Lock Solenoid
ALT
Stop Light Switch
Shift Lock Control ECU
SLS+
SLS-
STP
MAIN FL
Shift Lock Control Switch
P1
Key Interlock Solenoid
KLS+
P2
Battery
Stop Light
P
E
TY5029601011000X

Fig. 9 Shift lock system wiring circuit. 4Runner

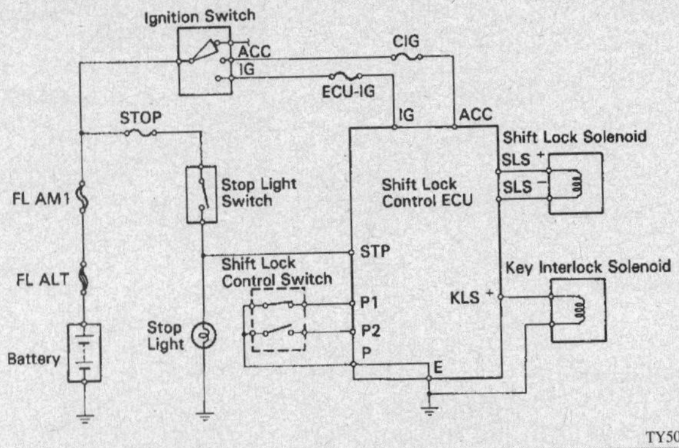
Ignition Switch
ACC
IG
CIG
ECU-IG
STOP
IG
ACC
Shift Lock Solenoid
SLS +
SLS -
FL AM1
Stop Light Switch
Shift Lock Control ECU
STP
FL ALT
Shift Lock Control Switch
Key Interlock Solenoid
KLS +
P1
P2
P
Battery
Stop Light
E
TY5029601012000X

Fig. 10 Shift lock system wiring circuit. Supra

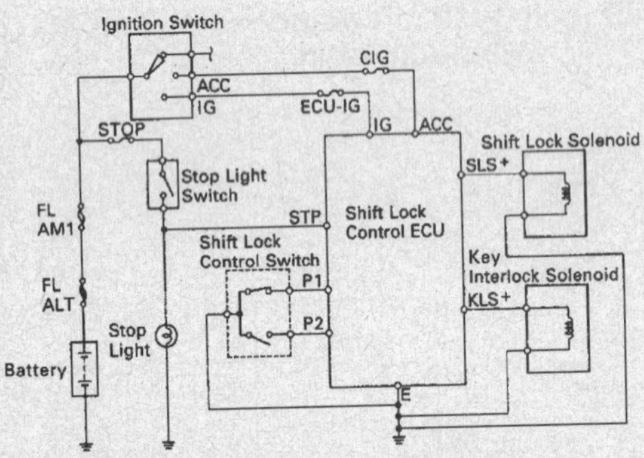
Ignition Switch
CIG
ACC
IG
ECU-IG
STOP
IG
ACC
Shift Lock Solenoid
SLS+
Stop Light Switch
FL AM1
STP
Shift Lock Control ECU
Shift Lock Control Switch
P1
Key Interlock Solenoid
KLS+
FL ALT
P2
Stop Light
Battery
E
TY5029601013000X

Fig. 11 Shift lock system wiring circuit. Tacoma w/column shift

4. **On A340H units,** transaxle drain and refill capacity is 4.0 US quarts.
5. **On all models,** start engine, move shift lever through all positions, ensuring smooth operation.
6. Allow engine to idle, then check fluid level, add up to COOL level.
7. Once fluid temperature reaches 158–176°F, recheck fluid level.

ADJUSTMENTS

SHIFT LINKAGE

1. Loosen shift linkage nut.
2. Push manual lever fully forward, then return lever to notches two the "Neutral" position.
3. While holding selector slightly toward "Reverse" range, tighten shift linkage nut.

NEUTRAL SAFETY SWITCH

1. Check that vehicle can only be started in either the "P" or "N" ranges.
2. If vehicle starts in any other position, adjust switch as follows:
   a. Loosen neutral start switch bolt and set shift lever to the "N" range.
   b. Align groove and neutral basic line as shown in **Fig. 41.**
   c. Hold in position and **torque** bolt to 9 ft. lbs.

THROTTLE CABLE

1. Fully depress accelerator pedal, then ensure throttle valve is fully open.
2. With accelerator pedal fully depressed, loosen throttle valve adjustment nuts, **Fig. 42.**
3. Adjust cable housing until distance between end of boot and stopper on cable is 0–.04 inch.
4. Tighten adjusting nuts, then recheck adjustment.

TRANSFER LINKAGE

1. Place transfer lever in "H2" position.
2. Disconnect No. 1 transfer linkage from cross shaft.
3. Position transfer indicator switch in "H2" position.
4. Connect No. 1 transfer linkage from cross shaft.

TRANSFER POSITION SWITCH

1. Loosen transfer position switch bolt, then place switch in "L4" position.
2. Disconnect electrical connector, then connect a suitable ohmmeter between terminals, **Fig. 43**
3. Adjust switch until there is no continuity between terminals.
4. Connect electrical connector, then torque bolt to 48 inch lbs.

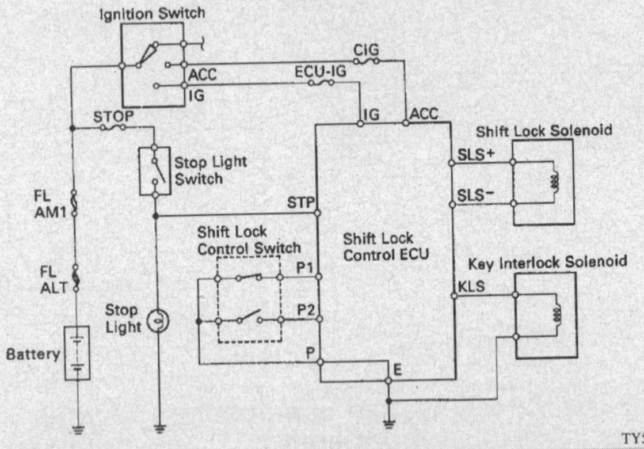
Ignition Switch
CIG
ACC
ECU-IG
IG
STOP
IG
ACC
Shift Lock Solenoid
SLS+
Stop Light Switch
SLS-
FL AM1
STP
Shift Lock Control Switch
Shift Lock Control ECU
P1
Key Interlock Solenoid
FL ALT
KLS
Stop Light
P2
Battery
P
E
TY5029601014000X

Fig. 12 Shift lock system wiring circuit. Tacoma w/floor shift

5. Ensure proper idle RPM.

IN-VEHICLE REPAIRS

VALVE BODY, REPLACE

Removal

1. **On models with coded audio anti-theft system,** obtain three digit code.
2. **On all models,** disconnect battery ground cable, then clean exterior of transmission.
3. Raise and support vehicle, then drain transmission fluid.
4. **On A340H models,** remove front stabilizer bar and front propeller shaft.
5. **On all models,** remove oil pan attaching bolts, then remove oil pan by inserting oil pan seal cutter, tool No. 09032-00100, or equivalent, between oil pan and transmission case and cut seal.
6. Being careful not to damage oil pan flange, remove oil pan by lifting transmission case.
7. Remove attaching bolts, then oil strainer and two gaskets.

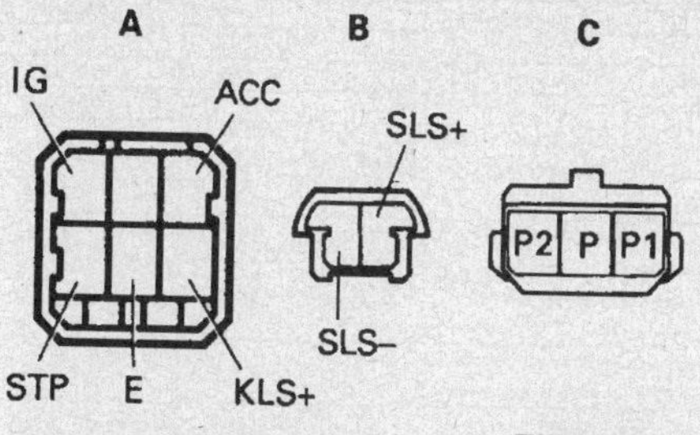
A
B
C
IG
ACC
SLS+
P2
P
P1
SLS–
STP
E
KLS+

TY5029601015000X

Fig. 13 Shift lock ECU connector. Pickup

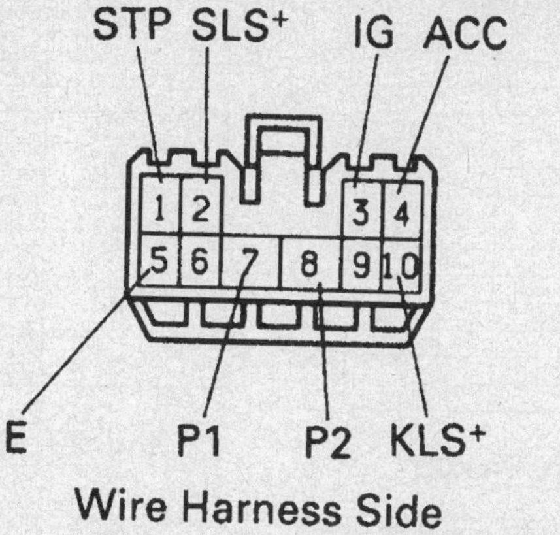
STP
SLS+
IG
ACC
1
2
3
4
5
6
7
8
9
10
E
P1
P2
KLS+
Wire Harness Side

TY5029601016000X

Fig. 14 Shift lock ECU connector. Tacoma w/column shift

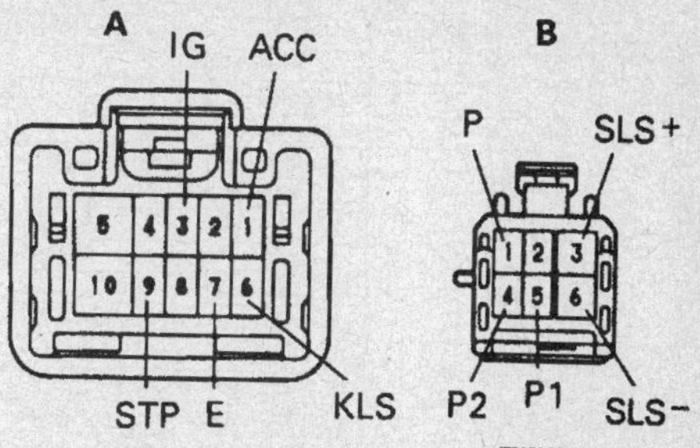
A
IG
ACC
B
P
SLS+
5
4
3
2
1
10
9
8
7
6
1
2
3
4
5
6
STP
E
KLS
P2
P1
SLS–

TY5029601017000X

Fig. 15 Shift lock ECU connector. Tacoma w/floor shift

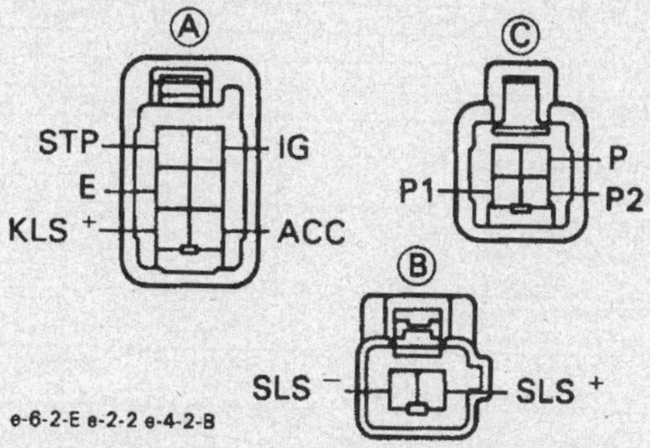
Ⓐ
Ⓒ
STP
IG
E
P
P1
P2
KLS +
ACC
Ⓑ
SLS –
SLS +
e-6-2-E e-2-2 e-4-2-B

TY5029601018000X

Fig. 16 Shift lock ECU connector. Supra

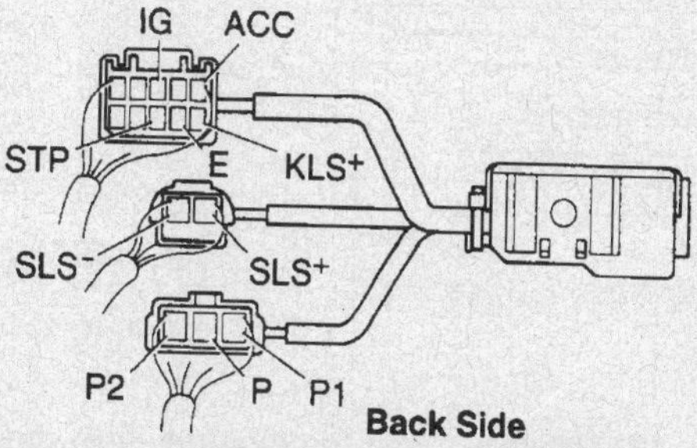
IG
ACC
STP
E
KLS+
SLS–
SLS+
P2
P
P1
Back Side

TY5029601019000X

Fig. 17 Shift lock ECU connector. 4Runner w/A340E

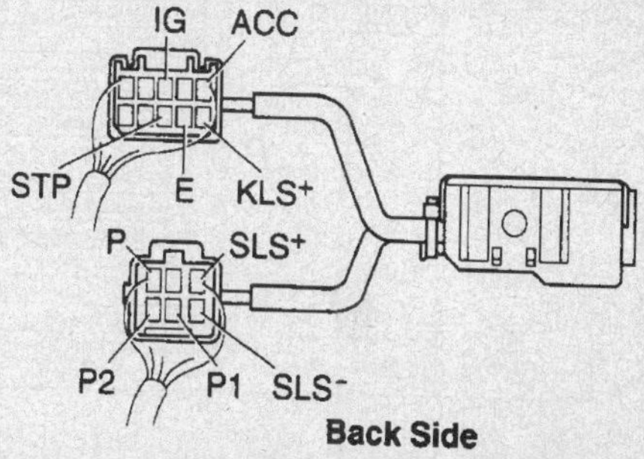
IG
ACC
STP
E
KLS+
P
SLS+
P2
P1
SLS–
Back Side

TY5029601020000X

Fig. 18 Shift lock ECU connector. 4Runner w/A340F

8. Note position of oil tubes to facilitate installation, then remove oil tubes.
9. Disconnect solenoid electrical connectors.
10. Remove attaching bolts, then disconnect throttle cable from the cam and remove the valve body.

Installation

1. Align groove of manual valve to pin of manual lever.
2. Connect throttle cable to cam, then ensure springs are correctly installed into the accumulator pistons.
3. Install valve body, then tighten to specifications.
4. Before installing solenoid wiring into the case, coat a new O-ring with ATF and install it into the grommet.
5. Insert solenoid wiring into the case, then install stopper plate.
6. Connect remaining connectors to No. 1, No. 2 and lock-up solenoids.
7. Using a plastic hammer, install oil tubes into position.
8. Install two new gaskets and oil strainer, then tighten to specifications and clamp the solenoid wire.
9. Install four magnets in the indentations of the oil pan.
10. Apply seal packing, tool No. 08826-00090, Three Bond 1281, or equivalent, to the oil pan.
11. Install oil pan, tighten to specifications.
12. Install drain plug, then tighten to specifications.
13. **On A340H models,** install front stabilizer bar and front propeller shaft.
14. **On all models,** add transmission fluid to specifications, then road test vehicle, noting that **on models with coded audio anti-theft systems,** rearm as outlined under "Precautions."

TRANSFER VALVE BODY, REPLACE

Removal

1. **On models with coded audio anti-theft system,** obtain three digit code.
2. **On all models** disconnect battery ground cable, then clean exterior of transfer case.
3. Raise and support vehicle, then drain transfer case fluid.
4. Support transmission, using suitable jack stands, then remove attaching bolts and disconnect rear support member from body.
5. Remove four attaching bolts, then the rear support member.
6. Remove four attaching bolts, then the member bracket from transfer case.
7. Remove transfer case oil pan attaching bolts, then the oil pan.
8. Disconnect No. 4 solenoid electrical connector, then the solenoid attaching bolt and solenoid.
9. Remove six valve body attaching bolts, then the valve body.

Installation

1. Align manual valve lever with manual valve, then install attaching bolts as shown, **Fig. 44,** then tighten to specifications. Attaching bolt lengths (mm) are indicated in **Fig. 44.**
2. Install No. 4 solenoid, then insert attaching bolt and tighten to specifications.
3. Connect solenoid electrical connector.
4. Clean contacting surfaces of oil pan and case, then apply a suitable sealant to surfaces. Install oil pan within 10 minutes of application of sealant, then insert attaching bolts and tighten to specifications.
5. Install drain plug, then tighten to specifications.
6. Assemble member bracket to case.
7. Install engine rear support member, then insert attaching bolts and **torque** to 31 ft. lbs.
8. Install rear support member onto body, then insert attaching bolts and tighten to specifications.
9. Fill transfer case to specifications, then ensure proper fluid level.
10. Remove transmission jack, then lower vehicle, noting that **on models with coded audio anti-theft systems,** rearm as outlined under "Precautions."
11. Road test vehicle.

THROTTLE CABLE, REPLACE

EXCEPT A340H UNIT

1. Disconnect cable housing from bracket on cylinder head cover, then the cable from throttle linkage.
2. Remove valve body as previously described.
3. Remove throttle cable mounting bolt from transmission case, then pull out cable.
4. Reverse procedure to install. Tighten

Connector	Terminal	Measuring condition		Voltage (V)
A	ACC – E	IG SW ACC position		10 – 14
	IG – E	IG SW ON position		10 – 14
	STP – E	Depress brake pedal		10 – 14
	KLS⁺ – E	①	IG SW ACC position and P position	0
		②	P → R, N, D, 2, L position	10 – 14
		③	↑ (Approx. after second)	6 – 9
B	SLS⁺ – SLS⁻	①	IG SW ON position and P position	0
		②	Depress brake pedal	10 – 14
		③	P → R, N, D, 2, L positions or release brake pedal	0
C	P1 – P	①	IG SW ON, P position and depress brake pedal	0
		②	R, N, D, 2, L positions	10 – 14
	P2 – P	①	IG SW ACC position and P position	10 – 14
		②	R, N, D, 2, L positions	0

TY5029601021000X

Fig. 19 Shift lock ECU inspection. Pickup

Terminal	Measuring Condition	Voltage (V)
ACC – E	Ignition switch ACC	10 – 14
IG – E	Ignition switch ON	10 – 14
STP – E	Depressing brake pedal	10 – 14
KLS⁺ – E	(1) Ignition switch ACC and P position	0
	(2) Ignition switch ACC and except P position	7.5 – 11
	(3) (After approx. 1 second)	6 – 9.5
SLS⁺ – SLS⁻	(1) Ignition switch ON and P position	0
	(2) Depress brake pedal	8 – 13.5
	(3) (After approx. 20 seconds)	6 – 8.5
	(4) Except P position	0
P1 – P	(1) Ignition switch ON, P position and depress brake pedal	0
	(2) Shift except P position under conditions above	9 – 13.5
P2 – P	(1) Ignition switch ACC, P position	9 – 13.5
	(2) Shift except P position under conditions above	0

TY5029601022000X

Fig. 20 Shift lock ECU inspection. 4Runner

Connector	Terminal	Measuring condition	Voltage (v)
Ⓐ	ACC – E	IG SW ACC	10 – 14
	IG – E	IG SW ON	10 – 14
	STP – E	Depress brake pedal	10 – 14
	KLS⁺ – E	① IG SW ACC and P position	0
		② R, N, D, 2, L position	7.5 – 11
		③ R, N, D, 2, L position (after 1second)	6 – 9.5
Ⓑ	SLS⁺ – SLS⁻	① IG SW ON and P position	0
		② Depress brake pedal	8 – 13.5
		③ Depress brake pedal (after 20 seconds)	6 – 8.5
		④ R, N, D, 2, L position	0
Ⓒ	P1 – P	① IG SW ON, P position and depress brake pedal	0
		② R, N, D, 2, L position	9 – 13.5
	P2 – P	① IG SW ACC and P position	9 – 13.5
		② R, N, D, 2, L position	0

TY5029601023000X

Fig. 21 Shift lock ECU inspection. Supra

Terminal	Measuring Condition	Voltage (V)
ACC – E	IG SW ACC	10 – 14
IG – E	IG SW ON	10 – 14
STP – E	Depressing brake pedal	10 – 14
KLS⁺ – E	① IG SW ACC and P position	0
	② IG SW ACC and except P position	10 – 14
	③ (After—approx. 1 second)	6 – 9
SLS⁺ – E	① IG SW ON and P position	0
	② Depress brake pedal	8.5 – 13.5
	③ Except P position	0
P1 – E	① IG SW ON, P position and depress brake pedal	0
	② Shift except P position under conditions above	9 – 13.5
P2 – E	① IG SW ACC and P position	9 – 13.5
	② Shift except P position under conditions above	0

TY5029601024000X

Fig. 22 Shift lock ECU inspection. Tacoma w/ column shift

throttle cable mount bolt to specifications and adjust cable as previously described.

A340H UNIT

1. Disconnect throttle cable from linkage.
2. Remove throttle cable clamp.
3. Drain transmission fluid.
4. Remove front stabilizer bar and front propeller shaft.
5. Remove oil pan attaching bolts, then install tool No. 09032–00100, or equivalent, between case and oil pan and remove gasket.
6. Disconnect solenoid electrical connectors.
7. Disconnect throttle cable from valve body.
8. Remove throttle cable attaching bolt, then pull from transmission case.
9. Reverse procedure to install. Tighten oil pan and drain plug to specifications. Adjust throttle cable as previously outlined.

PARKING LOCK PAWL, REPLACE

1. Remove valve body as previously described.
2. Remove parking lock pawl bracket.
3. Remove pivot pin spring, then the pivot and pin.
4. Reverse procedure to install.

EXTENSION HOUSING, REPLACE

1. **On models with coded audio anti-theft system,** obtain three digit code.
2. **On all models** disconnect battery ground cable, then raise and support vehicle.
3. Position a pan to catch any fluid that may drip.
4. Remove propeller shaft together with center bearing.
5. Remove exhaust front pipe together with converter, as required.
6. Disconnect speedometer cable, then remove speedometer driven gear and speed sensor.
7. Jack up transmission slightly to remove weight from rear support member.
8. Remove ground cable, then remove rear support member.
9. Remove extension housing and gasket.
10. Reverse procedure to install, noting that **on models with coded audio anti-theft systems,** rearm as outlined under "Precautions."

SENSOR ROTOR, REPLACE

1. Remove extension housing as previously described.
2. Using snap ring pliers, remove snap ring, then speedometer gear and lock ball.
3. Remove sensor rotor from output shaft.
4. Reverse procedure to install, ensuring that sensor rotor key is installed in groove.

REAR OIL SEAL, REPLACE

1. Raise vehicle, then position pan to catch any fluid that may drip.
2. Remove propeller shaft together with center bearing.
3. Remove oil seal with seal remover tool No. 09308-10010 or suitable equivalent.
4. Reverse procedure to install, using installation tool No. 09325-40010 or suitable equivalent, to install new seal.

TRANSMISSION

REPLACE

PICKUP, TACOMA & 4RUNNER

A340E

On models with coded audio anti-theft system, disarm as outlined under precautions.

On Pickup models, refer to **Fig. 45,** for transmission replacement. On 4Runner models, refer to **Fig. 46,** for transmission replacement.

On models with coded audio anti-theft systems, rearm as outlined under "Precautions."

A340F

1. **On models with coded audio anti-theft system,** obtain three digit code.
2. **On all models** disconnect battery ground cable.
3. Raise and support vehicle, then drain transaxle fluid.
4. Refer to **Fig. 47,** for removal and installation procedure, noting that **on models with coded audio anti-theft systems,** rearm as outlined under "Precautions."

A340H

On models with coded audio anti-theft system, disarm as outlined under "Precautions."

Refer to **Fig. 48,** for transmission replacement.

Connector	Terminal	Measuring condition	Voltage (V)
A	ACC – E	IG SW ACC	10 – 14
	IG – E	IG SW ON	10 – 14
	STP – E	Brake pedal depressed	10 – 14
	KLS – E	① IG SW ACC and P position	0
		② R, N, D, 2, L position	7.5 – 11
		③ R, N, D, 2, L position (After - approx. 1 second)	6 – 9.5
B	SLS+ – SLS−	① IG SW ON and P position	0
		② Brake pedal depressed	8 – 13.5
		③ Brake pedal depressed (After - approx. 20 seconds)	6 – 8.5
		④ R, N, D, 2, L position	0
	P1 – P	① IG SW ON, P position and depress brake pedal	0
		② R, N, D, 2, L position	9 – 13.5
	P2 – P	① IG SW ACC and P position	9 – 13.5
		② R, N, D, 2, L position	0

TY5029601030000X

Fig. 23 Shift lock ECU inspection. Tacoma w/floor shift

SLS+
SLS−
TY5029601025000X

Fig. 24 Shift lock solenoid connector. Pickup

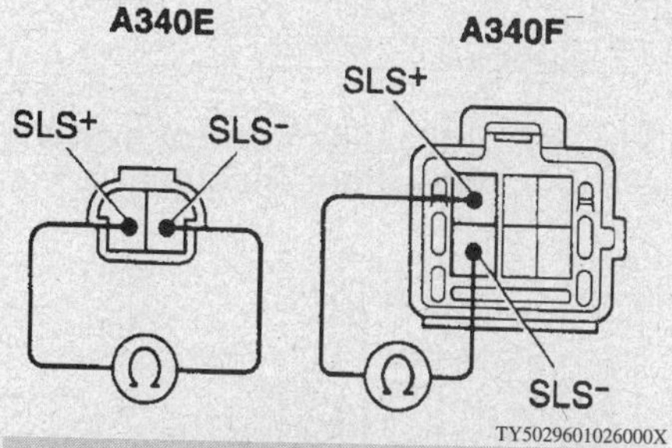
A340E
A340F
SLS+
SLS−
SLS+
SLS−
TY5029601026000X

Fig. 25 Shift lock solenoid connector. 4Runner

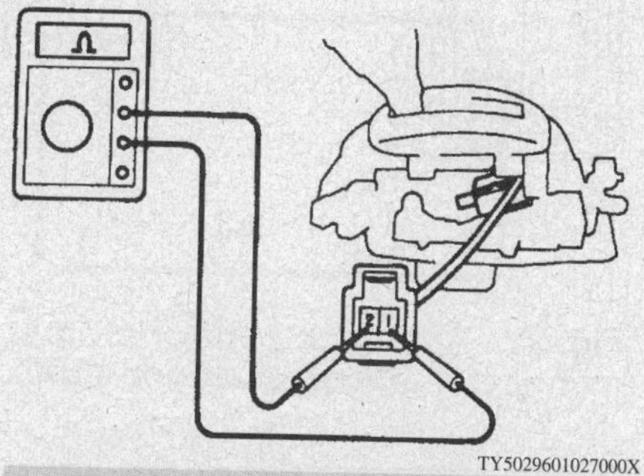
TY5029601027000X

Fig. 26 Shift lock solenoid connector. Supra

Column Shift

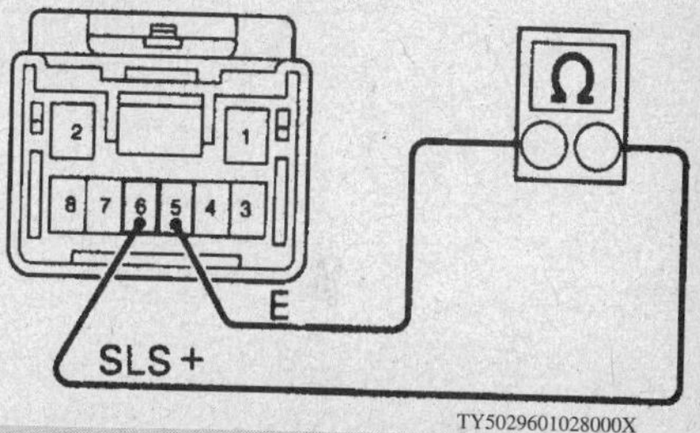
2
1
8
7
6
5
4
3
E
SLS +
TY5029601028000X

Fig. 27 Shift lock solenoid connector. Tacoma w/column shift

Floor Shift

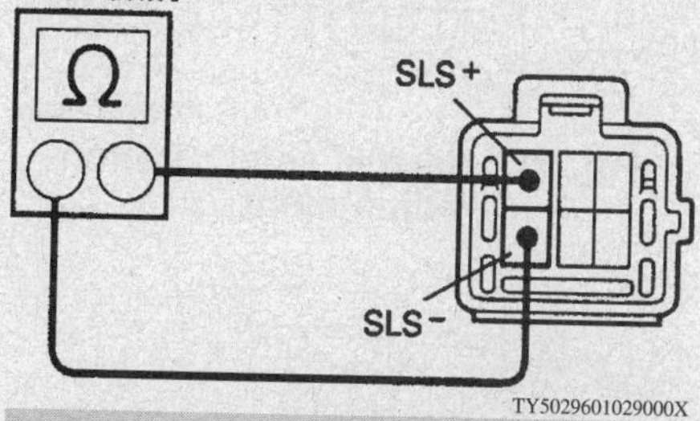
SLS+
SLS−
TY5029601029000X

Fig. 28 Shift lock solenoid connector. Tacoma w/floor shift

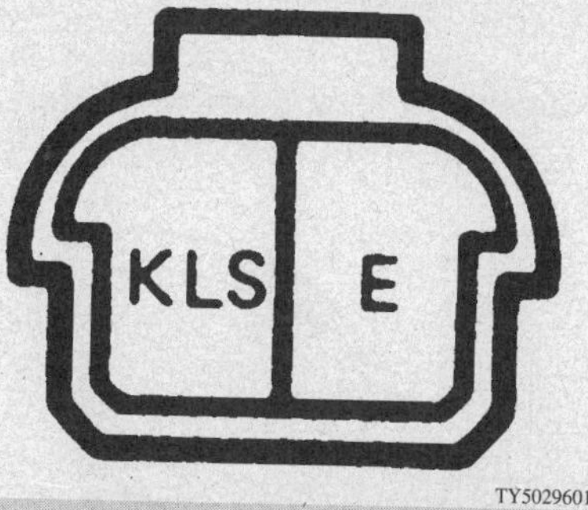
KLS
E
TY5029601031000X

Fig. 29 Key interlock solenoid connector. Pickup

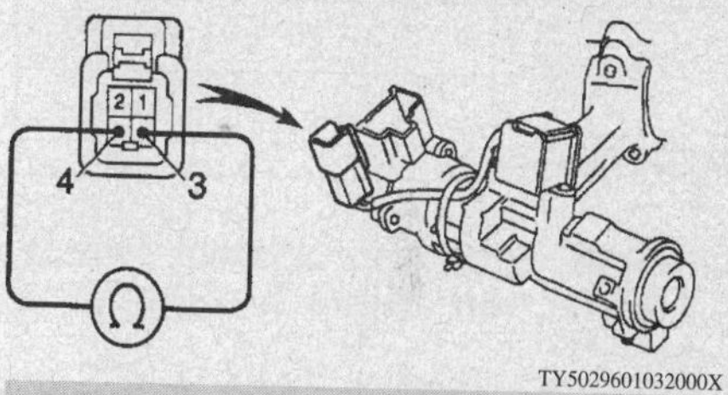
2
1
4
3
TY5029601032000X

Fig. 30 Key interlock solenoid connector. 4Runner

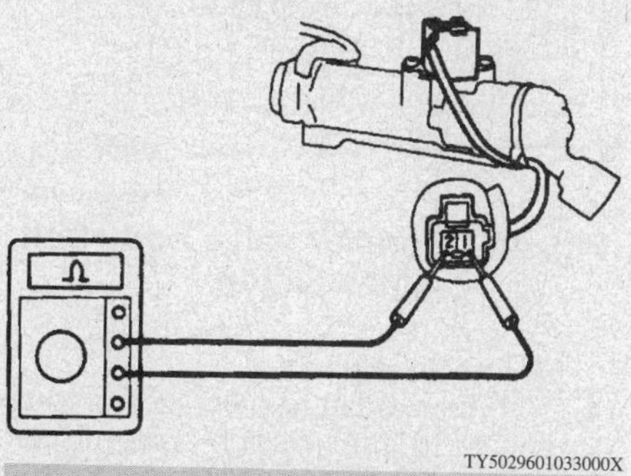
TY5029601033000X

Fig. 31 Key interlock solenoid connector. Supra

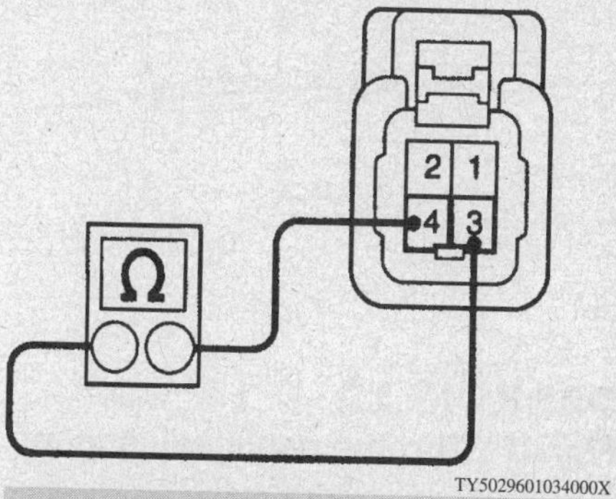
2
1
4
3
TY5029601034000X

Fig. 32 Key interlock solenoid connector. Tacoma

On models with coded audio anti-theft systems, rearm as outlined under "Precautions."

SUPRA

On models with coded audio anti-theft system, disarm as outlined under "Precautions."

Refer to **Fig. 49,** for transmission replacement.

On models with coded audio anti-theft systems, rearm as outlined under "Precautions."

T100

1. **On models with coded audio anti-theft system,** obtain three digit code.
2. **On all models** disconnect battery ground cable, then remove level gauge.
3. Remove engine undercover, then disconnect throttle cable.
4. **On A340F models,** remove transfer shift lever from inside vehicle.
5. **On all models,** remove filler tube mounting bolt, then jack up vehicle and

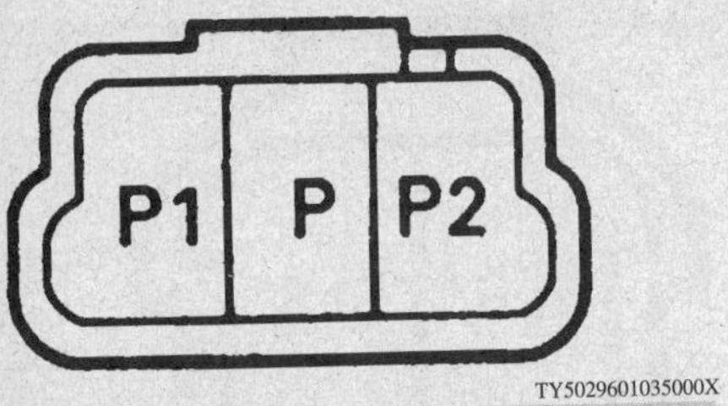
P1
P
P2
TY5029601035000X

Fig. 33 Shift lock control switch connector. Pickup

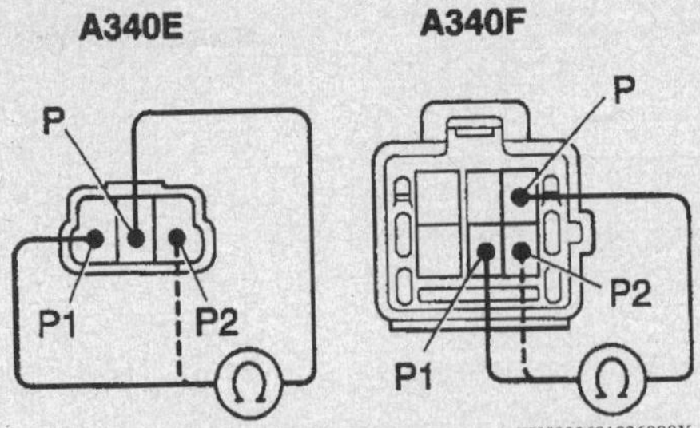
A340E
A340F
P
P1
P2
P
P1
P2
TY5029601036000X

Fig. 34 Shift lock control switch connector. 4Runner

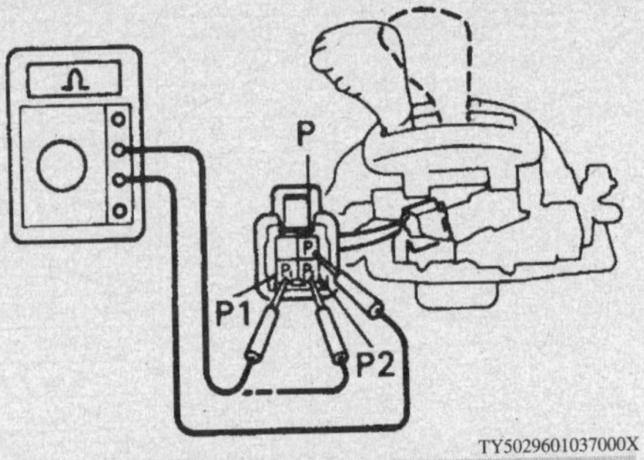
P
P1
P2
TY5029601037000X

Fig. 35 Shift lock control switch connector. Supra

Column Shift

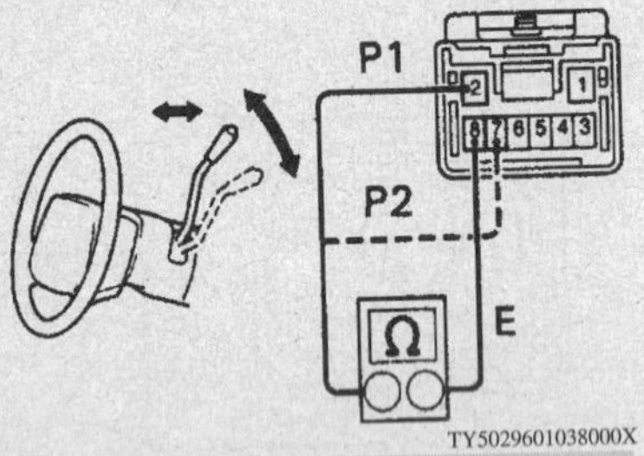
P1
P2
E
TY5029601038000X

Fig. 36 Shift lock control switch connector. Tacoma w/column shift

Floor Shift

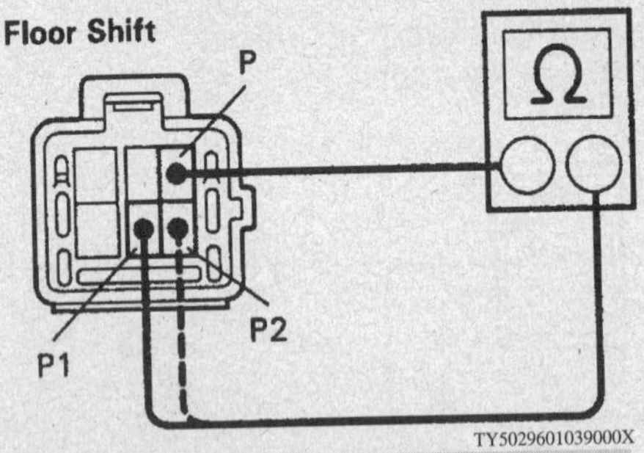
P
P2
P1
TY5029601039000X

Fig. 37 Shift lock control switch connector. Tacoma w/floor shift

Shift position	Tester condition to terminal	Specified value
P (Release button is not pushed)	P1 – P	Continuity
R, N, D, 2, L positions	P2 – P	Continuity

TY5029601040000X

Fig. 38 Shift lock control switch inspection. Pickup

Shift position	Tester condition to terminal number	Specified value
P position (Release button is not pushed)	P – P1	Continuity
P position (Release button is pushed)	P – P1 P – P2	Continuity
R, N, D, 2, L position	P – P2	Continuity

TY5029601041000X

Fig. 39 Shift lock control switch inspection. Supra & 4Runner

Shift position	Tester condition to terminal number	Specified value
[1] P position	P1 – P or E	Continuity
[2] P position	P1 – P or E P2 – P or E	Continuity
R, N, D, 2, L position	P2 – P or E	Continuity

TY5029601042000X

Fig. 40 Shift lock control switch inspection. Tacoma

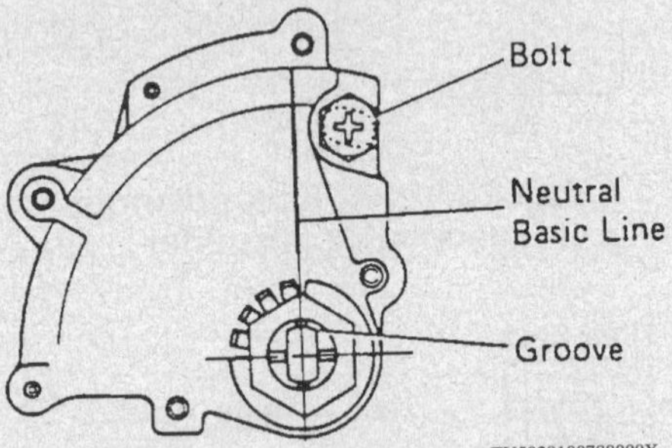
Bolt
Neutral
Basic Line
Groove
TY5029100788000X

Fig. 41 Neutral safety switch adjustment

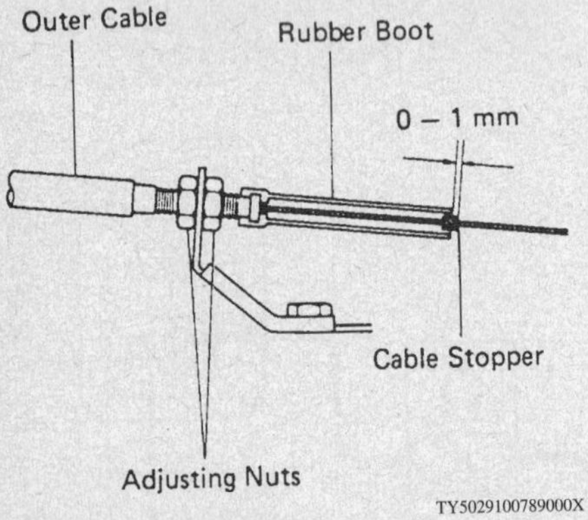
Outer Cable
Rubber Boot
0 – 1 mm
Cable Stopper
Adjusting Nuts
TY5029100789000X

Fig. 42 Throttle cable adjustment

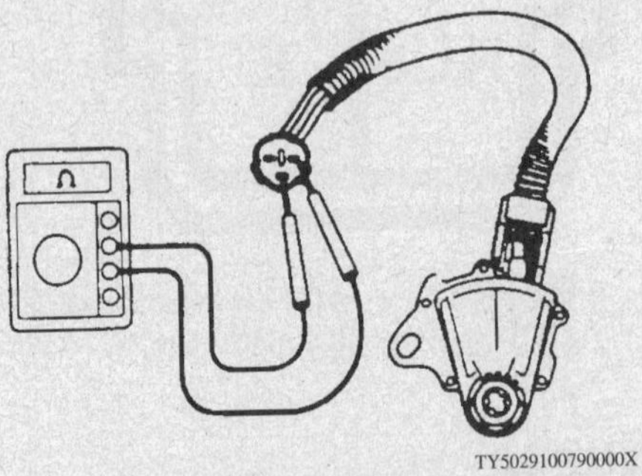
TY5029100790000X

Fig. 43 Transfer indicator switch adjustment

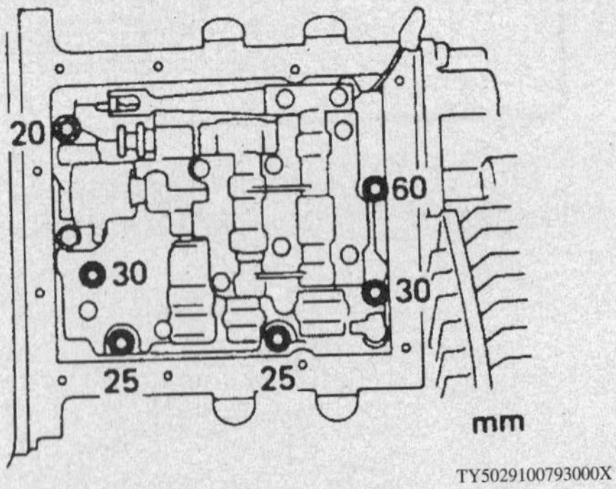
20
60
30
30
25
25
mm
TY5029100793000X

Fig. 44 Transfer valve body bolt installation

remove exhaust pipe.

6. Remove filler tube and propeller shaft on A340E models and both propeller shafts on A340F models.
7. Disconnect No. 1 and No. 2 speed sensor connectors and solenoid connectors.
8. Remove clip and disconnect shifting rod, then remove nut, four bolts and cross shaft.
9. Disconnect transmission fluid temperature sensor, then remove two oil cooler tubes.
10. Remove control shaft lever, then disconnect Park/Neutral position switch connector.
11. Remove starter connectors, then starter.
12. Remove stabilizer bar, both stiffener plates, converter cover and throttle cable clamp.
13. Disconnect rear mounting, then jack up transmission.
14. Turn crankshaft to gain access to six engine to transmission bolts, disconnect wire harness and connectors from transmission, then remove transmission.
15. Reverse procedure to install, noting that **on models with coded audio anti-theft systems,** rearm as outlined under "Precautions."

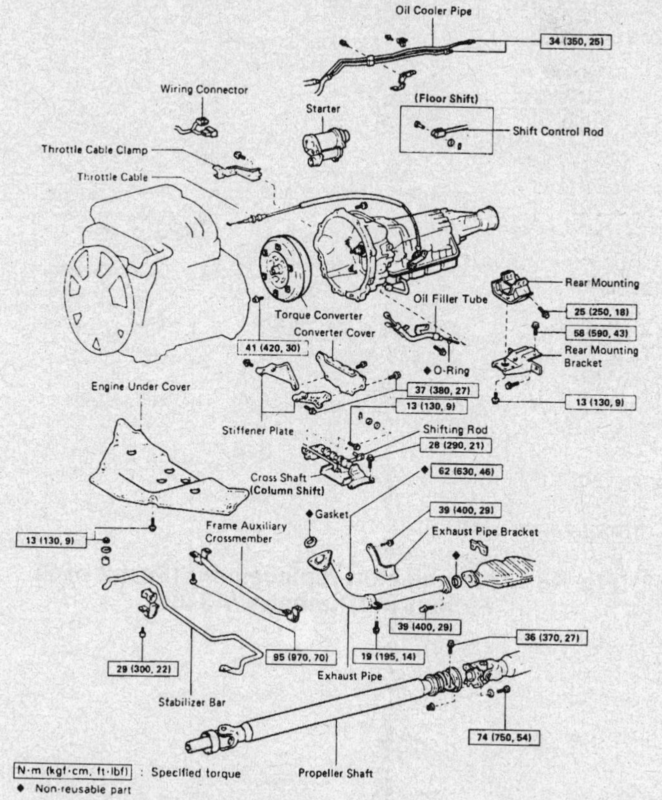

Oil Cooler Pipe
34 (350, 25)
Wiring Connector
(Floor Shift)
Starter
Shift Control Rod
Throttle Cable Clamp
Throttle Cable
Rear Mounting
Oil Filler Tube
Torque Converter
25 (250, 18)
58 (590, 43)
Converter Cover
Rear Mounting Bracket
41 (420, 30)
O-Ring
Engine Under Cover
37 (380, 27)
13 (130, 9)
13 (130, 9)
Stiffener Plate
Shifting Rod
28 (290, 21)
Cross Shaft (Column Shift)
62 (630, 46)
Gasket
39 (400, 29)
Frame Auxiliary Crossmember
Exhaust Pipe Bracket
13 (130, 9)
39 (400, 29)
36 (370, 27)
95 (970, 70)
19 (195, 14)
29 (300, 22)
Exhaust Pipe
Stabilizer Bar
74 (750, 54)
N·m (kgf·cm, ft·lbf) : Specified torque
◆ Non-reusable part
Propeller Shaft

TY5029100795000X

Fig. 45 Transmission replacement. 1995 Tacoma w/A340E

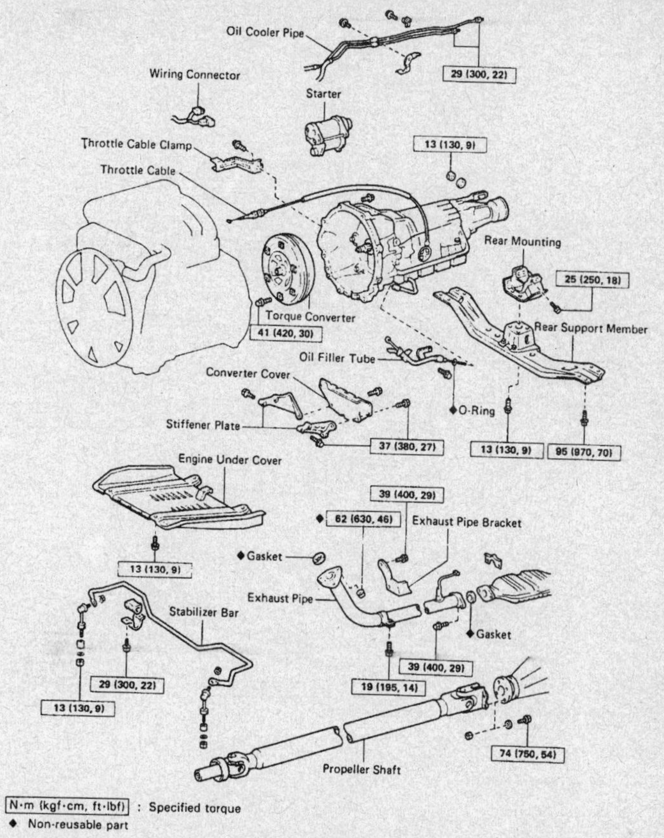

Oil Cooler Pipe
29 (300, 22)
Wiring Connector
Starter
Throttle Cable Clamp
13 (130, 9)
Throttle Cable
Rear Mounting
25 (250, 18)
Torque Converter
41 (420, 30)
Rear Support Member
Oil Filler Tube
Converter Cover
O-Ring
Stiffener Plate
37 (380, 27)
13 (130, 9)
95 (970, 70)
Engine Under Cover
39 (400, 29)
62 (630, 46)
Exhaust Pipe Bracket
Gasket
13 (130, 9)
Exhaust Pipe
Stabilizer Bar
Gasket
29 (300, 22)
39 (400, 29)
19 (195, 14)
13 (130, 9)
74 (750, 54)
Propeller Shaft
N·m (kgf·cm, ft·lbf) : Specified torque
◆ Non-reusable part

TY5029100796000X

Fig. 46 Transmission replacement. 1995 Tacoma w/A340E

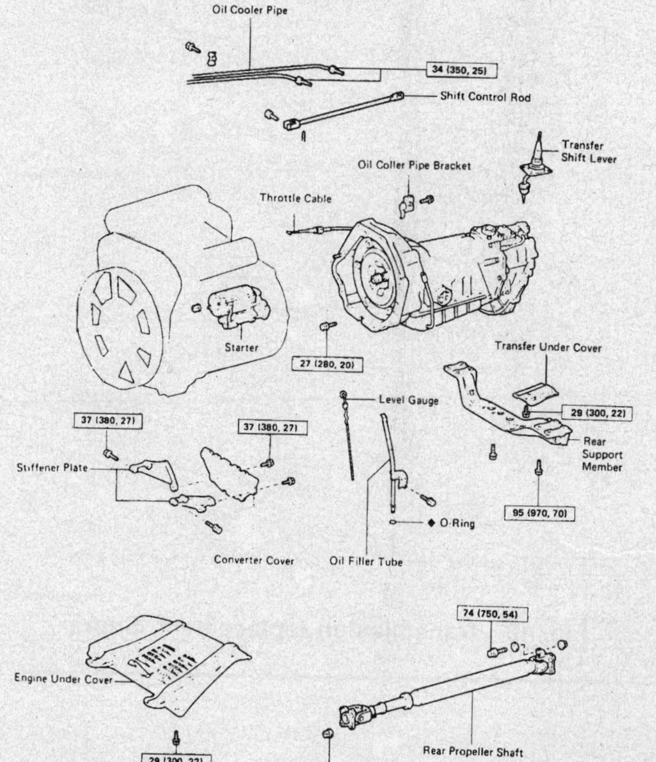

Oil Cooler Pipe
34 (350, 25)
Shift Control Rod
Transfer Shift Lever
Oil Coller Pipe Bracket
Throttle Cable
Starter
27 (280, 20)
Transfer Under Cover
Level Gauge
29 (300, 22)
37 (380, 27)
37 (380, 27)
Rear Support Member
Stiffener Plate
95 (970, 70)
O-Ring
Converter Cover
Oil Filler Tube
74 (750, 54)
Engine Under Cover
Rear Propeller Shaft
29 (300, 22)
74 (750, 54)
N·m (kgf·cm, ft·lbf) : Specified torque
◆ Non-reusable part

TY5029100797010X

Fig. 47 Transmission replacement (Part 1 of 2). Pickup, 4Runner & Tacoma w/A340F

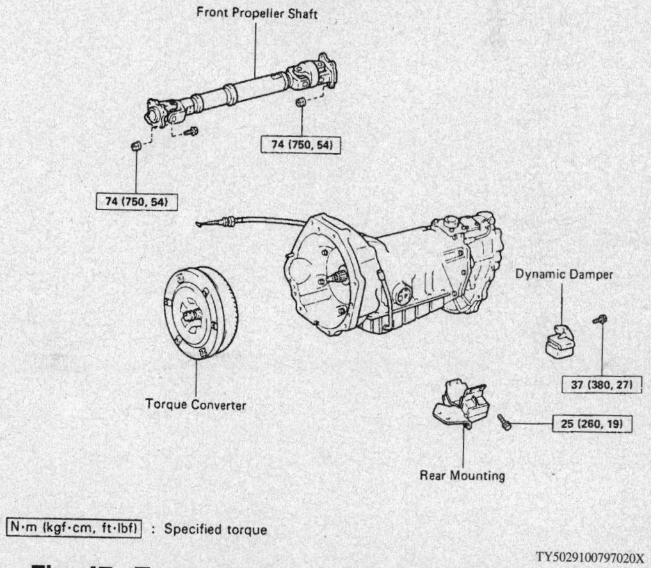

Front Propeller Shaft
74 (750, 54)
74 (750, 54)
Dynamic Damper
Torque Converter
37 (380, 27)
25 (260, 19)
Rear Mounting
N·m (kgf·cm, ft·lbf) : Specified torque

TY5029100797020X

Fig. 47 Transmission replacement (Part 2 of 2). Pickup, 4Runner & Tacoma w/A340F

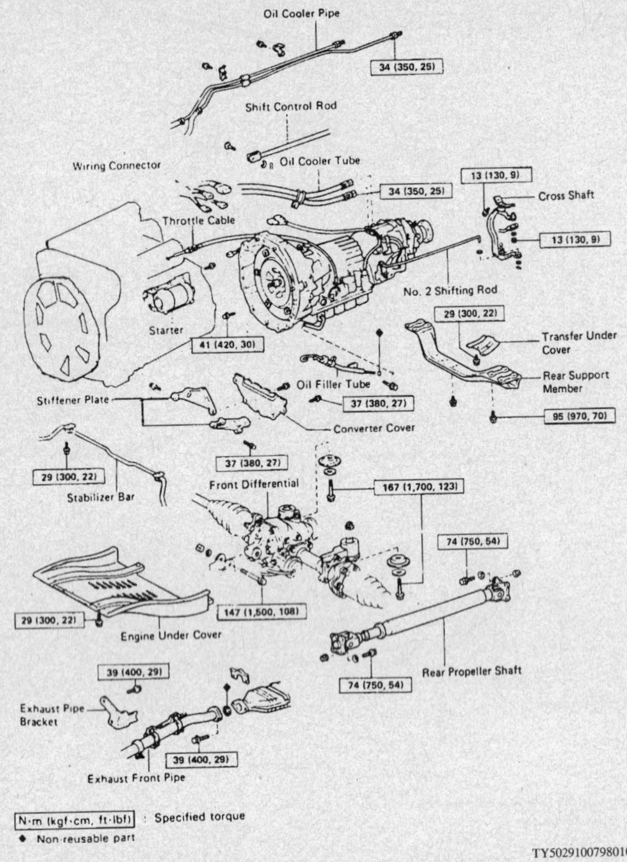

Oil Cooler Pipe
34 (350, 25)
Shift Control Rod
Wiring Connector
Oil Cooler Tube
34 (350, 25)
13 (130, 9)
Cross Shaft
Throttle Cable
13 (130, 9)
No. 2 Shifting Rod
Starter
29 (300, 22)
Transfer Under Cover
41 (420, 30)
Oil Filler Tube
Rear Support Member
Stiffener Plate
37 (380, 27)
95 (970, 70)
Converter Cover
37 (380, 27)
29 (300, 22)
Front Differential
Stabilizer Bar
167 (1,700, 123)
74 (750, 54)
147 (1,500, 108)
29 (300, 22)
Engine Under Cover
39 (400, 29)
Rear Propeller Shaft
74 (750, 54)
Exhaust Pipe Bracket
39 (400, 29)
Exhaust Front Pipe
N·m (kgf·cm, ft·lbf) : Specified torque
◆ Non-reusable part
TY5029100798010X

Fig. 48 Transmission replacement (Part 1 of 2). Pickup & 4Runner w/A340H

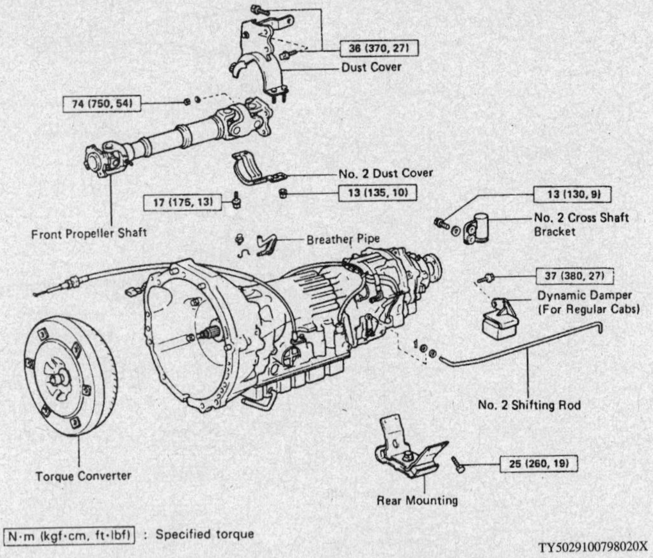

36 (370, 27)
Dust Cover
74 (750, 54)
No. 2 Dust Cover
17 (175, 13)
13 (135, 10)
13 (130, 9)
No. 2 Cross Shaft Bracket
Front Propeller Shaft
Breather Pipe
37 (380, 27)
Dynamic Damper (For Regular Cabs)
No. 2 Shifting Rod
25 (260, 19)
Torque Converter
Rear Mounting
N·m (kgf·cm, ft·lbf) : Specified torque
TY5029100798020X

Fig. 48 Transmission replacement (Part 2 of 2). Pickup & 4Runner w/A340H

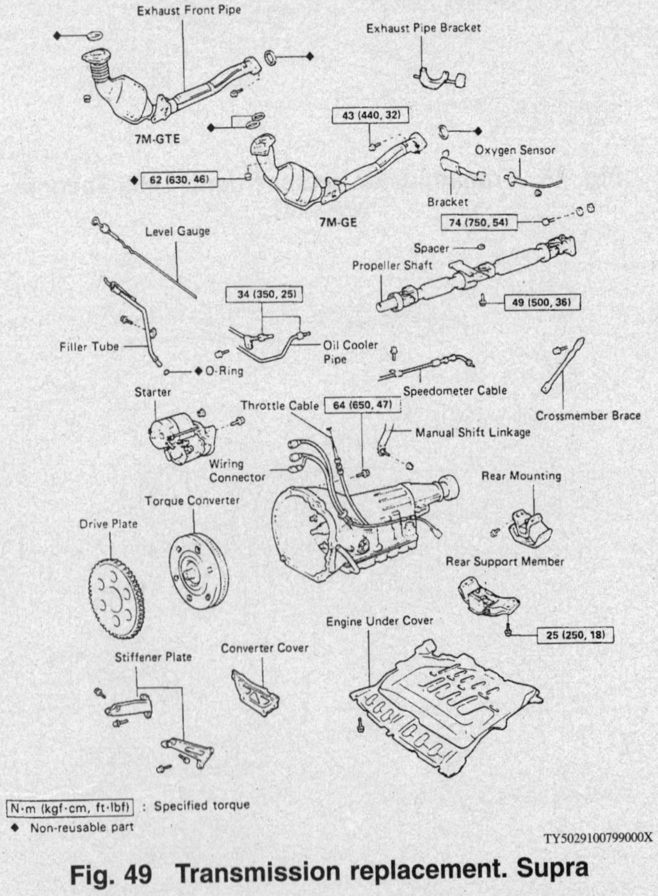

Exhaust Front Pipe
Exhaust Pipe Bracket
43 (440, 32)
7M-GTE
Oxygen Sensor
62 (630, 46)
Bracket
7M-GE
74 (750, 54)
Level Gauge
Spacer
Propeller Shaft
34 (350, 25)
49 (500, 36)
Filler Tube
Oil Cooler Pipe
O-Ring
Starter
Speedometer Cable
Throttle Cable
64 (650, 47)
Crossmember Brace
Manual Shift Linkage
Wiring Connector
Rear Mounting
Torque Converter
Drive Plate
Rear Support Member
Engine Under Cover
25 (250, 18)
Converter Cover
Stiffener Plate
N·m (kgf·cm, ft·lbf) : Specified torque
◆ Non-reusable part
TY5029100799000X

Fig. 49 Transmission replacement. Supra

TIGHTENING SPECIFICATIONS

Year	Component	Torque/ Ft. Lbs.
1993–96	Center Support Bolt	18
	Chain Case	25
	Control Shaft Lever	12
	Detent Spring To Valve Body (A340E & A340F)	7
	Detent Spring To Valve Body (A340H)	61①
	Driveplate To Crankshaft	②
	Extension Housing To Chain Rear Case	25
	Extension Housing To Transmission Case	27
	Fluid Temperature Sensor	11
	Front & Rear Companion Flanges	90
1993–96	Front Support To Transfer Case	25
	Neutral Start Switch (Bolt)	9
	Neutral Start Switch (Nut)	61①
	No. 4 Solenoid To Valve Body	7
	O/D Support To Transmission Case	19
	Oil Cooler Pipe Union Nut	25
	Oil Cooler Union	22
	Oil Drain Plug	15
	Oil Pan To Transfer Case	65①
	Oil Pan To Transmission	65①
	Oil Pump Body To Oil Pump Cover	7
	Oil Pump Body To Stator Shaft	7
	Oil Pump To Transmission Case	16
	Oil Strainer Case	7
	Oil Strainer To Chain Rear Case	61①
	Parking Lock Pawl Bracket	65①
	Solenoid To Valve Body	7
	Speed Sensor	12
	Speedometer Driven Gear Lock Plate	12
	Throttle Cable Bolt	7
	Torque Converter To Driveplate	30
	Transfer Case To Transmission Case	25
	Transfer Chain Oil Receiver To Chain Front Case	7
	Transfer Oil Cooler Tube Union Nut	25
	Transfer Oil Pump To Chain Rear Case	12
	Transfer Position Switch (Bolt)	9
	Transfer Position Switch (Nut)	35①
	Transfer Pressure Switch To Valve Body	61①
	Transmission Housing To Transmission Case (10 mm Bolt)	25
	Transmission Housing To Transmission Case (12 mm Bolt)	42
	Upper Valve Body To Lower Valve Body	56①
	Valve Body Bolts	7
	Valve Body To Transfer Case	7
	Valve Body To Transmission Case	7

① — Inch pounds.

② — Pickup, Tacoma & 4Runner, 61 ft. lbs.; T100, 30 ft. lbs.; Supra, 54 ft. lbs.

A440F & A442F Automatic Transmissions

INDEX

Page No.

Adjustments 48-297
Idle Speed (N Position) 48-297
Park/Neutral Position (Neutral Start) Switch 48-297
Throttle Cable 48-297
Transmission Shift Lever Position 48-297
In-Vehicle Repairs 48-297
Throttle Cable, Replace 48-297
Valve Body, Replace 48-297
Maintenance 48-297
Fluid Change 48-297
Fluid Check 48-297

Page No.

Precautions 48-296
Air Bag Systems 48-296
Audio Coded Anti-Theft System 48-296
Tightening Specifications 48-298
Transmission, Replace 48-297
Troubleshooting 48-296
Delayed Upshift Or Downshift In Forward Gears 48-296
Downshift Occurs Too Quick Or Late During Coast 48-296
Drag Or Bind In Forward Gears 48-296
Fluid Discolored Or Smells Burned 48-296

Page No.

Harsh Downshift 48-296
Harsh Engagement 48-296
Incorrect Shift Lever Position 48-296
No Downshift When Coasting 48-296
No Engine Brake In 2 Or L 48-297
No Kickdown In Downshift 48-296
No Lock-Up 48-296
Shift Lock System 48-296
Slips In Upshift Or Downshift In Forward Gears 48-296
Vehicle Does Not Hold In Park 48-297
Vehicle Does Not Move In Any Gear 48-296

PRECAUTIONS

AIR BAG SYSTEMS

Refer to "Air Bag System Precautions" in the front of this manual for system disarming and arming procedures.

AUDIO CODED ANTI-THEFT SYSTEM

Some models are equipped with an audio coded anti-theft system that will disable the radio when the battery cable is disconnected. The system can be identified by the "ANTI-THEFT SYSTEM" on the cassette lid. Obtain 3 digit code for input. Reset system after service as follows:

1. Obtain 3 digit audio theft code.
2. Depress 1 (PROG) while depressing righthand side of TUNE SEEK button, - - - will appear in tape operation display.
3. To enter the first digit, depress 1 (PROG) button repeatedly until the number of times depressed equals the first digit (depress the 1 button six times if the first digit if five, first press equals 0).
4. To enter second digit, depress 2 (APS) button repeatedly until the number of times depressed equals the second digit.
5. To enter third digit, depress 3 (RPT) button repeatedly until the number of times depressed equals the third digit.
6. If - - - is displayed after inputting digits, repeat procedure.
7. When code appears in display, depress and hold SCAN button until SEC appears.
8. When SEC disappears audio system is operative.
9. If Err is displayed, repeat procedure. **Attempting to input code more than 9 times may permanently disable audio system.**

TROUBLESHOOTING

SHIFT LOCK SYSTEM

Refer to "A343F Automatic Transmission" for shift lock system troubleshooting.

FLUID DISCOLORED OR SMELLS BURNED

1. Contaminated transmission fluid.
2. Faulty torque converter.
3. Faulty transmission.

VEHICLE DOES NOT MOVE IN ANY GEAR

1. Improperly adjusted linkage.
2. Faulty valve body or primary regulator.
3. Faulty parking pawl.
4. Faulty torque converter.
5. Broken converter driveplate.
6. Plugged oil pump intake strainer.
7. Faulty transmission.

INCORRECT SHIFT LEVER POSITION

1. Improperly adjusted manual linkage.
2. Faulty manual valve or lever.
3. Faulty transmission.

HARSH ENGAGEMENT

1. Improperly adjusted throttle cable.
2. Faulty valve body or primary regulator.
3. Faulty accumulator pistons.
4. Faulty transmission.

DELAYED UPSHIFT OR DOWNSHIFT IN FORWARD GEARS

1. Improperly adjusted throttle cable.
2. Faulty throttle cable and cam.
3. Faulty governor.
4. Faulty valve body.

SLIPS IN UPSHIFT OR DOWNSHIFT IN FORWARD GEARS

1. Improperly adjusted manual linkage.
2. Improperly adjusted throttle cable.
3. Faulty valve body.
4. Faulty transmission.

DRAG OR BIND IN FORWARD GEARS

1. Improperly adjusted manual linkage.
2. Faulty valve body.
3. Faulty transmission.

NO LOCK-UP

1. Faulty valve body.
2. Faulty torque converter.
3. Faulty transmission.

HARSH DOWNSHIFT

1. Improperly adjusted throttle cable.
2. Faulty throttle cable and cam.
3. Faulty accumulator piston.
4. Faulty valve body.
5. Faulty transmission.

NO DOWNSHIFT WHEN COASTING

1. Faulty governor.
2. Faulty valve body.

DOWNSHIFT OCCURS TOO QUICK OR LATE DURING COAST

1. Improperly adjusted throttle cable.
2. Faulty governor.
3. Faulty valve body.
4. Faulty transmission.

NO KICKDOWN IN DOWNSHIFT

1. Improperly adjusted throttle cable.
2. Faulty governor.
3. Faulty valve body.

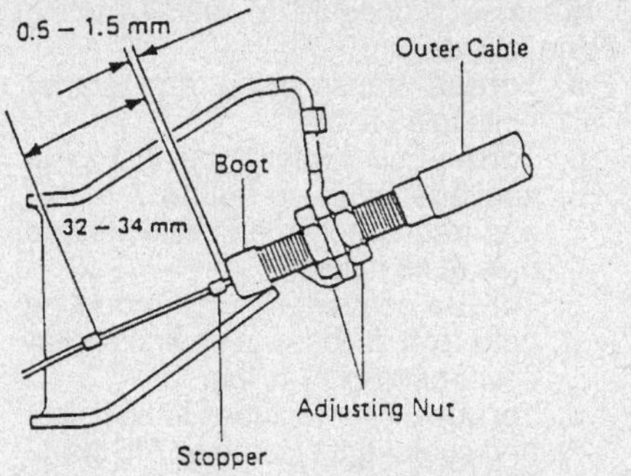
0.5 – 1.5 mm
Outer Cable
Boot
32 – 34 mm
Adjusting Nut
Stopper

TY5029100800000X

Fig. 1 Throttle cable adjustment

NO ENGINE BRAKE IN 2 OR L

1. Faulty valve body.
2. Faulty transmission.

VEHICLE DOES NOT HOLD IN PARK

1. Improperly adjusted manual linkage.
2. Faulty parking lock pawl or spring.

MAINTENANCE

FLUID CHECK

1. Ensure operating temperatures are 158–176°F.
2. Park vehicle on a level surface and set the parking brake.
3. With the engine idling, shift the shift lever through all positions, then return to park.
4. Remove the dipstick and wipe it off. Replace the dipstick, then remove it a second time.
5. Ensure fluid level is in the HOT range. If not add fluid as necessary.
6. Total dry fill capacity on models with oil cooler are 16.3 quarts, on models, less oil cooler 15.9 quarts.

FLUID CHANGE

1. Remove drain plug and drain fluid. Reinstall drain plug and **torque** to 20 ft. lbs.
2. With engine Off, add new fluid through the filler tube, using ATF Dexron II.
3. Fluid drain and refill capacity is 6.3 Us qts.
4. Start engine and shift into all positions, then return to P position. With the engine running, check the fluid level. Add fluid up to the Cool level on the dipstick.
5. Check the fluid level at operating temperatures, 158–176°F and add as necessary.

ADJUSTMENTS

THROTTLE CABLE

1. Ensure throttle cable is installed correctly and not bent.
2. With throttle valve fully closed, measure the distance between the boot end and cable stopper.

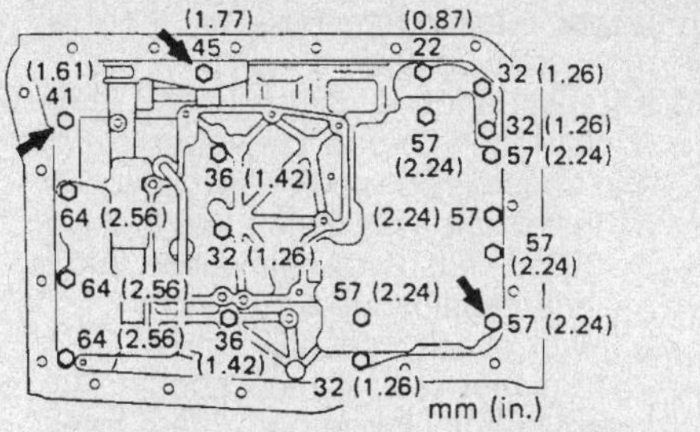
(1.77)
45
(0.87)
22
(1.61)
41
32 (1.26)
32 (1.26)
57 (2.24)
57
(2.24)
36 (1.42)
64 (2.56)
(2.24) 57
32 (1.26)
57
(2.24)
64 (2.56)
57 (2.24)
64 (2.56)
36
(1.42)
57 (2.24)
32 (1.26)
mm (in.)

TY5029100801000X

Fig. 2 Valve body bolt installation

3. Standard distance, when fully closed is 0–0.04 inch.
4. If the distance is not standard, make adjustment at adjusting nut, **Fig. 1.**

TRANSMISSION SHIFT LEVER POSITION

1. Ensure shift lever moves smoothly and accurately through all positions.
2. If the indicator is not correctly aligned, loosen the nut on the control rod.
3. Push the control shaft lever fully towards the rear of the vehicle, then return control shaft two notches (to N position).
4. Set the shift lever at N position and while holding the lever slightly towards the R position side, tighten the control rod nut.
5. Start engine, check transmission operation in all shift positions.

PARK/NEUTRAL POSITION (NEUTRAL START) SWITCH

1. Start vehicle, and ensure it will only start in N or P position. If it starts in any other position, make the following adjustments:
   a. Loosen the neutral start switch bolts and set the shift lever to the N position.
2. Align the groove and neutral basic line, then while holding in position, **torque** bolts to 9 ft. lbs.

IDLE SPEED (N POSITION)

Connecting a suitable tachometer test probe, check connector terminal IG (-), then inspect idle speed. Idle speed should be 650 RPM.

IN-VEHICLE REPAIRS

THROTTLE CABLE, REPLACE

1. **On models with coded audio anti-theft system,** obtain three digit code.
2. **On all models** raise vehicle, then disconnect battery ground cable.
3. Remove front propeller shaft, then disconnect throttle cable and cable housing from bracket.
4. Disconnect cable from throttle linkage, then from torque converter clutch housing.
5. Remove valve body and center support apply gaskets.
6. Remove frame crossmember bolts, then cable clamp from transmission housing.

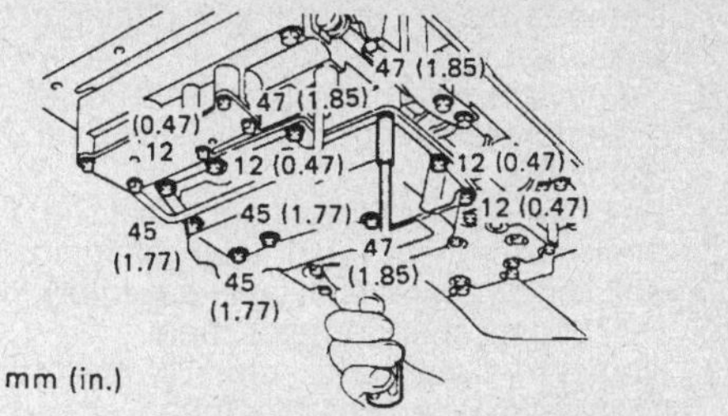
47 (1.85)
47 (1.85)
(0.47)
12
12 (0.47)
12 (0.47)
12 (0.47)
45 (1.77)
45
(1.77)
47
45
(1.85)
(1.77)
mm (in.)

TY5029100802000X

Fig. 3 Oil strainer bolt installation

7. Using a 10 mm socket driver, remove throttle cable by pushing retainer portion of throttle cable.
8. Reverse procedure to install noting the following:
   a. **Torque** frame crossmember set bolts to specifications.
   b. Ensure cable stroke is 1.26–1.34 inch.
   c. Fill and check automatic transmission fluid (ATF) level.
   d. **On models with coded audio anti-theft systems,** reset as outlined under "Precautions."

VALVE BODY, REPLACE

1. Remove cover from transmission and transfer unit, then clean transmission exterior.
2. Remove transmission drain plug and drain ATF into suitable container.
3. Remove oil pan protector, bolts, oil pan and gasket. Some fluid will remain in oil pan. **Be careful not to damage filler tube.**
4. Remove applied sealer with a suitable blade. **Be careful not to damage oil pan flange.**
5. Remove bolts and washers, then oil strainer and gasket.
6. Remove valve body bolts, then disconnect four connectors from solenoids.
7. Remove throttle cable from cam, then valve body.
8. Reverse procedure to install noting the following:
   a. **Torque** valve body bolts to specifications, **Fig. 2.**
   b. **Torque** oil strainer bolts to specifications, **Fig. 3.**
   c. **Torque** oil pan bolts and drain plug to specifications.
   d. Check transmission fluid level.

TRANSMISSION

REPLACE

1. **On models with coded audio anti-theft system,** obtain three digit code.
2. **On all models** disconnect battery cables, then remove battery and cover.
3. Loosen cooling fan shroud and disconnect throttle cable.
4. Disconnect starter connectors, then remove transmission control rod.
5. Remove transfer shift lever knob, then four console retaining screws and shift lever console.
6. Remove four shift lever boot retaining bolts, then the boot.

7. Remove three console box retaining bolts, then the console box.
8. Remove six transmission shift lever assembly retaining bolts and shift lever assembly.
9. Remove pin and disconnect shift rod, then four transfer shift lever retaining bolts and transfer shift lever assembly.
10. Disconnect speedometer cable.
11. Remove front and rear propeller shafts, starter and oil filler tube.
12. Disconnect oil cooler tube clamps and two oil cooler tubes.
13. Remove four undercover retaining bolts, then the undercover.
14. Remove end plate hole plug, then turn crankshaft to gain access to each of six torque converter mounting bolts. Remove six bolts.
15. Using a suitable floor jack, support transmission. Place wooden block between the jack and oil pan.
16. Remove frame crossmember attaching nuts and bolts, then remove.
17. Lower rear of transmission, then remove from vehicle.
18. If transmission is contaminated, thoroughly flush torque converter clutch and transmission cooler as follows:
    a. Install one-way clutch test tool No. 09351-32010, or equivalent, in the inner race of one-way clutch.
    b. With clutch converter on its side, turn test tool. Clutch should lock counterclockwise and rotate freely clockwise.
    c. Using a suitable indicator, measure driveplate runout. If greater than 0.0079 inch or if ring gear is damaged, replace driveplate.
    d. Using a suitable dial indicator, measure torque converter clutch sleeve runout. If greater than 0.0118 inch, reorient installation of converter clutch. If not corrected, replace torque converter clutch.
19. Reverse procedure to install, noting the following:
    a. **Torque** transmission and starter bolts to 53 ft. lbs.
    b. **Torque** oil cooler tube clamp to converter housing bolt to 7 ft. lbs. and frame crossmember bolts and nuts to 45 ft. lbs.
    c. **Torque** converter clutch mounting bolts to 40 ft. lbs. and engine undercover bolts to 21 ft. lbs.
    d. **Torque** oil cooler tubes to 25 ft. lbs. and cooler tube clamp to 7 ft. lbs.
    e. Tighten fan shroud of cooling fan to avoid damage to fan, then adjust and fill shift control rod with ATF. Refer to lubricant data at end of manual.
    f. **On models with coded audio anti-theft system,** reset as outlined under "Precautions."

TIGHTENING SPECIFICATIONS

Year	Component	Torque/ Ft. Lbs.
1993–94	Center Support Bolt	18
	Control Shaft To Transmission Case	9
	Crossmember Bolts	29
	Crossmember Nuts	43
	Engine To Transmission Bolts (14mm)	27
	Engine To Transmission Bolts (17mm)	53
	Engine Undercover	21
	Exhaust Front Pipe To Exhaust Manifold	46
	Exhaust Front Pipe To Exhaust Tail Pipe	29
	Frame Crossmember Set Bolts	45
	Front Accumulator Cover To Transmission Case	69①
	Governor Cover To Governor Valve Body Support	7
	Lock-Up Relay Valve Body Plate To Valve Body (8mm Bolt)	48①
	Lock-Up Relay Valve Body Plate To Valve Body (10mm Bolt)	7①
	Neutral Start Switch To Manual Valve Shaft	61①
	Neutral Start Switch To Transmission Case	9
	Oil Cooler Pipe To Oil Cooler Union	25
	Oil Cooler Pipe Union Nuts	25
	Oil Pan Drain Plug	20
	Oil Pan To Transmission	61①
	Oil Pump To Transmission Case	16
	Oil Strainer To Valve Body (8mm Head Bolt)	48①
	Oil Strainer To Valve Body (10mm Head Bolt)	7①
	Overdrive Case Set Bolt	18
	Parking Lock Pawl To Transfer Adapter	14
	Propeller Shaft To Differential	65
	Propeller Shaft To Transfer	65
	Rear Transmission Mount	43
	Torque Converter To Driveplate	21
	Transfer Adapter To Transmission Case	27

Continued

TIGHTENING SPECIFICATIONS—Continued

Year	Component	Torque/ Ft. Lbs.
1993–94	Transfer Shift Lever	13
	Transmission Control Rod	9
	Transmission Housing To Transmission Case	47
	Transmission Rear Cover To Transmission Case	69①
	Transmission Shift Lever Assembly	48①
	Valve Body To Transmission Case	7

① — Inch lbs.

A343F Automatic Transmission

INDEX

Page No.

Adjustments 48-301
Park/Neutral Position Switch 48-302
Shift Lever 48-302
Throttle Cable 48-301
In-Vehicle Repairs 48-302
Parking Lock Pawl, Replace 48-302
Speedometer Driven Gear 48-302
Throttle Cable, Replace 48-302
Valve Body, Replace 48-302
Maintenance 48-301
Fluid Change 48-301
Fluid Check 48-301
Precautions 48-299
Air Bag Systems 48-299
Audio Coded Anti-Theft System . 48-299
Tightening Specifications 48-303
Transmission, Replace 48-302
Troubleshooting 48-300
Harsh Engagement 1-2 48-301
Harsh Engagement 2-3 48-301
Harsh Engagement 2-3-O/D 48-301
Harsh Engagement 3-O/D 48-301
Harsh Engagement In Any Driving Position 48-301
Harsh Engagement N-D 48-301
Harsh Engagement N-L 48-301
Harsh Engagement N-R 48-301
Harsh Engagement O/D-3 48-301
Harsh Lock-Up Engagement 48-301
Large Shift Shock Or Engine Stalls When Starting Off Or Stopping 48-301
Lock-Up Does Not Disengage ... 48-301
Lock-Up Does Not Engage 48-300
No 2nd Start 48-301
No Downshift 48-300
No Engine Braking In 1st 48-301
No Engine Braking In 2nd 48-301
No Kickdown 48-301
No Pattern Select 48-301
No Upshift 48-300
Poor Acceleration 48-301
Shift Lock System 48-300
Shift Point Too High Or Too Low 48-301
Slip Or Shudder In Forward & Reverse 48-301
Upshifts To O/D From 3rd While Engine Is Cold 48-301
Upshifts To 2nd Or 3rd While In "L" Position 48-301
Vehicle Does Not Move In Any Forward Or Reverse Position . 48-300

PRECAUTIONS

AIR BAG SYSTEMS

Refer to "Air Bag System Precautions" in the front of this manual for system disarming and arming procedures.

AUDIO CODED ANTI-THEFT SYSTEM

Some models are equipped with an audio coded anti-theft system that will disable the radio when the battery cable is disconnected. The system can be identified by the "ANTI-THEFT SYSTEM" on the cassette lid. Obtain 3 digit code for input. Reset system after service as follows:

1. Obtain 3 digit audio theft code.
2. Depress 1 (PROG) while depressing righthand side of TUNE SEEK button, - - - will appear in tape operation display.
3. To enter the first digit, depress 1 (PROG) button repeatedly until the number of times depressed equals the first digit (depress the 1 button six times if the first digit if five, first press equals 0).
4. To enter second digit, depress 2 (APS) button repeatedly until the number of times depressed equals the second digit.
5. To enter third digit, depress 3 (RPT) button repeatedly until the number of times depressed equals the third digit.
6. If - - - is displayed after inputting digits, repeat procedure.
7. When code appears in display, depress and hold SCAN button until SEC appears.
8. When SEC disappears audio system is operative.
9. If Err is displayed, repeat procedure. **Attempting to input code more than**

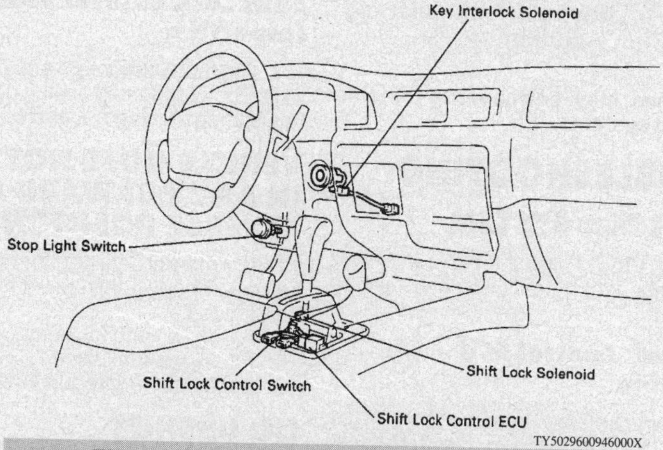
Key Interlock Solenoid
Stop Light Switch
Shift Lock Control Switch
Shift Lock Solenoid
Shift Lock Control ECU
TY5029600946000X

Fig. 1 Shift lock system components

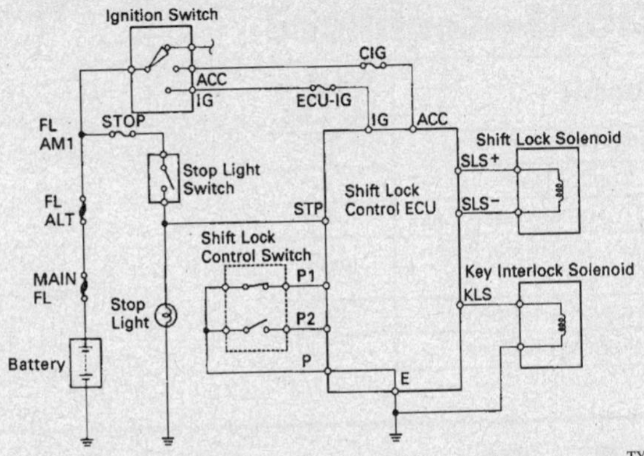
Ignition Switch
CIG
ACC
IG
ECU-IG
FL AM1
STOP
IG
ACC
Shift Lock Solenoid
SLS+
SLS−
Stop Light Switch
Shift Lock Control ECU
STP
FL ALT
Shift Lock Control Switch
P1
P2
Key Interlock Solenoid
KLS
MAIN FL
Stop Light
Battery
P
E

TY5029600947000X

Fig. 2 Shift lock system wiring diagram

Connector	Terminal	Measuring condition	Voltage (V)
A	ACC – E	IG SW ACC	10 – 14
	IG – E	IG SW ON	10 – 14
	STP – E	Depress brake pedal	10 – 14
	KLS – E	① IG SW ACC and shift lever P position	0
		② IG SW ACC and shift lever except P position	10 – 14
		③ ↑ (After - approx. 1 second)	6 – 9
B	SLS+ – SLS−	① IG SW ON and shift lever P position	0
		② Depress brake pedal	8.5 – 13.5
		③ ↑ (After - approx. 20 seconds)	5.5 – 9.5
		④ Shift lever except P position under condition above	0
C	P1 – P	① IG SW ON, shift lever P position and depress brake pedal	0
		② Shift lever except P position under condition above	9 – 13.5
	P2 – P	① IG SW ACC and shift lever at P position	9 – 13.5
		② Shift lever except P position under condition above	0

TY5029600949000X

Fig. 4 Shift lock control ECU inspection

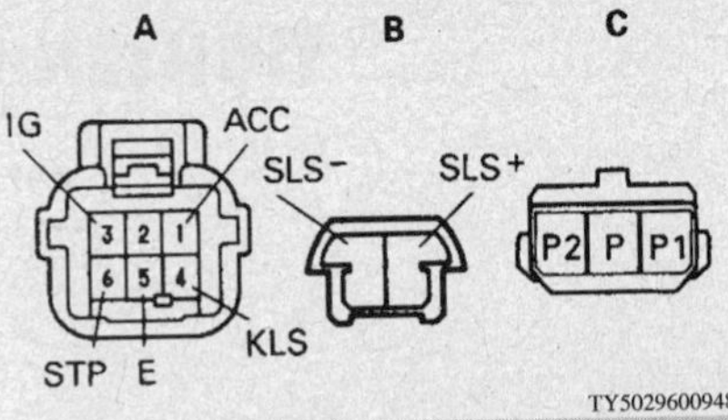
A
B
C
IG
ACC
SLS−
SLS+
3
2
1
6
5
4
P2
P
P1
KLS
STP
E

TY5029600948000X

Fig. 3 Shift lock ECU terminal identification

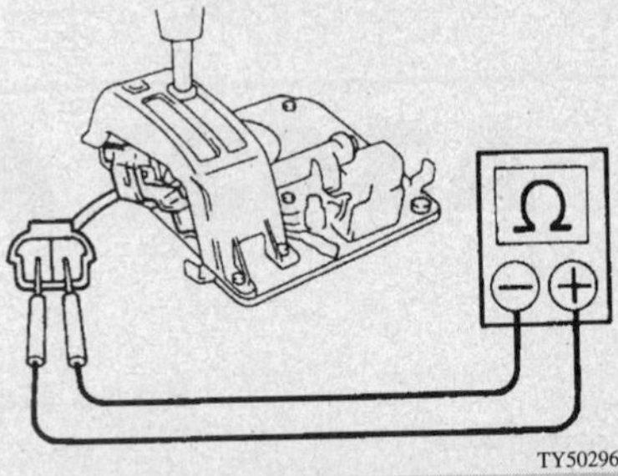
Ω

TY5029600950000X

Fig. 5 Shift lock solenoid inspection

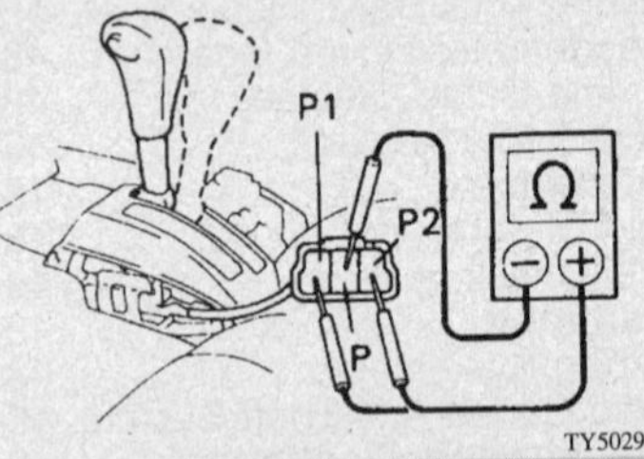
P1
P2
P
Ω

TY5029600952000X

Fig. 7 Shift lock control switch connector

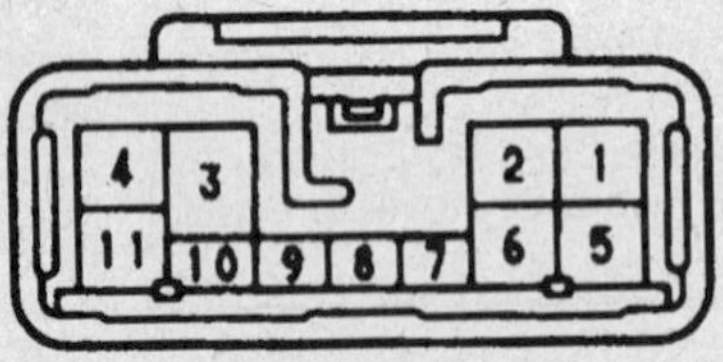
4
3
2
1
11
10
9
8
7
6
5

TY5029600951000X

Fig. 6 Key interlock solenoid connector

9 times may permanently disable audio system.

TROUBLESHOOTING

SHIFT LOCK SYSTEM

Refer to **Figs. 1 and 2** for shift lock system component locations and wiring diagram.

Shift Lock Control ECU Inspection

Using a voltmeter, measure the voltage at each terminal of the ECU, **Fig. 3.** Refer to **Fig. 4** for test conditions and voltage specifications.

Shift Lock Solenoid Inspection

1. Disconnect solenoid connector.
2. Using an ohmmeter, measure resistance between terminals, **Fig. 5.** Standard resistance is 20–28 Ohms.
3. Apply battery positive voltage between terminals and ensure solenoid operates.

Key Interlock Solenoid Inspection

Disconnect the key interlock solenoid and, using an ohmmeter, measure the resistance between terminals 7 and 8, **Fig. 6.** Resistance should be 12–17 Ohms.

Shift Lock Control Switch Inspection

Using an ohmmeter, ensure continuity exists between each switch connector terminal shown in **Figs. 7 and 8.**

VEHICLE DOES NOT MOVE IN ANY FORWARD OR REVERSE POSITION

1. Improperly adjusted throttle cable.
2. Improperly adjusted transmission control rod.
3. Faulty parking lock pawl.
4. Faulty manual valve.
5. Faulty primary regulator valve.

NO UPSHIFT

1. Faulty shift valve.
2. Fault in No. 1 vehicle speed sensor circuit.
3. Fault in No. 2 vehicle speed sensor circuit.
4. Fault in shift solenoid valve No. 1, No. 2 circuit.
5. Fault in throttle position sensor circuit.
6. Fault in park/neutral position switch circuit.
7. Faulty ECM.

8. Fault in O/D main switch and O/D OFF indicator circuit.
9. Fault in O/D cancel signal circuit.
10. Fault in engine coolant temperature sensor circuit.

NO DOWNSHIFT

1. Faulty shift valve.
2. Fault in No. 1 vehicle speed sensor circuit.
3. Fault in No. 2 vehicle speed sensor circuit.
4. Fault in shift solenoid valve No. 1, No. 2 circuit.
5. Fault in throttle position sensor circuit.
6. Faulty ECM.

LOCK-UP DOES NOT ENGAGE

1. Faulty lockup relay valve.
2. Fault in No. 1 vehicle speed sensor circuit.
3. Fault in No. 2 vehicle speed sensor circuit.
4. Fault in shift solenoid valve SL circuit.
5. Fault in throttle position sensor circuit.
6. Fault in park/neutral position switch circuit.
7. Faulty ECM.
8. Fault in stop lamp switch circuit.
9. Fault in engine coolant temperature sensor circuit.

Shift position	Tester condition to terminal number	Specified value
P position (Release button is not pushed)	P1 – P	Continuity
P position (Release button is pushed)	P1 – P P2 – P	Continuity
R, N, D, 2, L position	P2 – P	Continuity

TY5029600953000X

Fig. 8 Shift lock control switch inspection

LOCK-UP DOES NOT DISENGAGE

1. Faulty lockup relay valve.
2. Fault in No. 1 vehicle speed sensor circuit.
3. Fault in No. 2 vehicle speed sensor circuit.
4. Fault in throttle position sensor circuit.
5. Faulty ECM.
6. Fault in stop lamp switch circuit.

SHIFT POINT TOO HIGH OR TOO LOW

1. Fault in No. 1 vehicle speed sensor circuit.
2. Fault in No. 2 vehicle speed sensor circuit.
3. Fault in throttle position sensor circuit.
4. Pattern select switch circuit.
5. Faulty ECM.

UPSHIFTS TO 2ND OR 3RD WHILE IN "L" POSITION

1. Fault in park/neutral position switch circuit.
2. Faulty ECM.

UPSHIFTS TO O/D FROM 3RD WHILE ENGINE IS COLD

1. Fault in engine coolant temperature sensor circuit.
2. Faulty ECM.

HARSH ENGAGEMENT IN ANY DRIVING POSITION

1. Fault in No. 1 vehicle speed sensor circuit.
2. Fault in No. 2 vehicle speed sensor circuit.
3. Fault in shift solenoid SL circuit.
4. Fault in throttle position sensor circuit.
5. Faulty ECM.
6. Fault in ATF temperature sensor circuit.

HARSH ENGAGEMENT N-D

1. Faulty accumulator control valve.
2. Fault in shift solenoid SL circuit.
3. Fault in throttle position sensor circuit.
4. Fault in park/neutral position switch circuit.
5. Fault in ATF temperature sensor circuit.
6. Faulty ECM.

HARSH LOCK-UP ENGAGEMENT

1. Faulty lock-up relay valve.
2. Fault in No. 1 vehicle speed sensor circuit.

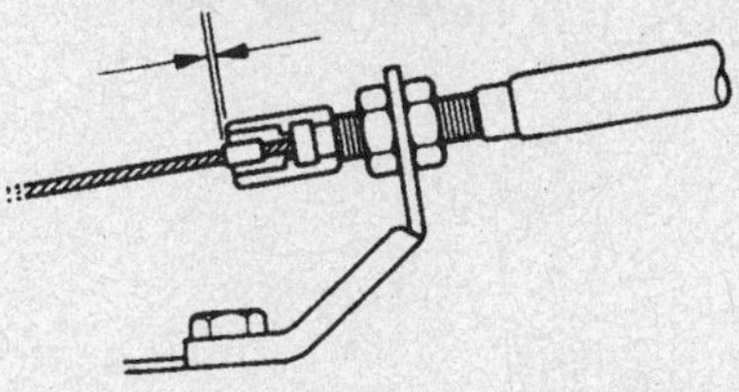
0 – 1 mm (0 – 0.04 in)

TY5029600943000X

Fig. 9 Throttle cable adjustment

3. Fault in No. 2 vehicle speed sensor circuit.
4. Fault in throttle position sensor circuit.
5. Faulty ECM.
6. Fault in shift solenoid SL circuit.

HARSH ENGAGEMENT N-R

1. Faulty accumulator control valve.
2. Faulty C_2 accumulator.

HARSH ENGAGEMENT N-L

1. Faulty low coast modulator valve.

HARSH ENGAGEMENT 1-2

1. Faulty accumulator control valve.
2. Faulty B_2 accumulator.

HARSH ENGAGEMENT 2-3-O/D

1. Faulty accumulator control valve.
2. Faulty throttle valve.

HARSH ENGAGEMENT 2-3

1. Faulty accumulator control valve.
2. Faulty C_2 accumulator.

HARSH ENGAGEMENT 3-O/D

1. Faulty accumulator control valve.
2. Faulty B_0 accumulator.

HARSH ENGAGEMENT O/D-3

1. Faulty accumulator control valve.
2. Faulty C_0 accumulator.

SLIP OR SHUDDER IN FORWARD & REVERSE

1. Improperly adjusted throttle cable.
2. Improperly adjusted transmission control rod.
3. Faulty oil strainer.
4. Faulty pressure relief valve.

NO ENGINE BRAKING IN 1ST

1. Faulty low coast modulator valve.

NO ENGINE BRAKING IN 2ND

1. Faulty 2nd coast modulator valve.

NO KICKDOWN

1. Faulty 1-2 shift valve.
2. Faulty 2-3 shift valve.
3. Fault in No. 1 vehicle speed sensor circuit.
4. Fault in shift solenoid No. 1, No. 2 circuit.
5. Fault in throttle position sensor circuit.
6. Faulty ECM.

NO PATTERN SELECT

1. Pattern select switch circuit.
2. Faulty ECM.

NO 2ND START

1. Fault in shift solenoid No. 1, No. 2 circuit.
2. Pattern select switch circuit.
3. Faulty ECM.

POOR ACCELERATION

1. Fault in No. 1 vehicle speed sensor circuit.
2. Fault in No. 2 vehicle speed sensor circuit.
3. Fault in shift solenoid No. 1, No. 2 circuit.
4. Fault in shift solenoid valve SL circuit.
5. Fault in throttle position sensor circuit.

LARGE SHIFT SHOCK OR ENGINE STALLS WHEN STARTING OFF OR STOPPING

1. Fault in shift solenoid valve SL circuit.
2. Fault in stop lamp switch circuit.
3. Faulty ECM.

MAINTENANCE

FLUID CHECK

1. Operate vehicle to allow transaxle fluid temperature to reach 158°–176°F.
2. Position vehicle on level surface and apply parking brake.
3. Allow engine to idle, depress brake pedal, then move shift lever through all positions.
4. Remove transaxle dipstick, wipe clean, then replace.
5. Remove dipstick and check fluid level in HOT range.

FLUID CHANGE

1. Drain transaxle fluid, then install drain plugs.
2. With engine off, add fluid through filler tube. **Do not overfill.**
3. Transmission dry capacity is 11.6 quarts.
4. Start engine and move shift lever through all positions, ensuring smooth operation.
5. Allow engine to idle, then check fluid level. Add fluid up to COOL level.

ADJUSTMENTS

THROTTLE CABLE

1. Ensure throttle valve is fully closed.
2. Ensure inner cable is not slack.
3. Measure distance between outer cable and stopper on cable, **Fig. 9.** Distance should be 0-.04 inch.

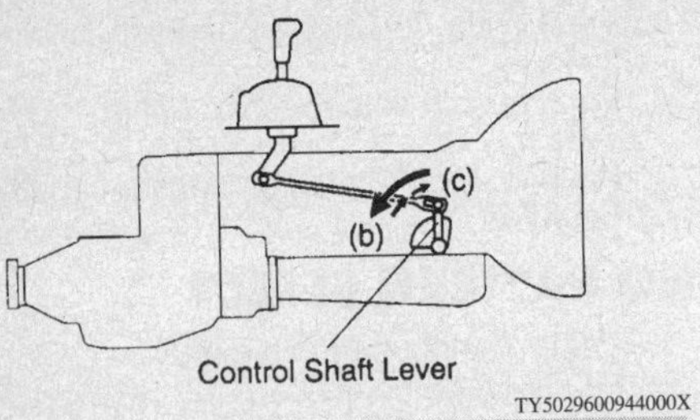
(c)
(b)
Control Shaft Lever
TY5029600944000X

Fig. 10 Shift lever adjustment

4. If distance is not within specifications, adjust cable by turning adjusting nuts.

SHIFT LEVER

Move the shift lever to each position. If the indicator does not align with the correct position, perform the following procedure.

1. Loosen nut on control rod.
2. Push control rod fully rearward.
3. Return control shaft lever 2 notches to "N" position.
4. Set shift lever to "N" position.
5. While holding shift lever lightly toward "R" position side, adjust control rod nut, **Fig. 10.**
6. **Torque** control rod nut to 9 ft. lbs.
7. Start engine and ensure vehicle moves forward when shifting lever from "N" to "D" position and reverses when shifting to "R" position.

PARK/NEUTRAL POSITION SWITCH

If the engine can be started with the shift lever in any position other than "N" or "P," perform the following adjustment procedure.

1. Loosen park/neutral position switch bolt and set shift lever to "N" position.
2. Align groove and neutral basic line, **Fig. 11.**
3. Hold in position and **torque** bolt to 9 ft. lbs.

IN-VEHICLE REPAIRS

VALVE BODY, REPLACE

1. Drain transmission fluid.
2. Remove transmission oil pan bolts.
3. Install blade of tool No. 09032-00100, or equivalent, between transmission case and oil pan.
4. Remove transmission oil pan.
5. Disconnect solenoid valve connectors.
6. Remove three solenoid valve mounting bolts.
7. Remove three solenoid valves.
8. Remove oil strainer bolts, oil strainer and gaskets.
9. Pry up both ends of oil pipe with suitable screwdriver and remove oil pipe.
10. Remove valve body bolts, **Fig. 12.** Valve body "A" bolts are .91 inch and "B" bolts are 1.26 inches.
11. Disconnect throttle cable from cam.
12. Remove valve body.
13. Reverse procedure to install, noting the following:
    a. **Torque** solenoid valve mounting bolts to 7 ft. lbs.

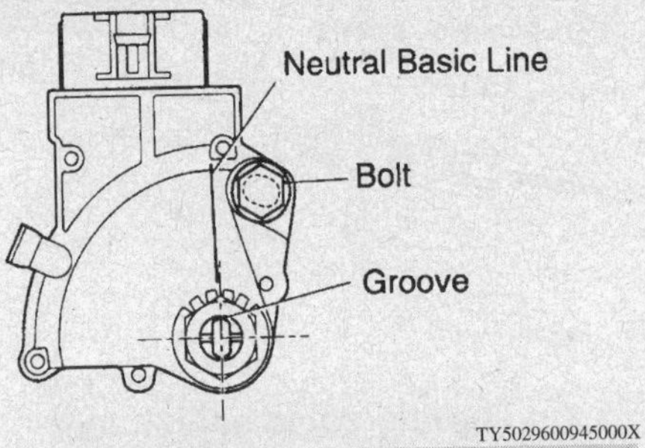
Neutral Basic Line
Bolt
Groove
TY5029600945000X

Fig. 11 Park/neutral position switch adjustment

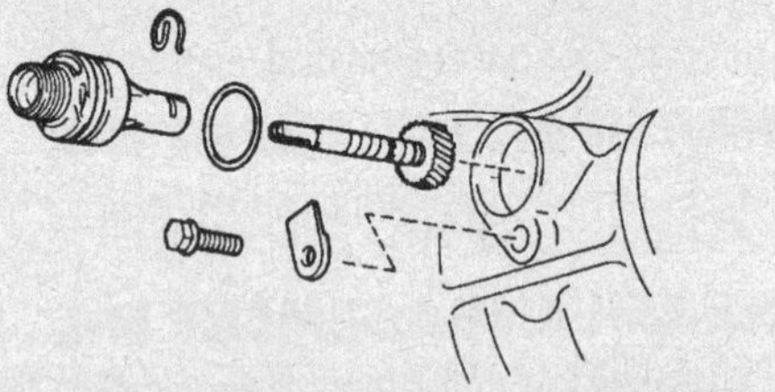
TY5029600955000X

Fig. 13 Speedometer driven gear removal

    b. **Torque** oil strainer bolts to 7 ft. lbs.
    c. **Torque** oil pan mounting bolts to 65 inch lbs.

PARKING LOCK PAWL, REPLACE

1. Remove valve body as described under "Valve Body, Replace."
2. Remove parking lock pawl bracket.
3. Remove spring from parking lock pawl and shaft.
4. Reverse procedure to install.

THROTTLE CABLE, REPLACE

1. Disconnect cable housing from bracket.
2. Disconnect cable from throttle linkage.
3. Disconnect cable clamp from torque converter clutch housing.
4. Remove valve body as described under "Valve Body, Replace."
5. Remove throttle body retaining bolt and pull out throttle cable.
6. Reverse procedure to install.

SPEEDOMETER DRIVEN GEAR

1. Loosen serrated collar with suitable pliers. **Do not lose felt dust protector and washer.**
2. Disconnect speedometer cable.
3. Remove bolt and locking plate. Pry out speedometer driven gear assembly, **Fig. 13.**
4. Remove O-ring from speedometer driven gear assembly.
5. Remove clip and speedometer driven gear from speedometer driven gear sleeve.
6. Remove speedometer driven gear oil seal using tool No. 09921-00010, or equivalent.
7. Reverse procedure to install, noting the following:
    a. Install new speedometer driven gear oil seal using tool No. 09201-10000, or equivalent.
    b. **Torque** retaining bolt with locking plate to 12 ft. lbs.

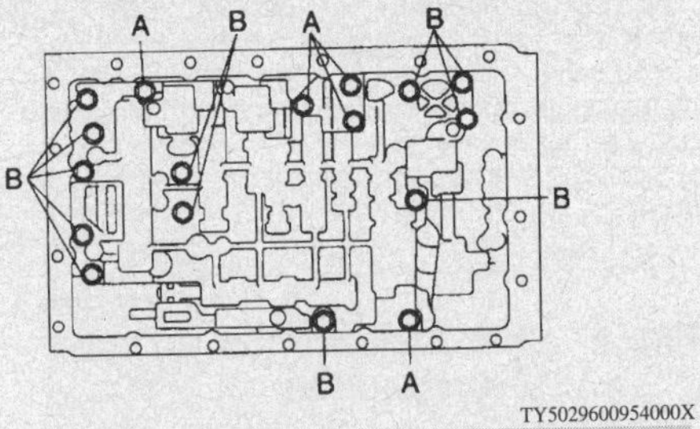
A
B
A
B
B
B
B
A
TY5029600954000X

Fig. 12 Valve body bolt locations

TRANSMISSION

REPLACE

1. Remove battery and battery tray, **Fig. 14.**
2. Remove upper cooling fan shroud bolts.
3. Loosen throttle cable adjusting nut and disconnect cable from bracket.
4. Disconnect throttle cable from linkage.
5. Remove upper starter mounting bolt.
6. Remove transfer shift lever clip, washer and wave washer and disconnect transfer shift lever link.
7. Remove transfer shift lever knob.
8. Remove four center shift console screws and the console.
9. Remove transfer shift lever boot.
10. Remove console box.
11. Disconnect three console electrical connectors.
12. Remove six screws and transmission shift lever assembly.
13. Remove transfer shift lever.
14. Remove cushions.
15. Disconnect Nos. 1 and 2 vehicle speed sensor connectors.
16. Disconnect park/neutral position switch connector.
17. Disconnect solenoid connector.
18. Disconnect ATF sensor connector.
19. Disconnect center differential lock indicator switch, L4 position switch, neutral position switch connectors and bleeder hose from transfer.
20. Remove front and rear propeller shaft.
21. Remove transmission dipstick and upper side mounting bolt.
22. Remove filler pipe.
23. Loosen oil cooler pipe union nuts.
24. Remove stabilizer bar bracket mounting bolts.
25. Remove engine under cover.
26. Remove torque converter hole plug.
27. Turn crankshaft to gain access to each torque converter clutch (TCC) mounting bolt.
28. Hold crankshaft pulley nut with wrench and remove six TCC bolts.
29. Disconnect front exhaust pipe assembly.
30. Loosen front exhaust pipe clamp bolt and disconnect clamp from support bracket.
31. Remove front exhaust support bracket.
32. Remove remaining front exhaust pipe

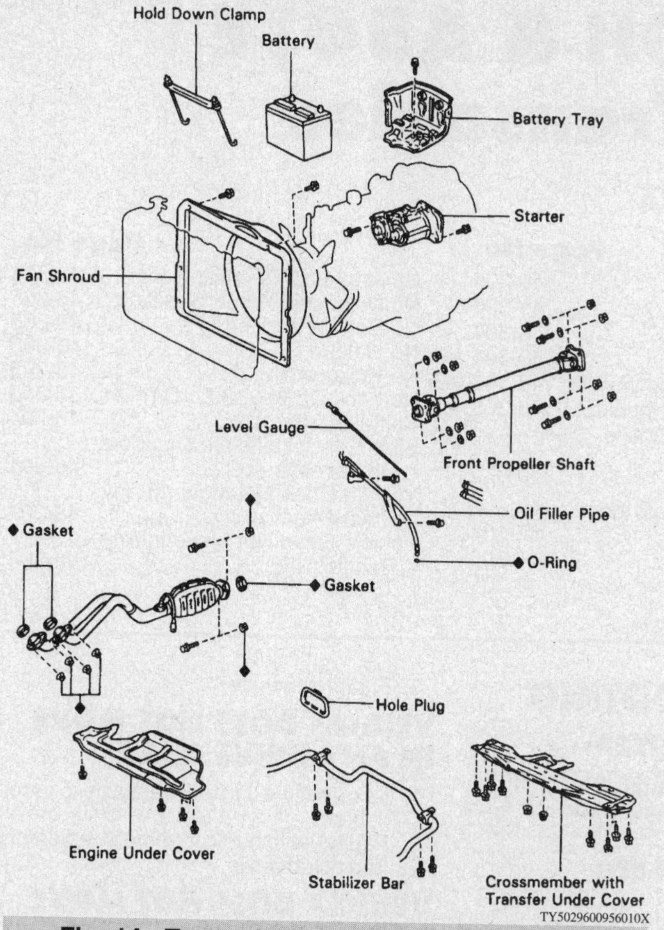
Hold Down Clamp
Battery
Battery Tray
Starter
Fan Shroud
Level Gauge
Front Propeller Shaft
Oil Filler Pipe
◆ Gasket
◆ O-Ring
◆ Gasket
Hole Plug
Engine Under Cover
Stabilizer Bar
Crossmember with Transfer Under Cover
TY5029600956010X

Fig. 14 Transmission removal (Part 1 of 2)

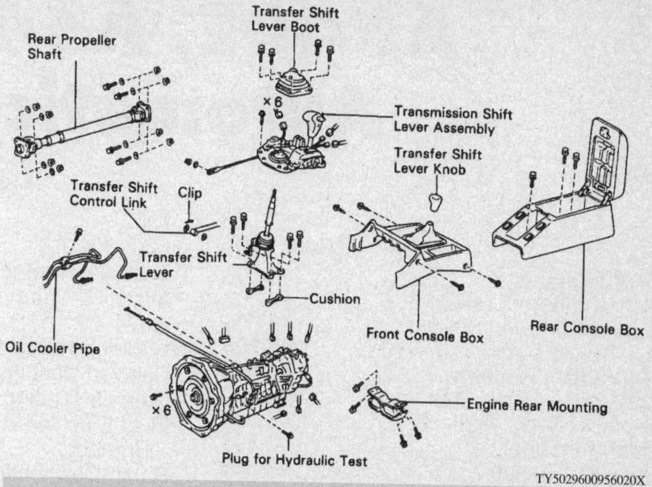
Transfer Shift Lever Boot
Rear Propeller Shaft
×6
Transmission Shift Lever Assembly
Transfer Shift Lever Knob
Transfer Shift Control Link
Clip
Transfer Shift Lever
Cushion
Oil Cooler Pipe
Front Console Box
Rear Console Box
×6
Engine Rear Mounting
Plug for Hydraulic Test
TY5029600956020X

Fig. 14 Transmission removal (Part 2 of 2)

fasteners and position front exhaust assembly aside.

33. Disconnect starter electrical connector and remove starter.
34. Support transmission with suitable jack.
35. Remove crossmember from under transmission.
36. Lower rear end of transmission.
37. Separate wire harness from transmission and transfer.
38. Remove oil cooler pipe mounting bolts from torque converter clutch housing, then disconnect oil cooler pipes from elbows.
39. Remove transmission to engine mounting bolts.
40. Remove transmission.
41. Inspect torque converter and drive plate as follows:
    a. Install one-way test tool No. 09350-30020, or equivalent, in inner race of one-way clutch.
    b. With clutch converter on its side, turn test tool. Clutch should lock counterclockwise and rotate freely clockwise.
    c. Using a suitable dial indicator, measure driveplate runout. If greater than .0079 inch or if ring gear is damaged, replace driveplate.
    d. Using a suitable dial indicator, measure torque converter clutch sleeve runout. If greater than .0118 inch, reorient installation of converter clutch. If not corrected, replace torque converter clutch.
42. Reverse procedure to install, noting the following:
    a. Tighten all bolts and nuts to specifications.
    b. After installation, adjust shift lever and throttle cable as described under "Adjustments."

TIGHTENING SPECIFICATIONS

Year	Component	Torque/ Ft. Lbs.
1996	Crossmember Bolts	45
	Crossmember Nuts	54
	Engine Under Cover Bolts	21
	Front Exhaust Support Bracket Bolts	17
	Stabilizer Bar Bracket Mounting Bolts	13
	Starter Mounting Bolts	29
	Torque Converter Clutch Clamp Bolt	14
	Torque Converter Clutch Mounting Bolts	40
	Transfer Shift Lever Retaining Bolts	13
	Transmission Mounting Bolts	53
	Transmission Shift Lever Assembly Bolts	48①
	Vehicle Speed Sensor Retaining Bolt	48①

① — Inch lbs.

A540E, A540H & A541E Automatic Transaxles

INDEX

Page No.

Adjustments 48-306
Manual Shift Lever............. 48-306
Neutral Safety Switch 48-306
Throttle Cable 48-306
In-Vehicle Repairs 48-306
Throttle Cable, Replace......... 48-306
Valve Body, Replace 48-306
Maintenance 48-305
Fluid Change 48-305
Fluid Check..................... 48-305
Precautions....................... 48-304
Air Bag Systems.................. 48-304
Audio Coded Anti-Theft System . 48-304
Tightening Specifications 48-308

Transaxle, Replace 48-306
Avalon & Camry 48-306
RAV4 48-307
Troubleshooting 48-304
Delayed Upshifts & Downshifts.. 48-304
Drag Or Binding On Upshifts.... 48-305
Fluid Discolored Or Smells Burned 48-304
Harsh Downshift 48-305
Harsh Engagement Into Any Drive Range 48-304
Incorrect Downshift 48-305
Incorrect Shift Lever Position.... 48-304

No Center Differential Control... 48-305
No Downshift When Coasting... 48-305
No Engine Braking In 2 48-305
No Hold In P.................... 48-305
No Kickdown 48-305
No Lock-Up In 2, 3 Or O/D 48-305
Shift Lock System 48-304
Slips On Upshifts Or Shudders On Takeoffs.................. 48-304
Vehicle Does Not Move In Any Drive Gear.................... 48-304
Vehicle Does Not Move In Any Range 48-304

PRECAUTIONS

AIR BAG SYSTEMS

Refer to "Air Bag System Precautions" in the front of this manual for system disarming and arming procedures.

AUDIO CODED ANTI-THEFT SYSTEM

Some models are equipped with an audio coded anti-theft system that will disable the radio when the battery cable is disconnected. The system can be identified by the "ANTI-THEFT SYSTEM" on the cassette lid. Obtain 3 digit code for input. Reset system after service as follows:

1. Obtain 3 digit audio theft code.
2. Depress 1 (PROG) while depressing righthand side of TUNE SEEK button, - - - will appear in tape operation display.
3. To enter the first digit, depress 1 (PROG) button repeatedly until the number of times depressed equals the first digit (depress the 1 button six times if the first digit if five, first press equals 0).
4. To enter second digit, depress 2 (APS) button repeatedly until the number of times depressed equals the second digit.
5. To enter third digit, depress 3 (RPT) button repeatedly until the number of times depressed equals the third digit.
6. If - - - is displayed after inputting digits, repeat procedure.
7. When code appears in display, depress and hold SCAN button until SEC appears.
8. When SEC disappears audio system is operative.
9. If Err is displayed, repeat procedure. **Attempting to input code more than 9 may permanently disable audio system.**

TROUBLESHOOTING

SHIFT LOCK SYSTEM

Refer to **Figs. 1 through 4** for shift lock system component locations and Fig. 5 for wiring circuit.

Shift Lock Control ECU Inspection

Using a suitable voltmeter, measure voltage at each ECU connector terminal, **Figs. 6 through 8.** Refer to **Figs. 9 and 10.** for ECU inspection.

Shift Lock Solenoid Inspection

1. Disconnect solenoid connector.
2. Using suitable ohmmeter, measure resistance between connector terminals.
3. Resistance should be 29–35 ohms on Avalon and Camry models, and 26–33 ohms on RAV4 models.
4. Apply battery positive voltage between terminals and ensure solenoid operating noise can be heard.

Key Interlock Solenoid Inspection

1. Disconnect solenoid connector.
2. Using suitable ohmmeter, measure resistance between connector terminals.
3. Resistance should be 12.5–16.5 ohms
4. Apply battery positive voltage between terminals and ensure solenoid operating noise can be heard.

Shift Lock Control Switch Inspection

Using a suitable ohmmeter, check for continuity between shift lock control switch connector terminals, **Figs. 11 through 13.**

FLUID DISCOLORED OR SMELLS BURNED

1. Contaminated fluid.
2. Faulty torque converter.
3. Faulty transaxle.

VEHICLE DOES NOT MOVE IN ANY DRIVE GEAR

1. Incorrectly adjusted transaxle control cable.
2. Faulty valve body or primary regulator.
3. Faulty transaxle.

VEHICLE DOES NOT MOVE IN ANY RANGE

1. Faulty park lock pawl.
2. Faulty valve body or Primary regulator.
3. Faulty torque converter.
4. Broken converter driveplate.
5. Blocked oil pump intake strainer.
6. Faulty transaxle.

INCORRECT SHIFT LEVER POSITION

1. Incorrectly adjusted transaxle control cable.
2. Faulty manual valve and lever.
3. Faulty transaxle.

HARSH ENGAGEMENT INTO ANY DRIVE RANGE

1. Incorrectly adjusted throttle cable.
2. Faulty valve body or primary regulator.
3. Faulty accumulator pistons.
4. Faulty transaxle.

DELAYED UPSHIFTS & DOWNSHIFTS

1. Faulty electronic control.
2. Faulty valve body.
3. Faulty solenoid valve.

SLIPS ON UPSHIFTS OR SHUDDERS ON TAKEOFFS

1. Incorrectly adjusted transaxle control cable.
2. Incorrectly adjusted throttle cable.
3. Faulty valve body.
4. Faulty transaxle.

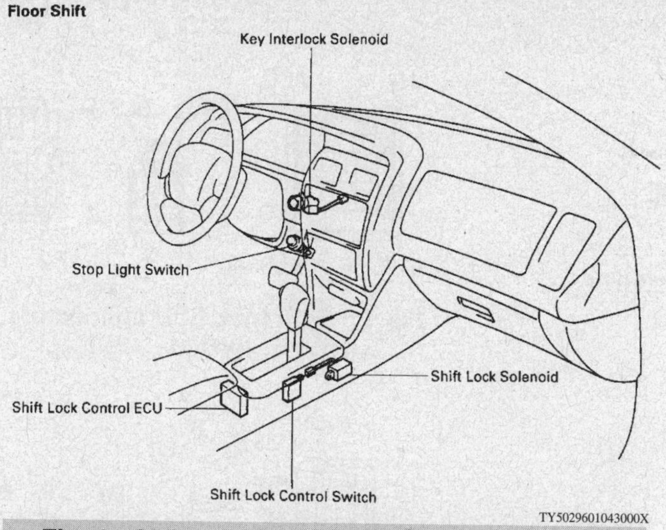
Floor Shift
Key Interlock Solenoid
Stop Light Switch
Shift Lock Solenoid
Shift Lock Control ECU
Shift Lock Control Switch
TY5029601043000X

Fig. 1 Shift lock system components. Avalon w/floor shift

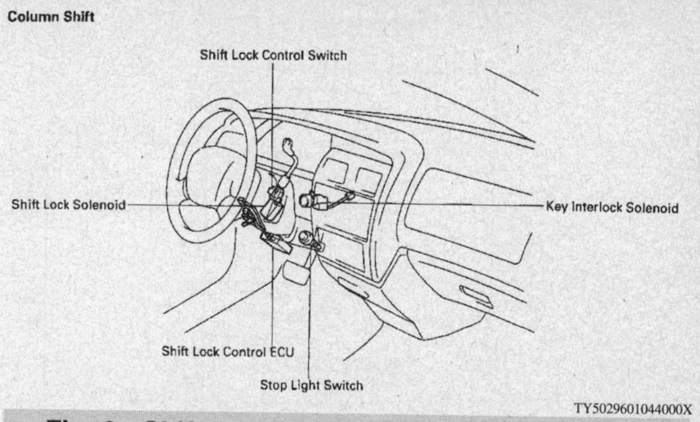
Column Shift
Shift Lock Control Switch
Shift Lock Solenoid
Key Interlock Solenoid
Shift Lock Control ECU
Stop Light Switch
TY5029601044000X

Fig. 2 Shift lock system components. Avalon w/column shift

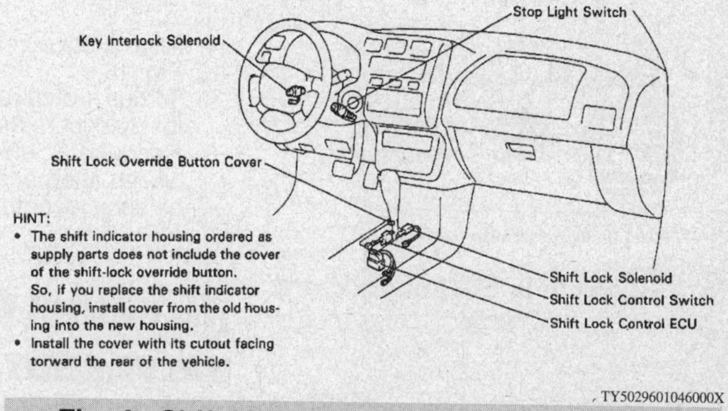
Stop Light Switch
Key Interlock Solenoid
Shift Lock Override Button Cover
HINT:
• The shift indicator housing ordered as supply parts does not include the cover of the shift-lock override button. So, if you replace the shift indicator housing, install cover from the old housing into the new housing.
• Install the cover with its cutout facing torward the rear of the vehicle.
Shift Lock Solenoid
Shift Lock Control Switch
Shift Lock Control ECU
TY5029601046000X

Fig. 4 Shift lock system components. RAV4

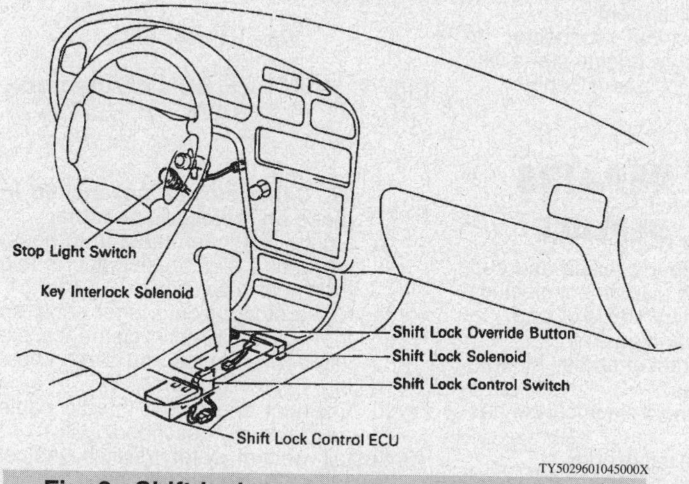
Stop Light Switch
Key Interlock Solenoid
Shift Lock Override Button
Shift Lock Solenoid
Shift Lock Control Switch
Shift Lock Control ECU
TY5029601045000X

Fig. 3 Shift lock system components. Camry

5. Faulty solenoid valve.

DRAG OR BINDING ON UPSHIFTS

1. Incorrectly adjusted transaxle control cable.
2. Faulty valve body.
3. Faulty transaxle.

NO LOCK-UP IN 2, 3 OR O/D

1. Faulty valve body.
2. Faulty transaxle.
3. Faulty solenoid valve.
4. Faulty electronic control.

HARSH DOWNSHIFT

1. Incorrectly adjusted throttle cable.
2. Faulty throttle cable and cam.
3. Faulty accumulator pistons.
4. Faulty valve body.
5. Faulty transaxle.

NO DOWNSHIFT WHEN COASTING

1. Faulty valve body.
2. Faulty solenoid valve.
3. Faulty electronic control.

INCORRECT DOWNSHIFT

1. Faulty throttle cable.
2. Faulty valve body.
3. Faulty transaxle.
4. Faulty solenoid valve.
5. Faulty electronic control.

NO KICKDOWN

1. Faulty valve body.
2. Faulty solenoid valve.
3. Faulty electronic control.

NO ENGINE BRAKING IN 2

1. Faulty valve body.
2. Faulty transaxle.
3. Faulty solenoid valve.
4. Faulty electronic control.

NO HOLD IN P

1. Incorrectly adjusted transaxle Control Cable.
2. Faulty parking lock pawl and rod.

NO CENTER DIFFERENTIAL CONTROL

1. Faulty valve body.
2. Faulty electronic control.
3. Faulty transfer.
4. Faulty hydraulic multi-plate clutch.

MAINTENANCE

FLUID CHECK

1. Operate vehicle, allow transaxle fluid temperature to reach 158–176°F.
2. Position vehicle on level surface, apply parking brake.
3. Allow engine to idle, depress brake pedal, then move shift lever through all positions.
4. Remove transaxle dipstick, wipe clean, then replace.
5. Remove again, then check fluid level in HOT range.
6. **On A540E units,** dry fill capacity is 6.2 quarts.
7. **On A540H units,** dry fill capacity is 7.4 quarts.

FLUID CHANGE

1. Drain transaxle fluid, then using tool No. 09043–38100, or equivalent, reinstall drain plug and new gasket.
2. Add fluid through filler tube. **Do not overfill.**
3. **On A540E units,** drain and refill capacity is 2.6 US quarts.

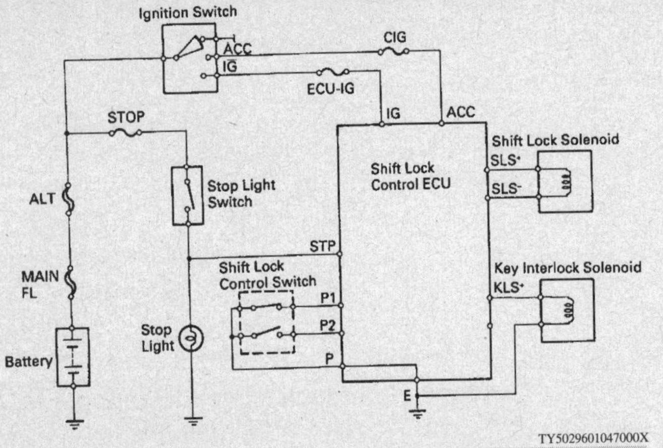

Ignition Switch
ACC
IG
CIG
ECU-IG
IG
ACC
STOP
Shift Lock Solenoid
SLS+
SLS-
Shift Lock Control ECU
ALT
Stop Light Switch
STP
Shift Lock Control Switch
Key Interlock Solenoid
KLS+
MAIN FL
P1
P2
P
Stop Light
Battery
E
TY5029601047000X

Fig. 5 Shift lock system wiring circuit

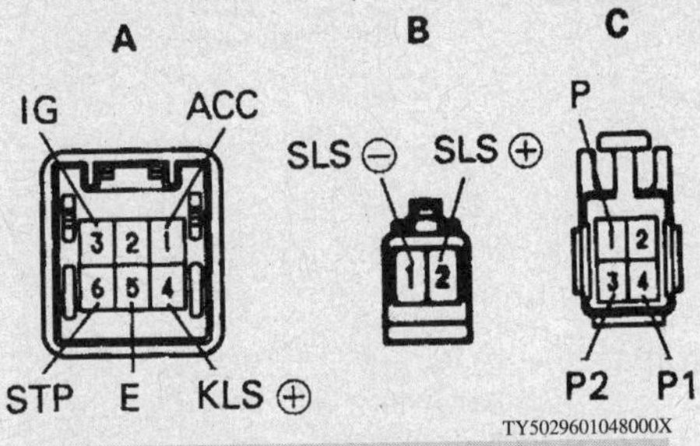

A
B
C
IG
ACC
SLS ⊖
SLS ⊕
P
3 2 1
6 5 4
1 2
1 2
3 4
STP
E
KLS ⊕
P2
P1
TY5029601048000X

Fig. 6 Shift lock ECU connectors. Avalon

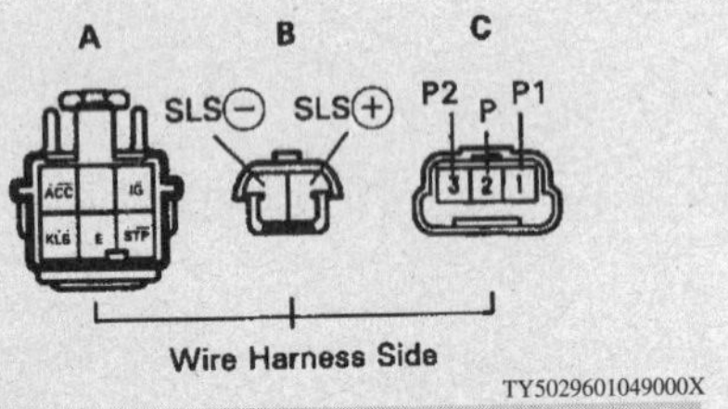

A
B
C
SLS⊖
SLS⊕
P2
P
P1
3 2 1
ACC
IG
KLS
E
STP
Wire Harness Side
TY5029601049000X

Fig. 7 Shift lock ECU connectors. Camry

4. **On A540H units,** drain and refill capacity is 3.5 US quarts.
5. **On all models,** start engine, move shift lever through all positions, ensuring smooth operation.
6. Allow engine to idle, then check fluid level, add up to COOL level.
7. Once fluid temperature reaches 158–176°F, recheck fluid level.

ADJUSTMENTS

MANUAL SHIFT LEVER

1. Loosen swivel nut on lever, then push manual lever fully toward right side of vehicle, **Fig. 14.**
2. Return lever two notches to Neutral position, then place selector lever in Neutral position.
3. Manually hold lever tightly toward R range, then tighten swivel nut.

THROTTLE CABLE

1. Hold accelerator pedal in fully depressed position, then loosen cable adjusting nuts, **Fig. 15.**
2. Adjust cable to obtain .04 inch between end of boot and stopper on cable, then tighten adjusting nut.
3. Fully depress accelerator pedal and recheck adjustment, then road test vehicle.

NEUTRAL SAFETY SWITCH

1. Loosen neutral safety switch attaching bolts.
2. Place selector lever in Neutral position.
3. Disconnect electrical connector.
4. Align groove in with neutral basic line, **Fig. 16.**
5. Torque switch retaining bolts to 48 inch lbs. to secure adjustment.
6. Reconnect electrical connector to switch, then ensure engine starts with selector lever in "N" and "P" only.

IN-VEHICLE REPAIRS

VALVE BODY, REPLACE

1. With vehicle properly raised and supported, label and disconnect electrical connectors from transaxle oil pan.
2. Remove oil pan and gasket.
3. Remove tube bracket and oil strainer.
4. Remove oil tubes.
5. Disconnect solenoid electrical connectors.
6. Remove manual valve body.
7. Remove connector clamp and tube retainer.
8. Remove S_3 apply tube.
9. Remove ten valve body attaching bolts, then the valve body.
10. Reverse procedure to install. Note the following:
    a. Hand tighten and then **torque** valve body bolts specifications.
    b. Align manual valve body with pin on the manual shaft lever.
    c. Hand tighten manual valve body bolts, then **torque** to specifications.

THROTTLE CABLE, REPLACE

Removal

1. Disconnect throttle cable from engine.
2. Remove neutral safety switch.
3. Remove valve body as previously described.
4. Remove throttle cable from transaxle case.

Installation

1. Insert cable into transaxle case.
2. Install valve body as previously described, then position cable stop for adjustment reference as follows:
    a. Bend cable to a radius of approximately 7.87 inches as shown, **Fig.**

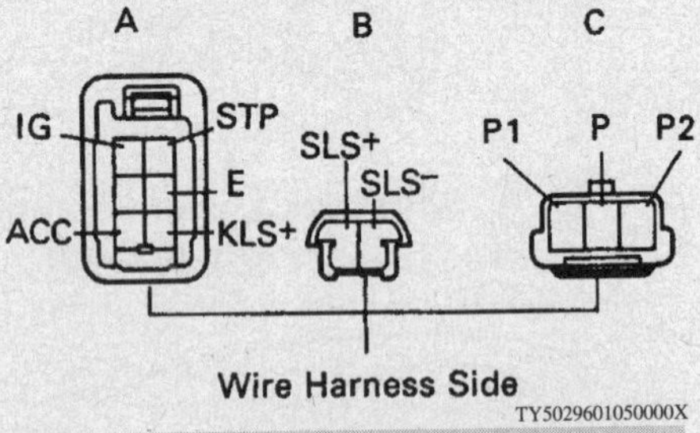

A
B
C
IG
STP
SLS+
SLS−
E
P1
P
P2
ACC
KLS+
Wire Harness Side
TY5029601050000X

Fig. 8 Shift lock ECU connectors. RAV4

17. Cable stop is not staked in place on replacement cable.

b. Lightly pull inner cable from housing until a slight resistance is felt, then hold in position.
c. Stake stopper onto inner cable so that .031–.059 inch clearance exists between stop and cable housing.
d. Connect and adjust throttle cable as previously described.

3. Install neutral safety switch. Adjust switch as previously described.
4. Ensure transaxle fluid level is to specifications, then road test vehicle.

TRANSAXLE

REPLACE

AVALON & CAMRY

1. **On models with coded audio anti-theft system,** obtain three digit code.
2. **On all models,** disconnect battery ground cable.
3. Remove air cleaner assembly and throttle cable.
4. **On models with cruise control,** remove cruise control actuator cover and disconnect connector from actuator.
5. **On all models,** remove ground earth terminal.
6. Remove starter.
7. Disconnect speed sensor connectors, Park/Neutral switch and solenoid connector.
8. Disconnect shift control cable and oil cooler hoses.
9. Remove two front side transaxle mounting bolts and engine mounting bolts.
10. Remove oil cooler clamping bolts from frame assembly.

Connector	Terminal	Measuring condition	Voltage (V)
A	ACC – E	Ignition switch ACC	10 – 14
	IG – E	Ignition switch ON	10 – 14
	STP – E	Depress brake pedal	10 – 14
	KLS – E	① Ignition switch ACC and P position	0
		② Ignition switch ACC and except P position	7.5 – 11
		③ (After approx. 1 second)	6 – 9
B	SLS⊕ – SLS⊖	① Ignition switch ON shift lever P position	0
		② Depress brake pedal	8.5 – 13.5
		③ Except P position	0
C	P1 – P	① Ignition switch ON, P position and depress brake pedal	0
		② Shift except P position under conditions above	9 – 13.5
	P2 – P	① Ignition switch ACC and shift lever at P position	9 – 13.5
		② Shift except P position under conditions above	0

TY5029601051000X

Fig. 9 Shift lock ECU inspection. Avalon & Camry

Connector	Terminal	Measuring condition	Voltage (V)
A	ACC – E	Ignition switch ACC	10 – 14
	IG – E	Ignition switch ON	10 – 14
	STP – E	Depress brake pedal	10 – 14
	KLS+ – E	1 Ignition switch ACC and P position	0
		2 Ignition switch ACC and except P position	7.5 – 11
		3 (After approx 1 second)	5.5 – 10
B	SLS+ – SLS−	1 Ignition switch ON and P position	0
		2 Depress brake pedal	8.5 – 14
		4 Except P position	0
C	P1 – P	1 Ignition switch ON, P position and depress brake pedal	0
		2 Shift except P position under condition above	10 – 14
	P2 – P	1 Ignition switch ACC and P position	10 – 14
		2 Shift except P position under condition above	0

TY5029601052000X

Fig. 10 Shift lock ECU inspection. RAV4

Shift position	Tester condition to terminal number	Specified value
P position (Release button is not pushed)	P – P 1	Continuity
P position (Release button is pushed)	P – P 1 P – P 2	Continuity
R, N, D, 2, L position	P – P 2	Continuity

TY5029601055000X

Fig. 13 Shift lock control switch inspection

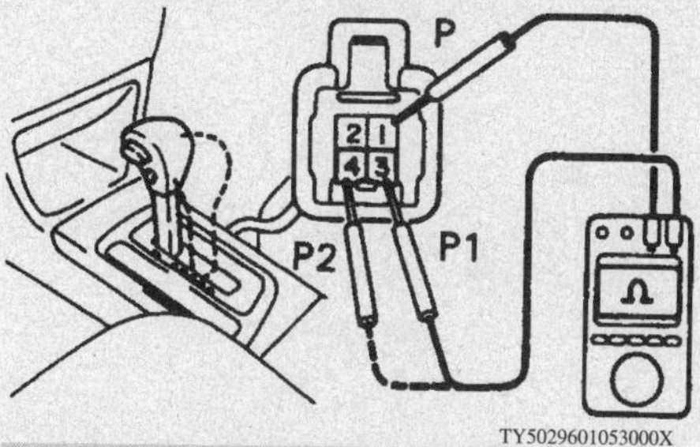
P
2 1
4 3
P2
P1
Ω

TY5029601053000X

Fig. 11 Shift lock control switch connector. Avalon

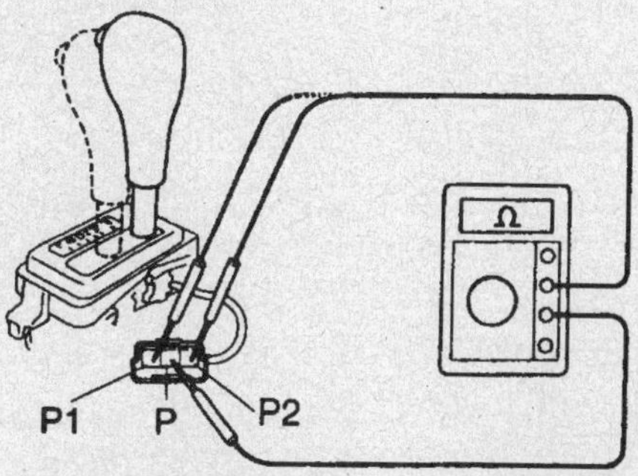
Ω
P1
P
P2

TY5029601054000X

Fig. 12 Shift lock control switch connector. Camry & RAV4

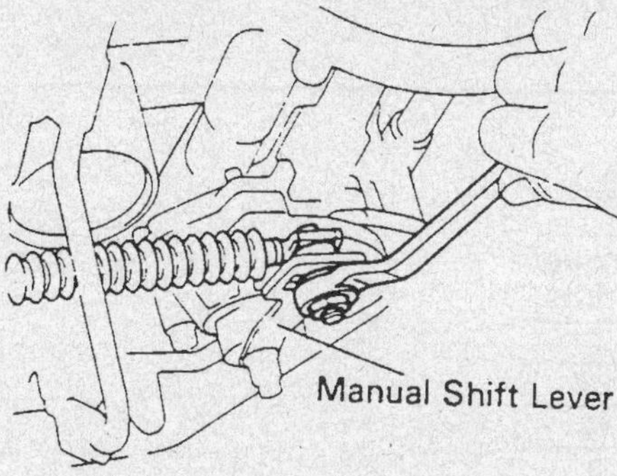
Manual Shift Lever

TY5029100803000X

Fig. 14 Manual shift lever adjustment

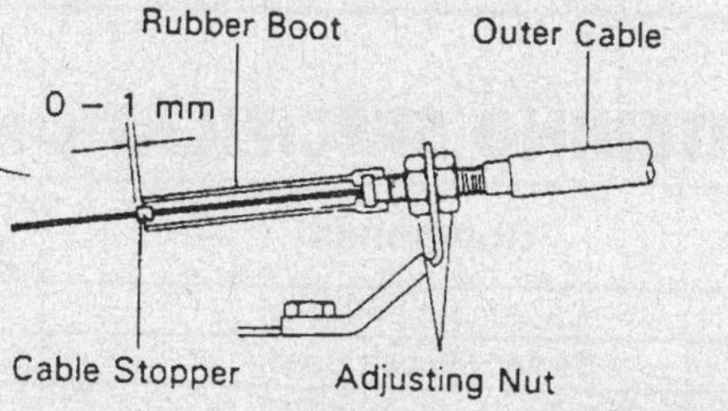
Rubber Boot
Outer Cable
0 – 1 mm
Cable Stopper
Adjusting Nut

TY5029100804000X

Fig. 15 Throttle cable adjustment

11. Remove three upper transaxle to engine bolts.
12. Install engine support fixture and tie steering gear housing to support fixture by suitable cord, or equivalent.
13. Raise and support vehicle then remove left front wheel.
14. Remove exhaust pipe.
15. Remove differential fluid drain plug and drain fluid into suitable container.
16. Remove engine side covers and front engine cover.
17. Remove driveshaft.
18. Remove front and rear side engine mounting bolts then left side transaxle mounting bolts.
19. Remove four bolts and disconnect stabilizer bar bush bracket from front frame assembly then steering gear housing bolts and steering gear housing.
20. Remove front frame assembly.
21. Hold transaxle with a jack and remove rear end plate.
22. Remove torque converter clutch mounting bolts.
23. Remove engine to transaxle bolts.
24. Remove transaxle assembly and torque converter clutch.
25. Reverse procedure to install, noting that **on models with coded audio anti-theft systems,** rearm as outlined under "Precautions."

RAV4

1. Remove transaxle with engine as described in engine section of "Toyota RAV4" chapter.
2. Remove starter, **Fig. 18.**
3. Remove stiffener plate.
4. Remove rear end plate.
5. Remove torque converter clutch mounting bolts. Turn crankshaft to gain access to bolts.
6. Disconnect transaxle wire harness connectors.
7. Remove CTR stiffener plate.
8. Remove transaxle with transfer assembly.
9. Remove five transaxle mounting bolts and separate transaxle assembly.
10. Reverse procedure to install. Tighten to specifications.

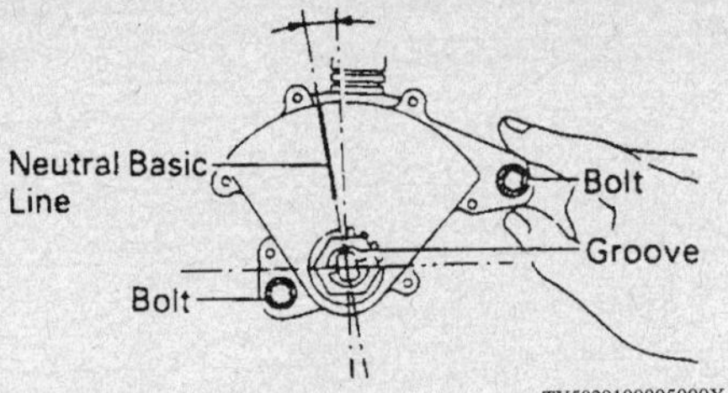
Neutral Basic Line
Bolt
Groove
Bolt

TY5029100805000X

Fig. 16 Neutral start switch adjustment

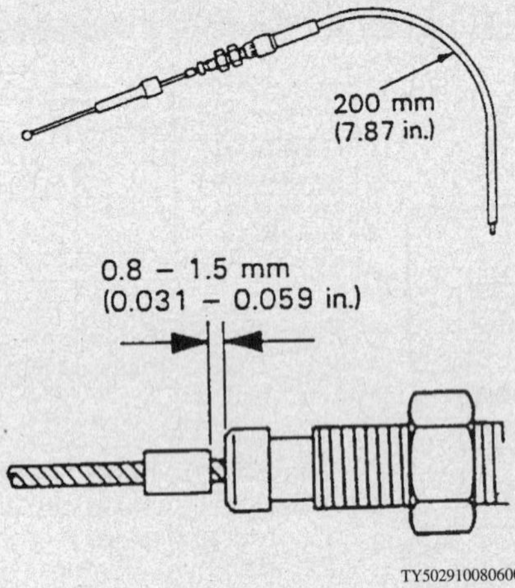
200 mm
(7.87 in.)
0.8 – 1.5 mm
(0.031 – 0.059 in.)

TY5029100806000X

Fig. 17 Throttle cable replacement

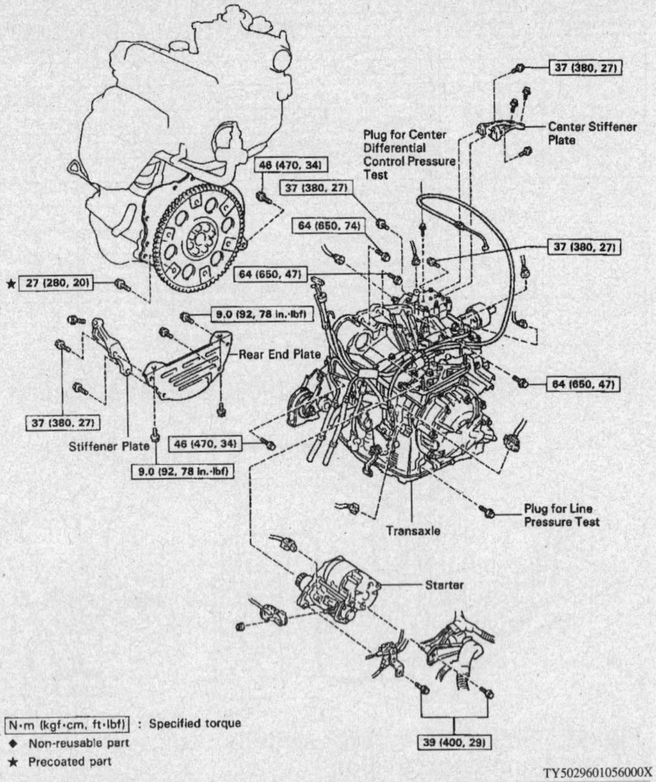
37 (380, 27)
Center Stiffener Plate
Plug for Center Differential Control Pressure Test
46 (470, 34)
37 (380, 27)
64 (650, 74)
37 (380, 27)
64 (650, 47)
★ 27 (280, 20)
9.0 (92, 78 in.·lbf)
Rear End Plate
64 (650, 47)
37 (380, 27)
Stiffener Plate
46 (470, 34)
9.0 (92, 78 in.·lbf)
Plug for Line Pressure Test
Transaxle
Starter
N·m (kgf·cm, ft·lbf) : Specified torque
◆ Non-reusable part
★ Precoated part
39 (400, 29)

TY5029601056000X

Fig. 18 Transaxle replacement. RAV4 w/A540H

TIGHTENING SPECIFICATIONS

Year	Component	Torque/ Ft. Lbs.
1993–96	Apply Tube Bracket	7
	Center Support Bearing	27
	Center Support Bolt	18
	Detent Spring	8
	Driveplate	61
	Engine Front Mounting Bolts	57
	Engine Mounting LH Stay	15
	Front Exhaust Pipe	46
	Front Frame (12 mm Bolt)	24
	Front Frame (19 mm Bolt)	134
	Front Frame (Nut)	27
	LH Transaxle Mount	38
	Manual Valve Body To Transaxle	8
	Neutral Start Switch (Bolt)	48①
	Neutral Start Switch Nut	61①
	Oil Cooler Pipe Union	20
	Oil Pan To Transaxle	43①
	Oil Strainer To Valve Body	8
	Oil Tube Retainers	8
	Propeller Shaft To Transfer Case	54
	Rear End Plate	27
	Rear Exhaust Pipe	32
	Rear Side Mount	48
	Starter	29
	Steering Gear Housing To Frame	134

Continued

TIGHTENING SPECIFICATIONS—Continued

Year	Component	Torque/ Ft. Lbs.
1993–96	Test Plug	65①
	Throttle Cable	11
	Torque Converter To Driveplate	20
	Transaxle Rear Cover To Case	27
	Transaxle To Engine (12 mm)	34
	Transaxle To Engine (14 mm)	47
	Valve Body To Transaxle	8

① — Inch pounds.

Front Wheel Drive Axles

NOTE: On Camry & Celica Models Equipped With The All Wheel Drive System, Refer To "All Wheel Drive System" For Service Procedures Not Found In This Section.

INDEX

Page No.

Description 48-309
Avalon, Camry & Celica......... 48-309
Corolla, Paseo & Tercel......... 48-309
Land Cruiser.................... 48-309
Pickup, Tacoma & T100 w/4WD, Previa w/AWD & 4Runner 48-309
RAV4.......................... 48-309
Driveshaft, Replace.............. 48-309
Avalon, Camry & Celica......... 48-309
Corolla, Paseo & Tercel......... 48-310
Land Cruiser.................... 48-310
Pickup, Tacoma, T100 w/4WD, Previa w/AWD & 1993–95 4Runner 48-311
RAV4.......................... 48-312
1996 4Runner 48-312
Driveshaft Service 48-312
Avalon, Camry & Celica......... 48-312
Corolla, Paseo & Tercel......... 48-313
Land Cruiser.................... 48-314
Pickup, Tacoma, T100 w/4WD, Previa w/AWD & 1993–95 4Runner 48-315
RAV4.......................... 48-314
1996 4Runner 48-315
Intermediate Shaft Service....... 48-317
Avalon & Camry w/V6 Engine... 48-317
Camry w/4 Cylinder Engine & Corolla....................... 48-317
Tightening Specifications 48-317

DESCRIPTION

AVALON, CAMRY & CELICA

These models use an intermediate (center) shaft to allow the use of equal length driveshafts. This shaft is supported at one end in the transaxle and the other end by a bearing and bearing carrier secured to the engine **Figs. 1 through 3.**

Two types of inner joint are used on these model. A tripod type and a constant velocity type.

COROLLA, PASEO & TERCEL

These models use unequal length driveshaft that connect directly to the output of the transaxle **Figs. 4 through 5.**

LAND CRUISER

This model uses a solid type front axle which incorporates axle shafts, joints and differential within a solid housing **Fig. 6.**

PICKUP, TACOMA & T100 W/4WD, PREVIA W/AWD & 4RUNNER

These models use equal length driveshafts connected to a center differential unit. This unit incorporates a side gear shaft and extension housing to compensate for differential offset, **Figs. 7 and 8.**

RAV4

These models use equal length driveshafts connected to a center differential unit, **Figs. 9 and 10.** The front driveshaft of the 2WD manual transaxle model uses the double offset type constant velocity joints (CVJs) on the differential side and Rzeppa type CVJs on the wheel side. The front driveshaft of the 4WD and 2WD automatic transaxle models use the tripod type CVJs on the differential side and Rzeppa type CVJs on the wheel side.

DRIVESHAFT

REPLACE

AVALON, CAMRY & CELICA

1. Raise and support vehicle, then remove front wheels as necessary and front fender apron seal.
2. Remove cotter pin, locknut cap and locknut from axle spline **Figs. 1 through 3.**
3. Drain transmission fluid, then using a suitable puller, disconnect tie rod end from steering knuckle.
4. Disconnect stabilizer bar link from lower control arm.
5. Disconnect ball joint from steering knuckle.
6. **On models with constant velocity type inner joints,** using paint or chalk, place match marks on driveshaft inner joint and side gear shaft or center driveshaft, then proceed as follows:
   a. Have an assistant apply brakes to prevent axle from turning.
   b. Use a suitable drive socket to loosen, **but do not remove,** six hexagon bolts connecting inner joint to side gear shaft or center drive shaft.
7. **On all models,** remove outer joint from hub by using a plastic hammer to gently tap drive shaft spline to separate joint from axle hub.
8. Push front axle hub toward outside of vehicle to remove shaft from hub. **Use a suitable hanger or jack stand to support shaft, do not allow shaft to hang from inner joint.**
9. To separate LH driveshaft from transmission, gently pry shaft out of transaxle with suitable tool, then remove snap ring from splined end of side gear shaft.
10. To separate RH driveshaft from transmission proceed as follows:
    a. **On Celica models,** remove two bolts and retainer holding center bearing into support.

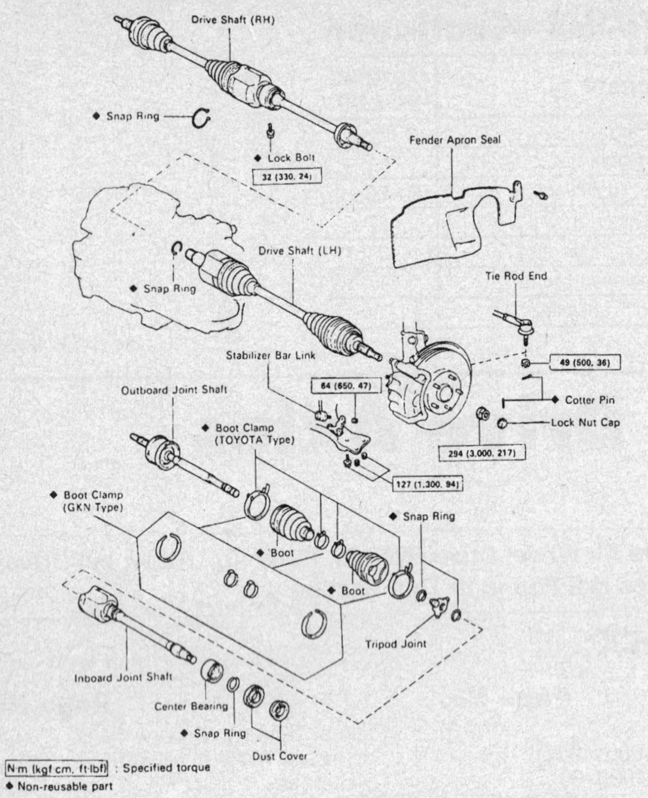
Drive Shaft (RH)
◆ Snap Ring
◆ Lock Bolt
32 (330, 24)
Fender Apron Seal
Drive Shaft (LH)
◆ Snap Ring
Tie Rod End
Stabilizer Bar Link
64 (650, 47)
49 (500, 36)
Outboard Joint Shaft
◆ Boot Clamp (TOYOTA Type)
◆ Cotter Pin
Lock Nut Cap
294 (3,000, 217)
127 (1,300, 94)
◆ Boot Clamp (GKN Type)
◆ Snap Ring
◆ Boot
◆ Boot
Tripod Joint
Inboard Joint Shaft
Center Bearing
◆ Snap Ring
Dust Cover
N·m (kgf·cm, ft·lbf) : Specified torque
◆ Non-reusable part
TY3039200024000X

Fig. 1 Exploded View of driveshaft & related components. Camry w/4 cylinder engine

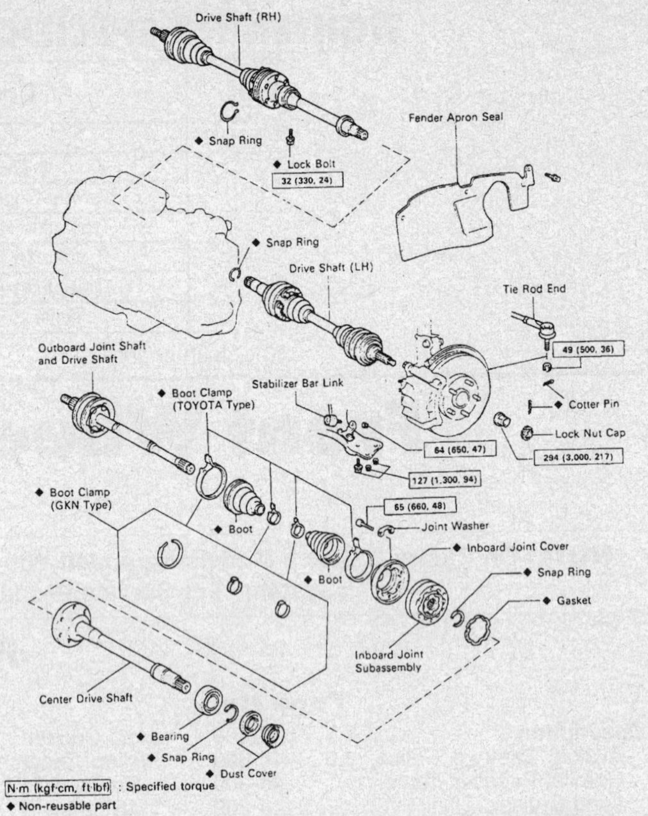
Drive Shaft (RH)
Fender Apron Seal
◆ Snap Ring
◆ Lock Bolt
32 (330, 24)
◆ Snap Ring
Drive Shaft (LH)
Tie Rod End
Outboard Joint Shaft and Drive Shaft
49 (500, 36)
◆ Boot Clamp (TOYOTA Type)
Stabilizer Bar Link
◆ Cotter Pin
Lock Nut Cap
64 (650, 47)
294 (3,000, 217)
127 (1,300, 94)
◆ Boot Clamp (GKN Type)
65 (660, 48)
◆ Boot
Joint Washer
◆ Inboard Joint Cover
◆ Boot
◆ Snap Ring
◆ Gasket
Inboard Joint Subassembly
Center Drive Shaft
◆ Bearing
◆ Snap Ring
◆ Dust Cover
N·m (kgf·cm, ft·lbf) : Specified torque
◆ Non-reusable part
TY3039200021000X

Fig. 2 Exploded View of driveshaft & related components. Avalon & Camry w/V6 engine

b. **Except Celica models,** remove center drive shaft support bearing lock bolt and snap ring.
c. Using a suitable pry bar and/or soft face hammer pry and/or tap center drive shaft with support bearing from transaxle and support bearing housing
d. Using suitable pliers, remove snap ring from splined end of center driveshaft.

11. Reverse procedure to install, noting the following:
    a. Always use new snap ring on splined end of shaft inserted into transaxle.
    b. Ensure positive engagement of snap ring into transaxle.
    c. Tighten fasteners to specifications.
    d. Fill transaxle to correct level using a suitable fluid.

COROLLA, PASEO & TERCEL

1. Raise and support vehicle, then remove wheels and engine undercover.
2. Drain transmission fluid, then remove cotter pin and lock cap. While applying brakes, remove axle spline nut **Figs. 4 through 5.**
3. Disconnect tie rod end from steering knuckle, then lower ball joint from lower control arm.
4. Remove brake disc if necessary, then using suitable puller, remove driveshaft outer joint from axle hub.
5. To remove driveshafts from transaxle, gently tap with hammer and brass drift to release shaft, or use a suitable pry bar to lever shaft from transaxle, then remove snap ring from transaxle end of shaft.
6. Reverse procedure to install, noting the following:
    a. Always use new snap ring on splined end of shaft inserted into transaxle.
    b. Ensure positive engagement of snap ring into transaxle.
    c. Tighten fasteners to specifications.
    d. Fill transaxle to correct level using a suitable fluid.

LAND CRUISER

REPLACEMENT

1. Raise and support vehicle, then remove tire and wheel assembly.
2. Remove axle hub.
3. Remove dust seal and gasket, then the dust cover, **Fig. 6.**
4. Remove knuckle spindle and gasket, then position flattened part of outer axle shaft upward and remove axle shaft.
5. Remove oil seal retainer, then disconnect drag link from knuckle arm.
6. Disconnect tie rod from knuckle arm, then remove knuckle arm and shim using a suitable brass brand hammer to tap cone washers loose.
7. Remove bearing cap and shim using pusher tool No. 09606-60020, or equivalent. Identify upper and lower bearings and shims for reference during assembly. **If original axle shaft is being reused, original shims may be used. If new axle shaft is to be installed, new shims must be used. Refer to "Adjustments" to determine shim thickness.**

ADJUSTMENT

Whenever axle housing or steering knuckle is replaced, the steering knuckle alignment and knuckle bearing preload should be adjusted using a suitable alignment and preload measurement tool set.

Axle Shaft Alignment

1. Assemble a suitable axle alignment tool using tool manufactures instructions to knuckle and axle housing.
2. Thickness of steering knuckle lower bearing shim will be distance between two scribe marks less .12 inch (3 mm).
3. Thickness of steering knuckle upper bearing shim will be difference between shim selected in step 4 and shim selected in step 6 under "Bearing Preload." Adjusting shims are available in .004 inch (.1 mm), .008 inch (.2 mm), .02 inch (.5 mm) and .04 inch (1 mm) thicknesses.

Bearing Preload

1. Using puller tool No. 09308-00010, or equivalent, remove oil seal.
2. Lubricate bearing with suitable grease, then install bearing and a suitable preload measurement tool into axle housing.

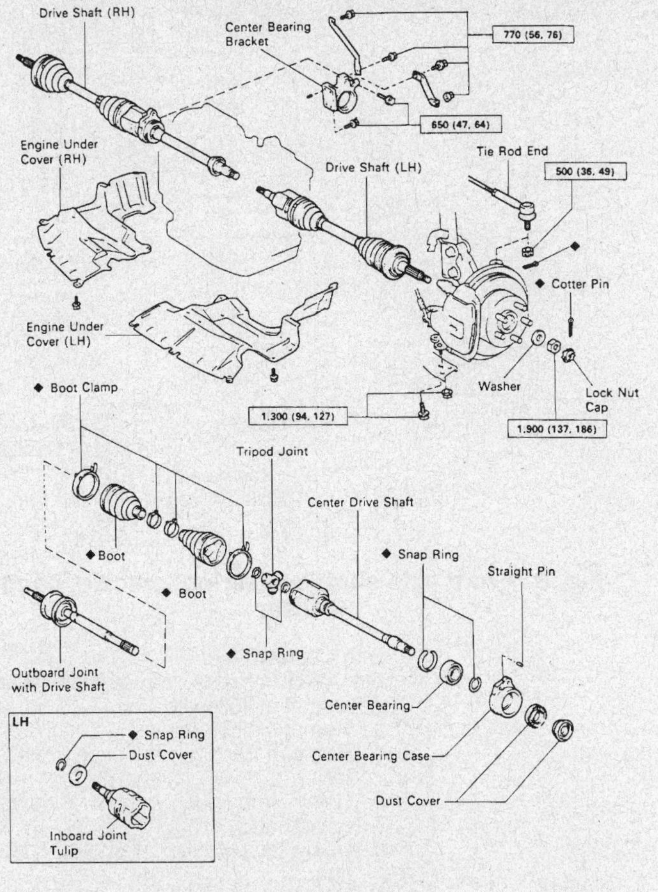
Drive Shaft (RH)
Center Bearing Bracket
770 (56, 76)
650 (47, 64)
Engine Under Cover (RH)
Drive Shaft (LH)
Tie Rod End
500 (36, 49)
◆ Cotter Pin
Engine Under Cover (LH)
Washer
Lock Nut Cap
1,300 (94, 127)
1,900 (137, 186)
◆ Boot Clamp
Tripod Joint
Center Drive Shaft
◆ Boot
◆ Snap Ring
Straight Pin
◆ Boot
◆ Snap Ring
Outboard Joint with Drive Shaft
Center Bearing
LH
◆ Snap Ring
Dust Cover
Center Bearing Case
Dust Cover
Inboard Joint Tulip
TY3039100032000X

Fig. 3 Exploded View of driveshaft & related components. Celica w/5S-FE engine

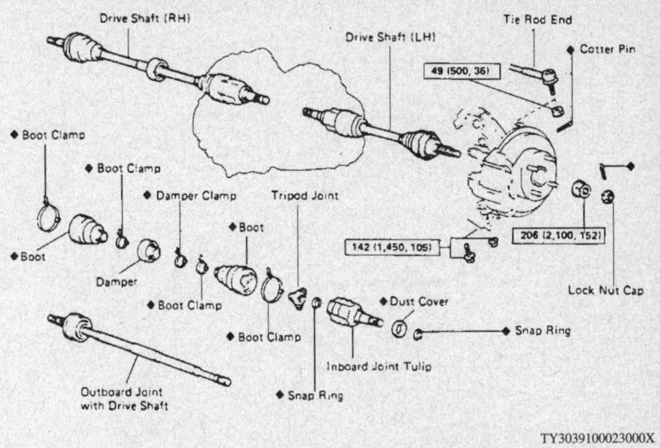
Drive Shaft (RH)
Tie Rod End
Drive Shaft (LH)
◆ Cotter Pin
49 (500, 36)
◆ Boot Clamp
◆ Boot Clamp
◆ Damper Clamp
Tripod Joint
◆ Boot
◆ Boot
142 (1,450, 105)
206 (2,100, 152)
Damper
Lock Nut Cap
◆ Boot Clamp
◆ Dust Cover
◆ Snap Ring
◆ Boot Clamp
Inboard Joint Tulip
Outboard Joint with Drive Shaft
◆ Snap Ring
TY3039100023000X

Fig. 4 Exploded view of driveshaft & related components. Corolla

3. Install a suitable spring scale and measure bearing preload.
4. Bearing preload should be 5.6–9.9 lbs. Tighten nut at top of suitable preload measurement tool until specified bearing preload is obtained.
5. Measure distance A as shown in **Fig. 11,** then measure distance B as shown in **Fig. 12.**
6. Subtract measurement A from measurement B to obtain total adjusting shim thickness required to maintain correct bearing preload.

PICKUP, TACOMA, T100 W/4WD, PREVIA W/AWD & 1993-95 4RUNNER

Removal

1. Raise and support vehicle, then remove tire and wheel assembly.
2. Depress brake pedal, then loosen six front driveshaft attaching nuts, **Fig. 7.**
3. Remove manual locking hub as follows:
   a. Place control handle to "Free" position.
   b. Remove cover attaching bolts, then the cover.
   c. Remove axle bolt with washer, then the hub body attaching nuts and washers.
   d. Remove cone washer by tapping on heads of bolts using a hammer and suitable drift.
   e. Remove manual locking hub body.
4. Remove automatic locking hub as follows:
   a. Remove hub cover.
   b. Remove axle bolt, then the washer.
   c. Remove hub body attaching nuts.
   d. Remove cone washer by tapping on heads of bolts, using a hammer and suitable drift.
   e. Remove automatic locking hub body.
5. **On models less locking hubs,** remove hub as follows:
   a. Remove grease cap from hub flange.
   b. Remove hub bolt and washer, then hub flange attaching nuts.
   c. Tap hub flange attaching studs with brass drift and hammer to remove cone washers.
   d. Install two bolts into hub flange opposite from each other, then tighten evenly to remove hub flange.
6. **On all models,** remove driveshaft snap ring, then the spacer.
7. Pull front shaft from side gear shaft, then pull from steering knuckle.

Installation

1. Apply molybdenum disulphide lithium base grease to outboard joint shaft, then insert it into steering knuckle and side gear shaft. Install 6 retaining nuts, **Fig. 7.**
2. Install spacer and snap ring to outboard joint shaft.
3. Install free wheeling hub as follows:
   a. Place new gasket on front axle hub.
   b. Install hub body with 6 cone washers and nuts, then **torque** attaching nuts to 23 ft. lbs.
   c. Install hub bolt with washer, then **torque** to 13 ft. lbs.
   d. Apply a suitable grease to inner hub splines, then place control handle in "Free" position.
   e. Install new gasket on cover, then install cover on body with follower pawl tabs aligned with non-toothed portions of body.
   f. Install cover attaching bolts and **torque** to 7 ft. lbs.
4. Install automatic locking hub as follows:
   a. Position new gasket on axle hub, then apply suitable multipurpose grease to automatic locking hub splines.
   b. Align spring ends of brake assembly in hub with hub flange alignment pins.
   c. Ensure locking hub outer cam stopper is securely in inner cam groove, then position inner cam protrusion so it is centered between outer cam protrusions and aligned with hub alignment pin holes.
   d. Install locking hub to axle hub ensuring inner cam protrusion is set between ends of hub brake spring.
   e. Install 6 cone washers and nuts and **torque** nuts to 23 ft. lbs. **If hub does not fit perfectly on axle hub, remove and reinstall.**
   f. Install axle bolt with washer, then **torque** to 13 ft. lbs.
   g. Install cover, then insert attaching bolts and **torque** to 7 ft. lbs.
5. **On models less locking hubs,** install hubs as follows:
   a. Position new gasket on axle hub, then install hub flange on axle.
   b. Install cone washers and attaching nuts. **Torque** attaching nuts to 23 ft. lbs.

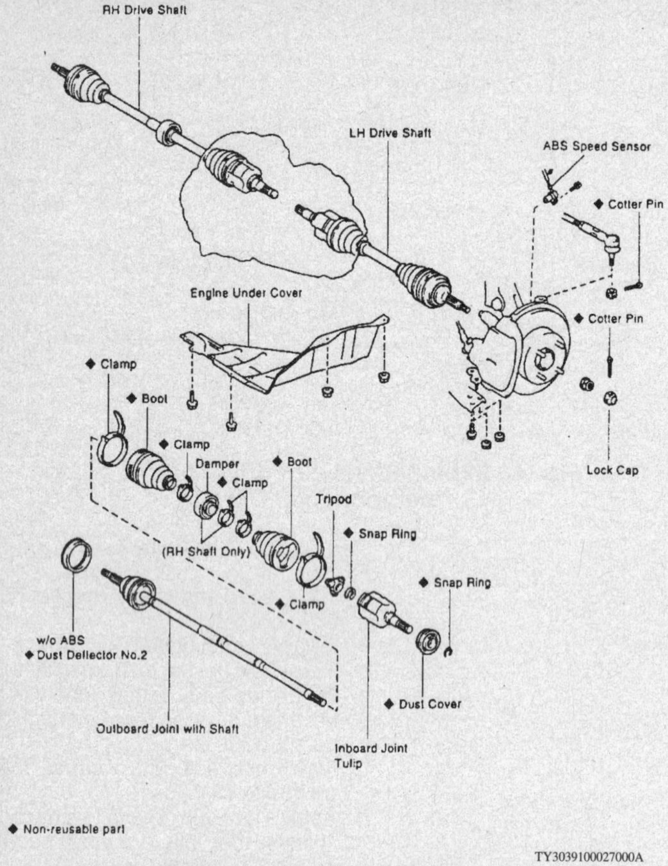
RH Drive Shaft
LH Drive Shaft
ABS Speed Sensor
◆ Cotter Pin
Engine Under Cover
◆ Cotter Pin
◆ Clamp
◆ Boot
◆ Clamp
Damper
◆ Boot
◆ Clamp
Lock Cap
Tripod
◆ Snap Ring
(RH Shaft Only)
◆ Snap Ring
◆ Clamp
w/o ABS
◆ Dust Deflector No.2
◆ Dust Cover
Outboard Joint with Shaft
Inboard Joint Tulip
◆ Non-reusable part
TY3039100027000A

Fig. 5 Exploded view of driveshaft & related components. Paseo & Tercel

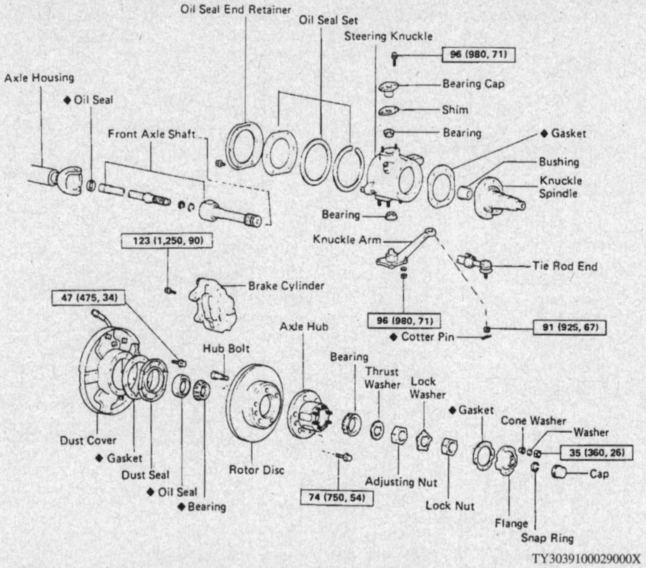
Oil Seal End Retainer
Oil Seal Set
Steering Knuckle
96 (980, 71)
Bearing Cap
Shim
Bearing
◆ Gasket
Axle Housing
◆ Oil Seal
Front Axle Shaft
Bushing
Knuckle Spindle
Bearing
Knuckle Arm
123 (1,250, 90)
Tie Rod End
Brake Cylinder
47 (475, 34)
Axle Hub
96 (980, 71)
◆ Cotter Pin
91 (925, 67)
Hub Bolt
Bearing
Thrust Washer
Lock Washer
◆ Gasket
Cone Washer
Washer
35 (360, 26)
Cap
Dust Cover
◆ Gasket
Dust Seal
◆ Oil Seal
◆ Bearing
Rotor Disc
Adjusting Nut
74 (750, 54)
Lock Nut
Flange
Snap Ring
TY3039100029000X

Fig. 6 Front axle shaft & steering knuckle. Land Cruiser

c. Install washer and bolt in driveshaft. **Torque** to 13 ft. lbs.
d. Install grease cap on hub flange.

6. **On all models,** while an assistant depresses brake pedal, **Torque** side gear shaft to driveshaft attaching nuts to 61 ft. lbs.

1996 4RUNNER

1. Raise and support vehicle, then remove front wheel.
2. Drain differential oil.
3. Using a screwdriver, remove grease cap, **Fig. 8.**
4. Remove driveshaft locknut cotter pin, lock cap and locknut.
5. Disconnect driveshaft using brass bar and hammer. If driveshaft is difficult to remove, tap screwdriver between differential tube/carrier and driveshaft.
6. Remove lower suspension arm cotter pin and nut.
7. Using tool No. 09628-62011, or equivalent, disconnect lower suspension arm.
8. Push steering knuckle outward and remove driveshaft.
9. Remove snap ring from inboard shaft.
10. Reverse procedure to install.

RAV4

1. Raise and support vehicle, then remove front wheel.
2. Remove engine under cover.
3. Drain gear oil.
4. **On models with ABS,** remove ABS speed sensor.
5. **On all models,** remove cotter pin, lock cap and driveshaft locknut.
6. Disconnect tie rod end from steering knuckle.
7. Disconnect stabilizer bar link from lower suspension arm.
8. Disconnect lower ball joint from lower suspension arm.
9. Disconnect driveshaft from axle hub.
10. **On 2WD models with manual transaxle,** remove RH driveshaft as follows:
    a. Using a screwdriver and hammer, remove snap ring from center bearing bracket.
    b. Remove bolt from center bearing bracket.
    c. Remove driveshaft with center driveshaft.
    d. Remove center bearing bracket.
11. **On 2WD models with automatic transaxle,** remove RH driveshaft as follows:
    a. Remove two center bearing bracket bolts and pull out driveshaft together with center bearing case and center driveshaft.
    b. Remove three bolts and the center bearing bracket.
12. **On all 2WD models,** remove LH side driveshaft using brass bar and hammer, then pry off snap ring with a screwdriver.
13. **On 4WD models,** remove RH side driveshaft using brass bar and hammer, then pry off snap ring and O-ring with a screwdriver.
14. **On 4WD models,** remove LH side driveshaft as follows:
    a. Remove air cleaner.
    b. Remove transmission case protector.
    c. Using hub nut wrench, remove driveshaft.
    d. Using screwdriver, remove snap ring.
15. **On all models,** reverse procedure to install, noting the following:
    a. After installation, ensure there is .08–.12 inch of play in axial direction.
    b. **Torque** driveshaft locknut to 159 ft. lbs.
    c. **Torque** ABS speed sensor bolt to 69 inch lbs.

DRIVESHAFT SERVICE

AVALON, CAMRY & CELICA

DISASSEMBLE

1. Check driveshaft for excessive wear and/or damage.
2. For righthand driveshaft, proceed as follows:
    a. **On driveshafts with constant velocity type joints,** remove bolts and disconnect center driveshaft, then remove boot clamps and pull back boot **Figs. 1 through 3.**
    b. **On driveshafts with constant velocity type joints,** pry off inboard joint cover, using suitable tools.
    c. **On driveshafts with tripod type joints,**remove boot clamps, pull back boot then, disconnect center driveshaft.
3. For lefthand driveshaft, proceed as follows:
    a. **On driveshafts with constant velocity type joints,** remove boot clamps and pull back boot.
    b. **On driveshafts with constant velocity type joints,** pry off inboard joint cover, using suitable tools.

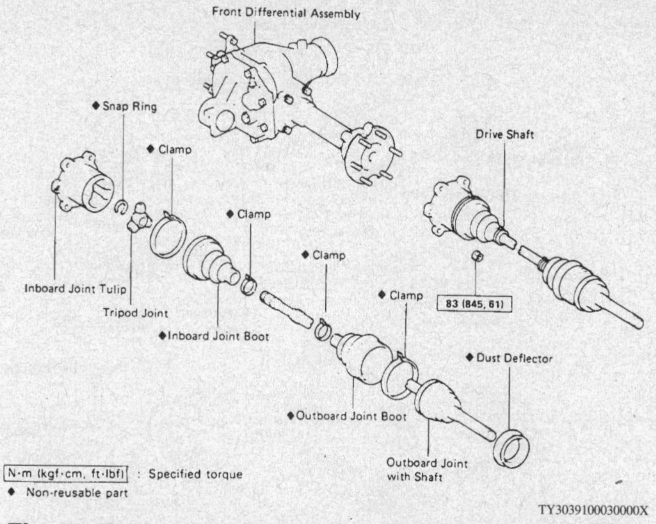

Front Differential Assembly
◆ Snap Ring
◆ Clamp
◆ Clamp
Drive Shaft
◆ Clamp
◆ Clamp
83 (845, 61)
Inboard Joint Tulip
Tripod Joint
◆ Inboard Joint Boot
◆ Dust Deflector
◆ Outboard Joint Boot
Outboard Joint with Shaft
N·m (kgf·cm, ft·lbf) : Specified torque
◆ Non-reusable part
TY3039100030000X

Fig. 7 Exploded view of front driveshaft assembly. Pickup, Tacoma & T100 w4WD, Previa w/AWD & 1993–95 4Runner

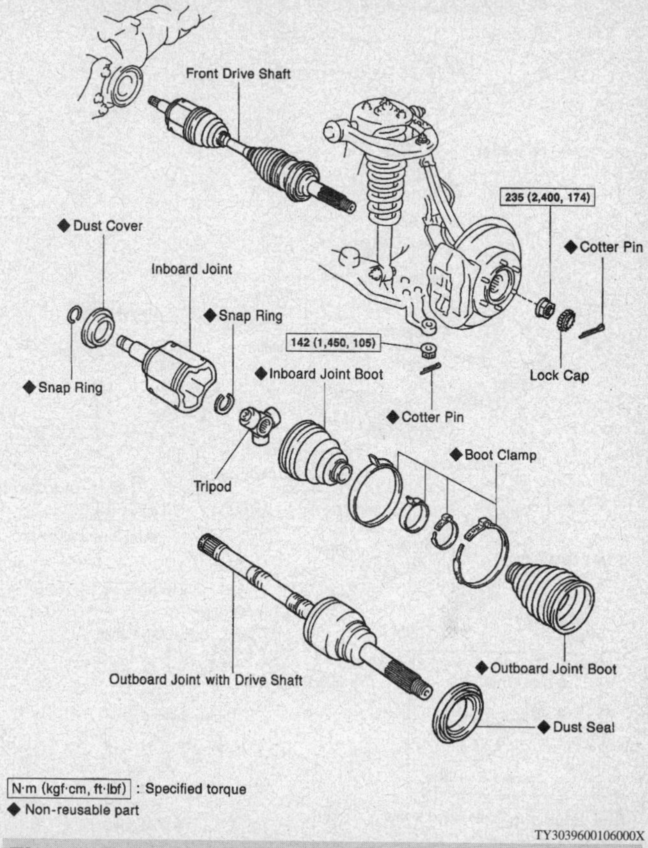

Front Drive Shaft
235 (2,400, 174)
◆ Dust Cover
◆ Cotter Pin
Inboard Joint
◆ Snap Ring
142 (1,450, 105)
◆ Inboard Joint Boot
Lock Cap
◆ Snap Ring
◆ Cotter Pin
◆ Boot Clamp
Tripod
◆ Outboard Joint Boot
Outboard Joint with Drive Shaft
◆ Dust Seal
N·m (kgf·cm, ft·lbf) : Specified torque
◆ Non-reusable part
TY3039600106000X

Fig. 8 Exploded view of front driveshaft assembly. 1996 4Runner

c. **On driveshafts with tripod type joints,**remove boot clamps, then pull back boot and remove outer housing.

4. **On all driveshafts,** place matchmarks on the shaft and inboard joint inner race.
5. Using suitable pliers, remove snap ring retaining inboard joint.
6. Using suitable press tools and press, remove inboard joint from driveshaft. **Mark position of chamfers on joints for later assembly.**
7. Remove any remaining inboard joint clips or washers.
8. Remove both boots by sliding off inboard end of shaft.
9. Outboard joints are serviced with shaft. **Do not remove outboard joints from shaft.**

ASSEMBLE

1. Install outboard joint boot and new boot clamps.
2. Using a suitable grease, pack boot and joint then assemble boot to outboard joint. **Do not tighten clamps at this time.**
3. Install new boot clamps and inboard joint boot.
4. **On driveshafts with constant velocity type joints,** assemble a new inboard joint cover to inboard joint. Align bolt holes of cover with those of the inboard joint, then insert attaching bolts. Using a suitable hammer, tap rim of the inboard joint cover into place.
5. Temporarily install the attaching nuts, bolts and washers to keep the inboard joint together during installation of joint to shaft. Tighten bolts hand tight.
6. **On all driveshafts,** install any required snap rings and washers, then assemble the inboard joint to shaft as follows:
   a. Align marks made during disassembly, then using a brass bar and hammer, tap inboard joint into the driveshaft. Ensure brass bar is contacting the inner race and not the bearing cage.
   b. Install inboard joint retaining snap ring, then using a suitable grease pack inboard joint and boot.
7. **On driveshafts with tripod type joints,** install outer housing to joint, then install boot.**Do not tighten clamps at this time.**
8. **On driveshafts with constant velocity type joints,** install boot to inboard joint cover.**Do not tighten clamps at this time.**
9. **On all driveshafts,** ensure the boots are properly located when installing. **On righthand driveshafts with constant velocity type joints,** install center driveshaft. Ensure the boot is not stretched or contracted when the driveshaft is at standard length.**Figs. 13 through 15**
10. Bend back boot band and lock it.
11. Check driveshaft for smooth operation. Ensure there is no play in the inboard joint and outboard joint. Ensure the inboard joint slides smoothly in the thrust direction.

COROLLA, PASEO & TERCEL

DISASSEMBLE

Before disassembling driveshaft, ensure there is no play in the inboard or outboard joints and that the inboard joint slides smoothly in the thrust direction.

1. Remove boot clamps, **Figs. 4 and 5.**
2. Place matchmarks on inboard joint. **Do not use a sharp tool to place matchmarks on inboard joint.**
3. Remove inboard joint from driveshaft.
4. Using snap ring pliers, remove snap ring.
5. Using a suitable punch and hammer, place matchmarks on driveshaft and tripod joint.
6. Using suitable press tools, press tripod joint from driveshaft.
7. Remove boots for inboard and outboard joints from shaft.
8. **Do not disassemble outboard joint, it is serviced as an assembly with the shaft.**

ASSEMBLE

Before installing boot, wrap vinyl tape around driveshaft splines.

1. Install outboard joint boot and new boot clamp onto shaft.
2. **On right side driveshaft** install damper assembly.
3. **On all shafts** install inboard joint boot and new boot clamp onto shaft. **The boot and clamp for the inboard joint are larger than those of the outboard joint.**
4. Assemble tripod joint as follows:
   a. Face the beveled side of tripod axial spline toward the outboard joint.
   b. Align matchmarks placed during disassembly.

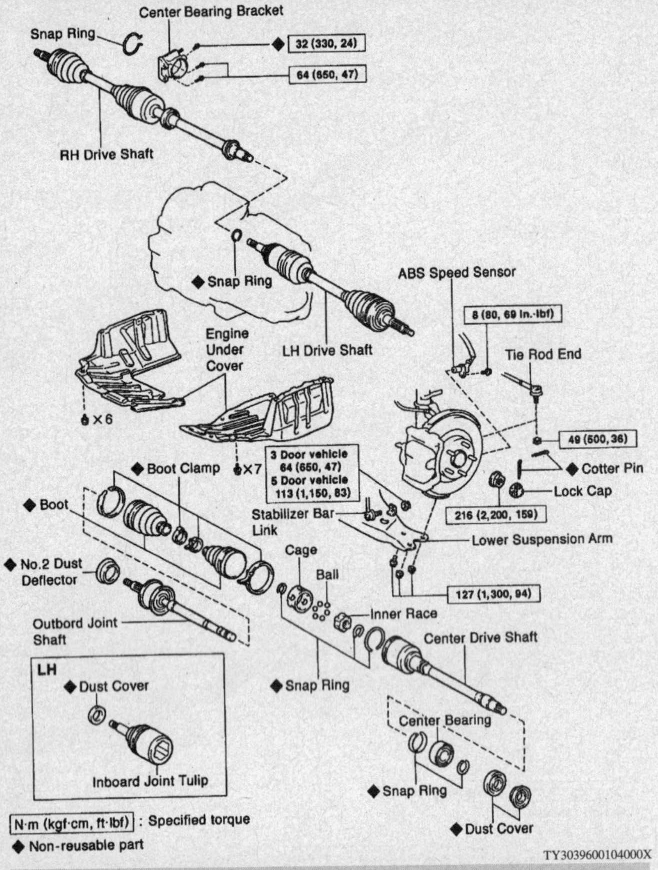

Center Bearing Bracket
Snap Ring
32 (330, 24)
64 (650, 47)
RH Drive Shaft
◆ Snap Ring
ABS Speed Sensor
Engine Under Cover
LH Drive Shaft
8 (80, 69 in.-lbf)
Tie Rod End
×6
◆ Boot Clamp
×7
3 Door vehicle 64 (650, 47) 5 Door vehicle 113 (1,150, 83)
49 (500, 36)
◆ Cotter Pin
Lock Cap
216 (2,200, 159)
◆ Boot
Stabilizer Bar Link
Lower Suspension Arm
Cage
Ball
◆ No.2 Dust Deflector
127 (1,300, 94)
Inner Race
Outbord Joint Shaft
Center Drive Shaft
LH
◆ Dust Cover
◆ Snap Ring
Center Bearing
Inboard Joint Tulip
◆ Snap Ring
◆ Dust Cover
N·m (kgf·cm, ft·lbf) : Specified torque
◆ Non-reusable part
TY3039600104000X

Fig. 9 Exploded view of front driveshaft assembly. RAV4 w/2WD manual transaxle

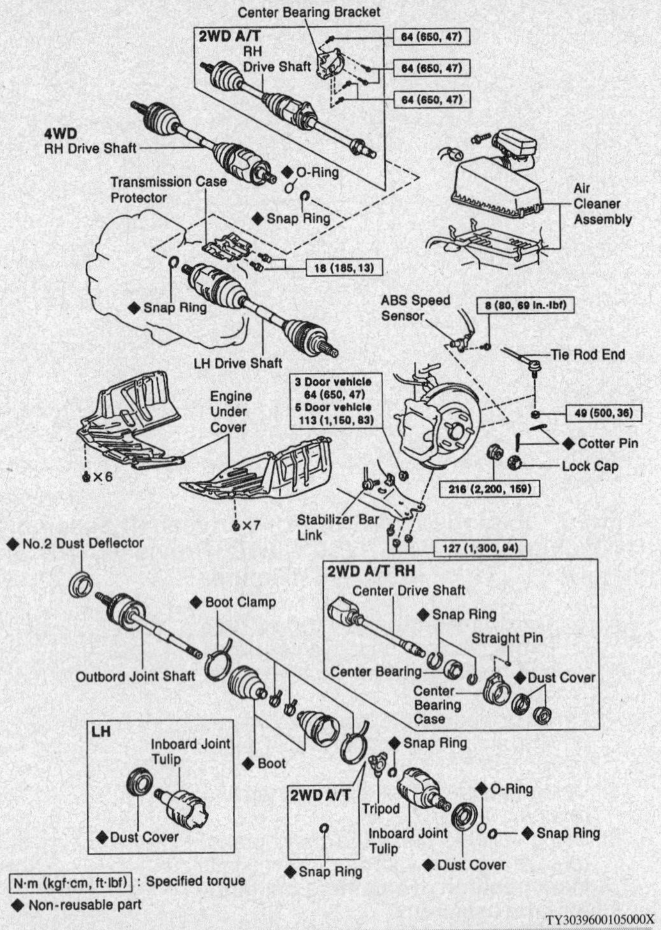

Center Bearing Bracket
2WD A/T
RH Drive Shaft
64 (650, 47)
64 (650, 47)
64 (650, 47)
4WD RH Drive Shaft
◆ O-Ring
Transmission Case Protector
◆ Snap Ring
Air Cleaner Assembly
18 (185, 13)
◆ Snap Ring
ABS Speed Sensor
8 (80, 69 in.-lbf)
Tie Rod End
LH Drive Shaft
Engine Under Cover
3 Door vehicle 64 (650, 47) 5 Door vehicle 113 (1,150, 83)
49 (500, 36)
◆ Cotter Pin
Lock Cap
×6
216 (2,200, 159)
◆ No.2 Dust Deflector
×7
Stabilizer Bar Link
127 (1,300, 94)
2WD A/T RH
Center Drive Shaft
◆ Boot Clamp
◆ Snap Ring
Straight Pin
Outbord Joint Shaft
Center Bearing
◆ Dust Cover
Center Bearing Case
LH
Inboard Joint Tulip
◆ Snap Ring
◆ Boot
2WD A/T
◆ O-Ring
Tripod
Inboard Joint Tulip
◆ Snap Ring
◆ Dust Cover
◆ Snap Ring
◆ Dust Cover
N·m (kgf·cm, ft·lbf) : Specified torque
◆ Non-reusable part
TY3039600105000X

Fig. 10 Exploded view of front driveshaft assembly. RAV4 w/2WD automatic transaxle & 4WD models

c. Using a suitable brass bar and hammer, tap tripod joint onto driveshaft.

5. Install a new snap ring onto driveshaft.
6. Pack inboard and outboard joints and boots with a suitable grease, then install boot and clamps onto outboard joint. **Do not tighten clamps at this time.**
7. Install inboard joint onto driveshaft, then install boot and clamps onto inboard joint.
8. Ensure boots are not stretched or damaged in any way and that driveshaft is at assembled length, **Fig. 14 and 15.**
9. Install both boot clamps onto boots. Ensure boot is on the driveshaft groove. Bend clamp band and lock.

LAND CRUISER

1. Place axle shaft in vise, then separate outer shaft from axle shaft using drift , **Fig. 6.**
2. Remove six ball bearings by rotating inner cage until bearings can be removed.
3. Remove cage and inner race from outer shaft. Remove inner race from cage.
4. Inspect all parts for damage or wear, then assemble inner race into cage as shown in **Fig. 16.**
5. Assemble cage and inner race onto outer shaft by positioning two large openings of cage against protruded parts of outer shaft.
6. Assemble inner race and cage, then install ball bearings. Lubricate outer shaft cavity with suitable grease.
7. Install new snap ring onto inner shaft then assemble inner and outer shafts.

RAV4

2WD W/MANUAL TRANSAXLE

Disassemble

1. Using a screwdriver, remove two inboard joint boot clamps, **Fig. 9.**
2. Using a side cutter, cut small outboard joint boot clamp and remove.
3. Using pliers, draw hooks together and remove large outboard joint boot clamp.
4. Place matchmarks on inboard joint tulip or center driveshaft and driveshaft.
5. Using a screwdriver, remove snap ring.
6. Remove inboard joint tulip from driveshaft.
7. Place matchmarks on driveshaft inner race and outer cage.
8. Remove six balls and cage.
9. Using a snap ring expander, remove snap ring.
10. Using brass bar and hammer, remove inner race.
11. Slide out inboard and outboard joint boots.
12. Using a press, remove dust cover from RH side center driveshaft.
13. Using tool No. 09950-00020, or equivalent, remove dust cover from LH side inboard joint tulip.
14. Using tool No. 09950-00020, or equivalent, remove dust cover from center driveshaft.
15. Using a snap ring expander, remove snap ring.
16. Using suitable press, remove bearing.
17. Mount outboard joint shaft in soft jaw vise and remove No. 2 dust deflector.

Assemble

1. Using tool Nos. 09309-36010 and 09316-20011, or equivalents, install new No. 2 dust deflector.
2. Using suitable press, install snap ring and bearing.
3. Using suitable press, install new dust cover.
4. Place new boot clamp on small ends of new outboard joint boot and install boot to driveshaft.

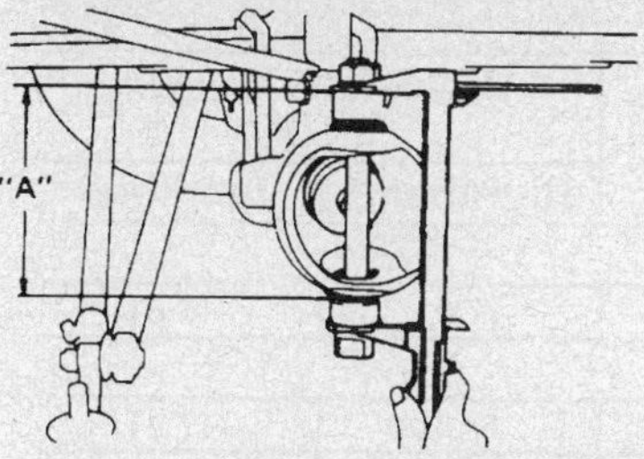
"A"
TY3039100036000X

Fig. 11 Axle housing dimension A inspection

5. Temporarily install new inboard joint boot to driveshaft.
6. Install cage with new snap ring to driveshaft.
7. Align matchmarks and install inner race to driveshaft using hammer and brass bar.
8. Install boot to outboard joint.
9. Pack boot and inboard joint tulip with grease.
10. Align matchmarks and install cage to inner race.
11. Install six balls.
12. Align matchmarks and install inboard joint tulip or center driveshaft to driveshaft.
13. Install new snap ring.
14. Temporarily install boot to the inboard joint tulip.
15. Ensure both boots are on shaft groove and place new boot clamps on inboard joint boot. Ensure boots are not stretched when driveshaft is at standard length, **Fig. 15.**
16. Secure clamps by drawing closing hooks together.
17. Place tool No. 09521-24010, or equivalent, onto clamp and tighten tool so that clamp is pinched.
18. Using tool No. 09240-00020, or equivalent, adjust clearance of clamp to .075 inch or less.

2WD W/AUTOMATIC TRANSAXLE & 4WD MODELS

Disassemble

1. Using a screwdriver, remove inboard and outboard joint boot clamps, **Fig. 10.**
2. Place matchmarks on tripod, inboard joint tulip or center driveshaft and driveshaft.
3. Remove inboard joint tulip from driveshaft.
4. Using a snap ring expander, remove snap ring.
5. Place matchmarks on driveshaft and tripod, then use brass bar and hammer to remove tripod from driveshaft.
6. Remove snap ring and slide out two inboard and outboard joint boots.
7. Using suitable press, remove dust cover from center driveshaft.
8. **On 4WD models and 2WD LH side driveshaft,** remove dust cover from inboard joint tulip using tool No. 09950-00020, or equivalent.
9. **On 2WD model RH side driveshaft,** disassemble center driveshaft as follows:

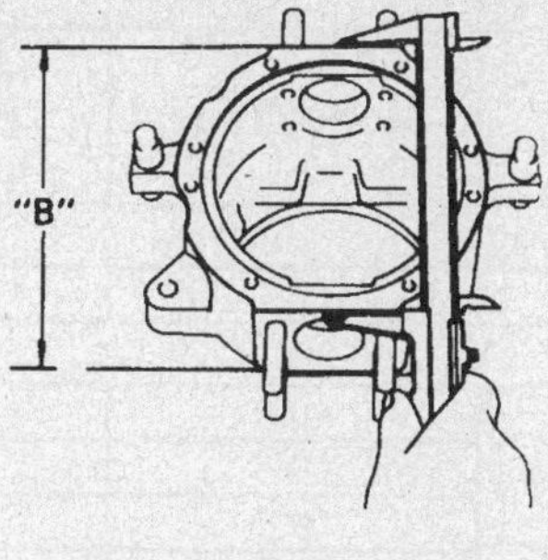
"B"
TY3039100037000X

Fig. 12 Steering knuckle dimension B inspection

a. Using a screwdriver, remove snap ring.
b. Using suitable press, remove bearing case.
c. Using pin punch and hammer, remove straight pin from bearing case.
d. Using tool No. 09950-00020, or equivalent and a suitable press, remove dust cover.
e. Using snap ring expander, remove snap ring.
f. Using suitable press, remove bearing.

10. **On all models,** mount outboard shaft in soft jaw vise.
11. Using screwdriver and hammer, remove No. 2 dust deflector.

Assemble

1. Using suitable press, install new No. 2 dust deflector.
2. Using pin punch and hammer, install straight pin into bearing case.
3. Using tool Nos. 09950-60010 and 09950-70010, or equivalents, install new bearing into bearing case.
4. Using a screwdriver, install new snap ring.
5. Using tool No. 09710-30021, or equivalent, install bearing with bearing case assembly to center driveshaft.
6. Using tool No. 09506-35010, or equivalent, an extension bar and press, install new dust cover.
7. Temporarily install new outboard joint boot to driveshaft.
8. Temporarily install new inboard joint boot to driveshaft.
9. Place beveled side of tripod axial spline toward outboard joint.
10. Align matchmarks and tap in tripod to driveshaft using brass bar and hammer.
11. Install new snap ring using snap ring expander.
12. Pack outboard joint and boot with grease and install boot to outboard joint.
13. Pack boot and inboard joint tulip with grease.
14. Align matchmarks and install inboard joint tulip or center driveshaft to drive shaft.
15. Temporarily install boot to inboard joint tulip.
16. Ensure both boots are on shaft groove and are not stretched or compressed

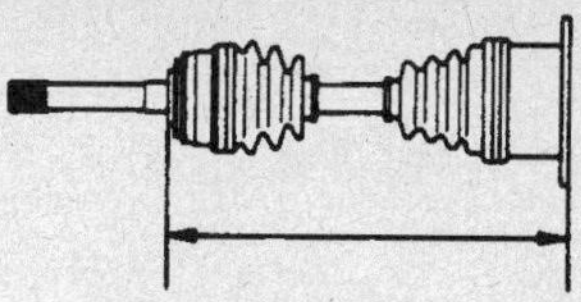
TY3039100026000X

Fig. 13 Front axle shaft assembled length measurement. Models with constant velocity type inner joints

when driveshaft is at standard length, **Fig. 15.**

17. Install four new boot clamps and bend clamp bands with a screwdriver to lock.

PICKUP, TACOMA, T100 W/4WD, PREVIA W/AWD & 1993-95 4RUNNER

1. Place axle shaft in a suitable vise, then make sure there is no play in inboard and outboard joints.
2. Ensure inboard boot slides smoothly in thrust direction and that there in no radial play in U-joints.
3. Check boots for damage, then remove inboard joint clamps **Fig. 7.**
4. Place matchmarks on inboard joint tulip and tripod, then separate inboard joint tulip from driveshaft.
5. Remove snap ring from tripod joint, then place matchmarks on shaft and tripod, using paint or chalk.
6. Remove tripod joint from shaft, using a hammer and brass drift.
7. Remove inboard joint boot, then the outboard joint boot clamps and boot. **Do not attempt to disassemble outboard joint.**
8. Remove dust deflector.
9. Temporarily install new dust deflector, then wrap vinyl tape around spline of shaft and install boot with new clamps to outboard joint.
10. Temporarily install boot with new clamps to inboard joint and driveshaft.
11. Place beveled side of tripod axial spline toward outboard joint, then align matchmarks previously marked. Tap tripod joint into driveshaft using a suitable drift, then install snap ring.
12. Apply .39–.41 lbs. of grease included with boot kit into boot, then assemble boot to outboard joint.
13. Apply .60–.62 lbs. of grease included in boot kit to inboard tulip and boot, then assemble inboard joint to inboard joint tulip. Align matchmarks, then insert inboard tulip to driveshaft. Install boot to inboard tulip.
14. Install both boot clamps, then bend bands rearward and close clamps.
15. Measure assembled length of axle without boots stretched or contracted, **Figs. 13 and 15.**

1996 4RUNNER

Disassemble

1. Using a screwdriver, remove inboard joint boot clamps, **Fig. 8.**

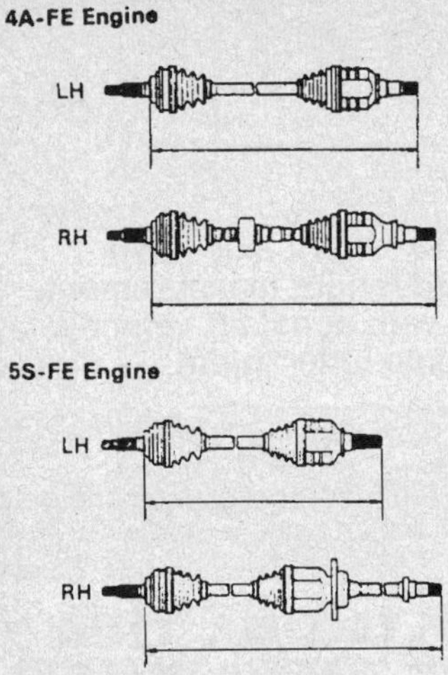
4A-FE Engine
LH
RH
5S-FE Engine
LH
RH

TY3039100034000X

Fig. 14 Front axle shaft standard length measurement. Celica, other models w/tripod joints similar

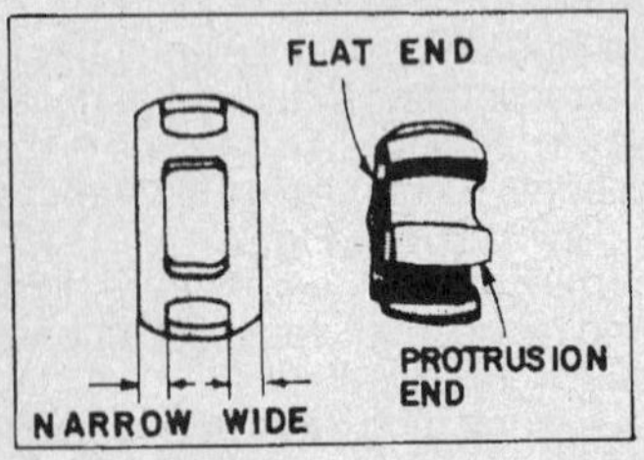
FLAT END
PROTRUSION END
NARROW
WIDE

TY3039100035000X

Fig. 16 Inner race into cage installation. Land Cruiser

2. Slide inboard joint boot toward outboard joint.
3. Place matchmarks on inboard joint and driveshaft.
4. Remove inboard joint tulip from driveshaft.
5. Using snap ring expander, remove tripod snap ring.
6. Place matchmarks on shaft and tripod.
7. Using brass bar and hammer, remove tripod.
8. Remove inboard joint boot from driveshaft.
9. Using a side cutter, cut two outboard boot clamps.
10. Remove outboard joint boot from driveshaft.
11. Using a screwdriver, remove dust seal from driveshaft.

Assemble

1. Using a screwdriver and hammer, install new dust cover and dust seal.
2. Place two new clamps to outboard joint boot and install to driveshaft.
3. Place beveled side of tripod axial spline toward outboard joint.
4. Align matchmarks and install tripod onto driveshaft using brass bar and hammer.
5. Install new snap ring.
6. Pack outboard joint and boot with grease and assemble boot to outboard joint.
7. Pack inboard joint and boot with grease, align matchmarks and install inboard joint tulip to driveshaft.

Year	Model/Type	Damper Position, Inch⑬	Driveshaft Length, Inch⑬	
			Righthand	Lefthand
AVALON				
1995–96	—	—	17.81	17.81
CAMRY				
1993–96	①③	—	17.81	17.81
	①②	—	17.95	17.95
	④②	—	34.10	23.94
	④③	—	34.68	23.98
CELICA				
1993	⑪⑩⑤	16.99	33.69	21.24
	⑪⑨⑤	16.99	33.97	21.30
	⑦⑤	16.99	33.28	21.99
	⑥	7.85	15.96	15.96
1994–96	⑦⑨	7.87	33.76	22.53
	⑦⑩	7.87	33.94	22.71
	⑧	15.45	34.54	22.02
COROLLA				
1993–96	②	14.14	33.17	20.80
	⑫	14.14	33.75	21.26
PASEO				
1993–96	—	16.36	30.88	21.81
PICKUP				
1993–96	—	—	15.70	15.70
PREVIA				
1993–96	⑥	—	19.35	19.35
RAV4				
1996	⑤⑩	—	33.25	21.59
	⑤⑨	—	33.19	21.36
	⑭	—	20.13	20.00
TACOMA				
1995–96	—	—	17.17	17.17
TERCEL				
1993–94	—	14.34	30.88	21.82
1995–96	—	14.34	30.90	21.42
T100				
1993–96	—	—	19.14	19.14
4RUNNER				
1993–95	—	—	15.70	15.70
1996	—	—	20.90	20.90

① — Models w/V6 engines.
② — Toyota type boot & clamp.
③ — GKN type boot & clamp.
④ — Models w/4 cylinder engines.
⑤ — 2WD.
⑥ — AWD.
⑦ — 5S-FE engine.
⑧ — 7A-FE engine.
⑨ — Manual transaxle.
⑩ — Automatic transaxle.
⑪ — 4A-FE engine.
⑫ — Saginaw type boot & clamp.
⑬ — ± .20 inches,
⑭ — 4WD

Fig. 15 Front driveshaft length specification chart

8. Temporarily install boot to inboard joint tulip.
9. Ensure both boots are in shaft groove and not stretched or contracted with driveshaft at standard length, **Fig. 15.**
10. Install new inboard joint boot clamps and bend the bands with a screwdriver to lock.

11. Install outboard joint boot clamps and pinch clamps to tighten. Use tool No. 09521-24010, or equivalent, to adjust clamp clearance to .031 inch or less.

INTERMEDIATE SHAFT SERVICE

CAMRY W/4 CYLINDER ENGINE & COROLLA

The following procedure applies only to the right side driveshaft on Camry models.

1. Using suitable tools, press out dust covers.
2. Remove snap ring.
3. Using press tool 09950-00020, or equivalent, remove bearing.
4. Remove the snap ring.
5. Install snap ring over shaft, then, using press tool 09527-20011, or equivalent, press on a new bearing.
6. Install new snap ring.
7. Using suitable press, press in a new dust cover on driveshaft side to a clearance of .04–.08 inch, ensuring that there is clearance between dust cover and bearing.
8. Using suitable press, press in a new dust cover on transaxle side to a distance of 3.39–3.43 inches from end of shaft.

AVALON & CAMRY W/V6 ENGINE

Disassemble

1. Using a suitable press, remove dust cover from transaxle side.
2. Using press tool 09950-00020, or equivalent and a suitable press, remove driveshaft side dust cover.
3. Remove snap ring.
4. Using a suitable press, remove bearing.

Assemble

1. Install snap ring to the center driveshaft.
2. Using a suitable press and a extension bar, press in the bearing.
3. Install a new snap ring.
4. Install dust covers, as follows:
   a. Using a suitable press, install driveshaft side dust cover. Clearance between the dust cover and the bearing should be .04–.08 inch.
   b. Using a suitable press, install transaxle side dust cover. Clearance between dust cover and transaxle end should be 3.94–3.98 inch.

TIGHTENING SPECIFICATIONS

Year	Component	Torque/Ft. Lbs.
CAMRY		
1993–96	Brake Caliper To Steering Knuckle	79
	Bearing Locknut	137
	Shock Absorber To Steering Knuckle	166
	Stabilizer Bar Link Nut	47
	Steering Knuckle Attaching Nuts	105
	Steering Knuckle To Lower Arm	83
	Tie Rod To Steering Knuckle	36
	Wheel Lug Nut	76
CELICA		
1993–96	Bearing Locknut	137
	Brake Caliper To Steering Knuckle	①
	Driveshaft To Differential Side Shaft	27
	Lower Arm To Steering Knuckle	94
	Tie Rod End To Steering Knuckle	36
	Wheel Lug Nuts	76
COROLLA		
1993–96	Bearing Locknut	137
	Brake Caliper To Steering Knuckle	18
	Driveshaft Locknut	159
	Shock Absorber To Steering Knuckle	105
	Stabilizer Bar Link Nut	47
	Steering Knuckle Attaching Nuts	105
	Steering Knuckle To Lower Arm	83
	Tie Rod To Steering Knuckle	36
	Wheel Lug Nut	76

Continued

TIGHTENING SPECIFICATIONS—Continued

Year	Component	Torque/Ft. Lbs.
LAND CRUISER		
1993–96	Disc Brake Cylinder To Axle Hub	90
	Flange To Axle Hub	26
	Front Axle Hub Bearing Locknut	65
	Shock Absorber To Axle Housing	51
	Shock Absorber To Body	51
	Steering Knuckle To Bearing Cap	71
	Steering Knuckle To Knuckle Arm	71
	Steering Knuckle To Knuckle Spindle	34
1993–96	Tie Rod End	67
	Wheel Lug Nuts	108
PASEO		
1993–96	Brake Caliper To Steering Knuckle	65
	Driveshaft To Axle Hub Nut	152
	Shock Absorber To Steering Knuckle	166
	Tie Rod Locknut	35
	Wheel Lug Nut	76
PICKUP, T100, TACOMA & 1993–95 4RUNNER		
1993–96	Driveshaft To Side Gear Shaft	61
	Hub Body Nuts	23
	Hub Body To Cover	7
	Hub Body To Driveshaft	13
	Wheel Lug Nuts	76
1996 4RUNNER		
1996	Driveshaft Locknut	174
	Lower Suspension Arm	105
	Wheel Lug Nuts	83
RAV4		
1996	ABS Speed Sensor Bolt	5.8
	Driveshaft Locknut	159
	Lower Ball Joint To Lower Suspension Arm	94
	Lower Ball Joint To Steering Knuckle Bolts	94
	Tie Rod End Locknut	36
TERCEL		
1993–96	Brake Caliper To Steering Knuckle	18
	Bearing Locknut	137
	Shock Absorber To Steering Knuckle	166
	Tie Rod Locknut	36
	Wheel Lug Nut	76

①–With 13 inch wheel, 18 ft. lbs.; w/14 & 15 inch wheel, 29 ft. lbs.

All-Wheel Drive Systems

INDEX

	Page No.
Description	48-319
Celica	48-319
Previa	48-319
Differential Service	48-320
Celica	48-320
PREVIA	48-322
Driveshaft Service	48-319
Front	48-319
Rear	48-319
Rear Axle Hub & Carrier Service	48-324
Axle Hub & Bearing, Replace	48-324
Replacement	48-324
Rear Axle Shaft, Replace	48-324
Installation	48-324
Removal	48-324
Transaxle Select Lever Service Positioning	48-319
Select Modes, Models w/ Viscous Coupling	48-319

DESCRIPTION

CELICA

1993

The E150F manual transmission, **Fig 1.** is equipped with a viscous coupling. The center differential, which compensates for the difference between the rotational speed of front and rear wheels, provides durability and reliability by utilizing beveled gears to distribute engine power from the transaxle to both front and rear driveshaft in a 50% split of engine power. The center differential has been equipped with a control coupling which functions similar to a limited slip differential.

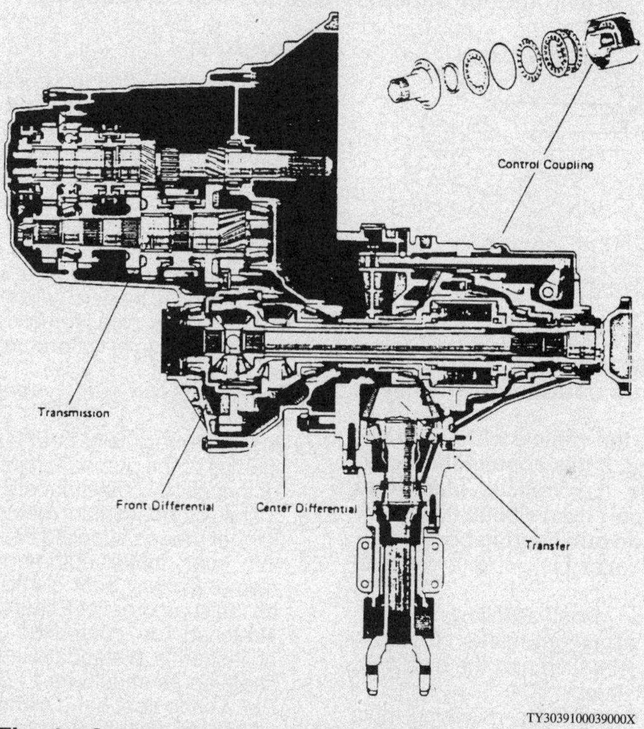

Control Coupling
Transmission
Front Differential
Center Differential
Transfer
TY3039100039000X

Fig. 1 Cross-sectional view of AWD transaxle case. Celica model transaxle E150F w/viscous coupling

PREVIA

1993

G57

The G57 manual transaxle, **Fig. 2** is a full time all wheel drive system that incorporates a viscous coupling, basic transaxle components, the center differential, front differential and the transfer assembly is built into the same quadruple case axle.

The center differential, which compensates for the difference between the rotational speed of the front and rear wheels, provides durability and reliability by utilizing beveled gears to distribute engine power from the transaxle to both front and rear driveshaft in a 50% split of engine power. The center differential has been equipped with a control coupling which functions similar to a limited slip differential.

A46DE, A46DF, A340E & A340F

These automatic transmissions are four-speed, electronically controlled transmissions developed for use with high performance engines.

The A46DF & A340F automatic transmissions are equipped with a full time four wheel drive transfer cases.

These transmissions are mainly composed of a torque converter, the overdrive planetary gear, a 3-speed planetary gear unit, a hydraulic control system and electronic control system.

A lock-up mechanism is built into the torque converter clutch.

TRANSAXLE SELECT LEVER SERVICE POSITIONING

SELECT MODES, MODELS W/VISCOUS COUPLING

1. Viscous mode. This mode is during normal driving. After completing inspection and or service to the vehicle, return the mode switch to position shown in **Fig. 3.**
2. Viscous free mode. This mode cuts off the driving force transmitted from the center differential to the control coupling, and makes the center differential free, **Fig. 4.** Never use this mode during normal vehicle operation.
3. FF mode. This mode cuts off the driving force transmitted from the center differential to the transfer unit and locks the center differential. However, when the lever is shifted to this mode, the driving force is transmitted only to the front wheels, **Fig. 5.** Do not use this during normal driving.

DRIVESHAFT SERVICE

FRONT

Refer to "Front Wheel Drive Axles" for front driveshaft repair procedures.

REAR

PREVIA

Refer to "Rear Axle & Suspension" section for rear axle service procedures.

CELICA

Removal

The hub bearing could be damaged if it is subjected to vehicle weight, as

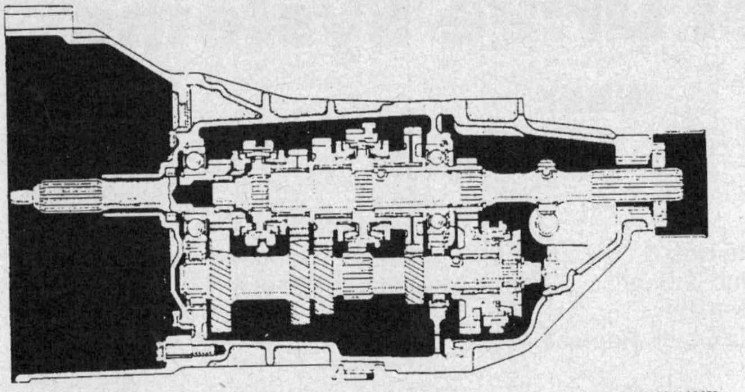

TY3039100041000X

Fig. 2 Cross-sectional view of AWD transaxle case. Previa model transaxle G57 w/viscous coupling

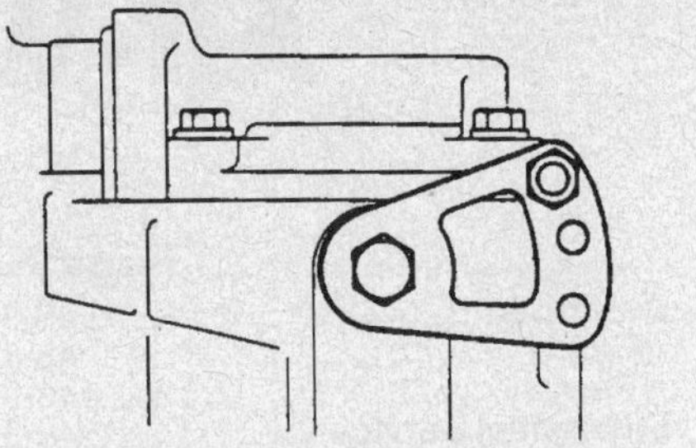

TY3039100042000X

Fig. 3 Transaxle select lever, viscous mode. Models w/viscous coupling transaxle

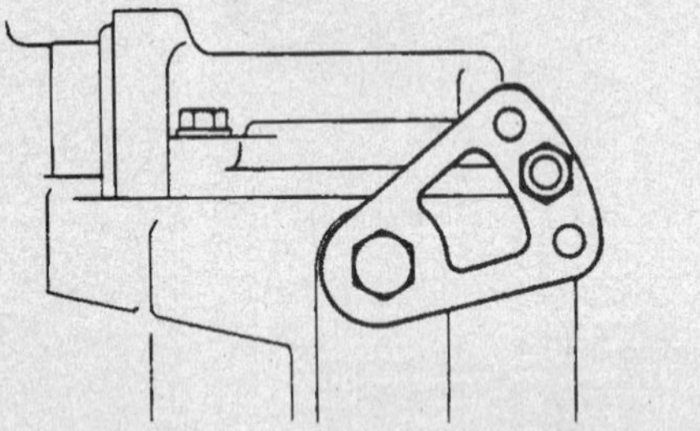

TY3039100043000X

Fig. 4 Transaxle select lever, viscous free mode. Models w/viscous coupling transaxle

when moving the vehicle with the driveshaft removed. If it is absolutely necessary to move the vehicle, place hub bearing support tool 09608-02020, or equivalent, into hub bearing bore.

1. Remove cotter pin, locknut cap and locknut.
2. Remove driveshaft as follows:
   a. Place alignment marks on the inboard joint tulip and the side gear shaft flange.
   b. Loosen the four attaching nuts holding the driveshaft to the side gear shaft.
   c. Disconnect the driveshaft from the side gear shaft, **Fig. 6.**
   d. Remove the driveshaft from the axle carrier.

Disassemble

1. Check driveshaft to ensure there is no play in the inboard and outboard joints. Ensure inboard joint slides smoothly on the thrust direction and there is no excessive play in the axial direction.
2. Remove inboard joint boot clamps.
3. Remove inboard joint boot from inboard joint tulip.
4. Remove inboard joint tulip from driveshaft. Place alignment marks on the inboard joint tulip and driveshaft for assembly reference. Do not punch the marks.
5. Remove tripod joint. Place alignment marks on the driveshaft and tripod joint for assembly reference.
6. Remove inboard joint boot and clamp.
7. Remove outboard joint boot.

Assemble

1. Temporarily install the boots and new boot clamps. **The boot and clamp for the outboard joint are smaller than those for the inboard joint.**
2. Install tripod joint. Align marks made during disassembly and tap tripod joint onto driveshaft. Install snap ring.
3. Install inboard joint tulip to driveshaft. Pack .40 lbs., of grease supplied in boot kit to the inboard tulip. Align marks made during disassembly and install the inboard joint tulip onto the driveshaft.
4. Install inboard joint boot to inboard joint tulip.
5. Install inboard joint boot clamps. The clamps of the outboard joint are smaller than those of the inboard joint.
6. Install outboard joint boot. Pack .26 lbs., of grease supplied by the boot kit into boot. Install outboard joint boot clamp. Ensure boot clamp is located on the shaft groove. Ensure boot is not stretched or contracted when the driveshaft is at standard length. Driveshaft length should be 21.957 inches.
7. Bend back boot band clamp and lock.
8. Check driveshaft. Ensure there is no play in the inboard joint and outboard joint. Ensure the inboard joint slides smoothly in the thrust direction.

Installation

1. Install driveshaft. Ensure not to damage boots during installation.
2. Install driveshaft to axle carrier assembly.
3. Align marks during removal on inboard joint tulip and side gear shaft flange.
4. Connect driveshaft to side gear shaft. **Torque** attaching bolts to 51 ft. lbs.
5. Install bearing locknut, locknut cap and cotter pin. **Torque** nut while depressing brake pedal to 137 ft. lbs. Install locknut cap, then a new cotter pin.

DIFFERENTIAL SERVICE

CELICA

Disassemble

1. Place differential carrier into a suitable working fixture.
2. Remove side gear shafts, **Fig. 7.**

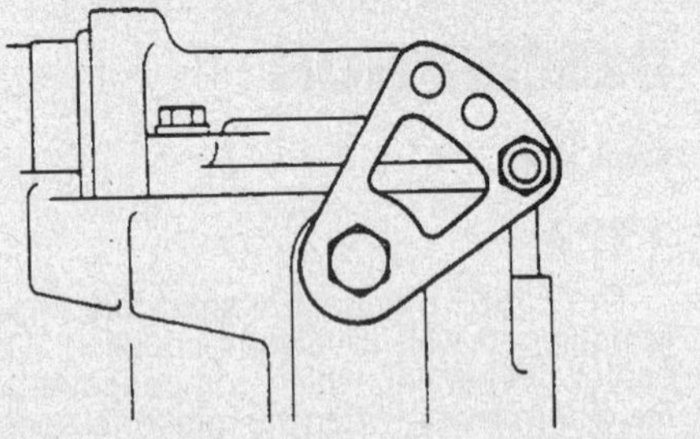

TY3039100044000X

Fig. 5 Transaxle select lever, FF mode. Models w/viscous coupling transaxle

3. Remove side gear shaft oil seals.
4. Using suitable tools, remove companion flange.
5. Remove front oil seal and oil slinger.
6. Remove front bearing and bearing spacer.
7. Remove differential case. Proceed as follows:
   a. Place alignment marks on the bearing cap and differential carrier.
   b. Remove the two bearing caps.
   c. Using tool 09504-22011, or equivalent, remove the two side bearing preload adjusting plate.
   d. Measure adjusting plate washer and note thickness.
   e. Remove differential case and bearing outer race from carrier.
   f. Tag bearing outer races for identification.
8. Remove drive pinion from differential carrier.
9. Remove drive pinion rear bearing, front and rear bearing outer races.
10. Remove ring gear and side bearings.
11. Remove straight pin, pinion shaft, two pinion gears, side gears and thrust washers from differential case.

Assemble

1. Assemble differential case as follows:
   a. Install thrust washers to the side gears.
   b. Install side gears with thrust washers and pinion gears with thrust washers.
   c. Install pinion shaft. Check side gear backlash. Measure backlash while holding one pinion gear toward the case. Backlash should be .0020–.079 inch. If backlash is not as specified, install side gear thrust

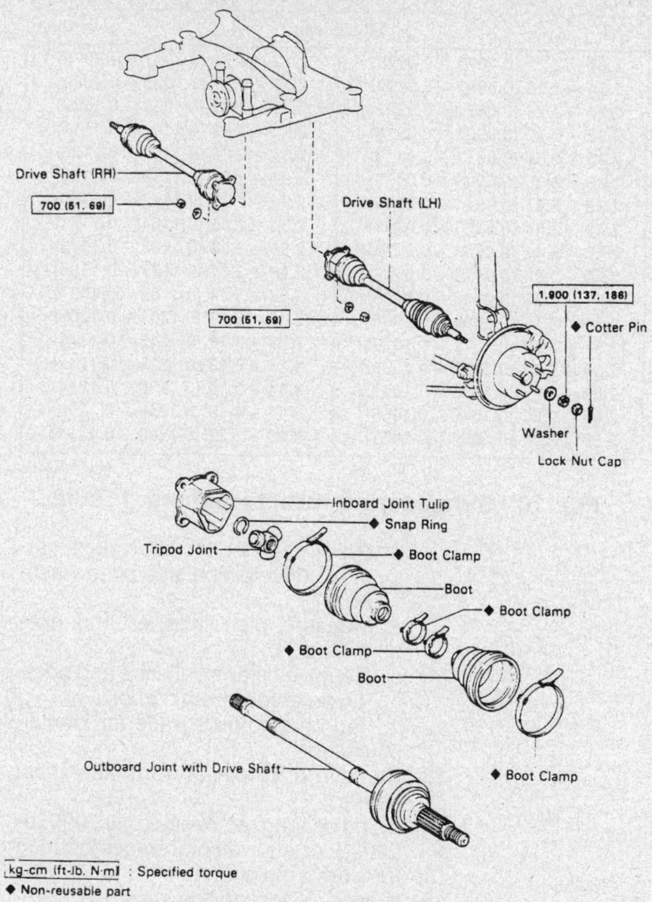
Drive Shaft (RH)
700 (51, 69)
Drive Shaft (LH)
1,900 (137, 186)
700 (51, 69)
◆ Cotter Pin
Washer
Lock Nut Cap
Inboard Joint Tulip
◆ Snap Ring
Tripod Joint
◆ Boot Clamp
Boot
◆ Boot Clamp
◆ Boot Clamp
Boot
Outboard Joint with Drive Shaft
◆ Boot Clamp
kg-cm (ft-lb, N·m) : Specified torque
◆ Non-reusable part
TY3039100049000X

Fig. 6 Exploded view of AWD rear driveshaft components. Celica

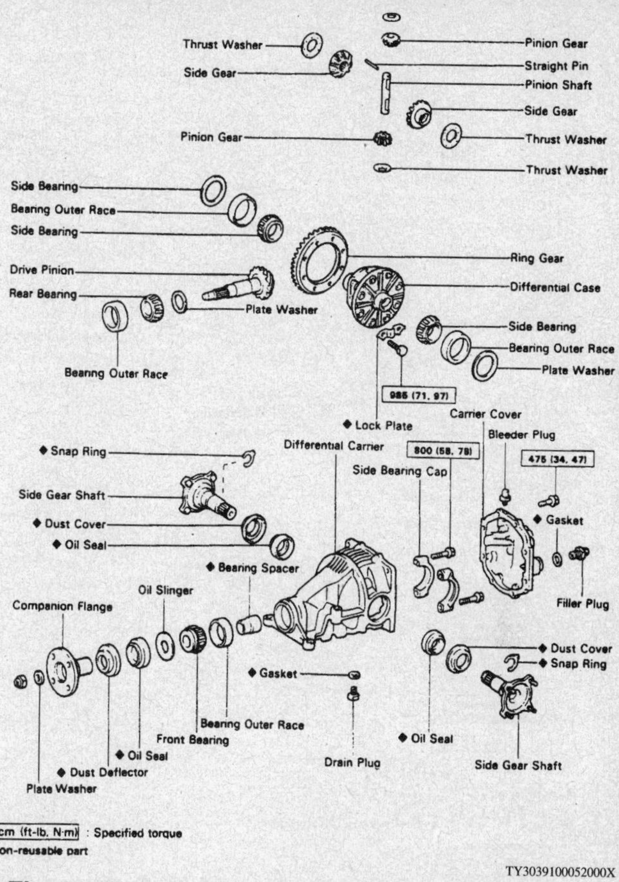
Thrust Washer
Side Gear
Pinion Gear
Straight Pin
Pinion Shaft
Side Gear
Pinion Gear
Thrust Washer
Thrust Washer
Side Bearing
Bearing Outer Race
Side Bearing
Drive Pinion
Rear Bearing
Plate Washer
Ring Gear
Differential Case
Side Bearing
Bearing Outer Race
Plate Washer
Bearing Outer Race
985 (71, 97)
◆ Lock Plate
Carrier Cover
Bleeder Plug
◆ Snap Ring
Differential Carrier
800 (58, 78)
Side Bearing Cap
475 (34, 47)
Side Gear Shaft
◆ Dust Cover
◆ Oil Seal
◆ Gasket
◆ Bearing Spacer
Oil Slinger
Companion Flange
Filler Plug
◆ Dust Cover
◆ Snap Ring
◆ Gasket
Bearing Outer Race
Front Bearing
◆ Oil Seal
◆ Dust Deflector
Plate Washer
Drain Plug
◆ Oil Seal
Side Gear Shaft
kg-cm (ft-lb, N·m) : Specified torque
◆ Non-reusable part
TY3039100052000X

Fig. 7 Disassembled view of AWD differential. Celica

washer of different thickness. The available washers are as follows, .037, .039, .041, .043, .045 and .047 inch.

d. Use washers of the same thickness on both right and left sides.
e. Install straight pin through case and hole in pinion shaft.
f. Stake case.

2. Install ring gear onto differential case. Heat gear to approximately 212°F, in oil bath before installing. Align marks on ring gear and differential case. Install and **torque** attaching bolts to 71 ft. lbs.
3. Stake lock plates. Stake one claw flush with the flat surface of the nut. For the claw contacting the protruding portion of the nut, stake only half on the tightening side.
4. Install side bearings.
5. Using a dial indicator, check ring gear runout. Ring gear runout should be .0028 inch.
6. Install front and rear bearing outer races.
7. Install rear bearing to drive pinion. Temporarily adjust drive pinion preload.
8. Install drive pinion and front bearing. Assemble the spacer, oil slinger and oil seal after adjusting gear contact pattern. Install companion flange. Adjust drive pinion preload by tightening companion flange nut. Using torque wrench, measure preload. Preload (at the start of tightening) should be 10.4–16.5 inch lbs. for new bearings or 5.2–8.7 inch lbs. for used bearings.
9. Install differential case into carrier. Place bearing outer races on their respective bearings. Ensure the left and right outer races are not interchanged.
10. Install the differential case into carrier.
11. Check ring gear backlash, backlash should be .0051–.0071 inch. If not, adjust backlash by either increasing or decreasing the number of washers on both sides by an equal amount. There should be no clearance between plate washer and case.
12. Adjust side bearing preload, as follows:
    a. Remove ring gear teeth side plate washer and measure thickness.
    b. Install a new plate washer approximately .0024–.0035 inch thicker than the removed washer.
    c. Select a washer that can be pressed in ⅔ of the way in by hand.
    d. Using a suitable tool, tap in side washer.
    e. Install side bearing caps. Align marks on cap and carrier. **Torque** attaching bolts to 58 ft. lbs.
    f. Check ring gear backlash. Backlash should be .0051–.0071 inch. Backlash will change approximately .0008 inch with a .0012 inch alteration of the side washer. If backlash is incorrect, adjust by either increasing or decreasing the number of washers on both sides by equal amounts.
13. Measure total preload. Total preload (at the start plus drive pinion preload) should be 2.6–4.3 inch.
14. Check ring gear tooth contact pattern. If teeth are not contacting properly, use proper washers for correction.
15. Remove companion flange and front bearing.
16. Install new bearing spacer and front bearing. Install oil slinger and a new oil seal.
17. Install companion flange. **Torque** attaching nut to 80 ft. lbs.
18. Check drive pinion bearing preload. Preload (at the start) should be 8.7–13.9 inch lbs. for new bearings or 4.3–6.9 inch lbs. for used bearings. If preload is greater than specified, replace bearing spacer. If preload is less than specified, tighten nut 9 ft. lbs. at a time until specified preload is reached. If maximum **torque** is exceeded (174 ft. lbs.) while tightening nut, replace bearing spacer and repeat preload procedure. Do not back off the pinion nut to reduce preload.
19. Check total preload.
20. Check ring gear backlash. Backlash should be .0051–.0071 inch.
21. Check tooth contact pattern.

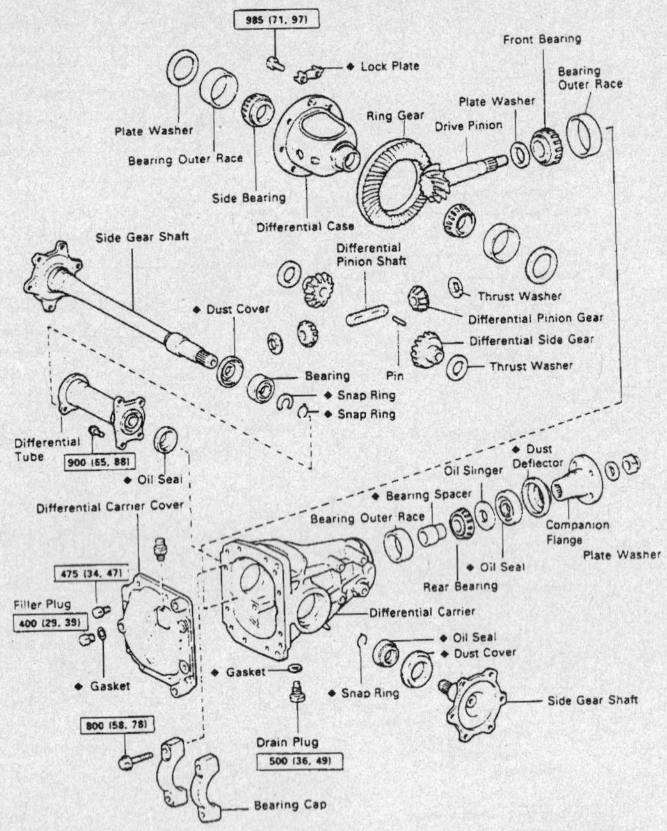
985 (71, 97)
Lock Plate
Front Bearing
Bearing Outer Race
Plate Washer
Ring Gear
Drive Pinion
Plate Washer
Bearing Outer Race
Side Bearing
Differential Case
Side Gear Shaft
Differential Pinion Shaft
Thrust Washer
Dust Cover
Differential Pinion Gear
Differential Side Gear
Thrust Washer
Bearing
Pin
Snap Ring
Snap Ring
Differential Tube
900 (65, 88)
Oil Seal
Dust Deflector
Oil Slinger
Bearing Spacer
Differential Carrier Cover
Bearing Outer Race
Companion Flange
Plate Washer
Oil Seal
475 (34, 47)
Rear Bearing
Filler Plug
400 (29, 39)
Differential Carrier
Oil Seal
Dust Cover
Gasket
Gasket
Snap Ring
Side Gear Shaft
800 (58, 78)
Drain Plug
500 (36, 49)
Bearing Cap

TY3039100053000X

Fig. 8 Disassembled view of AWD differential. Previa

Thickness	mm(in.)
2.21 – 2.23 (0.0870 – 0.0878)	2.72 – 2.74 (0.1071 – 0.1079)
2.24 – 2.26 (0.0881 – 0.0890)	2.75 – 2.77 (0.1083 – 0.1091)
2.27 – 2.29 (0.0894 – 0.0902)	2.78 – 2.80 (0.1095 – 0.1102)
2.30 – 2.32 (0.0906 – 0.0913)	2.81 – 2.83 (0.1106 – 0.1114)
2.33 – 2.35 (0.0917 – 0.0925)	2.84 – 2.86 (0.1118 – 0.1126)
2.36 – 2.38 (0.0929 – 0.0937)	2.87 – 2.89 (0.1130 – 0.1138)
2.39 – 2.41 (0.0941 – 0.0949)	2.90 – 2.92 (0.1142 – 0.1150)
2.42 – 2.44 (0.0953 – 0.0961)	2.93 – 2.95 (0.1154 – 0.1161)
2.45 – 2.47 (0.0965 – 0.0972)	2.96 – 2.98 (0.1165 – 0.1173)
2.48 – 2.50 (0.0976 – 0.0984)	2.99 – 3.01 (0.1177 – 0.1185)
2.51 – 2.53 (0.0988 – 0.0996)	3.02 – 3.04 (0.1189 – 0.1197)
2.54 – 2.56 (0.1000 – 0.1008)	3.05 – 3.07 (0.1201 – 0.1209)
2.57 – 2.59 (0.1012 – 0.1020)	3.08 – 3.10 (0.1213 – 0.1220)
2.60 – 2.62 (0.1024 – 0.1031)	3.11 – 3.13 (0.1224 – 0.1232)
2.63 – 2.65 (0.1035 – 0.1043)	3.14 – 3.16 (0.1236 – 0.1244)
2.66 – 2.68 (0.1047 – 0.1055)	3.17 – 3.19 (0.1248 – 0.1256)
2.69 – 2.71 (0.1059 – 0.1067)	3.20 – 3.22 (0.1260 – 0.1268)

TY3039100055000X

Fig. 10 Side bearing thrust washers. Previa

Thrust washer thickness
0.95 mm (0.037 in.)
1.00 mm (0.039 in.)
1.05 mm (0.041 in.)
1.10 mm (0.043 in.)
1.15 mm (0.045 in.)
1.20 mm (0.047 in.)

TY3039100054000X

Fig. 9 Side gear thrust washers. Previa

22. Check companion flange runout. Maximum lateral runout should be .0039 inch. Maximum radial runout should be .0039 inch.
23. Stake drive pinion nut.
24. Install new side gear shaft oil seals.
25. Install side gear shafts.
26. Install differential carrier cover. **Torque** attaching bolts to 34 ft. lbs.

PREVIA

Disassemble

1. Place differential carrier into a suitable working fixture.
2. Remove differential carrier cover, **Fig. 8.**
3. Measure side gear backlash while holding on pinion gear toward case. Backlash should be .0020–.0079 inch.
4. If backlash is not within specifications, install correct thrust washer, **Fig 9.**
5. Remove side gear shaft, differential tube and side gear shaft oil seals.
6. Using a dial indicator, measure ring gear runout. Maximum runout should be .0028 inch.
7. If runout is greater than maximum, replace ring gear and drive pinion as a set.
8. Check ring gear backlash as follows:
   a. Fix dial indicator on tooth surface at 90° angle.
   b. Holding drive pinion flange, measure ring gear backlash. Backlash should be .0051–.0071 inch.
   c. If backlash is not within specifications, adjust ring gear backlash. Measure from three of more places on circumference of ring gear.
   d. Inspect tooth contact between ring gear and drive pinion.
9. Using remover tool No. 09557-22022, or equivalent, remove companion flange.
10. Using oil seal puller tool No. 09308-00010, or equivalent, remove oil seal and oil slinger.
11. Using bearing remover tool No. 09556-22010, or equivalent, remove rear bearing and bearing spacer.
12. Remove differential case assembly as follows:
    a. Place alignment marks on bearing cap and differential carrier.
    b. Remove four bolts and two bearing caps.
    c. Using differential remover tool No. 09504-22011, or equivalent, remove drive pinion side plate washer.
    d. Measure plate washer and note thickness.
    e. Remove differential case and bearing outer race from carrier.
    f. Tag bearing outer race for identification.
13. Remove drive pinion from differential carrier.
14. Using bearing remover tool No. 09950-00020, or equivalent, remove bearing from drive pinion.
15. If drive pinion or ring gear are damaged, replace as a set.
16. Using a brass bar and hammer, drive out outer races from differential carrier.
17. Place marks on ring gear and differential case, then using a screwdriver unstake lock plate.
18. Remove eight bolts and four lock plates, then using plastic hammer tap on ring gear to separate it from differential case.
19. Check differential case runout as follows:
    a. Place bearing outer races on respective bearings. Ensure the left and right outer races are not interchanged.
    b. Install differential case in differential carrier.
    c. When there no play left in side bearings, install plate washers.
    d. Align marks on bearing cap and differential carrier.
    e. Install and uniformly tighten four bearing caps in several passes.
    f. Using dial indicator, measure differential case runout. Runout should be .016 inch.
    g. Remove differential case.
20. Using puller tool No. 09950-20017, or equivalent, remove side bearing from differential case.
21. Using pin punch and hammer, drive out straight pin.
22. Remove pinion shaft, pinion gear, pinion gear thrust washers, side gears and side gear thrust washers from differential case.

Thickness	mm(in.)
2.27 (0.0894)	2.51 (0.0988)
2.30 (0.0906)	2.54 (0.1000)
2.33 (0.0917)	2.57 (0.1012)
2.36 (0.0929)	2.60 (0.1024)
2.39 (0.0941)	2.63 (0.1035)
2.42 (0.0953)	2.66 (0.1047)
2.45 (0.0965)	2.69 (0.1059)
2.48 (0.0976)	

TY3039100056000X

Fig. 11 Tooth contact between ring gear & drive pinion. Previa

Thickness	mm(in.)
2.27 (0.0894)	2.51 (0.0988)
2.30 (0.0906)	2.54 (0.1000)
2.33 (0.0917)	2.57 (0.1012)
2.36 (0.0929)	2.60 (0.1024)
2.39 (0.0941)	2.63 (0.1035)
2.42 (0.0953)	2.66 (0.1047)
2.45 (0.0965)	2.69 (0.1059)
2.48 (0.0976)	

TY3039100057000X

Fig. 12 Tooth thrust washers. Previa

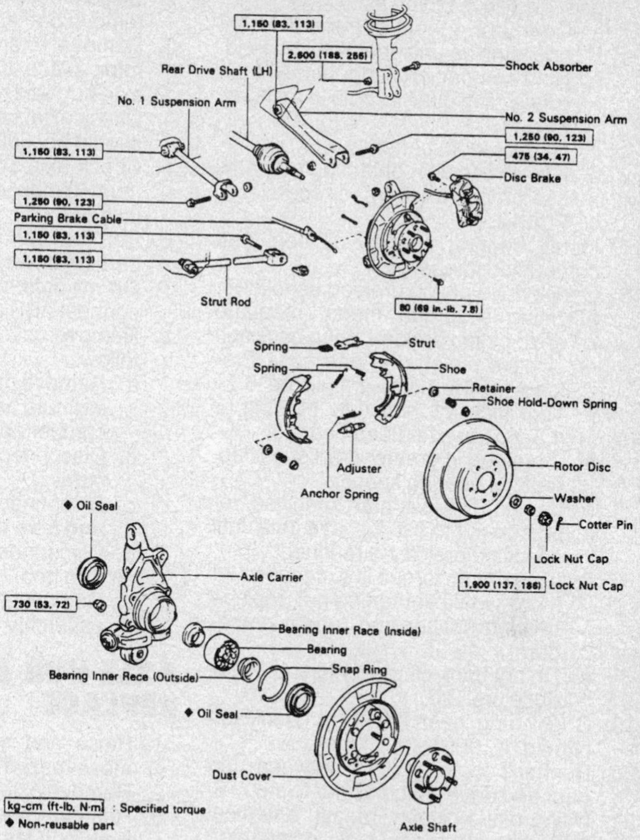
1,150 (83, 113)
2,600 (188, 255)
Rear Drive Shaft (LH)
Shock Absorber
No. 1 Suspension Arm
No. 2 Suspension Arm
1,250 (90, 123)
475 (34, 47)
Disc Brake
1,150 (83, 113)
1,250 (90, 123)
Parking Brake Cable
1,150 (83, 113)
1,150 (83, 113)
Strut Rod
80 (69 in.-lb, 7.8)
Spring
Strut
Spring
Shoe
Retainer
Shoe Hold-Down Spring
Adjuster
Anchor Spring
Rotor Disc
Washer
Cotter Pin
Lock Nut Cap
1,900 (137, 186) Lock Nut Cap
◆ Oil Seal
Axle Carrier
730 (53, 72)
Bearing Inner Race (Inside)
Bearing
Snap Ring
Bearing Inner Rece (Outside)
◆ Oil Seal
Dust Cover
kg-cm (ft-lb, N·m) : Specified torque
◆ Non-reusable part
Axle Shaft

TY3039100050000X

Fig. 13 Exploded view of AWD rear axle hub & carrier assembly. Celica

Assemble

1. Adjust differential side gear shaft backlash as follows:
   a. Install proper thrust washers on side gears.
   b. Refer to **Fig. 9,** select thrust washers which will ensure backlash is within specification.
   c. Install side gears, pinion gears, pinion gear thrust washers and pinion shaft in differential case.
   d. Align holes of differential case and pinion shaft.
   e. Push side gear shafts carefully into differential case by hand and install.
   f. Measure side gear backlash while holding on pinion gear toward differential case. Backlash should be .0020–.0079 inch.
   g. If backlash is not within specifications, install side gear thrust washers with differential thickness.
   h. Remove side gear shafts.
2. Using a hammer and punch, install straight pin through case and hole of pinion shaft.
3. Stake differential case.
4. Install side bearings into differential case.
5. Heat ring gear in boiling water. After moisture on ring gear has completely evaporated, install ring gear to differential case.
6. Align marks on ring gear and differential case, then temporarily install five new lock plates and ten bolts so that bolt holes in ring gear and differential case are not misaligned. **Ring gear set bolts should not be tightened until ring gear has cooled sufficiently. Torque** ring gear set bolt to 71 ft. lbs.
7. Stake lock plates. Stake one claw flush with the flat surface of the nut. For claw contacting the protruding portion of the nut, stake only half on the tightening side.
8. Using a dial indicator, check ring gear runout. Ring gear runout should be .0028 inch.
9. Install drive pinion front bearing.
10. Temporarily adjust drive pinion preload as follows:
    a. Install drive pinion, rear bearing and oil slinger.
    b. Assemble spacer and oil seal after adjusting gear contact pattern.
    c. Using companion flange replacer tool No. 09557-22022, or equivalent, install companion flange.
    d. Adjust drive pinion preload by tightening plate washer and companion flange nut.
    e. Using companion flange replacer tool No. 09557-22022, or equivalent, hold flange to tighten nut. **As there is no spacer, tighten nut little at a time, ensuring not to overtighten.**
    f. Using a torque meter, measure preload. Preload should be 8.7–13.9 inch lbs., for new bearing or 4.3–6.9 lbs., for used bearing.
11. Install differential case in differential carrier. Place bearing outer on their respective bearings. Ensure the left and right outer races are not interchanged.
12. Install differential case in the differential carrier.
13. Check ring gear backlash, backlash should be .0051–.0071 inch, If not, adjust backlash by either increasing or decreasing the number of washers on both sides by an equal amount. There should be no clearance between plate, washer and case, **Fig. 10.**
14. Adjust side bearing preload as follows:
    a. Remove drive pinion side plate washer, then measure thickness.
    b. Using backlash as a reference, install a new washer of .0024–.0035 inch thicker than washer removed.
    c. Select a washer which can be pressed in 2/3 of the way in by hand.
    d. Using suitable tool, tap in plate washer.
    e. Recheck ring gear backlash. Backlash should be .0051–.0071 inch. Backlash will change approximately .0008 inch with a .0012 inch alteration of the side washer. If backlash is incorrect, adjust by either increasing or decreasing the number of washers on both sides by equal amounts.
    f. Install bearing caps. Align marks on cap and carrier. **Torque** attaching bolts to 58 ft. lbs.
15. Measure total preload. Total preload at the (start plus drive pinion preload) should be 2.6–4.3 inch lbs.
16. Inspect tooth contact between ring

gear and drive pinion as follows:
a. Coat 3 or 4 teeth at three different positions on ring gear with red lead.
b. Hold companion flange firmly, then rotate ring gear in both directions, **Fig. 11.**
c. Inspect tooth pattern.
d. If teeth are not contacting properly, use proper washers for correction, **Fig. 12.**

17. Install bearing spacer, oil seal and companion flange.
18. Check drive pinion preload as follows:
    a. Using a torque meter, measure drive pinion preload using backlash of drive pinion and ring gear. Preload (at the start) should be 8.7–13.9 inch lbs., for new bearing or 4.3–6.9 lbs., for used bearing.
    b. If preload is greater than specified, replace bearing spacer.
    c. If preload is less than specified, retighten nut to 9 ft. lbs. at a time until specified preload is reached.
    d. If maximum torque is exceeded 174 ft. lbs. while tightening nut, replace bearing spacer and repeat procedure.
    e. Do not back off the pinion nut to reduce preload.
19. Check ring gear backlash. Backlash should be .0051–.0071 inch.
20. Recheck tooth contact between ring gear and drive pinion. Refer to step 16.
21. Using dial indicator, measure vertical and lateral runout of companion flange. Maximum runout should be .0039 inch. Maximum lateral runout should be .0039 inch.
22. If runout is greater than maximum, inspect bearings.
23. Stake drive pinion nut.
24. Install side gear shaft oil seals.
25. Install differential tube. **Torque** attaching bolt to 65 ft. lbs.
26. Install side gear shafts.
27. Install differential carrier cover. **Torque** attaching bolts to 34 ft. lbs.

REAR AXLE HUB & CARRIER SERVICE

REPLACEMENT

1. Remove cotter pin, bearing locknut cap and bearing locknut, **Fig. 13.**
2. Disconnect parking brake cable, then remove brake caliper.
3. Remove rotor disc. Before removing rotor, place alignment marks on the axle hub and rotor disc.
4. Check axial bearing play. Bearing play should be .0020 inch or less.
5. Check axle shaft flange runout. Maximum flange runout should be .0028 inch or less.
6. Remove parking brake assembly and parking brake cable.
7. **On models equipped with ABS,** disconnect ABS speed sensor.
8. Remove axle carrier with axle hub as follows:
    a. Remove the two axle carrier attaching nuts and the two bolts with the camber adjusting cam assembly.
    b. Disconnect strut rod from the axle carrier.
    c. Disconnect the No. 1 suspension arm from the axle carrier assembly.
    d. Disconnect the No. 2 suspension arm from the axle carrier.
    e. Remove the axle carrier and hub assembly.

AXLE HUB & BEARING, REPLACE

1. Raise and support vehicle, then remove rear wheel and brake drum.
2. Remove axle shaft from axle hub.
3. Remove bearing inner race (outer) from axle shaft.
4. Remove dust cover, then the inner and outer oil seals.
5. Remove hole snap ring.
6. Remove bearing.
7. Install bearing.
8. Install hole snap ring and outer seal.
9. Install dust cover, axle shaft and inner oil seal.
10. Install axle carrier with axle hub. Install carrier with axle hub. Place rear axle carrier to the shock absorber lower bracket. Install the two attaching bolts and nuts. **Torque** nuts to 188 ft. lbs.
11. Temporarily install the No. 2 suspension arm to the axle carrier and the No. 1 suspension arm to the axle carrier.
12. Temporarily install the strut rod to the axle carrier.
13. Install parking brake cable, parking brake assembly and rotor disc. Install brake caliper and **torque** attaching bolts to 34 ft. lbs.
14. Install plate washer, bearing locknut, bearing locknut cap and a new cotter pin. **Torque** attaching nut to 137 ft. lbs.
15. **Torque** strut rod to axle carrier mount bolts to 83 ft. lbs. **Torque** No. 1 and No. 2 suspension arm to axle carrier attaching bolts to 90 ft. lbs.

REAR AXLE SHAFT

REPLACE

REMOVAL

1. Remove rear wheels, then the brake drums.
2. Remove backing plate mounting nuts.
3. **On models equipped with ABS,** Remove ABS speed sensor.
4. **On all models,** using slide hammer No. 09520-00031, or equivalent, remove rear axle shaft. **Ensure care is taken not to damage oil seal when removing shaft.**
5. Disconnect brake line from wheel cylinder, then remove backing plate.
6. Remove end gasket from rear axle housing.

INSTALLATION

1. Apply suitable sealer to both sides of end gasket and retainer gasket.
2. Install end gasket on axle housing with notch facing downward.
3. **On models equipped with ABS,** install ABS speed sensor.
4. **On all models,** install backing plate on axle housing, then connect brake lineto wheel cylinder.
5. Install retainer gasket on axle shaft.
6. Install axle shaft, then the retaining nuts. **Torque** nuts to 48 ft. lbs.
7. Install brake drums, then bleed brake system.
8. Install wheels.

Drive Axles

INDEX

Page No.
Drive Axle Specifications 48-333
Identification.....................48-325
Integral Type Carrier Differential w/Independent Rear Suspension 48-329
Except Limited Slip 48-329
Limited Slip Differential 48-331
Removable Type Carrier Differential.......................48-325
Celica 48-325
Land Cruiser, Pickup, Previa, Tacoma, T100 & 4Runner.....48-327
RAV4..........................48-326

IDENTIFICATION

Refer to **Fig. 1** for drive axle identification.

REMOVABLE TYPE CARRIER DIFFERENTIAL

CELICA

Disassemble

1. Mount carrier assembly in a suitable holding fixture.
2. Loosen staked flange of pinion nut, then hold companion flange with holding tool No. 09330-00021, or equivalent and remove pinion nut and washer, **Fig. 2.**
3. Using holding tool No. 09557-22022, or equivalent, remove companion flange.
4. Using pulling tool No. 09308-10010, or equivalent, remove oil seal.
5. Remove oil slinger.
6. Remove front bearing, using holding tool No. 09556-22010, or equivalent, for 6.7 in. axle and holding tool No. 09556-30010, or equivalent, for 7.5 in. axle.
7. Punch alignment marks on bearing caps and carrier to prevent intermixing left and right bearing caps.
8. Remove following parts, **Fig. 3:**
   a. Lock plate mounting nut (1).
   b. Lock plate (2).
   c. Bearing cap mounting bolt (3).
   d. Bearing cap (4).
   e. Adjusting nut (5).
9. Remove differential case together with bearing cups.
10. Remove drive pinion and spacer.
11. Remove front and rear bearing cups with tool No. 09608-30011, or equivalent. Tool No. 09608-30030, or equivalent, must also be used on 6.7 in. axle.
12. Remove drive pinion rear bearing using suitable puller, use care not to deform the plate washer used to adjust pinion extension.
13. Remove side bearings from differential case using suitable puller.
14. Remove ring gear set bolts and lock plates, then separate ring gear from case by lightly tapping outer perimeter of ring gear with a soft faced mallet.
15. Disassemble differential case as follows:
   a. Drive out straight pin toward the ring gear mounting surface.
   b. Push out pinion shaft, and take out differential pinions, differential side gears, and thrust washers.

Assemble

Before assembling, apply hypoid gear oil to each part.

1. Assemble differential case as follows:
   a. Assemble side gears and thrust washers, with oil groove side positioned toward side gear, into differential case.
   b. Assemble differential pinions, and insert pinion shaft with straight pin holes aligned. **Install straight pin after completing side gear backlash adjustment.**
2. Adjust the differential side gear backlash.
   a. Place the dial gauge spindle against side gear tooth tip, and while holding one pinion fixed, measure backlash by moving side gear, **Fig. 4.** Backlash should be .0020–.0079 in. (.05–.20 mm).
   b. If required, adjust backlash by installing replacement thrust washers. If possible, select washers of equal thickness for each side, **Fig. 5.**
3. Drive in straight pin from ring gear mounting surface side, then peen case pin hole with a hammer.
4. Press differential side bearings onto the case.
5. Install ring gear on differential case.
   a. Cut off hexagon head from a separate ring gear set bolt, form a screwdriver slot on cut end, then screw bolt into gear to serve as guide pin for ring gear.
   b. Heat ring gear to around 194° to 230°F, and quickly fit into case.
   c. Screw on bolts over lock plates. **Torque** bolts to 66.5–76 ft. lbs.
   d. Lock bolts by prying up lock plate lips.
6. Install bearing cups into differential carrier with tool No. 09608-30011, or equivalent. Tool No. 09608-30030, or equivalent, must be used to press in rear bearing cup on 6.7 in axle.
7. Mount pinion assembly in housing, then install front bearing and companion flange on pinion. **Bearing spacer, oil slinger and seal are installed after assembly adjustments have been performed.**
8. Press companion flange onto pinion using tool No. 09557-22022, or equivalent, **Fig. 6,** then install washer and nut.
9. Hold companion flange and tighten pinion nut to obtain specified preload. **To prevent bearing damage, tighten nut in small increments, checking preload with torque wrench between each adjustment, Fig. 7.**
10. Install the differential case on the carrier.
   a. Assemble differential case, together with bearing cups, on carrier.
   b. Assemble adjusting nuts, making sure to fit threads on properly.
   c. Assemble bearing caps, and tighten bolts until spring washers just begin to take effect.
   d. Screw in adjusting nuts at both sides with tool No. 09504-00011, or equivalent, until bearing cups are properly seated in carrier.
   e. Tighten adjuster on rear side of ring gear until backlash is approximately 0.008 inch, then securely tighten adjuster on face side of ring gear and recheck backlash. **If tightening adjuster increases backlash, loosen nut until original backlash is restored.**
   f. Mount dial indicator with pointer against race of bearing opposite ring gear face, **Fig. 8.**
   g. Adjust for zero preload by tightening adjuster nut on gear face side until indicator needle just begins to move, then tighten nut an additional 1–1 ½ notches to set preload.
   h. Adjust ring gear backlash, **Fig. 9,** to 0.0051–0.0071 inch by turning both adjusters equal amounts in opposite directions. **Adjusters must be turned equally to maintain bearing preload.**
   i. **Torque** bearing cap bolts to 58 ft. lbs., then ensure backlash is still within specifications.
   j. Measure total assembly preload with torque wrench, **Fig. 7.** If total preload is not greater than pinion preload by 2.6–4.3 inch lbs., recheck differential installation.
11. Coat several ring gear teeth at 3 evenly spaced locations with lead marking compound.
12. Hold companion flange to place drag on assembly, rotate ring gear in both directions and inspect tooth contact pattern, **Fig. 10.**
13. Remove differential and pinion assemblies from carrier.

Model	Size①	Ratio
Land Cruiser	9.5	4.100
MR2⑨	15.343⑪	4.285
MR2⑩	⑫	⑬
Pickup 2WD	7.5	3.417
	8.0	3.071
Pickup & 1993–95 4Runner	8.0	②
RAV4	⑧	2.928
Tacoma	8.0	⑤
T100	8.0	③
Supra	8.0	④
1996 4Runner 2WD Models	8.0	⑥
1996 4Runner 4WD Models	8.0	⑦

① — Inches.
② — A340F transmission, 4.556; A340H transmission, 4.100; G58 transmission, 4.100; R150F transmission, 4.100; R150F transmission and 10.5R15 tire with 7JJ wheel, 4.556; W56 transmission, 4.100.
③ — 3RZ-FE engine w/manual transmission, 3.615; 3RZ-FE engine w/auto transmission, 3.916; 5VZ-FE engine w/manual transmission 2WD, 3.769; 5VZ-FE engine w/manual transmission 4WD, 3.909; 5VZ-FE engine w/manual transmission 4WD & 31 inch tires, 4.100.
④ — 2JZ-GE engine, W58 & A340E transmissions, 4.272; 2JZ-GTE engine, V160 manual transmission, 3.133; A340E automatic transmission, 3.769.
⑤ — 2RZ-FE engine w/manual transmission, 3.416; 3RZ-FE engine w/manual transmission, 3.583; 2RZ-FE engine w/auto transmission, 3.583; 3RZ-FE engine w/auto transmission, 3.410; 5VZ-FE engine w/manual transmission 2WD, 3.153; 5VZ-FE engine w/manual transmission 4WD, 3.909; 5VZ-FE engine w/manual transmission 4WD & 31 inch tires, 4.100.
⑥ — 3RZ-FE engine w/manual transmission & 5VZ-FE engine w/automatic transmission, 3.727; 3RZ-FE engine w/automatic transmission, 3.909.
⑦ — 3RZ-FE engine w/A340F & W59 transmissions, 4.100 (4.556 w/P265/70R16 Tire); 5VZ-FE engine w/R150 & A340F transmissions, 3.909 (4.100 w/P265/70R16 Tire).
⑧ — LH side, 21.787 inches; RH side, 23.598 inches.
⑨ — 3S-GTE engine.
⑩ — 5S-FE engine.
⑪ — LH side & RH side halfshafts.
⑫ — LH side, 21.272 inches; RH side, 32.732 inches.
⑬ — S54 manual transaxle, 4.176; A241 automatic transaxle, 3.034.

Fig. 1 Identification Chart

14. If tooth contact is incorrect, replace washer between rear bearing and pinion with one that will provide proper contact, **Fig. 11. If pinion depth adjustment is necessary, repeat steps 7–14 until proper contact has been obtained.**
15. Install selected thrust washer and press rear bearing onto pinion, then mount pinion assembly in carrier.
16. Install new bearing spacer, front bearing and oil slinger on pinion shaft.
17. Install oil seal to a depth of 0.157 inch on Celica and Supra using a suitable driver, **Fig. 12.**
18. Press companion flange onto pinion with tool No. 09557-22022, or equivalent, **Fig. 6.**
19. Install washer and new pinion nut, hold companion flange and **torque** nut to 80 ft. lbs.
20. Measure pinion preload, **Fig. 7.** If preload is greater than specified, replace bearing spacer. If preload is less than specified, continue tightening nut 5–10° at a time until specified preload is obtained. **If maximum torque of 174 ft. lbs. is exceeded when tightening nut, replace bearing spacer and repeat procedure. Do not back-off on nut to reduce torque or preload.**
21. Ensure companion flange runout is less than 0.004 inch, then stake pinion nut.
22. Install differential assembly and adjust preload and backlash as outlined in step 10.
23. Ensure total assembly preload is within specifications.
24. Select and install adjusting nut locks and **torque** lock retaining bolts to 9 ft. lbs.

RAV4

Disassemble

1. Using a hammer and chisel, unstake staked part of companion flange nut, **Fig. 13.**
2. Using tool No. 09330-00021, or equivalent, to hold flange, remove companion flange nut.
3. Using tool Nos. 09950-30010 and 09954-03010, or equivalents, remove companion flange.
4. Using tool No. 09308-10010, or equivalent, remove oil seal and oil slinger from housing.
5. Using tool No. 09556-22010, or equivalent, remove front bearing from drive pinion.
6. Remove bearing spacer.
7. **On models with torque sensing limited slip differential,** proceed as follows:
   a. Using tool No. 09520-24010, or equivalent, remove two side gear shafts from differential.
   b. Using a screwdriver, remove two snap rings from side gear shafts.
8. **On models with 2 pinion differential,** proceed as follows:
   a. Use needle nose pliers to remove two snap rings from side gear shafts.
   b. Remove side gear shafts.
9. **On all models,** use tool No. 09308-00010, or equivalent, to remove oil seals from housing.
10. Place matchmarks on bearing and differential carrier, then remove bearing caps.
11. Using tool No. 09504-22010, or equivalent, remove two plate washers.
12. Remove differential case and two bearing outer races from carrier.
13. Remove drive pinion from differential carrier.
14. Using tool No. 09950-00020, or equivalent and a suitable press, remove bearing from drive pinion.
15. Remove plate washer.
16. Remove front and rear bearing outer races using brass bar and hammer.
17. Place matchmarks on ring gear and differential case.
18. Using a screwdriver, unstake four ring gear lock plates.
19. Remove 8 ring gear set bolts and four lock plates.
20. Using a plastic hammer, tap on ring gear to separate it from differential case.
21. Remove side bearings from differential case using tool No. 09950-00020, or equivalent.
22. **On models with 2 pinion differential,** proceed as follows:
   a. Using pin punch and hammer, remove differential case straight pin.
   b. Remove pinion shaft, two pinion gears, two pinion gear thrust washers, two side gears and side gear thrust washers.

Assemble

1. **On models with 2 pinion differential,** proceed as follows:
   a. Install two proper thrust washers on two side gears. Select shim from selection chart, **Fig. 14,** to ensure side gear backlash is .0020–.0079 inch.
   b. Install two side gears, two pinion gears, two pinion gear thrust washers and pinion shaft into differential case.
   c. Measure side gear backlash while holding one pinion gear toward differential case. If backlash is not .0020–.0079 inch, install two side gear thrust washers of different

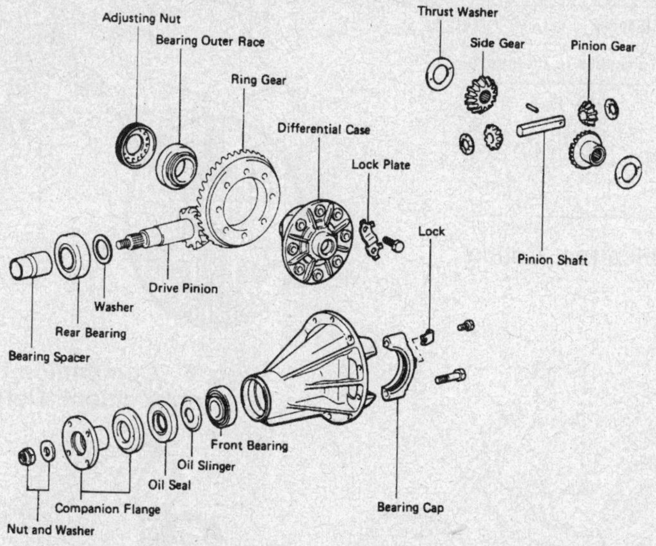
Adjusting Nut
Bearing Outer Race
Ring Gear
Differential Case
Lock Plate
Lock
Thrust Washer
Side Gear
Pinion Gear
Pinion Shaft
Drive Pinion
Washer
Rear Bearing
Bearing Spacer
Front Bearing
Oil Slinger
Oil Seal
Companion Flange
Nut and Washer
Bearing Cap
TY3039100058000X

Fig. 2 Exploded view of removable type carrier differential. Celica

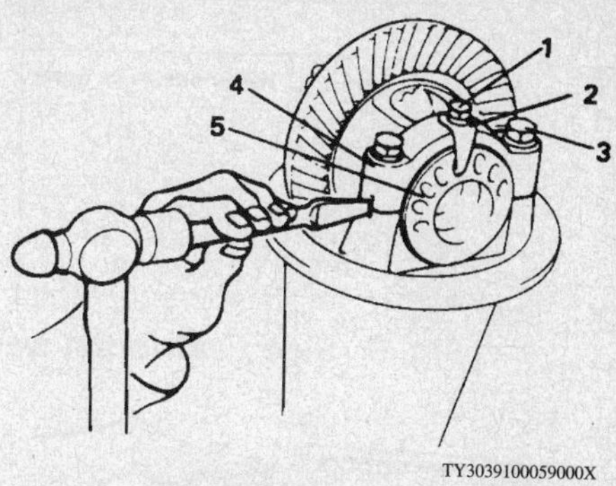
1
2
3
4
5
TY3039100059000X

Fig. 3 Differential case removal. Celica

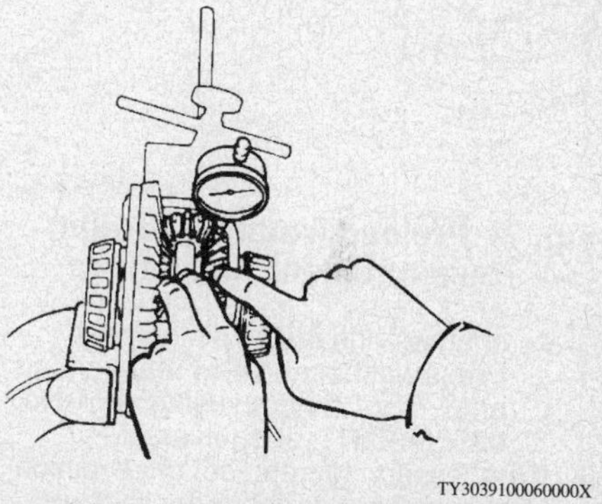
TY3039100060000X

Fig. 4 Differential side gear backlash measurement. Celica

thicknesses.
   d. Install straight pin and stake outside of differential case pin hole.
2. **On all models,** clean contact surfaces of differential case and ring gear.
3. Heat ring gear in boiling water.
4. Carefully remove ring gear from boiling water and install to differential case.
5. Align matchmarks on ring gear and differential case.
6. Temporarily install 4 lock plates and 8 bolts.
7. After ring gear has cooled, **torque** 8 lock plate bolts to 71 ft lbs.
8. Using a chisel and hammer, stake outside of differential case pin hole.
9. Using tool No. 09710-22021, or equivalent and a press, install two side bearings into differential case.
10. Install differential case on carrier and install 2 plate washers where no play exists in bearing.
11. Install bearing caps.
12. Using dial indicator, measure runout of ring gear. Maximum runout should be .0028 inch.
13. Remove two bearing caps, two plate washers and differential carrier.
14. Install front and rear bearing outer races.
15. Install reused washer on drive pinion.
16. Using tool No. 09506-30012, or equivalent and a press, install rear bearing onto drive pinion.
17. Install drive pinion and front bearing.
18. Using tool Nos. 09950-30010 and 09954-03010, or equivalents, install companion flange.
19. Adjust drive pinion preload by tightening companion flange nut.
20. Using tool No. 09330-00021, or equivalent, to hold flange, **torque** nut to 80 ft. lbs.
21. Using a torque wrench to measure preload, ensure preload is within specifications.
22. Place two bearing outer races in their respective bearings, then install differential case in carrier.
23. Adjust ring gear backlash as follows:
   a. Install plate washer on ring gear back side.
   b. Snug down washer and bearing by tapping on ring gear with plastic hammer.
   c. Using dial indicator, hold side bearing boss on teeth surface of ring gear and measure ring gear backlash. Backlash should be .0051 inch.
   d. Select ring gear back side plate washer to ensure backlash is correct.
   e. Select a ring gear teeth side washer with thickness that eliminates any clearance between outer race and case.
   f. Remove plate washer and differential case.
   g. Install plate washer into ring gear back side.
   h. Place outer plate washer onto differential case together with outer race.
   i. Install differential case with outer race onto carrier.
   j. Using a plastic hammer, snug down washer and bearing by tapping ring gear.
24. Remove companion flange and front bearing.
25. Install new bearing spacer and front bearing.
26. Install oil slinger and new front oil seal. Apply grease to oil seal lip.
27. Install companion flange, then check drive pinion preload. If preload is greater than specification, replace bearing spacer. If preload is less than specification, **retorque** nut 9 ft. lbs. at a time until proper preload is reached.
28. **Do not back off pinion nut to reduce preload.**
29. Stake drive pinion nut, then install side gear shaft oil seals.
30. Install side gear shafts with new snap rings.
31. **On models with 2 pinion differential,** install two side gear shafts to differential case with new snap rings.
32. **On all models,** install differential carrier cover. **Torque** to 34 ft. lbs.

LAND CRUISER, PICKUP, PREVIA, TACOMA, T100 & 4RUNNER

Disassemble

1. Place carrier assembly on a suitable workbench, **Fig. 15.**
2. Loosen staked portion of companion flange locknut, then retain flange using tool No. 09330-00021, or equivalent and remove nut.
3. Remove companion flange using tool No. 09557-22022, or equivalent.
4. Remove oil seal, using tool No. 09557-22022, or equivalent, then the oil slinger.
5. Remove front bearing front drive pinion, using tool No. 09556-30010, or equivalent, then the bearing spacer.
6. Mark relative position between bearing cap and differential carrier, then remove 2 adjusting locknuts, bearing caps, adjusting nuts, bearing outer races and differential case from carrier. **Tag components as to original location to facilitate installation.**
7. Remove drive pinion from differential carrier.
8. If necessary to replace drive pinion rear bearing, proceed as follows:
   a. Remove rear bearing from drive pinion, using tool No. 09950-00020, or equivalent.
   b. Install washer on drive pinion with

6.7 In.		7.5 In.	
Part No.	Thickness In In. (mm)	Part No.	Thickness In In. (mm)
41361-22140	.0374 (.95)	41361-30040	.0394 (1.0)
41361-22020	.0394 (1.0)	41361-30050	.0433 (1.1)
41361-22150	.0413 (1.05)	41361-30060	.0472 (1.2)
41361-22030	.0433 (1.1)	41361-30070	.0512 (1.3)
41361-22160	.0453 (1.15)		
41361-22040	.0472 (1.2)		

TY3039100061000X

Fig. 5 Side gear thrust washer identification. Celica

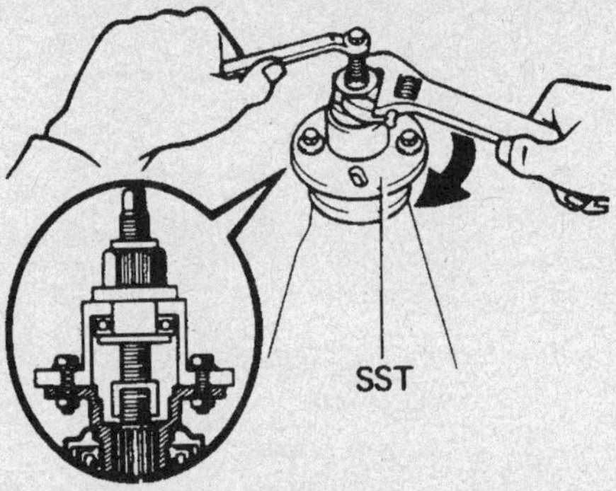
SST

TY3039100062000X

Fig. 6 Companion flange replacement. Celica

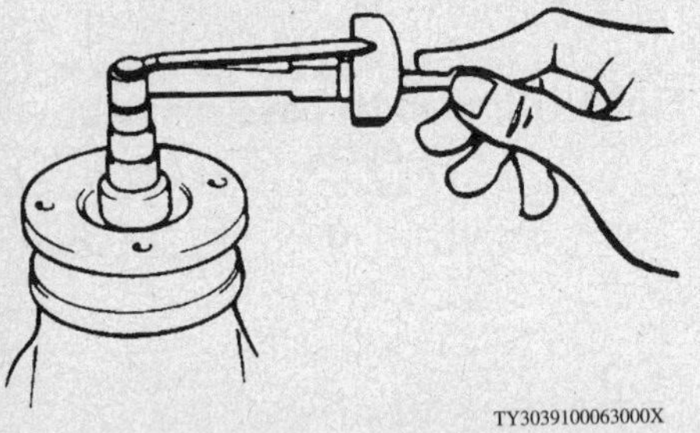

TY3039100063000X

Fig. 7 Preload (rotating torque) measurement. Celica

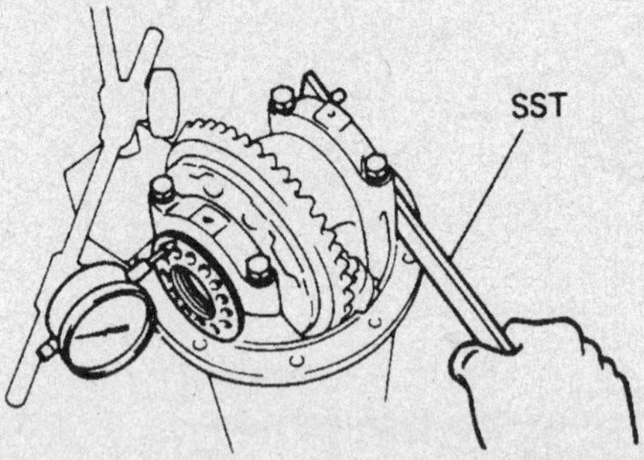
SST

TY3039100064000X

Fig. 8 Differential bearing preload adjustment. Celica

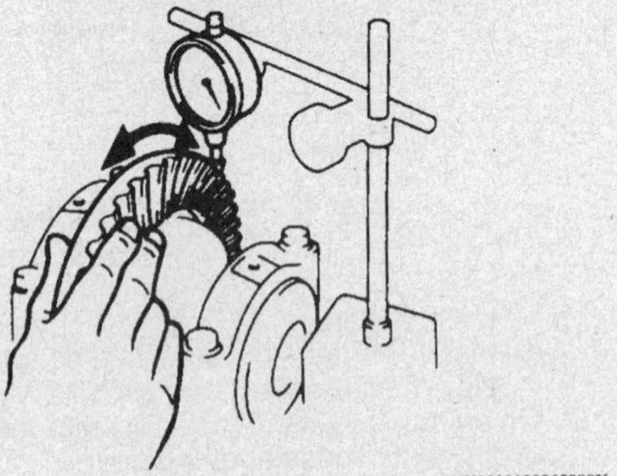

TY3039100065000X

Fig. 9 Ring gear & pinion backlash adjustment. Celica

chamfer end facing pinion gear.

c. Press washer and new rear bearing onto drive pinion, using tool No. 09506-30011, or equivalent.

9. If necessary to replace drive pinion front and rear bearing outer race, proceed as follows:
   a. Drive out outer bearing race using a hammer and suitable drift.
   b. Press in new outer race using suitable tool.
10. Remove side bearing from differential case using tool No. 09950-20016, or equivalent.
11. Remove ring gear attaching bolts and lock plates, then mark relative position between ring gear and differential case. Separate ring gear from case by tapping on ring gear, using a suitable mallet.
12. Drive out straight pin, then remove pinion shaft, two pinion gears, side gears and thrust washers from differential case.

Assemble

1. Select suitable thrust washers from chart, **Fig. 16** that will bring backlash to .0020–.0079 inch, then install thrust washers into differential case.
2. Drive in straight pin, using a hammer and suitable drift, through case and hole in pinion shaft, then stake pin to differential case.
3. Install side bearings using tool No. 09608-30012, or equivalent.
4. Clean mating surfaces of differential case, then heat ring gear in a suitable oil bath to approximately 212°F.
5. Install ring gear into differential case, aligning mating marks on gear and case.
6. Apply a suitable lubricant to ring gear, then install lock plates and attaching bolts. **Torque** bolts uniformly to 71 ft. lbs.
7. Stake lock plates using a hammer and suitable drift.
8. Check ring gear runout. Maximum runout should be .0028 inch on ½ ton Previa and Pickup models, or .0039 inch on 4WD Pickup and 4Runner models.
9. Temporarily adjust drive pinion preload as follows:
   a. Install drive pinion and front bearing.
   b. Install companion flange using tool No. 09557-22022, or equivalent.
   c. Retain companion flange using tool No. 09330-0021, or equivalent, then adjust drive pinion preload to 5.2–8.7 inch lbs. on ½ ton Pickup and Previa, 7.8–11.3 on 4WD Pickup and 4Runner models.
10. Place bearing outer races on their respective bearings, then insert case into carrier.
11. Install adjusting nuts on their respective carrier, ensuring backlash exists between ring gear and drive pinion.
12. Align mating marks on bearing caps and carrier, then rotate cap bolts 2–3 turns and manually depress cap.
13. Tighten cap bolts until adjusting nut on ring gear side until backlash is approximately .008 inch.
14. Tighten adjusting nut from drive pinion side as shown, **Fig. 8,** then check for backlash. If tightening nut causes backlash, loosen nut until backlash is eliminated.
15. Install a suitable dial indicator on top of adjusting nut, then adjust side bearing for zero preload, or until indicator begins to move. **Tighten nut 1 ½ notches from zero preload position.**
16. Adjust ring gear backlash to .0051–.0071 inch, by rotating both left and right adjusting nuts equal amounts, then **torque** bearing cap bolts to 58 ft. lbs.
17. Measure total preload. Preload should be 3.5–5.2 inch lbs., with a preload of .0051–.0071 inch.
18. Inspect gear tooth contact as shown, **Fig. 10.** If contacting pattern is not correct, select a suitable shim from chart, **Fig. 17,** that will ensure proper contact.
19. Install new bearing spacer and front bearing.
20. Install oil slinger, then drive in new oil seal to a depth of .059 inch on ½ ton Pickup and Previa or .039 inch on 4WD Pickup and 4Runner models.
21. Install companion flange, using tool No. 09557-22022, or equivalent, then apply a suitable lubricant to new nut. Retain companion flange, using tool No. 09330-00021, or equivalent, then install nut and **torque** to 80–173 ft. lbs. on ½ ton Pickup and Previa, 145–253 ft. lbs. on 1 ton and 4WD Pickup and 4Runner models.
22. Check drive pinion preload. Drive pinion preload should be 5.2–8.7 inch lbs. on ½ ton Pickup, 7.8–11.3 inch lbs. on 1 ton and 4WD Pickup and 4Runner models.
23. If preload is greater than specified, replace bearing spacer. If preload is less than specified **torque** nut 9 ft. lbs. at a time until specified preload is obtained. **If maximum torque is exceeded during tightening procedure, replace bearing spacer and repeat preload adjustment.**
24. Check companion flange deviation. Deviation in any direction should not exceed .0039 inch.
25. Stake drive pinion nut.
26. Install bearing cap nut lock, then **torque** attaching bolt to 9 ft. lbs.

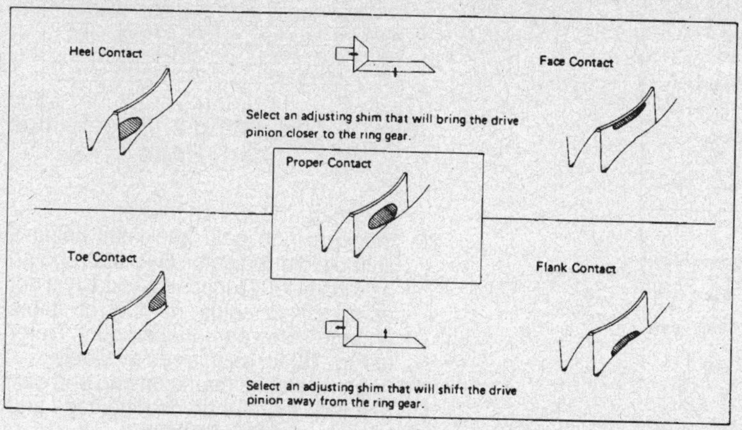
Heel Contact
Face Contact
Select an adjusting shim that will bring the drive pinion closer to the ring gear.
Proper Contact
Toe Contact
Flank Contact
Select an adjusting shim that will shift the drive pinion away from the ring gear.

TY3039100066000X

Fig. 10 Ring gear & pinion tooth contact inspection. Celica

Part No.	Thickness in In. (mm)
90201-35434①	.0882 (2.24)
90201-35435	.0894 (2.27)
90201-35436	.0906 (2.30)
90201-35437	.0917 (2.33)
90201-35396	.0929 (2.36)
90201-35397	.0941 (2.39)
90201-35398	.0953 (2.42)
90201-35399	.0965 (2.45)
90201-35400	.0976 (2.48)
90201-35401	.0988 (2.51)
90201-35402	.1000 (2.54)
90201-35403	.1012 (2.57)
90201-35404	.1024 (2.6)
90201-35438	.1036 (2.63)
90201-35439	.1048 (2.66)
90201-35440	.1059 (2.69)
90201-35441①	.1071 (2.72)

①—For 7.5 in. axle only.

TY3039100067000X

Fig. 11 Drive pinion washer identification. Celica

INTEGRAL TYPE CARRIER DIFFERENTIAL W/INDEPENDENT REAR SUSPENSION

EXCEPT LIMITED SLIP

SUPRA

Disassemble

1. Drain lubricant, then remove differential carrier cover attaching bolts and the cover, **Fig. 18.**
2. Using suitable dial indicator, measure ring gear runout. If runout exceeds .0028 inch, replace ring gear.
3. With dial indicator positioned 90° to ring gear teeth surface, hold drive pinion flange while measuring ring gear backlash. Backlash should be .0051–.0071 inch. If backlash is not within specifications, it must be adjusted.
4. Using suitable inch lbs. torque wrench mounted on pinion nut, **Fig. 7,** measure and record starting preload of the ring and pinion backlash. Preload should be 4.3–6.9 inch lbs.
5. With wrench positioned as above, measure and record the total starting preload of ring and pinion assembly. Total preload should be 3.5–5.2 inch lbs. plus drive pinion preload measured in step 4, above.
6. Using suitable hammer and chisel, unstake pinion nut.
7. While holding companion flange from turning with tool 09330-00021, remove pinion nut.
8. Remove companion flange with suitable puller.
9. Remove pinion oil seal and oil slinger from differential carrier.
10. Remove pinion rear bearing using suitable puller, then the spacer.
11. Remove side gear shaft from differential with puller tool No. 09520-24010, or equivalent.
12. Remove side gear shaft oil seal with puller tool No. 09308-00010, or equivalent.
13. Place reference marks between bearing caps and differential carrier, then remove bearing cap bolts and caps.
14. Remove two side bearing preload adjusting shims.
15. Lift differential case with bearing outer races from differential carrier.
16. Tag outer races to show which side they were removed from.
17. Remove drive pinion from differential carrier.
18. If necessary to replace drive pinion rear bearing, remove rear bearing from drive pinion, using press and tool No. 09950-00020, or equivalent. **If drive pinion or ring gear are damaged, they must be replaced as a set.**
19. If necessary to replace drive pinion

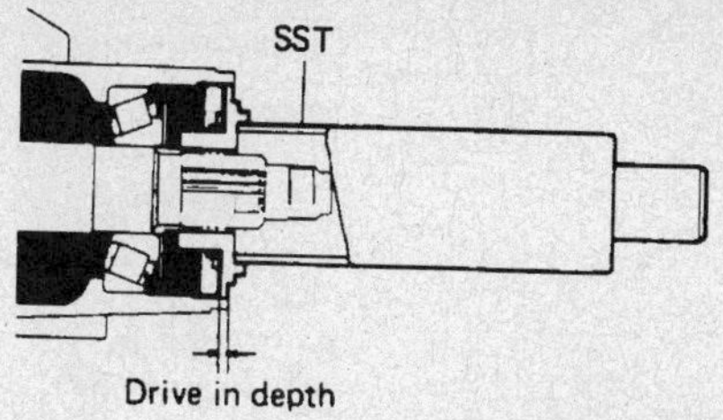
SST
Drive in depth

TY3039100068000X

Fig. 12 Pinion seal installation. Celica

front and rear bearing outer race, drive out outer bearing race using a hammer and suitable drift.

20. If necessary to replace differential side bearings, remove with puller tool No. 09950-20017, or equivalent.
21. If ring gear replacement is necessary, proceed as follows:
    a. Make reference marks between ring gear and differential case.
    b. Bend back attaching bolt lock plates, then remove ring gear attaching bolts and lock plates.
    c. Tap on ring gear with plastic mallet to separate it from differential case.

Differential Case Service

1. Make reference marks between left and right side differential case halves.
2. Remove 8 case halves attaching bolts, then separate halves by tapping with plastic hammer.
3. Remove two side gears, two side gear thrust washers, spider, four pinion gears and four pinion thrust washers.
4. Install side gear thrust washer on side gear, then install in right side of case.
5. Install four pinion gears and thrust washers to spider, then install spider in right side of case.
6. While holding side gear, measure side gear backlash. Backlash should be .002–.0079 inch. **Measure backlash at right side case and at left side case.**
7. If backlash is not within specifications, install a different thickness thrust washer. **Washers of same thickness must be used on both right and left sides.**
8. Install side gears and thrust washers to right side case.
9. Install pinion gears and spider to right side case.
10. Install side gear and thrust washer to left side case.
11. Lubricate differential case parts with gear oil.
12. Align right and left side case reference marks and position together.
13. Install 8 attaching bolts and **torque** to 35 ft. lbs.

Assemble

1. Place ring gear in oil bath heated to 212°F, then clean differential case to ring gear contact surface with suitable solvent. **Do not heat ring gear to more than 230°F.**
2. Align ring gear and differential case

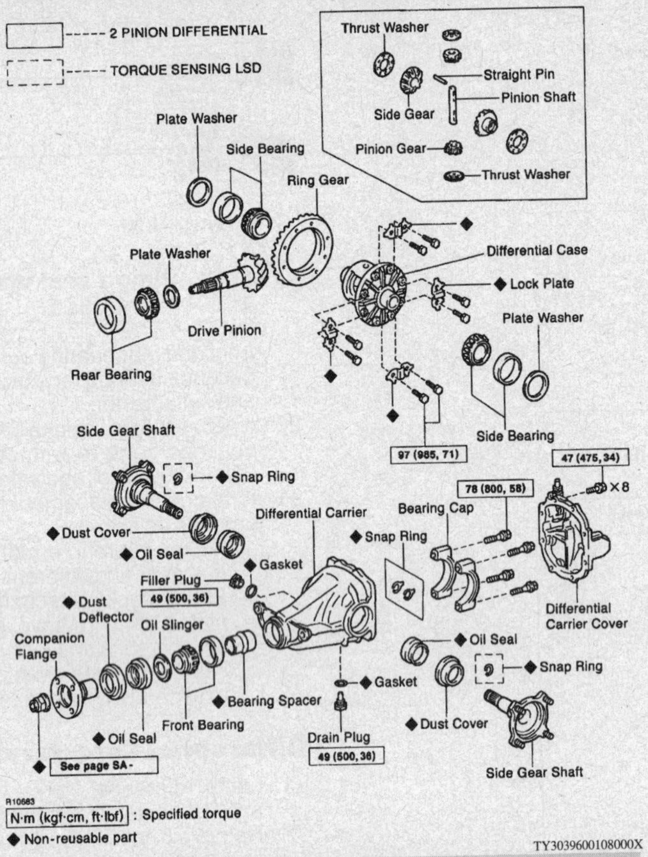
2 PINION DIFFERENTIAL
TORQUE SENSING LSD
Thrust Washer
Straight Pin
Pinion Shaft
Side Gear
Pinion Gear
Thrust Washer
Plate Washer
Side Bearing
Ring Gear
Plate Washer
Differential Case
Lock Plate
Plate Washer
Drive Pinion
Rear Bearing
Side Bearing
Side Gear Shaft
97 (985, 71)
47 (475, 34)
Snap Ring
78 (800, 58)
×8
Differential Carrier
Bearing Cap
Dust Cover
Snap Ring
Oil Seal
Gasket
Filler Plug
49 (500, 36)
Dust Deflector
Oil Slinger
Differential Carrier Cover
Companion Flange
Oil Seal
Snap Ring
Gasket
Bearing Spacer
Front Bearing
Oil Seal
Dust Cover
Drain Plug
49 (500, 36)
See page SA-
Side Gear Shaft
R10683
N·m (kgf·cm, ft·lbf) : Specified torque
Non-reusable part
TY3039600108000X

Fig. 13 Exploded view of differential carrier. RAV4

Thickness mm (in.)	Thickness mm (in.)
0.93–0.97 (0.0366–0.0382)	1.08–1.12 (0.0425–0.0441)
0.98–1.02 (0.0386–0.0402)	1.13–1.17 (0.0445–0.0461)
1.03–1.07 (0.0406–0.0421)	1.18–1.22 (0.0465–0.0480)

TY3039600107000X

Fig. 14 Adjusting shim selection chart. RAV4

alignment marks, then install ring gear on case.

3. Install ring gear attaching bolts and lock plates, then **torque** ring gear attaching bolts to 71 ft. lbs. Bend over lock plates.
4. Press on side bearings using press and tool Nos. 09316-60010 and 09608-30012, or equivalents.
5. Install differential case into carrier and tighten adjusting nut until all play is removed, then check ring gear runout. Maximum runout is .004 inch. Remove differential.
6. Press in pinion front and rear bearing outer races using tool No. 09608-35014, or equivalent.
7. Install washer on drive pinion with chamfer end facing pinion gear.
8. Install new rear bearing onto drive pinion, using press and tool No. 09506-30012, or equivalent.
9. Temporarily adjust drive pinion preload as follows:
   a. Install drive pinion and front bearing.
   b. Install companion flange using tool No. 09557-22022, or equivalent.
   c. Retain companion flange using tool No. 09330-00021, or equivalent, then adjust drive pinion preload to 8.7–13.9 inch lbs. for new bearings or 4.3–6.9 inch lbs. for used bearings.
10. Place bearing outer races on their respective bearings, then insert differential case into carrier.
11. Install shim on ring gear side of case side bearing, then ensure ring gear has backlash.
12. Tap on ring gear, using a suitable mallet to snug down washer and bearing, then retain side bearing boss on tooth surface and measure backlash. Backlash should be .0039 inch.
13. Select proper ring gear side of case side bearing shim, using backlash as reference.
14. Select ring gear side of case side bearing shim with a thickness that will eliminate clearance between outer race and carrier.
15. Remove shims and differential case, then install shim into lower part of carrier.
16. Place second shim onto differential case with outer races, then insert differential case, shim and outer races into carrier.
17. Snug down shim and bearing, by tapping on ring gear, using a suitable mallet.
18. Measure ring gear backlash, using a suitable dial indicator. Backlash should be .0051–.0071 inch. If backlash is not as specified, adjust number of shims on both sides an equal amount.
19. Adjust side bearing preload as follows:
    a. Remove ring gear side of case side bearing shim, then measure and record thickness.
    b. Install a new shim approximately .0024–.0035 inch thicker.
20. Measure ring gear backlash, using a suitable dial indicator. Backlash should be .0051–.0071 inch. If backlash is not as specified, adjust number of shims on both sides an equal amount. Refer to **Fig. 19,** for shim sizes available.
21. Align reference marks on cap and carrier, then install side bearing caps and **torque** evenly to 58 ft. lbs.
22. Measure total preload with inch lbs. wrench on pinion nut. Preload should be 3.5–5.2 inch lbs. in addition to drive pinion preload.
23. Paint 3 or 4 ring gear teeth at 3 different positions on ring gear with red lead paint, then hold companion flange firmly and rotate ring gear in either direction.
24. Inspect gear tooth contact as shown, **Fig. 10.** If contacting pattern is not correct, select a suitable shim from chart, **Fig. 20,** that will ensure proper contact.
25. Remove companion flange and front bearing.
26. Install new bearing spacer and front bearing.
27. Install oil slinger, then drive in new oil seal to a depth of .059 inch.
28. Install companion flange, using tool No. 09557-22022, or equivalent, then apply a suitable lubricant to new nut. Retain companion flange, using tool No. 09330-00021, or equivalent, then install nut and **torque** to 134 ft. lbs.
29. Check preload of backlash between ring and pinion (measure pinion preload). Preload should be 8.7–13.9 inch lbs. on new bearings or 4.3–6.9 inch lbs. on used bearings.
30. If preload is greater than specified, replace bearing spacer. If preload is less that specified, **torque** nut 9 ft. lbs. at a time until specified preload is obtained. **If a maximum torque** to 250 ft. lbs. is exceeded during tightening procedure, replace bearing spacer and repeat preload adjustment.
31. Check companion flange runout. Runout in any direction should not exceed .004 inch. If runout exceeds specifications, inspect pinion bearing.
32. Stake drive pinion nut.
33. Apply a suitable lubricant to new side gear shaft oil seal, then drive in new oil seal using tool Nos. 09608-10010 and 09608-35014, or equivalents, until flush with carrier end surface.
34. Install new snap ring on side gear shaft, then using tool No. 09520-24010, or equivalent, drive in side gear shaft until it contacts pinion shaft.
35. Check side gear shaft runout. If runout exceeds .008 inch in either direction, replace side gear shaft.
36. Install differential carrier cover. **Torque** attaching bolts to 34 ft. lbs.

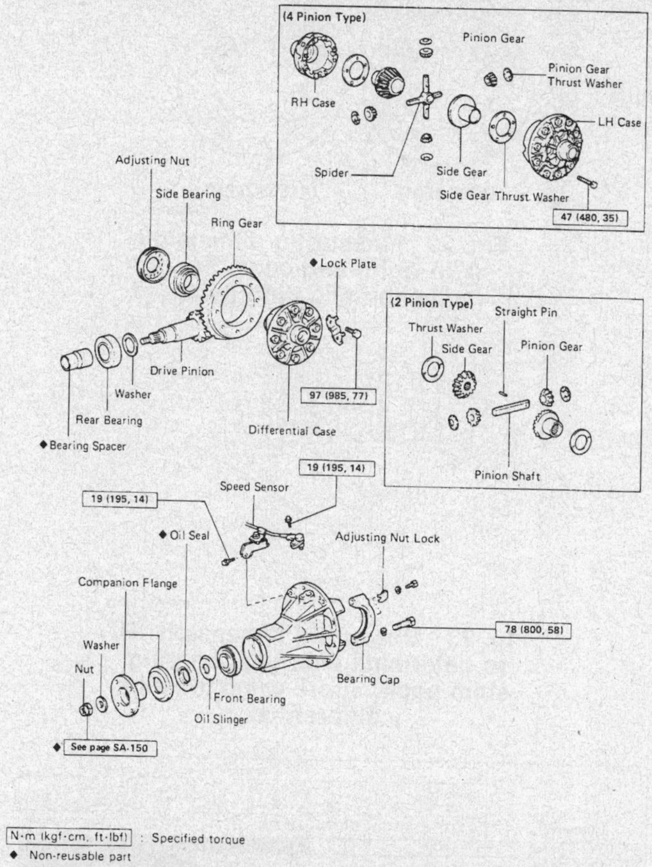
(4 Pinion Type)
Pinion Gear
Pinion Gear Thrust Washer
RH Case
LH Case
Spider
Side Gear
Side Gear Thrust Washer
47 (480, 35)
Adjusting Nut
Side Bearing
Ring Gear
◆ Lock Plate
(2 Pinion Type)
Straight Pin
Thrust Washer
Side Gear
Pinion Gear
Pinion Shaft
Drive Pinion
Washer
Rear Bearing
◆ Bearing Spacer
97 (985, 77)
Differential Case
19 (195, 14)
Speed Sensor
19 (195, 14)
◆ Oil Seal
Adjusting Nut Lock
Companion Flange
78 (800, 58)
Washer
Nut
Bearing Cap
Front Bearing
Oil Slinger
◆ See page SA-150
N·m (kgf·cm, ft·lbf) : Specified torque
◆ Non-reusable part

TY3039100072000X

Fig. 15 Exploded view of differential assembly. Land Cruiser, Pickup, Previa, Tacoma, T100 & 4Runner

Thickness mm (in)	
1/2 ton and 3/4 ton (except*)	C&C and 4WD (incl.*)
1.0 (0.039)	1.6 (0.063)
1.1 (0.043)	1.7 (0.067)
1.2 (0.047)	1.8 (0.071)
1.3 (0.051)	
*: Short wheel base, 22R Engine vehicle.	

TY3039100073000X

Fig. 16 Side gear thrust washer identification. Land Cruiser, Pickup, Previa, Tacoma, T100 & 4Runner

1/2 ton and 3/4 ton (except*)		C & C and 4WD (incl*)	
Thickness	mm (in.)	Thickness	mm (in.)
2.24	(0.0882)	1.70	(0.0669)
2.27	(0.0894)	1.73	(0.0681)
2.30	(0.0906)	1.76	(0.0693)
2.33	(0.0917)	1.79	(0.0705)
2.36	(0.0929)	1.82	(0.0717)
2.39	(0.0941)	1.85	(0.0728)
2.42	(0.0953)	1.88	(0.0740)
2.45	(0.0965)	1.91	(0.0752)
2.48	(0.0976)	1.94	(0.0764)
2.51	(0.0988)	1.97	(0.0776)
2.54	(0.1000)	2.00	(0.0787)
2.57	(0.1012)	2.03	(0.0799)
2.60	(0.1024)	2.06	(0.0811)
2.63	(0.1035)	2.09	(0.0823)
2.66	(0.1047)	2.12	(0.0835)
2.69	(0.1059)	2.15	(0.0846)
2.72	(0.1071)	2.18	(0.0858)
		2.21	(0.0870)
		2.24	(0.0882)
		2.27	(0.0894)
		2.30	(0.0906)
		2.33	(0.0917)
*: Short wheel base, 22R Engine Vehicle.			

TY3039100074000X

Fig. 17 Drive pinion shim identification. Land Cruiser, Pickup, Previa, Tacoma, T100 & 4Runner

LIMITED SLIP DIFFERENTIAL

For removal and installation of differential carrier, and adjustment of pinion depth, backlash and preload, refer to procedure for models "Except Limited Slip Differential."

SUPRA

Disassemble

1. Make reference marks on left and right side differential case halves, then place righthand case in suitable vise.
2. Loosen case halves attaching bolts a little at a time, then remove attaching bolts and separate lefthand case from righthand case, **Fig. 21.**
3. From lefthand side case, remove side gear, 5 side gear thrust washers and 4 clutch plates. **Keep disassembled parts in order.**
4. From righthand case, remove lefthand retainer, spring, spider with pinion gear, righthand retainer, side gear, 5 side gear thrust washers and 4 clutch plates. **Keep disassembled parts in order they were removed.**

Inspection & Adjustment

1. Inspect parts for signs of damage or wear. Replace as necessary. **If side gear requires replacement, replace the thrust washer that contacts it also.**
2. Inspect thrust washers for damage or wear. Ensure contact surface is even with no bare metal showing.
3. Using a suitable micrometer, measure thrust washer thickness. If less than .0685 (1.74 mm), replace thrust washers. If thrust washers require replacement, replace clutch plate that contacts thrust washer.
4. Check clutch plates for wear or damage and replace as necessary. **These differentials may be assembled with either of two type clutch plates, Fig. 21.** If clutch plates require replacement, they must be replaced with the same type that was removed.
5. Measure spring free length. Spring should be 1.232 inch (31.3 mm).
6. Measure and record right side case dimension "A, " **Fig. 22,** then determine required side bearing shim thickness as follows:
   a. Assemble thrust washers and clutch plates on side gear. **Do not assemble side gear shims at this time.**
   b. Using tool No. 09726-35010, or equivalent, apply approximately 22 lbs. of pressure to thrust washer and clutch pack while measuring dimension "B," **Fig. 23.**
   c. To determine side bearing shim thickness "C," use the following formula: "C"= "A"– "B"–.6358 inch (16.15 mm).
   d. Refer to **Figs. 24 and 25** to select proper shims.
   e. Install selected shim(s) between outer thrust washer and case.
7. Determine side bearing shim thickness for left side case by following procedures in step 6, above.

Assemble

1. Lubricate all components with limited slip differential lubricant.
2. Into righthand case, install adjusting shim, thrust washers and clutch plates. **Install thrust washer without oil groove on outer side so it makes contact with the side of the case with no oil groove.**
3. Into lefthand case, install adjusting shim, thrust washers and clutch plates. **Install thrust washer without oil groove on outer side so it makes contact with the side of the case with no oil groove.**
4. Install pinion gears and washers to spider, then align righthand retainer holes with spider lockpins and install retainer.
5. Install spider, pinion, washers and righthand retainer assembly to righthand case.
6. Secure side gear, then measure backlash while pushing on spider retainer. Backlash should be .002–.0079 inch

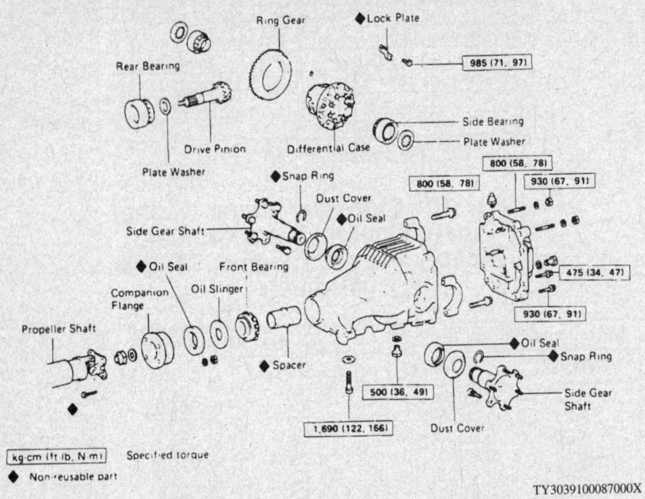
Ring Gear
◆Lock Plate
985 (71, 97)
Rear Bearing
Drive Pinion
Differential Case
Side Bearing
Plate Washer
Plate Washer
800 (58, 78)
◆Snap Ring
800 (58, 78)
930 (67, 91)
Dust Cover
◆Oil Seal
Side Gear Shaft
◆Oil Seal
Front Bearing
475 (34, 47)
Companion Flange
Oil Slinger
930 (67, 91)
Propeller Shaft
◆Oil Seal
◆Snap Ring
◆Spacer
500 (36, 49)
Side Gear Shaft
1,690 (122, 166)
Dust Cover
kg-cm (ft-lb, N-m) Specified torque
◆ Non-reusable part
TY3039100087000X

Fig. 18 Exploded view of differential assembly. Supra

Washer thickness

Thickness		mm (in.)
2.57 – 2.59 (0.1012 – 0.1020)	2.90 – 2.92 (0.1142 – 0.1150)	3.23 – 3.25 (0.1272 – 0.1280)
2.60 – 2.62 (0.1024 – 0.1031)	2.93 – 2.95 (0.1154 – 0.1161)	3.26 – 3.28 (0.1283 – 0.1291)
2.63 – 2.65 (0.1035 – 0.1043)	2.96 – 2.98 (0.1165 – 0.1173)	3.29 – 3.31 (0.1295 – 0.1303)
2.66 – 2.68 (0.1047 – 0.1055)	2.99 – 3.01 (0.1177 – 0.1185)	3.32 – 3.34 (0.1307 – 0.1315)
2.69 – 2.71 (0.1059 – 0.1067)	3.02 – 3.04 (0.1189 – 0.1197)	3.35 – 3.37 (0.1319 – 0.1327)
2.72 – 2.74 (0.1071 – 0.1079)	3.05 – 3.07 (0.1201 – 0.1209)	3.38 – 3.40 (0.1331 – 0.1339)
2.75 – 2.77 (0.1083 – 0.1091)	3.08 – 3.10 (0.1213 – 0.1220)	3.41 – 3.43 (0.1343 – 0.1350)
2.78 – 2.80 (0.1094 – 0.1102)	3.11 – 3.13 (0.1224 – 0.1232)	3.44 – 3.46 (0.1354 – 0.1362)
2.81 – 2.83 (0.1106 – 0.1114)	3.14 – 3.16 (0.1236 – 0.1244)	3.47 – 3.49 (0.1366 – 0.1374)
2.84 – 2.86 (0.1118 – 0.1126)	3.17 – 3.19 (0.1248 – 0.1256)	
2.87 – 2.89 (0.1130 – 0.1138)	3.20 – 3.22 (0.1260 – 0.1268)	

TY3039100088000X

Fig. 19 Side gear bearing shim identification chart. Supra

Washer thickness

Thickness		mm (in.)	
1.70	(0.0669)	2.03	(0.0799)
1.73	(0.0681)	2.06	(0.0811)
1.76	(0.0693)	2.09	(0.0823)
1.79	(0.0705)	2.12	(0.0835)
1.82	(0.0717)	2.15	(0.0846)
1.85	(0.0728)	2.18	(0.0858)
1.88	(0.0740)	2.21	(0.0870)
1.91	(0.0752)	2.24	(0.0882)
1.94	(0.0764)	2.27	(0.0894)
1.97	(0.0776)	2.30	(0.0906)
2.00	(0.0787)	2.33	(0.0917)

TY3039100089000X

Fig. 20 Drive pinion shim identification chart. Supra

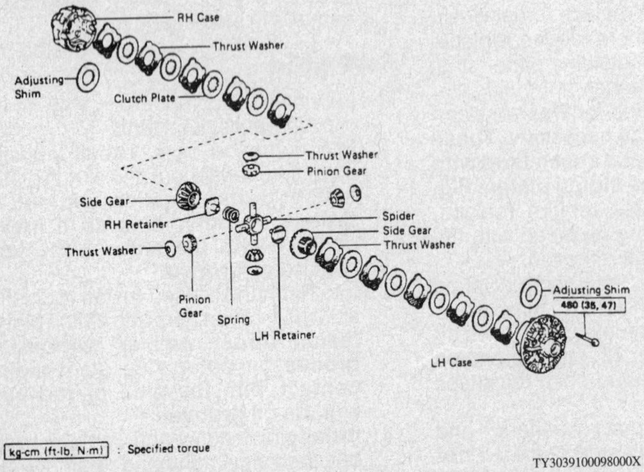
RH Case
Thrust Washer
Adjusting Shim
Clutch Plate
Thrust Washer
Pinion Gear
Side Gear
RH Retainer
Spider
Side Gear
Thrust Washer
Thrust Washer
Adjusting Shim
480 (35, 47)
Pinion Gear
Spring
LH Retainer
LH Case
kg-cm (ft-lb, N-m) : Specified torque
TY3039100098000X

Fig. 21 Exploded view of limited slip differential. Supra

(.05–.20 mm). If not within specifications, select suitable adjusting shim.

7. Measure backlash in left side case as outlined in step 6.

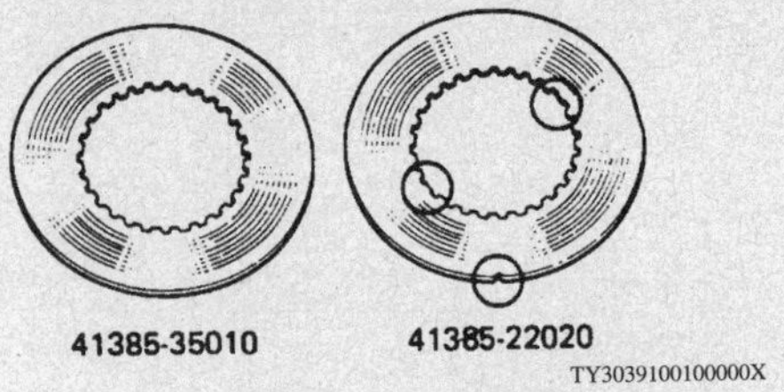
41385-35010
41385-22020
TY3039100100000X

Fig. 22 Measuring dimension "A" in righthand case. Supra w/limited slip differential

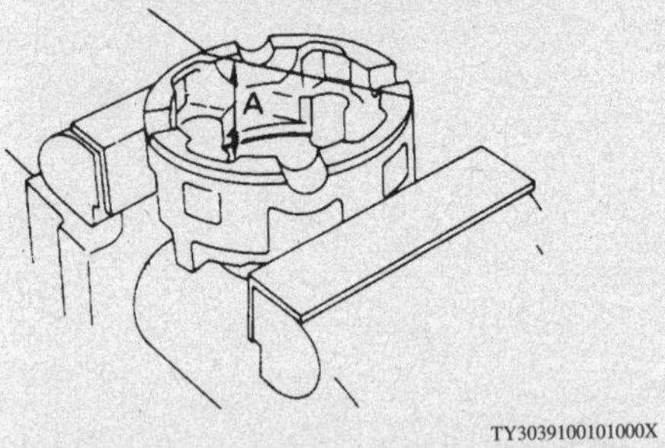
A
TY3039100101000X

Fig. 23 Measuring dimension "B" to determine side gear bearing shim pack. Supra w/limited slip differential

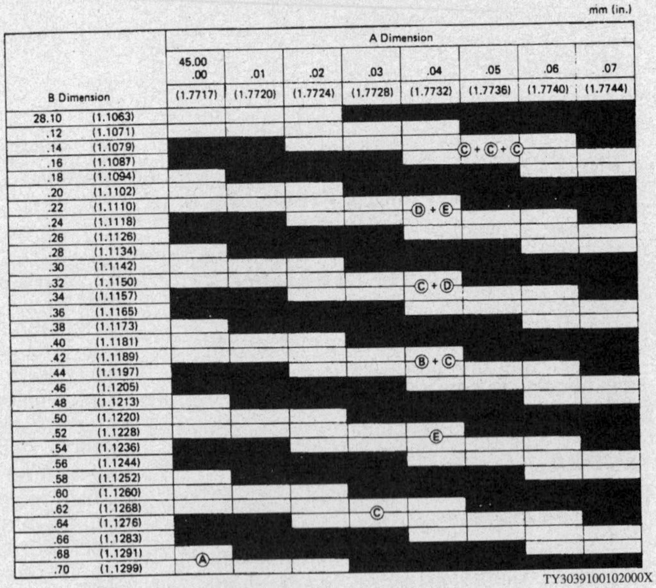
mm (in.)
A Dimension
45.00 .00 (1.7717)
.01 (1.7720)
.02 (1.7724)
.03 (1.7728)
.04 (1.7732)
.05 (1.7736)
.06 (1.7740)
.07 (1.7744)
B Dimension
28.10 (1.1063)
.12 (1.1071)
.14 (1.1079)
.16 (1.1087)
.18 (1.1094)
.20 (1.1102)
.22 (1.1110)
.24 (1.1118)
.26 (1.1126)
.28 (1.1134)
.30 (1.1142)
.32 (1.1150)
.34 (1.1157)
.36 (1.1165)
.38 (1.1173)
.40 (1.1181)
.42 (1.1189)
.44 (1.1197)
.46 (1.1205)
.48 (1.1213)
.50 (1.1220)
.52 (1.1228)
.54 (1.1236)
.56 (1.1244)
.58 (1.1252)
.60 (1.1260)
.62 (1.1268)
.64 (1.1276)
.66 (1.1283)
.68 (1.1291)
.70 (1.1299)
C + C + C
D + E
C + D
B + C
E
C
A
TY3039100102000X

Fig. 24 Adjusting shim selection chart. Supra w/limited slip differential

Mark	Thickness	Mark	Thickness
A	0.15 (0.0059)	D	0.30 (0.0118)
B	0.20 (0.0079)	E	0.35 (0.0138)
C	0.25 (0.0098)		

TY3039100103000X

Fig. 25 Adjusting shim sizes. Supra w/limited slip differential

8. Install spring and lefthand retainer in spider.
9. Align reference marks, then install lefthand case on righthand case.
10. Lightly oil attaching bolts, then install bolts and tighten evenly and gradually. When snug, **torque** to 35 ft. lbs.

DRIVE AXLE SPECIFICATIONS

Year	Model	Ring Gear & Pinion		Pinion Bearing Preload			Differential Bearing Preload		
		Backlash Method	Adjustment, Inch	Method	New Bearing In. Lbs.	Used Bearing In. Lbs.	Method	New Bearing In. Lbs.	Used Bearing In. Lbs.
1993	Celica③	Shim	.002–.008④	Spacer & Shims	6.9–13.9	4.3–8.7	—	—	—
	Celica⑤	Shim	.002–.008④	Shim	8.7–13.9	—	—	—	—
	Celica⑥	Shim	.002–.008	—	—	—	Shim	6.9–12.2	3.5–6.1
1993–95	Pickup⑫⑬	Threaded Adjust	.005–.007	Spacer & Shims	10.4–16.5	5.2–8.7	Threaded adj.	3.5–5.2①	3.5–5.2①
	Pickup⑭⑬	Threaded Adjust	.005–.007	Spacer & Shims	⑮	②	Threaded adj.	3.5–5.2①	3.5–5.2①
	Pickup⑦	Shim	.005–.007	Spacer & Shims	10.4–16.5	5.2–8.7	Shim	1.6–3.0①	1.6–3.0①
	4Runner⑦	Shim	.005–.007	Spacer & Shims	10.4–16.5	5.2–8.7	Shim	3.5–5.2①	3.5–5.2①
	4Runner⑬	Shim	.005–.007	Spacer & Shims	⑪	⑧	Shim	3.5–5.2①	3.5–5.2①
1993–96	Land Cruiser	Shims	.006–.008	Spacer & Shims	11.3–17.4	6.1–8.7	Shims	3.5–5.2①	3.5–5.2①
	Previa⑫⑬	Threaded Adjust	.005–.007	Spacer & Shims	10.4–16.5	5.2–8.7	Threaded adj.	3.5–5.2①	3.5–5.2①
	Supra	Shim	.002–.007	Spacer & Shims	17.3–21.7⑨	8.9–10.6⑩	Shim	3.5–5.2①⑩	3.5–5.2①⑩
	T100	Shim	.002-.008	Spacer & Shims	8.7-13.9	4.3-6.9	Shim	3.5–5.2①	3.5–5.2①
1995–96	Tacoma	Shim	.002-.008	Spacer & Shims	12.2-18.3	5.2-8.7	Shim	3.5–5.2①	3.5–5.2①
1996	RAV4	Shim	.005-.007	Spacer & Shim	8.7-13.9	4.3-6.9	Shim	2.6-4.3①	2.6-4.3①
	4Runner	Threaded Adgust	.002-.008	Spacer & Shims	8.7-13.9	4.3-6.9	Shims	3.5–5.2①	3.5–5.2①

① — Total preload, add this to drive pinion preload.
② — 2 pinion type, 7.8–11.3 inch lbs.; 4 pinion type, 4.3–6.9 inch lbs.
③ — C50 & C52 manual transaxles.
④ — Side gear backlash.
⑤ — S53 manual transaxle.
⑥ — Auto. trans. models.
⑦ — Front axle.
⑧ — Models w/22R-E engine, 7.8–11.3 inch lbs.; models w/3VZ-E engine, 4.3–9.6 inch lbs.
⑨ — Except 2JZ-GTE engine, 10.8–16.0 inch lbs.
⑩ — Except 2JZ-GTE engine, 4.3–6.9 inch lbs.
⑪ — Models w/22R-E engine, 16.5–22.6 inch lbs.; models w/3VZ-E engine, 8.7–13.9 inch lbs.
⑫ — 7.5 inch ring gear.
⑬ — Rear axle.
⑭ — 8 inch ring gear.
⑮ — 2 pinion type, 16.5–22.6 inch lbs.; 4 pinion type, 8.7–13.9 inch lbs.

Engine Rebuilding Specifications

INDEX

Page No.

Camshaft 48-338
Crankshaft, Bearings & Rods 48-339
Cylinder Block 48-342
Cylinder Head, Valve Guide & Valve Seats 48-334
Oil Pump 48-344
Pistons, Pins & Rings 48-340
Valve Springs 48-335
Valves 48-336

CYLINDER HEAD, VALVE GUIDE & VALVE SEATS

All measurements given are in inches unless otherwise specified.

Year	Engine Liters (ID Code)	Cylinder Head Warpage Limit	Valve Guides			Valve Seats		
			Standard Inside Diameter	Stem To Guide Clearance		Seat Angle, Degree	Seat Width	
				Intake	Exhaust		Intake	Exhaust
1993	1.5L (3E-E)	.002	.2366-.2374	.0010-.0024	.0012-.0026	45	.047-.063	.047-.063
	1.5L (5E-FE)	.020	.2366-.2374	.0010-.0024	.0012-.0026	45	.039-.055	.039-.055
	1.6L (4A-FE)	③	.2366-.2374	.0010-.0024	.0012-.0026	45	.047-.063	.047-.063
	1.8L (7A-FE)	③	.2366-.2374	.0010-.0024	.0012-.0026	45	.039-.055	.039-.055
	2.0L (3S-GTE)	⑤	.2362-.2369	.0010-.0023	.0012-.0025	45	.039-.055	.039-.055
	2.2L (5S-FE)	②	.2366-.2374	.0010-.0024	.0012-.0026	45	.039-.055	.039-.055
	2.4L (22R-E)	④	.3154-.3161	.0010-.0024	.0012-.0026	45	.047-.063	.047-.063
	2.4L (2TZ-FE)	④	.2366-.2374	.0010-.0024	.0012-.0026	45	.039-.055	.039-.055
	3.0L (3VZ-E)	.0039	.3154-.3161	.0010-.0024	.0012-.0026	45	.047-.063	.047-.063
	3.0L (3VZ-FE)	.0039	.2366-.2374	.0010-.0024	.0012-.0026	45	.039-.055	.039-.055
	4.5L (1FZ-FE)	①	.2760-.2768	.0010-.0024	.0012-.0026	45	.047-.063	.039-.055
1994	1.5L (3E-E)	.002	.2366-.2374	.0010-.0024	.0012-.0026	45	.047-.063	.047-.063
	1.5L (5E-FE)	.020	.2366-.2374	.0010-.0024	.0012-.0026	45	.039-.055	.039-.055
	1.6L (4A-FE)	③	.2366-.2374	.0010-.0024	.0012-.0026	45	.047-.063	.047-.063
	1.8L (7A-FE)	③	.2366-.2374	.0010-.0024	.0012-.0026	45	.039-.055	.039-.055
	2.0L (3S-GTE)	⑤	.2362-.2369	.0010-.0023	.0012-.0025	45	.039-.055	.039-.055
	2.2L (5S-FE)	②	.2366-.2374	.0010-.0024	.0012-.0026	45	.039-.055	.039-.055
	2.4L (22R-E)	④	.3154-.3161	.0010-.0024	.0012-.0026	45	.047-.063	.047-.063
	2.4L (2TZ-FE)	④	.2366-.2374	.0010-.0024	.0012-.0026	45	.039-.055	.039-.055
	2.7L (3RZ-FE)	②	.2366-.2374	.0010-.0024	.0012-.0026	45	.039-.055	.039-.055
	3.0L (3VZ-E)	.0039	.3154-.3161	.0010-.0024	.0012-.0026	45	.047-.063	.047-.063
	3.0L (1MZ-FE)	.0039	.2169-.2177	.0010-.0024	.0012-.0026	45	.039-.055	.039-.055
	3.0L (2JZ-GE)	.0039	.2366-.2374	.0010-.0024	.0012-.0026	45	.039-.055	.047-.063
	3.0L (2JZ-GTE)	.0039	.2366-.2374	.0010-.0024	.0012-.0026	45	.039-.055	.047-.063
	4.5L (1FZ-FE)	①	.2760-.2768	.0010-.0024	.0012-.0026	45	.047-.063	.039-.055
1995	1.5L (5E-FE)	.020	.2366-.2374	.0010-.0024	.0012-.0026	45	.039-.055	.039-.055
	1.6L (4A-FE)	③	.2366-.2374	.0010-.0024	.0012-.0026	45	.047-.063	.047-.063
	1.8L (7A-FE)	③	.2366-.2374	.0010-.0024	.0012-.0026	45	.039-.055	.039-.055
	2.0L (3S-GTE)	⑤	.2362-.2369	.0010-.0023	.0012-.0025	45	.039-.055	.039-.055
	2.2L (5S-FE)	②	.2366-.2374	.0010-.0024	.0012-.0026	45	.039-.055	.039-.055
	2.4L (22R-E)	④	.3154-.3161	.0010-.0024	.0012-.0026	45	.047-.063	.047-.063
	2.4L (2RZ-FE)	②	.2366-.2374	.0010-.0024	.0012-.0026	45	.039-.055	.039-.055
	2.4L (2TZ-FE & 2TZ-FZE)	④	.2366-.2374	.0010-.0024	.0012-.0026	45	.039-.055	.039-.055
	2.7L (3RZ-FE)	②	.2366-.2374	.0010-.0024	.0012-.0026	45	.039-.055	.039-.055
	3.0L (3VZ-E)	.0039	.3154-.3161	.0010-.0024	.0012-.0026	45	.047-.063	.047-.063
	3.0L (1MZ-FE)	.0039	.2169-.2177	.0010-.0024	.0012-.0026	45	.039-.055	.039-.055
	3.0L (2JZ-GE)	.0039	.2366-.2374	.0010-.0024	.0012-.0026	45	.039-.055	.047-.063
	3.0L (2JZ-GTE)	.0039	.2366-.2374	.0010-.0024	.0012-.0026	45	.039-.055	.047-.063
	3.4L (5VZ-FE)	.0039	.2348-.2356	.0010-.0024	.0012-.0026	45	.039-.055	.039-.055
	4.5L (1FZ-FE)	①	.2760-.2768	.0010-.0024	.0012-.0026	45	.047-.063	.039-.055

Continued

CYLINDER HEAD, VALVE GUIDE & VALVE SEATS—Continued

All measurements given are in inches unless otherwise specified.

Year	Engine Liters (ID Code)	Cylinder Head Warpage Limit	Valve Guides			Valve Seats		
			Standard Inside Diameter	Stem To Guide Clearance		Seat Angle, Degree	Seat Width	
				Intake	Exhaust		Intake	Exhaust
1996	1.5L (5E-FE)	.020	.2366-.2374	.0010-.0024	.0012-.0026	45	.039-.055	.039-.055
	1.6L (4A-FE)	③	.2366-.2374	.0010-.0024	.0012-.0026	45	.047-.063	.047-.063
	1.8L (7A-FE)	③	.2366-.2374	.0010-.0024	.0012-.0026	45	.039-.055	.039-.055
	2.0L (3S-FE)	②	.2366-.2374	.0010-.0024	.0012-.0026	45	.039-.055	.039-.055
	2.2L (5S-FE)	②	.2366-.2374	.0010-.0024	.0012-.0026	45	.039-.055	.039-.055
	2.4L (2RZ-FE)	②	.2366-.2374	.0010-.0024	.0012-.0026	45	.039-.055	.039-.055
	2.4L (2TZ-FZE)	④	.2366-.2374	.0010-.0024	.0012-.0026	45	.039-.055	.039-.055
	2.7L (3RZ-FE)	②	.2366-.2374	.0010-.0024	.0012-.0026	45	.039-.055	.039-.055
	3.0L (1MZ-FE)	.0039	.2169-.2177	.0010-.0024	.0012-.0026	45	.039-.055	.039-.055
	3.0L (2JZ-GE)	.0039	.2366-.2374	.0010-.0024	.0012-.0026	45	.039-.055	.047-.063
	3.0L (2JZ-GTE)	.0039	.2366-.2374	.0010-.0024	.0012-.0026	45	.039-.055	.047-.063
	3.4L (5VZ-FE)	.0039	.2348-.2356	.0010-.0024	.0012-.0026	45	.039-.055	.039-.055
	4.5L (1FZ-FE)	①	.2760-.2768	.0010-.0024	.0012-.0026	45	.047-.063	.039-.055

①— Cylinder block side, .0059 inch, manifold side .0039 inch.
②— Cylinder block side, .0020 inch, manifold side .0031 inch.
③— Cylinder block side, .0020 inch, manifold side .0039 inch.
④— Cylinder block side, .0059 inch, manifold side .0079 inch.
⑤— Cylinder block & intake manifold side, .0079 inch, exhaust manifold side .0118 inch.

VALVE SPRINGS

All measurements given are in inches, unless otherwise specified.

Year	Engine Liter (ID Code)	Valve Springs			
		Free Length	Installed Height	Pressure @ Installed Height	Out Of Square Limit
1993	1.5L (3E-E)	1.6346	1.3842	35.1	.079
	1.5L (5E-FE)	1.5669	1.252	33.3-36.8	.079
	1.6L (4A-FE)③	1.774	1.366	34.8	.079
	1.6L (4A-FE)④	1.5185	1.248	37.3	.079
	1.8L (7A-FE)	1.5185	1.248	37.3	.079
	2.0L (3S-GTE)	1.7492	1.354	45.2-53.1	.079
	2.2L (5S-FE)	1.5669	1.252	33.3-36.8	.079
	2.4L (22R-E)	1.909	1.594	66.1	.063
	2.4L (2TZ-FE)	1.6425	1.406	38.7	.079
	3.0L (3VZ-E)	①	1.575	57	.0484
	3.0L (3VZ-FE)	1.630	1.311	38.4-42.4	.075
	4.5L (1FZ-FE)	1.7299-1.7740	1.437	48.1-53.4	.079
1994	1.5L (3E-E)	1.6346	1.3842	35.1	.079
	1.5L (5E-FE)	1.5669	1.252	33.3-36.8	.079
	1.6L (4A-FE)③	1.774	1.366	34.8	.079
	1.6L (4A-FE)④	1.5185	1.248	37.3	.079
	1.8L (7A-FE)	1.5185	1.248	37.3	.079
	2.0L (3S-GTE)	1.7492	1.354	45.2-53.1	.079
	2.2L (5S-FE)	1.5669	1.252	33.3-36.8	.079
	2.4L (22R-E)	1.909	1.594	66.1	.063
	2.4L (2TZ-FE)	1.6425	1.406	38.7	.079
	2.7L (3RZ-FE)	—	1.406	—	.079

Continued

VALVE SPRINGS—Continued

All measurements given are in inches, unless otherwise specified.

Year	Engine Liter (ID Code)	Valve Springs			
		Free Length	Installed Height	Pressure @ Installed Height	Out Of Square Limit
1994	3.0L (3VZ-E)	①	1.575	57	.0484
	3.0L (1MZ-FE)	②	1.7913	33.8	.079
	3.0L (2JZ-GE)	②	1.358	34.5	.079
	3.0L (2JZ-GTE)	②	1.358	34.5	.079
	4.5L (1FZ-FE)	1.7299-1.7740	1.437	48.1-53.4	.079
1995	1.5L (5E-FE)	1.5669	1.252	33.3-36.8	.079
	1.6L (4A-FE)③	1.774	1.366	34.8	.079
	1.6L (4A-FE)④	1.5185	1.248	37.3	.079
	1.8L (7A-FE)	1.5185	1.248	37.3	.079
	2.0L (3S-GTE)	1.7492	1.354	45.2-53.1	.079
	2.2L (5S-FE)	1.5669	1.252	33.3-36.8	.079
	2.4L (22R-E)	1.909	1.594	66.1	.063
	2.4L (2RZ-FE)	—	1.406	39.7	.079
	2.4L (2TZ-FE)	1.6425	1.406	38.7	.079
	2.7L (3RZ-FE)	—	1.406	39.7	.079
	3.0L (3VZ-E)	①	1.575	57	.0484
	3.0L (1MZ-FE)	②	1.7913	33.8	.079
	3.0L (2JZ-GE)	②	1.358	34.5	.079
	3.0L (2JZ-GTE)	②	1.358	34.5	.079
	3.4L (5VZ-FE)	1.7630	1.311	41.9-46.3	.079
	4.5L (1FZ-FE)	1.7299-1.7740	1.437	48.1-53.4	.079
1996	1.5L (5E-FE)	1.5669	1.252	33.3-36.8	.079
	1.6L (4A-FE)③	1.774	1.366	34.8	.079
	1.6L (4A-FE)④	1.5185	1.248	37.3	.079
	1.8L (7A-FE)	1.5185	1.248	37.3	.079
	2.0L (3S-FE)	1.6520-1.6531	1.366	36.8-42.5	.079
	2.2L (5S-FE)	1.5669	1.252	33.3-36.8	.0079
	2.4L (2RZ-FE)	—	1.406	39.7	.079
1996	2.4L (2TZ-FZE)	1.6425	1.406	38.7	.079
	2.7L (3RZ-FE)	—	1.406	39.7	.079
	3.0L (1MZ-FE)	②	1.7913	33.8	.079
	3.0L (2JZ-GE)	②	1.358	34.5	.079
	3.0L (2JZ-GTE)	②	1.358	34.5	.079
	3.4L (5VZ-FE)	1.7630	1.311	41.9-46.3	.079
	4.5L (1FZ-FE)	1.7299-1.7740	1.437	48.1-53.4	.079

① — Green paint, 1.8508 inch; white paint, 1.8307 inch.
② — Blue paint, 1.6433 inch; yellow paint, 1.6417
③ — Celica.
④ — Corolla.

VALVES

All measurements given are in inches, unless otherwise specified.

Year	Engine Liter (ID Code)	Valves						
		Stem Diameter		Face Angle, Degree	Margin		Clearance	
		Int.	Exh.		Int.	Exh.	Int.	Exh.
1993	1.5L (3E-E)	.2350-.2356	.2348-.2354	44.5	.039	.039	.008	.008
	1.5L (5E-FE)	.2350-.2356	.2348-.2354	44.5	.031-.047	.031-.047	.006-.010	.012-.016
	1.6L (4A-FE)③	.2350-.2356	.2348-.2354	44.5	.031-47	.031-.047	.006-.010	.008-.012

Continued

VALVES—Continued

All measurements given are in inches, unless otherwise specified.

Year	Engine Liter (ID Code)	Valves						
		Stem Diameter		Face Angle, Degree	Margin		Clearance	
		Int.	Exh.		Int.	Exh.	Int.	Exh.
1993	1.6L (4A-FE)①	.2350-.2356	.2348-.2354	44.5	.031-47	.031-.047	.006-.010	.008-.012
	1.8L (7A-FE)	.2350-.2356	.2348-.2354	44.5	.031-47	.031-.047	.006-.010	.008-.012
	2.0L (3S-GTE)	.2346-.2352	.2344-.2350	44.5	.031-.047	.031-.047	.006-.010	.011-.015
	2.2L (5S-FE)	.2350-.2356	.2348-.2354	44.5	.031-.047	.031-.047	.007-.011	.011-.015
	2.4L (22R-E)	.3138-.3144	.3136-.3142	44.5	.039	.039	.008	.012
	2.4L (2TZ-FE)	.2350-.2356	.2348-.2354	44.5	.020②	.020②	.006-.010	.010-.014
	3.0L (3VZ-E)	.3138-.3144	.3136-.3412	44.5	.051-.067	.051-.067	.007-.011	.009-.013
	3.0L (3VZ-FE)	.2350-.2356	.2348-.2354	44.5	.0394	.0394	.005-.09	.011-.015
	4.5L (1FZ-FE)	.2744-.2750	.2742-.2748	44.5	.047	.047	.006-.010	.010-.014
1994	1.5L (3E-E)	.2350-.2356	.2348-.2354	44.5	.039	.039	.008	.008
	1.5L (5E-FE)	.2350-.2356	.2348-.2354	44.5	.031-.047	.031-.047	.006-.010	.012-.016
	1.6L (4A-FE)③	.2350-.2356	.2348-.2354	44.5	.031-47	.031-.047	.006-.010	.008-.012
	1.6L (4A-FE)①	.2350-.2356	.2348-.2354	44.5	.031-47	.031-.047	.006-.010	.008-.012
	1.8L (7A-FE)	.2350-.2356	.2348-.2354	44.5	.031-47	.031-47	.006-.010	.008-.012
	2.0L (3S-GTE)	.2346-.2352	.2344-.2350	44.5	.031-.047	.031-.047	.006-.010	.011-.015
	2.2L (5S-FE)	.2350-.2356	.2348-.2354	44.5	.031-.047	.031-.047	.007-.011	.011-.015
	2.4L (22R-E)	.3138-.3144	.3136-.3142	44.5	.039	.039	.008	.012
	2.4L (2TZ-FE)	.2350-.2356	.2348-.2354	44.5	.020②	.020②	.006-.010	.010-.014
	2.7L (3RZ-FE)	.2350-.2356	.2348-.2354	44.5	.039	.039	.006-.010	.010-.014
	3.0L (3VZ-E)	.3138-.3144	.3136-.3412	44.5	.051-.067	.051-.067	.007-.011	.009-.013
	3.0L (1MZ-FE)	.2154-.2159	.2152-.2157	44.5	.039	.039	.006-.010	.010-.014
	3.0L (2JZ-GE)	.2350-.2356	.2348-.2354	44.5	.031-.047	.031-.047	.006-.010	.010-.014
	3.0L (2JZ-GTE)	.2350-.2356	.2348-.2354	44.5	.031-.047	.031-.047	.006-.010	.010-.014
	4.5L (1FZ-FE)	.2744-.2750	.2742-.2748	44.5	.047	.047	.006-.010	.010-.014
1995	1.5L (5E-FE)	.2350-.2356	.2348-.2354	44.5	.031-.047	.031-.047	.006-.010	.012-.016
	1.6L (4A-FE)③	.2350-.2356	.2348-.2354	44.5	.031-47	.031-47	.006-.010	.008-.012
	1.6L (4A-FE)①	.2350-.2356	.2348-.2354	44.5	.031-47	.031-.047	.006-.010	.008-.012
	1.8L (7A-FE)	.2350-.2356	.2348-.2354	44.5	.031-47	.031-.047	.006-.010	.008-.012
	2.0L (3S-GTE)	.2346-.2352	.2344-.2350	44.5	.031-.047	.031-.047	.006-.010	.011-.015
	2.2L (5S-FE)	.2350-.2356	.2348-.2354	44.5	.031-.047	.031-.047	.007-.011	.011-.015
	2.4L (22R-E)	.3138-.3144	.3136-.3142	44.5	.039	.039	.008	.012
	2.4L (2RZ-FE)	.2350-.2356	.2348-.2354	44.5	.039	.039	.006-.010	.010-.014
	2.4L (2TZ-FE)	.2350-.2356	.2348-.2354	44.5	.020②	.020②	.006-.010	.010-.014
	2.7L (3RZ-FE)	.2350-.2356	.2348-.2354	44.5	.039	.039	.006-.010	.010-.014
	3.0L (3VZ-E)	.3138-.3144	.3136-.3412	44.5	.051-.067	.051-.067	.007-.011	.009-.013
	3.0L (1MZ-FE)	.2154-.2159	.2152-.2157	44.5	.039	.039	.006-.010	.010-.014
	3.0L (2JZ-GE)	.2350-.2356	.2348-.2354	44.5	.031-.047	.031-.047	.006-.010	.010-.014
	3.0L (2JZ-GTE)	.2350-.2356	.2348-.2354	44.5	.031-.047	.031-.047	.006-.010	.010-.014
	3.4L (5VZ-FE)	.2350-.2356	.2348-.2354	44.5	.020-.039	.020-.039	.001-003	.001-.004
	4.5L (1FZ-FE)	.2744-.2750	.2742-.2748	44.5	.047	.047	.006-.010	.010-.014
1996	1.5L (5E-FE)	.2350-.2356	.2348-.2354	44.5	.031-.047	.031-.047	.006-.010	.012-.016
	1.6L (4A-FE)③	.2350-.2356	.2348-.2354	44.5	.031-47	.031-47	.006-.010	.008-.012
	1.6L (4A-FE)①	.2350-.2356	.2348-.2354	44.5	.031-47	.031-47	.006-.010	.008-.012
	1.8L (7A-FE)	.2350-.2356	.2348-.2354	44.5	.031-47	.031-.047	.006-.010	.008-.012
	2.0L (3S-FE)	.2350-.2356	.2348-.2354	44.5	.031-.047	.031-.047	.007-.011	.011-.015
	2.2L (5S-FE)	.2350-.2356	.2348-.2354	44.5	.031-.047	.031-.047	.007-.011	.011-.015
	2.4L (2RZ-FE)	.2350-.2356	.2348-.2354	44.5	.039	.039	.006-.010	.010-.014
	2.4L (2TZ-FZE)	.2350-.2356	.2348-.2354	44.5	.020②	.020②	.006-.010	.010-.014
	2.7L (3RZ-FE)	.2350-.2356	.2348-.2354	44.5	.039	.039	.006-.010	.010-.014
	3.0L (1MZ-FE)	.2154-.2159	.2152-.2157	44.5	.039	.039	.006-.010	.010-.014
	3.0L (2JZ-GE)	.2350-.2356	.2348-.2354	44.5	.031-.047	.031-.047	.006-.010	.010-.014
	3.0L (2JZ-GTE)	.2350-.2356	.2348-.2354	44.5	.031-.047	.031-.047	.006-.010	.010-.014

Continued

VALVES—Continued

All measurements given are in inches, unless otherwise specified.

Year	Engine Liter (ID Code)	Valves						
		Stem Diameter		Face Angle, Degree	Margin		Clearance	
		Int.	Exh.		Int.	Exh.	Int.	Exh.
1996	3.4L (5VZ-FE)	.2350-.2356	.2348-.2354	44.5	.020-.039	.020-.039	.001-003	.001-.004
	4.5L (1FZ-FE)	.2744-.2750	.2742-.2748	44.5	.047	.047	.006-.010	.010-.014

① — Corolla. ② — Limit. ③ — Celica.

CAMSHAFT

All measurements given are in inches, unless otherwise specified.

Year	Engine Liters (ID Code)	Journal Dia.	Max. Journal Runout	Bearing Clearance	Camshaft Endplay	Lifter Dia.	Lifter To Bore Clearance
1993	1.5L (3E-E)	1.0622-1.0628	.0016	.0015-.0029	.0031-.0071	—	—
	1.5L (5E-FE)	①	.0016	.0014-.0028	.0018-.0039	1.1014-1.1018	.0006-.0018
	1.6L (4A-FE)⑤	①	.0016	.0014-.0028	②	1.1014-1.1018	.0008-.0020
	1.6L (4A-FE)④	.9822-.9829	.0016	.0014-.0028	②	1.2191-1.2195	.0009-.0023
	1.8L (7A-FE)	.9822-.9829	.0016	.0014-.0028	②	1.2191-1.2195	.0009-.0023
	2.0L (3S-GTE)	1.0614-1.0620	.0024	.0010-.0024	.0047-.0094	1.2195-1.2199	.0006-.0018
	2.2L (5S-FE)	1.0614-1.0620	.0016	.0010-.0024	③	1.1014-1.1018	.0006-.0018
	2.4L (22R-E)	1.2984-1.2992	.0080	.0004-.0020	.0031-.0071	—	—
	2.4L (2TZ-FE)	1.0614-1.0620	.0024	.0010-.0024	.0016-.0037	1.2191-1.2195	.0009-.0020
	3.0L (3VZ-E)	1.3370-1.3376	.0024	.0010-.0026	.0031-.0075	1.4930-1.4934	.0011-.0021
	3.0L (3VZ-FE)	1.0610-1.0616	.0024	.0014-.0028	.0013-.0031	1.2191-1.2195	.0009-.0020
	4.5L (1FZ-FE)	1.0614-1.0620	.0024	.0010-.0024	.0012-.0031	1.3372-1.3376	.0009-.0022
1994	1.5L (3E-E)	1.0622-1.0628	.0016	.0015-.0029	.0031-.0071	—	—
	1.5L (5E-FE)	①	.0016	.0014-.0028	.0018-.0039	1.1014-1.1018	.0006-.0018
	1.6L (4A-FE)⑤	①	.0016	.0014-.0028	②	1.1014-1.1018	.0008-.0020
	1.6L (4A-FE)④	.9822-.9829	.0016	.0014-.0028	②	1.2191-1.2195	.0009-.0023
	1.8L (7A-FE)	.9822-.9829	.0016	.0014-.0028	②	1.2191-1.2195	.0009-.0023
	2.0L (3S-GTE)	1.0614-1.0620	.0024	.0010-.0024	.0047-.0094	1.2195-1.2199	.0006-.0018
	2.2L (5S-FE)	1.0614-1.0620	.0016	.0010-.0024	③	1.1014-1.1018	.0006-.0018
	2.4L (22R-E)	1.2984-1.2992	.0080	.0004-.0020	.0031-.0071	—	—
	2.4L (2TZ-FE)	1.0614-1.0620	.0024	.0010-.0024	.0016-.0037	1.2191-1.2195	.0009-.0020
	2.7L (3RZ-FE)	1.0614-1.0620	.0024	.0010-.0024	.0016-.0037	1.1576-1.2195	.0009-.0022
	3.0L (3VZ-E)	1.3370-1.3376	.0024	.0010-.0026	.0031-.0075	1.4930-1.4934	.0011-.0021
	3.0L (1MZ-FE)	1.0610-1.0616	.0024	.0014-.0028	.0016-.0035	1.2191-2.195	.0009-.0020
	3.0L (2JZ-GE)	1.1397-1.1404	.0031	.0014-.0028	.0031-.0075	1.2191-1.2195	.0009-.0020
	3.0L (2JZ-GTE)	1.1397-1.1404	.0031	.0014-.0028	.0031-.0075	1.2191-1.2195	.0009-.0020
	4.5L (1FZ-FE)	1.0614-1.0620	.0024	.0010-.0024	.0012-.0031	1.3372-1.3376	.0009-.0022
1995	1.5L (5E-FE)	①	.0016	.0014-.0028	.0018-.0039	1.1014-1.1018	.0006-.0018
	1.6L (4A-FE)⑤	①	.0016	.0014-.0028	②	1.1014-1.1018	.0008-.0020
	1.6L (4A-FE)④	.9822-.9829	.0016	.0014-.0028	②	1.2191-1.2195	.0009-.0023
	1.8L (7A-FE)	.9822-.9829	.0016	.0014-.0028	②	1.2191-1.2195	.0009-.0023
	2.0L (3S-GTE)	1.0614-1.0620	.0024	.0010-.0024	.0047-.0094	1.2195-1.2199	.0006-.0018
	2.2L (5S-FE)	1.0614-1.0620	.0016	.0010-.0024	③	1.1014-1.1018	.0006-.0018
	2.4L (22R-E)	1.2984-1.2992	.0080	.0004-.0020	.0031-.0071	—	—
	2.4L (2RZ-FE)	1.0614-1.0620	.0024	.0010-.0024	.0016-.0037	1.1576-1.2195	.0009-.0022
	2.4L (2TZ-FE)	1.0614-1.0620	.0024	.0010-.0024	.0016-.0037	1.2191-1.2195	.0009-.0020
	2.7L (3RZ-FE)	1.0614-1.0620	.0024	.0010-.0024	.0016-.0037	1.1576-1.2195	.0009-.0022
	3.0L (3VZ-E)	1.3370-1.3376	.0024	.0010-.0026	.0031-.0075	1.4930-1.4934	.0011-.0021
	3.0L (1MZ-FE)	1.0610-1.0616	.0024	.0014-.0028	.0016-.0035	1.2191-2.195	.0009-.0020

Continued

CAMSHAFT—Continued

All measurements given are in inches, unless otherwise specified.

Year	Engine Liters (ID Code)	Journal Dia.	Max. Journal Runout	Bearing Clearance	Camshaft Endplay	Lifter Dia.	Lifter To Bore Clearance
1995	3.0L (2JZ-GE)	1.1397-1.1404	.0031	.0014-.0028	.0031-.0075	1.2191-1.2195	.0009-.0020
	3.0L (2JZ-GTE)	1.1397-1.1404	.0031	.0014-.0028	.0031-.0075	1.2191-1.2195	.0009-.0020
	3.4L (5VZ-FE)	1.0610-1.0616	.0024	.0014-.0028	.0008-.0079	1.2191-1.2195	.0009-.0020
	4.5L (1FZ-FE)	1.0614-1.0620	.0024	.0010-.0024	.0012-.0031	1.3372-1.3376	.0009-.0022
1996	1.5L (5E-FE)	①	.0016	.0014-.0028	.0018-.0039	1.1014-1.1018	.0006-.0018
	1.6L (4A-FE)⑤	①	.0016	.0014-.0028	②	1.1014-1.1018	.0008-.0020
	1.6L (4A-FE)④	.9822-.9829	.0016	.0014-.0028	②	1.2191-1.2195	.0009-.0023
	1.8L (7A-FE)	.9822-.9829	.0016	.0014-.0028	②	1.2191-1.2195	.0009-.0023
	2.0L (3S-FE)	1.0614-1.0620	.0016	.0010-.0024	.0008-.0079	1.2191-1.2195	.0009-.0020
	2.2L (5S-FE)	1.0614-1.0620	.0016	.0010-.0024	③	1.1014-1.1018	.0006-.0018
	2.4L (2RZ-FE)	1.0614-1.0620	.0024	.0010-.0024	.0016-.0037	1.1576-1.2195	.0009-.0022
	2.4L (2TZ-FZE)	1.0614-1.0620	.0024	.0010-.0024	.0016-.0037	1.2191-1.2195	.0009-.0020
	2.7L (3RZ-FE)	1.0614-1.0620	.0024	.0010-.0024	.0016-.0037	1.1576-1.2195	.0009-.0022
	3.0L (1MZ-FE)	1.0610-1.0616	.0024	.0014-.0028	.0016-.0035	1.2191-2.195	.0009-.0020
	3.0L (2JZ-GE)	1.1397-1.1404	.0031	.0014-.0028	.0031-.0075	1.2191-1.2195	.0009-.0020
	3.0L (2JZ-GTE)	1.1397-1.1404	.0031	.0014-.0028	.0031-.0075	1.2191-1.2195	.0009-.0020
	3.4L (5VZ-FE)	1.0610-1.0616	.0024	.0014-.0028	.0008-.0079	1.2191-1.2195	.0009-.0020
	4.5L (1FZ-FE)	1.0614-1.0620	.0024	.0010-.0024	.0012-.0031	1.3372-1.3376	.0009-.0022

① — No. 1 Exhaust, .9822-.9829 inch; all others, .9035-.9041 inch.
② — Intake, .0012-.0033 inch; exhaust, .0014-.0035 inch.
③ — Intake, .0018-.0039 inch; exhaust, .0012-.0033 inch.
④ — Corolla.
⑤ — Celica.

CRANKSHAFT, BEARINGS & RODS

All measurements given are in inches, unless otherwise specified.

Year	Engine Liters (ID Code)	Crankshaft Std. Journal Dia. ①		Bearing Clearance			Connecting Rod Side Clearance
		Main Bearing	Crank Pin	Main Bearing	Connecting Rod Bearing	Thrust Bearing	
1993	1.5L (3E-E)	⑤	1.6923-1.6929	.0006-.0014	.0006-.0019	.0008-.0087	.0059-.0138
	1.5L (5E-FE)	③	1.6923-1.6929	.0006-.0014	.0006-.0019	.0008-.0087	.0059-.0138
	1.6L (4A-FE)	1.8891-1.8898	1.5742-1.5748	.0006-.0013	.0008-.0020	.0008-.0087	.0059-.0098
	1.8L (7A-FE)	1.8891-1.8898	1.8891-1.8898	.0006-.0013	.0008-.0020	.0008-.0087	.0059-.0098
	2.0L (3S-GTE)	2.1653-2.1655	1.8892-1.8898	②	.0009-.0022	.0008-.0087	.0063-.0123
	2.2L (5S-FE)	2.1653-2.1655	2.0466-2.0472	②	.0009-.0022	.0008-.0087	.0063-.0123
	2.4L (22R-E)	2.3616-2.3622	2.0861-2.0866	.0010-.0022	.0010-.0022	.0008-.0087	.0063-.0102
	2.4L (2TZ-FE)	2.3617-2.3622	2.0861-2.0866	.0009-.0019	.0012-.0023	.0008-.0087	.0063-.0123
	3.0L (3VZ-E)	④	2.1648-2.1654	.0009-.0017	.0009-.0021	.0008-.0098	.0059-.0130
	3.0L (3VZ-FE)	2.5191-2.5197	2.1648-2.1654	.0011-.0022	.0011-.0026	.0008-.0087	.0059-.0130
	4.5L (1FZ-FE)	2.7158-2.7165	2.2434-2.2441	.0017-.0024	.0013-.0020	.0008-.0087	.0063-.0103
1994	1.5L (3E-E)	⑤	1.6923-1.6929	.0006-.0014	.0006-.0019	.0008-.0087	.0059-.0138
	1.5L (5E-FE)	③	1.6923-1.6929	.0006-.0014	.0006-.0019	.0008-.0087	.0059-.0138
	1.6L (4A-FE)	1.8891-1.8898	1.5742-1.5748	.0006-.0013	.0008-.0020	.0008-.0087	.0059-.0098
	1.8L (7A-FE)	1.8891-1.8898	1.8891-1.8898	.0006-.0013	.0008-.0020	.0008-.0087	.0059-.0098
	2.0L (3S-GTE)	2.1653-2.1655	1.8892-1.8898	②	.0009-.0022	.0008-.0087	.0063-.0123
	2.2L (5S-FE)	2.1653-2.1655	2.0466-2.0472	②	.0009-.0022	.0008-.0087	.0063-.0123
	2.4L (22R-E)	2.3616-2.3622	2.0861-2.0866	.0010-.0022	.0010-.0022	.0008-.0087	.0063-.0102
	2.4L (2TZ-FE)	2.3617-2.3622	2.0861-2.0866	.0009-.0019	.0012-.0023	.0008-.0087	.0063-.0123
	2.7L (3RZ-FE)	2.3617-2.3622	2.0861-2.0866	⑤	.0012-.0022	.0008-.0087	.0063-.0123
	3.0L (3VZ-E)	④	2.1648-2.1654	.0009-.0017	.0009-.0021	.0008-.0098	.0059-.0130

Continued

CRANKSHAFT, BEARINGS & RODS—Continued

All measurements given are in inches, unless otherwise specified.

Year	Engine Liters (ID Code)	Crankshaft Std. Journal Dia. ①		Bearing Clearance			Connecting Rod Side Clearance
		Main Bearing	Crank Pin	Main Bearing	Connecting Rod Bearing	Thrust Bearing	
1994	3.0L (1MZ-FE)	2.4011-2.4016	2.0864-2.0866	.0010-.0018	.0015-.0025	.0016-.0095	.0059-.0118
	3.0L (2JZ-GE)	2.4403-2.4409	2.0465-2.0472	.0010-.0016	.0014-.0021	.0008-.0087	.0098-.0158
	3.0L (2JZ-GTE)	2.4403-2.4409	2.0465-2.0472	.0010-.0016	.0014-.0021	.0008-.0087	.0098-.0158
	4.5L (1FZ-FE)	2.7158-2.7165	2.2434-2.2441	.0017-.0024	.0013-.0020	.0008-.0087	.0063-.0103
1995	1.5L (3E-E)	⑤	1.6923-1.6929	.0006-.0014	.0006-.0019	.0008-.0087	.0059-.0138
	1.5L (5E-FE)	③	1.6923-1.6929	.0006-.0014	.0006-.0019	.0008-.0087	.0059-.0138
	1.6L (4A-FE)	1.8891-1.8898	1.5742-1.5748	.0006-.0013	.0008-.0020	.0008-.0087	.0059-.0098
	1.8L (7A-FE)	1.8891-1.8898	1.8891-1.8898	.0006-.0013	.0008-.0020	.0008-.0087	.0059-.0098
	2.0L (3S-GTE)	2.1653-2.1655	1.8892-1.8898	②	.0009-.0022	.0008-.0087	.0063-.0123
	2.2L (5S-FE)	2.1653-2.1655	2.0466-2.0472	②	.0009-.0022	.0008-.0087	.0063-.0123
	2.4L (22R-E)	2.3616-2.3622	2.0861-2.0866	.0010-.0022	.0010-.0022	.0008-.0087	.0063-.0102
	2.4L (2RZ-FE)	2.3617-2.3622	2.0861-2.0866	⑤	.0012-.0022	.0008-.0087	.0063-.0123
	2.4L (2TZ-FE)	2.3617-2.3622	2.0861-2.0866	.0009-.0019	.0012-.0023	.0008-.0087	.0063-.0123
	2.7L (3RZ-FE)	2.3617-2.3622	2.0861-2.0866	⑤	.0012-.0022	.0008-.0087	.0063-.0123
	3.0L (3VZ-E)	④	2.1648-2.1654	.0009-.0017	.0009-.0021	.0008-.0098	.0059-.0130
	3.0L (1MZ-FE)	2.4011-2.4016	2.0864-2.0866	.0010-.0018	.0015-.0025	.0016-.0095	.0059-.0118
	3.0L (2JZ-GE)	2.4403-2.4409	2.0465-2.0472	.0010-.0016	.0014-.0021	.0008-.0087	.0098-.0158
	3.0L (2JZ-GTE)	2.4403-2.4409	2.0465-2.0472	.0010-.0016	.0014-.0021	.0008-.0087	.0098-.0158
	3.4L (5VZ-FE)	2.5191-2.5197	2.1648-2.1654	.0008-.0025	.0009-.0027	.0008-.0087	.0059-.0130
	4.5L (1FZ-FE)	2.7158-2.7165	2.2434-2.2441	.0017-.0024	.0013-.0020	.0008-.0087	.0063-.0103
1996	1.5L (5E-FE)	③	1.6923-1.6929	.0006-.0014	.0006-.0019	.0008-.0087	.0059-.0138
	1.6L (4A-FE)	1.8891-1.8898	1.5742-1.5748	.0006-.0013	.0008-.0020	.0008-.0087	.0059-.0098
	1.8L (7A-FE)	1.8891-1.8898	1.8891-1.8898	.0006-.0013	.0008-.0020	.0008-.0087	.0059-.0098
	2.0L (3S-FE)	2.1653-2.1655	2.0466-2.0472	.0006-.0013	.0009-.0022	.0008-.0087	.0063-.0123
	2.2L (5S-FE)	2.1653-2.1655	2.0466-2.0472	②	.0009-.0022	.0008-.0087	.0063-.0123
	2.4L (2RZ-FE)	2.3617-2.3622	2.0861-2.0866	⑤	.0012-.0022	.0008-.0087	.0063-.0123
	2.4L (2TZ-FZE)	2.3617-2.3622	2.0861-2.0866	.0009-.0019	.0012-.0023	.0008-.0087	.0063-.0123
	2.7L (3RZ-FE)	2.3617-2.3622	2.0861-2.0866	⑤	.0012-.0022	.0008-.0087	.0063-.0123
	3.0L (1MZ-FE)	2.4011-2.4016	2.0864-2.0866	.0010-.0018	.0015-.0025	.0016-.0095	.0059-.0118
	3.0L (2JZ-GE)	2.4403-2.4409	2.0465-2.0472	.0010-.0016	.0014-.0021	.0008-.0087	.0098-.0158
	3.0L (2JZ-GTE)	2.4403-2.4409	2.0465-2.0472	.0010-.0016	.0014-.0021	.0008-.0087	.0098-.0158
	3.4L (5VZ-FE)	2.5191-2.5197	2.1648-2.1654	.0008-.0025	.0009-.0027	.0008-.0087	.0059-.0130
	4.5L (1FZ-FE)	2.7158-2.7165	2.2434-2.2441	.0017-.0024	.0013-.0020	.0008-.0087	.0063-.0103

① — Max. taper and out of round, .0008 inch.
② — No. 3, .0010-.0017 inch; all others, .0006-.0013 inch.
③ — Mark 0, 1.9683-1.69685 inch; Mark 1, 1.9681-1.9683 inch; Mark 2, 1.9679-1.9681 inch.
④ — No. 0, 2.5195-2.5197 inch; No. 1, 2.5193-2.5195 inch; No. 2, 2.5191-2.5192 inch.
⑤ — No. 0, 1.9683-1.9685 inch; No. 1, 1.9681-1.9683 inch; No. 2, 1.9679-1.9681 inch.

PISTONS, PINS & RINGS

All measurements given are in inches, unless otherwise specified.

Year	Engine Liters (ID Code)	Piston Dia. Std.	Piston Clearance	Piston Pin Dia.	Piston Ring End Gap			Piston Ring Side Clearance	
					Top	Second	Oil	Top	Second
1993	1.5L (3E-E)	⑤	.0028-.0035	—	.0102-.0189	.0118-.0224	.0059-.0205	.0016-.0031	.0012-.0028
	1.5L (5E-FE)	⑥	.0035-.0043	—	.0102-.0189	.0118-.0224	.0059-.0197	.0016-.0031	.0012-.0028
	1.6L (4A-FE)⑪	⑦	.0024-.0031	—	.0098-.0177	.0059-.0157	.0039-.0276	.0016-.0032	.0012-.0028
	1.6L (4A-FE)⑫	⑬	.0033-.0041	—	.0098-.0177	.0138-.0197	.0059-.0177	.0018-.0033	.0012-.0028

Continued

PISTONS, PINS & RINGS—Continued

All measurements given are in inches, unless otherwise specified.

Year	Engine Liters (ID Code)	Piston Dia. Std.	Piston Clear-ance	Piston Pin Dia.	Piston Ring End Gap			Piston Ring Side Clearance	
					Top	Second	Oil	Top	Second
1993	1.8L (7A-FE)	④	.0033-.0041	—	.0098-.0177	.0138-.0197	.0059-.0177	.0018-.0033	.0012-.0028
	2.0L (3S-GTE)	⑧	.0028-.0035	.8660-.8665	.0130-.0217	.0177-.0264	.0079-.0236	.0016-.0031	.0012-.0028
	2.2L (5S-FE)	3.4193-3.4205	.0055-.0063	.8660-.8665	.0106-.0197	.0138-.0234	.0079-.0217	.0016-.0031	.0012-.0028
	2.4L (22R-E)	②	.0006-.0014	—	.0098-.0185	.0236-.0323	.0079-.0224	.0012-.0028	.0012-.0028
	2.4L (2TZ-FE)	3.7382-3.7386	.0012-.0020	.9449-.9452	.0118-.0169	.0177-.0236	.0051-.0150	.0008-.0028	.0012-.0028
	3.0L (3VZ-E)	①	.0051-.0059	—	.0091-.0130	.0150-.0189	.0059-.0157	.0012-.0028	.0012-.0028
	3.0L (3VZ-FE)	⑩	.0051-.0059	.8860-8864	.0110-.0197	.0150-.0236	.0059-.0224	.0004-.0031	.0012-.0028
	4.5L (1FZ-FE)	⑨	.0016-.0024	1.0236-1.0241	.0118-.0205	.0177-.0264	.0059-.0205	.0016-.0031	.0012-.0028
1994	1.5L (3E-E)	⑤	.0028-.0035	—	.0102-.0189	.0118-.0224	.0059-.0205	.0016-.0031	.0012-.0028
	1.5L (5E-FE)	⑥	.0035-.0043	—	.0102-.0189	.0118-.0224	.0059-.0197	.0016-.0031	.0012-.0028
	1.6L (4A-FE)⑪	⑦	.0024-.0031	—	.0098-.0177	.0059-.0157	.0039-.0276	.0016-.0032	.0012-.0028
	1.6L (4A-FE)⑫	④	.0033-.0041	—	.0098-.0177	.0138-.0197	.0059-.0177	.0018-.0033	.0012-.0028
	1.8L (7A-FE)	④	.0033-.0041	—	.0098-.0177	.0138-.0197	.0059-.0177	.0018-.0033	.0012-.0028
	2.0L (3S-GTE)	⑧	.0028-.0035	.8660-.8665	.0130-.0217	.0177-.0264	.0079-.0236	.0016-.0031	.0012-.0028
	2.2L (5S-FE)	3.4193-3.4205	.0055-.0063	.8660-.8665	.0106-.0197	.0138-.0234	.0079-.0217	.0016-.0031	.0012-.0028
	2.4L (22R-E)	②	.0006-.0014	—	.0098-.0185	.0236-.0323	.0079-.0224	.0012-.0028	.0012-.0028
	2.4L (2TZ-FE)	3.7382-3.7386	.0012-.0020	.9449-.9452	.0118-.0169	.0177-.0236	.0051-.0150	.0008-.0028	.0012-.0028
	2.7L (3RZ-FE)	3.7379-3.7379	.0019-.0024	—	.0118-.0157	.0157-.0194	.0157-.0194	.0008-.0028	.0012-.0028
	3.0L (3VZ-E)	①	.0051-.0059	—	.0091-.0130	.0150-.0189	.0059-.0157	.0012-.0028	.0012-.0028
	3.0L (1MZ-FE)	3.4412-3.4416	.0033-.0042	—	.0098-.0138	.0138-.0177	.0059-.0157	.0008-.0028	.0008-.0024
	3.0L (2JZ-GE)	3.3833-2.3837	.0022-.0031	—	.0118-.0185	.0138-.0205	.0051-.0177	.0004-.0028	.0012-.0028
	3.0L (2JZ-GTE)	3.3833-3.3837	.0022-.0031	—	.0118-.0157	.0138-.0178	.0051-.0150	.0016-.0031	.0012-.0028
	4.5L (1FZ-FE)	⑨	.0016-.0024	1.0236-1.0241	.0118-.0205	.0177-.0264	.0059-.0205	.0016-.0031	.0012-.0028
1995	1.5L (5E-FE)	⑥	.0035-.0043	—	.0102-.0189	.0118-.0224	.0059-.0197	.0016-.0031	.0012-.0028
	1.6L (4A-FE)⑪	⑦	.0024-.0031	—	.0098-.0177	.0059-.0157	.0039-.0276	.0016-.0032	.0012-.0028
	1.6L (4A-FE)⑫	④	.0033-.0041	—	.0098-.0177	.0138-.0197	.0059-.0177	.0018-.0033	.0012-.0028
	1.8L (7A-FE)	④	.0033-.0041	—	.0098-.0177	.0138-.0197	.0059-.0177	.0018-.0033	.0012-.0028
	2.0L (3S-GTE)	⑧	.0028-.0035	.8660-.8665	.0130-.0217	.0177-.0264	.0079-.0236	.0016-.0031	.0012-.0028
	2.2L (5S-FE)	3.4193-3.4205	.0055-.0063	.8660-.8665	.0106-.0197	.0138-.0234	.0079-.0217	.0016-.0031	.0012-.0028
	2.4L (22R-E)	②	.0006-.0014	—	.0098-.0185	.0236-.0323	.0079-.0224	.0012-.0028	.0012-.0028
	2.4L (2RZ-FE)	3.7371-3.7375	.0022-.0031	.9449-.9452	.0118-.0157	.0157-.0194	.0157-.0194	.0008-.0028	.0012-.0028
	2.4L (2TZ-FE)	3.7382-3.7386	.0012-.0020	.9449-.9452	.0118-.0169	.0177-.0236	.0051-.0150	.0008-.0028	.0012-.0028
	2.7L (3RZ-FE)	3.7375-3.7379	.0019-.0028	.9449-.9452	.0118-.0157	.0157-.0194	.0157-.0194	.0008-.0028	.0012-.0028
	3.0L (3VZ-E)	①	.0051-.0059	—	.0091-.0130	.0150-.0189	.0059-.0157	.0012-.0028	.0012-.0028
	3.0L (1MZ-FE)	3.4412-3.4416	.0033-.0042	—	.0098-.0138	.0138-.0177	.0059-.0157	.0008-.0028	.0008-.0024

Continued

PISTONS, PINS & RINGS—Continued

All measurements given are in inches, unless otherwise specified.

Year	Engine Liters (ID Code)	Piston Dia. Std.	Piston Clear-ance	Piston Pin Dia.	Piston Ring End Gap			Piston Ring Side Clearance	
					Top	Second	Oil	Top	Second
1995	3.0L (2JZ-GE)	3.3833-2.3837	.0022-.0031	—	.0118-.0185	.0138-.0205	.0051-.0177	.0004-.0028	.0012-.0028
	3.0L (2JZ-GTE)	3.3833-3.3837	.0022-.0031	—	.0118-.0157	.0138-.0178	.0051-.0150	.0016-.0031	.0012-.0028
	3.4L (5VZ-FE)	3.6754-3.6758	.0053-.0060	.8660-.8665	.0118-.0197	.0157-.0236	.0059-.0217	.0016-.0031	.0012-.0028
	4.5L (1FZ-FE)	⑨	.0016-.0024	1.0236-1.0241	.0118-.0205	.0177-.0264	.0059-.0205	.0016-.0031	.0012-.0028
1996	1.5L (5E-FE)	⑥	.0035-.0043	—	.0102-.0189	.0118-.0224	.0059-.0197	.0016-.0031	.0012-.0028
	1.6L (4A-FE)⑪	⑦	.0024-.0031	—	.0098-.0177	.0059-.0157	.0039-.0276	.0016-.0032	.0012-.0028
	1.6L (4A-FE)⑫	④	.0033-.0041	—	.0098-.0177	.0138-.0197	.0059-.0177	.0018-.0033	.0012-.0028
	1.8L (7A-FE)	④	.0033-.0041	—	.0098-.0177	.0138-.0197	.0059-.0177	.0018-.0033	.0012-.0028
	2.0L (3S-FE)	③	.0047-.0063	.8660-.8665	.0106-.0197	.0106-.0201	.0079-.0217	.0012-.0028	.0012-.0028
	2.2L (5S-FE)	3.4193-3.4205	.0055-.0063	.8660-.8665	.0106-.0197	.0138-.0234	.0079-.0217	.0016-.0031	.0012-.0028
	2.4L (2RZ-FE)	3.7371-3.7375	.0022-.0031	.9449-.9452	.0118-.0157	.0157-.0194	.0157-.0194	.0008-.0028	.0012-.0028
	2.4L (2TZ-FZE)	3.7382-3.7386	.0012-.0020	.9449-.9452	.0118-.0169	.0177-.0236	.0051-.0150	.0008-.0028	.0012-.0028
	2.7L (3RZ-FE)	3.7375-3.7379	.0019-.0028	.9449-.9452	.0118-.0157	.0157-.0194	.0157-.0194	.0008-.0028	.0012-.0028
	3.0L (1MZ-FE)	3.4412-3.4416	.0033-.0042	—	.0098-.0138	.0138-.0177	.0059-.0157	.0008-.0028	.0008-.0024
	3.0L (2JZ-GE)	3.3833-2.3837	.0022-.0031	—	.0118-.0185	.0138-.0205	.0051-.0177	.0004-.0028	.0012-.0028
	3.0L (2JZ-GTE)	3.3833-3.3837	.0022-.0031	—	.0118-.0157	.0138-.0178	.0051-.0150	.0016-.0031	.0012-.0028
	3.4L (5VZ-FE)	3.6754-3.6758	.0053-.0060	.8660-.8665	.0118-.0197	.0157-.0236	.0059-.0217	.0016-.0031	.0012-.0028
	4.5L (1FZ-FE)	⑨	.0016-.0024	1.0236-1.0241	.0118-.0205	.0177-.0264	.0059-.0205	.0016-.0031	.0012-.0028

① — Standard No. 1, 3.4394-3.4398 inch; No. 2, 3.4398-3.4402 inch; No. 3, 3.4402-3.4406 inch.
② — Standard No. 1, 3.6211-3.6214 inch; No. 2, 3.6214-3.6218 inch; No. 3, 3.6218-3.6222 inch.
③ — Standard No. 1, 3.3807-3.3811 inch; No. 2, 3.3811-3.3815 inch; No. 3, 3.3815-3.3819 inch.
④ — Mark 1, 3.1852-3.1856 inch; Mark 2, 3.1856-3.1860 inch; Mark 3, 3.1860-3.1864 inch.
⑤ — Mark 1, 2.8708-2.8712 inch; Mark 2, 2.8712-2.8716 inch; Mark 3, 2.8716-2.8720 inch.
⑥ — Mark 1, 2.9094-2.9098 inch; Mark 2, 2.9098-2.9102 inch; Mark 3, 2.9102-2.9106 inch.
⑦ — Mark 1, 3.1862-3.1866 inch; Mark 2, 3.1866-3.1870 inch; Mark 3, 3.1870-3.1874 inch.
⑧ — Mark 1, 3.3827-3.3831 inch; Mark 2, 3.3831-3.3835 inch; Mark 3, 3.3835-3.3839 inch.
⑨ — Mark 1, 3.9350-3.9354 inch; Mark 2, 3.9354-3.9358 inch; Mark 3, 3.9358-3.9362 inch.
⑩ — Mark 1, 3.4394-3.4398 inch; Mark 2, 3.4398-3.4402 inch; Mark 3, 3.4402-3.4405 inch.
⑪ — Celica.
⑫ — Corolla.

CYLINDER BLOCK

All measurements given are in inches unless otherwise specified.

Year	Engine Liters (ID Code)	Cylinder Bore Dia. (Std.)	Cylinder Bore Dia. (Max.)
1993	1.5L (3E-E)	2.8740-2.8752 ②	2.8831
	1.5L (5E-FE)	2.9134-2.9138	2.8831
	1.6L (4A-FE)	④	3.1982
	1.8L (7A-FE)	④	3.1982
	2.0L (3S-GTE)	⑤	3.3949
	2.2L (5S-FE)	⑥	3.4342
	2.4L (22R-E)	③	3.6312

Continued

CYLINDER BLOCK—Continued

All measurements given are in inches unless otherwise specified.

Year	Engine Liters (ID Code)	Cylinder Bore Dia. (Std.)	Cylinder Bore Dia. (Max.)
1993	2.4L (2TZ-FE)	3.3798-3.27402	3.7425
	3.0L (3VZ-E)	②	3.4539
	3.0L (3VZ-FE)	②	3.4549
	4.5L (1FZ-FE)	①	3.9461
1994	1.5L (3E-E)	2.8740-2.8752 ②	2.8831
	1.5L (5E-FE)	2.9134-2.9138	2.8831
	1.6L (4A-FE)	④	3.1982
	1.8L (7A-FE)	④	3.1982
	2.0L (3S-GTE)	⑤	3.3949
	2.2L (5S-FE)	⑥	3.4342
	2.4L (22R-E)	③	3.6312
	2.4L (2TZ-FE)	3.3798-3.27402	3.7425
	2.7L (3RZ-FE)	3.7398-3.7403	3.7425
	3.0L (3VZ-E)	②	3.4539
	3.0L (1MZ-FE)	3.4449-3.4453	3.4457
	3.0L (2JZ-GE)	3.3858-3.3863	3.3866
	3.0L (2JZ-GTE)	3.3858-3.3863	3.3866
	4.5L (1FZ-FE)	①	3.9461
1995	1.5L (5E-FE)	2.9134-2.9138	2.8831
	1.6L (4A-FE)	④	3.1982
	1.8L (7A-FE)	④	3.1982
	2.0L (3S-GTE)	⑤	3.3949
	2.2L (5S-FE)	⑥	3.4342
	2.4L (22R-E)	③	3.6312
	2.4L (2RZ-FE)	3.7398-3.7403	3.7425
	2.4L (2TZ-FE)	3.3798-3.27402	3.7425
	2.7L (3RZ-FE)	3.7398-3.7403	3.7425
	3.0L (3VZ-E)	②	3.4539
	3.0L (1MZ-FE)	3.4449-3.4453	3.4457
	3.0L (2JZ-GE)	3.3858-3.3863	3.3866
	3.0L (2JZ-GTE)	3.3858-3.3863	3.3866
	3.4L (5VZ-FE)	3.6811-3.6819	3.6902
	4.5L (1FZ-FE)	①	3.9461
1996	1.5L (5E-FE)	2.9134-2.9138	2.8831
	1.6L (4A-FE)	④	3.1982
	1.8L (7A-FE)	④	3.1982
	2.0L (3S-FE)	⑤	3.3949
	2.2L (5S-FE)	⑥	3.4342
	2.4L (2RZ-FE)	3.7398-3.7403	3.7425
	2.4L (2TZ-FZE)	3.3798-3.27402	3.7425
	2.7L (3RZ-FE)	3.7398-3.7403	3.7425
	3.0L (1MZ-FE)	3.4449-3.4453	3.4457
	3.0L (2JZ-GE)	3.3858-3.3863	3.3866
	3.0L (2JZ-GTE)	3.3858-3.3863	3.3866
	3.4L (5VZ-FE)	3.6811-3.6819	3.6902
	4.5L (1FZ-FE)	①	3.9461

① — Mark 1, 3.9370-3.9374 inch; Mark 2, 3.9374-3.9378 inch; Mark 3, 3.9378-3.9382 inch.

② — Mark 1, 3.4449-3.4453 inch; Mark 2, 3.4453-3.4457 inch; Mark 3, 3.4457-3.4461 inch.

③ — Standard No 1, 3.6220-3.6224 inch; No. 2, 3.6224-3.6228 inch; No. 3, 3.6228-3.6232 inch.

④ — Mark 1, 3.1890-3.1894 inch; Mark 2, 3.1894-3.1898 inch; Mark 3, 3.1898-3.1902 inch.

⑤ — Mark 1, 3.3858-3.3862 inch; Mark 2, 3.3862-3.3866 inch; Mark 3, 3.3866-3.3870 inch.

⑥ — Mark 1, 3.4252-3.4256 inch; Mark 2, 3.4256-3.4260 inch; Mark 3, 3.4260-3.4264 inch.

OIL PUMP

All measurements given are in inches, unless otherwise specified.

Year	Engine Liters (ID Code)	Gear Backlash	Gear To Body Clearance	Tip Clearance	Side Clearance
1993	1.5L (3E-E)	—	.0039-.0063	.0024-.0059	.0012-.0035
	1.5L (5E-FE)	—	.0039-.0083	.0024-.0059	.1146-.1169
	1.6L (4A-FE)	—	.0031-.0071	.0010-.0033	.0010-.0033
	1.8L (7A-FE)	—	.0031-.0071	.0010-.0033	.0010-.0033
	2.0L (3S-GTE)	—	.0039-.0063	.0016-.0063	—
	2.2L (5S-FE)	—	.0039-.0063	.0016-.0063	—
	2.4L (22R-E)	—	.0035-.0059	①	.0012-.0035
	2.4L (2TZ-FE)	—	.0039-.0069	.0043-.0094	.0012-.0035
	3.0L (3VZ-E)	—	.0039-.0051	.0043-.0094	.0012-.0035
	3.0L (3VZ-FE)	—	.0039-.0069	.0043-.0094	.0012-.0035
	4.5L (1FZ-FE)	—	.0039-.0067	.0012-.0063	.0012-.0035
1994	1.5L (3E-E)	—	.0039-.0063	.0024-.0059	.0012-.0035
	1.5L (5E-FE)	—	.0039-.0083	.0024-.0059	.1146-.1169
	1.6L (4A-FE)	—	.0031-.0071	.0010-.0033	.0010-.0033
	1.8L (7A-FE)	—	.0031-.0071	.0010-.0033	.0010-.0033
	2.0L (3S-GTE)	—	.0039-.0063	.0016-.0063	—
	2.2L (5S-FE)	—	.0039-.0063	.0016-.0063	—
	2.4L (22R-E)	—	.0035-.0059	①	.0012-.0035
	2.4L (2TZ-FE)	—	.0039-.0069	.0043-.0094	.0012-.0035
	2.7L (3RZ-FE)	—	.0039-.0069	.0043-.0094	.0012-.0035
	3.0L (3VZ-E)	—	.0039-.0051	.0043-.0094	.0012-.0035
	3.0L (1MZ-FE)	—	.0039-.0069	.0043-.0094	.0012-.0035
	3.0L (2JZ-GE)	—	.0039-.0069	.0122-.0193	.0012-.0035
	3.0L (2JZ-GTE)	—	.0039-.0069	.0022-.0128	.0007-.0026
	4.5L (1FZ-FE)	—	.0039-.0067	.0012-.0063	.0012-.0035
1995	1.5L (5E-FE)	—	.0039-.0083	.0024-.0059	.1146-.1169
	1.6L (4A-FE)	—	.0031-.0071	.0010-.0033	.0010-.0033
	1.8L (7A-FE)	—	.0031-.0071	.0010-.0033	.0010-.0033
	2.0L (3S-GTE)	—	.0039-.0063	.0016-.0063	—
	2.2L (5S-FE)	—	.0039-.0063	.0016-.0063	—
	2.4L (22R-E)	—	.0035-.0059	①	.0012-.0035
	2.4L (2RZ-FE)	—	.0039-.0069	.0043-.0094	.0012-.0035
	2.4L (2TZ-FE)	—	.0039-.0069	.0043-.0094	.0012-.0035
	2.7L (3RZ-FE)	—	.0039-.0069	.0043-.0094	.0012-.0035
	3.0L (3VZ-E)	—	.0039-.0051	.0043-.0094	.0012-.0035
	3.0L (1MZ-FE)	—	.0039-.0069	.0043-.0094	.0012-.0035
	3.0L (2JZ-GE)	—	.0039-.0069	.0122-.0193	.0012-.0035
	3.0L (2JZ-GTE)	—	.0039-.0069	.0022-.0128	.0007-.0026
	3.4L (5VZ-FE)		.0039-.0069	.0043-.0094	.0012-.0035
	4.5L (1FZ-FE)	—	.0039-.0067	.0012-.0063	.0012-.0035
1996	1.5L (5E-FE)	—	.0039-.0083	.0024-.0059	.1146-.1169
	1.6L (4A-FE)	—	.0031-.0071	.0010-.0033	.0010-.0033
	1.8L (7A-FE)	—	.0031-.0071	.0010-.0033	.0010-.0033
	2.0L (3S-FE)	—	.0039-.0063	.0016-.0063	—
	2.2L (5S-FE)	—	.0039-.0063	.0016-.0063	—
	2.4L (2RZ-FE)	—	.0039-.0069	.0043-.0094	.0012-.0035
	2.4L (2TZ-FZE)	—	.0039-.0069	.0043-.0094	.0012-.0035
	2.7L (3RZ-FE)	—	.0039-.0069	.0043-.0094	.0012-.0035
	3.0L (1MZ-FE)	—	.0039-.0069	.0043-.0094	.0012-.0035
	3.0L (2JZ-GE)	—	.0039-.0069	.0122-.0193	.0012-.0035
	3.0L (2JZ-GTE)	—	.0039-.0069	.0022-.0128	.0007-.0026
	3.4L (5VZ-FE)		.0039-.0069	.0043-.0094	.0012-.0035
	4.5L (1FZ-FE)	—	.0039-.0067	.0012-.0063	.0012-.0035

① — Drive gear to crescent, .0059-.0083; driven gear to crescent, .0087-.0098.

VOLKSWAGEN

INDEX OF SERVICE OPERATIONS

	Page No.
AIR BAG SYSTEM PRECAUTIONS	0-8
AUTOMATIC TRANSMISSIONS/ TRANSAXLES	49-136
BRAKES	
Anti-Lock Brakes	49-109
Disc Brakes	49-95
Drum Brakes	49-105
Hydraulic Brake Systems	49-107
Power Brake Units	49-109
CLUTCH & MANUAL TRANSMISSION/ TRANSAXLE	
Adjustments	49-53
Application Chart	49-53
Clutch, Replace	49-56
Clutch Cable, Replace	49-56
Hydraulic System Service	49-56
Precautions	49-53
Tightening Specifications	49-59
Transaxle, Replace	49-57
ELECTRICAL	
Air Bags	49-85
Air Conditioning	49-73
Alternator, Replace	49-9
Alternators	49-79
Blower Motor, Replace	49-14
Coil Pack, Replace	49-10
Combination Switch, Replace	49-12
Cooling Fans	49-76
Cruise Control	49-81
Dash Panels	49-89
Distributor, Replace	49-9
Evaporator Core, Replace	49-16
Fuel Pump Relay Location	49-8
Fuse Panel & Flasher Location	49-8
Headlamp Switch, Replace	49-11
Heater Core, Replace	49-15
Ignition Lock, Replace	49-10
Ignition Switch, Replace	49-11
Instrument Cluster, Replace	49-12
Neutral Safety Switch, Replace	49-11
Passive Restraints	49-85
Precautions	49-8
Radio, Replace	49-13
Relay Center Location	49-8
Speed Controls	49-81
Starter Motors	49-78
Starter, Replace	49-8
Steering Columns	49-91
Steering Wheel, Replace	49-12
Stop Light Switch, Replace	49-11
Turn Signal Switch, Replace	49-12
Wiper Motor, Replace	49-13
Wiper Switch, Replace	49-14
Wiper Transmission, Replace	49-14
ELECTRICAL SYMBOL IDENTIFICATION	0-139
FRONT SUSPENSION & STEERING	
Ball Joint, Replace	49-66
Coil Spring, Replace	49-67
Control Arm, Replace	49-68
Description	49-65
Hub & Bearing, Replace	49-66
Manual Steering Gear, Replace	49-69
Power Steering	49-93
Power Steering Gear, Replace	49-68
Precautions	49-65
Shock Absorber, Replace	49-68
Strut, Replace	49-67
Strut Service	49-67
Tightening Specifications	49-70
Wheel Bearing Housing, Replace	49-65
FRONT WHEEL DRIVE AXLES	49-144
REAR AXLE & SUSPENSION	
Precautions	49-61
Rear Axle, Replace	49-61
Shock Absorber, Replace	49-63
Strut, Replace	49-63
Strut Service	49-63
Tightening Specifications	49-64
Wheel Bearing, Adjust	49-62
SERVICE REMINDER & WARNING LAMP RESET PROCEDURES	0-10
SPECIFICATIONS	
Diesel Engine Performance Specifications	49-4
Engine Application Chart	49-2
Fluid Capacities & Cooling System Data	49-6
Front Wheel Alignment Specifications	49-4
General Engine Specifications	49-3
Lubricant Data	49-7
Rear Wheel Alignment Specifications	49-5
Tune Up Specifications	49-3
VEHICLE IDENTIFICATION	0-1
VEHICLE LIFT POINTS	0-34
VEHICLE MAINTENANCE SCHEDULES	0-69
WHEEL ALIGNMENT	
Front Wheel Alignment	49-71
Rear Wheel Alignment	49-72
Wheel Alignment Specifications	49-4
WIRE COLOR CODE IDENTIFICATION	0-144
1.8L & 2.0L ENGINES	
Camshaft, Replace	49-28
Compression Pressure	49-22
Cooling System Bleed	49-29
Crankshaft Rear Oil Seal, Replace	49-29
Cylinder Head, Replace	49-25
Engine Mount, Replace	49-23
Engine Rebuilding Specifications	49-148
Engine, Replace	49-23
Exhaust Manifold, Replace	49-25
Front Main Bearing Oil Seal, Replace	49-29
Fuel Pump, Replace	49-30
Hydraulic Lifter Inspection	49-26
Hydraulic Lifters, Replace	49-27
Intake Manifold, Replace	49-25
Main & Rod Bearings	49-28
Oil Pan, Replace	49-29
Piston & Rod Assembly	49-28
Pistons, Pins & Rings	49-28
Precautions	49-22
Radiator, Replace	49-30
Serpentine Drive Belt	49-29
Tightening Specifications	49-31
Timing Belt, Replace	49-27
Valve Adjustment	49-26
Valve Clearance Specifications	49-26
Valve Guides	49-26
Water Pump, Replace	49-29
1.9L TURBOCHARGED DIRECT INJECTION (TDI) DIESEL ENGINE	
Camshaft, Replace	49-46
Compression Pressure	49-44
Cooling System Bleed	49-47
Crankshaft Rear Oil Seal, Replace	49-47
Cylinder Head, Replace	49-45
Engine Mount, Replace	49-45
Engine Rebuilding Specifications	49-148
Engine, Replace	49-45
Front Main Bearing Oil Seal, Replace	49-47
Fuel Filter, Replace	49-48
Fuel Injection System	49-49
Glow Plug System	49-51
Hydraulic Lifter Inspection	49-45
Hydraulic Lifter, Replace	49-46
Idle Speed, Adjust	49-51
Injection Pump, Replace	49-48
Injection Pump Timing	49-48
Main & Rod Bearings	49-47
Oil Pan, Replace	49-47
Oil Pump, Replace	49-47
Oil Pump Service	49-47
Piston & Rod Assembly	49-46
Precautions	49-44
Radiator, Replace	49-48
Tightening Specifications	49-51
Timing Belt, Replace	49-46
Turbocharger, Replace	49-48
Valve Adjustment	49-45
Valve Clearance Specifications	49-45
Valve Guides	49-46
Water Pump, Replace	49-47
2.5L ENGINE	
Camshaft, Replace	49-36
Compression Pressure	49-34
Crankshaft Seal, Replace	49-37
Cylinder Head, Replace	49-36
Engine Mount, Replace	49-35
Engine Rebuilding Specifications	49-148
Engine, Replace	49-35
Exhaust Manifold, Replace	49-36
Fuel Filter, Replace	49-38
Fuel Pump, Replace	49-38
Hydraulic Lifters	49-36
Intake Manifold, Replace	49-35
Main & Rod Bearings	49-37
Oil Pan, Replace	49-38
Piston & Rod Assembly	49-37
Precautions	49-34
Radiator, Replace	49-38

Page No.

Tightening Specifications...... 49-38
Timing Belt, Replace.......... 49-36
Valve Adjustment 49-36
Valve Clearance Specifications................. 49-36
Valve Cover, Replace......... 49-36
Valve Guides 49-36

2.8L ENGINE

Camshaft, Replace 49-41
Compression Pressure........ 49-39
Cooling System Bleed 49-42
Crankshaft Rear Oil Seal, Replace 49-42
Crankshaft Seal, Replace..... 49-42
Cylinder Head, Replace....... 49-41
Engine Mount, Replace 49-39
Engine Rebuilding Specifications.................49-148
Engine, Replace 49-40
Fuel Pump, Replace 49-42
Oil Pan, Replace.............. 49-42
Oil Pump, Replace............ 49-42
Piston & Rod Assembly....... 49-42
Precautions................... 49-39
Radiator, Replace............ 49-42
Tightening Specifications...... 49-43
Timing Chain, Replace........ 49-41
Valve Adjustment 49-41
Valve Clearance Specifications................ 49-41
Valve Guides 49-41
Valve Timing, Adjust 49-41
Water Pump, Replace 49-42

Specifications

ENGINE APPLICATION CHART

Year	Engine Liter	Engine Code	Model
1993	1.8L	ABG	Fox
	1.8L	2H	Cabriolet
	2.0L 16-V	9A	Passat
	2.0L	ABA	Golf III
			Jetta III
	2.5L	AAF	Eurovan
	2.8L	AAA	Corrado
			Passat
1994	2.0L	ABA	Golf III
			Jetta III GL
	2.8L	AAA	Corrado
			Jetta III GLX
			Passat
1995	2.0L	ABA	Cabrio
			Golf III
			Jetta III GL
	2.8L	AAA	GTI
			Jetta III GLX
			Passat
1996	1.9L①	1Z	Golf III TDI
			Jetta III TDI
			Passat GLS TDI
	2.0L	ABA	Cabrio
			Golf III GL
			GTI
			Jetta III GL & GLS
			Passat GLS
	2.8L	AAA	GTI VR6
			Jetta III GLX
			Passat GLX

① — TDI (Turbocharged Direct Injection) diesel.

GENERAL ENGINE SPECIFICATIONS

Year	Engine Liter	Engine Code	Fuel System	Bore & Stroke, Inches	Comp. Ratio	Horsepower @ RPM	Torque Ft. Lbs. @ RPM	Normal Oil Pressure, Lbs.①
1993	1.8L	ABG	②	3.19 x 3.40	9.0	81 @ 5500	93 @ 3250	29
	1.8L	2H	②	3.19 x 3.40	10.0	94 @ 5400	100 @ 3000	29
	2.0L 16-V	9A	CIS-E Motronic	3.25 x 3.65	10.8	134 @ 5800	133 @ 4400	29
	2.0L	ABA	CIS-E Motronic	3.25 x 3.65	10.0	115 @ 5400	122 @ 3200	29
	2.5L	AAF	Digifant	3.19 x 3.76	8.5	109 @ 4500	140 @ 2200	29
	2.8L	AAA	Motronic	3.19 x 3.56	10.0	172 @ 5800	177 @ 4200	29
1994	2.0L	ABA	CIS-E Motronic	3.25 x 3.65	10.0	115 @ 5400	122 @ 3200	29
	2.8L	AAA	Motronic	3.19 x 3.56	10.0	172 @ 5800	177 @ 4200	29
1995	2.0L	ABA	CIS-E Motronic	3.25 x 3.65	10.0	115 @ 5400	122 @ 3200	29
	2.8L③	AAA	Motronic	3.19 x 3.56	10.0	172 @ 5800	177 @ 4200	29
	2.8L④	AAA	Motronic	3.19 x 3.56	10.0	172 @ 5400	173 @ 4200	29
1996	1.9L⑤	1Z	Mechanical Direct Injection	3.13 x 3.76	19.5	90 @ 3750	149 @ 1900	29
	2.0L	ABA	CIS-E Motronic	3.25 x 3.65	10.0	115 @ 5400	122 @ 3200	29
	2.8L	AAA	Motronic	3.19 x 3.56	10.0	172 @ 5800	177 @ 4200	29

①— Minimum @ 2000 RPM & normal operating temperature.
②— Digifant I, California models; Digifant II, except California models.
③— Except GTI-VR6.
④— GTI-VR6.
⑤— TDI (Turbocharged Direct Injection) diesel.

TUNE UP SPECIFICATIONS

Year	Engine Liter	Engine Code	Spark Plug Gap, Inch	Ignition Timing: Firing Order	Ignition Timing: Timing, °BTDC	Ignition Timing: Timing Mark Fig.	Curb Idle Speed, RPM: Man. Trans.	Curb Idle Speed, RPM: Auto. Trans.	Fuel System Pressure, psi	Valve Lash
1993	1.8L	ABG	.024–.032	1-3-4-2	①②⑦	A	⑤⑦⑨	⑤⑦⑨	③	④
	1.8L	2H	.024–.032	1-3-4-2	①②⑦	A	⑤⑦⑨	⑤⑦⑨	68.2–78.3	④
	2.0L 16-V	9A	.028–.032	1-3-4-2	①	A	700–900⑥	700–900⑥	88.4–95.7	④
	2.5L	AAF	.028–.031	1-2-4-5-3	①②	A	775–825⑥	775–825⑥	6.2–44.0	④
	2.8L	AAA	.028–.031	1-5-3-6-2-4	6⑧	—	650–750⑧	650–750⑧	50.75	④
1994	2.0L	ABA	.032	1-3-4-2	12⑧	A	840⑧	840N⑧	88.4–95.7	④
	2.8L	AAA	.030	1-5-3-6-2-4	6⑧	—	650–750⑧	650–750⑧	50.75	④
1995	2.0L	ABA	.032	1-3-4-2	12⑧	—	840⑧	840N⑧	88.4–95.7	④
	2.8L	AAA	.030	1-5-3-6-2-4	6⑧	—	700⑧	700N⑧	50.75	④
1996	2.0L	ABA	.032	1-3-4-2	12⑧	—	840⑧	840N⑧	88.4–95.7	④
	2.8L	AAA	.030	1-5-3-6-2-4	6⑧	—	700⑧	700N⑧	50.75	④

BTDC — Before Top Dead Center.
①— Checking value, 4–8°; adjusting value, 5–7°.
②— Values observed at 2000–2500 RPM w/engine at operating temperature & coolant temperature sensor disconnected.
③— At idle w/vacuum hose connected, 36 psi; at idle w/vacuum hose disconnected, 44 psi.
④— Hydraulic lifters, no adjustment required.
⑤— A/C switched off & radiator fan not running.
⑥— Idle speed controlled by idle speed stabilization & cannot be adjusted.
⑦— California emissions models w/ Digifant I, not adjustable.
⑧— Not adjustable.
⑨— Federal Emissions, 800–900; California emissions, 750–850.

DIESEL ENGINE PERFORMANCE SPECIFICATIONS

Year	Engine Code	Firing Order	Injection Pump Timing	Cylinder Compression: Cranking Pressure, psi	Cylinder Compression: Maximum Variation	Fuel Injectors: Spray Test, psi	Fuel Injectors: Leak Test, psi	Idle Speed	Max. Speed @ Zero Load, RPM	Valve Lash
1996	1Z	1-3-4-2	①④	493	72.5	2755–2900②	2175③	④	④	⑤

① — Refer to "1.9L Engine" for injection pump timing procedures.
② — Opening pressure new, wear limit 2465 psi.
③ — Maintain pressure for ten seconds with no fuel leakage.
④ — Computer controlled.
⑤ — Hydraulic lifters, no adjustment required.

FRONT WHEEL ALIGNMENT SPECIFICATIONS

EXCEPT EUROVAN

Year	Model	Caster Angle, Degrees①		Camber Angle, Degrees		Total Toe, Degrees		Toe Per Wheel, Degrees	Ball Joint Wear
		Limits	Desired	Limits	Desired	Limits	Desired		
1993	Cabriolet	+1 1/3 to +2 1/3	+1 5/6②	-1/6 to + 5/6	+1/3②	-1/12 to -1/2	-1/4	–	⑥
	Corrado	+2 11/12 to +3 11/12 ③	+3 5/12	-1 2/3 to -1⑤	-1 1/3	-1/6 to +1/6	0	–	⑥
	Fox	+1 2/3 to +2 1/3 ③	–	-5/6 to -1/6④	–	-1/3 to 0	–	–	⑥
	Golf III & Jetta III GL	+1 1/3 to +2 1/3	+1 5/6	-11/12 to -1/4	-7/12	-1/6 to +1/6	0	–	⑥
	Jetta III GLX	+2 23/30 to +3 23/30	+3 4/15	-1/6 to -5/6	-1/2	-1/6 to +1/6	0	–	⑥
	Passat GL	+1 1/6 to +2 1/6 ②	+1 2/3	-1 2/3 to -1⑤	-1 1/3	0 to +2/3	+1/6	–	⑥
	Passat GLX	+2 5/6 to +3 5/6 ③	+3 2/3	-1 1/2 to -5/6⑤	-1 1/6	0 to +2/3	+1/6	–	⑥
1994	Cabriolet	+1 1/3 to +2 1/3	+1 5/6②	-1/6 to +5/6	+1/3②	-1/12 to -1/2	-1/4	–	⑥
	Corrado 4 Cyl.	+1 1/12 to +2 1/12	+1 7/12	–1 to –1/3	–2/3	–1/6 to +1/6	0	–	⑥
	Corrado VR6	+2 11/12 to +3 11/12 ③	+3 5/12	-1 2/3 to -1⑤	-1 1/3	-1/6 to +1/6	0	–	⑥
	Golf III & Jetta III GL	+1 1/3 to +2 1/3	+1 5/6	-11/12 to -1/4	-7/12	-1/6 to +1/6	0	–	⑥
	Jetta III GLX	+2 23/30 to +3 23/30	+3 4/15	-1/6 to -5/6	-1/2	-1/6 to +1/6	0	–	⑥
	Passat GL	+1 1/6 to +2 1/6 ②	+1 2/3	-1 2/3 to -1⑤	-1 1/3	0 to +2/3	+1/6	–	⑥
	Passat GLX	+2 5/6 to +3 5/6 ③	+3 2/3	-1 1/2 to -5/6⑤	-1 1/6	0 to +2/3	+1/6	—	⑥
1995	Golf III & Jetta III GL	+1 1/3 to +2 1/3	+1 5/6	-11/12 to -1/4	-7/12	-1/6 to +1/6	0	–	⑥
	GTI & Jetta III GLX	+2 23/30 to +3 23/30	+3 4/15	-1/6 to -5/6	-1/2	-1/6 to +1/6	0	–	⑥
	Passat GL	+1 1/6 to +2 1/6 ②	+1 2/3	-1 2/3 to -1⑤	-1 1/3	-1/6 to +1/6	0	–	⑥
	Passat GLX	+2 5/6 to +3 5/6 ③	+3 1/3	-1 1/2 to -5/6⑤	-1 1/6	-1/6 to +1/6	0	–	⑥

Continued

FRONT WHEEL ALIGNMENT SPECIFICATIONS—Continued

EXCEPT EUROVAN

Year	Model	Caster Angle, Degrees①		Camber Angle, Degrees		Total Toe, Degrees		Toe Per Wheel, Degrees	Ball Joint Wear
		Limits	Desired	Limits	Desired	Limits	Desired		
1996	Golf III, GTI & Jetta III GL	+1 ⅓ to +2⅓	+1 ⅚	-11/12 to -¼	-7/12	-⅙ to +⅙	0	–	⑥
	Golf III TDI & Jetta III TDI	+1 ¼ to +2¼	+1 ¾	-⅙ to -⅚	-½	-⅙ to +⅙	0	–	⑥
	GTI-VR6 & Jetta III GLX	+2 23/30 to +3 23/30	+3 4/15	-⅙ to -⅚	-½	-⅙ to +⅙	0	–	⑥
	Passat GL & Passat GL TDI	+1 ⅙ to +2 ⅙ ②	+1 ⅔	-1 ⅔ to -1⑤	-1 ⅓	-⅙ to + ⅙	0	–	⑥
	Passat GLX	+2 ⅚ to +3 ⅚ ③	+3 ⅓	-1 ½ to -⅚⑤	-1 ⅙	-⅙ to +⅙	0	–	⑥

① — Not adjustable.
② — Maximum permissible difference between left and right, 1°.
③ — Maximum permissible difference between left and right, 1/2°.
④ — Maximum permissible difference between left and right, 1/4°.
⑤ — Maximum permissible difference between left and right, 1/3°.
⑥ — With suspension unloaded, no noticeable play.

EUROVAN

Year	Group No.①	Caster Angle, Degrees②			Camber Angle, Degrees③			Total Toe, Degrees③			Ball Joint Wear
		Empty	Half Load	Full Load	Empty	Half Load	Full Load	Empty	Half Load	Full Load	
1993	Groups 1 & 2	+1 ⅔	+1 ⅚	+2	+¼	–1/12	–⅓	+⅓	0	–⅓	④
	Group 3	+1 ⅔	+1 ⅚	+2	0	–⅙	–⅓	+⅙	0	–⅓	④
	Group 4	+1 ⅚	+1 11/12	+2	–⅙	–¼	–⅓	0	–⅙	–⅓	④

① — The vehicle group number sticker is located on the lefthand side A-pillar. The group number is located after the term Grund or Kom. Early vehicles not equipped with a group number sticker are considered to be group 1.
② — Plus or minus ½°.
③ — Plus or minus ⅓°.
④ — With suspension unloaded, no noticeable play

REAR WHEEL ALIGNMENT SPECIFICATIONS

EXCEPT EUROVAN

Year	Model	Camber Angle, Degrees		Total Toe, Degrees①	Toe Per Wheel, Degrees
		Limits	Desired		
1993	Cabriolet, Golf III, Jetta III & Passat	–1 ⅚ to –⅔	–1 ¼	–⅙ to +⅚	–
	Corrado	–1 ⅔ to –1 ⅓	–1 ½	+⅙ to +½	–
	Fox Sedan	–2 to –1	–1 ½	+¼ to +7/12	–
	Fox Wagon	–2 to –1	–1 ½	+⅙ to +⅗	–
1994	Cabriolet, Golf III, Jetta III & Passat	–1 ⅚ to –⅔	–1 ¼	–⅙ to +⅚	–
	Corrado	–1 ⅔ to –1 ⅓	–1 ½	+⅙ to +½	–
1995–96	Cabrio, Golf III, GTI, Jetta III & Passat	–1 ⅚ to –⅔	–1 ¼	–⅙ to +⅚	–

① — Toe-in (+); toe-out (-).

EUROVAN

Year	Group No.①	Camber Angle, Degrees②			Total Toe, Degrees③		
		Empty	Half Load	Full Load	Empty	Half Load	Full Load
1993	Group 1	−½	−1 ⅙	−1 7⁄12	+⅓	+⅔	+1
	Group 2	0	−⅔	−1 ⅙	+1⁄10	+⅖	+⅔
	Group 3	−½	−1 ⅙	−1 7⁄12	+⅓	+⅔	+1
	Group 4	−⅔	−1 ⅙	−1 ½	+⅖	+11⁄15	+9⁄10

① — The vehicle group number sticker is located on the left side A-pillar. The group number is located after the term Grund or Kom. Early vehicles not equipped with a group number sticker are considered to be group 1.
② — Plus or minus ½°.
③ — Plus or minus ⅓°.

FLUID CAPACITIES & COOLING SYSTEM DATA

Year	Model	Coolant System Capacity, Qts.	Rad. Cap Relief Pressure, Lbs.	Thermostat Opening Temp., °F	Fuel Tank Capacity, Gals.	Engine Oil Refill, Qts.①	Transmission Capacity		
							Manual, Pts.	Automatic: Trans., Qts.⑦	Automatic: Final Drive, Pts.
1993	Cabriolet	5.1	18–22	198	13.8	4.3	4.2	6.4⑧	1.6④
	Corrado	10.6	17–22	176	18.5	6.3	4.2	6.4⑧	1.6④
	Eurovan	12.2	18–22	189	21.1	5.9	6.4	5.9⑧	3.2④
	Fox	②	19–22	194	12.4	3.7	4.2	–	–
	Golf III & Jetta III	6.5	18–22	185	14.5	4.3	4.0	5.9⑧	1.6④
	Passat GL	7.3	18–22	185	18.5	4.3	4.2	5.9⑧	1.6④
	Passat GLX	9.6	17–22	176	18.5	7.4	4.2	5.9⑧	1.6④
1994	Cabriolet	5.1	18–22	198	13.8	4.3	4.2	6.4⑧	1.6④
	Corrado	10.6	17–22	176	18.5	6.3	4.2	5.9⑧	1.6④
	Golf III & Jetta III	6.5	18–22	185	14.5	4.3	4.0	5.9⑧	1.6④
	Jetta III GLX	9.5	17–22	176	14.5	7.3	4.2	5.9⑧	1.6④
	Passat GLX	9.6	17–22	176	18.5	7.4	4.2	5.9⑧	1.6④
1995	Cabrio, Golf III & Jetta III	6.5	18–22	185	14.5	4.3	4.0	5.6⑧	1.6④
	GTI & Jetta III GLX	9.5	17–22	185	14.5	7.3	4.2	5.6⑧	1.6④
	Passat GLX	9.6	17–22	176	18.5	7.4	4.2	5.9⑧	1.6④
1996	Cabrio, Golf III, GTI & Jetta III	6.5	18–22	185	14.5	4.8	4.0	5.6⑧	1.6④
	Golf III TDI & Jetta III TDI③	6.4	19–22	185	14.5	4.4	4.0	–	–
	GTI-VR6 & Jetta III GLX	8.5	17–22	176	14.5	5.8	4.2	5.6⑧	1.6④
	Passat TDI③	⑤	19–22	185	18.5	4.4	4.2	5.6⑤⑧	1.6④⑤
	Passat GLS	7.1	18–22	185	18.5	4.2	4.2	5.6⑧	1.6④
	Passat GLX	9.7	17–22	176	18.5	5.8	4.2	5.6⑧	1.6④

① — Includes filter.
② — Less A/C, 6.4 qts.; with A/C, 6.9 qts.
③ — Turbocharged Direct Injection (TDI) diesel.
④ — Filled for service life.
⑤ — Automatic Transaxle available in wagon only.
⑤ — Sedan, 4.4 qts.; wagon, 6.4 qts.
⑦ — Initial fill.
⑧ — Refill, add three qts, then adjust level per dipstick.

LUBRICANT DATA

Year	Model	Lubricant Type					
		Engine	Transmission			Power Steering	Brake System
			Manual	Automatic			
				Planetary	Differential		
1993	Cabriolet	⑤	GL-4①	②	G-50 SAE 75w/90 Synthetic	G 002 000④	DOT 4
	Corrado	⑤	③	Dexron	G-50 SAE 75w/90 Synthetic	G 002 000④	DOT 4
	Eurovan	⑤	③	Dexron	G-50 SAE 75w/90 Synthetic	G 002 000④	DOT 4
	Fox	⑤	GL-4 SAE 80W	–	–	G 002 000④	DOT 4
	Golf III, & Jetta III	⑤	③	Dexron	G-50 SAE 75w/90 Synthetic	G 002 000④	DOT 4
	Passat	⑤	③	Dexron	G-50 SAE 75w/90 Synthetic	G 002 000④	DOT 4
1994	Cabriolet	⑤	GL-4①	②	G-50 SAE 75w/90 Synthetic	G 002 000④	DOT 4
	Corrado	⑤	③	Dexron	G-50 SAE 75w/90 Synthetic	G 002 000④	DOT 4
	Golf III & Jetta III	⑤	③⑨	Dexron	G-50 SAE 75w/90 Synthetic	G 002 000④	DOT 4
	Passat	⑤	③	Dexron	G-50 SAE 75w/90 Synthetic	G 002 000④	DOT 4
1995	Cabrio, Golf III, GTI & Jetta III	⑤	③⑨	Dexron	G-50 SAE 75w/90 Synthetic	G 002 000④	DOT 4
	Passat	⑤	③⑨	Dexron	G-50 SAE 75w/90 Synthetic	G 002 000④	DOT 4
1996	Cabrio, Golf III, GTI & Jetta III	⑤	③⑨	Dexron	G-50 SAE 75w/90 Synthetic	G 002 000④	DOT 4
	Golf III TDI & Jetta III TDI⑦	⑥	③⑨	–	–	G 002 000④	DOT 4
	Passat	⑤	③⑨	Dexron	G-50 SAE 75w/90 Synthetic	G 002 000④	DOT 4
	Passat TDI⑦	⑥	③⑨	Dexron⑦	G-50 SAE 75w/90 Synthetic⑧	G 002 000④	DOT 4

① — SAE 80W or SAE 80w/90.
② — Dexron or Dexron II.
③ — GL-4 SAE 80W or G-50 SAE 75w/90 synthetic.
④ — Hydraulic oil, Volkswagen part number.
⑤ — API service SF or SG.
⑥ — API service CD.
⑦ — Turbocharged Direct Injection (TDI).
⑧ — Station wagon only.
⑨ — 01M transaxle use VW ATF part No. G 052 162 A2 only

Electrical

NOTE: On Air Bag Equipped Models, Refer To "Air Bag System Precautions" Located In The Front Of This Manual For System Disarming & Arming Procedures.

INDEX

	Page No.
Air Bags	49-85
Air Conditioning	49-73
Alternator, Replace	49-9
Alternators	49-79
Blower Motor, Replace	49-14
Cabriolet	49-14
Corrado	49-15
Eurovan	49-15
Fox	49-15
Passat	49-15
Coil Pack, Replace	49-10
Combination Switch, Replace	49-12
Cooling Fans	49-76
Cruise Control	49-81
Dash Panels	49-89
Distributor, Replace	49-9
1.8L & 2.0L 8-Valve Engines	49-9
2.0L 16-Valve & 2.5L Engines	49-10
Evaporator Core, Replace	49-16
Cabriolet	49-16
Corrado	49-16
Eurovan	49-17
Fox	49-17
Passat	49-17
Fuel Pump Relay Location	49-8
Fuse Panel & Flasher Location	49-8
Headlamp Switch, Replace	49-11
Cabrio, Golf III, GTI & Jetta III	49-11
Passat	49-11
Heater Core, Replace	49-15
Cabriolet	49-15
Corrado	49-16
Eurovan	49-16
Fox	49-16
Passat	49-16
Ignition Lock, Replace	49-10
Ignition Switch, Replace	49-11
Instrument Cluster, Replace	49-12
Cabrio, Golf III, GTI & Jetta III	49-13
Cabriolet	49-12
Corrado & Passat	49-12
Eurovan	49-13
Fox	49-13
Neutral Safety Switch, Replace	49-11
Passive Restraints	49-85
Precautions	49-8
Air Bag Systems	49-8
Audio Coded Anti-Theft System	49-8
Radio, Replace	49-13
Relay Center Location	49-8
Speed Controls	49-81
Starter Motors	49-78
Starter, Replace	49-8
Cabrio, Golf III, GTI, Jetta III & Passat	49-8
Cabriolet	49-9
Corrado	49-9
Eurovan	49-9
Fox	49-9
Steering Columns	49-91
Steering Wheel, Replace	49-12
Less Air Bag	49-12
With Air Bag	49-12
Stop Light Switch, Replace	49-11
Cabrio, Corrado, Eurovan, Golf, GTI, Jetta & Passat	49-11
Cabriolet & Fox	49-11
Turn Signal Switch, Replace	49-12
Wiper Motor, Replace	49-13
Front	49-13
Rear	49-14
Wiper Switch, Replace	49-14
Wiper Transmission, Replace	49-14

PRECAUTIONS

Do not use computer memory saver tool on air bag equipped models. Using the tool will keep the air bag system charged and may cause accidental activation of the air bag unit. Prior to disconnecting the battery negative cable, obtain the radio security code. After service has been completed and the battery negative cable has been reconnected, use security code to activate the radio.

AIR BAG SYSTEMS

Refer to "Air Bag System Precautions" in the front of this manual for system disarming and arming procedures.

AUDIO CODED ANTI-THEFT SYSTEM

Some models are equipped with a radio anti-theft system that will disable the system when battery power is interrupted, unless the system is reset the radio will not operate.

1. Turn radio to On position, SAFE should be displayed.
2. Depress and hold AM/FM and SCAN buttons until 1000 remains on display. If AM/FM and SCAN buttons are depressed too long or depressed again, radio will misinterpret the 1000 as an attempt at coding and one incorrect coding attempt will be logged. **After two incorrect attempts to reset system, radio will lock up electronically. If this occurs, leave radio On for approximately one hour, then reset radio as if battery power were disconnected.**
3. Enter radio code using first four program station buttons. Security code will appear on display.
4. Depress and hold AM/FM and SCAN buttons again until SAFE is displayed.
5. Release AM/FM and SCAN buttons. Display should change to a radio frequency and operate normally.

FUSE PANEL & FLASHER LOCATION

The fuse/relay panel is located under the left side of the instrument panel. The flasher relays are located at the fuse panel.

FUEL PUMP RELAY LOCATION

The fuel pump relay for gasoline engines is located in the fuse panel. Diesel engines do not use an electric fuel pump.

RELAY CENTER LOCATION

The relay/fuse panel is located under the left side of the instrument panel.

STARTER

REPLACE

CABRIO, GOLF III, GTI, JETTA III & PASSAT

1. Obtain audio coded anti-theft code, then disconnect battery ground cable.
2. Support engine/transaxle assembly using engine support tool No. 10-222A and leg set tool No. 10-222A/1, or equivalents, then raise and support vehicle.
3. Cut and discard cable ties used to secure wiring for starter.
4. Unclip and pull off white and black harness connectors from solenoid.
5. Disconnect electrical leads from starter solenoid.
6. Remove 8 mm nut securing hose support bracket to starter.
7. **On models with 1.9L diesel and 2.0L gasoline engines,** remove 12 mm bolt securing starter to engine support.
8. **On all models,** remove upper and lower starter mounting bolts, then the starter motor.

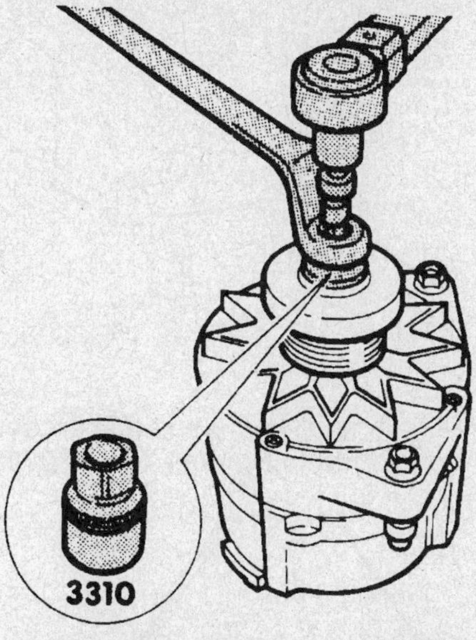
3310

VW1129300006000X

Fig. 1 Serpentine belt pulley removal

9. Reverse procedure to install, noting the following:
   a. **Torque** starter solenoid nut to 10 ft. lbs.
   b. **Torque** starter mounting bolts to 44 ft. lbs.
   c. **Torque** 8 mm nut for hose support bracket to 7 ft. lbs.
   d. **On models with 1.9L diesel and 2.0L engines, torque** 12 mm mounting bolt to 33 ft. lbs.
   e. **On all models,** reset audio coded anti-theft system as outlined under "Precautions."

CABRIOLET

1. Obtain audio coded anti-theft code, then disconnect battery ground cable.
2. Disconnect electrical leads from starter solenoid.
3. Remove starter mounting bolts, then the starter.
4. Reverse procedure to install, noting the following:
   a. **On models with manual transaxle, torque** starter mounting bolts to 43 ft. lbs.
   b. **On models with automatic transaxle, torque** starter mounting bolts to 14 ft. lbs.
   c. **On all models, torque** battery cable to solenoid nut to 10 ft. lbs.
   d. Reset audio coded anti-theft system as outlined under "Precautions."

CORRADO

Starter motor installation requires precise alignment of engine and related components. Removal procedures will cause these components to shift position if engine support is not used.

1. Obtain audio coded anti-theft code, then disconnect battery ground cable.
2. Support engine/transaxle assembly using engine support tool No. 10-222A and leg set tool No. 10-222A/1, or equivalents.
3. Disconnect electrical leads from starter solenoid, then pull leads out of retainer.
4. Unclip and disconnect harness connector.
5. Remove upper mounting nut and lower mounting bolt, then the starter motor.
6. Reverse procedure to install, noting the following:
   a. **Torque** starter solenoid nut to 11 ft. lbs.
   b. **Torque** solenoid ground connection nut to 7 ft. lbs.
   c. **Torque** starter mounting nut and bolt to 44 ft. lbs.
   d. Reset audio coded anti-theft system as outlined under "Precautions."

EUROVAN

1. Obtain audio coded anti-theft code, then disconnect battery ground cable, then raise and support vehicle.
2. Remove black plastic protective cap from starter solenoid, then the battery cable.
3. Disconnect remaining solenoid wiring, then remove starter mounting bolts and starter motor.
4. Reverse procedure to install, noting the following:
   a. **Torque** battery cable to solenoid nut to 10 ft. lbs.
   b. **Torque** starter mounting bolts to 15 ft. lbs.
   c. Reset audio coded anti-theft system as outlined under "Precautions."

FOX

1. Obtain audio coded anti-theft code, then disconnect battery ground cable.
2. **On models with A/C,** install engine/transaxle support tool No. VW 10-222, or equivalent, to support engine.
3. **On models with A/C,** remove right side engine mount and support.
4. **On all models,** disconnect electrical leads from starter solenoid, then remove clip.
5. Remove starter motor mounting bolts, then the starter motor.
6. Reverse procedure to install. **Torque** starter mounting bolts to 15 ft. lbs. Reset audio coded anti-theft system as outlined under "Precautions."

ALTERNATOR

REPLACE

1. Obtain audio coded anti-theft code, then disconnect battery ground cable.
2. Disconnect wiring connectors from alternator.
3. Remove serpentine drive belt as outlined in the appropriate engine section.
4. Remove alternator mounting bolts, then alternator.
5. Remove serpentine belt pulley using holder tool No. 3310, or equivalent, as shown in **Fig. 1.**
6. Reverse procedure to install, noting the following:

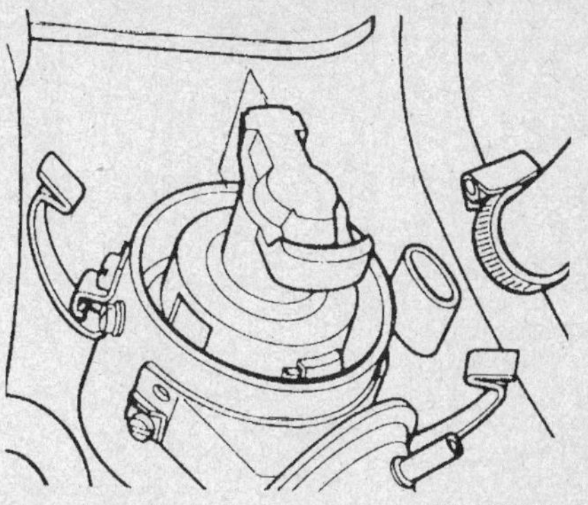

VW1119100001000X

Fig. 2 Distributor rotor alignment

   a. **Torque** drive belt pulley to 45–51 ft. lbs.
   b. **Torque** alternator mounting bolts to 18 ft. lbs.
   c. Tension drive belt as outlined in the appropriate engine section.
   d. Reset audio coded anti-theft system as outlined under "Precautions."

DISTRIBUTOR

REPLACE

1.8L & 2.0L 8-VALVE ENGINES

Removal

1. Obtain audio coded anti-theft code, then disconnect battery ground cable.
2. Disconnect electrical connector from distributor, then remove distributor cap.
3. Set engine to Top Dead Center (TDC) compression stroke, rotating engine in normal direction of rotation only.
4. Ensure center of rotor tip is aligned with centering mark on distributor housing, **Fig. 2.**
5. If alignment cannot be achieved, engine re-timing may be required as outlined under "1.8L & 2.0L Engines."
6. Remove distributor clamp bolt, then the distributor. Due to helical gears of distributor drive, rotor will turn slightly during removal. Note this position for later assembly.

Installation

1. Ensure engine is set to TDC compression stroke.
2. Replace distributor base sealing gasket or O-ring as necessary.
3. Rotate distributor shaft and rotor so that tip center is slightly to right of centering mark on distributor body (about width of rotor tip), **Fig. 2.**
4. **On 1.8L engines,** using a suitable long screwdriver, align oil pump drive slot so it points towards distributor mounting bolt hole.
5. **On 1.8 L engines,** insert distributor into engine, then ensure oil pump drive is fully engaged and rotor and centering mark are aligned.
6. **On 2.0L engines,** proceed as follows:

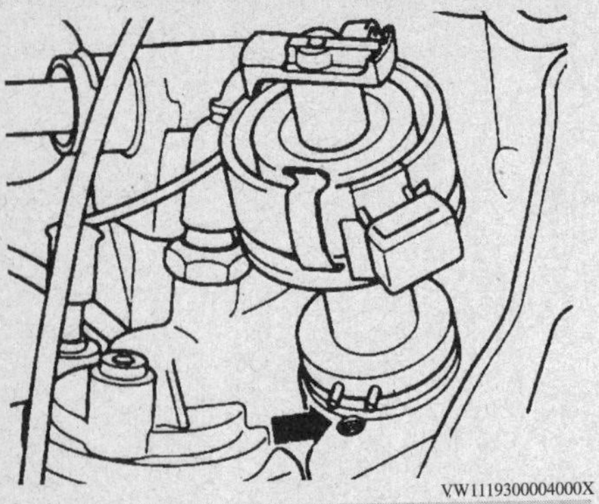
VW1119300004000X

Fig. 3 Distributor alignment. 2.0L engines

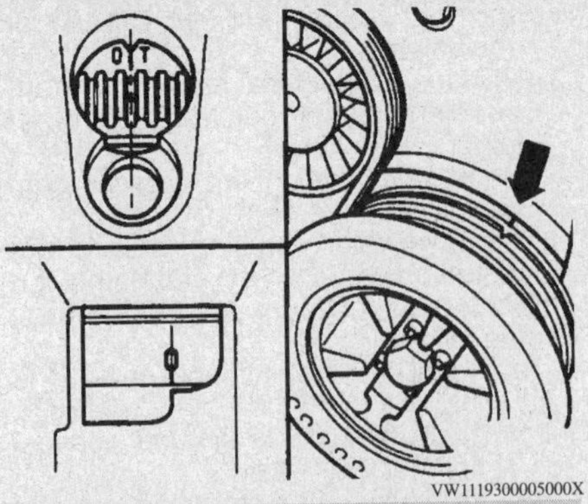
VW1119300005000X

Fig. 4 Crankshaft alignment for distributor timing. 2.5L engine

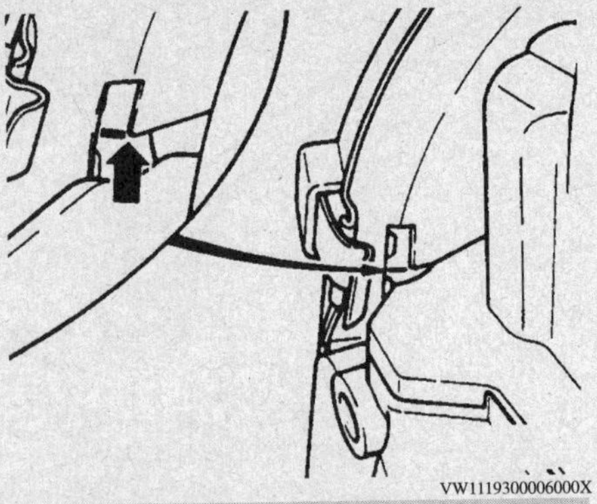
VW1119300006000X

Fig. 5 Camshaft alignment for distributor timing. 2.5L engine

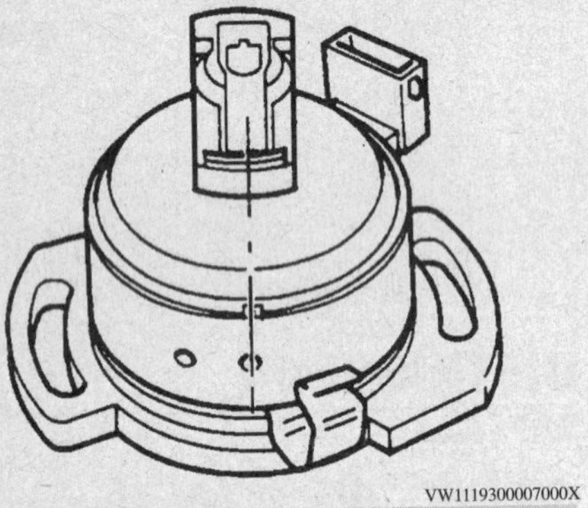
VW1119300007000X

Fig. 6 Rotor alignment for distributor timing. 2.5L engine

a. Using a suitable long screwdriver, align oil pump drive slot so it is parallel to the crankshaft.
b. Insert distributor into engine, then ensure oil pump drive is fully engaged, rotor and centering mark are aligned and locating pins on distributor body are centered over mounting bolt hole, **Fig. 3.**
c. If alignment cannot be achieved, remove timing belt from intermediate shaft sprocket as outlined under "1.8L & 2.0L Engines."
d. Turn intermediate shaft until alignment of crankshaft TDC, rotor tip centering and distributor locating pin can be achieved.
e. Install timing belt as outlined under "1.8L & 2.0L Engines."

7. **On all models,** install distributor hold-down clamp and bolt, **torque** to 18 ft. lbs.
8. Install wiring connectors and distributor cap.
9. Check ignition timing. Refer to "Specifications" for data.
10. Reset audio coded anti-theft system as outlined under "Precautions."

2.0L 16-VALVE & 2.5L ENGINES

1. Obtain audio coded anti-theft code, then disconnect battery ground cable.
2. Remove distributor cap and position aside, then disconnect distributor wiring.
3. Ensure flywheel is at TDC position, **Fig. 4,** camshaft timing mark is aligned, **Fig. 5,** and distributor rotor points toward cylinder No. 1 marking on distributor housing, **Fig. 6.**
4. If alignment cannot be achieved, engine re-timing may be required as outlined under "2.5L Engine."
5. Remove distributor hold-down bolts, then the distributor.
6. Reverse procedure to install, noting the following:
   a. **Torque** distributor hold-down bolts to 7 ft. lbs.
   b. Check ignition timing. Refer to "Specifications" for data.
   c. Reset audio coded anti-theft system as outlined under "Precautions."

COIL PACK

REPLACE

1. Note position of spark plug wires for later assembly.
2. Disconnect spark plug wires from coil pack.
3. Disconnect electrical connector from coil pack.
4. Remove mounting bolts, then coil pack.
5. Reverse procedure to install. **Torque** mounting bolts to 7 ft. lbs.

IGNITION LOCK

REPLACE

Refer to "Steering Columns" for illustrations for the following procedure. **Obtain new shear head bolt before starting procedure.**

1. Obtain audio coded anti-theft code, then disconnect battery ground cable.
2. **On Eurovan models,** remove steering column as outlined under "Steering Columns."
3. **On Eurovan models,** place steering column in a suitable vice as shown in **Fig. 7.** Ensure U-joint is supported on face of vice so steering shaft will not move down in column.
4. **On all models except Eurovan,** remove combination switch as outlined under "Combination Switch, Replace."
5. **On all models,** remove spacer or spring and locking washer, as equipped, from steering shaft using suitable tools.

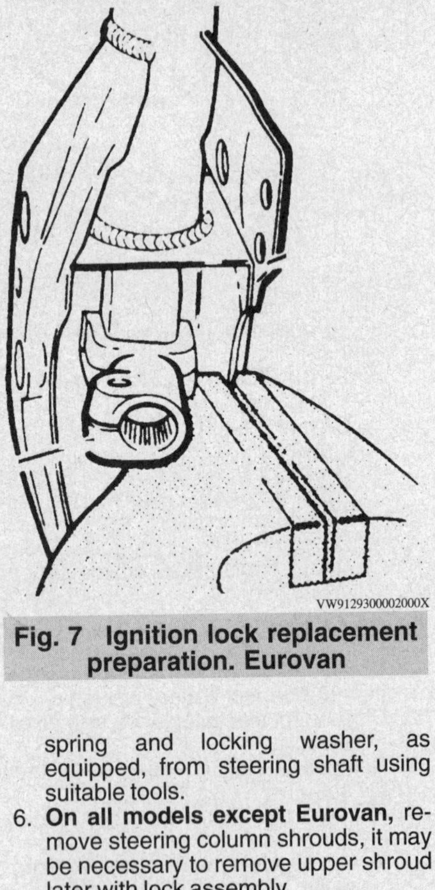
VW9129300002000X

Fig. 7 Ignition lock replacement preparation. Eurovan

6. **On all models except Eurovan,** remove steering column shrouds, it may be necessary to remove upper shroud later with lock assembly.
7. **On all models except Eurovan,** using suitable tools, clamp or block steering shaft so it will not slide down into steering column.
8. **On models with shifter lock cable,** disconnect shifter lock cable from ignition lock.
9. **On all models,** using a suitable chisel and hammer, back out end of shear head bolt retaining ignition lock to steering column on lefthand side. Alternatively, use a suitable drill motor to drill out shear head bolt retaining ignition lock to steering column on lefthand side.
10. Ensure body of shear head bolt is either drilled out or backed out sufficiently to clear mounting tab of steering column during lock removal.
11. **Unlock steering lock from column**

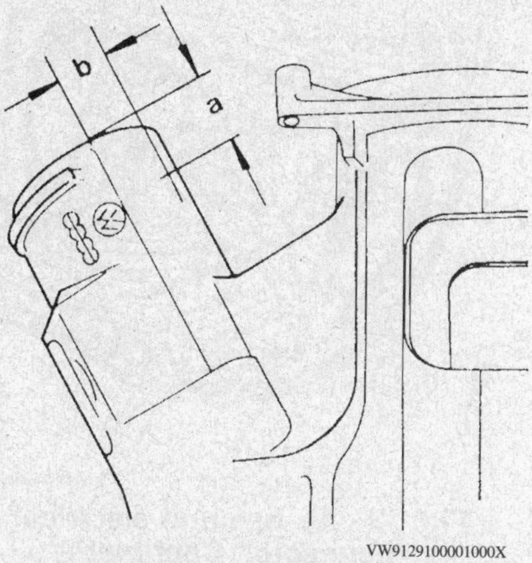
b
a
VW9129100001000X

Fig. 8 Ignition lock cylinder drilling dimensions

with ignition key prior to removing ignition lock.

12. Slide ignition lock, with upper trim if necessary, off steering column. Heat lock body with hot air blower if necessary.
13. **If unable to unlock ignition lock,** remove complete steering column if necessary, as outlined under "Steering Columns," then remove key tumbler as outlined below.
14. **If key tumbler removal or replacement is required,** proceed as follows:
    a. Insert ignition key into ignition lock cylinder.
    b. Using 1/8 inch drill bit, drill hole in lock housing approximately 1/8 inch deep as shown in **Fig. 8.** Dimension A = 0.47 inch, dimension B = .39 inch.
    c. Using a suitable drift punch, remove lock cylinder with key by pressing in check spring using hole previously drilled.
    d. When installing lock tumbler, ensure tumbler and lock assembly are in Off position.
15. Reverse procedure to install, noting the following:
    a. **On Eurovan models,** position ignition lock as shown in **Fig. 9.** Dimension A = 3.7 inches. Tighten shear bolt until head breaks off.
    b. **On Eurovan models,** position locking washer and spring as shown in **Fig. 10.** Dimension A = 2.5 inches.
    c. **On all models except Eurovan,** prior to final tightening of shear head bolt, assemble steering column completely.
    d. **On all models except Eurovan,** position ignition lock on column for proper clearance of slip ring contacts and trim shroud alignment.
    e. **On all models except Eurovan,** tighten shear bolt until head breaks off.
    f. **On models with shifter lock cable,** adjust shifter lock cable as outlined under "Automatic Transmissions/Transaxles."
    g. **On all models,** reverse remaining

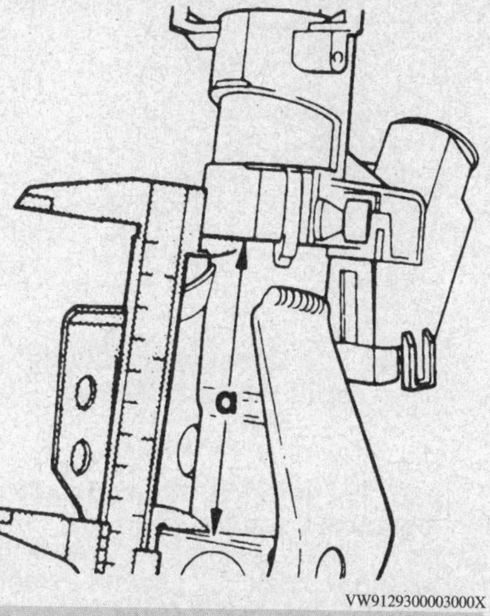
a
VW9129300003000X

Fig. 9 Ignition lock to column position. Eurovan

procedures to install. Reset audio coded anti-theft system as outlined under "Precautions."

IGNITION SWITCH

REPLACE

1. Remove ignition lock housing as outlined under "Ignition Lock, Replace."
2. Remove screw attaching ignition switch to lock housing assembly.
3. Remove ignition switch.
4. Reverse procedure to install. Reset audio coded anti-theft system as outlined under "Precautions."

NEUTRAL SAFETY SWITCH

REPLACE

The neutral safety switch is a part of the multi-function transaxle range switch. Refer to the appropriate transaxle section for procedures.

HEADLAMP SWITCH

REPLACE

CABRIO, GOLF III, GTI & JETTA III

1. Using a suitable flat tool, pry out trim plate to left of switch.
2. Using a suitable blunt pointed tool with a 90° bend, reach above and behind switch, in line with knob, and press in on release button, **Fig. 11.**
3. Pull switch from dash, then disconnect electrical connector.
4. Reverse procedure to install.

PASSAT

1. Insert a suitable thin flat tool, with a maximum thickness of .035 inch, between vent and switch at a point just above left end of dash lamp dimmer control.

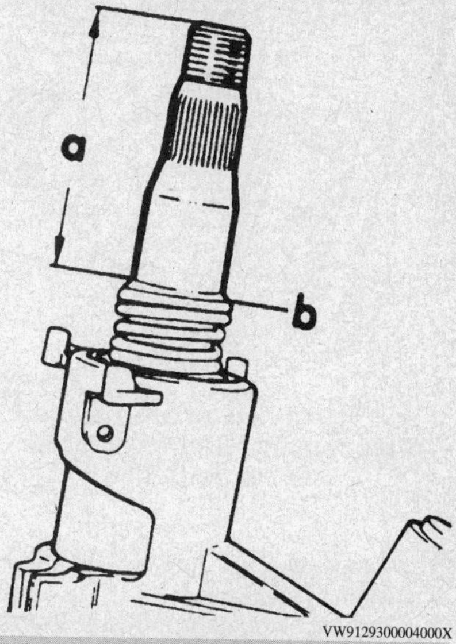
a
b
VW9129300004000X

Fig. 10 Steering shaft tension spring positioning. Eurovan

2. Move tool to right to disengage switch latch, **Fig. 12.**
3. Pull switch from dash, then disconnect electrical connector.
4. Reverse procedure to install.

STOP LIGHT SWITCH

REPLACE

CABRIOLET & FOX

The brake lamp switches are located at the master cylinder and are easily accessible from the engine compartment.

1. Disconnect wire connector from switch.
2. Remove switch from master cylinder.
3. Install new switch and connect electrical connector.
4. Top up master cylinder reservoir and bleed brake system.
5. Check master cylinder fluid level after bleeding brakes.

CABRIO, CORRADO, EUROVAN, GOLF, GTI, JETTA & PASSAT

Removal

The brake lamp switch is located on the brake pedal bracket at the top of the brake pedal.

1. Remove left underdash panels as necessary to access switch, then disconnect electrical connector from brake lamp switch.
2. Turn brake lamp switch 90° clockwise, then remove switch.

Installation

1. Pull switch plunger to its fullest extension.
2. Hold brake pedal down, then install new switch and turn 90° counterclockwise to fasten.

VW9019300001000X

Fig. 11 Headlamp switch replacement. Cabrio, Golf III, GTI & Jetta III

3. Pull brake pedal fully to rear to allow switch to auto adjust.
4. Connect electrical connector, then test brake lamp operation.
5. Reset audio coded anti-theft system as outlined under "Precautions."

COMBINATION SWITCH

REPLACE

1. Obtain audio coded anti-theft code, then disconnect battery ground cable.
2. Remove steering wheel as outlined under "Steering Wheel, Replace."
3. Remove lower and upper trim cover attaching screws, then trim covers, as necessary.
4. Remove attaching screws, then detach switch unit from steering column.
5. Disconnect multi-pin connectors, then remove switch unit.
6. Reverse procedure to install, noting the following:
   a. Lubricate turn signal cancelling ring with multi-purpose grease.
   b. Reset audio coded anti-theft system as outlined under "Precautions."

TURN SIGNAL SWITCH

REPLACE

1. Remove combination switch as outlined under "Combination Switch, Replace."
2. Carefully pry clips holding wiper switch and turn signal switch together, then separate switches.
3. Reverse procedure to install.

STEERING WHEEL

REPLACE

LESS AIR BAG

1. Place front wheels in straight ahead position, obtain audio coded anti-theft code, then disconnect battery ground cable.
2. Carefully pry out or pull off horn pad, then remove steering wheel retaining nut and spring washer. **Gently pry horn pad buttons from front of horn pad, if equipped, then disconnect electrical connectors.**
3. Mark steering wheel in relation to steering spindle, then remove steering wheel.
4. Reverse procedure to install, noting the following:
   a. Ensure wheels are in straight ahead position and signal lever is in Neutral position prior to installing wheel.
   b. **On Cabrio, Cabriolet, Golf III, GTI and Jetta III models,** ensure cancelling lug points to the left prior to installing wheel.
   c. **On all models,** align index marks made during removal.
   d. **On all models except Eurovan, torque** steering wheel retaining nut to 36 ft. lbs.
   e. **On Eurovan models, torque** steering wheel retaining nut to 52 ft. lbs.
   f. **On all models,** reset audio coded anti-theft system as outlined under "Precautions."

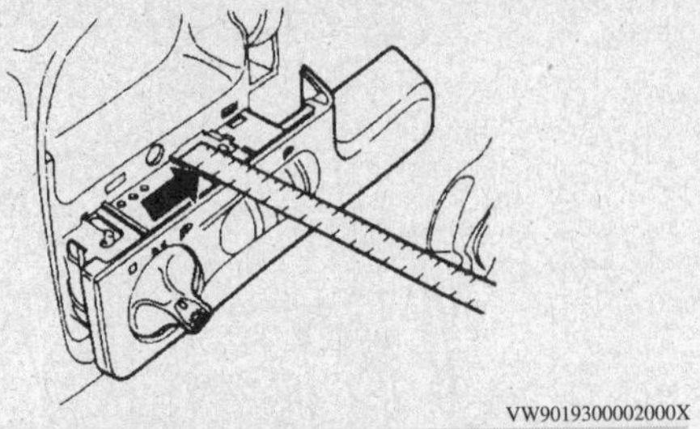

VW9019300002000X

Fig. 12 Headlamp switch replacement. Passat

WITH AIR BAG

1. Place front wheels in straight ahead position, obtain audio coded anti-theft code, then disconnect battery ground cable and cover negative terminal.
2. **Wait 20 minutes after disconnecting battery ground cable, before working on steering wheel to allow air bag system capacitor to discharge.**
3. Remove Torx screws from rear of horn pad.
4. Carefully detach air bag unit from steering wheel, then tilt downward. **Gently pry horn pad buttons from front of horn pad, if equipped, then disconnect electrical connectors.**
5. Disconnect electrical connector from air bag unit, **Fig 13,** then remove air bag unit. **Do not place air bag unit on its vinyl horn pad side. Always place unit on its metal housing.**
6. Remove steering wheel retaining nut and spring washer.
7. Remove lower steering column shroud, then disconnect connector from spiral spring assembly.
8. Mark steering wheel in relation to steering spindle.
9. Remove steering wheel. **Do not turn or release spiral spring assembly while steering wheel is removed.**
10. Reverse procedure to install, noting the following:
    a. Ensure wheels are in straight ahead position prior to installing wheel.
    b. Align index marks made during removal.
    c. Spiral spring assembly must be seated.
    d. **Torque** steering wheel retaining nut to 36 ft. lbs.
    e. Reset audio coded anti-theft system as outlined under "Precautions."

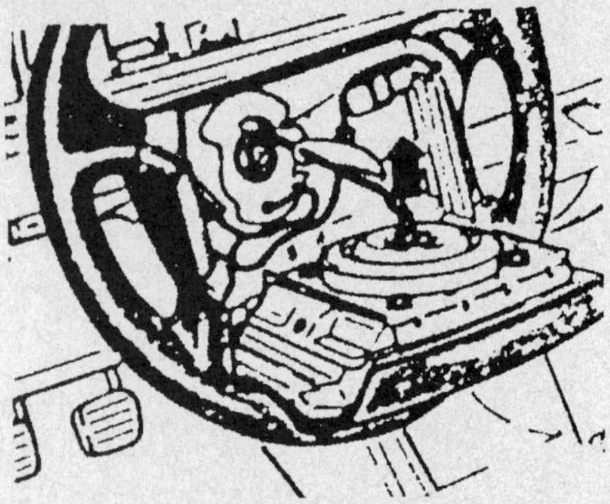

VW9049100001000X

Fig. 13 Air bag unit electrical connector. Cabriolet

INSTRUMENT CLUSTER

REPLACE

CABRIOLET

1. Obtain audio coded anti-theft code, then disconnect battery ground cable.
2. Remove steering wheel as outlined under "Steering Wheel, Replace."
3. Tilt shelf downward, then remove three screws and take off shelf.
4. Remove three screws, pry out clips, then remove instrument panel cover.
5. Remove two screws, then the instrument cluster insert trim.
6. Remove screw, then tilt instrument cluster forward.
7. Press lugs together and disconnect speedometer cable.
8. Disconnect multi-pin electrical connector, then remove instrument cluster.
9. Reverse procedure to install. Reset audio coded anti-theft system as outlined under "Precautions."

CORRADO & PASSAT

All components in instrument cluster, except printed circuit, may be removed from front without removing complete instrument cluster housing.

1. Obtain audio coded anti-theft code, then disconnect battery ground cable and remove steering wheel as outlined under "Steering Wheel, Replace."
2. Remove grille covers (1) and trim caps (2) covering screws, then remove screws from corners of cluster trim, **Fig. 14.**
3. Remove instrument cluster trim.
4. Unscrew trip odometer reset button,

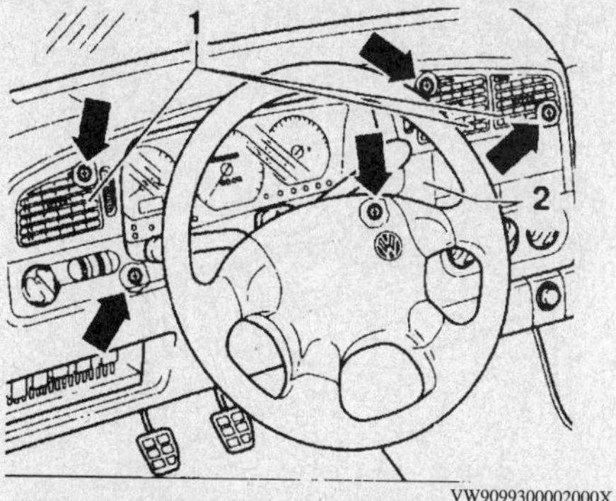
1
2
VW9099300002000X

Fig. 14 Instrument cluster removal. Passat

then remove instrument cluster cover retaining screws from rear outside of trim cover.
5. Remove cover from instrument cluster.
6. Instrument cluster components may be removed at this point. If entire cluster must be removed, proceed as follows:
   a. Remove instrument cluster housing mounting screws.
   b. Pull instrument cluster housing from instrument panel.
   c. Disconnect multi-pin connector, MFI vacuum sensor hose and speedometer drive cable.
   d. Remove instrument cluster housing.
7. Reverse procedure to install. Reset audio coded anti-theft system as outlined under "Precautions."

EUROVAN

1. Obtain audio coded anti-theft code, then disconnect battery ground cable.
2. Remove steering wheel as outlined under "Steering Wheel, Replace."
3. Remove radio or storage tray, heater control knobs, and control trim plate.
4. Remove screws securing instrument cluster bezel and pull bezel away from dash.
5. If equipped, press switches out of bezel and remove bezel.
6. Remove screws securing instrument cluster, disconnect wiring harness connectors and speedometer cable, then remove cluster.
7. Reverse procedure to install. Reset audio coded anti-theft system as outlined under "Precautions."

FOX

1. Obtain audio coded anti-theft code, then disconnect battery ground cable.
2. Remove steering wheel as outlined under "Steering Wheel, Replace."
3. Pry switch blanks from instrument cluster trim.
4. Using a suitable thin flat tool inserted between switch and instrument cluster, **Fig. 15,** depress clips and remove switch, then disconnect wiring connectors.
5. Using a suitable magnetic screwdriver through switch holes in cluster trim, remove retaining screws, then cluster trim.
6. Remove screws retaining cluster to instrument panel.
7. Release clips holding speedometer cable to cluster, then remove cluster.
8. Reverse procedure to install. Reset audio coded anti-theft system as outlined under "Precautions."

CABRIO, GOLF III, GTI & JETTA III

It is not necessary to remove the steering wheel when removing the instrument cluster.

Trim panels may be replaced by switch panels on some models, depending on vehicle equipment level.

1. Obtain audio coded anti-theft code, then disconnect battery ground cable.
2. Remove headlamp switch as outlined under "Headlamp Switch, Replace."
3. Remove trim panel from dash at right lower corner of instrument cluster.
4. Remove screws from lower steering column trim cover, then steering column upper cover.
5. Remove instrument cluster trim cover mounting screws as shown in **Fig. 16.**
6. Release instrument cluster trim cover side retainers by pulling firmly at top, then remove instrument cluster trim cover.
7. Remove instrument cluster mounting screws.
8. Tilt instrument cluster downward and disconnect electrical connectors from back of instrument cluster.
9. Remove instrument cluster.
10. Reverse procedure to install.

RADIO

REPLACE

Factory supplied radios use two distinct types of mountings and face plates, requiring two different removal tools. Refer to **Figs. 17 and 18** to determine, by the type of face plate, which tool will be required.

1. Obtain audio coded anti-theft code.
2. Determine removal tool required as outlined above.
3. Insert tools as shown in **Figs. 17 or 18** until they are felt to seat.
4. **On models using tool No. VW160,** after tool is inserted, press outward on tools while pulling radio out.
5. **On models using tool No. 3316,** after tool is inserted, pull straight out with no up/down, twist or side movements.
6. **On all models,** disconnect wiring connectors and antenna lead.
7. Release tool from radio by pressing in on radio mounting tabs while pulling on tool.
8. Reverse procedure to install, noting the following:
   a. While installing radio, ensure wiring will not be pinched and rear mounting post will be engaged.
   b. Reset audio coded anti-theft system as outlined under "Precautions."

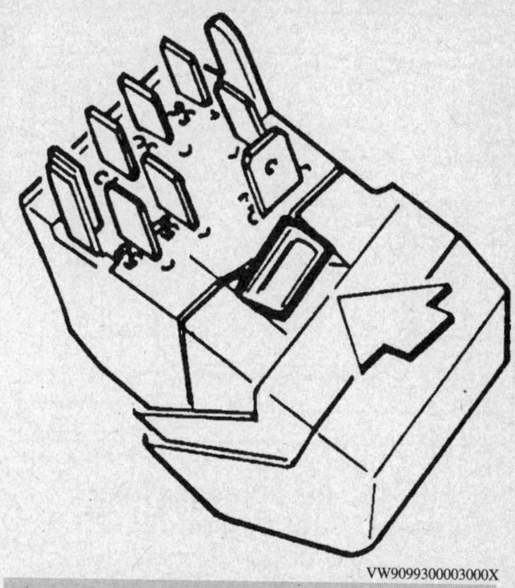
VW9099300003000X

Fig. 15 Switch latch clip location. Fox

WIPER MOTOR

REPLACE

FRONT

Refer to **Figs. 19 through 24** for front wiper configurations.

1. Open hood and remove any panels necessary to gain access to cowl area where wiper motor and linkage are mounted.
2. Disconnect wiper motor electrical connector.
3. Note Park position of wiper arms for later assembly.
4. **On models with wiper motor mounting bolts/nuts accessible through cowl,** disconnect wiper linkage rods from crank arm on motor, then remove mounting bolts/nuts and motor.
5. **On models where wiper motor mounting bolts/nuts are not accessible through cowl,** proceed as follows:
   a. Remove wiper assembly as outlined under "Wiper Transmission, Replace."
   b. Place assembly on suitable workspace.
   c. Disconnect wiper linkage rods from crank arm on motor.
   d. Remove mounting bolts/nuts and motor.
6. **On all models,** reverse procedure to install, noting the following:
   a. Prior to installing motor, connect motor to vehicle electrical connector, turn ignition on, then turn wiper on and off to ensure motor is in Park position.
   b. Turn ignition off, then disconnect electrical connector.
   c. Ensure wiper linkage is in Park position. If necessary, remove and position crank arm on motor to correct alignment.
   d. Install motor and mounting bolts/nuts, then **torque** to 14 ft. lbs.

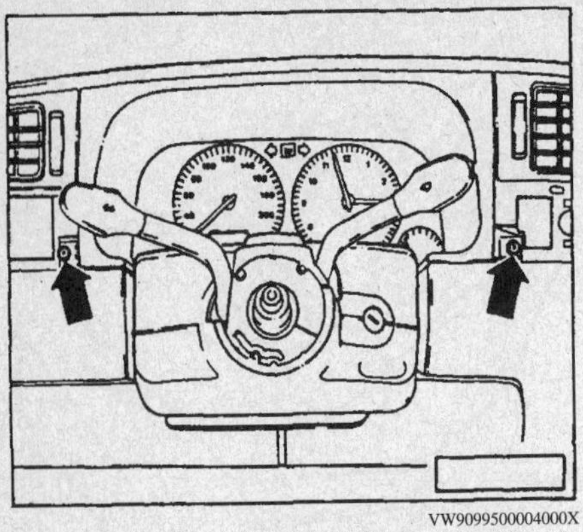
VW9099500004000X

Fig. 16 Instrument cluster removal. Cabrio, Golf III, GTI & Jetta III

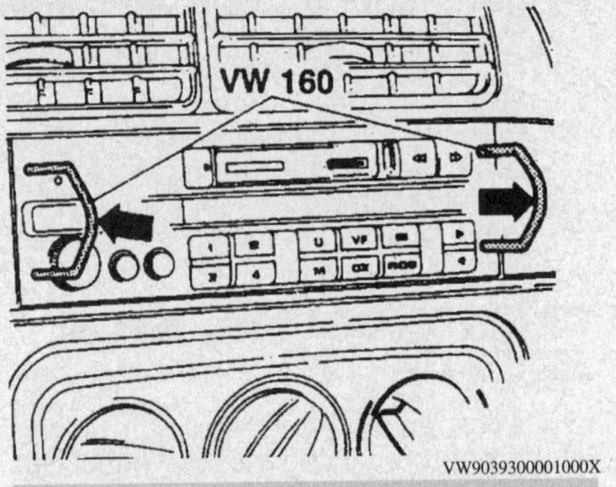
VW 160
VW9039300001000X

Fig. 17 Radio removal tool No. VW160

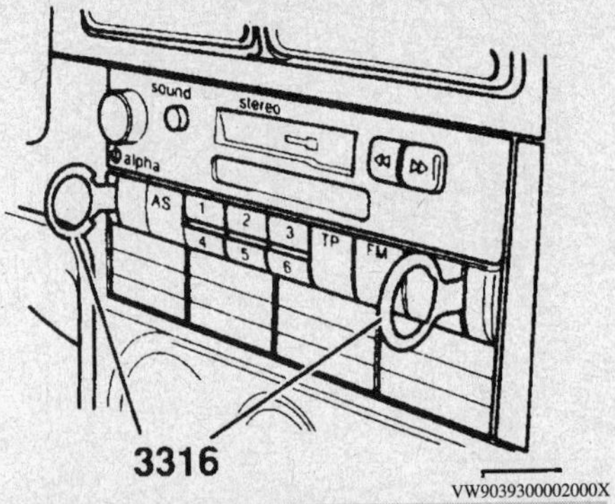
sound
stereo
alpha
AS
1
2
3
4
5
6
TP
FM
3316
VW9039300002000X

Fig. 18 Radio removal tool No. 3316

REAR

Refer to **Figs. 25 through 29** for rear wiper configurations.

1. Remove cap or cover at base of wiper arm. Use caution not to damage window washer nozzle.
2. Remove wiper arm retaining nut from pivot shaft.
3. Remove wiper arm and blade assembly. Note Park position of wiper arm for later assembly.
4. Remove any trim panels necessary to gain access to wiper motor.
5. Remove nut retaining wiper pivot shaft bushing to body. Note position of any washers, spacers and seals for later assembly.
6. Disconnect window washer hose.
7. Remove wiper motor attaching bolts/nuts, then disconnect electrical connector.
8. Remove wiper motor assembly, with brackets if equipped, from liftgate.
9. Use caution not to damage seals when withdrawing pivot bushing.
10. **On Eurovan models,** disconnect wiper linkage from wiper motor crank arm.
11. **On all models,** remove mounting bolts, then wiper motor from brackets, if equipped.
12. Reverse procedure to install, noting the following:
    a. Prior to installing motor, connect motor to vehicle electrical connector and turn ignition on.
    b. Turn wiper on and off to ensure motor is in Park position, then turn ignition off.
    c. **Torque** wiper motor mounting bolts/nuts to 44 inch lbs.
    d. **On Eurovan models, torque** wiper pivot shaft bushing mounting nut to 7 ft. lbs.
    e. **On models except Eurovan, torque** wiper pivot shaft bushing mounting nut to 62 inch lbs.
    f. **On all models, torque** wiper arm mounting nut to 12 ft. lbs.

WIPER SWITCH

REPLACE

1. Remove combination switch as outlined under "Combination Switch, Replace."
2. Carefully pry clips holding wiper switch and turn signal switch together, then separate switches.
3. Reverse procedure to install.

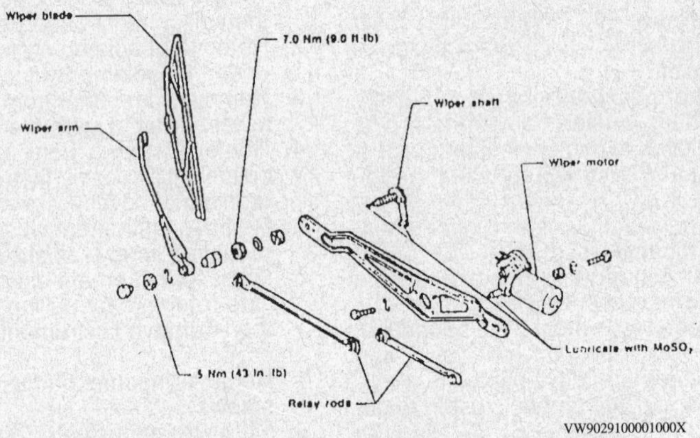
Wiper blade
7.0 Nm (9.0 ft lb)
Wiper shaft
Wiper arm
Wiper motor
5 Nm (43 in. lb)
Relay rods
VW9029100001000X

Fig. 19 Exploded view of front windshield wiper assembly. Cabriolet

WIPER TRANSMISSION

REPLACE

Refer to **Figs. 19 through 24** when replacing front linkages.

Refer to **Fig. 26** when replacing rear linkages.

1. Remove cap or cover at base of wiper arms, then remove wiper arm retaining nuts from pivot shafts.
2. Remove wiper arm and blade assemblies. Note Park position of wiper arms for later assembly.
3. **On models with front linkages,** open hood and remove any panels necessary to gain access to cowl area where wiper motor and linkage are mounted.
4. **On models with rear linkages,** remove trim panels necessary to access rear wiper assembly.
5. **On all models,** disconnect wiper motor electrical connector.
6. Remove nuts retaining wiper pivot shaft bushing to panel. Note position of any washers, spacers and seals for later assembly.
7. Remove any bolts/nuts retaining wiper frame assembly.
8. Remove wiper assembly from vehicle. Use caution not to damage seals when withdrawing pivot bushing.
9. Disconnect wiper linkage from motor crank arm and wiper pivot shafts.
10. Noting position of O-rings and washers, remove C-clip from pivot shaft, then slide pivot shaft out of bushings.
11. Remove motor mounting bolts/nuts, then motor.
12. Reverse procedure to install, noting the following:
    a. Prior to installing motor, connect motor to vehicle electrical connector, turn ignition on, then turn wiper on and off to ensure motor is in Park position.
    b. Turn ignition off, then disconnect electrical connector.
    c. Ensure wiper linkage is in Park position. If necessary, remove and position crank arm on motor to correct alignment.
    d. Install motor and mounting bolts/nuts, then **torque** to 14 ft. lbs.
    e. **Torque** wiper pivot shaft bushing mounting nut to 62 inch lbs.
    f. **Torque** wiper arm mounting nut to 12 ft. lbs.

BLOWER MOTOR

REPLACE

CABRIOLET

1. Obtain audio coded anti-theft code,

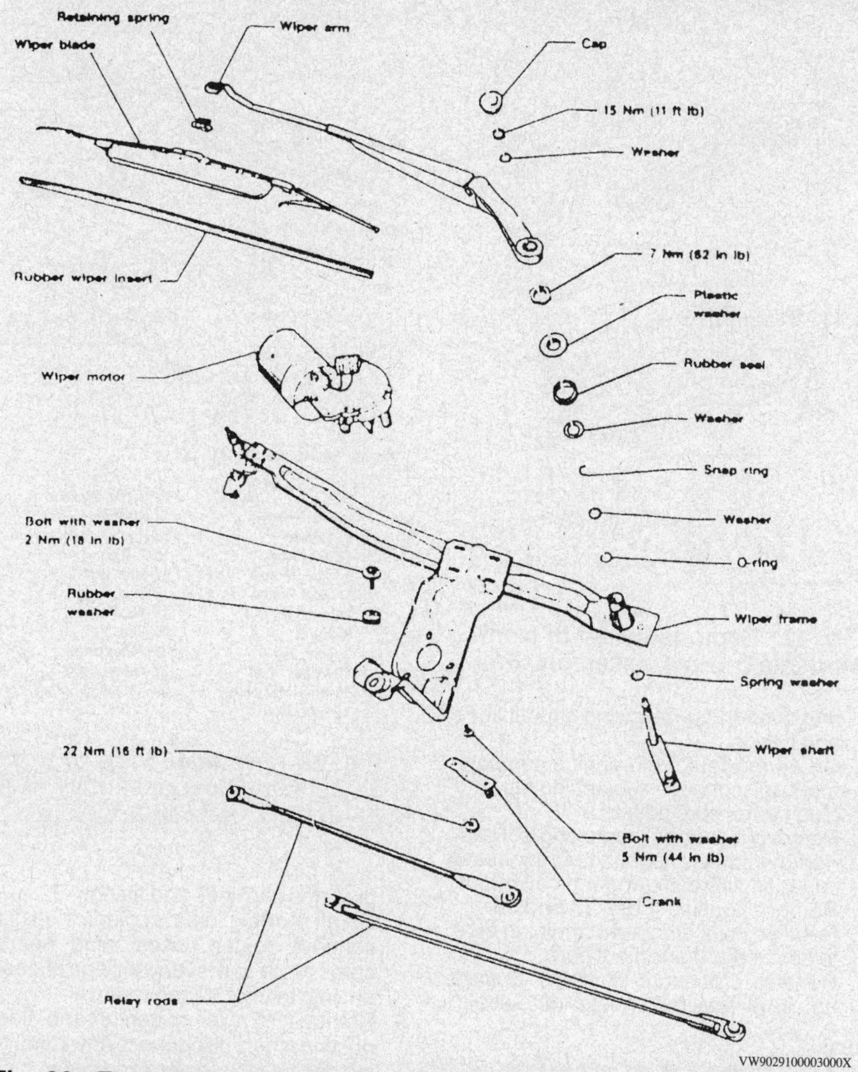
Retaining spring
Wiper arm
Wiper blade
Cap
15 Nm (11 ft lb)
Washer
Rubber wiper insert
7 Nm (62 in lb)
Plastic washer
Wiper motor
Rubber seal
Washer
Snap ring
Bolt with washer
2 Nm (18 in lb)
Washer
O-ring
Rubber washer
Wiper frame
Spring washer
22 Nm (16 ft lb)
Wiper shaft
Bolt with washer
5 Nm (44 in lb)
Crank
Relay rods
VW9029100003000X

Fig. 20 Exploded view of front windshield wiper assembly. Corrado

then disconnect battery ground cable.
2. Open hood and remove any panels necessary to gain access to cowl area.
3. **On models equipped with A/C,** remove screws securing air distribution flap housing to cowl and partially remove cover.
4. **On all models,** remove screws securing heater cover to cowl and remove cover.
5. Remove resistor retaining bolts and lay resistor aside.
6. Remove clamp and screws securing motor, then remove fan and motor assembly, **Fig. 30.**
7. Reverse procedure to install. Reset audio coded anti-theft system as outlined under "Precautions."

CORRADO

It may be necessary to remove glove compartment assembly to gain access to blower motor.

1. Obtain audio coded anti-theft code, then disconnect battery ground cable.
2. Disconnect electrical connector, then the blower motor retaining lug.
3. Turn motor clockwise, then pull from housing.
4. Reverse procedure to install. Reset audio coded anti-theft system as outlined under "Precautions."

EUROVAN

FRONT

1. Remove glove compartment, then disconnect wiring connectors from blower resistor (1), **Fig. 31.**
2. Remove right air duct.
3. Disengage retaining clamp (4), then turn blower motor in clockwise direction.
4. Pull blower unit (3) out of housing, then move to center of instrument panel to remove.
5. Reverse procedure to install.

REAR

Air Conditioning

1. Remove any seats and panels necessary to access rear A/C unit.
2. Disconnect electrical connector for motor.
3. Loosen and remove components to gain access to motor, **Fig. 32.**
4. Remove retainers, then motor.
5. Reverse procedure to install.

Heater

1. Raise and support vehicle.
2. Remove any splash panels necessary to access rear heater.
3. Disconnect wiring connector.
4. Remove screws from lefthand side of heater case retaining blower unit, **Figs. 33 and 34.**
5. Remove blower unit.
6. Reverse procedure to install.

FOX

1. Obtain audio coded anti-theft code, disconnect battery ground cable, then remove front cover sealing gasket.
2. Remove water deflector, then loosen fresh air housing cover retaining clips.
3. Remove fresh air housing.
4. **On models with A/C,** remove lock and disconnect air distribution flap levers.
5. **On all models,** remove fresh air housing cover (rear).
6. **On models with A/C,** disconnect vacuum system hoses, then the hoses from grommets in bottom of fresh air housing covers.
7. **On all models,** disconnect resistor and thermal circuit breaker from support.
8. Loosen blower motor mounting screw, then disconnect electrical connector.
9. Remove bottom of fresh air housing covers, then the blower motor housing cover.
10. Rotate blower motor toward front of vehicle, then remove.
11. Reverse procedure to install. Reset audio coded anti-theft system as outlined under "Precautions."

PASSAT

WITH A/C

1. Remove righthand lower shelf.
2. Remove glove compartment, then disconnect wiring connectors (1), **Fig. 35.**
3. Remove cable clamp (3), then the four mounting screws.
4. Pull blower unit (2) out of housing, then remove downward.
5. Reverse procedure to install.

LESS A/C

1. Remove righthand lower shelf.
2. Remove righthand lower duct cover, then disconnect wiring connector.
3. Push down retaining clips with a suitable screwdriver, **Fig. 36.**
4. Rotate blower unit clockwise, then lower from blower housing.
5. Reverse procedure to install.

HEATER CORE

REPLACE

CABRIOLET

1. Obtain audio coded anti-theft code, then disconnect battery ground cable and drain cooling system.

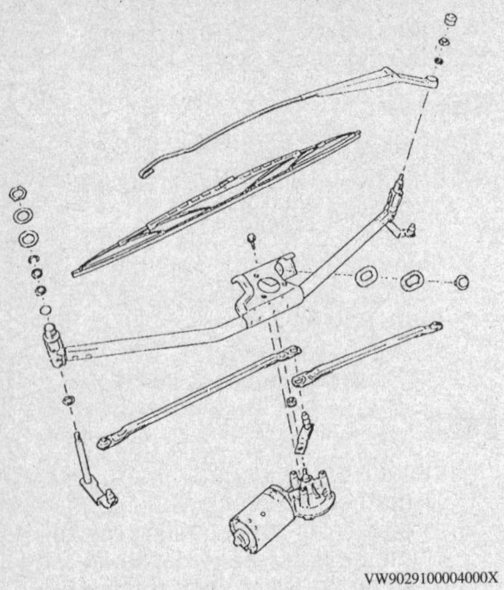

VW9029100004000X

Fig. 21 Exploded view of front windshield wiper assembly. Eurovan

2. Remove windshield washer reservoir from mounting bracket.
3. Remove ignition coil.
4. From inside engine compartment, disconnect heater hoses from heater core.
5. Pull knobs off heater control assembly to instrument panel attaching screws and the control assembly.
6. Remove console and dash trim panels as needed to gain access to fresh air housing.
7. Disconnect wiring harness electrical connectors from housing, then pry housing from retainers and remove lower housing.
8. Remove heater core cover from lefthand side of housing and pull out core.
9. Reverse procedure to install. Reset audio coded anti-theft system as outlined under "Precautions."

CORRADO

Refer to **Fig. 37** to aid in heater core replacement on these models.

EUROVAN

Front

Ensure heater core outlets are securely plugged to prevent coolant spillage into interior during removal procedures.

1. Remove glove compartment, then remove right heater duct.
2. From engine compartment, remove screws from air intake duct.
3. Remove center air outlet and duct if equipped.
4. Disconnect blower electrical connector.
5. Disconnect all control cables, connectors and lines.
6. Remove footwell air outlet and cover.
7. **On models with A/C,** recover refrigerant using a suitable recovery station, then disconnect evaporator drain hose.
8. **On models with A/C,** disconnect refrigerant lines from expansion valve

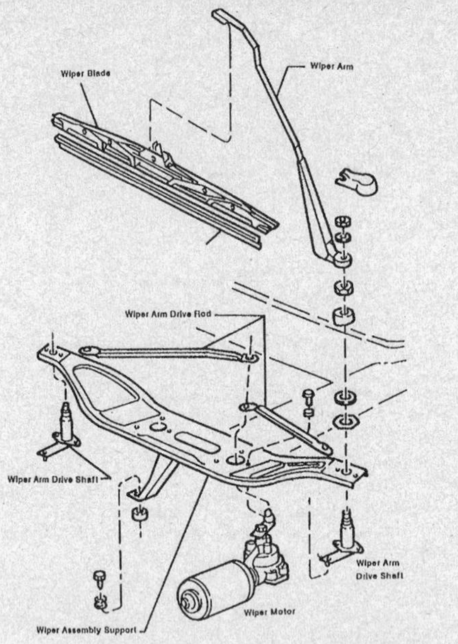
Wiper Blade
Wiper Arm
Wiper Arm Drive Rod
Wiper Arm Drive Shaft
Wiper Arm Drive Shaft
Wiper Assembly Support
Wiper Motor

VW9029100005000X

Fig. 22 Exploded view of front windshield wiper assembly. Fox

and evaporator, plug and cap all lines and fittings.

9. **On all models,** from engine compartment, disconnect coolant hoses and plug heater core outlets.
10. Remove two upper mounting screws.
11. Remove lower mounting screw found under engine compartment cover trim.
12. Remove housing, **Figs. 38 and 39.**
13. Remove clips or screws retaining core to assembly, then lift out core.
14. Reverse procedure to install. Ensure no air will leak past heater core seals.

Rear

1. Raise and support vehicle, then remove any splash panels necessary to access rear heater.
2. Disconnect coolant hoses from rear heater assembly, drain coolant into a suitable container.
3. **On Multivan models,** remove screws on lefthand side of heater case retaining heater core, **Fig. 33.**
4. **On GL models,** remove screws on right hand side of heater case retaining heater core, **Fig. 34**
5. Pull core from heater assembly.
6. Reverse procedure to install. Ensure no air will leak past heater core seals.

FOX

Refer to **Fig. 40** to aid in heater core replacement on these models.

PASSAT

During the following procedure, refer to **Figs. 41 and 42** to locate various components on models with and less A/C.

1. Remove instrument panel as outlined under "Dash Panel Service."
2. **On models with A/C,** recover refrigerant using a suitable recovery station.
3. **On models with A/C,** disconnect refrigerant lines from evaporator, then

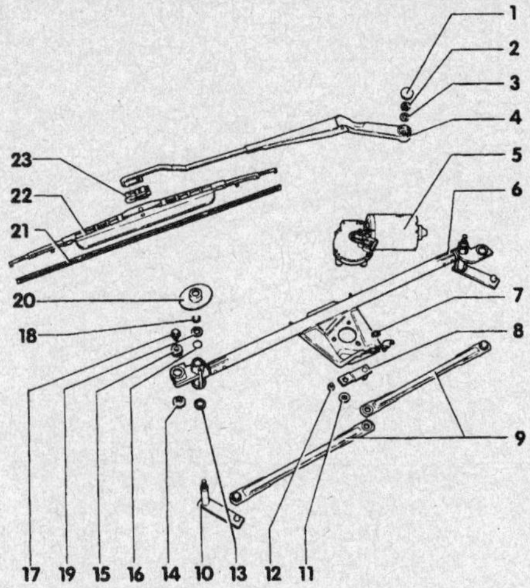
1
2
3
4
5
6
7
8
9
23
22
21
20
18
17 19 15 16 14 10 13 12 11

1-Cap	13-Spring Washer
2-8mm Hex Nut	14-Washer
3-Washer	15-Rubber Seal
4-Wiper Arm	16-O-Ring
5-Wiper Motor	17-6mm Bolt
6-Wiper Frame	18-Snap Ring
7-6mm Hex Nut	19-Washer
8-Crank	20-Cap
9-Relay Rods	21-Wiper Insert
10-Wiper Shaft	22-Wiper Blade
11-8mm Hex Nut	23-Retaining Spring
12-6mm Bolt	

VW9029300014000X

Fig. 23 Exploded view of front windshield wiper assembly. Golf III, GTI, Jetta III & Cabrio

plug and cap lines and fittings.

4. **On all models,** drain coolant, then disconnect heater hoses, plug heater core fittings to prevent spillage of coolant into interior during removal.
5. Remove remaining center and floor ducting, then disconnect any remaining cables, connectors and lines.
6. From under hood, remove air plenum cover, then the air inlet filter.
7. Remove heater and A/C housing mounting screws from air inlet filter housing, then mounting nuts from engine compartment side of firewall.
8. Remove heater and A/C housing from vehicle.
9. Disconnect retaining clips or remove mounting screws, as equipped, then lift heater core from air distribution housing.
10. Reverse procedure to install. Ensure no air will leak past heater core seals.

EVAPORATOR CORE

REPLACE

CABRIOLET

Refer to **Fig. 30** to aid in evaporator core replacement on these models.

CORRADO

Refer to **Fig. 37** to aid in evaporator core replacement on these models.

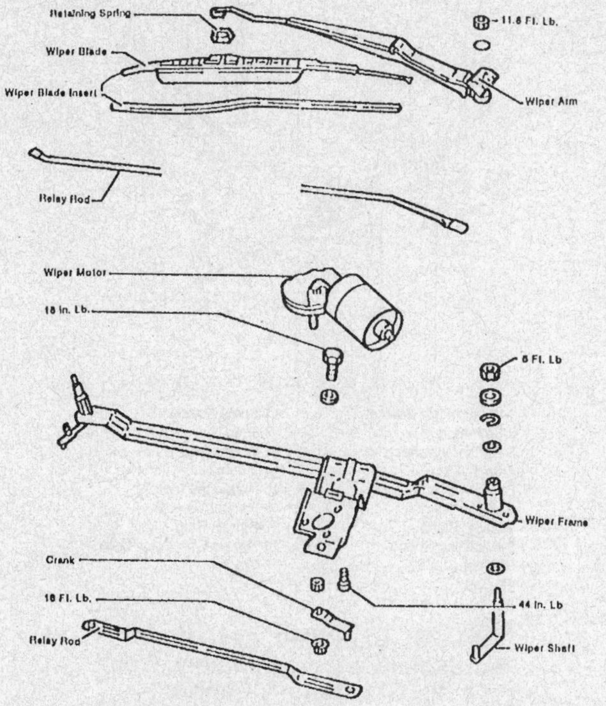
Retaining Spring
Wiper Blade
Wiper Blade Insert
11.8 Ft. Lb.
Wiper Arm
Relay Rod
Wiper Motor
18 In. Lb.
6 Ft. Lb
Wiper Frame
Crank
18 Ft. Lb.
44 In. Lb
Relay Rod
Wiper Shaft

VW9029100006000X

Fig. 24 Exploded view of front windshield wiper assembly. Passat

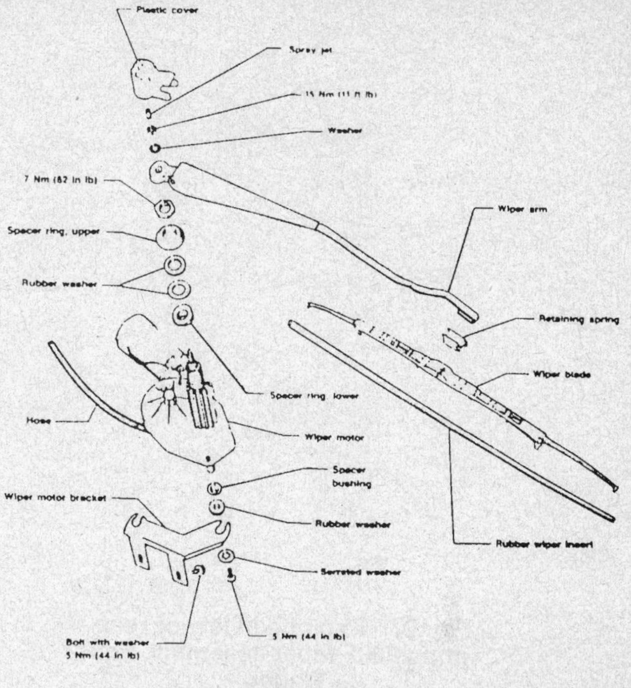
Plastic cover
Spray jet
15 Nm (11 ft lb)
Washer
7 Nm (62 in lb)
Spacer ring, upper
Rubber washer
Wiper arm
Retaining spring
Wiper blade
Spacer ring, lower
Hose
Wiper motor
Spacer bushing
Wiper motor bracket
Rubber washer
Rubber wiper insert
Serrated washer
Bolt with washer 5 Nm (44 in lb)
5 Nm (44 in lb)

VW9029100008000X

Fig. 25 Exploded view of rear windshield wiper assembly. Corrado

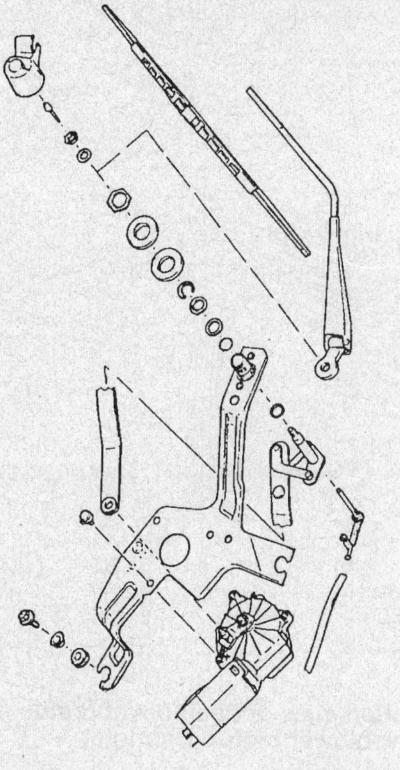

VW9029100009000X

Fig. 26 Exploded view of rear windshield wiper assembly. Eurovan

EUROVAN

Front

Ensure heater core outlets are securely plugged to prevent coolant spillage into interior during removal procedures.

1. Remove housing as outlined under "Heater Core, Replace."
2. Remove evaporator temperature sensor tube and switch. Use caution not to bend tube. **Note inserted depth and position of tube for later assembly.**
3. Disassemble housing to remove evaporator core, **Fig. 39.**
4. Reverse procedure to install, noting the following:
   a. Ensure no air can leak past evaporator core seals.
   b. Insert evaporator core temperature sensing tube 13 inches through case grommet and into core.
   c. Evacuate and recharge A/C.

Rear

1. Recover refrigerant using a suitable recovery station.
2. Access rear evaporator/housing as outlined under "Blower motor, Replace."
3. Disconnect refrigerant lines from expansion valve, then disconnect evaporator drain hose.
4. Disconnect remaining electrical connectors.
5. Disconnect ducting from evaporator/housing, then remove housing mounting screws.
6. Remove evaporator and housing, then any remaining components. **Note length and position of inserted part of evaporator core temperature sensing tube for later assembly.**
7. Reverse procedure to install.

FOX

Refer to **Fig. 40** to aid in evaporator core replacement on these models.

PASSAT

1. Remove heater and A/C housing as outlined under "Heater Core, Replace."
2. Separate evaporator housing from air distributor housing.
3. Remove blower motor by releasing clip then rotating clockwise.
4. Remove components necessary to allow separation of upper and lower housing.
5. Remove evaporator from housing.
6. Reverse procedure to install. Ensure no air will leak past evaporator
7. core seals.

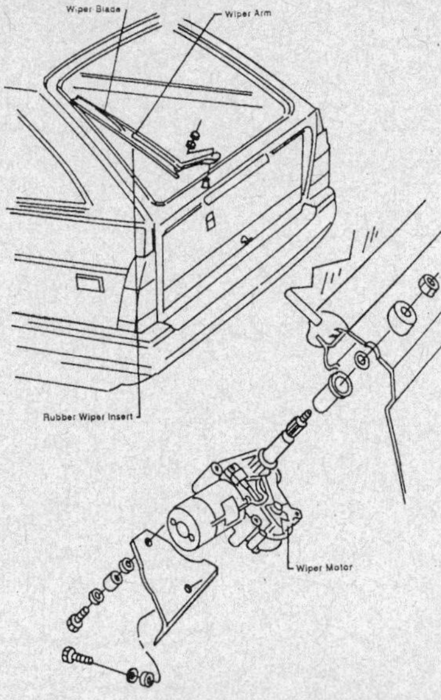
Wiper Blade
Wiper Arm
Rubber Wiper Insert
Wiper Motor

VW9029100010000X

Fig. 27 Exploded view of rear windshield wiper assembly. Fox Wagon

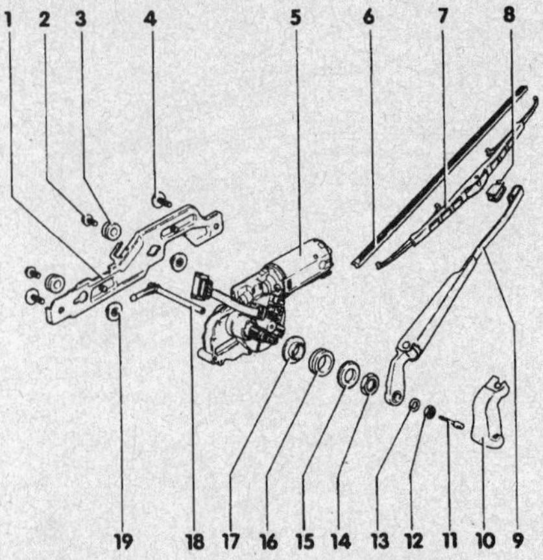
1 2 3 4 5 6 7 8
19 18 17 16 15 14 13 12 11 10 9

1-Wiper Motor Bracket
2-6mm Bolt
3-Rubber Washer
4-6mm Bolt
5-Rear Wiper Motor
6-Wiper Insert
7-Wiper Blade
8-Retaining Spring
9-Wiper Arm
10-Cap
11-Spray Nozzle
12-8mm Nut
13-Washer
14-16mm Nut
15-Plastic Washer
16-Rubber Washer
17-Spacer Ring
18-Nozzle Connector Tube
19-Washer

VW9029300015000X

Fig. 28 Exploded view of rear windshield wiper assembly. Golf III, GTI, Jetta & Cabrio

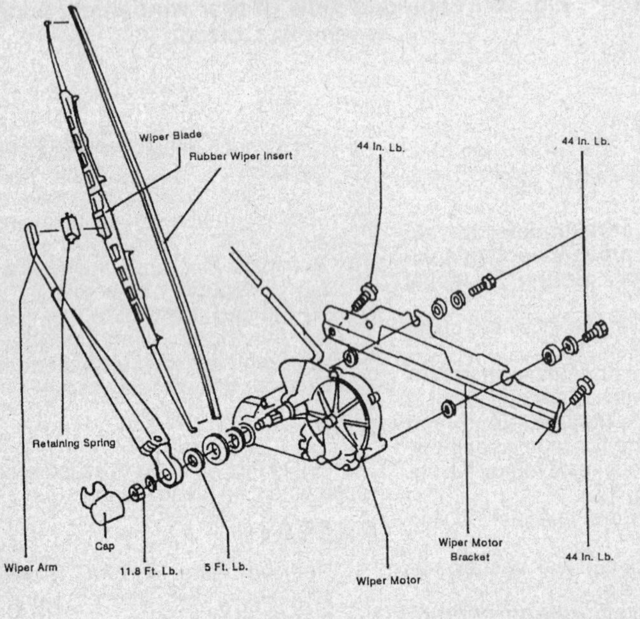
Wiper Blade
Rubber Wiper Insert
44 In. Lb.
44 In. Lb.
Retaining Spring
Cap
Wiper Arm
11.8 Ft. Lb.
5 Ft. Lb.
Wiper Motor
Wiper Motor Bracket
44 In. Lb.

VW9029100012000X

Fig. 29 Exploded view of rear windshield wiper assembly. Passat Wagon

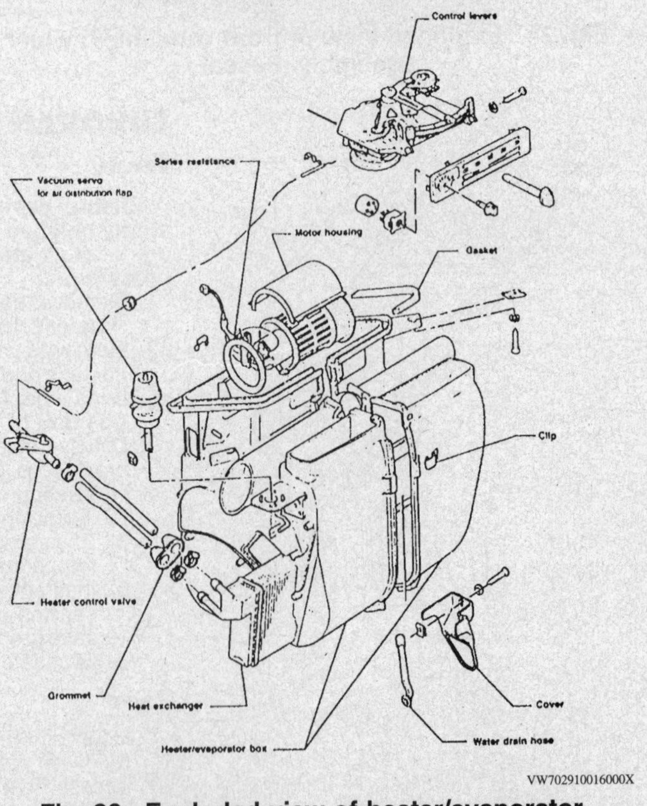
Control levers
Series resistance
Vacuum servo for air distribution flap
Motor housing
Gasket
Clip
Heater control valve
Grommet
Heat exchanger
Heater/evaporator box
Cover
Water drain hose

VW702910016000X

Fig. 30 Exploded view of heater/evaporator housing w/blower motor. Cabriolet

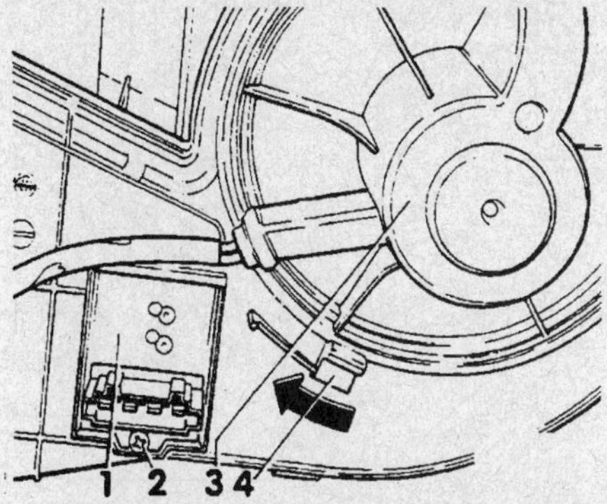
1
2
3
4

VW7029300025000X

Fig. 31 Front blower motor removal. Eurovan

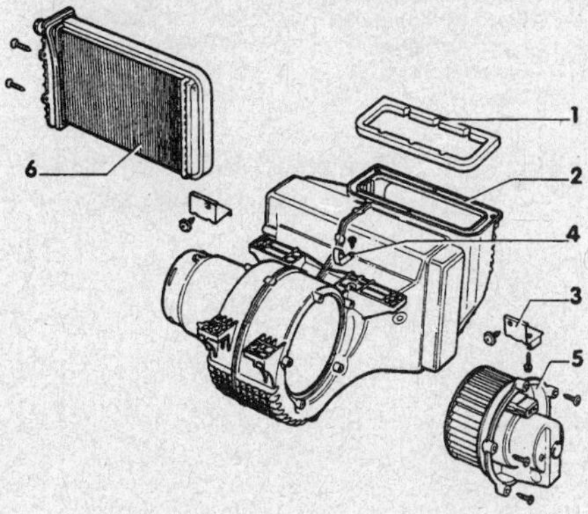
1
2
3
4
5
6

1-Gasket
2-Housing
3-Bracket
4-Clip
5-Blower Motor
6-Heater Core

VW7029300028000X

Fig. 34 Exploded view of rear heater. Eurovan GL

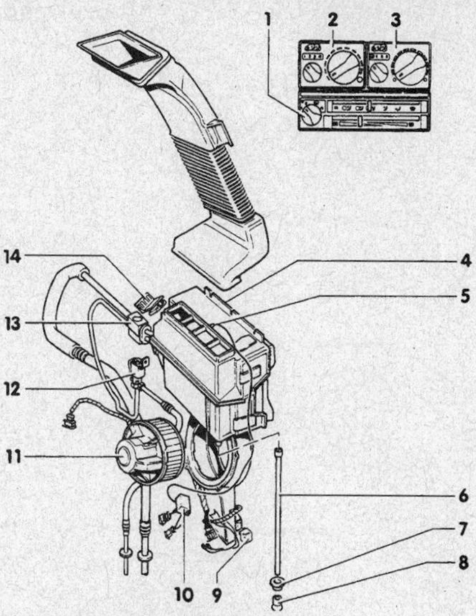
1
2
3
14
4
5
13
12
11
6
7
8
10
9

1-Front Heat A/C Blower Switch
2-Rear A/C Blower Switch
3-Rear Heater Blower Switch
4-Evaporator w/Case
5-Temperature Sensor For Rear A/C Evaporator
6-Rear Evaporator Water Drain Hose
7-Grommet
8-Rear Evaporator Water Drain Hose Check Valve
9-Blower Relay For Rear A/C
10-Programmer & Temperature Sensor Rear A/C
11-Rear A/C Blower Motor
12-Rear A/C Freon Shut Off Valve
13-Rear A/C Expansion Valve
14-Rear A/C Blower Resistor
15-Rear A/C Ducting

VW7029300026000X

Fig. 32 Rear A/C blower motor removal. Eurovan

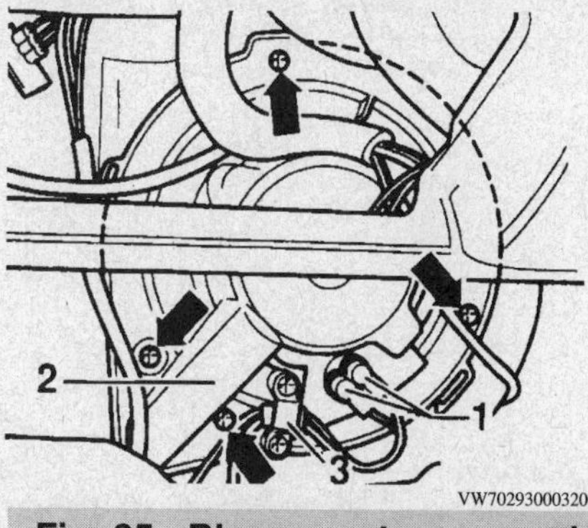
2
1
3

VW7029300032000X

Fig. 35 Blower motor removal. Passat w/A/C

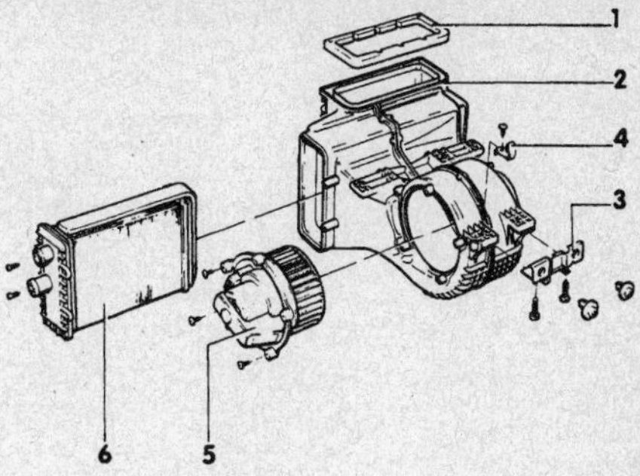
1
2
4
3
6
5

1-Gasket
2-Housing
3-Bracket
4-Clip
5-Blower Motor
6-Heater Core

VW7029300027000X

Fig. 33 Exploded view of rear heater. Eurovan Multivan

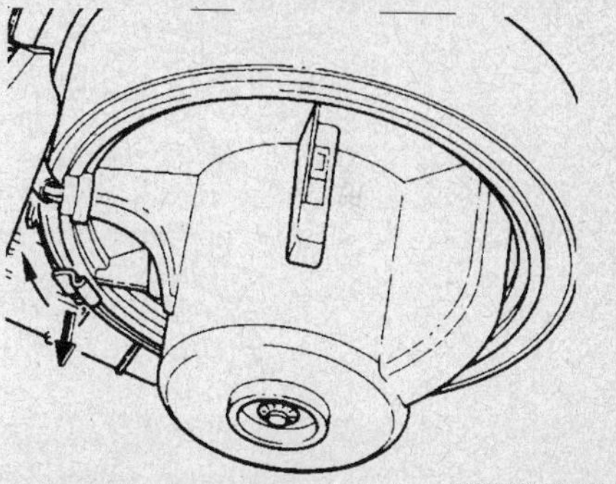

VW7029300031000X

Fig. 36 Blower motor removal. Passat less A/C

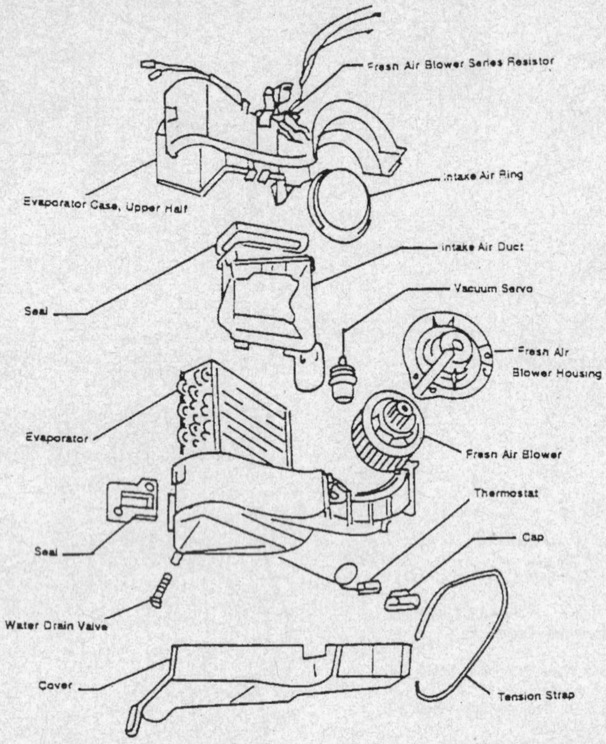
Fresh Air Blower Series Resistor
Intake Air Ring
Evaporator Case, Upper Half
Intake Air Duct
Seal
Vacuum Servo
Fresh Air Blower Housing
Evaporator
Fresh Air Blower
Thermostat
Seal
Cap
Water Drain Valve
Cover
Tension Strap

VW7029100019000X

Fig. 37 Exploded view of heater/evaporator housing w/blower motor. Corrado,

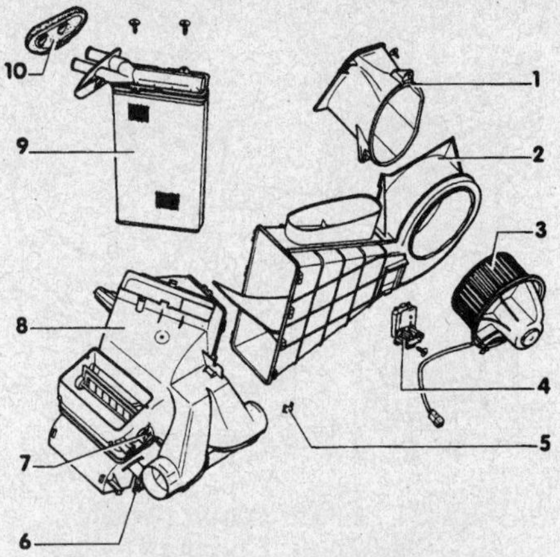
10
9
8
7
6
1
2
3
4
5

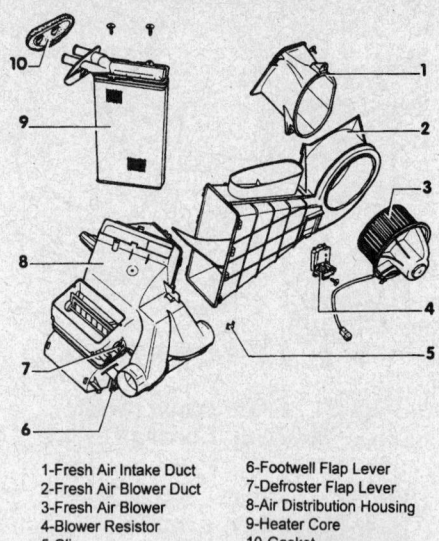

1-Fresh Air Intake Duct
2-Fresh Air Blower Duct
3-Fresh Air Blower
4-Blower Resistor
5-Clip
6-Footwell Flap Lever
7-Defroster Flap Lever
8-Air Distribution Housing
9-Heater Core
10-Gasket

VW7029300029000X

Fig. 38 Exploded view of front heater. Eurovan less A/C

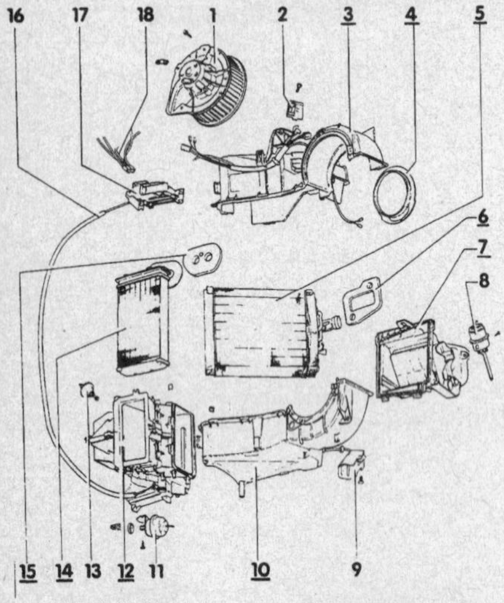
16 17 18 1 2 3 4 5
6
7
8
15 14 13 12 11 10 9

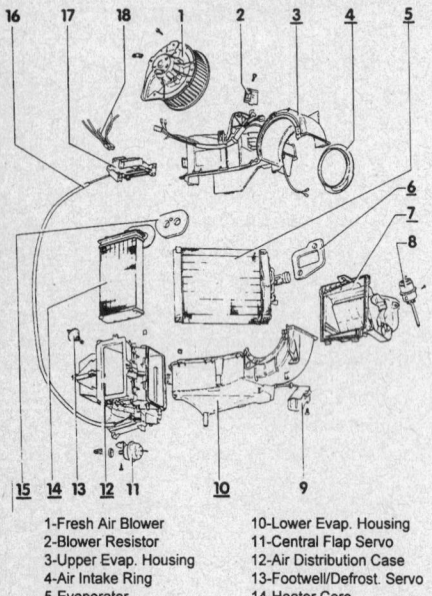

1-Fresh Air Blower
2-Blower Resistor
3-Upper Evap. Housing
4-Air Intake Ring
5-Evaporator
6-Seal
7-Air Intake Duct
8-Fresh Air/Recirc. Servo
9-A/C Evap. Temp. Switch
10-Lower Evap. Housing
11-Central Flap Servo
12-Air Distribution Case
13-Footwell/Defrost. Servo
14-Heater Core
15-Seal
16-Temperature Flap Cable
17-A/C Control Unit
18-Vacuum Hoses

VW7029300030000X

Fig. 39 Exploded view of front heater. Eurovan w/A/C

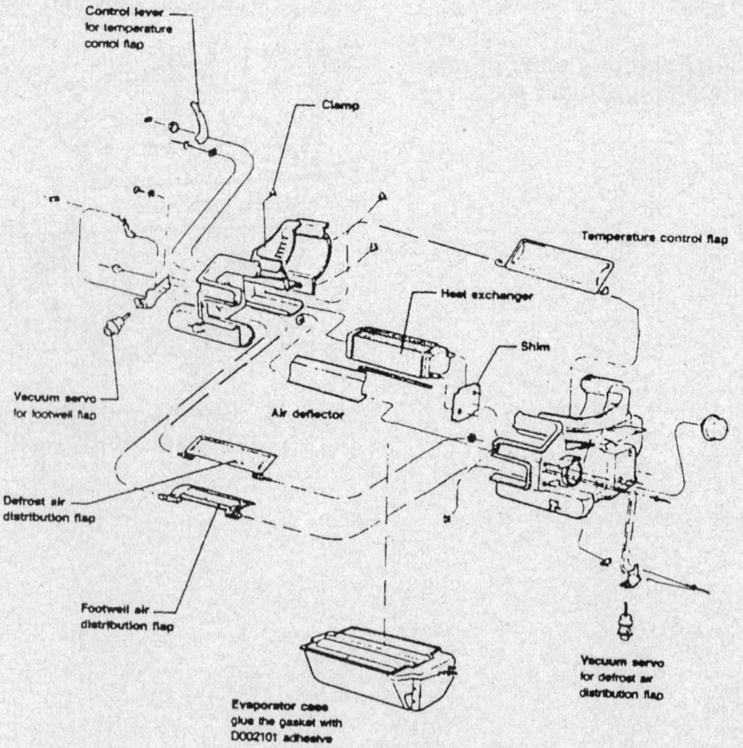
Control lever for temperature control flap
Clamp
Temperature control flap
Heat exchanger
Shim
Vacuum servo for footwell flap
Air deflector
Defrost air distribution flap
Footwell air distribution flap
Vacuum servo for defrost air distribution flap
Evaporator case glue the gasket with D002101 adhesive

VW7029100020000X

Fig. 40 Exploded view of heater/evaporator housing. Fox

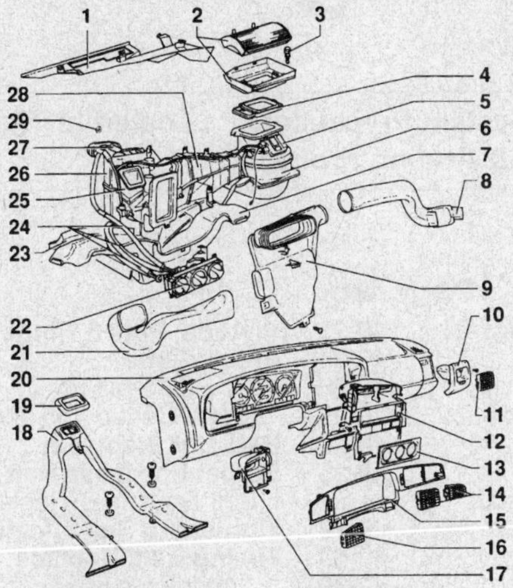
1
2
3
4
5
6
7
8
9
10
11
12
13
14
15
16
17
18
19
20
21
22
23
24
25
26
27
28
29

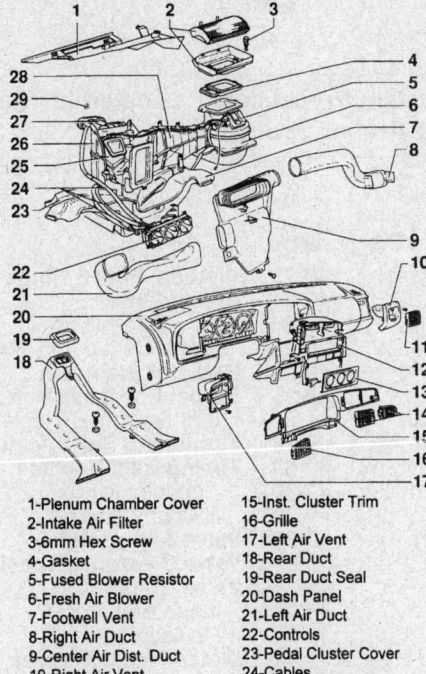

1-Plenum Chamber Cover	15-Inst. Cluster Trim
2-Intake Air Filter	16-Grille
3-6mm Hex Screw	17-Left Air Vent
4-Gasket	18-Rear Duct
5-Fused Blower Resistor	19-Rear Duct Seal
6-Fresh Air Blower	20-Dash Panel
7-Footwell Vent	21-Left Air Duct
8-Right Air Duct	22-Controls
9-Center Air Dist. Duct	23-Pedal Cluster Cover
10-Right Air Vent	24-Cables
11-Grille	25-Intermediate Duct
12-Center Vent	26-Air Dist. Housing
13-Control Panel Trim	27-Heater Core
14-Grilles	28-Air Duct w/Shut Off
	29-6mm Nut

VW7029300033000X

Fig. 41 Disassembled view of dash & heater assembly. Passat less A/C

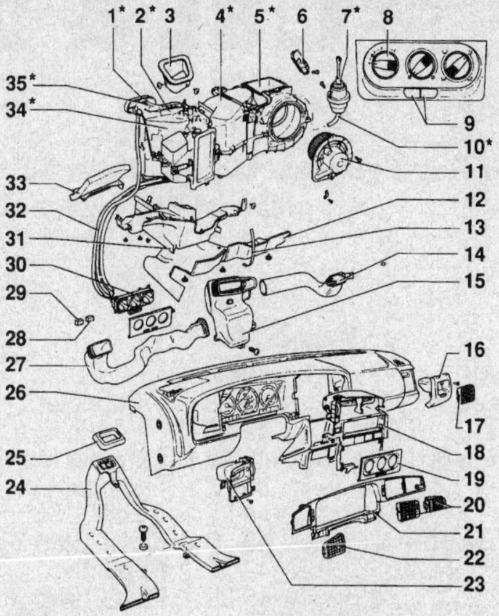
1*
2*
3
4*
5*
6
7*
8
9
10*
11
12
13
14
15
16
17
18
19
20
21
22
23
24
25
26
27
28
29
30
31
32
33
34*
35*

1-Gasket	19-Control Panel Trim
2-Heater Core	20-Grilles
3-Connecting Duct	21-Instrument Cluster Trim
4-Evaporator Housing	22-Grille
5-Air Intake	23-Left Air Vent
6-Blower Resistor	24-Rear Heater Duct
7-Fresh Air/Recirc. Servo	25-Gasket
8-Blower Switch	26-Dash Panel
9-Controls	27-Left Air Duct
10-Vacuum Lines	28-A/C Shut-Off Control
11-Fresh Air Blower	29-A/C Clutch Cut Out
12-Evap. Housing Cover	30-Controls
13-Retaining Strap	31-Footwell Outlet
14-Right Air Duct	32-Cables
15-Center Air Duct	33-Pedal Cluster Cover
16-Right Air Vent	34-Air Dist. Housing
17-Grille	35-Vacuum Line Connection
18-Center Vent	

VW7029300034000X

Fig. 42 Disassembled view of dash & heater assembly. Passat w/A/C

1.8L & 2.0L Engines

NOTE: On Air Bag Equipped Models, Refer To "Air Bag System Precautions" Located In The Front Of This Manual For System Disarming & Arming Procedures.

INDEX

	Page No.
Camshaft, Replace	49-28
Except 1993 Passat	49-28
1993 Passat	49-28
Compression Pressure	49-22
1.8L Engine	49-22
2.0L Engine	49-22
Cooling System Bleed	49-29
Except Fox	49-29
Fox	49-29
Crankshaft Rear Oil Seal, Replace	49-29
Cylinder Head, Replace	49-25
Engine Mount, Replace	49-23
Except Fox & Cabriolet	49-23
Fox	49-23
Engine Rebuilding Specifications	49-148
Engine, Replace	49-23
Cabrio, Golf III, GTI, Jetta III & Passat	49-23
Cabriolet	49-24
Fox	49-25
Exhaust Manifold, Replace	49-25
Except Fox & Cabriolet	49-25
Fox & Cabriolet	49-25
Front Main Bearing Oil Seal, Replace	49-29
Fuel Pump, Replace	49-30
Except In Tank	49-30
In Tank	49-30
Hydraulic Lifter Inspection	49-26
Hydraulic Lifters, Replace	49-27
Intake Manifold, Replace	49-25
Except Fox & Cabriolet	49-25
Fox & Cabriolet	49-25
Main & Rod Bearings	49-28
Oil Pan, Replace	49-29
Piston & Rod Assembly	49-28
Pistons, Pins & Rings	49-28
Precautions	49-22
Air Bag Systems	49-22
Audio Coded Anti-Theft System	49-22
Radiator, Replace	49-30
Serpentine Drive Belt	49-29
Belt Routing & Replacement	49-29
Tightening Specifications	49-31
Timing Belt, Replace	49-27
Cabriolet & Fox	49-27
Except Cabriolet & Fox	49-27
Valve Adjustment	49-26
Valve Clearance Specifications	49-26
Valve Guides	49-26
Inspection	49-26
Replace	49-26
Water Pump, Replace	49-29
Fox Less A/C	49-29
With A/C Except Fox	49-29

PRECAUTIONS

Do not use computer memory saver tool on air bag equipped models. Using the tool will keep the air bag system charged and may cause accidental activation of the air bag unit. Prior to disconnecting the battery negative cable, obtain the radio security code. After service has been completed and the battery negative cable has been reconnected, use security code to activate the radio.

AIR BAG SYSTEMS

Refer to "Air Bag System Precautions" in the front of this manual for system disarming and arming procedures.

AUDIO CODED ANTI-THEFT SYSTEM

Some models are equipped with a radio anti-theft system that will disable the system when battery power is interrupted, unless the system is reset the radio will not operate.

1. Turn radio to On position, SAFE should be displayed.
2. Depress and hold AM/FM and SCAN buttons until 1000 remains on display. If AM/FM and SCAN buttons are depressed too long or depressed again, radio will misinterpret the 1000 as an attempt at coding and one incorrect coding attempt will be logged. **After two incorrect attempts to reset system, radio will lock up electronically. If this occurs, leave radio on for approximately one hour, then reset radio as if battery power were disconnected.**
3. Enter radio code using first four program station buttons. Security code will appear on display.
4. Depress and hold AM/FM and SCAN buttons again until SAFE is displayed.
5. Release AM/FM and SCAN buttons. Display should change to a radio frequency and operate normally.

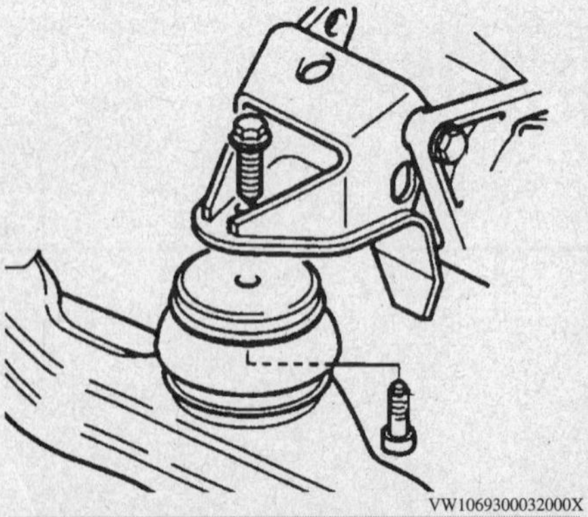
VW1069300032000X

Fig. 1 Front engine & transaxle mount

COMPRESSION PRESSURE

1.8L ENGINE

1. Perform compression test with engine at operating temperature, spark plugs removed, coolant temperature above 176°F and throttle plate completely open.
2. Disconnect coil high tension wire from distributor cap and connect to suitable ground.
3. Connect compression tester tool No. 1120, or equivalent, following manufacturer's instructions, then crank engine until compression tester shows no further increase in pressure.
4. **On all models except Cabriolet, Corrado and Fox,** compression should be 140.5–188.5 psi with a maximum difference between highest and lowest cylinder of 43.5 psi. Minimum compression should be 108.75 psi.
5. **On Cabriolet and Fox models,** compression should be 130.5–174 psi with a maximum difference between highest and lowest cylinder of 43.5 psi. Minimum compression should be 108.75 psi on Cabriolet models or 101.5 psi on Fox models.
6. **On Corrado models,** compression should be 116–174 psi with a maximum difference between highest and lowest cylinder of 43.5 psi. Minimum compression should be 87 psi.

2.0L ENGINE

1. Perform compression test with engine at operating temperature, spark plugs removed, coolant temperature at least 176°F and throttle plate completely open.
2. Disconnect power output stage of ignition coil high tension wire from distributor cap and connect to suitable ground.

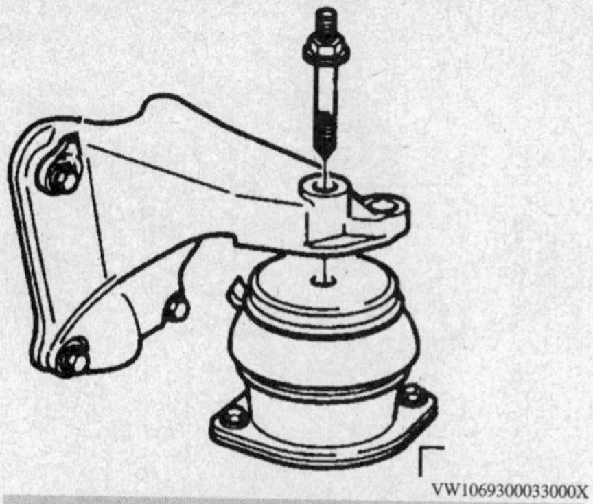
VW1069300033000X

Fig. 2 Right rear engine & transaxle mount

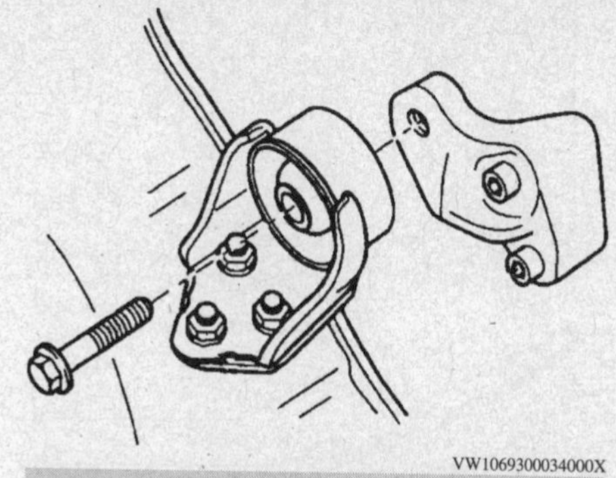
VW1069300034000X

Fig. 3 Right engine & transaxle mount. Cabrio

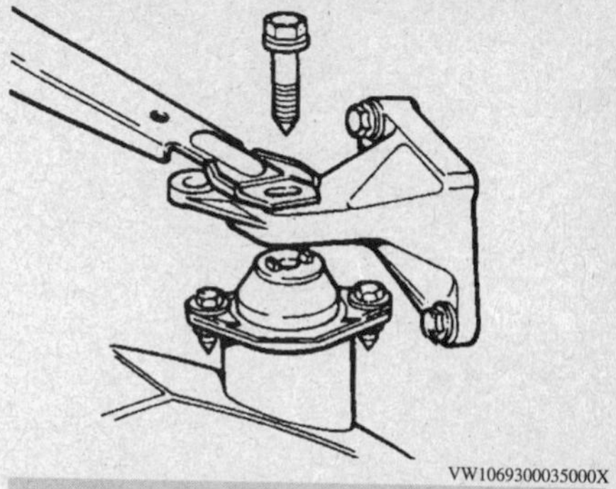
VW1069300035000X

Fig. 4 Left rear engine & transaxle mount. Except Passat

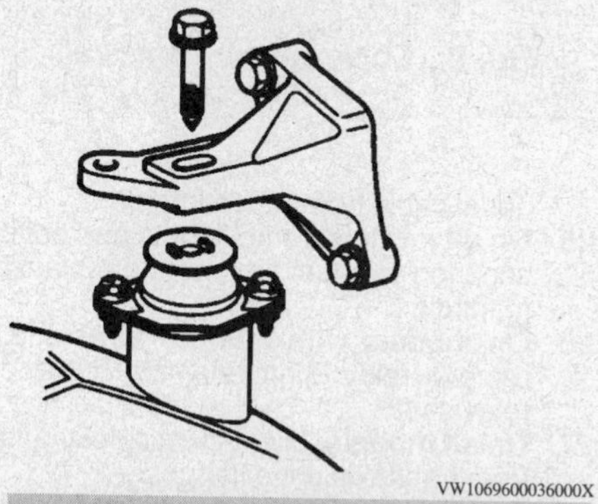
VW1069600036000X

Fig. 5 Left rear engine & transaxle mount. Passat w/manual transaxle

3. **On Passat models,** disconnect Hall sender electrical connector from ignition distributor.
4. **On all models,** connect compression tester tool No. US 1120, or equivalent, per manufacturer's instructions, then crank engine until compression tester shows no further increase in pressure.
5. Compression should be 140.5–188.5 psi with a maximum difference between highest and lowest cylinder of 43.5 psi. Minimum compression should be 108.75 psi.

ENGINE MOUNT

REPLACE

EXCEPT FOX & CABRIOLET

1. Attach a suitable engine lifting tool to engine, positioned to relieve pressure from mount to be replaced, then loosen engine mount center mounting bolt, **Figs. 1 through 6.**
2. Raise engine and transaxle assembly until weight is off mount, then remove center bolt from mount.
3. Remove remaining engine mount and subframe mounting bolts, then engine mount.
4. Reverse procedure to install.

FOX

1. Install suitable engine lifting tool, then loosen left/right engine mount to subframe bolts.
2. Raise engine/transaxle slightly to relieve weight off mounts then remove engine to subframe bolts.
3. Raise engine/transaxle, then remove bolts securing mounts to engine and mounts.
4. Reverse procedure to install.

ENGINE

REPLACE

CABRIO, GOLF III, GTI, JETTA III & PASSAT

The engine and transaxle (powertrain) are removed as an assembly through the front of these vehicles by removing the front end panels (lock carrier) and bumper.

1. Obtain audio coded anti-theft code.
2. Disconnect battery ground cable, then drain cooling system.
3. Remove air cleaner and ducting as necessary.
4. Raise and support vehicle, then disconnect drive axles from transaxle and support them aside.
5. Disconnect exhaust system and position aside.
6. Disconnect necessary lines, electrical connectors, clamps, cables, components and hoses to allow removal of lock carrier, **Figs. 7 through 9.**
7. **On models equipped with A/C,** disconnect additional components necessary to allow condenser with radiator and fans, receiver drier and compressor to be removed and supported aside without disconnecting lines, **Figs. 10 and 11.**
8. **On models equipped with power steering,** disconnect any additional components necessary to allow pump and lines to be removed and supported aside without disconnecting lines.
9. **On all models,** remove lock carrier, **Figs. 7 through 9,** then radiator, supporting aside A/C and power steering components, if equipped, **Figs. 10 and 11.**
10. Remove any additional drive belts and components needed for removal clearance.
11. **On Cabrio, Golf III and Jetta III models,** disconnect clutch cable and gearshift mechanism.

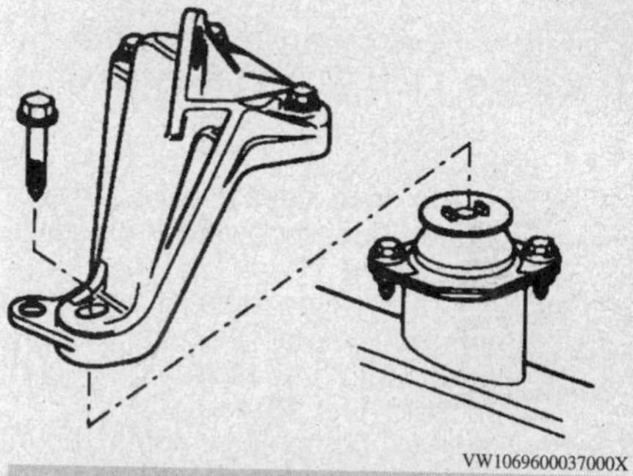
VW1069600037000X

Fig. 6 Left rear engine & transaxle mount. Passat w/ automatic transaxle

12. **On Passat models,** remove clutch slave cylinder from transaxle, without disconnecting fluid line, and support aside, then disconnect gearshift mechanism.
13. **On all models,** disconnect any remaining lines, cables, electrical connectors, hoses or components necessary to allow powertrain removal.
14. Connect lifting bar tool No. 2024A, or equivalent, **Figs. 12 and 13,** suitably adjusted to keep powertrain unit balanced during removal of engine.
15. Attach suitable lifting equipment to lifting bar, then raise powertrain slightly to relieve pressure from mounts, then disconnect mounts.
16. **On Passat models,** disconnect subframe, **Fig. 14,** by prying bracket from subframe rubber mountings.
17. **On all models,** remove powertrain from vehicle.
18. Place powertrain on a suitable surface, then remove starter and transaxle to engine bolts and nuts.
19. Remove transaxle from engine.
20. Reverse procedure to install, noting the following:
    a. Tighten to specifications.
    b. Ensure alignment dowels are in place when installing transaxle to engine.
    c. Lubricate transaxle input shaft splines, and if equipped, release bearing guide sleeve with a suitable grease.

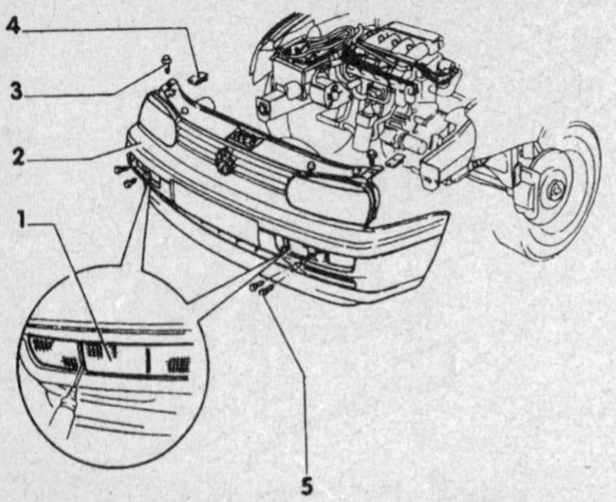

1-Cover For Towing Eye
2-Lock Carrier w/Attachments
3-Screw
4-Speed Nut
5-Hex Bolt

VW1069300038000X

Fig. 7 Lock carrier removal. Cabrio, Golf III, GTI & Jetta III

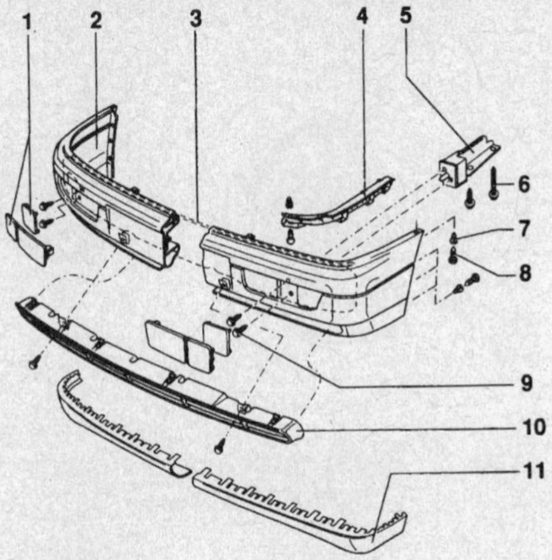

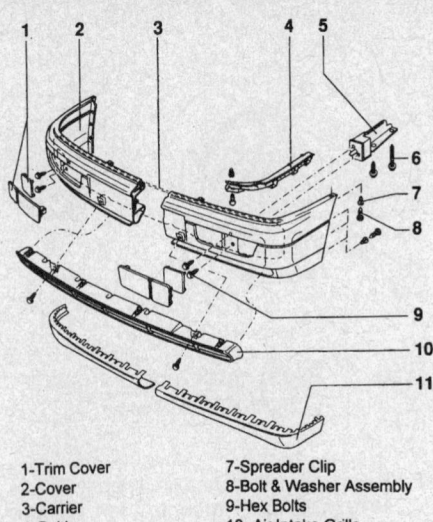

1-Trim Cover
2-Cover
3-Carrier
4-Guide
5-Bracket
6-Hex Bolts
7-Spreader Clip
8-Bolt & Washer Assembly
9-Hex Bolts
10- Air Intake Grille
11-Spoiler

VW1069300039000X

Fig. 8 Bumper components of lock carrier removal. Passat

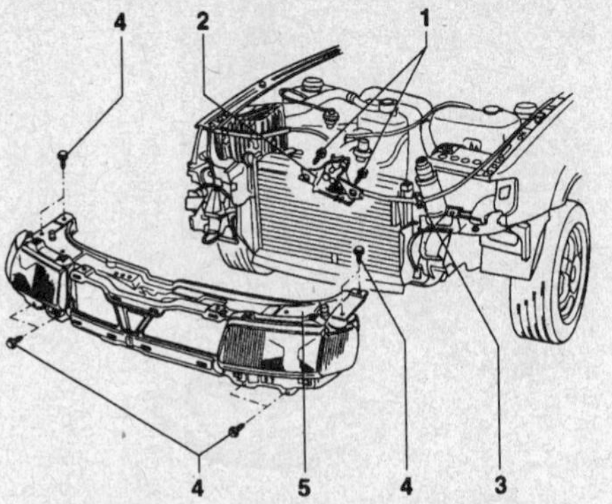

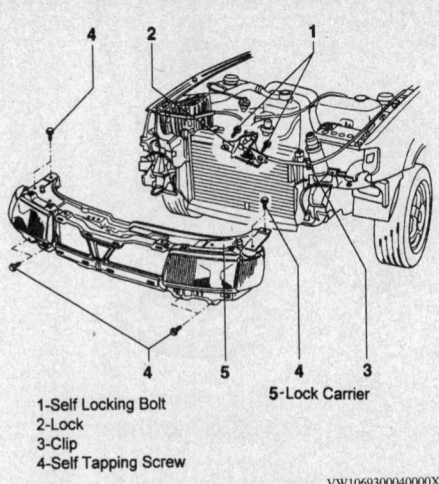

1-Self Locking Bolt
2-Lock
3-Clip
4-Self Tapping Screw
5-Lock Carrier

VW1069300040000X

Fig. 9 Lock carrier removal. Passat

d. Ensure drive axles are properly positioned during powertrain installation.
e. Ensure locating tabs of right rear and front motor mounts are engaged into recesses of mount brackets, **Fig. 15.**
f. Prior to tightening motor mount bolts, shake powertrain unit to relieve any stresses.
g. Ensure correct adjustment of headlamps.
h. Ensure correct adjustment of all cables.
i. Replace any cable ties cut during powertrain removal with suitable equivalents.
j. Reset audio coded anti-theft system as outlined under "Precautions."

CABRIOLET

Engine and transaxle are removed as an assembly on these vehicles.

1. Obtain audio coded anti-theft code, disconnect battery ground and positive cables, then wires connected to positive cable end and remove battery, if necessary.
2. **On models equipped with A/C,** proceed as follows:
   a. Remove crankshaft pulley attaching bolts, then disassemble pulley.
   b. Remove A/C compressor drive belt.
   c. Disconnect electrical connector from compressor.
   d. Remove alternator attaching bolts, then alternator.
   e. Remove timing belt cover, the preheat hose.
   f. Remove compressor mounting and support brace bolts, leaving hoses attached, position compressor assembly aside.
3. **On models equipped with automatic transaxle,** place shift selector in Park position.
4. **On all models,** open fuel filler cap to relieve tank pressure.
5. Remove air intake pipe between fuel distributor and throttle valve assembly.
6. Remove radiator cap.
7. Remove thermostat housing to engine attaching bolts, open heater control valve and drain cooling system.
8. Remove thermostat housing, then disconnect upper radiator hose.
9. Mark, then disconnect all electrical connectors from engine.
10. Remove radiator side retaining nuts.
11. Remove upper radiator clip, then the radiator upper clamp.
12. Remove radiator assembly with electric cooling fan from vehicle.
13. Remove preheater pipe, then disconnect vacuum hoses from distributor and EGR temperature valve.
14. Remove coil and coolant temperature sensor wires, then disconnect heater hoses from engine.
15. Disconnect fuel line from cold start valve and warm-up regulator.
16. **On models with automatic transaxle,** disconnect speedometer cable.
17. **On all models,** disconnect vacuum hoses from brake booster, front and rear vacuum amplifiers and vacuum booster, if equipped.
18. Disconnect PCV hose.
19. **On models with manual transaxle,** disconnect accelerator cable from linkage ball stud and cylinder head cover attaching bracket.
20. **On all models,** remove fuel injectors, fuel lines and vacuum hoses and position aside.
21. **On models with 16-valve engine,** remove intake manifold.
22. **On all models,** disconnect ground cable strap from transaxle.
23. **On models with manual transaxle,** disconnect clutch cable from clutch lever and speedometer cable from transaxle, then remove upper starter bolt.
24. **On models with automatic transaxle,** disconnect selector cable and accelerator pedal cable from transaxle bracket, then disconnect accelerator pedal cable from operating rod.
25. **On all models,** remove nuts and bolts securing exhaust flex pipe to exhaust manifold.
26. **On models with manual transaxle,** remove relay shaft retaining nut and relay shaft.
27. **On all models,** disconnect axle shafts from transaxle drive flanges.
28. **On models with manual transaxle,** remove starter.
29. **On all models,** remove horn assembly and position aside.
30. Remove front mount cup to body attaching bolts, then the front mount and cup.
31. Remove both axle shaft to bearing housing attaching bolts, then the ball joint lock bolts.
32. Separate both ball joints from bearing housings, then remove both axle shafts from vehicle. After removing axle shafts, connect ball joints and lock bolts to enable vehicle to be lowered.
33. Remove rear transaxle mount, right front wheel/tire assembly and alternator support.
34. Attach engine sling tool No. 2024A, or equivalent, and lift engine slightly with hoist.
35. **On models with manual transaxle,** disconnect all shift linkages that will interfere with engine/transaxle removal.
36. **On all models,** remove left and right side engine mount to body attaching bolts, then the mounts.
37. Lower engine/transaxle assembly onto floor dolly, raise vehicle, then remove engine/transaxle assembly out from underneath vehicle.
38. **On models with 16–valve engine,** attach engine sling tool No. 2024A, or equivalent, and lift engine/transaxle out (upward), rotating engine slightly at the same time.
39. **On all models,** reverse procedure to install. Tighten nuts and bolts to specifications. Reset audio coded anti-theft system as outlined under "Precautions."

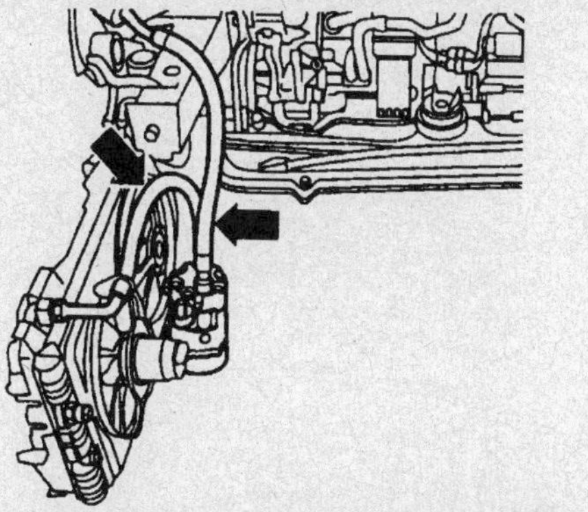

VW1069300041000X

Fig. 10 A/C components placed aside. Cabrio, Golf III, GTI & Jetta III

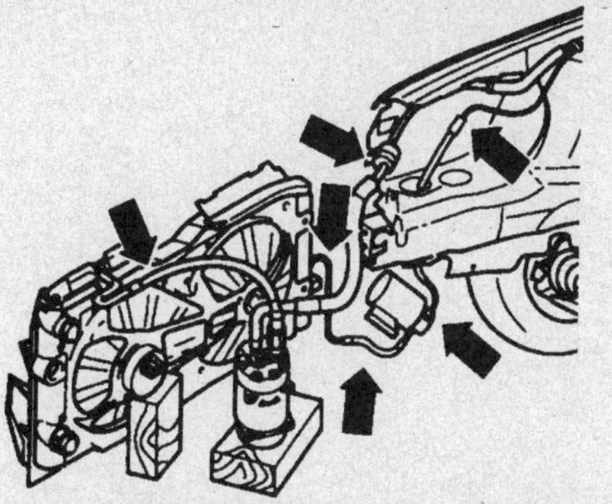

VW1069300042000X

Fig. 11 A/C components placed aside. Passat

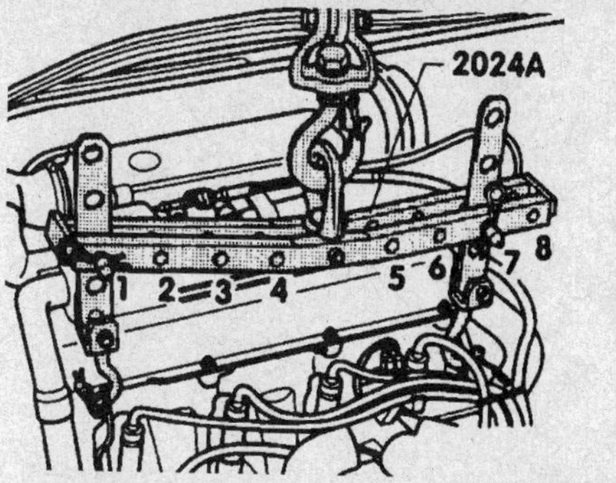
2024A
1 2 3 4 5 6 7 8

VW1069300043000X

Fig. 12 Lifting bar connection. Manual transaxle

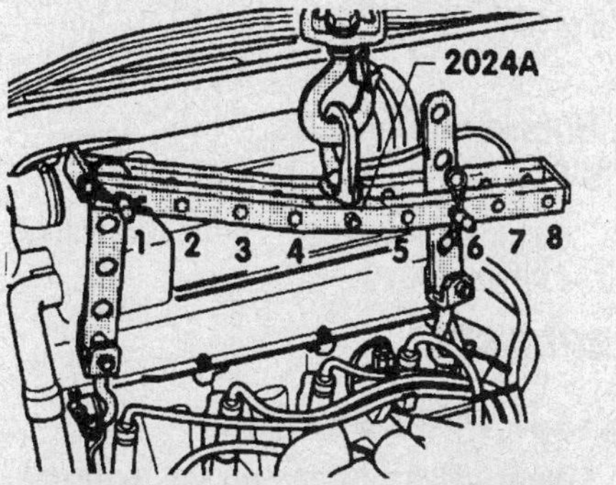
2024A
1 2 3 4 5 6 7 8

VW1069300044000X

Fig. 13 Lifting bar connection. Automatic transaxle

FOX

1. **On models equipped with A/C,** proceed as follows:
   a. Disconnect condenser from radiator, then remove radiator.
   b. Remove compressor mounting bolts, then the compressor and belt. **Secure compressor to body.**
2. **On all models,** obtain audio coded anti-theft code, disconnect battery ground cable, then open heating valve and cap on coolant expansion tank.
3. Disconnect lower radiator hose from engine and drain coolant, then the coolant hoses.
4. Disconnect electrical connectors from radiator fan and radiator thermo switch, then remove lower radiator mounting bolt.
5. Remove radiator side mounts and upper air duct, then the radiator fan and fan shroud.
6. Disconnect clutch cable, then the electrical connectors at alternator, oil pressure switches, oxygen sensor, water flange, auxiliary air regulator and cold start valve.
7. Disconnect vacuum hoses, then remove fuel injectors and install protective caps and plugs.
8. Remove cold start valve, leaving fuel line connected.
9. Release pressure in fuel system, then disconnect fuel hoses and return hoses.
10. Loosen charcoal filter clamp and move to rear of engine compartment.
11. Remove three upper engine/transaxle bolts, then the engine stop.
12. Remove air duct from intake manifold, the left and right engine mounting nuts.
13. Disconnect and label starter electrical connectors, then remove starter.
14. Remove two lower engine/transaxle bolts, then the cover plate bolts and plate.
15. Disconnect exhaust pipe from manifold at flange, then remove bolt from exhaust pipe support and pipe from manifold.
16. Install transaxle support bar tool No. VW 758/1, or equivalent, with a slight preload.
17. Install lifting chain tool No. US 1105, or equivalent, then lift engine until weight is taken off engine mounts.
18. Adjust support bar to contact transaxle, then remove upper engine/transaxle mounting bolts.
19. Separate engine from transaxle, then lift engine carefully and guide out of engine compartment.
20. Reverse procedure to install, noting the following:
    a. Prior to installing engine, ensure bushing is installed between oil pump shaft and distributor drive gear.
    b. Lubricate transaxle main shaft splines and contact area between clutch release bearing and pressure plate with No. MoS2 grease, or equivalent.
    c. Tighten nuts and bolts to specifications. Reset audio coded anti-theft system as outlined under "Precautions."

INTAKE MANIFOLD

REPLACE

FOX & CABRIOLET

1. Obtain audio coded anti-theft code, then disconnect battery ground cable, then accelerator cable.
2. Disconnect air cleaner housing horn from manifold, then wiring to intake air temperature sensor.
3. Disconnect fuel supply and return lines and vacuum hoses, then remove fuel rail and fuel injectors.
4. Remove intake manifold bolts, then intake manifold.
5. Reverse procedure to install. Reset audio coded anti-theft system as outlined under "Precautions."

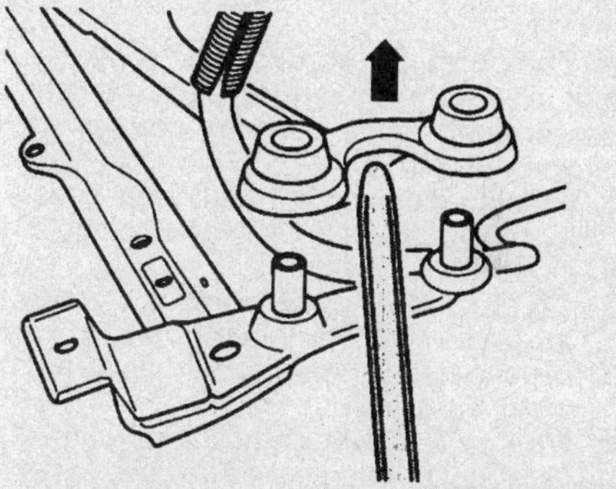

VW1069300045000X

Fig. 14 Subframe disconnection. Passat

EXCEPT FOX & CABRIOLET

Refer to **Figs. 16 and 17** for component locations during removal procedures.

EXHAUST MANIFOLD

REPLACE

FOX & CABRIOLET

Refer to **Figs. 18 and 19** for component locations during removal procedures.

EXCEPT FOX & CABRIOLET

Refer to **Figs. 20 and 21** for component locations during removal procedures.

When tightening exhaust pipe to manifold nuts refer to **Fig. 22** for sequence.

CYLINDER HEAD

REPLACE

On Passat with 16-valve engines, with the timing belt removed, avoid turning

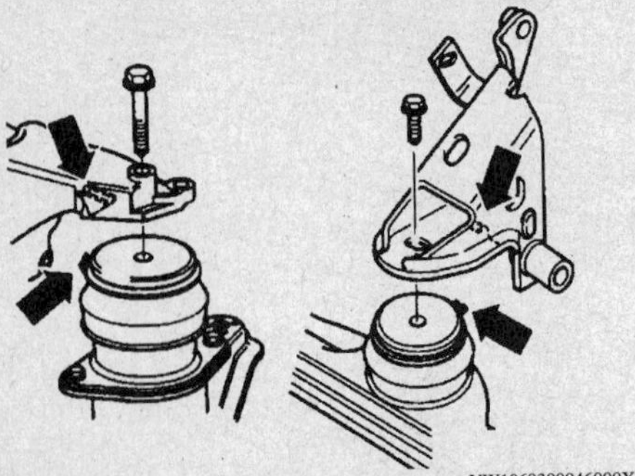
VW1069300046000X

Fig. 15 Motor mount tab alignment. Cabrio, Golf III, GTI, Jetta III & Passat

VW1059100001000X

Fig. 16 Upper intake manifold removal. 2.0L 16-valve engine

the camshaft or crankshaft. If movement is required, exercise extreme caution to avoid valve damage caused by piston contact.

1. Obtain audio coded anti-theft code, then disconnect battery ground cable.
2. Drain cooling system.
3. **On all models except Fox & Cabriolet,** remove upper intake manifold attaching bolts, then manifold as shown in "Intake Manifold, Replace."
4. **On Fox & Cabriolet models,** remove valve cover nuts, then the valve cover and camshaft cover.
5. **On all models,** loosen alternator adjusting bolt or drive belt tensioner as equipped, then remove alternator drive belt.
6. Remove any alternator mounting brackets and/or alternator that may interfere with cylinder head removal.
7. Disconnect all hoses, cables and wires that will interfere with cylinder head removal.
8. Disconnect exhaust manifold from exhaust pipe.
9. Remove timing belt as outlined under "Timing Belt, Replace."
10. **On all models except Fox & Cabriolet,** remove valve cover to cylinder head attaching nuts, then valve cover and gasket.
11. **On all models,** loosen cylinder head bolts in reverse order shown in **Fig. 23.**
12. Remove bolts and the cylinder head.
13. Reverse procedure to install. Tighten head bolts using sequence shown in **Fig. 23** as follows:
    a. Insert bolts 8 and 10 first to align cylinder head and gasket, then tighten all bolts hand tight.
    b. **Torque** cylinder head bolts in four stages: first to 30 ft. lbs.; then to 44 ft. lbs.; next tighten 1/4 (90°) turn; and finally, tighten an additional 1/4 (90°) turn.
    c. Reset audio coded anti-theft system as outlined under "Precautions."

VALVE CLEARANCE SPECIFICATIONS

All engines are equipped with hydraulic lifters. No adjustment provision is provided.

VALVE ADJUSTMENT

All engines are equipped with hydraulic lifters. No adjustment provision is provided.

HYDRAULIC LIFTER INSPECTION

Hydraulic valve lifters are non-adjustable. Noisy lifters may be replaced after the following check.

1. Run engine until radiator fan comes on at least once.
2. Raise engine speed to 2500 RPM, for two minutes.
3. If lifter(s) is still noisy, proceed as follows:
    a. **On all models except Fox & Cabriolet,** remove upper intake manifold.
    b. **On all models,** remove cylinder head cover.
    c. Turn crankshaft pulley bolt clockwise until cam lobes of cylinder to be checked, point upward.
    d. Press down lightly against valve lifter with a wooden stick. If lifter can be pushed down more than .004 inch (.1 mm), replace as outlined under "Hydraulic Lifter, Replace."

VALVE GUIDES

INSPECTION

1. Remove all carbon deposits from valve guide.
2. Set up a dial indicator on cylinder head to check suspected guide.
3. Insert new valve into valve guide. End of valve stem must be flush with valve guide end.
4. Rock valve back and forth against dial indicator.
5. Maximum for intake valves is .039 inch. Maximum for exhaust valves is .051 inch. Replace guide(s) if reading is beyond limit.

REPLACE

Except 1993 Passat

1. Worn valve guides can be removed using rod tool No. 10-206, or equivalent.
2. Press guides with collar out from combustion chamber side of cylinder head and cracked guides out from camshaft side of cylinder head.
3. Coat new guides with engine oil, then press into cold cylinder head from camshaft side.
4. Press guides in as far as they will go. Once valve guide shoulder is seated, do not use more than one ton of pressure or guide shoulder may break. Ream guides by hand using tool No. 3120, or equivalent, and a proper cutting lubricant.
5. Machine valve seats.

1993 Passat

1. Worn valve guides can be removed using rod tool No. 3121, or equivalent. Use tool No. 30-23, or equivalent, as a support.
2. Press guides out from combustion chamber side.
3. Coat new guides with engine oil, then press into cold cylinder head from camshaft side. **When pressing intake valve guides, use backing plate tool No. 3123, or equivalent.**
4. Press guides in as far as they will go. Once valve guide shoulder is seated, do not use more than one ton of pressure, or guide shoulder may break. Ream guides by hand using tool No. 10-215, or equivalent, and a proper cutting lubricant.
5. Machine valve seats.

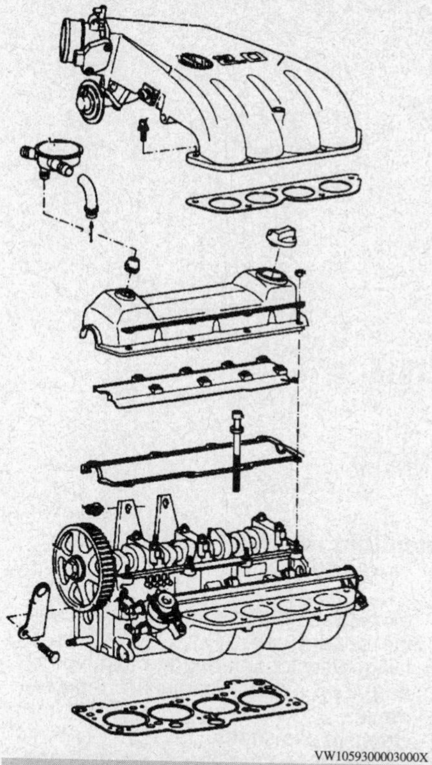
VW1059300003000X

Fig. 17 Upper intake manifold removal. 2.0L 8-valve engine

HYDRAULIC LIFTERS

REPLACE

After replacing hydraulic lifters, do not run engine for 30 minutes. This will allow lifters time to bleed down to proper adjustment.

1. Remove camshaft(s) as outlined under "Camshaft, Replace."
2. Replace defective lifter(s).
3. Install camshaft(s) as outlined under "Camshaft, Replace."

TIMING BELT

REPLACE

CABRIOLET & FOX

1. Obtain audio coded anti-theft code, then disconnect battery ground cable.
2. **On models with A/C,** remove A/C drive belt.
3. **On models less A/C,** loosen alternator drive belt.
4. **On all models,** remove water pump pulley retaining bolts, then the pulley.
5. Remove upper timing belt cover retaining bolts, then the cover.
6. Set engine to Top Dead Center (TDC) compression stroke, **Fig. 24. Do not turn engine counterclockwise using sprocket retaining bolt, as this may slightly loosen bolt.**
7. Remove crankshaft pulley, then lower timing belt cover.
8. Remove timing belt guide, if equipped.
9. If belt is to be reused, mark direction of rotation.
10. Loosen timing belt tensioner adjusting nut, then remove timing belt.
11. Ensure crankshaft pulley notch is aligned with intermediate sprocket mark at TDC pointer, **Fig. 24.**
12. Ensure camshaft sprocket mark is aligned with valve cover flange, **Fig. 24.**
13. Install timing belt onto sprockets, then tighten belt tensioner adjuster clockwise until belt can just be twisted 90° at mid-point between cam sprocket and intermediate shaft sprocket.
14. Tighten adjuster retaining nut.
15. Install timing belt guide, if equipped, then the lower timing belt cover.
16. Install crankshaft and water pump pulleys, then upper timing belt cover.
17. Install and tension drive belts.
18. Reset audio coded anti-theft system as outlined under "Precautions."

EXCEPT CABRIOLET & FOX

On Passat with 16-valve engines, with the timing belt removed, avoid turning the camshaft or crankshaft. If movement is required, exercise extreme caution to avoid valve damage caused by piston contact.

Removal

On Passat with 16-valve engines, to prevent piston and valve contact, if it becomes necessary to turn the camshafts with the timing belt removed, **ensure crankshaft is not at TDC.**

1. Obtain audio coded anti-theft code, then disconnect battery ground cable.
2. Remove power steering V-belt.
3. Remove serpentine belt as outlined under "Serpentine Drive Belt, Replace."
4. Remove upper timing belt cover.
5. Set engine to Top Dead Center (TDC) compression stroke using timing marks shown in **Figs. 25 and 26.**
6. Loosen belt tensioner, then remove timing belt from camshaft drive sprocket.
7. Remove crankshaft vibration damper/pulley. Note installed position for later assembly.
8. If timing belt is to be reused, mark with direction of rotation.
9. Remove lower timing belt cover, then belt.

Installation

On Passat with 16-valve engines, to prevent piston and valve contact, if it becomes necessary to turn the camshafts with the timing belt removed, **ensure crankshaft is not at TDC.**

1. Install the timing belt on crankshaft and intermediate shaft sprockets. **If a used belt is being installed, note direction of rotation mark made during removal.**
2. Install lower drive belt cover, then water pump pulley.
3. Install crankshaft vibration damper. Note offset mounting bolt holes for alignment of pulley to crankshaft.
4. Align mark on front of camshaft sprocket with arrow on valve cover (A), **Fig. 25.** If valve cover has been removed, align mark on rear of sprocket with cylinder head (B).
5. **On models with 8-valve engine,** align crankshaft and intermediate shaft as follows:
   a. With engine removed, align TDC mark on vibration damper with arrow on drive belt cover, **Fig. 26.**
   b. With engine installed, align TDC mark on flywheel with mark on clutch housing, **Fig. 26.**
   c. Remove distributor cap.
   d. While allowing belt to slip over crankshaft sprocket teeth, turn intermediate shaft sprocket to align rotor tip to mark on distributor body, **Fig. 27.**
6. **On all models,** mount drive belt on camshaft drive sprocket and over tensioner pulley.
7. Tighten belt tensioner eccentric adjuster by turning clockwise until belt can just be twisted 90° at mid-point between cam sprocket and intermediate shaft sprocket, **Fig. 28.**
8. Tighten tensioner locknut to specifications.
9. Rotate crankshaft twice in normal direction of rotation, then check tension adjustment. If adjustment is incorrect, repeat steps above. If adjustment is correct, proceed to next step.
10. Install upper drive belt cover, then drive belts.

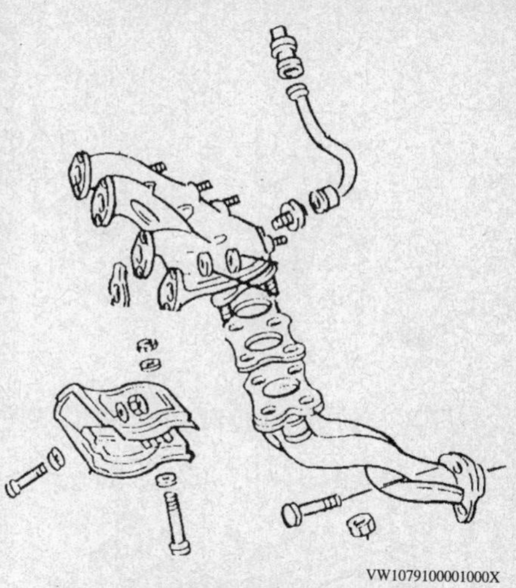
VW1079100001000X

Fig. 18 Exhaust manifold removal. Cabriolet

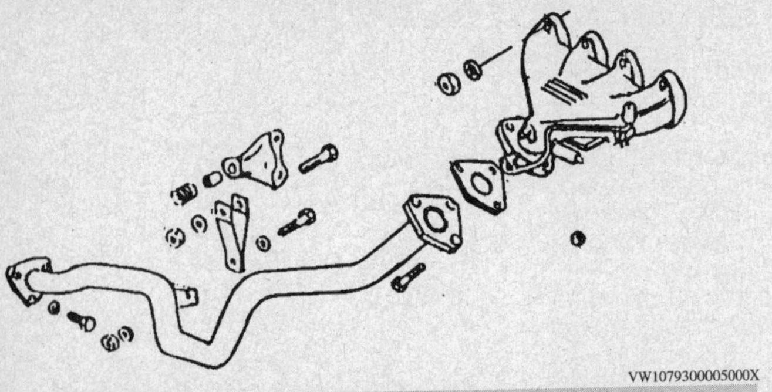
VW1079300005000X

Fig. 19 Exhaust manifold removal. Fox

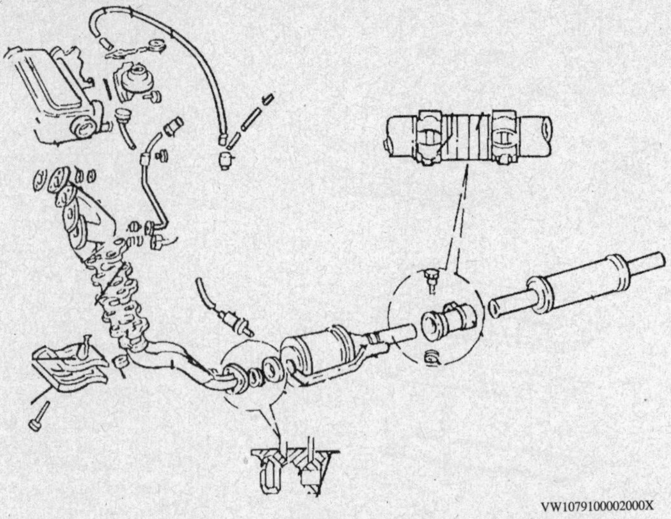
VW1079100002000X

Fig. 20 Exhaust manifold removal. 2.0L 16-valve engine

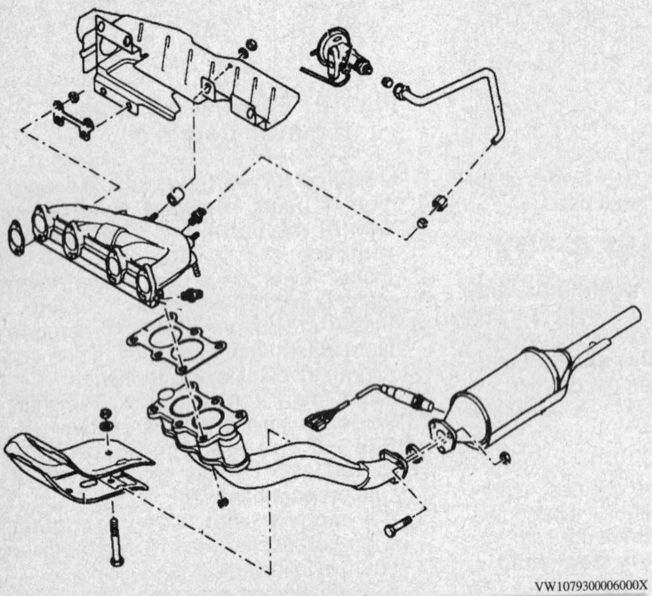
VW1079300006000X

Fig. 21 Exhaust manifold removal. 2.0L 8-valve engine

11. Reset audio coded anti-theft system as outlined under "Precautions."

CAMSHAFT

REPLACE

EXCEPT 1993 PASSAT

1. Remove valve cover to cylinder head attaching bolts, then the valve cover.
2. Remove timing belt as outlined under "Timing Belt, Replace."
3. Remove camshaft sprocket attaching bolt and the camshaft sprocket.
4. Working from front of engine, remove Nos. 5, 1 and 3 bearing caps.
5. Diagonally loosen, then remove, Nos. 2 and 4 bearing caps. **Numbered from front to rear.**
6. Remove camshaft from cylinder head.
7. Lubricate bearing shells, journals and contact surface of bearing caps with engine oil.
8. Position camshaft onto bearing saddles and install new camshaft oil seal.
9. Install bearing caps and ensure caps align correctly, **Fig. 29.**
10. Lightly tighten Nos. 2 and 4 bearing caps diagonally, then tighten all caps to specifications.
11. Install camshaft sprocket onto camshaft and tighten attaching bolt to specifications.
12. Align timing marks, then install timing belt, timing cover and valve cover.

1993 PASSAT

With the timing belt removed, avoid turning the camshaft or crankshaft. If movement is required, exercise extreme caution to avoid valve damage caused by piston contact.

1. Remove upper intake manifold.
2. Remove cylinder head valve cover.
3. Remove timing belt as outlined under "Timing Belt, Replace," then camshaft sprocket.
4. **Note position of timing marks on inter camshaft timing chain and sprockets for later assembly.**
5. Remove bearing cap Nos. 5 and 7 on intake camshaft, then the last bearing cap, **Fig. 30.**
6. Diagonally loosen bearing cap Nos. 6 and 8 on intake camshaft, then remove.
7. Remove bearing cap Nos. 1 and 3 on exhaust camshaft, then the first and last bearing cap.
8. Diagonally loosen bearing cap Nos. 2 and 4 on exhaust camshaft, then remove.
9. Remove camshafts.
10. Lubricate bearing shells, journals and contact surface of bearing caps with engine oil.
11. Ensure arrow on bearing caps face toward the intake side of cylinder head.
12. Install camshafts with chain so that timing marks on chain sprockets align.
13. Diagonally tighten bearing cap Nos. 6 and 8 on intake camshaft, then tighten to specifications.
14. Install remaining bearing caps on intake camshaft and tighten to specifications.
15. Diagonally tighten bearing cap Nos. 2 and 4 on exhaust camshaft, then tighten to specifications.
16. Install remaining bearing caps on exhaust camshaft and tighten to specifications.
17. Install camshaft sprocket and tighten to specifications.
18. Install drive belt, valve cover, intake manifold and timing belt cover.

PISTON & ROD ASSEMBLY

Assemble the piston to the rod with the arrow on the piston crown pointing toward the front of the engine and the casting marks on the rod facing the intermediate shaft.

PISTONS, PINS & RINGS

Pistons and rings are available in .010 inch, .020 inch and .040 inch oversizes. Oversize piston pins are not available.

MAIN & ROD BEARINGS

Main and connecting rod bearings are

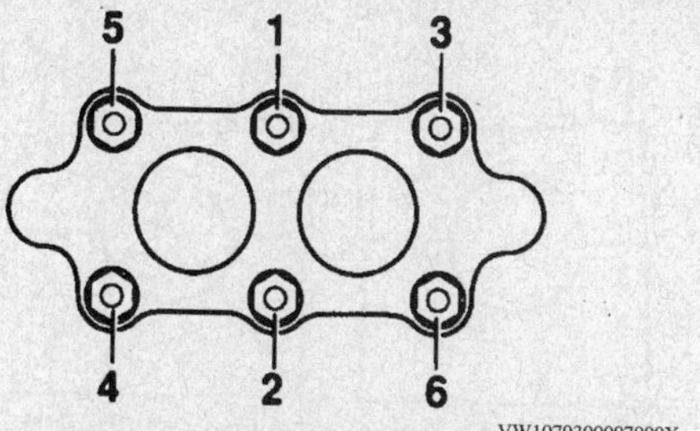
5
1
3
4
2
6
VW1079300007000X

Fig. 22 Exhaust manifold to pipe tightening sequence. 2.0L engines

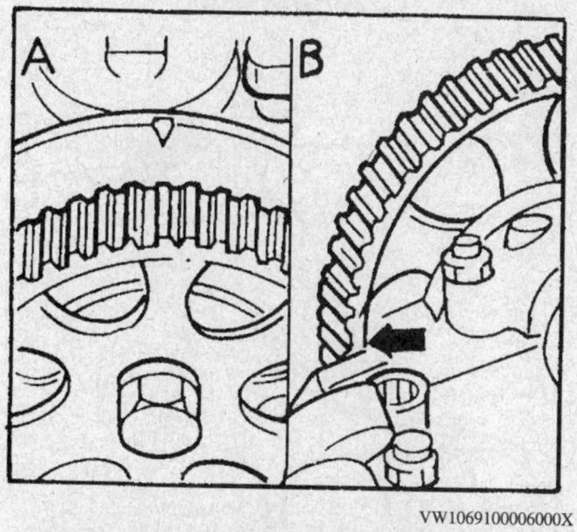
A
B
VW1069100006000X

Fig. 25 Camshaft alignment. Except Cabriolet & Fox

available in .010 inch, .020 inch and .030 inch undersizes.

CRANKSHAFT REAR OIL SEAL

REPLACE

1. **On models with manual transaxle,** remove transaxle, flywheel, pressure plate, clutch disc and intermediate plate.
2. **On models with automatic transaxle,** remove transaxle, torque converter and torque converter driveplate.
3. **On all models,** pry oil seal out of oil seal flange using a screwdriver, or equivalent.
4. Lubricate new seal, center seal in seal flange and press until fully seated.
5. Reverse procedure to complete installation.

FRONT MAIN BEARING OIL SEAL

REPLACE

1. Remove timing belt as outlined under "Timing Belt, Replace."
2. Remove crankshaft sprocket retaining bolt, then sprocket. **On 16-valve engines, do not allow crankshaft to turn as piston valve contact will occur.**
3. Using a suitable tool remove oil seal.
4. Lightly lubricate sealing lip and outer edge of new oil seal.

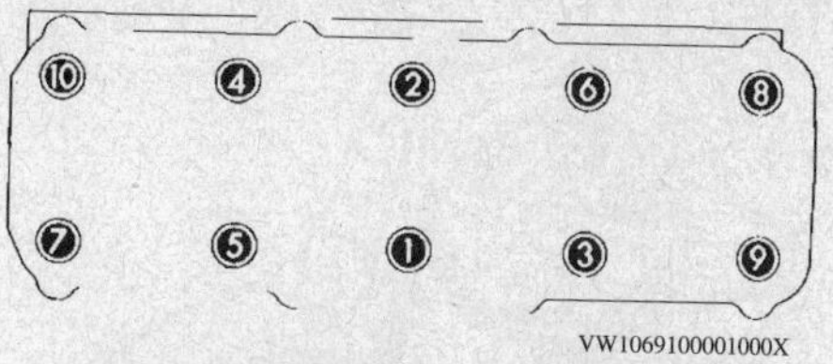
10
4
2
6
8
7
5
1
3
9
VW1069100001000X

Fig. 23 Cylinder head bolt tightening sequence

5. Place suitable guide sleeve onto crankshaft, then push oil seal over guide sleeve.
6. Using a suitable tool, press oil seal in until it reaches stop.
7. Reverse procedure to install. Use a suitable Loctite on crankshaft sprocket bolt and tighten to specifications.

OIL PAN

REPLACE

1. Remove oil pan drain plug and drain engine oil.
2. Remove oil pan to engine attaching bolts and the oil pan.
3. Reverse procedure to install. Tighten to specifications.

SERPENTINE DRIVE BELT

BELT ROUTING & REPLACEMENT

Refer to **Figs. 31 and 32** for serpentine drive belt routing and tensioner release tool placement.

1. Loosen power steering pump adjustment bolts, then remove V-belt.
2. Mark running direction of serpentine drive belt if it is to be reused.
3. Insert tensioner tool No. 3299, or equivalent, onto belt tensioner.
4. Rotate tensioner clockwise to release tension, then remove belt from alternator pulley.
5. Remove belt from remaining pulleys.
6. Reverse procedure to install. Note running direction of used belts.

COOLING SYSTEM BLEED

EXCEPT FOX

1. Slowly fill coolant expansion tank to Max mark, then install expansion tank cap.
2. Run engine until cooling fan comes on, then check coolant level.
3. Coolant level should be at or slightly above Max mark with engine at normal operating temperature, and between Min and Max marks with engine cold.
4. If necessary, add coolant to specified marking.

FOX

1. Disconnect thermo-time switch connector and remove thermo-time switch, then fully open heater valve.

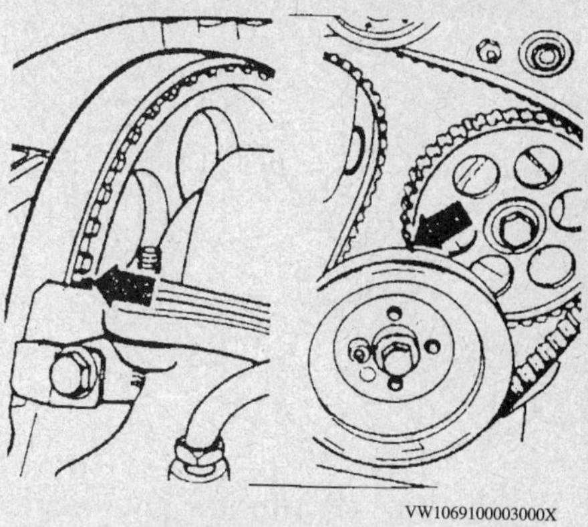
VW1069100003000X

Fig. 24 Timing mark alignment. Cabriolet & Fox

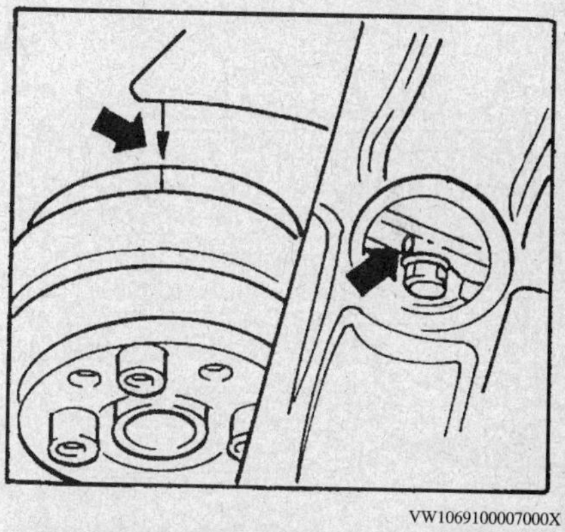
VW1069100007000X

Fig. 26 Vibration damper & flywheel alignment. Except Cabriolet & Fox

2. Add coolant to expansion tank until coolant flows from thermo-time switch opening, then install and connect thermo-time switch.
3. Fill coolant expansion tank to Max mark, then install expansion tank cap.
4. Run engine until cooling fan comes on, then check coolant level.
5. Coolant level should be at or slightly above Max mark with engine at normal operating temperature, and between Min and Max marks with engine cold.
6. If necessary, add coolant to specified marking.

WATER PUMP

REPLACE

WITH A/C EXCEPT FOX

1. Drain cooling system.
2. Remove timing belt as outlined under "Timing Belt, Replace."
3. Remove intermediate shaft sprocket.
4. Remove water pump to housing attaching bolts, then discard bolts.
5. Remove water pump and gasket.
6. Reverse procedure to install.

FOX LESS A/C

1. Obtain audio coded anti-theft code, then disconnect battery ground cable.
2. Drain cooling system, then disconnect hoses from coolant pump body.

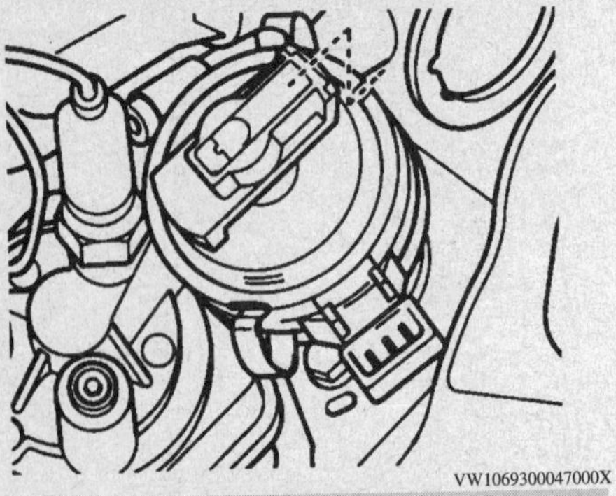
VW1069300047000X

Fig. 27 Distributor alignment. 2.0L 8-valve engines

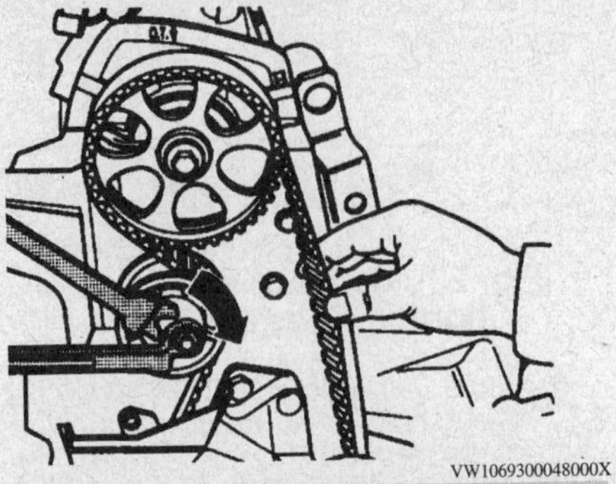
VW1069300048000X

Fig. 28 Timing belt tension. 2.0L engine

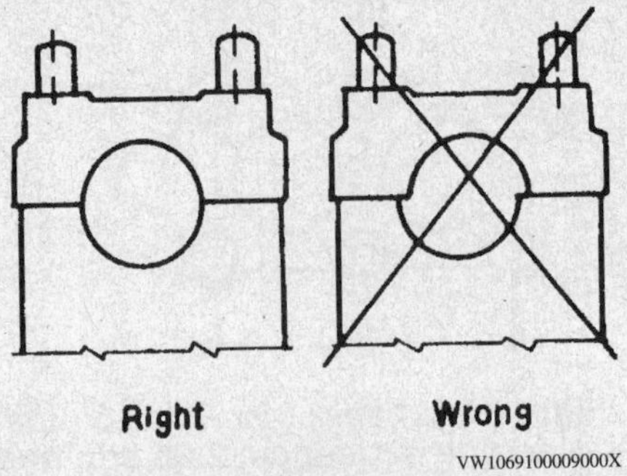
Right
Wrong
VW1069100009000X

Fig. 29 Camshaft bearing cap alignment

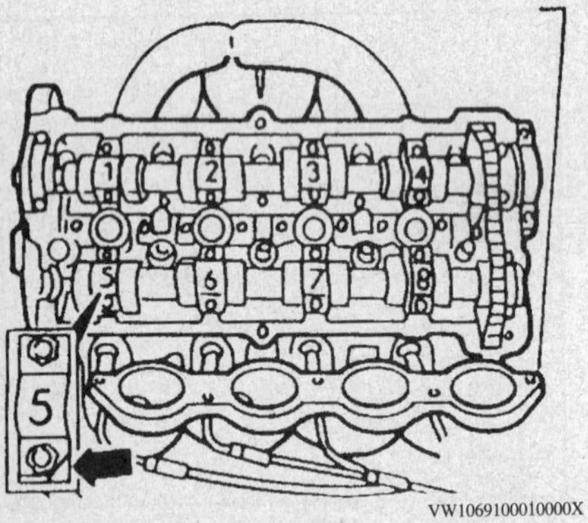
1
2
3
4
5
6
7
8
5
VW1069100010000X

Fig. 30 Camshaft & bearing caps. 1993 Passat

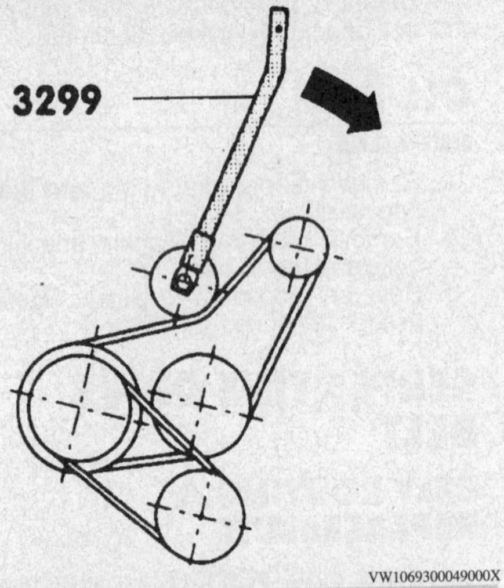
3299
VW1069300049000X

Fig. 31 Serpentine drive belt routing. 2.0L engines less A/C

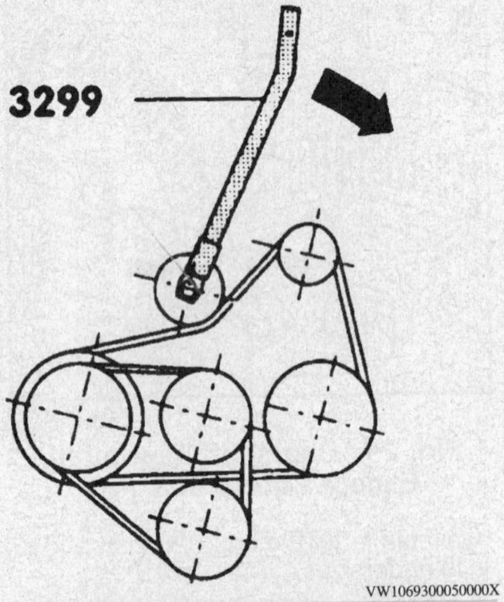
3299
VW1069300050000X

Fig. 32 Serpentine drive belt routing. 2.0L engines w/A/C

3. Remove belts as outlined under "Serpentine Drive Belt."
4. Remove water pump pulley.
5. Remove alternator from mounting bracket if clearance requires and position aside.
6. If equipped, remove any bolts attaching timing belt cover to pump body.
7. **On all models except Fox,** remove and discard mounting bracket/belt tensioner housing bolts.
8. Remove mounting bracket/belt tensioner housing.
9. **On all models,** remove and discard any remaining water pump housing bolts. **Note position of any special mounting bolts.**
10. Remove water pump housing from engine, then place onto a suitable work surface.
11. Remove and discard water pump cover bolts, then cover.
12. Reverse procedure to install, noting the following:
    a. Replace water pump body to block sealing O-ring.
    b. Tighten to specifications.
    c. Reset audio coded anti-theft system as outlined under "Precautions."

RADIATOR

REPLACE

1. Drain cooling system.
2. Disconnect battery ground cable.
3. Remove radiator cover and radiator mounting shroud.
4. Disconnect upper and lower radiator hoses.
5. Disconnect coolant expansion tank tube from radiator.
6. Remove cooling fan cowl with cooling fan(s).
7. **On models with automatic transaxle,** disconnect oil cooler hose.
8. **On all models,** remove thermo switch from radiator.
9. Remove radiator.
10. Reverse procedure to install.

FUEL PUMP

REPLACE

The fuel system is designed to retain a residual fuel pressure. When disconnecting lines use precautions to prevent any fuel spillage.

EXCEPT IN TANK

1. Remove fuel cap to release fuel vapor pressure.
2. Disconnect fuel lines from pump. Use a suitable clamping device on pump inlet line to prevent fuel siphon.
3. Disconnect mounting bracket from underbody, then the electrical connector from fuel pump.
4. Remove fuel pump from bracket.
5. Reverse procedure to install.

IN TANK

1. Remove fuel tank cap to relieve tank pressure.
2. Locate fuel pump access port from inside vehicle luggage compartment.
3. Remove screws, then pry up cover.
4. Clean fuel pump and fuel line unions thoroughly to prevent entry of dirt into fuel system.
5. Disconnect fuel lines and electrical connections from pump.
6. Place match marks on fuel pump flange and tank for later assembly.
7. Remove fuel pump flange retaining ring nut using wrench tool No. 3217, or equivalent.
8. Remove flange and seal.
9. Turn fuel pump module to left to disengage, then lift from tank. Use caution not to damage fuel level sender float arm.
10. Separate pump from module.
11. Reverse procedure to install, noting the following:
    a. When installing fuel pump module,

float arm will point to front of vehicle, offset to the left as follows:

b. Cabrio, Golf III, GTI & Jetta: 5°.

c. Passat Station Wagon: 5° to 10°.

d. Passat Sedan: 70° to 75°.

e. Ensure access port cover is properly sealed.

TIGHTENING SPECIFICATIONS

Year	Component	Torque/Ft. Lbs.
FOX		
1993	Axle Shaft To Transmission Flange Bolts	33
	Axle Shaft To Wheel Bearing Housing Nut	177
	Ball Joint To Wheel Bearing Housing Lockbolt	44
	Camshaft Bearing Cap To Cylinder Head Nuts	15
	Camshaft Sprocket To Camshaft Bolt	59
	Connecting Rod Nuts	22①
	Crankshaft Timing Belt Sprocket To Crankshaft Bolt	66④
	Cylinder Head Bolts	②
	Engine To Transmission Bolts, M12	41
	Exhaust Pipe To Exhaust Manifold Bolts	44
	Flywheel To Pressure Plate Bolts	15
	Flywheel To Crankshaft Bolts	74
	Front Main Oil Seal Housing To Block Bolts	7
	Fuel Line To Cold Start Valve	7
	Fuel Line To Control Pressure Regulator, Large Line	11
	Fuel Line To Control Pressure Regulator, Small Line	7
	Intermediate Shaft Oil Seal Flange To Block Bolts	18
	Intermediate Shaft Sprocket To Intermediate Shaft Bolt	59
	Lower Timing Belt Cover Bolts	7
	Main Bearing Cap Bolts	48
	Oil Cooler To Oil Filter Bracket Nut	18
	Oil Pan Drain Plug To Oil Pan	22
	Oil Pan To Block Bolts	15
	Oil Pressure Switch To Oil Filter Bracket	18
	Oil Pump Cover To Oil Pump Housing Bolts	7
	Oil Pump Pickup To Pump Bolts	7
	Oil Pump To Block Bolts	15
	Radiator Mounting Bolts	4
	Rear Timing Belt Cover To Block Middle Bolts	22
	Rear Timing Belt Cover To Block Threaded Bolt	22③
	Rear Timing Belt Cover To Block Upper Bolt	7
	Starter Mounting Bolts	34
	Thermostat Flange Bolts	7
	Timing Belt Tensioner Nut	33
	Upper Timing Belt Cover Bolts	7
	Vibration Damper (Pulley) To Crankshaft Timing Belt Sprocket Bolt	15
	Water Pump Housing To Block Bolts	16
	Water Pump Pulley To Water Bolts	15
	Water Pump To Water Pump Housing Bolts	7

Continued

TIGHTENING SPECIFICATIONS—Continued

Year	Component	Torque/Ft. Lbs.
CABRIOLET		
1993–94	Axle Shaft To Transmission Flange Bolts	33
	Axle Shaft To Wheel Bearing Housing Nut	177
	Ball Joint To Wheel Bearing Housing Lockbolt	37
	Camshaft Bearing Cap To Cylinder Head Nuts	15
	Camshaft Sprocket To Camshaft Bolt	59
	Clutch Pressure (Carrier) Plate To Crankshaft Bolts	74
	Connecting Rod Nuts	22①
	Crankshaft Timing Belt Sprocket To Crankshaft Bolt	148
	Cylinder Head Bolts	②
	Engine To Transmission Bolts, M10	33
	Engine To Transmission Bolts, M12	55
	Flexplate To Crankshaft Bolts	74
	Flexplate To Torque Converter Bolts	22
	Flywheel To Pressure Plate Bolts	15
	Front Main Oil Seal Housing To Block Bolts	7
	Fuel Line To Cold Start Valve	7
	Fuel Line To Control Pressure Regulator, Large Line	11
	Fuel Line To Control Pressure Regulator, Small Line	7
	Intermediate Shaft Oil Seal Flange To Block Bolts	18
	Intermediate Shaft Sprocket To Intermediate Shaft Bolt	59
	Lower Timing Belt Cover Bolts	7
	Main Bearing Cap Bolts	48
	Oil Cooler To Oil Filter Bracket Nut	18
	Oil Pan Drain Plug To Oil Pan	22
	Oil Pan To Block Bolts	15
	Oil Pressure Switch To Oil Filter Bracket	18
	Oil Pump Cover To Oil Pump Housing Bolts	7
	Oil Pump Pickup To Pump Bolts	7
	Oil Pump To Block Bolts	15
	Radiator Mounting Bolts	4
	Rear Main Oil Seal Housing To Block Bolts	7
	Rear Timing Belt Cover To Block Middle Bolts	22
	Rear Timing Belt Cover To Block Threaded Bolt	22③
	Rear Timing Belt Cover To Block Upper Bolt	7
	Starter Mounting Bolts	34
	Thermostat Flange Bolts	7
	Timing Belt Tensioner Nut	33
	Upper Timing Belt Cover Bolts	7
	Vibration Damper (Pulley) To Crankshaft Timing Belt Sprocket Bolt	15
	Water Pump Housing To Block Bolts	15
	Water Pump Pulley To Water Bolts	15
	Water Pump To Water Pump Housing Bolts	7

Continued

TIGHTENING SPECIFICATIONS—Continued

Year	Component	Torque/Ft. Lbs.
GOLF, GTI, JETTA, PASSAT & 1995–96 CABRIO		
1993–96	Axle Shaft To Transmission Flange Bolts	33
	Axle Nut	195
	Ball Joint To Suspension Arm Bolts	26
	Camshaft Bearing Cap To Cylinder Head Nuts	15
	Camshaft Sprocket To Camshaft Bolt	60-
	Clutch Pressure Plate (Driveplate) to Crankshaft	44①⑥
	Clutch Slave Cylinder	18⑦
	Connecting Rod Nuts	22①
	Crankshaft Timing Belt Sprocket To Crankshaft Bolt	66①
	Cylinder Head Cover To Cylinder Head Bolts	7
	Cylinder Head Bolts	②
	Engine To Transmission Bolts, M10	44
	Engine To Transmission Bolts, M12	59
	Exhaust Pipe To Exhaust Manifold Bolts	30
	Front Main Oil Seal Housing To Block Bolts	15
	Flywheel To Crankshaft Bolts	44①⑦
	Flywheel To Pressure Plate (Driveplate) Bolts	15⑥
	Intermediate Shaft Oil Seal Flange To Block Bolts	18
	Intermediate Shaft Sprocket To Intermediate Shaft Bolt	48
	Hub Nut	195
	Lower Timing Belt Cover Bolts	7
	Main Bearing Cap Bolts	48
	Oil Cooler To Oil Filter Bracket Nut	18
	Oil Pan Drain Plug To Oil Pan	22
	Oil Pan To Block Bolts	15
	Oil Pressure Switch To Oil Filter Bracket	18
	Oil Pump Cover To Oil Pump Housing Bolts	7
	Oil Pump Pickup To Pump Bolts	7
	Oil Pump To Block Bolts	15
	Oil Spray Nozzle To Block Bolt	7⑤⑦
	Power Steering Pump To Mounting Bracket Bolts	18
	Pressure Plate (Driveplate) to Crankshaft	44①⑥
	Pressure Plate to Flywheel	15⑦
	Radiator Mounting Bolts	7
	Rear Main Oil Seal Housing To Block Bolts	15
	Rear Timing Belt Cover To Block Bolts	22
	Rear Timing Belt Cover To Block Threaded Bolt	22③
	Thermostat Flange Bolts	7
	Timing Belt Tensioner Nut	33
	Upper Intake Manifold Bolts	15
	Upper Timing Belt Cover Bolts	4
	Vibration Damper (Pulley) To Crankshaft Timing Belt Sprocket Bolt	74

Continued

TIGHTENING SPECIFICATIONS—Continued

Year	Component	Torque/Ft. Lbs.
GOLF, GTI, JETTA, PASSAT & 1995–96 CABRIO		
1993–96	Water Pump Housing To Block Bolts	15
	Water Pump Pulley To Water Pump Bolts	15
	Water Pump To Water Pump Housing Bolts	7

① — Plus an additional 1/4 (90°) turn.
② — Refer to "Cylinder Head, Replace."
③ — Coat threads with D6 locking compound, or equivalent.
④ — Plus an additional 1/2 (180°) turn.
⑤ — Coat threads with locking compound No. AMV 188 100 02, or equivalent.
⑥ — Except Passat.
⑦ — Passat.

2.5L Engine

NOTE: On Air Bag Equipped Models, Refer To "Air Bag System Precautions" Located In The Front Of This Manual For System Disarming & Arming Procedures.

INDEX

	Page No.
Camshaft, Replace	49-36
Compression Pressure	49-34
Crankshaft Seal, Replace	49-37
Front	49-37
Rear	49-37
Cylinder Head, Replace	49-36
Engine Mount, Replace	49-35
Front	49-35
Left	49-35
Rear	49-35
Engine Rebuilding Specifications	49-148
Engine, Replace	49-35
Exhaust Manifold, Replace	49-36
Fuel Filter, Replace	49-38
Fuel Pump, Replace	49-38
Hydraulic Lifters	49-36
Inspection	49-36
Intake Manifold, Replace	49-35
Main & Rod Bearings	49-37
Oil Pan, Replace	49-38
Piston & Rod Assembly	49-37
Precautions	49-34
Air Bag Systems	49-34
Audio Coded Anti-Theft System	49-34
Radiator, Replace	49-38
Tightening Specifications	49-38
Timing Belt, Replace	49-36
Valve Adjustment	49-36
Valve Clearance Specifications	49-36
Valve Cover, Replace	49-36
Valve Guides	49-36
Inspection	49-36
Replacement	49-36

PRECAUTIONS

AIR BAG SYSTEMS

Refer to "Air Bag System Precautions" in the front of this manual for system disarming and arming procedures.

AUDIO CODED ANTI-THEFT SYSTEM

Some models are equipped with a radio anti-theft system that will disable the system when battery power is interrupted, unless the system is reset the radio will not operate.

1. Turn radio to On position, SAFE should be displayed.
2. Depress and hold AM/FM and SCAN buttons until 1000 remains on display. If AM/FM and SCAN buttons are depressed too long or depressed again, radio will misinterpret the 1000 as an attempt at coding and one incorrect coding attempt will be logged. **After two incorrect attempts to reset system, radio will lock up electronically. If this occurs, leave radio on for approximately one hour, then reset radio as if battery power were disconnected.**
3. Enter radio code using first four program station buttons. Security code will appear on display.
4. Depress and hold AM/FM and SCAN buttons again until SAFE is displayed.
5. Release AM/FM and SCAN buttons. Display should change to a radio frequency and operate normally.

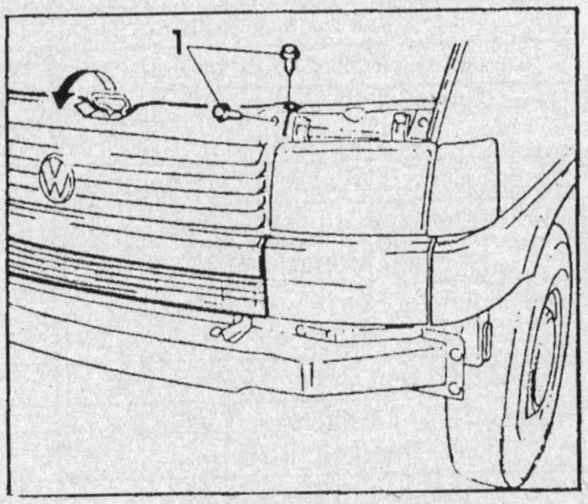
1
VW1069100014000X

Fig. 1 Radiator securing bolts

COMPRESSION PRESSURE

1. Perform compression test with engine at operating temperature, spark plugs removed, coolant temperature at minimum of 176°F and throttle plate completely open.
2. Disconnect coil high tension wire from distributor cap and connect to suitable ground.
3. Connect compression tester tool No. VAG 1381, or equivalent, following manufacturer's instructions, then crank engine until compression tester shows no further increase in pressure.
4. **Compression should be 130–174 psi with a maximum difference between highest and lowest cylinder of 43.5 psi. Minimum compression should be 108.75 psi.**

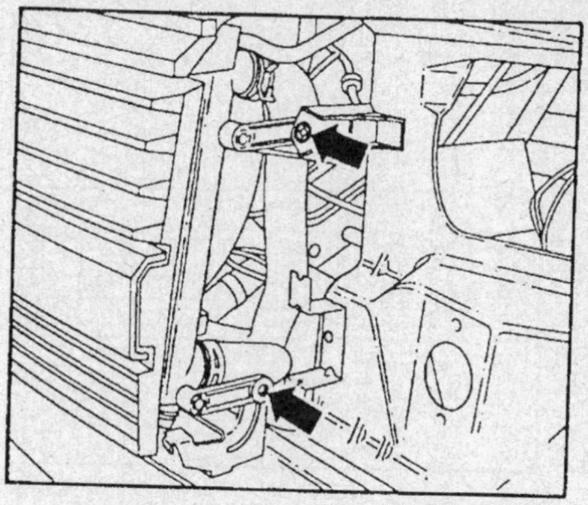
1

VW1069100015000X

Fig. 2 Radiator hinge pins removal

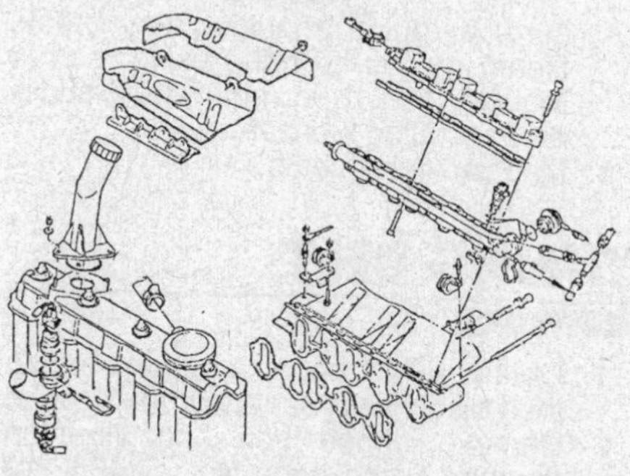

VW1059100002000X

Fig. 5 Intake manifold

ENGINE MOUNT

REPLACE

FRONT

1. Attach engine lifting tool No. 2024A, or equivalent, and loosen front engine mount center mounting bolt.
2. Raise engine and transaxle assembly until weight is off mount, then remove center bolt.
3. Remove center engine mount bolt, then remove subframe mounting bolts and engine mount.
4. Reverse procedure to install.

LEFT

1. Attach engine lifting tool No. 2024A, or equivalent, and loosen engine/transaxle center mount mounting bolt.
2. Raise engine and transaxle assembly until weight is off mount, then remove center mounting bolt.
3. Remove engine mount bolts from subframe, then engine mount.
4. Reverse procedure to install.

REAR

1. Attach engine lifting tool No. 2024A, or equivalent, and loosen center engine mount mounting bolt.
2. Raise engine and transaxle assembly until weight is off mount, then remove center mounting bolt.
3. Remove engine mount bolts from subframe, then engine mount.
4. Reverse procedure to install.

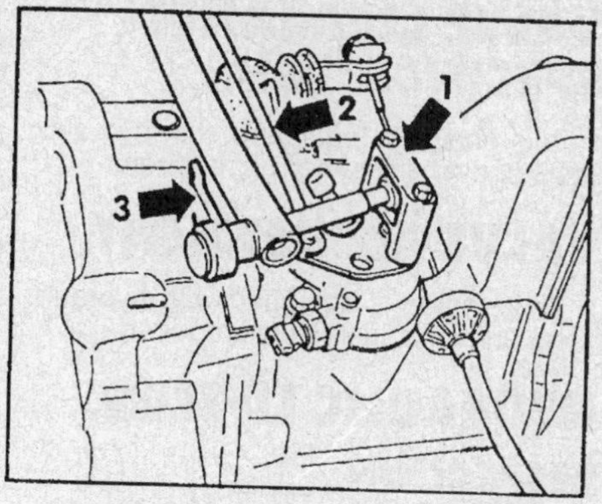
1
2
3

VW1069100016000X

Fig. 3 Transaxle gearshift disconnect

ENGINE

REPLACE

1. Obtain audio coded anti-theft code, disconnect battery ground cable, then raise and support vehicle.
2. Support right and left upper control arms by fitting support wedges tool No. 3240, or equivalent, then remove noise damping pan.
3. Drain coolant and remove securing bolts from left and right, **Fig. 1,** then move radiator and lock carrier forward.
4. Disconnect cooling fan and thermo switch.
5. Drive radiator hinge pins out of right and left side brackets, **Fig. 2,** then remove radiator assembly complete with lock carrier and coolant hoses.
6. Disconnect speedometer cable and accelerator cable at throttle body and support bracket.
7. Disconnect clutch cable, then engine, transaxle, alternator and starter wiring and secure away.
8. Disconnect all coolant, vacuum and intake hoses from engine, then disconnect fuel supply line at T-piece and return line at fuel rail.
9. Refer to **Fig. 3** when disconnecting gearshift from transaxle as follows:
   a. Remove clevis (1), then pry up shift lever at front from gear control lever (2).
   b. Disconnect selector rod from bearing block (3).
   c. Disconnect oil lines from power steering pump and drain hydraulic fluid.
10. Remove lefthand driveshaft and detach righthand driveshaft at transaxle.
11. Remove front exhaust pipe with oxygen sensor, then disconnect supply and return lines from power steering pump.
12. Secure engine take-up bracket tool No. 3227, or equivalent, to cylinder block, **torque** to 15 ft. lbs., then raise engine and transaxle slightly with lift tool No. VAG 1383A, or equivalent.
13. Remove both securing bolts from transaxle mounting bracket, **Fig. 4.**
14. Remove central bolts for engine and transaxle mounts on right and left side of engine compartment.

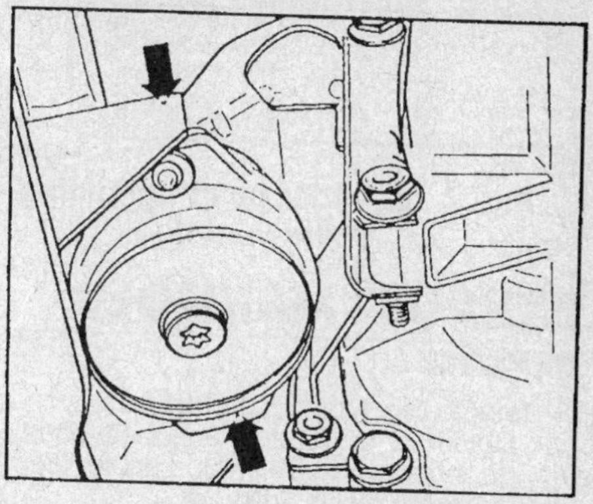

VW1069100017000X

Fig. 4 Transaxle mounting bolt location

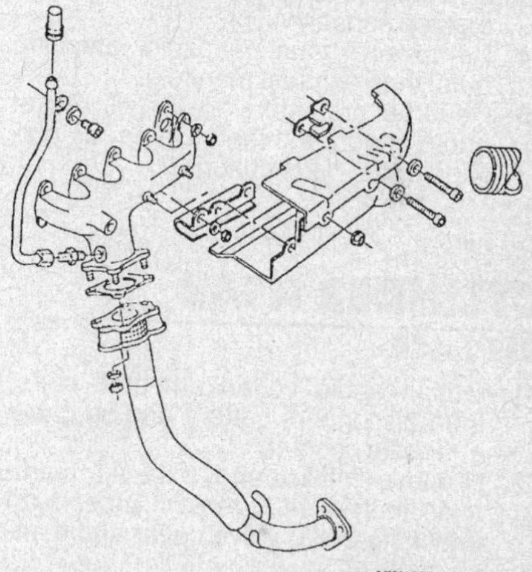

VW1079100004000X

Fig. 6 Exhaust manifold

15. Lower engine/transaxle assembly while guiding power steering pump oil return line away, then mount engine on appropriate repair stand.
16. Separate engine from transaxle.
17. Reverse procedure to install, noting the following:
   a. Ensure centering dowels are properly positioned in cylinder block.
   b. Reset audio coded anti-theft system as outlined under "Precautions."

INTAKE MANIFOLD

REPLACE

Refer to **Fig. 5** during procedure.

1. Obtain audio coded anti-theft code, then disconnect battery ground cable.
2. Remove oil filler pipe and bracket, then hot air stove.
3. Remove lower section of fuel rail, then harness for fuel injectors.
4. Remove upper fuel rail, then remove injectors.
5. Disconnect fuel pressure regulator and fuel supply line.
6. Disconnect T-connector and fuel return line, then remove intake manifold attaching nuts.
7. Reverse procedure to install. Reset audio coded anti-theft system as outlined under "Precautions."

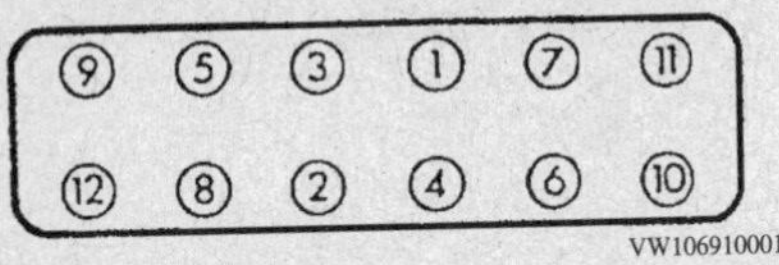
9 5 3 1 7 11
12 8 2 4 6 10

VW1069100018000X

Fig. 7 Cylinder head tightening sequence

EXHAUST MANIFOLD

REPLACE

Refer to **Fig. 6** during procedure.

1. Obtain audio coded anti-theft code, disconnect battery ground cable, then remove heat shield/stove.
2. Remove intake air hose on air cleaner housing.
3. Disconnect exhaust down pipe, then oxygen sensor.
4. Remove exhaust manifold attaching nuts, then exhaust manifold.
5. Reverse procedure to install. Reset audio coded anti-theft system as outlined under "Precautions."

CYLINDER HEAD

REPLACE

1. Obtain audio coded anti-theft code, then disconnect battery ground cable and drain coolant.
2. Remove intake and exhaust manifolds, then valve cover to cylinder head attaching bolts, valve cover and camshaft cover.
3. Loosen alternator adjusting bolt, then remove alternator drive belt.
4. Remove timing belt as outlined under "Timing Belt, Replace."
5. Remove camshaft drive sprocket using countering tool No. 3036, or equivalent, to loosen.
6. Remove distributor as outlined under "Distributor, Replace."
7. Disconnect all cables, hoses and wires that obstruct removal of cylinder head, then loosen cylinder head bolts following sequence in **Fig 7.**
8. Reverse procedure to install, noting the following:
   a. Using sequence shown in **Fig. 7, torque** cylinder head bolts in four steps as follows: first, to 30 ft. lbs.; second, to 44 ft. lbs.; third, tighten an additional 1/4 (90°) turn; and finally, tighten an additional 1/4 (90°) turn.
   b. Reset audio coded anti-theft system as outlined under "Precautions."

VALVE COVER

REPLACE

1. Remove oil filler tube, then timing belt cover.
2. Remove emission control valve, then the valve cover retaining nuts.
3. Remove valve cover.
4. Reverse procedure to install.

VALVE CLEARANCE SPECIFICATIONS

This engine is equipped with hydraulic lifters and no adjustment is required.

VALVE ADJUSTMENT

This engine is equipped with hydraulic lifters and no adjustment is required.

HYDRAULIC LIFTERS

INSPECTION

1. Start engine and let idle until radiator fan comes on at least once.
2. Raise engine speed to approximately 2500 RPM and hold for two minutes.
3. Listen to sound of engine. If valve noise is still present, check for malfunctioning lifters as follow:
   a. Remove valve cover as outlined under "Valve Cover, Replace."
   b. Turn crankshaft clockwise by hand until cam lobe for the valve to be checked is pointing away from and is perpendicular to lifter. Repeat with each valve.
4. Measure clearance between cam and lifter. .004 inch or less should be indicated. If not as indicated, replace lifter.
5. If no play is indicated, depress lifter using suitable wooden or plastic wedge. If freeplay is greater than .004 inches, replace lifter. **After installing new valve lifters, do not start engine for approximately 30 minutes to allow lifters to bleed down. If this precaution is not observed, possible damage from valves hitting piston crowns could result.**

VALVE GUIDES

INSPECTION

1. Remove all carbon deposits from valve guide.
2. Position a dial indicator on cylinder head to check guides.
3. Insert new valve into valve guide. End of valve stem must be flush with valve guide end.
4. Rock valve back and forth against dial indicator.
5. Maximum clearance is .039 inch for intake valves and .051 inch for exhaust valves . Replace guide(s) if reading is not within specifications.

REPLACEMENT

1. Worn valve guides can be removed using valve guide removal tool No. 10-206 3121, or equivalent.
2. Press guides outward from camshaft side. On guides with collar, press guides from combustion chamber side.
3. Coat new guides with engine oil, then press into cold cylinder head from camshaft side.
4. Press guides in as far as they will go. Once valve guide shoulder is seated, do not use more than one ton of pressure, or guide shoulder may break. Ream guides by hand using reamer tool No. 10-215, or equivalent, and a proper cutting lubricant.

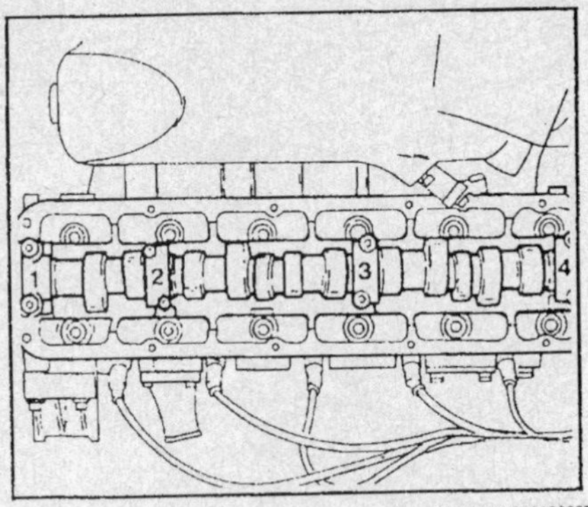
1
2
3
4

VW1069100019000X

Fig. 8 Camshaft bearing cap tightening sequence

5. Machine valve seats.

TIMING BELT

REPLACE

1. Obtain audio coded anti-theft code, then disconnect battery ground cable.
2. Remove ribbed belt and vibration damper using tool No. 3248A, or equivalent, then upper and lower belt guards.
3. Mark belt running direction, then loosen tensioner pulley and water pump.
4. Remove belt.
5. Reverse procedure to install, noting the following:
   a. Ensure crankshaft is at TDC.
   b. Coat center bolt threads and surface contacting portion of bolt with Loctite, or equivalent.
   c. Reset audio coded anti-theft system as outlined under "Precautions."

CAMSHAFT

REPLACE

1. Obtain audio coded anti-theft code, then disconnect battery ground cable.
2. Remove timing belt as outlined under "Timing Belt, Replace," then remove valve cover.
3. Loosen camshaft drive sprocket using countering tool No. 3036, or equivalent.
4. Rotate camshaft drive sprocket to TDC on No. 1 cylinder by manually rotating crankshaft, then mark camshaft sprocket to align with rear timing belt guard.
5. Remove camshaft drive sprocket using suitable puller, then woodruff key from camshaft.
6. Remove ignition distributor.
7. Remove first bearing caps 1 and 3, **Fig. 8,** then loosen bearing caps 4 and 4, alternately in a diagonal sequence.
8. Reverse procedure to install, noting the following:
   a. Install camshaft with lobes for cylinder No. 1 pointing upward.

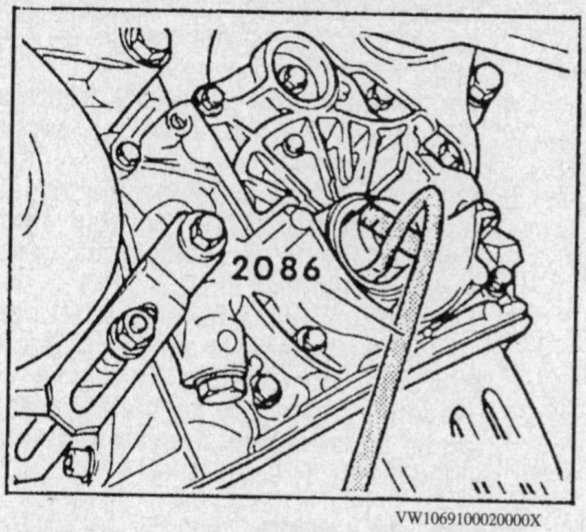
2086
VW1069100020000X

Fig. 9 Front crankshaft oil seal removal

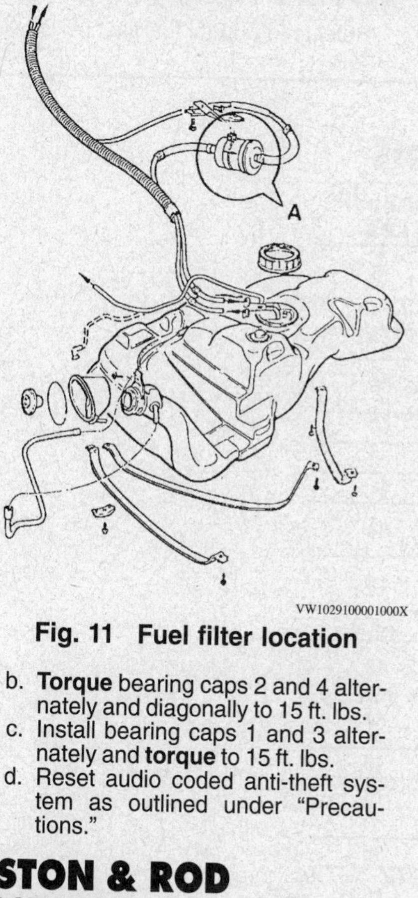
A
VW1029100001000X

Fig. 11 Fuel filter location

b. **Torque** bearing caps 2 and 4 alternately and diagonally to 15 ft. lbs.
c. Install bearing caps 1 and 3 alternately and **torque** to 15 ft. lbs.
d. Reset audio coded anti-theft system as outlined under "Precautions."

PISTON & ROD ASSEMBLY

1. Prior to removal, mark pistons and rods to match cylinder number.
2. Remove circlips from piston, press pin out by hand and separate assembly. **If pin is too tight in bore, heat piston to approximately 140°F.**
3. Check piston to cylinder wall clearance at right angles to piston pin, 3/8 inch from top and bottom and in center of travel.
4. Ensure ring end gaps are within specifications by installing ring approximately 9/16 inch from top of cylinder and centering with an inverted piston.
5. Assemble piston and rod combinations with casting marks on rod and markings on piston crown facing timing belt. **If piston pin is tight in pin bore, heat piston to approximately 140°F to aid installation. Ensure pin attaching locks are properly seated.**
6. Install piston rings with TOP markings facing piston crown. Side clearance for compression rings should measure .002–.004 inch on upper rings and .002–.003 inch on lower rings and must not exceed .008 inch. Side clearance for oil rings should measure .001–.002 inch and must not exceed .006 inch.
7. Install assemblies with piston marking facing timing belt, using a ring compressor. Ensure connecting rod side clearance is less than .004 inch. **Ensure "stretch" type connecting rod bolts are used. Bolts are not reusable, and must be replaced during assembly. During installation, tighten nuts to specifications, then turn each nut an additional ½ turn to obtain proper stretch.**

VW1089500001000X

Fig. 10 Radiator replacement. Eurovan

MAIN & ROD BEARINGS

Main and connecting rod bearings are available in .010 inch, .020 inch and .030 inch undersizes.

CRANKSHAFT SEAL

REPLACE

FRONT

1. Obtain audio coded anti-theft code, disconnect battery ground cable, then remove timing belt following procedure outlined under "Timing Belt, Replace."
2. Remove vibration damper and camshaft drive sprocket.
3. Use counter-hold tool No. 3248, or equivalent, to loosen center bolt.
4. Press out seal using tool No. 2086, or equivalent, **Fig. 9.**
5. Lightly oil sealing lip and outer edge of new seal, then fit seal over installation sleeve tool No. 2080A, or equivalent and press in as far as it will go using installation tool and bolt from vibration damper.
6. Reverse above steps 1 and 2 to complete installation. Reset audio coded anti-theft system as outlined under "Precautions."

REAR

1. Obtain audio coded anti-theft code, disconnect battery ground cable, then remove transaxle following procedure outlined under "Transaxle, Replace."
2. Remove flywheel, then the seal using pry tool No. 10-221, or equivalent.
3. Reverse procedure to install, noting the following:
   a. Clean seal recess in sealing flange, then evenly push new oil seal by

hand onto sealing flange and carefully remove fitting aid.

b. Reset audio coded anti-theft system as outlined under "Precautions."

OIL PAN

REPLACE

1. Raise and support vehicle, then remove sound damper.
2. Drain engine oil.
3. Remove oil pan securing bolts, then lower oil pan.
4. Reverse procedure to install.

RADIATOR

REPLACE

1. Drain engine coolant.
2. Remove hood lock carrier, **Fig. 10.**
3. Remove radiator grille.
4. Remove radiator air duct.
5. Remove radiator cowl with electric cooling fans and thermostatically controlled shutters.
6. Remove thermo switch from radiator.
7. Disconnect upper and lower radiator hoses.
8. Disconnect coolant expansion tank tube from radiator.
9. Remove radiator from vehicle.
10. Reverse procedure to install.

FUEL PUMP

REPLACE

1. Obtain audio coded anti-theft code, then disconnect battery ground cable.
2. Pull out carpeting around perforation to right of handbrake lever, then remove fuel pump cover plate.
3. Disconnect harness connector, supply and return lines from flange on fuel tank.
4. **On models with auxiliary heaters,** disconnect fuel line between supply and return lines.
5. **On all models,** unfasten union nuts using tool No. 3217, or equivalent, then pull flange and sealing ring out of fuel tank opening.
6. Loosen fuel pump from bayonet connection by twisting to left, then remove fuel pump from tank.
7. Reverse procedure to install. Reset audio coded anti-theft system as outlined under "Precautions."

FUEL FILTER

REPLACE

Refer to **Fig. 11** for fuel filter (A) location.

TIGHTENING SPECIFICATIONS

Year	Component	Torque/Ft. Lbs.
1993	Camshaft Bearing Cap To Cylinder Head Nuts	15
	Camshaft Sprocket To Camshaft Bolt	60-70
	Connecting Rod Nuts	22③
	Crankshaft Timing Belt Sprocket To Crankshaft Bolt	66
	Cylinder Head Bolts	②
	Engine To Transmission Bolts, M10	33
	Engine To Transmission Bolts, M12	41
	Exhaust Pipe To Exhaust Manifold Bolts	30
	Front Main Oil Seal Housing To Block Bolts	15
	Flywheel To Crankshaft Bolts	22①
	Intermediate Shaft Oil Seal Flange To Block Bolts	18
	Intermediate Shaft Sprocket To Intermediate Shaft Bolt	59
	Main Bearing Cap Bolts	48
	Oil Cooler To Oil Filter Bracket Nut	18
	Oil Pan Drain Plug To Oil Pan	30
	Oil Pan To Block Bolts	15
	Oil Pressure Switch To Oil Filter Bracket	18
	Oil Pump Cover To Oil Pump Housing Bolts	7
	Oil Pump Pickup To Pump Bolts	7
	Oil Pump To Block Bolts	15
	Oil Spray Nozzle To Block Bolt	7④
	Power Steering Pump To Mounting Bracket Bolts	18
	Radiator Mounting Bolts	7
	Rear Main Oil Seal Housing To Block Bolts	7
	Rear Timing Belt Cover To Block Middle Bolts	18
	Rear Timing Belt Cover To Block Upper Bolt	7

Continued

TIGHTENING SPECIFICATIONS—Continued

Year	Component	Torque/Ft. Lbs.
1993	Timing Belt Tensioner Nut	33
	Valve Cover Bolts	11
	Vibration Damper to Crankshaft Timing Belt Sprocket Bolts	18
	Water Pump Pulley To Water Pump Bolts	18
	Water Pump To Water Pump Housing Bolts	7

① — Plus an additional 1/4 (90°) turn.
② — Refer to "Cylinder Head, Replace."
③ — Plus an additional 1/2 (180°) turn.
④ — Coat threads with locking compound No. AMV 188 100 02, or equivalent.

2.8L Engine

NOTE: On Air Bag Equipped Models, Refer To "Air Bag System Precautions" Located In The Front Of This Manual For System Disarming & Arming Procedures.

INDEX

Page No.

Camshaft, Replace 49-41
Assemble 49-41
Disassemble 49-41
Compression Pressure 49-39
Cooling System Bleed 49-42
Crankshaft Rear Oil Seal, Replace 49-42
Crankshaft Seal, Replace 49-42
Cylinder Head, Replace 49-41
Engine Mount, Replace 49-39
Front 49-39
Left 49-40
Right 49-40
Engine Rebuilding Specifications 49-
Engine, Replace 49-40
Fuel Pump, Replace 49-42
Oil Pan, Replace 49-42
Oil Pump, Replace 49-42
Piston & Rod Assembly 49-42
Precautions 49-39
Air Bag Systems 49-39
Audio Coded Anti-Theft System . 49-39
Radiator, Replace 49-43
Tightening Specifications 49-44
Timing Chain, Replace 49-41
Valve Adjustment 49-41
Valve Clearance Specifications .. 49-41
Valve Guides 49-41
Inspection 49-41
Replacement 49-41
Valve Timing, Adjust 49-41
Water Pump, Replace 49-42

PRECAUTIONS

AIR BAG SYSTEMS

Refer to "Air Bag System Precautions" in the front of this manual for system disarming and arming procedures.

AUDIO CODED ANTI-THEFT SYSTEM

Some models are equipped with a radio anti-theft system that will disable the system when battery power is interrupted, unless the system is reset the radio will not operate.

1. Turn radio to On position, SAFE should be displayed.
2. Depress and hold AM/FM and SCAN buttons until 1000 remains on display. If AM/FM and SCAN buttons are depressed too long or depressed again, radio will misinterpret the 1000 as an attempt at coding and one incorrect coding attempt will be logged. **After two incorrect attempts to reset system, radio will lock up electronically. If this occurs, leave radio on for approximately one hour, then reset radio as if battery power were disconnected.**
3. Enter radio code using first four program station buttons. Security code will appear on display.
4. Depress and hold AM/FM and SCAN buttons again until SAFE is displayed.
5. Release AM/FM and SCAN buttons. Display should change to a radio frequency and operate normally.

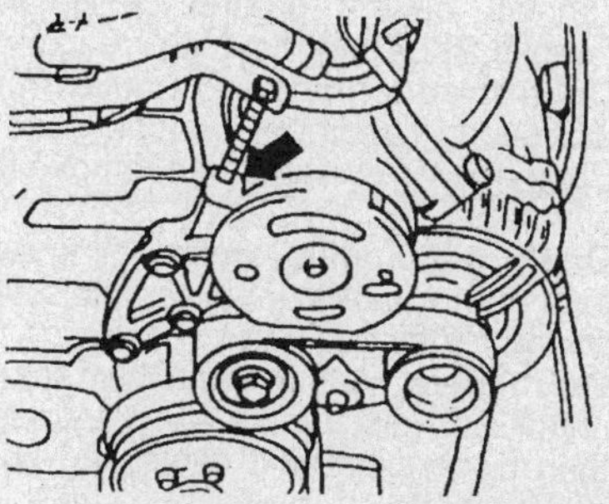

VW1069100021000X

Fig. 1 Belt tension release

COMPRESSION PRESSURE

1. Perform compression test with coolant temperature at minimum of 176°F, throttle plate completely open, fuse No. 18 removed and ignition coil lead removed from distributor.
2. Connect compression tester tool No. US 1120, or equivalent. Crank engine until gauge reaches highest level.
3. Correct compression specification is 160–189 psi with a maximum difference between cylinders of 43.5 psi. Minimum compression is 109 psi.

ENGINE MOUNT

REPLACE

FRONT

1. Attach engine lifting tool No. 2024A, or

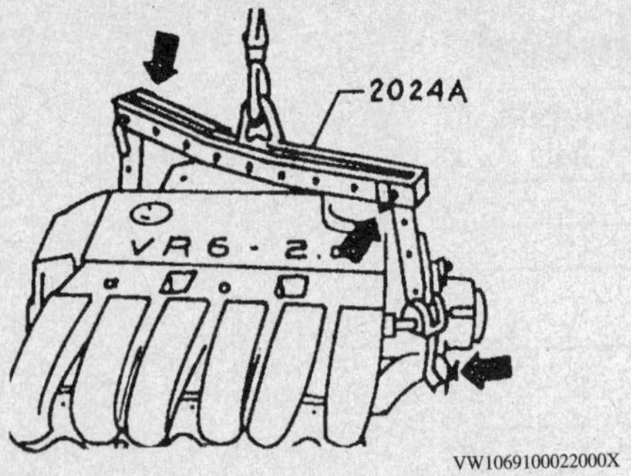
2024A
VR6 - 2.
VW1069100022000X

Fig. 2 Engine sling installation

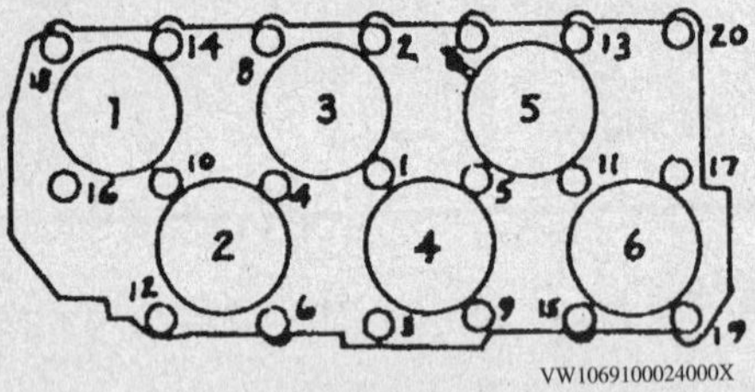
VW1069100024000X

Fig. 4 Cylinder head tightening sequence

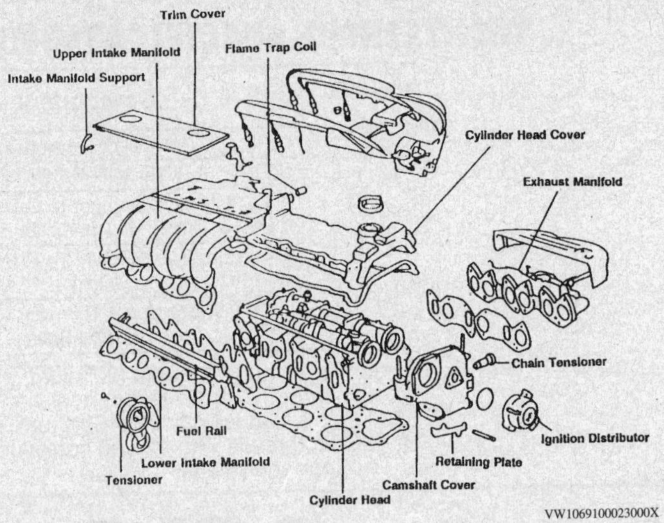
Trim Cover
Upper Intake Manifold
Flame Trap Coil
Intake Manifold Support
Cylinder Head Cover
Exhaust Manifold
Chain Tensioner
Fuel Rail
Ignition Distributor
Lower Intake Manifold
Retaining Plate
Tensioner
Camshaft Cover
Cylinder Head
VW1069100023000X

Fig. 3 Exploded view of cylinder head

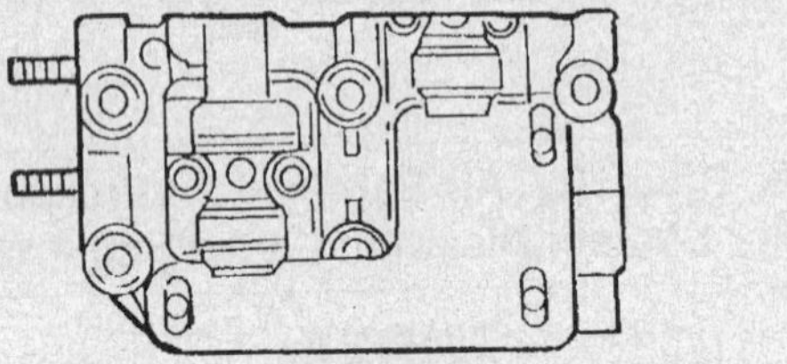
VW1069100025000X

Fig. 5 Camshaft guide tool

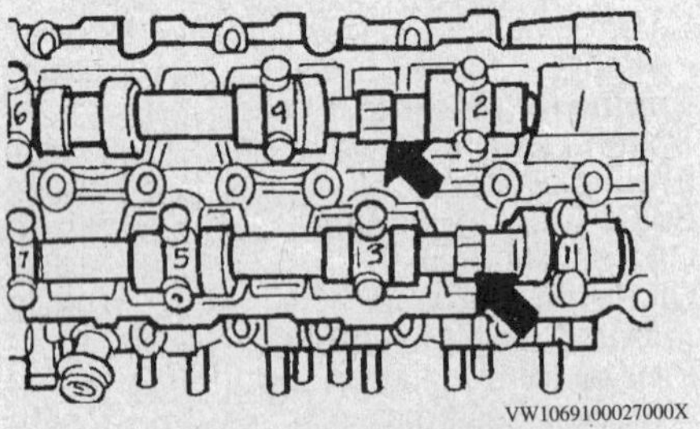
VW1069100027000X

Fig. 7 Camshaft bearing caps

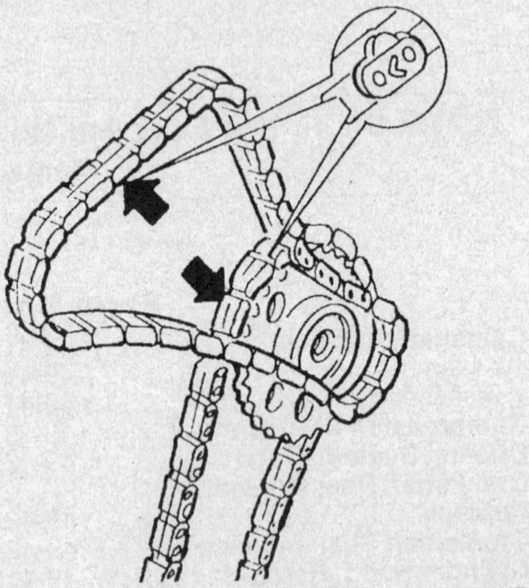
VW1069100026000X

Fig. 6 Running direction marking

equivalent, and loosen front engine mount center mounting bolt.

2. Raise engine and transaxle assembly until weight is off mount, then remove center bolt.
3. Remove center engine mount bolt, then remove subframe mounting bolts and engine mount.
4. Reverse procedure to install.

LEFT

1. Attach engine lifting tool No. 2024A, or equivalent, and loosen engine/transaxle center mount mounting bolt.
2. Raise engine and transaxle assembly until weight is off mount, then remove center mounting bolt.
3. Remove engine mount bolts from subframe, then engine mount.
4. Reverse procedure to install.

RIGHT

1. Attach engine lifting tool No. 2024A, or equivalent, and loosen center engine mount mounting bolt.
2. Raise engine and transaxle assembly until weight is off mount, then remove center mounting bolt.
3. Remove engine mount bolts from subframe, then engine mount.
4. Reverse procedure to install.

ENGINE

REPLACE

Wait at least 20 seconds after switching off ignition before disconnecting battery. This will allow the platinum hot wire in air mass sensor to burn itself clean.

Ensure the ignition switch is in the Off position whenever disconnecting or connecting battery or any part of Motronic ignition wiring system to prevent damage to Motronic control unit.

1. Obtain radio security code, ensure ignition switch is in Off position, then disconnect battery ground cable and remove air cleaner housing.
2. **On Corrado models,** remove front lock support and front bumper.
3. Drain cooling system, then remove radiator.
4. **On Passat models,** drain cooling system, then remove upper radiator support with attached parts.
5. **On models with manual transaxle,** unbolt and disconnect slave cylinder, then disconnect shift cable and support bracket.
6. **On models with automatic transaxle,** unclip and disconnect selector lever cable.
7. **On all models,** thread an 8 mm x 80 mm bolt into threaded hole on tensioner, **Fig. 1,** to release belt tension. **Thread in bolt only far enough to release tension on belt, otherwise, damage to tensioner may occur.**
8. Remove belt from power steering pump and A/C compressor, then the A/C compressor and secure to body or frame. **Do not disconnect or kink A/C refrigerant lines.**
9. Remove power steering pump from bracket and secure to body or frame. **Do not disconnect or kink power steering hoses.**
10. Remove ignition wire guides and ignition wires, then the distributor cap.
11. Remove cylinder head cover trim covers, then disconnect accelerator cable at throttle body and cable guide.
12. Disconnect 42-point electrical connector from engine electrical harness, then all other engine and transaxle electrical wiring as necessary, and position aside.
13. Disconnect all coolant, vacuum and intake hoses from engine, then the inlet and return fuel lines at fuel distributor. **Cap all open fuel lines.**
14. Disconnect oxygen sensor and front exhaust pipe, then the axle shafts and secure to body or frame.
15. Attach engine sling as shown in **Fig. 2,** then relieve engine weight using a suitable lift.
16. Unbolt engine from engine mounts, carefully guide engine and transaxle assembly from vehicle, then separate engine from transaxle.

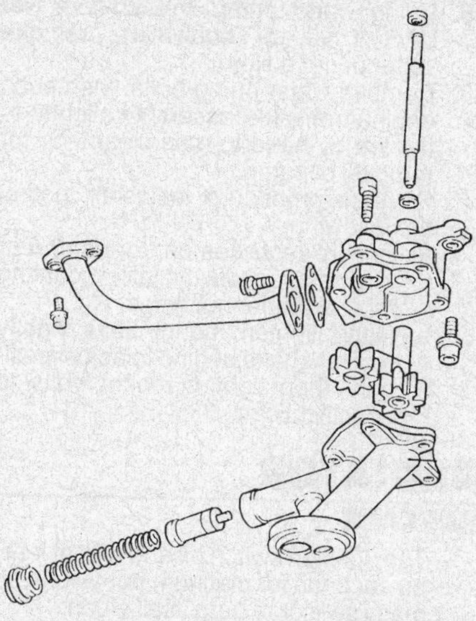

VW1099100001000X

Fig. 8 Oil pump pressure hose

17. Reverse procedure to install, noting the following:
    a. Ensure recesses on front and rear engine brackets fit into mounting tabs of rubber bushings.
    b. Hand tighten mount bolts, lightly rock or shake engine to adjust position, then tighten mount bolts to specifications.

CYLINDER HEAD

REPLACE

Prior to removing drive chains, mark direction of rotation with touch-up paint.

Refer to **Fig. 3** for cylinder head replacement, noting the following:

1. Adjust valve timing as outlined under "Valve Timing, Adjust," and tighten cylinder head bolts as follows:
    a. Install "new" cylinder head bolts hand tight.
    b. **Torque** bolts in sequence shown in **Fig. 4** to 29 ft. lbs.
    c. **Torque** bolts again in sequence shown in **Fig. 4** to 43 ft. lbs.
    d. **Torque** bolts again in sequence shown in **Fig. 4** an additional ½ (180°) turn.

VALVE TIMING

ADJUST

1. Rotate engine until piston for cylinder No. 1 is at TDC.
2. Align casting on sealing flange with TDC marking on flywheel, then remove ignition wire guides.
3. Remove upper intake manifold, then valve cover.
4. Install and align camshaft guide tool No. 3268, or equivalent onto cylinder head studs with both camshafts positioned snug in guide indentations, **Fig. 5. This alignment is only possible every second engine revolution.**

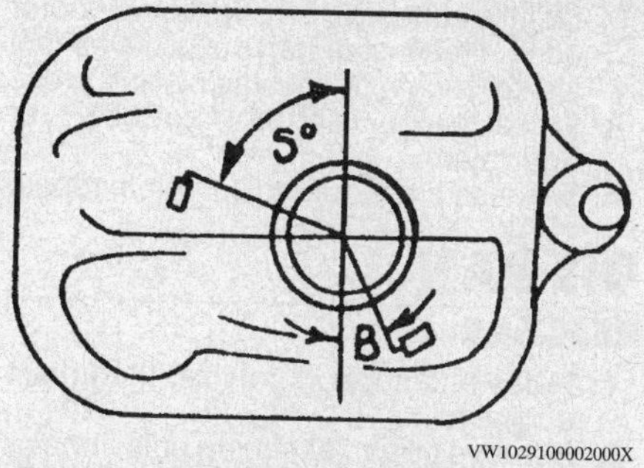

5°
B

VW1029100002000X

Fig. 9 Correct installation of fuel pump assembly

VALVE CLEARANCE SPECIFICATIONS

These engine are equipped with hydraulic lifters and no specifications are available.

VALVE ADJUSTMENT

These engines are equipped with hydraulic lifters. No procedure for adjustment is provided.

VALVE GUIDES

INSPECTION

1. Remove all carbon deposits from valve guide.
2. Position a dial indicator on cylinder head to check guides.
3. Insert new valve into valve guide. End of valve stem must be flush with valve guide end.
4. Rock valve back and forth against dial indicator.
5. Maximum clearance is .039 inch for intake valves and .051 inch for exhaust valves. Replace guide(s) if reading is not within specifications.

REPLACEMENT

1. Worn valve guides can be removed using rod tool No. 3121, or equivalent.
2. Lay cylinder head flat on work bench, then press guides out from combustion chamber side.
3. Coat new guides with engine oil, then press into cold cylinder head from camshaft side.
4. Press guides in as far as they will go. Once valve guide shoulder is seated, do not use more than one ton of pressure, or guide shoulder may break. Ream guides by hand using reamer tool No. 3120, or equivalent, and a proper cutting lubricant.
5. Machine valve seats.

TIMING CHAIN

REPLACE

Before removing timing chains, mark running direction using a felt tip pen at locations noted in **Fig. 6.**

1. Obtain audio coded anti-theft code, then disconnect battery ground cable.

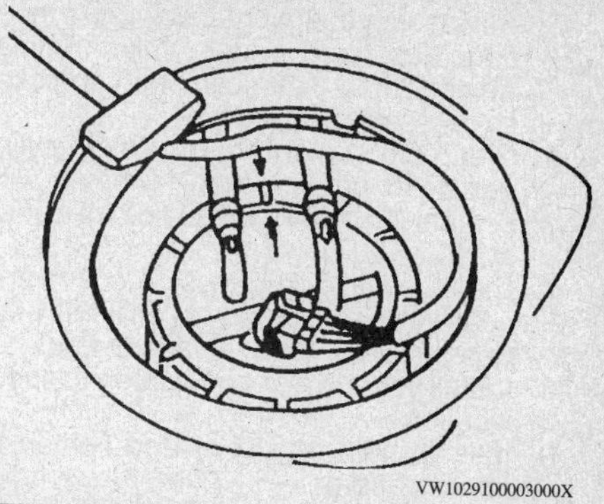

VW1029100003000X

Fig. 10 Fuel pump flange & tank alignment marks

2. Remove timing chain covers and valve cover.
3. Loosen all chain tensioners and remove, then sliding rail.
4. Remove camshaft sprockets, then timing chains.
5. Reverse procedure to install, tightening chain tensioners and sliding rail bolts to specifications.

CAMSHAFT

REPLACE

DISASSEMBLE

1. Obtain audio coded anti-theft code, then disconnect battery ground cable.
2. Remove ignition cable guide, then remove upper intake manifold. **Cover intake channels with a clean shop towel to avoid contamination.**
3. Set crankshaft to TDC on cylinder No. 1, then remove distributor.
4. Remove cylinder head cover and chain tensioner.
5. Remove camshaft sprocket cover, then the camshaft sprocket bolts.
6. **Before removing double chains, mark direction of rotation with touch-up paint.**
7. On cylinder Nos. 1, 3 & 5, proceed as follows:
    a. Remove bearing caps 1 and 7, **Fig. 7.**
    b. Remove bearing caps 3 and 5 alternately and diagonally.
8. On cylinder Nos. 2, 4 & 6 proceed as follows:
    a. Remove bearing cap 4.
    b. Loosen caps 2 and 6 alternately and diagonally.

ASSEMBLE

1. Install bearing caps ensuring marking can be read from exhaust manifold side and arrow points to vibration damper.
2. Install bearing caps 3 and 5 alternately and diagonally, then tighten to specifications.
3. Install bearing caps 1 and 7, then tighten to specifications.
4. Install bearing caps 2 and 6 alternately and diagonally, then tighten to specifications, then cap 4, and tighten to specifications.

5. Adjust valve timing following procedure described under "Valve Timing, Adjust," then clean camshaft sprocket cover sealing surface.
6. Clean old sealant from holes in cylinder head gasket, then fill holes with sealant No. AMV 188 001 02, or equivalent.
7. Clean sealing surfaces of cover and coat with sealant No. AMV 188 001 02, or equivalent, then replace O-ring.
8. Install valve cover and tighten to specifications.
9. Install chain tensioner and tighten to specifications.

PISTON & ROD ASSEMBLY

Mark installation portion and cylinder number. Install piston and rod assembly with highest side of piston crown facing center of cylinder block.

CRANKSHAFT SEAL

REPLACE

1. Remove ribbed belt, then using support bracket tool No. 3273, or equivalent, remove vibration dampener.
2. Unscrew inner portion of oil seal extractor tool No. 3203, or equivalent, three turns out of outer portion (approximately 4 mm) and lock in position with knurled screw.
3. Lubricate threaded head of oil seal extractor, place in position and push into seal as far as possible.
4. Loosen knurled screw, then turn inner part against crankshaft until oil seal is pulled out.
5. Clamp extractor in a vise and remove oil seal using pliers.
6. Lightly lubricate sealing lip and outer edge of new oil seal, then place guide sleeve from tool No. 3266/1, or equivalent, onto crankshaft pin and push oil seal over guide sleeve.
7. Press oil seal in with sleeve tool No. 3266, or equivalent, until stop using vibration dampener securing bolt.
8. Install vibration dampener using support bracket and tighten to specifications.
9. Install ribbed belt.

CRANKSHAFT REAR OIL SEAL

REPLACE

1. Obtain radio code and disconnect battery ground cable.
2. Raise and support vehicle then remove transaxle and clutch following procedure described under "Clutch, Replace."
3. Use flywheel holding tool No. 58, or equivalent, remove flywheel bolts, then remove flywheel.
4. **On models with automatic transaxle,** remove torque converter.
5. **On all models,** using seal puller tool No. 2086, or equivalent, remove crankshaft seal.
6. Lightly lubricate new seal lip and outer edge, then install with pull sleeves tool No. 2003/2A, or equivalent, and press in seal to stop using tool No. 2003/1, or equivalent.
7. Reverse procedure to complete repair.

OIL PAN

REPLACE

1. Raise and support vehicle, then drain engine oil.
2. Remove oil pan attaching nuts, then oil pan.
3. Reverse procedure to install.

OIL PUMP

REPLACE

1. Raise and support vehicle, then drain engine oil.
2. Remove oil pan following procedure described under "Oil Pan, Replace."
3. Remove attaching bolts from oil pressure hose to crankcase housing, **Fig. 8.**
4. Remove attaching bolts from oil pump to crankcase housing, then lower oil pump.
5. Reverse procedure to install.

COOLING SYSTEM BLEED

1. Slowly fill coolant expansion tank to Max mark, then install expansion tank cap.
2. Run engine until cooling fan comes on, then check coolant level.
3. Coolant level should be slightly above Max mark with engine at normal operating temperature, and between Min and Max marks with engine cold.
4. If necessary, add coolant to specified marking.

WATER PUMP

REPLACE

Wait at least 20 seconds after switching off ignition before disconnecting battery. This will allow the platinum hot wire in air mass sensor to burn itself clean.

Ensure the ignition switch is in the Off position whenever disconnecting or connecting battery or any part of Motronic ignition wiring system to prevent damage to Motronic control unit.

1. Obtain radio security code, then ensure ignition switch is in Off position and disconnect battery ground cable.
2. Drain cooling system, then disconnect front exhaust pipe at flange to catalyst.
3. Remove ribbed belt, then disconnect engine with bracket from front and rear rubber engine mounts.
4. Disconnect transaxle with bracket from rear transaxle rubber mount, then remove ignition cable guide.
5. Attach engine sling as shown in **Fig. 2,** then lift engine with transaxle using a suitable lift, to gain access to water pump.
6. Using water pump wrench tool No. VAG 1590, or equivalent, remove water pump pulley.
7. Remove water pump bolts, then push engine/transaxle assembly slightly to the left by hand to gain clearance for removal of pump.
8. Reverse procedure to install, noting the following:
   a. Ensure recesses on front and rear engine brackets fit into mounting tabs of rubber bushings.
   b. Hand tighten mount bolts, lightly rock or shake engine to adjust position, then tighten mount bolts to specifications.

RADIATOR

REPLACE

1. Turn ignition switch off and wait at least 20 seconds for platinum hot-wire in air mass sensor to burn itself clean.
2. Disconnect battery cables and remove battery.
3. Drain engine coolant.
4. Disconnect coolant hoses from radiator.
5. Disconnect thermo switch and cooling fan.
6. Remove radiator mounting bolts.
7. Remove front bumper.
8. Remove hood lock support.
9. **On models with A/C,** separate condenser from radiator and pull forward as far as possible.
10. **On all models,** remove radiator from top.
11. Reverse procedure to install.

FUEL PUMP

REPLACE

Wait at least 20 seconds after switching off ignition before disconnecting battery. This will allow the platinum hot wire in air mass sensor to burn itself clean.

Ensure the ignition switch is in the Off position whenever disconnecting or connecting battery or any part of Motronic ignition wiring system to prevent damage to Motronic control unit.

1. Obtain radio security code, ensure ignition switch is in Off position, then disconnect battery ground cable.
2. Remove cover plate in luggage compartment floor, then disconnect electrical connector and fuel lines from flange.
3. Unscrew flange nut using spanner tool No. 3217, or equivalent, then withdraw flange and O-ring from fuel tank.
4. Reverse procedure to install, noting the following:
   a. Ensure sender is not bent when installing.
   b. Fuel pump assembly is correctly installed when sender float angle from direction of travel A, **Fig. 9,** is 5°.
   c. Coat flange O-ring with fuel, then install flange with mark on flange aligned with mark on fuel tank, **Fig. 10.**

TIGHTENING SPECIFICATIONS

Year	Component	Torque/Ft. Lbs.
1993–96	Camshaft Sprocket Bolts	74
	Camshaft Sprocket Cover Bolts	18
	Connecting Rod Bolts	22①
	Cylinder Head Bolts	②
	Cylinder Head Cover Nuts	7
	Double Drive Chain Sprocket Bolt	74
	Driveshaft To Flange Bolts	33
	Engine Mounts To Engine Bolts	44
	Engine Mounts To Engine Rubber Mounts Bolt	44
	Engine Rubber Mount To Bracket Bolt, Front	41
	Engine Rubber Mount To Bracket Bolts, Right	18
	Engine Support To Body Bolts	37
	Engine To Transmission Bolts, M10	44
	Engine To Transmission Bolts, M12	59
	Flywheel Bolts	22③
	Front Crankshaft Seal Flange Bolts	7
	Front Crankshaft Seal Flange Bolts	15
	Front Crankshaft Seal Mounting Flange Bolts	18
	Front Exhaust Pipe To Catalytic Converter Bolts	18
	Front Exhaust Pipe To Exhaust Manifold Bolts	30
	Intermediate Shaft Guide Ring Bolts	7
	Main Bearing Cap Bolts	48
	Oil Cooler Cover Bolt	18
	Oil Drain Plug	37
	Oil Filter Housing Bolt	15
	Oil Injection Nozzle Bolts	87④
	Oil Pan Bolts	15
	Oil Pump Drive Cover Bolts	7
	Oil Pump To Block Bolts	18
	Oil Pressure Relief Valve To Block	44④
	Oil Pressure Switch	18
	Oil Temperature Sender	7
	Pressure Plate To Flywheel Bolts	15
	Rear Crankshaft Seal Flange Bolts	7
	Ribbed Belt Tension Roller Bolts	18
	Speed/Reference Sender Bolt	7
	Thermostat Housing Bolts	7
	Timing Chain Guide Rail Bolts	15
	Timing Chain Locating Pin w/Collar	18
	Timing Chain Pivot Pin	18
	Timing Chain Tensioner Bolt	15
	Timing Chain Tensioner w/Plate Bolts	7
	Transmission Mount To Transmission Bolts	18
	Transmission Mount To Transmission Rubber Mount Bolts	44
	Transmission Rubber Mount To Bracket Bolts	22

Continued

TIGHTENING SPECIFICATIONS—Continued

Year	Component	Torque/Ft. Lbs.
1993–96	Upper Intake Manifold Bolts	18
	Vibration Dampener Bolt	328
	Water Pump Bolts	15
	Water Pump Pulley To Water Pump Nuts	18

① — Plus an additional ½ (180°) turn.
② — Refer to "Cylinder Head, Replace."
③ — Plus an additional ¼ (90°) turn.
④ — Inch lbs.

1.9L Turbocharged Direct Injection (TDI) Diesel Engine

NOTE: On Air Bag Equipped Models, Refer To "Air Bag System Precautions" Located In The Front Of This Manual For System Disarming & Arming Procedures.

INDEX

	Page No.
Camshaft, Replace	49-46
Compression Pressure	49-44
Cooling System Bleed	49-47
Crankshaft Rear Oil Seal, Replace	49-47
Cylinder Head, Replace	49-45
Engine Mount, Replace	49-45
Engine Rebuilding Specifications	49-148
Engine, Replace	49-45
Front Main Bearing Oil Seal, Replace	49-47
Fuel Filter, Replace	49-48
Fuel Injection System	49-49
Fuel Shutoff Solenoid	49-49
Fuel Supply	49-49
Injection Pump	49-49
Injectors	49-49
Throttle Position Sensor	49-50
Glow Plug System	49-51
Testing	49-51
Hydraulic Lifter Inspection	49-45
Hydraulic Lifter, Replace	49-46
Idle Speed, Adjust	49-51
Injection Pump, Replace	49-48
Injection Pump Timing	49-48
Basic Injection Pump Timing	49-48
Dynamic Injection Pump Timing	49-48
Main & Rod Bearings	49-47
Oil Pan, Replace	49-47
Oil Pump Service	49-47
Oil Pump, Replace	49-47
Piston & Rod Assembly	49-46
Precautions	49-44
Air Bag Systems	49-44
Audio Coded Anti-Theft System	49-44
Radiator, Replace	49-48
Tightening Specifications	49-51
Timing Belt, Replace	49-46
Turbocharger, Replace	49-48
Valve Adjustment	49-45
Valve Clearance Specifications	49-45
Valve Guides	49-46
Inspection	49-46
Replacement	49-46
Water Pump, Replace	49-47

PRECAUTIONS

AIR BAG SYSTEMS

Refer to "Air Bag System Precautions" in the front of this manual for system disarming and arming procedures.

AUDIO CODED ANTI-THEFT SYSTEM

Some models are equipped with a radio anti-theft system that will disable the system when battery power is interrupted, unless the system is reset the radio will not operate.

1. Turn radio to On position, SAFE should be displayed.
2. Depress and hold AM/FM and SCAN buttons until 1000 remains on display. If AM/FM and SCAN buttons are depressed too long or depressed again, radio will misinterpret the 1000 as an attempt at coding and one incorrect coding attempt will be logged. **After two incorrect attempts to reset system, radio will lock up electronically. If this occurs, leave radio on for approximately one hour, then reset radio as if battery power were disconnected.**
3. Enter radio code using first four program station buttons. Security code will appear on display.
4. Depress and hold AM/FM and SCAN buttons again until SAFE is displayed.
5. Release AM/FM and SCAN buttons. Display should change to a radio frequency and operate normally.

COMPRESSION PRESSURE

1. Perform compression test with engine at normal operating temperature and coolant temperature at least 176°F.
2. Disconnect electrical wire from stop solenoid on injection pump and insulate end of wire.
3. Clean all unions and area near connections, then disconnect injector fuel lines using wrench tool No. 3035, or equivalent.
4. Remove all injectors and heat shields.
5. Mount suitable adapter tool in place of injectors, then insert old heat shield

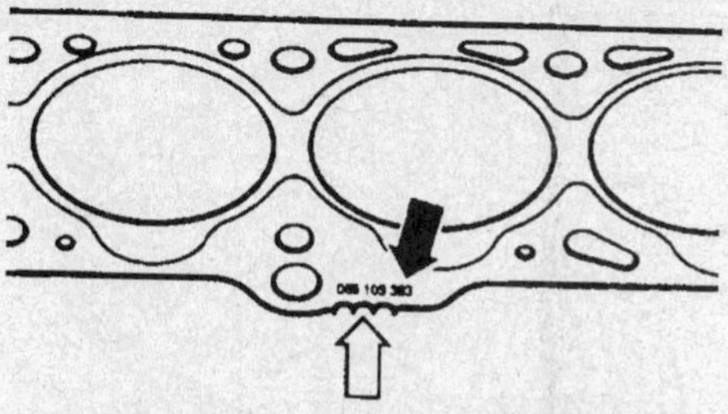
VW1069600049000X

Fig. 1 Cylinder head gasket selection

between adapter and cylinder head.

6. Screw compression tester tool No. VW 1381, or equivalent, into adapter by hand.
7. Operate starter until compression tester indicates no further rise in pressure.
8. Correct compression is 493 psi, with a maximum difference of 72.5 psi between highest and lowest cylinder. Minimum compression is 406 psi.
9. Install injectors and new heat shields. **Torque** injector retainers to specifications.
10. Connect injector fuel lines and **torque** to 18 ft. lbs.
11. Connect wire to stop solenoid on injection pump.
12. Start engine and accelerate several times to clear air bubbles.

ENGINE MOUNT

REPLACE

Refer to "1.8L & 2.0L Engines" for information and procedures.

ENGINE

REPLACE

Refer to "1.8L & 2.0L Engines" for information and procedures.

CYLINDER HEAD

REPLACE

With the timing belt removed, avoid turning the camshaft or crankshaft. If movement is required, exercise extreme caution to avoid valve damage caused by piston contact.

During the following procedure, the engine coolant must be drained completely and discarded. Refer to "Specifications" for cooling system capacities. **Do not reuse contaminated coolant.**

1. Obtain audio coded anti-theft code, then disconnect battery ground cable. Remove air cleaner and intercooler duct assembly.
2. Identify cylinder head gasket thickness by noting part number (black arrow) or number of notches/holes (white arrow), **Fig. 1.**
3. Remove expansion tank cap and drain cooling system by removing thermostat.
4. Disconnect all coolant hoses from cylinder head, then crankcase ventilation hoses which interfere with head removal.
5. Disconnect wiring harness connectors to temperature sensors and glow plugs, and remove wiring harness from cylinder head.
6. Disconnect and remove injector fuel pipe assemblies as a unit, then plug open fittings. **Do not alter shape of fuel pipe assemblies.**
7. If cylinder head is to be replaced, remove fuel injectors and glow plugs, then plug openings in cylinder head.
8. **Note No. 3 injector contains needle lift sensor and must be installed into No. 3 cylinder.**
9. Remove timing belt as outlined under "Timing Belt, Replace." **Do not rotate crankshaft or camshaft with timing belt removed, as engine damage may result.**
10. Raise and support vehicle. Disconnect exhaust pipe, oil drain lines and fittings from turbocharger, then lower vehicle.
11. Remove cylinder head retaining bolts in reverse order of tightening sequence, **Fig. 2.**
12. Ensure hoses, cables and wiring harness components are disconnected from cylinder head and that camshaft is properly secured, then remove head.
13. Remove camshaft as outlined in "Camshaft, Replace."
14. Remove lifters, noting original position if cam or head is to be reused, then valves, valve springs and valve guide seals using a suitable valve spring compressor.
15. Check valve guides as outlined in "Valve Guides, Inspection."
16. Thoroughly clean cylinder head and check for cracks. Check gasket surface for flatness. **Diesel engine cylinder heads cannot be resurfaced. If more than .004 inch warpage is measured, cylinder head must be replaced.**
17. The following procedure is used only when engine block or components are replaced or original gasket thickness cannot be determined. Check piston deck height to determine head gasket thickness as follows:
    a. Ensure TDC mark on flywheel is aligned with pointer, and measure piston projection using a dial indicator.
    b. Select head gasket thickness according to next step. **Cylinder head gaskets can be identified by part number and notches in edge of gasket. Install gasket with "OBEN" marking toward cylinder head.**
    c. With piston projection .0260–.0341 inch, one notch should be indicated, .0341–.0356 inch, two notches should be indicated and with piston projection .0356–.0402 inch, three notches should be indicated.
18. Install cylinder head gasket without sealer, ensure camshaft is locked and TDC mark on flywheel is properly aligned with pointer.

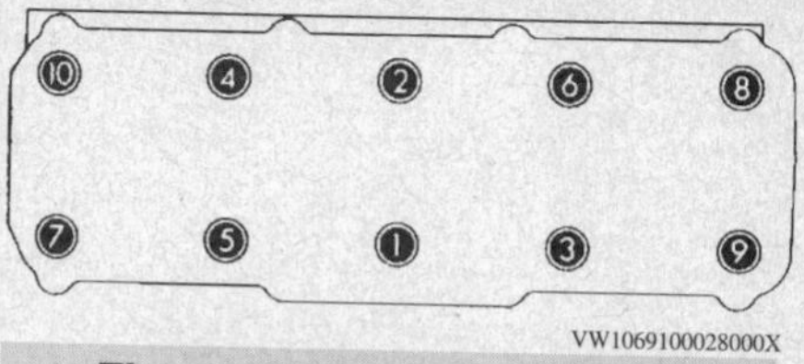
10
4
2
6
8
7
5
1
3
9
VW1069100028000X

Fig. 2 Cylinder head bolt tightening sequence

19. To aid in cylinder head and gasket alignment, insert guide pins from kit No. 3070, or equivalent, in outer holes on intake manifold side.
20. Mount cylinder head, insert bolts 1 through 7 and 9, **Fig. 2,** and tighten by hand.
21. Remove guide pins with tool from kit No. 3070, or equivalent, then install bolts 8 and 10.
22. Using sequence shown in **Fig. 2, torque** cylinder head bolts in four steps as follows (engine cold): first, to 30 ft. lbs.; second, to 44 ft. lbs.; third, tighten an additional 1/4 (90°) turn; and finally, tighten an additional 1/4 (90°) turn.
23. Reverse procedure to complete installation. Ensure injection pump timing is within specifications as outlined under "Injection Pump Timing."

VALVE CLEARANCE SPECIFICATIONS

These engines are equipped with hydraulic lifters. No procedure for adjustment is provided.

VALVE ADJUSTMENT

These engines are equipped with hydraulic lifters. No procedure for adjustment is provided.

HYDRAULIC LIFTER INSPECTION

Hydraulic valve lifters are non-adjustable. Noisy lifters may be replaced after the following check.

1. Run engine until radiator fan comes on at least once.
2. Raise engine speed to 2500 RPM, for two minutes.
3. If lifter(s) is still noisy, proceed as follows:
    a. Remove cylinder head cover.
    b. Turn crankshaft pulley bolt clockwise until cam lobes of cylinder to be checked, point upward.
    c. Press down lightly against valve lifter with a wooden stick. If lifter can be pushed down more than .004 inch (.1 mm), replace as outlined under "Hydraulic Lifter, Replace."

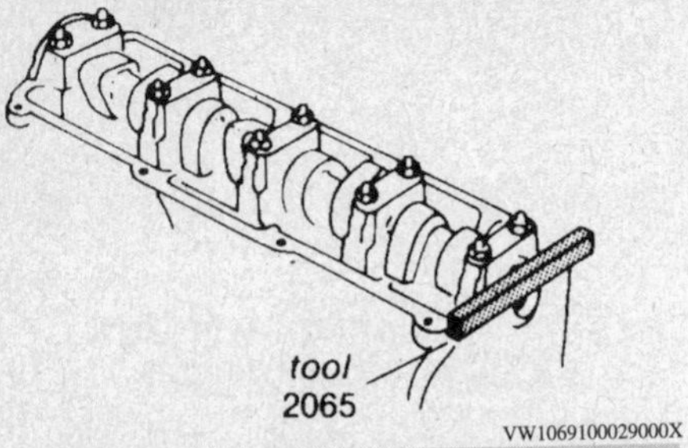
tool
2065
VW1069100029000X

Fig. 3 Camshaft locking tool installation

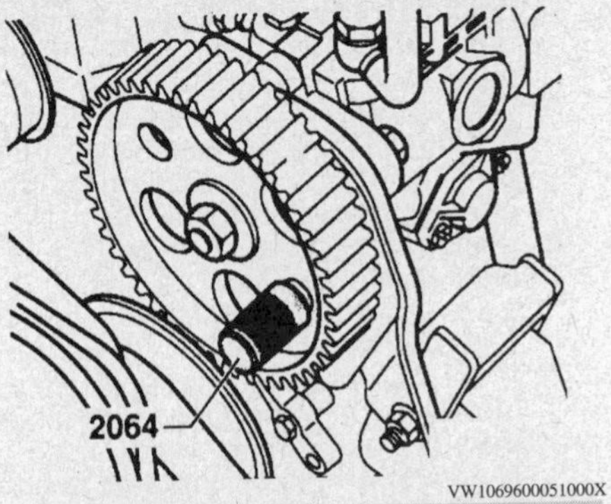
2064
VW1069600051000X

Fig. 4 Lockpin installation

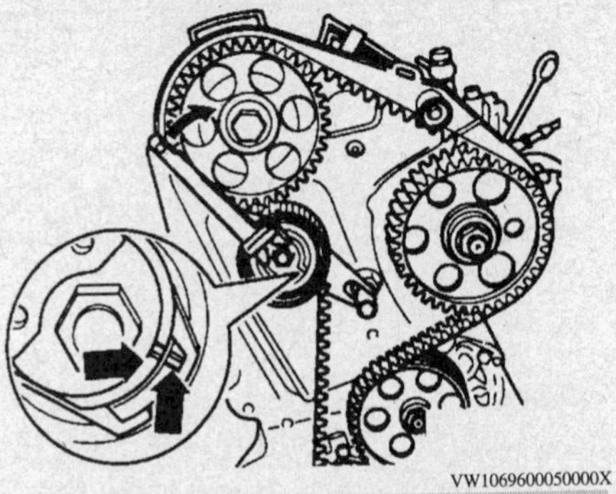
VW1069600050000X

Fig. 5 Timing belt tensioning

VALVE GUIDES

INSPECTION

1. Remove all carbon deposits from valve guide.
2. Set up a dial indicator on cylinder head to check suspected guide.
3. Insert new valve into valve guide. End of valve stem must be flush with valve guide end.
4. Rock valve back and forth against dial indicator.
5. Maximum is .051 inch for all valves. Replace guide(s) if reading is beyond limit.

REPLACEMENT

1. Worn valve guides can be removed using rod tool No. 10-206, or equivalent.
2. Press guides with collar out from combustion chamber side of cylinder head and worn guides out from camshaft side of cylinder head.
3. Coat new guides with engine oil, then press into cold cylinder head from camshaft side.
4. Press guides in as far as they will go. Once valve guide shoulder is seated, do not use more than one ton of pressure, or guide shoulder may break. Ream guides by hand using reamer tool No. 10-206, or equivalent, and a proper cutting lubricant.
5. Machine valve seats.

HYDRAULIC LIFTER

REPLACE

After replacing hydraulic lifters, do not run engine for 30 minutes. This will allow lifters time to bleed down to proper adjustment.

1. Remove camshaft(s) as outlined under "Camshaft, Replace."
2. Replace defective lifter(s).
3. Install camshaft(s) as outlined under "Camshaft, Replace."

TIMING BELT

REPLACE

With the timing belt removed, avoid turning the camshaft or crankshaft. If movement is required, exercise extreme caution to avoid valve damage caused by piston contact.

1. Remove drive belts to allow access to crankshaft pulley.
2. Remove upper timing belt cover, then the cylinder head cover.
3. **Do not rotate engine opposite normal direction of rotation (counterclockwise) using crankshaft center bolt, as torque setting may be disturbed allowing sprocket to loosen.**
4. Rotate crankshaft until cylinder No. 1 is at TDC compression stroke, **Fig. 3**, then lock camshaft using setting bar tool No. 2065A, or equivalent, on rear of camshaft. Align setting bar as follows:
   a. Turn camshaft until one end of setting bar touches cylinder head.
   b. Measure gap at other end of setting bar with a feeler gauge.
   c. Take half of measurement and insert a shim of this thickness between setting bar and cylinder head.
   d. Turn camshaft so that setting bar rests on shim.
   e. Insert a second shim of same thickness between other end of setting bar and cylinder head.
5. Insert locking pin No. 2064, or equivalent, into injector pump sprocket, **Fig. 4.** Ensure marks on sprocket, pump and bracket are properly aligned. Refer to "Injection Pump Timing."
6. Remove water pump pulley and crankshaft pulley. Note position of offset bolt hole for crankshaft pulley mounting to crankshaft sprocket.
7. Remove lower timing belt covers, then, if equipped, any timing belt guides.
8. Loosen timing belt tensioner and remove belt. **Do not rotate camshaft or crankshaft with belt removed, as engine damage will result.**
9. Prior to installation, ensure all timing marks are properly aligned and injection pump mounting bolts are centered in elongated holes of mounting bracket.
10. Loosen camshaft sprocket retaining bolt ½ turn and loosen sprocket on taper shaft by tapping with a hammer.
11. Install timing belt, tighten camshaft sprocket retaining bolt to specifications, then remove camshaft locking bar.
12. Remove locking pin from injection pump sprocket.
13. Adjust belt tension by turning tensioner until marks are aligned, **Fig. 5,** then tighten retaining nut to specification.
14. Check that injection pump timing is within specifications as outlined under "Injection Pump Timing," then reverse procedure to complete installation.

CAMSHAFT

REPLACE

With the timing belt removed, avoid turning the camshaft or crankshaft. If movement is required, exercise extreme caution to avoid valve damage caused by piston contact.

1. Remove timing belt as outlined under "Timing Belt, Replace."
2. Remove bearing caps 1, 3 and 5, then diagonally loosen caps 2 and 4.
3. Remove bearing caps 2 and 4, then the camshaft.
4. Install new camshaft with lobes for cylinder No. 1 facing upwards, then oil bearing surfaces.
5. Install bearing caps 2 and 4, noting offset and tighten to specifications diagonally.
6. Install bearing caps 1, 3 and 5. Locate bearing cap 5 by tapping lightly on end of camshaft.
7. Tighten bearing caps 1, 3 and 5 to specifications, then reinstall timing belt as outlined under "Timing Belt, Replace."

PISTON & ROD ASSEMBLY

1. Prior to removal, mark pistons and rods to match cylinder number.
2. Remove circlips from piston, press pin out by hand and separate assembly. **If pin is too tight in bore, heat piston to approximately 140°F.**
3. Check piston to cylinder wall clearance at right angles to piston pin, ⅜ inch from top and bottom and in center of travel.
4. Ensure ring end gaps are within specifications found under "Engine Rebuilding Specifications" by installing ring approximately 9/16 inch from top of cylinder and centering with an inverted piston.

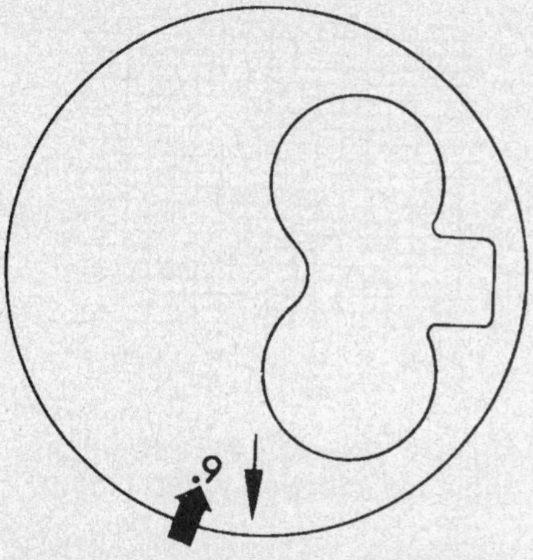
.9

VW1069100031000X

Fig. 6 Piston installation. Piston marked ".9" in direction of installation

5. Assemble piston and rod combinations with casting marks on rod and markings on piston crown, **Fig. 6,** facing timing belt. **If piston pin is tight in pin bore, heat piston to approximately 140°F to aid installation. Ensure pin attaching locks are properly seated.**
6. Install piston rings with TOP markings-facing piston crown. Side clearance for compression rings should measure .002–.004 inch on upper rings and .002–.003 inch on lower rings and must not exceed .008 inch. Side clearance for oil rings should measure .001–.002 inch and must not exceed .006 inch.
7. Install assemblies with piston marking facing timing belt, using a ring compressor. Ensure connecting rod side clearance is less than .004 inch. **Ensure "stretch" type connecting rod bolts are used. Bolts are not reusable, and must be replaced during assembly. During installation, tighten nuts to specified value, then turn each nut an additional ½ turn to obtain proper stretch.**

MAIN & ROD BEARINGS

Main and connecting rod bearings are available in .010 inch, .020 inch and .030 inch undersizes.

CRANKSHAFT REAR OIL SEAL

REPLACE

1. **On models with manual transaxle,** remove transaxle, flywheel, pressure plate, clutch disc and intermediate plate as outlined under "Clutch & Manual Transmission/Transaxle."
2. **On models with automatic transaxle,** remove transaxle, torque converter and torque converter driveplate

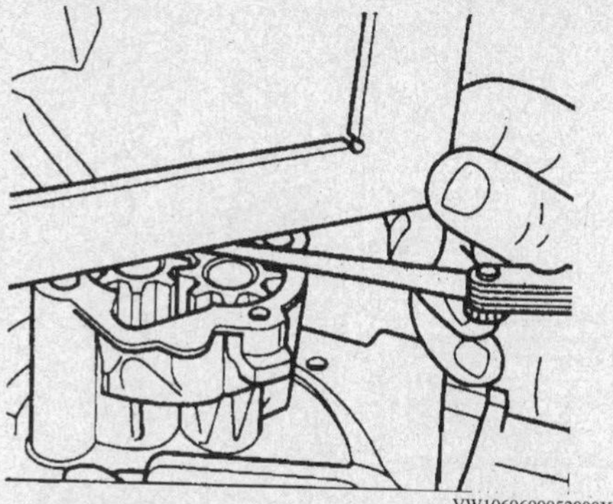

VW1069600052000X

Fig. 7 Oil pump wear check

as outlined under "Automatic Transmission/Transaxle."
3. **On all models,** pry oil seal out of oil seal flange using a screwdriver, or equivalent.
4. Lubricate new seal, center seal in seal flange and press until fully seated.
5. Reverse procedure to complete installation.

FRONT MAIN BEARING OIL SEAL

REPLACE

1. Remove timing belt as outlined under "Timing Belt, Replace."
2. Remove crankshaft sprocket retaining bolt, then sprocket. **Do not allow crankshaft to turn as piston valve contact will occur.**
3. Using a suitable tool, remove oil seal.
4. Lightly lubricate sealing lip and outer edge of new oil seal.
5. Place suitable guide sleeve onto crankshaft, then push oil seal over guide sleeve.
6. Using a suitable tool, press oil seal in until it reaches stop.
7. Reverse procedure to install. Tighten to specifications.

OIL PAN

REPLACE

1. Remove oil pan drain plug and drain engine oil.
2. Disconnect oil return line from turbocharger.
3. Remove oil pan to engine attaching bolts, then the oil pan, discarding gasket.
4. Reverse procedure to install, using new sealing washers. Tighten to specification.

OIL PUMP

REPLACE

1. Remove oil pan as outlined under "Oil Pan, Replace."
2. Remove oil pump pick-up tube retaining bolts.
3. Remove oil pump mounting bolts, then pump.
4. Reverse procedure to install, noting the following

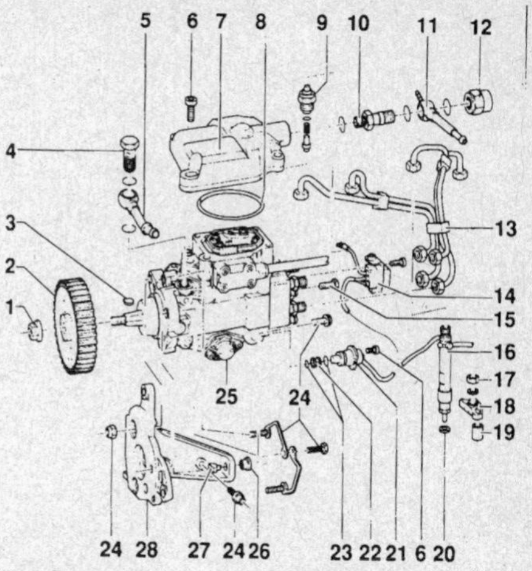
5 6 7 8 9 10 11 12
4
3
2
1
13
14
15
16
17
18
19
25 24
24 28 27 24 26 23 22 21 6 20

1-Sprocket Nut
2-Sprocket
3-Woodruff Key
4-Banjo Bolt Fuel Inlet
5-Fuel Inlet Line
6-Pump Cover Bolt
7-Pump Cover
8-Gasket
9-Fuel Shut Off Valve
10-Union/Reducer
11-Fuel Return Line
12-Cap Nut Fuel Return
13-Fuel Injector Pipe Set
14-Connector
15-Bolt
16-Fuel Injector
17-Nut
18-Injector Retainer
19-Spacer
20-Injector Heat Shield
21-Cold Start Injector
22-Strainer
23-O-ring
24-Bolt
25-Timing Control Cover
26-Tapered Sleeve
27-Tapered Nut
28-Pump Mount

VW1029600069000X

Fig. 8 Exploded view of injection system components. TDI diesel

a. Tighten to specifications.
b. Ensure oil pump driveshaft is properly engaged into vacuum pump drive.

OIL PUMP SERVICE

1. Remove oil pump cover plate and inspect plate for excessive wear.
2. Using a suitable feeler gauge, **Fig. 7,** check oil pump for gear backlash and endplay.
3. Refer to "Engine Rebuilding Specifications" for data.

COOLING SYSTEM BLEED

1. Slowly fill coolant expansion tank to Max mark, then install expansion tank cap.
2. Run engine until cooling fan comes on, then check coolant level.
3. Coolant level should be at or slightly above Max mark with engine at normal operating temperature, and between Min and Max marks with engine cold.
4. If necessary, add coolant to specified marking.

WATER PUMP

REPLACE

Refer to "1.8L & 2.0L Engines" for information and procedures.

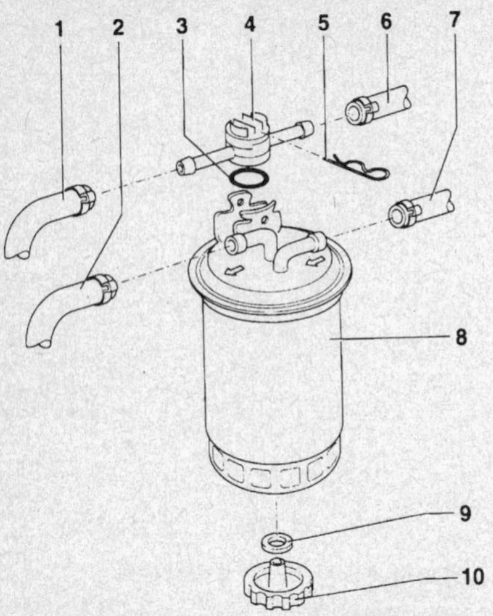
1
2
3
4
5
6
7
8
9
10

1-Fuel Return Line
2-Fuel Supply Line
3-O-Ring
4-Control Valve
5-Securing Clip
6-Fuel Return Line
7-Fuel Supply Line
8-Filter Element
9-Water Drain Gasket
10-Water Drain Plug

VW1029600070000X

Fig. 9 Fuel filter replacement

RADIATOR

REPLACE

1. Disconnect battery ground cable.
2. Drain engine coolant.
3. Remove radiator mounts.
4. Disconnect coolant hoses from radiator.
5. Disconnect coolant expansion tank tube from radiator.
6. Disconnect all radiator electrical connections.
7. Lift out radiator with cooling fan and shroud.
8. Separate cooling fan with shroud from radiator.
9. Reverse procedure to install.

TURBOCHARGER

REPLACE

1. Obtain audio coded anti-theft code, disconnect battery ground cable, then exhaust pipe from turbocharger.
2. Disconnect oil supply line and mounting clamp, then remove air hose between intake manifold/turbocharger and turbocharger/intercooler.
3. Disconnect oil return line from oil pan and support bracket on cylinder block, then remove mounting bolts and turbocharger from top.
4. Reverse procedure to install, noting the following:
   a. Tighten nuts and bolts to specifications.
   b. Prior to connecting oil supply line, fill connection on turbocharger with engine oil.
   c. After installing turbocharger, let engine idle for approximately one minute.

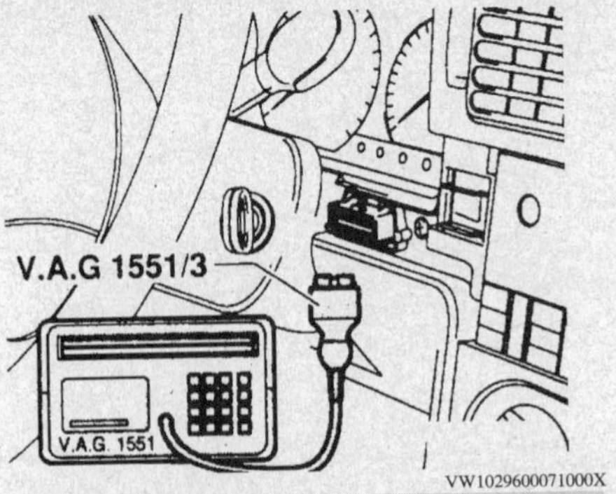
V.A.G 1551/3
V.A.G. 1551

VW1029600071000X

Fig. 10 Scan tool connection

INJECTION PUMP

REPLACE

1. Remove timing belt as outlined under "Timing Belt, Replace."
2. Loosen injection pump sprocket retaining bolt slightly, **Fig. 8.**
3. Install puller tool No. VW203b, or equivalent, so that jaws are at 90° angle to crossbar and facing direction of spindle rotation.
4. Carefully apply pressure to sprocket and tap puller spindle with a light hammer until sprocket is released from shaft taper. **Do not apply excessive force with puller, as sprocket at pump shaft will be damaged.**
5. Remove puller, retaining bolt and sprocket.
6. Disconnect fuel pipe assembly from pump and plug lines and open fittings.
7. Disconnect wiring connections from pump.
8. Remove lower bolt securing pump mounting plate, bolts securing pump to mounting plate and braces (if equipped) and remove pump. **Do not loosen bolts on fuel distributor head, as distributor will be damaged.**
9. Install pump on mounting bracket with marks on pump and bracket aligned. Tighten bolts to specifications.
10. Install pump sprocket and tighten retaining bolt to specifications. Align mark on pump sprocket with marks on pump and bracket and lock position with pin 2064.
11. Install timing belt as outlined under "Timing Belt, Replace." Check injection timing as outlined under "Injection Pump Timing."
12. Reverse procedure to complete installation.

FUEL FILTER

REPLACE

The filter element should be replaced at normal maintenance intervals to ensure reliable operation of the pump and injectors.

1. Remove securing clip, **Fig. 9,** then remove fuel return control valve from filter. Discard sealing O-ring.
2. Disconnect fuel supply lines from filter.
3. Fill new filter with clean diesel fuel (no further priming should be necessary when filter is full of fuel), replace filter.
4. Install new fuel return control valve O-ring, then valve and securing clip.
5. Connect and properly clamp fuel supply lines to filter.
6. Start engine, allow to idle until air self bleeds from filter, then check for fuel leaks at connections.

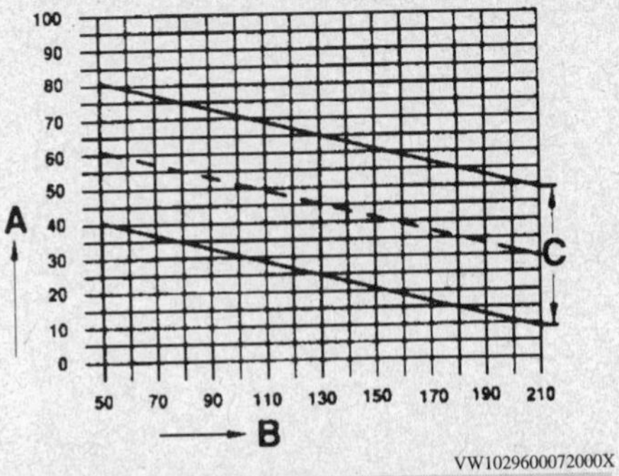
100
90
80
70
60
50
40
30
20
10
0
A
C
50
70
90
110
130
150
170
190
210
B

VW1029600072000X

Fig. 11 Temperature correction table for injection pump timing

INJECTION PUMP TIMING

BASIC INJECTION PUMP TIMING

1. Remove upper belt cover.
2. Set engine to TDC compression stroke as outlined under "Timing Belt, Replace."
3. Ensure marks on pump body and on pump sprocket are aligned with marks on pump bracket.
4. Ensure pump mounting bolts are centered in elongated slots in pump mounting bracket.
5. If required, adjust basic timing as outlined under "Injection Pump, Replace."
6. Proceed to "Dynamic Injection Pump Timing."

DYNAMIC INJECTION PUMP TIMING

1. Connect scan tool No. VAG1551 or VAG 1552, or equivalents, to the Diagnostic Link Connector (DCL) found to right of steering column, under left-hand side of instrument panel, **Fig. 10.**
2. With engine running at closed throttle idle, select "Engine Electronics" with "Address Word 01," on scan tool.
3. Select function 04, "Introduction Of Basic Setting, " then 00, "Display Group 00."
4. Read output figures from scan tool channel 2 (injection timing) and channel 9 (fuel temperature).
5. Injection timing is dependent on fuel temperature. Refer to table in **Fig. 11,** in which "A" equals injection timing and "B" equals fuel temperature. Zone "C" of table is acceptable range with no adjustment required.
6. If adjustment is required, proceed as follows:

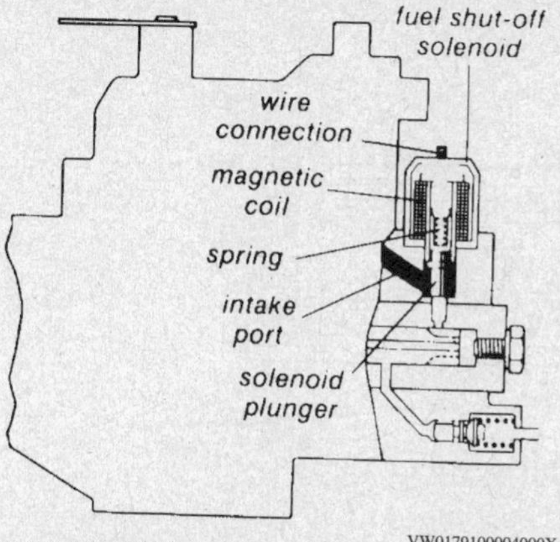
fuel shut-off solenoid
wire connection
magnetic coil
spring
intake port
solenoid plunger
VW0179100004000X

Fig. 12 Fuel shutoff solenoid

a. Shut off engine.
b. Remove upper timing belt cover.
c. Loosen injection pump mounting bolts until pump can be moved.
d. If timing was retarded move pump against direction of engine rotation. If advanced, move in direction of rotation.
e. Secure injection pump, then check timing. If necessary, repeat above steps until mean value of zone "C," **Fig. 11,** is reached.
f. Tighten pump mounting bolts to specifications.

7. Install upper belt cover, then remove scan tool.

FUEL INJECTION SYSTEM

Refer to **Fig. 8** for injection system components and locations.

FUEL SHUTOFF SOLENOID

Since diesels do not use spark ignition systems, the engine is switched off by a fuel shutoff solenoid on the injection pump.

Current is supplied to the fuel shutoff solenoid whenever the ignition key is on. The magnetic coil pulls the solenoid plunger up against the spring, opening the injection port for injection, **Fig. 12.**

Whenever the ignition key is turned off, the solenoid closes the intake port, cutting off the supply of fuel for injection from the vane pump.

The engine will not run if the fuel shutoff solenoid sticks closed. If it sticks open, the engine will continue to run after the ignition key is turned off.

FUEL SUPPLY

Fuel is drawn through the filter from the tank by the fuel supply pump located inside the injection pump, **Fig. 13.** The injection pump meters and distributes fuel under pressure to the injectors in the correct firing order.

Excess fuel from the pump and injectors returns to the feed side of the fuel system or tank through a separate line. This fuel circulation cools and lubricates the injection pump and injectors and also warms the fuel in the tank slightly to help prevent wax formation during cold weather.

INJECTORS

Diesel injectors spray fuel directly into the combustion chamber near the end of each compression stroke. The injectors are threaded into the cylinder head and are subject to the direct heat of combustion like a gasoline engine spark plug. Each injector is protected by a heat shield between the cylinder head and injector body. The heat shield acts as an insulating and sealing washer.

Fuel pressure from the injection pump into these dual spring injectors, forces the needle up against spring pressure, in two stages, so that the injector sprays a cone-shaped mist of diesel fuel at the proper time. A small quantity of fuel leaks around the injector needle to lubricate and cool the injector. This fuel returns to the tank through a separate fuel line.

Remove & Test

Always keep hands/arms away from nozzle end of injector when it is installed in the "pop" tester. The high pressure spray can penetrate skin and cause serious injury.

Note that No. 3 injector contains a needle lift sensor and must be installed into No. 3 cylinder.

1. Using compressed air, clean fuel connections and area around injectors.
2. Remove injector pipe assembly. **Do not use force or deform assembly.**
3. Remove injector retainers, injectors, then heat shields. Discard old heat shields.
4. Install injector on a "pop" tester, tool Nos. US1322 or US1111, or equivalents. Ensure knob is closed, **Fig. 14.**
5. Operate gauge lever with rapid strokes to prime tester and injector. Ensure injector sprays with even, compact pattern.
6. Operate lever with slow strokes. Injector should make creaking sound if nozzle is in good condition.
7. Turn knob out to open gauge and operate lever slowly. Note gauge reading when injector begins to spray.
8. Operate lever carefully to hold pressure specified for leak test. The injector should not drip within approximately ten seconds.
9. Refer to "Specifications" for injector opening pressures and leak test data.

Install

1. Install new injector heat shields with largest diameter sealing surface facing injector, **Fig. 15.**
2. Install injectors in cylinder head and tighten retainers to specifications. **No. 3 injector contains a needle lift sensor and must be installed in cylinder No. 3.**
3. Install injector pipe assembly. **Do not use force or deform assembly.** Tighten to specification.

Repair

Dual spring injectors used in TDI (Turbo Direct Injection) models are not serviceable in the field. Exchange is the only allowable method of repair.

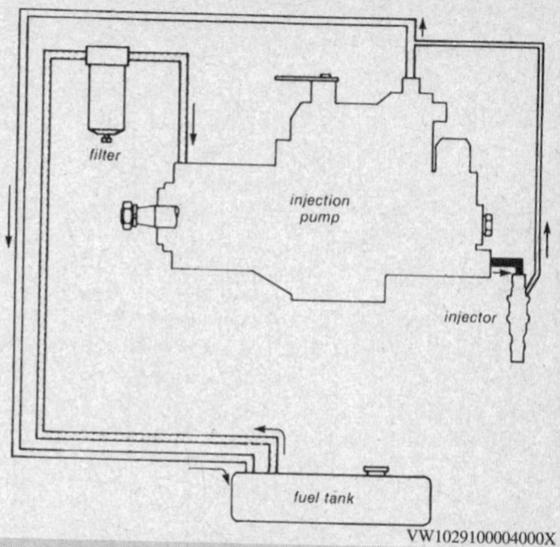
filter
injection pump
injector
fuel tank
VW1029100004000X

Fig. 13 Diesel fuel system

INJECTION PUMP

The injection pump, **Fig. 8,** is a single-plunger mechanical pump which meters and distributes fuel to the injectors in the correct firing order. The pump is driven by the camshaft spur belt at one-half engine speed. All internal pump components are lubricated by diesel fuel so the pump is maintenance free. Diesel pumps operate reliably for a long time if clean fuel is used. Idle speed and maximum speed are computer controlled and cannot be adjusted. Injection timing can be adjusted using a suitable scan tool. The fuel shutoff solenoid and fuel temperature sensor can be replaced separately, but generally, any internal problem means pump replacement. Since diesel pumps should not be disassembled, normal service consists only of troubleshooting to determine whether a pump may necessitate replacement.

Fuel Supply Pump

The rotary-vane fuel supply pump inside the injection pump draws fuel through the filter from the tank and supplies it to the distributor plunger, **Fig. 16.** The vane pump is driven by the engine camshaft spur belt. As the rotor spins, centrifugal force holds the vanes against the walls of the pressure chamber. The off center configuration of the rotor and pressure chamber "squeezes " fuel trapped between the vanes and forces it out the delivery port.

Vane pump delivery pressure varies depending on engine speed and is controlled by the regulating valve. The relief port is actually a series of small holes which open progressively to allow vane pump pressure to vary with engine speed. Vane pump pressure lubricates the internal components in the pump, supplies fuel to the distributor plunger for the injector and controls injection timing advance mechanism.

Injection pump manufacturers use a special test bench to set and check internal pump pressures. The vane pump and distributor plunger injection pressures cannot be checked easily with normal workshop equipment. If clean fuel is used, diesel injection pumps operate reliably for a long

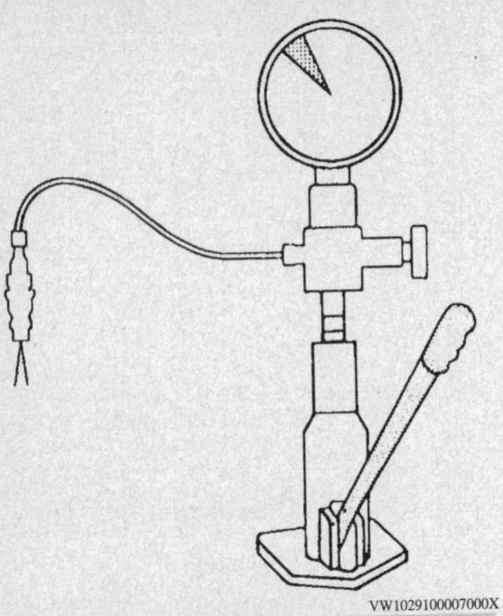
VW1029100007000X

Fig. 14 Injector testing

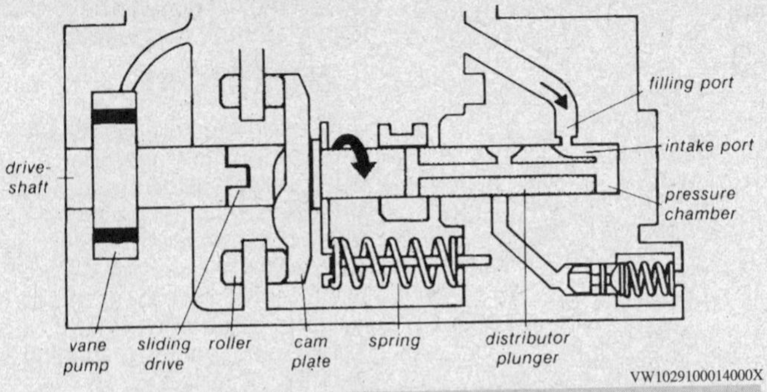
drive-
shaft
filling port
intake port
pressure
chamber
vane
pump
sliding
drive
roller
cam
plate
spring
distributor
plunger
VW1029100014000X

Fig. 17 Plunger & roller

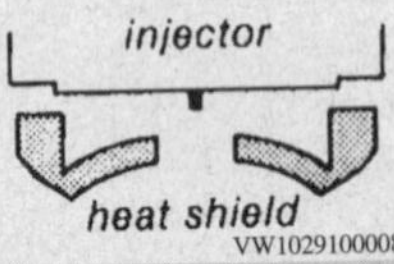
injector
heat shield
VW1029100008000X

Fig. 15 Heat shield installation

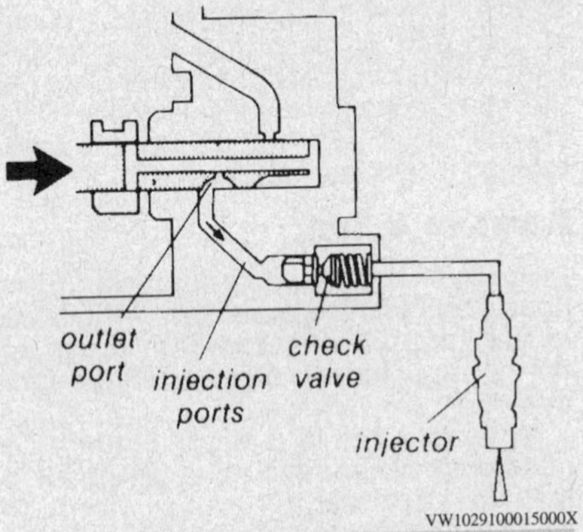
outlet
port
injection
ports
check
valve
injector
VW1029100015000X

Fig. 18 Plunger installation

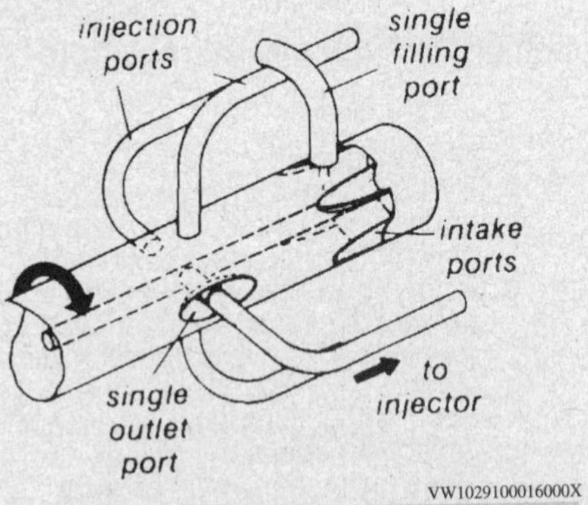
injection
ports
single
filling
port
intake
ports
to
injector
single
outlet
port
VW1029100016000X

Fig. 19 Plunger & ports

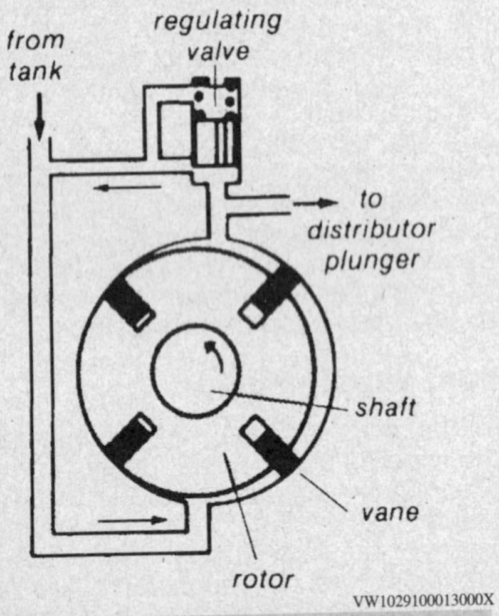
from
tank
regulating
valve
to
distributor
plunger
shaft
vane
rotor
VW1029100013000X

Fig. 16 Vane type fuel supply pump

time. Diesel pumps should not be disassembled or adjusted. Normal service consists only of troubleshooting to determine whether a pump might need replacement.

Injection & Distribution

The injection pump driveshaft turns the vane pump, distributor plunger, and cam plate as a unit. Springs hold the cam plate against stationary rollers. In this position, the plunger also moves back and forth as it turns.

Whenever an intake port in the plunger is inline with the filling port in the pump body, fuel from the vane pump fills the pressure chamber, **Fig. 17.** As the plunger turns, the intake port is covered up so that fuel is trapped in the pressure chamber. The cam plate and rollers push the plunger and pressurize the fuel to approximately 1800 psi.

As the plunger continues to turn, the outlet port in the plunger lines up with the injection passage in the pump body, opening the check valve and supplying high-pressure fuel to the injector, **Fig. 18.**

The pump and plunger are designed with ports to supply each injector with fuel in the proper firing order, **Fig. 19.**

Fuel Metering & Timing

Cold start functions, fuel metering, idle, engine speed limit and injection timing are computer controlled and cannot be adjusted.

THROTTLE POSITION SENSOR

The Throttle Position (TP) sensor provides the diesel Engine Control Module (ECM) with information about the vehicle operator demands.

Remove

1. Remove lefthand instrument panel pedal cluster cover, then disconnect wiring connector for TP sensor.
2. Remove clip, **Fig. 20,** pin, bushing and spring, then disconnect throttle pedal from cam.
3. Remove TP sensor mounting bracket nuts, then sensor and bracket.
4. Remove cam from TP sensor shaft, then disconnect TP sensor from mounting bracket.

Install

1. During component installation, refer to **Figs. 20 and 21** for component locations and basic settings.
2. Secure TP sensor to mounting bracket, then cam to sensor using **Fig. 21** for basic setting adjustments.
3. Secure bracket with sensor to vehicle, then install pedal, bushing, spring, pin and clip.
4. Connect wiring connector, then proceed to "Adjust."

Adjust

1. Connect scan tool VAG 1551 or VAG 1552, or equivalents, to Data Link Connector (DLC) found in lower lefthand side of instrument panel, to right of steering column.
2. Turn ignition on.
3. Select "Engine Electronics" on scan tool.
4. Select function 08, "Read Measuring Value Block."
5. Select function 02, "Display Group Number 2."
6. With throttle pedal fully released, reading should be 0%.
7. Slowly apply throttle to full position, reading should increase continuously until 100% is reached just before wide open throttle position.

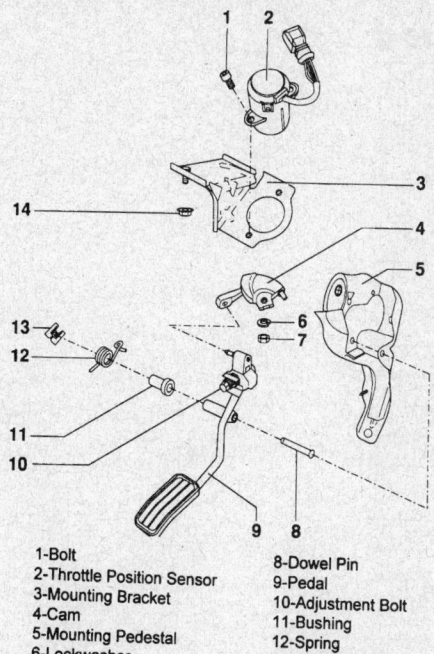

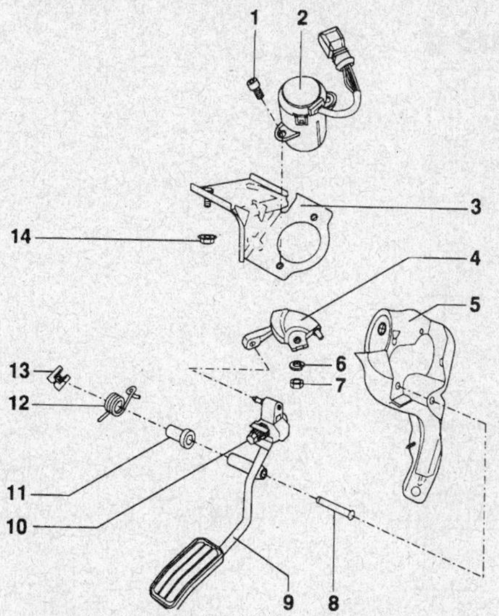
1
2
3
4
5
6
7
8
9
10
11
12
13
14
1-Bolt
2-Throttle Position Sensor
3-Mounting Bracket
4-Cam
5-Mounting Pedestal
6-Lockwasher
7-Nut
8-Dowel Pin
9-Pedal
10-Adjustment Bolt
11-Bushing
12-Spring
13-Circlip
14-Nut
VW1029600073000X

Fig. 20 Exploded view of throttle position sensor

8. Turn adjustment bolt on pedal or reposition cam as necessary until above conditions are met.

IDLE SPEED

ADJUST

Engine idle speed is computer controlled and cannot be adjusted.

GLOW PLUG SYSTEM

During cold starts, diesel compression heat is dissipated rapidly through the cold

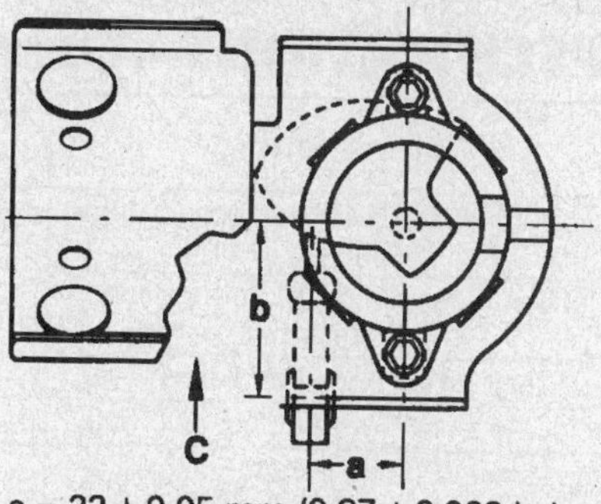
a
b
C
a = 22 ± 0.05 mm (0.87 ± 0.002 in.)
b = 41 ± 0.05 mm (1.61 ± 0.002 in.)
c = Forwards
VW1029600074000X

Fig. 21 Throttle position sensor initial setup

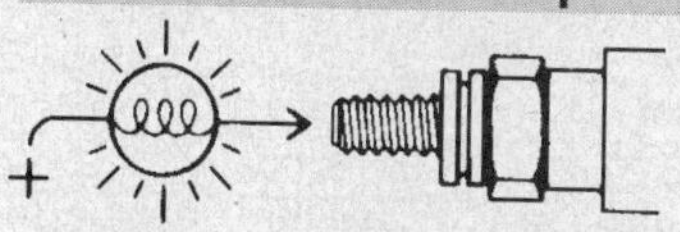
VW0179100003000X

Fig. 23 Glow plug continuity check

engine so that a preheating provision is necessary to ensure compression ignition. The glow plugs are threaded into the cylinder head so they project into each combustion chamber. A heating element in each plug gets red hot whenever current is applied to the plug terminals.

Current is supplied to the glow plugs directly from the battery by a relay that is controlled by the Turbocharged Direct Injection (TDI) diesel Engine Control Module (ECM). A temperature sensor connected to the ECM controls preheating time. The colder the temperature, the longer the preheating time. The glow plug light is on when the plugs are being heated and goes off when the engine is ready to start.

Defective glow plugs cause hard starting

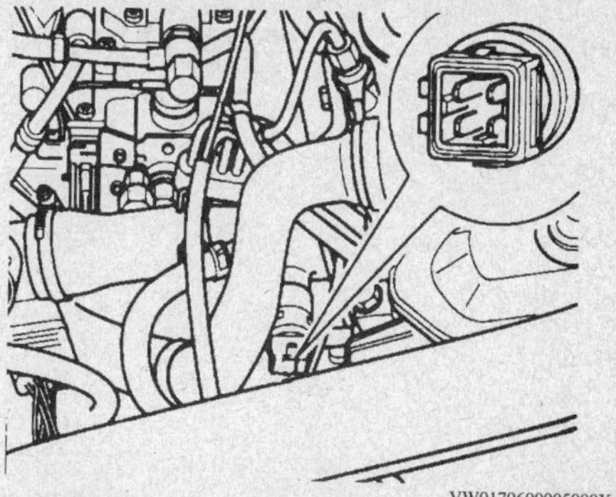
VW0179600005000X

Fig. 22 Glow plug temperature sensor disconnection

and rough running during warm-up. Carbon deposits can build up and insulate the heating element. If the system seems satisfactory, but the engine is hard to start, the glow plugs should be removed for cleaning.

Most problems in the preheat system can be found with a test light. Glow plugs can also be checked with an ohmmeter. The resistance value is about .25 ohms.

TESTING

1. With ignition switch in Off position, disconnect engine coolant temperature sensor on water outlet housing, **Fig. 22,** to simulate cold engine, then remove glow plug connectors.
2. Connect test light clip to ground and touch test light probe to any glow plug connection, turn on ignition switch.
3. Test light should light up for about 20 seconds if system is working properly.
4. Connect test light clip to battery positive post and probe to each glow plug connection. Test light should light up each time if heating elements are satisfactory, **Fig. 23.**

TIGHTENING SPECIFICATIONS

Year	Component	Torque/Ft. Lbs.
1996	Camshaft Bearing Cap To Cylinder Head Nuts	15
	Camshaft Sprocket To Camshaft Bolt	33
	Connecting Rod Nuts	22①
	Crankshaft Timing Belt Sprocket To Crankshaft Bolt	66①
	Cylinder Head Bolts	③
	Cylinder Head Cover To Cylinder Head Bolts	7
	Exhaust Pipe To Turbocharger Nuts	18
	Front Main Oil Seal Housing To Block Bolts	15
	Glow Plugs To Cylinder Head	11
	Injection Pump Bolts	18

Continued

TIGHTENING SPECIFICATIONS—Continued

Year	Component	Torque/Ft. Lbs.
1996	Injection Pump Bracket To Injection Pump Bolts	18
	Injection Pump Sprocket To Injection Pump Nut	41
	Injector Pipe Nuts To Injector	14
	Injector Retainer Nuts To Cylinder Head	15
	Intermediate Shaft Oil Seal Flange To Block Bolts	18
	Main Bearing Cap Bolts	48
	Oil Pan Drain Plug To Oil Pan	22
	Oil Pan To Block Bolts	15
	Oil Pressure Switch To Oil Filter Bracket	18
	Oil Pump Cover To Oil Pump Housing Bolts	7
	Oil Pump Pickup To Pump Bolts	7
	Oil Pump To Block Bolts	15
	Oil Return Line To Pan Bolt	37
	Oil Return Line To Turbocharger Nut	30
	Oil Spray Nozzle To Block Bolt	7④
	Pulley to Crankshaft Timing Belt Sprocket Bolt	15
	Timing Belt Tensioner Nut	33
	Turbocharger To Exhaust Manifold Bolts	33②
	Water Pump Pulley To Water Pump Bolts	15
	Water Pump To Water Pump Housing Bolts	7

① — Plus an additional 1/4 (90°) turn.

② — Coat threads & head contact surface with sealant No. G 000 500, or equivalent.

③ — Refer to "Cylinder Head, Replace."

④ — Coat threads with sealant No. AMV 188 100 02, or equivalent.

Clutch & Manual Transmission/ Transaxle

NOTE: On Air Bag Equipped Models, Refer To "Air Bag System Precautions" Located In The Front Of This Manual For System Disarming & Arming Procedures.

INDEX

	Page No.
Adjustments	49-53
Hydraulically Operated Clutch	49-53
Mechanically Operated Clutch	49-53
Shift Lever	49-53
Application Chart	49-53
Clutch, Replace	49-56
Except 020 Transaxle	49-57
020 Transaxle	49-56
Clutch Cable, Replace	49-56
Automatic Adjustment Cable	49-56
Manual Adjustment Cable	49-56
Hydraulic System Service	49-56
Clutch System Bleed	49-56
Precautions	49-53
Air Bag Systems	49-53
Audio Coded Anti-Theft System	49-53
Tightening Specifications	49-59
Transaxle, Replace	49-57
013 & 014 Transaxle	49-57
02A Transaxle	49-58
02B Transaxle	49-58
020 Transaxle	49-57

PRECAUTIONS

Do not use computer memory saver tool on air bag equipped models. Using the tool will keep the air bag system charged and may cause accidental activation of the air bag unit. Prior to disconnecting the battery negative cable, obtain the radio security code. After service has been completed and the battery negative cable has been reconnected, use security code to activate the radio.

AIR BAG SYSTEMS

Refer to "Air Bag System Precautions" in the front of this manual for system disarming and arming procedures.

AUDIO CODED ANTI-THEFT SYSTEM

Some models are equipped with a radio anti-theft system that will disable the system when battery power is interrupted, unless the system is reset the radio will not operate.

1. Turn radio to On position, SAFE should be displayed.
2. Depress and hold AM/FM and SCAN buttons until 1000 remains on display. If AM/FM and SCAN buttons are depressed too long or depressed again, radio will misinterpret the 1000 as an attempt at coding and one incorrect coding attempt will be logged. **After two incorrect attempts to reset system, radio will lock up electronically. If this occurs, leave radio on for approximately one hour, then reset radio as if battery power were disconnected.**
3. Enter radio code using first four program station buttons. Security code will appear on display.
4. Depress and hold AM/FM and SCAN buttons again until SAFE is displayed.
5. Release AM/FM and SCAN buttons. Display should change to a radio frequency and operate normally.

APPLICATION CHART

Model	Transaxle
1993	
Cabriolet	020
Corrado	02A
Eurovan	02B
Fox w/4–Speed	014
Fox w/5-Speed	015
Golf III	020
Jetta III	020
Passat	02A
1994	
Cabriolet	020
Corrado	02A
Golf III	020
Jetta III	020
Passat	02A
1995	
Cabrio	020
Golf III	020
GTI	02A
Jetta III	020
Jetta III GLX	02A
Passat	02A
1996	
Cabrio	020
Golf III	020
GTI	020
GTI-VR6	02A
Jetta III	020
Jetta III GLX	02A
Passat	02A

ADJUSTMENTS

HYDRAULICALLY OPERATED CLUTCH

The clutch operating system used on these vehicles is self adjusting.

MECHANICALLY OPERATED CLUTCH

MANUALLY ADJUSTED CLUTCH

Cabriolet

1. Fully depress clutch pedal approximately five times.
2. Loosen locknut, **Fig. 1.**
3. Install adjusting gauge tool No. US 5043, or equivalent, as shown in **Fig. 1.**
4. Raise clutch release lever at transaxle until resistance is felt.
5. Adjust adjusting sleeve, **Fig. 1,** until zero freeplay is obtained.
6. Tighten cable locknut to specifications, then remove adjusting tool.
7. Clutch freeplay at clutch release lever should be .236 inch plus or minus .012 inch.

Fox

1. Adjust freeplay on cable at left engine mount.
2. Clutch freeplay measured at clutch pedal should be .008–.024 inch.

SHIFT LEVER

013 TRANSAXLE

1. Shift into 1st gear, then push gearshift lever to left stop and release lever.
2. Lever must spring back ¼ to ⅜ inch to right.
3. If not, move gearshift lever housing slightly in slots.
4. Shift into 5th gear, then push gearshift

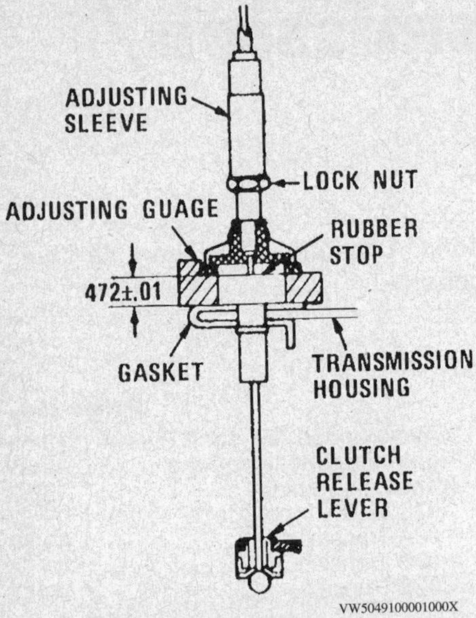
ADJUSTING SLEEVE
LOCK NUT
ADJUSTING GUAGE
RUBBER STOP
472±.01
GASKET
TRANSMISSION HOUSING
CLUTCH RELEASE LEVER
VW5049100001000X

Fig. 1 Clutch freeplay adjustment. Cabriolet

lever to right stop and release lever.
5. Lever must spring back 1/4 to 3/8 inch to left.
6. When gearshift lever is placed in 1st or 5th gear and lever is pushed to left or right stop and then released, lever must spring back approximately same distance.
7. If not, move gearshift lever housing slightly in slots sideways.
8. If this adjustment does not correct hard shifting problem, adjust gearshift lever as follows:
   a. Place gearshift lever in Neutral position, loosen clamp nut, **Fig. 2,** and ensure shift finger slides freely on shift rod.
   b. Remove lever knob and shift boot, then loosen bolts for gearshift lever housing slightly.
   c. Align centering holes of gearshift lever housing and gearshift lever bearing housing and tighten bolts.
   d. Install shift lever gauge tool No. 3057, or equivalent, with locating pin in front centering hole, then place gearshift lever in right cutout of slide 5/R and tighten lower knurled nut of gauge.
   e. Move slide with gearshift lever to right stop and tighten upper knurled nut of gauge.
   f. Push gearshift lever into left cutout slide 3/4, then tighten clamp nut.
9. Remove shift lever gauge, then engage 1st gear and press gearshift lever to left stop.
10. Release lever. Lever must spring back to right.
11. Engage 5th gear, then press gearshift lever to right stop.
12. Release lever. Lever must spring back to left.
13. When gearshift lever is placed in 1st or 5th gear and lever is pushed to left or right stop and then released, lever must spring back approximately same distance.

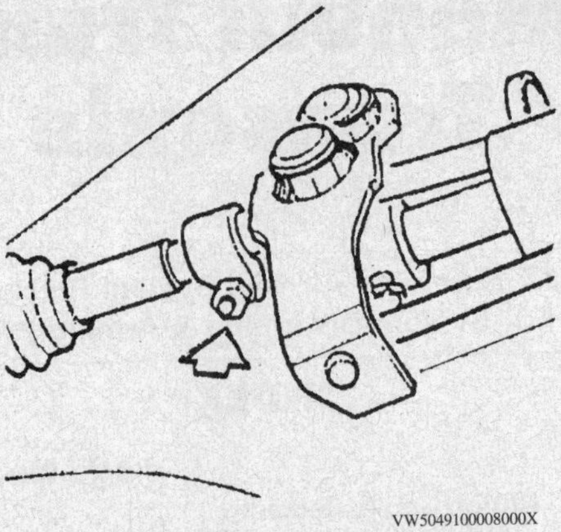
VW5049100008000X

Fig. 2 Shift rod clamp bolt location. Fox, Golf, GT & Jetta

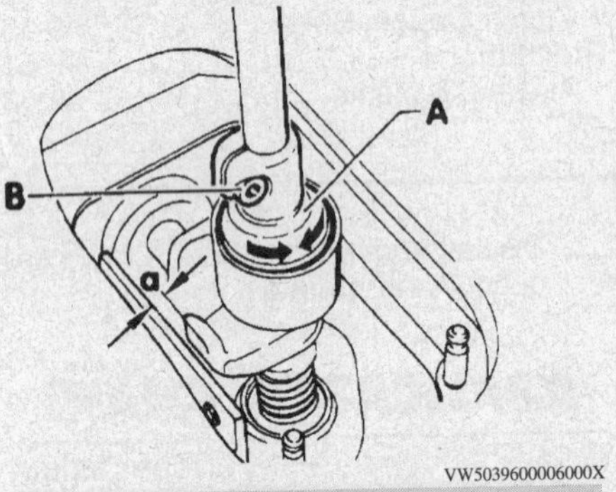
A
B
a
VW5039600006000X

Fig. 4 Shifter fine adjustment. Cabrio, Golf III, GTI & Jetta III w/020 transaxle

14. If not, move gearshift lever housing slightly in slots sideways.
15. Ensure all gears engage easily without jamming. Also check operation of reverse gear stop.

014 TRANSAXLE

1. Shift into 1st gear, then push gearshift lever to left stop and release lever.
2. Lever must spring back 1/4 to 3/8 inch to right.
3. If not, move gearshift lever housing slightly in slots.
4. If this adjustment does not correct hard shifting problem, adjust gearshift lever as follows:
   a. Place gearshift lever in Neutral position, then remove lever knob and shift boot.
   b. Loosen clamp nut, **Fig. 2,** and ensure shift finger slides freely on shift rod.
   c. Move gearshift lever to righthand side, between 3rd and 4th position. **Gearshift lever remains perpendicular to ball housing.**
   d. With inner shift lever in Neutral position and gearshift lever between 3rd and 4th gear, tighten clamp nut.
   e. Check engagement of all gears, including reverse. Gearshift lever must move freely.
   f. If necessary, adjust gearshift lever bearing housing by moving along slotted holes.

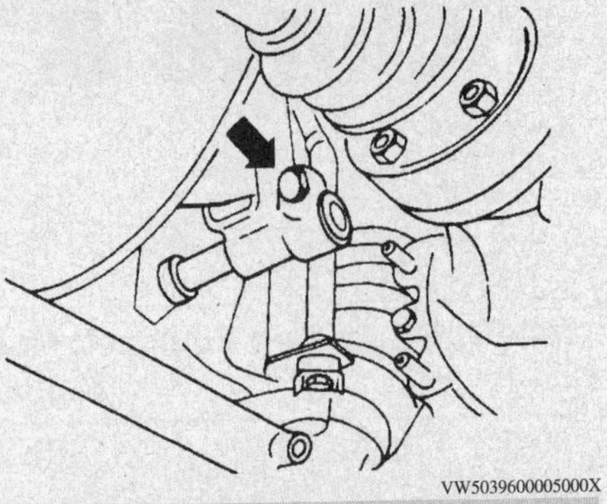
VW5039600005000X

Fig. 3 Shift rod clamp bolt. Cabrio, Golf III, GTI & Jetta III w/020 transaxle

020 TRANSAXLE

Cabrio, Golf III, GTI & Jetta III

1. Position gearshift lever in neutral.
2. Loosen shift rod clamp bolt, **Fig. 3,** then ensure selector lever moves freely on shaft.
3. Remove gearshift lever knob and boot.
4. Install adjustment gauge tool No. 3104, or equivalent.
5. With transaxle in neutral, align shift lever with gauge, then tighten shift rod clamp. **Shift linkage should not be under pressure during adjustment.**
6. Remove adjustment gauge and move gearshift lever through all gears, including reverse. Gears should engage smoothly and without jamming.
7. If jamming occurs, proceed as follows:
   a. Engage first gear, then take all play out of shifter by lightly pressing left at top of lever.
   b. Dimension "a," **Fig. 4,** should be .040–.060 inch.
   c. If adjustment is necessary, loosen clamp bolt "B, " then adjust eccentric "A" as necessary.

Cabriolet

1. Pull boot from lever housing and move aside, or remove cover plate only, if equipped.
2. Loosen shift rod clamp so selector lever moves easily on shift rod.
3. Adjust shift finger in center of lock out plate so front and rear spacing are equal.
4. Adjust shift rod end so that distance between shift finger and lock out bracket is 9/16 inch.
5. Tighten shift rod clamps to specifications.
6. Ensure gears engage easily without jamming. Ensure reverse lock out works properly.
7. If shift linkage is spongy or jams after adjustment, adjust shift rod end so that distance between shift finger and lock out bracket is 1/2 inch and recheck operation.
8. If shift linkage adjustment cannot be maintained, install a "new" clamp bolt and locknut.

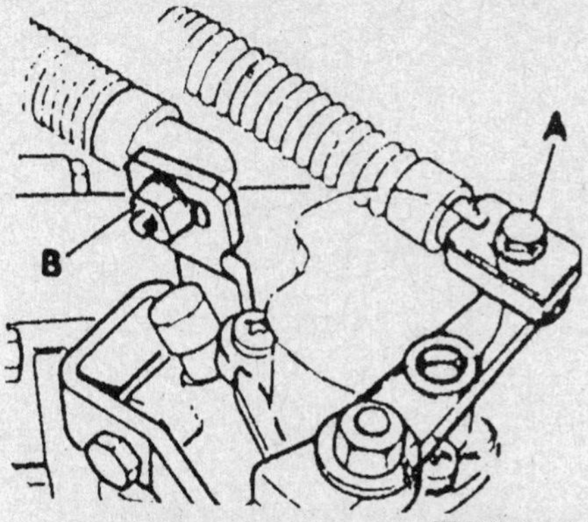
A
B
VW5049100004000X

Fig. 5 Gearshift lever operating cables. Corrado, GTI, Jetta III GLX & Passat w/02A transaxle

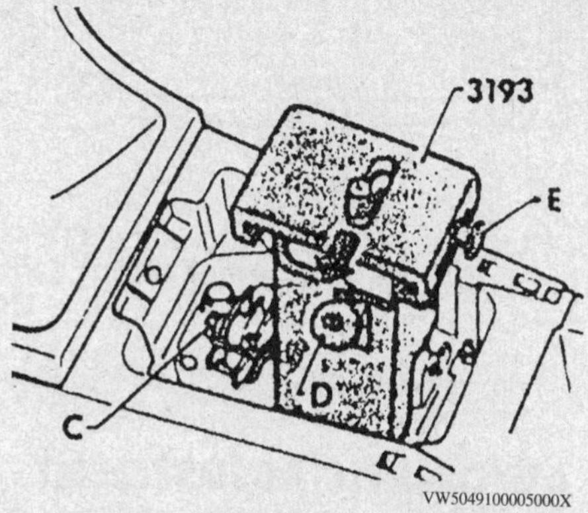
3193
E
C
D
VW5049100005000X

Fig. 6 Shift lever gauge installation. Corrado, GTI, Jetta III GLX & Passat w/02A transaxle

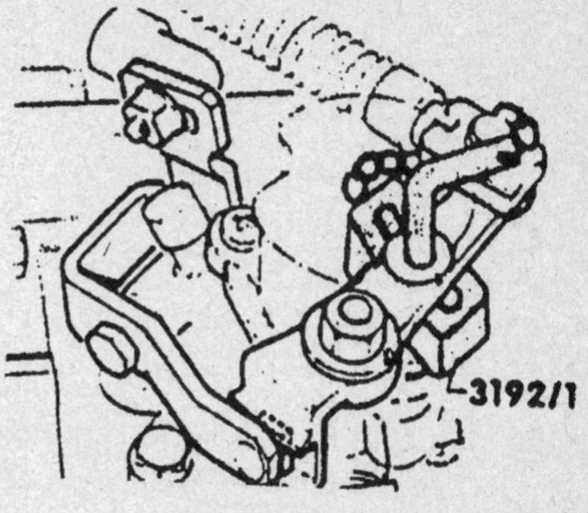
3192/1
VW5049100006000X

Fig. 7 Wedge & locating pin installation. Corrado, GTI, Jetta III GLX & Passat w/02A transaxle

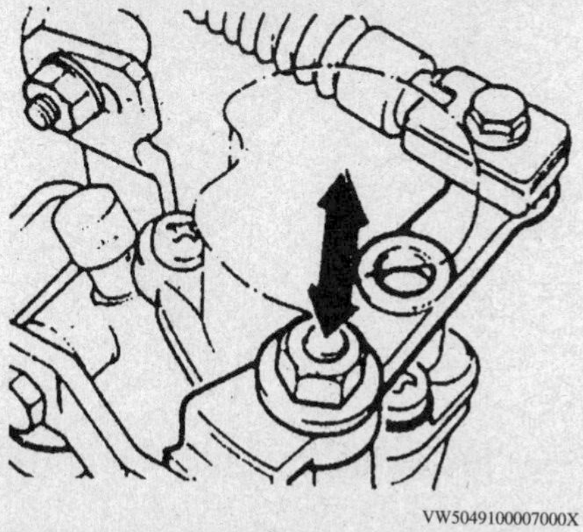
VW5049100007000X

Fig. 8 Transaxle rod travel check. Corrado, GTI, Jetta III GLX & Passat w/ 02A transaxle

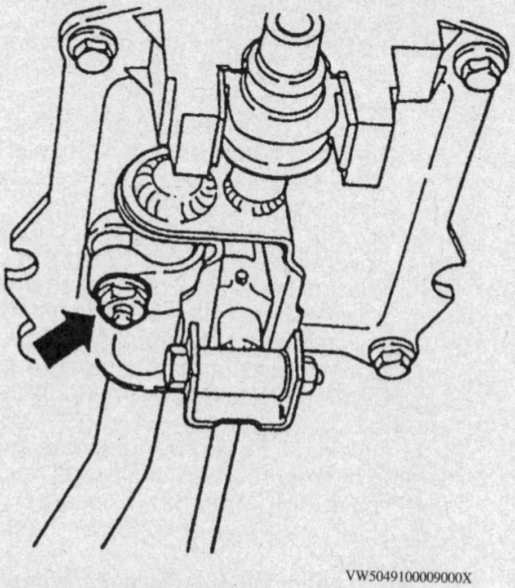
VW5049100009000X

Fig. 9 Shift linkage adjustment. Eurovan

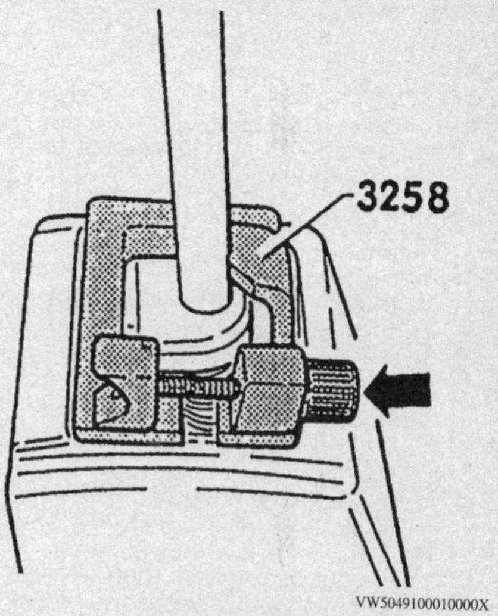
3258
VW5049100010000X

Fig. 10 Shift linkage adjusting tool. Eurovan

02A TRANSAXLE

To obtain a correct gearshift adjustment, shift linkage should be operating satisfactorily, shift/selector cable mounting components and cable boots should be in satisfactory condition, shift cables should be operating smoothly and transaxle and clutch should be in satisfactory condition.

1. Place gearshift lever in Neutral position, then remove the gearshift lever knob and shift boot.
2. Loosen bolt A and nut B until operating cables move freely in centering holes, **Fig. 5.**
3. Loosen bolt C, then install shift lever gauge tool No. 3193, or equivalent, **Fig. 6.**
4. Pivot locating pin (for attaching gauge) under bearing plate, then tighten nut D.
5. Press gearshift lever into left detent of slide, then press gearshift lever with slide to left stop (toward driver side), and tighten bolt E.
6. Move gearshift lever to right detent (toward passenger side), then tighten bolt C.
7. Install wedge and locating pin tool No. 3192/1, or equivalent, **Fig. 7,** then push wedge between gearshift lever and cover, until no play is present. **Wedge must not raise transaxle gearshift lever.**
8. Attach operating cables in this position, then check position of the wedge.
9. Remove wedge and pin, then the shift lever gauge.
10. **On Corrado models,** depress clutch pedal, then shift into all gears several times. Notice effectiveness of reverse gear lock.
11. **On Passat models,** start engine and depress clutch pedal, wait approximately three to six seconds until transaxle input shaft comes to a standstill, then shift into all gears several times. Notice effectiveness of reverse gear pawl.
12. **On all models,** if any gear binds or drags, check transaxle rod travel as follows:
    a. Shift into first gear.
    b. Press shift lever to left, up to stop, then release.
    c. Have an assistant watch shift rod on transaxle. Rod must travel approximately 3/64 inch in direction of arrow, **Fig. 8,** when activating shift lever.
13. If rod travel is not within specifications:
    a. Shift out of first gear, then loosen nut A at selector cable mounting lug. **Minimal cable play at lug is normal.**
    b. Reposition cable/lug slightly toward instrument panel to increase cable play and away from instrument panel to decrease cable play, then tighten nut.

02B TRANSAXLE

1. Place shifter in Neutral position.
2. Loosen clamp, **Fig. 9.** There must be free movement in gate selector rod/gearshift console connection.
3. Remove gearshift knob and cover, then frame with rubber gaiter.
4. Insert gauge tool No. 3258, or equivalent, as far as the stop and tighten knurled head screw, **Fig. 10.**
5. Align gate selector rod/gearshift console to be free of tension (transaxle in neutral), then tighten to specification.
6. Pull gear lever toward bench seat, loosen knurled head screw and remove gauge.
7. In neutral, the shift lever must be in 3rd/4th gear plane. The section of shift lever below the bend must be perpendicular.
8. Depress clutch, start engine, wait approximately three to six seconds until input shaft is stationary, then select all gears several times. Check function of reverse gear lock, then install frame

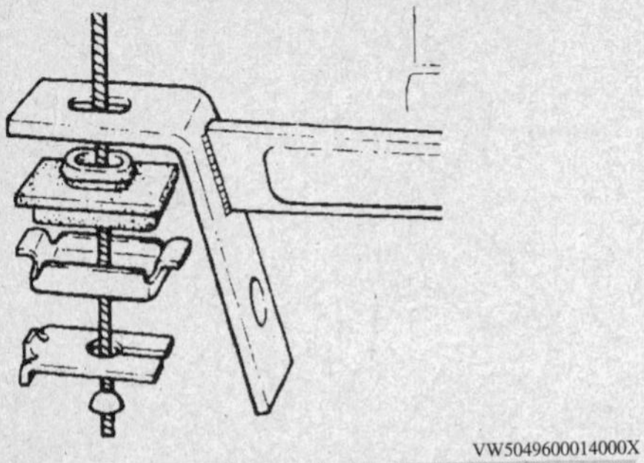
VW5049600014000X

Fig. 11 Clutch cable clip removal. 020 transaxle

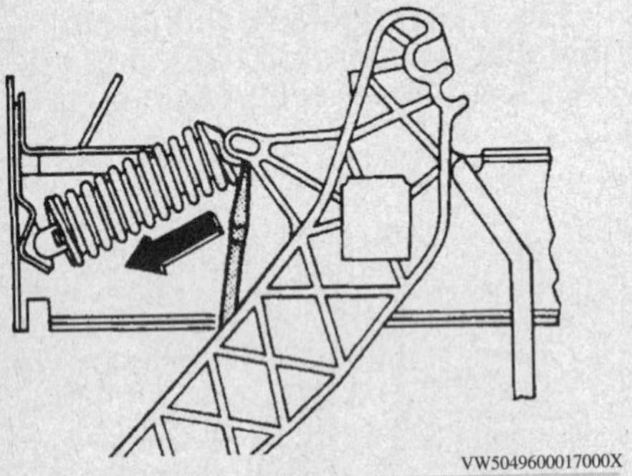
VW5049600017000X

Fig. 14 Overcenter spring removal

with rubber gaiter and shift knob with cover.

9. When repeating engagement of a gear and the gear sticks, proceed as follows:
   a. Engage 1st gear, then eliminate play in gearshift linkage by pressing gear lever with pressure of .14–.67 lbs. to the left against threads of gear lever knob with 1st gear engaged.
   b. The distance between shift lever stop and shifter housing stop must be .047–.090 inches. If not, disengage 1st gear and repeat adjusting procedure.

CLUTCH CABLE

REPLACE

MANUAL ADJUSTMENT CABLE

1. Release and back off cable adjuster sleeve locknut.
2. Turn adjuster sleeve until sufficient slack is created at clutch arm to allow cable clip to be disengaged from cable, **Fig. 11,** then remove clip and isolator pad from arm.
3. Remove any lefthand side lower instrument panels necessary to access top of clutch pedal.
4. Disengage cable from top of clutch pedal, then pull cable and outer housing through and out of firewall.
5. Reverse procedure to install. Ensure cable outer housing is properly seated

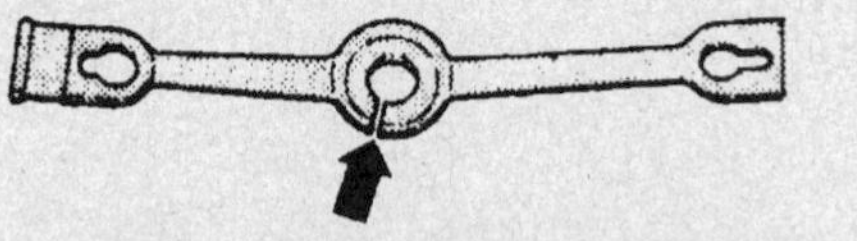
VW5049600015000X

Fig. 12 Tensioner strap

in firewall and clutch is properly adjusted.

AUTOMATIC ADJUSTMENT CABLE

1. Perform auto adjuster function check as follows:
   a. Press clutch pedal fully to stop at least five times.
   b. **On Eurovan models,** grasp outer cable sleeve at Transaxle and pull in direction away from transaxle, cable should move at least .40 inch.
   c. **On all models except Eurovan,** clutch release lever should freely move down .40 inch.
   d. **On all models,** function check movement can only be made one time for each time clutch pedal is pressed to stop five or more times.
2. If function check movement cannot be performed, adjuster is damaged and cable will have to be destroyed to be removed.
3. If function check is passed, locate existing or procure a new cable tensioner retaining strap, **Fig. 12.** If necessary, cut strap at arrow to install on cable adjuster.
4. Depress clutch five or more times, then attach tension retaining strap as shown in **Fig. 13.**
5. Remove clip and isolator pad from cable end at release lever, **Fig. 11.**
6. **Except Eurovan models,** remove clutch pedal overcenter spring as follows:
   a. Remove lower left interior trim panel, then the relay panel from bracket.
   b. Remove wiring from clip of guard plate mounted between relay panel and pedal cluster.
   c. Press snap detent on guard plate towards pedal cluster.
   d. Push guard plate up until free, then remove guard plate.
   e. Insert screwdriver between steering column and pedal and against overcenter spring, **Fig. 14.**
   f. Depress clutch pedal, then remove overcenter spring in direction of arrow, **Fig. 14.**
7. **On all models,** disconnect cable from pedal, then remove, **Fig. 15.**
8. Ensure a tensioning strap is installed on cable to be installed.
9. Reverse procedure to install. Remove tensioning strap after installation.

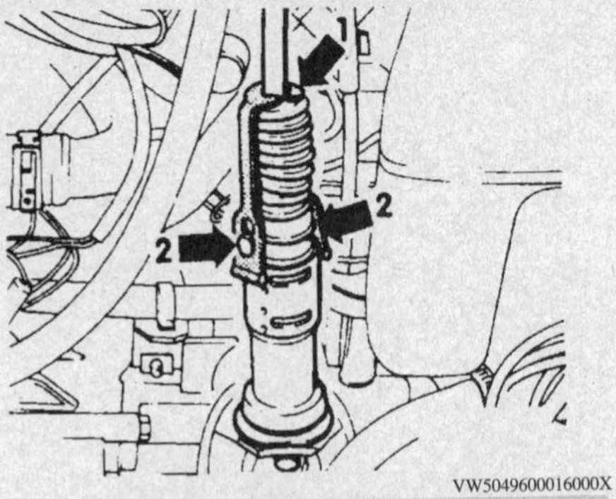
1
2
2
VW5049600016000X

Fig. 13 Tensioner strap installation

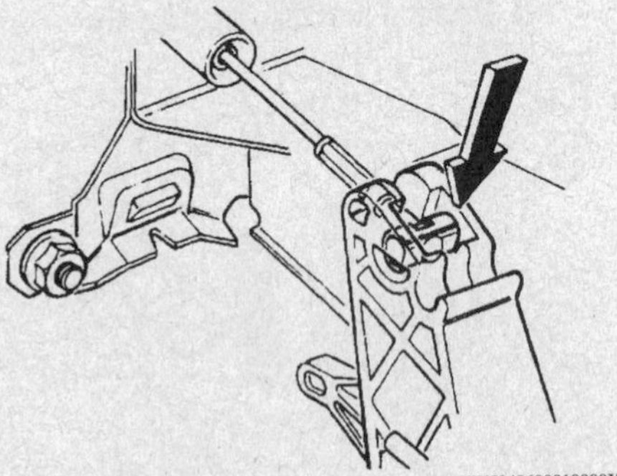
VW5049600018000X

Fig. 15 Cable from pedal removal

HYDRAULIC SYSTEM SERVICE

CLUTCH SYSTEM BLEED

Obtain a suitable brake pressure bleeder to bleed clutch hydraulic system. Follow manufacturer's instructions for bleeding procedures. Maximum working pressure should be 36 psi. Bleed master cylinder first, then clutch slave cylinder.

CLUTCH

REPLACE

020 TRANSAXLE

1. Remove transaxle as outlined under "Transaxle, Replace."
2. Install flywheel locking tool No. VW 558, or equivalent, then remove flywheel to pressure plate attaching bolts.
3. Remove flywheel, clutch disc, release plate retaining ring and the release plate, **Fig. 16.**
4. Lock pressure plate using tool No. VW 558, or equivalent, then remove pressure plate to crankshaft retaining bolts and the pressure plate.
5. To install, position pressure plate to crankshaft, coat retaining bolts with D6

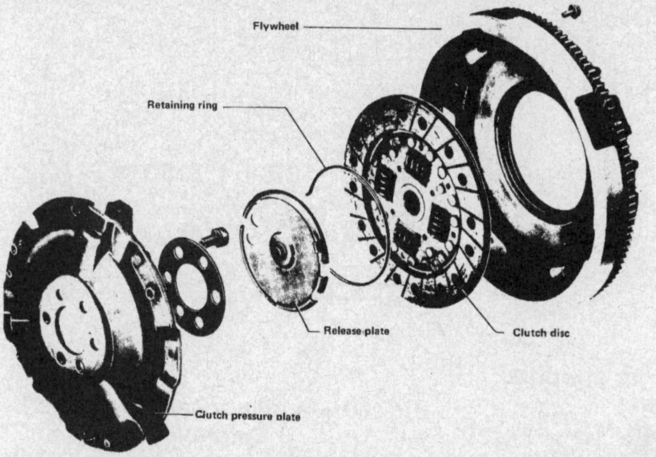
Flywheel
Retaining ring
Release plate
Clutch disc
Clutch pressure plate

VW5049100012000X

Fig. 16 Disassembled view of clutch assembly. Cabriolet w/1.8L engine & Cabrio, Golf III, Jetta III except GLX & 1996 GTI w/2.0L engine

thread locking compound, or equivalent, and install bolts finger tight.

6. Install pressure plate locking tool and tighten retaining bolts to specifications.
7. Lubricate release plate contact surface and pushrod socket with lithium grease, then install release plate and retaining ring to pressure plate.
8. Install clutch disc, flywheel and flywheel attaching bolts.
9. Using centering tool No. VW 547, or equivalent, center clutch disc in flywheel and tighten attaching bolts to specifications.
10. Install transaxle assembly.

EXCEPT 020 TRANSAXLE

1. Remove transaxle as outlined under "Transaxle, Replace."
2. Loosen pressure plate bolts in a diagonal sequence, **Fig. 17.**
3. To install, lock flywheel in place with holding tool No. 3067, or equivalent, then install disc and pressure plate using aligning tool No. 3190, or equivalent.
4. Tighten to specifications.

TRANSAXLE

REPLACE

013 & 014 TRANSAXLE

1. Obtain audio coded anti-theft code, disconnect battery ground cable, then remove upper engine/transaxle bolts.
2. Disconnect clutch cable from clutch lever, then the speedometer cable from transaxle.
3. Remove front exhaust pipe, then the engine stop bolts.
4. Disconnect axle shafts from transaxle flanges and wire up.
5. Disconnect wires from back-up light switch connector, then the upshift indicator switch, if equipped.
6. Remove cover plate, then the starter motor.
7. Remove bolt from shift rod coupling, pry off linkage coupling, then pull shift rod coupling off shift rod.
8. Position transaxle support under transaxle and raise slightly.
9. Loosen bolt 1, **Fig. 18,** then remove bolt 2 and pivot support 4 rearward.
10. Remove mount 3, then bolts 5.
11. Remove front mounting support, then the lower engine/transaxle bolts.
12. Pry transaxle away from engine, then lower and remove transaxle from vehicle.
13. Reverse procedure to install, noting the following:
    a. Ensure large cover plate is properly seated.
    b. Tighten nuts and bolts to specifications.
    c. Align engine/transaxle in mounts.
    d. Reset audio coded anti-theft system as outlined under "Precautions."

020 TRANSAXLE

Cabriolet

1. Obtain audio coded anti-theft code, then disconnect battery ground cable.
2. Install engine support bar tool No. 10-222A, or equivalent.
3. Remove left mount.
4. Disconnect wires from back-up light switch connector, then the clutch cable and speedometer drive cable and plug hole.
5. Remove upper transaxle to engine bolts.
6. Remove starter motor.
7. Turn engine until lug on flywheel aligns with boss on bell housing. The engine and transaxle can only be separated in this position.
8. Disconnect shift linkage by opening clips with screwdriver.
9. Remove front selector rod.
10. Remove exhaust pipe bracket.
11. Remove transaxle rear mount from body and transaxle.
12. Disconnect right and left side axle shafts from transaxle and wire up.
13. Remove bolts from large cover plate and bolt from small cover plate.
14. Remove remaining transaxle bolt or nut near the differential.
15. Pull transaxle away from engine and dowel sleeves.
16. Lower and remove transaxle from vehicle.
17. Reverse procedure to install, noting the following:
    a. Tighten nuts and bolts to specifications.
    b. Align engine/transaxle in mounts.
    c. Reset audio coded anti-theft system as outlined under "Precautions."

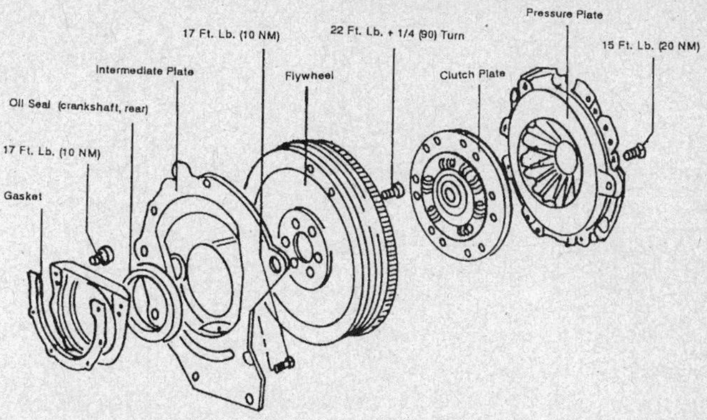
Pressure Plate
17 Ft. Lb. (10 NM)
22 Ft. Lb. + 1/4 (90) Turn
15 Ft. Lb. (20 NM)
Intermediate Plate
Flywheel
Clutch Plate
Oil Seal (crankshaft, rear)
17 Ft. Lb. (10 NM)
Gasket

VW5049100013000X

Fig. 17 Disassembled view of clutch assembly. Corrado, Eurovan, Fox, GTI-VR6, Jetta III GLX & Passat

Except Cabriolet

1. Obtain audio coded anti-theft code, then disconnect battery ground cable and wiring at transaxle.
2. Disconnect all electrical connectors and wiring from the transaxle.
3. Remove upper bolts attaching engine to transaxle, then disconnect clutch cable at clutch release lever and transaxle housing as outlined under "Clutch Cable, Replace."
4. **On all models except Cabrio,** remove right side engine support attaching bolts.
5. **On Cabrio models,** remove right side engine support and spacers from frame rail and engine.
6. **On all models,** disconnect short selector rod, then connecting rod from gearshift lever shaft.
7. Remove long selector rod from relay lever, then bolt from left transaxle mount.
8. Remove the two upper left side engine support attaching bolts.
9. **On Cabrio Models,** remove left side engine support from frame rail and transaxle.
10. **On all models,** install engine support bar tool No. 10-222A, or equivalent, onto engine.
11. Detach axle shafts from transaxle and support with wire.
12. Remove large clutch cover plate, small clutch cover plate behind right axle drive flange, then the starter motor.
13. Remove front mount assembly, then the remaining left side engine support

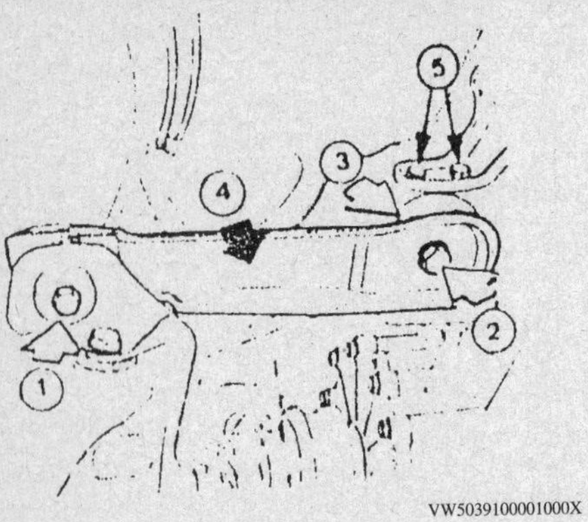

5
3
4
2
1
VW5039100001000X

Fig. 18 Transaxle support bolt locations. Fox

attaching bolt.

14. Lower transaxle housing slightly, then remove left transaxle mounting bolts.
15. Position engine/transaxle assembly as far to right as possible, then position a suitable transmission jack under transaxle and remove lower transaxle attaching bolts.
16. Separate transaxle from engine centering pins, then remove transaxle.
17. Reverse procedure to install, noting the following:
    a. Clean input shaft splines and lubricate lightly with No. MoS2 grease, or equivalent.
    b. Ensure clutch cover plate is positioned correctly.
    c. Tighten to specifications.
    d. Reset audio coded anti-theft system as outlined under "Precautions."

02A TRANSAXLE

1. Obtain audio coded anti-theft code, then disconnect battery ground strap and electrical connectors from transaxle.
2. Remove power steering reservoir from battery bracket if equipped.
3. Remove gearshift cable from gearshift lever, then the selector cable with linkage lever from the transaxle.
4. Remove cable support from transaxle.
5. Remove clutch slave cylinder and position aside. **Do not open hydraulic lines.**
6. Disconnect all electrical connectors and wiring from transaxle.
7. Remove engine to transaxle bolts from above. It may be necessary to remove intake hose from air flow sensor.
8. Remove three righthand side engine mount bolts, then the center bolt from lefthand engine mount. It may be necessary to remove coolant overflow bottle to gain access to bolt.
9. Remove fan, cover and mount, then the center nut from front transaxle bracket.
10. Install engine support bar tool No. 10-222 A, or equivalent, and bases tool No. 10-222 A/1, or equivalent.
11. Slightly tighten engine/transaxle support, then remove the starter and front transaxle bracket.
12. Remove transaxle support arm from

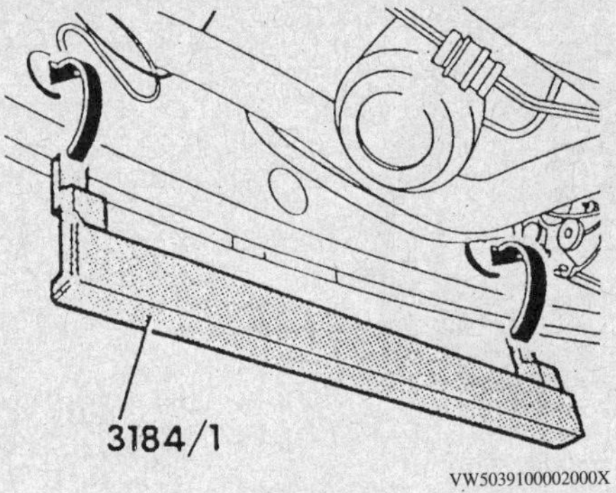

3184/1
VW5039100002000X

Fig. 19 Axle carrier support. Eurovan

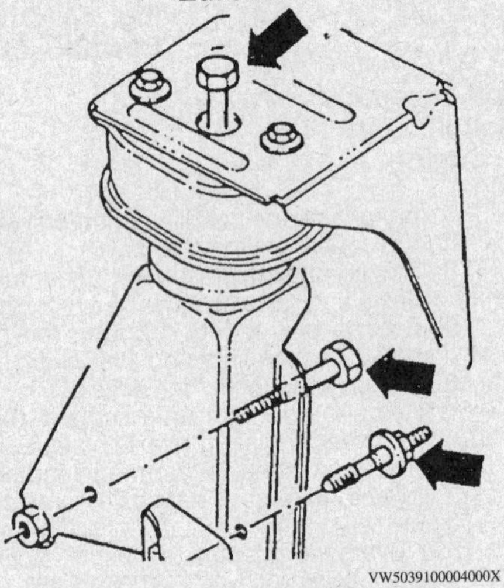

VW5039100004000X

Fig. 21 Transaxle bearing console. Eurovan

transaxle, then the balance weight from the mount.

13. Remove inner right constant velocity joint heat shield, then the axle shafts from the flanges. Wire axle shafts out of the way.
14. Remove transaxle bracket from transaxle, pry engine/transaxle mount rearward, then remove lower mounting bolt from transaxle bracket.
15. Push engine/transaxle mount as far as possible to the right, then lower slightly using spindle on support bar.
16. Remove gear carrier housing cover bolts and cover, position a transmission jack under transaxle, then remove lower engine/transaxle attachment bolt.
17. Carefully pry transaxle from bushings and lower from vehicle.
18. Reverse procedure to install, noting the following:
    a. Press clutch release lever toward transaxle housing, then secure by mounting pin or M8 X 22 bolt. **Remove pin after transaxle is installed.**
    b. Adjust shift linkage as previously described.
    c. Tighten nuts and bolts to specifications.
    d. Reset audio coded anti-theft system as outlined under "Precautions."

3184/1
3184
3230
VW5039100003000X

Fig. 20 Auxiliary carrier support. Eurovan

02B TRANSAXLE

1. Obtain audio coded anti-theft code, then disconnect battery ground cable.
2. Tilt radiator forward as outlined under "Engine, Replace."
3. Disconnect all electrical wiring from transaxle and starter.
4. Disconnect gearshift linkage as outlined under "Engine, Replace," then unscrew slave cylinder from transaxle and secure away with wire. **Do not open system or depress clutch pedal, otherwise the clutch will have to be bled.**
5. Remove brake booster/engine vacuum line from engine. Secure support tool No. 3250, or equivalent, then remove left driveshaft as follows:
    a. Loosen bolt drive driveshaft/wheel hub with the vehicle on its wheels.
    b. Remove wheel bearing housing/lower drive joint bolt, while supporting drive joint to prevent it from falling.
    c. Remove bolt for shock absorber and connecting stabilizer.
    d. Remove lower engine cover, then unbolt driveshaft from transaxle.
    e. Push shock absorber together completely, then remove driveshaft.
6. Disconnect right driveshaft from transaxle and tie up, then remove bolt for shock absorber and connecting rod/stabilizer on righthand side.
7. Disconnect ground cable from transaxle and console, then remove starter.
8. Remove alternator and disconnect A/C compressor without disconnecting hoses.
9. Remove mounting bolt for transaxle mounting bracket, then disconnect speedometer from bearing housing of right flange shaft.
10. Install catching fixture tool No. 3184, or equivalent, then install engine fixture tool No. 3227, or equivalent, to engine block.
11. Attach auxiliary carrier tool No. 3184/1, or equivalent, for catching fixture tool No. 3184, or equivalent, in end members, **Fig. 19,** if necessary after first removing wire harnesses and pipes.
12. Attach front end of catching fixture tool

No. 3184, or equivalent, in auxiliary carrier tool No. 3184/1, or equivalent, and rear end in transaxle carrier, **Fig. 20.** Guide pin of engine holder into bore of movable sled. **Sled will bear on righthand pipe when catching fixture is installed correctly.**

13. Tighten lift locks after installation of catching fixture.
14. Preload catching fixture with spindle, then loosen transaxle bearing console from transaxle mount on body, **Fig. 21.**
15. Lower transaxle to remove bearing console from transaxle, then push up stabilizer at both connecting rods as far as the stop for clearance for exhaust pipe.
16. Disconnect exhaust pipe from primary silencer, then remove engine/transaxle securing screws above bearing housing of output shaft/flange shaft on righthand side.
17. Place transaxle lifter tool No. VAG 1383, or equivalent, under transaxle and remove remaining engine/transaxle screws.
18. Secure transaxle and separate from engine and carefully lower from vehicle.
19. Reverse procedure to install, noting the following:
    a. Always transfer gearshift lever to new transaxle.
    b. Before installing transaxle, press clutch release lever towards transaxle housing and secure with dowel pin or M8 x 22 screw. Remove after installation of transaxle.
    c. Check for correct fit of cover when installing transaxle.
    d. **On models with power steering,** the bearing housing to transaxle carrier securing screws must be inserted in bores of bearing housing before installing transaxle.
    e. **On all models,** reset audio coded anti-theft system as outlined under "Precautions."

TIGHTENING SPECIFICATIONS

Year	Component	Torque/ Ft. Lbs.
013 & 014 TRANSAXLES		
1993	Axle Shaft To Transmission Flange Bolts	30
	Clutch Pressure Plate To Flywheel Bolts	18①
	Cover Plate To Transmission Bolts, 5-Speed Trans.	7
	Engine Stop To Block Bolts, 5-Speed Trans.	18
	Exhaust Pipe To Exhaust Manifold Bolts, 5-Speed Trans.	22
	Front Bracket To Transmission Bolts, 5-Speed Trans.	18
	Front Exhaust Pipe To Muffler/Catalytic Converter Bolts, 5-Speed Trans.	18
	Front Mount To Transmission Bolts, 4-Speed Trans.	18
	Gearshift Lever Bearing Housing To Gearshift Lever Housing Bolts, 4-Speed Trans.	7
	Mount To Front Support Bolt, 4-Speed Trans.	18
	Rubber Mount To Body Bolt	81
	Rubber Mount To Bracket Bolt, 5-Speed Trans.	81
	Shift Rod Clamp Nut & Bolt, 4-Speed Trans.	12
	Shift Rod Coupling Self-Locking Bolt	15
	Starter Motor Bolts, 5-Speed Trans.	15
	Subframe/Support To Body Bolts	48
	Transmission To Engine Bolts	41
020 TRANSAXLE, CABRIOLET		
1993–94	Axle Shaft To Transmission Flange Bolts	33
	Clutch Pressure Plate To Crankshaft Bolts	72①②
	Flywheel To Clutch Pressure Plate Bolts	22①
	Large Cover Plate To Transmission Bolts	7
	Lever Bearing Plate To Lever Housing Bolts	6
	Shift Rod Clamp Nut & Bolt	15
	Small Cover Plate To Transmission Bolts	7
	Starter Motor Bolts	33
	Transmission Rear Mount To Body Bolts	33
	Transmission Rear Mount To Transmission Bolts	33

Continued

TIGHTENING SPECIFICATIONS—Continued

Year	Component	Torque/ Ft. Lbs.
020 TRANSAXLE, CABRIOLET		
1993–94	Transmission To Engine Bolts	59
020 TRANSAXLE EXCEPT CABRIOLET		
1993–96	Axle Shaft To transmission Flange Bolts	33
	Clutch Pressure Plate To Crankshaft Bolts	44①③
	Flywheel To Clutch Pressure Plate Bolts	15
	Left Bracket To Engine Mount Bolt	44
	Left Bracket To Transmission Bolt	30
	Right Rear Bracket To Transmission Bolt	18
	Starter Motor to Transaxle Bolts	44
	Starter Motor to Front Mount Bolt	33
	Transmission To Engine Bolts (12 mm)	59
	Transmission To Engine Bolts (10 mm)	44
	Transmission To Engine Bolts (7 mm)	7
	Transmission To Engine Bolts (6 mm)	7
	Transmission Support To Transmission Bolt	18
02A TRANSAXLE		
1993–96	Axle Shaft To Transmission Flange Bolts	33
	Balance Weight To Mount Bolt	22
	Cable Support To Transmission Bolts	18
	Clutch Pressure Plate To Crankshaft Bolts	44①③
	Clutch Pressure Plate To Flywheel Bolts	15①
	Front Transmission Bracket To Rubber Bonded Bushing Bolt	44
	Left Transmission Bracket To Transmission Bolt	18
	Left Transmission Bracket & Transmission Support To Mount Bolt	44
	Right Rear Transmission Bracket To Mount Bolt	18
	Shifter Operating Cable Bolt	18
	Shifter Operating Cable Nut	11
	Slave Cylinder To Transmission Bolt	18
	Starter Motor Bolts	44
	Transmission Support To Engine & Transmission Bolt	33
	Transmission To Engine Bolts (12 mm)	59
	Transmission To Engine Bolts (10 mm)	44
	Transmission To Engine Bolts (7 mm)	7
02B TRANSAXLE		
1993	Axle Shaft To Transmission Flange Bolts, Except Syncro	33
	Axle Nut	144
	Clutch Pressure Plate To Flywheel Bolts	22③
	Front Left Transaxle Mount To Body	48
	Front Left Transaxle Mount To Transaxle	48
	Gearshift Lever Bearing Housing To Gearshift Lever Housing Bolts	7
	Hub Nut	144
	Rear Transaxle Mount (12 mm)	74
	Rear Transaxle Mount (10 mm)	30
	Rear Transaxle Mount To Bracket (16 mm)	148
	Shift Rod Clamp Nut & Bolt	18
	Starter To Transaxle	15
	Transaxle To Engine Bolts (12 mm)	59

Continued

TIGHTENING SPECIFICATIONS—Continued

Year	Component	Torque/ Ft. Lbs.
02B TRANSAXLE		
1993	Transaxle To Engine Bolts (8 mm)	18
	Transaxle Carrier To Engine Bolts (10 mm)	44
	Transaxle Carrier To Engine Bolts (8 mm)	18
	Transaxle Carrier To Transaxle Bolts	18

① — Loosen & tighten diagonally.
② — Coat threads w/D6 thread locking compound, or equivalent.
③ — Plus an additional 1/4 (90°) turn. This may be done in several steps.

Rear Axle & Suspension

NOTE: On Air Bag Equipped Models, Refer To "Air Bag System Precautions" Located In The Front Of This Manual For System Disarming & Arming Procedures.

INDEX

	Page No.
Precautions	49-61
Air Bag Systems	49-61
Audio Coded Anti-Theft System	49-61
Rear Axle, Replace	49-61
Cabrio, Corrado, Golf III, GTI, Jetta III & Passat	49-62
Cabriolet	49-61
Eurovan	49-62
Fox	49-62
Shock Absorber, Replace	49-63
Eurovan	49-63
Except Eurovan	49-63
Strut, Replace	49-63
Cabrio, Corrado, Golf III, GTI, Jetta III & Passat	49-63
Cabriolet	49-63
Fox	49-63
Strut Service	49-63
Tightening Specifications	49-64
Wheel Bearing, Adjust	49-62

PRECAUTIONS

Do not use computer memory saver tool on air bag equipped models. Using the tool will keep the air bag system charged and may cause accidental activation of the air bag unit. Prior to disconnecting the battery negative cable, obtain the radio security code. After service has been completed and the battery negative cable has been reconnected, use security code to activate the radio.

AIR BAG SYSTEMS

Refer to "Air Bag System Precautions" in the front of this manual for system disarming and arming procedures.

AUDIO CODED ANTI-THEFT SYSTEM

Some models are equipped with a radio anti-theft system that will disable the system when battery power is interrupted, unless the system is reset the radio will not operate.

1. Turn radio to On position, SAFE should be displayed.
2. Depress and hold AM/FM and SCAN buttons until 1000 remains on display. If AM/FM and SCAN buttons are depressed too long or depressed again, radio will misinterpret the 1000 as an attempt at coding and one incorrect coding attempt will be logged. **After two incorrect attempts to reset system, radio will lock up electronically. If this occurs, leave radio on for approximately one hour, then reset radio as if battery power were disconnected.**
3. Enter radio code using first four program station buttons. Security code will appear on display.
4. Depress and hold AM/FM and SCAN buttons again until SAFE is displayed.
5. Release AM/FM and SCAN buttons. Display should change to a radio frequency and operate normally.

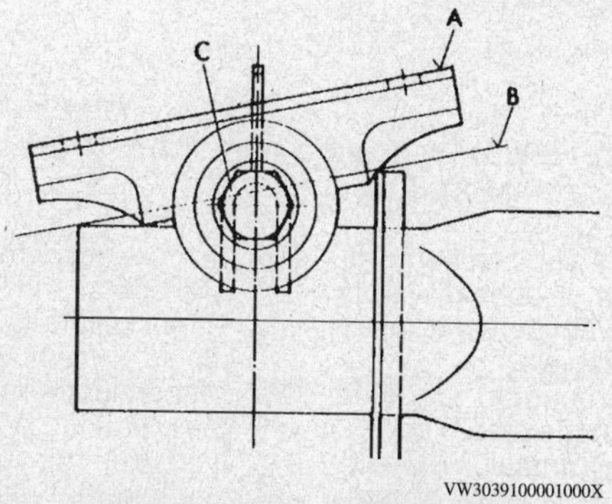
A
B
C
VW3039100001000X

Fig. 1 Rear axle mount alignment. Cabriolet

REAR AXLE

REPLACE

CABRIOLET

1. Obtain audio coded anti-theft code, then raise and support rear of vehicle.
2. Working from inside vehicle, disconnect parking brake cable from parking brake lever.
3. Disconnect and plug brake hoses.
4. Raise rear axle beam with a floor jack,

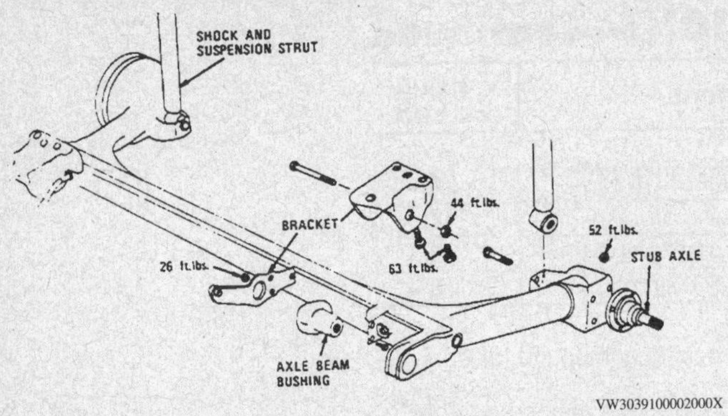
SHOCK AND
SUSPENSION STRUT
BRACKET
44 ft.lbs.
52 ft.lbs.
STUB AXLE
26 ft.lbs.
63 ft.lbs.
AXLE BEAM
BUSHING
VW3039100002000X

Fig. 2 Exploded view of rear axle assembly. Cabrio, Corrado, Golf III, GTI, Jetta III & Passat

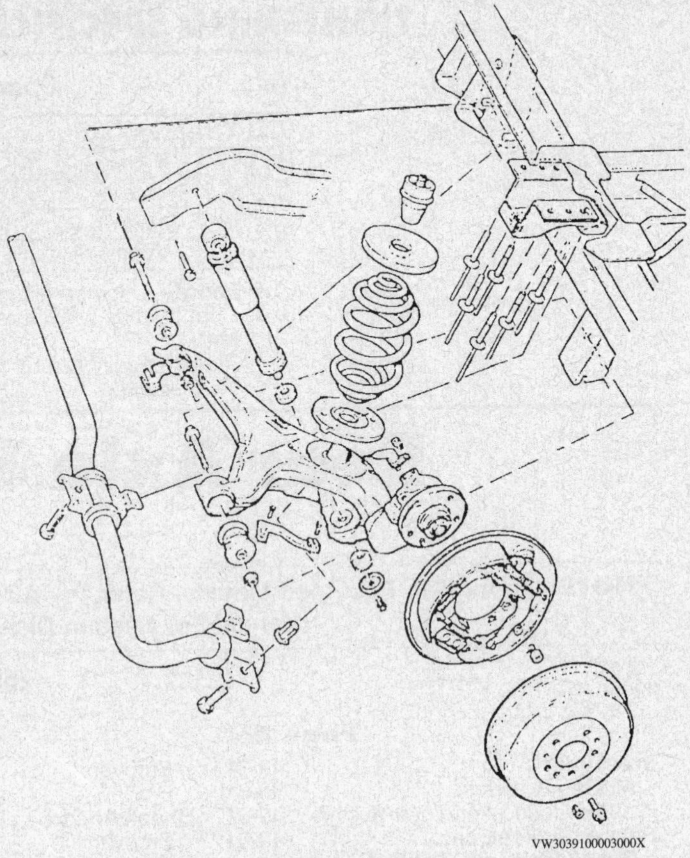
VW3039100003000X

Fig. 3 Exploded view of rear axle assembly. Eurovan

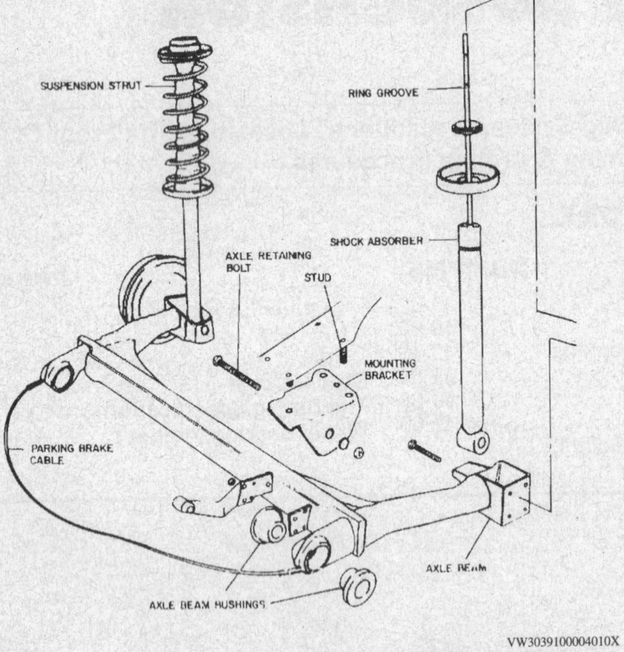
SUSPENSION STRUT
RING GROOVE
SHOCK ABSORBER
AXLE RETAINING
BOLT
STUD
MOUNTING
BRACKET
PARKING BRAKE
CABLE
AXLE BEAM BUSHINGS
VW3039100004010X

Fig. 4 Exploded view of rear axle assembly (Part 1 of 2). Fox

then remove upper strut to body attaching nut. Always disconnect struts one at a time to prevent personal injury and/or damage to vehicle.

5. Remove rear axle mount to rear axle attaching bolts, then the rear axle.
6. Reverse procedure to install. **When installing rear axle assembly, ensure upper edge of rear mount (A), Fig. 1, is parallel to line (B). If not, loosen nut (C), adjust mount as required, then tighten nut to specifications.** Reset audio coded anti-theft system as outlined under "Precautions."

CABRIO, CORRADO, GOLF III, GTI, JETTA III & PASSAT

1. Obtain audio coded anti-theft code, then raise and support rear of vehicle.
2. Raise and support vehicle, then remove wheels.
3. Disconnect rear brake pressure regulator spring if equipped, **Fig. 2.**
4. Remove rear brakes as outlined under "Drum Brakes."
5. Disconnect wheel speed sensors, if equipped, and brake fluid lines from wheel cylinders, then remove backing plates and spindles.
6. Disconnect and remove electrical cables, parking brake cables, and brake fluid lines from rear axle.
7. Support rear axle at rear, then disconnect rear struts.
8. Support rear axle at front, then disconnect from mounting bracket.
9. Remove axle from vehicle.
10. Reverse procedure to install, noting the following:
    a. Tighten to specifications.
    b. Bleed brakes as outlined under "Hydraulic Brake Systems."
    c. Adjust rear brake pressure, if equipped, with a rear brake pressure regulator, as outlined under "Hydraulic Brake Systems."
    d. Ensure mounting pads for spindles are clean and free of rust and scale.
    e. Reset audio coded anti-theft system as outlined under "Precautions."

EUROVAN

Refer to **Fig. 3** for rear axle replacement procedure.

FOX

1. Raise and support rear of vehicle.
2. Disconnect parking brake cable from pull rod, **Fig. 4.**
3. Disconnect and plug brake hoses. **If mounting brackets are to remain on body, remove axle retaining bolts. When installing bolts, ensure axle is horizontal and level prior to tightening bolts.**
4. Disconnect brake equalizer, then remove mounting bracket nuts, leaving one nut installed on each side.
5. Loosen exhaust pipe attaching rings, then lower vehicle while supporting axle with a jack.
6. Disconnect strut upper mounts, then remove remaining nut from both mount brackets.
7. Raise rear of vehicle slowly. Lift parking brake cable over exhaust pipe and slide axle assembly from under vehicle.
8. Reverse procedure to install, noting the following:
    a. Install mounting brackets on axle at an angle of 15–19°.
    b. Bleed brake system.
    c. Check total toe of rear axle.

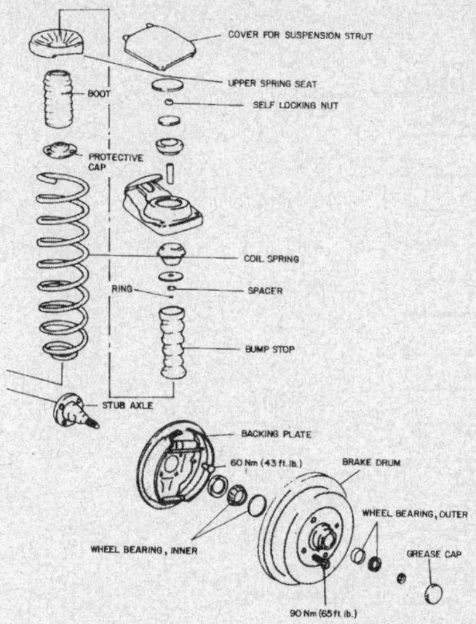
COVER FOR SUSPENSION STRUT
UPPER SPRING SEAT
SELF LOCKING NUT
BOOT
PROTECTIVE CAP
COIL SPRING
RING
SPACER
BUMP STOP
STUB AXLE
BACKING PLATE
60 Nm (43 ft. lb.)
BRAKE DRUM
WHEEL BEARING, OUTER
WHEEL BEARING, INNER
GREASE CAP
90 Nm (65 ft. lb.)
VW3039100004020X

Fig. 4 Exploded view of rear axle assembly (Part 2 of 2). Fox

d. Tighten nuts and bolts to specifications.

WHEEL BEARING

ADJUST

1. Raise and support rear of vehicle, then remove the wheel/tire assembly.
2. Remove grease cap, then the cotter pin and locknut.
3. Tighten adjusting nut while turning wheel to settle bearings.
4. Loosen, then retighten adjusting nut, until thrust washer can be moved slightly with screwdriver.
5. Install locknut and new cotter pin, then the grease cap.
6. Install wheel/tire assembly and lower vehicle to ground.

STRUT

REPLACE

Whenever replacing struts, always remove then install one strut at a time to prevent personal injury and/or damage to vehicle.

CABRIOLET

1. Raise and support rear of vehicle.
2. Position a floor jack under axle beam, then remove upper strut to body attaching nut.
3. Carefully lower floor jack, then remove strut to axle beam mounting bolt.

CABRIO, CORRADO, GOLF III, GTI, JETTA III & PASSAT

1. Raise and support vehicle, then loosen but do not remove lower strut mounting bolts, **Fig. 2.**

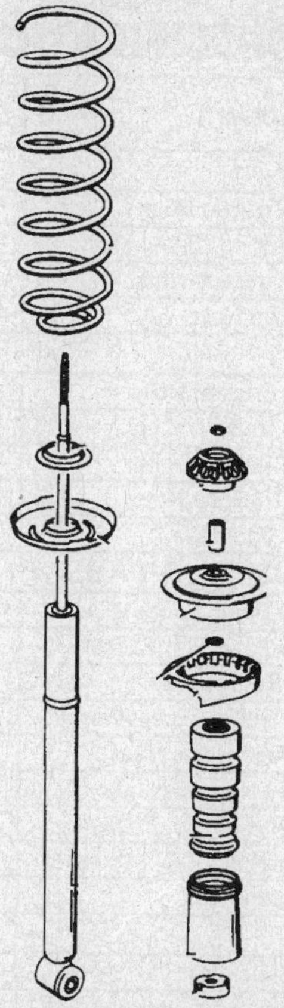
VW2039300001000X

Fig. 5 Exploded view of rear strut. Cabrio, Golf III, GTI & Jetta III

2. Support axle beam at rear ends with struts in fully extended position.
3. From inside vehicle, locate and disconnect upper strut mounting for one side. **Remove and install struts one side at a time.**
4. Remove lower strut mounting bolt, then strut.
5. Reverse procedure to install. Tighten to specifications.

FOX

1. Remove shock absorber upper cover, then disconnect strut from body, **Fig. 4.**
2. Raise rear of vehicle slowly and remove strut to axle attaching bolt.
3. Disconnect strut from lower mounting while pressing down on wheel slightly.

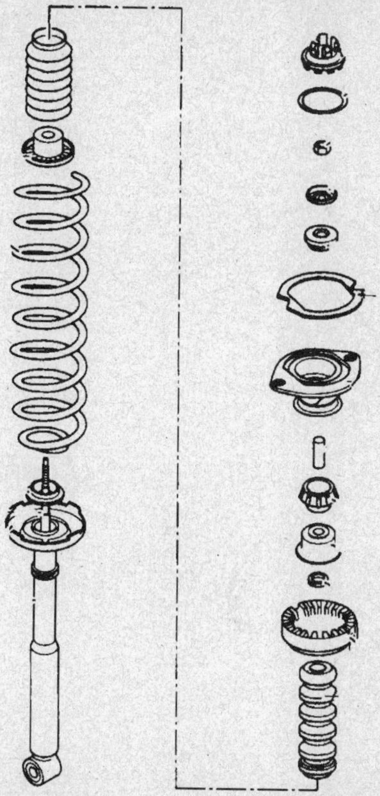
VW2039300002000X

Fig. 6 Exploded view of rear strut. Passat

4. Guide strut assembly out between wheel and wheel housing.
5. Reverse procedure to install.

STRUT SERVICE

Refer to **Figs. 5 and 6** for component location locations during strut service.

1. Remove strut from vehicle as outlined under "Strut, Replace."
2. Secure strut/coil spring assembly in a suitable coil spring compressor, remove nut, then spring and components.
3. Assemble spring and components to new strut.
4. Reverse procedure to complete installation.

SHOCK ABSORBER

REPLACE

EUROVAN

Refer to **Fig. 3** to aid in removal and installation of shock absorber.

EXCEPT EUROVAN

Refer to "Strut Service" for procedures.

TIGHTENING SPECIFICATIONS

Year	Component	Torque/ Ft. Lbs.
CABRIOLET		
1993–94	Lower Strut To Axle Bolts	33
	Stabilizer Bar Retaining Clamp Nuts	22
	Upper Strut To Body Nuts	23
	Wheel Lug Nuts	81
FOX		
1993	Axle To Axle Bracket Bolts	44
	Axle Bracket To Body Nuts	33
	Lower Strut To Axle Bolts	43
	Upper Strut To Body Nuts	15
	Wheel Lug Nuts	81
CORRADO, GOLF, GTI, JETTA & PASSAT		
1993–96	Axle To Axle Bracket Bolts, Except Passat	44
	Axle To Axle Bracket Bolts, Passat	59
	Axle Bracket To Body Bolts	52
	Lower Strut To Axle Bolts, Except Passat	52
	Lower Strut To Axle Bolts, Passat	77
	Strut Assembly Nuts, Passat	18
	Upper Strut To Body Bolts, Passat	18
	Upper Strut To Body Nuts, Except Passat	11
	Wheel Lug Nuts	81
EUROVAN		
1993	Upper Shock Bolt	74
	Lower Shock absorber to Control arm Bolt	33
	Stabilizer Bar Bolts	22
	Wheel Lug Nuts	118

Front Suspension & Steering

NOTE: On Air Bag Equipped Models, Refer To "Air Bag System Precautions" Located In The Front Of This Manual For System Disarming & Arming Procedures.

INDEX

Page No.

Ball Joint, Replace 49-66
Cabriolet 49-66
Eurovan 49-66
Except Cabriolet, Eurovan & Fox 49-66
Fox 49-67
Coil Spring, Replace 49-67
Control Arm, Replace 49-68
Cabriolet 49-68
Eurovan 49-68
Except Cabriolet, Eurovan & Fox 49-68
Fox 49-68
Description 49-65
Eurovan 49-65
Except Eurovan 49-65
Hub & Bearing, Replace 49-66
Installation 49-66
Removal 49-66
Manual Steering Gear, Replace 49-69
Golf III & Jetta III 49-69
Power Steering 49-93
Power Steering Gear, Replace 49-68
Cabrio, Golf III, GTI, Jetta III & Passat 49-69
Cabriolet 49-68
Corrado 49-68
Eurovan 49-69
Precautions 49-65
Air Bag Systems 49-65
Shock Absorber, Replace 49-68
Eurovan 49-68
Except Eurovan 49-68
Strut, Replace 49-67
Except Fox 49-67
Fox 49-67
Strut Service 49-67
Tightening Specifications 49-70
Wheel Bearing Housing, Replace 49-65
Cabrio, Corrado, Golf III, GTI, Jetta III & Passat 49-65
Cabriolet 49-65
Eurovan 49-65
Fox 49-66

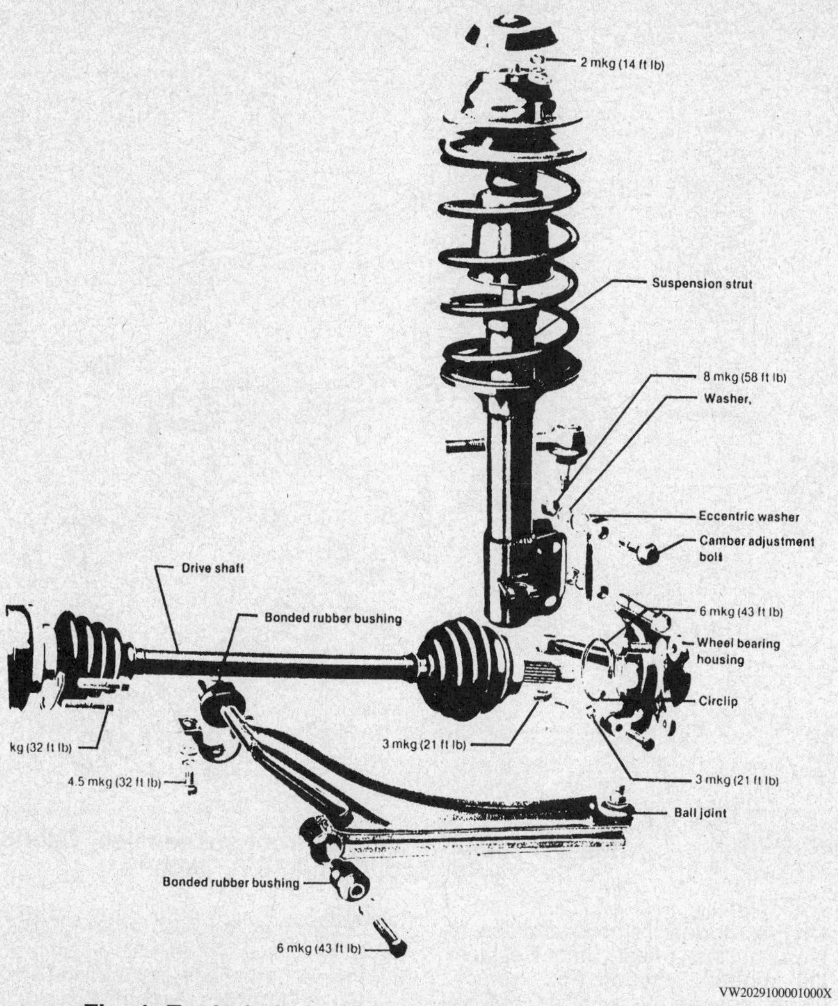
2 mkg (14 ft lb)
Suspension strut
8 mkg (58 ft lb)
Washer,
Eccentric washer
Camber adjustment bolt
Drive shaft
Bonded rubber bushing
6 mkg (43 ft lb)
Wheel bearing housing
Circlip
kg (32 ft lb)
3 mkg (21 ft lb)
4.5 mkg (32 ft lb)
3 mkg (21 ft lb)
Ball joint
Bonded rubber bushing
6 mkg (43 ft lb)
VW2029100001000X

Fig. 1 Exploded view of front suspension. Cabriolet

PRECAUTIONS

AIR BAG SYSTEMS

Refer to "Air Bag System Precautions" in the front of this manual for system disarming and arming procedures.

DESCRIPTION

EXCEPT EUROVAN

These vehicles use a McPherson strut type front suspension. The upper part of strut is attached to the upper fender reinforcement. On Fox models, the wheel bearing housing is integral with the strut assembly and is attached to the lower control arm through a ball joint. On all models except Fox, the strut and wheel bearing housing are separate and distinct parts, with the strut attached to the housing with through bolts. The assembly is attached to the lower control arm through a ball joint, **Figs. 1 through 3.** During steering maneuvers, the strut and housing rotate as an assembly.

The axle shafts are attached inboard to the transaxle output drive flanges and outboard to the driven wheel hub.

EUROVAN

The Eurovan has a shock absorber/torsion bar front suspension system, **Fig. 4.** The shock and wheel bearing housing are separate and distinct parts, with the shock attached to the housing with through bolts.

The axle shafts are attached inboard to the transaxle output drive flanges and outboard to the driven wheel hub.

WHEEL BEARING HOUSING

REPLACE

CABRIOLET

Removal

1. Remove axle shaft to hub retaining nut.
2. Raise and support vehicle. Remove wheel assembly.
3. Remove brake caliper and support using a length of wire.
4. Remove brake rotor.
5. Remove tie rod to wheel bearing housing retaining nut, then separate tie rod from wheel bearing housing.
6. Remove ball joint to wheel bearing housing clamp bolt, then separate ball joint from wheel bearing housing.
7. Mark location of camber adjusting bolt, then remove the camber and through bolts, **Fig. 1.**
8. Support axle shaft, pull housing from strut and remove housing from vehicle.

Installation

1. Insert axle shaft into hub, then install wheel bearing housing onto strut bracket. Install cam and through bolts. Align reference marks on cam bolt and tighten through bolt to specifications.
2. Install ball joint and clamp bolt. Tighten clamp bolt to specifications.
3. Connect tie rod to wheel bearing housing and tighten retaining nut to specifications. Install new cotter pin.
4. Install brake rotor and caliper.
5. Install wheel, then axle shaft to hub retaining nut, lower vehicle and tighten to specifications.

CABRIO, CORRADO, GOLF III, GTI, JETTA III & PASSAT

Refer to **Figs. 2 and 3** to aid in removal and installation of wheel bearing housing.

Removal

1. Remove axle shaft to hub retaining nut.
2. Raise and support vehicle. Remove wheel assembly.
3. Remove brake caliper and support using a length of wire.
4. Remove brake rotor.
5. Remove tie rod to wheel bearing housing retaining nut, then separate tie rod from wheel bearing housing.
6. Remove bolts retaining ball joint to lower control arm, then ball joint from control arm.
7. Mark location of camber adjusting bolt, if installed, then remove the bolts, **Figs. 2 and 3.**
8. Support axle shaft, pull housing from strut and remove housing from vehicle.

Installation

1. Insert axle shaft into hub, then install wheel bearing housing onto strut bracket. Install cam bolts, if installed, and through bolts. Align reference marks on cam bolt and tighten through bolt to specifications.
2. Install ball to control arm, then tighten bolts to specifications.
3. Connect tie rod to wheel bearing housing and tighten retaining nut to specifications. Install new cotter pin.
4. Install brake rotor and caliper.
5. Install wheel and axle shaft to hub retaining nut, then lower vehicle and tighten to specifications.

EUROVAN

Refer to **Fig. 4** to aid in removal and installation of wheel bearing housing.

To prevent component damage or personal injury always install upper control arm support tool No. 3250, or

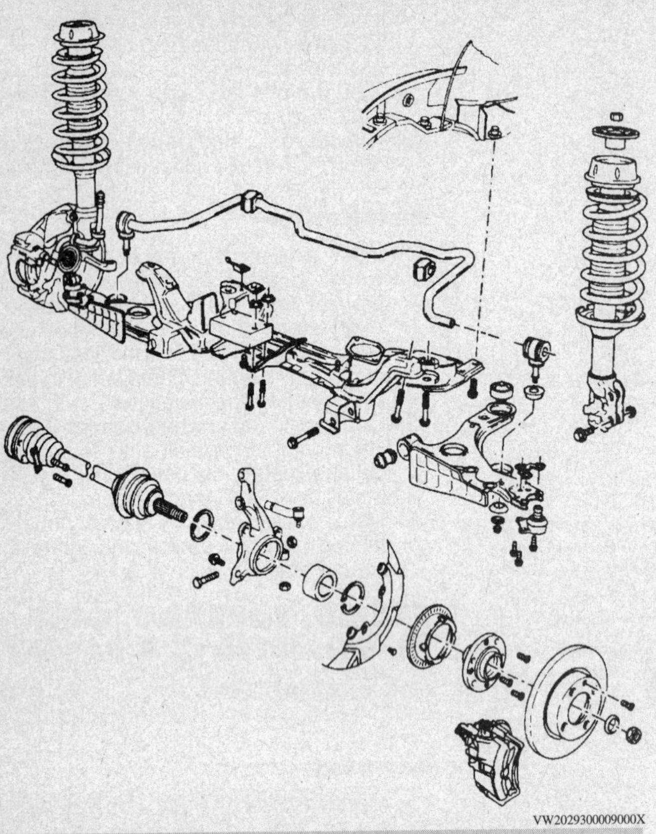
VW2029300009000X

Fig. 2 Component view of front suspension. Passat

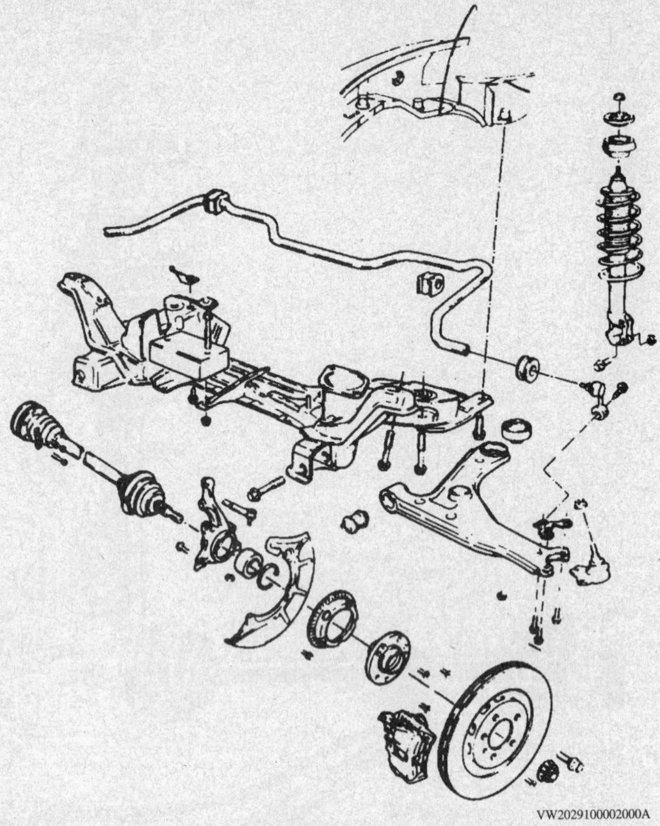
VW2029100002000A

Fig. 3 Exploded view of front suspension. Cabrio, Corrado, Golf III, GTI, Jetta III

equivalent, Fig. 5, to suspension or release tension from torsion bars before disassembling suspension components.

1. Install upper control arm support tool No. 3250, or equivalent, on both sides, then loosen axle shaft bolt with vehicle on wheels.
2. Remove wheel, then raise and support vehicle.
3. Remove link rod bolt, then caliper and secure away with wire.
4. Remove brake disc and splash shield.
5. Press tie rod off steering arm, then remove bolts securing wheel bearing housing/lower ball joint.
6. Mark position of eccentric bushing to wheel bearing housing.
7. Separate wheel bearing housing/upper ball joint, then remove wheel bearing housing.
8. Reverse procedure to install.

FOX

Since the wheel bearing housing is integral with the strut assembly, it is necessary to remove the strut assembly to service the housing. Refer to "Strut, Replace."

HUB & BEARING

REPLACE

REMOVAL

Damage will occur to the wheel bearing as hub is pressed from the housing. Therefore, it will be necessary to install a new bearing.

1. **On Fox models,** remove strut assembly as outlined under "Strut, Replace."
2. **On models except Fox,** remove wheel bearing housing as outlined under "Wheel Bearing Housing, Replace."
3. **On all models,** press hub from wheel bearing housing.
4. Using a suitable puller, remove wheel bearing inner race from hub.
5. Remove brake dust shield from wheel bearing housing.
6. Remove retaining clips, then press bearing from wheel bearing housing.

INSTALLATION

1. Install outer retaining clip, then press new bearing into housing. Ensure press tool bears only against outer race of bearing assembly.
2. Install inner retaining clip.
3. Install brake dust shield on wheel bearing housing.
4. Press hub assembly into wheel bearing housing. Ensure press tool properly supports inner bearing races of bearing assembly.
5. Install strut or wheel bearing housing.

BALL JOINT

REPLACE

EXCEPT CABRIOLET, EUROVAN & FOX

1. Raise and support vehicle, then remove front wheel.
2. **On Passat models,** remove ball joint to wheel bearing housing clamp bolt, then separate ball joint from housing.
3. **On all models except Passat,** remove ball joint nut, then using a suitable tool, separate taper shaft from wheel bearing housing.
4. **On all models,** mark position of ball joint in control arm for later assembly.
5. Remove bolts, then ball joint from control arm
6. Position new ball joint to control arm and install retaining bolts, spring washers and nuts and tighten to specifications.
7. Reverse procedure to complete installation.

CABRIOLET

1. Raise and support vehicle, then remove front wheel.
2. Remove ball joint to wheel bearing housing clamp bolt, then separate ball joint from housing.
3. Using a 1/4 inch drill bit, drill out rivets, then chisel off rivet heads and remove ball joint from control arm.
4. Position new ball joint to control arm, install retaining bolts, spring washers and nuts and tighten to specifications.
5. Reverse procedure to complete installation.

EUROVAN

Refer to "Wheel Bearing Housing, Replace" for ball joint removal.

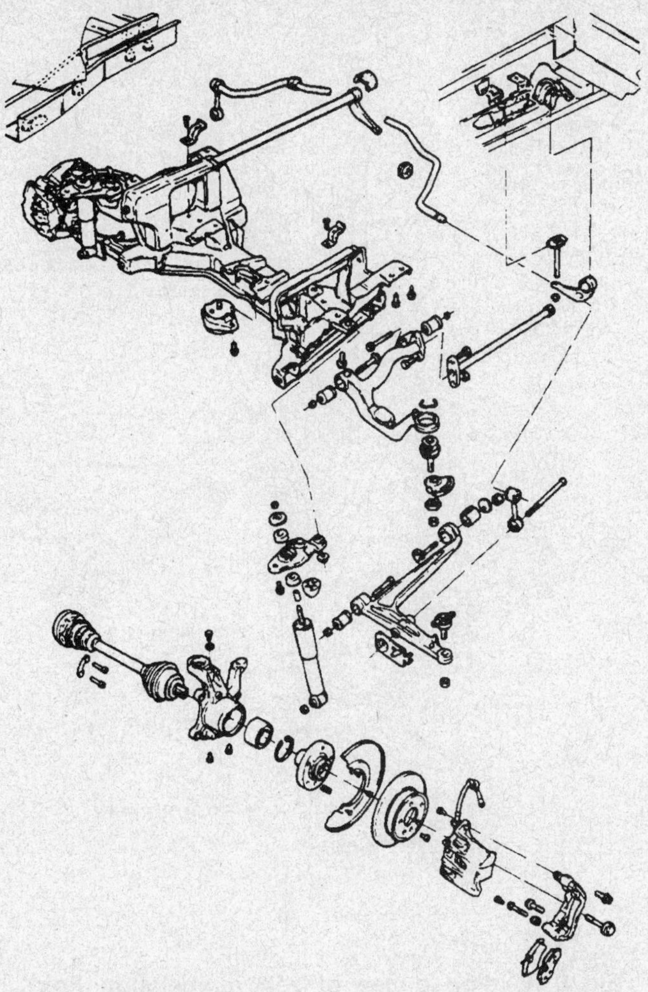
VW2029300010000X

Fig. 4 Exploded view of front suspension. Eurovan

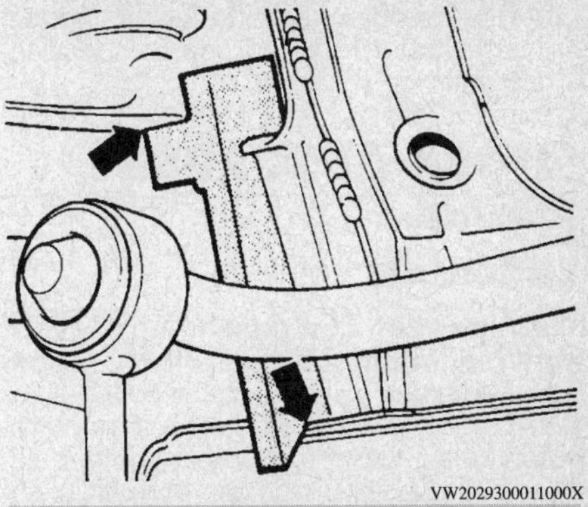
VW2029300011000X

Fig. 5 Supporting front suspension. Eurovan

1. Raise and support vehicle, then remove front wheels.
2. Disconnect caliper brake hose from brake line support on strut.
3. Mark position of strut to wheel bearing housing.
4. Support control arm and wheel bearing housing assembly with a suitable jack, then remove strut to wheel bearing housing bolts.
5. Lower wheel bearing housing assembly and disconnect from strut.
6. **On Cabriolet models,** remove two retaining nuts from inner fender strut tower.
7. **On all models except Cabriolet,** remove the upper nut and stop plate.
8. **On all models,** remove the strut assembly.
9. Reverse procedure to install. Tighten to specifications.

FOX

1. Loosen axle shaft nut and wheel lug nuts, **Fig. 6,** then raise and support front of vehicle and remove front wheel.
2. Remove brake caliper attaching bolts and brake caliper, then the brake line bracket.
3. Remove wheel bearing housing to ball joint clamp bolt. Then, using a suitable puller, press tie rod end off of strut steering arm.
4. Disconnect stabilizer bar from lower control arm.
5. Remove axle nut, then push control arm down and disconnect axle shaft from wheel bearing housing.
6. Remove upper mounting nut, then carefully lower strut from vehicle.
7. Reverse procedure to install.

FOX

1. Raise and support vehicle, then remove front wheel.
2. Scribe mark where ball joint flange meets lower control arm to aid installation.
3. Remove ball joint to wheel bearing housing clamp bolt, then separate ball joint from wheel bearing housing.
4. Disconnect stabilizer bar from lower control arm.
5. Remove ball joint to lower control arm retaining bolts and the ball joint.
6. Install new ball joint to control arm, align scribe mark and tighten retaining bolts to specifications.
7. Reverse procedure to complete installation.

COIL SPRING

REPLACE

1. Remove strut assembly as outlined under "Strut, Replace." **Mark position of upper mount in relation to strut. Scribe mark on upper mount to aid installation.**
2. Using tool No. US 4475, or equivalent, compress coil spring.
3. Hold shock absorber shaft with hex key, then remove attaching nut.
4. Carefully release tension on spring compressor, then remove retainer, end collar and mount, rubber damper, bearing, upper spring seat and the coil spring.
5. Inspect rubber components for deterioration, retainers and seats for cracks or distortion and bearing for binding. Replace if necessary.
6. Position coil spring onto strut and compress, using tool US 4475, or equivalent.
7. Install upper spring seat, bearing rubber damper, end collar and mount, then the retainer and nut. Tighten nut to specifications.
8. Remove spring compressor.

STRUT

REPLACE

EXCEPT FOX

Mark position of strut to hub cam bolt, if installed, to aid installation.

STRUT SERVICE

These vehicles incorporate an integral, non-serviceable shock absorber cartridge built into the strut assembly.

1. Remove coil spring as outlined previously.
2. Secure strut assembly in a vise, then remove the strut tube threaded cap.
3. Remove strut cartridge from strut assembly.

4. Reverse procedure to install. Tighten strut tube threaded cap to specifications.

SHOCK ABSORBER

REPLACE

EUROVAN

To prevent component damage or personal injury always install upper control arm support tool No. 3250, or equivalent, Fig. 5, to suspension or release tension from torsion bars before disassembling suspension components.

1. Install upper control arm support tool No. 3250, or equivalent, on both sides.
2. Remove lower shock absorber bolt, then remove from upper mounting.
3. Reverse procedure to install.

EXCEPT EUROVAN

Refer to "Strut Service."

CONTROL ARM

REPLACE

CABRIOLET

Manual Transmission

1. Raise and support vehicle, then remove front wheel.
2. Remove lower control arm to frame attaching bolts, then disconnect control arm from frame.
3. Remove ball joint to wheel bearing housing clamp bolt, then separate ball joint from housing.
4. Disconnect stabilizer bar from control arm, if equipped, then remove control arm from vehicle.
5. Reverse procedure to install.

Automatic Transmission

1. Raise and support vehicle, then remove front wheel.
2. Remove left front engine mount, then the rear mount attaching nut.
3. Remove engine mount support, then install engine support bar tool No. 10-222, or equivalent, across engine compartment.
4. Lift engine with support bar until lower control arm attaching bolts can be removed.
5. Remove control arm to frame attaching bolts.
6. Remove ball joint to wheel bearing housing clamp bolt, then separate ball joint from housing.
7. Disconnect stabilizer bar from control arm, if equipped, then remove control arm.
8. Reverse procedure to install.

EXCEPT CABRIOLET, EUROVAN & FOX

Refer to **Figs. 2 and 3** to aid in removal and installation of lower control arm.

1. Raise and support vehicle, then remove wheel.
2. Disconnect stabilizer bar from control arm.

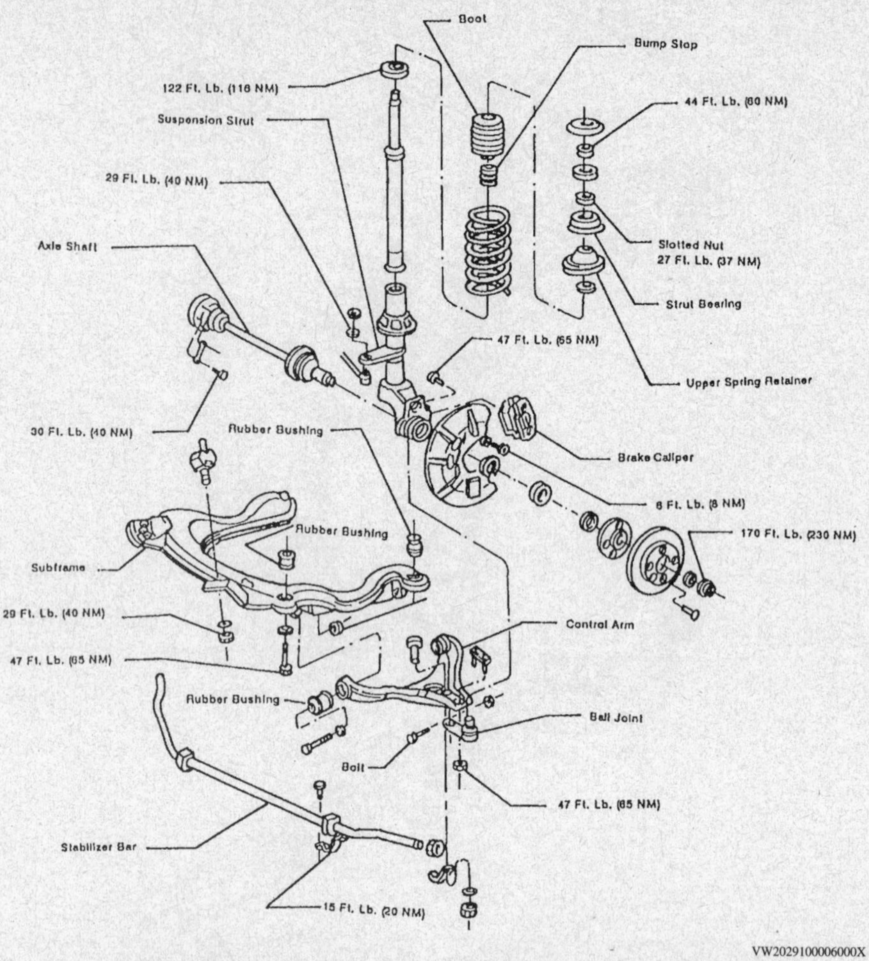

Boot
Bump Stop
122 Ft. Lb. (116 NM)
Suspension Strut
44 Ft. Lb. (60 NM)
29 Ft. Lb. (40 NM)
Axle Shaft
Slotted Nut
27 Ft. Lb. (37 NM)
Strut Bearing
47 Ft. Lb. (65 NM)
Upper Spring Retainer
30 Ft. Lb. (40 NM)
Rubber Bushing
Brake Caliper
6 Ft. Lb. (8 NM)
Rubber Bushing
170 Ft. Lb. (230 NM)
Subframe
29 Ft. Lb. (40 NM)
Control Arm
47 Ft. Lb. (65 NM)
Rubber Bushing
Ball Joint
Bolt
47 Ft. Lb. (65 NM)
Stabilizer Bar
15 Ft. Lb. (20 NM)
VW2029100006000X

Fig. 6 Exploded view of front suspension. Fox

3. Mark position of control arm to ball joint, then remove ball joint mounting bolts.
4. Remove control arm to subframe mounting bolts, then control arm.
5. Reverse procedure to install. Tighten to specification.

EUROVAN

To prevent component damage or personal injury always install upper control arm support tool No. 3250, or equivalent, Fig. 5, to suspension or release tension from torsion bars before disassembling suspension components.

Refer to **Fig. 7** to aid in removal and installation of lower control arm.

FOX

Refer to **Fig. 6** to aid in removal and installation of lower control arm.

POWER STEERING GEAR

REPLACE

CABRIOLET

1. Disconnect battery ground cable.
2. Raise and support vehicle, then disconnect power steering pressure hose and drain system.
3. Disconnect both tie rods from steering arms, then remove transaxle mount with bracket.
4. Remove exhaust manifold, then pressure and return lines at steering gear.
5. Remove gearshift linkage bracket from steering gear housing.
6. Remove ground wire and clamps from steering gear.
7. Remove steering gear by moving as far to the right as possible. Swing left tie rod downward, then pull steering gear out.
8. Reverse procedure to install.

CORRADO

1. Raise and support vehicle, then remove tie rods using Kukko commercial puller tool No. 128/2, or equivalent.
2. Remove suction hose at power steering pump and drain.
3. Remove lock bolts for universal joint shaft, then remove nuts and take power steering gear assembly off mounting.
4. Disconnect pressure and return lines from steering gear.
5. Support engine/transaxle with support tool No. 10-222A, or equivalent, and tool No. 10-222A/1, or equivalent.
6. Remove bolts for subframe and move

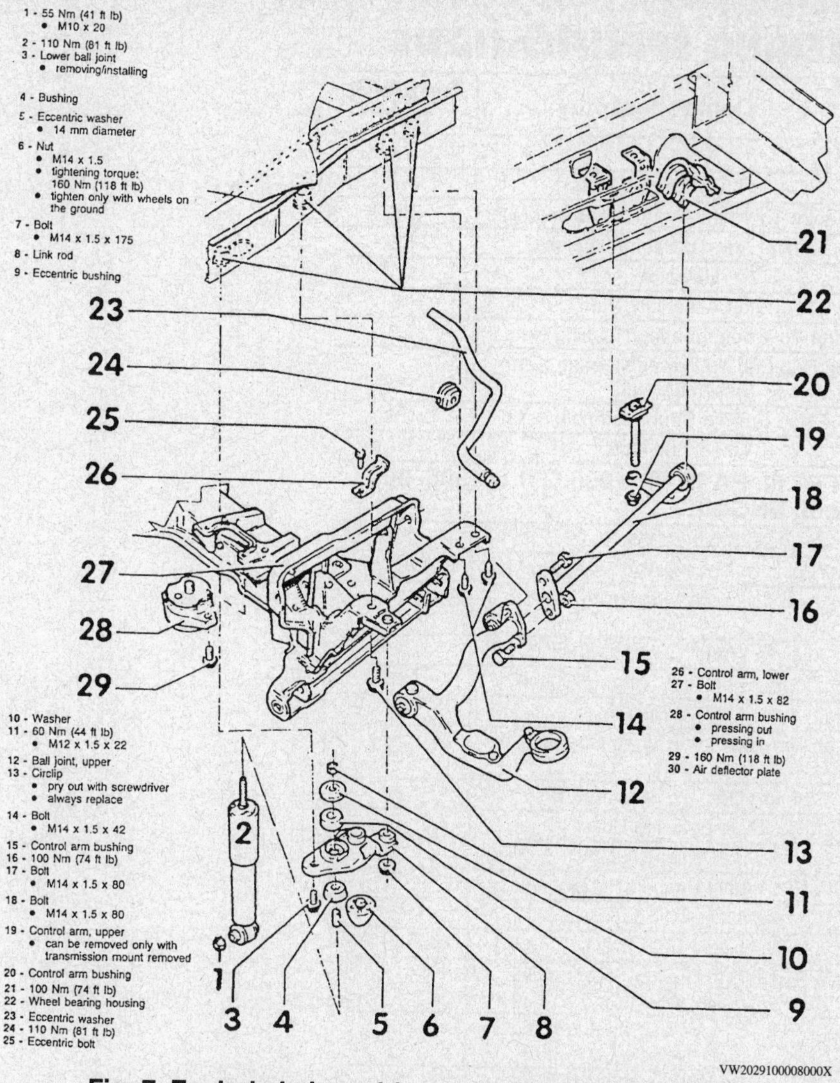
1 - 55 Nm (41 ft lb)
• M10 x 20
2 - 110 Nm (81 ft lb)
3 - Lower ball joint
• removing/installing
4 - Bushing
5 - Eccentric washer
• 14 mm diameter
6 - Nut
• M14 x 1.5
• tightening torque: 160 Nm (118 ft lb)
• tighten only with wheels on the ground
7 - Bolt
• M14 x 1.5 x 175
8 - Link rod
9 - Eccentric bushing
10 - Washer
11 - 60 Nm (44 ft lb)
• M12 x 1.5 x 22
12 - Ball joint, upper
13 - Circlip
• pry out with screwdriver
• always replace
14 - Bolt
• M14 x 1.5 x 42
15 - Control arm bushing
16 - 100 Nm (74 ft lb)
17 - Bolt
• M14 x 1.5 x 80
18 - Bolt
• M14 x 1.5 x 80
19 - Control arm, upper
• can be removed only with transmission mount removed
20 - Control arm bushing
21 - 100 Nm (74 ft lb)
22 - Wheel bearing housing
23 - Eccentric washer
24 - 110 Nm (81 ft lb)
25 - Eccentric bolt
26 - Control arm, lower
27 - Bolt
• M14 x 1.5 x 82
28 - Control arm bushing
• pressing out
• pressing in
29 - 160 Nm (118 ft lb)
30 - Air deflector plate
VW2029100008000X

Fig. 7 Exploded view of front suspension. Eurovan

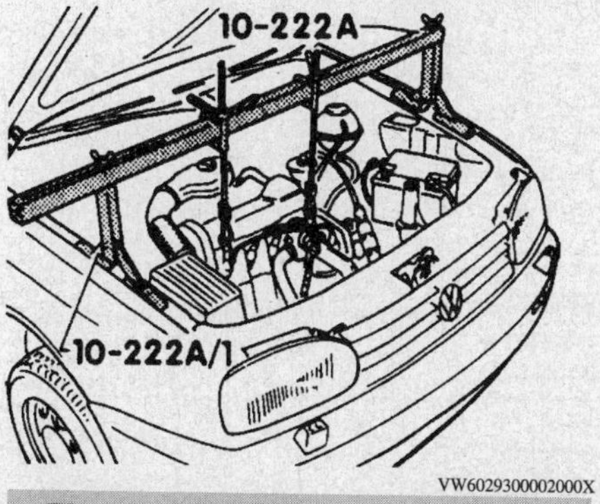
10-222A
10-222A/1
VW6029300002000X

Fig. 9 Engine support during steering gear removal. Cabrio, Golf III, GTI, Jetta III & Passat

steering gear towards rear.
7. Reverse procedure to install.

CABRIO, GOLF III, GTI, JETTA III & PASSAT

1. Raise and support vehicle, then disconnect tie rod ends from steering arms.
2. From under lefthand side of instrument panel, remove connecting bolts from steering shaft, **Fig. 8.**
3. Drain oil from steering system at suction line of pump.
4. Support engine and transaxle using support frame tool No. VW10-222A and leg set tool No. VW 10-222A/1, or equivalents, **Fig. 9.**
5. Disconnect steering shaft boot from steering gear.
6. Remove subframe to body bolts, then lower assembly until steering shaft can be separated.
7. Disconnect fluid lines from steering gear, cap or plug all lines or fittings.
8. Remove steering gear mounting bolts. Note that bolts will stay in subframe.

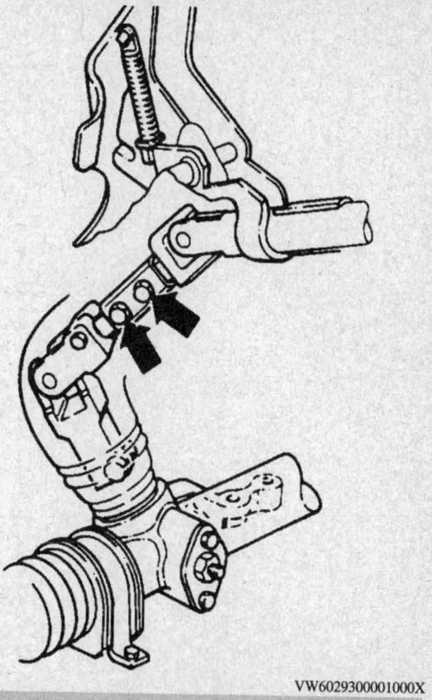
VW6029300001000X

Fig. 8 Steering shaft bolts removal. Cabrio, Golf III, GTI, Jetta III & Passat

9. Remove steering gear towards rear of vehicle.
10. Reverse procedure to install.

EUROVAN

1. Raise and support vehicle, then remove lower insulation pan.
2. Remove front exhaust pipe.
3. **On early production models,** remove heat shield above power steering gear.
4. **On all models,** loosen banjo bolt on power steering pump and drain fluid.
5. Disconnect hydraulic lines at steering gear and seal openings with plastic plugs and tape.
6. Disconnect tie rod from steering gear, then remove stabilizer clamps from subframe.
7. Remove universal joint bolt on steering pinion, then disconnect power steering gear from subframe.
8. Press stabilizer upward, then move steering gear slightly to right to remove pinion from universal joint.
9. Remove steering gear by moving to left, then out toward the rear.
10. Reverse procedure to install.

MANUAL STEERING GEAR

REPLACE

GOLF III & JETTA III

Follow procedure described under "Power Steering Gear, Replace."

TIGHTENING SPECIFICATIONS

Year	Component	Torque/Ft. Lbs.
CABRIOLET		
1993–94	Axle Shaft To Hub Nuts	177
	Ball Joint To Wheel Bearing Housing Nuts	36
	Control Arm To Subframe Bolts	52
	Hub Nut	177
	Strut Assembly Nut	15
	Strut To Wheel Bearing Housing Nuts	59
	Tie Rod End To Power Steering Gear Assembly Nuts	
	Tie Rod End To Strut Assembly Nuts	22
	Wheel Lug Nuts	81
GOLFIII, JETTA III, PASSAT, 1996 GTI & 1995–96 CABRIO w/2.0L ENGINE		
1993–96	Axle Shaft To Hub Nuts	195
	Ball Joint To Control Arm Nuts, Passat	25
	Ball Joint To Control Arm Nuts, Golf, GTI & Jetta	25
	Ball Joint To Wheel Bearing Housing Nuts	37
	Control Arm To Subframe Bolts	96
	Hub Nut	195
	Stabilizer Bar Link Rod To Control Arm Nuts	18
	Steering Gear To Subframe Bolts	22
	Steering Shaft Bolts	18
	Strut Assembly Nut	30
	Strut To Wheel Bearing Housing Nuts	70
	Subframe To Body Bolts	52②
	Subframe Rear Bracket	48
	Tie Rod End To Power Steering Gear Assembly Nuts	59
	Tie Rod End To Wheel Bearing Housing Nuts	26
	Wheel Lug Nuts	81
CORRADO, GTI-VR6, JETTA III GLX & PASSAT w/2.8L ENGINE		
1993–96	Axle Shaft To Hub Nuts	66①
	Ball Joint To Control Arm Nuts, Corrado & Passat	26
	Ball Joint To Control Arm Nuts, Golf, GTI & Jetta	25
	Ball Joint To Wheel Bearing Housing Nuts	37
	Control Arm To Subframe Bolts	96
	Hub Nut	66①
	Stabilizer Bar Link Rod To Control Arm Nuts	18
	Steering Gear To Subframe Bolts	22
	Steering Shaft Bolts	18
	Strut Assembly Nut	30
	Strut To Wheel Bearing Housing Nuts	70
	Subframe To Body Bolts	52②
	Subframe Rear Bracket	48
	Tie Rod End To Power Steering Gear Assembly Nuts	59
	Tie Rod End To Wheel Bearing Housing Nuts	26
	Wheel Lug Nuts	81

Continued

TIGHTENING SPECIFICATIONS—Continued

Year	Component	Torque/Ft. Lbs.
EUROVAN		
1993	Axle Shaft To Hub Nut	144
	Ball Joint To Control Arm Bolts	26
	Ball Joint To Wheel Bearing Housing Nuts	33
	Control Arm To Subframe Bolts	81
	Shock Absorber To Wheel Bearing Housing Nuts	41
	Tie Rod End To Power Steering Gear Assembly Nuts	42
	Tie Rod End To Wheel Bearing Housing Nuts	30
	Torsion Bar Bolts	74
	Wheel Lug Nuts	118
FOX		
1993	Axle Shaft To Hub Nuts	170
	Ball Joint To Control Arm Nuts	48
	Ball Joint To Wheel Bearing Housing Nuts	44
	Control Arm To Subframe Bolts	40
	Stabilizer Bar Clamp To Control Arm Nuts	15
	Stabilizer Bar Clamp To Subframe Nuts	15
	Strut Assembly Nut	27
	Strut Tube Threaded Cap	122
	Tie Rod End To Strut Assembly Nuts	29
	Wheel Lug Nuts	81

① — Plus an additional 1/8 (45°) turn.
② — Plus an additional 1/4 (90°) turn.

Wheel Alignment

INDEX

	Page No.
Front Wheel Alignment	49-71
Camber Adjustment	49-71
Caster Adjustment	49-71
Toe Setting Adjustment	49-72
Rear Wheel Alignment	49-72
Camber Adjustment	49-72
Toe Setting Adjustment	49-72
Wheel Alignment Specifications	49-4
Front	49-4
Rear	49-5

FRONT WHEEL ALIGNMENT

CASTER ADJUSTMENT

Except Eurovan

The caster angle on these vehicles cannot be adjusted.

Eurovan

Eccentric bolt should be replaced if caster adjusting nut has been replaced. Refer to **Fig. 1** to set caster. Loosen nut "a" and turn eccentric bolt "b" until specification has been reached.

CAMBER ADJUSTMENT

Cabriolet

Loosen nuts on wheel bearing housing/suspension strut, then turn eccentric bolt until required camber is obtained. Tighten nuts.

Cabrio, Golf III, GTI, Jetta III & Passat w/2.0L Engine

Camber should never be adjusted by moving position of ball joint in control arm.

1. Loosen bolts securing suspension strut to wheel bearing housing.
2. Move top of wheel/tire in or out to achieve proper camber.
3. **On Cabrio, Corrado, Golf III, GTI and Jetta III models, torque** bolts to 59 ft. lbs., then recheck camber.
4. **On Passat models, torque** bolts to 70 ft. lbs., then recheck camber.
5. **On all models,** if camber is out of specified range, use replacement bolt, part No. N 101 740.01, or equivalent. This will allow 1° of camber adjustment.
6. Using original bolt in lower position, pivot top of wheel/tire in or out to achieve proper camber.
7. If more movement is required for specified camber, replace original bolt with part No. N 101 740.01, or equivalent.
8. **On Cabrio, Corrado, Golf III, GTI and Jetta III models, torque** bolts to 59 ft. lbs., then recheck camber.
9. **On Passat models, torque** bolts to 70 ft. lbs., then recheck camber.

Corrado & Passat w/2.8L Engine

1. Remove brake hose from bracket on strut, then install tool No. 3270, or equivalent, between wheel and body near strut and tighten slightly, **Fig. 2.**
2. Loosen strut to wheel bearing housing

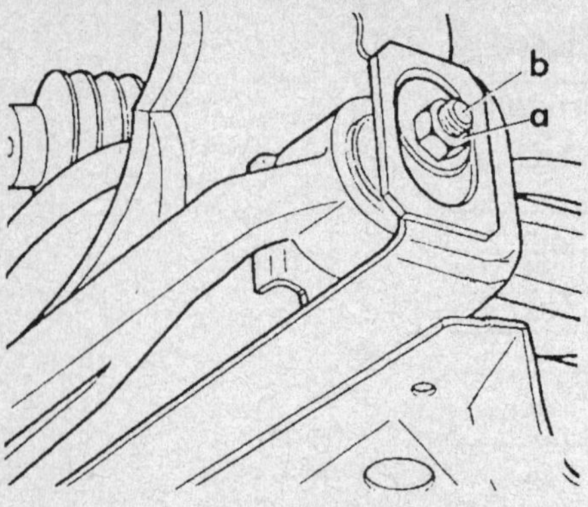
b
a
VW2049100003000X

Fig. 1 Caster adjustment. Eurovan

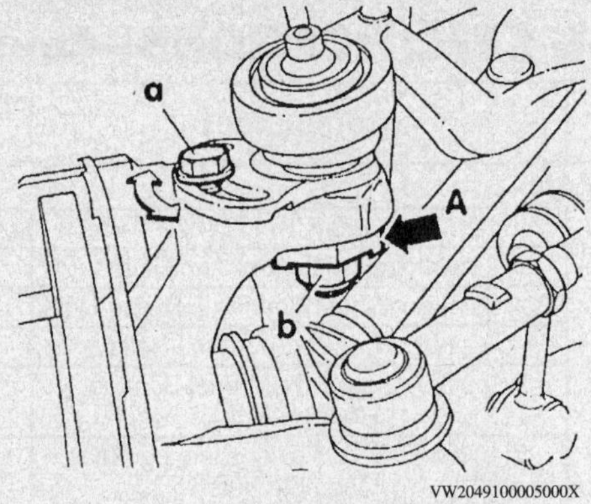
a
A
b
VW2049100005000X

Fig. 3 Camber adjustment. Eurovan

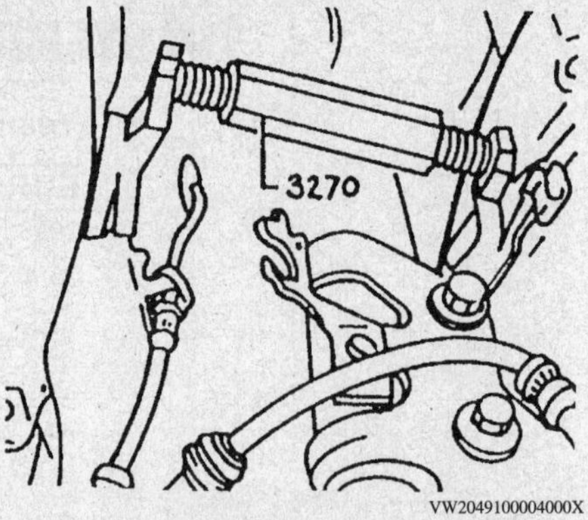
3270
VW2049100004000X

Fig. 2 Camber adjustment. Corrado & Passat w/2.8L engine

bolts, then adjust camber by turning tool spindle. **Slight diagonal positioning of tool may be necessary.**

Eurovan

Refer to **Fig. 3** to aid in camber adjustment.

1. Loosen bolts "a" and "b." Then, using tool No. 3252, or equivalent, turn eccentric washer (arrow "A") until setting for camber is reached.
2. **Torque** bolt "a" to 44 ft. lbs.
3. **Torque** bolt "b" to 81 ft. lbs.

Fox

1. Loosen both ball joint mounting nuts on lower control arm, then bounce vehicle lightly to break ball joints loose.
2. Install adjusting wrench tool No. US 067, or equivalent, from front on right side and from rear on left side.
3. Move ball joint with adjusting wrench until required camber is obtained.
4. **Torque** outboard ball joint mounting nut to 47 ft. lbs.
5. Recheck camber and correct if necessary, then remove adjusting wrench or tools and **torque** inboard ball joint mounting nut to 47 ft. lbs.

TOE SETTING ADJUSTMENT

Cabriolet

Toe adjustment is done on right side only, left side tie rod is not adjustable as original equipment. However, part No. 175 419 804, or equivalent, is available as an adjustable replacement.

Adjust toe by turning right side tie rod while holding rubber boot to avoid twisting.

Eurovan

1. Center steering wheel, then loosen both tie rod counter nuts.
2. Turn both tie rods until setting for toe-in is reached. **Ensure steering gear boots are not twisted.**

Fox

1. Remove front bolt from steering rack cover, then attach centering tool No. 3075, or equivalent, over mounting nut of left tie rod.
2. Remove bolt from spacer on chain of centering tool, then put spacer under hole marked "L" and insert bolt through hole and hole in spacer and tighten to steering gear. **On vehicles with power steering, it is advisable to install bolt from underside of vehicle.**
3. Measure and divide total toe in half, then loosen clamps and outer locknuts on both tie rods.
4. Turn both tie rods until specified setting for toe is obtained.
5. Tighten clamps and locknuts on tie rods, then remove centering tool and **torque** front bolt from steering rack cover to 15 ft. lbs.

REAR WHEEL ALIGNMENT

CAMBER ADJUSTMENT

Camber on rear axle assembly is not adjustable.

TOE SETTING ADJUSTMENT

Except Eurovan

Rear axle assembly is not adjustable.

Eurovan

Loosen nut on trailing arm. With vehicle standing on ground, adjust toe by moving trailing arm to front or rear.

Air Conditioning

INDEX

	Page No.
A/C Specifications	49-75
Charging System	49-74
Discharging System	49-74
Freon Recovery Procedures	49-74
Leak Test	49-74
Oil Charge	49-74
Performance Test	49-73
R-12 System	49-73
R-134a System	49-73
Precautions	49-73

PRECAUTIONS

R-12 and R-134a refrigerant are not compatible. Never add R-12 refrigerant to an R-134a system or refrigerant or R-134a to a R-12 system. If the refrigerants are mixed, total system contamination will occur and compressor failure may result.

Refrigerant oils used for the R-134a system and R-12 system are also not compatible. Use only the specified synthetic oil Polyalkylene Glycol/PAG for the R-134a refrigerant system. Do not use R-134a system oil in the R-12 system or R-12 oil in a R-134a system. If the oils are mixed system contamination will occur and compressor failure may result.

R-134a refrigerant system oil (PAG oil) absorbs moisture very rapidly. Moisture combines with the refrigerant to form acids which will damage the system. Use only the specified oil from a sealed container and always reseal oil container immediately after use. Do not use oil that has been contaminated with moisture. Immediately plug open connections on A/C components to prevent dirt and moisture contamination. Like wise do not remove new components from packaging until ready to install. Immediately tighten components after installation.

PERFORMANCE TEST

R-12 SYSTEM

CABRIOLET

1. Connect gauge and manifold set.
2. Connect tachometer and set engine speed at 2500 RPM.
3. Insert thermometer fully in lefthand fresh air vent and close all other outlets.
4. Set controls at maximum cooling and maximum fan speed.
5. With all doors, windows and sunroof closed, park vehicle out of direct sunlight.
6. Read pressures with compressor on and engine running at 2500 RPM.
7. Compare readings to specifications. Low pressure gauge reading is dependent on evaporator temperature, **Fig. 1,** and high pressure gauge reading is dependent on ambient temperature of engine compartment, **Fig. 2.** Ideal test pressures are shown by dotted line boxes.
8. If temperatures and pressures are not within acceptable range, refer to "A/C System Troubleshooting."

CORRADO & PASSAT

Test Preparations

1. Do not park car in sunlight.
2. Ensure condenser and radiator are clean.
3. Drive belt is properly tensioned and in good condition.
4. Air ducts are properly installed and all cables properly adjusted.
5. A/C compressor clutch functions properly.
6. Connect pressure gauge set to service valves, then open all dash air outlets.
7. Run engine to operating temperature, then set engine speed at 2000 RPM.
8. Set blower to High, set control lever to Max-A/C and temperature lever to Cold.
9. Close windows and doors.

Lefthand Vent Temperature To Ambient Temperature

1. Check the outside temperature against the vent output temperatures as follows:
   a. At 68°F, 45–52°F.
   b. At 77°F, 42–49°F.
   c. At 86°F, 40–47°F.
   d. At 95°F, 38–45°F.
   e. At 104°F, 36–43°F.
2. If results do not fall within specifications, refer to "High Pressure Check" and "Low Pressure Check."

High Pressure Check

Compare results with **Fig. 3.**

1. Letters on graph refer to the following:
   a. A-high side discharge pressure.
   b. B-ambient or outside temperature.
   c. C-radiator cooling fan on low speed.
   d. D-radiator cooling fan on high speed with switches Off.
   e. E-radiator cooling fan on high speed with switches On.

Low Pressure Check

Compare results with **Fig. 4.**

1. Letters on graph refer to the following:
   a. A-low side suction side.
   b. B-ambient or outside temperature.
   c. C-A/C thermostat. Switch closes at upper level arrow, A/C compressor On. Switch opens at lower level arrow, A/C compressor Off.

CABRIO, EUROVAN, GOLF III, GTI & JETTA III

1. Connect gauge and manifold set.
2. Open at least 1 front window and all dash air outlets, and insert thermometer into center air outlet.
3. Place temperature selector in COLD position, depress VENT button, turn on ignition and set blower to run at high speed.
4. Record ambient temperature, start engine and set to run at fast idle.
5. Depress MAX A/C button, and note discharge temperature after 1 minute. Air discharge temperature should be at least 15°F less than ambient temperature recorded in step 4.
6. Allow system to operate for approximately 10 minutes and note gauge readings.
7. Low (suction) side readings for relative ambient temperatures should be as follows:
   a. 59°F, 16–27 psi.
   b. 68°F, 21–32 psi.
   c. 77°F, 23–35 psi.
   d. 86°F, 29–40 psi.
   e. 95°F, 36–50 psi.
8. High (discharge) side readings for relative ambient temperatures should be as follows:
   a. 59°F, 130–159 psi.
   b. 68°F, 162–190 psi.
   c. 77°F, 192–224 psi.
   d. 86°F, 226–258 psi.
   e. 95°F, 275–310 psi.
9. If discharge temperature does not drop by at least 15°F, and/or if system pressures are not as specified, check air distribution system as outlined and refer to "A/C System Troubleshooting."

R-134a SYSTEM

TEST CONDITIONS & PREPARATIONS

1. Ambient temperature is between 68–86°F, vehicle in shade.
2. Ensure condenser and radiator are clean.
3. Drive belt is properly tensioned and in good condition.
4. Air ducts are properly installed and all cables properly adjusted.
5. A/C compressor clutch functions properly.
6. Connect pressure gauge set to service valves, then open all dash air outlets.
7. Close windows and doors.

TEST 1 TEMPERATURE FROM CENTER VENT

1. Start engine, warm to operating temperature and allow to idle.

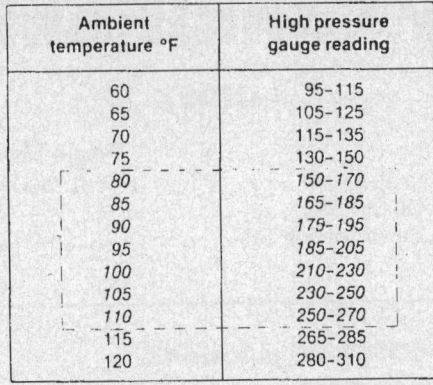

Low pressure gauge reading	Evaporator temperature °F
10	2
12	6
14	10
16	14
18	18
20	20
22	22
24	24
26	27
28	29
30	32
35	36
40	42
45	48
50	53
55	58
60	62
65	66
70	70

VW7029100021000X

Fig. 1 Relationship of low pressure gauge reading to evaporator temperature. Cabriolet

2. Set air distribution to instrument panel outlets.
3. Set temperature control to Full Cold.
4. Set Blower to second speed (2nd. position).
5. Place suitable thermometer in center air outlet.
6. Switch A/C On with NORM A/C button.
7. Raise engine speed to 2000 RPM, maintain during test.
8. Outlet air temperature should drop to below 50°F in less than one minute.
9. If results are not as expected perform "Test 2" and "Test 3," then compare results with table **Fig. 5.**

TEST 2, HIGH PRESSURE CHECK

1. Connect suitable High/Low pressure gauge set to service valves, if not previously connected. Refer to "A/C Specifications" for locations.
2. Disconnect electrical connector to radiator cooling fans.
3. Set air distribution to footwell.
4. Set temperature control to Full Hot.
5. Set Blower to high speed (4th. position).
6. Start engine, then turn On A/C with MAX A/C button.
7. Raise engine speed to 1500 RPM, maintain during test.
8. System high pressure should rise to about 232 psi in less than 30 seconds.
9. If results are not as expected perform "Test 1" and "Test 3," then compare results with table **Fig. 5.**

TEST 3, LOW PRESSURE CHECK

1. Connect suitable High/Low pressure gauge set to service valves, if not previously connected. Refer to "A/C Specifications" for locations.
2. Set air distribution to instrument panel outlets.
3. Set temperature control to Full Cold.
4. Set Blower to low speed (1st. position).
5. Start engine, then turn On A/C with NORM A/C button.
6. Raise engine speed to 1500 RPM, maintain during test.

Ambient temperature °F	High pressure gauge reading
60	95-115
65	105-125
70	115-135
75	130-150
80	150-170
85	165-185
90	175-195
95	185-205
100	210-230
105	230-250
110	250-270
115	265-285
120	280-310

VW7029100022000X

Fig. 2 Relationship of high pressure gauge reading to engine compartment ambient temperature. Cabriolet

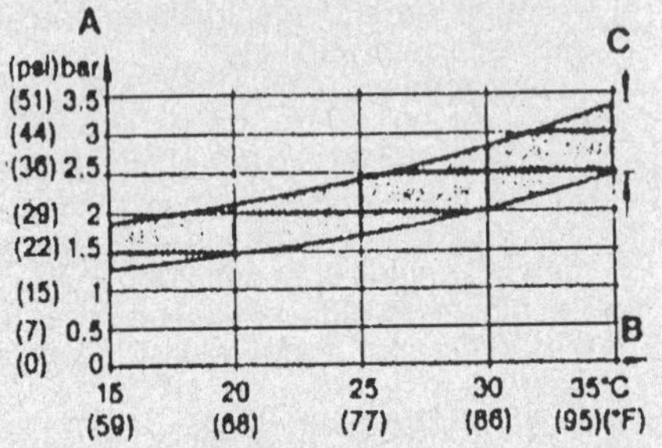
A
C
(psi)bar
(51) 3.5
(44) 3
(36) 2.5
(29) 2
(22) 1.5
(15) 1
(7) 0.5
(0) 0
B
15 (59)
20 (68)
25 (77)
30 (86)
35°C (95)(°F)

VW7029100024000X

Fig. 4 Low pressure check chart. Corrado & Passat

7. System low pressure should drop to about 22–38 psi in less than 30 seconds.
8. If results are not as expected perform "Test 1" and "Test 2," then compare results with table **Fig. 5.**

LEAK TEST

Use halogen leak detector Hitec HI400A-TEL or equivalent to check for refrigerant leaks.

Refrigerant gas dissipates very quickly. Avoid drafty or windy areas when checking for leaks. If the refrigerant system is empty, charge system with approximately 3.5 oz. of refrigerant in order to check for leaks. Check A/C systems for leaks following the leak detector manufacturer's instructions.

DISCHARGING SYSTEM

Ensure initial set-up had been performed on the refrigerant recovery/recycling/recharging unit before discharging A/C system.

1. Connect red high pressure hose of recovery/recycling unit to high side fitting on vehicle and open coupler valve.
2. Connect blue low pressure hose of refrigerant recovery/recycling unit to low side fitting on vehicle and open coupler valve.
3. Following refrigerant recovery/recycling/recharging unit manufacturer's instructions, discharge A/C system into recovery/recycling unit.

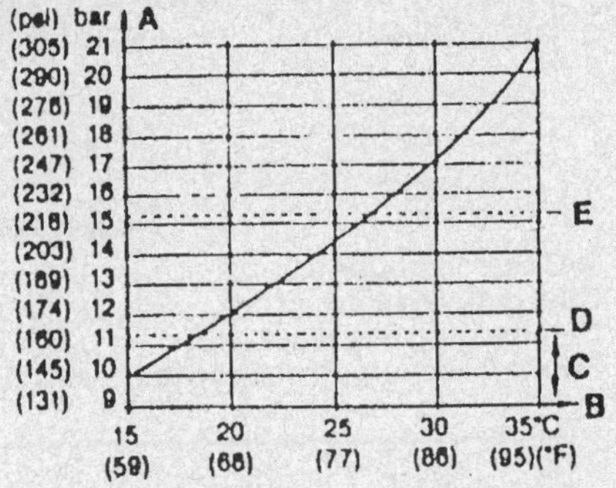
(psi) bar A
(305) 21
(290) 20
(276) 19
(261) 18
(247) 17
(232) 16
(218) 15
(203) 14
(189) 13
(174) 12
(160) 11
(145) 10
(131) 9
E
D
C
B
15 (59)
20 (68)
25 (77)
30 (86)
35°C (95)(°F)

VW7029100023000X

Fig. 3 High pressure check chart. Corrado & Passat

4. Close manifold gauge valves when refrigerant is fully discharged.
5. Disconnect power supply from A/C clutch to prevent accidental compressor operation with A/C discharged.

CHARGING SYSTEM

Follow refrigerant recharging unit manufacturers instructions for evacuating and recharging the A/C system. After system recharge, manually rotate A/C compressor 10 turns before starting the engine. Start engine with A/C off and allow to idle for at least two minutes with A/C on before raising engine speed.

OIL CHARGE

See "Specifications" chart for oil charge amount on each model.

FREON RECOVERY PROCEDURES

Automotive refrigerant containing CFCs is hazardous to the earth's atmosphere. To protect our environment, use an Underwriter's Laboratory (UL) approved refrigerant recovery/recycling unit such as Kent-Moore ACR3 or equivalent, whenever discharging an A/C system.

The A/C system should be serviced only by trained personnel familiar with equipment use, related safety precautions and regulations governing the discharging/handling/disposal of automotive refrigerants.

Always wear safety goggles when charging or discharging system. Use caution so that refrigerant does not come in contact with your skin or eyes. If refrigerant comes in contact with skin or eyes, do not rub, flush immediately with cool water, then seek medical attention. Keep refrigerant away from open flames, R12 exposure to open flame will produce poisonous gas.

1. Close both valves on A/C manifold gauge set, then connect hose from low pressure gauge to low pressure service valve.
2. Connect hose from high pressure

Test 1 Temperature from center air vent*	Test 2 High pressure	Test 3 Low pressure	Possible causes of incorrect readings	Corrective measures
Normal	Normal	Normal	None	—
Too high	Normal	Normal	Temperature flap position incorrect	Adjust temperature flap cable
Too high	Too low	Normal	Compressor	Replace compressor
Normal	Too low	Normal	Compressor	Replace compressor
Normal	Normal	Too high or too low	Expansion valve or compressor	Replace expansion valve or compressor
Too high	Normal	Too high or too low	Expansion valve or compressor	Replace expansion valve or compressor
Normal	Too high or too low	Too high or too low	Expansion valve or compressor	Replace expansion valve or compressor

* Normal air outlet temperature approx. 43°F (6°C).

VW7029300035000X

Fig. 5 A/C performance test diagnostic table. R-134a system

gauge to high pressure service valve, then the manifold gauge hose to inlet connection on refrigerant recovery/recycling unit.

3. Follow refrigerant recovery/recycling unit manufacturer's instructions to discharge A/C system into recovery/recycling unit.
4. Close manifold gauge valves when refrigerant is fully discharged.
5. Disconnect power supply from compressor clutch to prevent damage to system if compressor is accidentally switched On with refrigerant system discharged.

A/C SPECIFICATIONS

Year	Model	Refrigerant		Refrigerant Oil		Service Valve Location
		Type	Capacity, Oz.	Viscosity	Total System Capacity, Oz.	
1993	Cabriolet	R12	38.0–42.0	①	4.75	⑤
	Corrado	R12	37.1–40.5	①	4.6	⑦
	Eurovan	R134a	②	④	③	⑦
	Fox	R12	40.5–42.3	①	6.2	⑥
	Golf III	R12	37.1–40.5	①	4.6	⑦
	Jetta III	R12	37.1–40.5	①	4.6	⑦
	Passat	R134a	40.6–42.4	SP-10④	3.9–4.4	⑦
1994	Cabriolet	R12	38.0–42.0	①	4.75	⑤
	Corrado	R12	37.1–40.5	①	4.6	⑦
	Golf III	R134a	28.2–30.0	SP-10④	3.9	⑦
	Jetta III	R134a	28.2–30.0	SP-10④	3.9	⑦
	Passat	R134a	40.6–42.4	SP-10④	3.9–4.4	⑦
1995–96	Cabrio	R134a	–	SP-10④	–	⑦
	Golf III	R134a	28.2–30.0	SP-10④	3.9	⑦
	GTI	R134a	28.2–30.0	SP-10④	3.9	⑦
	Jetta III	R134a	28.2–30.0	SP-10④	3.9	⑦
	Passat	R134a	40.6–42.4	SP-10④	3.9–4.4	⑦

① — Use A/C refrigerant oil that meets the specifications of the following oils: Shell Clavus G 100, Sunoil Suniso 5 GS, Texaco DEA Capella MS 100 or Capella WF 100, Indemitsu Dens Oil 6 or Fuchs Reniso KES 100.

② — Models w/one evaporator, 33.5–35.3 oz.; models w/two evaporators, 47.6–49.4 oz.

③ — Models w/one evaporator, 4.6 oz.; models w/two evaporators, 8.1 oz.

④ — Special Polyalkaline Glycol (PAG) lubricant required.

⑤ — High pressure service valve on high pressure line near condenser. Low pressure valve on low pressure line between evaporator and compressor.

⑥ — Mounted on compressor.

⑦ — Located in RH rear of engine compartment near firewall.

Cooling Fans

INDEX

	Page No.		Page No.		Page No.
Component Replacement	49-77	Cabriolet	49-76	Fox	49-76
Description	49-76	Corrado	49-76	Passat	49-76
Cabrio, Golf III, GTI & Jetta III	49-76	Eurovan	49-76		

DESCRIPTION

CABRIOLET

The two speed electric cooling fan can be controlled by three devices as equipped. A thermo switch mounted in the radiator will turn on low speed when a coolant temperature of 203°F is reached and high speed when 221°F is reached. The A/C control relay will turn on low speed whenever the A/C system is switched on and high speed whenever the A/C high pressure switch is tripped. A cooling fan after run control unit will allow the low speed to run for a predetermined period of time after the ignition is cut off if the coolant thermo switch is tripped, to prevent hot soak starting problems.

CORRADO

The electric cooling fan uses a thermoswitch to control fan motor operation. The fan operates at 1st (low) speed when engine coolant temperature is 198°–207°F. The fan operates at 2nd (medium) speed when coolant temperature is 210°–221°F. The fan operates at 3rd (high) speed when coolant temperature is 234°F. The A/C system will also switch on various fan speeds dependent on coolant temperature and freon pressure.

EUROVAN

Less A/C

The electric cooling fan uses a radiator thermoswitch to control fan motor operation. The fan operates at first speed when engine coolant temperature is 192°F. The fan operates at second speed when coolant temperature is 203°F. Additionally, thermostatically controlled fan shutters are used to control air flow through the radiator. The shutters are controlled by a unit located between the fan units, mounted on the fan shroud.

With A/C

The electric cooling fan uses a radiator mounted thermoswitch and a second thermoswitch mounted in the coolant manifold to control fan motor operation. The fan operates at low speed when engine coolant temperature is 183°–192°F. The fan operates at medium speed when coolant temperature is 193°–203°F. The fan operates at high speed when coolant temperature is 234°F. The A/C system will also switch on various fan speeds dependent on coolant temperature and freon pressure.

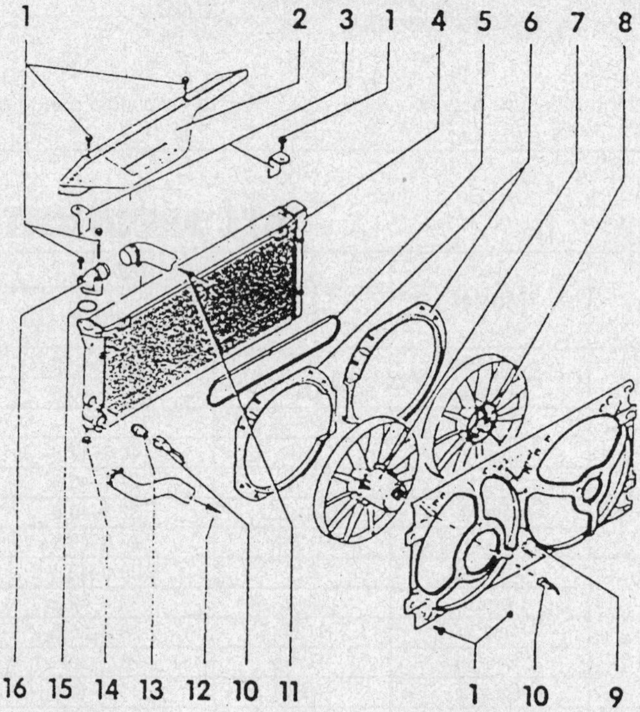

1
2
3
1
4
5
6
7
8
16
15
14
13
12
10
11
1
10
9

1. Screws
2. Cover
3. Upper radiator mount
4. Radiator
5. V-belt
6. Guide rings
7. Fan
8. Additional fan
9. Fan shroud
10. Connector
11. Upper coolant hose
12. Lower coolant hose
13. Thermoswitch
14. Washer mount
15. O-ring
16. Upper radiator hose flange

VW1089500002000X

Fig. 1 Cooling fan replacement. Corrado

FOX

The electric cooling fan uses a temperature switch to control 1st and 2nd speed fan motor operation. The fan operates at 1st speed with A/C off and engine coolant temperature 183°–203°F. The fan operates at 2nd speed with A/C on and coolant temperature 196°–216°F.

CABRIO, GOLF III, GTI & JETTA III

1.9L & 2.0L Engines Less A/C

The electric cooling fan uses a thermoswitch to control fan motor operation. The fan operates at low speed when engine coolant temperature is 197°–205°F. The fan operates at high speed when coolant temperature is 210°–221°F.

1.9L, 2.0L & 2.8L Engines With A/C

Refer to "Passat."

PASSAT

The three speed electric cooling fan is controlled by the cooling fan control module through a coolant temperature sensor mounted in the radiator and a second thermosensor mounted in the coolant manifold and by the A/C control system and the after run control module, if equipped. Various fan speeds are chosen dependent on coolant temperature and refrigerant pressure when the A/C system is On. The coolant fan can also be switched on after the ignition is switched Off if coolant temperature rises above 198°F by the after run control module to prevent hot soak starting problems.

Fan speeds will be, 1st (low) speed when

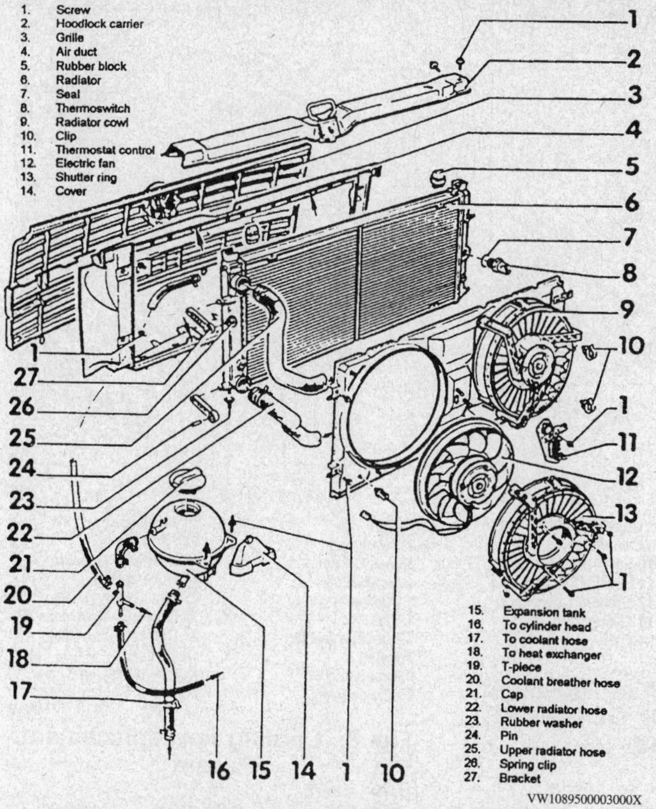
1. Screw
2. Hoodlock carrier
3. Grille
4. Air duct
5. Rubber block
6. Radiator
7. Seal
8. Thermoswitch
9. Radiator cowl
10. Clip
11. Thermostat control
12. Electric fan
13. Shutter ring
14. Cover
15. Expansion tank
16. To cylinder head
17. To coolant hose
18. To heat exchanger
19. T-piece
20. Coolant breather hose
21. Cap
22. Lower radiator hose
23. Rubber washer
24. Pin
25. Upper radiator hose
26. Spring clip
27. Bracket

VW1089500003000X

Fig. 2 Cooling fan replacement. Eurovan

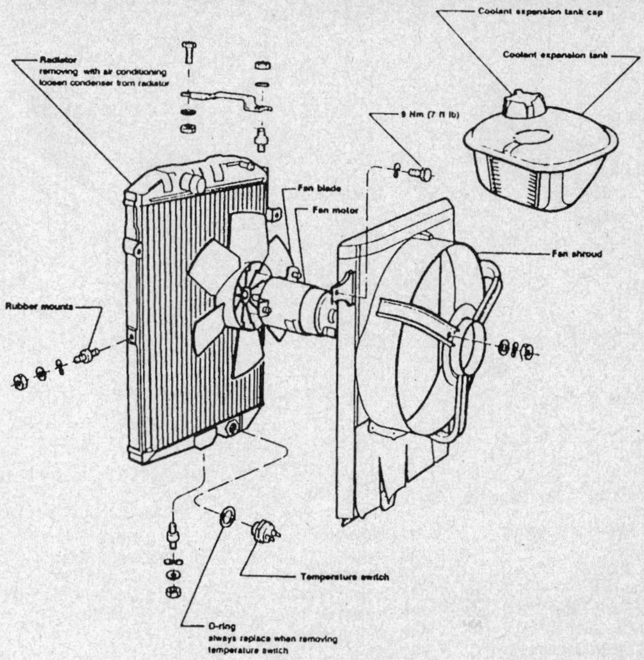
Coolant expansion tank cap
Coolant expansion tank
Radiator
removing with air conditioning
loosen condenser from radiator
9 Nm (7 ft lb)
Fan blade
Fan motor
Fan shroud
Rubber mounts
Temperature switch
O-ring
always replace when removing
temperature switch

VW1089500004000X

Fig. 3 Cooling fan replacement. Fox

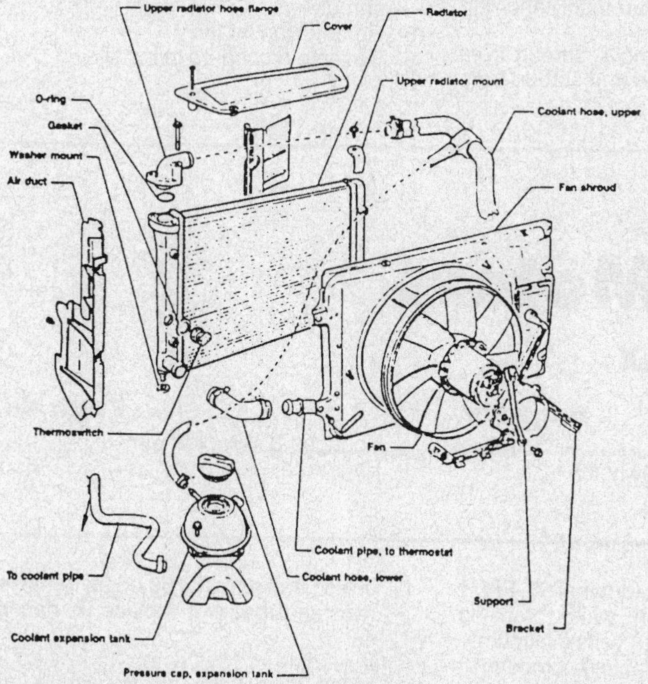
Upper radiator hose flange
Cover
Radiator
O-ring
Gasket
Washer mount
Air duct
Upper radiator mount
Coolant hose, upper
Fan shroud
Thermoswitch
Fan
To coolant pipe
Coolant pipe, to thermostat
Coolant hose, lower
Support
Bracket
Coolant expansion tank
Pressure cap, expansion tank

VW1089500005000X

Fig. 4 Cooling fan replacement. Cabriolet

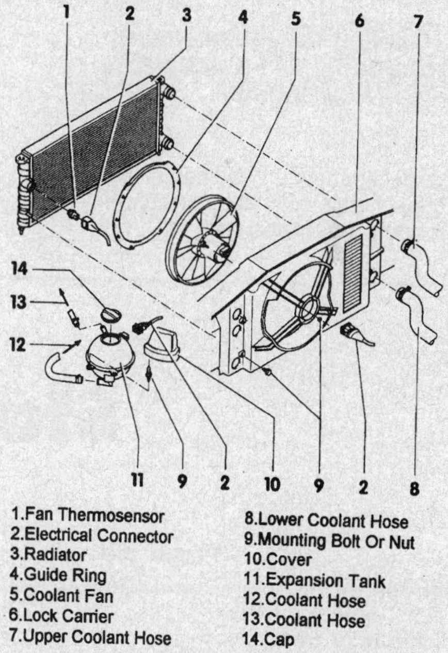
1.Fan Thermosensor
2.Electrical Connector
3.Radiator
4.Guide Ring
5.Coolant Fan
6.Lock Carrier
7.Upper Coolant Hose
8.Lower Coolant Hose
9.Mounting Bolt Or Nut
10.Cover
11.Expansion Tank
12.Coolant Hose
13.Coolant Hose
14.Cap

VW1089600007000X

Fig. 5 Cooling fan replacement. Golf III & Jetta III w/1.9L TDI engine

engine coolant temperature is 198°–207°F, 2nd (medium) speed when coolant temperature is 210°–221°F and 3rd (high) speed when coolant temperature is 234°F. The fan will run at 1st (low) speed whenever the A/C is turned On and at 2nd (medium) speed whenever refrigerant pressure rises above 232 psi regardless of coolant temperature.

COMPONENT REPLACEMENT

Refer to **Figs. 1 through 8** for cooling fan replacement.

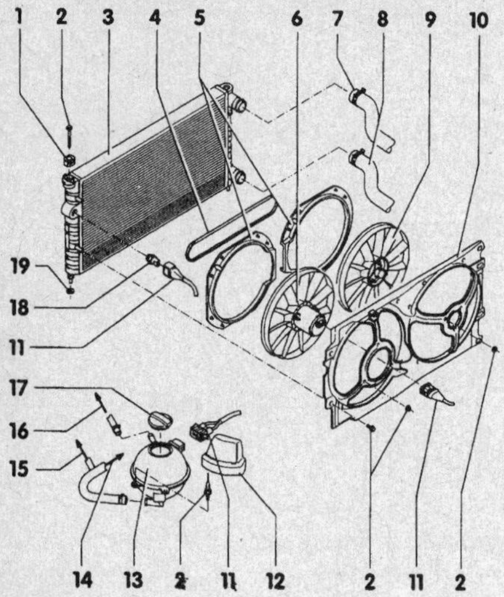

1. Radiator Mounting
2. Bolt
3. Radiator
4. V-Belt
5. Guide Ring
6. Coolant Fan
7. Upper Coolant Hose
8. Lower Coolant Hose
9. Auxilliary Fan
10. Fan Shroud
11. Connector
12. Cover
13. Expansion Tank
14. Coolant Hose
15. Coolant Hose
16. Coolant Hose
17. Cap
18. Fan Thermosensor
19. Rubber Bushing

VW1089300008000X

Fig. 6 Cooling fan replacement. Cabrio, Golf III, GTI & Jetta III w/2.0L engine

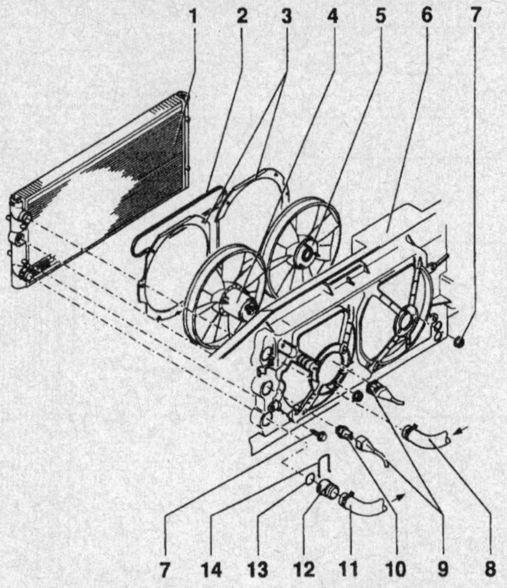

1. Radiator
2. V-Belt
3. Guide Ring
4. Coolant Fan
5. Auxilliary Fan
6. Lock Carrier
7. Bolt
8. Upper Coolant Hose
9. Connector
10. Fan Thermoswitch
11. Lower Coolant Hose
12. Coolant Connector
13. O-ring
14. Clip

VW1089500009000X

Fig. 7 Cooling fan replacement. GTI-VR6 & Jetta III GLX w/2.8L engine

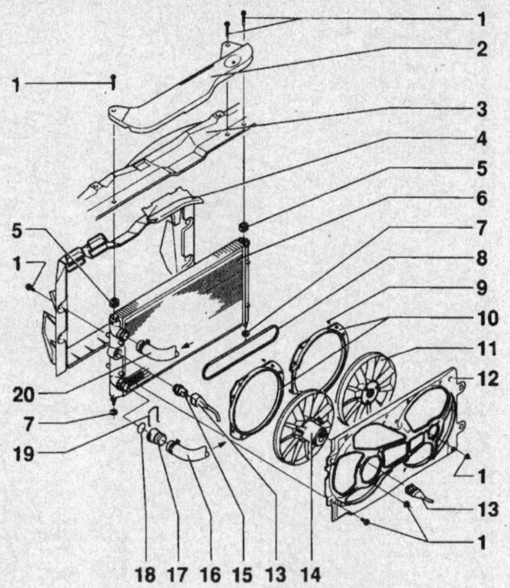

1. Bolt
2. Cover
3. Lock Carrier
4. Air Ducting
5. Bracket
6. Radiator
7. Rubber Washer
8. V-Belt
9. Expanding Pin
10. Guide Ring
11. Auxilliary Fan
12. Fan Ring
13. Eletrical Connector
14. Cooling Fan
15. Fan Thermoswitch
16. Lower Coolant Hose
17. Coolant Connector
18. O-ring
19. Retaining Clip
20. Upper Coolant Hose

VW1089500006000A

Fig. 8 Cooling fan replacement. Passat

1. Disconnect battery ground cable, then disconnect fan electrical connector.
2. **On models equipped with A/C,** disconnect resistor connector and fan relay.
3. **On all models,** remove shroud from radiator, then the fan and shroud from the vehicle.
4. Remove nuts securing fan motor to shroud.
5. Remove fan motor.
6. Reverse procedure to install.

Starter Motors

INDEX

	Page No.
Troubleshooting	49-78
Does Not Turn Engine When Ignition/Starter Switch Is Operated	49-78
Turns Engine Too Slowly Or Engages & Will Not Turn Engine	49-79

TROUBLESHOOTING

DOES NOT TURN ENGINE WHEN IGNITION/STARTER SWITCH IS OPERATED

Use SUN VAT-40 or SUN VAT-60, or equivalents, for measurements.

1. Ensure solenoid switch connections are satisfactory, ground straps between engine and body are tight and free of corrosion and that battery is fully charged.
2. Measure voltage at terminal 50, **Fig. 1,** of solenoid switch while cranking. Reading should be 8 volts minimum.
3. If reading is satisfactory, proceed to step 7.
4. If there is no voltage, or voltage is less than 8, measure voltage at terminal 50, **Fig. 2,** of ignition/starter switch. Reading should be 8 volts minimum.
5. If there is no voltage, replace ignition/starter switch.
6. If voltage is satisfactory, Inspect wiring between terminal 50 on ignition/starter switch and terminal 50 on starter solenoid and repair or replace as necessary.
7. If reading is satisfactory from step 3, measure voltage at connection 4, **Fig.1,** for field winding on solenoid switch. Reading should be 8 volts minimum.
8. If there is no voltage, replace solenoid switch.
9. If voltage is satisfactory, replace starter.

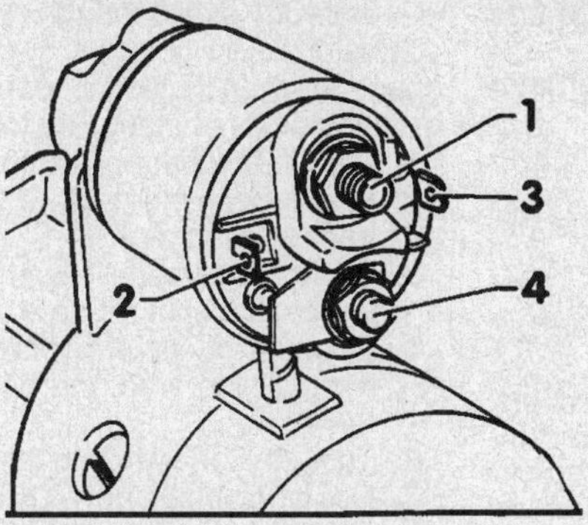
1
3
2
4

1 - Terminal **30 - B+**, from battery
2 - Terminal **15a**
3 - Terminal **50** - from starter switch
4 - Connection for field windings

VW1129100001000A

Fig. 1 Starter solenoid terminal identification

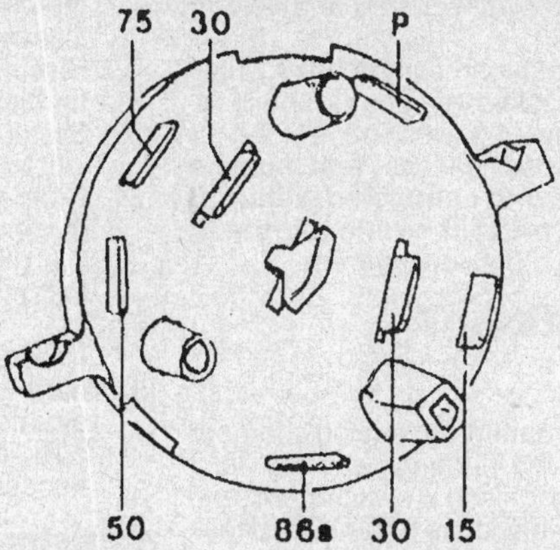
75
30
P
50
86s
30
15

VW1129100002000X

Fig. 2 Starter switch terminal identification

TURNS ENGINE TOO SLOWLY OR ENGAGES & WILL NOT TURN ENGINE

1. Ensure engine is filled with oil of recommended viscosity, then check V-belt tension, wire connections, battery voltage and charge if necessary and clean battery terminals.
2. Crank engine.
3. If starter turns engine, system is operating properly.
4. If starter does not turn engine, clean starter terminals and tighten connections, then clean and tighten ground strap connections between transaxle and body at transaxle.
5. Crank engine.
6. If starter turns engine, system is operating properly.
7. If starter does not turn engine, starter is defective, replace starter.

Alternators

INDEX

	Page No.
Alternator Specifications	49-80
Diagnosis & Testing	49-79
Exciter Circuit	49-80
Output Test	49-79
Troubleshooting	49-79
Alternator Indicator Light	49-79

TROUBLESHOOTING

ALTERNATOR INDICATOR LIGHT

Does Not Illuminate w/ Ignition On (Engine Not Started)

Possible open circuit between alternator D + and indicator light.

1. Remove alternator cover, then disconnect D + wire from alternator.
2. Connect a jumper wire between D + and ground, then turn ignition switch to On position.
3. If indicator light illuminates, proceed as follows:
   a. Check for improper alternator ground, worn carbon brushes, defective voltage regulator or rotor.
   b. If alternator grounding and brushes are defective, make necessary corrections. If light now illuminates, system is operating properly.
   c. If alternator grounding and brushes are satisfactory, replace voltage regulator. If light still fails to illuminate, replace alternator.
4. If indicator light does not illuminate, proceed as follows:
   a. Indicator bulb is burned out.
   b. Disconnect battery ground cable, replace bulb, reconnect ground cable and turn ignition switch to On position.
   c. If indicator light illuminates, system is operating properly.
   d. If indicator light does not illuminate, wiring between alternator D + and indicator light is open, repair as necessary.

Light Illuminated w/Ignition Off

Alternator diode(s) defective (rectifier bridge), replace alternator.

Light Does Not Go Out When RPM Increases

Check for slipping fan belt, short to ground between alternator D + and indicator light or alternator is defective, replace.

Possible Short To Ground Between Alternator D + & Indicator Light

1. Disconnect alternator wiring, then turn ignition switch to On position.
2. If indicator light illuminates, there is a short to ground between alternator D+ and indicator light. Repair as necessary.
3. If indicator light does not illuminate, test alternator output and voltage regulator. Replace defective component.

DIAGNOSIS & TESTING

OUTPUT TEST

Use SUN VAT-40 or SUN VAT-60 or their equivalents for test.

1. Connect black clamp from VAT to battery ground cable, then red clamp from VAT to battery positive cable.
2. Connect green clamp from VAT (inductive pickup) to alternator D +; either at alternator or battery.

3. Start engine, raise speed and hold at 2000 RPM.
4. Slowly adjust load control of VAT until highest possible reading is obtained. Reading must be within 10% of manufacturer's specifications. **Test must be performed and completed within 15 seconds to avoid overloading and damaging electrical system.**

EXCITER CIRCUIT

Inspection

If complaint "battery isn't being charged" is received even though warning light comes on when ignition is switched On and goes out when ignition is turned Off, check exciter circuit as follows:

1. Verify that battery voltage is approximately 12 volts minimum, then charge if necessary.
2. Disconnect blue wire from alternator terminal 61.
3. Switch multimeter US 1119 or equivalent to 200 mA range.
4. Connect multimeter between disconnected blue wire and terminal 61.
5. Turn ignition switch to On position.
6. Current must fall between 150 and 185 mA.
7. If reading is lower than 150 mA, check blue wire between alternator and instrument panel or replace printed circuit in instrument cluster as is necessary.

Resistance Check

If complaint "battery isn't being charged" is received even though warning light comes on when ignition is switched On and goes out when ignition is turned Off, check exciter circuit resistance as follows:

1. Disconnect battery ground cable.
2. Disconnect blue wire (D +/61) from back of alternator.
3. Switch multimeter US 1119 or equivalent to 200 ohm range.
4. Connect multimeter between disconnected blue wire and battery positive terminal.
5. Turn ignition switch to On position.
6. Reading should be 140–160 ohms.
7. If reading is infinite, reverse probes and recheck.
8. If reading is still infinite, printed circuit must be replaced.

ALTERNATOR SPECIFICATIONS

Year	Model	Alternator Type	Rated Hot Output	
			Amps	Volts
1993	Cabriolet	Bosch	②	14
	Corrado	Bosch	120	14
	Eurovan	Bosch/Valeo	③	14
	Fox	Bosch	②	14
	Golf III	Bosch/Valeo	①	14
	Jetta III GL & GLS	Bosch/Valeo	①	14
	Jetta GLX	Bosch/Valeo	120	14
	Passat	Bosch/Valeo	90	14
	Passat GLX	Bosch/Valeo	120	14
1994	Cabriolet	Bosch	②	14
	Corrado	Bosch	120	14
	Golf III	Bosch	①	14
	Jetta III GL & GLS	Bosch	①	14
	Jetta GLX	Bosch	120	14
	Passat	Bosch	90	14
	Passat GLX	Bosch	120	14
1995	Cabrio	Bosch	①	14
	Golf III GL & Sport	Bosch	①	14
	GTI-VR6	Bosch	120	14
	Jetta III GL & GLS	Bosch	①	14
	Jetta III GLX	Bosch	120	14
	Passat GLX	Bosch	120	14
1996	Cabrio	Bosch	①	14
	Golf III GL	Bosch	①	14
	Golf III TDI	Bosch	120	14
	GTI & GTI-VR6	Bosch	90	14
	Jetta III GL & GLS	Bosch	①	14
	Jetta GLX	Bosch	90	14
	Jetta TDI	Bosch	120	14
	Passat GLS	Bosch	90	14
	Passat GLX & TDI	Bosch	120	14

① — Less A/C, 70 amps; with A/C, 90 amps.

② — Less A/C, 65 amps; with A/C, 90 amps.

③ — Less A/C, 90 amps; with A/C, 120 amps.

Speed Control Systems

INDEX

	Page No.
Activate Speed Control	49-81
Models w/Turbocharged Direct Injection (TDI) Diesel Engine	49-81
Adjustments	49-81
Cabriolet	49-81
Except Cabriolet & Models w/Turbocharged Direct Injection (TDI) Diesel Engine	49-81
Component Replacement	49-83
Cabriolet	49-83
Except Cabriolet & Models w/Turbocharged Direct Injection (TDI) Diesel Engine	49-83
System Diagnosis & Testing	49-81
Cabriolet	49-81
Except Cabriolet, Eurovan & Models w/Diesel Engine	49-81
Passat w/Turbocharged Direct Injection (TDI) Diesel Engine	49-83

ACTIVATE SPEED CONTROL

MODELS w/ TURBOCHARGED DIRECT INJECTION (TDI) DIESEL ENGINE

In the event that speed control function become blocked in the Engine Control Module (ECM), use the following procedure to activate the speed control system.

1. Connect scan tool No. VAG 1551, or equivalent, to the Diagnostic Link Connector (DLC), located on the LH lower side of the instrument panel to right of the steering column.
2. Follow scan tool manufacturer's instructions to access "Engine Electronics."
3. Follow scan tool manufacturer's instructions to "Log In."
4. Enter code 11463 to encode "Activate Speed Control " into ECU.
5. After encoding "Activate Speed Control" into ECU, disconnect scan tool and road test vehicle for speed control functions.

ADJUSTMENTS

EXCEPT CABRIOLET & MODELS w/ TURBOCHARGED DIRECT INJECTION (TDI) DIESEL ENGINE

Throttle Control Element

1. Remove trim panels and covers necessary to access throttle control element, near throttle pedal.
2. Release adjusting sleeve (2), **Fig. 1,** by turning counter clockwise, then pushing forward.
3. Ensure throttle cable (3) is properly adjusted, pedal is fully returned and throttle control element (1) is fully released.
4. Pull adjusting sleeve to rear until free play is removed then lock sleeve to element by turning clockwise.

CABRIOLET

Vacuum Servo

1. Allow engine to reach operating temperature.

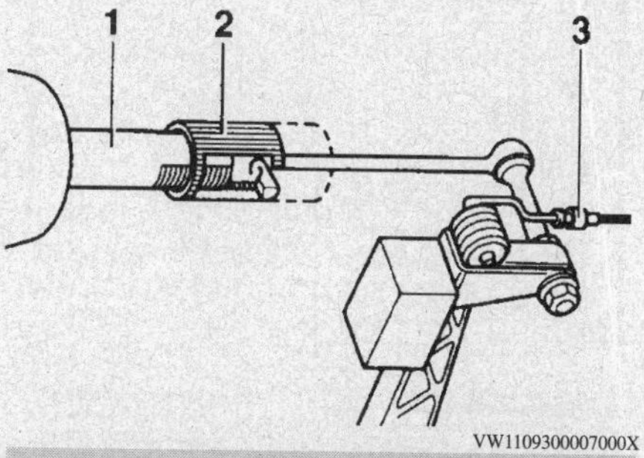

1
2
3
VW1109300007000X

Fig. 1 Throttle control element adjusting. Except Cabriolet & models w/Turbocharged Direct Injection (TDI) diesel engine

2. With engine at idle, loosen the ball stud nut.
3. Adjust the linkage until a clearance of .0039–.0120 inch is achieved between the bushing and stop plate.

SYSTEM DIAGNOSIS & TESTING

EXCEPT CABRIOLET, EUROVAN & MODELS w/DIESEL ENGINE

Refer to wiring diagrams, **Figs. 2 and 3,** and component identification diagram, **Fig. 4,** when troubleshooting these systems.

VACUUM SYSTEM LEAK TEST

Refer to component identification diagram, **Fig. 4,** when testing for vacuum leaks.

1. Remove trim panels and covers necessary to access throttle control element, near throttle pedal.
2. Disconnect vacuum line at pump and plug.
3. Hold down brake pedal to open vacuum vent valve.
4. Push in throttle control element diaphragm in and hold while releasing brake pedal to close vacuum vent valve.
5. Release throttle control element diaphragm, element must not move.
6. If element moves, repeat above test after isolating each component and circuit until leak is located.

CABRIOLET

LESS VOLTMETER

When performing the following tests, refer to **Fig. 5** for control unit electrical connector terminal identification

On models with automatic transaxle, position gear select lever to Drive or 2nd when performing test procedures.

No Ground Circuit To Control Unit

1. Disconnect control unit electrical connector **Fig. 5.**
2. Connect test light between terminal No. 8 and battery positive.
3. If test light does not illuminate, repair broken wire in ground circuit.
4. If test light illuminates, proceed to next test.

On/Off Switch Does Not Work

1. Connect test light between terminal No. 1 and ground.
2. Turn the ignition switch and cruise control switch on.
3. If test light does not illuminate, repair broken wire.
4. If test light illuminates, proceed to next test.

Vacuum Vent Valves Do Not Work

1. Connect test light between terminal No. 3 and ground.
2. Turn the ignition switch, and cruise control switch on.
3. Press and release the brake pedal. If equipped, press and release the clutch pedal.
4. If test light turns off, proceed to next test.
5. If test light does not turn off, check the following:
   a. Repair broken wire.
   b. Adjust vacuum vent valve.
   c. Replace vacuum vent valve.

Cruise Control Switch Does Not Work

1. Connect test light between terminal No. 6 and ground.
2. Turn the ignition switch, and cruise control switch on.
3. Press the resume switch.

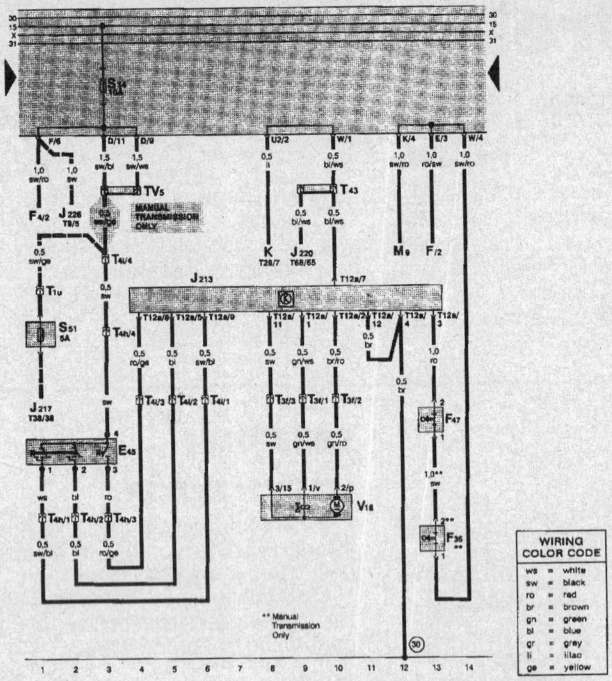
WIRING COLOR CODE
ws = white
sw = black
ro = red
br = brown
gn = green
bl = blue
gr = grey
li = lilac
ge = yellow
** Manual Transmission Only

E45 – Cruise Control Switch
F – Brake Light Switch
F4 – Back-Up Light Switch
F36 – Cruise Control Clutch Pedal Position Switch
F47 – Cruise Control Brake Pedal Position Switch
J213 – Cruise Control Module
J217 – Transmission Control Module (TCM)
J220 – Motronic Engine Control Module (ECM)
J226 – Park/Neutral Position (PNP) Relay
K – Instrument Cluster
M9 – Brake Light, Left
S51 – Fuse
V18 – Cruise Control Vacuum Pump
T1u – Connector, Single, behind fuse/relay panel
T3f – Connector, 3 Pin, below left side of dash
T4h – Connector, 4 Pin, behind steering column switch trim
T4l – Connector, 4 Pin, behind fuse/relay panel
T9 – Connector, 9 Pin, on Park/Neutral Position (PNP) Relay
T12a – Connector, 12 Pin, on Cruise Control Module
T28 – Connector, 28 Pin, instrument cluster
T38 – Connector, 38 Pin, below right front seat, on Transmission Control Module (TCM)
T43 – Connector, vehicle speed signal
T68 – Connector, 68 Pin, under right side of hood, on Motronic Engine Control Module (ECM)
TV5 – Connector, terminal 15a
(30) – Ground connection – beside fuse/relay panel
– – – Automatic transmission only

VW1109300004000X

Fig. 2 Speed control wiring diagram. Cabrio, Golf III, GTI & Jetta III except TDI

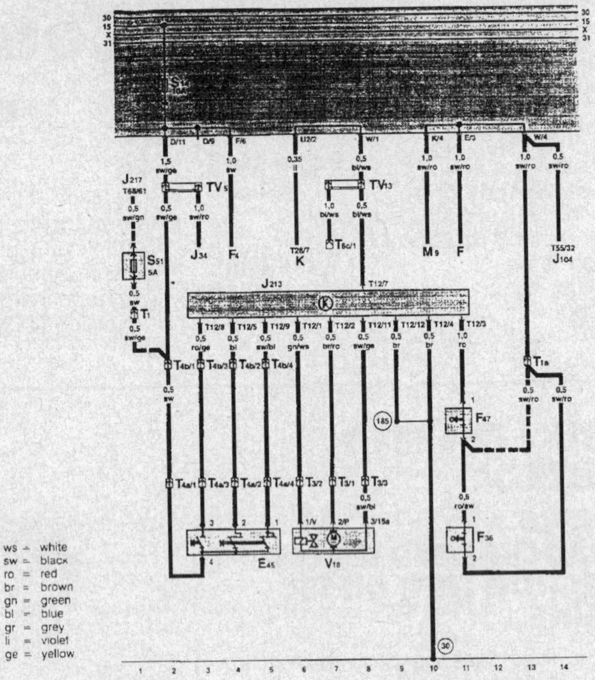
ws = white
sw = black
ro = red
br = brown
gn = green
bl = blue
gr = grey
li = violet
ge = yellow

E45 – Cruise Control Switch
F – Brake Light Switch
F4 – Back-Up Light Switch
F36 – Clutch Vacuum Vent Valve Switch*
F47 – Brake Vacuum Vent Valve Switch
J34 – Seat Belt Warning System Relay
J104 – ABS Control Module (w/EDL)
J213 – Cruise Control, Control Module, behind console
J217 – Transmission Control Module (TCM)
K – Instrument Cluster
M9 – Left Brake Light
S51 – Fuse for cruise control, above fuse/relay panel
T1 – Single Connector, behind fuse/relay panel
T1a – Single Connector, behind fuse/relay panel
T3 – 3-Pin Connector, behind fuse/relay panel
T4a – 4-Pin Connector, behind steering column switch cover
T4b – 4-Pin Connector, near steering column
T6c – 6-Pin Connector, behind fuse/relay panel
T12 – 12-Pin Connector
T28 – 28-Pin Connector, on instrument cluster
T55 – 55-Pin Connector, on ABS Control Module (w/EDL)
T68 – 68-Pin Connector, on Transmission Control Module (TCM)
TV5 – Terminal 15a Wire Connector, above fuse/relay panel
TV13 – Vehicle Speed Signal Wire Connector, above fuse/relay panel
V18 – Cruise Control Vacuum Pump
(30) – Ground connection, –1–, beside fuse/relay panel
(185) – Ground connection, in cruise control wiring harness
* – Manual transmission only
▬ ▬ – Automatic transmission only

VW1109500005000X

Fig. 3 Speed control wiring diagram. Passat except TDI

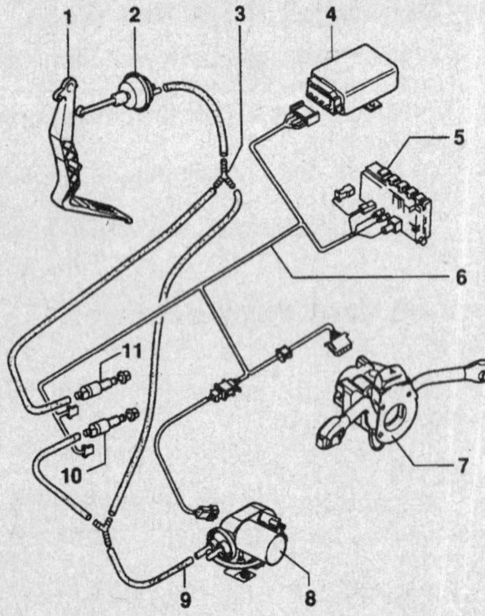
1
2
3
4
5
6
7
8
9
10
11

1.Accelerator Pedal
2.Throttle Control Element
3.T-connector
4.Cruise Control Module
5.Relay Panel
6.Wiring Harness
7.Cruise Control Switch
8.Vacuum Pump
9.Vacuum Hose
10.Clutch Switch
11.Brake Switch

VW1109300006000X

Fig. 4 Component diagram. Except Cabriolet, Eurovan & models w/diesel engine

4. If test light does not illuminate, check the following:

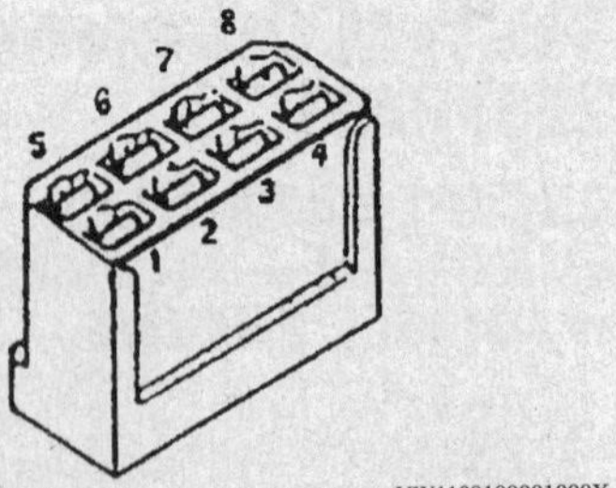
1
2
3
4
5
6
7
8

VW1109100001000X

Fig. 5 Control unit connector terminal identification. Cabriolet

a. Repair broken wire.
b. Replace switch.

5. If test light illuminates, proceed as follows:
   a. Connect test light between terminal No. 2 and ground.
   b. Press the set switch.
   c. If test light does not illuminate, repair broken wire or replace switch.
   d. If test light illuminates, proceed to next test.

Vacuum Control Motor Does Not Work

1. Connect jumper wire between terminal No. 4 and ground.

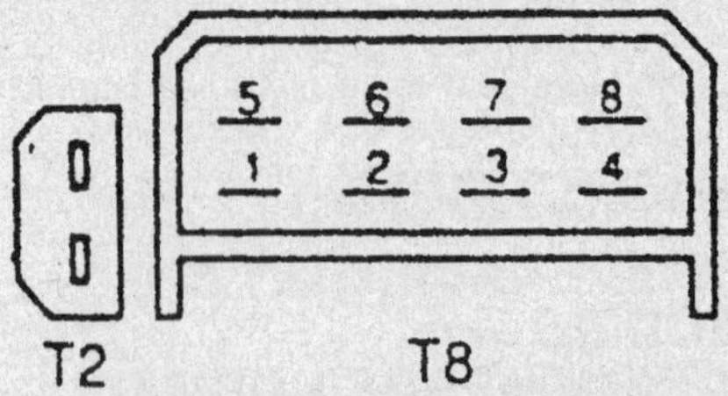
5
6
7
8
1
2
3
4
T2
T8

VW1109500002000X

Fig. 6 Cruise control harness connector terminal identification

2. If pump does not run, replace it.
3. If pump runs, proceed to next test.

Vacuum Control Motor Vent Valve Does Not Work

1. Connect a jumper wire to terminal No. 7 and touch it briefly to ground.
2. If vent valve clicks, proceed to next test.
3. If vent valve does not click, check the following:
   a. Repair broken wire.
   b. Replace vacuum control motor.

Speed Sensor Does Not Work

1. Turn ignition switch off.

Connector Terminals	Condition	Result	Area To Check If Result Not Obtained
1 & Ground	Drive Vehicle Above 20 mph In D, 3, Or 2	Battery Voltage	Check For No Signal Condition At Cruise Control Switch
	Ignition Switch On. Bridge Fuse S51 With Jumper, Turn On Cruise Control	Battery Voltage	Fuse & Cruise Control Switch Wiring
1 & 8	Cruise Control On	Battery Voltage	Control Unit Ground
1 & 3	Cruise Control On	Battery Voltage	Brake Switch, Cruise Control Switch & Brake Light Ground
	Cruise Control On	0 V	Brake Pedal Switch & Wiring
	Cruise Control Off	0 V	Cruise Control Switch & Wiring
6 & 8	Press RESUME	Battery Voltage	Cruise Control Switch & Wiring
2 & 8	Cruise Control On, Select SET	Battery Voltage	Cruise Control Switch & Wiring
5 & 8	Cruise Control On, Raise Front Wheel & Rotate By Hand In Driving Direction	0-10.5 V	VSS, Speedometer, Voltage Stabilizer For Instruments & Wiring
No Voltmeter Connections	Ignition Switch ON But Do Not Start Engine. Cruise Control On. Install Jumpers Between Terminals (7 & 8), (8 & 4) & (1 & T2 Black/Blue Wire Terminal)	Throttle Opens Fully	Vacuum Servo & Vacuum Circuit For Leakage
	Depress Brake Pedal (Jumpers Remain Connected)	Throttle Closes	Brake Vent Switch
	Release Brake Pedal (Jumpers Remain Connected)	Throttle Opens Fully	—
	Remove Jumper Between 8 & 4	Pump Shuts Off & Throttle Stays Open	Vacuum Servo & Vacuum Circuit For Leakage
	Remove Remaining Jumpers	Throttle Closes Smoothly	Vacuum Pump Motor

Fig. 7 Cruise control system diagnosis

2. Connect multimeter to terminal 5 and ground.
3. Set multimeter to ohms scale. If reading is not 90–110 ohms, replace speed sensor.
4. If reading is 90–110 ohms, replace cruise control main control unit.

WITH VOLTMETER

Disconnect harness connector, **Fig. 6,** from cruise control unit and use a voltmeter to perform connector terminal tests, **Fig. 7.**

PASSAT w/ TURBOCHARGED DIRECT INJECTION (TDI) DIESEL ENGINE

DIAGNOSIS

1. Connect scan tool No. VAG 1551, or equivalent, to the Diagnostic Link Connector (DLC), located on the LH lower side of the instrument panel to right of the steering column.
2. Follow scan tool manufacturer's instructions to access Diagnostic Trouble Codes (DTCs).
3. Refer to "Speed Control Diagnosis Trouble Code Table," **Fig. 8,** for information on any speed control DTC accessed.

TESTING

Speed Control Switch

In the event a display value of 255 is shown in display field four of the scan tool during the following procedure, refer to "Activate Speed Control, Models w/Turbocharged Direct Injection (TDI) Diesel Engine."

1. Connect scan tool No. VAG 1551, or equivalent, to the Diagnostic Link Connector (DLC), located on the LH lower side of the instrument panel to right of the steering column.
2. Follow scan tool manufacturer's instructions to access "Engine Electronics."
3. Follow scan tool manufacturer's instructions to access "Read Measuring Block Value."Follow scan tool manufacturer's instructions to access "Display Group 06."
4. Refer to **Fig. 9** for scan tool display values for each test condition and their possible fault correction procedures.

COMPONENT REPLACEMENT

EXCEPT CABRIOLET & MODELS w/ TURBOCHARGED DIRECT INJECTION (TDI) DIESEL ENGINE

Cruise Control Switch

Refer to "Electrical" section for procedure.

Throttle Control Element

1. Remove lower instrument panel covers.
2. Disconnect vacuum line from element.
3. Disconnect actuator rod from pedal.
4. Remove element mounting nut, then element.
5. Reverse procedure to install, adjust element as described under "Adjustments."

Vent Valves

To prevent trapping vacuum in throttle control element and inadvertent racing of engine, ensure throttle pedal is fully returned before connecting vacuum line to vent valve.

1. Remove lower instrument panel covers.
2. Disconnect vacuum line and electrical connectors from valve.
3. Unscrew valve from bracket.
4. Reverse procedure to install, ensure pedal for valve is fully returned to stop after valve is installed.

Speed Control Vacuum Pump

1. Remove battery, then if necessary the windshield washer bottle.
2. Disconnect wiring connector and vacuum line.
3. Disconnect pump from mounting, then remove pump.
4. Reverse procedure to install.

CABRIOLET

Control Unit

1. Disconnect battery ground cable.
2. Remove passenger side trim cover from the instrument panel.

DTC	Related Component	Fault Indication	Possible Fault Cause
00513	Engine Speed Sensor	Implausible Signal	Sensor Faulty, Distance Between Speed Sensor And Sensor Wheel Excessive, Metal Chips On Sensor, Sensor Mounting Base Loose
		No Signal	Sensor Faulty, Open Circuit In Wiring
00542	Needle Lift Sensor	Inlet Open	Sensor Faulty, Open Circuit In Wiring
		No Signal	Sensor Faulty, Injector Line Bad, Air In Fuel System, Fuel Shortage
00652	Vehicle Speed Sensor Or Electronic Speedometer	Implausible Signal	With Electronic Speedometer, No Signal From Speedometer Or Speedometer Vehicle Speed Sensor. With Mechanical Speedometer No Signal from Vehicle Speed Sensor
00671	Cruise Control Switch	Undefined Switch State	Cruise Control Switch Faulty, Open Or Short Circuit In Wiring
00741	Brake Light Switch Or Brake Pedal Switch	Implausible Signal	Brake Light Switch Faulty, Brake Pedal Switch Faulty, Switching Points Of Both Switches Not Synchronized
65535	Control Module	–	Internal Fault In Control Module

Fig. 8 Speed Control Diagnosis Trouble Code Table. Passat w/TDI diesel engine

Display Group	Display Field	Designation	Test conditions	Display	Fault correction
06	2 3	Brake pedal switch for cruise control (F47), clutch pedal switch (F36)	Brake and clutch pedal in rest position	000 000000	– Check wiring to brake pedal switch for cruise control (F47) and clutch pedal switch (F36) using wiring diagram – Check electrical function of cruise control switch (F47) and clutch pedal switch (F36) ·at brake pedal
		Brake pedal switch for cruise control (F47)	Brake pedal depressed	011 010000	
		Clutch pedal switch (F36)	Clutch pedal depressed	100 100000	
06	3	Cruise control switch (E45)	E45 In OFF position	000000	– Check wiring to cruise control switch (E45) using wiring diagram
		Cruise control switch (E45)	E45 in ON position	000001	– Check wiring to cruise control switch (E45) using wiring diagram
		Cruise control switch (E45)	E45 in ON position, SET button pressed	000101	
		Cruise control switch (E45)	E45 pushed toward left into RES position	001001	
	4	Cruise control status	Cruise control blocked	255	– Cruise control system activated
		Cruise control status	Cruise control activated	0	

VW1109300008000X

Fig. 9 Speed control testing scan tool values. Passat Turbocharged Direct Injection (TDI) diesel

3. Disconnect control unit electrical connector.
4. Remove retaining screws, then the control unit.
5. Reverse procedure to install.

Speedometer Sender

1. Disconnect battery ground cable.
2. Remove instrument cluster.
3. Remove retaining screws, then the sensor.
4. Reverse procedure to install.

Cruise Control Switch

1. Disconnect battery ground cable.
2. Remove steering wheel.
3. Disconnect switch electrical connector.
4. Remove retaining screws and the switch.
5. Reverse procedure to install.

Vacuum Vent Valves

1. Disconnect battery ground cable.
2. Remove driver side trim cover from the instrument panel.
3. Disconnect vent valve vacuum hose, and electrical connector.

Air Bag System

NOTE: On Air Bag Equipped Models, Refer To "Air Bag System Precautions" Located In The Front Of This Manual For System Disarming & Arming Procedures.

INDEX

	Page No.
Air Bag System Disarming & Arming	49-85
Arming	49-85
Disarming	49-85
Collision Inspection	49-86
Component Locations	49-86
Component Service	49-86
Air Bag Assembly Disposal	49-87
Air Bag Module, Replace	49-86
Control Module/Unit Replace	49-87
Spiral Spring, Replace	49-87
Description & Operation	49-85
Diagnosis & Testing	49-86
Precautions	49-85
Scheduled Maintenance	49-85
Technical Service Bulletins	49-88
Phantom SRS Lamp Lighting	49-88
SRS Control Module & Wiring Harness Revisions	49-88
SRS ECM Safety Lock Connector Replacement	49-88
Steering Wheel Off Center	49-88
Use Of Stabilant 22A On Electrical Connections	49-88
Tightening Specifications	49-89
Wiring Diagrams	49-85

AIR BAG SYSTEM DISARMING & ARMING

Disarming

Do not use the computer memory saver tool on air bag equipped models. Using this tool will keep the system charged and may cause unwanted air bag unit activation. Obtain the radio security code prior to disconnecting the battery ground cable. After service has been completed and the cable connected, use this code to activate the radio.

1. Disconnect battery ground cable.
2. **Wait 20 minutes to allow air bag/ Supplemental Restraint System (SRS) capacitor to discharge prior to performing any service procedures.**

Arming

1. **Ensure nobody is in vehicle, then connect battery ground cable.**
2. Turn ignition On and note air bag warning lamp operation. Lamp should light for approximately three to eight seconds, then go off. If lamp fails to light or remains lit after eight seconds, refer to "Diagnosis & Testing."

DESCRIPTION & OPERATION

The Supplemental Restraint System (SRS), **Fig. 1,** is designed to supplement protection offered by seat belts in a frontal impact collision.

The SRS incorporates an on-board diagnostic feature. System faults or diagnostic trouble codes (DTCs) detected are stored in the control unit memory, located behind the center console. DTCs can be extracted from the memory using a scan tool No. VAG 1551, or equivalent.

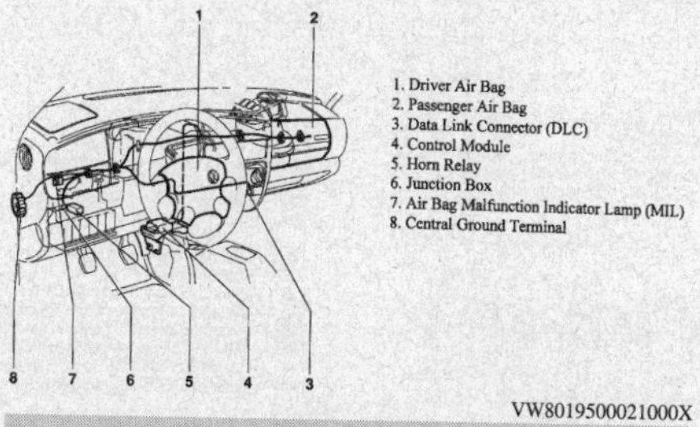
1
2
1. Driver Air Bag
2. Passenger Air Bag
3. Data Link Connector (DLC)
4. Control Module
5. Horn Relay
6. Junction Box
7. Air Bag Malfunction Indicator Lamp (MIL)
8. Central Ground Terminal
8
7
6
5
4
3
VW8019500021000X

Fig. 1 SRS components

PRECAUTIONS

1. The SRS must be disarmed prior to disconnecting any system electrical connectors, servicing any system components or other items located near any system electrical connectors. Refer to "Air Bag System Arming & Disarming."
2. Obtain radio security code prior to disconnecting battery ground cable. After service has been completed and cable connected, use this code to activate radio.
3. **Never perform SRS inspections while control module is installed and connected.**
4. Air bag units have an expiration date, which can be found on a sticker behind driver's sun visor. After 10 years, SRS must be replaced. For safety reasons, all other components must also be replaced at this time.
5. SRS inspection is never conducted with a test light, voltmeter or analog Ohmmeter. Use air bag tester VAG 1551, or equivalent, and inspect system in an installed condition.
6. SRS components must not be opened or repaired. Always use new components.
7. If air bag unit or triggering unit has been dropped from a height of 18 inches or more, do not install component into vehicle. These units must be replaced.
8. Always replace SRS components which have been mechanically damaged (bubbles, cracks, etc.).
9. Do not use a computer memory saver tool on air bag equipped models. Using the tool will keep system charged and may cause accidental unit activation.
10. Do not leave an undeployed air bag unit unattended if work is interrupted. Install air bag into vehicle as soon as unit is removed from packaging.
11. Always place a removed air bag unit so it rests on its metal housing and the horn pad faces upward.
12. Air bag unit must not be exposed to grease, or cleaned with any type of cleaning agent.
13. Do not paint air bag unit to correct cosmetic flaws. It must be replaced.
14. Do not expose air bag units to temperatures above 194°F for even brief periods. Keep units clear of all heat sources.
15. Deployed air bag units do not have to be disposed of as hazardous waste, but may be discarded with other automotive metal scrap for recycling.
16. Triggering units contain a mercury switch and must be disposed of in an approved manner.

SCHEDULED MAINTENANCE

Air bag units have an expiration date located on a label attached to the rear of the driver's sun visor. If label is missing, use the vehicle build date listed on a label on the driver's side door pillar. After 10 years, the air bag unit must be replaced. For safety reasons all other air bag system components must also be replaced at this time. Refer to "Component Service" for replacement procedures. After replacing components, install a new air bag date sticker, with

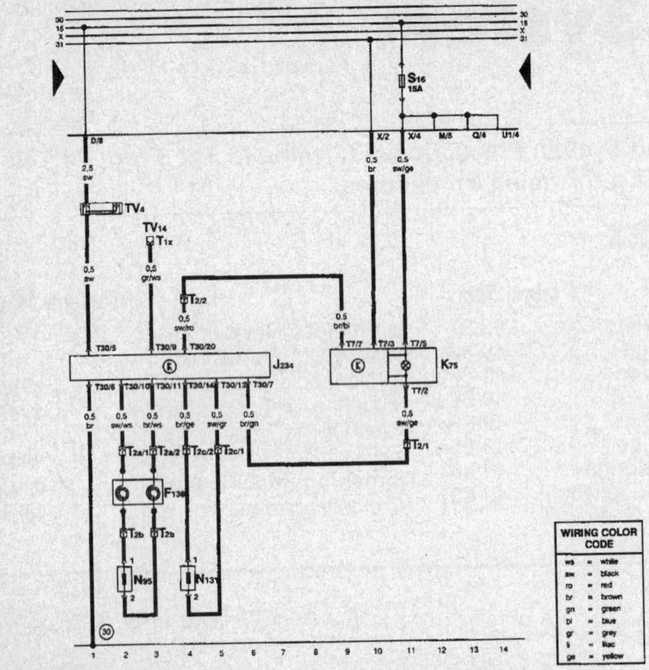
WIRING COLOR CODE
ws = white
sw = black
ro = red
br = brown
gn = green
bl = blue
gr = grey
li = lilac
ge = yellow

F138 – Airbag Spiral Spring/Return Spring With Slop Ring
J234 – Airbag Control Module
K75 – Airbag Malfunction Indicator Lamp (MIL)
N95 – Driver's Side Airbag Igniter (00588)
N131 – Passenger's Side Airbag Igniter 1 (00589)
T2a – Double Connector, behind instrument panel, center
T2b – Double Connector, behind steering column switch cover
T2c – Double Connector, behind Airbag-unit
T2 – Double Connector, behind Airbag-unit
T7 – 7-Pin Connector, near Airbag-unit
T30 – 30-Pin Connector on Airbag Control Module
TV4 – Terminal 15 Wire Connector, above fuse/relay panel
TV14 – Data Link Connector (DLC) wire Connector, above fuse/relay panel
(30) – Ground connection –1–, beside fuse/relay panel

VW8019500022000A

Fig. 2 SRS wiring circuit. Cabrio, 1994–95 Golf III & Jetta III

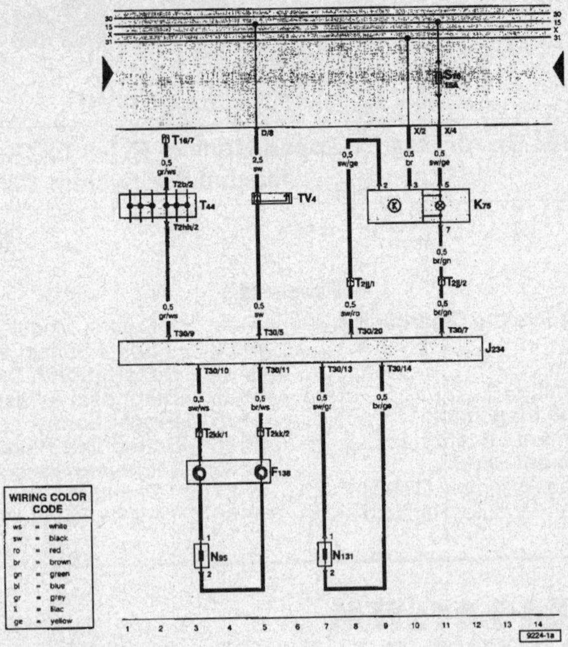
WIRING COLOR CODE
ws = white
sw = black
ro = red
br = brown
gn = green
bl = blue
gr = grey
li = lilac
ge = yellow
9224-1a

F138 – Airbag Spiral Spring
J234 – Airbag Control Module
K75 – Airbag Malfunction Indicator Lamp (MIL)
N95 – Driver's Side Airbag Ignitor
N131 – Passenger Side Airbag Ignitor 1
T2b – Double Connector, on junction connector (T44) above fuse/relay panel
T2hh – Double Connector, on junction connector (T44) above fuse/relay panel
T16 – Data Link Connector (DLC), behind center of dash panel
T2jj – Double Connector, behind fuse/relay panel
T2kk – Double Connector, behind fuse/relay panel
T30 – 30-Pin Connector, on Airbag Control Module
T44 – Junction Box for on Board Diagnosis, above fuse/relay panel
TV4 – Terminal 15 Wire Connector

VW8019600024000X

Fig. 3 SRS wiring circuit. 1996 Golf III & Jetta III

the expiration date punched out, on the driver's sun visor.

WIRING DIAGRAMS

Refer to **Figs. 2 through 4** for SRS wiring diagrams.

COMPONENT LOCATIONS

Refer to **Fig. 1** for SRS component locations.

DIAGNOSIS & TESTING

Refer to MOTOR'S Air Bag Manual for complete Diagnosis & Testing information.

COLLISION INSPECTION

On vehicles which have experienced an air bag system deployment, certain system components must be replaced. To determine which components require replacement, refer to the "General Information" section located at the front of this manual.

To ensure proper system operation on any vehicle involved in a collision, perform procedures outlined under "Diagnosis & Testing." All system components should be inspected for dents, cracks, exposure to excessive heat and other damage. All air bag system wiring should be inspected for chafing and interference with other vehicle components. The instrument should also be inspected. The system should be disarmed as described under "Air Bag System Disarming & Arming " when repairing the vehicle. Do not expose components or wiring to heat guns, welding or spray guns when performing service procedures.

COMPONENT SERVICE

The air bag system must be disarmed prior to disconnecting any air bag system electrical connectors or servicing any system components or other components located near any air bag system electrical connectors. Refer to "Air Bag System Arming & Disarming."

Do not use a computer memory saver tool on air bag equipped models. Using this tool will keep the air bag system charged and may cause accidental unit activation.

Obtain the radio security code prior to disconnecting the battery ground cable. After service has been completed and the cable connected, use this code to activate the radio.

AIR BAG MODULE, REPLACE

DRIVER'S

Remove

1. Disarm air bag system as described under "Air Bag System Disarming & Arming."
2. Ensure front wheels are in straight-ahead position.
3. If necessary, remove horn pad using screwdriver. **Do not pull with fingers.**
4. Remove socket-head bolts, then carefully lift air bag unit from wheel, **Fig. 5.**
5. Disconnect red connector from air bag unit.
6. **Place air bag unit so it rests on its metal housing with horn pad facing upward.**

Install

1. Connect electrical connector to air bag unit, then position unit to steering wheel.
2. Install fasteners and tighten bolts to specifications.
3. Arm SRS as described under "Air Bag System Disarming & Arming."

PASSENGER'S

1. Disarm SRS as described under "Air Bag System Disarming & Arming."
2. Remove screws, upper tabs and right hand kneebar, then screws and air vent housing.
3. **On Cabrio, Golf III, GTI and Jetta III models,** remove hex bolts, then slide air bag cover to right and remove, **Fig. 6.**
4. **On Passat models,** remove hex bolts, then unhook retaining tabs and open

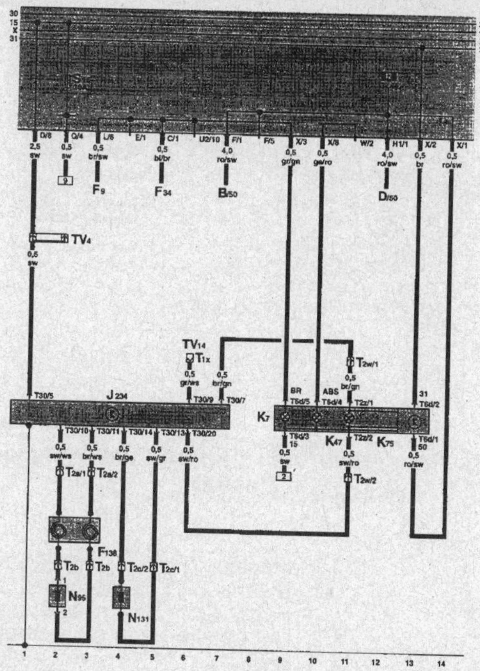

ws = white
sw = black
ro = red
br = brown
gn = green
bl = blue
gr = grey
li = violet
ge = yellow

B – Starter
D – Ignition/Starter Switch
F9 – Parking Brake Warning Light Switch (01114)
F34 – Brake Fluid Level Warning Switch
F138 – Airbag Spiral Spring/Return Spring With Slip Ring
J234 – Airbag Control Module, behind console
K7 – Brake and Parking Brake Warning Light
K47 – ABS Warning Light
K75 – Airbag Malfunction Indicator Lamp (MIL)
N95 – Driver's Side Airbag Igniter (00588)
N131 – Passenger's Side Airbag Igniter 1 (00589)
T1x – Single Connector, on Data Link Connector (DLC) Wire Connector
T2a – Double Connector, behind steering column switch cover
T2b – Double Connector, in steering wheel
T2c – Double Connector, behind instrument panel, right
T2w – Double Connector, behind fuse/relay panel
T2z – Double Connector
T6d – 6-Pin Connector
T30 – 30-Pin Connector
TV14 – Data Link Connector (DLC) Wire Connector, behind console

VW8019500023000A

Fig. 4 SRS wiring circuit. Passat

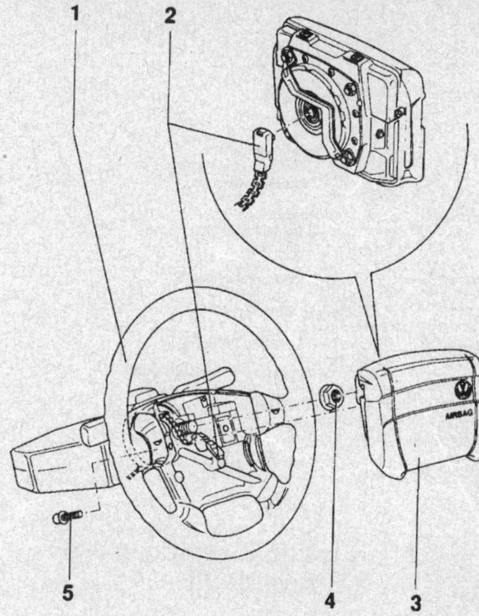
1
2
5
4
3

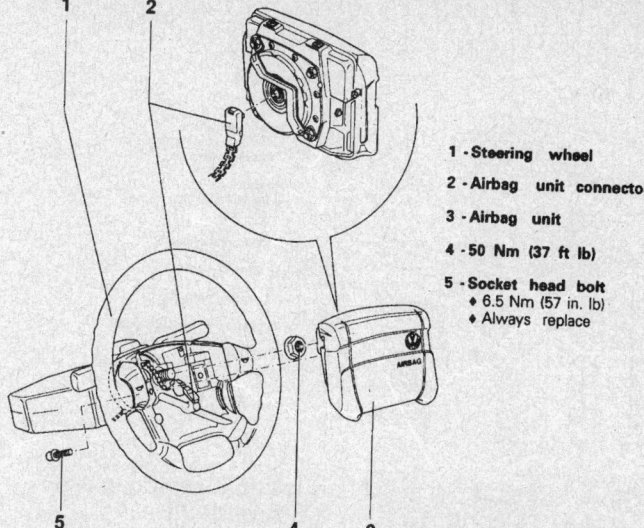

1 - Steering wheel
2 - Airbag unit connector
3 - Airbag unit
4 - 50 Nm (37 ft lb)
5 - Socket head bolt
- 6.5 Nm (57 in. lb)
- Always replace

VW8019500025000X

Fig. 5 Driver's air bag module replacement

cover, then remove screws and cover with retaining frame, **Fig. 7.**

5. **On all models,** remove hex bolts, then lift air bag module and disconnect electrical connector.
6. Reverse procedure to install, tightening bolts to specifications and arm SRS as described under "Air Bag System Disarming & Arming."

SPIRAL SPRING, REPLACE

1. Disarm SRS as described under "Air Bag System Disarming & Arming."
2. Remove air bag unit as described under "Air Bag Module, Replace."
3. Place alignment marks on the steering wheel hub and steering shaft for use during installation.
4. Remove lower steering column trim, then pull foam tube off and separate connector.
5. Remove steering wheel retaining nut and washer, then remove wheel with suitable steering wheel puller tool.
6. Remove horn connector from air bag spiral spring.
7. Remove screws and air bag spiral spring.
8. Reverse procedure to install, tighten bolts to specifications and arm SRS as described under "Air Bag System Disarming & Arming."

CONTROL MODULE/UNIT REPLACE

1. Disarm SRS as described under "Air Bag System Disarming & Arming."
2. **On Passat models,** remove parking brake handle and trim.
3. **On all models,** remove center console and footwell air outlet.
4. Cut carpeting and insulation in module mounting bracket area if necessary.
5. Move connector lock and remove connector from module.
6. Remove nuts and module.
7. Reverse procedure to install, tighten bolts to specifications and arm SRS as described under "Air Bag System Disarming & Arming."

AIR BAG ASSEMBLY DISPOSAL

When handling a deployed air bag assembly, a face shield and rubber gloves should be worn. Vehicle interior and all HVAC ducts should be vacuumed. If sinus or throat irritation is encountered during air bag removal, exit vehicle and breathe fresh air. If skin irritation is encountered, flush affected area with cool water. If any type of irritation continues, consult a physician. Wash hands and rinse thoroughly with water after handling a deployed air bag assembly.

DEPLOYED AIR BAG MODULE

A deployed air bag should be removed as described under "Air Bag Module, Replace." Prior to removing a deployed air bag assembly, place tape over air bag exhaust vents. After unit has been removed, it should be placed in a heavy duty plastic bag, sealed securely, then placed with automotive scrap.

Air bag units that have not been deployed must be deployed prior to scrapping. Refer to "Undeployed Air Bag Module."

UNDEPLOYED AIR BAG MODULE

Air bag modules must be deployed prior to scrapping vehicle.

Driver's

1. Locate vehicle in an open outdoor area with no strong winds or breezes with doors closed.
2. Disarm SRS as described under "Air Bag System Disarming & Arming."
3. Remove driver's air bag module as described under "Air Bag Module, Replace."
4. Disconnect red air bag module connector and connect suitable activation cable, then install air bag.
5. Connect special air bag igniter tool No. VAG 1821 and cable connector tool No. 1594A, or equivalents, activation cable two-pin connector.
6. Run igniter cable trough door gap toward front of vehicle and connect to external, fully charged 12 volt battery at least 33 feet from vehicle.
7. **Ensure no people, animals or objects are within 33 feet of the vehicle prior to deployment.**
8. Follow air bag igniter tool instructions to deploy air bag module.
9. **If air bag fails to deploy, contact**

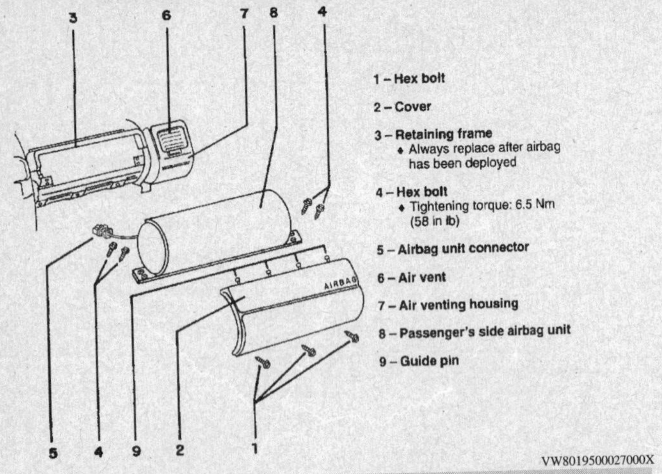
3
6
7
8
4
1 – Hex bolt
2 – Cover
3 – Retaining frame
♦ Always replace after airbag has been deployed
4 – Hex bolt
♦ Tightening torque: 6.5 Nm (58 in lb)
5 – Airbag unit connector
6 – Air vent
7 – Air venting housing
8 – Passenger's side airbag unit
9 – Guide pin
AIRBAG
5
4
9
2
1
VW8019500027000X

Fig. 6 Passenger's air bag module replacement. Cabrio, Golf III, GTI & Jetta III

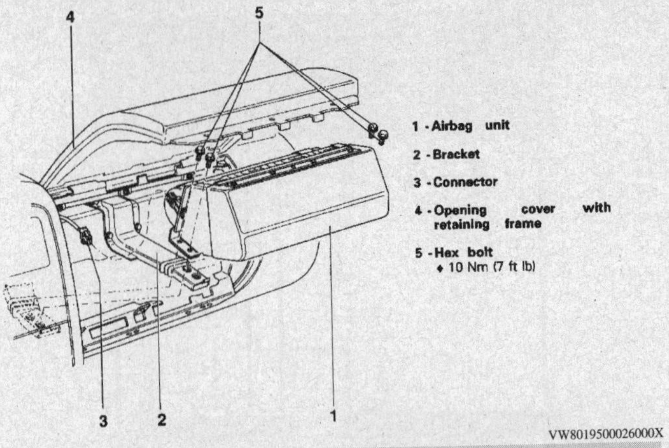
4
5
1 - Airbag unit
2 - Bracket
3 - Connector
4 - Opening cover with retaining frame
5 - Hex bolt
♦ 10 Nm (7 ft lb)
3
2
1
VW8019500026000X

Fig. 7 Passenger's air bag module replacement. Passat

Volkswagen for further instructions.

Passenger's

1. Locate vehicle in an open outdoor area with no strong winds or breezes with doors closed.
2. Disarm SRS as described under "Air Bag System Disarming & Arming."
3. **On Cabrio, Golf III, GTI and Jetta III models,** remove front passenger side shelf, then unclip and separated connector.
4. **On Passat models,** remove knee bar and open cover as described under "Air Bag Module, Replace."
5. **On all models,** cut off air bag module connector.
6. Connect special air bag igniter tool No. VAG 1821, or equivalent.
7. Run igniter cable trough door gap toward front of vehicle and connect to external, fully charged 12 volt battery at least 33 feet from vehicle.
8. **Ensure no people, animals or objects are within 33 feet of the vehicle prior to deployment.**
9. Follow air bag igniter tool instructions to deploy air bag module.
10. **If air bag fails to deploy, contact Volkswagen for further instructions.**

TECHNICAL SERVICE BULLETINS

PHANTOM SRS LAMP LIGHTING

1994 Golf & Jetta Except GLX

On these models, phantom SRS indicator lamp lighting may occur after adding additional horns. Only a single horn was standard equipment.

To avoid phantom SRS lamp lighting, do not add any additional horns to these vehicles.

STEERING WHEEL OFF CENTER

1994-96 Golf III & Jetta III

On these models, the steering wheel may not be centered when the vehicle is driven straight on a level surface.

To correct this condition, proceed as follows:

1. Disarm SRS as described under "Air Bag System Disarming & Arming."
2. Remove driver's air bag module as described under "Air Bag Module, Replace."
3. Remove screws holding spiral spring to wheel.
4. Unplug horn connection, then remove wheel retaining nut.
5. **Spiral spring assembly must remain in place on column. Reach behind wheel and hold spring in place while sliding wheel off with other hand.**
6. Slide wheel off just enough to clear shaft splines, then position as needed.
7. Turn spiral spring assembly to align its holes as wheel goes back onto shaft. **Do not turn wheel until all attachments are complete.**
8. Tighten bolts to specifications.
9. Arm SRS as described under "Air Bag System Disarming & Arming."

SRS ECM SAFETY LOCK CONNECTOR REPLACEMENT

1994-95 Golf III, GTI & Jetta III

On these models, the air bag electronic control module (ECM) connector plug has a locking safety catch to ensure proper retention and engagement. In the past, the entire air bag harness required replacement if this catch was broken. However, the plug housing with catch is now available separately.

To replace housing, proceed as follows:

1. Disarm SRS as described under "Air Bag System Disarming & Arming."
2. Cut tie strap and slide off plastic end cap.
3. Slide entire connector plug housing off of pin retainer.
4. Slide new housing onto pin retainer, then install end cap and new tie strap.
5. After completing installation, arm SRS as described under "Air Bag System Disarming & Arming."

SRS CONTROL MODULE & WIRING HARNESS REVISIONS

1995 Golf III, GTI & Jetta III

On these models, the SRS control module and its mounting bracket have been changed, resulting in additional wiring harness revisions.

On models built through August 1994, a Temic brand module was original equipment.

On models built after August 1994, a Siemens brand module has been installed.

Since November 1994, the module's wiring harness has been changed to eliminate brown ground wire. This new harness and Siemens module are the only replacement parts now available. A Siemens module may be installed into a vehicle which was equipped with the Temic module, but the wiring harness must also be replaced.

USE OF STABILANT 22A ON ELECTRICAL CONNECTIONS

On these models, always use Stabilant 22A contact enhancer on all SRS wiring connections and terminals whenever these are replaced or separated.

Stabilant 22A should also be used whenever a harness replacement is performed.

TIGHTENING SPECIFICATIONS

Component	Torque/Ft. Lbs.
Air Bag Module, Driver's	57①
Air Bag Module Bolts, Passenger's (Passat)	7
Air Bag Module Bolts, Passenger's (Cabrio, Golf III, GTI & Jetta III)	58①
Air Bag Module Cover Screws, Passenger's	13①
Control Unit Mounting Bolts	15
Knee Bar Screws	57①
Steering Wheel Retaining Nut	37

① — Inch lbs.

Dash Panel Service

NOTE: On Air Bag Equipped Models, Refer To "Air Bag System Precautions" Located In The Front Of This Manual For System Disarming & Arming Procedures.

NOTE: Refer To The "Electronic Instrumentation" Section In MOTOR'S "Imported Engine Performance & Driveability Manual" For Information Related To Electronic Instrumentation.

INDEX

	Page No.
Dash Panel, Replace	49-89
Cabrio, Golf III, GTI & Jetta III	49-90
Cabriolet	49-89
Corrado	49-90
Eurovan	49-90
Fox	49-90
Passat	49-91
Precautions	49-89
Air Bag Systems	49-89
Audio Coded Anti-Theft System	49-89

PRECAUTIONS

Do not use computer memory saver tool on air bag equipped models. Using the tool will keep the air bag system charged and may cause accidental activation of the air bag unit. Prior to disconnecting the battery negative cable, obtain the radio security code. After service has been completed and the battery negative cable has been reconnected, use security code to activate the radio.

AIR BAG SYSTEMS

Refer to "Air Bag System Precautions" in the front of this manual for system disarming and arming procedures.

AUDIO CODED ANTI-THEFT SYSTEM

Some models are equipped with a radio anti-theft system that will disable the system when battery power is interrupted, unless the system is reset the radio will not operate.

1. Turn radio to On position, SAFE should be displayed.
2. Depress and hold AM/FM and SCAN buttons until 1000 remains on display. If AM/FM and SCAN buttons are depressed too long or depressed again, radio will misinterpret the 1000 as an attempt at coding and one incorrect coding attempt will be logged. **After two incorrect attempts to reset system radio will lock up electronically, if this occurs leave radio On for approximately 1 hour, then reset radio as if battery power were disconnected.**
3. Enter radio code using first four program station buttons, security code will appear on display.
4. Depress and hold AM/FM and SCAN buttons again until SAFE is displayed.
5. Release AM/FM and SCAN buttons, display should change to a radio frequency and operate normally.

DASH PANEL

REPLACE

CABRIOLET

1. Obtain audio coded anti-theft code and disarm as described under "Precautions."
2. Disconnect battery ground cable, then remove steering wheel as described under "Electrical" section.
3. Tilt shelf under steering column downward, remove screws, then the shelf.
4. Remove screws, pry out clips, then remove instrument panel cover.
5. Remove screws, then the shelf on passengers side.
6. Pry out clips below glove box, then pull lower instrument panel cover out of guides.
7. Remove screws, then pull lower part of console to rear.
8. Remove heater/fresh air control knobs, two screws, then pull upper part of console off slightly.
9. Disconnect electrical connections from console, then remove upper console.
10. Remove screws and pull off instrument panel insert trim, then the screws for instrument gauge cluster and tip forward.
11. Pull off vacuum hose, disconnect multi-pin connector and speedometer cable from instrument gauge cluster.
12. Remove instrument gauge cluster, then push switch forward out of instrument panel.
13. Pull air ducts off side vents, then disconnect electrical connections from ashtray and wiring harness from instrument panel.

14. Open glove box and remove screws for instrument panel, then the screws on right and left end of instrument panel.
15. Pry off E-clip and disconnect flap cable, then pull off instrument panel and remove to right side.
16. Reverse procedure to install. Reset audio coded anti-theft system as outlined under "Precautions."

CORRADO

1. Obtain audio coded anti-theft code, disconnect battery ground cable, then remove shelf screws, plastic nuts and pull out tray.
2. Turn rotating clips, pull out storage box, unscrew oval head screw and multi-purpose screws and remove cover.
3. Remove steering wheel as described in "Electrical " section.
4. Pry off cover cap, then remove screws and trim plate for instrument gauge cluster.
5. Pry out vents with a screwdriver, then remove radio or glove box.
6. Pry off trim plate, remove screws and pull out cassette storage box.
7. Pull off temperature control knobs and sliding levers, pry out trim plate and remove heating and ventilation controls.
8. Remove screws and pull out center trim plate, then the instrument panel cover.
9. Remove combination switch as described in "Electrical " section.
10. pry off left and right instrument panel caps, then remove mounting bolts.
11. Remove mounting nuts in plenum panel, then slightly pull off instrument panel.
12. Loosen cables, disconnect electrical connectors and remove instrument panel.
13. Reverse procedure to install. Reset audio coded anti-theft system as outlined under "Precautions."

EUROVAN

1. Obtain audio coded anti-theft code and disarm as described under "Precautions," then disconnect battery ground cable
2. From the engine compartment, remove the hex bolt from the air inlet duct.
3. Remove combination switch as described in the "Electrical " section.
4. Remove instrument cluster trim, then disconnect speedometer and electrical connectors from instrument cluster.
5. Remove right, center and left air outlets as follows:
   a. Unclip and pry out louver unit from vent.
   b. Through louver opening, remove screw retaining lower edge of vent to dash panel.
   c. Pry down on clips retaining top edge of vent, then remove vent.
6. Pry headlight switch from dash panel, then disconnect electrical connector.
7. **On models with instrument panel speakers,** disconnect left speaker through headlight switch mounting hole and right speaker through right air vent mounting hole.
8. **On all models,** remove left side under dash storage tray, then pry screw cap from left end of dash panel and remove mounting screw.
9. Pry out and disconnect any dash mounted switches as equipped.
10. Remove heater and A/C knobs by pulling straight out of control unit.
11. Pry heater and A/C control unit trim from dash panel, then disconnect heater blower switch.
12. Remove radio if equipped as described in the "Electrical " section.
13. Remove screws retaining front edge of heater and A/C control unit to dash panel (control unit remains in vehicle when dash removed).
14. **On models with center footwell air duct,** remove console, then remove mounting screws from lower edge of dash panel.
15. **On all models,** remove glove compartment, then pry screw cap from right end of dash panel and remove mounting screw.
16. Remove dash panel, then any components from dash as necessary to complete repair.
17. Reverse procedure to install.

FOX

1. Obtain audio coded anti-theft code, disconnect battery ground cable, then remove gearshift knob.
2. Remove console mounting screws behind and in front of handbrake lever, then pull out and remove console storage box.
3. Disconnect heater duct hoses inside console area, then remove ashtray.
4. Disconnect ashtray light, then shift into second gear, pull console toward rear and remove.
5. Tip vent grille in at top, remove mounting screw, tip in at bottom, pry up release tabs and remove vent grille assembly.
6. Pull off heater control knobs and face plate, then remove control light.
7. Remove screws, disconnect electrical connector from fan switch and remove switch.
8. Disconnect cigarette lighter, remove air duct to heater housing, radio face plate and remove radio.
9. Remove screws at bottom of instrument panel, then the steering wheel as described in "Electrical" section.
10. Carefully remove covers from vacant switch positions, then remove switches by inserting a ⅛ inch screwdriver blade behind switch to release spring retainer.
11. Remove screws at instrument gauge cluster, then the combination switch as described in "Electrical" section.
12. Remove instrument gauge cluster mounting screws, then disconnect speedometer cable at counter box.
13. Separate left side air vent assembly with air duct from under left side of instrument panel, then pull instrument gauge cluster away and down, disconnect electrical connects and remove. **Cover end of steering shaft to prevent scratching face of instrument gauge cluster during removal.**
14. Remove screw at back of glove box, then the glove box lamp.
15. Remove two nuts in plenum chamber, then separate right side air vent assembly with air duct from under right side of instrument panel.
16. Drill out rivets at both sides of instrument panel, then remove instrument panel mounting screws.
17. Remove instrument panel by pulling firmly on both sides, disconnect any remaining hoses or wires. **Avoid damage to defroster deflection piece by using screwdriver to guide deflector past heat exchanger.**
18. Reverse procedure to install. Reset audio coded anti-theft system as outlined under "Precautions."

CABRIO, GOLF III, GTI & JETTA III

1. Obtain audio coded anti-theft code and disarm as described under "Precautions," then disconnect battery ground cable.
2. **On models with air bags,** remove center console as follows:
   a. Remove cap plugs from sides of console extension, then remove screws.
   b. Pull out and disconnect rear lid opening switch connector.
   c. Pull console extension with storage compartment to rear then lift off console.
   d. Remove shift knob and trim.
   e. Remove hex nuts retaining console to floor and screws retaining console to dash.
   f. Lift console off mounting studs, then remove console, disconnecting any electrical connectors as equipped. **Note position of mounting stud spacers.**
3. **On models less air bags,** remove center console as follows:
   a. Remove rear ash tray, then remove hex nuts.
   b. Lift and pull rear cover to rear while disconnecting any electrical connectors as equipped.
   c. Remove shift knob and trim.
   d. Remove hex nuts retaining console to floor and screws retaining console to dash.
   e. Lift console off mounting studs, then remove console, disconnecting any electrical connectors as equipped. **Note position of mounting stud spacers.**
4. **On all models,** remove combination switch as described in the "Electrical" section.
5. Remove the radio, if equipped, as described in the "Electrical" section.
6. Remove relay cover, then the left side lower dash cover.
7. Remove tray on right side lower dash.
8. **On models less passengers air bag,** remove glove compartment.

9. **On models with passengers air bag,** remove passenger air bag.
10. **On all models,** pull off temperature control trim plate, remove temperature control unit mounting screws, then push into dash (control unit remains in vehicle when dash removed).
11. Remove and disconnect any switches from instrument panel trim plate, as equipped.
12. Remove instrument panel trim plate screws, then the trim plate.
13. Remove the instrument cluster as described in the "Electrical" section.
14. Remove mounting screws from lower edge of dash panel, then mounting nuts from air inlet plenum from under hood. Note position of all sealing washers.
15. Partially remove dash panel, then disconnect any remaining electrical connectors and cables.
16. Remove dash panel from vehicle.
17. Reverse procedure to install. Reset audio coded anti-theft system as outlined under "Precautions."

PASSAT

1. Obtain audio coded anti-theft code, disconnect battery ground cable.
2. Remove the radio as described in the "Electrical" section.
3. Remove steering wheel as described in the "Electrical" section.
4. **On models with air bags,** remove passengers air bag as described in "Air Bag Systems."
5. **On models less air bags,** remove screws from passenger side storage tray, then the tray at a downward angle. **Do not damage pins.**
6. **On models less air bags,** turn fittings for drivers side storage tray 90°, remove pin, unclip tray, then remove.
7. **On models less air bags,** remove screws and take out storage tray housing at a downward angle.
8. **On models with air bags,** remove left knee bar unit, then remove right knee bar unit.
9. **On all models,** remove front and rear consoles.
10. Remove trim plate for heater control unit, screws from instrument panel, then press control unit inward and under instrument panel (control unit remains in vehicle when dash removed).
11. Drill out shear bolts and lower steering column, then disconnect electrical connectors and grounds as required.
12. Disconnect connectors on fuse/relay panel from instrument panel wiring harness, then remove cover caps and mounting screws on both ends of instrument panel.
13. Pull out retainers on air intake housing upward, then remove front screws on support, slacken rear screws and fold back supports.
14. Remove instrument panel.
15. Reverse procedure to install. Reset audio coded anti-theft system as outlined under "Precautions."

Steering Columns

NOTE: On Air Bag Equipped Models, Refer To "Air Bag System Precautions" Located In The Front Of This Manual For System Disarming & Arming Procedures.

INDEX

	Page No.
Precautions	49-91
Air Bag Systems	49-91
Audio Coded Anti-Theft System	49-91
Steering Column Service	49-91

PRECAUTIONS

Do not use computer memory saver tool on air bag equipped models. Using the tool will keep the air bag system charged and may cause accidental activation of the air bag unit. Prior to disconnecting the battery negative cable, obtain the radio security code. After service has been completed and the battery negative cable has been reconnected, use security code to activate the radio.

AIR BAG SYSTEMS

Refer to "Air Bag System Precautions" in the front of this manual for system disarming and arming procedures.

AUDIO CODED ANTI-THEFT SYSTEM

Some models are equipped with a radio anti-theft system that will disable the system when battery power is interrupted, unless the system is reset the radio will not operate.

1. Turn radio to On position, SAFE should be displayed.
2. Depress and hold AM/FM and SCAN buttons until 1000 remains on display. If AM/FM and SCAN buttons are depressed too long or depressed again, radio will misinterpret the 1000 as an attempt at coding and one incorrect coding attempt will be logged. **After two incorrect attempts to reset system, radio will lock up electronically, if this occurs leave radio On for approximately 1 hour, then reset radio as if battery power were disconnected.**
3. Enter radio code using first four program station buttons, security code will appear on display.
4. Depress and hold AM/FM and SCAN buttons again until SAFE is displayed.
5. Release AM/FM and SCAN buttons, display should change to a radio frequency and operate normally.

STEERING COLUMN SERVICE

Prior to removing steering column, ensure correct shear head bolts are available. If shear bolts are not replaced with correct components, steering column collapse functions may be impaired.

For steering column service, refer to **Figs. 1 through 5,** for component locations. Refer also to ignition lock procedures found in the "Electrical" section.

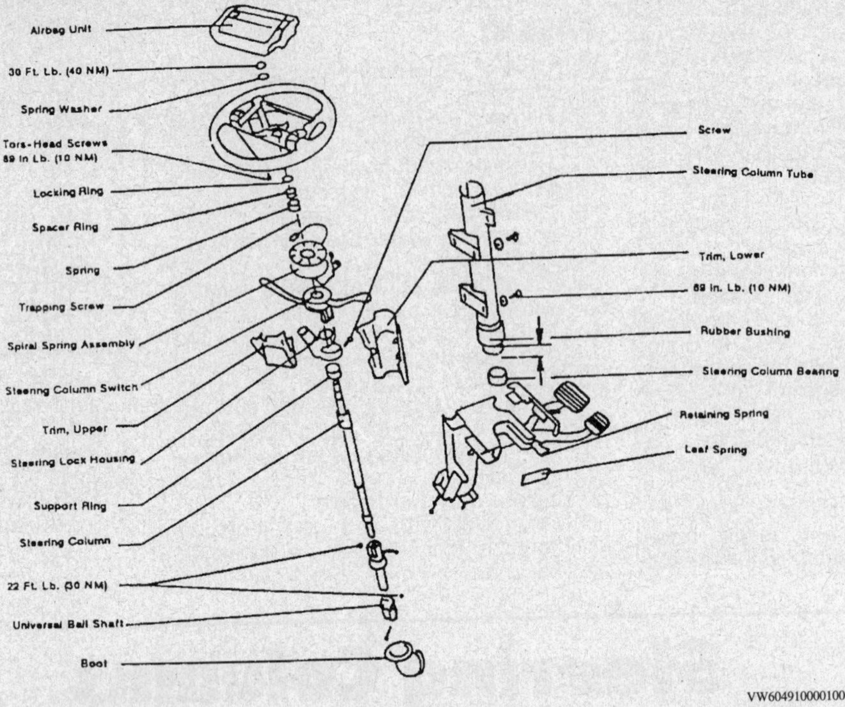
Airbag Unit
30 Ft. Lb. (40 NM)
Spring Washer
Tors-Head Screws
89 In. Lb. (10 NM)
Locking Ring
Spacer Ring
Spring
Trapping Screw
Spiral Spring Assembly
Steering Column Switch
Trim, Upper
Steering Lock Housing
Support Ring
Steering Column
22 Ft. Lb. (30 NM)
Universal Ball Shaft
Boot
Screw
Steering Column Tube
Trim, Lower
89 In. Lb. (10 NM)
Rubber Bushing
Steering Column Bearing
Retaining Spring
Leaf Spring
VW6049100001000X

Fig. 1 Exploded view of steering column assembly. Cabriolet

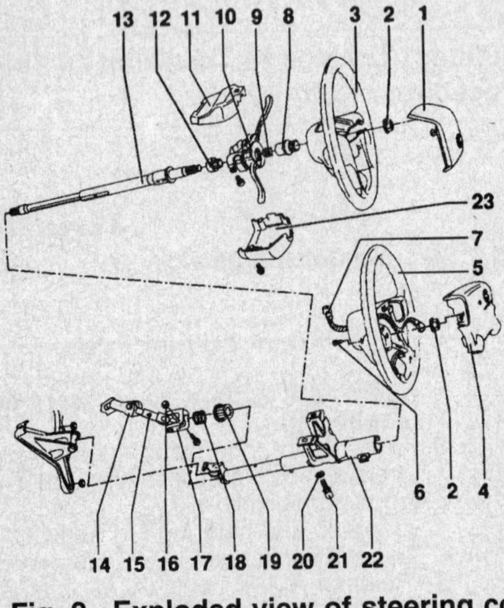
13 12 11 10 9 8 3 2 1
23
7
5
6 2 4
14 15 16 17 18 19 20 21 22

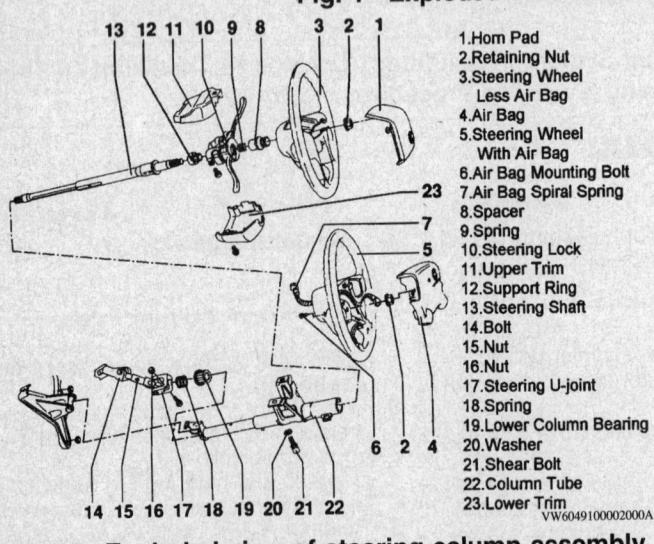

1. Hom Pad
2. Retaining Nut
3. Steering Wheel Less Air Bag
4. Air Bag
5. Steering Wheel With Air Bag
6. Air Bag Mounting Bolt
7. Air Bag Spiral Spring
8. Spacer
9. Spring
10. Steering Lock
11. Upper Trim
12. Support Ring
13. Steering Shaft
14. Bolt
15. Nut
16. Nut
17. Steering U-joint
18. Spring
19. Lower Column Bearing
20. Washer
21. Shear Bolt
22. Column Tube
23. Lower Trim

VW6049100002000A

Fig. 2 Exploded view of steering column assembly. Passat shown, Corrado similar

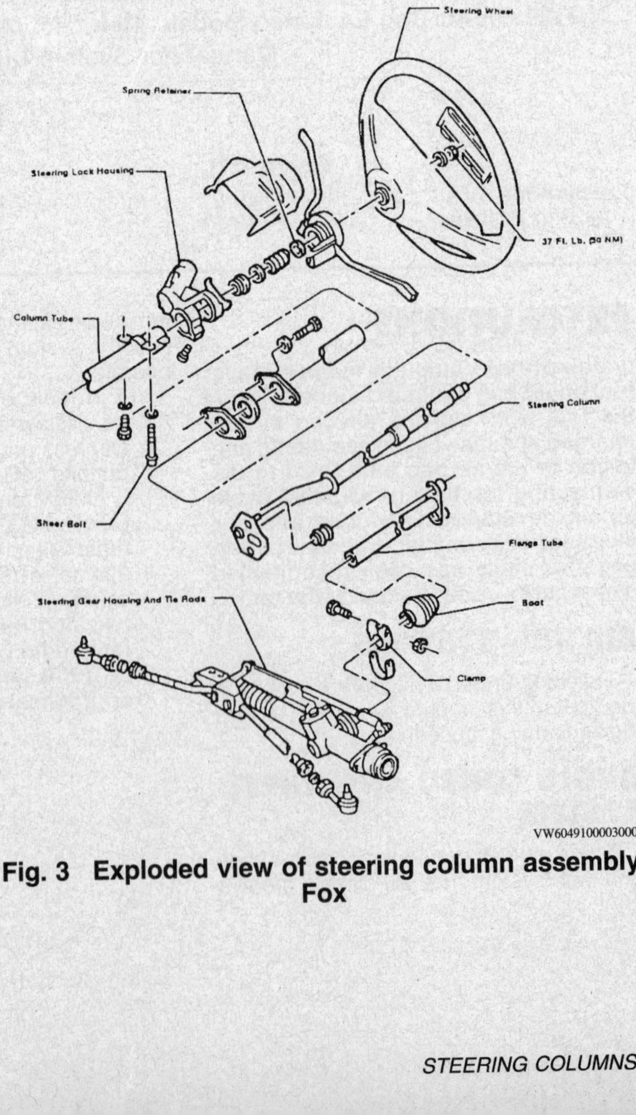
Steering Wheel
Spring Retainer
Steering Lock Housing
37 Ft. Lb. (50 NM)
Column Tube
Steering Column
Sheer Bolt
Flange Tube
Steering Gear Housing And Tie Rods
Boot
Clamp
VW6049100003000X

Fig. 3 Exploded view of steering column assembly. Fox

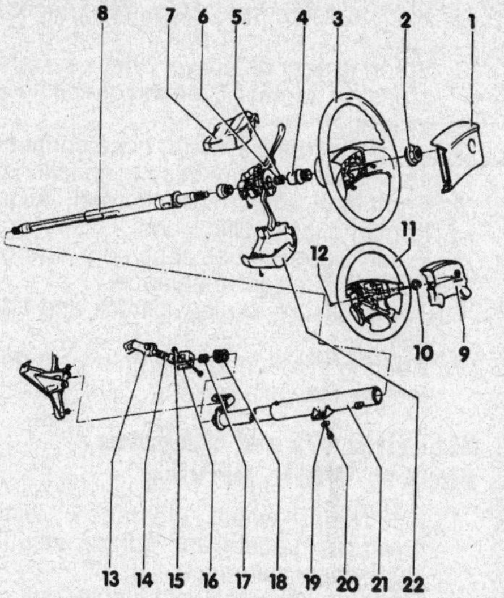

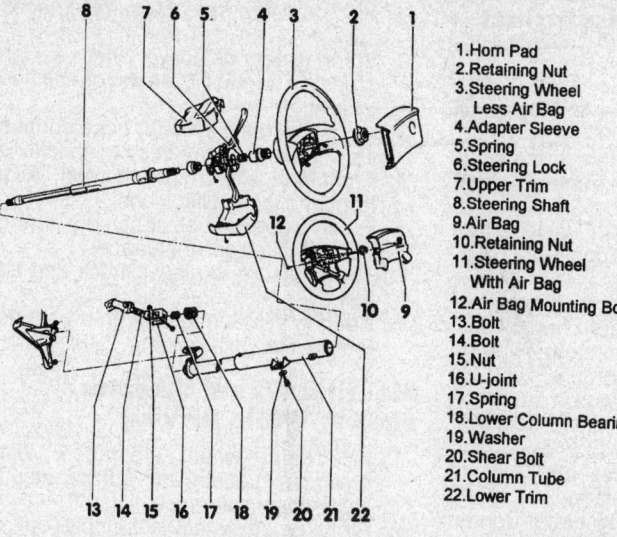

1. Horn Pad
2. Retaining Nut
3. Steering Wheel Less Air Bag
4. Adapter Sleeve
5. Spring
6. Steering Lock
7. Upper Trim
8. Steering Shaft
9. Air Bag
10. Retaining Nut
11. Steering Wheel With Air Bag
12. Air Bag Mounting Bolt
13. Bolt
14. Bolt
15. Nut
16. U-joint
17. Spring
18. Lower Column Bearing
19. Washer
20. Shear Bolt
21. Column Tube
22. Lower Trim

VW6049100004000A

Fig. 4 Exploded view of steering column assembly. Golf III, GTI & Jetta III

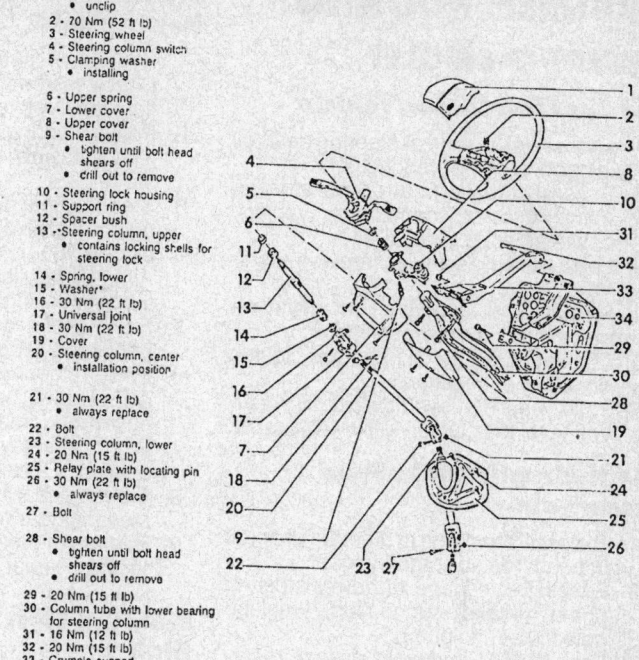

1 - Cover
- unclip

2 - 70 Nm (52 ft lb)
3 - Steering wheel
4 - Steering column switch
5 - Clamping washer
- installing

6 - Upper spring
7 - Lower cover
8 - Upper cover
9 - Shear bolt
- tighten until bolt head shears off
- drill out to remove

10 - Steering lock housing
11 - Support ring
12 - Spacer bush
13 - Steering column, upper
- contains locking shells for steering lock

14 - Spring, lower
15 - Washer*
16 - 30 Nm (22 ft lb)
17 - Universal joint
18 - 30 Nm (22 ft lb)
19 - Cover
20 - Steering column, center
- installation position

21 - 30 Nm (22 ft lb)
- always replace

22 - Bolt
23 - Steering column, lower
24 - 20 Nm (15 ft lb)
25 - Relay plate with locating pin
26 - 30 Nm (22 ft lb)
- always replace

27 - Bolt

28 - Shear bolt
- tighten until bolt head shears off
- drill out to remove

29 - 20 Nm (15 ft lb)
30 - Column tube with lower bearing for steering column
31 - 16 Nm (12 ft lb)
32 - 20 Nm (15 ft lb)
33 - Crumple support
34 - Mounting plate

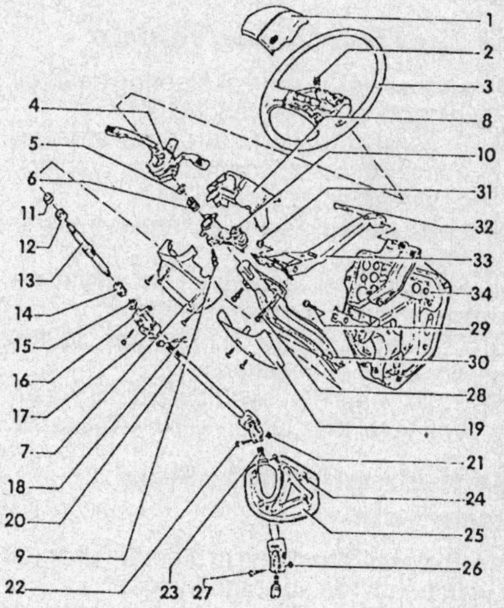

VW6049100005000X

Fig. 5 Exploded view of steering column assembly. Eurovan

Power Steering

INDEX

	Page No.
Diagnosis & Testing	49-95
Power Steering Pump Pressure Check	49-95
System Pressure Check	49-95
Power Steering Pressure	
Specifications	49-93
Power Steering System Bleed	49-95
Adjustments	49-95
Cabriolet	49-95
Except Cabriolet & Eurovan	49-95
Component Service	49-95
Power Steering System Service	49-95
Troubleshooting	49-94
Cabriolet	49-94
Except Cabriolet	49-94

POWER STEERING PRESSURE SPECIFICATIONS

Year	Model	System/Pump Pressure, psi①
1993	Cabriolet	1015-1160
	Corrado & Passat	1232–1377
	Golf III & Jetta III	1233-1378
	Eurovan	1310–1595
1994	Cabriolet	1015-1160
	Corrado & Passat	1232–1377
	Golf III & Jetta III	1233-1378
1995-96	Cabrio, Golf III, GTI & Jetta III	1233-1378
	Passat	1232–1377

① — Install pressure gauge in high pressure line, shut flow off no more than 5 seconds while reading maximum pressure.

TROUBLESHOOTING

EXCEPT CABRIOLET

Oil Spotting Under Vehicle

1. Excessive leakage at steering gear (oil in boot), replace steering gear.
2. Excessive leakage at power steering pump (intake connection), replace power steering pump.
3. Leak at fluid reservoir, replace reservoir.
4. Hydraulic oil hose/line defective, replace hydraulic oil hose/line.
5. Leak at hydraulic oil hose/line, tighten hose/line connections.
6. Fluid reservoir overflowing, fill reservoir level to between MIN/MAX marks.

No Hydraulic Oil In Fluid Reservoir

1. Excessive leakage at steering gear (oil in boot), replace steering gear.
2. Excessive leakage at power steering pump (intake connection), replace power steering pump.
3. Leak at fluid reservoir, replace reservoir.
4. Hydraulic oil hose/line defective, replace hydraulic oil hose/line.
5. Leak at hydraulic oil hose/line, tighten hose/line connections.

Hydraulic Oil Level In Fluid Reservoir Too Low

1. Excessive leakage at steering gear (oil in boot), replace steering gear.
2. Excessive leakage at power steering pump (intake connection), replace power steering pump.
3. Leak at fluid reservoir, replace reservoir.
4. Hydraulic oil hose/line defective, replace hydraulic oil hose/line.
5. Leak at hydraulic oil hose/line, tighten hose/line connections.

Hydraulic Oil In Fluid Reservoir Had To Be Replaced A Second Time

1. Hydraulic oil hose/line defective, replace hydraulic oil hose/line.
2. Leak at hydraulic oil hose/line, tighten hose/line connections.

Hydraulic Oil Spray In Engine Compartment

1. Leak at fluid reservoir, replace reservoir.
2. Hydraulic oil hose/line defective, replace hydraulic oil hose/line.
3. Leak at hydraulic oil hose/line, tighten hose/line connections.
4. Fluid reservoir overflowing, fill reservoir level to between MIN/MAX marks.

Hydraulic Oil In Fluid Reservoir Milky Or Foamy

1. Leak at hydraulic oil hose/line, tighten hose/line connections.
2. Air leak in system, check and tighten hose connections, add hydraulic oil.

Steering Difficult/Insufficient Power Assist

1. Hydraulic oil level too low/oil loss. Check system for leaks and repair, fill fluid reservoir to "MAX."
2. Power steering pump defective. Check feed pressure, replace pump if necessary.
3. Steering gear defective. Check system pressure, replace Steering gear if necessary.
4. Air in hydraulic system, hose connections loose. Tighten hose connections.
5. Front end alignment incorrect. Align front end to specifications.
6. Power steering belt tension incorrect. Adjust drive belt tension, check belt/pulley for damage.
7. Front wheel/wheel assembly out of balance. Correct imbalance.
8. Steering gear mounting loose. Tighten steering gear mounting.
9. Bearing in steering column switch defective. Replace bearing.

Steering Effort Occasionally High

1. Hydraulic oil level too low/oil loss. Check system for leaks and repair, fill fluid reservoir to "MAX."
2. Power steering belt tension incorrect. Adjust drive belt tension, check belt/pulley for damage.
3. Power steering pump defective. Check feed pressure, replace pump if necessary.
4. Steering gear defective. Check system pressure, replace Steering gear if necessary.
5. Air in hydraulic system, hose connections loose. Tighten hose connections.
6. Steering gear mounting loose. Tighten steering gear mounting.

Steering Wheel Jerks At Full Lock

1. Hydraulic oil level too low/oil loss. Check system for leaks and repair, fill fluid reservoir to "MAX."
2. Power steering belt tension incorrect. Adjust drive belt tension, check belt/pulley for damage.
3. Power steering pump defective. Check feed pressure, replace pump if necessary.
4. Steering gear defective. Check system pressure, replace Steering gear if necessary.
5. Air in hydraulic system, hose connections loose. Tighten hose connections.
6. Tire pressure too low. Check and adjust.
7. Steering gear mounting loose. Tighten steering gear mounting.
8. Steering gear mounted under tension. Loosen and retighten steering column mounting bolts.

Steering In Center Position Difficult/Poor Straight Line Driving

1. Power steering pump defective. Check feed pressure, replace pump if necessary.
2. Steering gear defective. Check system pressure, replace Steering gear if necessary.
3. Air in hydraulic system, hose connections loose. Tighten hose connections.
4. Front end alignment incorrect. Align front end to specifications.
5. Front wheel/wheel assembly out of balance. Correct imbalance.
6. Tire pressure too low. Check and adjust.
7. Bearing in steering column switch defective. Replace bearing.

Steering Wheel Vibrates/ Shakes While Driving

1. Insufficient wheel clearance, wide tires/rims. Locate and correct insufficient wheel clearance.
2. Front wheel/wheel assembly out of balance. Correct imbalance.

CABRIOLET

Fluid Level In Reservoir Low

1. Air trapped in steering system has escaped during normal operation. Fill reservoir to "MAX" mark.
2. Valve housing seal leaking, fluid leaks out at steering gear pinion. Replace seal and O-rings.
3. Leaks at connections on steering gear, hoses, pump or reservoir. Check system for leaks and repair.

Fluid Level In Reservoir Low Again, No External Leaks Visible

1. Additional air trapped in steering system has escaped during normal operation. Fill reservoir to "MAX" mark.
2. Steering rack seal defective, fluid found inside boot. Replace seal, install complete repair kit.

Steering Effort Becomes Greater As Wheel Is Turned

1. Dirt/foreign material restricting pump delivery capacity. Replace pump.
2. Insufficient pump pressure. Check pump pressure, replace if necessary.
3. Pressure/flow limiting valve in pump housing sticking. Replace pump.
4. Dirt/foreign material in valve control slot. Replace steering gear.

Noises In Power Steering System

1. Fluid level in reservoir low. Fill reservoir to "MAX" mark.
2. Incorrect idle speed. Correct idle speed.
3. Pump mounting loose. Tighten pump bolts.
4. Belt pulley loose on pump. Tighten pulley.
5. Loose connection at pump drawing air into system, fluid foaming in reservoir. Tighten pump connections.
6. Belt pulley hub rubbing against pump housing. Replace pump.

Hissing Noises w/Any Movement Of Steering Wheel

1. Dirt/foreign material in steering gear valve. Replace steering gear.

Cracking Noises In Steering Gear

1. Steering gear mounted under tension. Loosen and retighten steering column and steering gear mounting bolts.

DIAGNOSIS & TESTING

POWER STEERING PUMP PRESSURE CHECK

1. Disconnect pressure line from pump, then install adapters VW 1402/1A, VW 1402/2 and US 1074/4 A, as necessary, and pressure gauge US 1074B, or equivalents. Ensure valve on pressure gauge is in open position.
2. Start engine, and if necessary, top up fluid in reservoir.
3. With engine running at idle, close valve on gauge and check pressure. **Do not leave valve closed for longer than five seconds or system damage may occur.**
4. If pressure is not within specifications, replace power steering pump.

SYSTEM PRESSURE CHECK

1. Disconnect pressure line from pump, then install adapters VW 1402 1A and US 1074/4 A and pressure gauge US 1074B, or equivalents. Ensure valve on pressure gauge is in open position.
2. Start engine, and if necessary, top up fluid in reservoir.
3. With engine running at idle close valve open, rotate steering wheel from lock to lock and hold to check pressure in each position. **Do not hold against stop longer than five seconds or system damage may occur.**
4. If pressure is not within specifications, replace power steering gear assembly.

POWER STEERING SYSTEM SERVICE

POWER STEERING SYSTEM BLEED

Replacement power steering pumps must be filled with part No. G002–000 hydraulic oil, or equivalent, and rotated by hand to prevent possible damage.

Fill system with a suitable hydraulic oil, start engine and allow to idle. Turn steering wheel lock to lock several times to release trapped air from system. If fluid becomes aerated, allow to settle before adjusting level.

Component Service

Power steering gear on these vehicles should be replaced as a unit.

Adjustments

EXCEPT CABRIOLET & EUROVAN

Two technicians are necessary to perform the following adjustment.

1. Ensure engine is Off, vehicle is on ground and wheels are in a straight ahead position.
2. Move steering wheel back and forth approximately 30° from center position while listening for rattling and/or popping noises from steering gear.
3. Have second technician turn adjusting screw clockwise until rattling and/or popping noises are no longer heard from inside vehicle.
4. Test drive vehicle, and readjust if necessary. Ensure steering returns to a straight ahead position on its own after turning.

CABRIOLET

1. Remove steering gear from vehicle as described under "Front Suspension & Steering."
2. Loosen crown nut, then turn adjusting bolt until pinion can be turned by hand without binding.

Disc Brakes

INDEX

	Page No.
Application Chart	49-96
Girling Framed Single Piston Caliper w/Dual Mounting Bolts, Front	49-96
Girling Single Piston w/Dual Mounting Bolts, Front	49-98
Single Piston Rear Disc Brake	49-103
Teves/ATE Single Piston w/Dual Mounting Bolts, Front	49-100
Volkswagen Single Piston w/Dual Mounting Bolts, Front	49-102

Application Chart

Year	Model	Application
Front		
1993	Cabriolet & Fox	Volkswagen Single Piston w/Dual Mounting Bolts
	Corrado Golf III, Jetta III & Passat	Girling Single Piston w/Dual Mounting Bolts
	Eurovan	Girling Framed Caliper w/Dual Mounting Bolts
1994	Cabriolet	Volkswagen Single Piston w/Dual Mounting Bolts
	Corrado, Golf III, Jetta III & Passat	Girling Single Piston w/Dual Mounting Bolts
1995	Cabriolet	Volkswagen Single Piston w/Dual Mounting Bolts
	Golf III, GTI, Jetta III	Girling Single Piston w/Dual Mounting Bolts
	Passat	Teves/ATE Single Piston w/Dual Mounting Bolts
1996	Cabrio, Golf III, Jetta III & GTI Except 2.8L Engine	Girling Single Piston w/Dual Mounting Bolts
	GTI, Jetta III GLX & Passat w/2.8L Engine	Teves/ATE Single Piston w/Dual Mounting Bolt
Rear		
1993–94	Corrado	Single Piston Disc Brake
	Jetta III GLX	Single Piston Disc Brake
	Passat	Single Piston Disc Brake
1995	Golf III Sport	Single Piston Disc Brake
	GTI	Single Piston Disc Brake
	Jetta III GLX	Single Piston Disc Brake
	Passat	Single Piston Disc Brake
1996	GTI-VR6	Single Piston Disc Brake
	Jetta III GLX	Single Piston Disc Brake
	Passat	Single Piston Disc Brake

Girling Framed Single Piston Caliper w/Dual Mounting Bolts, Front

INDEX

	Page No.
Brake Pad Service	49-96
Brake Rotor, Replace	49-97
Caliper Service	49-96
Overhaul	49-96
Disc Brake Specifications	49-97
Tightening Specifications	49-97

BRAKE PAD SERVICE

Always remove some brake fluid from master cylinder reservoir prior to installing new pads. When caliper piston is pushed back, fluid is forced out of caliper and into reservoir. After pads are installed and seated, refill reservoir to MAX mark.

1. Raise and support vehicle, then remove front wheels.
2. Remove lock spring from brake pad retaining pins **Fig. 1.**
3. Drive brake pad retaining pins from pads and brake pad carrier using a suitable pin punch and hammer.
4. Pry and slide caliper bridge outward about width of one pad.
5. Remove inner, then outer pad, prying loose adhesive backing from caliper.
6. Clean caliper of rust, scale and old adhesive, lubricate with a suitable brake grease.
7. Push piston back into caliper housing.
8. Install inner (pad without adhesive backing) brake pad into position, then partially insert pad retaining pins to hold inner pad in position.
9. Remove protective backing from outer pad, position into caliper, then insert retaining pins fully into place.
10. Install lock spring into pad retaining pins.
11. Depress brake pedal several times to position caliper piston and seat brake pads.
12. Reverse remaining procedure, tighten to specification.

CALIPER SERVICE

OVERHAUL

Refer to **Fig. 2** when servicing caliper.

1. Remove brake pad carrier **Fig. 1,** to allow clearance.
2. Place wooden block between caliper piston and caliper housing, then apply compressed air to brake line bore to force piston from housing.
3. Remove piston seal from caliper piston bore using a plastic rod. **If either caliper piston or caliper piston bore is**

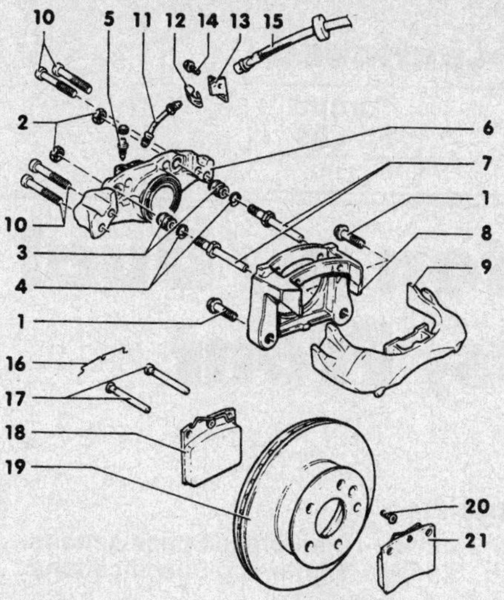
10
5
11
12
14
13
15
2
6
7
1
8
9
10
3
4
1
16
17
18
19
20
21

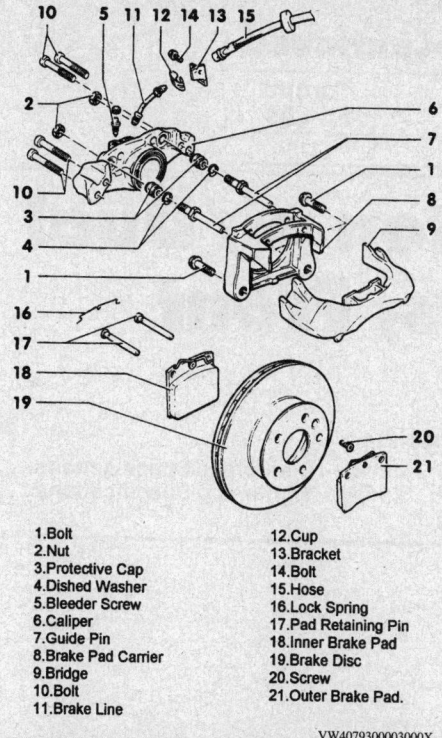

1.Bolt
2.Nut
3.Protective Cap
4.Dished Washer
5.Bleeder Screw
6.Caliper
7.Guide Pin
8.Brake Pad Carrier
9.Bridge
10.Bolt
11.Brake Line
12.Cup
13.Bracket
14.Bolt
15.Hose
16.Lock Spring
17.Pad Retaining Pin
18.Inner Brake Pad
19.Brake Disc
20.Screw
21.Outer Brake Pad.

VW4079300003000X

Fig. 1 Component view of front brake

corroded, pitted or scored, affected part must be replaced.

4. Slide dust cap onto piston, then lubricate piston and caliper piston bore lightly with a suitable brake cylinder paste.
5. Install piston into caliper bore and insert inner lip of dust cap into groove on caliper.
6. Open bleeder screw, then press caliper piston into caliper as far as possible, ensuring outer lip of dust cap slips into groove in piston.

BRAKE ROTOR

REPLACE

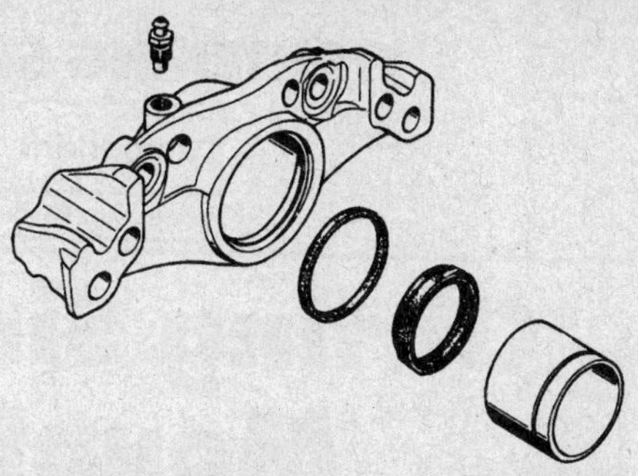

VW4079300004000X

Fig. 2 Exploded view of caliper

1. Raise and support vehicle, then remove front wheels.
2. Remove brake caliper, then remove brake disc securing screw.
3. Remove brake disc.
4. Reverse procedure to install, tighten to specification.

DISC BRAKE SPECIFICATIONS

Model	Thickness			Lateral Runout (T.I.R.)
	New	Wear Limit①	Thickness Variation (Parallelism)	
1993				
Eurovan	—	—	.0004	.0012

① — Refer to minimum thickness stamped on disc.

TIGHTENING SPECIFICATIONS

Component	Torque/ Ft. Lbs.
Brake Pad Carrier Guide Pin Nuts	53
Brake Caliper To Bridge Bolt	66
Brake Hose Bracket Bolt	7
Caliper Assembly Mounting Bolts	199
Splash Shield Bolts	7
Rotor To Hub Screw	4
Wheel Speed Sensor Bolt	7

Continued

TIGHTENING SPECIFICATIONS—Continued

Component	Torque/ Ft. Lbs.
Wheel Lug Bolts	118

Girling Single Piston w/Dual Mounting Bolts, Front

INDEX

	Page No.
Brake Pad Service	49-98
Brake Rotor, Replace	49-98
Caliper Service	49-98
Overhaul	49-98
Disc Brake Specifications	49-99
Tightening Specifications	49-99

BRAKE PAD SERVICE

Always remove some brake fluid from master cylinder reservoir prior to installing new pads. When caliper piston is pushed back, fluid is forced out of caliper and into reservoir. After pads are installed and seated, refill reservoir to MAX mark.

1. Raise and support vehicle, then remove front wheels.
2. Using open end wrench to hold guide pin head, **Fig. 1,** remove lower caliper mounting bolt.
3. Swing caliper upward, then remove brake pads.
4. Push piston back into caliper housing.
5. Install brake pads and heat shield with shield facing piston, then swing caliper downward and install "new" lower self-locking mounting bolt. Use an open end wrench to hold guide pin in position when tightening lower mounting bolt. Tighten bolt to specifications.
6. Depress brake pedal several times to position caliper piston and seat brake pads.
7. Reverse remaining procedure, tighten to specification.

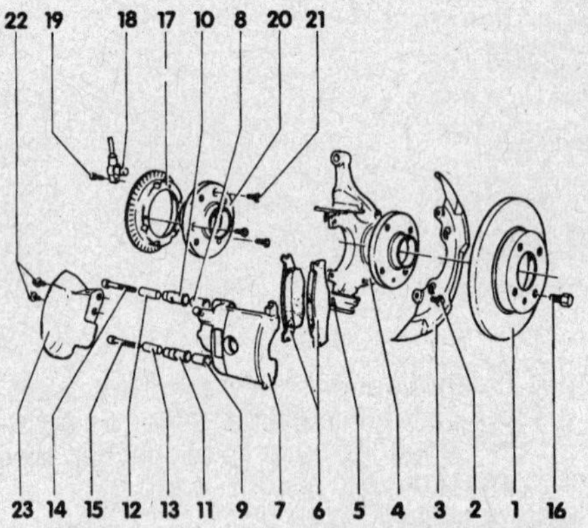

22 19 18 17 10 8 20 21
23 14 15 12 13 11 9 7 6 5 4 3 2 1 16

1.Brake Disc
2.Bolt
3.Disc Shield
4.Hub & Knuckle
5.Pad Retaining Spring
6.Brake Pad
7.Caliper
8.Upper Sleeve
9.Lower Sleeve
10.Upper Bushing
11.Lower Bushing
12.Upper Spacer Sleeve
13.Lower Spacer Sleeve
14.Upper Mountig Bolt
15.Lower Mounting Bolt
16.Lug Bolt
17.Brake Disc
18.ABS Speed Sensor
19.Bolt
20.Hub
21.Screw
22.Bolt
23.Air Deflector

VW4079300005000X

Fig. 1 Component view of front brake

CALIPER SERVICE

OVERHAUL

Refer to **Fig. 2,** when servicing caliper.

1. Place wooden block between caliper piston and caliper housing, then apply compressed air to brake line bore to force piston from housing.
2. Remove piston seal from caliper piston bore using a plastic rod. **If either caliper piston or caliper piston bore is corroded, pitted or scored, affected part must be replaced.**
3. Slide dust cap onto piston, then lubricate piston and caliper piston bore lightly with a suitable brake cylinder paste.

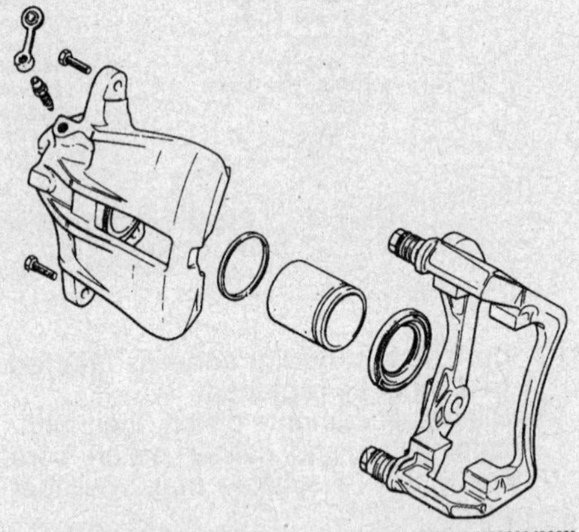

VW4079300006000X

Fig. 2 Exploded view of caliper

4. Install piston into caliper bore and insert inner lip of dust cap into groove on caliper.
5. Open bleeder screw, then press caliper piston into caliper as far as possible, ensuring outer lip of dust cap slips into groove in piston.

BRAKE ROTOR

REPLACE

1. Raise and support vehicle, then remove front wheels.
2. Remove brake caliper, then remove brake disc securing screw.
3. Remove brake disc.
4. Reverse procedure to install, tighten to specification.

DISC BRAKE SPECIFICATIONS

Model	Thickness			Lateral Runout (T.I.R.)
	New	Wear Limit①	Thickness Variation (Parallelism)	
1993-94				
Corrado	.866	.787	.0004	.0012
Golf III & Jetta III②	.472	.394	.0004	.0012
Golf III & Jetta III③	.787	.708	.0004	.0012
Passat	.788	.709	.0004	.0012
1995				
Cabrio, Golf III & Jetta III③	.787	.708	.0004	.0012
Golf III & Jetta III②	.472	.394	.0004	.0012
GTI & Jetta III GTX	.866	.787	.0011	.0020
1996				
Cabrio, Golf III & Jetta III③	.787	.708	.0004	.0012
Golf III & Jetta III②	.472	.394	.0004	.0012
Passat②	.512	.433	.0004	.0012
Passat③	.788	.709	.0004	.0012

① — Refer to minimum thickness stamped on disc.

② — With solid rotors.

③ — With ventilated rotors & 1.9L or 2.0 L engine.

TIGHTENING SPECIFICATIONS

Component	Torque/ Ft. Lbs.
Brake Pad Carrier Lower & Upper Bolts	26
Brake Pad Carrier Center Bolt	92
Splash Shield Bolts	7
Wheel Speed Sensor Bolt	7

Teves/ATE Single Piston w/Dual Mounting Bolts, Front

INDEX

	Page No.
Brake Pad Service	49-100
Brake Rotor, Replace	49-100
Caliper Service	49-100
Overhaul	49-100
Disc Brake Specifications	49-100
Tightening Specifications	49-101

BRAKE PAD SERVICE

Brake pads used in this caliper are directional, if pads are to be reinstalled mark them for location prior to removal.

Always remove some brake fluid from master cylinder reservoir prior to installing new pads. When caliper piston is pushed back, fluid is forced out of caliper and into reservoir. After pads are installed and seated, refill reservoir to MAX mark.

1. Raise and support vehicle, then remove front wheels.
2. Using a suitable pry bar, pry off brake pad retaining spring, **Fig. 1.**
3. Remove protective caps from caliper guide pin bushings.
4. Using a suitable Allen wrench, remove upper and lower guide pins from caliper and bushing.
5. Pull caliper from frame and support aside without placing brake fluid hose under a strain.
6. Remove pads from caliper frame and/ or caliper housing.
7. Clean rust, scale and old adhesive from caliper, frame and slider surfaces, then lubricate slider surfaces and guide pins using a suitable brake grease.
8. Using a suitable piston compressor, push piston back into caliper housing.
9. Install brake pads, inner pad is installed to caliper, outer pad is installed to frame.
10. **Arrow marked on each pad must be pointed down, Fig. 2.**
11. Remove foil backing on outer brake pad only.

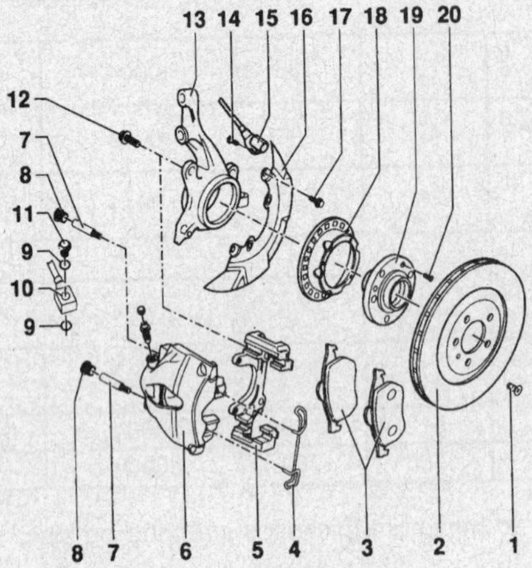

13 14 15 16 17 18 19 20
12
7
8
11
9
10
9
8 7 6 5 4 3 2 1

1.Screw
2.Brake Disc
3.Brake Pad
4.Retaining Spring
5.Brake Carrier
6.Caliper Housing
7.Guide Pins
8.Protective Cap
9.Seal
10.Brake Hose
11.Banjo Bolt
12.Ribbed Bolt
13.Knuckel
14.Bolt
15.ABS Speed Sensor
16.Disc Shield
17.Bolt
18.Speed Sensor Rotor
19.Hub
20.Bolt

VW4079500007000X

Fig. 1 Component view of front brake

12. Place caliper in place onto frame, install caliper guide pins, then tighten to specifications.
13. Depress brake pedal several times to position caliper piston and seat brake pads.
14. Reverse remaining procedure, tighten to specification.

CALIPER SERVICE

OVERHAUL

Refer to **Fig. 3** when servicing caliper.

1. Place wooden block between caliper piston and caliper housing, then apply compressed air to brake line bore to force piston from housing.
2. Remove piston seal from caliper piston bore using a plastic rod. **If either caliper piston or caliper piston bore is corroded, pitted or scored, affected part must be replaced.**
3. Slide dust cap onto piston, then lubricate piston and caliper piston bore lightly with a suitable brake cylinder paste.
4. Install piston into caliper bore and insert inner lip of dust cap into groove on caliper.
5. Open bleeder screw, then press caliper piston into caliper as far as possible, ensuring outer lip of dust cap slips into groove in piston.

BRAKE ROTOR

REPLACE

1. Raise and support vehicle, then remove front wheels.
2. Remove brake caliper, then remove brake disc securing screw.
3. Remove brake disc.
4. Reverse procedure to install, tighten to specification.

DISC BRAKE SPECIFICATIONS

Model	Thickness: New	Thickness: Wear Limit①	Thickness: Thickness Variation (Parallelism)	Lateral Runout (T.I.R.)
1995				
Passat	.985	.906	—	—
1996				
GTI-VR6 & Jetta III GTX	—	—	—	—
Passat	.985	.906	—	—

① — Refer to minimum thickness stamped on disc.

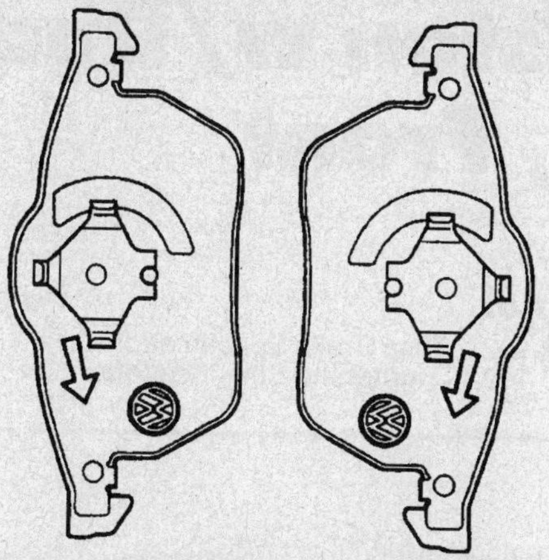
VW4079500009000X

Fig. 2 Brake pad installation direction

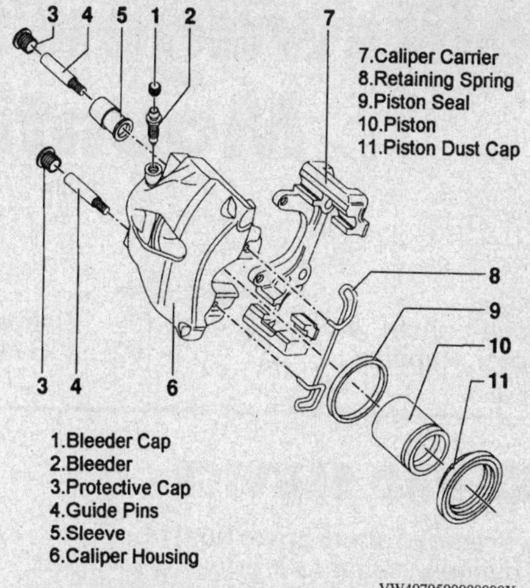
3
4
5
1
2
7
7.Caliper Carrier
8.Retaining Spring
9.Piston Seal
10.Piston
11.Piston Dust Cap
8
9
10
11
3
4
6
1.Bleeder Cap
2.Bleeder
3.Protective Cap
4.Guide Pins
5.Sleeve
6.Caliper Housing
VW4079500008000X

Fig. 3 Exploded view of caliper

TIGHTENING SPECIFICATIONS

Component	Torque/ Ft. Lbs.
Caliper Guide Pins	18
Brake Hose Banjo Bolt	22
Caliper Assembly Mounting Bolts	92
Splash Shield Bolts	7
Rotor To Hub Screw	4
Wheel Speed Sensor Bolt	7
Wheel Lug Bolts	81

Volkswagen Single Piston w/Dual Mounting Bolts, Front

INDEX

	Page No.
Brake Pad Service	49-102
Brake Rotor, Replace	49-102
Caliper Service	49-102
Overhaul	49-102
Disc Brake Specifications	49-102
Tightening Specifications	49-103

BRAKE PAD SERVICE

Always remove some brake fluid from master cylinder reservoir prior to installing new pads. When caliper piston is pushed back, fluid is forced out of caliper and into reservoir. After pads are installed and seated, refill reservoir to MAX mark.

1. Raise and support vehicle, then remove front wheels.
2. Disconnect retaining springs at top and bottom of caliper, then remove upper and lower guide pins.
3. Remove caliper, then the brake pads from carrier.
4. Push piston back into caliper housing.
5. Clean rust and scale from caliper, frame and slider surfaces, then lubricate slider surfaces and guide pins using a suitable brake grease.
6. Install brake pads, then the caliper.
7. Install guide pins, then tighten pins to specifications.
8. Install retaining springs, then depress brake pedal several times to position caliper piston and seat brake pads.

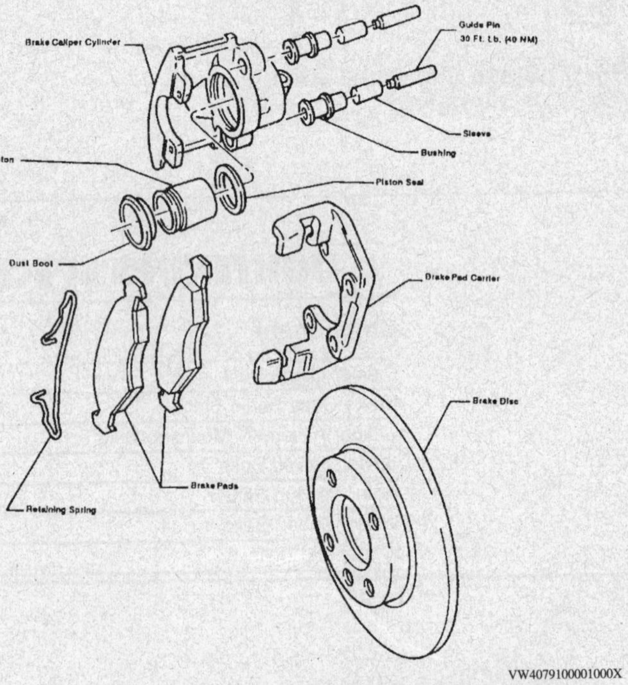
Brake Caliper Cylinder
Guide Pin
30 Ft. Lb. (40 NM)
Sleeve
Bushing
Piston
Piston Seal
Dust Boot
Brake Pad Carrier
Brake Disc
Brake Pads
Retaining Spring
VW4079100001000X

Fig. 1 Exploded view of caliper. Fox shown, Cabriolet similar

CALIPER SERVICE

OVERHAUL

Refer to **Fig. 1** when servicing caliper.

Refer to "Girling Single Piston w/Dual Mounting Bolts, Front" for service procedure.

BRAKE ROTOR

REPLACE

1. Raise and support vehicle, then remove front wheels.
2. Remove brake caliper, then remove brake disc securing screw.
3. Remove brake disc.
4. Reverse procedure to install, tighten to specification.

DISC BRAKE SPECIFICATIONS

Year	Model	Nominal Thickness	Minimum Refinish Thickness	Lateral Runout (T.I.R.)
1993-94	Cabriolet	.787	.709①	.002
	Fox	.472	.393①	.002

① — Refer to minimum thickness stamped on disc.

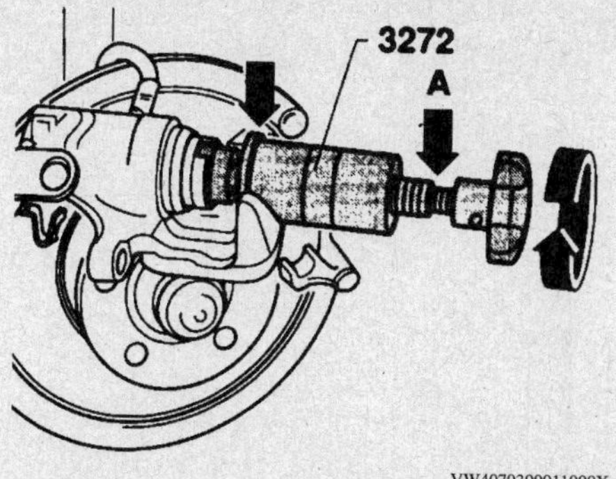
3272
A
VW4079300011000X

Fig. 2 Caliper piston returning

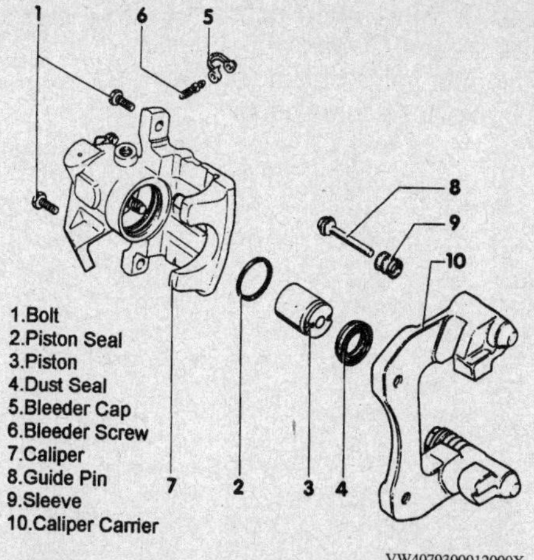
1
6
5
8
9
10
1.Bolt
2.Piston Seal
3.Piston
4.Dust Seal
5.Bleeder Cap
6.Bleeder Screw
7.Caliper
8.Guide Pin
9.Sleeve
10.Caliper Carrier
7
2
3
4
VW4079300012000X

Fig. 3 Exploded view of caliper

TIGHTENING SPECIFICATIONS

Component	Torque/Ft. Lbs.
Brake Caliper Mounting Bolts	48
Splash Shield	6

Single Piston Rear Disc Brake

INDEX

Page No.
Adjustments 49-103
Parking Brake 49-103
Brake Caliper Pre-Bleeding 49-103
Brake Pad Service 49-103
Brake Rotor, Replace 49-103
Caliper Service 49-103
Overhaul 49-103
Disc Brake Specifications 49-104
Tightening Specifications 49-104

BRAKE PAD SERVICE

This caliper uses an internal screw type parking brake self adjusting mechanism. If the caliper piston is pushed back into caliper this mechanism will be destroyed. Always return piston by rotating it clockwise using a suitable tool.

Always remove some brake fluid from master cylinder reservoir prior to installing new pads. When caliper piston is pushed back, fluid is forced out of caliper and into reservoir. After pads are installed and seated, refill reservoir to MAX mark.

1. Raise and support vehicle, then remove rear wheels.
2. Disconnect parking cables from caliper, **Fig. 1.**
3. Remove mounting bolts, then the caliper.
4. Screw piston into housing using caliper piston seating tool No. 3272, or equivalent, **Fig. 2,** by turning clockwise while pushing in firmly.
5. Install brake pads onto carrier, then the caliper and "new" self-locking mounting bolts. Tighten mounting bolts to specifications.
6. Reconnect parking brake cable, then adjust parking brake as described under "Parking Brake, Adjust."

CALIPER SERVICE

OVERHAUL

Refer to **Fig. 3** when servicing caliper.

1. Secure caliper in a suitable soft-jawed vise, then remove piston from bore by turning counterclockwise with caliper piston seating tool No. 3272, or equivalent, **Fig. 2.**
2. Pry piston seals from groove, being careful not to score the piston bore.
3. Slide outer dust boot onto piston.
4. Lubricate piston and cylinder bore lightly with a suitable brake cylinder paste.
5. Insert inner lip of dust boot into groove of brake cylinder.
6. Press piston down, while turning clockwise. Turn piston in as far as possible. Outer lip of dust cap must slip into groove of piston.

ADJUSTMENTS

PARKING BRAKE

1. Ensure parking brake lever is in OFF position, then tighten adjusting nut until levers on calipers just move off their stops. **Maximum permissible distance from stop is .059 inch.**
2. Apply and release parking brake and ensure both wheels rotate freely.

BRAKE ROTOR

REPLACE

1. Raise and support vehicle, then remove front wheels.
2. Remove brake caliper, then remove brake disc securing screw.
3. Remove brake disc.
4. Reverse procedure to install, tighten to specification.

BRAKE CALIPER PRE-BLEEDING

1. Place caliper so that piston bore is facing down.

2. Open bleeder valve, then connect a suitable hose and fill with brake fluid through bleeder valve until fluid flows out from brake hose connection.

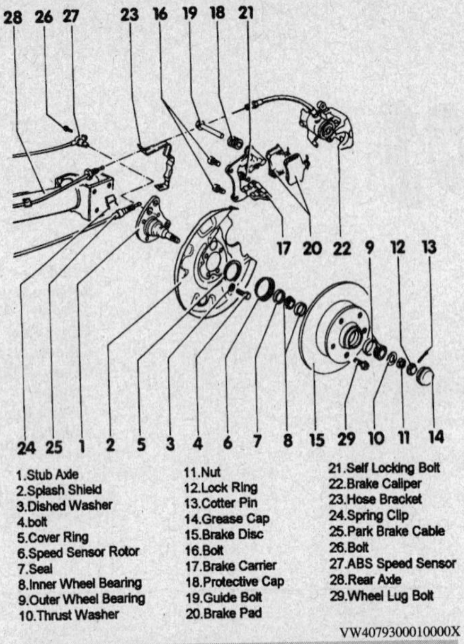
28 26 27 23 16 19 18 21
17 20 22 9 12 13
24 25 1 2 5 3 4 6 7 8 15 29 10 11 14
1.Stub Axle
2.Splash Shield
3.Dished Washer
4.bolt
5.Cover Ring
6.Speed Sensor Rotor
7.Seal
8.Inner Wheel Bearing
9.Outer Wheel Bearing
10.Thrust Washer
11.Nut
12.Lock Ring
13.Cotter Pin
14.Grease Cap
15.Brake Disc
16.Bolt
17.Brake Carrier
18.Protective Cap
19.Guide Bolt
20.Brake Pad
21.Self Locking Bolt
22.Brake Caliper
23.Hose Bracket
24.Spring Clip
25.Park Brake Cable
26.Bolt
27.ABS Speed Sensor
28.Rear Axle
29.Wheel Lug Bolt
VW4079300010000X

Fig. 1 Component view of rear brake

DISC BRAKE SPECIFICATIONS

Year	Nominal Thickness	Minimum Refinish Thickness	Lateral Runout (T.I.R.)
1993-95	.394	.315①	.002

① — Refer to minimum thickness stamped on disc.

TIGHTENING SPECIFICATIONS

Component	Torque/Ft. Lbs.
Disc Brake Shield Bolts	7
Rear Brake Pad Carrier Bolts	41
Rear Carrier To Brake Pad Carrier Bolts	21
Wheel Lug Nuts	81

Drum Brakes

INDEX

Page No.		Page No.		Page No.	
Adjustments	49-105	Shoes, Replace	49-105	**Drum Brake Specifications**	49-106
Parking Brake Cable	49-105	Wheel Cylinder Overhaul	49-105	**Tightening Specifications**	49-106
Brake Service	49-105				

Application Chart

Year	Model
1993	Cabriolet
	Eurovan
	Fox
	Golf III
	Jetta III GL & GLS
1994	Cabriolet
	Golf III
	Jetta III GL & GLS
1995-96	Cabrio
	Golf III
	Jetta III GL & GLS

BRAKE SERVICE

SHOES, REPLACE

Failure to follow described procedures may lead to a reduction in parking brake efficiency.

1. **On Fox models,** remove heat deflector plate, then disconnect parking brake cable from compensator bar.
2. **On all models,** remove one wheel bolt, then push self adjusting wedge upwards with a suitable screwdriver through wheel bolt hole to back off brake shoes, **Fig. 1.**
3. Reinstall wheel bolt and tighten to specifications, then remove grease cap with puller tool No. VW 637/2, or equivalent.
4. Remove cotter pin and axle nut, then pull off brake drum.
5. Remove spring retainer by pressing it against spring and turning ¼ turn.
6. Disconnect brake shoes from anchor pins, then remove return spring.
7. Disconnect parking brake cable from lever, then the spring for adjusting wedge and upper return spring using suitable pliers.
8. Remove brake shoes.
9. Install pushrod and brake shoe in a suitable soft jaw vise, then disconnect tensioning spring.
10. Install "new" brake shoe in vise, slide on pushrod, then connect tensioning spring on pushrod and brake shoe.
11. Insert adjusting wedge. Lug on adjusting wedge faces backing plate and must be in initial position.
12. Attach other brake shoe with lever to pushrod, then install upper return spring.

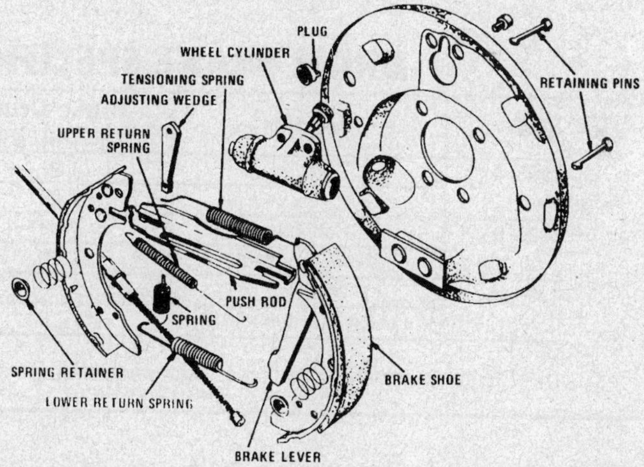

PLUG
WHEEL CYLINDER
TENSIONING SPRING
ADJUSTING WEDGE
UPPER RETURN SPRING
RETAINING PINS
PUSH ROD
SPRING
SPRING RETAINER
LOWER RETURN SPRING
BRAKE SHOE
BRAKE LEVER
VW4089100001000X

Fig. 1 Exploded view of brake assembly

13. Connect parking brake cable onto lever, then place brake shoes onto brake cylinder pistons.
14. Connect lower return spring onto brake shoes, then mount brake shoes onto retaining pins.
15. Connect spring for adjusting wedge onto adjusting wedge and brake shoe, then install retaining springs and spring retainers.
16. Install brake drum and adjust wheel bearings as described in "Rear Axle & Suspension" section.
17. Apply brake pedal firmly once to set self-adjusting mechanism.
18. **On Fox models,** install heat deflector plate and parking brake cable in compensator bar, then adjust parking brake cable as described under "Parking Brake Cable, Adjust."

WHEEL CYLINDER OVERHAUL

Refer to **Fig. 2** to aid in overhaul of wheel cylinder.

ADJUSTMENTS

PARKING BRAKE CABLE

Cabriolet & Fox

1. **On Fox models,** remove heat deflector plate.

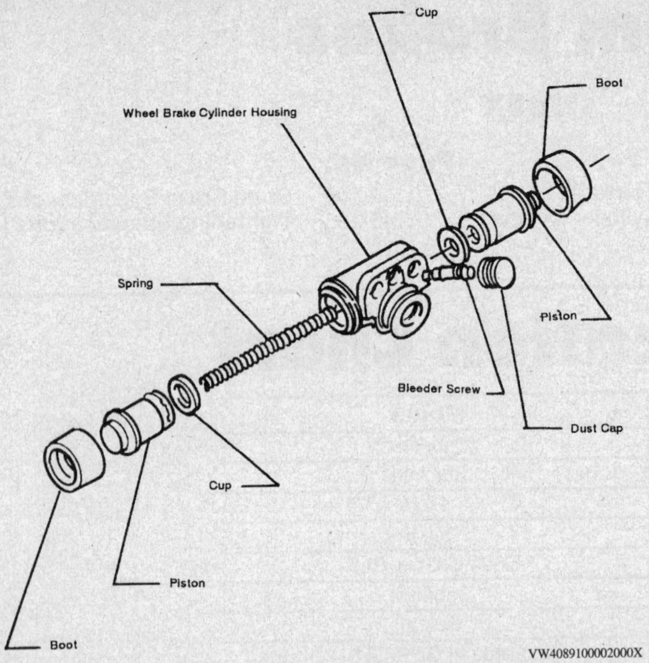
Cup
Boot
Wheel Brake Cylinder Housing
Spring
Piston
Bleeder Screw
Dust Cap
Cup
Piston
Boot
VW4089100002000X

Fig. 2 Exploded view of wheel cylinder assembly

2. **On all models,** apply brake pedal firmly once, then pull parking brake lever to second tooth.
3. Tighten adjusting nuts until neither rear wheel can be turned by hand.
4. Release parking brake and ensure wheels rotate freely, then tighten lock nuts.
5. **On Fox models,** install heat deflector plate.

Cabrio & Golf III, GTI & Jetta III w/1.9L & 2.0L Engines

1. Apply brake pedal firmly once, then pull parking brake lever to fourth tooth.
2. Tighten adjusting nuts until both wheels can JUST be turned by hand.
3. Release parking brake and ensure wheels rotate freely, then tighten lock nuts.

Eurovan

Due to self adjusting rear brakes, readjustment of parking brake is usually not necessary. Readjustment is necessary if the parking brake cables or backing plates are replaced.

1. Raise and support vehicle, then remove both brake drums.
2. Tighten adjusting nut until brake lever moves .079 inches away from brake shoe.
3. Install brake drum, then check if wheel rotates freely. If not, repeat adjusting procedure.

DRUM BRAKE SPECIFICATIONS

Year	Model	Brake Drum Inside Dia. Inches	Maximum Refinish Dia. Inches①
1993	Eurovan	10	10.06
	Fox	7.087	7.106
1993–94	Cabriolet	7.087	7.106
	Golf III & Jetta III	7.9	7.96
1995-96	Cabrio	7.9	7.96
	Golf III & Jetta III	7.9	7.96

① — Refer to minimum thickness stamped on drum.

TIGHTENING SPECIFICATIONS

Year	Component	Torque/ Ft. Lbs.
CABRIOLET		
1993–94	Brake Cylinder Mounting Bolts	7
	Brake Assembly To Axle Mounting Bolt	43
	Wheel Lug Nuts	65
FOX		
1993	Brake Cylinder Bolt	6
	Brake Assembly To Axle Mounting Bolts	42
	Wheel Lug Nuts	81
GOLF III, GTI & JETTA III w/1.9L OR 2.0L ENGINE & 1995-96 CABRIO		
1993-96	Brake Cylinder Mounting Bolts	7
	Brake Assembly To Axle Mounting Bolt	44
	Wheel Lug Nuts	81

Continued

TIGHTENING SPECIFICATIONS—Continued

Year	Component	Torque/ Ft. Lbs.
EUROVAN		
1993	Brake Cylinder Mounting Bolt	44①
	Brake Line Screw	14
	Wheel Lug Nuts	118

Hydraulic Brake Systems

INDEX

Page No.
Adjustments 49-107
Brake Pressure Regulator....... 49-107
Brake System Bleed 49-108

Page No.
Less Anti-Lock Brakes 49-108
With Anti-Lock Brakes 49-108

Page No.
Component Replacement........ 49-108
Master Cylinder................. 49-108

ADJUSTMENTS

BRAKE PRESSURE REGULATOR

LESS ANTI-LOCK BRAKES

Cabriolet

Brake pressure regulator is mounted on body, and operated by a spring attached to the rear axle.

1. Remove bleeder screw on right front caliper and connect gauge US 1016 or equivalent.
2. Remove bleeder screw on left rear wheel cylinder/caliper and connect gauge US 1016 or equivalent.
3. Bleed both hoses and gauges with bleeding screws on gauges, then depress brake pedal firmly several times.
4. Depress brake pedal until gauge of right front caliper reads 797 psi. Gauge of left rear wheel cylinder/caliper must read 565–623 psi.
5. Increase pressure to brake pedal until gauge of right front caliper reads 1450 psi. Gauge of left rear wheel cylinder/caliper must read 739–826 psi.
6. Repeat procedure for other brake circuit.
7. If specifications are not obtained, replace brake pressure regulator.
8. Disconnect pressure gauges and bleed brakes as described previously.

Corrado, Fox & Passat

Brake pressure regulator is mounted on body, and operated by a spring attached to the rear axle.

Check with vehicle empty, fuel tank full and a driver in vehicle.

1. Firmly depress brake pedal once, with car on the ground.
2. Release pedal suddenly and ensure lever on pressure regulator lever moves.
3. Raise and support vehicle.
4. Remove bleeder screw on right front caliper and connect gauge US 1016 or equivalent.
5. Remove bleeder screw on left rear wheel cylinder or caliper and connect gauge US 1016 or equivalent.
6. Bleed both hoses and gauges with bleeding screws on gauges, then lower vehicle and bounce rear of vehicle several times.
7. Depress brake pedal until gauge of right front caliper reads 725 psi. Gauge of left rear wheel cylinder or caliper must read as follows:
   a. 391–478 psi on Corrado, 435–522 psi on Passat.
   b. 392–479 psi on Fox Wagon, and 537–609 on Fox Coupe and Sedan.
8. Increase pressure to brake pedal until gauge of right front caliper reads 1450 psi. Gauge of left rear wheel cylinder or caliper must read as follows:
   a. 696–783 psi on Corrado, 740–827 psi on Passat.
   b. 754–841 psi on Fox Wagon, and 725–958 psi on Fox Coupe and Sedan.
9. Release brake pedal.
10. **On models except Fox Coupe and Sedan,** if pressure is too high, decrease spring tension on regulator, then recheck.
11. **On all models,** if pressure is too low, increase spring tension on regulator, then recheck.
12. **Do not adjust pressure regulator with brake pedal depressed.**
13. If pressure cannot be adjusted, replace pressure regulator.
14. **On Fox Coupe and Sedan models,** if readings are not within specifications, replace proportioning valves.
15. **On all models,** disconnect pressure gauges and bleed brakes as described previously.

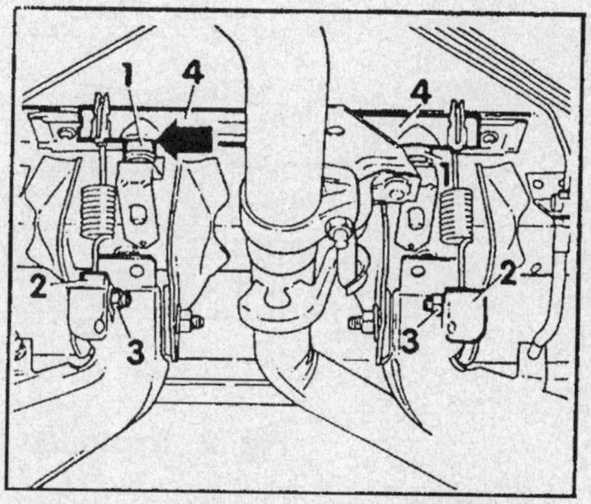

1
4
4
2
2
3
3

VW4099100001010X

Fig. 1 Brake pressure regulator adjustment (Part 1 of 2). Eurovan

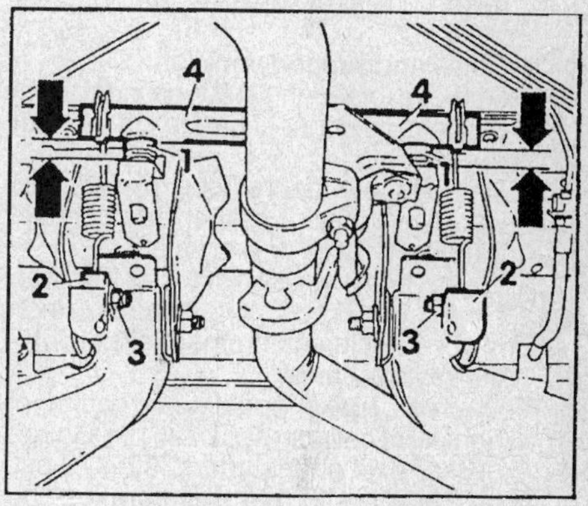

4
4
2
2
3
3

VW4099100001020X

Fig. 1 Brake pressure regulator adjustment (Part 2 of 2). Eurovan

Eurovan

1. Connect pressure gauge tool No. VAG 1310, or equivalent, to right front caliper and left rear wheel cylinder.
2. Bleed both gauges, then depress brake pedal and obtain specified pressure at front axle and read measured pressure at rear axle:
   a. Front axle 725 psi.
   b. Rear axle 290–319.
3. Refer to **Fig. 1** during the following adjustment procedures:
   a. Screw back both buffer stops (1).
   b. Mark position of mounting (2) on

trailing arm, then loosen bolts **3** and slide mounting (2).
  c. Sliding mounting (2) downward increases pressure. Upward decreases pressure.
4. The adjustment of second sliding mount (2) is only necessary if horizontal beam (4) is more than .157 inches from horizontal beam (arrows). A .039 inch adjustment upward or downward of sliding mounting (2) will alter rear axle pressure by approximately 58 psi.
5. Correct pressure regulator setting at second mounting (2).
6. Counter hold and tighten bolt (3).

Golf III, GTI & Jetta III

The brake pressure regulator is mounted on a bracket, and operated by a spring attached to the rear axle.

Check with vehicle empty of occupants and the fuel tank full.

1. Firmly depress brake pedal once, with car on the ground.
2. Release pedal suddenly and ensure lever on pressure regulator lever moves.
3. Raise and support vehicle.
4. Remove bleeder screw on right front caliper and connect gauge US 1016 or equivalent.
5. Remove bleeder screw on left rear wheel cylinder or caliper and connect gauge US 1016 or equivalent.
6. Bleed both hoses and gauges with bleeding screws on gauges, then lower vehicle and bounce rear of vehicle several times.
7. Depress brake pedal until gauge of right front caliper reads 725 psi. Gauge of rear axle should read 392–479 psi. on models with rear drum brakes and 348–435 psi. on models with rear disc brakes.
8. Increase pressure to brake pedal until gauge of right front caliper reads 1450 psi. Gauge of rear axle should read 696–783 psi. on models with rear drum brakes and 667–754 psi. on models with rear disc brakes.
9. Release brake pedal.
10. Adjust regulator spring tension.
11. If test pressure is too high, decrease spring tension.
12. If test pressure is too low, increase spring tension.
13. Recheck regulator pressures and adjust if necessary.
14. Disconnect pressure gauges and bleed brakes as described under "Brake System Bleed."

COMPONENT REPLACEMENT

MASTER CYLINDER

Refer to **Fig. 2** during replacement procedures.

1. Disconnect battery ground cable.
2. Siphon brake fluid from reservoir, then disconnect brake lines from master cylinder and electrical connectors from brake light switches.
3. Remove master cylinder to firewall or

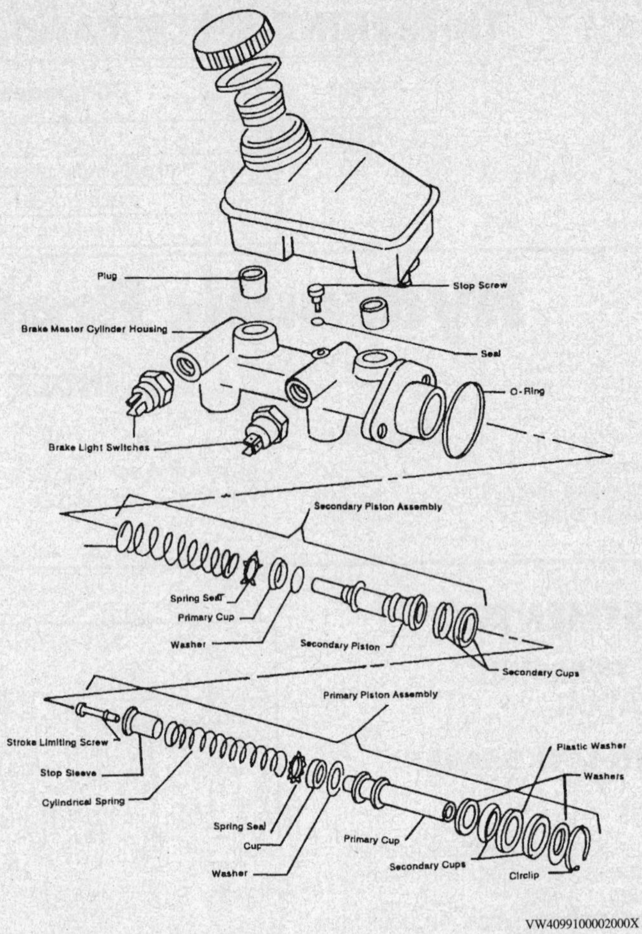
Plug
Stop Screw
Brake Master Cylinder Housing
Seal
O-Ring
Brake Light Switches
Secondary Piston Assembly
Spring Seat
Primary Cup
Washer
Secondary Piston
Secondary Cups
Primary Piston Assembly
Stroke Limiting Screw
Stop Sleeve
Cylindrical Spring
Plastic Washer
Washers
Spring Seal
Cup
Primary Cup
Washer
Secondary Cups
Circlip
VW4099100002000X

Fig. 2 Exploded view of master cylinder

brake booster, if equipped, attaching nuts, then the master cylinder and seal.
4. Position new master cylinder and seal to firewall or brake booster, then install attaching nuts.
5. Transfer brake light switches to new master cylinder, then connect brake lines and electrical connectors.
6. Fill fluid reservoir with clean brake fluid and bleed brake system.

BRAKE SYSTEM BLEED

LESS ANTI-LOCK BRAKES

EXCEPT FOX

To bleed brake system, use bottle with a transparent hose attached so that brake fluid can be checked for air bubbles.

1. Connect brake filling and bleeding tool US 1116 or equivalent per manufacturers instructions.
2. **On models with brake booster,** ensure engine is Off, then disconnect vacuum hose/check valve from brake booster.
3. **On models with brake pressure regulator,** push lever on brake pressure regulator in direction of rear axle.
4. **On all models,** bleed brakes in following sequence:
  a. Right rear wheel cylinder/caliper, left rear wheel cylinder/caliper, right front caliper, then left front caliper.
  b. After bleeding, fill reservoir to maximum mark.
5. **On models with brake booster,** reconnect vacuum hose/check valve to brake booster.

FOX

To bleed brake system, use bottle with a transparent hose attached so that brake fluid can be checked for air bubbles.

1. Ensure engine is Off, then disconnect vacuum hose/check valve from brake booster.
2. Push lever on brake pressure regulator in direction of rear axle.
3. Bleed brakes in following sequence:
  a. Right rear wheel cylinder, left rear wheel cylinder, right front caliper, then left front caliper.
  b. After bleeding, fill reservoir to maximum mark.
4. Reconnect vacuum hose/check valve to brake booster.

WITH ANTI-LOCK BRAKES

To bleed brake system, use bottle with a transparent hose attached so that brake fluid can be checked for air bubbles.

Always attempt to bleed brakes in the conventional manner first. If bleeding cannot be performed then refer to "Bleeding w/Scan Tool."

BLEEDING w/SCAN TOOL

1. Connect a suitable scan tool to the Diagnostic Link Connector (DLC) as described under "Diagnosis & Testing."
2. Connect a suitable pressure brake bleeder, following pressure bleeder manufacturer's instructions.
3. Access "Brake Electronics," then "Basic Settings" using scan tool.
4. Follow step by step procedure of scan tool to bleed brakes.

CONVENTIONAL BLEEDING

Front

1. Ensure engine is Off, then depress brake pedal approximately 20 times to reduce pressure in reservoir.
2. Connect brake filling and pressure brake bleeder tool No. US 1116, or equivalent, per manufacturer's instructions, then switch On.
3. Connect hose from bleeder bottle to left front caliper and open bleeder screw.
4. Depress brake pedal slowly until brake fluid flows without air bubbles.
5. Close bleeder screw and release pedal.
6. Repeat steps 3, 4 and 5 to bleed right front caliper.
7. Remove pressure bleeder.

Rear

1. Ensure engine is Off, then depress brake pedal approximately 20 times to reduce pressure in reservoir.
2. Connect brake filling and pressure brake bleeder tool No. US 1116, or equivalent, per manufacturer's instructions, then switch On.
3. Connect hose from bleeder bottle to right rear caliper and open bleeder screw.
4. Turn ignition switch to On position, then press lever of pressure regulator in direction of rear axle until brake fluid flows without air bubbles. **ABS system pump must not be in operation for longer than 120 seconds at a time during this procedure. If running time exceeds 120 seconds, a cool down period of ten minutes is required.**
5. Repeat above steps to bleed left rear caliper.
6. Turn ignition switch On until pump shuts Off, then fill brake fluid reservoir up to MAX mark.

Power Brake Units

INDEX

	Page No.
Power Brake Unit Service	49-109
Brake Booster Check	49-109
Brake Booster, Replace	49-109

POWER BRAKE UNIT SERVICE

BRAKE BOOSTER, REPLACE

Except Fox

1. Remove master cylinder as previously described.
2. Disconnect vacuum line(s) from booster.
3. Remove brake booster attaching bolts.
4. Disconnect booster pushrod from brake pedal.
5. Reverse procedure to install.

Fox

1. Disconnect vacuum line(s) from booster.
2. Remove brake booster attaching bolts.
3. Disconnect booster pushrod from brake pedal.
4. Remove brake booster with master cylinder.
5. Reverse procedure to install.

BRAKE BOOSTER CHECK

1. Depress brake pedal firmly approximately 20 times with engine Off.
2. Depress brake pedal and hold.
3. Start engine, if brake booster is working properly, pedal will fall slightly and then hold.

Anti-Lock Brakes

INDEX

	Page No.
Description	49-110
Diagnosis & Testing	49-110
Accessing Diagnostic Trouble Codes	49-110
Clearing Diagnostic Trouble Codes	49-110
Testing	49-110
Diagnostic Trouble Code Interpretation	49-110
Diagnostic Chart Index	49-113
Precautions	49-109
Air Bag Systems	49-109
Audio Coded Anti-Theft System	49-109
Brake Fluid	49-110
System Service	49-110
Brake System Bleed	49-110
Component Replacement	49-110
Coding Teves Type 20 Control Module	49-112
Control Module	49-113
Hydraulic Modulator Replace.	49-110
Troubleshooting	49-110

PRECAUTIONS

AIR BAG SYSTEMS

Refer to "Air Bag System Precautions" in the front of this manual for system disarming and arming procedures.

AUDIO CODED ANTI-THEFT SYSTEM

Some models are equipped with a radio anti-theft system that will disable the system when battery power is interrupted, unless the system is reset the radio will not operate.

1. Turn radio to On position, SAFE should be displayed.

2. Depress and hold AM/FM and SCAN buttons until 1000 remains on display. If AM/FM and SCAN buttons are depressed too long or depressed again, radio will misinterpret the 1000 as an attempt at coding and one incorrect coding attempt will be logged. **After two incorrect attempts to reset system radio will lock up electronically, if this occurs leave radio On for approximately 1 hour, then reset radio as if battery power were disconnected.**
3. Enter radio code using first four program station buttons, security code will appear on display.
4. Depress and hold AM/FM and SCAN buttons again until SAFE is displayed.
5. Release AM/FM and SCAN buttons, display should change to a radio frequency and operate normally.

BRAKE FLUID

Do not allow brake fluid to come in contact with painted surfaces.

Brake fluid absorbs moisture from the air and should therefore be replaced every two years.

Do not use silicone based brake fluid (DOT 5). Even the smallest traces may cause corrosion in the brake system.

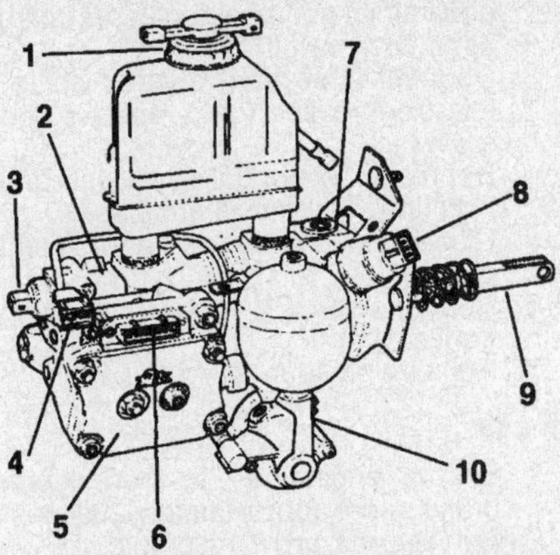
1
2
3
4
5
6
7
8
9
10

1 - Brake fluid level warning switch/ABS fluid level warning switch
2 - Tandem master cylinder
3 - ABS main valve
4 - Connection for hydraulic pump
5 - Solenoid valve block
6 - Connection for solenoid valves
7 - Hydraulic brake servo
8 - Multi-function switch
9 - Brake actuator
10 - Hydraulic pump

VW4029300072000X

Fig. 1 ABS Components. Corrado & 1993-94 Passat

DESCRIPTION

Refer to **Figs. 1 through 6** to identify ABS system components and type.

TROUBLESHOOTING

Refer to "Diagnosis & Testing" for ABS troubleshooting.

DIAGNOSIS & TESTING

Accessing Diagnostic Trouble Codes

The ABS control unit has a permanent fault memory. If problems occur at electrically monitored sensors or components they are stored in memory.

Faults are stored with varying priorities, solenoid faults have the highest priority and are displayed first. Faults which occur occasionally, or sporadic faults have the lowest priority and are displayed last.

Do not drive vehicle with VAG 1551 or equivalent scan tool connected.

1. Connect a suitable scan tool to the Diagnostic Link Connector (DLC). Refer to **Figs. 7 through 11** for DLC locations and types.
2. Follow scan tool manufacturer instructions to access Anti-Lock Brake System (ABS) Electronic Control Unit (ECU) Diagnostic Trouble Codes (DTCs).
3. Record all DTCs, then refer to "Diagnostic Chart Index" to locate correct DTC tables for vehicle.

Diagnostic Trouble Code Interpretation

Refer to "Accessing Diagnostic Trouble Codes" to find any Diagnostic Trouble Code (DTC), then refer to the "Diagnostic Chart Index" to locate the correct DTC table, Figs. 12 through 61, for vehicle.

Refer to Diagnostic Trouble Code (DTC) tables to locate fault and any additional testing or recommended correction.

Teves model 20 ABS control modules are coded to the vehicle. If a DTC is accessed that requires coding of control module, refer to "Coding Teves Type 20 Control Module" for procedures.

Clearing Diagnostic Trouble Codes

Follow scan tool manufacturer instructions to clear DTCs.

TESTING

ELECTRICAL TESTING

When performing electrical testing, refer to wiring diagrams **Figs. 62 through 68**, and "Test Steps" **Figs. 69 through 71.**

Wiring Diagrams

Test Steps

Obtain the following test equipment: pin out test box tool No. VAG 1598, **Fig. 72**, adapter tool No. VAG 1598/3, test kit connector tool No. VAG 1594 and multimeter tool No. US 1119, or equivalents.

Connect ABS control unit multi-pin electrical connector to pin out tester tool No. VAG 1598 using adapter tool No. VAG 1598/3, test kit connector tool No. VAG 1594, or equivalents. **The terminal numbering on the pin out tester tool No. VAG 1598 test box is identical to the numbering of the control unit.**

When using these tests in conjunction with a scan tool, perform only those tests recommended in the DTC tables.

When using these tests without a scan tool or on vehicles for which the self-diagnosis feature does not determine the problem source, perform all steps in sequence.

Ensure fuses and ground wires for control unit are in satisfactory condition, and that ignition switch remains in Off position during all test steps.

SYSTEM SERVICE

Brake System Bleed

Refer to "Hydraulic Brake Systems" for bleeding procedure.

Component Replacement

Teves model 20 ABS control modules are coded to the vehicle. Replacement control modules must be coded after installation. Refer to "Coding Teves Type 20 Control Module" for procedures.

Prior to servicing the ABS system, always turn the ignition off, disconnect battery negative cable.

On 1993–94 Corrado and Passat models reduce pressure in the booster system by pressing the brake pedal at least 25–35 times. The reduction in pressure can be felt when pedal effort increases. Serious injury may result if the system is serviced without reducing pressure.

The ABS control unit must never be exposed to temperatures greater than 185°F for more than two hours, or 203°F for even short time periods. The ABS control unit must be unplugged if an electric welder is to be used on the vehicle.

HYDRAULIC MODULATOR REPLACE

When replacing hydraulic components, ensure all areas to be disassembled are clean before starting. Place all removed parts on a clean surface. Always cover and plug components if the repair cannot be completed immediately. Ensure all replacement parts are thoroughly cleaned before installation. Use care not to allow brake fluid to contact painted surfaces or electrical connectors.

Ensure all components and lines are connected in their original position, do not allow lines to become crossed.

1993-94 CORRADO & PASSAT

Some models are equipped with a dual port brake pressure regulator. Replacement ABS hydraulic modulators are only

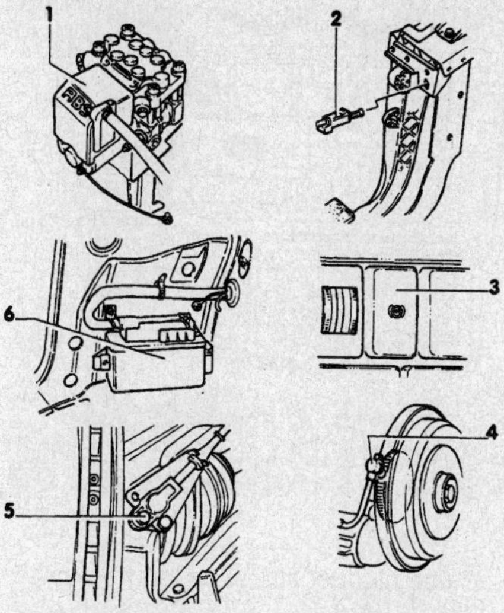

1.Hydraulic Modulator
2.Brake Light Switch
3.ABS Warning Light
4.Rear ABS Speed Sensor
5.Front ABS Speed Sensor
6.ABS Control Module

VW4029300073000X

Fig. 2 ABS Components. Eurovan

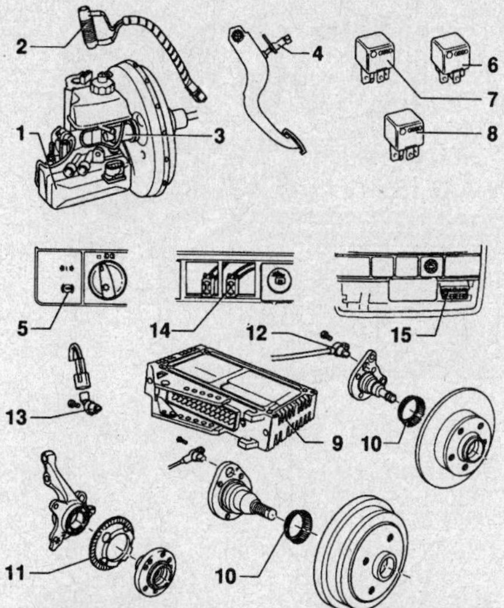

1.Hydraulic Modulator
2.Differential Lock Resistor (Optional)
3.Brake Pedal Position Sensor
4.Brake Light Switch
5.ABS Warning Light
6.ABS Relay
7.ABS Pump Relay
8.Differential Lock Relay (Optional)
9.ABS Control Module
10.Rear Impulse Rotor
11.Front Impulse Rotor
12.Rear Speed Sensor
13.Front Speed Sensor
14.Data Link Connector Early 1993
15.Data Link Connector Late 1993 & On

VW4029300076000X

Fig. 3 ABS Components. Cabrio, Golf III, GTI & Jetta III w/Teves type 04

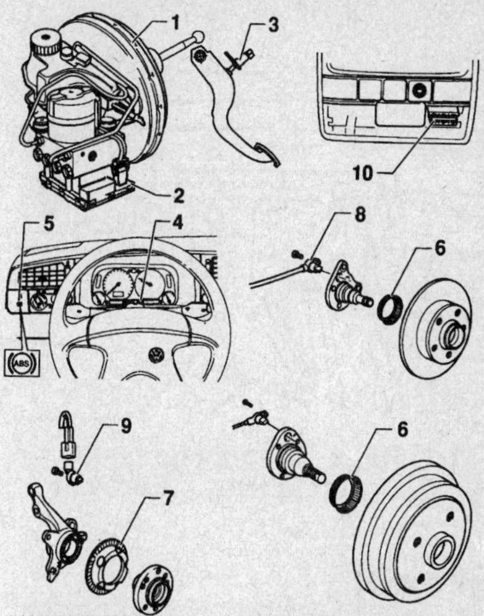

1.Hydraulic Modulator
2.Control Module
3.Brake Light Switch
4.Brake Warning Light
5.ABS Warning Light
6.Rear Impulse Rotor
7.Front Impulse Rotor
8.Rear Speed Sensor
9.Front Speed Sensor
10.Data Link Connector

VW4029300077000X

Fig. 4 ABS Components. Cabrio, Golf III, GTI & Jetta III w/Teves type 20

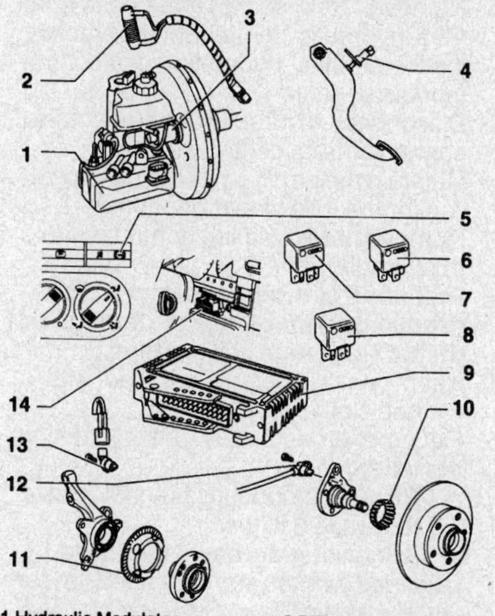

1.Hydraulic Modulator
2.Differential Lock Resistor (Optional)
3.Brake Pedal Position Sensor
4.Brake Light Switch
5.ABS Warning Light
6.ABS Relay
7.ABS Pump Relay
8.Differential Lock Relay (Optional)
9.ABS Control Module
10.Rear Impulse Rotor
11.Front Impulse Rotor
12.Rear Speed Sensor
13.Front Speed Sensor
14.Data Link Connector

VW4029500074000X

Fig. 5 ABS Components. 1995-96 Passat w/Teves type 04

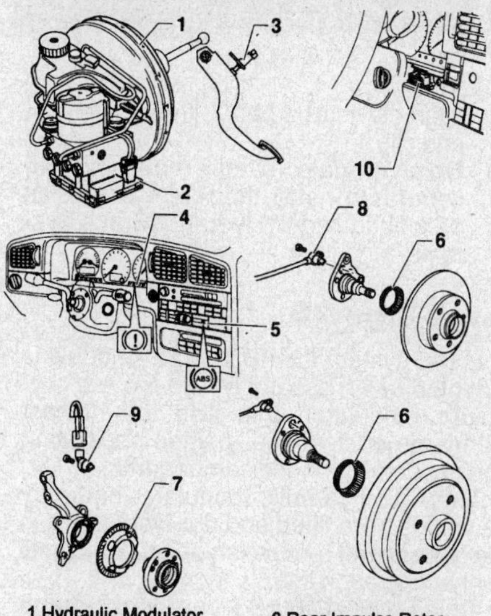

1.Hydraulic Modulator
2.Control Module
3.Brake Light Switch
4.Brake Warning Light
5.ABS Warning Light
6.Rear Impulse Rotor
7.Front Impulse Rotor
8.Rear Speed Sensor
9.Front Speed Sensor
10.Data Link Connector

VW4029500075000X

Fig. 6 ABS Components. 1995-96 Passat w/Teves type 20

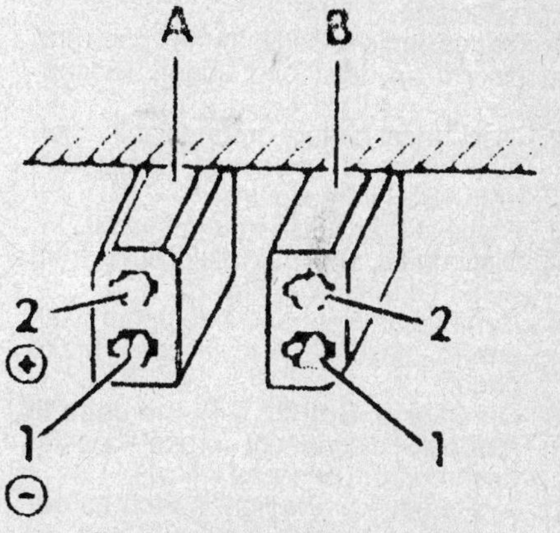
A
B
2
+
1
−
2
1

VW4029100001000X

Fig. 7 Diagnostic Link Connectors (DLC). Corrado & 1993–94 Passat

available with a single port brake pressure regulator. Therefore a T-bracket must be installed at the front of the brake pressure regulator to accommodate the two brake lines.

Refer to **Fig. 73** during replacement procedures.

1. Turn the ignition off.
2. Disconnect the battery negative cable.
3. Press brake pedal, 25–35 times, to reduce pressure in the accumulator. **Serious injury may result if unit is serviced without reducing pressure.**
4. Disconnect ABS unit cable terminals and ground connection.
5. Using a suction bottle, drain brake fluid from the reservoir.
6. Disconnect ABS unit brake lines, then plug the bores.
7. Remove driver side shelf from under the instrument panel.
8. Remove attaching bolts and safety bolt from pushrod clevis.
9. Remove lock nuts, then the hydraulic modulator.
10. Reverse procedure to install, noting the following:
    a. **Torque** new hydraulic modulator to cross panel nuts to 18 ft. lbs.
    b. **Torque** brake lines to hydraulic modulator to 18 ft. lbs.
11. Bleed brake system as described under "Hydraulic Brake Systems".

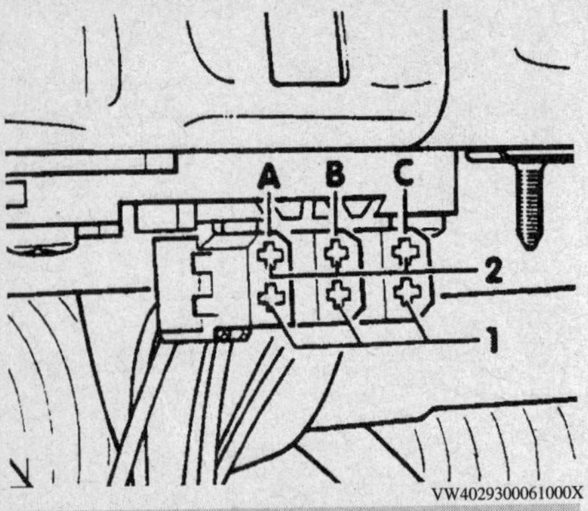
A
B
C
2
1
VW4029300061000X

Fig. 8 Diagnostic Link Connectors (DLC). Eurovan

EUROVAN

Refer to **Fig. 74,** when servicing the hydraulic modulator or components

EXCEPT EUROVAN & 1993–94 CORRADO & PASSAT

Teves Type 04

For ease of service it is recommended that the modulator unit be removed and installed as an assembly with the brake vacuum booster.

1. Obtain audio coded anti-theft code and disarm as described under "Precautions."
2. Disconnect battery ground cable, then disconnect all electrical connectors from ABS hydraulic unit.
3. Remove brake fluid from reservoir.
4. Disconnect and plug fluid lines from ABS hydraulic unit, **Fig. 75.**
5. Remove any lefthand side under dash panels necessary to access brake pedal.
6. **On Cabrio, Golf III, GTI and Jetta III Models,** disconnect brake booster pushrod from pedal as follows:
   a. Remove brake light switch as described under "Electrical. "
   b. Push down on brake pedal and hold, then install pushrod disconnector tool No. 3289, or equivalent, as shown in **Fig. 76.**
   c. Pull tool towards rear and into pedal socket until seated, while holding pedal stationary.
   d. Pull tool and pedal together to rear until pedal pops off ball of booster pushrod.
7. **On Passat models,** disconnect clip from clevis pin, remove pin, then pull pedal from pushrod clevis.
8. **On all models,** remove nuts retaining booster to bulkhead, then remove assembly.
9. Remove and install components from assembly as necessary to effect repair.
10. Install assembly to bulkhead, install mounting nuts, then **torque** nuts to 18 ft. lbs.
11. **On Cabrio, Golf III, GTI and Jetta III Models,** to install pedal to pushrod, align ball and socket, then push in until they pop together.
12. **On Passat models,** to install pushrod, align clevis and pedal, then install pin and clip.
13. **On all models,** reverse remaining procedures to install, then bleed brakes as described under "Hydraulic Brake Systems."

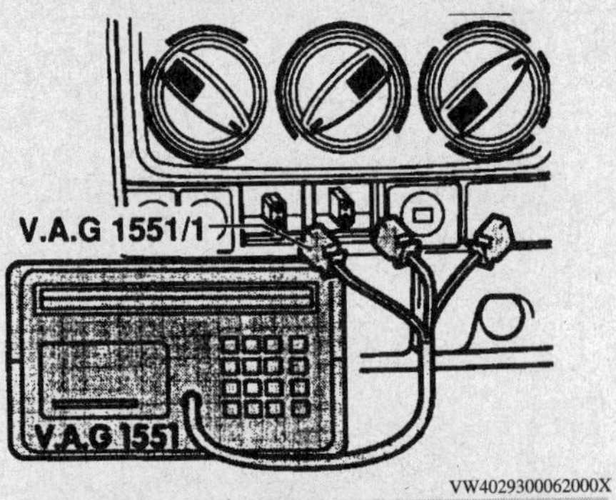
V.A.G 1551/1
V.A.G 1551
VW4029300062000X

Fig. 9 Diagnostic Link Connectors (DLC). 1993 Golf III & Jetta III

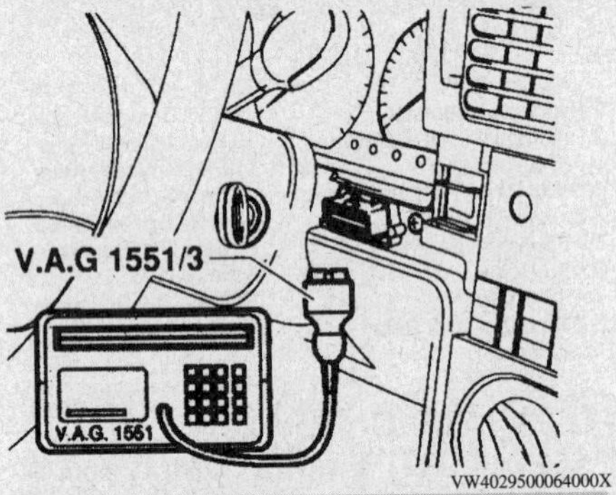
V.A.G 1551/3
V.A.G. 1551
VW4029500064000X

Fig. 11 Diagnostic Link Connectors (DLC). 1995–96 Passat

Teves Type 20

In this system the ABS control module is mounted as an assembly with the ABS hydraulic modulator unit. Use the highest standards of cleanliness when separating and assembling these components.

The ABS hydraulic modulator unit may be shipped pre filled and pre bled. If this is the case do not remove shipping plugs until connecting each line.

Teves model 20 ABS control modules are coded to the vehicle. Replacement control modules must be coded after installation. Refer to "Coding Teves Type 20 Control Module" for procedures.

1. Obtain audio coded anti-theft code and disarm as described under "Precautions."
2. Disconnect battery ground cable, then disconnect all electrical connectors from ABS hydraulic unit.
3. Disconnect coolant expansion tank and position aside.
4. Raise and support vehicle and connect a bleeder hose and bottle to left front brake caliper bleeder screw, then open bleeder.
5. Depress brake pedal at least 2 3/8 inches, then block pedal to hold in this position.

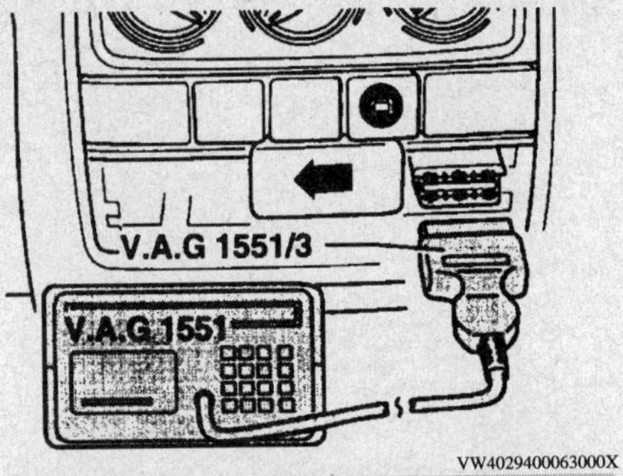
V.A.G 1551/3
V.A.G 1551
VW4029400063000X

Fig. 10 Diagnostic Link Connectors (DLC). 1994–96 Golf III & Jetta III & 1995–96 Cabrio & GTI

6. Close bleeder screw on left front caliper.
7. Remove heat shield from master cylinder **Fig. 77.**
8. Remove fluid lines from master cylinder and hydraulic modulator. **Cap and plug all lines and fittings, note position of all lines for later assembly.**
9. Remove "Torx" socket head bolts from ABS hydraulic unit mounting bracket, then remove hydraulic unit/control module assembly.
10. Disconnect hydraulic unit electrical connector from control module.
11. Maintain assembly in its installed position for the following procedures.
12. Remove nuts retaining control module to hydraulic unit.
13. **Pull control module straight off hydraulic unit so as not to damage or disturb solenoid assemblies.**
14. Keep control module covered with a lint free cloth until assembly.
15. Reverse procedure to install, noting the following:
    a. **Torque** mounting bracket "Torx" screws to 6 ft. lbs.
    b. Do not intermix brake fluid lines.
    c. Bleed brakes as described under "Hydraulic Brake Systems."

CODING TEVES TYPE 20 CONTROL MODULE

Teves model 20 ABS control modules are coded to the vehicle. Replacement control modules must be coded after installation.

1. Connect a suitable scan tool, as described under "Accessing Diagnostic Trouble Codes."
2. Follow manufacturer's instructions to access control module coding function of scan tool.
3. Unless documentation accompanies replacement control modules with updated information code control modules as follows:
   a. **On 1995–96 Passat models,** enter code 04505.
   b. **Except 1995–96 Passat models,** enter code 03604.
4. **On all models,** complete service that required control module coding.

CONTROL MODULE

Always connect a suitable scan tool to ABS system and check for any stored Diagnostic Trouble Codes (DTC) before disconnecting control module.

Teves model 20 ABS control modules are coded to the vehicle. Replacement control modules must be coded after installation. Refer to "Coding Teves Type 20 Control Module" for procedures.

CABRIO, GOLF III, GTI & JETTA III

Teves Type 04 ABS

On early 1993 models, ABS control unit is located under the floor covering of the footwell for righthand front seat. After early 1993 models, ABS control unit is located under the righthand side rear seat.

1. Disconnect battery ground cable.
2. Pull outward on sheet metal straps near the control unit.
3. Pull control unit out.
4. Release connector latch, then disconnect.
5. Reverse procedure to install.

Teves Type 20 ABS

The Teves type 20 ABS control module is in unit with the hydraulic unit. Refer to "Hydraulic Modulator Replace" for procedures.

Teves model 20 ABS control modules are coded to the vehicle. Replacement control modules must be coded after installation. Refer to "Coding Teves Type 20 Control Module" for procedures.

EUROVAN

ABS control unit is located near lower lefthand side "A" pillar.

PASSAT

1993–94 & 1995–96 w/ Teves Type 04 ABS

On 1993–94 models ABS control unit is located under the lefthand side rear seat. On 1995–96 models ABS control unit is located under the righthand side rear seat.

1. Remove ABS control unit retaining screws.
2. Remove control unit.
3. Press clip on control unit downward, then remove main connector.
4. Reverse procedure to install.

Teves Type 20 ABS

The Teves type 20 ABS control module is in unit with the hydraulic unit. Refer to "Hydraulic Modulator Replace" for procedures.

Teves type 20 ABS control modules are coded to the vehicle. Replacement control modules must be coded after installation. Refer to "Coding Teves Type 20 Control Module" for procedures.

DIAGNOSTIC CHART INDEX

Code	Description	Page No.	Fig. No.
CORRADO			
0000	End Of Output Response	49-116	12
1111	Control Unit Defective	49-116	12
1112	Front Left ABS Inlet Valve	49-116	12
1114	Front Right ABS Inlet Valve	49-116	12
1122	Rear ABS Inlet Valve	49-116	12
1132	Front Left ABS Outlet Valve	49-116	12
1134	Front Right ABS Outlet Valve	49-116	12
1142	Rear ABS Outlet Valve	49-116	12
1222	Main ABS Valve	49-116	12
1233	Front Left Wheel Speed Sensor	49-116	12
1241	Front Right Wheel Speed Sensor	49-116	12
1243	Rear Right Wheel Speed Sensor	49-116	12
1311	Rear Left Wheel Speed Sensor	49-116	12
1312	Low Pressure Warning Switch/Low Fluid Level Switch	49-116	12
4444	No Fault Recognized	49-116	12
EUROVAN w/FOUR DIGIT DTC			
1111	Control Module Faulty	49-118	23
1221	Front Left ABS Inlet/Outlet Valve	49-117	13
1233	Front Left Vehicle Speed Sensor	49-117	14
1234	Front Right ABS Inlet/Outlet Valve	49-117	15
1241 (Part 1)	Front Right Vehicle Speed Sensor	49-117	15
1241 (Part 2)	Front Right Vehicle Speed Sensor	49-117	16
1242	Rear Left ABS Inlet/Outlet Valve	49-117	16
1243	Rear Right Vehicle Speed Sensor	49-117	17
1244	Rear Right ABS Inlet/Outlet Valve	49-117	18
1311 (Part 1)	Rear Left Vehicle Speed Sensor	49-117	18
1311 (Part 2)	Rear Left Vehicle Speed Sensor	49-118	19
1334	Return Feed Pump For ABS	49-118	20
1341	Relay For ABS Solenoid Valve	49-118	21
2131	Brake Light Switch	49-118	22
2234	Solenoid Valves	49-118	22
4444	No Malfunction Recognized	49-117	13

Continued

DIAGNOSTIC CHART INDEX—Continued

Code	Description	Page No.	Fig. No.
EUROVAN w/FIVE DIGIT DTC			
Code 00000	No Malfunction Recognized	49-117	13
00277	Front Left ABS Inlet/Outlet Valve	49-117	13
00283	Front Left Vehicle Speed Sensor	49-117	14
00284	Front Right ABS Inlet/Outlet Valve	49-117	15
00285 (Part 1)	Front Right Vehicle Speed Sensor	49-117	15
00285 (Part 2)	Front Right Vehicle Speed Sensor	49-117	16
00286	Rear Left ABS Inlet/Outlet Valve	49-117	16
00287	Rear Right Vehicle Speed Sensor	49-117	17
00289	Rear Right ABS Inlet/Outlet Valve	49-117	18
00290 (Part 1)	Rear Left Vehicle Speed Sensor	49-117	18
00290 (Part 2)	Rear Left Vehicle Speed Sensor	49-118	19
00301	Return Feed Pump For ABS	49-118	20
00302	Relay For ABS Solenoid Valve	49-118	21
00526	Brake Light Switch	49-118	22
00532	Solenoid Valves	49-118	22
00597	Different Wheel Speed Pulses	49-118	23
65535	Control Module Faulty	49-118	23
CABRIO, GOLF III, GTI & JETTA III w/TEEVES TYPE 04 ABS & FOUR DIGIT DTC			
1111	Control Module Malfunctioning	49-120	36
1112	Front Left ABS Inlet Valve	49-118	24
1114	Front Right ABS Inlet Valve	49-118	24
1132	Front Left ABS Outlet Valve	49-119	25
1134	Front Right ABS Outlet Valve	49-119	25
1211	Rear Right ABS Inlet Valve	49-119	25
1212	Rear Left ABS Inlet Valve	49-119	25
1213	Rear Right ABS Outlet Valve	49-119	26
1214	Rear Left ABS Outlet Valve	49-119	26
1223	Differential Lock Valve	49-119	26
1224	Differential Lock Valve	49-119	26
1233	Front Left Wheel Speed Sensor	49-119	27
1241	Front Right Wheel Speed Sensor	49-119	28
1243	Rear Right Wheel Speed Sensor	49-119	29
1311	Rear Left Wheel Speed Sensor	49-119	30
1313	Hydraulic Energy Supply Pressure Level	49-119	31
2234	Battery Supply Voltage	49-119	31
2133	ABS Pressure Control Switch	49-119	32
3231	Brake Pedal Position Sensor	49-120	35
4133	ABS Hydraulic Pump	49-120	36
4444	No DTC Recognized	49-118	24
CABRIO, GOLF III, GTI & JETTA III w/TEEVES TYPE 04 ABS & FIVE DIGIT DTC			
00000	No DTC Recognized	49-118	24
00257	Front Left ABS Inlet Valve	49-118	24
00259	Front Right ABS Inlet Valve	49-118	24
00265	Front Left ABS Outlet Valve	49-119	25
00267	Front Right ABS Outlet Valve	49-119	25
00273	Rear Right ABS Inlet Valve	49-119	25
00274	Rear Left ABS Inlet Valve	49-119	25
00275	Rear Right ABS Outlet Valve	49-119	26
00276	Rear Left ABS Outlet Valve	49-119	26
00279	Differential Lock Valve	49-119	26
00280	Differential Lock Valve	49-119	26
00283	Front Left Wheel Speed Sensor	49-119	27
00285	Front Right Wheel Speed Sensor	49-119	28
00287	Rear Right Wheel Speed Sensor	49-119	29
00290	Rear Left Wheel Speed Sensor	49-119	30
00292	Hydraulic Energy Supply Pressure Level	49-119	31

Continued

DIAGNOSTIC CHART INDEX—Continued

Code	Description	Page No.	Fig. No.
CABRIO, GOLF III, GTI & JETTA III w/TEEVES TYPE 04 ABS & FIVE DIGIT DTC			
00532	Battery Supply Voltage	49-119	31
00547	ABS Pressure Control Switch	49-119	32
00599	Plausibility Pressure/Brake Light Switch	49-120	33
00634	Series Resistance	49-120	34
00793	Brake Pedal Position Sensor	49-120	35
01276	ABS Hydraulic Pump	49-120	36
65535	Control Module Malfunctioning	49-120	36
CABRIO, GOLF III, GTI & JETTA III w/TEEVES TYPE 20 ABS			
00000	No DTC Recognized	49-120	37
00283	Front Left Wheel Speed Sensor	49-120	38
00285	Front Right Wheel Speed Sensor	49-120	39
00287	Rear Right Wheel Speed Sensor	49-120	40
00290	Front Left Wheel Speed Sensor	49-121	41
00668	Battery Supply Voltage	49-121	41
01044	Control Module Incorrectly Coded	49-121	41
01130	ABS Operation	49-121	42
01276	ABS Hydraulic Pump	49-121	42
65535	Control Module Malfunctioning	49-121	42
1995–96 PASSAT w/TEEVES TYPE 04 ABS			
00000	No DTC Recognized	49-121	43
00257	Front Left ABS Inlet Valve	49-121	43
00259	Front Right ABS Inlet Valve	49-121	43
00265	Front Left ABS Outlet Valve	49-121	44
00267	Front Right ABS Outlet Valve	49-121	44
00273	Rear Right ABS Inlet Valve	49-121	44
00274	Rear Left ABS Inlet Valve	49-121	44
00275	Rear Right ABS Outlet Valve	49-121	45
00276	Rear Left ABS Outlet Valve	49-121	45
00279	Differential Lock Valve	49-121	45
00280	Differential Lock Valve	49-121	45
00283	Front Left Wheel Speed Sensor	49-121	46
00285	Front Right Wheel Speed Sensor	49-122	47
00287	Rear Right Wheel Speed Sensor	49-122	48
00290	Rear Left Wheel Speed Sensor	49-122	49
00292	Hydraulic Energy Supply Pressure Level	49-122	50
00532	Battery Supply Voltage	49-122	50
00547	ABS Pressure Control Switch	49-122	51
00599	Plausibility Pressure/Brake Light Switch	49-122	52
00634	Series Resistance	49-122	53
00793	Brake Pedal Position Switch	49-122	54
01276	ABS Hydraulic Pump	49-123	55
65535	Control Module Malfunctioning	49-123	55
1995–96 PASSAT w/TEEVES TYPE 20 ABS			
00000	No DTC Recognized	49-123	56
00283	Front Left Wheel Speed Sensor	49-123	57
00285	Front Right Wheel Speed Sensor	49-123	58
00287	Rear Right Wheel Speed Sensor	49-123	59
00290	Rear Left Wheel Speed Sensor	49-123	60
00668	Battery Supply Voltage	49-123	60
01044	Control Module Incorrectly Coded	49-123	60
01130	ABS Operation	49-123	61
01276	ABS Hydraulic Pump	49-123	61
65535	Control Module Malfunctioning	49-123	61

Flash Code	Fault Readout	Possible Cause(s)	Corrective Action(s)
0000	"End of output" response during initial fault retrieval, with indicator light constantly "ON"	Inadequate battery voltage Defective control unit	Check battery voltage and charge as required Replace control unit, as necessary
1111	Control unit defective	Electrical interference from outside sources Poor ground connection Control unit defective	Check wires, plug-type terminals, and ground wire to control unit. Repair/replace as necessary Check battery voltage and charge as required If necessary, replace control unit
1112	ABS inlet valve, front left	Circuit, plug-type terminal, or valve coil defective Control unit defective	Test①: circuits, plug-type terminals, and valve coil (Steps 28, 11, 37). Repair/replace as necessary If all tests are negative, replace control unit
1114	ABS inlet valve, front right	Circuit, plug-type terminal, or valve coil defective Control unit defective	Test①: circuits, plug-type terminals, and valve coil (Steps 27, 11, 36). Repair/replace as necessary If all tests are negative, replace control unit
1122	ABS inlet valve, rear	Circuit, plug-type terminal, or valve coil defective Control unit defective	Test①: circuits, plug-type terminals, and valve coil (Steps 26, 11, 35). Repair/replace as necessary If all tests are negative, replace control unit
1132	ABS outlet valve, front left	Circuit, plug-type terminal, or valve coil defective Control unit defective	Test①: circuits, plug-type terminals, and valve coil (Steps 31, 11, 37). Repair/replace as necessary If all tests are negative, replace control unit
1134	ABS outlet valve, front right	Circuit, plug-type terminal, or valve coil defective Control unit defective	Test①: circuits, plug-type terminals, and valve coil (Steps 30, 11, 36). Repair/replace as necessary If all tests are negative, replace control unit
1142	ABS outlet valve, rear	Circuit, plug-type terminal, or valve coil defective Control unit defective	Test①: circuits, plug-type terminals, and valve coil (Steps 29, 11, 35). Repair/replace as necessary If all tests are negative, replace control unit
1222	Main ABS valve	Circuit, plug-type terminal, or valve coil defective	Test①: circuits, plug-type terminals on main valve and inlet/outlet valves, and valve coil (Steps 25, 33). Repair/replace as necessary If all tests are negative, replace control unit
1233	Wheel speed sensor, front left	Short circuit, open circuit, loose connection in: speed sensor line, plug-type terminal, speed sensor coil Wrong air gap between speed sensor and pulse wheel (signal inaccurate) Control unit defective	Test①: circuits, plug-type terminals, speed sensor, and ground wire to control unit (Steps 19, 23, 8) Check speed sensor/pulse wheel installation: clean as necessary If all tests are negative, replace control unit

①—Refer to electrical testing troubleshooting chart.

VW4029100002010X

Fig. 12 Code 0000 Through 1233: DTC table. Corrado & 1993–94 Passat

Flash Code	Fault Readout	Possible Cause(s)	Corrective Action(s)
1241	Wheel speed sensor, front right	Short circuit, open circuit, loose connection in: speed sensor line, plug-type terminal, speed sensor coil Wrong air gap between speed sensor and pulse wheel (signal inaccurate) Control unit defective	Test①: circuits, plug-type terminals, speed sensor, and ground wire to control unit (Steps 18, 22, 7) Check speed sensor/pulse wheel installation: clean as necessary If all tests are negative, replace control unit
1243	Wheel speed sensor, rear right	Short circuit, open circuit, loose connection in: speed sensor line, plug-type terminal, speed sensor coil Wrong air gap between speed sensor and pulse wheel (signal inaccurate) Control unit defective	Test①: circuits, plug-type terminals, speed sensor, and ground wire to control unit (Steps 16, 20, 5) Check speed sensor/pulse wheel installation: clean as necessary If all tests are negative, replace control unit
1311	Wheel speed sensor, rear left	Short circuit, open circuit, loose connection in: speed sensor line, plug-type terminal, speed sensor coil Wrong air gap between speed sensor and pulse wheel (signal inaccurate) Control unit defective	Test①: circuits, plug-type terminals, speed sensor, and ground wire to control unit (Steps 17, 21, 6) Check speed sensor/pulse wheel installation: clean as necessary If all tests are negative, replace control unit
1312	Low pressure warning switch Low fluid level switch	ABS control unit circuit drawing excess battery voltage between terminals 9 and 10	Inspect/connect wiring routing between terminals 9 and 10. Connect multi-pin terminal from ABS control unit to VAG 1598 and multi-meter US 1119. Check voltage between terminals 9 and 1, and 10 and 1 •must be: 0.1V Repair/replace as necessary
4444	"No fault recognized" readout, despite ABS problems		Continue troubleshooting, using ABS Electrical Tests①

①—Refer to electrical testing troubleshooting chart.

VW4029100002020X

Fig. 12 Code 1241 Through 4444: DTC table. Corrado & 1993–94 Passat

00000 **4444** No malfunction recognized!	— If this display appears, On-Board Diagnostic **(OBD)** has ended. — If complaint is still present, although no malfunction has been recognized by control module:
00277 **1221** Front left ABS inlet/ outlet valve **(N 137)**	— Open in wiring or short circuit to positive; ground between hydraulic unit **(N 55)**, terminal 1, and control unit **(J 104)**, terminal 2 — Inlet/outlet valve **(N 137)** faulty

VW4029300012000X

Fig. 13 Code 00000 Or 00277 / Code 4444 Or 1221: DTC Table. Eurovan

00283 **1233** Front left Vehicle Speed Sensor **(VSS) (G 47)** *Open in wiring/short circuit to positive	— Open in wiring or short circuit to positive between **(G 47)** and control module **(J 104)**, terminals **4** and **5** — **(G 47)** faulty
*No malfunction recognized! **Note:** — Malfunction location not possible — May be incorrectly indicated if a wheel turns at more than 6 km/hr with ignition switched **ON**	— Short circuit to ground between **(G 47)** and control unit **(J 104)**, terminals **4** and **5** — Rotor dirty or damaged — Play in wheel bearing — **(G 47)** installation position — **(G 47)** faulty

VW4029300013000X

Fig. 14 Code 00283 / Code 1233: Front Left Vehicle Speed Sensor. Eurovan

00284 **1234** Front right ABS inlet/outlet valve **(N 138)**	— Open in wiring or short circuit to positive; ground between hydraulic unit **(N 55)**, terminal **3**, and control module **(J 104)**, terminal **35** — Inlet/outlet valve **(N 138)** faulty
00285 **1241** Front right Vehicle Speed Sensor **(VSS) (G 45)** *Open in wiring/short circuit to positive	— Open in wiring or short circuit to positive between **(G 45)** and control module **(J 104)**, terminals **11** and **21**

VW4029300014000X

Fig. 15 Code 00284 Or 00285 (Part 1) / Code 1234 Or 1241 (Part 1): DTC Table. Eurovan

00285 **1241** *No malfunction recognized! **Note:** Malfunction location not possible. May be incorrectly indicated if a wheel turns at more than 6 km/hr with ignition switched **ON**.	— **(G 45)** defective — Short circuit to **GND** between **(G 45)** and control module **(J 104)**, terminals **11** and **21** — Short circuit to **GND** between **(G 47)** and control unit **(J 104)**, terminals **4** and **5** — Rotor dirty or damaged — Play in wheel bearing — **(G 45)** installation position — **(G 45)** faulty
00286 **1242** Rear left ABS inlet/ outlet valve **(N 139)**	— Open in wiring or short circuit to positive; **GND** between hydraulic unit **(N 55)**, contact **5**, and control module **(J 104)**, terminal **18** — Inlet/outlet valve **(N 139)** faulty

VW4029300015000X

Fig. 16 Code 00285 (Part 2) Or 00286 / Code 1241 (Part 2) Or 1242: DTC Table. Eurovan

00287 **1243** Rear right Vehicle Speed Sensor **(VSS) (G 44)** *Open in wiring/short circuit to positive	— Open in wiring or short circuit to positive between **(G 44)** and control unit **(J 104)**, terminals **24** and **26**
*No malfunction recognized! **Note:** Malfunction location not possible. May be incorrectly indicated if a wheel turns at more than 6 km/hr with ignition switched **ON**.	— **(G 44)** faulty — Short circuit to ground between **(G 44)** and control module **(J 104)**, terminals **24** and **26** — Rotor dirty or damaged — Play in wheel bearing — **(G 44)** installation position — **(G 44)**

VW4029300016000X

Fig. 17 Code 00287 / Code 1243: Rear Right Vehicle Speed Sensor. Eurovan

00289 **1244** Right rear ABS inlet/outlet valve **(N 140)**	— Open in wiring or short circuit to positive; ground between hydraulic unit **(N 55)**, terminal **7**, and control module **(J 104)**, terminal **19** — Inlet/outlet valve **(N 140)** faulty
00290 **1311** Rear left Vehicle Speed Sensor **(VSS) (G 46)** *Open in wiring/short circuit to positive Continued on next page	— Open in wiring or short circuit to positive between **(G 46)** and control module **(J 104)**, terminals **7** and **9**

VW4029300017000X

Fig. 18 Code 00289 Or 00290 (Part 1) / Code 1244 Or 1311 (Part 1): DTC Table. Eurovan

00290 1311	— (G 46) faulty
*No malfunction recognized!	— Short circuit to ground between (G 46) and control module (J 104), terminals 7 and 9
Note:	
*Malfunction location not possible	— Rotor dirty or damaged
*May be incorrectly indicated if a wheel turns at more than 6 km/hr with ignition switched **ON**	— Play in wheel bearing
	— (G 46) installation position
	— (G 46)

VW4029300018000X

Fig. 19 Code 00290 (Part 2) / Code 1311 (Part 2): Rear Left Vehicle Speed Sensor. Eurovan

00301 1334	
Return feed pump for ABS (V 39)	— Open in wiring or contact resistance in ground connection or positive connection to return feed pump (V 39): hydraulic unit (N 55), terminal 10 — Open in wiring or short circuit to positive/ground in wiring between relay for return feed pump (J 105) and control module (J 104), terminals 14, 17 and 28 — Relay (J 105), return feed pump (V 39) or hydraulic unit (N 55) faulty

VW4029300019000X

Fig. 20 Code 00301 / Code 1334: Return Feed Pump For ABS. Eurovan

00302 1341	
Relay for ABS solenoid valve (J 106)	— Open in wiring or contact resistance in positive connection to relay (J 106): hydraulic unit (N 55) terminal 6 — Open in wiring or short circuit to positive/ground in wiring between relay for solenoid valves (J 106) and control module (J 104), terminals 17, 27 and 32 — Relay (J 106) or hydraulic unit (N 55) faulty

VW4029300020000X

Fig. 21 Code 00302 / Code 1341: Relay For ABS Solenoid Valve. Eurovan

00526 2131	
Brake light switch (F)	— Open in wiring between brake light switch/brake lights and control module (J 104), terminal 25 — Open in brake light system
00532 2234	— Insufficient supply voltage at solenoid valves: Voltage at control module (J 104), terminal 32, is only 7.5-9.0 volts

VW4029300021000X

Fig. 22 Code 00526 Or 00532 / Code 2131 Or 2234: DTC Table. Eurovan

00597	
Different wheel speed pulses	No signal or incorrect pulse from one of 4 Vehicle Speed Sensors (VSS):
Note:	— 1 rotor with incorrect number of teeth installed
*Wheel assignment not possible	— Rotors dirty or damaged
*Malfunction location not possible	— 1 VSS installation position wrong
*May be incorrectly indicated if a wheel turns at more than 6 km/hr with ignition switched on	— Play in wheel bearing or wheel bearing faulty
	— 1 VSS faulty
65535 1111	
Control module faulty	— Contact resistance in ground or positive wire to control module (J 104)
Note: If malfunction "Return feed pump for ABS - V 39" is indicated at same time, eliminate this malfunction first	— Control module (J 104) faulty

VW4029300022000X

Fig. 23 Code 00597 Or 65535 / Code – Or 1111: DTC Table. Eurovan

00000 4444		
No DTC recognized	If "No DTC recognized" is displayed after carrying out repairs, On Board Diagnostic (OBD) program sequence has ended. If, despite "No DTC recognized" being displayed, the ABS system does not operate properly, then proceed as follows: 1. Carry out road test exceeding 40 km/h (24 mph). 2. Again check DTC memory. If there is still no DTC stored: 3. Troubleshoot without On Board Diagnostic (OBD) and work through the complete electrical test	
00257 1112		
ABS Inlet Valve,LF –N101	Faulty wire, connector or valve winding	– Check wiring, connectors and valve winding Test steps 17 and 37[1)]
00259 1114		
ABS Inlet Valve,RF –N99	Faulty wire, connector or valve winding	– Check wiring, connectors and valve winding Test steps 18 and 38[1)]

[1)] Electrical test

VW4029300035000X

Fig. 24 Code 00000 Through 00259 / Code 4444 & 1112 Through 1114: DTC Table. Cabrio, Golf III, GTI & Jetta III w/Teves Type 04 ABS

00265 1132 ABS Outlet Valve,LF –N102	Faulty wire, connector or valve winding	– Check wiring, connectors and valve winding Test steps 21 and 37[1]
00267 1134 ABS Outlet Valve,RF –N100	Faulty wire, connector or valve winding	– Check wiring, connectors and valve winding Test steps 22 and 38[1]
00273 1211 ABS Inlet Valve,RR –N133	Faulty wire, connector or valve winding	– Check wiring, connectors and valve winding Test steps 20 and 40[1]
00274 1212 ABS Inlet Valve,LR –N134	Faulty wire, connector or valve winding	– Check wiring, connectors and valve winding Test steps 19 and 39[1]

[1] Electrical test

VW4029300023000X

Fig. 25 Code 00265 Through 00274 / Code 1132 Through 1212: DTC Table. Cabrio, Golf III, GTI & Jetta III w/Teves Type 04 ABS

00275 1213 ABS Outlet Valve,RR –N135	Faulty wire, connector or valve winding	– Check wiring, connectors and valve winding Test steps 24 and 40[1]
00276 1214 ABS Outlet Valve,LR –N136	Faulty wire, connector or valve winding	– Check wiring, connectors and valve winding Test steps 23 and 39[1]
00279 1223 Differential Lock Valve 1–N125	Faulty wire, connector or valve winding	– Check wiring, connectors and valve winding Test steps 25 and 41[1]
00280 1224 Differential Lock Valve 2–N126	Faulty wire, connector or valve winding	– Check wiring, connectors and valve winding Test steps 26 and 41[1]

[1] Electrical test

VW4029300024000X

Fig. 26 Code 00275 Through 00280 / Code 1213 Through 1224: DTC Table. Cabrio, Golf III, GTI & Jetta III w/Teves Type 04 ABS

00283 1233		
ABS Wheel Speed Sensor,LF–G47	Open circuit, short circuit or loose connection in: ♦ ABS wheel speed sensor wire ♦ Connector ♦ ABS wheel speed sensor winding	– Check wiring, connectors, ABS wheel speed sensor, Ground (GND) wiring to ABS control module and also capacitor for correct Ground (GND) connection Test steps 7, 11 and 34[1]
Mechanical malfunction[2]	Excessive or insufficient air gap between ABS wheel speed sensor and impulse rotor (signal not OK)	– Check installation of ABS wheel speed sensor and impulse rotor; clean if necessary
Signal outside tolerances[2]	Impulse rotor and ABS wheel speed sensor dirty or damaged	

[1] Electrical test

[2] Type of malfunction.

VW4029300025000X

Fig. 27 Code 00283 / Code 1233: Front Left Wheel Speed Sensor. Cabrio, Golf III, GTI & Jetta III w/Teves Type 04 ABS

00285 1241		
ABS Wheel Speed Sensor,RF–G45	Open circuit, short circuit or loose connection in: ♦ ABS wheel speed sensor wire ♦ Connector ♦ ABS wheel speed sensor winding	– Check wiring, connectors, ABS wheel speed sensor, Ground (GND) wiring to ABS control module and also capacitor for correct Ground (GND) connection Test steps 6, 10 and 33[1]
Mechanical malfunction[2]	Excessive or insufficient air gap between ABS wheel speed sensor and impulse rotor (signal not OK)	– Check installation of ABS wheel speed sensor and impulse rotor; clean if necessary
Signal outside tolerances[2]	Impulse rotor and ABS wheel speed sensor dirty or damaged	

[1] Electrical test

[2] Type of malfunction.

VW4029300026000X

Fig. 28 Code 00285 / Code 1241: Front Right Wheel Speed Sensor. Cabrio, Golf III, GTI & Jetta III w/Teves Type 04 ABS

00287 1243		
ABS Wheel Speed Sensor,RR–G44	Open circuit, short circuit or loose connection in: ♦ ABS wheel speed sensor wire ♦ Connector ♦ ABS wheel speed sensor winding	– Check wiring, connectors, ABS wheel speed sensor, Ground (GND) wiring to ABS control module and also capacitor for correct Ground (GND) connection Test steps 8, 12 and 31[1]
Mechanical malfunction[2]	Excessive or insufficient air gap between ABS wheel speed sensor and impulse rotor (signal not OK)	– Check installation of ABS wheel speed sensor and impulse rotor; clean if necessary
Signal outside tolerances[2]	Impulse rotor and ABS wheel speed sensor dirty or damaged	

[1] Electrical test

[2] Type of malfunction.

VW4029300027000X

Fig. 29 Code 00287 / Code 1243: Rear Right Wheel Speed Sensor. Cabrio, Golf III, GTI & Jetta III w/Teves Type 04 ABS

00290 1311		
ABS Wheel Speed Sensor,LR–G46	Open circuit, short circuit or loose connection in: ♦ ABS wheel speed sensor wire ♦ Connector ♦ ABS wheel speed sensor winding	– Check wiring, connectors, ABS wheel speed sensor, Ground (GND) wiring to ABS control module and also capacitor for correct Ground (GND) connection Test steps 9, 13 and 32[1]
Mechanical malfunction[2]	Excessive or insufficient air gap between ABS wheel speed sensor and impulse rotor (signal not OK)	– Check installation of ABS wheel speed sensor and impulse rotor; clean if necessary
Signal outside tolerances[2]	Impulse rotor and ABS wheel speed sensor dirty or damaged	

[1] Electrical test

[2] Type of malfunction.

VW4029300028000X

Fig. 30 Code 00290 / Code 1311: Rear Left Wheel Speed Sensor. Cabrio, Golf III, GTI & Jetta III w/Teves Type 04 ABS

00292 1313		
Hydraulic Energy Supply Pressure Level	Pressure loss through leaks or air in the hydraulic unit and brake system	– Bleed brake system
Mechanical malfunction[2]	ABS hydraulic pump -V64- not producing sufficient pressure	– If necessary, replace ABS hydraulic unit and tandem master cylinder – After repairs, erase DTC memory with VAG 1551 scan tool
00532 2234		
Supply Voltage (B+)	Faulty wiring, connectors, fuse -S4-, ABS valves fuse -S54- or ABS relay -J102-	– Check fuses, wiring, connectors, Ground (GND) wiring and the voltage supply to ABS control module Test steps 1–4, 14 and 30[1]

[1] Electrical test.

[2] Type of malfunction.

VW4029300029000X

Fig. 31 Code 00292 Or 00532 / Code 1313 Or 2234: DTC Table. Cabrio, Golf III, GTI & Jetta III w/Teves Type 04 ABS

VAG 1551 scan tool printout	Possible cause of malfunction	Repairing malfunction
00547 2133		
ABS Pressure Control Switch–F137[2]	Wire between terminal 13 and terminal 26 of ABS control module -J104- with ABS pressure control switch -F137- has connection to battery + or battery –	– Visual check of wiring between terminal 13 and terminal 26 – Disconnect multi-pin connector from ABS control module, connect to test box and use multimeter to measure voltage between terminals: 13 and 1 = max. 0.1 V 26 and 1 = max. 0.1 V Test step 29[1]

[1] Electrical test

[2] Applies to ABS control module 1H0 907 379A only.

VW4029300030000X

Fig. 32 Code 00547 / Code 2133: ABS Pressure Control Switch. Cabrio, Golf III, GTI & Jetta III w/Teves Type 04 ABS

00599		
Plausibility Pressure/ Brake Light Switch	Faulty wiring, connectors, ABS pressure control switch -F137-, fuse -S20- or brake light switch -F-	– Visual check of wire routing from brake light switch -F-, ABS pressure control switch -F137- and fuse -S20- Test steps 5 and 29[1]
	Time delay between brake light switch signal and pressure control switch signal excessive	– Ensure that the brake light switch signal enters the ABS control module before the pressure control switch signal, if necessary adjust brake light switch

[1] Electrical test

VW4029300031000X

Fig. 33 Code 005994: Plausibility Pressure/Brake Light Switch. Cabrio, Golf III, GTI & Jetta III w/Teves Type 04 ABS

00793 3231		
Brake Pedal Pos. Sensor–G100 Mechanical malfunction[2]	Faulty wiring, connectors, brake pedal position sensor -G100- or short to battery positive (B+) or Ground	– Check wiring, connectors and brake pedal position sensor -G100- Test steps 28[1] – Unplug multi-pin connector from ABS control module, connect to test box with adapter and use multimeter to measure voltage between the terminals: 16 and 1 = max. 0.1 V 41 and 1 = max. 0.1 V

[1] Electrical test

[2] Type of malfunction.

VW4029300033000X

Fig. 35 Code 00793 / Code 3231: Brake Pedal Position Sensor. Cabrio, Golf III, GTI & Jetta III w/Teves Type 04 ABS

00000	
No DTC recognized	If "No DTC recognized" is displayed after carrying out repairs, On Board Diagnostic (OBD) program sequence has ended. If, despite "No DTC recognized" being displayed, the ABS system does not operate properly, then proceed as follows: 1. Carry out road test exceeding 20 km/h (12 mph). 2. Again check DTC memory. If there is still no DTC stored: 3. Troubleshoot without On Board Diagnostic (OBD) and work through the complete electrical test

VW4029300036000X

Fig. 37 Code 00000: No DTC Recognized. Cabrio, Golf III, GTI & Jetta III w/Teves Type 20 ABS

00285		
ABS Wheel Speed Sensor,LF–G47	Open circuit, short circuit or loose connection in: ♦ ABS wheel speed sensor wire ♦ Connector ♦ ABS wheel speed sensor winding	– Check wiring, connectors, ABS wheel speed sensor and Ground (GND) wiring to ABS control module
	Short circuit in ABS wheel speed sensor	Test steps 5 and 9[1]
Mechanical malfunction[2]	Excessive air gap between ABS wheel speed sensor and impulse rotor (signal not OK)	– Check installation of ABS wheel speed sensor and impulse rotor; clean if necessary Read measuring value block, function 08. Display field 2
Signal outside tolerances[2]	Impulse rotor and ABS wheel speed sensor dirty or damaged	

[1] Electrical test.

[2] Type of malfunction; this malfunction is only recognized above 20 km/h (12 mph); test drive.

VW4029300038000X

Fig. 39 Code 00285: Front Right Wheel Speed Sensor. Cabrio, Golf III, GTI & Jetta III w/Teves Type 20 ABS

00634		
Series Resistance -N159	Faulty wiring, connectors, EDL relay -J310- or EDL series resistance -N159-	– Check wiring, connectors, EDL relay -J310- and EDL series resistance -N159- Test steps 15, 35 and 36[1] – Check EDL series resistance -N159- for continuity (using connector test kit and multimeter in 200 ohm resistance range); Specification: max. 2 Ω, replace if necessary

[1] Electrical test.

VW4029300032000X

Fig. 34 Code 00634: Series Resistance. Cabrio, Golf III, GTI & Jetta III w/Teves Type 04 ABS

01276 4133		
ABS Hydraulic Pump–V64 Signal outside tolerances[2]	Faulty wiring, connectors, ABS hydraulic pump relay -J185-, ABS hydraulic pump -V64- or hydraulic pump sender -G101-	– Check wiring, connectors, ABS hydraulic pump relay -J185-, ABS hydraulic pump -V64- and hydraulic pump sender -G101- Test steps 15, 27, 35 and 36[1]
65535 1111		
Control Module Malfunctioning	Electrical malfunctions caused by outside interference, poor Ground (GND) connections, poor positive connections to ABS control module -J104-	– Check wiring, connectors and Ground (GND) wires to ABS control module and voltage supply Test steps 1–4, 14 and 30[1]
	ABS control module faulty	– Replace ABS control module if necessary

[1] Electrical test

[2] Type of malfunction.

VW4029300034000X

Fig. 36 Code 01276 Or 65535 / Code 1111 Or 4133: DTC Table. Cabrio, Golf III, GTI & Jetta III w/Teves Type 04 ABS

00283		
ABS Wheel Speed Sensor,LF–G47	Open circuit, short circuit or loose connection in: ♦ ABS wheel speed sensor wire ♦ Connector ♦ ABS wheel speed sensor winding	– Check wiring, connectors, ABS wheel speed sensor and Ground (GND) wiring to ABS control module
	Short circuit in ABS wheel speed sensor	Test steps 6 and 10[1]
Mechanical malfunction[2]	Excessive air gap between ABS wheel speed sensor and impulse rotor (signal not OK)	– Check installation of ABS wheel speed sensor and impulse rotor; clean if necessary Read measuring value block, function 08. Display field 2
Signal outside tolerances[2]	Impulse rotor and ABS wheel speed sensor dirty or damaged	

[1] Electrical test

[2] Type of malfunction; this malfunction is only recognized above 20 km/h (12 mph); test drive.

VW4029300037000X

Fig. 38 Code 00283: Front Left Wheel Speed Sensor. Cabrio, Golf III, GTI & Jetta III w/Teves Type 20 ABS

00287		
ABS Wheel Speed Sensor,LF–G47	Open circuit, short circuit or loose connection in: ♦ ABS wheel speed sensor wire ♦ Connector ♦ ABS wheel speed sensor winding	– Check wiring, connectors, ABS wheel speed sensor and Ground (GND) wiring to ABS control module
	Short circuit in ABS wheel speed sensor	Test steps 7 and 11[1]
Mechanical malfunction[2]	Excessive air gap between ABS wheel speed sensor and impulse rotor (signal not OK)	– Check installation of ABS wheel speed sensor and impulse rotor; clean if necessary ⇒ Read measuring value block, function 08. Display field 2
Signal outside tolerances[2]	Impulse rotor and ABS wheel speed sensor dirty or damaged	

[1] Electrical test

[2] Type of malfunction; this malfunction is only recognized above 20 km/h (12 mph); test drive.

VW4029300039000X

Fig. 40 Code 00287 : Rear Right Wheel Speed Sensor. Cabrio, Golf III, GTI & Jetta III w/Teves Type 20 ABS

00290		
ABS Wheel Speed Sensor,LF–G47	Open circuit, short circuit or loose connection in: ♦ ABS wheel speed sensor wire ♦ Connector ♦ ABS wheel speed sensor winding	– Check wiring, connectors, ABS wheel speed sensor and Ground (GND) wiring to ABS control module
	Short circuit in ABS wheel speed sensor	Test steps 8 and 12 [1]
Mechanical malfunction [2]	Excessive air gap between ABS wheel speed sensor and impulse rotor (signal not OK)	– Check installation of ABS wheel speed sensor and impulse rotor; clean if necessary
Signal outside tolerances [2]	Impulse rotor and ABS wheel speed sensor dirty or damaged	Read measuring value block, function 08. Display field 2
00668		
Battery Positive Voltage (B+) Term.30	Faulty voltage supply wires, connections, fuses 1 and/or 2 for control module–ABS, -S123- and/or -S124-	– Check fuses, wires, connections as well as battery positive voltage (B+) supply to ABS control module Test step 2 [1]
01044		
Control Module incorrectly coded	An incorrect code number has been entered via VAG 1551 scan tool	– Check ABS control module coding
	Open or short circuit in wiring harness between terminals 15 and terminal 21	– Check wiring in harness Test step 13 [1]

[1] Electrical test.

[2] Type of malfunction; this malfunction is only recognized above 20 km/h (12 mph); test drive.

VW4029300040000X

Fig. 41 Code 00290 Through 01044: DTC Table. Cabrio, Golf III, GTI & Jetta III w/Teves Type 20 ABS

01130		
ABS operation	Electrical interference from external sources (high frequency radiation; e.g. non-insulated ignition cable)	Sequence: – Check all wiring and connections for short to positive or Ground (GND) – Erase DTC memory – Carry out a test drive exceeding 20 km/h (12 mph) – Check DTC memory again
Signal outside tolerance [2]		
01276		
ABS hydraulic pump–V64 Signal outside tolerance [2]	♦ Connection electric motor to ABS control module ♦ Short to positive or Ground (GND) or open circuit ♦ Pump motor faulty	– Check wiring, connections ⇒ output Diagnostic Test Mode (DTM), function 03.
65535		
Control Module Malfunctioning	ABS control module faulty	– Replace ABS control module

[1] Electrical test.

[2] Type of malfunction; this malfunction is only recognized above 20 km/h (12 mph); test drive.

VW4029300041000X

Fig. 42 Code 01130 Through 65535: DTC Table. Cabrio, Golf III, GTI & Jetta III w/Teves Type 20 ABS

00000		
No DTC recognized	If "No DTC recognized" is displayed after carrying out repairs, On Board Diagnostic (OBD) program sequence has ended. If, despite "No DTC recognized" being displayed, the ABS system does not operate properly, then proceed as follows: 1. Carry out road test exceeding 40 km/h (24 mph). 2. Again check DTC memory. If there is still no DTC stored: 3. Troubleshoot without On Board Diagnostic (OBD) and work through the complete electrical test	
00257		
ABS Inlet Valve,LF –N101	Faulty wire, connector or valve winding	– Check wiring, connectors and valve winding Test steps 17 and 37 [1]
00259		
ABS Inlet Valve,RF –N99	Faulty wire, connector or valve winding	– Check wiring, connectors and valve winding Test steps 18 and 38 [1]

[1] Electrical test

VW4029500042000X

Fig. 43 Code 00000 Through 00259: DTC Table. 1995–96 Passat w/Teves Type 04 ABS

00265		
ABS Outlet Valve,LF –N102	Faulty wire, connector or valve winding	– Check wiring, connectors and valve winding Test steps 21 and 37 [1]
00267		
ABS Outlet Valve,RF –N100	Faulty wire, connector or valve winding	– Check wiring, connectors and valve winding Test steps 22 and 38 [1]
00273		
ABS Inlet Valve,RR –N133	Faulty wire, connector or valve winding	– Check wiring, connectors and valve winding Test steps 20 and 40 [1]
00274		
ABS Inlet Valve,LR –N134	Faulty wire, connector or valve winding	– Check wiring, connectors and valve winding Test steps 19 and 39 [1]

[1] Electrical test

VW4029500043000X

Fig. 44 Code 00265 Through 00274: DTC Table. 1995–96 Passat w/Teves Type 04 ABS

VAG 1551 scan tool printout	Possible cause of malfunction	Repairing malfunction
00275		
ABS Outlet Valve,RR –N135	Faulty wire, connector or valve winding	– Check wiring, connectors and valve winding Test steps 24 and 40 [1]
00276		
ABS Outlet Valve,LR –N136	Faulty wire, connector or valve winding	– Check wiring, connectors and valve winding Test steps 23 and 39 [1]
00279		
Differential Lock Valve 1–N125	Faulty wire, connector or valve winding	– Check wiring, connectors and valve winding Test steps 25 and 41 [1]
00280		
Differential Lock Valve 2–N126	Faulty wire, connector or valve winding	– Check wiring, connectors and valve winding Test steps 26 and 41 [1]

[1] Electrical test

VW4029500044000X

Fig. 45 Code 00275 Through 00280: DTC Table. 1995–96 Passat w/Teves Type 04 ABS

00283		
ABS Wheel Speed Sensor,LF–G47	Open circuit, short circuit or loose connection in: ♦ ABS wheel speed sensor wire ♦ Connector ♦ ABS wheel speed sensor winding	– Check wiring, connectors, ABS wheel speed sensor, Ground (GND) wiring to ABS control module and also capacitor for correct Ground (GND) connection Test steps 7, 11 and 34 [1]
Mechanical malfunction [2]	Excessive or insufficient air gap between ABS wheel speed sensor and impulse rotor (signal not OK)	– Check installation of ABS wheel speed sensor and impulse rotor; clean if necessary
Signal outside tolerances [2]	Impulse rotor and ABS wheel speed sensor dirty or damaged	

[1] Electrical test

[2] Type of malfunction.

VW4029500045000X

Fig. 46 Code 00283: Front Left Wheel Speed Sensor. 1995–96 Passat w/Teves Type 04 ABS

00285		
ABS Wheel Speed Sensor,RF–G45	Open circuit, short circuit or loose connection in: ♦ ABS wheel speed sensor wire ♦ Connector ♦ ABS wheel speed sensor winding	– Check wiring, connectors, ABS wheel speed sensor, Ground (GND) wiring to ABS control module and also capacitor for correct Ground (GND) connection Test steps 6, 10 and 33[1]
Mechanical malfunction[2]	Excessive or insufficient air gap between ABS wheel speed sensor and impulse rotor (signal not OK)	– Check installation of ABS wheel speed sensor and impulse rotor; clean if necessary
Signal outside tolerances[2]	Impulse rotor and ABS wheel speed sensor dirty or damaged	

1) Electrical test

2) Type of malfunction.

VW4029500046000X

Fig. 47 Code 00285: Front Right Wheel Speed Sensor. 1995–96 Passat w/Teves Type 04 ABS

00287		
ABS Wheel Speed Sensor,RR–G44	Open circuit, short circuit or loose connection in: ♦ ABS wheel speed sensor wire ♦ Connector ♦ ABS wheel speed sensor winding	– Check wiring, connectors, ABS wheel speed sensor, Ground (GND) wiring to ABS control module and also capacitor for correct Ground (GND) connection Test steps 8, 12 and 31[1]
Mechanical malfunction[2]	Excessive or insufficient air gap between ABS wheel speed sensor and impulse rotor (signal not OK)	– Check installation of ABS wheel speed sensor and impulse rotor; clean if necessary
Signal outside tolerances[2]	Impulse rotor and ABS wheel speed sensor dirty or damaged	

1) Electrical test

2) Type of malfunction.

VW4029500047000X

Fig. 48 Code 00287: Rear Right Wheel Speed Sensor. 1995–96 Passat w/Teves Type 04 ABS

00290		
ABS Wheel Speed Sensor,LR–G46	Open circuit, short circuit or loose connection in: ♦ ABS wheel speed sensor wire ♦ Connector ♦ ABS wheel speed sensor winding	– Check wiring, connectors, ABS wheel speed sensor, Ground (GND) wiring to ABS control module and also capacitor for correct Ground (GND) connection Test steps 9, 13 and 32[1]
Mechanical malfunction[2]	Excessive or insufficient air gap between ABS wheel speed sensor and impulse rotor (signal not OK)	– Check installation of ABS wheel speed sensor and impulse rotor; clean if necessary
Signal outside tolerances[2]	Impulse rotor and ABS wheel speed sensor dirty or damaged	

1) Electrical test

2) Type of malfunction.

VW4029500048000X

Fig. 49 Code 00290: Rear Left Wheel Speed Sensor. 1995–96 Passat w/Teves Type 04 ABS

00292		
Hydraulic Energy Supply Pressure Level	Pressure loss through leaks or air in the hydraulic unit and brake system	– Bleed brake system
Mechanical malfunction[2]	ABS hydraulic pump -V64- not producing sufficient pressure	– If necessary, replace ABS hydraulic unit and tandem master cylinder – After repairs, erase DTC memory
00532		
Supply Voltage (B+)	Faulty wiring, connectors, fuse -S22-, ABS valves fuse -S54- or ABS relay -J102-	– Check fuses, wiring, connectors, Ground (GND) wiring and the voltage supply to ABS control module Test steps 1–4, 14 and 30[1]

1) ⇒ Electrical test, page 01-39.

2) Type of malfunction.

VW4029500049000X

Fig. 50 Code 00292 Or 00532: DTC Table. 1995–96 Passat w/Teves Type 04 ABS

00547		
ABS Pressure Control Switch–F137[2]	Wire between terminal 13 and terminal 26 of ABS control module -J104- with ABS pressure control switch -F137- has connection to battery (+) or battery (–)	– Visual check of wiring between terminal 13 and terminal 26 – Disconnect multi-pin connector from ABS control module, connect to test box and use multimeter to measure voltage between terminals: 13 and 1 = max. 0.1 V 26 and 1 = max. 0.1 V Test step 29[1]

1) Electrical test

2) Applies to ABS control module 1H0 907 379A only.

VW4029500050000X

Fig. 51 Code 00547: ABS Pressure Control Switch. 1995–96 Passat w/Teves Type 04 ABS

00599		
Plausibility Pressure/ Brake Light Switch[2]	Faulty wiring, connectors, ABS pressure control switch -F137-, fuse -S16- or brake light switch -F-	– Visual check of wire routing from brake light switch -F-, ABS pressure control switch -F137- and fuse -S16- Test steps 5 and 29[1]
	Time delay between brake light switch signal and pressure control switch signal excessive	– Ensure that the brake light switch signal enters the ABS control module before the pressure control switch signal, if necessary adjust brake light switch

1) Electrical test

2) Applies to ABS control module 1H0 907 379A only.

VW4029500051000X

Fig. 52 Code 00599: Plausibility Pressure/Brake Light Switch. 1995–96 Passat w/Teves Type 04 ABS

00634		
Series Resistance –N159	Faulty wiring, connectors, EDL relay -J310- or EDL series resistance -N159-	– Check wiring, connectors, EDL relay -J310- and EDL series resistance -N159- ⇒ Test steps 15, 35 and 36[1] – Check EDL series resistance -N159- for continuity (using VW 1594 connector test kit and multimeter (Fluke 83 or equivalent) in 200 ohm resistance range); Specification: max. 2 Ω, replace if necessary

1) Electrical test

VW4029500052000X

Fig. 53 Code 00634: Series Resistance. 1995 Passat w/Teves–96 Type 04 ABS

00793		
Brake Pedal Pos. Sensor–G100	Faulty wiring, connectors, brake pedal position sensor -G100- or short to battery positive (B+) or Ground	– Check wiring, connectors and brake pedal position sensor -G100- – Test steps 28[1]
Mechanical malfunction[2]		– Unplug multi-pin connector from ABS control module, connect to test box to measure voltage between the terminals: 16 and 1 = max. 0.1 V 41 and 1 = max. 0.1 V

1) Electrical test

2) Type of malfunction.

VW4029500053000X

Fig. 54 Code 00793: Brake Pedal Position Switch. 1995–96 Passat w/Teves Type 04 ABS

01276		
ABS Hydraulic Pump-V64 Signal outside tolerances[2]	Faulty wiring, connectors, ABS hydraulic pump relay -J185-, ABS hydraulic pump -V64- or hydraulic pump sender -G101-	– Check wiring, connectors, ABS hydraulic pump relay -J185-, ABS hydraulic pump -V64- and hydraulic pump sender -G101- Test steps 15, 27, 35 and 36[1]
65535		
Control Module Malfunctioning	Electrical malfunctions caused by outside interference, poor Ground (GND) connections, poor positive connections to ABS control module -J104-	– Check wiring, connectors and Ground (GND) wires to ABS control module and voltage supply Test steps 1–4, 14 and 30[1]
	ABS control module faulty	– Replace ABS control module if necessary

[1] Electrical test

[2] Type of malfunction.

VW4029500054000X

Fig. 55 Code 01276 Or 65535: DTC Table. 1995–96 Passat w/Teves Type 04 ABS

00000	
No DTC recognized	If "No DTC recognized" is displayed after carrying out repairs, On Board Diagnostic (OBD) program sequence has ended. If, despite "No DTC recognized" being displayed, the ABS system does not operate properly, then proceed as follows: 1. Carry out road test exceeding 20 km/h (12 mph). 2. Again check DTC memory. If there is still no DTC stored: 3. Troubleshoot without On Board Diagnostic (OBD) and work through the complete electrical test.

VW4029500055000X

Fig. 56 Code 00000: No DTC Recognized. 1995–96 Passat w/Teves Type 20 ABS

00283		
ABS Wheel Speed Sensor,LF-G47	Open circuit, short circuit or loose connection in: • ABS wheel speed sensor wire • Connector • ABS wheel speed sensor winding	– Check wiring, connectors, ABS wheel speed sensor and Ground (GND) wiring to ABS control module
	Short circuit in ABS wheel speed sensor	– Electrical test. Test steps 6 and 10
Mechanical malfunction[1]	Excessive air gap between ABS wheel speed sensor and impulse rotor (signal not OK)	– Check installation of ABS wheel speed sensor and impulse rotor; clean if necessary Read measuring value block, function 08, Display field 1
Signal outside tolerances[1]	Impulse rotor and ABS wheel speed sensor dirty or damaged	

[1] Type of malfunction; this malfunction is only recognized above 20 km/h (12 mph); test drive.

VW4029500056000X

Fig. 57 Code 00283: Front Left Wheel Speed Sensor. 1995–96 Passat w/Teves Type 20 ABS

00287		
ABS Wheel Speed Sensor,RR-G44	Open circuit, short circuit or loose connection in: • ABS wheel speed sensor wire • Connector • ABS wheel speed sensor winding	– Check wiring, connectors, ABS wheel speed sensor and Ground (GND) wiring to ABS control module
	Short circuit in ABS wheel speed sensor	– Electrical test. Test steps 7 and 11
Mechanical malfunction[1]	Excessive air gap between ABS wheel speed sensor and impulse rotor (signal not OK)	– Check installation of ABS wheel speed sensor and impulse rotor; clean if necessary Read measuring value block, function 08, Display field 4
Signal outside tolerances[1]	Impulse rotor and ABS wheel speed sensor dirty or damaged	

[1] Type of malfunction; this malfunction is only recognized above 20 km/h (12 mph); test drive.

VW4029500057000X

Fig. 58 Code 00285: Front Right Wheel Speed Sensor. 1995–96 Passat w/Teves Type 20 ABS

00285		
ABS Wheel Speed Sensor,RF-G45	Open circuit, short circuit or loose connection in: • ABS wheel speed sensor wire • Connector • ABS wheel speed sensor winding	– Check wiring, connectors, ABS wheel speed sensor and Ground (GND) wiring to ABS control module
	Short circuit in ABS wheel speed sensor	– Electrical test, page 01-129 Test steps 5 and 9
Mechanical malfunction[1]	Excessive air gap between ABS wheel speed sensor and impulse rotor (signal not OK)	– Check installation of ABS wheel speed sensor and impulse rotor; clean if necessary Read measuring value block, function 08. Display field 2
Signal outside tolerances[1]	Impulse rotor and ABS wheel speed sensor dirty or damaged	

[1] Type of malfunction; this malfunction is only recognized above 20 km/h (12 mph); test drive.

VW4029500058000X

Fig. 59 Code 00287: Rear Right Wheel Speed Sensor. 1995–96 Passat w/Teves Type 20 ABS

00290		
ABS Wheel Speed Sensor,LR-G46	Open circuit, short circuit or loose connection in: • ABS wheel speed sensor wire • Connector • ABS wheel speed sensor winding	– Check wiring, connectors, ABS wheel speed sensor and Ground (GND) wiring to ABS control module
	Short circuit in ABS wheel speed sensor	Electrical test, Test steps 8 and 12
Mechanical malfunction[1]	Excessive air gap between ABS wheel speed sensor and impulse rotor (signal not OK)	– Check installation of ABS wheel speed sensor and impulse rotor; clean if necessary Read measuring value block, function 08, Display field 3
Signal outside tolerances[1]	Impulse rotor and ABS wheel speed sensor dirty or damaged	
00668		
Battery Positive Voltage (B+) Term.30	Faulty voltage supply wires, connections, fuses -S124-	– Check fuses, wires, connections as well as battery positive voltage (B+) supply to ABS control module Electrical test, Test step 2
01044		
Control Module incorrectly coded	An incorrect code number has been entered via VAG 1551 scan tool	– Check ABS control module coding
	Open or short circuit in wiring harness between terminals 15 and terminal 21	– Check wiring in harness Electrical test, Test step 13

[1] Type of malfunction; this malfunction is only recognized above 20 km/h (12 mph); test drive.

VW4029500059000X

Fig. 60 Code 00290 Through 01044: DTC Table. 1995–96 Passat w/Teves Type 20 ABS

01130		
ABS operation Signal outside tolerance[1]	Electrical interference from external sources (high frequency radiation; e.g. non-insulated ignition cable)	Sequence: – Check all wiring and connections for short to positive or Ground (GND) – Erase DTC memory – Carry out a test drive exceeding 20 km/h (12 mph) – Check DTC memory again
01276		
ABS hydraulic pump-V64 Signal outside tolerance[1]	• Connection electric motor to ABS control module • Short to positive or Ground (GND) or open circuit • Pump motor faulty	– Check wiring, connections
65535		
Control Module Malfunctioning	ABS control module faulty	– Replace ABS control module

[1] Type of malfunction; this malfunction is only recognized above 20 km/h (12 mph); test drive.

VW4029500060000X

Fig. 61 Code 01130 Through 65535: DTC Table. 1995–96 Passat w/Teves Type 20 ABS

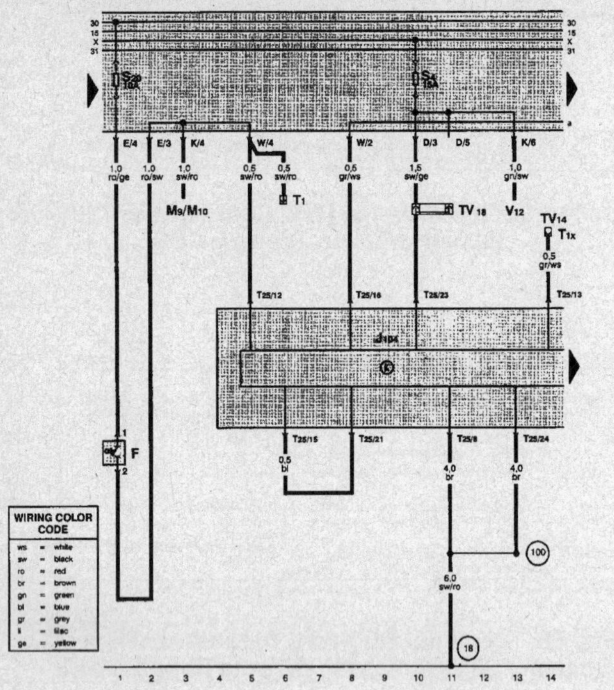

WIRING COLOR CODE
ws = white
sw = black
ro = red
br = brown
gn = green
bl = blue
gr = grey
li = lilac
ge = yellow
Ms/M10
T1
TV 18
V12
TV14
T1x
J104
F
100
18

F – Brake Light Switch (00526–2131)
J104 – ABS Control Module (w/EDL), in engine compartment, left
M9 – Left Brake Light
M10 – Right Brake Light
T1 – Single Connector, above fuse/relay panel
T25 – 25-Pin Connector
TV14 – Data Link Connector (DLC) Wire Connector, above fuse/relay panel
TV18 – Distributor for terminal Xa, above fuse/relay panel
V12 – Rear Window Wiper Motor

(18) – Ground connection, on engine block
(100) – Ground connection –1–, in ABS wiring harness

VW4029500065010X

Fig. 62 ABS wiring diagram (Part 1 of 3). Cabrio

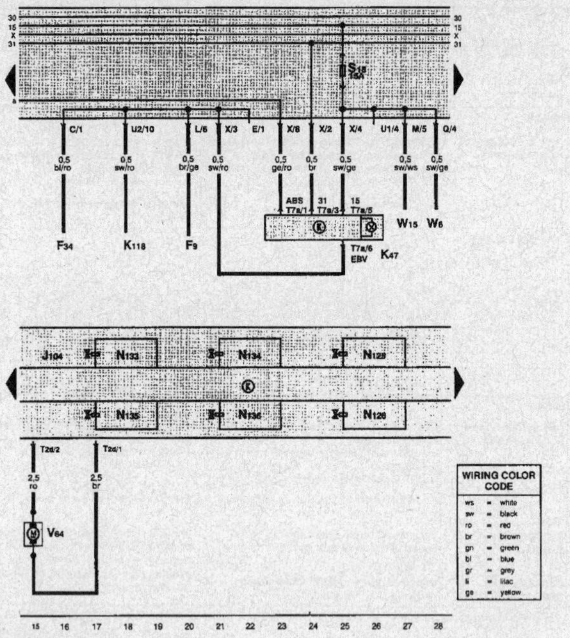

WIRING COLOR CODE
ws = white
sw = black
ro = red
br = brown
gn = green
bl = blue
gr = grey
li = lilac
ge = yellow
F34
K118
F9
W15
W6
K47
J104
N133
N134
N129
N135
N136
N128
V64

F9 – Parking Brake Warning Light Switch (01114)
F34 – Brake Fluid Level Warning Switch
J104 – ABS Control Module (w/EDL), in engine compartment, left
K – Instrument Cluster
K47 – ABS Warning Light
N125 – Differential Lock Valve 1
N126 – Differential Lock Valve 2
N133 – Right Rear ABS Inlet Valve (00273–1211)
N134 – Left Rear ABS Inlet Valve (00274–1212)
N135 – Right Rear ABS Outlet Valve (00275–1213)
N136 – Left Rear ABS Outlet Valve (00276–1214)
T7a – 7-Pin Connector
W6 – Glove Compartment Light
W15 – Interior Light with Delay Switch
V64 – ABS Hydraulic Pump

VW4029500065020X

Fig. 62 ABS wiring diagram (Part 2 of 3). Cabrio

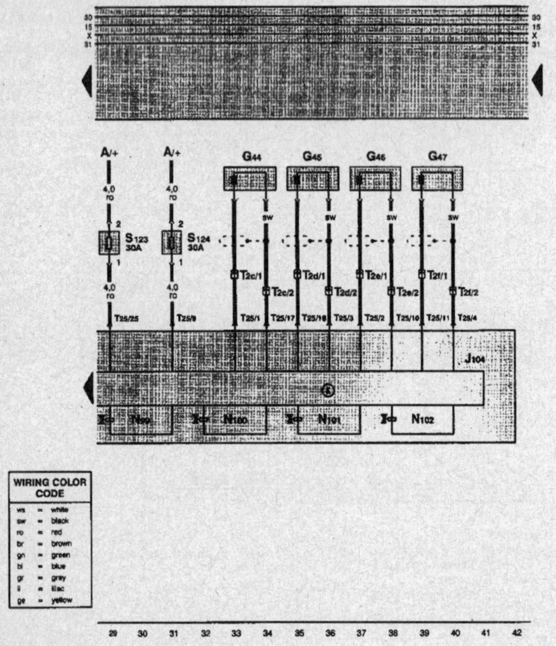

A/+
A/+
G44
G45
G46
G47
S123 30A
S124 30A
J104
N99
N100
N101
N102
WIRING COLOR CODE
ws = white
sw = black
ro = red
br = brown
gn = green
bl = blue
gr = grey
li = lilac
ge = yellow

A – Battery
G44 – Right Rear ABS Wheel Speed Sensor (00287–1243)
G45 – Right Front ABS Wheel Speed Sensor (00285–1241)
G46 – Left Rear ABS Wheel Speed Sensor (00290–1311)
G47 – Left Front ABS Wheel Speed Sensor (00283–1233)
J104 – ABS Control Module (w/EDL) , in engine compartment, left
N99 – Right Front ABS Inlet Valve (00259–1114)
N100 – Right Front ABS Outlet Valve (00267–1134)
N101 – Left Front ABS Inlet Valve (00257–1112)
N102 – Left Front ABS Outlet Valve (00265–1132)
S123 – Fuse 1 for control module – ABS in engine compartment, left
S124 – Fuse 2 for control module – ABS in engine compartment, left
T2 – Double Connector, below rear seat bench
T2 – Double Connector, behind suspension strut, right
T2 – Double Connector, below rear seat bench
T2 – Double Connector, behind suspension strut, left
T25 – 25-Pin Connector, on ABS Control Module

VW4029500065030X

Fig. 62 ABS wiring diagram (Part 3 of 3). Cabrio

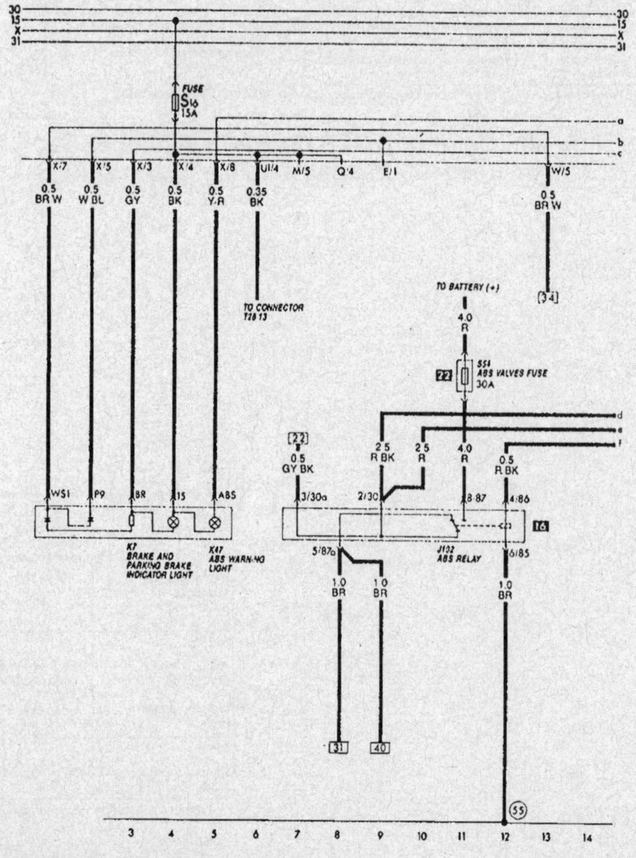

FUSE
S16
15A
TO CONNECTOR T28 13
TO BATTERY (+)
S51
ABS VALVES FUSE
30A
K7
BRAKE AND PARKING BRAKE INDICATOR LIGHT
K47
ABS WARNING LIGHT
J102
ABS RELAY

VW4029100005010X

Fig. 63 ABS wiring diagram (Part 1 of 3). Corrado

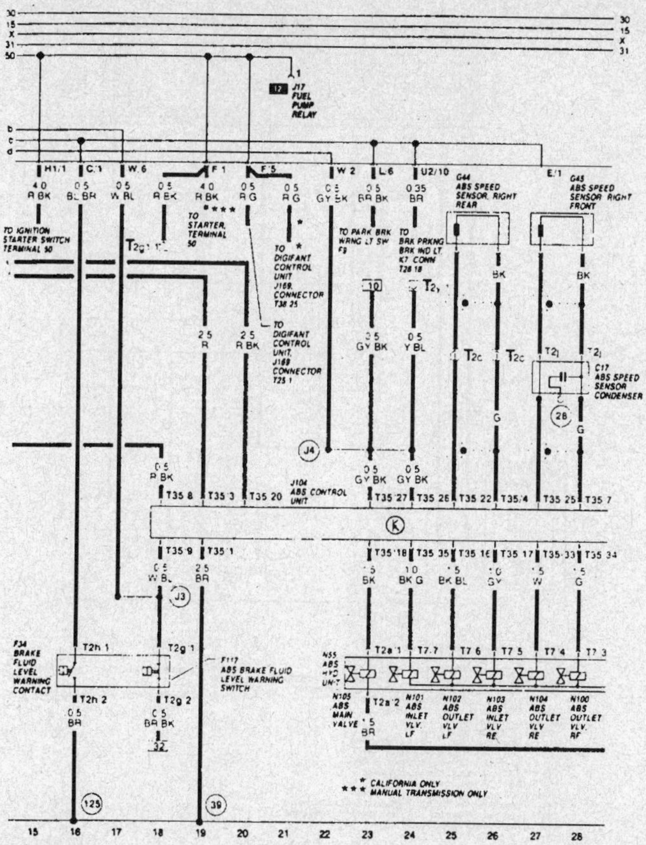

VW4029100005020X

Fig. 63 ABS wiring diagram (Part 2 of 3). Corrado

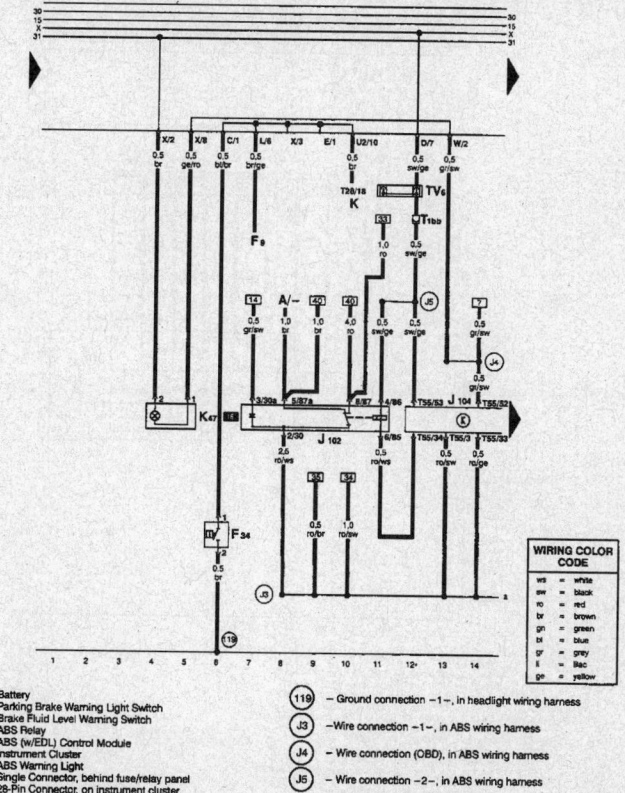

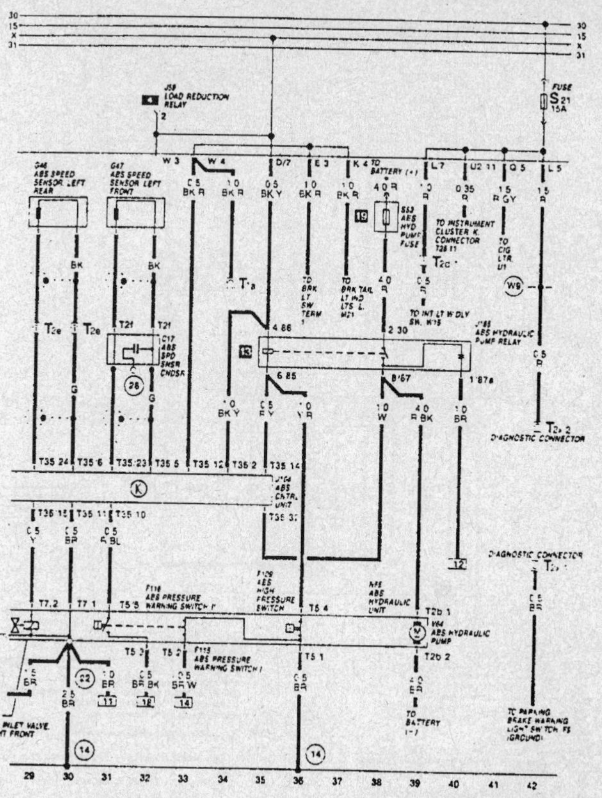

VW4029100005030X

Fig. 63 ABS wiring diagram (Part 3 of 3). Corrado

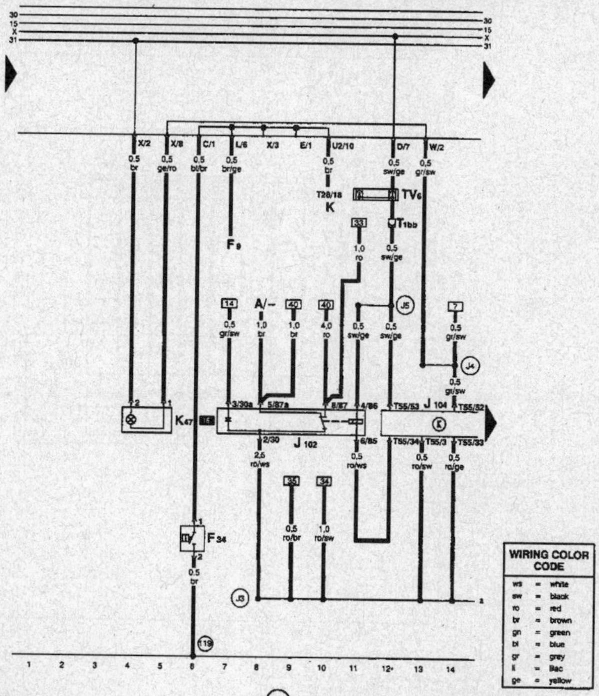

WIRING COLOR CODE		
ws	=	white
sw	=	black
ro	=	red
br	=	brown
gn	=	green
bl	=	blue
gr	=	grey
li	=	lilac
ge	=	yellow

A – Battery
F9 – Parking Brake Warning Light Switch
F34 – Brake Fluid Level Warning Switch
J102 – ABS Relay
J104 – ABS (w/EDL) Control Module
K – Instrument Cluster
K47 – ABS Warning Light
T1bb – Single Connector, behind fuse/relay panel
T28 – 28-Pin Connector, on instrument cluster
T55 – 55-Pin Connector, on ABS Control Module
TV6 – Terminal X Wire Connector

(119) – Ground connection –1–, in headlight wiring harness
(J3) –Wire connection –1–, in ABS wiring harness
(J4) – Wire connection (OBD), in ABS wiring harness
(J5) – Wire connection –2–, in ABS wiring harness

VW4029300066010X

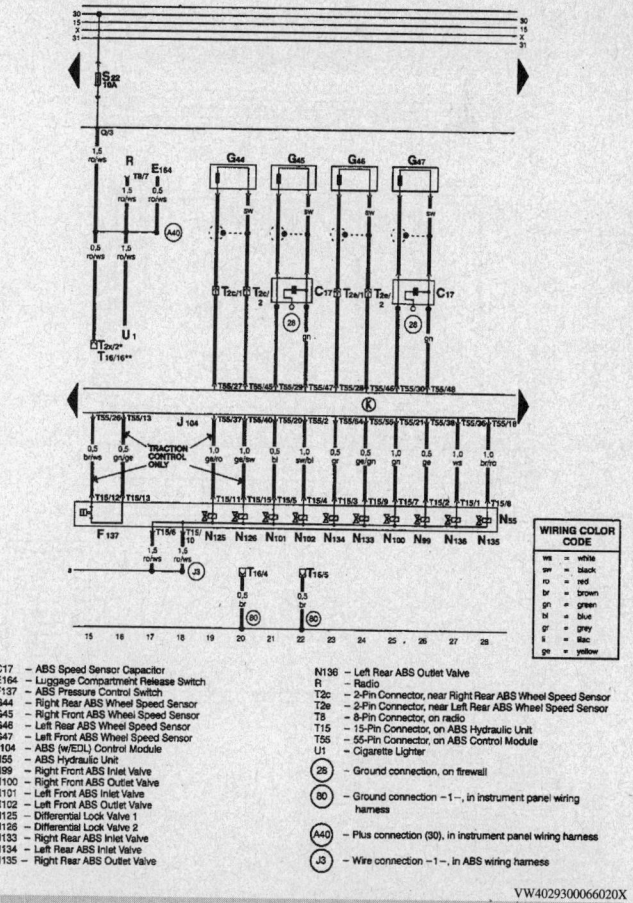

Fig. 64 ABS wiring diagram (Part 1 of 3). 1993–95 Golf III & Jetta III & 1995 GTI

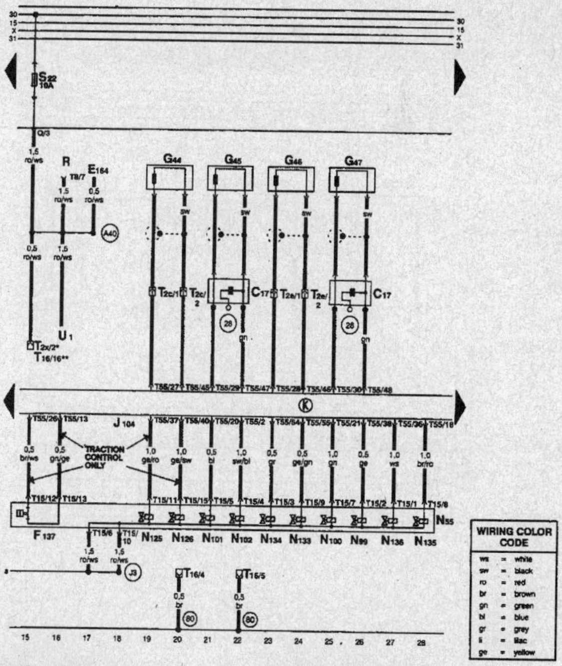

WIRING COLOR CODE		
ws	=	white
sw	=	black
ro	=	red
br	=	brown
gn	=	green
bl	=	blue
gr	=	grey
li	=	lilac
ge	=	yellow

C17 – ABS Speed Sensor Capacitor
E164 – Luggage Compartment Release Switch
F137 – ABS Pressure Control Switch
G44 – Right Rear ABS Wheel Speed Sensor
G45 – Right Front ABS Wheel Speed Sensor
G46 – Left Rear ABS Wheel Speed Sensor
G47 – Left Front ABS Wheel Speed Sensor
J104 – ABS (w/EDL) Control Module
N55 – ABS Hydraulic Unit
N99 – Right Front ABS Inlet Valve
N100 – Right Front ABS Outlet Valve
N101 – Left Front ABS Inlet Valve
N102 – Left Front ABS Outlet Valve
N125 – Differential Lock Valve 1
N126 – Differential Lock Valve 2
N133 – Right Rear ABS Inlet Valve
N134 – Left Rear ABS Inlet Valve
N135 – Right Rear ABS Outlet Valve
N136 – Left Rear ABS Outlet Valve
R – Radio
T2c – 2-Pin Connector, near Right Rear ABS Wheel Speed Sensor
T2e – 2-Pin Connector, near Left Rear ABS Wheel Speed Sensor
T8 – 8-Pin Connector, on radio
T15 – 15-Pin Connector, on ABS Hydraulic Unit
T55 – 55-Pin Connector, on ABS Control Module
U1 – Cigarette Lighter

(28) – Ground connection, on firewall
(80) – Ground connection –1–, in instrument panel wiring harness
(A40) – Plus connection (30), in instrument panel wiring harness
(J3) – Wire connection –1–, in ABS wiring harness

VW4029300066020X

Fig. 64 ABS wiring diagram (Part 2 of 3). 1993–95 Golf III & Jetta III & 1995 GTI

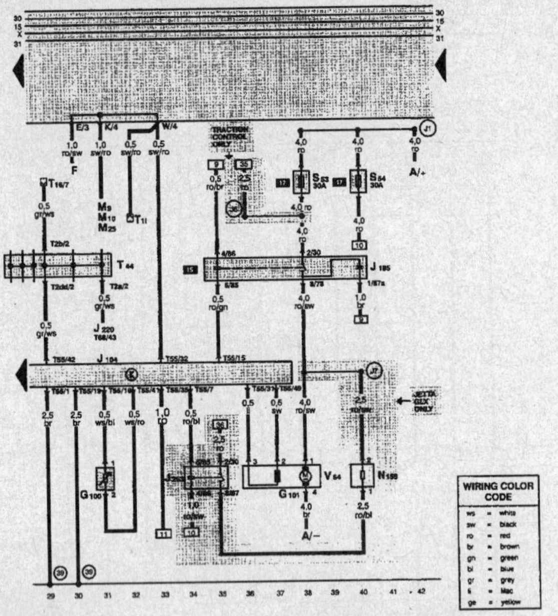
WIRING COLOR CODE
ws = white
sw = black
ro = red
br = brown
gn = green
bl = blue
gr = grey
li = lilac
ge = yellow

A – Battery
F – Brake Light Switch
G100 – Brake Pedal Position Sensor
G101 – Hydraulic Pump Sensor
J104 – ABS (w/EDL) Control Module
J185 – ABS Hydraulic Pump Relay
J220 – Motronic Engine Control Module (ECM)
J263 – Electronic Differential Lock Cut-Off Relay
M9 – Left Brake Light
M10 – Right Brake Light
M25 – High-Mount Brake Light
N159 – Electronic Differential Lock Series Resistance
S53 – ABS Hydraulic Pump Fuse
S54 – ABS Valves Fuse
T1l – Single Connector, behind fuse/relay panel
T2a – Double Connector, on junction connector (T44) above fuse/relay panel
T2b – Double Connector, on junction connector (T44) above fuse/relay panel
T2dd – Double Connector, on junction connector (T44) behind fuse/relay panel
T44 – 44-Pin Connector, Junction Box for on board diagnosis, above fuse/relay panel
T55 – 55-Pin Connector, on ABS Control Module
T68 – 68-Pin Connector, right side of engine compartment, on Motronic Engine Control Module (ECM)
V64 – ABS Hydraulic Pump Fuse
(39) – Ground connection, below rear seat bench, left
(J1) – Plus connection (30) in ABS wiring harness
(J6) – Plus connection –2– (30), in ABS wiring harness
(J7) – Wire connection –3–, in ABS wiring harness

VW4029300066030X

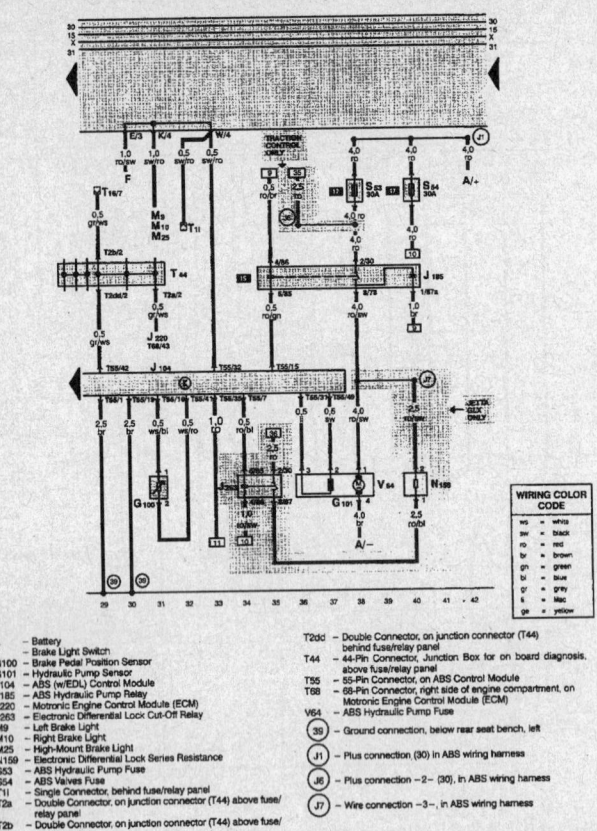

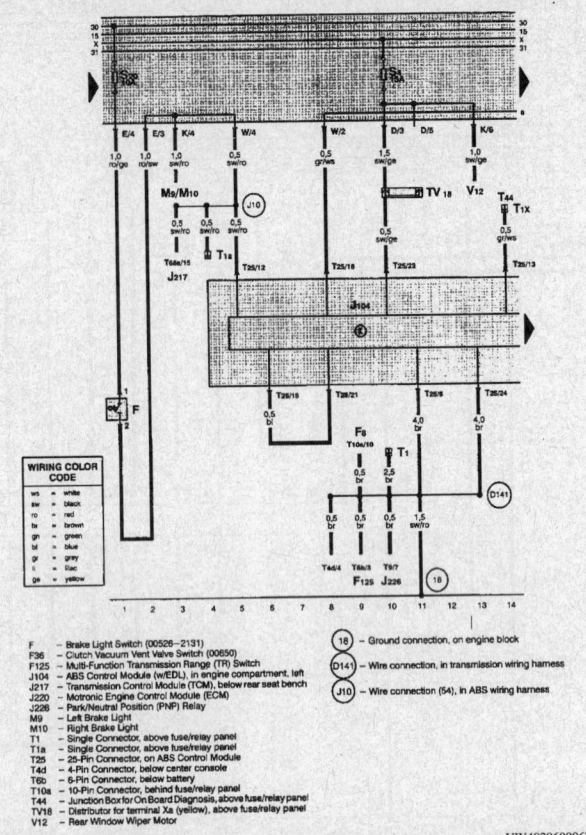

Fig. 64 ABS wiring diagram (Part 3 of 3). 1993–95 Golf III & Jetta III & 1995 GTI

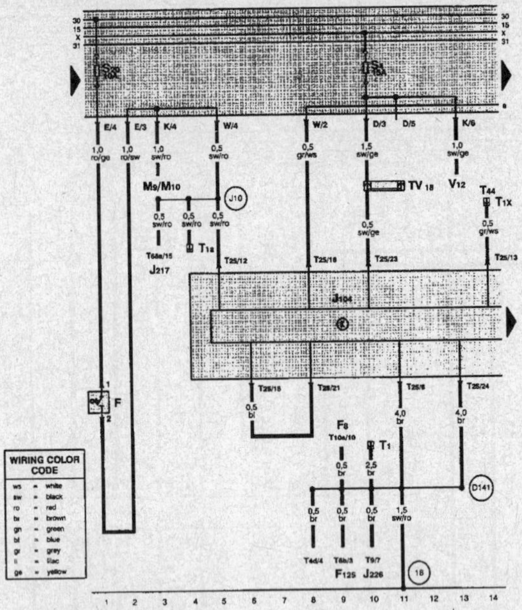
WIRING COLOR CODE
ws = white
sw = black
ro = red
br = brown
gn = green
bl = blue
gr = grey
li = lilac
ge = yellow

F – Brake Light Switch (00526–2131)
F36 – Clutch Vacuum Vent Valve Switch (00650)
F125 – Multi-Function Transmission Range (TR) Switch
J104 – ABS Control Module (w/EDL), in engine compartment, left
J217 – Transmission Control Module (TCM), below rear seat bench
J220 – Motronic Engine Control Module (ECM)
J226 – Park/Neutral Position (PNP) Relay
M9 – Left Brake Light
M10 – Right Brake Light
T1 – Single Connector, above fuse/relay panel
T1a – Single Connector, above fuse/relay panel
T25 – 25-Pin Connector, on ABS Control Module
T4d – 4-Pin Connector, below center console
T6b – 6-Pin Connector, below battery
T10a – 10-Pin Connector, behind fuse/relay panel
T44 – Junction Box for On Board Diagnosis, above fuse/relay panel
TV18 – Distributor for terminal Xa (yellow), above fuse/relay panel
V12 – Rear Window Wiper Motor
(18) – Ground connection, on engine block
(D141) – Wire connection, in transmission wiring harness
(J10) – Wire connection (54), in ABS wiring harness

VW4029600067010X

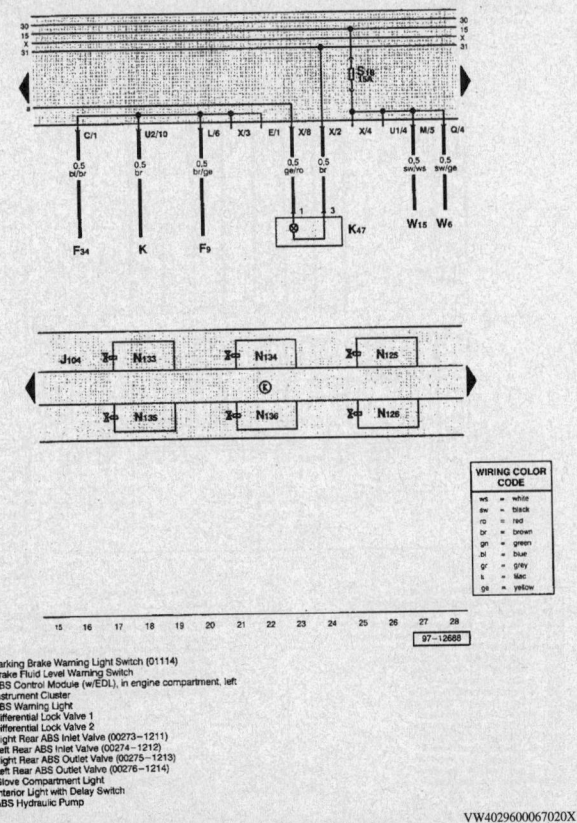

Fig. 65 ABS wiring diagram (Part 1 of 3). 1996 Golf III, GTI & Jetta III

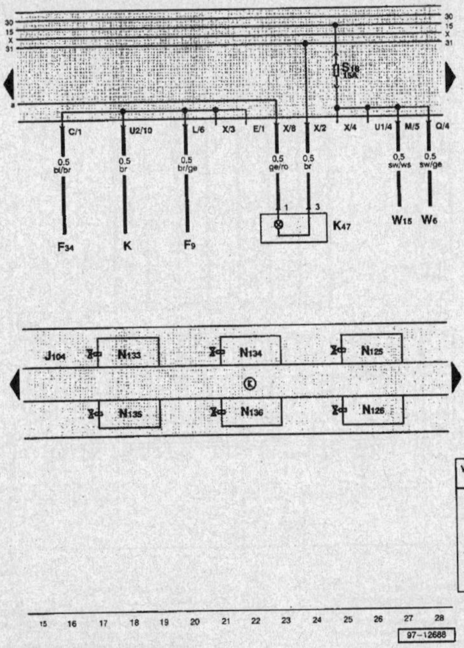
WIRING COLOR CODE
ws = white
sw = black
ro = red
br = brown
gn = green
bl = blue
gr = grey
li = lilac
ge = yellow
97-12688

F9 – Parking Brake Warning Light Switch (01114)
F34 – Brake Fluid Level Warning Switch
J104 – ABS Control Module (w/EDL), in engine compartment, left
K – Instrument Cluster
K47 – ABS Warning Light
N125 – Differential Lock Valve 1
N126 – Differential Lock Valve 2
N133 – Right Rear ABS Inlet Valve (00273–1211)
N134 – Left Rear ABS Inlet Valve (00274–1212)
N135 – Right Rear ABS Outlet Valve (00275–1213)
N136 – Left Rear ABS Outlet Valve (00276–1214)
W6 – Glove Compartment Light
W15 – Interior Light with Delay Switch
V64 – ABS Hydraulic Pump

VW4029600067020X

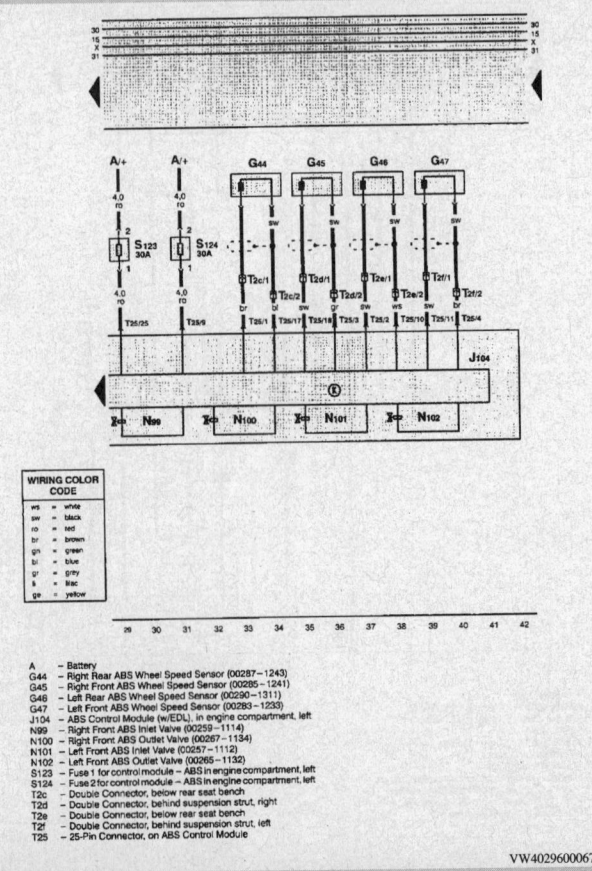

Fig. 65 ABS wiring diagram (Part 2 of 3). 1996 Golf III, GTI & Jetta III

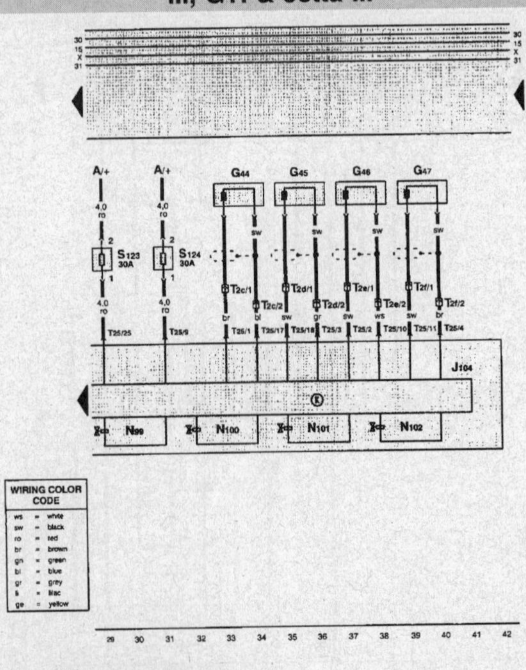
WIRING COLOR CODE
ws = white
sw = black
ro = red
br = brown
gn = green
bl = blue
gr = grey
li = lilac
ge = yellow

A – Battery
G44 – Right Rear ABS Wheel Speed Sensor (00287–1243)
G45 – Right Front ABS Wheel Speed Sensor (00285–1241)
G46 – Left Rear ABS Wheel Speed Sensor (00290–1311)
G47 – Left Front ABS Wheel Speed Sensor (00283–1233)
J104 – ABS Control Module (w/EDL), in engine compartment, left
N99 – Right Front ABS Inlet Valve (00259–1114)
N100 – Right Front ABS Outlet Valve (00267–1134)
N101 – Left Front ABS Inlet Valve (00257–1112)
N102 – Left Front ABS Outlet Valve (00265–1132)
S123 – Fuse 1 for control module – ABS in engine compartment, left
S124 – Fuse 2 for control module – ABS in engine compartment, left
T2c – Double Connector, below rear seat bench
T2d – Double Connector, behind suspension strut, right
T2e – Double Connector, below rear seat bench
T2f – Double Connector, behind suspension strut, left
T25 – 25-Pin Connector, on ABS Control Module

VW4029600067030X

Fig. 65 ABS wiring diagram (Part 3 of 3). 1996 Golf III, GTI & Jetta III

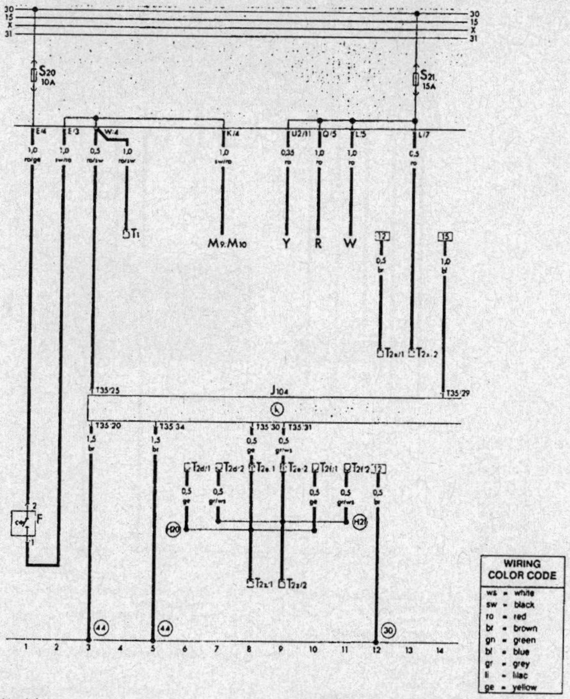
WIRING
COLOR CODE
ws = white
sw = black
ro = red
br = brown
gn = green
bl = blue
gr = grey
li = lilac
ge = yellow

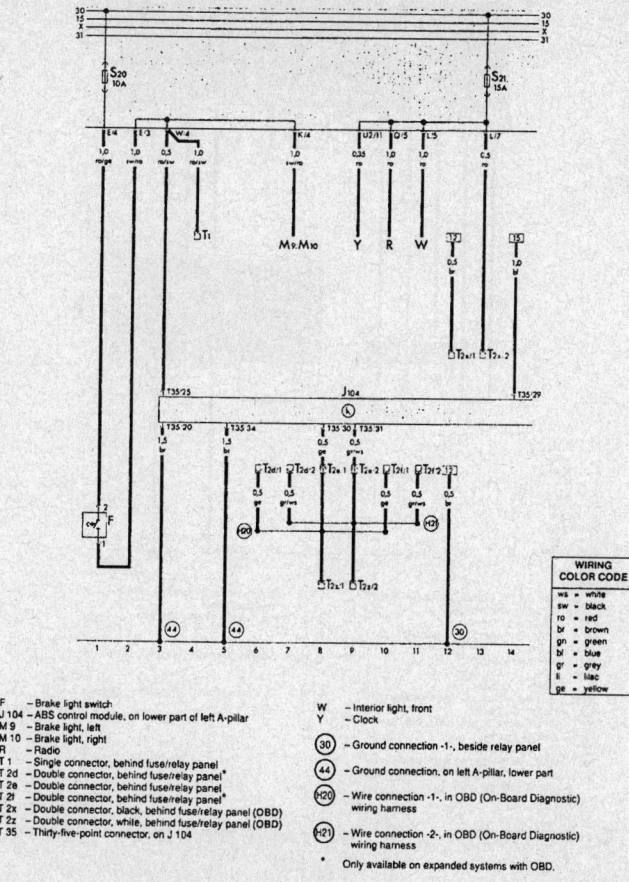

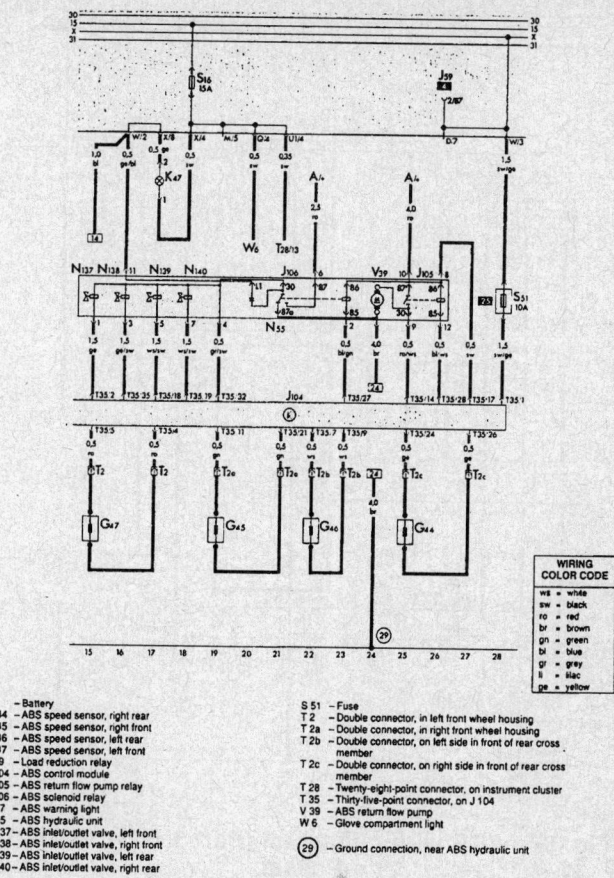

F – Brake light switch
J 104 – ABS control module, on lower part of left A-pillar
M 9 – Brake light, left
M 10 – Brake light, right
R – Radio
T 1 – Single connector, behind fuse/relay panel
T 2d – Double connector, behind fuse/relay panel*
T 2e – Double connector, behind fuse/relay panel
T 2f – Double connector, behind fuse/relay panel*
T 2x – Double connector, black, behind fuse/relay panel (OBD)
T 2z – Double connector, white, behind fuse/relay panel (OBD)
T 35 – Thirty-five-point connector, on J 104

W – Interior light, front
Y – Clock

(30) – Ground connection -1-, beside relay panel
(44) – Ground connection, on left A-pillar, lower part
(H20) – Wire connection -1-, in OBD (On-Board Diagnostic) wiring harness
(H21) – Wire connection -2-, in OBD (On-Board Diagnostic) wiring harness
* Only available on expanded systems with OBD.

VW4029300003010X

Fig. 66 ABS wiring Diagram (Part 1 of 2). Eurovan

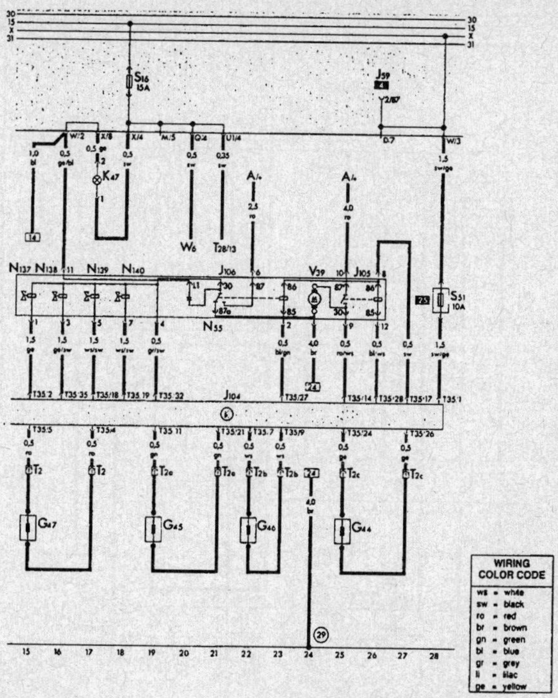
WIRING
COLOR CODE
ws = white
sw = black
ro = red
br = brown
gn = green
bl = blue
gr = grey
li = lilac
ge = yellow

A – Battery
G 44 – ABS speed sensor, right rear
G 45 – ABS speed sensor, right front
G 46 – ABS speed sensor, left rear
G 47 – ABS speed sensor, left front
J 59 – Load reduction relay
J 104 – ABS control module
J 105 – ABS return flow pump relay
J 106 – ABS solenoid relay
K 47 – ABS warning light
N 55 – ABS hydraulic unit
N 137 – ABS inlet/outlet valve, left front
N 138 – ABS inlet/outlet valve, right front
N 139 – ABS inlet/outlet valve, left rear
N 140 – ABS inlet/outlet valve, right rear

S 51 – Fuse
T 2 – Double connector, in left front wheel housing
T 2a – Double connector, in right front wheel housing
T 2b – Double connector, on left side in front of rear cross member
T 2c – Double connector, on right side in front of rear cross member
T 28 – Twenty-eight-point connector, on instrument cluster
T 35 – Thirty-five-point connector, on J 104
V 39 – ABS return flow pump
W 6 – Glove compartment light

(29) – Ground connection, near ABS hydraulic unit

VW4029300003020X

Fig. 66 ABS wiring Diagram (Part 2 of 2). Eurovan

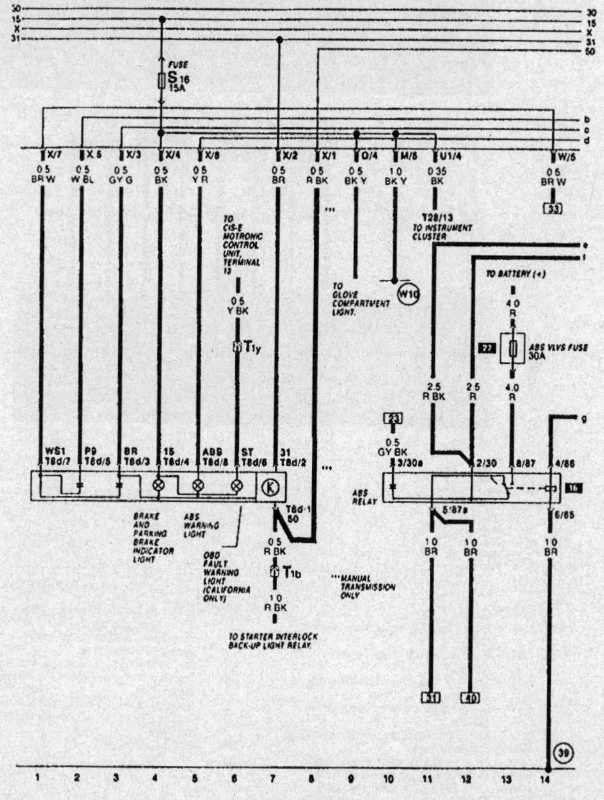

VW4029100006010X

Fig. 67 ABS wiring diagram (Part 1 of 3). 1993–94 Passat

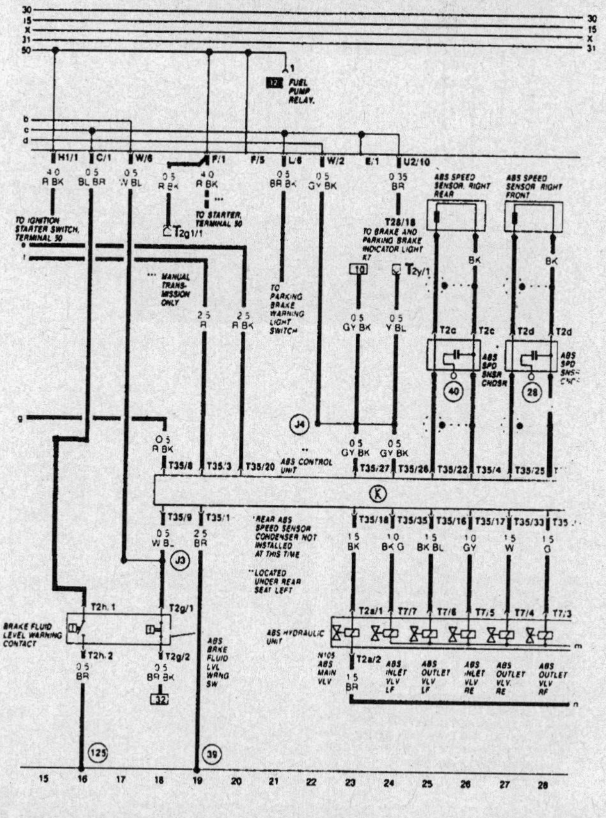

VW4029100006020X

Fig. 67 ABS wiring diagram (Part 2 of 3). 1993–94 Passat

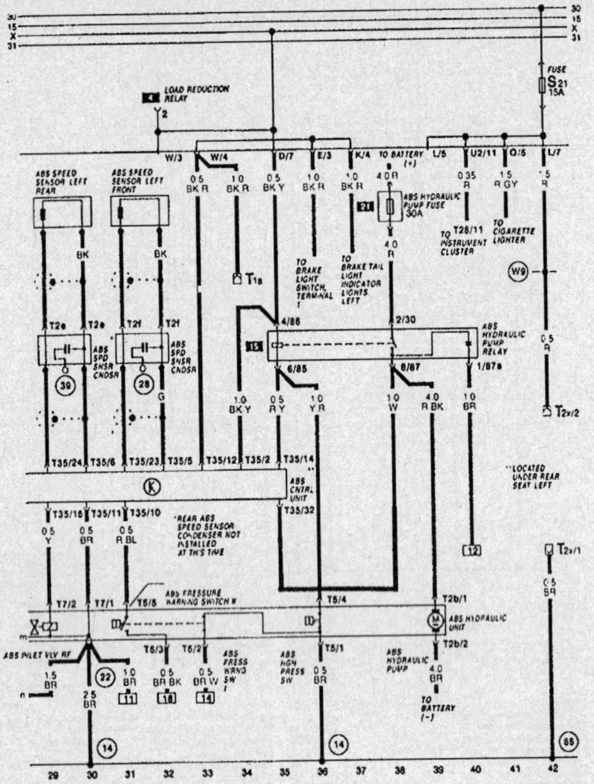

VW4029100006030X

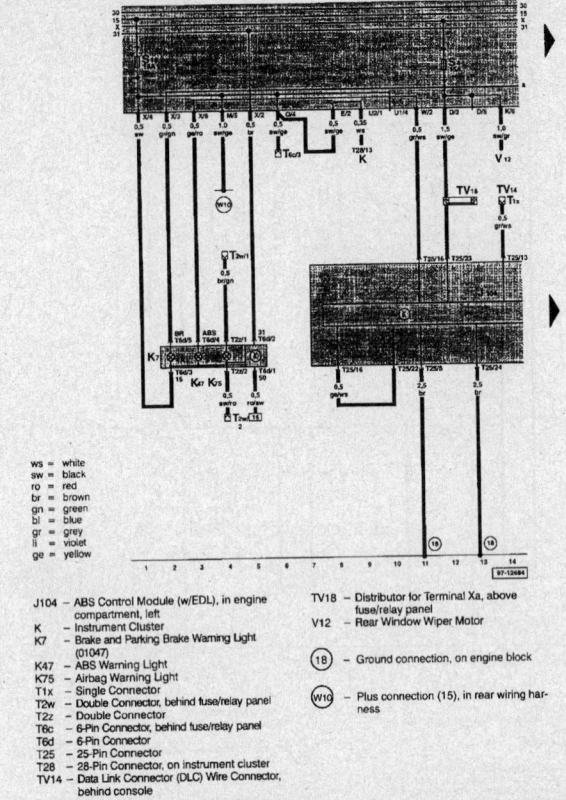

Fig. 67 ABS wiring diagram (Part 3 of 3). 1993–94 Passat

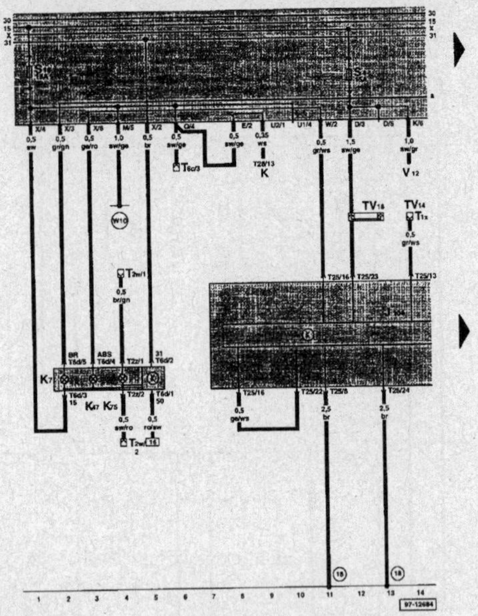

ws = white
sw = black
ro = red
br = brown
gn = green
bl = blue
gr = grey
li = violet
ge = yellow

J104 – ABS Control Module (w/EDL), in engine compartment, left
K – Instrument Cluster
K7 – Brake and Parking Brake Warning Light (01047)
K47 – ABS Warning Light
K75 – Airbag Warning Light
T1x – Single Connector
T2w – Double Connector, behind fuse/relay panel
T2z – Double Connector
T6c – 6-Pin Connector, behind fuse/relay panel
T6d – 6-Pin Connector
T25 – 25-Pin Connector
T28 – 28-Pin Connector, on instrument cluster
TV14 – Data Link Connector (DLC) Wire Connector, behind console
TV18 – Distributor for Terminal Xa, above fuse/relay panel
V12 – Rear Window Wiper Motor
(18) – Ground connection, on engine block
(W10) – Plus connection (15), in rear wiring harness

VW4029500068010X

Fig. 68 ABS wiring diagram (Part 1 of 3). 1995–95 Passat

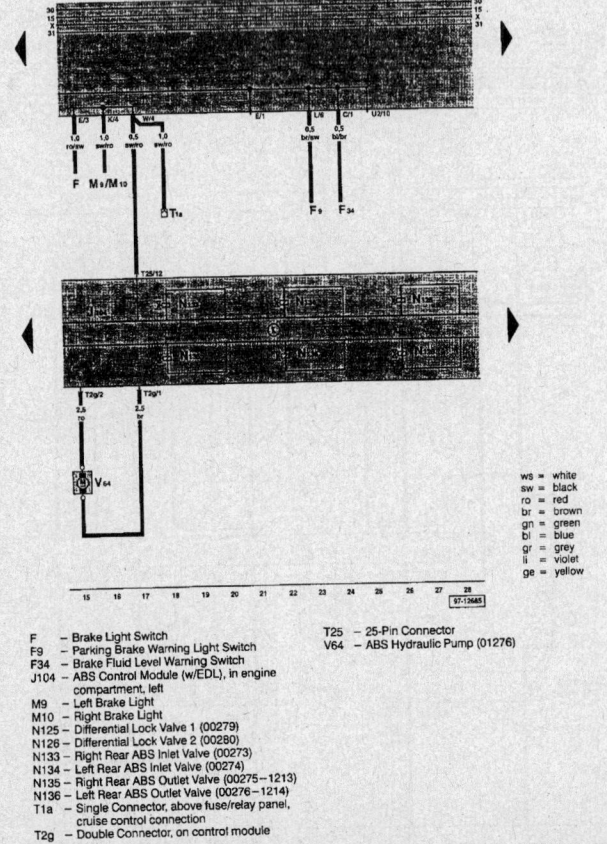

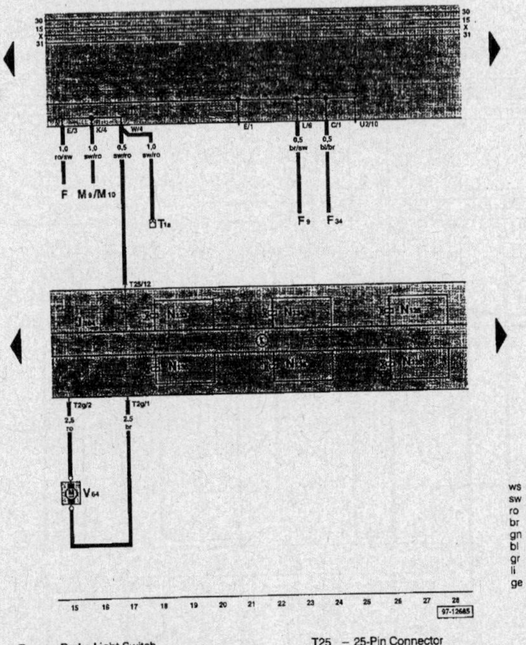

ws = white
sw = black
ro = red
br = brown
gn = green
bl = blue
gr = grey
li = violet
ge = yellow

F – Brake Light Switch
F9 – Parking Brake Warning Light Switch
F34 – Brake Fluid Level Warning Switch
J104 – ABS Control Module (w/EDL), in engine compartment, left
M9 – Left Brake Light
M10 – Right Brake Light
N125 – Differential Lock Valve 1 (00279)
N126 – Differential Lock Valve 2 (00280)
N133 – Right Rear ABS Inlet Valve (00273)
N134 – Left Rear ABS Inlet Valve (00274)
N135 – Right Rear ABS Outlet Valve (00275–1213)
N136 – Left Rear ABS Outlet Valve (00276–1214)
T1a – Single Connector, above fuse/relay panel, cruise control connection
T2g – Double Connector, on control module
T25 – 25-Pin Connector
V64 – ABS Hydraulic Pump (01276)

VW4029500068020X

Fig. 68 ABS wiring diagram (Part 2 of 3). 1995–95 Passat

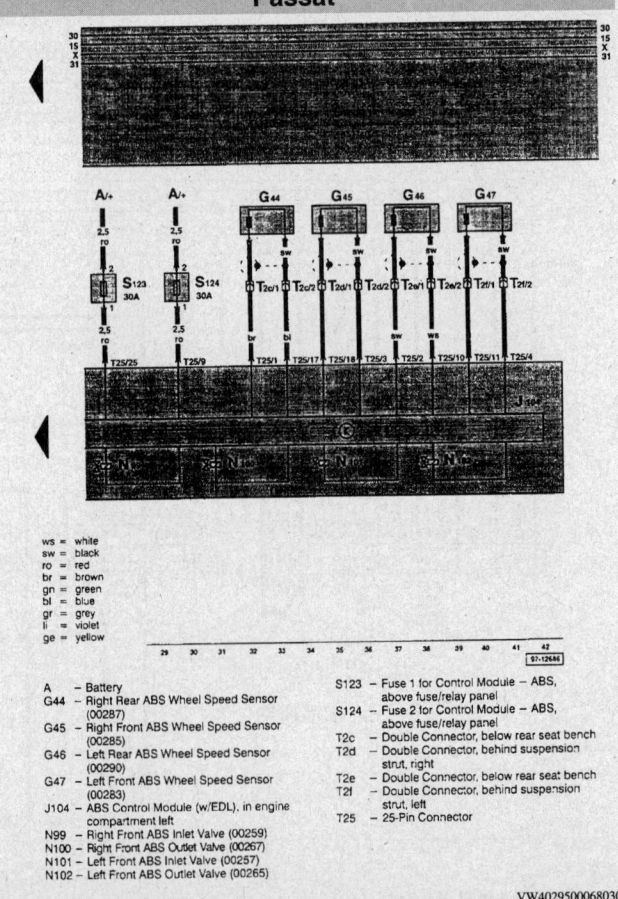

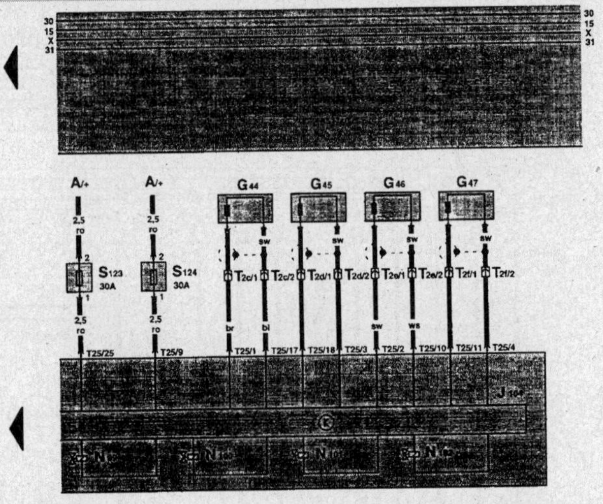

ws = white
sw = black
ro = red
br = brown
gn = green
bl = blue
gr = grey
li = violet
ge = yellow

A – Battery
G44 – Right Rear ABS Wheel Speed Sensor (00287)
G45 – Right Front ABS Wheel Speed Sensor (00285)
G46 – Left Rear ABS Wheel Speed Sensor (00290)
G47 – Left Front ABS Wheel Speed Sensor (00283)
J104 – ABS Control Module (w/EDL), in engine compartment left
N99 – Right Front ABS Inlet Valve (00259)
N100 – Right Front ABS Outlet Valve (00267)
N101 – Left Front ABS Inlet Valve (00257)
N102 – Left Front ABS Outlet Valve (00265)
S123 – Fuse 1 for Control Module – ABS, above fuse/relay panel
S124 – Fuse 2 for Control Module – ABS, above fuse/relay panel
T2c – Double Connector, below rear seat bench
T2d – Double Connector, behind suspension strut, right
T2e – Double Connector, below rear seat bench
T2f – Double Connector, behind suspension strut, left
T25 – 25-Pin Connector

VW4029500068030X

Fig. 68 ABS wiring diagram (Part 3 of 3). 1995–95 Passat

Test Step	VAG 1598 Terminals	Component Tested	Test Requirements	Result Specifications	Additional Steps If Results Not Within Specs
1	2 - 1	ABS control unit, voltage supply	•Switch ignition ON	Battery voltage (approximate) Note: take reading on 20 V scale	•Check wire from terminal 1 to ground •Check wire from terminal 2 to terminal D-7 (relay board)
2	3 - 1	ABS relay, function	•Switch ignition ON •Remove fuse S16 •Bridge sockets 2 and 8 on VAG 1598 After testing: •Disconnect connections from terminals 2 and 8 •Install fuse S16	Battery voltage (approximate)	•Check fuse S54 •Check wire from terminal 1 to ground •Check wire from terminal 3, via ABS relay, to battery positive •Perform test step 9 •Perform test step 24
3	12 – 1	Brake light switch, function	•Switch ignition ON •Actuate brake pedal	Battery voltage (approximate)	•Check fuse S20 and brake light switch •Check wire from terminal 1 to ground •Check wire from terminal 2 to terminal W-4 (relay board)
4	32 - 1	ABS relay for hydraulic pump, function	•Fuse S53 OK •Switch ignition OFF •Pull plug terminal T2 from hydraulic pump •Press brake pedal to floor 20 times •Switch ignition ON After testing, reconnect plug terminal T2	Battery voltage (approximate)	•Check wire from terminal 1 to ground •Check wire from terminal 32, via hydraulic pump and fuse S53, to battery positive •Perform test step 12 •Perform test step 32
5	4 - 22	Wheel speed sensor, right rear, voltage	•Switch ignition OFF •Raise and support vehicle •Rotate right rear wheel, approximately 1 rotation per second	75 mV ac (minimum) Note: take reading on 2 V scale	•Check installation of sensor •Check plug-type terminal T2 •Perform test step 16 •Perform test step 20
6	6 - 24	Wheel speed sensor, left rear, voltage	•Switch ignition OFF •Raise and support vehicle •Rotate left rear wheel, approximately 1 rotation per second	75 mV ac (minimum)	•Check installation of sensor •Check plug-type terminal T2 •Perform test step 17 •Perform test step 21

VW4029100007010X

Fig. 69 ABS electrical testing chart (Part 1 of 5). Corrado & 1993–94 Passat

Test Step	VAG 1598 Terminals	Component Tested	Test Requirements	Result Specifications	Additional Steps If Results Not Within Specs
7	7 + 25	Wheel speed sensor, right front, voltage	•Switch ignition OFF •Raise and support vehicle •Rotate right front wheel, approximately 1 rotation per second	75 mV ac (minimum)	•Check installation of sensor •Check plug-type terminal T2 •Perform test step 18 •Perform test step 22
8	5 + 23	Wheel speed sensor, left front, voltage	•Switch ignition OFF •Raise and support vehicle •Rotate left front wheel, approximately 1 rotation per second	75 mV ac (minimum)	•Check installation of sensor •Check plug-type terminal T2 •Perform test step 19 •Perform test step 23
9	1 - 3	ABS relay continuity	•Switch ignition OFF	1.5 Ohms (maxi- mum) Note: take reading on 200 Ohm scale	•Check circuit from terminal 3, via ABS relay, to hydraulic unit ground •Check wire from terminal 1 to ground •If no open circuits exist, Replace ABS relay
10	1 - 20	ABS relay continuity	•Switch ignition OFF	1.5 Ohms (maxi- mum)	•Check circuit from terminal 20, via ABS relay, to hydraulic unit ground •Check wire from terminal 1 to ground •If no open circuits exist, Replace ABS relay
11	1 + 11	Inlet valve, ground Outlet valve, ground	•Switch ignition OFF	1.5 Ohms (maxi- mum)	•Check circuit from terminal 11, via hydraulic unit, to ground •Check wire from terminal 1 to ground
12	1 - 14	Hydraulic pump relay, ground via high pressure switch	•Switch ignition ON •Wait until pump stops running •Switch ignition OFF •Press brake pedal to floor, 20 times	1.5 Ohms (maxi- mum)	•Check circuit from terminal 14, to hydraulic pump, and via high pressure switch, to ground •Check wire from terminal 1 to ground •Check continuity on high pressure switch
13	9 - 10	Low pressure warning switch, continuity Brake fluid level warning contact, continuity	•Check for correct brake fluid level •Switch ignition ON •Wait until pump switches OFF (reservoir filled)	1.5 Ohms (maxi- mum)	•Check circuit from terminal 9, via brake fluid level warning contact and low pressure warning switch, to terminal 10 •Perform test step 14 •Perform test step 15
14	9 + 10	Low pressure warning switch, function	•Check for correct brake fluid level •Switch ignition OFF •Press brake pedal to floor, 20 times (reservoir emptied)	100 K Ohms (minimum) Note: take reading on 200 K Ohm scale	•Check if low pressure warning switch has continuity between terminals 3 and 5, of hydraulic unit's 5-pin terminal. If YES, low pressure warning switch is defective. Replace •Perform test step 15

VW4029100007020X

Fig. 69 ABS electrical testing chart (Part 2 of 5). Corrado & 1993–94 Passat

Test Step	VAG 1598 Terminals	Component Tested	Test Requirements	Result Specifications	Additional Steps If Results Not Within Specs
15	9 + 10	Brake fluid level warning contact	•Switch ignition ON •Wait until pump switches OFF (reservoir filled) •Switch ignition OFF •Remove warning contact from reservoir	100 K Ohms (minimum), when warning contact float has been removed from fluid (simulating level below minimum)	•Check brake fluid level warning contact, when removed, for continuity. If YES, brake fluid level warning contact is defective. Replace.
16	4 - 22	Wheel speed sensor, right rear, resistance	•Switch ignition OFF	0.8–1.4 K Ohms Note: take reading on 2 K Ohm scale	•Check plug connector T2 •Check speed sensor resistance (0.8–1.4 K Ohms) •Check wire to wheel speed sensor •Perform test step 20
17	6 + 24	Wheel speed sensor, left rear, resistance	•Switch igniti on OFF	0.8–1.4 K Ohms	•Check plug connector T2 •Check speed sensor resistance (0.8–1.4 K Ohms) •Check wire to wheel speed sensor •Perform test step 21
18	7 + 25	Wheel speed sensor, right front, resistance	•Switch ignition OFF	0.8–1.4 K Ohms	•Check plug connector T2 •Check speed sensor resistance (0.8–1.4 K Ohms) •Check wire to wheel speed sensor •Perform test step 22
19	5 + 23	Wheel speed sensor, left front, resistance	•Switch ignition OFF	0.8–1.4 K Ohms	•Check plug connector T2 •Check speed sensor resistance (0.8–1.4 K Ohms) •Check wire to wheel speed sensor •Perform test step 23
20	1 - 4	Shielded wire to right rear wheel speed sensor, insulator resistance	•Switch ignition OFF	20 K Ohms (minimum) Note: take reading on 200 K Ohm scale	•Check wire for damaged insulation
21	1 + 6	Shielded wire to left rear wheel speed sensor, insulator resistance	•Switch ignition OFF	20 K Ohms (minimum)	•Check wire for damaged insulation
22	1 + 7	Shielded wire to right front wheel speed sensor, insulator resistance	•Switch ignition OFF	20 K Ohms (minimum)	•Check wire for damaged insulation

VW4029100007030X

Fig. 69 ABS electrical testing chart (Part 3 of 5). Corrado & 1993–94 Passat

Test Step	VAG 1598 Terminals	Component Tested	Test Requirements	Result Specifications	Additional Steps If Results Not Within Specs
23	1 + 5	Shielded wire to left front wheel speed sensor, insulator resistance	•Switch ignition OFF	20 K Ohms (minimum)	•Check wire for damaged insulation
24	1 + 8	ABS relay, resistance	•Switch ignition OFF	50-100 Ohms Note: take reading on 200 Ohm scale	•Check wire from terminal 8, via ABS relay, to ground •Check coil resistance (50-100 Ohms). Replace ABS relay, if necessary
25	1 + 18	ABS main valve, resistance	•Switch ignition OFF	2-5 Ohms	•Check wire from terminal 18, via ABS main valve, to ground •Check ABS main valve coil resistance (2-5 Ohms). If defective, replace hydraulic unit *Perform test step 33
26	11 + 17	Inlet valve, rear, resistance	•Switch ignition OFF	5-7 Ohms	•Check wire from terminal 17, via inlet valve, rear, to ground •Test inlet valve, rear, resistance (5-7 Ohms). If defective, replace hydraulic unit
27	11 + 15	Inlet valve, right front, resistance	•Switch ignition OFF	5-7 Ohms	•Check wire from terminal 15, via inlet valve, right front, to ground •Check inlet valve, right front, resistance (5-7 Ohms). If defective, replace hydraulic unit
28	11 + 35	Inlet valve, left front, resistance	•Switch ignition OFF	5-7 Ohms	•Check wire from terminal 35, via inlet valve, left front, to ground •Check inlet valve, left front, resistance (5-7 Ohms). If defective, replace hydraulic unit
29	11 + 33	Outlet valve, rear, resistance	•Switch ignition OFF	3-5 Ohms	•Check wire from terminal 33, via outlet valve, rear, to ground •Check outlet valve, rear, resistance (3-5 Ohms). If defective, replace hydraulic unit
30	11 + 34	Outlet valve, right front, resistance	•Switch ignition OFF	3-5 Ohms	•Check wire from terminal 34, via outlet valve, right front, to ground •Check outlet valve, right front, resistance (3-5 Ohms). If defective, replace hydraulic unit
31	11 + 16	Outlet valve, left front, resistance	•Switch ignition OFF	3-5 Ohms	•Check wire from terminal 16, via outlet valve, left front, to ground •Check outlet valve, left front, resistance (3-5 Ohms). If defective, replace hydraulic unit
32	2 + 14	ABS hydraulic pump relay, resistance	•Switch ignition OFF •Remove fuse S6	50-100 Ohms	•Check wire from terminal 2, via ABS hydraulic pump relay, to contact 14 •Check coil resistance (50-100 Ohms). Replace ABS hydraulic pump relay, if necessary

VW4029100007040X

Fig. 69 ABS electrical testing chart (Part 4 of 5). Corrado & 1993–94 Passat

Test Step	VAG 1598 Terminals	Component Tested	Test Requirements	Result Specifications	Additional Steps If Results Not Within Specs
33	Bridge 2-18	ABS main valve, function	•Switch ignition OFF •Press brake pedal to floor and hold •Switch ignition ON	Pulsation from brake pedal should be felt at foot	For defective ABS main valve: •replace hydraulic unit
34	—	ABS hydraulic pump, function	•Switch ignition OFF •Pump brake pedal 20 times to discharge reservoir •Mark filud level on reservoir •Switch ignition ON	Fluid level in reservoir drops approximately 0.6 inch	•Check wire from battery positive, via fuse S53 and ABS hydraulic pump relay and ABS hydraulic pump, back to battery. If no opens exist, replace ABS hydraulic pump
35	Bridge 2-17-33	Inlet and outlet valve, rear, function	•Raise and support vehicle •Switch ignition OFF •Depress brake pedal	Rear wheels must lock	•Replace defective hydraulic unit
			•Switch ignition ON •Depress brake pedal	Rear wheels must rotate freely	
36	Bridge 2-15-34	Inlet and outlet valve, right front, function	•Raise and support vehicle •Switch ignition OFF •Depress brake pedal	Right front wheel must lock	•Replace defective hydraulic unit
			•Switch ignition ON •Depress brake pedal	Right front wheel must rotate freely	
37	Bridge 2-16-35	Inlet and outlet valve, left front, function	•Raise and support vehicle •Switch ignition OFF •Depress brake pedal	Left front wheel must lock	•Replace defective hydraulic unit
			•Switch ignition ON •Depress brake pedal	Left front wheel must rotate freely	

VW4029100007050X

Fig. 69 ABS electrical testing chart (Part 5 of 5). Corrado & 1993–94 Passat

Switch to voltage measuring range — 20 V					
Test step	**VAG 1598 sockets**	**Test of**	**• Test conditions – Additional operations**	**Specified value**	**Repairing malfunction**
1 EDL	35 + 1	Voltage supply (terminal 30) at ABS control module -J104-	• Ignition switched off	10.0 – 14.5 V	– Check wire from terminal 1 to Ground (GND) point – Check wire from terminal 35 via ABS valves fuse -S54- to battery pos. (B+)
2	53 + 1	Voltage supply (terminal 15) at ABS control module -J104-	• Ignition switched off	10.0 – 14.5 V	– Check wire from terminal 1 to Ground (GND) point – Check wire from terminal 53 to terminal D/7 (relay panel)

VW4029300070010X

Fig. 70 ABS electrical testing chart (Part 1 of 26). Teves type 04 ABS

Switch to voltage measuring range — 20 V					
Test step	**VAG 1598 sockets**	**Test of**	**• Test conditions – Additional operations**	**Specified value**	**Repairing malfunction**
3	33 + 1	• Function of ABS relay -J102- • Voltage supply at ABS control module -J104-	• Ignition switched off – Bridge sockets 19 and 34 on VAG 1598 – Switch ignition on: ABS relay -J102- operates – Remove bridge after check	10.0 – 14.5 V ABS warning light -K47- goes out	– Check wire from terminal 1 to Ground (GND) point – Check wire from terminal 33 via -J102- and -S54- to battery positive (B+) If ABS relay -J102- does not operate, check activation: – Check wire from terminal 34 to -J102- terminal 4 and -J102-

VW4029300070020X

Fig. 70 ABS electrical testing chart (Part 2 of 26). Teves type 04 ABS

Switch to voltage measuring range — 20 V					
Test step	**VAG 1598 sockets**	**Test of**	**• Test conditions – Additional operations**	**Specified value**	**Repairing malfunction**
4	3 + 1	Function of ABS relay -J102- (Reference voltage)	• Ignition switched off – Bridge sockets 19 and 34 on VAG 1598 – Switch ignition on: ABS relay -J102- operates – Remove bridge after the check	10.0 – 14.5 V ABS warning light -K47- goes out	– Check wire from terminal 3 via -J102- and -S54- to battery positive (B+) If -J102- does not operate, check activation: – Check wire from terminal 34 to -J102- terminal 4 and ABS relay -J102-
5	32 + 1	Function of brake light switch -F-	• Ignition switched off – Depress and hold brake pedal	After operating the brake light switch: 10.0 – 14.5V	– Check fuse and brake light switch -F- – Check wire from terminal 1 to Ground (GND) point – Check wire from terminal 32 to terminal W/4 (relay panel)

VW4029300070030X

Fig. 70 ABS electrical testing chart (Part 3 of 26). Teves type 04 ABS

Switch to resistance measuring range — 2 kΩ					
Test step	**VAG 1598 sockets**	**Test of**	**• Test conditions – Additional operations**	**Specified value**	**Repairing malfunction**
6	47 + 29	Resistance of right front ABS wheel speed sensor -G45-	• Ignition switched off	1.0 – 1.3 kΩ	– Check connector T2 – Check resistance of speed sensor (1.0 – 1.2 kΩ) – Check wire to speed sensor, move wire while checking (loose connection)
7	48 + 30	Resistance of left front ABS wheel speed sensor -G47-	• Ignition switched off	1.0 – 1.3 kΩ	– Check connector T2 – Check resistance of speed sensor (1.0 – 1.2 kΩ) – Check wire to speed sensor, move wire while checking (loose connection)

VW4029300070040X

Fig. 70 ABS electrical testing chart (Part 4 of 26). Teves type 04 ABS

Switch to resistance measuring range — 2 kΩ					
Test step	**VAG 1598 sockets**	**Test of**	**• Test conditions – Additional operations**	**Specified value**	**Repairing malfunction**
8	45 + 27	Resistance of right rear ABS wheel speed sensor -G44-	• Ignition switched off	1.0 – 1.3 kΩ	– Check connector T2 – Check resistance of speed sensor (1.0 – 1.2 kΩ) – Check wire to speed sensor, move wire while checking (loose connection)
9	46 + 28	Resistance of left rear ABS wheel speed sensor -G46-	• Ignition switched off	1.0 – 1.3 kΩ	– Check connector T2 – Check resistance of speed sensor (1.0 – 1.2 kΩ) – Check wire to speed sensor, move wire while checking (loose connection)

VW4029300070050X

Fig. 70 ABS electrical testing chart (Part 5 of 26). Teves type 04 ABS

Switch to resistance measuring range — 2 MΩ					
Test step	**VAG 1598 sockets**	**Test of**	**• Test conditions – Additional operations**	**Specified value**	**Repairing malfunction**
10	1 + 29	Insulation resistance of shielding for right front ABS wheel speed sensor -G45-	• Ignition switched off	Min. 2 MΩ 2)	– Check shielding for damage (chafing), move wire while checking (loose connection)
11	1 + 30	Insulation resistance of shielding for left front ABS wheel speed sensor -G47-	• Ignition switched off	Min. 2 MΩ 2)	– Check shielding for damage (chafing), move wire while checking (loose connection)

2) Multimeter (Fluke 83 or equivalent) indicating "1" signifies infinite resistance and is OK.

VW4029300070060X

Fig. 70 ABS electrical testing chart (Part 6 of 26). Teves type 04 ABS

Switch to resistance measuring range — 2 MΩ					
Test step	**VAG 1598 sockets**	**Test of**	**• Test conditions – Additional operations**	**Specified value**	**Repairing malfunction**
12	1 + 27	Insulation resistance of shielding for right rear ABS wheel speed sensor -G44-	• Ignition switched off	Min. 2 MΩ 2)	– Check shielding for damage (chafing), move wire while checking (loose connection)
13	1 + 28	Insulation resistance of shielding for left rear ABS wheel speed sensor -G46-	• Ignition switched off	Min. 2 MΩ 2)	– Check shielding for damage (chafing), move wire while checking (loose connection)

2) If multimeter (Fluke 83 or equivalent) indicates "1", this signifies infinite resistance and is OK.

VW4029300070070X

Fig. 70 ABS electrical testing chart (Part 7 of 26). Teves type 04 ABS

Switch to resistance measuring range — 200 Ω					
Test step	**VAG 1598 sockets**	**Test of**	**• Test conditions – Additional operations**	**Specified value**	**Repairing malfunction**
14	53 + 34	Winding resistance of ABS relay -J102-	• Ignition switched off	50 – 100 Ω	– Check wire from terminal 53 without -J102- to terminal 34 – Check -J102- winding resistance (50 – 100 Ω), replace if necessary
15	15 + 33	Winding resistance of ABS hydraulic pump relay -J185-	• Ignition switched off	50 – 100 Ω	– Check wire from terminal 33 without -J185- to terminal 15 – Check -J185- winding resistance (50 – 100 Ω), replace if necessary
16 EDL	7 + 33	Winding resistance of EDL relay -J310-	• Ignition switched off	50 – 100 Ω	– Check wire from terminal 33 without -J185- to terminal 7 – Check -J310- winding resistance (50 – 100 Ω), replace if necessary

VW4029300070080X

Fig. 70 ABS electrical testing chart (Part 8 of 26). Teves type 04 ABS

Switch to resistance measuring range — 200 Ω					
Test step	**VAG 1598 sockets**	**Test of**	**• Test conditions – Additional operations**	**Specified value**	**Repairing malfunction**
17	20 + 3	Resistance of left front ABS inlet valve -N101-	• Ignition switched off	6.5 – 10 Ω	– Check wire from terminal 20 without -N101- to terminal 3 – Check resistance of -N101- (6.5 – 8 Ω), if necessary replace ABS hydraulic unit
18	38 + 3	Resistance of right front ABS inlet valve -N99-	• Ignition switched off	6.5 – 10 Ω	– Check wire from terminal 38 without -N99- to terminal 3 – Check resistance of -N99- (6.5 – 8 Ω), if necessary replace ABS hydraulic unit

VW4029300070090X

Fig. 70 ABS electrical testing chart (Part 9 of 26). Teves type 04 ABS

Switch to resistance measuring range — 200 Ω					
Test step	**VAG 1598 sockets**	**Test of**	**• Test conditions – Additional operations**	**Specified value**	**Repairing malfunction**
19	54 + 3	Resistance of left rear ABS inlet valve -N134-	• Ignition switched off	6.5 – 10 Ω	– Check wire from terminal 54 without -N134- to terminal 3 – Check resistance of -N134- (6.5 – 8 Ω), if necessary replace ABS hydraulic unit
20	55 + 3	Resistance of right rear ABS inlet valve -N133-	• Ignition switched off	6.5 – 10 Ω	– Check wire from terminal 55 without -N133- to terminal 3 – Check resistance of -N133- (6.5 – 8 Ω), if necessary replace ABS hydraulic unit

VW4029300070100X

Fig. 70 ABS electrical testing chart (Part 10 of 26). Teves type 04 ABS

Switch to resistance measuring range — 200 Ω					
Test step	**VAG 1598 sockets**	**Test of**	**• Test conditions – Additional operations**	**Specified value**	**Repairing malfunction**
21	2 + 3	Resistance of left front ABS outlet valve -N102-	• Ignition switched off	3 – 7 Ω	– Check wire from terminal 2 without -N102- to terminal 3 – Check resistance of -N102- (3 – 5 Ω), if necessary replace ABS hydraulic unit
22	21 + 3	Resistance of right front ABS outlet valve -N100-	• Ignition switched off	3 – 7 Ω	– Check wire from terminal 21 without -N100- to terminal 3 – Check resistance of -N100- (3 – 5 Ω), if necessary replace ABS hydraulic unit

VW4029300070110X

Fig. 70 ABS electrical testing chart (Part 11 of 26). Teves type 04 ABS

Switch to resistance measuring range — 200 Ω					
Test step	**VAG 1598 sockets**	**Test of**	**• Test conditions – Additional operations**	**Specified value**	**Repairing malfunction**
23	36 + 3	Resistance of left rear ABS outlet valve -N136-	• Ignition switched off	3 – 7 Ω	– Check wire from terminal 36 without -N136- to terminal 3 – Check resistance of -N136- (3 – 5 Ω), if necessary replace ABS hydraulic unit
24	18 + 3	Resistance of right rear ABS outlet valve -N135-	• Ignition switched off	3 – 7 Ω	– Check wire from terminal 18 without -N135- to terminal 3 – Check resistance of -N135- (3 – 5 Ω), if necessary replace ABS hydraulic unit

VW4029300070120X

Fig. 70 ABS electrical testing chart (Part 12 of 26). Teves type 04 ABS

Switch to resistance measuring range — 200 Ω					
Test step	VAG 1598 sockets	Test of	• Test conditions – Additional operations	Specified value	Repairing malfunction
25 EDL	37 + 3	Resistance of differential lock valve 1 -N125-	• Ignition switched off	6 – 10 Ω	– Check wire from terminal 37 without -N125- to terminal 3 – Check resistance of -N125- (6 – 8 Ω), if necessary replace ABS hydraulic unit
26 EDL	40 + 3	Resistance of differential lock valve 2 -N126-	• Ignition switched off	6 – 10 Ω	– Check wire from terminal 40 without -N126- to terminal 3 – Check resistance of -N126- (6 – 8 Ω), if necessary replace ABS hydraulic unit

VW4029300070130X

Fig. 70 ABS electrical testing chart (Part 13 of 26). Teves type 04 ABS

Switch to resistance measuring range — 200 Ω					
Test step	VAG 1598 sockets	Test of	• Test conditions – Additional operations	Specified value	Repairing malfunction
27	31 + 49	Resistance of hydraulic pump sensor -G101-	• Ignition switched off	29 – 40 Ω	– Check wire from terminal 49 without -G101- to terminal 31 – Check resistance of -G101- (29 – 40 Ω), if necessary replace ABS hydraulic unit

VW4029300070140X

Fig. 70 ABS electrical testing chart (Part 14 of 26). Teves type 04 ABS

Switch to resistance measuring range — 200 Ω					
Test step	VAG 1598 sockets	Test of	• Test conditions – Additional operations	Specified value	Repairing malfunction
28	16 + 41	Resistance of brake pedal position sensor -G100-	• Ignition switched off		– Check wire from terminal 16 without -G100- to terminal 41
			-G100- has variable resistance. The following resistance values are specified, depending on pedal position as the pedal is depressed from rest:		– Check resistance of -G100- (with adapter cable VW 1594/23), if faulty, replace brake pedal position sensor
			–Stage 1 (Rest position)	230 – 270 Ω	
			–Stage 2	410 – 460 Ω	
			–Stage 3	540 – 600 Ω	
			–Stage 4	650 – 730 Ω	
			–Stage 5	770 – 860 Ω	
			–Stage 6	980 –1100 Ω	
			–Stage 7	2)	

2) Stage 7 is only achieved if a malfunction exists (pressure loss); Specification: min. 2MΩ.

VW4029300070150X

Fig. 70 ABS electrical testing chart (Part 15 of 26). Teves type 04 ABS

Switch to resistance measuring range — 200 Ω (Note change to 2 MΩ range during test step 29)					
Test step	VAG 1598 sockets	Test of	• Test conditions – Additional operations	Specified value	Repairing malfunction
29 EDL	13 + 26	Function of ABS pressure control switch -F137-3)	• Ignition switched off		– Check wire from terminal 13 without -F137- to terminal 26
			• Brake pedal not depressed – Select (2 MΩ) measuring range on multimeter (Fluke 83 or equivalent)	Min. 1.5 Ω	– If resistance is not attained, replace ABS hydraulic unit
			– Depress brake pedal fully and hold	Min. 2 M Ω	
30	1 + 3 1 + 33	Resistance of ABS relay -J102-	• Ignition switched off	Max. 1.5 Ω	– Check wire from terminal 3 and terminal 33 without -J102- to Ground (GND)
	1 + 19	Resistance of Ground (GND) connections			– Check wire from terminal 1 and terminal 19 via Ground connections2) to battery – (GND)

VW4029300070160X

Fig. 70 ABS electrical testing chart (Part 16 of 26). Teves type 04 ABS

Switch to voltage measuring range — 2 V					
Test step	VAG 1598 sockets	Test of	• Test conditions – Additional operations	Specified value	Repairing malfunction
31	45 + 27	Right rear ABS wheel speed sensor -G44- voltage signal	• Vehicle raised • Ignition switched off		– Check connector T2, installation of speed sensor and impulse wheel
			– Rotate rear right wheel at approx. 1 rev./sec.	Min. 65 mV alternating voltage	– Check whether speed sensor has been interchanged
32	46 + 28	Left rear ABS wheel speed sensor -G46- voltage signal	• Vehicle raised • Ignition switched off		– Check connector T2, installation of speed sensor and impulse wheel
			– Rotate rear left wheel at approx. 1 rev./sec.	Min. 65 mV alternating voltage	– Check whether speed sensor has been interchanged

VW4029300070170X

Fig. 70 ABS electrical testing chart (Part 17 of 26). Teves type 04 ABS

Switch to voltage measuring range — 2 V					
Test step	VAG 1598 sockets	Test of	• Test conditions – Additional operations	Specified value	Repairing malfunction
33	47 + 29	Right front ABS wheel speed sensor -G45- voltage signal	• Vehicle raised • Ignition switched off		– Check connector T2, installation of speed sensor and impulse wheel
			– Rotate front right wheel at approx. 1 rev./sec.	Min. 65 mV alternating voltage	– Check whether speed sensor has been interchanged
34	48 + 30	Left front ABS wheel speed sensor -G47- voltage signal	• Vehicle raised • Ignition switched off		– Check connector T2, installation of speed sensor and impulse wheel
			– Rotate front left wheel at approx. 1 rev./sec.	Min. 65 mV alternating voltage	– Check whether speed sensor has been interchanged

VW4029300070180X

Fig. 70 ABS electrical testing chart (Part 18 of 26). Teves type 04 ABS

Functional check: ABS hydraulic pump -V64- *CAUTION!: On no account must the brake pedal be depressed during this check!*					
Test step	VAG 1598 sockets	Test of	• Test conditions – Additional operations	Specified value	Repairing malfunction
35	Bridge: 19 = 34 19 = 15	Function of ABS hydraulic pump -V64-	• Ignition switched off	After switching ignition on:	– Check wire from battery positive (B+) via ABS hydraulic pump fuse -S53-, -J185- and -V64- to battery – (GND)
			– Switch ignition on for max. 30 sec. – Remove bridge after test	ABS hydraulic pump -V64- must run audibly	– If no open circuit, replace ABS hydraulic unit
36 EDL	Bridge: 19 = 34 19 = 7	EDL function of ABS hydraulic pump -V64-	• Ignition switched off	After switching ignition on:	– Check wire from battery positive (B+) via ABS hydraulic pump fuse -S53-, -J310-, -N159- and -V64- to battery – (GND)
			– Switch ignition on for max. 30 sec. – Remove bridge after test	ABS hydraulic pump -V64- must run audibly	– If no open circuit, replace ABS hydraulic unit

VW4029300070190X

Fig. 70 ABS electrical testing chart (Part 19 of 26). Teves type 04 ABS

Functional check: Left front ABS inlet and outlet valves -N101-/-N102-					
Test step	VAG 1598 sockets	Test of	• Test conditions – Additional operations	Specified value	Repairing malfunction
37	Bridge: 19 = 34 19 = 20 19 = 2	Function of left front ABS inlet and outlet valves (-N101-/-N102-)	• Vehicle raised • Ignition switched off		– Check that brake lines are correctly connected
			– Depress brake pedal and hold	Left front wheel locks	– ABS hydraulic unit faulty; replace
			– Switch ignition on for max. 30 sec. – Depress brake pedal and hold	Left front wheel must rotate freely; pedal must not give	
			– Remove bridge after check		

VW4029300070200X

Fig. 70 ABS electrical testing chart (Part 20 of 26). Teves type 04 ABS

Functional check: Right front ABS inlet and outlet valves -N99-/-N100-					
Test step	VAG 1598 sockets	Test of	• Test conditions – Additional operations	Specified value	Repairing malfunction
38	Bridge: 19 = 34 19 = 21 19 = 38	Function of right front ABS inlet and outlet valves (-N99-/-N100-)	• Vehicle raised • Ignition switched off		– Check that brake lines are correctly connected
			– Depress brake pedal and hold	Right front wheel locks	– ABS hydraulic unit faulty, replace
			– Switch ignition on for max. 30 sec.		
			– Depress brake pedal and hold	Right front wheel must rotate freely; pedal must not give	
			– Remove bridge after check		

VW4029300070210X

Fig. 70 ABS electrical testing chart (Part 21 of 26). Teves type 04 ABS

Functional check: Left rear ABS inlet and outlet valves -N134-/-N136-					
Test step	VAG 1598 sockets	Test of	• Test conditions – Additional operations	Specified value	Repairing malfunction
39	Bridge: 19 = 34 19 = 36 19 = 54	Function of left rear ABS inlet and outlet valves (-N134-/-N136-)	• Vehicle raised • Ignition switched off		– Check that brake lines are correctly connected
			– Depress brake pedal and hold	Left rear wheel locks	– ABS hydraulic unit faulty, replace
			– Switch ignition on for max. 30 sec.		
			– Depress brake pedal and hold	Left rear wheel must rotate freely; pedal must not give	
			– Remove bridge after check		

VW4029300070220X

Fig. 70 ABS electrical testing chart (Part 22 of 26). Teves type 04 ABS

Functional check: Right rear ABS inlet and outlet valves -N133-/-N135-					
Test step	VAG 1598 sockets	Test of	• Test conditions – Additional operations	Specified value	Repairing malfunction
40	Bridge: 19 = 55 19 = 34 19 = 18	Function of rear right ABS inlet and outlet valves (-N133-/-N135-)	• Vehicle raised • Ignition switched off		– Check that brake lines are correctly connected
			– Operate brake pedal and hold	Right rear wheel locks	– ABS hydraulic unit faulty, replace
			– Switch ignition on for max. 30 sec.		
			– Operate brake pedal and hold	Right rear wheel must rotate freely; pedal must not give	
			– Remove bridge after check		

VW4029300070230X

Fig. 70 ABS electrical testing chart (Part 23 of 26). Teves type 04 ABS

Functional check: Differential lock valves 1 + 2 -N125-/-N126-					
Test step	VAG 1598 sockets	Test of	• Test conditions – Additional operations	Specified value	Repairing malfunction
41	Bridge: 1 = 7 1 = 34 1 = 40 1 = 37	Functional check of differential lock valves 1, 2 (-N125-, -N126-)	• Vehicle raised		– ABS hydraulic unit faulty, replace
EDL			– Switch ignition on for max. 30 sec.	It must not be possible to turn front wheels	
			– Remove bridge after check		

VW4029300070240X

Fig. 70 ABS electrical testing chart (Part 24 of 26). Teves type 04 ABS

Switch to voltage measuring range 20 V in test step 42 Resistance measuring range (20 Ω) in test step 43					
Test step	VAG 1598 sockets	Test of	• Test conditions – Additional operations	Specified value	Repairing malfunction
42	–	Voltage supply for VAG 1551 scan tool, data link connector T16	– Connect multimeter (Fluke 83/equivalent) to T16 using adapter cables from VW 1594 connector test kit		– Check wire from T16/4 to Ground (GND) – Check wire from T16/16 via -S22- to terminal 30
			♦ Terminal 4: Ground ♦ Terminal 16: positive (B+)	10.0 – 14.5 V	
43	–	Resistance of K wire for OBD data link connector T16, terminal 7	• Ignition switched off		– Check wire from T2d to terminal 42
			– Connect multimeter (Fluke 83/equivalent) to VAG 1598 test box socket 42 and data link connector T16 terminal 7 using adapter cables from VW 1594 connector test kit	Max. 1.5 Ω	– Check wire from T16/7 via TV14 to terminal 42

VW4029300070250X

Fig. 70 ABS electrical testing chart (Part 25 of 26). Teves type 04 ABS

Functional check: ABS warning light -K47-					
Test step	VAG 1598 sockets	Test of	• Test conditions – Additional operations	Specified value	Repairing malfunction
44	–	Function of ABS warning light -K47-	• Ignition switched off		– Check wire from terminal W/2 (relay panel) via ABS relay -J102- (diode) to Ground (GND)
			– Switch ignition on	ABS warning light -K47- lights up	– Check wire from terminal X/8 (relay panel) via -K47- to terminal X/4 (relay panel), -K47- (12 V, 1,2 W) replace if necessary
			– Bridge VAG 1598 test box sockets 1 and 34 (-J102- operates)	ABS warning light -K47- goes out	– Check wire from terminal 52 to terminal W/2 (relay panel)
			– Bridge sockets 1 and 52 on VAG 1598	ABS warning light -K47- lights up	
			– Remove bridge after check		

VW4029300070260X

Fig. 70 ABS electrical testing chart (Part 26 of 26). Teves type 04 ABS

Switch to voltage measuring range — 20 V					
Test step	**VAG 1598/21 sockets**	**Test of**	**• Test conditions – Additional operations**	**Specified value**	**Repairing malfunction**
1	8 + 25	Voltage supply for ABS hydraulic pump motor (terminal 30) on ABS control module -J104-	• Ignition switched off	10.0 – 14.5 V	– Check wire from terminal 8 to Ground (GND) – Check wire from terminal 25 via fuse 1 for control module – ABS -S123- to battery positive (B+)
2	9 + 24	Voltage supply for the inlet and outlet solenoid valves (terminal 30) on ABS control module -J104-	• Ignition switched off	10.0 – 14.5 V	– Check wire from terminal 24 to Ground (GND) – Check wire from terminal 9 via fuse 2 for control module – ABS -S124- to battery positive (B+)

VW4029300071010X

Fig. 71 ABS electrical testing chart (Part 1 of 8). Teves type 20 ABS

Switch to voltage measuring range — 20 V					
Test step	**VAG 1598/21 sockets**	**Test of**	**• Test conditions – Additional operations**	**Specified value**	**Repairing malfunction**
3	8 + 23	Voltage supply (terminal X) on ABS control module -J104-	• Ignition switched on	10.0 – 14.5 V	– Check wire from terminal 8 to Ground (GND) – Check wire from terminal 23 to terminal D/3 (relay panel)
4	8 + 12	Function of brake light switch -F-	• Ignition switched off – Brake pedal not depressed – Depress brake pedal	0.0 – 0.5 V 10.0 – 14.5 V	– Check fuse -S20- and brake light switch -F-. – Check wire from terminal 8 to Ground (GND) – Check wire from terminal 12 to terminal W/4 (relay panel)

VW4029300071020X

Fig. 71 ABS electrical testing chart (Part 2 of 8). Teves type 20 ABS

Switch to resistance measuring range — 2 kΩ					
Test step	**VAG 1598/21 sockets**	**Test of**	**• Test conditions – Additional operations**	**Specified value**	**Repairing malfunction**
5	3 + 18	Resistance of right front ABS wheel speed sensor -G45-	• Ignition switched off	1.0 – 1.3 kΩ	– Check connector T2d – Check resistance of ABS wheel speed sensor (1.0 – 1.3 kΩ) – Check wire to ABS wheel speed sensor, move wire while checking (loose connection)
6	4 + 11	Resistance of left front ABS wheel speed sensor -G47-	• Ignition switched off	1.0 – 1.3 kΩ	– Check connector T2f – Check resistance of ABS wheel speed sensor (1.0 – 1.3 kΩ) – Check wire to ABS wheel speed sensor, move wire while checking (loose connection)

VW4029300071030X

Fig. 71 ABS electrical testing chart (Part 3 of 8). Teves type 20 ABS

Switch to resistance measuring range — 2 kΩ					
Test step	**VAG 1598/21 sockets**	**Test of**	**• Test conditions – Additional operations**	**Specified value**	**Repairing malfunction**
7	1 + 17	Resistance of right rear ABS wheel speed sensor -G44-	• Ignition switched off	1.0 – 1.3 kΩ	– Check connector T2c – Check resistance of ABS wheel speed sensor (1.0 – 1.3 kΩ) – Check wire to ABS wheel speed sensor, move wire while checking (loose connection)
8	2 + 10	Resistance of left rear ABS wheel speed -G46-	• Ignition switched off	1.0 – 1.3 kΩ	– Check connector T2e – Check resistance of ABS wheel speed sensor (1.0 – 1.3 kΩ) – Check wire to ABS wheel speed sensor, move wire while checking (loose connection)

VW4029300071040X

Fig. 71 ABS electrical testing chart (Part 4 of 8). Teves type 20 ABS

Switch to voltage measuring range — 2 V					
Test step	**VAG 1598/21 sockets**	**Test of**	**• Test conditions – Additional operations**	**Specified value**	**Repairing malfunction**
9	3 + 18	Right front ABS wheel speed sensor -G45- voltage signal	• Vehicle raised • Ignition switched off – Rotate right rear wheel at approx. 1 rev./sec.	Min. 65 mV alternating voltage	– Check installation of ABS wheel speed sensor and impulse rotor – Check whether ABS wheel speed sensor has been interchanged Read measuring value block,
10	4 + 11	Left front ABS wheel speed sensor -G47- voltage signal	• Vehicle raised • Ignition switched off – Rotate left front wheel at approx. 1 rev./sec.	Min. 65 mV alternating voltage	– Check installation of ABS wheel speed sensor and impulse rotor – Check whether ABS wheel speed sensor has been interchanged ·Reading measured value

VW4029300071050X

Fig. 71 ABS electrical testing chart (Part 5 of 8). Teves type 20 ABS

Switch to voltage measuring range — 2 V, Resistance measurement — 200 Ω for test step 13					
Test step	**VAG 1598/21 sockets**	**Test of**	**• Test conditions – Additional operations**	**Specified value**	**Repairing malfunction**
11	1 + 17	Right rear ABS wheel speed sensor -G44- voltage signal	• Vehicle raised • Ignition switched off – Rotate right front wheel at approx. 1 rev./sec.	190 mV to 1140 mV	– Check installation of ABS wheel speed sensor and impulse rotor – Check whether ABS wheel speed sensor has been interchanged ⇒ Read measuring value block.
12	2 + 10	Left rear ABS wheel speed sensor -G46- voltage signal	• Vehicle raised • Ignition switched off – Rotate left front wheel at approx. 1 rev./sec.	190 mV to 1140 mV	– Check installation of ABS wheel speed sensor and impulse rotor – Check whether ABS wheel speed sensor has been interchanged ⇒ Read measuring value block,
13	15 + 21	Coding bridge	• Ignition switched off	0.0 –1.0 Ω	– Check wire and wiring connections in harness connector – Replace if value deviates from specifications

VW4029300071060X

Fig. 71 ABS electrical testing chart (Part 6 of 8). Teves type 20 ABS

Switch to voltage measuring range — 20 V for test step 14, Resistance measurement — 200 Ω for test step 15					
Test step	**VAG 1598/21 sockets**	**Test of**	**• Test conditions – Additional operations**	**Specified value**	**Repairing malfunction**
14	–	Voltage supply for VAG 1551 scan tool, data link connector T16	– Connect multimeter (Fluke 83/equivalent) to T16 (black) using adapter cables from VW 1594 connector test kit ♦ Terminal 4 : Ground ♦ Terminal 16 : positive (B+)	10.0 – 14.5 V	– Check wire from T16/4 to Ground (GND) – Check wire from T16/16 via -S22- to terminal 30
15	–	Resistance of K wire for On Board Diagnostic (OBD) data link connector T16	• Ignition switched off – Connect multimeter (Fluke 83/equivalent) to VAG 1598/21 test box socket 6 and data link connector T16, terminal 7. using adapter cables from VW 1594 connector test kit	Max. 1.5 Ω	– Check wire from TV14 to terminal 13 – Check wire from T16/7 via TV14 to terminal 13

VW4029300071070X

Fig. 71 ABS electrical testing chart (Part 7 of 8). Teves type 20 ABS

Functional check: ABS warning light -K47-					
Test step	**VAG 1598/21 sockets**	**Test of**	**• Test conditions – Additional operations**	**Specified value**	**Repairing malfunction**
16	–	Function of ABS warning light -K47-	• Ignition switched off – Switch ignition on	Warning light -K47- lights up	– Check wire from terminal W/2 (relay panel) to Ground (GND) – Check wire from terminal X/8 (relay panel) via -K47- to terminal X/3 (relay panel), -K47- (12 V; 1.2 W) replace if necessary – Check wire from terminal 16 to terminal W/2 (relay panel)
17	–	Function of warning light for brake system -K118-	• Ignition switched off – Switch ignition on	Warning light for brake system -K118- lights up	– Check wire from terminal U2/10 (replay plate) to Ground (GND) – Check wire from terminal U2/10 (relay panel) via -K47- to terminal W/2 – Check wire from terminal 16 to terminal W/2 (relay panel) – Check wire from terminal U2/10 to terminal 28/18 (instrument cluster connector)

VW4029300071080X

Fig. 71 ABS electrical testing chart (Part 8 of 8). Teves type 20 ABS

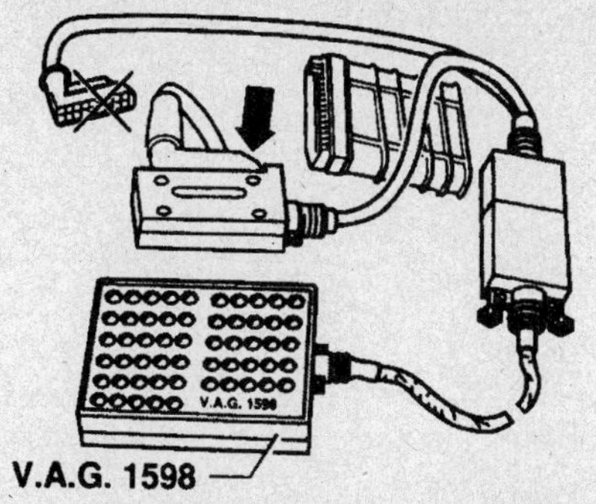
V.A.G. 1598
V.A.G. 1598

VW4029300069000X

Fig. 72 Pin out tester

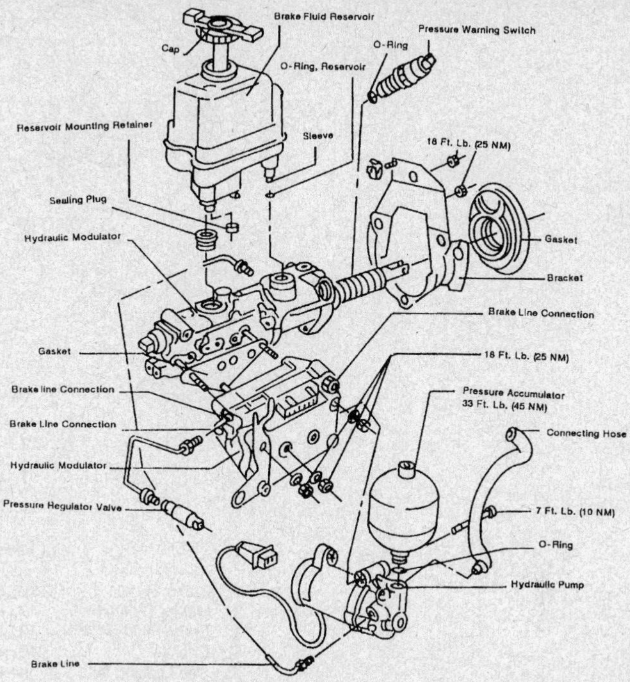
Brake Fluid Reservoir
Pressure Warning Switch
Cap
O-Ring
O-Ring, Reservoir
Reservoir Mounting Retainer
Sleeve
18 Ft. Lb. (25 NM)
Sealing Plug
Hydraulic Modulator
Gasket
Bracket
Brake Line Connection
Gasket
18 Ft. Lb. (25 NM)
Brake line Connection
Pressure Accumulator
33 Ft. Lb. (45 NM)
Brake Line Connection
Connecting Hose
Hydraulic Modulator
Pressure Regulator Valve
7 Ft. Lb. (10 NM)
O-Ring
Hydraulic Pump
Brake Line

VW4029100011000X

Fig. 73 Component view of hydraulic modulator assembly. 1993–94 Corrado & Passat

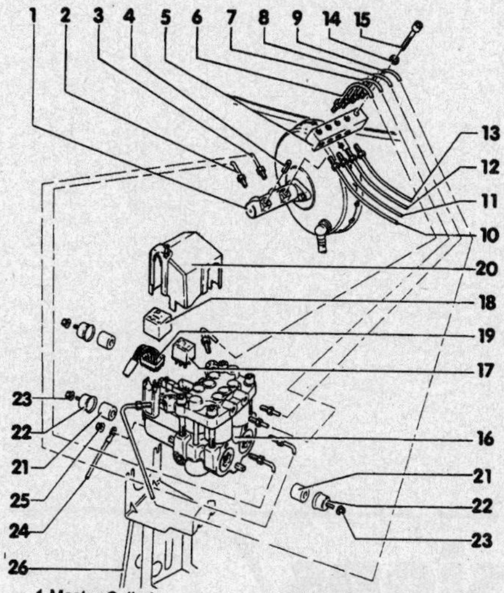
1 2 3 4 5 6 7 8 9 14 15
13
12
11
10
20
18
19
17
23
22
21
25
24
26
16
21
22
23

1. Master Cylinder
2. Brake Line
3. Brake Line
4. Spring Pin
5. Intermediate Piece
6. Brake Line VR
7. Brake Line HR
8. Brake Line HL
9. Brake Line VL
10. Brake Line RH Front
11. Brake Line RH Rear
12. Brake Line LH Rear
13. Brake Line LH Front
14. Washer
15. Bolt
16. Hydraulic Modulator
17. Solenoid Valve Relay
18. Return Pump Realy
19. Wiring Harness
20. Cover
21. Buffer
22. Bushing
23. Ground Wire
24. Nut
25. Console

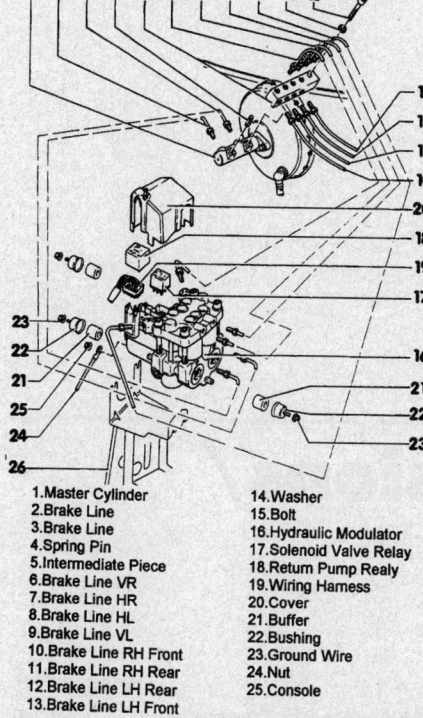

VW4029300078000X

Fig. 74 Component view of hydraulic modulator. Eurovan

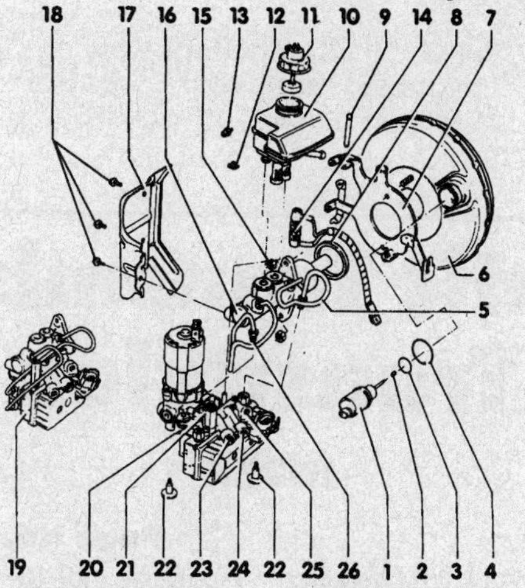
18 17 16 15 13 12 11 10 9 14 8 7
6
5
19 20 21 22 23 24 22 25 26 1 2 3 4

1. Pedal Position Sensor
2. Spacer Cap
3. O-ring
4. Cir-clip
5. Hydraulic Line
6. Brake Booster
7. Bracket
8. Seal
9. Pin
10. Reservoir
11. Cap
12. Clip
13. Screw
14. Diff. Lock Resistor (Optional)
15. Nut
16. Master Cylinder
17. Shield
18. Bolt
19. Hydraulic Modulator
20. Hydraulic Modulator w/Diff. Lock
21. Hydraulic Connection
22. Bolt□

VW4029300080000X

Fig. 75 Component view of hydraulic modulator. Teves type 04 ABS

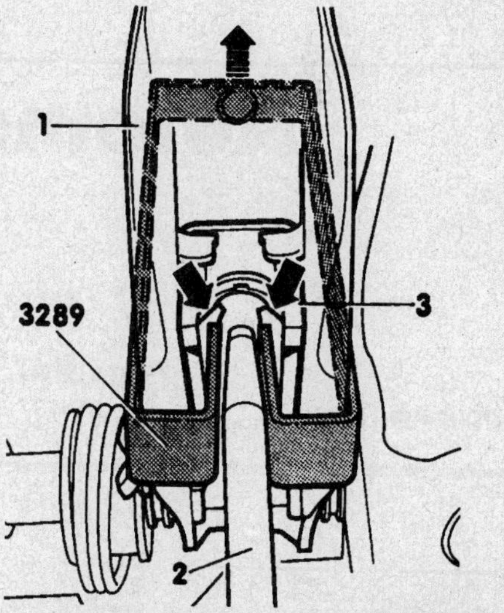
1
3289
3
2

VW4029300079000X

Fig. 76 Booster from brake pedal disconnecting. Cabrio, Golf III, GTI & Jetta III w/Teves type 04 ABS

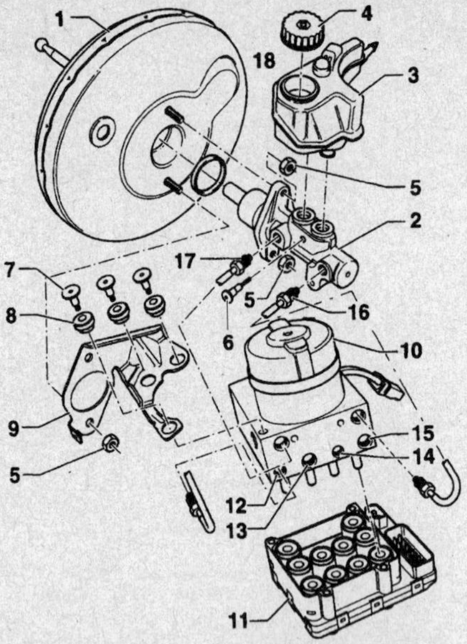
1
2
3
4
5
6
7
8
9
10
11
12
13
14
15
16
17
18
5
5

1. Brake Servo
2. Master Cylinder
3. Brake Fluid Reservoir
4. Cap
5. Self Locking Nut
6. Torx Bolt
7. Torx Bolt
8. Rubber Damper
9. Retainer
10. ABS Hydraulic Unit
11. ABS Control Module
12. Brake Line Connection
13. Brake Line Connection
14. Brake Line Connection
15. Brake Line Connection
16. Brake Line
17. Brake Line

VW4029300081000X

Fig. 77 Component view of hydraulic modulator & control unit. Teves type 20 ABS

Automatic Transmissions/ Transaxles

INDEX

Page No.	Page No.	Page No.
Application Chart 49-137	096 & 01M Automatic Transaxle..49-137	098 Automatic Transaxle.........49-142

Application Chart

Year	Model	Transmission
1993	Cabriolet	096
	Corrado	096
	Eurovan	098
	Golf III & Jetta III	096
	Passat	096 & 01M
1994	Cabriolet	096
	Corrado	096
	Golf III & Jetta III	096
	Passat	096 & 01M
1995	Cabrio	096
	Corrado	096
	Golf III & Jetta III	096 & 01M
	Passat	096 & 01M
1996	Cabrio	096
	Corrado	096
	Golf III, GTI & Jetta III	096 & 01M
	Passat	096 & 01M

096 & 01M Automatic Transaxles

INDEX

	Page No.
Adjustments	49-141
Ignition Lock Cable	49-141
Shift Lock Solenoid	49-141
Throttle Cable	49-141
Description	49-137
Identification	49-137
Maintenance	49-139
Final Drive Gear Oil Level Inspection	49-140
Fluid Check	49-140
Tightening Specifications	49-142
Transaxle, Replace	49-141
Corrado	49-141
Except Corrado	49-141
Troubleshooting	49-137
Main Pressure	49-139
Shift Points	49-137
Stall Speed	49-137

IDENTIFICATION

The model identification numbers are located on the lefthand side of transaxle. code letters are on the upper front part and type numbers are in the center.

Refer to **Figs. 1 and 2** to locate transaxle code No. (1) and transaxle model No. (2).

DESCRIPTION

The 096 and 01M transaxles are fully automatic, four speed automatic transaxles.

TROUBLESHOOTING

Refer to **Fig. 3** for troubleshooting procedures.

SHIFT POINTS

Locate transaxle code as described under "Identification," then refer to **Figs. 4 and 5** to locate shift point table that applies to vehicle being tested.

After locating the correct table, note that the capitol letter following the shift (M or H) indicates whether the shift is to be performed (M) manually or (H) hydraulically.

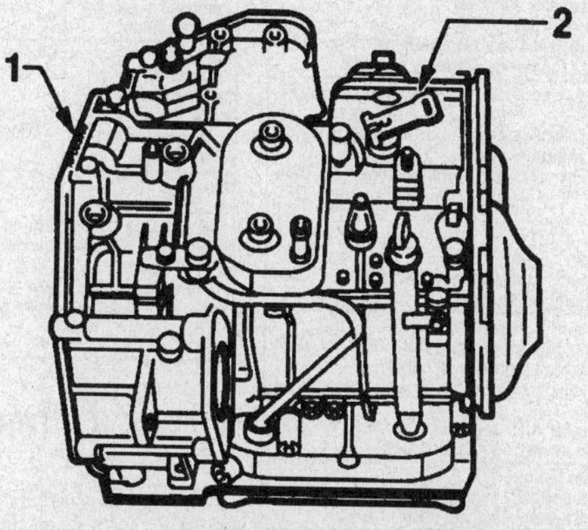
1
2

VW5029300005000X

Fig. 1 Code & model number locations. 096 transaxle

Tables for transaxles with shift program selection built into the control module, (control module senses how fast accelerator pedal is pushed down to choose between SPOrt or ECOnomy modes) show only kick down speeds.

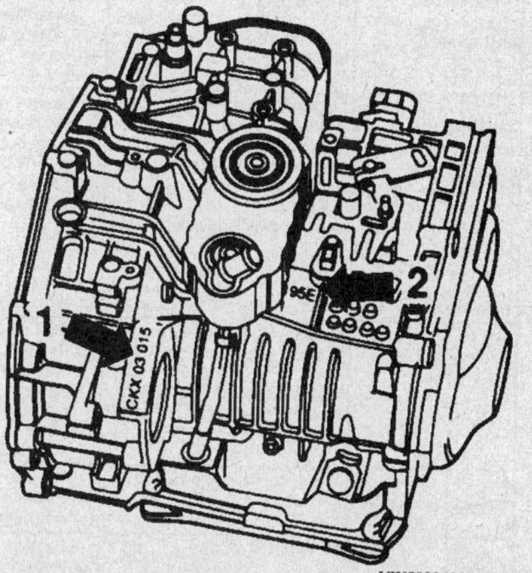
1
2

VW5029400006000X

Fig. 2 Code & model number locations. 01M transaxle

STALL SPEED

Locate transaxle code as described under "Identification," then refer to **Figs. 6**

Condition	Possible cause	Correction
No. 1 Drive disc (drive plate) cracked	Engine/transmission centralizing bushes missing	– Replace engine/transmission centering bushings and drive plate
No. 2 Transmission oily	Transmission leaking	– Clean engine/transmission and determine where engine or transmission is leaking, if necessary use leak detector. – Seal or replace faulty components on leaky transmissions – Replace sealing rings, seals, screw connections or transmission housing (torque converter housing) ⇒ Repair automatic transmission 096 or 098
	ATF overfilled	– Clean transmission, check ATF level, if necessary extract ⇒ Repair automatic transmission 096 or 098; checking ATF level and topping up
	Gear oil overfilled	– Clean transmission, check gear oil level, if necessary extract ⇒ Repair automatic transmission 096 or 098; checking gear oil in final drive
No. 3 ATF leak in area of torque converter	Drive disc (drive plate) clearance dimension not OK	– Adjust drive plate clearance dimension
	Torque converter bushing faulty	– Replace torque converter ⇒ Repair automatic transmission 096 or 098; torque converter identification
	Torque converter oil seal faulty	– Replace torque converter oil seal, if bearing surface or torque converter is damaged then additionally replace torque converter ⇒ Repair automatic transmission 096 or 098; removing and installing torque converter oil seal
	ATF pump leaking	– Disassemble ATF pump, replace faulty components and then reassemble ⇒ Repair automatic transmission 096 or 098; disassembling and assembling planetary gearbox
No. 4 ATF in coolant or coolant in ATF	ATF cooler faulty	– Replace ATF cooler and coolant and replace ATF – If too much coolant is in ATF then the planetary gearbox as well as the clutches must be disassembled, cleaned and reassembled ⇒ Repair automatic transmission 096 or 098; disassembling and assembling planetary gearbox
No. 5 ATF and gear oil mixed	ATF level or gear oil level too low, no visible leaks on transmission exterior	– Correct ATF and gear oil levels – Carry out a longer test drive and again check ATF and gear oil levels, if levels have changed replace drive pinion oil seal and bearing support ring O–ring ⇒ Repair automatic transmission 096 or 098; removing and installing drive pinion

VW5029500004010X

Fig. 3 Transaxle troubleshooting (Part 1 of 4)

Condition	Possible cause	Correction
No. 6 Gear selector mechanism difficult to operate	Gear selector mechanism difficult (exterior to transmission) Gear selector mechanism difficult (within transmission)	– Remove selector lever cable at lever/selector shaft – If selector mechanism is stiff up to transmission exterior, then service stiff selector mechanism ⇒ Repair automatic transmission 096 or 098; servicing selector mechanism – Selector mechanism stiff within the transmission, disassemble and assemble parking lock ⇒ Repair automatic transmission 096 or 098; disassembling and assembling parking lock
No. 7 Selector lever position: 1 Automatic transmission will not select: 1st Gear (no drive)	1st to 3rd Gear clutch –K1– or reverse Gear brake –B1– faulty	– Service 1st to 3rd gear clutch –K1– or reverse gear –B1– ⇒ Repair automatic transmission 096 or 098; disassembling and assembling planetary gearbox
No. 8 Selector lever position: D, 3 or 2 Automatic transmission will not select: 1st Gear (no drive)	1st to 3rd Gear clutch –K1– or freewheel faulty	– Service 1st to 3rd gear clutch –K1– or freewheel ⇒ Repair automatic transmission 096 or 098; disassembling and assembling planetary gearbox
No. 9 Selector lever position: D, 3 or 2 Automatic transmission will not select: 2nd Gear	2nd and 4th Gear brake –B2– faulty	– Service 2nd and 4th gear brake –B2– ⇒ automatic transmission 096 or 098; disassembling and assembling planetary gearbox
No. 10 Selector lever position: D or 3 Automatic transmission will not select: 3rd Gear	Reverse Gear clutch –K2– faulty	– Service reverse gear clutch –K2– ⇒ Repair automatic transmission 096 or 098; disassembling and assembling planetary gearbox
No. 11 Selector lever position: D Automatic transmission will not select: 4th Gear	4th Gear (3rd and 4th Gear [1]) Clutch –K3– or 2nd and 4th Gear brake –B2– faulty	– Service 4th gear (3rd and 4th gear [1]) clutch or 2nd and 4th gear brake –B2– ⇒ Repair automatic transmission 096 or 098; disassembling and assembling planetary gearbox
No. 12 Selector lever position: R Automatic transmission will not select: Reverse gear	Reverse gear clutch –K2– faulty Reverse gear brake –B1– faulty	– Service reverse gear clutch –K2– or reverse gear brake –B1– ⇒ Repair automatic transmission 096 or 098; disassembling and assembling planetary gearbox

[1] Transmissions manufactured up to December 92 with program switch

VW5029500004020X

Fig. 3 Transaxle troubleshooting (Part 2 of 4)

Condition	Possible cause	Correction
No. 13 Selector lever position: D, 3, 2 or 1 No drive in all gears	1st to 3rd Gear clutch –K1– faulty Freewheel or reverse gear brake –B1– faulty	– Service 1st to 3rd gear clutch –K1– or freewheel or reverse gear brake –B1– ⇒ Repair automatic transmission 096 or 098; disassembling and assembling planetary gearbox
No. 14 Gear selections not taking place	Valves or solenoid valves in valve body stuck	– Replace valve body ⇒ Repair automatic transmission 096 or 098; removing and installing valve body
No. 15 Uncontrolled or harsh shifts	Short circuit between valve wiring or cable guide rail Valve in valve body or solenoid valve faulty	– Replace valve body ⇒ Repair automatic transmission 096 or 098; removing and installing valve body
No. 16 Shifts: When changing gear one shift is harsh	Check in which gear the harsh shifting occurs Relevant selector elements faulty	– Check selector element activation ⇒ Repair automatic transmission 096 or 098; transmission with selector elements – Replace selector element ⇒ Repair automatic transmission 096 or 098; disassembling and assembling planetary gearbox
No. 17 Transmission selects emergency running mode	Incorrect control module installed Conductor strip (cable guide rail) faulty valve in valve body stuck	– Select Control Module according to parts catalogue and if necessary replace – Carry out OBD and electrical check and then replace wiring or components if necessary ⇒ Repair automatic transmission 096 or 098; self–diagnosis or – Replace valve body ⇒ Repair automatic transmission 096 or 098; removing and installing valve body
No. 18 Parking lock will not engage	Selector lever cable defective or incorrectly adjusted Locking lever, parking lock wheel or locking lever mechanism faulty	– Replace selector lever cable and adjust ⇒ Repair automatic transmission 096 or 098; checking and adjusting selector lever cable – Service locking lever, parking lock wheel and locking lever mechanism ⇒ Repair automatic transmission 096 or 098; disassembling and assembling parking lock
No. 19 Noises in final drive	Taper roller bearing loud	– Replace taper roller bearing ⇒ Repair automatic transmission 096 or 098; disassembling and assembling final drive
	Drive pinion loud	– Replace drive pinion ⇒ Repair automatic transmission 096 or 098; removing and installing drive pinion
	Output gear loud	– Replace output gear ⇒ Repair automatic transmission 096 or 098; removing and installing drive pinion
	Input gear loud	– Replace input gear ⇒ Repair automatic transmission 096 or 098; removing and installing input gear
	Differential loud	– Replace differential ⇒ Repair automatic transmission 096 or 098; removing and installing differential

VW5029500004030X

Fig. 3 Transaxle troubleshooting (Part 3 of 4)

Condition	Possible cause	Correction
No. 20 Poor driving characteristics (bucking or idling)	Throttle valve housing leaking (sometimes only when engine/transmission moves)	– Check throttle valve housing and air ducting for leaks
No. 21 Engine speed drops when selecting a driving range	Engine Control Module faulty	– Replace engine Control Module
No. 22 Vehicle will not start or starts in incorrect selector lever position	Park/Neutral position switch faulty	– Replace switch
No. 23 Selector lever can be moved from "N" or "P" or these positions are not blocked	Shiftlock solenoid –N110 faulty Transmission Control Module –J217 defective	– Replace shiftlock solenoid –N110 ⇒ Repair automatic transmission 096 or 098; disassembling and assembling selector mechanism – Replace TCM –J217 ⇒ Repair automatic transmission 096 or 098; On Board Diagnostic (OBD)
No. 24 Multifunction Transmission Range (TR) Switch –F125– contacts overheated	TR Switch faulty Wiring guide and connecters overheated Wiring as well as wiring guide seals faulty TR Switch contacts corroded	– Replace TR Switch ⇒ Repair automatic transmission 096 or 098; disassembling and assembling parking lock – Replace wiring and connections – The TR Switch contact assignment must be changed on transmissions 096 or 098 up to February 1994

VW5029500004040X

Fig. 3 Transaxle troubleshooting (Part 4 of 4)

and 7 to locate stall speed table that applies to vehicle being tested.

1. Connect a suitable engine tachometer to vehicle.
2. Run vehicle until it is at normal operating temperature.
3. Block wheels and set parking brake.
4. Start engine, then while holding down on brake pedal, apply full throttle for no more than five seconds and read torque converter stall speed from the engine tachometer.
5. Compare reading with table.
   a. If stall speed reading is over 200 RPM high, check for a damaged forward clutch or one way clutch.
   b. If stall speed reading is up to 200 RPM low, check for poor engine performance.

Transmission code letters	Gearshifts	Wide Open Throttle		Kickdown
		km/h (mph)	km/h (mph)	km/h (mph)
CFA 128 kW (172 hp) engine	1 H – 2 H	30 – 36 (19 – 23)	52 – 58 (33 – 36)	52 – 58 (33 – 36)
	2 H – 3 H	65 – 71 (41 – 44)	92 – 98 (58 – 61)	92 – 98 (58 – 61)
	3 H – 3 M	92 – 98 (58 – 61)	133 – 139 (83 – 87)	133 – 139 (83 – 87)
	3 M – 4 M	126 – 132 (79 – 83)	156 – 162 (98 – 101)	156 – 162 (98 – 101)
	4 M – 3 M	103 – 97 (64 – 61)	132 – 124 (83 – 78)	155 – 149 (97 – 93)
	3 M – 3 H	54 – 48 (34 – 30)	60 – 54 (38 – 34)	91 – 85 (57 – 53)
	3 H – 2 H	51 – 45 (32 – 28)	51 – 45 (32 – 28)	91 – 85 (57 – 53)
	2 H – 1 H	16 – 10 (10 – 6)	30 – 24 (19 – 15)	30 – 24 (29 – 25)
CFC 85 kW (115 hp) engine	1 H – 2 H	28 – 34 (18 – 21)	44 – 50 (28 – 31)	44 – 50 (28 – 31)
	2 H – 3 H	58 – 64 (36 – 40)	84 – 90 (53 – 56)	84 – 90 (53 – 56)
	3 H – 3 M	84 – 90 (53 – 56)	122 – 128 (76 – 80)	122 – 128 (76 – 80)
	3 H – 4 M	125 – 131 (78 – 82)	142 – 148 (89 – 93)	142 – 148 (89 – 93)
	4 M – 3 M	87 – 81 (54 – 51)	123 – 117 (77 – 73)	142 – 136 (89 – 85)
	3 M – 3 H	58 – 52 (36 – 33)	63 – 57 (39 – 36)	82 – 76 (51 – 48)
	3 H – 2 H	51 – 45 (32 – 28)	51 – 45 (32 – 28)	82 – 76 (51 – 48)
	2 H – 1 H	12 – 6 (8 – 4)	28 – 22 (18 – 14)	44 – 38 (28 – 24)
CFD 66 kW (90 hp) engine	1 H – 2 H	27 – 33 (17 – 21)	43 – 49 (27 – 31)	43 – 49 (27 – 31)
	2 H – 3 H	62 – 68 (39 – 43)	79 – 85 (49 – 53)	79 – 85 (49 – 53)
	3 H – 3 M	79 – 85 (49 – 53)	114 – 120 (71 – 75)	114 – 120 (71 – 75)
	3 M – 4 M	118 – 124 (74 – 78)	136 – 142 (85 – 89)	136 – 142 (85 – 89)
	4 M – 3 M	100 – 94 (63 – 59)	116 – 110 (73 – 69)	136 – 130 (85 – 81)
	3 M – 3 H	54 – 48 (34 – 30)	58 – 52 (36 – 33)	78 – 72 (49 – 45)
	3 H – 2 H	51 – 45 (32 – 28)	51 – 45 (32 – 28)	78 – 72 (49 – 45)
	2 H – 1 H	10 – 4 (6 – 3)	28 – 22 (18 – 14)	43 – 37 (27 – 23)

VW5029300007010X

Fig. 4 Shift point table (Part 1 of 2). 096 transaxle

Transmission code letters	Gearshifts	Kickdown km/h (mph)
CFF 128 kW (172 hp) engine	1 H – 2 H	61 – 67 (38 – 42)
	2 H – 3 H	122 – 128 (76 – 80)
	3 H – 4 M	176 – 182 (109 – 113)
	4 M – 3 H	178 – 172 (111 – 107)
	3 H – 2 H	119 – 113 (74 – 70)
	2 H – 1 H	50 – 44 (31 – 27)
CFH, CNK 85 kW (115 hp) engine	1 H – 2 H	51 – 57 (32 – 35)
	2 H – 3 H	99 – 107 (62 – 66)
	3 H – 4 M	144 – 153 (89 – 95)
	4 M – 3 H	147 – 140 (91 – 87)
	3 H – 2 H	98 – 92 (61 – 57)
	2 H – 1 H	46 – 40 (29 – 25)
CFK, CRR 66 kW (90 hp) engine	1 H – 2 H	47 – 53 (29 – 33)
	2 H – 3 H	93 – 98 (58 – 61)
	3 H – 4 M	135 – 142 (84 – 88)
	4 M – 3 H	137 – 131 (85 – 81)
	3 H – 2 H	92 – 85 (57 – 53)
	2 H – 1 H	44 – 38 (27 – 24)

VW5029300007020X

Fig. 4 Shift point table (Part 2 of 2). 096 transaxle

Transmission Code Letter	Shift	Kickdown km/h (mph)
CLB	1 H – 1 M	60 – 66 (37 – 41)
	1 M – 2 H	60 – 66 (37 – 41)
	2 H – 2 M	122 –128 (76 – 80)
	2 M – 3 H	122 –128 (76 – 80)
	3 H – 3 M	179 –185 (111 – 115)
	3 M – 4 H	179 –185 (111 –115)
	4 H – 4 M	179 –185 (111 – 115)
	4 M – 4 H	180 –174 (112 –108)
	4 H – 3 M	180 –174 (112 –108)
	3 M – 3 H	121 –115 (75 – 71)
	3 H – 2 M	121 –115 (75 –71)
	2 M – 2 H	121 –115 (75 – 71)
	2 H – 1 M	51 – 45 (32 – 28)
	1 M – 1 H	51 – 45 (32 – 28)

VW5029400008010X

Fig. 5 Shift point table (Part 1 of 2). 01M transaxle

Transmission Code Letter	Shift	Kickdown km/h (mph)
CLK	1 H – 1 M	49 – 55 (30 – 34)
	1 M – 2 H	49 – 55 (30 – 34)
	2 H – 2 M	98 –104 (61 – 65)
	2 M – 3 H	98 –104 (61 – 65)
	3 H – 3 M	137–143 (85 – 89)
	3 M – 4 H	137–143 (85 – 89)
	4 H – 4 M	137–143 (85 – 89)
	4 M – 4 H	139 –133 (86 – 83)
	4 H – 3 M	139 –133 (86 – 83
	3 M – 3 H	98 – 92 (61 – 57)
	3 H – 2 M	98 – 92 (61 – 57)
	2 M – 2 H	98 – 92 (61 – 57)
	2 H – 1 M	42 – 36 (26 – 22)
	1 M – 1 H	42 – 36 (26 – 22)
CKX	1 H – 1 M	46 – 52 (29 – 32)
	1 M – 2 H	46 – 52 (29 – 32)
	2 H – 2 M	90 – 96 (56 – 60)
	2 M – 3 H	90 – 96 (56 – 60)
	3 H – 3 M	105 –111 (65 – 69)
	3 M – 4 H	131 –137 (81 – 85)
	4 H – 4 M	131 –137 (81 – 85)
	4 M – 4 H	132 –126 (82 – 78)
	4 H – 3 M	132 –126 (82 – 78)
	3 M – 3 H	99 – 93 (61 – 58)
	3 H – 2 M	89 – 83 (55 – 51)
	2 M – 2 H	89 – 83 (55 – 51)
	2 H – 1 M	39 – 33 (24 – 20)
	1 M – 1 H	39 – 33 (24 – 20)

VW5029400008020X

Fig. 5 Shift point table (Part 2 of 2). 01M transaxle

Transmission code letters Automatic transmission 096	Torque converter Code letters	Stall speed rpm
CFA	QCCR	2400 – 2700
CFC	QACA	2700 – 3000
CFD	QACA	2550 – 2850
CFF	QCCR	2350 – 2650
CFH, CNK	QACA	2750 – 3050
CFK, CRR	QACA	2350 – 2650

VW5029300009000X

Fig. 6 Stall speed specifications. 096 transaxle

c. If stall speed reading is over 200 RPM low, check for a faulty torque converter.

MAIN PRESSURE

The following procedure will set a Diagnostic Trouble Code (DTC) into the control module memory. It will be necessary to have a suitable scan tool available to erase this DTC at completion of test.

Prior to performing the following procedure it is recommended that a suitable scan tool be connected to the vehicle as described under "Anti-Lock Brakes" in the "Diagnosis & Testing " section, then check for and repair any transaxle DTC. Check for other possible stored DTC for other vehicle systems.

If possible perform the following procedure on a chassis dynamometer.

If tests show pressure out of specification the following areas should be inspected.

Engine idle too high or too low.
ATF pump faulty.
Sticking valve in valve body.

1. Connect a suitable transaxle pressure gauge to main pressure port on transaxle, **Fig. 8.**
2. Ensure transaxle oil is at normal operating temperature.
3. Start vehicle and allow to idle.
4. Place shifter in D position and read pressure.
5. Pressure should be between 49–55 psi.
6. Place shifter in R position and read pressure.
7. Pressure should be between 94–109 psi.
8. Disconnect transaxle solenoid valve electrical connector from transaxle.
9. Place shifter in D position, raise engine speed to 2000 RPM and read pressure.
10. Pressure should be between 146–164 psi.
11. Place shifter in R position, raise engine speed to 2000 RPM and read pressure.
12. Pressure should be between 334–348 psi.
13. Stop engine, then remove pressure gauge.
14. Connect transaxle solenoid valve electrical connector to transaxle.
15. Connect a suitable scan tool to vehicle, then erase stored DTC.

MAINTENANCE

On transaxle model 01M use only ATF VW G 052 162 A2, or equivalent, for topping up or replacing fluid.

Note that Volkswagen original equipment transaxle oil is yellowish in color. It is

Transmission Code Letter	Torque Converter Code Letter	Stall speed rpm
CLB	QCDV	2050 – 2350
CLK	QADB	2550 – 2850
CKX	QADB	2250 – 2550
CKZ	QCDB	...

VW5029400010000X

Fig. 7 Stall speed specifications. 01M transaxle

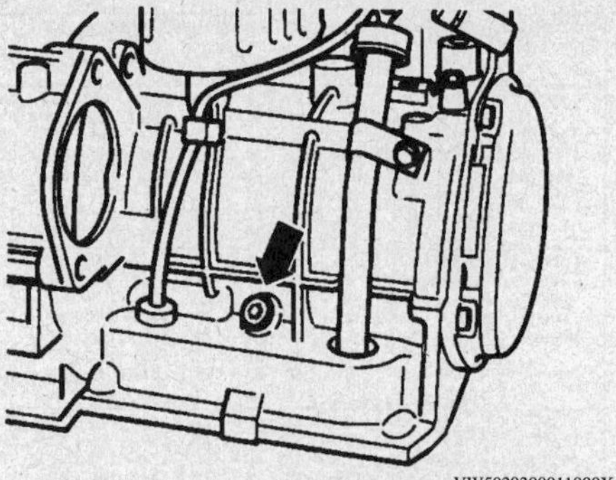
VW5029300011000X

Fig. 8 Transaxle main oil pressure port location

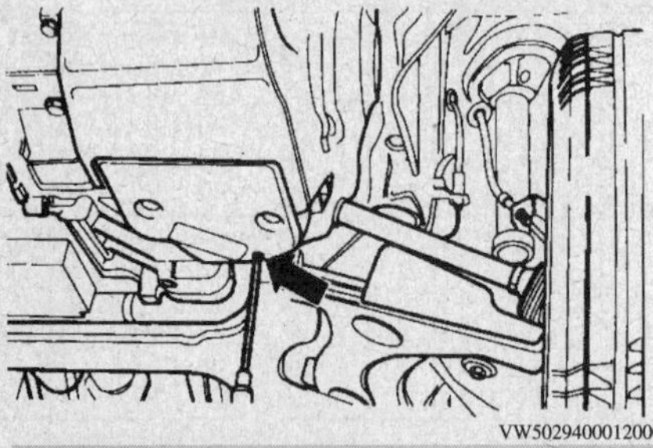
VW5029400012000X

Fig. 9 Level tube plug removal. 01M transaxle

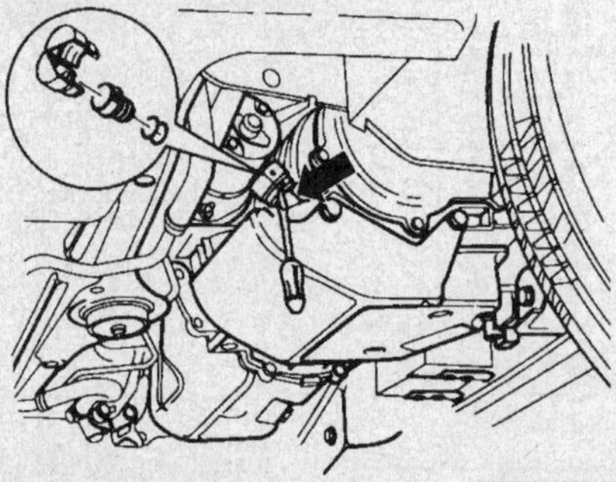
VW5029400013000X

Fig. 10 Filler tube cap removal. 01M transaxle

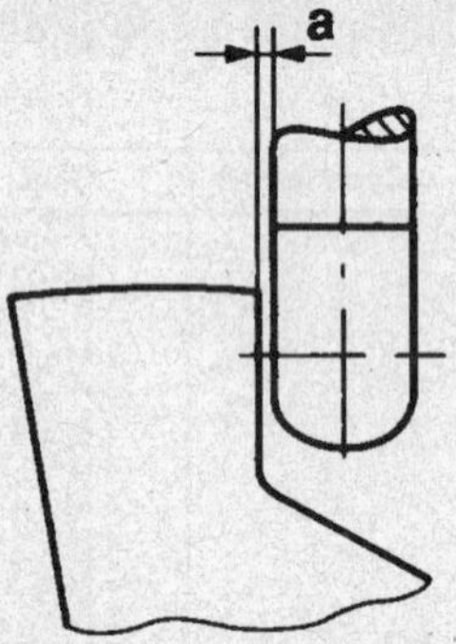
a
VW5029300014000X

Fig. 11 Shift lock solenoid adjustment

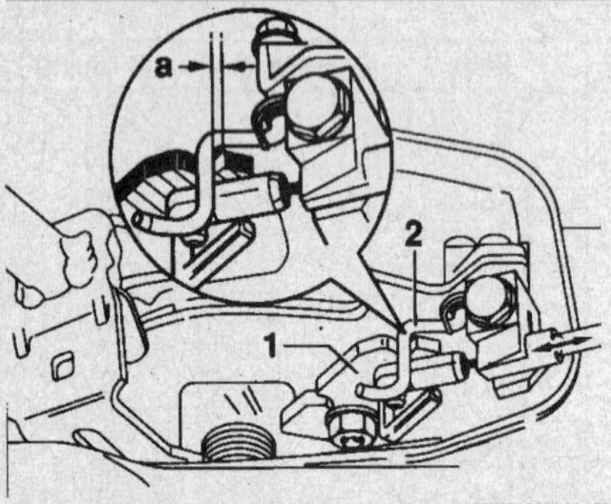
a
2
1
VW5029300015000X

Fig. 12 Ignition lock cable adjustment

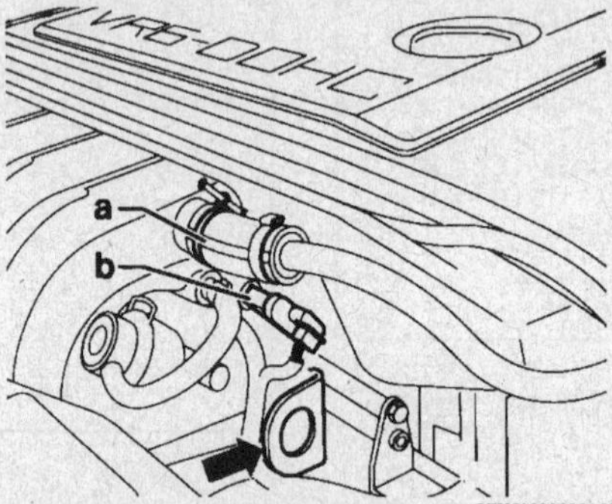
a
b
VW5029300016000X

Fig. 13 Vacuum hose disconnecting. 2.8L engine

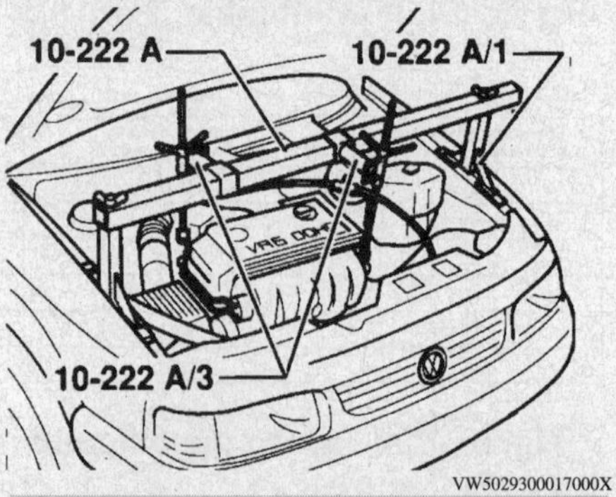
10-222 A
10-222 A/1
10-222 A/3
VW5029300017000X

Fig. 14 Engine support installation

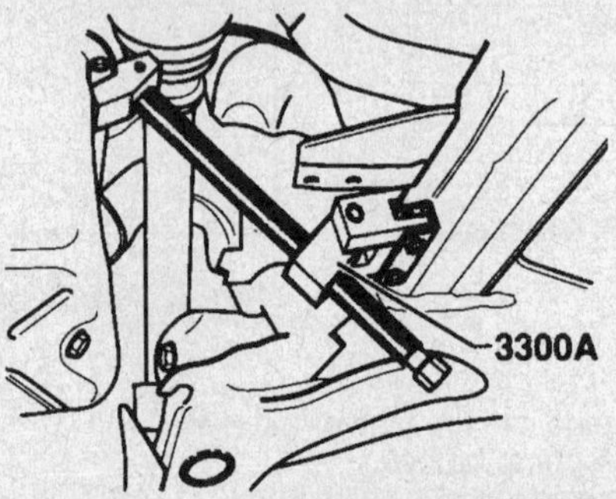
3300A
VW5029300018000X

Fig. 15 Engine tilting forward w/support device

not necessary to replace the transaxle oil based on color alone.

FLUID CHECK

096 Transaxle

1. Drive vehicle approximately 6 miles to bring transaxle to operating temperature.
2. Park vehicle on flat surface, place selector lever in park and apply parking brake.
3. Check fluid level on dipstick. Fluid level should be between the minimum and maximum marks on dipstick, if needed add Dexron ATF fluid.

01M Transaxle

Use only ATF VW G 052 162 A2 or equivalent for topping up or replacing fluid.

1. Raise and support vehicle.
2. Connect a suitable scan tool to Data Link Connector (DLC), found under left side of dash panel, to right of steering column.
3. Follow scan tool manufacturer's instructions to access "Transaxle Electronics," then advance to transaxle oil temperature measurement.
4. Transaxle oil cannot be above 30° C to begin oil level test.
5. Remove ATF level plug from oil pan, **Fig. 9,** discarding seal, a small amount of fluid in tube should run out.
6. Run vehicle until transaxle temperature reaches 35–45°C, ATF should "drip" out of level overflow tube.
7. If fluid drips out replace level plug with new gasket and tighten to specification, level check is complete.
8. If Fluid does not drip out proceed as follows:
   a. Pry securing cap off filler tube plug **Fig. 10** discard securing cap. (Note on some models a reusable securing cap with spring clip was used.)
   b. Remove filler tube plug, fill transaxle with suitable ATF until fluid runs out of level plug hole.
   c. Install level tube plug using a new gasket.
   d. Install filler plug, then filler plug securing cap.

FINAL DRIVE GEAR OIL LEVEL INSPECTION

The oil level for the final drive gear is checked with the transaxle installed.

1. Remove speedometer driveshaft from transaxle and wipe clean.
2. Install driveshaft into transaxle, then remove and check oil level on shaft.
3. Oil level must be between minimum and maximum marks on the shaft. If

necessary add synthetic gear oil G50 SAE 75W90, or equivalent.

ADJUSTMENTS

THROTTLE CABLE

Corrado

1. Fully depress accelerator to floor and ensure throttle valve just reaches full throttle position with a maximum of .039 inch play at throttle lever.
2. If not, remove retaining clip and reposition slotted portion of cable until .039 inch maximum play is met.
3. Re-insert retaining clip and verify that play is .039 inch.

Except Corrado

1. Place spacer of 0.60 inch between accelerator pedal and pedal stop.
2. Fully depress accelerator until it contacts spacer and hold in position.
3. Open throttle by pulling on accelerator cable sleeve, then secure in this position using retainer clip.
4. Connect multimeter tool No. US1119, or equivalent, to kickdown switch using adapter switch tool No. VW 1594, or equivalent, switch must read infinite ohms.
5. Slowly depress accelerator pedal until full throttle is reached, after kickdown pressure point is reached resistance must drop to 0 ohms.
6. At this point accelerator pedal must be just short of the pedal stop.

SHIFT LOCK SOLENOID

Adjustment

1. Access shift lock solenoid by removing console and shifter components as necessary.
2. Loosen solenoid mounting, then slide solenoid on elongated mounting slots and adjust as follows:
   a. Place selector lever in "N" position.
   b. Refer to **Fig. 11** adjust position of solenoid until clearance (a) of .018 inch is achieved between rod and solenoid lever.
3. Perform "Functional Check."

Functional Check

1. Ensure ignition cable lock is disengaged.
2. Place selector lever in "P" position.
3. Disconnect connector for solenoid and connect solenoid to a suitable 12 volt source.
4. It must not be possible to move shifter into any gear position.
5. Disconnect 12 volt source, shifter must move to all gear positions.
6. Repeat above steps with lever in position "N."

IGNITION LOCK CABLE

Ignition lock cable can only be adjusted after it has been completely installed.

1. Access ignition lock cable and lever by removing console and shifter components as necessary.
2. Place shift lever in "1" position, then release cable clamp bolt.
3. Turn ignition switch to start position, then release.
4. Refer to **Fig. 12,** adjust dimension (a) between lever (1) and locking pin (2) to .025 – .030 inch.
5. Tighten cable clamp bolt to specification.
6. Place selector lever into "P" position and remove ignition key.
7. It must not be possible to remove ignition key with shift lever in any but "P" position.
8. It must not be possible to move shift lever from "P" position with ignition key removed.

TRANSAXLE

REPLACE

CORRADO

1. Disconnect battery ground cable.
2. Loosen upper air cooler connecting pipe clamps, then remove brake disc air duct.
3. Loosen air cooler lower clamps, then remove upper connecting pipes.
4. Remove speedometer drive from transaxle, then the engine/transaxle connecting bolts.
5. Clamp off coolant hoses at transaxle cooler using tool 3094 or equivalent, then disconnect hoses.
6. Install engine support bar 10-222 and retainer 3180 or their equivalents.
7. Remove upper starter motor bolt, then place selector lever in park and remove cable.
8. Remove left transaxle mount, then disconnect electrical connectors from transaxle.
9. Remove front assembly mounting, then the starter motor.
10. Remove axle shaft protective cap, then disconnect right axle shaft from transaxle flange.
11. Remove left axle shaft from vehicle as described in "Front Wheel Drive Axles" section.
12. Remove torque converter bolts, then the lower support bar.
13. Slide engine and transaxle to right, then install transmission jack.
14. Remove lower engine/transaxle bolts, separate transaxle from engine, then lower transaxle.
15. Reverse procedure to install, noting the following. Tighten nuts and bolts to specifications.

EXCEPT CORRADO

1. Disconnect battery ground cable.
2. Disconnect speedometer, then place selector in "P" position and remove selector cable from lever.
3. Disconnect electrical connectors from transaxle.
4. Remove Multi-Function Transaxle Range (TR) switch.
5. Using a suitable clamp, pinch off, then remove coolant hoses at transaxle cooler.
6. **On models with 2.8L engines,** disconnect vacuum line (a) and electrical connector (b), **Fig. 13,** then radiator fan connector.
7. **On all models,** install a suitable engine support, **Fig. 14.**
8. Disconnect and remove front engine mount.
9. Dismount an position aside coolant expansion tank.
10. Remove complete left engine mount.
11. **On models with 2.8L engines,** remove drive belt cover for clearance when lowering engine.
12. **On all models,** remove starter, then upper engine/transaxle bolts.
13. Remove protective plate for transaxle if equipped, then torque converter cover plate and torque converter mounting bolts.
14. Remove vibration weight from subframe if equipped, then disconnect axle shafts at transaxle flange and raise and secure right side shaft aside.
15. **Models with tripod type inner joint,** remove left axle shaft from vehicle, refer to "Front Wheel Drive Axles" for identification and procedure.
16. **Models less tripod type inner joint,** mark then loosen lower ball joint, then swing out to allow clearance.
17. **On all models,** remove bracket for power steering hose if equipped.
18. Place support device tool No. 3300A, or equivalent, into place, **Fig. 15,** then tilt engine forward.
19. Lower engine and transaxle using engine support unit until transaxle removal clearance is achieved
20. Position suitable transmission jack under transaxle.
21. Remove lower engine/transaxle bolts, separate transaxle from engine, then lower transaxle.
22. Reverse procedure to install, noting the following:
    a. Tighten nuts and bolts to specifications.
    b. Check and adjust selector cable if necessary.

TIGHTENING SPECIFICATIONS

Year	Component	Torque/ Ft. Lbs.
CORRADO		
1993–94	Axle Nut	②
	Axle Shaft To Transmission Flange Bolts	33
	Cover Plate To Transmission Bolts	11
	Driveshaft Nut	②
	Front Bracket To Mount Bolts	44
	Hub Nut	②
	Left Side Bracket To Transmission Bolts	18
	Torque Converter To Drive Plate Bolts	44
	Transmission To Engine Bolts, M10	44
	Transmission To Engine Bolts, M12	59
EXCEPT CORRADO		
1993–96	Axle Nut	②
	Axle Shaft To Transmission Flange Bolts	37
	Ball Join To Control Arm	26
	Cover Plate To Transmission Bolts	11
	Driveshaft Nut	②
	Front Bracket To Mount Bolts	44
	Ignition Lock Cable Clamp Bolt	53①
	Hub Nut	②
	Left Side Bracket To Transaxle Bolts	18
	Left Side Mount To Transaxle Bolts	44
	Starter To Transaxle	44
	Torque Converter To Drive Plate Bolts	44
	Transmission To Engine Bolts, M10	44
	Transmission To Engine Bolts, M12	59
	Wheel Lug Bolts	81

① — Inch lbs.
② — 66 ft. lbs. plus an additional 1/8 turn.

098 Automatic Transaxle

INDEX

	Page No.
Description	49-142
Identification	49-142
Maintenance	49-142
Final Drive Gear Oil Level Inspection	49-142
Fluid Check	49-142
Tightening Specifications	49-143
Transmission, Replace	49-142

IDENTIFICATION

The identification numbers are located on the lefthand side of transaxle. Code letters are on the upper front part and type numbers are in the center.

DESCRIPTION

The 098 transaxle is a fully automatic, four speed automatic transaxle.

MAINTENANCE

FLUID CHECK

1. Drive Vehicle approximately 6 miles to bring transaxle to operating temperature.
2. Park vehicle on flat surface, place selector lever in park and apply parking brake.
3. Check fluid level on dipstick. Fluid level should be between the minimum and maximum marks on dipstick, if needed add Dexron ATF fluid.

FINAL DRIVE GEAR OIL LEVEL INSPECTION

1. Raise and support vehicle.
2. Remove either bolt on top of gearbox or bolt on torque converter housing to check oil level.
3. Top up with gear oil G50 if necessary, then install plug(s) and **torque** to 14 ft. lbs.

TRANSMISSION

REPLACE

1. Obtain radio security code, then disconnect battery ground cable.
2. Tilt radiator in forward position as described under "Engine, Replace."

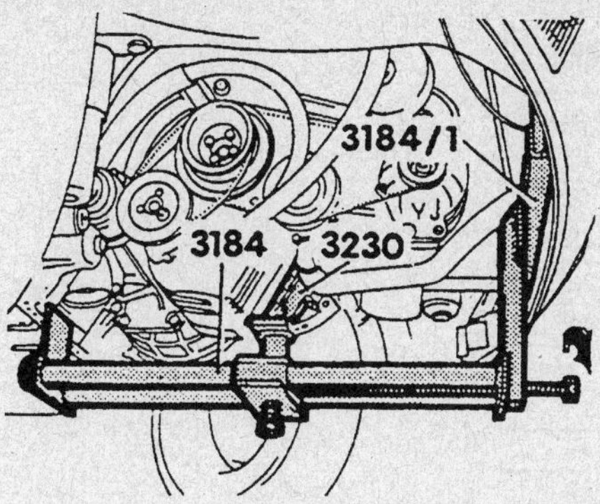
3184/1
3184
3230
VW5029100001000X

Fig. 1 Support tools

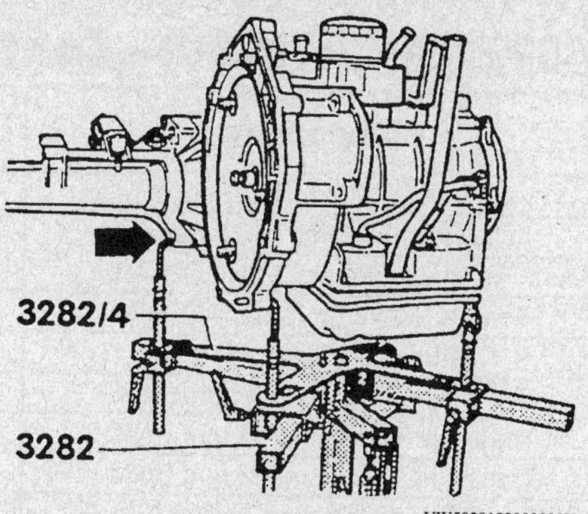
3282/4
3282
VW5029100002000X

Fig. 2 Transaxle support mount

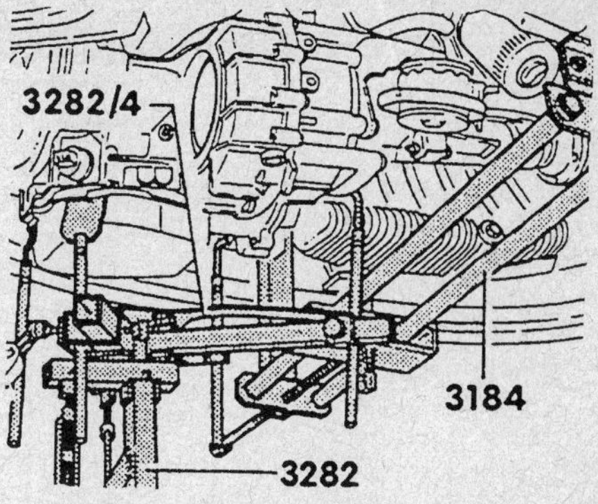
3282/4
3184
3282
VW5029100003000X

Fig. 3 Transaxle lifter tool w/transaxle mount below transaxle & support

3. Raise and support vehicle, then remove sound damper.
4. Detach cap covering left horn, then disconnect following electrical connections:
   a. Plug connection to valve body.
   b. Vehicle speed sensor.
   c. Multi-function switch.
5. Disconnect oxygen sensor connection above subframe.
6. Remove front exhaust pipe, then disconnect transaxle support from engine and bearing housing.
7. Remove bolt for cover plate, then unscrew nut from torque converter using tool No. V 175, or equivalent.
8. Relieve tension on torsion bars on both sides by slackening nut with tool No. 3257, or equivalent.
9. Detach left shock absorber from bottom if suspension link and push together. Disconnect both drive shafts from transaxle.
10. Loosen alternator and unscrew tensioning bar for alternator from engine.
11. Insert support tool No. 3184, or equivalent, in order to support engine/transaxle at engine.
12. Install engine mount device tool No. 3227, or equivalent, then attach auxiliary support tool No. 3184/1, or equivalent, for supporting device tool No. 3184, or equivalent, into end member.
13. Attached supporting device tool No. 3184, or equivalent, into auxiliary support tool No. 3184/1, or equivalent, and into subframe. Screw spindle into hole of engine mount.
14. Align supporting device so that slide is resting against righthand tube.
15. Secure supporting device to subframe and to auxiliary support device by screwing angle plates tight. Relieve load on subframe by raising engine/transaxle by means of spindle and mount tool No. 3230, or equivalent.
16. Disconnect engine mount at rear of subframe.
17. Loosen bearing bracket for transaxle from mount at body.
18. Carefully swivel engine/transaxle forward and lower **Fig. 1. Do not damage left drive shaft and selector cable when proceeding with the following:**
    a. Turn spindle to left to swivel assembly forward.
    b. To swivel back, turn spindle to right.
19. Remove circlips for selector lever cable, then detach cable from transaxle.
20. Clamp coolant hose at ATF cooler with tool No. 3094, or equivalent, and disconnect from ATF cooler.
21. Disconnect securing bolt of bearing housing for inserting of transaxle mount tool No. 3282, or equivalent. Set up mount with adjusting plate tool No. 3282/4, or equivalent, for removing transaxle, **Fig. 2.**
22. Move lifter tool No. 3282, or equivalent, with transaxle mount tool No. 3184 or equivalent below transaxle and support, **Fig. 3.**
23. Remove attaching bolts on bottom of engine/transaxle assembly, then carefully separate transaxle from engine. **Secure torque converter to prevent dropping and damaging.**
24. Swivel transaxle and lower carefully. **It is important to ensure right articulated flange does not strike against support device tool No. 3184, or equivalent.**
25. Reverse procedure to install, noting the following
    a. Ensure dowel sleeves are correctly aligned.
    b. When swiveling transaxle, position both driveshafts into flanged shaft and articulated flange.
    c. Install engine/transaxle mounting by aligning supporting device tool No. 3184, or equivalent.

TIGHTENING SPECIFICATIONS

Year	Component	Torque/ Ft. Lbs.
1993	Assembly Mounting To Carrier	148
	Assembly Mounting To Torque Convertor 10 mm	30
	Assembly Mounting To Torque Convertor 12 mm	74
	Axle Nut	148
	Axle Shaft To Transaxle Flange Bolts	52
	Drive Shaft Nut	148
	Exhaust Pipe To Manifold 6 mm	8
	Exhaust Pipe To Manifold 8 mm	18
	Exhaust Pipe To Manifold 10 mm	30
	Hub Nut	148

Continued

TIGHTENING SPECIFICATIONS—Continued

Year	Component	Torque/ Ft. Lbs.
1993	Left Motor Mount To Bracket	48
	Left Mount Bracket To Transaxle	48
	Mount To Torque Converter Housing 10 mm	33
	Torque Converter To Drive Plate	44
	Transaxle Cover Plate	15
	Transaxle To Engine 8 mm Bolts	15
	Transaxle To Engine 10 mm Bolts	44
	Transaxle To Engine 12 mm Bolts	59
	Wheel Bearing Housing To Axle Joint	41

Front Wheel Drive Axles

INDEX

	Page No.
Driveshaft, Replace	49-144
Eurovan	49-144
Except Fox, Cabriolet & Eurovan	49-144
Fox & Cabriolet	49-144
Driveshaft Service	49-144
Constant Velocity Joint Boot, Replace	49-146
Inner Constant Velocity Joint	49-145
Outer Constant Velocity Joint	49-145
Tuned Absorber (Balance Weight), Replace	49-145
Tightening Specifications	49-147

DRIVESHAFT

REPLACE

FOX & CABRIOLET

1. With vehicle on ground, remove drive axle retaining nut from wheel assembly.
2. Remove drive axle to transaxle drive flange attaching bolts.
3. **On models except Fox with manual transaxle,** separate ball joint from wheel bearing housing.
4. **On Fox models equipped with manual transaxle,** mark position of ball joint to right and left side control arm and separate ball joint from control arm.
5. **On all models,** pull wheel and tire assembly outward and remove drive axle from vehicle.
6. Reverse procedure to install.

EUROVAN

Manual Transaxles

1. Install support tool No. 3250, or equivalent, to upper control arm.
2. With car on ground, loosen axle shaft bolts, then remove bolt securing wheel bearing housing to lower ball joint.
3. Remove bolt for shock absorber/ stabilizer link rod.
4. Remove axle shaft from drive flange of transaxle.
5. Compress shock absorber completely, then remove axle shaft.
6. Reverse procedure to install.

Automatic Transaxles

1. Install support tool No. 3250, or equivalent, to support upper control arm on left and right sides.
2. Loosen axle shaft bolt with vehicle on ground.
3. Remove left shock absorber from lower control arm and compress.
4. Remove bolts and separate wheel bearing housing/lower ball joint.
5. Remove plug from multi-function switch, then axle shaft from transaxle drive flange.
6. Reverse procedure to install.
7.

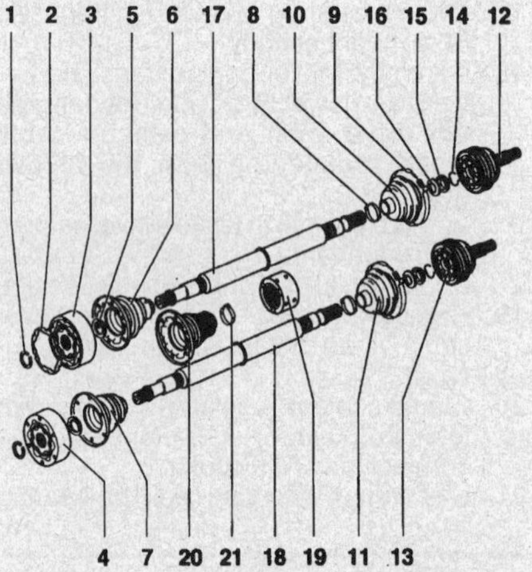

1 2 3 5 6 17 8 10 9 16 15 14 12
4 7 20 21 18 19 11 13

1.Circlip
2.Gasket
3.Inner CV Joint (100mm)
4.Inner CV Joint (94mm)
5.Dished Washer
6.Inner Boot (100mm)
7.Inner Boot (94mm)
8.Clamp
9.Clamp
10.Outer Boot (90mm)
11.Outer Boot (81mm)
12.Outer CV Joint (90mm)
13.Outer CV Joint (81mm)
14.Snap Ring
15.Thrust Washer
16.Dished Washer
17.Axle Shaft
18.Axle Shaft
19.Balance Weight
20.Inner Boot (100mm)
21.Clamp

VW3039300011000X

Fig. 1 Exploded view of driveshaft. Cabrio, Golf III, GTI & Jetta III

EXCEPT FOX, CABRIOLET & EUROVAN

1. With vehicle on ground, remove drive axle retaining nut from wheel assembly.
2. Raise and support vehicle, then remove wheel.
3. Mark position of bolts attaching ball joints to control arms, then remove bolts and separate ball joint from control arm.
4. Remove drive axle to transaxle drive flange attaching bolts.
5. Mount puller 3283 or equivalent onto hub assembly and press axle shaft out of hub.
6. Remove axle shaft from vehicle.
7. Reverse procedure to install. Apply locking compound D 185 400 A2 or equivalent to splines of axle shaft in two 3 mm beads.

DRIVESHAFT SERVICE

When servicing driveshafts, refer to **Figs. 1through 5,** for component location and identification.

The surface of the axle shaft is covered with a special coating designed to prevent stress cracks from forming due to rust and abrasion. Use caution not to damage this surface while servicing unit.

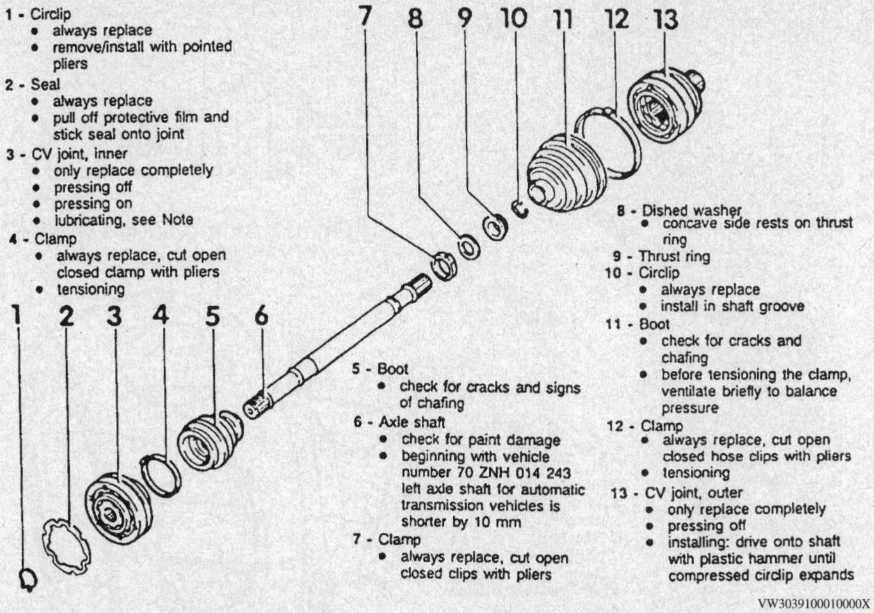
1 - Circlip
• always replace
• remove/install with pointed pliers
2 - Seal
• always replace
• pull off protective film and stick seal onto joint
3 - CV joint, inner
• only replace completely
• pressing off
• pressing on
• lubricating, see Note
4 - Clamp
• always replace, cut open closed clamp with pliers
• tensioning
5 - Boot
• check for cracks and signs of chafing
6 - Axle shaft
• check for paint damage
• beginning with vehicle number 70 ZNH 014 243 left axle shaft for automatic transmission vehicles is shorter by 10 mm
7 - Clamp
• always replace, cut open closed clips with pliers
8 - Dished washer
• concave side rests on thrust ring
9 - Thrust ring
10 - Circlip
• always replace
• install in shaft groove
11 - Boot
• check for cracks and chafing
• before tensioning the clamp, ventilate briefly to balance pressure
12 - Clamp
• always replace, cut open closed hose clips with pliers
• tensioning
13 - CV joint, outer
• only replace completely
• pressing off
• installing: drive onto shaft with plastic hammer until compressed circlip expands
1
2
3
4
5
6
7
8
9
10
11
12
13
VW3039100010000X

Fig. 2 Exploded view of driveshaft. Eurovan

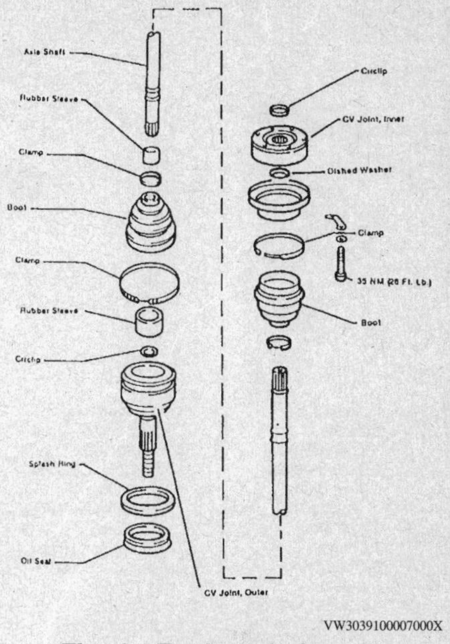
VW3039100007000X

Fig. 3 Exploded view of driveshaft. Fox

TUNED ABSORBER (BALANCE WEIGHT), REPLACE

EXCEPT CABRIOLET, EUROVAN & FOX

1. Raise and support vehicle.
2. Remove axle as outlined under "Driveshaft, Replace."
3. Remove drift pin securing both halves, then remove absorber (weight).
4. Ensure axle shaft paint and friction tape on I.D. of weight are in good condition.
5. Refer to **Fig. 6** position and install balance weight as follows:
   a. **On Corrado models,** dimension (a) is 17.815 inch.
   b. **On Cabrio, Golf III, GTI & Jetta III models,** dimension (a) is 21.260 to 21.340 inch.
   c. **On Passat models,** dimension (a) is 20.487 to 20.567 inch for right axle shaft and if equipped 10.362 to 10.442 inch for left axle shaft.
6. Reverse procedure to install, tighten to specification.

OUTER CONSTANT VELOCITY JOINT

REPLACE

1. Remove driveshaft as described under "Driveshaft, Replace."
2. Remove large boot clamp, then slide boot back from joint.
3. Clean area where shaft enters joint and determine whether joint has circlip or internal snap ring.
4. **On models using circlip retention of joint** proceed as follows:
   a. Clamp axle shaft into a suitable soft jaw vice.
   b. Using suitable circlip pliers, expand and hold circlip.
   c. Using a suitable soft face hammer, tap on inner race of joint to start joint off axle spline.
   d. Pull and tap to remove joint from shaft, note position of dished washer and thrust washer for later assembly.
   e. Remove and discard circlip.
5. **On models using internal snap ring retention of joint** proceed as follows:
   a. Clamp axle shaft into a suitable soft jaw vice.
   b. Hold joint parallel to shaft, then strike body of joint **Fig. 7**with a suitable soft face hammer to unseat internal snap ring.
   c. Pull and tap to remove joint from shaft, note position of dished washer and thrust washer for later assembly.
   d. Remove and discard snap ring from axle shaft.
6. **On all models,** reverse procedure to install, noting the following:
   a. Use new snap ring or circlip.
   b. Clean and inspect boot and shaft splines for damage.
   c. Ensure boot and joint are packed with correct quantity of a suitable CV joint grease.

SERVICE

1. Remove joint from axle shaft as described under "Replace," then clean joint thoroughly.
2. Mark position of ball hub in relation to cage and housing prior to disassembling.
3. Pivot and remove ball hub and cage, then remove balls **Fig. 8. Do not interchange balls from one cage with balls from another.**
4. Turn cage until two rectangular openings are even with joint edge **Fig. 9,** then remove cage from the hub.
5. Turn hub until one segment can be pushed into rectangular opening of cage, then tilt hub out of cage. Check housing, hub, cage and balls for pitting or scoring. **Do not replace joint due to a polished appearance or because of visible ball track.**
6. Fill joint with 45 grams of G6.2 grease (half of total amount).
7. Install cage with hub, into housing. Balls must be installed from opposite side. **Marked position of hub, cage and housing must match.**
8. Install new snap ring on shaft or circlip into joint, then fill joint with remaining grease.

INNER CONSTANT VELOCITY JOINT

Some vehicles may use a tripod type inner joint. Repair or replacement of tripod joint or boot can only be done as an assembly with axle shaft.

REPLACE

Tripod Type Joint

1. Remove outer CV joint as described under "Outer Constant Velocity Joint," then remove outer CV joint boot.
2. Reverse procedure to install.

Less Tripod Type Joint

1. Remove axle as outlined under "Driveshaft, Replace."
2. Pull CV joint boot and shield back and away from joint.
3. Remove and discard circlip retaining joint to axle.
4. Place axle in a stable press, supporting inner race of joint on a suitable press plate.
5. Press shaft from inner race of joint.
6. Reverse procedure to install, noting the following:
   a. Clean and inspect boot and shaft splines for damage.
   b. Press joint onto axle using suitable press tools as shown in **Fig. 10.**

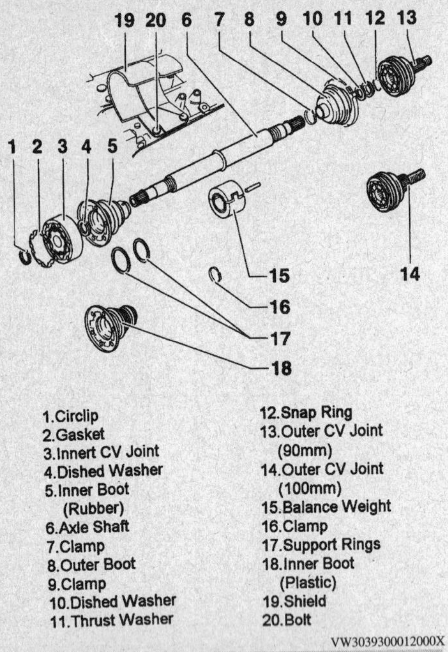
19 20 6 7 8 9 10 11 12 13
1 2 3 4 5
15
14
16
17
18
1.Circlip
2.Gasket
3.Innert CV Joint
4.Dished Washer
5.Inner Boot (Rubber)
6.Axle Shaft
7.Clamp
8.Outer Boot
9.Clamp
10.Dished Washer
11.Thrust Washer
12.Snap Ring
13.Outer CV Joint (90mm)
14.Outer CV Joint (100mm)
15.Balance Weight
16.Clamp
17.Support Rings
18.Inner Boot (Plastic)
19.Shield
20.Bolt
VW3039300012000X

Fig. 4 Exploded view of driveshaft. Passat & 1993–94 Corrado

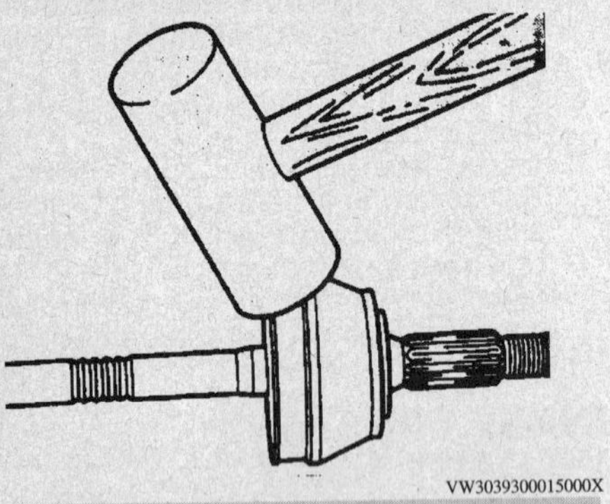
VW3039300015000X

Fig. 7 Outer CV joint removal

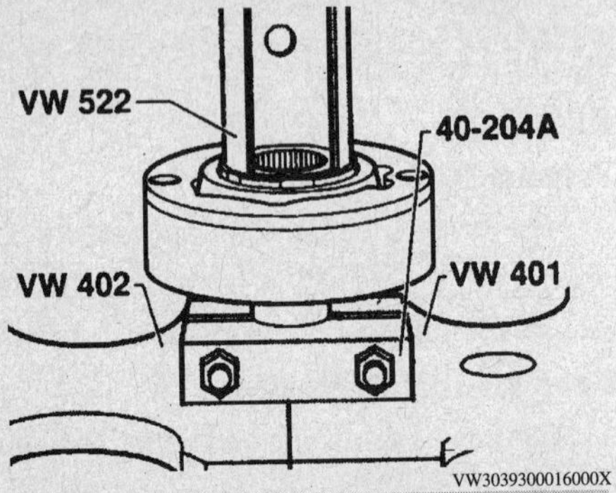
VW 522
40-204A
VW 402
VW 401
VW3039300016000X

Fig. 10 Inner CV joint to shaft installation

c. Use new circlip.
d. Ensure boot and joint are packed with correct quantity of a suitable CV joint grease.

SERVICE

Tripod Type Joint

The tripod type inner joint cannot yet be serviced in the field. Replacement of the joint with shaft is the only acceptable repair.

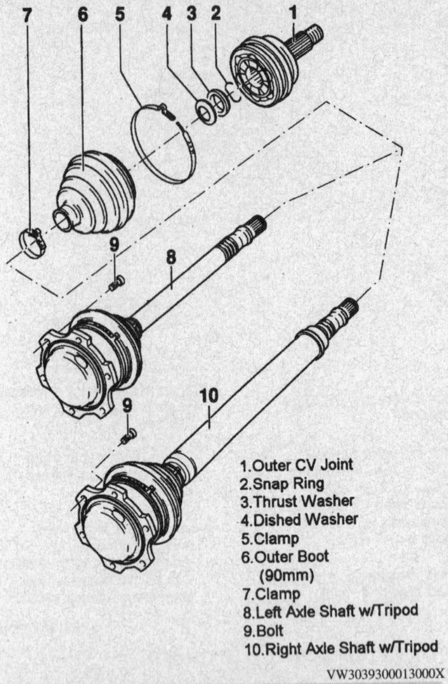
7 6 5 4 3 2 1
9
8
9
10
1.Outer CV Joint
2.Snap Ring
3.Thrust Washer
4.Dished Washer
5.Clamp
6.Outer Boot (90mm)
7.Clamp
8.Left Axle Shaft w/Tripod
9.Bolt
10.Right Axle Shaft w/Tripod
VW3039300013000X

Fig. 5 Exploded view of driveshaft. Models w/tripod inner constant velocity joints

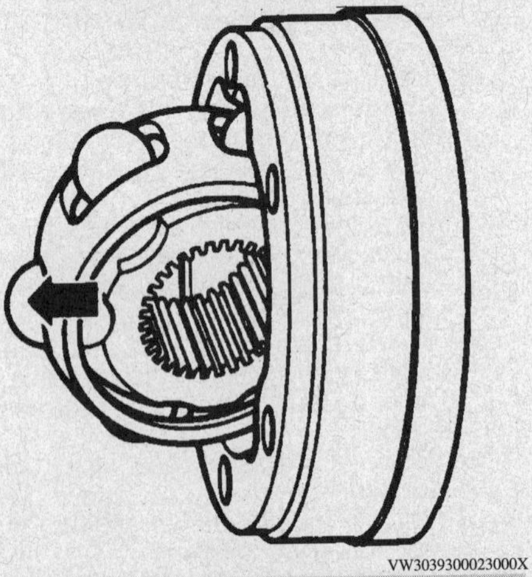
VW3039300023000X

Fig. 8 Pivot ball hub & cage removal

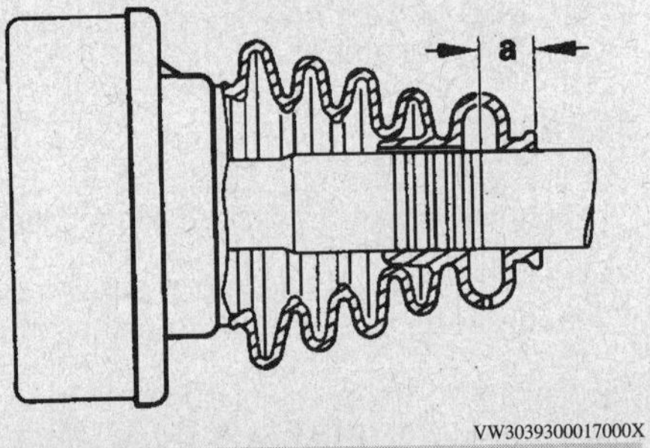
a
VW3039300017000X

Fig. 11 Left inner CV joint boot positioning. Cabrio, Golf III, GTI, Jetta III & Passat

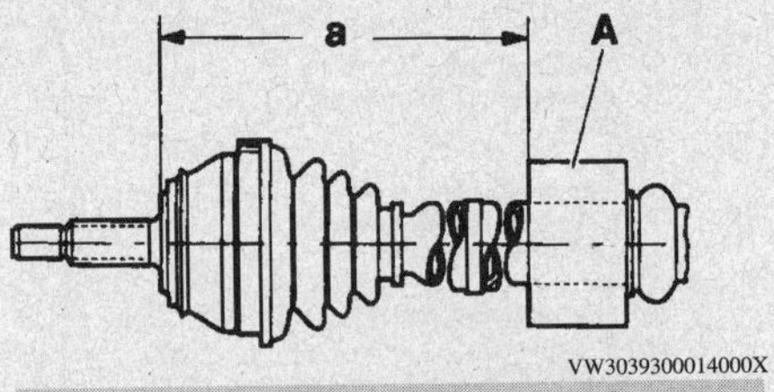
a
A
VW3039300014000X

Fig. 6 Axle balance weight locating

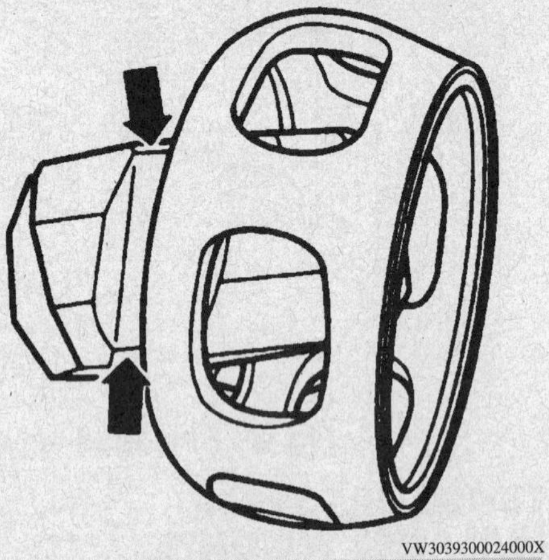
VW3039300024000X

Fig. 9 CV joint hub from cage removal

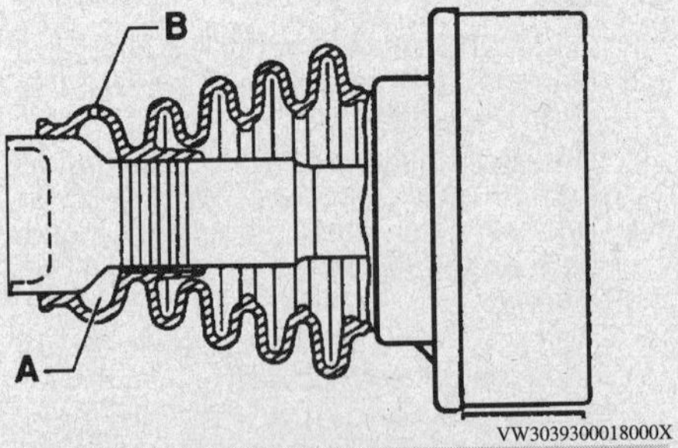
B
A
VW3039300018000X

Fig. 12 Right inner CV joint boot positioning. Cabrio, Golf III, GTI, Jetta III & Passat

Less Tripod Type Joint

1. Remove joint as described above.
2. Service joint as described in "Outer Constant Velocity Joint."

CONSTANT VELOCITY JOINT BOOT, REPLACE

CABRIO, GOLF III, GT, JETTA III & PASSAT

1. Remove constant velocity joint as described.
2. Remove inner boot clamp, then boot.
3. Position inner end of boot onto axle shaft as follows:

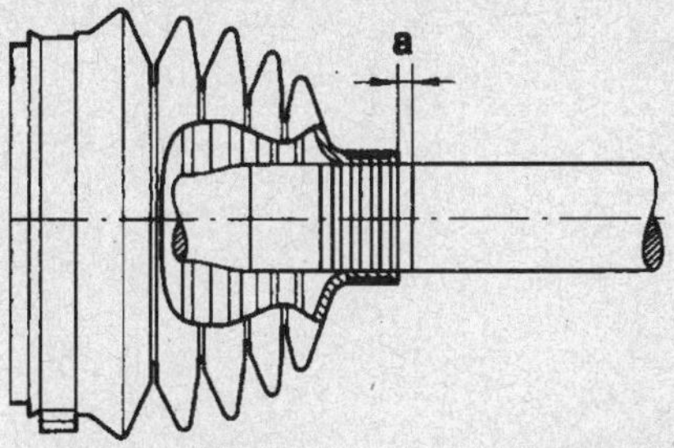
a

VW3039300019000X

Fig. 13 Left outer CV joint boot positioning. Cabrio, Golf III, GTI, Jetta III & Passat w/27 mm axle shaft

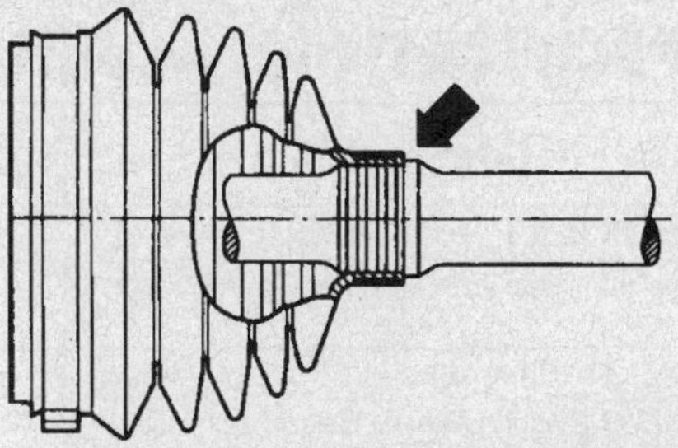

VW3039300021000X

Fig. 14 Left outer CV joint boot positioning. Cabrio, Golf III, GTI, Jetta III & Passat w/22 mm axle shaft

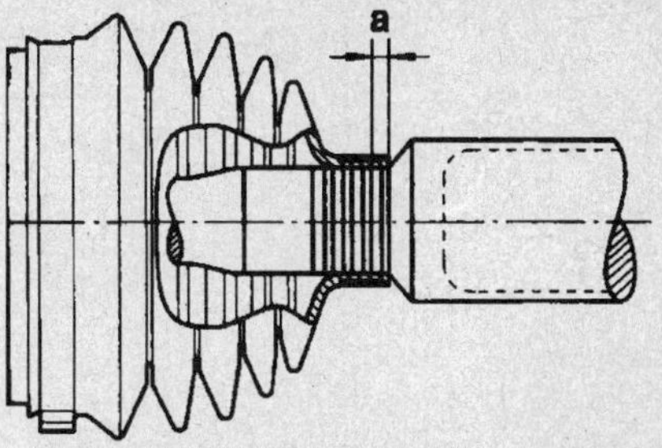
a

VW3039300022000X

Fig. 15 Right outer CV joint boot positioning. Cabrio, Golf III, GTI, Jetta III & Passat

a. Left inner boot **Fig. 11,** dimension (a) equals .670 inch.
b. Right inner boot **Fig. 12.**
c. Left outer boot on 27 mm driveshaft **Fig. 13,** dimension (a) equals ½ to 1½ grooves visible.
d. Left outer boot on 22 mm driveshaft, **Fig. 14,** end of boot butts against shoulder.
e. Right outer boot, **Fig. 15,** dimension (a) equals up to ½ groove visible.

4. Install constant velocity joint.
5. Install boot to joint, ensure boot is fully relaxed, then position clamps.
6. Crimp boot clamps, using crimping pliers tool No. VAG 1682 and a suitable torque wrench, or equivalents, **Fig. 16.**
7. **Torque** crimping pliers drive bolt to 18 ft. lbs.

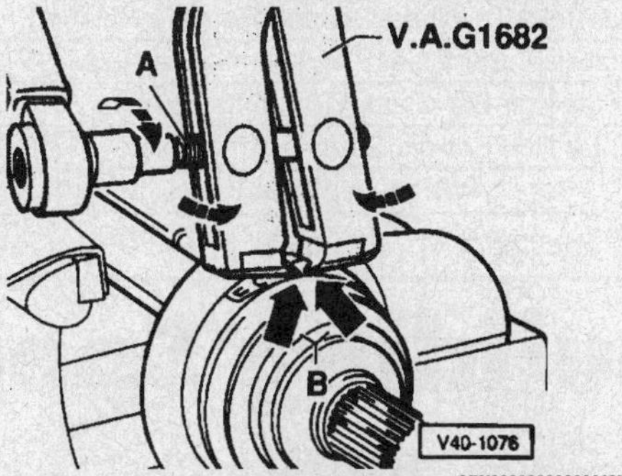
V.A.G1682
A
B
V40-1076

VW3039300020000X

Fig. 16 CV joint boot clamp crimping

TIGHTENING SPECIFICATIONS

Year	Component	Torque/ Ft. Lbs.
CABRIOLET		
1993–94	Axle Shaft To Hub Nuts	177
	Ball Joint To Wheel Bearing Housing Nuts	36
	Driveshaft Nut	177
	Hub Nut	177
	Strut To Wheel Bearing Housing Nuts	59
	Tie Rod End To Strut Assembly Nuts	22
	Wheel Lug Nuts	81
EUROVAN		
1993	Axle Shaft To Flange	41
	Axle Shaft To Wheel Hub	148
	Driveshaft Nut	148
	Hub Nut	148
	Shock Absorber To Control Arm	118
	Subframe mount	33
	Wheel Bearing Housing To Ball Joint	41
	Wheel Lug Nuts	118
EXCEPT CABRIOLET, FOX & EUROVAN		
1993–96	Axle Nut	66①
	Axle To Transaxle Flange	33
	Ball Joint To Control Arm Bolts	26
	Ball Joint To Wheel Bearing Housing Nuts	33
	Driveshaft Nut	66①
	Hub Nut	66①

Continued

TIGHTENING SPECIFICATIONS—Continued

Year	Component	Torque/ Ft. Lbs.
EXCEPT CABRIOLET, FOX & EUROVAN		
1993–96	Stabilizer Bar Link Rod To Control Arm Nuts	18
	Strut To Wheel Bearing Housing Nuts	70
	Tie Rod End To Wheel Bearing Housing Nuts	26
	Wheel Lug Nuts	81
FOX		
1993	Axle Shaft To Hub Nuts	170
	Ball Joint To Control Arm Nuts	48
	Ball Joint To Wheel Bearing Housing Nuts	44
	Stabilizer Bar Clamp To Control Arm Nuts	15
	Stabilizer Bar Clamp To Subframe Nuts	15
	Tie Rod End To Strut Assembly Nuts	29
	Wheel Lug Nuts	81

① — Plus an additional ⅛ (45°) turn.

Engine Rebuilding Specifications

INDEX

	Page No.
Camshaft	49-149
Crankshaft, Bearings & Rods	49-149
Cylinder Block	49-150
Cylinder Head, Valve Guide & Valve Seats	49-148
Oil Pump	49-150
Pistons, Pins & Rings	49-149
Valves	49-148

CYLINDER HEAD, VALVE GUIDE & VALVE SEATS

All Measurements Given In Inches, Unless Otherwise Specified.

Engine Liter	Year	Cylinder Head		Valve Stem To Guide Clearance②		Valve Seats		
		Warpage Limit	Minimum Height	Intake	Exhaust	Seat Angle, Degrees	Seat Width Intake	Seat Width Exhaust
1.8L	1993	.004	5.220	.039	.051	45	.079	.094
1.9L TDI①	1996	.004	–	.051	.051	45	.106	.087
2.0L 8V	1993–96	.004	–	.039	.051	45	.079	.094
2.0L 16V	1993–96	.004	4.650	.039	.051	45	–	–
2.5L	1993	.004	–	.039	.051	45	.079	.094
2.8L	1993–96	.004	–	.039	.051	45	.055	.079

① — Diesel.

② — Use dial indicator against head of valve to measure valve rock w/valve tip lifted flush with end of guide.

VALVES

All Measurements Given In Inches, Unless Otherwise Specified.

Engine Liter	Year	Valve Stem Diameter		Valve Installed Height⑤		Valve Face Angle, Degrees	Valve Clearance	
		Intake	Exhaust	Intake	Exhaust		Intake	Exhaust
1.8L	1993	.314	.313	—	—	45	②	③
1.9L TDI ①	1996	.314	.313	1.409	1.421	45	④	④
2.0L 8V	1993–96	.314	.313	1.331	1.343	45	④	④

Continued

VALVES—Continued

All Measurements Given In Inches, Unless Otherwise Specified.

Engine Liter	Year	Valve Stem Diameter		Valve Installed Height⑤		Valve Face Angle, Degrees	Valve Clearance	
		Intake	Exhaust	Intake	Exhaust		Intake	Exhaust
2.0L 16V	1993	.2744	.2732	—	—	45	④	④
2.5L	1993	.314	.313	1.313	1.343	45	④	④
2.8L	1993–96	.2744	.2736	1.336	1.343	45	④	④

① — Diesel.
② — Cold, .006–.010 inch; warm, .008–.012 inch.
③ — Cold, .014–.018 inch; warm, .016–.020 inch.
④ — Hydraulic lifters, no adjustment required.
⑤ — Minimum allowable distance, measured from tip of valve stem to level of valve cover surface.

CAMSHAFT

All Measurements Given In Inches, Unless Otherwise Specified.

Engine Liter	Year	Camshaft Bearing Clearance	Camshaft Endplay
1.8L	1993	.004	.006
1.9L TDI ①	1996	.004	.006
2.0L 8V	1993–96	.004	.006
2.0L 16V	1993	.004	.006
2.5L	1993	.004	.006
2.8L	1993–96	.004	.006

① — Diesel.

CRANKSHAFT, BEARINGS & RODS

All Measurements Given In Inches, Unless Otherwise Specified.

Engine Liter	Year	Crankshaft			Bearing Clearance		Connecting Rods	
		Standard Journal Diameter		End Play	Main Bearings	Connecting Rod Bearings	Piston Pin Bore Diameter	Side Clearance
		Main Bearing	Crank Pin					
1.8L	1993	2.1243–2.1251	1.8802–1.8810	.003–.007	.0010–.0030	.0047②	.787	.015②
1.9L TDI①	1996	2.1251–2.1244	1.8810–1.8803	.003–.007	.0012–.0031	.0031②	–	.0146②
2.0L 8V	1993–96	2.1251–2.1244	1.8810–1.8803	.003–.007	.0008–.0024	.0004–.0024	–	.002–.012
2.0L 16V	1993	2.1251–2.1276	1.8802–1.8810	.001	.0007–.0020	.0004–.0040	–	.0019–.0120
2.5L	1993	2.2843–2.2835	1.8825–1.8816	–	–	–	–	–
2.8L	1993–96	2.3251–2.3259	2.1243–2.1251	–	–	–	–	–

① — Diesel.
② — Wear limit.

PISTONS, PINS & RINGS

All Measurements Given In Inches, Unless Otherwise Specified.

Engine Liter	Year	Piston Diameter (Std.)	Piston Clearance	Piston Pin Diameter	Piston Ring End Gap		Piston Ring Side Clearance	
					Comp.	Oil	Comp.	Oil
1.8L	1993	3.1881	.0016	.787	.012–.018	.010–.0180	.0010–.0020	.0010–.0020

Continued

PISTONS, PINS & RINGS—Continued

All Measurements Given In Inches, Unless Otherwise Specified.

Engine Liter	Year	Piston Diameter (Std.)	Piston Clearance	Piston Pin Diameter	Piston Ring End Gap		Piston Ring Side Clearance	
					Comp.	Oil	Comp.	Oil
1.9L TDI①	1996	3.1291	.0012	1.020	.008–.016	.010–.020	②	.0012–.0024
2.0L 8V	1993–96	3.2474	.0010	.827	.008–.016	.010–.020	.0008–.0020	.0008–.0020
2.0L 16V	1993	3.2472	.0016	–	.007–.015	.009–.019	.0007–.0027	.0007–.0023
2.5L	1993	3.1884	.0016	–	.008–.016	.010–.020	.0007–.0019	.0007–.0019
2.8L	1993–96	3.1884	–	–	.008–.056	.010–.020	.0008–.0028	.0008–.0024

① — Diesel.
② — Top ring, .0035–.0050; second ring, .0020–.0031.

CYLINDER BLOCK

All Measurements Given In Inches, Unless Otherwise Specified.

Engine Liter	Year	Cylinder Bore Diameter (Std.)	Cylinder Bore Out Of Round (Max.)
1.8L	1993	3.1893	.0030
1.9L TDI①	1996	3.1303	.0039
2.0L 8V	1993–96	3.2484	.0015
2.0L 16V	1993	3.2484	.003
2.5L	1993	3.1893	.0015
2.8L	1993–96	3.1893	.0015

① — Diesel.

OIL PUMP

All Measurements Given In Inches, Unless Otherwise Specified.

Engine Liter	Year	Backlash		Axial Play
		New	Wear Limit	
1.8L	1993	.002	.008	.006
1.9L TDI	1996	.002	.006	.006
2.0L	1993–96	.002	.008	.006
2.5L	1993	—	—	—
2.8L	1993–96	.002	.008	.006

VOLVO

INDEX OF SERVICE OPERATIONS

	Page No.
AIR BAG SYSTEM PRECAUTIONS	0-8
AUTOMATIC TRANSMISSIONS/ TRANSAXLES	50-93
BRAKES	
Anti-Lock Brakes	50-77
Disc Brakes	50-73
Hydraulic Brake Systems	50-76
Power Brake Units	50-77
CLUTCH & MANUAL TRANSMISSION	
Adjustments	50-23
Clutch, Replace	50-24
Hydraulic System Service	50-23
Precautions	50-23
Tightening Specifications	50-25
Transaxle, Replace	50-24
Transmission, Replace	50-24
DRIVE AXLES	50-105
ELECTRICAL	
Air Bags	50-56
Air Conditioning	50-40
Alternators	50-52
Blower Motor, Replace	50-8
Coil Pack, Replace	50-7
Cooling Fans	50-46
Cruise Control	50-53
Dash Gauges	50-49
Dash Panel Service	50-66
Distributor, Replace	50-6
Evaporator Core, Replace	50-9
Fuel Pump Relay Location	50-6
Fuse Panel & Flasher Location	50-6
Headlamp Switch, Replace	50-7
Heater Core, Replace	50-8
Ignition Switch, Replace	50-7
Instrument Cluster, Replace	50-7
Neutral Safety Switch, Replace	50-7
Passive Restraints	50-56
Precautions	50-6
Relay Center Location	50-6
Speed Controls	50-53
Starter Motors	50-51
Starter, Replace	50-6
Steering Columns	50-67
Steering Wheel, Replace	50-7
Stop Light Switch, Replace	50-7
Turn Signal Switch, Replace	50-7
Wiper Motor, Replace	50-7
Wiper Switch, Replace	50-8
ELECTRICAL SYMBOL IDENTIFICATION	0-139
ENGINE	
Belt Tension Data	50-20
Camshaft Oil Seal, Replace	50-19
Camshaft, Replace	50-18
Compression Pressures	50-10
Cooling System Bleed	50-20
Crankshaft Seal, Replace	50-19
Cylinder Head, Replace	50-13
Engine Mount, Replace	50-10
Engine Rebuilding Specifications	50-107
Engine, Replace	50-11
Exhaust Manifold, Replace	50-13
Front Cover, Replace	50-17
Fuel Filter, Replace	50-21
Fuel Pump, Replace	50-21
Intake Manifold, Replace	50-13
Main & Rod Bearings	50-19
Oil Pan, Replace	50-20
Oil Pump, Replace	50-20
Piston & Rod Assembly	50-19
Pistons, Pins & Rings	50-19
Precautions	50-10
Radiator, Replace	50-21
Serpentine Drive Belt	50-20
Thermostat, Replace	50-21
Tightening Specifications	50-21
Timing Belt, Replace	50-17
Valve Adjustment	50-16
Valve Clearance Specifications	50-16
Valve Guides	50-16
Water Pump, Replace	50-21
FRONT SUSPENSION & STEERING	
Ball Joint Inspection	50-34
Ball Joint, Replace	50-34
Coil Spring, Replace	50-34
Control Arm Bushing, Replace	50-36
Control Arm, Replace	50-35
Power Steering	50-68
Power Steering Gear, Replace	50-36
Power Steering Pump, Replace	50-37
Precautions	50-34
Shock Absorber, Replace	50-34
Stabilizer Bar, Replace	50-36
Tightening Specifications	50-37
Wheel Bearing, Adjust	50-34
REAR AXLE & SUSPENSION	
Coil Spring, Replace	50-28
Control Arm, Replace	50-28
Differential Housing Bushings, Replace	50-31
Hub & Bearing, Replace	50-27
Reaction Rod & Bushings, Replace	50-27
Rear Axle, Replace	50-26
Rear Axle Link, Replace	50-31
Rear Axle Shaft, Replace	50-27
Shock Absorber, Replace	50-27
Stabilizer Bar, Replace	50-29
Support Arm, Replace	50-30
Tightening Specifications	50-32
Torque Rod & Bushings, Replace	50-27
Track Rod, Replace	50-29
Trailing Arm, Replace	50-29
Transverse Arm Mount, Replace	50-31
Upper Rear Axle Member Bushings, Replace	50-31
SERVICE REMINDER & WARNING LAMP RESET PROCEDURES	0-10
SPECIFICATIONS	
Engine, Transaxle/ Transmission & Rear Suspension Applications	50-2
Fluid Capacities & Cooling System Data	50-4
Front Wheel Alignment Specifications	50-4
General Engine Specifications	50-2
Lubricant Data	50-5
Rear Wheel Alignment Specifications	50-4
Tune Up Specifications	50-3
VEHICLE IDENTIFICATION	0-1
VEHICLE LIFT POINTS	0-34
VEHICLE MAINTENANCE SCHEDULES	0-69
WHEEL ALIGNMENT	
Front Wheel Alignment	50-38
Rear Wheel Alignment	50-40
Wheel Alignment Specifications	50-4
WIRE COLOR CODE IDENTIFICATION	0-144

Specifications

ENGINE, TRANSAXLE/TRANSMISSION & REAR SUSPENSION APPLICATIONS

Model	Engine Code/Liter	Man. Trans.	Auto. Trans.	Rear Suspension
1993				
240	B230F/2.3L	M47	AW-70	4-L Live
850	B5254FS/2.4L	M56	AW-42	Delta-Link
940	B230F/2.3L	—	AW-71	C-T Live
940 Turbo	B230FT/2.3L Turbo	—	AW-71	C-T Live
960 4-Door	B6304F/2.9L	—	AW-40	Multi-Link
960 5-Door	B6304F/2.9L	—	AW-40	C-T Live
1994				
850	B5254FS/2.4L	M56	AW-42	Delta-Link
940	B230F/2.3L	—	AW-71	C-T Live
940 Turbo	B230FT/2.3L Turbo	—	AW-71	C-T Live
960 4-Door	B6304F/2.9L	—	AW-40	Multi-Link
960 5-Door	B6304F/2.9L	—	AW-40	C-T Live
1995				
850	B5254FS/2.4L	M56	AW-42	Delta-Link
850 Turbo	B5234T/2.4L	M56	AW-42	Delta-Link
850R Turbo①	B5254FT/2.3L	M56	AW-42	Delta-Link
940	B230F/2.3L	—	AW-71	C-T Live
940 Turbo	B230FT/2.3L Turbo	—	AW-71	C-T Live
960	B6304F/2.9L		AW-40	Multi-Link
1996				
850	B5254FS/2.4L	M56	AW-42	Delta-Link
850 Turbo	B5234T/2.3L	M56	AW-42	Delta-Link
960	B6304F/2.9L	—	AW-40	Multi-Link

C-T Live — Constant-Trak live axle rear suspension.
Delta-Link — Fully independent multi-link rear suspension.
Multi-Link — Fully independent multi-link rear suspension.
4-L Live — 4-Link live axle semi-floating rear suspension.
① — California.

GENERAL ENGINE SPECIFICATIONS

Year	Model	Engine Liter	Fuel System	Bore & Stroke	Compression Ratio	Maximum Brake HP @ RPM	Maximum Torque Lbs. Ft. @ RPM	Normal Oil Pressure, psi
1993	240 Series	2.3L	MFI	3.780 X 3.150 (96 X 80 mm)	9.8	114 @ 5400	136 @ 2700	14.5–43.5
	850	2.4L	MFI	3.267 X 3.543 (83 X 90 mm)	10.5	168 @ 6200	162 @ 3300	14.5–43.5
	940	2.3L	MFI	3.780 X 3.150 (96 X 80 mm)	9.8	114 @ 5400	134 @ 2500	14.5–43.5
	940 Turbo	2.3L	MFI	3.780 X 3.150 (96 X 80 mm)	8.7	162 @ 4800	195 @ 3450	14.5–43.5
	960	2.9L	MFI	3.267 X 3.543 (83 X 90 mm)	10.7	201 @ 6000	197 @ 4300	14.5–43.5

Continued

GENERAL ENGINE SPECIFICATIONS—Continued

Year	Model	Engine Liter	Fuel System	Bore & Stroke	Compression Ratio	Maximum Brake HP @ RPM	Maximum Torque Lbs. Ft. @ RPM	Normal Oil Pressure, psi
1994	850	2.4L ①	MFI	3.267 X 3.543 (83 X 90 mm)	10.5	168 @ 6200	162 @ 3300	14.5–43.5
	940	2.3L	MFI	3.780 X 3.150 (96 X 80 mm)	9.8	114 @ 5400	136 @ 2150	14.5–43.5
	940 Turbo	2.3L	MFI	3.780 X 3.150 (96 X 80 mm)	8.7	162 @ 4800	195 @ 3450	14.5–43.5
	960	2.9L	MFI	3.267 X 3.543 (83 X 90 mm)	10.7	181 @ 5200	199 @ 4100	14.5–43.5
1995	850	2.4L	SFI	3.267 X 3.543 (83 X 90 mm)	③	①	②	14.5–43.5
	850R	2.3L	SFI	3.190 X 3.543 (81 X 90 mm)	8.5	240 @ 5600	221 @ 2100	14.5–43.5
	940	2.3L	SFI	3.780 X 3.150 (96 X 80 mm)	9.8	114 @ 5400	136 @ 2150	14.5–43.5
	940 Turbo	2.3L	SFI	3.780 X 3.150 (96 X 80 mm)	8.7	162 @ 4800	195 @ 3450	14.5–43.5
	960	2.9L	SFI	3.267 X 3.543 (83 X 90 mm)	10.7	181 @ 5200	199 @ 4100	14.5–43.5
1996	850	2.4L	SFI	3.267 X 3.543 (83 X 90 mm)	③	①	②	14.5–43.5
	850 Turbo	2.3L	SFI	3.190 X 3.543 (81 X 90 mm)	8.5	222 @ 5600	221 @ 2100	14.5–43.5
	960	2.9L	SFI	3.267 X 3.543 (83 X 90 mm)	10.7	181 @ 5200	199 @ 4100	14.5–43.5

① — Models equipped w/ M/T, 168 @ 6200; models equipped w/ A/T, 168 @ 6100.

② — Models equipped w/ M/T, 162 @ 3300; models equipped w/ A/T, 162 @ 4700.

③ — Models equipped w/ M/T, 10.5; models equipped w/ A/T, 10.3.

TUNE UP SPECIFICATIONS

Year	Engine	Spark Plug Gap, Inch	Ignition Timing			Curb Idle Speed②		Fuel Pressure, psi	Valve Clearance, Inch
			Firing Order	Timing, °BTDC	Timing Mark Fig.	Man. Trans.	Auto. Trans.		
1993	2.3L③	.030	1-3-4-2	12	A	750①	750①	36	.014–.018
	2.3L Turbo③	.030	1-3-4-2	12	A	700/800①	700/800①	42	.014–.018
	2.4L	.030	1-2-4-5-3	10	—	800	800	43	⑥
	2.9L	.030	1-5-3-6-2-4	5	—	750	750	43	⑥
1994	2.3L③	.030	1-3-4-2	12	A	775①	775①	36	.014–.018
	2.3L Turbo③	.030	1-3-4-2	12	A	750①	750①	42	.014–.018
	2.3L Turbo④⑤	.030	1-2-4-5-3	6	—	850①	850①	43	⑥
	2.4L	.030	1-2-4-5-3	10	—	800①	800①	43	⑥
	2.9L	.030	1-5-3-6-2-4	5	—	750①	750①	43	⑥
1995–96	2.3L③	.030	1-3-4-2	12	A	775①	775①	36	.014–.018
	2.3L Turbo④	.030	1-2-4-5-3	3-7	—	850①	850①	43	⑥
	2.4L	.030	1-2-4-5-3	10	—	800①	800①	43	⑥
	2.9L	.030	1-5-3-6-2-4	7-11	—	750①	750①	43	⑥

BTDC: Before Top Dead Center.

① — Controlled by Constant Idle Speed (CIS) system.

② — Where two speeds are listed, second speed is w/ A/C on. When adjusting idle speed, set parking brake & chock drive wheels.

③ — 4-cylinder engine.

④ — 5-cylinder engine.

⑤ — 850R models.

⑥ — Equipped with hydraulic lash adjusters; no adjustment is necessary.

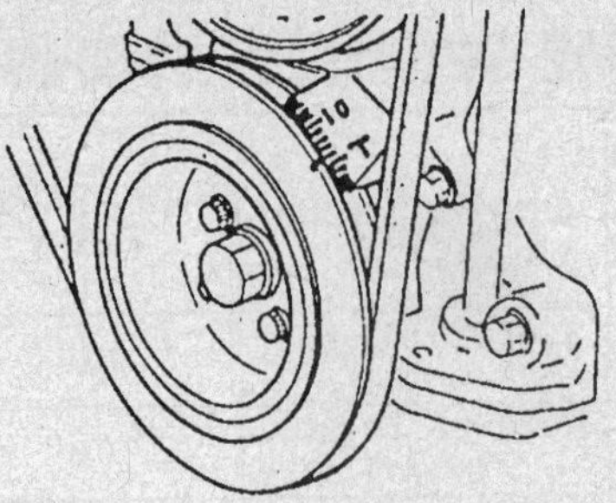

VV1139100017000X

Fig. A

FRONT WHEEL ALIGNMENT SPECIFICATIONS

Year	Model	Caster Angle, Degrees		Camber Angle, Degrees				Toe-In, Inch	Ball Joint Wear
				Limits		Desired			
		Limits	Desired	Left	Right	Left	Right		
1993	240	+3 to +4	+3 ½	+¼ to +¼	+¼ to +¾	+½	+½	⅙	①
	850	+2.35 to +4.35	+3.35	–1 to +1	–1 to +1	0	0	⅓	①
	940	+3 to +4	+3 ½	+¼ to +¾	+¼ to +¾	+½	+½	⅙	①
	960	+4 ½ to +6 ½	+5	–⅕ to +⅘	–⅕ to +⅘	3/10	3/10	3/10	①
1994–95	850	+2.35 to +4.35	+3.35	–1 to +1	–1 to +1	0	0	⅓	①
	940	+3 to +4	+3 ½	+¼ to +¾	+¼ to +¾	+½	+½	⅙	①
	960	+4 ½ to +6 ½	+5	–⅕ to +⅘	–⅕ to +⅘	3/10	3/10	3/10	①
1996	850	+2.35 to +4.35	+3.35	–1 to +1	–1 to +1	0	0	⅓	①
	960	+4 ½ to +6 ½	+5	–⅕ to +⅘	–⅕ to +⅘	3/10	3/10	3/10	①

① — Refer to "Ball Joint Inspection" under "Front Suspension & Steering."

REAR WHEEL ALIGNMENT SPECIFICATIONS

Year	Model	Camber Angle, Degrees		Toe-In, Inch
		Limits	Desired	
1993–96	850 Series	–1 ½ to –½	–1	0–.07
	960 4-Door	—	—	0–.03

FLUID CAPACITIES & COOLING SYSTEM DATA

Model	Engine	Cooling Capacity, Qts.	Radiator Cap Relief Pressure, Lbs.	Thermo Opening Temp., °F	Fuel Tank, Gals.	Engine Oil Refill, Qts.①	Transmission Oil		Axle Oil, Pints
							5 Speed, Pints	Auto. Trans, Qts.②	
1993									
240 Series	B230F	10	9–12	187–190	15.8	4.7	3.2	7.8	③
850	B5254FS	7.6	21.7	189	19.3	5.3	4.5	3.2	—
940	B230F	9.0	14.0	187–190	19.8	4.7	—	4.1	④
940 Turbo	B230FT	9.0	21.0	187–190	19.8	4.7	—	4.1	④
960	B6304F	11.3	21.0	189	⑤	6.0	—	3.3	④

Continued

FLUID CAPACITIES & COOLING SYSTEM DATA—Continued

Model	Engine	Cooling Capacity, Qts.	Radiator Cap Relief Pressure, Lbs.	Thermo Opening Temp., °F	Fuel Tank, Gals.	Engine Oil Refill, Qts.①	Transmission Oil		Axle Oil, Pints
							5 Speed, Pints	Auto. Trans, Qts.②	
1994–95									
850	B5254FS	7.6	22	189	19.3	5.3	4.5	8	—
850 Turbo	B5234T	7.4	22	189	19.3	5.6	4.4	8	—
850R Turbo	B5254FT	7.4	22	189	19.3	5.6	4.4	8	—
940	B230F	9	14	189	19.8	4	—	7.9	④
940 Turbo	B230FT	9	14	198	19.8	4⑥	—	7.9	④
960	B6304F	11.3	22	189	20.8	6	—	8.2	④
1996									
850	B5254FS	7.6	22	189	19.3	6.1	4.5	8	—
850 Turbo	B5234FT	7.6	22	189	19.3	5.6	4.4	8	—
960	B6304F	11.3	22	189	20.8	6	—	8.2	④

① — With filter change.
② — Approximate, make final check w/dipstick.
③ — Type 1030, 2.8; type 1031 or 1031F, 3.4.
④ — Type 1030 & 1045, 2.8; type 1031, 3.4; type 1035, 3.0 or type 1041, 3.1.
⑤ — 4-door models, 21.8 gals.; 5-door models, 19.8 gals.
⑥ — Oil cooler capacity is an additional .7 qts.

LUBRICANT DATA

Year	Model	Lubricant Type				
		Transmission		Rear Axle	Power Steering	Brake System
		Manual	Automatic			
1993–94	All	ATF Type F Or G	Dexron II	API GL-5	ATF Type A Or F	DOT 4
1995–96	940 & 960	①	Dexron IID/IIE/II/ Mercon	②	ATF Type F/G or Dexron IID/IIE/III	DOT 4+
	850	①	Dexron IID/IIE/II/ Mercon	—	ATF Type F/G or Dexron II/IIE/III	DOT 4+

① — Synthetic gear oil Volvo part No. 11 61423–7.

② — Ambient temperature above -10°F, 90 GL-5; below -10°F, 80 GL-5.

Electrical

NOTE: On Air Bag Equipped Models, Refer To "Air Bag System Precautions" Located In The Front Of This Manual For System Disarming & Arming Procedures.

INDEX

	Page No.
Air Bags	50-56
Air Conditioning	50-40
Alternators	50-52
Blower Motor, Replace	50-8
240	50-8
850	50-8
940 & 960	50-8
Coil Pack, Replace	50-7
2.9L Engine	50-7
Cooling Fans	50-54
Cruise Control	50-53
Dash Gauges	50-49
Dash Panel Service	50-66
Distributor, Replace	50-6
Installation	50-7
Removal	50-6
Evaporator Core, Replace	50-9
240	50-9
850	50-9
940 & 960	50-9
Fuel Pump Relay Location	50-6
240	50-6
850	50-6
940 & 1993–94 960	50-6
1995–96 960	50-6
Fuse Panel & Flasher Location	50-6
240	50-6
850	50-6
940 & 1993–94 960	50-6
1995–96 960	50-6
Headlamp Switch, Replace	50-7
240	50-7
940 & 960	50-7
Heater Core, Replace	50-8
240	50-8
850	50-8
940 & 960	50-8
Ignition Switch, Replace	50-7
240	50-7
940 & 960	50-7
Instrument Cluster, Replace	50-7
240	50-7
850	50-7
940 & 960	50-7
Neutral Safety Switch, Replace	50-7
Passive Restraints	50-56
Precautions	50-6
Air Bag Systems	50-6
Microprocessor Radios	50-6
Relay Center Location	50-6
240	50-6
850	50-6
940 & 960	50-6
Speed Controls	50-53
Starter Motors	50-51
Starter, Replace	50-6
Steering Columns	50-67
Steering Wheel, Replace	50-7
Stop Light Switch, Replace	50-7
Turn Signal Switch, Replace	50-7
240, 940 & 960	50-7
850	50-7
Wiper Motor, Replace	50-7
240	50-7
850	50-8
940 & 960	50-8
Wiper Switch, Replace	50-8
240, 940 & 960	50-8
850	50-8

PRECAUTIONS

AIR BAG SYSTEMS

Refer to "Air Bag System Precautions" in the front of this manual for system disarming and arming procedures.

MICROPROCESSOR RADIOS

On models equipped with microprocessor radios, always switch radio off before disconnecting or connecting battery ground cable to prevent damage to the radio.

FUSE PANEL & FLASHER LOCATION

240

The fuse panel is behind the driver side kick panel, and the flasher is behind the center console.

940 & 1993-94 960

The fuse panel and flasher are behind the ashtray in the center console.

850

The fuse panel is located in the lefthand rear corner of the engine compartment.

1995-96 960

The fuse panel is behind the far lefthand corner of the instrument panel, and the flasher is behind the instrument panel on the righthand side of the steering wheel.

FUEL PUMP RELAY LOCATION

240

The fuel pump relay is located behind the lefthand side of the instrument panel, to the left of the steering column.

850

The fuel pump relay is located in the fuse/relay box, to the rear lefthand side of the engine compartment.

940 & 1993-94 960

The fuel pump relay is located in the fuse/relay box, behind the ashtray in the center of the instrument panel.

1995-96 960

The fuel pump relay is located in the fuse/relay box, to the lefthand side of the instrument panel.

RELAY CENTER LOCATION

240

The relay panel is located behind the driver side kick panel.

940 & 960

The relay panel is located behind the center of the instrument panel, behind the ashtray.

850

The engine compartment relay panel is located in the rear lefthand corner of the engine compartment. The passenger compartment relay panel is located under the steering column, behind the soundproofing panel.

STARTER

REPLACE

1. Disconnect battery cable.
2. Disconnect starter leads.
3. Remove two starter mounting bolts, then the starter.
4. Reverse procedure to install.

DISTRIBUTOR

REPLACE

REMOVAL

1. Remove distributor cap, then turn engine until rotor arm is aligned with timing mark on distributor housing.
2. Mark housing position in direction to cylinder block.
3. Loosen attaching bolts, then remove distributor.

INSTALLATION

1. Turn rotor arm to position approximately 30° after mark.
2. Mount distributor in position, ensuring drive gears engage.
3. Ensure rotor arm and housing are aligned with appropriate marks.

COIL PACK

REPLACE

2.9L ENGINE

1. Disconnect battery ground cable.
2. Remove ignition coil cover screws and cover.
3. Mark positions of ignition coils, **Fig. 1**, then remove coil retaining bolts.
4. Disconnect coil electrical connectors and remove coils.
5. Reverse procedure to install.

6
5
4
3
2
1

VV11191000260000X

Fig. 1 Ignition coils. 2.9L engine

IGNITION SWITCH

REPLACE

240

1. Disconnect battery ground cable.
2. Remove noise insulation panel and center side panel.
3. Disconnect terminal block from ignition switch.
4. Remove ignition switch.

940 & 960

1. Disconnect battery ground cable.
2. Remove noise insulation panel below instrument panel, then disconnect electrical connector from switch.
3. Remove upper steering column cover and casing around switch.
4. Loosen switch mounting screw, then install key and position switch in Start position.
5. Working through hole beneath holder, depress catch and remove switch from vehicle.
6. Insert key into new switch, depress locking tab, the remove key.
7. Position switch in holder and reinsert key to release locking tab.
8. Tighten switch mounting screw, then install column casing and cover.
9. Connect electrical connector, then install noise insulation panel.

NEUTRAL SAFETY SWITCH

REPLACE

The switch is located inside the passenger compartment and is mounted directly beneath the gear shift selector. Remove the selector cover and loosen the two retaining bolts to adjust or replace the switch.

HEADLAMP SWITCH

REPLACE

240

1. Disconnect defroster hose from defroster outlet.
2. Remove screws retaining outlet.
3. Pull out switch knob.
4. Lift out defroster outlet.
5. Remove nut and lift out switch.

940 & 960

1. Disconnect battery ground cable.
2. Remove trim panel under dashboard, then disconnect switch wires.
3. Remove switch retaining nut and switch.

STOP LIGHT SWITCH

REPLACE

1. Disconnect battery ground cable.
2. Disconnect switch wires.
3. Remove switch retaining nut. Remove switch.
4. When installing switch, be sure that distance between brake pedal when fully released, and thread bronze hub on switch is 4 mm (.008). If necessary, adjust by loosening bracket attaching screw and moving bracket.

TURN SIGNAL SWITCH

REPLACE

240, 940 & 960

1. Remove screws holding upper and lower switch covers and remove covers.
2. Where necessary, remove overdrive switch bracket.
3. Remove turn signal switch mounting screws and remove switch.

850

1. Park vehicle on a level surface, then turn ignition switch to Off position and disconnect battery ground cable.
2. Remove steering wheel as outlined under "Steering Wheel, Replace," then the steering column covers.
3. Remove turn signal switch.
4. Reverse procedure to install.

STEERING WHEEL

REPLACE

1. Remove two Torx screws from rear of steering wheel, then disconnect electrical connector and remove air bag assembly, **Fig. 2.**
2. Remove center attaching screw from steering wheel.
3. Loosen screw at end of plastic strap from Park position in steering wheel.
4. Place screw in pin on contact reel. Screw will now lock contact reel in zero position. **Be careful not to turn steering wheel. Otherwise it will shear head off lockpin.**
5. Remove steering wheel.
6. Remove upper and lower column casing attaching screws, then remove casings.
7. Reverse procedure to install, noting the following:
   a. Position steering wheel so contact reel pin is in center of hole in steering wheel.
   b. **Torque** center bolt to 24 ft. lbs.
   c. **Torque** Torx screws to 8 ft. lbs.
   d. Ensure wires are not kinked or pinched.

INSTRUMENT CLUSTER

REPLACE

240

1. Remove covers over the steering column.
2. Remove attaching screws for the bracket and allow it to drop down toward the steering column. Remove the cluster attaching screws.
3. Disconnect speedometer cable.
4. Take hold of back side of the speedometer unit and press upward and out until the snap lock in the upper edge releases.
5. Lift out the cluster and disconnect the electrical leads.

940 & 960

1. Remove insulation and sound proofing from under instrument panel.
2. Remove two attaching screws and catches, located at both ends of instrument cluster.
3. Press cluster forward to remove from catches, then lift up and partially pull out cluster.
4. Disconnect speedometer and electrical connections from cluster, then remove cluster.

850

1. Disconnect battery ground cable, then remove instrument panel as outlined in "Dash Panel Service."
2. Disconnect instrument cluster electrical connectors, then release two spring catches on upper edge of cluster and lift cluster out.
3. Reverse procedure to install.

WIPER MOTOR

REPLACE

240

1. Disconnect battery ground cable, then remove side panel.
2. Remove glove compartment.

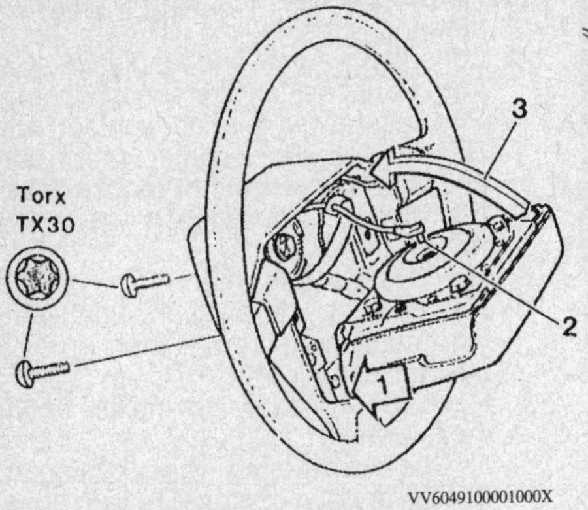
Torx
TX30
3
2
1
VV6049100001000X

Fig. 2 Steering wheel replacement

3. Disconnect the linkage to motor retaining nut and remove retaining bolts. Lift motor off of firewall.

940 & 960

1. Remove wiper arm, then lift hood and disconnect battery ground cable.
2. Remove cover plate attaching screws and clips, then lift out cover plate.
3. Close hood and remove motor cover located below the windshield.
4. Disconnect all electrical connections, then remove attaching screws and wiper assembly.
5. Remove motor from wiper assembly.

850

1. Disconnect battery ground cable and ensure wiper motor is in Park position.
2. Remove wiper arms as follows:
   a. Loosen wiper arm nut a few turns, then release wiper arm from splines by levering against nut and pressing arm up using a pair of adjustable pliers.
   b. Remove nut and arm.
3. Remove cover plate, then disconnect two drainage tubes.
4. Remove wiper assembly securing screws, then pull assembly outward to release it from its socket.
5. Disconnect electrical connectors, then remove wiper assembly.
6. Turn wiper assembly upside down, then mark connecting rod and remove.
7. Remove wiper motor from assembly.
8. Reverse procedure to install. **Torque** wiper arm nuts to 12 ft. lbs.

WIPER SWITCH

REPLACE

240, 940 & 960

1. Remove covers over steering column.
2. Remove switch retaining screws.
3. Transfer wires to new switch and install retaining screws and covers.

850

1. Park vehicle on a level surface, then turn ignition switch to Off position and disconnect battery ground cable.

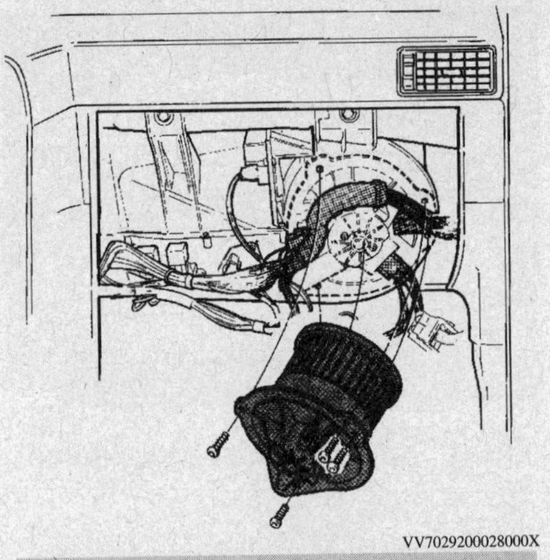
VV7029200028000X

Fig. 3 Blower motor replacement. 850

2. Remove steering wheel as outlined previously, then the steering column covers.
3. Remove wiper switch.
4. Reverse procedure to install.

BLOWER MOTOR

REPLACE

240

1. Disconnect battery ground cable.
2. Remove trim panels from both sides of center console.
3. Snap off retaining clips for both side covers of heater unit.
4. Slip retaining clips off turbine wheels on each side of the heater.
5. Move the heater control valve capillary tube to one side.
6. Remove the lefthand inner end of the central unit.
7. Remove the motor retainer, disconnect the wires and lift out the motor.

940 & 960

1. Disconnect battery ground cable.
2. Remove trim panel under glove compartment.
3. Remove blower motor attaching screws, then lower motor and disconnect all hoses and electrical connections.
4. Remove fan and blower motor.

850

1. Remove passenger side sound wall, then the glove compartment and glove compartment panel.
2. Disconnect blower motor electrical connector, then the cable duct from blower motor.
3. Disconnect two connectors from their brackets, then remove blower motor, **Fig. 3.**
4. Reverse procedure to install.

HEATER CORE

REPLACE

240

1. Drain coolant, then disconnect battery

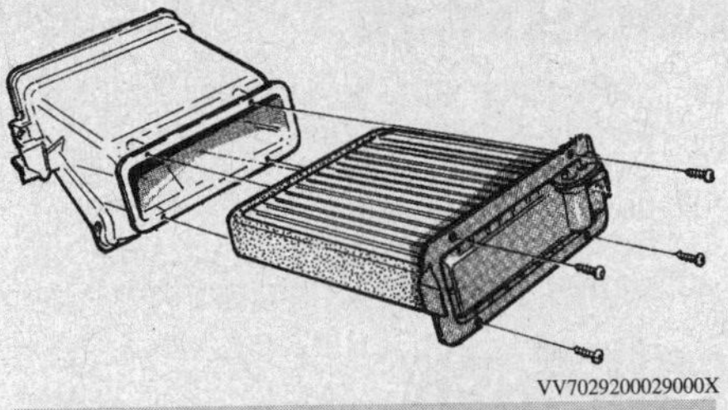
VV7029200029000X

Fig. 4 Heater core removal. 850

ground cable.
2. Remove heater hoses from connections at firewall and plug connections.
3. **On models equipped with A/C,** remove holding clamps from evaporator hoses. **Do not discharge the air conditioning system, simply loosen the retaining clamps to allow removal of the firewall door.**
4. **On all models,** remove instrument cluster.
5. Disconnect air ducts and vacuum hoses.
6. Remove unit mounting bolts.
7. Carry out steps 2–6 under "Blower Motor, Replace" procedure.
8. Remove evaporator from central unit without disconnecting evaporator hoses.
9. Disconnect heater valve hoses and remove the heater core.

940 & 960

1. Drain coolant, then disconnect battery ground cable.
2. Remove heater hose from connections at fire wall and plug connections.
3. Remove ashtray and holder, lighter and storage compartment, then remove center console.
4. Remove lefthand side trim panel from under dash, then remove air duct under steering column.
5. Remove glove compartment and electrical connections, then upper console side panels.
6. Remove radio compartment attaching bolts, then radio compartment.
7. Remove panel around heater control, radio console and control panel attaching screws.
8. Remove control panel cables and electrical connections, then remove control panel.
9. Remove center panel vents, distribution unit attaching screws and remaining air ducts.
10. Remove vacuum motor hoses, then aspirator hoses, if equipped with Automatic Climate Control (ACC).
11. Remove distribution unit, then four heater core attaching bolts and heater core.

850

1. Close off heater hoses using hose pliers, then remove righthand and lefthand sound wall.
2. Remove carpet support plates, then the amplifier, if equipped, and amplifier bracket.
3. Remove drain hose, then the heater

exchanger screws.
4. Place an appropriate amount of absorbent paper under heat exchanger pipe flange to soak up any escaping coolant, then remove heat exchanger pipe flange screws.
5. Disconnect pipes from heater, then remove heater and cover by pulling backward toward selector lever and twisting slightly upward at the same time.
6. Remove heater core from heater cover, **Fig. 4.**
7. Reverse procedure to install, noting the following:
   a. Refill coolant as necessary and check for leaks.

EVAPORATOR CORE

REPLACE

240

1. Disconnect battery ground cable.
2. Discharge refrigerant into an approved recovery/recycling device compatible with refrigerant type.
3. Remove glove compartment and panel beneath glove compartment.
4. Remove side panel next to heater.
5. Remove righthand defroster vent and air duct.
6. Remove expansion valve, insulation and cover.
7. Disconnect evaporator connections, then remove evaporator.
8. Reverse procedure to install. **Torque** refrigerant hose to 22 ft. lbs. Evacuate refrigerant into an approved container, recharge system and check for leaks.

940 & 960

1. Disconnect battery ground cable.
2. Discharge refrigerant into an approved recovery/recycling device compatible with refrigerant type.
3. Disconnect evaporator connections in engine compartment and plug all openings.
4. Remove panel beneath glove compartment, then the glove compartment.
5. Disconnect electrical connectors for fan motor and resistor, if equipped.
6. Remove screws securing lower fan housing cover. **Two screws are hidden beneath fan housing and evaporator housing.**
7. Remove cover and lift out evaporator.
8. Reverse procedure to install. **Torque** hose to evaporator to 13–15 ft. lbs. **Torque** hose to condenser to 11–13 ft. lbs.
9. Evacuate refrigerant into an approved container, recharge system and check for leaks.

850

1. Disconnect battery ground cable, then remove instrument panel as outlined in "Dash Panel Service" section.
2. Discharge refrigerant into an approved recovery/recycling device compatible with refrigerant type.
3. Disconnect pipes to evaporator using snap-on connector remover tool No. 5385-5472, or equivalent, then plug pipes.
4. Remove cover plate and rubber gasket on bulkhead opening.
5. Close off heater hoses using hose pliers, then disconnect quick-release couplings on hoses by pressing catches together and pulling hose out.
6. Plug heater pipes, then remove cover plate and rubber gasket from firewall opening.
7. Disconnect blower motor electrical connection, recirculation damper motor electrical connection, blower motor resistor connector and connectors on brackets.
8. Remove cable duct from blower motor, then the blower relay and relay base from relay shelf and the relay shelf.
9. Open control box and disconnect control lighting connector, then close control box.
10. Remove console as follows:
    a. Remove ashtray and cigarette lighter bracket, then the console securing screws.
    b. Place selector lever in neutral and apply parking brake, then remove parking brake socket cover plate.
    c. Remove console by lifting up and moving slightly forward at the same time.
11. Remove carpet backing boards, then disconnect rear floor ducts.
12. Remove amplifier, if equipped, then the amplifier bracket.
13. Remove drain hose.
14. **On models with Manual Climate Control (MCC),**disconnect cable to righthand temperature damper.
15. **On all models,** disconnect cruise control vacuum cylinder from climate control unit, if equipped, then remove climate control unit.
16. Remove evaporator cover, then the evaporator core.
17. Reverse procedure to install, noting the following:
    a. Refill coolant as necessary and check for leaks.
    b. Fill A/C system with refrigerant and check for leaks. Refer to "Air Conditioning" section.

Engine

NOTE: On Air Bag Equipped Models, Refer To "Air Bag System Precautions" Located In The Front Of This Manual For System Disarming & Arming Procedures.

INDEX

	Page No.
Belt Tension Data	50-20
Camshaft Oil Seal, Replace	50-19
Except 2.3L 4-Cylinder Engine	50-19
Camshaft, Replace	50-18
Except 2.3L 4-Cylinder Engine	50-19
2.3L 4-Cylinder Engine	50-18
Compression Pressures	50-10
Cooling System Bleed	50-20
Except 2.3L 4-Cylinder Engine	50-20
2.3L 4-Cylinder Engine	50-20
Crankshaft Seal, Replace	50-19
Front	50-19
Rear	50-20
Cylinder Head, Replace	50-13
2.3L 4-Cylinder Engines	50-13
2.4L & 2.3L 5-Cylinder Engines	50-14
2.9L Engine	50-15
Engine Mount, Replace	50-10
240	50-10
850	50-10
940	50-10
960	50-11
Engine Rebuilding Specifications	50-107
Engine, Replace	50-11
240	50-11
850	50-12
940	50-11
960	50-12
Exhaust Manifold, Replace	50-13
2.3L 4-Cylinder Engine	50-13
2.4L & 2.3L 5-Cylinder Engines	50-13
2.9L Engine	50-13
Front Cover, Replace	50-17
2.3L 4-Cylinder Engine	50-17
2.4L & 2.3L 5-Cylinder Engine	50-17
2.9L Engine	50-17
Fuel Filter, Replace	50-21
2.3L 4-Cylinder & 2.9L Engines	50-21
2.4L & 2.3L 5-Cylinder Engines	50-21
Fuel Pump, Replace	50-21
2.3L & 2.4L 5-Cylinder Engines	50-21
2.3L 4-Cylinder & 2.9L Engines	50-21
Intake Manifold, Replace	50-13
2.3L 4-Cylinder Engine	50-13
2.4L & 2.3L 5-Cylinder Engines	50-13
2.9L Engine	50-13
Main & Rod Bearings	50-19
Except 2.3L 4-Cylinder Engine	50-19
2.3L 4-Cylinder Engine	50-19
Oil Pan, Replace	50-20
Except 2.3L 4-Cylinder Engines	50-20
2.3L 4-Cylinder Engine	50-20
Oil Pump, Replace	50-20
Except 2.3L 4-Cylinder Engine	50-20
2.3L 4-Cylinder Engine	50-20
Piston & Rod Assembly	50-19
Except 2.3L 4-Cylinder Engine	50-19
2.3L 4-Cylinder Engine	50-19
Pistons, Pins & Rings	50-19
Except 2.3L 4-Cylinder Engine	50-19
2.3L 4-Cylinder Engine	50-19
Precautions	50-10
Air Bag Systems	50-10
Microprocessor Radios	50-10
Radiator, Replace	50-21
Serpentine Drive Belt	50-20
Belt Routing	50-20
Thermostat, Replace	50-21
Tightening Specifications:	50-21
2.3L 4-Cylinder Engine	50-21
2.3L & 2.4L 5-Cylinder Engine	50-22
2.9L Engine	50-23
Timing Belt, Replace	50-17
2.3L 4-Cylinder Engine	50-17
2.4L & 2.3L 5-Cylinder Engines	50-17
2.9L Engine	50-18
Valve Adjustment	50-16
Except 2.3L 4-Cylinder Engine	50-16
2.3L 4-Cylinder Engine	50-16
Valve Clearance Specifications	50-16
Except 2.3L 4-Cylinder Engine	50-16
2.3L 4-Cylinder Engine	50-16
Valve Guides	50-16
Except 2.3L 4-Cylinder Engine	50-17
2.3L 4-Cylinder Engine	50-16
Water Pump, Replace	50-21
Except 2.3L 4-Cylinder Engine	50-21
2.3L 4-Cylinder Engine	50-21

PRECAUTIONS

AIR BAG SYSTEMS

Refer to "Air Bag System Precautions" in the front of this manual for system disarming and arming procedures.

MICROPROCESSOR RADIOS

On models equipped with microprocessor radios, always switch radio off before disconnecting or connecting battery ground cable to prevent damage to the radio.

COMPRESSION PRESSURES

1. Disconnect timing pick-up connector.
2. Remove ignition wiring cover.
3. Lock throttle in fully open position.
4. Remove spark plugs and connect starter switch (part No. 1158263, or equivalent) between alternator positive terminal and service socket of control unit box.
5. Using compression gauge tool No. 9689, or equivalent, and extension sleeve (part No. 1158540, or equivalent), measure compression in all cylinders.
6. **On 2.3L 4-cylinder engine,** compression pressure should measure 128–156 psi with engine hot.
7. **On 2.3L 5-cylinder turbocharged engine,** compression pressure should be 156–185 psi with engine hot.
8. **On 2.4L engine,** compression pressure should measure 188–218 psi with engine hot.
9. **On 2.9L engine,** compression pressure should measure 197–213 psi with engine hot.
10. **On all models,** the maximum difference between cylinder compression pressures should be 28 psi.

ENGINE MOUNT

REPLACE

240

1. Disconnect battery ground cable, then release tension from mounts using lifting beam tool No. 5006, or equivalent, two support rails tool No. 5033, or equivalent, and lifting hook tool No. 5115, or equivalent.
2. Remove oil filter, if necessary, then the righthand or lefthand mount, as necessary.
3. Reverse procedure to install.

940

1. Disconnect battery ground cable, then remove mount nuts.
2. Cut strap for power steering hose, if necessary, then release tension from mounts using lifting beam tool No. 5006, or equivalent, two support rails tool No. 5033, or equivalent, and lifting hook tool No. 5115, or equivalent.
3. Remove righthand or lefthand mount as necessary.
4. Reverse procedure to install.

850

FRONT MOUNT

Manual Transmission

1. Remove upper torque arm bolt from engine, then loosen upper torque arm bolt in body mounting and push arm to one side.
2. Remove front mount nut, splashguard

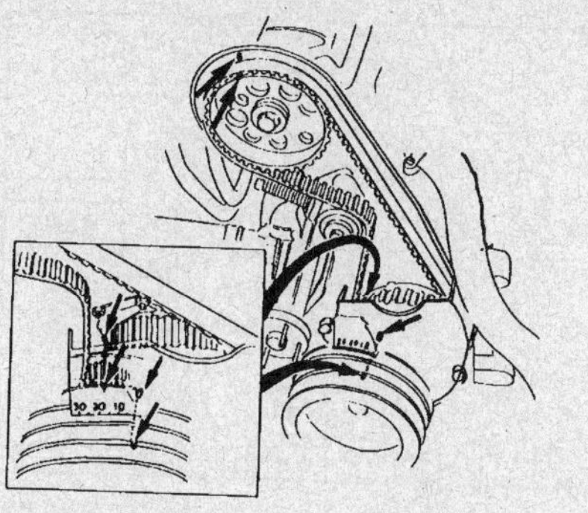

VV1069100001000X

Fig. 1 Aligning timing marks. 2.3L 4-cylinder engine

under engine, lower torque arm bolt and front mount bolt.
3. Raise engine slightly using assembly hoist tool No. 998 5972, or equivalent, then remove front mount.
4. Reverse procedure to install. **Torque** upper and lower torque arm bolts to 37 ft. lbs.

Automatic Transmission

1. Remove splashguard under engine, lower torque arm bolt and front mount bolt.
2. Remove electric cooling fan and upper torque arm bolt from engine, then loosen upper torque arm bolt in body mounting and push arm to one side.
3. Remove front mount nut, then raise engine slightly and remove front mount.
4. Reverse procedure to install. **Torque** upper and lower torque arm bolts to 37 ft. lbs.

RIGHTHAND MOUNT

1. Remove righthand front wheel, then the inner fender liner as required to gain access to mount.
2. Remove mount bolts, then raise engine slightly and remove mount.
3. Reverse procedure to install. **Torque** bolts to 18 ft. lbs.

REAR MOUNT

1. Remove mount nut, then the upper torque arm bolt.
2. Remove splashguard under engine, lower torque arm bolt and mount bolt.
3. Raise engine a maximum of 1.181 inches (30 mm) using assembly hoist tool No. 998 5972 9, or equivalent, then remove two engine mounting bracket bolts and loosen third bolt slightly. **Do not raise engine more than specified or damage to inner universal joint on lefthand side may result.**
4. Remove mount by lifting engine mounting bracket and shield slightly.
5. Reverse procedure to install. **Torque** upper and lower torque arm bolts to 37 ft. lbs.

960

LEFTHAND MOUNT

1. Disconnect battery ground cable, then

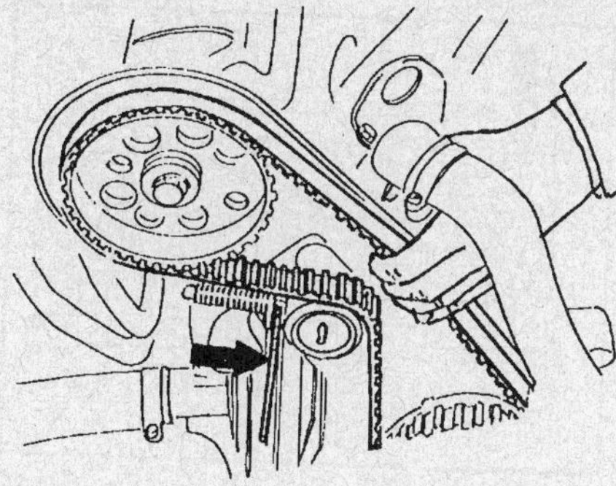

VV1069100002000X

Fig. 2 Locking tensioner spring. 2.3L 4-cylinder engine

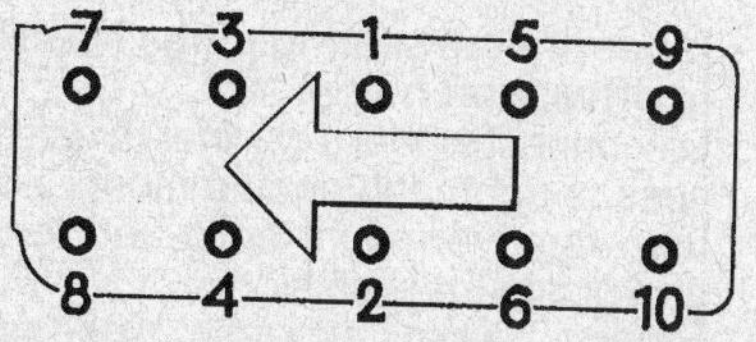
7 3 1 5 9
8 4 2 6 10

VV1069100004000X

Fig. 4 Cylinder head tightening sequence. 2.3L 4-cylinder engine

remove mount top nut.
2. Using lifting beam tool No. 5006, or equivalent, two support rails tool No. 5033, or equivalent, and lifting hook tool No. 5115, or equivalent, with a 15 mm spacer between lifting yoke and hook, raise engine using the lefthand front lifting lug.
3. Remove splashguard under engine, then the mount nuts and bolt.
4. Remove mount with bracket toward front holding lower edge, then the mount from bracket.
5. Reverse procedure to install. **Torque** mount top nut to 37 ft. lbs.

RIGHTHAND MOUNT

1. Remove mount top nut.
2. Using lifting beam tool No. 5006, or equivalent, two support rails tool No. 5033, or equivalent, and lifting hooks tool Nos. 5115 and 5186, or equivalents, line up lifting lug, then raise engine using the righthand front lifting lug.
3. Remove splashguard under engine, then the mount nuts and bolt.
4. Remove mount with bracket toward rear, then the mount from bracket.
5. Reverse procedure to install. **Torque** mount top nut to 37 ft. lbs.

ENGINE

REPLACE

240

The engine and transmission are removed as an assembly.

1. Open hood, then scribe hood hinge locations and remove hood.
2. Disconnect battery ground cable.
3. Remove air filter.
4. Drain coolant from radiator and oil from engine.

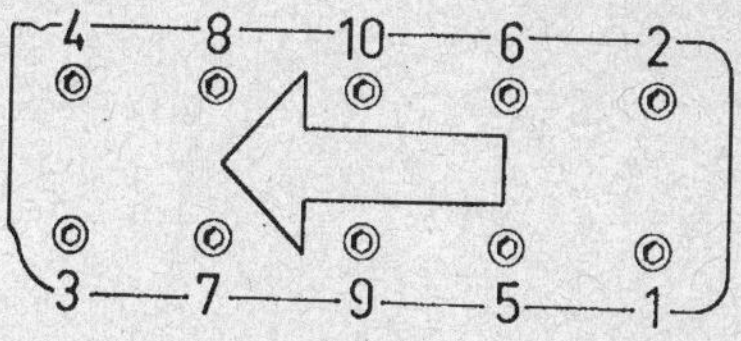
4 8 10 6 2
3 7 9 5 1

VV1069100003000X

Fig. 3 Cylinder head loosening sequence. 2.3L 4-cylinder engine

5. Disconnect radiator hoses, then remove radiator and fan cover.
6. **On turbocharged models,** loosen attaching bolts, then disconnect exhaust pipe from turbocharger assembly.
7. **On models with A/C,** remove attaching bolts, then move servo pump and A/C compressor aside. **Do not disconnect lines and/or hoses.**
8. **On all models,** label, then disconnect all necessary vacuum lines, fuel lines, electrical connectors and water hoses from engine.
9. Raise and support front of vehicle.
10. Remove engine splash guard attaching bolts, then the splash guard.
11. **On naturally aspirated models,** disconnect exhaust pipe from manifolds.
12. **On all models,** remove engine to front axle crossmember mount bolts.
13. Remove front exhaust pipe support from transmission.
14. **On models with manual transmission,** disconnect clutch cable, then remove gearshift lever.
15. **On models with automatic transmission,** disconnect selector linkage from transmission.
16. **On all models,** disconnect speedometer cable from transmission.
17. Disconnect driveshaft from transmission.
18. Position a suitable jack under transmission assembly, then remove transmission crossmember.
19. Disconnect electrical connectors from transmission.
20. Install lifting sling tool No. 5035 and lifting yoke tool No. 2810, or equivalents.
21. Carefully lift engine and transmission assembly from vehicle.
22. Reverse procedure to install.

940

The engine and transmission are removed as an assembly.

1. Disconnect battery ground cable, then drain cooling system and crankcase.
2. Remove distributor cap, if necessary.
3. Remove preheating hose and fan shroud.
4. **On turbo models,** disconnect exhaust pipe at turbocharger assembly.
5. **On models equipped with power steering and A/C,** remove attaching bolts and position power steering pump and A/C compressor aside. **Do not disconnect lines and/or hoses.**
6. **On all models,** disconnect all electrical wires, hoses, lines and cables that will interfere will engine removal. Label all vacuum hoses to aid in installation.
7. Raise and support vehicle, then remove engine splash guard attaching

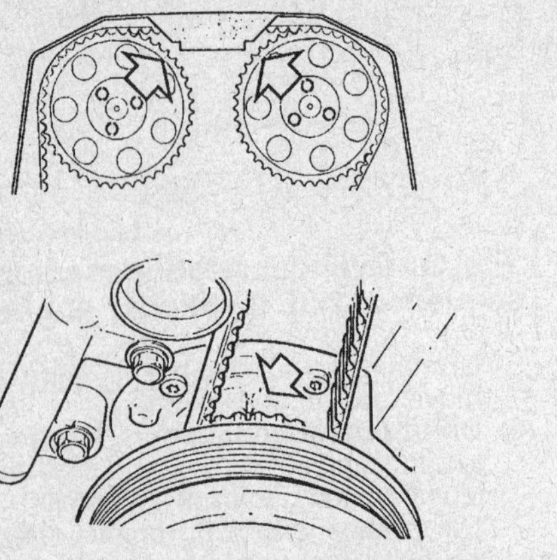

VV1069100008000X

Fig. 5 Aligning timing marks. Except 2.3L 4-cylinder engine

screws and guard.

8. **On naturally aspirated models,** disconnect exhaust pipe from manifold.
9. **On all models,** remove engine mount to front crossmember attaching bolts.
10. Remove front exhaust pipe support from transmission.
11. **On models equipped with manual transmission,**disconnect clutch cable and remove gearshift lever.
12. **On models equipped with automatic transmission,**disconnect selector linkage from transmission.
13. **On all models,** disconnect speedometer cable, then remove driveshaft from transmission. On some models, the front U-joint is insulated for vibration with a rubber mount. Use care when separating joint from output flange to prevent damage to rubber mounting.
14. Support transmission with suitable jack, remove rear crossmember, then disconnect all electrical connectors from transmission.
15. Install lifting sling tool No. 5035 and lifting yoke tool No. 2810, or equivalents, then carefully lift engine/transmission assembly from vehicle.
16. Reverse procedure to install.

850

The engine and transmission are removed as an assembly.

1. Remove coolant expansion tank cap, then raise and support vehicle.
2. Remove splashguard and air baffle under engine, then open drain cocks on cylinder block and radiator and drain coolant.
3. Remove front wheel, disconnect steering arm/wheel spindle joints, then remove nuts securing ball joints to support arms.
4. Remove ABS lead and brake pipe/hose bracket retaining bolt, then the lefthand driveshaft. **Use lever tool No. 5462, or equivalent, to free shaft.**
5. Disconnect thin black hoses from EVAP canister and white hose from vacuum reservoir.
6. Remove righthand driveshaft and intermediate bearing cap. **Place components carefully on steering servo**

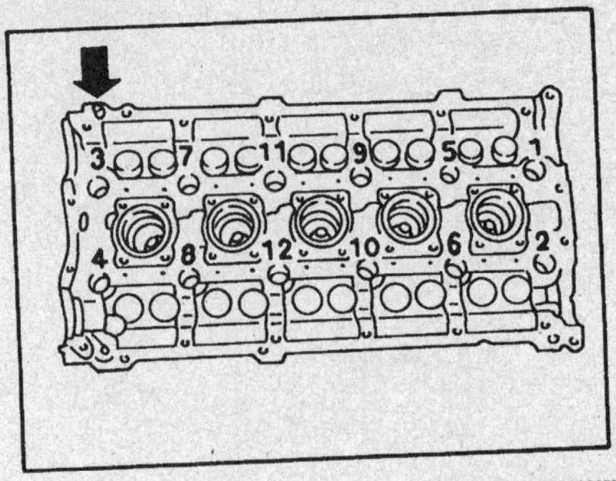
3
7
11
9
5
1
4
8
12
10
6
2

VV1069100009000X

Fig. 6 Cylinder head bolt loosening sequence. 2.4L & 2.3L 5-cylinder engines

pipes. Install sealing plugs No. 5488 in driveshaft holes.

7. Disconnect wheel arch liner to gain access to righthand engine mount bolts, then remove mount bolts and torque arm bolt in transmission.
8. Remove front exhaust pipe nuts, springs and bolts and transmission/engine mounting shield bolt, then disconnect speedometer connector and lower vehicle.
9. Remove battery and battery shelf, fresh air hose between air intake and air cleaner housing, high tension lead between distributor and ignition coil and throttle pulley cover, then disconnect mass air flow sensor electrical connector and cruise control vacuum hose and electrical connector, if equipped.
10. Disconnect intake hose at throttle body and idle air control valve hose and vacuum hose and crankcase ventilation hose from intake hose.
11. Disconnect vacuum hoses and electrical connector from solenoid valve, heater hose and throttle cable from throttle pulley, then remove air cleaner housing and torque arm.
12. Disconnect heater hoses at firewall, brake servo hose and heated oxygen sensor connectors, then remove upper nut on rear engine mount.
13. Disconnect gear selector cables from mounting bracket on transmission, then remove rubber mounted section of cable bracket.
14. **On models equipped with automatic transmission,**disconnect connector, gear selector cables from transmission and oil cooler hoses from cooler.
15. **On all models,** remove clutch slave cylinder retaining ring, then disconnect slave cylinder from transmission, battery ground cable from engine and lower radiator hose at radiator.
16. Remove rubber mount from air cleaner mounting bracket, withdraw clutch slave cylinder through front hole in bracket, then place bracket and cylinder aside.
17. Remove both relays from fan shroud, then disconnect electrical connectors and place wiring aside.
18. Remove control module box cooling

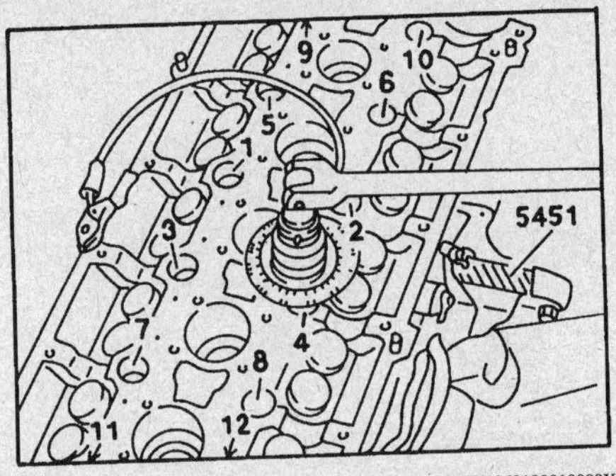
5451

VV1069100010000X

Fig. 7 Cylinder head tightening sequence. 2.4L & 2.3L 5-cylinder engines

air ducts, fan shroud screws from radiator, slide fan housing back slightly, then remove air intakes and fan assembly.

19. Remove long mounting bolts from A/C compressor. Leave compressor in position at this time.
20. Remove front engine mount nut and cable duct bracket mounting bolts, then the intake manifold and starter motor support brackets.
21. Disconnect upper radiator hose from thermostat housing, coolant hose between expansion tank and thermostat housing, expansion tank lower hose from engine and temperature sensor lead from bracket on servo pump.
22. Remove auxiliary drive belts, then the servo pump mounting bolts. Leave pump in position at this time.
23. Remove protective cover over fuel distribution manifold, upper and lower fuel pipe clips and fuel distribution manifold bolts, then disconnect braided ground strap from engine.
24. Secure injectors with holders tool No. 5465, or equivalent, then remove fuel distribution manifold complete with injectors and place aside.
25. Disconnect all electrical connectors from engine, then remove wiring harness.
26. Remove spark plug cover and attach lifting lugs tool No. 5459, or equivalent, and tool No. 5464, or equivalent, then place servo pump and A/C compressor aside.
27. Using lifting yokes tool No. 2810, or equivalent, and tool No. 5428, or equivalent, remove engine and transmission assembly from vehicle.
28. Reverse procedure to install.

960

The engine and transmission are removed as an assembly.

1. Disconnect battery ground cable, wiring connected to positive terminal, battery positive cable, ground connection to body at top of side member, clip at side member, then remove battery.
2. Remove auxiliary drive belt and cooling fan, then the upper bolts and disconnect connector at relay in front of battery.
3. Disconnect ground cable at righthand

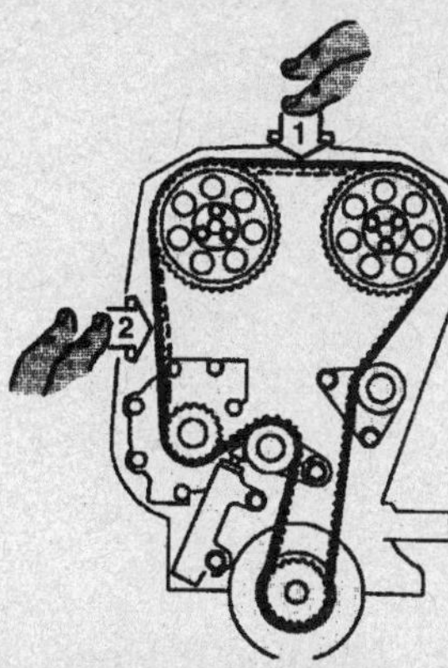
1
2

VV1069600023000X

Fig. 8 Timing belt installation. 2.4L & 2.3L 5-cylinder engines

ground terminal, then drain coolant.
4. Disconnect upper and lower coolant hoses from engine, expansion vessel hose from radiator and return pipe and transmission cooling pipes from radiator.
5. Remove top nut on righthand and lefthand engine mounts.
6. Disconnect large and small crankcase ventilation hoses, idling hose and idling valve electrical connector, EVAP valve hoses at intake manifold, air mass meter electrical connector and air preheater hose, then remove throttle pulley cover.
7. Remove servo pump, then disconnect fuel return line at regulator, fuel line at bulkhead, throttle cable, cruise control vacuum hose and fuel line snap catches.
8. Remove cover, then disconnect engine wiring harness connector, relay connectors and remove harness duct mounting nuts.
9. Disconnect cooling hoses at bulkhead, ECC hoses at intake manifold, camshaft sensor and timing pickup electrical connectors and brake servo vacuum hose.
10. Using support rails tool No. 5033, or equivalent, lifting beam tool No. 5006, or equivalent, and lifting hook tool Nos. 5115 and 5428, or equivalents, attach lifting lug No. 5429, or equivalent, to rear of engine and support engine.
11. Remove splashguard and air baffle under engine, radiator mounting bolts, then drain engine oil.
12. Disconnect oil thermostat hoses at thermostat in cylinder block, then remove A/C compressor, set aside and support from side member.
13. Disconnect exhaust pipe flange at manifold, remove lower section of air preheater pipe, then the exhaust pipe shield.
14. Disconnect and plug oil pipe connections at transmission, remove clips between selector lever and control rod/reaction arm, then the rods from mounting.
15. Disconnect oxygen sensor connector, then remove lead from connector.
16. Mark, then separate front and rear propeller shaft couplings, then remove transmission support member.
17. Place a jack under transmission and remove lifting support rails, lifting beam, lifting hook and lifting yoke.
18. Remove radiator upper bolts, then the radiator and transmission cooling pipes.
19. Using lifting tool No. 2810, or equivalent, adjust lifting yoke to ensure engine is balanced, then remove jack under transmission.
20. Remove engine and transmission assembly from vehicle.
21. Reverse procedure to install.

INTAKE MANIFOLD

REPLACE

2.3L 4-CYLINDER ENGINE

1. Drain coolant level below intake manifold.
2. Remove intake manifold from cylinder head.
3. Reverse procedure to install.

2.4L & 2.3L 5-CYLINDER ENGINES

1. Remove throttle pulley and injector covers, then disconnect throttle cable and electrical connectors from injectors.
2. Remove both clips securing fuel pipes and fuel distribution manifold mounting screws, secure injectors using holders tool No. 5465, or equivalent, then remove injectors and distribution manifold from intake.
3. Remove fan shroud retaining screws and control module box cooling air ducts, then bend shroud slightly aside, lift relay holder and disconnect fan electrical connectors.
4. Remove control module box and air cleaner intakes, then the fan assembly.
5. Disconnect idle air control valve and throttle position potentiometer electrical connectors, crankcase ventilation and EVAP canister hoses, servo reservoir and intake manifold vacuum servo hoses, then remove intake hose.
6. Remove upper intake manifold bolts, oil dipstick and bracket lower manifold bolts and manifold bracket bolts, then the intake manifold from cylinder head.
7. Reverse procedure to install. **Torque** intake manifold bolts to 15 ft. lbs.

2.9L ENGINE

1. Disconnect battery ground cable, then the electrical connector at air mass meter.
2. Disconnect idling valve electrical connector and air hose, then remove flame trap holder and intake hose.
3. Remove throttle pulley cover, then disconnect throttle switch electrical connector, throttle cable, cruise control vacuum servo, cable bracket at throttle pulley and vacuum hoses at throttle housing.
4. Remove injector cover plate and distribution manifold retaining bolts, then disconnect injector electrical connectors, pressure regulator vacuum hose and fuel line bracket and remove injector/distribution manifold assembly.
5. Remove air preheater inlet hose and manifold bottom mounting, then disconnect lefthand and righthand power stage connectors on bottom of manifold.
6. Disconnect vacuum hoses under manifold and brake servo vacuum hose, then cut away clamps securing rubber sleeves between manifold sections, and discard.
7. Remove outer section of manifold, then the inner section of manifold.
8. Reverse procedure to install. **Torque** intake manifold bolts to 15 ft. lbs.

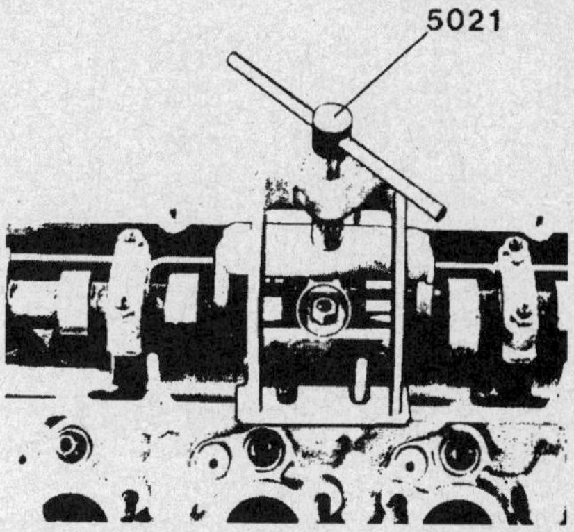
5021

VV1069100015000X

Fig. 9 Camshaft tensioning tool. 2.3L 4-cylinder engine

EXHAUST MANIFOLD

REPLACE

2.3L 4-CYLINDER ENGINE

1. Disconnect exhaust pipe from exhaust manifold.
2. **On models equipped with turbo,** remove turbocharger.
3. **On all models,** remove exhaust manifold from cylinder head.
4. Reverse procedure to install.

2.4L & 2.3L 5-CYLINDER ENGINES

1. Disconnect front exhaust pipe, then remove heat shields from manifold.
2. Lift manifold off studs, turn 90° to right, then remove from vehicle.
3. Reverse procedure to install.

2.9L ENGINE

1. Disconnect front exhaust pipes, then remove heat shield from manifolds.
2. Remove manifolds from cylinder head.
3. Reverse procedure to install.

CYLINDER HEAD

REPLACE

2.3L 4-CYLINDER ENGINES

Removal

1. Disconnect battery ground cable, then

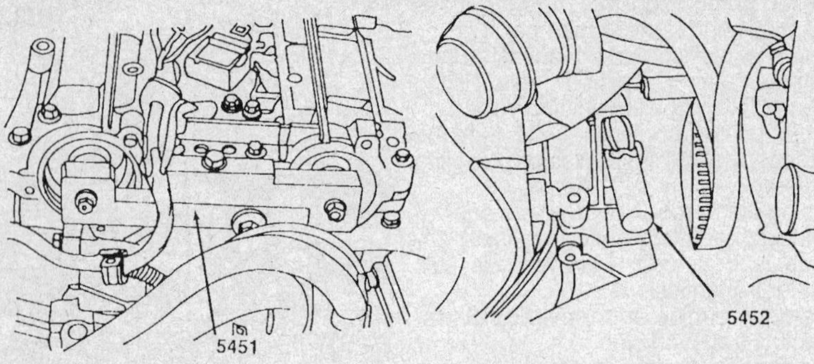
5451
5452

VV1069100016000X

Fig. 10 Locking tool installation. Except 2.3L 4-cylinder engine

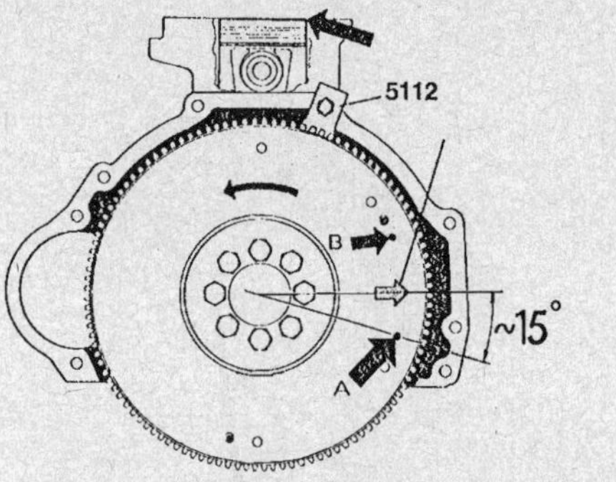
5112
B
A
~15°

VV1069100017000X

Fig. 11 Aligning flywheel. 2.3L 4-cylinder engine

drain coolant by opening nipple on righthand side of engine, rear.
2. Remove fan, clamp for preheater hose and fan shroud.
3. Remove drive belts and water pump pulley.
4. Remove valve cover and gasket, then all other necessary components from cylinder head and intake manifold.
5. Remove upper timing belt cover, then set camshaft and crankshaft timing marks as follows:
   a. Rotate crankshaft using center bolt and set camshaft so that marking on pulley is opposite marking on inner timing gear cover and crankshaft marking is opposite 0 on cover, **Fig. 1.**
   b. On engines equipped with side mounted distributor, remove distributor cap and ensure rotor is opposite marking, **Fig. 1.**
6. Remove timing belt tensioner nut and washer, pull on timing belt to depress tensioner spring, then use a 3 mm drill bit to lock tensioner spring, **Fig. 2.**
7. Remove timing belt, then the camshaft gear and spacer washer using counterhold tool No. 5034, or equivalent.
8. Remove stud for timing belt tensioner, then loosen cylinder head bolts in sequence shown in **Fig. 3.**
9. Remove cylinder head.

Installation

1. Check position of crankshaft and camshaft and ensure No. 1 piston is at TDC and camshaft is at TDC firing for No. 1 cylinder.
2. Install cylinder head and gasket, ensuring O-ring for water pump is sitting correctly in groove.
3. Oil and install cylinder head bolts, then **torque** bolts in sequence shown in **Fig. 4,** in three stages. First to 14 ft. lbs., then to 43 ft. lbs. and finally tighten an additional 90°.
4. Install camshaft gear and spacer washer using counterhold tool No. 5034, or equivalent.
5. Install stud for belt tensioner, belt tensioner, washer and nut.
6. Ensure timing basic setting is as outlined in steps 5a and 5b under "Removal" procedure.
7. Place belt around crankshaft gear and intermediate shaft gear, then stretch belt and place it over camshaft gear and belt tensioner.
8. Remove drill bit from belt tensioner, then ensure timing belt is correctly positioned and timing marks are aligned correctly.
9. Stretch timing belt as follows:
   a. Rotate engine until at TDC.
   b. Loosen belt tensioner nut approximately one turn and allow spring to tension timing belt, then retighten nut.
10. Install upper timing belt cover, then check and if necessary, adjust valve clearances. Refer to "Valve Adjustment."
11. Install valve cover and gasket, then all other necessary components to cylinder head and intake manifold.
12. Warm up engine, then check and, if necessary, adjust ignition timing, idle speed and CO content. Check cooling system for leaks.

2.4L & 2.3L 5-CYLINDER ENGINES

Removal

1. Disconnect battery ground cable, then remove coolant expansion tank cap and splashguard under engine.
2. Open drain cocks on cylinder block and radiator and drain coolant. Close drain cocks, then disconnect front exhaust pipe from exhaust manifold.
3. Remove exhaust manifold as outlined under "Exhaust Manifold, Replace," then the timing belt as follows:
   a. Remove spark plug cover, fuel line clips, coolant expansion tank, front timing belt cover and auxiliary drive belt.
   b. Remove righthand front wheel, arch liner and vibration damper guard, then turn crankshaft until all timing marks are aligned, **Fig. 5.**
   c. Place gauge tool No. 998 8500, or equivalent, between exhaust camshaft drive pulley and water pump and read gauge with aid of a mirror. If belt tension is correct, reading should be between 3.5 and 4.6 units. If tension is incorrect, replace tensioner.
   d. Remove tensioner upper mounting bolt and slacken lower mounting bolt, then twist tensioner to free pulley.
   e. Remove lower bolt, tensioner, upper timing belt cover and timing belt.
   f. Spin idler pulleys and check for bearing noise, check pulley surfaces that contact belt and ensure they are clean and smooth, ensure tensioner pulley arm has not seized, then check idler pulley mounting torques.
   g. Inspect tensioner for signs of leakage. Compress tensioner using tool No. 5456, or equivalent. Mount tensioner in tool and tighten center nut fully. Wait until compression has taken place and insert a 2 mm locking pin in plunger.
4. Remove intake manifold as outlined under "Intake Manifold, Replace," then disconnect braided ground straps from engine.
5. Disconnect upper radiator hose from thermostat housing, then mark and remove camshaft pulleys using counterhold tool No. 5199, or equivalent.
6. Remove inner timing belt cover bolt under exhaust camshaft pulley, air cleaner housing and hoses, camshaft position sensor and shutter, distributor cap, rotor and ignition lead clip, torque arm and brackets.
7. Remove bolts in upper half of cylinder head, starting at outer edge and working inward, then the upper half of cylinder head by tapping carefully upward with a copper mallet at parting lugs and at camshaft pulley end.
8. Mark and remove camshafts, then the coolant pipe bolts.
9. Remove cylinder head bolts starting at outer edge and working inward, **Fig. 6,** then the cylinder head and gasket.
10. Clean mating surfaces between exhaust manifold and cylinder head, cylinder block joint face, coolant pipe joint face and joint faces between top and bottom halves of cylinder head. **Do not use a metal scraper. Use a soft putty blade and gasket solvent No. 1 161 340-3.**

Installation

1. Remove starter motor and protective plug on block, then mount crankshaft locking tool No. 5451, or equivalent, and turn crankshaft counterclockwise until stopped by tool.
2. Install lower half of cylinder head, then

oil and install cylinder head bolts. **Torque** cylinder head bolts starting inside and working outward, **Fig. 7,** to 15 ft. lbs., then to 44 ft. lbs., and finally another 130° using angle gauge tool No. 951 2050, or equivalent.

3. Install coolant pipe and new O-rings in spark plug wells, then remove No. 1 and 5 spark plugs.
4. Using a roller, apply liquid sealing compound tool No. 1 161 059-9, or equivalent, to upper section of cylinder head. Install camshafts and secure with front end holder tool No. 5453, or equivalent, and rear end locking tool No. 5452, or equivalent. **Ensure sealing compound does not penetrate oil passages. A thin coating is sufficient.**
5. Position upper cylinder head and press onto lower section using press tool No. 5454, or equivalent. Tighten mounting bolts to specifications starting from inside and working outward. Remove press tool and camshaft front end holder.
6. Grease camshaft front seals, then tap into position using drift tool No. 5449, or equivalent.
7. Place upper timing belt cover in position, then mount camshaft pulleys and align timing marks. Insert two bolts in each pulley. Screw in bolts until they just contact pulleys, then remove upper timing belt cover.
8. Install timing belt tensioner and tighten bolts to specifications. Place timing belt over camshaft pulleys, around water pump and press over tensioner pulley. Loosen pulley bolts, then remove locking pin from tensioner.
9. Insert third bolt in each camshaft pulley, then tighten bolts to specifications. Install inner timing belt cover bolt below exhaust camshaft pulley and upper timing belt cover.
10. Remove crankshaft locking tool and install protective plug. Install starter motor, then remove camshaft locking tool.
11. Turn crankshaft through two revolutions and ensure timing marks on crankshaft and camshaft pulleys are correctly aligned, then install outer timing belt cover.
12. Grease camshaft rear seals, then press into position using drift tool No, 5450, or equivalent. **Seal is normally installed flush with inside edge of chamfer. If shaft is worn, seal may be located 2 mm further in by reversing tool.**
13. Install torque arm and switch brackets, distributor rotor and ignition lead clip, camshaft position sensor and shutter, spark plugs, distributor cap and ignition leads and air cleaner housing.
14. Install exhaust manifold as outlined under "Exhaust Manifold, Replace," intake manifold as outlined under "Intake Manifold, Replace," engine braided ground straps, exhaust pipe and splashguard under engine.
15. Reconnect battery ground cable, change engine oil, then fill coolant system. Run engine until thermostat opens, then top up coolant as necessary and inspect engine for leaks.

2.9L ENGINE

Removal

1. Disconnect battery ground cable, then remove coolant expansion tank cap.
2. Open drain cock on righthand side of engine and drain coolant, then close drain cock.
3. Remove exhaust manifold as outlined under "Exhaust Manifold, Replace," then the coolant pipe bolts.
4. Remove timing belt and tensioner as follows:
   a. Remove auxiliary drive belt, front timing belt cover, splashguard under engine, vibration damper guard and ignition coil cover.
   b. Turn crankshaft clockwise until timing marks on camshaft pulleys/timing belt cover mounting plate and crankshaft pulley/oil pump housing are aligned, **Fig. 5,** then remove upper timing belt cover.
   c. Place gauge tool No. 998 8500, or equivalent, between exhaust camshaft drive pulley and water pump and read gauge. If belt tension is correct, reading should be between 3.5 and 4.6 units. If tension is incorrect, replace tensioner.
   d. Remove tensioner upper mounting bolt and loosen lower mounting bolt, then twist tensioner to free plunger.
   e. Remove lower bolt, tensioner and timing belt.
   f. Spin idler pulleys and check for bearing noise, check pulley surfaces that contact belt and ensure they are clean and smooth, then check tensioner pulley arm and idler pulley mounting torques.
   g. Inspect tensioner for signs of leakage. Compress tensioner using tool No. 5456, or equivalent. Mount tensioner in tool and tighten center nut fully. Wait until compression has taken place and insert a 2 mm lock kingpin in plunger.
5. Remove timing belt cover mounting plate bolt, then disconnect battery ground cable and electrical connector at air mass meter.
6. Disconnect idling valve electrical connector and air hose, then remove flame trap holder and intake hose.
7. Remove throttle pulley cover, then disconnect throttle switch electrical connector, throttle cable, cruise control vacuum servo, cable bracket at throttle pulley and vacuum hoses at throttle housing.
8. Remove injector cover plate and distribution manifold retaining bolts, then disconnect injector electrical connectors, pressure regulator vacuum hose and fuel line bracket and remove injector/distribution manifold assembly.
9. Cut away clamps securing rubber sleeves between manifold sections, and discard, then remove outer section of intake manifold.
10. Remove coolant temperature sensor, then disconnect coolant hose from thermostat housing.
11. Mark positions and remove ignition coils, then the camshaft pulleys using counterhold tool No. 5199, or equivalent.
12. Remove camshaft position sensor, switch mounting bracket, ground terminals 1 and 2, temperature sensor connector and coolant hoses at rear of engine.
13. Remove mounting bolts for top half of cylinder head, then the top half of cylinder head by tapping carefully upward with copper mallet at joint lugs and front ends.
14. Remove camshafts, then the cylinder head bolts starting at outer edge and working inward.
15. Remove cylinder head and gasket.
16. Clean mating surfaces between exhaust manifold and cylinder head, cylinder block joint face, coolant pipe joint face and joint faces between top and bottom halves of cylinder head. **Do not use a metal scraper. Use a soft putty blade and gasket solvent No. 1 161 340-3.**

Installation

1. Remove starter motor and protective plug on block, then mount crankshaft locking tool No. 5451, or equivalent, and turn crankshaft counterclockwise until stopped by tool.
2. Install lower half of cylinder head, then oil and install cylinder head bolts. **Torque** cylinder head bolts starting inside and working outward, to 15 ft. lbs., then to 44 ft. lbs., and finally another 130°.
3. Install new O-rings in spark plug wells, then oil camshaft bearing seats.
4. Using a roller, apply liquid sealing compound tool No. 1 161 059-9, or equivalent, to upper section of cylinder head. Install camshafts and secure with front end holder tool No. 5453, or equivalent, and rear end locking tool No. 5452, or equivalent. **Ensure sealing compound does not penetrate oil passages. A thin coating is sufficient.**
5. Position upper cylinder head and press onto lower section using press tool No. 5454, or equivalent. Tighten mounting bolts to specifications starting from inside and working outward. Remove press tools and camshaft front end holder.
6. Grease camshaft front seals, then tap into position using drift tool No. 5449, or equivalent.
7. Place upper timing belt cover in position, then mount camshaft pulleys and align timing marks. Tighten each pulley with two bolts, then remove upper timing belt cover.
8. Install timing belt cover mounting plate bolt, then place timing belt around crankshaft and righthand idler. Place timing belt over camshaft pulleys, around water pump and press over tensioner pulley.
9. Install timing belt tensioner and tighten

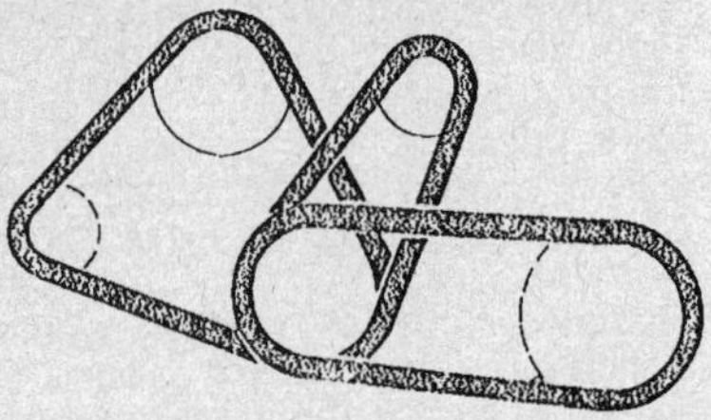

1069100018000X

Fig. 12 Belt routing. 2.3L 4-cylinder engine

to specifications, then loosen camshaft pulley bolts, and remove tensioner locking pin.

10. Insert third bolt in each camshaft pulley, then tighten bolts alternately to specifications.
11. Remove crankshaft locking tool and install protective plug. Install starter motor, then remove camshaft locking tool.
12. Install upper timing belt cover, then ensure timing marks on crankshaft and camshaft pulleys are correctly aligned.
13. Grease camshaft rear seals, then press into position using drift tool No. 5450, or equivalent. **Seal is normally installed flush with inside edge of chamfer. If shaft is worn, seal may be located 2 mm further in by reversing tool.**
14. Install temperature sensor connector, ground terminals 1 and 2, cover, switch mounting bracket, shutter, camshaft position sensor and coolant hoses at rear of engine.
15. Install ignition coils spark plug cover, front timing belt cover, auxiliary drive belt, vibration damper guard and splashguard under engine.
16. Pass wiring between 2nd and 3rd branches of inner intake manifold, then position outer section of intake manifold and crankcase ventilation hoses.
17. Insert manifold branches in rubber sleeves, then fit and secure with new Oetiker clamps.
18. Connect vacuum hoses and brake servo hose, then tighten manifold lower mounting.
19. Connect power stage connectors and air preheater hose, then inspect injector O-rings and lubricate with water-free vaseline.
20. Connect fuel pressure regulator vacuum hose, then press fuel distribution manifold into position and tighten manifold.
21. Connect injector electrical connectors and ECC vacuum hoses, then install injector cover.
22. Connect crankcase ventilation hoses, idling valve lead and air hose, air mass meter and throttle housing connector, then install cable bracket at throttle pulley.
23. Connect coolant hose to thermostat housing, then the coolant temperature sensor.
24. Install coolant pipe, then the exhaust manifold as outlined under "Exhaust Manifold, Replace."
25. Install heat shield and front exhaust pipe. **Unbolt joint after catalytic converter and retighten to specifications to prevent stress on exhaust system.**
26. Reconnect battery ground cable, change engine oil, then fill coolant system. Run engine until thermostat opens, then top up coolant as necessary and inspect engine for leaks.

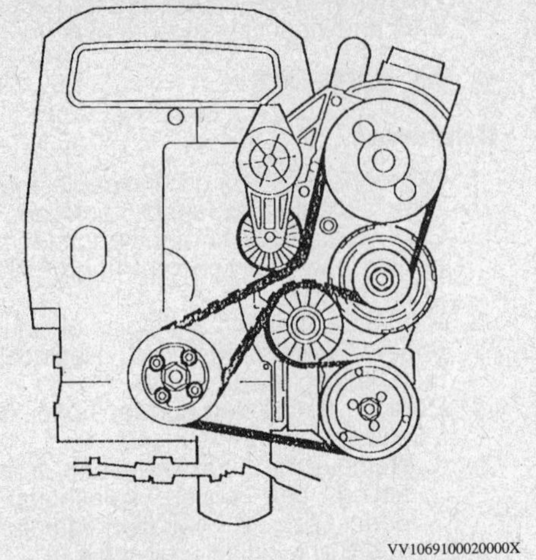

VV1069100020000X

Fig. 13 Serpentine belt routing. 2.4L & 2.3L 5-cylinder engines

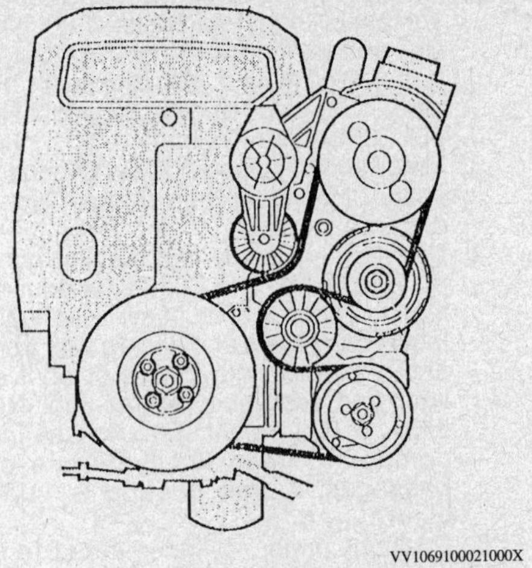

VV1069100021000X

Fig. 14 Serpentine belt routing. 2.9L engine

VALVE CLEARANCE SPECIFICATIONS

EXCEPT 2.3L 4-CYLINDER ENGINE

These engine are equipped with hydraulic valve lash adjusters and no adjustment is required.

2.3L 4-CYLINDER ENGINE

Intake Cold	Exhaust Cold	Intake Hot	Exhaust Hot
INSPECTION			
.012–.016	.012–.016	.014–.018	.014–.018
ADJUSTMENT			
.014–.016	.014–.016	.016–.018	.016–.018

VALVE ADJUSTMENT

EXCEPT 2.3L 4-CYLINDER ENGINE

No provision for adjustment is provided.

2.3L 4-CYLINDER ENGINE

1. Remove valve cover, then set No. 1 cylinder at TDC on its compression stroke. **Camshaft lobes for No. 1 cylinder must slant upward, and timing mark on pulley must be at 0°.**
2. Measure and note valve clearances for No. 1 cylinder, then compare with specifications listed under "Valve Clearance Specifications."
3. If clearance is incorrect, proceed as follows:
   a. Rotate tappets so that groove is completely to side, then depress tappets using press tool No. 5022, or equivalent, and remove adjustment washer using pliers tool No. 5026, or equivalent.
   b. Measure thickness of existing washer, then select adjustment washer of correct thickness. **Washers are available in thicknesses from 0.130 to 0.180 inch in increments of .002 inch. Use only new washers.**
   c. Oil and install new washer. Turn washer with marking facing downward, then remove press tool.
4. Check and, if necessary, adjust valve clearance of remaining cylinders 3, 4 and 2. In that order.
5. Turn engine over a few times with starter motor, then recheck clearances and adjust if necessary.
6. Install valve cover using a new gasket, then check and, if necessary, adjust ignition timing, CO content and idle speed.

VALVE GUIDES

2.3L 4-CYLINDER ENGINE

1. Heat cylinder head to 194–230°F, then using drift tool No. 5218, or equivalent, press out old guide toward combustion chamber. Ensure guide has not seized during removal. If so, valve guide bore must be reamed to oversize.
2. Ensure new guide has same number of grooves as old guide unless replacing with an oversize guide, then with cylinder head at room temperature, press in guide using drift tool No. 5027, or equivalent, for intake guides or drift tool No. 5028, or equivalent, for exhaust guides until drift contacts cylinder head to obtain correct height. **Press force must be at least 2000 lbs. If press force is lower, guide must be removed and reamed out for fitting oversized guide.**
3. Clean inside of valve guide using reamer tool No. 5224 or 5164, or equivalents, then grind valve and seat after replacing guide.

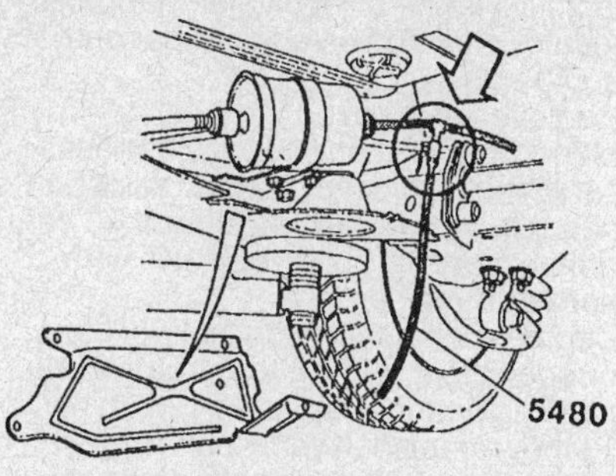
5480

VV1069100022000X

Fig. 15 Fuel filter location. 2.4L & 2.3L 5-cylinder engines

EXCEPT 2.3L 4-CYLINDER ENGINE

1. Mount cylinder head on fixture tool No. 5363, or equivalent. Adjust angle of inclination using holes at top of fixture ends. Clamp head to fixture using locating hole No. 2 on face. Use four sleeves as spacers for cylinder head bolts.
2. Using drift tool No. 5364, or equivalent, slowly press guide until drift bears against valve spring seat, then using drift tool No. 5365, or equivalent, slowly press guide until drift bears against valve seat. Remove valve guide and inspect upper section of guide bore.
3. Place new guide on drift tool No. 999 5505, or equivalent, and slowly press guide into head until drift bears against valve spring seat. Top of guide should project by 0.50–.52 inch. **Press force must be at least 2025 lbs. If press force is lower, guide must be removed and reamed out for fitting oversized guide.**
4. Ream guide using reamer tool No. 999 5373, or equivalent, from combustion chamber side, then grind valve and seat after replacing guide.

FRONT COVER

REPLACE

2.3L 4-CYLINDER ENGINE

1. Disconnect battery ground cable.
2. Remove cooling fan, preheater hose clamp below fan shroud, if applicable, then the fan shroud.
3. Remove drive belts and water pump pulley.
4. Remove upper timing cover, then the lower cover.
5. Reverse procedure to install.

2.4L & 2.3L 5-CYLINDER ENGINE

1. Remove spark plug cover, fuel line clips and coolant expansion tank, then the front timing belt cover.
2. Remove righthand front wheel, arch liner and vibration damper guard, then turn crankshaft until all timing marks are aligned, **Fig. 5.**
3. Remove upper timing belt cover.
4. Reverse procedure to install.

2.9L ENGINE

1. Remove auxiliary drive belt, front timing cover, splashguard under engine, vibration damper guard and ignition coil cover.
2. Turn crankshaft clockwise until timing marks on camshaft pulleys/timing belt cover mounting plate and crankshaft pulley/oil pump housing are aligned, **Fig. 5,** then remove upper timing cover.
3. Reverse procedure to install.

TIMING BELT

REPLACE

2.3L 4-CYLINDER ENGINE

With the timing belt removed, avoid turning the camshaft or crankshaft. If movement is required, exercise extreme caution to avoid valve damage caused by piston contact.

Removal

1. Disconnect battery ground cable.
2. Remove cooling fan, clamp for preheating hose below fan shroud, then the fan shroud.
3. Remove all drive belts, then the water pump pulley.
4. Remove upper timing belt cover, then set camshaft and crankshaft timing marks as follows:
   a. Rotate crankshaft using center bolt and set camshaft so that marking on pulley is opposite marking on inner timing gear cover and crankshaft marking is opposite 0 on cover, **Fig. 1.**
   b. **On engine with side mounted distributor,** remove distributor cap and ensure rotor is opposite marking, **Fig. 1.**
5. Remove belt tensioner retaining nut and washer, then install tool No. 5284, or equivalent, onto vibration damper and tensioner stud.
6. Remove bolt for vibration damper, then tool No. 5284, or equivalent. Check and, if necessary, adjust 0 marking on vibration damper, then remove damper and lower timing cover.
7. Pull on timing belt to depress tensioner spring, then use a 3 mm drill bit to lock tensioner spring, **Fig. 2.**
8. Remove timing belt. **Do not turn crankshaft with timing belt removed.**
9. Rotate tensioner roller and listen for abnormal noises from bearing. Also, ensure belt contact face is free of cracks and rubber deposits.

Installation

1. Ensure pulleys are positioned correctly, then place timing belt on crankshaft pulley and intermediate shaft pulley. Two lines on timing belt should be opposite crankshaft marking.
2. Stretch timing belt and install it on camshaft and belt tensioner pulleys. Ensure timing belt is correctly positioned and timing marks are correct.

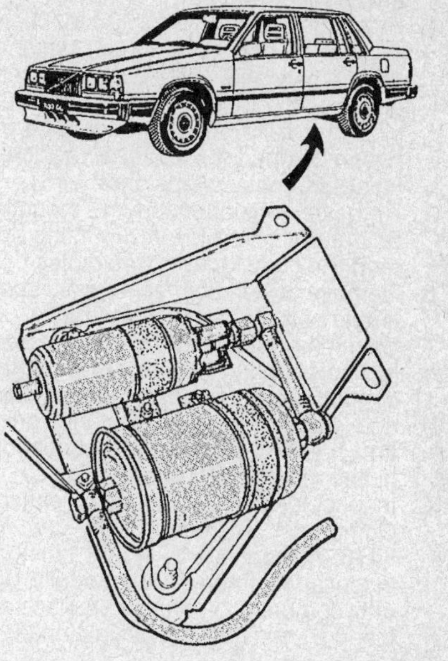

VV1029100001000X

Fig. 16 Fuel filter location. 2.3L 4-cylinder & 2.9L engines

3. Pull on timing belt to depress belt tensioner spring, then remove drill bit.
4. Install lower timing belt cover and vibration damper, ensuring guide plate is correctly positioned.
5. Remove belt tensioner retaining nut and washer, then install tool No. 5284, or equivalent, onto vibration damper and tensioner stud.
6. **Torque** vibration damper bolt first to 44 ft. lbs., then an additional 60°. Remove tool No. 5284, or equivalent, and install nut and washer on belt tensioner.
7. Turn engine to TDC, slacken belt tensioner nut, allowing spring to tension timing belt, then tighten belt tensioner nut.
8. Install upper timing belt cover, water pump pulley, drive belts, fan shroud, preheater hose clamp and cooling fan.
9. Connect battery ground cable, then check and, if necessary, adjust ignition timing, idle speed and CO content.
10. Check cooling system for leaks, then adjust timing belt tension as follows:
    a. Remove rubber plug from timing belt cover, perform step 7, then install rubber plug.

2.4L & 2.3L 5-CYLINDER ENGINES

With the timing belt removed, avoid turning the camshaft or crankshaft. If movement is required, exercise extreme caution to avoid valve damage caused by piston contact.

Removal

1. Disconnect battery ground cable.
2. Remove spark plug cover, fuel line clips, coolant expansion tank, front timing belt cover and auxiliary drive belt.
3. Remove righthand front wheel, arch liner and vibration damper guard, then turn crankshaft until all timing marks

are aligned, **Fig. 5.**

4. Place gauge tool No. 998 8500, or equivalent, between exhaust camshaft drive pulley and water pump and read gauge with aid of a mirror. If belt tension is correct, reading should be between 3.5 and 4.6 units. If tension is incorrect, replace tensioner.
5. Remove tensioner upper mounting bolt and slacken lower mounting bolt, then twist tensioner to free pulley.
6. Remove lower bolt, tensioner, upper timing belt cover and timing belt.
7. Spin idler pulleys and check for bearing noise, check pulley surfaces that contact belt and ensure they are clean and smooth, ensure tensioner pulley arm has not seized, then check idler pulley mounting torques.
8. Inspect tensioner for signs of leakage. Compress tensioner using tool No. 5456, or equivalent. Mount tensioner in tool and tighten center nut fully. Wait until compression has taken place and insert a 2 mm locking pin in plunger.

Installation

1. Install belt tensioner and tighten to specifications, then place belt around crankshaft pulley and righthand idler pulley, over camshaft pulleys, around water pump pulley and press over tensioner pulley, **Fig. 8.**
2. Remove locking pin from tensioner, install upper timing belt cover, then turn crankshaft through two revolutions and ensure timing marks on crankshaft and camshaft pulleys are correctly aligned.
3. Install fuel pipe clips, front timing belt cover, auxiliary drive belt, spark plug cover, coolant expansion tank, vibration damper guard and wheel arch liner.
4. Test run engine and check operation.

2.9L ENGINE

With the timing belt removed, avoid turning the camshaft or crankshaft. If movement is required, exercise extreme caution to avoid valve damage caused by piston contact.

Removal

1. Disconnect battery ground cable.
2. Remove auxiliary drive belt, front timing belt cover, splashguard under engine, vibration damper guard and ignition coil cover.
3. Turn crankshaft clockwise until timing marks on camshaft pulleys/timing belt cover mounting plate and crankshaft pulley/oil pump housing are aligned, **Fig. 5,** then remove upper timing belt cover.
4. Place gauge No. 998 8500 between exhaust camshaft drive pulley and water pump and read gauge. If belt tension is correct, reading should be between 3.5 and 4.6 units. If tension is incorrect, replace tensioner.
5. Remove tensioner upper mounting bolt and loosen lower mounting bolt, then twist tensioner to free plunger.
6. Remove lower bolt, tensioner and timing belt.
7. Spin idler pulleys and check for bearing noise, check pulley surfaces that contact belt and ensure they are clean and smooth, then check tensioner pulley arm and idler pulley mounting torques.
8. Inspect tensioner for signs of leakage. Compress tensioner using tool No. 5456, or equivalent. Mount tensioner in tool and tighten center nut fully. Wait until compression has taken place and insert a 2 mm locking pin in plunger.

Installation

1. Place belt around crankshaft pulley and righthand idler pulley, over camshaft pulleys, around water pump pulley and press over tensioner pulley.
2. Install belt tensioner and tighten to specifications, remove locking pin from tensioner, install upper timing belt cover, then turn crankshaft through two revolutions and ensure timing marks on crankshaft and camshaft pulleys are correctly aligned.
3. Install ignition coil cover, front timing belt cover, auxiliary drive belt, vibration damper guard and splashguard under engine.
4. Test run engine and check operation.

CAMSHAFT

REPLACE

When camshaft is replaced due to wear, it is essential that the engine be flushed clean before installing new components. Replace engine oil and filter, run engine for approximately ten minutes, then drain engine oil and remove filter. After camshaft has been replaced, install new oil filter and fill engine with new oil.

2.3L 4-CYLINDER ENGINE

Removal

1. Disconnect battery ground cable, then remove cooling fan, clamp for preheating hose below fan shroud and fan shroud.
2. Remove all drive belts, then the water pump pulley.
3. Remove upper timing belt cover, then set camshaft and crankshaft timing marks as follows:
   a. Rotate crankshaft using center bolt and set camshaft so that marking on pulley is opposite marking on inner timing gear cover and crankshaft marking is opposite 0 on cover, **Fig. 1.**
   b. **On engine with side mounted distributor,** remove distributor cap and ensure rotor is opposite marking, **Fig. 1.**
4. Remove belt tensioner retaining nut and washer, pull on timing belt to depress tensioner spring, then use a 3 mm drill bit to lock tensioner spring, **Fig. 2.**
5. Remove timing belt from camshaft pulley, then remove camshaft pulley using tool No. 5034, or equivalent, and distributor mounted on engine rear end, if applicable.
6. Remove valve cover.
7. Mark camshaft bearing caps as necessary, then remove center camshaft bearing cap. **If cap is difficult to remove, carefully pry cap off with a screwdriver.**
8. Depress camshaft using tool No. 5021, or equivalent, **Fig. 9,** then remove remaining bearing caps.
9. Remove camshaft with seal.
10. Check camshaft end float as follows:
    a. Remove valve tappets, then place camshaft into cylinder head.
    b. Install rear bearing cap, then slide camshaft back and forth.
    c. Check end float clearance with a feeler gauge. Clearance should be .004–.016 inch.
    d. If clearance is excessive, replace rear bearing cap.

Installation

1. Oil bearing shells, cams and adjustment washers on tappets, then install tappets.
2. Coat sealing surface toward cylinder head of front and rear bearing caps with sealing compound tool No. 1161027-6, or equivalent, then position camshaft and rear bearing cap on cylinder head. Guide pin on camshaft should point upward.
3. Using tool No. 5021, or equivalent, and rear bearing cap to guide, depress camshaft, then loosely tighten rear bearing cap.
4. Oil and install three bearing caps and loosely tighten nuts.
5. Remove tool No. 5021, equivalent, then oil and install the center bearing cap.
6. Tighten bearing cap nuts to specifications.
7. Grease front oil seal and shaft, then install front oil seal using sleeve tool No. 5025, or equivalent. **Ensure rubber lip on seal does not become damaged.**
8. Install camshaft pulley and spacer washer using tool No. 5034, or equivalent. Tighten camshaft pulley bolt to specifications.
9. If applicable, install distributor on engine rear end.
10. Ensure pulleys are positioned correctly, then place timing belt on crankshaft pulley and intermediate shaft pulley. Two lines on timing belt should be opposite crankshaft marking.
11. Stretch timing belt and install it on camshaft and belt tensioner pulleys. Ensure timing belt is correctly positioned and timing marks are correct.
12. Install belt tensioner nut and washer, pull on timing belt to depress belt tensioner spring, then remove drill bit. Tensioner spring will tension timing belt. Tighten tensioner nut.
13. Install upper timing belt cover, pulley, drive belts loosely, fan shroud, clamp for preheating hose and fan.
14. Tension drive belts, then check and, if necessary, adjust valve clearance.

15. Run engine until warm, then check and, if necessary, adjust ignition timing, CO content, idle speed, cooling system level and timing belt tension.

EXCEPT 2.3L 4-CYLINDER ENGINE

1. Remove timing belt as outlined under "Timing Belt, Replace," then the camshaft pulleys using counterhold tool No. 5199, or equivalent.
2. Remove bolts from top half of cylinder head starting at outside and working inward, then the top half of cylinder head by tapping gently with a plastic mallet adjacent to lugs and front end of camshafts.
3. Remove camshafts by twisting and lifting simultaneously.
4. Reverse procedure to install, noting the following:
   a. Install top half of cylinder head using press tool No. 5454, or equivalent.
   b. Tighten fasteners to specifications.

CAMSHAFT OIL SEAL

REPLACE

EXCEPT 2.3L 4-CYLINDER ENGINE

If replacing rear seal(s) only, perform only steps 4 through 6.

1. Remove timing belt as outlined under "Timing Belt, Replace," then the camshaft pulleys using counterhold tool No. 5199, or equivalent.
2. Using a screwdriver, remove front camshaft seal(s). Ensure sealing surface is not damaged.
3. Coat new seal(s) with grease, then install seal(s) using drift tool No. 5449, or equivalent.
4. **If replacing rear seal(s) only,** remove camshaft position sensor and shutter.
5. Using a screwdriver, remove rear camshaft seal(s). Ensure sealing surface is not damaged.
6. Coat new seal(s) with grease, then install seal(s) using drift tool No. 5450, or equivalent. **Seal is normally installed flush with inside edge of chamfer. If shaft is worn, seal may be located .080 inch (2 mm) further in by reversing tool.**
7. **If front and rear seals, or front seals only were replaced,** proceed as follows:
   a. **On 2.4L engines,** remove air cleaner housing and hoses, distributor cap, rotor, and ignition lead clip and cooling fan.
   b. **On both engines,** remove camshaft position sensor and shutter and starter motor.
   c. Remove protective plug on block behind starter motor and mount crankshaft locking tool No. 5451, or equivalent, in position, **Fig. 10.** Turn crankshaft clockwise until stopped by tool, then mount camshaft locking tool No. 5452, or equivalent, at rear of camshafts.
   d. Install camshaft pulleys. Insert two bolts in each pulley until just in contact with pulleys. **Ensure camshaft bolt holes are centered in pulley holes.**
   e. Install timing belt as outlined under "Timing Belt, Replace,"
   f. Loosen two bolts in camshaft pulleys, install third bolt, then tighten bolts alternately to specifications using counterhold.
   g. remove locking tools, then install upper timing cover.
   h. Rotate crankshaft through two revolutions and ensure timing marks are still aligned.
   i. Install camshaft position sensor and shutter, distributor rotor and cover, air cleaner housing and hoses, ignition coil cover, spark plug cover, starter motor, cooling fan, wheel arch and liner.
8. Test run engine and check operation.

PISTON & ROD ASSEMBLY

2.3L 4-CYLINDER ENGINE

Assemble connecting rods to pistons with arrow on piston crown facing forward and numerical designation stamp on connecting rod facing toward oil filter side.

EXCEPT 2.3L 4-CYLINDER ENGINE

Assemble connecting rods to pistons with arrow on piston crown facing forward and numerical designation stamp on connecting rod facing toward intake side of block.

PISTONS, PINS & RINGS

2.3L 4-CYLINDER ENGINE

Pistons and rings are available in .012 inch (.30 mm) and .024 inch (.60 mm) oversizes.

Oversize piston pins are not available. However, connecting rod bushing may be replaced if rod bore is worn.

EXCEPT 2.3L 4-CYLINDER ENGINE

Pistons, pins and rings are not available in oversizes.

Oversize piston pins are not available. However, connecting rod bushing may be replaced if rod bore is worn.

MAIN & ROD BEARINGS

2.3L 4-CYLINDER ENGINE

Main and rod bearings are available in .010 inch (.25 mm) and .020 inch (.50 mm) undersizes.

EXCEPT 2.3L 4-CYLINDER ENGINE

Main bearings are not available in undersizes.

Connecting rod bearings are available in .010 inch (.25 mm) and .020 inch (.50 mm) undersizes.

CRANKSHAFT SEAL

REPLACE

FRONT

2.3L 4-Cylinder Engine

Before suspecting that the crankshaft front seal is leaking, check engine flame guard, if equipped. A restricted flame guard will cause the engine oil dipstick to jump out of the pipe seat, engine knock and oil leakage at front seals. If any of these symptoms are encountered, thoroughly clean flame guard and engine assembly, then check for oil leaks.

1. Remove timing belt as outlined under "Timing Belt, Replace," then the pulley at seal to be replaced using tool No. 5034, or equivalent.
2. Remove tensioner and inner timing belt cover.
3. Use a screwdriver to pry out oil seal, being careful not to damage contact face.
4. Inspect and clean sealing contact faces.
5. Grease seal and seat, then press in new seal using sleeve tool No. 5025, or equivalent, for camshaft or intermediate shaft seal or sleeve tool No. 5283, or equivalent, for crankshaft seal. **Ensure seal is not distorted or damaged during installation.**
6. Install inner timing belt cover, timing belt tensioner and applicable pulley(s). Position guide plates of camshaft pulley so they incline outward from pulley. Position intermediate shaft pulley with marking (a cavity) outward.
7. Install timing belt as outlined under "Timing Belt, Replace."

Except 2.3L 4-Cylinder Engine

1. Remove timing belt as outlined under "Timing Belt, Replace."
2. Remove guard plate, then the vibration damper using counterhold tool No. 5433, or equivalent.
3. Remove crankshaft belt pulley using a universal puller and two vibration damper bolts. **Finger tighten bolts as far as possible in pulley, then attach puller so that arms act on bolts, not on pulley.**
4. Use a screwdriver to pry out oil seal, then clean sealing face.
5. Grease oil seal, install seal on tool No. 5455, or equivalent, then press into place using crankshaft center nut.
6. Install timing belt as outlined under "Timing Belt, Replace," then the vibration damper. Tighten nut to specifications.

REAR

2.3L 4-Cylinder Engine

1. Remove transmission, and if applicable, clutch assembly. Refer to appropriate transmission section for procedure.
2. Lock flywheel in place with gear sector tool No. 5112, or equivalent, then remove flywheel.
3. Use a screwdriver to pry out oil seal, being careful not to damage sealing surfaces on holder or crankshaft. **Note seal position in relation to sealing flange so correct position is known when installing new seal.**
4. Inspect and clean sealing surfaces in holder and on crankshaft.
5. Oil sealing lips and contact face of seal against holder, install seal on handle tool No. 1801 and drift tool No. 5276, or equivalents, then tap in seal until drift contacts crankshaft. **If there is a wear surface on crankshaft, press seal further into flange than before. Remove one spacer ring from drift if old seal was flush with flange. Remove two spacer rings from drift if old seal was .012 inch (3 mm) inside flange. Leave both spacer rings in drift if crankshaft is undamaged.**
6. Install flywheel as follows:
   a. Turn crankshaft to TDC on compression stroke, **Fig. 1,** then position flywheel on crankshaft so that pins A and B, **Fig. 11,** are located 15° on either side of horizontal position.
   b. Apply sealing compound No. 1 161 056-6 to threads of new flywheel bolts, then install bolts.
   c. Install gear sector No. 5112 to lock flywheel, then tighten flywheel bolts to specifications and remove gear sector.
7. If applicable, install clutch assembly, then the transmission. Refer to appropriate transmission section for procedure.

Except 2.3L 4-Cylinder Engine

1. Remove transmission, and if applicable, clutch assembly. Refer to appropriate transmission section for procedure.
2. Lock flywheel in place with gear sector No. 5112, then remove flywheel.
3. Use a screwdriver to pry out oil seal, being careful not to damage sealing surfaces on holder or crankshaft.
4. Inspect and clean sealing surfaces in holder and on crankshaft.
5. Oil lips of seal, install seal onto handle tool No. 1801 and drift tool No. 5430, or equivalents, then tap in seal until drift bottoms on crankshaft.
6. Install gear sector No. 5112 to lock flywheel, then tighten new flywheel bolts, coated with thread locking compound, to specifications and remove gear sector.
7. If applicable, install clutch assembly, then the transmission. Refer to appropriate transmission section for procedure.

OIL PAN

REPLACE

2.3L 4-CYLINDER ENGINE

240

1. Raise and support vehicle and drain oil. Replace drain plug and tighten to specifications.
2. Remove splashguard under engine, then the engine mount nuts from underside of crossmember.
3. Disconnect steering shaft at steering gear. On vehicles with manual steering gear, pull shield up. On all models, remove lower bolt and loosen upper bolt, then slide flange assembly up steering shaft.
4. Using engine support tool Nos. 5033, 5006 and 5115, or equivalents, raise engine slightly and support.
5. Remove lefthand side engine mount.
6. Support front crossmember, remove retaining bolts, then lower crossmember and remove support bracket at rear of oil pan.
7. Remove oil pan from vehicle by turning front of oil pan toward left and lowering oil pan.
8. Reverse procedure to install.

940

1. Raise and support vehicle and drain oil. Replace drain plug and tighten to specifications.
2. Remove splashguard under engine.
3. Disconnect battery ground cable, then disconnect exhaust pipe from front muffler flange and remove engine mount retaining nuts.
4. Remove steering shaft lower clamp bolt and loosen upper bolt, then slide flange assembly up steering shaft.
5. Loosen fan shroud, remove dipstick, then raise and support engine using tool No. 5033, 5115 and 5006, or equivalents.
6. Remove power steering hose retaining strap, then remove lefthand side engine mount.
7. Remove front crossmember attaching bolts, disconnect hoses from power steering fluid reservoir, then remove reinforcing bracket and lower crossmember.
8. Remove retaining bolts, then turn oil pan and remove from vehicle.
9. Reverse procedure to install. Tighten oil pan bolts and steering shaft coupling to specifications.

EXCEPT 2.3L 4-CYLINDER ENGINES

1. Raise and support vehicle, then drain engine oil.
2. Remove engine oil filter.
3. **On 2.9L engine,** disconnect flame trap return line.
4. **On all models,** remove oil pan retaining bolts.
5. Tap pan loose from engine block with a rubber mallet.
6. Clean old gasket material from oil pan and engine block mating surfaces.
7. Apply suitable liquid gasket to oil pan and install. Tighten oil pan bolts to specifications.

OIL PUMP

REPLACE

2.3L 4-CYLINDER ENGINE

1. Remove oil pan as outlined under "Oil Pan, Replace."
2. Remove oil pump retaining bolts and remove pump together with delivery pipe.
3. When installing oil pump, always use new seals on delivery pipe. Attach oil trap drain hose clamp, if applicable, to one of the pump retaining bolts. Ensure hose is properly positioned behind oil pump shoulder.

EXCEPT 2.3L 4-CYLINDER ENGINE

1. Remove crankshaft front seal as outlined under "Crankshaft Seal, Replace."
2. Remove oil pump.
3. Reverse procedure to install, noting the following:
   a. Use tool No. 5455, or equivalent, and crankshaft center nut to press pump into place. Use bolts as guides.
   b. Tighten pump bolts to specifications.

BELT TENSION DATA

When belt tension is correct, belts may be depressed .20–.40 inch (5–10 mm) halfway between pulleys.

SERPENTINE DRIVE BELT

BELT ROUTING

Refer to **Figs. 12 through 14** for proper belt routing.

COOLING SYSTEM BLEED

2.3L 4-CYLINDER ENGINE

1. Disconnect vacuum hose from heating system water valve.
2. Fill cooling system through expansion tank.
3. Start engine and allow to reach normal operating temperatures.
4. Top up coolant as necessary, then connect vacuum hose to heating system water valve.

EXCEPT 2.3L 4-CYLINDER ENGINE

1. Fill system through coolant expansion tank.
2. Start engine and allow to reach normal operating temperatures.
3. Top up coolant as necessary.

THERMOSTAT

REPLACE

1. Drain coolant to below level of thermostat housing, then replace thermostat.
2. Refill coolant system.

WATER PUMP

REPLACE

2.3L 4-CYLINDER ENGINE

1. Drain cooling system and remove radiator shroud retaining screws and move shroud to rear. Remove fan and fan clutch.
2. Loosen and remove accessory drive belts.
3. Remove fan pulley.
4. Remove timing cover.
5. Remove lower radiator hose.
6. Remove coolant pipe retaining bolt and pull pipe rearward.
7. Remove water pump.
8. Reverse procedure to install.

EXCEPT 2.3L 4-CYLINDER ENGINE

1. Open drain cock on righthand side of engine block, remove coolant expansion tank cap, and drain cooling system.
2. Remove timing belt as outlined under "Timing Belt, Replace."
3. Remove water pump.
4. Reverse procedure to install.

RADIATOR

REPLACE

1. Remove expansion tank cap, then remove guard from under radiator.
2. Drain coolant from radiator.
3. Remove electric cooling fan, then disconnect radiator hoses.
4. **On models equipped with A/C,** remove condenser to radiator mounting bolts, then condenser.
5. **On all models,** remove radiator mounting bolts, then radiator.
6. Reverse procedure to install.

FUEL PUMP

REPLACE

2.3L 4-CYLINDER & 2.9L ENGINES

The main fuel pump may be located on the lefthand side of the fuel tank, or attached to a bracket underneath vehicle under the rear seat.

1. Clamp off the tank to pump hose with suitable pliers. Disconnect fuel lines from pump.
2. Disconnect wire connector from pump.
3. Remove pump retaining bolts, then the pump.
4. Reverse procedure to install. Tighten fasteners to specifications.

2.3L & 2.4L 5-CYLINDER ENGINES

1. Drain fuel system as follows:
   a. Remove throttle pulley cover, fuel distribution manifold cover and shield over valve on fuel distribution manifold.
   b. Connect hose/union tool No. 999 5484, or equivalent, to fuel drainage unit tool Nos. 981 2270, 2273 and 2282, or equivalents, and start fuel drainage unit.
   c. Connect union on fuel drainage unit to valve on fuel distribution manifold, then raise and support vehicle.
   d. Remove fuel filter cover and shield over valve at fuel filter, then use key tool No. 999 5480, or equivalent, to open vent cock upstream of fuel filter, **Fig. 15.**
2. Tilt righthand rear seat forward, then remove luggage compartment mat and cover over pump unit nut in tank.
3. Remove righthand luggage compartment panel, then disconnect fuel pump electrical connector.
4. Mark position, then disconnect quick release couplings on delivery and return lines using a screwdriver to lift outer sleeve carefully.
5. Remove pump unit nut using spanner tool No. 999 5485, or equivalent, then fabricate a tool to aid in pump removal by fitting two quick release couplings tool No. 3517 139-6, or equivalent, to a tube tool No. 1266 870-3, or equivalent.
6. Connect couplings to delivery and return lines, lift out pump unit and rubber seal, then reinstall pump unit nut on branch on tank.
7. Disconnect upper clip on fuel hose, then the electrical leads.
8. Twist lower section of unit to right, then pull pump base downward while working fuel hose downward.
9. Separate pump retaining halves, then remove spring and rubber spacer and disconnect fuel hose from pump.
10. Reverse procedure to install. Tighten fasteners to specifications.

FUEL FILTER

REPLACE

2.3L 4-CYLINDER & 2.9L ENGINES

Fuel filter is located next to fuel pump, **Fig. 16.** Disconnect filter couplings by pushing sleeves back with a 17 mm open end wrench.

2.4L & 2.3L 5-CYLINDER ENGINES

1. Drain fuel system as follows:
   a. Remove throttle pulley cover, fuel distribution manifold cover and shield over valve on fuel distribution manifold.
   b. Connect hose/union tool No. 999 5484, or equivalent, to fuel drainage unit tool Nos. 981 2270, 2273 and 2282, or equivalents, and start fuel drainage unit.
   c. Connect union on fuel drainage unit to valve on fuel distribution manifold, then raise and support vehicle.
   d. Remove fuel filter cover and shield over valve at fuel filter, then use key tool No. 999 5480, or equivalent, to open vent cock upstream of fuel filter, **Fig. 15.**
2. Disconnect filter quick release couplings using an open spanner to push sleeves back, then remove screw securing filter clip.
3. Remove filter.
4. Reverse procedure to install.

TIGHTENING SPECIFICATIONS

2.3L 4-CYLINDER ENGINE

Year	Component	Torque/Ft. Lbs.
1993–96	Camshaft Bearing Cap Bolts	15
	Camshaft Pulley Bolt	37
	Connecting Rod Cap Nuts	①
	Crankshaft Bolt	②
	Cylinder Head Bolts	③
	Flywheel Bolts	50

Continued

Year	Component	Torque/Ft. Lbs.
1993–96	Intermediate Shaft Pulley Bolt	36
	Main Bearing Cap Bolts	80
	Oil Drain Plug	43
	Oil Pan Bolts	8
	Steering Shaft Bolts	14.5–21.5

① — Tighten in two stages. First to 15 ft. lbs., then an additional 90°.

② — Tighten in two stages. First to 44 ft. lbs., then an additional 60°.

③ — Refer to "Cylinder Head, Replace."

2.3L & 2.4L 5-CYLINDER ENGINES

Year	Component	Torque/Ft. Lbs.
1993–96	Camshaft Gear Bolts	15
	Carrier Plate Bolts	①
	Connecting Rod Bearing Cap Nuts	②
	Cylinder Head	③
	Exhaust Manifold Bolts	17
	Flywheel Bolts	④
	Fuel Distribution Manifold Bolts	⑤
	Intake Manifold Bolts	12
	Oil Pan Bolts	13
	Oil Pump Bolts	7
	Oil Suction Line	12
	Oil Sump Bolts	13
	Oil Sump Plug	25
	Oil Trap	11
	Timing Belt Damper Unit Bolt	18
	Timing Belt Idler Pulley Bolt	18
	Timing Belt Tensioning Pulley Bolt	28
	Transmission To Engine Bolts	36
	Vibration Damper Flange Bolts	⑥
	Vibration Damper Nut	132
	Water Pump Bolts	12

① — Tighten in two stages. First to 33 ft. lbs., then an additional 50°.

② — Tighten in two stages. First to 15 ft. lbs., then an additional 90°.

③ — Refer to "Cylinder Head, Replace."

④ — Tighten in two stages. First to 33 ft. lbs., then an additional 65°.

⑤ — Tighten in two stages. First to 7 ft. lbs., then an additional 75°.

⑥ — Tighten in two stages. First to 18 ft. lbs., then an additional 30°.

Continued

2.9L ENGINE

Year	Component	Torque/ Ft. Lbs.
1993–96	Camshaft Gear Bolt	15
	Carrier Plate Bolts	①
	Connecting Rod Bearing Cap Nuts	②
	Cylinder Head	③
	Flywheel Bolts	①
	Fuel Distribution Manifold Bolts	④
	Oil Pan Bolts	15
	Oil Suction Pipe	13
	Oil Sump Bolts	15
	Oil Sump Plug	28
	Oil Trap	11
	Timing Belt Damper Unit Bolt	18
	Timing Belt Idler Pulley Bolt	18
	Timing Belt Tensioning Pulley Bolt	29
	Vibration Damper Flange Bolts	⑤
	Vibration Damper Nut	222
	Water Pump Bolts	13

①— Tighten in two stages. First to 33 ft. lbs., then an additional 50°.
②— Tighten in two stages. First to 15 ft. lbs., then an additional 90°.
③— Refer to "Cylinder Head, Replace."
④— Tighten in two stages. First to 7 ft. lbs., then an additional 75°.
⑤— Tighten in two stages. First to 26 ft. lbs., then an additional 60°.

Clutch & Manual Transmission

NOTE: On Air Bag Equipped Models, Refer To "Air Bag System Precautions" Located In The Front Of This Manual For System Disarming & Arming Procedures.

INDEX

	Page No.
Adjustments	50-23
Clutch Pedal	50-23
Clutch, Replace	50-24
240	50-24
850	50-24
Hydraulic System Service	50-23
Clutch Master Cylinder, Replace	50-23
Clutch System Bleed	50-24
Slave Cylinder, Replace	50-24
Precautions	50-23
Air Bag Systems	50-23
Tightening Specifications	50-25
Transaxle, Replace	50-24
850	50-24
Transmission, Replace	50-24
240	50-24

PRECAUTIONS

AIR BAG SYSTEMS

Refer to "Air Bag System Precautions" in the front of this manual for system disarming and arming procedures.

ADJUSTMENTS

CLUTCH PEDAL

Models w/Mechanical Actuation

On vehicles with clutch pedal return spring mounted on the clutch pedal assembly, check clearance by pressing fork toward rear of vehicle. Clearance should be .039–.118 inch (1–3 mm). If necessary, adjust clearance using nut on cable.

On vehicles with clutch pedal return spring mounted on the clutch fork, check clearance by pressing fork forward. Clearance should be .039–.118 inch (1–3 mm). If necessary, adjust clearance using nuts on cable.

Models w/Hydraulic Actuation

This system is designed so clutch fork and throw-out bearing touch lightly on pressure plate. No provision for adjustment is provided.

HYDRAULIC SYSTEM SERVICE

CLUTCH MASTER CYLINDER, REPLACE

240

1. Remove panel from under dash, then the locking spring and pin from clutch pedal assembly.
2. Disconnect fluid pipe from master cylinder, then place a container under cylinder to collect fluid.
3. Remove master cylinder attaching bolts and master cylinder.
4. Reverse procedure to install. Ensure

.04 inch clearance exists between pushrod and piston, then bleed hydraulic system.

850

1. Remove air cleaner, bracket retaining screws, then cable tie to drain hose and move to one side.
2. Place suitable shop towel under clutch master cylinder to protect paint.
3. Drain brake fluid from reservoir into suitable container, then disconnect brake line from clutch master cylinder.
4. Remove lower instrument panel, then the knee guard.
5. Fold carpeting back, remove clip securing clutch master cylinder pushrod to clutch pedal.
6. Remove nut and bolt securing clutch master cylinder to firewall, then clutch master cylinder.
7. Reverse procedure to install, noting the following:
   a. Tighten fasteners to specifications.
   b. Bleed system using clutch bleeder unit tool No. 998 5876-3, or equivalent, following manufacturer's instructions.

SLAVE CYLINDER, REPLACE

1. Disconnect hose from pipe and bracket.
2. Remove slave cylinder to bellhousing attaching bolts, then the slave cylinder.
3. Reverse procedure to install, then bleed hydraulic system.

CLUTCH SYSTEM BLEED

240

1. Check reservoir fluid level and add brake fluid if necessary.
2. Attach a hose to bleed screw on slave cylinder, then insert free end in clean container with sufficient clean brake fluid to cover end of tube.
3. Have an assistant depress clutch pedal, open bleed screw, then close screw with clutch still depressed.
4. Release clutch pedal, then repeat step 3 until air bubbles can no longer be observed.
5. Top up reservoir to correct level.

CLUTCH

REPLACE

240

1. Remove transmission as outlined under "Transmission, Replace."
2. Install centering drift tool No. 5111, or equivalent, to support clutch disc, then remove pressure plate mounting bolts in a cross directional pattern, a couple of turns at a time, to prevent warping of the pressure plate.
3. Remove pressure plate and clutch disc.
4. Reverse procedure to install.

850

1. Remove transaxle as outlined under "Transmission, Replace."
2. Install tool No. 999 5112, or equivalent, to immobilize flywheel, then loosen pressure plate bolts in rotation and remove clutch disc and pressure plate.
3. Install clutch disc and pressure plate using drift tool No. 999 5487, or equivalent, to center disc, then tighten pressure plate bolts to specifications carefully in rotation.
4. Remove drift and immobilizing tools, then install transaxle as outlined under "Transmission, Replace."

TRANSMISSION

REPLACE

240

1. Remove front support for exhaust pipe, then disconnect clutch cable, shift lever and speedometer cable.
2. Remove propeller shaft, then the transmission crossmember. Support transmission with a jack.
3. Disconnect transmission electrical connectors, then remove transmission.
4. Reverse procedure to install.

TRANSAXLE

REPLACE

850

1. Move steering wheel to highest position.
2. Place shift lever in Neutral position, remove battery, air cleaner and air intake, battery shelf, then air cleaner bracket retaining screws.
3. Remove selector cables from bracket and levers, then selector link plate by tapping out pin.
4. Remove back-up light switch connector.
5. Remove cable tie from engine cable harness, then ground lead from transaxle.
6. Remove circlip from clutch slave cylinder to transaxle, then clutch slave cylinder.
7. Loosen nut on rear engine mounting/splash guard, remove five bolts securing starter and transaxle, then remove cover over spark plug wires. Lift coolant expansion tank off bracket and place aside.
8. Remove tie bar between torque arm and engine, then disconnect ground lead from cable harness.
9. Install lifting tool No. 999 5459, or equivalent, on valve cover using two bolts from tie bar.
10. Install lifting lug tool No. 999 5464, or equivalent, with center bolt to manifold heat guard. Install lifting yoke tool No. 999 5428, or equivalent, then adjust lifting yoke to lifting lugs.
11. Place support tool No. 999 5033, or equivalent, onto fender. Install lifting beam tool No. 999 5006, or equivalent onto support. Place lifting beam directly above lugs on lifting yoke.
12. Install lifting hook tool No. 999 5460, or equivalent. Extend hook approximately 5 mm to relieve the weight on engine mounting.
13. Raise and support vehicle, remove tire and wheels, then ABS sensor from lefthand outboard shaft.
14. Disconnect brake line and ABS cable brackets on both sides.
15. Remove fasteners from lefthand fenderwell.
16. Remove hub center nut locking device, then install tool No. 9995461, or equivalent and remove nut.
17. Remove front splash guard bolts, push guard forward so locating pins on back come loose, then disconnect front of guard and remove.
18. Remove nuts attaching link arms and ball joints, then disconnect link arm and ball joints.
19. Remove roll bar, then any vacuum or electrical connectors as needed.
20. Remove steering gear line bracket, then two bolts securing the steady bar bracket to transaxle.
21. Drain transaxle into suitable container.
22. Remove righthand driveshaft bearing cap, driveshaft, then twist MacPherson strut out of way.
23. Loosen bolts holding steering gear to engine mounting one turn, remove nuts holding steering gear to subframe.
24. Position a jack tool No. 998 5972-0, or equivalent, under lefthand side of subframe, then gently tighten.
25. Remove fixing bolts to subframe brackets on both sides, then unscrew two bolts holding subframe to body on righthand by 15 mm.
26. Lower subframe, let frame hang free from bolts on righthand side.
27. Remove bolts to engine mounting subframe and nut on top of engine mounting, then remove engine mounting. **Ensure steering gear is hanging properly on hook so that lower steering wheel shaft section does not slip out of steering column.**
28. Disconnect heated oxygen sensor cable terminals, then remove cover from rear engine mounting and rear mounting from transaxle.
29. Twist lefthand MacPherson strut and pull out. Tap lefthand driveshaft end with plastic mallet and pull shaft out of hub.
30. Using tool No. 999 5462, or equivalent remove driveshaft from transaxle.
31. Lower engine and transaxle using lifting hook until approximately 130 mm of hook thread is clear.
32. Install universal tool No. 999 5972 and transaxle fixture tool No. 999 5463, or equivalents, then attach transaxle fixture to transaxle using fixing bolts from steady bar bracket. At same time position support plate tool No. 5463-2, or equivalent, on fixture.

33. Raise engine, then remove seven remaining transaxle to engine attaching bolts.
34. Pull transaxle away from engine, then lower jack and transaxle.
35. Reverse procedure to install noting the following:
    a. Tighten fasteners to specifications.
    b. When installing lefthand driveshaft, ensure driveshaft circlip snaps into place.

TIGHTENING SPECIFICATIONS

Year	Component	Torque/ Ft. Lbs.
240		
1993	Bellhousing Bolts	28–37
	Countershaft Bolts (M47 Trans.)	26–33
	Driveplate Nuts, M16 (M46 Trans.)	122-133
	Driveplate Nuts, M16 (M47 Trans.)	52-66
	Driveplate Nuts, M20 (M47 Trans.)	66-81
	Gear Lever Carrier Bolts	30
	Oil Drain Plugs	20–30
	Rear Housing Nut (M46 Trans.)	9–13
	Transmission Cover Bolts	11–18
	5th Gear Synchromesh Nut (M47 Trans.)	89
850		
1993–96	Bellhousing To Engine Bolts	37
	Bellhousing To Transmission Bolts	18
	Clutch Master Cylinder Nut & Bolt	18
	Clutch Pressure Plate Bolts	18
	Firewall Harness Grommet	4.4
	Gear Selector Bracket Bolts	18
	Inductive Sensor	7
	Input Shaft	37
	Knee Guard	15
	Lever Bracket	18
	Oil Drain Plugs	26
	Release Bearing Sleeve	7
	Reverse Gear Detent Holder	18
	Reverse Light Switch	18
	Ring Gear	22①
	Starter Motor Bolts	30

① — Plus an additional 90°.

Rear Axle & Suspension

NOTE: Refer To "Engine, Transaxle/Transmission & Rear Suspension Application" In The "Specifications" Section For Rear Suspension Applications.

INDEX

	Page No.
Coil Spring, Replace	50-28
Control Arm, Replace	50-28
Lower	50-28
Upper	50-28
Differential Housing Bushings, Replace	50-31
Multi-Link Independent Suspension	50-31
Hub & Bearing, Replace	50-27
Delta-Link Independent Suspension	50-27
Reaction Rod & Bushings, Replace	50-27
4-Link Live Axle	50-27
Rear Axle, Replace	50-26
Constant-Track Live Axle	50-26
Multi-Link Independent Suspension	50-26
4-Link Live Axle	50-26
Rear Axle Link, Replace	50-31
Delta-Link Independent Suspension	50-31
Rear Axle Shaft, Replace	50-27
4-Link & Constant-Track Live Axles	50-27
Shock Absorber, Replace	50-27
Delta-Link Independent Suspension	50-27
Stabilizer Bar, Replace	50-29
Constant Track Live Axle	50-29
Delta-Link Independent Suspension	50-29
Support Arm, Replace	50-30
Multi-Link Independent Suspension	50-30
Tightening Specifications:	50-32
Constant-Track Live Axle	50-32
Delta-Link Independent Suspension	50-32
Multi-Link Active Suspension	50-32
4-Link Live Axle	50-32
Torque Rod & Bushings, Replace	50-27
Constant Track Live Axle	50-27
Track Rod, Replace	50-29
Multi-Link Independent Suspension	50-29
4-Link & Constant Track Live Axles	50-29
Trailing Arm, Replace	50-29
Constant Track Live Axle	50-29
4-Link Live Axle	50-29
Transverse Arm Mount, Replace	50-31
Delta-Link Independent Suspension	50-31
Upper Rear Axle Member Bushings, Replace	50-31
Multi-Link Independent Suspension	50-31

REAR AXLE

REPLACE

4-LINK LIVE AXLE

1. Raise and support vehicle, then remove rear wheels.
2. Disconnect rear axle ventilation hose and brake pipe brackets, then remove collision guard and bake calipers. Secure calipers to upper spring mounts.
3. Remove brake shoes, then withdraw driveshafts with brake discs.
4. Position support fixture tool No. 2714, or equivalent, and a jack beneath rear axle, then remove exhaust pipe, if necessary.
5. Disconnect reaction and track rods, propeller shaft, parking brake cables, shock absorbers at lower mount and anti-roll bar, **Fig. 1.**
6. Release trailing arm mounts at front and lower axle until springs are free, then remove trailing arm mounts.
7. Remove rear axle assembly from vehicle.
8. Reverse procedure to install.

CONSTANT-TRACK LIVE AXLE

1. Raise and support vehicle, then remove rear wheels.
2. Remove brake caliper, then hang calipers from springs.
3. Remove brake discs and parking brake shoes, then disconnect parking brake cable from equalizing arms and clips on axle.
4. Loosen torque arms in frame, then disconnect torque arms from axle, **Fig. 2.**
5. Position support fixture tool No. 2714, or equivalent, and a jack under axle and raise rear axle assembly slightly.
6. Remove exhaust pipe, if necessary, then disconnect track rod and speedometer cable.
7. Disconnect propeller shaft, upper torque arm, dampers from lower mountings in support arms, support arm front brackets, then pry support arms loose from front mountings.
8. Remove anti-roll bar, righthand and lefthand support arms, then the rear axle assembly.
9. Reverse procedure to install.

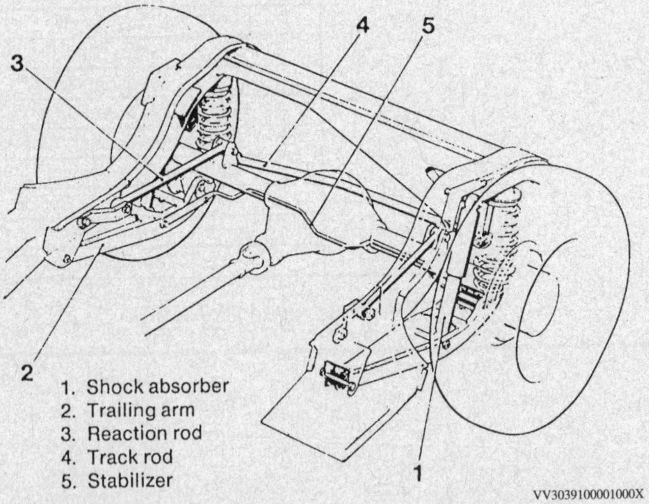

3
4
5
2
1
1. Shock absorber
2. Trailing arm
3. Reaction rod
4. Track rod
5. Stabilizer
VV3039100001000X

Fig. 1 4-Link Live Axle rear suspension. 240

MULTI-LINK INDEPENDENT SUSPENSION

1. Raise and support vehicle, then remove rear wheels, support arm guards and bolts securing support arms at front and rear, **Fig. 3.** Tap out rear end of support arms from wheel bearing housings.
2. Position support fixture tool No. 5972, or equivalent, and a jack under support arms and lock support arms with fixture arms.

3. Slightly relieve tension on shock absorbers and remove bolts from upper shock mountings, then remove support arms complete with springs and shocks.
4. Remove calipers and secure with wire, then mark relation of propeller shaft to axle flange and disconnect propeller shaft.
5. Position support fixture tool No. 5972, or equivalent, and a jack under axle, remove bolts securing axle to floor and lower axle slightly.
6. Disconnect speedometer cable from inspection cover, then remove screws securing cable to axle.
7. Disconnect parking brake cable, then remove rear axle assembly.
8. Reverse procedure to install.

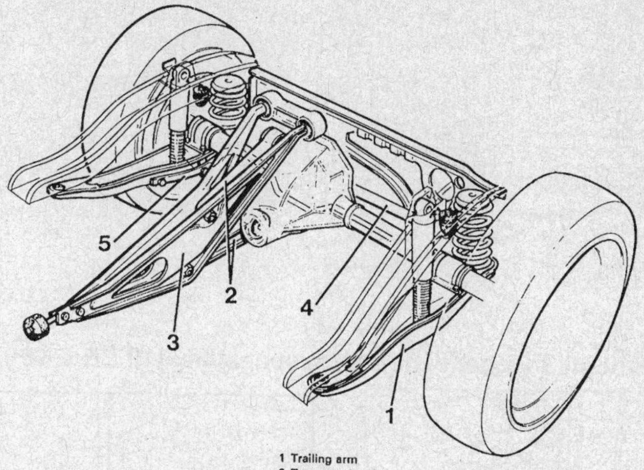
5
2
4
3
1
1 Trailing arm
2 Torque rods
3 Sub frame
4 Track rod
5 Anti-roll bar
VV3039100002000X

Fig. 2 Constant Track Live Axle rear suspension. 940 & 960 5-Door

REAR AXLE SHAFT

REPLACE

4-LINK & CONSTANT-TRACK LIVE AXLES

1. Raise and support vehicle, then remove rear wheel.
2. **On 240 models,** disconnect brake pipe mounting brackets, then remove collision guard.
3. **On all models,** remove brake caliper and secure to spring.
4. Remove brake disc and shoes.
5. **On 850, 940 and 960 models,** remove pressure plate bolts.
6. **On all models,** invert brake disc and secure to axle with tapered end of lug nuts facing outward.
7. Remove axle shaft using brake disc to withdraw shaft.
8. Remove inner seal using a long screwdriver, then clean inside of rear axle tube.
9. Remove bearing and outer seal using press tool No. 5212, or equivalent, and a hydraulic press.
10. Install bearing and outer seal using support tool No. 5010, or equivalent, standard handle tool No. 1801, or equivalent, and a hydraulic press.
11. Install inner seal using drift tool No. 5243, or equivalent, and standard handle tool No. 1801, or equivalent, then reverse removal steps to install axle shaft.

HUB & BEARING

REPLACE

DELTA-LINK INDEPENDENT SUSPENSION

1. Raise and support vehicle, then remove wheel.
2. Disconnect brake pipes from clip on rear axle, then the three way connector from lefthand trailing arm.
3. Remove caliper and hang from strut with wire, then disconnect parking brake shoe adjuster.
4. Remove guide pin, brake disc, protecting cover, hub nut and hub.
5. Remove ABS sensor, then the parking brake shoes.
6. Remove screw for brake wire in backing plate and bracket for wire's guide sleeve.
7. Remove screws on backing plate and brake shoe retaining springs, then the backing plate.
8. Pull guide sleeve forward on parking brake wire and disconnect wire from parking brake segment, then remove segment.
9. Remove bolts locating wheel axle end piece, then the axle.
10. Reverse procedure to install, noting the following:
    a. Use a soft brush to clean ABS sensor before installing.
    b. If necessary to replace ABS toothed wheel, use mandrel tool No. 5351, spacer tool No. 5350, counterhold tool No. 5340, or equivalents, and a hydraulic press to press wheel off hub. Use mandrel tool No. 5351, counterhold tool No. 2861, or equivalents, and a hydraulic press to install wheel. **Ensure wheel sits square in hub.**
    c. Install hub protecting cover using mandrel tool No. 5225, or equivalent.
    d. Tighten all fasteners to specifications.

REACTION ROD & BUSHINGS

REPLACE

4-LINK LIVE AXLE

1. Raise and support vehicle, then remove reaction rod.
2. Replace bushings using drift tool No. 5086, or equivalent, sleeve tool No. 5087, or equivalent, and a hydraulic press. **Position bushings in rod so that flat sides are parallel to rod.**
3. Install reaction rod and lower vehicle.

TORQUE ROD & BUSHINGS

REPLACE

CONSTANT TRACK LIVE AXLE

1. Raise and support vehicle, then remove torque rod.
2. Replace bushings in large end using drift tool No. 5239, or equivalent, a V-block and a hydraulic press. **Press bushings in squarely.**
3. Replace bushings in small end using drift tool No. 5239, or equivalent, plate tool No. 5240, or equivalent, supported on a V-block and a hydraulic press.
4. Install torque rod and lower vehicle.

SHOCK ABSORBER

REPLACE

DELTA-LINK INDEPENDENT SUSPENSION

1. Fold rear seat backs forward, then undo luggage area carpet at front edge.
2. Remove cover plate under front edge of carpet, then undo righthand side panel at front edge and fold to one side. Remove seat back catch and panel attachment clip.
3. Raise rear of vehicle until wheels are off ground, remove upper shock absorber mounting bolts on righthand side, then disconnect electrical connector retainer and position wiring and connector away from shock mount.
4. Raise and support vehicle.
5. Remove load from shock absorber by pressing trailing arm upward. Use a jack placed against recess for spring mounting bolt.
6. Disconnect shock absorber from lower mount, then remove spring mounting nut and spring.

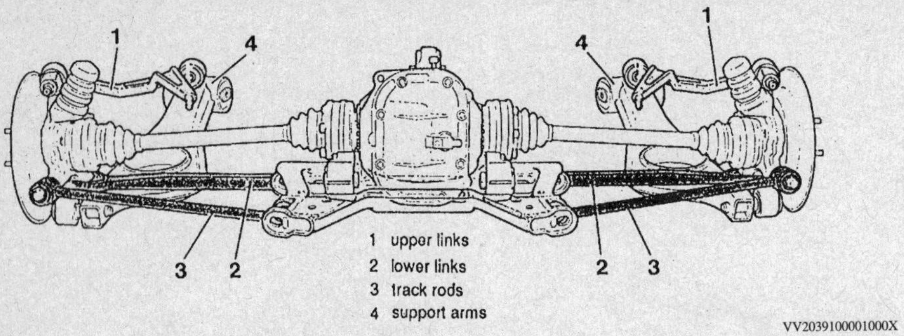
1
4
1
4
1 upper links
2 lower links
3 track rods
4 support arms
3 2
2 3
VV2039100001000X

Fig. 3 Multi-Link Independent rear suspension. 940 SE & 960 4-Door

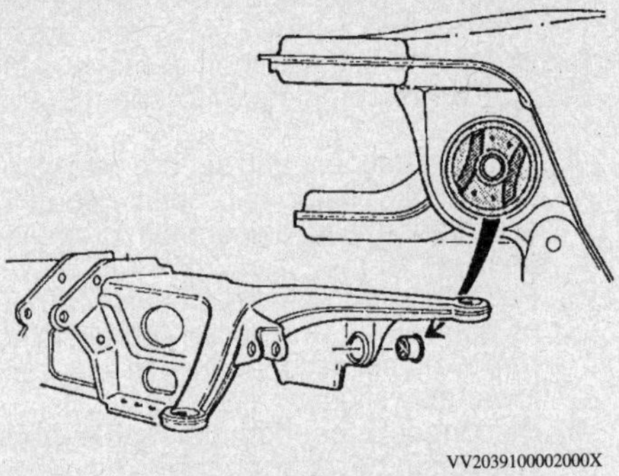
VV2039100002000X

Fig. 4 Upper control arm bushing orientation. Multi-Link Independent rear suspension

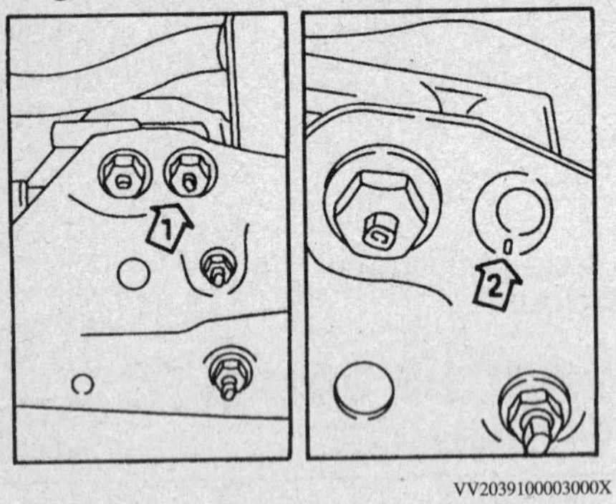
1
2
VV2039100003000X

Fig. 5 Transverse arm bolt removal. Delta-Link Independent rear suspension

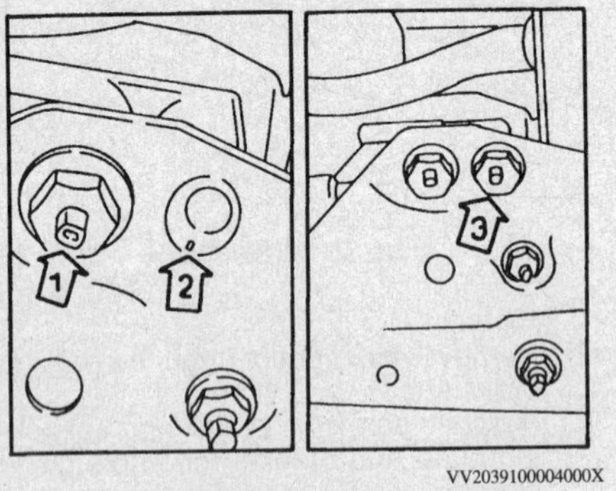
1
2
3
VV2039100004000X

Fig. 6 Transverse arm bolt installation. Delta-Link Independent rear suspension

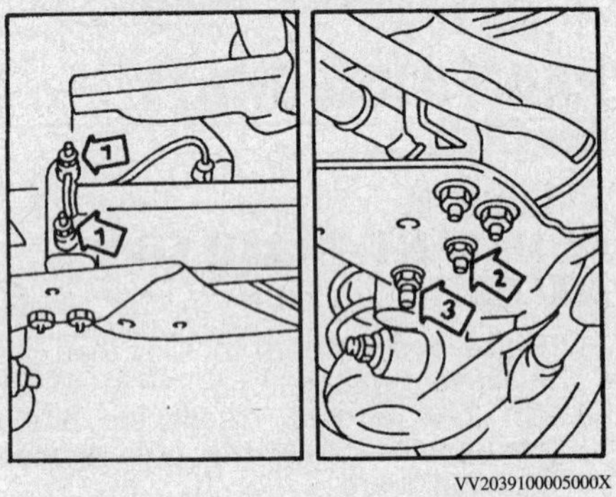
1
1
2
3
VV2039100005000X

Fig. 7 Transverse arm bolt tightening sequence. Delta-Link Independent rear suspension

7. Lower vehicle, then lift out shock absorber with upper mount.
8. Place shock absorber mount in a vise, then remove nut using sleeve tool No. 5498, or equivalent, and spanner tool No. 5499, or equivalent, for standard shock absorbers or sleeve tool No. 5500, or equivalent, and spanner tool No. 5501, or equivalent, for Nivomat ride-height control shock absorbers.
9. Install new shock absorber in mount and tighten new nut to specifications, then install shock absorber and tighten upper mounting bolts a few turns.
10. Raise and support vehicle, then insert end of spring into trailing arm recess and attaching washer guide pin into hole in trailing arm. Tighten to specifications.
11. Press trailing arm upward using a jack placed against recess for spring mounting bolt, then connect shock absorber to lower mount and tighten to specifications.
12. Lower vehicle, then tighten upper shock absorber mounting bolts to specifications and connect electrical connector with a strip clamp.
13. Refit carpets and panels. Lock seat back catch plunger with locking fluid and tighten to specifications.

COIL SPRING

REPLACE

Refer to “Shock Absorber, Replace” for coil spring replacement.

CONTROL ARM

REPLACE

UPPER

Multi-Link Independent Suspension

1. Raise and support vehicle, remove wheel, then the caliper and hang from spring with wire.
2. Disconnect support arm, lower control arm, track rod and upper control arm from wheel bearing housing. Use a small puller and a 12 mm x 50 mm bolt to disconnect track rod from housing. Retain spacers located between upper control arm and wheel bearing housing.
3. Remove nut securing control arm to rear axle member at rear, bolt and nut securing control arm to rear axle member at front, then the control arm.
4. Mount control arm in a vise, then use a chisel to pry up edge of outer bushing.
5. Mount control arm in a hydraulic press using two V-blocks as counterholds, then press out outer bushing using drift tool No. 5345, or equivalent.
6. Press in new outer bushing using drift tool No. 5090, or equivalent, counterhold tool No. 5087, or equivalent, and a hydraulic press.
7. Mount control arm in a vise, then use a chisel to pry up edge of inner front bushing.
8. Mount control arm in a hydraulic press, then press out inner front bushing using drift tool No. 5345, or equivalent, counterhold tool No. 5343, or equivalent, and drift tool No. 5347, or equivalent.
9. Press in new inner front bushing using drift tool No. 2731, or equivalent, counterhold tool No. 2904, or equivalent, and a hydraulic press.
10. **If replacing lefthand inner rear bushing,** lower support arm slightly.
11. Press out inner rear bushing using press tool No. 5343, or equivalent.
12. Press in new inner rear bushing using press tool No. 5353, or equivalent. Note orientation of bushing, **Fig. 4.**
13. Install control arm, bolt and nut securing control arm to rear axle member, spacers between upper control arm and wheel bearing housing, then the nut securing control arm to wheel bearing housing.
14. Pull top of wheel bearing housing outward while tightening upper control arm nut to specifications.
15. Pull wheel bearing housing outward and insert lower control arm, then pull wheel bearing housing inward toward differential while tightening control arm nut to specifications.
16. Connect support arm and track rod, then install brake caliper and wheel.

LOWER

Multi-Link Independent Suspension

1. Raise and support vehicle, remove wheel, then the caliper and hang from spring with wire.
2. Remove brake disc and parking brake

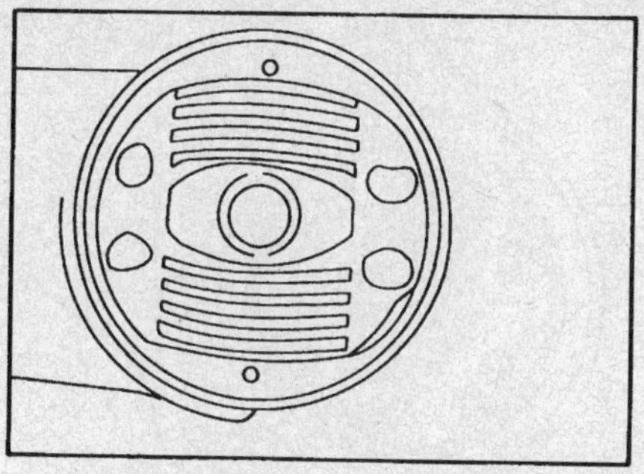
VV2029100001000X

Fig. 8 Support arm bushing orientation. Multi-Link Independent rear suspension

pads, then disconnect parking brake cable.

3. Disconnect support arm and lower control arm from wheel bearing housing and lower control arm from rear axle member, then remove lower control arm.
4. Use a small puller and a 12 mm x 50 mm bolt to disconnect track rod from housing.
5. Remove hub nut and nut securing upper support arm to wheel bearing housing, then the hub assembly. **Retain spacers between upper support arm and wheel bearing housing.**
6. Replace control rod bushing using a 1.318–1.358 inches (33.5–34.5 mm) outside diameter sleeve, counterhold tool No. 5090, or equivalent, and a hydraulic press. **Bushing should project .40 inch (10 mm) on either side.**
7. Mount hub assembly in a vise, then chisel off bushing edges to provide a seat for counterhold.
8. Press out bushing using a 1.318–1.358 inches (33.5–34.5 mm) diameter sleeve, counterhold tool No. 5343, or equivalent, and a hydraulic press.
9. Press in bushing using drift tool No. 5310, or equivalent, counterhold tool No. 5342, or equivalent, and a hydraulic press.
10. Install hub assembly on halfshaft, hub nut, spacers between upper control arm and wheel bearing housing, wheel bearing housing on upper control arm, then the upper control arm nut and tighten to specifications while pulling outward on top of wheel bearing housing.
11. Pull wheel bearing housing outward and insert lower control arm, install a new lower control arm bolt and tighten to specifications while pulling inward toward differential.
12. Connect support arm, track rod and parking brake cable, then install parking brake pads, brake disc, brake caliper and wheel.
13. Lower vehicle then tighten hub nut to specifications.

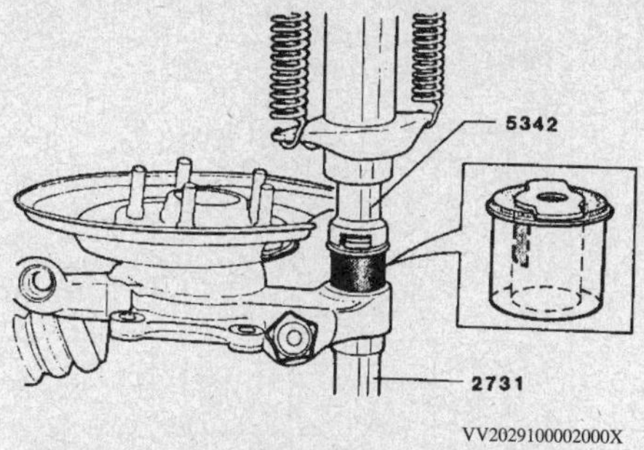
5342
2731
VV2029100002000X

Fig. 9 Positioning support arm bushing in wheel bearing housing. Multi-Link Independent rear suspension

TRAILING ARM

REPLACE

4-LINK LIVE AXLE

1. Raise and support vehicle, position a jack under rear axle and raise rear axle slightly to off load spring and shock absorber, then remove wheel.
2. Remove lower shock absorber bolt and spring bottom nut, then the trailing arm.
3. Replace front bushings using drift tool No. 5088, or equivalent, counterhold tool No. 5087, or equivalent, and a hydraulic press.
4. Replace rear bushings using press tool No. 5078, or equivalent, and spacer Sleeve tool No. 5079, or equivalent. **Install bushing in bracket from inside. Bushing has recesses which should be in horizontal position when installed. Larger rubber area should be at bottom.**
5. Install trailing arm, front first, then rear and lower vehicle. **Tighten nuts for arm after vehicle has been lowered and settles.**
6. Raise jack and guide spring into position, then install nut on bottom of spring and bolt on lower shock absorber.
7. Install wheel and lower vehicle.

CONSTANT TRACK LIVE AXLE

1. Raise and support vehicle, then remove wheel and caliper. Hang caliper from rear spring.
2. Scribe alignment marks on propeller shaft, remove rear flange bolts, then lower shaft slightly.
3. Support trailing arm on a jack stand, then remove bolts from both sides of anti-roll bar.
4. Remove shock absorber lower bolt and loosen bolt on opposite side.
5. Loosen bracket nuts crosswise, then remove bracket and rubber supports.
6. Remove bolts from front bracket, nut and bracket, then the trailing arm.
7. Replace bushing using drift tool No. 2704, or equivalent, support tool No. 5082, or equivalent, and a hydraulic press. Bushing tapered hole should face upward and bushing must be evenly spaced in arm.
8. Reverse removal procedure to install. Tighten fasteners to specifications.

STABILIZER BAR

REPLACE

CONSTANT TRACK LIVE AXLE

1. Raise and support vehicle, then use a jack stand to unload shock absorbers.
2. Remove nut from bracket, shock absorber lower bolt, then the anti-roll bar.
3. Reverse procedure to install. Tighten fasteners to specifications.

DELTA-LINK INDEPENDENT SUSPENSION

1. Raise and support vehicle, then remove lefthand rubber muffler support. Hang muffler with a strip clamp so that muffler is up as high as possible.
2. Remove outer nut (1) for transverse arm attachment, then the bolt, **Fig. 5.**
3. Mark position on righthand transverse arm attachment in relation to lefthand trailing arm's hole (2), **Fig. 5.** Center punch attachment at edge of hole, then remove attachments second bolt. **It is crucial that marking is correct, otherwise rear wheel toe-in will be incorrect.**
4. Remove anti-roll bar mounting bolts, then the anti-roll bar.
5. Reverse procedure to install, noting the following:
   a. Use new nuts and bolts.
   b. Install transverse arm attachment on trailing arm. Install inner bolt (1) and nut, **Fig. 6.**Adjust in anchorage according to previous marking (2). Tighten nut so that position may be fixed, then install nut and bolt (3).
   c. Tighten anti-roll bar attachment bolts, **Fig. 7,** to specifications.

TRACK ROD

REPLACE

4-LINK & CONSTANT TRACK LIVE AXLES

1. Raise and support vehicle, then remove track rod.
2. Replace axle side bushings using drift tool No. 2731, or equivalent, counterhold tool No. 2733, or equivalent, and a hydraulic press. **Press in new bushing with counterhold inverted.**
3. Replace body side bushings using drift tool No. 2706, or equivalent, counterhold tool No. 2733, or equivalent, and a hydraulic press. **Press in new bushing with counterhold inverted.**
4. Install track rod and lower vehicle.

MULTI-LINK INDEPENDENT SUSPENSION

1. Raise and support vehicle, remove wheel, then the track rod.
2. Replace bushings using drift tool No.

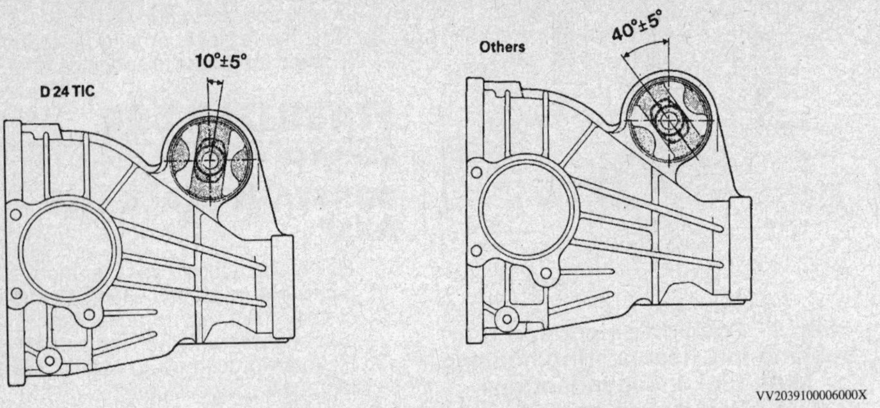
D 24 TIC
10°±5°
Others
40°±5°
VV2039100006000X

Fig. 10 Differential housing bushing orientation. Multi-Link Independent rear suspension

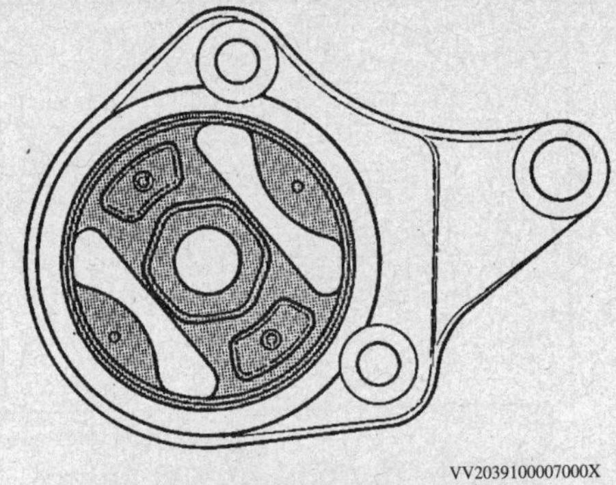
VV2039100007000X

Fig. 11 Differential housing bushing bracket bushing orientation. Multi-Link Independent rear suspension

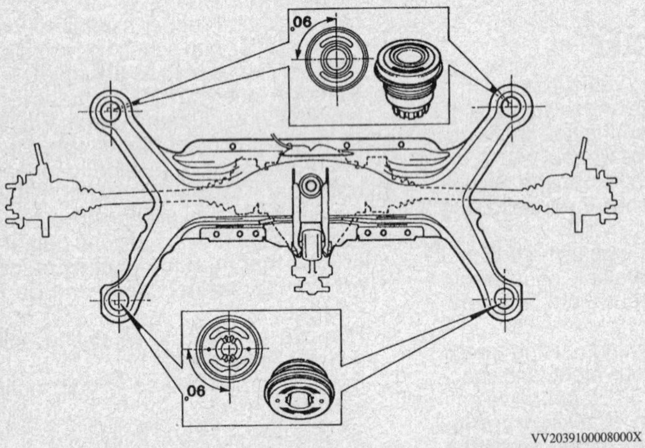
.06
.06
VV2039100008000X

Fig. 12 Upper rear axle member bushing orientation. Multi-Link Independent rear suspension

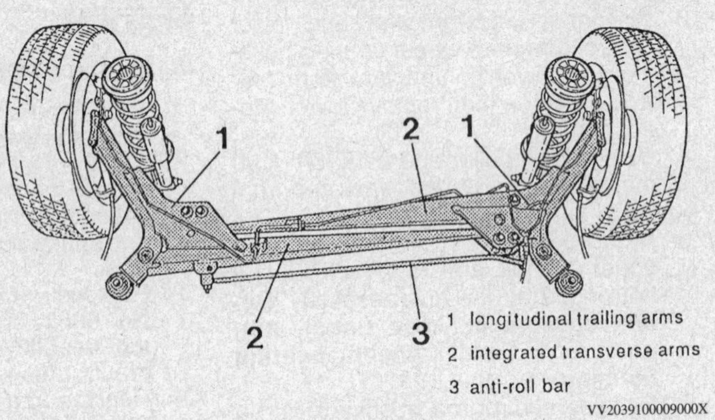
1
2
1
2
3
1 longitudinal trailing arms
2 integrated transverse arms
3 anti-roll bar
VV2039100009000X

Fig. 13 Delta-Link Independent rear suspension. 850 series

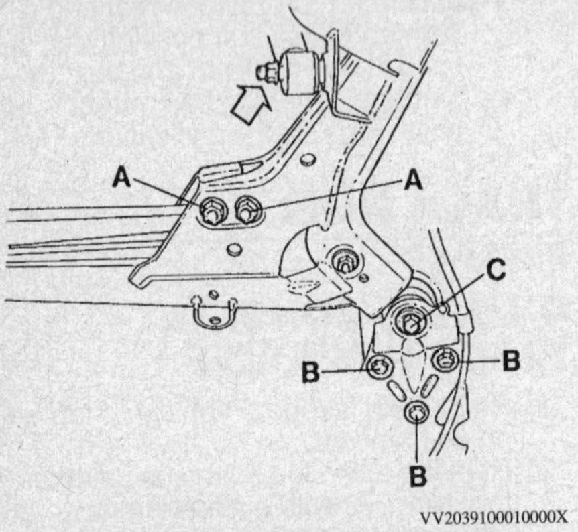
A
A
C
B
B
B
VV2039100010000X

Fig. 14 Transverse arm anchorage bolt removal. Delta-Link Independent rear suspension

5345, or equivalent, counterhold tool No. 5349, or equivalent, and a hydraulic press.

3. Install track rod and wheel, then lower vehicle.

SUPPORT ARM

REPLACE

MULTI-LINK INDEPENDENT SUSPENSION

1. Replace support arm assembly as follows:
   a. Perform steps 1 through 3 as outlined under "Rear Axle, Replace," then remove spring and rubber seats and shock absorber.
   b. Reverse step 1a to install.
2. Replace front support arm bushings as follows:
   a. Remove support arm, then the bracket at front of support arm.
   b. Note position of bushings, **Fig. 8**, then position spacer tool No. 5348, or equivalent, between bushings.
   c. Using drift tool No. 5347, or equivalent, handle tool No. 1801, or equivalent, counterhold tool No. 5346, or equivalent, and a hydraulic press, remove one bushing at a time.
   d. Press in bushings from each side using drift, handle, counterhold and a hydraulic press. **Ensure bushings are orientated correctly.**
   e. Install bracket at front of support arm, then the support arm.
3. Replace rear support arm bushings as follows:
   a. Remove brake caliper and hang from spring with wire.
   b. Remove brake disc and brake pads, then disconnect parking brake cable at wheel bearing housing.
   c. Remove bolt and nut securing lower support arm and bolt securing track rod to wheel bearing housing, then use a small puller and a 12 mm x 50 mm bolt to disconnect track rod from housing.
   d. Remove hub nut and nut securing upper support arm to wheel bearing housing, then the hub assembly. **Retain spacers between upper support arm and wheel bearing housing.**
   e. Mount wheel bearing housing in a vise, remove brake shield mounting bolts, then chisel off bushing edges to provide a seat for counterhold.
   f. Remove bushing using 1.632–

1.675 inches (41.45–42.55 mm) diameter sleeve, counterhold tool No. 5343, or equivalent, and a hydraulic press.

g. Install bushing using drift tool No. 5342, or equivalent, counterhold tool No. 2731, or equivalent, and a hydraulic press. Bushing must be positioned with slot at top, **Fig. 9.**
h. Install brake shield, hub assembly on halfshaft, hub nut, spacers between upper control arm and wheel bearing housing, then the nut at top of upper control arm and tighten to specifications while pulling outward on top of wheel bearing housing.
i. Pull wheel bearing housing outward and insert lower control arm, install a new lower control arm bolt and tighten to specifications while pulling inward toward differential.
j. Connect parking brake cable to wheel bearing housing, then install brake pads, brake disc, brake caliper and track rod.

DIFFERENTIAL HOUSING BUSHINGS

REPLACE

MULTI-LINK INDEPENDENT SUSPENSION

1. Raise and support vehicle, then remove wheels and bolts attaching support arms to wheel bearing housings. Tap out arms.
2. Remove bolts and nuts securing lower control arms to wheel bearing housings, then the support arm bolt from one side.
3. Disconnect track rods from wheel bearing housings using a small puller and a 12 mm x 50 mm bolt to disconnect track rod from each housing.
4. Remove bolts securing upper and lower sections of rear axle member, then pull wheel bearing housings outward and remove lower section of rear axle member complete with track rods and control arms.
5. Remove bolts in propeller shaft/differential coupling, then place a jack and fixture tool No. 5972, or equivalent, under differential.
6. Remove three bolts securing differential to rear axle member, then lower differential slightly.
7. Replace upper bushing using press tool No. 5354, or equivalent. Note orientation of bushing, **Fig. 10.**
8. Remove lower bushing and bracket, then replace lower bushing using drift tool No. 5349, or equivalent, a V-block and a hydraulic press. Note orientation of bushing, **Fig. 11.**
9. Install lower bushing and bracket, then lift differential into position and tighten bolts attaching differential to rear axle member to specifications.
10. Install bolts in propeller shaft and tighten to specifications, then raise lower section of rear axle member and loosely install bolts securing upper and lower sections of rear axle member.
11. Install to 12 mm bolts or drifts into rear axle member centering holes, then tighten rear axle member assembly bolts to specifications.
12. Install bolts securing control arms to wheel bearing housings and tighten to specifications while pulling inward toward differential.
13. Install support arms, track rods and wheels.

UPPER REAR AXLE MEMBER BUSHINGS

REPLACE

MULTI-LINK INDEPENDENT SUSPENSION

1. Raise and support vehicle, remove wheels, then the caliper and hang from spring with wire.
2. Remove support arm guards, bolts and nuts at front of support arms and bolts at rear of support arms.
3. Disconnect support arms at rear, then the propeller shaft at differential.
4. Position fixture tool No. 5972, or equivalent, and a jack underneath rear axle assembly, then remove bolts securing upper section of rear axle member to floor and lower rear axle slightly.
5. Replace front bushings using press tool No. 5344, or equivalent. Note orientation of bushings, **Fig. 12.**
6. Replace rear bushings using press tool No. 5352, or equivalent. Note orientation of bushings, **Fig. 12.**
7. Raise assembly and install lower attachment bolts and tighten to specifications.
8. Install propeller shaft bolts, then the front nuts and bolts in support arms. Tighten to specifications.
9. Tap in support arms at rear and tighten bolts to specifications, then install support arm guards, calipers and wheels.

TRANSVERSE ARM MOUNT

REPLACE

DELTA-LINK INDEPENDENT SUSPENSION

1. Fold rear seat back forward, then undo luggage area carpet at front edge.
2. Remove cover plate under front edge of carpet, then undo righthand side panel at front edge and fold to one side. Remove seat back catch and panel attachment clip.
3. Raise rear of vehicle until wheels are off ground, remove upper shock absorber mounting bolts on righthand side, then disconnect electrical connector retainer and position wiring and connector away from shock mount.
4. Raise and support vehicle.
5. Remove righthand wheel and protecting plate at bracket for rear axle link, then disconnect anti-roll bar mount at righthand side, **Fig. 13.**
6. Disconnect brake pipe bracket on righthand trailing arm, then the ABS pipe and brake pipe from clip on righthand trailing arm.
7. Remove load from shock absorber by pressing trailing arm upward. Use a jack placed against recess for spring mounting bolt.
8. Disconnect shock absorber from lower mount, then remove spring mounting nut and spring.
9. Reinstall shock absorber and tighten nut a few turns, then remove bolts A for transverse arm mounts on both sides, then bolts B and C on righthand side, **Fig. 14.**
10. Position a jack under lefthand spring seat and raise seat a few centimeters, then disconnect trailing arm mount from body guide pin on righthand side.
11. Press out righthand trailing arm, lefthand trailing arm remains in position.
12. Install a new transverse arm mount for righthand trailing arm and tighten to specifications.
13. Align attachment with mount in lefthand trailing arm. Ensure trailing arm maintains same position relative to body, then tighten to specifications.
14. Adjust lefthand trailing arm position with jack, then install righthand transverse arm with attachment in its mount without inserting bolts.
15. Replace attachment for lefthand transverse arm and tighten to specifications.
16. Install transverse arm with attachment in its mount without inserting bolts, then connect righthand trailing arm to body guide pins using new bolts and tighten to specifications. Bolt C, which goes through rear axle link and bracket, should be tightened first then the brackets three bolts B, **Fig. 14.**
17. Install new bolts A for transverse arm attachments, then disconnect righthand shock absorber.
18. Install spring, then connect righthand shock absorber and tighten to nuts specifications.
19. Connect brake pipe and ABS cable to trailing arm attachment, brake pipe bracket to trailing arm attachment lug, then the anti-roll bar to trailing arm. Tighten to specifications.
20. Install protecting plate and wheel, the tighten lug nuts crosswise to specifications.
21. Tighten upper shock absorber mount to specifications, then connect electrical connector with a strip clamp.
22. Refit carpets and panels. Lock seat back catch plunger with locking fluid and tighten to specifications.

REAR AXLE LINK

REPLACE

DELTA-LINK INDEPENDENT SUSPENSION

1. Raise and support vehicle.
2. Remove nut attaching rear axle link to trailing arm, then knock out attachment bolt using a copper mallet.
3. Remove muffler bracket bolt and disconnect brake pipe from clips on lefthand side, then remove bolts retaining

trailing arm bracket. Let bracket remain in place in brake cables attachment lug.

4. Raise righthand trailing arm a bit with a jack, then force apart link on lefthand side from body guide pin using a lever. Ensure trailing arm link is free from guide pin in body.
5. Replace bushing in trailing arm using press tool No. 5497, or equivalent, then replace nut and bolt for rear axle link in trailing arm. **Do not tighten nut yet.**
6. Connect trailing arm to body guide pin, then install bolts for trailing arm bracket loosely.
7. Tighten rear axle link bracket through bolt, three bracket bolts and bolt passing through trailing arm rear axle link to specifications.
8. Connect brake pipe to clips, then install muffler bracket bolt.

TIGHTENING SPECIFICATIONS

Year	Component	Torque/Ft. Lbs.
CONSTANT-TRACK LIVE AXLE		
1993–96	Anti-Roll Bar To Bracket Bolts	33
	Brake Caliper Bolts	43
	Shock Absorber Lower Bolt	63
	Subframe To Front Bushing Bolts	63
	Torque Rod Bolts	103
	Track Rod Bolts	63
	Trailing Arm Front Bracket Bolt	35
	Trailing Arm Front Bracket Nut	63
	Wheel Lug Nuts	63
MULTI-LINK ACTIVE SUSPENSION		
1993–96	Brake Caliper Bolts	44
	Differential/Propeller Shaft Bolts	37
	Rear Axle Damper Upper Mount	63
	Rear Axle Member Assembly Bolts	51①
	Rear Axle Member To Floor Bolts	52②
	Shock Absorber Lower Mounting Bolt	41
	Lower Control Arm Bolt	37③
	Support Arm Bracket Bolts	91④
	Support Arm Front Bolts	35
	Support Arm Front Large Nut	51③
	Support Arm Rear Bolt	44③
	Track Rod To Rear Axle Member Bolt	51
	Track Rod To Wheel Bearing Housing Bolt	62
	Upper Control Arm Top Nut	84
	Upper Control Inner Front Bolt & Nut	51②
	Upper Control Inner Rear Nut	62
	Wheel Hub Nut	102②
	Wheel Lug Nuts	62
4-LINK LIVE AXLE		
1993	Brake Caliper Bolts	42
	Reaction Rod Nuts	65
	Shock Absorber Mounting Nuts	65
	Spring Lower Mounting Nut	15
	Spring Upper Mounting Nut	30
	Stabilizer Bar Front Attachments	65
	Stabilizer Bar Rear Attachments	30
	Track Rod To Axle Bolt	45
	Track Rod To Body Bolt	65
	Trailing Arm Mounting Bolts	85
	Wheel Lug Nuts	85
DELTA-LINK INDEPENDENT SUSPENSION		
1993–96	ABS Sensor Screws	7
	Anti-Roll Bar Nut 1	37
	Anti-Roll Bar Nut 2	37④

Continued

TIGHTENING SPECIFICATIONS—Continued

Year	Component	Torque/Ft. Lbs.
DELTA-LINK INDEPENDENT SUSPENSION		
1993–96	Anti-Roll Bar Nut 3	66
	Anti-Roll Bar To Trailing Arm Nuts	37
	Seat Back Catch Plunger	15
	Brake Backing Plate Lower Screws	15
	Brake Backing Plate Upper Screws	18
	Brake Caliper Bolts	44
	Brake Disc Guide Pin	7
	LH Trailing Arm Mount	59
	LH Transverse Arm Mount	59
	Rear Axle Link Bracket Bolts	48②
	Rear Axle Link Bracket Through Bolt	77③
	Rear Axle Link/Trailing Arm Through Bolt	48④
	RH Trailing Arm Bracket Bolts	48②
	RH Trailing Arm Bracket Through Bolt	77③
	RH Trailing Arm Mount	59
	Shock Absorber Lower Mounting Bolt	59
	Shock Absorber Upper Mounting Bolt	18
	Shock Absorber Upper Mount To Shock Absorber, Ride-Height Control	60
	Shock Absorber Upper Mount To Shock Absorber, Standard	30
	Transverse Arm Mount To Trailing Nuts & Bolts	37⑤
	Wheel Axle Bolts	26②
	Wheel Hub Nut	88①
	Wheel Lug Nuts	81

① — Plus an additional 30°.
② — Plus an additional 60°.
③ — Plus an additional 90°.
④ — Plus an additional 120°.
⑤ — Plus an additional 150°.

Front Suspension & Steering

NOTE: On Air Bag Equipped Models, Refer To "Air Bag System Precautions" Located In The Front Of This Manual For System Disarming & Arming Procedures.

INDEX

	Page No.
Ball Joint Inspection	50-34
Ball Joint, Replace	50-34
240	50-34
850	50-34
940 & 960	50-34
Coil Spring, Replace	50-34
Control Arm Bushing, Replace	50-36
240	50-36
940 & 960	50-36
Control Arm, Replace	50-35
240	50-35
850	50-36
940 & 960	50-35
Power Steering	50-68
Power Steering Gear, Replace	50-36
240	50-36
850	50-36
940 & 960	50-36
Power Steering Pump, Replace	50-37
240	50-37
850	50-37
940 & 960	50-37
Precautions	50-34
Air Bag Systems	50-34
Shock Absorber, Replace	50-34
240	50-34
850	50-35
940 & 960	50-35
Stabilizer Bar, Replace	50-36
240, 940 & 960	50-36
850	50-36
Tightening Specifications:	50-37
240	50-37
850	50-37
940 & 960	50-37
Wheel Bearing, Adjust	50-34
240	50-34
940 & 960	50-34

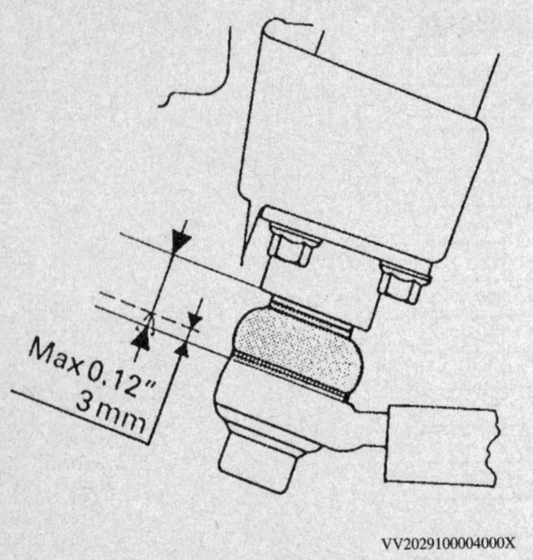
Max 0.12"
3mm
VV2029100004000X

Fig. 1 Ball joint inspection

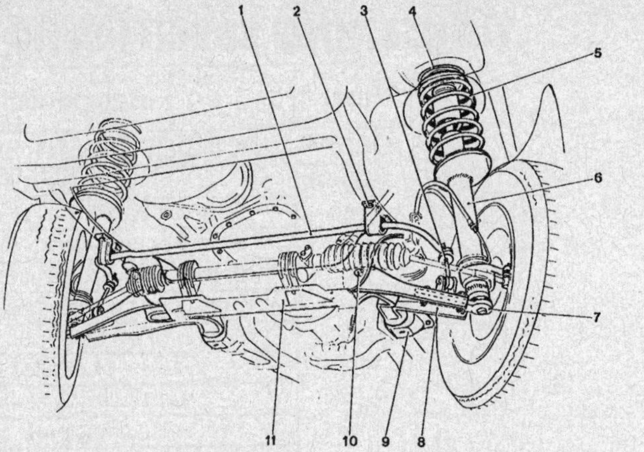
1
2
3
4
5
6
7
11
10
9
8

1 Anti-roll bar
2 Anti-roll bar bracket
3 Anti-roll bar link
4 Shock absorber upper mount
5 Spring
6 Spring strut
7 Ball joint
8 Control arm
9 Rear control arm bracket
10 Front control arm attachment
11 Front cross member

VV2029100003000X

Fig. 2 Front suspension. 240

PRECAUTIONS

AIR BAG SYSTEMS

Refer to "Air Bag System Precautions" in the front of this manual for system disarming and arming procedures.

WHEEL BEARING

ADJUST

240

12 Or 20 Slot Castle Nut

1. Thoroughly grease stub axle threads and nut, then **torque** castle nut to 41 ft. lbs. while rotating wheel.
2. Loosen castle nut ½ turn and ensure outer bearing's inner race is stuck, then tighten castle nut until it is only just possible to move axial washer radially with a screwdriver.
3. Loosen castle nut approximately a half-hexagon so that cotter pin can be installed in nearest hole. **Hub should rotate easily, without any play.**
4. Half fill grease cap with grease and install using tool No. 2715, or equivalent.

20 Slot Castle Nut w/Integral Washer

1. Thoroughly grease stub axle threads and nut, then **torque** castle nut to 37–47 ft. lbs. while rotating wheel.
2. Loosen castle nut ½ turn and ensure outer bearing's inner race is stuck, then **torque** castle nut to 0.97–1.50 ft. lbs. (finger tight).
3. Turn castle nut to nearest hole and insert cotter pin. **Hub should rotate easily, without any play.**
4. Half fill grease cap with grease and install using tool No. 2715, or equivalent.

940 & 960

Torque nut to 42 ft. lbs. while rotating wheel, then loosening nut ½ turn. **Retorque** nut to 1.1 ft. lbs. (finger tight) and install cotter pin. If slot in nut does not align with hole in spindle, tighten nut to the next notch.

BALL JOINT INSPECTION

Measure ball joint radial and axial play, **Fig. 1.** If axial play exceeds .12 inch, or radial play exceeds .02 inch, replace ball joint.

BALL JOINT

REPLACE

240

1. Raise and support vehicle, then remove front wheel.
2. Remove ball joint housing to strut retaining bolts and lock washers (if applicable), then separate housing from strut.
3. Remove ball joint and housing assembly to control arm retaining nuts and bolts, then separate and remove joint assembly from control arm.
4. Position ball joint and housing on suitable bench, remove retaining nut, then press ball joint from housing.
5. Install new ball joint into housing and tighten retaining nut to specifications. **Different ball joints are used for lefthand and righthand sides of vehicle. Ensure correct one is used when replacing joints.**
6. Install ball joint housing to strut, using new bolts and lock washers (if applicable). Tighten retaining bolts to specifications.
7. Install ball joint to control arm, then tighten attaching nuts to specifications.

940 & 960

1. Raise and support vehicle.
2. Remove anti-roll bar link to control arm attaching bolt.
3. Remove ball joint stud cotter pin and nut.
4. Press ball joint out of control arm using ball joint replacement tool No. 5259, or equivalent.
5. Remove ball joint to strut attaching bolts, then press control arm down and remove ball joint.
6. Reverse procedure to install. Tighten to specifications.

850

1. Raise and support vehicle, then remove nuts securing ball joint to control arm.
2. Remove bolt between axle shaft and ball joint, then the ball joint.
3. Reverse procedure to install. Tighten nuts and bolt to specifications.

COIL SPRING

REPLACE

Refer to "Shock Absorber, Replace" for coil spring replacement.

SHOCK ABSORBER

REPLACE

The following procedures allow servicing of the shock absorbers without removing the strut assembly from vehicle.

240

1. Raise vehicle and place stands under jacking points, then remove wheel.
2. Using spanner tool No. 5039 (hydraulic shocks) or 5173 (gas shocks), or equivalents, loosen shock absorber retaining nut several turns.
3. Disconnect steering rod from steering arm using puller tool No. 5043, or equivalent.
4. Disconnect stabilizer bar from link attachment.
5. Disconnect brake line bracket.
6. Remove cover for spring and strut assembly upper attachment.
7. Using socket tool Nos. 5036 and 5037, or equivalents, loosen center nut.
8. Place alignment marks on nut plate and wheel housing, then remove strut

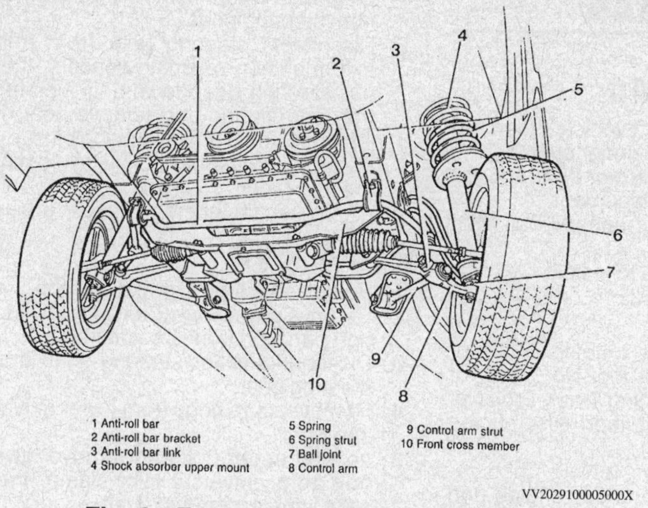
1
2
3
4
5
6
7
8
9
10
1 Anti-roll bar
2 Anti-roll bar bracket
3 Anti-roll bar link
4 Shock absorber upper mount
5 Spring
6 Spring strut
7 Ball joint
8 Control arm
9 Control arm strut
10 Front cross member
VV2029100005000X

Fig. 3 Front suspension. 940 & 960

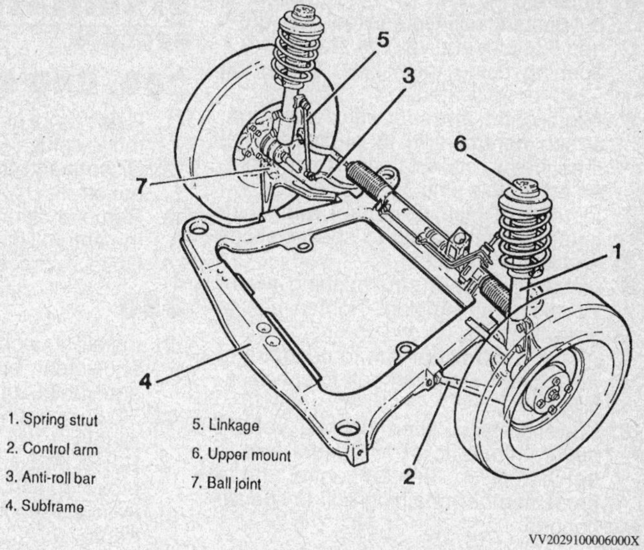
1. Spring strut
2. Control arm
3. Anti-roll bar
4. Subframe
5. Linkage
6. Upper mount
7. Ball joint
1
2
3
4
5
6
7
VV2029100006000X

Fig. 4 Front suspension. 850

upper retaining nuts. Lower jack, support strut assembly when lowering jack so that brake lines and hoses do not become damaged. Attach retaining hook tool No. 5045, or equivalent, to strut assembly and stabilizer bar.
9. Install two No. 5040 spring compressors. Be sure compressor spans five coils or spring will not be sufficiently compressed. Tighten compressors.
10. Remove center nut using tools mentioned above, then remove spring seat, rubber bumper and shock absorber protector.
11. Loosen spring compressors and remove coil spring.
12. Remove shock absorber retaining nut. Use a pipe wrench to hold the outer housing. Be sure to place the pipe wrench on the weld of the housing.
13. Pull shock absorber out of housing.
14. Reverse procedure to install. Ensure marks on nut plate and wheel housing are aligned. Tighten strut upper retaining nuts to specifications.

940 & 960

1. Raise and support front of vehicle and remove wheel.
2. Disconnect steering rod from steering arm.
3. Support control arm with a suitable jack, then disconnect anti-roll bar from link attachment.
4. Remove brake line bracket attaching bolt, then disconnect brake lines from retaining clips.
5. Remove rubber boot from upper strut nut, then disconnect high tension lead from ignition coil.
6. Loosen strut center nut.
7. Mark position of upper mount, then remove mount attaching nuts and washers.
8. Lower jack while supporting strut assembly to avoid damage to brake lines and fender. Attach retaining hook tool No. 5045, or equivalent, to strut and anti-roll bar.
9. Install two spring compressors tool No. 5040, or equivalents. Position compressors so that claws span three spring coils and compress each side alternately.
10. Remove strut center nut, then the upper mount, spring retainer, spring and rubber bumper, or rubber bellows and disc on gas pressure shocks.
11. Remove shock absorber retaining nut, then the shock absorber.
12. Reverse procedure to install.

850

1. Raise and support vehicle, then remove wheel.
2. Disconnect anti-roll bar link from spring strut, then remove ABS sensor lead from spring strut and brake bracket. **Do not disconnect connector.**
3. Install support tool No. 5466, or equivalent, under link arm to avoid damaging driveshaft.
4. Remove nuts securing spring strut to body, then the bolts securing spring strut to axle shaft.
5. Remove spring strut and clamp in a vise.
6. Compress spring using spring clamps tool No. 5407, or equivalent, then remove bolt and washer using socket tool No. 5467, or equivalent, and counterhold tool No. 5468, or equivalent.
7. Remove bolt on shock absorber using socket tool No. 5469, or equivalent, and counterhold tool No. 5468, or equivalent.
8. Remove spring seating, rubber bump stop with gaiter and spring.
9. Reverse procedure to assemble and install. Tighten fasteners to specifications.

CONTROL ARM

REPLACE

240

1. Raise and support front of vehicle and remove wheel.
2. Disconnect stabilizer link and ball joint from control arm, **Fig. 2.**
3. Remove rear bushing bracket to side member attaching bolts.
4. Remove front retaining bolt, then the control arm together with rear bushing bracket. Separate control arm from bracket.
5. Using press tool Nos. 5085 and 5091, or equivalents, positioned in a vise, press out control arm bushing. Press in new bushing using tools Nos. 5084 and 5085 or equivalents.
6. Using press tool Nos. 5082, 5083 and 1801, or equivalents, press bushing from rear bracket. Press in new bushing using tools Nos. 5081, 5082 and 1801, or equivalents.
7. Connect rear bushing bracket to control arm, then install washer and retaining nut. Tighten nut sufficiently, while still allowing rotation of washer.
8. Install control arm and front retaining bolt. Do not tighten nut at this time.
9. Guide stabilizer link into position, then connect ball joint to control arm and tighten attaching nuts to specifications.
10. Attach rear bushing bracket to side member, then install attaching bolts and tighten to specifications.
11. Tighten stabilizer link at control arm, lower vehicle, then bounce vehicle several times to allow control arm to set in position.
12. Tighten control arm to rear bushing bracket attaching nut to specifications and control arm front retaining bolt to specifications.

940 & 960

1. Raise and support front of vehicle and remove wheel.
2. Remove ball joint stud cotter pin and nut.
3. Remove anti-roll bar link and control arm strut attaching bolt, **Fig. 3,** then drive out front bushing.
4. Press ball joint out of control arm using ball joint replacement tool No. 5259, or equivalent, then remove control arm from crossmember.

5. Secure control arm in a vise and press out bushing using press tool Nos. 5091 and 5240, or equivalents. Press in rear bushing using tools Nos. 2904 and 5240, or equivalents.
6. Align control arm strut with control arm, attach control arm to crossmember, then install retaining bolt. Do not tighten bolt at this time.
7. Install ball joint to control arm, then tighten attaching nut to specifications and install cotter pin.
8. Install control arm strut bushing, washer and retaining bolt. Tighten bolt to specifications.
9. Attach anti-roll bar link to control arm and tighten retaining bolt to specifications.
10. Lower vehicle, then bounce vehicle several times to allow control arm to set in position. Tighten control arm to crossmember retaining bolt to specifications.

850

1. Raise and support vehicle, then remove nuts securing ball joint to control arm.
2. Remove control arm mounting bolts, then the control arm, **Fig. 4.**
3. Clean rust from bushing outer sleeves and note position of outer sleeves in relation to control arms.
4. Replace bushings using drift tool No. 5481, or equivalent, counterhold tool No. 5482, or equivalent, and a hydraulic press.
5. Check position of bushings using gauge tool No. 5483, or equivalent.
6. Install control arm and control arm mounting bolts, then the ball joint to control arm nuts. Tighten nuts to specifications.
7. Lower vehicle and bounce up and down a few times, then tighten control arm bolts to specifications.

CONTROL ARM BUSHING

REPLACE

240

Refer to "Control Arm Replace" for bushing replacement.

940 & 960

1. Raise and support front of vehicle and remove wheel.
2. Remove strut to control arm attaching bolt, then detach strut and remove bushing.
3. Remove strut rear mount attaching bolt, then remove strut from vehicle.
4. Press rear bushing out of strut.
5. Reverse procedure to install. Press rear bushing into strut using press tool No. 2731, or equivalent, and a V-block. Tighten strut to control arm attaching bolt to specifications. Tighten rear mount attaching bolt to specifications.

STABILIZER BAR

REPLACE

240, 940 & 960

1. Raise and support vehicle, then remove splash guard under engine.
2. Disconnect anti-roll bar from anti-roll bar strut's upper attachment.
3. Remove clamps for anti-roll bar, then the anti-roll bar.
4. Reverse procedure to install.

850

1. Install support rails tool No. 5033, or equivalent, bracket tool No. 5006, or equivalent, and lifting hook tool No. 5115, or equivalent, then raise engine slightly.
2. Raise and support vehicle, then remove splashguard under engine and five nuts securing steering gear to subframe.
3. Disconnect hydraulic fluid line brackets from subframe at front and rear edges, then place a jack under rear crossmember.
4. Remove four bolts securing subframe brackets to body on both sides, then the two bolts together with brackets and washers.
5. Loosen subframe front bolts approximately .60–.80 inch (15–20 mm), lower frame at rear edge and ensure steering gear bolts come away from frame.
6. Disconnect anti-roll bar from links, then remove anti-roll bar caps and the anti-roll bar.
7. Reverse procedure to install, noting the following:
   a. Press subframe up at rear edge using jack while installing steering gear mounting bolts into frame.
   b. Install new bolts on subframe loosely, move jack to front edge of frame, tighten bolts on lefthand side of frame to specifications, then the bolts on righthand side of frame to specifications.

POWER STEERING GEAR

REPLACE

240

1. Raise and support vehicle, then disconnect tie rods from steering arms using puller tool No. 5043, or equivalent.
2. Remove splash guard under engine, then loosen screws for hydraulic hoses a few turns. Leave screws in place.
3. Place a container under steering gear, then turn steering wheel from lock to lock until steering gear is empty. **Engine must not be running.**
4. Drain power steering fluid reservoir.
5. Loosen lower flange from steering gear, then disconnect hydraulic hoses from steering gear.
6. Disconnect steering gear from front axle member, retaining spacers, then pull steering gear down until it comes free from flange and remove gear on lefthand side. Retain locating pins.
7. Reverse procedure to install, noting the following:
   a. Tighten fasteners to specifications.

940 & 960

1. Raise and support front of vehicle.
2. Remove splash pan, then the jack support panel on front crossmember.
3. Disconnect lower steering shaft from steering gear.
4. Remove snap rings from lower universal joint.
5. Loosen upper bolt and remove lower bolt from universal joint clamp, then slide joint up steering shaft.
6. Remove ball joint nut, then disconnect tie rods.
7. Disconnect oil lines from steering gear.
8. Remove steering gear attaching bolts, then the steering gear from vehicle.
9. Reverse procedure to install, noting the following:
   a. Tighten fasteners to specifications.

850

1. Install support rails tool No. 5033, or equivalent, bracket tool No. 5006, or equivalent, and lifting hook tool No. 5115, or equivalent, then raise engine slightly.
2. Raise and support vehicle, then remove front wheels.
3. Disconnect tie rod ends using puller tool No. 5259, or equivalent, then measure length of tie rod on one side in relation to steering gear housing and record measurement.
4. Remove splashguard under engine, then disconnect bracket and clamps of hydraulic fluid pipes at front and rear edges.
5. Remove five nuts securing steering gear to subframe, then place a jack under rear crossmember.
6. Remove four bolts securing subframe brackets to body on both sides, then the two bolts together with brackets and washers.
7. Loosen subframe front bolts approximately .60–.80 inch (15–20 mm), lower subframe at rear edge, then place a spacer between frame and body at rear edge so that frame does not spring up.
8. Place an oil pan under steering gear, then disconnect hydraulic fluid pipes from steering gear.
9. Remove steering column joint bolt, press joint up from steering gear, then remove bolt securing steering gear to rear engine pad.
10. Remove steering gear to right.
11. Reverse procedure to install, noting the following:
    a. Ensure tie rod is in same position as

when removed.

b. Tighten fasteners to specifications.

POWER STEERING PUMP

REPLACE

240

1. Raise and support vehicle, then remove splash guard under engine.
2. Loosen belt tensioner, then remove power steering belt.
3. Place rags under pump, then place locking hose clamp pliers on hoses from reservoir and remove hoses from pump.
4. Remove power steering pump.
5. Reverse procedure to install.

940 & 960

1. Raise and support vehicle, then remove splash guard under engine.
2. Remove mounting bracket bolt and nut, then loosen power steering belt.
3. Place a drip pan underneath pump, then remove hoses from pump.
4. Remove retaining bolts and drive belts, then lower pump slightly and disconnect filler hose.
5. Remove power steering pump.
6. Reverse procedure to install. Tighten fasteners to specifications.

850

1. Drain approximately 3.2 quarts of coolant, then disconnect radiator hose from thermostat housing.
2. Remove holder for oil hoses from dipstick, then the air cooling hose from control module box.
3. Disconnect drive belt from pump, then remove bolt and spacing sleeve of plate.
4. Loosen pressure hose fitting 1/4 turn, then the plate lower mount nut a few turns.
5. Remove pump mounting bolts. Three through holes in pulley and two on left-hand side.
6. Remove power steering pump.
7. Reverse procedure to install. Tighten fasteners to specifications.

TIGHTENING SPECIFICATIONS

Year	Component	Torque/Ft. Lbs.
240		
1993	Ball Joint Housing To Spring Strut Bolts	13.3–20.5
	Ball Joint To Control Arm	73.8–95.8
	Ball Joint To Housing Nut	34.2–54.2
	Control Arm Front Bushing Bolt	40.6–70.0
	Control Arm Rear Bushing Bracket To Side Member	22.2–36.8
	Control Arm Rear Bushing Nut	36.9–44.1
	Power Steering Gear Flange Lockbolt	14.8–22.0
	Power Steering Gear Return Hose Screws	30.9
	Power Steering Gear U-Bolt Nuts	11.1–18.3
	Steering Strut To Steering Arm	36.9–51.5
	Steering Strut Upper Mounting Nuts	15
	Tie Rod End To Steering Arm	44
	Wheel Lug Nuts	85
940 & 960		
1993–96	Anti-Roll Bar Link To Control Arm	63
	Ball Joint To Control Arm	44
	Ball Joint To Strut	22①
	Control Arm Strut Front Mount	70
	Control Arm Strut Rear Mount	63
	Power Steering Gear Flange Lockbolt	16
	Power Steering Gear Hose Screws	30
	Power Steering Gear Mounting Bolts	32
	Power Steering Pump Hose Screw	31
	Shock Absorber Upper Nut	111
	Spring Strut Upper Mounting Nuts	30
	Tie Rod End To Steering Arm	44
	Wheel Lug Nuts	63
850		
1993–96	Anti-Roll Bar Link To Spring Strut	37
	Ball Joint To Control Arm	13②
	Ball Joint To Steering Knuckle	37
	Control Arm To Subframe	48②
	Power Steering Gear Center Mount Bolt	59
	Power Steering Gear Flange Lockbolt	15
	Power Steering Gear To Engine Pad	37

Continued

TIGHTENING SPECIFICATIONS—Continued

Year	Component	Torque/Ft. Lbs.
850		
1993–96	Power Steering Pump Mounting Bolts	18
	Shock Absorber Upper Nuts	52
	Spring Strut To Steering Knuckle	48①
	Spring Strut Upper Mounting Nuts	18
	Subframe Bracket Bolts	37
	Subframe Mounting Bolts	77②
	Tie Rod End To Steering Knuckle	52
	Wheel Lug Nuts	81

① — Plus an additional 90°.
② — Plus an additional 120°.

Wheel Alignment

INDEX

	Page No.
Front Wheel Alignment	50-38
240	50-38
850	50-39
940 & 960	50-39
Rear Wheel Alignment	50-40
850	50-40
960	50-40
Wheel Alignment Specifications	50-4

FRONT WHEEL ALIGNMENT

240

Caster

Caster is not adjustable. If caster angle is not within specifications, check for damaged or worn suspension components and replace as needed.

Camber

1. Bounce vehicle up and down several times to set control arms in normal position.
2. Loosen upper strut attaching nuts.
3. Adjust camber using adjustment tool No. 5038, or equivalent, **Fig. 1.**
4. Tighten strut attaching nuts, then recheck caster angle.

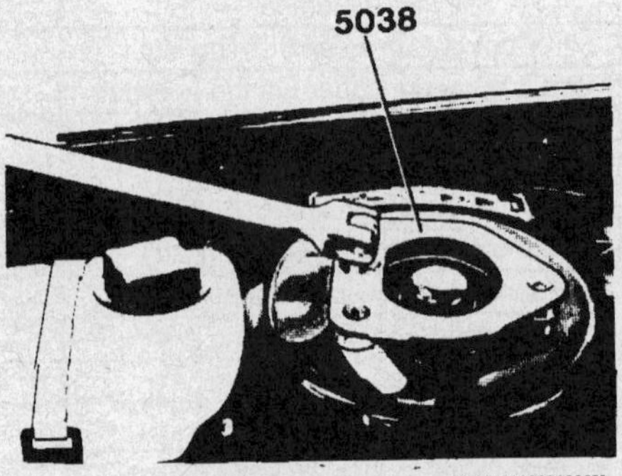
5038
VV2049100001000X

Fig. 1 Camber adjustment. 240

Toe-In

1. Loosen locknut on each tie rod.
2. Turn each tie rod to obtain proper toe-in. Length of tie rods may not differ more than .080 inch (2 mm), measured between wrench grip and locknut.
3. If after toe-in adjustment, steering wheel is not properly centered, proceed as follows:
   a. Place car on a level surface and ensure front wheels are straight, then disconnect battery ground cable and turn ignition switch to Off position.
   b. Remove Torx bolts at rear of steering wheel, disconnect air bag electrical connector, then remove air bag assembly.
   c. Connect special tool No. 998 8695, or equivalent, in place of air bag assembly so that vehicle may be driven without generating a fault code.
   d. Loosen, but do not remove nut in center of steering wheel, then check that steering wheel is straight.
   e. Connect battery ground cable, then drive vehicle straight ahead on a smooth surface to ensure front wheels are pointing perfectly straight ahead.
   f. Disconnect battery ground cable, remove special tool No. 998 8695, or equivalent, and nut in center of wheel.
   g. Remove locking screw at end of plastic ribbon from its parking hole in steering wheel (leave screw in ribbon), then lift off wheel and pull wiring, plastic ribbon and locking screw through opening in wheel.
   h. Set contact reel to zero by turning contact reel fully to right, then turning back three turns to left. Ensure screw hole is at six o'clock, then lock contact reel in this position with screw in plastic ribbon. **Do not turn steering wheel, or contact reel pin will be sheared off, and entire contact reel will have to be replaced.**
   i. Pass contact reel lead through hole in steering wheel, install steering wheel nut finger tight, remove screw in end of plastic ribbon and install in parking hole in steering wheel, reconnect special tool No. 998 8695, or equivalent, then connect battery ground cable and drive vehicle on level ground and ensure steering wheel is straight.
   j. Tighten wheel center nut 44.2 ft. lbs., ensure air bag warning lamp has gone out (no fault codes present), then disconnect battery ground cable and remove special tool No. 998 8695, or equivalents.
   k. Rest bottom of air bag assembly on steering wheel, connect electrical connector, place air bag assembly in position and **torque** righthand Torx bolt to 4.4 ft. lbs., then the lefthand bolt. **Ensure cable does not get pinched on reassembly.**
   l. Check that steering wheel turns easily and steering lock operates. Ensure air bag assembly is mounted securely.
   m. Turn ignition switch to On position, connect battery ground cable and check air bag lamp. If a fault code is displayed, refer to "Air Bag System" section for procedures to cancel fault code.

940 & 960

Caster

Caster angle can be adjusted by replacing control arm strut. A shorter strut reduces caster angle by 0.8°, and a longer strut increases caster angle by 0.8°.

Camber

Camber angle can be adjusted by altering the hole position for front fixing bolt of upper spring strut mount. To correct angle, proceed as follows:

1. Remove front nut in upper retaining plate of spring strut, then knock front press bolt out of retaining plate with a soft-headed hammer.
2. Loosen rear bolt in retaining plate, then set wrench tool No. 5038, or equivalent, on rear bolt and hold against retaining plate.
3. Turn suspension assembly to correct camber angle, turn spring strut so that hole in retaining plate passes hole in suspension tower by at least .12 inch (3 mm). Mark position when hole disappears, then turn .12 inch (3 mm) further.
4. Mark position of new hole with a punch, then **torque** rear nut to 35 ft. lbs. so that spring strut will not move out of position.
5. Drill a new hole in retaining plate, .41 inch (10.3 mm) in diameter, through hole in top of suspension tower. **Drill motor must be held at right angles to retaining plate and not to suspension tower top. Blow out metal shavings and apply rustproof compound to hole. Hole in top of suspension tower must not be damaged.**
6. Install front press bolt from underside, up through new hole in retaining plate and hole in top of suspension tower. Place a few washers on bolt and tighten slightly using a nut without compression ring.
7. Tighten bolt in retaining plate with a nut, then remove original nut and washers. Replace with new nut with compression ring and **torque** to 35 ft. lbs.

Toe-In

1. Loosen locknut on each tie rod, then turn each tie rod to obtain proper toe-in. Length of tie rods must not differ more than .080 inch (2 mm), measured between edge of thread and locknut.
2. If after toe-in adjustment, steering wheel is not properly centered, proceed as follows:
   a. Place car on a level surface and ensure front wheels are straight, then disconnect battery ground cable and turn ignition switch to Off position.
   b. Remove Torx bolts at rear of steering wheel, disconnect air bag electrical connector, then remove air bag assembly.
   c. Connect special tool No. 998 8695, or equivalent, in place of air bag assembly so that vehicle may be driven without generating a fault code.
   d. Loosen, but do not remove nut in center of steering wheel, then check that steering wheel is straight.
   e. Connect battery ground cable, then drive vehicle straight ahead on a smooth surface to ensure front wheels are pointing perfectly straight ahead.
   f. Disconnect battery ground cable, remove special tool No. 998 8695, or equivalent, and nut in center of wheel.
   g. Remove locking screw at end of plastic ribbon from its parking hole in steering wheel (leave screw in ribbon), then lift off wheel and pull wiring, plastic ribbon and locking screw through opening in wheel.
   h. **On 940 and 960 series,** set contact reel to zero by turning contact reel fully to right, then turning back approximately three turns to left. Ensure screw hole is at eight o'clock, then lock contact reel in this position with screw in plastic ribbon. **Do not turn steering wheel, or contact reel pin will be sheared off, and entire contact reel will have to be replaced.**
   i. **On all models,** pass contact reel lead through hole in steering wheel, position steering wheel so that contact reel pin is in center hole on wheel, install steering wheel nut finger tight, remove screw in end of plastic ribbon and install in parking hole in steering wheel, reconnect special tool No. 998 8695, or equivalent, then connect battery ground cable and drive vehicle on level ground and ensure steering wheel is straight.
   j. Tighten wheel center nut 24 ft. lbs., ensure air bag warning lamp has gone out (no fault codes present), then disconnect battery ground cable and remove special tool No. 998 8695, or equivalent.
   k. Rest bottom of air bag assembly on steering wheel, connect electrical connector, place air bag assembly in position and **torque** Torx bolts to 4.4 ft. lbs. **Ensure cable does not get pinched on reassembly.**
   l. Check that steering wheel turns easily and steering lock operates. Ensure air bag assembly is mounted securely.
   m. Turn ignition switch to On position, connect battery ground cable and check air bag lamp. If a fault code is displayed, refer to "Air Bag System" section for procedures to cancel fault code.

850

Caster

Caster is not adjustable. If caster angle is not within specifications, check for damaged or worn suspension components and replace as needed.

Camber

Camber angle can be adjusted by modifying spring struts. To correct angle, proceed as follows:

1. Disconnect spring strut from steering knuckle, then drill out upper holes in shock absorber attachment to .55 inch (14 mm). Clean burrs from holes after drilling.
2. Install washer tool No. 3 546 451-0, or equivalent, with an old bolt and nut in lower hole. Do not tighten fully.
3. Install fixing plug tool No. 3 546 450-2, or equivalent, in upper hole, then drill a .16 inch (4 mm) hole through washer and shock absorber attachment. Drill at center of washer, then knock clamping pin tool No. 951 950-5, or equivalent, into hole.
4. Install spring strut using eccentric bolt tool No. 3 546 449-4, or equivalent, in upper hole and new bolt tool No. 977 267-4, or equivalent, in lower hole. Tighten bolts very lightly.
5. Adjust camber angle by turning upper bolt, then **torque** both nuts to 48 ft. lbs., plus an additional 90°.

Toe-In

1. Loosen locknut on each tie rod.
2. Turn each tie rod to obtain proper toe-in. Length of tie rods may not differ more than .080 inch (2 mm), measured between edge of thread and locknut.
3. If after toe-in adjustment, steering wheel is not properly centered, proceed as follows:
   a. Place car on a level surface and ensure front wheels are straight, then disconnect battery ground cable and turn ignition switch to Off position.
   b. Remove Torx bolts at rear of steering wheel, disconnect air bag electrical connector, then remove air bag assembly.
   c. Connect special tool No. 998 8695, or equivalent, in place of air bag assembly so that vehicle may be driven without generating a fault code.
   d. Loosen, but do not remove nut in center of steering wheel, then check that steering wheel is straight.
   e. Connect battery ground cable, then drive vehicle straight ahead on a smooth surface to ensure front wheels are pointing perfectly straight ahead.
   f. Disconnect battery ground cable, remove special tool No. 998 8695, or equivalent, and nut in center of wheel.
   g. Remove locking screw at end of plastic ribbon from its parking hole in steering wheel (leave screw in ribbon), then insert and tighten screw in contact reel.
   h. Lift off wheel and allow plastic ribbon and lead to pass through opening in wheel.
   i. Set contact reel to zero by turning contact reel fully to right, then turning back three turns to left. Ensure screw hole is at one o'clock, then

lock contact reel in this position with screw in plastic ribbon. **Do not turn steering wheel, or contact reel pin will be sheared off, and whole contact reel will have to be replaced.**

j. Pass contact reel lead through hole in steering wheel, install steering wheel nut finger tight, remove screw in end of plastic ribbon and install in parking hole in steering wheel, reconnect special tool No. 998 8695, or equivalent, then connect battery ground cable and drive vehicle on level ground and ensure steering wheel is straight.
k. **Torque** wheel center nut 30 ft. lbs., ensure air bag warning lamp has gone out (no fault codes present), then disconnect battery ground cable and remove special tool No. 998 8695, or equivalent.
l. Rest bottom of air bag assembly on steering wheel, connect electrical connector, place air bag assembly in position and **torque** righthand Torx bolt to 7.5 ft. lbs., then the lefthand Torx bolt. **Ensure cable does not get pinched on reassembly.**
m. Check that steering wheel turns easily and steering lock operates. Ensure air bag assembly is mounted securely.
n. Turn ignition switch to On position, connect battery ground cable and check air bag lamp. If a fault code is displayed, refer to "Air Bag System" section for procedures to cancel fault code.

REAR WHEEL ALIGNMENT

960

MULTI-LINK INDEPENDENT SUSPENSION

Camber

Camber angle can be adjusted with eccentric bolts in lower inner link mountings. Using level scale tool Nos. 5493 or 8691, or equivalents, measure lower link angles to adjust camber as follows:

1. Loosen nut on lower link eccentric bolt so eccentric bolt can just be turned.
2. Use channel lock pliers to pull link inward, then turn eccentric bolt until bubble in level scale is centered.

Toe-In

1. Loosen nut for track rod eccentric bolt so bolt can just be turned. Turn bolt so smallest part of washer points inward.
2. Use channel lock pliers to pull rod inward, then turn eccentric bolt until toe-in is within specifications.

850

DELTA-LINK INDEPENDENT SUSPENSION

Camber

Camber angle cannot be adjusted. If angle is not within specifications, check trailing arms for damage.

Toe-In

If toe-in measurement is not within specifications, loosen nuts connecting transverse arms to trailing arms and adjust by moving transverse arms forward or rearward in their anchorages until correct value is obtained.

Air Conditioning

INDEX

	Page No.
A/C Specifications	50-45
Discharging System	50-40
Oil Charge	50-40
Performance Test	50-40
Precautions	50-40
A/C Systems	50-40
Air Bag Systems	50-40
Troubleshooting	50-40

PRECAUTIONS

AIR BAG SYSTEMS

Refer to "Air Bag System Precautions"in the front of this manual for system disarming and arming procedures.

A/C SYSTEMS

R134a refrigerant is used in A/C systems. An R134a A/C system may be identified by a decal on the righthand front wheelhouse and a yellow plastic ring around the filler valve marked "R134a" This refrigerant must not be mixed or used in A/C systems where other refrigerants are specified. In addition, other types of refrigerant R-12 should never be used in an R134a system. Using the wrong type of refrigerant will result in serious damage to the compressor.

Always wear safety goggles and gloves when working with any type of refrigerant. Frostbite may occur if refrigerant comes into contact with the skin or eyes.

TROUBLESHOOTING

Refer to **Fig. 1,** for general troubleshooting, **Fig. 2,** for pressure testing troubleshooting and **Fig. 3** for A/C system noise troubleshooting.

PERFORMANCE TEST

1. Set temperature switch to full cooling and turn A/C switch On.
2. Set mode control to Ventilation.
3. Set recirculation switch to Recirculation.
4. Set fan switch to full speed.
5. Close hood, doors and windows.
6. **On 850, 940 and 960 models,** run engine at 1500–1600 RPM.
7. **On 240 models,** run engine at 2000 RPM.
8. **On all models,** place thermometer in instrument panel center A/C vent.
9. Allow system to stabilize for about 8 minutes, then check temperature in center I/P vent.
10. Refer to **Fig. 4** for performance test procedure.

DISCHARGING SYSTEM

1. Block front wheels and set parking brake.
2. Connect low pressure hose of recovery station Part No. 9511000-3, or equivalent, to A/C system service valve.
3. Slowly open service valve to prevent oil from being drawn out of the compressor. Turn switch on recovery station to "Recovery."
4. Evacuation should take approximately 15–20 minutes.
5. When pressure gauges read zero, close valves.
6. Disconnect hose from service valve and install cap.
7. When the system is empty, the low pressure gauge should show a vacuum (less than zero).

OIL CHARGE

1. Discharge A/C system as described in "Discharging System."
2. After approximately five minutes the pressure in the recovery station will equalize.
3. Check recovery station drain valve for any oil that may have come out of the A/C system during system discharge.
4. Measure amount of oil in sight gauge and add an equal amount of oil to system.
5. To add oil directly to the A/C system,

No cooling	Poor cooling	Intermittent cooling	Noise	Possible cause	Remedy
				Electrical faults:	
X				Blown fuse	Check fuses
X				Poor connection or short (compressor does not operate)	Check all cables
X				Compressor coupling burnt	Replace coupling
X				Fan motor (blower), does not operate	Check cables and motor
	X	X		Fan motor (blower), poor operation (loose or cracked motor)	Check/replace
		X	X	Broken or poor connection in compressor clutch winding (clutch moves in and out)	Replace clutch
			X	Fan motor screeches or contacts fan shroud	Check
				Mechanical faults	
X	X		X	Drive belt too loose or cracked	Tension or replace belt.
X	X			Heater control valve leaks in "COOL"	Check valve.
	X			Air ducts blocked	Check and clean
	X			Air inlet in front of windscreen/shield blocked	Check and clean
			X	Clutch bearing worn or off-centre	Replace bearing.
	X		X	Compressor worn or loose	Recondition compressor.
				System faults	
X				Evaporator thermostat does not disengage compressor.	Check/replace thermostat.
X				Expansion valve stuck in open position	Replace.
X				Leakage	Top-up system. Find leakage and repair.
X				Blocked hose or component	Check flow through each component
X				No refrigerant in system	Add refrigerant.
	X			Air flow through condenser blocked	Clean condenser
	X			Evaporator blocked on air cooling side	Clean off dirt etc.
	X			Evaporator thermostat incorrectly adjusted	Check thermostat.
	X		X	Insufficient refrigerant (whistling noise from evaporator near expansion valve, bubbles in sight glass)	Drain and refill system.
	X			Expansion valve capillary tube damaged.	Replace.
	X			Receiver/dryer blocked	Replace.
	X	X		Moisture in system. Cooling capacity good at start (few minutes) then poor. Or poor operation at high ambient temperatures	Drain system, replace receiver/dryer or drying agent, fill with refrigerant.
	X			Air in system (bubbles in sight glass)	Drain system, replace receiver/dryer or drying agent, fill with refrigerant.
		X		Ice on evaporator air cooling side (thermostat adjusted too low or fan not operating)	Check evaporator thermostat. Test with fan on
		X		Loose evaporator thermostat	Check/replace.
		X		Poor contact between expansion valve capillary tube and evaporator outlet or poor insulation	Check
		X		Too large a difference between off and on for evaporator thermostat	Replace.
			X	System overfull causes crashing noise or vibrations from high pressure lines, clicking noise from compressor, excessive compressor pressure and suction pressure, hissing noise from expansion valve, bubbles or vapour in sight glass. If compressor valves damaged by overfilling, compressor pressure will be too low	Drain System. Refill
			X	Moisture in system, can cause noise from expansion valve	Drain system, replace/receiver/dryer or drying agent, fill with refrigerant.

VV7029100022000X

Fig. 1 General troubleshooting

Switch compressor on and off by switching between 'A/C setting on/off' on the dashboard.

Noise persists when compressor is switched off:

Noise is not coming from compressor.
System is OK.

Noise disappears when compressor is off:

Check drive belt.

VV7029200030010X

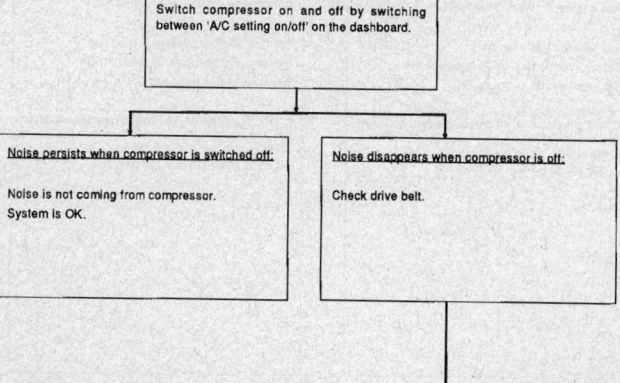

Fig. 3 A/C noise troubleshooting (Part 1 of 4)

Low pressure side	High pressure side	Cause	Remedy
Low	Normal	1. Expansion valve blocked or seized in closed position. 2. Expansion valve capillary tube damage – liquid loss. 3. Moisture in system, causes ice in expansion valve.	*1. Remove blockage. Replace valve if necessary. *2. Replace expansion valve. 3. Drain system. Replace receiver/dryer. Evacuate system and fill.
Low	Low	1. Not enough refrigerant.	*1. Drain system, Evacuate and fill.
Low	High	1. Blockage in receiver/dryer or connecting pipes.	1. Replace. Remove blockage.
High	Normal	1. Expansion valve seized in open position. 2. Expansion valve coil against evaporator outlet, loose or poorly insulated. 3. Not enough refrigerant. Possibly bubbles in sight glass.	*1. Replace. 2. Secure coil and insulate. 3. Drain system. Evacuate and fill.
High	Low	1. Defective compressor.	1. Repair/replace. Replace receiver/dryer.
Normal – High	High	1. Too much refrigerant. 2. No cold air reaches condenser. 3. Blockage in high pressure side. 4. Engine radiator overheated. 5. Air in system. Poor evacuation and filling of refrigerant.	1. Drain system. Evacuate and fill. 2. Remove obstruction. Check cooling fan and belts. 3. Remove blockage. 4. Improve cooling. 5. Drain system. Replace receiver/dryer. Evacuate and fill according to instructions.
Normal	Normal	1. Moisture in system, occasional formation of ice. Low pressure side pressure varies. Cooling ability OK in cool conditions but poor or non existent in hot weather.	1. Drain system. Replace receiver/dryer. Evacuate and fill according to instructions.

*USA vehicles:
To conform with Warranty policy, the receiver/dryer must be replaced each time the system is opened.

VV7029100023000X

Fig. 2 Pressure testing troubleshooting

Drive belt faulty:
Replace belt.
Check if noise persists with compressor on.

Drive belt OK:

Noise disappears:
System is OK.

Noise persists:
Check that compressor runs continuously with passenger compartment fan at maximum speed.

Compressor cuts in and out at intervals of less than five seconds:
Loose contact in sheath on compressor connection or in some connector.

Compressor runs continuously:

VV7029200030020X

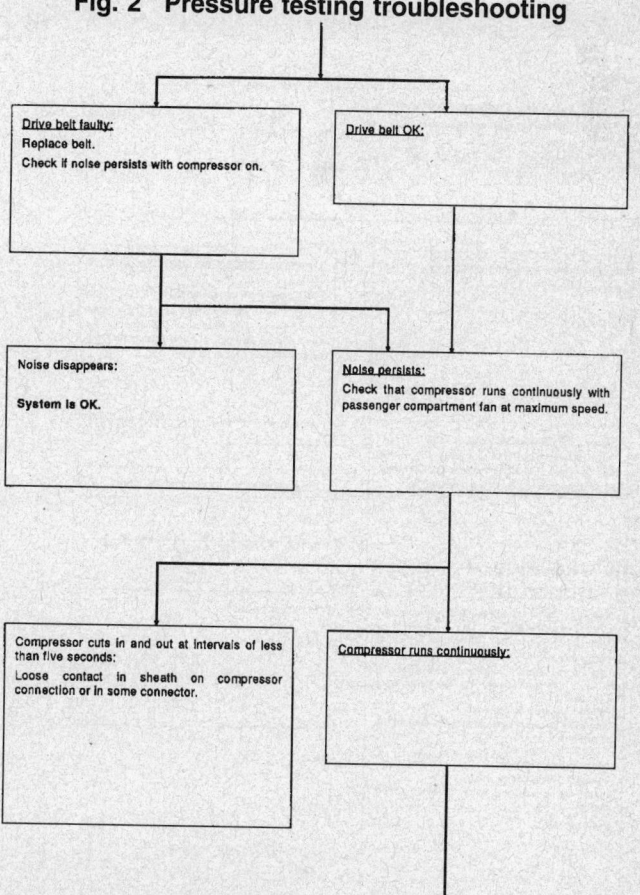

Fig. 3 A/C noise troubleshooting (Part 2 of 4)

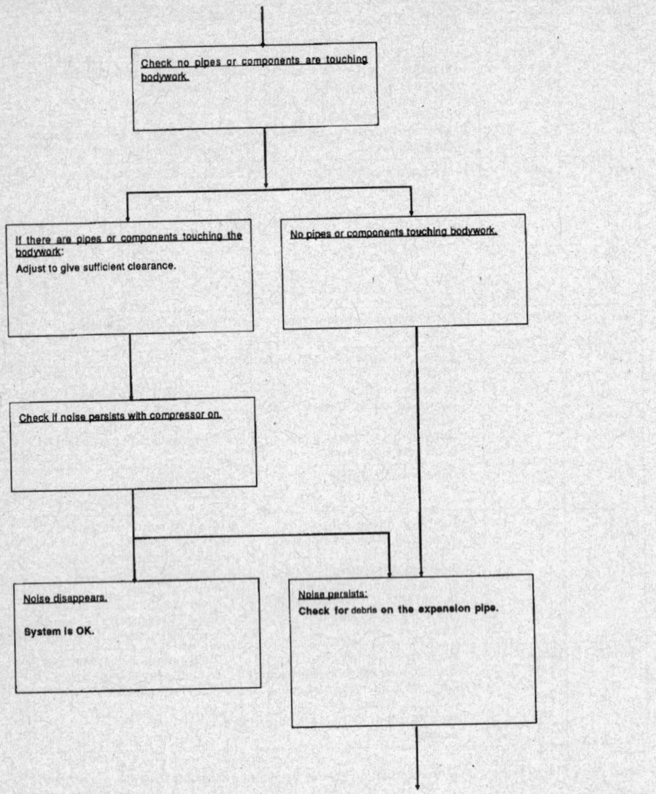

Check no pipes or components are touching bodywork.
If there are pipes or components touching the bodywork: Adjust to give sufficient clearance.
No pipes or components touching bodywork.
Check if noise persists with compressor on.
Noise disappears. System is OK.
Noise persists: Check for debris on the expansion pipe.

VV7029200030030X

Fig. 3 A/C noise troubleshooting (Part 3 of 4)

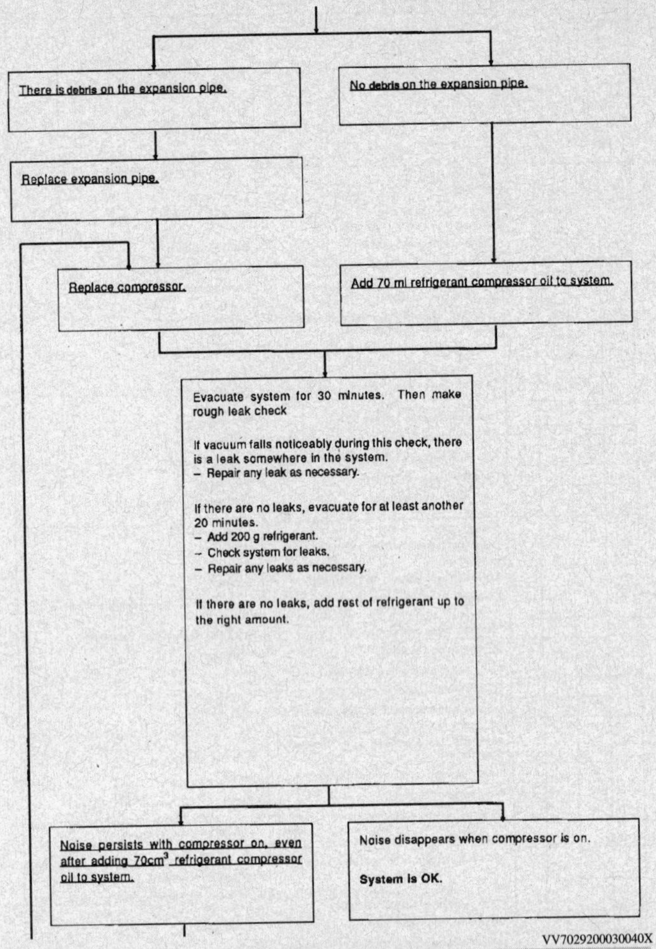

There is debris on the expansion pipe.
No debris on the expansion pipe.
Replace expansion pipe.
Replace compressor.
Add 70 ml refrigerant compressor oil to system.
Evacuate system for 30 minutes. Then make rough leak check
If vacuum falls noticeably during this check, there is a leak somewhere in the system.
– Repair any leak as necessary.
If there are no leaks, evacuate for at least another 20 minutes.
– Add 200 g refrigerant.
– Check system for leaks.
– Repair any leaks as necessary.
If there are no leaks, add rest of refrigerant up to the right amount.
Noise persists with compressor on, even after adding 70cm³ refrigerant compressor oil to system.
Noise disappears when compressor is on. System is OK.

VV7029200030040X

Fig. 3 A/C noise troubleshooting (Part 4 of 4)

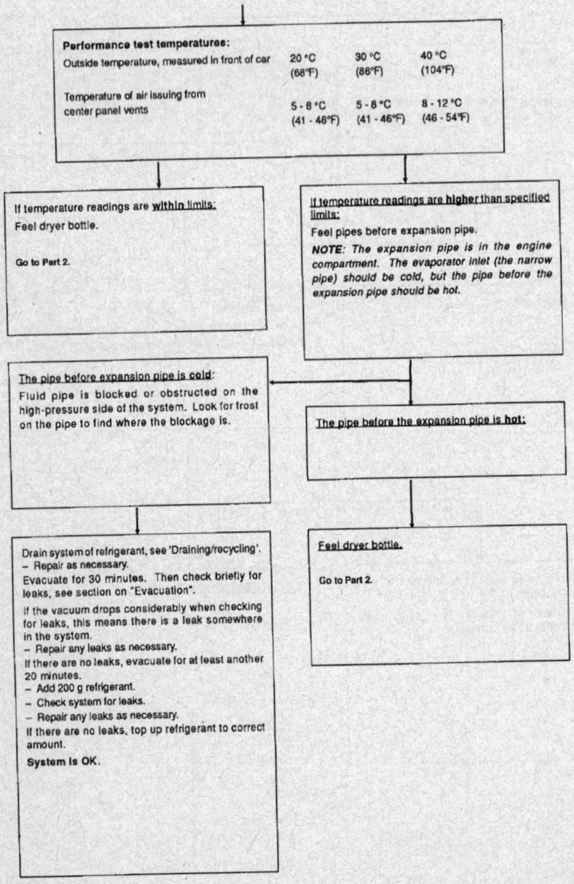

Performance test temperatures:
Outside temperature, measured in front of car
20 °C (68°F)
30 °C (86°F)
40 °C (104°F)
Temperature of air issuing from center panel vents
5 - 8 °C (41 - 46°F)
5 - 8 °C (41 - 46°F)
8 - 12 °C (46 - 54°F)
If temperature readings are within limits: Feel dryer bottle. Go to Part 2.
If temperature readings are higher than specified limits: Feel pipes before expansion pipe.
NOTE: The expansion pipe is in the engine compartment. The evaporator inlet (the narrow pipe) should be cold, but the pipe before the expansion pipe should be hot.
The pipe before expansion pipe is cold: Fluid pipe is blocked or obstructed on the high-pressure side of the system. Look for frost on the pipe to find where the blockage is.
The pipe before the expansion pipe is hot:
Drain system of refrigerant, see 'Draining/recycling'.
– Repair as necessary.
Evacuate for 30 minutes. Then check briefly for leaks, see section on "Evacuation".
If the vacuum drops considerably when checking for leaks, this means there is a leak somewhere in the system.
– Repair any leaks as necessary.
If there are no leaks, evacuate for at least another 20 minutes.
– Add 200 g refrigerant.
– Check system for leaks.
– Repair any leaks as necessary.
If there are no leaks, top up refrigerant to correct amount.
System is OK.
Feel dryer bottle. Go to Part 2.

VV7029200031010X

Fig. 4 A/C system performance test (Part 1 of 10)

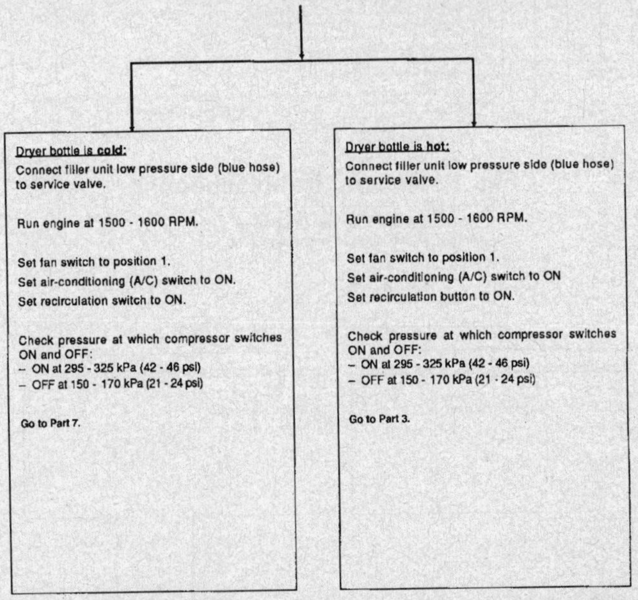

Dryer bottle is cold:
Connect filler unit low pressure side (blue hose) to service valve.
Run engine at 1500 - 1600 RPM.
Set fan switch to position 1.
Set air-conditioning (A/C) switch to ON.
Set recirculation switch to ON.
Check pressure at which compressor switches ON and OFF:
– ON at 295 - 325 kPa (42 - 46 psi)
– OFF at 150 - 170 kPa (21 - 24 psi)
Go to Part 7.
Dryer bottle is hot:
Connect filler unit low pressure side (blue hose) to service valve.
Run engine at 1500 - 1600 RPM.
Set fan switch to position 1.
Set air-conditioning (A/C) switch to ON
Set recirculation button to ON.
Check pressure at which compressor switches ON and OFF:
– ON at 295 - 325 kPa (42 - 46 psi)
– OFF at 150 - 170 kPa (21 - 24 psi)
Go to Part 3.

VV7029200031020X

Fig. 4 A/C system performance test (Part 2 of 10)

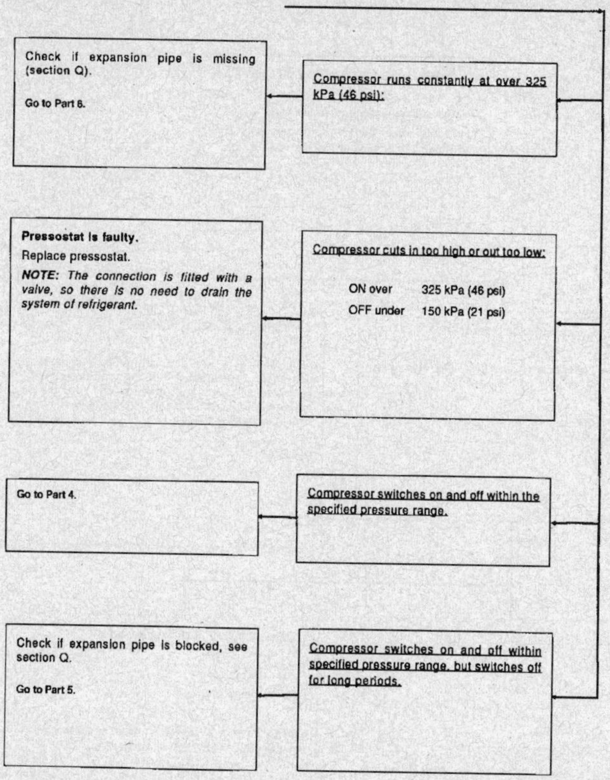
Check if expansion pipe is missing (section Q).
Go to Part 6.
Compressor runs constantly at over 325 kPa (46 psi):
Pressostat is faulty.
Replace pressostat.
NOTE: The connection is fitted with a valve, so there is no need to drain the system of refrigerant.
Compressor cuts in too high or out too low:
ON over 325 kPa (46 psi)
OFF under 150 kPa (21 psi)
Go to Part 4.
Compressor switches on and off within the specified pressure range.
Check if expansion pipe is blocked, see section Q.
Go to Part 5.
Compressor switches on and off within specified pressure range, but switches off for long periods.

VV7029200031030X

Fig. 4 A/C system performance test (Part 3 of 10)

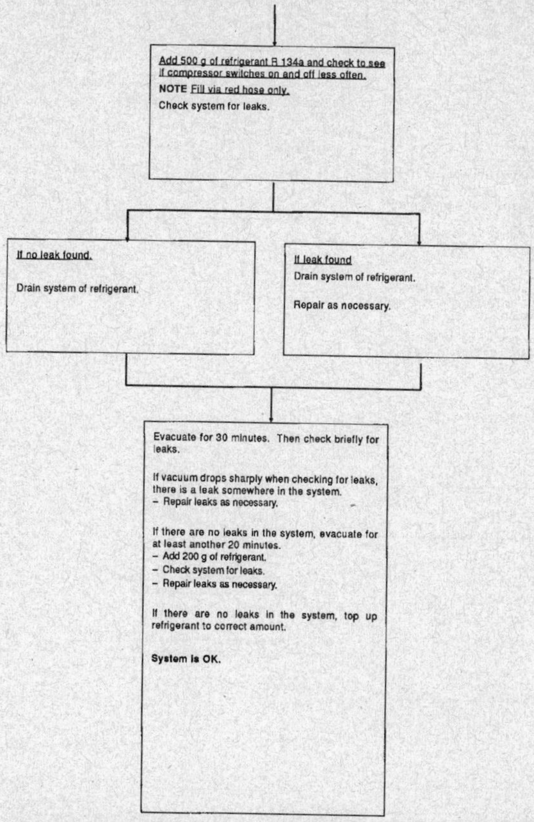
Add 500 g of refrigerant R 134a and check to see if compressor switches on and off less often.
NOTE Fill via red hose only.
Check system for leaks.
If no leak found.
Drain system of refrigerant.
If leak found
Drain system of refrigerant.
Repair as necessary.
Evacuate for 30 minutes. Then check briefly for leaks.
If vacuum drops sharply when checking for leaks, there is a leak somewhere in the system.
– Repair leaks as necessary.
If there are no leaks in the system, evacuate for at least another 20 minutes.
– Add 200 g of refrigerant.
– Check system for leaks.
– Repair leaks as necessary.
If there are no leaks in the system, top up refrigerant to correct amount.
System is OK.

VV7029200031040X

Fig. 4 A/C system performance test (Part 4 of 10)

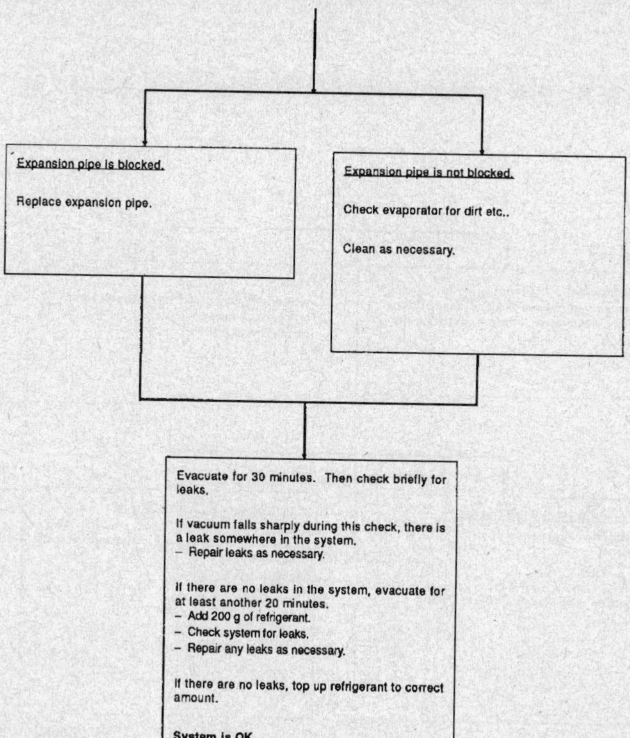
Expansion pipe is blocked.
Replace expansion pipe.
Expansion pipe is not blocked.
Check evaporator for dirt etc..
Clean as necessary.
Evacuate for 30 minutes. Then check briefly for leaks.
If vacuum falls sharply during this check, there is a leak somewhere in the system.
– Repair leaks as necessary.
If there are no leaks in the system, evacuate for at least another 20 minutes.
– Add 200 g of refrigerant.
– Check system for leaks.
– Repair any leaks as necessary.
If there are no leaks, top up refrigerant to correct amount.
System is OK.

VV7029200031050X

Fig. 4 A/C system performance test (Part 5 of 10)

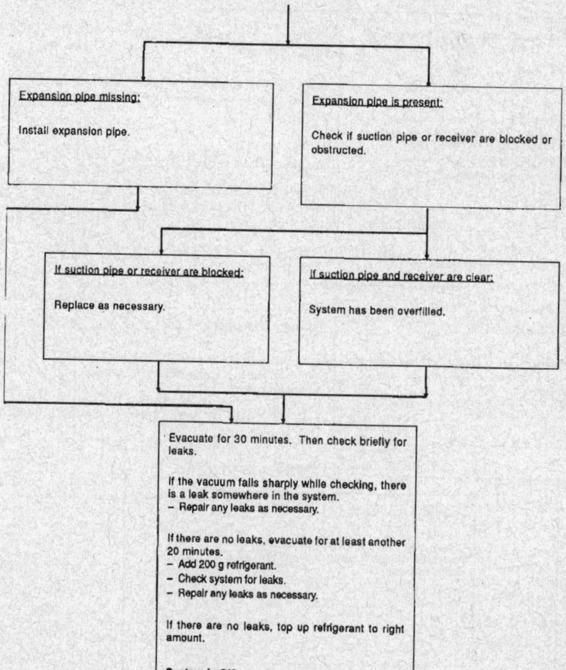
Expansion pipe missing:
Install expansion pipe.
Expansion pipe is present:
Check if suction pipe or receiver are blocked or obstructed.
If suction pipe or receiver are blocked:
Replace as necessary.
If suction pipe and receiver are clear:
System has been overfilled.
Evacuate for 30 minutes. Then check briefly for leaks.
If the vacuum falls sharply while checking, there is a leak somewhere in the system.
– Repair any leaks as necessary.
If there are no leaks, evacuate for at least another 20 minutes.
– Add 200 g refrigerant.
– Check system for leaks.
– Repair any leaks as necessary.
If there are no leaks, top up refrigerant to right amount.
System is OK.

VV7029200031060X

Fig. 4 A/C system performance test (Part 6 of 10)

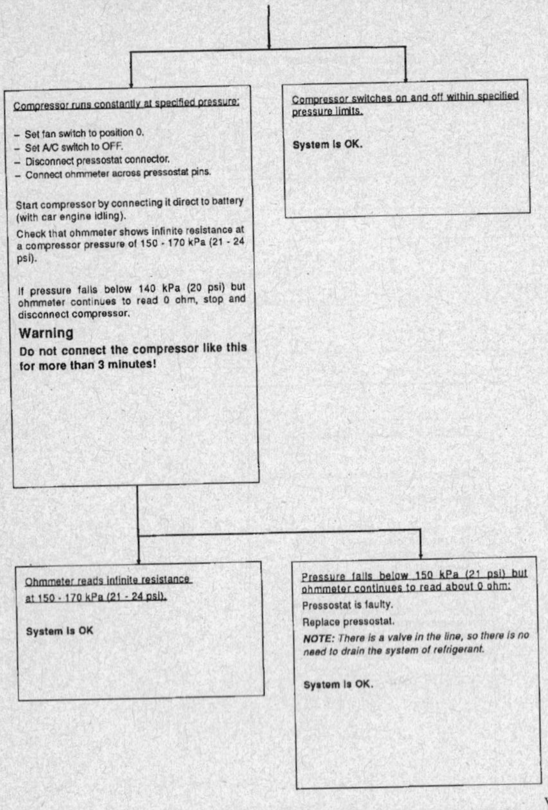
Compressor runs constantly at specified pressure:
- Set fan switch to position 0.
- Set A/C switch to OFF.
- Disconnect pressostat connector.
- Connect ohmmeter across pressostat pins.
Start compressor by connecting it direct to battery (with car engine idling).
Check that ohmmeter shows infinite resistance at a compressor pressure of 150 - 170 kPa (21 - 24 psi).
If pressure falls below 140 kPa (20 psi) but ohmmeter continues to read 0 ohm, stop and disconnect compressor.
Warning
Do not connect the compressor like this for more than 3 minutes!
Compressor switches on and off within specified pressure limits.
System is OK.
Ohmmeter reads infinite resistance at 150 - 170 kPa (21 - 24 psi).
System is OK
Pressure falls below 150 kPa (21 psi) but ohmmeter continues to read about 0 ohm:
Pressostat is faulty.
Replace pressostat.
NOTE: There is a valve in the line, so there is no need to drain the system of refrigerant.
System is OK.
VV7029200031070X

Fig. 4 A/C system performance test (Part 7 of 10)

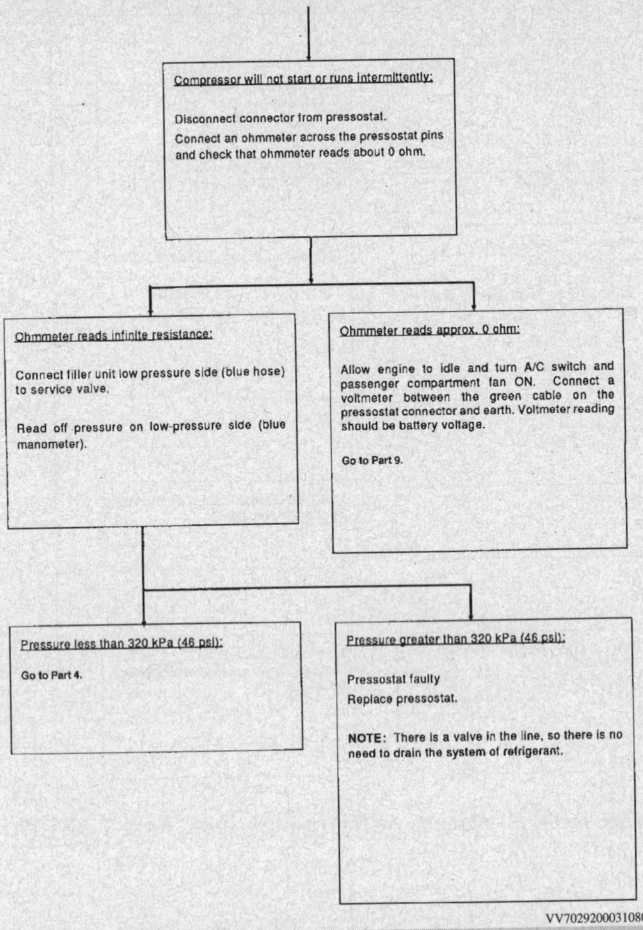
Compressor will not start or runs intermittently:
Disconnect connector from pressostat.
Connect an ohmmeter across the pressostat pins and check that ohmmeter reads about 0 ohm.
Ohmmeter reads infinite resistance:
Connect filler unit low pressure side (blue hose) to service valve.
Read off pressure on low-pressure side (blue manometer).
Ohmmeter reads approx. 0 ohm:
Allow engine to idle and turn A/C switch and passenger compartment fan ON. Connect a voltmeter between the green cable on the pressostat connector and earth. Voltmeter reading should be battery voltage.
Go to Part 9.
Pressure less than 320 kPa (46 psi):
Go to Part 4.
Pressure greater than 320 kPa (46 psi):
Pressostat faulty
Replace pressostat.
NOTE: There is a valve in the line, so there is no need to drain the system of refrigerant.
VV7029200031080X

Fig. 4 A/C system performance test (Part 8 of 10)

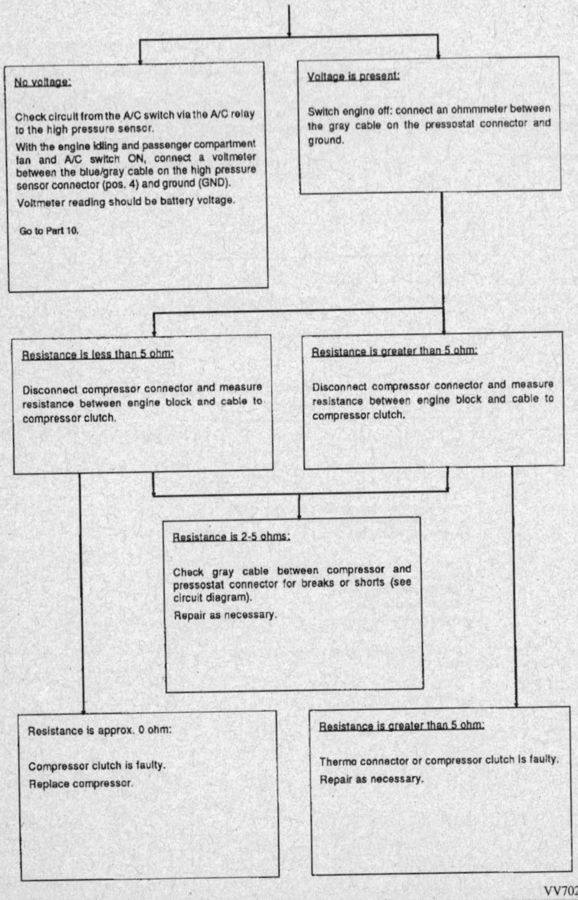
No voltage:
Check circuit from the A/C switch via the A/C relay to the high pressure sensor.
With the engine idling and passenger compartment fan and A/C switch ON, connect a voltmeter between the blue/gray cable on the high pressure sensor connector (pos. 4) and ground (GND).
Voltmeter reading should be battery voltage.
Go to Part 10.
Voltage is present:
Switch engine off: connect an ohmmmeter between the gray cable on the pressostat connector and ground.
Resistance is less than 5 ohm:
Disconnect compressor connector and measure resistance between engine block and cable to compressor clutch.
Resistance is greater than 5 ohm:
Disconnect compressor connector and measure resistance between engine block and cable to compressor clutch.
Resistance is 2-5 ohms:
Check gray cable between compressor and pressostat connector for breaks or shorts (see circuit diagram).
Repair as necessary.
Resistance is approx. 0 ohm:
Compressor clutch is faulty.
Replace compressor.
Resistance is greater than 5 ohm:
Thermo connector or compressor clutch is faulty.
Repair as necessary.
VV7029200031090X

Fig. 4 A/C system performance test (Part 9 of 10)

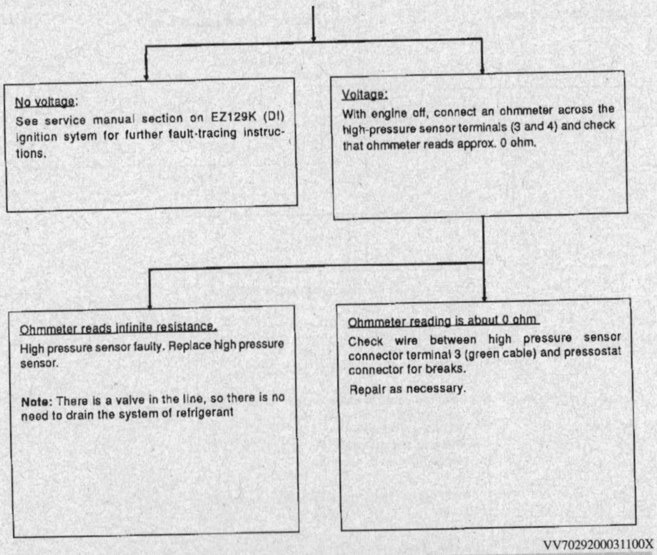
No voltage:
See service manual section on EZ129K (DI) ignition sytem for further fault-tracing instructions.
Voltage:
With engine off, connect an ohmmeter across the high-pressure sensor terminals (3 and 4) and check that ohmmeter reads approx. 0 ohm.
Ohmmeter reads infinite resistance.
High pressure sensor faulty. Replace high pressure sensor.
Note: There is a valve in the line, so there is no need to drain the system of refrigerant
Ohmmeter reading is about 0 ohm.
Check wire between high pressure sensor connector terminal 3 (green cable) and pressostat connector for breaks.
Repair as necessary.
VV7029200031100X

Fig. 4 A/C system performance test (Part 10 of 10)

use valve extractor tool No. 981 1994-4, or equivalent, to remove Schraeder valve.

6. Using a clean syringe, measure how much oil needs to be added to the system, **Fig. 5.**
7. Add needed oil and replace Schrader valve.

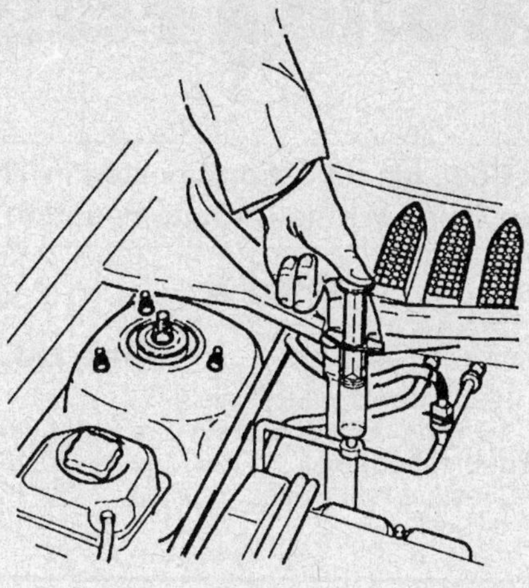

VV70291000260000X

Fig. 5 A/C system fluid level inspection

A/C SPECIFICATIONS

Model	Refrigerant Type	Refrigerant Capacity, Lbs.	Refrigerant Oil		Charging Valve Locations	
			Viscosity	Total System Capacity, Ounces	High Press.	Low Press.
1993						
240	R134a	1.65	①	②	④	③
850	R134a	⑤	⑥	6.8	—	—
940	R134a	2.1	⑥	⑦	—	—
960	R134a	2.0	⑥	⑦	—	—
1994–95						
850	R134a	⑤	⑥	6.8	—	—
940	R134a	2.1	⑥	⑦	—	—
960	R134a	2.0	⑥	⑦	—	—
1996						
850	R134a	⑤	⑥	6.8	—	—
960	R134a	2.0	⑥	⑦	—	—

① — PAG oil, part No. 1161426–0.
② — .23 quarts.
③ — On upper RH side of accumulator.
④ — On compressor.
⑤ — Cold climates, 1.8 lbs.; warm climates, 1.65 lbs.
⑥ — Volvo part No. 8708581 (ZXL 100 PG).
⑦ — Senden SD 510 compressor, 4.56 ounces; Senden SD 709 compressor, 8.11 ounces; Seiko-Seiki SS 121 DS5 compressor, 7.43 ounces.

Cooling Fans

NOTE: Electrical Symbol & Wire Color Code Identification Located In The Front Of This Manual May Be Used As An Aid When Using Wiring Circuits Found In This Section.

INDEX

	Page No.
Component Replacement	50-47
Engine Cooling Fan	50-47
System Diagnosis & Testing	50-46
Except 1996 Models w/Motronic 4.4 Engine Control System	50-46
1996 Models w/Motronic 4.4 Engine Control System	50-46
Troubleshooting	50-46
Constant Half Speed	50-46
Constant High Speed	50-46
No High Speed	50-46
No Low Speed Or High Speed	50-46
No Low Speed	50-46

TROUBLESHOOTING

CONSTANT HALF SPEED

1. Short circuit to ground in low speed signal cable.
2. Defective engine cooling fan relay.

CONSTANT HIGH SPEED

1. Short circuit to ground in high speed signal cable.
2. Defective engine cooling fan relay.

NO LOW SPEED

1. Defective fan or cooling fan relay.

NO HIGH SPEED

1. Open circuit in high speed signal cable.
2. Defective engine cooling fan relay or cooling fan.

NO LOW SPEED OR HIGH SPEED

1. Open circuit in power cable to ground lead.
2. Defective engine cooling fan relay or cooling fan.

SYSTEM DIAGNOSIS & TESTING

When performing the following tests, refer to wiring circuits in **Figs. 1 through 4.**

EXCEPT 1996 MODELS w/MOTRONIC 4.4 ENGINE CONTROL SYSTEM

Engine Cooling Fan & Relay

1. Turn ignition to ON position.
2. Connect a suitable jumper wire between thermal switch electrical connector terminals. **Do not disconnect electrical connector.**
3. With jumper wire properly installed, the engine cooling fan should activate.
4. If fan does not operate, visually check relay, wiring and electrical connector for open and/or short circuits, relay for correct installation, incorrectly grounded and/or damaged electrical connector. After conducting repairs on either the wiring, relay or electrical connector, repeat step 3.
5. If fan still does not operate, replace relay and repeat test procedure.

Thermal Switch

1. Connect a suitable ohmmeter onto thermal switch terminals.
2. Place thermal switch into a container filled with oil. Submerge thermal switch in oil up to its flange. Do not completely submerge thermal switch. **When an oil bath solution is used to heat the thermal switch, ensure thermal switch does not come in contact with container bottom or its side or thermal switch damage will result.**
3. Place a suitable thermometer into the oil bath as close to the thermal switch as possible.
4. Heat the oil bath solution and observe both thermometer and ohmmeter readings.
5. The thermal switch should activate (as indicated by a small deflection by the ohmmeter needle) with oil bath solution heated to approximately 207–216°F.
6. Allow thermal switch to cool from approximately 207°F to 198°F. At approximately 198°F, the thermal switch should deactivate (as indicated by a large deflection on ohmmeter needle).
7. If the thermal switch does not operate as specified in steps 5 and 6, replace thermal switch assembly.

1996 MODELS w/MOTRONIC 4.4 ENGINE CONTROL SYSTEM

High Speed Signal Cable Inspection

1. Connect test box and check ground terminals as follows:
   a. Turn ignition off and wait at least 3 minutes before disconnecting ECM.
   b. Connect adapter tool No. 9511351, or equivalent, into ECM connector, then connect test box (tool No. 9813190, or equivalent) to adapter, **Fig. 5.**
   c. Turn off all lights and electrical accessories that use battery power.
   d. Connect an ohmmeter between battery ground terminal and terminal A13 on test box and measure resistance.
   e. Connect an ohmmeter between battery ground terminal and terminal A28 on test box and measure resistance.
   f. Connect an ohmmeter between battery ground terminal and terminal A42 on test box and measure resistance.
   g. Resistance should be approximately 0 ohms for all measurements.
   h. If resistance is incorrect, check both ground terminals at rear of engine and their wires for an open circuit. Also check for open circuit in ground lead between engine and chassis.
2. Disconnect terminal B from engine cooling fan relay.
3. Connect an ohmmeter between coupling B connector No. 2, **Fig. 6,** and No. 22 (A22) on test box.
4. Resistance should be approximately 0 ohms.
5. If resistance is incorrect, check wire for open circuit between cooling fan relay terminal B2 and ECM.

Cooling Fan Motor High Speed Inspection

1. Turn ignition off.
2. Disconnect terminal C from cooling fan relay.
3. Connect an ohmmeter between terminal C2 and ground.
4. Resistance should be 0–10 ohms.
5. If resistance is within specifications but fan does not operate at high speed, replace cooling fan relay.
6. If resistance is not within specifications, replace cooling fan/motor.

1/1	Battery
2/11	Relay, el. cooling fan
4/23	Control unit, LH-jetronic 2.4
6/29	Electric cooling fan
7/14	Thermostat, el. cooling fan
7/38	Low-speed pressure sensor, el. cooling fan
7/40	High-speed pressure sensor, el. cooling fan
31/1	Ground connection right front fender
31/2	Ground connection left front fender
31/64	Ground connection el. cooling fan
A	Connector at right suspension tower, 3-pin
*)	Fuse

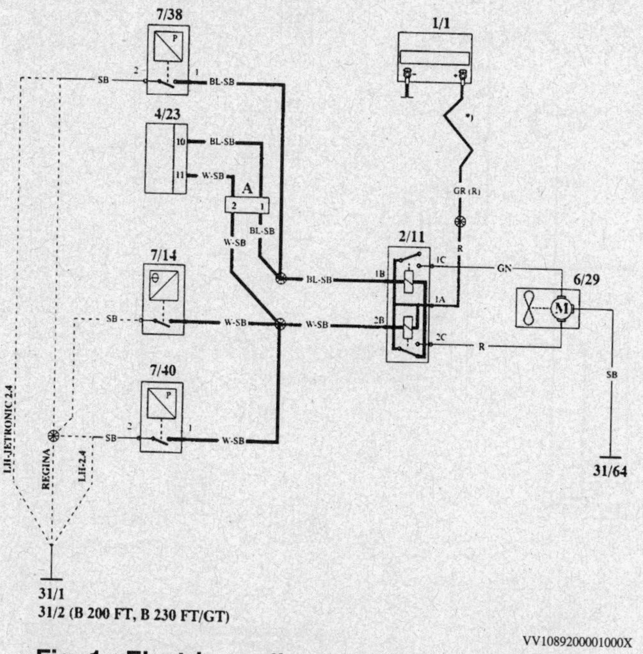
7/38
1/1
4/23
A
2/11
6/29
7/14
7/40
LH-JETRONIC 2.4
REGINA
LH-2.4
31/64
31/1
31/2 (B 200 FT, B 230 FT/GT)
VV1089200001000X

Fig. 1 Electric cooling fan wiring circuit. 960

1/1	Battery
2/11	Relay, electric cooling fan
4/12	Control unit, Motronic
6/29	Electric cooling fan
7/38	Low-speed pressure sensor, electric cooling fan
7/40	High-speed pressure sensor, electric cooling fan
31/1	Ground connection, right front wing
31/64	Ground connection, electric cooling fan
B	Connector, left A-post
C	Connector, right A-post
*)	Fuse-element (fuse)

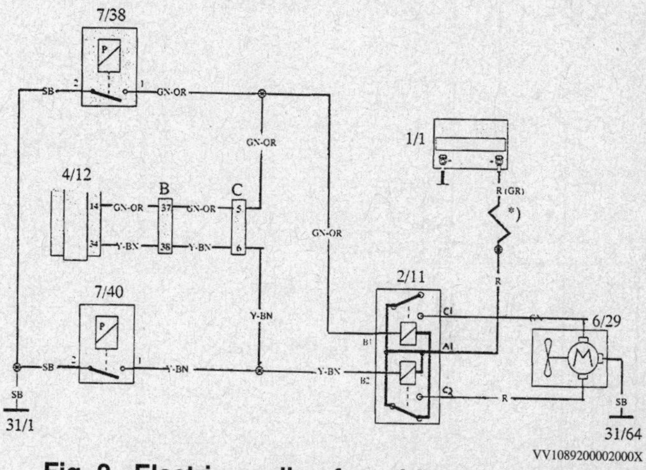
7/38
1/1
4/12
B
C
2/11
7/40
6/29
31/1
31/64
VV1089200002000X

Fig. 2 Electric cooling fan wiring circuit. 940

Cooling Fan Motor Low Speed Inspection

1. Turn ignition off.
2. Disconnect terminal C from cooling fan relay.
3. Connect an ohmmeter between terminal C1 and ground.
4. Resistance should be 0–10 ohms.
5. If resistance is within specifications but fan does not operate at low speed, replace cooling fan relay.
6. If resistance is not within specifications, replace cooling fan/motor.

Cooling Fan Ground Inspection

1. Turn ignition off an disconnect cooling fan electrical connector (C/EA single pin ground lead), **Fig. 7.**
2. Connect an ohmmeter between single pin connector and ground.
3. Resistance should be approximately 0 ohms.
4. If resistance is within specifications but fan does not operate, perform cooling fan motor high speed and low speed inspections.
5. If resistance is not within specifications, replace cooling fan.

Cooling Fan Relay Low Speed Inspection

1. Turn ignition off and disconnect terminal B from engine cooling fan relay.
2. If cooling fan cuts out, check wire between relay terminal B1 and ECM terminal A7 for a short circuit.
3. If cooling fan does not cut out, replace cooling fan relay.

Cooling Fan Relay High Speed Inspection

1. Turn ignition off and disconnect terminal B from engine cooling fan relay.
2. If cooling fan cuts out, check wire between relay terminal B2 and ECM terminal A22 for a short circuit.
3. If cooling fan does not cut out, replace cooling fan relay.

COMPONENT REPLACEMENT

ENGINE COOLING FAN

1. Open hood, then disconnect battery ground cable.
2. Remove grille, if necessary.
3. Remove radiator, if necessary.
4. Disconnect electrical connectors from fan assembly.
5. Remove fan and fan shroud assembly.
6. Separate fan from fan shroud assembly.
7. Reverse procedure to install.

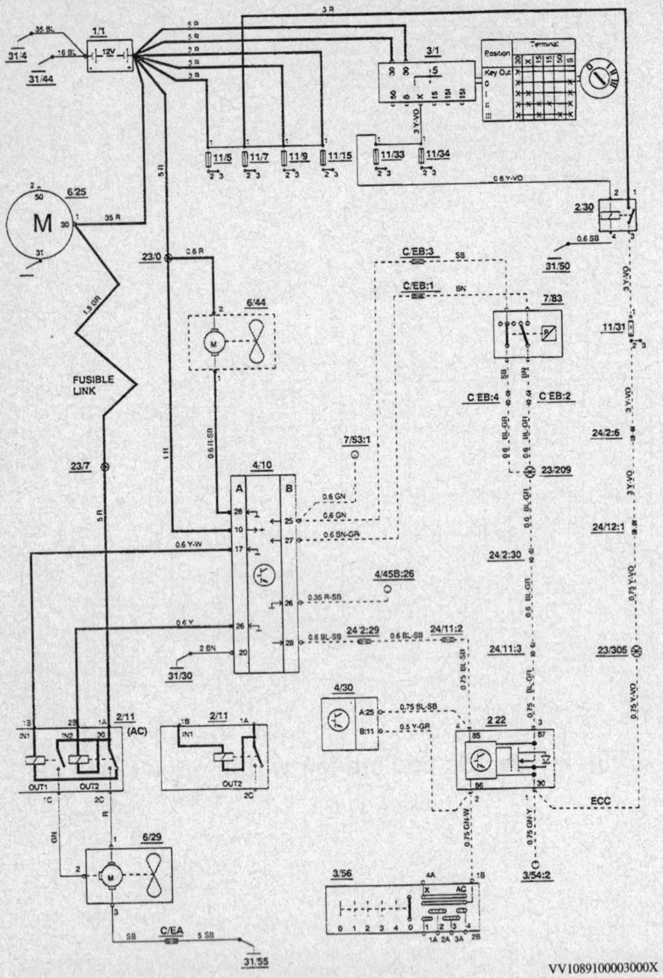
FUSIBLE LINK
M
ECC

VV1089100003000X

Fig. 3 Electric cooling fan wiring circuit. 1993–95 850

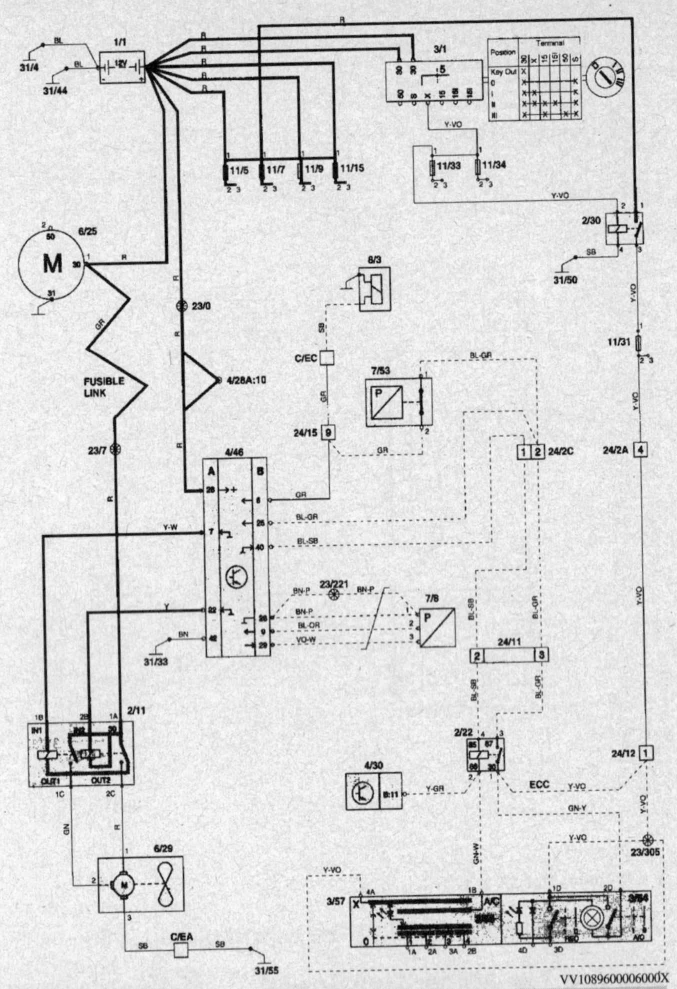
FUSIBLE LINK
M
ECC

VV1089600006000X

Fig. 4 Electric cooling fan wiring circuit. 1996 850

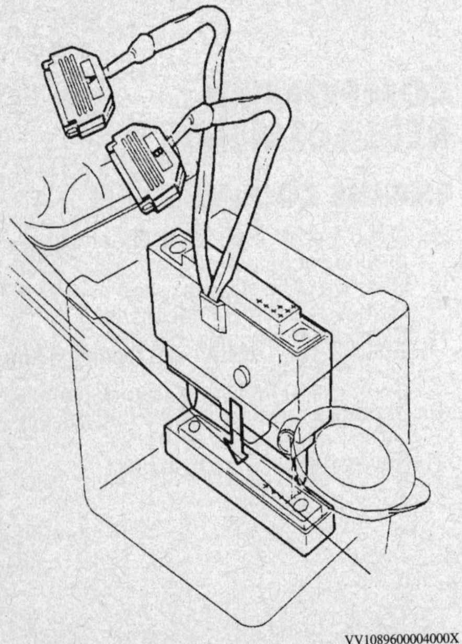

VV1089600004000X

Fig. 5 Test box & adapter installation. 1996 w/Motronic 4.4 engine control system

C B A
2
2
1
1

VV1089600005000X

Fig. 6 Cooling fan relay terminal identification. 1996 w/Motronic 4.4 engine control system

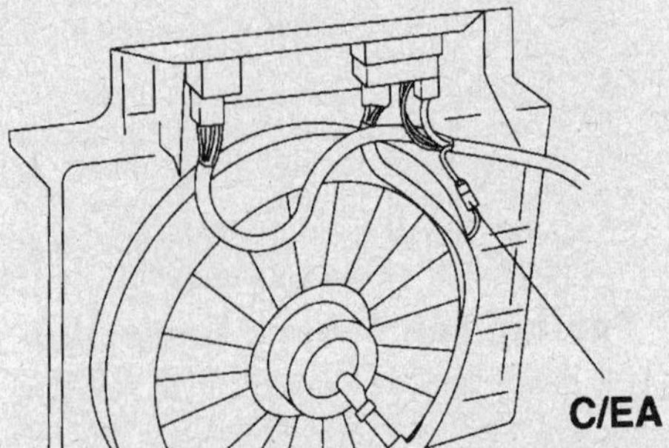
C/EA

VV1089600007000X

Fig. 7 Cooling fan ground connector (C/EA)

Dash Gauges

NOTE: On Air Bag Equipped Models, Refer To "Air Bag System Precautions" Located In The Front Of This Manual For System Disarming & Arming Procedures.

NOTE: Refer To The "Dash Panel Service" Section For Dash Panel Removal Procedures.

NOTE: Refer To The "Electronic Instrumentation" Section In MOTOR'S "Imported Engine Performance & Driveability Manual" For Information Related To Electronic Instrumentation.

INDEX

	Page No.
Gauges	50-49
Fuel	50-49
Tachometer	50-50
Temperature	50-49
Precautions	50-49
Air Bag Systems	50-49
Speedometer	50-50
Inspection	50-50
Troubleshooting	50-50
Wiring Diagram	50-50

PRECAUTIONS

AIR BAG SYSTEMS

Refer to "Air Bag System Precautions" in the front of this manual for system disarming and arming procedures.

WIRING DIAGRAM

Refer to **Fig. 1** for instrument cluster wiring diagram.

GAUGES

FUEL

GAUGE NOT WORKING AT ALL

An inoperative fuel gauge may be caused by one or more of the following:

1. Open circuit in sensor ground connection.
2. Sensor ground connection shorted to battery potential.
3. Open circuit in sensor signal wiring.
4. Sensor signal wiring shorted to ground.
5. Open circuit in sensor.
6. Sensor short circuited.
7. Defective fuel gauge.
8. Sensor stuck in lowest position.

GAUGE READING INCORRECT

The fuel gauge may display an incorrect reading due to one or more of the following:

1. Sensor ground connection has incorrect ground potential.
2. Sensor is sticking.
3. Sensor at incorrect resistance.
4. Instrument cluster has incorrect ground potential.
5. Defective fuel gauge.

INSPECTION

Fuel Level Sensor Check

1. Turn ignition off and disconnect battery ground cable.
2. Fold down righthand backrest on rear seat, then remove luggage compartment mat, **Fig. 2.**
3. Remove righthand luggage compartment panel.
4. Remove fuel pump and sensor plastic cover.
5. Remove fuel pump and sensor cover caps.
6. Disconnect electrical connectors and unscrew plastic nut from fuel level sensor, **Fig. 3.**
7. Lift up fuel level sensor while feeding wire through.
8. Connect an ohmmeter to sensor connector. Resistance should read 7–327 ohms depending on how much fuel is in the tank.
9. If resistance is within specifications, check sensor ground connection.
10. If resistance is not within specifications, replace sensor.

Sensor Ground Connection Check

1. Using an ohmmeter, measure resistance between sensor connector to harness (yellow/red), and ground.
2. Resistance should be approximately 0 ohms.
3. If resistance is correct, check sensor signal.
4. If resistance is incorrect, check for open circuits in wiring between connector (yellow/red), and 30-pole connector on instrument cluster (A4).

Sensor Signal Check

1. On connector leading to harness, connect a voltmeter between point 1 (yellow/gray) and ground.
2. Turn ignition switch on.
3. Voltmeter should read approximately 7 volts.
4. If voltmeter reads 0 volts, check wiring between connector point 1 (yellow/gray) and 30-pole connector on instrument cluster (A3) for open or short circuit.
5. If voltmeter reads battery voltage, check wiring between connector point 1 (yellow/gray) and 30-pole connector on instrument cluster (A5) for short circuit to battery potential.
6. If voltmeter reads 7 volts, replace instrument cluster.

TEMPERATURE

GAUGE NOT WORKING AT ALL

The coolant temperature gauge may become inoperative due to one or more of the following:

1. Fuel injection system not receiving any signal from temperature sensor.
2. Open circuit forwarding temperature signal from fuel system control module.
3. Temperature signal wiring from fuel system control module short circuited to ground or battery potential.
4. Defective temperature gauge.

GAUGE READING INCORRECT

The temperature gauge may give an incorrect reading due to the following:

1. Instrument cluster has defective ground potential.
2. Defective temperature sensor.

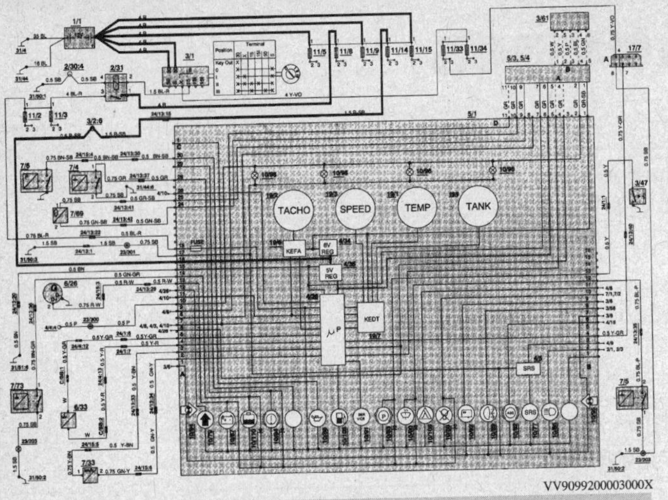
TACHO
SPEED
TEMP
TANK
KEFA
KEDT
SRS
VV9099200003000X

Fig. 1 Instrument cluster wiring diagram

3. Defective temperature gauge.

TACHOMETER

TACHOMETER NOT WORKING AT ALL

The tachometer may become inoperative due to one or more of the following:

1. Open circuit in tachometer signal wiring from ignition control module.
2. Tachometer signal wiring from ignition control module short circuited to ground or battery potential.
3. Defective tachometer.
4. Defective ignition control module.

TACHOMETER READING INCORRECT

The temperature gauge may give an incorrect reading due to the following:

1. Instrument cluster has incorrect ground potential.
2. Defective tachometer.

INSPECTION

Gauge Check

1. If tachometer does not work at all, check wiring between 30-pole connector on instrument cluster A11 (white/black) and ignition control module connector B29 for short circuit.
2. If no short is found, replace instrument cluster.
3. If tachometer gives an inaccurate reading, check instrument cluster signal ground connection by inspecting wiring between 30-pin connector on instrument cluster (A15/brown) and ground point 31/51:6 on wiring diagram.

SPEEDOMETER

TROUBLESHOOTING

Speedometer Not Working At All

1. Open circuit in vehicle speed sensor ground connection.
2. Vehicle speed sensor ground connection short circuited to ground or battery potential.
3. Open circuit in speed sensor signal wiring.
4. Vehicle speed sensor signal wiring short circuited to ground or battery potential.
5. Open circuit in speed sensor.
6. Short circuit in speed sensor.
7. Speedometer defective.

Speedometer Reading Incorrect

1. Vehicle speed sensor position in relation to toothed wheel is incorrect.
2. Instrument cluster has incorrect ground potential.
3. Defective speedometer.
4. Vehicle speed sensor ground connection has incorrect ground potential.

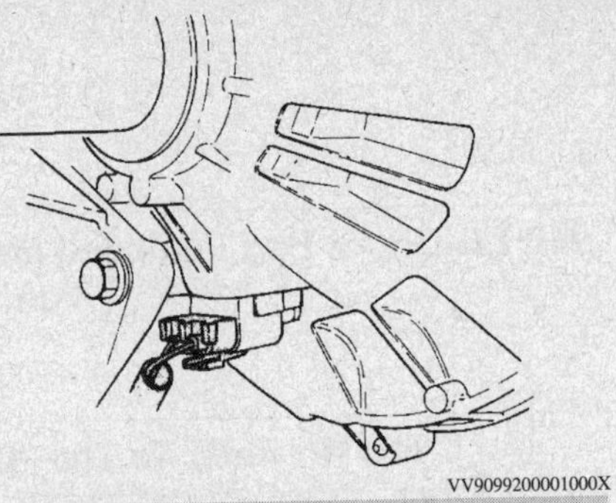
VV9099200001000X

Fig. 2 Fuel level sensor access

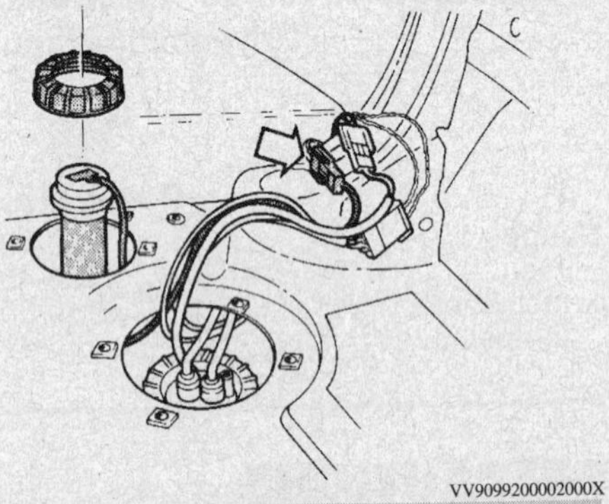
VV9099200002000X

Fig. 3 Fuel level sensor connectors

INSPECTION

Vehicle Speed Sensor Check

1. Turn ignition off and disconnect connector from vehicle speed sensor.
2. Connect an ohmmeter across sensor.
3. Resistance should be 640–1000 ohms.
4. If resistance is incorrect, replace vehicle speed sensor.
5. If resistance is within specifications, check sensor ground connection.

Sensor Ground Connection Check

1. Connect an ohmmeter between vehicle speed sensor connector 2 (green/yellow) and ground.
2. Resistance should be approximately 0 ohms.
3. If resistance is incorrect, check wiring between connector 2 (green/yellow) and 30-pole connector on instrument cluster (A2) for open circuits.

Starter Motors

INDEX

	Page No.
Diagnosis & Testing	50-51
No Load Test	50-51
Pull In Test	50-51
Starter Specifications	50-51
Troubleshooting	50-51
Control Solenoid Does Not Engage	50-51
Control Solenoid Engages But Starter Motor Does Not	50-51
Drive Does Not Return To Rest When Voltage Is Interrupted	50-51
Drive Returns To Rest Position Before Break In Voltage	50-51
Heavy Sparking, Low RPM	50-51
Long Overrun Time For Starter Motor When Ignition Key Is Released	50-51
Low RPM & Low Current Draw	50-51
Low RPM & High Current Draw	50-51

TROUBLESHOOTING

LOW RPM & LOW CURRENT DRAW

1. Discharged battery.
2. High resistance, caused by dirt in commutator.
3. Worn brushes or spring force.

LOW RPM & HIGH CURRENT DRAW

1. Short circuit in coil.
2. Armature drags against pole shoes due to worn bushing(s) or bent shaft.

HEAVY SPARKING, LOW RPM

1. Weak spring force due to worn brushes or springs.
2. Short circuit or open circuit in armature coil.

DRIVE RETURNS TO REST POSITION BEFORE BREAK IN VOLTAGE

1. Poor connection at terminal 50 or fault in control solenoid.

DRIVE DOES NOT RETURN TO REST WHEN VOLTAGE IS INTERRUPTED

1. The drive is jammed on the armature shaft.

CONTROL SOLENOID ENGAGES BUT STARTER MOTOR DOES NOT

1. Defective control solenoid.
2. Poor connection at carbon brushes.
3. Open circuit in field coil.
4. Armature seized in bushing.

LONG OVERRUN TIME FOR STARTER MOTOR WHEN IGNITION KEY IS RELEASED

1. Worn brushes.
2. Weak brush spring force.

CONTROL SOLENOID DOES NOT ENGAGE

1. Defective control solenoid.
2. Fault in circuit between terminal 50 on starter motor and ignition switch.
3. Faulty ignition switch.

DIAGNOSIS & TESTING

PULL IN TEST

1. With starter removed from vehicle.
2. Connect battery as shown in **Fig. 1.**
3. When circuit is completed, the drive pinion should extend.
4. If drive pinion does not operate as specified, repair or replace solenoid as necessary.

NO LOAD TEST

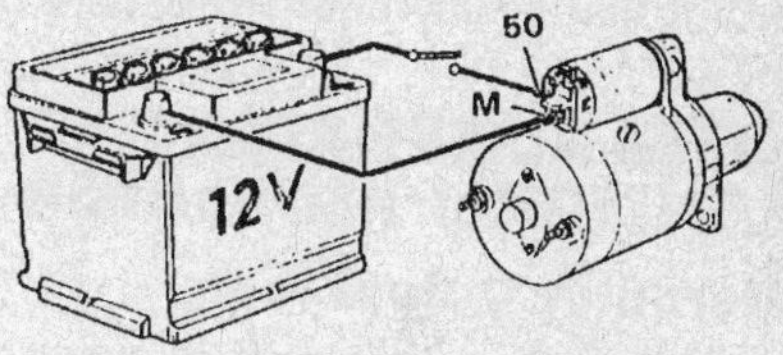
50
M
12V

VV1129100001000X

Fig. 1 Control solenoid inspection

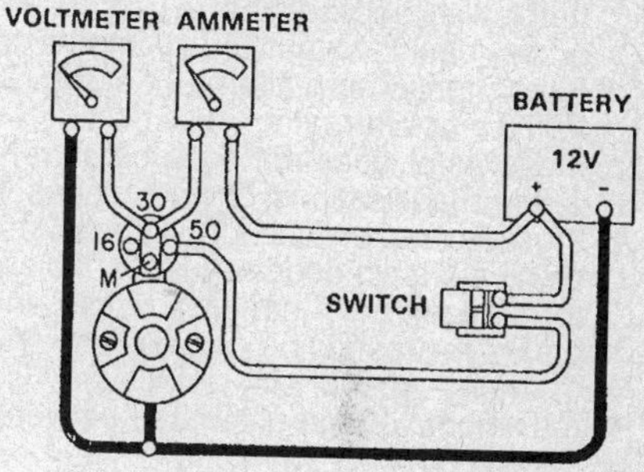
VOLTMETER
AMMETER
BATTERY
12V
+
-
30
16
50
M
SWITCH

VV1129100002000X

Fig. 2 No load test

1. Connect starter motor as shown in **Fig. 2.**
2. Turn switch On, measure voltmeter and ammeter readings.
3. Compare readings to "Starter Specifications" chart.
4. If reading are not as specified, repair or replace starter motor as necessary.

STARTER SPECIFICATIONS

Year	Part No.	Brush Spring Tension, Ounces	No Load Test			Torque Test	
			Amperes	Volts	RPM	Amperes	Volts
1993–96	Bosch GE	3.1–3.5	30–50	11.5	5800–7800	185–220	9
	Bosch JF	5.1–5.5	65–95	11.5	6500–8500	—	—
	Bosch 0001362	—	95	11.5	6500	700–800①	4.5①
	Bosch 00013111	—	70	11.5	7500	410–490①	6.5①
	Bosch 0001108030	—	80	11.5	6500	700–880①	4.5①
	Hitachi S114-232A	—	60	12	7000	650	6.0①
	Hitachi S13-91	—	140	11	3900	880①	3.0①

① — Locked starter motor current consumption.

Alternators

INDEX

Page No.

Alternator Specifications 50-53
Diagnosis & Testing 50-52
Bosch Alternator w/Integral Regulator 50-52

DIAGNOSIS & TESTING

When testing an alternator, it is important that a fully charged battery be used.

BOSCH ALTERNATOR w/INTEGRAL REGULATOR

Alternator Output Test

1. With alternator at normal operating temperature, run engine at 3000 RPM for 3 minutes.
2. Using a suitable shunt or loading alternator with accessories to require 40 amps, check output and compare to **Fig. 1**, for 55 amp alternator or **Fig. 2**, for 70 amp alternator.
3. If alternator does not produce current within specifications, check brushes. If brushes are satisfactory, repeat test using a known good regulator. Indicator on dash must not glow during any part of the testing procedure, if so one or more diodes are defective. Also maximum voltage difference between B+ and D+/61 is ½ volt.

Voltage Regulator Test

1. Run alternator until normal operating temperature is reached.
2. With the engine running at 3000 RPM, measure the voltage between B+ and D− terminals on back of alternator.
3. Correct reading should be 13.4–14.2 volts. If voltage is incorrect, make sure alternator brush length is correct. Minimum brush length is .2 inch (5 mm). If brush length is satisfactory, replace regulator.

Temperature Sensor Test

Some model vehicles use an external temperature sensor located underneath the battery. This sensor, directly connected to the voltage regulator, senses battery temperature and relays this information to the regulator. During cold weather operation, the alternator delivers higher voltage to the battery, thereby charging it at a faster rate. As the battery warms, the charging rate is reduced to prevent excessive gassing. To check sensor operation, proceed as follows:

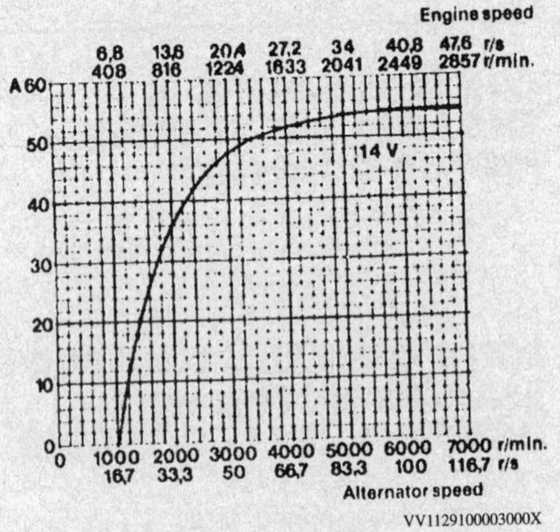

Engine speed
6,8 13,6 20,4 27,2 34 40,8 47,6 r/s
408 816 1224 1633 2041 2449 2857 r/min.
A 60
50
40
30
20
10
0
14 V
0 1000 2000 3000 4000 5000 6000 7000 r/min.
16,7 33,3 50 66,7 83,3 100 116,7 r/s
Alternator speed
VV1129100003000X

Fig. 1 Alternator output test. Bosch 55 amp alternator w/ integral regulator

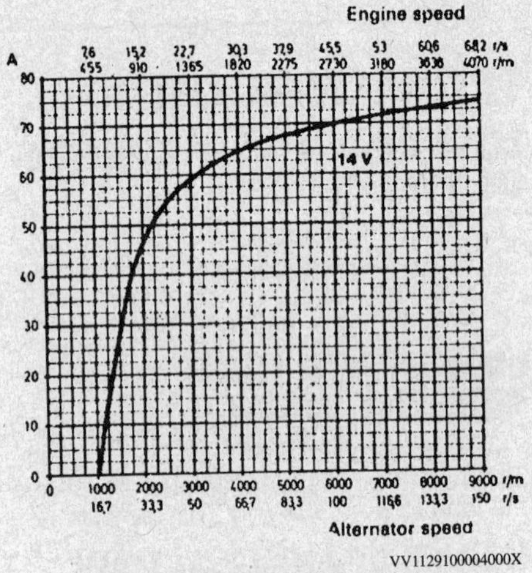

Engine speed
A
14 V
Alternator speed
VV1129100004000X

Fig. 2 Alternator output test. Bosch 70 amp alternator w/ integral regulator

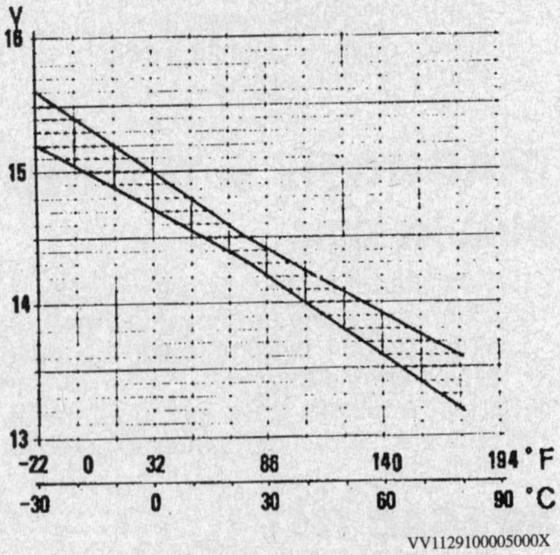

V
16
15
14
13
-22 0 32 86 140 194 °F
-30 0 30 60 90 °C
VV1129100005000X

Fig. 3 Charging voltage graph (w/external temperature sensor connected)

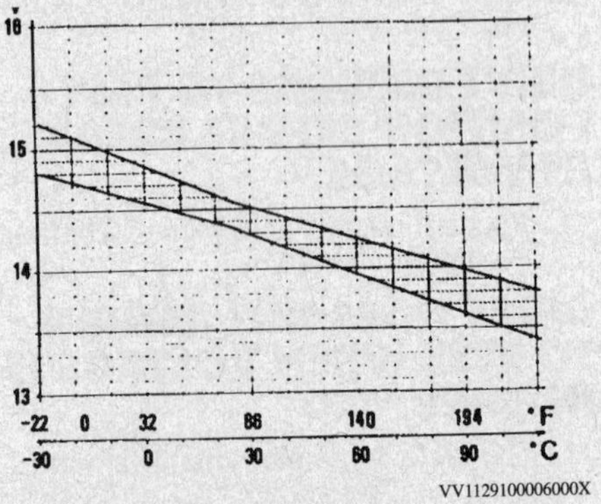

16
15
14
13
-22 0 32 86 140 194 °F
-30 0 30 60 90 °C
VV1129100006000X

Fig. 4 Charging voltage graph (w/external temperature sensor disconnected)

1. Note and record battery temperature.
2. Connect voltmeter across battery terminals, then with all accessories off, start engine and allow to run at 2000 RPM. Observe charging voltage.
3. With battery temperature as noted in step 1, charging voltage should be within shaded areas of graph, **Fig. 3.** If voltage is as specified, temperature sensor is functioning properly. If not, proceed to next step.
4. Disconnect external temperature sensor from regulator, then repeat steps 1 and 2. With battery temperature as noted, charging voltage should be within shaded areas of graph, **Fig. 4.** If voltage is as specified, replace temperature sensor. If voltage is not as specified, replace voltage regulator.

ALTERNATOR SPECIFICATIONS

Year	Alternator				Regulator	
	Model	Rated Hot Output Amps	Field Winding Resistance Ohms	Output @ 14 Volts 6000 RPM Amps	Type	Voltage @ 125°F
1993–96	Bosch N1	80	2.6	80/100	Integral	13.8–14.6
	Bosch N1	100	2.6	100/100	Integral	13.8–14.6
	Bosch KC	80	2.6	80/100	Integral	13.8- 14.6
	Bosch NC	100	2.6	100/100	Integral	13.8- 14.6
	Nippondenso	80	2.9	108/100	Integral	13.8- 14.6

Speed Control Systems

NOTE: On Air Bag Equipped Models, Refer To "Air Bag System Precautions" Located In The Front Of This Manual For System Disarming & Arming Procedures.

NOTE: Electrical Symbol & Wire Color Code Identification Located In The Front Of This Manual May Be Used As An Aid When Using Wiring Circuits Found In This Section.

INDEX

	Page No.
Component Diagnosis & Testing	50-55
Speed Control Switch	50-55
Description	50-53
Precautions	50-53
Air Bag Systems	50-53
System Diagnosis & Testing	50-53
Less Electronic Tester	50-53
With Electronic Tester	50-54

PRECAUTIONS

AIR BAG SYSTEMS

Refer to "Air Bag System Precautions" in the front of this manual for system disarming and arming procedures.

DESCRIPTION

This speed control system is electrically controlled and vacuum operated. The speed control module stores the exact speed of the vehicle the moment the set button is pressed and released. This system adjusts the throttle position eight times per second to hold vehicle speed within one mph of the speed set.

This system uses a vacuum reservoir to maintain the set speed when climbing a hill. The rapid deceleration cutoff is used to turn off the system if vehicle speed drops by more than 10 mph even if there is no indication that the brakes have been applied. The wheel spin cutoff will turn the system off if the set, resume, brake or clutch switches do not close and reopen when activated or if a wiring malfunction occurs in these circuits. This prevents the system from operating in an unexpected manner because of a system malfunction.

Test #	Switch Position	Tester Lamps						
		RESUME	SET	BRAKE/CLUTCH	IGNITION	SPEED	VAC	VENT
1	OFF	OFF	OFF	OFF	ON	OFF	OFF	OFF
2	ON	OFF	ON	OFF	ON	OFF	ON	ON
3	RESUME	ON	ON	OFF	ON	OFF	ON	ON
4	SET	ON	OFF	OFF	ON	OFF	ON	ON
5	BRAKE/CLUTCH*	OFF	ON	DIMLY LIT	ON	OFF	ON	ON

* Check each separately.

VV1109100001000X

Fig. 1 Speed control diagnosis chart

SYSTEM DIAGNOSIS & TESTING

LESS ELECTRONIC TESTER

1. Check that brake lights work and that the brake switch is properly adjusted. The control unit is grounded through the brake lights. If both brake lights are blown, the control unit will not function.
2. Remove lower dash panel from left side footwell.
3. Check that air valves at brake and clutch pedals are correctly adjusted and do not leak. The valves should be closed when the pedals are up and open when pedals are depressed.
4. Check that vacuum servo hoses and air valve hoses are correctly connected and not kinked.
5. Ensure vacuum hose connected to intake manifold is not blocked or punctured.
6. Disconnect hose from connection marked "VACUUM"on valve housing. Start engine and place thumb on end of hose. Suction should be felt. If no suction is felt, check hose and connection at intake manifold.
7. Reconnect hose, start engine and leave running for about 30 seconds to establish vacuum.
8. Turn engine off and disconnect hose marked "VACUUM " from the valve housing. A hissing sound should be heard. If no sound is heard, there is a vacuum leak in the system. Repair as necessary.

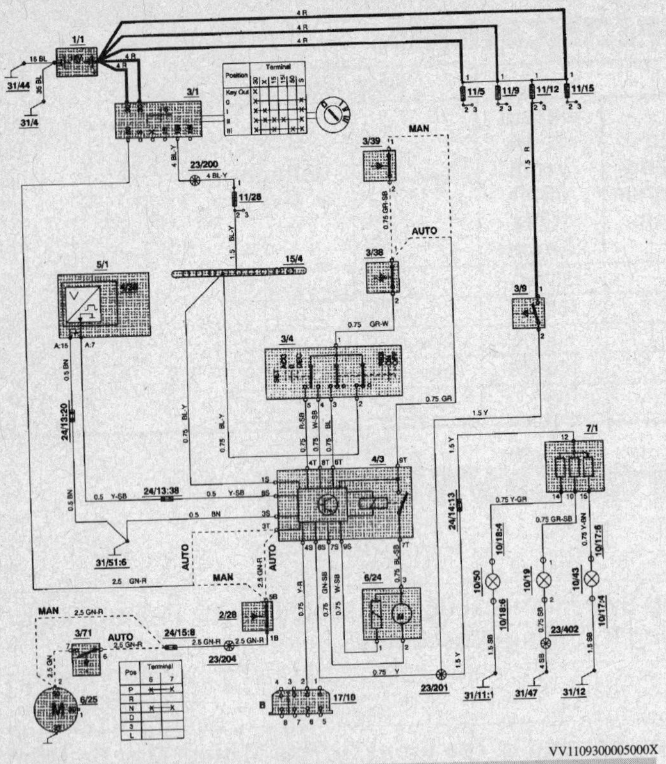

Fig. 2 Speed control wiring diagram. 1993 850

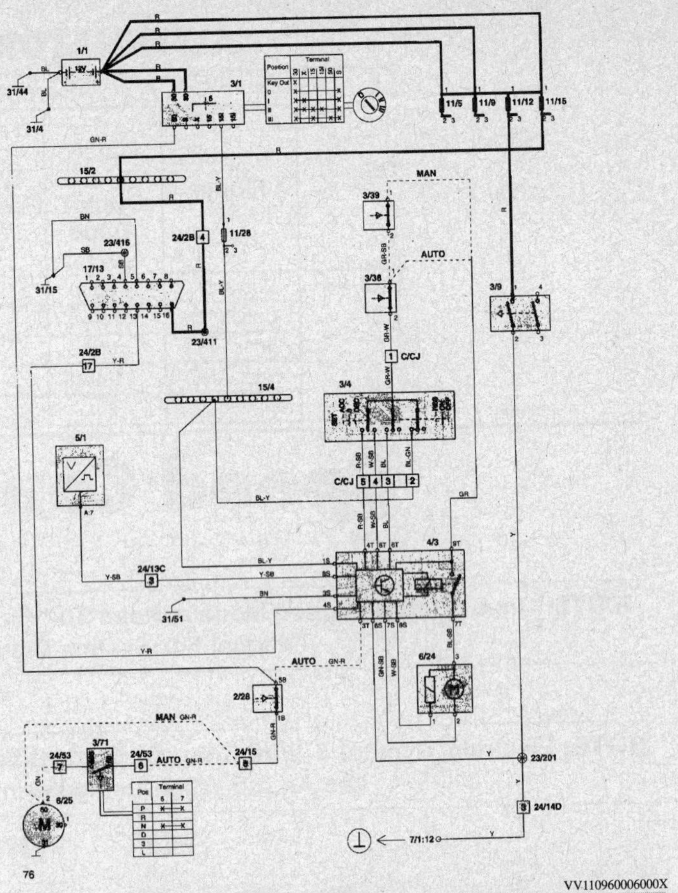

Fig. 3 Speed control wiring diagram. 1994–96 850

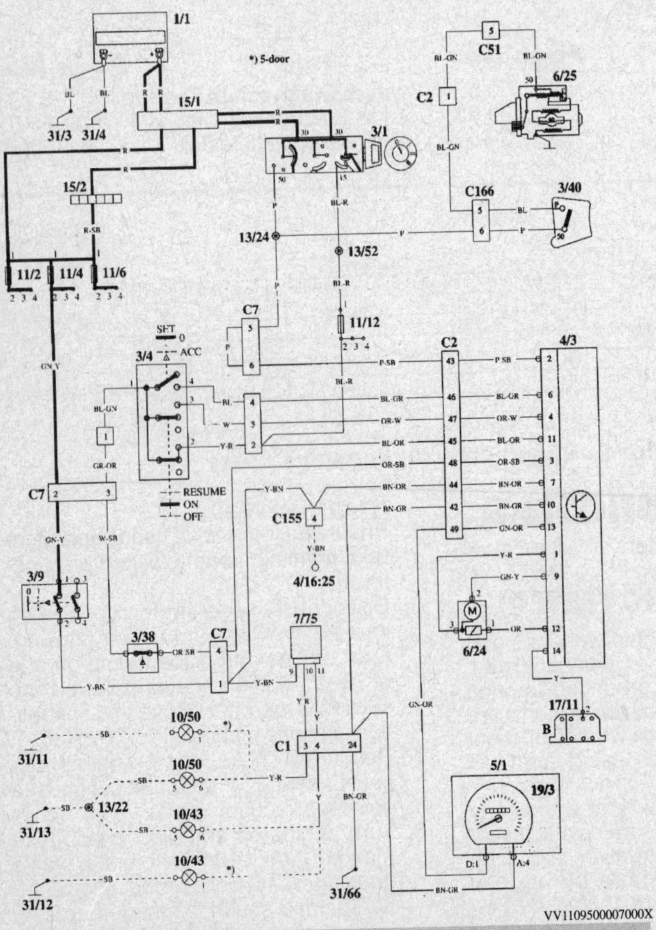

Fig. 4 Speed control wiring diagram. 940

WITH ELECTRONIC TESTER

The most accurate method of fault tracing this speed control system requires the use of test unit, tool No. 9990943-4, or equivalent. This test unit will check the functions of all components including the control unit. Refer to **Figs. 1 through 5,** when testing this system.

1. Connect speed control tester as follows:
   a. Remove lower dash panel from drivers side.
   b. Disconnect speed control harness from control unit.
   c. Connect tester lead to the control unit.
   d. Connect speed control wiring harness to tester unit.
2. Switch tester to position "1." Turn ignition switch on, but do not start engine.
3. Check each switch position of the speed control system and compare as shown in **Fig. 1.**
4. If tester lamps do not light in the correct sequence, proceed as follows:
   a. Check fuse No. 12 and wiring, **Figs. 2 through 5.**
   b. For "Resume and Set" lamps, check yellow and green wires between control unit and switch, **Fig. 6.** If not satisfactory, locate and repair open circuit in wires. If satisfactory, replace switch.

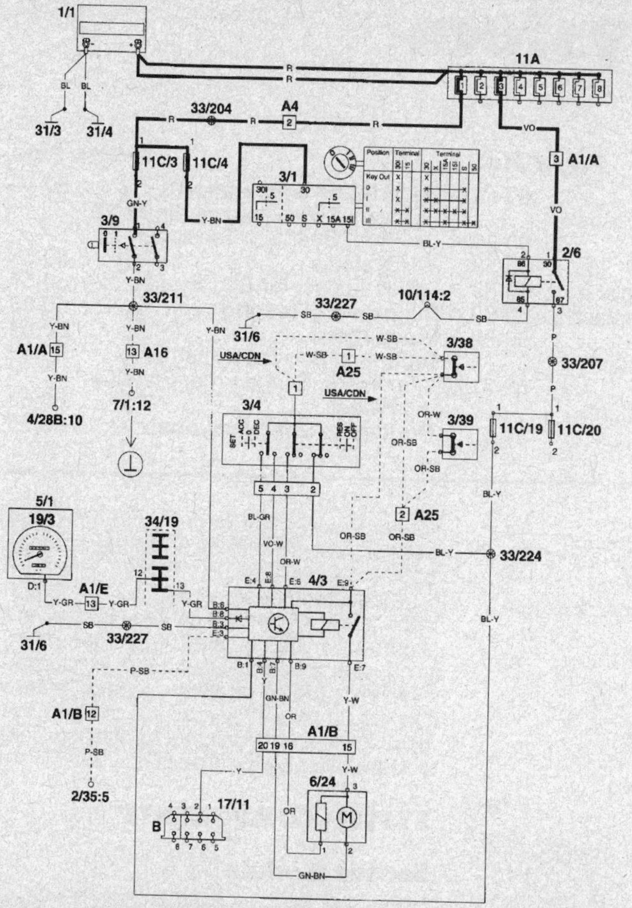
1/1
11A
31/3
31/4
33/204
A4
11C/3
11C/4
3/1
A1/A
3/9
2/6
33/211
33/227
10/114:2
A1/A
A16
31/6
USA/CDN
3/38
A25
33/207
4/28B:10
7/1:12
3/4
USA/CDN
3/39
11C/19
11C/20
5/1
19/3
34/19
A25
33/224
A1/E
4/3
31/6
33/227
A1/B
A1/B
2/35:5
6/24
17/11

VV1109600008000X

Fig. 5 Speed control wiring diagram. 960

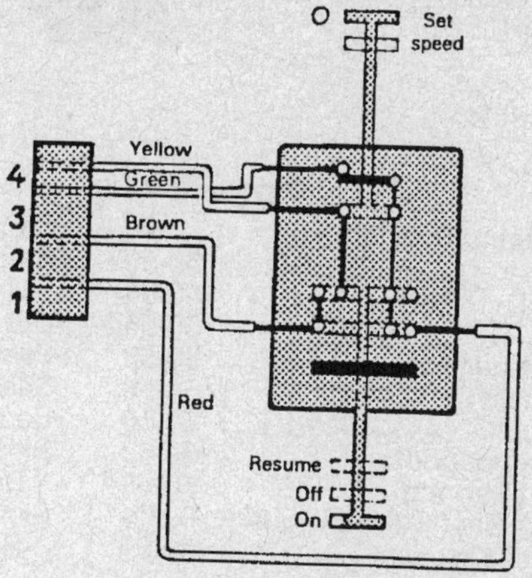
Set speed
4
3
2
1
Yellow
Green
Brown
Red
Resume
Off
On

VV1109100003000X

Fig. 6 Speed control switch wiring circuit

Wire color	Cruise control switch position			
	OFF	ON	ON and SET SPEED depressed	RESUME
	Test light indication			
Brown	off	on	on	on
Green	off	on	off	on
Yellow	off	off	on	on

VV1109100004000X

Fig. 7 Speed control switch diagnosis chart

c. For "Brake/Clutch" lamp, check adjustment of switches on pedals. Check wiring and brake light operation. If not satisfactory, repair as necessary.

d. For the "Speed" lamp, verify proper operation of the speedometer. Check connection of orange wire at the rear of the instrument cluster. If not satisfactory, repair as necessary.

e. For "Vac and Vent" light, check three wires going to the servo valve under the hood. If not satisfactory, repair as necessary.

5. **On models less limited-slip differential,** raise left rear wheel off the ground. Rotate wheel slowly while watching "Speed" light on tester. Light should blink on and off with low light intensity.
6. **On models equipped with limited-slip differential,** raise both rear wheels off the ground and set transmission to "Neutral." Rotate wheels slowly while watching "Speed" light on tester. Light should blink on and off with low light intensity.
7. **On all models,** set speed control to the "OFF" position and start engine. Allow engine to run for approximately 30 seconds to establish vacuum.
8. Turn engine off, then turn ignition switch to "ON " and speed control to "ON." Depress "VAC" and "VENT" buttons on the tester simultaneously. Throttle pedal should be pulled down. If throttle pedal is not pulled down, proceed as follows:
   a. Release the "VAC" button on tester and keep "VENT" button depressed for a minimum of 15 seconds. Throttle pedal should remain steady. If not, the vacuum system has a leak. Repair as necessary.
   b. If vacuum supply is satisfactory, replace control unit.

COMPONENT DIAGNOSIS & TESTING

SPEED CONTROL SWITCH

1. Disconnect electrical connector from speed control switch.
2. Connect a jumper wire from a 12 volt current source to red wire terminal in connector.
3. Connect a test light across ground and the three wires shown in **Fig. 6.**
4. Compare results with those shown in **Fig. 7.**
5. If indications are not satisfactory, replace switch.

Air Bag System

INDEX

Page No.

Air Bag System Disarming & Arming 50-56
Arming 50-56
Disarming 50-56
Collision Inspection 50-58
SIPS System 50-58
SRS System 50-58
Component Locations 50-58
Component Service 50-58
Air Bag Or Seat Belt Tensioner Assembly Disposal 50-61
Contact Reel, Replace 50-59
Crash Sensor & Standby Power Unit 50-60
Drivers Air Bag, Replace 50-58
Passengers Air Bag, Replace 50-59
Seat Belt Tensioners, Replace 50-60
Sensor Module, Replace 50-59
Side Impact Air Bag System Disposal 50-61
Side Impact Air Bag System, Replace 50-60
Description & Operation 50-56
Drivers & Passengers Air Bag & Front Seat Belt Tensioner Systems 50-56
Side Impact Air Bag System 50-57
Diagnosis & Testing 50-58
Precautions 50-57
Technical Service Bulletins 50-62
Springing Sound From Steering Wheel 50-62
Tightening Specifications: 50-65

AIR BAG SYSTEM DISARMING & ARMING

Disarming

On models equipped with microprocessor radios,always turn them off before disconnecting or connecting the battery ground cable to prevent radio damage.

To disarm air bag/Supplemental Restraint System (SRS), turn ignition Off, then disconnect battery ground cable. Wait at least 10 seconds after disconnection prior to performing any service procedures. The SRS is designed to retain enough deployment voltage for a short time even after the battery ground cable has been disconnected. Performing service before the minimum 10 second lapse may cause unwanted deployment and possible injury.

When beginning service operations on vehicles with side impact air bags (SIPS) always lock the (SIPS) bag with the transport safety device. Lift up the seat pocket then lift the front edge and push the seat pocket backward. Remove the safety device from its holder and attach it to the sensor unit as shown in Fig. 1. Failure can cause damage to the crash sensor.

Arming

1. Connect battery ground cable.
2. **On models equipped with SIPS bag,** remove transport safety device from sensor.
3. **On all models,** wait at least 10 minutes, then place ignition switch in the ON position.
4. Warning lamp should illuminate for approximately 10 seconds and then go off.
5. If warning lamp operates as specified, air bag system is functioning properly. If lamp does not operate as specified, refer to MOTOR's Air Bag Manual for diagnosis of the air bag system.

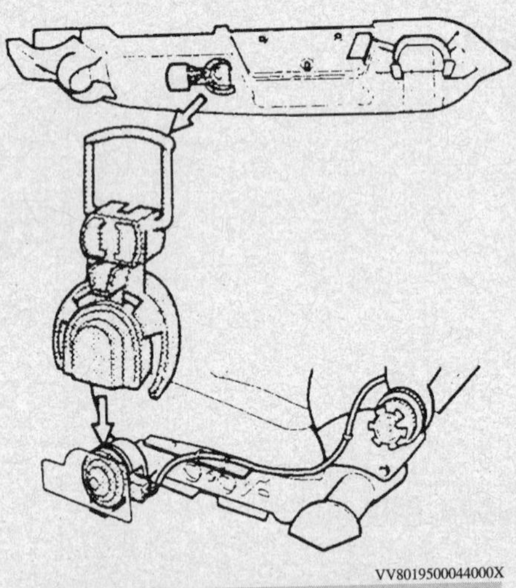
VV8019500044000X

Fig. 1 SIPS bag transport safety device installation

DESCRIPTION & OPERATION

DRIVERS & PASSENGERS AIR BAG & FRONT SEAT BELT TENSIONER SYSTEMS

The Supplemental Restraint System (SRS), **Figs. 2 and 3,** consists of inflatable air bag assemblies, mounted in the center of the steering wheel and in the righthand portion of the instrument panel. The rear of each assembly incorporates a gas generator which inflates the air bag. A crash sensor records deceleration of the car. A standby power unit supplies the system with power to inflate the bag if the normal power supply is interrupted.

Front seat belt tensioners are also used. The tensioners are activated at the same time the air bags are deployed. Upon activation, the front seat belt tensioners will take up any slack in the belt to restrict the forward movement of the driver and passenger. The system also includes a knee bolster.

If deceleration recorded by the crash sensor is sufficiently high, the unit delivers a current which triggers the gas generator, producing a quantity of non-toxic nitrogen which fills the air bag and triggers the tensioners. Immediately after the collision, the gas is released through a ventilation hole and the bag slowly collapses.

SYSTEM COMPONENTS

Sensor Module

The sensor module also functions as a diagnostic unit. The sensor module incorporates piezoelectric sensor elements to detect deceleration, microprocessors, a memory function which retains information even after the power supply has failed and a standby power supply. To ensure proper operation of the sensor module, it is essential the device be properly secured to the floor. Otherwise the device will record only its own deceleration rather than the value measured from the moment of impact. The device is grounded through a terminal connected to one of its mounting screws. It is essential that there is good contact to the floor panel. The air bag system is monitored continuously by a microprocessor in the sensor module.

The sensor module also contains a back-up power supply which stores sufficient energy to operate system even if the battery fails. This may occur, for example, if a lead is pinched or if the battery is damaged in a collision. Energy is stored only for about a second after the power supply has failed and is sufficient to trigger the gas generator in the event of a collision.

Air Bag Assembly

The air bag assembly consists of an inflatable bag and a gas generator. When the connector is opened, the terminals are

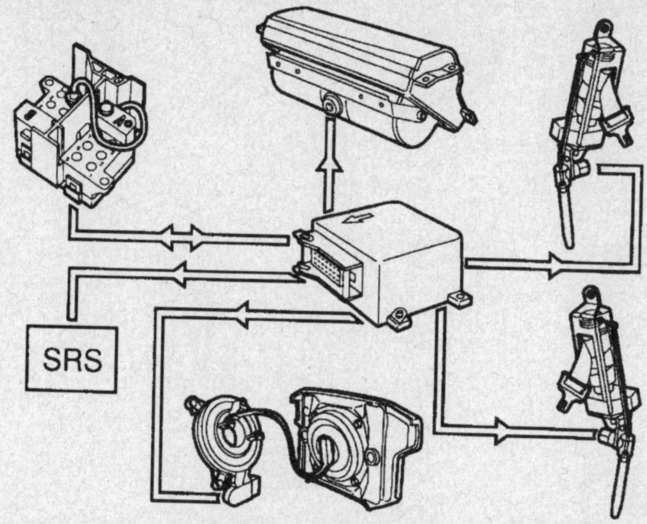
SRS

VV8019400047000X

Fig. 2 Air bag system/SRS. 1994–95

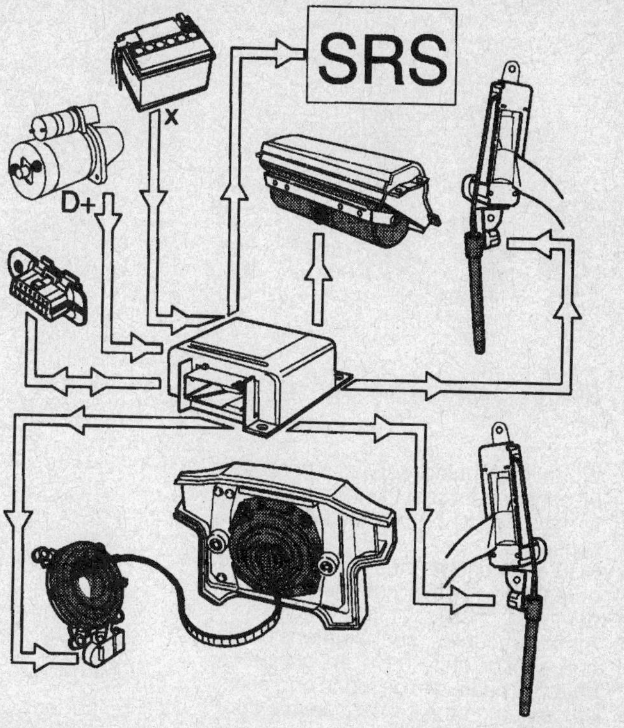
SRS
X
D+

VV8019600142000X

Fig. 3 Air bag system/SRS. 1996

short-circuited to prevent inadvertent system operation by static electricity or careless handling. The bag assembly must never be disassembled.

Inflatable Bag

The volume of the inflated bag is approximately 18 gallons for the drivers air bag, and 42 gallons for the passengers air bag. The bag is folded on top of the gas generator. The rear of the bag is provided with an opening through which gas is discharged.

Inflator

The inflator consists of a gas generator and an igniter. It contains a material, which when ignited, generates the nitrogen gas which inflates the bag. As already described, the bag is rapidly inflated by this gas. The inflator is a sealed unit, made of aluminum or steel.

Seat Belt Tensioners

The seat belt tensioners are attached to the belt reel at each of the B-pillars. Upon activation the belts are tightened by means of cables acting on the seat belt reels. The maximum degree of tightening is three and one half inches.

Contact Reel

The contact reel consists of a spirally wound wire coil to ensure the most reliable contact between the gas generator and crash sensor. This reel is mounted on the steering column.

Wiring Between Crash Sensor & Air Bag Modules

If a connector in the circuit between the air bag module(s) and crash sensor is opened, the terminals nearest the bag assembly are automatically short-circuited by a spring. The terminal pins are gold plated for maximum conductivity.

SRS Warning Lamp

The system is monitored continuously by a microprocessor in the crash sensor. Any fault or condition which occurs is stored in memory, while the instrument panel warning lamp also lights. The warning lamp lights together with other lamps on the panel to test its integrity when the ignition is turned On. When the engine is started the lamp goes off, indicating the system is operating properly.

If the engine is not started after turning the ignition On, the lamp will go off after approximately 10 seconds. If the lamp remains lit while driving, an SRS condition is indicated. Once a condition has been detected, the warning lamp will remain lit until the condition has been corrected and the memory cleared. If the lamp fails to light, this indicates a faulty bulb or a shorted lead.

SIDE IMPACT AIR BAG SYSTEM

On some 1995 850 models, and all 1996 models, a side impact air bag system, **Fig. 4,**is available. The system is located on the outside edges of the seat back on the driver and front passenger seats. **This system is mechanically triggered, requires no electrical hook up, and does not incorporate a diagnostic system or a warning lamp.** All components are contained in the seats. If a side impact of sufficient force is encountered, the seat base mounted sensor will trigger the system. When contacted by the door, the pressure plate will deform the aluminum cover, pushing on the firing pin, releasing the ignition charge. This charge creates an impulse which is routed through the firing circuit. The charge ignites a power charge in the gas generator. The gas charge is routed through the firing chamber tube, inflating the air bag. Approximately three milliseconds after the first gas generator has been activated, the second gas generator is activated to maintain pressure and volume of the inflated air bag module. A vent hole in the bag cushion will allow the bag to slowly collapse after the activation.

PRECAUTIONS

Prior to disconnecting any SRS electrical connector or servicing any system components or other components located near an SRS electrical connector, the system must be disarmed. Refer to "Air Bag System Disarming & Arming" for procedure.

1. **On models equipped with microprocessor radios,**always switch radio off before disconnecting or connecting battery ground cable to prevent damage to radio.
2. **On all models,** when disconnecting or connecting SRS electrical connectors, the ignition switch must be in the off position and the battery ground cable must be disconnected.
3. The contact reel must not be turned more than three turns in either direction as damage to contact reel may result.
4. When making welding repairs, always disconnect the driver side air bag, passenger side air bag and seat belt tensioner electrical connectors.

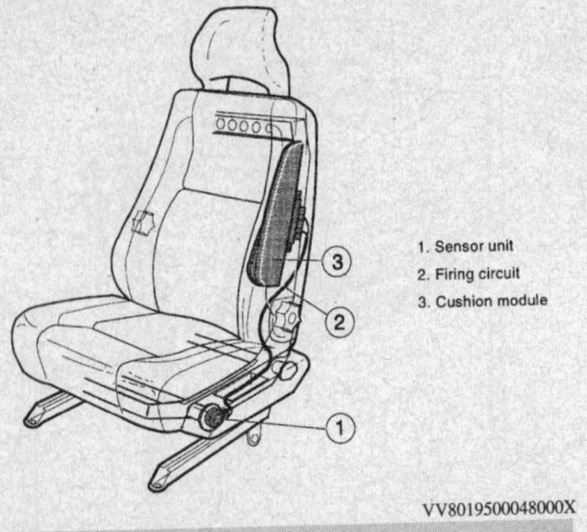
1. Sensor unit
2. Firing circuit
3. Cushion module
VV8019500048000X

Fig. 4 Side impact air bag system

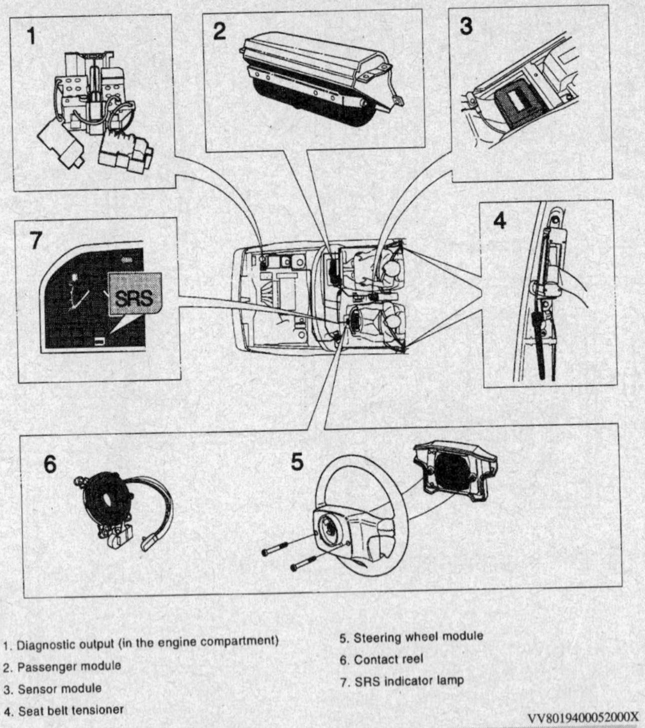
SRS
1. Diagnostic output (in the engine compartment)
2. Passenger module
3. Sensor module
4. Seat belt tensioner
5. Steering wheel module
6. Contact reel
7. SRS indicator lamp
VV8019400052000X

Fig. 5 Air bag/SRS components. 1993–95 850

5. When preforming service operations on or near front seat the transport safety device must be connected to SIPS sensor.
6. SRS components must not be opened or repaired. Always install new components.
7. Air bag modules, seat belt tensioners and sensor units have an expiration date. This date can be found on a sticker located on the center console door or the lefthand B pillar.
8. Gold plated connector terminals cannot be repaired. If lead becomes dislodged from connector, the wiring harness must be replaced.
9. SRS wiring cannot be repaired or spliced. If damaged, replace wiring harness.
10. Do not use ohmmeter or other current producing device to measure resistance.
11. Prior to checking resistance of system components or wiring, disconnect air bag modules and seat belt tensioners.
12. If air bag module, seat belt tensioner or sensor unit has been dropped, do not install component into vehicle.
13. Do not leave an undeployed air bag module or seat belt tensioner unattended if work is interrupted. Install into vehicle as soon as unit is removed from packaging.
14. Always place a removed air bag module so that the horn pad or air bag cover is facing upward.
15. Air bag modules and seat belt tensioners must not be exposed to grease, or cleaned with any type of cleansing agent.
16. Do not expose air bag modules or seat belt tensioners to high temperatures even for brief periods. Keep unit clear of all heat sources.

COMPONENT LOCATIONS

Refer to **Figs. 5 through 8** for air bag/SRS component locations.

DIAGNOSIS & TESTING

Refer to MOTOR's Air Bag Manual for system diagnosis and testing.

COLLISION INSPECTION

SRS SYSTEM

If deployment has taken place, the driver side air bag, passenger side air bag, instrument panel cover, seat belt tensioners including belts, steering wheel, cable reel, crash sensor and knee bolsters must be replaced. If SRS wiring or electrical connectors are damaged, replace SRS wiring harness.

SIPS SYSTEM

If the Side Impact Protection System (SIPS) has deployed, it must be replaced. If this system has not deployed, inspect system components as follows:

1. Lift front edge of seat pocket and push pocket rearward.
2. Remove safety device from holder inside pocket, **Fig. 9,** then attach safety device to sensor unit.
3. Visually inspect exposed system components for damage to firing tube and protective sleeve.
4. Remove sensor unit as described under "Side Impact Air Bag System, Replace."
5. Remove safety device from sensor unit.
6. Using a suitable caliper, measure sensor unit height, **Fig. 10.**
7. Sensor unit height must be at least 1.06 inches.
8. If any side impact system components are damaged, the complete system must be replaced.
9. Install sensor unit as described under "Side Impact Air Bag System, Replace."

On 1996 models, there are two additional inspection procedures to determine if the seat belt tensioners have deployed.

Begin by pulling out and releasing the seat belts. If a belt rolls in and out normally, it is operating properly. If a belt sticks, jerks, rolls up improperly or does not roll at all, there probably has been a deployment. For the second procedure, proceed as follows:

1. Disarm SRS as described under "Air Bag System Disarming and Arming."
2. Remove "B" post inner panel.
3. **On 850 models,** push a wire into bottom of belt tensioner tube, **Fig. 11.**
4. **On 960 models,** push a wire into top of belt tensioner tube, **Fig. 12.**
5. If a tensioner has been deployed, replace both tensioner assemblies.

COMPONENT SERVICE

DRIVERS AIR BAG, REPLACE

1. Disarm SRS as described under "Air Bag System Disarming and Arming."
2. **On 1994–95 models,** remove air bag module to steering wheel Torx attaching screws from rear of steering wheel.
3. **On 1996 models, loosen, but do not remove** the T30 Torx screws from their countersunk holes in rear of steering wheel.
4. **On all models,** carefully pull module from steering wheel, then disconnect connector, **Fig. 13.**
5. Connect test resistor No. 998 8695 to air bag connector.
6. Loosen, but do not remove steering

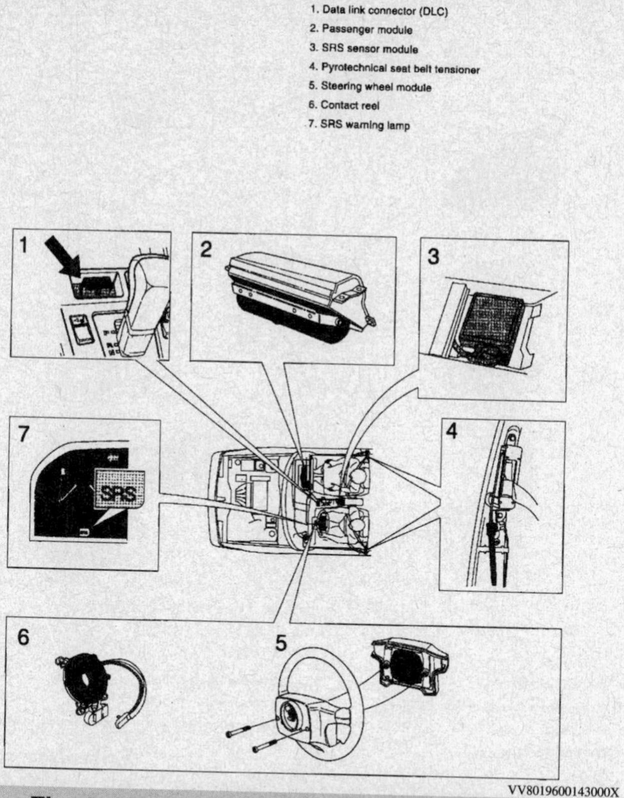
1. Data link connector (DLC)
2. Passenger module
3. SRS sensor module
4. Pyrotechnical seat belt tensioner
5. Steering wheel module
6. Contact reel
7. SRS warning lamp
1
2
3
4
5
6
7
SRS
VV8019600143000X

Fig. 6 Air bag/SRS components. 1996 850

wheel center bolt. **Do not turn steering wheel when contact reel is locked,** or the reel pin will break off.

7. Reverse procedure to install. Tighten air bag module attaching screws to specifications. After completing installation, arm SRS as described under "Air Bag System Disarming and Arming."

PASSENGERS AIR BAG, REPLACE

850 Series

1. Disarm SRS as described under "Air Bag System Disarming and Arming."
2. Remove glove compartment door, then remove attaching screws and compartment.
3. Disconnect air bag module connector.
4. From glove compartment opening, remove air bag module attaching screws, **Fig. 14.**
5. Remove defroster outlet retaining screws, **Fig. 15.**
6. **On 1994–95 models,** remove both air duct nozzles from righthand side of instrument panel.
7. **On 1996 models,** remove both air duct nozzles from righthand side and the driver side window defroster vent from instrument panel.
8. **On all models,** remove radio speakers from lefthand and righthand side of instrument panel.
9. Remove retaining screws located under radio speakers, **Fig. 16.**
10. Remove upper pad attaching screws, then remove pad and air bag, **Fig. 17.**
11. Remove eight Torx screws and six nuts retraining air bag to instrument panel pad, **Fig. 18.**
12. Reverse procedure to install, noting the following:
    a. Position two ft. of electrical wire through straps, **Fig. 19**
    b. Position air bag into place while keeping wire stretched tight.
    c. Place screws in module to secure position, then release and remove wire.
    d. Tighten attaching bolts and nuts to torque listed in "Tightening Specifications."
    e. After completing installation, arm SRS as described under "Air Bag System Disarming and Arming."

960

1. Disarm SRS as described under "Air Bag System Disarming and Arming."
2. Remove trim from above glove compartment.
3. Disconnect connector from below passengers air bag.
4. Remove two air bag unit attaching screws, then remove air bag module, **Figs. 20 and 21.**
5. Reverse procedure to install. After completing installation, arm SRS as described under "Air Bag System Disarming and Arming."

CONTACT REEL, REPLACE

1. Position front wheels in the straight–ahead position.
2. Disarm SRS as described under "Air Bag System Disarming and Arming."
3. **On 1996 models, loosen, but do not remove** the T30 Torx screws from their countersunk holes in the rear of steering wheel.
4. **On all models,** remove drivers air bag as described under "Drivers Air Bag, Replace."
5. **Prior to removing steering wheel, ensure front wheels are in the straight–ahead position, then place alignment marks on steering shaft and steering wheel hub for use during installation.**
6. Remove steering wheel retaining nut, then remove wheel.
7. Remove steering column upper and lower covers.
8. Disconnect contact reel connector and horn wire.
9. Remove three contact reel attaching screws and reel.
10. Reverse procedure to install, noting the following:
    a. **On 1994–95 models,** prior to installation, rotate contact reel fully to right, then rotate to left three turns. **On 850 and 960 models,** contact reel screw hole should be at the one O'clock position, **Fig. 22. On 940 models,** contact reel screw hole should be at the eight O'clock position, **Fig. 23.** Tighten lock screw to hold in this position.
    b. **On 1996 models,** prior to installation, rotate contact reel fully to left, then two full turns to the right. Continue turning ¾ turn to the screw hole, which should now be at the one O'clock position. Tighten lock screw to hold in this position.
    c. **On all models,** when installing steering wheel, align hub and shaft marks made during removal.
    d. Tighten contact reel attaching screws and steering wheel nut specifications.
    e. After completing installation, arm SRS as described under "Air Bag System Disarming and Arming."

SENSOR MODULE, REPLACE

850

1. Disarm SRS as described under "Air Bag System Disarming and Arming."
2. Turn ignition Off, then disconnect battery ground cable.
3. Remove ashtray, cigarette lighter holder and center console, **Fig. 24.**
4. Remove sensor module attaching screws, then module.
5. **Never touch sensor module pins: static discharge may damage module.**
6. Reverse procedure to install, noting the following:
    a. Ensure arrow on sensor module faces toward front of vehicle. Tighten attaching screws to specifications. **Sensor must be well grounded and mounted securely to ensure proper air bag operation.**
    b. After completing installation, arm

SRS as described under "Air Bag System Disarming and Arming."

c. Clear DTCs.

1994–95 940 & 960

1. Disarm SRS as described under "Air Bag System Disarming and Arming."
2. Remove drivers seat rail retaining screws, then tilt seat backward.
3. Fold back carpet, then move air duct to allow access to sensor module attaching screws.
4. Remove sensor module attaching screws, then module.
5. **Never touch sensor module pins: static discharge may damage module.**
6. Reverse procedure to install, noting the following:
   a. Tighten attaching screws to specifications. **Sensor must be mounted securely to ensure proper air bag operation.**
   b. After completing installation, arm SRS as described under "Air Bag System Disarming and Arming."
   c. Clear DTCs.

1996 960

1. Disarm SRS as described under "Air Bag System Disarming and Arming."
2. Secure the Side Impact Protection System (SIPS) with transport safety device, **Fig. 25.**
3. Remove driver side front seat assembly.
4. Roll back floor carpet, remove three T30 Torx module mounting screws, then the module.
5. **Never touch sensor module pins: static discharge may damage module.**
6. Reverse procedure to install, noting the following:
   a. Install module connector as shown, **Fig. 26, before module is mounted into place.**
   b. Mount module into place with arrow facing front of vehicle.
   c. Tighten attaching screws to specifications.
   d. After completing installation, arm SRS as described under "Air Bag System Disarming and Arming."

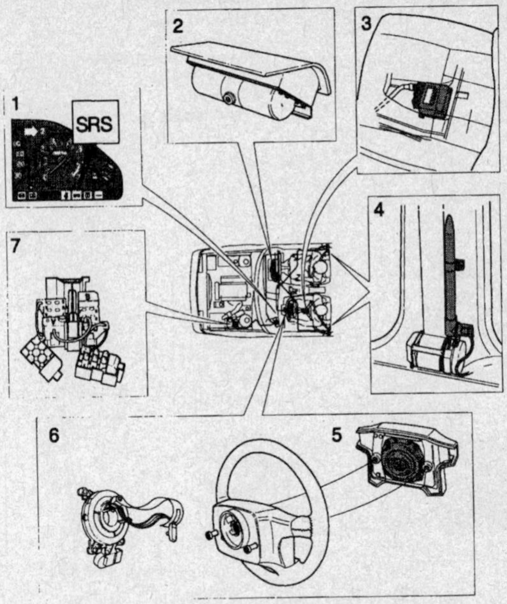
SRS
1
2
3
4
5
6
7

1. SRS indicator lamp
2. Passenger module (certain models)
3. Sensor unit
4. Seat belt tensioner
5. Steering wheel module
6. Contact reel
7. Diagnostic output (in the engine compartment)

VV8019400053000X

Fig. 7 Air bag/SRS components. 1993–95 940/960

CRASH SENSOR & STANDBY POWER UNIT

240

The crash sensor has an eight digit identification number which must always be quoted when ordering new parts. Ground connection is direct by a short black lead secured by one retaining screw. It is extremely important the screw makes good contact to body. Remove crash sensor and standby power unit as follows:

1. Turn ignition switch to Off position, then disconnect battery ground cable.
2. Loosen drivers seat bolt, then tilt backwards. Lift carpet to reach crash sensor and wiring.
3. Disconnect electrical connectors at center console. **Never disconnect connector from crash sensor. This is extremely important to maintain maximum reliability of contact.**
4. Remove tape from standby power unit, then disconnect electrical connector and clip, **Fig. 27.**
5. Remove crash sensor retaining screws and release cable clamp.
6. Remove crash sensor and wiring harness.
7. Reverse procedure to install, noting the following:
   a. Use original screws. **Torque** to 8 ft. lbs.
   b. Crash sensor connector is held in place by a fixture which is part of the body where it bolts. Place carefully to avoid damaging connector.
   c. Check for fault codes as described under "Fault Tracing (SRS) System."

SEAT BELT TENSIONERS, REPLACE

1. Disarm SRS as described under "Air Bag System Disarming and Arming."
2. Push front seat forward.
3. Remove B-pillar inner panel.
4. Remove seat side pocket, lift at front and push rearward.
5. Remove seat belt collar bolt.
6. Disconnect belt tensioner connector.
7. Remove seat belt reel to B–pillar attaching bolts.
8. Remove plunger tube attaching screw.
9. Thread seat belt through slot in B–pillar panel.
10. Reverse procedure to install, noting the following:
    a. Tighten attaching screws to specification.
    b. After completing installation, arm SRS as described under "Air Bag System Disarming and Arming."

SIDE IMPACT AIR BAG SYSTEM, REPLACE

1. Disarm SRS as described under "Air Bag System Disarming and Arming."
2. Lift front edge of seat pocket and push pocket rearward.
3. Remove safety device from holder inside pocket, **Fig. 9,** then attach safety device to sensor unit.
4. Remove cover (B) from front edge of front seat rail, **Fig. 28.**
5. Remove four front seat rail attaching bolts.
6. Disconnect connectors to seat heater and seat belt buckle.
7. Lift front seat upward and out of vehicle.
8. Remove three screws from each side of seat, then detach seat back from bottom cushion. Remove seat back angle and lumbar support adjustment knobs.
9. Remove upholstery clamps from outside upholstery and between upholstery and padding.
10. Cut both firing tube ties, **Fig. 29. Note routing of tube and tie locations for use during installation.**
11. Remove two Torx screws attaching air bag module to seat back frame, then remove air bag module, **Fig. 29.**
12. Remove sensor unit Torx attaching screw.

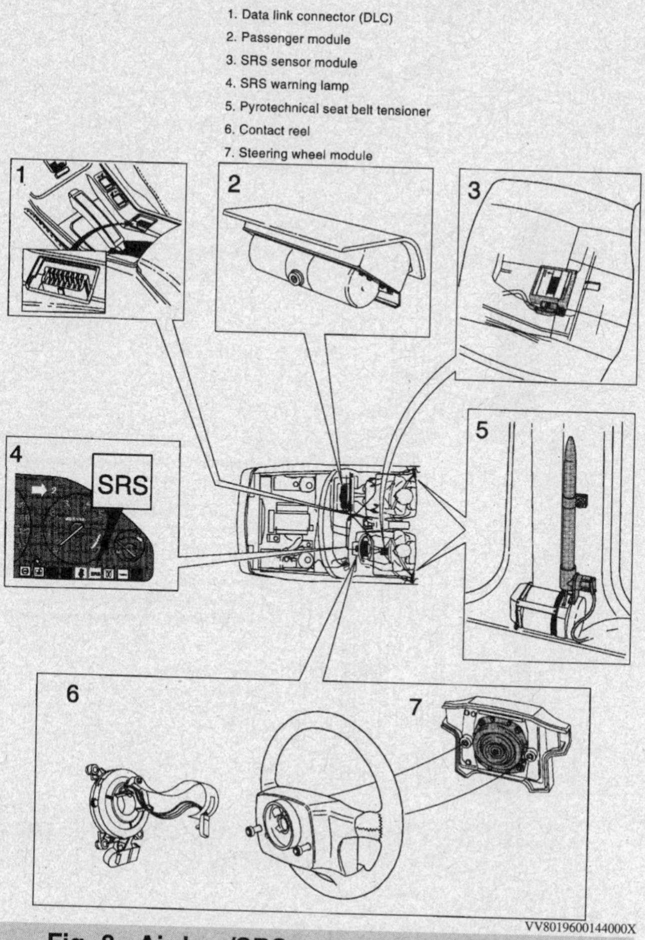
1. Data link connector (DLC)
2. Passenger module
3. SRS sensor module
4. SRS warning lamp
5. Pyrotechnical seat belt tensioner
6. Contact reel
7. Steering wheel module
1
2
3
4
SRS
5
6
7
VV8019600144000X

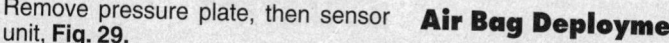

Fig. 8 Air bag/SRS components. 1996 960

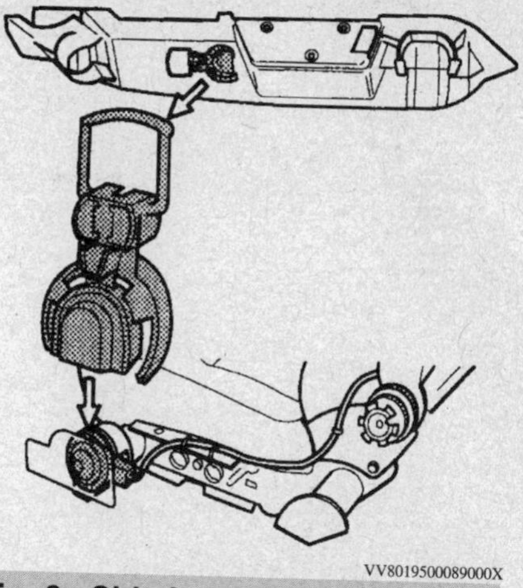
VV8019500089000X

Fig. 9 Side impact air bag safety device installation

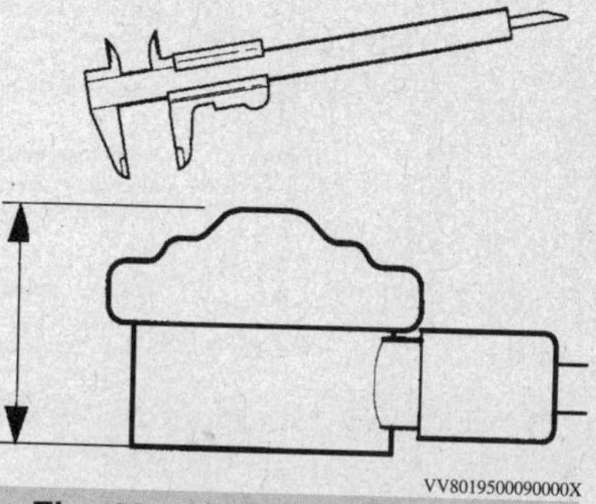
VV8019500090000X

Fig. 10 Side impact air bag sensor unit height measurement

13. Remove pressure plate, then sensor unit, **Fig. 29.**
14. Remove side impact air bag system from seat.
15. Reverse procedure to install, noting the following:
    a. Tighten attaching screws to specifications. **Tighten outer rear bolt last.**
    b. Do not remove manual seat adjuster rail cotter pin: this will affect SIPS bag function.
    c. After completing installation, arm SRS as described under "Air Bag System Disarming and Arming."
    d. Remove safety device from sensor unit.

AIR BAG OR SEAT BELT TENSIONER ASSEMBLY DISPOSAL

In the event an air bag assembly or seat belt tensioner must be disposed of, it is recommended that the unit be triggered without removing the system from the vehicle. **Adequate eye and ear protection should be worn at all times when conducting the following procedures.**

Air Bag Deployment

1. Place vehicle outdoors, then disconnect battery ground cable.
2. Open all windows and doors.
3. Ensure air bag assembly is firmly mounted to vehicle and there is no loose debris around unit.
4. Connect two 20 ft. long wires to twin terminal ignition connector of air bag module to be deployed.
5. Working from 20 ft away, connect wires to terminals of a 12 volt power source to trigger the inflator. **Ensure no people, animals or objects are within 20 feet of vehicle when air bag deploys.**
6. If air bag or seat belt tensioner does do not deploy, disconnect wires from power source. Use extreme care when inspecting wiring.
7. In some cases the drivers air bag contact reel is damaged, and it may be necessary to splice the wires going directly to air bag assembly. However, unit must remain securely mounted in steering wheel while being deployed.

Seat Belt Tensioner Deployment

1. Place vehicle outdoors, then disconnect battery ground cable.
2. Open all windows and doors.
3. **On 960 models,** remove B–pillar trim panel
4. **On all models,** disconnect belt tensioner connector.
5. Ensure seat belt tensioner is firmly mounted to vehicle.
6. Connect two 20 ft. long wires to twin terminal ignition connector of seat belt tensioner to be deployed.
7. Working from 20 ft away, connect wires to terminals of a 12 volt power source to trigger the inflator. **Ensure no people, animals or objects are within 20 feet of vehicle when unit deploys.**
8. If unit does not deploy, disconnect wires from power source. Use extreme care to inspect wiring and repeat procedure.

SIDE IMPACT AIR BAG SYSTEM DISPOSAL

Adequate eye and ear protection

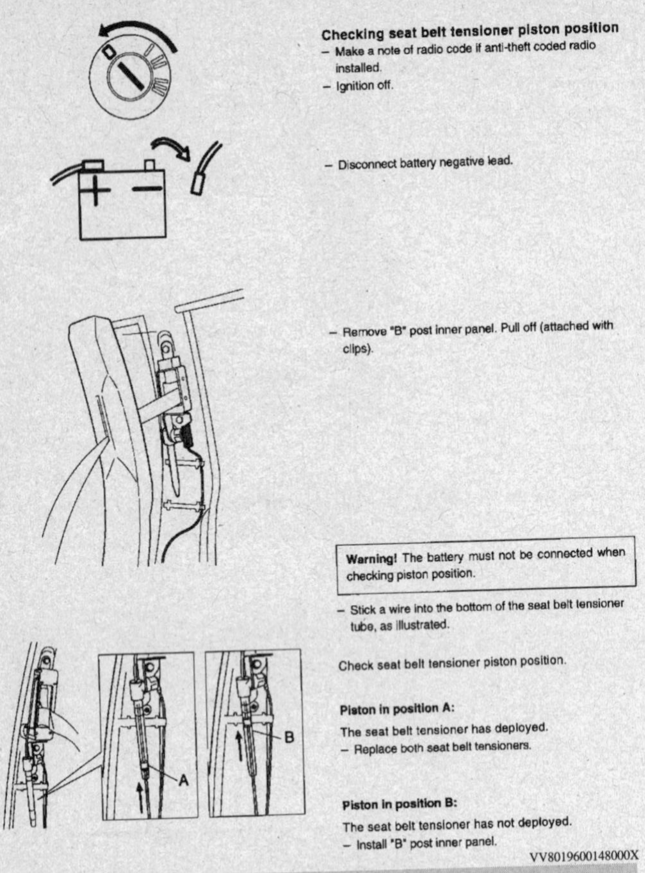
Checking seat belt tensioner piston position
– Make a note of radio code if anti-theft coded radio installed.
– Ignition off.
– Disconnect battery negative lead.
– Remove "B" post inner panel. Pull off (attached with clips).
Warning! The battery must not be connected when checking piston position.
– Stick a wire into the bottom of the seat belt tensioner tube, as illustrated.
Check seat belt tensioner piston position.
Piston in position A:
The seat belt tensioner has deployed.
– Replace both seat belt tensioners.
Piston in position B:
The seat belt tensioner has not deployed.
– Install "B" post inner panel.
A
B
VV8019600148000X

Fig. 11 Seat belt tensioner deployment inspection. 1996 850

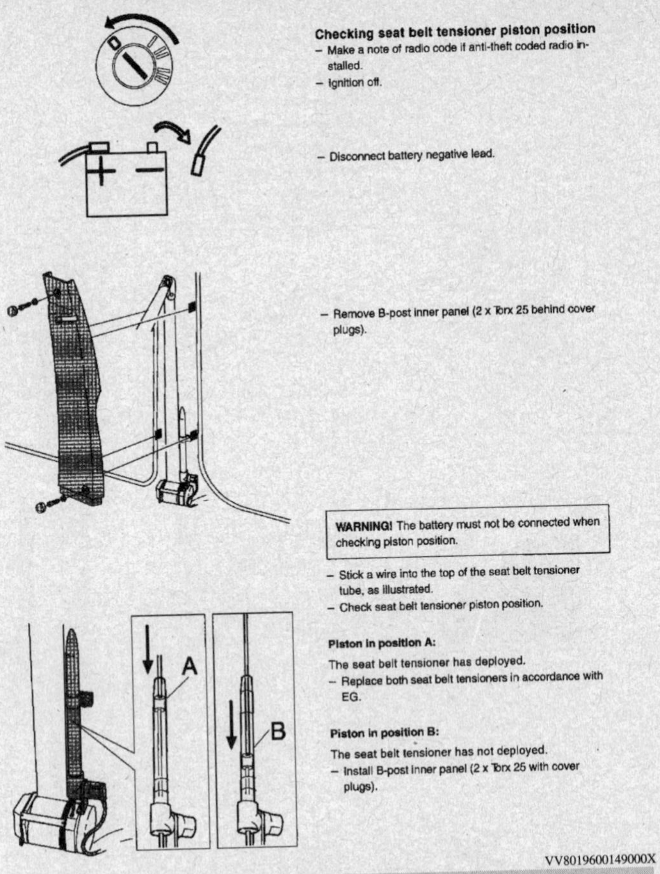
Checking seat belt tensioner piston position
– Make a note of radio code if anti-theft coded radio installed.
– Ignition off.
– Disconnect battery negative lead.
– Remove B-post inner panel (2 x Torx 25 behind cover plugs).
WARNING! The battery must not be connected when checking piston position.
– Stick a wire into the top of the seat belt tensioner tube, as illustrated.
– Check seat belt tensioner piston position.
Piston in position A:
The seat belt tensioner has deployed.
– Replace both seat belt tensioners in accordance with EG.
Piston in position B:
The seat belt tensioner has not deployed.
– Install B-post inner panel (2 x Torx 25 with cover plugs).
A
B
VV8019600149000X

Fig. 12 Seat belt tensioner deployment inspection. 1996 960

should be worn at all times when performing the following procedures.

With Side Impact Air Bag System Installed On Vehicle

The following procedure should be performed if vehicle is to be scrapped:

1. Turn ignition Off.
2. Lift front edge of seat pocket and push pocket rearward.
3. Remove safety device from holder inside pocket, **Fig. 9,** then attach device to sensor unit.
4. Remove sensor unit from seat.
5. Free firing cables from ties and clips.
6. Close front doors and windows.
7. Position sensor unit on floor behind front seat, **Fig. 30.**
8. Remove safety device from sensor unit.
9. Ensure no people, animals or objects are inside or around vehicle.
10. While standing outside vehicle, strike middle of sensor unit with a hammer, **Fig. 31.**

With Side Impact Air Bag System Removed From Vehicle

1. Ensure safety device is attached to sensor unit.
2. Secure air bag module in a suitable vise. Position air unit so that cushion is facing away from sensor unit.
3. Ensure no people or animals are near air bag unit, and that no loose objects are nearby.
4. Position sensor unit as far away from air bag unit as possible.
5. While standing as far away from air bag unit as possible, strike middle of sensor unit with a hammer, **Fig. 31.**

TECHNICAL SERVICE BULLETINS

SPRINGING SOUND FROM STEERING WHEEL

960, 1993-94 850 & 940

On these models, the drivers air bag may make springing noises.

To correct this condition, proceed as follows:

1. Remove air bag module. Refer to "Component Service" for procedure.
2. Replace four Torx bolts, (part No. 9157407-9) in retainers one at a time using old, thin plastic washers.
3. **Torque** bolts to 3.7 ft. lbs.

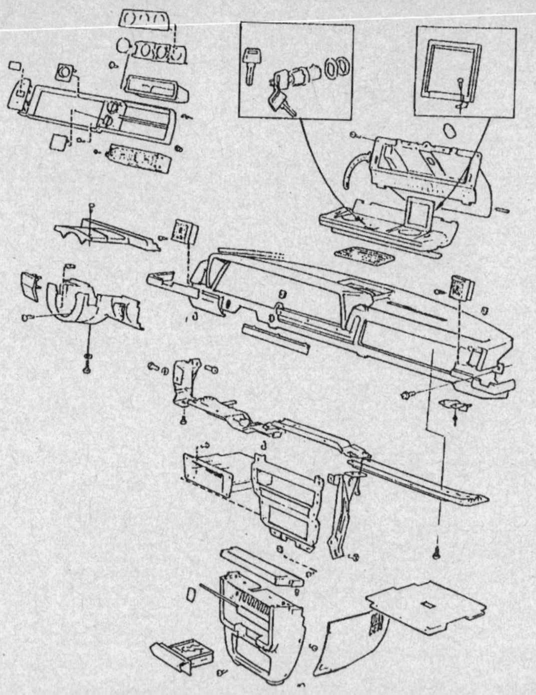
VV9149100001000X

Fig. 1 Exploded view of instrument panel. 240

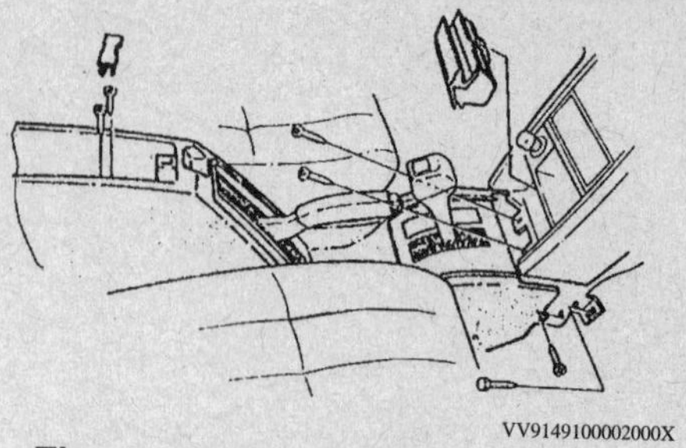
VV9149100002000X

Fig. 2 Center console removal. 940 & 960

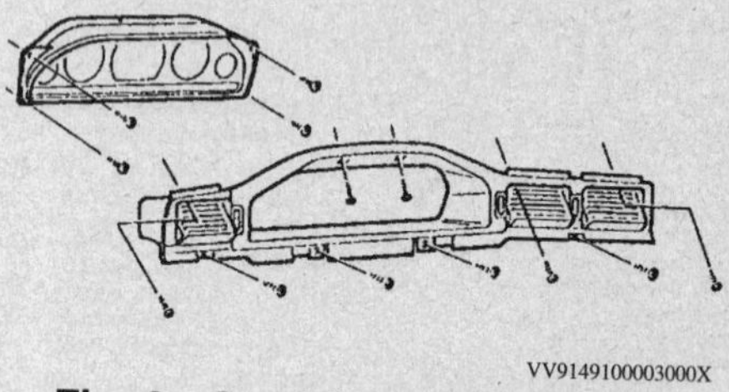
VV9149100003000X

Fig. 3 Combined instrument assembly removal. 940 & 960

Steering Columns

NOTE: On Air Bag Equipped Models, Refer To "Air Bag System Precautions" Located In The Front Of This Manual For System Disarming & Arming Procedures.

INDEX

	Page No.
Precautions	50-67
Air Bag Systems	50-67
Microprocessor Radios	50-67
Steering Column, Replace	50-67
850	50-67
940 & 960	50-67
Steering Column Service	50-68

PRECAUTIONS

AIR BAG SYSTEMS

Refer to "Air Bag System Precautions" in the front of this manual for system disarming and arming procedures.

MICROPROCESSOR RADIOS

On models equipped with microprocessor radios, always switch radio off before disconnecting or connecting battery ground cable to prevent damage to the radio.

STEERING COLUMN

REPLACE

940 & 960

1. Disconnect battery ground cable.
2. Remove upper and lower steering shaft joint clamp attaching screws and snap ring.
3. Push steering shaft in toward cowl to release it.
4. Remove steering wheel as described under "Steering Wheel, Replace." in the electrical section.
5. Remove upper and lower steering column casings.
6. Remove indicator and wiper switch levers.
7. Remove electrical connectors for indicators, wiper switch and horn.
8. Remove lower panel, heater hose under dashboard, then panel around ignition switch and heater controls.
9. Remove shear head bolts for steering column lock as follows:
   a. Center punch bolts and drill a hole of suitable diameter and depth for screw extractor tool.
   b. Remove attaching bolts.
10. Remove attaching screws for bearing plate, then loosen support bracket bolts.
11. Remove steering column lock as follows:
    a. Insert key and turn to position, then remove retaining screw.
    b. Press in locking tab and withdraw lock, then remove key and wiring electrical connector.
12. Pull down on bracket and lift out steering column guide, then remove steering column.
13. Reverse procedure to install.

850

1. Disconnect battery ground cable, then remove steering wheel as described in "Electrical" section.
2. Remove upper and lower steering column covers, controls for indicators and wipers, slip ring and ignition lock connector.
3. Insert ignition key into lock, turn key to position 1, press in lock lug using a 2 mm drift, then pull out ignition lock.

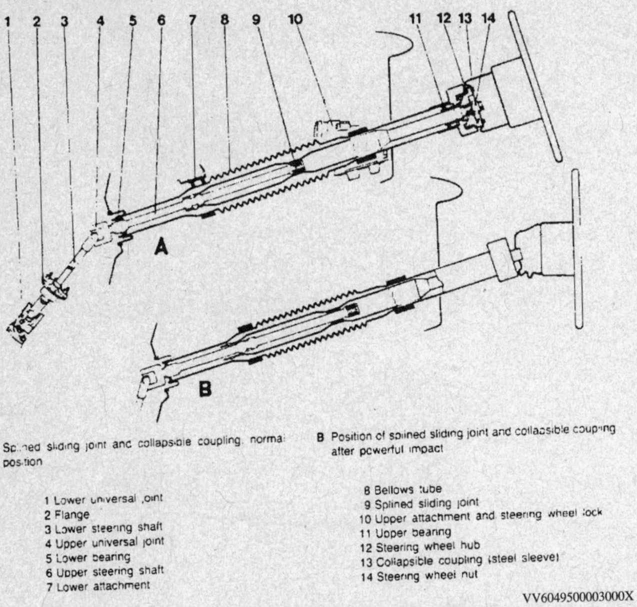
1 2 3 4 5 6 7 8 9 10 11 12 13 14
A
B
A Splined sliding joint and collapsible coupling, normal position
B Position of splined sliding joint and collapsible coupling after powerful impact
1 Lower universal joint
2 Flange
3 Lower steering shaft
4 Upper universal joint
5 Lower bearing
6 Upper steering shaft
7 Lower attachment
8 Bellows tube
9 Splined sliding joint
10 Upper attachment and steering wheel lock
11 Upper bearing
12 Steering wheel hub
13 Collapsible coupling (steel sleeve)
14 Steering wheel nut
VV6049500003000X

Fig. 1 Steering column. 240

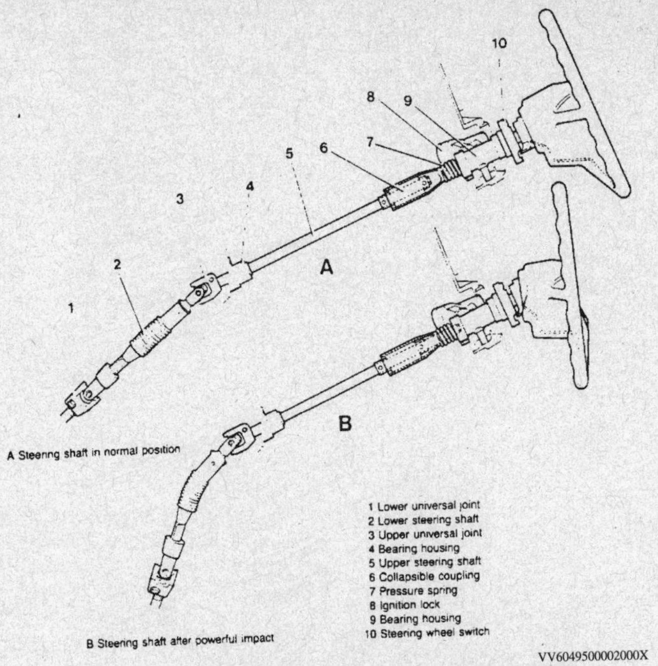
1 2 3 4 5 6 7 8 9 10
A
B
A Steering shaft in normal position
B Steering shaft after powerful impact
1 Lower universal joint
2 Lower steering shaft
3 Upper universal joint
4 Bearing housing
5 Upper steering shaft
6 Collapsible coupling
7 Pressure spring
8 Ignition lock
9 Bearing housing
10 Steering wheel switch
VV6049500002000X

Fig. 2 Steering column. 850, 940 & 960

4. Remove connector holder, then lower steering column cable harness in center.
5. Remove panel above pedals and the two nuts for steering column attachment, then bend support plate up slightly and remove washers.
6. Remove steering column from vehicle.
7. Reverse procedure to install.

STEERING COLUMN SERVICE

Refer to **Figs. 1 and 2,** for steering column service.

Power Steering

NOTE: On Air Bag Equipped Models, Refer To "Air Bag System Precautions" Located In The Front Of This Manual For System Disarming & Arming Procedures.

INDEX

	Page No.
Cam Gear Type	50-68
240	50-68
850	50-70
940 & 960	50-71
Precautions	50-68
Air Bag Systems	50-68
Microprocessor Radios	50-68
Tightening Specifications	50-73
ZF Type	50-72
Assemble	50-72
Disassemble	50-72

PRECAUTIONS

AIR BAG SYSTEMS

Refer to "Air Bag System Precautions" in the front of this manual for system disarming and arming procedures.

MICROPROCESSOR RADIOS

On models equipped with microprocessor radios, always switch radio off before disconnecting or connecting battery ground cable to prevent damage to the radio.

CAM GEAR TYPE

240

Disassemble

1. Remove steering rack assembly and, with fixture tool No. 5046, or equivalent, mount the unit in a vise.
2. Loosen left side rubber bellow and drain oil.
3. Loosen locknut, unscrew and remove left ball stud, locknut and bellow.
4. Unstake and unscrew left steering rod. Repeat steps 2-4 for right side.
5. Remove oil pipes.
6. Remove cover for pre-tensioning device. Remove pre-tensioning piston, O-ring and spring, **Fig. 1.**
7. Remove lower cover and spacer sleeve for pinion, bend up locking tab and remove nut. Unscrew inner bearing race with ball-retainer and outer race from pinion with tool No. 5049, or equivalent.
8. Remove valve housing cover, remove spring and lift off the valve housing.
9. Lift out the pinion.
10. Remove lock bolt for the right side housing, **Fig. 2.**
11. Pull off housing and connecting tube

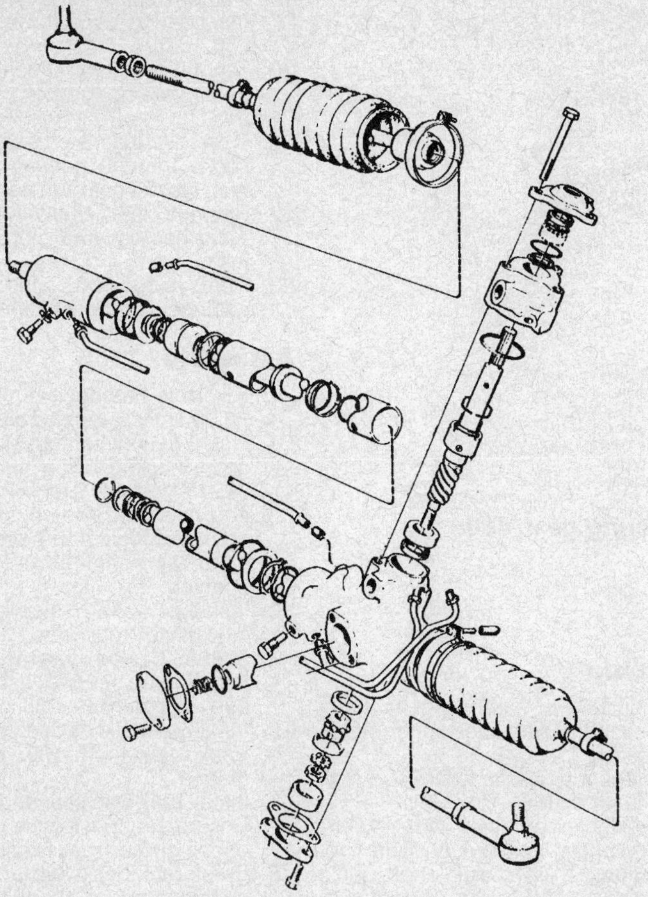

VV6029100001000X

Fig. 1 Exploded view of Cam Gear power steering gear. 240

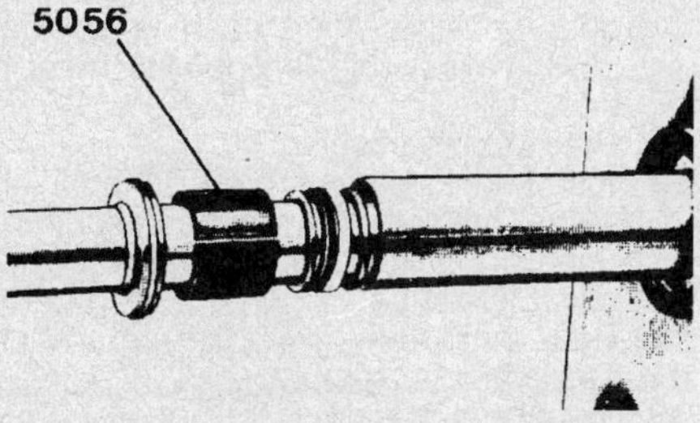
5056

VV6029100003000X

Fig. 3 Rack with seal & spacer rings installation. 240 w/Cam Gear power steering

from outer tube.

12. Pull out rack and bearing sleeve. Remove bearing sleeve from rack.
13. Remove lock bolt for left side housing. Pull outer tube from housing.
14. Pull inner tube out of housing.
15. Remove bushings, seals and O-rings.

Assemble

1. After installing new bushings, seals and O-rings, install inner tube and spacer in housing. Insert rack with seal and spacer rings in inner tube. Use tool No. 5056, or equivalent, as a spacer, **Fig. 3.** Press in seal and spacer rings using rack and tool No. 5056, or equivalent. Remove tool and install lock ring.

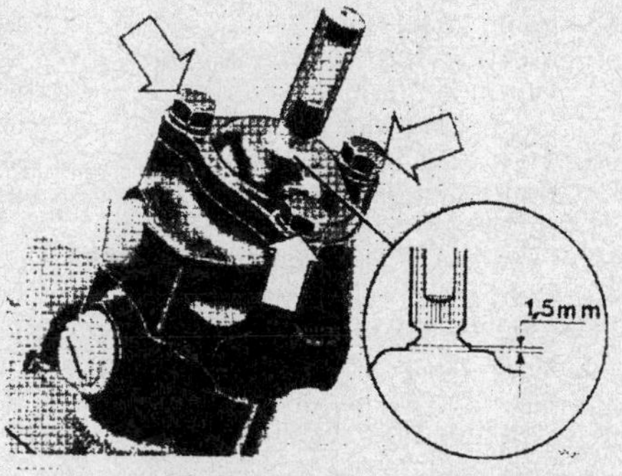
1,5mm

VV6029100004000X

Fig. 4 Shaft shoulder to cover face clearance. 240 w/Cam Gear power steering

2. Insert outer tube in left side housing.
3. Install lock bolt. Insert bearing sleeve in outer tube. Align hole in sleeve so it coincides with lock bolt hole in housing.
4. Install seal and plastic ring in bearing sleeve.
5. Insert connecting tube with rubber seal in right side housing.
6. Install right side housing with connecting tube and seal. Align hole in housing so it coincides with lock bolt hole in the outer tube. Install lock bolt.

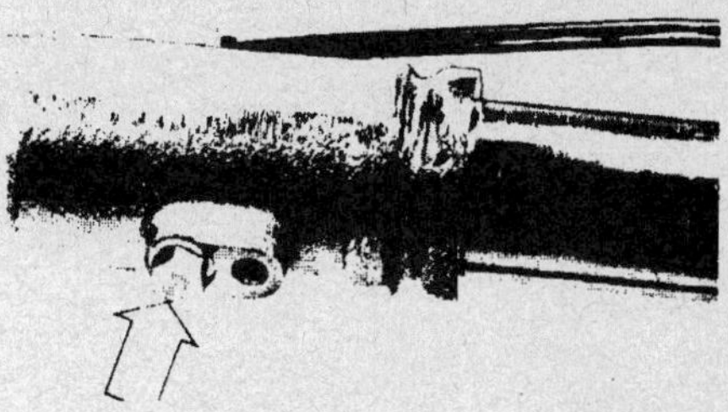

VV6029100002000X

Fig. 2 Lock bolt removal. 240 w/Cam Gear power steering

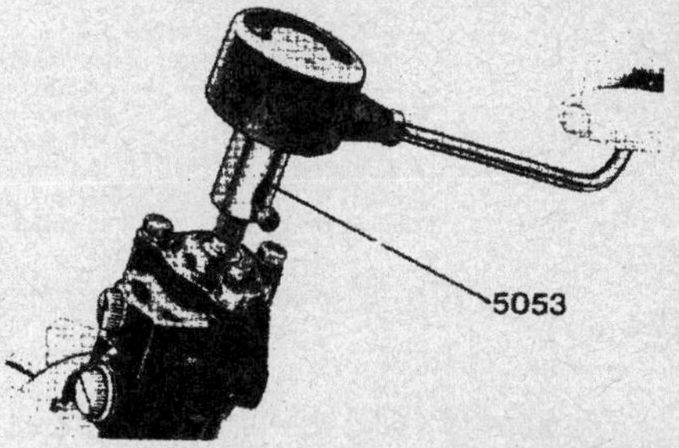
5053

VV6029100005000X

Fig. 5 Pinion torque inspection. 240

7. Install outer race for pinion lower bearing. Insert pinion.
8. Fit inner race and ball retainer on pinion using tool No. 5049, or equivalent. Install lock ring and nut. Do not lock the nut.
9. Install outer race and spacer sleeve. Measure distance between spacer ring and the machined surface of the housing. Selective thickness gaskets are available.
10. Install the proper gasket and install tool No. 5054, or equivalent, in place of the cover; install valve housing and coil spring big end first.
11. Install valve housing cover. Shaft shoulder should be 1.5 mm (.060 inch) above cover face, **Fig. 4.** Adjust position by moving lower bearing inner race with tool No. 5049, or equivalent.
12. Place pre-tensioning piston, without O-ring, in housing. Measure clearance between housing and piston faces while pressing piston against rack.
13. Select shims to equal clearance obtained in step 12 plus .05–.15 mm (.002–.006 inch). Install O-ring and spring for pre-tensioning piston. Install shims and cover.
14. Check pinion torque. Connect a torque gauge to the input shaft. Use tool No. 5053, or equivalent, to crank back and forth between end positions, **Fig. 5. Torque** should be 8–14 inch lbs. If torque in any place is excessive, stop rack in that position and readjust the pre-tensioning device. If rack jams with pre-tensioning device removed, rack is warped and must be replaced.
15. Install oil tubes.
16. Complete reassembly by installing steering rods, bellows and ball studs.

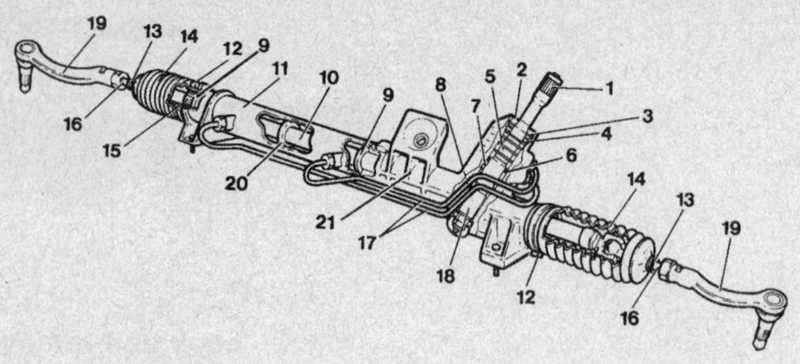

1. Input shaft (pinion shaft)
2. Dust cap
3. Seal
4. Roller bearing
5. Valve sleeve
6. Seal
7. Journal bearing
8. Preload piston
9. Rack seal
10. Rack
11. Cylindrical tube
12. Clamp
13. Clip
14. Protective boot (gaiter)
15. Journal bearing
16. Tie rod (track rod)
17. Fluid lines
18. Gear (pinion)
19. Outer ball bearing
20. Piston
21. Steering gear housing

VV6029200008000X

Fig. 6 Rack & pinion cam type steering gear. 850

Be sure to stake the steering rod ball joints.

Power Balance Test

1. Connect test equipment. Position pressure gauge at cowl so it can be read from the drivers seat.
2. Fill fluid reservoir. Start engine and turn steering wheel slowly from side to side to bleed the system. Refill reservoir, if necessary.
3. Remove steering wheel impact cover and attach a torque wrench to the steering wheel retaining nut. Start engine and turn torque wrench clockwise while watching the pressure gauge. Read torque the moment the pressure gauge approaches 170 psi. Repeat the procedure while turning to the left (counterclockwise).
4. If the torque difference between the left and right turns exceeds 8.8 inch lbs. shut the engine off and remove the locknut and lock washer from the pinion lower bearing. Install tool No. 5054, or equivalent.
5. If torque should be increased for left side and decreased for right side, unfold lock washer tab which was previously bent against the adjusting nut. Bend in the next tab to the left of the previously bent tab. To change pressure in the opposite direction, bend the tab to the right of the previously bent one. Turn adjustment nut so the lock can be installed. Bending the next tab to the left increases torque 4 inch lbs. for the left side and decreases equally for the right side. Use tool No. 5049, or equivalent. When reinstalling the lock, do not bend the tab tightly against the nut. Recheck the power balance as outlined in step 3. When balance is correct, bend the tab tightly against the nut, remove tool No. 5054, or equivalent, and replace the cover.

850

Disassemble

1. Clean outside of steering gear, then disconnect pressure lines and remove O-rings.
2. Mount steering gear in fixture tool No. 9995046, or equivalent.
3. Place suitable container under steering gear and drain through fluid line connections. Turn pinion shaft back and forth with socket wrench to pump out fluid.
4. Adjust rack to approximate middle position.
5. Remove outer ball joints, boot clamps, boots and seal rings, **Fig. 6.**
6. Remove lefthand side tie rod and loosen righthand tie rod a few turns.
7. Remove sealant covering rack bushing locking wire hole.
8. Turn end sleeve with hook spanner until locking wire emerges and can be removed.
9. Remove rack bushing locking wire.
10. Hold pinion shaft with socket wrench (socket No. 9995179, or equivalent). Blow compressed air through outer pipe connection until bushing and seal emerge. Tie rod will act as stop to prevent escape of bushing.
11. Remove tie rod, bushing and seal.
12. Using pin spanner tool No. 9995333, or equivalent, to remove preload assembly cover.
13. Remove preload assembly spring and piston.
14. Remove piston dust seal and snap ring.
15. Insert chisel and tap off pinion cover.
16. Using socket No. 9995179, or equivalent, hold pinion shaft while removing locknut.
17. Use brass drift and hammer to tap out pinion assembly from lower end.
18. Withdraw rack carefully to avoid damage to internal surfaces of rack and housing.
19. Remove snap ring and tap out pinion ball bearing from above with suitable drift.
20. Tap out pinion lower seal and bushing from underneath using an extension bar.
21. Insert two extension bars and suitable socket through steering gear housing, then tap out seal and backing ring.
22. Replace piston seal only if damaged or if car has covered more than 25,000 miles.
23. Remove dust seal, snap ring, seal and roller bearing from pinion.

Assemble

1. If vehicle has been driven more than 25,000 miles, replace piston seal.
2. Install new pinion bushing in steering gear housing using handle tool No. 9991801 and drift tool No. 9995277, or equivalents. Ensure bushing is seated against shoulder in housing by visual observation through preload assembly opening.
3. Install new seal in steering gear housing using tool Nos. 9991801 and 9995393, or equivalents.
4. Install ball bearing using tool Nos. 9991801 and 9995388, or equivalents.
5. Install seal and backing ring on rack.
6. Pack rack teeth with steering gear grease.
7. Install rack with seal and backing ring. Ensure seal position is past center of opening when rack is fully home.
8. Press rack backward until end barely projects beyond housing opening. Do not press further or seal will be damaged by teeth.
9. Install seal and bushing on rack.
10. Install O-ring on bushing.
11. Install bushing and seal in steering gear housing. Align bushing so that locking wire hole is opposite hole in housing.
12. Press home bushing.
13. Insert locking wire hook in bushing hole. Turn bushing with hook spanner until wire is in position. Seal hole with suitable sealant.
14. Pack pinion teeth with grease and install pinion assembly.
15. Install pinion locknut.
16. To ensure rack is not seizing, turn pinion a few times from left to right end limits.
17. Install pinion shaft bearing.
18. Mount upper seal on pinion shaft.
19. Install pinion dust seal.
20. Fill pinion cover with grease, then install new pinion cover.
21. Install preload assembly components. Apply locking fluid to threads of new cover.
22. Adjust rack to mid position and tighten preload bolt to 3.7–4.1 ft. lbs., then loosen 50–55° using angle gauge tool No. 9512050, or equivalent.
23. Install tie rod and press ball joint edges into recesses in rack.
24. Pack each boot with grease, then install both boots and ball joints.
25. Remove steering gear from support

fixture and connect pressure lines.

940 & 960

Disassemble

1. Remove steering gear assembly from vehicle.
2. Remove and cap power steering gear lines.
3. Place fixture 5046 on to steering gear, then place assembly into a suitable vise.
4. Drain fluid from steering gear assembly.
5. Visually check inner and outer ball joints for wear and/or damage.
6. Remove clamps from bellows. Wipe clean grease from shaft.
7. Disconnect steering rods from rack as follows:
   a. **On late type assemblies,** use suitable pliers to remove steering rods from rack.
   b. **On early type assemblies,** use a 32 mm open end wrench to remove steering rods rack.
   c. **On all assemblies,** prevent rack assembly from moving with an adjustable spanner wrench. Install spanner wrench on to outermost flats.
   d. Disconnect left steering rod completely, then loosen right side and leave connected to rack assembly.
8. Remove lock sleeve locking wire from right side.
9. Using compressed air, blow air through outer tube connector to free lock sleeve and brushing.
10. Remove steering rod.
11. Remove lock sleeve, plastic ring and bushing.
12. Remove pretension cover, adjusting shims, gasket, spring and piston assembly.
13. Remove dust cover and pinion lock ring.
14. Remove pinion cover.
15. Secure shaft with socket tool No. 5179, or equivalent, then remove pinion nut.
16. Gently remove pinion and spool valve assembly. If necessary, gently tap lower portion of pinion using a brass drift and hammer to remove assembly.
17. Remove rack assembly.
18. Release lock ring, then remove pinion lower bearing.
19. Remove lower seal and guide sleeve.
20. Remove rack seal and spacer from tube housing.
21. Remove piston seal. **Replace piston seal only if seal is damaged or vehicle has been driven 25,000 miles or more.**
22. Remove socket tool No. 5179, or equivalent, dust cover, locking ring, seal and ball bearing.
23. Remove four Teflon rings from spool valve.
24. Clean and check all parts for excessive wear and/or damage. Replace all seals. If pinion or spool valve is damaged, replace complete assembly. Replace rack bearing and pinion guide sleeve. Check bellows and replace, if necessary.

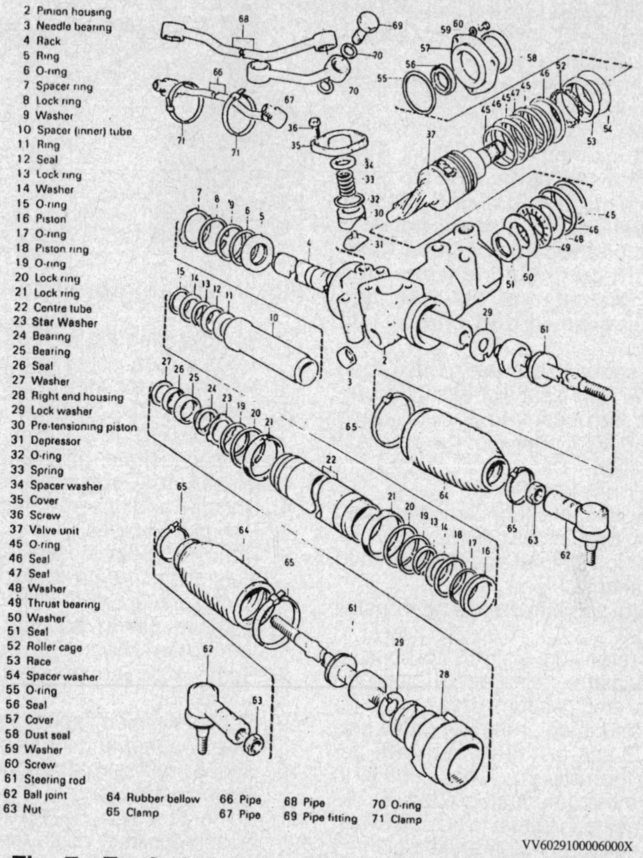
2 Pinion housing
3 Needle bearing
4 Rack
5 Ring
6 O-ring
7 Spacer ring
8 Lock ring
9 Washer
10 Spacer (inner) tube
11 Ring
12 Seal
13 Lock ring
14 Washer
15 O-ring
16 Piston
17 O-ring
18 Piston ring
19 O-ring
20 Lock ring
21 Lock ring
22 Centre tube
23 Star Washer
24 Bearing
25 Bearing
26 Seal
27 Washer
28 Right end housing
29 Lock washer
30 Pre-tensioning piston
31 Depressor
32 O-ring
33 Spring
34 Spacer washer
35 Cover
36 Screw
37 Valve unit
45 O-ring
46 Seal
47 Seal
48 Washer
49 Thrust bearing
50 Washer
51 Seal
52 Roller cage
53 Race
54 Spacer washer
55 O-ring
56 Seal
57 Cover
58 Dust seal
59 Washer
60 Screw
61 Steering rod
62 Ball joint
63 Nut
64 Rubber bellow
65 Clamp
66 Pipe
67 Pipe
68 Pipe
69 Pipe fitting
70 O-ring
71 Clamp
VV6029100006000X

Fig. 7 Exploded view of ZF power steering gear. 240

Assemble

1. Lubricate all components as necessary.
2. Install O-ring, then Teflon ring. **If Teflon ring is difficult to install, heat ring to approximately 100–120°F.**
3. Place guide sleeve and seal into housing.
4. Install lower ball bearing.
5. Install seal and spacer onto rack.
6. Install the following:
   a. Install seal, with lip facing piston seal.
   b. Install tapered spacer, with tapered side facing seal.
   c. Install flat spacer.
7. Press the two spacers together.
8. Coat rack teeth with suitable lubricant.
9. Install rack, seals and spacers as follows:
   a. With rack teeth facing upward, carefully insert rack into housing. Avoid scratching inner surface.
   b. When rack seats, push it further inward until lock seal and spacers are in correct position.
   c. Carefully tap rack end with a plastic mallet.
10. Check seal seating as follows:
    a. **On early type gear assemblies,** place an old lock sleeve without seal and O-ring into position. Measure distance between rack end and cage. Distance should be .351 inch. If not seal is incorrectly seated.
    b. **On late type gear assemblies,** look through pressure tube opening and check that at least half of piston seal retainer has passed the center of the opening.
11. Push back on rack assembly so that rack end is approximately .8 inch from housing. **Do not push rack further into housing or seals may be damaged.**
12. Install bushing and plastic spacer as follows:
    a. Clean rack end with wet abrasive (sand) paper. Remove all dirt, then wrap suitable adhesive tape around edge.
    b. Lubricate all components.
    c. Install bushing seal facing outward.
    d. Use a small screwdriver to lift edge of seal over end of rack assembly.
    e. Install plastic spacer with bevelled side facing inward, then remove tape.
13. Position lock sleeve with cutout sections facing end of rack assembly. Lock wire opening should be aligned with elongated hole in tube assembly.
14. Install lock wire by connecting on to lock sleeve. Turn sleeve until wire is correctly positioned in groove.
15. Center rack in housing. Pack teeth with grease, then place into housing with flat side facing either the 2, 3, or 4 o'clock position. Place rack into housing so that rack end protrudes 2.2 inches on late models, or 2.4 inches on early models with pinion in position.

Ensure pinion and rack mesh and flat side of pinion is in either 2, 3, or 4 o'clock position.

16. Apply adhesive tape to pinion splines, then lubricate tape.
17. Install the following:
    a. Install bearing onto pinion. Turn bevelled side down, then tap bearing into position. **Use drift 5048, or equivalent, and a plastic hammer to tap bearing into position. Modify drift by drilling inner section to a diameter of .87 inch and grinding down drift end to 1.34 inch.**
    b. Coat seal with suitable grease, then install with seal lip facing downward. Tap seal into position using drift 5048, or equivalent, and a plastic mallet.
    c. Install lock ring.
    d. Apply suitable lubricant onto dust cover, then install cover.
18. Install pinion locknut and tighten nut to specifications.
19. Pack plug seal with grease, then install plug.
20. Place pretension piston into housing and measure clearance between housing and piston. Use a feeler gauge and steel ruler for measurements. Press piston toward rack assembly, then slide rack back and forth and note maximum clearance. Thickness of adjusting shim to be used must equal measured clearance obtained between pretension piston and housing. If necessary, add one extra adjusting shim (.002–.006 inch) to obtain correct endplay.
21. Install spring, adjusting shims and gasket. Install cover. Tighten cover attaching bolts to specifications.
22. Check pinion torque as follows:
    a. Install torque gauge 9177, or equivalent, on to pinion shaft using adapter 5179, or equivalent. Move rack assembly back and forth between end positions.
    b. Correct **torque** value obtained should be 5–15 inch lbs.
    c. If torque is too high at any position of rack, stop rack in that position and readjust pretension. If rack binds with the pretension piston removed, rack assembly may be warped and should be replaced.
    d. Remove torque gauge and adapter.
23. Install steering rods. **During installation of steering rods, rack must be prevented from rotating or pinion will be damaged.**
24. Install and lock steering rods onto rack assembly.
25. Install bellows. Fill each bellow with approximately .7 ounces of suitable lubricant. Position bellows and secure with clamps.
26. Install rack assembly into vehicle.

ZF TYPE

DISASSEMBLE

Some ZF steering gears come with a removable valve housing.

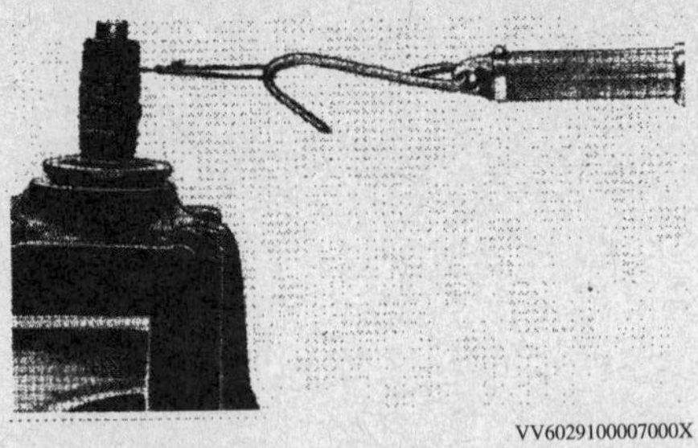
VV6029100007000X

Fig. 8 Bearing preload inspection

1. Remove steering rack assembly from vehicle, then using tool No. 5046, or equivalent, mount unit in vise.
2. Loosen both side rubber bellows and drain oil, **Fig. 7.**
3. Loosen locknut, unscrew and remove left ball stud, locknut and bellow.
4. Unstake and unscrew steering rod.
5. Remove oil pipes.
6. Remove cover for pre-tensioning device. Remove pre-tensioning piston, O-ring and spring.
7. Remove pinion housing dust shield from pinion shaft.
8. Remove pinion housing cover, seal and O-ring.
9. Remove pinion, upper roller bearing, lower washer and thrust bearing.
10. Scribe marks on center tube and housing for installation.
11. Using tool No. 5178, or equivalent, loosen locking collar next to pinion housing, then place right side housing in vise and remove lock collar and center tube.
12. Remove O-rings from center tube.
13. Remove rack and spacer tube as a unit.
14. Remove washer from right side of pinion housing.
15. Using tool No. 1819, or equivalent, remove seal from pinion housing.
16. Using a suitable punch, remove needle bearing from inside of housing. **Bearing should only be removed if it requires replacement.**
17. Remove lock rings, thrust washers and piston from rack. Fill lock ring grooves with grease and slide tube away from rack teeth.
18. Using tool No. 1819, or equivalent, remove inner tube seal and narrow brass bushing.
19. Remove O-ring and washer from spacer tube.
20. Remove star washer, bearings and seal from right side housing.
21. Remove seal and O-ring from pinion housing cover.
22. Remove O-ring and depressor from pretension piston.
23. Remove rings from pinion valve unit.

ASSEMBLE

1. Clean all parts and inspect for wear and damage, replace as necessary. **Valve housing should not be disassembled. Replace if defective.**
2. Lubricate needle bearing using suitable lubricant. Using a suitable drift, install needle bearing. **Bearing bottom should be flush with housing. If bearing is set too far, pinion preload will be affected.**
3. Install lower washers and thrust bearing.
4. Install pinion assembly, roller bearing and pinion housing cover.
5. Adjust pinion using one of the following methods:
    a. Using adapter No. 5179 and torque wrench, check torque of pinion, **Fig. 5. Torque** should be 1.3–2.2 inch lbs.
    b. Using suitable spring gauge, check pinion torque, **Fig. 8.** Scale should read 3.7–6.5 lbs.
    c. Preload is adjusted by altering the bearing washer under the cover. Washers are available in various sizes.
6. Remove pinion assembly, bearings and spacers.
7. Install all rings on valve body grooves.
8. Install seal and spacer ring in pinion housing.
9. Install bronze bushing in spacer tube, chamfered side down.
10. Install spacer tube seal in spacer tube.
11. Install O-ring and washer on spacer tube.
12. Install seal, bearings and star washer in right side housing.
13. Fill lock ring grooves and coat surrounding area with suitable grease, then slide spacer tube into steering rack from smooth end and pass it quickly over lock ring grooves.
14. Install piston, thrust washers and lock ring on rack.
15. Install center tube locking collars and lock rings. Also apply a suitable lubricant on collar threads and lock rings.
16. Place right side housing in a vise and using tool No. 5178, or equivalent, attached to a torque wrench, install center tube on right side housing. Tighten retaining collar to specifications. Ensure scribe marks made previously are aligned.
17. Install rack and spacer tube as a unit in pinion housing.
18. Using tool No. 5178, or equivalent, attached to a torque wrench, install center tube to pinion housing. Tighten retaining collar to specifications. Ensure scribe marks made previously are aligned.
19. Punch a mark in aluminum housing at one of the recesses on each housing to lock retaining collars.
20. Install pre-tensioning piston, without O-ring, in housing.
21. Set up pretension measuring fixture tool No. 5865, or equivalent, using one cover bolt hole fitted with a 45 mm x 8 mm bolt. Assemble tool with pretension spring between bolt head and tool.
22. Move gear from lock to lock and ensure it does not bind or jam.
23. Using a suitable micrometer, measure distance between housing face and piston top, checking measurement at three different points of steering rack. Subtract .004–.006 inch from smallest reading obtained and select a washer

of the approximate thickness. Washers are available in thickness of .083–.114 inch in increments of .0019 inch.

24. Remove tool No. 5865, or equivalent, and install O-ring and spring for pretension piston. Install selected washer and cover. Tighten cover bolts to specifications.
25. Reverse procedures 1 through 5 of disassembly procedure for remainder of assembly and note the following:
    a. Tighten pressure pipe fittings to specifications.
    b. Fill rubber bellows with 3–4 ounces of suitable lubricant.

TIGHTENING SPECIFICATIONS

Year	Component	Torque/Ft. Lbs.
1993–96	Cover Bolts	12
	Pinion Locknut	27
	Pressure Pipe Fittings	15
	Retaining Collar	88
	Steering Arm To Outer Ball Joints	44
	Steering Gear To Crossmember	32
	Steering Rod To Outer Ball Joints	52

Disc Brakes

INDEX

Page No.

Brake Pad Service 50-73
Front 50-73
Rear............................. 50-73
Caliper Service 50-73
Front 50-73
Rear............................. 50-74
Disc Brake Specifications 50-75
Parking Brake Service 50-74
Parking Brake, Adjust........... 50-74
Parking Brake Shoes, Replace.. 50-74
Tightening Specifications 50-76

BRAKE PAD SERVICE

FRONT

240

1. Raise car and remove wheels.
2. Remove hairpin shaped locking clips for guide pins. Tap out one of guide pins while holding damper springs in place. Remove springs and other guide pin.
3. Pull out pads using puller tool No. 2917, or equivalent.
4. Carefully clean out cavity in which pads are located. Replace any dust covers that are damaged. If dirt has penetrated into cylinder due to a damaged cover, recondition brake caliper. Check brake disc and resurface if necessary.
5. Press caliper pistons back into their bores with press tool No 2809, or equivalent. Use caution if a screwdriver is used to avoid damage to rubber dust covers. When pistons are pressed back into their bores, brake fluid in master cylinder can overflow.
6. Reverse procedure to install, noting the following:
    a. If caliper has previously been equipped with intermediate shims, rubber coated spacers or damper washers, they should be reinstalled. In the case of round damper washers, smaller contact face should face pad. Do not install spacers or shims with round damper washers.

940 & 960

1. Raise vehicle and remove wheels.
2. Using a 17 mm wrench, hold caliper guide pin and remove lower caliper attaching bolt.
3. Loosen upper caliper attaching bolt, then lift caliper and remove springs and pads. **Do not depress brake pedal when caliper is removed.**
4. Press caliper pistons back into bores using suitable clamp.
5. Install new brake pads with springs and lower caliper, then install lower attaching bolt. Tighten bolts to specifications.
6. Install wheels and lower vehicle. After replacing pads on any disc brake system, caliper pistons will be retracted in their bores and will require one full application of brakes to assume correct position. **Do not attempt to move car until a firm brake pedal has been achieved.**

850

1. Raise and support vehicle, then remove wheel.
2. Carefully remove retaining spring, **Fig. 1,** then the protective caps from guide pin bolts.
3. Remove guide pin bolts using a 7 mm Allen key, then the caliper. **Suspend caliper from front spring with wire.**
4. Remove brake pads.
5. Reverse procedure to install. Tighten fasteners to specifications.

REAR

The following procedures are applicable to all models. Some models may use either Girling or ATE type rear caliper assemblies, **Figs. 2 and 3.**

1. Raise and support rear of vehicle, then remove rear wheels and tires.
2. Using a suitable punch, remove lockpins and spring clips, then remove pads.
3. Using a suitable clamp, press pistons back into bore.
4. Install new pads, then replace lockpins and spring clips.
5. Install wheels and lower vehicle. After replacing pads on any disc brake system, caliper pistons will be retracted in their bores and will require at least one full application of brakes to assume correct position. **Do not attempt to move car until a firm brake pedal has been achieved.**

CALIPER SERVICE

FRONT

REMOVAL & OVERHAUL

240

1. Raise vehicle and remove wheels.

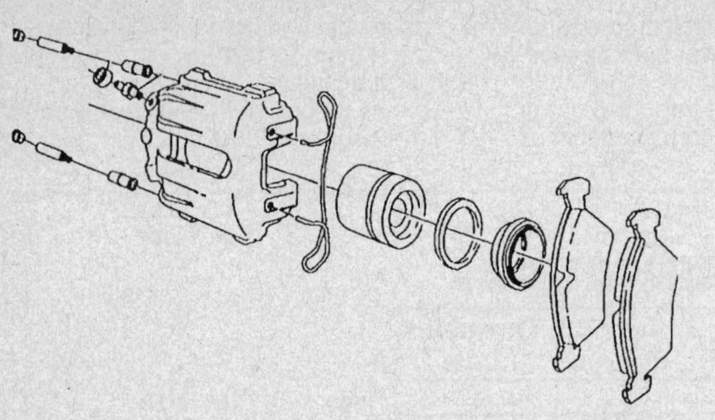
VV4079100001000X

Fig. 1 Front caliper assembly. 850

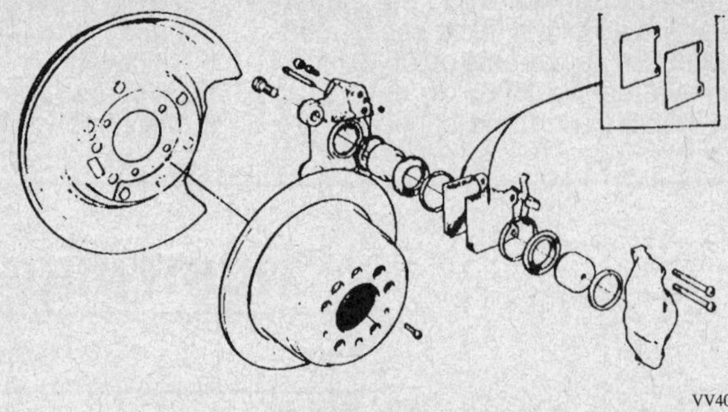
VV4079100002000X

Fig. 2 ATE rear caliper assembly

2. Disconnect brake lines. Before loosening mounting bolts, loosen all bleeder screws.
3. Remove caliper mounting bolts and remove caliper. Do not loosen bridge bolts.
4. Remove retaining ring and rubber dust cover from each caliper piston, **Fig. 4.** Place a thick piece of wood between pistons and apply air pressure to brake line connection of caliper to blow pistons out. Remove seals. The caliper must not be separated or leaks may result after reassembly.
5. Coat pistons and cylinders with brake fluid before assembling.
6. Install seals in cylinders, then install pistons, dust covers and lock rings.
7. Reinstall calipers and bleed system. Tighten caliper retaining bolts to specifications.

940 & 960

1. Raise vehicle and remove wheels.
2. Mark hoses, then disconnect from brake pipes.
3. Remove caliper to spring strut attaching bolts, then the caliper.
4. Remove rubber dust cover from each piston, **Fig. 5.** Place a thick shop towel between pistons and outer portion of caliper, then apply air pressure to brake line connection of caliper to blow pistons out. Remove inner seals.
5. Clean all passages with compressed air, then coat pistons and cylinders with brake fluid before assembling.
6. Install inner seals into cylinders.
7. Position dust covers onto lower edges of pistons, then pull covers outward so that they are fully extended.
8. Insert lower edge of dust covers onto groove in cylinders, then press pistons fully inward.
9. Inspect guide pins and bushings for excessive wear or damage. Replace as necessary.
10. Reinstall calipers and bleed system. Tighten caliper attaching bolts to specifications.

850

1. Raise and support vehicle, then remove wheel.
2. Clean caliper, then remove dust cap from bleed nipple and open nipple.
3. Lock brake pedal in its lowest position using a pedal jack. Collect any brake fluid spillage.
4. Loosen brake hose ½ turn, then remove brake pads as previously described.
5. Disconnect caliper from brake hose, then drain remaining brake fluid.
6. Place a wooden block in front of piston, then blow out piston using compressed air.
7. Remove dust boot, then the sealing ring using a weatherstrip tool.
8. Remove rubber sleeves and bleed nipple.
9. Clean components in mineral spirits, then inspect for wear, damage, cracks or rust.
10. Clean passages with compressed air, then coat cylinder walls, piston and new sealing ring with brake fluid.
11. Install lubricated sealing ring into groove in cylinder, then replace dust boot at end of piston.
12. Install dust boot into groove in cylinder and carefully push in piston. **Ensure dust boot is located in its groove and is properly seated.**
13. Replace bleed nipple.
14. Reverse steps 1 through 5 to install caliper.

REAR

REMOVAL & OVERHAUL

1. Raise and support rear of vehicle, then remove rear tires.
2. Disconnect brake lines, then remove two caliper attaching bolts and caliper.
3. Remove piston dust cover, then place a piece of wood or suitable material between both pistons. Force pistons out of bore using low pressure compressed air.
4. Using a suitable screwdriver, remove sealing rings, then bleeder screw. **Do not separate brake caliper into two separate halves.**
5. Clean caliper assembly thoroughly using brake fluid or denatured alcohol.
6. Remove any surface rust on cylinder using fine sandpaper.
7. Before assembly, coat all parts with power steering fluid, then install new seal rings and pistons.
8. **On ATE calipers,** check to be sure caliper pistons are in proper position to avoid squeals. Piston recess should incline 20° in relation to lower guide area of caliper. Inspect using template tool No. 2919, or equivalent, **Fig. 6.** If necessary, rotate piston with adjustment tool No. 2918, or equivalent.
9. Install new dust cover and bleeder screw.

PARKING BRAKE SERVICE

PARKING BRAKE SHOES, REPLACE

1. Loosen parking brake cable adjusting screw. Refer to "Parking Brake Adjustment."
2. Raise and support vehicle, then remove rear wheels.
3. Remove caliper.
4. Remove brake disc, then remove brake shoe springs, brake shoes and adjuster, if applicable. On some models, it may be necessary to work through holes in axle shaft flange to gain access to springs.
5. Before assembly, apply a thin layer of heat resistant graphite grease, or equivalent, on brake shoe sliding surface.
6. Install brake shoes, springs and adjuster, if applicable.
7. Install brake disc and caliper.
8. Adjust parking brake as outlined under "Parking Brake Adjustment."

PARKING BRAKE, ADJUST

240, 940 & 960

1. Remove rear ashtray.
2. Working through ashtray hole, tighten adjusting nut at rear of parking lever so that brake is fully applied after 2–5 notches, **Fig. 7.**

850

Remove square cover plate under arm rest in console, then turn adjustment screw on parking brake lever so that full braking is obtained between second and eighth notch.

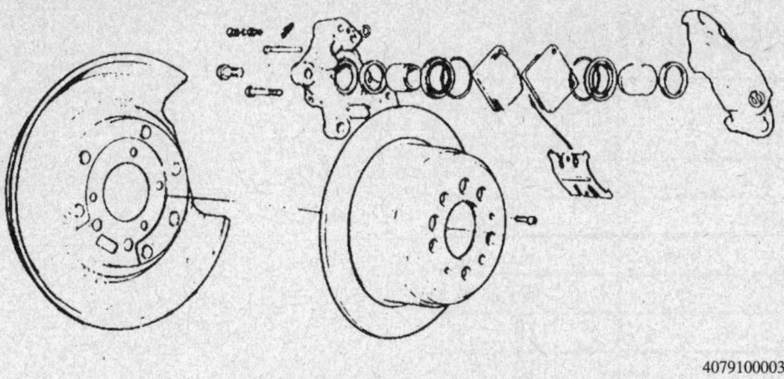

4079100003000X

Fig. 3 Girling rear caliper assembly

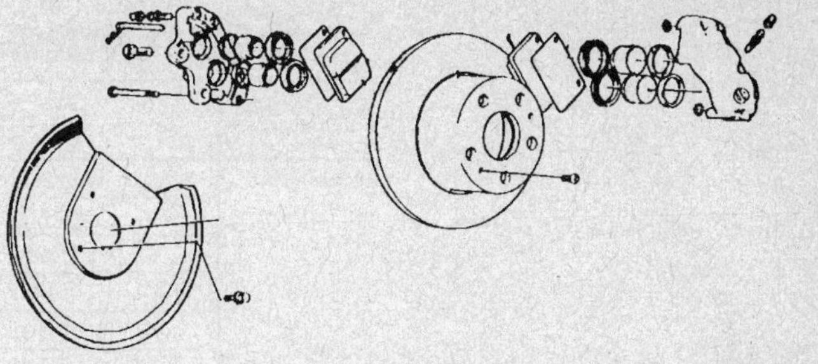

VV4079100004000X

Fig. 4 Girling front caliper assembly. 240

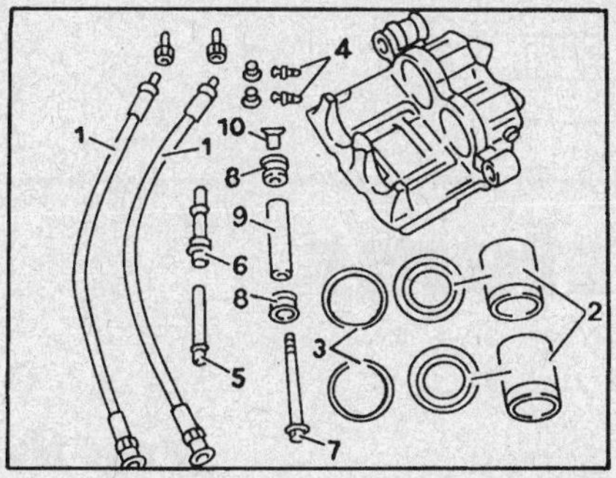
1
1
4
10
8
9
6
8
3
2
5
7

VV4079100005000X

Fig. 5 Exploded view of Girling front caliper assembly. 940 & 960

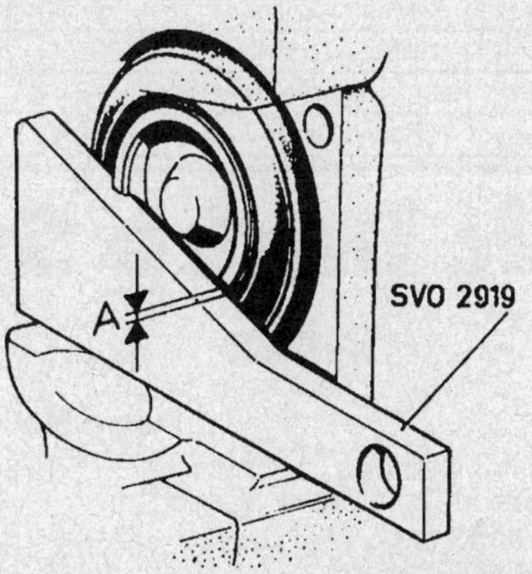
A
SVO 2919

VV4079100006000X

Fig. 6 Caliper piston position inspection. ATE rear caliper

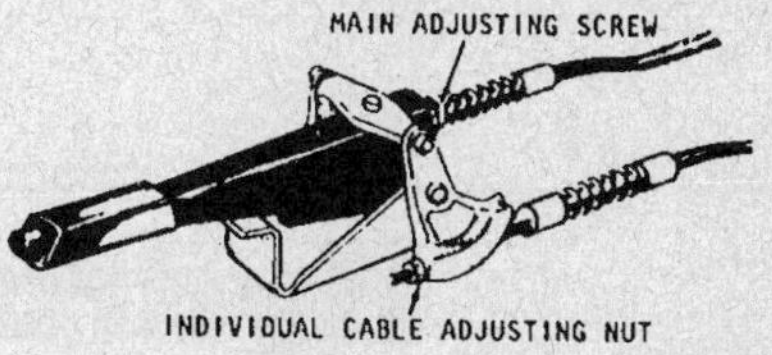
MAIN ADJUSTING SCREW
INDIVIDUAL CABLE ADJUSTING NUT

VV4079100007000X

Fig. 7 Parking brake adjustment

DISC BRAKE SPECIFICATIONS

Model	Type	Nominal Thickness	Minimum Refinish Thickness	Thickness Variation (Parallelism)	Lateral Runout (T.I.R.)
FRONT					
240	ATE	.946	.898	.0008	.002
	Girling	.867	.804	.0004	.002
	Solid	.563	.500	.0001	.002
940 & 960	I	.867	.778	.0003	—
	II	1.024	.906	.0003	—
850	—	1.024	.906	.0003	.002
REAR					
240	—	.378	.331	.0005	.002
940 & 960	I①	.378	.331	.0005	—
	II②	.394	.315	.0003	—
850	—	.378	.350	.0003	.003

① — C-T live rear suspension.
② — Multi-Link rear suspension.

TIGHTENING SPECIFICATIONS

Year	Component	Torque/Ft. Lbs.
1993–96	Brake Caliper Slide Pin	25
	Brake Hoses To Nipple	12
	Brake Pipe Unions	10
	Caliper Bracket	35
	Front Brake Calipers Bolts	74
	Front Dust Shield	18
	Lower Caliper Bolts	25
	Master Cylinder	22
	Nipple To Caliper	12
	Rear Brake Caliper Bolts	43
	Rear Dust Shield	29

Hydraulic Brake Systems

INDEX

	Page No.
Brake System Bleed	50-76
240, 940 & 960	50-76
850	50-77
Component Replacement	50-76
Master Cylinder	50-76
Pressure Differential Warning Valve	50-76
Regulating Valve	50-76
Component Service	50-76
Master Cylinder Overhaul	50-76
Description	50-76

DESCRIPTION

The function of hydraulic brake system is to transmit pressure from the master cylinder to caliper pistons. The system will operate properly if fluid is tight and brake fluid cannot be compressed. Normally, brake fluid cannot be compressed. If however the fluid overheats sufficiently it can partially change to a vapor form. Vapor can be compressed and since the master cylinder has a specific volume with which to build up pressure, the compression of vapor can result in excess brake pedal travel before the system has time to develop adequate braking pressure.

Brake fluid is hygroscopic in nature (absorbs water vapor from the air). For this reason it is important to keep brake fluid in a tightly sealed container. If only a small amount of fluid is required, it should be purchased in small cans. Avoid storing small quantities of fluid in bulk containers.

Only brake fluid which meets standard DOT 4 should be used. The boiling point for brake fluid depends on several factors including the ages of the fluid and climatic conditions. Any brake fluid efficiency will deteriorate as it ages. It should be changed at least every three years for cars in normal service.

COMPONENT REPLACEMENT

MASTER CYLINDER

1. Place a cover over the fender to protect paint from brake fluid.
2. Disconnect brake lines and cap openings.
3. Remove retaining nuts, then the master cylinder.
4. Reverse procedure to install. Bleed master cylinder prior to installation.

REGULATING VALVE

The regulating valve must be replaced as an assembly.

1. Disconnect brake pipe from valve, replace unions if necessary.
2. Remove valve from bracket, then disconnect brake hose from valve.
3. Install new valve and bleed system.
4. Ensure there are no leaks.

PRESSURE DIFFERENTIAL WARNING VALVE

1. Remove attaching screw, then disconnect electrical lead.
2. Place a suitable container beneath valve, then disconnect brake lines.
3. Install new valve and connect brake lines and electrical lead.
4. Bleed system and ensure there are no leaks.

COMPONENT SERVICE

MASTER CYLINDER OVERHAUL

Disassemble

1. Remove reservoir from master cylinder.
2. Drain fluid from reservoir, then remove seals.
3. Remove circlip and withdraw pistons and return spring.

Cleaning & Inspection

1. Polish inner surface of the master cylinder with a honing tool (cylinder grinding tool).
2. Clean all pistons parts and cylinder with methylated spirits.
3. Using compressed air, blow air into the equalizer and overflow holes.
4. Check master cylinder bore for scoring, replace as necessary. Replace both pistons, with connecting sleeve and seals as an assembly.
5. Apply brake fluid to master cylinder and lubricate piston seals with suitable grease.

Assemble

1. Assemble pistons, spring seat and spring.
2. Position master cylinder over pistons and spring, then install circlip.
3. Install seals into master cylinder, replace seals if necessary.
4. Connect brake pipes, then install brake fluid reservoir.
5. Fill reservoir with brake fluid, then bleed system.

BRAKE SYSTEM BLEED

240, 940 & 960

A diaphragm type pressure bleeder should be used to bleed system. Bleed system with wheels on vehicle.

1. Raise vehicle and fill brake fluid reservoir to MAX mark.

2. Install automatic filler cap.
3. Use only upper nipple for bleeding vehicles equipped with Multi-Link.
4. Begin by bleeding one of rear wheels as follows:
   a. Connect bleeder tool to one of the bleed nipples. Connect bleeder unit.
   b. Connect air hose to other side of unit.
   c. Open bleed nipple and close it when no bubbles remain in fluid flowing out.
5. Repeat procedure on other rear wheel and both front wheels. On front wheels, open upper nipple first.
6. Check for air in system by depressing brake pedal with force equivalent, to a sudden stop.
7. Pedal should not feel spongy and travel should not exceed two inches.
8. Install protective plugs on bleeder nipples and lower vehicle.

850

1. Turn ignition switch to Off position, then raise and support vehicle.
2. Clean area around brake fluid reservoir cap, then remove cap.
3. Connect bleeding unit to brake fluid reservoir. **Follow manufacturer's instruction for connecting and operating bleeding unit.**
4. Depress brake pedal several times to remove any air bubbles from clutch master cylinder.
5. Remove dust cap from bleed nipple on one of the rear wheels and connect hose from overflow bottle.
6. Open bleed nipple, then close and tighten nipple when no further air bubbles can be seen in fluid flowing out. Remove hose and replace dust cap.
7. Bleed other rear wheel, right front wheel, then the left front wheel using procedure described in steps 4 through 6.
8. Remove bleeding unit connector from brake fluid reservoir, then check to see if there is air in system by depressing brake pedal with a force corresponding to an abrupt braking. Pedal travel must not exceed 1.574 inch (40 mm) and warning indicator on dashboard must not flash or light up.
9. If pedal travel exceeds limit, bleed system again and check pedal travel again.
10. Ensure fluid level is not over Max mark, then lower vehicle.

Power Brake Units

INDEX

	Page No.
Power Brake Unit Service	50-77
Check Valve, Replace	50-77
Power Brake Booster, Replace	50-77

POWER BRAKE UNIT SERVICE

POWER BRAKE BOOSTER, REPLACE

1. Remove master cylinder, then disconnect vacuum hose from power brake unit.
2. Disconnect link arm from brake pedal, then remove bracket with clutch pedal stop.
3. Remove nuts attaching power brake unit to dash panel.
4. Pull power brake unit forward, then disconnect fork from link arm and remove brake unit.

CHECK VALVE, REPLACE

1. Disconnect vacuum hose from check valve.
2. Pry out check valve using two screwdrivers, then remove seal.
3. Install new seal, ensuring flange is properly aligned in cylinder.
4. Lubricate seal with grease, then press valve carefully into place.
5. Ensure seal does not move out of its position.
6. Connect vacuum hose, ensure highest point is at attachment to valve.

Anti-Lock Brakes

NOTE: On Air Bag Equipped Models, Refer To "Air Bag System Precautions" Located In The Front Of This Manual For System Disarming & Arming Procedures.

NOTE: Electrical Symbol & Wire Color Code Identification Located In The Front Of This Manual May Be Used As An Aid When Using Wiring Circuits Found In This Section.

INDEX

	Page No.
Description	50-78
Diagnosis & Testing	50-80
Accessing Fault Codes	50-80
Clearing Diagnostic Trouble Codes	50-89
Intermittent Faults	50-89
Trouble Code Interpretation	50-80
Precautions	50-78
Air Bag Systems	50-78
Microprocessor Radios	50-78
System Service	50-89
Brake System Bleed	50-89
240, 940 & 960	50-89
850	50-89

Page No.		Page No.		Page No.	
Component Replacement	50-90	Hydraulic Modulator, Replace	50-90	**Troubleshooting**	50-78
Control Module, Replace	50-90	Rear Sensor, Replace	50-92	Component Fault Tracing	50-78
Front Sensor, Replace	50-92				

PRECAUTIONS

AIR BAG SYSTEMS

Refer to "Air Bag System Precautions" in the front of this manual for system disarming and arming procedures.

MICROPROCESSOR RADIOS

On models equipped with microprocessor radios, always switch radio off before disconnecting or connecting battery ground cable to prevent damage to the radio.

DESCRIPTION

The Anti-Lock Brake System (ABS) uses a control unit, hydraulic modulator, transient surge protector, front speed sensors and a speedometer sensor to control wheel lock-up. The control unit receives vehicle speed, wheel speed and wheel acceleration information from the sensors, then sends the information to the hydraulic modulator. The hydraulic modulator uses this information to ensure correct hydraulic pressure is maintained at each wheel.

If a lock-up condition should occur, the hydraulic modulator reduces pressure to that particular wheel cylinder by pumping brake fluid from the wheel cylinder back to the master cylinder. If an (ABS) malfunction occurs, the system will shutdown completely and a warning light will come on. The Vehicle can still be driven safely as the normal operation of the brake system will continue.

TROUBLESHOOTING

COMPONENT FAULT TRACING

240, 940 & 960

All procedures must be completed to avoid damaging the control unit.

Refer to wiring diagram and component locations in **Figs. 1 through 3,** during fault tracing procedures.

1. Check fuse in transient surge protector
2. Check all connectors, wires and ground connections for ABS System.
3. Switch ignition off.
4. Disconnect connector from control unit by depressing lock spring and swinging connector out.
5. Remove cover from hydraulic modulator.
6. Remove cover from control unit connector.
7. Remove white protective moldings from sides of connector.
8. Check ground connections in connector.
   a. Always check connectors through holes in side of connector.
   b. Connection numbers are stamped into side of connector
9. Connect ohmmeter between ground and terminals 10, 20, 32 and 34.
   a. Resistance should be zero for all terminals.
   b. If values are not zero, check that wires are undamaged and correctly connected.
10. If a fault is found at terminal 32, test a new solenoid relay (mounted on hydraulic modulator).
11. Switch ignition on.
12. Check transient surge protector as follows:
    a. Connect voltmeter between ground and terminal 1 on control unit connector.
    b. Voltage should be 12 V.
    c. If no voltage is registered, take measurement directly on transient surge protector connector.
    d. Terminals 1, 2 and 4 should be energized and terminal 3 grounded.
    e. If only terminals 1 and 4 are energized when terminal 3 is grounded, transient surge protector is defective and should be replaced.
13. Check power supply to control unit connector by connecting voltmeter between ground and following terminal:
    a. Terminal 25, depress brake pedal at same time.
    b. Terminal 27.
    c. Terminal 28.
    d. Terminal 29.
14. Voltmeter reading obtained should be 12 volts at all terminals except terminal 29. Voltage reading at terminal 29 should be .5–1.0 V.
15. Start engine, voltmeter reading obtained should be 12 volts at terminal 25.
16. If no reading was obtained at:
    a. Terminal 25, check brake light switch, replace if necessary.
    b. Terminal 27, solenoid relay is defective, replace.
    c. Terminal 28, pump relay defective, replace.
    d. Terminal 29, if reading at terminal 27 is correct, reading at terminal 29 should be .5–1.0 V. If not, replace solenoid relay.
17. Switch ignition off.
18. Check voltage to hydraulic modulator connector.
19. Disconnect connector from modulator.
20. Switch ignition on.
21. Connect voltmeter between ground and terminals 6, 7, 10 and 12. Voltmeter should indicate 12 V.
22. If there is no voltage to terminals, perform following checks and make sure wires are undamaged.
    a. Terminal 6. Check wires.
    b. Terminal 7. Connect connector, ABS light should come on. If not, replace bulb.
    c. Terminal 10. Transient surge protector defective, replace.
    d. Terminal 12. Check wires.
23. Switch ignition off.
24. Connect electrical connector and check front sensors as follows:
    a. Connect ohmmeter to control unit electrical connector.
    b. Connect instrument between terminals 4 and 6 for left front sensor, and between terminals 11 and 21 for right front sensor.
    c. Reading obtained should be between .9–2.2 K-ohms.
    d. If reading is not as specified, measure resistance between corresponding terminals of connectors at wheel housings in the engine compartment.
    e. If readings still differ, check that the wiring is intact. If incorrect readings persist, replace sensor.
25. Check pulse wheels for defects. Maximum radial runout is .006 inch.
26. Check rear sensor as follows:
    a. Connect ohmmeter between terminals 7 and 9.
    b. Resistance should be 0.6–1.6 K-ohms. If other readings are obtained, take reading at sensor connector on filler pipe on boot.
    c. If readings are still incorrect, replace sensor.
27. **On vehicles less Multi-Link,** check wiring to sensors.
28. Check hydraulic modulator solenoid valves as follows:
    a. Connect one of ohmmeter test leads to terminal 32 on control unit connector. Move other test lead from terminal 2 to 18 and then to 35.
    b. Readings should be 0.7–1.7 ohms. If not, take reading directly at hydraulic modulator. If reading is still incorrect, replace modulator.
29. Switch ignition on.
30. Check pump relay in hydraulic modulator as follows:
    a. Connect a lead between terminal 28 and ground. **Do not connect for more than 2 seconds.** Modulator should then start.
    b. If modulator does not start, check that the wiring in intact. If fault persists, try connecting by installing a new pump relay.
31. Check valve relay in hydraulic modulator as follows:
    a. Connect voltmeter between pin 32 and ground. Connect a wire between ground and pin 27.
    b. Valve relay should switch on and voltmeter should indicate 12 V.
    c. If volts are not as indicated, test with new relay.
32. Switch ignition off.

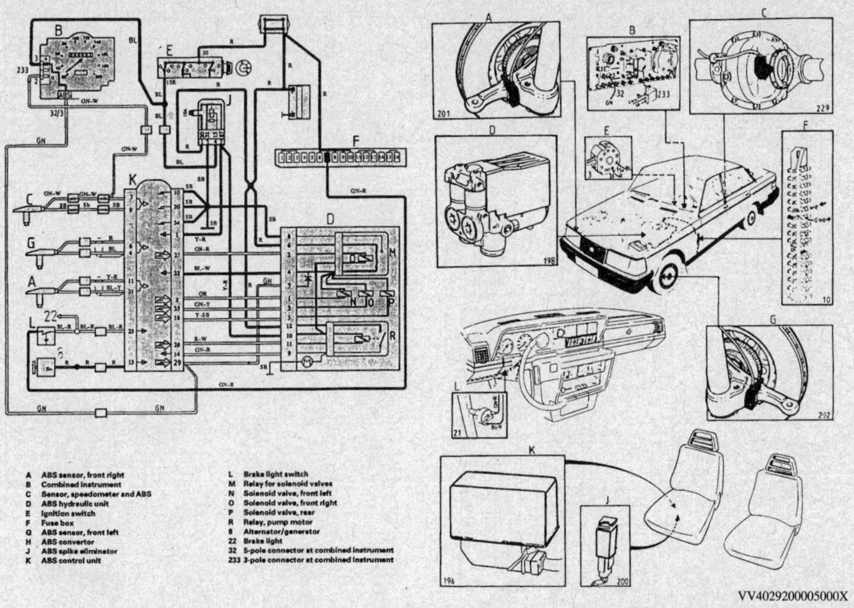
A ABS sensor, front right
B Combined instrument
C Sensor, speedometer and ABS
D ABS hydraulic unit
E Ignition switch
F Fuse box
G ABS sensor, front left
H ABS convertor
J ABS spike eliminator
K ABS control unit
L Brake light switch
M Relay for solenoid valves
N Solenoid valve, front left
O Solenoid valve, front right
P Solenoid valve, rear
R Relay, pump motor
S Alternator/generator
22 Brake light
32 5-pole connector at combined instrument
233 3-pole connector at combined instrument
VV4029200005000X

Fig. 1 ABS wiring circuit & electrical components. 240

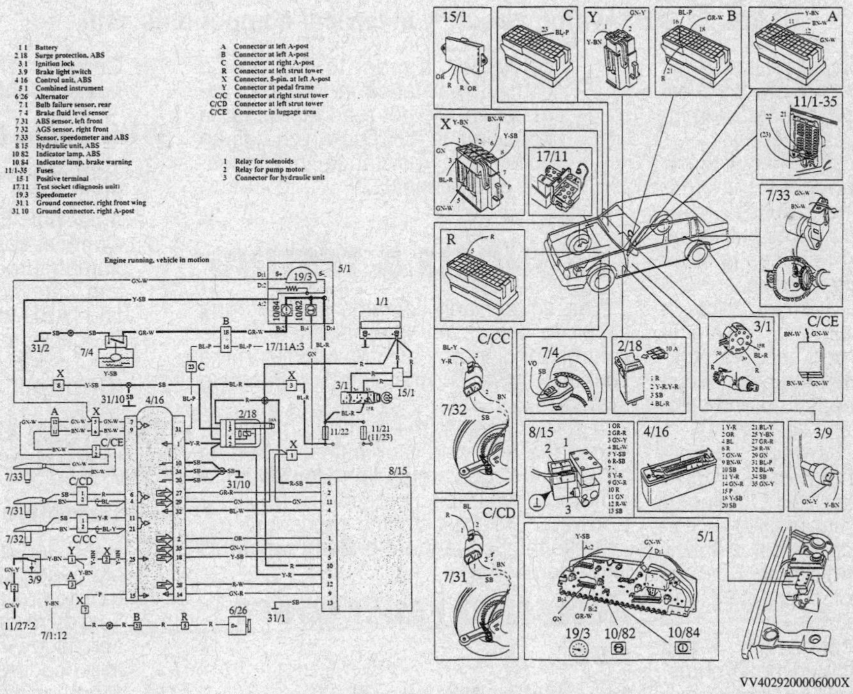
1 1 Battery
2 18 Surge protection, ABS
3 1 Ignition lock
3 9 Brake light switch
4 16 Control unit, ABS
5 1 Combined instrument
6 26 Alternator
7 1 Bulb failure sensor, rear
7 4 Brake fluid level sensor
7 31 ABS sensor, left front
7 32 ABS sensor, right front
7 33 Sensor, speedometer and ABS
8 15 Hydraulic unit, ABS
10 82 Indicator lamp, ABS
10 84 Indicator lamp, brake warning
11/1-35 Fuses
15 1 Positive terminal
17 11 Test socket (diagnosis unit)
19 3 Speedometer
31 1 Ground connector, right front wing
31 10 Ground connector, right A-post
A Connector at left A-post
B Connector at left A-post
C Connector at right A-post
R Connector at left strut tower
X Connector, 8-pin, at left A-post
Y Connector at pedal frame
C/C Connector at right strut tower
C/CD Connector at left strut tower
C/CE Connector in luggage area
1 Relay for solenoids
2 Relay for pump motor
3 Connector for hydraulic unit
Engine running, vehicle in motion
VV4029200006000X

Fig. 2 ABS wiring circuit & electrical components. 960

33. Disconnect test equipment.
34. If no faults were detected during fault tracing, test with new control unit.

850

Refer to wiring diagram and component locations in **Figs. 4 and 5,** during fault tracing procedures.

Testing Wiring

1. Visually inspect terminals as follows:
   a. Whenever a connector is disconnected for measurements or checks, terminals should be visually inspected.
   b. Check for oxidation affecting contact in terminals.
   c. Check terminal pins and ensure copper conductor makes good contact with pin.
2. Check for breaks in the circuit as follows:
   a. An open circuit is indicated by the loss of a function. Worn wiring or terminals which have come loose are common causes of faults.
   b. Disconnect connectors at both ends of wiring, measure resistance between ends of wiring. Ohmmeter should read 0 ohms on wiring without a break.
3. Check for grounding of the circuit as follows:
   a. Grounding is often indicated by the fuse blowing when a voltage is passed through the wiring.
   b. Activate all switches and sensors in circuit and check to see if fuse blows.
   c. Gently shake wiring and pull terminals while taking readings in order to detect intermittent faults.
   d. Disconnect circuit component connectors so that these do not affect readings.
   e. Measure resistance between wiring and ground to detect any grounding. Ohmmeter should read infinite resistance when no components are connected.

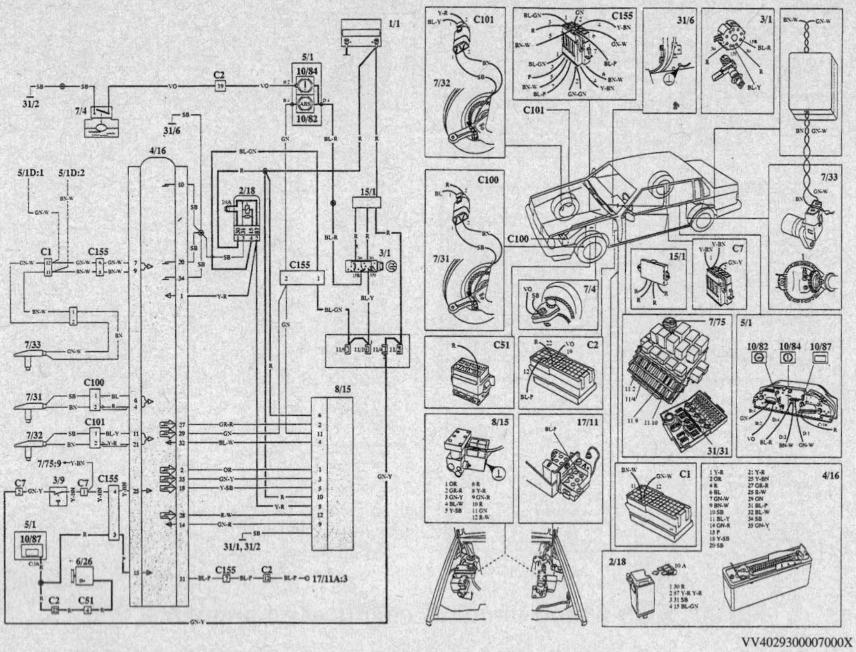
VV4029300007000X

Fig. 3 ABS wiring circuit & electrical components. 940

4. Check for short circuits as follows:
   a. Short circuits do not always blow the fuse. The fault is most often indicated by loss of a function.
   b. Gently shake wiring and pull terminals while taking readings in order to detect intermittent faults.
   c. Gently shake wiring and pull terminals while taking readings in order to detect intermittent faults.
   d. Take readings at various points in circuit using a voltmeter while activating switches and sensors. Voltage indicated depends on circuit which is being measured and position of switches and sensors.
   e. Take readings between suspect wires using an ohmmeter in order to locate short circuits. Ohmmeter should read infinite resistance between wires which are not connected to each other in circuit.
5. Check resistance of connectors and terminals as follows:
   a. Resistance of connectors, wiring and terminals should be 0 ohms. However there may be some resistance because of poorly connected wiring, oxidation on terminals and wear. If resistance becomes too great, functions will be interrupted. The magnitude that this resistance must reach before there is interference varies with the load on the circuit. A guideline is a few ohms.
   b. Gently shake wiring and pull terminals while taking readings in order to detect intermittent faults.
   c. Using a loose female connector, test to see if it provides a good contact and if it and the pin stay together when the male connector is pulled lightly.
   d. Take readings between ends of wires using an ohmmeter. Also take readings with switches and sensors connected in order to detect high contact resistance in these. Ohmmeter should not read more than a few ohms in a circuit which has an acceptable resistance in connectors and terminals.

DIAGNOSIS & TESTING

The control unit contains a monitoring circuit to detect any internal faults in the control unit and any electrical faults in the sensors, hydraulic modulator or signaling system.

If a fault occurs, the control unit disengages the ABS and illuminates a warning light. When the warning light comes on, a complete fault tracing procedure should be followed. The fault tracing procedure assumes that the standard braking system is fully operational.

ACCESSING FAULT CODES

850

Less Volvo Diagnostic Key

1. Connect diagnostic lead to position 3 on diagnostic output A, **Fig. 4,** then turn ignition switch to On position.
2. Press button once, briefly but firmly. System is now in test mode 1 "On-Board Diagnostic (OBD)" and will display trouble codes.

Reading Diagnostic Trouble Codes

1. Count number of times LED flashes and write down code.
2. Pressing button once more will indicate if there are any further codes stored.
3. When code which was displayed first is displayed again, there are no further codes stored.
4. Correct any faults, then delete diagnostic trouble codes.

With Volvo Diagnostic Key

1. Turn ignition switch to Off position, then insert memory cassette for car model into Diagnostic Key.
2. Connect connector lead to diagnostic output, turn ignition switch to Off position, then use the and arrow keys to find "ABS-800" in the display window.
3. Follow instructions in window to get to test mode 1 "On-Board Diagnostic (OBD)" and obtain trouble codes.

TROUBLE CODE INTERPRETATION

F. Intermittent Faults

1. Read and delete any diagnostic trouble codes stored in ABS/TRACS system control module.
2. Test drive vehicle and duplicate driving conditions in which fault appears, refer to procedure "H. Test Drive."
3. Stop vehicle and read any diagnostic trouble codes stored in ABS/TRACS system control module. Refer to "G. Diagnostic Trouble Code (DTC) Table" for trouble code interpretation. If no diagnostic trouble codes have been stored, then Refer to "K. Symptoms/ Diagnosis Table."

G. Diagnostic Trouble Code (DTC) Table

Refer to **Figs. 6 and 7** for diagnostic trouble codes (DTC).

H. Test Drive

Brake problems can make vehicle difficult to operate. Test drive must be performed under safe and controlled conditions.

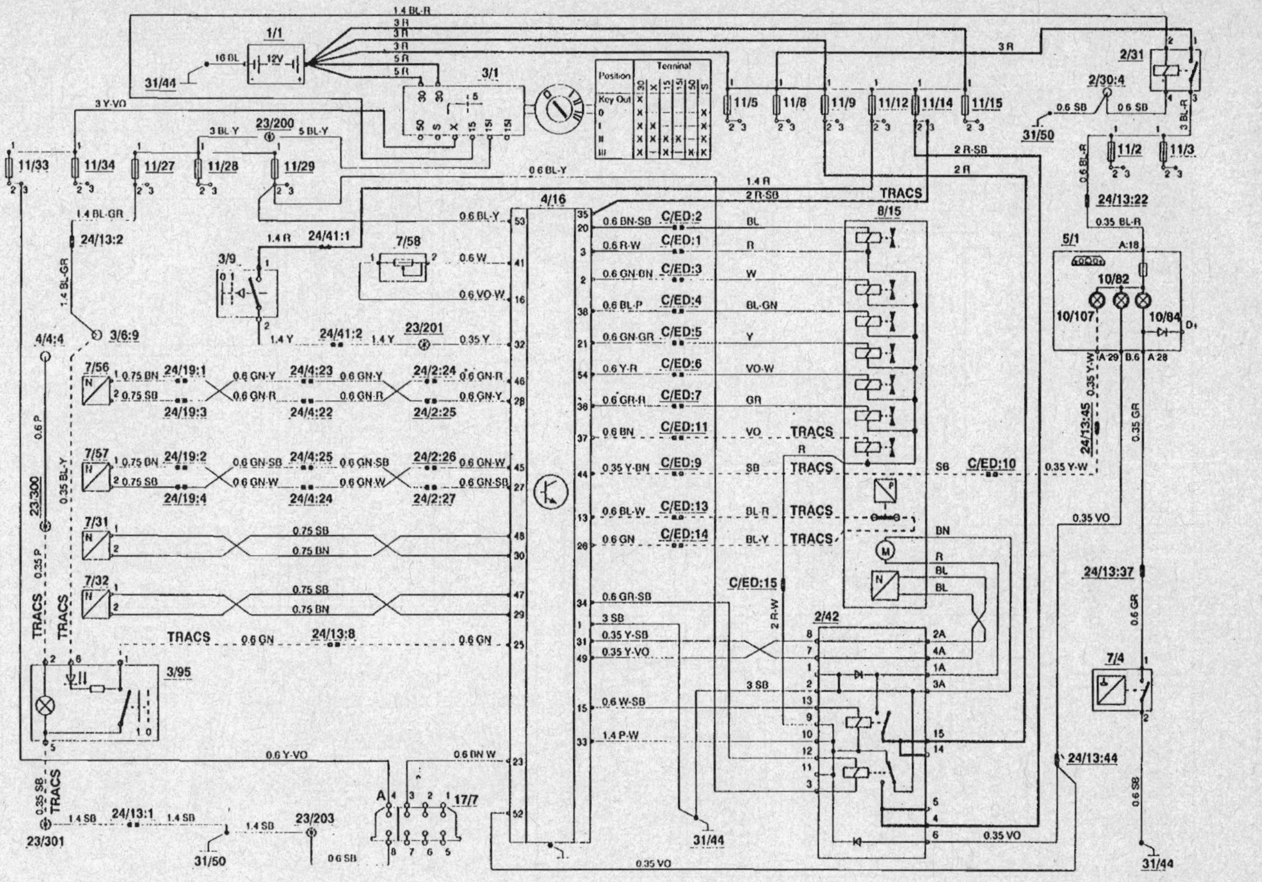
1/1
31/44
3/1
4/16
7/58
3/9
3/6:9
4/4:4
7/56
7/57
7/31
7/32
3/95
17/7
23/301
31/50
23/203
31/44
2/42
8/15
2/31
2/30:4
31/50
5/1
10/82
10/107
10/84
7/4
24/13:44
31/44
TRACS
C/ED:10
C/ED:15
VV4029100001010X

Fig. 4 ABS wiring circuit & electrical components (Part 1 of 2). 1993-95 850

1. Read any codes stored in control module and delete then turn ignition switch to On position.
2. Start engine and observe brake warning indicator. If indicator is lit, car should not be driven. Perform diagnosis procedure "NF. Brake Warning Indicator Does Not Go Out."
3. Drive at least 25 mph to exit diagnostic mode. ABS warning indicator should go out. If not, stop vehicle and read and record codes registered. Refer to "J. Diagnostic Trouble Code (DTC)/ Diagnosis Table. "
4. Brake to a stop several times from a reasonable speed on a smooth, dry road. Listen for unusual noises or note if vehicle handles unusually. Pay close attention to clicking or popping noises, observe if vehicle pulls to one side, or if brake pedal feels strange. If ABS warning indicator lights, stop vehicle read and record any codes. Note condition under which indicator lights.
5. Read codes and ensure code 1-1-1 is displayed.

J. Diagnostic Trouble Code (DTC)/Diagnosis Table

Refer to **Fig. 8,** for Diagnosis Table.

K. Symptoms/Diagnosis Table

Refer to **Fig. 9,** for Symptoms/Diagnosis Table.

L. Mechanical Components, Fault Tracing

Refer to **Fig. 10,** for fault tracing on mechanical components.

MA. Diagnostic Trouble Codes (DTC), Wheel Sensors

1. Ensure ignition switch is in Off position, then disconnect battery ground cable.
2. Disconnect control module electrical connector, then connect adapter 981 3196 to control module connector.
3. Connect test box 981 3190 to adapter, then the battery ground cable.
4. Connect an ohmmeter between suspect wheel sensor terminals. Left front sensor, terminals 30 and 48. Right front sensor, terminals 29 and 47. Left rear sensor, terminals 28 and 46. Right rear sensor, terminals 27 and 45.
5. Ohmmeter should read between 1040 and 1160 ohms. If reading is incorrect, proceed to step 10. If reading is correct, proceed to next step.
6. Connect ohmmeter between suspect wheel sensor input terminal and ground. Left front sensor, terminal 48. Right front sensor, terminal 47. Left rear sensor, terminal 46. Right rear sensor, terminal 45.
7. Ohmmeter should indicate an open circuit. If reading is incorrect, proceed to step 11. If reading is correct, proceed to next step.
8. Connect a voltmeter and measure AC voltage between suspect wheel sensor terminals while turning wheel by hand. Left front sensor, terminals 30 and 48. Right front sensor, terminals 29 and 47. Left rear sensor, terminals 28 and 46. Right rear sensor, terminals 27 and 45.
9. Voltmeter should read ca. 0.05 to 0.9 V AC. If reading is incorrect, check pulse wheel and sensor for excess dirt or damage. If pulse wheel is satisfactory, wheel sensor should be replaced. If reading is correct, proceed to step 12.
10. Raise and support vehicle, then remove wheel so that suspect sensor is easily accessible. Carefully clean area around sensor connector and brush off any dirt on sensor and pulse wheel with a soft bristle brush. Connect an ohmmeter between terminals 1 and 2 on sensor. Ohmmeter should read between 1040 and 1160 ohms. If reading is incorrect, replace wheel sensor. If reading is correct, check wiring for an open circuit.
11. Raise and support vehicle, then remove wheel so that suspect sensor is easily accessible. Carefully clean area around sensor connector and brush off any dirt on sensor and pulse wheel with a soft bristle brush. Connect ohmmeter between connector terminal 1 and ground. Ohmmeter should indicate an

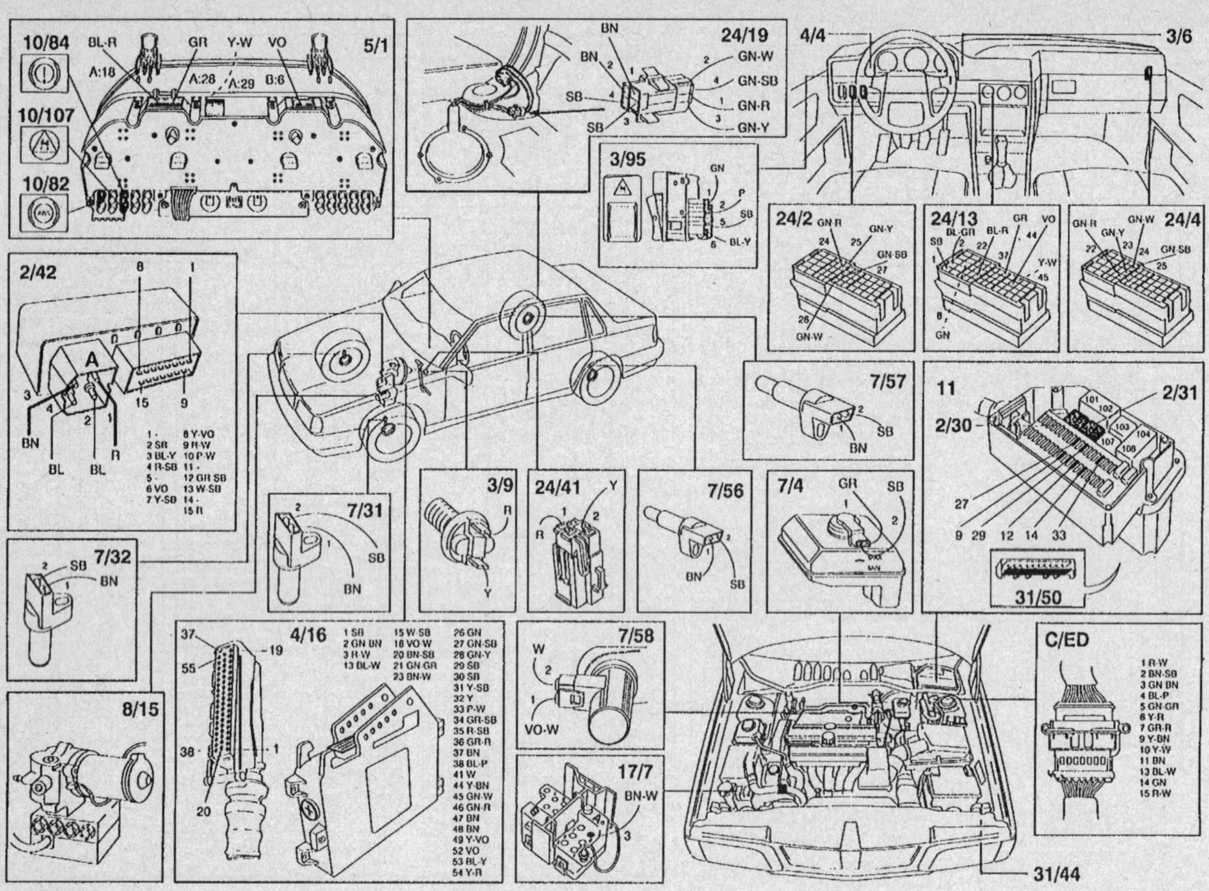

VV4029100001020X

Fig. 4 ABS wiring circuit & electrical components (Part 2 of 2). 1993-95 850

open circuit. If reading is incorrect, replace wheel sensor. If reading is correct, check wiring for short circuits.

12. Check for interference as follows:
    a. Connect ohmmeter between control module housing and ground. Ohmmeter should indicate a closed circuit.
    b. Connect ohmmeter between terminal 1 on test box and ground. Ohmmeter should indicate a closed circuit.
    c. Check that sensor wiring is not too close to sources of interference (electric motors, ignition leads, etc.).
    d. Check that wiring of suspect sensor is not loose.
    e. Check that pulse wheel is not damaged.
    f. If tests or components tested in steps a through e are satisfactory, replace control module.

MB. Diagnostic Trouble Code (DTC) 1-4-1

1. Ensure ignition switch is in Off position, then disconnect battery ground cable.
2. Disconnect control module electrical connector, then connect adapter 981 3196 to control module connector.
3. Connect test box 981 3190 to adapter, then the battery ground cable.
4. Connect jumpers between terminals 1, 2, 21, 34 and 36, then an ohmmeter between terminals 16 and 41. Ohmmeter should read between 224.1 and 273.9 ohms.
5. Turn ignition switch to On position, depress brake pedal as far as it will go and hold, then turn ignition switch to Off position. **So valves do not overheat, ignition must not be switched On for more than 20 seconds. Wait at least 30 seconds before next test.**
6. Release brake pedal slowly while at the same time taking readings from ohmmeter. It should be possible to observe seven distinct resistance readings. **In position 1 brake pedal is fully released. In position 7 brake pedal is fully depressed.**
7. In position 7 resistance should be infinite. In position 6 resistance should be between 928.8 and 1135.2 ohms. In position 5 resistance should be between 735.3 and 898.7 ohms. In position 4 resistance should be between 621 and 759 ohms. In position 3 resistance should be between 507.7 and 619.3 ohms. In position 2 resistance should be between 392.4 and 479.6 ohms. In position 1 resistance should be between 224.1 and 273.9 ohms.
8. If one of the resistance readings is incorrect, check wiring for short circuits. If wiring is satisfactory, pedal sensor must be replaced. Compare color of pedal sensor spacer sleeve with power brake booster color code. If all resistance readings are correct, replace control module.

MC. Diagnostic Trouble Code (DTC) 1-4-2

1. Check that brake lights work. If brake lights do not work, ensure bulbs are not defective. If bulbs are satisfactory, proceed to step 6. If brake lights work, proceed to next step.
2. Ensure ignition switch is in Off position, then disconnect battery ground cable.
3. Disconnect control module electrical connector, then connect adapter 981 3196 to control module connector.
4. Connect test box 981 3190 to adapter, then the battery ground cable.
5. Connect a voltmeter between terminal 32 and terminal 1, then depress brake pedal. Voltmeter should read battery voltage. If reading is incorrect, check for open or shorted circuit. If reading is correct, delete code and test drive vehicle. If fault occurs again, replace control module.
6. Remove contact pins from brake light contact, then connect voltmeter between contact pin 1 and ground. Voltmeter should read battery voltage. If reading is incorrect, check for break in fuse or wiring. If reading is correct, proceed to next step.

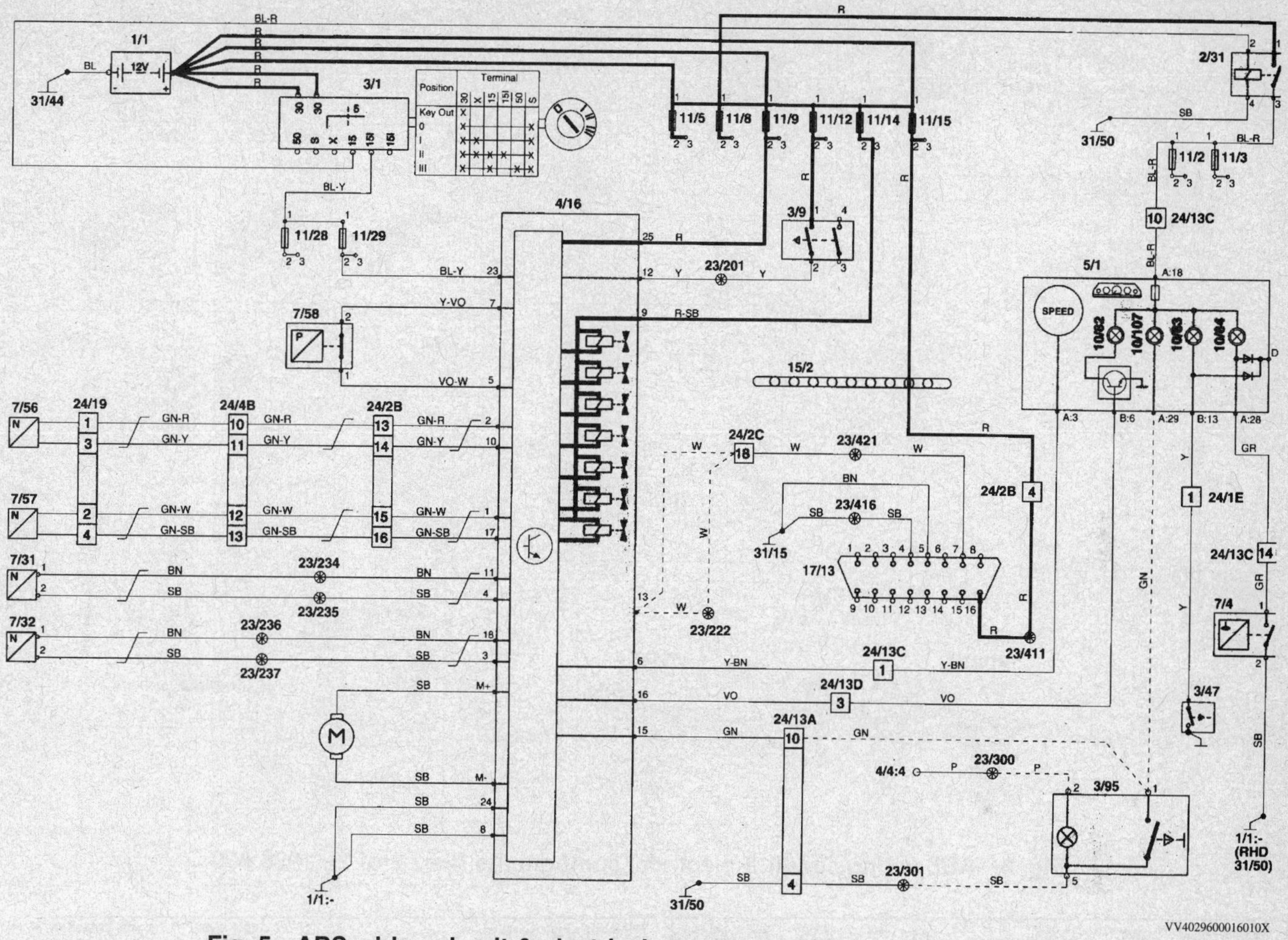
1/1
12V
31/44
BL
BL-R
R
3/1
Position
Terminal
Key Out
0
I
II
III
30
50
15
X
4/16
11/5
11/8
11/9
11/12
11/14
11/15
2/31
31/50
SB
11/2
11/3
24/13C
5/1
A:18
SPEED
10/82
10/107
10/63
10/64
15/2
BL-Y
11/28
11/29
3/9
25
12
Y
23/201
Y-VO
7/58
9
R-SB
VO-W
7/56
24/19
24/4B
24/2B
GN-R
GN-Y
7/57
GN-W
GN-SB
7/31
BN
23/234
23/235
7/32
23/236
23/237
M+
M-
24
8
1/1:-
24/2C
W
23/421
23/416
31/15
17/13
13
23/222
23/411
24/13C
Y-BN
24/13D
VO
24/13A
GN
23/300
4/4:4
P
3/95
23/301
31/50
24/1E
GR
7/4
3/47
1/1:-
(RHD
31/50)
VV4029600016010X

Fig. 5 ABS wiring circuit & electrical components (Part 1 of 2). 1996 850

7. Bridge contact pin 1 and contact pin 2 with a wire. Brake light should light. If brake light functions correctly, check that brake light contact is properly adjusted. If contact is properly adjusted, replace brake light contact. If brake light does not function correctly, check that wiring to brake light bulbs is intact.

MD. Diagnostic Trouble Code (DTC) 1-4-4

Code 1-4-4 is posted when the control module detects that the TRACS system has been used to such an extent that there is a risk of the brakes overheating. In this case, the TRACS system is automatically disengaged and the TRACS warning indicator is lit. When the control module calculates that brake temperature is normal again, the TRACS function is engaged and the TRACS warning indicator goes out.

Visually inspect front brakes for signs of overheating damage. Delete code.

ME. Diagnostic Trouble Codes (DTC), Valves

1. Ensure ignition switch is in Off position, then disconnect battery ground cable.
2. Disconnect control module electrical connector, then connect adapter 981 3196 to control module connector.
3. Connect test box 981 3190 to adapter, then the battery ground cable.
4. Connect an ohmmeter between terminal 3 and left front inlet valve terminal 20, right front inlet valve terminal 38, rear inlet valve terminal 54 and TRACS valve terminal 37. Resistance should be 6–8 ohms for all measurements. Connect ohmmeter between terminal 3 and left front return valve terminal 2, right front return valve terminal 21 and rear return valve terminal 36. Resistance should be 3–5 ohms for all measurements.
5. If readings are incorrect, check for open circuit in wiring. If wiring is satisfactory, replace hydraulic modulator. If readings are correct, proceed to next step.
6. Remove 15-pole connector from combination relay. Connect ohmmeter between terminal 1 and left front inlet valve terminal 20, right front inlet valve terminal 38, rear inlet valve terminal 54 and TRACS valve terminal 37. Connect ohmmeter between terminal 1 and left front return valve terminal 2, right front return valve terminal 21 and rear return valve terminal 36. Ohmmeter should indicate an open circuit for all measurements.
7. If readings are incorrect, check for short circuit in wiring. If wiring is satisfactory, replace hydraulic modulator. If reading are correct, replace control module.

MF. Diagnostic Trouble Code (DTC) 4-2-4

1. Ensure ignition switch is in Off position, then disconnect battery ground cable.
2. Disconnect control module electrical connector, then connect adapter 981 3196 to control module connector.
3. Connect test box 981 3190 to adapter, then the battery ground cable.
4. Connect an ohmmeter between terminal 13 and terminal 26. Ohmmeter should read ca. 0 ohms. Connect ohmmeter between terminal 26 and ground. Ohmmeter should indicate an open circuit.
5. If one of the readings is incorrect, check for open or short circuit in wiring. If wiring is satisfactory, replace hydraulic modulator. If reading are correct, proceed to next step.
6. Connect an ohmmeter between terminal 13 and terminal 26, then depress brake pedal. Ohmmeter should indicate an open in the circuit.

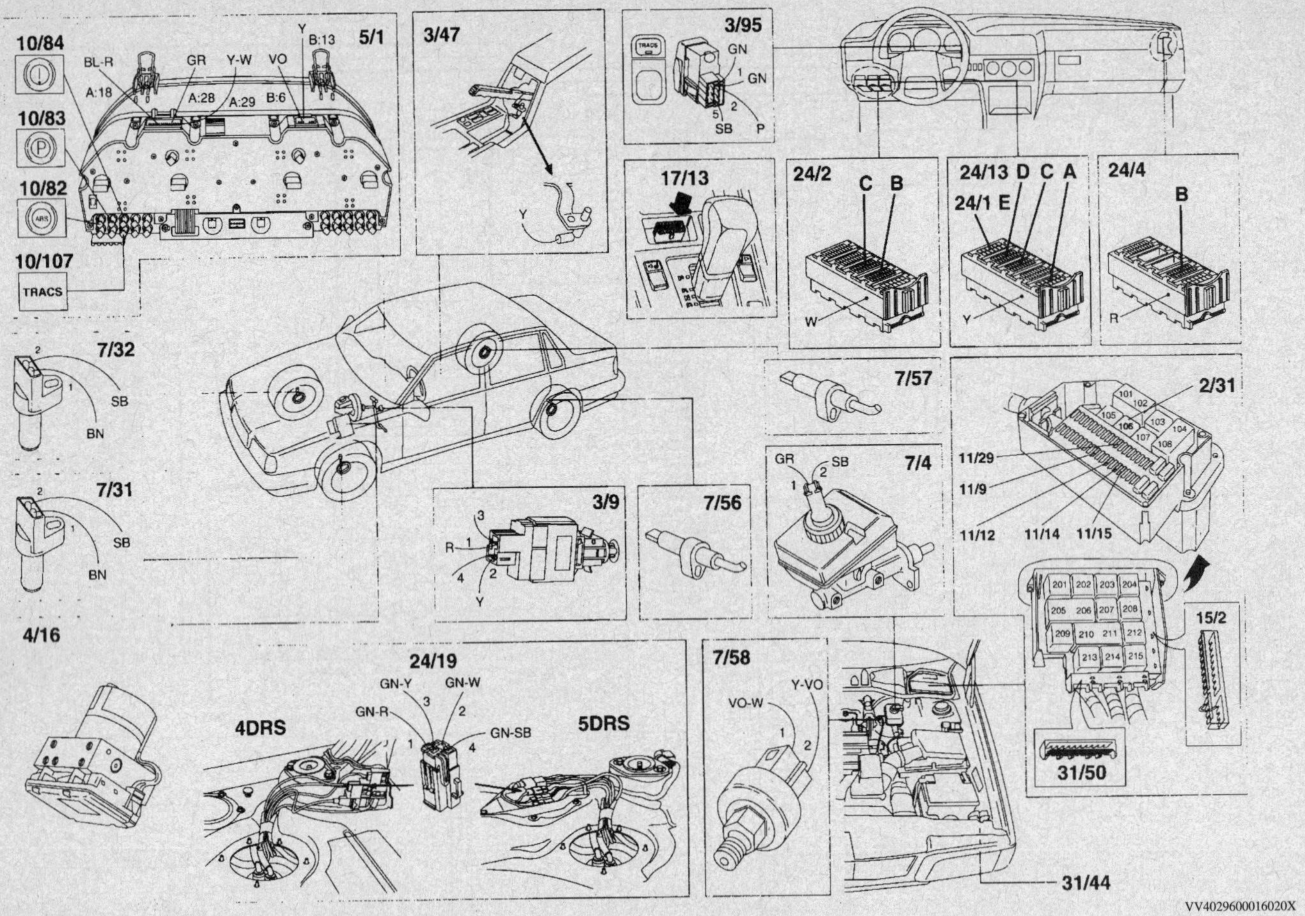

10/84
10/83
10/82
10/107
TRACS
BL-R
A:18
GR
Y-W
VO
A:28
A:29
B:6
Y
B:13
5/1
3/47
3/95
GN
SB
P
17/13
24/2
C B
W
24/13 D C A
24/1 E
24/4
B
R
7/32
7/31
BN
4/16
7/57
2/31
7/4
11/29
11/9
11/12
11/14
11/15
3/9
7/56
24/19
GN-Y
GN-W
GN-R
GN-SB
4DRS
5DRS
7/58
Y-VO
VO-W
15/2
31/50
31/44

VV4029600016020X

Fig. 5 ABS wiring circuit & electrical components (Part 2 of 2). 1996 850

Diagnostic trouble code (DTC)	Fault registered	ABS lamp	ABS function	TRACS lamp	TRACS function
444	No supply to hydraulic unit valves	On	Off	On	Off
443	Pump motor, electrical or mechanical fault	On	Off	On	Off
442	Pump pressure too low	On	Off	On	Off
441	Control module fault	On	Off	On	Off
424	TRACS pressure switch, faulty or short circuited	Off	On	On	Off
423	TRACS valve, open-circuit or short-circuit	On	Off	On	Off
422	Rear wheel circuit return valve, open-circuit or short-circuit	On	Off	On	Off
421	Rear wheel circuit inlet valve, open-circuit or short-circuit	On	Off	On	Off
414	Right front wheel return valve, open-circuit or short-circuit	On	Off	On	Off
413	Right front wheel inlet valve, open-circuit or short-circuit	On	Off	On	Off
412	Left front wheel return valve, open-circuit or short-circuit	On	Off	On	Off
411	Left front wheel inlet valve, open-circuit or short-circuit	On	Off	On	Off
324	Right rear wheel sensor, intermittent disturbance at speeds > 40 km/h (25mph)	On	Off	On	Off
323	Left rear wheel sensor, intermittent disturbance at speeds > 40 km/h (25mph)	On	Off	On	Off
322	Right front wheel sensor, intermittent disturbance at speeds > 40 km/h (25mph)	On	Off	On	Off
321	Left front wheel sensor, intermittent disturbance at speeds > 40 km/h (25mph)	On	Off	On	Off
314	Right rear wheel sensor, open-circuit or short-circuit	On	Off	On	Off
313	Left rear wheel sensor, open-circuit or short-circuit	On	Off	On	Off
312	Right front wheel sensor, open-circuit or short-circuit	On	Off	On	Off
311	Left front wheel sensor, open-circuit or short-circuit	On	Off	On	Off

Diagnostic trouble code (DTC)	Fault registered	ABS lamp	ABS function	TRACS lamp	TRACS function
224	Right rear wheel sensor, signal absent in ABS function	On	Off	On	Off
223	Left rear wheel sensor, signal absent in ABS function	On	Off	On	Off
222	Right front wheel sensor, signal absent in ABS function	On	Off	On	Off
221	Left front wheel sensor, signal absent in ABS function	On	Off	On	Off
214	Right rear wheel sensor, signal absent when moving off	On	Off	On	Off
213	Left rear wheel sensor, signal absent when moving off	On	Off	On	Off
212	Right front wheel sensor, signal absent when moving off	On	Off	On	Off
211	Left front wheel sensor, signal absent when moving off	On	Off	On	Off
144	Brake discs overheated	Off	On	On	Off
143	Control module fault	Off	On	Off	On
142	Faulty brake light switch, open-circuit or short-circuit	Off	On	Off	On
141	Faulty pedal sensor, short circuit to ground (GND) or supply	On	Off	On	Off
124	Right rear wheel sensor, circuit fault below 40 km/h (25 mph)	On *	Off	On	Off
123	Left rear wheel sensor, circuit fault below 40 km/h (25 mph)	On *	Off	On	Off
122	Right front wheel sensor, circuit fault below 40 km/h (25 mph)	On *	Off **	On	Off
121	Left front wheel sensor, circuit fault below 40 km/h (25 mph)	On *	Off **	On	Off
111	No faults detected	Off	On	Off	On

* ABS warning indicator does not light at speeds lower than 20 km/h.

** ABS function remains on the rear wheels.

VV4029100008000

Fig. 6 ABS diagnostic trouble codes. 1993-95 850

DTC	Fault text	Note
ABS–141	EBD–pressure sensor signal, circuit fault	Switches on warning light ABS Switches on warning light TRACS
ABS–142	Brake light switch signal	
ABS–143	Road speed signal, circuit fault	
ABS–144	Brake discs on front wheels overheating	Cars with TRACS only Switches on TRACS warning light Only while temperature is still high
ABS–211	Wheel sensor signal LH front wheel wheel speed incorrect	Switches on ABS warning light Switches on TRACS warning light
ABS–212	Wheel sensor signal RH front wheel wheel speed incorrect	Switches on ABS warning light Switches on TRACS warning light
ABS–213	Wheel sensor signal LH rear wheel wheel speed incorrect	Switches on ABS warning light Switches on TRACS warning light
ABS–214	Wheel sensor signal RH rear wheel wheel speed incorrect	Switches on ABS warning light Switches on TRACS warning light
ABS–221	Wheel sensor signal LH front wheel ABS control phase too long	Switches on ABS warning light Switches on TRACS warning light
ABS–222	Wheel sensor signal RH front wheel ABS control phase too long	Switches on ABS warning light Switches on TRACS warning light
ABS–223	Wheel sensor signal LH rear wheel ABS control phase too long	Switches on ABS warning light Switches on TRACS warning light
ABS–224	Wheel sensor signal RH rear wheel ABS control phase too long	Switches on ABS warning light Switches on TRACS warning light
ABS–311	Wheel sensor signal LH front wheel circuit fault	Switches on ABS warning light Switches on TRACS warning light
ABS–312	Wheel sensor signal RH front wheel circuit fault	Switches on ABS warning light Switches on TRACS warning light
ABS–313	Wheel sensor signal LH rear wheel circuit fault	Switches on ABS warning light Switches on TRACS warning light
ABS–314	Wheel sensor signal RH rear wheel circuit fault	Switches on ABS warning light Switches on TRACS warning light
ABS–321	Wheel sensor signal LH front wheel extrapolation counter	Switches on ABS warning light Switches on TRACS warning light
ABS–322	Wheel sensor signal RH front wheel extrapolation counter	Switches on ABS warning light Switches on TRACS warning light
ABS–323	Wheel sensor signal LH rear wheel extrapolation counter	Switches on ABS warning light Switches on TRACS warning light
ABS–324	Wheel sensor signal RH rear wheel extrapolation counter	Switches on ABS warning light Switches on TRACS warning light

VV4029600015010X

Fig. 7 ABS diagnostic trouble codes (Part 1 of 2). 1996 850

DTC	Fault text	Note
ABS–411	Inlet valve LH front wheel, fault in valve terminal circuit	Switches on ABS warning light Switches on TRACS warning light
ABS–412	Outlet valve LH front wheel, fault in valve terminal circuit	Switches on ABS warning light Switches on TRACS warning light
ABS–413	Inlet valve RH front wheel, fault in valve terminal circuit	Switches on ABS warning light Switches on TRACS warning light
ABS–414	Outlet valve HR front wheel, fault in valve terminal circuit	Switches on ABS warning light Switches on TRACS warning light
ABS–421	Inlet valve rear wheel,fault in valve terminal circuit	Switches on ABS warning light Switches on TRACS warning light
ABS–422	Outlet valve rear wheel, fault in valve terminal circuit	Switches on ABS warning light Switches on TRACS warning light
ABS-423	Inlet valve TRACS, fault in valve terminal circuit	Cars with TRACS only
ABS–431	Control module - general hardware fault	Switches on ABS warning light Switches on TRACS warning light
ABS–432	Control module - general interference fault	Switches on ABS warning light Switches on TRACS warning light
ABS–433	Battery voltage too high	Switches on ABS warning light Switches on TRACS warning light
ABS–441	Main control module relay	Switches on ABS warning light Switches on TRACS warning light
ABS–442	Control module - creeping powers	Switches on ABS warning light Switches on TRACS warning light
ABS–443	Pump motor electrical or mechanical fault	Switches on ABS warning light Switches on TRACS warning light
ABS–444	Control module - valve reference power	Switches on ABS warning light Switches on TRACS warning light
ABS–445	Control module - general valve fault	Switches on ABS warning light Switches on TRACS warning light

VV4029600015020X

Fig. 7 ABS diagnostic trouble codes (Part 2 of 2). 1996 850

7. If reading is incorrect, check for short circuit. If circuit is satisfactory, replace hydraulic modulator. If readings are correct, check for properly operating brake light contact. If brake light contact is operating properly, delete code and test drive vehicle. If code appears again, replace control module.

MG. Diagnostic Trouble Code (DTC) 4-4-1

1. Ensure ignition switch is in Off position, then disconnect battery ground cable.
2. Disconnect control module electrical connector, then connect adapter 981 3196 to control module connector.
3. Connect test box 981 3190 to adapter, then the battery ground cable.
4. Connect an ohmmeter between control module housing and ground. Ohmmeter should indicate a closed circuit. Connect ohmmeter between terminal 1 and ground. Ohmmeter should indicate a closed circuit.
5. If reading is correct, check that wheel sensor is not too close to sources of interference, (electric motors, telephone lines, etc.). Delete code and test drive vehicle. If fault occurs again, replace control module.

MH. Diagnostic Trouble Code (DTC) 4-4-3

1. Disconnect 15-pole connector from combination relay, then connect a voltmeter between terminal 15 and

DTC	Diagnosis, carry out procedure: MJ. Diagnostic trouble code (DTC) 4-4-4	MH. Diagnostic trouble code (DTC) 4-4-3	MG. Diagnostic trouble code (DTC) 4-4-1	MF. Diagnostic trouble code (DTC) 4-2-4	ME. Diagnostic trouble codes (DTC), valves.	MD. Diagnostic trouble codes (DTC) 1-4-4	MC. Diagnostic trouble codes (DTC) 1-4-2	MB. Diagnostic trouble codes 1-4-1	MA. Diagn. trouble codes (DTC), wheel sensors.	RK. Bleeding brakes.	Delete diagn. trouble codes (DTC) and test drive, see proc. H. Test drive.	TD. Hydraulic modulator, replacement.	TC. Control module, replacement.
Code 444	■												
Code 443		■											
Code 442										Do no. 1	Do no. 2	Do no. 3	
Code 441			■										
Code 424				■									
Code 411, 412, 413, 414, 421, 422 or 423					■								
Code211, 212, 213, 214, 221, 222, 223, 224, 311, 312, 313, 314, 321, 322, 323, or 324									■				
Code 144						■							
Code 143											Do no. 1		Do no. 2
Code 142							■						
Code 141								■					
Code 121, 122, 123, or 124									■				

After repairs have been completed delete diagnostic trouble codes (DTC) so that 1-1-1 is displayed and test drive the vehicle (see procedure H. Test drive). Carry out procedure E. ABS/TRACS Function check to ensure that the function is operating properly.

VV4029100009000X

Fig. 8 ABS Diagnostic Trouble Code (DTC)/ Diagnosis Table. 850

Symptom	Diagnosis, carry out procedure: NA. ABS warning indocator does not light.	NB. ABS warning indicator lit, no diagnostic trouble codes (DTC) displayed.	NC. TRACS warning indicator does not light.	ND. TRACS warning indicator lit, no trouble codes (DTC) displayed.	NG. Diagnostic trouble codes (DTC cannot be read.	L. Mechanical components, fault tracing.	NH. Poor braking.	NJ. Both the fornt wheels wholly or partially locked.	NK. No TRACS function.
ABS warning indicator does not light.	■								
ABS warning indicator lit, no diagnostic trouble codes (DTC) displayed.		■							
TRACS warning indicator does not light.			■						
TRACS warning indicator lit, no diagnostic trouble codes (DTC) displayed.				■					
Diagnostic trouble codes cannot be read.					■				
Poor braking.						Do no. 1	Do no. 2		
Brakes binding.								■	
No TRACS function.									■
Excessive pedal travel.						■			
Brake pedal bottoms.						■			
Brakes pull to one side.						■			
Brakes grab.						■			
Brakes squeal						■			

After repairs have been completed delete diagnostic trouble codes (DTC) so that 1-1-1 is displayed and test drive the vehicle (see procedure H. Test drive). Carry out procedure E. ABS/TRACS Function check to ensure that the function is operating properly.

VV4029100010000X

Fig. 9 ABS Symptoms/Diagnosis Table. 850

Fault: Cause	Remedy
Excessive pedal travel, "spongy" brakes	
Pedal travel excessive due to lateral brake disc run-out.	Check the disc and replace if necessary.
Air in the braking system.	Bleed the braking system.
Brake fluid level low.	Check for leaks, fill and bleed the system.
Brake pedal bottoms	
Brake fluid level.	Check for leaks, fill and bleed the system.
Air in the braking system.	Bleed the braking system.
Leak in the braking system.	Check the braking system, repair the leak and bleed the system.
Faulty clutch master cylinder.	Replace clutch master cylinder.
Leaking hose.	Replace hose.
Worn seal.	Overhaul the brake caliper.
Poor braking	
Moisture on the pads and discs.	Brake several times to dry the pads.
Grease or oil on the pads.	Replace brake pads and check adjacent seals.
Faulty power brake booster non-return valve.	Replace non-return valve.
Faulty power brake booster.	Check the vacuum and the condition of the power brake booster.
	Replace the power brake booster or hoses if necessary.

VV4029100011010X

Fig. 10 ABS Mechanical Components, Fault Tracing (Part 1 of 2). 850

ground. Voltmeter should indicate battery voltage.

2. If reading is incorrect, check for break in fuse or wiring. If reading is correct, proceed to next step.
3. Connect voltmeter between terminal 15 and terminal 2. Voltmeter should indicate battery voltage.
4. If reading is incorrect, check that wiring to ground is not shorted or broken. If reading is correct, proceed to next step.
5. Disconnect 4-pole connector from combination relay, then connect an ohmmeter between terminal 2 and terminal 4. Ohmmeter should read between 10 and 40 ohms. Connect ohmmeter between terminal 2 and ground. Ohmmeter should indicate a broken circuit.
6. If one of the readings is incorrect, replace hydraulic modulator. If both readings are correct, proceed to next step.
7. Using two wire bridges, bridge terminal 2 on 15-pole connector and terminal 3 on 4-pole connector, then terminal 15 on 15-pole connector and terminal 1 on 4-pole connector. Pump motor should operate.
8. If pump motor does not operate, replace hydraulic modulator. If pump motor operates, leave bridges in place and proceed to next step.
9. Connect voltmeter between terminal 4 and terminal 2 on 4-pole connector. Voltmeter should read over 0.5 V AC while pump motor is running. Remove bridges.
10. If reading is incorrect, replace hydraulic modulator. If reading is correct, proceed to next step.
11. Connect ohmmeter between terminal 1 on 4-pole connector and terminal 15 on 15-pole connector. Ohmmeter should indicate an open circuit. Connect ohmmeter between terminal 3 on 4-pole connector and terminal 2 on 15-pole connector. Ohmmeter should read 0 ohms. Connect ohmmeter between terminal 2 on 4-pole connector and terminal 8 on 15-pole connector. Ohmmeter should read 0 ohms. Connect ohmmeter between terminal 4 on 4-pole connector and terminal 7 on 15-pole connector. Ohmmeter should read 0 ohms. Connect ohmmeter between terminal 10 and terminal 13 on 15-pole connector. Ohmmeter should read between 45 and 90 ohms.
12. If one of the readings is incorrect, replace combination relay. If all readings are correct, replace connectors, then proceed to next step.
13. Ensure ignition switch is in Off position, then disconnect battery ground cable.
14. Disconnect control module electrical connector, then connect adapter 981 3196 to control module connector.
15. Connect test box 981 3190 to adapter, then the battery ground cable.
16. Connect a wire between terminal 15 on test box and battery positive terminal. Pump motor should operate.
17. If pump motor does not operate, check combination relay for shorted or an open in wiring. If wiring is satisfactory, replace combination relay. If pump motor operates, proceed to next step.
18. Connect ohmmeter between terminal 49 and terminal 31. Ohmmeter should read between 10 and 40 ohms.
19. If reading is incorrect, check for a an open in wiring. If reading is correct, proceed to next step.
20. Connect ohmmeter between terminal 49 and terminal 1, then terminal 31 and terminal 1. Ohmmeter should indicate an open in circuit in both cases.
21. If readings are incorrect, check for grounding. If circuit is not grounded, replace combination relay. If readings are correct, replace control module.

MJ. Diagnostic Trouble Code (DTC) 4-4-4

1. Ensure ignition switch is in Off position, then disconnect battery ground cable.
2. Disconnect control module electrical connector, then connect adapter 981 3196 to control module connector.
3. Connect test box 981 3190 to adapter, then the battery ground cable.
4. Disconnect 15-pole connector from

combination relay, then connect an ohmmeter between ground and terminal 3 on test box, terminal 33 on test box and terminal 34 on test box. Ohmmeter should indicate an open circuit for each check.

5. If one of the readings is incorrect, check for short circuit in wiring. If readings are correct, proceed to next step.
6. Connect ohmmeter between terminal 3 on test box and terminal 9 on 15-pole connector. Ohmmeter should read ca. 0 ohms.
7. If readings are incorrect, proceed to step 16. If readings are correct, proceed to next step.
8. Connect ohmmeter between terminal 34 on test box and terminal 12 on 15-pole connector. Ohmmeter should read ca. 0 ohms.
9. If readings are incorrect, check for break in wiring. If readings are correct, proceed to next step.
10. Turn ignition switch to On position. Connect a voltmeter between terminal 3 on 15-pole connector and ground. Connect voltmeter between terminal 4 on 15-pole connector and ground. Turn ignition switch to Off position. Both readings should battery voltage.
11. If readings are incorrect, ensure wiring is intact. If readings are correct, proceed to next step.
12. Connect ohmmeter between terminal 9 and terminal 10 on 15-pole connector. Ohmmeter should read 0 ohms. Connect ohmmeter between terminal 3 and terminal 12 on 15-pole connector. Ohmmeter should read between 45 and 90 ohms.
13. If one of the readings is incorrect, replace combination relay. If both readings are correct, proceed to next step.
14. Connect 15-pole connector, turn ignition switch to On position, connect a jumper between test box terminals 34 and 1, then connect voltmeter between terminal 3 and terminal 1. Voltmeter should indicate battery voltage. Turn ignition switch to Off position.
15. If readings are incorrect, replace combination relay. If readings are correct, replace control module.
16. Disconnect 15-pole connector from hydraulic modulator, then connect ohmmeter between terminal 15 and terminal 1. Ohmmeter should read ca. 0 ohms.
17. If readings are incorrect, replace hydraulic modulator. If readings are correct, proceed to next step.
18. Connect ohmmeter between terminal 1 on hydraulic modulator connector and terminal 3 on test box. Ohmmeter should read ca. 0 ohms.
19. If readings are incorrect, ensure there are no breaks in wiring. If readings are correct, ensure wiring is intact between terminal 15 on hydraulic modulator connector and terminal 9 on 15-pole relay connector.

Fault	
Cause	Remedy
Brakes pull to one side	
Grease or oil on brake pads.	Replace brake pads and check adjacent seal.
Faulty brake caliper.	Overhaul the brake caliper.
Wrong tire pressure.	Adjust tire pressure.
Uneven tire wear.	Check/adjust wheel alignment.
Wrongly aligned front suspension.	Align front suspension.
Tires not mounted with DOT marking facing out.	Mount tires on rims with DOT marking facing out in order to counter conicity forces.
Brakes grab	
Moisture on pads and discs.	Brake several times to dry the pads.
Wheel hub play.	Replace the wheel hub.
Brake pads worn out.	Replace brake pads.
Vibrations in the brake pedal (caused by variations in the thickness of the brake disc).	Machine* or replace brake disc.(*check warranty conditions)
Brake caliper loose.	Tighten brake caliper.
Brakes squeal	
Affected by weather conditions.	Brake several times to dry.
Brake pads worn out.	Replace brake pads.
Rear brake caliper brake pads vibrate.	Check the brake disc. Replace if necessary.
Brakes binding	
Handbrake cable sticking .	Replace cable.
Wrongly adjusted handbrake .	Adjust the handbrake.
Faulty clutch master cylinder.	Replace clutch master cylinder.
Deformed brake pipes.	Replace brake pipes.

VV4029100011020X

Fig. 10 ABS Mechanical Components, Fault Tracing (Part 2 of 2). 850

NA. ABS-Warning Indicator Does Not Light

1. Ensure ignition switch is in Off position, then disconnect battery ground cable.
2. Disconnect control module electrical connector, then connect adapter 981 3196 to control module connector.
3. Connect test box 981 3190 to adapter, then the battery ground cable.
4. Disconnect 15-pole connector from combination relay, connect a voltmeter between terminals 52 and 1, then turn ignition switch to On position. Voltmeter should indicate battery voltage. Turn ignition switch to Off position.
5. If reading is incorrect, ensure wiring to bulb and bulb are intact. If bulb and wiring to bulb are satisfactory, replace combination instrument. If readings are correct, proceed to next step.
6. Turn ignition switch to On position, then connect a jumper between terminal 6 on 15-pole connector and ground. ABS warning indicator should light. Turn ignition switch to Off position. **If fuse blows, check wiring for short circuit.**
7. If indicator does not light, check for breaks in wiring. If indicator lights, a double fault may have occurred, proceed to next step.
8. Connect positive lead of a diode tester to relay terminal 6 and negative lead to relay terminal 2 on 15-pole combination relay connector. Diode tester should indicate continuity. Change polarity on diode tester. Diode tester should indicate a break.
9. If readings are incorrect, replace combination relay and continue to next step. If readings are correct, leave relay connector disconnected and proceed to next step.
10. Connect a jumper between terminal 52 and terminal 1, then turn ignition switch to On position. ABS warning indicator should light. Turn ignition switch to Off position.
11. If indicator does not light, check for breaks in wiring. If indicator lights, reconnect system and ensure ABS warning indicator is operating properly. If indicator still does not light, replace control module.

NB. ABS-Warning Indicator Lit, No Diagnostic Trouble Codes (DTC) Displayed

1. Drive vehicle at a speed of at least 25 mph. If ABS warning indicator does not go out, proceed to next step.
2. Ensure ignition switch is in Off position, then disconnect battery ground cable.
3. Disconnect control module electrical connector, then connect adapter 981 3196 to control module connector.

4. Connect test box 981 3190 to adapter, then the battery ground cable.
5. Connect a jumper between terminal 34 and terminal 1, a voltmeter between terminal 33 and terminal 1, then turn ignition switch to On position. Voltmeter should indicate battery voltage.
6. In reading is incorrect, check for an open in wiring. If wiring is satisfactory, replace combination relay. If reading is correct, leave jumper in place and proceed to next step.
7. With ignition switch in On position, connect an ohmmeter between terminal 52 and terminal 1. Ohmmeter should indicate an open circuit.
8. If reading is incorrect, proceed to next step. If reading is correct, replace control module.
9. Turn ignition switch to Off position, disconnect 15-pole connector from combination relay, then connect ohmmeter between terminal 52 and terminal 1. Ohmmeter should indicate an open circuit.
10. If reading is incorrect, check for short circuit in combination instrument wiring. If reading is correct, replace combination relay.

NC. TRACS Warning Indicator Does Not Light

1. Check that control module is intended for TRACS (blue label).
2. Ensure ignition switch is in Off position, then disconnect battery ground cable.
3. Disconnect control module electrical connector, then connect adapter 981 3196 to control module connector.
4. Connect test box 981 3190 to adapter, then the battery ground cable.
5. Connect a jumper between terminal 44 and terminal 1, then turn ignition switch to On position. TRACS warning indicator should light. Turn ignition switch to Off position.
6. If indicator did not light, ensure wiring to bulb and bulb are intact. If bulb and wiring to bulb are satisfactory, replace combination instrument. If readings are correct, replace control module.

ND. TRACS Warning Indicator Lit, No Diagnostic Trouble Codes (DTC) Displayed

1. Check that control module is intended for TRACS (blue label).
2. Ensure ignition switch is in Off position, then disconnect battery ground cable.
3. Disconnect control module electrical connector, then connect adapter 981 3196 to control module connector.
4. Connect test box 981 3190 to adapter, then the battery ground cable.
5. Turn ignition switch to On position, then connect an ohmmeter between terminal 44 and terminal 1. Ohmmeter should indicate a broken circuit. Turn Ignition switch to Off position.
6. If reading is incorrect, check for a short circuit in combination instrument wiring. If reading is correct, replace control module.

NE. Brake Warning Indicator Does Not Light

1. **If brake warning indicator does not light when ignition is switched On,** proceed as follows:
   a. Disconnect connector from brake fluid level switch, connect a jumper between terminals 1 and 2, start engine or remove D+ connector from alternator, then ensure charge indicator goes out. Brake warning indicator should light. Turn engine Off or connect D+ connector.
   b. If indicator does not light, ensure bulb is intact and there are no opens in wiring to fluid level switch. If bulb and wiring to bulb are satisfactory, replace combination instrument. If indicator lights, replace combination instrument.
2. **If brake warning indicator does not light when brake fluid level is too low,** proceed as follows:
   a. Disconnect connector from brake fluid level switch, connect a jumper between terminals 1 and 2, start engine or remove D+ connector from alternator. ensure charge indicator goes out. Brake warning indicator should light. Turn engine Off or connect D+ connector.
   b. If indicator does not light, check for an open in brake fluid warning level switch wiring. If indicator lights, replace brake fluid level switch.

NF. Brake Warning Indicator Does Not Go Out

1. Check brake fluid level. Reservoir should be full.
2. Disconnect connector from brake fluid level switch, start engine or remove D+ connector from alternator. Brake warning indicator should go out. Turn engine Off or connect D+ connector.
3. If indicator stayed On, ensure wiring to switch is not grounded. If circuit is not shorted, replace combination instrument. If indicator went out, replace brake fluid level switch.

NG. Diagnostic Trouble Codes (DTC) Cannot Be Read

1. Ensure ignition switch is in Off position, then disconnect battery ground cable.
2. Disconnect control module electrical connector, then connect adapter 981 3196 to control module connector.
3. Connect test box 981 3190 to adapter, then the battery ground cable.
4. Remove diagnostic output from its connector, turn ignition switch to On position, then connect a voltmeter between terminal 53 and terminal 1. Voltmeter should indicate battery voltage.
5. If reading is incorrect, ensure fuse 11/29 and wiring are intact. If reading is correct, proceed to next step.
6. Connect an ohmmeter between terminal 23 and terminal 1, remove diagnostic key or disconnect selector lead from diagnostic output. Ohmmeter should indicate an open circuit.
7. If reading is incorrect, check wiring for a short circuit. If reading is correct, proceed to next step.
8. Connect ohmmeter between terminal 23 on test box and terminal A3 on diagnostic output connector. Ohmmeter should read ca. 0 ohms.
9. If reading is incorrect, check for an open in wiring. If reading is correct, proceed to next step.
10. Turn ignition switch to On position, then connect voltmeter between terminal A4 on diagnostic output connector and ground. Voltmeter should indicate battery voltage.
11. If reading is incorrect, ensure fuse 11/33 and wiring are intact. If reading is correct, proceed to next step.
12. Connect voltmeter between terminals A8 and A4 on diagnostic output connector. Voltmeter should indicate battery voltage. Turn ignition switch to Off position.
13. If reading is incorrect, ensure wiring is intact. If reading is correct, check diagnostic key or diagnostic output on another system. If diagnostic key or diagnostic output are not faulty, replace control module.

NH. Poor Braking

1. Raise and support vehicle enough to allow its wheels to turn freely, release parking brake and place shift lever in Neutral, depress brake pedal and release it again, then turn wheel with suspect valve by hand. Wheel should turn.
2. If wheel did not turn, check that brake caliper is not frozen, parking brake cable is released and brake pads, springs and other components are not sticking or frozen. If wheel turned, proceed to next step.
3. Ensure ignition switch is in Off position, then disconnect battery ground cable.
4. Disconnect control module electrical connector, then connect adapter 981 3196 to control module connector.
5. Connect test box 981 3190 to adapter, then the battery ground cable.
6. Connect a jumper between terminals 34 and 1 of test box and between left front return valve terminal 2, right front return valve terminal 21 or rear return valve terminal 36 and terminal 1. Depress brake pedal and keep it down, turn ignition switch to On position, then turn wheel with suspect valve by hand. Wheel should turn. Turn ignition switch to Off position. **So valves do not overheat, ignition must not be switched On for more than 20 seconds. Wait at least 30 seconds before next test.**
7. If wheel did not turn, replace hydraulic modulator. If wheel turned, proceed to next step.
8. Connect jumper between left front inlet valve terminal 20, right front inlet valve terminal 38 or rear inlet valve terminal 54 and terminal 1. Turn ignition switch to On position, depress brake pedal and keep it down, then turn wheel with suspect valve by hand. Wheel should turn. Turn ignition switch to Off position. **So valves do not overheat, ignition must not be switched On for**

more than 20 seconds. Wait at least 30 seconds before next test.

9. If wheel did not turn, replace hydraulic modulator. If wheel turned, the suspect hydraulic modulator valve operates properly. Problem may be intermittent, refer to "F. Intermittent Faults."

NJ. Both Front Wheels Are Wholly Or Partially Locked

1. Check that both front wheels are locked or binding equally.
2. If wheels are not locked or binding, proceed to next step. If wheels are locked or binding, refer to "L. Mechanical Components, Fault Tracing."
3. Ensure ignition switch is in Off position, then disconnect battery ground cable.
4. Disconnect control module electrical connector, then connect adapter 981 3196 to control module connector.
5. Connect test box 981 3190 to adapter, then the battery ground cable.
6. Connect jumpers between terminals 34 and 1, terminals 21 and 1 and terminals 2 and 1, then turn ignition switch to On position. Wheels should turn. Turn ignition switch to Off position. Visually inspect brakes. **So valves do not overheat, ignition must not be switched On for more than 20 seconds. Wait at least 30 seconds before next test.**
7. If wheels turn, replace hydraulic modulator. If wheels do not turn, fault is mechanical. Refer to "L. Mechanical Components, Fault Tracing."

NK. No TRACS Function

1. TRACS switch must be On for TRACS to operate. Turn ignition switch to On position, set TRACS switch To On position. Indicator lamp should light. Turn ignition switch to Off position.
2. If indicator does not light, check wiring to switch for breaks. If wiring is satisfactory, replace switch. If indicator does light, proceed to next step.
3. Ensure ignition switch is in Off position, then disconnect battery ground cable.
4. Disconnect control module electrical connector, then connect adapter 981 3196 to control module connector.
5. Connect test box 981 3190 to adapter, then the battery ground cable.
6. Turn ignition switch to On position, connect a jumper between terminal 25 and terminal 1. Indicator lamp should light. Turn ignition switch to Off position.
7. If indicator does not light, check wiring to switch for breaks. If wiring is satisfactory, replace switch. If indicator does light, check that fault is not intermittent. Refer to "F. Intermittent Faults. " If fault remains, replace control module.

P. Signal Description, Control Module

1. Ensure ignition switch is in Off position, then disconnect battery ground cable.
2. Disconnect control module electrical connector, then connect adapter 981 3196 to control module connector.
3. Connect test box 981 3190 to adapter, then the battery ground cable.
4. Perform checks as shown in **Fig. 11.**

INTERMITTENT FAULTS

1. In case of intermittent faults, the On-Board Diagnostic (OBD) can be used in the following manner to help to ascertain which circuit is faulty:
   a. Read, note and delete any codes stored in control module.
   b. Test drive vehicle and try to repeat conditions under which fault appears. Refer to "H. Test Drive." A description of driving conditions at time fault occurred may aid in fault tracing.
   c. Stop vehicle and read codes stored. When codes have been stored, "G. Diagnostic Trouble Code (DTC) Table" should be used to decide which circuits may be faulty.
   d. If no codes are stored, fault tracing must be carried out using "K. Symptoms/Diagnosis Table."
   e. If fault does not appear during test drive, a good description of behavior of vehicle at time fault occurred may help in locating most probable faulty circuit. "K. Symptoms/ Diagnosis Table" may also be used for fault tracing.
2. Most intermittent problems can be caused by faults in connectors or wiring. Suspect circuits should be checked for the following:
   a. Poor contact between connectors or wiring connections which have not been properly connected.
   b. Poorly connected or damaged connectors.
   c. Poor connection between connectors and wiring.
   d. Most faults occurring in the system disengage the system entirely when vehicle is being driven, even if fault disappears before ignition is turned Off. In certain intermittent fault cases, ABS function may return if fault disappears before ignition is turned Off.
3. If ABS warning indicator lights temporarily, the following circuits for input signals to control module should be examined:
   a. Low system voltage. If system voltage is low, control module will light ABS warning indicator. Indicator will remain lit until system voltage returns to normal. When system voltage to control module is correct, system returns to normal function.
   b. Power Cut. If there is a power cut to control module or hydraulic modulator, ABS warning indicator lights temporarily. Affected circuits are main relay, pump motor relay, fuses and related wiring.

CLEARING DIAGNOSTIC TROUBLE CODES

850

1. Check that all codes stored have been read. Codes cannot be deleted until all codes have been displayed at least once and the first code has reappeared.
2. Hold button down for at least 5 seconds and release it. Three seconds after button is released, LED will light up.
3. While LED is lit press button again. Hold button down for at least 5 seconds, then release it. LED will go out.
4. Turn ignition switch to Off position.
5. Turn ignition switch to On position and check that all codes have been deleted by pressing button briefly but firmly.
6. If code 1-1-1 is displayed, codes have been deleted.
7. If codes have not been deleted, repeat "Accessing Diagnostic Trouble Codes," "Reading Diagnostic Trouble Codes" and "Deleting Diagnostic Trouble Codes."
8. When codes are deleted and code 1-1-1 has been displayed, drive vehicle at least 25 mph. ABS warning indicator should go out.
9. If ABS warning indicator does not go out check that no new codes have been posted.
10. Carry out a system check as a guideline for normal function. Refer to **Fig. 12,** for procedures.
11. Check ABS/TRACS, refer to **Fig. 13,** for procedures.

SYSTEM SERVICE

Brake System Bleed

240, 940 & 960

A diaphragm type pressure bleeder should be used to bleed system. Bleed system with wheels on vehicle.

1. Raise vehicle and fill brake fluid reservoir to MAX mark.
2. Install automatic filler cap.
3. Use only upper nipple for bleeding vehicles equipped with Multi-Link.
4. Begin by bleeding one of rear wheels as follows:
   a. Connect bleeder tool to one of the bleed nipples. Connect bleeder unit.
   b. Connect air hose to other side of unit.
   c. Open bleed nipple and close it when no bubbles remain in fluid flowing out.
5. Repeat procedure on other rear wheel and both front wheels. On front wheels, open upper nipple first.
6. Check for air in system by depressing brake pedal with force equivalent, to a sudden stop.
7. Pedal should not feel spongy and travel should not exceed two inches.
8. Install protective plugs on bleeder nipples and lower vehicle.

850

1. Turn ignition switch to Off position, then raise and support vehicle.
2. Clean area around brake fluid reservoir cap, then remove cap.
3. Connect bleeding unit to brake fluid

Note! All readings shown are between the terminal in column 1 and terminal 1 (Signal ground (GND)). Ensure, therefore, that this ground (GND) point is properly connected to the battery negative terminal before readings are taken.

Con-nection	Signal type Function	Ignition Off		On	
		U (V)	R (Ω)	U (V)	R (Ω)
1	Signal ground (GND)	U_{low}	0	U_{low}	0
2	Output to the return valve (left front wheel), in the hydraulic modulator.	U_{low}	3-5	U_{bat}	∞
3	Power supply to all valves in the hydraulic modulator.	U_{low}	0	U_{bat}	∞
4-12	Not used.		-	-	-
13	Input from the pressure switch (TRACS) in the hydraulic modulator. Normally closed, opens on activation.	U_{low}	-	6-10	∞
14	Not used.	-	-	-	-
15	Output for activation of pump motor relay.	U_{low}	45-90	U_{bat}	∞
16	Terminal for the pedal position sensor in the power brake booster.	U_{low}	249 ± 10 %	0-2	∞
17-19	Not used.	-	-	-	-
20	Output to inlet valve (left front wheel), in the hydraulic modulator.	U_{low}	6-8	U_{bat}	∞
21	Output to return valve (right front wheel), in the hydraulic modulator.	U_{low}	3-5	U_{bat}	∞
22	Not used.	-	-	-	-
23	Input and output for diagnostic output.	U_{low}	-	8-11	∞
24	Not used.	-	-	-	-
25	Input from TRACS switch	U_{low}	∞	U_{bat}	∞
26	Output to (TRACS) pressure switch in the hydraulic modulator. Normally closed, opens on activation.	U_{low}	-	6-10	∞
27	Negative reference for right rear wheel sensor.	U_{low}	0	U_{low}	6-8
28	Negative reference for left rear wheel sensor.	U_{low}	0	U_{low}	6-8
29	Negative reference for right front wheel sensor.	U_{low}	0	U_{low}	6-8
30	Negative reference for left front wheel sensor.	U_{low}	0	U_{low}	6-8
31	Negative reference for pump motor sensor in the hydraulic modulator.	U_{low}	12000	0-2	∞

VV4029100012010X

Fig. 11 ABS Control Module Signal Description (Part 1 of 2). 850

U = Voltage (V) U_{bat} = Battery voltage U_{low} = voltage almost 0 V

R = Resistance in ohm (Ω) ∞ = Infinite resistance

Con-nection	Signal type Function	Ignition Off		On	
		U (V)	R (Ω)	U (V)	R (Ω)
32	Input from brake light contact. High signal indicates braking.	U_{low}	0-2	U_{low}	
33	Input for main relay function check.	U_{low}	0	U_{bat}	∞
34	Output main relay activation. Low signal operates the relay.	U_{low}	45-90	0-2	-
35	30-supply. The power supply from the battery to the control module, for calculating brake temperature.	U_{bat}	∞	U_{bat}	∞
36	Output to return valve in the hydraulic modulator.	U_{low}	3-5	U_{bat}	∞
37	Output to the TRACS valve. A low signal activates the valve.	U_{low}	6-9	U_{bat}	∞
38	Output to inlet valve (right front wheel), in the hydraulic modulator.	U_{low}	6-8	U_{bat}	∞
39-40	Not used.	-	-	-	-
41	Terminal for pedal position sensor in the power brake booster.	U_{low}	0	U_{low}	6-9
42-43	Not used.	-	-	-	-
44	Output to TRACS warning indicator. A low signal lights the lamp.	U_{low}	-	U_{bat}	∞
45	Positive reference for right rear wheel sensor.	U_{low}	1100	U_{bat}	∞
46	Positive reference for left rear wheel sensor.	U_{low}	1100	U_{bat}	∞
47	Positive reference for right front wheel sensor.	U_{low}	1100	U_{bat}	∞
48	Positive reference for left front wheel sensor.	U_{low}	1100	U_{bat}	∞
49	Positive reference for pump motor sensor in the hydraulic modulator.	U_{low}	12000	0-2	∞
50-51	Not used.	-	-	-	-
52	Output to ABS warning indicator. A low signal lights the lamp.	U_{low}	-	U_{bat}	∞
53	15I-supply. The power supply from the ignition switch to the control module.	U_{low}	1-3	U_{bat}	∞
54	Output to the inlet valve (rear wheels), in the hydraulic modulator.	U_{low}	6-8	U_{bat}	∞
55	Not used.	-	-	-	-

VV4029100012020X

Fig. 11 ABS Control Module Signal Description (Part 2 of 2). 850

reservoir. **Follow manufacturer's instruction for connecting and operating bleeding unit.**

4. Depress brake pedal several times to remove any air bubbles from clutch master cylinder.
5. Remove dust cap from bleed nipple on one of the rear wheels and connect hose from overflow bottle.
6. Open bleed nipple, then close and tighten nipple when no further air bubbles can be seen in fluid flowing out. Remove hose and replace dust cap.
7. Bleed other rear wheel, right front wheel, then the left front wheel using procedure described in steps 4 through 6.
8. Remove bleeding unit connector from brake fluid reservoir, then check to see if there is air in system by depressing brake pedal with a force corresponding to an abrupt braking. Pedal travel must not exceed 1.574 inch (40 mm) and warning indicator on dashboard must not flash or light up.
9. If pedal travel exceeds limit, bleed system again and check pedal travel again.
10. Ensure fluid level is not over Max mark, then lower vehicle.

Component Replacement

CONTROL MODULE, REPLACE

240, 940 & 960

1. Disconnect battery ground cable.
2. Ensure ignition is off.
3. Remove sound proofing under instrument panel.
4. Loosen band holding control module and lift module out.
5. Remove control module connector.
6. Reverse procedure to install.

850

1993–95

1. Turn ignition switch to Off position, then disconnect battery ground cable.
2. **On 1996 models,** remove air filter case and hose to air heater.
3. **On 1993–95 models,** clean area around connector, then disconnect module connector.
4. **On 1996 models,** clean area around connector, then remove control module connection by first pressing in the catch on back of cover (toward wheel housing), then carefully turn cover upwards to release the catches.
5. Remove mounting screws, then carefully lift module out of vehicle.
6. Reverse procedure to install. Read diagnostic trouble codes (DTC) and ensure code 1-1-1 is displayed.

1996

1. Turn ignition switch to Off position, then disconnect battery ground cable.
2. Remove air filter case and hose to air heater.
3. Clean area around connector, then remove control module connection by first pressing in the catch on back of cover (toward wheel housing), then carefully turn cover upwards to release the catches.
4. Disconnect ABS hydraulic pump motor connector.
5. Remove four bolts and the control module.
6. Reverse procedure to install. **Torque** to 1.3 ft. lbs.

HYDRAULIC MODULATOR, REPLACE

240, 940 & 960

1. Disconnect battery ground cable.

Carry out a system check as a guideline for normal function. See the fault tracing procedure if other results are obtained.

Do	Normal function	Fault tracing in case of fault
Start mode Ignition: off		
Ignition: On Engine off.	ABS warning indicator (and TRACS warning indicator) lit for 1 to 2 seconds, then go out.	Carry out procedure E. ABS/TRACS - Function check.
	Brake warning indicator lit.	Carry out procedure NE. Brake warning indicator does not light.
Start the engine.	ABS warning indicator (and TRACS warning indicator) lit for 1 to 2 seconds, then go out.	Carry out procedure E. ABS/TRACS - Function check
	Brake warning indicator goes out.	Carry out procedure NF. Brake warning indicator does not go out.

Note! If the car is not fitted with TRACS, only the ABS warning indicator should light.

VV4029100013000X

Fig. 12 ABS System Check, Normal Function. 850

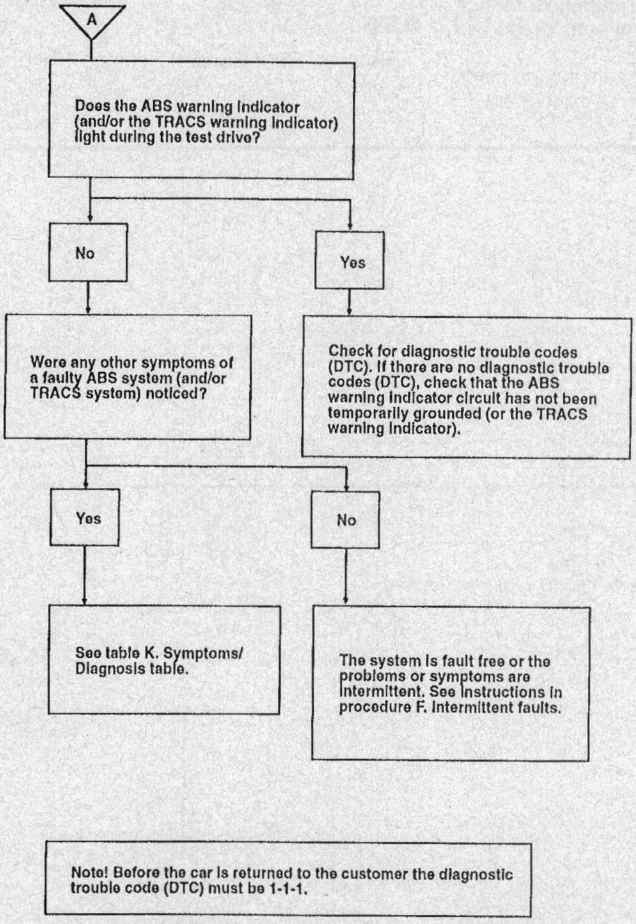
A
Does the ABS warning indicator (and/or the TRACS warning indicator) light during the test drive?
No
Yes
Were any other symptoms of a faulty ABS system (and/or TRACS system) noticed?
Check for diagnostic trouble codes (DTC). If there are no diagnostic trouble codes (DTC), check that the ABS warning indicator circuit has not been temporarily grounded (or the TRACS warning indicator).
Yes
No
See table K. Symptoms/ Diagnosis table.
The system is fault free or the problems or symptoms are intermittent. See instructions in procedure F. Intermittent faults.
Note! Before the car is returned to the customer the diagnostic trouble code (DTC) must be 1-1-1.

VV4029100014020X

Fig. 13 ABS/TRACS Function Check (Part 2 of 2). 850

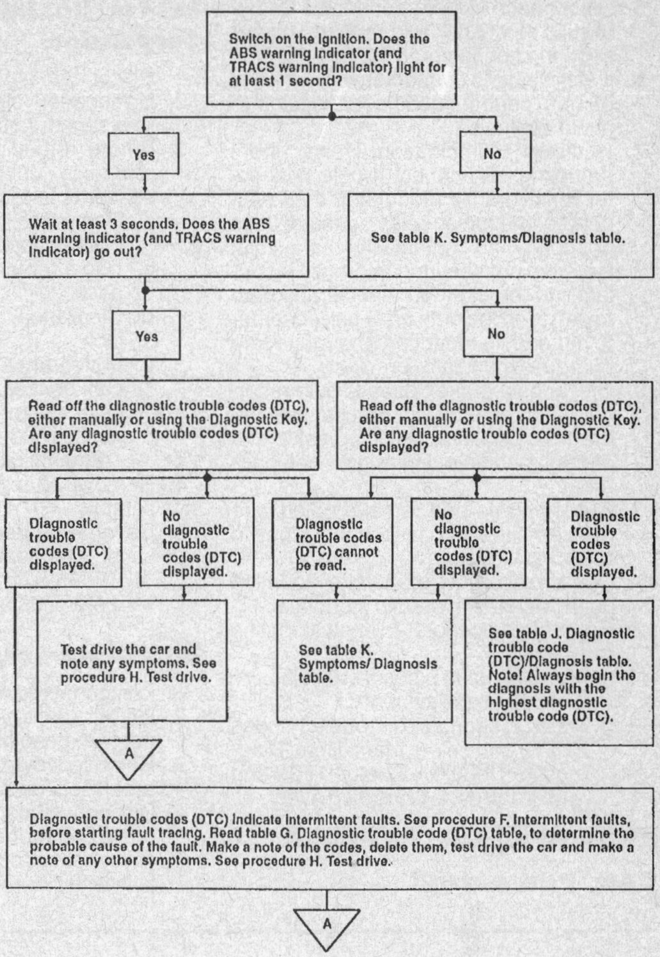
Switch on the ignition. Does the ABS warning indicator (and TRACS warning indicator) light for at least 1 second?
Yes
No
Wait at least 3 seconds. Does the ABS warning indicator (and TRACS warning indicator) go out?
See table K. Symptoms/Diagnosis table.
Yes
No
Read off the diagnostic trouble codes (DTC), either manually or using the Diagnostic Key. Are any diagnostic trouble codes (DTC) displayed?
Read off the diagnostic trouble codes (DTC), either manually or using the Diagnostic Key. Are any diagnostic trouble codes (DTC) displayed?
Diagnostic trouble codes (DTC) displayed.
No diagnostic trouble codes (DTC) displayed.
Diagnostic trouble codes (DTC) cannot be read.
No diagnostic trouble codes (DTC) displayed.
Diagnostic trouble codes (DTC) displayed.
Test drive the car and note any symptoms. See procedure H. Test drive.
See table K. Symptoms/ Diagnosis table.
See table J. Diagnostic trouble code (DTC)/Diagnosis table. Note! Always begin the diagnosis with the highest diagnostic trouble code (DTC).
A
Diagnostic trouble codes (DTC) indicate intermittent faults. See procedure F. Intermittent faults, before starting fault tracing. Read table G. Diagnostic trouble code (DTC) table, to determine the probable cause of the fault. Make a note of the codes, delete them, test drive the car and make a note of any other symptoms. See procedure H. Test drive.
A

VV4029100014010X

Fig. 13 ABS/TRACS Function Check (Part 1 of 2). 850

2. Remove cover over hydraulic modulator.
3. Remove both relays and connector.
4. Disconnect ground lead from modulator
5. Remove hydraulic lines to modulator noting position for installation.
6. Remove screw from support and push support to right. Remove hydraulic modulator
7. Reverse procedure to install, transferring three rubber pads to new modulator.

850

1. Turn ignition switch to Off position, then drain system of brake fluid.
2. Clean area around brake hose and pipe connectors on modulator and clutch master cylinder, then lay out rags under clutch master cylinder to protect paint.
3. Remove air cleaner, then disconnect battery ground cable.
4. Disconnect brake pipes to reducing valve from clutch master cylinder, then the brake pipes on side of hydraulic modulator. **Plug pipes and connectors on modulator to prevent entry of dirt or contaminants.**

5. Disconnect 15-pole connector for hydraulic modulator and remove screws securing connector to its mounting.
6. Twist wiring to connector with wiring to 55 pin control module connector to avoid confusion.
7. Remove combination relay from mounting, disconnect 4-pole connector for hydraulic modulator, then suspend combination relay so that it does not come into contact with brake fluid.
8. Remove nut securing hydraulic modulator to bracket on shock absorber tower, then the nuts on shock absorber tower and lift mounting enough to free hydraulic modulator bracket.
9. Disconnect brake hoses to fluid reservoir, then carefully lift bracket with hydraulic modulator, reducing valve and control module out of engine compartment.
10. Cut wiring tie and remove rolled wire from bracket, then disconnect pipes to reducing valve.
11. Remove hydraulic modulator mounting bolts, then the hydraulic modulator.
12. Reverse procedure to install, noting the following:
    a. **Torque** brake pipes to 10 ft. lbs.
    b. Bleed braking system.
    c. Read Diagnostic Trouble Codes (DTC) and delete them. Read Diagnostic Trouble Codes (DTC) and ensure code 1-1-1 is displayed.

REAR SENSOR, REPLACE

240, 940 & 960

Less Multi-Link Rear Suspension

1. Disconnect battery ground cable.
2. Disconnect electrical connector for rear sensor (located in trunk).
3. Before removing speed sensor from rear axle, check clearance between sensor tip and pulse wheel as follows:
    a. Remove oil plug from axle assembly inspection cover.
    b. Use a feeler gauge to check clearance.
    c. Clearance should be .023–.024 inch.
    d. If clearance is not as specified, it can be adjusted by replacing the shim. Shims are available in thicknesses .0394–.0709 inches, in increments of .008 inch.
4. Remove speed sensor form axle assembly.
5. Reverse procedure to install. Apply a small amount of lubricant No. 11610375-5, or equivalent, to the sensor before installation.

Multi-Link Suspension

1. Disconnect battery ground cable.
2. Lift out spare wheel and fold back carpet to expose filler pipe.
3. Remove covers over filler pipe and break seal on sensor cable connector.
4. Disconnect connector and press out cable and rubber grommet.
5. Raise rear section of vehicle and place jack with fixture 5972, or equivalent, under rear axle.
6. Remove four bolts which hold member to body.
7. Lower rear axle slightly. **Driveshaft must not press against fuel tank.**
8. Disconnect right hand brake wire from attachment.
9. Remove sensor cable from clamps, noting placement for installation.
10. Clean area around sensor and remove sensor assembly.
11. Reverse procedure to install, using new O-ring on sensor.

850

1. Turn ignition switch to Off position, then disconnect battery ground cable.
2. Remove wheel, then the sensor mounting bolt.
3. Remove sensor mounting bolt and pull out sensor, then disconnect connector.
4. Reverse procedure to install, noting the following:
    a. Clean dirt and rust from sensor seat so sensor locates properly against pulse wheel.
    b. **Torque** sensor mounting bolt to 7 ft. lbs.

FRONT SENSOR, REPLACE

850

Refer to "Rear Sensor, Replace." for procedure.

Automatic Transmissions

NOTE: On Air Bag Equipped Models, Refer To "Air Bag System Precautions" Located In The Front Of This Manual For System Disarming & Arming Procedures.

INDEX

	Page No.
Adjustments	50-95
AW 30-40	50-96
AW 50-42	50-96
AW 70, 70L, 71 & 72L	50-95
ZF 4-HP-22	50-95
Application Chart	50-93
Description	50-93
AW 70, 70L, 71 & 72L	50-93
ZF 4-HP-22	50-93
Identification	50-93
AW 70, 70L, 71 & 72L	50-93
ZF 4-HP-22	50-93
In-Vehicle Repairs	50-97
AW 30-40	50-98
AW 50-42	50-101
AW 70, 70L, 71 & 72L	50-97
ZF 4-HP-22	50-97
Maintenance	50-95
AW 30-40	50-95
AW 50-42	50-95
AW 70, 70L, 71 & 72L	50-95
ZF 4-HP-22	50-95
Precautions	50-93
Air Bag Systems	50-93
Tightening Specifications	50-103
Transmission, Replace	50-102
AW 30-40	50-102
AW 50-42	50-103
AW 70, 70L, 71 & 72L	50-102
ZF 4-HP-22	50-102
Troubleshooting	50-93
AW 50–42	50-94
AW 70, 70L, 71 & 72L	50-93
ZF 4-HP-22	50-94

APPLICATION CHART

Model	Transmission
1993	
240	Aisin Warner 70
850	Aisin Warner 50-42
940	Aisin Warner 70L, 71 & ZF 4 HP-22
960	Aisin Warner 71, 30-40 & ZF 4 HP-22
1994–95	
850	Aisin Warner 50-42
940	Aisin Warner 70L, 71 & ZF 4 HP-22
960	Aisin Warner 71, 30-40 & ZF 4 HP-22
1996	
850	Aisin Warner 50-42
960	Aisin Warner 71, 30-40 & ZF 4 HP-22

PRECATUIONS

AIR BAG SYSTEMS

Refer to "Air Bag System Precautions" in the front of this manual for system disarming and arming procedures.

IDENTIFICATION

AW 70, 70L, 71 & 72L

The identification plate is located on the lower left side of the transmission, above the filler tube connection.

ZF 4-HP-22

The identification plate is located on the lower left side of transmission, above the filler tube connection.

DESCRIPTION

AW 70, 70L, 71 & 72L

The AW 70/71 and AW 70L/72L models are four speed transmissions, where fourth gear is effectively an overdrive. The AW 70L model incorporates a lock-up torque converter clutch. The AW 71 transmission is similar to the AW 70. The AW 72L transmission is a reinforced and modified version of the AW 71. The AW 72L differs from the AW 71 in the following areas: It has a new torque converter with higher torque amplification and a lock-up clutch; a split sun gear shaft in the planetary gear; modified ratios in 1st, 2nd, and 4th gears; recalibrated governor; new F2 freewheel with wider locking rollers; B2 brake with lighter brake bands and heavier steel plates and an additional air-cooled oil cooler.

ZF 4-HP-22

The ZF 4-HP-22 is a four speed automatic transmission incorporating a torque converter with a lock-up clutch. Fourth gear is effectively an overdrive.

TROUBLESHOOTING

AW 70, 70L, 71 & 72L

Parking Lock Fails Or Is Delayed

1. Check gear shift control in all positions for proper operation.
2. Check gear selector adjustment.
3. Check parking brake components, replace defective parts as necessary.
4. Defective front ring gear in planetary gear assembly.

No Movement In Any Forward Gear

1. Check fluid level and condition, correct as necessary.
2. Check kickdown cable adjustment.
3. Check adjustment and operation of shift linkage.
4. Check line pressure.

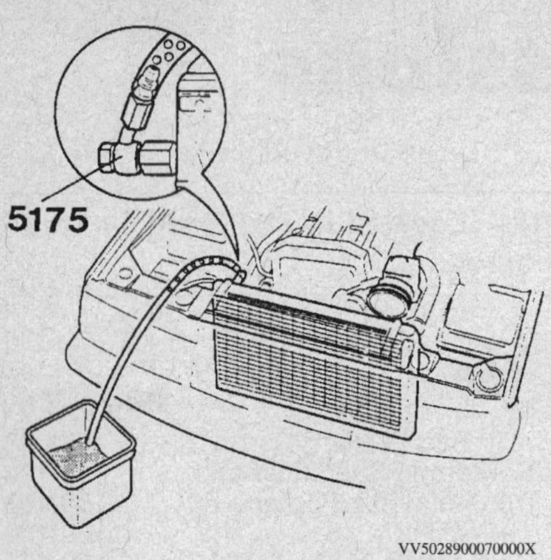
5175
VV5028900070000X

Fig. 1 Fitting installation

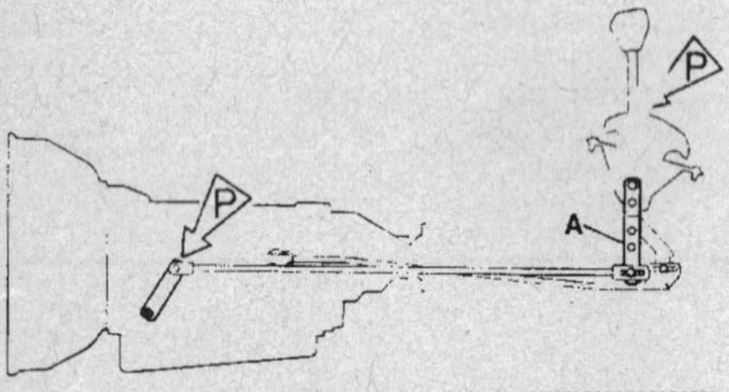
P
A
VV5028900058000X

Fig. 4 Shift linkage adjustment. Position P

5. Check one-way clutches as follows:
   a. Disconnect propeller shaft from drive flange.
   b. Rotate output shaft clockwise then counterclockwise. A much greater force will be needed to turn output shaft clockwise.
   c. If force needed to turn output shaft is same in both directions, one-way clutch 2 is defective.
   d. If output shaft turns clockwise. Clutch 1 is defective.
6. Check pan for solid particles.
   a. Solid particles in pan indicates a defective clutch 1.
   b. If no particles are found, clean or replace valve body and filter.
   c. Check gear selector unit for proper operation.

No Movement In 2 & D

1. Check fluid level and condition, correct as necessary.
2. Check kickdown cable and shift linkage adjustment.
3. Check line pressure.
4. Check one-way clutches.
5. Check fluid pan for solid particles.
   a. Solid particles in pan indicates a defective brake and/or clutch hydraulic circuit.
   b. If no particles are found, clean or replace valve body and filter.
   c. Check secondary regulator valve. Replace valve if necessary.

No Movement In R

1. Check fluid level and condition, correct as necessary.
2. Check kickdown cable adjustment.

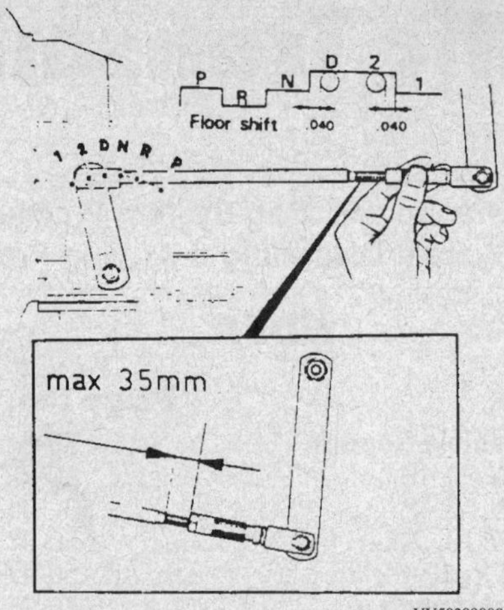
P R N D 2 1
Floor shift .040 .040
max 35mm
VV5028900006000X

Fig. 2 Gear shift linkage adjustment

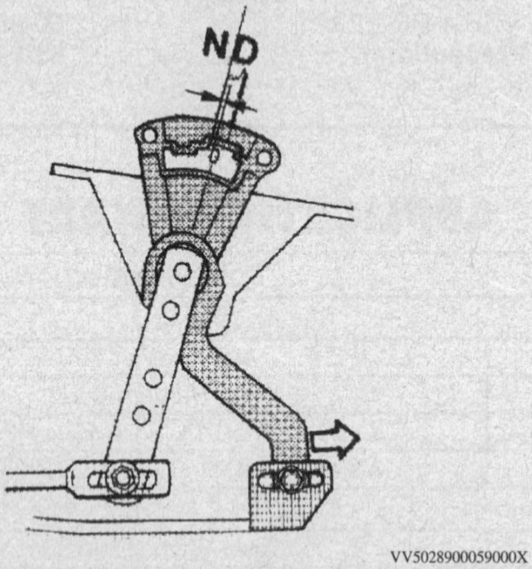
ND
VV5028900059000X

Fig. 5 Shift linkage adjustment. Position D & N

3. Check operation and adjustment of shift linkage.
4. Check line pressure.
5. Check fluid pan for solid particles:
   a. Solid particles in pan may indicate a broken flywheel drive flange, torque converter contacting cover and torque converter incorrectly installed onto engine.
   b. If no particles are found, replace valve body. Clean and check primary regulator valve, shift valve 2-3 and control valve for rear brake B3.
   c. Check accumulator piston C2.

Vehicle Starts In 2 Or 3

1. Check fluid level and condition, correct as necessary.
2. Check kickdown cable adjustment.
3. Check operation and adjustment of shift linkage.
4. Check line pressure.
5. Ensure governor pressure varies with speed.

Harsh Engagement, Noisy Disengagement

1. Check fluid level and condition, correct as necessary.
2. Check kickdown cable adjustment.
3. Check operation and adjustment of shift linkage.
4. Check line pressure.
5. Check accumulator piston, replace if necessary.
6. Check valve body, replace if necessary.

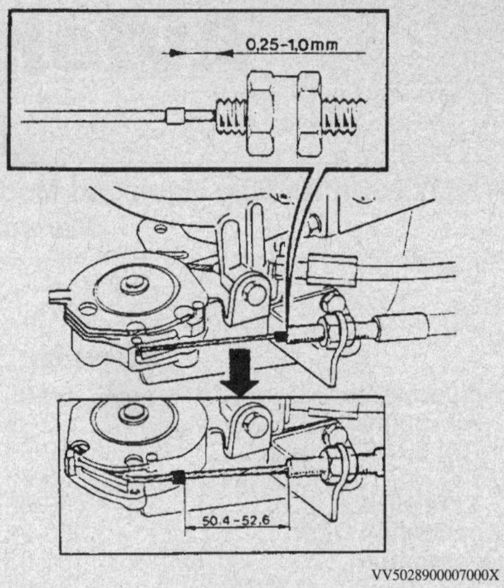
0.25-1.0mm
50.4-52.6
VV5028900007000X

Fig. 3 Kickdown cable adjustment

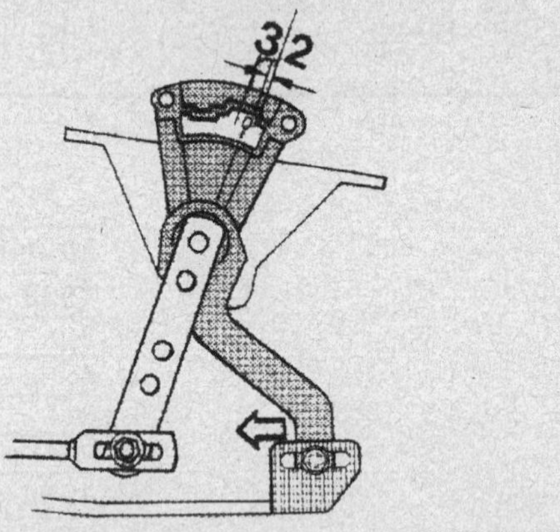
3 2
VV5028900060000X

Fig. 6 Shift linkage adjustment. Position 2 & 3

ZF 4-HP-22

When troubleshooting the ZF 4 HP-22 transmission, ensure the following:

1. Engine is in perfect mechanical condition.
2. Fault, program and range indicators are functioning properly.
3. Battery, plugs and ground points are in good condition.
4. Transmission fluid level is correct.

AW 50-42

Loud Whining Noise In Gear Position N Or P

1. Incorrect oil level.
2. Torque converter malfunction.
3. Oil pump malfunction.
4. Internal transaxle malfunction.

Grating Noise In Gear Position N Or P

1. Loosen carrier plate screws.
2. Torque converter casing improperly mounted on engine.
3. Broken carrier plate.
4. Torque converter scraping against casing.
5. Internal malfunction.

Squeaking Noise While In Gear

1. Worn bushing in oil pump.
2. Internal transaxle malfunction.

Prominent Knock Or Metallic Noise In Any Gear Other Than 4TH

1. Internal transaxle malfunction.

Oil Leak When Stationary

1. Leaky seals or seal seams.

Oil Leak When Stationary, w/Engine Running

1. Oil leak at front edge of transaxle, adjacent to engine:
   a. High oil level.
   b. Torque converter casing improperly mounted to engine.
   c. Pump bushing damaged/loose.
   d. O-ring in oil pump damaged.
   e. Torque converter throat damaged.

MAINTENANCE

AW 70, 70L, 71 & 72L

Fluid Check

1. With vehicle on level surface, engine idling and gear selector in Park; move shifter through all gear positions, stopping in each approximately 4–5 seconds.
2. Return selector to Park and wait two minutes before removing dipstick.
3. Fluid level should be between marks on hot side of dipstick.

ZF 4-HP-22

Fluid Check

1. With vehicle on level surface and engine idling, place selector lever in Park.
2. Move selector lever through each gear position, stopping in each position for 4–5 seconds.
3. Return to Park and wait two minutes before removing dipstick.
4. Fluid level should be between two marks on hot side of dipstick.

AW 30-40

Fluid Check

The dipstick is accessible from the engine compartment using a long extension with a ½ inch socket drive. Socket drive engages top part of dipstick. Turn dipstick a quarter turn to free spring catch.

1. Park vehicle on level surface, then apply parking brake.
2. Run engine at idle speed with transmission in Park.
3. Move gear selector through all positions, pausing 5 seconds in each position.
4. Move gear selector back to Park and wait about 2 minutes before checking fluid level.
5. With engine at operating temperature, fluid level should be between Hot marks.

Fluid Change

1. Remove drain plug from transmission pan, then allow fluid to drain into suitable container.
2. Install drain plug and **torque** to 15 ft. lbs.
3. Remove upper fluid cooler pipe from cooler. Always use a spanner wrench to prevent movement of hexagonal coupling.
4. Install fitting part No. 5175, or equivalent, as shown in **Fig. 1.** Use nipple and seals from special tool part No. 5320, or equivalent.
5. Install transparent plastic hose to fitting, then place container under hose to catch fluid.
6. Apply parking brake and put gear selector in Park.
7. Add 4 quarts of fluid as follows:
   a. Add 2 quarts of fluid to transmission, then start and idle engine.
   b. Stop engine when bubbles appear in tubing.
   c. Add another 2 quarts of fluid to transmission, then start and idle engine again.
   d. Stop engine when bubbles appear in tubing.
   e. Remove nipple and fitting from cooler, then reconnect pipe to cooler.
8. Add another 2.3 quarts of fluid to transmission.
9. Apply parking brake, then start and idle engine.
10. Move gear selector through all positions, pausing 5 seconds in each position.
11. Move gear selector back to Park and wait about 2 minutes before checking fluid level.
12. Top off fluid, if necessary.

AW 50-42

Fluid Check

1. Park vehicle on flat surface with parking brake set.
2. Idle engine with gear selector in Park position.
3. Move gear selector through all positions, stopping in each position for 3 seconds.
4. Return gear position selector to Park and wait 2 minutes before checking oil level.
5. Check oil level with dipstick. The cold range on the dipstick (104°F) is reached after approximately 5 minutes of idling. The hot range on the dipstick (176°F) is reached after about 30 minutes of highway driving.
6. Transaxle oil temperature can be checked using Volvo diagnostic key, test function 5.
7. Ensure oil level is between the MAX and MIN lines of the appropriate temperature range. Difference between MAX and MIN is ½ quart.

Fluid Change

1. Remove splash guard beneath engine.
2. Remove transaxle drain plug and drain oil into suitable container.
3. Replace drain plug seal washer and install drain plug. **Torque** to 30 ft. lbs.
4. Disconnect return hose from control system cover.
5. Install transparent hose on oil return hose connection.
6. Apply parking brake and move gear selector lever to Park.
7. Add approximately 2.1 quarts of oil to transaxle.
8. Start engine and run at idle.
9. Turn off engine when air bubbles become visible in transparent hose.
10. Add additional 2.1 quarts to transaxle.
11. Start engine and run at idle.
12. Turn off engine when air bubbles become visible in transparent hose.
13. Remove transparent hose from connection and connect oil return hose.
14. Add additional 2.1 quarts to transaxle, then start engine and move gear selector through all positions, stopping at each position for 4–5 seconds.
15. Place gear selector in Park and wait 2 minutes with engine idling.
16. Check oil level and fill if necessary. Transaxle oil capacity is 8 quarts.

ADJUSTMENTS

AW 70, 70L, 71 & 72L

Gear Shift Linkage

Adjust shift rod so there is equal clearance between gear lever and its stop, when lever is in D and in 2 position, **Fig. 2.**

Kickdown Cable

1. Pull cable out until a slight resistance is felt. Hold cable in this position and install cable clip .01–.04 inch from cable sheath end, **Fig. 3.**
2. Adjust cable sheath position so clip is pulled out approximately 1.98–2.07 inch when throttle pedal is completely depressed, **Fig. 3.**

ZF 4-HP-22

Gear Shift Linkage

1. Place gear selector in position P, then loosen locknuts for actuator rod and reaction rod.
2. Ensure transmission lever is in P, then put gear linkage lever (A) in vertical position, **Fig. 4,** and tighten locknut to specifications.
3. Push reaction lever lightly backwards until a slight resistance is felt. **Torque** locknut to 3.5 ft. lbs.
4. Check clearance between positions D and N, **Fig. 5,** and between positions 3

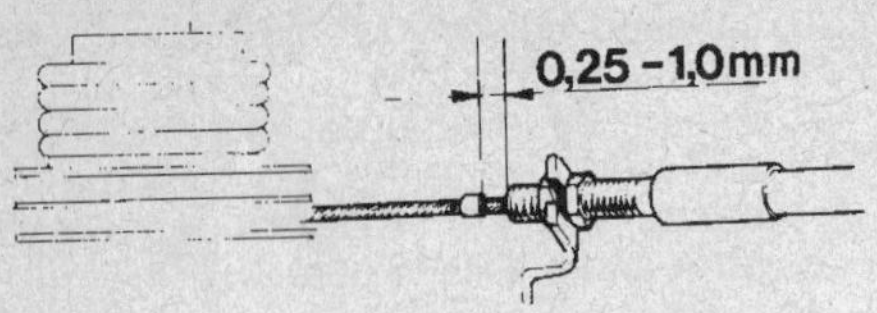
0,25 -1,0mm

VV5028900061000X

Fig. 7 Cable sheath end clearance

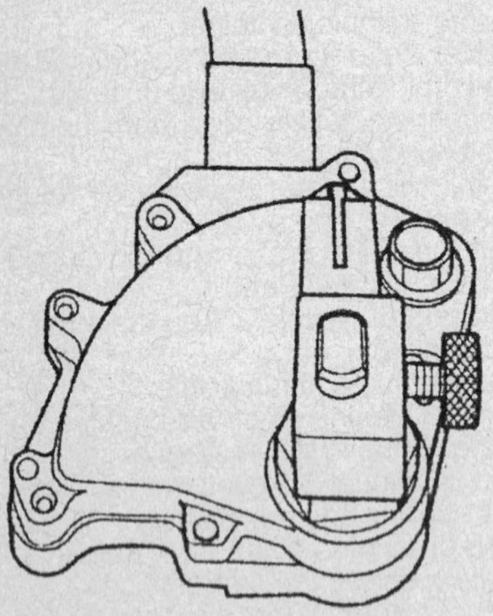

VV5028900094000X

Fig. 10 Gear position sensor adjustment

and 2, **Fig. 6.** Ensure clearance between positions D and N is same or less than clearance between positions 2 and 3.

5. If clearance is correct, **torque** adjusting locknut to 12–17 ft. lbs.
6. If there is no clearance at position D, move shift rod arm rearward approximately .08 inch and tighten locknut to specifications.
7. If there is no clearance at position 3, move shift rod arm forward approximately .012 inch and tighten locknut to specifications.
8. Ensure vehicle starts in positions P and N and that reverse lamp lights in position R.

Kickdown Cable

1. Pull cable out until a slight resistance is felt. Hold cable in this position and install cable clip .010–0.04 inch from cable sheath end, **Fig. 7.**
2. Adjust cable sheath position so clip is pulled out approximately 1.99–2.07 inch when throttle pedal is completely depressed, **Fig. 8.**

AW 30-40

Gear Selector

1. Move gear selector lever to Park position.
2. Loosen control rod and reaction strut nuts.
3. Ensure selector link arm on transmission is in Park position (rearmost position). **Gear selector lever will interfere with instrument panel if arm is adjusted too far back.**

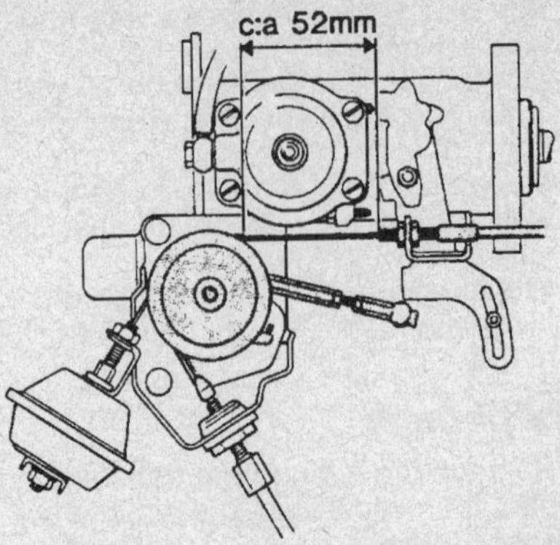
c:a 52mm

VV5028900062000X

Fig. 8 Kickdown cable pulley clearance

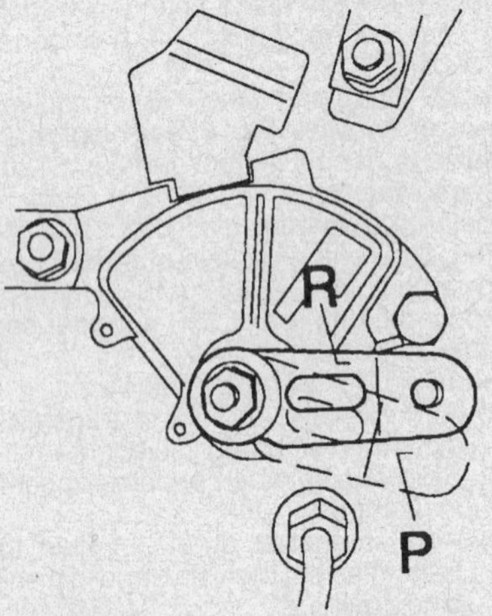
R
P

VV5029500117000X

Fig. 11 Transaxle cable adjustment

4. Ensure gear lever arm, (A) is vertical or slightly forward, **Fig. 9.** Install locknut on gear lever arm.
5. Press reaction arm (B) gently backwards until slight resistance is felt, **Fig. 9. Torque** nut to 4 ft. lbs.

Gear Position Sensor

1. Disconnect battery ground cable.
2. Release oxygen sensor wire from transmission support member routing clip and transmission fluid pan. Disconnect oxygen sensor electrical connectors.
3. Remove front exhaust pipe and front heat shield.
4. With gear selector in Neutral position, loosen gear position fixing/adjusting bolt slightly so sensor can be turned relative to shaft.
5. Position template tool No. 5475, or equivalent, outside nut on gear selector shaft.
6. Turn gear position sensor until groove on template is pointing directly towards lug on gear position sensor as shown in **Fig. 10.**
7. **Torque** fixing/adjusting bolt to 10 ft. lbs.

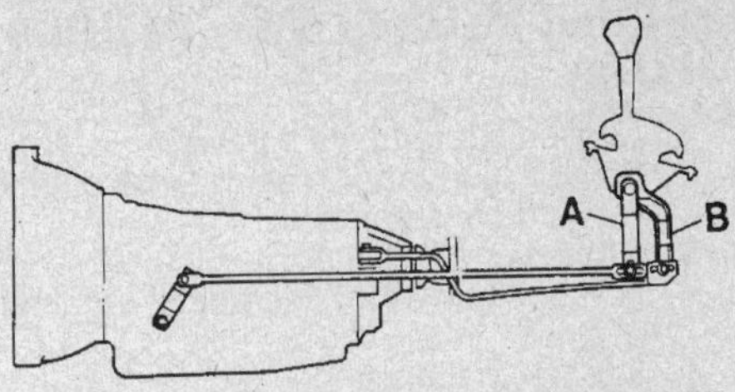
A
B

VV5028900090000X

Fig. 9 Gear selector adjustment

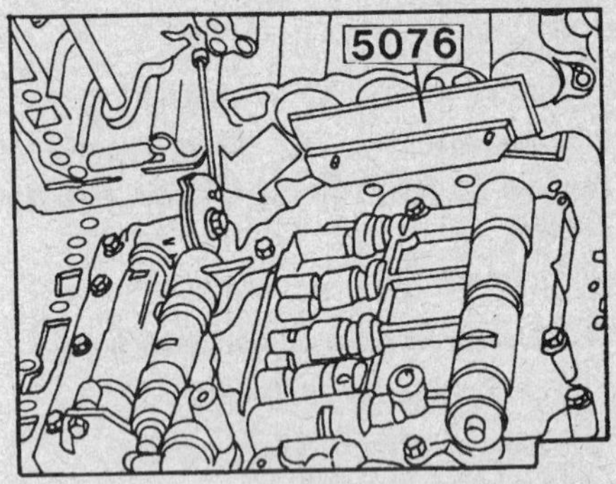
5076

VV5028900008000X

Fig. 12 Accumulator piston retainer

8. Install heat shield and front exhaust pipe.
9. Connect oxygen sensor connectors and secure to transmission support member and fluid pan.
10. Connect Volvo Diagnostic Key to diagnostic output and delete any stored trouble codes. The code 1-1-1 should be displayed when all trouble codes have been deleted.

AW 50-42

Gear Position Sensor

1. Remove battery, tray and air intake manifold.
2. Disconnect transaxle cable from rod arm.
3. Remove rod arm.
4. Insert tool No. 9995475, or equivalent, into control shaft.
5. Check that shaft is set to N position.
6. Disconnect dipstick pipe bracket.
7. Remove gear position sensor screws.
8. Rotate gear position sensor so that mark on switch aligns with identification on tool.
9. **Torque** switch screws to 18 ft. lbs.
10. Install dipstick pipe bracket. **Torque** to 17.5 ft. lbs.
11. Install rod arm on control shaft. **Torque** to 18 ft. lbs.
12. Attach transaxle cable to rod arm, using washer and locking clip.

Transaxle Cable

1. Set gear lever to R position.
2. Push rod arm on transaxle forward to P position, **Fig. 11.**
3. Turn rod arm to next position (R).
4. Apply grease to rod arm pin and install cable on studs and rod arm pin. **Torque** nuts to 18 ft. lbs.

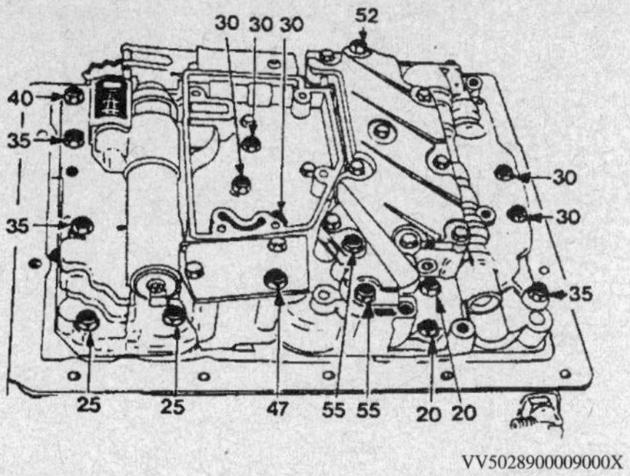
30 30 30
52
40
35
35
30
30
35
25
25
47
55 55
20 20
VV5028900009000X

Fig. 13 Valve body attaching bolt locations

5. Install washers and locking clip on rod arm.

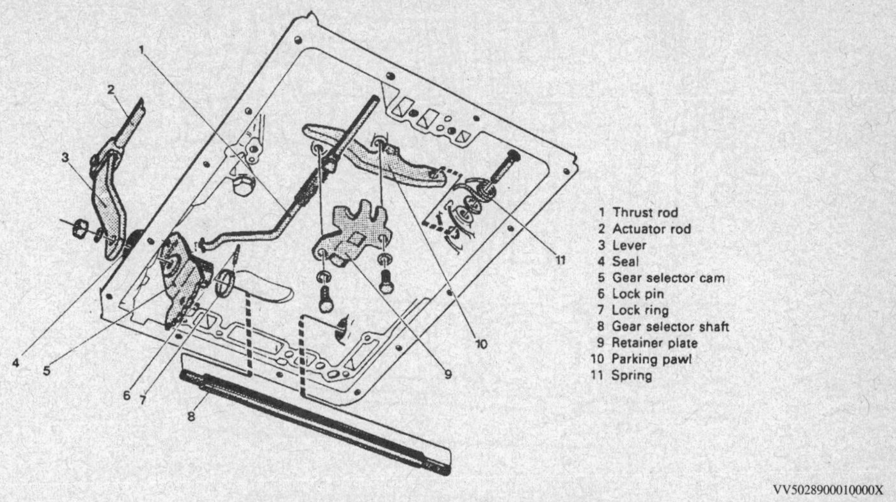
1 Thrust rod
2 Actuator rod
3 Lever
4 Seal
5 Gear selector cam
6 Lock pin
7 Lock ring
8 Gear selector shaft
9 Retainer plate
10 Parking pawl
11 Spring
VV5028900010000X

Fig. 14 Gear selector components

IN-VEHICLE REPAIRS

AW 70, 70L, 71 & 72L

VALVE BODY, REPLACE

1. Disconnect battery ground cable and remove air cleaner.
2. Disconnect kickdown cable from throttle pulley.
3. Drain fluid and remove filler tube.
4. Remove fluid pan, gasket, filter and spacer (if equipped), then remove magnet located in pan.
5. Carefully pry off two oil tubes using a suitable screwdriver.
6. Remove valve body attaching bolts. **Do not remove screw behind cam spring at this time, Fig. 12.**
7. Loosen cam screw slightly, then install accumulator piston retainer No. 5076, or equivalent, **Fig. 12.**
8. Remove cam screw, then disconnect kickdown cable from throttle cam and remove valve body assembly.
9. Reverse procedure to install, noting the following:
   a. Align gear selector cam pin with valve groove.
   b. Ensure valve body attaching bolts are correctly installed, **Fig. 13.** Bolt lengths are shown in millimeters.
   c. **Torque** valve body attaching bolts to 7 ft. lbs.
   d. **Torque** filter attaching bolts to 3.6 ft. lbs.
   e. **Torque** pan attaching bolts to 4 ft. lbs.
   f. **Torque** filler tube to 66 ft. lbs.
   g. Attach kickdown cable to throttle pulley, refer to "Adjustments" for kickdown cable adjustment procedure.

GEAR SELECTOR UNIT

1. Disconnect battery ground cable.
2. Remove valve body as described under "Valve Body, Replace."
3. Remove parking pawl rod plate, then parking pawl rod, **Fig. 14.**
4. Disconnect control rod from regulator shaft.
5. Using a suitable drift and hammer, drive lockpin from throttle cam.
6. Remove regulator shaft and regulator shaft seals. **On some models, a 3/4 inch hole must be drilled in left floor pan to remove regulator shaft.**
7. Clean and inspect all parts. Replace defective parts as required.
8. Install new seals onto regulator shaft.
9. Reverse procedure to install.

ACCUMULATOR PISTONS, REPLACE

1. Disconnect battery ground cable.
2. Remove valve body as described under "Valve Body, Replace."
3. Mark accumulator piston location for installation, if original pistons are to be reused.
4. Remove accumulator pistons from piston bores, **Fig. 15.** If accumulator pistons are stuck, apply compressed air into air holes indicated by arrows and remove pistons.
5. Clean and inspect accumulator pistons and springs. Replace pistons if they were stuck. Replace damaged or worn pistons as required.
6. Reverse procedure to install, using new O-rings. **Be sure to install pistons into their original locations if same pistons are used.**

OVERDRIVE SOLENOID, REPLACE

1. Disconnect battery ground cable.
2. Disconnect electrical connector from gear selector, then pull wire from sheath and unhook from bracket.
3. Clean, then remove solenoid and O-rings.
4. Connect a suitable ohmmeter to solenoid. Correct resistance is 13 ohms. If not, replace solenoid.
5. Reverse procedure to install, using new O-rings.

ZF 4-HP-22

KICKDOWN CABLE, REPLACE

1. Disconnect battery ground cable.
2. Position gear selector in N, then disconnect kickdown cable from throttle pulley, **Fig. 16.**
3. Drain fluid from transmission, then remove oil pan and disconnect fluid filler tube.
4. Rotate cam into position and lock it using a suitable screwdriver. Disconnect cable and remove screwdriver.
5. Using drift No. 5279, or equivalent, **Fig. 17,** push out cable sheath. Ensure taper on drift compresses entire holder.
6. Reverse procedure to install noting the following:
   a. **Torque** oil pan bolts to 4.3 ft. lbs.
   b. **Torque** fluid filler tube to 72 ft. lbs.
   c. Refer to "Adjustments" for kickdown cable adjustment procedure.

VALVE BODY, REPLACE

1. Disconnect battery ground cable.
2. Remove filter as previously described.
3. Remove valve body assembly attaching bolts, **Fig. 18.**
4. Ensure channel seals, springs and snap ring remain in place, **Fig. 19.**
5. Install valve body assembly, then screws. Do not tighten screws to specifications at this time.
6. Position gauge No. 5278, or equivalent, between pin on throttle valve and machined surface on valve body, **Fig. 20.** Press valve body assembly lightly against gauge until you feel a resistance, throttle valve in contact with cam, then **torque** screws to 5.8 ft. lbs.
7. Install oil strainer O-ring and oil strainer.
8. Install oil pan, and **torque** bolts to 4.3 ft. lbs., then connect fluid filler tube and **torque** to 72 ft. lbs.

START INHIBITOR SWITCH/ REVERSING LAMP SWITCH, REPLACE

1. Disconnect battery ground cable.
2. Remove ashtray, then panel in center console.
3. Remove gear selector trim and prism (A), **Fig. 21.**
4. Disconnect electrical connector, then remove inhibitor switch attaching screws, then inhibitor switch.
5. Reverse procedure to install.

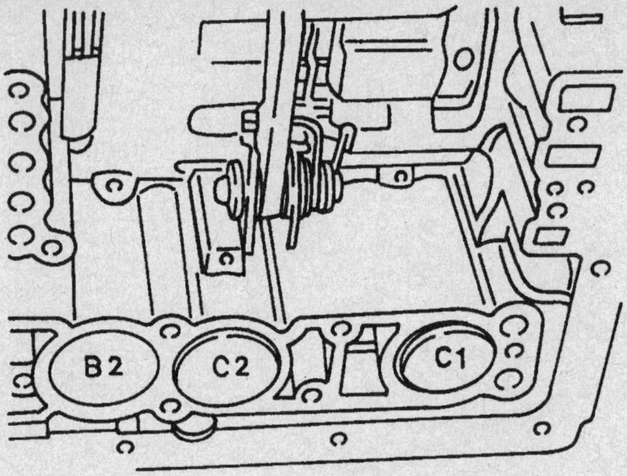
B2
C2
C1

VV5028900011000X

Fig. 15 Accumulator pistons

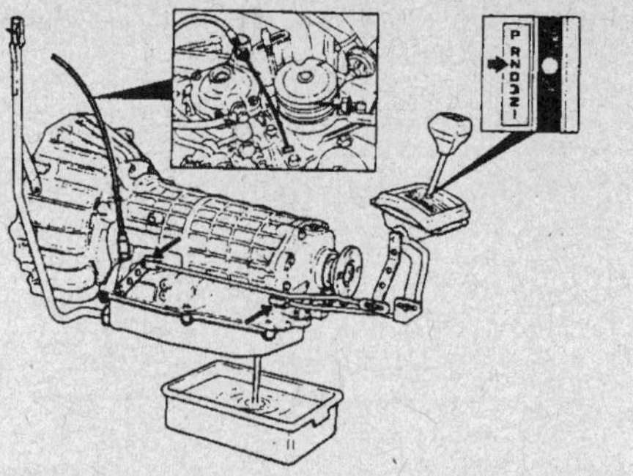

VV5028900063000X

Fig. 16 Kickdown cable removal

5279

VV5028900064000X

Fig. 17 Kickdown cable sheath removal

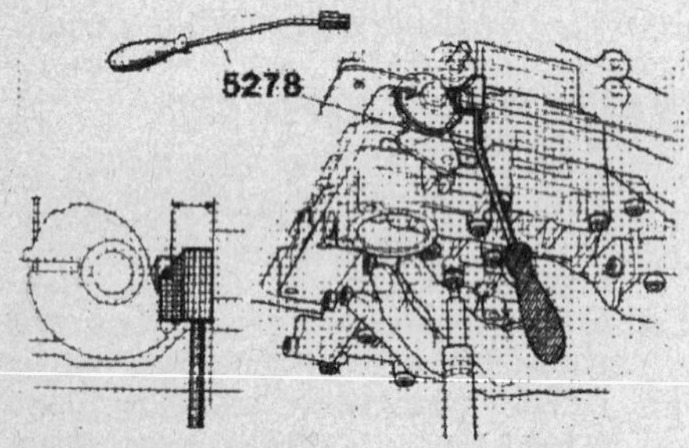
5278

VV5028900067000X

Fig. 20 Valve body assembly adjustment

AW 30-40

REAR EXTENSION HOUSING SEAL, REPLACE

Removal

1. Using socket tool No. 5244, or equivalent, remove four propeller shaft drive flange bolts.
2. Lift propeller shaft to side and secure with suitable wire or rope.
3. Separate drive flange from output shaft as follows:
   a. Using a punch, remove clamping from output shaft nut.
   b. Remove output shaft nut. To prevent output shaft rotation, secure with counterhold tool No. 5149, or equivalent.
   c. Separate drive flange from output shaft, using remove tool No. 5304, or equivalent, if necessary.
   d. Remove drive flange O-ring.
   e. Ensure drive flange sealing surfaces are free of defects.
4. Remove rear extension housing seal using seal removal tool No. 5069, or equivalent.

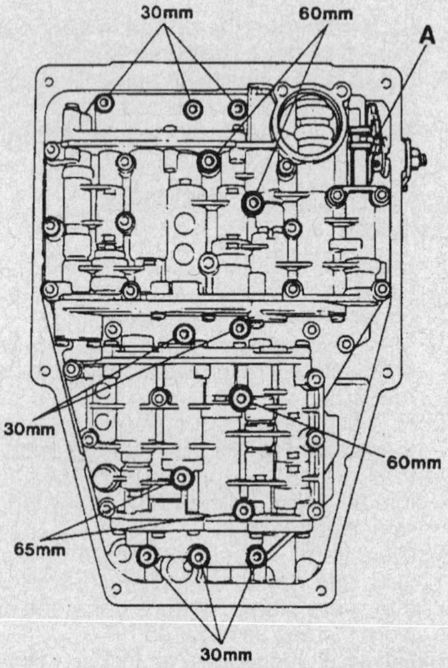
30mm
60mm
A
30mm
60mm
65mm
30mm

VV5028900065000X

Fig. 18 Valve body mounting bolt location

Installation

1. Apply small amount of grease to lip of new seal.
2. Install seal using drift tool No. 5492, or equivalent. Tap into position until drift bottoms on rear extension housing.
3. Install drive flange as follows:
   a. Apply a small amount of grease to new drive flange O-ring.
   b. Install drive flange a new nut coated with locking fluid part No. 116103-2, or equivalent. Prevent drive flange from rotating using counterhold tool No. 5149, or equivalent.
   c. **Torque** drive flange nut to 91 ft. lbs.
   d. Secure nut with a punch.
4. Connect propeller shaft to drive flange using new nuts and bolts. **Torque** alternately to 37 ft. lbs.

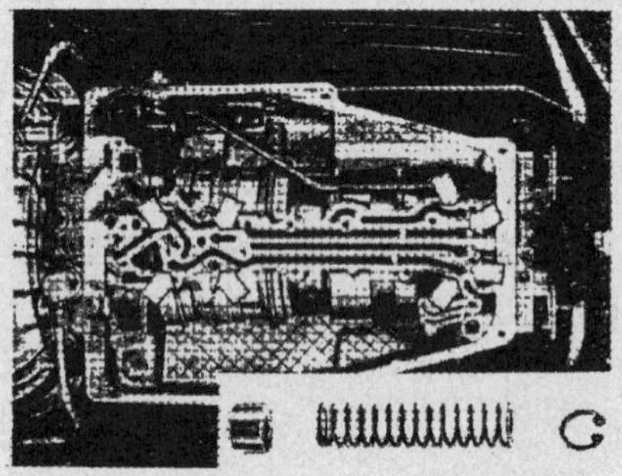

VV5028900066000X

Fig. 19 Oil channel seals, springs & snap ring location

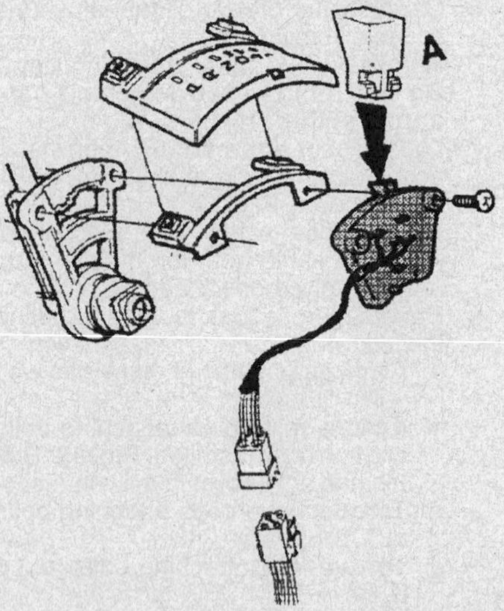
A

VV5028900068000X

Fig. 21 Gear selector components

REAR EXTENSION HOUSING BEARING, REPLACE

1. Drain transmission fluid.
2. Support transmission with suitable transmission jack, then release oxygen sensor cable from transmission support member.
3. Remove transmission support member.
4. Disconnect propeller shaft from drive flange using socket tool No. 5244, or equivalent. Suspend propeller shaft to one side with wire or rope.

5. Remove four bolts from support bracket, then the support bracket.
6. Remove torque strut circlips and washer.
7. Separate drive flange from output shaft as described under "Rear Extension Housing Seal, Replace."
8. Remove rear extension housing as follows:
   a. Remove six mounting bolts.
   b. Free housing by prying with two screwdrivers under two cast lugs.
   c. Remove rear extension housing.
9. Pry out seal and remove bearing circlip.
10. Press bearing out of housing using a suitable press and drift tool No. 5088, or equivalent.
11. Reverse procedure to install, noting the following:
    a. Press new bearing into rear housing using suitable press and drift tool No. 5496, or equivalent.
    b. Ensure bearing is installed in correct direction. The end with sheet metal seal must face inward. Outer end has two grooves on the inner ring.
    c. Apply a small amount of grease to lip of seal. Install seal using drift tool No 5492, or equivalent.
    d. Apply liquid sealant to rear extension housing contact surfaces.
    e. **Torque** six rear extension housing mounting bolts to 25 ft. lbs. and drive flange bolts to 91 ft. lbs.
    f. **Torque** propeller shaft to drive flange bolts to 37 ft. lbs.
    g. **Torque** transmission support bracket bolts to 35 ft. lbs.

GEAR SELECTOR SHAFT, REPLACE

1. Disconnect battery ground cable.
2. Release oxygen sensor cable from transmission support member and fluid pan. Disconnect oxygen sensor electrical connectors.
3. Remove front exhaust pipe.
4. Remove front heat shield.
5. Disconnect and plug rear transmission fluid line.
6. Remove gear position sensor as follows:
   a. Remove nut, locking washer and rubber washer from gear selector shaft.
   b. Disconnect sensor lead to prevent damage.
   c. Remove gear position sensor securing bolt.
   d. Remove sensor from gear selector shaft and move to one side.
7. Use a screwdriver to pry right side seal out of position.
8. To remove left side seal, remove nut and selector link arm, then remove seal by using a screwdriver to pry out of position.
9. Reverse procedure to install, noting the following:
   a. Apply a small amount of grease to new seals.
   b. Install left side seal using drift tool No. 5476, or equivalent.
   c. **Torque** link arm to 13 ft. lbs.

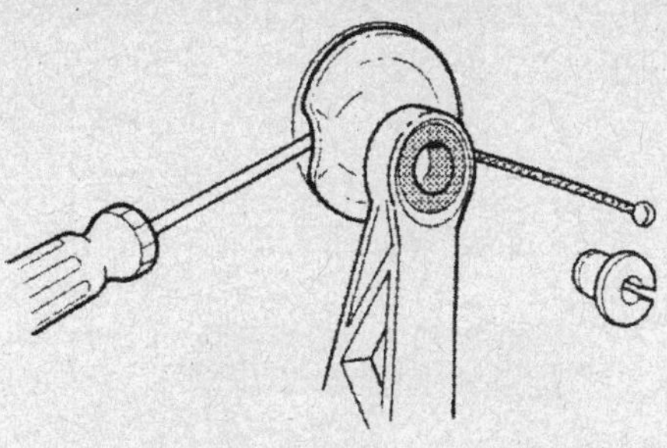
VV5028900091000X

Fig. 22 Kickdown switch installation

GEAR SELECTOR SOLENOID, REPLACE

1. Remove gear selector housing and gear lever.
2. Move gear selector lever to Park position and disconnect P-shift lock solenoid latch.
3. Remove P-shift lock solenoid from gear selector housing.
4. Using suitable pliers, release clip securing P-shift lock solenoid.
5. Reverse procedure to install, noting the following:
   a. Move gear selector to Park position, then place bottom edge of P-shift lock solenoid into slot position.
   b. Press solenoid rearward until upper edge snaps into position.
   c. Check gear selector lever movement. Adjust as described under "Adjustments."

PROGRAM SELECTOR, REPLACE

1. Disconnect battery ground cable.
2. Release latch at each end of program selector using a small screwdriver.
3. Disconnect program selector electrical connector.
4. Reverse procedure to install.

KICKDOWN SWITCH & THROTTLE CABLE, REPLACE

Removal

1. Remove throttle control cover as follows:
   a. Remove cable tensioner locking clip.
   b. Disconnect cable from throttle control pulley and remove from bracket.
   c. Disconnect kickdown switch electrical connector.
2. Remove control unit as described under "Control Unit, Replace."
3. Disconnect accelerator cable from pedal, then remove kickdown switch from cable.

Installation

1. Squeeze rubber seal together and secure with electrical tape. Leave approximately four inches of tape hanging free, **Fig. 22.**
2. Insert kickdown switch with connector facing upwards.
3. Ensure latch lugs on kickdown switch engage bulkhead correctly.
4. Remove tape and ensure rubber seal seats on bulkhead sound insulation.
5. Hook cable with holder on accelerator pedal, ensuring end bead ends firmly at bottom of holder.
6. Replace cable tensioner locking clip, then connect cable onto throttle control pulley.
7. Insert a 0.14 inch (3.5 mm) spacer on idling stop on throttle control pulley, **Fig. 23.**
8. Ensure locking clip is firmly against bracket. Adjust cable until it is pulled slightly tight.
9. Remove spacer, then attach throttle control pulley to bracket with locking clip.
10. Install control unit and soundproofing panel A.
11. Connect Volvo Diagnostic Key to diagnostic output and delete any stored trouble codes. The code 1-1-1 should be displayed when all trouble codes have been deleted.

CONTROL UNIT, REPLACE

1. Disconnect battery ground cable and remove fuse No. 24.
2. Remove soundproofing material from driver side panel A, **Fig. 24.**
3. **On models with air bag,** remove knee bolster.
4. **On all models,** remove control unit from mounting bracket using a screwdriver to gently pry bracket free of securing clip.
5. Disconnect control unit electrical connectors.
6. Reverse procedure to install, noting the following:
   a. Connect Volvo Diagnostic Key to diagnostic output and delete any stored trouble codes. The code 1-1-1 should be displayed when all trouble codes have been deleted.
   b. Reset control unit adaptive function to normal values using test functions 5 and 6 following Volvo Diagnostic Key instructions.

SPEED SENSOR, REPLACE

1. Disconnect battery ground cable.
2. Disconnect speed sensor electrical connector and cable.
3. Remove speed sensor.
4. Reverse procedure to install, noting the following:
   a. **Torque** speed sensor to 4 ft. lbs.
   b. Connect Volvo Diagnostic Key to diagnostic output and delete any stored trouble codes. The code 1-1-1 should be displayed when all trouble codes have been deleted.

FLUID TEMPERATURE SENSOR, REPLACE

1. Disconnect battery ground cable.
2. Release oxygen sensor wire from transmission support member routing clip. Disconnect oxygen sensor electrical connectors.
3. Remove front exhaust pipe.
4. Disconnect fluid temperature sensor connector and disconnect wire from front fluid pipe.
5. Disconnect fluid temperature sensor

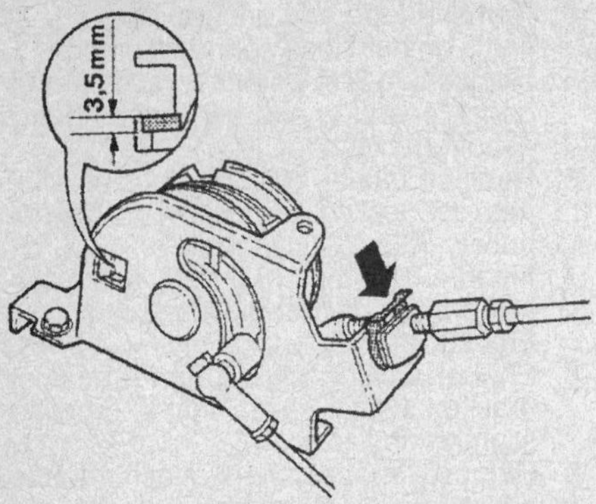
3,5 mm

VV5028900092000X

Fig. 23 Throttle control pulley spacer

from front fluid pipe.

6. Reverse procedure to install, noting the following:
   a. Apply a small amount of transmission fluid to new temperature sensor O-ring.
   b. **Torque** temperature sensor to 7 ft. lbs.
   c. Connect Volvo Diagnostic Key to diagnostic output and delete any stored trouble codes. The code 1-1-1 should be displayed when all trouble codes have been deleted.

GEAR POSITION SENSOR, REPLACE

1. Disconnect battery ground cable.
2. Release oxygen sensor wire from transmission support member routing clip and transmission fluid pan. Disconnect oxygen sensor electrical connectors.
3. Remove front exhaust pipe and front heat shield.
4. Disconnect link arm from gear selector shaft on left side of transmission.
5. Release gear position sensor lead from cable clips on both sides of transmission.
6. Disconnect gear position sensor electrical connector.
7. Disconnect and plug transmission fluid lines.
8. Remove gear position sensor as follows:
   a. Remove gear position sensor nut with locking washer and rubber washer.
   b. Remove gear position sensor fixing/adjusting bolt.
   c. Pull sensor and wire off gear selector shaft.
9. Reverse procedure to install, noting the following:
   a. **Torque** gear position sensor locking washer and nut to 5 ft. lbs.
   b. **Torque** link arm on gear selector to 13 ft. lbs.

SOLENOID VALVES, REPLACE

1. Disconnect battery ground cable.
2. Drain transmission fluid and disconnect oxygen sensor lead from fluid pan.
3. Remove fluid pan and dipstick tube.
4. Release cable holder from valve body.

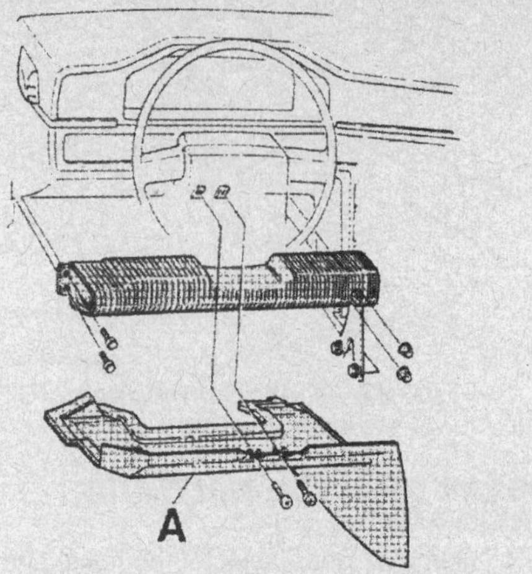
A

VV5028900093000X

Fig. 24 Driver side panel A removal

Disconnect solenoid valve connectors.

5. Disconnect external solenoid connector from transmission.
6. Remove solenoid valves S1 and S2, **Fig. 25,** as follows:
   a. Remove solenoid valve holder.
   b. Pull out solenoid valves S1 and S2 and remove from valve body.
7. Remove solenoid valves SL and STH, **Fig. 25,** as follows:
   a. Remove fluid filter.
   b. Remove solenoid holder.
   c. Pull out solenoid valves SL and STH and remove from valve body.
8. Reverse procedure to install, noting the following:
   a. Apply a small amount of grease to new solenoid valve O-rings.
   b. **Torque** solenoid valves and fluid filter retaining bolts to 7 ft. lbs.
   c. Apply liquid sealant to fluid pan contact surfaces. **Torque** pan attaching bolts to 5 ft. lbs.
   d. Connect Volvo Diagnostic Key to diagnostic output and delete any stored trouble codes. The code 1-1-1 should be displayed when all trouble codes have been deleted.

VALVE BODY, REPLACE

Removal

1. Disconnect battery ground cable and drain transmission fluid.
2. Disconnect oxygen sensor wire from transmission fluid pan.
3. Remove fluid pan and filter, then disconnect solenoid valve connectors.
4. Loosen remaining valve body bolts to valve body is lowered approximately 0.20–0.24 inch (5–6 mm).
5. Remove two bolts at "A" shown in **Fig. 26.** Remove two bolts at "B" and one bolt at "C."
6. At position "A" **Fig. 26,** insert retainer tool No. 5493, or equivalent, between valve body and transmission housing to keep accumulator pistons No. B2, C2 and B0 in correct position. Secure retainer tool to transmission with a fluid pan bolt.
7. At position "B," insert retainer tool No.

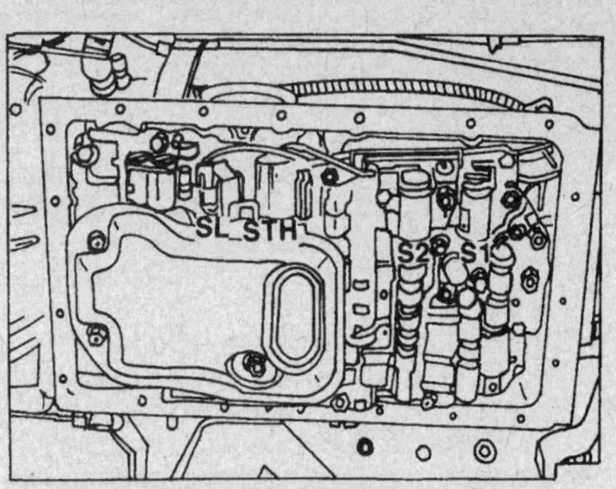
SL STH
S2 S1

VV5028900095000

Fig. 25 Solenoid valve replacement

5495, or equivalent, to keep accumulator piston No. C0 in correct position. Secure retainer tool to transmission with a fluid pan bolt.

8. At position "C," secure retainer tool No. 5494, or equivalent, to keep non-return valve in correct position.
9. Remove remaining valve body mounting bolts, then remove valve body.

Installation

1. Align pin on gear selector cam with slot in gear selector valve.
2. Install valve body bolts as follows:
   a. First mount valve body and secure in position with two mounting bolts. Only tighten bolts enough to hold valve body in position.
   b. Remove retainer tools securing accumulator pistons and non-return valve in position.
   c. Install valve body bolts, ensuring different length bolts are installed in correct position, as shown in **Fig. 27.**
   d. Starting from center, **torque** bolts alternately to 7 ft. lbs.
3. Install solenoid valve connectors and wiring harness cable holder. **Torque** cable holder bolts to 7 ft. lbs.
4. Install new fluid filter. **Torque** bolts to 7 ft. lbs.
5. Place particle magnet in fluid pan depression. Apply liquid gasket material to fluid pan sealing surfaces.
6. Install fluid pan. **Torque** bolts to 7 ft. lbs.
7. **Torque** drain plug to 15 ft. lbs.
8. Connect battery ground cable, then connect Volvo Diagnostic Key to diagnostic output and delete any stored trouble codes. The code 1-1-1 should be displayed when all trouble codes have been deleted.

ACCUMULATOR PISTONS, REPLACE

1. Remove valve body as described under "Valve Body, Replace."
2. Remove non-return valve housing with spring.
3. Remove accumulator pistons B2, C2 and B0 with springs as follows:
   a. Carefully remove retainer tool, securing accumulator pistons in position.
   b. Remove accumulator pistons B2,

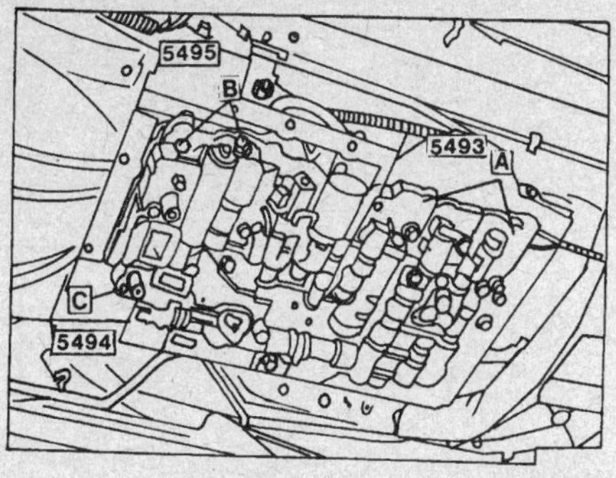
5495
B
5493
A
C
5494
VV5028900096000X

Fig. 26 Valve body removal

C2 and B0 with springs, **Fig. 28.**

c. If accumulator pistons are difficult to remove, apply compressed air to fluid passage to force pistons out.

4. Remove accumulator piston C0 with springs as follows:
   a. Carefully remove retainer tool, securing accumulator piston C0 in position.
   b. Remove accumulator piston C0 with springs, **Fig. 28.**
   c. If accumulator piston is difficult to remove, apply compressed air to fluid passage to force piston out.
5. Clean and inspect accumulator pistons, non-return valve and all springs. Replace any stiff or worn pistons.
6. Reverse procedure to install, noting the following:
   a. Use new O-rings coated with a small amount of new transmission fluid.
   b. Connect Volvo Diagnostic Key to diagnostic output and delete any stored trouble codes. The code 1-1-1 should be displayed when all trouble codes have been deleted.

PARKING LOCK PAWL, REPLACE

1. Remove valve body as described under "Valve Body, Replace."
2. Remove three bolts securing parking lock pawl retaining plate to transmission.
3. Remove parking lock pawl spring and shaft.
4. Reverse procedure to install. **Torque** parking lock pawl retaining plate bolts to 5 ft. lbs.

BRAKE B2 SEAL SLEEVE, REPLACE

1. Remove valve body as described under "Valve Body, Replace."
2. Remove tube with seal for brake B2.
3. Remove sleeve using suitable circlip pliers.
4. Reverse procedure to install. Apply a small amount of transmission fluid to new sleeve seal and insert sleeve with seal pointing up towards brake B2.

BRAKE CYLINDER B1, REPLACE

1. Remove valve body as described under "Valve Body, Replace."
2. Remove piston cover circlip, then pull cover out, using pliers to grip flange.
3. Remove piston by carefully blower

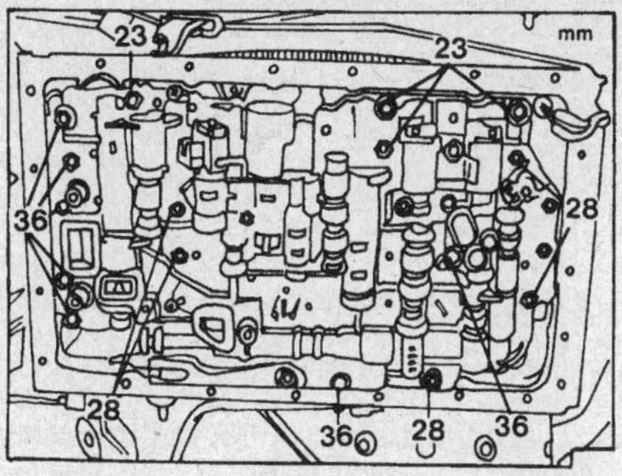
23
23
mm
36
28
28
36
28
36
VV5028900097000X

Fig. 27 Valve body bolt length & location

compressed air into hole while retaining cover with fingers.

4. Piston rods are available in four different lengths. If replacing piston rod, ensure new rod is same length as original rod.
5. Reverse procedure to install, noting the following:
   a. Replace seal and two O-rings on cover. Apply a small amount of transmission fluid to seal and O-rings.
   b. **Install piston so piston rod seats correctly on brake band attachment.**
   c. Connect Volvo Diagnostic Key to diagnostic output and delete any stored trouble codes. The code 1-1-1 should be displayed when all trouble codes have been deleted.

AW 50-42

OIL PUMP SEAL RING, REPLACE

1. Using seal ring extractor tool No. 9995069, or equivalent, remove seal ring from transaxle.
2. Install new oil seal ring using tool No. 9995117, or equivalent.

DRIVESHAFT SEAL, REPLACE

1. Remove brake hose and ABS cable bracket and let bracket hang loose.
2. Disconnect linkage from anti-roll bar.
3. Disconnect ball joint from link.
4. Using disconnecting tool No. 9995462, or equivalent, between transaxle and inside of left side driveshaft, remove driveshaft. Let driveshaft end rest on subframe.
5. Remove splash guard from beneath engine.
6. Remove bearing cap for right side driveshaft support bearings.
7. Press out inner portion of right side driveshaft and fold out spring strut.
8. Allow right side drive shaft to rest on steering gear hose.
9. Use crowbar or suitable pry too to remove seal ring from transaxle housing.
10. Apply small amount of grease to sealing lip and, using suitable drift and handle, carefully tap in new seal ring.
11. Install right driveshaft. Install bearing cap and **torque** to 18 ft. lbs.
12. Install left side driveshaft. Press driveshaft firmly in firmly so it locks onto differential gear.

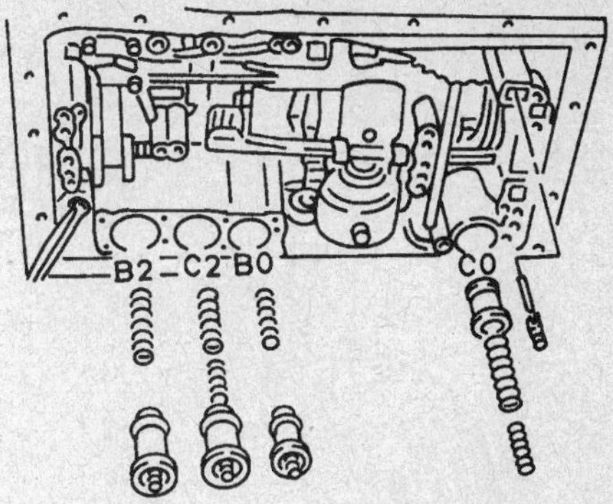
B2
C2
B0
C0
VV5028900098000X

Fig. 28 Accumulator pistons replacement

13. Ensure driveshaft lock ring fits in its groove.
14. Install link in ball joint on both sides. Apply suitable rust-proofing compound to area between ball joint, link and nuts.
15. Install link to anti-roll bar on both sides. **Torque** to 37 ft. lbs.
16. Install engine splash guard.
17. Install brake hose/ABS cable bracket.

ENGINE SPEED SENSOR, REPLACE

1. Remove battery cables and battery.
2. Remove air cleaner with intake manifold.
3. Remove battery tray.
4. Remove air cleaner bracket.
5. Disassemble transaxle connector.
6. Remove connector from transaxle.
7. Remove cable clamps around cable harness and rubber grommet.
8. Remove sockets from connector casing.
9. Remove socket for RPM sensor cables from connector.
10. Remove engine speed sensor.
11. Apply vaseline to new sensor O-ring and install new sensor.
12. Assemble transaxle connector and install into connector casing.
13. Install connector in vehicle.
14. Install air cleaner bracket, battery tray and air cleaner with intake manifold and connections.
15. Install battery.

OIL TEMPERATURE SENSOR, REPLACE

1. Remove battery cables and battery.
2. Remove air cleaner with intake manifold.
3. Remove battery tray.
4. Remove air cleaner bracket.
5. Disassemble transaxle connector.
6. Detach oil sensor wiring pins from connector socket.
7. Remove under-engine protective cover.
8. Drain oil from transaxle and insert oil plug with new seal. **Torque** plug to 30 ft. lbs.
9. Remove sensor.
10. Apply vaseline to O-ring of new sensor and install new sensor.
11. Push wiring pins into socket.

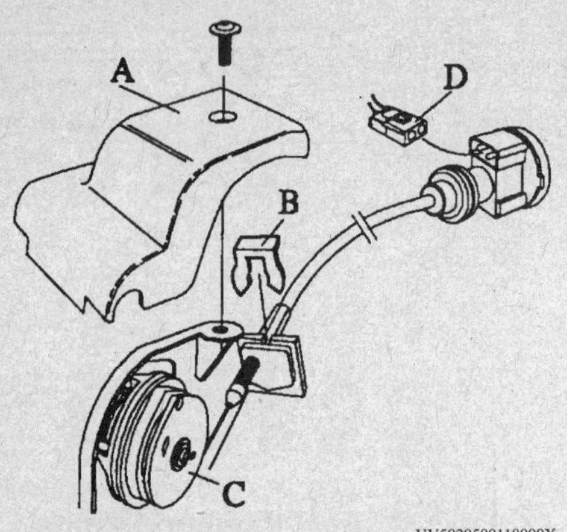
A
B
C
D
VV5029500118000X

Fig. 29 Throttle cable replacement

12. Install protective cover under engine.
13. Assemble connector wiring sockets in connector casing.
14. Install connector in vehicle.
15. Install air cleaner bracket, battery tray and air cleaner with intake manifold and connections.
16. Install battery.

TRANSAXLE CABLE, REPLACE

1. Park vehicle on level surface. Do not apply parking brake.
2. Remove air cleaner, battery and battery tray.
3. Remove locking clip and washers from transaxle control rod arm.
4. Disconnect transaxle cable from rod arm.
5. Remove cigar lighter panel.
6. Remove cover plate below parking brake lever.
7. Remove glove compartment cover.
8. Disconnect center console connectors and remove center console (4 screws).
9. Remove transaxle cable from gear lever mechanism.
10. Fold down carpeting and fold aside side panel around tunnel.
11. Remove screws from cable grommet through cowl panel and.
12. Remove transaxle cable.
13. Reverse procedure to install. **Torque** cable grommet in cowl panel screws to 4.5 ft. lbs.

KICKDOWN SWITCH/THROTTLE CABLE, REPLACE

1. Remove throttle control lever (A), **Fig. 29.**
2. Remove locking clip (B), **Fig. 29,** on cable tensioner.
3. Unhook cable from throttle control pulley (C), **Fig. 29,** and remove it from bracket.
4. Remove kickdown switch (D), **Fig. 29.**
5. Remove sound insulation pad and knee bolster on drivers side.
6. Detach throttle cable from accelerator pedal. Free latch lugs holding kickdown switch in place at cowl panel, then push out switch with throttle cable.
7. Reverse procedure to install.

TRANSMISSION

REPLACE

AW 70, 70L, 71 & 72L

1. Disconnect battery ground cable.
2. Move selector lever to position 2.
3. Remove air cleaner assembly and disconnect kickdown cable from throttle pulley.
4. Raise and support vehicle, then drain fluid.
5. Disconnect shift control rod from shift lever.
6. Disconnect shift reaction rod from transmission housing.
7. Disconnect electrical connector from overdrive unit.
8. Disconnect propeller shaft and remove crossmember assembly.
9. Remove rear engine mount and exhaust pipe bracket. Disconnect exhaust pipe from exhaust manifold.
10. **On diesel engine models,** remove starter motor.
11. **On gasoline engine models,** remove starter retaining bolts and position starter aside. Remove cover bolts, then cover.
12. **On gasoline engine models,** remove cover plate from torque converter housing.
13. **On all units,** disconnect fluid lines and speedometer cable.
14. Remove two upper bolts from torque converter cover.
15. Remove fluid filler tube.
16. Position a suitable jack under transmission.
17. Remove transmission to engine mounting bolts.
18. Remove torque converter mounting bolts, then pry converter away from driveplate.
19. Remove transmission and torque converter assembly from vehicle. Do not tilt forward when removing from vehicle.
20. Reverse procedure to install, noting the following:
    a. **Torque** converter housing to engine M10 bolts to 25–36 ft. lbs.
    b. **Torque** converter housing to engine M12 bolts to 40–65 ft. lbs.
    c. **Torque** driveplate to converter M10 bolts to 30–36 ft. lbs.
    d. **Torque** driveplate to converter M8 bolts (diesel engine only) to 12–20 ft. lbs.

ZF 4-HP-22

1. Disconnect battery ground cable.
2. Disconnect kickdown cable from throttle pulley.
3. Raise and support vehicle.
4. Position gear selector in N, then disconnect shift control rod from transmission gear lever and shift reaction rod from transmission housing.
5. Remove starter motor attaching bolts, then starter motor.
6. Remove filler tube, then oil cooler pipes.
7. Loosen bolts on exhaust pipe joint.
8. Disconnect propeller shaft from transmission.

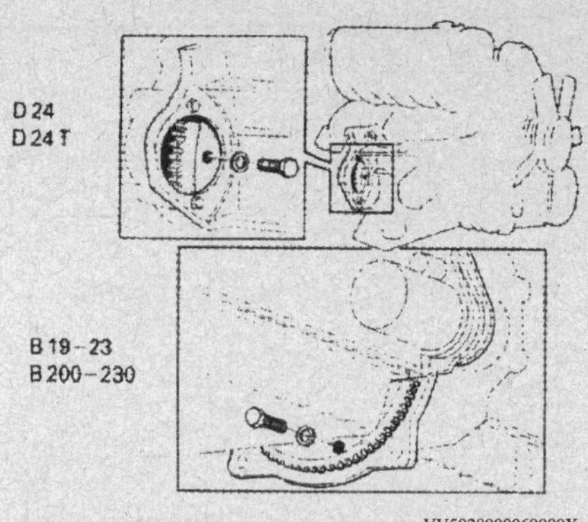
D 24
D 24 T
B 19-23
B 200-230
VV5028900069000X

Fig. 30 Coupling flange removal

9. Remove crossmember assembly from vehicle.
10. **On diesel engine models,** remove bolts from coupling flange through hole for starter motor, **Fig. 30.**
11. **On gasoline engine models,** remove flywheel inspection plate, then bolts from coupling flange **Fig. 30.**
12. **On all models,** remove bolts securing torque converter casing with engine, then remove transmission with torque converter. **Do not tilt transmission forward when removing from vehicle.**
13. Reverse procedure to install noting the following:
    a. **Torque** coupling flange bolts to 16 ft. lbs.
    b. **Torque** fluid filler tube to 72 ft. lbs.

AW 30-40

1. Disconnect negative battery ground cable.
2. Attach lifting lug tool No. 5429, or equivalent, and lifting yoke tool No. 5428, or equivalent, to engine.
3. Place support rails tool No. 5053, or equivalent, on wing edges of fenders and attach lifting beam tool No. 5115, or equivalent, to relieve weight from transmission bracket.
4. Remove splash guard from under engine, air preheater pipe, then lateral strut.
5. Disconnect electrical connectors from oxygen sensor, starter motor, then open clips on transmission and remove two clips on transmission support member.
6. Remove three connectors from bracket on torque converter housing.
7. Remove front exhaust pipe, disconnect propeller shaft from transmission using socket tool No. 5244, or equivalent. Disconnect control rod and reaction arm from gear selector mechanism by removing circlips and washers.
8. Remove heat shield, then disconnect fluid lines from transmission. Plug pipe end to prevent contamination of fluid.
9. Remove transmission support member, then lower rear of engine as far as possible. Ensure no electrical wires or hoses are trapped between engine and bulkhead.
10. Remove torque converter bolts, then

place suitable lift under transmission.

11. Remove transmission to engine mounting bolts, push transmission backwards while holding torque converter in place, then lower unit from vehicle.
12. Reverse procedure to install noting the following:
    a. Ensure carrier plate is not cracked or warped.
    b. Ensure torque converter is properly positioned by placing a straightedge across converter housing and measure distance between converter mounting lug. Distance should be approximately 0.55 inch.
    c. **Torque** converter housing bolts to 35 ft. lbs., and the two starter mounting bolts to 30 ft. lbs.
    d. When tightening converter bolts, tighten until head of bolts are against carrier plate, then **torque** to 22 ft. lbs.
    e. **Torque** propeller shaft attaching bolts to 37 ft. lbs.
    f. Clear diagnostic codes as outlined under "Clearing Diagnostic Trouble Codes."

AW 50-42

1. Undo steering wheel adjustment lever and push wheel as far in and as far up as possible. Lock steering wheel with lever.
2. Place gear selector into N position.
3. Disconnect battery cables and remove battery.
4. Remove air cleaner assembly with intake.
5. Remove battery tray.
6. **On turbo models,** proceed as follows:
    a. Disconnect control valve from air cleaner.
    b. Disconnect charge air manifold clamp and hose from manifold.
    c. Remove air cleaner intake to turbocharger.
7. **On all models,** Disconnect transaxle cable from transaxle.
8. Disconnect transaxle connector.
9. Remove wire harness/ground lead clamp on control system cover.
10. Disconnect transaxle ventilation hose from clamp, if equipped.
11. Unhook wiring conduit from transaxle.
12. Disconnect oxygen sensor connector from bracket on transaxle.
13. Disconnect inlet hose at upper cooler quick connector, and return hose at transaxle.
14. Drain transaxle oil.
15. Remove dipstick pipe.
16. Disconnect hoses from EGR valve, if equipped.
17. **On turbo models,** remove control pulley cover.
18. **On all models,** remove intake to throttle body and pull intake to one side.
19. Disconnect upper oil cooler hose from engine oil cooler and plug oil cooler and hose ports.
20. Remove rear engine mounting nut and transaxle to engine screws.
21. Remove transaxle to starter screws.
22. Disconnect ground lead from transaxle.
23. Lift radiator overflow tank from mounting and allow to hang free.
24. Disconnect ground strap from firewall.
25. Install supports (tool No. 999–5033, or equivalent) on fenders.
26. Install lifting beam tool No. 999–5006, or equivalent, on supports. Place beam directly over eyelet on lifting yoke.
27. Install lifting hook tool No. 999–5460, or equivalent.
28. Pull hook enough to unload engine mountings.
29. Remove front wheels.
30. Remove ABS sensor from left side of axle shaft. **Do not disconnect electrical connector.**
31. Remove brake line brackets and allow to hang.
32. Remove front plastic fender wheelwell liners.
33. Remove left driveshaft nut.
34. Install counterhold tool No. 999–5461, or equivalent, for 4 wheel nuts, or tool No. 999–5540, or equivalent, for 5 wheel nuts.
35. Pull end of driveshaft from hub.
36. Remove front splash guard.
37. Remove nuts from control arms and ball joints, then separate control arms from ball joints.
38. Remove carbon filter container and hoses from subframe. Cut bundle tie holding hoses and hand holder on body.
39. Disconnect exhaust pipe clamp behind catalytic converter.
40. Remove oil pipe bracket.
41. Remove two torque rod holder mounting screws on transaxle.
42. Remove righthand driveshaft bearing cap.
43. Pull off righthand driveshaft inner section and fold out spring strut.
44. Install seal plug No. 999–5488, or equivalent, in transaxle.
45. Let driveshaft rest on subframe and oil pipes.
46. Loosen engine mounting/steering gear screw one turn.
47. Remove steering gear mounting nuts in subframe.
48. Position suitable jack under lefthand side of subframe.
49. Remove subframe support bracket screws on body.
50. Lower subframe and remove jack, allowing frame to hang free.
51. Hang steering gear with hook No. 9995045, or equivalent, in hole on the flange of frame member.
52. Remove oxygen sensor wiring clamps from cover.
53. Disconnect vehicle speed sensor connector.
54. Remove cover at rear engine mounting.
55. Remove rear engine mounting from transaxle.
56. Twist and fold out left spring strut.
57. Knock out end of left driveshaft with plastic or copper mallet and pull left driveshaft out of hub.
58. Remove left driveshaft from transaxle.
59. Install seal plug tool No. 999–5462, or equivalent, into transaxle.
60. Lower engine and transaxle until distance between lifting beam and spark plug cover is 12.6 inches. If engine is lowered too far, exhaust pipe may press onto steering gear.
61. Install universal tool No. 999–5972, or equivalent, and transaxle fixture tool No. 9995463, or equivalent, on jack.
62. Raise jack so it is lightly in contact with transaxle.
63. Remove six torque converter bolts using Torx TX50 socket.
64. Remove lower plastic nut and fold out righthand fender liner.
65. Remove transaxle to engine mounting bolts while turning crankshaft with socket wrench.
66. Remove transaxle. Ensure torque converter comes out with transaxle and does not slip off stator shaft.
67. Reverse procedure to install, noting the following:
    a. **Torque** transaxle to engine mounting bolts to 37 ft. lbs.
    b. **Torque** torque converter bolts to 22 ft. lbs.
    c. **Torque** subframe mounting bolts to 78 ft. lbs.
    d. **Torque** rear engine mounting bolts to 37 ft. lbs.
    e. Install torque rod mounting to transaxle and **torque** new screws to 26 ft. lbs. + 40° on late models, and 13 ft. lbs. + 90° on early models.
    f. **Torque** ABS sensor to 7.4 ft. lbs.

TIGHTENING SPECIFICATIONS

Component	Torque/Ft. Lbs
AW 30-40, 70, 70L, 71 & 72L	
Blind Plug	5-9
Center Support To Transmission	①

Continued

TIGHTENING SPECIFICATIONS—Continued

Component	Torque/Ft. Lbs
AW 30-40, 70, 70L, 71 & 72L	
Companion Flange To Output Shaft	40-50
Control System To Transmission	8-12
Coolant Pipe Nipple	22
Cover Plate To Transmission	6-9
Drain Plug	18-23
Drive Plate To Torque Converter	②
Gear Selector Lever	12
Locking Plate Over Parking Prawl	6-9
Oil Cooler Connection	20-30
Oil Strainer To Lower Valve Housing	5-6
Oil Sump To Transmission	4-5
Pump Cover To Pump	6-9
Pump To Transmission Case	22-28
Rear Extension To Transmission	27-47
Solenoid Valve	10-16
Speedometer Drive Gear	4-6
Torque Converter To Engine	③
Torque Converter To Transmission	27-42
Transmission To Oil Filler Pipe	④
AW 50-42	
Coolant Pipe Nipple	22
Drain Plug	30
Drive Plate To Torque Converter	21
Gear Selector Cable To Shaft	22
Torque Converter To Engine	35
Transmission To Oil Filler Pipe	18
ZF 4 HP-22	
Companion Flange To Output Shaft	63-85
Cylinder B4 To Transmission	6.6-8.1
Drive Plate To Torque Converter	⑤
Lock Plate To Parking Lock	6.6-8.1
Oil Filler Pipe To Oil Sump	63-85
Oil Pump To Connecting Plate	6.6-8.1
Oil Strainer To Valve Body Assembly	5.2-6.6
Oil Sump Plug	10-13
Oil Sump To Transmission	4-5
Plug To Connecting Plate	⑥
Rear Housing To Transmission	15-19
Torque Converter To Connecting Plate	30-38
Torque Converter To Engine	⑦
Valve Body Assembly To Transmission	5.2-6.6

① — Torque bolts in an alternate pattern, in steps of 7 ft. lbs. up to 24–28 ft. lbs.

② — 940 & 960 models, 21 ft. lbs.; 240 models 41–50 ft. lbs.

③ — 940 & 960 models, 35 ft. lbs.; 240 models 35–50 ft. lbs.

④ — 940 & 960 models, 18 ft. lbs.; 240 models 65–70 ft. lbs.

⑤ — 8 mm bolts, 13–20 ft. lbs.; 10 mm bolts, 30–37 ft. lbs.

⑥ — 14 mm bolts, 25–34 ft. lbs.; 20 mm bolts, 32–42 ft. lbs.

⑦ — 10 mm bolts, 26–37 ft. lbs.; 12 mm bolts, 41–66 ft. lbs.

Drive Axles

INDEX

	Page No.
Assemble	50-105
Disassemble	50-105

DISASSEMBLE

1. Remove rear axle assembly from vehicle, **Fig. 1,** and install in a suitable holding fixture with pinion flange facing downward.
2. Remove axle shafts.
3. Remove differential cover. If the unit is being reconditioned because of noise, the contact pattern should be checked before disassembly.
4. Before disassembly, check markings on carrier and caps. If marks are difficult to read, mark caps with a punch to insure proper assembly. Remove caps.
5. Install expander tool No. 2394 or other suitable spreader in holes in carrier housing. Hold tool in place with retainers 2601, **Fig. 2,** Tighten tool tension bolt until all freeplay is eliminated. Turn tension bolt 3 to 3 ½ additional turns. **Do not turn tension bolt more than 3 ½ turns.**
6. Using prying tool No. 2337, or equivalent, remove differential assembly from housing. Loosen tension bolt of expander tool No. 2394, or equivalent, and remove tool.
7. Invert axle case and drain oil.
8. Using a suitable wrench and socket, remove flange nut.
9. Using puller tool No. 2261, or equivalent, remove flange.
10. Using a plastic mallet, drive out pinion from differential housing. Hold pinion with one hand to prevent damage while pinion is driven out.
11. Using handle and drift tool Nos. 1801 and 2599, or equivalents, remove front pinion bearing, washer and oil seal from axle case.
12. Remove rear pinion bearing outer race. On type 1030 axle, use tool Nos. 1801 and 2598, or equivalents, to remove rear pinion bearing outer race. On type 1031 axle, use tool Nos. 1801 and 2843, or equivalents, to remove outer race.
13. **On type 1030 axle,** use puller tool No. 5215, or equivalent, to remove rear pinion bearing. On type 1031 axle, use ring tool No. 5214 and puller tool No. 5216, or equivalents, to remove rear pinion bearing.
14. Using puller tool No. 2483, or equivalent, remove differential carrier bearings. Record position of shims and bearings for reassembly.
15. **On models without limited slip differential,**remove lock plate from ring gear bolts, loosen ring gear bolts about halfway and tap on bolt heads to loosen ring gear, then remove bolts and ring gear. Drive out lockpin, **Fig. 3,** and push out shaft for differential gears. Lift out block, differential gears and thrust washers.
16. **On models with limited slip differential,** place marks on differential gear shafts and differential carrier to ensure parts are installed in the same manner as when removed. Remove differential carrier bolts. **Limited slip differential model type 1030, has bolts with left-hand threads.**
17. **On all models,** remove differential carrier and gear plates.
18. Remove ring gear bolts and ring gear. Discard old bolts.

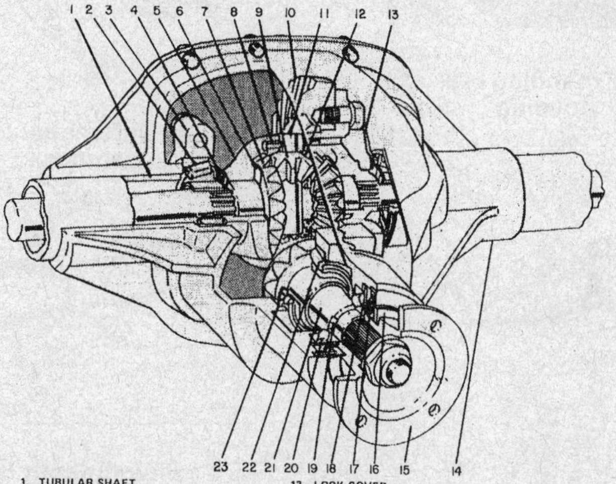

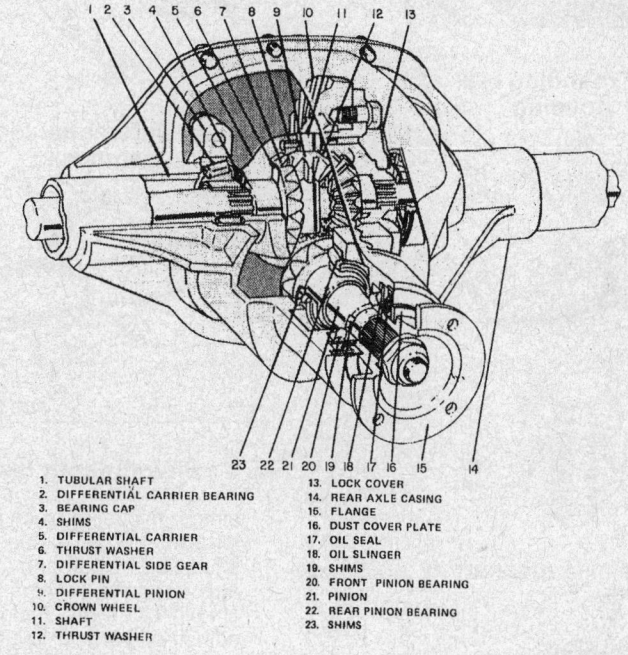

1. TUBULAR SHAFT
2. DIFFERENTIAL CARRIER BEARING
3. BEARING CAP
4. SHIMS
5. DIFFERENTIAL CARRIER
6. THRUST WASHER
7. DIFFERENTIAL SIDE GEAR
8. LOCK PIN
9. DIFFERENTIAL PINION
10. CROWN WHEEL
11. SHAFT
12. THRUST WASHER
13. LOCK COVER
14. REAR AXLE CASING
15. FLANGE
16. DUST COVER PLATE
17. OIL SEAL
18. OIL SLINGER
19. SHIMS
20. FRONT PINION BEARING
21. PINION
22. REAR PINION BEARING
23. SHIMS

VV3039100003000X

Fig. 1 Exploded view of rear axle assembly

ASSEMBLE

1. **On models less limited slip differential,** install thrust washers and large differential gears into case using suitable nut, bolt and washers to retain them. Tighten nuts to compress thrust washers. Install small differential gears and thrust washers into housing as an assembly and remove nut, bolt and washers. Install differential gear shaft and lockpin.
2. **On models without limited slip differential,**install ring gear onto carrier assembly. Using new bolts, **torque** standard head bolts to 50–58 ft. lbs., **torque** flanged head bolts to 65–80 ft. lbs.
3. **On models with limited slip differential,** install ring gear onto carrier assembly. Coat new bolt threads with a suitable sealing compound and install bolts. **Torque** standard head bolts to 50–58 ft. lbs., **torque** flanged head bolts to 65–80 ft. lbs. Install shafts, gears and discs into differential housing. **Torque** bolts to 44–55 ft. lbs.
4. **On type 1030 axle,** install adjusting ring 2685 and wrench 2841 or 5157 onto pinion, **Fig. 4.** On type 1031 axle, install adjusting ring 2840 and wrench 2841 or 5157 onto pinion.
5. Install pinion into housing. **Ensure screw head on adjusting ring faces the larger part of the differential carrier. Ensure adjusting ring pin is in the differential carrier recess.**
6. Check pinion depth with dial gauge holder tool No. 2284, or equivalent, and measuring tool No. 2393, or equivalent, and a dial indicator as follows:
   a. Place gauge plug on machined surface of pinion, install tool No. 2393, or equivalent, in housing in place of carrier and place dial indicator in tool No. 2284, or equivalent, then

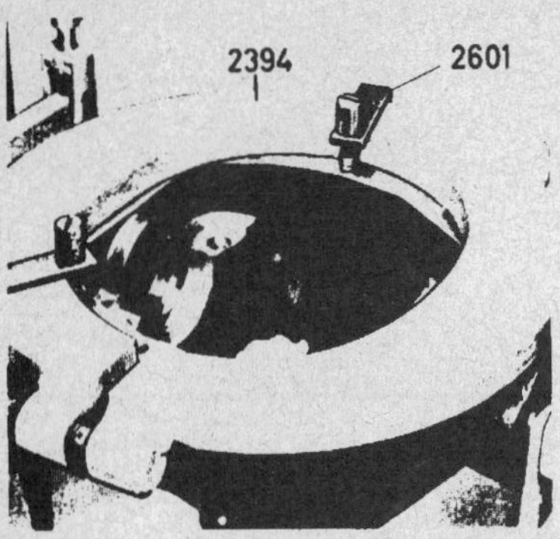
2394
2601

VV3039100004000X

Fig. 2 Expanding rear axle housing

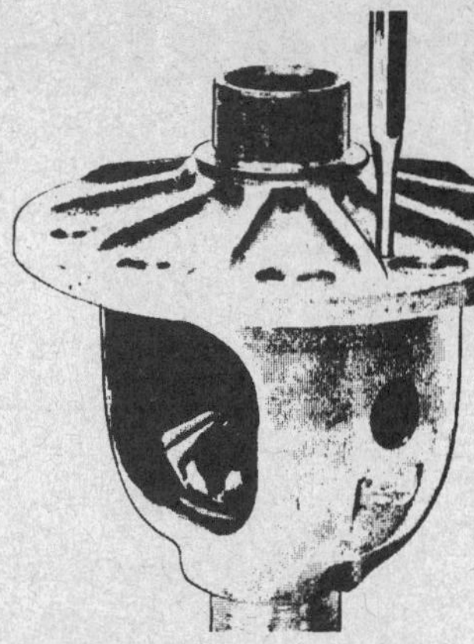

VV3039100005000X

Fig. 3 Differential lockpin removal

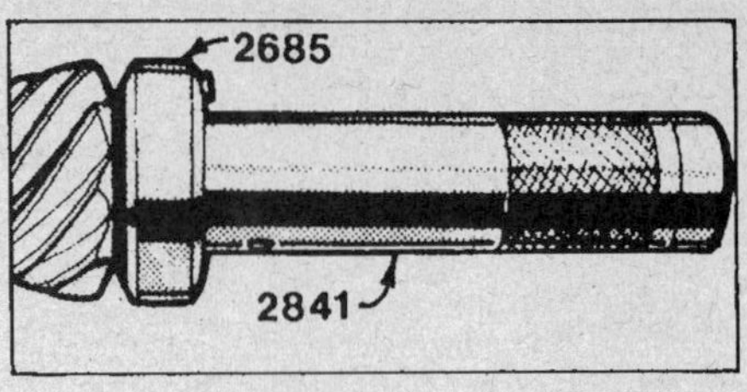
2685
2841

VV3039100006000X

Fig. 4 Adjusting ring & tool for pinion location

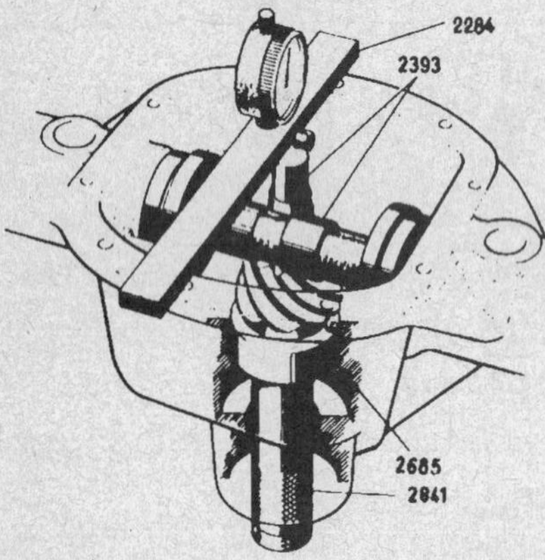
2284
2393
2685
2841

VV3039100007000X

Fig. 5 Rear axle measuring tools

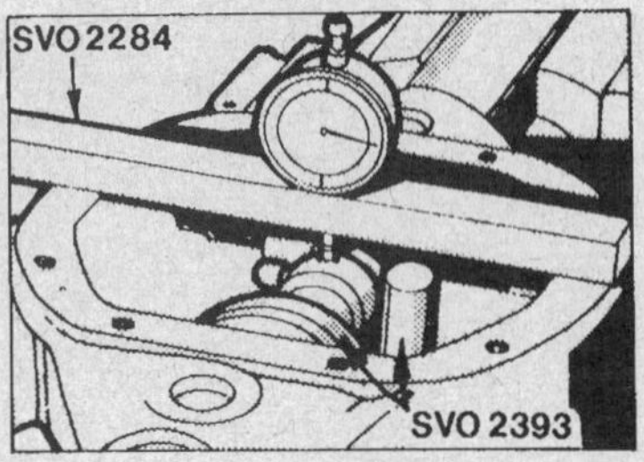
SVO 2284
SVO 2393

VV3039100008000X

Fig. 6 Pinion depth inspection

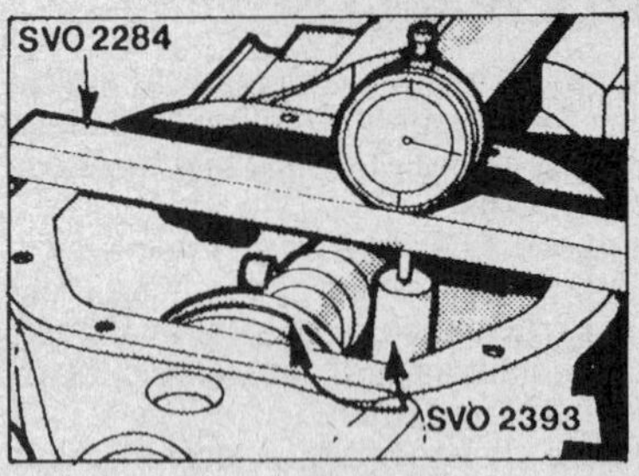
SVO 2284
SVO 2393

VV3039100009000X

Fig. 7 Pinion location measurement

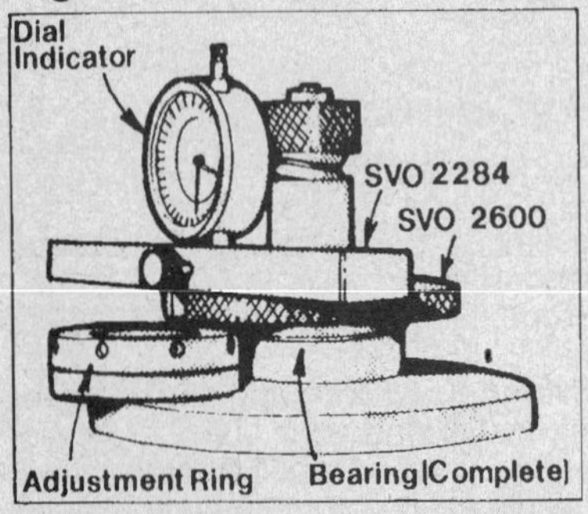
Dial
Indicator
SVO 2284
SVO 2600
Adjustment Ring
Bearing(Complete)

VV3039100010000X

Fig. 8 Adjusting ring & bearing measurement

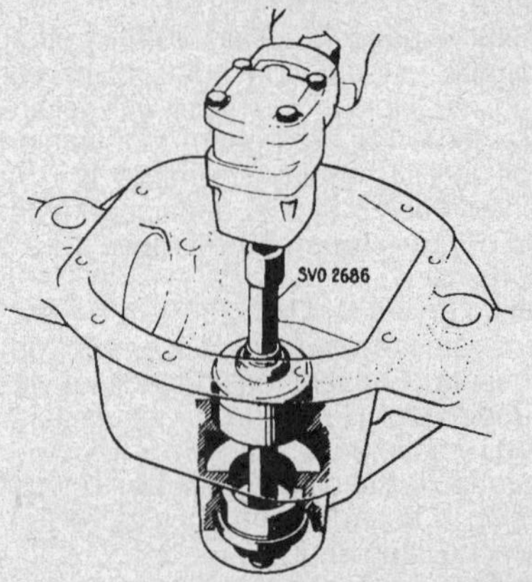
SVO 2686

VV3039100011000X

Fig. 9 Bearing race installation

place tool across machined surface of housing, **Fig. 5.**

b. Place dial indicator on tool, **Fig. 6,** and zero indicator. Move indicator retainer so that indicator comes in contact with gauge plug. The machined surface of the pinion is marked with a nominal dimension. The reading taken in **Fig. 7,** should equal the nominal dimension as marked on pinion.

c. If pinion, for example, is marked 33, gauge plug should be .33 mm (.013 inch) under adjusting fixture. Nominal dimensions on pinion are in metric measurements on all late units, however, some early units are marked in thousandths of an inch. Metric units have no plus or minus sign. Inch units are marked plus or minus. On inch units, if pinion is marked (–) minus, gauge plug should be higher than adjusting fixture. If marked (+) plus, gauge plug should be lower. Pinion height is adjusted to proper value by turning wrench tool No. 2841, or equivalent, until height is correct. Lock the lock screw on the adjusting ring. Remove adjusting ring from pinion.

7. Place the complete rear pinion bearing with the outer ring in fixture tool No. 2600, or equivalent, **Fig. 8.** Turn bearing back and forth to seat rollers. Tighten knurled nut down to hold bearing fully seated. Place adjusting ring in fixture, **Fig. 8.**
8. Use dial indicator and dial gauge holding tool No. 2284, or equivalent, to check difference in height between adjusting ring and bearing. This is the correct thickness for the pinion bearing shims. Measure out the correct shim thickness with a micrometer. **It is almost impossible to obtain a shim with exactly the correct thickness. Shims must not be more than .02 mm (.0082 inch) thicker than the measured value, but can be up to .05 mm (.002 inch) thinner.**
9. Press rear pinion bearing onto pinion.
10. The measured shims obtained are installed in the housing under the bearing race for the rear pinion bearing. Do not install washer that was under bearing cup originally. The measured shims will provide proper pinion depth.
11. Install both bearing races with press tool No. 2686, or equivalent, on type 1030 axles or 2842, or equivalent, on type 1031 axles, **Fig. 9.**
12. Insert pinion into housing, then install three .75 mm (.030 inch) shims and front pinion bearing. Using press tool No. 1845, or equivalent, and wrench tool No. 2404, or equivalent, pull in pinion.
13. Replace press tool No. 1845, or equivalent, with washer and nut. **Torque** nut to 185 ft. lbs.
14. Using the dial indicator and dial gauge holder tool No. 2284, or equivalent, check pinion endplay.
15. Remove pinion. Reduce thickness of front shim pack according to dial indicator reading plus .0035 inch (.09 mm) for new bearings. On used bearings, reduce thickness of front shim pack according to dial indicator reading plus .0028 inch (.07 mm).
16. Using the above shim pack, install pinion as outlined in Step 13. Check the torque necessary to rotate the pinion. For used bearings, 13–22 inch lbs. should rotate the pinion. For new bearings, 22–31 inch lbs. Higher torque on new units may occur. Higher torque is not a cause for concern, but if torque

does not meet minimum values, reduce the front bearing shim pack to obtain the correct torque.

17. Lubricate the inside of adjusting rings 2595 and install them on the differential carrier in place of the carrier bearings. The ring with the black oxidized ring should be placed on the ring gear side. Install the differential assembly in the housing.
18. Turn the adjusting rings to adjust the ring gear position to obtain a gear backlash of .15 mm (.006 inch). Tighten the lock screws to specifications. **Previously, the gear contact pattern could be used to determine correct installation of the gears. This is no longer possible because of altered manufacturing and test procedures. The pinion should always be installed according to its number marking regardless of the contact pattern.**
19. Install each carrier bearing assembly in measurement tool No. 2600, or equivalent. Follow procedure outlined to determine the proper shim thickness for each carrier bearing. Place the right bearing in the tool and measure the adjusting ring that was on the right side of the carrier. When each shim pack has been determined, add .07 mm (.003 inch) to each side for preload. Install shims on carrier and press on the carrier bearings.
20. Install expander tool No. 2394, or equivalent, on the housing. Expand the tool until the tool pins are tight in the holes in the housing, then turn the tensioning screw an additional 3 to 3 ½ turns. Install the differential and bearing rings.
21. Remove tool No. 2394, or equivalent.
22. Install the caps according to their markings and **torque** to 36–50 ft. lbs.
23. Remove tool No. 2404, or equivalent, from pinion. Install oil seal.
24. Press on the flange with press tool Nos. 1845 or 5156, or equivalents.
25. Install washer and nut. **Torque** nut to 185 ft. lbs.
26. Install differential cover with a new gasket.
27. Install axle shafts.

Engine Rebuilding Specifications

INDEX

	Page No.
Camshaft	50-108
Crankshaft, Bearings & Rods	50-109
Cylinder Block	50-110
Cylinder Head, Valve Guide & Valve Seats	50-107
Oil Pump	50-110
Pistons, Pins & Rings	50-109
Valves	50-107
Valve Springs	50-107

CYLINDER HEAD, VALVE GUIDE & VALVE SEATS

All Measurements Given In Inches Unless Otherwise Specified.

Engine Model	Engine Liter	Cylinder Head		Valve Guides			Valve Seats			Valve Clearance	
		Warpage Limit	Minimum Height	Standard Inside Diameter	Stem To Guide Clearance: Intake	Stem To Guide Clearance: Exhaust	Seat Angle	Seat Width: Intake	Seat Width: Exhaust	Intake	Exhaust
1993–95											
B230F	2.3L	①	5.732	.3150-.3158	.0012-.0024	.0024-.0035	45°	.051-.075	.067-.090	②	②
B230FT	2.3L Turbo	①	5.732	.3150-.3158	.0012-.0024	.0024-.0035	45°	.051-.075	.067-.090	②	②
B5254FT	2.3L Turbo T-5R	④	5.066	.4720	.0012-.0024	.0012-.0024	45°	.055-.071	.055-.071	③	③
B5254FS	2.4L	④	5.066	.4720	.0012-.0024	.0012-.0024	45°	.055-.071	.055-.071	③	③
B6304F	2.9L	④	5.066	.4720	.0024	.0024	45°	.055-.071	.071-.087	③	③
1996											
B5234FT	2.3L Turbo	④	5.066	.4720	.0012-.0024	.0012-.0024	45°	.055-.071	.055-.071	③	③
B5254FS	2.4L	④	5.066	.4720	.0012-.0024	.0012-.0024	45°	.055-.071	.055-.071	③	③
B6304FS	2.9L	④	5.066	.4720	.0024	.0024	45°	.055-.071	.071-.087	③	③

① — .020 inch lengthwise or .010 inch crosswise.
② — Checking cold, .012–.016 inch; checking hot, .014–.018 inch; adjusting cold, .014–.016 inch; adjusting hot, .016–.018 inch.
③ — Equipped w/ hydraulic valve lash adjusters, no adjustment required.
④ — .020 inch lengthwise or .008 inch crosswise.

VALVE SPRINGS

All Measurements Given In Inches Unless Otherwise Specified.

Engine Model	Engine Liter	Valve Springs	
		Free Length	Compressed Pressure Pounds @ Inches
1993–95			
B230F	2.3L	1.69	158-176 @ 1.08
B230FT	2.3L Turbo	1.69	158-176 @ 1.08
B5254FT	2.3L Turbo T-5R	1.67	143-158 @ .964
B5254FS	2.4L	1.67	143-158 @ .964
B6304F	2.9L	1.69	147-154 @ .964
1996			
B5234T	2.3L Turbo	1.67	143-158 @ .964
B5254FS	2.4L	1.67	143-158 @ .964
B6304FS	2.9L	1.69	147-154 @ .964

VALVES

All Measurements Given In Inches Unless Otherwise Specified.

Engine Model	Engine Liter	Valves		
		Stem Diameter		Face Angle
		Intake	Exhaust	
1993–95				
B230F	2.3L	.3126	.3126	44.5
B230FT	2.3L Turbo	.3126	.3126	44.5
B5254FT	2.3L Turbo T-5R	.2743	.2743	44.5
B5254FS	2.4L	.2743	.2743	44.5
B6304FS	2.9L	.2743	.2743	44.5
1996				
B5234FT	2.3L Turbo	.2743	.2743	44.5
B5254FS	2.4L	.2743	.2743	44.5
B6304FS	2.9L	.2743	.2743	44.5

CAMSHAFT

All Measurements Given In Inches Unless Otherwise Specified.

Engine Model	Engine Liter	Camshaft Journal Dia.	Camshaft Bearing Clearance	Camshaft Endplay	Lifter Dia.	Lifter To Bore Clearance
1993–95						
B230F	2.3L	1.1791-1.1799	.0012-.0028	.0008-.0020	1.4557-1.4565	.0012-.0030
B230FT	2.3L Turbo	1.1791-1.1799	.0012-.0028	.0008-.0020	1.4557-1.4565	.0012-.0029
B5254FT	2.3L Turbo T-5R	—	—	.0020-.0079	1.3409-1.3789	—
B5254FS	2.4L	—	—	.0020-.0079	1.3409-1.3789	—
B6304FS	2.9L	—	—	.0020-.0079	1.259	—
1996						
B5234FT	2.3L Turbo	—	—	.0020-.0079	1.3409-1.3789	—
B5254FS	2.4L	—	—	.0020-.0079	1.3409-1.3789	—
B6304FS	2.9L	—	—	.0020-.0079	1.259	—